MW01201100

Standard Catalog of ® WORLD COINS 1701-1800

4th OFFICIAL Edition

Colin R. Bruce II
Senior Editor

Thomas Michael
Market Analyst

Harry Miller
U.S. Market Analyst

George Cuhaj
Editor

Merna Dudley
Coordinating Editor

Deborah McCue
Database Specialist

Randy Thern
Numismatic Cataloging Supervisor

Special Contributors

Wade Hinderling **Tom Jacobs**
Paul Montz **N. Douglas Nicol**
Bill Noyes **Gastone Polacco**
Remy Said **Daniel Frank Sedwick**
Alexander Shapiro **Mehmet Tolga Tanner**

Bullion Value (BV) Market Valuations

Valuations for all platinum, gold, palladium and silver coins of the more common, basically bullion types, or those possessing only modest numismatic premiums are presented in this edition based on the market levels of:

$1,300 per ounce for **platinum**

$675 per ounce for **gold**

$335 per ounce for **palladium**

$12.75 per ounce for **silver**

Published by

700 East State Street • Iola, WI 54990-0001
715-445-2214 • 888-457-2873
www.krausebooks.com

Our toll-free number to place an order or obtain
a free catalog is (800) 258-0929.

ISSN 1078-8816

ISBN-13: 978-0-89689-561-4
ISBN-10: 0-89689-561-0

Designed by Sally Olson
Edited by Randy Thern

Printed in the United States of America

TABLE OF CONTENTS

Title Page I
Copyright Page II
Introduction IV
Acknowledgements VI
Country Index VIII
How To Use XII
Foreign Exchange XVII
German States Instant Identifier XXI
Illustrated Guide to Eastern Mint Names XXV
Standard International Numeral Systems XXXIV
Hejira Date Conversion Chart XXXVI
18th Century Legends 1273

ADVERTISING INDEX

Ponterio and Associates, Inc. V
Smythe & Co. VII
J & F Rubenstein Rare Coins XIII
Jean Elsen s.a. XXIV

INTRODUCTION

We are pleased to present the completely revised and updated 4th Edition of the *Standard Catalog of World Coins* – 1701-1800. Not only does this edition contain nearly 5 years of market adjustments, it provides expanded descriptions, pricing in up to *5* grades of preservation, and hundreds of new images.

This volume contains a wealth of data for early China, the German States and the Holy Roman Empire, Transylvania, the Papal States, France, Spain, India, Turkey and many, many other countries. Concise listings of minors and fractional issues which have generally been available to collectors and dealers only in long out-of-print, difficult to locate, non-English references are presented here in a new, easy to use format, making this catalog an excellent alternative to the acquisition of a large and prohibitively expensive library.

Intriguing issues documented in this volume are virtually endless, the study of which could certainly conjure up visions of the treasure troves preyed upon by the highwaymen and pirates of the era.

In keeping with the traditions that have been held in focus with the *Standard Catalog of World Coins* from the very first edition, this volume is organized in a user-friendly format. A new alphabetical sort order has been incorporated for countries of issue. An effort has been made to indicate each change in political structure and its associated coinage. The listings are generally arranged by denomination, which now appear with each type. Coins are heavily illustrated by basic types, to the point that there is a virtual certainty you will find a photo match to the designs, or at least a clear word description of any 18th century coins that may come into your possession. To facilitate the easy identification and attribution of coins of the era, this volume features numerous helpful illustrated mint and privy mark charts, denomination and legend abbreviation indexes, along with German States shield instant identifier compilations. This edition also features our 9-page *Illustrated Guide to Eastern Mint Names.*

The *Standard Catalog of World Coins – 1701-1800 Edition* is the result of over 35 years of research by more than 200 respected numismatic experts around the world. True to the stated objective of the original *Standard Catalog of World Coins* (published in 1971), this edition augments the current family of five 'century' reference catalogs, which conveniently replace a shelf of often-elusive specialized books, many of which were obscure and when found, very expensive.

The new 4th Edition provided an opportunity for focus on some specific areas long in need of heavy revision, including pricing throughout. More detail and improved descriptions are found in every country. The result is a nearly 1400-page book complete with detailed information no collector or dealer can do without.

Does this mean this *Standard Catalog of World Coins* - 1701-1800 volume represents unquestioned completeness of coverage for the era? No.

Is it a definitive work, on the basis of authoritativeness and exhaustiveness? Yes.

Is it the ultimate word on the subject that will ever be published? We certainly hope not.

What this is, in effect, is a living and breathing book. This is a reference that will grow and benefit your future interests, in the presentation of successor editions, to the measure of what you, the user, contribute to make it something more than it presently is. Toward that end, you are invited — make that encouraged — to point up errors and omissions, and challenge any contents you have reason to question.

We hope you find this new edition meets your collecting needs. Enjoy your hobby.

Colin R. Bruce II
Krause Publications

ACKNOWLEDGMENTS

Many numismatists have contributed countless changes, which have been incorporated in this edition. While all cannot be acknowledged here, special appreciation is extended to the following individuals and organizations who have exhibited a special dedication — revising and verifying historical and technical data and coin listings, reviewing market valuations and loaning coins to photograph— for this edition.

Jan Olav Aamlid
Dr. Lawrence A. Adams
Stephen Album
Antonio Alessandrini
Esko Alroth
Don Bailey
Mitchell A. Battino
Dr. Bernd Becker
Allen G. Berman
Wolfgang Bertsch
Shailendra Bhandare
Joseph Boling
Al Boulanger
Klaus Bronny
Xavier Calico
Doru Calin
Ralph A. Cannito
Adolfo Cayon
Henry Chan
Raul Chirila
Scott Cordry
Jerry Crain
Vincent Craven-Bartl
Jed Crump
Raymond Czahor
Howard A. Daniel III
Eric G. Dawson, M.D.
Jean-Paul Divo
Mike Dunigan
Wilhelm Eglseer
Jack Erb
George Falcke
John Ferm
Thomas Fitzgerald
Arthur Friedberg
Kent Froseth
Tom Galway
Stan Goron
Ron Guth
Marcel Häberling
Brian Hannon
Flemming Lyngbeck Hansen
Hans Herrli
Wade Hinderling
Serge Huard
Clyde Hubbard
Louis Hudson
Ton Jacobs
Lorenzo Jimenez
Robert Johnston
Robert W. Julian
Børge R. Juul
Alex Kaglyan
Christine Karstedt
Craig Keplinger
Lawrence C. Korchnak
Dmitry Korzhkov
Peter Kraneveld
Ronachai Krisadaolarn
Prashant Kulkarni
Samson Kin Chiu Lai
Joseph E. Lang
Thomas Lautz
Nirat Lertchitvikul
Jan Janusz Lingen
Richard Lobel
Ma Tak Wo
Enrico Manara
Ranko Mandic
John Means
Franck Medina
Jürgen Mikeska
Juozas Minikevicius
Robert Mish
Paul Montz
Edward Moschetti
Horst-Dieter Müller
Glenn Murray
N. Douglas Nicol
Arkady Nakhimovsky
Vladimir Nastich
Bill Noyes
Frank Passic
Marc Pelletier
Jens Pilegaard
Gastone Polacco
Kent Ponterio
Rick Ponterio
Mircea Raicopol
Kavan Ratnatunga
Nicholas Rhodes
Dana Roberts
William Rosenblum
Sanjay Sahadev
Remy Said
Gerhard Schön
Dr. Wolfgang Schuster
Daniel Frank Sedwick
Olav Sajeroe
Ladislav Sin
Alexander Shapiro
Saran Singh
Jørgen Sømod
Gylfi Snorrason
Richard Stuart
Vladimir Suchy
Alim A. Sumana
Barry Tabor
Gilbert Tan
Mehmet Tolga Tanner
M. Louis Teller
Gunnar Thesen
Frank Timmerman
Archie Tonkin
Anthony Tumonis
J. L. Van der Schueren
Erik J. Van Loon
Jesus Vico
Helen Wallace
Justin C. Wang
Paul C. Welz
Stewart Westdal
Ertekin Yenisey
Isaac Zadeh
Joseph Zaffern

AUCTION HOUSES

Bruun Rasmussen
Dix-Noonan-Webb
Jean Elsen S. A.
Frankfurter Münzhandlung GmbH
Gorny & Mosch - Giessener Münzhandlung
Heritage World Coin Auctions
Hess-Divo AG
Gerhard Hirsch
Thomas Høiland Møntauktion
Fritz Rudolf Künker
Münzenhandlung Harald Möller, GmbH
Münz Zentrum
Noble Numismatics, Pty. Ltd.
Numismatik Lanz (München)
Ponterio & Associates
Laurens Schulman, b.v.
Stack's - Coin Galleries
Superior Galleries
UBS, AG
World-Wide Coins of California

SOCIETIES and INSTITUTIONS

American Numismatic Association
American Numismatic Society
British Museum
Numismatics International
Russian Numismatic Society
Smithsonian Institution

PUBLICATIONS

The Stateman's Year-Book - The Politics, Culture and Economics of the World, 2004
140th Edition
by Barry Turner, editor, Palgrave Macmillan Ltd., Houndsmills, Basingstoke, Hampshire, RG21 6XS, England.
(Statistical and Historical Annual of the States of the World)
The World Factbook, 2006, by Central Intelligence Agency.

COUNTRY INDEX

A

Aachen 248
Aalen 249
Afghanistan 1
Aire 243
Alessandria 862
Algeria 15
Algiers 15
Alwar 767
Angola 17
Anhalt-Bernburg 249
Anhalt-Bernburg-Schaumburg-Hoym 252
Anhalt-Kothen 253
Anhalt-Zerbst 253
Appenzell 1185
Aragon 1166
Arakan 724
Arcot 767
Arenberg 255
Armenia 19
Assam 725
Auersperg 52
Augsburg 255
Austria 20
Austrian Netherlands 75
Austrian States 52
Awadh 769
Azerbaijan 82
Azores 84

B

Bacaim 807
Baden 260
Bahawalpur 775
Bamberg 264
Banjarmasin 1082
Banswara 775
Barbados 85
Barcelona 1166
Baroda 776
Basel 1186
Batthyani 52
Bavaria 266
Belgiojoso 862
Belmonte 862
Bengal Presidency 815
Bentheim-Tecklenburg-Rheda 278
Bermuda 86
Bern 1191
Beromuenster 1197
Bharatpur 776
Bhatgaon, Kingdom of 1043
Bhaunagar 778
Bhopal 778
Bhutan 87
Biberach 279
Bikanir 778
Bindraban 779
Bocholt 279
Bohemia 87
Bolivia 97
Bombay Presidency 820
Brabant 1167
Brandenburg-Ansbach 279
Brandenburg-Ansbach-Bayreuth 289
Brandenburg-Bayreuth 289
Braunau 296
Brazil 106
Bremen 297
Breslau 300
Bretzenheim 300
British Virgin Islands 116
Brixen 53
Broach 780
Brunswick-Blankenburg 301
Brunswick-Luneburg-Calenberg-Hannover 302
Brunswick-Luneburg-Celle 323
Brunswick-Wolfenbuttel 324
Buchhorn 346
Bukhara 118
Bundi 780
Burgau 53
Burma 116

C

Cagliari 862
Cannanore 780
Casale Monferrato 862
Castiglione Dei Gatti 862
Central Asia 117
Ceylon 118
Chhatarpur 781
Chile 120
China 124
Chur 1198
Cisalpine Republic 862
Cleves 346
Cochin 781
Coesfeld 347
Colloredo-Mansfeld 54
Cologne 348
Colombia 136
Connecticut 1253
Constance 353
Cooch Behar 733
Coorg 782
Corsica 863
Corvey 354
Courland 142
Crailsheim 356
Crimea (Krim) 143
Cuba 144
Curacao 144

D

Damao 807
Danish West Indies 144
Danzig 145
Darband 82
Datia 782
Denmark 147
Deventer 1055
Dholpur 782
Dietrichstein 54
Disentis 1200
Diu 808
Dominica 156
Dortmund 356

E

East Friesland 357
East Prussia 1104
Eger 55
Egypt 157
Eichstatt 361
Einbeck 363
Einsiedeln 1200
Elbing 1105
Ellwangen 363
Empire 125
Erbach 363
Erfurt 363
Essen 364
Essequibo & Demerary 162
Esslingen 364
Eszterhazy 55
Ethiopia 162

F

Fagnolle 81
Farrukhabad 734
Fischingen 1200
Flanders 1168
France 163
Franconian Circle 364
Frankfurt Am Main 364
Freiburg 1200
Freiburg Im Breisgau 370
Freising 372

French Colonies 244
French Guiana 244
French States 243
Friedberg 372
Friesland 1055
Fugger 373
Fugger-Pfirt 373
Fulda 373
Furstenberg 377
Furstenberg-Purglitz 377
Furstenberg-Stuhlingen 377
Further Austria 378

G

Galicia & Lodomeria 1106
Ganja 82
Garhwal 783
Gelderland 1055
Geneva 1201
Genoa 863
Georgia 244
German States 247
Gluckstadt 156
Gnesen 1106
Goa 810
Gold Coast 629
Gorizia 867
Goslar 379
Great Britain 629
Grenada 647
Groningen And Ommeland 1059
Grosswardein 1235
Guadeloupe 647
Guastalla 868
Guatemala 647
Gurkha Kingdom 735
Gwalior 783

H

Haiti 652
Haldenstein 1204
Hall 381
Hamburg 383
Hamm 388
Hanau 388
Hanau-Lichtenberg 388
Hanau-Munzenberg 389
Harar 162
Heilbronn 391
Hejaz 653
Hejaz & Nejd 1150
Henneberg 391
Henneberg-Ilmenau 391
Henneberg-Schleusingen 392
Hesse-Cassel 392
Hesse-Darmstadt 401
Hesse-Homburg 405
Hildesheim 405
Hohenlohe 408
Hohenlohe-Bartenstein 409
Hohenlohe-Bartenstein-Pfedelbach 409
Hohenlohe-Ingelfingen 409
Hohenlohe-Kirchberg 409
Hohenlohe-Langenburg 410
Hohenlohe-Neuenstein Oehringen 410
Hohenlohe-Neuenstein-Weikersheim 411
Hohenlohe-Pfedelbach 412
Hohenlohe-Waldenburg-Schillingsfurst 412
Hohenzollern-Hechingen 413
Holland 1059
Holstein-Gottorp-Rendsborg 156
Hungary 654
Hyderabad 786
Hyderabad Feudatories-Elichpur 787
Hyderabad Feudatories-Firoznagar 787
Hyderabad Feudatories-Gadwal 787
Hyderabad Feudatories-Kalayani 787
Hyderabad Feudatories-Narayanpett 787

I

India-British 815
India-Danish, Tranquebar 801
India-Dutch 806
India-French 803
India-Independent Kingdoms 723
India Mughal Empire 668
India-Portuguese 807
India-Princely States 765
Indore 788
Indore Feudatory 789
Iran 827
Iraq 857
Ireland 858
Isle De Bourbon 859
Isle Of Man 859
Isny 413
Italian States 861

J

Jaintiapur 735
Jaipur 790
Jaisalmir 791
Jamaica 960
Jammu 735
Janid Khanate 118
Janjira Island 793
Jaora 793
Japan 962
Java 1082
Jever 413
Jind 793
Jodhpur 793
Jodhpur Feudatory -Kuchawan 794
Julich-Berg 414

K

Kachar 736
Kaga 966
Kaithal 794
Kalsia 794
Karabagh 83
Karauli 795
Kaufbeuren 418
Kedah 1003
Kempten 418
Khevenhuller-Metsch 55
Kingdom Of Bhatgaon 1043
Kingdom Of Kathmandu 1043
Kingdom Of Patan 1045
Kinsky 55
Kirchberg 419
Kishangarh 795
Kolhapur 795
Konigsegg-Rothenfels 419
Korea 966
Kosel 419
Koshu 966
Kotah 795
Krakow 1106
Kumaon 737
Kutch 737

L

Ladakh 796
Landau 419
Lauenburg 420
Leutkirch 421
Libya 994
Liechtenstein 996
Liege 1000
Lille 243
Limbourg Province-Maastricht 1063
Lindau 421
Lippe-Detmold 421
Lithuania 1000
Livonia 1000
Livonia & Estonia 1001
Livorno 868
Lobkowitz-Sternstein 96
Lorraine 426
Lowenstein-Wertheim-Rochefort 429

Lowenstein-Wertheim-Virneburg 431
Lowenstein-Wertheim-Virneburg & Rochefort 433
Lubeck 433
Lucca 869
Luneburg 438
Luxembourg 1002
Luzern 1205

M

Madras Presidency 824
Madurai 738
Mainz 438
Majorca 1166
Malay Peninsula 1003
Maldive Islands 1005
Maler Kotla 796
Malta, Order Of 1006
Manipur 739
Mansfeld 445
Mansfeld-Bornstedt 445
Mansfeld-Eisleben 445
Mantua 870
Maratha Confederacy 740
Martinique 1016
Massa-Carrara 872
Massachusetts 1254
Mecca 653
Mecklenburg-Schwerin 446
Mecklenburg-Strelitz 449
Memmingen 452
Mewar 796
Mexico 1018
Milan 872
Mimasaka 966
Modena 876
Moldavia & Wallachia 1031
Monaco 1032
Montfort 452
Montserrat 1033
Morocco 1034
Mozambique 1040
Mughal Empire-India 668
Muhlhausen Alsace 455
Muhlhausen Thuringen 456
Munster 457
Muri 1208
Mysore 746

N

Nabha 798
Namur 1169
Naples & Sicily 877
Narwar 798
Nassau 462
Navarre 1166
Nawanagar 799
Nepal 1041
Netherlands 1053
Netherlands East Indies 1078
Netherlands West Indies 1085
Neuchatel 1208
New Hampshire 1254
New Jersey 1254
New York 1255
Nijmegen 1064
Norway 1085
Nostitz-rieneck 55
Nurnberg 462

O

Oldenburg 469
Olmutz 56
Orange 243
Orbetello 882
Orchha 799
Orezzo 882
Orsini-rosenberg 60
Osnabruck 470
Ottingen 473
Ottingen-Ottingen 473
Ottingen-Wallerstein-Spielberg 473
Overyssel 1064

P

Paar 60
Paderborn 474
Panna 800
Papal States 882
Papal States-Ancona 901
Papal States-Ascoli 901
Papal States-Bologna 902
Papal States-Civitavecchia 910
Papal States-Fano 910
Papal States-Fermo 910
Papal States-Ferrara 911
Papal States-Foligno 913
Papal States-Gubbio 913
Papal States-Macerata 917
Papal States-Matelica 917
Papal States-Montalto 917
Papal States-Pergola 917
Papal States-Perugia 917
Papal States-Ravenna 918
Papal States-Ronciglione 919
Papal States-San Severino 919
Papal States-Spoleto 920
Papal States-Terni 920
Papal States-Tivoli 920
Papal States-Viterbo 920
Parma 920
Partabgarh 800
Passau 476
Patan, Kingdom of 1045
Patiala 800
Penang 1003
Peru 1089
Pfalz 478
Pfalz-Birkenfeld-Zweibrucken 478
Pfalz-Neuburg 480
Pfalz-Sulzbach 482
Philippines 1098
Piacenza 922
Piedmont Republic 922
Pisa 923
Poland 1098
Pomerania 489
Pontianak 1083
Porcia 923
Portugal 1107
Prussia 491
Prussian Gelderland 1058
Pudukkottai 757
Puerto Rico 1115
Pyrmont 511

Q

Qubba 83
Quedlinburg 511

R

Ragusa 1115
Ratlam 800
Reckheim 81
Regensburg 512
Reggio Emilia 923
Reichenau-tamins 1210
Retegno 923
Reuss 525
Reuss-Ebersdorf 525
Reuss-Gera 525
Reuss-Lobenstein 526
Reuss-Obergreiz 526
Reuss-Schleiz 528
Reuss-Untergreiz 528
Rheinau 1210
Rietberg 529
Rohilkhand 757
Roman Republic 923
Roman Republic -ancona 925
Roman Republic-ascoli 925
Roman Republic-civitavecchia 925
Roman Republic-clitunno 925
Roman Republic-fermo 926
Roman Republic-foligno 926
Roman Republic-gubbio 927
Roman Republic-macerata 927

Roman Republic-pergola 927
Roman Republic-perugia 927
Rostock 530
Rothenburg 531
Russia 1117
Russia-Siberia 1146

S

Saint Alban 532
Saint Eustatius 1148
Saint Gall 1210
Saint Helena 1148
Saint Lucia 1149
Saint Martin 1149
Saint Vincent 1149
Salm 532
Salm-Kyrburg 532
Salzburg 61
San Georgio 928
San Martino 928
Sardinia 928
Saudi Arabia 1150
Savoy 934
Saxe-Coburg-Saalfeld 532
Saxe-Eisenach 536
Saxe-Eisenberg 536
Saxe-Gotha-Altenburg 536
Saxe-Hildburghausen 540
Saxe-Meiningen 543
Saxe-Saalfeld 544
Saxe-Weimar 546
Saxe-Weimar, Middle 546
Saxe-Weimar-Eisenach 547
Saxe-Weissenfels 550
Saxony 550
Sayn-Altenkirchen 571
Schaumburg-Hessen 572
Schaumburg-Lippe 572
Schleswig-Holstein 573
Schleswig-Holstein-Gottorp 574
Schleswig-Holstein-Ploen 575
Schlick 97
Schmalkalden 575
Schonau 575
Schwarzburg 576
Schwarzburg-Arnstadt 576
Schwarzburg-Rudolstadt 576
Schwarzburg-Sondershausen 577
Schwarzenberg 578
Schweinfurt 579
Schwyz 1213
Scotland 1150
Selam 801
Sendai 966
Shah Dynasty-Nepal 1049
Sheki 83
Shemakhi 84
Siberia 1146
Sicily 934
Sierra Leone 1151
Sikh Empire 760
Sikh Feudatory Najibabad 762
Silesia 580
Sinkiang Province 135
Sinzendorf 74
Sitten 1214
Sivaganga 762
Soest 585
Solms 586
Solms-braunfels 586
Solms-laubach 586
Solothurn 1215
Soragna 938
South Prussia 1106
Spain-Local 1166
Spain 1151
Spanish Netherlands 1167
Speyer 587
Sprinzenstein 74
Stolberg 588
Stolberg-Gedern 588
Stolberg-Rossla 588
Stolberg-Stolberg 588
Stolberg-Wernigerode 594
Stolberg-Wernigerode-Gedern 596
Stralsund 596
Strassburg 597
Sumatra, Island Of 1084
Suriname 1170
Swabian Circle 597
Sweden 1170
Swiss Cantons 1185
Switzerland 1225
Syria 1226

T

Tajima 966
Tanjore 762
Teutonic Order 598
Thailand 1226
Thorn 1107
Thurn And Taxis 598
Tibet 1227
Tinnevelly 762
Tobago 1228
Tortola 116
Tournai 1170
Town Of Le Cap 652
Transylvania 1229
Trautson 74
Travancore 801
Trengganu 1004
Trento 938
Trier 599
Trinidad 1235
Tripoli 994
Tripura 762
Tunis 1236
Tunisia 1235
Turkey 1238
Tuscany 938
Ulm 604

U

United States 1250
Unterwalden 1217
Uri 1218
Uri, Schwyz & Unterwalden 1218
Utrecht 1065

V

Vasto 942
Venice 942
Ventimiglia 960
Vermont 1256
Vienna 75
Vieques Island 1115
Vietnam 1267
Vietnam 1272
Vijayanagar 764

W

Waldeck 605
Waldeck-Pyrmont 607
Werden & Helmstaedt 607
West Friesland 1070
Wiedenbruck 610
Wied-Neuwied 608
Wied-Runkel 609
Windisch-Gratz 75
Windward Islands 1272
Wismar 610
Worms 611
Wurttemberg 611
Wurttemberg-Oels 619
Wurzburg 620

Y

Yemen 1272

Z

Zeeland 1074
Zoefingen 1219
Zug 1219
Zurich 1220

HOW TO USE THIS CATALOG

This catalog series is designed to serve the needs of both the novice and advanced collectors. It provides a comprehensive guide to over 400 years of world coinage. It is generally arranged so that persons with no more than a basic knowledge of world history and a casual acquaintance with coin collecting can consult it with confidence and ease. The following explanations summarize the general practices used in preparing this catalog's listings. However, because of specialized requirements, which may vary by country and era, these must not be considered ironclad. Where these standards have been set aside, appropriate notations of the variations are incorporated in that particular listing.

ARRANGEMENT

Countries are arranged alphabetically. Political changes within a country are arranged chronologically. In countries where Rulers are the single most significant political entity a chronological arrangement by Ruler has been employed. Distinctive subgeographic regions are listed alphabetically following the countries main listings. A few exceptions to these rules may exist. Refer to the Country Index.

Diverse coinage types relating to fabrication methods, revaluations, denomination systems, non-circulating categories and such have been identified, separated and arranged in logical fashion. Chronological arrangement is employed for most circulating coinage, i.e., Hammered coinage will normally precede Milled coinage, monetary reforms will flow in order of their institution. Non-circulating types such as Essais, Pieforts, Patterns, Trial Strikes, Mint and Proof sets will follow the main listings, as will Medallic coinage and Token coinage.

Within a coinage type coins will be listed by denomination, from smallest to largest. Numbered types within a denomination will be ordered by their first date of issue.

IDENTIFICATION

The most important step in the identification of a coin is the determination of the nation of origin. This is generally easily accomplished where English-speaking lands are concerned, however, use of the country index is sometimes required. The coins of Great Britain provide an interesting challenge. For hundreds of years the only indication of the country of origin was in the abbreviated Latin legends. In recent times there have been occasions when there has been no indication of origin. Only through the familiarity of the monarchical portraits, symbols and legends or indication of currency system are they identifiable.

The coins of many countries beyond the English-language realm, such as those of French, Italian or Spanish heritage, are also quite easy to identify through reference to their legends, which appear in the national languages based on Western alphabets. In many instances the name is spelled exactly the same in English as in the national language, such as France; while in other cases it varies only slightly, like Italia for Italy, Belgique or Belgie for Belgium, Brasil for Brazil and Danmark for Denmark.

This is not always the case, however, as in Norge for Norway, Espana for Spain, Sverige for Sweden and Helvetia for Switzerland. Some other examples include:

DEUTSCHES REICH - Germany 1873-1945
BUNDESREPUBLIC DEUTSCHLAND -
Federal Republic of Germany.
DEUTSCHE DEMOKRATISCHE REPUBLIK -
German Democratic Republic.
EMPIRE CHERIFIEN MAROC - Morocco.
ESTADOS UNIDOS MEXICANOS -
United Mexican States (Mexico).
ETAT DU GRAND LIBAN -
State of Great Lebanon (Lebanon).

Thus it can be seen there are instances in which a little schooling in the rudiments of foreign languages can be most helpful. In general, colonial possessions of countries using the Western alphabet are similarly identifiable as they often carry portraits of their current rulers, the familiar lettering, sometimes in combination with a companion designation in the local language.

Collectors have the greatest difficulty with coins that do not bear legends or dates in the Western systems. These include coins bearing Cyrillic lettering, attributable to Bulgaria, Russia, the Slavic states and Mongolia, the Greek script peculiar to Greece, Crete and the Ionian Islands; The Amharic characters of Ethiopia, or Hebrew in the case of Israel. Dragons and sunbursts along with the distinctive word characters attribute a coin to the Oriental countries of China, Japan, Korea, Tibet, Viet Nam and their component parts.

The most difficult coins to identify are those bearing only Persian or Arabic script and its derivatives, found on the issues of nations stretching in a wide swath across North Africa and East Asia, from Morocco to Indonesia, and the Indian subcontinent coinages which surely are more confusing in their vast array of Nagari, Sanskrit, Ahom, Assamese and other local dialects found on the local issues of the Indian Princely States. Although the task of identification on the more modern issues of these lands is often eased by the added presence of Western alphabet legends, a feature sometimes adopted as early as the late 19th Century, for the earlier pieces it is often necessary for the uninitiated to laboriously seek and find.

Except for the cruder issues, however, it will be found that certain characteristics and symbols featured in addition to the predominant legends are typical on coins from a given country or group of countries. The toughra monogram, for instance, occurs on some of the coins of Afghanistan, Egypt, the Sudan, Pakistan, Turkey and other areas of the late Ottoman Empire. A predominant design feature on the coins of Nepal is the trident; while neighboring Tibet features a lotus blossom or lion on many of their issues.

To assist in identification of the more difficult coins, we have assembled the Instant Identifier section presented on the following pages designed to provide a point of beginning for collectors by allowing them to compare unidentified coins with photographic details from typical issues.

We also suggest reference to the comprehensive Country Index.

DATING

Coin dating is the final basic attribution consideration. Here, the problem can be more difficult because the reading of a coin date is subject not only to the vagaries of numeric styling, but to calendar variations caused by the observance of various religious eras or regal periods from country to country, or even within a country. Here again with the exception of the sphere from North Africa through the Orient, it will be found that most countries rely on Western date numerals and Christian (AD) era reckoning, although in a few instances, coin dating has been tied to the year of a reign or government. The Vatican, for example dates its coinage according to the year of reign of the current pope, in addition to the Christian-era date.

Countries in the Arabic sphere generally date their coins to the Muslim era (AH), which commenced on July 16, 622 AD (Julian calendar), when the prophet Mohammed fled from Mecca

to Medina. As their calendar is reckoned by the lunar year of 354 days, which is about three percent (precisely 2.98%) shorter than the Christian year, a formula is required to convert AH dating to its Western equivalent. To convert an AH date to the approximate AD date, subtract three percent of the AH date (round to the closest whole number) from the AH date and add 622. A chart converting all AH years from 1010 (July 2, 1601) to 1421 (May 25, 2028) is presented as the Heijra Chart elsewhere in this volume.

The Muslim calendar is not always based on the lunar year (AH), however, causing some confusion, particularly in Afghanistan and Iran, where a calendar based on the solar year (SH) was introduced around 1920. These dates can be converted to AD by simply adding 621. In 1976 the government of Iran implemented a new solar calendar based on the foundation of the Iranian monarchy in 559 BC. The first year observed on the new calendar was 2535 (MS), which commenced March 20, 1976. A reversion to the traditional SH dating standard occurred a few years later.

Several different eras of reckoning, including Christian and Muslim (AH), have been used to date coins of the Indian subcontinent. The two basic systems are the Vikrama Samvat (VS), which dates from Oct. 18, 58 BC, and the Saka era, the origin of which is reckoned from March 3, 78 AD. Dating according to both eras appears on various coins of the area.

Coins of Thailand (Siam) are found dated by three different eras. The most predominant is the Buddhist era (BE), which originated in 543 BC. Next is the Bangkok or Ratanakosindsok (RS) era, dating from 1781 AD; followed by the Chula- Sakarat (CS) era, dating from 638 AD. The latter era originated in Burma and is used on that country's coins.

Other calendars include that of the Ethiopian era (EE), which commenced seven years, eight months after AD dating; and that of the Jewish people, which commenced on Oct. 7, 3761 BC. Korea claims a legendary dating from 2333 BC, which is acknowledged in some of its coin dating. Some coin issues of the Indonesian area carry dates determined by the Javanese Aji Saka era (AS), a calendar of 354 days (100 Javanese years equal 97 Christian or Gregorian calendar years), which can be matched to AD dating by comparing it to AH dating.

The following table indicates the year dating for the various eras, which correspond to 2003 in Christian calendar reckoning, but it must be remembered that there are overlaps between the eras in some instances.

Christian era (AD)	2007
Muslim era (AH)	AH1428
Solar year (SH)	SH1385
Monarchic Solar era (MS)	MS2566
Vikrama Samvat (VS)	VS2064
Saka era (SE)	SE1929
Buddhist era (BE)	BE2550
Bangkok era (RS)	RS226
Chula-Sakarat era (CS)	CS1369
Ethiopian era (EE)	EE2001
Korean era	4340
Javanese Aji Saka era (AS)	AS1940
Fasli era (FE)	FE1417
Jewish era (JE)	JE5767

Coins of Asian origin - principally Japan, Korea, China, Turkestan and Tibet and some modern gold issues of Turkey - are generally dated to the year of the government, dynasty, reign or cyclic eras, with the dates indicated in Asian characters which usually read from right to left. In recent years, however, some dating has been according to the Christian calendar and in Western numerals. In Japan, Asian character dating was reversed to read from left to right in Showa year 23 (1948 AD).

More detailed guides to less prevalent coin dating systems, which are strictly local in nature, are presented with the appropriate listings.

Some coins carry dates according to both locally observed and Christian eras. This is particularly true in the Arabic world, where the Hejira date may be indicated in Arabic numerals and the Christian date in Western numerals, or both dates in either form.

The date actually carried on a given coin is generally cataloged here in the first column (Date). Dates listed alone in the date column which do not actually appear on a given coin, or dates which are known, but do not appear on the coin, are generally enclosed by parentheses with 'ND' at the left, for example ND(1926).

Timing differentials between some era of reckoning, particularly the 354-day Mohammedan and 365-day Christian years, cause situations whereby coins which carry dates for both eras exist bearing two year dates from one calendar combined with a single date from another.

Countermarked Coinage is presented with both 'Countermark Date' and 'Host Coin' date for each type. Actual date representation follows the rules outlined above.

NUMBERING SYSTEM

Some catalog numbers assigned in this volume are based on established references. This practice has been observed for two reasons: First, when world coins are listed chronologically they are basically self-cataloging; second, there was no need to confuse collectors with totally new numeric designations where appropriate systems already existed. As time progressed we found many of these established systems incomplete and inadequate and have now replaced many with new KM numbers. When numbers change appropriate cross-referencing has been provided.

Some of the coins listed in this catalog are identified or cross-referenced by numbers assigned by R.S. Yeoman (Y#), or slight adaptations thereof, in his Modern World Coins, and Current Coins of the World. For the pre-Yeoman dated issues, the numbers assigned by William D. Craig (C#) in his Coins of the World (1750-1850 period), 3rd edition, have generally been applied.

In some countries, listings are cross-referenced to Robert Friedberg's (FR#) Gold Coins of the World or Coins of the British World. Major Fred Pridmore's (P#) studies of British colonial coinage are also referenced, as are W.H. Valentine's (V#) references on the Modern Copper Coins of the Muhammadan States. Coins issued under the Chinese sphere of influence are assigned numbers from E. Kann's (K#) Illustrated Catalog of Chinese Coins and T.K. Hsu's (Su) work of similar title. In most cases, these cross- reference numbers are presented in the descriptive text for each type.

DENOMINATIONS

The second basic consideration to be met in the attribution of a coin is the determination of denomination. Since denominations are usually expressed in numeric, rather than word form on a coin, this is usually quite easily accomplished on coins from nations, which use Western numerals, except in those instances where issues are devoid of any mention of face value, and denomination must be attributed by size, metallic composition or weight. Coins listed in this volume are generally illustrated in actual size. Where size is critical to proper attribution, the coin's millimeter size is indicated.

The sphere of countries stretching from North Africa through the Orient, on which numeric symbols generally unfamiliar to Westerners are employed, often provide the collector with a much greater challenge. This is particularly true on nearly all pre-20th Century issues. On some of the more modern issues and increasingly so as the years progress, Western-style numerals usually

presented in combination with the local numeric system are becoming more commonplace on these coins.

Determination of a coin's currency system can also be valuable in attributing the issue to its country of origin.

The included table of Standard International Numeral Systems presents charts of the basic numeric designations found on coins of non- Western origin. Although denomination numerals are generally prominently displayed on coins, it must be remembered that these are general representations of characters, which individual coin engravers may have rendered in widely varying styles. Where numeric or script denominations designation forms peculiar to a given coin or country apply, such as the script used on some Persian (Iranian) issues. They are so indicated or illustrated in conjunction with the appropriate listings.

MINTAGES

Quantities minted of each date are indicated where that information is available, generally stated in millions, and usually rounded off to the nearest 10,000 pieces. On quantities of a few thousand or less, actual mintages are generally indicated. For combined mintage figures the abbreviation "Inc. Above" means Included Above, while "Inc. Below" means Included Below. "Est." beside a mintage figure indicates the number given is an estimate or mintage limit.

MINT AND PRIVY MARKS

The presence of distinctive, but frequently inconspicuously placed, mintmarks indicates the mint of issue for many of the coins listed in this catalog. An appropriate designation in the date listings notes the presence, if any, of a mint mark on a particular coin type by incorporating the letter or letters of the mint mark adjoining the date, i.e., 1883CC or 1890H.

The presence of mint and/or mintmaster's privy marks on a coin in non-letter form is indicated by incorporating the mint letter in lower case within parentheses adjoining the date; i.e. 1827(a). The corresponding mark is illustrated or identified in the introduction of the country.

In countries such as France and Mexico, where many mints may be producing like coinage in the same denomination during the same time period, divisions by mint have been employed. In these cases the mint mark may appear next to the individual date listings and/or the mint name or mint mark may be listed in the Note field of the type description.

Where listings incorporate mintmaster initials, they are always presented in capital letters separated from the date by one character space; i.e., 1850 MF. The different mintmark and mintmaster letters found on the coins of any country, state or city of issue are always shown at the beginning of listings.

METALS

Each numbered type listing will contain a description of the coins metallic content. The traditional coinage metals and their symbolic chemical abbreviations sometimes used in this catalog are:

Platinum - (PT)	Copper - (Cu)
Gold - (Au)	Brass -
Silver - (Ag)	Copper-nickel- (CN)
Billion -	Lead - (Pb)
Nickel - (Ni)	Steel -
Zinc - (Zn)	Tin - (Sn)
Bronze - (Ae)	Aluminum - (Al)

During the 18th and 19th centuries, most of the world's coins were struck of copper or bronze, silver and gold. Commencing in the early years of the 20th century, however, numerous new coinage metals, primarily non-precious metal alloys, were introduced. Gold has not been widely used for circulation coinages since World War I, although silver remained a popular coinage metal in most parts of the world until after World War II. With the disappearance of silver for circulation coinage, numerous additional compositions were introduced to coinage applications.

OFF-METAL STRIKES

Off-metal strikes previously designated by "(OMS)" which also included the wide range of error coinage struck in other than their officially authorized compositions have been incorporated into Pattern listings along with special issues, which were struck for presentation or other reasons.

Collectors of Germanic coinage may be familiar with the term "Abschlag" which quickly identifies similar types of coinage.

PRECIOUS METAL WEIGHTS

Listings of weight, fineness and actual silver (ASW), gold (AGW), platinum or palladium (APW) content of most machine-struck silver, gold, platinum and palladium coins are provided in this edition. This information will be found incorporated in each separate type listing, along with other data related to the coin.

The ASW, AGW and APW figures were determined by multiplying the gross weight of a given coin by its known or tested fineness and converting the resulting gram or grain weight to troy ounces, rounded to the nearest ten-thousandth of an ounce. A silver coin with a 24.25-gram weight and .875 fineness for example, would have a fine weight of approximately 21.2188 grams, or a .6822 ASW, a factor that can be used to accurately determine the intrinsic value for multiple examples.

The ASW, AGW or APW figure can be multiplied by the spot price of each precious metal to determine the current intrinsic value of any coin accompanied by these designations.

Coin weights are indicated in grams (abbreviated "g") along with fineness where the information is of value in differentiating between types. These weights are based on 31.103 grams per troy (scientific) ounce, as opposed to the avoirdupois (commercial) standard of 28.35 grams. Actual coin weights are generally shown in hundredths or thousands of a gram; i.e., 2.9200 g., SILVER, 0.500 oz.

WEIGHTS AND FINENESSES

As the silver and gold bullion markets have advanced and declined sharply in recent years, the fineness and total precious metal content of coins has become especially significant where bullion coins - issues which trade on the basis of their intrinsic metallic content rather than numismatic value - are concerned. In many instances, such issues have become worth more in bullion form than their nominal collector values or denominations indicate.

Establishing the weight of a coin can also be valuable for determining its denomination. Actual weight is also necessary to ascertain the specific gravity of the coin's metallic content, an important factor in determining authenticity.

TROY WEIGHT STANDARDS

24 Grains = 1 Pennyweight
480 Grains = 1 Ounce
31.103 Grams = 1 Ounce

UNIFORM WEIGHTS

15.432 Grains = 1 Gram
0.0648 Gram = 1 Grain

AVOIRDUPOIS STANDARDS

27-11/32 Grains = 11 Dram
437-1/2 Grains = 1 Ounce
28.350 Grams = 1 Ounce

FOREIGN EXCHANGE TABLE

The latest foreign exchange rates below apply to trade with banks in the country of origin. The left column shows the number of units per U.S. dollar at the official rate. The right column shows the number of units per dollar at the free market rate.

Country	Official #/$	Market #/$
Afghanistan (New Afghani)	49.6	–
Albania (Lek)	93	–
Algeria (Dinar)	69	–
Andorra uses Euro	.757	–
Angola (Readjust Kwanza)	80	–
Anguilla uses E.C. Dollar	2.7	–
Antigua uses E.C. Dollar	2.7	–
Argentina (Peso)	3.06	–
Armenia (Dram)	365	–
Aruba (Florin)	1.79	–
Australia (Dollar)	1.273	–
Austria (Euro)	.757	–
Azerbaijan (Manat)	4,600	–
Bahamas (Dollar)	1.0	–
Bahrain Is. (Dinar)	.377	–
Bangladesh (Taka)	70	–
Barbados (Dollar)	2.0	–
Belarus (Ruble)	2,140	–
Belgium (Euro)	.757	–
Belize (Dollar)	1.97	–
Benin uses CFA Franc West	490	–
Bermuda (Dollar)	1.0	–
Bhutan (Ngultrum)	45	–
Bolivia (Boliviano)	7.99	–
Bosnia-Herzegovina (Conv. marka)	1.47	–
Botswana (Pula)	6.05	–
British Virgin Islands uses U.S. Dollar	1.00	–
Brazil (Real)	2.14	–
Brunei (Dollar)	1.54	–
Bulgaria (Lev)	1.47	–
Burkina Faso uses CFA Fr.West	490	–
Burma (Kyat)	6.42	1,250
Burundi (Franc)	1,040	–
Cambodia (Riel)	4,050	–
Cameroon uses CFA Franc Central	490	–
Canada (Dollar)	1.149	–
Cape Verde (Escudo)	83.1	–
Cayman Is.(Dollar)	0.82	–
Central African Rep.	490	–
CFA Franc Central	490	–
CFA Franc West	490	–
CFP Franc	90	–
Chad uses CFA Franc Central	490	–
Chile (Peso)	525	–
China, P.R. (Renminbi Yuan)	7.825	–
Colombia (Peso)	2,280	–
Comoros (Franc)	370	–
Congo uses CFA Franc Central	490	–
Congo-Dem.Rep. (Congolese Franc)	490	–
Cook Islands (Dollar)	1.73	–
Costa Rica (Colon)	517	–
Croatia (Kuna)	5.74	–
Cuba (Peso)	1.00	27.00
Cyprus (Pound)	.43	–
Czech Republic (Koruna)	21.1	–
Denmark (Danish Krone)	5.65	–
Djibouti (Franc)	178	–
Dominica uses E.C. Dollar	2.7	–
Dominican Republic (Peso)	32.8	–
East Caribbean (Dollar)	2.7	–
Ecuador uses U.S. Dollar		
Egypt (Pound)	5.72	–
El Salvador (U.S. Dollar)	1.00	–
England (Sterling Pound)	.512	–
Equatorial Guinea uses CFA Franc Central	490	–
Eritrea (Nafka)	15	–
Estonia (Kroon)	11.9	–
Ethiopia (Birr)	8.75	–
Euro	.757	–
Falkland Is. (Pound)	.512	–
Faroe Islands (Krona)	5.65	–
Fiji Islands (Dollar)	1.67	–
Finland (Euro)	.757	–
France (Euro)	.757	–
French Polynesia uses CFP Franc	90	–
Gabon (CFA Franc)	490	–
Gambia (Dalasi)	28	–
Georgia (Lari)	1.73	–
Germany (Euro)	.757	–
Ghana (Cedi)	9,200	–
Gibraltar (Pound)	.512	–
Greece (Euro)	.757	–
Greenland uses Danish Krone	5.65	–
Grenada uses E.C. Dollar	2.7	–
Guatemala (Quetzal)	7.63	–
Guernsey uses Sterling Pound	.512	–
Guinea Bissau (CFA Franc)	490	–
Guinea Conakry (Franc)	5,550	–
Guyana (Dollar)	200	–
Haiti (Gourde)	38.9	–
Honduras (Lempira)	18.9	–
Hong Kong (Dollar)	7.773	–
Hungary (Forint)	195	–
Iceland (Krona)	69.5	–
India (Rupee)	44.7	–
Indonesia (Rupiah)	9,075	–
Iran (Rial)	9,230	–
Iraq (Dinar)	1,425	–
Ireland (Euro)	.757	–
Isle of Man uses Sterling Pound	.512	–
Israel (New Sheqalim)	4.19	–
Italy (Euro)	.757	–
Ivory Coast uses CFA Franc West	490	–
Jamaica (Dollar)	67	–
Japan (Yen)	116.3	–
Jersey uses Sterling Pound	.512	–
Jordan (Dinar)	.71	–
Kazakhstan (Tenge)	130	–
Kenya (Shilling)	70	–
Kiribati uses Australian Dollar	1.273	–
Korea-PDR (Won)	2.2	500
Korea-Rep. (Won)	920	–
Kuwait (Dinar)	.289	–
Kyrgyzstan (Som)	39	–
Laos (Kip)	9720	–
Latvia (Lats)	.53	–
Lebanon (Pound)	1,510	–
Lesotho (Maloti)	7.09	–
Liberia (Dollar)	53.3	–
Libya (Dinar)	1.27	–
Liechtenstein uses Swiss Franc	1.205	–
Lithuania (Litas)	2.62	–
Luxembourg (Euro)	.757	–
Macao (Pataca)	8.0	–
Macedonia (New Denar)	46	–
Madagascar (Franc)	2,040	–
Malawi (Kwacha)	140	–
Malaysia (Ringgit)	3.55	–
Maldives (Rufiya)	12.8	–
Mali uses CFA Franc West	490	–
Malta (Lira)	3.1	–
Marshall Islands uses U.S.Dollar		
Mauritania (Ouguiya)	270	–
Mauritius (Rupee)	32.5	–
Mexico (Peso)	10.82	–
Moldova (Leu)	13.1	–
Monaco uses Euro	.757	–
Mongolia (Tugrik)	1,165	–
Montenegro uses Euro	.757	–
Montserrat uses E.C. Dollar	2.7	–
Morocco (Dirham)	8.44	–
Mozambique (New Metical)	26.3	–
Myanmar (Burma) (Kyat)	6.42	1,250
Namibia (Rand)	7.09	–
Nauru uses Australian Dollar	1.456	–
Nepal (Rupee)	71.6	–
Netherlands (Euro)	.757	–
Netherlands Antilles (Gulden)	1.79	–
New Caledonia uses CFP Franc	90	–
New Zealand (Dollar)	1.493	–
Nicaragua (Cordoba Oro)	17.9	–
Niger uses CFA Franc West	490	–
Nigeria (Naira)	128	–
Northern Ireland uses Sterling Pound	.512	–
Norway (Krone)	6.16	–
Oman (Rial)	.385	–
Pakistan (Rupee)	60.9	–
Palau uses U.S.Dollar		
Panama (Balboa) uses U.S.Dollar		
Papua New Guinea (Kina)	3.02	–
Paraguay (Guarani)	5,400	–
Peru (Nuevo Sol)	3.21	–
Philippines (Peso)	50	–
Poland (Zloty)	2.9	–
Portugal (Euro)	.757	–
Qatar (Riyal)	3.64	–
Romania (New Leu)	2.6	–
Russia (New Ruble)	26.3	–
Rwanda (Franc)	550	–
St. Helena (Pound)	.512	–
St. Kitts uses E.C. Dollar	2.7	–
St. Lucia uses E.C. Dollar	2.7	–
St. Vincent uses E.C. Dollar	2.7	–
San Marino uses Euro	.757	–
Sao Tome e Principe (Dobra)	6,780	–
Saudi Arabia (Riyal)	3.75	–
Scotland uses Sterling Pound	.512	–
Senegal uses CFA Franc West	490	–
Serbia (Dinar)	59.9	–
Seychelles (Rupee)	5.59	6.40
Sierra Leone (Leone)	2,990	–
Singapore (Dollar)	1.55	–
Slovakia (Sk. Koruna)	26.8	–
Slovenia (Tolar)	180	–
Solomon Is.(Dollar)	7.63	–
Somalia (Shilling)	1,370	–
Somaliland (Somali Shilling)	1,800	4,000
South Africa (Rand)	7.09	–
Spain (Euro)	.757	–
Sri Lanka (Rupee)	110	–
Sudan (Dinar)	200	300
Surinam (Dollar)	2.75	–
Swaziland (Lilangeni)	7.09	–
Sweden (Krona)	6.87	–
Switzerland (Franc)	1.205	–
Syria (Pound)	52.2	–
Taiwan (NT Dollar)	32.4	–
Tajikistan (Somoni)	3.40	–
Tanzania (Shilling)	1,280	–
Thailand (Baht)	35.5	–
Togo uses CFA Franc West	490	–
Tonga (Pa'anga)	1.99	–
Transdniestra (Ruble)	6.51	–
Trinidad & Tobago (Dollar)	6.28	–
Tunisia (Dinar)	1.3	–
Turkey (New Lira)	1.43	–
Turkmenistan (Manat)	5,200	–
Turks & Caicos uses U.S. Dollar		
Tuvalu uses Australian Dollar	1.273	–
Uganda (Shilling)	1,800	–
Ukraine (Hryvnia)	5.03	–
United Arab Emirates (Dirham)	3.673	–
Uruguay (Peso Uruguayo)	24.3	–
Uzbekistan (Sum)	1,235	–
Vanuatu (Vatu)	106	–
Vatican City uses Euro	.757	–
Venezuela (Bolivar)	2,150	2,300
Vietnam (Dong)	16,050	–
Western Samoa (Tala)	2.66	–
Yemen (Rial)	198	–
Zambia (Kwacha)	4,050	–
Zimbabwe (revalued Dollar)	250	–

HOMELAND TYPES

Homeland types are coins which colonial powers used in a colony, but do not bear that location's name. In some cases they were legal tender in the homeland, in others not. They are listed under the homeland and cross-referenced at the colony listing.

COUNTERMARKS/COUNTERSTAMPS

There is some confusion among collectors over the terms "countermark" and "counterstamp" when applied to a coin bearing an additional mark or change of design and/or denomination.

To clarify, a countermark might be considered similar to the "hall mark" applied to a piece of silverware, by which a silversmith assured the quality of the piece. In the same way, a countermark assures the quality of the coin on which it is placed, as, for example, when the royal crown of England was countermarked (punched into) on segmented Spanish reales, allowing them to circulate in commerce in the British West Indies. An additional countermark indicating the new denomination may also be encountered on these coins.

Countermarks are generally applied singularly and in most cases indiscriminately on either side of the "host" coin.

Counterstamped coins are more extensively altered. The counterstamping is done with a set of dies, rather than a hand punch. The coin being counterstamped is placed between the new dies and struck as if it were a blank planchet as found with the Manila 8 reales issue of the Philippines.

PHOTOGRAPHS

To assist the reader in coin identification, every effort has been made to present actual size photographs of every coinage type listed. Obverse and reverse are illustrated, except when a change in design is restricted to one side, and the coin has a diameter of 39mm or larger, in which case only the side required for identification of the type is generally illustrated. All coins up to 60mm are illustrated actual size, to the nearest 1/2mm up to 25mm, and to the nearest 1mm thereafter. Coins larger than 60mm diameter are illustrated in reduced size, with the actual size noted in the descriptive text block. Where slight change in size is important to coin type identification, actual millimeter measurements are stated.

TRADE COINS

From approximately 1750-1940, a number of nations, particularly European colonial powers and commercial traders, minted trade coins to facilitate commerce with the local populace of Africa, the Arab countries, the Indian subcontinental, Southeast Asia and the Far East. Such coins generally circulated at a value based on the weight and fineness of their silver or gold content, rather than their stated denomination. Examples include the sovereigns of Great Britain and the gold ducat issues of Austria, Hungary and the Netherlands. Trade coinage will sometimes be found listed at the end of the domestic issues.

VALUATIONS

Values quoted in this catalog represent the current market and are compiled from recommendations provided and verified through various source documents and specialized consultants. It should be stressed, however, that this book is intended to serve only as an aid for evaluating coins, actual market conditions are constantly changing and additional influences, such as particularly strong local demand for certain coin series, fluctuation of international exchange rates and worldwide collection pat-

COIN ALIGNMENT

MEDAL ALIGNMENT

COIN VS MEDAL ALIGNMENT

Some coins are struck with obverse and reverse aligned at a rotation of 180 degrees from each other. When a coin is held for vertical viewing with the obverse design aligned upright and the index finger and thumb at the top and bottom, upon rotation from left to right for viewing the reverse, the latter will be upside down. Such alignment is called "coin rotation." Other coins are struck with the obverse and reverse designs mated on an alignment of zero or 360 degrees. If such an example is held and rotated as described, the reverse will appear upright. This is the alignment, which is generally observed in the striking of medals, and for that reason coins produced in this manner are considered struck in "medal rotation". In some instances, often through error, certain coin issues have been struck to both alignment standards, creating interesting collectible varieties, which will be found noted in some listings. In addition, some countries are now producing coins with other designated overse to reverse alignments which are considered standard for this type.

terns must also be considered. Publication of this catalog is not intended as a solicitation by the publisher, editors or contributors to buy or sell the coins listed at the prices indicated.

All valuations are stated in U.S. dollars, based on careful assessment of the varied international collector market. Valuations for coins priced below $100.00 are generally stated in full amounts - i.e. 37.50 or 95.00 - while valuations at or above that figure are rounded off in even dollars - i.e. $125.00 is expressed 125. A comma is added to indicate thousands of dollars in value.

It should be noted that when particularly select uncirculated or proof-like examples of uncirculated coins become available they can be expected to command proportionately high premiums. Such examples in reference to choice Germanic Thalers are referred to as "erst schlage" or first strikes.

TOKEN COINAGE

At times local economic conditions have forced regular coinage from circulation or found mints unable to cope with the demand for coinage, giving rise to privately issued token coinage substitutes. British tokens of the late 1700s and early 1880s, and the German and French and French Colonial emergency emissions of the World War I era are examples of such tokens being freely accepted in monetary transactions over wide areas. Tokens were likewise introduced to satisfy specific restricted needs, such as the leper colony issues of Brazil, Colombia and the Philippines.

This catalog includes introductory or detailed listings with "Tn" prefixes of many token coinage issues, particularly those which enjoyed wide circulation and where the series was limited in diversity. More complex series, and those more restricted in scope of circulation are generally not listed, although a representative sample may be illustrated and a specialty reference provided.

MEDALLIC ISSUES

All medallic issues can be found in the current edition of Unusual World Coins.

RESTRIKES, COUNTERFEITS

Deceptive restrike and counterfeit (both contemporary and modern) examples exist of some coin issues. Where possible, the existence of restrikes is noted. Warnings are also incorporated in instances where particularly deceptive counterfeits are known to exist. Collectors who are uncertain about the authenticity of a coin held in their collection, or being offered for sale, should take the precaution of having it authenticated by the American Numismatic Association Authentication Bureau, 818 N. Cascade, Colorado Springs, CO 80903. Their reasonably priced certification tests are widely accepted by collectors and dealers alike.

EDGE VARIETIES

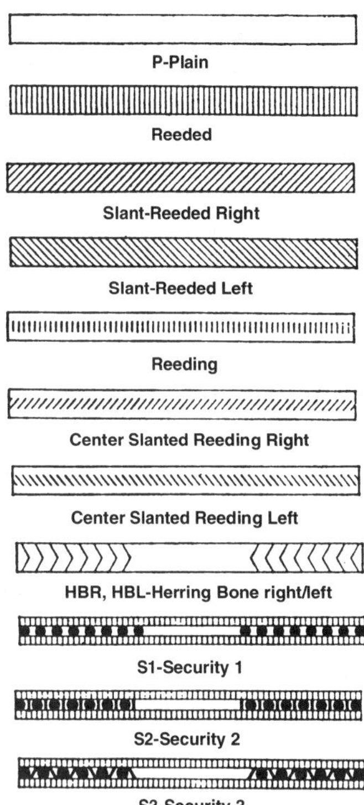

SETS

Listings in this catalog for specimen, proof and mint sets are for official, government-produced sets. In many instances privately packaged sets also exist.

Mint Sets/Fleur de Coin Sets: Specially prepared by worldwide mints to provide banks, collectors and government dignitaries with examples of current coinage. Usually subjected to rigorous inspection to insure that top quality specimens of selected business strikes are provided. One of the most popular mint set is that given out by the monarch of Great Britain each year on Maunday Thursday. This set contains four special coins in denominations of 1, 2, 3 and 4 pence, struck in silver and contained in a little pouch. They have been given away in a special ceremony for the poor for more than two centuries.

Specimen Sets: Forerunners of today's proof sets. In most cases the coins were specially struck, perhaps even double struck, to produce a very soft or matte finish on the effigies and fields, along with high, sharp, "wire" rims. The finish is rather dull to the naked eye.

The original purpose of these sets was to provide VIPs, monarchs and mintmasters around the world with samples of the highest quality workmanship of a particular mint. These were usually housed in elaborate velvet-lined leather and metal cases.

Proof Sets: This is undoubtedly among the most misused terms in the hobby, not only by collectors and dealers, but also by many of the world mints.

A true proof set must be at least double-struck on specially prepared polished planchets and struck using dies (often themselves polished) of the highest quality.

Listings for proof sets in this catalog are for officially issued proof sets so designated by the issuing authority, and may or may not possess what are considered modern proof quality standards.

It is necessary for collectors to acquire the knowledge to allow them to differentiate true proof sets from would-be proof sets and proof- like sets which may be encountered.

CONDITIONS/GRADING

Wherever possible, coin valuations are given in four or five grades of preservation. For modern commemoratives, which do not circulate, only uncirculated values are usually sufficient. Proof issues are indicated by the word "Proof" next to the date, with valuation proceeded by the word "value" following the mintage. For very recent circulating coins and coins of limited value, one, two or three grade values are presented.

There are almost no grading guides for world coins. What follows is an attempt to help bridge that gap until a detailed, illustrated guide becomes available.

In grading world coins, there are two elements to look for: 1) Overall wear, and 2) loss of design details, such as strands of hair, feathers on eagles, designs on coats of arms, etc.

The age, rarity or type of a coin should not be a consideration in grading.

Grade each coin by the weaker of the two sides. This method appears to give results most nearly consistent with conservative American Numismatic Association standards for U.S. coins. Split grades, i.e., F/VF for obverse and reverse, respectively, are normally no more than one grade apart. If the two sides are more than one grade apart, the series of coins probably wears differently on each side and should then be graded by the weaker side alone.

Grade by the amount of overall wear and loss of design detail evident on each side of the coin. On coins with a moderately small design element, which is prone to early wear, grade by that design alone. For example, the 5-ore (KM#554) of Sweden has a crown above the monogram on which the beads on the arches show wear most clearly. So, grade by the crown alone.

For Brilliant Uncirculated (BU) grades there will be no visible signs of wear or handling, even under a 30-power microscope. Full mint luster will be present. Ideally no bags marks will be evident.

For Uncirculated (Unc.) grades there will be no visible signs of wear or handling, even under a 30-power microscope. Bag marks may be present.

For Almost Uncirculated (AU), all detail will be visible. There will be wear only on the highest point of the coin. There will often be half or more of the original mint luster present.

On the Extremely Fine (XF or EF) coin, there will be about 95% of the original detail visible. Or, on a coin with a design with no inner detail to wear down, there will be a light wear over nearly all the coin. If a small design is used as the grading area, about 90% of the original detail will be visible. This latter rule stems from the logic that a smaller amount of detail needs to be present because a small area is being used to grade the whole coin.

The Very Fine (VF) coin will have about 75% of the original detail visible. Or, on a coin with no inner detail, there will be moderate wear over the entire coin. Corners of letters and numbers may be weak. A small grading area will have about 66% of the original detail.

For Fine (F), there will be about 50% of the original detail visible. Or, on a coin with no inner detail, there will be fairly heavy wear over all of the coin. Sides of letters will be weak. A typically uncleaned coin will often appear as dirty or dull. A small grading area will have just under 50% of the original detail.

On the Very Good (VG) coin, there will be about 25% of the original detail visible. There will be heavy wear on all of the coin.

The Good (G) coin's design will be clearly outlined but with substantial wear. Some of the larger detail may be visible. The rim may have a few weak spots of wear.

On the About Good (AG) coin, there will typically be only a silhouette of a large design. The rim will be worn down into the letters if any.

Strong or weak strikes, partially weak strikes, damage, corrosion, attractive or unattractive toning, dipping or cleaning should be described along with the above grades. These factors affect the quality of the coin just as do wear and loss of detail, but are easier to describe.

In the case of countermarked/counterstamped coins, the condition of the host coin will have a bearing on the end valuation. The important factor in determining the grade is the condition, clarity and completeness of the countermark itself. This is in reference to countermarks/counterstamps having raised design while being struck in a depression.

Incuse countermarks cannot be graded for wear. They are graded by the clarity and completeness including the condition of the host coin which will also have more bearing on the final grade/valuation determined.

STANDARD INTERNATIONAL GRADING TERMINOLOGY AND ABBREVIATIONS

	PROOF	UNCIRCULATED	EXTREMELY FINE	VERY FINE	FINE	VERY GOOD	GOOD	POOR
U.S. and ENGLISH SPEAKING LANDS	PRF	UNC	EF or XF	VF	F	VG	G	PR
BRAZIL	—	(1)FDC or FC	(3) S	(5) MBC	(7) BC	(8) BC/R	(9) R	UT GeG
DENMARK	M	0	01	1+	1	1÷	2	3
FINLAND	00	0	01	1+	1	1?	2	3
FRANCE	FB Flan Bruni	FDC Fleur de Coin	SUP Superbe	TTB Très très beau	TB Très beau	B Beau	TBC Très Bien Conservée	BC Bien Conservée
GERMANY	PP Polierte Platte	STG Stempelglanz	VZ Vorzüglich	SS Sehr schön	S Schön	S.G.E. Sehr gut erhalten	G.E. Gut erhalten	Gering erhalten
ITALY	FS Fondo Specchio	FDC Fior di Conio	SPL Splendido	BB Bellissimo	MB Molto Bello	B Bello	M	—
JAPAN	—	未使用	極美品	美品	並品	—	—	—
NETHERLANDS	— Proef	FDC Fleur de Coin	Pr. Prachtig	Z.f. Zeer fraai	Fr. Fraai	Z.g. Zeer goed	G	—
NORWAY	M	0	01	1+	1	1÷	2	3
PORTUGAL	—	Soberba	Bela	MBC	BC	MREG	REG	MC
SPAIN	Prueba	SC	EBC	MBC	BC+	BC	RC	MC
SWEDEN	Polerad	0	01	1+	1	1?	2	—

GERMAN STATES INSTANT IDENTIFIER

Aachen

Anhalt
(Joint Coinage)

Anhalt-Bernberg

Arenberg

Augsburg

Augsburg

Baden

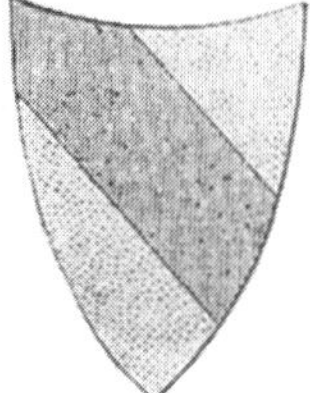
Baden

Bamberg

Bamberg

Bavaria

Bentheim

Berlin

Biberach

Brandenburg
Old City

Brandenburg
New City

Brandenburg
Ansbach

Bremen

Bretzenheim

Brunswick

Brunswick-
Luneburg

Brunswick-
Wolfenbuttel

Chur Pfalz

Cologne

Constance

Dessau

Dortmund

Eichstadt

Emden

Erfurt
Mainz

Erfurt

Essen

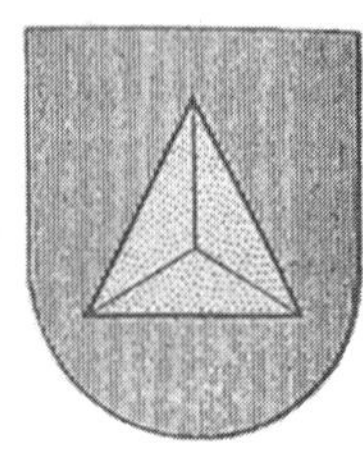
Frankenthal

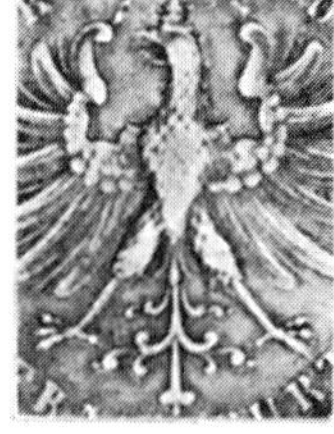
Frankfurt am Main

Frankfurt am Main

Frankfurt
am Oder

Friedberg

Fugger

Fulda

Fulda

Furstenberg

Furth

GERMAN STATES INSTANT IDENTIFIER

German Empire

German New Guinea

Glogau

Gorlitz

Goslar

Gottingen

Greifswald

Hagenau

Hall in Swabia

Hall in Swabia

Hamburg

Hamburg

Hamm

Hanau

Hanau-Munzenberg

Hannover

Hannover

Hannover

Heilbronn

Herford

Hersfeld

Hesse-Cassel

Hesse-Cassel

Hesse-Darmstadt

Hesse-Homburg

Hildesheim

Hildesheim

Hohenlohe-Neuenstein-Oehringen

Hohenzollern

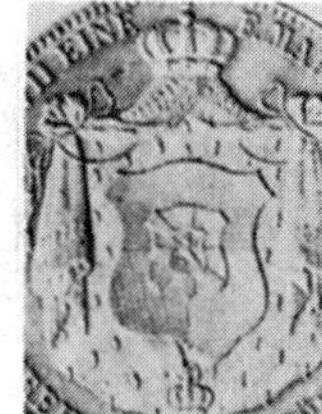
Hohenzollern-Hechingen

Jever

Julich-Berg

Kaufbeuren

Kempten

Landau

Liegnitz

Lindau

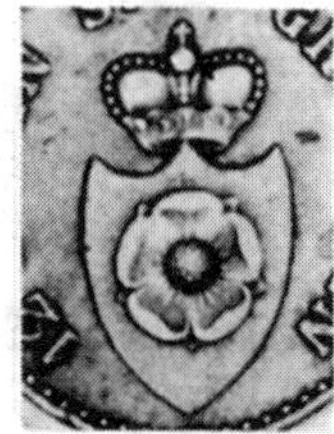
Lippe-Detmold

Lowenstein-Wertheim

Lubeck

Lubeck

Luneburg

GERMAN STATES INSTANT IDENTIFIER

Magdeburg

Mainz

Mainz

Mecklenburg-Strelitz

Memmingen

Muhlhausen

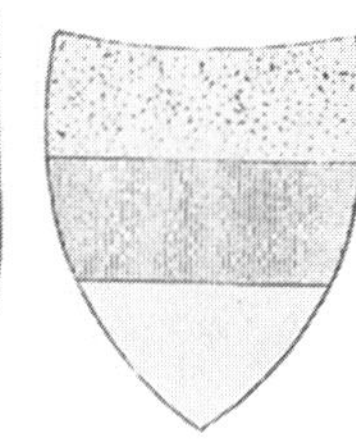
Munster

Munsterberg

Nassau

Nordhausen

Nurnberg

Oldenburg

Oldenburg

Oldenburg

Osnabruck

Paderborn

Paderborn

Passau

Passau

Prussia

Quedlinburg

Regensburg

Reuss-Greiz

Rhenish Confederation

Rostock

Rostock

Rothenburg

Rottweil

Saint Alban

Saxe-Altenburg

Saxe-Coburg-Gotha

Saxe-Meiningen

Saxe-Saalfield

Saxe-Weimar

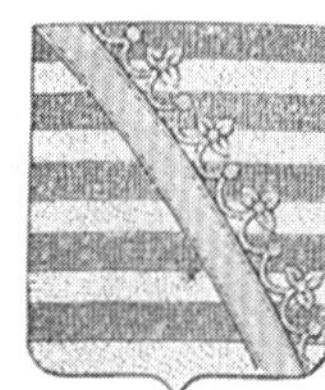
Saxony

Saxony

Schaumburg-Lippe

Schmalkalden

Schwarzburg

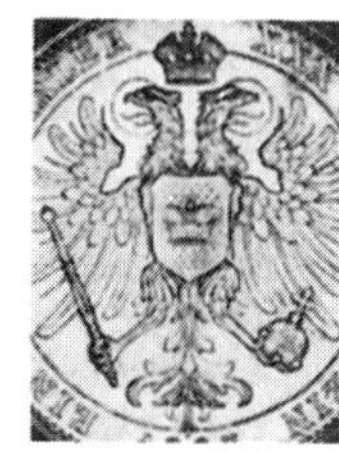
Schwarzburg-Rudolstadt

Schwarzburg-Sondershausen

Schwarzenberg

GERMAN STATES INSTANT IDENTIFIER

Solms-Laubach

Speyer

Stade

Stolberg-Stolberg

Stralsund

Teutonic Order

Trier

Waldeck-Pyrmont

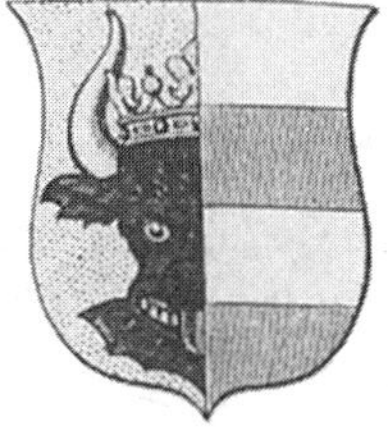
Wismar

Wismar

Worms

Wurttemberg

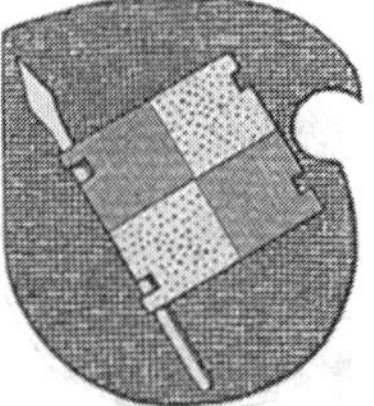
Wurzburg

Wurzburg

ILLUSTRATED GUIDE TO EASTERN MINT NAMES

Compiled by Dr. N. Douglas Nicol, 2006

Abarquh (Iran)	ابرقوه
'Abdullahnagar (Pihani)	عبدالله نگر
Abivard	ابي ورد ابيورد باورد
Abu Arish (the Yemen)	ابو عريش
Abushahr (Bushire - Iran)	ابو سهر
'Adan (Aden-the Yemen)	عدن
Adoni (Imtiyazgarh-Mughal)	ادوني
Adrana (see Edirne)	
Advani (Adoni - Mughal)	ادواني
Afghanistan	افغانستان
Agra (Mughal)	اگره
Ahmadabad (Gujarat Sultanate, Mughal, Maratha, Bombay Presidency, Baroda)	احمداباد
Ahmadnagar (Ahmadnagar Sultanate, Mughal)	احمدنگر
Ahmadnagar Farrukhabad (state, Afghanistan)	احمدنگر فرخ اباد
Ahmadpur (Bahawalpur, Afghanistan)	احمدپور
Ahmadshahi (Qandahar-Afghanistan)	احمدشاهي
Ahsanabad (Kulbarga - Mughal)	احسن اباد
Ajman (United Arab Emirates)	عجمان
Ajmer (Salimabad - Mughal, Maratha, Gwalior, Jodhpur)	اجمير
Ajmer Salimabad (Mughal)	اجمير سليم اباد
Akalpurakh (Kashmir, Sikh)	اكال پورخ
Akbarabad (Agra - Mughal, Maratha, Bharatpur)	اكبراباد
Akbarnagar (Rajmahal - Mughal)	اكبرنگر
Akbarpur (Tanda - Mughal)	اكبرپور
Akbarpur Tanda (Mughal)	اكبرپور تانده
Akhshi, Akhshikath (Central Asia)	اخشي اخشيكاث
Akhtarnagar (Awadh - Mughal)	اخترنگر
'Akka (Ottoman Turkey)	عكّا عكّة
Aksu (China - Sinkiang)	اقسو اقصو
al-Aliya	العالية
'Alamgirnagar (Mughal, Koch Bihar)	عالمگيرنگر
'Alamgirpur (Bhilsa, Vidisha-Mughal, Gwalior)	عالم گيرپور
Amul (Iran)	آمل
al-'Arabiya as-Sa'udiya (Saudi Arabia)	العربية السعودية
al-'Ara'ish (Larache - Morocco)	العرائش
Algeria (al-Jaza'ir)	الجزائر
'Alinagar (Calcutta - Mughal)	علي نگر
'Alinagar Kalkatah (Calcutta - Bengal Pres.)	علي نگر كلكته
Allahabad (Mughal, Awadh)	الله اباد
Almora (Gurkha)	
Alwar (Mughal)	الوار
Amaravati (Hyderabad)	امراوتي
Amasya (Amasia - Turkey)	اماسية
Amid (Turkey)	آمد
Amritsar (Ambratsar - Sikh)	امبرت سر امرت سر
Amirkot (Umarkot - Mughal)	اميركوت
Anandgharh (Anandpur - Mughal)	انندگهره
Andijan (Andigan - Central Asia)	اندجان اندگان
Anhirwala Pattan (Mughal)	انحيروالا پتن
Ankaland (Bi-Ankaland - in England, Birmingham and London mints for Morocco)	انكلند بانكلند
Ankara (Anguriya, Engüriye - Turkey)	انگورية انقرية انقرة
Anupnagar Shahabad (Mughal)	انوپنگر شاه باد
Anwala (Anola - Mughal, Rohilkhand, Afghanistan)	انوله
Aqsara (Aqsaray, Aksara - the Yemen)	اقصرا اقصراي اكصرا
Ardabil (Iran)	اردبيل
Ardanuç (Turkey)	اردنوچ اردانيچ
Ardanush (Iran)	اردنوش
Arjish (Iran)	ارجيش
Arkat (Arcot - Mughal, French India, Madras Presidency)	اركات
Asafabad (Bareli - Mughal, Awadh)	اصف اباد
Asafabad Bareli (Mughal, Awadh)	اصفاباد
Asafnagar (Aklooj - Mughal, Rohilkhand, Awadh)	اصف نگر اصفنگر
Asfarayin (Central Asia, Iran)	اسفراين
Asfi (Safi - Morocco)	اسفي
Asir (Asirgarh - Mughal)	اسير
Astarabad (Central Asia, Iran)	استراباد
Atak (Attock - Mughal, Afghanistan)	اتك
Atak Banaras (Mughal)	اتك بنارس
Atcheh (Sultanate, Netherlands East Indies)	اچه
Athani (Maratha)	اثاني
Aurangabad (Khujista Bunyad - Mughal, Hyderabad)	اورنگ اباد
Aurangnagar (Mughal, Maratha)	اورنگ نگر
Ausa (Mughal)	اوسا
Awadh (Oudh, Khitta - Awadh state)	اوده
Awbah (Central Asia)	اوبه
Ayasluk (Ayasoluq, Ephesus - Turkey)	اياسلق اياثلق
Aydaj (Iran)	ايدج
Azak (Azow - Turkey)	آزاق آزق
A'zamnagar (Gokak - Mughal)	اعظم نگر
A'zamnagar Bankapur (Mughal)	اعظم نگر بنكاپور
A'zamnagar Gokak (Belgaum - Mughal, Kolhapur)	اعظم نگر گوكاك
'Azimabad (Patna - Mughal, Bengal Presidency)	عظيم اباد
Badakhshan (Mughal, Central Asia, Afghanistan)	بدخشان
Bagalkot (Maratha)	بگلكوت
Bagchih Serai (Krim)	باغچه سراي
Baghdad (Bagdad - Iraq)	بغداد

Bahadurgarh (Mughal)	بهادرگره
Bahawalpur (Bahawalpur state, Afghanistan)	بهاولپور
Bahraich (Mughal)	بهرايچ بهريچ
Bahrain (al-Bahrayn)	البحرين
Bairata (Mughal)	بيراتة
Bakhar (Bakkar, Bakhar, Bhakhar, Bhakkar - Mughal, Sind, Afghanistan)	بهكّر بهكهر
Baku (Bakuya - Iran)	باكو باكويه
Balanagor Gadha (Mandla - Maratha)	بالانگر گدها
Balapur (two places - one in Kandesh, one in Sira - Mughal)	بالاپور
Balhari (Bellary - Mysore)	بلهاري
Balikesir (Turkey)	بالكسير
Balkh (Mughal, Central Asia, Afghanistan)	بلخ
Balwantnagar (Jhansi - Mughal, Maratha, Gwalior)	بلونت نگر
Banaras (Benares, Varanasi - Mughal, Bengal Presidency, Awadh)	بنارس
Banda Malwari (Maratha)	بنده ملواري
Bandar (Iran)	بندر
Bandar Abbas (Iran)	بندر عباس
Bandar Abu Shahr (Iran)	بندر ابو شهر
Bandar Shahi (Mughal)	بندرشاهي
Bandhu (Qila - Mughal)	بندحو
Bangala (Mughal)	بنگالة
Banjarmasin (Netherlands East Indies)	بنجرمسن
Bankapur (Mughal)	بنكپ بنكاپور
Baramati (Sultanate, Mughal)	بنده ملواري
Bareli (Bareilly - Mughal, Rohilkhand, Awadh, Afghanistan)	بريلي
Bariz (Paris, in Paris - Morocco)	باريز بباريز
Baroda (Vadodara - Baroda state)	بروده
Basoda (Gwalior)	بسوده
al-Basra (Basra - Iraq)	البصرة
Batan (Baltistan? - Ladakh)	بتان
Bela (Las Bela state)	بيله
Belgrad (Turkey)	بنگالور
Bengalur (Bangalor - Mysore)	بنگالور
Berar (Mughal)	برار
Berlin (for Morocco)	برلين
Bhakkar, Bhakhar (See Bakkar)	
Bharatpur (Braj Indrapur)	بهرت پور
Bhaunagar (Mughal)	بهاونگر
Bhelah (See Bela)	بهله
Bhilsa (Alamgirpur - Mughal)	بهيلسة
Bhilwara (Mewar)	بهيلوارا
Bhopal (Bhopal state)	بهوپال
Bhuj (Kutch)	بهوج
Bhujnagar (Bhuj - Kutch)	بهوج نگر
Bidlis (Bitlis - Turkey)	بدليس بتليس
Bidrur (Mughal)	بدرور
Bihbihan (Behbehan - Iran)	بهبهان
Bijapur (Bijapur Sultanate, Mughal)	بيجاپور
Bikanir (Mughal, Bikanir state)	بيكانير
Bindraban (Vrindavan - Mughal, Bindraban state)	بندربن
Bisauli (Rohilkhand)	بسولے بسولي
Bistam (Central Asia)	بسطام
Biyar (Iran)	بيار
Borujerd (Iran)	بروجرد
Bosna (Sarajevo - Turkey)	بوسنه
Bosna Saray (Sarajevo - Turkey)	بوسنة سراي
Braj Indrapur (Bharatpur)	برج اندرپور
Broach (Baroch, Bharoch - Mughal, Broach state, Gwalior)	بروني
Brunei (Malaya)	بروني
Bukhara (Central Asia)	بخارا
Bukhara-yi Sharif (Central Asia)	بخاراي شريف
Bundi (Bundi state)	بوندي
Burhanabad (Mughal)	برهان اباد
Burhanpur (Mughal, Maratha, Gwalior)	برهانپور
Bursa (Brusa - Turkey)	برسه بروسه
Bushanj (Iran)	بوشنج
Bushire (see Abushahr)	
Çaniçe (Chanicha - Turkey)	چانيچه چاينيچه
Chakan (Maratha)	چاكن
Champanir (Gujarat Sultanate)	چانپانير
Chanda (Maratha)	چانده
Chanderi (Gwalior)	چنديري
Chandor (Maratha, Indore)	چاندور
Chhachrauli (Kalsia)	چحچرولي
Chhatarpur (Chhatarpur state)	چترپور
Chikodi (Maratha)	چكودي
Chinapattan (Madras - Mughal)	چيناپتن
Chinchwar (Maratha)	چنچور
Chitor (Akbarpur - Mughal)	چيتور
Chunar (Mughal)	چنار
Cuttack (see Katak)	
Dadiyan (Iran)	داديان
Dalipnagar (Datia)	دليپ نگر
Damarvar (Mysore)	دماروار
Damghan (Central Asia)	دامغان
al-Damigh (the Yemen)	الدامغ
Damla (Mughal)	داملا
Darband (Derbent - Azerbaijan, Iran)	دربند
Darfur (see al-Fashir)	
Darur (Mughal)	درور دارر
Daulatabad (Deogir - Mughal, Hyderabad)	دولت اباد دولتاباد
Daulat Anjazanchiya (see Comoros)	دولة انجزنچية
Daulatgarh (Rahatgarh - Bharatpur, Gwalior)	دولت گره

Daulat Qatar (State of Qatar - Qatar) دولة قطر

Dawar (Iran) داور

al-Dawla al-Mughribiya (Empire of Morocco) الدولة المغربية

Dawlatabad (Iran) دولتاباد

Dawraq (Iran) دورق

Dehdasht (Iran) دهدشت

Dehli (Shahjahanabad - Mughal, Afghanistan) دهلي

Deli (Netherlands East Indies) دلي

Deogarh (Partabgarh) ديوگره

Deogir (Daulatabad - Mughal) ديوگير

Dera (Derah - Mughal, Sikh, Afghanistan) ديره

Derajat (Mughal, Sikh, Afghanistan) ديره جات

Dewal Bandar (Mughal) ديول بندر

Dezful (Iran) دزفول

Dhamar (the Yemen) ذمار ذمر

Dharwar (Mysore) دهاروار

Dholapur (Dholapur state) دهولپور دہولپور

Dicholi (Mughal, Maratha) ديچولي

Dilshadabad (Mughal, Narayanpett) دلشاداباد

Dimashq (Damascus - Syria) دمشق

Diyar Bakr (Turkey) جيبوتي

Djibouti (Jaibuti - French Somaliland) جيبوتي

Dogam (Dogaon - Mughal) دوگام

Dogaon (Mughal) دوگاون

Edirne (Adrianople - Turkey) ادرنه

Elichpur (Mughal, Hyderabad) ايلچپور

Erzurum (Theodosiopolis - Turkey) ارزروم

Faiz Hisar (Gooty - Mysore) فعز حصار

Farahabad (Iran) فرح اباد

Farkhanda Bunyad (Hyderabad - Mughal) فرخنده بنياد

Farrukhabad (Ahmadnagar - Mughal, Bengal Presidency) فرخ اباد

Farrukhi (Feroke - Mysore) فرخي

Farrukhnagar (Mughal) فرخ نگر

Farrukhyab Hisar (Chitradurga - Mysore) فرخياب حصار

Fas (Fez - Morocco) فاس

Fas al-Jadid (see al-Madina al-Bayda' - Morocco) فاش الجديد

al-Fashir (Darfur, Sudan) الفشير

Fathabad Dharur (Mughal) فبح اباد دهرور

Fathnagar (Aurangabad - فتحنگر

Fathpur (Nusratabad, Sikri - Mughal) فتحپور

Fedala (Fadalat al-Muhammadiya - Morocco) فضالة

Fergana (Central Asia) فرغانة

Filastin (Palestine) فاسطين

Filibe (Philipopolis, Plovdiv - Turkey) فيليب فلبه

Firozgarh (Yadgir - Mughal) فيروزگره

Firoznagar (Mughal, Hyderabad) فيروزنگر

al-Fujaira (United Arab Emir- الفجيرة

Fuman (Iran) فومان

Gadraula (Mughal) گدرولة

Gadwal (Hyderabad) گدوال

Gajjikota (Mughal) گجيكوتا

Ganja (Ganjah, Genje - Elizabethpol, Kirovabad in Azerbaijan, Iran, Turkey) گنجه

Ganjikot (Genjikot - Mughal) گنجيكوت

Gargaon (Assam) گرگاو

Garha (Mughal) گارحة

Gelibolu (Gallipoli - Turkey) گليبولي

Ghazni (Afghanistan) غزني

al-Ghurfa (Hadhramaut) الغرفة

Gilan (Iran) گنلان

Gobindpur (Mughal) گوبندپور

Gohad (Mughal, Dholapur) گوهد

Gokak (Belgaum, 'Azamnagar - Mughal) گوكاك

Gokul (Bindraban) گوكل

Gokulgarh (Mughal) گوكل گره

Gorakpur (Muazzamabad - Mughal) گوركپور

Gözlü (see Shahr-Gözlü - Krim) گوزلو

Gulbarga (Kulbarga, Ahsanabad - Mughal) گلبرگة

Gulkanda (Golkona - Sultanate, Mughal) گلكندة

Gulshanabad (Nasik - Mughal, Maratha) گلشن اباد

Gümüsh-hane (Turkey) گمشخانه

Guti (Gooty - Mughal, Mysore) گوتي

Guzelhisar (Turkey) گوزلحصر

Gwaliar (Mughal, Gwalior state, گواليار

Hafizabad (Mughal) هافظاباد

Haidarabad (Hyderabad, Haidrabad, Farkhanda Bunyad - Golkanda Sultanate, Mughal, Hyderabad state, Sind, Afghanistan) حيدراباد

Haidarnagar (Bednur, Nagar - Mysore) حيدرنگر

Hajipur (Mughal) حجيپور

Halab (Aleppo - Syria) بلب

Hamadan (Iran) همدان

Hansi (Qanauj - Mughal, Awadh) هانسي

al-Haramayn ash-Sharifayn (Mecca and Medina in Arabia - Ottoman Turkey) الشريفين الحرمين

al-Harar (Ethiopia) الهرر

Hardwar (Haridwar, Tirath - Mughal, Saharanpur) هاردوار

Harput, Harburt (see Khartapirt)

Harran (Turkey) حران

Hasanabad (Mughal) حسن اباد

Hathras (Mughal, Awadh) هاتهرس

Hathrasa (Hathras) هاتهرسا

Hawran (Horan - Syria) حوران

Hawta (the Yemen) حوطة

Hawz (Morocco) حوز

al-Hejaz (Saudi Arabia) الحجاز

Herat (Afghanistan, Central Asia, Iran) — هراة هرات

al-Hilla (Hille - Iraq) — الحلة

Hinganhat (Maratha) — حنگنهات

Hisar (Central Asia) — حصر حصار

Hisar Firoza (Mughal) — حصار فيروزة

al-Hisn (el-Hisin - Turkey) — الحصن

Hizan (Khizan - Turkey) — هزان خيزان

Hukeri (Mughal, Maratha) — هوكري

Husaingarh (Mughal) — حسين گره

Huwayza (Iran) — حويزة

Ibb (the Yemen) — ايب

Ilahabad (Allahabad) — اله اباد

Ilahabas (Mughal) — اله اباس

Ili (China - Sinkiang) — الي

al-Imarat al-'Arabiya al-Muttahida (United Arab Emirates) — امتيازگره

Imtiyazgarh (Adoni - Mughal) — امتيازگره

Indore (Indore state) — اندور

Inebolu (Turkey) — اينه بولى

Inegöl (Turkey) — اينه كول

Iran — ايران

al-Iraq

Iravan (Eravan, Erewan, Revan – Iran, Yeravan – Armenia) — ايروان

'Isagarh (Gwalior) — عيسى گره

Isfahan (Iran) — اصفهان

Islamabad (Mathura – Mughal, Bindraban — اسلام اباد

Islam Bandar (Rajapur – Mughal) — اسلام بندر

Islambul (Istanbul – Turkey) — اسلامبول

Islamnagar (Navanagar – Mughal) — اسلام نگر

Ismailgarh (Mughal) — اسمعيل گره

Italian Somaliland (Somalia) — الصومال الايطاليانية

Itawa (Mughal, Maratha, Rohilkhand, Awadh — اتاوا اتاوه

Izmir (Turkey) — ازمير ازمر

Jabbalpur (Mughal) — جَبالپور

Ja'farabad urf Chandor (Indore) — جعفراباد عرف چاندور

Jahangirnagar (Dacca - Mughal, Bengal Presidency) — جهانگيرنگر

Jaipur (Sawai - Mughal) — جي پور

Jaisalmir (Jaisalmir state) — جيسلمير

Jalalnagar (Mughal) — جلال نگر

Jalalpur (Mughal) — جلالپور

Jalaun (Jalon - Maratha) — جلون

Jalesar (Mughal) — جليسار

Jallandar (Jullundur - Mughal) — جالندر جلّندر

Jalnapur (Jalna - Mughal) — جالنة پور

Jambusar (Baroda) — جمبوسر

Jammu (Jamun - Kashmir) — جمون

Jaora (Jaora state) — جاوره

Jaunpur (Mughal) — جونپور

Java (Netherlands East Indies) — جاو جاوا

Jaytapur (Jaiyatpur - Mughal) — جيت پور

Jaza'ir (Algiers) — جزائر

Jaza'ir Gharb (Algiers) — جزائر غرب

al-Jaza'ir-i Gharb (Algiers) — الجزائر غرب

Jelu (Jelou - Iran) — جلو

Jerba (Cerbe, Gabes - — جربة

Jering (Jaring, Jerin - Thai- — جريج جرين

Jhalawar (Jhalawar state) — جهالاوار

Jinji (Nusratgarh - — جنجي

Jind (Jind state) — جيند

Jodhpur (Mughal, Jodhpur state) — جودهپور

Jordan (al-Urdunn) — الاردن

al-Jumhuriya al-'Arabiya al-Muttahida (The United Arab Republic - Egypt, Syria and the Yemen) — الجمهورية العربية المتحدة

al-Jumhuriya al-'Arabiya al-Suriya (The Arab Republic of Syria) — الجمهورية العربية السورية

al-Jumhuriya al-'Arabiya al-Yamaniya (The Arab Republic of the Yemen) — الجمهورية العربية اليمنية

al-Jumhuriya al-'Iraqiya (The Republic of Iraq) — الجمهورية العراقية

al-Jumhuriya al-Libiya (The Republic of Libya) — الجمهورية الليبية

al-Jumhuriya al-Lubnaniya (The Republic of Leba- — الجمهورية اللبنانية

al-Jumhuriya as-Somal (The Republic of Somalia) — الجمهورية الصومال

al-Jumhuriya as-Sudan (The Republic of the Sudan) — الجمهورية السودان

al-Jumhuriya as-Sudan al-Dimuqratiya (The Democratic Republic of the Sudan) — الجمهورية السودان الديمقراطية

al-Jumhuriya as-Suriiya (The Republic of Syria) — الجمهورية السورية

al-Jumhuriya at-Tunisiya (The Republic of Tunisia) — الجمهورية العراقية

al-Jumhuriya al-Yaman al-Dimuqratia al-Shu'ubiya (The Peoples' Democratic Republic of the Yemen) — الجمهورية اليمن الديمقراطية الشعبية

Jumhuriyeti Turkiye (The Republic of Turkey) — جمهوريتى توركيه

Junagarh (Junagadh - Mughal) — جونة گره

al-Junub al-Arabi (South Arabia) — الجنوب العربي

Kabul (Mughal, Afghanistan) — كابل

Kaffa (Krim) — كفّة

Kalanur (Mughal) — كالانور

Kalat (Kalat state) — قلات كلات

Kalian (Kalayani - Hydera- — كليان

Kalikut (Calicut, Kozhikode - Mysore) — كليكوت

Kalkatah (Calcutta, Alinagar - Mughal, Bengal Presidency) — كلكته

Kalpi (Mughal, Maratha) — كلپي

Kanauj (Qanauj - Mughal, Awadh) — قنوج

Kanauj urf Shahgarh (Qanauj - Mughal, Awadh) — قنوج عرف شاه گره

Kanbayat (Kambayat, Kanbat, Khambayat - Mughal, Cambay state) — كمبايت كهنبايت كنبات كنبايت

Kandahar (see Qandahar)

Kangun (Hosakote - Mughal) — كنگون

Kanji (Conjeeveram - Mughal) — كنجي

Kankurti (Mughal, Maratha) — كانكرتي

Kara Amid (Turkey) — قره آمد

Karahisar (Qara-Hisar - Turkey) — قراحصار قره حسار

Kararabad (Karad - Mughal) — كراراباد

Karatova (Kratova - Turkey) — قراطوه قراطوه

Karauli (Karauli state) — كرولي

Karimabad (Mughal)	كريم اباد
Karmin (Central Asia)	كرمين
Karnatak (Carnatic - Mughal)	كرناتك
Karpa (Kurpa - Mughal)	كرپا
Kars (Qars - Turkey)	قارص قارس
Kashan (Iran)	كاشان
Kashgar (China - Sinkiang)	كاشغر كشقر
Kashmir (Srinagar - Kashmir Sultanate, Mughal, Sikh, Afghanistan)	كشمير
Kastamonu (Turkey)	قسطمونى
Katak (Cuttack - Mughal, Maratha)	كتك
Katak Banaras (Mughal)	كتك بنارس
Kawkaban (the Yemen)	كوكبان
Kayeri (Turkey)	قيصري قيسري
Kedah (Straits Settlements, Malaya)	كداه
Kelantan (Straits Settlements, Malaya)	كلنتن
Kemasin (Straits Settlements, Malaya)	كماسن
Khairabad (Mughal)	خيراباد
Khairnagar (Mughal)	خيرنگر
Khairpur (Mughal, Sind)	خيرپور
Khaliqabad (Dindigal - Mysore)	خالق اباد
Khambayat (Kanbayat - Mughal)	كمنبايت
Khanabad (Afghanistan)	خان اباد
Khanja (Canca, Hanca - Turkey)	خانجة خانجا
Khanpur (Bahawalpur)	خانپور
Khartapirt (Harput, Harburt - Turkey)	خرتبرت خربت خربرت
Khizan (Turkey)	خيزان
Khoqand (Central Asia)	خوقند
Khotan (Khutan, China - Sinkiang)	خوتن ختن
Khoy (Khoi, Khui - Iran)	خوي
Khujista Bunyad (Aurangabad - Mughal, Hyderabad)	خجسته بنياد
al-Khurfa (the Yemen)	الخرفاة
Khurshid Sawad (Mysore)	خورشيد سواد
Khwarizm (Central Asia)	خوارزم
Kighi (Turkey)	كيغي
Kirman (Kerman - Iran)	كرمان
Kirmanshahan (Kermanshah - Iran)	كرمانساهان
Kish (Central Asia)	كش
Kishangar (Kishangar state)	كشنگره
Kishtwar (Mughal)	كشتوار
Koçaniye (Kochana - Turkey)	قوچانية
Koilkunda (Mughal)	كويلكونده
Kolapur (Mughal, Kolhapur)	كولاپور كلاپور
Konya (Turkey)	قونية
Kora (Mughal, Maratha, Awadh)	كورا
Kosantina (see Qusantinia)	
Kosova (Kosovo - Turkey)	قوصوه قوسوه
Kostantaniye (see Qustantaniya)	
Kotah (Kotah state)	كوته
Kotah urf Nandgaon	كوته عرف نندگانو
Kubrus (Cyprus - Turkey)	قبرص
Kuch Hijri (Kunch)	كوچ حجري
Kuchaman (Mughal)	كچامن
Kuche (China - Sinkiang)	كوچا
Kufan (Kufin - Central Asia)	كوفن كوفين
Kulbarga (see Gulbarga)	
Kumber (Kumbar - see Maha Indrapur)	
Kunar (Maratha)	كنار
Kunch (Maratha)	كونچ
Kurdasht (Azerbaijan)	كرداشت كردشت
Kuwait (al-Kuwayt)	الكويت
Ladakh (Ladakah - Kashmir, Afghanistan)	لداكه لداخ
Lahej (the Yemen)	لحج
Lahijan (Iran)	لاهيجان
Lahore (Lahur - Mughal, Sikh, Afghanistan)	لاهور
Lahri Bandar (Mughal)	لهري بندر
Langar (Central Asia)	لنگر
Lar (Iran)	لار
Larenda (Turkey)	لارندة
Lashkar (Gwalior)	لاشكار
Lebanon (Lubnan)	لبنان
Legeh (Thailand)	لغكه
Libya	ليبيا
Lucknow (Lakhnau - Mughal, Awadh)	لكهنو
Machhli Bandar (Masulipatam)	مچهلي بندر
Machhlipatan (Masulipatam - Mughal, French India, Madras Pres.)	مچهلي پتن
Madankot (Mughal)	مدنكوت
al-Madina al-Bayda' (see Fas al-Jadid - Morocco)	المدينة البيضاء
Madrid (for Morocco)	مدريد
al-Maghrib (Morocco)	المغرب
Maha Indrapur (Dig, Kumbar - Mughal, Bharatpur)	مهه اندرپور
Mahle (Male - Maldive Islands)	محلي
Mahmud Bandar (Porto Novo - Mughal)	محمودبندر
Mahoba (Maratha)	مهوبة
Mailapur (Madras - Mughal)	ميلاپور
Makhsusabad (Murshidabad - Mughal)	مخصوص اباد
Malharnagar (Indore, also for Maheshwar)	ملهارنگر
Malher (Malhar, Mulher - Mughal)	ملهر
Maliknagar (Mughal)	ملك نگر
Malnapur (Mughal)	مالناپور
Malpur (Mughal)	مالپور
Maluka (Netherlands East Indies)	ملوكة
al-Mamlaka al-'Arabiya as-Sa'udiya (The Kingdom of Saudi Arabia)	المملكة العربية السعودية
al-Mamlaka al-Libiya (The Kingdom of Libya)	المملكة الليبية
al-Mamlaka al-Maghribiya (The Kingdom of Morocco)	المملكة المغربية
al-Mamlaka al-Misriya (The Kingdom of Egypt)	المملكة المصرية
al-Mamlaka al-Mutawakkiliya al-Yamaniya (The Mutawakkilite Kingdom of the Yemen)	المملكة المتوكلية اليمنية

al-Mamlaka al-Tunisiya (The Kingdom of Tunisia) المملكة التونسية

al-Mamlaka al-Urdunniya al-Hashimiya (The Hashimite Kingdom of Jordan) الاردنية الهاسمية

Manastir (Turkey) مناستر

Mandasor (Gwalior) منديسور

Mandla (Maratha) مندلا

Mandu (Mughal) مندو

Mangarh (Mughal) مانگره

Manghir (Monghyr - Bihar) مانگهير

Manikpur (Mughal) مانكپور

Maragha (Azerbaijan, Iran) مراغة

Marakesh (Marrakech - Morocco) مراكش

Mar'ash (Turkey) مرعش

Mardin (Turkey) ماردين

Marv (Central Asia, Iran) ماروار

Marwar (Jodhpur, Nagor, Pali, Sojat) ماروار

al-Mu'askar (Mascara - Algeria) المعسكر

Mashhad (Iran) مشهد

Mashhad Imam Rida (Iran) مشهد امام رضى

Mathura (Islamabad - Mughal, Bindraban) متهره

Mazandaran (Iran) مازندران

Mecca (Makkah - al-Hejaz) مكّة

Medea (Algeria) مدية

Meknes (Miknas - Morocco) مكناس

Menangkabau (Netherlands East Indies) منقكابو

Merta (Mirath - Mughal, Jodhpur) ميرتة ميرتا

Misr (Egypt, Turkey) مصر

Modava (Moldava - Turkey) مداوه موداوه

Mombasa (Kenya) ممباسة

Mosul (al-Mawsil - Iraq) الموصل موصل

Muazzamabad (Gorakpur - Mughal, Awadh) معظم اباد

Muhammadabad (Udaipur - Mughal) محمداباد

Muhammadabad Banaras (Mughal, Awadh, Bengal Presidency, fictitious for Lucknow) محمداباد بنارس

Muhammadabad urf Kalpi (Kalpi) محمداباد عرف كلپي

al-Muhammadiya (al-Masila - Morocco) المحمدية

al-Muhammadiya ash-Sharifa (Morocco) المحمدية الشريفة

Muhammadnagar Tandah (Awadh) محمدنگر تانده

Muhiabad Poona (Maratha) محيى اباد پونه

Mujahidabad (Mughal) مجاهداباد

Mujibalanagar (Rohilkhand) مجى بالانگر

al-Mukala (the Yemen) المكلا

Mukha (Mocca - the Yemen) مخا

Mukhtara (the Yemen) مختارة

Müküs (Turkey) مكس

Multan (Mughal, Sikh, Afghanistan) ملتان

Muminabad (Bindraban) مؤمن اباد

Munbai (Mumbai, Bombay - Mughal, Bombay Presidency) منبي

Mungir (Mughal) مهنگير

Muradabad (Mughal, Rohilkhand, Awadh, Afghanistan) مراداباد

Murshidabad (Makhsusabad - Mughal, French India, Bengal Pres.) مرشداباد

Murtazabad (Mughal) مرتضاباد

Muscat (Oman) مسقط

Mustafabad (Rampur - Rohilkhand) مصطفاباد

Muzaffargarh (Jhajjar - Mughal) مظفرگره

Mysore (Mahisur - Mysore state) مهي سور مهيسور

Nabha (Sirkar - Nabha state) سركار نابهه

Nagar (Ahmadnagar, Bednur - Maratha, Mysore) نگر

Nagar Ijri (Srinagar in Bundelkand) نگر يجري

Nagor (Mughal, Jodhpur) ناگور

Nagpur (Maratha) ناگپور

Nahan (Sirmur) ناهن

Nahtarnagar (Trichinopoly - Arcot) نهتر نگر

Najafgarh (Mughal, Rohilkhand) نجف گره

Najibabad (Mughal, Sikh, Rohilkhand, Awadh, Afghanistan) نجيب اباد نجيباباد

Nakhjuvan (Iran, Azerbaijan) نخجوان

Nandgaon (Nandgano - Kotah) نندگانو

Nandgaon urf Kotah نندگانو عرف كوته

Narnol (Mughal) نارنول

Narwar (Sipri - Mughal, Gwalior, Narwar state) نرور

Nasaf (Central Asia) نسف

Nasirabad (Sagar, Wanparti - Hyderabad) نصر اباد

Nasirabad (Dharwar - Mughal) نصيراباد

Nasiri (Iran) ناصري

Nasrullahnagar (Rohilkhand) نصرالله نگر

Nazarbar (Mysore) نظربار

Nejd (Saudi Arabia) نجد

Nigbolu (Turkey) نگبولو

Nihavand (Iran) نهاوند

Nimak (Sikh) نمك

Nimruz (Central Asia, Iran) نيمروز نمرز

Nipani (Maratha) نپني

Nisa (Iran) نسا

Nishapur (Naysabur - Iran) نيشاپور

Novabirda (Novoberda - Turkey) نوابرده

Novar (Turkey) نوار

Nukhwi (Iran, Azerbaijan) نخوي

Nusratabad (Dharwar, Nasratabad, Fathpur - Mughal) نصرت اباد

Nusratgarh (Jinji - Mughal) نصرت گره

Ohri (Okhri, Ochrida - Turkey) اوخرى

Oman ('Uman) عمان

Omdurman (Umm Durman - the Sudan) ام درمان

Orchha (Orchha state) اورچه

Ordu-Bagh (Iran) اوردوباغ

Ordu-yi Humayun (Turkey) اردو همايون

Orissa (Mughal) اوريسة

Pahang (Straits Settlements) فاحغ

Pakistan پاكستان

Palembang (Netherlands East Indies) فلمبغ

Palestine (see Filastin)

Pali (Jodhpur) پالي

Panahabad (Iran, Karabagh) پناه اباد

Panipat (Mughal) پاني پت

Parenda (Purenda - Mughal) پرينده پرنده

Parnala (Qila) (Mughal) پرنالا (قلع)

Patan (Seringapatan - Mysore) پتن

al-Patani (Patani - Thailand) الفطاني

Pathankot پثنكوت

Patna (Azimabad - Mughal, Bengal Presidency) پتنة

Pattan (Anhirwala - Mughal) پتن

Pattan Deo (Somnath – Mughal) پتن ديو

Perak (Straits Settlements, Malaya) فيرق

Peshawar (Mughal, Sikh, Afghanistan, Iran) پشاور

Petlad (Baroda) پتلاد

Phonda (Mughal) پهونده

Pondichery (Pholcheri - French India) پهلچري

Pondichery (Porcheri - French India) پرچري

Poona (Punah, Pune, Muhiabad - Mughal, Maratha) پونه

Pulu Malayu (IslandoftheMalays-Sumatra, Netherlands East Indies) فولو ملايو

Pulu Penang (Penang, Prince of Wales Island - Straits Settlements, Malaya) فولو فنيغ

Pulu Percha (Island of Sumatra - Netherlands East Indies) فولو فرچ

Punamali (Mughal) پونامالي

Punch (Mughal) پونچ

Purbandar (Porbandar - Mughal) پوربندر

Qafsa (Capsa - Tunis, Tunisia) قفصة

al-Qahira (Cairo - Egypt) القاهرة

Qaiti (the Yemen) القعياطي

Qamarnagar (Karnul - Mughal) قمرنگر

Qanauj (see Kanauj)

Qandahar (Ahmadshahi - Mughal, Afghanistan, Iran) قندهار

Qarshi (Central Asia) قرشي

Qasbah Panipat (Rohilkhand) قصبة پاني پت

Qatar wa Dubai (Qatar and Dubai - Qatar) قطر و دبي

Qayin (Central Asia) قاين

Qazvin (Iran) قزوين

Qubba (Azerbaijan) قبة

Qumm (Qomm - Iran) قم

Qunduz (Central Asia) قندوز

Qusantinia (Qustantina, Qusantina - Constantine, Algiers) قسنطينية قسطنطينة قسنطينة

Qustantaniya (Constantinople - Turkey) قسطنطنية

Rabat (Morocco) رباط

Rabat al-Fath (Rabat - Morocco) رباط الفتح

Rada' (the Yemen) راداء

Radhanpur (Radhanpur state) رادهنپور

Rajapur (Islam Bandar - Mughal) راجاپور

Rajgarh (Alwar) راج گره

Ramhurmuz (Iran) رامهرمز

Ra'nash (Ramhurmuz - Iran) رعنش

Rangpur (Assam) رنگپور

Ranthor (Ranthambhor - Mughal) رنتهور

Ras al-Khaima (United Arab Emirates) رأس الخيمة

Rasht (Resht - Iran) رشت

Ratlam (Ratlam state) رتلام

Ravishnagar Sagar (Garhakota - Maratha - Gwalior) روش نگر ساگر

Rehman (Reman - Thailand) رحمن

Revan (Iravan - Armenia) روان

Rewan (Rewa) ريوان

Reza'iyeh (Urumi - Iran) رضائية

Rikab (Rekab - Afghanistan, Iran) ركاب

Rohtas (Rohtak - Mughal) رحتاس رهتاس

Rudana (Taroudant - Morocco) ردانة

Ruha (al-Ruha - Turkey) الرها رها رهى

Sa'adnagar (Aklaj - Mughal) سعدنگر

Sabzavar (Iran) سبزوار

Sa'da (the Yemen) صعدة

Sagar (Maratha, Bengal Pres.) ساگر

Saharanpur (Mughal) سهارنپور

Sahibabad Hansi (Hansi state) صاحب اباد هنسي

Sahrind (Sarhind - Mughal, Cis-Sutlej Patiala, Afghanistan) سرهند سهرند

Sailana (Sailana state) سيلانه

Saimur (Mughal) سيمور

al-Saiwi (Sai, Saiburi, Teluban - Thailand) السيوي

Sakiz (Saqyz, Scio - Turkey) سكيز ساقز

Sakkhar (Mughal) سكهر

Sala (Sale - Morocco) سلا

Salamabad (Satyamangalam - Mysore) سلام اباد

Salimabad (Ajmer - Mughal) سليم اباد

Samandra (Turkey) سمندره

Samarqand (Central Asia) سمرقند

San'a (the Yemen) صنعاء

Sanbal (Sambhal - Mughal) سنبل

Sanbhar (Sambhar - Mughal) سانبهر

Sangamner (Mughal) سنگمنر

Sangli (Maratha) سنگلي

al-Saniya (Turkey) السنية

Sarakhs (Iran) سرخس

Sarangpur (Mughal) سارنگپور

Saray (Turkey) سراي

Sari (Iran) ساري

Sari Pol (Afghanistan) سر پل

Sarhind (see Sahrind)

Sashti (in Devanagari) (Maratha)

Satara (Mughal) ستارا

Saudi Arabia (see al-Hejaz, Nejd) العربية السعودية

Sawai Jaipur (Jaipur, fictitious for Karauli) سواي جيپور

Sawai Madhopur (Jaipur, fictitious for Sikar) سواي مادهوپور

Sawuj Balaq (Iran) ساوج بلاق

Selam (Selam state) سيلم

Selanghur (Selangor - Straits Settlements, Malaya) سلاغور

Selanik (Salonika - Turkey) سلانيك

Selefke (Turkey) سلفكه

Semnan (Simnan - Iran) سمنان

Serbernik (Turkey) سربرنيك

Serez (see Siroz - Turkey) سرز سريز

Seringapatan (Mysore)

Shadiabad Urf Mandu (Mughal) شادياباد ارف مندو

Shadman (Central Asia) شادمان

Shadora (Gwalior) شادهوره

Shahabad (Awadh) شاه اباد قنوج شاهاباد

Shahabad Qanauj (Mughal, Rohilkhand, Awadh) شاه اباد قنوج

Shahgarh Qanauj (Mughal) شاه گره قنوج

Shahjahanabad (Dehli - Mughal, Bhilwara, Bindraban, Chitor, Mathura, Shapura, Udaipur, also fictitious for Bagalkot, Jaisalmir, Satara-EIC) شاه جهان اباد

Shahr-Gözlü (see Gözlü - Krim) شهرگوزلو

Shakola (Mughal) شكولا

Shamakhi (Shamakha, Shemakhi - Iran, Azerbaijan) شماخي شماخه

Sharakat Almaniya (German East Africa Co.) شراكة المانيا

ash-Sharja (Sharja - United Arab Emirates) الشارجة

Shekki (Iran) شكّى

Sheopur (Gwalior) شيوپور

Shergarh (Shirgarh - Mughal) شيرگره

Sherkot (Mughal) شيركوت

Sherpur (Shirpur - Mughal) شيرپور

Shikarpur (Sind) شكارپور

Shiraz (Iran) شيراز

Shirvan (Azerbaijan, Iran, Turkey) شيروان شروان

Sholapur (Mughal) شولاپور

Shustar (Iran) شوستر

Siak (Netherlands East Indies) سيك

Sidrekipsi (Turkey) بسدره قپسى

Siirt (Sa'irt - Turkey) سعرت

Sijilmasa (Sizilmassa - Morocco) سجلماسة

Sikakul (Chicacole - Mughal) سيكاكل

Sikandarah (Sikandra – Mughal) سكندره

Sind (Mughal, Sind state, Afghanistan, Iran) سند

Singgora (Thailand) سڠگورا

Sira (Mughal) سيرة

Sironj (Mughal, Indore, Tonk) سرونج

Siroz (see Serez - Turkey) سيروز

Sistan (Iran) سيستان

Sitamau (Sitamo) سيتامو

Sitapur (Mughal) سيتاپور

Sitpur (Sidhpur in Gujarat? - Mughal) سيتپور

Sivas (Siwas - Turkey) سيواس

Sofia (Turkey) صوفية

Sojat (Jodhpur) سوجت

al-Somal al-Italyaniya (Italian Somaliland, Somalia) الصومال الايطاليانية

Sreberniçe (Serbernichna - Turkey) سربرنيچه

Sri (Amritsar) سري

Sri Akalpur (Malkarian) سري اكلپور

Srinagar (Mughal, Garhwal, Kashmir) سرينگر

Srinagar (in Bundelkhand - Maratha) سرينگر

Sultanabad (Iran) سلطاناباد

Sultanpur (Mughal) سلطانپور

Sumenep (Netherlands East Indies) سمنف

Surat (Mughal, French India, Bombay Presidency, fictitious for Chand) سورت

Suriya (Syria) سورية

al-Suwair/al-Suwaira (Essaouir, Essaouira - Mogador, Morocco) السوير الصويرة

Tabaristan (Iran) طبرستان

Tabriz (Iran, Turkey) تبريز

Tadpatri (Mughal) تدپتري

Ta'izz (the Yemen) تعز

Tanah Malayu (Land of the Malays - Sumatra, Malacca, Straits Settlements) تانة ملايو

Tana Ugi (Land of the Bugis - Netherlands East Indies) تانة اغيسى

Tanda (Akbarpur - Bengal Sultanate, Mughal, Awadh) تانده

Tanja (Tangier - Morocco) طنجة

Tappal (Mughal) ابرقوه

Taqidemt (Algiers) تاقدمت

Tarablus (Tripoli in Lebanon) طرابلس

Tarablus Gharb (Tripoli West - in Libya) طرابلس غرب

Tarapatri (Mughal) تراپتري

Tarim (the Yemen) تريم

Tashkand (Tashkent - Central Asia) تشكند

Tashqurghan (Afghanistan) تاشقورغان

Tatta (Tattah - Mughal, Sind, Afghanistan) تته

Tehran (Iran) طهران

Tellicherry (French India, Bombay Presidency) تلجري تالچري

Termez (Central Asia) ترمذ

Tetuan (Tetouan, Titwan - Morocco) تطوان

Tibet (Mughal, Ladakh) تبت

Tiflis (Georgia, Iran) تفليس

Tilimsan (Tlemcen, Aghadir - Algiers) تلمسان

Tirat Hardwar (Hardwar) تيرتهردوار

Tire (Turkey) تيره

Tokat (Tuqat - Turkey) توقاط توقات دوقات طوقات

Tonk (Tonk state) تونك

Toragal (Mughal, Maratha) تورگل توراگال

Trabzon (Trebizond - Turkey) طرابزون طرابزن

Trengganu (Straits Settlements, Malaya) ترغگانو

Tun (Central Asia) تون

Tunis (Tunisia) تونس

Turbat (Central Asia) تربت

Tuyserkan (Iran) توي سركان

Udaipur (Muhammadabad - Mughal) اديپور اوديپور

Udgir (Mughal) اجين

Ujjain (Mughal, Gwalior) اجين

Ujjain Dar al-Fath (Gwalior) اجين دارالفتح

Ujjainpur (Mughal) اجين پور

Umarkot (Mughal) امركوت

Umm al-Qaiwain (United Arab Emirates) ام القيوين

United Arab Emirates (see al-Imarat al-'Arabiya al-Muttahida)

Urdu (Camp mint - Mughal, Central Asia, Iran) اردو

Urdu Dar Rahi-i-Dakkin (Mughal) اردو دار راه دكين

Urdu Zafar Qirin (Mughal) اردو ظفر قرين

al-Urdunn (Jordan) الاردن

Urumchi (China - Sinkiang) ارومچي

Urumi (Urumia, Urmia, Reza'iya - Iran) ارومي ارومية ارمية

Ushi (China - Sinkiang) اوش

Usküp (Uskub, Skopje, Kosovo - Turkey) اسكوپ

Van (Wan - Turkey, Armenia) وان

Varne (Turkey) ورنه

al-Yaman (the Yemen) اليمن

Yarkand (China - Sinkiang) يارقند

Yarkhissarmaran (China - Sinkiang) ياركسارمرن

Yazd (Iran) يزد

Yazur (Cemtral Asia) يازر

Yenishehr (Larissa - Turkey) ينكى شهر

Za (Taorirt - Morocco) صا

Zabid (the Yemen) زبيد

Zafarabad (Bidar - Mughal, Gurramkonda - Mysore) ظفراباد

Zafarnagar (Fathabad - Mughal) ظفرنگر

Zafarpur (Mughal) ظفرپور

Zain-ul-Bilad (Ahmadabad) زين البلاد

Zanjibar (Zanjibara - Zanzibar) زنجبارا زنجبار

Zebabad (Mughal, Sardhanah) زيب اباد

Zegam (Zigam - Iran) زگام

Zinjan (Zanjan - Iran) زنجان

al-Zuhra (the Yemen) الزهرة

MINT EPITHETS

Geographical Terms:

Baldat (City - Agra, Allahabad, Burhanpur, Bikanir, Patna, Sarhind, Ujjain) بلدات

Bandar (Port - Dewal, Hari, Surat, Machhlipatan) بندر

Dakhil (Breach, Entrance - Chitor) داخل

Dawla/Daula (State, State of) دولة

Hazrat (Royal Residence - Fas, Marakesh, Dehli) حضرة

Khitta (District - Awadh, Kalpi, Kashmir, Lakhnau) خطة

Negri (State of - Straits Settlements, Malaya, Netherlands East Indies, Thailand) نكري

Qasba (Town - Panipat, Sherkot) قصبة

Qila (Fort - Agra, Alwar, Bandhu, Gwalior, Punch) قلع قلعة

Qila Muqam (Fort Residence - Gwalior) قلعة مقام

Qita (District - Bareli) قطة

Sarkar (County - Lakhnau, Torgal) سركار

Shahr (City - Anhirwala Pattan) شهر

Suba (Province - Awadh) سوبة

Tirtha (Shrine - Hardwar) ترتة

Poetic Allusion:

Ashraf al-Bilad (Most Noble of Cities - Qandahar/Ahmadshahi) اشراف البلاد

Baldat-i-Fakhira (Splendid City - Burhanpur) بلدات فخيرة

Bandar-i-Mubarak (Blessed Port - Surat) بندر مبارك

Dar-ul-Aman (Abode of Security - Agra, Jammu, Multan, Sarhind) دار الامان

Dar-ul-Barakat (Abode of Blessings - Jodhpur, Nagor) دار البركات

Dar-ul-Fath (Seat of Conquest - Ujjain) دار الفتح

Dar-ul-Islam (Abode of Islam - Bahawalpur, Dogaon, Mandisor) دار الاسلام

Dar-ul-Jihad (Seat of Holy War - Hyderabad) دار الجهاد

Dar-ul-Khair (Abode of Beneficence - Ajmer) دار الخير

Dar-ul-Khilafa (Abode of the Caliphate - Agra, Ahmadabad, Akbarabad, Akbarpur Tanda, Awadh, Bahraich, Daulatabad, Dogaon, Gorakpur, Gwalior, Jaunpur, Kanauj, Lahore, Lakhnau, Malpur, Shahgarh, Shahjahanabad, Tehran, the Yemen) دار الخلافة

Dar-ul-Mansur (Abode of the Victorious - Ajmer, Jodhpur) دار المنصور

Dar-ul-Mulk (Seat of Kingship - Dehli, Fathpur, Kabul) دار الملك

Dar an-Nusrat (Abode of Succor - Herat) دار النصرات

Dar-ur-Riyasa (Seat of the Chief of State - Jaisalmir) دار الرياسة

Dar-us-Salam (Abode of Peace - Dogaon, Mandisor, Legeh) دار السلام

Dar-us-Saltana (Seat of the Sultanate - Ahmadabad, Burhanpur, Fathpur, Herat, Kabul, Kora, Lahore) دار السلطنة

Dar-ul-Surur (Abode of Happiness - Bahawalpur, Burhanpur, Saharanpur) دار السرور

Dar-uz-Zafar (Seat of Victory - Advani, Bijapur) دار الظفر

Dar-uz-Zarb (Seat of the Mint - Jaunpur, Kalpi, Patna) دار الضرب

Farkhanda Bunyad (Of Auspicious Foundation - Hyderabad) فرخنده بنياد

Hazrat (Venerable - Dehli) حضرت

Khujista Bunyad (Of Fortunate Foundation - Aurangabad) خجستة بنياد

Mustaqarr-ul-Khilafa (Residence of the Caliphate - Akbarabad, Ajmer) مستقر الخلافة

Mustaqarr-ul-Mulk (Abode of Kingship - Akbarabad, Azimabad) مستقر الملك

Sawai (One-fourth, i.e. "a notch better" - Jaipur) سواي

Umm al-Bilad (Mother of Cities - Balkh) ام البلاد

Zain-ul-Bilad (The Most-Beautiful of Cities – Ahmadabad) زين البلاد

STANDARD INTERNATIONAL NUMERAL SYSTEMS

Prepared especially for the ***Standard Catalog of World Coins***© 2007 by Krause Publications

Western	0	½	1	2	3	4	5	6	7	8	9	10	50	100	500	1000
Roman			I	II	III	IV	V	VI	VII	VIII	IX	X	L	C	D	M
Arabic-Turkish	٠	١/٢	١	٢	٣	٤	٥	٦	٧	٨	٩	١٠	٥٠	١٠٠	٥٠٠	١٠٠٠
Malay-Persian	٠	١/٢	١	٢	٣	۴	۵	٦ or ۶	٧	٨	٩	١٠	۵٠	١٠٠	۵٠٠	١٠٠٠
Eastern Arabic	۰	۱/۲	۱	۲	۳	۴	۵	۶	۷	۸	۹	۱۰	۵۰	۱۰۰	۵۰۰	۱۰۰۰
Hyderabad Arabic	۰	١/٢	١	٢	٣	۴	۵	۶	۷	۸	۹	۱۰	۵۰	۱۰۰	۵۰۰	۱۰۰۰
Indian (Sanskrit)	०	१/२	१	२	३	४	५	६	७	८	९	१०	५०	१००	५००	१०००
Assamese	০	১/২	১	২	৩	৪	৫	৬	৭	৮	৯	১০	৫০	১০০	৫০০	১০০০
Bengali	০	১/২	১	২	৩	৪	৫	৬	৭	৮	৯	১০	৫০	১০০	৫০০	১০০০
Gujarati	૦	૧/૨	૧	૨	૩	૪	૫	૬	૭	૮	૯	૧૦	૫૦	૧૦૦	૫૦૦	૧૦૦૦
Kutch	०	१/२	१	२	३	४	५	६	७	८	९	१०	५०	१००	५००	१०००
Devavnagri	०	१/२	१	२	३	४	५	६ or ६	७	८	९ or ९	१०	५०	१००	५००	१०००
Nepalese	०	१/२	१	२	३	४	५	६	७	८	९	१०	५०	१००	५००	१०००
Tibetan	༠	༡/༢	༡	༢	༣	༤	༥	༦	༧	༨	༩	༡༠	༥༠	༡༠༠	༥༠༠	༡༠༠༠
Mongolian	᠐	᠑/᠒	᠑	᠒	᠓	᠔	᠕	᠖	᠗	᠘	᠙	᠑᠐	᠕᠐	᠑᠐᠐	᠕᠐᠐	᠑᠐᠐᠐
Burmese	၀	၁/၂	၁	၂	၃	၄	၅	၆	၇	၈	၉	၁၀	၅၀	၁၀၀	၅၀၀	၁၀၀၀
Thai-Lao	๐	๑/๒	๑	๒	๓	๔	๕	๖	๗	๘	๙	๑๐	๕๐	๑๐๐	๕๐๐	๑๐๐๐
Lao-Laotian	໐		໑	໒	໓	໔	໕	໖	໗	໘	໙	໑໐				
Javanese	꧐		꧑	꧒	꧓	꧔	꧕	꧖	꧗	꧘	꧙	꧑꧐	꧕꧐	꧑꧐꧐	꧕꧐꧐	꧑꧐꧐꧐
Ordinary Chinese Japanese-Korean	零	半	一	二	三	四	五	六	七	八	九	十	十五	百	百五	千
Official Chinese			壹	贰	叁	肆	伍	陸	柒	捌	玖	拾	拾伍	佰	佰伍	仟
Commercial Chinese			〡	〢	〣	〤	〥	〦	〧	〨	〩	十	〥十	〡百	〥百	〡千
Korean		반	일	이	삼	사	오	육	칠	팔	구	십	오십	백	오백	천
Georgian			ა	ბ	გ	დ	ე	ვ	ზ	ჱ	თ	ი	ნ	რ	ჶ	ჩ
			11 [illegible]	20 კ	30 ლ	40 მ	60 ჲ	70 ო	80 პ	90 ჟ	200 ს	300 ტ	400 ჳ	600 ქ	700 ღ	800 ყ
Ethiopian	◆		፩	፪	፫	፬	፭	፮	፯	፰	፱	፲	፶	፻	፭ ፻	፲ ፻
				20 ፳	30 ፴	40 ፵	60 ፷	70 ፸	80 ፹	90 ፺						
Hebrew			א	ב	ג	ד	ה	ו	ז	ח	ט	י	נ	ק	תק	
				20 כ	30 ל	40 מ	60 ס	70 ע	80 פ	90 צ	200 ר	300 ש	400 ת	600 תר	700 תש	800 תת
Greek			Α	Β	Γ	Δ	Ε	Τ	Ζ	Η	Θ	Ι	Ν	Ρ	Φ	Α
				20 Κ	30 Λ	40 Μ	60 Ξ	70 Ο	80 Π		200 Σ	300 Τ	400 Υ	600 Χ	700 Ψ	800 Ω

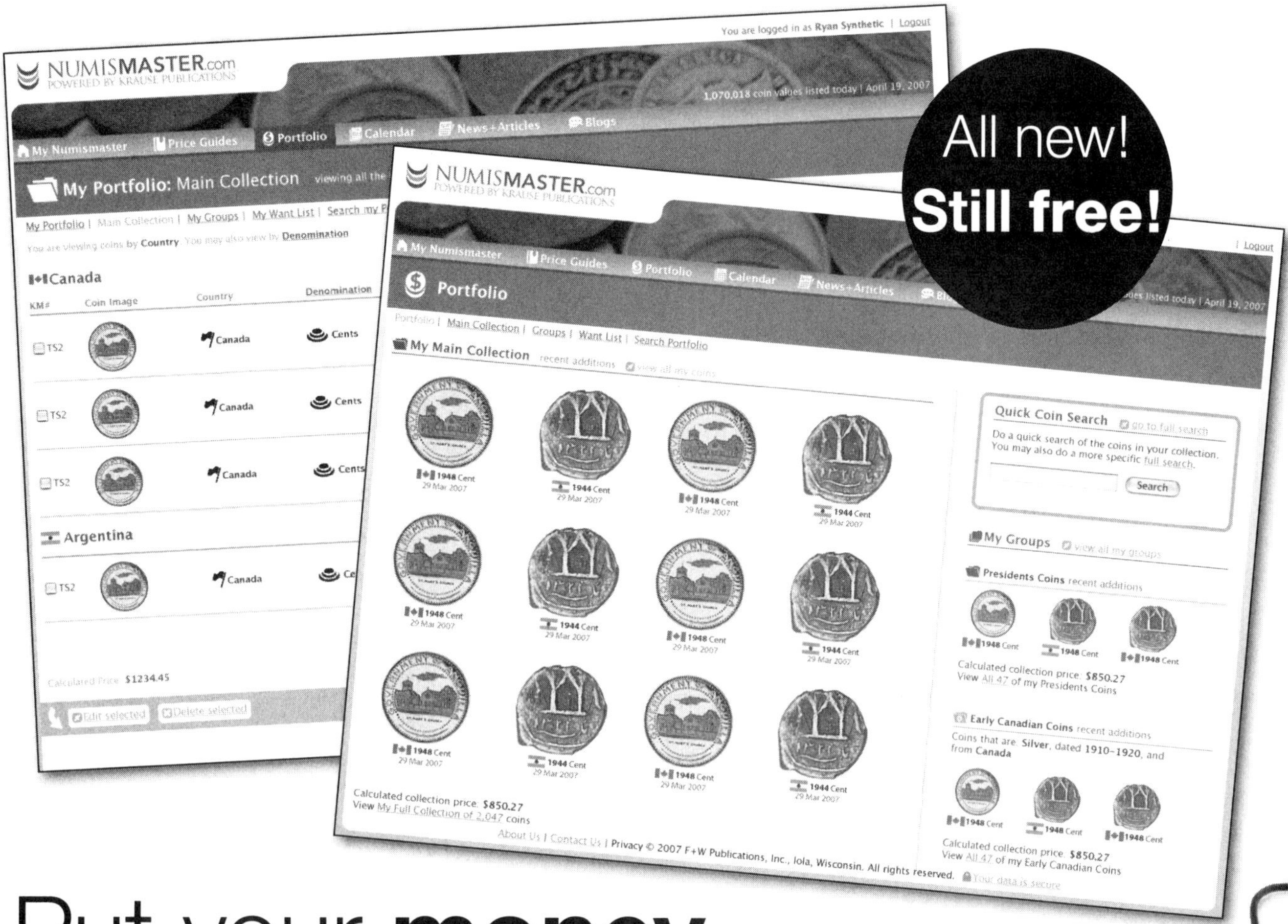

HEJIRA DATE CONVERSION CHART

HEJIRA (Hijira, Hegira), the name of the Muslim era (A.H. = Anno Hegirae) dates back to the Christian year 622 when Mohammed "fled" from Mecca, escaping to Medina to avoid persecution from the Koreish tribemen. Based on a lunar year the Muslim year is 11 days shorter.

*=Leap Year (Christian Calendar)

AH Hejira	AD Christian Date
1010	1601, July 2
1011	1602, June 21
1012	1603, June 11
1013	1604, May 30
1014	1605, May 19
1015	1606, May 19
1016	1607, May 9
1017	1608, April 28
1018	1609, April 6
1017	1608, April 28
1018	1609, April 6
1019	1610, March 26
1020	1611, March 16
1021	1612, March 4
1022	1613, February 21
1023	1614, February 11
1024	1615, January 31
1025	1616, January 20
1026	1617, January 9
1027	1617, December 29
1028	1618, December 19
1029	1619, December 8
1030	1620, November 26
1031	1621, November 16
1032	1622, November 5
1033	1623, October 25
1034	1624, October 14
1035	1625, October 3
1036	1626, September 22
1037	1627, Septembe 12
1038	1628, August 31
1039	1629, August 21
1040	1630, July 10
1041	1631, July 30
1042	1632, July 19
1043	1633, July 8
1044	1634, June 27
1045	1635, June 17
1046	1636, June 5
1047	1637, May 26
1048	1638, May 15
1049	1639, May 4
1050	1640, April 23
1051	1641, April 12
1052	1642, April 1
1053	1643, March 22
1054	1644, March 10
1055	1645, February 27
1056	1646, February 17
1057	1647, February 6
1058	1648, January 27
1059	1649, January 15
1060	1650, January 4
1061	1650, December 25
1062	1651, December 14
1063	1652, December 2
1064	1653, November 22
1065	1654, November 11
1066	1655, October 31
1067	1656, October 20
1068	1657, October 9
1069	1658, September 29
1070	1659, September 18
1071	1660, September 6
1072	1661, August 27
1073	1662, August 16
1074	1663, August 5
1075	1664, July 25
1076	1665, July 14
1077	1666, July 4
1078	1667, June 23
1079	1668, June 11
1080	1669, June 1
1081	1670, May 21
1082	1671, may 10
1083	1672, April 29
1084	1673, April 18
1085	1674, April 7

AH Hejira	AD Christian Date
1086	1675, March 28
1087	1676, March 16*
1088	1677, March 6
1089	1678, February 23
1090	1679, February 12
1091	1680, February 2*
1092	1681, January 21
1093	1682, January 10
1094	1682, December 31
1095	1683, December 20
1096	1684, December 8*
1097	1685, November 28
1098	1686, November 17
1099	1687, November 7
1100	1688, October 26*
1101	1689, October 15
1102	1690, October 5
1103	1691, September 24
1104	1692, September 12*
1105	1693, September 2
1106	1694, August 22
1107	1695, August 12
1108	1696, July 31*
1109	1697, July 20
1110	1698, July 10
1111	1699, June 29
1112	1700, June 18
1113	1701, June 8
1114	1702, May 28
1115	1703, May 17
1116	1704, May 6*
1117	1705, April 25
1118	1706, April 15
1119	1707, April 4
1120	1708, March 23*
1121	1709, March 13
1122	1710, March 2
1123	1711, February 19
1124	1712, Feburary 9*
1125	1713, January 28
1126	1714, January 17
1127	1715, January 7
1128	1715, December 27
1129	1716, December 16*
1130	1717, December 5
1131	1718, November 24
1132	1719, November 14
1133	1720, November 2*
1134	1721, October 22
1135	1722, October 12
1136	1723, October 1
1137	1724, September 19
1138	1725, September 9
1139	1726, August 29
1140	1727, August 19
1141	1728, August 7*
1142	1729, July 27
1143	1730, July 17
1144	1731, July 6
1145	1732, June 24*
1146	1733, June 14
1147	1734, June 3
1148	1735, May 24
1149	1736, May 12*
1150	1737, May 1
1151	1738, April 21
1152	1739, April 10
1153	1740, March 29*
1154	1741, March 19
1155	1742, March 8
1156	1743, Febuary 25
1157	1744, February 15*
1158	1745, February 3
1159	1746, January 24
1160	1747, January 13
1161	1748, January 2
1162	1748, December 22*
1163	1749, December 11
1164	1750, November 30
1165	1751, November 20
1166	1752, November 8*
1167	1753, October 29
1168	1754, October 18
1169	1755, October 7
1170	1756, September 26*
1171	1757, September 15
1172	1758, September 4
1173	1759, August 25
1174	1760, August 13*
1175	1761, August 2
1176	1762, July 23

AH Hejira	AD Christian Date
1177	1763, July 12
1178	1764, July 1*
1179	1765, June 20
1180	1766, June 9
1181	1767, May 30
1182	1768, May 18*
1183	1769, May 7
1184	1770, April 27
1185	1771, April 16
1186	1772, April 4*
1187	1773, March 25
1188	1774, March 14
1189	1775, March 4
1190	1776, February 21*
1191	1777, February 91
1192	1778, January 30
1193	1779, January 19
1194	1780, January 8*
1195	1780, December 28*
1196	1781, December 17
1197	1782, December 7
1198	1783, November 26
1199	1784, November 14*
1200	1785, November 4
1201	1786, October 24
1202	1787, October 13
1203	1788, October 2*
1204	1789, September 21
1205	1790, September 10
1206	1791, August 31
1207	1792, August 19*
1208	1793, August 9
1209	1794, July 29
1210	1795, July 18
1211	1796, July 7*
1212	1797, June 26
1213	1798, June 15
1214	1799, June 5
1215	1800, May 25
1216	1801, May 14
1217	1802, May 4
1218	1803, April 23
1219	1804, April 12*
1220	1805, April 1
1221	1806, March 21
1222	1807, March 11
1223	1808, February 28*
1224	1809, February 16
1225	1810, Febauary 6
1226	1811, January 26
1227	1812, January 16*
1228	1813, Janaury 26
1229	1813, December 24
1230	1814, December 14
1231	1815, December 3
1232	1816, November 21*
1233	1817, November 11
1234	1818, October 31
1235	1819, October 20
1236	1820, October 9*
1237	1821, September 28
1238	1822, September 18
1239	1823, September 18
1240	1824, August 26*
1241	1825, August 16
1242	1826, August 5
1243	1827, July 25
1244	1828, July 14*
1245	1829, July 3
1246	1830, June 22
1247	1831, June 12
1248	1832, May 31*
1249	1833, May 21
1250	1834, May 10
1251	1835, April 29
1252	1836, April 18*
1253	1837, April 7
1254	1838, March 27
1255	1839, March 17
1256	1840, March 5*
1257	1841, February 23
1258	1842, February 12
1259	1843, February 1
1260	1844, January 22*
1261	1845, January 10
1262	1845, December 30
1263	1846, December 20
1264	1847, December 9
1265	1848, November 27*
1266	1849, November 17
1267	1850, November 6

AH Hejira	AD Christian Date
1268	1851, October 27
1269	1852, October 15*
1270	1853, October 4
1271	1854, September 24
1272	1855, September 13
1273	1856, September 1*
1274	1857, August 22
1275	1858, August 11
1276	1859, July 31
1277	1860, July 20*
1278	1861, July 9
1279	1862, June 29
1280	1863, June 18
1281	1864, June 6*
1282	1865, May 27
1283	1866, May 16
1284	1867, May 5
1285	1868, April 24*
1286	1869, April 13
1287	1870, April 3
1288	1871, March 23
1289	1872, March 11*
1290	1873, March 1
1291	1874, February 18
1292	1875, Febuary 7
1293	1876, January 28*
1294	1877, January 16
1295	1878, January 5
1296	1878, December 26
1297	1879, December 15
1298	1880, December 4*
1299	1881, November 23
1300	1882, November 12
1301	1883, November 2
1302	1884, October 21*
1303	1885, October 10
1304	1886, September 30
1305	1887, September 19
1306	1888, September 7*
1307	1889, August 28
1308	1890, August 17
1309	1891, August 7
1310	1892, July 26*
1311	1893, July 15
1312	1894, July 5
1313	1895, June 24
1314	1896, June 12*
1315	1897, June 2
1316	1898, May 22
1317	1899, May 12
1318	1900, May 1
1319	1901, April 20
1320	1902, april 10
1321	1903, March 30
1322	1904, March 18*
1323	1905, March 8
1324	1906, February 25
1325	1907, February 14
1326	1908, February 4*
1327	1909, January 23
1328	1910, January 13
1329	1911, January 2
1330	1911, December 22
1332	1913, November 30
1333	1914, November 19
1334	1915, November 9
1335	1916, October 28*
1336	1917, October 17
1337	1918, October 7
1338	1919, September 26
1339	1920, September 15*
1340	1921, September 4
1341	1922, August 24
1342	1923, August 14
1343	1924, August 2*
1344	1925, July 22
1345	1926, July 12
1346	1927, July 1
1347	1928, June 20*
1348	1929, June 9
1349	1930, May 29
1350	1931, May 19
1351	1932, May 7*
1352	1933, April 26
1353	1934, April 16
1354	1935, April 5
1355	1936, March 24*
1356	1937, March 14
1357	1938, March 3
1358	1939, February 21
1359	1940, February 10*

AH Hejira	AD Christian Date
1360	1941, January 29
1361	1942, January 19
1362	1943, January 8
1363	1943, December 28
1364	1944, December 17*
1365	1945, December 6
1366	1946, November 25
1367	1947, November 15
1368	1948, November 3*
1369	1949, October 24
1370	1950, October 13
1371	1951, October 2
1372	1952, September 21*
1373	1953, September 10
1374	1954, August 30
1375	1955, August 20
1376	1956, August 8*
1377	1957, July 29
1378	1958, July 18
1379	1959, July 7
1380	1960, June 25*
1381	1961, June 14
1382	1962, June 4
1383	1963, May 25
1384	1964, May 13*
1385	1965, May 2
1386	1966, April 22
1387	1967, April 11
1388	1968, March 31*
1389	1969, march 20
1390	1970, March 9
1391	1971, February 27
1392	1972, February 16*
1393	1973, February 4
1394	1974, January 25
1395	1975, January 14
1396	1976, January 3*
1397	1976, December 23*
1398	1977, December 12
1399	1978, December 2
1400	1979, November 21
1401	1980, November 9*
1402	1981, October 30
1403	1982, October 19
1404	1984, October 8
1405	1984, September 27*
1406	1985, September 16
1407	1986, September 6
1409	1987, August 26
1409	1988, August 14*
1410	1989, August 3
1411	1990, July 24
1412	1991, July 13
1413	1992, July 2*
1414	1993, June 21
1415	1994, June 10
1416	1995, May 31
1417	1996, May 19*
1418	1997, May 9
1419	1998, April 28
1420	1999, April 17
1421	2000, April 6*
1422	2001, March 26
1423	2002, March 15
1424	2003, March 5
1425	2004, February 22*
1426	2005, February 10
1427	2006, January 31
1428	2007, January 20
1429	2008, January 10*
1430	2008, December 29
1431	2009, December 18
1432	2010, December 8
1433	2011, November 27*
1434	2012, November 15
1435	2013, November 5
1436	2014, October 25
1437	2015, October 15*
1438	2016, October 3
1439	2017, September 22
1440	2018, September 12
1441	2019, September 11*
1442	2020, August 20
1443	2021, August 10
1444	2022, July 30
1445	2023, July 19*
1446	2024, July 8
1447	2025, June 27
1448	2026, June 17
1449	2027, June 6*
1450	2028, May25

The Islamic State of Afghanistan, which occupies a mountainous region of Southwest Asia, has an area of 251,825 sq. mi. (652,090 sq. km.) and a population of 25.59 million. Presently, about a fifth of the total population lives in exile as refugees, (mostly in Pakistan). Capital: Kabul. It is bordered by Iran, Pakistan, Turkmenistan, Uzbekistan, Tajikistan, and China's Sinkiang Province. Agriculture and herding are the principal industries; textile mills and cement factories add to the industrial sector. Cotton, wool, fruits, nuts, oil, sheepskin coats and hand-woven carpets are normally exported but foreign trade has been interrupted since 1979.

Previous to 1747, Afghan Kings ruled not only in Afghanistan, but also in India, of which Sher Shah Suri was one. Ahmad Shah Abdali, founder of the Durrani dynasty, established his rule at Qandahar in 1747. His clan was known as Saddozai. He conquered large territories in India and eastern Iran, which were lost by his grandson Shah Zaman. A new family, the Barakzai, drove the Durrani king out of Kabul, the capital, in 1819, but the Durranis were not eliminated completely until 1858. Further conflicts among the Barakzai prevented full unity until the reign of Abdur Rahman beginning in 1880.

Afghanistan's traditional coinage was much like that of its neighbors Iran and India. There were four major mints: Kabul, Qandahar, Balkh and Herat. The early Durranis also controlled mints in Iran and India. On gold and silver coins, the inscriptions in Persian (called *Dari* in Afghanistan) included the name of the mint city and, normally, of the ruler recognized there, but some issues are anonymous. The arrangement of the inscriptions, and frequently the name of the ruler, was different at each mint. Copper coins were controlled locally and usually did not name any ruler. For these reasons the coinage of each mint is treated separately. The relative values of gold, silver, and copper coins were not fixed but were determined in the marketplace.

RULERS

Names of rulers are shown in Perso-Arabic script in the style usually found on their coins; they are not always in a straight line.

DURRANI OR SADDOZAI DYNASTY

Ahmad Shah,
AH1160-1186/1747-1772AD

Taimur Shah, as Nizam,
AH1170-1186/1757-1772AD

Sulaiman Shah, pretender,
AH1186/1772AD

or

Taimur Shah, as King,
AH1186-1207/1772-1793AD

Humayun, at Qandahar
AH1207/1793AD

Shah Zaman, AH1207-1216/1793-1801AD

MINT NAMES

Coins were struck at numerous mints in Afghanistan and adjacent lands. These are listed below, together with their honorific titles, and shown in the style ordinarily found on the coins.

Afghanistan — افغانستان

Ahmadnagar-Farrukhabad — احمدنگر فرخ اباد

Ahmadshahi, — احمدشاهي
see Qandahar

Until AH 1273, this mint was almost always given on the coins as *Ahmadshahi*, a name given it by Ahmad Shah in honor of himself in AH1171, often with the honorific *Ashraf as-Bilad* (meaning 'Most Noble of Cities'). On later issues, after AH1271, the traditional name *Qandahar* is generally used.

Although Qandahar was Ahmad Shah's capital throughout his reign, he did not issue coins from there until AH1171 (1758AD).

Anwala — انوله

Attock — اتك

Balkh — بلخ

Located in northern Afghanistan, Balkh bore the honorary epithet of *Umm al-Bilad*, 'Mother of Cities', because of its great age. It was taken by Ahmad Shah from the Amir of Bukhara in AH1180 (1765AD) and lost by Taimur Shah to the Uzbeks in AH1206 (1792AD).

Bareli — بريلي

Bhakkar — بهكر بهكهر

The mint is found variously spelled, as *Bhakhar* (most common), *Bakhar*, and *Bakkar*.

Dehli, — دهلي
see Shahjahanabad

Dera, — ديره

The mint of Dera was located at Dera Ghazi Khan, taken by the Sikhs in AH1235 (1819AD), and now within Pakistan.

Derajat, — ديره جات
Dera Isma'il Khan

The mint of Derajat was located at Dera Ismail Khan, which fell to the Sikhs in AH1236 (1820-21AD). Issues in the name of Mahmud Shah dated AH1236 and later are actually Sikh issues. The Sikhs formally annexed Derajat in AH1281 (1835AD).

Haidarabad Sind — حيدراباد

Herat — هراة هرات

Kabul, — كابل

Kashmir — كشمير

Lahore — لاهور

Mashhad — مشهد

Mashhad, entitled Muqaddas (holy), was the chief city of Iranian Khorasan. From AH1161/1748AD until AH1218/1803AD, it was the capital of the Afsharid principality which remained under nominal Durrani suzerainty from AH1163/1750AD onwards. Coins were struck in the name of Durrani rulers in AH1163, 1168-1186, 1198-1218.

Multan — ملتان

Multan was annexed by Ahmad Shah in AH1165/1752AD, and held under Afghan rule until lost to the Sikhs in AH1233/1818AD, except for an interval of Maratha control in AH1173/1759AD and Sikh control from AH1185-1194/1771-1780AD.

Muradabad — مراداباد

Najibabad — نجيب اباد

Peshawar — پشاور

Peshawar passed to Ahmad Shah after the death of Nadir Shah Afshar, who had seized it from the Mughals in AH1151/1738AD. It was lost to the Sikhs in AH1250/1834AD. Although the winter capital of the Durranis, it was never granted an honorific epithet.

Qandahar, — قندهار
see Ahmadshahi

Issues of this mint are listed together with those of Ahmadshahi, which was a name of Qandahar granted in honor of Ahmad Shah, founder of the Durrani Kingdom.

Rikab, — ركاب

The Camp mint brought *Mubarak* with the royal entourage while traveling.

Sahrind, — سرهند سهرند
(Sarhind)

Shahjahanabad, — شاه جهان اباد
see Delhi

Shahjahanabad was the Mughal name for Delhi, which was twice seized by Ahmad Shah, once for a couple of months in AH1170/winter 1756-1757AD, a second time in AH1173-1174/1760-1761AD for thirteen months.

Sind — سند

Tatta — تته

MINT EPITHETS

اشراف البلاد
'Ashraf al-Bilad',
Most Noble of Cities

دار السلطنة
'Dar as-Sultanat',
Abode of the Sultanate

ام البلاد
'Umm al-Bilad',
Mother of Cities

NAMED HAMMERED COINAGE

Unlike the anonymous copper coinage, which was purely local, the silver and gold coins, as well as some of the early copper coins, bear the name or characteristic type of the ruler. Because the sequence of rulers often varied at different mint cities, each ruled by different princes, the coins are best organized according to mint. Each mint employed characteristic types and calligraphy, which continued from one ruler to the next. It is hoped that this system will facilitate identification of these coins.

The following listings include not only the mints situated in contiguous territories under Durrani and Barakzai rule for extended periods of time, but also mints in Kashmir or in other parts of India which the Afghans occupied for relatively brief intervals.

KINGDOM

ANONYMOUS HAMMERED COINAGE

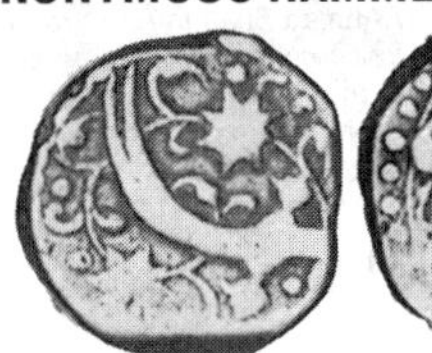

Mint: Ahmadshahi
KM# 4 FALUS
Copper **Obv:** Scimitar and star **Rev:** Inscription

Date	Mintage	Good	VG	F	VF	XF
AH1190 (1776)	—	8.00	15.00	25.00	40.00	—

Mint: Ahmadshahi
KM# 6 FALUS
Copper **Obv:** Sword and scabbard **Rev:** Inscription

Date	Mintage	Good	VG	F	VF	XF
AH1198 (1783)	—	8.00	15.00	25.00	40.00	—

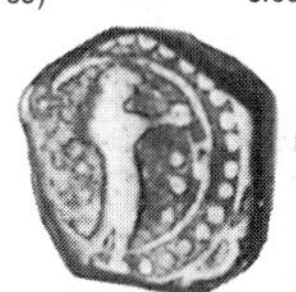

Mint: Ahmadshahi
KM# 8 FALUS
Copper **Obv:** Sword **Rev:** Inscription

Date	Mintage	Good	VG	F	VF	XF
AH1205 (1790)	—	8.00	15.00	25.00	40.00	—

Mint: Ahmadshahi
KM# 10 FALUS
Copper **Obv:** Sword within dotted circles **Rev:** Inscription

Date	Mintage	Good	VG	F	VF	XF
AH1211 (1796)	—	15.00	30.00	45.00	75.00	—

Mint: Kabul
KM# A53 FALUS
Copper **Obv:** Flower between crossed swords **Rev:** Inscription

Date	Mintage	Good	VG	F	VF	XF
AH1201 (1786)	—	8.00	15.00	25.00	40.00	—

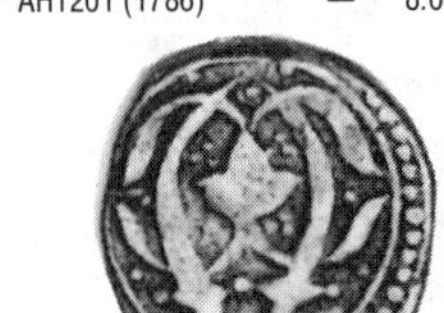

Mint: Kabul
KM# B53 FALUS
Copper **Obv:** Flower between two swords **Rev:** Inscription

Date	Mintage	Good	VG	F	VF	XF
AH1213 (1798)	—	12.00	17.00	25.00	40.00	—

Ahmad Shah

AH1148-1186 / 1735-1772AD

HAMMERED COINAGE

Mint: Bhakhar
KM# 280 FALUS
Copper **Obv:** Inscription **Rev:** Inscription **Note:** Weight varies: 16.60-19.50 grams.

Date	Mintage	Good	VG	F	VF	XF
AH1161//2 (1748)	—	10.00	15.00	25.00	40.00	—
AH1162//1(1748)	—	8.00	12.00	20.00	35.00	—
AH1162//3 (1749)	—	10.00	15.00	25.00	40.00	—
AH1163//3 (1749)	—	8.00	12.00	20.00	35.00	—
AH116x//7 (1753)	—	8.00	12.00	20.00	35.00	—
AH1168//8 (1754)	—	8.00	12.00	20.00	35.00	—
AH1169//8 (1755)	—	8.00	12.00	20.00	35.00	—

Mint: Derajat
KM# 346 FALUS
Copper

Date	Mintage	VG	F	VF	XF	Unc
AH1176 (1762) Rare	—	—	—	—	—	—

Mint: Kabul Mint
KM# 422 FALUS
Copper **Obv:** Inscription **Rev:** Inscription

Date	Mintage	Good	VG	F	VF	XF
AH1169 (1755)	—	—	—	—	—	—

Mint: Multan
KM# 640 FALUS
Copper, 23 mm. **Obv:** "Dur-e-Durrane" **Note:** Weight varies: 13.60-13.80 grams.

Date	Mintage	Good	VG	F	VF	XF
AH1170//10 (1756)	—	10.00	15.00	25.00	40.00	—
AH1172//12 (1758)	—	8.00	12.00	22.00	35.00	—

Mint: Multan
KM# 641 FALUS
Copper **Obv:** "Ahmad Shahe" **Note:** Weight varies: 13.60-13.80 grams.

Date	Mintage	Good	VG	F	VF	XF
AH1175//15 (1761)	—	12.00	18.00	27.00	45.00	—
AH1176//16 (1762)	—	12.00	18.00	27.00	45.00	—

Mint: Peshawar
KM# 690 FALUS
Copper, 20 mm. **Obv. Legend:** Inscription **Rev. Legend:** Inscription **Note:** Weight varies: 11.60-11.70 grams.

Date	Mintage	Good	VG	F	VF	XF
ND//4 (1750)	—	10.00	15.00	25.00	40.00	—
AH116x//5 (1752)	—	10.00	15.00	25.00	40.00	—
ND//7 (1753)	—	10.00	15.00	25.00	40.00	—
AH1177//17 (1763)	—	10.00	15.00	25.00	40.00	—

Mint: Dera
KM# 310 FALUS
Copper, 20-28 mm. **Obv:** Inscription **Rev:** Inscription **Note:** Weight varies: 13.00-18.50g. Size varies.

Date	Mintage	Good	VG	F	VF	XF
AH1161//1 (1748)	—	8.00	12.00	22.00	35.00	—
AH1162//1 (1748)	—	8.00	12.00	22.00	35.00	—
AH1163//1 (1749)	—	8.00	12.00	22.00	35.00	—
AH1165//5 (1751)	—	8.00	12.00	22.00	35.00	—
AH1166 (1752)	—	8.00	12.00	22.00	35.00	—
AH1167//7 (1753)	—	8.00	12.00	22.00	35.00	—
AH1168//7 (1754)	—	8.00	12.00	22.00	35.00	—
AH11xx//10 (1756)	—	8.00	12.00	22.00	35.00	—

Mint: Kashmir
KM# 550 DAM
Copper

Date	Mintage	Good	VG	F	VF	XF
ND//23 (1769)	—	10.00	15.00	25.00	40.00	—
AH1187 (sic) (1773) Error	—	12.00	20.00	30.00	45.00	—

Mint: Peshawar
KM# 691 1/10 RUPEE
Silver **Obv:** Inscription **Rev:** Inscription **Note:** Weight varies: 1.10-1.15 grams

Date	Mintage	Good	VG	F	VF	XF
AH1167//7 (1753)	—	—	15.00	35.00	55.00	75.00

Mint: Shahjahanabad
KM# 759 1/8 RUPEE
Silver **Note:** Weight varies: 1.34-1.45 grams

Date	Mintage	Good	VG	F	VF	XF
AH1170//11 (1757) Rare	—	—	—	—	—	—

Mint: Herat
KM# 377 1/4 RUPEE
2.8000 g., Silver **Obv:** Inscription **Rev:** Inscription

Date	Mintage	Good	VG	F	VF	XF
AH1163 (1749)	—	—	25.00	50.00	75.00	100

Mint: Shahjahanabad
KM# 761 NISAR
4.0000 g., Silver **Obv:** Small beaded circle at center of inscription **Rev:** Beaded circle surrounds inscription

Date	Mintage	Good	VG	F	VF	XF
AH117x//14 (1760) Rare	—	—	—	—	—	—

Mint: Shahjahanabad
KM# 762 1/2 RUPEE
Silver **Note:** Weight varies: 5.65-5.70 grams

Date	Mintage	Good	VG	F	VF	XF
AH(11)70//11 (1757) Rare	—	—	—	—	—	—

Mint: Ahmadnagar-Farrukhabad
KM# 103 RUPEE
Silver **Obv:** Inscription **Rev:** Inscription **Note:** Weight varies: 11.20-11.40 grams

Date	Mintage	Good	VG	F	VF	XF
AH1174//14 (1760)	—	—	35.00	70.00	90.00	130
AH1176//15 (1761)	—	—	35.00	70.00	90.00	130

Mint: Ahmadshahi
KM# 113 RUPEE

Silver **Obv:** Inscription **Rev:** Inscription **Note:** Weight varies: 11.40-11.60 grams.

Date	Mintage	Good	VG	F	VF	XF
AH11xx//10 (1756)	—	—	10.00	20.00	30.00	40.00
AH1171//11 (1757)	—	—	15.00	30.00	38.00	55.00
AH1172//12 (1758)	—	—	10.00	22.00	30.00	40.00
AH1172//13 (1759)	—	—	10.00	22.00	30.00	40.00
AH117x//16 (1762)	—	—	10.00	20.00	25.00	35.00
AH117x//17 (1763)	—	—	10.00	20.00	25.00	35.00
AH1178//18 (1764)	—	—	10.00	22.00	30.00	40.00
AH1180//20 (1766)	—	—	10.00	22.00	30.00	40.00
AH1182//22 (1768)	—	—	10.00	22.00	30.00	40.00
AH1182//23 (1768)	—	—	10.00	22.00	30.00	40.00
AH1183//23 (1769)	—	—	10.00	22.00	30.00	40.00
AH1184//23 (1769)	—	—	10.00	22.00	30.00	40.00
AH118x//25 (1771)	—	—	10.00	22.00	30.00	40.00
AH118x//26 (1772)	—	—	10.00	22.00	30.00	40.00

Mint: Anwala
KM# 228.1 RUPEE

Silver **Obv:** Inscription **Rev:** Quatrefoil in Arabic "S", mint name at bottom **Note:** Weight varies: 11.00-11.20 grams

Date	Mintage	Good	VG	F	VF	XF
AH1173//14 (1760)	—	—	7.50	14.00	22.50	35.00
AH1174//14 (1760	—	—	17.50	35.00	60.00	—

Mint: Anwala
KM# 228.2 RUPEE

Silver **Obv:** Inscription **Rev:** Mint name at top **Note:** Weight varies: 11.00-11.20 grams

Date	Mintage	Good	VG	F	VF	XF
AH1173//14 (1760)	—	—	15.00	35.00	50.00	70.00

Mint: Anwala
KM# 228.3 RUPEE

Silver **Obv:** Inscription **Rev:** Hexafoil in Arabic S **Note:** Weight varies: 11.00-11.20 grams

Date	Mintage	Good	VG	F	VF	XF
AH1174//14 (1760)	—	—	8.00	16.00	25.00	35.00

Mint: Attock
KM# 233 RUPEE

Silver **Note:** Weight varies: 11.00-11.40 grams

Date	Mintage	Good	VG	F	VF	XF
AH116x//9 (1755)	—	—	9.00	17.00	25.00	35.00
AH1170//11 (1756)	—	—	9.00	17.00	25.00	35.00
AH1171//11 (1757)	—	—	9.00	17.00	25.00	35.00
AH1170//12 (1757)	—	—	9.00	17.00	25.00	35.00
AH1172//12 (1758)	—	—	9.00	17.00	25.00	35.00
AH1173//13 (1759)	—	—	9.00	17.00	25.00	35.00
AH1174//14 (1760)	—	—	9.00	17.00	25.00	35.00
AH117x//19 (1764)	—	—	9.00	17.00	25.00	35.00
AH1177//81 (1764)	—	—	9.00	17.00	25.00	35.00
Note: Error for 18						
AH1179 (1765)	—	—	9.00	17.00	25.00	35.00
AH11xx//20 (1766)	—	—	9.00	17.00	25.00	35.00
AH1180//21 (1767)	—	—	9.00	17.00	25.00	35.00
AH1181//21 (1767)	—	—	9.00	17.00	25.00	35.00
AH1182//22 (1768)	—	—	9.00	17.00	25.00	35.00

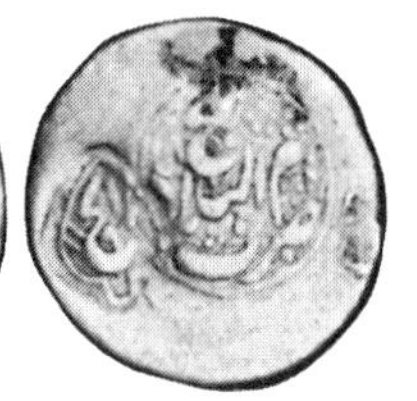

Mint: Balkh
KM# 268 RUPEE

Silver **Obv:** Inscription **Rev:** Inscription **Note:** Weight varies: 11.40-11.60 grams

Date	Mintage	Good	VG	F	VF	XF
AH1180 (1766)	—	—	30.00	60.00	100	150

Mint: Bareli
KM# 278 RUPEE

Silver, 21 mm. **Obv:** Inscription **Rev:** Inscription **Note:** Weight varies: 11.00-11.60 grams

Date	Mintage	Good	VG	F	VF	XF
AH1173//14 (1760)	—	—	10.00	20.00	35.00	50.00
AH1174//14 (1760)	—	—	10.00	20.00	35.00	50.00

Mint: Bhakhar
KM# 282 RUPEE

Silver **Obv:** Couplet in three or four lines **Rev:** Inscription in three lines **Note:** Legends arranged in various ways, weight varies: 11.20-11.60 grams

Date	Mintage	Good	VG	F	VF	XF
AH116x//3 (1749)	—	—	20.00	40.00	50.00	60.00
AH1164//4 (1750)	—	—	20.00	40.00	50.00	60.00
AH1165//5 (1751)	—	—	20.00	40.00	50.00	60.00
AH1166//7 (1753)	—	—	20.00	40.00	50.00	60.00
AH116x//8 (1754)	—	—	20.00	40.00	—	—

Mint: Bhakhar
KM# 283.1 RUPEE

Silver **Obv:** Couplet arranged around central cartouche **Rev:** Legend within small cartouche **Note:** Weight varies: 11.20-11.60 grams

Date	Mintage	Good	VG	F	VF	XF
AH116x//7 (1753)	—	—	12.50	22.50	35.00	50.00
AH116x//8 (1754)	—	—	12.50	22.50	35.00	50.00
AH1169//9 (1755)	—	—	12.50	22.50	35.00	50.00
AH1170//8 (1756)	—	—	12.50	22.50	35.00	50.00
AH1171 (1757)	—	—	12.50	22.50	35.00	50.00
AH1172 (1758)	—	—	12.50	22.50	35.00	50.00
AH1173 (1759)	—	—	12.50	22.50	35.00	50.00
AH1174 (1760)	—	—	12.50	22.50	35.00	50.00
AH1175 (1761)	—	—	12.50	22.50	35.00	50.00
AH1176 (1762)	—	—	12.50	22.50	35.00	50.00
AH1178 (1764)	—	—	—	—	—	—

Mint: Bhakhar
KM# 283.2 RUPEE

Silver **Obv:** Inscription **Rev:** Legend within large cartouche **Note:** Weight varies: 11.20-11.60 grams

Date	Mintage	Good	VG	F	VF	XF
AH1177 (1763)	—	—	12.50	22.50	35.00	50.00
AH1178 (1764)	—	—	12.50	22.50	35.00	50.00
AH1179 (1765)	—	—	12.50	22.50	35.00	50.00
AH1180 (1766)	—	—	12.50	22.50	35.00	50.00
AH1181 (1767)	—	—	12.50	22.50	35.00	50.00
AH1182 (1768)	—	—	12.50	22.50	35.00	50.00

Date	Mintage	Good	VG	F	VF	XF
AH1183 (1769)	—	—	12.50	22.50	35.00	50.00
AH1184 (1770)	—	—	12.50	22.50	35.00	50.00
AH1185 (1771)	—	—	13.00	23.00	40.00	65.00

Mint: Derajat
KM# 348.2 RUPEE

Silver **Obv:** Inscription **Rev:** Inscription **Note:** Crude style. Retrograde 6 in date. Weight varies: 10.80-11.60 grams

Date	Mintage	Good	VG	F	VF	XF
AH1168 (1754)	—	—	—	—	—	—
AH1180 (1766)	—	—	—	—	—	—

Mint: Derajat
KM# 348.1 RUPEE

Silver **Obv:** Inscription in three lines **Rev:** Inscription **Note:** Weight varies: 10.80-11.60 grams

Date	Mintage	Good	VG	F	VF	XF
AH116x//5 (1751)	—	—	10.00	18.00	28.00	40.00
AH1166 (1752)	—	—	10.00	18.00	28.00	40.00
AH1168 (1754)	—	—	10.00	18.00	28.00	40.00
AH1170 (1756)	—	—	10.00	18.00	28.00	40.00
AH1171 (1757)	—	—	10.00	18.00	28.00	40.00
AH1173 (1759)	—	—	10.00	18.00	28.00	40.00
AH1180 (1766)	—	—	10.00	18.00	28.00	40.00
AH1181 (1767)	—	—	10.00	18.00	28.00	40.00
AH1183//23 (1769)	—	—	10.00	18.00	28.00	40.00
AH118x (1770)	—	—	10.00	18.00	28.00	40.00

Mint: Herat
KM# 378 RUPEE

11.4000 g., Silver **Obv:** Inscription **Rev:** Inscription

Date	Mintage	Good	VG	F	VF	XF
AH1168//8 (1754)	—	—	15.00	35.00	45.00	60.00
AH1171 (1757)	—	—	15.00	35.00	45.00	60.00

Mint: Kabul Mint
KM# 423 RUPEE

Silver **Obv:** Inscription in four lines **Rev:** Inscription in three lines **Note:** Weight varies: 11.20-11.40 grams

Date	Mintage	Good	VG	F	VF	XF
AH116x//1 (1747)	—	—	10.00	20.00	30.00	40.00
AH116x//3 (1749)	—	—	10.00	20.00	30.00	40.00
AH1163 (1749)	—	—	—	—	—	—
AH116x//5 (1751)	—	—	10.00	20.00	30.00	40.00
AH1166//6 (1752)	—	—	10.00	20.00	30.00	40.00
AH116x//8 (1754)	—	—	10.00	20.00	30.00	40.00
AH1170 (1756)	—	—	10.00	20.00	30.00	40.00
AH1171 (1757)	—	—	10.00	20.00	30.00	40.00
AH1170//1173 (1759)	—	—	10.00	20.00	30.00	40.00
AH1173 (1759)	—	—	10.00	20.00	30.00	40.00
AH1174 (1760)	—	—	10.00	20.00	30.00	40.00
AH1175//15 (1761)	—	—	10.00	20.00	30.00	40.00
AH1176//16 (1762)	—	—	10.00	20.00	30.00	40.00
AH1177//17 (1763)	—	—	10.00	20.00	30.00	40.00
AH1178//18 (1764)	—	—	10.00	20.00	30.00	40.00
AH1179//19 (1765)	—	—	10.00	20.00	30.00	40.00
AH1180//20 (1766)	—	—	10.00	20.00	30.00	40.00
AH1181//21 (1767)	—	—	10.00	20.00	30.00	40.00
AH1182//22 (1768)	—	—	10.00	20.00	30.00	40.00
AH1183//23 (1769)	—	—	10.00	20.00	30.00	40.00
AH1184//23 (1770)	—	—	10.00	20.00	30.00	40.00
AH1184//24 (1770)	—	—	10.00	20.00	30.00	40.00
AH1185//24 (1771)	—	—	10.00	20.00	30.00	40.00
AH1186//25 (1772)	—	—	10.00	20.00	30.00	40.00

Mint: Kabul Mint
KM# 424 RUPEE
Silver **Obv:** Couplet around central cartouche **Rev:** Inscription **Note:** Weight varies: 11.20-11.40 grams

Date	Mintage	Good	VG	F	VF	XF
AH116x//8 (1754)	—	—	20.00	50.00	60.00	90.00

Mint: Kashmir
KM# 553 RUPEE
Silver **Obv:** Inscription **Rev:** Inscription **Note:** Weight varies: 11.20-11.40 grams

Date	Mintage	Good	VG	F	VF	XF
AH1176//14 (1762)	—	—	10.00	18.00	30.00	45.00
AH1176//15 (1762)	—	—	10.00	18.00	30.00	45.00
AH1177//15 (1763)	—	—	10.00	18.00	30.00	45.00
AH1177//16 (1763)	—	—	10.00	18.00	30.00	45.00
AH1178//17 (1764)	—	—	10.00	18.00	30.00	45.00
AH1179//18 (1765)	—	—	10.00	18.00	30.00	45.00
AH1179//19 (1765)	—	—	10.00	18.00	30.00	45.00
AH11xx//20 (1766)	—	—	10.00	18.00	30.00	45.00
AH118x//21 (1767)	—	—	10.00	18.00	30.00	45.00
AH1181//21 (1767)	—	—	10.00	18.00	30.00	45.00
AH1182//22 (1768)	—	—	10.00	18.00	30.00	45.00
AH1184//23 (1770)	—	—	10.00	18.00	30.00	45.00
AH1184//24 (1770)	—	—	10.00	18.00	30.00	45.00
AH1185//24 (1771)	—	—	10.00	18.00	30.00	45.00
AH1186//25 (1772)	—	—	10.00	18.00	30.00	45.00

Mint: Lahore
KM# 622 RUPEE
Silver **Obv:** Inscription in four lines **Rev:** Inscription in four lines **Note:** Weight varies: 11.20-11.40 grams

Date	Mintage	Good	VG	F	VF	XF
AH1161//1 (1748)	—	—	30.00	70.00	100	125

Mint: Lahore
KM# 623 RUPEE
Silver **Note:** Weight varies: 11.20-11.40 grams. Struck at Lahore Mint.

Date	Mintage	Good	VG	F	VF	XF
AH1165//5 (1751)	—	—	20.00	35.00	50.00	75.00
AH1170//10 (1756)	—	—	10.00	15.00	20.00	30.00
AH1170//11 (1757)	—	—	10.00	15.00	20.00	30.00
AH1173//13 (1759)	—	—	10.00	15.00	20.00	30.00
AH1173//14 (1760)	—	—	10.00	15.00	20.00	30.00
AH1173//15 (1760)	—	—	10.00	15.00	20.00	30.00
AH1174//15 (1761)	—	—	10.00	15.00	20.00	30.00
AH1175//15 (1761)	—	—	10.00	15.00	20.00	30.00
AH1175//16 (1762)	—	—	10.00	15.00	20.00	30.00
AH1176//16 (1762)	—	—	10.00	15.00	20.00	30.00
AH1176//17 (1763)	—	—	10.00	15.00	20.00	30.00
AH1177//17 (1763)	—	—	10.00	15.00	20.00	30.00
AH1177//18 (1764)	—	—	10.00	15.00	20.00	30.00
AH1178//18 (1764)	—	—	10.00	15.00	20.00	30.00
AH1178//19 (1765)	—	—	10.00	15.00	20.00	30.00
AH1179//19 (1765)	—	—	10.00	15.00	20.00	30.00
AH1180//21 (1767)	—	—	10.00	15.00	20.00	30.00

Mint: Multan
KM# 643 RUPEE
Silver **Obv:** Inscription in four lines **Rev:** Inscription in three lines **Note:** Weight varies: 11.20-11.50 grams

Date	Mintage	Good	VG	F	VF	XF
AH1165//5 (1751)	—	—	10.00	15.00	25.00	40.00
AH1166//5 (1752)	—	—	10.00	15.00	25.00	40.00
AH1166//6 (1752)	—	—	10.00	15.00	25.00	40.00
AH1167//6 (1753)	—	—	10.00	15.00	25.00	40.00
AH1167//7 (1753)	—	—	10.00	15.00	25.00	40.00
AH1168//7 (1754)	—	—	10.00	15.00	25.00	40.00
AH1168//8 (1754)	—	—	10.00	15.00	25.00	40.00
AH1170//10 (1756)	—	—	15.00	25.00	35.00	45.00

Mint: Multan
KM# 644 RUPEE
Silver **Obv:** Name in central cartouche **Rev:** Inscription **Note:** Weight varies: 11.40-11.50 grams

Date	Mintage	Good	VG	F	VF	XF
AH1168//8 (1754)	—	—	10.00	25.00	35.00	50.00
AH1169//8 (1755)	—	—	10.00	25.00	35.00	50.00
AH1169//9 (1755)	—	—	10.00	25.00	35.00	50.00

Mint: Multan
KM# A645 RUPEE
Silver **Obv:** Inscription **Rev:** Epithet "Dar al-Aman" added **Note:** Weight varies: 11.40-11.50 grams

Date	Mintage	Good	VG	F	VF	XF
AH1170//9 (1756)	—	—	12.50	25.00	35.00	45.00
AH1170//10 (1756)	—	—	12.50	25.00	35.00	45.00

Mint: Muradabad
KM# 683 RUPEE
Silver **Obv:** Inscription **Rev:** Inscription **Note:** Weight varies: 11.20-11.40 grams

Date	Mintage	Good	VG	F	VF	XF
AH1173//14 (1760)	—	—	10.00	17.00	30.00	45.00

Mint: Najibabad
KM# 688 RUPEE
Silver **Obv:** Inscription **Rev:** Inscription **Note:** Weight varies: 11.00-11.40 grams

Date	Mintage	Good	VG	F	VF	XF
AH1180//21 (1767)	—	—	40.00	70.00	100	125

Mint: Peshawar
KM# 693 RUPEE
Silver **Obv:** Inscription in four lines **Rev:** Inscription in three lines **Note:** Weight varies: 11.20-11.40 grams

Date	Mintage	Good	VG	F	VF	XF
AH1160 (1747)	—	—	12.00	18.00	30.00	45.00
AH1161//1 (1748)	—	—	10.00	15.00	25.00	35.00
AH1161//2 (1748)	—	—	10.00	15.00	25.00	35.00
AH1162//2 (1748)	—	—	10.00	15.00	25.00	35.00
AH1164//3 (1750)	—	—	10.00	15.00	25.00	35.00
AH116x//4 (1750)	—	—	10.00	15.00	25.00	35.00
AH1166//5 (1752)	—	—	10.00	15.00	25.00	35.00
AH1166//6 (1752)	—	—	10.00	15.00	25.00	35.00
AH1168//9 (1755)	—	—	10.00	15.00	25.00	35.00
AH1170//10 (1756)	—	—	10.00	15.00	25.00	35.00
AH1171//11 (1757)	—	—	10.00	15.00	25.00	35.00
AH1172//12 (1758)	—	—	10.00	15.00	25.00	35.00
AH117x//14 (1760)	—	—	10.00	15.00	25.00	35.00
AH117x//15 (1761)	—	—	10.00	15.00	25.00	35.00
AH1176//16 (1762)	—	—	10.00	15.00	25.00	35.00
AH1177//17 (1763)	—	—	10.00	15.00	25.00	35.00
AH117x//18 (1764)	—	—	10.00	15.00	25.00	35.00
AH117x//19 (1765)	—	—	10.00	15.00	25.00	35.00
AH118x//22 (1768)	—	—	10.00	15.00	25.00	35.00
AH1183//23 (1769)	—	—	10.00	15.00	25.00	35.00
AH1184//24 (1770)	—	—	10.00	15.00	25.00	35.00
AH1185//25 (1771)	—	—	10.00	15.00	25.00	35.00
AH1186//26 (1772)	—	—	10.00	15.00	25.00	35.00

Mint: Sarhind
KM# 753 RUPEE
Silver, 21.5 mm. **Obv:** Inscription in three lines **Rev:** Inscription in three lines **Note:** Weight varies: 10.60-11.20 grams

Date	Mintage	Good	VG	F	VF	XF
AH116x//1 (1747)	—	—	10.00	17.50	25.00	35.00
AH1164//4 (1750)	—	—	10.00	17.50	25.00	35.00
AH1173 (1759)	—	—	10.00	17.50	25.00	35.00
AH1174//14 (1760)	—	—	10.00	17.50	25.00	35.00
AH1174//15 (1761)	—	—	10.00	17.50	25.00	35.00
AH1175//16 (1762)	—	—	10.00	17.50	25.00	35.00
AH1176//15 (1762)	—	—	10.00	17.50	25.00	35.00
AH1176//16 (1762)	—	—	10.00	17.50	25.00	35.00
AH1177 (sic)//21 (1767)	—	—	10.00	17.50	25.00	35.00

Mint: Shahjahanabad
KM# 763 RUPEE
Silver **Obv:** Inscription **Rev:** Inscription **Note:** Weight varies: 11.30-11.40 grams

Date	Mintage	Good	VG	F	VF	XF
AH1170//11 (1757)	—	—	45.00	100	150	200
AH1173//14 (1760)	—	—	45.00	100	150	200
AH1174//15 (1760)	—	—	45.00	100	150	200

Mint: Sind
KM# 771 RUPEE
Silver **Obv:** Inscription **Rev:** Inscription **Note:** Weight varies: 11.00-11.50 grams

Date	Mintage	Good	VG	F	VF	XF
AH1173 (1759)	—	—	40.00	85.00	110	150

Mint: Tatta
KM# 783 RUPEE
Silver **Obv:** Inscription **Rev:** Inscription **Note:** Weight varies: 11.40-11.60 grams

Date	Mintage	Good	VG	F	VF	XF
AH1170 (1756)	—	—	20.00	40.00	55.00	70.00
AH1171 (1757)	—	—	20.00	40.00	55.00	70.00
AH1174//14 (1760)	—	—	20.00	40.00	55.00	70.00

Mint: Dera
KM# 313 RUPEE
Silver **Obv:** Inscription **Rev:** Inscription in four lines

Note: Obverse and reverse dies are often carelessly paired, which accounts for the discrepancies between AH dates and regnal years. Other dates may exist. Weight varies: 11.30-11.50 grams.

Date	Mintage	Good	VG	F	VF	XF
AH1168//8 (1754)	—	—	12.50	20.00	30.00	45.00
AH1169//9 (1755)	—	—	12.50	20.00	30.00	45.00
AH1170//10 (1756)	—	—	12.50	20.00	30.00	45.00
AH1173//13 (1759)	—	—	12.50	20.00	30.00	45.00
AH1173//14 (1760)	—	—	12.50	20.00	30.00	45.00
AH1174//14 (1761)	—	—	12.50	20.00	30.00	45.00
AH1174//15 (1761)	—	—	12.50	20.00	30.00	45.00
AH1175//15 (1761)	—	—	12.50	20.00	30.00	45.00
AH1175//16 (1762)	—	—	12.50	20.00	30.00	45.00
AH1177//17 (1763)	—	—	12.50	20.00	30.00	45.00
AH1178//18 (1764)	—	—	12.50	20.00	30.00	45.00
AH1179//19 (1765)	—	—	12.50	20.00	30.00	45.00
AH1180//20 (1766)	—	—	12.50	20.00	30.00	45.00
AH1180//21 (1768)	—	—	12.50	20.00	30.00	45.00
AH1180//22 (1768)	—	—	12.50	20.00	30.00	45.00
AH1182//22 (1768)	—	—	12.50	20.00	30.00	45.00
AH1182//23 (1769)	—	—	12.50	20.00	30.00	45.00
AH1182//24 (1770)	—	—	12.50	20.00	30.00	45.00
AH1184//24 (1770)	—	—	12.50	20.00	30.00	45.00
AH1184//25 (1770)	—	—	12.50	20.00	30.00	45.00
AH1185//25 (1771)	—	—	12.50	20.00	30.00	45.00
AH1184//26 (1772)		—	12.50	20.00	30.00	45.00

Mint: Dera
KM# B315 RUPEE
Silver **Note:** Weight varies: 10.70-11.00g

Date	Mintage	Good	VG	F	VF	XF
AH11xx//Yr9 (1722)	—	—	—	—	—	—

Mint: Dera
KM# A313 RUPEE
Silver **Obv:** Inscription in four lines **Rev:** Inscription in three lines **Note:** Weight varies: 11.30-11.50 grams

Date	Mintage	Good	VG	F	VF	XF
AH116x//1 (1747)	—	—	12.50	20.00	30.00	45.00
AH1163 (1749)	—	—	12.50	20.00	30.00	45.00
AH1166//5 (1752)	—	—	12.50	20.00	30.00	45.00
AH1167//6 (1753)	—	—	12.50	20.00	30.00	45.00
AH1167//7 (1753)	—	—	12.50	20.00	30.00	45.00
AH1168//7 (1754)	—	—	12.50	20.00	30.00	45.00

Mint: Shahjahanabad
KM# 764 NAZARANA RUPEE
11.3000 g., Silver, 38 mm. **Obv:** Inscription in four lines **Rev:** Inscription in three lines

Date	Mintage	Good	VG	F	VF	XF
AH1173//14 (1760) Rare	—	—	—	—	—	—
AH1174//15 (1760)	—	—	—	—	1,500	1,800

Mint: Dera
KM# 314 HEAVY RUPEE
13.6800 g., Silver **Obv:** Lion left **Rev:** Inscription

Date	Mintage	Good	VG	F	VF	XF
AH116x//2 (1748)	—	—	175	300	400	550

Mint: Kabul
KM# A422 1-1/4 RUPEE
Silver **Shape:** Teardrop flan **Note:** Similar to Mashad Mint Rupee KM#636

Date	Mintage	Good	VG	F	VF	XF
AH1163 (1749) Rare	—	—	—	—	—	—

Mint: Ahmadshahi
KM# 114 ASHRAFI
3.5000 g., Gold

Date	Mintage	Good	VG	F	VF	XF
AH1171//11 (1757) Rare	—	—	—	—	—	—
AH118x//22 (1768) Rare	—	—	—	—	—	—
AH118x//23 (1769) Rare	—	—	—	—	—	—

Mint: Bhakhar
KM# 284 ASHRAFI
3.5000 g., Gold

Date	Mintage	Good	VG	F	VF	XF
AH1168//8 (1754) Rare	—	—	—	—	—	—

Mint: Shahjahanabad
KM# 768 1/2 MOHUR
Gold **Obv:** Inscription within cartouche **Rev:** Inscription **Note:** Weight varies: 5.35-5.42 grams.

Date	Mintage	Good	VG	F	VF	XF
AH1170//11 (1757) Rare	—	—	—	—	—	—

Mint: Ahmadnagar-Farrukhabad
KM# 105 MOHUR
Gold **Obv:** Inscription **Rev:** Inscription **Note:** Weight varies: 10.80-11.00 grams.

Date	Mintage	Good	VG	F	VF	XF
AH1176//15 (1761)	—	—	300	550	800	1,150

Mint: Ahmadshahi
KM# 115 MOHUR
Gold **Obv:** Inscription in four lines **Rev:** Inscription **Note:** Weight varies: 10.90 grams.

Date	Mintage	Good	VG	F	VF	XF
AH1177 (1763) Rare	—	—	—	—	—	—
AH118x//22 (1768)	—	—	—	—	450	500
AH118x//23 (1769)	—	—	—	—	450	500

Mint: Attock
KM# 235 MOHUR
Gold **Obv:** Inscription **Rev:** Inscription **Note:** Weight varies: 10.80-10.90 grams.

Date	Mintage	Good	VG	F	VF	XF
AH1175//15 (1761) Rare	—	—	—	—	—	—
AH1181//21 (1767) Rare	—	—	—	—	—	—

Mint: Bhakhar
KM# 285 MOHUR
10.9000 g., Gold **Obv:** Inscription **Rev:** Inscription

Date	Mintage	Good	VG	F	VF	XF
AH1177 (1763) Rare	—	—	—	—	—	—

Mint: Derajat
KM# 349 MOHUR
Gold **Obv:** Inscription in four lines **Rev:** Inscription **Note:** Weight varies: 10.80-10.90 grams

Date	Mintage	Good	VG	F	VF	XF
AH1161 (1748) Rare	—	—	—	—	—	—
AH1170 (1756) Rare	—	—	—	—	—	—
AH1180 (1766) Rare	—	—	—	—	—	—
AH118x//23 (1769) Rare	—	—	—	—	—	—

Mint: Herat
KM# 379 MOHUR
Gold **Obv:** Inscription in four lines **Rev:** Inscription on beaded background **Note:** Weight varies: 10.90-11.00 grams.

Date	Mintage	Good	VG	F	VF	XF
ND (1747)	—	—	275	450	700	1,000

Mint: Kabul Mint
KM# 426 MOHUR
Gold, 20-21.5 mm. **Note:** Weight varies: 10.80-10.90 grams. Size varies.

Date	Mintage	Good	VG	F	VF	XF
AH1161//1 (1748) Rare	—	—	—	—	—	—
AH1161//1 (1748) Rare	—	—	—	—	—	—
AH1170//10 (1756) Rare	—	—	—	—	—	—
AH1174//(1)4 (1760) Rare	—	—	—	—	—	—
AH1181//21 (1767)	—	—	200	325	500	700
AH1185//25 (1771)	—	—	200	325	500	700
AH1186//25 (1772)	—	—	200	325	500	700

Mint: Kashmir
KM# 555 MOHUR
10.9000 g., Gold

Date	Mintage	Good	VG	F	VF	XF
AH1167//6 (1754) Rare	—	—	—	—	—	—

Mint: Lahore
KM# 626 MOHUR
Gold **Obv:** Inscription in four lines **Rev:** Inscription in three lines **Note:** Similar to Rupee, KM#623. Weight varies: 10.70-11.00 grams.

Date	Mintage	Good	VG	F	VF	XF
AH1170 (1756)	—	—	300	525	800	1,150
AH1175//15 (1761)	—	—	300	525	800	1,150
AH1175//16 (1762)	—	—	300	525	800	1,150

Mint: Lahore
KM# 625 MOHUR
Gold **Obv:** Inscription in four lines **Rev:** Inscription in four lines
Note: Weight varies: 10.70-11.00 grams.

Date	Mintage	Good	VG	F	VF	XF
AH1161//1 (1748) Rare	—	—	—	—	—	—

Mint: Multan
KM# 645.1 MOHUR
Gold **Obv:** Inscription, small cartouche at center **Rev:** Inscription within large cartouche **Note:** Weight varies: 10.90-11.00 grams.

Date	Mintage	Good	VG	F	VF	XF
AH1165//5 (1751)	—	—	400	650	1,000	1,600
AH1166//5 (1752)	—	—	400	650	1,000	1,600
AH1167//6 (1753)	—	—	400	650	1,000	1,600
AH116x//8 (1754)	—	—	400	650	1,000	1,600
AH1169//9 (1755)	—	—	400	650	1,000	1,600
AH1170//9 (1756)	—	—	400	650	1,000	1,600
AH1170//10 (1756)	—	—	400	650	1,000	1,600

Mint: Multan
KM# 645.2 MOHUR
Gold **Obv:** Inscription **Rev:** Inscription **Note:** Weight varies: 10.90-11.00 grams.

Date	Mintage	Good	VG	F	VF	XF
AH1170//9 (1756)	—	—	450	750	1,200	1,750

Mint: Najibabad
KM# 689 MOHUR
Gold **Obv:** Inscription **Rev:** Inscription **Note:** Weight varies: 10.80-11.00 grams.

Date	Mintage	Good	VG	F	VF	XF
AH1180//21 (1767) Rare	—	—	—	—	—	—

Mint: Peshawar
KM# 695 MOHUR
Gold, 20 mm. **Obv:** Inscription in three lines **Rev:** Inscription in three lines **Note:** Weight varies: 10.80-11.00 grams.

Date	Mintage	Good	VG	F	VF	XF
AH1161//1 (1748)	—	—	175	300	450	700
AH116x//3 (1749)	—	—	175	300	450	700
AH116x//6 (1752)	—	—	175	300	450	700
AH116x//9 (1755)	—	—	175	300	450	700
AH1177//17 (1763)	—	—	175	300	450	700

Mint: Rikab
KM# 742 MOHUR
11.0000 g., Gold

Date	Mintage	Good	VG	F	VF	XF
AH1173 (1759) Rare	—	—	—	—	—	—

Mint: Sarhind
KM# 755 MOHUR
Gold **Note:** Weight varies: 10.80-10.90 grams.

Date	Mintage	Good	VG	F	VF	XF
AH116x//1 (1747) Rare	—	—	—	—	—	—

Date	Mintage	Good	VG	F	VF	XF
AH1172 (1758) Rare	—	—	—	—	—	—
AH117x//16 (1762) Rare	—	—	—	—	—	—

Mint: Shahjahanabad
KM# 765 MOHUR
Gold **Obv:** Inscription **Rev:** Inscription **Note:** Weight varies: 10.70-10.85 grams.

Date	Mintage	Good	VG	F	VF	XF
AH1170//11 (1757)	—	—	—	375	525	650
AH1173//14 (1760)	—	—	—	375	525	650
AH1174//14 (1760)	—	—	—	375	525	650

Mint: Shahjahanabad
KM# 766 MOHUR
Gold **Obv:** Inscription in four lines **Rev:** Inscription **Note:** Weight varies: 10.70-10.85 grams.

Date	Mintage	Good	VG	F	VF	XF
AH1174//15 (1760)	—	—	350	550	800	1,000

Mint: Dera
KM# A315 MOHUR
Gold **Obv:** Inscription **Rev:** Inscription

Date	Mintage	Good	VG	F	VF	XF
1168//8 (1754)	—	—	—	—	—	—

Mint: Dera
KM# 315 MOHUR
Gold **Obv:** Inscription **Rev:** Inscription within large cartouche **Note:** Weight varies: 10.90-11.00 grams. Several varieties exist.

Date	Mintage	Good	VG	F	VF	XF
AH1162//2 (1748)	—	—	175	300	450	700
AH1166//5 (1752)	—	—	175	300	450	700
AH116x//8 (1754)	—	—	175	300	450	700
AH116x//9 (1755)	—	—	175	300	450	700
AH1170//10 (1756)	—	—	175	300	450	700
AH1171//11 (1757)	—	—	175	300	450	700
AH1175//15 (1761)	—	—	175	300	450	700
AH1175//16 (1762)	—	—	175	300	450	700
AH1184//25 (1771)	—	—	175	300	450	700

Mint: Kabul Mint
KM# 427 NAZARANA MOHUR
10.9200 g., Gold, 35 mm. **Obv:** Inscription **Rev:** Inscription

Date	Mintage	Good	VG	F	VF	XF
AH1175 (1761)	—	—	—	1,500	2,500	3,500
AH1175/4//14 (1761)	—	—	—	—	—	—

Mint: Shahjahanabad
KM# 767 NAZARANA MOHUR
Gold, 34-37 mm. **Obv:** Inscription in four lines **Rev:** Inscription
Note: Weight varies: 10.70-11.00 grams. Size varies.

Date	Mintage	Good	VG	F	VF	XF
AH1173//14 (1760) Rare	—	—	—	—	—	—
AH1174//15 (1761) Rare	—	—	—	—	—	—

Ahmad Shah
AH1163 / 1750AD
HAMMERED COINAGE

Mint: Lahore
KM# 636 1-1/4 RUPEE
Silver **Obv:** Inscription **Rev:** Inscription **Shape:** Teardrop flan
Note: Struck in the name of Shahrokh, the local Afsharid prince. Weight varies: 13.80-14.00 grams

Date	Mintage	Good	VG	F	VF	XF
AH1163 (1750) Rare	—	—	—	—	—	—

Ahmad Shah
AH1186 / 1755AD
HAMMERED COINAGE

Mint: Lahore
KM# 637 SHAHI
Silver **Obv:** Inscription **Rev:** Inscription **Note:** Weight varies: 1.00-1.15 grams

Date	Mintage	Good	VG	F	VF	XF
AH1168//8 (1754)	—	—	15.00	35.00	50.00	70.00
AH1170 (1756)	—	—	40.00	55.00	75.00	100
AH1181 (1767)	—	—	15.00	35.00	50.00	70.00

Mint: Lahore
KM# 638 RUPEE
Silver **Obv:** Inscription **Rev:** Inscription within circle **Note:** Weight varies: 11.00-11.50 grams

Date	Mintage	Good	VG	F	VF	XF
AH1168//8 (1754)	—	—	17.50	40.00	60.00	80.00
AH116x//9 (1755)	—	—	15.00	30.00	45.00	60.00
AH1170//(10) (1756)	—	—	17.50	40.00	60.00	80.00
AH1171//11 (1757)	—	—	17.50	40.00	60.00	80.00
AH1186 (1772)	—	—	17.50	40.00	60.00	80.00

Note: After Ahmad's death in AH1186/1772AD, Shahrukh resumed minting coins in his own name; coins are known dated AH1187-1197 (rupees and mohurs)

Mint: Lahore
KM# A639 ASHRAFI

3.5000 g., Gold **Obv:** Inscription **Rev:** Inscription within 8-pointed star

Date	Mintage	Good	VG	F	VF	XF
AH1168//8 (1754)	—	—	120	200	300	475

Mint: Lahore
KM# 639 ASHRAFI

3.5000 g., Gold **Obv:** Inscription **Rev:** Inscription **Note:** Weight varies: 10.60-11.00 grams.

Date	Mintage	Good	VG	F	VF	XF
AH116x//8 (1754)	—	—	—	—	275	350
AH116x//9 (1755)	—	—	—	—	275	350
AH117x//11 (1757)	—	—	—	—	275	350

Taimur Shah

AH1170-1186 / 1757-1772AD - Nizam

HAMMERED COINAGE

Mint: Multan
KM# 650 FALUS

Copper **Obv:** Inscription **Rev:** Inscription **Note:** AH dates and regnal years are usually mismatched. Weight varies: 11.30-13.70 grams.

Date	Mintage	Good	VG	F	VF	XF
AH1181 (1772) Error date	—	9.00	15.00	25.00	38.00	—
AH1194//3 (1780)	—	8.00	12.00	22.00	35.00	—
AH1196 (1781)	—	8.00	12.00	22.00	35.00	—
AH1197//6 (1782)	—	8.00	12.00	22.00	35.00	—
AH1200//7 (1785)	—	8.00	12.00	22.00	35.00	—
AH120x//8 (1786)	—	8.00	12.00	22.00	35.00	—
AH1201//10 (1786)	—	8.00	12.00	22.00	35.00	—
AH1202//10 (1787)	—	8.00	12.00	22.00	35.00	—
AH1203//10 (1788)	—	8.00	12.00	22.00	35.00	—
AH1204 (1789)	—	8.00	12.00	22.00	35.00	—
AH1205//19 (1790)	—	8.00	12.00	22.00	35.00	—
AH1206//19 (1791)	—	8.00	12.00	22.00	35.00	—
AH1206//20 (1792)	—	8.00	12.00	22.00	35.00	—
AH1207//19 (1792)	—	8.00	12.00	22.00	35.00	—

Mint: Dera
KM# 316 FALUS

Copper **Obv:** Inscription **Rev:** Inscription **Note:** Weight varies: 12.00-13.00 grams.

Date	Mintage	Good	VG	F	VF	XF
AH1172//3 (1758)	—	10.00	15.00	25.00	45.00	—

Mint: Bhakhar
KM# 292.2 RUPEE

Silver **Note:** Retrograde date. Weight varies: 11.20-11.60 grams

Date	Mintage	Good	VG	F	VF	XF
AH1180 (1766)	—	—	—	—	—	—

Mint: Bhakhar
KM# 292.1 RUPEE

Silver **Note:** Weight varies: 11.20-11.60 grams

Date	Mintage	Good	VG	F	VF	XF
AH1173 (1759)	—	—	20.00	40.00	50.00	65.00
AH1175 (1761)	—	—	20.00	40.00	50.00	65.00
AH1177 (1763)	—	—	20.00	40.00	50.00	65.00
AH1178 (1764)	—	—	20.00	40.00	50.00	65.00
AH1180 (1766)	—	—	20.00	40.00	50.00	65.00
AH1181 (1767)	—	—	20.00	40.00	50.00	65.00
AH1182 (1768)	—	—	20.00	40.00	50.00	65.00
AH1183 (1769)	—	—	20.00	40.00	50.00	65.00
AH1184 (1770)	—	—	20.00	40.00	50.00	65.00
AH1185 (1771)	—	—	20.00	40.00	50.00	65.00
AH1186 (1772)	—	—	20.00	40.00	50.00	65.00

Mint: Haidarabad Sind
KM# 420 RUPEE

Silver **Obv:** Inscription **Rev:** Inscription

Date	Mintage	Good	VG	F	VF	XF
AH(1186-1207) (1772)	—	—	25.00	50.00	80.00	125

Note: Mint name appears as Haidarabad Sind; this city was founded by Ghulam Shah Kalhora in 1768AD and became the capital of the Talpur Mirs in 1786AD, both being feudatories of Taimur Shah Durrani; also see coins of Sind Mint

Mint: Lahore
KM# 628 RUPEE

Silver **Obv:** Inscription **Rev:** Inscription **Note:** Weight varies: 11.20-11.40 grams

Date	Mintage	Good	VG	F	VF	XF
AH1170//1 (1756)	—	—	12.50	28.00	40.00	55.00
AH1171//1 (1757)	—	—	12.50	28.00	40.00	55.00
AH1172//1 (1758)	—	—	12.50	28.00	40.00	55.00
AH1173//3 (1759)	—	—	12.50	28.00	40.00	55.00
AH1174//4 (1760)	—	—	12.50	28.00	40.00	55.00

Mint: Multan
KM# 652.1 RUPEE

Silver **Obv:** Inscription **Rev:** Inscription **Note:** Weight varies: 11.40-11.50 grams

Date	Mintage	Good	VG	F	VF	XF
AH1170//1 (1757)	—	—	12.00	25.00	35.00	45.00
AH1171//1 (1757)	—	—	12.00	25.00	35.00	45.00
AH1172//2 (1758)	—	—	12.00	25.00	35.00	45.00

Mint: Multan
KM# 652.2 RUPEE

Silver **Obv:** With mint epithet **Rev:** Inscription **Note:** Weight varies: 11.40-11.50 grams

Date	Mintage	Good	VG	F	VF	XF
AH1173//2 (1759)	—	—	12.00	25.00	35.00	45.00
AH1173//3 (1759)	—	—	12.00	25.00	35.00	45.00
AH1174//3 (1760)	—	—	12.00	25.00	35.00	45.00
AH1174//4 (1760)	—	—	12.00	25.00	35.00	45.00
AH1175//4 (1761)	—	—	12.00	25.00	35.00	45.00
AH1175//5 (1761)	—	—	12.00	25.00	35.00	45.00
AH1176//5 (1762)	—	—	12.00	25.00	35.00	45.00
AH1176//6 (1762)	—	—	12.00	25.00	35.00	45.00
AH1177//7 (1763)	—	—	12.00	25.00	35.00	45.00
AH1177//8 (1764)	—	—	12.00	25.00	35.00	45.00
AH1178//8 (1764)	—	—	12.00	25.00	35.00	45.00
AH1178//9 (1765)	—	—	12.00	25.00	35.00	45.00

Mint: Multan
KM# 652.4 RUPEE

Silver **Obv:** Mint name above "ZERB" wtihin cartouche **Rev:** Inscription **Note:** Weight varies: 11.40-11.50 grams

Date	Mintage	Good	VG	F	VF	XF
AH1181//11 (1767)	—	—	25.00	50.00	70.00	90.00
AH1182 (1769)	—	—	25.00	50.00	70.00	90.00

Mint: Multan
KM# 652.3 RUPEE

Silver **Obv:** Inscription **Rev:** Ornamented quatrefoil in linear and beaded circles **Note:** Weight varies: 11.40-11.50 grams.

Date	Mintage	Good	VG	F	VF	XF
AH1179//9 (1765)	—	—	12.00	25.00	35.00	45.00
AH1179//10 (1766)	—	—	12.00	25.00	35.00	45.00
AH1180//10 (1766)	—	—	12.00	25.00	35.00	45.00
AH1180//11 (1767)	—	—	12.00	25.00	35.00	45.00
AH1181//11 (1767)	—	—	12.00	25.00	35.00	45.00
AH1181//12 (1768)	—	—	12.00	25.00	35.00	45.00
AH1182//12 (1768)	—	—	12.00	25.00	35.00	45.00
AH1182//13 (1769)	—	—	12.00	25.00	35.00	45.00
AH1183//13 (1769)	—	—	12.00	25.00	35.00	45.00
AH1183//14 (1770)	—	—	12.00	25.00	35.00	45.00
AH1184//14 (1770)	—	—	12.00	25.00	35.00	45.00
AH1184//15 (1771)	—	—	12.00	25.00	35.00	45.00
AH1185//15 (1771)	—	—	12.00	25.00	35.00	45.00
AH1185//16 (1772)	—	—	12.00	25.00	35.00	45.00

Mint: Sind
KM# 773 RUPEE

Silver **Obv:** Inscription **Rev:** Inscription **Note:** Weight varies: 11.00-11.50 grams

Date	Mintage	Good	VG	F	VF	XF
AH1170//1 (1757)	—	—	25.00	60.00	85.00	115

Mint: Dera
KM# 318 RUPEE

Copper, 21.5 mm. **Obv:** Inscription within beaded circle **Rev:** Inscription **Note:** Weight varies: 11.40-11.60 grams

Date	Mintage	Good	VG	F	VF	XF
AH1170//1 (1757)	—	—	14.00	30.00	40.00	50.00
ND//2 (1757)	—	—	14.00	30.00	40.00	50.00
ND//3 (1758)	—	—	14.00	30.00	40.00	50.00

Mint: Lahore
KM# 629 MOHUR

Gold **Obv:** Inscription **Rev:** Inscription **Note:** Weight varies: 10.80-11.00 grams.

Date	Mintage	Good	VG	F	VF	XF
AH1170//1 (1757)	—	—	225	400	600	800
AH1171//1 (1757)	—	—	225	400	600	800

Mint: Multan
KM# 655 MOHUR

Gold **Note:** Weight varies: 10.85-11.00 grams. Size varies: 19-20.5 milimeters.

Date	Mintage	Good	VG	F	VF	XF
AH1170//1 (1757)	—	—	225	400	600	900
AH1173//2 (1759)	—	—	225	400	600	900
AH1176//6 (1762)	—	—	225	400	600	900
AH1178//8 (1764)	—	—	225	400	600	900
AH117x//9 (1765)	—	—	225	400	600	900
AH1182//12 (1768)	—	—	225	400	600	900

Mint: Dera
KM# 319 MOHUR
11.0000 g., Gold **Obv:** Inscription **Rev:** Inscription

Date	Mintage	Good	VG	F	VF	XF
AH1170//1 (1757) Rare	—	—	—	—	—	—
AH117x//3 (1758) Rare	—	—	—	—	—	—

Sulaiman Shah
AH1186 / 1772AD
HAMMERED COINAGE

Mint: Ahmadshahi
KM# 118 RUPEE
Silver **Obv:** Inscription **Rev:** Inscription **Note:** Weight varies: 11.40-11.60 grams.

Date	Mintage	Good	VG	F	VF	XF
AH1186//1 (1772)	—	—	50.00	110	160	240

Mint: Kabul Mint
KM# 428 RUPEE
Silver, 21.5 mm. **Obv:** Inscription **Rev:** Inscription **Note:** Weight varies: 11.40-11.50 grams

Date	Mintage	Good	VG	F	VF	XF
AH1186//1 (1772)	—	—	55.00	100	150	225

Mint: Kashmir
KM# 558 RUPEE
Silver **Obv:** Inscription **Rev:** Inscription **Note:** Weight varies: 10.90-11.00

Date	Mintage	Good	VG	F	VF	XF
AH1186//1 (1772)	—	—	65.00	140	200	250

Mint: Peshawar
KM# 699 RUPEE
11.4000 g., Silver **Obv:** Inscription **Rev:** Inscription

Date	Mintage	Good	VG	F	VF	XF
AH1186//1 (1772)	—	—	75.00	140	185	250

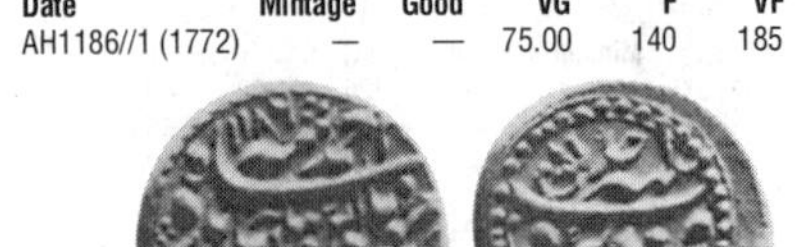

Mint: Dera
KM# 322 RUPEE
Silver **Obv:** Full couplet **Rev:** Inscription **Note:** Weight varies: 11.40-11.60 grams

Date	Mintage	Good	VG	F	VF	XF
AH1186//1 (1772)	—	—	60.00	150	200	265

Mint: Dera
KM# 323 RUPEE
Silver **Obv:** "Dur-i-Durran" **Rev:** Inscription **Note:** Weight varies: 11.40-11.60 grams

Date	Mintage	Good	VG	F	VF	XF
AH1186//1 (1772)	—	—	60.00	150	200	265

Mint: Kabul Mint
KM# 429 MOHUR
10.8500 g., Gold **Obv:** Inscription **Rev:** Inscription

Date	Mintage	Good	VG	F	VF	XF
AH1186//1 (1772) Rare	—	—	—	—	—	—

Taimur Shah
AH1186-1207 / 1772-1793AD - King
HAMMERED COINAGE

Mint: Balkh
KM# 270 FALUS
Copper **Obv:** Inscription **Rev:** Single sword **Note:** Weight varies: 7.00-10.50 grams.

Date	Mintage	Good	VG	F	VF	XF
AH1197 (1782)	—	8.00	12.00	22.00	35.00	—
AH1202 (1787)	—	7.00	10.00	16.00	30.00	—
Note: AH1202 is ordinarily found written as AH1220						
AH1205 (1790)	—	7.00	10.00	16.00	30.00	—
AH1206 (1791)	—	10.00	20.00	25.00	40.00	—

Mint: Balkh
KM# 271 FALUS
Copper **Obv:** Inscription **Rev:** Double sword **Note:** Weight varies: 7.00-10.50 grams.

Date	Mintage	Good	VG	F	VF	XF
AH1206 (1791)	—	8.00	12.00	22.00	35.00	—

Mint: Bhakhar
KM# 290 FALUS
Copper **Obv:** Inscription **Rev:** Inscription **Note:** Weight varies: 12.00-16.20 grams.

Date	Mintage	Good	VG	F	VF	XF
AH1188 (1774)	—	12.00	18.00	30.00	45.00	—
AH1189//8 (1775)	—	12.00	18.00	30.00	45.00	—
AH119x//9 (1780)	—	12.00	18.00	30.00	45.00	—
AH1194 (1780)	—	12.00	18.00	30.00	45.00	—
AH1196 (1781)	—	12.00	18.00	30.00	45.00	—
AH1197 (1782)	—	12.00	18.00	30.00	45.00	—
AH1198 (1783)	—	12.00	18.00	30.00	45.00	—

Mint: Peshawar
KM# 700 FALUS
Copper **Obv:** Inscription **Rev:** Inscription **Note:** Weight varies: 10.20-12.60 grams.

Date	Mintage	Good	VG	F	VF	XF
AH1186//1 (1772)	—	10.00	15.00	25.00	40.00	—
AH11xx//4 (1775)	—	10.00	15.00	25.00	40.00	—
AH119x//8 (1779)	—	10.00	15.00	25.00	40.00	—

Mint: Peshawar
KM# 701 FALUS
Copper, 18-20 mm. **Rev:** Foliated design **Note:** Weight varies: 7.80-8.00 grams. Size varies.

Date	Mintage	Good	VG	F	VF	XF
ND (1772)	—	10.00	17.00	28.00	45.00	—

Mint: Dera
KM# 326 FALUS
Copper **Obv:** Inscription **Rev:** Inscription **Note:** Weight varies: 11.30-12.20 grams.

Date	Mintage	Good	VG	F	VF	XF
AH119x//6 (1777)	—	8.00	12.00	22.00	35.00	—
AH1199 (1784)	—	8.00	12.00	22.00	35.00	—
AH1201//16 (1786)	—	8.00	12.00	22.00	35.00	—
AH120x//18 (1788)	—	8.00	12.00	22.00	35.00	—

Mint: Kashmir
KM# 560 DAM
Copper **Obv:** Inscription **Rev:** Inscription **Note:** Weight varies: 16.00-19.00 grams

Date	Mintage	Good	VG	F	VF	XF
AH118x//1 (1772)	—	9.00	14.00	25.00	45.00	—
AH119x//9 (1780)	—	9.00	14.00	25.00	45.00	—
AH1195 (1780)	—	9.00	14.00	25.00	45.00	—
AH1197 (1782)	—	9.00	14.00	25.00	45.00	—

Mint: Kashmir
KM# 561 DAM
Copper **Obv:** Inscription **Rev:** Inscription **Note:** Weight varies: 16.00-19.00 grams

Date	Mintage	Good	VG	F	VF	XF
AH1199//12 (1784)	—	8.00	13.00	22.00	40.00	—
AH1200//12 (1785)	—	8.00	13.00	22.00	40.00	—
AH1200//13 (1785)	—	7.00	12.00	20.00	35.00	—
AH1201//13 (1786)	—	7.00	12.00	20.00	35.00	—
AH1201//14 (1786)	—	7.00	12.00	20.00	35.00	—
AH1201//15 (1786)	—	7.00	12.00	20.00	35.00	—
AH1202//15 (1787)	—	7.00	12.00	20.00	35.00	—
AH1203//16 (1788)	—	7.00	12.00	20.00	35.00	—
AH1204//17 (1789)	—	7.00	12.00	20.00	35.00	—

Mint: Herat
KM# 381 1/12 RUPEE
0.9000 g., Silver, 13 mm. **Obv:** Full couplet **Rev:** Mint name, date

Date	Mintage	Good	VG	F	VF	XF
AH1211 (1796) Rare	—	—	—	—	—	—

Mint: Mashhad
KM# A640 SHAHI
Silver **Obv:** Inscription **Rev:** Inscription within cartouche

Date	Mintage	Good	VG	F	VF	XF
ND (1784)	—	—	—	—	—	—

Mint: *Ahmadshahi/Qandahar Mint*
KM# 123 RUPEE
Silver **Obv:** Inscription **Rev:** Long legend **Note:** Weight varies: 11.40-11.60 grams.

Date	Mintage	Good	VG	F	VF	XF
AH1187//2 (1773)	—	—	10.00	17.50	25.00	35.00
AH1187//3 (1774)	—	—	10.00	17.50	25.00	35.00
AH1189 (1775)	—	—	10.00	17.50	25.00	35.00
AH1190//5 (1776)	—	—	10.00	17.50	25.00	35.00
AH1191 (1777)	—	—	10.00	17.50	25.00	35.00
AH1192 (1778)	—	—	10.00	17.50	25.00	35.00
AH1193//21 (1779)	—	—	10.00	17.50	25.00	35.00
AH1194//9 (1780)	—	—	10.00	17.50	25.00	35.00
AH1195 (1780)	—	—	10.00	17.50	25.00	35.00
AH1197//12 (1782)	—	—	10.00	17.50	25.00	35.00
AH1198 (1783)	—	—	10.00	17.50	25.00	35.00

Mint: Ahmadshahi
KM# 124 RUPEE
Silver **Obv:** Inscription **Rev:** Shorter legend **Note:** Weight varies: 11.40-11.60 grams.

Date	Mintage	Good	VG	F	VF	XF
AH1204//18 (1788)	—	—	—	10.00	15.00	25.00
AH1205//19 (1789)	—	—	—	10.00	15.00	25.00
AH1206//19 (1790)	—	—	—	10.00	15.00	25.00
AH1206//20 (1791)	—	—	—	10.00	15.00	25.00
AH1026 (sic) (1791)	—	—	—	—	—	—
AH1207 (sic)//20 (1791)	—	—	—	10.00	15.00	25.00
AH1207//20 (1792)	—	—	—	10.00	15.00	25.00
AH1027//21 (1792)	—	—	—	—	—	—
AH1207 (sic)//12 (1792)	—	—	—	10.00	15.00	25.00

Error for year 21

Mint: Attock
KM# 238 RUPEE
Silver **Obv:** Inscription **Rev:** Inscription **Note:** Weight varies: 11.00-11.40 grams

Date	Mintage	Good	VG	F	VF	XF
AH1186//1 (1772)	—	—	10.00	20.00	30.00	40.00
AH1187//2 (1773)	—	—	10.00	20.00	30.00	40.00
AH1188//2 (1774)	—	—	10.00	20.00	30.00	40.00
AH1188 (sic)//4 (1774)	—	—	10.00	20.00	30.00	40.00
AH1190//4 (1776)	—	—	10.00	20.00	30.00	40.00
AH1192//4 (1778)	—	—	10.00	20.00	30.00	40.00
AH1193//8 (1779)	—	—	10.00	20.00	30.00	40.00
AH1195//10 (1780)	—	—	10.00	20.00	30.00	40.00
AH1195//8 (1780)	—	—	10.00	20.00	30.00	40.00
AH1196//10 (1781)	—	—	10.00	20.00	30.00	40.00
AH1197//12 (1782)	—	—	10.00	20.00	30.00	40.00
AH1197//11 (1782)	—	—	10.00	20.00	30.00	40.00
AH1197//14 (1782)	—	—	10.00	20.00	30.00	40.00
AH1198//12 (1783)	—	—	10.00	20.00	30.00	40.00
AH1198 (sic)//14 (1784)	—	—	10.00	20.00	30.00	40.00
AH120x//16 (1786)	—	—	10.00	20.00	30.00	40.00

Mint: Bakhar
KM# 294 RUPEE
Silver **Obv:** Without cartouche **Rev:** Without cartouche **Note:** Weight varies: 11.20-11.60 grams.

Date	Mintage	Good	VG	F	VF	XF
AH1205 (1790)	—	—	50.00	75.00	95.00	120

Mint: Balkh
KM# 273 RUPEE
Silver **Obv:** Inscription **Rev:** Inscription within circle **Note:** Weight varies: 11.00-11.60 grams

Date	Mintage	Good	VG	F	VF	XF
AH1195 (1780)	—	—	35.00	60.00	75.00	100
AH1198 (1783)	—	—	35.00	60.00	75.00	100
AH1200 (1785)	—	—	35.00	60.00	75.00	100
AH1201 (1786)	—	—	35.00	60.00	75.00	100
AH1205 (1790)	—	—	35.00	50.00	75.00	100

Mint: Bhakhar
KM# 293b RUPEE
Silver

Date	Mintage	Good	VG	F	VF	XF
ND (1792)	—	—	—	—	—	—

Mint: Bhakhar
KM# B293 RUPEE
Silver **Note:** Chevron border, star above.

Date	Mintage	Good	VG	F	VF	XF
AH1190 (1776)	—	—	—	—	—	—

Mint: Bhakhar
KM# 293 RUPEE
Silver **Obv:** Inscription **Rev:** Inscription **Note:** Weight varies: 11.20-11.60 grams.

Date	Mintage	Good	VG	F	VF	XF
AH1186 (1772)	—	—	12.50	20.00	28.00	38.00
AH1187 (1773)	—	—	12.50	20.00	28.00	38.00
AH1188 (1774)	—	—	12.50	20.00	28.00	38.00
AH1189 (1775)	—	—	12.50	20.00	28.00	38.00
AH1190 (1776)	—	—	12.50	20.00	28.00	38.00
AH1191 (1777)	—	—	12.50	20.00	28.00	38.00
AH1192 (1778)	—	—	12.50	20.00	28.00	38.00
AH1193 (1779)	—	—	12.50	20.00	28.00	38.00
AH1195 (1780)	—	—	12.50	20.00	28.00	38.00
AH1196 (1781)	—	—	12.50	20.00	28.00	38.00
AH1197 (1782)	—	—	12.50	20.00	28.00	38.00
AH1198 (1783)	—	—	12.50	20.00	28.00	38.00
AH1199 (1784)	—	—	12.50	20.00	28.00	38.00
AH1200 (1785)	—	—	12.50	20.00	28.00	38.00
AH1201 (1786)	—	—	12.50	20.00	28.00	38.00
AH1202 (1787)	—	—	12.50	20.00	28.00	38.00
AH1203 (1788)	—	—	12.50	20.00	28.00	38.00
AH1204 (1789)	—	—	12.50	20.00	28.00	38.00

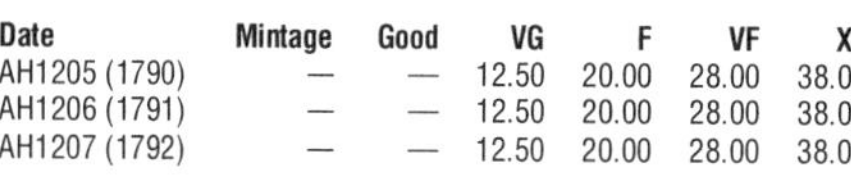

Date	Mintage	Good	VG	F	VF	XF
AH1205 (1790)	—	—	12.50	20.00	28.00	38.00
AH1206 (1791)	—	—	12.50	20.00	28.00	38.00
AH1207 (1792)	—	—	12.50	20.00	28.00	38.00

Mint: Bhakhar
KM# 293a RUPEE
Silver **Obv:** Inscription **Rev:** Mint and date in dotted circle **Note:** Weight varies: 11.20-11.60 grams.

Date	Mintage	Good	VG	F	VF	XF
AH1190 (1776)	—	—	40.00	65.00	90.00	110
AH1191 (1777)	—	—	40.00	65.00	90.00	110

Mint: Derajat
KM# 353 RUPEE
Silver **Obv:** Inscription **Rev:** Inscription **Note:** Weight varies: 10.80-11.20 grams

Date	Mintage	Good	VG	F	VF	XF
AH1187 (1773)	—	—	15.00	20.50	40.00	55.00
AH1192//6 (1778)	—	—	10.00	20.00	30.00	40.00
AH1192 (sic)//8 (1779)	—	—	10.00	20.00	30.00	40.00
AH1194//7 (1780)	—	—	10.00	20.00	30.00	40.00
AH1196//10 (1781)	—	—	10.00	20.00	30.00	40.00
AH1197//11 (1782)	—	—	10.00	20.00	30.00	40.00
AH1198//12 (1783)	—	—	10.00	20.00	30.00	40.00
AH1199//13 (1784)	—	—	10.00	20.00	30.00	40.00
AH1199 (sic)//15 (1785)	—	—	10.00	20.00	30.00	40.00
AH1200//15 (1785)	—	—	10.00	20.00	30.00	40.00
AH1201//16 (1786)	—	—	10.00	20.00	30.00	40.00
AH1202//17 (1787)	—	—	10.00	20.00	30.00	40.00
AH1202 (sic)//18 (1788)	—	—	10.00	20.00	30.00	40.00
AH1203//18 (1788)	—	—	10.00	20.00	30.00	40.00
AH1204//18 (1789)	—	—	10.00	20.00	30.00	40.00
AH1205//19 (1790)	—	—	10.00	20.00	30.00	40.00
AH1206//19 (1790)	—	—	10.00	20.00	30.00	40.00
AH1206//20 (1791)	—	—	10.00	20.00	30.00	40.00
AH120x//21 (1791)	—	—	10.00	20.00	30.00	40.00
AH1207//20 (1792)	—	—	10.00	20.00	30.00	40.00
AH1207//22 (1792)	—	—	17.50	35.00	50.00	70.00
AH1208 (1793)	—	—	17.50	35.00	50.00	70.00

Note: Posthumous issues, bearing no regnal year

Date	Mintage	Good	VG	F	VF	XF
AH1209 (1794)	—	—	17.50	35.00	50.00	70.00

Note: Posthumous issues, bearing no regnal year

Mint: Herat
KM# 383.2 RUPEE
Silver **Obv:** Inscription **Obv. Inscription:** "Taimur Shah..." **Rev:** Mint and epithet **Note:** Posthumous issue struck by Mahmud Shah. Weight varies: 11.20-11.60 grams.

Date	Mintage	Good	VG	F	VF	XF
AH1201 (1786)	—	—	7.00	14.00	20.00	28.00
AH1202 (1787)	—	—	7.00	14.00	20.00	28.00
AH1203 (1788)	—	—	7.00	14.00	20.00	28.00
AH1204 (1789)	—	—	6.00	10.00	12.50	20.00
AH1205 (1790)	—	—	6.00	10.00	12.50	20.00
AH1206 (1791)	—	—	6.00	10.00	12.50	20.00
AH1207 (1792)	—	—	6.00	10.00	12.50	20.00
AH1208 (1793)	—	—	6.00	12.00	18.00	25.00
AH1209 (1794)	—	—	6.00	12.00	18.00	25.00
AH1210 (1795)	—	—	6.00	12.00	18.00	25.00
AH1211 (1796)	—	—	6.00	12.00	18.00	25.00
AH1216 (1801)	—	—	6.00	12.00	20.00	30.00
AH1221 (1806)	—	—	6.00	12.00	20.00	30.00

Mint: Herat
KM# 383.1 RUPEE

Silver **Obv:** Inscription **Rev:** Formula and mint **Rev. Legend:** "Julus" **Note:** Weight varies: 11.20-11.60 grams

Date	Mintage	Good	VG	F	VF	XF
AH1184 (1770)	—	—	7.00	14.00	20.00	28.00
AH1187 (1773)	—	—	7.00	14.00	20.00	28.00
AH1188 (1774)	—	—	7.00	14.00	20.00	28.00
AH1189 (1775)	—	—	7.00	14.00	20.00	28.00
AH1190 (1776)	—	—	7.00	14.00	20.00	28.00
AH1191 (1777)	—	—	7.00	14.00	20.00	28.00
AH1192 (1778)	—	—	7.00	14.00	20.00	28.00
AH1193 (1779)	—	—	7.00	14.00	20.00	28.00
AH1194 (1780)	—	—	7.00	14.00	20.00	28.00
AH1195 (1780)	—	—	7.00	14.00	20.00	28.00
AH1196 (1781)	—	—	7.00	14.00	20.00	28.00
AH1197 (1782)	—	—	7.00	14.00	20.00	28.00
AH1198 (1783)	—	—	7.00	14.00	20.00	28.00
AH1199 (1784)	—	—	7.00	14.00	20.00	28.00
AH1200 (1785)	—	—	7.00	14.00	20.00	28.00

Mint: Kabul Mint
KM# 433.1 RUPEE

Silver **Obv:** Inscription with ruler's name and titles in three lines **Rev:** Full year in "L" of "Kabul", regnal year below **Note:** Weight varies: 11.00-11.65 grams

Date	Mintage	Good	VG	F	VF	XF
AH1186//1 (1772)	—	—	12.00	20.00	30.00	40.00
AH1187//1 (1773)	—	—	12.00	20.00	30.00	40.00
AH1187//2 (1773)	—	—	12.00	20.00	30.00	40.00
AH1188//2 (1774)	—	—	12.00	20.00	30.00	40.00
AH1188//3 (1774)	—	—	12.00	20.00	30.00	40.00
AH1189//3 (1775)	—	—	12.00	20.00	30.00	40.00

Mint: Kabul Mint
KM# 433.3 RUPEE

Silver **Obv:** Similar to KM#433.2, inscription with ruler name and titles in four lines, year in bottom line **Rev:** Similar to KM#433.1, but only regnal year **Note:** Weight varies: 11.00-11.65 grams

Date	Mintage	Good	VG	F	VF	XF
AH1190//4 (1776)	—	—	12.00	20.00	30.00	40.00
AH1191//4 (1777)	—	—	12.00	20.00	30.00	40.00
AH1191//5 (1777)	—	—	12.00	20.00	30.00	40.00
AH1192//6 (1778)	—	—	12.00	20.00	30.00	40.00
AH1193//6 (1779)	—	—	12.00	20.00	30.00	40.00
AH1193//7 (1779)	—	—	12.00	20.00	30.00	40.00
AH1194//8 (1780)	—	—	12.00	20.00	30.00	40.00
AH1195//9 (1780)	—	—	12.00	20.00	30.00	40.00
AH1197//11 (1782)	—	—	12.00	20.00	30.00	40.00
AH119x//12 (1782)	—	—	12.00	20.00	30.00	40.00
AH1200//13 (1785)	—	—	12.00	20.00	30.00	40.00
AH120x//15 (1785)	—	—	12.00	20.00	30.00	40.00
AH1201 (1786)	—	—	12.00	20.00	30.00	40.00
AH120x//16 (1786)	—	—	12.00	20.00	30.00	40.00
AH1203//17 (1788)	—	—	12.00	20.00	30.00	40.00

Mint: Kabul Mint
KM# 433.4 RUPEE

Silver **Obv:** Inscription **Rev:** Inscription **Note:** Weight varies: 11.00-11.65 grams

Date	Mintage	Good	VG	F	VF	XF
AH1204//18 (1789)	—	—	8.00	12.50	18.00	25.00
AH1204//19 (1789)	—	—	8.00	12.50	18.00	25.00
AH1205//19 (1790)	—	—	8.00	12.50	18.00	25.00
AH1205//20 (1790)	—	—	8.00	12.50	18.00	25.00
AH1206//20 (1791)	—	—	8.00	12.50	18.00	25.00
AH1207//20 (1792)	—	—	8.00	12.50	18.00	25.00
AH1207//21 (1792)	—	—	8.00	12.50	18.00	25.00

Note: Some rupees are exceptionally well struck on wide planchets, up to 34mm; flans over 30mm command a substantial premium

Mint: Kabul Mint
KM# 433.2 RUPEE

Silver **Obv:** Inscription with ruler's name and titles in four lines, year in bottom line **Rev:** Inscription with mint name, regnal year in bottom line **Note:** Weight varies: 11.00-11.65 grams.

Date	Mintage	Good	VG	F	VF	XF
AH1189//3 (1775)	—	—	12.00	20.00	30.00	40.00

Mint: Kashmir
KM# 563 RUPEE

Silver **Obv:** Inscription in three lines **Rev:** Inscription **Note:** Weight varies: 10.80-11.00 grams

Date	Mintage	Good	VG	F	VF	XF
AH1187//1 (1773)	—	—	15.00	25.00	35.00	50.00
AH118x//3 (1774)	—	—	8.00	15.00	25.00	40.00
AH1190//4 (1776)	—	—	8.00	15.00	25.00	40.00
AH1191//5 (1777)	—	—	8.00	15.00	25.00	40.00
AH1192//5 (1778)	—	—	8.00	15.00	25.00	40.00
AH1193//6 (1779)	—	—	8.00	15.00	25.00	40.00
AH1194//7 (1780)	—	—	8.00	15.00	25.00	40.00
AH1195//7 (1780)	—	—	8.00	15.00	25.00	40.00
AH1195//8 (1780)	—	—	8.00	15.00	25.00	40.00
AH1196//9 (1781)	—	—	8.00	15.00	25.00	40.00
Note: Contains a different arrangement of the reverse legend						
AH1197//9 (1782)	—	—	8.00	15.00	25.00	40.00
Note: Contains a different arrangement of the reverse legend						
AH1197//10 (1782)	—	—	8.00	15.00	25.00	40.00
AH1198//6 (1783)	—	—	8.00	15.00	25.00	40.00
AH1198//7 (1783)	—	—	8.00	15.00	25.00	40.00
AH1198//10 (1784)	—	—	8.00	15.00	25.00	40.00
AH1198//11 (1784)	—	—	8.00	15.00	25.00	40.00
AH1199//12 (1784)	—	—	8.00	15.00	25.00	40.00
Note: Contains a different arrangement of the reverse legend						
AH1200//12 (1785)	—	—	8.00	15.00	25.00	40.00
Note: Contains a different arrangement of the reverse legend						
AH1200//13 (1786)	—	—	8.00	15.00	25.00	40.00
AH1201//13 (1786)	—	—	8.00	15.00	25.00	40.00
AH1201//14 (1787)	—	—	8.00	15.00	25.00	40.00
AH1202//14 (1787)	—	—	8.00	15.00	25.00	40.00
AH1202//15 (1788)	—	—	8.00	15.00	25.00	40.00
AH1203//15 (1788)	—	—	8.00	15.00	25.00	40.00
AH1203//16 (1789)	—	—	8.00	15.00	25.00	40.00
AH1204//16 (1789)	—	—	8.00	15.00	25.00	40.00
AH1204//17 (1790)	—	—	8.00	15.00	25.00	40.00
AH1205//17 (1790)	—	—	8.00	15.00	25.00	40.00
AH1206//19 (1791)	—	—	8.00	15.00	25.00	40.00
AH1207//19 (1792)	—	—	8.00	15.00	25.00	40.00
AH1207//20 (1793)	—	—	8.00	15.00	25.00	40.00
AH1208//20 (1793)	—	—	8.00	15.00	25.00	40.00

Mint: Kashmir
KM# 564 RUPEE

Silver **Obv:** Inscription **Rev:** "Khitta Kashmir" **Note:** Weight varies: 10.80-11.00 grams. Struck at Kashmir Mint.

Date	Mintage	Good	VG	F	VF	XF
AH1208//20 (1793)	—	—	10.00	15.00	25.00	35.00

Mint: Mashhad
KM# C640 RUPEE

Silver **Note:** Posthumous issue. Struck by Mahmud Shah in the name of his deceased father. In AH1210/1797AD, Mashhad was seized by Agha Mohammad Shah of Iran and held for a few weeks. Coins dated AH1211 are known. Weight varies: 11.00-11.50 grams.

Date	Mintage	Good	VG	F	VF	XF
AH1208 (1793)	—	—	20.00	45.00	65.00	100

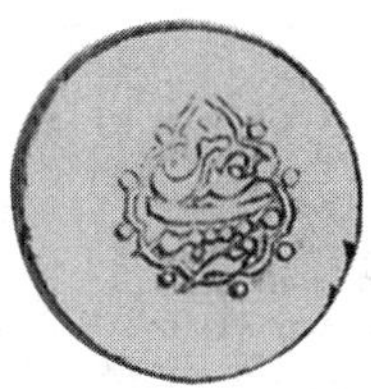

Mint: Mashhad
KM# B640 RUPEE

Silver **Obv:** Inscription **Rev:** Inscription within beaded cartouche **Note:** Weight varies: 11.00-11.50 grams

Date	Mintage	Good	VG	F	VF	XF
AH119x (1776)	—	—	17.50	35.00	50.00	70.00
AH1201 (1786)	—	—	17.50	35.00	50.00	70.00
AH1202 (1787)	—	—	17.50	35.00	50.00	70.00
AH1203 (1788)	—	—	17.50	35.00	50.00	70.00
AH1204 (1789)	—	—	17.50	35.00	50.00	70.00
AH1205 (1790)	—	—	17.50	35.00	50.00	70.00
AH12(0)7 (1792)	—	—	17.50	35.00	50.00	70.00

Mint: Multan
KM# 653 RUPEE

Silver, 21.5 mm. **Obv:** Inscription **Rev:** Inscription **Note:** Local regnal years

Date	Mintage	Good	VG	F	VF	XF
AH1194//3 (1780)	—	—	11.00	20.00	30.00	45.00
AH1195//4 (1781)	—	—	11.00	20.00	30.00	45.00
AH1197//5 (1782)	—	—	11.00	20.00	30.00	45.00
AH1198//5 (1783)	—	—	11.00	20.00	30.00	45.00
AH1198//6 (1783)	—	—	11.00	20.00	30.00	45.00
AH1198//7 (1784)	—	—	11.00	20.00	30.00	45.00
AH1199//7 (1784)	—	—	11.00	20.00	30.00	45.00
AH1200//7 (1785)	—	—	11.00	20.00	30.00	45.00
AH1201//7 (1786)	—	—	11.00	20.00	30.00	45.00
AH1203//9 (1788)	—	—	11.00	20.00	30.00	45.00
AH1203//10 (1789)	—	—	11.00	20.00	30.00	45.00
AH1204//10 (1789)	—	—	11.00	20.00	30.00	45.00

Note: Rupees of AH1194-1204 (KM#653) are struck on small, thick flans, and have mismatched regnal years, due to the Sikh occupation of Multan from AH1185-94; In AH1204, (KM#654) the flan was made broader, the design changed and the regnal years made to conform with Taimur's other mints; Weight varies: 11.40-11.60 grams

Mint: Multan
KM# 654 RUPEE

Silver **Note:** Normal regnal years. Weight varies: 11.40-11.60 grams

Date	Mintage	Good	VG	F	VF	XF
AH1204//18 (1789)	—	—	17.50	35.00	50.00	70.00
AH1205//18 (1789)	—	—	17.50	35.00	50.00	70.00
AH1205//19 (1790)	—	—	17.50	35.00	50.00	70.00
AH1206//19 (1791)	—	—	17.50	35.00	50.00	70.00
AH1207//20 (1792)	—	—	17.50	35.00	50.00	70.00

Mint: Peshawar
KM# 703 RUPEE

Silver **Obv:** King's name at top **Rev:** Inscription **Note:** Weight varies: 11.20-11.40 grams

Date	Mintage	Good	VG	F	VF	XF
AH1186//1 (1772)	—	—	10.00	15.00	25.00	40.00
AH1187//1 (1773)	—	—	10.00	15.00	25.00	40.00
AH1187//2 (1773)	—	—	10.00	15.00	25.00	40.00
AH1188//2 (1774)	—	—	10.00	15.00	25.00	40.00
AH1188//3 (1774)	—	—	10.00	15.00	25.00	40.00
AH1189//4 (1775)	—	—	10.00	15.00	25.00	40.00
AH1190//5 (1776)	—	—	10.00	15.00	25.00	40.00
AH1191 (1777)	—	—	10.00	15.00	25.00	40.00
AH1193//8 (1779)	—	—	10.00	15.00	25.00	40.00
AH1194//8 (1780)	—	—	10.00	15.00	25.00	40.00
AH1195//10 (1780)	—	—	10.00	15.00	25.00	40.00
AH1195//9 (1780)	—	—	10.00	15.00	25.00	40.00
AH1196//10 (1781)	—	—	10.00	15.00	25.00	40.00
AH1196//11 (1781)	—	—	10.00	15.00	25.00	40.00
AH1197//10 (1782) Muling	—	—	10.00	15.00	25.00	40.00
AH1197//11 (1782)	—	—	10.00	15.00	25.00	40.00
AH1197//12 (1782)	—	—	10.00	15.00	25.00	40.00
AH1198//12 (1783)	—	—	10.00	15.00	25.00	40.00
AH1199//12 (1783)	—	—	10.00	15.00	25.00	40.00
AH1199//13 (1784)	—	—	10.00	15.00	25.00	40.00
AH1200//13 (1785)	—	—	10.00	15.00	25.00	40.00

Date	Mintage	Good	VG	F	VF	XF
AH1201//15 (1786)	—	—	10.00	15.00	25.00	40.00
AH1203//17 (1788)	—	—	10.00	15.00	25.00	40.00

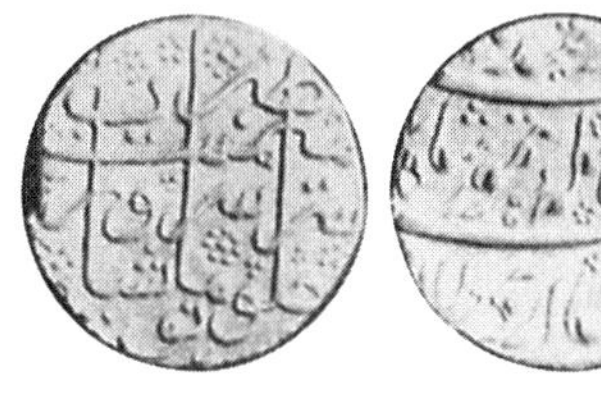
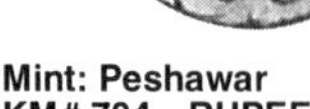

Mint: Peshawar
KM# 704 RUPEE
Silver **Obv:** King's name in middle line **Rev:** Inscription **Note:** Weight varies: 11.40-11.60 grams

Date	Mintage	Good	VG	F	VF	XF
AH120x//18 (1788)	—	—	10.00	20.00	30.00	45.00
AH120x//19 (1788)	—	—	10.00	20.00	30.00	45.00
AH1206//20 (1791)	—	—	10.00	20.00	30.00	45.00
AH1207//20 (1792)	—	—	10.00	20.00	30.00	45.00

Mint: Rikab
KM# 743 RUPEE
Silver, 23-25 mm. **Obv:** Inscription **Rev:** Full legend **Note:** Weight varies: 11.40-11.60 grams. Size varies

Date	Mintage	Good	VG	F	VF	XF
AH119x//11 (1781)	—	—	40.00	90.00	125	150

Mint: Rikab
KM# 744 RUPEE
Silver, 23-25 mm. **Obv:** Inscription **Rev:** Short legend in circle **Note:** Weight varies: 11.40-11.60 grams. Size varies

Date	Mintage	Good	VG	F	VF	XF
AHxxxx (1772)	—	—	40.00	90.00	125	150

Mint: Sind
KM# 774 RUPEE
Silver **Obv:** Inscription **Rev:** Inscription **Note:** Lightweight posthumous issues exist dated AH124-57, and are listed under Sind. Weight varies: 11.00-11.50 grams.

Date	Mintage	Good	VG	F	VF	XF
AH119x//6 (1777)	—	—	17.50	40.00	60.00	90.00
AH1198 (1783)	—	—	17.50	40.00	60.00	90.00

Mint: Tatta
KM# 788 RUPEE
11.8000 g., Silver, 22 mm. **Obv:** Inscription **Rev:** Inscription

Date	Mintage	Good	VG	F	VF	XF
AH120x (1785)	—	—	20.00	40.00	60.00	80.00

Mint: Dera
KM# 328 RUPEE
Silver **Obv:** Inscription and date **Rev:** Inscription, flower at top **Note:** Weight varies: 11.20-11.60 grams

Date	Mintage	Good	VG	F	VF	XF
AH1186//1 (1772)	—	—	10.00	20.00	28.00	38.00
AH1188//2 (1774)	—	—	10.00	20.00	28.00	38.00
AH1188//3 (1774)	—	—	10.00	20.00	28.00	38.00
AH1189//3 (1775)	—	—	10.00	20.00	28.00	38.00
AH1190//4 (1776)	—	—	10.00	20.00	28.00	38.00
AH1191//5 (1777)	—	—	10.00	20.00	28.00	38.00
AH1192//6 (1778)	—	—	10.00	20.00	28.00	38.00
AH1193//7 (1779)	—	—	10.00	20.00	28.00	38.00

Date	Mintage	Good	VG	F	VF	XF
AH1194//8 (1780)	—	—	10.00	20.00	28.00	38.00
AH1195//9 (1780)	—	—	10.00	20.00	28.00	38.00
AH1196//10 (1781)	—	—	10.00	20.00	28.00	38.00
AH1197//11 (1782)	—	—	10.00	20.00	28.00	38.00
AH1198//12 (1783)	—	—	10.00	20.00	28.00	38.00
AH1199//13 (1784)	—	—	10.00	20.00	28.00	38.00
AH1200//14 (1785)	—	—	10.00	20.00	28.00	38.00
AH1200//15 (1785)	—	—	10.00	20.00	28.00	38.00
AH1201//16 (1786)	—	—	10.00	20.00	28.00	38.00
AH1202//17 (1787)	—	—	10.00	20.00	28.00	38.00
AH1203//18 (1788)	—	—	10.00	20.00	28.00	38.00
AH1204//19 (1789)	—	—	10.00	20.00	28.00	38.00
AH1205//20 (1790)	—	—	10.00	20.00	28.00	38.00
AH1206//21 (1791)	—	—	10.00	20.00	28.00	38.00
AH1207//21 (1792)	—	—	10.00	20.00	28.00	38.00

Mint: Ahmadshahi
KM# 126 MOHUR
Gold **Obv:** Inscription **Rev:** Legend at top **Note:** Weight varies: 10.70-10.90 grams.

Date	Mintage	Good	VG	F	VF	XF
ND (1772)	—	—	—	—	350	425

Mint: Attock
KM# 239 MOHUR
10.9000 g., Gold, 20.5 mm.

Date	Mintage	Good	VG	F	VF	XF
AH1188//2 (1774) Rare	—	—	—	—	—	—

Mint: Bakhar
KM# 296 MOHUR
Gold **Obv:** Inscription **Rev:** Inscription **Note:** Weight varies: 10.90-11.00 grams.

Date	Mintage	Good	VG	F	VF	XF
AH1204//18 (1789) Rare	—	—	—	—	—	—

Mint: Bhakhar
KM# 295 MOHUR
Gold **Note:** Weight varies: 10.90-11.00 grams.

Date	Mintage	Good	VG	F	VF	XF
AH1196 (1781) Rare	—	—	—	—	—	—
AH1204 (1789) Rare	—	—	—	—	—	—

Mint: Herat
KM# 385 MOHUR
Gold **Obv:** Inscription **Rev:** Inscription **Note:** Retrograde date.

Date	Mintage	Good	VG	F	VF	XF
AH1190 (1776)	—	—	—	—	—	—

Mint: Herat
KM# 386 MOHUR
Gold **Obv:** Inscription **Rev:** Inscription **Note:** Weight varies: 10.80-10.90 grams.

Date	Mintage	Good	VG	F	VF	XF
AH1190 (1776)	—	—	150	250	400	550
AH1192 (1778)	—	—	150	250	400	550
AH1194 (1780)	—	—	150	250	400	550
AH1195 (1780)	—	—	150	250	400	550
AH1200 (1785)	—	—	150	250	400	550
AH1203 (1788)	—	—	150	250	400	550
AH1205 (1790)	—	—	150	250	400	550
AH1206 (1791)	—	—	150	250	400	550
AH1207 (1792)	—	—	150	250	400	550
AH1207//1208 (1792)	—	—	150	250	400	550

Date	Mintage	Good	VG	F	VF	XF
Note: Posthumous issues						
AH1208 (1793)	—	—	150	250	400	550
Note: Posthumous issues						

Mint: Kabul Mint
KM# 435 MOHUR
Gold **Obv:** Inscription **Rev:** Inscription **Note:** Weight varies: 10.70-11.00 grams.

Date	Mintage	Good	VG	F	VF	XF
AH1186//1 (1772)	—	—	100	165	250	350
AH1187//1 (1773)	—	—	100	165	250	350
AH1188//3 (1774)	—	—	100	165	250	350
AH1189//3 (1775)	—	—	100	165	250	350
AH1190//4 (1776)	—	—	125	200	325	450
AH1192//6 (1778)	—	—	125	200	325	450
AH1194//8 (1780)	—	—	125	200	325	450
AH1197//11 (1782)	—	—	125	200	325	450
AH1199//13 (1784)	—	—	125	200	325	450
AH1201//15 (1786)	—	—	125	200	325	450
AH120x//16 (1786)	—	—	125	200	325	450
AH1204//18 (1789)	—	—	125	200	325	450
AH1209 (sic)//21 (1791)	—	—	125	200	325	450

Mint: Kashmir
KM# 568 MOHUR
Gold, 23-24 mm. **Obv:** Inscription **Rev:** Inscription **Note:** Weight varies: 10.90-11.00 grams. Size varies.

Date	Mintage	Good	VG	F	VF	XF
AH119x//12 (1781) Rare	—	—	—	—	—	—

Mint: Kashmir
KM# 569 MOHUR
Gold, 23-24 mm. **Obv:** Inscription **Rev:** Inscription **Note:** Weight varies: 10.90-11.00 grams. Size varies.

Date	Mintage	Good	VG	F	VF	XF
AH1203//15 (1788) Rare	—	—	—	—	—	—

Mint: Multan
KM# 656 MOHUR
Gold **Note:** Weight varies: 10.80-11.00 grams.

Date	Mintage	Good	VG	F	VF	XF
AH1199//7 (1784)	—	—	225	400	600	900
AH1203//9 (1788)	—	—	225	400	600	900
AH1203//10 (1789)	—	—	225	400	600	900

Mint: Peshawar
KM# 706 MOHUR
Gold **Obv:** Inscription **Rev:** Inscription, mint mark **Note:** Posthumous issue. Weight varies: 10.80-10.90 grams.

Date	Mintage	Good	VG	F	VF	XF
AH1186//1 (1772)	—	—	150	250	400	625
AH118x//2 (1773)	—	—	150	250	400	625
AH1189//4 (1775)	—	—	150	250	400	625
AH1191//5 (1777)	—	—	150	250	400	625
AH1193//7 (1779)	—	—	150	250	400	625
AH1194//8 (1780)	—	—	150	250	400	625
AH1196//11 (1781)	—	—	150	250	400	625
AH119x//12 (1782)	—	—	150	250	400	625
AH1202//15 (1787)	—	—	150	250	400	625

Date	Mintage	Good	VG	F	VF	XF
AH1204//17 (1788)	—	—	150	250	400	625
AH1204//17 (1789)	—	—	150	250	400	625
AH1205//18 (1790)	—	—	150	250	400	625
AH1209//21 (1794)	—	—	150	250	400	625

Note: Posthumous.

Mint: Qandahar
KM# 125 MOHUR
Gold, 21.5-23 mm. **Obv:** Inscription **Rev:** Inscription **Note:** Weight varies: 10.70-10.90 grams. Size varies.

Date	Mintage	Good	VG	F	VF	XF
AH1186//1 (1772)	—	—	—	—	325	400
AH1190//2 (1776)	—	—	—	—	325	400
AH1197//12 (1782)	—	—	—	—	325	400
ND//14 (1784)	—	—	—	—	325	400
ND//15 (1785)	—	—	—	—	325	400
AH1204//18 (1788)	—	—	—	—	325	400
AH1207//21 (1791)	—	—	—	—	325	400

Mint: Rikab
KM# 745 MOHUR
Gold **Obv:** Inscription in three lines **Rev:** Inscription **Note:** Weight varies: 10.80-10.90 grams.

Date	Mintage	Good	VG	F	VF	XF
AH1191//5 (1777) Rare	—	—	—	—	—	—

Mint: Dera
KM# 329 MOHUR
10.9000 g., Gold **Obv:** Inscription **Rev:** Inscription

Date	Mintage	Good	VG	F	VF	XF
AH118x//1 (1772)	—	—	175	300	450	700
AH1202//17 (1787)	—	—	175	300	450	700
AH1204//19 (1789)	—	—	175	300	450	700
AH1207//22 (1792)	—	—	175	300	450	700

Humayun
AH1207 / 1793AD
HAMMERED COINAGE

Mint: Qandahar
KM# 128 RUPEE
Silver **Obv:** Inscription **Rev:** Inscription

Date	Mintage	Good	VG	F	VF	XF
AH1207//(1) (1793)	—	—	60.00	140	200	300

Mint: Ahmadshahi
KM# 129 MOHUR
Gold **Obv:** Inscription **Rev:** Inscription **Note:** Weight varies: 11.40-11.60 grams.

Date	Mintage	Good	VG	F	VF	XF
AH1207 (1793) Rare	—	—	—	—	—	—

Shah Zaman
AH1207-1216 / 1793-1801AD
HAMMERED COINAGE

Mint: Bakhar
KM# 300 FALUS
Copper **Obv:** Inscription **Rev:** Inscription within beaded circle **Note:** Weight varies: 14.00-15.00 grams.

Date	Mintage	Good	VG	F	VF	XF
ND (1793)	—	10.00	15.00	25.00	45.00	—

Mint: Kashmir
KM# 572.2 FALUS
Copper **Obv:** Date above "Shah" at top **Rev:** Inscription **Note:** Weight varies: 10.60-10.90 grams.

Date	Mintage	Good	VG	F	VF	XF
AH1212//5 (1797)	—	8.00	15.00	25.00	40.00	—
AH1212//6 (1798)	—	8.00	15.00	25.00	40.00	—
AH1213//6 (1798)	—	8.00	15.00	25.00	40.00	—
AH1213//7 (1799)	—	8.00	15.00	25.00	40.00	—

Mint: Kashmir
KM# 573 FALUS
Copper **Obv:** Inscription **Rev:** Inscription **Note:** Weight varies: 10.80-13.80 grams.

Date	Mintage	Good	VG	F	VF	XF
AH1214//7 (1799)	—	8.00	15.00	25.00	40.00	—
AH1214//8 (1800)	—	8.00	15.00	25.00	40.00	—
AH1215//8 (1800)	—	8.00	15.00	25.00	40.00	—

Mint: Kashmir
KM# 571 FALUS
Copper **Obv:** Inscription within star outline **Rev:** Inscription **Note:** Weight varies: 7.10-10.90 grams.

Date	Mintage	Good	VG	F	VF	XF
AH1212//5 (1797)	—	8.00	15.00	25.00	40.00	—

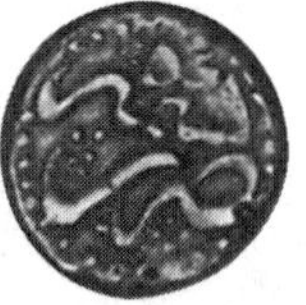

Mint: Kashmir
KM# 572.1 FALUS
Copper **Obv:** Date at right of "Zaman" **Rev:** Inscription **Note:** Weight varies: 7.10-10.90 grams.

Date	Mintage	Good	VG	F	VF	XF
AH1212//5 (1797)	—	10.00	17.00	28.00	45.00	—

Mint: Kashmir
KM# 570 FALUS
Copper **Obv:** Inscription **Rev:** Inscription **Note:** Weight varies: 9.20-12.40 grams.

Date	Mintage	Good	VG	F	VF	XF
AH1210//3 (1795)	—	8.00	15.00	25.00	40.00	—
AH1212 (1797)	—	8.00	15.00	25.00	40.00	—

Mint: Multan
KM# 660 FALUS
Copper, 21.5-23 mm. **Obv:** Flower **Rev:** Inscription **Note:** Weight varies: 11.50-12.20 grams. Size varies.

Date	Mintage	Good	VG	F	VF	XF
AH1208//1 (1793)	—	9.00	15.00	25.00	35.00	—
AH1209//2 (1794)	—	8.00	13.00	22.00	32.00	—
AH1210//4 (1796)	—	8.00	12.00	20.00	30.00	—
AH1211//4 (1796)	—	8.00	12.00	20.00	30.00	—
AH1212//5 (1797)	—	8.00	12.00	20.00	30.00	—
AH1215//8 (1800)	—	8.00	12.00	20.00	30.00	—

Mint: Dera
KM# 330 FALUS
Copper **Obv:** Inscription **Rev:** Inscription **Note:** Weight varies: 9.80-10.00 grams.

Date	Mintage	Good	VG	F	VF	XF
AH1209//2 (1794)	—	8.00	12.00	22.00	35.00	—

Mint: Kashmir
KM# 574 DAM
17.3000 g., Copper, 23 mm.

Date	Mintage	Good	VG	F	VF	XF
AH1208 (1793)	—	10.00	17.00	28.00	45.00	—

Mint: Ahmadshahi
KM# 131 1/4 RUPEE
Silver **Obv:** Inscription **Rev:** Inscription **Note:** Weight varies: 2.80-3.00 grams.

Date	Mintage	Good	VG	F	VF	XF
AH1214//8	—	—	20.00	40.00	60.00	80.00

Mint: Kabul Mint
KM# 441 1/4 RUPEE
2.8500 g., Silver, 14 mm. **Obv:** Inscription **Rev:** Inscription

Date	Mintage	Good	VG	F	VF	XF
AH1211 (1797)	—	—	18.00	40.00	60.00	80.00
AH1211//5 (1797)	—	—	18.00	40.00	60.00	80.00

Mint: Kabul Mint
KM# 442 1/2 RUPEE
Silver **Obv:** Inscription **Rev:** Inscription **Note:** Weight varies: 5.40-5.60 grams

Date	Mintage	Good	VG	F	VF	XF
AH1211//5 (1797)	—	—	20.00	40.00	60.00	80.00
AH1212 (1797)	—	—	20.00	40.00	60.00	80.00

Mint: *Ahmadshahi/Qandahar Mint*
KM# B134 RUPEE

Silver **Obv:** First couplet **Rev:** Second couplet added in margin

Date	Mintage	Good	VG	F	VF	XF
AH1214//7 (1799)	—	—	7.50	14.00	20.00	30.00
AH1214//8 (1800)	—	—	7.50	14.00	20.00	30.00
AH1215//7 (1800)	—	—	—	—	—	—
AH1215//8 (1800)	—	—	7.50	14.00	20.00	30.00

Mint: Ahmadshahi
KM# A134 RUPEE

Silver **Obv:** Second couplet **Rev:** Inscription

Date	Mintage	Good	VG	F	VF	XF
AH1211//4 (1796)	—	—	7.50	14.00	20.00	30.00
AH1212//5 (1797)	—	—	7.50	14.00	20.00	30.00
AH1212//5 (1797)	—	—	7.50	14.00	20.00	30.00
AH1213//5 (1798)	—	—	7.50	14.00	20.00	30.00
AH1214//6 (1799)	—	—	7.50	14.00	20.00	30.00

Mint: Ahmadshahi
KM# 133 RUPEE

Silver **Obv:** First couplet **Rev:** Inscription **Note:** Weight varies: 11.40-11.60 grams.

Date	Mintage	Good	VG	F	VF	XF
AH1207 (1792)	—	—	6.00	12.00	18.00	25.00
AH1208 (1793)	—	—	6.00	12.00	18.00	25.00
AH1209//2 (1794)	—	—	6.00	12.00	18.00	25.00
AH1210//3 (1795)	—	—	6.00	12.00	18.00	25.00
AH1201// (1795)	—	—	—	—	—	—
Note: Error for 1210						
AH1211//2 (1796)	—	—	—	—	—	—
AH1211//4 (1796)	—	—	6.00	12.00	18.00	25.00
AH1212 (1797)	—	—	6.00	12.00	18.00	25.00
AH1213//6 (1798)	—	—	6.00	12.00	18.00	25.00

Mint: Bakhar
KM# 303 RUPEE

Silver **Obv:** Inscription **Rev:** Inscription **Note:** Weight varies: 11.40-11.60 grams.

Date	Mintage	Good	VG	F	VF	XF
AH1209 (1794)	—	—	15.00	28.00	40.00	60.00
AH1211 (1796)	—	—	15.00	28.00	40.00	60.00
AH1212 (1797)	—	—	15.00	28.00	40.00	60.00
AH1215 (1800)	—	—	15.00	28.00	40.00	60.00
AH1216 (1801)	—	—	12.00	24.00	40.00	60.00

Mint: Derajat
KM# 358 RUPEE

Silver **Obv:** Inscription **Rev:** Inscription **Note:** Weight varies: 10.80-11.20 grams.

Date	Mintage	Good	VG	F	VF	XF
AH1207//1 (1793)	—	—	12.50	30.00	40.00	50.00
AH1208//1 (1793)	—	—	12.50	30.00	40.00	50.00
AH1209//2 (1794)	—	—	12.50	30.00	40.00	50.00
Note: The regnal year 2 was retained for 5 years, for reasons unknown today						
AH1210//2 (1795)	—	—	12.50	30.00	40.00	50.00
AH1211//2 (1796)	—	—	12.50	30.00	40.00	50.00
AH1212//2 (1797)	—	—	12.50	30.00	40.00	50.00
AH1212//6 (1798)	—	—	12.50	30.00	40.00	50.00
AH1213//7 (1799)	—	—	12.50	30.00	40.00	50.00
AH1214//7 (1799)	—	—	12.50	30.00	40.00	50.00
AH1214//8 (1800)	—	—	12.50	30.00	40.00	50.00
AH1215//8 (1801)	—	—	12.50	30.00	40.00	50.00

Mint: Herat
KM# 388 RUPEE

Silver, 21.5 mm. **Obv:** Inscription **Rev:** Inscription **Note:** Weight varies: 11.40-11.60 grams. Some AH1212 and AH1213 obverses are muled with reverses of other dates. These command no premium.

Date	Mintage	Good	VG	F	VF	XF
AH1212 (1797)	—	—	—	7.50	12.50	20.00
AH1213 (1798)	—	—	—	7.50	12.50	20.00
AH1214 (1799)	—	—	—	7.50	12.50	20.00
AH1215 (1800)	—	—	—	7.50	12.50	20.00

Mint: Kabul Mint
KM# B444 RUPEE

Silver **Obv:** First couplet with new arrangement in inscription **Note:** Occasionally found on wide planchets. Weight varies: 11.40-11.65 grams.

Date	Mintage	Good	VG	F	VF	XF
AH1215//7 (1800)	—	5.00	7.00	12.00	20.00	30.00
AH1215//8 (1800)	—	5.00	7.00	12.00	20.00	30.00
AH1216//8 (1801)	—	5.00	7.00	12.00	20.00	30.00

Mint: Kabul Mint
KM# 443 RUPEE

Silver **Obv:** First couplet **Rev:** Inscription **Note:** Weight varies: 11.40-11.65 grams

Date	Mintage	Good	VG	F	VF	XF
AH1207//1 (1793)	—	—	9.00	15.00	20.00	28.00
AH1208//1 (1793)	—	—	9.00	15.00	20.00	28.00
AH1208//2 (1794)	—	—	9.00	15.00	20.00	28.00
AH1209//2 (1794)	—	—	9.00	15.00	20.00	28.00
AH1209//3 (1795)	—	—	9.00	15.00	20.00	28.00
AH1210//4 (1796)	—	—	9.00	15.00	20.00	28.00
AH1211//4 (1796)	—	—	9.00	15.00	20.00	28.00
AH1212//4 (1797)		—	9.00	15.00	20.00	28.00
Note: Muling with old die						

Mint: Kabul Mint
KM# A444 RUPEE

Silver **Obv:** Second couplet **Rev:** Inscription **Note:** Weight varies: 11.40-11.65 grams

Date	Mintage	Good	VG	F	VF	XF
AH1211//5 (1797)	—	—	9.00	15.00	20.00	28.00
AH1212//5 (1797)	—	—	9.00	15.00	20.00	28.00
AH1212//6 (1798)	—	—	9.00	15.00	20.00	28.00
AH1213//6 (1798)	—	—	9.00	15.00	20.00	28.00
AH1213//7 (1799)	—	—	9.00	15.00	20.00	28.00

Mint: Kashmir
KM# 575 RUPEE

Silver **Obv:** Inscription **Rev:** Mont and "Julus" formula **Note:** Weight varies: 10.70-11.20 grams

Date	Mintage	Good	VG	F	VF	XF
AH1208//2 (1794)	—	—	10.00	15.00	25.00	35.00
AH1209//2 (1794)	—	—	10.00	15.00	25.00	35.00
AH1209//3 (1795)	—	—	10.00	15.00	25.00	35.00
AH1210//3 (1795)	—	—	10.00	15.00	25.00	35.00
AH1211//4 (1796)	—	—	10.00	15.00	25.00	35.00
AH1211//5 (1797)	—	—	10.00	15.00	25.00	35.00
AH1212//5 (1797)	—	—	10.00	15.00	25.00	35.00

Mint: Kashmir
KM# 576 RUPEE

Silver **Obv:** Inscription **Rev:** "Khitta Kashmir" fills area **Note:** Weight varies: 10.70-11.20 grams

Date	Mintage	Good	VG	F	VF	XF
AH1211//5 (1797)	—	—	10.00	17.00	27.00	40.00
AH1212//5 (1797)	—	—	10.00	17.00	27.00	40.00
AH1213//6 (1798)	—	—	10.00	17.00	27.00	40.00

Mint: Kashmir
KM# 577 RUPEE

Silver **Rev:** Legend in circle **Note:** Weight varies: 10.70-11.20 grams

Date	Mintage	Good	VG	F	VF	XF
AH1213//6 (1798)	—	—	11.50	25.00	40.00	55.00
AH1213//7 (1799)	—	—	11.50	25.00	40.00	55.00
AH1214//7 (1799)	—	—	11.50	25.00	40.00	55.00

Mint: Kashmir
KM# 578 RUPEE

Silver **Rev:** Legend in lozenge **Note:** Weight varies: 10.70-11.20 grams

Date	Mintage	Good	VG	F	VF	XF
AH1214//7 (1799)	—	—	10.00	20.00	30.00	40.00
AH1214//8 (1800)	—	—	10.00	20.00	30.00	40.00
AH1215//8 (1800)	—	—	10.00	20.00	30.00	40.00

Mint: Lahore
KM# 633 RUPEE

Silver **Obv:** First couplet **Rev:** Inscription **Note:** Weight varies: 11.50-11.60 grams

Date	Mintage	Good	VG	F	VF	XF
AH1211//4 (1796)	—	—	20.00	50.00	70.00	90.00

Mint: Lahore
KM# 634 RUPEE

Silver **Obv:** Second couplet **Rev:** Inscription **Note:** Weight varies: 11.50-11.60 grams

Date	Mintage	Good	VG	F	VF	XF
AH1213//6 (1798)	—	—	25.00	60.00	80.00	100

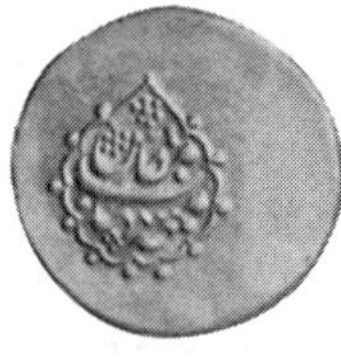

Mint: Mashhad
KM# E640 RUPEE
Silver **Obv:** Inscription **Rev:** Inscription within beaded teardrop **Note:** Weight varies: 11.00-11.50 grams

Date	Mintage	Good	VG	F	VF	XF
AH1212 (1797)	—	—	50.00	100	125	160
AH1214 (1799)	—	—	50.00	100	125	160

Mint: Multan
KM# 663 RUPEE
Silver, 20.5 mm. **Note:** It is not known why the first regnal year was retained so long at Multan. Weight varies: 11.50-11.60 grams.

Date	Mintage	Good	VG	F	VF	XF
AH1207//1 (1793)	—	—	20.00	40.00	60.00	80.00
AH1208//1 (1793)	—	—	20.00	40.00	60.00	80.00
AH1209//1 (1794)	—	—	20.00	40.00	60.00	80.00
AH1210//1 (1795)	—	—	20.00	40.00	60.00	80.00
AH1215//8 (1800)	—	—	20.00	40.00	60.00	80.00

Mint: Peshawar
KM# 712 RUPEE
Silver **Obv:** First couplet in three lines **Rev:** Inscription **Note:** Weight varies: 11.40-11.60 grams

Date	Mintage	Good	VG	F	VF	XF
AH1207//1 (1793)	—	—	10.00	14.00	20.00	30.00
AH1208//1 (1793)	—	—	10.00	14.00	20.00	30.00
AH1207//2 (1793)	—	—	10.00	14.00	20.00	30.00
ND//2 (1794)	—	—	10.00	14.00	20.00	30.00
AH1211//3 (1796)	—	—	10.00	14.00	20.00	30.00
AH1211//4 (1796)	—	—	10.00	14.00	20.00	30.00
AH1212//4 (1797)	—	—	10.00	14.00	20.00	30.00

Mint: Peshawar
KM# A713 RUPEE
Silver **Obv:** Second couplet in three lines **Rev:** Inscription **Note:** Weight varies: 11.40-11.60 grams

Date	Mintage	Good	VG	F	VF	XF
AH121x//4 (1796)	—	—	9.00	12.00	18.00	25.00
AH1211//5 (1797)	—	—	9.00	12.00	18.00	25.00
AH1212//5 (1797)	—	—	9.00	12.00	18.00	25.00
AH1213//6 (1798)	—	—	9.00	12.00	18.00	25.00
AH1214//6 (1799)	—	—	9.00	12.00	18.00	25.00
AH1214//8 (1800)	—	—	9.00	12.00	18.00	25.00
AH1215//8 (1800)	—	—	9.00	12.00	18.00	25.00

Mint: Peshawar
KM# 713 RUPEE
Silver **Obv:** First couplet in circle, second in margin **Note:** Weight varies: 11.40-11.60 grams.

Date	Mintage	Good	VG	F	VF	XF
AH1215//8 (1800)	—	3.50	9.00	18.00	30.00	45.00
AH1215//9 (1801)	—	6.00	9.00	18.00	30.00	45.00
AH1216//9 (1801)	—	6.00	9.00	18.00	30.00	45.00

Mint: Dera
KM# 333 RUPEE
Silver, 19-21.5 mm. **Obv:** Inscription **Rev:** Inscription **Note:** Weight varies: 11.20-11.60 grams. Size varies.

Date	Mintage	Good	VG	F	VF	XF
AH1208//1 (1793)	—	—	14.00	30.00	40.00	50.00
AH1208//2 (1794)	—	—	14.00	30.00	40.00	50.00
AH1209 (1794)	—	—	14.00	30.00	40.00	50.00
AH1210//3 (1795)	—	—	14.00	30.00	40.00	50.00
AH1211//4 (1796)	—	—	14.00	30.00	40.00	50.00
AH1211//3 (1796)	—	—	14.00	30.00	40.00	50.00
AH1213//5 (1798)	—	—	14.00	30.00	40.00	50.00
AH1214//6 (1799)	—	—	14.00	30.00	40.00	50.00
AH1215//7 (1800)	—	—	14.00	30.00	40.00	50.00

Mint: Kabul Mint
KM# C444 NAZARANA RUPEE
Silver **Obv:** First couplet **Rev:** Inscription **Note:** Weight varies: 11.40-11.65 grams

Date	Mintage	Good	VG	F	VF	XF
AH1211//4 (1796)	—	—	90.00	150	170	185

Mint: Ahmadshahi
KM# 134 2 RUPEES
Silver, 28 mm. **Note:** Weight varies: 22.60-23.20 grams.

Date	Mintage	Good	VG	F	VF	XF
AH121x//7 (1799)	—	—	150	250	450	750
AH1214//8 (1800)	—	—	150	250	450	750

Mint: Kabul Mint
KM# 444 2 RUPEES
Silver **Obv:** Inscription **Rev:** Inscription **Note:** Weight varies: 23.00-23.30 grams

Date	Mintage	Good	VG	F	VF	XF
AH1212//5 (1797)	—	—	75.00	125	200	300
AH1212//6 (1797)	—	—	75.00	125	200	300
AH1213//6 (1798)	—	—	75.00	125	200	300
AH121x//7 (1799)	—	—	75.00	125	200	300

Mint: Ahmadshahi
KM# A137 MOHUR
Gold **Note:** Similar to Rupee, KM#A134.

Date	Mintage	Good	VG	F	VF	XF
AH1215//7 (1800) Rare	—	—	—	—	—	—

Mint: Ahmadshahi
KM# 136 MOHUR
Gold, 21.5-23 mm. **Note:** Weight varies: 10.80-10.90 grams. Size varies.

Date	Mintage	Good	VG	F	VF	XF
AH1209//2 (1794)	—	—	350	600	900	1,350
AH1215//7 (1800)	—	—	350	600	900	1,350
AH1215//8 (1800)	—	—	350	600	900	1,350

Mint: Bakhar
KM# 305 MOHUR
10.9000 g., Gold

Date	Mintage	Good	VG	F	VF	XF
AH1209 (1793) Rare	—	—	—	—	—	—

Mint: Derajat
KM# 359 MOHUR
Gold **Obv:** Inscription **Rev:** Inscription **Note:** Weight varies: 10.80-10.90 grams.

Date	Mintage	Good	VG	F	VF	XF
AH1211//2 (1796) Rare	—	—	—	—	—	—

Mint: Herat
KM# 389 MOHUR
10.9000 g., Gold **Obv:** Inscription **Rev:** Inscription on beaded background

Date	Mintage	Good	VG	F	VF	XF
AH1212 (1797)	—	—	150	250	400	600
AH1214 (1799)	—	—	150	250	400	600
AH1215 (1800)	—	—	150	250	400	600

Mint: Kabul Mint
KM# 445 MOHUR
Gold **Obv:** First couplet **Rev:** Inscription **Note:** Weight varies: 10.80-11.00 grams

Date	Mintage	Good	VG	F	VF	XF
AH1208//1 (1793)	—	—	200	325	500	700
AH1209//2 (1794)	—	—	200	325	500	700
AH1209//3 (1795)	—	—	200	325	500	700
AH1211//4 (1796)	—	—	200	325	500	700

Mint: Kabul Mint
KM# 446 MOHUR
Gold **Obv:** Second couplet **Note:** Weight varies: 10.80-11.00 grams.

Date	Mintage	Good	VG	F	VF	XF
AH12xx//5 (1797)	—	—	200	325	500	700
AH1213//6 (1798)	—	—	200	325	500	700
AH1215//7 (1800)	—	—	200	325	500	700

Mint: Lahore
KM# 635 MOHUR
Gold **Obv:** Inscription **Rev:** Inscription **Note:** Weight varies: 10.80-11.00 grams

Date	Mintage	Good	VG	F	VF	XF
AH1211//4 (1796)	—	—	600	1,000	1,600	2,500

Mint: Multan
KM# 665 MOHUR
Gold, 20 mm. **Note:** Weight varies: 10.80-11.00 grams

Date	Mintage	Good	VG	F	VF	XF
AH1210//1 (1795) Rare	—	—	—	—	—	—

Mint: Peshawar
KM# 715 MOHUR
Gold, 22-24 mm. **Obv:** First couplet in three lines **Rev:** Inscription **Note:** Weight varies: 10.80-10.90 grams. Size varies.

Date	Mintage	Good	VG	F	VF	XF
AH120x//2 (1794)	—	—	200	325	500	800
AH12xx//3 (1795)	—	—	200	325	500	800

Mint: Peshawar
KM# 716 MOHUR
Gold, 22-24 mm. **Obv:** First couplet in circle, second in margin **Rev:** Inscription **Note:** Weight varies: 10.80-10.90 grams. Size varies.

Date	Mintage	Good	VG	F	VF	XF
AH1215//8 (1800)	—	—	225	400	600	900

Mint: Qandahar
KM# 137 MOHUR
Gold **Obv:** Inscription **Rev:** Inscription

Date	Mintage	Good	VG	F	VF	XF
AH1211//5 (1797) Rare	—	—	—	—	—	—

Mint: Dera
KM# 335 MOHUR
Gold, 19 mm. **Obv:** Inscription **Rev:** Inscription **Note:** Weight varies: 10.90-11.00 grams.

Date	Mintage	Good	VG	F	VF	XF
AH1208//1 (1793)	—	—	250	400	600	1,000
AH1208//2 (1794)	—	—	250	400	600	1,000
AH1210//3 (1795)	—	—	250	400	600	1,000
AH1211//4 (1796)	—	—	250	400	600	1,000

ALGERIA

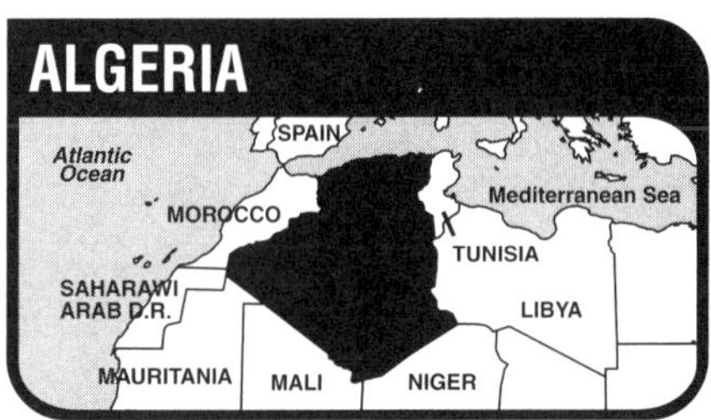

The Democratic and Popular Republic of Algeria, a North African country fronting on the Mediterranean Sea between Tunisia and Morocco, has an area of 919,595 sq. mi. (2,381,740 sq. km.) and a population of 31.6 million. Capital: Algiers (Alger). Most of the country's working population is engaged in agriculture although a recent industrial diversification, financed by oil revenues, is making steady progress. Wines, fruits, iron and zinc ores, phosphates, tobacco products, liquified natural gas, and petroleum are exported.

Algiers, the capital and chief seaport of Algeria, was the site of Phoenician and Roman settlements before the present Moslem city was founded about 950. Nominally part of the sultanate of Tilimsan, Algiers had a large measure of independence under the amirs of its own. In 1492 the Jews and Moors who had been expelled from Spain settled in Algiers and enjoyed an increasing influence until the imposition of Turkish control in 1518. For the following three centuries, Algiers was the headquarters of the notorious Barbary pirates as Turkish control became more and more nominal. The French took Algiers in 1830, and after a long and wearisome war completed the conquest of Algeria and annexed it to France, 1848. Following the armistice signed by France and Nazi Germany on June 22, 1940, Algeria fell under Vichy Government control until liberated by the Allied invasion forces under the command of Gen. D. D. Eisenhower on Nov. 8, 1942. The inability to obtain equal rights with Frenchmen led to an organized revolt which began on Nov. 1, 1954 and lasted until a ceasefire was signed on July l, 1962. Independence was proclaimed on July 5, 1962, following a self-determination referendum, and the Republic was declared on September 25, 1962.

RULERS
Ottoman, until 1830
Abd-el-Kader (rebel), AH1250-1264/1834-1847AD

ALGIERS

MINT NAMES

جزائر

Jaza'ir

جزائر غرب

Jaza'Ir Gharb
, AH1012-1115/1603-1703AD

MONETARY SYSTEM
(Until 1847)
14-1/2 Asper (Akche, Dirham Saghir)
= 1 Kharub
2 Kharuba = 1 Muzuna
24 Muzuna = 3 Batlaka (Pataka) = 1 Budju

NOTE: Coin denominations are not expressed on the coins, and are best determined by size and weight. The silver Budju weighed about 13.5 g until AH1236/1821AD, when it was reduced to about 10.0 g. The fractional pieces varied in proportion to the Budju. They had secondary names, which are given in the text. In 1829 three new silver coins were introduced and Budju became Tugrali-rial, Tugrali-batlaka = 1/3 Rial = 8 Muzuna and Tugralinessflik = 1/2 Batlaka = 4 Muzuna. The gold Sultani was officially valued at 108 Muzuna, but varied in accordance with the market price of gold expressed in silver. It weighed 3.20-3.40 g. The Zeri Mahbub was valued at 80 Muzuna & weighed 2.38-3.10 g.

OTTOMAN

Mustafa II
AH1106-1115/1695-1703AD

HAMMERED COINAGE

KM# 13 SULTANI
3.4500 g., Gold, 21 mm.

Date	Mintage	VG	F	VF	XF	Unc
AH1110	—	—	—	—	—	—

Ahmed III
AH1115-1143/1703-1730AD

HAMMERED COINAGE

KM# 15 1/2 SULTANI
1.4900 g., Gold, 17.5 mm.

Date	Mintage	VG	F	VF	XF	Unc
AH1143 Rare	—	300	—	—	—	—
AH1144 Rare	—	300	—	—	—	—

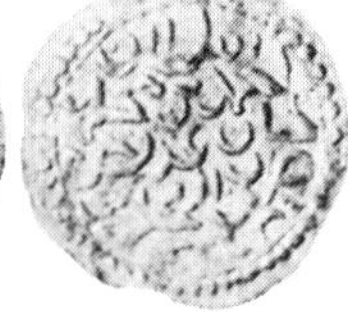

KM# 16.1 SULTANI
3.4000 g., Gold, 23-24 mm. **Obv:** Inscription **Rev:** Inscription **Note:** Mint is al-Jaza'ir Gharb. Size varies.

Date	Mintage	VG	F	VF	XF	Unc
AH1124	—	175	225	500	750	—
AH1126	—	175	225	500	750	—
AH1129	—	175	225	500	750	—
AH1131	—	175	225	500	750	—
AH1132	—	175	225	500	750	—
AH1133	—	175	225	500	750	—
AH1134	—	175	225	500	750	—
AH1136	—	175	225	500	750	—
AH1137	—	175	225	500	750	—
AH1138	—	175	225	500	750	—
AH1140	—	175	225	500	750	—
AH1141	—	175	225	500	750	—

KM# 16.2 SULTANI
Gold, 23-24 mm. **Obv:** Inscription **Rev:** Inscription **Note:** Mint is al-Jaza'ir. Size varies. Weight varies 3.25-3.44 grams.

Date	Mintage	VG	F	VF	XF	Unc
AH1136	—	175	225	500	750	—
AH1140	—	175	225	500	750	—
AH1141	—	175	225	500	750	—
AH1147	—	175	225	500	750	—

Mahmud I
AH1143-1168/1730-1754AD

HAMMERED COINAGE

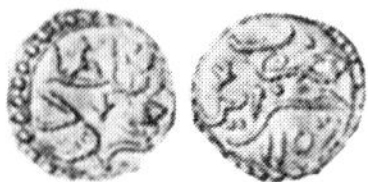

KM# 18 1/4 SULTANI
Gold **Obv:** Inscription **Rev:** Inscription **Note:** Weight varies: 0.75-0.85 grams.

Date	Mintage	VG	F	VF	XF	Unc
AH1144	—	150	200	250	325	—
AH1145	—	150	200	250	325	—
AH1146	—	150	200	250	325	—
AH1147	—	150	200	250	325	—
AH1148	—	150	200	250	325	—
AH1149	—	150	200	250	325	—
AH1154	—	150	200	250	325	—
AH1155	—	150	200	250	325	—
AH1156	—	150	200	250	325	—
AH1157	—	150	200	250	325	—
AH1160	—	150	200	250	325	—
AH1161	—	150	200	250	325	—
AH1165	—	150	200	250	325	—
AH1166	—	150	200	250	325	—
AH1168	—	150	200	250	325	—
AH1171	—	150	200	250	325	—

Note: Coins dated AH1171 were struck posthumously

KM# 19 1/2 SULTANI
Gold, 16-18 mm. **Obv:** Inscription **Rev:** Inscription **Note:** Weight varies: 1.68-1.71 grams. Size varies.

Date	Mintage	VG	F	VF	XF	Unc
AH1143	—	100	150	200	300	—
AH1144	—	100	150	200	300	—
AH1145	—	100	150	200	300	—
AH1147	—	100	150	200	300	—
AH1148	—	100	150	200	300	—
AH1150	—	100	150	200	300	—
AH1151	—	100	150	200	300	—
AH1152	—	100	150	200	300	—
AH1154	—	100	150	200	300	—
AH1156	—	100	150	200	300	—
AH1157	—	100	150	200	300	—
AH1158	—	100	150	200	300	—
AH1159	—	100	150	200	300	—
AH1160	—	100	150	200	300	—
AH1161	—	100	150	200	300	—
AH1162	—	100	150	200	300	—
AH1163	—	100	150	200	300	—
AH1164	—	100	150	200	300	—
AH1165	—	100	150	200	300	—
AH1168	—	100	150	200	300	—

KM# 20 SULTANI
Gold, 23-25.5 mm. **Obv:** Inscription **Rev:** Inscription **Note:** Weight varies: 3.20-3.40g. Size varies. Varieties exist with lines dividing obverse and reverse legends.

Date	Mintage	VG	F	VF	XF	Unc
AH1143	—	200	275	375	500	—
AH1161	—	200	275	375	500	—
AH1162	—	200	275	375	500	—
AH1164	—	200	275	375	500	—
AH1165	—	200	275	375	500	—
AH1166	—	200	275	375	500	—
AH1167	—	200	275	375	500	—
AH1168	—	200	275	375	500	—

Osman III
AH1168-1171/1754-1757AD

HAMMERED COINAGE

KM# 24 1/4 SULTANI
0.0850 g., Gold, 13-14.4 mm. **Obv:** Inscription **Rev:** Inscription **Note:** Size varies.

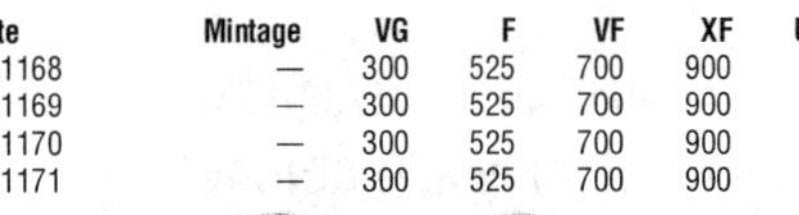

Date	Mintage	VG	F	VF	XF	Unc
AH1168	—	300	525	700	900	—
AH1169	—	300	525	700	900	—
AH1170	—	300	525	700	900	—
AH1171	—	300	525	700	900	—

KM# 22 1/2 SULTANI

Gold, 17-18 mm. **Obv:** Inscription **Rev:** Inscription **Note:** Weight varies: 1.63-1.70 g. Size varies.

Date	Mintage	VG	F	VF	XF	Unc
AH1168	—	200	275	375	500	—
AH1169	—	300	350	450	750	—
AH1170	—	300	350	450	750	—
AH1171	—	300	350	450	750	—

KM# 23 SULTANI

Gold **Obv:** Inscription **Rev:** Inscription **Note:** Weight varies: 3.15-3.40g.

Date	Mintage	VG	F	VF	XF	Unc
AH1168 Rare	—	—	—	—	—	—
AH1169 Rare	—	—	—	—	—	—
AH1172 Rare	—	—	—	—	—	—

Mustafa III

AH1171-1187/1757-1774AD

HAMMERED COINAGE

KM# 30 1/8 BUDJU (3 Mazuna)

Silver **Obv:** Legend is three lines **Rev:** Legend has two lines in octagram **Note:** Weight varies 1.56-1.96 grams.

Date	Mintage	VG	F	VF	XF	Unc
AH1173 (1759)	—	25.00	50.00	75.00	150	—
AH1174 (1760)	—	25.00	50.00	75.00	150	—
AH1178 (1764)	—	25.00	50.00	75.00	150	—
AH1179 (1765)	—	25.00	50.00	75.00	150	—
AH1180 (1766)	—	25.00	50.00	75.00	150	—
AH1183 (1769)	—	25.00	50.00	75.00	150	—

KM# 31 1/8 BUDJU (3 Mazuna)

Silver **Obv:** Inscription **Rev:** Without octagram **Note:** Coins dated 1100-91 of this type were struck posthumously. Coins dated AH1174 exist with date left of mint mark. Weight varies 1.56-1.96 grams.

Date	Mintage	VG	F	VF	XF	Unc
AH1174 (1760)	—	25.00	50.00	75.00	150	250
AH1178 (1764)	—	25.00	50.00	75.00	150	250
AH1179 (1765)	—	25.00	50.00	75.00	150	250
AH1180 (1766)	—	25.00	50.00	75.00	150	250
AH1183 (1769)	—	25.00	50.00	75.00	150	250
AH1184 (1770)	—	25.00	50.00	75.00	150	250
AH1185 (1771)	—	25.00	50.00	75.00	150	250
AH1186 (1772)	—	25.00	50.00	75.00	150	250
AH1187 (1773)	—	25.00	50.00	75.00	150	250
AH1188 (1774)	—	25.00	50.00	90.00	150	250
AH1190 (1776)	—	30.00	60.00	90.00	175	275
AH1191 (1777)	—	30.00	60.00	90.00	175	275

KM# 26 1/4 BUDJU

Silver **Obv:** Inscription **Rev:** Legend in octogram **Note:** Weight varies: 2.50-3.30 grams.

Date	Mintage	VG	F	VF	XF	Unc
AH1172 (1758)	—	50.00	90.00	125	175	—
AH1173 (1759)	—	60.00	100	150	200	—

KM# 27 1/4 BUDJU

3.3600 g., Silver **Obv:** Inscription **Rev:** Inscription

Date	Mintage	VG	F	VF	XF	Unc
AH1173 (1759)	—	45.00	65.00	100	165	270
Note: Coins dated AH1173 exist with date left of mint mark						
AH1174 (1760)	—	45.00	65.00	100	165	270
Note: Coins dated AH1174 exist with date left of mint mark						
AH1176 (1762)	—	45.00	65.00	100	165	270
AH1177 (1763)	—	45.00	65.00	100	165	270
AH1180 (1766)	—	45.00	65.00	100	165	270
AH1182 (1768)	—	45.00	65.00	100	165	270
AH1184 (1770)	—	45.00	65.00	100	165	270
AH1185 (1771)	—	45.00	65.00	100	165	270
AH1186 (1772)	—	45.00	65.00	100	165	270
AH1187 (1773)	—	45.00	65.00	100	165	270
AH1188 (1774)	—	45.00	65.00	100	165	270
Note: Coins dated AH1188 of this type were struck posthumously						

KM# 28 1/4 SULTANI

Gold **Obv:** Inscription **Note:** Weight varies: 0.79-0.83 grams.

Date	Mintage	VG	F	VF	XF	Unc
AH1171	—	100	150	200	275	—
AH1172	—	100	150	200	275	—
AH1173	—	100	150	200	275	—
AH1176	—	100	150	200	275	—
AH1177	—	100	150	200	275	—
AH1186	—	100	150	200	275	—
AH1187	—	100	150	200	275	—

KM# 29 1/2 SULTANI

1.6900 g., Gold, 17-18 mm. **Obv:** Inscription **Rev:** Inscription **Note:** Weight varies: 1.64-1.96 grams. Size varies.

Date	Mintage	VG	F	VF	XF	Unc
AH1171	—	100	150	200	275	—
AH1172	—	100	150	200	275	—
AH1173	—	100	150	200	275	—
AH1174	—	100	150	200	275	—
AH1175	—	100	150	200	275	—
AH1176	—	100	150	200	275	—
AH1180	—	100	150	200	275	—
AH1183	—	100	150	200	275	—
AH1186	—	100	150	200	275	—

KM# 25 1/2 SULTANI

Gold **Obv:** Inscription **Rev:** Inscription

Date	Mintage	VG	F	VF	XF	Unc
AH1172	—	—	—	—	—	—

KM# 32 SULTANI

Gold **Obv:** Legend in four lines **Rev:** Legend in four lines **Note:** Weight varies 3.23-3.41 grams.

Date	Mintage	VG	F	VF	XF	Unc
AH1171	—	500	750	1,000	1,200	—
AH1177	—	200	275	375	500	—
AH1183	—	200	275	375	500	—
AH1184	—	200	275	375	500	—
AH1185	—	500	750	1,000	1,200	—

KM# 33 1/2 ZERI MAHBUB

1.2900 g., Gold **Obv:** Inscription **Rev:** Inscription

Date	Mintage	VG	F	VF	XF	Unc
AH1176 Rare	—	—	—	—	—	—

Abdul Hamid I

AH1187-1203/1774-1789AD

HAMMERED COINAGE

KM# 35 1/8 BUDJU (3 Mazuna)

1.6000 g., Silver **Obv:** Inscription **Rev:** Inscription **Note:** Weight varies 1.59-1.72 grams.

Date	Mintage	VG	F	VF	XF	Unc
AH1188 (1774)	—	35.00	50.00	85.00	160	—
AH1189 (1775)	—	35.00	50.00	85.00	160	—
AH1191 (1777)	—	35.00	50.00	100	180	—
AH1192 (1778)	—	35.00	50.00	100	180	—
AH1193 (1779)	—	35.00	50.00	100	180	—
AH1195 (1780)	—	35.00	50.00	100	180	—
AH1196 (1781)	—	35.00	50.00	100	180	—
AH1198 (1783)	—	35.00	50.00	100	180	—
AH1199 (1784)	—	35.00	50.00	100	180	—
AH1200 (1785)	—	35.00	50.00	90.00	165	—
AH1201 (1786)	—	35.00	50.00	90.00	165	—
AH1202 (1787)	—	35.00	55.00	100	165	—
AH1203 (1788)	—	35.00	55.00	100	165	—

KM# 36 1/4 BUDJU

Silver **Obv:** Inscription **Rev:** Inscription **Note:** Weight varies: 2.42-3.72 grams.

Date	Mintage	VG	F	VF	XF	Unc
AH1188 (1774)	—	25.00	50.00	100	180	—
AH1189 (1775)	—	25.00	50.00	100	180	—
AH1190 (1776)	—	25.00	50.00	100	180	—
AH1191 (1777)	—	25.00	50.00	100	180	—
AH1193 (1779)	—	25.00	50.00	100	180	—
AH1195 (1780)	—	25.00	50.00	100	180	—
AH1196 (1781)	—	25.00	50.00	100	180	—
AH1197 (1782)	—	25.00	50.00	100	180	—
AH1198 (1783)	—	25.00	50.00	100	180	—
AH1199 (1784)	—	25.00	50.00	100	180	—
AH1200 (1785)	—	25.00	50.00	100	180	—
AH1201 (1786)	—	25.00	50.00	100	180	—
AH1202 (1787)	—	25.00	50.00	100	180	—
AH1203 (1788)	—	25.00	50.00	100	180	—

KM# 37 1/4 SULTANI

0.8500 g., Gold **Obv:** Inscription **Rev:** Inscription

Date	Mintage	VG	F	VF	XF	Unc
AH1192	—	65.00	100	150	225	—
AH1193	—	65.00	100	150	225	—
AH1194	—	65.00	100	150	225	—
AH1195	—	65.00	100	150	225	—

KM# 38 1/2 SULTANI

1.7000 g., Gold, 14 mm. **Obv:** Inscription **Rev:** Inscription

Date	Mintage	VG	F	VF	XF	Unc
AH1197	—	100	150	250	350	—

KM# 34 SULTANI

Gold, 23-25 mm. **Obv:** Inscription **Rev:** Inscription **Note:** Weight varies: 3.30-3.40g. Size varies.

Date	Mintage	VG	F	VF	XF	Unc
AH1187	—	200	275	375	500	—
AH1188	—	200	275	375	500	—
AH1189	—	200	275	375	500	—
AH1190	—	200	275	375	500	—
AH1191	—	200	275	375	500	—
AH1192	—	200	275	375	500	—
AH1193	—	200	275	375	500	—
AH1194	—	200	275	375	500	—
AH1196	—	200	275	375	500	—
AH1197	—	200	275	375	500	—
AH1198	—	200	275	375	500	—
AH1199	—	200	275	375	500	—
AH1200	—	200	275	375	500	—
AH1201	—	200	275	375	500	—
AH1202	—	200	275	375	500	—
AH1203	—	200	275	375	500	—

Selim III

AH1203-1222/1789-1807AD

HAMMERED COINAGE

KM# 43 FELS

2.2000 g., Copper, 13-14 mm. **Obv:** Legend has Sultan Selim **Rev:** Mint name Jaza'ir above date **Note:** Size varies.

Date	Mintage	VG	F	VF	XF	Unc
AH1206 (1791)	—	80.00	120	—	—	—

KM# 40 1/8 BUDJU (3 Mazuna)

Silver **Obv:** Inscription **Rev:** Inscription **Note:** Weight varies: 1.65-1.70 grams.

Date	Mintage	VG	F	VF	XF	Unc
AH1200 Error	—	25.00	50.00	75.00	150	—
AH1204	—	20.00	40.00	60.00	100	—
AH1206	—	20.00	40.00	60.00	100	—
AH1207	—	20.00	30.00	60.00	100	—

Date	Mintage	VG	F	VF	XF	Unc
AH1208	—	20.00	30.00	60.00	100	—
AH1209	—	20.00	30.00	60.00	100	—
AH1210	—	20.00	30.00	60.00	100	—
AH1211	—	20.00	30.00	60.00	100	—
AH1212	—	20.00	30.00	60.00	100	—
AH1213	—	20.00	30.00	60.00	100	—
AH1214	—	20.00	40.00	60.00	100	—
AH1215	—	20.00	40.00	60.00	100	—

KM# 42 1/4 BUDJU

Silver, 19-20 mm. **Obv:** Inscription **Rev:** Inscription **Note:** Weight varies: 2.90-3.40 grams. Size varies.

Date	Mintage	VG	F	VF	XF	Unc
AH1204	—	20.00	35.00	60.00	100	—
AH1205	—	20.00	35.00	60.00	100	—
AH1206	—	16.00	30.00	60.00	100	—
AH1207	—	20.00	35.00	60.00	100	—
AH1208	—	20.00	35.00	60.00	100	—
AH1209	—	25.00	35.00	50.00	80.00	—
AH1210	—	20.00	35.00	60.00	100	—
AH1211	—	16.00	30.00	60.00	100	—
AH1212	—	20.00	35.00	60.00	100	—
AH1213	—	15.00	25.00	30.00	45.00	—
AH1214	—	15.00	25.00	30.00	45.00	—
AH1215	—	20.00	35.00	60.00	100	—

KM# 45 1/2 BUDJU

Silver **Note:** Weight varies: 5.80-6.80 grams.

Date	Mintage	VG	F	VF	XF	Unc
AH1206	—	60.00	100	150	225	—
AH1211	—	60.00	100	150	225	—
AH1213	—	60.00	100	150	225	—
AH1214	—	60.00	100	150	225	—
AH1215	—	60.00	100	150	225	—

KM# 44 1/4 SULTANI

0.8500 g., Gold, 15-16 mm. **Obv:** Legend has 2 lines **Rev:** Mintname above date. **Note:** Size varies.

Date	Mintage	VG	F	VF	XF	Unc
AH1209	—	65.00	100	200	250	—
AH1213	—	65.00	100	200	250	—
AH1214	—	65.00	100	200	250	—

KM# 46 1/2 SULTANI

Gold, 18-19 mm. **Obv:** Inscription within beaded circle **Rev:** Inscription within beaded circle **Note:** Weight varies: 1.54-1.70g. SIze varies

Date	Mintage	VG	F	VF	XF	Unc
AH1215	—	100	150	200	275	—

KM# 41 SULTANI

Gold, 22-25 mm. **Obv:** Star of Solomon **Rev:** Inscription **Note:** Weight varies: 3.25-3.40g. Size varies.

Date	Mintage	VG	F	VF	XF	Unc
AH1203	—	125	175	225	350	—
AH1204	—	200	275	375	500	—
AH1205	—	200	275	375	500	—
AH1206	—	200	275	375	500	—
AH1207	—	200	275	375	500	—
AH1208	—	200	275	375	500	—
AH1209	—	200	275	375	500	—
AH1210	—	200	275	375	500	—
AH1213	—	200	275	375	500	—
AH1214	—	200	275	375	500	—
AH1215	—	200	275	375	500	—

ANGOLA

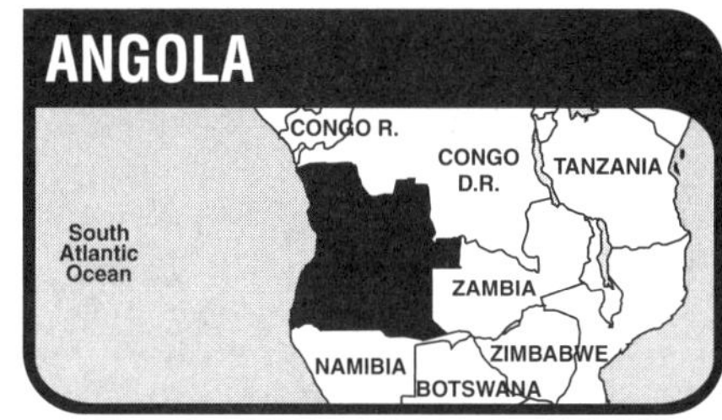

The Republic of Angola, a country on the west coast of southern Africa bounded by Congo Democratic Republic, Zambia, and Namibia (Southwest Africa), has an area of 481,351 sq. mi. (1,246,700 sq. km.) and a population of 12.78 million, predominantly Bantu in origin. Capital: Luanda. Most of the people are engaged in subsistence agriculture. However, important oil and mineral deposits make Angola potentially one of the richest countries in Africa. Iron and diamonds are exported.

The Portuguese navigator, Diogo Cao, discovered Angola in 1482 Angola. Portuguese settlers arrived in 1491, and established Angola as a major slaving center, which sent about 3 million slaves to the New World.

A revolt, characterized by guerrilla warfare, against Portuguese rule began in 1961 and continued until 1974, when a new regime in Portugal offered independence. The independence movement was actively supported by three groups; the National Front, based in Zaire, the Soviet-backed Popular Movement, and the moderate National Union. Independence was proclaimed on Nov. 11, 1975, and the Portuguese departed, leaving the Angolan people to work out their own political destiny. Within hours, each of the independence groups proclaimed itself Angola's sole ruler. A bloody intertribal civil war erupted in which the Communist Popular Movement, assisted by Soviet arms and Cuban mercenaries, was the eventual victor.

RULER

Portuguese until 1975

MINT MARK

KN - King's Norton

PORTUGUESE COLONY

COLONIAL COINAGE

KM# 6 5 REIS (V)

Copper **Obv:** Rosettes flank crowned denomination **Rev:** Sash brosses lined globe

Date	Mintage	VG	F	VF	XF	Unc
1752	—	25.00	70.00	210	350	—
1753	232,000	10.00	30.00	80.00	175	—
1757	—	22.00	60.00	120	275	—

KM# 19 5 REIS (V)

Copper **Obv:** Denomination and 5 rosettes within beaded circle **Rev:** Crowned arms on globe

Date	Mintage	VG	F	VF	XF	Unc
1770	400,000	7.00	15.00	50.00	90.00	—
1771	533,000	8.00	18.00	55.00	100	—

KM# 7 10 REIS (X)

Copper

Date	Mintage	VG	F	VF	XF	Unc
1752	—	40.00	90.00	350	550	—
1753	397,000	10.00	22.00	65.00	125	—
1757	—	22.00	60.00	210	375	—

KM# 10 1/4 MACUTA

Copper **Obv:** Crowned arms on globe **Rev:** Rosettes and denomination within beaded circle

Date	Mintage	VG	F	VF	XF	Unc
1762	—	15.00	35.00	110	200	—
1763	—	7.00	15.00	32.00	75.00	—
1770	268,000	7.00	15.00	32.00	75.00	—
1771	280,000	18.00	35.00	165	285	—

KM# 27 1/4 MACUTA

Copper **Rev:** Rosettes and denomination within beaded circle

Date	Mintage	VG	F	VF	XF	Unc
1783 Rare	—	—	—	—	—	—
1785	13,000	12.00	25.00	65.00	135	—
1786	151,000	—	—	—	—	—

KM# 29 1/4 MACUTA

Copper **Rev:** Rosettes and denomination within beaded circle **Note:** Similar to 1/2 Macuta, KM#30.

Date	Mintage	VG	F	VF	XF	Unc
1789	152,000	12.00	28.00	50.00	90.00	—

KM# 8 20 REIS (XX)

Copper **Note:** Similar to 10 Reis, KM#8.

Date	Mintage	VG	F	VF	XF	Unc
1752	—	25.00	100	210	375	—
1753	134,000	10.00	25.00	55.00	120	—
1757	—	15.00	35.00	110	200	—

KM# 11 1/2 MACUTA

Copper **Obv:** Crowned arms on globe **Rev:** Rosettes and denomination within beaded circle **Note:** Similar to 1 Macuta, KM#12.

Date	Mintage	VG	F	VF	XF	Unc
1762	—	25.00	50.00	135	275	—
1763	133,000	12.00	25.00	50.00	90.00	—
1770	140,000	7.00	15.00	30.00	60.00	—

KM# 28 1/2 MACUTA

Copper **Rev:** Rosettes and denomination within beaded circle **Note:** Similar to 1/4 Macuta, KM#27.

Date	Mintage	VG	F	VF	XF	Unc
1783 Rare	—	—	—	—	—	—
1785	154,000	18.00	30.00	55.00	120	—
1786	158,000	18.00	35.00	60.00	135	—

KM# 30 1/2 MACUTA

Copper **Rev:** Rosettes and denomination within beaded circle

Date	Mintage	VG	F	VF	XF	Unc
1789	125,000	12.00	30.00	50.00	100	—

KM# 9 40 REIS (XL)

Copper **Note:** Similar to 10 Reis, KM#8.

Date	Mintage	VG	F	VF	XF	Unc
1753	22,000	12.00	25.00	50.00	100	—
1757	—	12.00	25.00	50.00	100	—

KM# 12 MACUTA

Copper **Obv:** Crowned arms on globe **Rev:** Rosettes and denomination within beaded circle

Date	Mintage	VG	F	VF	XF	Unc
1762	—	60.00	200	350	550	—
1763	—	15.00	30.00	60.00	125	—
1770	67,000	12.00	25.00	55.00	120	—

KM# 20 MACUTA

Copper **Obv:** Crowned arms **Rev:** Denomination within laurel wreath **Note:** Similar to 4 Macutas, KM#14.

Date	Mintage	VG	F	VF	XF	Unc
1783	5,386	250	450	750	1,250	—
1785	194,000	12.00	25.00	50.00	90.00	—
1786	81,000	20.00	40.00	80.00	185	—

KM# 31 MACUTA

Copper **Obv:** Crowned arms **Rev:** Denomination within laurel wreath **Note:** Similar to 10 Macutas, KM#36.

Date	Mintage	VG	F	VF	XF	Unc
1789	100,000	15.00	30.00	60.00	125	—

KM# 13 2 MACUTAS

2.9500 g., 0.9170 Silver **Obv:** Crowned arms **Rev:** Denomination within laurel wreath

Date	Mintage	VG	F	VF	XF	Unc
1762	—	25.00	55.00	80.00	140	—
1763	20,000	12.50	25.00	55.00	120	—
1770 Rare	—	—	—	—	—	—

KM# 21 2 MACUTAS

2.9500 g., 0.9170 Silver **Obv:** Crowned arms **Rev:** Denomination within laurel wreath

Date	Mintage	VG	F	VF	XF	Unc
1783	10,000	25.00	50.00	75.00	130	—

KM# 35 2 MACUTAS

2.9500 g., 0.9170 Silver **Obv:** Crowned arms **Rev:** Denomination within laurel wreath

Date	Mintage	VG	F	VF	XF	Unc
1796	20,000	20.00	30.00	55.00	120	—

KM# 14 4 MACUTAS

5.7000 g., 0.9170 Silver **Obv:** Crowned arms **Rev:** Denomination within laurel wreath

Date	Mintage	VG	F	VF	XF	Unc
1762	—	20.00	50.00	85.00	165	—
1763	—	20.00	50.00	85.00	165	—
1770	10,000	75.00	200	355	550	—

KM# 22 4 MACUTAS

5.7000 g., 0.9170 Silver **Obv:** Crowned arms **Rev:** Denomination within laurel wreath

Date	Mintage	VG	F	VF	XF	Unc
1783	10,000	90.00	185	325	600	—
1784	30,000	30.00	90.00	175	350	—

KM# 32 4 MACUTAS

5.7000 g., 0.9170 Silver **Obv:** Crowned arms **Rev:** Denomination within laurel wreath

Date	Mintage	VG	F	VF	XF	Unc
1789	5,000	50.00	100	175	350	—
1796	20,000	20.00	55.00	110	180	—

KM# 15 6 MACUTAS

8.7500 g., 0.9170 Silver **Obv:** Crowned arms **Rev:** Denomination within laurel wreath

Date	Mintage	VG	F	VF	XF	Unc
1762	—	250	500	950	1,500	—
1763	—	35.00	65.00	115	200	—
1770	10,000	30.00	55.00	100	180	—

KM# 26 6 MACUTAS

8.7500 g., 0.9170 Silver **Obv:** Crowned arms **Rev:** Denomination within laurel wreath **Note:** Similar to 8 Macutas, KM#23.

Date	Mintage	VG	F	VF	XF	Unc
1784	10,000	35.00	65.00	115	180	—

KM# 33 6 MACUTAS

8.7500 g., 0.9170 Silver **Obv:** Crowned arms **Rev:** Denomination within laurel wreath **Note:** Similar to 12 Macutas, KM#37.

Date	Mintage	VG	F	VF	XF	Unc
1789	4,998	50.00	100	200	320	—
1796	20,000	35.00	70.00	140	200	—

KM# 16 8 MACUTAS

11.7000 g., 0.9170 Silver

Date	Mintage	VG	F	VF	XF	Unc
1762	—	65.00	125	250	400	—
1763	—	40.00	80.00	150	285	—
1770	5,000	55.00	110	165	300	—

KM# 23 8 MACUTAS

11.7000 g., 0.9170 Silver **Obv:** Crowned arms **Rev:** Denomination within laurel wreath

Date	Mintage	VG	F	VF	XF	Unc
1783	30,000	40.00	80.00	160	290	—

KM# 34 8 MACUTAS

11.7000 g., 0.9170 Silver **Obv:** Crowned arms **Rev:** Denomination within laurel wreath **Note:** Similar to 12 Macutas, KM#37.

Date	Mintage	VG	F	VF	XF	Unc
1789	6,250	50.00	175	265	475	—
1796	25,000	40.00	100	165	300	—

KM# 17 10 MACUTAS

14.5500 g., 0.9170 Silver **Obv:** Crowned arms **Rev:** Denomination within laurel wreath

Date	Mintage	VG	F	VF	XF	Unc
1762	—	275	700	1,200	2,000	—
1763	—	75.00	135	275	400	—
1770	6,000	90.00	185	350	500	—

KM# 24 10 MACUTAS

14.5500 g., 0.9170 Silver **Obv:** Crowned arms **Rev:** Denomination within laurel wreath **Note:** Similar to 8 Macutas, KM#23.

Date	Mintage	VG	F	VF	XF	Unc
1783	28,000	50.00	100	250	400	—

KM# 36 10 MACUTAS

14.5500 g., 0.9170 Silver **Obv:** Crowned arms **Rev:** Denomination within laurel wreath

Date	Mintage	VG	F	VF	XF	Unc
1796	24,000	50.00	100	275	450	—

KM# 18 12 MACUTAS

17.5000 g., 0.9170 Silver **Obv:** Crowned arms **Rev:** Denomination within laurel wreath

Date	Mintage	VG	F	VF	XF	Unc
1762	—	300	900	1,350	2,250	—
1763	—	150	350	500	850	—
1770	13,000	85.00	200	350	500	—

KM# 25 12 MACUTAS

17.5000 g., 0.9170 Silver **Obv:** Crowned arms **Rev:** Denomination within laurel wreath

Date	Mintage	VG	F	VF	XF	Unc
1783	30,000	55.00	135	275	425	—

KM# 37 12 MACUTAS

17.5000 g., 0.9170 Silver **Obv:** Crowned arms **Rev:** Denomination within laurel wreath

Date	Mintage	VG	F	VF	XF	Unc
1789	8,334	100	250	375	600	—
1796	27,000	65.00	145	275	425	—

ARMENIA

The Republic of Armenia (formerly Armenian S.S.R.) is bounded in the north by Georgia, to the east by Azerbaijan and to the south and west by Turkey and Iran. It has an area of 11,506 sq. mi. (29,800 sq. km) and an estimated population of 3.66 million. Capital: Yerevan. Agriculture including cotton, vineyards and orchards, hydroelectricity, chemicals - primarily synthetic rubber and fertilizers, vast mineral deposits of copper, zinc and aluminum, and production of steel and paper are major industries.

The earliest history of Armenia records continuous struggles with expanding Babylonia and later Assyria. In the sixth century B.C. it was called Armina. Later under the Persian empire it enjoyed the position of a vassal state. Conquered by Macedonia, it later defeated the Seleucids and Greater Armenia was founded under the Artaxis dynasty. Christianity was established in 303 A.D. which led to religious wars with the Persians and Romans who divided it into two zones of influence. The Arabs succeeded the Persian Empire of the Sassanids which later allowed the Armenian princes to conclude a treaty in 653 A.D. In 862 A.D. Ashot V was recognized as the "prince of princes" and established a throne recognized by Baghdad and Constantinople in 886 A.D. The Seljuks overran the whole country and united with Kurdistan which eventually ran the new government. In 1240 A.D. onward the Mongols occupied almost all of western Asia until their downfall in 1375 A.D. when various Kurdish, Armenian and Turkoman independent principalities arose. After the defeat of the Persians in 1516 A.D. the Ottoman Turks gradually took control over a period of some 40 years, with Kurdish tribes settling within Armenian lands. In 1605 A.D. the Persians moved thousands of Armenians as far as India developing prosperous colonies. Persia and the Ottoman Turks were again at war, with the Ottomans once again prevailing. The Ottomans later gave absolute civil authority to a Christian bishop allowing them free enjoyment of their religion and traditions.

Russia occupied Armenia in 1801 until the Russo-Turkish war of 1878. British intervention excluded either side from remaining although the Armenians remained more loyal to the Ottoman Turks, but in 1894 the Ottoman Turks sent in an expeditionary force of Kurds fearing a revolutionary movement. Large massacres were followed by retaliations, then amnesty was proclaimed which led right into WW I and once again occupation by Russian forces in 1916. After the Russian revolution the Georgians, Armenians and Azerbaijanis formed the short lived Transcaucasian Federal Republic on Sept. 20, 1917 which broke up into three independent republics on May 26, 1918. Communism developed and in Sept. 1920 the Turks attacked the Armenian Republic; the Russians soon followed suit from Azerbaijan routing the Turks. On Nov. 29, 1920 Armenia was proclaimed a Soviet Socialist Republic. On March 12, 1922, Armenia, Georgia and Azerbaijan were combined to form the Transcaucasian Soviet Federated Socialist Republic, which on Dec. 30, 1922, became a part of U.S.S.R. On Dec. 5, 1936, the Transcaucasian federation was dissolved and Armenia became a constituent Republic of the U.S.S.R. A new constitution was adopted in April 1978. Elections took place on May 20, 1990. The Supreme Soviet adopted a declaration of sovereignty in Aug. 1991, voting to unite Armenia with Nagorno-Karabakh. This newly constituted "Republic of Armenia" became fully independent by popular vote in Sept. 1991. It became a member of the CIS in Dec. 1991.

Fighting between Christians in Armenia and Muslim forces of Azerbaijan escalated in 1992 and continued through early 1994. Each country claimed the Nagorno-Karabakh, an Armenian ethnic enclave, in Azerbaijan. A temporary cease-fire was announced in May, 1994.

RULERS

Persian, until 1724
Ottoman, 1724-1735

MINT NAME

روان

Revan, (Erevan, now Yerevan)

MONETARY SYSTEM

1/4 Abbasi (Abazi) = 4 Para
1/2 Abbasi = 8 Para
Abbasi = 16 Para

OTTOMAN EMPIRE

OTTOMAN COINAGE

KM# 15 1/4 ABBASI

1.2500 g., Silver, 14 mm. **Ruler:** Ahmed III **Obv:** Toughra

Date	Mintage	VG	F	VF	XF	Unc
AH1115	—	400	550	750	1,000	—

KM# 16 1/2 ABBASI

2.6700 g., Silver, 17 mm. **Ruler:** Ahmed III **Obv:** Toughra

Date	Mintage	VG	F	VF	XF	Unc
AH1115	—	250	350	450	600	—

KM# 17 ABBASI

Silver, 23-25 mm. **Ruler:** Ahmed III **Obv:** Toughra **Note:** Weight varies 4.90-5.44g.

Date	Mintage	VG	F	VF	XF	Unc
AH1115	—	85.00	115	150	200	—

Note: Border varieties exist; Strikes on 1/2 Abbasi planchets exist

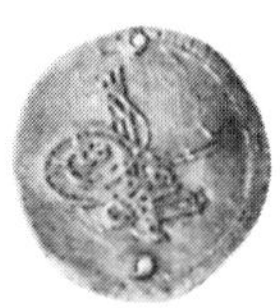 

KM# 18 CEDID ZINCIRLI

Gold, 18-20 mm. **Ruler:** Ahmed III **Obv:** Toughra **Note:** Weight varies 3.35-3.50g.

Date	Mintage	VG	F	VF	XF	Unc
AH1115 Rare	—	—	—	—	—	—

KM# 19 ALTUN

3.1000 g., Gold, 26 mm. **Ruler:** Ahmed III **Obv:** Toughra

Date	Mintage	VG	F	VF	XF	Unc
AH1115 Rare	—	—	—	—	—	—

AUSTRIA

The Republic of Austria, a parliamentary democracy located in mountainous central Europe, has an area of 32,374 sq. mi. (83,850 sq. km.) and a population of 8.08 million. Capital: Wien (Vienna). Austria is primarily an industrial country. Machinery, iron, steel, textiles, yarns and timber are exported.

The territories later to be known as Austria were overrun in pre-Roman times by various tribes, including the Celts. Upon the fall of the Roman Empire, the country became a margravate of Charlemagne's Empire. Premysl II of Otakar, King of Bohemia, gained possession in 1252, only to lose the territory to Rudolf of Habsburg in 1276. Thereafter, until World War I, the story of Austria was conducted by the ruling Habsburgs.

During the 17th century, Austrian coinage reflected the geopolitical strife of three wars. From 1618-1648, the Thirty Years' War between northern Protestants and southern Catholics produced low quality, "kipperwhipper" strikes of 12, 24, 30, 60, 75 and 150 Kreuzer. Later, during the Austrian-Turkish War, 1660-1664, coinages used to maintain soldier's salaries also reported the steady division of Hungarian territories. Finally, between 1683 and 1699, during the second Austrian-Turkish conflict, new issues of 3, 6 and 15 Kreuzers were struck, being necessary to help defray mounting expenses of the war effort.

During World War I, the Austro-Hungarian Empire was one of the Central Powers with Germany, Bulgaria and Turkey. At the end of the war, the Empire was dismembered and Austria established as an independent republic. In March, 1938, Austria was incorporated into Hitler's short-lived Greater German Reich. Allied forces of both East and West occupied Austria in April 1945, and subsequently divided it into 4 zones of military occupation. On May 15, 1955, the 4 powers formally recognized Austria as a sovereign independent democratic state.'

Francis I died on August 18, 1765. His wife Maria Theresa, decreed on July 21, 1766 that coins would be issued with the portrait of Francis and bearing the year of his death (1765). Also to be included were letters of the alphabet to indicate the actual year of issue: i.e. A-1766, G-1772, P-1780.

The posthumous coins were issued rather erratically as to denominations, years and mints. 5 denominations were made and 7 mints were used. Only the Ducat and 20 Kreuzer were made until 1780, the year in which Maria Theresa died. The other denominations were 3, 10 and 17 Kreuzer.

RULERS

Leopold I, 1657-1705
Joseph I, 1705-1711
Charles VI, 1711-1740
Maria Theresa, 1740-1780
with Franz I, 1745-1765
as widow, 1765-1780
Joseph II, joint with his Mother, 1765-1780
Alone, 1780-1790
Leopold II, 1790-1792
Franz II (I), 1792-1835
(as Franz II, Holy Roman Emperor, 1792-1806)
(as Franz I, Austrian Emperor, 1806-1835)

MINT MARKS

A, W, WI - Vienna (Wien)
(a) - Vienna (Wien)
AI,AL-IV,C-A,E,GA - Karlsburg (Alba Iulia, Transylvania)
B,K,KB - Kremnica (Kremnitz, Hungary)
CB,CI,CI-BI(NI),CW,H,HS - Hermannstadt (Sibiu) (Transylvania)
CV (1693-94),FT,KV (1694-1700) - Klausenburg (Cluy, Transylvania)
D - Salzburg
D,G,GR - Graz (Styria)
E – Karlsburg (Alba Iula)
F, HA - Hall
G,H,P-R - Gunzburg
GM - Mantua (Mantova)
(h) Shield - Vienna (Wien)
M - Milan (Milano, Lombardy)
NB - Nagybanya (Baia Mare, Hungary)
O - Oravicza (Oravita, Hungary)
S - Schmollnitz (Smolnik, Hungary)
V - Venice (Venice, Venetia)
(v) Eagle - Hall
W - Breslau (Wroclaw, Vratislav, Poland)

MINT IDENTIFICATION

To aid in determining an Austrian (Habsburg) coin's mint it is necessary to first check the coat of arms. In some cases the coat of arms will dominate the reverse. The Hungarian Madonna and child is a prime example. On more traditional Austrian design types the provincial coat of arms will be the only one on the imperial eagle's breast. When a more complicated coat of arms is used the provincial arms will usually be found in the center or at the top center usually overlapping neighboring arms.

Legend endings frequently reflect the various provincial coats of arms. Sometimes mint marks appear on coins such as the letter W for Breslau. Mintmaster's and mint officials' initials or symbols also appear and can be used to confirm the mint identity.

The following pages will present the mint name, illustrate or describe the provincial coats of arms, legend endings, mint marks, and mint officials' initials or symbols with which the mint identity can be determined.

AUGSBURG MINT

(In Bavaria)

MINT MARKS

A - Augsburg, 1713-1714

MINT OFFICIALS' INITIALS & PRIVY MARKS

Initials	Privy marks	Years	Names
(hs)	Horse shoes	1713-14	J. Christian Holeisen

BRUSSELS MINT

MINT OFFICIALS' INITIALS

Initials	Years	Names
H	1725-64	F. Harrewyn
R	1719-32	Philipp Roettiers
R	1732-72	Jacques Roettiers

GUNZBURG MINT

(in Burgau)

MINT MARKS

G - 1764-1765
H - 1766-1771, 1791-1797

MINT OFFICIALS' INITIALS

Initials	Years	Names
FS	1780	Ward J. Faby and Stehr Franz
PS, IF	1780	?
SC	1765-74	Tobias Schobl, Jos. V. Clotz, warden
SF	1776-77, 1780	Tobias Schobl, Ward J. Faby
ST, SF	1780	Schobl Tobias, Stehr Franz
TS, IF	1780	Tobias Schobl, Josef Faby

HALL MINT

(in Tyrol)

Coat of arms are on eagle's breast. Legends usually end: TYR or TYROL.

MINT MARKS

F - 1765-1767, 1771, 1775-1777, 1795-1797
F, H - 1765
HA - 1749-1765

MINT OFFICIALS' INITIALS

Initials	Years	Names
As, AS	1765-74	Ludw. Aschpacher, Joh. Josef Stockner, warden
IAK	1693-1701, 1704, 1706	Joh. Anton Konig, die-cutter
S	1768	Joh. Josef Stockner, warden
VCS	1774-77	Josef Hub. Von Clotz, Joh. Josef Stockner, warden

HERMANNSTADT

(in Transylvania)

Coat of arms usually on breast of imperial eagle. Legend usually ends TRANS or TRANSSYLVANIAE.

MINT MARKS

 (c) - crowned coat of arms

 (h) - crowned AHR monogram

(MINT OFFICIALS' INITIALS

Initials	Years	Names
FT	1701-08	?
IFK	1709-11	Johann Franz Kropf
MIHS	1709	Miller Henricus

KARLSBURG MINT

(in Transylvania)

For coat of arms and legend endings, see Hermannstadt.

MINT MARKS

C - 1762
CA - 1747-1753, 1758-1759
E - 1797, 1819-1824, 1830-1833, 1857-1868

MINT OFFICIALS' INITIALS

Initials	Years	Names
AHGS	-	A.J. Hammerschmidt, G. Schickmayer, warden

KASCHAU MINT

(Kosice)
(in Hungary)

Coat of arms is Madonna and child above small Hungarian arms like Kremnitz.

MINT MARK

CM – 1691-1704

KLAGENFURT MINT

(in Province of Carinthia)

Coat of arms usually found in legend or as the middle arms on the imperial eagle's breast. Legend usually ends CAR or CARINTHIAE.

MINT OFFICIALS' INITIALS

PS - P. Sigharter

KREMNITZ MINT

(Hungary)

Small Hungarian arms and Madonna and child in legends usually at 3 and 9 o'clock.

MINT MARKS

B, K, KB

MINT OFFICIALS' INITIALS

Initials	Years	Names
EvMD	1767-72	Ignaz Krammer Edler v. Munzburg, P. Joseph v. Damiani
SKPD	1775-80	Sigmund A. Klemmer, P. Josef v. Damiani

MUNICH MINT

MINT OFFICIALS' PRIVY MARKS

(S) - Star

NAGYBANYA MINT

(Hungary)

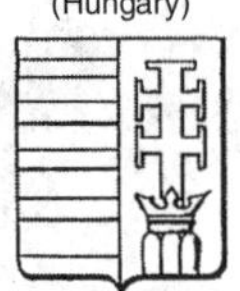

Coat of arms on imperial eagle's breast.

MINT MARKS

G – 1797, 1813-14, 1819-26
NB

MINT OFFICIALS' INITIALS

Initials	Years	Names
IB, ICB	1698-1728	J.C. Block

PRESSBURG MINT

(in Hungary)

MINT MARKS

CH – 1697-1718

MINT OFFICIALS' INITIALS & PRIVY MARKS

Initials	Privy marks	Years	Names
BPW		1717-18	PH. Ch. Becker, die-cutter and Paul Wodrodi, warden
IGS		1705-10, 1712, 1715	Joh. Georg Seidlitz
PW		1709-21	Paul Wodrodi
(csh)		1705-08	Christoph Sigm. Hunger

SANKT VEIT MINT

(in Carinthia)

Coat of arms, see Klagenfurt, are usually found on top center of the massive coat of arms on the imperial eagle's breast. Legend usually ends CAR or CARINTHIAE.

MINT OFFICIALS' INITIALS

Initials	Years	Names
IP, IIP	1699-1717	Johann Josef Preiss

VIENNA MINT

Coat of arms, usually found in the legend or as the middle arms on a multiple arms shield or alone on the imperial eagle's breast. Legend usually ends TY, TYR or TYROL.

MINT MARKS

A – 1765-

WI – 1746-53, 1756

MINT OFFICIALS' INITIALS & PRIVY MARKS

Initials	Privy marks	Years	Names
AW		1764	A. Widmann, die-cutter
GTK		1761	?
ICFA		1774-80	Joh. August v. Cronberg, Franz Aicherau, warden
ICSK		1766-74	Johann August v. Cronberg, Sigmund Klemmer
ECSK		1766	(error) ICSK
IKSC		1767	(error) ICSK
IMH, MH		1705-12	Joh. Michael Hofmann
IZV		1761-65	Joh. Zanobio Weber
(mm)	MM monogram	1703-05, 1707-08	Matthias Mittermayer

MONETARY SYSTEM

Before 1857

8 Heller = 4 Pfennig = 1 Kreuzer
60 Kreuzer = 1 Florin (Gulden)
2 Florin = 1 Species or Convention Thaler

MINTAGES

The mintage figures listed for the Hall Mint in the Tyrol represent the combined emissions for Maria Theresa and Franz I from 1745 to 1765 and Maria Theresa with Joseph II from 1765 to 1780. It was a frequent practice at Hall to strike coins with dies made in and bearing the date of earlier years. See Tyrol for mintages of Maria Theresa issues having no counterpart date and denomination of Franz I or Joseph II.

EMPIRE

STANDARD COINAGE

KM# 1417 PFENNIG

Silver **Ruler:** Joseph I **Mint:** Munich **Obverse:** Value in heart on double-headed eagle, date below **Note:** Uniface. Prev. KM#1180.

Date	Mintage	VG	F	VF	XF	Unc
1705	—	7.50	15.00	30.00	60.00	—

KM# 1111 PFENNIG

Billon **Ruler:** Leopold I **Mint:** Saint Veit **Obverse:** Carinthian arms in diamond, one digit of date on each side **Note:** Uniface. Prev. KM#1635.

Date	Mintage	VG	F	VF	XF	Unc
1705	—	4.00	8.00	17.50	35.00	—

KM# 1419 PFENNIG

Billon **Ruler:** Joseph I **Mint:** Vienna **Obverse:** Crowned imperial eagle, crown divides date **Note:** Uniface. Prev. KM#1900.

Date	Mintage	VG	F	VF	XF	Unc
1705	—	6.00	12.50	25.00	55.00	—
1706	—	6.00	12.50	25.00	55.00	—
1707	—	6.00	12.50	25.00	55.00	—
1708	—	6.00	12.50	25.00	55.00	—
1710	—	6.00	12.50	25.00	55.00	—
1711	—	6.00	12.50	25.00	55.00	—

KM# 1418 PFENNIG

Silver **Ruler:** Joseph I **Mint:** Munich **Obverse:** Value in circle **Note:** Prev. KM#1181.

Date	Mintage	VG	F	VF	XF	Unc
1706	—	7.50	15.00	35.00	75.00	—
1707	—	7.50	15.00	35.00	75.00	—
1708	—	7.50	15.00	35.00	75.00	—
1709	—	7.50	15.00	35.00	75.00	—
1710	—	7.50	15.00	35.00	85.00	—
1711	—	7.50	15.00	35.00	85.00	—

KM# 1482 PFENNIG

Billon **Ruler:** Joseph I **Mint:** Saint Veit **Obverse:** Carinthian arms in diamond, one digit of date on each side **Note:** Uniface. Prev. KM#1665.

Date	Mintage	VG	F	VF	XF	Unc
1707	—	25.00	50.00	100	200	—

KM# 1481 PFENNIG

Billon **Ruler:** Joseph I **Mint:** Graz **Note:** Uniface.Prev. KM#480.

Date	Mintage	VG	F	VF	XF	Unc
1707	—	9.00	18.00	40.00	85.00	—
1711 Rare	—	—	—	—	—	—

KM# 1514 PFENNIG

Billon **Ruler:** Karl (Charles) VI **Mint:** Vienna **Obverse:** Value in circle on eagle's breast **Note:** Uniface. Prev. KM#1915.

Date	Mintage	VG	F	VF	XF	Unc
1712	—	6.00	14.00	30.00	65.00	—

KM# 1513 PFENNIG

Silver **Ruler:** Karl (Charles) VI **Mint:** Munich **Note:** Uniface. Prev. KM#1187.

Date	Mintage	VG	F	VF	XF	Unc
1712	—	10.00	20.00	55.00	120	—
1713	—	10.00	20.00	55.00	120	—
1714	—	10.00	20.00	55.00	120	—

KM# 1532 PFENNIG

Billon **Ruler:** Karl (Charles) VI **Mint:** Vienna **Obverse:** Value in heart on eagle's breast **Note:** Prev. KM#1916.

Date	Mintage	VG	F	VF	XF	Unc
1713	—	6.00	14.00	30.00	65.00	—
1714 Rare	—	—	—	—	—	—
1723	—	6.00	14.00	30.00	65.00	—
1726	—	6.00	14.00	30.00	65.00	—
1738 Rare	—	—	—	—	—	—
1740	—	6.00	14.00	30.00	65.00	—

KM# 1531 PFENNIG

Billon **Ruler:** Karl (Charles) VI **Mint:** Graz **Obverse:** Crowned imperial eagle, crown divides date **Note:** Varieties exist. Uniface. Prev. KM#490.

Date	Mintage	VG	F	VF	XF	Unc
1713	—	8.00	16.00	35.00	75.00	—
1718 Rare	—	—	—	—	—	—
1723	—	7.00	15.00	30.00	65.00	—
1727	—	7.00	15.00	30.00	65.00	—

KM# 1622 PFENNIG

Billon **Ruler:** Karl (Charles) VI **Mint:** Graz **Obverse:** Crowned arms in cartouche, date divided at top **Note:** Prev. KM#491.

Date	Mintage	VG	F	VF	XF	Unc
1728	—	5.00	10.00	20.00	50.00	—
1730	—	5.00	10.00	20.00	50.00	—
1731	—	5.00	10.00	20.00	50.00	—
1733	—	5.00	10.00	20.00	50.00	—
1740	—	5.00	10.00	20.00	50.00	—

KM# 1337 2 PFENNIG

Silver **Ruler:** Leopold I **Mint:** Vienna **Obverse:** Three shields of arms - one above two, divided date in arc **Note:** Varieties exist. Uniface. Prev. KM#1851.

Date	Mintage	VG	F	VF	XF	Unc
1701	—	5.00	10.00	20.00	40.00	—
1707	—	5.00	10.00	20.00	40.00	—

KM# 1131 2 PFENNIG

Billon **Ruler:** Leopold I **Mint:** Graz **Obverse:** Three shields of arms **Note:** Varieties exist. Uniface. Prev. KM#447.

Date	Mintage	VG	F	VF	XF	Unc
1702	—	4.00	8.00	16.00	35.00	—

KM# 1228 2 PFENNIG

Silver **Ruler:** Leopold I **Mint:** Saint Veit **Obverse:** Bottom shields round **Note:** Uniface. Prev. KM#1637.

Date	Mintage	VG	F	VF	XF	Unc
1705	—	6.00	12.00	25.00	55.00	—

KM# 1483 2 PFENNIG

Silver **Ruler:** Joseph I **Mint:** Munich **Obverse:** Crowned imperial double eagle with value on breast **Note:** Uniface. Prev. KM#1182.

Date	Mintage	VG	F	VF	XF	Unc
1707	—	15.00	30.00	65.00	125	—
1709	—	15.00	30.00	65.00	125	—
1710	—	15.00	30.00	65.00	125	—

KM# 1566 2 PFENNIG

Silver **Ruler:** Karl (Charles) VI **Mint:** Munich **Note:** Uniface. Prev. KM#1188.

Date	Mintage	VG	F	VF	XF	Unc
1714	—	15.00	30.00	65.00	130	—

KM# 1685 1/4 KREUZER (Quadrans)

Billon **Ruler:** Maria Theresa **Mint:** Hall **Obverse:** Tyrolean eagle **Reverse:** Value in three lines, date below **Note:** Prev. KM#705.

Date	Mintage	VG	F	VF	XF	Unc
1742	874,000	5.00	10.00	20.00	35.00	—
1743	718,000	5.00	10.00	20.00	35.00	—
1744	724,000	5.00	10.00	20.00	35.00	—
1745	804,000	5.00	10.00	20.00	35.00	—
1746	718,000	5.00	10.00	20.00	35.00	—
1747	799,000	5.00	10.00	20.00	35.00	—

KM# 1760 1/4 KREUZER (Quadrans)

Billon **Ruler:** Maria Theresa **Mint:** Hall **Obverse:** Crowned imperial eagle with Tyrolean arms on breast, value below **Note:** Uniface. Prev. KM#706.

Date	Mintage	VG	F	VF	XF	Unc
1748	758,000	6.00	12.00	25.00	50.00	—
1749	809,000	6.00	12.00	25.00	50.00	—

KM# 1777 1/4 KREUZER (Quadrans)

Billon **Ruler:** Maria Theresa **Mint:** Hall **Obverse:** Date above Tyrolean eagle **Reverse:** Blank **Note:** Prev. KM#707.

Date	Mintage	VG	F	VF	XF	Unc
1750	625,000	10.00	15.00	30.00	60.00	—

KM# 1778 1/4 KREUZER (Quadrans)

Billon **Ruler:** Maria Theresa **Mint:** Hall **Obverse:** Date above Tyrolean eagle **Reverse:** Large fraction **Note:** Prev. KM#708.

Date	Mintage	VG	F	VF	XF	Unc
1750	Inc. above	5.00	10.00	20.00	40.00	—
1751	438,000	5.00	10.00	20.00	40.00	—
1752	599,000	5.00	10.00	20.00	40.00	—
1753	473,000	5.00	10.00	20.00	40.00	—
1754	377,000	5.00	10.00	20.00	40.00	—
1755	288,000	5.00	10.00	20.00	40.00	—
1756	277,000	5.00	10.00	20.00	40.00	—
1758	204,000	5.00	10.00	20.00	40.00	—
1759	128,000	5.00	10.00	20.00	40.00	—

KM# 1485 1/2 KREUZER

Silver **Ruler:** Joseph I **Mint:** Graz **Obverse:** Three shields, one above two, date divided at top **Note:** Uniface. Prev. KM#481.

Date	Mintage	VG	F	VF	XF	Unc
1707	—	8.00	16.00	35.00	75.00	—
1708	—	8.00	16.00	35.00	75.00	—
1711	—	8.00	16.00	35.00	75.00	—

KM# 1486 1/2 KREUZER

Billon **Ruler:** Joseph I **Mint:** Vienna **Obverse:** Three shields - one above two, date divided at top **Note:** Uniface. Prev. KM#1901.

Date	Mintage	VG	F	VF	XF	Unc
1707	—	7.50	15.00	30.00	65.00	—

KM# 1504 1/2 KREUZER

Billon **Ruler:** Joseph I **Mint:** Vienna **Note:** Uniface. Prev. KM#1902.

Date	Mintage	VG	F	VF	XF	Unc
1709	—	10.00	20.00	40.00	85.00	—

KM# 1534 1/2 KREUZER

Billon **Ruler:** Karl (Charles) VI **Mint:** Vienna **Obverse:** Date in straight line divided by top shield **Reverse:** Crowned eagle with center shield **Note:** Uniface. Prev. KM#1917.

Date	Mintage	VG	F	VF	XF	Unc
1713	—	10.00	20.00	40.00	50.00	—
1714	—	10.00	20.00	40.00	50.00	—

KM# 1533 1/2 KREUZER

Silver **Ruler:** Karl (Charles) VI **Mint:** Graz **Obverse:** Crowned imperial eagle, value divides date at bottom **Note:** Varieties exist. Uniface. Prev. KM#492.

Date	Mintage	VG	F	VF	XF	Unc
1713	—	4.00	8.00	17.50	45.00	—
1714	—	4.00	8.00	17.50	45.00	—
1715	—	4.00	8.00	17.50	45.00	—
1716	—	4.00	8.00	17.50	45.00	—
1717	—	4.00	8.00	17.50	45.00	—
1718	—	7.00	15.00	30.00	65.00	—
1723	—	4.00	8.00	17.50	45.00	—
1726 Rare	—	—	—	—	—	—
1727	—	4.00	8.00	17.50	45.00	—
1728	—	4.00	8.00	17.50	45.00	—
1729	—	4.00	8.00	17.50	45.00	—

KM# 1567 1/2 KREUZER

Billon **Ruler:** Karl (Charles) VI **Mint:** Vienna **Obverse:** Three shields - one above two, date divided at top in arc near border **Note:** Prev. KM#1918.

Date	Mintage	VG	F	VF	XF	Unc
1714	—	5.00	10.00	20.00	40.00	—
1715	—	5.00	10.00	20.00	40.00	—
1716	—	5.00	10.00	20.00	40.00	—
1717	—	5.00	10.00	20.00	40.00	—
1718	—	5.00	10.00	20.00	40.00	—
1719	—	5.00	10.00	20.00	40.00	—
1720	—	5.00	10.00	20.00	40.00	—

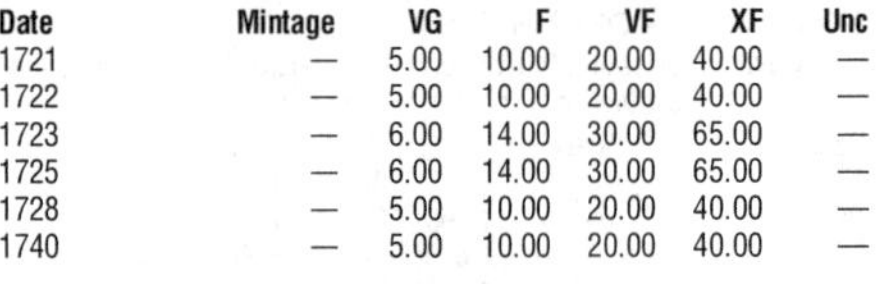

Date	Mintage	VG	F	VF	XF	Unc
1721	—	5.00	10.00	20.00	40.00	—
1722	—	5.00	10.00	20.00	40.00	—
1723	—	6.00	14.00	30.00	65.00	—
1725	—	6.00	14.00	30.00	65.00	—
1728	—	5.00	10.00	20.00	40.00	—
1740	—	5.00	10.00	20.00	40.00	—

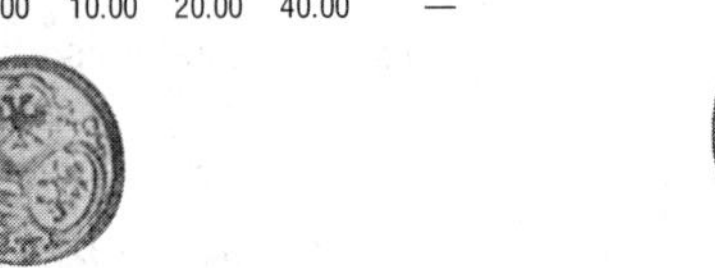

KM# 1637 1/2 KREUZER

Billon **Ruler:** Karl (Charles) VI **Mint:** Graz **Obverse:** Three shields **Note:** Varieties exist. Prev. KM#493.

Date	Mintage	VG	F	VF	XF	Unc
1730	—	5.00	10.00	20.00	50.00	—
1731 Rare	—	—	—	—	—	—
1733 Rare	—	—	—	—	—	—
1738	—	5.00	10.00	20.00	50.00	—
1739	—	5.00	10.00	20.00	50.00	—
1740	—	5.00	10.00	20.00	50.00	—

KM# 1671 1/2 KREUZER

Silver **Ruler:** Maria Theresa **Mint:** Graz **Obverse:** Crowned arms in branches, crown divides M - T; date at bottom **Note:** Prev. KM#515.

Date	Mintage	VG	F	VF	XF	Unc
1741	—	5.00	10.00	20.00	40.00	—
1742	—	3.00	7.50	15.00	30.00	—

KM# 1707 1/2 KREUZER

Silver **Ruler:** Maria Theresa **Mint:** Graz **Obverse:** Crowned large arms in branches, crown divides date, value at bottom **Note:** Prev. KM#516.

Date	Mintage	VG	F	VF	XF	Unc
1744	—	3.00	7.50	15.00	30.00	—
1745	—	3.00	7.50	15.00	30.00	—

KM# 1751 1/2 KREUZER

Silver **Ruler:** Maria Theresa **Mint:** Graz **Obverse:** Three shields, top shield divides date, value between bottom two **Note:** Prev. KM#517.

Date	Mintage	VG	F	VF	XF	Unc
1747	—	3.00	7.50	15.00	30.00	—
1748	—	3.00	7.50	15.00	30.00	—
1749	—	3.00	7.50	15.00	30.00	—

KM# 1229 KREUZER

Silver **Ruler:** Leopold I **Mint:** Vienna **Note:** Varieties exist. Prev. KM#1852.

Date	Mintage	VG	F	VF	XF	Unc
1701	—	7.00	15.00	30.00	60.00	—
1702	—	7.00	15.00	30.00	60.00	—

KM# 1240 KREUZER

Silver **Ruler:** Leopold I **Mint:** Graz **Obverse:** Portrait and titles of Leopold I **Reverse:** Date divided below arms **Note:** Varieties exist. Prev. KM#449.

Date	Mintage	VG	F	VF	XF	Unc
1702	—	7.00	15.00	30.00	60.00	—
1703	—	7.00	15.00	30.00	60.00	—
1705	—	7.00	15.00	30.00	60.00	—

KM# 1423 KREUZER

Silver **Ruler:** Joseph I **Mint:** Hall **Obverse:** Bust right **Obv. Legend:** IOSEPHUS • D • G • R • I • S • ... **Note:** Varieties exist. Prev. KM#660.

Date	Mintage	VG	F	VF	XF	Unc
ND	2,705,000	5.00	10.00	20.00	45.00	—

KM# 1422 KREUZER

Silver **Ruler:** Joseph I **Mint:** Augsburg **Obverse:** Bust right **Reverse:** Crowned imperial eagle with value on breast, date divided at top **Note:** Prev. KM#137.

Date	Mintage	VG	F	VF	XF	Unc
1705	—	8.00	15.00	35.00	70.00	—
1706	—	8.00	15.00	35.00	70.00	—
1707	—	8.00	15.00	35.00	70.00	—
1708	—	8.00	15.00	35.00	70.00	—
1709	—	8.00	15.00	35.00	70.00	—
1710	—	8.00	15.00	35.00	70.00	—

KM# 1424 KREUZER

Silver **Ruler:** Joseph I **Mint:** Munich **Obverse:** Bust right **Reverse:** Crowned imperial double eagle with value on breast **Note:** Prev. KM#1183.

Date	Mintage	VG	F	VF	XF	Unc
1705 (s)	—	9.00	18.00	40.00	100	—
1706 (s)	—	9.00	18.00	40.00	100	—
1707 (s)	—	9.00	18.00	40.00	100	—
1708 (s)	—	9.00	18.00	40.00	100	—
1709 (s)	—	9.00	18.00	40.00	100	—
1710 (s)	—	9.00	18.00	40.00	100	—

KM# 1425 KREUZER

Silver **Ruler:** Joseph I **Mint:** Vienna **Obverse:** Laureate bust right in inner circle **Reverse:** Crowned imperial eagle in inner circle, date in legend **Note:** Prev. KM#1903.

Date	Mintage	VG	F	VF	XF	Unc
1705	—	5.00	10.00	22.50	45.00	—
1706	—	—	—	—	—	—
Note: Reported, not confirmed						
1707	—	4.00	8.00	17.50	35.00	—
1709	—	—	—	—	—	—
Note: Reported, not confirmed						

KM# 1461 KREUZER

Silver **Ruler:** Joseph I **Mint:** Graz **Obverse:** Laureate bust right in inner circle, value below **Reverse:** Arms on cross of St. George and St. Andrew in inner circle, date below **Note:** Prev. KM#482.

Date	Mintage	VG	F	VF	XF	Unc
1706 IA	—	7.00	15.00	30.00	65.00	—
1707 IA	—	7.00	15.00	30.00	65.00	—
1708 IA	—	7.00	15.00	30.00	65.00	—
1709 IA	—	7.00	15.00	30.00	65.00	—
1710 IA	—	7.00	15.00	30.00	65.00	—
1711 IA	—	7.00	15.00	30.00	65.00	—
ND	—	7.00	15.00	30.00	65.00	—

KM# 1487 KREUZER

Silver **Ruler:** Joseph I **Mint:** Saint Veit **Obverse:** Bust right in inner circle, value below **Obv. Legend:** IOSEPHVS • D • G • R • I • S • A • ... **Reverse:** Arms on cross of St. George and St. Andrew in inner circle, date below **Note:** Prev. KM#1666.

Date	Mintage	VG	F	VF	XF	Unc
1707 IP	—	25.00	50.00	100	200	—

KM# 1511 KREUZER

Silver **Ruler:** Karl (Charles) VI **Mint:** Vienna **Obverse:** Laureate bust right **Reverse:** Crowned imperial eagle, date in legend **Note:** Prev. KM#1919.

Date	Mintage	VG	F	VF	XF	Unc
ND	—	7.50	15.00	32.00	70.00	—

KM# 1510 KREUZER

Silver **Ruler:** Karl (Charles) VI **Mint:** Hall **Obverse:** Bust right **Reverse:** Crowned imperial double eagle with arms on breast **Note:** Varieties exist. Prev. KM#676.

Date	Mintage	VG	F	VF	XF	Unc
ND	655,000	3.00	7.50	15.00	35.00	—
1713	738,000	3.00	7.50	15.00	35.00	—
1714	6,507,000	5.00	10.00	20.00	40.00	—
1724	6,176,000	5.00	10.00	20.00	45.00	—

KM# 1516 KREUZER

Silver **Ruler:** Karl (Charles) VI **Mint:** Munich **Obverse:** Bust right **Obv. Legend:** CAR • VI • D • G • R • ... **Reverse:** Crowned imperial double eagle with arms on breast **Note:** Prev. KM#1189.

Date	Mintage	VG	F	VF	XF	Unc
1712 (s)	—	8.00	16.00	35.00	75.00	—

KM# 1515 KREUZER

Silver **Ruler:** Karl (Charles) VI **Mint:** Augsburg **Obverse:** Bust right **Note:** Prev. KM#B145.

Date	Mintage	VG	F	VF	XF	Unc
1712	—	10.00	20.00	40.00	80.00	—

KM# 1537 KREUZER

Silver **Ruler:** Karl (Charles) VI **Mint:** Saint Veit **Obverse:** Laureate bust right in inner circle, value below **Note:** Prev. KM#1675.

Date	Mintage	VG	F	VF	XF	Unc
1713	—	25.00	50.00	100	200	—

KM# 1538 KREUZER

Silver **Ruler:** Karl (Charles) VI **Mint:** Saint Veit **Reverse:** Crowned imperial eagle in inner circle, crown divides date **Note:** Prev. KM#1676.

Date	Mintage	VG	F	VF	XF	Unc
1713	—	25.00	50.00	100	200	—

KM# 1536 KREUZER

Silver **Ruler:** Karl (Charles) VI **Mint:** Graz **Obverse:** Bust right within inner circle **Obv. Legend:** CAROL • VI • D • G • R • I • ... **Reverse:** Crowned imperial double eagle with arms on breast within circle **Rev. Legend:** ARCHID : AVS : DVXBVRG : STYRIÆ • **Note:** Varieties exist. Prev. KM#494.

Date	Mintage	VG	F	VF	XF	Unc
1713	—	5.00	10.00	20.00	45.00	—
1715	—	5.00	10.00	20.00	45.00	—
1717	—	5.00	10.00	20.00	45.00	—
1718	—	5.00	10.00	20.00	45.00	—
1720	—	5.00	10.00	20.00	45.00	—
1721	—	5.00	10.00	20.00	45.00	—
1722	—	5.00	10.00	20.00	45.00	—
1723	—	5.00	10.00	20.00	45.00	—
1724	—	5.00	10.00	20.00	45.00	—
1725	—	5.00	10.00	20.00	45.00	—
1726	—	5.00	10.00	20.00	45.00	—
1727	—	5.00	10.00	20.00	45.00	—
1728	—	5.00	10.00	20.00	45.00	—
1729	—	5.00	10.00	20.00	45.00	—
1730	—	5.00	10.00	20.00	45.00	—
1731	—	5.00	10.00	20.00	45.00	—

KM# 1638 KREUZER

Silver **Ruler:** Karl (Charles) VI **Mint:** Graz **Obverse:** Without inner circle **Reverse:** Without inner circle **Note:** Varieties exist. Prev. KM#495.

Date	Mintage	VG	F	VF	XF	Unc
1730	—	4.00	8.00	16.00	40.00	—
1732	—	4.00	8.00	16.00	40.00	—
1733	—	4.00	8.00	16.00	40.00	—
1734	—	4.00	8.00	16.00	40.00	—
1735	—	4.00	8.00	16.00	40.00	—
1736	—	4.00	8.00	16.00	40.00	—
1737	—	4.00	8.00	16.00	40.00	—
1738	—	4.00	8.00	16.00	40.00	—
1739	—	4.00	8.00	16.00	40.00	—
1740	—	4.00	8.00	16.00	40.00	—

KM# 1509 KREUZER

Silver **Ruler:** Karl (Charles) VI **Mint:** Hall **Obverse:** Bust right **Reverse:** Crowned imperial double eagle with arms on breast **Note:** Varieties exist. Prev. KM#675.

Date	Mintage	VG	F	VF	XF	Unc
ND(1711)	Inc. below	3.00	7.50	15.00	35.00	—

KM# 1688 KREUZER

Billon **Ruler:** Maria Theresa **Mint:** Hall **Obverse:** Bust right, value below shoulder **Reverse:** Eagle in cartouche **Note:** Mint records show 252,000 for 1744, almost certainly dated 1742-43. Prev. KM#711.

Date	Mintage	VG	F	VF	XF	Unc
1742	Inc. above	5.00	10.00	20.00	45.00	—
1743	215,000	5.00	10.00	20.00	45.00	—

KM# 1689 KREUZER

Billon **Ruler:** Maria Theresa **Mint:** Vienna **Obverse:** Bust right **Obv. Legend:** MAR•THERES•D•G•REG•HU•BO•**Reverse:** Multi-fold shield in cartouche **Note:** Varieties exist in shield design. Prev. KM#1935.

Date	Mintage	VG	F	VF	XF	Unc
1742	—	3.00	6.00	12.00	30.00	—
1743	—	3.00	6.00	12.00	30.00	—
1744	—	3.00	6.00	12.00	30.00	—
1745	—	3.00	6.00	12.00	30.00	—

KM# 1686 KREUZER

Billon **Ruler:** Maria Theresa **Mint:** Hall **Obverse:** Bust right **Reverse:** Large eagle, value below **Note:** Prev. KM#709.

Date	Mintage	VG	F	VF	XF	Unc
1742	248,000	6.00	12.00	25.00	50.00	—

KM# 1687 KREUZER

Billon **Ruler:** Maria Theresa **Mint:** Hall **Obverse:** Tyrolean eagle in crowned cartouche, value below **Note:** Prev. KM#710.

Date	Mintage	VG	F	VF	XF	Unc
1742	Inc. above	6.00	12.00	25.00	50.00	—

KM# 1701 KREUZER

Silver **Ruler:** Maria Theresa **Mint:** Graz **Obverse:** Bust right **Obv. Legend:** MAR • THERES • D • G • REG • HUN • BO • **Reverse:** Crowned multi-fold shield **Rev. Legend:** ARCH • AUS • DUX • ... **Note:** Prev. KM#518.

Date	Mintage	VG	F	VF	XF	Unc
1743	—	6.50	13.50	27.50	55.00	—

KM# 1708 KREUZER

Silver **Ruler:** Maria Theresa **Mint:** Graz **Rev. Legend:** BUR. & STYR. **Note:** Prev. KM#519.

Date	Mintage	VG	F	VF	XF	Unc
1744	—	5.00	10.00	20.00	40.00	—

KM# 1718 KREUZER

Silver **Ruler:** Maria Theresa **Mint:** Graz **Obverse:** Bust right **Reverse:** Crowned shield **Rev. Legend:** ARCH • AUS... **Note:** Prev. KM#520.

Date	Mintage	VG	F	VF	XF	Unc
1745	—	4.00	8.00	17.50	35.00	—

KM# 1719 KREUZER

Billon **Ruler:** Maria Theresa **Mint:** Hall **Reverse:** Eagle in cartouche, value below **Note:** Prev. KM#712.

Date	Mintage	VG	F	VF	XF	Unc
1745	243,000	5.00	10.00	20.00	45.00	—
1746	169,000	5.00	10.00	20.00	45.00	—
1747	351,000	5.00	10.00	20.00	45.00	—

KM# 1735 KREUZER

Billon **Ruler:** Maria Theresa **Mint:** Vienna **Reverse:** Imperial eagle with shield **Note:** Prev. KM#1936.

Date	Mintage	VG	F	VF	XF	Unc
1746	—	3.00	6.00	12.00	25.00	—
1747/6	—	3.50	7.50	15.00	35.00	—
1747	—	3.00	6.00	12.00	25.00	—
1748	—	3.00	6.00	12.00	25.00	—
1749	—	3.00	6.00	12.00	25.00	—
1750	—	3.00	6.00	12.00	25.00	—
1751	—	3.00	6.00	12.00	25.00	—
1752	—	3.00	6.00	12.00	25.00	—
1753	—	3.00	6.00	12.00	25.00	—
1755	—	7.00	15.00	30.00	50.00	—
1759	—	—	—	—	—	—

Note: Reported, not confirmed; For later issues refer to Uniform Coinage

KM# 1752 KREUZER

Silver **Ruler:** Maria Theresa **Mint:** Graz **Obverse:** Bust right **Obv. Legend:** M • THER • D • G • R • I • GER • HUN • ... **Reverse:** Imperial double eagle with arms on breast, value below **Rev. Legend:** ARCH • AVST • DUX • BURG • ... **Note:** Prev. KM#521.

Date	Mintage	VG	F	VF	XF	Unc
1747	—	3.00	7.50	15.00	30.00	—
1748	—	3.00	7.50	15.00	30.00	—

KM# 1761.1 KREUZER

Billon **Ruler:** Maria Theresa **Mint:** Hall **Obverse:** Bust right without value below shoulder **Reverse:** Crowned imperial eagle with Tyrolean arms on breast, value below **Note:** Prev. KM#713.1.

Date	Mintage	VG	F	VF	XF	Unc
1748	231,000	3.00	6.00	15.00	35.00	—
1750	121,000	3.00	6.00	15.00	35.00	—
1752	1,231,000	3.00	6.00	10.00	25.00	—
1753	992,000	3.00	6.00	10.00	25.00	—
1754	205,000	3.00	6.00	10.00	25.00	—
1755	225,000	3.00	6.00	10.00	25.00	—
1756	155,000	3.00	6.00	10.00	25.00	—
1757	83,000	3.00	6.00	10.00	25.00	—

KM# 1771 KREUZER

Silver **Ruler:** Maria Theresa **Mint:** Graz **Obverse:** Bust right **Reverse:** Crowned imperial double eagle with arms on breast, value below **Rev. Legend:** ARCHID... **Note:** Prev. KM#522.

Date	Mintage	VG	F	VF	XF	Unc
1749	—	3.00	7.50	15.00	30.00	—
1751	—	5.00	10.00	20.00	40.00	—
1753	—	3.00	7.50	15.00	30.00	—
1754	—	—	—	—	—	—

Note: Reported, not confirmed

KM# 1761.2 KREUZER

Billon **Ruler:** Maria Theresa **Mint:** Hall **Reverse:** Cross after date **Note:** Mint records show 150,000 for 1758, probably struck with dies from earlier years. Varieties exist. Prev. KM#713.2.

Date	Mintage	VG	F	VF	XF	Unc
1751	—	12.00	25.00	50.00	80.00	—

KM# 1818 KREUZER

Silver **Ruler:** Maria Theresa **Mint:** Graz **Rev. Legend:** AUS... and BUR... **Note:** Prev. KM#523.

Date	Mintage	VG	F	VF	XF	Unc
1755 Division DU-X	—	3.00	7.50	15.00	30.00	—
1755 Division R-I GE	—	3.00	7.50	15.00	30.00	—

KM# 1820 KREUZER

Silver **Ruler:** Maria Theresa **Mint:** Graz **Obverse:** Bust right **Reverse:** Crowned imperial double eagle with arms on breast, value below **Note:** Prev. KM#524.

Date	Mintage	VG	F	VF	XF	Unc
1756	—	3.00	7.50	15.00	30.00	—
1757	—	4.00	8.00	17.50	35.00	—
1758/7	—	5.00	10.00	20.00	40.00	—
1758	—	3.00	7.50	15.00	30.00	—
1762	—	—	—	—	—	—

KM# 1412 3 KREUZER

Silver **Ruler:** Leopold I **Mint:** Hall **Obverse:** Bust right in inner circle **Reverse:** Two plain shields, crown above divides date **Note:** Prev. KM#627.

Date	Mintage	VG	F	VF	XF	Unc
1701 Rare	103,000	—	—	—	—	—

KM# 1116 3 KREUZER

Silver **Ruler:** Leopold I **Mint:** Saint Veit **Obverse:** Bust right in inner circle **Obv. Legend:** LEOPOLDVS • D • G • R • I • .... **Reverse:** Three shields in inner circle **Note:** Varieties exist. Prev. KM#1639.

Date	Mintage	VG	F	VF	XF	Unc
1701 IP	—	10.00	20.00	40.00	90.00	—
1702 IP	—	10.00	20.00	40.00	90.00	—
1703 IP	—	10.00	20.00	40.00	90.00	—
1704 IP	—	10.00	20.00	40.00	90.00	—
1705 IP	—	10.00	20.00	40.00	90.00	—
1706	—	12.00	25.00	50.00	100	—

Note: Coins dated 1706 are a posthumous issue

KM# 1115 3 KREUZER

Silver **Ruler:** Leopold I **Mint:** Graz **Obverse:** Portrait right and titles of Leopold I **Reverse:** Three shields in inner circle, date at top **Note:** Varieties exist. Prev. KM#450.

Date	Mintage	VG	F	VF	XF	Unc
1702 IA	—	7.00	15.00	30.00	60.00	—
1703 IA	—	7.00	15.00	30.00	60.00	—
1704 IA	—	7.00	15.00	30.00	60.00	—
1705 IA	—	7.00	15.00	30.00	60.00	—

KM# 1428 3 KREUZER

Silver **Ruler:** Joseph I **Mint:** Augsburg **Obverse:** Bust right **Note:** Prev. KM#138.

Date	Mintage	VG	F	VF	XF	Unc
1705	—	10.00	20.00	40.00	80.00	—
1706	—	10.00	20.00	40.00	80.00	—
1707	—	10.00	20.00	40.00	80.00	—
1708	—	10.00	20.00	40.00	80.00	—
1709	—	10.00	20.00	40.00	80.00	—
1710	—	10.00	20.00	40.00	80.00	—
1711	—	10.00	20.00	40.00	80.00	—

KM# 1430 3 KREUZER

Silver **Ruler:** Joseph I **Mint:** Munich **Obverse:** Bust right **Reverse:** Crowned imperial double eagle with arms on breast **Note:** Prev. KM#1184.

Date	Mintage	VG	F	VF	XF	Unc
1705 (s)	—	10.00	20.00	45.00	120	—
1706 (s)	—	10.00	20.00	45.00	120	—
1707 (s)	—	10.00	20.00	45.00	120	—
1708 (s)	—	10.00	20.00	45.00	120	—
1709 (s)	—	10.00	20.00	45.00	120	—
1710 (s)	—	10.00	20.00	45.00	120	—
1711 (s)	—	10.00	20.00	45.00	120	—

KM# 1463 3 KREUZER

Silver **Ruler:** Joseph I **Mint:** Graz **Obverse:** Laureate bust right in inner circle, value below **Reverse:** Three shields within inner circle **Note:** Prev. KM#483.

Date	Mintage	VG	F	VF	XF	Unc
1706 IA	—	6.00	12.00	25.00	60.00	—
1707 IA	—	6.00	12.00	25.00	60.00	—
1708 IA	—	6.00	12.00	25.00	60.00	—
1709 IA	—	6.00	12.00	25.00	60.00	—
1710 IA	—	6.00	12.00	25.00	60.00	—
1711 IA	—	6.00	12.00	25.00	60.00	—

KM# 1462 3 KREUZER

Silver **Ruler:** Leopold I **Mint:** Graz **Note:** Posthumous issue. Prev. KM#451.

Date	Mintage	VG	F	VF	XF	Unc
1706 IA	—	6.00	12.00	25.00	55.00	—

KM# 1489 3 KREUZER

Silver **Ruler:** Joseph I **Mint:** Saint Veit **Obverse:** Laureate bust right in inner circle, value below **Reverse:** Three shields - one above two with ornamentation in angles in inner circle, date at top in legend **Note:** Varieties exist. Prev. KM#1667.

Date	Mintage	VG	F	VF	XF	Unc
1707 IP	—	20.00	40.00	85.00	175	—
1708 IP	—	20.00	40.00	85.00	175	—
1709 IP	—	20.00	40.00	85.00	175	—
1710 IP	—	20.00	40.00	85.00	175	—
1711 IP	—	20.00	40.00	85.00	175	—

KM# 1488 3 KREUZER

Silver **Ruler:** Joseph I **Mint:** Hall **Obverse:** Bust right **Obv. Legend:** IOSEPHUS • D • G • ... **Reverse:** Crowned two-fold shield **Note:** Prev. KM#661.

Date	Mintage	VG	F	VF	XF	Unc
1707	178,000	60.00	125	200	350	—

KM# 1519 3 KREUZER

Silver **Ruler:** Karl (Charles) VI **Mint:** Augsburg **Obverse:** Bust right **Note:** Legend varieties exist. Prev. KM#A143.

Date	Mintage	VG	F	VF	XF	Unc
1712	—	12.00	25.00	50.00	100	—
1713	—	12.00	25.00	50.00	100	—
1714	—	12.00	25.00	50.00	100	—

KM# 1520 3 KREUZER

Silver **Ruler:** Karl (Charles) VI **Mint:** Munich **Note:** Varieties exist. Prev. KM#1190.

Date	Mintage	VG	F	VF	XF	Unc
1712 (s)	—	15.00	30.00	65.00	125	—
1713	—	15.00	30.00	65.00	125	—
1714	—	15.00	30.00	70.00	135	—

KM# 1540 3 KREUZER

Silver **Ruler:** Karl (Charles) VI **Mint:** Graz **Obverse:** Laureate bust right in inner circle, value below **Reverse:** Crowned imperial eagle in inner circle, crown divides date **Note:** Varieties exist. Prev. KM#496.

Date	Mintage	VG	F	VF	XF	Unc
1713	—	5.00	10.00	20.00	45.00	—
1714	—	5.00	10.00	20.00	45.00	—
1715	—	5.00	10.00	20.00	45.00	—
1716	—	5.00	10.00	20.00	45.00	—
1717	—	5.00	10.00	20.00	45.00	—
1718	—	5.00	10.00	20.00	45.00	—
1719	—	5.00	10.00	20.00	45.00	—
1720	—	5.00	10.00	20.00	45.00	—
1721	—	5.00	10.00	20.00	45.00	—
1722	—	5.00	10.00	20.00	45.00	—
1724	—	5.00	10.00	20.00	45.00	—
1725 Rare	—	—	—	—	—	—
1727	—	5.00	10.00	20.00	45.00	—
1728	—	5.00	10.00	20.00	45.00	—

KM# 1541 3 KREUZER

Silver **Ruler:** Karl (Charles) VI **Mint:** Saint Veit **Obverse:** Bust right **Obv. Legend:** CAROLUS • VI • D: G • R • I • S • A • ... **Reverse:** Double eagle with shield on breast **Rev. Legend:** ARCHIDVX • AVS • & • CARINTH • **Note:** Varieties exist. Prev. KM#1677.

Date	Mintage	VG	F	VF	XF	Unc
1713	—	20.00	40.00	85.00	175	—
1714	—	20.00	40.00	85.00	175	—

KM# 1568 3 KREUZER

Silver **Ruler:** Karl (Charles) VI **Mint:** Vienna **Obverse:** Laureate bust right in inner circle, value below **Obv. Legend:** CAROL • VI • D • G • RO • ... **Reverse:** Crowned imperial eagle in inner circle, crown divides date **Rev. Legend:** ARCHIDVX • AVST: DVX • BVR • CO • TYR • **Note:** Prev. KM#1920.

Date	Mintage	VG	F	VF	XF	Unc
1714	—	4.00	9.00	20.00	50.00	—
1715	—	4.00	9.00	20.00	50.00	—
1716	—	4.00	9.00	20.00	50.00	—
1717	—	4.00	9.00	20.00	50.00	—
1718/7	—	4.00	9.00	20.00	35.00	—
1718	—	4.00	9.00	20.00	50.00	—
1719	—	4.00	9.00	20.00	50.00	—
1720	—	4.00	9.00	20.00	50.00	—

KM# 1587 3 KREUZER

Silver **Ruler:** Karl (Charles) VI **Mint:** Hall **Obverse:** Bust right **Reverse:** Crowned imperial double eagle with arms on breast, value encircled below **Note:** Varieties exist. Prev. KM#677.

Date	Mintage	VG	F	VF	XF	Unc
1716	14,000	7.50	15.00	30.00	75.00	—
1724	—	—	—	—	—	—
Note: Reported, not confirmed						
1725	—	—	—	—	—	—
Note: Reported, not confirmed						
1726	—	4.00	8.00	16.00	45.00	—
1727	56,000	4.00	8.00	16.00	45.00	—
1728	22,000	4.00	8.00	16.00	45.00	—
1729	25,000	—	—	—	—	—
1730	215,000	—	—	—	—	—
1731	503,000	4.00	8.00	16.00	45.00	—
1733	217,000	4.00	8.00	16.00	45.00	—
1734	187,000	4.00	8.00	16.00	45.00	—
1736	142,000	4.00	8.00	16.00	45.00	—
1737	257,000	4.00	8.00	16.00	45.00	—
1739	226,000	4.00	8.00	16.00	45.00	—
1740	117,000	20.00	35.00	75.00	125	—

KM# 1606 3 KREUZER

Silver **Ruler:** Karl (Charles) VI **Mint:** Vienna **Obverse:** Large laureate bust right **Reverse:** Crowned imperial eagle, value below, date in legend **Note:** Varieties exist. Prev. KM#1921.

Date	Mintage	VG	F	VF	XF	Unc
1721	—	4.00	9.00	20.00	50.00	—
1722	—	4.00	9.00	20.00	50.00	—
1723	—	4.00	9.00	20.00	50.00	—
1724	—	4.00	9.00	20.00	50.00	—
1725	—	4.00	9.00	20.00	50.00	—
1726	—	4.00	9.00	20.00	50.00	—
1727	—	4.00	9.00	20.00	50.00	—
1728	—	4.00	9.00	20.00	50.00	—
1729	—	4.00	9.00	20.00	50.00	—
1730	—	4.00	9.00	20.00	50.00	—
1731	—	4.00	9.00	20.00	50.00	—
1732	—	4.00	9.00	20.00	50.00	—
1733	—	4.00	9.00	20.00	50.00	—
1734	—	4.00	9.00	20.00	50.00	—
1735	—	4.00	9.00	20.00	50.00	—
1736	—	4.00	9.00	20.00	50.00	—
1737	—	4.00	9.00	20.00	50.00	—
1738	—	4.00	9.00	20.00	50.00	—
1739	—	4.00	9.00	20.00	50.00	—
1740	—	4.00	9.00	20.00	50.00	—

KM# 1627 3 KREUZER

Silver **Ruler:** Karl (Charles) VI **Mint:** Graz **Obverse:** Large laureate bust right **Reverse:** Crowned imperial eagle, value below, crown divides date **Note:** Prev. KM#497.

Date	Mintage	VG	F	VF	XF	Unc
1729	—	6.00	12.50	25.00	55.00	—
1730	—	6.00	12.50	25.00	55.00	—
1732	—	6.00	12.50	25.00	55.00	—
1734	—	6.00	12.50	25.00	55.00	—
1738	—	6.00	12.50	25.00	55.00	—
1739	—	6.00	12.50	25.00	55.00	—
1740	—	6.00	12.50	25.00	55.00	—

KM# 1659 3 KREUZER

Silver **Ruler:** Karl (Charles) VI **Mint:** Hall **Obverse:** Bust right **Obv. Legend:** CAR • VI • D • G • R • I • S • A • G • HI • H • B • REX • **Reverse:** Crowned imperial double eagle with arms on breast, value encircled below **Note:** Prev. KM#678.

Date	Mintage	VG	F	VF	XF	Unc
1738	186,000	4.00	8.00	16.00	45.00	—

KM# 1660 3 KREUZER

Silver **Ruler:** Karl (Charles) VI **Mint:** Hall **Obverse:** Value below bust **Note:** Prev. KM#679.

Date	Mintage	VG	F	VF	XF	Unc
1739	Inc. above	12.50	25.00	50.00	100	—

KM# 1672 3 KREUZER

1.7000 g., 0.3440 Silver .0188 oz. ASW **Ruler:** Maria Theresa **Mint:** Vienna **Obverse:** Young bust right **Reverse:** Crowned arms with Austrian shield **Note:** Prev. KM#1937.

Date	Mintage	VG	F	VF	XF	Unc
1741	—	15.00	35.00	75.00	150	—

KM# 1691 3 KREUZER

1.7000 g., 0.3440 Silver .0188 oz. ASW **Ruler:** Maria Theresa **Mint:** Vienna **Reverse:** Crowned arms in branches **Note:** Prev. KM#1938.

Date	Mintage	VG	F	VF	XF	Unc
1742	—	4.00	7.00	15.00	40.00	—
1743	—	4.00	7.00	15.00	40.00	—
1744	—	4.00	7.00	15.00	40.00	—
1745	—	4.00	7.00	15.00	40.00	—

KM# 1690 3 KREUZER

Silver **Ruler:** Maria Theresa **Mint:** Graz **Obverse:** Bust right **Reverse:** Crowned multi-fold shield in cartouche, value below **Note:** Prev. KM#525.

Date	Mintage	VG	F	VF	XF	Unc
1742	—	8.00	16.00	37.50	80.00	—

KM# 1702 3 KREUZER

Silver **Ruler:** Maria Theresa **Mint:** Graz **Obverse:** Mature bust right **Note:** Prev. KM#526.

Date	Mintage	VG	F	VF	XF	Unc
1743	—	7.50	15.00	32.00	65.00	—

KM# 1709 3 KREUZER

Silver **Ruler:** Maria Theresa **Mint:** Graz **Obverse:** Young bust right **Obv. Legend:** MAR • THERESIA D: G • REG • HI • HU • & BOH • **Reverse:** Crowned multi-fold arms **Note:** Prev. KM#527.

Date	Mintage	VG	F	VF	XF	Unc
1744	—	7.50	15.00	35.00	75.00	—
1745	—	10.00	20.00	40.00	85.00	—

KM# 1720 3 KREUZER

Billon **Ruler:** Maria Theresa **Mint:** Hall **Obverse:** Bust right **Reverse:** Crowned arms in branches, value below **Note:** Prev. KM#714.

Date	Mintage	VG	F	VF	XF	Unc
1745	—	3.00	6.00	12.00	25.00	—

KM# 1721 3 KREUZER

Billon **Ruler:** Maria Theresa **Mint:** Hall **Reverse:** Crowned arms in flowers, value below **Note:** Roller die coins. Mint records show 308,000 for 1745-47, probably all dated 1745. Prev. KM#715.

Date	Mintage	VG	F	VF	XF	Unc
1745	—	8.00	12.50	20.00	30.00	—

KM# 1736 3 KREUZER

1.7000 g., 0.3440 Silver .0188 oz. ASW **Ruler:** Maria Theresa **Mint:** Vienna **Obv. Legend:** Ends: REG. **Reverse:** Crowned eagle with heart-shaped shield on breast **Note:** Prev. KM#1939.

Date	Mintage	VG	F	VF	XF	Unc
1746	—	5.00	10.00	20.00	50.00	—
1747	—	5.00	10.00	20.00	50.00	—
1748	—	5.00	10.00	20.00	50.00	—
1749	—	5.00	10.00	30.00	70.00	—

KM# 1762.1 3 KREUZER

Billon **Ruler:** Maria Theresa **Mint:** Hall **Obverse:** Crowned bust right **Obv. Legend:** M • THERES • D: G • R • I • GE • HU • BO • REG • **Reverse:** Crowned imperial double eagle with arms on breast, value below **Rev. Legend:** ARCH • AUST • DUX • BU • COM • TYR • **Note:** Prev. KM#716.1.

Date	Mintage	VG	F	VF	XF	Unc
1748	223,000	4.00	7.50	15.00	35.00	—
1749	126,000	4.00	7.50	15.00	35.00	—
1750	182,000	4.00	7.50	15.00	35.00	—

KM# 1772 3 KREUZER

Silver **Ruler:** Maria Theresa **Mint:** Graz **Obverse:** Bust right **Reverse:** Crowned imperial double eagle with crowned arms on breast, encircled value below **Note:** Prev. KM#528.

Date	Mintage	VG	F	VF	XF	Unc
1749	—	7.50	15.00	30.00	60.00	—
1750	—	7.50	15.00	35.00	75.00	—

KM# 1779 3 KREUZER

1.7000 g., 0.3440 Silver .0188 oz. ASW **Ruler:** Maria Theresa **Mint:** Vienna **Obverse:** Smaller head **Reverse:** Crowned eagle with spade-shaped shield on breast **Note:** Prev. KM#1940.

Date	Mintage	VG	F	VF	XF	Unc
1750	—	20.00	40.00	80.00	120	—

KM# 1791 3 KREUZER
1.7000 g., 0.3440 Silver .0188 oz. ASW **Ruler:** Maria Theresa **Mint:** Vienna **Reverse:** Cross after date **Note:** Prev. KM#1941.

Date	Mintage	VG	F	VF	XF	Unc
1751	—	4.00	6.00	15.00	50.00	—
1752	—	4.00	6.00	15.00	50.00	—
1753	—	4.00	6.00	15.00	40.00	—
1754	—	4.00	6.00	15.00	50.00	—
1755	—	4.00	6.00	15.00	50.00	—
1756/5	—	4.00	6.00	17.50	45.00	—
1756	—	4.00	6.00	15.00	40.00	—
1757	—	4.00	6.00	15.00	40.00	—
1759	—	4.00	6.00	15.00	40.00	—
1760	—	6.00	15.00	25.00	50.00	—
1761	—	4.00	6.00	15.00	50.00	—
1762	—	6.00	15.00	25.00	40.00	—
1763	—	4.00	6.00	15.00	40.00	—
1764/3	—	4.00	7.50	17.50	45.00	—
1764	—	4.00	6.00	15.00	40.00	—
1765	—	4.00	6.00	15.00	40.00	—

Note: For later issues refer to Uniform Coinage

KM# 1790 3 KREUZER
Silver **Ruler:** Maria Theresa **Mint:** Graz **Reverse:** Cross after date **Note:** Prev. KM#529.

Date	Mintage	VG	F	VF	XF	Unc
1751	—	7.50	15.00	35.00	75.00	—
1752	—	12.50	25.00	50.00	100	—
1754	—	10.00	20.00	45.00	90.00	—

KM# 1762.2 3 KREUZER
Billon **Ruler:** Maria Theresa **Mint:** Hall **Reverse:** Cross after date **Note:** Varieties exist. Prev. KM#716.2.

Date	Mintage	VG	F	VF	XF	Unc
1752	—	—	—	—	—	—
Note: Reported, not confirmed						
1753	384,000	4.00	7.50	15.00	30.00	—
1754	113,000	4.00	7.50	15.00	30.00	—
1755	90,000	4.00	7.50	15.00	30.00	—
1760	102,000	10.00	20.00	40.00	90.00	—
1762	300,000	15.00	30.00	60.00	125	—
1763	125,000	4.00	7.50	15.00	30.00	—
1764	122,000	4.00	7.50	15.00	30.00	—
1765	82,000	4.00	7.50	15.00	30.00	—

KM# 1832 3 KREUZER
Silver **Ruler:** Maria Theresa **Mint:** Graz **Reverse:** Legend rotated 180 degrees **Note:** Prev. KM#530.

Date	Mintage	VG	F	VF	XF	Unc
1765	—	12.50	25.00	55.00	110	—

KM# 1833 5 KREUZER
2.3300 g., 0.4380 Silver .0328 oz. ASW **Ruler:** Maria Theresa **Mint:** Vienna **Obverse:** Young bust right in wreath **Reverse:** Eagle, value below **Note:** Prev. KM#1942.

Date	Mintage	VG	F	VF	XF	Unc
1765	—	20.00	40.00	85.00	150	—

KM# 1863 5 KREUZER
2.3300 g., 0.4380 Silver .0328 oz. ASW **Ruler:** Maria Theresa **Mint:** Vienna **Obverse:** Veiled bust right in wreath **Obv. Legend:** M • THERESIA • D • G • R • IMP • HU • BO • REG • **Reverse:** Crowned imperial double eagle with arms on breast **Rev. Legend:** ARCHID • AUST • DUX • BURG • CO • TYR • **Note:** Prev. KM#1943.

Date	Mintage	VG	F	VF	XF	Unc
1772 C-K	—	20.00	45.00	85.00	175	—
1778 C-A	—	20.00	35.00	65.00	125	—
1779 C-A	—	20.00	35.00	65.00	125	—

Note: For later issues refer to Uniform Coinage

KM# 1870 5 KREUZER
Billon **Ruler:** Maria Theresa **Mint:** Hall **Obverse:** Veiled bust right in wreath **Reverse:** Crowned imperial eagle with Tyrolean arms at center **Note:** Prev. KM#717.

Date	Mintage	VG	F	VF	XF	Unc
1778 VC-S	—	30.00	60.00	125	250	—
1779 VC-S	187,000	30.00	60.00	125	250	—

KM# 1491 6 KREUZER
Silver **Ruler:** Joseph I **Mint:** Hall **Obverse:** Bust right **Obv. Legend:** IOSEPHUS • D: G: ROM: IMP: ... **Reverse:** Crowned two-fold shield **Note:** Prev. KM#662.

Date	Mintage	VG	F	VF	XF	Unc
1707	357,000	40.00	80.00	160	275	—
1711/07	87,000	40.00	80.00	160	275	—
1711	Inc. above	40.00	80.00	160	275	—

KM# 1569 6 KREUZER
Silver **Ruler:** Karl (Charles) VI **Mint:** Hall **Obverse:** Crowned imperial double eagle with arms on breast, value below **Obv. Legend:** CAROLUS • VI • D: G: R: I: S: A: G: H: H: B: R: **Rev. Legend:** ARCHIDUX • AVST • DUX • BV • CO • TYR • **Note:** Varieties exist. Prev. KM#680.

Date	Mintage	VG	F	VF	XF	Unc
1714	120,000	7.50	20.00	50.00	100	—
1715	267,000	7.50	15.00	35.00	75.00	—
1717	169,000	7.50	20.00	50.00	100	—
1718	264,000	7.50	20.00	50.00	100	—
1719	244,000	7.50	15.00	35.00	75.00	—
1720	188,000	7.50	15.00	35.00	75.00	—
1721	419,000	7.50	15.00	35.00	75.00	—
1722	307,000	7.50	15.00	35.00	75.00	—
1723	505,000	7.50	15.00	35.00	75.00	—
1724	410,000	7.50	15.00	35.00	75.00	—

KM# 1588 6 KREUZER
Silver **Ruler:** Karl (Charles) VI **Mint:** Saint Veit **Obverse:** Bust right **Obv. Legend:** CAROLVS • VI • D: G • R • I • ... **Reverse:** Crowned imperial double eagle with arms on breast **Rev. Legend:** ARCHIDVX • AVS • & • CARINTHIAE • **Note:** Prev. KM#1678.

Date	Mintage	VG	F	VF	XF	Unc
1716	—	60.00	120	250	450	—

KM# 1615 6 KREUZER
Silver **Ruler:** Karl (Charles) VI **Mint:** Hall **Obverse:** Armored bust right **Obv. Legend:** CAR • VI • D • G • R • I • S • A • G • E • HI • HV • BO • REX • **Reverse:** Crowned imperial double eagle with arms on breast, value below **Rev. Legend:** ARCHID • AUSTR • DUX • BV • COM • TYROL • **Note:** Varieties exist. Prev. KM#681.

Date	Mintage	VG	F	VF	XF	Unc
1724	Inc. above	7.50	15.00	35.00	75.00	—
1725	412,000	7.50	15.00	35.00	75.00	—
1726	—	7.50	15.00	35.00	75.00	—
1728	833,000	7.50	15.00	35.00	75.00	—
1729	629,000	7.50	15.00	35.00	75.00	—
1730	512,000	7.50	15.00	35.00	75.00	—
1731	367,000	7.50	15.00	35.00	75.00	—
1732	255,000	7.50	15.00	35.00	75.00	—
1734 Rare	224,000	—	—	—	—	—
1735	157,000	7.50	15.00	35.00	75.00	—
1736	716,000	6.50	12.50	32.00	70.00	—
1737	770,000	6.50	12.50	32.00	70.00	—
1738	464,000	6.50	12.50	32.00	70.00	—
1739	375,000	6.50	12.50	32.00	70.00	—
1740	362,000	6.50	12.50	32.00	70.00	—

KM# 1623 6 KREUZER
Silver **Ruler:** Karl (Charles) VI **Mint:** Graz **Obverse:** Laureate bust right **Reverse:** Crowned imperial eagle, value below, date in legend **Note:** Prev. KM#498.

Date	Mintage	VG	F	VF	XF	Unc
1728	—	60.00	120	200	350	—

KM# 1661 6 KREUZER
Silver **Ruler:** Karl (Charles) VI **Mint:** Hall **Obverse:** Legend begins at lower left **Obv. Inscription:** CAR • VI • D • G • R • I • S • A • GE • HI • HV • B • REX • **Reverse:** Crowned imperial double eagle with arms on breast, value below **Rev. Legend:** ARCHID • AVST • DVX • BV • COM • TYR • **Note:** Prev. KM#682.

Date	Mintage	VG	F	VF	XF	Unc
1739	Inc. above	7.50	15.00	35.00	75.00	—

KM# 1673 6 KREUZER
3.2900 g., 0.4380 Silver .0463 oz. ASW **Ruler:** Maria Theresa **Mint:** Vienna **Obverse:** Bust right **Obv. Legend:** MAR • THERESIA D: G • REG • HUNG • BOH • **Reverse:** Crowned four-fold arms within cartouche **Rev. Legend:** ARCH • AUST • DUX BUR • CO • TYR • **Note:** Varieties in legend abbreviations and positioning exist. Prev. KM#1944.

Date	Mintage	VG	F	VF	XF	Unc
1741	—	7.50	15.00	35.00	70.00	—
1742	—	7.50	15.00	30.00	60.00	—
1743	—	7.50	15.00	30.00	60.00	—
1744	—	7.50	15.00	30.00	60.00	—
1745	—	7.50	15.00	35.00	70.00	—

KM# 1692 6 KREUZER
Billon **Ruler:** Maria Theresa **Mint:** Hall **Obverse:** Bust right **Obv. Legend:** MAR • THERESIA • D: G • REG • HUNG • BOH • **Reverse:** Crowned four-fold arms within cartouche **Rev. Legend:** ARCHID • AUST • DUX BUR • COM • TYR • **Note:** Varieties exist in legend abbreviations and cartouche. Prev. KM#718.

Date	Mintage	VG	F	VF	XF	Unc
1742	691,000	5.00	10.00	20.00	45.00	—
1745	647,000	5.00	10.00	20.00	45.00	—
1746	843,000	15.00	35.00	75.00	150	—

KM# 1703 6 KREUZER
Silver **Ruler:** Maria Theresa **Mint:** Graz **Obverse:** Bust right **Obv. Legend:** MAR • THERESIA • D: G • REG • HUNG • & BOH • **Reverse:** Crowned four-fold arms within sprays **Rev. Legend:** ARCHID • AUS • DUX BURG & STYR • **Note:** Prev. KM#531.

Date	Mintage	VG	F	VF	XF	Unc
1743	—	13.50	27.50	55.00	125	—

KM# 1704 6 KREUZER
Billon **Ruler:** Maria Theresa **Mint:** Hall **Obverse:** Smaller bust **Note:** Prev. KM#719.

Date	Mintage	VG	F	VF	XF	Unc
1743	860,000	5.00	10.00	20.00	45.00	—

KM# 1711 6 KREUZER
Billon **Ruler:** Maria Theresa **Mint:** Hall **Obverse:** Legend ends: ET. BO. **Note:** Varieties exist in legend abbreviations. Prev. KM#720.

Date	Mintage	VG	F	VF	XF	Unc
1744	987,000	5.00	10.00	20.00	40.00	—

KM# 1710 6 KREUZER

Silver **Ruler:** Maria Theresa **Mint:** Graz **Obverse:** Bust right **Reverse:** Crowned four-fold arms within cartouche **Note:** Varieties exist. Prev. KM#532.

Date	Mintage	VG	F	VF	XF	Unc
1744	—	10.00	20.00	45.00	100	—
1745	—	10.00	20.00	45.00	100	—

KM# 1724 6 KREUZER

Billon **Ruler:** Maria Theresa **Mint:** Hall **Obverse:** Modified bust, legend begins opposite forehead **Reverse:** Crowned imperial eagle with Tyrolean arms at center **Note:** Varieties exist in legend abbreviations. Prev. KM#723.

Date	Mintage	VG	F	VF	XF	Unc
1745	Inc. above	4.00	8.00	12.50	25.00	—

KM# 1722 6 KREUZER

Billon **Ruler:** Maria Theresa **Mint:** Hall **Obverse:** Bust drapes without tassels **Note:** Prev. KM#721.

Date	Mintage	VG	F	VF	XF	Unc
1745	647,000	4.00	8.00	12.50	25.00	—

KM# 1723 6 KREUZER

Billon **Ruler:** Maria Theresa **Mint:** Hall **Reverse:** Crowned cartouche in branches **Note:** Prev. KM#722.

Date	Mintage	VG	F	VF	XF	Unc
1745	Inc. above	4.00	8.00	12.50	25.00	—

KM# 1738 6 KREUZER

3.2900 g., 0.4380 Silver .0463 oz. ASW **Ruler:** Maria Theresa **Mint:** Vienna **Reverse:** Crowned eagle **Note:** Prev. KM#1945.

Date	Mintage	VG	F	VF	XF	Unc
1746	—	25.00	50.00	100	150	—
1747	—	20.00	40.00	60.00	100	—

Note: For later issues refer to Uniform Coinage

KM# 1753 6 KREUZER

Silver **Ruler:** Maria Theresa **Mint:** Graz **Obverse:** Bust right **Obv. Legend:** MAR • THERES • D: G • R • IMP • GER • HV • H • BO • REG • **Reverse:** Crowned imperial eagle with panther shield on breast, value below **Rev. Legend:** ARCHID • AUSTR • DVX • BURG • & • STYR • **Note:** Prev. KM#533.

Date	Mintage	VG	F	VF	XF	Unc
1747	—	10.00	15.00	25.00	45.00	—

KM# 1754 6 KREUZER

Billon **Ruler:** Maria Theresa **Mint:** Hall **Obverse:** Bust drapes without tassels **Reverse:** Tyrolean eagle with multi-fold arms at center **Note:** Prev. KM#724.

Date	Mintage	VG	F	VF	XF	Unc
1747	905,000	5.00	10.00	20.00	45.00	—

KM# 1763 6 KREUZER

Billon **Ruler:** Maria Theresa **Mint:** Hall **Obverse:** Bust right **Reverse:** Crowned imperial eagle with Tyrolean arms on breast, value below **Note:** Prev. KM#725.

Date	Mintage	VG	F	VF	XF	Unc
1748	550,000	5.00	10.00	20.00	45.00	—

KM# 1780 6 KREUZER

Billon **Ruler:** Maria Theresa **Mint:** Hall **Obverse:** Bust with embroidered drapes **Note:** Prev. KM#726.

Date	Mintage	VG	F	VF	XF	Unc
1750	109,000	15.00	35.00	75.00	150	—

KM# 1781 6 KREUZER

Billon **Ruler:** Maria Theresa **Mint:** Hall **Reverse:** Tyrolean eagle with multi-fold arms at center **Note:** Prev. KM#727.

Date	Mintage	VG	F	VF	XF	Unc
1750	Inc. above	25.00	50.00	90.00	175	—

KM# 1794 7 KREUZER

3.2400 g., 0.4200 Silver .0437 oz. ASW **Ruler:** Maria Theresa **Mint:** Vienna **Obverse:** Draped bust right **Obv. Legend:** M • THERES • D: G • R • IMP • GE • HU • BO • REG • **Reverse:** Crowned imperial double eagle with crowned arms on breast **Rev. Legend:** ARCH • AUST • DUX • BUR • CO • TYR • **Note:** Prev. KM#1946.

Date	Mintage	VG	F	VF	XF	Unc
1751	—	60.00	125	200	300	—
1752	—	40.00	80.00	150	250	—
1753	—	40.00	80.00	150	250	—
1765	—	25.00	50.00	150	175	—

Note: For later issues refer to Uniform Coinage

KM# 1792 7 KREUZER

Silver **Ruler:** Maria Theresa **Mint:** Graz **Obverse:** Bust right **Reverse:** Crowned imperial eagle with complex arms and Styrian center shield, value below **Note:** Prev. KM#534.

Date	Mintage	VG	F	VF	XF	Unc
1751	—	45.00	85.00	175	350	—

KM# 1793 7 KREUZER

Billon **Ruler:** Maria Theresa **Mint:** Hall **Obverse:** Similar to KM#1805 but bust with long hair on shoulder **Note:** Prev. KM#728.

Date	Mintage	VG	F	VF	XF	Unc
1751	49,000	20.00	45.00	90.00	185	—

KM# 1805 7 KREUZER

Billon **Ruler:** Maria Theresa **Mint:** Hall **Obverse:** Draped bust right **Obv. Legend:** M • THERESIA • D: G • R • IMP • GE • HU • BO • REG • **Reverse:** Crowned imperial double eagle with crowned arms on breast, value below **Rev. Legend:** ARCHID • AUST • DUX BUR • CO • TYR • **Note:** Varieties exist in legend abbreviations and shield shape. Prev. KM#729.

Date	Mintage	VG	F	VF	XF	Unc
1752	49,000	40.00	70.00	125	200	—
1753	145,000	20.00	45.00	85.00	170	—
1754	38,000	40.00	70.00	125	200	—
1760	140,000	15.00	35.00	75.00	145	—
1761	133,000	15.00	35.00	75.00	145	—
1762	147,000	15.00	35.00	75.00	145	—
1763	164,000	15.00	35.00	75.00	135	—

KM# 1810 10 KREUZER

3.8900 g., 0.5000 Silver .0625 oz. ASW **Ruler:** Maria Theresa **Mint:** Vienna **Obverse:** Bust in wreath **Reverse:** Crowned eagle on pedestal **Note:** Prev. KM#1947.

Date	Mintage	VG	F	VF	XF	Unc
1754	—	7.50	15.00	40.00	80.00	—
1755	—	7.50	15.00	40.00	80.00	—
1756	—	7.50	15.00	40.00	80.00	—
1757	—	7.50	15.00	45.00	90.00	—
1758	—	7.50	15.00	40.00	80.00	—
1759	—	7.50	15.00	40.00	80.00	—
1760	—	7.50	15.00	40.00	80.00	—
1763	—	7.50	15.00	40.00	80.00	—
1764	—	7.50	15.00	35.00	75.00	—
1765	—	7.50	15.00	35.00	75.00	—

KM# 1809 10 KREUZER

Silver **Ruler:** Maria Theresa **Mint:** Hall **Obverse:** Crowned bust right within wreath of palm and laurel **Obv. Legend:** M • THERESIA • D: G • R • IMP • HU • BO • REG • **Reverse:** Crowned imperial double eagle with arms on breast atop pedestal **Rev. Legend:** ARCHID • AUST • DUX • BURG • CO • STYR • **Note:** Varieties exist in legend abbreviations and shield shape. Prev. KM#730.

Date	Mintage	VG	F	VF	XF	Unc
1754	2,055,000	8.00	15.00	35.00	75.00	—
1755	264,000	12.50	25.00	50.00	110	—
1761	54,000	12.50	25.00	50.00	110	—
1763	—	10.00	20.00	40.00	80.00	—
1764	—	10.00	20.00	40.00	80.00	—
1765	153,000	8.00	15.00	35.00	75.00	—

KM# 1808 10 KREUZER

Silver **Ruler:** Maria Theresa **Mint:** Graz **Obverse:** Bust right in arched branches **Reverse:** Crowned imperial eagle with panther shield, value within **Note:** Varieties exist. Prev. KM#1808.

Date	Mintage	VG	F	VF	XF	Unc
1754	—	7.50	15.00	35.00	75.00	—
1755	—	7.50	15.00	35.00	75.00	—
1756	—	7.50	15.00	35.00	75.00	—
1758	—	7.50	15.00	35.00	75.00	—
1763	—	12.50	25.00	50.00	100	—
1764	—	7.50	15.00	30.00	65.00	—
1765	—	7.50	15.00	30.00	55.00	—

KM# 1855 10 KREUZER

3.8900 g., 0.5000 Silver .0625 oz. ASW **Ruler:** Maria Theresa **Mint:** Vienna **Obverse:** Draped bust right within wreath of palm and laurel **Obv. Legend:** M • THERESIA • D: G • R • IMP • HU • BO • REG • **Reverse:** Crowned imperial double eagle with arms on breast atop pedestal **Rev. Legend:** ARCHID • AUST• DUX • BURG • CO • TYR • **Note:** Prev. KM#1948.

Date	Mintage	VG	F	VF	XF	Unc
1768 C-K	—	6.00	12.50	35.00	75.00	—
1769 C-K	—	30.00	60.00	100	150	—
1769 IC-SK	—	6.00	12.50	35.00	75.00	—
1770 C-K	—	6.00	12.50	35.00	75.00	—
1771 C-K	—	6.00	12.50	35.00	75.00	—
1772/1 C-K	—	6.00	12.50	35.00	80.00	—
1772 C-K	—	6.00	12.50	35.00	75.00	—
1773 C-K	—	6.00	12.50	35.00	75.00	—
1773 IC-SK	—	30.00	60.00	100	150	—
1774 C-A	—	6.00	12.50	35.00	75.00	—
1775 C-A	—	6.00	12.50	35.00	75.00	—
1776 C-A	—	6.00	12.50	35.00	75.00	—
1777 C-A	—	6.00	12.50	35.00	75.00	—
1778 C-A	—	6.00	12.50	35.00	75.00	—
1779 C-A	—	6.00	12.50	35.00	75.00	—
1780 C-A	—	6.00	12.50	35.00	75.00	—

Note: For later issues refer to Uniform Coinage

KM# 1862 10 KREUZER

Silver **Ruler:** Maria Theresa **Mint:** Hall **Obverse:** Veiled head right in wreath **Reverse:** Crowned imperial double eagle, arms on breast, value below date in legend **Note:** Prev. KM#731.

Date	Mintage	VG	F	VF	XF	Unc
1770 AS	31,000	15.00	30.00	60.00	125	—
1771 AS	156,000	10.00	20.00	45.00	90.00	—
1772 AS	115,000	10.00	20.00	45.00	90.00	—
1773 AS	113,000	15.00	30.00	60.00	125	—
1774 AS	79,000	12.50	25.00	50.00	110	—
1774 VC-S	Inc. above	20.00	45.00	90.00	175	—
1775 VC-S	—	10.00	20.00	40.00	80.00	—
1776 VC-S	30,000	15.00	30.00	60.00	120	—
1777 VC-S	23,000	10.00	20.00	40.00	80.00	—
1778 VC-S	777,000	10.00	20.00	40.00	80.00	—
1778 VC-S	Inc. above	10.00	15.00	35.00	75.00	—
1779 VC-S	57,000	15.00	30.00	60.00	125	—
1780 VC-S	37,000	20.00	45.00	90.00	175	—

KM# 1302 15 KREUZER

Silver **Ruler:** Leopold I **Mint:** Saint Veit **Obverse:** Bust right, value in Roman numerals **Reverse:** Crowned imperial eagle **Note:** Varieties exist. Prev. KM#1649.

Date	Mintage	VG	F	VF	XF	Unc
1701	—	16.50	35.00	65.00	125	—

KM# 1624 15 KREUZER

Silver **Ruler:** Karl (Charles) VI **Mint:** Graz **Obverse:** Draped bust right **Obv. Legend:** CAR • VI • D: G • R • I • S • A • GE • HI • HU • BO • REX • **Reverse:** Crowned imperial double eagle with arms on breast, value below **Rev. Legend:** • ARCHID • AUSTR • DUX • BURG • & • STRYIÆ • **Note:** Prev. KM#499.

Date	Mintage	VG	F	VF	XF	Unc
1728	—	25.00	50.00	100	200	—

KM# 1654 15 KREUZER

Silver **Ruler:** Karl (Charles) VI **Mint:** Hall **Obverse:** Laureate bust right **Reverse:** Crowned imperial eagle, value below, date in legend **Note:** Prev. KM#683.

Date	Mintage	VG	F	VF	XF	Unc
1734	—	—	—	—	—	—

KM# 1674 15 KREUZER

6.4000 g., 0.5630 Silver .1158 oz. ASW **Ruler:** Maria Theresa **Mint:** Vienna **Obverse:** Young bust right **Reverse:** Crowned arms, cartouche above value **Note:** Prev. KM#1949.

Date	Mintage	VG	F	VF	XF	Unc
1741	—	15.00	35.00	70.00	140	—
1742/1	—	15.00	40.00	80.00	160	—
1742	—	15.00	35.00	70.00	140	—

KM# 1693 15 KREUZER
Silver **Ruler:** Maria Theresa **Mint:** Graz **Obverse:** Young draped bust right **Obv. Legend:** MAR • THERESIA • D: G • REG • HUNG & • BOH • **Reverse:** Crowned four-fold arms within sprays **Rev. Legend:** ARCHID • AUSTR • DUX • BURG • & • STYRIÆ • **Note:** Prev. KM#536.

Date	Mintage	VG	F	VF	XF	Unc
1742	—	13.50	27.50	60.00	140	—

KM# 1755 15 KREUZER
6.4000 g., 0.5630 Silver .1158 oz. ASW **Ruler:** Maria Theresa **Mint:** Vienna **Obverse:** Older, small bust right **Reverse:** Eagle with Austrian shield, value below **Note:** Prev. KM#1950.

Date	Mintage	VG	F	VF	XF	Unc
1747	—	12.50	25.00	60.00	120	—
1748	—	12.50	25.00	60.00	120	—
1749	—	12.50	25.00	60.00	120	—
1750	—	40.00	80.00	150	180	—

Note: For later issues refer to Uniform Coinage

KM# 1764 15 KREUZER
Silver **Ruler:** Maria Theresa **Mint:** Graz **Obverse:** Draped bust right **Obv. Legend:** M: THERES: D: G: R: I: GER: HUNG: & • BOH: REG: **Reverse:** Crowned imperial double eagle with arms on breast, value below **Rev. Legend:** • ARCHID: AUSTR: DUX: BURG: ET: STYRIÆ • **Note:** Varieties exist in reverse legend. Prev. KM#537.

Date	Mintage	VG	F	VF	XF	Unc
1748	—	30.00	60.00	125	200	—
1749	—	30.00	60.00	125	200	—
1750	—	30.00	60.00	125	200	—

KM# 1765 15 KREUZER
Silver **Ruler:** Maria Theresa **Mint:** Hall **Obverse:** Bust right **Reverse:** Crowned imperial eagle with crowned arms on breast, value below **Note:** Varieties exist. Prev. KM#732.

Date	Mintage	VG	F	VF	XF	Unc
1748	62,000	30.00	60.00	125	250	—
1749	255,000	30.00	60.00	125	250	—
1750	218,000	25.00	50.00	100	200	—

KM# 1782 17 KREUZER
6.1200 g., 0.5420 Silver .1066 oz. ASW **Ruler:** Maria Theresa **Mint:** Vienna **Obverse:** Draped bust with tassels right **Obv. Legend:** M • THERESIA • D • G • R • IMP • GE • HU • BO • REG • **Reverse:** Crowned imperial double eagle with Austrian arms on breast, value below **Rev. Legend:** ARCHID • AUST • DUX • BURG • CO • TYR • **Note:** Varieties exist in legend positioning. Prev. KM#1951.

Date	Mintage	VG	F	VF	XF	Unc
1750	—	—	—	—	—	—
Note: Reported, not confirmed						
1751	—	7.50	15.00	35.00	85.00	—
1752	—	7.50	15.00	35.00	85.00	—
1753	—	7.50	15.00	35.00	85.00	—
1754	—	15.00	30.00	60.00	120	—
1761	—	7.50	15.00	25.00	85.00	—
1762	—	7.50	15.00	25.00	70.00	—
1763	—	7.50	15.00	25.00	70.00	—
1765	—	10.00	20.00	40.00	90.00	—

KM# 1795 17 KREUZER
Silver **Ruler:** Maria Theresa **Mint:** Graz **Obverse:** Draped bust right **Obv. Legend:** M • THERESIA • D: G • R • I • GER • HU • & • BO • REG • **Reverse:** Crowned imperial double eagle with crowned arms on breast, value below **Rev. Legend:** ARCHID • AUSTR • DUX - BURG • & • STYR • **Note:** Varieties exist. Prev. KM#538.

Date	Mintage	VG	F	VF	XF	Unc
1751	—	—	—	—	—	—
Note: Reported, not confirmed						
1752	—	12.00	20.00	45.00	90.00	—
1753	—	12.00	20.00	45.00	90.00	—
1754	—	12.00	20.00	45.00	90.00	—
1760	—	12.00	20.00	45.00	90.00	—
1761	—	12.00	20.00	45.00	90.00	—
1762	—	12.00	20.00	45.00	90.00	—
1763	—	12.00	20.00	45.00	90.00	—
1764	—	—	—	—	—	—
Note: Reported, not confirmed						
1765	—	—	—	—	—	—
Note: Reported, not confirmed						

KM# 1796 17 KREUZER
Silver **Ruler:** Maria Theresa **Mint:** Hall **Obverse:** Bust right **Reverse:** Crowned imperial eagle with crowned arms on breast, value below **Note:** Varieties exist. Prev. KM#733.

Date	Mintage	VG	F	VF	XF	Unc
1751	139,000	15.00	30.00	60.00	120	—
1753	1,085,000	15.00	30.00	60.00	120	—
1754	177,000	15.00	30.00	60.00	120	—
1757	—	15.00	35.00	70.00	140	—
1761	750,000	10.00	20.00	40.00	80.00	—
1762	208,000	10.00	25.00	50.00	100	—
1763	135,000	15.00	25.00	70.00	140	—

KM# 1825 17 KREUZER
6.1200 g., 0.5420 Silver .1066 oz. ASW **Ruler:** Maria Theresa **Mint:** Vienna **Obverse:** Bust with armor on shoulder **Note:** Prev. KM#1952.

Date	Mintage	VG	F	VF	XF	Unc
1762	—	40.00	85.00	150	250	—

Note: For later issues refer to Uniform Coinage

KM# 1814 20 KREUZER
6.6800 g., 0.5830 Silver .1252 oz. ASW **Ruler:** Maria Theresa **Mint:** Vienna **Obverse:** Bust right within wreath of laurel and palm **Obv. Legend:** M • THERESIA • D: G • R • IMP • GE • HU • BO • REG • **Reverse:** Crowned imperial double eagle with arms on breast atop pedestal **Rev. Legend:** ARCHID • AUST • DUX • BURG • CO • TYR • **Note:** Prev. KM#1953.

Date	Mintage	VG	F	VF	XF	Unc
1754	—	4.00	8.00	15.00	30.00	—
1755	—	4.00	8.00	15.00	30.00	—
1756/5	—	10.00	17.00	35.00	70.00	—
1756	—	4.00	8.00	15.00	30.00	—
1757	—	4.00	8.00	15.00	30.00	—
1758	—	4.00	8.00	15.00	30.00	—
1759	—	4.00	8.00	15.00	30.00	—
1760	—	5.00	10.00	20.00	40.00	—
1761	—	5.00	10.00	20.00	40.00	—
1762	—	8.00	15.00	30.00	60.00	—
1763	—	3.00	4.00	9.00	18.00	—
1764	—	3.00	4.00	9.00	18.00	—
1765	—	3.00	4.00	9.00	18.00	—
1766/5	—	8.00	15.00	30.00	60.00	—
1766	—	8.00	15.00	30.00	60.00	—

KM# 1813 20 KREUZER
Silver **Ruler:** Maria Theresa **Mint:** Hall **Obverse:** Bust right in branches **Reverse:** Crowned imperial eagle with Tyrolean arms on breast, value below **Note:** Shield varieties exist. Prev. KM#734.

Date	Mintage	VG	F	VF	XF	Unc
1754	583,000	5.00	10.00	20.00	40.00	—
1755	622,000	7.50	12.50	25.00	50.00	—
1756	558,000	7.50	12.50	25.00	50.00	—
1758	549,000	5.00	10.00	20.00	40.00	—
1759	340,000	5.00	10.00	20.00	40.00	—
1760	70,000	5.00	10.00	20.00	40.00	—
1761	199,000	5.00	10.00	20.00	40.00	—
1763	30,000	5.00	10.00	20.00	40.00	—
1764	161,000	7.50	12.50	25.00	50.00	—
1765	132,000	5.00	7.50	10.00	25.00	—

KM# 1812 20 KREUZER
Silver **Ruler:** Maria Theresa **Mint:** Graz **Obverse:** Bust right in wreath **Reverse:** Crowned imperial eagle with panther shield on breast, value within **Note:** Varieties exist. Prev. KM#539.

Date	Mintage	VG	F	VF	XF	Unc
1754	—	6.50	8.50	15.00	30.00	—
1755	—	6.50	8.50	15.00	30.00	—
1756	—	6.50	8.50	15.00	30.00	—
1757	—	6.50	8.50	15.00	30.00	—
1758	—	6.50	8.50	15.00	30.00	—
1759	—	6.50	8.50	15.00	30.00	—
1760	—	6.50	8.50	15.00	30.00	—
1761	—	6.50	8.50	15.00	30.00	—
1765	—	6.50	8.50	15.00	30.00	—
1765 IK	—	6.50	8.50	15.00	30.00	—
1765 GK	—	6.50	8.50	15.00	30.00	—

KM# 540x 20 KREUZER
Silver **Ruler:** Maria Theresa **Mint:** Graz **Obverse:** Veiled head right **Reverse:** Crowned imperial eagle on pedestal, value in pedestal **Note:** Prev. KM#540.

Date	Mintage	VG	F	VF	XF	Unc
1767 CG-AK	—	10.00	12.00	15.00	30.00	—
1768 CvG-QK	—	10.00	12.00	15.00	30.00	—
1769 CvG-AK	—	10.00	12.00	15.00	30.00	—
1770 CvG-AK	—	10.00	12.00	15.00	30.00	—
1771 CvG-AK	—	10.00	12.00	15.00	30.00	—
1772 CvG-AK	—	10.00	12.00	15.00	30.00	—

KM# 1856 20 KREUZER
Silver **Ruler:** Maria Theresa **Mint:** Hall **Obverse:** Veiled head right in wreath **Reverse:** Crowned imperial eagle, arms on breast, value below, date in legend **Note:** Prev. KM#735.

Date	Mintage	VG	F	VF	XF	Unc
1768 AS	246,000	6.00	8.50	12.50	25.00	—
1769 AS	259,000	6.00	8.50	12.50	25.00	—
1770 AS	280,000	6.00	8.50	12.50	25.00	—
1771 AS	164,000	6.00	8.50	12.50	25.00	—
1772 AS	153,000	6.00	8.50	12.50	25.00	—
1773 AS	418,000	6.00	8.50	12.50	25.00	—
1774 AS	307,000	6.00	8.50	12.50	25.00	—
1774 VC-S	Inc. above	7.50	15.00	35.00	70.00	—
1775 VC-S	—	6.00	8.50	12.50	25.00	—
1776 VC-S	388,000	6.00	8.50	12.50	25.00	—
1777 VC-S	337,000	6.00	8.50	12.50	25.00	—
1778 VC-S	4,569,000	3.00	5.00	10.00	20.00	—
1779 VC-S	788,000	6.00	8.50	12.50	25.00	—
1780 VC-S	300,000	6.00	8.50	12.50	25.00	—

KM# 1658 30 KREUZER
Silver **Ruler:** Karl (Charles) VI **Mint:** Vienna **Obverse:** Bust right **Obv. Legend:** CAROL • VI • D • G • R • I • S • A • GE • HI • H • B • REX • **Reverse:** Crowned imperial double eagle with arms on breast **Rev. Legend:** ARCHID • AUST • DUX • ... **Note:** Prev. KM#1922.

Date	Mintage	VG	F	VF	XF	Unc
1737	—	55.00	110	225	450	—

KM# 1694 30 KREUZER
Silver **Ruler:** Maria Theresa **Mint:** Vienna **Obverse:** Young bust right divides date, value below, all within square outline **Obv. Legend:** MARIA THERESIA D: G • REG • HUNG • BOH • **Reverse:** Crowned Arms within palm and laurel spray, square outline surrounds **Rev. Legend:** ARCHID AUSTRIÆ DUX ... **Note:** Prev. KM#1954.

Date	Mintage	VG	F	VF	XF	Unc
1742	—	10.00	20.00	40.00	80.00	—
1743	—	15.00	25.00	55.00	110	—
1744	—	20.00	40.00	75.00	150	—
1745	—	20.00	40.00	75.00	150	—

KM# 1712 30 KREUZER
Silver **Ruler:** Maria Theresa **Mint:** Graz **Obverse:** Bust right divides date, value below, square outline surrounds **Obv. Legend:** MARIA • THERESIA • D: G • REGINA • HUNG & BOH • **Reverse:** Crowned arms within wreath of palm and laurel, square outline surrounds **Rev. Legend:** ARCHID • AUSTRIÆ • DUX • BURG • ET • STYRIÆ • **Note:** Prev. KM#541.

Date	Mintage	VG	F	VF	XF	Unc
1744	—	10.00	17.50	35.00	100	—
1745/4	—	10.00	25.00	50.00	125	—
1745	—	10.00	17.50	35.00	100	—

KM# 1740 30 KREUZER
Silver **Ruler:** Maria Theresa **Mint:** Vienna **Obverse:** Bust right in rhombus **Reverse:** Eagle in rhombus **Note:** Prev. KM#1956.

Date	Mintage	VG	F	VF	XF	Unc
1746	—	40.00	85.00	175	280	—
1747/6	—	40.00	85.00	175	280	—
1749	—	40.00	85.00	175	280	—
1750	—	40.00	85.00	175	280	—

KM# 1939 30 KREUZER
Silver **Ruler:** Maria Theresa **Mint:** Graz **Note:** Varieties exist. Prev. KM#542.

Date	Mintage	VG	F	VF	XF	Unc
1746	—	10.00	20.00	40.00	120	—
1747	—	10.00	20.00	40.00	120	—
1748	—	10.00	20.00	40.00	120	—

KM# 1766 30 KREUZER
Silver **Ruler:** Maria Theresa **Mint:** Hall **Note:** Prev. KM#736.

Date	Mintage	VG	F	VF	XF	Unc
1748	53,000	15.00	25.00	50.00	100	—
1749	118,000	15.00	25.00	50.00	100	—
1750	—	15.00	25.00	50.00	100	—

KM# 1806 30 KREUZER
Silver **Ruler:** Maria Theresa **Mint:** Hall **Obverse:** Value in cartouche **Reverse:** Cross after date **Note:** Prev. KM#737.

Date	Mintage	VG	F	VF	XF	Unc
1752	—	25.00	45.00	90.00	175	—

KM# 1824 30 KREUZER
Silver **Ruler:** Maria Theresa **Mint:** Hall **Obverse:** Value in diamond below bust right, square outline surrounds all **Obv. Legend:** MARIA THERESIA D: G • R • I • GE • HU • BO • REG • **Reverse:** Cross after date **Rev. Legend:** ARCHID • AUST • DUX BU • CO • TYR • **Note:** Prev. KM#738.

Date	Mintage	VG	F	VF	XF	Unc
1760	—	20.00	35.00	65.00	140	—

KM# 1834 30 KREUZER
6.6800 g., 0.5830 Silver .1252 oz. ASW **Ruler:** Maria Theresa **Mint:** Vienna **Reverse:** Cross after date **Note:** Prev. KM#1957.

Date	Mintage	VG	F	VF	XF	Unc
1765	—	25.00	50.00	100	175	—

KM# 1835 30 KREUZER
Silver **Ruler:** Maria Theresa **Mint:** Vienna **Obverse:** Draped bust right, value below, square outline surrounds all **Obv. Legend:** MARIA THERESIA D: G • R • IMP • HU • BO • REG • **Reverse:** Crowned imperial double eagle with arms on breast within square outline **Rev. Legend:** AR • AUST • DUX • BURG • COM • TYR • **Note:** Prev. KM#1958.

Date	Mintage	VG	F	VF	XF	Unc
1765 IC-SK	—	25.00	50.00	85.00	145	—
1765 C-K	—	25.00	50.00	85.00	145	—
1766 IC-SK	—	20.00	40.00	75.00	130	—
1767 IC-SK	—	20.00	40.00	75.00	130	—
1768 IC-SK	—	10.00	20.00	45.00	90.00	—
1769 IC-SK	—	10.00	20.00	40.00	85.00	—
1770 IC-SK	—	10.00	20.00	45.00	90.00	—
1773 IC-SK	—	30.00	60.00	100	175	—

Note: For later issues refer to Uniform Coinage

KM# 1664 1/12 THALER
Silver **Ruler:** Karl (Charles) VI **Mint:** Hall **Obverse:** Bust right **Reverse:** Value below eagle, date in legend **Note:** Varieties exist. Prev. KM#684.

Date	Mintage	VG	F	VF	XF	Unc
1740	12,000	40.00	75.00	150	275	—

KM# 1675 1/12 THALER
Silver **Ruler:** Maria Theresa **Mint:** Hall **Note:** Prev. KM#739.

Date	Mintage	VG	F	VF	XF	Unc
1741	19,000	35.00	65.00	140	275	—

KM# 1665 1/8 THALER
Silver **Ruler:** Karl (Charles) VI **Mint:** Hall **Obverse:** Laureate bust right **Reverse:** Crowned imperial eagle, value below, date in legend **Note:** Prev. KM#685.

Date	Mintage	VG	F	VF	XF	Unc
1740 Rare	—	—	—	—	—	—

KM# 1415 1/4 THALER
Silver **Ruler:** Leopold I **Mint:** Saint Veit **Obverse:** Laureate bust right in inner circle, value below **Obv. Legend:** LEOPOLDVS • D • G • R • I • S • A • ... **Reverse:** Crowned imperial eagle in inner circle, crown divides date **Rev. Legend:** ARCHI • DVX • ... **Note:** Prev. KM#1650.

Date	Mintage	VG	F	VF	XF	Unc
1704 I-P	—	200	350	575	700	—

KM# 1416 1/4 THALER
Silver **Ruler:** Leopold I **Mint:** Saint Veit **Obverse:** Laureate bust right in diamond above inner circle, value at bottom **Reverse:** Crowned imperial eagle in diamond above inner circle, date divided at top **Rev. Legend:** ARCHID • AVST • DVX • ... **Note:** Prev. KM#1651.

Date	Mintage	VG	F	VF	XF	Unc
1704	—	200	350	575	700	—

KM# 1492 1/4 THALER
Silver **Ruler:** Joseph I **Mint:** Hall **Obverse:** Armored bust right **Obv. Legend:** IOSEPHUS • D: G: ROM: IMP: S • ... **Reverse:** Crowned arms within order chain **Rev. Legend:** ARCHIDV: AVST: DVX: .... **Note:** Prev. KM#663.

Date	Mintage	VG	F	VF	XF	Unc
ND	—	75.00	135	275	400	—

KM# 1493 1/4 THALER
Silver **Ruler:** Joseph I **Mint:** Saint Veit **Note:** Prev. KM#1668.

Date	Mintage	VG	F	VF	XF	Unc
1707	—	300	600	900	1,200	—

KM# 1577.1 1/4 THALER
Silver **Ruler:** Karl (Charles) VI **Mint:** Hall **Obverse:** Laureate armored bust right **Obv. Legend:** CAROL: VI: D: G: ROM: IMP: S: A: G: H: H: B: REX • **Reverse:** Crowned imperial double eagle with arms on breast, value within oval below **Rev. Legend:** ARCHIDUX • AVST: DUX • -BVRG... **Note:** Prev. KM#686.1.

Date	Mintage	VG	F	VF	XF	Unc
ND	33,000	75.00	135	275	400	—

KM# 1577.2 1/4 THALER
Silver **Ruler:** Karl (Charles) VI **Mint:** Hall **Obverse:** Laureate armored bust right **Obv. Legend:** CAROLUS • VI • D: G: ROM: IMP: S: A: G: H: H: B: R • **Reverse:** Crowned imperial double eagle with arms on breast, value within oval below **Rev. Legend:** ARCH(sic) • DUX • AUSTRIAE • DVX • BURG ... **Note:** Prev. KM#686.2.

Date	Mintage	VG	F	VF	XF	Unc
ND	Inc. above	75.00	135	275	400	—

KM# 1577.3 1/4 THALER
Silver **Ruler:** Karl (Charles) VI **Mint:** Hall **Obverse:** Laureate armored bust right **Reverse:** Crowned imperial double eagle with arms on breast, value within oval below **Rev. Legend:** ARCHIDUX • AUSTRIAE **Note:** Reduced size. Varieties exist. Prev. KM#686.3.

Date	Mintage	VG	F	VF	XF	Unc
ND	Inc. above	75.00	135	275	400	—

KM# 1576 1/4 THALER

Silver **Ruler:** Karl (Charles) VI **Mint:** Graz **Obverse:** Laureate bust right in inner circle **Reverse:** Crowned imperial eagle, date in legend **Note:** Prev. KM#1576.

Date	Mintage	VG	F	VF	XF	Unc
1715 Rare	—	—	—	—	—	—
1729 Rare	—	—	—	—	—	—

KM# 1618.1 1/4 THALER

Silver **Ruler:** Karl (Charles) VI **Mint:** Hall **Obverse:** Laureate armored bust right **Obv. Legend:** CAROL • VI • D • G • R • I • S • A • G • HI • HU • B • REX • **Reverse:** Small shield with eagle in Order chain on large crowned eagle's breast **Rev. Legend:** ARCHIDUX • AVST • DUX • BVRG • ... **Note:** Prev. KM#687.1.

Date	Mintage	VG	F	VF	XF	Unc
1725	11,000	35.00	65.00	125	275	—

KM# 1642 1/4 THALER

Silver **Ruler:** Karl (Charles) VI **Mint:** Graz **Obverse:** Large bust without inner circle **Note:** Prev. KM#501.

Date	Mintage	VG	F	VF	XF	Unc
1731 Rare	—	—	—	—	—	—
1739 Rare	—	—	—	—	—	—

KM# 1618.2 1/4 THALER

Silver **Ruler:** Karl (Charles) VI **Mint:** Hall **Obverse:** Armored bust right **Obv. Legend:** CAROL • VI • D • G • R • I • S • A • GE • HI • HU • BO • REX • **Reverse:** Small eagle in Order chain on large crowned eagle's breast **Rev. Legend:** ARCHID • AUST • DUX • BU • ... **Note:** Prev. KM#687.2.

Date	Mintage	VG	F	VF	XF	Unc
1734	27,000	35.00	65.00	125	275	—

KM# 1666 1/4 THALER

Silver **Ruler:** Karl (Charles) VI **Mint:** Hall **Obverse:** Laureate bust right **Obv. Legend:** CAROL • VI • D • G • R • I • S • A • GE • HI • HU • BO • REX • **Reverse:** Crowned imperial double eagle with crowned arms on breast, value encircled below **Rev. Legend:** ARCHID • AUST • DUX • BU: COM • TYROL • **Note:** Varieties exist. Prev. KM#688.

Date	Mintage	VG	F	VF	XF	Unc
1740	42,000	20.00	40.00	80.00	175	—
1740/1	—	20.00	40.00	80.00	175	—

KM# 1695 1/4 THALER

7.2050 g., 0.8750 Silver .2027 oz. ASW **Ruler:** Maria Theresa **Mint:** Hall **Obverse:** Draped bust right **Obv. Legend:** MARIA • THERESIA D: G • REG • HUNG • BOH • **Reverse:** Crowned arms within cartouche, value below **Rev. Legend:** ARCHID • AVST • DUX • BU.... **Note:** Varieties exist. Prev. KM#740.

Date	Mintage	VG	F	VF	XF	Unc
1742	—	20.00	40.00	60.00	125	—
1743	—	20.00	40.00	60.00	125	—
1744	—	20.00	40.00	60.00	125	—
1745	—	20.00	40.00	60.00	125	—

KM# 1368 1/2 THALER

0.8330 Silver **Ruler:** Leopold I **Mint:** Vienna **Obverse:** Thin bust right in inner circle **Reverse:** Crowned imperial eagle in inner circle, crown divides date **Note:** Varieties exist. Prev. KM#1867.

Date	Mintage	VG	F	VF	XF	Unc
1702	—	40.00	100	175	300	—

KM# 1433 1/2 THALER

Silver **Ruler:** Joseph I **Mint:** Hall **Obverse:** Armored bust right **Obv. Legend:** IOSEPHUS • D: G: ROM: IMP .... **Reverse:** Crowned arms within order chain **Rev. Legend:** ARCHIDVX: AVSTRI: DVX: .... **Note:** Prev. KM#664.

Date	Mintage	VG	F	VF	XF	Unc
ND	—	50.00	100	200	350	—

KM# 1547 1/2 THALER

Silver **Ruler:** Karl (Charles) VI **Mint:** Hall **Obverse:** Laureate armored bust right **Obv. Legend:** CAROLUS • VI • D: G: ROM: IMP: SE: AV: G: H: H: B: REX • **Reverse:** Crowned imperial double eagle with crowned arms on breast **Rev. Legend:** ARCHIDUX • AVSTRIÆ • DUX • BVRGUN... **Note:** Varieties exist. Prev. KM#689.

Date	Mintage	VG	F	VF	XF	Unc
ND	46,000	85.00	175	350	485	—

KM# 1546 1/2 THALER

Silver **Ruler:** Karl (Charles) VI **Mint:** Graz **Obverse:** Armored bust right **Obv. Legend:** CAROL VI • D • G • R: I: GER: HISP: ... **Reverse:** Crowned imperial double eagle with arms on breast **Note:** Prev. KM#502.

Date	Mintage	VG	F	VF	XF	Unc
1713	—	65.00	135	250	400	—
1714	—	65.00	135	250	400	—
1728	—	65.00	135	250	400	—

KM# 1544 1/2 THALER

Silver **Ruler:** Karl (Charles) VI **Mint:** Augsburg **Obverse:** Armored bust right **Obv. Legend:** CAROL • VI • D • G • ROM • IMP • S • A • G • H • H • B • REX • **Reverse:** Crowned imperial double eagle with arms in Order chain on breast **Rev. Legend:** ARCHIDUX • AUSTRIÆ • ... **Note:** Prev. KM#C145.

Date	Mintage	VG	F	VF	XF	Unc
1713A	—	65.00	125	200	350	—

KM# 1543 1/2 THALER

Silver **Ruler:** Karl (Charles) VI **Mint:** Augsburg **Obverse:** Bust right **Reverse:** Austrian double eagle **Note:** Prev. KM#A144.

Date	Mintage	VG	F	VF	XF	Unc
1713A	—	—	—	—	—	—

KM# 1616.1 1/2 THALER

Silver **Ruler:** Karl (Charles) VI **Mint:** Hall **Obverse:** Laureate armored bust right **Obv. Legend:** CAROL • VI • D • G • R • ... **Reverse:** With "S • A •" in legend behind bust **Rev. Legend:** ARCHID • AUST • DUX • .... **Note:** Prev. KM#690.1.

Date	Mintage	VG	F	VF	XF	Unc
1724	68,000	35.00	75.00	150	300	—

KM# 1643 1/2 THALER

Silver **Ruler:** Karl (Charles) VI **Mint:** Graz **Obverse:** Larger armored bust right **Obv. Legend:** CAROL • VI • D • G • R • I • S • A • G • E • HI • HU • BO • REX • **Reverse:** Crowned imperial double eagle with arms on breast **Rev. Legend:** ARCHID • AUST • DUX • ... **Note:** Varieties exist. Prev. KM#503.

Date	Mintage	VG	F	VF	XF	Unc
1731	—	65.00	135	250	400	—
1738	—	65.00	135	250	400	—
1739	—	65.00	135	250	400	—

KM# 1616.2 1/2 THALER

Silver **Ruler:** Karl (Charles) VI **Mint:** Hall **Obverse:** Laureate armored bust right **Obv. Legend:** CAROLVS • D • G • R • I • S • A • ... **Reverse:** With "S • A •" in legend in front of bust **Rev. Legend:** ARCHID • AUST • DUX • ... **Note:** Varieties exist. Prev. KM#690.2.

Date	Mintage	VG	F	VF	XF	Unc
1733	21,000	35.00	75.00	150	300	—

KM# 1677 1/2 THALER

14.4100 g., 0.8750 Silver .8108 oz. ASW **Ruler:** Maria Theresa **Mint:** Vienna **Obverse:** Bust right with décolletage **Obv. Legend:** MAR • THERESIA D: G • REG • HUNG • BOH • **Reverse:** Crowned arms **Rev. Legend:** ARCHID • AUST • DUX BURG ... **Note:** Prev. KM#1959.

Date	Mintage	VG	F	VF	XF	Unc
1741	—	65.00	145	275	500	—
1742	—	65.00	145	275	500	—
1743	—	65.00	145	275	500	—

KM# 1713 1/2 THALER

14.4100 g., 0.8750 Silver .8108 oz. ASW **Ruler:** Maria Theresa **Mint:** Vienna **Obverse:** Bust right with décolletage **Obv. Legend:** MAR • THERESIA • D • G • REG • HUNG • BOH • **Reverse:** Crowned arms with griffin supporters **Rev. Legend:** ARCHID • AUST • DUX BURG ... **Note:** Prev. KM#1960.

Date	Mintage	VG	F	VF	XF	Unc
1744	—	50.00	120	250	475	—
1745	—	50.00	120	250	475	—

KM# 1741 1/2 THALER

14.4100 g., 0.8750 Silver .8108 oz. ASW **Ruler:** Maria Theresa **Mint:** Vienna **Obverse:** Bust right with décolletage **Obv. Legend:** M • THERESIA • D • G • R • IMP • GE • HU • BO • REG • **Reverse:** Crowned imperial double eagle with crowned arms on breast **Rev. Legend:** ARCHID • AUST • DUX • BURG ... **Note:** Prev. KM#1961.

Date	Mintage	VG	F	VF	XF	Unc
1746	—	50.00	120	250	450	—
1747	—	50.00	120	250	450	—
1749	—	50.00	120	250	450	—
1751	—	45.00	110	225	400	—
1752	—	45.00	110	225	400	—
1753	—	45.00	110	225	400	—

KM# 1773 1/2 THALER

14.4100 g., Silver **Ruler:** Maria Theresa **Mint:** Graz **Obverse:** Bust right with décolletage **Obv. Legend:** MAR • THERESIA • D • G • R • IMP • GE • HU • BO • REG • **Reverse:** Crowned imperial double eagle with crowned arms on breast **Rev. Legend:** ARCHID: AUST: DUX BURG .... **Note:** Prev. KM#543.

Date	Mintage	VG	F	VF	XF	Unc
1749	—	55.00	100	150	300	—
1750	—	55.00	100	150	300	—

KM# 1797 1/2 THALER

14.0300 g., Silver **Ruler:** Maria Theresa **Mint:** Graz **Obverse:** Bust right with décolletage **Obv. Legend:** MAR • THERESIA • D • G • R • IMP • GE • HU • BO • REG • **Reverse:** Similar to KM#1773 but with cross after date **Rev. Legend:** ARCHID AUST DUX BURG ... **Note:** Varieties exist in legend abbreviations. Prev. KM#544.

Date	Mintage	VG	F	VF	XF	Unc
1751	—	55.00	100	150	285	—
1752	—	55.00	100	150	285	—
1753	—	55.00	100	150	285	—
1754	—	55.00	100	150	285	—

KM# 1815 1/2 THALER

14.0300 g., 0.8330 Silver .3758 oz. ASW **Ruler:** Maria Theresa **Mint:** Vienna **Note:** Legend varieties exist. Prev. KM#1961a.

Date	Mintage	VG	F	VF	XF	Unc
1754	—	45.00	110	225	400	—
1755	—	45.00	110	225	400	—
1756	—	45.00	110	225	400	—
1757	—	45.00	110	225	400	—

KM# 1821 1/2 THALER

14.0300 g., 0.8330 Silver .3758 oz. ASW **Ruler:** Maria Theresa **Mint:** Hall **Obverse:** Bust right with décolletage **Obv. Legend:** M • THERESIA • D • G • R • IMP • GE • HU • BO • REG • **Rev. Legend:** ARCHID • AUST • DUX • BU • COM • ... **Rev. Designer:** Crowned imperial double eagle with crowned arms on breast **Note:** 1/2 Convention Thaler. Prev. KM#741.

Date	Mintage	VG	F	VF	XF	Unc
1756	—	35.00	65.00	125	200	—
1757	—	35.00	65.00	125	200	—
1759	—	35.00	65.00	125	200	—
1760	—	35.00	65.00	125	200	—
1761	—	35.00	65.00	125	200	—
1762	—	35.00	65.00	125	200	—
1763	—	35.00	65.00	125	200	—
1764	—	35.00	65.00	125	200	—
1765	—	35.00	65.00	125	200	—

KM# 1822 1/2 THALER

14.0300 g., 0.8330 Silver .3758 oz. ASW **Ruler:** Maria Theresa **Mint:** Vienna **Obverse:** More mature bust right, more curls on neck **Obv. Legend:** M • THERESIA • D • G • R • IMP • GE • HU • BO • REG • **Reverse:** Crowned imperial double eagle with crowned arms on breast **Rev. Legend:** ARCHID • AUST • DUX • BURG • ... **Note:** Varieties exist. Prev. KM#1962.

Date	Mintage	VG	F	VF	XF	Unc
1758	—	35.00	75.00	125	250	—
1759	—	35.00	75.00	125	250	—
1760	—	35.00	75.00	125	250	—
1761	—	35.00	75.00	125	250	—
1762	—	35.00	75.00	125	250	—
1763	—	35.00	75.00	125	250	—
1764	—	35.00	75.00	125	250	—
1765	—	35.00	75.00	125	250	—

KM# 1848 1/2 THALER

14.0300 g., 0.8330 Silver .3758 oz. ASW **Ruler:** Maria Theresa **Mint:** Hall **Obverse:** Veiled bust right **Obv. Legend:** M • THERESIA • D: G • R • IMP • HU • BO • REG • **Reverse:** Crowned imperial double eagle with crowned arms on breast **Rev. Legend:** ARCHID • AUST • DUX • BURG • ... **Note:** Prev. KM#742.

Date	Mintage	VG	F	VF	XF	Unc
1766 AS	—	25.00	45.00	75.00	155	—
1767 AS	—	25.00	45.00	75.00	155	—
1768 AS	—	25.00	45.00	75.00	155	—
1769 AS	—	25.00	45.00	75.00	155	—
1770 AS	—	25.00	45.00	75.00	155	—
1771 AS	—	25.00	45.00	75.00	155	—
1772 AS	—	25.00	45.00	75.00	155	—
1773 AS	—	25.00	45.00	75.00	155	—
1774 VC-S	—	25.00	45.00	75.00	155	—
1775 VC-S	—	25.00	45.00	75.00	155	—
1776 VC-S	—	25.00	45.00	75.00	155	—
1777 VC-S	—	25.00	45.00	75.00	155	—

KM# 1846 1/2 THALER

14.0300 g., 0.8330 Silver .3758 oz. ASW **Ruler:** Maria Theresa **Mint:** Vienna **Obverse:** Veiled bust right **Obv. Legend:** M • THERESIA • D: G • R • IMP • HU • BO • REG • **Reverse:** Crowned imperial double eagle with crowned arms on breast **Rev. Legend:** ARCHID • AUST • DUX • BURG • ... **Note:** 1/2 Convention Thaler. Prev. KM#1963.

Date	Mintage	VG	F	VF	XF	Unc
1766 IC-SK	—	22.00	50.00	75.00	150	—
1767 IC-SK	—	22.00	50.00	75.00	150	—
1768 IC-SK	—	22.00	50.00	75.00	150	—
1769 IC-SK	—	22.00	50.00	75.00	150	—
1770 IC-SK	—	22.00	50.00	75.00	150	—
1771 IC-SK	—	22.00	50.00	75.00	150	—

KM# 1864 1/2 THALER

14.0300 g., 0.8330 Silver .3758 oz. ASW **Ruler:** Maria Theresa **Mint:** Vienna **Obverse:** Beaded brooch on shoulder **Note:** Prev. KM#1990.

Date	Mintage	VG	F	VF	XF	Unc
1772 IC-SK	—	22.00	50.00	75.00	150	—

KM# 1867 1/2 THALER

14.0300 g., 0.8330 Silver .3758 oz. ASW **Ruler:** Maria Theresa **Mint:** Vienna **Obverse:** Oval brooch on shoulder **Obv. Legend:** M • THERESIA • D • G • R • IMP • HU • BO • REG • **Reverse:** Crowned imperial double eagle with crowned arms on breast **Rev. Legend:** ARCHID • AUST • DUX • BURG • ... **Note:** Prev. KM#1991.

Date	Mintage	VG	F	VF	XF	Unc
1773 IC-SK	—	22.00	50.00	75.00	150	—
1774 IC-FA	—	22.00	50.00	75.00	150	—
1775 IC-FA	—	22.00	50.00	75.00	150	—
1776 IC-FA	—	22.00	50.00	75.00	150	—
1777 IC-FA	—	22.00	50.00	75.00	150	—
1778 IC-FA	—	22.00	50.00	75.00	150	—
1779 IC-FA	—	22.00	50.00	75.00	150	—
1780 IC-FA	—	30.00	65.00	100	185	—

Note: For later issues refer to Uniform Coinage

KM# 1413 THALER

Silver **Ruler:** Leopold I **Mint:** Vienna **Obverse:** Bust right **Reverse:** Crowned imperial eagle, date at right of crown **Note:** Dav. #1001. Prev. KM#1872.

Date	Mintage	VG	F	VF	XF	Unc
1701	—	25.00	55.00	100	175	—
1702	—	25.00	55.00	100	175	—
1703	—	25.00	55.00	100	175	—
1704	—	25.00	55.00	100	175	—
1705	—	25.00	55.00	100	175	—

KM# 1303.4 THALER

Silver **Ruler:** Leopold I **Mint:** Hall **Obverse:** Old laureate bust right in inner circle **Obv. Legend:** LEOPOLDVS • D: G: ROM: IMP: SE: A: G: H: B: REX • **Reverse:** Crowned arms within Order chain **Rev. Legend:** ARCHID: AVST: DVX: BV: COM: TYR: **Note:** Dav. #3245. Varieties exist. Prev. KM#644.4.

Date	Mintage	VG	F	VF	XF	Unc
1701	—	25.00	85.00	145	300	—
1701 IAK	—	25.00	85.00	145	300	—
1703	—	25.00	85.00	145	300	—
1704	—	25.00	85.00	145	300	—
1704 IAK	—	25.00	85.00	145	300	—

KM# 1386.2 THALER

Silver **Ruler:** Leopold I **Mint:** Brieg **Obverse:** Laureate bust right in inner circle **Obv. Legend:** LEOPOLDUS. DG: ROM: IMPERATOR... **Note:** Dav. #3305. Prev. KM#177.2.

Date	Mintage	VG	F	VF	XF	Unc
1705 CB	—	200	375	600	900	—

KM# 1444 THALER

Silver **Ruler:** Joseph I **Mint:** Vienna **Obverse:** Armored bust right **Obv. Legend:** IOSEPHUS • D: G • RO :IMP • S: A: GER: HV • BO • REX • **Reverse:** Crowned imperial double eagle with crowned arms on breast **Rev. Legend:** ARCHIDVX • AVSTRIÆ • DVX • BVR • COM • TYROL • **Note:** Varieties exist. Dav. #1013. Prev. KM#1904. Letters IMH in garment fold.

Date	Mintage	VG	F	VF	XF	Unc
1705 IMH	—	40.00	80.00	150	250	—
1706 IMH	—	40.00	80.00	150	250	—
1707 IMH	—	40.00	80.00	150	250	—
1708 IMH	—	40.00	80.00	150	250	—
1709 IMH	—	40.00	80.00	150	250	—
1710 IMH	—	40.00	80.00	150	250	—

KM# 1436 THALER

Silver **Ruler:** Joseph I **Mint:** Brieg **Obverse:** Laureate bust right **Reverse:** Crowned imperial eagle **Note:** Similar to 1/2 Thaler, KM#1432. Dav. #1032. Prev. KM#189.

Date	Mintage	VG	F	VF	XF	Unc
1705 CB	—	175	350	575	850	—
1706 CB	—	—	—	—	—	—

Note: Reported, not confirmed

KM# 1437 THALER

Silver **Ruler:** Leopold I **Mint:** Graz **Obverse:** Laureate bust right in inner circle **Reverse:** Crowned imperial double eagle with crowned arms on breast **Note:** Varieties exist. Dav. #1002. Prev. KM#A465.3.

Date	Mintage	Good	VG	F	VF	XF
1705	—	—	30.00	55.00	125	250

KM# 1435.1 THALER

Silver **Ruler:** Joseph I **Mint:** Augsburg **Obverse:** Armored bust right, tassles on end of scarf **Obv. Legend:** IOSEPHVS • D • G • R • I • S • A • G • H • B • Rx • **Reverse:** Continuous legend **Rev. Legend:** ARCHIDVX * AVSTRIÆ ... **Note:** Austrian Administration. Dav. #1033. Prev. KM#139.1.

Date	Mintage	VG	F	VF	XF	Unc
1705	—	100	300	600	1,000	—

KM# 1438.1 THALER

Silver **Ruler:** Joseph I **Mint:** Hall **Obverse:** Laureate armored bust right **Obv. Legend:** IOSEPHUS • D: G: ROM: IMP: SE: AV: G: HV: BO: REX • **Reverse:** Arms within Order chain **Rev. Legend:** ARCHID: AVST: DVX: BV: COM: TYR • **Note:** Dav. #1018. Prev. KM#665.1.

Date	Mintage	VG	F	VF	XF	Unc
1705	150,000	80.00	170	280	425	—
1706	157,000	80.00	170	280	425	—
1706 IAK	Inc. above	80.00	170	280	425	—
1707	429,000	80.00	170	280	425	—
1710/07	—	80.00	170	280	425	—

KM# 1439 THALER

Silver **Ruler:** Joseph I **Mint:** Munich **Obverse:** Bust similar to KM#1440 with two lines of armor on right arm **Reverse:** Eagle's tail feathers divide legend **Note:** Dav. #1033. Prev. KM#1176.

Date	Mintage	VG	F	VF	XF	Unc
1705 (s)	—	200	350	600	1,000	—

KM# 1435.2 THALER

Silver **Ruler:** Joseph I **Mint:** Augsburg **Obverse:** Clothing like KM#1435.3 **Reverse:** Crowned imperial double eagle with arms on breast **Note:** Dav. #1033. Prev. KM#139.2.

Date	Mintage	VG	F	VF	XF	Unc
1705	—	100	300	600	1,000	—

KM# 1440 THALER

Silver **Ruler:** Joseph I **Mint:** Munich **Obverse:** Bust wtih four lines of armor on right arm **Note:** Dav. #1033A. Prev. KM#1177.

Date	Mintage	VG	F	VF	XF	Unc
1705	—	200	350	600	1,000	—

KM# 1441 THALER

Silver **Ruler:** Joseph I **Mint:** Munich **Obverse:** Laureate armored bust right **Obv. Legend:** IOSEPHVS • D • G • R • I • S • A • G • H • B • Rx • **Reverse:** Eagle's tail feathers within legend **Rev. Legend:** ARCHIDVX * AVSTRIÆ & 17-05 * **Note:** Dav. #1033B. Prev. KM#1178.

Date	Mintage	VG	F	VF	XF	Unc
1705 (s)	—	200	350	600	1,000	—

KM# 1442 THALER

Silver **Ruler:** Joseph I **Mint:** Munich **Obverse:** Modified bust with changed robe **Note:** Dav. #1034. Prev. KM#1179.

Date	Mintage	VG	F	VF	XF	Unc
1705 (s)	—	200	350	600	1,000	—

KM# 1435.3 THALER

Silver **Ruler:** Joseph I **Mint:** Augsburg **Obverse:** Finished end of scarf **Obv. Legend:** IOSEPHVS • D • G • R • I • S • A • G • H • B • Rx • **Reverse:** Broken legend **Rev. Legend:** ARCHIDVX - AVSTRIAE & • 17 - 05 * **Note:** Dav. #1034. Prev. KM#139.3.

Date	Mintage	VG	F	VF	XF	Unc
1705	—	100	300	600	1,000	—

KM# 1443 THALER

Silver **Ruler:** Joseph I **Mint:** Munich **Obverse:** Armored bust right **Obv. Legend:** IOSEPHVS • D • G • R • I • S • A • G • H • B • R • **Reverse:** Eagle's tail feathers divide legend **Rev. Legend:** ARCHIDVX - AVSTRIÆ & • 17 - 05 * **Note:** Dav. #1034A. Prev. KM#1185.

Date	Mintage	VG	F	VF	XF	Unc
1705 (s)	—	200	350	600	1,000	—

KM# 1464 THALER

Silver **Ruler:** Joseph I **Mint:** Graz **Obverse:** Armored bust right **Obv. Legend:** IOSEPHVS • D: G: ROm: IMP: S: A: GER: HV: ET: BO: REX • **Reverse:** Arms within Order chain **Rev. Legend:** ARCHIS: AVST: DVX: BVRGV: STYRIÆ•EC• **Note:** Dav. #1015. Prev. KM#484.

Date	Mintage	VG	F	VF	XF	Unc
1706	—	60.00	125	200	325	—

KM# 1438.2 THALER

Silver **Ruler:** Joseph I **Mint:** Hall **Obverse:** Finer design in curls and harness **Obv. Legend:** IOSEPHUS • D: G: ROM: IMP: SE: AV: G: HV: BO: REX • **Reverse:** Crowned arms within Order chain **Rev. Legend:** ARCHID: AVST: DVX: BV: COM: TYR • **Note:** Dav. #1018A. Prev. KM#665.2.

Date	Mintage	VG	F	VF	XF	Unc
1710	150,000	80.00	170	280	425	—

KM# 1505 THALER

Silver **Ruler:** Joseph I **Mint:** Vienna **Obverse:** Armored bust right without inner circle **Obv. Legend:** IOSEPHUS • D: G: RO IMP • S • A • GER • HV: BO: REX • **Reverse:** Without inner circle **Rev. Legend:** ARCHIDVX • AUSTRIÆ • DVX • BVR • COM • TYROL • **Note:** Varieties exist. Dav. #1014. Prev. KM#1905. Letters IMH and HMA in garment fold.

Date	Mintage	VG	F	VF	XF	Unc
1710 IMH	—	40.00	80.00	150	250	—
1711 IMH	—	40.00	80.00	150	250	—
1711 HMA	—	40.00	80.00	150	250	—

KM# 1438.3 THALER

Silver **Ruler:** Joseph I **Mint:** Hall **Obverse:** Laureate bust right **Reverse:** Crowned arms within Order chain **Note:** Prev. KM#665.3.

Date	Mintage	VG	F	VF	XF	Unc
1711	154,000	80.00	170	280	425	—

KM# 1522 THALER

Silver **Ruler:** Karl (Charles) VI **Mint:** Vienna **Obverse:** Armored bust right **Obv. Legend:** CAROL • vi • D: G: RO: IMP: S: A: GER: HISP: HU BO REX • **Reverse:** Crowned imperial double eagle with crowned arms on breast **Rev. Legend:** • ARCHIDVX • AVSTRIÆ • DVX • BVRG • COM • TYROL • **Note:** Varieties exist. Dav. #1035. Prev. KM#1923.

Date	Mintage	VG	F	VF	XF	Unc
1712 MH	—	35.00	75.00	150	275	—
1713	—	35.00	75.00	150	275	—
1714	—	35.00	75.00	150	275	—
1715/2	—	35.00	75.00	150	275	—
1715/4	—	35.00	75.00	150	275	—
1715	—	35.00	75.00	150	275	—
1716/3	—	35.00	75.00	150	275	—
1716	—	35.00	75.00	150	275	—
1717/6	—	35.00	75.00	150	275	—
1717	—	35.00	75.00	150	275	—
1718	—	35.00	75.00	150	275	—

KM# 1553 THALER

Silver **Ruler:** Karl (Charles) VI **Mint:** Saint Veit **Obverse:** Armored bust right **Obv. Legend:** CAROLVS: VI • D: G • ROM • IMP • S • A • GERM • HISP • HVNG • BOH • REX • **Reverse:** Date divided by crown **Rev. Legend:** ARCHIDVX: AVSTRIÆ: ET CARINTHIÆ **Note:** Dav. #1046. Prev. KM#1679.

Date	Mintage	VG	F	VF	XF	Unc
1713	—	700	1,150	1,750	2,500	—

KM# 1554 THALER

Silver **Ruler:** Karl (Charles) VI **Mint:** Saint Veit **Reverse:** Date divided by crown **Rev. Legend:** ...& CARINTHIAE **Note:** Dav. #1047. Prev. KM#1680.

Date	Mintage	VG	F	VF	XF	Unc
1713	—	700	1,150	1,750	2,500	—

KM# 1551 THALER

Silver **Ruler:** Karl (Charles) VI **Mint:** Graz **Obverse:** Armored bust right **Obv. Legend:** CAROL • VI • D: G: RO: IMP: S: A: GER: HISP: HV: ET: BO: REX • **Reverse:** Crowned imperial double eagle with crowned arms on breast **Rev. Legend:** • ARCHIDVX AVSTRIÆ • DVX • BVRG: ET STYRIÆ • EC • **Note:** Dav. #1039. Varieties exist. Prev. KM#504.

Date	Mintage	VG	F	VF	XF	Unc
1713	—	60.00	120	200	350	—
1718	—	60.00	120	200	350	—

KM# 1548 THALER

Silver **Ruler:** Karl (Charles) VI **Mint:** Augsburg **Obverse:** Laureate armored bust right **Obv. Legend:** CAROL • VI • D • G • ROM • IMP • S • A • G • H • H • B • REX • **Reverse:** Crowned imperial double eagle with arms on breast **Rev. Legend:** ARCHIDUX • AUSTRIÆ • DUX • COM • TYR • **Note:** Dav. #1107. Prev. KM#145.

Date	Mintage	VG	F	VF	XF	Unc
1713A	—	100	250	500	900	—
1714A	—	100	250	500	900	—

KM# 1552 THALER

Silver **Ruler:** Karl (Charles) VI **Mint:** Hall **Obverse:** Legend begins at upper right **Obv. Legend:** CAROLVS • VI • D: G: ROM: IMP: SE: A: G: HIS: HV: BO: REX • **Reverse:** Legend around small crowned imperial eagle **Rev. Legend:** ARCHIDUX • AVSTRIÆ • DUX • BVRG: COM: TYROL: **Note:** Dav. #1050. Prev. KM#691.

Date	Mintage	VG	F	VF	XF	Unc
1713	116,000	50.00	100	200	300	—
1714	111,000	50.00	100	200	300	—

KM# 1570 THALER

Silver **Ruler:** Karl (Charles) VI **Mint:** Hall **Obverse:** Legend begins at lower left **Obv. Legend:** CAROLUS • VI • D: G: ROM: IMP: S: A: G: HI: HU: B: REX **Reverse:** Imperial double eagle with arms on breast **Rev. Legend:** ARCHIDUX • AVSTRIÆ • DUX • BVRG: COM: TYROLIS • **Note:** Dav. #1051. Prev. KM#A692.

Date	Mintage	VG	F	VF	XF	Unc
1714	Inc. above	50.00	100	200	300	—
1715	248,000	50.00	100	200	300	—
1716	119,000	50.00	100	200	300	—
1717	131,000	50.00	100	200	300	—
1718	124,000	50.00	100	200	300	—

KM# 1571 THALER

Silver **Ruler:** Karl (Charles) VI **Mint:** Saint Veit **Reverse:** Date in legend left of crown **Note:** Dav. #1048. Prev. KM#1681.

Date	Mintage	VG	F	VF	XF	Unc
1711	—	400	800	1,400	2,000	—

KM# 1579.1 THALER

Silver **Ruler:** Karl (Charles) VI **Mint:** Vienna **Obverse:** Armored bust right **Obv. Legend:** CAROL: VI • D: G: R: I: S: A: GE: HI: HU: BO: REX • **Reverse:** Crowned imperial double eagle with crowned arms on breast **Rev. Legend:** ARCHID: AUST: DUX • BU: COM: TYROL: **Note:** Dav. #1036. Prev. KM#1924.1.

Date	Mintage	VG	F	VF	XF	Unc
1716A	—	35.00	75.00	175	325	—
1719A	—	35.00	75.00	150	275	—
1720A	—	35.00	75.00	150	275	—
1721A	—	35.00	75.00	150	275	—
1722A	—	35.00	75.00	150	275	—

KM# 1594 THALER

Silver **Ruler:** Karl (Charles) VI **Mint:** Hall **Obverse:** Legend begins at lower left **Obv. Legend:** CAROLUS • VI • D: G: ROM: IMP: S: A: G: HI: HU: B: REX • **Reverse:** Legend divided by large crowned imperial eagle **Rev. Legend:** ARCHID: AUST: DUX • BU: COM: TYROL: **Note:** Dav. #1053. Prev. KM#692.

Date	Mintage	VG	F	VF	XF	Unc
1719	118,000	50.00	100	200	300	—
1720	132,000	50.00	100	200	300	—
1721	411,000	50.00	100	200	300	—
1724	145,000	75.00	150	350	500	—
1725	216,000	75.00	100	200	300	—
1730	231,000	75.00	100	200	300	—
1734	153,000	50.00	100	200	300	—

KM# 1579.2 THALER

Silver **Ruler:** Karl (Charles) VI **Mint:** Vienna **Obverse:** Modified bust **Obv. Legend:** CAROL: VI: D: G: R: I: S: A: GE: HI: HU: BO: REX • **Reverse:** Crowned imperial double eagle with crowned arms within Order chain on breast **Rev. Legend:** ARCHID: AUST: DUX • BU: COM: TYROL: **Note:** Dav. #1037. Prev. KM#1924.2.

Date	Mintage	VG	F	VF	XF	Unc
1720	—	35.00	75.00	150	275	—
1721	—	35.00	75.00	150	275	—
1722	—	50.00	100	200	400	—
1723	—	35.00	75.00	150	275	—
1724	—	35.00	75.00	150	275	—
1725	—	35.00	75.00	150	275	—
1726	—	35.00	75.00	150	275	—
1727	—	35.00	75.00	150	275	—
1728	—	50.00	100	200	400	—
1729	—	35.00	75.00	150	275	—
1730	—	50.00	100	225	425	—
1731	—	35.00	75.00	150	275	—
1732	—	35.00	75.00	150	275	—
1733	—	35.00	75.00	150	275	—
1734	—	35.00	75.00	150	275	—
1735	—	35.00	75.00	150	275	—

KM# 1610.1 THALER

Silver **Ruler:** Karl (Charles) VI **Mint:** Graz **Obverse:** Legend begins at 9 o'clock **Obv. Legend:** CAROL • VI • D: G: R: I: - S: A: GE: HI: HV: BO: REX • **Reverse:** Crowned imperial double eagle with arms within Order chain on breast **Rev. Legend:** • ARCHIDVX AVSTRIÆ • DVX • BVRG: ET STYRIÆ • EC • **Note:** Dav. #1040. Prev. KM#505.1.

Date	Mintage	VG	F	VF	XF	Unc
1723	—	50.00	100	175	300	—
1728	—	50.00	100	175	300	—
1729	—	50.00	100	175	300	—

KM# 1617 THALER

Silver **Ruler:** Karl (Charles) VI **Mint:** Hall **Obverse:** Legend begins at upper right **Obv. Legend:** CAROL • VI • D • G • R • I • S • A • GE • HI • HU • BO • REX • **Reverse:** Curve-sided shield **Rev. Legend:** ARCHID • AUST • DUX • BU • COM • TYROL • **Note:** Dav. #1054. Varieties exist. Prev. KM#693.

Date	Mintage	VG	F	VF	XF	Unc
1724	Inc. above	50.00	100	200	300	—
1725	Inc. above	50.00	100	200	300	—
1727	245,000	50.00	100	200	300	—
1728	231,000	50.00	100	200	275	—
1729	415,000	50.00	100	200	300	—
1732	196,000	50.00	100	200	300	—
1733	Inc. above	50.00	100	200	300	—
1734	Inc. above	50.00	100	200	300	—

KM# 1629 THALER

Silver **Ruler:** Karl (Charles) VI **Mint:** Hall **Obverse:** Modified bust **Obv. Legend:** CAROL • VI • D • G • R • I • S • A • GE • HI • HU • BO • REX • **Reverse:** Straight-sided shield **Rev. Legend:** ARCHID • AUST • DUX • COM • TYROL • **Note:** Dav. #A1054. Prev. KM#694.

Date	Mintage	VG	F	VF	XF	Unc
1729	Inc. above	50.00	100	200	300	—

KM# 1639.1 THALER

Silver **Ruler:** Karl (Charles) VI **Mint:** Hall **Obverse:** Mature bust right **Obv. Legend:** CAROL • VI • D • G • R • I • S • A • GE • HI • HU • BO • REX • **Reverse:** Crowned imperial double eagle with crowned arms within Order chain on breast **Rev. Legend:** ARCHID • AUST • DUX BU • COM • TYROL • **Note:** Dav. #1055. Prev. KM#695.1.

Date	Mintage	VG	F	VF	XF	Unc
1730	Inc. above	50.00	100	200	300	—
1733	152,000	50.00	100	200	300	—
1734	Inc. above	50.00	100	200	300	—
1736	131,000	50.00	100	200	300	—
1737	246,000	50.00	100	200	300	—
1738	299,000	50.00	100	200	300	—

KM# 1610.2 THALER

Silver **Ruler:** Karl (Charles) VI **Mint:** Graz **Obverse:** Laureate armored bust right **Obv. Legend:** CAR • VI • D: G • R • I • S • A • - GE • HI • HU • BO • REX • **Reverse:** Curve-sided shield on eagle's breast **Rev. Legend:** ARCHID: AUST: DUX: BUR: ET: STYRIAE: **Note:** Prev. KM#505.2.

Date	Mintage	VG	F	VF	XF	Unc
1732	—	50.00	100	175	300	—

KM# 1579.3 THALER

Silver **Ruler:** Karl (Charles) VI **Mint:** Vienna **Obverse:** Older bust right **Obv. Legend:** CAR: VI: D: G: R: I: S: A: GE: HI: HU: BO: REX: **Reverse:** Crowned imperial double eagle with crowned arms within Order chain on breast **Rev. Legend:** ARCHID: AUST: DUX•BU: COM: TYROL: **Note:** Varieties exist. Dav. #1038. Prev. KM#1924.3.

Date	Mintage	VG	F	VF	XF	Unc
1735	—	35.00	75.00	150	275	—
1736	—	35.00	75.00	150	275	—
1737	—	35.00	75.00	150	275	—
1738	—	35.00	75.00	150	275	—
1739	—	35.00	75.00	150	275	—
1740	—	35.00	75.00	150	275	—

KM# 1610.3 THALER

Silver **Ruler:** Karl (Charles) VI **Mint:** Graz **Obverse:** Different armor and drapery **Obv. Legend:** CAR: VI: D: G: R: I: S: A: GE: HI: HU: BO: REX: **Reverse:** Crowned imperial double eagle with crowned arms on breast **Rev. Legend:** ARCHID: AUST: DUX: BURG: ET: STYRIAE: **Note:** Dav. #1042. Prev. KM#505.3.

Date	Mintage	VG	F	VF	XF	Unc
1735	—	50.00	100	175	300	—
1737	—	50.00	100	175	300	—
1738	—	50.00	100	175	300	—

KM# 1639.2 THALER

Silver **Ruler:** Karl (Charles) VI **Mint:** Hall **Obverse:** Numeral below bust **Obv. Legend:** CAR • VI • D • G • R • I • S • A • GE • HI • HU • BO • REX • **Reverse:** Curve-sided shield **Rev. Legend:** ARCHID • AUST • DUX • BU • COM • TYROL • **Note:** Dav. #1056. Mintage included in KM#1639.1. Prev. KM#695.2.

Date	Mintage	VG	F	VF	XF	Unc
1737	Inc. above	50.00	100	200	300	—
Note: With 1 below bust						
1737	Inc. above	50.00	100	200	300	—
Note: With 2 below bust						
1737	Inc. above	50.00	100	200	300	—
Note: With 3 below bust						
1737	Inc. above	75.00	150	300	450	—
Note: With 4 below bust						
1737	Inc. above	50.00	100	200	300	—
Note: With 5 below bust						

KM# 1610.4 THALER

Silver **Ruler:** Karl (Charles) VI **Mint:** Graz **Obverse:** Armored bust right **Obv. Legend:** CAR: VI: D: G: R: I: S: A: GE: HI: HU: BO: REX: **Reverse:** Crowned imperial double eagle with arms on breast **Rev. Legend:** ARCHID: AUST • DU - X: BUR: ET: STYRIAE • **Note:** Dav. #1043. Prev. KM#505.4.

Date	Mintage	VG	F	VF	XF	Unc
1740	—	50.00	100	175	300	—

KM# 1678 THALER

28.8200 g., 0.8750 Silver .8108 oz. ASW **Ruler:** Maria Theresa **Mint:** Vienna **Obverse:** Bust right **Obv. Legend:** MAR: THERESIA • D: G: REG: HUNG: BOH: **Reverse:** Crowned arms within cartouche, tassels at right and left **Rev. Legend:** ARCHID: AUST: DUX BURG: COM: TYR: **Note:** Dav. #1109. Prev. KM#1964.

Date	Mintage	VG	F	VF	XF	Unc
1741	—	60.00	125	350	400	—
1742	—	60.00	125	350	400	—
1743	—	60.00	125	350	400	—
1744	—	60.00	125	350	400	—

KM# 1714 THALER

28.8200 g., 0.8750 Silver .8108 oz. ASW **Ruler:** Maria Theresa **Mint:** Vienna **Obverse:** Bust right with décolletage **Obv. Legend:** MAR • THERESIA D • G • REG • HUNG • BOH • **Reverse:** Griffin supporters **Rev. Legend:** ARCHID • AUST • DUX • BURG • COM • TYR • **Note:** Dav. #1110. Prev. KM#1965.

Date	Mintage	VG	F	VF	XF	Unc
1744	—	90.00	175	450	600	—
1745	—	90.00	175	450	600	—

KM# 1966x THALER

28.8200 g., 0.8750 Silver .8108 oz. ASW **Ruler:** Maria Theresa **Mint:** Vienna **Obverse:** Diademed young bust right **Reverse:** Crowned imperial eagle with arms on breast **Note:** Dav. #1111. Varieties exist. Prev. KM#1966.

Date	Mintage	VG	F	VF	XF	Unc
1746	—	45.00	75.00	125	225	—
1747	—	45.00	75.00	125	225	—
1748	—	45.00	75.00	125	225	—
1749	—	45.00	75.00	125	225	—
1750	—	45.00	75.00	125	225	—
1751	—	45.00	75.00	125	225	—
1752	—	45.00	75.00	125	225	—

KM# 1742 THALER

28.8200 g., 0.8750 Silver .8109 oz. ASW **Ruler:** Maria Theresa **Mint:** Hall **Obverse:** Bust right in decorated gown **Obv. Legend:** M • THERESIA • D: G • R • IMP • GE • HU • BO • REG • **Reverse:** Crowned imperial double eagle with crowned arms on breast **Rev. Legend:** ARCHID • AUST • DUX • BU • COM • TYR • **Note:** Varieties exist. Dav. #1120. Prev. KM#743.

Date	Mintage	VG	F	VF	XF	Unc
1746	—	150	250	350	525	—
1749	—	150	250	350	525	—
1750	—	150	250	350	525	—
1751	—	150	250	350	525	—
1753	—	150	250	350	525	—
1754	—	150	250	350	525	—
1760	—	150	250	350	525	—
1763	—	150	250	350	525	—
1764	—	150	250	350	525	—
1765	—	150	250	350	525	—

KM# 1799 THALER
28.0600 g., 0.8330 Silver .7515 oz. ASW **Ruler:** Maria Theresa **Mint:** Hall **Obverse:** Mature armored bust right **Obv. Legend:** M • THERESIA • D: G • R • IMP • GE • HU • BO • REG • **Reverse:** Crowned imperial double eagle with crowned arms on breast **Rev. Legend:** ARCHID • AUST • DUX • BU • COM • TYR • **Note:** Dav. #1122. Varieties exist. Prev. KM#746.

Date	Mintage	VG	F	VF	XF	Unc
1751	—	60.00	120	200	375	—
1752	—	60.00	120	200	375	—
1764	—	60.00	120	200	375	—
1765	—	60.00	120	200	375	—
1765 AS	—	60.00	120	200	375	—

KM# 1798 THALER
28.8200 g., 0.8750 Silver .8109 oz. ASW **Ruler:** Maria Theresa **Mint:** Hall **Obverse:** Bust right with plain gown **Obv. Legend:** M: THERESIA: D: G: R: IMP: GE: HU: BO: REG: **Reverse:** Crowned imperial double eagle with crowned arms on breast **Rev. Legend:** ARCHID: AUST: DUX: BU: COM: TYR: **Note:** Convention Thaler. Dav. #1121. Prev. KM#744.

Date	Mintage	VG	F	VF	XF	Unc
1751	—	60.00	120	200	475	—
1752	—	60.00	120	200	475	—
1753	—	60.00	120	200	475	—

KM# 1807 THALER
28.8200 g., 0.8750 Silver .8108 oz. ASW **Ruler:** Maria Theresa **Mint:** Vienna **Obverse:** More mature armored bust right **Obv. Legend:** M • THERESIA • D: G • R • IMP • GE • HU • BO • REG • **Reverse:** Crowned imperial double eagle with crowned arms on breast **Rev. Legend:** ARCHID • AUST • DUX • BURG • CO • TYR • **Note:** Dav. #1112. Prev. KM#1967.

Date	Mintage	VG	F	VF	XF	Unc
1753	—	40.00	75.00	125	200	—

KM# 1816 THALER
28.0600 g., 0.8330 Silver .7515 oz. ASW **Ruler:** Maria Theresa **Mint:** Hall **Note:** Dav. #1121. Varieties exist. Prev. KM#745.

Date	Mintage	VG	F	VF	XF	Unc
1754	—	60.00	120	200	375	—
1755	—	60.00	120	200	375	—
1756	—	60.00	120	200	375	—
1757	—	60.00	120	200	375	—
1758	—	60.00	120	200	375	—
1759	—	60.00	120	200	375	—
1760	—	60.00	120	200	375	—
1761	—	60.00	120	200	375	—
1762	—	60.00	120	200	375	—
1763	—	60.00	120	200	375	—
1764	—	60.00	120	200	375	—
1765	—	60.00	120	200	375	—

KM# 1817 THALER
28.0600 g., 0.8330 Silver .7515 oz. ASW **Ruler:** Maria Theresa **Mint:** Vienna **Note:** Varieties exist. Prev. KM#1967a.

Date	Mintage	VG	F	VF	XF	Unc
1754	—	40.00	75.00	125	200	—
1755	—	40.00	75.00	125	200	—
1756	—	40.00	75.00	125	200	—
1757	—	40.00	75.00	125	200	—
1758	—	40.00	75.00	125	200	—
1759	—	40.00	75.00	125	200	—
1760	—	40.00	75.00	125	200	—
1761	—	40.00	75.00	125	200	—
1762	—	40.00	75.00	125	200	—
1763	—	40.00	75.00	125	200	—
1764	—	40.00	75.00	125	200	—
1765	—	40.00	75.00	125	200	—

KM# 1823 THALER
28.0600 g., 0.8330 Silver .7515 oz. ASW **Ruler:** Maria Theresa **Mint:** Vienna **Obverse:** Bust right with décolletage **Obv. Legend:** M • THERESIA • D • G • R • IMP • GE • HU • BO • REG • **Reverse:** Two-part arms, crossed hammers below eagle **Rev. Legend:** S • ANNÆ FUND GRUBEN - AUSB • THA • IN • N • OE • **Note:** Mining Thaler. Dav. #1113. Varieties exist. Prev. KM#1968.

Date	Mintage	VG	F	VF	XF	Unc
1758	—	200	375	750	1,250	—
1765	—	200	375	750	1,250	—

KM# 1838 THALER
28.0600 g., 0.8330 Silver .7515 oz. ASW **Ruler:** Maria Theresa **Mint:** Hall **Obverse:** Veiled bust right **Note:** Similar to 1/2 Thaler, KM#1848. Dav. #1123. Prev. KM#747.

Date	Mintage	VG	F	VF	XF	Unc
1765 F	—	40.00	65.00	125	200	—
1765 AS	—	40.00	65.00	125	200	—
1766 AS	—	40.00	65.00	125	200	—
1767 AS	—	40.00	65.00	125	200	—
1768 AS	—	40.00	65.00	125	200	—
1768 S	—	40.00	65.00	125	200	—
1769 AS	—	40.00	65.00	125	200	—
1771 AS	—	40.00	65.00	125	200	—
1772 AS	—	40.00	65.00	125	200	—

KM# 1836 THALER
Silver **Ruler:** Maria Theresa **Mint:** Graz **Obverse:** Draped bust with décolletage right **Obv. Legend:** M • THERESIA • D: G • R • IMP • GE • HU • BO • REG • **Reverse:** Crowned imperial double eagle with arms on breast **Rev. Legend:** ARCHID • AUST • DUX • BURG • & • STYR • **Note:** Dav. #1118. Prev. KM#545.

Date	Mintage	VG	F	VF	XF	Unc
1765	—	175	350	650	1,250	—

KM# 1837 THALER
Silver **Ruler:** Maria Theresa **Mint:** Graz **Obverse:** Bust with décolletage right **Obv. Legend:** M • THERESIA • D: G • R • IMP • GE • HU • BO • REG • **Reverse:** Crowned imperial double eagle with crowned arms on breast **Rev. Legend:** ARCHID • AUST • DUX • BURG • & • STYR • **Note:** Dav. #1119. Prev. KM#546.

Date	Mintage	VG	F	VF	XF	Unc
1765	—	175	350	650	1,250	—

KM# 1839 THALER
28.0600 g., 0.8330 Silver .7515 oz. ASW **Ruler:** Maria Theresa **Mint:** Vienna **Obverse:** Veiled bust right **Obv. Legend:** M • THERESIA • D: G • R • IMP • HU • BO • REG • **Reverse:** Crowned imperial double eagle with crowned arms on breast **Rev. Legend:** ARCHID • AUST • DUX • BURG • ... **Note:** Convention Thaler. Dav. #1113. Varieties exist. Prev. KM#1969.

Date	Mintage	VG	F	VF	XF	Unc
1765A	—	35.00	65.00	125	185	—
1766A	—	35.00	65.00	125	185	—
1766	—	35.00	65.00	125	185	—
1766 IC-SK	—	35.00	65.00	125	185	—
1766 EC-SK	—	35.00	65.00	125	185	—
1767 IC-SK	—	35.00	65.00	125	185	—

KM# 1849 THALER
28.0600 g., 0.8330 Silver .7515 oz. ASW **Ruler:** Maria Theresa **Mint:** Vienna **Obverse:** Different veiled bust right **Obv. Legend:** M • THERESIA • D: G • R • IMP • HU • BO • REG • **Reverse:** Crowned imperial double eagle with crowned arms on breast **Rev. Legend:** ARCHID • AUST • DUX • BURG • CO ... **Note:** Dav. #1115. Prev. KM#1970.

Date	Mintage	VG	F	VF	XF	Unc
1767 IK-SC	—	35.00	65.00	125	185	—
1767 IC-SK	—	35.00	65.00	125	185	—
1768 IC-SK	30,000	35.00	65.00	125	185	—

Date	Mintage	VG	F	VF	XF	Unc
1769 IC-SK	—	35.00	65.00	125	185	—
1770 IC-SK	—	35.00	65.00	125	185	—
1771 IC-SK	—	35.00	65.00	125	185	—
1772 IC-SK	—	35.00	65.00	125	185	—

KM# 1861 THALER

28.0600 g., 0.8330 Silver .7515 oz. ASW **Ruler:** Maria Theresa **Mint:** Vienna **Obverse:** Veiled head right with jeweled bust **Note:** Ordens Thaler. Prev. KM#1972.

Date	Mintage	VG	F	VF	XF	Unc
1769 IC-SK	—	100	225	300	425	—

Note: For later issues refer to Uniform Coinage

KM# 1865 THALER

28.0600 g., 0.8330 Silver .7515 oz. ASW **Ruler:** Maria Theresa **Mint:** Hall **Obverse:** Smaller veil on bust **Reverse:** Initials **Note:** Dav. #1124. Prev. KM#748.

Date	Mintage	VG	F	VF	XF	Unc
1772 AS	—	150	300	500	1,000	—
1773 AS	—	40.00	65.00	125	200	—
1774 AS	—	40.00	65.00	125	200	—
1774 VC-S	—	40.00	65.00	125	200	—
1775 VC-S	—	40.00	65.00	125	200	—
1776 VC-S	—	40.00	65.00	125	200	—

KM# 1866.1 THALER

28.0600 g., 0.8330 Silver .7515 oz. ASW **Ruler:** Maria Theresa **Mint:** Vienna **Obverse:** Smaller veiled head right **Obv. Legend:** M • THERESIA • D • G • R • IMP • HU • BO • REG • **Reverse:** Crowned imperial double eagle with crowned arms on breast **Rev. Legend:** ARCHID • AUST • DUX • BURG • ... **Note:** Dav. #1116. Prev. KM#1971.1.

Date	Mintage	VG	F	VF	XF	Unc
1772 IC-SK	—	35.00	65.00	125	185	—
1773 IC-SK	—	35.00	65.00	125	185	—
1774 IC-SK	—	35.00	65.00	125	185	—
1774 IC-FA	—	35.00	65.00	125	185	—
1775 IC-FA	—	35.00	65.00	125	185	—
1776 IC-FA	—	35.00	65.00	125	185	—
1777 IC-FA	116,000	35.00	65.00	125	185	—
1778 IC-FA	83,000	35.00	65.00	125	185	—
1779 IC-FA	134,000	35.00	65.00	125	185	—

KM# 1866.2 THALER

28.0600 g., 0.8330 Silver .7515 oz. ASW **Ruler:** Maria Theresa **Mint:** Vienna **Obverse:** Larger veiled bust with décolletage right **Obv. Legend:** M • THERESIA • D • G • R • IMP • HU • BO • REG • **Reverse:** Crowned imperial double eagle with crowned arms on breast **Rev. Legend:** ARCHID • AVST • DUX • BURG • CO • TYR • **Note:** Dav. #1117. Prev. KM#1971.2.

Date	Mintage	VG	F	VF	XF	Unc
1780 IC-FA	—	15.00	27.50	50.00	100	—

Note: Coins dated 1780 were restruck until 1984 with minor changes

KM# 1445 2 THALER

Silver **Ruler:** Joseph I **Mint:** Hall **Obverse:** Laureate armored bust right **Obv. Legend:** IOSEPHUS • D: G: ROM: IMP: SE: AV - G: HV: BO: REX • **Reverse:** Imperial eagle **Rev. Legend:** ARCHIDVX: AVST: DVX: BVR: COM: TYROLIS **Note:** Dav. #1016. Prev. KM#666.

Date	Mintage	VG	F	VF	XF	Unc
ND	—	300	600	1,000	1,450	—

KM# 1446 2 THALER

Silver **Ruler:** Joseph I **Mint:** Hall **Obverse:** Inner circle added **Note:** Dav. #1017. Prev. KM#667.

Date	Mintage	VG	F	VF	XF	Unc
ND	—	300	600	1,000	1,450	—

KM# 1447 2 THALER

Zinc **Ruler:** Joseph I **Mint:** Hall **Note:** Dav. #1017A. Klippe. Prev. KM#668.

Date	Mintage	VG	F	VF	XF	Unc
ND Rare	—	—	—	—	—	—

KM# 1523 2 THALER

Silver **Ruler:** Karl (Charles) VI **Mint:** Hall **Obverse:** Laureate armored bust right **Obv. Legend:** CAROLUS • VI • D: G: RO: IMP: S: A: G: H: H: B: REX • **Reverse:** Crowned imperial double eagle with arms on breast **Rev. Legend:** ARCHIDVX • AUSTRIÆ • DVX • BURGVNDIÆ • COM: TYR • **Note:** Dav. #1049. Prev. KM#696.

Date	Mintage	VG	F	VF	XF	Unc
ND	834	300	500	700	900	—

KM# 1555 2 THALER

Silver **Ruler:** Karl (Charles) VI **Mint:** Saint Veit **Obverse:** Bust right in inner circle **Reverse:** Crowned imperial eagle, crown divides date **Note:** Dav. #1045. Thick planchet. Prev. KM#1682.

Date	Mintage	VG	F	VF	XF	Unc
1713	—	1,800	3,600	5,600	7,500	—

KM# 1595 2 THALER

Silver **Ruler:** Karl (Charles) VI **Mint:** Hall **Reverse:** Date in legend **Note:** Dav. #1052. Prev. KM#697.

Date	Mintage	VG	F	VF	XF	Unc
1719	2,500	500	700	900	1,100	—

KM# 1556 3 THALER

Silver **Ruler:** Karl (Charles) VI **Mint:** Saint Veit **Obverse:** Bust right in inner circle **Reverse:** Crowned imperial eagle, crown divides date **Note:** Dav. #1044. Thick planchet. Prev. KM#1683.

Date	Mintage	VG	F	VF	XF	Unc
1713 Rare	—	—	—	—	—	—

UNIFORM SERIES

KM# 1975 HELLER

Copper **Obverse:** Crowned arms **Reverse:** 1/HEL/LER and date

Date	Mintage	VG	F	VF	XF	Unc
1763	—	1.75	3.50	15.00	30.00	45.00
1765	—	1.75	3.50	15.00	30.00	45.00

KM# 1976 HELLER

Copper **Ruler:** Joseph II **Obverse:** Modified crowned arms **Reverse:** Denomination

Date	Mintage	VG	F	VF	XF	Unc
1768	—	1.75	3.50	15.00	30.00	45.00

KM# 1977 HELLER

Copper **Ruler:** Joseph II **Obverse:** Crowned arms **Reverse:** 1/HELLER and date

Date	Mintage	VG	F	VF	XF	Unc
1777	—	1.75	3.50	15.00	30.00	45.00
1778	—	1.75	3.50	15.00	30.00	45.00
1779	—	1.75	3.50	15.00	30.00	45.00

KM# 1978 PFENNIG

Copper **Ruler:** Maria Theresa **Obverse:** Bust of Maria Theresa **Reverse:** Value and date in cartouche

Date	Mintage	VG	F	VF	XF	Unc
1748W	—	7.50	15.00	30.00	75.00	125
1749W	—	5.00	10.00	20.00	60.00	110
1750W	—	7.50	15.00	30.00	75.00	125

KM# 2000 PFENNIG

Copper **Ruler:** Franz I **Obverse:** Head right **Reverse:** Value and date in cartouche

Date	Mintage	VG	F	VF	XF	Unc
1748W	—	5.00	10.00	20.00	60.00	110
1749W	—	5.00	10.00	20.00	60.00	110

KM# 2001 PFENNIG

Copper **Ruler:** Franz I **Reverse:** Crowned arms of Lorraine, value and date below

Date	Mintage	VG	F	VF	XF	Unc
NDCA	—	5.00	10.00	20.00	50.00	80.00
1759HA	—	2.50	5.00	7.50	20.00	35.00
1759WI	—	2.50	5.00	7.50	20.00	35.00
1764WI	—	2.50	5.00	7.50	20.00	35.00
1765HA	—	2.50	5.00	7.50	20.00	35.00
1765WI	—	2.50	5.00	7.50	20.00	35.00

KM# 1979 PFENNIG

Copper **Ruler:** Maria Theresa **Obverse:** Diademed young bust of Maria Theresa right **Obv. Legend:** M • THERES • D • G • RO • I • G • HU • BO • REG • **Reverse:** Crowned arms, value divides date at bottom **Note:** Varieties exist.

Date	Mintage	VG	F	VF	XF	Unc
1759	—	5.00	10.00	20.00	60.00	110
1760	—	5.00	10.00	20.00	60.00	110
1764	—	5.00	10.00	20.00	60.00	110
1765	—	5.00	10.00	20.00	60.00	110

KM# 2002 PFENNIG

Copper **Ruler:** Maria Theresa **Reverse:** Crowned Austrian arms, value and date below

Date	Mintage	VG	F	VF	XF	Unc
1765	—	7.50	15.00	40.00	65.00	100

KM# 1980 1/4 KREUZER

Billon **Obverse:** Crowned imperial eagle with Austrian arms, value in cartouche **Note:** Uniface.

Date	Mintage	VG	F	VF	XF	Unc
1746	—	10.00	20.00	35.00	60.00	100

KM# 2003 1/4 KREUZER

Billon **Obverse:** Crowned imperial eagle with arms of Lorraine, value in cartouche below **Note:** Uniface.

Date	Mintage	VG	F	VF	XF	Unc
1746	—	10.00	20.00	50.00	100	185

KM# 2004 1/4 KREUZER

Billon **Obverse:** Crowned imperial eagle, value without cartouche **Note:** Uniface.

Date	Mintage	VG	F	VF	XF	Unc
1748	—	15.00	30.00	80.00	145	250
1749	—	15.00	30.00	80.00	145	250

KM# 2005 1/4 KREUZER

Billon **Obverse:** Crowned arms of Lorraine, date and value in cartouche below **Note:** Uniface.

Date	Mintage	VG	F	VF	XF	Unc
1750WI	—	12.00	25.00	50.00	80.00	150
1751WI	—	12.00	25.00	50.00	80.00	150

KM# 1981 1/4 KREUZER

Billon **Obverse:** Crowned Austrian arms, date and value in cartouche below

Date	Mintage	VG	F	VF	XF	Unc
1750WI	—	25.00	50.00	100	150	250
1751WI	—	50.00	75.00	125	200	300

KM# 2050 1/4 KREUZER

Copper **Ruler:** Joseph II **Obverse:** Head right, as joint ruler **Obv. Legend:** IOS • II • D • G • R • I • S • A • GER • IER • REX • **Reverse:** Value and date

Date	Mintage	VG	F	VF	XF	Unc
1772W	—	2.50	5.00	15.00	35.00	55.00
1777S	—	2.50	5.00	15.00	35.00	55.00

KM# 1982 1/4 KREUZER

Copper **Ruler:** Maria Theresa **Obverse:** Veiled head **Reverse:** Value

Date	Mintage	VG	F	VF	XF	Unc
ND Rare	—	—	—	—	—	—

KM# 1983 1/4 KREUZER

Copper **Ruler:** Maria Theresa **Obverse:** Veiled head right **Obv. Legend:** M • THERESIA • D: G • R • I • H • B • R • A • AUST • **Reverse:** Value and date in cartouche

Date	Mintage	VG	F	VF	XF	Unc
1777S	—	2.00	4.00	10.00	25.00	45.00
1779	—	2.00	4.00	10.00	25.00	45.00
1779K	—	5.00	7.50	15.00	38.00	60.00

KM# 1984 1/4 KREUZER

Copper **Reverse:** Value and date in wreath

Date	Mintage	VG	F	VF	XF	Unc
1780	—	10.00	20.00	35.00	60.00	100
1780W	—	10.00	20.00	35.00	60.00	100

KM# 2051.1 1/4 KREUZER

Copper **Ruler:** Joseph II **Obverse:** Head right, as sole ruler **Obv. Legend:** IOS • II • D • G • R • I • S • A • G • E • ... **Reverse:** Value and date

Date	Mintage	VG	F	VF	XF	Unc
1781A	—	2.50	5.00	8.00	20.00	35.00
1781B	—	2.50	5.00	8.00	20.00	35.00
1781F	—	10.00	20.00	40.00	80.00	125
1781S	—	2.50	5.00	8.00	20.00	35.00
1782A	—	2.50	5.00	8.00	20.00	35.00
1782B	—	2.50	5.00	8.00	20.00	35.00
1782F	—	2.50	5.00	10.00	25.00	40.00
1782S	—	2.50	5.00	8.00	20.00	35.00
1783A	—	9.00	15.00	20.00	40.00	60.00
1783F	—	9.00	15.00	20.00	40.00	60.00
1785F	—	10.00	20.00	40.00	80.00	125
1790F	—	2.50	5.00	10.00	25.00	40.00

KM# 2051.2 1/4 KREUZER

Copper **Ruler:** Joseph II **Obverse:** Letter U instead of V in HU **Reverse:** Value and date

Date	Mintage	VG	F	VF	XF	Unc
1783F Rare	—	—	—	—	—	—

KM# 2105 1/4 KREUZER

Copper **Ruler:** Franz II (I) **Obverse:** Crowned imperial double eagle **Obv. Legend:** FRANC • II • D • G • R • I • S • A • ... **Reverse:** Value and date **Note:** KM#2105 struck until 1809 with 1800 date.

Date	Mintage	F	VF	XF	Unc
1800A	—	3.50	7.00	15.00	40.00
1800B	—	—	—	—	—

Note: Reported, not confirmed

KM# 1985 1/2 KREUZER

Copper **Ruler:** Maria Theresa **Obverse:** Young head right **Obv. Legend:** M • THERES • D: G • RO • I • G • HU • BO • REG • **Reverse:** Value within cartouche

Date	Mintage	VG	F	VF	XF	Unc
ND(1760)	—	3.00	6.00	14.00	30.00	55.00
1764CA	—	5.00	9.00	20.00	45.00	70.00

KM# 2006 1/2 KREUZER

Copper **Ruler:** Franz I **Obverse:** Bust right **Reverse:** Value and date in cartouche

Date	Mintage	VG	F	VF	XF	Unc
ND	—	2.00	4.00	9.00	17.00	30.00
1764	—	3.00	6.00	12.00	28.00	40.00
1764CA	—	3.00	6.00	12.00	28.00	40.00

KM# 1986 1/2 KREUZER

Copper **Ruler:** Maria Theresa **Obverse:** Veiled head **Reverse:** Value

Date	Mintage	VG	F	VF	XF	Unc
ND Rare	—	—	—	—	—	—

KM# 1987 1/2 KREUZER

Copper **Ruler:** Maria Theresa **Obverse:** Veiled head right **Obv. Legend:** M • THERESIA • D • G • R • I • H • B • R • A • AUST **Reverse:** Value and date within cartouche

Date	Mintage	VG	F	VF	XF	Unc
1772W	—	5.00	9.00	18.00	38.00	60.00
1776S	—	2.25	4.50	9.00	20.00	35.00
1777S	—	2.25	4.50	9.00	20.00	35.00
1779	—	2.25	4.50	9.00	20.00	35.00
1779K	—	5.00	9.00	18.00	38.00	60.00

KM# 2052 1/2 KREUZER

Copper **Ruler:** Joseph II **Obverse:** Bust right, as joint ruler **Obv. Legend:** IOS • II • D • G • R • I • S • A • GER • IER • REX • **Reverse:** Value and date within cartouche

Date	Mintage	VG	F	VF	XF	Unc
1772W	—	1.00	3.00	5.00	22.00	35.00
1773S	—	5.00	10.00	20.00	55.00	85.00
1774S	—	1.00	3.00	5.00	22.00	35.00
1775S	—	2.00	5.00	10.00	32.00	55.00
1776S	—	2.00	5.00	10.00	37.00	60.00
1779	—	5.00	10.00	20.00	55.00	85.00

KM# 2053 1/2 KREUZER

Copper **Ruler:** Joseph II **Obverse:** Bust right, as sole ruler **Note:** Varieties exist for 1783 date, obverse legend HU or HV.

Date	Mintage	VG	F	VF	XF	Unc
1780W	—	5.00	10.00	20.00	45.00	75.00
1781A	—	4.50	7.50	15.00	35.00	60.00
1781B	8,283,000	4.50	7.50	15.00	35.00	60.00
1781G	—	20.00	40.00	65.00	120	200
1781S	—	4.50	7.50	15.00	35.00	60.00
1781W	—	5.00	10.00	20.00	45.00	75.00
1782A	—	4.50	7.50	15.00	35.00	60.00
1782B	360,000	4.50	7.50	15.00	35.00	60.00
1782F	—	7.00	12.50	25.00	55.00	85.00
1782S	—	4.50	7.50	15.00	35.00	60.00
1783	—	—	—	—	—	—

Note: Reported, not confirmed

Date	Mintage	VG	F	VF	XF	Unc
1783F	—	4.50	7.50	15.00	35.00	60.00
1790F	—	7.00	12.50	25.00	55.00	85.00

KM# 1988 1/2 KREUZER

Copper **Ruler:** Maria Theresa **Obverse:** Veiled head right **Obv. Legend:** M • THERESIA • D • G • R • I • HU • BO • R • A • A • **Reverse:** Value and date within wreath of palm and laurel

Date	Mintage	VG	F	VF	XF	Unc
1780W	—	5.00	10.00	20.00	45.00	70.00

KM# 2108 1/2 KREUZER

Copper **Ruler:** Franz II (I) **Note:** Struck until 1809 with 1800 date.

Date	Mintage	VG	F	VF	XF	Unc
1800A	—	1.50	3.00	9.00	27.00	
1800B	—	12.50	25.00	50.00	110	
1800C	—	3.00	6.00	20.00	75.00	
1800D	—	15.00	30.00	60.00	120	
1800E	—	15.00	30.00	60.00	120	
1800F	—	6.00	12.00	25.00	85.00	
1800G Rare	—	—	—	—	—	
1800S Rare	—	—	—	—	—	

KM# 2008 KREUZER

Billon **Ruler:** Franz I **Obverse:** Large bust right **Reverse:** Crowned imperial eagle, value below

Date	Mintage	VG	F	VF	XF	Unc
1746	—	10.00	15.00	30.00	75.00	125

KM# 2009.1 KREUZER

Billon **Ruler:** Franz I **Obverse:** Bust right **Obv. Legend:** FRANC • D • G • R • I • S • A • ... **Reverse:** Crowned imperial double eagle **Rev. Legend:** IN TE DOMINE SPERAVI **Note:** Varieties exist.

Date	Mintage	VG	F	VF	XF	Unc
1747W	—	3.00	6.00	12.50	25.00	40.00
1748HA	231,000	5.00	8.00	15.00	30.00	50.00

Note: Includes Maria Theresa coins of same date and denomination; See Tyrol listings

Date	Mintage	VG	F	VF	XF	Unc
1748WI	—	3.00	6.00	12.50	25.00	40.00
1749WI	—	3.00	6.00	12.50	25.00	40.00
1750HA	121,000	5.00	8.00	15.00	30.00	50.00

Note: Includes Maria Theresa coins of same date and denomination; See Tyrol listings

Date	Mintage	VG	F	VF	XF	Unc
1750WI	—	3.00	6.00	12.50	25.00	40.00
1751WI	—	3.00	6.00	12.50	25.00	40.00
1752HA	1,231,000	5.00	8.00	15.00	30.00	50.00

Note: Includes Maria Theresa coins of same date and denomination; See Tyrol listings

Date	Mintage	VG	F	VF	XF	Unc
1752WI	—	3.00	6.00	12.50	25.00	40.00
1753GR	—	6.50	10.00	20.00	40.00	65.00
1753HA	992,000	5.00	8.00	15.00	30.00	50.00

Note: Includes Maria Theresa coins of same date and denomination; See Tyrol listings

Date	Mintage	VG	F	VF	XF	Unc
1753/2WI	—	5.00	8.00	20.00	35.00	60.00
1753WI	—	3.00	6.00	12.50	25.00	40.00
1754GR	—	6.50	10.00	20.00	40.00	65.00
1754HA	205,000	5.00	8.00	15.00	30.00	50.00

Note: Includes Maria Theresa coins of same date and denomination; See Tyrol listings

Date	Mintage	VG	F	VF	XF	Unc
1755GR	—	6.50	10.00	20.00	40.00	65.00
1755HA	225,000	5.00	8.00	15.00	30.00	50.00

Note: Includes Maria Theresa coins of same date and denomination; See Tyrol listings

Date	Mintage	VG	F	VF	XF	Unc
1755PR	—	15.00	30.00	60.00	125	235
1755WI	—	6.50	10.00	20.00	40.00	65.00
1756GR	—	6.50	10.00	20.00	40.00	65.00
1756/5HA	155,000	5.00	8.00	20.00	35.00	55.00

Note: Includes Maria Theresa coins of same date and denomination; See Tyrol listings

Date	Mintage	VG	F	VF	XF	Unc
1756HA	Inc. above	5.00	8.00	15.00	30.00	50.00
1756KB	1,084,000	5.00	8.00	15.00	30.00	50.00
1757KB	63,000	5.00	8.00	15.00	30.00	50.00
1758GR	—	8.00	12.00	25.00	50.00	80.00
1758KB	455,000	5.00	8.00	15.00	30.00	50.00
1758NB	—	10.00	20.00	35.00	70.00	120
1759HA	64,000	20.00	40.00	70.00	150	250
1759KB	266,000	5.00	8.00	15.00	30.00	50.00
1760KB	253,000	5.00	8.00	15.00	30.00	50.00

KM# 1992 KREUZER

Copper **Ruler:** Maria Theresa **Obverse:** Bust right **Reverse:** Value in cartouche

Date	Mintage	VG	F	VF	XF	Unc
1749W	—	60.00	90.00	150	250	400
1750W	—	60.00	90.00	150	250	400

KM# 2007 KREUZER

Copper **Ruler:** Franz I **Obverse:** Bust right **Reverse:** Value within cartouche

Date	Mintage	VG	F	VF	XF	Unc
1749W	—	80.00	120	200	325	500
1760H	—	2.00	5.00	10.00	30.00	50.00
Note: Included in mintage for KM#1993						
1760K	2,337,000	7.50	15.00	30.00	80.00	135
1760P	—	25.00	40.00	70.00	120	225
1760W	—	2.00	5.00	10.00	30.00	50.00
1761C	—	5.00	10.00	20.00	45.00	70.00
1761G	—	5.00	10.00	20.00	45.00	70.00
1761K	—	7.50	15.00	30.00	80.00	135
1761NB	—	5.00	10.00	20.00	45.00	70.00
1761W	—	5.00	10.00	20.00	45.00	70.00
1762C	—	5.00	10.00	20.00	45.00	70.00
1762G	—	5.00	10.00	20.00	45.00	70.00
1762NB	—	5.00	10.00	20.00	45.00	70.00
1762W	—	2.00	5.00	10.00	30.00	50.00
1763C	—	7.50	15.00	30.00	65.00	100
1763NB	—	5.00	10.00	20.00	45.00	70.00
1763W	—	3.00	6.00	12.00	35.00	55.00
1764C	—	7.50	15.00	30.00	65.00	100
1765H	—	2.00	5.00	10.00	30.00	50.00
Note: Included in mintage for KM#1993						

KM# 2009.2 KREUZER

Billon **Ruler:** Franz I **Obverse:** Bust right **Reverse:** Cross after date

Date	Mintage	VG	F	VF	XF	Unc
1751HA	143,000	10.00	20.00	35.00	60.00	90.00

KM# 1993 KREUZER

Copper **Ruler:** Maria Theresa **Obverse:** Bust right **Obv. Legend:** M • THERESIA • D: G • R • I • H • B • R • A • AUST **Reverse:** Value in cartouche

Date	Mintage	VG	F	VF	XF	Unc
1760H	2,775,000	4.00	7.00	15.00	40.00	60.00
1760NB	—	6.00	12.00	20.00	50.00	80.00
1760P	—	3.00	6.00	10.00	30.00	50.00
1760W	—	4.00	7.00	15.00	40.00	60.00
1761C	—	4.00	7.00	15.00	45.00	70.00
1761G	—	3.00	6.00	10.00	32.00	55.00
1761K	22,923,000	3.00	7.00	10.00	32.00	55.00
1761NB	—	4.00	7.00	15.00	50.00	80.00
1761P	—	3.00	6.00	10.00	30.00	50.00
1761W	—	5.00	10.00	25.00	55.00	90.00
1762C	—	4.00	7.00	15.00	45.00	70.00
1762G	—	3.00	6.00	10.00	32.00	55.00
1762K	27,139,000	3.00	7.00	10.00	32.00	55.00
1762NB	—	4.00	7.00	15.00	50.00	80.00
1762P	—	3.00	6.00	10.00	30.00	50.00
1762W	—	5.00	10.00	20.00	40.00	60.00
1763C	—	4.00	7.00	15.00	45.00	70.00
1763G	—	3.00	6.00	10.00	32.00	55.00
1763K	2,244,000	4.00	8.00	15.00	40.00	60.00
1763NB	—	4.00	7.00	15.00	50.00	80.00
1763P	—	5.00	10.00	20.00	45.00	70.00
1763S	—	3.00	6.00	10.00	30.00	50.00
1763W	—	4.00	7.00	15.00	45.00	70.00
1764C	—	4.00	7.00	15.00	45.00	70.00
1764P	—	15.00	30.00	40.00	70.00	120
1765H	Inc. above	4.00	7.00	15.00	45.00	70.00

KM# 1994 KREUZER

Copper **Ruler:** Maria Theresa **Obverse:** Veiled bust right **Obv. Legend:** M • THERESIA • D: G • R • I • H • B • R • A • AUST • **Reverse:** Value and date within cartouche

Date	Mintage	VG	F	VF	XF	Unc
1772W	—	3.50	7.00	15.00	35.00	55.00
1775S	—	3.50	7.00	15.00	35.00	55.00
1775W	—	5.00	10.00	20.00	45.00	70.00
1779	—	3.50	7.00	15.00	35.00	55.00
1779G	—	3.50	7.00	15.00	35.00	55.00
1779H	343,000	5.00	10.00	20.00	45.00	70.00

KM# 2054 KREUZER

Copper **Ruler:** Joseph II **Obverse:** Head right, as joint ruler **Reverse:** Value and date in cartouche

Date	Mintage	VG	F	VF	XF	Unc
1772W	—	4.00	8.00	16.00	40.00	60.00
1773S	—	4.00	10.00	25.00	65.00	100
1774S	—	4.00	10.00	20.00	55.00	85.00
1775S	—	4.00	10.00	30.00	80.00	135
1779	—	4.00	10.00	25.00	65.00	100

KM# 2055 KREUZER

Billon **Reverse:** Value and date in wreath

Date	Mintage	VG	F	VF	XF	Unc
1780NB	—	6.00	15.00	40.00	85.00	145
1780S	—	7.50	15.00	30.00	70.00	120
1780W	—	4.00	10.00	25.00	55.00	85.00

KM# 1995 KREUZER

Copper **Ruler:** Maria Theresa **Obverse:** Veiled bust right **Obv. Legend:** M • THERESIA • D • G • R • I • ... **Reverse:** Value and date within wreath of palm and laurel **Note:** Varieties exist.

Date	Mintage	VG	F	VF	XF	Unc
1780	—	3.50	7.00	15.00	35.00	55.00
1780H	2,208,000	3.50	7.00	15.00	35.00	55.00
1780K	—	5.00	10.00	20.00	45.00	70.00
1780NB	—	6.00	12.00	25.00	55.00	85.00
1780S	—	2.50	5.00	15.00	35.00	55.00
1780W	—	3.50	7.00	15.00	35.00	55.00

KM# 2056 KREUZER

Copper-Billon **Ruler:** Joseph II **Obverse:** Head right, as sole ruler

Date	Mintage	VG	F	VF	XF	Unc
1780B	229,516,000	—	—	—	—	—
Note: Reported, not confirmed						
1780C	—	2.50	5.00	10.00	30.00	50.00
1780G	—	—	—	—	—	—
Note: Reported, not confirmed						
1780W	—	5.00	10.00	20.00	55.00	85.00
1781A	—	2.50	5.00	10.00	30.00	50.00
1781B	18,191,000	2.50	5.00	10.00	30.00	50.00
1781B.	Inc. above	2.50	5.00	10.00	30.00	50.00
1781C	—	—	—	—	—	—
Note: Reported, not confirmed						
1781F	—	5.00	10.00	20.00	55.00	85.00
1781G	—	5.00	10.00	20.00	55.00	85.00
1781H	—	3.50	7.00	15.00	40.00	60.00
1781S	—	2.50	5.00	10.00	30.00	50.00
1782A	—	2.50	5.00	10.00	30.00	50.00
1782B	—	2.50	5.00	12.00	30.00	50.00
1782B.	—	2.50	5.00	10.00	30.00	50.00
1782C	—	2.50	5.00	10.00	30.00	50.00
1782G	—	2.50	5.00	10.00	60.00	90.00
1782H	—	6.00	12.00	25.00	60.00	90.00
1782S	—	3.50	7.00	15.00	40.00	60.00
1788A	—	4.50	9.00	17.50	45.00	70.00
1790A	—	2.50	5.00	10.00	30.00	50.00
1790B	22,912,000	6.00	12.00	25.00	65.00	100
1790F	—	2.50	5.00	10.00	30.00	50.00
1790G	—	—	—	—	—	—
Note: Reported, not confirmed						
1790S	—	1.00	3.00	7.00	20.00	35.00

KM# 2111 KREUZER

Billon **Ruler:** Franz II (I) **Obverse:** Head right **Obv. Legend:** FRANC • II • D • G • R • I • S • A • G E • HV • BO • REX • A • A • **Reverse:** Value on breast of crowned double eagle **Note:** Struck until 1809 with 1800 date. Uniface strikes exist.

Date	Mintage	F	VF	XF	Unc
1800A	—	1.00	4.00	8.00	25.00
1800B	86,919,000	1.00	5.00	10.00	30.00
1800C	—	1.00	4.00	12.00	25.00
1800D	—	15.00	40.00	80.00	125
1800E	—	6.00	12.00	24.00	50.00
1800F	—	6.00	12.00	24.00	50.00
1800G	—	8.00	17.50	30.00	55.00
1800S	—	1.00	4.00	8.00	25.00

KM# 2011 3 KREUZER

Billon **Ruler:** Franz I **Obverse:** Armored bust right **Obv. Legend:** FRANC • D: G • R • I • S • A • GER • IER • REX • **Reverse:** Crowned imperial double eagle **Rev. Legend:** IN TE DOMINE SPERAVI •

Date	Mintage	VG	F	VF	XF	Unc
1746	—	5.00	10.00	20.00	40.00	60.00
1747	—	5.00	10.00	20.00	40.00	60.00

KM# 2012 3 KREUZER

Billon **Ruler:** Franz I **Obverse:** Armored bust right **Obv. Legend:** FRANC • D: G • R • I • S • A • GER • IER • REX • **Reverse:** Crowned imperial double eagle **Rev. Legend:** IN TE DOMINE SPERAVI •

Date	Mintage	VG	F	VF	XF	Unc
1747WI	—	5.00	10.00	20.00	40.00	60.00
1749GR	—	10.00	20.00	45.00	90.00	150
1749WI	—	6.00	12.50	25.00	55.00	85.00
1750GR	—	10.00	20.00	45.00	90.00	150
1750PR	—	10.00	20.00	45.00	90.00	150
1750WI	—	6.00	12.50	25.00	50.00	80.00

KM# 2013.1 3 KREUZER

Billon **Reverse:** Without cartouche around denomination

Date	Mintage	VG	F	VF	XF	Unc
1748KB	—	25.00	40.00	75.00	130	235
1748WI	—	5.50	11.00	22.50	45.00	70.00
1749WI	—	8.00	15.00	30.00	60.00	90.00
1750NB	—	35.00	50.00	80.00	140	250

KM# 2014 3 KREUZER

Billon **Ruler:** Franz I **Obverse:** Pleated drapes over shoulder **Reverse:** Without cartouche around denomination **Note:** Includes Maria Theresa coins of same date and denomination. See Tyrol listings.

Date	Mintage	VG	F	VF	XF	Unc
1748HA	223,000	20.00	35.00	65.00	110	200
1749HA	126,000	25.00	40.00	75.00	130	235
1750HA	182,000	25.00	40.00	75.00	130	235
1762HA	300,000	6.00	12.50	25.00	50.00	80.00

KM# 2015.1 3 KREUZER

Billon **Ruler:** Franz I **Reverse:** Without cartouche around denomination but with cross after date **Note:** Includes Maria Theresa coins of same date and denomination. See Tyrol listings. Mint mark placement varieties exist for this issue.

Date	Mintage	VG	F	VF	XF	Unc
1750HA	—	50.00	100	200	300	500
Note: Mintage included with KM#2014						
1752HA	—	5.50	11.00	22.50	45.00	70.00
1752WI	—	6.00	12.50	25.00	55.00	85.00
1753HA	384,000	5.50	11.00	22.50	45.00	70.00
1753WI	—	11.00	22.50	45.00	85.00	160
1754HA	113,000	5.50	11.00	22.50	45.00	70.00
1754WI	—	8.00	15.00	30.00	60.00	90.00
1755HA	90,000	2.50	6.00	15.00	30.00	50.00
1755WI	—	8.00	15.00	30.00	60.00	90.00
1756HA	121,000	2.50	6.00	15.00	30.00	50.00
1756WI	—	15.00	25.00	45.00	85.00	160
1759HA	29,000	2.50	6.00	15.00	30.00	50.00
1760HA	102,000	2.50	6.00	15.00	30.00	50.00
1761HA	497,000	2.50	6.00	15.00	30.00	50.00

Date	Mintage	VG	F	VF	XF	Unc
1762HA	—	5.00	10.00	20.00	40.00	60.00

Note: Mintage included with KM#2014

Date	Mintage	VG	F	VF	XF	Unc
1763HA	125,000	5.00	10.00	20.00	40.00	60.00

KM# 2013.2 3 KREUZER

Billon **Ruler:** Franz I **Reverse:** Cross after date

Date	Mintage	VG	F	VF	XF	Unc
1751GR	—	10.00	20.00	35.00	70.00	120
1751WI	—	8.00	15.00	30.00	60.00	90.00
1753PR	—	25.00	40.00	75.00	130	235
1754GR	—	10.00	20.00	35.00	70.00	120
1754PR	—	11.00	22.50	45.00	90.00	150
1761PR	—	25.00	40.00	75.00	130	235

KM# 2016.2 3 KREUZER

Billon **Obverse:** Legend ends: "...M. H. D."

Date	Mintage	VG	F	VF	XF	Unc
1751KB	—	15.00	30.00	55.00	100	190
1752KB	—	15.00	30.00	55.00	100	190
1757KB	—	10.00	20.00	35.00	70.00	120
1758KB	—	10.00	20.00	40.00	80.00	150
1759KB	—	10.00	20.00	35.00	70.00	120
1760KB	—	10.00	20.00	40.00	80.00	150
1761KB	—	10.00	20.00	40.00	80.00	150
1762KB	—	10.00	20.00	40.00	80.00	150
1763KB	—	10.00	20.00	40.00	80.00	150
1764KB	—	10.00	20.00	40.00	80.00	150
1765KB	—	10.00	20.00	40.00	80.00	150

KM# 2016.1 3 KREUZER

Billon **Obverse:** Drapes over shoulder without pleats **Note:** Mint mark placement varieties exist for this issue.

Date	Mintage	VG	F	VF	XF	Unc
1752NB	—	17.50	35.00	70.00	120	225
1756HA	—	2.50	6.00	12.50	25.00	40.00
1757NB	—	17.50	35.00	70.00	120	225
1757WI	—	8.00	15.00	30.00	55.00	85.00
1758NB	—	17.50	35.00	70.00	120	225
1759NB	—	17.50	35.00	70.00	120	225
1760HA	—	2.50	6.00	12.50	25.00	40.00
1760NB	—	17.50	35.00	70.00	120	225
1760WI	—	10.00	20.00	35.00	65.00	100
1761HA	—	2.50	6.00	12.50	25.00	40.00

Note: Mintage included in KM#2015

Date	Mintage	VG	F	VF	XF	Unc
1763HA	—	2.50	6.00	12.50	25.00	40.00

Note: Mintage included in KM#2015

Date	Mintage	VG	F	VF	XF	Unc
1764NB	—	17.50	35.00	70.00	120	225
1765HA	82,000	5.00	10.00	20.00	40.00	60.00
1765NB	—	20.00	35.00	70.00	120	225

KM# 2015.2 3 KREUZER

Billon **Ruler:** Franz I **Obverse:** Legend ends: "...M. H. D." **Note:** Mint mark placement varieties exist for this issue.

Date	Mintage	VG	F	VF	XF	Unc
1753KB	—	15.00	30.00	60.00	110	200
1754KB	—	15.00	30.00	60.00	110	200
1755KB	—	15.00	30.00	60.00	110	200
1756KB	—	15.00	30.00	60.00	110	200
1758KB	—	15.00	30.00	60.00	110	200

KM# 2017 3 KREUZER

Billon **Ruler:** Maria Theresa **Obverse:** Bust of Franz right **Reverse:** Crowned imperial eagle, value below **Note:** Posthumous issue.

Date	Mintage	VG	F	VF	XF	Unc
1765 C-EVM-D(1768)	—	15.00	30.00	60.00	120	225
1765 D-EVM-D(1769)	—	15.00	30.00	60.00	120	225
1765 E-EVM-D(1770)	—	17.50	35.00	70.00	135	245
1765 F-EVM-D(1771)	—	12.50	25.00	55.00	110	200
1765 G-EVM-D(1772)	—	15.00	30.00	60.00	120	225
1765 H-EVM-D(1773)	—	15.00	30.00	60.00	120	225

KM# 1996 3 KREUZER

Billon **Ruler:** Maria Theresa **Obverse:** Veiled bust right **Obv. Legend:** M • THERES • D • G • R • I • HV • BO • REG • **Reverse:** Crowned imperial double eagle, value on breast **Rev. Legend:** ARCH • AUST • DUX • BU • CO • TYR •

Date	Mintage	VG	F	VF	XF	Unc
1765	—	3.50	8.00	20.00	35.00	55.00
1766 C-K	—	3.50	8.00	20.00	35.00	55.00
1767 C-K	—	3.50	8.00	20.00	35.00	55.00
1768 C-K	—	3.50	8.00	20.00	35.00	55.00
1769 C-K	—	3.50	8.00	20.00	50.00	80.00
1770 C-K	—	3.50	8.00	20.00	35.00	55.00
1771 C-K	—	3.50	8.00	30.00	35.00	55.00
1772 C-K	—	3.50	8.00	20.00	35.00	55.00
1773 C-K	—	3.50	8.00	20.00	35.00	55.00
1774 C-A	—	3.50	8.00	20.00	35.00	55.00
1774 C-K	—	10.00	20.00	40.00	70.00	120
1775 C-A	—	7.00	15.00	30.00	50.00	80.00
1776 C-A	—	3.50	8.00	20.00	35.00	55.00
1777 C-A	—	3.50	8.00	20.00	35.00	55.00
1778 C-A	—	5.00	15.00	35.00	60.00	90.00
1779 C-A	—	3.50	8.00	20.00	35.00	55.00
1780 C-A	—	3.50	8.00	20.00	35.00	55.00

KM# 2057.1 3 KREUZER

Billon **Ruler:** Joseph II **Obverse:** Bust right with lion face on shoulder **Reverse:** Crowned imperial eagle

Date	Mintage	VG	F	VF	XF	Unc
1766B EVM-D	—	17.50	35.00	75.00	150	250
1767B EVM-D	—	17.50	35.00	75.00	150	250
1768B EVM-D	—	17.50	35.00	70.00	135	245
1768E H-G	—	20.00	40.00	80.00	145	250
1768F H-G	32,000	17.50	35.00	75.00	140	245
1769B EVM-D	—	17.50	35.00	70.00	135	245
1770B EVM-D	—	40.00	85.00	150	225	325
1770F A-S	50,000	15.00	30.00	60.00	120	225
1771B EVM-D	—	17.50	35.00	70.00	135	245
1773B EVM-D	—	17.50	35.00	70.00	135	245
1773E H-G	—	17.50	35.00	75.00	150	250
1773A A-S	19,000	17.50	35.00	70.00	135	245
1774E H-G	—	17.50	35.00	70.00	135	245
1775C VS-K	—	17.50	35.00	75.00	140	245
1776C VS-K	—	17.50	35.00	70.00	135	245
1776F VC-S	15,000	17.50	35.00	70.00	135	245
1777C VS-K	—	17.50	45.00	90.00	165	275
1777E H-G	—	20.00	45.00	85.00	150	250
1778C VS-K	—	17.50	35.00	70.00	135	245
1779C VS-K	—	17.50	35.00	65.00	130	240

KM# 2057.2 3 KREUZER

Billon **Ruler:** Joseph II **Obverse:** Without lion face on shoulder **Reverse:** Crowned imperial eagle

Date	Mintage	VG	F	VF	XF	Unc
1767A C-K	—	10.00	20.00	40.00	75.00	125
1768A C-K	—	10.00	20.00	40.00	75.00	125
1770A C-K	—	10.00	20.00	40.00	75.00	125
1771A C-K	—	10.00	20.00	45.00	85.00	135
1773A C-K	—	10.00	20.00	45.00	85.00	135
1774A C-A	—	15.00	25.00	50.00	95.00	150
1775A C-A	—	10.00	20.00	40.00	75.00	125
1776A C-A	—	10.00	20.00	40.00	80.00	130
1777A C-K	—	10.00	20.00	40.00	75.00	125
1777A C-A	—	10.00	20.00	35.00	70.00	120
1778A C-A	—	10.00	20.00	40.00	75.00	125
1779A C-A	—	10.00	20.00	35.00	70.00	120
1780A C-A	—	10.00	20.00	40.00	75.00	125

KM# 2058.1 3 KREUZER

Billon **Ruler:** Joseph II **Obverse:** Bust right; legend ends: "... REX." **Note:** Varieties exist with letter "U" instead of "V" in "HU".

Date	Mintage	VG	F	VF	XF	Unc
1780A	—	25.00	55.00	110	150	250
1781A	—	17.50	35.00	70.00	100	190
1781B	—	20.00	40.00	80.00	120	225
1782B	—	20.00	40.00	80.00	120	225
1783B	—	25.00	50.00	100	150	250
1784B	—	20.00	40.00	80.00	120	225

KM# 2058.2 3 KREUZER

Billon **Obverse:** Bust right with lion on shoulder; Legend ends: "... REX." **Rev. Legend:** ARCH....

Date	Mintage	VG	F	VF	XF	Unc
1781E	—	30.00	60.00	110	180	285
1781F	12,000	20.00	40.00	80.00	140	245
1783F	—	—	—	—	—	—

Note: Reported, not confirmed

KM# 2059 3 KREUZER

Billon **Ruler:** Joseph II **Obverse:** Head right **Obv. Legend:** IOS • II • D • G • R • I • S • A • GE • ... **Reverse:** Crowned imperial double eagle **Rev. Legend:** ARCH • A • D • HV • ...

Date	Mintage	VG	F	VF	XF	Unc
1782A	—	7.50	15.00	30.00	60.00	90.00
1783A	—	6.00	12.00	20.00	40.00	60.00
1783C	—	—	—	—	—	—

Note: Reported, not confirmed

Date	Mintage	VG	F	VF	XF	Unc
1783E	—	7.50	15.00	35.00	70.00	120
1783G	—	40.00	100	200	350	550
1784A	—	6.00	12.00	20.00	40.00	60.00
1785E	—	7.50	15.00	35.00	70.00	120
1786A	—	6.00	12.00	20.00	40.00	60.00
1786B	—	7.50	15.00	35.00	70.00	120
1786E	—	7.50	15.00	35.00	70.00	120
1787A	—	6.00	12.00	20.00	40.00	60.00
1787B	—	7.50	15.00	30.00	60.00	90.00
1787G	—	7.50	15.00	35.00	70.00	120
1788A	—	6.00	12.00	20.00	40.00	60.00
1788B	—	6.00	12.00	20.00	40.00	60.00
1789A	—	6.00	12.00	20.00	40.00	60.00
1790A	—	7.50	15.00	35.00	70.00	120
1790B	—	6.00	12.00	25.00	50.00	80.00

KM# 2095 3 KREUZER

0.3460 Silver **Ruler:** Leopold II **Obverse:** Head right **Obv. Legend:** LEOP • II • D • G • R • I • S • A • GE • HV • BO • REX • **Reverse:** Crowned imperial double eagle with value on breast **Rev. Legend:** ARCH • A • D • BVRG • LOTH • M • D • H •

Date	Mintage	F	VF	XF	Unc
1790A	—	15.00	40.00	100	175
1791A	—	15.00	40.00	100	175
1791B	—	15.00	40.00	100	175

Note: Varieties exist for 1791 with larger letter X after date

Date	Mintage	F	VF	XF	Unc
1792A	—	15.00	40.00	100	175

Note: Varieties exist for 1792 with smaller numbers

Date	Mintage	F	VF	XF	Unc
1792B	—	15.00	40.00	100	175
1792G	—	30.00	65.00	150	225

KM# 2114 3 KREUZER

0.3460 Silver **Ruler:** Franz II (I) **Obverse:** Head right **Obv. Legend:** FRANC • II • D • G • R • I • S • A • GE • HV • BO • REX • **Reverse:** Crowned imperial double eagle with value on breast **Rev. Legend:** ARCH • A • D • BVRG • LOTH • M • D • H •

Date	Mintage	F	VF	XF	Unc
1792B	—	20.00	40.00	90.00	180
1792G Rare	—	—	—	—	—
1793B	—	20.00	40.00	90.00	180
1793F	12,000	25.00	50.00	120	200
1793G Rare	—	—	—	—	—
1794A	—	30.00	60.00	120	225
1794B	—	20.00	40.00	90.00	180
1795/2B	—	10.00	20.00	40.00	90.00
1795B	—	10.00	25.00	55.00	110
1796A Rare	—	—	—	—	—
1796B	—	15.00	30.00	75.00	150
1796E	—	30.00	60.00	120	225
1796F	14,000	20.00	45.00	95.00	200
1796G Rare	—	—	—	—	—
1797A Rare	37,000	—	—	—	—
1798A	14,000	35.00	65.00	130	250
1799A Rare	1,420	—	—	—	—

KM# 2115.1 3 KREUZER

17.0700 g., Copper **Ruler:** Franz II (I) **Obverse:** Head right **Obv. Legend:** FRANC • D • G • R • I • S • A • GER • HVN • BOH • REX • ... **Reverse:** Crowned imperial double eagle, value on breast

Date	Mintage	F	VF	XF	Unc
1799A	—	12.50	25.00	70.00	120
1799B	48,459,000	10.00	20.00	60.00	120
1799C	—	35.00	75.00	150	300

KM# 2115.2 3 KREUZER

8.7500 g., Copper **Ruler:** Franz II (I) **Obverse:** Head right **Reverse:** Crowned imperial double eagle, value on breast **Note:** Reduced weight.

Date	Mintage	F	VF	XF	Unc
1800A	—	1.50	4.00	8.00	25.00

KM# 2115.3 3 KREUZER

8.7500 g., Copper **Ruler:** Franz II (I) **Obverse:** Head right **Obv. Legend:** REX. **Reverse:** Crowned imperial double eagle, value on breast **Note:** Varieties of tail feathers and heads exist.

Date	Mintage	F	VF	XF	Unc
1800B	74,558,000	2.50	5.00	12.50	40.00
1800C	—	2.50	5.00	12.50	40.00
1800D	—	50.00	100	200	—
1800E	—	6.00	15.00	45.00	90.00
1800F	—	6.00	12.50	30.00	60.00
1800G	—	5.00	10.00	20.00	40.00
1800S	—	3.00	6.00	12.00	25.00

KM# 2060 5 KREUZER

2.3300 g., 0.4380 Silver .0328 oz. ASW **Ruler:** Joseph II **Obverse:** Head right in wreath

Date	Mintage	VG	F	VF	XF	Unc
1783A	—	35.00	75.00	125	200	300

KM# 2061 5 KREUZER

2.3300 g., 0.4380 Silver .0328 oz. ASW **Ruler:** Joseph II **Obverse:** Wreath open above head

Date	Mintage	VG	F	VF	XF	Unc
1788A	—	15.00	25.00	50.00	100	190
1790A	—	7.50	15.00	35.00	70.00	120

KM# 2018 6 KREUZER

3.2900 g., 0.4380 Silver .0463 oz. ASW **Ruler:** Franz I **Obverse:** Draped bust right **Obv. Legend:** FRANC • D: G • R • I • S: A • GER • IER: REX • **Reverse:** Crowned imperial double eagle, shield on breast **Rev. Legend:** IN TE DOMINE SPERAVI

Date	Mintage	VG	F	VF	XF	Unc
1747HA	905,000	7.50	15.00	30.00	55.00	85.00

Note: Includes Maria Theresa coins of same date and denomination; See Tyrol listings

Date	Mintage	VG	F	VF	XF	Unc
1747PR	—	50.00	150	250	400	600
1747WI	—	7.50	15.00	30.00	60.00	90.00
1748HA	550,000	7.50	15.00	30.00	60.00	90.00

Note: Includes Maria Theresa coins of same date and denomination; See Tyrol listings

Date	Mintage	VG	F	VF	XF	Unc
1748PR	—	50.00	150	250	400	600
1748WI	—	10.00	20.00	40.00	80.00	135

KM# 2019 6 KREUZER

3.2900 g., 0.4380 Silver .0463 oz. ASW **Ruler:** Franz I **Obverse:** Bust with armor on shoulder

Date	Mintage	VG	F	VF	XF	Unc
1747HA	—	10.00	20.00	35.00	70.00	120

Note: Mintage included in KM#2018

KM# 2020 6 KREUZER

3.2900 g., 0.4380 Silver .0463 oz. ASW **Obverse:** Modified bust

Date	Mintage	VG	F	VF	XF	Unc
1748HA	—	—	—	—	—	—

Note: Mintage included in KM#2018

KM# 2127 6 KREUZER

3.2900 g., 0.4380 Silver .0463 oz. ASW

Date	Mintage	F	VF	XF	Unc
1795A	—	5.00	10.00	25.00	50.00
1795B	36,127,000	5.00	10.00	25.00	50.00
1795C Rare	—	—	—	—	—
1795E	—	50.00	100	200	300
1795F	3,090,000	30.00	60.00	100	150

Note: Struck through 1800 with 1795 date

Date	Mintage	F	VF	XF	Unc
1795G	—	35.00	70.00	125	200

KM# 2128 6 KREUZER

Copper **Ruler:** Franz II (I) **Obverse:** Head right **Obv. Legend:** FRANZ • II • ROM • KAI • KON • Z • HU • U • BO • ERZH • Z • OEST • **Reverse:** Crowned imperial double eagle with value on breast **Rev. Legend:** SECUS • KREUTZER • ERBLAN....

Date	Mintage	F	VF	XF	Unc
1800A	—	2.00	6.00	12.00	25.00
1800B	225,017,000	2.00	6.00	12.00	25.00
1800C	—	2.00	6.00	12.00	25.00
1800C FRANC	—	—	—	—	—
1800D	—	30.00	60.00	120	250
1800E	—	2.00	6.00	12.00	25.00
1800F	—	8.00	16.00	30.00	80.00
1800G	—	15.00	30.00	75.00	150
1800S	—	2.00	6.00	12.00	25.00

KM# 2022 7 KREUZER

3.2400 g., 0.4200 Silver .0437 oz. ASW **Ruler:** Franz I **Obverse:** Bust with pleated drapes without armor

Date	Mintage	VG	F	VF	XF	Unc
1751HA	49,000	25.00	50.00	100	150	250

KM# 2021 7 KREUZER

3.2400 g., 0.4200 Silver .0437 oz. ASW **Ruler:** Franz I **Obverse:** Bust right **Obv. Legend:** FRANC • D: G • R • I • S • A • GE • IER • R • LO • B • M • H • D • **Reverse:** Crowned imperial double eagle with shield on breast **Rev. Legend:** IN TE DOMINE SPERAVI • **Note:** Varieties exist.

Date	Mintage	VG	F	VF	XF	Unc
1751GR Unique	—	—	—	—	—	—
1751WI	—	50.00	100	160	225	350
1752HA	49,000	7.50	15.00	25.00	45.00	70.00

Note: Includes Maria Theresa coins of same date and denomination; See Hall listings

Date	Mintage	VG	F	VF	XF	Unc
1753HA	145,000	7.50	15.00	30.00	55.00	85.00

Note: Includes Maria Theresa coins of same date and denomination; See Hall listings

Date	Mintage	VG	F	VF	XF	Unc
1753/2WI Unique	—	—	—	—	—	—
1754KB	—	—	—	—	—	—

Note: Reported, not confirmed

Date	Mintage	VG	F	VF	XF	Unc
1754PR Unique	—	—	—	—	—	—
1755KB	—	7.50	15.00	30.00	60.00	90.00
1756KB	—	7.50	15.00	30.00	60.00	90.00
1758HA	43,000	7.50	15.00	30.00	55.00	85.00
1758KB	—	35.00	75.00	100	175	285
1759KB	—	7.50	15.00	25.00	50.00	80.00
1760HA	140,000	5.00	10.00	20.00	40.00	60.00

Note: Includes Maria Theresa coins of same date and denomination; See Hall listings

Date	Mintage	VG	F	VF	XF	Unc
1760KB	—	5.00	10.00	20.00	45.00	70.00
1761/0HA	133,000	12.00	25.00	50.00	100	190

Note: Includes Maria Theresa coins of same date and denomination; See Hall listings

Date	Mintage	VG	F	VF	XF	Unc
1761HA	Inc. above	7.50	15.00	25.00	50.00	80.00
1761KB	—	5.00	10.00	20.00	45.00	70.00
1762HA	147,000	10.00	20.00	35.00	70.00	120

Note: Includes Maria Theresa coins of same date and denomination; See Hall listings

Date	Mintage	VG	F	VF	XF	Unc
1762KB	—	5.00	10.00	20.00	45.00	70.00
1762PR	—	5.00	10.00	20.00	45.00	70.00
1763HA	164,000	10.00	20.00	35.00	65.00	100

Note: Includes Maria Theresa coins of same date and denomination; See Hall listings

Date	Mintage	VG	F	VF	XF	Unc
1763KB	—	5.00	10.00	20.00	45.00	70.00
1763PR	—	5.00	10.00	20.00	45.00	70.00
1764KB	—	7.50	15.00	30.00	55.00	85.00
1764PR	—	7.50	15.00	30.00	55.00	85.00
1765KB	—	5.00	10.00	20.00	40.00	60.00

KM# 2062 7 KREUZER

3.2400 g., 0.4200 Silver .0437 oz. ASW **Ruler:** Joseph II **Obverse:** Bust right, as joint ruler **Note:** Varieties exist.

Date	Mintage	VG	F	VF	XF	Unc
1768A C-K	—	20.00	30.00	60.00	170	275
1769A C-K	—	20.00	30.00	60.00	170	275
1770/69A C-K	—	35.00	75.00	110	200	300
1770A C-K	—	15.00	20.00	50.00	130	245
1771A C-K	—	15.00	20.00	50.00	120	225
1776A C-A	—	50.00	100	150	225	350

KM# C1973 7 KREUZER

3.2400 g., 0.4200 Silver .0437 oz. ASW **Ruler:** Maria Theresa

Date	Mintage	VG	F	VF	XF	Unc
1768 C-K	—	10.00	20.00	35.00	70.00	120
1769 C-K	—	10.00	20.00	35.00	70.00	120
1770 C-K	—	10.00	20.00	35.00	70.00	120
1771 C-K	—	7.50	15.00	30.00	60.00	90.00
1772 C-K	—	10.00	20.00	35.00	70.00	120
1773 C-K	—	10.00	20.00	35.00	70.00	120
1774/3 C-A	—	10.00	20.00	40.00	80.00	135
1774 C-A	—	7.50	15.00	30.00	60.00	90.00
1775 C-A	—	7.50	15.00	30.00	60.00	90.00
1776/5 C-A	—	10.00	20.00	40.00	80.00	135
1776 C-A	—	7.50	15.00	30.00	60.00	90.00
1777 C-A	—	10.00	20.00	35.00	70.00	120

KM# 2023 10 KREUZER

3.8900 g., 0.5000 Silver .0625 oz. ASW **Ruler:** Franz I **Obverse:** Bust within wreath **Obv. Legend:** FRANC • D • G • R • IMP • S • A • G • ER • IER • REX • LO • B • M • H • D • **Reverse:** Crowned double eagle above boxed value **Rev. Legend:** INTE DOMINE - SPERAVI

Date	Mintage	VG	F	VF	XF	Unc
1754WI	—	7.50	17.50	40.00	60.00	90.00
1755GR	—	7.50	22.50	50.00	90.00	145
1755HA	264,000	7.50	12.50	30.00	50.00	80.00

Note: Includes Maria Theresa coins of same date and denomination; See Hall listings

Date	Mintage	VG	F	VF	XF	Unc
1755KB	—	7.50	20.00	45.00	70.00	120
1755WI	—	7.50	17.50	40.00	60.00	90.00
1756HA	143,000	7.50	20.00	45.00	70.00	120
1756WI	—	7.50	22.50	50.00	90.00	145
1757GR	—	7.50	22.50	50.00	90.00	145
1757HA	119,000	7.50	20.00	45.00	70.00	120
1758GR	—	7.50	12.50	30.00	50.00	80.00
1758KB	—	7.50	22.50	50.00	90.00	145
1758PR	—	7.50	22.50	50.00	90.00	145
1759KB	—	7.50	22.50	50.00	90.00	145
1759PR	—	7.50	20.00	45.00	70.00	120
1760KB	—	7.50	20.00	45.00	70.00	120
1761/57HA	54,000	7.50	20.00	45.00	70.00	120

Note: Includes Maria Theresa coins of same date and denomination; See Hall listings

Date	Mintage	VG	F	VF	XF	Unc
1761HA	Inc. above	7.50	20.00	45.00	70.00	120
1761PR	—	7.50	20.00	50.00	90.00	145
1762HA	—	7.50	20.00	45.00	70.00	120
1763GR	—	7.50	17.50	40.00	60.00	90.00
1763HA	—	7.50	20.00	45.00	70.00	120
1763PR	—	7.50	20.00	45.00	70.00	120
1764GR	—	7.50	12.50	30.00	50.00	80.00
1764HA	—	7.50	12.50	30.00	50.00	80.00
1764KB	—	7.50	12.50	30.00	50.00	80.00
1765GR	—	7.50	12.50	30.00	50.00	80.00
1765HA	153,000	7.50	12.50	30.00	50.00	80.00

Note: Includes Maria Theresa coins of same date and denomination; See Hall listings

Date	Mintage	VG	F	VF	XF	Unc
1765KB	—	7.50	12.50	30.00	50.00	80.00
1765WI	—	7.50	20.00	45.00	70.00	120
1766GR	—	50.00	100	150	250	400

KM# 2024 10 KREUZER

3.8900 g., 0.5000 Silver .0625 oz. ASW **Ruler:** Maria Theresa **Obverse:** Bust of Franz right within wreath **Reverse:** Crowned double eagle above boxed value **Note:** Posthumous issue. Similar to KM#2023.

Date	Mintage	VG	F	VF	XF	Unc
1765B A-EVM-D(1766)	—	15.00	30.00	60.00	120	220
1765B B-EVM-D(1767)	—	15.00	30.00	60.00	120	220
1765B D-EVM-D(1769)	—	15.00	30.00	60.00	120	220

KM# 2063 10 KREUZER

3.8900 g., 0.5000 Silver .0625 oz. ASW **Ruler:** Joseph II **Obverse:** Bust right in wreath, as joint ruler

Date	Mintage	VG	F	VF	XF	Unc
1765B EVM D	—	12.50	35.00	70.00	140	240
1766B EVM D	—	12.50	35.00	70.00	140	240
1767A C-K	—	12.50	30.00	60.00	125	220
1767B EVM-D	247,000	12.50	30.00	60.00	125	220
1768A C-K	—	12.50	30.00	60.00	125	220
1768B EVM-D	142,000	12.50	35.00	70.00	140	240
1768C VS-S	—	12.50	35.00	75.00	150	250
1768H S-C	—	12.50	25.00	55.00	110	200
1769A C-K	—	12.50	30.00	60.00	125	220
1769B EVM-D	22,000	25.00	50.00	100	200	300
1770A C-K	—	12.50	30.00	60.00	125	220
1770E H-G	—	12.50	30.00	65.00	130	230
1770F A-S	31,000	12.50	30.00	60.00	125	220

Note: Includes Maria Theresa coins of same date and denomination; See Hall listings

Date	Mintage	VG	F	VF	XF	Unc
1771A C-K	—	12.50	25.00	50.00	100	190
1771F A-S	156,000	12.50	30.00	60.00	125	220

Note: Includes Maria Theresa coins of same date and denomination; See Hall listings

Date	Mintage	VG	F	VF	XF	Unc
1772A C-K	—	12.50	25.00	50.00	100	190
1772/1F A-S	115,000	12.50	35.00	70.00	140	240

Note: Includes Maria Theresa coins of same date and denomination; See Hall listings

Date	Mintage	VG	F	VF	XF	Unc
1772F A-S	Inc. above	12.50	30.00	60.00	125	220
1772H S-C	—	12.50	25.00	55.00	110	200
1773A C-K	—	12.50	25.00	50.00	100	190
1773F A-S	113,000	12.50	30.00	60.00	125	220

Note: Includes Maria Theresa coins of same date and denomination; See Hall listings

Date	Mintage	VG	F	VF	XF	Unc
1773H S-C	—	12.50	25.00	55.00	110	200
1774F A-S	79,000	12.50	30.00	60.00	125	220

Note: Includes Maria Theresa coins of same date and denomination; See Hall listings

Date	Mintage	VG	F	VF	XF	Unc
1774F VC-S	Inc. above	12.50	35.00	70.00	140	240
1774H S-C	—	12.50	25.00	55.00	110	200
1775E H-G	—	12.50	30.00	65.00	130	230
1775F A-S	—	—	—	—	—	—

Note: Reported, not confirmed

Date	Mintage	VG	F	VF	XF	Unc
1775F VC-S	—	12.50	30.00	60.00	125	220
1776E H-G	—	12.50	30.00	65.00	130	230
1777C VS-K	—	12.50	35.00	75.00	150	250
1777F VC-S	23,000	12.50	30.00	60.00	125	220

Note: Includes Maria Theresa coins of same date and denomination; See Hall listings

Date	Mintage	VG	F	VF	XF	Unc
1778A C-A	—	12.50	25.00	50.00	100	190
1778C VS-K	—	12.50	35.00	75.00	150	250
1778E H-S	—	12.50	30.00	65.00	130	230
1778F VC-S	777,000	12.50	30.00	60.00	125	220

Note: Includes Maria Theresa coins of same date and denomination; See Hall listings

Date	Mintage	VG	F	VF	XF	Unc
1779A C-A	—	12.50	25.00	50.00	100	190

Date	Mintage	VG	F	VF	XF	Unc
1779C VS-K	—	12.50	35.00	75.00	150	250
1779G IB-IV	—	15.00	35.00	70.00	140	240
1780E H-S	—	12.50	30.00	65.00	130	230

KM# 2064 10 KREUZER

3.8900 g., 0.5000 Silver .0625 oz. ASW **Ruler:** Joseph II
Obverse: Bust right in wreath, as sole ruler

Date	Mintage	VG	F	VF	XF	Unc
1781C	—	20.00	40.00	75.00	130	230
1782C	—	20.00	40.00	75.00	130	230
1782E	—	20.00	45.00	85.00	150	250
1783E	—	20.00	45.00	85.00	150	250
1783G	—	20.00	45.00	85.00	150	250
1783H	—	15.00	35.00	65.00	120	220
1784H	—	30.00	60.00	100	175	275
1785F	—	20.00	45.00	85.00	150	250
1785H	—	—	—	—	—	—
Note: Reported, not confirmed						
1787F	34,000	20.00	45.00	85.00	150	250
1787H	—	15.00	35.00	65.00	120	220
1788H	—	20.00	45.00	85.00	150	250
1790F	—	—	—	—	—	—
Note: Reported, not confirmed						

KM# 2065 10 KREUZER

3.8900 g., 0.5000 Silver .0625 oz. ASW **Ruler:** Joseph II
Obverse: Head right in closed wreath **Reverse:** Crowned imperial eagle above date

Date	Mintage	VG	F	VF	XF	Unc
1782A	—	3.50	7.50	15.00	30.00	50.00
1783A	—	3.50	7.50	15.00	30.00	50.00
1785B	170,000	10.00	15.00	30.00	50.00	80.00
1787B	2,806,000	10.00	25.00	50.00	75.00	125
1787E	—	15.00	30.00	65.00	100	190
1788B	2,023,000	10.00	15.00	30.00	50.00	80.00
1788E	—	15.00	30.00	65.00	100	190

KM# 2066 10 KREUZER

3.8900 g., 0.5000 Silver .0625 oz. ASW **Ruler:** Joseph II
Obverse: Open wreath above head

Date	Mintage	VG	F	VF	XF	Unc
1784A	—	15.00	30.00	60.00	80.00	135
1785A	—	20.00	40.00	75.00	120	220
1786A	—	10.00	20.00	40.00	60.00	90.00
1787A	—	7.50	15.00	30.00	50.00	80.00
1787B	Inc. above	10.00	25.00	50.00	75.00	125
1788A	—	7.50	15.00	30.00	50.00	80.00
1788B	Inc. above	7.50	15.00	30.00	50.00	80.00
1788E	—	—	—	—	—	—
Note: Reported, not confirmed						
1789A	—	15.00	35.00	75.00	120	220
1789B	2,626,000	7.50	15.00	30.00	50.00	80.00
1789E	—	15.00	30.00	65.00	100	190
1790A	—	15.00	30.00	65.00	100	190
1790B	2,513,000	7.50	15.00	30.00	50.00	80.00
1790E	—	15.00	30.00	65.00	100	190

KM# 2096 10 KREUZER

0.5000 Silver **Ruler:** Leopold II **Obverse:** Bust right within wreath **Obv. Legend:** LEOP • II • D • G • R • I • S • A • GERM • HV • BO • REX • **Reverse:** Crowned imperial double eagle

Date	Mintage	F	VF	XF	Unc
1790A	—	20.00	45.00	85.00	150
1791A	—	20.00	45.00	85.00	150
1791B	1,254,000	25.00	50.00	100	175
1791H Rare	—	—	—	—	—
1792A	—	35.00	65.00	125	200
1792B	1,095,000	20.00	45.00	85.00	150
1792E Rare	—	—	—	—	—

KM# 2130 10 KREUZER

0.5000 Silver **Ruler:** Franz II (I) **Obverse:** Bust right within wreath **Reverse:** Crowned imperial double eagle

Date	Mintage	F	VF	XF	Unc
1792A	—	25.00	50.00	100	175
1792B	356,000	25.00	50.00	100	175
1792E Rare	—	—	—	—	—
1792F Rare	—	—	—	—	—
1793A	—	20.00	45.00	90.00	165
1794B	452,000	20.00	40.00	80.00	150
1794E	—	30.00	60.00	120	250
1795B Unique	101,000	—	—	—	—
1795C	—	40.00	80.00	160	300
1795E	—	25.00	55.00	110	200
1795G Rare	—	—	—	—	—
1796B	124,000	30.00	60.00	120	250
1796E	—	20.00	45.00	85.00	160
1797E	—	25.00	50.00	100	175

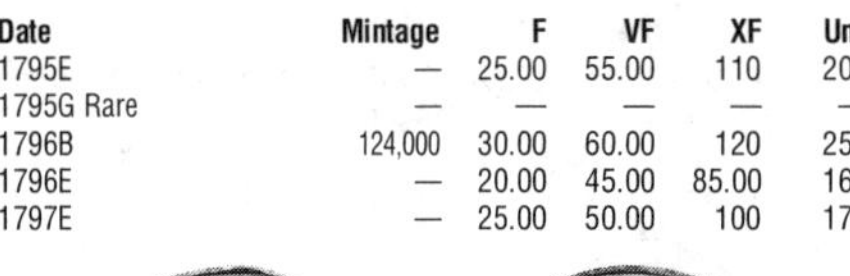

KM# 2137 12 KREUZER

4.6800 g., 0.2500 Silver .0376 oz. ASW **Ruler:** Franz II (I)
Obverse: Crowned imperial double eagle **Obv. Legend:** SCHEID • MUNZ • KAI • KON • ERBLANDISCHE • **Reverse:** Denomination and date above sprays of palm and laurel **Note:** Uniface pieces exist, struck through 1800.

Date	Mintage	F	VF	XF	Unc
1795A	—	5.00	12.00	32.00	65.00
1795B	85,036,000	5.00	15.00	40.00	80.00
1795C	—	10.00	25.00	60.00	120
1795E	—	10.00	30.00	70.00	140
1795F	10,340,000	10.00	20.00	50.00	100
1795G	—	10.00	30.00	70.00	135

KM# 2025 15 KREUZER

6.4000 g., 0.5630 Silver .1158 oz. ASW **Ruler:** Franz I **Obverse:** Armored bust right **Obv. Legend:** FRANC: D: G: R: I: S: A: GER: IER: R: LO: B: M: H: D: **Reverse:** Crowned imperial double eagle **Rev. Legend:** IN TE DOMINE SPERAVI • **Note:** Varieties exist.

Date	Mintage	VG	F	VF	XF	Unc
1747CA	—	25.00	50.00	95.00	160	265
1747GR	—	20.00	40.00	80.00	150	250
1747KB	—	7.50	15.00	30.00	60.00	100
1747NB	—	15.00	30.00	60.00	120	220
1747PR	—	10.00	20.00	40.00	80.00	145
1747WI	—	7.50	15.00	30.00	60.00	100
1748GR	—	20.00	40.00	80.00	150	250
1748HA	62,000	20.00	40.00	80.00	150	250
Note: Includes Maria Theresa coins of same date and denomination; See Hall listings						
1748KB	—	7.50	15.00	30.00	60.00	100
1748NB	—	17.50	35.00	75.00	130	230
1748PR	—	7.50	15.00	30.00	60.00	100
1748WI	—	7.50	15.00	30.00	60.00	100
1749HA	255,000	12.50	25.00	50.00	100	200
Note: Includes Maria Theresa coins of same date and denomination; See Hall listings						
1749KB	—	7.50	15.00	30.00	60.00	100
1749NB	—	50.00	100	150	200	300
1749PR	—	7.50	15.00	30.00	60.00	100
1749WI	—	7.50	15.00	30.00	60.00	100
1750CA	—	40.00	60.00	110	200	300
1750GR	—	15.00	30.00	60.00	120	220
1750HA	218,000	15.00	30.00	60.00	120	220
Note: Includes Maria Theresa coins of same date and denomination; See Hall listings						
1750KB	—	7.50	15.00	30.00	60.00	100
1750PR	—	7.50	15.00	30.00	60.00	100
1750WI	—	7.50	15.00	30.00	60.00	100

KM# 2026.1 17 KREUZER

6.1200 g., 0.5420 Silver .1066 oz. ASW **Ruler:** Franz I **Obverse:** Draped bust right **Obv. Legend:** FRANC • D • G • R • I • S • A • GE • IER • R • LO • B • M • H • D • **Reverse:** Crowned imperial double eagle **Rev. Legend:** INTEDOMINE SPERAVI • **Note:** Varieties exist in eagle's tail, mint mark placement, and size of letters in legend.

Date	Mintage	VG	F	VF	XF	Unc
1751CA	—	10.00	20.00	40.00	80.00	145
1751GR	—	10.00	25.00	50.00	100	200
1751HA	Est. 139,000	7.50	15.00	30.00	60.00	100
Note: Includes Maria Theresa coins of same date and denomination; See Tyrol listings						
1751KB	1,833,000	5.00	10.00	22.50	45.00	70.00
1751NB	—	45.00	75.00	125	200	300
1751PR	—	6.00	12.50	25.00	50.00	80.00
1751WI	—	10.00	22.50	45.00	90.00	165
1752GR	—	10.00	25.00	50.00	100	200
1752HA	703,000	10.00	20.00	40.00	80.00	145
1752KB	1,759,000	5.00	10.00	22.50	45.00	70.00
1752NB	—	45.00	75.00	125	200	300
1752PR	—	10.00	20.00	40.00	80.00	145
1752WI	—	10.00	22.50	45.00	90.00	165
1753/2GR	—	10.00	25.00	50.00	100	200
1753GR	—	10.00	25.00	50.00	100	200
1753HA	Est. 1,085,000	5.00	10.00	22.50	45.00	70.00
Note: Includes Maria Theresa coins of same date and denomination; See Tyrol listings						
1753KB	1,786,000	5.00	10.00	22.50	45.00	70.00
1753NB	—	7.50	15.00	30.00	60.00	100
1753PR	—	10.00	20.00	40.00	80.00	145
1753WI	—	12.50	25.00	50.00	90.00	165
1754GR	—	10.00	25.00	50.00	100	200
1754HA	Est. 177,000	5.00	10.00	22.50	45.00	70.00
Note: Includes Maria Theresa coins of same date and denomination; See Tyrol listings						
1754KB	1,849,000	5.00	10.00	22.50	45.00	70.00
1754NB	—	7.50	15.00	30.00	60.00	100
1754PR	—	10.00	20.00	40.00	80.00	145
1755KB	—	5.00	10.00	22.50	45.00	70.00
1755NB	—	7.50	15.00	30.00	60.00	100
1756KB	1,117,000	5.00	10.00	22.50	45.00	70.00
1757KB	944,000	5.00	10.00	22.50	45.00	70.00
1758HA	36,000	5.00	10.00	22.50	45.00	70.00
1758KB	1,074,000	5.00	10.00	22.50	45.00	70.00
1759KB	946,000	5.00	10.00	22.50	45.00	70.00
1760GR	—	10.00	25.00	50.00	100	200
1760KB	1,071,000	5.00	10.00	22.50	45.00	70.00
1761GR	—	10.00	25.00	50.00	100	200
1761HA	Est. 750,000	5.00	10.00	22.50	45.00	70.00
Note: Includes Maria Theresa coins of same date and denomination; See Tyrol listings						
1761KB	1,765,000	5.00	10.00	22.50	45.00	70.00
1762GR	—	8.00	25.00	50.00	100	200
1762HA	Est. 208	5.00	10.00	22.50	45.00	70.00
Note: Includes Maria Theresa coins of same date and denomination; See Tyrol listings						
1762KB	4,091,999	5.00	10.00	22.50	45.00	70.00
1762NB	—	5.00	10.00	22.50	45.00	70.00
1762PR	—	5.00	10.00	22.50	45.00	70.00
1763GR	—	7.00	15.00	35.00	75.00	125
1763/2HA	Est. 135	10.00	20.00	35.00	65.00	110
Note: Includes Maria Theresa coins of same date and denomination; See Tyrol listings						
1763HA	Inc. above	5.00	10.00	22.50	45.00	70.00
1763KB	542,000	5.00	10.00	22.50	45.00	70.00
1763NB	—	7.50	15.00	30.00	60.00	100
1763PR	—	5.00	10.00	22.50	45.00	70.00
1764GR	—	45.00	75.00	125	200	300
1764KB	1,178,000	5.00	10.00	22.50	45.00	70.00
1764NB	—	5.00	10.00	22.50	45.00	70.00
1765KB	2,432,000	5.00	10.00	22.50	45.00	70.00
1765NB	—	5.00	10.00	22.50	45.00	70.00

KM# 2026.2 17 KREUZER

6.1200 g., 0.5420 Silver .1066 oz. ASW **Ruler:** Franz I **Obverse:** Draped bust right **Reverse:** Legend begins at 7 o'clock position

Date	Mintage	VG	F	VF	XF	Unc
1760HA	70,000	12.50	25.00	45.00	75.00	125

KM# 2027 17 KREUZER

6.1200 g., 0.5420 Silver .1066 oz. ASW **Ruler:** Maria Theresa **Obverse:** Draped bust right **Reverse:** Crowned imperial double eagle **Note:** Posthumous issue. Similar to KM#2026.1

Date	Mintage	VG	F	VF	XF	Unc
1765 A(1766)NB	—	35.00	75.00	150	250	350

KM# 2028 20 KREUZER

6.6800 g., 0.5830 Silver .1252 oz. ASW **Ruler:** Franz I **Obverse:** Laureate head right in wreath **Obv. Legend:** FRANC • D • G • R • IMP • S • A • GE • IER • REX • LO • B • M • H • D • **Reverse:** Imperial eagle on pedestal containing value, flanked by branches **Rev. Legend:** INTEDOMINE SPERAVI • **Note:** Varieties exist.

Date	Mintage	VG	F	VF	XF	Unc
1754	—	5.00	10.00	20.00	40.00	60.00
1754GR	—	8.00	16.00	30.00	65.00	100
1754HA	Est. 583,000	3.50	7.50	15.00	30.00	50.00
Note: Includes Maria Theresa coins of same date and denomination; See Hall listings						
1754PR	—	3.50	7.50	15.00	30.00	50.00
1754WI	—	3.50	7.50	15.00	30.00	50.00
1755GR	—	8.00	16.00	30.00	65.00	100

Date	Mintage	VG	F	VF	XF	Unc
1755HA	Est. 622,000	3.50	7.50	15.00	30.00	50.00
Note: Includes Maria Theresa coins of same date and denomination; See Hall listings						
1755KB	—	6.00	12.50	25.00	50.00	80.00
1755NB	—	5.00	10.00	20.00	40.00	60.00
1755PR	—	3.50	7.50	15.00	30.00	50.00
1755WI	—	3.50	7.50	15.00	30.00	50.00
1756GR	—	8.00	16.00	30.00	65.00	100
1756HA	Est. 558,000	3.50	7.50	15.00	30.00	50.00
Note: Includes Maria Theresa coins of same date and denomination; See Hall listings						
1756NB	—	5.00	10.00	20.00	40.00	60.00
1756PR	—	3.50	7.50	15.00	30.00	50.00
1756WI	—	5.00	10.00	20.00	40.00	60.00
1757GR	—	8.00	16.00	30.00	65.00	100
1757HA	Est. 296,000	3.50	7.50	15.00	30.00	50.00
Note: Includes Maria Theresa coins of same date and denomination; See Hall listings						
1757NB	—	5.00	10.00	20.00	40.00	60.00
1757PR	—	3.50	7.50	15.00	30.00	50.00
1757WI	—	5.00	10.00	20.00	40.00	60.00
1758GR	—	8.00	16.00	30.00	65.00	100
1758HA	Est. 549,000	3.50	7.50	15.00	30.00	50.00
Note: Includes Maria Theresa coins of same date and denomination; See Hall listings						
1758KB	—	6.00	12.50	25.00	50.00	80.00
1758NB	—	5.00	10.00	20.00	40.00	60.00
1758PR	—	3.50	7.50	15.00	30.00	50.00
1759GR	—	8.00	16.00	30.00	65.00	100
1759HA	Est. 340,000	5.00	10.00	20.00	40.00	60.00
Note: Includes Maria Theresa coins of same date and denomination; See Hall listings						
1759KB	—	5.00	10.00	20.00	40.00	60.00
1759NB	—	5.00	10.00	20.00	40.00	60.00
1759PR	—	3.50	7.50	15.00	30.00	50.00
1760GR	—	8.00	16.00	30.00	65.00	100
1760HA	Est. 70,000	5.00	10.00	20.00	40.00	60.00
Note: Includes Maria Theresa coins of same date and denomination; See Hall listings						
1760KB	—	5.00	10.00	20.00	40.00	60.00
1760/59NB	—	—	—	—	—	—
1760NB	—	3.50	7.50	15.00	30.00	50.00
1760PR	—	3.50	7.50	15.00	30.00	50.00
1761GR	—	3.50	7.50	15.00	30.00	50.00
1761/57HA	Est. 199,000	5.00	10.00	20.00	40.00	60.00
Note: Includes Maria Theresa coins of same date and denomination; See Hall listings						
1761HA	Inc. above	3.50	7.50	15.00	30.00	50.00
1761KB	—	5.00	10.00	20.00	40.00	60.00
1761NB	—	3.50	7.50	15.00	30.00	50.00
1762NB	—	5.00	10.00	20.00	40.00	60.00
1762WI	—	5.00	10.00	20.00	40.00	60.00
1763HA	Est. 30,000	5.00	10.00	20.00	40.00	60.00
Note: Includes Maria Theresa coins of same date and denomination; See Hall listings						
1763KB	—	3.50	7.50	15.00	30.00	50.00
1763NB	—	5.00	10.00	20.00	40.00	60.00
1763PR	—	5.00	10.00	20.00	40.00	60.00
1763WI	—	3.50	7.50	15.00	30.00	50.00
1764HA	Est. 161,000	5.00	10.00	20.00	40.00	60.00
Note: Includes Maria Theresa coins of same date and denomination; See Hall listings						
1764KB	—	3.50	7.50	15.00	30.00	50.00
1764WI	—	3.50	7.50	15.00	30.00	50.00
1765GR	—	8.00	16.00	30.00	65.00	100
1765HA	Est. 132,000	3.50	7.50	15.00	30.00	50.00
Note: Includes Maria Theresa coins of same date and denomination; See Hall listings						
1765KB	—	3.50	7.50	15.00	30.00	50.00
1765NB	—	3.50	7.50	15.00	30.00	50.00
1765PR	—	5.00	10.00	20.00	40.00	60.00
1765WI	—	3.50	7.50	15.00	30.00	50.00

KM# 1997 20 KREUZER

6.6800 g., 0.5830 Silver .1252 oz. ASW **Ruler:** Maria Theresa **Obverse:** Bust within wreath **Reverse:** Imperial eagle on pedestal containing value, flanked by branches

Date	Mintage	VG	F	VF	XF	Unc
1759	—	35.00	75.00	125	175	275

KM# 1998 20 KREUZER

6.6800 g., 0.5830 Silver .1252 oz. ASW **Ruler:** Maria Theresa **Obverse:** Similar to KM#1999 but veil not folded behind neck

Date	Mintage	VG	F	VF	XF	Unc
1765B	—	12.50	25.00	50.00	100	200
1766B IC-SK	—	10.00	20.00	40.00	75.00	145
1767B IC-SK	—	5.00	10.00	20.00	40.00	70.00

KM# 2031 20 KREUZER

6.6800 g., 0.5830 Silver **Obverse:** Laureate head right within wreath **Reverse:** Similar to KM#1998 **Note:** Appears to be mule of posthumous Franz I obverse with Maria Theresa KM#1998 reverse.

Date	Mintage	VG	F	VF	XF	Unc
1765B H-IC-SK(1773)	—	7.50	15.00	30.00	60.00	90.00

KM# 2030 20 KREUZER

6.6800 g., 0.5830 Silver .1252 oz. ASW **Ruler:** Maria Theresa **Obverse:** Laureate head right within wreath **Obv. Legend:** FRANC • D • G • R • IMP • S • A • GE • IER • REX • LO • B • M • H • D • **Reverse:** Imperial eagle on pedestal containing value, flanked by branches **Rev. Legend:** IN TE DOMINE • SPERAVI • **Note:** Posthumous issue.

Date	Mintage	VG	F	VF	XF	Unc
1765B A-EVM-D(1766)	—	5.00	10.00	20.00	40.00	60.00
1765B B-EVM-D(1767)	—	5.00	10.00	20.00	40.00	60.00
1765B B-EVM-D(1767)	—	5.00	10.00	20.00	40.00	60.00
1765B D-EVM-D(1769)	—	5.00	10.00	20.00	40.00	60.00
1765B BD/BC EVM-D (1769/68)	—	10.00	25.00	40.00	60.00	90.00
1765B E-EVM-D(1770)	—	5.00	10.00	20.00	40.00	60.00
1765B F-EVM-D(1771)	—	5.00	10.00	20.00	40.00	60.00
1765B G-EVM-D(1772)	—	5.00	10.00	20.00	40.00	60.00
1765B H-EVM-D(1773)	—	5.00	10.00	20.00	40.00	60.00
1765B I-EVM-D(1774)	—	5.00	10.00	20.00	40.00	60.00
1765B I-SK-PD(1774)	—	5.00	10.00	20.00	40.00	60.00
1765B K-SK-PD(1775)	—	5.00	10.00	20.00	40.00	60.00
1765B L-SK-PD(1776)	—	5.00	10.00	20.00	40.00	60.00
1765B M-SK-PD(1777)	—	5.00	10.00	20.00	40.00	60.00
1765B N-SK-PD(1778)	—	5.00	10.00	20.00	40.00	60.00
1765B O-SK-PD(1779)	—	5.00	10.00	20.00	40.00	60.00
1765B P-SK-PD(1780)	—	5.00	10.00	20.00	40.00	60.00

KM# 2029 20 KREUZER

6.6800 g., 0.5830 Silver .1252 oz. ASW **Ruler:** Maria Theresa **Obverse:** Similar to KM#2028, but letter below bust signifying year of minting **Note:** Posthumous issue.

Date	Mintage	VG	F	VF	XF	Unc
1765CA A(1766)	—	20.00	40.00	70.00	100	190
1765GR A(1766)	—	6.00	12.50	25.00	50.00	80.00
1765GR B(1767)	—	6.00	12.50	25.00	50.00	80.00
1765HA A(1766)	253,000	10.00	20.00	40.00	75.00	125
1765HA B(1767)	318,000	10.00	20.00	40.00	75.00	125
1765HA C(1768)	Est. 246,000	10.00	20.00	40.00	75.00	125
Note: Includes Maria Theresa coins of same date and denomination; See Hall listings						
1765NB B(1767)	—	5.00	10.00	20.00	40.00	60.00
1765NB C(1768)	—	5.00	10.00	20.00	40.00	60.00
1765NB D(1769)	—	5.00	10.00	20.00	40.00	60.00
1765NB E(1770)	—	5.00	10.00	20.00	40.00	60.00
1765PR A(1766)	—	5.00	10.00	20.00	40.00	60.00
1765PR B(1767)	—	5.00	10.00	20.00	40.00	60.00

KM# 2067.1 20 KREUZER

6.6800 g., 0.5830 Silver **Ruler:** Joseph II **Obverse:** Bust right as joint ruler, lion face on shoulder **Obv. Legend:** IOSEPH • II • D • G • R • I • S • A • GE • REX • A • A • LO • & • M • H • D • **Reverse:** Crowned imperial double eagle, shield on breast, value below **Rev. Legend:** VIRTUTE ET EXEMPLO

Date	Mintage	VG	F	VF	XF	Unc
1765A	—	10.00	20.00	40.00	80.00	135
1765E H-G	—	5.00	10.00	20.00	40.00	60.00
1766A IC-SK	—	10.00	20.00	40.00	80.00	145
1766E H-G	—	5.00	10.00	20.00	40.00	60.00
1767A IC-SK	—	5.00	10.00	25.00	50.00	80.00
1767B EVM-D	—	5.00	10.00	15.00	30.00	50.00
1767C EVS-AS	—	5.00	10.00	20.00	40.00	60.00
1767D CG-AK	—	10.00	15.00	25.00	50.00	80.00
1767G IB-FL	—	5.00	10.00	20.00	40.00	60.00
1767H S-C	—	5.00	10.00	20.00	40.00	60.00
1767 EVS-AS	—	15.00	25.00	45.00	90.00	165
1768A IC-SK	—	5.00	10.00	20.00	40.00	60.00
1768A C-K	—	10.00	15.00	35.00	70.00	120
1768B EVM-D	—	5.00	10.00	15.00	30.00	50.00
1768C EVS-AS	—	5.00	10.00	15.00	30.00	50.00
1768E H-G	—	5.00	10.00	20.00	40.00	60.00
1768G IB-FL	—	5.00	10.00	15.00	30.00	50.00
1769A IC-SK	—	5.00	10.00	15.00	30.00	50.00
1769B EVM-D	—	5.00	10.00	15.00	30.00	50.00
1769C EVS-AS	—	5.00	10.00	15.00	30.00	50.00
1769D CVG-AK	—	5.00	10.00	25.00	50.00	80.00
1769E H-G	—	5.00	10.00	15.00	30.00	50.00
1769F A-S	Est. 259,000	5.00	10.00	15.00	30.00	50.00
Note: Includes Maria Theresa coins of same date and denomination; See Hall listings						
1769G IB-FL	—	5.00	10.00	15.00	30.00	50.00
1769H S-C	—	5.00	10.00	20.00	40.00	60.00
1770A IC-SK	—	5.00	10.00	15.00	30.00	50.00
1770B EVM-D	—	5.00	10.00	15.00	30.00	50.00
1770C EVS-AS	—	5.00	10.00	15.00	30.00	50.00
1770D CG-AK	—	10.00	20.00	40.00	80.00	145
1770D CVG-AK	—	10.00	15.00	30.00	60.00	90.00
1770E H-G	—	5.00	10.00	15.00	30.00	50.00
1770F A-S	Est. 280,000	5.00	10.00	15.00	30.00	50.00
Note: Includes Maria Theresa coins of same date and denomination; See Hall listings						
1770G IB-FL	—	5.00	10.00	15.00	30.00	50.00
1770H S-C	—	5.00	10.00	20.00	40.00	60.00
1771A IC-SK	—	5.00	10.00	20.00	40.00	60.00
1771B EVM-D	—	5.00	10.00	15.00	30.00	50.00
1771C EVS-AS	—	7.50	15.00	25.00	45.00	70.00
1771C EVS-AS	—	5.00	10.00	15.00	30.00	50.00
1771D CVG-AK	—	10.00	15.00	30.00	60.00	90.00
1771E H-G	—	5.00	10.00	20.00	40.00	60.00
1771F A-S	Est. 164,000	5.00	10.00	15.00	30.00	50.00
Note: Includes Maria Theresa coins of same date and denomination; See Hall listings						
1771G IB-FL	—	5.00	10.00	15.00	30.00	50.00
1771H S-C	—	5.00	10.00	20.00	40.00	60.00
1772A IC-SK	—	5.00	10.00	20.00	40.00	60.00
1772B EVM-D	—	5.00	10.00	15.00	30.00	50.00
1772C EVS-AS	—	5.00	10.00	15.00	30.00	50.00
1772F A-S	Est. 153,000	5.00	10.00	15.00	30.00	50.00
Note: Includes Maria Theresa coins of same date and denomination; See Hall listings						
1772G IB-FL	—	5.00	10.00	15.00	30.00	50.00
1772G IB-IV	—	5.00	10.00	15.00	30.00	50.00
1772H S-C	—	10.00	15.00	30.00	50.00	80.00
1772 CVG-AK	—	10.00	20.00	40.00	80.00	145
1773/2B EVM-D	—	5.50	11.50	16.50	32.50	55.00
1773A IC-SK	—	—	—	—	—	—
1773B EVM-D	—	5.00	10.00	15.00	30.00	50.00
1773C EVS-AS	—	5.00	10.00	20.00	40.00	60.00
1773C EVS-IK	—	15.00	25.00	45.00	90.00	165
1773E H-G	—	5.00	10.00	20.00	40.00	60.00
1773F A-S	Est. 418,000	5.00	10.00	15.00	30.00	50.00
Note: Includes Maria Theresa coins of same date and denomination; See Hall listings						
1773G IB-IV	—	5.00	10.00	15.00	30.00	50.00
1773G B-V	—	15.00	25.00	45.00	90.00	165
1773H S-C	—	5.00	10.00	20.00	40.00	60.00
1774A IC-SK	—	5.00	10.00	20.00	40.00	60.00
1774A IC-FA	—	5.00	10.00	20.00	40.00	60.00
1774B EVM-D	—	10.00	15.00	25.00	50.00	80.00
1774B SK-PD	—	5.00	8.00	12.00	25.00	45.00
1774C EVS-IK	—	5.00	10.00	15.00	30.00	50.00
1774E H-G	—	5.00	10.00	20.00	40.00	60.00
1774F VC-S	Est. 307,000	10.00	15.00	30.00	60.00	90.00
Note: Includes Maria Theresa coins of same date and denomination; See Hall listings						
1774F A-S	Inc. above	5.00	10.00	20.00	40.00	60.00
1774G IB-IV	—	5.00	10.00	15.00	30.00	50.00
1774G B-V	—	10.00	15.00	25.00	50.00	80.00
1774H S-F	—	15.00	25.00	45.00	90.00	165
1775A IC-FA	—	10.00	20.00	40.00	80.00	145
1775B SK-PD	—	5.00	10.00	15.00	30.00	50.00
1775C EVS-IK	—	5.00	10.00	20.00	40.00	60.00
1775E H-G	—	5.00	10.00	20.00	40.00	60.00
1775F VC-S	—	5.00	10.00	20.00	40.00	60.00
1775G IB-IV	—	5.00	10.00	15.00	30.00	50.00
1776B SK PD		5.00	8.00	12.00	25.00	45.00
1776C EVS-IK	—	5.00	10.00	20.00	40.00	60.00
1776F VC-S	Est. 388,000	5.00	10.00	15.00	30.00	50.00
Note: Includes Maria Theresa coins of same date and denomination; See Hall listings						
1776G IB-IV	—	5.00	10.00	15.00	30.00	50.00
1777B SK-PD	—	5.00	8.00	12.00	25.00	45.00
1777C EVS-IK	—	5.00	10.00	20.00	40.00	60.00
1777F VC-S	Est. 337,000	5.00	10.00	20.00	40.00	60.00
Note: Includes Maria Theresa coins of same date and denomination; See Hall listings						
1777G IB-IV	—	5.00	10.00	15.00	30.00	50.00
1777H S-F	—	10.00	15.00	25.00	50.00	80.00
1778B SK-PD	—	5.00	10.00	15.00	30.00	50.00
1778C EVS-IK	—	5.00	10.00	20.00	40.00	60.00
1778F VC-S	Est. 4,569,000	5.00	10.00	15.00	30.00	50.00
Note: Includes Maria Theresa coins of same date and denomination; See Hall listings						
1778G IB-IV	—	5.00	10.00	20.00	40.00	60.00
1778H S-F	—	10.00	15.00	25.00	50.00	80.00
1779B SK-PD	—	5.00	10.00	15.00	30.00	50.00
1779C EVS-IK	—	5.00	10.00	20.00	40.00	60.00
1779F VC-S	Est. 788,000	5.00	10.00	20.00	40.00	60.00
Note: Includes Maria Theresa coins of same date and denomination; See Hall listings						
1779G B-V	—	5.00	10.00	15.00	30.00	50.00
1780B SK-PD	—	5.00	10.00	15.00	30.00	50.00
1780C EVS-IK	—	5.00	10.00	20.00	40.00	60.00
1780F VC-S	Est. 300,000	5.00	10.00	20.00	40.00	60.00
Note: Includes Maria Theresa coins of same date and denomination; See Hall listings						
1780G IB-IV	—	5.00	10.00	15.00	30.00	50.00

KM# 1999 20 KREUZER

6.6800 g., 0.5830 Silver .1252 oz. ASW **Ruler:** Maria Theresa **Obverse:** Bust right within wreath **Obv. Legend:** M • THERESIA • D • G • R • IMP • HU • BO • REG • **Reverse:** Crowned imperial double eagle **Rev. Legend:** ARCHID • AUST • DUX • BURG • CO • TYR •

Date	Mintage	VG	F	VF	XF	Unc
1767B IC-SK	—	5.00	10.00	20.00	40.00	60.00
1768B IC-SK	—	5.00	10.00	20.00	40.00	60.00
1769B IC-SK	—	3.00	7.50	15.00	30.00	50.00
1770B IC-SK	—	3.00	7.50	15.00	30.00	50.00
1771/0B IC-SK	—	3.50	9.00	18.50	35.00	55.00
1771B IC-SK	—	3.00	7.50	15.00	30.00	50.00
1772B IC-SK	—	3.00	7.50	15.00	30.00	50.00
1773B IC-SK	—	3.00	7.50	15.00	30.00	50.00
1774B IC-SK	—	5.00	10.00	20.00	40.00	60.00
1774B IC-FA	—	3.00	7.50	15.00	30.00	50.00
1775B IC-FA	—	5.00	10.00	20.00	40.00	60.00
1776B IC-FA	—	5.00	10.00	20.00	40.00	60.00
1777B IC-FA	—	3.00	7.50	15.00	30.00	50.00
1778B IC-FA	—	3.00	4.00	8.00	20.00	35.00
1779B IC-FA	—	5.00	10.00	20.00	40.00	60.00
1780B IC-FA	—	5.00	10.00	20.00	40.00	60.00

KM# 2067.2 20 KREUZER

6.6800 g., 0.5830 Silver **Ruler:** Joseph II **Obverse:** Bust without lion's face on shoulder; as joint ruler

Date	Mintage	VG	F	VF	XF	Unc
1776A IC-FA	—	10.00	20.00	40.00	80.00	145
1777A IC-FA	—	10.00	20.00	40.00	80.00	145
1777E H-S	—	5.00	10.00	20.00	40.00	60.00
1778A IC-FA	—	10.00	20.00	40.00	80.00	145
1778E H-S	—	5.00	10.00	20.00	40.00	60.00
1779A IC-FA	—	7.50	15.00	30.00	60.00	90.00
1779E H-S	—	5.00	10.00	20.00	40.00	60.00
1780E IC-FA	—	7.50	15.00	30.00	60.00	90.00
1780 H-S	—	4.00	8.00	15.00	30.00	50.00

KM# 2068.1 20 KREUZER

6.6800 g., 0.5830 Silver .1252 oz. ASW **Ruler:** Joseph II **Obverse:** Armored bust right, without lion's face on shoulder **Rev. Legend:** Begins: ARCH... **Note:** As sole ruler.

Date	Mintage	VG	F	VF	XF	Unc
1780A	—	10.00	20.00	40.00	80.00	145
1781A	—	5.00	10.00	20.00	40.00	60.00
1781E	—	5.00	10.00	20.00	40.00	60.00
1781G	—	5.00	10.00	20.00	40.00	60.00
1782E	—	5.00	10.00	20.00	40.00	60.00
1782G	—	5.00	10.00	20.00	40.00	60.00

KM# 2068.2 20 KREUZER

6.6800 g., 0.5830 Silver .1252 oz. ASW **Ruler:** Joseph II **Obverse:** Armored bust right, lion face on shoulder **Note:** As sole ruler. Varieties exist.

Date	Mintage	VG	F	VF	XF	Unc
1781B	3,367,000	5.00	10.00	20.00	40.00	60.00
1781C	—	7.50	15.00	30.00	60.00	90.00
1781F	363,000	5.00	10.00	20.00	40.00	60.00
1782B	3,019,000	5.00	10.00	20.00	40.00	60.00
1782C	—	5.00	10.00	20.00	40.00	60.00
1782F	379,000	5.00	10.00	20.00	40.00	60.00
1782H	—	7.50	15.00	30.00	60.00	90.00
1783B	2,259,000	5.00	10.00	20.00	40.00	60.00
1783F	400,000	5.00	10.00	20.00	40.00	60.00
1784F	389,000	5.00	10.00	20.00	40.00	60.00
1785F	494,000	5.00	10.00	20.00	40.00	60.00
1786F	509,000	5.00	10.00	20.00	40.00	60.00
1786/2H	—	5.00	10.00	20.00	40.00	60.00
1786H	—	5.00	10.00	20.00	40.00	60.00
1787F	472,000	5.00	10.00	20.00	40.00	60.00
1787H	—	5.00	10.00	20.00	40.00	60.00

KM# 2069 20 KREUZER

6.6800 g., 0.5830 Silver .1252 oz. ASW **Ruler:** Joseph II **Obverse:** Head right within wreath **Obv. Legend:** IOSEPH • II • D • G • R • ... **Reverse:** Crowned imperial double eagle, shield on breast, value below **Rev. Legend:** ARCH • A • D • B • LOTH • ... **Note:** Varieties exist.

Date	Mintage	VG	F	VF	XF	Unc
1781A	—	—	—	—	—	—

Note: Reported, not confirmed

Date	Mintage	VG	F	VF	XF	Unc
1782A	—	5.00	8.00	15.00	30.00	50.00
1782C	1,057,000	5.00	10.00	20.00	40.00	60.00
1782E	—	10.00	15.00	20.00	40.00	60.00
1782G	—	10.00	15.00	20.00	40.00	60.00
1783A	—	5.00	8.00	15.00	30.00	50.00
1783B	—	4.00	6.00	8.00	17.50	30.00

Note: Mintage included in KM#2068

Date	Mintage	VG	F	VF	XF	Unc
1783C	—	5.00	8.00	15.00	30.00	50.00
1783E	—	5.00	8.00	15.00	30.00	50.00
1783G	—	5.00	10.00	15.00	30.00	50.00
1784A	—	5.00	8.00	15.00	30.00	50.00
1784B	2,861,000	4.00	6.00	8.00	17.50	30.00
1784C	—	5.00	8.00	15.00	30.00	50.00
1784E	—	5.00	8.00	15.00	30.00	50.00
1784G	—	5.00	10.00	15.00	30.00	50.00
1785A	—	5.00	8.00	15.00	30.00	50.00
1785B	3,763,000	4.00	6.00	8.00	17.50	30.00
1785E	—	5.00	10.00	20.00	40.00	60.00
1785G	—	7.50	15.00	20.00	40.00	60.00
1786A	—	5.00	8.00	15.00	30.00	50.00
1786B	4,751,000	4.00	6.00	8.00	17.50	30.00
1786E	—	5.00	10.00	20.00	40.00	60.00
1786G	—	5.00	10.00	15.00	30.00	50.00
1786	—	12.50	25.00	50.00	100	190
1787A	—	5.00	8.00	15.00	30.00	50.00
1787B	18,667,000	4.00	6.00	8.00	17.50	30.00
1787E	—	5.00	8.00	15.00	30.00	50.00
1787F	—	5.00	10.00	20.00	40.00	60.00

Note: Mintage included with KM#2068

Date	Mintage	VG	F	VF	XF	Unc
1787F HETR Rare	—	—	—	—	—	—
1787G	—	5.00	10.00	15.00	30.00	50.00
1787H	—	5.00	10.00	20.00	40.00	60.00
1788B	7,644,000	4.00	6.00	8.00	17.50	30.00
1788E	—	5.00	8.00	15.00	30.00	50.00
1788F	421,000	5.00	10.00	15.00	30.00	50.00
1788G	—	5.00	10.00	15.00	30.00	50.00
1788H	—	5.00	10.00	20.00	40.00	60.00
1789F	434,000	5.00	10.00	15.00	30.00	50.00
1789G	—	5.00	10.00	15.00	30.00	50.00
1789H	—	5.00	10.00	20.00	40.00	60.00
1790F	248,000	5.00	10.00	15.00	30.00	50.00
1790G	—	7.50	15.00	30.00	60.00	90.00

KM# 2070 20 KREUZER

6.6800 g., 0.5830 Silver .1252 oz. ASW **Ruler:** Joseph II **Obverse:** Open wreath above head

Date	Mintage	VG	F	VF	XF	Unc
1786A	—	7.50	15.00	30.00	60.00	90.00
1787A	—	7.50	15.00	30.00	60.00	90.00
1788A	—	7.50	15.00	30.00	60.00	90.00
1788B	145,000	5.00	10.00	20.00	40.00	60.00
1788/7E	—	7.50	15.00	30.00	60.00	90.00
1788E	—	7.50	15.00	30.00	60.00	90.00
1789A	—	7.50	15.00	30.00	60.00	90.00
1789E	—	7.50	15.00	30.00	60.00	90.00
1790A	—	7.50	15.00	35.00	70.00	120
1790E	—	7.50	15.00	30.00	60.00	90.00
1790G	—	7.50	15.00	30.00	60.00	120

KM# 2097 20 KREUZER

6.6800 g., 0.5830 Silver .1252 oz. ASW **Ruler:** Leopold II **Obverse:** Head right within wreath **Obv. Legend:** LEOP • II • D • G • R • I • S • A • GERM • HV • BO • REX • **Reverse:** Crowned imperial double eagle **Rev. Legend:** ARCH • AVSTR • BVRG • ...

Date	Mintage	F	VF	XF	Unc
1790A	—	40.00	85.00	135	225
1791A	—	15.00	30.00	60.00	120
1791B	3,568,000	10.00	20.00	40.00	80.00
1791E	—	15.00	30.00	60.00	120
1791F	259,000	17.50	35.00	75.00	150
1791G	—	15.00	30.00	60.00	120
1791H	—	17.50	35.00	75.00	150
1792A	—	10.00	20.00	40.00	80.00
1792B	3,388,000	10.00	20.00	40.00	80.00
1792E	—	35.00	70.00	110	200
1792F	311,000	20.00	40.00	75.00	150
1792G	—	20.00	40.00	75.00	150
1792H	—	35.00	70.00	110	200

KM# 2139 20 KREUZER

6.6800 g., 0.5830 Silver .1252 oz. ASW **Ruler:** Franz II (I) **Obverse:** Laureate head right within wreath **Obv. Legend:** FRANC • II • D • G • R • I • S • A • GERM • HV • BO • REX • **Reverse:** Crowned imperial double eagle **Rev. Legend:** ARCH • AVST • D • BVRG • LOTH • M • ...

Date	Mintage	F	VF	XF	Unc
1792A	—	15.00	30.00	65.00	130
1792B	2,005,000	10.00	20.00	40.00	90.00
1792E	—	15.00	30.00	60.00	120
1792H	—	15.00	35.00	75.00	120
1793A	—	7.00	15.00	35.00	80.00
1793B	3,833,000	7.00	15.00	30.00	65.00
1793E	—	20.00	40.00	80.00	160
1793F	350,000	15.00	30.00	60.00	100
1793G	—	9.00	20.00	40.00	80.00
1793H	—	9.00	15.00	35.00	75.00
1794B	2,981,000	7.00	15.00	30.00	70.00
1794E	—	9.00	20.00	40.00	80.00
1794F	315,000	12.00	25.00	55.00	110
1794G	—	9.00	20.00	45.00	90.00
1794H	—	12.00	25.00	50.00	100
1795B	4,544,000	7.00	15.00	27.50	60.00
1795C	—	20.00	40.00	85.00	170
1795E	—	9.00	20.00	40.00	90.00
1795F	270,000	7.00	15.00	35.00	70.00
1795G	—	7.00	15.00	35.00	70.00
1795H	—	35.00	60.00	100	175
1796B	1,099,000	7.00	15.00	27.50	60.00
1796C	42,000	15.00	35.00	70.00	140
1796E	—	9.00	20.00	40.00	90.00
1796F	473,000	9.00	20.00	40.00	80.00
1796G	—	9.00	20.00	45.00	90.00
1796H	—	12.00	25.00	50.00	100
1797B	Inc. above	15.00	35.00	70.00	120
1797C	662,000	9.00	20.00	45.00	90.00
1797E	—	7.00	15.00	35.00	80.00
1797F	192,000	20.00	45.00	85.00	150
1797G	—	7.00	15.00	30.00	60.00
1797H	—	9.00	20.00	40.00	85.00

KM# 2148 24 KREUZER

9.3500 g., 0.2500 Silver .0751 oz. ASW **Ruler:** Franz II (I) **Obverse:** Crowned imperial double eagle **Obv. Legend:** FRANZ • II • ROM • KAI • KON • ZU • HU • U • BO • ERZH • ZU • OEST • **Reverse:** Value and date above sprays **Note:** Most of these coins were overstruck as 2 Lire coins for the occupation of Venice in 1801.

Date	Mintage	F	VF	XF	Unc
1800A	—	20.00	50.00	100	200
1800B	—	40.00	100	200	350
1800C	—	30.00	75.00	150	300

KM# 2031.1 30 KREUZER

Silver **Ruler:** Franz I **Obverse:** Draped bust right within square outline **Obv. Legend:** FRANC D: G: ROM: I: S: A: GER: IER: R: LO: B: M: H: D: **Reverse:** Without cross after date **Rev. Legend:** TU DOMINE SPES MEA

Date	Mintage	VG	F	VF	XF	Unc
1746GR	—	75.00	150	275	425	650

KM# 2031.2 30 KREUZER

Silver **Ruler:** Franz I **Obverse:** Draped bust right within square outline **Obv. Legend:** FRANC D : G • R • I • S • A • GE • IER • R • LO • B • M • H • D • **Reverse:** Without cross after date **Rev. Legend:** IN TE DOMINE SPERAVI

Date	Mintage	VG	F	VF	XF	Unc
1746WI	—	20.00	40.00	80.00	140	240
1747WI	—	20.00	40.00	80.00	140	240
1748HA	53,000	15.00	30.00	60.00	120	220
1749HA	118,000	15.00	30.00	60.00	110	210
1749NB	—	20.00	40.00	85.00	150	250
1749WI	—	20.00	40.00	80.00	140	240
1750HA	—	10.00	20.00	40.00	75.00	125
1750KB	—	20.00	45.00	95.00	170	275
1750NB	—	20.00	45.00	95.00	170	275

KM# 2032 30 KREUZER

Silver **Ruler:** Franz I **Obverse:** Draped bust right within square outline **Reverse:** Crowned imperial double eagle **Note:** Similar to KM#2033 but date on obverse.

Date	Mintage	VG	F	VF	XF	Unc
1747	—	25.00	50.00	100	185	285
1748	—	20.00	40.00	90.00	160	265
1765KB	—	30.00	60.00	120	200	300

KM# 2033 30 KREUZER

Silver **Ruler:** Franz I **Obverse:** Draped bust right within square outline **Obv. Legend:** FRANC • D • G • R • I • S • A • GE • IER • R • LO • B • M • H • D • **Reverse:** Cross after date **Rev. Legend:** IN TE DOMINE SPERAVI **Note:** Varieties exist.

Date	Mintage	VG	F	VF	XF	Unc
1751KB	—	20.00	40.00	85.00	150	250
1751NB	—	15.00	30.00	60.00	110	210
1752HA	Est. 37,000	10.00	20.00	40.00	80.00	145

Note: Includes Maria Theresa coins of same date and denomination; See Hall listing

Date	Mintage	VG	F	VF	XF	Unc
1752KB	—	20.00	45.00	95.00	170	275
1752NB	—	20.00	45.00	95.00	170	275
1753/2HA	61,000	8.00	15.00	35.00	70.00	120
1753HA	Inc. above	8.00	15.00	35.00	70.00	120
1758/7HA	6,000	20.00	40.00	80.00	140	240
1758HA	Inc. above	20.00	40.00	80.00	140	240
1760/58HA	—	20.00	40.00	80.00	140	240
1760HA	—	20.00	40.00	80.00	140	240
1765WI	—	20.00	40.00	85.00	150	250

KM# 2071 30 KREUZER

Silver **Ruler:** Joseph II **Obverse:** Armored bust right within square outline **Obv. Legend:** IOSEPH • II • D • G • R • I • S • A • GE • REX • A • A • LO & M H • D • **Reverse:** Crowned imperial double eagle **Rev. Legend:** VIRTUTE ET EXEMPLO

Date	Mintage	VG	F	VF	XF	Unc
1767A IC-SK	—	20.00	40.00	75.00	130	230
1768/7A IC-SK	—	12.50	25.00	50.00	90.00	165
1768A IC-SK	—	12.50	25.00	50.00	90.00	165
1768A	—	25.00	55.00	110	180	285
1769A IC-SK	—	12.50	25.00	50.00	90.00	165

KM# 2034 1/4 THALER

Silver **Ruler:** Franz I **Obverse:** Laureate bust right **Reverse:** Crowned imperial eagle with arms on breast

Date	Mintage	VG	F	VF	XF	Unc
1746WI	—	35.00	50.00	85.00	135	245

KM# 2035 1/2 THALER

14.4100 g., Silver **Ruler:** Franz I **Obverse:** Armored bust right **Obv. Legend:** FRANC • D • G • R • I • S • A • GE • IER • R • LO • B • M • H • D • **Reverse:** Crowned imperial double eagle **Rev. Legend:** IN TE DOMINE SPERAVI

Date	Mintage	VG	F	VF	XF	Unc
1746WI	—	45.00	80.00	150	275	425
1747WI	—	45.00	80.00	150	275	425
1748KB	—	40.00	75.00	125	225	375
1749GR	—	40.00	75.00	125	225	375
1749KB	—	40.00	75.00	125	225	375
1749WI	—	45.00	80.00	150	275	425
1750GR	—	45.00	80.00	150	275	425
1750WI	—	45.00	80.00	150	275	425

KM# 2036 1/2 THALER

14.0700 g., Silver **Ruler:** Franz II (I) **Obverse:** Bust right **Obv. Legend:** FRANC • D : G • R •(O) • I • S • A • GR • IER • R • LO • B • M • H • D • **Reverse:** Imperial eagle **Rev. Legend:** IN TE DOMINE-SPERAVI **Note:** Dav. #1153, 1155, 1157-1160.

Date	Mintage	VG	F	VF	XF	Unc
1751GR	—	45.00	80.00	125	225	375
1751KB	—	35.00	65.00	100	185	300
1751WI	—	45.00	80.00	125	225	375
1752GR	—	45.00	80.00	125	225	375
1752WI	—	45.00	80.00	125	225	375
1753CA	—	45.00	80.00	125	225	375
1753GR	—	45.00	80.00	125	225	375
1754GR	—	45.00	80.00	125	225	375
1754HA	—	35.00	65.00	100	185	300
1754KB	—	35.00	65.00	100	185	300
1755HA	—	35.00	65.00	100	185	300
1755KB	—	35.00	65.00	100	185	300
1756HA	—	35.00	65.00	100	185	300
1757HA	—	35.00	65.00	100	185	300
1757KB	—	35.00	65.00	100	185	300
1758HA	—	35.00	65.00	100	185	300
1758KB	—	35.00	65.00	100	185	300
1759KB	—	35.00	65.00	100	185	300
1760KB	—	35.00	65.00	100	185	300
1761KB	—	35.00	65.00	100	185	300
1762HA	—	35.00	65.00	100	185	300
1763HA	—	35.00	65.00	100	185	300
1763KB	—	35.00	65.00	100	185	300
1764KB	—	35.00	65.00	100	185	300
1765GR	—	45.00	80.00	125	225	375
1765WI	—	45.00	80.00	125	225	375

KM# 2072 1/2 THALER

14.0700 g., Silver **Obverse:** Bust of Joseph II right, as joint ruler

Date	Mintage	VG	F	VF	XF	Unc
1768A IC-SK	—	60.00	125	175	250	400

KM# 2073 1/2 THALER

14.0700 g., Silver **Ruler:** Joseph II **Obverse:** Head right **Obv. Legend:** IOSEPH • II • D • G • R • I • S • A • GER • ... **Reverse:** Crowned imperial double eagle **Rev. Legend:** ARCH • AVST • D • BVRG • ...

Date	Mintage	VG	F	VF	XF	Unc
1781A	—	75.00	150	200	275	450
1782A	—	75.00	150	200	275	450
1784A	—	75.00	150	200	275	450
1785A	—	75.00	150	200	275	450
1786A	—	75.00	150	200	275	450
1787A	—	75.00	150	200	275	450
1788A	—	75.00	150	200	275	450
1789A Rare	—	—	—	—	—	—
1790A	—	75.00	150	200	275	450

KM# 2098 1/2 THALER

14.0300 g., 0.8330 Silver .3757 oz. ASW **Ruler:** Leopold II **Obverse:** Head right **Obv. Legend:** LEOPOLDVS • II • D • G • R • IMP • SA • GERM • HV • BO • REX • **Reverse:** Crowned imperial double eagle **Rev. Legend:** ARCH • AVST • D • BVRG • LOTH • M • D • HET •

Date	Mintage	F	VF	XF	Unc
1790	—	375	850	1,450	2,400
1792	—	300	750	1,200	2,000

KM# A2149 1/2 THALER

14.0300 g., 0.8330 Silver .3757 oz. ASW **Ruler:** Franz II (I) **Obv. Legend:** FRANCISCVS II. D. G. R. IMP...

Date	Mintage	F	VF	XF	Unc
1792A	—	300	400	800	1,000
1793A	—	100	225	350	500
1794A	—	100	225	350	500
1795A	—	60.00	125	250	400
1796A	—	400	700	1,100	1,500
1797A	—	100	200	350	500
1798A	—	60.00	125	250	400
1799A	—	50.00	100	250	400
1800A	—	100	200	350	400

KM# 2037 THALER

28.8200 g., Silver **Ruler:** Franz I **Obverse:** Armored bust right **Obv. Legend:** FRANC • D : G : R • I • S • A • GE • IER • R • LO • B • M • H • D • **Reverse:** Crowned imperial double eagle **Rev. Legend:** IN TE DOMINE SPERAVI **Note:** Dav. #1152. Varieties exist.

Date	Mintage	VG	F	VF	XF	Unc
1746KB	—	35.00	75.00	125	175	275
1746PR	—	35.00	75.00	125	175	275
1746WI	—	35.00	75.00	125	175	275
1747CA	—	35.00	75.00	125	175	275
1747KB	—	35.00	75.00	125	175	275
1747PR	—	35.00	75.00	125	175	275
1747WI	—	35.00	75.00	125	175	275
1748CA	—	35.00	75.00	125	175	275
1748KB	—	35.00	75.00	125	175	275
1748WI	—	35.00	75.00	125	175	275
1749CA	—	35.00	75.00	125	175	275
1749HA	—	35.00	75.00	125	175	275
1749PR	—	35.00	75.00	125	175	275
1749WI	—	35.00	75.00	125	175	275
1750CA	—	35.00	75.00	125	175	275
1750HA	—	35.00	75.00	125	175	275
1750KB	—	35.00	75.00	125	175	275
1750PR	—	35.00	75.00	125	175	275
1750WI	—	35.00	75.00	125	175	275

KM# 2038 THALER

28.8200 g., Silver **Ruler:** Franz I **Obverse:** Armored bust right **Obv. Legend:** FRANC • D • G • R • I • S • A • GE • IER • R • LO • B • M • H • D • **Reverse:** Crowned imperial double eagle **Rev. Legend:** IN TE DOMINE SPERAVI • **Note:** Dav. #1153. Varieties exist.

Date	Mintage	VG	F	VF	XF	Unc
1751HA	—	35.00	75.00	125	175	275
1751KB	—	35.00	75.00	125	175	275
1751PR	—	35.00	75.00	125	175	275
1751WI	—	35.00	75.00	125	175	275
1752KB	—	35.00	75.00	125	175	275
1752PR	—	35.00	75.00	125	175	275
1753CA	—	35.00	75.00	125	175	275
1753HA	—	35.00	75.00	125	175	275
1753KB	—	35.00	75.00	125	175	275
1753PR	—	35.00	75.00	125	175	275
1753WI	—	35.00	75.00	125	175	275
1754HA	—	35.00	75.00	125	175	275
1754KB	—	35.00	75.00	125	175	275
1754PR	—	35.00	75.00	125	175	275
1755HA	—	35.00	75.00	125	175	275
1755KB	—	35.00	75.00	125	175	275
1755PR	—	35.00	75.00	125	175	275
1756HA	—	35.00	75.00	125	175	275
1756KB	—	35.00	75.00	125	175	275
1756WI	—	35.00	75.00	125	175	275
1757HA	—	35.00	75.00	125	175	275
1757KB	—	35.00	75.00	125	175	275
1757PR	—	35.00	75.00	125	175	275
1758KB	—	35.00	75.00	125	175	275
1759HA	—	35.00	75.00	125	175	275
1759KB	—	35.00	75.00	125	175	275
1759PR	—	35.00	75.00	125	175	275
1760HA	—	35.00	75.00	125	175	275
1760KB	—	35.00	75.00	125	175	275
1760PR	—	35.00	75.00	125	175	275
1761HA	—	35.00	75.00	125	175	275
1761KB	—	35.00	75.00	125	175	275
1761PR	—	35.00	75.00	125	175	275
1762HA	—	35.00	75.00	125	175	275
1762KB	—	35.00	75.00	125	175	275
1762PR	—	35.00	75.00	125	175	275
1763HA	—	35.00	75.00	125	175	275
1763KB	—	35.00	75.00	125	175	275
1763WI	—	35.00	75.00	125	175	275
1764HA	—	35.00	75.00	125	175	275
1764KB	—	35.00	75.00	125	175	275
1765KB	—	35.00	75.00	125	175	275

KM# 2039 THALER

28.1400 g., Silver **Ruler:** Franz I **Obverse:** Similar to KM#2038, but with three letters below bust **Note:** Dav. #1154. Varieties exist.

Date	Mintage	VG	F	VF	XF	Unc
1761 GTK	—	35.00	75.00	125	175	275
1761 IZV	—	35.00	75.00	125	175	275
1763 IZV	—	35.00	75.00	125	175	275
1764 IZV	—	35.00	75.00	125	175	275
1764 AW	—	35.00	75.00	125	175	275
1765 IZV	—	35.00	75.00	125	175	275

KM# 2074.2 THALER

Silver **Obverse:** Bust right **Reverse:** Imperial eagle **Note:** Dav. #1164-1166.

Date	Mintage	VG	F	VF	XF	Unc
1765F S	—	—	—	—	—	—
1765F A-S	—	—	—	—	—	—
1766F	—	—	—	—	—	—
1766F A-S	—	—	—	—	—	—
1766H S-C	—	—	—	—	—	—
1767F S	—	—	—	—	—	—
1767F A-S	—	—	—	—	—	—
1767H S-C	—	—	—	—	—	—
1768H S-C	—	—	—	—	—	—
1769H S-C	—	—	—	—	—	—
1770C EvS-AS	—	—	—	—	—	—
1771F A-S	—	—	—	—	—	—
1771H S-C	—	—	—	—	—	—
1773C EvS-AS	—	—	—	—	—	—
1774C EvS-LK	—	—	—	—	—	—
1775C EvS-LK	—	—	—	—	—	—
1775F VC-S	—	—	—	—	—	—
1776F VC-S	—	—	—	—	—	—
1777F VC-S	—	—	—	—	—	—

KM# 2074.1 THALER

28.1400 g., Silver **Ruler:** Joseph II **Mint:** Vienna **Obverse:** Armored bust right, as joint ruler **Obv. Legend:** JOSEPH • II • D • G • R • I • S • A • COR • & • HER • R • H • B • & C **Reverse:** Crowned imperial double eagle **Rev. Legend:** ARCH • AUST • D • BURG • LOTH • M • D • HET • **Note:** Convention Thaler. Dav. #1161. Prev. KM#2074.

Date	Mintage	VG	F	VF	XF	Unc
1765A	—	60.00	135	175	275	425
1766A	—	60.00	135	175	275	425
1766A IC-SK	—	60.00	135	175	275	425
1767A IC-SK	—	60.00	135	175	275	425
1769A IC-SK	—	60.00	135	175	275	425
1770A IC-SK	—	60.00	135	175	275	425
1771A IC-SK	—	60.00	135	175	275	425
1772A IC-SK	—	60.00	135	175	275	425

KM# 2076 THALER

28.1400 g., Silver **Ruler:** Joseph II **Mint:** Vienna **Obverse:** Armored bust of with Order sash over shoulder, as joint ruler **Note:** Ordens Thaler. Dav. #1162.

Date	Mintage	VG	F	VF	XF	Unc
1768A IC-SK Rare	—	—	—	—	—	—
1769A IC-SK Rare	—	—	—	—	—	—

KM# 2075 THALER

28.1400 g., Silver **Ruler:** Joseph II **Mint:** Vienna **Obverse:** Armored laureate bust right **Obv. Legend:** IOSEPH : II • D : G • R • I • S • A • COR • & • HER • R • H • B • & c• **Reverse:** Crowned imperial double eagle **Rev. Legend:** ARCH • AUST • D • BURG LOTH • M • D • HET • **Note:** Dav. #1163.

Date	Mintage	VG	F	VF	XF	Unc
1773A IC-SK	—	60.00	135	175	275	425
1774A IC-SK	—	60.00	135	175	275	425
1774A IC-FA	—	60.00	135	175	275	425
1775A IC-FA	—	60.00	135	175	275	425
1776A IC-FA	—	60.00	135	175	275	425
1778A IC-FA	—	60.00	135	175	275	425
1779A IC-FA	—	60.00	135	175	275	425
1780A IC-FA	—	60.00	135	175	275	425

KM# 2077 THALER

28.1400 g., Silver **Ruler:** Joseph II **Mint:** Vienna **Obverse:** Laureate head right, as sole ruler **Note:** Convention Thaler. Dav. #1167.

Date	Mintage	VG	F	VF	XF	Unc
1781A	—	100	200	375	650	950
1782A	—	100	200	375	650	950
1784A	—	100	200	375	650	950
1784A	—	100	200	375	650	950
1785A	—	100	200	375	650	950
1786A	—	100	200	375	650	950
1787A	—	100	200	375	650	950
1788A	—	100	200	375	650	950
1789A	—	100	200	375	650	950
1790A	—	100	200	375	650	950

KM# 2099 THALER

28.0600 g., 0.8330 Silver .7514 oz. ASW **Ruler:** Leopold II **Mint:** Vienna **Obverse:** Head right as King of Hungary and Bohemia **Obv. Legend:** LEOPOLDVS II • D • G • HUNGAR • BOHEM • GALLIC • LODOM • REX • **Reverse:** Crowned arms with supporters **Rev. Legend:** ARCHIDVX AVST DVX BVRG • ET LOTH • MAG • DVX • HETR • **Note:** Dav. #1171.

Date	Mintage	F	VF	XF	Unc
1790A	—	350	600	1,000	1,500

KM# 2100 THALER

28.0600 g., 0.8330 Silver .7514 oz. ASW **Ruler:** Leopold II **Mint:** Vienna **Obverse:** Head right as Emperor **Obv. Legend:** LEOPOLDVS II • D • G • R • IMP • S • A • GERM • HV • BO • REX • **Reverse:** Crowned imperial eagle **Rev. Legend:** ARCH • AVST • D • BVRG • LOTH • M • D • HET • **Note:** Dav. #1173.

Date	Mintage	F	VF	XF	Unc
1790A	—	400	750	1,250	2,000
1791A	—	600	1,000	1,650	2,000
1792A	—	400	750	1,250	2,000

KM# 2157 THALER

28.0600 g., 0.8330 Silver .7514 oz. ASW **Ruler:** Franz II (I) **Mint:** Vienna **Obverse:** Laureate head right **Obv. Legend:** FRANCISCVS • D • G • HVNGAR • BOHEM • GALLIC • LODEM • REX • **Reverse:** Crowned arms with supporters **Rev. Legend:** ARCHIDVX AVST • DVX • BVRG • ET LOTH • MAG • DVX HETR • **Note:** Dav. #1176.

Date	Mintage	F	VF	XF	Unc
1792A	—	475	800	1,600	2,400

KM# 2158 THALER

28.0600 g., 0.8330 Silver .7514 oz. ASW **Ruler:** Franz II (I) **Mint:** Vienna **Obverse:** Head right, long loose hair **Obv. Legend:** FRANCISCVS II. D. G. R. IMP. S.A... **Reverse:** Crowned imperial double eagle with heads in haloes **Note:** Dav. #1178.

Date	Mintage	F	VF	XF	Unc
1792A	—	200	400	800	1,200
1793A	—	200	400	800	1,200
1794A	—	175	325	650	950
1795A	—	85.00	175	325	650
1796A	—	125	250	475	950
1797A Rare	—	—	—	—	—
1798A	—	75.00	150	275	550
1799A	1,187	85.00	175	325	650
1800A	—	85.00	175	325	650

TRADE COINAGE

KM# 1630 1/16 DUCAT

0.2188 g., 0.9860 Gold .0069 oz. AGW **Ruler:** Karl (Charles) VI **Mint:** Graz **Obverse:** Laureate head right **Reverse:** Crowned imperial eagle **Note:** Prev. KM#506.

Date	Mintage	VG	F	VF	XF	Unc
1729	—	70.00	100	250	600	—

KM# 1495 1/8 DUCAT

0.4375 g., 0.9860 Gold .0139 oz. AGW **Ruler:** Joseph I **Mint:** Vienna **Obverse:** Laureate bust right **Reverse:** Crowned imperial eagle in inner circle **Note:** Prev. KM#1906.

Date	Mintage	VG	F	VF	XF	Unc
1707	—	100	180	300	650	—

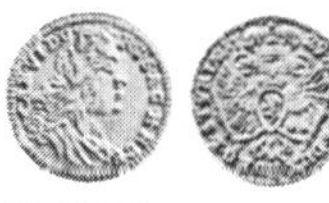

KM# 1631 1/8 DUCAT

0.4375 g., 0.9860 Gold .0139 oz. AGW **Ruler:** Karl (Charles) VI **Mint:** Graz **Obverse:** Bust right **Reverse:** Crowned imperial double eagle **Note:** Prev. KM#507.

Date	Mintage	VG	F	VF	XF	Unc
1729	—	80.00	120	225	450	—

KM# 1496 1/4 DUCAT

0.8750 g., 0.9860 Gold .0277 oz. AGW **Ruler:** Joseph I **Mint:** Vienna **Obverse:** Laureate bust right, value at shoulder **Reverse:** Crowned imperial eagle in inner circle **Note:** Prev. KM#1907.

Date	Mintage	VG	F	VF	XF	Unc
1707	—	70.00	140	275	650	—

KM# 1605 1/4 DUCAT

0.8750 g., 0.9860 Gold .0277 oz. AGW **Ruler:** Karl (Charles) VI **Mint:** Graz **Obverse:** Laureate bust right **Reverse:** Crowned imperial eagle **Note:** Prev. KM#508.

Date	Mintage	VG	F	VF	XF	Unc
1720	—	80.00	140	275	700	—
1728	—	80.00	140	275	700	—
1729	—	80.00	140	275	700	—

KM# 1653 1/4 DUCAT

0.8750 g., 0.9860 Gold .0277 oz. AGW **Ruler:** Karl (Charles) VI **Mint:** Vienna **Obverse:** Laureate head right **Obv. Legend:** CAROL • VI • ... **Reverse:** Crowned imperial double eagle **Note:** Prev. KM#1925.

Date	Mintage	VG	F	VF	XF	Unc
1733	—	80.00	160	325	800	—

KM# 1819 1/4 DUCAT

0.8750 g., 0.9860 Gold .0277 oz. AGW **Ruler:** Franz I **Obverse:** Laureate head right **Obv. Legend:** FRANC • D • G • R • I • S • A • ... **Reverse:** Crowned imperial double eagle **Rev. Legend:** TU DOMINE SPES MEA • **Note:** Varieties exist. Prev. KM#2040.

Date	Mintage	VG	F	VF	XF	Unc
1755NB	—	60.00	100	185	350	550
1757G B-V	—	60.00	100	185	350	550
1759NB	—	60.00	100	185	350	550
1760NB	—	60.00	100	185	350	550
1761NB	—	60.00	100	185	350	550
1762NB	—	60.00	100	185	350	550
1764NB	—	60.00	100	185	350	550
1765NB	—	60.00	100	185	350	550

KM# 1840 1/4 DUCAT

0.8750 g., 0.9860 Gold .0277 oz. AGW **Ruler:** Joseph II **Obverse:** Large bust right, as joint ruler **Reverse:** Crowned imperial eagle **Note:** Prev. KM#2078.

Date	Mintage	VG	F	VF	XF	Unc
1765NB	—	80.00	120	185	350	550

KM# 1497 1/2 DUCAT

1.7500 g., 0.9860 Gold .0555 oz. AGW **Ruler:** Joseph I **Mint:** Hall **Obverse:** Laureate bust right **Reverse:** Crowned imperial eagle **Note:** Prev. KM#669.

Date	Mintage	VG	F	VF	XF	Unc
1707	—	200	300	500	900	—

KM# 1645 1/2 DUCAT

1.7500 g., 0.9860 Gold .0555 oz. AGW **Ruler:** Karl (Charles) VI **Mint:** Vienna **Obverse:** Laureate head right **Reverse:** Crowned imperial eagle, value below **Note:** Prev. KM#1926.

Date	Mintage	VG	F	VF	XF	Unc
1731	—	70.00	140	275	650	—
1732	—	70.00	140	275	650	—
1738	—	70.00	140	275	650	—
1740	—	70.00	140	275	650	—

KM# 1841 3/4 DUCAT

2.5568 g., 0.9860 Gold .0830 oz. AGW **Note:** Prev. KM#2091.

Date	Mintage	VG	F	VF	XF	Unc
1765	—	—	—	—	—	—

KM# 1414 DUCAT

3.5000 g., 0.9860 Gold .1109 oz. AGW **Ruler:** Leopold I **Mint:** Saint Veit **Obverse:** Laureate bust right in inner circle **Reverse:** Crowned imperial eagle; crown divides date **Note:** Prev. KM#1658.

Date	Mintage	VG	F	VF	XF	Unc
1702	—	175	375	750	1,600	—
1704	—	175	375	750	1,600	—
1704 IP	—	175	375	750	1,600	—

KM# 1325 DUCAT

3.5000 g., 0.9860 Gold .1109 oz. AGW **Ruler:** Leopold I **Mint:** Vienna **Obverse:** Large laureate bust right divides legend **Reverse:** Crowned imperial eagle, crown divides date **Note:** Prev. KM#1890.

Date	Mintage	VG	F	VF	XF	Unc
1702	—	120	325	650	1,200	—
1703	—	120	325	650	1,200	—
1704	—	120	325	650	1,200	—

KM# 1454 DUCAT

3.5000 g., 0.9860 Gold .1109 oz. AGW **Ruler:** Joseph I **Mint:** Vienna **Obverse:** Laureate armored bust right **Reverse:** Crowned imperial eagle, date in legend **Note:** Prev. KM#1908.

Date	Mintage	VG	F	VF	XF	Unc
1705	—	175	375	800	1,750	—
1706	—	175	375	800	1,750	—
1708	—	175	375	800	1,750	—
1709	—	175	375	800	1,750	—
1710	—	175	375	800	1,750	—
1711	—	175	375	800	1,750	—

KM# 1450 DUCAT

3.4900 g., 0.9860 Gold .1106 oz. AGW **Ruler:** Joseph I **Mint:** Augsburg **Obverse:** Armored and laureate bust of right **Reverse:** Crowned imperial eagle with oval arms on breast, crown divides date **Note:** Prev. KM#135.

Date	Mintage	VG	F	VF	XF	Unc
1705	—	400	900	1,600	2,500	—

Date	Mintage	VG	F	VF	XF	Unc
1706	—	400	900	1,600	2,500	—
1707	—	400	900	1,600	2,500	—
1708	—	400	900	1,600	2,500	—
1709	—	400	900	1,600	2,500	—
1710	—	400	900	1,600	2,500	—

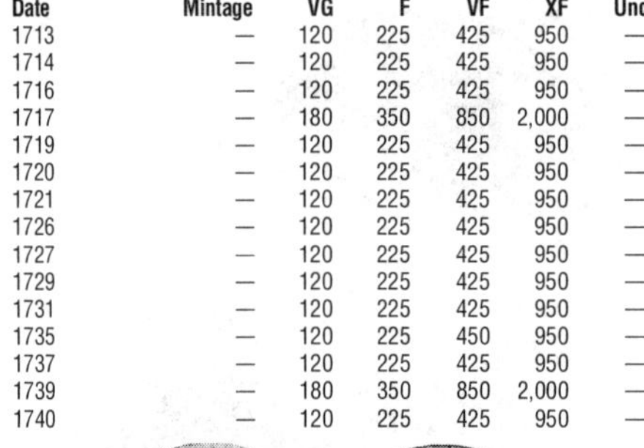

KM# 1453 DUCAT
3.5000 g., 0.9860 Gold .1109 oz. AGW **Ruler:** Joseph I **Mint:** Munich **Obverse:** Bust right **Reverse:** Crowned imperial double eagle **Note:** Prev. KM#1186.

Date	Mintage	VG	F	VF	XF	Unc
1705 (s)	—	250	600	1,450	2,750	—
1706 (s)	—	250	600	1,450	2,750	—
1707 (s)	—	250	600	1,450	2,750	—
1708 (s)	—	250	600	1,450	2,750	—
1709 (s)	—	250	600	1,450	2,750	—
1710 (s)	—	250	600	1,450	2,750	—

KM# 1452 DUCAT
3.5000 g., 0.9860 Gold .1109 oz. AGW **Ruler:** Joseph I **Mint:** Hall **Obverse:** Laureate armored bust right **Reverse:** Crowned arms in Order collar **Note:** Prev. KM#670.

Date	Mintage	VG	F	VF	XF	Unc
ND	—	500	1,200	4,000	8,000	—

KM# 1471 DUCAT
3.5000 g., 0.9860 Gold .1109 oz. AGW **Ruler:** Joseph I **Mint:** Graz **Obverse:** Laureate bust right in inner circle **Obv. Legend:** IOSEPHVS • D • G • ... **Reverse:** Crowned imperial eagle in inner circle, crown divides date **Rev. Legend:** ARCHID • AUS • D • B • STYRIÆ • **Note:** Prev. KM#485.

Date	Mintage	VG	F	VF	XF	Unc
1706	—	250	600	1,250	2,500	—

KM# 1506 DUCAT
3.5000 g., 0.9860 Gold .1109 oz. AGW **Ruler:** Joseph I **Mint:** Saint Veit **Obverse:** Laureate armored bust right **Reverse:** Crowned arms in Order collar **Note:** Prev. KM#1669.

Date	Mintage	VG	F	VF	XF	Unc
1710 IIP	—	250	600	1,400	2,500	—
1711 IIP	—	250	600	1,400	2,500	—

KM# 1526 DUCAT
3.5000 g., 0.9860 Gold .1109 oz. AGW **Ruler:** Karl (Charles) VI **Mint:** Munich **Obverse:** Bust right **Reverse:** Heraldic imperial eagle **Note:** Prev. KM#1191.

Date	Mintage	VG	F	VF	XF	Unc
1712 (s)	—	100	200	450	850	—

KM# 1524 DUCAT
3.4900 g., 0.9860 Gold .1106 oz. AGW **Ruler:** Karl (Charles) VI **Mint:** Augsburg **Reverse:** Heart-shaped arms on breast **Note:** Prev. KM#A135.

Date	Mintage	VG	F	VF	XF	Unc
1712 Rare	—	—	—	—	—	—

KM# 1558 DUCAT
3.5000 g., 0.9860 Gold .1109 oz. AGW **Ruler:** Karl (Charles) VI **Mint:** Saint Veit **Obverse:** Laureate head right **Reverse:** Crowned imperial eagle, crown divides date **Note:** Prev. KM#1684.

Date	Mintage	VG	F	VF	XF	Unc
1713	—	250	475	975	1,750	—

KM# 1559 DUCAT
3.5000 g., 0.9860 Gold .1109 oz. AGW **Ruler:** Karl (Charles) VI **Mint:** Vienna **Obverse:** Laureate head right **Obv. Legend:** CAROL VI D G ROM IMP SAGE R HISP HUB REX **Reverse:** Crowned imperial eagle, date in legend **Rev. Legend:** ARCHIDVX AVSTRIÆ DVX BUR CO TYR **Note:** Prev. KM#1927.

Date	Mintage	VG	F	VF	XF	Unc
1713	—	120	225	425	950	—
1714	—	120	225	425	950	—
1716	—	120	225	425	950	—
1717	—	180	350	850	2,000	—
1719	—	120	225	425	950	—
1720	—	120	225	425	950	—
1721	—	120	225	425	950	—
1726	—	120	225	425	950	—
1727	—	120	225	425	950	—
1729	—	120	225	425	950	—
1731	—	120	225	425	950	—
1735	—	120	225	450	950	—
1737	—	120	225	425	950	—
1739	—	180	350	850	2,000	—
1740	—	120	225	425	950	—

KM# 1557 DUCAT
3.5000 g., 0.9860 Gold .1109 oz. AGW **Ruler:** Karl (Charles) VI **Mint:** Graz **Obverse:** Laureate head right **Obv. Legend:** CAROL • VI • D: G: ROM • IMP: S: A: G: E: R: HIS: H: B: REX • **Reverse:** Crowned imperial eagle, crown divides date **Rev. Legend:** ARCHIDVX AVSTRIÆ DVX BVRG STYRIÆ **Note:** Prev. KM#509.

Date	Mintage	VG	F	VF	XF	Unc
1713	—	120	225	475	1,000	—
1720	—	120	225	475	1,000	—
1722	—	120	225	475	1,000	—
1728	—	120	225	475	1,000	—
1738	—	120	225	475	1,000	—
1739	—	120	225	475	1,000	—
1740	—	120	225	475	1,000	—

KM# 1612 DUCAT
3.5000 g., 0.9860 Silver .1109 oz. ASW **Ruler:** Karl (Charles) VI **Mint:** Hall **Obverse:** Young laureate armored bust right **Reverse:** Crowned imperial eagle **Note:** Prev. KM#698.

Date	Mintage	VG	F	VF	XF	Unc
ND	—	400	800	2,000	4,000	—
1723	—	150	350	750	1,500	—

KM# 1655 DUCAT
3.5000 g., 0.9860 Silver .1109 oz. ASW **Ruler:** Karl (Charles) VI **Mint:** Hall **Obverse:** Bust right **Obv. Legend:** CAROL • VI • D • G • R • I • S • A • GE • HI • HU • BO • REX • **Reverse:** Crowned imperial double eagle **Rev. Legend:** ARCHID • AUST • DUX • BU • COM • TYROL • **Note:** Prev. KM#699.

Date	Mintage	VG	F	VF	XF	Unc
1734	—	120	250	600	1,100	—
1737	—	120	250	600	1,100	—
1739	—	120	250	600	1,100	—
1740	—	120	250	600	1,100	—

KM# 1679 DUCAT
3.5000 g., 0.9860 Gold .1109 oz. AGW **Ruler:** Maria Theresa **Mint:** Hall **Obverse:** Crude wide bust right **Reverse:** Crowned arms in ornamental cartouche **Note:** Prev. KM#749.

Date	Mintage	VG	F	VF	XF	Unc
1741	—	150	225	325	550	—

KM# 1696 DUCAT
3.5000 g., 0.9860 Gold .1109 oz. AGW **Ruler:** Maria Theresa **Mint:** Hall **Obverse:** Bust right **Reverse:** Crowned large arms in ornamental cartouche **Note:** Varieties exist. Prev. KM#750.

Date	Mintage	VG	F	VF	XF	Unc
1742	—	150	200	275	500	—
1744	—	150	200	275	500	—

KM# 1705 DUCAT
3.5000 g., 0.9860 Gold .1109 oz. AGW **Ruler:** Maria Theresa **Mint:** Graz **Obverse:** Bust right **Reverse:** Crowned arms **Note:** Prev. KM#547.

Date	Mintage	VG	F	VF	XF	Unc
1743	—	125	250	500	750	—
1744	—	125	250	500	750	—
1745	—	125	250	500	750	—

KM# 1725.1 DUCAT
3.4909 g., 0.9860 Gold .1106 oz. AGW **Obverse:** Draped bust right **Reverse:** Crowned imperial double eagle **Rev. Legend:** IN TE DOMINE SPERAVI **Note:** Similar to KM#1725.2. Prev. KM#2041.1.

Date	Mintage	VG	F	VF	XF	Unc
1745HA S/IE	—	140	200	300	625	950

KM# 1725.2 DUCAT
3.4909 g., 0.9860 Gold .1106 oz. AGW **Ruler:** Franz I **Obv. Legend:** FRANC • D • G • R • I • S • A • GER • IER • REX • **Rev. Legend:** TU DOMINE SPES MEA • **Note:** Varieties exist. Prev. KM#2041.2.

Date	Mintage	VG	F	VF	XF	Unc
1745CA	—	80.00	160	275	550	850
1746HA	—	80.00	160	275	550	850
1746PR	—	80.00	160	275	550	850
1746WI	—	80.00	160	275	550	850
1746CA	—	80.00	160	275	550	850
1747GR	—	80.00	160	275	550	850
1747NB	—	80.00	160	275	550	850
1747WI	—	80.00	160	275	550	850
1747CA	—	80.00	160	275	550	850
1748PR	—	80.00	160	275	550	850
1748WI	—	80.00	160	275	550	850
1748CA	—	80.00	160	275	550	850
1749GR	—	80.00	160	275	550	850
1749HA	—	80.00	160	275	550	850
1749NB	—	80.00	160	275	550	850
1749PR	—	80.00	160	275	550	850
1749WI	—	80.00	160	275	550	850
1749CA	—	80.00	160	275	550	850
1750CA	—	80.00	160	275	550	850
1750GR	—	80.00	160	275	550	850
1750NB	—	80.00	160	275	550	850
1750PR	—	80.00	160	275	550	850
1750WI	—	80.00	160	275	550	850
1751CA	—	80.00	160	275	550	850
1751NB	—	80.00	160	275	550	850
1751PR	—	80.00	160	275	550	850
1751WI	—	80.00	160	275	550	850
1752CA	—	80.00	160	275	550	850
1752HA	—	80.00	160	275	550	850
1752NB	—	80.00	160	275	550	850
1752PR	—	80.00	160	275	550	850
1752WI	—	80.00	160	275	550	850
1753CA	—	80.00	160	275	550	850
1753GR	—	80.00	160	275	550	850
1753NB	—	80.00	160	275	550	850
1753PR	—	80.00	160	275	550	850
1753WI	—	80.00	160	275	550	850
1754CA	—	80.00	160	275	550	850
1754GR	—	80.00	160	275	550	850
1754NB	—	80.00	160	275	550	850
1754PR	—	80.00	160	275	550	850
1754WI	—	80.00	160	275	550	850
1755CA	—	80.00	160	275	550	850
1755GR	—	80.00	160	275	550	850
1755NB	—	80.00	160	275	550	850
1755PR	—	80.00	160	275	550	850
1755WI	—	80.00	160	275	550	850
1756CA	—	80.00	160	275	550	850
1756GR	—	80.00	160	275	550	850
1756NB	—	80.00	160	275	550	850
1756PR	—	80.00	160	275	550	850
1756WI	—	80.00	160	275	550	850
1757CA	—	80.00	160	275	550	850
1757GR	—	80.00	160	275	550	850
1757NB	—	80.00	160	275	550	850
1757WI	—	80.00	160	275	550	850
1758CA	—	80.00	160	275	550	850
1758GR	—	80.00	160	275	550	850
1758NB	—	80.00	160	275	550	850
1758WI	—	80.00	160	275	550	850
1759CA	—	80.00	160	275	550	850
1759NB	—	80.00	160	275	550	850
1760CA	—	80.00	160	275	550	850
1760NB	—	80.00	160	275	550	850
1761CA	—	80.00	160	275	550	850
1761HA	—	80.00	160	275	550	850
1761NB	—	80.00	160	275	550	850
1762GR	—	80.00	160	275	550	850
1762HA	—	80.00	160	275	550	850
1762NB	—	80.00	160	275	550	850
1763NB	—	80.00	160	275	550	850
1764GR	—	80.00	160	275	550	850

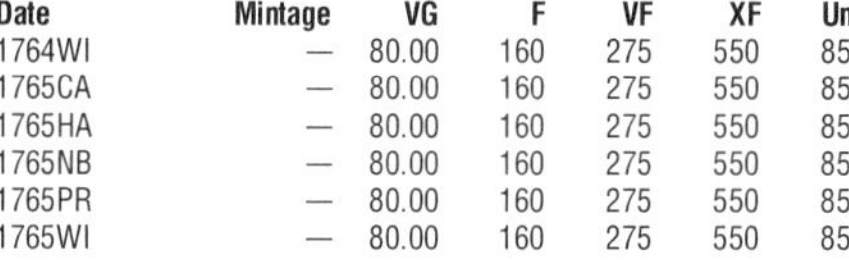

Date	Mintage	VG	F	VF	XF	Unc
1764WI	—	80.00	160	275	550	850
1765CA	—	80.00	160	275	550	850
1765HA	—	80.00	160	275	550	850
1765NB	—	80.00	160	275	550	850
1765PR	—	80.00	160	275	550	850
1765WI	—	80.00	160	275	550	850

KM# 1744 DUCAT

3.5000 g., 0.9860 Gold .1109 oz. AGW **Ruler:** Maria Theresa **Mint:** Hall **Obverse:** Bust right **Obv. Legend:** M • THERES • D • G • R • IMP • ... **Reverse:** Crowned imperial double eagle **Rev. Legend:** ARCH • AUST • DUX • ... **Note:** Varieties exist. Prev. KM#751.

Date	Mintage	VG	F	VF	XF	Unc
1746	—	125	175	250	500	—
1748	—	125	175	250	500	—

KM# 1756 DUCAT

3.5000 g., 0.9860 Gold .1109 oz. AGW **Ruler:** Maria Theresa **Mint:** Graz **Obverse:** Bust right **Obv. Legend:** M • THERES • D • G • R • IMP • GER • HU • BO • REG • **Reverse:** Crowned imperial double eagle **Rev. Legend:** ARCHID • AUSTR • DUX • BURG • & • STYRIÆ • **Note:** Varieties exist. Prev. KM#548.

Date	Mintage	VG	F	VF	XF	Unc
1747	—	80.00	175	400	600	—
1749	—	80.00	175	400	600	—
1750	—	80.00	175	400	600	—
1751	—	80.00	175	400	600	—
1752	—	80.00	175	400	600	—
1753	—	80.00	175	400	600	—
1754	—	80.00	175	400	600	—
1755	—	80.00	175	400	600	—
1756	—	80.00	175	400	600	—
1758	—	80.00	175	400	600	—
1759	—	80.00	175	400	600	—
1760	—	80.00	175	400	600	—
1761	—	80.00	175	400	600	—
1762	—	80.00	175	400	600	—
1765	—	80.00	175	400	600	—

KM# 1784 DUCAT

3.4909 g., 0.9860 Gold .1106 oz. AGW **Ruler:** Maria Theresa **Obverse:** Draped bust right **Obv. Legend:** FRANC • D : G • R • I • S • A • GER • IER • REX • **Reverse:** Legend begins at lower left, date below eagle **Rev. Legend:** TUDOMINE SPESMEA **Note:** Prev. KM#2049.

Date	Mintage	VG	F	VF	XF	Unc
1750NB	—	80.00	160	275	550	850

KM# 1783 DUCAT

3.5000 g., 0.9860 Gold .1109 oz. AGW **Ruler:** Maria Theresa **Mint:** Hall **Obverse:** Mature bust right **Reverse:** Crowned imperial eagle with crowned complex arms on breast **Note:** Varieties exist. Prev. KM#752.

Date	Mintage	VG	F	VF	XF	Unc
1750	—	125	175	375	600	—
1752	—	125	175	375	600	—
1753	—	125	175	375	600	—
1754	—	125	175	375	600	—
1756	—	125	175	375	600	—
1760	—	125	175	375	600	—
1762	—	125	175	375	600	—
1764	—	125	175	375	600	—
1765	—	125	175	375	600	—

KM# 1831 DUCAT

3.4909 g., 0.9860 Gold .1106 oz. AGW **Ruler:** Joseph II **Obverse:** Laureate bust of Joseph II right, royal title only **Obv. Legend:** IOSEPHUS • II • D • G • ROM • REX • S • A • G • R • **Reverse:** Crowned arms supported by griffins **Rev. Legend:** ARCHID • AUSTR • 1764 • HUNG • BO • & • PRINC • HER • **Note:** Prev. KM#2079.

Date	Mintage	VG	F	VF	XF	Unc
1764	—	160	325	500	900	1,350

KM# 1844 DUCAT

3.4909 g., 0.9860 Gold .1106 oz. AGW **Ruler:** Joseph II **Obverse:** Bust right **Obv. Legend:** IOSEPHVS • II • D • G • ROM • REX • S • A • G • R • **Reverse:** Crowned arms with supporters **Rev. Legend:** ARCHID • AUSTR • 1765 • HUNG • BOH • & • PRINC • HER • **Note:** Prev. KM#2080.

Date	Mintage	VG	F	VF	XF	Unc
1765A	—	160	325	500	900	1,350

KM# 1842 DUCAT

3.4909 g., 0.9860 Gold .1106 oz. AGW **Note:** Prev. KM#B1974.

Date	Mintage	VG	F	VF	XF	Unc
1765	—	120	200	325	625	950
1766 C-K	—	120	200	325	625	950
1767	—	120	200	325	625	950
1768 C-K	—	120	200	325	625	950
1769	—	120	200	325	625	950
1770 C-K	—	120	200	325	625	950
1771 C-K	—	120	200	325	625	950
1772 C-K	—	120	200	325	625	950
1773 C-K	—	120	200	325	625	950
1774 C-A	—	120	200	325	625	950
1775 C-A	—	120	200	325	625	950
1776 C-A	—	120	200	325	625	950
1777 C-A	—	120	200	325	625	950
1778 C-A	—	120	200	325	625	950
1779 C-A	—	120	200	325	625	950
1780 C-A	—	120	200	325	625	950

KM# 1843 DUCAT

3.4909 g., 0.9860 Gold .1106 oz. AGW **Ruler:** Maria Theresa **Note:** Similar to KM#1725.2. Prev. KM#2042.

Date	Mintage	VG	F	VF	XF	Unc
1765NB A(1766)	—	80.00	160	275	550	850
1765NB B(1767)	—	80.00	160	275	550	850
1765 B-IK(1767)	—	80.00	160	275	550	850
1765 F-CK(1771)	—	80.00	160	275	550	850
1765 G-CK(1772)	—	80.00	160	275	550	850
1765 H-CK(1773)	—	80.00	160	275	550	850
1765 I-CA(1774)	—	80.00	160	275	550	850
1765 K-CA(1775)	—	80.00	160	275	550	850
1765 L-CA(1776)	—	80.00	160	275	550	850
1765 M-CA(1777)	—	80.00	160	275	550	850
1765 N-CA(1778)	—	80.00	160	275	550	850
1765 O-CA(1779)	—	80.00	160	275	550	850
1765 P-CA(1780)	—	80.00	160	275	550	850
1765GR B(1767)	—	80.00	160	275	550	850
1765WI C-CK(1768)	—	80.00	160	275	550	850
1765WI D-CK(1769)	—	80.00	160	275	550	850
1765WI E-CK(1770)	—	80.00	160	275	550	850
1765WI F-CK(1771)	—	80.00	160	275	550	850

KM# 1859 DUCAT

3.4909 g., 0.9860 Gold .1106 oz. AGW **Ruler:** Joseph II **Obverse:** Draped bust right **Obv. Legend:** IOS • II • D • G • R • I • S • A • GER • IER • REX • **Reverse:** Crowned imperial double eagle **Rev. Legend:** VIRTUTE ET EXEMPLO **Note:** Prev. KM#2081.

Date	Mintage	VG	F	VF	XF	Unc
1768A C-K	—	120	200	325	625	950
1768E H-G	—	120	200	325	625	950
1769A C-K	—	120	200	325	625	950
1769C VS-S	—	120	200	325	625	950
1769E H-G	—	120	200	325	625	950
1769F A-S	—	120	200	325	625	950
1769G B-L	—	120	200	325	625	950
1770C VS-S	—	120	200	325	625	950
1770D G-K	—	120	200	325	625	950
1770E H-G	—	120	200	325	625	950
1771C VS-S	—	120	200	325	625	950
1771D G-K	—	120	200	325	625	950
1771E H-G	—	120	200	325	625	950
1772A C-K	—	120	200	325	625	950
1772C VS-S	—	120	200	325	625	950
1772E H-G	—	120	200	325	625	950
1772G B-L	—	120	200	325	625	950
1772G B-V	—	120	200	325	625	950
1773A C-K	—	120	200	325	625	950
1773C VS-S	—	120	200	325	625	950
1773E H-G	—	120	200	325	625	950
1773G B-V	—	120	200	325	625	950
1774E H-G	—	120	200	325	625	950
1774G B-V	—	120	200	325	625	950
1775A C-A	—	120	200	325	625	950
1775E H-G	—	120	200	325	625	950
1775G B-V	—	120	200	325	625	950
1776A C-A	—	120	200	325	625	950
1776C VS-K	—	120	200	325	625	950
1776E H-G	—	120	200	325	625	950
1776G B-V	—	120	200	325	625	950
1777C VS-K	—	120	200	325	625	950
1777E H-G	—	120	200	325	625	950
1777E H-S	—	120	200	325	625	950
1777F VC-S	—	120	200	325	625	950
1777G B-V	—	120	200	325	625	950
1778A C-A	—	120	200	325	625	950
1778C VS-K	—	120	200	325	625	950
1778G B-V	—	120	200	325	625	950
1779A C-A	—	120	200	325	625	950
1779C VS-K	—	120	200	325	625	950
1779E H-S	—	120	200	325	625	950
1779G B-V	—	120	200	325	625	950
1780E H-S	—	120	200	325	625	950
1780F VC-S	—	120	200	325	625	950
1780G IB-IV	—	120	200	325	625	950

KM# 1858 DUCAT

3.5000 g., 0.9860 Gold .1109 oz. AGW **Ruler:** Maria Theresa **Mint:** Hall **Obverse:** Veiled head right **Reverse:** Crowned imperial eagle with Tyrolean arms on breast **Note:** Prev. KM#753.

Date	Mintage	VG	F	VF	XF	Unc
1768 AS	—	100	175	375	600	—
1770 AS	—	100	175	375	600	—
1771 AS	—	100	175	375	600	—
1773 AS	—	100	175	375	600	—
1774 VC-S	—	100	175	375	600	—
1775 VC-S	—	100	175	375	600	—
1777 VC-S	—	100	175	375	600	—
1778 VC-S	—	100	175	375	600	—
1779 VC-S	—	100	175	375	600	—

KM# 1857 DUCAT

3.5000 g., 0.9860 Gold .1109 oz. AGW **Ruler:** Maria Theresa **Mint:** Graz **Obverse:** Veiled head right **Reverse:** Crowned imperial eagle, arms on breast **Note:** Prev. KM#549.

Date	Mintage	F	VF	XF	Unc
1768 G-K	—	175	350	550	1,000
1769 G-K	—	175	350	550	1,000

KM# 1872 DUCAT

3.4909 g., 0.9860 Gold .1106 oz. AGW **Ruler:** Joseph II **Obverse:** Balding bust right **Note:** Prev. KM#2083.

Date	Mintage	VG	F	VF	XF	Unc
1780A	—	80.00	120	200	350	550
1781A	—	80.00	120	200	350	550
1781E	—	80.00	120	200	350	550
1781G	—	80.00	120	200	350	550
1782E	—	80.00	120	200	350	550
1782G	—	80.00	120	200	350	550

KM# 1873 DUCAT

3.4909 g., 0.9860 Gold .1106 oz. AGW **Ruler:** Joseph II **Obverse:** Laureate head right **Obv. Legend:** IOS • II • D • G • R • I • S • A • GE • HV • BO • REX • **Reverse:** Crowned imperial double eagle with crowned shield on breast **Rev. Legend:** ARCH • A • D • BVRG • LOTH • M • D • H • **Note:** Prev. KM#2084.

Date	Mintage	VG	F	VF	XF	Unc
1780A	—	80.00	100	150	285	450
1782A	—	80.00	100	150	285	450
1783A	—	80.00	100	150	285	450
1783E	—	80.00	100	150	285	450
1783G	—	80.00	100	150	285	450
1784A	—	80.00	100	150	285	450
1784E	—	80.00	100	150	285	450
1784G	—	80.00	100	150	285	450
1785A	—	80.00	100	150	285	450
1786A	—	80.00	100	150	285	450
1786B	128,000	80.00	100	150	285	450
1786G	—	80.00	100	150	285	450
1786E	—	80.00	100	150	285	450
1787A	—	80.00	100	150	285	450
1787B	220,000	80.00	100	150	285	450
1787E	—	80.00	100	150	285	450
1787F	—	80.00	100	150	285	450
1787G	—	80.00	100	150	285	450
1788A	—	80.00	100	150	285	450
1788B	257,000	80.00	100	150	285	450
1788E	—	80.00	100	150	285	450
1788F	—	80.00	100	150	285	450
1788G	—	80.00	100	150	285	450
1789A	—	80.00	100	150	285	450
1789B	205,000	80.00	100	150	285	450

Date	Mintage	VG	F	VF	XF	Unc
1789E	—	80.00	100	150	285	450
1789F	—	80.00	100	150	285	450
1789G	—	80.00	100	150	285	450
1790A	—	80.00	100	150	285	450
1790B	172,000	80.00	100	150	285	450
1790E	—	80.00	100	150	285	450
1790F	8,171	80.00	100	150	285	450
1790G	—	80.00	100	150	285	450

KM# 1874 DUCAT

3.4909 g., 0.9860 Gold .1106 oz. AGW **Ruler:** Joseph II **Obverse:** Younger laureate military bust right, as sole ruler **Obv. Legend:** IOS • II • D : G • R • I • S • A • GE • HU • BO • REX • **Reverse:** Crowned imperial double eagle with crowned shield on breast **Rev. Legend:** ARCH • AUST • D • BV • LO • M • DUX • HET • **Note:** Prev. KM#2082.

Date	Mintage	VG	F	VF	XF	Unc
1781C	—	80.00	120	200	350	550
1781F	2,143	80.00	120	200	350	550
1782C	—	80.00	120	200	350	550
1782F	1,731	80.00	120	200	350	550
1783C	—	80.00	120	200	350	550
1783F	3,989	80.00	120	200	350	550
1784C Unique	—	—	—	—	350	550
1784F	—	80.00	120	200	350	550
1785F	3,145	80.00	120	200	350	550
1786F	—	80.00	120	200	350	550

KM# 1882 DUCAT

3.4909 g., 0.9860 Gold .1106 oz. AGW **Ruler:** Leopold II **Obverse:** Laureate head right, as King of Hungary and Bohemia **Reverse:** Crowned arms in collar of the Golden Fleece **Note:** Prev. KM#2101.

Date	Mintage	F	VF	XF	Unc
1790A	—	350	850	1,250	1,800

KM# 1883 DUCAT

3.4909 g., 0.9860 Gold .1106 oz. AGW **Ruler:** Leopold II **Obverse:** Head right **Obv. Legend:** LEOP • II • D • G • R • IMP • S • A • GE • HV • BO • REX • **Reverse:** Crowned imperial double eagle with crowned shield on breast **Rev. Legend:** ARCH • A • D • BVRG • LOTH • M • D • H • **Note:** Prev. KM#2102.

Date	Mintage	F	VF	XF	Unc
1790A	—	225	550	850	1,100
1791A	—	300	700	1,000	1,350
1791B	—	275	650	950	1,250
1791E	—	225	550	850	1,100
1791F	—	300	700	1,000	1,350
1791G	—	275	650	950	1,250
1792E	—	225	550	850	1,100
1792F	1,417	300	700	1,000	1,350
1792G	—	250	600	900	1,200

KM# 1885 DUCAT

3.4909 g., 0.9860 Gold .1106 oz. AGW **Obverse:** Bust right **Reverse:** Crowned shield **Note:** Prev. KM#2104.

Date	Mintage	F	VF	XF	Unc
1792A	—	900	1,800	2,600	3,750

KM# 1886 DUCAT

3.4909 g., 0.9860 Gold .1106 oz. AGW **Ruler:** Franz II (I) **Obverse:** Laureate head right **Obv. Legend:** FRANCISVS • D • G • HVNG • BOHEM • GAL • LOD • REX • **Reverse:** Crowned imperial double eagle **Rev. Legend:** ARCH • A • D • BVRG • LOTH • M • D • H • **Note:** Prev. KM#2166.

Date	Mintage	F	VF	XF	Unc
1792A	—	110	180	260	400
1792B	—	110	180	275	400
1792E	—	100	160	250	375
1793A	—	110	180	260	400
1793E	—	110	180	275	400
1793G	—	100	160	250	375
1793A	—	110	170	250	375
1794A	—	110	180	260	400
1794B	—	110	180	275	400
1794E	—	100	160	250	375

Date	Mintage	F	VF	XF	Unc
1794G	—	110	170	210	375
1795A	—	110	180	260	400
1795E	—	100	160	250	375
1795G	—	110	170	250	375
1796A	—	110	180	260	400
1796B	—	110	180	275	400
1796E	—	110	190	275	400
1796G	—	110	170	250	375
1797A	—	110	180	260	400
1797B	—	125	225	325	475
1797C	—	110	190	275	400
1797E	—	100	160	250	375
1797G	—	110	170	250	375
1798A	—	110	180	260	400
1798B	—	110	180	275	400
1798E	—	100	160	250	375
1798G	—	125	225	325	475
1799A	—	110	180	260	400
1799E	—	110	190	275	400
1799G	—	110	170	250	375
1800A	—	110	180	260	400
1800B	—	500	750	1,000	1,250
1800E	—	100	160	250	375
1800G	—	110	170	250	375

KM# 1498 2 DUCAT

7.0000 g., 0.9860 Gold .2219 oz. AGW **Ruler:** Joseph I **Mint:** Vienna **Obverse:** Laureate bust right **Reverse:** Crowned imperial eagle, date in legend **Note:** Klippe. Prev. KM#1909.

Date	Mintage	VG	F	VF	XF	Unc
1707	—	600	1,200	3,500	8,500	—

KM# 1507 2 DUCAT

7.0000 g., 0.9860 Gold .2219 oz. AGW **Ruler:** Joseph I **Mint:** Saint Veit **Obverse:** Laureate bust in inner circle **Reverse:** Crowned imperial eagle in inner circle, crown divides date **Note:** Prev. KM#1670.

Date	Mintage	VG	F	VF	XF	Unc
1710 IIP	—	600	1,200	3,500	8,500	—

KM# 1581 2 DUCAT

7.0000 g., 0.9860 Silver .2219 oz. ASW **Ruler:** Karl (Charles) VI **Mint:** Hall **Obverse:** Laureate bust right **Reverse:** Crowned imperial eagle, date in legend **Note:** Prev. KM#700.

Date	Mintage	VG	F	VF	XF	Unc
ND	—	600	1,450	4,250	8,500	—

KM# 1580 2 DUCAT

7.0000 g., 0.9860 Gold .2219 oz. AGW **Ruler:** Karl (Charles) VI **Mint:** Graz **Obverse:** Laureate bust right **Reverse:** Crowned imperial eagle, date in legend **Note:** Prev. KM#510.

Date	Mintage	VG	F	VF	XF	Unc
1715	—	500	950	2,750	7,250	—
1732	—	500	950	2,750	7,250	—

KM# 1656 2 DUCAT

7.0000 g., 0.9860 Gold .2219 oz. AGW **Ruler:** Karl (Charles) VI **Mint:** Vienna **Obverse:** Laureate bust right **Reverse:** Crowned imperial eagle, date in legend **Note:** Prev. KM#1928.

Date	Mintage	VG	F	VF	XF	Unc
1735	—	550	1,150	4,000	8,500	—

KM# 1727 2 DUCAT

7.0000 g., 0.9860 Gold .2219 oz. AGW **Ruler:** Franz I **Obverse:** Laureate head right **Reverse:** Crowned imperial eagle with arms on breast **Note:** Prev. KM#2043.

Date	Mintage	VG	F	VF	XF	Unc
1745	—	600	1,200	2,000	4,250	6,500

KM# 1726 2 DUCAT

7.0000 g., 0.9860 Gold .2219 oz. AGW **Ruler:** Maria Theresa **Mint:** Hall **Obverse:** Bust right **Reverse:** Crowned imperial eagle with crowned Tyrolean arms on breast **Note:** Prev. KM#754.

Date	Mintage	VG	F	VF	XF	Unc
1746 Rare	—	—	—	—	—	—

KM# 1745 2 DUCAT

7.0000 g., 0.9860 Gold .2219 oz. AGW **Ruler:** Franz I **Note:** Similar to 1 Ducat, KM#1725.1, but double thickness. Prev. KM#2044.

Date	Mintage	VG	F	VF	XF	Unc
1746HA	—	725	1,450	2,500	4,750	7,250

KM# 1860 2 DUCAT

7.0000 g., 0.9860 Gold .2219 oz. AGW **Ruler:** Joseph II **Obverse:** Bust right **Obv. Legend:** IOS • II • D • G • R • I • S • A • GER • IER • REX • **Reverse:** Crowned imperial double eagle, value encircled below **Rev. Legend:** VIRTUTE • ET EXEMPLO • **Note:** Prev. KM#2085.

Date	Mintage	VG	F	VF	XF	Unc
1768E H-G	—	175	325	600	950	1,500
1769E H-G	—	175	325	600	950	1,500
1770E H-G	—	175	325	600	950	1,500
1771E H-G	—	175	325	600	950	1,500
1772E H-G	—	175	325	600	950	1,500
1773E H-G	—	175	325	600	950	1,500
1774E H-G	—	175	325	600	950	1,500
1775E H-G	—	175	325	600	950	1,500
1776E H-G	—	175	325	600	950	1,500
1777E H-G	—	175	325	600	950	1,500

KM# 1869 2 DUCAT

7.0000 g., 0.9860 Gold .2219 oz. AGW **Ruler:** Joseph II **Obverse:** Laureate bust right **Obv. Legend:** IOS • II • D : G • R • I • S • A • GER • IER • REX • **Reverse:** Crowned imperial double eagle, value encircled below **Rev. Legend:** VIRTUTE • ET EXEMPLO • **Note:** Prev. KM#2086.

Date	Mintage	VG	F	VF	XF	Unc
1777E	—	175	325	600	950	1,500
1778E	—	175	325	600	950	1,500
1779E	—	175	325	600	950	1,500
1780E	—	175	325	600	950	1,500

KM# 1875 2 DUCAT

7.0000 g., 0.9860 Gold .2219 oz. AGW **Ruler:** Joseph II **Obverse:** Laureate bust right **Obv. Legend:** IOS • II • D : G • ROM • IMP • S • A • GER • HUNG • BOH • REX • **Reverse:** Crowned imperial double eagle, value encircled below **Rev. Legend:** ARCH • AUST • D • B • LOTH • M • D • HETR • **Note:** Similar to KM#1869 but longer legend. Prev. KM#2087.

Date	Mintage	VG	F	VF	XF	Unc
1781E	—	150	300	575	900	1,450
1782	—	150	300	575	900	1,450

KM# 1876 2 DUCAT

7.0000 g., 0.9860 Gold .2219 oz. AGW **Ruler:** Joseph II **Obverse:** Laureate bust right **Obv. Legend:** IOSEPH • II • D • G • R • I • S • A • GERM • HV • BO • REX • **Reverse:** Crowned imperial double eagle, value encircled below **Rev. Legend:** ARCH • AVST • D • BVRG • LOTH • M • D • HET • **Note:** Prev. KM#2088.

Date	Mintage	VG	F	VF	XF	Unc
1783E	—	150	300	575	900	1,450
1784A	—	150	300	575	900	1,450
1786A	—	150	300	575	900	1,450
1786B	58,000	150	300	575	900	1,450
1786E	—	150	300	575	900	1,450
1787A	—	150	300	575	900	1,450
1787B	20,000	150	300	575	900	1,450
1787E	—	150	300	575	900	1,450

KM# 1888 2 DUCAT

7.0000 g., 0.9860 Gold .2219 oz. AGW **Ruler:** Franz II (I) **Obverse:** Head right **Obv. Legend:** FRANC • II • D • G • R • IMP • S • A • GE • HV • BO • REX • **Reverse:** Crowned imperial double eagle **Rev. Legend:** ARCH • AVST • D • BVRG • LOTH • M • D • HET • **Note:** Prev. KM#2173.

Date	Mintage	VG	F	VF	XF	Unc
1799A	68,000	250	400	950	1,650	2,750
1803A Rare	—	—	—	—	—	—

KM# 1508 3 DUCAT

10.5000 g., 0.9860 Gold .3329 oz. AGW **Ruler:** Joseph I **Mint:** Saint Veit **Obverse:** Laureate bust right in inner circle **Reverse:** Crowned imperial eagle in inner circle **Note:** Prev. KM#1671.

Date	Mintage	VG	F	VF	XF	Unc
1710 IP	—	650	1,400	4,250	8,500	—

KM# 1657 3 DUCAT

10.5000 g., 0.9860 Gold .3329 oz. AGW **Ruler:** Karl (Charles) VI **Mint:** Vienna **Obverse:** Laureate bust right **Reverse:** Crowned imperial eagle in inner circle **Note:** Prev. KM#1929.

Date	Mintage	VG	F	VF	XF	Unc
1735	—	600	1,200	4,200	7,750	—
1737	—	600	1,200	4,200	7,750	—
1738	—	600	1,200	4,200	7,750	—

KM# 1868 3 DUCAT

10.5000 g., 0.9860 Gold .3329 oz. AGW **Ruler:** Joseph II **Obverse:** Armored laureate bust right **Obv. Legend:** IOSEPHUS • II • D: G • R • I • S • A • GER • IER • REX • **Reverse:** Crowned imperial double eagle, shield on breast **Rev. Legend:** VIRTUTE • ET EXEMPLO • **Note:** Prev. KM#2089.

Date	Mintage	VG	F	VF	XF	Unc
1773E	—	600	1,350	3,500	6,000	9,000
1776E	—	600	1,350	3,500	6,000	9,000
1778E	—	600	1,350	3,500	6,000	9,000

KM# 1561 4 DUCAT

14.0000 g., 0.9860 Gold .4438 oz. AGW **Ruler:** Karl (Charles) VI **Mint:** Graz **Note:** Struck with 1/2 Thaler dies, KM#1546. Prev. KM#511.

Date	Mintage	VG	F	VF	XF	Unc
1713 Rare	—	—	—	—	—	—

KM# 1871 4 DUCAT

14.0000 g., 0.9860 Gold .4438 oz. AGW **Ruler:** Maria Theresa **Obverse:** Veiled head right **Reverse:** Crowned imperial eagle, value below **Note:** Prev. KM#A1998.

Date	Mintage	VG	F	VF	XF	Unc
1778 IC-FA	—	650	1,450	3,850	6,500	9,500
1779 IC-FA	—	650	1,450	3,850	6,500	9,500

KM# 1881 4 DUCAT

14.0000 g., 0.9860 Gold .4438 oz. AGW **Ruler:** Joseph II **Obverse:** Laureate bust right **Note:** Prev. KM#2090.

Date	Mintage	VG	F	VF	XF	Unc
1786A	—	650	1,450	3,850	6,500	9,500

KM# 1884 4 DUCAT

14.0000 g., 0.9860 Gold .4438 oz. AGW **Ruler:** Leopold II **Obverse:** Laureate bust of right **Note:** Prev. KM#2103.

Date	Mintage	VG	F	VF	XF	Unc
1790A Rare	—	—	—	—	—	—

KM# 1887 4 DUCAT

14.0000 g., 0.9860 Gold .4438 oz. AGW **Ruler:** Franz II (I) **Obv. Legend:** FRANCISCVS II. D. G. R. IMP... **Rev. Legend:** ...LOTH. M. D. HET. **Note:** Prev. KM#2174.

Date	Mintage	F	VF	XF	Unc
1793A	—	400	1,100	2,750	3,500
1794A	—	550	1,150	2,750	3,500
1795A	—	350	900	2,150	3,000
1796A	—	400	950	2,500	3,500
1797A	—	350	950	2,500	3,250
1798A	—	550	1,150	2,750	3,500
1799A	—	350	950	2,500	3,500
1800A	—	350	950	2,500	3,500

KM# 1572 5 DUCAT

17.5000 g., 0.9860 Gold .5545 oz. AGW **Ruler:** Karl (Charles) VI **Mint:** Graz **Note:** Struck with 1/2 Thaler dies, KM#1546. Prev. KM#513.

Date	Mintage	VG	F	VF	XF	Unc
1714 Rare	—	—	—	—	—	—

KM# 1680 5 DUCAT

17.5000 g., 0.9860 Gold .5547 oz. AGW **Ruler:** Maria Theresa **Mint:** Vienna **Note:** Struck with 1/2 Thaler dies, KM#1677. Prev. KM#A1973.

Date	Mintage	VG	F	VF	XF	Unc
1741	—	425	800	1,500	2,500	—
1742	—	425	800	1,500	2,500	—
1743	—	425	800	1,500	2,500	—

KM# 1728 5 DUCAT

17.5000 g., 0.9860 Gold .5547 oz. AGW **Ruler:** Maria Theresa **Mint:** Vienna **Note:** Struck with 1/2 Thaler dies, KM#1713. Prev. KM#A1974.

Date	Mintage	VG	F	VF	XF	Unc
1745	—	425	800	1,500	2,500	—

KM# 1729 5 DUCAT

17.5000 g., 0.9860 Gold .5548 oz. AGW **Ruler:** Franz I **Obverse:** Laureate head right **Reverse:** Crowned imperial eagle with arms on breast **Note:** Prev. KM#2045.

Date	Mintage	VG	F	VF	XF	Unc
1745 AS/IE	—	1,500	3,000	5,500	8,000	11,500

KM# 1746 5 DUCAT

17.5000 g., 0.9860 Gold .5547 oz. AGW **Ruler:** Maria Theresa **Mint:** Vienna **Note:** Struck with 1/2 Thaler dies, KM#1741. Prev. KM#C1974.

Date	Mintage	VG	F	VF	XF	Unc
1746	—	425	800	1,500	2,500	—
1748	—	425	800	1,500	2,500	—

KM# 1758 5 DUCAT

17.5000 g., 0.9860 Gold .5548 oz. AGW **Ruler:** Franz I **Obverse:** Laureate head right **Note:** Prev. KM#2046.

Date	Mintage	VG	F	VF	XF	Unc
1747WI	—	1,500	3,000	5,500	8,000	11,500
1750CA Rare	—	—	—	—	—	—

KM# 1757 5 DUCAT

17.5000 g., 0.9860 Gold .5548 oz. AGW **Ruler:** Maria Theresa **Obverse:** Veiled head right **Obv. Legend:** M • THERESIA • D • G • R • IMP • HU • BO • REG • **Reverse:** Crowned imperial double eagle **Rev. Legend:** ARCHID • AUST • DUX • BURG • COM • TYR • **Note:** Prev. KM#A1999.

Date	Mintage	VG	F	VF	XF	Unc
1777 IC-FA Rare	—	—	—	—	—	—

KM# 1573 6 DUCAT

21.0000 g., 0.9860 Gold .6657 oz. AGW **Ruler:** Karl (Charles) VI **Mint:** Graz **Note:** Struck with 1/2 Thaler dies, KM#1546. Prev. KM#514.

Date	Mintage	VG	F	VF	XF	Unc
1714 Rare	—	—	—	—	—	—

KM# 1681 6 DUCAT

21.0000 g., 0.9860 Gold .6657 oz. AGW **Ruler:** Maria Theresa **Mint:** Vienna **Note:** Struck with 1/2 Thaler dies, KM#1677. Prev. KM#B1973.

Date	Mintage	VG	F	VF	XF	Unc
1741	—	550	950	1,750	3,000	—
1742	—	550	950	1,750	3,000	—
1743	—	550	950	1,750	3,000	—

KM# 1759 6 DUCAT

21.0000 g., 0.9860 Gold .6658 oz. AGW **Ruler:** Franz I **Obverse:** Bust right **Note:** Prev. KM#2047.

Date	Mintage	VG	F	VF	XF	Unc
1747WI Rare	—	—	—	—	—	—

KM# 1845 6 DUCAT

21.0000 g., 0.9860 Gold .6658 oz. AGW **Ruler:** Maria Theresa **Obverse:** Draped bust right **Obv. Legend:** M • THERESIA • D : G • R • IMP • GE • HU • BO • REG • **Reverse:** Crowned imperial double eagle with crowned shield on breast **Rev. Legend:** ARCHID • AUST • DUX • BURG • COM • TYR • **Note:** Prev. KM#2048.

Date	Mintage	VG	F	VF	XF	Unc
1765WI Rare	—	—	—	—	—	—

KM# 1455 10 DUCAT

35.0000 g., 0.9860 Gold 1.1090 oz. AGW **Ruler:** Joseph I **Mint:** Vienna **Note:** Struck with 1 Thaler dies, KM#1444. Prev. KM#1913.

Date	Mintage	VG	F	VF	XF	Unc
1705 IMH Rare	—	—	—	—	—	—
1707 IMH Rare	—	—	—	—	—	—
1708 IMH Rare	—	—	—	—	—	—

KM# 1574 10 DUCAT

35.0000 g., 0.9860 Gold 1.1090 oz. AGW **Ruler:** Karl (Charles) VI **Mint:** Vienna **Note:** Struck with 1 Thaler dies, KM#1522. Prev. KM#1930.

Date	Mintage	VG	F	VF	XF	Unc
1714 Rare	—	—	—	—	—	—
1716 Rare	—	—	—	—	—	—
1717 Rare	—	—	—	—	—	—

KM# 1632 10 DUCAT

35.0000 g., 0.9860 Gold 1.1090 oz. AGW **Ruler:** Karl (Charles) VI **Mint:** Vienna **Note:** Struck with 1 Thaler dies, KM#1579.1. Prev. KM#1931.

Date	Mintage	VG	F	VF	XF	Unc
1729 Rare	—	—	—	—	—	—

KM# 1706 10 DUCAT

35.0000 g., 0.9860 Gold 1.1095 oz. AGW **Ruler:** Maria Theresa **Mint:** Vienna **Obverse:** Veiled bust right **Obv. Legend:** M • THERESIA • D • G • R • IMP • HU • BO • REG • **Reverse:** Crownd imperial double eagle with shield on breast **Rev. Legend:** ARCHID • AUST • DUX • BURG • CO • TYR • **Note:** Struck with 1/2 Thaler dies, KM#1678. Prev. KM#1973.

Date	Mintage	VG	F	VF	XF	Unc
1743 Rare	—	—	—	—	—	—

KM# 1730 10 DUCAT

35.0000 g., 0.9860 Gold 1.1095 oz. AGW **Ruler:** Maria Theresa **Mint:** Vienna **Obverse:** Veiled bust right **Obv. Legend:** M • THERES • D • G • R • IMP • HU • BO • REG • **Reverse:** Crowned imperial double eagle, crowned shield on breast **Rev. Legend:** ARCHID • AUST • DUX • BURG • COM • TYR • **Note:** Struck with 1/2 Thaler dies, KM#1714. Prev. KM#1974.

Date	Mintage	VG	F	VF	XF	Unc
1745 Rare	—	—	—	—	—	—

KM# 1767 10 DUCAT

35.0000 g., 0.9860 Gold 1.1095 oz. AGW **Ruler:** Maria Theresa **Mint:** Vienna **Note:** Struck with 1/2 Thaler dies, KM#1743. Prev. KM#D1974.

Date	Mintage	VG	F	VF	XF	Unc
1748 Rare	—	—	—	—	—	—

KM# 1663 20 DUCAT

70.0000 g., 0.9860 Gold 2.2180 oz. AGW **Ruler:** Karl (Charles) VI **Mint:** Vienna **Note:** Struck with 1 Thaler dies, KM#1579.1. Prev. KM#1934.

Date	Mintage	VG	F	VF	XF	Unc
1739 Rare	—	—	—	—	—	—

PATTERNS

Including off metal strikes

KM#	Date	Mintage	Identification	Mkt Val
PnGR15	1702	—	Pfennig. Gold. KM#446	—
PnGR16	1713	—	Kreuzer. Gold. KM#494; weight of 1/2 Ducat.	—
PnGR20	1715	—	1/2 Kreuzer. Gold. KM#492	—
PnGR21	1715	—	Kreuzer. Gold. KM#494; weight of 1/4 Ducat.	—
PnGR22	1727	—	Pfennig. Gold. KM#490; weight of 1/4 Ducat.	—
PnPR40	1720	—	Ducat. Silver. KM#1510.	400
PnPR41	1722	—	5 Ducat. Silver. KM#1516.	—
PnPR42	1725	—	2 Ducat. Silver. KM#1515.	450
PnPR43	1754	—	3 Kreuzer. Pewter. Siege coins.	—
PnPR44	1754	—	17 Kreuzer. Pewter. KM#1532.	—
PnPR45	1757	—	20 Kreuzer. Pewter. Siege coins.	—
Pn31	1795A	—	12 Kreuzer. With value only.	—
Pn32	1795C	—	12 Kreuzer. With value only.	—
Pn33	1796E	—	1/2 Ducat. Gold.	1,250
Pn34	1798C	—	Ducat. Gold. KM#2166	—
Pn35	1799B	—	Ducat. Gold. KM#2166	—
Pn36	1800A	—	24 Kreuzer. Copper.	—

AUERSPERG

The Auersperg princes were princes of estates in Austrian Carniola, a former duchy with estates in Laibach and Silesia, a former province in southwestern Poland and Swabia, one of the stem-duchies of medieval Germany. They were elevated to princely rank in 1653, and the following year were made dukes of Muensterberg, which they ultimately sold to Prussia.

PRINCIPALITY

STANDARD COINAGE

KM# 4 THALER

Silver **Ruler:** Heinrich **Obv:** Bust right, "A. WIDEMAN" below **Rev:** Crowned and mantled arms **Note:** Dav. #1181.

Date	Mintage	VG	F	VF	XF	Unc
1762	260	350	550	900	1,500	—

BATTHYANI

The name of a royal Hungarian family, princes of domains in Austria, Styria and Bohemia, who were granted the coining privilege in 1763.

RULERS
Carl, 1761-1772
Ludwig, 1788-1806

MONETARY SYSTEM
120 Kreuzer = 1 Convention Thaler

ALITY

STANDARD COINAGE

KM# 12 20 KREUZER

Silver **Ruler:** Ludwig **Obv:** Draped bust right **Obv. Legend:** LVDOVICVS S • R • I • PRINCEPS DE ... **Rev:** Helmeted and supported arms within crowned mantle

Date	Mintage	VG	F	VF	XF	Unc
1790	—	35.00	75.00	125	200	—

KM# 10 1/2 THALER

Silver **Ruler:** Ludwig **Obv:** Draped bust right **Obv. Legend:** LVDOVICVS S • R • I • PRINCEPS DE ... **Rev:** Helmeted and supported arms within crowned mantle

Date	Mintage	VG	F	VF	XF	Unc
1789	—	75.00	125	175	250	—

KM# A1 1/2 THALER (Convention)

Silver **Ruler:** Carl **Obv:** Armored bust right **Obv. Legend:** CAROL. S.R.I.P DE. BATTHYAN.A.U.E.G.C.M. **Rev:** Crowned and supported oval arms in baroque frame, date at end of legend **Rev. Legend:** FIDELITATE ET FORTITUDINE.(date).

Date	Mintage	VG	F	VF	XF	Unc
1764	—	100	200	400	600	—

KM# 1 1/2 THALER (Convention)

Silver **Ruler:** Carl **Obv:** Armored bust right **Obv. Legend:** CAROL S • R • I • PRINC DE ... **Rev:** Helmeted and supported arms within crowned mantle

Date	Mintage	VG	F	VF	XF	Unc
1765	—	100	200	400	600	—

KM# 7 1/2 THALER (Convention)

Silver **Ruler:** Carl **Obv:** Armored bust right **Obv. Legend:** CAROL S • R • I • PRINC DE ... **Rev:** Crowned and mantled arms within Order chain

Date	Mintage	VG	F	VF	XF	Unc
1770	—	100	200	400	600	—

KM# 8 THALER

Silver **Ruler:** Ludwig **Obv:** Draped bust right **Obv. Legend:** LVDOVICVS S • R • I • PRINCEPS DE ... **Rev:** Helmeted and supported arms within crowned mantle **Note:** Dav. #1184.

Date	Mintage	VG	F	VF	XF	Unc
1788	—	150	250	350	575	—

KM# 2 THALER (Convention)

Silver **Ruler:** Carl **Obv:** Armored bust right **Obv. Legend:** CAROL S • R • I • PRINC DE ... **Rev:** Helmeted and supported arms within crowned mantle **Note:** Dav. #1182.

Date	Mintage	VG	F	VF	XF	Unc
1764	4,000	90.00	175	325	500	—

KM# 6 THALER (Convention)

Silver **Ruler:** Carl **Obv:** Armored bust right **Obv. Legend:** CAROL S • R • I • PRINC DE ... **Rev:** Crowned and mantled arms within Order chain **Note:** Dav. #1183. The KM#6 dated Thaler was apparently struck in 1770.

Date	Mintage	VG	F	VF	XF	Unc
1768	300	175	300	475	800	—

TRADE COINAGE

KM# 3 DUCAT

3.5000 g., 0.9860 Gold .1109 oz. AGW **Ruler:** Carl **Obv:**

Armored bust right **Obv. Legend:** CAROL S • R • I • P: DE ...
Rev: Crowned and mantled arms in Order chain

Date	Mintage	VG	F	VF	XF	Unc
1764	—	250	550	1,200	2,000	—
1765	—	250	550	1,200	2,000	—
1770	—	250	550	1,200	2,000	—

KM# 13 DUCAT
3.5000 g., 0.9860 Gold .1109 oz. AGW **Ruler:** Ludwig **Obv:** Bust **Rev:** Crowned mantled arms

Date	Mintage	F	VF	XF	Unc	BU
1791/0	—	300	650	1,350	2,250	—

KM# 4 5 DUCAT
17.5000 g., 0.9860 Gold .5548 oz. AGW **Ruler:** Carl **Obv:** Armored bust right **Rev:** Crowned and mantled arms wtih griffin supporters

Date	Mintage	VG	F	VF	XF	Unc
1764	—	1,250	2,500	5,000	9,000	—

KM# 11 5 DUCAT
17.5000 g., 0.9860 Gold .5548 oz. AGW **Ruler:** Ludwig **Obv:** Bust **Rev:** Crowned mantled arms

Date	Mintage	F	VF	XF	Unc	BU
1789	—	900	1,750	3,250	5,500	—

KM# 5 10 DUCAT
35.0000 g., 0.9860 Gold 1.1095 oz. AGW **Ruler:** Carl **Obv:** Armored bust right **Rev:** Crowned and mantled arms with griffin supporters

Date	Mintage	VG	F	VF	XF	Unc
1764 Rare	—	—	—	—	—	—

KM# 9 10 DUCAT
35.0000 g., 0.9860 Gold 1.1095 oz. AGW **Ruler:** Ludwig **Obv:** Bust **Rev:** Crowned mantled arms

Date	Mintage	F	VF	XF	Unc	BU
1788 Rare	—	—	—	—	—	—

BRIXEN

A city near the Brenner Pass that was the seat of a bishopric from 992. The bishops were given the coinage right in 1179. Brixen was given to Austria in 1802.

RULERS
Caspar Ignaz von Kuenigl, 1702-1747
Leopold, Graf Spaur, 1747-1778
Sede Vacante, 1778-1779

NOTE: Ruler listing includes only coin issuers and not all bishops.

BISHOPRIC

STANDARD COINAGE

KM# 22 THALER
Silver **Ruler:** Caspar Ignaz von Kuenigl **Note:** Dav. #1203.

Date	Mintage	VG	F	VF	XF	Unc
1710	—	750	1,500	2,750	4,750	—

KM# 31 2 THALER
Silver **Ruler:** Sede Vacante **Obv:** Legend and date in circle of 15 shields **Rev:** Eagle in circle **Note:** Dav. #1204.

Date	Mintage	VG	F	VF	XF	Unc
1779	—	3,500	5,000	8,000	12,500	—

TRADE COINAGE

KM# 26 DUCAT
3.5000 g., 0.9860 Gold .1109 oz. AGW **Ruler:** Caspar Ignaz von Kuenigl **Obv:** Mitre above 2 shields of arms

Date	Mintage	VG	F	VF	XF	Unc
1717	—	1,250	2,500	4,500	7,500	—

KM# 27 DUCAT
3.5000 g., 0.9860 Gold .1109 oz. AGW **Ruler:** Caspar Ignaz von Kuenigl **Obv:** Hat above 2 shields of arms

Date	Mintage	VG	F	VF	XF	Unc
1745	—	850	1,750	3,500	6,500	—

KM# 29 DUCAT
3.5000 g., 0.9860 Gold .1109 oz. AGW **Ruler:** Leopold, Graf Spaur **Obv:** Bust of Leopold Maria Josef right **Rev:** Crowned and mantled arms; date divided at bottom

Date	Mintage	VG	F	VF	XF	Unc
1768	—	750	1,550	3,200	6,000	—

KM# 24 10 DUCAT
35.0000 g., 0.9860 Gold 1.1095 oz. AGW **Ruler:** Caspar Ignaz von Kuenigl **Note:** Struck with 1 Thaler dies, KM#22.

Date	Mintage	VG	F	VF	XF	Unc
1710 Rare	—	—	—	—	—	—

KM# 25 20 DUCAT
37.0000 g., 0.9860 Gold 2.2190 oz. AGW **Ruler:** Caspar Ignaz von Kuenigl **Note:** Struck with 1 Thaler dies, KM#22.

Date	Mintage	VG	F	VF	XF	Unc
1710 Rare	—	—	—	—	—	—

BURGAU

An Austrian possession near Ulm in Germany from 1618 to 1805 at which time it passed to Bavaria. The Günzburg Mint is located in Burgau. For other issues of the Günzburg Mint, see Austria.

RULER
Maria Theresa, 1740-1780

MINT MARKS
GB, GH, H - Günzburg

MINTMASTERS' INITIALS
C - J.H.V. Clotz
F, IF - J. Faby
S, TS - T. Schobl

COUNTY

STANDARD COINAGE

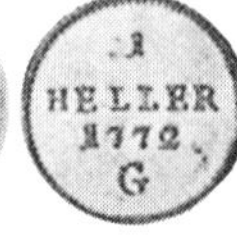

KM# 5 HELLER
Copper **Ruler:** Maria Theresa **Obv:** Arms of Austria-Burgau **Rev:** Denomination, date

Date	Mintage	VG	F	VF	XF	Unc
1768G	—	3.00	10.00	25.00	85.00	—
1772G	—	3.00	10.00	15.00	65.00	—
1773G	—	3.00	10.00	25.00	85.00	—
1774G	—	3.00	10.00	25.00	85.00	—
1777G	—	3.00	10.00	15.00	65.00	—
1778G	—	3.00	10.00	25.00	85.00	—
1780G	—	3.00	10.00	25.00	85.00	—

KM# 6 1/4 KREUZER
Copper **Ruler:** Maria Theresa **Obv:** Crowned arms **Rev:** Denomination

Date	Mintage	VG	F	VF	XF	Unc
1772G	—	3.00	5.00	15.00	65.00	—
1774G	—	3.00	10.00	25.00	85.00	—
1777G	—	3.00	10.00	25.00	85.00	—
1778G	—	3.00	10.00	25.00	85.00	—

KM# 7 1/2 KREUZER
Copper **Ruler:** Maria Theresa **Obv:** Arms of Austria-Burgau **Rev:** Denomination and date

Date	Mintage	VG	F	VF	XF	Unc
1772G	—	7.50	20.00	45.00	100	—

KM# 8 KREUZER
Copper **Ruler:** Maria Theresa **Obv:** Crowned arms **Rev:** Denomination within cartouche

Date	Mintage	VG	F	VF	XF	Unc
1771G	—	—	—	—	—	—
Note: Reported, not confirmed						
1772G	—	2.75	8.00	20.00	50.00	—
1773G	—	2.75	12.00	30.00	75.00	—
1774G	—	2.75	12.00	30.00	75.00	—
1779G	—	2.75	12.00	30.00	75.00	—

KM# 9 1/48 THALER (Convention - 2-1/2 Kreuzer)
Billon **Ruler:** Maria Theresa **Obv:** Crowned arms **Obv. Legend:** M • THER • D • G • .... **Rev:** Denomination, date

Date	Mintage	VG	F	VF	XF	Unc
1772G	—	10.00	20.00	35.00	70.00	—
1773G	—	10.00	20.00	40.00	85.00	—
1774G	—	10.00	25.00	45.00	90.00	—
1779G	—	—	—	—	—	—
Note: Reported, not confirmed						

KM# 10 5 KREUZER (Convention)
Silver **Ruler:** Maria Theresa **Obv:** Young head in wreath **Rev:** Crowned imperial eagle with Austrian arms; "G" above pedestal below

Date	Mintage	VG	F	VF	XF	Unc
1764	—	30.00	65.00	130	220	—
1765 SC	—	30.00	60.00	120	200	—

KM# 17 5 KREUZER (Convention)
Silver **Ruler:** Maria Theresa **Obv:** Veiled head in wreath **Rev:** Crowned imperial eagle with Burgau arms, value below

Date	Mintage	VG	F	VF	XF	Unc
1770 SC	—	—	75.00	150	275	—
1772 SC	—	—	65.00	125	200	—
1773 SC	—	—	65.00	125	200	—
1774 SC	—	—	75.00	150	275	—
1775 SF	—	—	75.00	150	250	—

KM# 11 10 KREUZER (Convention)
Silver **Ruler:** Maria Theresa **Obv:** Young head in wreath **Rev:** Crowned imperial eagle with Austrian arms, "G" above pedestal below

Date	Mintage	VG	F	VF	XF	Unc
1764	—	20.00	40.00	80.00	150	—
1765	—	20.00	40.00	80.00	150	—

KM# 18 10 KREUZER (Convention)
Silver **Ruler:** Maria Theresa **Obv:** Draped bust within wreath of laurel and palm **Obv. Legend:** M • THERESIA • D • G • R • ... **Rev:** Crowned imperial double eagle **Rev. Legend:** ARCHID • AUST • DUX • BURG: CO • T • Y • R • 1772

Date	Mintage	VG	F	VF	XF	Unc
1772 SC	—	40.00	70.00	125	200	—
1774 SC	—	40.00	70.00	125	200	—
1775 SF	—	40.00	70.00	125	200	—
1776 SF	—	40.00	70.00	125	200	—
1777 SF	—	40.00	70.00	125	200	—

KM# 12 20 KREUZER (Convention)
Silver **Ruler:** Maria Theresa **Obv:** Young head in wreath **Rev:** Crowned imperial eagle with Austrian arms, "G" above pedestal below

Date	Mintage	VG	F	VF	XF	Unc
1764	—	25.00	50.00	100	200	—
1765	—	25.00	50.00	110	225	—
1765 SC	—	25.00	50.00	110	200	—

KM# 19 20 KREUZER (Convention)
Silver **Ruler:** Maria Theresa **Obv:** Head in branches **Rev:** Crowned imperial eagle, value below, sprays at sides

Date	Mintage	VG	F	VF	XF	Unc
1765 SC	—	15.00	40.00	100	200	—
1767 SC	—	15.00	40.00	100	200	—
1768 SC	—	15.00	40.00	100	200	—
1769 SC	—	15.00	40.00	100	200	—
1772 SC	—	15.00	30.00	75.00	150	—
1773 SC	—	15.00	40.00	100	200	—

Date	Mintage	VG	F	VF	XF	Unc
1774 SF	—	15.00	40.00	100	200	—
1775 SF	—	15.00	40.00	100	200	—
1777 SF	—	15.00	40.00	100	200	—
1778 SF	—	15.00	40.00	100	200	—
1779 SF	—	15.00	40.00	100	200	—
1780 SF	—	15.00	40.00	100	200	—

KM# 13 30 KREUZER

Silver **Ruler:** Maria Theresa **Obv:** Bust right in rhombus **Rev:** Crowned imperial eagle with Austrian center shield, "G" below in cartouche, all in rhombus

Date	Mintage	F	VF	XF	Unc	BU
1764	—	125	300	700	1,000	—

KM# 14 1/2 THALER

Silver **Ruler:** Maria Theresa **Obv:** Bust right **Rev:** Crowned imperial eagle with Austrian center shield, "G" below in cartouche

Date	Mintage	F	VF	XF	Unc	BU
1764	—	75.00	150	300	600	—
1765	—	60.00	125	250	500	—
1765 SC	—	60.00	125	250	500	—

KM# 20 1/2 THALER

Silver **Ruler:** Maria Theresa **Obv:** Heavily veiled bust **Rev:** Crowned imperial eagle

Date	Mintage	F	VF	XF	Unc	BU
1768 SC	—	50.00	100	200	400	—
1769 SC	—	50.00	100	200	400	—
1771 SC	—	50.00	100	200	400	—
1772 SC	—	50.00	100	200	400	—
1773 SC	—	50.00	100	200	400	—
1774 SC	—	50.00	100	200	400	—

KM# 15 THALER (Convention)

Silver **Ruler:** Maria Theresa **Obv:** Armored bust right **Obv. Legend:** M • THERESIA • D : G • R • IMP ... **Rev:** G below eagle in cartouche **Rev. Legend:** ARCHID • AUST • DUX • BURG • CO • T • Y • R • **Note:** Dav. #1147.

Date	Mintage	F	VF	XF	Unc	BU
1764	—	60.00	120	250	500	—
1765	—	50.00	100	200	400	—
1765 SC	—	50.00	100	200	400	—

KM# 21 THALER (Convention)

Silver **Ruler:** Maria Theresa **Obv:** Veiled bust right **Rev:** Crowned imperial eagle **Note:** Dav. #1149.

Date	Mintage	F	VF	XF	Unc	BU
1765 SC	—	75.00	125	175	350	—
1767 SC	—	75.00	125	175	350	—
1768 SC	—	75.00	125	175	350	—
1769 SC	—	75.00	125	175	350	—
1770 SC	—	75.00	125	175	350	—
1771 SC	—	75.00	125	175	350	—
1772 SC	—	75.00	125	175	350	—

KM# 16 THALER (Convention)

Silver **Ruler:** Maria Theresa **Obv:** Crowned supported arms **Obv. Legend:** M • THERESIA • D : G • R • IMP • HU • BO • REG • **Rev:** Legend in sprays **Rev. Legend:** ARCHID • AUST • D • BURG • MARGGR • ... **Note:** Dav. #1148.

Date	Mintage	F	VF	XF	Unc	BU
1766 .	—	50.00	75.00	125	500	—
1766 .SC	—	50.00	75.00	125	500	—
1767 .SC	—	50.00	75.00	125	500	—

KM# 22 THALER (Convention)

Silver **Ruler:** Maria Theresa **Obv:** Bust with small veil **Obv. Legend:** M. THERESIA • D • G • R • IMP. HU. BO • REG • **Rev:** Crowned imperial double eagle **Rev. Legend:** ARCHID • AUST • DUX • BURG • CO • TYR **Note:** Dav. #1150.

Date	Mintage	F	VF	XF	Unc	BU
1773 SC	—	75.00	125	175	350	—
1774 SC	—	75.00	125	175	350	—
1775 SC	—	75.00	125	175	350	—
1775 SF	—	75.00	125	175	350	—
1776 SF	—	75.00	125	175	350	—
1777 SF	—	75.00	125	175	350	—
1778 SF	—	75.00	125	175	350	—
1779 SF	—	75.00	125	175	350	—
1780 SF	—	35.00	60.00	100	200	—

KM# 23 THALER (Convention)

Silver **Ruler:** Maria Theresa **Obv:** Large, mature bust right **Obv. Legend:** M • THERESIA • D • G • R • IMP • HU • BO • REG • **Rev:** Crowned imperial double eagle **Rev. Legend:** ARCHID • AVST • DUX • .... **Note:** Dav, #1151. There are many minor differences between types from the various mints. The reverse arms on coins from Vienna, Prague, Karlsburg, Kremnitz and the TS-IF type from Gunzburg are similar to those on regular thalers from the Vienna Mint except the colors of Burgau now appear in the lower right quadrant of the shield of arms. For more recent restrikes dated 1780 SF / \ X see KM#T1 listed under Trade Coins/Austria.

Date	Mintage	F	VF	XF	Unc	BU
1780 IC-FA	—	65.00	100	150	450	—
1780 SF/\ X \	—	35.00	60.00	100	300	—
1780 SF\X\ Restrike	—	BV	BV	10.00	20.00	—
1780 FS	—	600	1,000	1,500	2,000	—
1780 TS-IF	—	35.00	60.00	100	300	—
1780 ST/SF	—	175	300	500	1,000	—
1780 PS-IK	—	35.00	60.00	100	300	—
1780 B-SK-PD	—	175	300	500	1,000	—
1780 AH-GS	—	35.00	60.00	100	300	—

COLLOREDO-MANSFELD

The Colloredo's, a German-Italian family, attained the rank of count of the Austro-Hungarian Empire in 1724, and of prince in 1763. Prince Franz Gundacker acquired the titles of the predominant German Mansfeld family, (which was seated at Mansfeld in Saxony from the 11th to the 18th century), in 1780 by marriage.

RULER

Franz Gundacker, 1788-1807

PRINCIPALITY

STANDARD COINAGE

KM# 3 THALER (Convention)

Silver **Ruler:** Franz Gundacker **Obv:** St. George slaying the dragon **Rev:** Crowned, draped arms **Note:** Dav. #1185.

Date	Mintage	F	VF	XF	Unc	BU
1794 Restrike	—	—	—	500	700	—

TRADE COINAGE

KM# 1 DUCAT

3.5000 g., 0.9860 Gold .1109 oz. AGW **Ruler:** Franz Gundacker **Obv:** St. George slaying the dragon **Rev:** Crowned, draped arms

Date	Mintage	F	VF	XF	Unc	BU
1792	—	350	700	1,200	2,250	—

KM# 2 DUCAT

3.5000 g., 0.9860 Gold .1109 oz. AGW **Ruler:** Franz Gundacker **Note:** Curved die break.

Date	Mintage	F	VF	XF	Unc	BU
1792 Restrike	—	150	300	500	900	—

PATTERNS

Including off metal strikes

KM#	Date	Mintage	Identification	Mkt Val
Pn1	1791	—	Ducat. Copper.	350
Pn2	1791	—	Ducat. Silver.	—

DIETRICHSTEIN

A noble Carinthian family traceable from 1000, it was not until after 1500 that the first coins were made. The coinage was sporadic and Karl Ludwig was the last to issue coins in 1726.

RULERS

Pulsgau Line

Karl Ludwig, 1698-1732

NOTE: Ruler listing includes only coin issuers and not all rulers of the various line of this family.

COUNTY

STANDARD COINAGE

KM# 15 1/2 KREUZER

Silver **Ruler:** Karl Ludwig **Obv:** Crowned oval arms, date, denomination **Note:** Uniface.

Date	Mintage	VG	F	VF	XF	Unc
1731	—	25.00	45.00	85.00	160	—

KM# 16 KREUZER

Silver **Ruler:** Karl Ludwig **Obv:** Armored bust right **Rev:** Crowned oval arms

Date	Mintage	VG	F	VF	XF	Unc
1731	—	40.00	70.00	125	220	—

KM# 17 THALER

Silver **Ruler:** Karl Ludwig **Obv:** Armored bust right **Obv. Legend:** CAR: LUD: S • R • ICOM .... **Rev:** Crowned arms **Rev. Legend:** ...LIBER BARO IN HOLLENB... **Note:** Struck at Vienna Mint. Dav. #1186.

Date	Mintage	VG	F	VF	XF	Unc
1726	500	400	800	1,500	2,150	—

TRADE COINAGE

KM# 18 DUCAT

3.5000 g., 0.9860 Gold .1109 oz. AGW **Ruler:** Karl Ludwig **Obv:** Armored bust right **Rev:** Crowned arms in ornamental cartouche, date in legend

Date	Mintage	VG	F	VF	XF	Unc
1726	—	350	750	1,850	3,250	—

EGER

A town located west-northwest of Prague. The district of Eger is first mentioned as a part of East Franconia. After changing hands many times, it became a permanent part of Bohemia in 1350.

Obsidional minor coins were struck here in 1742 during the War of the Austrian Succession.

TOWN

SIEGE COINAGE

KM# 5 KREUZER

Tin **Obv:** Shielded arms **Rev:** Shielded arms

Date	Mintage	VG	F	VF	XF	Unc
1743	—	75.00	110	165	300	—

KM# 6 3 KREUZER

Tin **Obv:** Shielded arms **Rev:** Shielded arms **Note:** Similar to 1 Kreuzer, KM#5.

Date	Mintage	VG	F	VF	XF	Unc
1743	—	85.00	125	175	350	—

ESZTERHAZY

A rich and famous old Hungarian family. The name Eszterhazy established in 1584. Became princes in 1687. Nikolas Joseph was a patron of Haydn for 30 years and the only member of the family to exercise the coinage right.

RULER

Nikolas Joseph, 1762-1790

PRINCIPALITY

STANDARD COINAGE

KM# 1 1/2 THALER (Convention)

Silver **Ruler:** Nikolas Joseph **Obv:** Armored bust right **Obv. Legend:** NICOL • S • R • I • PRINC • ESZTERHAZY DE ... **Rev:** Crowned and mantled arms

Date	Mintage	F	VF	XF	Unc	BU
1770	—	225	400	800	1,500	—

KM# 2 THALER (Convention)

Silver **Ruler:** Nikolas Joseph **Obv:** Armored bust right **Obv. Legend:** NICOL • S • R • I • PRINC • ESZTERHAZY DE ... **Rev:** Crowned and mantled arms **Note:** Dav. #1187.

Date	Mintage	F	VF	XF	Unc	BU
1770	406	300	600	1,150	2,250	—

TRADE COINAGE

KM# 3 DUCAT

3.5000 g., 0.9860 Gold .1109 oz. AGW **Ruler:** Nikolas Joseph **Obv:** Armored bust right **Obv. Legend:** NICOL • S • R • I • PR • ESZTERHAZY DE ... **Rev:** Crowned and mantled arms in Order chain

Date	Mintage	F	VF	XF	Unc	BU
1770	—	650	1,250	2,250	4,000	—

KHEVENHULLER-METSCH

A prominent family of Carinthia which regained power after the anti-reformation wars and became counts in 1673. Elevated to Princes in 1763.

RULERS

Johann Joseph

As Count, 1742-1763

As Prince, 1763-1776

COUNTY

STANDARD COINAGE

KM# 1 THALER (Convention)

Silver **Ruler:** Johann Joseph as Count **Obv:** Armored bust right **Rev:** Helmeted and supported arms **Note:** Dav. #1188.

Date	Mintage	F	VF	XF	Unc	BU
1761	—	300	500	750	1,350	—

KM# 2 THALER (Convention)

Silver **Ruler:** Johann Joseph as Prince **Obv:** Armored bust right **Rev:** Crowned and mantled arms **Note:** Dav. #1189.

Date	Mintage	F	VF	XF	Unc	BU
1771	200	325	550	850	1,500	—

TRADE COINAGE

KM# 3 DUCAT

3.5000 g., 0.9860 Gold .1109 oz. AGW **Ruler:** Johann Joseph as Count **Obv:** Armored bust right **Rev:** Crowned and supported arms

Date	Mintage	F	VF	XF	Unc	BU
1761	—	750	1,450	3,000	5,500	—

KINSKY

A principality in Bohemia.

RULER

Leopold Ferdinand, 1741-1760

PRINCIPALITY

STANDARD COINAGE

KM# 5 1/2 THALER

Silver **Ruler:** Leopold Ferdinand **Obv:** Crowned monogram **Rev:** Crowned ornate arms

Date	Mintage	VG	F	VF	XF	Unc
ND(1741)	—	45.00	90.00	165	285	—

PATTERNS

Including off metal strikes

KM#	Date	Mintage	Identification	Mkt Val
Pn1	ND(1741)	—	1/2 Thaler. Copper. KM#5.	—

NOSTITZ-RIENECK

Nostitz was a Bohemian family first mentioned in 1454. Johann Hartwig was made a count in 1641 and purchased Rieneck in 1673. He was made a count of the empire and given the mint right in 1673. He died at Vienna in 1683 during the Turkish siege. The only coins of this house were made in 1719. The properties were mediatized early in the Napoleonic era.

RULER

Anton Johann, 1683-1736

COUNTY

STANDARD COINAGE

KM# 5 1/2 THALER
Silver **Ruler:** Anton Johann **Obv:** Armored bust right **Obv. Legend:** ANT • IOH • S • R • I • COM • DE • ... **Rev:** Crowned arms with griffon supporters, swan above crown, date divided below arms

Date	Mintage	VG	F	VF	XF	Unc
1719	—	500	750	1,000	1,650	—

KM# 6 THALER
Silver **Ruler:** Anton Johann **Obv:** Armored bust right **Obv. Legend:** ANTONI • IOH • S • R • I • COM • DE ... **Rev:** Crowned arms with griffon supporters, swan above crown, date divided below arms **Note:** Dav. #1191

Date	Mintage	VG	F	VF	XF	Unc
1719 GFN	—	600	1,000	1,250	1,850	—

TRADE COINAGE

FR# 1797 DUCAT
3.5000 g., 0.9860 Gold .1109 oz. AGW **Ruler:** Anton Johann **Obv:** Armored bust right **Obv. Legend:** ANT • IOH • S • R • I • COM • DE • ... **Rev:** Crowned arms with griffon supporters, swan above crown, date divided below arms

Date	Mintage	VG	F	VF	XF	Unc
1719	—	650	1,350	2,500	4,500	—

OLMUTZ

In Moravia

Olmütz (Olomouc) a town in the eastern part of the Czech Republic which was, until 1640, the recognized capital of Moravia, obtained the right to mint coinage in 1144, but exercised it sparingly until the 17th century, when it became an archbishopric.

RULERS

Karl III Josef Herzog von Lothringen, 1695-1711
Wolfgang von Schrattenbach, 1711-1738
Jakob Ernst von Liechtenstein-Castelcorn, 1738-1745
Ferdinand Julius, Graf von Troyer, 1745-1758
Leopold II Friedrich von Egkh, 1758-1760 (no coinage)
Maximilian von Hamilton, 1761-1776, (no coinage)
Anton Theodor, Graf von Colloredo, 1777-1811

BISHOPRIC

STANDARD COINAGE

KM# 105.1 KREUZER
Silver **Ruler:** Karl III Josef **Obv:** Bust right **Rev:** Crowned arms on cross with inner circles

Date	Mintage	VG	F	VF	XF	Unc
1701	—	2.50	5.00	10.00	25.00	—
1702	—	2.50	5.00	10.00	25.00	—
1704	—	2.50	5.00	10.00	25.00	—
1705	—	2.50	6.00	12.00	30.00	—

KM# 105.2 KREUZER
Silver **Ruler:** Karl III Josef **Obv:** Without inner circles **Rev:** Without inner circles **Note:** Type 105.2 has more than 13 minor varieties.

Date	Mintage	VG	F	VF	XF	Unc
1701	—	2.50	5.00	10.00	25.00	—
1702	—	2.50	5.00	10.00	25.00	—
1705	—	2.50	5.00	10.00	25.00	—
1707	—	2.50	5.00	10.00	25.00	—
1708	—	5.00	10.00	18.00	40.00	—

KM# 102 3 KREUZER
Silver **Ruler:** Karl III Josef **Obv:** Bust right **Rev:** Crowned arms on cross **Note:** Type 102 has more than 5 minor varieties.

Date	Mintage	VG	F	VF	XF	Unc
1706	—	5.00	12.00	25.00	60.00	—

KM# 113 6 KREUZER
Silver **Ruler:** Karl III Josef **Obv:** Bust right **Obv. Legend:** D G CAROLVS EPVS - OLOMVCENSIS **Rev:** Crowned arms on cross **Note:** Type 113 has more than 12 minor varieties.

Date	Mintage	VG	F	VF	XF	Unc
1706	—	8.00	15.00	35.00	70.00	—
1708	—	5.00	10.00	20.00	45.00	—
1709	—	5.00	10.00	20.00	45.00	—
1710	—	5.00	10.00	20.00	45.00	—
1711	—	5.00	10.00	20.00	45.00	—

KM# 125.1 6 KREUZER
Silver **Ruler:** Wolfgang **Obv:** Bust right **Obv. Legend:** WOLFGANG .... **Rev:** Cardinal's hat above cross dividing mitre and crown above round arms

Date	Mintage	VG	F	VF	XF	Unc
1712	—	10.00	20.00	45.00	80.00	—

KM# 125.2 6 KREUZER
Silver **Ruler:** Wolfgang **Obv:** Bust right **Obv. Legend:** WOLFGANG D: G: ... **Rev:** Oval arms, cardinal hat above mitre, crown and cross

Date	Mintage	VG	F	VF	XF	Unc
1712	—	5.00	10.00	20.00	45.00	—
1713	—	5.00	10.00	20.00	45.00	—
1714	—	5.00	10.00	20.00	45.00	—
1715	—	5.00	10.00	20.00	45.00	—
1716	—	10.00	20.00	35.00	50.00	—

KM# 185 10 KREUZER
Silver **Ruler:** Anton Theodor **Obv:** Bust right **Rev:** Arms

Date	Mintage	VG	F	VF	XF	Unc
1779	6,000	20.00	50.00	70.00	120	—

KM# 114 15 KREUZER
Silver **Ruler:** Karl III Josef **Obv:** Armored bust right **Obv. Legend:** D: G: CAROLVS ... **Rev:** Crowned arms on cross

Date	Mintage	VG	F	VF	XF	Unc
1706	—	15.00	25.00	45.00	85.00	—
1708	—	15.00	25.00	45.00	85.00	—
1709	—	15.00	25.00	45.00	85.00	—
1710	—	15.00	25.00	45.00	85.00	—
1711	—	15.00	25.00	45.00	85.00	—

KM# 126.1 15 KREUZER
Silver **Ruler:** Wolfgang **Obv:** Bust right **Rev:** Round arms with mitre and crown

Date	Mintage	VG	F	VF	XF	Unc
1712	—	20.00	45.00	90.00	175	—

KM# 126.2 15 KREUZER
Silver **Ruler:** Wolfgang **Obv:** Bust right **Obv. Legend:** WOLFGANG D: G: .... **Rev:** Oval arms with cardinal hat and cross

Date	Mintage	VG	F	VF	XF	Unc
1712	—	15.00	25.00	45.00	75.00	—
1713	—	20.00	40.00	70.00	100	—
1714	—	15.00	25.00	45.00	75.00	—
1715	—	20.00	40.00	70.00	100	—
1716	—	15.00	25.00	45.00	75.00	—

KM# 186 20 KREUZER
Silver **Ruler:** Anton Theodor **Obv:** Bust right **Obv. Legend:** ANT • THEODOR • D • G • ... **Rev:** Cardinal's hat above cross dividing mitre and crown above arms **Rev. Legend:** ...COLLOREDO & WALD • CO •

Date	Mintage	VG	F	VF	XF	Unc
1779	900	50.00	85.00	150	250	—

KM# 173 30 KREUZER
Silver **Ruler:** Ferdinand Julius **Obv:** Bust right **Rev:** Arms

Date	Mintage	VG	F	VF	XF	Unc
1750	—	30.00	50.00	75.00	125	—

KM# 174 1/2 CONVENTION THALER

Silver **Ruler:** Ferdinand Julius **Obv:** Bust right **Rev:** Arms

Date	Mintage	VG	F	VF	XF	Unc
1752	—	100	150	200	350	—

KM# 187 1/2 CONVENTION THALER

Silver **Ruler:** Anton Theodor **Obv:** Bust right **Obv. Legend:** ANT • THEODOR • D • G • ... **Rev:** Cardinal's hat above cross dividing mitre and crown above arms **Rev. Legend:** ...COLLOREDO & WALD • CO •

Date	Mintage	VG	F	VF	XF	Unc
1779	300	100	180	300	500	—

KM# 107 1/2 THALER

Silver **Ruler:** Karl III Josef **Obv:** Armored bust right **Obv. Legend:** DG CAROLVS:EPISCOPVSOLOMVCENSIS **Rev:** Curved center shield

Date	Mintage	VG	F	VF	XF	Unc
1702	—	60.00	100	200	400	—
1703	—	40.00	80.00	150	350	—

KM# 109 1/2 THALER

Silver **Ruler:** Karl III Josef **Obv:** Armored bust right **Obv. Legend:** DGCAROLVSEPISCOPVSOLO ... **Rev:** Angular center shield

Date	Mintage	VG	F	VF	XF	Unc
1703	—	35.00	65.00	125	250	—
1704	—	35.00	65.00	125	250	—
1705	—	35.00	65.00	125	250	—
1707	—	35.00	65.00	125	250	—

KM# 131 1/2 THALER

Silver **Ruler:** Wolfgang **Obv:** Bust right **Rev:** Round arms with mitre and crown

Date	Mintage	VG	F	VF	XF	Unc
1712	—	50.00	90.00	180	300	—

KM# 135 1/2 THALER

Silver **Ruler:** Wolfgang **Obv:** Bust right **Rev:** Oval arms with cardinal hat

Date	Mintage	VG	F	VF	XF	Unc
1717	—	30.00	60.00	100	200	—
1722	—	20.00	40.00	80.00	150	—
1724	—	20.00	40.00	80.00	150	—
1725	—	20.00	40.00	80.00	150	—

KM# 140 1/2 THALER

Silver **Ruler:** Wolfgang **Obv:** Bust right **Rev:** 3 ornate arms

Date	Mintage	VG	F	VF	XF	Unc
1727	—	15.00	30.00	65.00	125	—
1728	—	15.00	30.00	65.00	125	—
1729	—	15.00	30.00	65.00	125	—
1730	—	15.00	30.00	65.00	125	—
1731	—	15.00	30.00	65.00	125	—
1733	—	35.00	65.00	125	250	—
1734	—	35.00	65.00	125	250	—
1735	—	35.00	65.00	125	250	—
1737	—	35.00	65.00	125	250	—

KM# 161.1 1/2 THALER

Silver **Ruler:** Jakob Ernst **Obv:** Draped bust right **Obv. Legend:** IACOBUS • ERNESTUS • D: G: ... **Rev:** Arms with mitre and crown, date at left

Date	Mintage	VG	F	VF	XF	Unc
1739	—	40.00	90.00	180	350	—
1740	—	40.00	90.00	180	350	—
1742	—	40.00	90.00	180	350	—

KM# 161.2 1/2 THALER

Silver **Ruler:** Jakob Ernst **Obv:** Draped bust right **Rev:** Arms with mitre and crown, date on top

Date	Mintage	VG	F	VF	XF	Unc
1744	—	40.00	90.00	180	350	—

KM# 106 THALER

Silver **Ruler:** Karl III Josef **Obv:** Bust right **Rev:** Crowned oval arms on cross in sprays, date 17-01 in crown **Note:** Dav. #1205.

Date	Mintage	VG	F	VF	XF	Unc
1701	—	80.00	150	250	450	—

KM# 108 THALER

Silver **Ruler:** Karl III Josef **Obv:** Armored bust right **Obv. Legend:** D: G: CAROLVS • EPVSOLOM... **Rev:** Crown above oval arms on 8-pointed cross with crowned eagles left and right, date in legend **Rev. Legend:** DVX • LOTHAR • ET • BAR • S • R • I • ... **Note:** Dav. #1206. Without inner circles.

Date	Mintage	VG	F	VF	XF	Unc
1702	—	60.00	100	200	375	—

KM# 110 THALER

Silver **Ruler:** Karl III Josef **Obv:** Armored bust right **Obv. Legend:** D: G: CAROLVS ... **Rev:** Crown above oval arms on 8-pointed cross with crowned eagles at right and left **Rev. Legend:** DVX • LOTHAR • ET • BAR • S • R • I • ... **Note:** Dav. #1207. With inner circles.

Date	Mintage	VG	F	VF	XF	Unc
1703	—	35.00	65.00	125	250	—

KM# 103 THALER

Silver **Ruler:** Karl III Josef **Obv:** Armored bust right **Obv. Legend:** DEI GRATIA CAROLVS.... **Rev:** Crown above arms on 8-pointed cross, crowned eagles at left and right **Rev. Legend:** DVX • LOTHAR • ET • BAR • .... **Note:** Dav. #1208.

Date	Mintage	VG	F	VF	XF	Unc
1704	—	35.00	65.00	125	250	—

KM# 115 THALER

Silver **Ruler:** Karl III Josef **Obv:** Armored bust right **Obv. Legend:** DEI GRATIACAROLVSEPISCOPUSOLOMUCENSIS **Rev:** Crown divides date **Rev. Legend:** DUX • LOTHAR : ETBAR : S : R : I : ... **Note:** Dav. #1209.

Date	Mintage	VG	F	VF	XF	Unc
1705	—	30.00	60.00	100	240	—

KM# 116 THALER

Silver **Ruler:** Karl III Josef **Obv.** Armored bust right **Obv. Legend:** DEI GRATIACAROLVSEPISCOPUSOLOMUCENSIS

Rev: Crown above arms on 8-pointed cross, crowned eagles at right and left **Rev. Legend:** DUX LOTHAR ET BAR ... **Note:** Dav. #1211.

Date	Mintage	VG	F	VF	XF	Unc
1706	—	35.00	65.00	125	250	—
1707	—	35.00	65.00	125	250	—

KM# 118 THALER

Silver **Ruler:** Karl III Josef **Obv. Legend:** D. G. CAROLUS.. **Note:** Dav. #1212.

Date	Mintage	VG	F	VF	XF	Unc
1709	—	35.00	65.00	125	250	—
1710	—	35.00	65.00	125	250	—

KM# 120 THALER

Silver **Ruler:** Karl III Josef **Rev. Legend:** ...BO: COM **Note:** Similar to KM#115. Dav. #1213.

Date	Mintage	VG	F	VF	XF	Unc
1711	—	45.00	80.00	150	300	—

KM# 127 THALER

Silver **Ruler:** Wolfgang **Obv:** Bust right in beaded border **Obv. Legend:** WOLFGANGVS D:G: EPVS • OLOMVCENSIS DVX: S: R: I: PRCEPS **Rev:** Crowned and mitred arms in border **Rev. Legend:** REG • CAP • BO • ET DE SCHRATTENBACH COMES 1712 **Note:** Dav. #1214.

Date	Mintage	VG	F	VF	XF	Unc
1712	—	40.00	80.00	160	250	—

KM# 128 THALER

Silver **Ruler:** Wolfgang **Obv:** Capped bust right in beaded border **Obv. Legend:** WOLFGANG D: G: S: R: E: CARD: DE SCHRATTEMBACH EP: OLOM: **Rev:** Cardinal's hat above cross dividing mitre and crown above arms, date divided by star above **Rev. Legend:** DVX S: R: I: PCPS REG - CAP • BOHEM • COMES: **Note:** Dav. #1215.

Date	Mintage	VG	F	VF	XF	Unc
1713	—	35.00	75.00	150	225	—
1714/3	—	35.00	75.00	150	225	—

KM# 130 THALER

Silver **Ruler:** Wolfgang **Obv:** Capped bust right **Obv. Legend:** WOLFFG: D: G: S: R: E: PRESB: CARD ... **Rev:** Date not divided above hat **Rev. Legend:** DVX S: R: I: PS: R: C: B: COM • CON • GER • ... **Note:** Dav. #1216.

Date	Mintage	VG	F	VF	XF	Unc
1716	—	35.00	75.00	150	225	—

KM# 133 THALER

Silver **Ruler:** Wolfgang **Obv:** Bust right **Obv. Legend:** WOLFFG • D: G: S: R: E: PRESB • CARD • DE SCHRATTEMBACH EP • OLO • **Rev:** Hatted, mitred, and crowned arms divides date **Rev. Legend:** DVX S: R: I: P: C: B: COM • CON • .... **Note:** Dav. #1218.

Date	Mintage	VG	F	VF	XF	Unc
1718	—	30.00	60.00	125	200	—
1719	—	30.00	60.00	125	200	—
1720	—	30.00	60.00	125	200	—
1721	—	30.00	60.00	125	200	—
1722	—	30.00	60.00	125	200	—
1724	—	30.00	60.00	125	200	—
1725	—	30.00	60.00	125	200	—

KM# 139 THALER

Silver **Ruler:** Wolfgang **Rev:** 3 arms below crown, mitre and hat, date divided by bottom arm **Note:** Dav. #1219.

Date	Mintage	VG	F	VF	XF	Unc
1726	—	40.00	80.00	160	250	—
1727	—	40.00	80.00	160	250	—

KM# 141 THALER

Silver **Ruler:** Wolfgang **Obv:** Bust right **Obv. Legend:** WOLFFG: D: G: S: R: E: PRESBCARD.... **Rev:** 3 oval arms, date divided at top by cardinal's hat **Rev. Legend:** S: R: I: PS: R: C: B: C: PROTEC • GER • ... **Note:** Dav. #1220.

Date	Mintage	VG	F	VF	XF	Unc
1728	—	40.00	80.00	160	250	—

KM# 144 THALER

Silver **Ruler:** Wolfgang **Rev:** Episcopal arms divide date 1-7-2-9 **Note:** Dav. #1221.

Date	Mintage	VG	F	VF	XF	Unc
1729	—	70.00	120	250	350	—

KM# 150 THALER

Silver **Ruler:** Wolfgang **Obv:** St. Wenzeslaus seated on a cloud between 2 angels, 2 shields below **Rev:** St. Cyrill seated left holding book with IHS, arms at right **Note:** Dav. #1222.

Date	Mintage	VG	F	VF	XF	Unc
1730 Rare	—	—	—	—	—	—

KM# 151 THALER

Silver **Ruler:** Wolfgang **Obv:** Capped bust right **Rev:** Episcopal arms, date left of cardinal's hat **Note:** Dav. #1223.

Date	Mintage	VG	F	VF	XF	Unc
1730	—	70.00	120	250	350	—
1733	—	60.00	100	200	300	—
1734	—	60.00	100	200	300	—
1735	—	60.00	100	200	300	—
1736/35	—	100	130	180	300	—

KM# 152 THALER

Silver **Ruler:** Wolfgang **Obv:** Bust right **Obv. Legend:** WOLF: D: G: ... **Rev:** Date divided by cardinal's hat **Rev. Legend:** S • R • I • PS: R: C: B: C: PROT • GER: .... **Note:** Dav. #1224.

Date	Mintage	VG	F	VF	XF	Unc
1731	—	70.00	120	250	350	—

KM# 154 THALER

Silver **Ruler:** Wolfgang **Obv:** Bust right, JD below bust **Obv. Legend:** WOLFFG: D: G: S: R: E: ... **Rev:** Episcopal arms divide date, three shields **Rev. Legend:** S: R: I: PS: R: C: B: C: PROT • GER: ... **Note:** Dav. #1225.

Date	Mintage	VG	F	VF	XF	Unc
1736	—	50.00	90.00	175	275	—

KM# 155 THALER

Silver **Ruler:** Wolfgang **Rev:** Date left of cardinal's hat **Note:** Dav. #1226.

Date	Mintage	VG	F	VF	XF	Unc
1736	—	50.00	90.00	175	275	—
1737	—	80.00	100	180	300	—
1738	—	80.00	100	180	300	—

KM# 162 THALER

Silver **Ruler:** Jakob Ernst **Obv:** Bust right **Obv. Legend:** IAC: ERN: D: G: EPUS: OLOMUCENSIS: DUX • S: R: I: PCPS • **Rev:** Arms with mitre and crown, date at left **Rev. Legend:** REG: CAP: BO: ET: DE: LIECHTENSTEIN COMES **Note:** Dav. #1227.

Date	Mintage	VG	F	VF	XF	Unc
1739	—	85.00	175	300	450	—
1740	—	85.00	175	300	450	—

KM# 163 THALER

Silver **Ruler:** Jakob Ernst **Obv:** Smaller bust **Rev:** Date above crown **Note:** Dav. #1228.

Date	Mintage	VG	F	VF	XF	Unc
1741	—	75.00	150	250	350	—

KM# 164 THALER

Silver **Ruler:** Jakob Ernst **Rev:** Mitred and crowned arms divide date at sides **Note:** Dav. #1229.

Date	Mintage	VG	F	VF	XF	Unc
1742	—	75.00	150	250	350	—

KM# 165 THALER

Silver **Ruler:** Jakob Ernst **Obv:** Bust right **Obv. Legend:** IAC: ERN: D: G: EPVS: OLOMVC: DVX • S: R: I: PCPS **Rev:** Date divided at top **Rev. Legend:** REG: CAP: BO: ET: DE • LIECHTENSTEIN ... **Note:** Dav. #1230.

Date	Mintage	VG	F	VF	XF	Unc
1742	—	75.00	150	250	350	—
1743	—	75.00	150	250	350	—
1744	—	75.00	150	250	350	—
1745	—	75.00	150	250	350	—

KM# 171 THALER

Silver **Ruler:** Ferdinand Julius **Obv:** Bust right **Rev:** Hatted, mitred and crowned arms, date divided near bottom **Note:** Dav. #1232.

Date	Mintage	VG	F	VF	XF	Unc
1746	—	250	400	750	1,250	—
1749	—	250	400	750	1,250	—
1752	—	250	400	750	1,250	—
1756	—	250	400	750	1,250	—

KM# 188 THALER

Silver **Ruler:** Anton Theodor **Obv:** Bust right **Obv. Legend:** ANT • THEODOR • D • G • PRIM • A • EP • OLOMU • DUX • **Rev:** Cardinal's hat above cross dividing mitre and crown atop arms **Rev. Legend:** S • R • I • PR • RE • CAP • BOH • & A COLLOREDO & WALD • CO: **Note:** Dav. #1233.

Date	Mintage	VG	F	VF	XF	Unc
1779	200	175	300	600	900	—

KM# 136 2 THALER

Silver **Ruler:** Wolfgang **Note:** Similar to 1 Thaler, KM#133. Dav. #1217.

Date	Mintage	VG	F	VF	XF	Unc
1722 Rare	—	—	—	—	—	—

TRADE COINAGE

KM# 100 1/8 DUCAT

0.4375 g., 0.9860 Gold .0139 oz. AGW **Ruler:** Karl III Josef **Obv:** Bust right **Rev:** Arms

Date	Mintage	VG	F	VF	XF	Unc
ND	—	350	500	700	1,000	—

KM# 104 1/4 DUCAT

0.8750 g., 0.9860 Gold .0277 oz. AGW **Ruler:** Karl III Josef **Obv:** Bust right **Rev:** Arms on cross

Date	Mintage	VG	F	VF	XF	Unc
1704	—	200	350	700	1,450	—

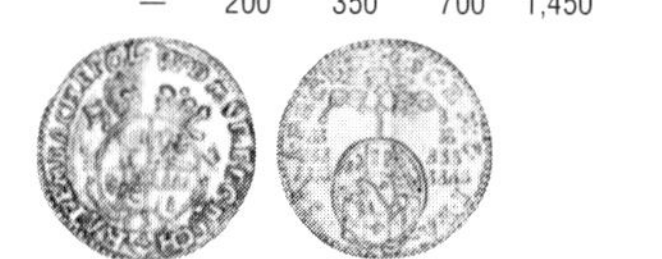

KM# 119 1/4 DUCAT

0.8750 g., 0.9860 Gold .0277 oz. AGW **Ruler:** Wolfgang **Obv:** Olmutz arms **Rev:** Bishop arms

Date	Mintage	VG	F	VF	XF	Unc
ND(1728-30)	—	125	200	350	750	—

KM# 142 1/4 DUCAT

0.8750 g., 0.9860 Gold .0277 oz. AGW **Ruler:** Wolfgang **Obv:** Bust right, value below **Rev:** 3 shields of arms

Date	Mintage	VG	F	VF	XF	Unc
ND(1728-30)	—	85.00	150	275	500	—

KM# 143 1/4 DUCAT

0.8750 g., 0.9860 Gold .0277 oz. AGW **Ruler:** Wolfgang **Obv:** Bust right **Rev:** Cardinal hat above oval arms

Date	Mintage	VG	F	VF	XF	Unc
ND(1728-30)	—	125	200	400	800	—

KM# 166 1/4 DUCAT

0.8750 g., 0.9860 Gold .0277 oz. AGW **Ruler:** Jakob Ernst **Obv:** Bust right **Rev:** Crowned and mitred arms

Date	Mintage	VG	F	VF	XF	Unc
ND(1741)	—	150	250	425	850	—

KM# 101 DUCAT

3.5000 g., 0.9860 Gold .1109 oz. AGW **Ruler:** Karl III Josef **Obv:** Bust right **Rev:** Crowned arms

Date	Mintage	VG	F	VF	XF	Unc
ND	—	250	400	1,000	2,000	—
1701	—	250	400	1,000	2,000	—

KM# 138 DUCAT

3.5000 g., 0.9860 Gold .1109 oz. AGW **Ruler:** Wolfgang **Obv:** Bust right **Rev:** Arms below cardinal's hat

Date	Mintage	VG	F	VF	XF	Unc
ND(1715-16)	—	250	450	900	1,750	—
1725	—	250	450	900	1,750	—
1726	—	250	450	900	1,750	—
1728	—	250	450	900	1,750	—
1736	—	250	450	900	1,750	—
1737	—	250	450	850	1,650	—

KM# 167 DUCAT

3.5000 g., 0.9860 Gold .1109 oz. AGW **Ruler:** Jakob Ernst **Obv:** Bust right **Rev:** Arms topped by mitre and crown

Date	Mintage	VG	F	VF	XF	Unc
1739	—	700	1,500	3,000	5,000	—
1740	—	700	1,500	3,000	5,000	—
1743	—	700	1,500	3,000	5,000	—
1744	—	700	1,500	3,000	5,000	—

KM# 172 DUCAT

3.5000 g., 0.9860 Gold .1109 oz. AGW **Ruler:** Ferdinand Julius **Obv:** Bust right **Rev:** Arms

Date	Mintage	VG	F	VF	XF	Unc
1747 Rare	—	—	—	—	—	—

KM# 189 DUCAT

3.5000 g., 0.9860 Gold .1109 oz. AGW **Ruler:** Anton Theodor **Obv:** Bust right **Rev:** Arms

Date	Mintage	VG	F	VF	XF	Unc
1779	500	450	950	1,750	3,000	—

KM# 111 2 DUCAT

7.0000 g., 0.9860 Gold .2219 oz. AGW **Ruler:** Karl III Josef **Obv:** Bust right **Rev:** Crowned arms on cross between twigs **Note:** Struck with 1/2 Thaler dies, KM#107.

Date	Mintage	VG	F	VF	XF	Unc
1703	—	450	950	1,750	3,000	—

KM# A113 2 DUCAT

7.0000 g., 0.9860 Gold .2219 oz. AGW **Ruler:** Karl III Josef **Note:** Struck with 1/2 Thaler dies, KM#109.

Date	Mintage	VG	F	VF	XF	Unc
1703	—	450	950	1,750	3,000	—
1704	—	—	—	—	—	—
Note: Reported, not confirmed						
1705	—	—	—	—	—	—
Note: Reported, not confirmed						

Date	Mintage	VG	F	VF	XF	Unc
1707	—	—	—	—	—	—

Note: Reported, not confirmed

KM# 112 2 DUCAT

7.0000 g., 0.9860 Gold .2219 oz. AGW **Ruler:** Karl III Josef **Obv:** Bust right **Rev:** Crowned arms on cross without twigs

Date	Mintage	VG	F	VF	XF	Unc
ND	—	450	950	1,750	3,000	—

KM# 180 2 DUCAT

7.0000 g., 0.9860 Gold .2219 oz. AGW **Ruler:** Maximilian von Hamilton **Obv:** Bust left **Rev:** 2 oval arms

Date	Mintage	VG	F	VF	XF	Unc
1762 Rare	—	—	—	—	—	—

KM# 117 3 DUCAT

10.5000 g., 0.9860 Gold .3329 oz. AGW **Ruler:** Karl III Josef **Obv:** Bust right **Rev:** Crowned arms **Note:** Struck with 1/2 Thaler dies, KM#109.

Date	Mintage	VG	F	VF	XF	Unc
1704	—	—	—	—	—	—
Note: Reported, not confirmed						
1705	—	—	—	—	—	—
Note: Reported, not confirmed						
1707	—	900	2,000	3,750	6,500	—

KM# 132 3 DUCAT

10.5000 g., 0.9860 Gold .3329 oz. AGW **Ruler:** Wolfgang **Obv:** Bust right **Obv. Legend:** WOLFFG D G S R I ... **Rev:** Cardinal's hat above cross dividing mitre and crown atop arms **Note:** Struck with 1/2 Thaler dies, KM#131.2.

Date	Mintage	VG	F	VF	XF	Unc
1717	—	750	1,450	3,000	5,500	—
1725	—	750	1,450	3,000	5,500	—

KM# A139 3 DUCAT

10.5000 g., 0.9860 Gold .3329 oz. AGW **Ruler:** Wolfgang **Note:** Struck with 1/2 Thaler dies, KM#135.

Date	Mintage	VG	F	VF	XF	Unc
1725	—	750	1,450	3,000	5,500	—

KM# A144 3 DUCAT

10.5000 g., 0.9860 Gold .3329 oz. AGW **Ruler:** Wolfgang **Note:** Struck with 1/2 Thaler dies, KM#140.

Date	Mintage	VG	F	VF	XF	Unc
1728	—	750	1,450	3,000	5,500	—

KM# A156 3 DUCAT

10.5000 g., 0.9860 Gold .3329 oz. AGW **Ruler:** Wolfgang **Note:** Struck with 1/2 Thaler dies, KM#153.

Date	Mintage	VG	F	VF	XF	Unc
1734	—	800	1,500	3,200	5,750	—

KM# 169 3 DUCAT

10.5000 g., 0.9860 Gold .3228 oz. AGW **Ruler:** Jakob Ernst **Note:** Struck with 1/2 Thaler dies, KM#161.

Date	Mintage	VG	F	VF	XF	Unc
1740 Rare	—	—	—	—	—	—

KM# 129 4 DUCAT

14.0000 g., 0.9860 Gold .4438 oz. AGW **Ruler:** Wolfgang **Obv:** Bust right in inner circle **Rev:** Arms topped by mitre and crown **Note:** Struck with 1 Thaler dies, KM#128.

Date	Mintage	VG	F	VF	XF	Unc
1713	—	1,000	2,500	4,000	7,000	—

KM# A103 5 DUCAT

17.5000 g., 0.9860 Gold .5545 oz. AGW **Ruler:** Karl III Josef **Obv:** Bust right **Rev:** Crowned arms on cross with eagle supporters

Date	Mintage	VG	F	VF	XF	Unc
ND	—	1,250	2,400	4,000	7,500	—

KM# C113 5 DUCAT

17.5000 g., 0.9860 Gold .5545 oz. AGW **Ruler:** Karl III Josef **Note:** Struck with 1 Thaler dies, KM#110.

Date	Mintage	VG	F	VF	XF	Unc
1703	—	1,400	3,000	5,000	8,500	—

KM# B113 5 DUCAT

17.5000 g., 0.9860 Gold .5545 oz. AGW **Ruler:** Karl III Josef **Obv:** Bust right **Rev:** Crowned arms **Note:** Struck with 1/2 Thaler dies, KM#109.

Date	Mintage	VG	F	VF	XF	Unc
1703	—	1,600	3,200	5,500	9,000	—
1704	—	1,600	3,200	5,500	9,000	—
1705	—	1,600	3,200	5,500	9,000	—
1707	—	1,600	3,200	5,500	9,000	—

KM# A115 5 DUCAT

17.5000 g., 0.9860 Gold .5545 oz. AGW **Ruler:** Karl III Josef **Note:** Struck with 1 Thaler dies, KM#103.

Date	Mintage	VG	F	VF	XF	Unc
1704	—	1,400	3,000	5,000	8,500	—

KM# A118 5 DUCAT

17.5000 g., 0.9860 Gold .5545 oz. AGW **Ruler:** Karl III Josef **Note:** Struck with 1 Thaler dies, KM#116.

Date	Mintage	VG	F	VF	XF	Unc
1707	—	1,600	3,200	5,500	9,000	—

KM# A119 5 DUCAT

17.5000 g., 0.9860 Gold .5545 oz. AGW **Ruler:** Karl III Josef **Note:** Struck with 1 Thaler dies, KM#118.

Date	Mintage	VG	F	VF	XF	Unc
1710	—	1,600	3,200	5,500	9,000	—

KM# A130 5 DUCAT

17.5000 g., 0.9860 Gold .5547 oz. AGW **Ruler:** Wolfgang **Note:** Struck with 1 Thaler dies, KM#128.

Date	Mintage	VG	F	VF	XF	Unc
1713	—	1,200	2,500	4,500	7,500	—

KM# 134 5 DUCAT

17.5000 g., 0.9860 Gold .5547 oz. AGW **Ruler:** Wolfgang **Note:** Struck with 1 Thaler dies, KM#133.

Date	Mintage	VG	F	VF	XF	Unc
1722	—	1,200	2,500	4,500	7,500	—
1725	—	1,200	2,500	4,500	7,500	—

KM# 170 5 DUCAT

17.5000 g., 0.9860 Gold .5547 oz. AGW **Ruler:** Jakob Ernst **Note:** Struck with 1 Thaler dies, KM#162.

Date	Mintage	VG	F	VF	XF	Unc
1740 Rare	—	—	—	—	—	—

KM# B118 6 DUCAT

21.0000 g., 0.9860 Gold .6657 oz. AGW **Ruler:** Karl III Josef **Note:** Struck with 1 Thaler dies, KM#116.

Date	Mintage	VG	F	VF	XF	Unc
1707 Rare	—	—	—	—	—	—

KM# A153 6 DUCAT

21.0000 g., 0.9860 Gold .6657 oz. AGW **Ruler:** Wolfgang **Note:** Struck with 1 Thaler dies, KM#152.

Date	Mintage	VG	F	VF	XF	Unc
1731 Rare	—	—	—	—	—	—

KM# C118 8 DUCAT

28.0000 g., 0.9860 Gold .8872 oz. AGW **Ruler:** Karl III Josef **Note:** Struck with 1 Thaler dies, KM#116.

Date	Mintage	VG	F	VF	XF	Unc
1707 Rare	—	—	—	—	—	—

KM# 137 12 DUCAT

42.0000 g., 0.9860 Gold 1.3316 oz. AGW **Ruler:** Wolfgang **Obv:** Bust right **Rev:** Oval arms

Date	Mintage	VG	F	VF	XF	Unc
ND(1722-25) Rare	—	—	—	—	—	—

PATTERNS

Including off metal strikes

KM#	Date	Mintage	Identification	Mkt Val
Pn11	1704	—	1/2 Thaler. Pewter.	—
Pn23	1712	—	1/2 Thaler. Pewter.	—
Pn29	1725	—	Thaler. Pewter.	—
Pn36	1762	—	2 Ducat. Silver.	250

ORSINI-ROSENBERG

The Princes of Orsini-Rosenberg were members of the Carinthian family who, in 1648, were given the rank of counts of the Austro-Hungarian Empire. Count Wolfgang Franz Xaver, who was made a prince in 1790, exercised his minting privilege to prepare a convention thaler in 1793 that was not actually struck until 1853.

RULER

Prince Franz, 1739-1796

PRINCIPALITY

STANDARD COINAGE

KM# 1 THALER

Silver **Ruler:** Prince Franz **Obv:** Bust right **Obv. Legend:** FRANCISVS • VRSIN • S • R • I • PRINCEPS • ROSENBERG • **Rev:** Arms with bear supporters within crowned mantle **Rev. Legend:** MONETA • NOVA • AD • NORMAN • CONVENTIONIS • **Note:** Dav. #1192.

Date	Mintage	VG	F	VF	XF	Unc
1793 Struck 1853	—	200	350	650	1,150	—

PAAR

The Princes of Paar were members of an Italian family that for nearly three centuries held office as hereditary Austrian postmaster general. They attained the rank of counts in 1629, and of princes, with the minting privilege, in 1769.

RULERS

Johann Wenzel
as Count, 1741-1769
as Prince, 1769-1792
Prince Wenzel 1792-1812

PRINCIPALITY

STANDARD COINAGE

KM# 1 1/2 CONVENTION THALER

14.0000 g., Silver **Ruler:** Johann Wenzel as Prince **Obv:** Bust right **Obv. Legend:** IOH • WEN • S • R • I • M • P • PRINCEPS • A • PAAR • **Rev:** Crowned imperial double eagle, crowned arms within Order chain on breast

Date	Mintage	VG	F	VF	XF	Unc
1771	700	70.00	125	250	400	—

KM# 5 1/2 CONVENTION THALER

14.0000 g., Silver **Ruler:** Prince Wenzel **Obv:** Bust right **Obv.**

Legend: WENCESLAVS • S • RO ... **Rev:** Crowned imperial double eagle, crowned arms on breast **Rev. Legend:** ...SVP • IMP • AVLREG • HER •

Date	Mintage	VG	F	VF	XF	Unc
1794	400	80.00	145	275	450	—

KM# 2 THALER

14.0000 g., Silver **Ruler:** Johann Wenzel as Prince **Obv:** Armored bust right **Obv. Legend:** IOH • WEN • S • R • I • M • P • PRINCEPS A • PAAR **Rev:** Crowned imperial double eagle, crowned arms within Order chain on breast **Rev. Legend:** ...GE • H • POST • MAG • **Note:** Dav. #1193. 500 additional pieces were struck in 1781.

Date	Mintage	VG	F	VF	XF	Unc
1771	200	200	350	600	950	1,500

KM# 6 THALER

14.0000 g., Silver **Ruler:** Prince Wenzel **Obv:** Bust right **Rev:** Imperial eagle **Note:** Similar to 1/2 Thaler, KM#5. Dav. #1194.

Date	Mintage	VG	F	VF	XF	Unc
1794	250	200	350	650	1,100	—

TRADE COINAGE

KM# 3 DUCAT

3.5000 g., 0.9860 Gold .1109 oz. AGW **Ruler:** Johann Wenzel as Prince **Obv:** Bust right **Rev:** Crowned imperial eagle

Date	Mintage	VG	F	VF	XF	Unc
1771	—	350	550	1,250	2,250	—

KM# 4 DUCAT

3.5000 g., 0.9860 Gold .1109 oz. AGW **Ruler:** Johann Wenzel as Prince **Obv:** Armored bust right **Obv. Legend:** IOH • WEN • S • H • I • M • P • PRINCEPS A • PAAR • **Rev:** Crowned imperial double eagle, crowned arms on breast **Rev. Legend:** S • I • AUL • REG • HER • ...

Date	Mintage	VG	F	VF	XF	Unc
1781	—	300	500	1,200	2,200	—

KM# 7 DUCAT

3.5000 g., 0.9860 Gold .1109 oz. AGW **Ruler:** Prince Wenzel **Obv:** Head right **Obv. Legend:** WENCESLAVS • S • ROM • IMP • PRINCEPS • A • PAAR • **Rev:** Crowned imperial double eagle, crowned arms on breast **Rev. Legend:** SVP • IMP • AVI : REG • HER • ...

Date	Mintage	VG	F	VF	XF	Unc
1794	—	200	375	850	1,500	—

KM# 8 5 DUCAT

17.5000 g., 0.9860 Gold .5548 oz. AGW **Ruler:** Prince Wenzel **Obv:** Head right **Rev:** Crowned arms **Note:** Struck with 1/2 Thaler dies, KM#5.

Date	Mintage	VG	F	VF	XF	Unc
1794 Rare	—	—	—	—	—	—

KM# 9 10 DUCAT

35.0000 g., 0.9860 Gold 1.1095 oz. AGW **Ruler:** Prince Wenzel **Obv:** Head right **Rev:** Crowned arms **Note:** Struck with 1/2 Thaler dies, KM#5.

Date	Mintage	VG	F	VF	XF	Unc
1794 Rare	—	—	—	—	—	—

SALZBURG

A town on the Austro-Bavarian frontier which grew up around a monastery and bishopric that was founded circa 700. It was raised to the rank of archbishopric in 798. In 1803 Salzburg was secularized and given to Archduke Ferdinand of Austria. In 1805 it was annexed to Austria. Salzburg was part of Bavaria from 1809 to 1813, returning to Austria in the latter year. It became a crownland in 1849, remaining so until becoming part of the Austrian Republic in 1918.

RULERS

Johann Ernst, Graf von Thun u. Hohenstein 1687-1709
Franz Anton, Graf u. Fürst von Harrach 1709-1727
Leopold Anton, Graf von Firmian 1727-1744
Jakob Ernst, Graf von Lichtenstein 1745-1747
Andreas Jakob, Graf von Dietrichstein 1747-1753
Sigismund III, Graf von Schrattenbach 1753-1771
Hieronymus, Graf von Colloredo-Walsee 1772-1803

ENGRAVERS' INITIALS

Initials	Years	Officials
(star)	1677-1718	Philipp Heinrich Müller, die-cutter in Augsburg
B	1702-43	Philipp Christoph von Becker, die-cutter in Vienna
G	ca.1713-27	Maria Antonio di Gennaro, die-cutter in Vienna
D	ca.1726-28	Georg Raphael Donner, die-cutter in Vienna
FMF, FMK, MK	1738-55	Franz Xavier Matzenkopf, Sr. die-cutter
FM, M	1755-1805	Franz Xavier Matzenkopf, Jr. die-cutter

MONETARY SYSTEM

4 Pfenning = 1 Kreuzer
120 Kreuzer = 1 Convention Thaler

ARCHBISHOPRIC

STANDARD COINAGE

KM# 291 PFENNING

Silver **Ruler:** Franz Anton **Obv:** Date above 2 shields, "FA" below **Note:** Uniface.

Date	Mintage	VG	F	VF	XF	Unc
1709	—	2.00	5.00	10.00	20.00	—
1710	—	2.00	5.00	10.00	20.00	—
1711	—	2.00	5.00	10.00	20.00	—
1712	—	2.00	5.00	10.00	20.00	—
1713	—	2.00	5.00	10.00	20.00	—
1714	—	2.00	5.00	10.00	20.00	—
1715	—	2.00	5.00	10.00	20.00	—
1716	—	2.00	5.00	10.00	20.00	—
1717	—	2.00	5.00	10.00	20.00	—
1719	—	2.00	5.00	10.00	20.00	—
1721	—	2.00	5.00	10.00	20.00	—
1722	—	2.00	5.00	10.00	20.00	—
1723	—	2.00	5.00	10.00	20.00	—
1724	—	2.00	5.00	10.00	20.00	—
1725	—	2.00	5.00	10.00	20.00	—
1726	—	2.00	5.00	10.00	20.00	—
1727	—	2.00	5.00	10.00	20.00	—

KM# 324 PFENNING

Silver **Ruler:** Leopold Anton **Obv:** Date above 2 shields, L below **Note:** Uniface

Date	Mintage	VG	F	VF	XF	Unc
1728	—	2.00	5.00	10.00	20.00	—
1729	—	2.00	5.00	10.00	20.00	—
1730	—	2.00	5.00	10.00	20.00	—
1731	—	2.00	5.00	10.00	20.00	—
1732	—	2.00	5.00	10.00	20.00	—
1733	—	2.00	5.00	10.00	20.00	—
1734	—	2.00	5.00	10.00	20.00	—
1735	—	2.00	5.00	10.00	20.00	—
1736	—	2.00	5.00	10.00	20.00	—
1737	—	2.00	5.00	10.00	20.00	—
1738	—	2.00	5.00	10.00	20.00	—
1739	—	2.00	5.00	10.00	20.00	—
1740	—	2.00	5.00	10.00	20.00	—
1741	—	2.00	5.00	10.00	20.00	—
1742	—	2.00	5.00	10.00	20.00	—
1743	—	2.00	5.00	10.00	20.00	—
1744	—	2.00	5.00	10.00	20.00	—

KM# 340 PFENNING

Silver **Ruler:** Jakob Ernst **Obv:** Date above 2 shields, "I" below **Note:** Uniface.

Date	Mintage	VG	F	VF	XF	Unc
1745	—	3.00	6.00	12.00	25.00	—
1746	—	3.00	6.00	12.00	25.00	—
1747	—	3.00	6.00	12.00	25.00	—

KM# 352 PFENNING

Billon **Ruler:** Andreas Jakob **Obv:** Date above 2 adjacent shields, "A" below **Note:** Uniface.

Date	Mintage	VG	F	VF	XF	Unc
1748	—	2.00	5.00	10.00	20.00	—
1750	—	3.00	6.00	12.00	25.00	—
1752	—	2.00	5.00	10.00	20.00	—

KM# 366 PFENNING

Billon **Ruler:** Sigismund III **Obv:** Date above 2 shields, S below **Note:** Uniface.

Date	Mintage	VG	F	VF	XF	Unc
1753	—	1.50	3.00	6.00	13.00	—
1755	—	1.50	3.00	6.00	13.00	—
1756	—	1.50	3.00	6.00	13.00	—
1760	—	1.50	3.00	6.00	13.00	—
1763	—	1.50	3.00	6.00	13.00	—
1765	—	1.50	3.00	6.00	13.00	—
1768	—	3.00	5.00	10.00	20.00	—
1769	—	1.50	3.00	6.00	13.00	—
1770	—	1.50	3.00	6.00	13.00	—
1771	—	3.00	5.00	10.00	20.00	—

KM# 441 PFENNING

Copper **Ruler:** Hieronymus **Obv:** Oval shield within frame divides S B **Rev:** Value, date

Date	Mintage	VG	F	VF	XF	Unc
1775	—	2.50	4.50	9.00	18.00	—
1777	—	2.50	5.00	10.00	20.00	—
1778	—	2.50	4.50	9.00	18.00	—
1779	—	2.50	4.50	9.00	18.00	—
1780	—	2.50	4.50	9.00	18.00	—
1781	—	2.50	4.50	9.00	18.00	—

KM# 454 PFENNING

Copper **Ruler:** Hieronymus **Obv:** Oval arms within frame divides S B **Rev:** Value, date within wreath

Date	Mintage	VG	F	VF	XF	Unc
1783	—	3.00	6.00	12.00	25.00	—

KM# 455 PFENNING

Copper **Ruler:** Hieronymus **Obv:** Oval shield in frame divides S B **Rev:** Value, date within wreath

Date	Mintage	VG	F	VF	XF	Unc
1783	—	3.00	6.00	12.00	25.00	—
1784	—	3.00	6.00	12.00	25.00	—

KM# 456 PFENNING

Copper **Ruler:** Hieronymus **Obv:** Round shield above sprigs, S B below **Rev:** Value, date within wreath **Note:** Varieties in ribbon design exist.

Date	Mintage	VG	F	VF	XF	Unc
1786	—	2.50	4.50	9.00	18.00	—
1789	—	2.50	4.50	9.00	18.00	—
1790	—	2.50	4.50	9.00	18.00	—

KM# 473 PFENNING

Copper **Ruler:** Hieronymus **Obv:** Shield within sprigs divides S B below **Rev:** Value, date within wreath

Date	Mintage	VG	F	VF	XF	Unc
1792	—	3.50	7.50	15.00	30.00	—

KM# 474 PFENNING

Copper **Ruler:** Hieronymus **Obv:** Shielded arms above spray **Rev:** Crossed palm branches below date

Date	Mintage	VG	F	VF	XF	Unc
1792	—	3.00	5.00	9.00	18.00	—
1793	—	3.00	5.00	9.00	18.00	—
1794	—	3.00	5.00	9.00	18.00	—
1795	—	3.00	6.00	12.00	25.00	—
1796	—	3.00	5.00	9.00	18.00	—
1797	—	3.00	5.00	9.00	18.00	—
1798	—	3.00	5.00	9.00	18.00	—
1799	—	3.00	5.00	9.00	18.00	—
1800	—	3.00	5.00	9.00	18.00	—

KM# 268 2 PFENNING

Silver **Ruler:** Johann Ernst **Obv:** Date above 2 shields, "IE" below **Note:** Uniface.

Date	Mintage	VG	F	VF	XF	Unc
1701	—	4.00	8.00	16.00	30.00	—
1702	—	4.00	8.00	16.00	30.00	—
1703	—	4.00	8.00	16.00	30.00	—
1704	—	4.00	8.00	16.00	30.00	—
1705	—	4.00	8.00	16.00	30.00	—
1706	—	4.00	8.00	16.00	30.00	—
1707	—	4.00	8.00	16.00	30.00	—
1708	—	4.00	8.00	16.00	30.00	—
1709	—	4.00	8.00	16.00	30.00	—

KM# 445 2 PFENNING

Copper **Ruler:** Hieronymus **Obv:** Oval shield within frame divides S B **Rev:** Value, date, rosettes

Date	Mintage	VG	F	VF	XF	Unc
1777	—	3.50	6.50	10.00	20.00	—
1781	—	3.50	6.50	10.00	20.00	—
1782	—	3.50	6.50	10.00	20.00	—

KM# 446 2 PFENNING

Copper **Ruler:** Hieronymus **Obv:** Oval shield within frame divides S B **Rev:** Value, date with ornamental design below

Date	Mintage	VG	F	VF	XF	Unc
1777	—	3.50	6.50	10.00	20.00	—

KM# 457 2 PFENNING

Copper **Ruler:** Hieronymus **Obv:** Oval shield within sprigs above S B **Rev:** Value, date within wreath

Date	Mintage	VG	F	VF	XF	Unc
1786	—	4.00	7.50	15.00	30.00	—
1791	—	4.00	7.50	15.00	30.00	—

KM# 472 2 PFENNING

Copper **Ruler:** Hieronymus **Obv:** Shield within sprigs above S B **Rev:** Value date

Date	Mintage	VG	F	VF	XF	Unc
1791	—	3.00	6.00	12.00	25.00	—
1793	—	3.00	6.00	12.00	25.00	—
1794	—	3.00	6.00	12.00	25.00	—
1795	—	4.00	7.50	15.00	30.00	—
1796	—	3.00	6.00	12.00	25.00	—
1797	—	3.00	6.00	12.00	25.00	—
1798	—	3.00	6.00	12.00	25.00	—
1799	—	3.00	6.00	12.00	25.00	—
1800	—	3.00	6.00	12.00	25.00	—

KM# 476.1 2 PFENNING

Copper **Ruler:** Hieronymus **Obv:** Shield within sprigs above S B **Rev:** Value, date above sprigs

Date	Mintage	VG	F	VF	XF	Unc
1793	—	3.00	6.00	12.00	28.00	—

KM# 476.2 2 PFENNING

Copper **Ruler:** Hieronymus **Obv:** Shield within sprigs above S B **Rev:** Value, date above sprigs

Date	Mintage	VG	F	VF	XF	Unc
1794	—	3.00	6.00	12.00	28.00	—

KM# 247 1/2 KREUZER

Silver **Ruler:** Johann Ernst **Obv:** Value divides date above 2 shields , "IE" below **Note:** Uniface.

Date	Mintage	VG	F	VF	XF	Unc
1701	—	4.00	8.00	16.00	30.00	—
1702	—	4.00	8.00	16.00	30.00	—
1703	—	4.00	8.00	16.00	30.00	—
1704	—	4.00	8.00	16.00	30.00	—
1705	—	4.00	8.00	16.00	30.00	—
1706	—	4.00	8.00	16.00	30.00	—
1707	—	4.00	8.00	16.00	30.00	—
1708	—	4.00	8.00	16.00	30.00	—
1709	—	4.00	8.00	16.00	30.00	—

KM# 292 1/2 KREUZER

Silver **Ruler:** Franz Anton **Obv:** Value divides date above 2 shields of arms, "FA" below

Date	Mintage	VG	F	VF	XF	Unc
1709	—	2.00	5.00	10.00	20.00	—
1710	—	2.00	5.00	10.00	20.00	—
1711	—	2.00	5.00	10.00	20.00	—
1712	—	2.00	5.00	10.00	20.00	—
1713	—	2.00	5.00	10.00	20.00	—
1714	—	2.00	5.00	10.00	20.00	—
1715	—	2.00	5.00	10.00	20.00	—
1716	—	2.00	5.00	10.00	20.00	—
1717	—	2.00	5.00	10.00	20.00	—
1718	—	2.00	5.00	10.00	20.00	—
1719	—	2.00	5.00	10.00	20.00	—
1720	—	2.00	5.00	10.00	20.00	—
1721	—	2.00	5.00	10.00	20.00	—
1722	—	2.00	5.00	10.00	20.00	—
1724	—	2.00	5.00	10.00	20.00	—
1725	—	2.00	5.00	10.00	20.00	—
1727	—	2.00	5.00	10.00	20.00	—

KM# 333 1/2 KREUZER

Silver **Ruler:** Leopold Anton **Obv:** Value divides date above 2 shields , "L" below **Note:** Uniface.

Date	Mintage	VG	F	VF	XF	Unc
1729	—	2.00	5.00	10.00	20.00	—
1730	—	2.00	5.00	10.00	20.00	—
1732	—	2.00	5.00	10.00	20.00	—
1733	—	2.00	5.00	10.00	20.00	—
1734	—	2.00	5.00	10.00	20.00	—
1735	—	2.00	5.00	10.00	20.00	—
1736	—	2.00	5.00	10.00	20.00	—
1737	—	2.00	5.00	10.00	20.00	—
1739	—	2.00	5.00	10.00	20.00	—
1741	—	2.00	5.00	10.00	20.00	—
1743	—	2.00	5.00	10.00	20.00	—

KM# 341 1/2 KREUZER

Silver **Ruler:** Jakob Ernst **Obv:** Value divides date above 2 shields of arms, "I" below

Date	Mintage	VG	F	VF	XF	Unc
1745	—	5.00	10.00	20.00	40.00	—

KM# 353 1/2 KREUZER

Billon **Ruler:** Andreas Jakob **Obv:** Date divided by value above 2 oval shields, "A" below **Note:** Uniface.

Date	Mintage	VG	F	VF	XF	Unc
1748	—	3.00	5.00	12.00	25.00	—
1752	—	3.00	5.00	12.00	25.00	—

KM# 367 1/2 KREUZER

Billon **Ruler:** Sigismund III **Note:** Uniface. Similar to KM#353 but "S" below shields.

Date	Mintage	VG	F	VF	XF	Unc
1753	—	6.00	10.00	20.00	35.00	—
1758	—	6.00	10.00	20.00	35.00	—
1760	—	6.00	10.00	20.00	35.00	—

KM# 248 KREUZER

Silver **Ruler:** Johann Ernst **Obv:** Oval arms with cardinals' hat above **Obv. Legend:** IO : ERNEST : D : G : ARCHIEP **Rev:** Round shield within double cross and circle

Date	Mintage	VG	F	VF	XF	Unc
1701	—	4.00	8.00	16.00	30.00	—
1702	—	4.00	8.00	16.00	30.00	—
1703	—	4.00	8.00	16.00	30.00	—
1704	—	4.00	8.00	16.00	30.00	—
1705	—	4.00	8.00	16.00	30.00	—
1706	—	4.00	8.00	16.00	30.00	—
1707	—	4.00	8.00	16.00	30.00	—
1708	—	4.00	8.00	16.00	30.00	—

KM# 293 KREUZER

Silver **Ruler:** Franz Anton **Obv. Legend:** FR ANT D G ARCHIE PR. **Rev:** Double-cross with Saltsburg arms in center

Date	Mintage	VG	F	VF	XF	Unc
1709	—	4.00	8.00	17.50	35.00	—
1710	—	4.00	8.00	17.50	35.00	—
1711	—	4.00	8.00	17.50	35.00	—

KM# 373 KREUZER

Billon **Ruler:** Sigismund III **Obv:** Oval arms with Cardinals' hat and garland above **Obv. Legend:** SIGISM : D : G : ... **Rev:** Oval, ornate arms, date above

Date	Mintage	VG	F	VF	XF	Unc
1754	—	1.50	3.00	7.50	15.00	—
1755	—	1.50	3.00	7.50	15.00	—
1756	—	1.50	3.00	7.50	15.00	—
1757	—	1.50	3.00	7.50	15.00	—
1758	—	1.50	3.00	7.50	15.00	—
1759	—	1.50	3.00	7.50	15.00	—

KM# 392 KREUZER

Billon **Ruler:** Sigismund III **Obv:** Bust right **Obv. Legend:** SIGISMUND • D • G • ... **Rev:** Oval, ornate arms, value below

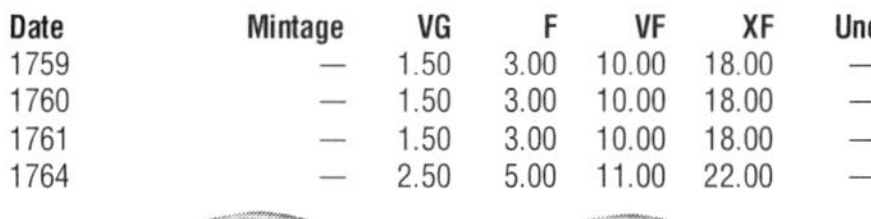

Date	Mintage	VG	F	VF	XF	Unc
1759	—	1.50	3.00	10.00	18.00	—
1760	—	1.50	3.00	10.00	18.00	—
1761	—	1.50	3.00	10.00	18.00	—
1764	—	2.50	5.00	11.00	22.00	—

KM# 451 KREUZER

Copper **Ruler:** Hieronymus **Obv:** Oval shield within frame divides S B **Rev:** Value, date, rosettes within wreath

Date	Mintage	VG	F	VF	XF	Unc
1782	—	3.50	7.50	15.00	30.00	—
1783	—	3.50	7.50	15.00	30.00	—
1784	—	3.50	7.50	15.00	30.00	—

KM# 458 KREUZER

Copper **Ruler:** Hieronymus **Obv:** Round shield within sprigs above S B **Rev:** Value, date within wreath

Date	Mintage	VG	F	VF	XF	Unc
1786	—	3.50	7.50	15.00	30.00	—
1790	—	3.50	7.50	15.00	30.00	—

KM# 470 KREUZER

Copper **Ruler:** Hieronymus **Obv:** Shield within sprigs above S B **Rev:** Value, date above sprigs

Date	Mintage	VG	F	VF	XF	Unc
1790	—	2.00	3.00	5.00	16.00	—
1793	—	2.00	3.00	5.00	16.00	—
1794	—	2.00	3.00	5.00	16.00	—
1795	—	2.00	3.00	5.00	16.00	—
1797	—	2.00	3.00	5.00	16.00	—
1798	—	2.00	3.00	5.00	16.00	—
1799	—	2.00	3.00	5.00	16.00	—
1800	—	2.00	3.00	5.00	16.00	—

KM# 478.1 KREUZER

Copper **Ruler:** Hieronymus **Obv:** Shield above sprigs and S B **Rev:** Value, date within wreath

Date	Mintage	VG	F	VF	XF	Unc
1790	—	4.00	8.00	17.50	38.00	—

KM# 478.2 KREUZER

Copper **Ruler:** Hieronymus **Obv:** Shield above sprigs and S B **Rev:** Value, date above sprigs

Date	Mintage	VG	F	VF	XF	Unc
1794	—	4.00	8.00	17.50	38.00	—

KM# 290 2 KREUZER (1/2 Batzen)

Silver **Ruler:** Franz Anton **Obv:** Oval shield with Cardinals' hat above **Obv. Legend:** FRAN ANT D G ARCHIES PR **Rev:** Round shield within frame and beaded circle, divided date above

Date	Mintage	VG	F	VF	XF	Unc
1708	—	3.00	6.00	12.50	25.00	—
1709	—	3.00	6.00	12.50	25.00	—
1710	—	3.00	6.00	12.50	25.00	—
1711	—	3.00	6.00	12.50	25.00	—
1712	—	3.00	6.00	12.50	25.00	—
1713	—	3.00	6.00	12.50	25.00	—
1714	—	3.00	6.00	12.50	25.00	—
1715	—	3.00	6.00	12.50	25.00	—
1716	—	3.00	6.00	12.50	25.00	—
1717	—	3.00	6.00	12.50	25.00	—
1718	—	3.00	6.00	12.50	25.00	—
1721	—	3.00	6.00	12.50	25.00	—
1723	—	3.00	6.00	12.50	25.00	—
1725	—	3.00	6.00	12.50	25.00	—
1726	—	3.00	6.00	12.50	25.00	—

KM# 335 2 KREUZER (1/2 Landbatzen)

Silver **Ruler:** Leopold Anton **Obv:** Hat above 2 shields of arms, value below **Rev. Legend:** SALZB/LAND/MINE/1731

Date	Mintage	VG	F	VF	XF	Unc
1731	—	3.00	7.50	15.00	30.00	—

KM# 342 2 KREUZER (1/2 Landbatzen)

Billon **Ruler:** Jakob Ernst **Obv:** Hatabore 2 oval shields of arms, 2 in cartouche in bottom

Date	Mintage	VG	F	VF	XF	Unc
1745 error date	—	10.00	20.00	35.00	65.00	—
1747	—	6.00	12.00	25.00	45.00	—

KM# A352 2 KREUZER (1/2 Landbatzen)

Billon **Ruler:** Andreas Jakob **Obv:** Hat above 2 oval shields of arms, value 2 in cartouche at bottom **Rev:** 3-line legend, date below **Note:** Struck with reverse die of previous reign.

Date	Mintage	VG	F	VF	XF	Unc
1747	—	6.00	12.00	25.00	45.00	—

KM# 368 2 KREUZER (1/2 Landbatzen)

Billon **Ruler:** Sigismund III **Obv:** 2 oval shields below Cardinals' hat, value below **Rev:** Inscription, date

Date	Mintage	VG	F	VF	XF	Unc
1753	—	12.50	25.00	50.00	80.00	—

KM# 374 2 KREUZER (1/2 Landbatzen)

Billon **Ruler:** Sigismund III **Obv:** Oval , ornate shield **Rev:** Date above inscription

Date	Mintage	VG	F	VF	XF	Unc
1754	—	2.50	5.00	10.00	20.00	—
1755	—	2.50	5.00	10.00	20.00	—
1756	—	2.50	5.00	10.00	20.00	—

KM# 389 2 KREUZER (1/2 Landbatzen)

Billon **Ruler:** Sigismund III **Obv:** Arms in cartouche **Rev:** 2 in center cartouche divides date

Date	Mintage	VG	F	VF	XF	Unc
1758	—	3.00	6.00	12.50	25.00	—
1759	—	3.00	6.00	12.50	25.00	—
1760	—	3.00	6.00	12.50	25.00	—

KM# 280 2 KREUZER (1/2 Reichsbatzen)

Silver **Ruler:** Johann Ernst **Obv:** Cardinals' hat above oval shield **Rev:** Oval shield within frame and circle with divided date above, value below

Date	Mintage	VG	F	VF	XF	Unc
1701	—	6.00	12.00	25.00	40.00	—
1702	—	6.00	12.00	25.00	40.00	—
1703	—	6.00	12.00	25.00	40.00	—
1704	—	6.00	12.00	25.00	40.00	—
1705	—	6.00	12.00	25.00	40.00	—
1706	—	6.00	12.00	25.00	40.00	—
1707	—	6.00	12.00	25.00	40.00	—
1708	—	6.00	12.00	25.00	40.00	—
1709	—	6.00	12.00	25.00	40.00	—

KM# 325 2 KREUZER (1/2 Reichsbatzen)

Silver **Ruler:** Leopold Anton **Obv. Legend:** LEOPOLD D G ARCH & PR **Rev:** Shield of arms in cartouche, value below

Date	Mintage	VG	F	VF	XF	Unc
1728	—	3.00	6.00	12.50	25.00	—
1729	—	3.00	6.00	12.50	25.00	—
1730	—	3.00	6.00	12.50	25.00	—

KM# 375 3 KREUZER

Billon **Ruler:** Sigismund III **Obv:** Cardinals' hat above 2 oval shields, value below **Obv. Legend:** SIGISMUND • .... **Rev:** Seated Pope, facing

Date	Mintage	VG	F	VF	XF	Unc
1754	—	5.00	10.00	20.00	45.00	—
1754 SALISBUG	—	10.00	15.00	35.00	75.00	—

KM# 382 3 KREUZER

Billon **Ruler:** Sigismund III **Obv:** Bust right **Obv. Legend:** SIGISM • D • G • ... **Rev:** Cardinals' hat above 2 oval shields

Date	Mintage	VG	F	VF	XF	Unc
1755	—	10.00	20.00	45.00	95.00	—

KM# 315 4 KREUZER (Batzen)

Silver **Ruler:** Franz Anton **Obv:** Cardinals' hat above oval shield within frame **Obv. Legend:** • FRAN • ANT • D:G • ARCH & PR • **Rev:** Oval shield within frame, divided date above, value below

Date	Mintage	VG	F	VF	XF	Unc
1718	—	3.00	7.50	15.00	30.00	—
1719	—	3.00	7.50	15.00	30.00	—
1720	—	3.00	7.50	15.00	30.00	—
1721	—	3.00	7.50	15.00	30.00	—
1722	—	3.00	7.50	15.00	30.00	—
1723	—	3.00	7.50	15.00	30.00	—
1724	—	3.00	7.50	15.00	30.00	—
1725	—	3.00	7.50	15.00	30.00	—
1726	—	3.00	7.50	15.00	30.00	—
1727	—	3.00	7.50	15.00	30.00	—

KM# 322 4 KREUZER (Batzen)

Silver **Ruler:** Leopold Anton **Obv:** Cardinals' hat above shield **Obv. Legend:** LEOPOLD • D:G • ARCH : & PR • **Rev:** Oval shield within frame, divided date above in legend

Date	Mintage	VG	F	VF	XF	Unc
1727	—	3.00	7.50	15.00	30.00	—
1728	—	3.00	7.50	15.00	30.00	—
1729	—	3.00	7.50	15.00	30.00	—
1730	—	3.00	7.50	15.00	30.00	—
1731	—	3.00	7.50	15.00	30.00	—
1732	—	3.00	7.50	15.00	30.00	—
1733	—	3.00	7.50	15.00	30.00	—

KM# 336 4 KREUZER (Landbatzen)
Silver **Ruler:** Leopold Anton **Obv:** Cardinals' hat above 2 oval shields, value below **Rev:** Inscription above date **Rev. Inscription:** SALZB/ LAND/ MINZ/ 1731

Date	Mintage	VG	F	VF	XF	Unc
1731	—	4.00	8.00	17.50	35.00	—

KM# 344 4 KREUZER (Landbatzen)
Silver **Ruler:** Jakob Ernst **Obv:** Cardinals' hat above 2 oval shields, value in cartouche below **Rev:** Inscription, date **Rev. Inscription:** SALZB/ LAND/ MINZ/ 1745

Date	Mintage	VG	F	VF	XF	Unc
1745	—	5.00	10.00	20.00	40.00	—

KM# 350 4 KREUZER (Landbatzen)
Billon **Ruler:** Andreas Jakob **Obv:** Cardinals' hat above 2 oval shields, value in cartouche below **Rev:** Inscription, date **Rev. Inscription:** SALZB/ LAND/ MINZ/ 1747

Date	Mintage	VG	F	VF	XF	Unc
1747	—	6.00	12.00	25.00	45.00	—
1750	—	6.00	12.00	25.00	45.00	—

KM# 369 4 KREUZER (Landbatzen)
Billon **Ruler:** Sigismund III **Obv:** 2 shields of arms below bishop's hat **Rev:** 3-line legend, date below

Date	Mintage	VG	F	VF	XF	Unc
1753	—	15.00	30.00	55.00	95.00	—

KM# 413 5 KREUZER
Billon **Ruler:** Sigismund III **Obv:** Crowned arms in ornamental shield **Rev:** Date and value in wreath

Date	Mintage	VG	F	VF	XF	Unc
1766	—	15.00	30.00	60.00	175	—
1770	—	15.00	30.00	60.00	175	—
1771/0	—	15.00	30.00	60.00	175	—

KM# 438 5 KREUZER
Billon **Ruler:** Hieronymus **Obv:** Crowned, oval shield in sprigs **Rev:** Date, inscription above value within sprigs **Rev. Inscription:** CCXL/EINE/FEINE/MARK

Date	Mintage	VG	F	VF	XF	Unc
1773	—	15.00	30.00	60.00	175	—
1775	—	15.00	30.00	60.00	175	—
1778	—	15.00	30.00	60.00	175	—
1781	—	10.00	20.00	45.00	130	—
1784	—	15.00	30.00	60.00	175	—

KM# 459 5 KREUZER
Billon **Ruler:** Hieronymus **Obv:** Oval arms

Date	Mintage	VG	F	VF	XF	Unc
1786	—	10.00	20.00	40.00	110	—
1788	—	10.00	20.00	40.00	110	—

KM# 475 5 KREUZER
Billon **Ruler:** Hieronymus **Obv:** Square arms

Date	Mintage	VG	F	VF	XF	Unc
1792	—	25.00	55.00	90.00	150	—

KM# 477 5 KREUZER
Billon **Ruler:** Hieronymus **Obv:** Crowned shield within sprigs, value below **Rev:** Inscription, date above sprigs **Rev. Inscription:** CCXL/EINE/FEINE/MARC

Date	Mintage	VG	F	VF	XF	Unc
1793	—	7.50	20.00	50.00	130	—
1794	—	7.50	20.00	50.00	130	—
1795	—	7.50	20.00	50.00	130	—
1796	—	7.50	20.00	50.00	130	—
1797	—	7.50	20.00	50.00	130	—
1798	—	7.50	20.00	50.00	130	—
1799	—	7.50	20.00	50.00	130	—
1800	—	7.50	20.00	50.00	130	—

KM# 376 10 KREUZER
Silver **Ruler:** Sigismund III **Obv:** Cardinals' hat above 2 oval shields **Obv. Legend:** SIGISM ... **Rev:** Bust of Pope facing, value within squared mantle below **Note:** Convention Kreuzer.

Date	Mintage	VG	F	VF	XF	Unc
1754	—	10.00	15.00	22.50	40.00	—
1755	—	15.00	35.00	70.00	140	—
1756	—	10.00	25.00	50.00	100	—
1757	—	10.00	20.00	45.00	90.00	—
1758	—	10.00	25.00	50.00	100	—
1761/0	—	15.00	20.00	35.00	65.00	—
1761	—	10.00	15.00	22.50	50.00	—

KM# 390 10 KREUZER
Silver **Ruler:** Sigismund III **Obv:** Cardinals' hat above 2 oval shields **Obv. Legend:** SIGISM • D • G • ... **Rev:** Bust of Pope facing, value within boxed mantle below **Note:** Convention Kreuzer.

Date	Mintage	VG	F	VF	XF	Unc
1758	—	10.00	20.00	45.00	90.00	—

KM# 408 10 KREUZER
Silver **Ruler:** Sigismund III **Obv:** Bust right **Obv. Legend:** SIGM • D • G • ... **Rev:** Cardinals' hat above oval, mantled shield, crown above **Note:** Convention Kreuzer.

Date	Mintage	VG	F	VF	XF	Unc
1765	—	25.00	50.00	100	200	—
1767	—	25.00	50.00	100	200	—
1768	—	25.00	50.00	100	200	—
1770	—	25.00	50.00	100	200	—
1771	—	25.00	50.00	100	200	—

KM# 409 10 KREUZER
Silver **Ruler:** Sigismund III **Rev:** Date above arms **Note:** Convention Kreuzer.

Date	Mintage	VG	F	VF	XF	Unc
1765	—	25.00	50.00	110	225	—
1766/5	—	25.00	50.00	110	225	—
1766	—	25.00	50.00	110	225	—
1767	—	25.00	50.00	110	225	—

KM# 430 10 KREUZER
3.8900 g., 0.5000 Silver .0625 oz. ASW **Ruler:** Hieronymus **Obv:** Large head right **Rev:** Crowned and mantled oval arms, value 10 divides date at bottom

Date	Mintage	VG	F	VF	XF	Unc
1772 M	—	30.00	60.00	125	250	—

KM# 439 10 KREUZER
3.8900 g., 0.5000 Silver .0625 oz. ASW **Ruler:** Hieronymus **Obv:** Bust right **Obv. Legend:** HIERONYMVS D • G • A • ... **Rev:** Cardinals' hat above oval, mantled shield, crown above

Date	Mintage	VG	F	VF	XF	Unc
1773 M	—	20.00	40.00	80.00	160	—
1774 M	—	20.00	40.00	80.00	160	—
1775 M	—	20.00	40.00	80.00	160	—

KM# 442 10 KREUZER
3.8900 g., 0.5000 Silver .0625 oz. ASW **Ruler:** Hieronymus **Obv:** Bust right **Obv. Legend:** HIERONYMVS D • G • A • ... **Rev:** Cardinals' hat above oval, mantled shield, crown above, value divides date below

Date	Mintage	VG	F	VF	XF	Unc
1776 M	—	15.00	30.00	55.00	110	—
1777 M	—	15.00	35.00	65.00	130	—
1778 M	—	15.00	35.00	65.00	130	—
1779 M	—	15.00	35.00	65.00	130	—
1780 M	—	15.00	35.00	65.00	130	—
1782 M	—	15.00	35.00	65.00	130	—
1784 M	—	15.00	35.00	65.00	130	—
1786 M	—	15.00	35.00	65.00	130	—

KM# 464 10 KREUZER
3.8900 g., 0.5000 Silver .0625 oz. ASW **Ruler:** Hieronymus **Obv:** Bust right **Obv. Legend:** HIERONYMVS D • G • A • ... **Rev:** Cardinals' hat above mantled crowned shield, crown above, value divides date below

Date	Mintage	VG	F	VF	XF	Unc
1788 M	—	15.00	35.00	65.00	130	—
1791 M	—	15.00	35.00	65.00	130	—
1792 M	—	15.00	35.00	65.00	130	—
1793 M	—	15.00	35.00	65.00	130	—
1794 M	—	15.00	35.00	65.00	130	—
1795 M	—	15.00	35.00	65.00	130	—
1796 M	—	15.00	35.00	65.00	130	—
1797 M	—	15.00	35.00	65.00	130	—
1798 M	—	15.00	35.00	65.00	130	—
1799 M	—	15.00	35.00	65.00	130	—
1800 M	—	15.00	30.00	55.00	110	—

KM# A471 10 KREUZER
3.8900 g., 0.5000 Silver .0625 oz. ASW **Ruler:** Hieronymus **Obv:** Bust right **Rev:** Crowned arms flanked by 2 lion supporters, date divided at bottom

Date	Mintage	VG	F	VF	XF	Unc
1790 Rare	—	—	—	—	—	—

KM# 377 17 KREUZER
Silver **Ruler:** Sigismund III **Obv:** Cardinals' hat above oval, ornate shield, value below **Obv. Legend:** SIGISM • D • G • ... **Rev:** Seated Pope, facing

Date	Mintage	VG	F	VF	XF	Unc
1754	—	25.00	45.00	95.00	180	—

KM# 378 20 KREUZER

Silver **Ruler:** Sigismund III **Obv:** Bust right, on boxed mantle with value within **Obv. Legend:** SIGISM : D : G : A : ... **Rev:** Cardinals' hat above 2 oval shields, divided date in legend **Note:** Convention Kreuzer.

Date	Mintage	VG	F	VF	XF	Unc
1754	—	12.50	25.00	50.00	125	—
1755	—	12.50	25.00	50.00	125	—
1756	—	12.50	25.00	50.00	125	—

KM# 386 20 KREUZER

Silver **Ruler:** Sigismund III **Obv:** Bust right **Obv. Legend:** SIGISM • D • G • ... **Rev:** Cardinals' hat above 2 oval shields, value in boxed mantle below, divided date in legend **Note:** Convention Kreuzer.

Date	Mintage	VG	F	VF	XF	Unc
1757	—	20.00	40.00	85.00	170	—
1758	—	30.00	60.00	120	240	—
1759	—	20.00	40.00	85.00	170	—
1760	—	30.00	60.00	120	240	—
1761	—	30.00	60.00	120	240	—
1762	—	30.00	60.00	120	240	—
1763	—	30.00	60.00	120	240	—
1764	—	30.00	60.00	120	240	—

KM# 410.1 20 KREUZER

Silver **Ruler:** Sigismund III **Obv:** Bust right **Obv. Legend:** SIGM • D • G • ... **Rev:** Cardinals' hat above oval, mantled shield, crown above **Note:** Convention Kreuzer.

Date	Mintage	VG	F	VF	XF	Unc
1765	—	17.50	35.00	75.00	150	—
1767	—	15.00	30.00	70.00	140	—
1768	—	17.50	35.00	75.00	150	—
1769	—	20.00	40.00	85.00	170	—
1770	—	17.50	35.00	75.00	150	—
1771/0	—	15.00	30.00	70.00	140	—
1771	—	15.00	30.00	70.00	140	—

KM# 410.2 20 KREUZER

Silver **Ruler:** Sigismund III **Obv:** Bust right **Obv. Legend:** SIGISM • D • G • ... **Rev:** Cardinals' hat above oval, mantled shield, crown above, value below **Note:** Convention Kreuzer.

Date	Mintage	VG	F	VF	XF	Unc
1770	—	—	—	—	—	—

KM# 410.3 20 KREUZER

6.6800 g., 0.5830 Silver .1252 oz. ASW **Ruler:** Hieronymus **Note:** Similar to 10 Kreuzer, KM#430.

Date	Mintage	VG	F	VF	XF	Unc
1772 M	—	50.00	100	200	400	—

KM# 410.4 20 KREUZER

6.6800 g., 0.5830 Silver .1252 oz. ASW **Ruler:** Hieronymus **Note:** Similar to 10 Kreuzer, KM#439.

Date	Mintage	VG	F	VF	XF	Unc
1773 M	—	40.00	85.00	175	350	—

KM# 431 20 KREUZER

6.6800 g., 0.5830 Silver .1252 oz. ASW **Ruler:** Hieronymus **Obv:** Bust right **Obv. Legend:** HIERONYMVS D • G • A • ... **Rev:** Cardinals' hat above oval, mantled shield, crown above, value divides date below **Note:** Varieties exist.

Date	Mintage	VG	F	VF	XF	Unc
1774 M	—	3.00	6.00	15.00	50.00	—
1775 M	—	3.00	6.00	15.00	50.00	—
1776 M	—	3.00	6.00	15.00	50.00	—
1777 M	—	3.00	6.00	15.00	50.00	—
1778 M	—	3.00	6.00	15.00	50.00	—
1779 M	—	3.00	6.00	15.00	50.00	—
1780 M	—	3.00	6.00	15.00	50.00	—
1781 M	—	3.00	6.00	15.00	50.00	—
1782 M	—	3.00	6.00	15.00	50.00	—
1783 M	—	3.00	6.00	15.00	50.00	—
1784 M	—	3.00	6.00	15.00	50.00	—
1785 M	—	3.00	6.00	15.00	50.00	—
1786 M	—	3.00	6.00	15.00	50.00	—

KM# 460 20 KREUZER

6.6800 g., 0.5830 Silver .1252 oz. ASW **Ruler:** Hieronymus **Obv:** Bust right **Obv. Legend:** HIERONYMVS D • G • A • ... **Rev:** Cardinals' hat above pear-shaped, mantled shield, crown above, value divides date below **Note:** Varieties exist.

Date	Mintage	VG	F	VF	XF	Unc
1787 M	—	3.00	6.00	15.00	45.00	—
1788/7 M	—	5.00	15.00	20.00	55.00	—
1788 M	—	3.00	6.00	15.00	45.00	—
1789 M	—	3.00	6.00	15.00	45.00	—
1790 M	—	3.00	6.00	15.00	40.00	—
1791 M	—	3.00	6.00	15.00	40.00	—
1792 M	—	3.00	6.00	15.00	40.00	—
1793 M	—	3.00	6.00	15.00	40.00	—
1794 M	—	3.00	6.00	15.00	40.00	—
1795 M	—	3.00	6.00	15.00	40.00	—
1796 M	—	3.00	6.00	15.00	40.00	—
1797 M	—	3.00	6.00	15.00	40.00	—
1798 M	—	3.00	6.00	15.00	40.00	—
1799 M	—	3.00	6.00	15.00	40.00	—
1800 M	—	3.00	6.00	15.00	40.00	—

KM# B471 20 KREUZER

6.6800 g., 0.5830 Silver .1252 oz. ASW **Ruler:** Hieronymus **Obv:** Bust right **Rev:** Crowned arms flanked by 2 lion supporters, date divided at bottom

Date	Mintage	VG	F	VF	XF	Unc
1790 Rare	—	—	—	—	—	—

KM# 379 30 KREUZER

Silver **Ruler:** Sigismund III **Obv:** Bust right divides date, value below, all within diamond shape **Obv. Legend:** SIGISM : D : G : ARCH : ... **Rev:** Cardinals' hat above oval shield within diamond shape

Date	Mintage	VG	F	VF	XF	Unc
1754	—	15.00	20.00	35.00	75.00	—
1760	—	30.00	70.00	100	175	—

KM# 282 1/4 THALER

Silver **Ruler:** Johann Ernst **Obv:** Madonna and Child above shield of arms in inner circle **Rev:** St. Rupert above value and arms in inner circle, date in legend

Date	Mintage	VG	F	VF	XF	Unc
1703	—	30.00	60.00	125	250	—
1704	—	30.00	60.00	125	250	—
1705	—	30.00	60.00	125	250	—
1706	—	30.00	60.00	125	250	—
1707	—	30.00	60.00	125	250	—
1708	—	30.00	60.00	125	250	—

KM# 294 1/4 THALER

Silver, 30 mm. **Ruler:** Franz Anton **Subject:** Enthronement of the archbishop **Obv:** Bust of Franz Anton right, star below bust **Rev:** Legend, date below **Rev. Legend:** IN MANV DOMINI SORTS MEA

Date	Mintage	VG	F	VF	XF	Unc
1709 Rare	—	—	—	—	—	—

KM# 305.1 1/4 THALER

Silver **Ruler:** Franz Anton **Obv:** Madonna and child over hat above Harrach family arms **Rev:** St. Rudbert, Salzburg arms at bottom with "1/4" in circle immediately above

Date	Mintage	VG	F	VF	XF	Unc
1710	—	45.00	85.00	170	325	—

KM# 306 1/4 THALER

Silver **Ruler:** Franz Anton **Obv:** Bust of Franz Anton right, star below bust **Rev:** Hat above shield of arms, value below, date above hat

Date	Mintage	VG	F	VF	XF	Unc
1710	—	40.00	80.00	160	325	—
1711	—	40.00	80.00	160	325	—
1712	—	40.00	80.00	160	325	—
1715	—	40.00	80.00	160	325	—

KM# 305.2 1/4 THALER

Silver **Ruler:** Franz Anton **Obv:** Madonna and child over hat above Harrach family arms **Rev:** St. Rudbert seated facing to left, Salzburg arms to lower right, "1/4" in cartouche to bottom

Date	Mintage	VG	F	VF	XF	Unc
1712	—	35.00	75.00	150	300	—
1713	—	35.00	75.00	150	300	—
1715	—	35.00	75.00	150	300	—

KM# 312 1/4 THALER

Silver **Ruler:** Franz Anton **Obv:** Without star below bust

Date	Mintage	VG	F	VF	XF	Unc
1715	—	50.00	100	200	400	—

KM# 326 1/4 THALER

Silver **Ruler:** Leopold Anton **Obv:** Madonna and Child above shield of arms in inner circle **Obv. Legend:** LEOPOLDUS D G ... **Rev:** St. Rupert in inner circle, date in legend

Date	Mintage	VG	F	VF	XF	Unc
1728	—	40.00	80.00	175	350	—
1730	—	40.00	80.00	175	350	—

KM# 414 1/4 THALER

Silver **Ruler:** Sigismund III **Obv:** Bust right **Obv. Legend:** SIGM • D • G • ... **Rev:** Cardinals' hat above mantled shield, crown above, value divides date below

Date	Mintage	VG	F	VF	XF	Unc
1766	—	35.00	65.00	135	275	—

KM# 417 1/4 THALER

Silver **Ruler:** Sigismund III **Obv:** Bust right with value below within diamond shape **Obv. Legend:** SIGISM : D : G : ARCH :

... **Rev:** Cardinals' hat above mantled shield, divided date, crown above, all within diamond shape

Date	Mintage	VG	F	VF	XF	Unc
1767	—	25.00	50.00	100	200	—

KM# 253 1/2 THALER

Silver **Ruler:** Johann Ernst **Obv:** Hat above shield of arms, date divided near bottom in inner circle **Rev:** SS. Rupert and Virgil

Date	Mintage	VG	F	VF	XF	Unc
1702	—	40.00	75.00	150	265	—
1703	—	40.00	75.00	150	265	—
1705	—	40.00	75.00	150	265	—
1706	—	40.00	75.00	150	265	—
1707	—	40.00	75.00	150	265	—
1708	—	40.00	75.00	150	265	—

KM# 307 1/2 THALER

Silver **Ruler:** Franz Anton **Obv:** Bust right **Obv. Legend:** FRANC • ANTON • S • R • I • ... **Rev:** Cardinals' hat above pear-shaped shield, date above in legend

Date	Mintage	VG	F	VF	XF	Unc
1710	—	200	400	700	1,200	—
1711	—	200	400	700	1,200	—
1712	—	200	400	700	1,200	—
1714	—	200	400	700	1,200	—
1716	—	200	400	700	1,200	—
1717	—	200	400	700	1,200	—
1718	—	200	400	700	1,200	—
1720	—	200	400	700	1,200	—

KM# 310 1/2 THALER

Silver **Ruler:** Franz Anton **Obv:** Madonna and child over shield of arms in inner circle **Rev:** St. Rupert in inner circle, date in legend

Date	Mintage	VG	F	VF	XF	Unc
1712	—	200	400	700	1,200	—
1715	—	200	400	700	1,200	—
1718	—	200	400	700	1,200	—
1720	—	200	400	700	1,200	—
1725	—	200	400	700	1,200	—

KM# 313 1/2 THALER

Silver **Ruler:** Franz Anton **Obv:** Bust of Franz Anton right, without star below bust **Rev:** Hat above shield of arms, date above hat

Date	Mintage	VG	F	VF	XF	Unc
1715	—	200	400	700	1,200	—
1717	—	200	400	700	1,200	—

KM# 316 1/2 THALER

Silver **Ruler:** Franz Anton **Obv:** Hat above shield of arms divide date in inner circle **Rev:** Saints Rupert and Virgil

Date	Mintage	VG	F	VF	XF	Unc
1718	—	200	400	700	1,200	—

KM# 327 1/2 THALER

Silver **Ruler:** Leopold Anton **Obv:** Madonna and child above Cardinals' hat and oval shield **Obv. Legend:** LEOPOLDUS • D : G : ... **Rev:** St. Rupert, oval shield in frame, date in legend **Rev. Legend:** S • RUDBERTUS • ...

Date	Mintage	VG	F	VF	XF	Unc
1728	—	150	250	425	750	—

KM# 363 1/2 THALER

Silver **Ruler:** Andreas Jakob **Note:** Similar to Thaler, KM#364. Convention 1/2 Thaler.

Date	Mintage	VG	F	VF	XF	Unc
1752	—	200	450	750	1,000	—

KM# 387.1 1/2 THALER

Silver **Ruler:** Sigismund III **Obv:** Bust right **Obv. Legend:** SIGISMUNDUS • D • G • ... **Rev:** Cardinals' hat above oval shield

Date	Mintage	VG	F	VF	XF	Unc
1757	—	50.00	100	150	250	—

KM# 387.2 1/2 THALER

Silver **Ruler:** Sigismund III **Obv:** Bust right **Obv. Legend:** SIGISMUNDUS • D • G • ... **Rev:** Cardinals' hat above pear-shaped shield, divided date above in legend

Date	Mintage	VG	F	VF	XF	Unc
1760	—	65.00	125	175	350	—

KM# 415 1/2 THALER

Silver **Ruler:** Sigismund III **Obv:** Bust right **Obv. Legend:** SIGM • D • G • A • ... **Rev:** Cardinals' hat above mantled shield, crown above, divided date below

Date	Mintage	VG	F	VF	XF	Unc
1766	—	80.00	150	250	450	—
1768	—	80.00	150	250	450	—

KM# 419 1/2 THALER

Silver **Ruler:** Sigismund III **Obv:** Bust right **Obv. Legend:** SIGM • D • G • A • ... **Rev:** Cardinals' hat above mantled shield, crown above

Date	Mintage	VG	F	VF	XF	Unc
1769	—	80.00	150	250	450	—

KM# 425 1/2 THALER

Silver **Ruler:** Sigismund III **Obv:** Bust right **Obv. Legend:** SIGISMUNDUS .... **Rev:** Cardinals' hat above mantled shield, crown above

Date	Mintage	VG	F	VF	XF	Unc
1770	—	80.00	150	250	450	—
1770 FM	—	80.00	150	250	450	—
1771	—	90.00	175	275	500	—
1771 FM	—	90.00	175	275	500	—

KM# 432 1/2 THALER

14.0300 g., 0.8330 Silver .3757 oz. ASW **Ruler:** Hieronymus **Obv:** Bust right **Obv. Legend:** HIERONYMVS D • G • A • ... **Rev:** Cardinals' hat above oval, mantled shield, crown above, date below

Date	Mintage	VG	F	VF	XF	Unc
1772 FM	—	50.00	100	200	350	—
1773 M	—	50.00	100	200	350	—
1775 M	—	50.00	100	200	350	—
1778 M	—	50.00	100	200	350	—
1779 M	—	50.00	100	200	350	—
1780 M	—	50.00	100	200	350	—
1782 M	—	50.00	100	200	350	—

KM# 461 1/2 THALER

14.0300 g., 0.8330 Silver .3757 oz. ASW **Ruler:** Hieronymus **Obv:** Bust right **Obv. Legend:** HIERONYMVS D • G • A • ... **Rev:** Cardinals' hat above pear-shaped, mantled shield, crown above, date below

Date	Mintage	VG	F	VF	XF	Unc
1787 M	—	50.00	100	175	325	—
1792 M	—	50.00	100	175	325	—
1797 M	—	50.00	100	175	325	—

KM# 254 THALER

Silver **Ruler:** Johann Ernst **Obv:** Madonna and child above Cardinals' hat and shield **Obv. Legend:** IO: ERNEST: D:G: ...

Rev: St. Rupert above shield in frame, date in legend **Rev. Legend:** S: RUDBERTUS: EPS .... **Note:** Dav.#1234.

Date	Mintage	F	VF	XF	Unc	BU
1701	—	75.00	135	275	500	—
1702	—	75.00	135	275	500	—
1703	—	75.00	135	275	500	—
1704	—	75.00	135	275	500	—
1705	—	75.00	135	275	500	—
1706	—	75.00	135	275	500	—
1707	—	75.00	135	275	500	—
1708	—	75.00	135	275	500	—
1709	—	75.00	135	275	500	—

KM# 295 THALER

Silver **Ruler:** Franz Anton **Obv:** Hat above oval arms in inner circle **Obv. Legend:** FRANC: ANTO: D: **Rev:** Legend in branches **Rev. Legend:** ANNO/DNI MDCCIX/ET/REGIMINIS/PRIMO/F.F. **Note:** Dav.#1235.

Date	Mintage	F	VF	XF	Unc	BU
1709 R.N. Rare	—	—	—	—	—	—

KM# 296 THALER

Silver **Ruler:** Franz Anton **Obv:** Madonna and child above Cardinals' hat and crowned shield in frame **Obv. Legend:** FRANC • ANTON • D:G • ARCH • ... **Rev:** St. Rupert above shield in frame, date in legend **Rev. Legend:** S: RVDBERTUS: EP: ... **Note:** Dav.#1236.

Date	Mintage	F	VF	XF	Unc	BU
1709	—	210	350	550	850	—
1711	—	210	350	550	850	—

KM# 308 THALER

Silver **Ruler:** Franz Anton **Obv:** Bust right **Obv. Legend:** FRANCISCVS ANTON • ... **Rev:** Cardinals' hat above pear-shaped shield, date in legend above **Note:** Dav.#1237.

Date	Mintage	F	VF	XF	Unc	BU
1710	—	360	600	900	1,500	—
1711	—	360	600	900	1,500	—
1712	—	360	600	900	1,500	—
1714	—	360	600	900	1,500	—
1715	—	360	600	900	1,500	—
1716	—	360	600	900	1,500	—
1717	—	360	600	900	1,500	—
1718	—	360	600	900	1,500	—
1719	—	360	600	900	1,500	—
1720	—	360	600	900	1,500	—

KM# 311 THALER

Silver **Ruler:** Franz Anton **Obv:** Madonna and child above Cardinals' hat and crowned oval shield **Obv. Legend:** FRANC : ANTO : D:G • ARCHI : ... **Rev:** St. Rupert with oval shield **Rev. Legend:** S • RUDBERTUS • ESP • ... **Note:** Dav.#1238.

Date	Mintage	F	VF	XF	Unc	BU
1712	—	210	350	550	950	—
1714	—	210	350	550	950	—
1715	—	210	350	550	950	—
1716	—	210	350	550	950	—
1717	—	210	350	550	950	—
1718	—	210	350	550	950	—
1722	—	210	350	550	950	—

KM# 314 THALER

Silver **Ruler:** Franz Anton **Obv:** Without star below bust **Note:** Similar to KM#308.

Date	Mintage	F	VF	XF	Unc	BU
1716	—	360	600	950	1,600	—
1717	—	360	600	950	1,600	—
1725	—	360	600	950	1,600	—

KM# 320 THALER

Silver **Ruler:** Franz Anton **Obv:** Bust right **Obv. Legend:** FRANC : ANT : S : R : I : PRINC • AB HARRACH **Rev:** Cardinals' hat above crowned pear-shaped shield **Note:** Similar to KM#308. Dav.#1239.

Date	Mintage	F	VF	XF	Unc	BU
1723 G	—	360	600	900	1,500	—
1724 G	—	360	600	900	1,500	—
1725 B	—	360	600	900	1,500	—
1726 D	—	360	600	900	1,500	—
1727 G	—	360	600	900	1,500	—

KM# 328 THALER

Silver **Ruler:** Leopold Anton **Obv:** Bust right **Obv. Legend:** LEOPOLDUS • D • G • ARCH ... **Rev:** Cardinals' hat above shield, date above in legend **Rev. Legend:** SALISBURG .... **Note:** Dav.#1240.

Date	Mintage	F	VF	XF	Unc	BU
1728 B	—	600	1,000	1,500	2,250	—

KM# 329 THALER

Silver **Ruler:** Leopold Anton **Obv:** Madonna and child above Cardinals' hat and shield **Obv. Legend:** LEOPOLDUS • D:G • ARCHI : ... **Rev:** St. Rupert with oval shield **Rev. Legend:** S : RUDBERTUS • ... **Note:** Dav.#1241.

Date	Mintage	F	VF	XF	Unc	BU
1728	—	180	300	475	750	—
1729	—	180	300	475	750	—
1730	—	180	300	475	750	—
1731	—	180	300	475	750	—
1732	—	180	300	475	750	—
1733	—	180	300	475	750	—
1734	—	180	300	475	750	—
1735	—	180	300	475	750	—

KM# 338 THALER

Silver **Ruler:** Leopold Anton **Obv:** Bust right **Obv. Legend:** LEOPOLDUS • D:G • ARCH • ET • PRINCEPS **Rev:** Cardinals' hat above ornate shield **Rev. Legend:** SALISBURG • S .... **Note:** Dav.#1242.

Date	Mintage	F	VF	XF	Unc	BU
1738 FMK	—	450	750	1,200	1,800	—
1739 FMK	—	450	750	1,200	1,800	—
1740 FMK	—	450	750	1,200	1,800	—
1742 FMK	—	450	750	1,200	1,800	—
1744 FMK	—	450	750	1,200	1,800	—

KM# 345 THALER

Silver **Ruler:** Jakob Ernst **Obv:** Madonna and child seated on cloud, Cardinals' hat above oval shield at left **Obv. Legend:** IACOBUSE.... **Rev:** St. Rupert seated on cloud **Rev. Legend:** SRUPERTUS ... **Note:** Dav.#1243.

Date	Mintage	F	VF	XF	Unc	BU
1745 FMK	—	500	800	1,250	2,000	—

KM# 348 THALER

Silver **Ruler:** Jakob Ernst **Obv:** Bust right **Obv. Legend:** IACOBUSERN : D : G : ARCH • ETPRINCEPS **Rev:** Cardinals' hat above ornate shield, divided date above **Rev. Legend:** SALISBURG • S • SED • .... **Note:** Dav.#1244.

Date	Mintage	F	VF	XF	Unc	BU
1746 FMK	—	600	1,000	1,600	2,500	—

KM# 354 THALER

Silver **Ruler:** Andreas Jakob **Obv:** Bust right **Obv. Legend:** ANDREAS • D : G • ARCH .... **Rev:** Cardinals' hat above pear-shaped, ornate shield **Rev. Legend:** SALISBURG • S • SED • ... **Note:** Dav.#1245. Convention Thaler.

Date	Mintage	F	VF	XF	Unc	BU
1748 FMK	—	300	600	800	1,200	—
1750 FMK	—	425	850	1,100	1,600	—

KM# 364 THALER

Silver **Ruler:** Andreas Jakob **Obv:** Radiant Madonna and child, Cardinals' hat above oval shield at left **Obv. Legend:** ANDREAS • D : G • ARCH .... **Rev:** St. Rupert seated with oval shield **Rev. Legend:** SALISBURGENS .... **Note:** Dav.#1246. Convention Thaler.

Date	Mintage	F	VF	XF	Unc	BU
1752	—	350	700	1,000	1,500	—

KM# 370 THALER

Silver **Ruler:** Sigismund III **Obv:** Bust right **Obv. Legend:** SIGISMUNDUS • D • G • ... **Rev:** Cardinals' hat above oval, ornate shield on mantle **Rev. Legend:** SALISB: S: S: AP: LEG: ..... **Note:** With or without die-cutter's initials FMK, MK or FM. Dav.#1247.

Date	Mintage	F	VF	XF	Unc	BU
1753	—	125	175	275	550	—
1754	—	125	175	275	550	—
1755	—	125	175	275	550	—
1756	—	125	175	275	550	—
1758	—	125	175	275	550	—
1761	—	125	175	275	550	—

KM# 380 THALER

Silver **Ruler:** Sigismund III **Obv:** Madonna and child within square, Cardinals' hat above oval shield at right, angel at left **Obv. Legend:** SIGISMUND • D • G • ... **Rev:** St. Rupert seated with oval shield in frame **Rev. Legend:** RUPERTUS • EPISCOP : SALISBURGENS • **Note:** Dav.#1248.

Date	Mintage	F	VF	XF	Unc	BU
1754	—	100	150	250	500	—

KM# 388 THALER

Silver **Ruler:** Sigismund III **Obv:** Bust right **Obv. Legend:** SIGISMUNDUS • D • G • ... **Rev:** St. Rupert seated with Cardinals' hat above oval shield at left **Rev. Legend:** SAP • SLEG • NATUS • GERM • PRIMAS • **Note:** Dav.#1249.

Date	Mintage	F	VF	XF	Unc	BU
1757 FM	—	125	200	300	600	—

KM# 391 THALER

Silver **Ruler:** Sigismund III **Obv:** Madonna and child within square, Cardinals' hat above oval shield at right, angel at left **Obv. Legend:** SIGISMUND • D • G • ... **Rev:** St. Rupert standing with oval shield at left **Rev. Legend:** S • RUPERTUS • EPISCOP : SALISBURGENS : **Note:** Dav.#1250.

Date	Mintage	F	VF	XF	Unc	BU
1758	—	90.00	150	225	450	—

KM# 393 THALER

Silver **Ruler:** Sigismund III **Obv:** Bust right **Obv. Legend:** SIGISMUNDUS • D • G • ... **Rev:** St. Rupert seated on cloud **Rev. Legend:** S • RUPERTUS • .... **Note:** Dav.#1251.

Date	Mintage	F	VF	XF	Unc	BU
1759 MK	—	90.00	150	275	450	—

KM# 395.1 THALER

Silver **Ruler:** Sigismund III **Obv:** Bust right **Obv. Legend:** SIGISMUNDUS D G A & P ... **Rev:** St. Rupert seated with small Madonna and child at left, Cardinals' hat above oval shield at lower left **Rev. Legend:** S • RUPERTUS • ... **Note:** Dav.#1253.

Date	Mintage	F	VF	XF	Unc	BU
1759	—	100	150	225	450	—
1759 MK	—	100	150	225	450	—
1760 MK	—	100	150	225	450	—

KM# 394 THALER

Silver **Ruler:** Sigismund III **Obv:** Cardinals' hat above 2 oval shields **Obv. Legend:** SIGISMUND • D • G • ... **Rev:** St. Rupert seated on cloud **Rev. Legend:** S • RUPERTUS • EPISCOP : ... **Note:** Dav.#1252.

Date	Mintage	F	VF	XF	Unc	BU
1759	—	90.00	150	275	450	—

KM# 402 THALER

Silver **Ruler:** Sigismund III **Obv:** Bust right **Obv. Legend:** SIGM • D • G • ... **Rev:** Cardinals' hat above mantled shield, crown above, divided date below **Note:** Dav.#1259.

Date	Mintage	F	VF	XF	Unc	BU
1761	—	110	175	275	550	—
1765 FM	—	110	175	275	550	—
1765 FMK	—	110	175	275	550	—
1766	—	110	175	275	550	—
1767	—	110	175	275	550	—
1767 FM	—	110	175	275	550	—
1768	—	110	175	275	550	—
1769	—	110	175	275	550	—

KM# 395.3 THALER

Silver **Ruler:** Sigismund III **Obv:** Bust right **Obv. Legend:** SIGISMUNDUS • D • G • ... **Rev:** St. Rupert seated with small Madonna and child at left, Cardinals' hat above shield at lower left **Rev. Legend:** S • RUPERTUS • EPISCOP : ... **Note:** Dav#1254A.

Date	Mintage	F	VF	XF	Unc	BU
1761	—	100	150	225	450	—
1762 FM	—	100	150	225	450	—

Note: SALISPURGENS (error)

KM# 401.1 THALER

Silver **Ruler:** Sigismund III **Obv:** Bust right **Obv. Legend:** SIGISMUNDUS • D • G • ... **Rev:** Cardinals' hat above 2 oval shields **Rev. Legend:** S • A • S • LEG • NATUSGERM • PRIMAS • **Note:** Dav.#1255.

Date	Mintage	F	VF	XF	Unc	BU
1761	—	150	200	275	550	—

KM# 401.2 THALER

Silver **Ruler:** Sigismund III **Rev. Legend:** S.R.I.PR. SALISB **Note:** Dav.#1256.

Date	Mintage	F	VF	XF	Unc	BU
1761	—	150	200	275	550	—

KM# 403.1 THALER

Silver **Ruler:** Sigismund III **Obv:** Bust right **Obv. Legend:** SIGISMUND • D • G • ... **Rev:** Angel above 2 oval shields with small Cardinals' hat at left, all within crowned mantle **Rev. Legend:** S • A • S • LEG • NATUS • ... **Note:** Dav.#1257.

Date	Mintage	F	VF	XF	Unc	BU
1762 FMK	—	135	225	325	650	—
1763	—	135	225	325	650	—
1764 MK	—	135	225	325	650	—

KM# 403.2 THALER

Silver **Ruler:** Sigismund III **Rev:** Date above crowned and mantled arms **Note:** Dav.#1258.

Date	Mintage	F	VF	XF	Unc	BU
1765	—	125	200	300	600	—

KM# 418 THALER

Silver **Ruler:** Sigismund III **Obv:** Bust right **Obv. Legend:** SIGISMUNDUS • D • G • ... **Rev:** Cardinals' hat above mantled shield, crown above, divided date below **Note:** Dav.#1260.

Date	Mintage	F	VF	XF	Unc	BU
1767	—	150	250	350	700	—

KM# 395.2 THALER

Silver **Ruler:** Sigismund III **Obv:** Bust right **Obv. Legend:** SIGISMUND • D • G • ... **Rev:** St. Rupert seated with small Madonna and child at left, Cardinals' hat above oval shield at lower left **Rev. Legend:** S • RUPERTUS • .... **Note:** Dav.#1254.

Date	Mintage	F	VF	XF	Unc	BU
1761	—	100	150	225	450	—

KM# 420 THALER

Silver **Ruler:** Sigismund III **Obv:** Bust right **Obv. Legend:** SIGISM • D • G • ... **Rev:** Cardinals' hat above mantled shield, crown above, divided date below **Note:** Dav.#1261.

Date	Mintage	F	VF	XF	Unc	BU
1769 FM	—	90.00	150	225	450	—
1770 FM	—	90.00	150	225	450	—

KM# 426 THALER

Silver **Ruler:** Sigismund III **Obv:** Bust right **Obv. Legend:** SIGISM • D • G • ... **Rev:** Cardinals' hat above mantled shield, crown above, date below **Note:** Dav#1261A.

Date	Mintage	F	VF	XF	Unc	BU
1770 FM	—	90.00	150	225	450	—

KM# 429 THALER

Silver **Ruler:** Sigismund III **Obv:** Bust right **Obv. Legend:** SIGISM • D • G • ... **Rev:** Cardinals' hat above mantled shield, crown above, divided date below **Note:** Dav#1261B.

Date	Mintage	F	VF	XF	Unc	BU
1771 FM	—	90.00	150	225	450	—

KM# 433.1 THALER

28.0600 g., 0.8330 Silver .7516 oz. ASW **Ruler:** Hieronymus **Obv:** Bust right **Obv. Legend:** HIERONYMUS D • G • A • ... **Rev:** Cardinals' hat above oval, mantled shield, crown above, divided date below **Note:** Dav.#1262.

Date	Mintage	F	VF	XF	Unc	BU
1772 FM close date	—	200	600	900	1,500	—
1772 FMF wide date	—	200	600	900	1,500	—

KM# 435 THALER

28.0600 g., 0.8330 Silver .7516 oz. ASW **Ruler:** Hieronymus **Obv:** Bust right **Obv. Legend:** HIERONYMUS D • G • A • ... **Rev:** Cardinals' hat above oval, mantled shield, crown above, divided date below **Note:** Varieties exist. Dav.#1263.

Date	Mintage	F	VF	XF	Unc	BU
1772 FM	—	65.00	100	150	325	—
1773 FM	—	65.00	100	150	325	—
1773	—	65.00	100	150	325	—
1773 M	—	65.00	100	150	325	—
1774 M	—	65.00	100	150	325	—
1775 M	—	65.00	100	150	325	—
1776 M	—	65.00	100	150	325	—
1777 M	—	65.00	100	150	325	—
1778 M	—	65.00	100	150	325	—
1779 M	—	65.00	100	150	325	—
1780 M	—	65.00	100	150	325	—
1781 M	—	65.00	100	150	325	—
1782 M	—	65.00	100	150	325	—
1783 M	—	65.00	100	150	325	—
1784 M	—	65.00	100	150	325	—
1785 M	—	65.00	100	150	325	—
1786 M	—	65.00	100	150	325	—

KM# 433.2 THALER

28.0600 g., 0.8330 Silver .7516 oz. ASW **Ruler:** Hieronymus **Obv:** Bust right **Obv. Legend:** HIERONYMUS D • G • A • ... **Rev:** Cardinals' hat above oval, mantled shield, crown above, date below **Note:** Dav#1262B.

Date	Mintage	F	VF	XF	Unc	BU
1772 FMF	—	200	600	900	1,500	—

KM# 434 THALER

28.0600 g., 0.8330 Silver .7516 oz. ASW **Ruler:** Hieronymus **Obv:** Bust right **Obv. Legend:** HIERONYMVS D • G • A • ... **Rev:** Cardinals' hat above oval , mantled shield, crown above, date below **Note:** Dav#1262A.

Date	Mintage	F	VF	XF	Unc	BU
1772 FMF	—	250	550	850	1,400	—

KM# 462 THALER

28.0600 g., 0.8330 Silver .7516 oz. ASW **Ruler:** Hieronymus **Obv:** Bust right **Obv. Legend:** HIERONYMVS D • G • A • ... **Rev:** Cardinals' hat above pear-shaped, mantled shield, crown above, date below **Note:** Dav.#1264.

Date	Mintage	F	VF	XF	Unc	BU
1787 M	—	65.00	110	150	325	—
1788 M	—	65.00	110	150	325	—
1789 M	—	65.00	110	150	325	—

KM# 465 THALER

28.0600 g., 0.8330 Silver .7515 oz. ASW **Ruler:** Hieronymus **Obv:** Bust right **Obv. Legend:** HIERONVMVS .... **Rev:** Cardinals' hat above mantled shield, crown above, date below **Note:** Varieties exist. Dav.#1265.

Date	Mintage	F	VF	XF	Unc	BU
1789	—	65.00	110	150	325	—
1789 M	—	65.00	110	150	325	—
1790 M	—	65.00	110	150	325	—
1791 M	—	65.00	110	150	325	—
1792 M	—	65.00	110	150	325	—
1793 M	—	65.00	110	150	325	—
1794 M	—	65.00	110	150	325	—
1795 M	—	65.00	110	150	325	—
1796 M	—	65.00	110	150	325	—
1797 M	—	65.00	110	150	325	—
1798 M	—	65.00	110	150	325	—
1799 M	—	65.00	110	150	325	—
1800 M	—	65.00	110	150	325	—

KM# 471 THALER
28.0600 g., 0.8330 Silver .7516 oz. ASW **Ruler:** Hieronymus **Obv:** Bust right **Obv. Legend:** HIERONYMVS D • G • A • ... **Rev:** Crowned shield with supporters on mantle, divided date below **Note:** Dav.#1266.

Date	Mintage	F	VF	XF	Unc	BU
1790 FM Rare	200	—	—	—	—	—

TRADE COINAGE

KM# 255 1/4 DUCAT
0.8750 g., 0.9860 Gold .0277 oz. AGW **Ruler:** Johann Ernst **Obv:** Cardinals' hat above oval shield **Obv. Legend:** IO ERNEST... **Rev:** St. Rupert, value within oval circle below

Date	Mintage	VG	F	VF	XF	Unc
1704	—	50.00	90.00	185	285	—
1705	—	50.00	90.00	185	285	—
1707	—	50.00	90.00	185	285	—

KM# 297 1/4 DUCAT
0.8750 g., 0.9870 Gold .0277 oz. AGW **Ruler:** Franz Anton **Obv:** Cardinals' hat above oval shield **Obv. Legend:** FRAN ANT ... **Rev:** St. Rupert above value within oval circle

Date	Mintage	VG	F	VF	XF	Unc
1709	—	60.00	120	250	350	—
1712	—	60.00	120	250	350	—
1713	—	60.00	120	250	350	—
1714	—	60.00	120	250	350	—
1718	—	60.00	120	250	350	—
1719	—	60.00	120	250	350	—
1725	—	60.00	120	250	350	—

KM# 330 1/4 DUCAT
0.8750 g., 0.9870 Gold .0277 oz. AGW **Ruler:** Leopold Anton **Obv:** Cardinals' hat above shield **Obv. Legend:** LEOPOLDUS ... **Rev:** St. Rupert above value within oval circle

Date	Mintage	VG	F	VF	XF	Unc
1728	—	60.00	80.00	185	300	—
1734	—	60.00	80.00	185	300	—
1740	—	60.00	80.00	185	300	—

KM# 346 1/4 DUCAT
0.8750 g., 0.9870 Gold .0277 oz. AGW **Ruler:** Jakob Ernst **Obv:** Cardinals' hat above shield **Obv. Legend:** IACOB ERN ... **Rev:** St. Rupert above value within oval circle

Date	Mintage	VG	F	VF	XF	Unc
1745	—	100	200	450	700	—

KM# 356 1/4 DUCAT
0.8750 g., 0.9870 Gold .0277 oz. AGW **Ruler:** Andreas Jakob **Obv:** Cardinals' hat above pear-shaped shield **Rev:** St. Rupert above value within oval circle

Date	Mintage	VG	F	VF	XF	Unc
1749	—	100	200	350	700	—

KM# 361 1/4 DUCAT
0.8750 g., 0.9870 Gold .0277 oz. AGW **Ruler:** Andreas Jakob **Obv:** Bust right **Rev:** Cardinals' hat above pear-shaped shield

Date	Mintage	VG	F	VF	XF	Unc
1751	—	150	300	650	1,250	—

KM# 371 1/4 DUCAT
0.8750 g., 0.9860 Gold .0277 oz. AGW **Ruler:** Sigismund III **Obv:** Arms **Rev:** St. Rupert seated, value below

Date	Mintage	VG	F	VF	XF	Unc
1753	—	75.00	150	300	550	—

KM# 383 1/4 DUCAT
0.8750 g., 0.9860 Gold .0277 oz. AGW **Ruler:** Sigismund III **Obv:** Bust right **Obv. Legend:** SIGISM • D • G • ... **Rev:** Cardinals' hat above oval shield

Date	Mintage	VG	F	VF	XF	Unc
1755	—	65.00	125	225	400	—

KM# 427 1/4 DUCAT
0.8750 g., 0.9860 Gold .0277 oz. AGW **Ruler:** Sigismund III **Obv:** Small bust of Sigismund right

Date	Mintage	VG	F	VF	XF	Unc
1770	—	60.00	100	200	350	—

KM# 443 1/4 DUCAT
0.8750 g., 0.9860 Gold .0277 oz. AGW **Ruler:** Hieronymus **Obv:** Bust right **Obv. Legend:** HIER D • G • A • ... **Rev:** Cardinals' hat above oval, mantled shield

Date	Mintage	VG	F	VF	XF	Unc
1776	—	50.00	80.00	175	285	—
1777	—	50.00	80.00	175	285	—
1782	—	50.00	80.00	175	285	—

KM# 256 1/2 DUCAT
1.7500 g., 0.9860 Gold .0555 oz. AGW **Ruler:** Johann Ernst **Obv:** Cardinals' hat above oval shield **Obv. Legend:** IO : ERNEST : D : G : ... **Rev:** St. Rupert **Rev. Legend:** SALISBVRG • 1705 • S: RVD....

Date	Mintage	VG	F	VF	XF	Unc
1705	—	70.00	110	250	450	—
1707	—	70.00	110	250	450	—

KM# 298 1/2 DUCAT
1.7500 g., 0.9860 Gold .0555 oz. AGW **Ruler:** Franz Anton **Obv:** Cardinals' hat above shield **Obv. Legend:** FRANC : ANTO : ... **Rev:** St. Rupert **Rev. Legend:** SALISBVRG ....

Date	Mintage	VG	F	VF	XF	Unc
1709	—	125	225	450	950	—
1715	—	125	225	450	950	—
1720	—	125	225	450	950	—
1722	—	125	225	450	950	—

KM# 331 1/2 DUCAT
1.7500 g., 0.9860 Gold .0555 oz. AGW **Ruler:** Leopold Anton **Obv:** Cardinals' hat above shield **Obv. Legend:** LEOPOLDUS ... **Rev:** St. Rupert

Date	Mintage	VG	F	VF	XF	Unc
1728	—	175	275	600	1,000	—

KM# 357 1/2 DUCAT
1.7500 g., 0.9860 Gold .0555 oz. AGW **Ruler:** Andreas Jakob **Obv:** Cardinals' hat above shield, value below **Obv. Legend:** ANDREAS • D : G • ... **Rev:** St. Rupert **Rev. Legend:** S • RVBERTVS ....

Date	Mintage	VG	F	VF	XF	Unc
1749	—	150	325	750	1,450	—

KM# 362 1/2 DUCAT
1.7500 g., 0.9860 Gold .0555 oz. AGW **Ruler:** Andreas Jakob **Obv:** Bust right **Obv. Legend:** ANDREAS • D : G • ARCH .... **Rev:** Cardinals' hat above shield, value below

Date	Mintage	VG	F	VF	XF	Unc
1751	—	150	325	700	1,350	—

KM# 384 1/2 DUCAT
1.7500 g., 0.9860 Gold .0555 oz. AGW **Ruler:** Sigismund III **Obv:** Bust right **Obv. Legend:** SIGISMUS • D • G • ... **Rev:** Cardinals' hat above oval shield, value below

Date	Mintage	VG	F	VF	XF	Unc
1755	—	75.00	150	300	550	—
1761	—	75.00	150	300	550	—

KM# 444 1/2 DUCAT
1.7500 g., 0.9860 Gold .0555 oz. AGW **Ruler:** Hieronymus **Obv:** Bust right **Obv. Legend:** HIERONYMVS D • G • A • ... **Rev:** Cardinals' hat above oval, mantled shield, crown above, date below

Date	Mintage	VG	F	VF	XF	Unc
1776	—	125	250	500	800	—

KM# 257 DUCAT
3.5000 g., 0.9860 Gold .1109 oz. AGW **Ruler:** Johann Ernst **Obv:** Cardinals' hat above oval shield **Obv. Legend:** IO : ERNEST : .... **Rev:** St. Rupert **Rev. Legend:** S: RVDBERTVS • EPS • SALISBVRG •

Date	Mintage	VG	F	VF	XF	Unc
1701	—	120	250	650	1,250	—
1702	—	120	250	650	1,250	—
1703	—	120	250	650	1,250	—
1704	—	120	250	650	1,250	—
1705	—	120	250	650	1,250	—
1706	—	120	250	650	1,250	—
1707	—	120	250	650	1,250	—
1708	—	120	250	650	1,250	—

KM# 299 DUCAT

3.5000 g., 0.9860 Gold .1109 oz. AGW **Ruler:** Franz Anton **Obv:** Cardinals' hat above crowned oval shield **Obv. Legend:** FRANC : ANTO : ... **Rev:** St. Rupert **Rev. Legend:** S: RVDBERTVS • EPS • SALISBVRG •

Date	Mintage	VG	F	VF	XF	Unc
1709	—	250	450	1,250	2,250	—
1710	—	250	450	1,250	2,250	—
1711	—	250	450	1,250	2,250	—
1712	—	250	450	1,250	2,250	—
1713	—	250	450	1,250	2,250	—
1715	—	250	450	1,250	2,250	—
1716	—	250	450	1,250	2,250	—
1717	—	250	450	1,250	2,250	—
1718	—	250	450	1,250	2,250	—
1719	—	250	450	1,250	2,250	—
1720	—	250	450	1,250	2,250	—
1721	—	250	450	1,250	2,250	—
1722	—	250	450	1,250	2,250	—
1723	—	250	450	1,250	2,250	—
1724	—	250	450	1,250	2,250	—
1725	—	250	450	1,250	2,250	—
1726	—	250	450	1,250	2,250	—

KM# 309 DUCAT

3.5000 g., 0.9860 Gold .1109 oz. AGW **Ruler:** Franz Anton **Obv:** Bust right **Obv. Legend:** FRANC • ANTO • ... **Rev:** Cardinals' hat above pear-shaped shield **Rev. Legend:** SALISBVRG • S • S • A • L • D • G • ARCH....

Date	Mintage	VG	F	VF	XF	Unc
1710	—	350	550	1,450	2,650	—
1711	—	350	550	1,450	2,650	—
1712	—	350	550	1,450	2,650	—
1713	—	350	550	1,450	2,650	—
1714	—	350	550	1,450	2,650	—
1715	—	350	550	1,450	2,650	—
1716	—	350	550	1,450	2,650	—
1718	—	350	550	1,450	2,650	—
1719	—	350	550	1,450	2,650	—
1720	—	350	550	1,450	2,650	—
1721	—	350	550	1,450	2,650	—
1724	—	350	550	1,450	2,650	—
1725	—	350	550	1,450	2,650	—

KM# 321 DUCAT

3.5000 g., 0.9860 Gold .1109 oz. AGW **Ruler:** Franz Anton **Obv:** Older bust of Franz Anton right

Date	Mintage	VG	F	VF	XF	Unc
1726	—	400	600	1,650	2,850	—

KM# 323 DUCAT

3.5000 g., 0.9860 Gold .1109 oz. AGW **Ruler:** Leopold Anton **Obv:** Cardinals' hat above pear-shaped shield **Obv. Legend:** LEOPOLD ... **Rev:** St. Rupert **Rev. Legend:** S: RUDBERTUS • EPS • SALISBURG •

Date	Mintage	VG	F	VF	XF	Unc
1727	—	150	250	500	900	—
1728	—	150	250	500	900	—
1729	—	150	250	500	900	—
1730	—	150	250	500	900	—
1731	—	150	250	500	900	—
1732	—	150	250	500	900	—
1733	—	150	250	500	900	—
1734	—	150	250	500	900	—
1735	—	150	250	500	900	—
1736	—	150	250	500	900	—
1737	—	150	250	500	900	—
1738	—	150	250	500	900	—
1739	—	150	250	500	900	—
1740	—	150	250	500	900	—

KM# 332 DUCAT

3.5000 g., 0.9860 Gold .1109 oz. AGW **Ruler:** Leopold Anton **Obv:** Bust right **Obv. Legend:** LEOPOLDUS • D • G • ... **Rev:** Cardinals' hat above shield **Note:** Varieties exist.

Date	Mintage	VG	F	VF	XF	Unc
1728 D	—	250	450	1,250	2,500	—
1738 FMK	—	250	450	1,500	2,750	—
1739 FMK	—	250	450	1,500	2,750	—
1740 FMK	—	250	450	1,500	2,750	—
1741 FMK	—	250	450	1,500	2,750	—
1742 FMK	—	250	450	1,500	2,750	—
1743 FMK	—	250	450	1,500	2,750	—
1744 FMK	—	250	450	1,500	2,750	—

KM# 347 DUCAT

3.5000 g., 0.9860 Gold .1109 oz. AGW **Ruler:** Jakob Ernst **Obv:** Arms below hat **Obv. Legend:** IACOBUS ERN ... **Rev:** St. Rupert seated facing

Date	Mintage	VG	F	VF	XF	Unc
1745	—	200	500	1,350	2,500	—
1746	—	200	500	1,350	2,500	—

KM# 349 DUCAT

3.5000 g., 0.9860 Gold .1109 oz. AGW **Ruler:** Jakob Ernst **Obv:** Bust right **Obv. Legend:** IACOBUS ERN D G ... **Rev:** Cardinals' hat above pear-shaped shield

Date	Mintage	VG	F	VF	XF	Unc
1746	—	175	400	1,150	2,250	—
1747	—	175	400	1,150	2,250	—

KM# 351 DUCAT

3.5000 g., 0.9860 Gold .1109 oz. AGW **Ruler:** Andreas Jakob **Obv:** Cardinals' hat above pear-shaped shield **Obv. Legend:** ANDREAS • D : G • ARCH .... **Rev:** St. Rupert **Rev. Legend:** S • RUPERTUS ...

Date	Mintage	VG	F	VF	XF	Unc
1747	—	125	250	900	1,600	—
1748	—	125	250	900	1,600	—
1749	—	125	250	900	1,600	—
1751	—	125	250	900	1,600	—
1752	—	125	250	900	1,600	—

KM# 355 DUCAT

3.5000 g., 0.9860 Gold .1109 oz. AGW **Ruler:** Andreas Jakob **Obv:** Bust right **Obv. Legend:** ANDREAS • D : G • ARCH .... **Rev:** Cardinals' hat above pear-shaped shield **Rev. Legend:** SALISBURG ..... **Note:** Varieties with and without die-cutter's initials MK exist.

Date	Mintage	VG	F	VF	XF	Unc
1748	—	175	325	1,200	1,850	—
1749	—	175	325	1,200	1,850	—
1750	—	175	325	1,200	1,850	—
1751	—	175	325	1,200	1,850	—

KM# 372 DUCAT

3.5000 g., 0.9860 Gold .1109 oz. AGW **Ruler:** Sigismund III **Obv:** Cardinals' hat above ornate shield **Obv. Legend:** SIGISMUND • D • G • ... **Rev:** St. Rupert, date in legend **Rev. Legend:** S • RUPERTUS • EPS • SALISBURG •

Date	Mintage	VG	F	VF	XF	Unc
1753	—	150	250	650	1,150	—

KM# 381 DUCAT

3.5000 g., 0.9860 Gold .1109 oz. AGW **Ruler:** Sigismund III **Obv:** Bust right **Obv. Legend:** SIGISMUNDUS • D • G • ... **Rev:** Cardinals' hat above oval shield, divided date above

Date	Mintage	VG	F	VF	XF	Unc
1754 MK	—	100	175	450	800	—
1755 MK	—	100	175	450	800	—
1756 MK	—	100	175	450	800	—
1757 MK	—	100	175	450	800	—
1758 MK	—	100	175	450	800	—
1759 MK	—	100	175	450	800	—
1760 MK	—	100	175	450	800	—
1761 MK	—	100	175	450	800	—
1762 MK	—	100	175	450	800	—
1763 MK	—	100	175	450	800	—

KM# 404 DUCAT

3.5000 g., 0.9860 Gold .1109 oz. AGW **Ruler:** Sigismund III **Obv:** Crowned and mantled arms

Date	Mintage	VG	F	VF	XF	Unc
1762	—	125	175	500	900	—
1763	—	125	175	500	900	—

KM# 405 DUCAT

3.5000 g., 0.9860 Gold .1109 oz. AGW **Ruler:** Sigismund III **Obv:** Arms **Rev:** St. Rupert holding Madonna

Date	Mintage	VG	F	VF	XF	Unc
1763	—	125	175	500	900	—

KM# 406 DUCAT

3.5000 g., 0.9860 Gold .1109 oz. AGW **Ruler:** Sigismund III **Obv:** Bust right **Rev:** Crowned and mantled arms, crown divides date

Date	Mintage	VG	F	VF	XF	Unc
1764	—	125	175	500	900	—

KM# 407 DUCAT

3.5000 g., 0.9860 Gold .1109 oz. AGW **Ruler:** Sigismund III **Obv:** Bust right **Obv. Legend:** SIGM ... **Rev:** Cardinals' hat above oval, mantled shield, crown above, divided date below

Date	Mintage	VG	F	VF	XF	Unc
1764	—	100	175	450	800	—
1765	—	100	175	450	800	—
1766	—	100	175	450	800	—
1767	—	100	175	450	800	—
1768	—	100	175	450	800	—
1769	—	100	175	450	800	—
1770	—	100	175	450	800	—
1771	—	100	175	450	800	—

KM# 411 DUCAT

3.5000 g., 0.9860 Gold .1109 oz. AGW **Ruler:** Sigismund III **Rev:** Date above arms

Date	Mintage	VG	F	VF	XF	Unc
1765	—	125	175	500	900	—

KM# 436 DUCAT

3.5000 g., 0.9860 Gold .1109 oz. AGW **Ruler:** Hieronymus **Obv:** Oval, ornate shield **Obv. Legend:** SALISBURG .... **Rev:** St. Rupert **Rev. Legend:** S • RUPERTUS • EPISCOPUS • SALISBURGENSIS • **Note:** Sede Vacante issue.

Date	Mintage	VG	F	VF	XF	Unc
1772	—	150	300	700	1,200	—

KM# 437 DUCAT

3.5000 g., 0.9860 Gold .1109 oz. AGW **Ruler:** Hieronymus **Obv:** Bust right **Obv. Legend:** HIERONYMVS D • G • A • ... **Rev:** Cardinals' hat above oval, mantled shield, crown above, date below **Note:** Varieties with narrow and wide dates exist, also with or without die-cutter's initials.

Date	Mintage	VG	F	VF	XF	Unc
1772 M	—	100	225	500	900	—
1773 M	—	75.00	125	250	450	—
1774 M	—	75.00	125	250	450	—
1775 M	—	75.00	125	250	450	—
1776 M	—	75.00	125	250	450	—
1777 M	—	75.00	125	250	450	—
1778 M	—	75.00	125	250	450	—
1779 M	—	75.00	125	250	450	—
1780 M	—	75.00	125	250	450	—
1781 M	—	75.00	125	250	450	—
1782 M	—	75.00	125	250	450	—
1783 M	—	75.00	125	250	450	—
1784 M	—	75.00	125	250	450	—
1785 M	—	75.00	125	250	450	—
1786 M	—	75.00	125	250	450	—

KM# 452 DUCAT

3.5000 g., 0.9860 Gold .1109 oz. AGW, 21.2 mm. **Ruler:** Hieronymus **Subject:** 1,200th Anniversary of the Bishopric **Obv:** Bust right **Obv. Legend:** HIERONYMVS D • G • A • ... **Rev:** Holy door with date below **Rev. Legend:** PRINCEPS POPULUSO IUVAVIENS **Note:** Ancient Roman Numeral date bottom reverse.

Date	Mintage	VG	F	VF	XF	Unc
(1782) M	—	125	275	800	1,250	—

KM# 463 DUCAT

3.5000 g., 0.9860 Gold .1109 oz. AGW **Ruler:** Hieronymus **Obv:** Bust right **Obv. Legend:** HIERON • D • G • A • ... **Rev:** Cardinals' hat above mantled shield, crown above, divided date below

Date	Mintage	VG	F	VF	XF	Unc
1787 M	—	85.00	125	250	450	—
1788 M	—	85.00	125	250	450	—
1789 M	—	85.00	125	250	450	—
1790 M	—	85.00	125	250	450	—
1791 M	—	85.00	125	250	450	—
1792 M	—	85.00	125	250	450	—
1793 M	—	85.00	125	250	450	—
1794 M	—	85.00	125	250	450	—
1795 M	—	85.00	125	250	450	—
1796 M	—	85.00	125	250	450	—
1797 M	—	85.00	125	250	450	—
1798 M	—	85.00	125	250	450	—
1799 M	—	85.00	125	250	450	—
1800 M	—	85.00	125	250	450	—

KM# 271 2 DUCAT

7.0000 g., 0.9860 Gold .2219 oz. AGW **Ruler:** Johann Ernst **Obv:** Arms **Obv. Legend:** IO ERNEST... **Rev:** Saint Rupert on throne

Date	Mintage	VG	F	VF	XF	Unc
1707	—	250	550	1,350	2,500	—
1708	—	250	550	1,350	2,500	—

KM# 300 2 DUCAT

7.0000 g., 0.9860 Gold .2219 oz. AGW **Ruler:** Franz Anton **Obv. Legend:** FRANC ANTO ... **Note:** Klippe.

Date	Mintage	VG	F	VF	XF	Unc
1709	—	1,000	2,000	4,000	6,500	—

KM# 337 2 DUCAT

7.0000 g., 0.9860 Gold .2219 oz. AGW **Ruler:** Leopold Anton **Obv. Legend:** LEOPOLD ...

Date	Mintage	VG	F	VF	XF	Unc
1734	—	450	950	2,450	4,500	—
1735	—	450	950	2,450	4,500	—

KM# 360 2 DUCAT

7.0000 g., 0.9860 Gold .2219 oz. AGW **Ruler:** Andreas Jakob **Note:** Similar to Ducat, KM#355.

Date	Mintage	VG	F	VF	XF	Unc
1750 MK	—	700	1,350	4,000	6,500	—

KM# 365 2 DUCAT

7.0000 g., 0.9860 Gold .2219 oz. AGW **Ruler:** Andreas Jakob **Obv:** Cardinals' hat above shield **Obv. Legend:** ANDREAS • D : G • ARCH .... **Rev:** St. Rupert, date in legend **Rev. Legend:** S • RUPERTUS • ...

Date	Mintage	VG	F	VF	XF	Unc
1752	—	600	1,200	3,250	6,000	—

KM# 385 2 DUCAT

7.0000 g., 0.9860 Gold .2219 oz. AGW **Ruler:** Sigismund III **Obv:** Bust of Sigismund right **Rev:** Arms, bishop's hat divides date

Date	Mintage	VG	F	VF	XF	Unc
1755	—	250	500	1,300	2,250	—

KM# A412 2 DUCAT

7.0000 g., 0.9860 Gold .2218 oz. AGW **Ruler:** Sigismund III **Obv:** Bust right **Rev:** 2 adjacent mantled shields of arms under electoral hat, angel's head and wings at top, value 2 in cartouche at bottom

Date	Mintage	VG	F	VF	XF	Unc
1764	—	250	500	1,300	2,000	—

KM# 412 2 DUCAT

7.0000 g., 0.9860 Gold .2219 oz. AGW **Ruler:** Sigismund III **Obv:** Bust right **Obv. Legend:** SIGISMUNDUS • D • G • ... **Rev:** Cardinals' hat above oval, mantled shield, crown above, divided date below

Date	Mintage	VG	F	VF	XF	Unc
1765	—	200	400	850	1,250	—
1766/5	—	200	400	850	1,250	—
1767	—	200	400	850	1,250	—
1768	—	200	400	850	1,250	—
1769	—	200	400	850	1,250	—
1770	—	200	400	850	1,250	—
1771	—	200	400	850	1,250	—

KM# 428 2 DUCAT

7.0000 g., 0.9860 Gold .2219 oz. AGW **Ruler:** Sigismund III **Rev:** Crowned and mantled ecclesiastical arms, date and value below

Date	Mintage	VG	F	VF	XF	Unc
1770	—	250	500	1,300	2,000	—
1771	—	250	500	1,300	2,000	—

KM# 440 2 DUCAT

7.0000 g., 0.9860 Gold .2219 oz. AGW **Ruler:** Hieronymus **Obv:** Bust right **Rev:** Crowned and mantled oval arms, value below

Date	Mintage	VG	F	VF	XF	Unc
1773 M	—	900	1,850	3,500	6,000	—

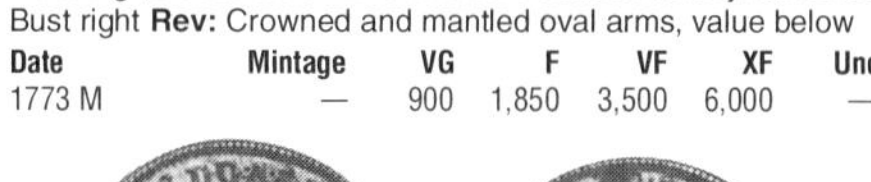

KM# 453 2 DUCAT

7.0000 g., 0.9860 Gold .2219 oz. AGW, 21.2 mm. **Ruler:** Hieronymus **Subject:** 1,200th Anniversary of the Bishopric **Obv:** Bust right **Obv. Legend:** HIERONYMVS D • G • A • ... **Rev:** Holy door **Rev. Legend:** PRINCEPS .... **Note:** Ancient Roman Numeral date at bottom reverse.

Date	Mintage	VG	F	VF	XF	Unc
(1782) M	—	400	800	2,500	4,000	—

KM# 416 3 DUCAT

10.5000 g., 0.9860 Gold .3329 oz. AGW **Ruler:** Sigismund III **Obv:** Bust right **Obv. Legend:** SIGM • D • G • ... **Rev:** Interior view of the mint **Note:** Installation of new machinery at mint.

Date	Mintage	VG	F	VF	XF	Unc
1766	—	1,250	2,500	5,000	8,000	—

KM# 301 5 DUCAT

17.5000 g., 0.9860 Gold .5548 oz. AGW **Ruler:** Franz Anton **Obv:** Arms below hat **Obv. Legend:** FRANC ANTON ... **Rev:** 2 saints seated, facing each other with croziers, church in foreground

Date	Mintage	VG	F	VF	XF	Unc
1709 Rare	—	—	—	—	—	—

KM# A301 5 DUCAT

17.5000 g., 0.9860 Gold .5548 oz. AGW **Ruler:** Franz Anton **Note:** Strike of 1/4 Thaler KM#294 in gold.

Date	Mintage	VG	F	VF	XF	Unc
1709 Rare	—	—	—	—	—	—

KM# A350 5 DUCAT

17.5000 g., 0.9860 Gold .5547 oz. AGW **Ruler:** Jakob Ernst **Obv:** Bust of Jakob Ernst right **Rev:** Arms below hat **Rev. Legend:** DOMINUS AUTEM ASSUMPSIT ME

Date	Mintage	VG	F	VF	XF	Unc
1745 Rare	—	—	—	—	—	—

KM# A381 5 DUCAT

17.5000 g., 0.9860 Gold .5548 oz. AGW **Ruler:** Sigismund III **Obv:** Bust of Sigismund III right **Rev:** Arms

Date	Mintage	VG	F	VF	XF	Unc
1753 Rare	—	—	—	—	—	—

KM# 396 5 DUCAT

17.5000 g., 0.9860 Gold .5548 oz. AGW **Ruler:** Sigismund III **Obv:** Bust right **Obv. Legend:** SIGISMUNDUS • D • G • ... **Rev:** St. Rupert seated with Cardinals' hat above oval shield **Rev. Legend:** S • RUPERTUS ...

Date	Mintage	VG	F	VF	XF	Unc
1759 FMK	—	1,650	3,000	6,500	10,000	—

KM# B381 6 DUCAT

21.0000 g., 0.9860 Gold .6658 oz. AGW **Ruler:** Sigismund III **Obv:** Bust of Sigismund III right **Rev:** Arms

Date	Mintage	VG	F	VF	XF	Unc
1753 Rare	—	—	—	—	—	—

KM# 400 6 DUCAT

21.0000 g., 0.9860 Gold .6658 oz. AGW **Ruler:** Sigismund III **Obv:** Bust of Sigismund III right **Rev:** St. Rupert seated left before statue of Madonna and Child

Date	Mintage	VG	F	VF	XF	Unc
1760 FMK Rare	—	—	—	—	—	—

KM# 448 6 DUCAT

21.0000 g., 0.9860 Gold .6658 oz. AGW **Ruler:** Hieronymus **Subject:** 1,200th Anniversary of the Bishopric **Note:** Similar to Ducat, KM#452.

Date	Mintage	VG	F	VF	XF	Unc
1782 M Rare	—	—	—	—	—	—

KM# 302 10 DUCAT
35.0000 g., 0.9860 Gold 1.1095 oz. AGW **Ruler:** Franz Anton **Obv:** Cardinals' hat above oval ornate shield, divided date below, all within roped wreath **Obv. Legend:** FRANC : ANTON : ... **Rev:** Standin Saints within roped wreath **Rev. Legend:** :RVDBERTUS ET VIRGILIUS PATRONI ....

Date	Mintage	VG	F	VF	XF	Unc
1709 Rare	—	—	—	—	—	—

KM# C381 10 DUCAT
35.0000 g., 0.9860 Gold 1.1095 oz. AGW **Ruler:** Sigismund III **Obv:** Bust of Sigismund III right **Rev:** 2 figures with arms

Date	Mintage	VG	F	VF	XF	Unc
1753	—	—	—	12,500	17,500	—

KM# A419 10 DUCAT
35.0000 g., 0.9860 Gold 1.1095 oz. AGW **Ruler:** Sigismund III **Obv:** Bust of Sigismund III **Rev:** City gate

Date	Mintage	VG	F	VF	XF	Unc
1767 Rare	—	—	—	—	—	—

KM# A382 12 DUCAT
42.0000 g., 0.9860 Gold 1.3314 oz. AGW **Ruler:** Sigismund III **Obv:** Bust of Sigismund III **Rev:** Crowned and mantled 2 shields

Date	Mintage	VG	F	VF	XF	Unc
1755 Rare	—	—	—	—	—	—

KM# 449 12 DUCAT
54.0000 g., 0.9860 Gold 1.3314 oz. AGW **Ruler:** Hieronymus **Subject:** 1,200th Anniversary of the Bishopric **Note:** Similar to Ducat, KM#452.

Date	Mintage	VG	F	VF	XF	Unc
1782 Rare	—	—	—	—	—	—

KM# 303 20 DUCAT
70.0000 g., 0.9860 Gold 2.219 oz. AGW **Ruler:** Franz Anton **Obv:** Arms below hat **Obv. Inscription:** FRANC ANTON **Rev:** 2 saints seated, facing each other with croziers, church in foreground

Date	Mintage	VG	F	VF	XF	Unc
1709 Rare	—	—	—	—	—	—

KM# B350 20 DUCAT
70.0000 g., 0.9860 Gold 2.2190 oz. AGW **Ruler:** Jakob Ernst **Note:** Similar to 5 Ducat, KM#A350.

Date	Mintage	VG	F	VF	XF	Unc
1745 Rare	—	—	—	—	—	—

KM# 304 25 DUCAT
87.5000 g., 0.9860 Gold 2.7738 oz. AGW, 46 mm. **Ruler:** Franz Anton **Obv:** Arms below hat **Obv. Inscription:** FRANC ANTON **Rev:** 2 saints, seated, facing each other with croziers, church in foreground

Date	Mintage	VG	F	VF	XF	Unc
1709 Rare	—	—	—	—	—	—

PATTERNS

Including off metal strikes

KM#	Date	Mintage	Identification	Mkt Val
Pn10	1753	—	10 Ducat. Silver. KM#C381.	500
Pn11	1761	—	20 Kreuzer. Silver. Without indication of value.	—

KM#	Date	Mintage	Identification	Mkt Val
Pn12	(1782)	—	Ducat. Silver. KM#452. Ancient Roman Numeral date.	—

KM#	Date	Mintage	Identification	Mkt Val
Pn13	(1782)	—	2 Ducat. Silver. KM#453. Ancient Roman Numeral date.	—

SINZENDORF

COUNTY

TRADE COINAGE

FR# 3290 DUCAT
3.5000 g., 0.9860 Gold .1109 oz. AGW **Ruler:** Philipp Ludwig **Obv:** Bust right **Obv. Legend:** PHILIP LUD ... **Rev:** Crowned arms within cartouche

Date	Mintage	VG	F	VF	XF	Unc
1726	—	500	1,000	2,500	4,000	—

C# 1 DUCAT
3.5000 g., 0.9860 Gold .1109 oz. AGW **Ruler:** Johann Wilhelm **Obv:** Bust right **Rev:** Arms within Order chain **Note:** Fr.#3291.

Date	Mintage	VG	F	VF	XF	Unc
1753	—	300	650	1,250	2,000	3,500

SPRINZENSTEIN

In 1529, Paul Riccio obtained the lordship of Sprinzenstein in Upper Austria from the bishop of Passau. He was elevated to the rank of hereditary freiherr the following year.

His son Hieronimus obtained the lordship of Neuhaus. Descendants of his oldest son were made counts of the Empire in 1646 and Ferdinand Max received the coinage right. He died without sons and the only coins of Sprinzenstein were struck at the Augsburg Mint by his nephew and the latter's nephew.

RULERS
Franz Ignaz, 1639-1705
Johann Ehrenreich, 1705-1729

COUNTY

STANDARD COINAGE

KM# 5 THALER
Silver **Ruler:** Franz Ignaz **Obv:** Armored bust right **Obv. Legend:** FRANC • IGNAT • S • R • I • C • & DOM • DE ET IN SPRINZENSTEIN ET NEUHAUS * **Rev:** Helmeted arms **Rev. Legend:** ARCHI • MONETARIVS HÆREDITARI • VTRIVSQ • AVSTRIAE **Note:** Dav. #1198.

Date	Mintage	VG	F	VF	XF	Unc
1705	—	450	750	1,250	2,150	—

KM# 10 THALER
Silver **Ruler:** Johann Ehrenreich **Obv:** Armored bust right **Obv. Legend:** IOAN • ERNRICUS S • R • I • C • & DOM • DE ET IN SPRINZENSTEIN ET NEUHAUS * **Rev:** Helmeted arms **Rev. Legend:** ARCHI • MONETARI • HAEREDITARI • UTRIUSQ: ARCHIDUCAT • AUSTRIAE * **Note:** Dav. #1199.

Date	Mintage	VG	F	VF	XF	Unc
1717	—	350	550	950	1,650	—

TRAUTSON

An old Tyrolean family that traced its lineage back to 1134. During the reign of Paul Sixtus I (1589-1621), who was Imperial Governor of the Tyrol, the mint right was given to this house. Members of this house held high imperial offices until 1775 when the house passed to Auersperg.

RULERS
Franz Eusebius, 1663-1728
Johann Leopold, 1663-1724

PRINCIPALITY

STANDARD COINAGE

KM# 31 THALER
Silver **Ruler:** Franz Eusebius **Obv:** Bust right **Obv. Legend:** FRANC • EUSEB • TRAVTHSON COM • IN FALKHENSTAIN **Rev:** Helmeted arms divide date at bottom **Rev. Legend:** • L • B • IN SPRECHEN: ET SCHROVENSTEIN • **Note:** Dav. #1200.

Date	Mintage	VG	F	VF	XF	Unc
1708	—	150	250	400	750	—
1715	—	150	250	400	750	—

KM# 34 THALER
Silver **Ruler:** Johann Leopold **Obv:** Bust right **Obv. Legend:** LEOP • S • R • I • PRINCEPS TRAVTSON • COM • IN • FALKENSTEIN **Rev:** Helmeted, crowned and mantled arms **Rev. Legend:** AVR • VELL • EQV • S • C • & CAT • MAI • INTIM • & CONFERENT • CONSILIAR • **Note:** Dav. #1201.

Date	Mintage	VG	F	VF	XF	Unc
1719	—	150	250	400	750	—

TRADE COINAGE

KM# 32 DUCAT
3.5000 g., 0.9860 Gold .1109 oz. AGW **Ruler:** Franz Eusebius **Obv:** Bust right **Obv. Legend:** FRA • EUS: TRAV THSON: CO: ... **Rev:** Angel above crowned arms **Rev. Legend:** • L B IN SPRECHEN: ET SCHROVENSTEIN •

Date	Mintage	VG	F	VF	XF	Unc
1708	—	450	850	2,000	3,250	—
1715	—	450	850	2,000	3,250	—

KM# 35 DUCAT
3.5000 g., 0.9860 Gold .1109 oz. AGW **Ruler:** Johann Leopold **Obv:** Draped bust **Rev:** Helmeted and draped arms

Date	Mintage	VG	F	VF	XF	Unc
1719	—	350	700	1,650	2,850	—

KM# 36 10 DUCAT
35.0000 g., 0.9860 Gold 1.1090 oz. AGW **Ruler:** Johann Leopold **Note:** Struck with 1 Thaler dies, KM#34.

Date	Mintage	VG	F	VF	XF	Unc
1719 Rare	—	—	—	—	—	—

PATTERNS

Including off metal stirkes

KM#	Date	Mintage	Identification	Mkt Val
Pn1	1719	—	Ducat. Silver. KM#35	—
Pn2	1719	—	Ducat. Copper. KM#35	—

VIENNA

Wien

Became a bishopric in 1471. The bishop became a prince in 1631 and Vienna was made an archbishopric in 1722.

RULER
Christoph Anton, Graf. v. Migazzi, 1757-1803

ARCHBISHOPRIC

STANDARD COINAGE

KM# 1 THALER (Convention)
Silver **Ruler:** Christoph Anton, Graf v. Migazzi **Obv:** Bust right **Obv. Legend:** CHRISTOPHORVS•D•N•S•R•E•CARDINALIS • DE MIGAZZI • **Rev:** Arms within crowned mantle, Cardinal's hat above **Rev. Legend:** ARCHIEP • VIEN • S • R • I • P • EP • VACIEN • ADM • S • STEPH • R • A • M • C • E • **Note:** Dav. #1267.

Date	Mintage	VG	F	VF	XF	Unc
1781	2,000	125	200	285	500	—

TRADE COINAGE

KM# 2 DUCAT
3.5000 g., 0.9860 Gold .1109 oz. AGW **Ruler:** Christoph Anton, Graf v. Migazzi **Obv:** Bust right **Rev:** Crowned and mantled arms below bishop's hat

Date	Mintage	VG	F	VF	XF	Unc
1781	—	350	700	1,250	2,200	—

WINDISCH-GRATZ

A family descended from the counts of Weimar with holdings in Styria. Made "free barons" in 1551. They became counts during the reign of Emperor Leopold I and received the coin right in 1730. First coins were made in 1732, the last in 1777.

RULERS
Leopold Victor Johann, 1727-1746
Joseph Nicholas, 1746-1802

COUNTY

STANDARD COINAGE

KM# 10 20 KREUZER
Silver **Ruler:** Joseph Nicholas **Obv:** Bust right **Obv. Legend:** IOS • NIC • S • R • I • .... **Rev:** Helmeted and supported arms **Rev. Legend:** SUP • PER STYR • STAB • PRAEFECTUS • HAERED •

Date	Mintage	F	VF	XF	Unc	BU
1777	—	40.00	70.00	120	200	—

KM# 11 1/2 THALER (Convention)
Silver **Ruler:** Joseph Nicholas **Obv:** Bust right **Obv. Legend:** IOS • NIC • S • R • I • ... **Rev:** Helmeted and supported arms **Rev. Legend:** SUP • PER STYR: STAB PRÆFECTUS ...

Date	Mintage	F	VF	XF	Unc	BU
1777	—	125	250	400	675	—

KM# 5 THALER
Silver **Ruler:** Leopold Victor Johann **Obv:** Bust right **Obv. Legend:** LEOPOLD • VICT • IO • S • R • I • COMES • A • WINDISCHGRATZ • **Rev:** Helmeted and supported arms **Rev. Legend:** S • C • M • CONS • STATUS • INT & HAERED • PER • STYR • SUP • STAB • PRAEFECTUS **Note:** Dav. #1202.

Date	Mintage	VG	F	VF	XF	Unc
1732	—	200	350	650	1,000	—

TRADE COINAGE

KM# 6 DUCAT
3.5000 g., 0.9860 Gold .1109 oz. AGW **Ruler:** Leopold Victor Johann **Obv:** Draped bust right **Rev:** Arms topped by 3 helmets; wolfhound supporters

Date	Mintage	VG	F	VF	XF	Unc
1732	—	550	1,250	2,500	4,500	—
1733	—	550	1,250	2,500	4,500	—

KM# 12 DUCAT
3.5000 g., 0.9860 Gold .1109 oz. AGW **Ruler:** Joseph Nicholas **Obv:** Bust right **Obv. Legend:** IOS • NIC • S • .... **Rev:** Helmeted and supported arms

Date	Mintage	F	VF	XF	Unc	BU
1777	—	450	1,000	2,250	4,000	—

KM# 7 5 DUCAT
17.5000 g., 0.9860 Gold .5547 oz. AGW **Ruler:** Leopold Victor Johann **Obv:** Bust right **Rev:** Helmeted and supported arms **Note:** Struck with 1 Thaler dies, KM#5.

Date	Mintage	VG	F	VF	XF	Unc
1732 Rare	—	—	—	—	—	—

KM# 13 5 DUCAT
17.5000 g., 0.9860 Gold .5547 oz. AGW **Ruler:** Joseph Nicholas **Obv:** Bust right **Rev:** Helmeted and supported arms **Note:** Struck with 1/2 Thaler dies, KM#11.

Date	Mintage	VG	F	VF	XF	Unc
1777 Rare	—	—	—	—	—	—

KM# 8 10 DUCAT
35.0000 g., 0.9860 Gold 1.1095 oz. AGW **Ruler:** Leopold Victor Johann **Note:** Similar to 5 Ducat, KM#7. Struck with 1 Thaler dies, KM#5.

Date	Mintage	VG	F	VF	XF	Unc
1732 Rare	—	—	—	—	—	—

KM# A8 20 DUCAT
75.0000 g., 0.9860 Gold 2.2190 oz. AGW **Ruler:** Leopold Victor Johann **Note:** Similar to 5 Ducat, KM#7. Struck with 1 Thaler dies, KM#5.

Date	Mintage	VG	F	VF	XF	Unc
1732 Rare	—	—	—	—	—	—

AUSTRIAN NETHERLANDS

The Austrian Netherlands, which corresponds roughly to present-day Belgium, came into being on April 11, 1713, when the Treaty of Utrecht awarded the lands to Austria as part settlement following the war with Spain. It passed to France in 1795, was part of the Kingdom of Netherlands from 1815 to 1830, and became the present Belgium as the result of the revolution of 1830 against William I, Prince of Orange and King of the Netherlands.

RULERS
Maria Theresa, 1740-1780
with Franz I, 1745-1765
Widow, 1765-1780
Joseph II, 1780-1790
Insurrection, 1790
Leopold II, 1790-1792
Franz II, 1792-1835

MINT MARKS
A - Vienna
(b) - Brussels (angel face)
B - Kremnitz
C - Prague
E - Karlsburg
F - Hall
G - Nagybanya
H - Gunzburg
(h) - Antwerp (hand)
(l) -Bruges (lion)
V - See note after KM#63-64
(w) Vienna

NOTE: For similar coins with M mint mark, refer to Italian States - Milan.

MINT OFFICIALS' INITIALS

Brussels

Initials	Years	Officials
R	1732-72	Jaques Roettiers, Engraver
IC	1765-74	Joseph Aug. Cronberg
SK	1774-80	Sig. Ant. Klemmer, Warden
FA	1774-80	F. Aycherau, Warden

MONETARY SYSTEM

4 Liards = 1 Sol
6 Sols = 1 Escalin
20 Sols = 1 Florin
54 Sols = 1 Kronentaler
60 Sols = 1 Ducaton
7 Florins, 13 Sols = 1 Souverain d'or

NOTE: In February 1786 the denomination of Souverain d'or was changed to 1/2 Souverain d'or except for the Antwerp pieces which retained their original 1 and 2 Souverain d'or denominations.

MINTAGES

NOTE: Mintages given as Inc. Ab. are included in the prior listing of that same mint.

POSSESSION
of Austrian Empire
STANDARD COINAGE

KM# 1 LIARD (Oord)

Copper **Ruler:** Maria Theresa with Franz I **Obv:** Young head right **Obv. Legend:** MAR • TH • D • G • HUNG • BOH • R • AR • AUS • D • BURG **Rev:** 4-line inscription date and mint mark below

Date	Mintage	VG	F	VF	XF	Unc
1744(h)	5,687,000	2.00	4.00	8.00	20.00	—
1744(l)	1,665,000	2.00	4.00	8.00	20.00	—
1744(b)	5,527,000	2.00	4.00	8.00	20.00	—
1745(h)	Inc. above	2.00	4.00	8.00	20.00	—
1745(l)	Inc. above	2.00	4.00	8.00	20.00	—
1745(b)	Inc. above	2.00	4.00	8.00	20.00	—

KM# 2 LIARD (Oord)

Copper **Ruler:** Maria Theresa with Franz I **Obv:** Bust with pearl necklace right

Date	Mintage	VG	F	VF	XF	Unc
1749(h)	6,988,000	2.00	4.00	8.00	20.00	—
1749(l)	—	2.00	4.00	8.00	20.00	—
1750(h)	Inc. above	2.00	4.00	8.00	20.00	—
1750(l)	—	2.00	4.00	8.00	20.00	—
1751(h)	Inc. above	2.00	4.00	8.00	20.00	—
1751(l)	—	2.00	4.00	8.00	20.00	—
1752(h)	Inc. above	2.00	4.00	8.00	20.00	—
1752(l)	—	2.00	4.00	8.00	20.00	—

KM# 28 LIARD (Oord)

Copper **Ruler:** Maria Theresa Widow **Obv:** Veiled bust right **Rev:** 4-Line inscription, date and mint mark below

Date	Mintage	VG	F	VF	XF	Unc
1776(b)	—	2.00	4.00	8.00	20.00	—
1777(b)	2,769,000	2.00	4.00	8.00	20.00	—
1778(b)	3,957,000	2.00	4.00	8.00	20.00	—
1780(b)	—	2.00	4.00	8.00	20.00	—

KM# 30 LIARD (Oord)

Copper **Ruler:** Joseph II **Obv:** Bust right **Obv. Legend:** JOS • II • D • G • R • IMP • D • B • **Rev:** 4-Line inscription, date and mint mark below

Date	Mintage	VG	F	VF	XF	Unc
1781(b)	1,656,000	2.00	4.00	8.00	20.00	—
1782(b)	Inc. above	2.00	4.00	8.00	20.00	—
1787(b)	135,000	2.00	4.00	10.00	25.00	—
1788/7(b)	—	2.00	4.00	10.00	25.00	—
1788(b)	1,185	2.00	4.00	8.00	20.00	—
1789(b)	655,000	2.00	4.00	8.00	20.00	—

KM# 52 LIARD (Oord)

Copper **Ruler:** Leopold II **Obv:** Draped bust right

Date	Mintage	VG	F	VF	XF	Unc
1791(b)	480,000	3.00	8.00	25.00	50.00	—
1792(b)	266,000	3.00	10.00	30.00	55.00	—

KM# 56 LIARD (Oord)

Copper **Ruler:** Franz II **Obv:** Bust right **Rev:** 4-Line inscription, date and mint mark below

Date	Mintage	VG	F	VF	XF	Unc
1792(b)	128,000	4.00	15.00	30.00	45.00	—
1793(b)	—	2.50	5.00	10.00	25.00	—
1794(b)	—	2.50	5.00	10.00	25.00	—

KM# 3 2 LIARDS (2 Oorden)

Copper **Ruler:** Maria Theresa with Franz I **Obv:** Bust with pearl necklace right **Rev:** 4-line inscription, date and mint mark below, all in wreath

Date	Mintage	VG	F	VF	XF	Unc
1749(h)	2,473,000	2.50	5.00	12.00	28.00	—
1749(l)	—	2.50	5.00	12.00	28.00	—
1750(h)	Inc. above	2.50	5.00	12.00	28.00	—
1750(l)	—	2.50	5.00	12.00	28.00	—
1751(h)	Inc. above	2.50	5.00	12.00	28.00	—
1751(l)	—	2.50	5.00	12.00	28.00	—
1752(l)	—	2.50	5.00	12.00	28.00	—
1753(h)	139,000	2.50	5.00	12.00	28.00	—

KM# 29 2 LIARDS (2 Oorden)

Copper **Ruler:** Maria Theresa Widow **Obv:** Veiled bust right **Rev:** 4-Line inscription, date and mint mark below, all within wreath

Date	Mintage	VG	F	VF	XF	Unc
1777(b)	1,371,000	2.50	5.00	12.00	28.00	—
1778(b)	1,443,000	2.50	5.00	12.00	28.00	—
1780(b)	—	2.50	5.00	12.00	28.00	—

KM# 31 2 LIARDS (2 Oorden)

Copper **Ruler:** Joseph II **Obv:** Draped bust right

Date	Mintage	VG	F	VF	XF	Unc
1781(b)	—	2.50	5.00	10.00	25.00	—
1782(b)	3,898,000	2.50	5.00	10.00	25.00	—
1787(b)	67,000	2.50	6.00	15.00	38.00	—
1788(b)	729,000	2.50	5.00	10.00	25.00	—
1789(b)	195,000	2.50	5.00	10.00	25.00	—

KM# 53 2 LIARDS (2 Oorden)

Copper **Ruler:** Leopold II **Obv:** Draped bust right **Obv. Legend:** LEOP•II•D•G•R•IMP•D•B• **Rev:** AD/USUM/BELGII/AUSTR, date within wreath

Date	Mintage	VG	F	VF	XF	Unc
1791(b)	210,000	6.00	12.00	35.00	60.00	—
1792(b)	83,000	8.00	20.00	55.00	75.00	—

KM# 57 2 LIARDS (2 Oorden)

Copper **Ruler:** Franz II **Obv:** Collared bust right **Rev:** 4-Line inscription, date and mint mark below, all within wreath

Date	Mintage	VG	F	VF	XF	Unc
1792(b) Rare	—	—	—	—	—	—
1793(b)	—	2.00	4.00	10.00	25.00	—
1794(b)	—	2.00	4.00	10.00	25.00	—

KM# 12 10 LIARDS (10 Oorden)

Billon **Ruler:** Maria Theresa with Franz I **Obv:** Titles of Maria Theresa **Obv. Legend:** MAR•TH•D: G•R•IMP•.... **Rev:** Crowned arms within sprays **Rev. Legend:** ARCH: AUS • DUX • ...

Date	Mintage	VG	F	VF	XF	Unc
1750(h)	2,333,000	7.00	20.00	40.00	100	—
1750(l)	—	7.00	20.00	40.00	100	—
1751(h)	Inc. above	7.00	20.00	40.00	100	—
1751(l)	722,000	7.00	20.00	40.00	100	—
1752(h)	Inc. above	7.00	20.00	40.00	100	—
1752(l)	Inc. above	7.00	20.00	40.00	100	—
1753(h)	209,000	7.00	20.00	40.00	100	—
1754(h)	34,000	7.00	20.00	40.00	100	—

KM# 36 10 LIARDS (10 Oorden)

Billon **Ruler:** Joseph II **Obv:** Burgundian cross, titles of Joseph II **Rev:** Crowned arms in order collar

Date	Mintage	VG	F	VF	XF	Unc
1788(h)	206,000	6.00	15.00	35.00	85.00	—
1789(h)	225,000	6.00	15.00	32.50	75.00	—

KM# 54 10 LIARDS (10 Oorden)

Billon **Ruler:** Leopold II **Obv:** Titles of Leopold II

Date	Mintage	VG	F	VF	XF	Unc
1791(b)	106,000	25.00	65.00	130	225	—

KM# 58 10 LIARDS (10 Oorden)

0.4150 Billon **Ruler:** Franz II **Obv:** Titles of Frances II **Obv. Legend:** FRANC • II • D • G • R • IMP • S • A • G • .... **Rev:** Arms within crowned Order chain **Rev. Legend:** ARCH • AUS • D • BURG • LOTH • ... **Note:** Patterns exist

Date	Mintage	VG	F	VF	XF	Unc
1792(b)	61,000	50.00	125	250	500	—

KM# 18 14 LIARDS (14 Oorden)

Billon **Ruler:** Maria Theresa with Franz I **Obv:** Burgundian cross divides value, mint mark below. Titles of Maria Theresa **Rev:** Arms on breast of crowned imperial eagle

Date	Mintage	VG	F	VF	XF	Unc
1755(h)	327,000	8.00	25.00	60.00	150	—
1756(h)	274,000	8.00	25.00	60.00	150	—
1757(h)	259,000	8.00	25.00	60.00	150	—
1758(b)	291,000	8.00	25.00	60.00	150	—
1759(b)	324,000	8.00	25.00	60.00	150	—
1760(b)	322,000	8.00	25.00	60.00	150	—
1761(b)	469,000	8.00	25.00	60.00	150	—
1762(b)	590,000	8.00	25.00	60.00	150	—
1763(b)	359,000	8.00	25.00	60.00	150	—
1772(b)	743,000	8.00	25.00	60.00	150	—
1773(b)	176,000	8.00	25.00	60.00	150	—
1775(b)	106,000	8.00	25.00	60.00	150	—
1776(b)	707,000	8.00	25.00	60.00	150	—
1777(b)	1,508,000	8.00	25.00	60.00	150	—
1778(b)	888,000	8.00	25.00	60.00	150	—

KM# 37 14 LIARDS (14 Oorden)

Billon **Ruler:** Joseph II **Obv:** Titles of Joseph II **Obv. Legend:** IOS • II • D • G • .... **Rev:** Crowned imperial double eagle with crowned arms on breast

Date	Mintage	VG	F	VF	XF	Unc
1788(b)	71,000	10.00	25.00	50.00	100	—
1789(b)	266,000	10.00	20.00	40.00	80.00	—

KM# 39 14 LIARDS (14 Oorden)

Billon **Ruler:** Leopold II **Obv:** Titles of Leopold II **Rev:** Crowned imperial double eagle with crowned arms on breast

Date	Mintage	VG	F	VF	XF	Unc
1790(b)	63,000	60.00	125	250	450	—
1791(b)	297,000	15.00	30.00	60.00	100	—
1792(b)	272,000	15.00	30.00	60.00	125	—

KM# 59 14 LIARDS (14 Oorden)

0.5380 Silver **Ruler:** Franz II **Obv:** Titles of Franz II **Obv. Legend:** FRANC • II • D • G • R • IMP • S • A • .... **Rev:** Crowned imperial eagle with crowned arms on breast **Rev. Legend:** ARCH • AUST • D • BURG • ....

Date	Mintage	VG	F	VF	XF	Unc
1792(b)	52,000	30.00	80.00	225	400	—
1793(b)	642,000	8.00	20.00	45.00	90.00	—
1794(b)	374,000	8.00	20.00	45.00	90.00	—

KM# 13 20 LIARDS (20 Oorden, 5 Sols, 5 Stuivers)

Billon **Ruler:** Maria Theresa with Franz I **Obv:** Burgundian cross, date below **Rev:** Crowned arms in branches, mint mark below

Date	Mintage	VG	F	VF	XF	Unc
1750(h)	1,176	10.00	20.00	50.00	130	—
1750(l)	—	—	—	—	—	—
Note: Reported, not confirmed						
1751(h)	Inc. above	10.00	20.00	50.00	130	—
1751(l)	421,000	10.00	20.00	60.00	150	—
1752(h)	Inc. above	—	—	—	—	—
Note: Reported, not confirmed						
1752(l)	Inc. above	10.00	20.00	60.00	150	—
1753(h)	324,000	10.00	20.00	50.00	130	—
1754(h)	47,000	10.00	20.00	50.00	130	—

KM# 4 ESCALIN (Schelling)

Silver **Ruler:** Maria Theresa with Franz I

Date	Mintage	VG	F	VF	XF	Unc
1749(h)	5,390	6.00	12.00	25.00	60.00	—
1750(h) R	Inc. above	6.00	12.00	25.00	60.00	—
1750(l)	2,016	6.00	12.00	25.00	60.00	—

KM# 15 ESCALIN (Schelling)

Silver **Ruler:** Maria Theresa with Franz I **Obv:** Lion's shield divided **Rev:** Crowned arms within cartouche **Note:** Similar to 2 Escalins, KM#16.

Date	Mintage	VG	F	VF	XF	Unc
1751(h)	Inc. above	6.00	12.00	25.00	60.00	—
1751(l)	Inc. above	6.00	12.00	25.00	60.00	—
1752(h) R	Inc. above	6.00	12.00	25.00	60.00	—
1752(l)	Inc. above	6.00	12.00	25.00	60.00	—
1753(h) R	1,680	6.00	12.00	25.00	60.00	—
1753(l)	426,000	6.00	12.00	25.00	60.00	—
1754(h) R	223,000	6.00	12.00	25.00	60.00	—
1763(b)	781,000	6.00	12.00	25.00	60.00	—
1764(b)	582,000	6.00	12.00	25.00	60.00	—
1765(b)	320,000	6.00	12.00	25.00	60.00	—
1766(b)	151,000	6.00	12.00	25.00	60.00	—
1767(b)	933,000	6.00	12.00	25.00	60.00	—
1768(b)	16,000	6.00	12.00	25.00	60.00	—

KM# 16 2 ESCALINS (2 Schellings)

Silver **Ruler:** Maria Theresa with Franz I **Obv:** Rampant lion left holding sword in right paw and shield in left paw **Rev:** Crowned arms within cartouche

Date	Mintage	VG	F	VF	XF	Unc
1751(h)	266,000	12.00	18.00	40.00	100	—
1751(l)	155,000	12.00	25.00	65.00	130	—
1752(h)	Inc. above	12.00	18.00	40.00	100	—
1752(l)	Inc. above	12.00	25.00	65.00	130	—
1753(h)	894,000	12.00	18.00	40.00	100	—
1753(l)	19,000	12.00	25.00	65.00	130	—

KM# 5 1/8 DUCATON

Silver **Ruler:** Maria Theresa with Franz I

Date	Mintage	VG	F	VF	XF	Unc
1749(h) R	1,638,000	12.00	25.00	50.00	120	—
1750(h) R	Inc. above	12.00	25.00	50.00	120	—
1751(h) R	Inc. above	12.00	25.00	50.00	120	—
1751(l) R	100,000	12.00	25.00	50.00	120	—
1752(h) R	Inc. above	12.00	25.00	50.00	120	—
1752(l) R	Inc. above	12.00	25.00	50.00	120	—
1753(h) R	210,000	12.00	25.00	50.00	120	—
1753(l) R	140,000	12.00	25.00	50.00	120	—

KM# 6 1/4 DUCATON

Silver **Ruler:** Maria Theresa with Franz I **Obv:** Bust left with décolletage **Obv. Legend:** MAR • TH • D • G • R • IMP • G • HUN • BOH • R • **Rev:** Crowned ornate arms **Rev. Legend:** ARCH • AUS • DUX BURG • BRAB • C • F • **Note:** Similar to 1/8 Ducaton, KM#5.

Date	Mintage	VG	F	VF	XF	Unc
1749(h) R	1,136,000	20.00	40.00	80.00	120	—
1750(h) R	Inc. above	20.00	40.00	80.00	120	—
1751(h) R	Inc. above	20.00	40.00	80.00	120	—
1751(l) R	210,000	25.00	50.00	100	150	—
1752(h) R	Inc. above	20.00	40.00	80.00	120	—
1752(l) R	Inc. above	25.00	50.00	100	150	—
1753(h) R	422,000	20.00	40.00	80.00	120	—
1753(l) R	18,000	25.00	50.00	100	150	—
1754(h) R	154,000	20.00	40.00	80.00	120	—

KM# 7 1/2 DUCATON

Silver **Ruler:** Maria Theresa with Franz I **Obv:** Bust left with décolletage **Obv. Legend:** MAR: TH: D: G: R: IMP: G: HUN: BOH: R:

Date	Mintage	VG	F	VF	XF	Unc
1749(h) R	450,000	10.00	40.00	80.00	150	—
1750(h) R	Inc. above	10.00	40.00	80.00	150	—
1750(l) R	—	12.00	50.00	100	200	—
1751(h) R	Inc. above	10.00	40.00	80.00	150	—
1751(l) R	34,000	12.00	50.00	100	200	—
1752(h) R	Inc. above	10.00	40.00	80.00	150	—
1752(l) R	Inc. above	12.00	50.00	100	200	—
1753(h) R	78,000	10.00	40.00	80.00	150	—
1753(l) R	19,000	12.00	50.00	100	200	—
1754(h) R	278,000	10.00	40.00	80.00	150	—
1754(l) R	111,000	12.00	50.00	100	200	—

KM# 8 DUCATON

Silver **Ruler:** Maria Theresa with Franz I **Obv:** Bust left with décolletage **Obv. Legend:** MAR • TH • D • G • R • IMP • G • HUN • BOH • R • **Rev:** Crowned ornate arms **Rev. Legend:** ARCH • AUS • DUX BURG • ... **Note:** Dav. #1280

Date	Mintage	VG	F	VF	XF	Unc
1749(h) R	285,000	60.00	120	200	400	—
1750(h) R	Inc. above	60.00	120	200	400	—
1750(l) R	—	70.00	140	250	500	—
1751(h) R	Inc. above	60.00	120	200	400	—
1751(l) R	—	70.00	140	250	500	—
1752(h) R	Inc. above	60.00	120	200	400	—
1753(h) R	21,000	60.00	120	200	400	—
1754(h) R	299,000	60.00	120	200	400	—
1754(l) R	41,000	70.00	140	250	500	—

KM# 8.2 DUCATON

Silver **Ruler:** Maria Theresa with Franz I **Note:** Dav. #1281

Date	Mintage	VG	F	VF	XF	Unc
1750	—	—	—	—	—	—
1754	—	—	—	—	—	—

KM# 38 1/4 KRONENTHALER

7.3600 g., 0.8730 Silver .2066 oz. ASW **Ruler:** Joseph II **Obv:** Head right **Obv. Legend:** IOSEPH • II • D • G • R • I • S • A • GER • .... **Rev:** Floriated cross with 3 crowns in upper angles **Rev. Legend:** ARCH • AVST • DVX • BVRG • ....

Date	Mintage	VG	F	VF	XF	Unc
1788A	—	9.00	14.00	30.00	65.00	—
1788B	—	10.00	18.00	35.00	75.00	—
1788H Rare	—	—	—	—	—	—
1789A	—	9.00	14.00	30.00	65.00	—
1789B	—	9.00	14.00	30.00	65.00	—
1790A	—	9.00	14.00	30.00	60.00	—
1790B	—	9.00	14.00	30.00	60.00	—

KM# 40 1/4 KRONENTHALER

7.3600 g., 0.8730 Silver .2066 oz. ASW **Ruler:** Leopold II **Obv:** Head right **Obv. Legend:** LEOP • II • D • G • R • I • S • A • GER • .... **Rev:** Floriated cross with 3 crowns in upper angles **Rev. Legend:** ARCH • AVST • DVX • BVRG • LOTH • BRAB • ...

Date	Mintage	VG	F	VF	XF	Unc
1790A	—	12.00	22.00	50.00	100	—
1791A	—	12.00	22.00	50.00	100	—
1791B	—	12.00	22.00	50.00	100	—
1791H	—	12.00	22.00	50.00	100	—
1792A	—	12.00	22.00	60.00	120	—

Date	Mintage	VG	F	VF	XF	Unc
1792B	—	12.00	22.00	50.00	100	—
1792H	—	12.00	22.00	60.00	120	—

KM# 60 1/4 KRONENTHALER

7.3600 g., 0.8730 Silver .2066 oz. ASW **Ruler:** Franz II **Obv:** Laureate head right **Obv. Legend:** FRANC • II • D • G • R • I • S • A • GER • HIE • HVN • BOH • REX • **Rev:** Floriated cross with 3 crowns in upper angles **Rev. Legend:** ARCH • AVST • DVX • BVRG • LOTH • BRAB • COM • FLAN • **Note:** Varieties exist.

Date	Mintage	VG	F	VF	XF	Unc
1792A	—	7.00	10.00	20.00	40.00	—
1792B	—	7.00	10.00	20.00	50.00	—
1793A	—	6.00	10.00	20.00	40.00	—
1793B	—	6.00	8.00	15.00	30.00	—
1794A	—	6.00	8.00	15.00	30.00	—
1794B	—	7.00	15.00	25.00	70.00	—
1795A	—	6.00	8.00	15.00	30.00	—
1795B	—	6.00	8.00	15.00	30.00	—
1795C	—	7.00	10.00	18.00	35.00	—
1795G	—	7.00	20.00	65.00	100	—
1796A	—	7.00	10.00	20.00	40.00	—
1796B	—	6.00	10.00	20.00	50.00	—
1796C	—	7.00	15.00	25.00	70.00	—
1797A	—	8.00	30.00	75.00	125	—
1797B	—	6.00	10.00	15.00	30.00	—
1797C	—	6.00	12.00	18.00	35.00	—
1797E	—	7.00	15.00	20.00	50.00	—
1797G	—	8.00	15.00	20.00	55.00	—

KM# 19 1/2 KRONENTHALER

Silver **Ruler:** Maria Theresa with Franz I **Obv:** Floriated cross with crowns at angles **Obv. Legend:** MAR • THERESIA • D • G • R • IMP • GERM • HUNG • ... **Rev:** Crowned imperial double eagle with crowned shield on breast **Rev. Legend:** ARCH • AUST • DUX • BURG • BRAB • ....

Date	Mintage	VG	F	VF	XF	Unc
1755(h)	190,000	15.00	30.00	50.00	90.00	—
1756(h)	427,000	15.00	30.00	50.00	90.00	—
1757(h)	403,000	15.00	30.00	50.00	90.00	—
1758(b)	456,000	15.00	30.00	50.00	90.00	—
1759(b)	253,000	15.00	30.00	50.00	90.00	—
1760(b)	175,000	15.00	30.00	50.00	90.00	—
1761(b)	171,000	15.00	30.00	50.00	90.00	—
1762(b)	165,000	15.00	30.00	50.00	90.00	—
1763(b)	863,000	15.00	30.00	50.00	90.00	—
1764(b)	495,000	15.00	30.00	50.00	90.00	—
1765(b)	801,000	15.00	30.00	50.00	90.00	—
1766(b)	860,000	15.00	30.00	50.00	90.00	—
1767(b)	780,000	15.00	30.00	50.00	90.00	—
1768(b)	663,000	15.00	30.00	50.00	90.00	—
1769(b)	415,000	15.00	30.00	50.00	90.00	—
1770(b)	166,000	15.00	30.00	50.00	90.00	—
1771(b)	267,000	15.00	30.00	50.00	90.00	—
1772(b)	107,000	15.00	30.00	50.00	90.00	—
1773(b)	204,000	15.00	30.00	50.00	90.00	—
1774(b)	237,000	15.00	30.00	50.00	90.00	—
1775(b)	273,000	15.00	30.00	50.00	90.00	—
1776(b)	164,000	15.00	30.00	50.00	90.00	—
1777(b)	62,000	15.00	30.00	50.00	90.00	—
1779(b)	93,000	15.00	30.00	50.00	90.00	—

KM# 20 1/2 KRONENTHALER

Silver **Ruler:** Maria Theresa with Franz I **Obv:** Crowned double-headed eagle with shield of arms on breast in Order collar **Rev:** Floriated St. Andrew's cross with 3 crowns in upper angles, Golden Fleece in 4th

Date	Mintage	VG	F	VF	XF	Unc
1755(a)	Inc. above	20.00	40.00	65.00	125	—
1756(a)	Inc. above	20.00	40.00	65.00	125	—
1757(a)	Inc. above	20.00	40.00	65.00	125	—
1758(a)	Inc. above	20.00	40.00	65.00	125	—
1758(b)	Inc. above	20.00	40.00	65.00	125	—
1759(b)	Inc. above	20.00	40.00	65.00	125	—
1760(b)	Inc. above	20.00	40.00	65.00	125	—
1761(b)	Inc. above	20.00	40.00	65.00	125	—
1762(b)	Inc. above	20.00	40.00	65.00	125	—
1763(b)	Inc. above	20.00	40.00	65.00	125	—
1765(b)	Inc. above	20.00	40.00	65.00	125	—

KM# 34 1/2 KRONENTHALER

14.7200 g., 0.8730 Silver .4132 oz. ASW **Ruler:** Joseph II **Obv:** Head right **Obv. Legend:** IOSEPH • II • D • G • R • I • S • A • GER • HIE • HVN • BOH • REX • **Rev:** Floriated cross with 3 crowns in upper angles **Rev. Legend:** ARCH • AVST • DVX • BVRG • LOTH • BRAB • ...

Date	Mintage	VG	F	VF	XF	Unc
1786(b)	61,000	50.00	125	275	375	—
1788(b)	14,000	60.00	150	300	425	—
1788A	—	12.00	25.00	45.00	80.00	—
1788B	—	15.00	30.00	55.00	100	—
1789(b)	24,000	50.00	125	275	375	—
1789B	—	12.00	25.00	45.00	80.00	—
1790A	—	12.00	25.00	45.00	80.00	—

KM# 41 1/2 KRONENTHALER

14.7200 g., 0.8730 Silver .4132 oz. ASW **Ruler:** Leopold II **Obv:** Head right **Obv. Legend:** LEOPOLD • II • D • G • R • I • S • A • GER • HIE • HVN • BOH • REX • **Rev:** Floriated cross with 3 crowns in upper angles **Rev. Legend:** ARCH • AVST • DVX • BVRG • LOTH • BRAB • ...

Date	Mintage	VG	F	VF	XF	Unc
1790A	—	18.00	35.00	60.00	100	—
1791H	—	18.00	32.00	55.00	90.00	—
1792H	—	18.00	35.00	60.00	100	—

KM# 61.1 1/2 KRONENTHALER

14.7200 g., 0.8730 Silver .4132 oz. ASW **Ruler:** Franz II **Obv:** Laureate head right **Obv. Legend:** FRANC • II • D • G • R • I • S • A • GER • HIE • HVN • BOH • REX • **Rev:** Similar to Kronenthaler, KM#62.1; date at upper left **Edge Lettering:** LEGE ET FIDE

Date	Mintage	VG	F	VF	XF	Unc
1792A	—	17.50	40.00	75.00	145	—
1792H	—	20.00	50.00	95.00	160	—
1793A	—	12.50	40.00	80.00	150	—
1794A	—	12.50	20.00	40.00	75.00	—
1795A	—	12.50	20.00	40.00	75.00	—
1795C	—	20.00	32.50	55.00	95.00	—
1795G	—	35.00	75.00	150	250	—
1796A	—	12.50	20.00	35.00	65.00	—
1796C	—	25.00	47.50	90.00	155	—
1796F	—	25.00	40.00	75.00	145	—
1797A	—	9.00	17.50	32.50	60.00	—
1797C	—	7.50	12.50	20.00	50.00	—
1797E	—	25.00	35.00	70.00	135	—

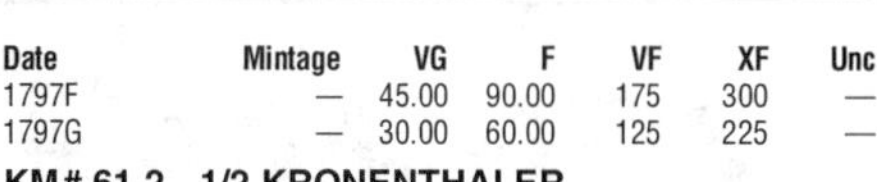

Date	Mintage	VG	F	VF	XF	Unc
1797F	—	45.00	90.00	175	300	—
1797G	—	30.00	60.00	125	225	—

KM# 61.2 1/2 KRONENTHALER

14.7200 g., 0.8730 Silver .4132 oz. ASW **Ruler:** Franz II **Edge Lettering:** FIDE ET LEGE

Date	Mintage	VG	F	VF	XF	Unc
1793B	—	10.00	15.00	30.00	80.00	—
1794B	—	10.00	30.00	50.00	150	—
1795B	—	20.00	40.00	60.00	250	—
1796B	—	8.00	10.00	20.00	50.00	—
1797B	—	8.00	10.00	20.00	50.00	—

KM# 21 KRONENTHALER

Silver **Ruler:** Maria Theresa with Franz I **Obv:** 4 crowns in the angles of a floriated St. Andrew's cross **Obv. Legend:** MAR • THERESIA • D: G • R • IMP • GERM • HUNG • BOH • REG: **Rev:** Crowned imperial eagle with shield on breast **Rev. Legend:** ARCH • AUST • DUX • BURG - BRAB • ... **Note:** Dav. #1282.

Date	Mintage	VG	F	VF	XF	Unc
1755(h)	191,000	25.00	40.00	60.00	125	—
1756(h)	427,000	25.00	40.00	60.00	125	—
1757(h)	403,000	25.00	40.00	60.00	125	—
1758(b)	456,000	25.00	40.00	60.00	125	—
1759(b)	253,000	25.00	40.00	60.00	125	—
1760(b)	175,000	25.00	40.00	60.00	125	—
1761(b)	121,000	25.00	40.00	60.00	125	—
1762(b)	165,000	25.00	40.00	60.00	125	—
1763(b)	863,000	25.00	40.00	60.00	125	—
1764(b)	495,000	25.00	40.00	60.00	125	—
1765(b)	801,000	25.00	40.00	60.00	125	—
1766(b)	860,000	25.00	40.00	60.00	125	—
1767(b)	780,000	25.00	40.00	60.00	125	—
1768(b)	663,000	25.00	40.00	60.00	125	—
1769(b)	415,000	25.00	40.00	60.00	125	—
1770(b)	166,000	25.00	40.00	60.00	125	—
1771(b)	267,000	25.00	40.00	60.00	125	—
1772(b)	107,000	25.00	40.00	60.00	125	—
1773(b)	204,000	25.00	40.00	60.00	125	—
1774(b)	237,000	25.00	40.00	60.00	125	—
1775(b)	273,000	25.00	40.00	60.00	125	—
1776(b)	164,000	25.00	40.00	60.00	125	—
1777(b)	62,000	25.00	40.00	60.00	125	—
1779(b)	—	25.00	40.00	60.00	125	—

KM# 22 KRONENTHALER

Silver **Ruler:** Maria Theresa with Franz I **Obv:** Crowned double-headed eagle with shield of arms on breast in Order collar **Rev:** Floriated St. Andrew's cross with 3 crowns in upper angles, Golden Fleece in 4th **Note:** Dav. #1283.

Date	Mintage	VG	F	VF	XF	Unc
1755(a)	Inc. above	30.00	45.00	70.00	135	—
1756(a)	Inc. above	30.00	45.00	70.00	135	—

Date	Mintage	VG	F	VF	XF	Unc
1757(a)	Inc. above	30.00	45.00	70.00	135	—
1758(a)	Inc. above	30.00	45.00	70.00	135	—
1758(b)	Inc. above	30.00	45.00	70.00	135	—
1759(b)	Inc. above	30.00	45.00	70.00	135	—
1760(b)	Inc. above	30.00	45.00	70.00	135	—
1761(b)	Inc. above	30.00	45.00	70.00	135	—
1762(b)	Inc. above	30.00	45.00	70.00	135	—
1763(b)	Inc. above	30.00	45.00	70.00	135	—
1764(b)	Inc. above	30.00	45.00	70.00	135	—
1765(b)	Inc. above	30.00	45.00	70.00	135	—

KM# 32 KRONENTHALER

29.4400 g., 0.8730 Silver .8264 oz. ASW **Ruler:** Joseph II **Obv:** Bust right **Obv. Legend:** IOSEPH • II • D • G • R • IMP • .... **Rev:** Floriated cross with 3 crowns in upper angles **Rev. Legend:** ARCH • AUST • DUX • BURG • LOTH • BRAB • ... **Note:** Dav. #1284. Varieties exist for 1784(b) dated coins.

Date	Mintage	VG	F	VF	XF	Unc
1781(b)	44,000	25.00	50.00	80.00	150	—
1782(b)	30,000	27.50	55.00	140	200	—
1783A	—	18.00	25.00	45.00	110	—
1783(b)	172,000	20.00	40.00	75.00	145	—
1784A	—	18.00	25.00	45.00	110	—
1784(b)	928,000	18.00	25.00	45.00	110	—
1785(b)	1,351	18.00	25.00	45.00	110	—
1786(b)	1,386	18.00	25.00	45.00	110	—
1787(b)	256,000	20.00	40.00	70.00	140	—
1788A	—	18.00	25.00	45.00	110	—
1788B	1,197,000	18.00	25.00	45.00	110	—
1788(b)	87,000	27.50	55.00	110	200	—
1789A	—	18.00	25.00	45.00	110	—
1789(b)	356,000	20.00	40.00	70.00	140	—
1790A	—	18.00	25.00	45.00	110	—

KM# 42 KRONENTHALER

29.4400 g., 0.8730 Silver .8264 oz. ASW **Ruler:** Leopold II **Obv:** Head right **Rev:** Floriated cross with 3 crowns in upper angles **Note:** Similar to KM#32.

Date	Mintage	VG	F	VF	XF	Unc
1790A	—	35.00	65.00	125	220	—
1791H	—	35.00	60.00	95.00	155	—
1792H	—	35.00	60.00	95.00	155	—

KM# 62.1 KRONENTHALER

29.4400 g., 0.8730 Silver .8264 oz. ASW **Ruler:** Franz II **Rev:** Date at upper left **Note:** Dav. #1180. Varieties exist for 1796F dated coins.

Date	Mintage	VG	F	VF	XF	Unc
1792A	—	20.00	35.00	90.00	145	—
1793A	—	18.00	25.00	50.00	110	—
1793H	—	20.00	37.50	90.00	145	—
1794A	—	25.00	35.00	55.00	110	—
1794H	—	18.00	27.50	55.00	110	—
1795A	—	18.00	27.50	55.00	110	—
1795C	—	18.00	20.00	35.00	75.00	—
1795F	—	40.00	85.00	160	250	—
1795H	—	18.00	20.00	35.00	75.00	—
1796A	—	18.00	20.00	35.00	75.00	—
1796C	—	18.00	20.00	35.00	75.00	—
1796F	—	20.00	55.00	95.00	165	—
1796H	—	18.00	20.00	45.00	80.00	—
1797A	—	20.00	60.00	110	200	—
1797C	—	20.00	30.00	55.00	90.00	—
1797E	—	20.00	50.00	85.00	160	—
1797F	—	20.00	50.00	85.00	140	—
1797G	—	20.00	37.50	75.00	125	—
1797H	—	18.00	20.00	35.00	75.00	—
1798A Rare	—	—	—	—	—	—

KM# 62.2 KRONENTHALER

29.4400 g., 0.8730 Silver .8264 oz. ASW **Ruler:** Franz II **Edge Lettering:** FIDE ET LEGE

Date	Mintage	VG	F	VF	XF	Unc
1793B	—	20.00	35.00	70.00	120	—
1794B	—	18.00	25.00	45.00	85.00	—
1795B	—	18.00	40.00	75.00	135	—
1796B	—	18.00	20.00	35.00	70.00	—
1797B	—	18.00	20.00	35.00	70.00	—

KM# 62.3 KRONENTHALER

29.4400 g., 0.8730 Silver .8264 oz. ASW **Ruler:** Franz II **Obv:** Laureate head right **Obv. Legend:** FRANC • II • D • G • R • IMP • S • A • GER • HIER • HUNG • BOH • REX • **Rev:** Date divided at top **Rev. Legend:** ARCH • AUST • DUX • BURG - LOTH • BRAB • COM • FLAN • **Note:** Dav. #1286.

Date	Mintage	VG	F	VF	XF	Unc
1794(b)	281,000	100	160	300	425	—

TRADE COINAGE

KM# 9 1/2 SOUVERAIN D'OR

5.5300 g., 0.9190 Gold .1634 oz. AGW, 25 mm. **Ruler:** Maria Theresa with Franz I **Obv:** Bust with décolletage right **Obv. Legend:** MAR • TH • D • G • R • IMP • HUNG • BOH • R • **Rev:** Crowned arms **Rev. Legend:** ARCH • AUST • DUX • BURG • BRAB • C • FL •

Date	Mintage	VG	F	VF	XF	Unc
1749(h) R	1,676	200	400	600	950	—

KM# 14 1/2 SOUVERAIN D'OR

5.5300 g., 0.9190 Gold .1634 oz. AGW, 22 mm. **Ruler:** Maria Theresa with Franz I **Obv:** Bust with décolletage right **Obv. Legend:** MAR • TH • D • G • R • IMP • G • HUN • BOH • R • **Rev:** Crowned arms **Rev. Legend:** ARCH • AUS • DUX • BURG • BRAB • C • FL •

Date	Mintage	VG	F	VF	XF	Unc
1750(h) R	—	150	300	425	650	—
Note: Mintage included in KM#9						
1750(l) R	424,000	150	300	425	650	—
1751(h) R	—	150	300	425	650	—
Note: Mintage included in KM#9						
1751(l) R	—	150	300	425	650	—
1752(h) R	—	150	300	425	650	—
Note: Mintage included in KM#9						

KM# 17 1/2 SOUVERAIN D'OR

5.5300 g., 0.9190 Gold .1634 oz. AGW **Ruler:** Maria Theresa with Franz I **Obv:** Bust with décolletage right **Obv. Legend:** MAR • TH • D: G • R • IMP • G • HUN • BOH • R • **Rev:** Crowned arms

Date	Mintage	VG	F	VF	XF	Unc
1751(l) R	—	150	300	425	650	—
1752(h) R	—	150	300	425	650	—
1752(l) R	—	150	300	425	650	—
1753(h) R	317,000	150	300	425	650	—
1753(l) R	22,000	150	300	425	650	—
1754(h) R	174,000	150	300	425	650	—
1754(l) R	24,000	150	300	425	650	—
1755(h) R	227,000	150	300	425	650	—
1756(h) R	197,000	150	300	425	650	—
1757(h) R	99,000	150	300	425	650	—
1764(b) R	38,000	150	300	425	650	—
1765(b) R	24,000	150	300	425	650	—

KM# 26 1/2 SOUVERAIN D'OR

5.5300 g., 0.9190 Gold .1634 oz. AGW **Ruler:** Maria Theresa Widow **Obv:** Veiled mature bust right **Obv. Legend:** MAR • TH • D: G • R • IMP • G • HUNG • BOH • R • **Rev:** Crowned ornate arms **Rev. Legend:** ARCH • AUST • DUX • BURG • BRAB • C • FL •

Date	Mintage	VG	F	VF	XF	Unc
1770(b) R	13,000	225	350	500	750	—
1773(b) R	18,000	225	350	500	750	—
1773(w) CK	—	225	350	500	750	—
1774(b)	37,000	225	350	500	750	—
1775(b)	28,000	225	350	500	750	—
1776/5(b)	—	225	350	500	750	—
1776(b)	24,000	225	350	500	750	—
1777(b)	17,000	225	350	500	750	—

KM# 35 1/2 SOUVERAIN D'OR

5.5300 g., 0.9190 Gold .1634 oz. AGW **Ruler:** Joseph II **Obv:** Laureate head right **Obv. Legend:** IOSEPH • II • D • G • R • IMP • S • A • ... **Rev:** Crowned arms within Order chain **Rev. Legend:** ARCH • AVST • DVX • BVRG • LOTH • BRAB • ...

Date	Mintage	VG	F	VF	XF	Unc
1786	2,186	1,000	2,000	5,000	8,500	—
1786A	—	125	200	300	500	—
1786F	—	225	300	400	1,000	—
1787A	—	175	250	350	600	—
1787F	—	225	300	400	1,000	—
1788 Rare	986	—	—	—	—	—
1788A	—	175	250	350	600	—
1788F	4,847	300	500	700	1,200	—
1789A	—	175	250	350	600	—
1789F	1,382	375	600	1,000	1,800	—
1790A	—	225	300	400	1,000	—
1790F	1,350	375	600	1,000	1,800	—

KM# 55 1/2 SOUVERAIN D'OR

5.5300 g., 0.9190 Gold .1634 oz. AGW **Ruler:** Leopold II **Obv:** Laureate head right **Rev:** Crowned arms within Order chain **Note:** Similar to KM#35.

Date	Mintage	VG	F	VF	XF	Unc
1791A	—	225	300	400	1,000	—
1792A	—	225	300	400	1,000	—
1792B	21,000	225	300	400	1,000	—
1792E	—	225	300	400	1,000	—

KM# 63 1/2 SOUVERAIN D'OR

5.5300 g., 0.9190 Gold .1634 oz. AGW **Ruler:** Franz II **Obv:** Head right **Obv. Legend:** FRANC • II • D • G • R • IMP • S • A • GE • HIE • HV • BO • REX • **Rev:** Crowned arms within Order chain **Rev. Legend:** ARCH • AVST • DVX • BVRG • LOTH • BRAB • COM • FLAN • **Note:** Coins dated 1793V were struck in 1823 at Gunzberg. For similar coins with M mint mark, refer to Italian States - Milan listings.

Date	Mintage	VG	F	VF	XF	Unc
1792A	—	150	225	350	525	—
1793A	—	125	200	300	500	—
1793B	11,000	125	200	300	500	—
1793(b) Rare	—	—	—	—	—	—
1793H	60,000	175	250	400	600	—
1793V	—	300	700	1,700	3,500	—
1794A	—	175	250	400	600	—
1794B	56,000	125	200	300	500	—
1795A	—	125	200	300	500	—
1795B	51,000	125	200	300	500	—
1796A	—	125	200	300	500	—
1796B	29,000	125	200	300	500	—
1797A	—	125	200	300	500	—
1798A	—	150	225	350	525	—

KM# 65 1/2 SOUVERAIN D'OR

5.5300 g., 0.9190 Gold .1634 oz. AGW **Ruler:** Franz II **Obv:** Head right **Obv. Legend:** FRANC • II • D • G • R • IMP • S • A • GER • HIE • HV • BO • REX • **Rev:** Crowned arms within Order chain **Rev. Legend:** ARCH • AVST • DVX • BVRG • LOTH • BRAB • COM • FLAN •

Date	Mintage	VG	F	VF	XF	Unc
1793F	1,892	175	250	450	800	—
1794F	1,636	250	400	600	850	—
1795F	1,503	300	500	800	1,000	—
1796F	3,355	175	250	425	775	—

KM# 10 SOUVERAIN D'OR

11.0600 g., 0.9190 Gold .3268 oz. AGW **Ruler:** Maria Theresa with Franz I **Obv:** Crowned bust right **Rev:** Crowned arms with mint mark and date below

Date	Mintage	VG	F	VF	XF	Unc
1749(h) R	610,000	500	850	1,250	2,000	—
1749(l) R	—	600	1,100	1,500	2,250	—

KM# 11 SOUVERAIN D'OR

11.0600 g., 0.9190 Gold .3268 oz. AGW, 27 mm. **Ruler:** Maria Theresa with Franz I **Obv:** Crowned bust right **Rev:** Crowned arms with mm and date below **Note:** Similar to KM#10.

Date	Mintage	VG	F	VF	XF	Unc
1749(h) R	—	300	500	800	1,250	—
Note: Mintage included in KM#10						
1750(h) R	—	300	500	800	1,250	—
Note: Mintage included in KM#10						
1750(l) R	—	350	600	1,000	1,600	—
1751(h) R	—	300	500	800	1,250	—
Note: Mintage included in KM#10						
1751(l) R	16,000	350	600	1,000	1,600	—

KM# 23 SOUVERAIN D'OR

11.0600 g., 0.9190 Gold .3268 oz. AGW **Ruler:** Maria Theresa with Franz I **Obv:** Crowned narrow bust right **Obv. Legend:** MAR • TH • D • G • R • IMP • S • HUNG • BOH • R •

Date	Mintage	VG	F	VF	XF	Unc
1756 W-Wi	—	300	550	1,000	1,600	—
1757 W-Wi	—	300	550	1,000	1,600	—
1758 W-Wi	—	300	550	1,000	1,600	—
1759 W-Wi	—	300	550	1,000	1,600	—
1760 W-Wi	—	300	550	1,000	1,600	—
1761 W-Wi	—	300	550	1,000	1,600	—

KM# 24 SOUVERAIN D'OR

11.0600 g., 0.9190 Gold .3268 oz. AGW **Ruler:** Maria Theresa with Franz I **Obv:** Mature bust right **Obv. Legend:** MAR • TH • D: G • R • IMP • G • HUNG • BOH • R • **Rev:** Crowned ornate arms **Rev. Legend:** ARCH • AUST • DUX • BURG • BRAB • C • FL •

Date	Mintage	VG	F	VF	XF	Unc
1757(h) R	38,000	300	500	800	1,250	—
1758(b) R	303,000	250	400	600	1,000	—
1759(b) R	190,000	250	400	600	1,000	—
1760(b) R	163,000	250	400	600	1,000	—
1761(b) R	300,000	250	400	600	1,000	—
1762(b) R	269,000	250	400	600	1,000	—
1763(b) R	119,000	250	400	600	1,000	—
1766(b) R	135,000	250	400	600	1,000	—

KM# 25 SOUVERAIN D'OR

11.0600 g., 0.9190 Gold .3268 oz. AGW **Ruler:** Maria Theresa Widow **Obv:** Veiled mature bust right **Obv. Legend:** MAR • TH • D: G • R • IMP • G • HUNG • BOH • R • **Rev:** Crowned ornate arms **Rev. Legend:** ARCH • AUST • DUX • BURG • BRAB • C • FL •

Date	Mintage	VG	F	VF	XF	Unc
1767(b) R	22,000	300	600	1,000	1,600	—
1768(b) R	13,000	300	600	1,000	1,600	—
1769(b)	9,000	300	600	1,000	1,600	—
1771(b)	10,000	300	600	1,000	1,600	—
1772(b)	7,000	300	600	1,000	1,600	—
1773(b)	3,000	—	—	—	—	—
1778(b)	83,000	300	550	800	1,250	—
1779(b)	77,000	300	550	800	1,250	—
1780(b)	3,000	300	750	1,200	1,850	—

KM# 27 SOUVERAIN D'OR

11.0600 g., 0.9190 Gold .3268 oz. AGW **Ruler:** Maria Theresa Widow **Obv:** Bust right **Obv. Legend:** MAR • TH • D • G • R • IMP • HUNG • BOH • R • **Rev:** Crowned ornate arms **Rev. Legend:** ARCH • AUS • DUX • BURG • BRAB • C • FL •

Date	Mintage	VG	F	VF	XF	Unc
1772(w) IC-SK	—	300	550	1,000	1,600	—
1773(w) IC-SK	—	300	550	1,000	1,600	—
1774(w) IC-FA	—	300	550	1,000	1,600	—
1780(w) IC-FA	—	300	550	1,000	1,600	—

KM# 33 SOUVERAIN D'OR

11.0600 g., 0.9190 Gold .3268 oz. AGW **Ruler:** Joseph II **Obv:** Laureate head right **Obv. Legend:** IOSEPH • II • D • G • R • IMP • S • A • GER • HIER • HUNG • BOH • REX • **Rev:** Crowned arms within Order chain **Rev. Legend:** ARCH • AUST • DUX • BURG • LOTH • BRAB • COM • FLAN •

Date	Mintage	VG	F	VF	XF	Unc
1781(b)	4,338	300	700	1,300	2,000	—
1782(b)	3,012	300	700	1,300	2,000	—
1783(b)	5,309	300	700	1,300	2,000	—
1783A	—	300	500	900	1,200	—
1784(b)	5,944	300	700	1,300	2,000	—
1784A	—	250	400	600	900	—
1785(b)	3,949	300	700	1,300	2,000	—
1785A	—	250	400	600	900	—
1786(b)	16,071	300	700	1,300	2,000	—
1786A	—	250	400	600	800	—
1786F	—	250	400	600	1,800	—
1787(b) Rare	1,053	—	—	—	—	—
1787A	—	250	400	600	900	—
1788(b)	8,632	300	700	1,300	2,000	—
1788A	—	250	400	600	900	—
1789(b)	—	300	700	1,300	2,000	—
1789A	—	400	700	1,000	1,600	—

KM# 43 SOUVERAIN D'OR

11.0600 g., 0.9190 Gold .3268 oz. AGW **Ruler:** Leopold II **Note:** Similar to KM#25.

Date	Mintage	VG	F	VF	XF	Unc
1790A	—	300	500	700	900	—
1791A	—	300	500	700	900	—
1792B	—	300	500	700	900	—
1792E	—	450	700	1,000	1,500	—
1792F	1,250	550	800	1,200	2,000	—

KM# 64 SOUVERAIN D'OR

11.0600 g., 0.9190 Gold .3268 oz. AGW **Ruler:** Franz II **Obv:** Head right **Obv. Legend:** FRANC • II • D • G • R • IMP • S • A • GE • HIE • HV • BO • REX • **Rev:** Crowned arms within Order chain **Rev. Legend:** ARCH • AVST • DVX • BVRG • LOTH • BRAB • COM • FLAN • **Note:** Coins dated 1793V were struck in 1823 at Gunzberg. For similar coins with M mint mark, refer to Italian States - Milan listings.

Date	Mintage	VG	F	VF	XF	Unc
1792A	—	250	450	750	1,500	—
1793A	—	250	450	600	1,000	—
1793(b)	1,763	1,000	2,000	4,000	7,000	—
1793H	60,000	250	450	750	1,250	—
1793V	—	250	500	1,200	2,500	—
1794A	—	250	450	750	1,500	—
1795A	—	650	1,000	1,500	3,000	—
1795B	—	200	350	550	850	—
1796A	—	650	1,000	1,500	3,000	—
1796B	—	200	350	550	850	—

Date	Mintage	VG	F	VF	XF	Unc
1796F	—	300	600	1,300	2,800	—
1797A	—	650	1,000	1,500	3,000	—
1798A	—	900	1,500	2,000	3,500	—

KM# 66 SOUVERAIN D'OR

11.0600 g., 0.9190 Gold .3268 oz. AGW, 27 mm. **Ruler:** Franz II **Obv. Legend:** FRANCISC. II..

Date	Mintage	VG	F	VF	XF	Unc
1796F	2,357	300	500	800	1,500	—

INSURRECTION COINAGE

1790

KM# 44 LIARD (Oord)

Copper **Obv:** 4-Line inscription, date and mint mark below **Rev:** Rampant lion right holding staff

Date	Mintage	VG	F	VF	XF	Unc
1790(b)	359,000	2.50	7.50	12.00	25.00	—

KM# 45 2 LIARDS (2 Oorden)

Copper **Obv:** 4-Line inscription, date and mint mark below **Rev:** Rampant lion right with staff

Date	Mintage	VG	F	VF	XF	Unc
1790(b)	763,000	4.00	10.00	17.50	30.00	—

KM# 46 10 SOLS (10 Stuivers)

Silver **Obv:** Rampant lion right **Obv. Legend:** MON • NOV • ARG • PROV • FOED • BELG • **Rev:** Arrows back of grasped hands at center **Rev. Legend:** IN VNIONE SALVS •

Date	Mintage	VG	F	VF	XF	Unc
1790(b)	53,000	30.00	60.00	150	250	—

KM# 47 10 SOLS (10 Stuivers)

Silver **Obv:** Rampant lion right **Obv. Legend:** DOMINI • EST • REGNVM • **Rev:** Arrows back of grasped hands at center **Rev. Legend:** ET • IPSE • DOMINABITVR • GENTIVM

Date	Mintage	VG	F	VF	XF	Unc
1790(b)	8,162	60.00	150	250	500	—

KM# 48 FLORIN (Gulden)

Silver **Obv:** Rampant lion right **Obv. Legend:** MON • NOV • ARG • PROV • FOED • BELG • **Rev:** Arrows back of grasped hands at center **Rev. Legend:** IN VNIONE SALVS •

Date	Mintage	VG	F	VF	XF	Unc
1790(b)	52,000	50.00	120	175	280	—

KM# 49 FLORIN (Gulden)

Silver **Obv:** Rampant lion right **Obv. Legend:** DOMINI • EST • REGNVM • **Rev:** Arrows back of grasped hands at center **Rev. Legend:** ET • IPSE • DOMINABITVR • GENTIVM

Date	Mintage	VG	F	VF	XF	Unc
1790(b)	15,000	60.00	130	200	350	—

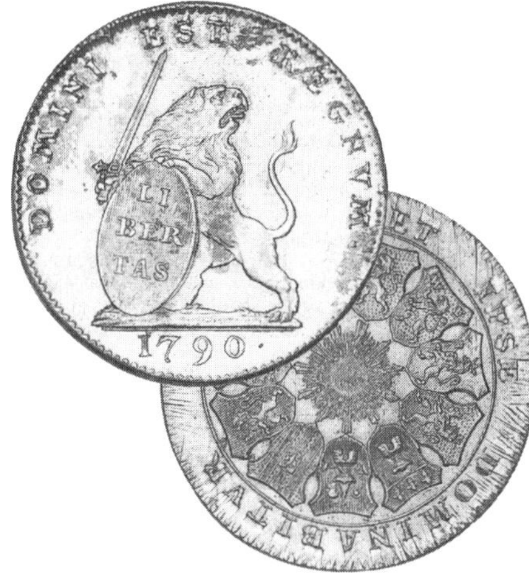

KM# 50 3 FLORINS (3 Guldens)

Silver **Obv:** Rampant lion right holding sword in right paw and shield in left paw **Obv. Legend:** DOMINI EST REGNVM **Rev:** 11 Shields surround central radiant design **Rev. Legend:** ET IPSE DOMINABITVR GENTIVM **Note:** Dav. #1285.

Date	Mintage	VG	F	VF	XF	Unc
1790(b)	44,000	—	250	400	750	—

KM# 51 14 FLORINS (14 Guldens)

0.9860 Gold **Obv:** Rampant lion right holding sword in right paw and shield in left paw **Obv. Legend:** DOMINI EST REGNVM • **Rev:** 11 Shields surround central radiant design **Rev. Legend:** ET IPSE DOMINABITVR GENTIVM

Date	Mintage	VG	F	VF	XF	Unc
1790(b)	3,805	650	1,250	2,750	5,500	—

PATTERNS

Including off metal strikes

KM#	Date	Mintage	Identification	Mkt Val
Pn1	1751(h)	—	5 Souverain D'Or. Gold. 55.5100 g.	—
Pn2	1751(h)	—	5 Souverain D'Or. Gold. 55.4800 g.	—

KM#	Date	Mintage	Identification	Mkt Val
Pn3	ND(1751)	—	Thaler. Silver. 33.3700 g.	1,800
Pn4	1794B	—	Sovereign D'Or. 0.9190 Gold. KM#64.	—
Pn5	1795E	—	1/2 Sovereign D'Or. 0.9190 Gold. KM#63.	—

FAGNOLLE

A small village located in the southern Belgian province of Namur. Prince Charles Joseph the Ligne, as the lord, obtained the right to strike coins in 1770 when his principality was recognized as part of the Holy Roman Empire. The French occupied Fagnolle from 1794-95.

RULER

Charles Joseph of Ligne, 1770-1803

PRINCIPALITY

TRADE COINAGE

KM# 94 DUCAT

3.5000 g., 0.9860 Gold .1109 oz. AGW **Ruler:** Charles Joseph of Ligne **Obv:** Bust left **Rev:** Crowned and mantled arms **Note:** Struck in Durlach, Germany.

Date	Mintage	VG	F	VF	XF	Unc
ND	50	1,000	2,500	4,000	5,500	—

RECKHEIM

A barony in Limburg which was raised to a county in 1624. Was in the hands of the van Lynden family and mediatized in 1803.

RULERS

Francois-Gobert and Ferdinand-Gobert of Aspremont-Lynden, 1665-1703
Ferdinand-Gobert of Aspremont-Lynden, 1703-1708
Joseph-Gobert of Aspremont-Lynden, 1708-1720
Charles-Gobert of Aspremont-Lynden, 1720-1749
Jean-Gobert of Aspremont-Lynden, 1749-1792

COUNTY

STANDARD COINAGE

KM# 110 2 KREUZERS

Billon **Ruler:** Joseph-Gobert **Obv:** Shield of arms **Obv. Legend:** IOS. GOB. COM. IN. ASPERM ET RS **Rev:** Orb **Rev. Legend:** CAROLVS. VI. I.. S. A. 1720

Date	Mintage	VG	F	VF	XF	Unc
1720 Rare	—	—	—	—	—	—

The Republic of Azerbaijan (formerly Azerbaijan S.S.R.) includes the Nakhichevan Autonomous Republic. Situated in the eastern area of Transcaucasia, it is bordered in the west by Armenia, in the north by Georgia and Dagestan, to the east by the Caspian Sea and to the south by Iran. It has an area of 33,430 sq. mi. (86,600 sq. km.) and a population of 7.8 million. Capital: Baku. The area is rich in mineral deposits of aluminum, copper, iron, lead, salt and zinc, with oil as its leading industry. Agriculture and livestock follow in importance.

Ancient home of Scythian tribes and known under the Romans as Albania and to the Arabs as Arran, the country of Azerbaijan was formed at the time of its invasion by Seliuk Turks and grew into a prosperous state under Persian suzerainty. From the 16th century the country was a theatre of fighting and political rivalry between Turkey, Persia and later Russia. Baku was first annexed to Russia by Czar Peter I in 1723 and remained under Russian rule for 12 years. After the Russian retreat the whole of Azerbaijan north of the Aras River became a khanate under Persian control. Czar Alexander I, after an eight-year war with Persia, annexed it in 1813 to the Russian empire.

Until the Russian Revolution of 1905, there was no political life in Azerbaijan. A Mussavat (Equality) party was formed in 1911 by Mohammed Emin, Rasulzade, a former Social Democrat. After the Russian Revolution of March 1917, the party started a campaign for independence. Baku, however, the capital with its mixed population, constituted an alien enclave in the country While a national Azerbaijani government was established at Gandzha (Elizavetpol), a Communist controlled council assumed power at Baku with Stepan Shaumian, an Armenian, at its head. The Gandzha government joined first, on Sept. 20, 1917, a Transcaucasian federal republic, but on May 28, 1918, proclaimed the independence of Azerbaijan. On June 4, 1918, at Batum, a peace treaty was signed with Turkey. Turko-Azerbaijani forces started an offensive against Baku, occupied since Aug. 17, 1918 by 1,400 British troops coming by sea from Anzali, Persia. On Sept. 14 the British evacuated Baku, returning to Anzali, and three days later the Azerbaijan government, headed by Fath Khoysky, established itself at Baku.

After the collapse of the Ottoman Empire, the British returned to Baku, at first ignoring the Azerbaijan government. A general election with universal suffrage for the Azerbaijan constituent assembly took place on Dec. 7, 1918 and out of 120 members there were 84 Mussavat supporters. On Jan. 15, 1920, the Allied powers recognized Azerbaijan de facto, but on April 27 of the same year the Red army invaded the country, and a Soviet republic of Azerbaijan was proclaimed the next day. Later it became a member of the Transcaucasian Federation joining the U.S.S.R. on Dec. 30, 1922, it became a self-constituent republic in 1936.

The Azerbaijan Communist party held its first congress at Baku in Feb. 1920. From 1921 to 1925 its first secretary was a Russian, S.M. Kirov, who directed a mass deportation to Siberia of about 120,000 Azerbaijani "nationalist deviationists," among them the country's first two premiers.

In 1990 it adopted a declaration of republican sovereignty and in Aug. 1991 declared itself formally independent. This action was approved by a vote of referendum in Jan. 1992. It announced its intention of joining the CIS in Dec. 1991, but a parliamentary resolution of Oct. 1992 declined to confirm its involvement. On Sept. 20, 1993, Azerbaijan became a member of the CIS. Communist President Mutaibov was relieved of his office in May 1992. On June 7, in the first democratic election in the country's history, a National Council replaced Mutaibov with Abulfez Elchibey. Surat Huseynov led a military coup against Elchibey and seized power on June 30, 1993. Huseynov became prime minister with former communist Geidar Aliyev, president.

Fighting commenced between Muslim forces of Azerbaijan and Christian forces of Armenia in 1992 and continued through early 1994. Each faction claimed the Nagorno-Karabakh, an Armenian ethnic enclave, in Azerbaijan. A cease-fire was declared in May 1994.

OTTOMAN EMPIRE

DARBAND

Darband (Derbent) is the principal city in Daghistan, now the extreme southeastern portion of Russia. Generally connected to Iran from early Islamic time, it was conquered by the Russians in 1722 but restored to Iran in 1735 under Nadir Shah., After the death of Nadir in 1747, Darband became quasi-independent, adjoined with Qubba, and seems to have begun its local coinage around 1780. Darband was briefly seized by the Russians in 1796 and finally conquered on July 3, 1806 (16 Rabi' II 1221).

The coinage of Darband between 1780 and 1806 never mentions the local ruler, but bears the Arabic phrase, ya'alî.

MINT

دربند

Darband

CITY

ANONYMOUS HAMMERED COINAGE

KM# 1 ABBASI

2.3000 g., Silver **Obv:** Ya Sahib al-Zaman **Rev:** Mint, date and inscription **Rev. Inscription:** Ya' Aziz **Note:** Additional dates are said to exist in the Baku Museum.

Date	Mintage	Good	VG	F	VF	XF
AH1200	—	40.00	70.00	125	—	—
AH1201	—	40.00	70.00	125	—	—
ND	—	25.00	40.00	70.00	—	—

GANJA

Ganja has been an important city since pre-Islamic times, and became an Islamic mint about 705 AD. It was part of the Safavid Empire, though occasionally occupied by the Ottomans for short intervals. After the death of Nadir Shah in 1747, it gained independence under Shah Verdi Khan, and local coinage started about 1755. It remained independent until 1805, when acquired by Russia, though it was briefly under Georgian control 1780-1783 and partially under Iranian control between 1790 and 1802.

RULERS

(Part of Iran until AH1137/1724AD)

OTTOMAN

Ahmed III, AH1137-1143/1724-1730AD

Mahmud I, AH1143-1148/1730-1735AD

(Once again under Iran, AH1148-1168/1735-1755AD)

LOCAL RULERS

Shah Verdi Khan, AH1160-1174/1747-1760 AD (effectively independent from 1168/1755)

Muhammad Shah Khan, AH1174-1195/1760-1780AD

(Georgian occupation, AH1193-1198/1780-1783AD)

Hajji Beg, AH1198-1200/1783-1785AD

Ja'far al-Jawwad, ca. 1200-1220/1785-1805AD (partly under Iranian control 1204-1217, see types KM632, 738 and 724 under Iran).

MINT

گنجه

Ganja

KHANATE

Ahmed III

AH1115-1141 / 1703-1730AD

HAMMERED COINAGE

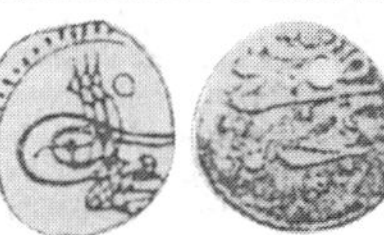

KM# 10 1/4 ABBASI

1.3100 g., Silver **Obv:** Toughra **Rev:** Legend

Date	Mintage	Good	VG	F	VF	XF
AH1115 (1703)	—	—	400	550	750	1,000

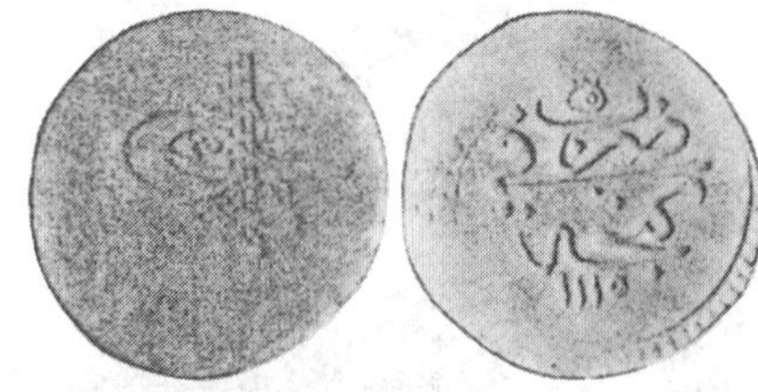

KM# 11 ABBASI

5.3400 g., Silver **Obv:** Toughra **Rev:** duriba Genge

Date	Mintage	Good	VG	F	VF	XF
AH1115 (1703)	—	—	110	150	200	265

Mahmud I

AH1143-1148 / 1730-1735AD

HAMMERED COINAGE

KM# 15 1/2 ABBASI

Silver **Obv:** Toughra **Rev:** duriba Genge **Note:** Weight varies 2.55 - 2.72 grams.

Date	Mintage	Good	VG	F	VF	XF
AH1143 (1730)	—	—	400	550	750	1,000

KM# 16 ABBASI

5.3200 g., Silver **Obv:** Toughra **Rev:** duribe Genge

Date	Mintage	Good	VG	F	VF	XF
AH1143 (1730)	—	—	120	165	225	300

Shah Verdi Khan

AH1160-1174 / 1747-1760AD

HAMMERED COINAGE

KM# 20 1/2 ABBASI

2.3000 g., Silver **Obv:** al-Sultan Nadir **Rev:** Mint and date

Date	Mintage	Good	VG	F	VF	XF
AH1173 (1759)	—	—	60.00	80.00	100	140

KM# 21 ABBASI

4.6000 g., Silver **Obv:** al-Sultan Nadir **Rev:** Mint and date **Note:** Similar to KM#20.

Date	Mintage	Good	VG	F	VF	XF
AH1155 (1754)	—	—	20.00	30.00	45.00	65.00
Note: Coins dated 1155 were actually struck from about 1168-1178; i.e.: between the last Iranian issues in the name of Shahrukh and the 1172 issues of this type.						
AH1172 (1758)	—	—	25.00	35.00	50.00	75.00
AH1173 (1759)	—	—	25.00	35.00	50.00	75.00
AH1174 (1760)	—	—	25.00	35.00	50.00	75.00

Muhammad Hasan Khan

AH1174-1195 / 1760-1780AD

HAMMERED COINAGE

KM# 24 1/4 ABBASI

1.1500 g., Silver **Obv:** al-Sultan Nadir **Rev:** Mint and date **Note:** Similar to KM#20.

Date	Mintage	Good	VG	F	VF	XF
AH1178 (1764)	—	—	50.00	60.00	75.00	100
AH1181 (1767)	—	—	50.00	60.00	75.00	100
AH1187 (1773)	—	—	50.00	60.00	75.00	100

KM# 30 1/4 ABBASI

0.9500 g., Silver **Obv:** Couplet of Karim Khan Zand **Rev:** Mint, date and 'ya-karim'

Date	Mintage	Good	VG	F	VF	XF
AH1186 (1772)	—	—	50.00	75.00	100	150
AH1188 (1774)	—	—	50.00	75.00	100	150

KM# 34 1/2 ABBASI

1.0000 g., Silver **Obv:** Ya Sahib al-Zaman **Rev:** Mint, date and 'ya karim' **Note:** Denomination uncertain.

Date	Mintage	Good	VG	F	VF	XF
AH1189 (1775) Rare	—	—	—	—	—	—

KM# 28 ABBASI

4.6000 g., Silver **Obv:** Shiite formula **Rev:** Mint, date and 'ya karim'

Date	Mintage	Good	VG	F	VF	XF
AH1174 (1760)	—	—	45.00	55.00	80.00	105
AH1176 (1762)	—	—	35.00	45.00	65.00	90.00
AH1179 (1765)	—	—	35.00	45.00	65.00	90.00

KM# 26 ABBASI

4.6000 g., Silver **Obv:** al-Sultan Nadir **Rev:** Mint and date **Note:** Similar to KM#20. Coins dated 1187 and 1188 may be errors for 1178 and 1177 or re-issue for those years, but no hard evidence has been found to confirm this.

Date	Mintage	Good	VG	F	VF	XF
AH1175 (1761)	—	—	25.00	35.00	50.00	70.00
AH1176 (1762)	—	—	25.00	35.00	50.00	70.00
AH1177 (1763)	—	—	25.00	35.00	50.00	70.00
AH1178 (1764)	—	—	25.00	35.00	50.00	70.00
AH1179 (1765)	—	—	30.00	40.00	60.00	85.00
AH1180 (1766)	—	—	30.00	40.00	60.00	85.00
AH1181 (1767)	—	—	30.00	40.00	60.00	85.00
AH1187 (1773)	—	—	25.00	35.00	50.00	70.00

Date	Mintage	Good	VG	F	VF	XF
AH1188 (1774)	—	—	25.00	35.00	50.00	70.00

KM# 32 ABBASI

4.6000 g., Silver **Obv:** Couplet of Karim Khan Zand **Rev:** Mint, date and 'ya karim'

Date	Mintage	Good	VG	F	VF	XF
AH1181 (1767)	—	—	35.00	45.00	65.00	80.00
AH1182 (1768)	—	—	30.00	40.00	55.00	70.00
AH1183 (1769)	—	—	30.00	40.00	55.00	70.00
AH1184 (1770)	—	—	30.00	40.00	55.00	70.00
AH1185 (1771)	—	—	35.00	45.00	65.00	80.00
AH1186 (1772)	—	—	30.00	40.00	55.00	70.00
AH1187 (1773)	—	—	30.00	40.00	55.00	70.00
AH1188 (1774)	—	—	35.00	45.00	65.00	80.00

KM# 36.1 ABBASI

3.0500 g., Silver **Obv:** Ya Sahib al-Zaman **Rev:** Mint, date and 'ya karim'

Date	Mintage	Good	VG	F	VF	XF
AH1189 (1775)	—	—	25.00	35.00	50.00	70.00
AH1190 (1776)	—	—	35.00	45.00	65.00	85.00
AH1191 (1777)	—	—	35.00	45.00	65.00	85.00
AH1192 (1778)	—	—	35.00	45.00	65.00	85.00
AH1193 (1779)	—	—	35.00	45.00	65.00	85.00
AH1195 (1780)	—	—	35.00	45.00	65.00	85.00

KM# 36.2 ABBASI

3.0000 g., Silver **Obv:** Ya Sahib al-Zaman **Rev:** Mint, date and 'ya karim' **Note:** Similar to KM#36.1. Struck during Georgian Occupation, AH1195-1198.

Date	Mintage	Good	VG	F	VF	XF
AH1198 (1783) Rare	—	—	—	—	—	—

KM# 100.8 KAZBEG

Copper **Note:** Unknown type. Normal weight varies: 7-9g.

Date	Mintage	Good	VG	F	VF	XF
AH1216	—	—	—	—	—	—

Note: Struck from before AH1181 until at least AH1216

Hajji Beg
AH1198-1200 / 1783-1785AD
HAMMERED COINAGE

KM# 40 ABBASI

Silver **Obv:** Couplet of Karim Khan Zand **Rev:** Mint, date and 'ya Karim' (same as KM#32)

Date	Mintage	Good	VG	F	VF	XF
AH1198 (1783)	—	—	70.00	90.00	135	—
AH1199 (1784)	—	—	70.00	90.00	135	—

Ja'far al-Jawwad
AH1200-1220 / 1785-1805AD
HAMMERED COINAGE

KM# 43 ABBASI

Silver **Obv:** Shiite formula **Rev:** Mint, date and 'ya Karim'

Date	Mintage	Good	VG	F	VF	XF
AH1203 (1788)	—	—	70.00	90.00	135	—
AH1211 (1796)	—	—	70.00	90.00	135	—

Anonymous
Struck from before AH1181 until at least AH1216
HAMMERED COINAGE

KM# 100.1 KAZBEG

Copper **Obv:** Lion right **Rev:** Mint & date **Note:** Weight varies: 7-9g.

Date	Mintage	Good	VG	F	VF	XF
AH1181 (1767)	—	—	10.00	17.50	25.00	—

KM# 100.2 KAZBEG

Copper **Obv:** Elephant left **Rev:** Mint and date **Note:** Weight varies: 7-9g.

Date	Mintage	Good	VG	F	VF	XF
AH1182 (1768)	—	—	12.50	20.00	30.00	—

KM# 100.3 KAZBEG

Copper **Obv:** "Quadruped" right **Rev:** Mint and date **Note:** Weight varies: 7-9g.

Date	Mintage	Good	VG	F	VF	XF
AH1188 (1774)	—	—	10.00	17.50	25.00	—

KM# 100.4 KAZBEG

Copper **Rev:** Mint & date **Note:** Weight varies: 7-9g. Obverse design unknown for this type.

Date	Mintage	Good	VG	F	VF	XF
AH1196 (1781)	—	—	—	—	—	—
AH1203 (1788)	—	—	—	—	—	—
AH1204 (1789)	—	—	—	—	—	—
AH1206 (1791)	—	—	—	—	—	—
AH1208 (1793)	—	—	—	—	—	—

KM# 100.5 KAZBEG

Copper **Obv:** Sunface **Rev:** Mint and date **Note:** Weight varies: 7-9g.

Date	Mintage	Good	VG	F	VF	XF
AH1205 (1790)	—	—	15.00	22.50	30.00	—

KM# 100.6 KAZBEG

Copper **Obv:** Goose left **Rev:** Mint and date **Note:** Weight varies: 7 0g.

Date	Mintage	Good	VG	F	VF	XF
AH1207 (1792)	—	—	12.50	20.00	30.00	—

KM# 100.7 KAZBEG

Copper **Obv:** 2-blade sword **Rev:** Mint and date **Note:** Weight varies: 7-9g.

Date	Mintage	Good	VG	F	VF	XF
AH1215 (1800)	—	—	12.50	20.00	30.00	—

KARABAGH

Karabagh, a former Khanate in Azerbaijan was under the control of the Ottomans until 996AD when Persia regained control. The principal mint was located in Panahabad, now the town of Shusha. The hereditary Jewanshir family then broke away from Persia in the second half of the 1700's and abandoned their principality to the Russians in 1822. For the remainder of the Czarist period it formed part of the Muslim governorship of Baker until 1868, when it was transfered to Elizabetpol.

It now forms part of The Nagorno-Karabakh-Oblast which was established as an autonomous region with Azerbaijan in 1923. They elected for independence in the C.I.S. in 1991.

RULER

Ibrahim Khalil Khan, AH1177-1221/1763-1806AD

MINT NAME

پناه اباد

Panahabad (Shusha)

MONETARY SYSTEM

Derived from the Safavid Persian System

1 Bisti = 20 Dinars

1 Abbasi = 200 Dinars

All coins are anonymous except KM#5, which is in the name of Fath'ali Shah of Iran.

The silver abbasi of Karabagh circulated widely in Iran, where it came to be known as a "Panabadi", a term later used for the half Kran in Iran.

KHANATE

Ibrahim Khalil Khan
AH1177-1221 / 1763-1806AD
HAMMERED COINAGE

KM# 1 1/2 BISTI

Copper **Obv:** Sunface rising above lion left **Rev:** Text

Date	Mintage	Good	VG	F	VF	XF
ND (1782)	—	12.50	16.00	25.00	45.00	—

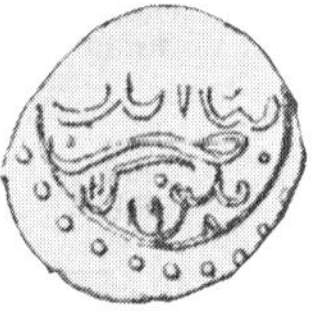

KM# 2 1/2 BISTI

Copper **Obv:** Sunface rising above lion right **Rev:** Text

Date	Mintage	Good	VG	F	VF	XF
AH1198 (1783)	—	12.50	16.00	25.00	45.00	—

KM# 3 1/2 ABBASI

Silver **Obv:** Shiite formula, sometimes with date **Rev:** Mint, date and the phrase 'ya Allah'

Date	Mintage	Good	VG	F	VF	XF
AH1209 (1794)	—	40.00	55.00	75.00	100	—

KM# 5 ABBASI

4.4500 g., Silver **Obv:** Inscription, mint name and date **Obv. Inscription:** "Fath'ali Shah" **Rev:** Shiite formula

Date	Mintage	Good	VG	F	VF	XF
AH1214	—	—	—	—	—	—

KM# 4 ABBASI

Silver **Note:** Weight is about 4.5 grams.

Date	Mintage	Good	VG	F	VF	XF
AH1214	—	—	—	50.00	75.00	120

QUBBA

Qubba is now the upland city of Kuba in the north of Azerbaijan. It was part of Daghistan and frequently associated with Darband, from time to time partially or fully independent. The local ruler, Fath 'Ali Khan (1771-1203/1758-1788AD), acquired Darband, probably about 1775, but Darband regained its autonomy after his death. Coinage commenced in the late 1770's. Like Darband, Qubba was briefly seized by the Russians in 1796, and then formally acquired in July 1806. However, unlike Darband it was apparently permitted to continue its local coinage until AH1223/1808AD.

Coins of Qubba can readily be distinguished from that of Darband by the name of the mint and phrase "a 'aziz" instead of "ya 'alī".

MINT

Qubba

CITY

ANONYMOUS HAMMERED COINAGE

KM# 1 ABBASI

2.3000 g., Silver **Obv. Inscription:** "Ya sahib al-zaman" **Rev:** Mint, date and inscription **Rev. Inscription:** ya'ali **Note:** Other dates may exist for this type, but are yet unreported.

Date	Mintage	Good	VG	F	VF	XF
AH1191 (1777)	—	40.00	70.00	125	—	—
AH1213 (1798)	—	40.00	70.00	125	—	—
AH1214 (1799)	—	40.00	70.00	125	—	—
AH1223	—	50.00	80.00	140	—	—
ND (date missing)	—	20.00	40.00	70.00	—	—

Note: The Baku Museum is said to contain examples dated AH1215-1222, as well as AH1223, which is illustrated in their catalog

KM# 1 ABBASI

2.3000 g., Silver **Obv. Inscription:** "Ya sahib al-zaman" **Rev:** Mint, date and inscription **Rev. Inscription:** ya'ali **Note:** Other dates may exist for this type, but are yet unreported.

Date	Mintage	Good	VG	F	VF	XF
AH1191 (1777)	—	40.00	70.00	125	—	—
AH1213 (1798)	—	40.00	70.00	125	—	—
AH1214 (1799)	—	40.00	70.00	125	—	—
AH1223	—	50.00	80.00	140	—	—
ND (date missing)	—	20.00	40.00	70.00	—	—

Note: The Baku Museum is said to contain examples dated AH1215-1222, as well as AH1223, which is illustrated in their catalog

SHEKI

Sheki, with its capital Nukha was a former khanate in Russian Caucasia, and in 1578 was part of Shirwan (under Ottoman rule). It was occupied in 1806 when the Russians invested Ja'far Quli Khan as governor and then annexed by Russia in 1819. Sheki is now part of Azerbaijan, which joined the Commonwealth of Independent States in December 1991.

RULER

Muhammad Hasan Khan, AH1212-1217/1797-1802AD

MINT NAME

Nukha (Nukhwi)

MONETARY SYSTEM

200 Dinars = 1 Abbasi

20 Dinars = 1 Bisti

KHANATE

Muhammad Hasan Khan
AH1212-1217 / 1797-1802AD
HAMMERED COINAGE

KM# 3 ABBASI

2.2000 g., Silver **Obv:** The couplet of Karim Khan Zand **Rev:** Mint name and date

Date	Mintage	Good	VG	F	VF	XF
AH1213	—	20.00	30.00	50.00	80.00	—
AH1214	—	20.00	30.00	50.00	80.00	—
AH1215	—	20.00	30.00	50.00	80.00	—

SHEMAKHI

Schemakhi, later the capital of Shirwan, is a former khanate located in Azerbaijan. It was taken by the Ottomans in 1578. Restored to Persian rule in 1607, it remained so throughout much of its later history until the Khan Mustafa submitted to the Russians in 1805 and later occupied by the Russians who annexed the khanate in 1813. After destruction in 1859 by earthquake, it came under the government of Baker. Presently it is part of Azerbaijan, C.I.S.

RULERS

Persian until about AH1170/1757AD, then quasi-autonomous until AH1177/1763AD.
Muhammad Sa'id Khan, AH1177-1180/1763-1766AD
Fath Ali Khan, AH1180-1203/1766-1788AD
Asker Khan, AH1203/1788AD
Qasim Khan, AH1203-1209/1788-1794AD
Mustafa Khan, AH1209-1236/1794-1820AD

NOTE: All coins of Schemakhi lack the ruler's name, but are traditionally assigned to ruler by date. Undated examples or examples with date off flan cannot be assigned to a ruler.

MINT NAME

Shamakha

MONETARY SYSTEM

20 Dinars = 1 Bisti
10 Bisti = 1 Abbasi

AUTONOMOUS PERIOD
AH1170-1177

HAMMERED COINAGE

KM# 1 ABBASI

4.5000 g., Silver **Obv:** Shiite formula **Rev:** Mint, date and inscription **Rev. Inscription:** ya karim **Note:** The date was frozen and used prior to the accession of Muhammad Sa'id in AH1177.

Date	Mintage	Good	VG	F	VF	XF
AH1170 (1762)	—	—	25.00	35.00	55.00	80.00

KHANATE
AH1177-1220

Muhammad Sa'id Khan
AH1177-1180 / 1763-1766AD

HAMMERED COINAGE

KM# 2 ABBASI

Silver **Note:** Same type as KM#1; weight is about 4.5 grams (1 mithqal).

Date	Mintage	Good	VG	F	VF	XF
AH1177 (1763)	—	—	25.00	35.00	50.00	75.00
AH1178 (1764)	—	—	25.00	35.00	50.00	75.00
AH1179 (1765)	—	—	25.00	35.00	50.00	75.00

Fath 'Ali Khan
AH1180-1203 / 1766-1788AD

HAMMERED COINAGE

KM# 4.1 KAZBEG

Copper **Obv:** Various designs **Rev:** Mint and date **Note:** When date is off flan, types KM#4 & KM#15 cannot be distinguished. Copper coins allegedly 1/2 Kazbeg are actually lightweight examples of the full Kazbeg. Weight varies: 4-7g.

Date	Mintage	Good	VG	F	VF	XF
ND (1766) Date off flan	—	—	7.50	12.50	25.00	—
AH1189 (1775)	—	—	—	—	—	—
AH1202 (1788)	—	—	—	—	—	—

KM# 4.2 KAZBEG

Copper **Obv:** Lion **Rev:** Mint and date **Note:** When date is off flan, types KM#4 & KM#15 cannot be distinguished. Copper coins allegedly 1/2 Kazbeg are actually lightweight examples of the full Kazbeg. Weight varies: 4-7g.

Date	Mintage	Good	VG	F	VF	XF
AH1196 (1781)	—	—	15.00	25.00	40.00	—

KM# 5 ABBASI

Silver **Obv:** Inscription in Persian **Obv. Inscription:** Ya Sâheb oz-Zamân **Rev:** Inscription in Persian - mint name and date **Rev. Inscription:** ya karim **Note:** Weight is approximately 3.7 grams (5/6 mithqal).

Date	Mintage	Good	VG	F	VF	XF
ND (1766) Date missing	—	—	10.00	13.50	20.00	35.00
AH1181 (1767)	—	—	25.00	35.00	50.00	85.00
AH1182 (1768)	—	—	25.00	35.00	50.00	85.00
AH1184 (1770)	—	—	20.00	30.00	40.00	65.00
AH1185 (1771)	—	—	25.00	35.00	50.00	85.00
AH1186 (1772)	—	—	20.00	30.00	40.00	65.00
AH1187 (1773)	—	—	25.00	35.00	50.00	85.00

KM# 6 ABBASI

Silver **Obv:** Arabic - ya-sahib al zaman **Rev:** Arabic - mint, date and ya-karim **Note:** Weight approximately 3.0-3.1g (4/6 mithqal).

Date	Mintage	Good	VG	F	VF	XF
ND (1773) Date missing	—	—	10.00	13.50	20.00	35.00
AH1188 (1774)	—	—	20.00	30.00	40.00	65.00
AH1189 (1775)	—	—	20.00	30.00	40.00	65.00
AH1190 (1776)	—	—	25.00	35.00	50.00	85.00
AH1191 (1777)	—	—	25.00	35.00	50.00	85.00
AH1192 (1778)	—	—	25.00	35.00	50.00	85.00
AH1193 (1779)	—	—	25.00	35.00	50.00	85.00
AH1194 (1780)	—	—	25.00	35.00	50.00	85.00
AH1195 (1780)	—	—	25.00	35.00	50.00	85.00
AH1196 (1781)	—	—	25.00	35.00	50.00	85.00

KM# 7 ABBASI

Silver **Note:** Weight approximately 2.6g. (7/12 mithqal), same design as KM#5 and KM#6.

Date	Mintage	Good	VG	F	VF	XF
ND (1782) Date missing	—	—	12.50	20.00	25.00	40.00
AH1198 (1783)	—	—	30.00	40.00	55.00	85.00
AH1200 (1785)	—	—	30.00	40.00	55.00	85.00
AH1201 (1786)	—	—	30.00	40.00	55.00	85.00
AH1202 (1787)	—	—	30.00	40.00	55.00	85.00
AH1203 (1788)	—	—	30.00	40.00	55.00	85.00

Note: Russian collectors traditionally assign this year to Asker Khan, but they may have been struck under any of the three rulers on the throne that year

Qasim Khan
AH1203-1209 / 1788-1794AD

HAMMERED COINAGE

KM# 9 KAZBEG

Copper **Rev:** Mint and date **Note:** Weight approximately 5-6g.

Date	Mintage	Good	VG	F	VF	XF
AH1205 (1790)	—	—	—	—	—	—

KM# 10 ABBASI

Silver **Obv:** Arabic text **Obv. Inscription:** Ya Sâhib al-Zamân. **Rev:** Arabic text, mint name and date. **Note:** Weight varies: 2.30-3g. Coins without date or date off flan cannot be differentiated from examples of type KM#20. Obverse and reverse designs similar to KM#5.

Date	Mintage	Good	VG	F	VF	XF
AH1204 (1789)	—	—	20.00	30.00	40.00	65.00
AH1205 (1790)	—	—	20.00	30.00	40.00	65.00
AH1207 (1792)	—	—	20.00	30.00	40.00	65.00
AH1208 (1793)	—	—	20.00	30.00	40.00	65.00

Mustafa Khan
AH1209-1235 / 1794-1820AD

ANONYMOUS HAMMERED COINAGE

KM# 15 KAZBEG

Copper **Obv:** Various designs **Rev:** Mint name and date

Date	Mintage	Good	VG	F	VF	XF
AH1212	—	12.50	15.00	25.00	35.00	—
AH1213	—	12.50	15.00	25.00	35.00	—

HAMMERED COINAGE

KM# 16 ABBASI

Silver **Note:** Weight approximately 1.85 grams (5/12 mithqal); similar to KM#5.

Date	Mintage	Good	VG	F	VF	XF
AH1209 (1794)	—	—	18.50	25.00	35.00	55.00
AH1210 (1795)	—	—	18.50	25.00	35.00	55.00
AH1211 (1796)	—	—	18.50	25.00	35.00	55.00
AH1212 (1797)	—	—	18.50	25.00	35.00	55.00

KM# 20 ABBASI

Silver **Note:** Weight approximately 2.25 grams (3/6 mithqal), heavier weight of pre-AH1209 restored; similar to KM#5.

Date	Mintage	Good	VG	F	VF	XF
AH1214	—	—	18.50	25.00	35.00	55.00
AH1215	—	—	18.50	25.00	35.00	55.00

AZORES

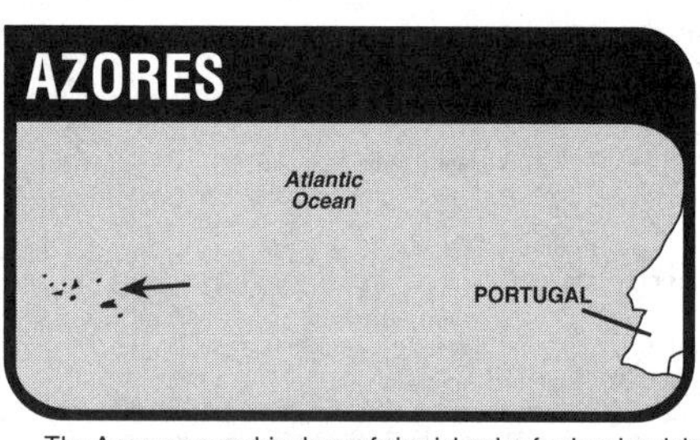

The Azores, an archipelago of nine islands of volcanic origin, are located in the Atlantic Ocean 740 miles (1,190 km.) west of Cape de Roca, Portugal. They are the westernmost region of Europe under the administration of Portugal and have an area of 902 sq. mi. (2,305 sq. km.) and a population of 236,000. Principal city: Ponta Delgada. The natives are mainly of Portuguese descent and earn their livelihood by fishing, wine making, basket weaving and the growing of fruit, grains and sugar cane. Pineapples are the chief item of export. The climate is particularly temperate, making the islands a favorite winter resort.

The Azores were discovered about 1427 by the Portuguese navigator Diogo de Sevill. Portugal secured the islands in the 15th century and established the first settlement on Santa Maria about 1439. From 1580 to 1640 the Azores were subject to Spain.

The Azores' first provincial coinage was ordered by law of August 19, 1750. Copper coins were struck for circulation in both the Azores and Madeira Islands, keeping the same technical specifications but with different designs. In 1795 a second provincial coinage was introduced but the weight was reduced by 50 percent.

Angra on Terceira Island became the capital of the captaincy-general of the Azores in 1766 and it was here in 1826 that the constitutionalists set up a pro-Pedro government in opposition to King Miguel in Lisbon. The whole Portuguese fleet attacked Terceira and was repelled at Praia, after which Azoreans, Brazilians and British mercenaries defeated Miguel in Portugal. Maria de Gloria, Pedro's daughter, was proclaimed queen of Portugal on Terceira in 1828.

A U.S. naval base was established at Ponta Delgada in 1917.

After World War II, the islands acquired a renewed importance as a refueling stop for transatlantic air transport. The United States maintains defense bases in the Azores as part of the collective security program of NATO.

In 1976 the archipelago became the Autonomous Region of Azores.

Note: Portuguese 50 Centavos and 1 Escudo pieces dated 1935 were issued for circulation in Azores. These are found under the appropriate listing in Portugal.

RULER

Portuguese

MONETARY SYSTEM

1000 Reis (Insulanos) = 1 Milreis

PORTUGUESE ADMINISTRATION

PROVINCIAL COINAGE

KM# A1 3 REIS

Copper **Obv:** Crowned arms within wreath **Rev:** Crowned pillars divide date

Date	Mintage	VG	F	VF	XF	Unc
1750	—	350	550	950	1,600	—

KM# 1 5 REIS

Copper **Obv:** Crowned pillars divide date, value below **Obv. Legend:** IOSEPHUS • I • D • G • PORT • ET • ALG • REX **Rev:** Crowned arms within wreath **Rev. Legend:** PECUNIA INS...

Date	Mintage	VG	F	VF	XF	Unc
1750	—	15.00	30.00	70.00	165	—
1751	—	20.00	40.00	90.00	185	—

KM# 9 5 REIS

Copper, 25 mm. **Obv:** Arms **Obv. Legend:** MARIA I.... **Rev:** Value in wreath, legend **Note:** Reduced size.

Date	Mintage	VG	F	VF	XF	Unc
1795	301,000	6.00	12.00	25.00	45.00	—
1797	Inc. above	6.00	12.00	25.00	45.00	—
1798	Inc. above	7.50	15.00	30.00	55.00	—

KM# 2 10 REIS

Copper **Obv:** Crowned pillars divide date, value below **Obv. Legend:** IOSEPHUS • I • D • G • PORT • ET • ALG • REX **Rev:** Crowned arms within wreath **Rev. Legend:** PECUNIA INS...

Date	Mintage	VG	F	VF	XF	Unc
1750	—	10.00	20.00	50.00	100	—

KM# 5 10 REIS

Copper **Obv:** Arms **Obv. Legend:** MARIA I.... **Rev:** Value in wreath, legend **Note:** Overstrikes on Portuguese 5 Reis, KM#305, dated 1791 exist.

Date	Mintage	VG	F	VF	XF	Unc
1795	116,000	8.00	16.00	35.00	70.00	—
1796	—	8.00	16.00	35.00	70.00	—

KM# 4 20 REIS

Copper **Note:** Error dates.

Date	Mintage	VG	F	VF	XF	Unc
1190(1790)	—	60.00	120	200	400	—
1196(1796)	—	28.00	50.00	80.00	200	—

KM# 3 20 REIS

Copper **Obv:** Crowned arms within cartouche **Obv. Legend:** MARIA ... **Rev:** Value and date within wreath **Rev. Legend:** PORTUGAL.... **Note:** Overstrikes on Portuguese 10 Reis, KM#306, exist.

Date	Mintage	VG	F	VF	XF	Unc
1790	137,000	25.00	50.00	175	350	—
1795	Inc. above	4.00	8.00	20.00	40.00	—
1796	Inc. above	5.00	10.00	25.00	50.00	—
1798 Unique	—	—	—	—	—	—

KM# 6 75 REIS

Silver **Obv:** Crowned arms divide date and value **Obv. Legend:** MARIA • I • D • G • PORT • ET • ALG • REGINA **Rev:** Florals in angles of Maltese cross **Rev. Legend:** IN HOC SIGNO VINCES

Date	Mintage	VG	F	VF	XF	Unc
1794	—	17.50	35.00	55.00	110	180
1795	—	20.00	40.00	60.00	120	185

KM# 7 150 REIS

Silver **Obv:** Denomination **Obv. Legend:** MARIA I D.G. PORT. ET ALG. REGINA. **Rev:** Cross **Rev. Legend:** IN HOC....

Date	Mintage	VG	F	VF	XF	Unc
1794	—	15.00	45.00	95.00	155	225
1795	—	12.50	30.00	55.00	130	180
1798	—	20.00	55.00	95.00	180	240

KM# 8 300 REIS

Silver **Obv:** Crowned arms divide value and date **Obv. Legend:** MARIA • I • D • G • PORT • ET • ALG • REGINA • **Rev:** Florals in angles of Maltese cross **Rev. Legend:** IN HOC SIGNO VINCES

Date	Mintage	VG	F	VF	XF	Unc
1794	—	27.50	35.00	70.00	145	185
1795	—	27.50	35.00	70.00	145	185
1797	—	40.00	60.00	115	185	260

COUNTERMARKED COINAGE

Series of 1795-1798

KM# 31 5 REIS

Copper **Countermark:** Raised 5 in indent **Note:** Countermark on Portuguese III Reis, KM#260.

CM Date	Host Date	Good	VG	F	VF	XF
ND(1795-98)	ND(1777-78) Rare	—	—	—	—	—

KM# 32 10 REIS

Copper **Countermark:** Raised 10 in indent **Note:** Countermark on Portuguese V Reis, KM#305.

CM Date	Host Date	Good	VG	F	VF	XF
ND(1795-98)	ND(1791-97) Rare	—	—	—	—	—
ND(1795-98)	ND(1791-97) Rare	—	—	—	—	—

KM# 40.3 20 REIS

Copper **Countermark:** Raised flower/20 in indent **Note:** Countermark on X Reis, KM#306.

CM Date	Host Date	Good	VG	F	VF	XF
ND(1795-98)	ND(1791-92) Rare	—	—	—	—	—

PATTERNS

Including off metal strikes

KM#	Date	Mintage	Identification	Mkt Val

KM#	Date	Mintage	Identification	Mkt Val
Pn1	1750	—	3 Reis. Copper. Crowned pillars divide date, value below. Crowned arms within wreath.	—
Pn2	1798	—	40 Reis. Copper. Crowned arms within cartouche. Value witin wreath. Maria I	2,750

TRIAL STRIKES

KM#	Date	Mintage	Identification	Mkt Val

KM#	Date	Mintage	Identification	Mkt Val
TS1	1798	—	5 Reis. Tin. Uniface, reverse KM#9.	90.00

BARBADOS

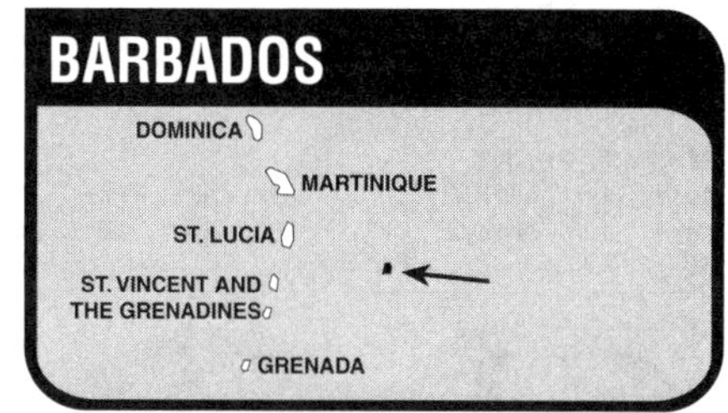

Barbados, an independent state within the British Commonwealth, is located in the Windward Islands of the West Indies east of St. Vincent. The coral island has an area of 166 sq. mi. (430 sq. km.) and a population of 269,000. Capital: Bridgetown. The economy is based on sugar and tourism. Sugar, petroleum products, molasses, and rum are exported.

Barbados was named by the Portuguese who achieved the first landing on the island in 1563. British sailors landed at the site of present-day Holetown in 1624. Barbados was under uninterrupted British control from the time of the first British settlement in 1627 until it obtained independence on Nov. 30, 1966. It is a member of the Commonwealth of Nations. Elizabeth II is Head of State as Queen of Barbados.

Unmarked side cut pieces of Spanish and Spanish Colonial 1, 2 and 8 reales were the principal coinage medium of 18th-century Barbados. The "Neptune" tokens issued by Sir Phillip Gibbs, a local plantation owner, circulated freely but were never established as legal coinage. The coinage and banknotes of the British Caribbean Territories (Eastern Group) were employed prior to 1973 when Barbados issued a decimal coinage.

RULER
British

INDEPENDENT SOVEREIGN STATE
within the British Commonwealth

COUNTERMARKED COINAGE

KM# 8 2 REALES

Silver **Countermark:** Pineapple in relief **Note:** Countermark on plugged Spanish or Spanish Colonial 8 Reales.

CM Date	Host Date	Good	VG	F	VF	XF
ND	ND(1791-99) Rare	—	—	—	—	—

KM# 9 8 REALES

Silver **Countermark:** Pineapple in relief **Note:** Countermark on plugged Spanish or Spanish Colonial 8 Reales.

CM Date	Host Date	Good	VG	F	VF	XF
ND	ND(1791-99) Rare	—	—	—	—	—

Note: The plug is usually missing

TOKEN COINAGE

KM# Tn9 1/2 PENNY

Copper **Obv:** Neptune in chariot **Obv. Legend:** BARBADOES • HALFPENNY **Rev:** Crowned head left

Date	Mintage	VG	F	VF	XF	Unc
1792	47,000	25.00	50.00	125	250	—
1792 (Restrike): Proof	—	Value: 200				

KM# Tn9a 1/2 PENNY

Silver **Obv:** Neptune in chariot **Rev:** Crowned head left

Date	Mintage	VG	F	VF	XF	Unc
1792 (Restrike); Proof	—	Value: 725				

KM# Tn4 PENNY

Copper **Obv:** Small pineapple, date below **Obv. Legend:** BARBADOES • PENNY • **Rev:** Crowned head left **Note:** Type I, small head, small pineapple, P#10.

Date	Mintage	VG	F	VF	XF	Unc
1788 Proof	—	Value: 350				

KM# Tn5 PENNY

Copper **Note:** Type II, small head, larger pineapple, P#11.

Date	Mintage	VG	F	VF	XF	Unc
1788	5,376	20.00	30.00	100	200	—
1788 Proof	—	Value: 250				

KM# Tn6 PENNY

Copper **Obv:** "I MILTON F" in relief on truncation, P#19

Date	Mintage	VG	F	VF	XF	Unc
1788 (Restrike); Proof	—	Value: 300				

KM# Tn8 PENNY

Copper **Obv:** Pineapple, date below **Obv. Legend:** BARBADOES • PENNY • **Rev:** Crowned head left **Note:** Type III, large head, large pineapple, wiry hair, P#14.

Date	Mintage	VG	F	VF	XF	Unc
1788	Est. 200,000	6.00	15.00	25.00	50.00	—

KM# TnA9 PENNY

Copper **Obv:** Small pineapple, P#20 **Obv. Legend:** BARBADOES • PENNY • **Rev:** Crowned head left

Date	Mintage	VG	F	VF	XF	Unc
1788 (Restrike); Proof	—	Value: 325				

KM# TnA9a PENNY

Silver **Obv:** Pineapple **Rev:** Crowned head left

Date	Mintage	VG	F	VF	XF	Unc
1788 (Restrike); Proof, Rare	—	—	—	—	—	—

KM# Tn10 PENNY

Copper **Obv:** Neptune in chariot **Obv. Legend:** BARBADOES • PENNY **Rev:** Crowned head left

Date	Mintage	VG	F	VF	XF	Unc
1792	39,000	20.00	50.00	100	200	—
1792 Proof	—	Value: 275				

KM# Tn10a PENNY

Silver **Obv:** Neptune in chariot **Rev:** Crowned head left **Note:** Proof restrikes were struck on thick and thin flans in collared dies while originals were not.

Date	Mintage	VG	F	VF	XF	Unc
1792 (Restrike); Proof	—	Value: 800				

BERMUDA

The Parliamentary British Colony of Bermuda, situated in the western Atlantic Ocean 660 miles (1,062 km.) east of North Carolina, has an area of 20.6 sq. mi. (53 sq. km.) and a population of 61,600. Capital: Hamilton. Concentrated essences, beauty preparations, and cut flowers are exported. Most Bermudians derive their livelihood from tourism.

Bermuda was discovered by Juan de Bermudez, a Spanish navigator, in about 1503. British influence dates from 1609 when a group of Virginia-bound British colonists under the command of Sir George Somers was shipwrecked on the islands for 10 months. The islands were settled in 1612 by 60 British colonists from the Virginia Colony and became a crown colony in 1684. The earliest coins issued for the island were the "Hogge Money" series of 2, 3, 6 and 12 pence, the name derived from the pig in the obverse design, a recognition of the quantity of such animals then found there. The next issue for Bermuda was the Birmingham coppers of 1793; all locally circulating coinage was demonetized in 1842, when the currency of the United Kingdom became standard. Internal autonomy was obtained by the constitution of June 8, 1968.

In February, 1970, Bermuda converted from its former currency, which was sterling, to a decimal currency, the dollar unit which is equal to one U.S. dollar. On July 31, 1972, Bermuda severed its monetary link with the British pound sterling and pegged its dollar to be the same gold value as the U.S. dollar.

RULER

British

BRITISH ADMINISTRATION

STANDARD COINAGE

KM# 5 PENNY

Copper **Ruler:** George III **Obv:** "DROZ F." incuse on shoulder **Obv. Legend:** GEORGIVS III • D • G • REX **Rev:** Three masted ship at sea **Note:** 2 varieties exist with single or double pennant.

Date	Mintage	Good	VG	F	VF	XF
1793	72,000	—	15.00	30.00	75.00	200

KM# 5a PENNY

Copper **Ruler:** George III **Obv:** Laureate head right **Rev:** Three masted ship at sea **Note:** Bronzed.

Date	Mintage	F	VF	XF	Unc	BU
1793 Proof	50	Value: 450				

KM# 6 PENNY

Copper **Ruler:** George III **Rev:** Rope removed between tip of bowsprit over the spritsail to foremast

Date	Mintage	F	VF	XF	Unc	BU
1793 Proof, rare	—	—	—	—	—	—

KM# 7 PENNY

Copper **Ruler:** George III **Obv:** "DROZ. F" removed from shoulder

Date	Mintage	F	VF	XF	Unc	BU
1793 Proof, restrike	—	Value: 200				

KM# 7a PENNY

Silver **Ruler:** George III **Note:** Mulings of English penny obverse dies with this reverse are fantasies.

Date	Mintage	F	VF	XF	Unc	BU
1793	—	Value: 1,000				

KM# 8 PENNY

Silver **Ruler:** George III **Obv:** "DROZ. F" incuse on shoulder, diamonds separate "III. D. G. REX"

Date	Mintage	F	VF	XF	Unc	BU
1793 Proof, restrike	—	Value: 300				

KM# 8a PENNY

Aluminum **Ruler:** George III **Obv:** "DROZ. F" incuse on shoulder, diamonds separate "III. D. G. REX"

Date	Mintage	F	VF	XF	Unc	BU
1793 Proof, restrike, rare	—	—	—	—	—	—

KM# 8b PENNY

Gilt **Ruler:** George III **Obv:** "DROZ. F" incuse on shoulder, diamonds separate "III. D. G. REX"

Date	Mintage	F	VF	XF	Unc	BU
1793 Proof, restrike, rare	—	—	—	—	—	—

KM# 8c PENNY

Pewter **Ruler:** George III **Obv:** "DROZ. F" incuse on shoulder, diamonds separate "III. D. G. REX"

Date	Mintage	F	VF	XF	Unc	BU
1793 Proof, restrike, rare	—	—	—	—	—	—

KM# 9 PENNY

Silver **Ruler:** George III **Obv:** Similar to KM#5 but extra curl below shoulder

Date	Mintage	F	VF	XF	Unc	BU
1793 Proof, restrike, rare	—	—	—	—	—	—

KM# 8d PENNY

Silver **Ruler:** George III

Date	Mintage	F	VF	XF	Unc	BU
1793 Proof, restrike, rare	—	—	—	—	—	—

KM# 8e PENNY

Gold **Ruler:** George III **Obv:** "DROZ. F" incuse on shoulder, diamonds separate "III. D. G. REX"

Date	Mintage	F	VF	XF	Unc	BU
1793 Proof, restrike, rare	—	—	—	—	—	—

KM# 10 PENNY

Silver **Obv:** Laureate bust right, broad rim with legend incuse "SOHO" below **Note:** Mule.

Date	Mintage	F	VF	XF	Unc	BU
ND Proof, restrike, rare	—	—	—	—	—	—

KM# 10a PENNY

Gold **Obv:** Laureate bust right, broad rim with legend incuse "SOHO" below **Note:** Mule.

Date	Mintage	F	VF	XF	Unc	BU
ND Proof, restrike, rare	—	—	—	—	—	—

KM# 11 PENNY

Copper **Obv:** Laureate bust right, broad rim with legend incuse "SOHO" below **Note:** Mule.

Date	Mintage	F	VF	XF	Unc	BU
ND Restrike, rare	—	—	—	—	—	—

KM# 11a PENNY

Silver **Obv:** Laureate bust right, broad rim with legend incuse "SOHO" below **Note:** Mule.

Date	Mintage	F	VF	XF	Unc	BU
ND Restrike, rare	—	—	—	—	—	—

KM# 12 PENNY

Gold **Obv:** Crowned draped bust right, without rim **Note:** Mule.

Date	Mintage	F	VF	XF	Unc	BU
ND Restrike, rare	—	—	—	—	—	—

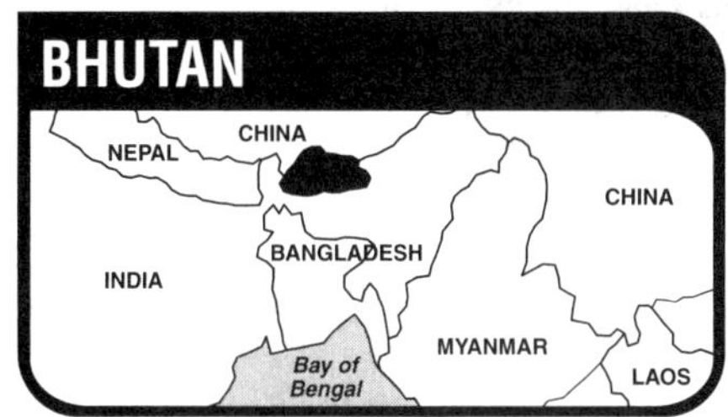

The Kingdom of Bhutan, a landlocked Himalayan country bordered by Tibet and India, has an area of 18,150 sq. mi. (47,000 sq. km.) and a population of *2.03 million. Capital: Thimphu. Virtually the entire population is engaged in agricultural and pastoral activities. Rice, wheat, barley, and yak butter are produced in sufficient quantity to make the country self-sufficient in food. The economy of Bhutan is primitive and many transactions are conducted on a barter basis.

Bhutan's early history is obscure, but is thought to have resembled that of rural medieval Europe. The country was conquered by Tibet in the 9th century, and a dual temporal and spiritual rule developed which operated until the mid-19th century, when the southern part of the country was occupied by the British and annexed to British India. Bhutan was established as a hereditary monarchy in 1907, and in 1910 agreed to British control of its external affairs. In 1949, India and Bhutan concluded a treaty whereby India assumed Britain's role in subsidizing Bhutan and guiding its foreign affairs. In 1971 Bhutan became a full member of the United Nations.

KINGDOM

HAMMERED COINAGE

Period I, 1790-1840AD

KM# 1 1/2 RUPEE (Deb)
Silver **Obv:** Letter "ma" at top right

Date	Mintage	Good	VG	F	VF	XF
ND(1790-1840)	—	—	—	25.00	45.00	60.00

KM# A1 1/2 RUPEE (Deb)
Silver **Rev:** Hook in letter "cha"

Date	Mintage	Good	VG	F	VF	XF
ND(1790-1840)	—	—	—	15.00	25.00	35.00

KM# 2.1 1/2 RUPEE (Deb)
Silver **Obv:** Letter "sa" above the end of "nd" of the syllable "ndra"; one dot each left and right of "ndra" **Rev:** Hook in letter "cha"

Date	Mintage	Good	VG	F	VF	XF
ND(1790-1840)	—	—	—	15.00	25.00	35.00

KM# 2.2 1/2 RUPEE (Deb)
Base Metal **Obv:** Letter "sa" above the end of "nd" of the syllable "ndra" **Rev:** No hook in letter "cha"

Date	Mintage	Good	VG	F	VF	XF
ND(1790-1840)	—	—	—	5.00	10.00	15.00

KM# 2.3 1/2 RUPEE (Deb)
Copper **Obv:** Letter "sa" above the end of "nd" of the syllable "ndra", one dot each left and right of "ndra" **Rev:** Hook in letter "cha"

Date	Mintage	Good	VG	F	VF	XF
ND(1790-1840)	—	—	—	5.00	10.00	15.00

KM# 3.1 1/2 RUPEE (Deb)
Silver **Obv:** Letter "sa" above the end of "ra" of the syllable "ndra", one dot right of "ndra" **Rev:** Tree at top left exists

Date	Mintage	Good	VG	F	VF	XF
ND(1790-1840)	—	—	—	10.00	20.00	25.00

KM# 3.2 1/2 RUPEE (Deb)
Base Metal **Obv:** Two dots right of "ndra" **Rev. Designer:** Tree at top left

Date	Mintage	Good	VG	F	VF	XF
ND(1790-1840)	—	—	—	2.00	5.00	8.00

KM# 3.3 1/2 RUPEE (Deb)
Silver **Obv:** Letter "sa" before the end of "ra" of the syllable "ndra", one dot right of "ndra"

Date	Mintage	Good	VG	F	VF	XF
ND(1790-1840)	—	—	—	10.00	20.00	25.00

KM# 4.1 1/2 RUPEE (Deb)
Silver **Obv:** One dot above the end of "ra" under the letter "na" is "x" over a small arch

Date	Mintage	Good	VG	F	VF	XF
ND(1790-1840)	—	—	—	5.00	10.00	15.00

KM# 5.1 1/2 RUPEE (Deb)
Base Metal **Obv:** Leaf spray before the end of "ra"

Date	Mintage	Good	VG	F	VF	XF
ND(1790-1840)	—	—	—	5.00	10.00	18.00

KM# 5.2 1/2 RUPEE (Deb)
Copper **Obv:** Leafy spray before the end of "ra"

Date	Mintage	Good	VG	F	VF	XF
ND(1790-1840)	—	—	—	5.00	7.00	12.00

KM# 4.2 1/2 RUPEE (Deb)
Silver **Obv:** One dot left and right of the syllable "ndra" under the letter "na" is "x" over a small arch **Note:** Silver coins without one or two dots belong to Rajendra Narayan (1770-1772) of Cooch Behar.

Date	Mintage	Good	VG	F	VF	XF
ND(1790-1840)	—	—	—	5.00	10.00	15.00

KM# 6 1/2 RUPEE (Deb)
Copper **Obv:** Swastika above the end of "ra" **Note:** Swastika reverse in KM#9.2.

Date	Mintage	Good	VG	F	VF	XF
ND(1790-1840)	—	—	—	5.00	10.00	15.00

KM# 3.4 1/2 RUPEE (Deb)
Base Metal **Obv:** Letter "sa" before the end of "ra" of the syllable "ndra", one dot right of "ndra" **Rev:** Tree at top right **Note:** Variety exists with two dots of "ndra".

Date	Mintage	Good	VG	F	VF	XF
ND(1790-1840)	—	—	—	2.00	5.00	8.00

KM# A23 RUPEE
11.6000 g., Silver

Date	Mintage	Good	VG	F	VF	XF
ND(1790-1840)	—	—	—	—	400	—

Böhmen

The large and important Kingdom of Bohemia is located in Central Europe between Bavaria and Austria on the south, Saxony and Silesia on the north, Franconia and the Upper Palatinate to the west, and the Margraviate of Moravia to the east. The region was early settled by the Celtic Boii and controlled by the Czechs, a Slavic people, from the fifth century. Bohemia was at first a duchy and produced a series of rulers dating from the late 9th century. The first hereditary king was Wladislaw II, who ruled 1140-1173. During the later Middle Ages, the kingdom was acquired through marriage to various dynasties of the region, notably the Margraves of Moravia, the Electors of Brandenburg and emperors as well. By the late 15th century, the ruler was another Wladislaw II, a son of the King of Poland, and he was also the King of Hungary. His son, Ludwig, was killed in 1526 at the Battle of Mohacz, fighting against the Turks. His sister was the wife of Emperor Ferdinand I and thus, Bohemia passed to the Hapsburgs.

Bohemia, however, was an electoral monarchy and the king was chosen by the leading nobles at the capital, Prague. In most instances, the succession of one emperor to the next made electing the new emperor as king of Bohemia a mere formality. Very often, the heir apparent to the emperor was elected King of Bohemia prior to his father's passing. By the early 17th century, Protestantism had made great inroads among the Czech nobility and anti-Catholic/anti-Hapsburg sentiments were at a peak. Before Emperor Matthias died in 1619, the nobles had been forced to elect Archduke Ferdinand (II) in 1617. When two governors, appointed by Matthias, were thrown from a window of the palace in Prague in May 1618, in what became known as the Defenestration of Prague, the event precipitated a revolt by the Bohemian Estates (Die böhmischen Stände). The Estates were constituted of the noble lords, the knights and the cities, who deposed Emperor Ferdinand II as king and elected the Protestant Friedrich V, Count Palatine and Elector of the Rhine, in his place. Hostilities had already begun between some of the Protestant German princes and the Emperor, but the elevation of Friedrich to the Bohemian throne galvanized imperial resolve and made the new king's reign very short. Coinage was struck under the authority of firstly, the Estates, and then King Friedrich. The Hapsburgs regained Bohemia in 1620 and except for the later short reign of Karl Albrecht of Bavaria in 1741-42, continued until 1918, although it ceased to be viewed as a separate entity after the dissolution of the Holy Roman Empire by Napoleon in 1806.

RULERS
Leopold I, 1657-1705
Josef I, 1705-11
Karl VI, 1711-40
Karl VII Albrecht, 1741-42, d.1745
Maria Theresia, 1742-80
Franz I, 1742-65
Josef II, 1765-90
Leopold II, 1790-92
Franz II, 1792-1806 (1835)

MINT MARKS
A – Vienna Mint
(c) – crossed hammers, Kuttenberg Mint, 1695, 1711-12
C – Prague, 1766-80
P – Prague, 1760-63
S – Schmöllnitz Mint

MINT OFFICIALS' INITIALS & PRIVY MARKS

PRAGUE MINT
(Praha)
(in Bohemia)

Coat of arms on imperial eagle's breast. Legend usually ends BO, BOH, BOHEMIAE REX.

Letters or Initials	Date	Name
PM	1694, 1710-11	Prague mint, during vacancies
GE	1694-1710	Gregor Egerer, mintmaster
IAP	1711-13	Ignaz Anton Putz, mintmaster
IGR	1713-14	Johann Georg Ritter, die-cutter
FS (sometimes in ligature)	1713-46	Ferdinand Scharff, mintmaster
IIL	1717	Johann Joseph Loth, die-cutter
EvS, VS, vS, PS	1766-90	Paul Erdmann von Schwingerschuh, mintmaster
AS, S	1768-73	A. Stöhr, warden
IK, K	1773-80	I. Kendler, warden
P – R	1746-67	Prague mint
P	1760-63	Prague mint
C	1766-1857	Prague mint

KUTTENBERG MINT
(Kutna Hora)

Letters or Initials	Privy mark	Date	Name
(jj) =	K or K	1677-1702	Christoph Kroh, mintmaster
(kk) =	(KM)	1702, 1707	Vacant
(ll) =		1678-1726	Kuttenberg mint
(mm) =	B W	1702-16	Bernard Wonsidler, mintmaster
(nn) =	or W	1716-26	Johann Franz Weyer, mintmaster

ARMS
Crowned lion rampant, usually to left.

KINGDOM

STANDARD COINAGE

KM# 696 PFENNIG
Billon **Ruler:** Charles VI **Obv:** Crowned arms in cartouche divide "C-VI" at top and date near bottom **Note:** Uniface. Prev. KM#1140.

Date	Mintage	VG	F	VF	XF	Unc
1720	—	15.00	30.00	65.00	125	—

KM# 780 PFENNIG
Copper **Ruler:** Franz I **Obv:** Crowned Bohemian lion left **Rev:** Value above date **Note:** Prev. KM#285.

Date	Mintage	VG	F	VF	XF	Unc
1757	—	5.00	10.00	22.00	50.00	—
1758/7	—	10.00	15.00	25.00	40.00	—
1758	—	5.00	10.00	22.00	50.00	—

KM# 789 GROESCHL
Copper, 17.5 mm. **Ruler:** Franz I **Obv:** Three oval arms, two above one, in baroque frame, crown above **Rev:** EIN/GRESCHL/date in cartouche **Note:** Prev. KM#290.

Date	Mintage	VG	F	VF	XF	Unc
1759	—	25.00	50.00	100	200	—

KM# 791 GROESCHL
Copper, 23-24 mm. **Ruler:** Franz I **Obv:** Crowned arms, two above one **Rev.** Value and date in cartouche **Note:** Varieties exist. Prev. KM#291.

Date	Mintage	VG	F	VF	XF	Unc
1760	—	2.00	5.00	10.00	18.00	—
1761	—	1.50	3.00	10.00	35.00	—
1763	—	2.50	5.00	20.00	50.00	—
1764	—	1.50	3.00	10.00	35.00	—
1765	—	1.50	3.00	10.00	35.00	—
1767	—	1.50	2.50	10.00	35.00	—
1768	—	1.50	3.50	10.00	35.00	—

KM# 797 GROESCHL

Copper **Ruler:** Franz I **Obv:** Three oval arms, two above one, crown above **Rev:** EIN/GRESCHL/date in cartouche

Date	Mintage	VG	F	VF	XF	Unc
1763S	—	—	—	—	—	—
1767S	—	—	—	—	—	—

KM# 818 GROESCHL

Copper **Ruler:** Josef II **Obv:** Crowned three-fold arms, Bohemia above, Moravia and Silesia below **Rev:** EIN/GROESCHL/date/mint mark in wreath **Note:** Prev. KM#299.

Date	Mintage	VG	F	VF	XF	Unc
1781A	—	5.00	10.00	20.00	35.00	—
1782A	—	5.00	10.00	20.00	35.00	—

KM# 1142 2 PFENNIG

Billon **Ruler:** Charles VI **Obv:** Crowned arms in cartouche, crown divides "C-VI", date divided near bottom **Note:** Uniface.

Date	Mintage	VG	F	VF	XF	Unc
1717	—	12.00	25.00	50.00	100	—
1718	—	12.00	25.00	50.00	100	—
1719	—	12.00	25.00	50.00	100	—
1720	—	12.00	25.00	50.00	100	—
1721	—	12.00	25.00	50.00	100	—
1722	—	12.00	25.00	50.00	100	—
1723	—	12.00	25.00	50.00	100	—
1724	—	12.00	25.00	50.00	100	—
1726	—	12.00	25.00	50.00	100	—

KM# 697 2 PFENNIG

Billon **Ruler:** Charles VI **Note:** Date at bottom. Varieties exist. Prev. KM#1475.

Date	Mintage	VG	F	VF	XF	Unc
1720	—	6.00	12.00	25.00	55.00	—
1721	—	6.00	12.00	25.00	55.00	—
1722	—	6.00	12.00	25.00	55.00	—
1723	—	6.00	12.00	25.00	55.00	—
1724	—	6.00	12.00	25.00	55.00	—
1725	—	6.00	12.00	25.00	55.00	—
1726	—	6.00	12.00	25.00	55.00	—
1727	—	6.00	12.00	25.00	55.00	—
1728	—	6.00	12.00	25.00	55.00	—
1729	—	6.00	12.00	25.00	55.00	—
1730	—	6.00	12.00	25.00	55.00	—
1731	—	6.00	12.00	25.00	55.00	—
1732	—	6.00	12.00	25.00	55.00	—
1733	—	6.00	12.00	25.00	55.00	—
1734	—	—	—	—	—	—
Note: Reported, not confirmed						
1735	—	6.00	12.00	25.00	55.00	—
1736	—	6.00	12.00	25.00	55.00	—
1763 Error 1736	—	6.00	12.00	25.00	55.00	—
1737	—	6.00	12.00	25.00	55.00	—
1738	—	6.00	12.00	25.00	55.00	—
1739	—	6.00	12.00	25.00	55.00	—
1740	—	6.00	12.00	25.00	55.00	—

KM# 664 1/4 KREUZER

Billon **Ruler:** Charles VI **Obv:** Crowned oval Bohemian arms in baroque frame divide "C-VI" near top and date near bottom **Note:** Uniface. Prev. KM#1470.

Date	Mintage	VG	F	VF	XF	Unc
1713	—	10.00	25.00	65.00	150	—
Note: Without 1/4						
1720	—	—	—	—	—	—
Note: Reported, not confirmed						
1722	—	10.00	25.00	65.00	150	—
1723	—	10.00	25.00	65.00	150	—

KM# 674 1/4 KREUZER

Silver **Ruler:** Charles VI **Obv:** Crowned oval Bohemian arms in baroque frame divide "C-VI" near top and date near bottom **Note:** Prev. KM#1140.

Date	Mintage	VG	F	VF	XF	Unc
1720	—	15.00	30.00	65.00	125	—

KM# 711 1/4 KREUZER

Billon **Ruler:** Charles VI **Obv:** Crown divides arched date **Note:** Uniface. Prev. KM#1471.

Date	Mintage	VG	F	VF	XF	Unc
1727	—	10.00	25.00	60.00	135	—
1730	—	10.00	25.00	60.00	135	—

KM# 714 1/4 KREUZER

Billon **Ruler:** Charles VI **Obv:** Without "C-VI" **Note:** Uniface. Prev. KM#1472.

Date	Mintage	VG	F	VF	XF	Unc
1728	—	10.00	25.00	65.00	150	—

KM# 618 1/2 KREUZER

Silver **Ruler:** Leopold I **Obv:** Crown above two shields, "L" in left shield, "1/2" in center **Note:** Uniface. Prev. KM#1426.

Date	Mintage	VG	F	VF	XF	Unc
1701	—	10.00	20.00	40.00	75.00	—

KM# 490 1/2 KREUZER

Silver **Ruler:** Leopold I **Obv:** Crowned Bohemian lion left **Note:** Uniface. Varieties exist. Prev. KM#1115.

Date	Mintage	VG	F	VF	XF	Unc
1701 (jj)	—	4.00	9.00	18.00	30.00	—
1702 (II)	—	4.00	9.00	18.00	30.00	—
1703 (II)	—	4.00	9.00	18.00	30.00	—
1704 (II)	—	4.00	9.00	18.00	30.00	—
1705 (II)	—	4.00	9.00	18.00	30.00	—

KM# 602 1/2 KREUZER

Silver **Ruler:** Leopold I **Obv:** Crowned rampant lion left, "L-I" divided by lion's head, date down right side **Note:** Uniface. Varieties exist. Prev. KM#1425.

Date	Mintage	VG	F	VF	XF	Unc
1701 GE	—	5.00	10.00	20.00	40.00	—
1702 GE	—	5.00	10.00	20.00	40.00	—
1703 GE	—	5.00	10.00	20.00	40.00	—
Note: Reported, not confirmed						
1704 GE	—	5.00	10.00	20.00	40.00	—
1705 GE	—	5.00	10.00	20.00	40.00	—

KM# 626 1/2 KREUZER

Silver **Ruler:** Joseph I **Obv:** Crowned rampant lion left "I-I" divided at top, date down right side **Note:** Uniface. Prev. KM#1135.

Date	Mintage	VG	F	VF	XF	Unc
1705 (II) Rare	—	—	—	—	—	—
1706 (II)	—	12.00	25.00	45.00	80.00	—
1707 (II)	—	12.00	25.00	45.00	80.00	—
1708 (II)	—	12.00	25.00	45.00	80.00	—
1709 (II)	—	12.00	25.00	45.00	80.00	—
1710 (II)	—	12.00	25.00	45.00	80.00	—
1711 (II)	—	12.00	25.00	45.00	80.00	—

KM# 634 1/2 KREUZER

Silver **Ruler:** Joseph I **Obv:** Crowned Bohemian lion right, "I-I" divided at left **Note:** Uniface. Struck on thick flan. Prev. KM#1456.

Date	Mintage	VG	F	VF	XF	Unc
1706 GE	—	5.00	15.00	45.00	100	—

KM# 635 1/2 KREUZER

Silver **Ruler:** Joseph I **Obv:** Crowned Bohemian lion left, date at right **Note:** Uniface. Varieties exist. Prev. KM#1455.

Date	Mintage	VG	F	VF	XF	Unc
1706 GE	—	12.00	25.00	45.00	80.00	—
1707 GE	—	12.00	25.00	45.00	80.00	—
1708 GE	—	12.00	25.00	45.00	80.00	—
1709 GE	—	12.00	25.00	45.00	80.00	—
1710 PM	—	12.00	25.00	45.00	80.00	—
1711 PM	—	12.00	25.00	45.00	80.00	—
1711 IAP	—	12.00	25.00	45.00	80.00	—

KM# 645 1/2 KREUZER

Silver **Ruler:** Charles VI **Obv:** Crowned arms in cartouche; "C-VI" divided near top; arched date divided at bottom **Note:** Varieties exist. Prev. KM#1474.

Date	Mintage	VG	F	VF	XF	Unc
1710	—	5.00	12.00	25.00	55.00	—
1713	—	5.00	12.00	25.00	55.00	—
1718	—	—	—	—	—	—
Note: Reported, not confirmed						
1719	—	5.00	12.00	25.00	55.00	—

KM# 653 1/2 KREUZER

Silver **Ruler:** Charles VI **Obv:** Crowned Bohemian lion left divides "C-VI" at head, date downwards at right **Note:** Uniface. Varieties exist. Prev. KM#1141.

Date	Mintage	VG	F	VF	XF	Unc
1712 (II)	—	12.00	25.00	50.00	100	—
1712 (mm)	—	12.00	25.00	50.00	100	—
1713 (II)	—	12.00	25.00	50.00	100	—
1713	—	12.00	25.00	50.00	100	—
1714	—	12.00	25.00	50.00	100	—
1714 (II)	—	12.00	25.00	50.00	100	—
1715 (II)	—	12.00	25.00	50.00	100	—
1716 (II)	—	12.00	25.00	50.00	100	—
1719 (II)	—	12.00	25.00	50.00	100	—

KM# 652 1/2 KREUZER

Silver **Ruler:** Charles VI **Obv:** •C:VI•/date **Rev:** Crowned Bohemian lion left **Note:** Prev. KM#1473.

Date	Mintage	VG	F	VF	XF	Unc
1712 IAP	—	10.00	25.00	65.00	150	—

KM# 684 1/2 KREUZER

Silver **Ruler:** Charles VI **Obv:** Crowned oval Bohemian arms in baroque frame, "C-VI" divided at crown, date divided to lower left and right **Note:** Uniface.

Date	Mintage	VG	F	VF	XF	Unc
1716	—	—	—	—	—	—
1717	—	—	—	—	—	—

KM# 679 1/2 KREUZER

Silver **Ruler:** Charles VI **Obv:** Crowned oval Bohemian arms in baroque frame, "C-VI" divided at crown, date divided to lower left and right

Date	Mintage	VG	F	VF	XF	Unc
1717 (II)	—	7.00	15.00	30.00	65.00	—
1718 (II)	—	7.00	15.00	30.00	65.00	—
1719 (II)	—	7.00	15.00	30.00	65.00	—
1720 (II)	—	7.00	15.00	30.00	65.00	—
1721 (II)	—	7.00	15.00	30.00	65.00	—
1722 (II)	—	7.00	15.00	30.00	65.00	—
1723 (II)	—	7.00	15.00	30.00	65.00	—
1724 (II)	—	7.00	15.00	30.00	65.00	—

KM# 676 1/2 KREUZER

Silver **Ruler:** Charles VI

Date	Mintage	VG	F	VF	XF	Unc
1720	—	5.00	12.00	25.00	55.00	—
1721	—	5.00	12.00	25.00	55.00	—
1722	—	5.00	12.00	25.00	55.00	—
1723	—	5.00	12.00	25.00	55.00	—
1724	—	5.00	12.00	25.00	55.00	—
1725	—	5.00	12.00	25.00	55.00	—
1726	—	5.00	12.00	25.00	55.00	—
1727	—	5.00	12.00	25.00	55.00	—
1728	—	5.00	12.00	25.00	55.00	—
1729	—	5.00	12.00	25.00	55.00	—
1730	—	5.00	12.00	25.00	55.00	—
1731	—	5.00	12.00	25.00	55.00	—
1732	—	5.00	12.00	25.00	55.00	—
1733	—	5.00	12.00	25.00	55.00	—
1734	—	—	—	—	—	—
Note: Reported, not confirmed						
1735	—	5.00	12.00	25.00	55.00	—
1736	—	5.00	12.00	25.00	55.00	—
1763	—	5.00	12.00	25.00	55.00	—
Note: Error for 1736						
1737	—	5.00	12.00	25.00	55.00	—
1738	—	5.00	12.00	25.00	55.00	—
1739	—	5.00	12.00	25.00	55.00	—
1740	—	5.00	12.00	25.00	55.00	—

KM# 703 1/2 KREUZER

Silver **Ruler:** Charles VI **Obv:** Crowned Bohemian arms in baroque frame

Date	Mintage	VG	F	VF	XF	Unc
1726 (II)	—	—	—	—	—	—

KM# 733 1/2 KREUZER

Silver **Ruler:** Maria Theresa **Obv:** Crowned Bohemian arms in baroque frame, date divided by crown at top, Titles of Maria Theresa **Obv. Legend:** M.T.D.G.R.H.B **Note:** Uniface. Prev. KM#1520.

Date	Mintage	VG	F	VF	XF	Unc
1743	—	10.00	20.00	35.00	65.00	—
1744	—	10.00	20.00	35.00	65.00	—
1745	—	10.00	20.00	35.00	65.00	—

KM# 746 1/2 KREUZER

Silver **Ruler:** Maria Theresa **Obv:** Crowned Bohemian arms in baroque frame, value below arms, date divided by crown **Note:** Uniface. Prev. KM#1521.

Date	Mintage	VG	F	VF	XF	Unc
1745	—	7.00	15.00	25.00	55.00	—
1746	—	7.00	15.00	25.00	55.00	—
1748	—	7.00	15.00	25.00	55.00	—
1749	—	7.00	15.00	25.00	55.00	—
1750	—	7.00	15.00	25.00	55.00	—
1751	—	7.00	15.00	25.00	55.00	—
1752	—	7.00	15.00	25.00	55.00	—
1753	—	7.00	15.00	25.00	55.00	—
1754	—	7.00	15.00	25.00	55.00	—
1755	—	7.00	15.00	25.00	55.00	—
1756	—	7.00	15.00	25.00	55.00	—
1758	—	7.00	15.00	25.00	55.00	—
1759	—	7.00	15.00	25.00	55.00	—

KM# 781 1/2 KREUZER

Silver **Ruler:** Maria Theresa

Date	Mintage	VG	F	VF	XF	Unc
1757	—	15.00	30.00	65.00	125	—
1758/7	—	15.00	30.00	65.00	125	—
1758	—	15.00	30.00	65.00	125	—

KM# 839 1/2 KREUZER

Copper **Ruler:** Franz II **Obv:** Laureate bust right, titles of Franz II **Rev:** Crowned imperial eagle divides date, "1/2" in oval on breast

Date	Mintage	VG	F	VF	XF	Unc
1800 C	—	4.00	10.00	20.00	38.00	—

KM# 582 KREUZER

Silver **Ruler:** Leopold I **Obv:** Older laureate bust right, "1" below

Rev: Crowned imperial eagle, crown divides date **Note:** Varieties exist. Prev. KM#1117.

Date	Mintage	VG	F	VF	XF	Unc
1701 (jj)	—	7.00	15.00	30.00	65.00	—
1702 (ll)	—	7.00	15.00	30.00	65.00	—
1702 (kk)	—	7.00	15.00	30.00	65.00	—
1703 (ll)	—	7.00	15.00	30.00	65.00	—
1704 (ll)	—	7.00	15.00	30.00	65.00	—
1705 (ll)	—	7.00	15.00	30.00	65.00	—
1707 (kk)	—	7.00	15.00	30.00	65.00	—

Note: Coins dated 1707 were a posthumous issue

KM# 603 KREUZER

Silver **Ruler:** Leopold I **Obv:** Young laureate bust right with long wig, value in oval below, titles of Leopold I **Rev:** Crowned imperial eagle holding sword and scepter in talons, oval Bohemian arms on breast, date divided by crown **Note:** Varieties exist. Prev. KM#1427.

Date	Mintage	VG	F	VF	XF	Unc
1701 GE	—	6.00	12.00	25.00	50.00	—
1702 GE	—	6.00	12.00	25.00	50.00	—

Note: Reported, not confirmed

Date	Mintage	VG	F	VF	XF	Unc
1703 GE	—	6.00	12.00	25.00	50.00	—
1704 GE	—	6.00	12.00	25.00	50.00	—
1705 GE	—	6.00	12.00	25.00	50.00	—

KM# 627 KREUZER

Silver **Ruler:** Joseph I **Obv:** Titles of Josef I **Note:** Prev. KM#1457.

Date	Mintage	VG	F	VF	XF	Unc
1705 GE	—	—	—	—	—	—

Note: Reported, not confirmed

Date	Mintage	VG	F	VF	XF	Unc
1706 GE	—	10.00	25.00	60.00	125	—
1710 PM	—	10.00	25.00	60.00	125	—

KM# 628 KREUZER

Silver **Ruler:** Joseph I **Obv:** Laureate bust right in inner circle, value below **Rev:** Crowned imperial eagle in inner circle, crown divides date **Note:** Varieties exist. Prev. KM#1136.

Date	Mintage	VG	F	VF	XF	Unc
1705 (ll) Rare	—	—	—	—	—	—
1706 (ll)	—	10.00	20.00	40.00	90.00	—
1707 (ll)	—	10.00	20.00	40.00	90.00	—
1708 (ll)	—	10.00	20.00	40.00	90.00	—
1709 (ll)	—	10.00	20.00	40.00	90.00	—
1710 (ll)	—	10.00	20.00	40.00	90.00	—

KM# 654 KREUZER

Silver **Ruler:** Charles VI **Obv:** Bust right, value "1" in oval below, titles of Karl VI **Rev:** Crowned imperial eagle, Bohemian arms on breast, date divided at top, titles continuous **Note:** Varieties exist. Prev. KM#1143.

Date	Mintage	VG	F	VF	XF	Unc
1712 (ll)	—	7.00	15.00	25.00	55.00	—
1713 (ll)	—	7.00	15.00	25.00	55.00	—
1714 (ll)	—	7.00	15.00	25.00	55.00	—
1715 (ll)	—	7.00	15.00	25.00	55.00	—
1716 (ll)	—	7.00	15.00	25.00	55.00	—
1717 (ll)	—	7.00	15.00	25.00	55.00	—
1718 (ll)	—	7.00	15.00	25.00	55.00	—
1719 (ll)	—	7.00	15.00	25.00	55.00	—

KM# 665 KREUZER

Silver **Ruler:** Charles VI **Obv:** Bust right, value below **Rev:** Crowned imperial eagle, Bohemian arms on breast, date at end of legend **Note:** Varieties exist. Prev. KM#1476.

Date	Mintage	VG	F	VF	XF	Unc
1712 IAP	—	—	—	—	—	—

Note: Reported, not confirmed

Date	Mintage	VG	F	VF	XF	Unc
1713	—	—	—	—	—	—

Note: Reported, not confirmed

Date	Mintage	VG	F	VF	XF	Unc
1717	—	18.00	40.00	70.00	115	—
1718	—	—	—	—	—	—

Note: Reported, not confirmed

Date	Mintage	VG	F	VF	XF	Unc
1721	—	—	—	—	—	—

Note: Reported, not confirmed

Date	Mintage	VG	F	VF	XF	Unc
1729	—	18.00	40.00	70.00	115	—
1731	—	18.00	40.00	70.00	115	—
1740	—	18.00	40.00	70.00	115	—

KM# 698 KREUZER

Silver **Ruler:** Charles VI **Obv:** Without inner circles **Rev:** Without inner circles **Note:** Varieties exist. Prev. KM#1144.

Date	Mintage	VG	F	VF	XF	Unc
1720 (ll)	—	15.00	30.00	60.00	120	—
1721 (ll)	—	15.00	30.00	60.00	120	—
1722 (ll)	—	15.00	30.00	60.00	120	—
1723 (ll)	—	15.00	30.00	60.00	120	—
1724 (ll)	—	15.00	30.00	60.00	120	—
1725 (ll)	—	15.00	30.00	60.00	120	—

KM# 708 KREUZER

Silver **Ruler:** Charles VI **Obv:** Larger bust **Rev:** Crowned imperial eagle, Bohemian arms on breast, date at end of legend **Note:** Prev. KM#1145.

Date	Mintage	VG	F	VF	XF	Unc
1726 (ll)	—	20.00	40.00	85.00	165	—

KM# 704 KREUZER

Silver **Ruler:** Charles VI **Obv:** Bust right **Rev:** Crowned imperial eagle **Note:** Prev. KM#1145.

Date	Mintage	VG	F	VF	XF	Unc
1726 (ll)	—	—	—	—	—	—

KM# 1522 KREUZER

Billon **Ruler:** Maria Theresa **Obv:** Bust right **Rev:** Crowned imperial eagle with Bohemian arms on breast; value below

Date	Mintage	VG	F	VF	XF	Unc
1744	—	—	—	—	—	—
1755	—	5.00	10.00	20.00	35.00	—
1757	—	6.50	12.50	25.00	50.00	—
1759	—	5.00	10.00	20.00	35.00	—
1760	—	5.00	10.00	20.00	35.00	—

KM# 742 KREUZER

Silver **Ruler:** Maria Theresa **Note:** Prev. KM#1552.

Date	Mintage	VG	F	VF	XF	Unc
1744	—	—	—	—	—	—

KM# 772 KREUZER

Silver **Ruler:** Maria Theresa **Obv:** Bust right, titles of Maria Theresa **Rev:** Crowned imperial eagle, Bohemian arms on breast, value "1" below, date in legend

Date	Mintage	VG	F	VF	XF	Unc
1755	—	7.00	15.00	25.00	55.00	—
1757	—	7.00	15.00	25.00	55.00	—
1759	—	7.00	15.00	25.00	55.00	—
1760	—	7.00	15.00	25.00	55.00	—

KM# 773 KREUZER

Silver **Ruler:** Franz I **Obv:** Laureate bust right, titles of Franz I **Rev:** Crowned imperial eagle, two-fold arms of Lothringen-Tuscany on breast, value "1" below, "IN TE DOMINE SPERA VI" and date

Date	Mintage	VG	F	VF	XF	Unc
1755 P-R	—	15.00	32.00	65.00	100	—

KM# 1522a KREUZER

Copper **Ruler:** Maria Theresa

Date	Mintage	VG	F	VF	XF	Unc
1760	—	3.00	7.50	15.00	50.00	—
1761	—	3.00	7.50	15.00	50.00	—
1762	—	3.00	7.50	15.00	50.00	—
1763	—	3.00	7.50	15.00	50.00	—

KM# 792 KREUZER

Copper **Ruler:** Maria Theresa **Obv:** Bust right, titles of Maria Theresa **Rev:** EIN/KREUTZER/date in baroque frame **Note:** Prev. KM#1552a.

Date	Mintage	VG	F	VF	XF	Unc
1760	—	2.00	5.00	15.00	32.00	—
1760 P	—	2.00	5.00	15.00	32.00	—
1761 P	—	2.00	5.00	15.00	32.00	—
1762 P	—	2.00	5.00	15.00	32.00	—
1763 P	—	2.00	5.00	15.00	32.00	—
1764 P	—	—	—	—	—	—

Note: Reported, not confirmed

KM# 823 KREUZER

Copper **Ruler:** Josef II **Obv:** Laureate bust right, titles of Josef II **Rev:** EIN/KREUTZER/date/mint mark in wreath of palm and laurel

Date	Mintage	VG	F	VF	XF	Unc
1782 C	—	4.00	10.00	22.00	45.00	—

KM# 840 KREUZER

Copper **Ruler:** Franz II **Obv:** Value in oval on eagle's breast

Date	Mintage	VG	F	VF	XF	Unc
1800 C	—	3.00	8.00	20.00	38.00	—
ND C	—	3.00	8.00	20.00	38.00	—

KM# 709 3 KREUZER

Silver **Ruler:** Charles VI **Obv:** Legend begins on left side, laureate bust **Note:** Varieties exist. Prev. KM#1481.

Date	Mintage	VG	F	VF	XF	Unc
1726 FS	—	10.00	20.00	35.00	65.00	—
1727 FS	—	10.00	20.00	35.00	65.00	—
1728 FS	—	10.00	20.00	35.00	65.00	—
1728	—	10.00	20.00	35.00	65.00	—
1729 FS	—	10.00	20.00	35.00	65.00	—
1729	—	10.00	20.00	35.00	65.00	—
1730	—	10.00	20.00	35.00	65.00	—
1731	—	10.00	20.00	35.00	65.00	—
1732	—	10.00	20.00	35.00	65.00	—
1733	—	10.00	20.00	35.00	65.00	—
1738	—	10.00	20.00	35.00	65.00	—
1739	—	10.00	20.00	35.00	65.00	—
1740	—	10.00	20.00	35.00	65.00	—

KM# 606 3 KREUZER

Silver **Ruler:** Leopold I **Obv:** Laureate bust right in inner circle **Note:** Varieties exist. Prev. KM#1120.

Date	Mintage	VG	F	VF	XF	Unc
1697 (jj)	—	7.00	12.00	25.00	55.00	—
1698 (jj)	—	7.00	12.00	25.00	55.00	—
1699 (jj)	—	7.00	12.00	25.00	55.00	—
1700 (jj)	—	7.00	12.00	25.00	55.00	—
1701 (jj)	—	7.00	12.00	25.00	55.00	—
1704 (ll)	—	7.00	12.00	25.00	55.00	—
1705 (mm)	—	10.00	20.00	35.00	65.00	—

KM# 590 3 KREUZER

Silver **Ruler:** Leopold I **Obv:** Bust left in long wig **Rev:** Crowned imperial arms with sword and scepter **Note:** Varieties exist. Prev. KM#1430.

Date	Mintage	VG	F	VF	XF	Unc
1701 GE	—	7.00	15.00	30.00	60.00	—
1702 GE	—	7.00	15.00	30.00	60.00	—
1720 GE Error 1702	—	7.00	15.00	30.00	60.00	—
1703 GE	—	7.00	15.00	30.00	60.00	—
1704 GE	—	7.00	15.00	30.00	60.00	—
1705 GE	—	7.00	15.00	30.00	60.00	—
1707 GE	—	7.00	15.00	30.00	60.00	—

Note: Reported, not confirmed

Date	Mintage	VG	F	VF	XF	Unc
1708 GE	—	7.00	15.00	30.00	60.00	—
1709 GE	—	7.00	15.00	30.00	60.00	—

Note: Reported, not confirmed

KM# 630 3 KREUZER

Silver **Ruler:** Joseph I **Obv:** Laureate bust right with long wig, value in oval below **Rev:** Crowned imperial eagle, oval Bohemian arms on breast **Note:** Varieties exist. Prev. KM#1137.

Date	Mintage	VG	F	VF	XF	Unc
1705 (mm)	—	5.00	10.00	22.00	45.00	—
1706 (mm)	—	5.00	10.00	22.00	45.00	—
1707 (mm)	—	5.00	10.00	22.00	45.00	—
1708 (mm)	—	5.00	10.00	22.00	45.00	—
1709 (mm)	—	5.00	10.00	22.00	45.00	—
1710 (mm)	—	5.00	10.00	22.00	45.00	—
1711 (mm)	—	5.00	10.00	22.00	45.00	—

KM# 629 3 KREUZER

Silver **Ruler:** Joseph I **Obv:** Bust left in long wig, titles of Josef I **Rev:** Crowned imperial arms with sword and scepter **Note:** Varietes exist. Prev. KM#1458.

Date	Mintage	VG	F	VF	XF	Unc
1705 GE	—	5.00	10.00	22.00	45.00	—
1706 GE	—	5.00	10.00	20.00	50.00	—
1707 GE	—	5.00	10.00	20.00	50.00	—
1708 GE	—	5.00	10.00	20.00	50.00	—
1709 GE	—	5.00	10.00	20.00	50.00	—
1710/00 GE	—	5.00	10.00	25.00	55.00	—
1710 GE	—	5.00	10.00	20.00	50.00	—
1710 PM	—	7.00	15.00	28.00	55.00	—
1711 PM	—	7.00	15.00	28.00	55.00	—
1711 IAP	—	7.00	15.00	28.00	55.00	—

KM# 656 3 KREUZER

Silver **Ruler:** Charles VI **Obv:** Laureate bust right in inner circle; value below **Rev:** Crowned imperial eagle in inner circle, crown divides date **Note:** Varieties exist. Prev. KM#1146.

Date	Mintage	VG	F	VF	XF	Unc
1712 (mm)	—	5.00	12.00	25.00	50.00	—
1713 (mm)	—	5.00	12.00	25.00	50.00	—
1714 (mm)	—	5.00	12.00	25.00	50.00	—
1715 (mm)	—	5.00	12.00	25.00	50.00	—
1716	—	5.00	12.00	25.00	50.00	—
1717 (mm)	—	—	—	—	—	—

Note: Reported, not confirmed

Date	Mintage	VG	F	VF	XF	Unc
1718 (ll)	—	5.00	12.00	25.00	50.00	—

KM# 657 3 KREUZER

Silver **Ruler:** Charles VI **Rev:** Date in legend **Note:** Prev. KM#1147.

Date	Mintage	VG	F	VF	XF	Unc
171Z (mm)	—	15.00	30.00	60.00	120	—

KM# 655 3 KREUZER

Silver **Ruler:** Charles VI **Obv:** Laureate bust right in inner circle, value below, titles of Karl VI **Rev:** Crowned imperial eagle in inner circle, date in legend **Note:** Prev. KM#1477. Varieties exist.

Date	Mintage	VG	F	VF	XF	Unc
1712	—	7.00	15.00	28.00	55.00	—
1712 IAP	—	7.00	15.00	28.00	55.00	—
1714 FS	—	7.00	15.00	28.00	55.00	—
1716	—	7.00	15.00	28.00	55.00	—

KM# 666 3 KREUZER

Silver **Ruler:** Charles VI **Obv:** Bust with long wig, no laurel wreath, no circles around central designs **Rev:** Crown divides date, no circles around central designs **Note:** Prev. KM#1478.

Date	Mintage	VG	F	VF	XF	Unc
1713	—	10.00	20.00	35.00	65.00	—
1714 FS	—	10.00	20.00	35.00	65.00	—
1715	—	10.00	20.00	35.00	65.00	—
1716	—	10.00	20.00	35.00	65.00	—

Date	Mintage	VG	F	VF	XF	Unc
1717	—	10.00	20.00	35.00	65.00	—
1718	—	10.00	20.00	35.00	65.00	—
1719	—	10.00	20.00	35.00	65.00	—

KM# 680 3 KREUZER

Silver **Ruler:** Charles VI **Obv:** Eagle holds sword and scepter in talons **Note:** Varieties exist. Prev. KM#1480.

Date	Mintage	VG	F	VF	XF	Unc
1717	—	8.00	18.00	40.00	75.00	—
1719	—	8.00	18.00	40.00	75.00	—
1720 FS	—	8.00	18.00	40.00	75.00	—
1721 FS	—	8.00	18.00	40.00	75.00	—
1722 FS	—	8.00	18.00	40.00	75.00	—
1723 FS	—	8.00	18.00	40.00	75.00	—
1724 FS	—	8.00	18.00	40.00	75.00	—
1725 FS	—	8.00	18.00	40.00	75.00	—
1726 FS	—	8.00	18.00	40.00	75.00	—

KM# 734 3 KREUZER

Silver **Ruler:** Maria Theresa **Obv:** Bust right, titles of Maria Theresa **Rev:** Four-fold arms with central shield of Bohemia in baroque frame, large crown above, value "3" in oval below, titles continuous and date **Note:** Prev. KM#1523.

Date	Mintage	VG	F	VF	XF	Unc
1743	—	25.00	50.00	100	175	—
1745	—	—	—	—	—	—

Note: Reported, not confirmed

KM# 748 3 KREUZER

Silver **Ruler:** Maria Theresa **Obv:** Bust right, titles of Maria Theresa **Rev:** Crowned imperial eagle, Bohemian arms on breast; value "3" in small shield below, titles continued and date **Note:** Varieties exist. Prev. KM#1519.

Date	Mintage	VG	F	VF	XF	Unc
1746	—	8.00	18.00	40.00	75.00	—
Note: Reported, not confirmed						
1747	—	8.00	18.00	40.00	75.00	—
Note: Reported, not confirmed						
1750	—	8.00	18.00	40.00	75.00	—
1752	—	8.00	18.00	40.00	75.00	—
1753	—	8.00	18.00	40.00	75.00	—
1758	—	8.00	18.00	40.00	75.00	—
1761	—	8.00	18.00	40.00	75.00	—
1762	—	8.00	18.00	40.00	75.00	—
1762/1	—	8.00	18.00	40.00	75.00	—
1764	—	8.00	18.00	40.00	75.00	—
1765	—	8.00	18.00	40.00	75.00	—

KM# 783 3 KREUZER

Silver **Ruler:** Maria Theresa **Obv:** Armored bust **Note:** Prev. KM#1524.

Date	Mintage	VG	F	VF	XF	Unc
1758 Rare	—	—	—	—	—	—

KM# 811 3 KREUZER

Silver **Ruler:** Maria Theresa **Obv:** Bust right wearing head covering, titles of Maria Theresa **Rev:** Crowned imperial eagle, "3" in oval on breast, titles continuous and date **Note:** Prev. KM#1525.

Date	Mintage	VG	F	VF	XF	Unc
1776 C/VSK	—	15.00	30.00	65.00	135	—
1777 C/VSK	—	15.00	30.00	65.00	135	—
1777 VSK Without mint mark	—	15.00	30.00	65.00	135	—
1778 C/VSK	—	15.00	30.00	65.00	135	—
1779 C/VSK	—	15.00	30.00	65.00	135	—

KM# 760 3 KREUZER (Groschen)

Silver **Ruler:** Maria Theresa **Obv:** Value "3" in small shield at bottom

Date	Mintage	VG	F	VF	XF	Unc
1750 P-R	—	—	—	—	—	—
1753 P-R	—	—	—	—	—	—
1754 P-R	—	—	—	—	—	—
1761 P-R	—	—	—	—	—	—

KM# 810 3 KREUZER (Groschen)

Silver **Ruler:** Josef II **Obv:** Laureate bust right, titles of Josef II **Rev:** Crowned imperial eagle, "3" in oval on breast, VIRTUTE ET EXEMPLO, date

Date	Mintage	VG	F	VF	XF	Unc
1775 C-VS-K	—	—	—	—	—	—
1776 C-VS-K	—	—	—	—	—	—
1777 C-VS-K	—	—	—	—	—	—
1778 C-VS-K	—	—	—	—	—	—
1779 C-VS-K	—	—	—	—	—	—

KM# 837 3 KREUZER (Groschen)

Copper **Ruler:** Josef II **Obv:** Value in oval on eagle's breast

Date	Mintage	VG	F	VF	XF	Unc
1799 C	—	2.50	5.00	10.00	25.00	—
1800 C	—	2.50	5.00	10.00	25.00	—

KM# 722 6 KREUZER

Silver **Ruler:** Charles VI **Obv:** Laureate bust right, titles of Karl VI **Rev:** Crowned imperial eagle holding sword and scepter in talons, crowned Bohemian arms on breast, value "VI" in cartouche at bottom, date in legend **Note:** Prev. KM#1482.

Date	Mintage	VG	F	VF	XF	Unc
1732	—	7.00	15.00	28.00	55.00	—
1733	—	7.00	15.00	28.00	55.00	—
1734	—	7.00	15.00	28.00	55.00	—
1735	—	7.00	15.00	28.00	55.00	—
1736	—	7.00	15.00	28.00	55.00	—
1740	—	7.00	15.00	28.00	55.00	—

KM# 735 6 KREUZER

Silver **Ruler:** Maria Theresa **Obv:** Bust right **Rev:** Crowned arms in cartouche; value below **Note:** Varieties exist. Prev. KM#1526.

Date	Mintage	VG	F	VF	XF	Unc
1743	—	12.00	30.00	65.00	115	—
1744	—	12.00	30.00	65.00	115	—

KM# 736 6 KREUZER

Silver **Ruler:** Maria Theresa **Rev:** Value "VI" below arms **Note:** Prev. KM#1527.

Date	Mintage	VG	F	VF	XF	Unc
1746	—	18.00	40.00	70.00	120	—
1747	—	18.00	40.00	70.00	120	—

KM# 753 6 KREUZER

Silver **Ruler:** Franz II **Rev:** Value "VI" at bottom

Date	Mintage	VG	F	VF	XF	Unc
1747 P-R	—	—	—	—	—	—
1748 P-R	—	—	—	—	—	—

KM# 827 6 KREUZER

Silver **Ruler:** Franz II **Obv:** Crowned imperial eagle, Austria-Lothringen arms on breast, titles of Franz II **Rev:** 6/KRAUZER /date/mint mark, crossed palm and laurel branches below

Date	Mintage	VG	F	VF	XF	Unc
1795 C	—	28.00	60.00	100	165	—

KM# 841 6 KREUZER

Silver **Ruler:** Franz II **Obv:** Value "6" in oval on eagle's breast

Date	Mintage	VG	F	VF	XF	Unc
1800 C	—	3.00	6.00	15.00	28.00	—

KM# 795 7 KREUZER

Silver **Ruler:** Franz I **Rev:** Value "VII" at bottom

Date	Mintage	VG	F	VF	XF	Unc
1762 P-R	—	18.00	40.00	70.00	120	—
1763 P-R	—	18.00	40.00	70.00	120	—
1764 P-R	—	18.00	40.00	70.00	120	—
1765 P-R	—	18.00	40.00	70.00	120	—

KM# 767 10 KREUZER

Silver **Ruler:** Franz I **Obv:** Bust and titles of Franz I **Rev:** IN TE...

Date	Mintage	VG	F	VF	XF	Unc
1754 P-R	—	—	—	—	—	—
Note: Reported, not confirmed						
1755 P-R	—	—	—	—	—	—
Note: Reported, not confirmed						
1756 P-R	—	—	—	—	—	—
Note: Reported, not confirmed						
1757 P-R	—	—	—	—	—	—
Note: Reported, not confirmed						
1758 P-R	—	10.00	20.00	35.00	65.00	—
1759 P-R	—	10.00	20.00	35.00	65.00	—
1760 P-R	—	—	—	—	—	—
Note: Reported, not confirmed						
1761 P-R	—	10.00	20.00	35.00	65.00	—
1762 P-R	—	—	—	—	—	—
Note: Reported, not confirmed						
1763 P-R	—	10.00	20.00	35.00	65.00	—
1764 P-R	—	10.00	20.00	35.00	65.00	—

KM# 784 10 KREUZER

Silver **Ruler:** Maria Theresa **Obv:** Bust right between palm and laurel branches, titles of Maria Theresa **Rev:** Crowned imperial eagle, Bohemian arms on breast above pedestal, date in legend

Date	Mintage	VG	F	VF	XF	Unc
1758	—	8.00	18.00	40.00	75.00	—
1759	—	8.00	18.00	40.00	75.00	—
1760	—	8.00	18.00	40.00	75.00	—
1763	—	8.00	18.00	40.00	75.00	—
1764	—	8.00	18.00	40.00	75.00	—
1765	—	8.00	18.00	40.00	75.00	—
1766/5	—	8.00	18.00	40.00	75.00	—
1766	—	8.00	18.00	40.00	75.00	—
1768	—	8.00	18.00	40.00	75.00	—

KM# 1528 10 KREUZER

Silver **Ruler:** Maria Theresa **Note:** Varieties exist.

Date	Mintage	VG	F	VF	XF	Unc
1758	—	20.00	40.00	75.00	150	—
1759	—	15.00	30.00	65.00	110	—
1760	—	5.00	12.50	30.00	80.00	—
1763	—	5.00	12.50	30.00	80.00	—
1764	—	5.00	12.50	30.00	80.00	—
1765	—	5.00	12.50	30.00	80.00	—

KM# 813 10 KREUZER

Silver **Ruler:** Maria Theresa **Obv:** Bust right between palm and laurel branches, titles of Maria Theresa **Rev:** Crowned imperial eagle, Bohemian arms on breast above pedestal, date in legend **Note:** Prev. KM#1529.

Date	Mintage	VG	F	VF	XF	Unc
1777 VSK	—	—	—	—	—	—
1778 VSK	—	—	—	—	—	—
1779 VSK	—	—	—	—	—	—
1780 VSK	—	—	—	—	—	—

KM# 814 10 KREUZER

Silver **Ruler:** Josef II **Obv:** Bust and titles of Josef II **Rev:** VIRTUTE...

Date	Mintage	VG	F	VF	XF	Unc
1777 C/VS-K	—	—	—	—	—	—
1778 C/VS-K	—	—	—	—	—	—
1779 C/VS-K	—	—	—	—	—	—

KM# 819 10 KREUZER

Silver **Ruler:** Josef II **Obv:** Titles continuous **Rev:** Date

Date	Mintage	VG	F	VF	XF	Unc
1781 C	—	—	—	—	—	—
1782 C	—	—	—	—	—	—

KM# 828 10 KREUZER

Silver **Ruler:** Franz II **Obv:** Bust and titles of Franz II

Date	Mintage	VG	F	VF	XF	Unc
1795 C	—	45.00	100	175	300	—

KM# 829 12 KREUZER

Silver **Ruler:** Franz II **Rev:** Value

Date	Mintage	VG	F	VF	XF	Unc
1795 C	—	10.00	20.00	35.00	65.00	—

KM# 715 15 KREUZER

Silver **Ruler:** Charles VI **Rev:** Value in Roman numerals at bottom **Note:** Prev. KM#1483.

Date	Mintage	VG	F	VF	XF	Unc
1728	—	12.00	30.00	65.00	115	—
1732	—	12.00	30.00	65.00	115	—
1733	—	12.00	30.00	65.00	115	—
1734	—	12.00	30.00	65.00	115	—
1736	—	12.00	30.00	65.00	115	—
1737	—	12.00	30.00	65.00	115	—
1738	—	12.00	30.00	65.00	115	—
1740	—	12.00	30.00	65.00	115	—

KM# 724 15 KREUZER

Silver **Ruler:** Charles VI **Rev:** Value in Arabic numerals, "15" at bottom **Note:** Prev. KM#1484.

Date	Mintage	VG	F	VF	XF	Unc
1735	—	12.00	30.00	65.00	115	—

KM# 737 15 KREUZER

Silver **Ruler:** Maria Theresa **Obv:** Bust right **Rev:** Crowned arms in branches, value at bottom **Note:** Prev. KM#1530.

Date	Mintage	VG	F	VF	XF	Unc
1743	—	12.00	30.00	65.00	115	—
1744/3	—	12.00	30.00	65.00	115	—
1744	—	12.00	30.00	65.00	115	—
1745	—	12.00	30.00	65.00	115	—

KM# 754 15 KREUZER

Silver **Ruler:** Maria Theresa **Rev:** Crowned imperial eagle with crowned Bohemian arms on breast, value below **Rev. Legend:** COM TYR **Note:** Prev. KM#1531.1.

Date	Mintage	VG	F	VF	XF	Unc
1747	—	12.00	30.00	65.00	115	—
1748	—	12.00	30.00	65.00	115	—

KM# 755 15 KREUZER

Silver **Ruler:** Franz I **Rev:** "XV" at bottom **Note:** Varieties exist. Prev. KM#1531.1.

Date	Mintage	VG	F	VF	XF	Unc
1747 P-R	—	22.00	50.00	95.00	155	—
1748 P-R	—	22.00	50.00	95.00	155	—
1749 P-R	—	22.00	50.00	95.00	155	—
1750 P-R	—	22.00	50.00	95.00	155	—

KM# 758 15 KREUZER

Silver **Ruler:** Maria Theresa **Rev. Legend:** SI.M.MO **Note:** Varieties exist. Prev. KM#1531.2.

Date	Mintage	VG	F	VF	XF	Unc
1749	—	12.00	30.00	65.00	115	—
1750	—	12.00	30.00	65.00	115	—
1752	—	—	—	—	—	—

Note: Reported, not confirmed

KM# 763 17 KREUZER

Silver **Ruler:** Franz I **Rev:** "XVII" at bottom **Note:** Prev. KM#1532.

Date	Mintage	VG	F	VF	XF	Unc
1751 P-R	—	10.00	25.00	45.00	80.00	—
1752 P-R	—	10.00	25.00	45.00	80.00	—
1753 P-R	—	10.00	25.00	45.00	80.00	—
1754 P-R	—	10.00	25.00	45.00	80.00	—
1762 P-R	—	10.00	25.00	45.00	80.00	—
1763 P-R	—	10.00	25.00	45.00	80.00	—

KM# 762 17 KREUZER

Silver **Ruler:** Franz I **Obv:** Bust right **Rev:** Crowned imperial eagle, arms on breast, value "XVII" or "20" at bottom **Note:** Varieties exist. Prev. KM#1532.

Date	Mintage	VG	F	VF	XF	Unc
1751	—	10.00	20.00	35.00	65.00	—
1752	—	10.00	20.00	35.00	65.00	—
1753	—	10.00	20.00	35.00	65.00	—
1754	—	10.00	20.00	35.00	65.00	—
1755	—	10.00	20.00	35.00	65.00	—
1761	—	10.00	20.00	35.00	65.00	—
1762	—	10.00	20.00	35.00	65.00	—
1763/2	—	10.00	20.00	35.00	65.00	—
1763	—	10.00	20.00	35.00	65.00	—

KM# 769 20 KREUZER

Silver **Ruler:** Franz I **Obv:** Bust of Franz I **Rev:** IN TE... **Note:** Dates 1761-65 are reporterd but not confirmed for this type.

Date	Mintage	VG	F	VF	XF	Unc
1754 P-R	—	7.00	15.00	28.00	55.00	—
1755 P-R	—	7.00	15.00	28.00	55.00	—
1756 P-R	—	7.00	15.00	28.00	55.00	—
1757 P-R	—	7.00	15.00	28.00	55.00	—
1758 P-R	—	7.00	15.00	28.00	55.00	—
1759 P-R	—	7.00	15.00	28.00	55.00	—
1760 P-R	—	7.00	15.00	28.00	55.00	—

KM# 768 20 KREUZER

Silver **Ruler:** Franz I **Rev:** Value "20" on pedestal **Note:** Varieties exist. Prev. KM#1533.

Date	Mintage	VG	F	VF	XF	Unc
1754	251,000	5.00	10.00	22.00	45.00	—
1755	521,000	5.00	10.00	22.00	45.00	—
1756	822,000	5.00	10.00	22.00	45.00	—
1757	840,000	5.00	10.00	22.00	45.00	—
1758	1,413,000	5.00	10.00	22.00	45.00	—
1759	615,000	5.00	10.00	22.00	45.00	—
1760	831,000	5.00	10.00	22.00	45.00	—
1761	1,123,000	5.00	10.00	22.00	45.00	—
1763	2,485,000	5.00	10.00	22.00	45.00	—
1764/3	1,353,000	5.00	10.00	22.00	45.00	—
1764	Inc. above	5.00	10.00	22.00	45.00	—
1765	934,000	5.00	10.00	22.00	45.00	—

KM# 799 20 KREUZER

Silver **Ruler:** Josef II **Rev:** Value at bottom

Date	Mintage	VG	F	VF	XF	Unc
1766 C/EvS-AS	—	7.00	15.00	28.00	55.00	—
1767 C/EvS-AS	—	7.00	15.00	28.00	55.00	—
1767 EvS-AS	—	7.00	15.00	28.00	55.00	—
1768 C/EvS-AS	—	7.00	15.00	28.00	55.00	—
1769 C/EvS-AS	—	7.00	15.00	28.00	55.00	—
1770 C/EvS-AS	—	7.00	15.00	28.00	55.00	—
1771 C/EvS-AS	—	7.00	15.00	28.00	55.00	—
1772 C/EvS-AS	—	7.00	15.00	28.00	55.00	—
1773 C/EvS-AS	—	7.00	15.00	28.00	55.00	—
1773 C/EvS-IK	—	7.00	15.00	28.00	55.00	—
1774 C/EvS-IK	—	7.00	15.00	28.00	55.00	—
1775 C/EvS-IK	—	7.00	15.00	28.00	55.00	—
1776 C/EvS-IK	—	7.00	15.00	28.00	55.00	—
1777 C/EvS-IK	—	7.00	15.00	28.00	55.00	—
1778 C/EvS-IK	—	7.00	15.00	28.00	55.00	—
1779 C/EvS-IK	—	7.00	15.00	28.00	55.00	—
1780 C/EvS-IK	—	7.00	15.00	28.00	55.00	—

KM# 800 20 KREUZER

Silver **Ruler:** Maria Theresa **Rev:** Value "20" below arms **Note:** Prev. KM#1534.

Date	Mintage	VG	F	VF	XF	Unc
1768 EvS-AS	1,120,000	4.00	8.00	18.00	38.00	—
1769 EvS-AS	1,163,000	4.00	8.00	18.00	38.00	—
1770 EvS-AS	1,276,000	4.00	8.00	18.00	38.00	—
1771 EvS-AS	1,480,000	4.00	8.00	18.00	38.00	—
1772 EvS-AS	1,249,000	4.00	8.00	18.00	38.00	—
1773 EvS-AS	Inc. above	4.00	8.00	18.00	38.00	—
1773/2 EvS-AS	1,069,000	4.00	8.00	18.00	38.00	—
1774 EvS-IK	1,059,000	5.00	10.00	22.00	45.00	—
1775 EvS-IK	728,000	5.00	10.00	22.00	45.00	—
1776 EvS-IK	1,195,000	5.00	10.00	22.00	45.00	—
1777 EvS-IK	1,163,000	5.00	10.00	22.00	45.00	—
1778 EvS-IK	1,458,000	5.00	10.00	22.00	45.00	—
1779 EvS-IK	786,000	5.00	10.00	22.00	45.00	—
1780 EvS-IK	1,117,000	5.00	10.00	22.00	45.00	—

KM# 820 20 KREUZER

Silver **Ruler:** Josef II **Rev:** Date in legend

Date	Mintage	VG	F	VF	XF	Unc
1781 C	—	5.00	12.00	25.00	50.00	—
1782 C	—	5.00	12.00	25.00	50.00	—

KM# 824 20 KREUZER

Silver **Ruler:** Josef II **Obv:** Bare bust **Rev:** Date in legend

Date	Mintage	VG	F	VF	XF	Unc
1782 C	—	5.00	12.00	25.00	50.00	—
1783 C	—	5.00	12.00	25.00	50.00	—
1784 C	—	5.00	12.00	25.00	50.00	—

KM# 830 20 KREUZER

Silver **Ruler:** Franz II **Obv:** Bust and titles of Franz II

Date	Mintage	VG	F	VF	XF	Unc
1795 C	—	4.00	7.00	16.00	35.00	—
1796 C	—	4.00	7.00	16.00	35.00	—
1797 C	—	4.00	7.00	16.00	35.00	—

KM# 843 24 KREUZER

Silver **Ruler:** Franz II **Rev:** Value (24)

Date	Mintage	VG	F	VF	XF	Unc
1800 C	—	75.00	140	225	360	—

KM# 785 30 KREUZER

Silver **Ruler:** Maria Theresa **Obv:** Bust right, value below in rhombus, titles of Maria Theresa along four segments of rhombus **Rev:** Crowned imperial eagle, Bohemian arms on breast in rhombus, titles continuous and date in segments **Note:** Prev. KM#1549.

Date	Mintage	VG	F	VF	XF	Unc
1758	—	22.00	50.00	95.00	155	—
1763	—	22.00	50.00	95.00	155	—
1764	—	22.00	50.00	95.00	155	—
1765	—	22.00	50.00	95.00	155	—
1765 Rare	—	22.00	50.00	95.00	155	—

Note: Without value

KM# 798 30 KREUZER

Silver **Ruler:** Franz I **Rev:** Without value

Date	Mintage	VG	F	VF	XF	Unc
1764	—	—	—	—	—	—
1765	—	—	—	—	—	—

KM# 683 1/4 THALER

Silver **Ruler:** Charles VI **Obv:** Laureate armored bust with long wig right, titles of Karl VI **Rev:** Crowned imperial eagle with central shield of Bohemia on breast, date in legend **Note:** Prev. KM#1148.

Date	Mintage	VG	F	VF	XF	Unc
1715 (II)	—	45.00	90.00	175	350	—
1719 (II)	—	45.00	90.00	175	350	—

KM# 718 1/4 THALER

Silver **Ruler:** Charles VI **Obv:** Bust right with plain cloak and shorter hair **Rev:** Crowned imperial eagle; date in legend **Note:** Prev. KM#1485.1.

Date	Mintage	VG	F	VF	XF	Unc
1729	—	275	600	1,000	1,650	—
1730	—	275	600	1,000	1,650	—

KM# 720 1/4 THALER

Silver **Ruler:** Charles VI **Obv:** Value added below bust **Note:** Prev. KM#1485.2.

Date	Mintage	VG	F	VF	XF	Unc
1731	—	350	725	1,125	1,800	—
1732	—	350	725	1,125	1,800	—
1736	—	350	725	1,125	1,800	—

KM# 723 1/4 THALER

Silver **Ruler:** Charles VI **Note:** Error: Value "1/2" below bust. Prev. KM#1487.

Date	Mintage	VG	F	VF	XF	Unc
1732 Rare	—	—	—	—	—	—

KM# 728 1/4 THALER

Silver **Ruler:** Charles VI **Obv:** Modified bust and shield **Note:** Prev. KM#1486.

Date	Mintage	VG	F	VF	XF	Unc
1739	—	75.00	175	375	650	—
1740	—	75.00	175	375	650	—

KM# 744 1/4 THALER

Silver **Ruler:** Maria Theresa **Obv:** Bust right **Rev:** Crowned 4-fold arms, lion on center shield in cartouche, no indication of value **Note:** Prev. KM#1535.

Date	Mintage	VG	F	VF	XF	Unc
1744 Rare	—	—	—	—	—	—

KM# 770 1/4 THALER

Silver **Ruler:** Maria Theresa **Rev:** Crowned imperial eagle with square manifold arms on breast **Note:** Prev. KM#1536.

Date	Mintage	VG	F	VF	XF	Unc
1754 Rare	—	—	—	—	—	—
1759 Rare	—	—	—	—	—	—

KM# 831 1/4 THALER

Silver **Ruler:** Franz II **Obv:** Laureate bust right, titles of Franz II **Rev:** Ornate cross in X position, three crowns and Order of the Golden Fleece in angles, date in legend

Date	Mintage	VG	F	VF	XF	Unc
1795 C	—	18.00	40.00	70.00	1,120	—
1796 (C)	—	18.00	40.00	70.00	1,120	—
1797 (C)	—	18.00	40.00	70.00	1,120	—

KM# 620 1/2 THALER

Silver **Ruler:** Leopold I **Obv:** Tall laureate bust **Note:** Varieties exist. Prev. KM#1438.3.

Date	Mintage	VG	F	VF	XF	Unc
1702 GE	—	65.00	125	250	425	—
1703 GE	—	65.00	125	250	425	—
1704 GE	—	65.00	125	250	425	—

KM# 642 1/2 THALER

Silver **Ruler:** Joseph I **Obv:** Large laureate bust right, titles of Josef I **Rev:** Crowned imperial eagle holding sword and scepter **Note:** Prev. KM#642.

Date	Mintage	VG	F	VF	XF	Unc
1709 GE	—	75.00	150	250	400	—
1710 PM	—	75.00	150	250	400	—

KM# 658 1/2 THALER

Silver **Ruler:** Charles VI **Obv:** Laureate bust right **Rev:** Crowned imperial eagle, oval Bohemian shield on breast; date in legend **Note:** Prev. KM#1149.

Date	Mintage	VG	F	VF	XF	Unc
1712 (mm)	—	120	275	550	925	—

KM# 668 1/2 THALER

Silver **Ruler:** Charles VI **Obv:** Inner circle added **Rev:** Inner circle added **Note:** Prev. KM#1150.

Date	Mintage	VG	F	VF	XF	Unc
1713 (II)	—	65.00	120	200	325	—
1714 (II)	—	65.00	120	200	325	—
1715 (II)	—	65.00	120	200	325	—
1716 (II)	—	65.00	120	200	325	—
1717 (II)	—	90.00	200	375	800	—

KM# 667 1/2 THALER

Silver **Ruler:** Charles VI **Obv:** Laureate armored bust with long wig right **Rev:** Crowned imperial eagle with central shield of Bohemia on breast **Note:** Prev. KM#1488.

Date	Mintage	VG	F	VF	XF	Unc
1713	—	125	325	575	1,000	—
1714	—	125	325	575	1,000	—
1716	—	125	325	575	1,000	—

KM# 688 1/2 THALER

Silver **Ruler:** Charles VI **Obv:** Bust draped with antique cloak **Note:** Varieties exist. Prev. KM#1151.

Date	Mintage	VG	F	VF	XF	Unc
1717	—	65.00	120	200	325	—
1718 (II)	—	65.00	120	200	325	—
1719	—	65.00	120	200	325	—
1720/19	—	65.00	120	200	325	—
1721/0	—	65.00	120	200	325	—
1721 (II)	—	65.00	120	200	325	—
1722 (nn)	—	65.00	120	200	325	—
1723 (nn)	—	65.00	120	200	325	—
1724 (nn)	—	65.00	120	200	325	—
1725/4	—	65.00	120	200	325	—
1725 (nn)	—	65.00	120	200	325	—
1726 (nn)	—	65.00	120	200	325	—

KM# 691 1/2 THALER

Silver **Ruler:** Charles VI **Obv:** Undraped bust

Date	Mintage	VG	F	VF	XF	Unc
1720 (II)	—	65.00	120	200	325	—

KM# 713 1/2 THALER

Silver **Ruler:** Charles VI **Obv:** Bare bust **Note:** Varieties exist. Prev. KM#1490.

Date	Mintage	VG	F	VF	XF	Unc
1726 FS	—	65.00	120	200	325	—
1727 FS	—	65.00	120	200	325	—
1728	—	90.00	200	375	800	—
1729	—	90.00	200	375	800	—
1730	—	90.00	200	375	800	—
1731	—	90.00	200	375	800	—
1732	—	90.00	200	375	800	—
1735	—	90.00	200	375	800	—
1737	—	90.00	200	375	800	—
1738	—	90.00	200	375	800	—
1739	—	90.00	200	375	800	—

KM# 730 1/2 THALER

Silver **Ruler:** Charles VI **Obv:** Laureate armored bust with shorter hair **Note:** Reduced size. Called "Notgulden". Struck in 1742 from low alloy silver. Prev. KM#1491.

Date	Mintage	VG	F	VF	XF	Unc
1740	—	85.00	160	275	600	—

KM# 738 1/2 THALER

Silver **Ruler:** Maria Theresa **Obv:** Bust right **Rev:** Crowned arms in branches with central shield of Bohemia in baroque frame, date in legend **Note:** Varieties exist. Prev. KM#1537.

Date	Mintage	VG	F	VF	XF	Unc
1742	—	98.00	200	375	800	—
1743	—	98.00	200	375	800	—
1744	—	98.00	200	375	800	—
1745	—	98.00	200	375	800	—

KM# 764 1/2 THALER

Silver **Ruler:** Maria Theresa **Rev:** Crowned imperial eagle with large manifold arms on breast **Note:** Prev. KM#1538.

Date	Mintage	VG	F	VF	XF	Unc
1751	—	35.00	75.00	150	300	—
1754	—	35.00	75.00	150	300	—
1758	—	35.00	75.00	150	300	—
1759	—	35.00	75.00	150	300	—
1761	—	35.00	75.00	150	300	—
1765	—	35.00	75.00	150	300	—

KM# 832 1/2 THALER

Silver **Ruler:** Franz II **Obv:** Laureate bust right

Date	Mintage	VG	F	VF	XF	Unc
1795 C	—	115	—	—	—	—
1796 C	—	115	—	—	—	—
1797 C	—	115	—	—	—	—

KM# 621 THALER

Silver **Ruler:** Leopold I **Obv:** Narrow bust **Rev:** Eagle with oval arms **Note:** Dav. #1006. Prev. KM#1440.3.

Date	Mintage	VG	F	VF	XF	Unc
1702 GE	—	85.00	145	275	650	—

KM# 624 THALER

Silver **Ruler:** Leopold I **Obv:** New bust with different armor **Rev:** Eagle with thicker tail **Note:** Dav. #1007. Prev. KM#1440.4.

Date	Mintage	VG	F	VF	XF	Unc
1703 GE	—	85.00	145	275	650	—
1704 GE	—	85.00	145	275	650	—

KM# 631 THALER

Silver **Ruler:** Leopold I **Obv:** Different bust with more curls in longer hair **Rev:** Smaller eagle, tail not breaking border **Note:** Prev. KM#1440.5. Dav. #1008. Varieties exist.

Date	Mintage	VG	F	VF	XF	Unc
1705 GE	—	85.00	145	275	650	—

KM# 636 THALER

Silver **Ruler:** Joseph I **Obv:** Laureate bust right, titles of Josef I **Obv. Legend:** IOSEPHUS.D:G:ROMAN:IM-P:SEMPERA.A: **Rev:** Similar to KM#1460.3 **Note:** Prev. KM#1460.1. Dav. #1024.

Date	Mintage	VG	F	VF	XF	Unc
1706 GE	—	150	275	450	750	—

KM# 637 THALER

Silver **Ruler:** Joseph I **Obv. Legend:** D:G.-ROMAN:IMP:-SEMPER.AV **Rev:** G.E. in different cartouche **Note:** Prev. KM#1460.2. Dav. #1025.

Date	Mintage	VG	F	VF	XF	Unc
1706	—	100	185	325	550	—
1707	—	100	185	325	550	—

KM# 640 THALER
Silver **Ruler:** Joseph I **Obv. Legend:** D:G:ROMAN:IMP: **Rev:** Large arms **Note:** Prev. KM#1460.3.

Date	Mintage	VG	F	VF	XF	Unc
1707 GE	—	100	185	325	550	—

KM# 643 THALER
Silver **Ruler:** Joseph I **Obv. Legend:** IOSEPHUS.D:G:-ROM:IMP:-SEMP:AU **Rev. Legend:** GERMAN:HUNG:-ET.BOHEMIAE.REX **Note:** Prev. KM#1460.4. Dav. #1026. Varieties exist.

Date	Mintage	VG	F	VF	XF	Unc
1709 GE	—	90.00	165	275	450	—
1710 PM	—	90.00	165	275	450	—

KM# 648 THALER
Silver **Ruler:** Joseph I **Obv:** Laureate bust right in inner circle **Note:** Prev. KM#1138.

Date	Mintage	VG	F	VF	XF	Unc
1711 (mm)	—	250	500	800	1,100	—

KM# 649 THALER
Silver **Ruler:** Charles VI **Obv:** Bust right, legend below bust **Rev:** Crowned double-headed eagle with complex arms on breast, date in legend **Note:** Dav. #1065. Prev. KM#1492.

Date	Mintage	VG	F	VF	XF	Unc
1711 Rare	—	—	—	—	—	—

KM# 659 THALER
Silver **Ruler:** Charles VI **Obv:** Laureate bust right **Note:** Dav. #1066. Prev. KM#1493.1.

Date	Mintage	VG	F	VF	XF	Unc
1712 IAP	—	75.00	150	275	475	—

KM# 660 THALER
Silver **Ruler:** Charles VI **Obv:** Legend ends AV **Rev:** Date is 171Z **Note:** Dav. #1067. Varieties exist. Prev. KM#1493.2.

Date	Mintage	VG	F	VF	XF	Unc
1712 IAP	—	75.00	150	275	475	—

KM# 661 THALER
Silver **Ruler:** Charles VI **Obv:** Laureate, armored bust **Rev:** Smaller arms on breast of eagle **Note:** Dav. #1088. Prev. KM#1152.

Date	Mintage	VG	F	VF	XF	Unc
1712 (mm)	—	250	450	750	1,250	—
1715 (mm)	—	—	—	—	—	—

Note: Reported, not confirmed

KM# 1494 THALER
Silver **Ruler:** Charles VI **Obv:** Legend begins at left **Rev:** Crown divides date **Note:** Dav. #1068.

Date	Mintage	VG	F	VF	XF	Unc
1713	—	100	200	350	550	—

KM# 1495 THALER
Silver **Ruler:** Charles VI **Obv:** Legend begins at top right and continues below bust **Obv. Legend:** CAROLUS • VI • D: G: R: I: .... **Rev:** Oval shield on eagle's breast **Note:** Dav. #1069. Varieties exist.

Date	Mintage	VG	F	VF	XF	Unc
1713 IGR	—	85.00	150	250	400	—
1714 IGR	—	85.00	150	250	400	—

KM# 1496 THALER
Silver **Ruler:** Charles VI **Obv:** Bust right in beaded circle **Rev:** Shield on eagle's breast **Note:** Dav/ #1070.

Date	Mintage	VG	F	VF	XF	Unc
1715	—	75.00	100	200	375	—
1716	—	75.00	100	200	375	—

KM# 1497 THALER
Silver **Ruler:** Charles VI **Obv:** Without beaded circle **Rev:** Shield on eagle's breast **Note:** Dav. #1071. Varieties exist with 2 rosettes after date. These command a premium of about twice the regular value. Reverse legend varieties exist with "SIL" or "SILE".

Date	Mintage	VG	F	VF	XF	Unc
1716	—	75.00	100	200	375	—
1717	—	75.00	100	200	375	—

KM# 1498.1 THALER
Silver **Ruler:** Charles VI **Obv:** Thinner bust **Obv. Legend:** CAROLVI • D: G: R: I: S: A: GE: HI: HU: BO: REX• **Rev:** Shield within Order collar on eagle's breast **Note:** Dav. #1072.

Date	Mintage	VG	F	VF	XF	Unc
1717	—	85.00	150	250	400	—

KM# 1498.2 THALER

Silver **Ruler:** Charles VI **Obv:** Different bust, without star after legend **Note:** Dav. #1073. Varieties exist with 2 rosettes after date. These command a premium of about twice the regular value.

Date	Mintage	VG	F	VF	XF	Unc
1717 IIL	—	100	200	350	550	—

KM# 1499 THALER

Silver **Ruler:** Charles VI **Obv:** Laureate bust right **Rev:** Two shields on eagle's breast **Note:** Mining Thaler. Dav. #1074.

Date	Mintage	VG	F	VF	XF	Unc
1717	—	450	750	1,200	2,000	—
1718 Rare	—	—	—	—	—	—

KM# 1501.1 THALER

Silver **Ruler:** Charles VI **Obv:** Armored bust right **Rev:** Shield within Order collar on eagle's breast **Note:** Dav. #1075.

Date	Mintage	VG	F	VF	XF	Unc
1718	—	85.00	150	250	400	—

KM# 1501.2 THALER

Silver **Ruler:** Charles VI **Obv:** Smaller bust and head **Note:** Dav. #1076. Varieties exist.

Date	Mintage	VG	F	VF	XF	Unc
1718	—	85.00	150	250	400	—

KM# 1500 THALER

Silver **Ruler:** Charles VI **Obv:** Legend begins at upper right **Rev:** Two shields on eagle's breast **Note:** Dav. #1077.

Date	Mintage	VG	F	VF	XF	Unc
1718	—	450	750	1,200	2,000	—

KM# 1502.2 THALER

Silver **Ruler:** Charles VI **Obv:** Laureate bust right **Obv. Legend:** CAR VI D.G.R.I.S.A.G.. **Rev:** Tail extends to edge of coin **Note:** Dav. #1079.

Date	Mintage	VG	F	VF	XF	Unc
1719	—	85.00	150	250	400	—

KM# 694 THALER

Silver **Ruler:** Charles VI **Obv:** Bust without drapery **Note:** Dav. #1080. Prev. KM#1502.3.

Date	Mintage	VG	F	VF	XF	Unc
1719	—	125	200	350	600	—
1720	—	125	200	350	600	—

KM# 700 THALER

Silver **Ruler:** Charles VI **Obv:** Armored bust right, legend begins at upper right **Rev:** Tail spread wide, legend and FS monogram below **Note:** Dav. #1081. Prev. KM#1502.4.

Date	Mintage	VG	F	VF	XF	Unc
1720	—	100	200	350	550	—
1720 FS	—	100	200	350	550	—
1721 FS	—	100	200	350	550	—
1722 FS	—	100	200	350	550	—
1724 FS	—	100	200	350	550	—

KM# 1502.5 THALER

Silver **Ruler:** Charles VI **Obv:** Bust right with low neck on armor **Obv. Legend:** CAROL.VI **Rev:** Different shaped arms on eagle, different tail **Note:** Dav. #1082.

Date	Mintage	VG	F	VF	XF	Unc
1723	—	85.00	150	250	400	—

KM# 1502.6 THALER

Silver **Ruler:** Charles VI **Obv:** Shorter bust **Obv. Legend:** CAR.vi D.G **Note:** Dav. #1083.

Date	Mintage	VG	F	VF	XF	Unc
1725 FS	—	85.00	150	250	400	—

KM# 1502.7 THALER

Silver **Ruler:** Charles VI **Obv:** Armored bust right, legend begins at 8 o'clock **Obv. Legend:** CAROL:VI **Note:** Dav. #1083.

Date	Mintage	VG	F	VF	XF	Unc
1726 FS	—	75.00	100	200	375	—
1727 FS	—	75.00	100	200	375	—

KM# 1502.8 THALER

Silver **Ruler:** Charles VI **Rev:** Tail extends to rim of coin, without monogram **Note:** Dav. #1085. Varieties exist.

Date	Mintage	VG	F	VF	XF	Unc
1727	—	60.00	90.00	175	300	—
1728	—	60.00	90.00	175	300	—

KM# 1503.1 THALER

Silver **Ruler:** Charles VI **Obv:** Armored laureate bust right **Rev:** Shield on eagle's breast **Note:** Dav. #1086.

Date	Mintage	VG	F	VF	XF	Unc
1728	—	60.00	90.00	175	300	—
1729	—	60.00	90.00	175	300	—
1730	—	60.00	90.00	175	300	—
1731	—	60.00	90.00	175	300	—
1732	—	60.00	90.00	175	300	—
1733	—	60.00	90.00	175	300	—
1735	—	60.00	90.00	175	300	—
1736	—	60.00	90.00	175	300	—
1739	—	60.00	90.00	175	300	—
1740	—	60.00	90.00	175	300	—

KM# 1503.2 THALER

Silver **Ruler:** Charles VI **Obv. Legend:** CAR:VI: **Note:** Dav. #1087. Varieties exist.

Date	Mintage	VG	F	VF	XF	Unc
1736	—	60.00	90.00	175	300	—
1737	—	60.00	90.00	175	300	—
1738	—	60.00	90.00	175	300	—
1739	—	60.00	90.00	175	300	—
1740	—	60.00	90.00	175	300	—

KM# 750 THALER

Silver **Ruler:** Franz I **Obv:** Laureate bust and titles of Franz I **Rev. Legend:** IN TE DOMINE SPERAVI

Date	Mintage	VG	F	VF	XF	Unc
1746 P-R	—	—	—	—	—	—
1747 P-R	—	—	—	—	—	—
1748 P-R	—	—	—	—	—	—
1749 P-R	—	—	—	—	—	—
1750 P-R	—	—	—	—	—	—
1751 P-R	—	—	—	—	—	—
1752 P-R	—	—	—	—	—	—
1753 P-R	—	—	—	—	—	—
1754 P-R	—	—	—	—	—	—
1755 P-R	—	—	—	—	—	—
1757 P-R	—	—	—	—	—	—
1759 P-R	—	—	—	—	—	—
1760 P-R	—	—	—	—	—	—
1761 P-R	—	—	—	—	—	—
1762 P-R	—	—	—	—	—	—

KM# 749 THALER

Silver **Ruler:** Maria Theresa **Obv:** Bust right **Rev:** Crowned imperial eagle with crowned arms on breast, arms rounded on bottom **Note:** Species Thaler. Dav. #1136. Prev. KM#1539.

Date	Mintage	VG	F	VF	XF	Unc
1746	—	75.00	100	200	375	—
1748	—	75.00	100	200	375	—
1749	—	75.00	100	200	375	—
1750	—	75.00	100	200	375	—

KM# 765 THALER

Silver **Ruler:** Maria Theresa **Note:** Prev. KM#1540. Convention Thaler. Similar to KM#1539 but "X" after date on reverse. Dav. #1136A. Varieties exist.

Date	Mintage	VG	F	VF	XF	Unc
1751	—	75.00	100	150	225	—

Date	Mintage	VG	F	VF	XF	Unc
1752 Rare	—	—	—	—	—	—
1753	—	75.00	100	150	225	—
1754	—	75.00	100	150	225	—
1755	—	75.00	100	150	225	—
1757	—	75.00	100	150	225	—
1759 Rare	—	—	—	—	—	—
1760	—	75.00	100	150	225	—

KM# 787 THALER

Silver **Ruler:** Maria Theresa **Obv:** Mature bust right, titles of Maria Theresa **Rev:** Crowned imperial eagle with crowned arms of St. Joachim and Bohemia on breast **Note:** Mining Thaler. Dav. #1137. Prev. KM#1541.

Date	Mintage	VG	F	VF	XF	Unc
1758	—	150	225	300	500	—
1759	—	150	225	300	500	—

KM# 802 THALER

Silver **Ruler:** Maria Theresa **Obv:** Veiled head right, titles of Maria Theresa **Rev:** Crowned imperial eagle, four-fold arms with central shield of Austria on breast, date in legend **Note:** Dav. #1138. Prev. KM#1542.

Date	Mintage	VG	F	VF	XF	Unc
1769	—	50.00	80.00	125	200	—
1770 EvS-AS	—	50.00	80.00	125	200	—
1771 EvS-AS	—	50.00	80.00	125	200	—

KM# 806 THALER

Silver **Ruler:** Josef II **Obv:** Laureate bust right, titles of Josef II **Rev:** Crowned imperial eagle, four-fold arms with central shield of Austria-Burgundy on breast, date in legend

Date	Mintage	VG	F	VF	XF	Unc
1770 C/EvS-AS	—	—	—	—	—	—
1771 C/EvS-AS	—	—	—	—	—	—
1772 C/EvS-AS	—	—	—	—	—	—
1773 C/EvS-AS	—	—	—	—	—	—
1774 C/EvS-IK	—	—	—	—	—	—
1775 C/EvS-IK	—	—	—	—	—	—

KM# 808 THALER

Silver **Ruler:** Maria Theresa **Obv:** Head right with smaller veil **Note:** Dav. #1139. Prev. KM#1543.

Date	Mintage	VG	F	VF	XF	Unc
1772 EvS-AS	—	50.00	80.00	125	200	—
1773 Evs-AS	—	50.00	80.00	125	200	—
1774 EvS-IK	—	50.00	80.00	125	200	—
1775 EvS-IK	—	50.00	80.00	125	200	—

KM# 816 THALER

Silver **Ruler:** Maria Theresa **Obv:** Large veiled head right **Note:** Dav. #1140. Prev. KM#1544. Varieties exist. For restrikes of this coin with "PS-IK" see Austrian States-Burgau.

Date	Mintage	VG	F	VF	XF	Unc
1780 EvS-IK	—	65.00	110	150	250	—
1780 PS-IK	—	65.00	110	150	250	—

KM# 833 THALER

Silver **Ruler:** Franz II **Obv:** Laureate bust right, titles of Franz II

Date	Mintage	VG	F	VF	XF	Unc
1795 C	—	—	—	—	—	—
1796 C	—	—	—	—	—	—
1797 C	—	—	—	—	—	—

TRADE COINAGE

KM# 598 1/4 DUCAT

0.8750 g., 0.9860 Gold .0277 oz. AGW **Ruler:** Leopold I **Obv:** Older laureate bust right in long wig **Rev:** Crowned imperial eagle with sword and scepter **Note:** Prev. KM#1441.

Date	MIntage	VG	F	VF	XF	Unc
1694 PM	—	125	275	450	800	—
1694 GE	—	125	275	450	800	—
1695 GE	—	125	275	450	800	—
1702 GE	—	125	275	450	800	—
1703 GE	—	125	275	450	800	—

KM# 638 1/4 DUCAT

0.8750 g., 0.9860 Gold .0277 oz. AGW **Ruler:** Joseph I **Obv:** Laureate bust right, titles of Josef I **Rev:** Crowned imperial eagle, date divided at top **Note:** Prev. KM#1461.

Date	Mintage	VG	F	VF	XF	Unc
1706 GE	—	125	200	375	700	—
1708 GE	—	125	200	375	700	—
1710 PM	—	125	200	375	700	—

KM# 669 1/4 DUCAT

0.8750 g., 0.9860 Gold .0277 oz. AGW **Ruler:** Charles VI **Obv:** Young bust right, titles of Karl VI **Rev:** Crowned imperial eagle **Note:** Prev. KM#1504.

Date	Mintage	VG	F	VF	XF	Unc
1713	—	100	150	200	350	—
1718	—	100	150	200	350	—

KM# 701 1/4 DUCAT

0.8750 g., 0.9860 Gold .0277 oz. AGW **Ruler:** Charles VI **Obv:** Older bust right **Rev:** Crowned imperial eagle, date at end of legend **Note:** Prev. KM#1505.

Date	Mintage	VG	F	VF	XF	Unc
1720	—	100	150	275	450	—
1725	—	100	150	275	450	—
1726	—	100	150	275	450	—
1729	—	100	150	275	450	—
1730	—	100	150	275	450	—
1732	—	100	150	275	450	—
1733	—	100	150	275	450	—
1734	—	100	150	275	450	—
1737	—	100	150	275	450	—

KM# 599 DUCAT

3.5000 g., 0.9860 Gold .1109 oz. AGW **Ruler:** Leopold I **Obv:** Older laureate bust right without inner circle **Rev:** Crowned imperial eagle with sword and scepter without inner circle **Note:** Prev. KM#1445. Varieties exist.

Date	Mintage	VG	F	VF	XF	Unc
1701 GE	—	150	250	600	1,000	—
1702 GE	—	150	250	600	1,000	—
1704 GE	—	150	250	600	1,000	—
1705 GE	—	150	250	600	1,000	—

KM# 639 DUCAT

3.5000 g., 0.9860 Gold .1109 oz. AGW **Ruler:** Joseph I **Obv:** Laureate bust right, titles of Josef I **Rev:** Crowned eagle without inner circle **Note:** Prev. KM#1462.

Date	Mintage	VG	F	VF	XF	Unc
1706 GE	—	200	400	900	1,600	—
1707 GE	—	200	400	900	1,600	—
1708 GE	—	200	400	900	1,600	—
1709 GE	—	200	400	900	1,600	—
1710 PM	—	200	400	900	1,600	—

KM# 647 DUCAT

3.5000 g., 0.9860 Gold .1109 oz. AGW **Ruler:** Joseph I **Obv:** Full-length figure 3/4 right holding orb and scepter **Obv. Legend:** JOSEPHUS-D.G.R-I.S.A.G.H.B.R.A.D.A **Note:** Prev. KM#1463.

Date	Mintage	VG	F	VF	XF	Unc
1710 PM	—	200	400	900	1,600	—

KM# 646 DUCAT

3.5000 g., 0.9860 Gold .1109 oz. AGW **Ruler:** Joseph I **Obv:** Full-length armored figure facing holding orb and scepter, titles of Josef I **Obv. Legend:** JOSEPHUS.D.G.RO-IMPERATOR.S.A **Rev:** Crowned eagle without inner circle **Note:** Prev. KM#1464.

Date	Mintage	VG	F	VF	XF	Unc
1710 PM	—	200	400	900	1,600	—
1711 IAP	—	200	400	900	1,600	—

KM# 651 DUCAT

3.5000 g., 0.9860 Gold .1109 oz. AGW **Ruler:** Charles VI **Obv:** Full-length figure 3/4 right holding orb and scepter, titles of Karl VI **Note:** Prev. KM#1506.

Date	Mintage	VG	F	VF	XF	Unc
1711 IAP	—	1,250	1,750	2,250	3,000	—
1712 IAP	—	1,250	1,750	2,250	3,000	—

KM# 663 DUCAT

3.5000 g., 0.9860 Gold .1109 oz. AGW **Ruler:** Charles VI **Rev:** Owl with wings closed **Note:** Prev. KM#1508.

Date	Mintage	VG	F	VF	XF	Unc
1712 (MDCCXII)	—	300	750	1,500	2,500	—
1713 (MDCCXIII)	—	300	750	1,500	2,500	—
1714 (MDCCXIIII)	—	300	750	1,500	2,500	—
1715 (MDCCXV)	—	300	750	1,500	2,500	—

KM# 670 DUCAT

3.5000 g., 0.9860 Gold 0.111 oz. AGW **Ruler:** Charles VI **Obv:** Oval shield of crowned imperial eagle to lower left **Rev:** Globe in clouds, owl on sun below, double legend around with R.N. dates **Note:** Prev. KM#1506

Date	Mintage	VG	F	VF	XF	Unc
1712(MDCCXII)	—	300	750	1,500	2,500	—
1713(MDCCXIII)	—	300	750	1,500	2,500	—
1714(MDCCXIIII)	—	300	750	1,500	2,500	—
1715(MDCCXV)	—	300	750	1,500	2,500	—

KM# 662 DUCAT

3.5000 g., 0.9860 Gold .1109 oz. AGW **Ruler:** Charles VI **Obv:** Oval shield of crowned imperial eagle to lower left **Rev:** Globe in clouds, owl with wings spread above sun, double legend around **Note:** Prev. KM1507.

Date	Mintage	VG	F	VF	XF	Unc
1712 (MDCCXII) IAP	—	300	750	1,500	2,500	—
1713 (MDCCXIII) IAP	—	300	750	1,500	2,500	—

KM# 671 DUCAT

3.5000 g., 0.9860 Gold .1109 oz. AGW **Ruler:** Charles VI **Obv:** Laureate bust right, titles of Karl VI **Rev:** Date in legend **Note:** Prev. KM#1509.

Date	Mintage	VG	F	VF	XF	Unc
1713	—	200	400	900	1,600	—
1714	—	200	400	900	1,600	—
1715	—	200	400	900	1,600	—
1729	—	200	400	900	1,600	—

KM# 677 DUCAT

3.5000 g., 0.9860 Gold .1109 oz. AGW **Ruler:** Charles VI **Obv:** Charles VI standing right without inner circle **Note:** Prev. KM#1510. Varieties exist.

Date	Mintage	VG	F	VF	XF	Unc
1716	—	150	250	450	700	—
1719	—	150	250	450	700	—
1720	—	150	250	450	700	—
1721	—	150	300	700	1,200	—
1722	—	150	250	450	700	—
1723	—	150	250	450	700	—
1724	—	150	250	450	700	—
1725	—	150	250	450	700	—
1726	—	150	250	450	700	—
1727	—	15.00	250	450	700	—
1728	—	200	400	800	1,400	—
1729	—	150	250	450	700	—
1731	—	150	250	450	700	—
1732	2,352	150	250	450	700	—
1733	3,265	150	250	450	700	—
1734	4,819	150	250	450	700	—
1736	9,641	150	250	450	700	—
1737	4,825	150	250	450	700	—
1738	4,508	150	250	450	700	—
1739	7,854	150	250	450	700	—

KM# 705 DUCAT

3.5000 g., 0.9860 Gold .1109 oz. AGW **Ruler:** Charles VI **Obv:** Charles VI, heart-shaped Bohemian arms to lower left **Rev:** St. John Nepomuk in clouds, sun divides date in exergue **Rev. Legend:** HOC PATROCINIO RESTA VRATVR **Note:** Prev. KM#1511.

Date	Mintage	VG	F	VF	XF	Unc
1725	—	—	—	—	—	—
Note: Reported, not confirmed						
1727	—	—	—	—	—	—
Note: Reported, not confirmed						
1729	—	200	400	900	1,600	—

KM# 725 DUCAT

Gold **Ruler:** Charles VI **Obv:** Emperor facing **Note:** Prev. KM#1512, 1513.

Date	Mintage	VG	F	VF	XF	Unc
1735	3,287	200	400	900	1,600	—
1740	—	—	—	—	—	—

KM# 739 DUCAT

3.5000 g., 0.9860 Gold .1109 oz. AGW **Ruler:** Maria Theresa **Obv:** Full-length facing figure of Empress holding orb and scepter, titles of Maria Theresia **Rev:** Crowned four-fold arms with central shield of Bohemia in baroque frame, date in legend **Note:** Prev. KM#1545.

Date	Mintage	VG	F	VF	XF	Unc
1743	—	135	275	425	750	—
1744	—	135	275	425	750	—
1745	—	135	275	425	750	—

KM# 751 DUCAT

Gold **Ruler:** Franz I **Rev. Legend:** TU DOMINE SPES MEA

Date	Mintage	VG	F	VF	XF	Unc
1746 P-R	—	85.00	175	325	550	—
1748 P-R	—	85.00	175	325	550	—
1749 P-R	—	85.00	175	325	550	—
1750 P-R	—	85.00	175	325	550	—
1751 P-R	—	85.00	175	325	550	—
1752 P-R	—	85.00	175	325	550	—
1753 P-R	—	85.00	175	325	550	—
1754 P-R	—	85.00	175	325	550	—
1755 P-R	—	85.00	175	325	550	—
1756 P-R	—	85.00	175	325	550	—
1765 P-R	—	85.00	175	325	550	—

KM# 756 DUCAT

3.5000 g., 0.9860 Gold .1109 oz. AGW **Ruler:** Maria Theresa **Obv:** Bust right, titles of Maria Theresa **Rev:** Crowned imperial eagle with crowned Bohemian arms on breast, date in legend **Note:** Prev. KM#1546. Varieties exist.

Date	Mintage	VG	F	VF	XF	Unc
1747	—	100	225	375	600	—
1748	—	100	225	375	600	—
1749	—	100	225	375	600	—
1750	—	100	225	375	600	—
1751	—	100	225	375	600	—
1752	—	100	225	375	600	—
1753	—	100	225	375	600	—
1754	—	100	225	375	600	—
1755	—	100	225	375	600	—
1756	—	100	225	375	600	—
1757	—	100	225	375	600	—
1758	—	100	225	375	600	—
1759	—	100	225	375	600	—
1760	—	100	225	375	600	—
1761	—	100	225	375	600	—
1764	—	125	250	450	800	—
1765	—	125	250	450	800	—

KM# 803 DUCAT

3.5000 g., 0.9860 Gold .1109 oz. AGW **Ruler:** Maria Theresa **Obv:** Veiled head right **Rev:** Crowned arms **Note:** Prev. KM#1547.

Date	Mintage	VG	F	VF	XF	Unc
1769 vS-S	—	150	275	400	675	—
1770 vS-S	—	150	275	400	675	—
1771 vS-S	—	150	275	400	675	—
1772 vS-S	—	150	275	400	675	—
1773 vS-S	—	150	275	400	675	—
1773 vS-K	—	150	275	400	675	—
1774 vS-K	—	150	275	400	675	—
1776 vS-K	—	150	275	400	675	—
1777 Rare	—	—	—	—	—	—
1778 vS-K Rare	—	—	—	—	—	—
1779 vS-K	—	150	275	400	675	—
1780 vS-K	—	150	275	400	675	—

KM# 804 DUCAT

Gold **Ruler:** Josef II **Obv:** Laureate bust right, titles of Josef II **Rev:** Crowned imperial eagle, two-fold arms of Austria-Lothringen on breast, VIRTUTE etc., date

Date	Mintage	VG	F	VF	XF	Unc
1769 C/vS-S	—	150	275	400	675	—
1770 C/vS-S	—	150	275	400	675	—
1771 C/vS-S	—	150	275	400	675	—
1772 C/vS-S	—	150	275	400	675	—
1773 C/vS-S	—	150	275	400	675	—
1776 C/vS-S	—	150	275	400	675	—
1777 C/vS-S	—	150	275	400	675	—
1778 C/vS-S	—	150	275	400	675	—
1779 C/vS-S	—	150	275	400	675	—

KM# 821 DUCAT

Gold **Ruler:** Josef II **Obv:** Laureate bust right, titles of Josef II **Rev:** Titles continuous, date in legend

Date	Mintage	VG	F	VF	XF	Unc
1781 C	—	85.00	175	325	550	—
1782 C	—	85.00	175	325	550	—
1783 C	—	85.00	175	325	550	—
1784 C	—	85.00	175	325	550	—

KM# 835 DUCAT

Gold **Ruler:** Franz II **Obv:** Laureate bust right, titles of Franz II **Rev:** Crowned imperial eagle, arms of Austria-Lothringen on breast, date in legend

Date	Mintage	VG	F	VF	XF	Unc
1797 C	—	150	275	400	675	—
1798 C	—	—	—	—	—	—

Note: Reported, not confirmed

KM# 673 2 DUCAT

7.0000 g., 0.9860 Gold .2219 oz. AGW **Ruler:** Ferdinand II **Note:** Fr. #48. Prev. KM#1514.

Date	Mintage	VG	F	VF	XF	Unc
1715	—	1,250	2,250	4,000	6,500	—
1719	—	1,250	2,250	4,000	6,500	—
1722	—	1,250	2,250	4,000	6,500	—

KM# 706 2 DUCAT

7.5000 g., 0.9860 Gold .1109 oz. AGW **Ruler:** Charles VI **Note:** Prev. KM#1515.

Date	Mintage	VG	F	VF	XF	Unc
1725	—	—	—	—	—	—
1727	—	—	—	—	—	—

KM# 685 5 DUCAT

17.5000 g., 0.9860 Gold .5548 oz. AGW **Ruler:** Charles VI **Note:** Prev. KM#1517. Struck with 1/2 Thaler dies, KM#689.

Date	Mintage	VG	F	VF	XF	Unc
1717	—	2,000	3,000	5,000	8,000	—

KM# 702 5 DUCAT

17.5000 g., 0.9860 Gold .5548 oz. AGW **Ruler:** Charles VI **Obv:** Charles VI standing right, shield at left **Rev:** St. John in clouds above mining scene **Note:** Prev. KM#1518.

Date	Mintage	VG	F	VF	XF	Unc
1722	—	1,250	2,000	3,500	6,000	—

SIEGE COINAGE

1754-1757

Struck by Austrian defenders during the siege of Prague.

KM# 274a KREUZER (Kipper Munze)

Pewter **Ruler:** Franz I

Date	Mintage	VG	F	VF	XF	Unc
1757	—	75.00	95.00	135	250	—

KM# 270b 3 KREUZER

Pewter **Ruler:** Franz I

Date	Mintage	VG	F	VF	XF	Unc
1754	—	75.00	135	195	300	—

Note: Struck in 1757.

KM# 286a 10 KREUZER

Pewter **Ruler:** Franz I

Date	Mintage	VG	F	VF	XF	Unc
1757	—	75.00	135	200	325	—

KM# 283a 20 KREUZER

Pewter **Ruler:** Franz I

Date	Mintage	VG	F	VF	XF	Unc
1757	—	75.00	135	200	325	—

KM# 281a 1/2 THALER

Pewter **Ruler:** Franz I

Date	Mintage	VG	F	VF	XF	Unc
1754	—	100	200	400	600	—

Note: Struck in 1757.

ESSAIS

KM#	Date	Mintage	Identification	Mkt Val
E1	1759	—	Ducat. Copper.	—
E2	1764	—	Kreuzer. Silver.	—
E3	1765	—	Ducat. Copper.	—

PATTERNS

Including off metal strikes

KM#	Date	Mintage	Identification	Mkt Val
Pn37	1710 PM	—	Ducat. Silver. KM#1463.	550
Pn38	1711 PM	—	1/2 Kreuzer. Copper. KM#1455.	—
Pn39	1717	—	1/2 Thaler. Gold. KM#1488, weight of 5 Ducat.	—
Pn40	1720	—	Ducat. Silver. KM#1510.	400
Pn41	1722	—	5 Ducat. Silver. KM#1516.	—
Pn42	1725	—	2 Ducat. Silver. KM#1515.	450
Pn44	1754	—	17 Kreuzer. Pewter. KM#1532.	—

LOBKOWITZ-STERNSTEIN

The Bohemian lords of Lobkowitz had long distinguished themselves in the service of the Holy Roman Empire. For his role on the side of the emperor in the opening phase of the Thirty Years' War, Dzenko Adalbert was given the countship of Sternstein in Upper Bavaria in 1623 and raised to the rank of Prince of the Empire. The lands in Bavaria were mediatized in 1805.

RULERS

Ferdinand August Leopold, 1677-1715
Philipp Hyacinth, 1715-1734
Wenseslaus Ferdinand Karl, 1734-1739 and
Ferdinand Philipp Joseph, 1734-1784
Franz Joseph Maximilian, 1784-1816
(Under regency of his mother, Maria Gabriele of Savoy-Carignan, and his cousin, ..August, until 1794)

MINT MARKS

VI = Vienna Mint

PRINCIPALITY

STANDARD COINAGE

KM# 10 20 KREUZER

Silver **Ruler:** Franz Joseph Maximilian **Obv:** Bust right **Rev:** 2 Shields within crowned mantle **Note:** Convention 20 Kreuzer.

Date	Mintage	VG	F	VF	XF	Unc
1794	—	25.00	55.00	80.00	125	—

KM# 11 THALER

Silver **Ruler:** Franz Joseph Maximilian **Obv:** Draped bust right **Rev:** 2 Shields within crownd mantle **Note:** Convention Thaler. Dav. #1190.

Date	Mintage	VG	F	VF	XF	Unc
1794 VI	300	275	350	500	850	—

TRADE COINAGE

KM# 6 DUCAT

3.5000 g., 0.9860 Gold .1109 oz. AGW **Ruler:** Ferdinand August Leopold **Obv:** Armored bust right **Rev:** Crowned arms

Date	Mintage	VG	F	VF	XF	Unc
ND	—	1,500	2,500	4,250	6,500	—

KM# 12 DUCAT

3.5000 g., 0.9860 Gold .1109 oz. AGW **Ruler:** Ferdinand August Leopold **Obv:** Bust right **Rev:** 2 Shields within crowned mantle

Date	Mintage	VG	F	VF	XF	Unc
1794	—	950	1,750	3,000	5,000	—

SCHLICK

A county in Bohemia, was raised to the rank of count in 1437. They were given the mint right in 1520 by the Czech Parliament, but King Ferdinand I took it away in 1528. Silver was mined in the Michaelsberg and Joachimsthal Mines in the area.

The "Joachimsthalers", the ancestor of all later dollars, were struck by this family beginning in 1517.

RULERS

Franz Josef, 1675-1740
Franz Heinrich, 1740-1766
Leopold Heinrich, 1766-1770

COUNTY

STANDARD COINAGE

KM# 28 THALER

Silver **Ruler:** Franz Josef **Obv:** Madonna and child with St. Anne in cloud above crowned arms dividing date, with legends around **Obv. Legend:** Titles of Franz Josef **Rev:** Crowned double-headed imperial eagle with shield on breast **Rev. Legend:** Titles of Charles **Note:** Dav. #1195.

Date	Mintage	VG	F	VF	XF	Unc
1716	2,112	200	350	650	1,000	—

KM# 30 THALER

Silver **Ruler:** Franz Heinrich **Obv:** Crowned imperial double eagle with arms on breast **Obv. Legend:** Titles of Maria Theresia **Rev:** Crowned arms **Rev. Legend:** Titles of Franz Heinrich **Note:** Ctoss-reference number Dav. #1196.

Date	Mintage	VG	F	VF	XF	Unc
1759	—	125	250	450	850	—

KM# 35 THALER

Silver **Ruler:** Leopold Heinrich **Obv:** Crowned imperial double eagle with shield on breast **Obv. Legend:** Titles of Maria Theresia **Rev:** Crowned arms with Madonna and child above **Rev. Legend:** Titles of Leopold Heinrich **Note:** Dav. #1197

Date	Mintage	VG	F	VF	XF	Unc
1767	—	100	175	350	550	—

TRADE COINAGE

KM# 27 DUCAT

3.5000 g., 0.9860 Gold .1109 oz. AGW **Ruler:** Franz Josef **Obv:** St. Anne standing **Rev:** Crowned imperial eagle, titles of Charles

Date	Mintage	VG	F	VF	XF	Unc
1716	—	750	1,500	2,750	4,500	—

KM# 31 DUCAT

3.5000 g., 0.9860 Gold .1109 oz. AGW **Ruler:** Franz Heinrich **Obv:** St. Anne and crown above arms separating date **Rev:** Crowned imperial eagle with arms on breast, titles of Maria Theresia

Date	Mintage	VG	F	VF	XF	Unc
1759	—	750	1,500	2,750	4,500	—

KM# 36 DUCAT

3.5000 g., 0.9860 Gold .1109 oz. AGW **Ruler:** Leopold Heinrich **Obv:** Crowned imperial eagle with arms on breast, titles of Maria Theresia **Rev:** St. Anne and crown above arms separating date **Rev. Legend:** Titles of Leopold Heinrich

Date	Mintage	VG	F	VF	XF	Unc
1767	—	700	1,400	2,500	4,250	—

BOLIVIA

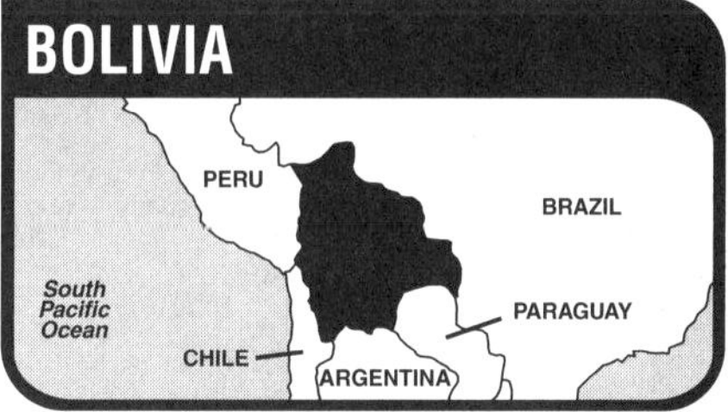

The Republic of Bolivia, a landlocked country in west central South America, has an area of 424,165 sq. mi. (1,098,580 sq. km.) and a population of *8.33 million. Its capitals are: La Paz (administrative) and Sucre (constitutional). Principal exports are tin, zinc, antimony, tungsten, petroleum, natural gas, cotton and coffee.

Much of present day Bolivia was first dominated by the Tiahuanaco Culture ca.400 BC. It had in turn been incorporated into the Inca Empire by 1440AD prior to the arrival of the Spanish, in 1535, who reduced the Indian population to virtual slavery. When Joseph Napoleon was placed upon the throne of occupied Spain in 1809, a fervor of revolutionary activity quickened throughout Alto Peru - culminating in the 1809 Proclamation of Liberty. Sixteen bloody years of struggle ensued before the republic, named for the famed liberator Simon Bolivar, was established on August 6, 1825. Since then Bolivia has survived more than 16 constitutions, 78 Presidents, 3 military juntas and over 160 revolutions.

The Imperial City of Potosi, founded by Villarroel in 1546, was established in the midst of what is estimated to have been the world's richest silver mines (having produced in excess of 2 billion dollars worth of silver).

The first mint, early in 1574, used equipment brought over from Lima. Before that it had been used at La Plata where the operation failed. The oldest type was a cob with the Hapsburg arms on the obverse and cross with quartered castles and lions on the reverse. To the heraldic right of the shield (at the left as one faces it) is a "p" and, under it, the assayer's initial, although in some early examples the "P" and assayer can appear to the right of the shield. While production at the "Casa de Moneda" was enormous, the quality of the coinage was at times so poor that some 50 were condemned to death by their superiors.

Therefore, by royal decree of February 17, 1651, the design was changed to the quartered castles and lions for the obverse and two crowned pillars of Hercules floating above the waves of the sea for the reverse. A new transitional series was introduced in 1651-1652 followed by a new standard design in 1652 and as the last cob type continued on for several years along with the milled pillars and bust pieces from 1767 through 1773. In the final years under Charles III the planchet is compact and dumpy, very irregular and of poor style, contrasting sharply with their counterpart denominations of the pillar and bust types.

Rarely, and at very high prices, we may be offered almost perfectly round cobs, with the dies well-centered, showing the legend and date completely. These have gained importance in the last decades and are known as "royal" or "presentation" pieces. Every year a few of these specimens were coined, using dies in excellent condition and a specially prepared round planchet, to prove the quality of the minting to the Viceroy or even to the King. Another very unusual and rare variety is specially struck specimens on heart-shaped flans. While many heart-shaped examples are encountered in today's market, a careful examination will reveal that most are underweight and were created after striking for jewelry and souvenir purposes. Most surviving specimens are holed, plugged or countermarked as found in Guatemala listings. The rest of the production was of primitive quality due to the shortage of equipment, skilled laborers and the volume to be struck.

Most pre-decimal coinage of independent Bolivia carries the assayers' initials on the reverse near the rim to the left of the date, in 4 to 5 o'clock position. The mint mark or name appears in the 7 to 8 o'clock area.

RULER

Spanish until 1825

MINT MARKS

PTA monogram - La Plata (Sucre)
P or PTS monogram - Potosi

ASSAYERS' INITIALS

Initial	Date	Name
C	1742-44	Jose Carnizer
C	1753-54	Jose Maria Caballero
E	1733-37; 1750-51	Esteban Gutierrez de Escalante
J	1767-73	Jose de Bargas Flores
M	1721-22; 1727-32	Jose de Matienzo
M	1737-40	Pedro Geronimo Manrique de Guzman
P	1740-42	Diego del Pui
P	1776-1802	Pedro de Mazondo
P	1795-1824	Pedro Martin de Albizu
Q	1744-60	Luis De Quintanilla
Q	1746-60	?
R	1767-95	Raimundo de Iturriaga
V	1760-73	Jose de Vargas y Flores
Y	1701-28	Diego de Ybarbouro
Y	1760-73	Raimundo de Yturriago
YA	1732-33	?

MONETARY SYSTEM

16 Reales = 1 Escudo

COLONIAL

COLONIAL COB COINAGE

KM# 24 2 REALES

6.7682 g., 0.9310 Silver .2026 oz. ASW **Ruler:** Charles II **Obv:** Cross of Jerusalem, castles and lions in quarters **Obv. Legend:** CAROLVS II **Rev:** Crowned pillars of Hercules and waves, value at top center

Date	Mintage	Good	VG	F	VF	XF
1701/0P F Rare	—	—	—	—	—	—
1701P F	—	55.00	100	150	225	—
1701P Y/F Rare	—	—	—	—	—	—
1701P Y	—	55.00	100	150	225	—

KM# 25 4 REALES

13.5365 g., 0.9310 Silver .4052 oz. ASW **Ruler:** Charles II **Obv:** Cross of Jerusalem, castles and lions at quarters **Rev:** Crowned pillars of Hercules and waves, value at top center

Date	Mintage	Good	VG	F	VF	XF
1701P F	—	175	250	400	575	—

Date	Mintage	Good	VG	F	VF	XF
1701P Y	—	175	250	400	575	—

KM# 30a 4 REALES

13.5337 g., 0.9170 Silver .3990 oz. ASW **Ruler:** Philip V

Date	Mintage	Good	VG	F	VF	XF
ND(1729-47)P Date off flan	—	60.00	85.00	140	200	—
1729P M	—	125	200	325	475	—
1730P M	—	175	250	400	525	—
1731P M	—	100	175	275	375	—
1732P M	—	175	250	400	575	—
1733/2P YA Rare	—	—	—	—	—	—
1733P E	—	125	200	325	475	—
1733P YA	—	200	300	475	650	—
1734P E	—	175	250	400	575	—
1735P E	—	175	250	400	575	—
1736P E	—	100	175	275	375	—
1737P E	—	125	200	325	475	—
1737P M	—	125	200	325	475	—
1738P M	—	100	175	275	375	—
1739P M	—	100	175	275	375	—
1740P M	—	175	250	400	575	—
1740P P	—	175	250	400	575	—
1741P P	—	100	175	275	375	—
1742P C/P Rare	—	—	—	—	—	—
1742P C	—	125	200	325	475	—
1742P P	—	175	250	400	575	—
1743P C	—	125	200	325	475	—
1744P C	—	125	200	325	475	—
1744P q	—	125	200	325	475	—
1745P q	—	125	200	325	475	—
1746P q	—	175	250	400	575	—
1747P q	—	175	250	400	575	—

KM# 26 8 REALES

27.0703 g., 0.9310 Silver .8103 oz. ASW **Ruler:** Charles II **Obv:** Cross of Jerusalem, castles and lions in quarters **Obv. Legend:** CAROLVS II D.G. HISPANIA **Rev:** Crowned pillars of Hercules and waves, value at top center

Date	Mintage	Good	VG	F	VF	XF
1701P F	—	100	200	325	475	—
1701P Y/F	—	100	200	325	475	—
1701P Y	—	100	200	325	475	—

COB COINAGE

KM# 27 1/2 REAL

1.6917 g., 0.9310 Silver .0506 oz. ASW **Ruler:** Philip V

Date	Mintage	Good	VG	F	VF	XF
ND(1701-28)P Date off flan	—	7.00	10.00	15.00	25.00	—
1701P	—	18.50	30.00	55.00	90.00	—
1702P	—	15.00	25.00	50.00	80.00	—
1703P	—	15.00	25.00	50.00	80.00	—
1704P	—	15.00	25.00	50.00	80.00	—
1705P	—	18.50	30.00	55.00	90.00	—
1706P	—	15.00	25.00	50.00	80.00	—
1707P	—	18.50	30.00	55.00	90.00	—
1708P	—	18.50	30.00	55.00	90.00	—
1709P	—	18.50	30.00	55.00	90.00	—
1710P	—	15.00	25.00	50.00	80.00	—
1711P	—	15.00	25.00	50.00	80.00	—
1712P	—	18.50	30.00	55.00	90.00	—
1713P	—	15.00	25.00	50.00	80.00	—
1714/3P Rare	—	—	—	—	—	—
1714P	—	15.00	25.00	50.00	80.00	—
1715P	—	15.00	25.00	50.00	80.00	—
1716P	—	15.00	25.00	50.00	80.00	—
1717P	—	15.00	25.00	50.00	80.00	—
1718P	—	18.50	30.00	55.00	90.00	—
1719P	—	10.00	25.00	50.00	80.00	—
1720P	—	10.00	25.00	50.00	80.00	—
1721P	—	18.50	30.00	55.00	90.00	—
1722P	—	15.00	25.00	50.00	80.00	—
1723P	—	25.00	35.00	60.00	110	—
1724P	—	15.00	25.00	50.00	80.00	—
1727P Rare	—	—	—	—	—	—
1728P	—	15.00	25.00	50.00	80.00	—

KM# 32 1/2 REAL

1.6921 g., 0.9170 Silver .0499 oz. ASW **Ruler:** Luis I **Obv:** Louis I monogram, date below

Date	Mintage	Good	VG	F	VF	XF
ND(1725-27)P Date off flan	—	25.00	40.00	60.00	90.00	—
1725P	—	40.00	70.00	100	150	—
1726P	—	40.00	70.00	100	150	—
1727P	—	40.00	70.00	100	150	—

KM# 27a 1/2 REAL

1.6921 g., 0.9170 Silver .0498 oz. ASW **Ruler:** Philip V

Date	Mintage	Good	VG	F	VF	XF
ND(1729-47)P Date off flan	—	7.00	10.00	15.00	25.00	—
1729P	—	15.00	25.00	50.00	80.00	—
1730P	—	15.00	25.00	50.00	80.00	—
1731P	—	15.00	25.00	50.00	80.00	—
1732P	—	15.00	25.00	50.00	80.00	—
1733P	—	15.00	25.00	50.00	80.00	—
1734P	—	15.00	25.00	50.00	80.00	—
1735P	—	15.00	25.00	50.00	80.00	—
1736P	—	15.00	25.00	50.00	80.00	—
1737P	—	15.00	25.00	50.00	80.00	—
1738P	—	15.00	25.00	50.00	80.00	—
1739P	—	15.00	25.00	50.00	80.00	—
1740P	—	15.00	25.00	50.00	80.00	—
1741/0P Rare	—	—	—	—	—	—
1741P	—	15.00	25.00	50.00	80.00	—
1741P Rare	—	—	—	—	—	—
1742P	—	15.00	25.00	50.00	90.00	—
1743P	—	17.50	30.00	55.00	80.00	—
1744P	—	17.50	25.00	50.00	80.00	—
1745P	—	17.50	25.00	50.00	80.00	—
1746P	—	17.50	25.00	50.00	80.00	—
1747P	—	20.00	35.00	60.00	90.00	—

KM# 36 1/2 REAL

1.6921 g., 0.9170 Silver .0499 oz. ASW **Ruler:** Ferdinand VI **Obv:** Cross of Jerusalem, lions and castles in quarters **Rev:** FERDINANDVS monogram, date below

Date	Mintage	Good	VG	F	VF	XF
ND(1747-60)P Date off flan	—	12.00	16.50	20.00	35.00	—
1747P	—	22.50	35.00	60.00	90.00	—
1748P	—	20.00	30.00	55.00	85.00	—
1749P	—	20.00	30.00	55.00	85.00	—
1750P	—	20.00	30.00	55.00	85.00	—
1751P	—	20.00	30.00	55.00	85.00	—
1752P	—	22.50	35.00	60.00	90.00	—
1753P	—	22.50	35.00	60.00	90.00	—
1754/3P Rare	—	—	—	—	—	—
1754P	—	20.00	30.00	55.00	85.00	—
1755P	—	20.00	30.00	55.00	85.00	—
1756P	—	20.00	30.00	55.00	85.00	—
1757P	—	20.00	30.00	55.00	85.00	—
1758P	—	20.00	30.00	55.00	85.00	—
1759P	—	20.00	30.00	55.00	85.00	—
1760P	—	25.00	40.00	75.00	110	—

KM# 41 1/2 REAL

1.6921 g., 0.9170 Silver .0499 oz. ASW **Ruler:** Charles III **Obv:** Cross of Jerusalem, lions and castles in quarters **Rev:** CAROLUS III monogram, date below

Date	Mintage	Good	VG	F	VF	XF
ND(1760-73)P Date off flan	—	8.00	15.00	25.00	35.00	—
1760P	—	18.00	25.00	35.00	55.00	—
1761P	—	18.00	25.00	35.00	55.00	—
1762P	—	18.00	25.00	35.00	55.00	—
1763P	—	18.00	25.00	35.00	55.00	—
1764P	—	18.00	25.00	35.00	55.00	—
1765P	—	18.00	25.00	35.00	55.00	—
1766P	—	18.00	25.00	35.00	55.00	—
1767P	—	20.00	30.00	55.00	85.00	—
1768P	—	25.00	45.00	75.00	125	—
1769P	—	20.00	30.00	55.00	85.00	—
1770/69P Rare	—	—	—	—	—	—
1770P	—	20.00	30.00	55.00	85.00	—
1771P	—	20.00	30.00	55.00	85.00	—
1772P	—	25.00	45.00	75.00	125	—
1773P	—	40.00	60.00	90.00	150	—

KM# 28 REAL

3.3834 g., 0.9310 Silver .1013 oz. ASW **Ruler:** Philip V **Obv:** Cross of Jerusalem, castles and lions in quarters **Obv. Legend:** PHILIPVS V **Rev:** Crowned pillars of Hercules and waves, value at top center

Date	Mintage	Good	VG	F	VF	XF
ND(1702-28)P Date off flan	—	7.50	15.00	30.00	60.00	—
1702P Y	—	12.00	25.00	75.00	120	—
1703P Y	—	12.00	25.00	75.00	120	—
1704P Y	—	12.00	25.00	75.00	120	—
1705P Y	—	12.00	25.00	75.00	120	—
1706P Y	—	12.00	25.00	75.00	120	—
1707P Y	—	12.00	25.00	75.00	120	—
1708P Y	—	12.00	25.00	75.00	120	—
1709P Y	—	12.00	25.00	75.00	120	—
1710P Y	—	15.00	30.00	80.00	125	—
1711P Y	—	15.00	30.00	80.00	125	—
1712P Y	—	15.00	30.00	80.00	125	—
1713P Y	—	15.00	30.00	80.00	125	—
1714P Y	—	17.50	25.00	75.00	120	—
1715/4P Y Rare	—	—	—	—	—	—
1715P Y	—	12.50	25.00	75.00	120	—
1716P Y	—	12.50	25.00	75.00	120	—
1717P Y	—	12.50	25.00	75.00	120	—
1718P Y	—	12.50	25.00	75.00	120	—
1719P Y	—	12.50	25.00	75.00	120	—
1720P Y	—	12.50	25.00	75.00	120	—
1721P Y	—	12.50	25.00	75.00	120	—
1722P Y	—	12.50	25.00	75.00	120	—
1723P Y	—	12.50	25.00	75.00	120	—
1724P Y	—	12.50	25.00	75.00	120	—
1728P M	—	12.50	25.00	75.00	120	—

KM# 33 REAL

3.3841 g., 0.9170 Silver .0998 oz. ASW **Ruler:** Luis I **Obv:** Cross of Jerusalem, lions and castles in quarters **Obv. Legend:** LVIS PR

Date	Mintage	Good	VG	F	VF	XF
1725P Y	—	50.00	90.00	150	275	—
1726P Y	—	50.00	90.00	150	275	—
1727P Y	—	50.00	90.00	150	275	—

KM# 28a REAL

3.3834 g., 0.9170 Silver .0998 oz. ASW **Ruler:** Philip V **Obv:** Cross of Jerusalem, castles and lions in quarters **Obv. Legend:** PHILIPVS V **Rev:** Crowned pillars of Hercules and waves, value at top center

Date	Mintage	Good	VG	F	VF	XF
ND(1729-47)P Date off flan	—	7.50	15.00	30.00	60.00	—
1729P M	—	12.50	25.00	75.00	120	—
1730P M	—	12.50	25.00	75.00	120	—
1731P M	—	12.50	25.00	75.00	120	—
1732P M	—	12.50	25.00	75.00	120	—
1732P YA	—	40.00	75.00	135	250	—
1733P E	—	15.00	30.00	80.00	125	—
1733P YA	—	40.00	75.00	135	250	—
1734P E	—	12.50	25.00	75.00	120	—
1735P E	—	12.50	25.00	75.00	120	—
1736P E	—	12.50	25.00	75.00	120	—
1737P E	—	12.50	25.00	75.00	120	—
1737P M	—	12.50	25.00	75.00	120	—
1738P M	—	12.50	25.00	75.00	120	—
1739P M	—	12.50	25.00	75.00	120	—
1740P M	—	12.50	25.00	75.00	120	—
1740P P	—	12.50	25.00	75.00	120	—
1741//(17)40P P Rare	—	—	—	—	—	—
1741P P	—	12.50	25.00	75.00	120	—
1742P C	—	12.50	25.00	75.00	120	—
1742P C	—	12.50	25.00	75.00	120	—
1742P C/P Rare	—	—	—	—	—	—
1743P C	—	12.50	25.00	75.00	120	—
1744P C	—	12.50	25.00	75.00	120	—
1744P q/C Rare	—	—	—	—	—	—
1744P q	—	12.50	25.00	75.00	120	—
1745P q	—	12.50	25.00	75.00	120	—
1746P q	—	12.50	25.00	75.00	120	—
1747P q	—	15.00	30.00	80.00	125	—

KM# 37 REAL

3.3841 g., 0.9170 Silver .0998 oz. ASW **Ruler:** Philip III **Obv:** Cross of Jerusalem, lions and castles in quarters **Obv. Legend:** FERNANDVS VI **Rev:** Pillars, PLVS VLTRA, date

Date	Mintage	Good	VG	F	VF	XF
ND(1748-60)P Date off flan	—	7.50	15.00	30.00	60.00	—
1748P q	—	15.00	30.00	80.00	125	—
1749/8P q Rare	—	—	—	—	—	—
1749P q	—	15.00	30.00	80.00	125	—
1750/49P q Rare	—	—	—	—	—	—
1750P q	—	15.00	30.00	80.00	125	—

Date	Mintage	Good	VG	F	VF	XF
1750P E	—	15.00	30.00	80.00	125	—
1751//(17)50P q Rare	—	—	—	—	—	—
1751P q	—	15.00	30.00	80.00	125	—
1751P E	—	15.00	30.00	80.00	125	—
1751P q/E Rare	—	—	—	—	—	—
1752P q	—	15.00	30.00	80.00	125	—
1753P C/q Rare	—	—	—	—	—	—
1753P C	—	15.00	30.00	80.00	125	—
1753P q	—	15.00	30.00	80.00	125	—
1754P C, q Rare	—	—	—	—	—	—
1754P C	—	15.00	30.00	80.00	125	—
1754P q	—	15.00	30.00	80.00	125	—
1755P q	—	12.50	25.00	75.00	120	—
1756P q	—	12.50	25.00	75.00	120	—
1757P q	—	12.50	25.00	75.00	120	—
1758P q	—	12.50	25.00	75.00	120	—
1759P q	—	12.50	25.00	120	120	—
1760/59P q Rare	—	—	—	—	—	—
1760P q	—	15.00	30.00	80.00	125	—

KM# 42 REAL

3.3841 g., 0.9170 Silver .0998 oz. ASW **Ruler:** Charles III **Obv:** Cross of Jerusalem, lions and castles in quarters **Obv. Legend:** CAROLVS TERTIVS **Rev:** Pillars, PLVS VLTRA, date

Date	Mintage	Good	VG	F	VF	XF
ND(1760-73)P Date off flan	—	7.50	15.00	30.00	60.00	—
1760P V, Y	—	15.00	30.00	80.00	125	—
1761P V, Y	—	12.50	25.00	75.00	120	—
1762P V, Y	—	12.50	25.00	75.00	120	—
1763P V, Y	—	12.50	25.00	75.00	120	—
1764P V, Y	—	12.50	25.00	75.00	120	—
1765P V, Y	—	12.50	25.00	75.00	120	—
1766P V, Y	—	12.50	25.00	75.00	120	—
1767P V, Y	—	12.50	25.00	75.00	120	—
1768P V, Y	—	12.50	25.00	75.00	120	—
1769P V, Y	—	12.50	25.00	75.00	120	—
1770P V, Y	—	12.50	25.00	75.00	120	—
1771P V, Y	—	12.50	25.00	75.00	120	—
177TP Error; Rare	—	—	—	—	—	—
1771/0P V,Y	—	30.00	60.00	100	175	—
1772/1P V, Y Rare	—	—	—	—	—	—
1772P V,Y	—	12.50	25.00	75.00	120	—
1773P V, Y	—	12.50	25.00	75.00	120	—

KM# 29 2 REALES

6.7668 g., 0.9310 Silver .2026 oz. ASW **Ruler:** Philip V **Obv:** Cross of Jerusalem, castles and lions in quarters **Obv. Legend:** PHILIPVS V D.G. **Rev:** Crowned pillars of Hercules and waves, value at top center

Date	Mintage	Good	VG	F	VF	XF
ND(1702-28)P Date off flan	—	20.00	30.00	50.00	75.00	—
1702//(17)01P Y Rare	—	—	—	—	—	—
1702P Y	—	50.00	90.00	135	220	—
1703P Y	—	50.00	90.00	135	220	—
1704P Y	—	45.00	85.00	130	210	—
1705P Y	—	45.00	85.00	130	210	—
1706P Y	—	45.00	85.00	130	210	—
1706P Y	—	45.00	85.00	130	210	—
1707//(17)06P Y Rare	—	—	—	—	—	—
1707P Y	—	45.00	85.00	130	210	—
1708P Y	—	45.00	85.00	130	210	—
1709P Y	—	50.00	90.00	135	220	—
1710P Y	—	50.00	90.00	135	220	—
1711P Y	—	55.00	95.00	135	220	—
1712P Y	—	45.00	85.00	130	210	—
1713P Y	—	45.00	85.00	130	210	—
1714P Y	—	45.00	85.00	130	210	—
1715P Y	—	45.00	85.00	130	210	—
1716P Y	—	45.00	85.00	130	210	—
1717P Y	—	45.00	85.00	130	210	—
1718P Y	—	45.00	85.00	130	210	—
1719P Y	—	50.00	90.00	130	210	—
1720/19P Y Rare	—	—	—	—	—	—
1720P Y	—	50.00	90.00	130	210	—
1721P Y	—	50.00	90.00	130	210	—
1722P Y	—	50.00	90.00	130	210	—
1723P Y	—	45.00	85.00	130	210	—
1724P Y	—	45.00	85.00	130	210	—
1726 Y	—	—	85.00	130	210	—

Date	Mintage	Good	VG	F	VF	XF
1728P M	—	45.00	85.00	130	210	—

KM# 34 2 REALES

6.7668 g., 0.9170 Silver .1995 oz. ASW **Ruler:** Luis I **Obv. Legend:** LVIS PR

Date	Mintage	Good	VG	F	VF	XF
ND(1725-27)P	—	50.00	70.00	100	135	—
1725P Y	—	150	250	375	500	—
1726P Y	—	100	200	300	400	—
1727P Y	—	100	200	300	400	—

KM# 29a 2 REALES

6.7668 g., 0.9170 Silver .1995 oz. ASW **Ruler:** Philip V **Obv:** Cross of Jerusalem, castles and lions in quarters **Rev:** Crowned pillars of Hercules and waves, value at top center

Date	Mintage	Good	VG	F	VF	XF
ND(1729-47)P Date off flan	—	7.50	10.00	15.50	22.50	—
1729P M	—	45.00	85.00	130	210	—
1730P M	—	45.00	85.00	130	210	—
1731//30P M Rare	—	—	—	—	—	—
1731P M	—	45.00	85.00	130	210	—
1732P M	—	45.00	85.00	130	210	—
1732P YA	—	60.00	100	180	375	—
1733P YA	—	60.00	100	180	375	—
1733P E	—	45.00	85.00	130	210	—
1734P E	—	45.00	85.00	130	210	—
1735P E	—	45.00	85.00	130	210	—
1736P E	—	45.00	85.00	130	210	—
1737/6P E Rare	—	—	—	—	—	—
1737//(17)36P E Rare	—	—	—	—	—	—
1737P E	—	45.00	85.00	130	210	—
1737P M	—	45.00	85.00	130	210	—
1738P M	—	45.00	85.00	130	210	—
1739//(17)38P M Rare	—	—	—	—	—	—
1739P M	—	45.00	85.00	130	210	—
1740P M	—	50.00	90.00	135	220	—
1740P P	—	45.00	85.00	130	210	—
1741P P	—	45.00	85.00	130	210	—
1742P C/P Rare	—	—	—	—	—	—
1742P C	—	45.00	85.00	130	210	—
1742P P	—	—	—	—	—	—
1743P C	—	45.00	85.00	130	210	—
1744P q	—	45.00	85.00	130	210	—
1744P C	—	45.00	85.00	130	210	—
1745P q	—	45.00	85.00	130	210	—
1746P q	—	45.00	85.00	130	210	—
1747P q	—	50.00	90.00	135	220	—

KM# 38 2 REALES

6.7668 g., 0.9170 Silver .1995 oz. ASW **Ruler:** Ferdinand VI **Obv:** Cross of Jerusalem, castles and lions at quarters **Obv. Legend:** FERNANDVS VI **Rev:** Crowned pillars of Hercules and waves, value at top center

Date	Mintage	Good	VG	F	VF	XF
ND(1747-60)P Date off flan	—	200	30.00	50.00	75.00	—
1747P q	—	60.00	100	150	225	—
1748P q	—	50.00	90.00	135	220	—
1749/8P q Rare	—	—	—	—	—	—
1749P q	—	50.00	90.00	135	220	—
1750P q	—	50.00	90.00	135	220	—
1750P E/q	—	50.00	90.00	135	220	—
1750P E, q	—	50.00	90.00	135	220	—
1750P E	—	50.00	90.00	135	220	—
1751P q/E	—	60.00	100	175	225	—
1751P E	—	50.00	90.00	135	220	—
1751P q	—	50.00	90.00	135	220	—
1752P q	—	50.00	90.00	135	220	—
1753P C/q Rare	—	—	—	—	—	—
1753P C	—	50.00	90.00	135	220	—
1753P q	—	50.00	90.00	135	220	—
1754P C, q Rare	—	—	—	—	—	—
1754P C	—	50.00	90.00	135	220	—
1754P q/C Rare	—	—	—	—	—	—
1754P q	—	50.00	90.00	135	220	—
1755P q	—	45.00	85.00	130	210	—
1756P q	—	45.00	85.00	130	210	—
1757/6P q	—	45.00	85.00	130	210	—
1757P q	—	45.00	85.00	130	210	—
1758P q	—	45.00	85.00	130	210	—
1759P q	—	45.00	85.00	130	210	—
1760/59P q Rare	—	—	—	—	—	—
1760P q	—	50.00	90.00	135	220	—
1760P q, Y Reported, not confirmed	—	—	—	—	—	—

KM# 43 2 REALES

6.7682 g., 0.9170 Silver .1995 oz. ASW **Ruler:** Charles III **Obv. Legend:** CAROLVS TERTIVS

Date	Mintage	Good	VG	F	VF	XF
ND(1760-73)P Date off flan	—	20.00	30.00	50.00	75.00	—
1760P V/q Rare	—	—	—	—	—	—
1760P V , Y	—	50.00	90.00	130	220	—
1760P Y, V Rare	—	—	—	—	—	—
1761/0/9P V, Y Rare	—	—	—	—	—	—
1761P V, Y	—	40.00	80.00	120	190	—
1762P V, Y	—	40.00	80.00	120	190	—
1763P V, Y	—	40.00	80.00	120	190	—
1764P V, Y	—	40.00	80.00	120	190	—
1765P V , Y	—	40.00	80.00	120	190	—
1766//(17)65P V, Y Rare	—	—	—	—	—	—
1766P V, Y	—	40.00	80.00	120	190	—
1767P V, Y	—	40.00	80.00	120	190	—
1768P V, Y	—	40.00	80.00	120	190	—
1769P V, Y	—	40.00	80.00	120	190	—
1770/69P V, Y Rare	—	—	—	—	—	—
1770P V, Y	—	40.00	80.00	120	190	—
1771/70/69P V, Y Rare	—	—	—	—	—	—
1771P V, Y	—	40.00	80.00	120	190	—
1772/1P V, Y Rare	—	—	—	—	—	—
1772P V	—	40.00	80.00	120	190	—
1773/2P V, Y Rare	—	—	—	—	—	—
1773P V	—	60.00	100	150	225	—

KM# 30 4 REALES

13.5365 g., 0.9170 Silver .4052 oz. ASW **Ruler:** Philip V **Obv. Legend:** PHILIPPVS V

Date	Mintage	Good	VG	F	VF	XF
ND(1702-28)P Date off flan	—	60.00	85.00	140	200	—
1702P Y	—	175	250	400	575	—
1703P Y	—	125	200	325	475	—
1704P Y	—	125	200	325	475	—
1705P Y	—	175	250	400	575	—
1706P Y	—	125	200	325	475	—
1707P Y	—	175	250	400	575	—
1708P Y	—	125	200	325	475	—
1709P Y	—	125	200	325	475	—
1710P Y	—	175	250	400	575	—
1711P Y	—	175	250	400	575	—
1712P Y	—	125	200	325	475	—
1713P Y	—	125	200	325	475	—
1714P Y	—	125	200	325	475	—
1715P Y	—	125	200	325	475	—
1716P Y	—	125	200	325	475	—
1717P Y	—	125	200	325	475	—
1718P Y	—	175	250	400	575	—
1719P Y	—	200	275	450	626	—
1720P Y	—	175	250	400	575	—
1721P Y	—	175	250	400	575	—
1722P Y	—	175	250	400	575	—
1723P Y	—	175	250	400	575	—
1724P Y	—	125	200	325	475	—
1728P M	—	125	200	325	475	—

KM# A35 4 REALES

13.5337 g., 0.9310 Silver .4051 oz. ASW **Ruler:** Luis I **Obv:** Cross of Jerusalem, castles and lions in quarters **Obv. Legend:** LVIS PR.... **Rev:** Crowned pillars of Hercules and waves, value at top center **Rev. Legend:** POTOSI ANO.... **Note:** Inscription on reverse reads...PLV - SVL - TRA.

Date	Mintage	Good	VG	F	VF	XF
1725P Y Rare	—	—	—	—	—	—
1726P Y	—	250	375	500	750	—
1727P Y	—	250	375	500	750	—

KM# 39 4 REALES

13.5365 g., 0.9170 Silver .3991 oz. ASW **Ruler:** Philip V **Obv:** Cross of Jerusalem, lions and castles in quarters **Obv. Legend:** FERNANDVS VI **Rev:** Crowned pillars of Hercules and waves, value at top center

Date	Mintage	Good	VG	F	VF	XF
ND(1748-60)P Date off flan	—	60.00	85.00	140	200	—
1748P q	—	125	200	325	475	—
1749P q	—	125	200	325	475	—
1750P E	—	175	250	400	575	—
1750P q Rare	—	—	—	—	—	—
1751P q/E Rare	—	—	—	—	—	—
1751P E	—	125	200	325	475	—
1751P q	—	175	250	400	575	—
1752P q	—	125	200	325	475	—

Date	Mintage	Good	VG	F	VF	XF
1753P C/q Rare	—	—	—	—	—	—
1753P C	—	100	175	275	400	—
1753P q	—	125	200	325	475	—
1754P C, q Rare	—	—	—	—	—	—
1754P C	—	175	250	400	575	—
1754P q	—	125	200	325	475	—
1755P q	—	125	200	325	475	—
1756P q	—	125	200	325	475	—
1757P q	—	125	200	325	475	—
1758P q	—	125	200	325	475	—
1759P q	—	175	250	400	575	—
1760P q, Y	—	—	—	—	—	—
Note: Reported, not confirmed						
1760P q	—	175	250	400	575	—

KM# 44 4 REALES

13.5365 g., 0.9170 Silver .3991 oz. ASW **Ruler:** Philip V **Obv:** Cross of Jerusalem, castles and lions in quarters **Obv. Legend:** CAROLVS TERTIVS **Rev:** Crowned pillars of Hercules and waves, value at top center

Date	Mintage	Good	VG	F	VF	XF
ND(1760-73)P Date off flan	—	60.00	85.00	140	200	—
1760P V, Y	—	175	250	400	575	—
1760P Y, V Rare	—	—	—	—	—	—
1761P V, Y	—	125	200	325	475	—
1762P V, Y	—	125	200	325	475	—
1763P V, Y	—	100	175	275	375	—
1764P V, Y	—	100	175	275	375	—
1765P V, Y	—	100	175	275	375	—
1766P V, Y	—	100	175	275	375	—
1767P V, Y	—	100	175	275	375	—
1768P V, Y	—	100	175	275	375	—
1769P V, Y	—	100	175	275	375	—
1770P V, Y	—	175	250	400	575	—
1771/0P V, Y Rare	—	—	—	—	—	—
1771P V, Y	—	100	175	275	375	—
1772/1P V, Y Rare	—	—	—	—	—	—
1772P V, Y	—	100	175	275	375	—
1773/2P V, Y Rare	—	—	—	—	—	—
1773P V, Y	—	175	250	400	575	—

KM# 31 8 REALES

27.0730 g., 0.9310 Silver .8103 oz. ASW **Ruler:** Philip V **Obv:** Cross of Jerusalem, lions and castles in quarters **Obv. Legend:** PHILIPPVS V D.G.... **Rev:** Crowned pillars of Hercules and waves, value at top center **Rev. Legend:** POTOSI ANO (date) EL PERV

Date	Mintage	Good	VG	F	VF	XF
ND(1702-28)P Date off flan	—	75.00	125	175	225	—
1702P Y	—	100	200	300	420	—
1703P Y	—	100	200	300	420	—
1704P Y	—	100	200	300	420	—
1705P Y	—	100	200	300	420	—
1706P Y	—	100	200	300	420	—
1707P Y	—	100	200	300	420	—
1708P Y	—	100	200	300	420	—
1709P Y	—	110	220	340	500	—
1710P Y	—	110	220	340	500	—
1711P Y	—	110	220	340	500	—
1712P Y	—	110	220	340	500	—
1713P Y	—	110	220	340	500	—
1714P Y	—	100	200	300	420	—
1715P Y	—	100	200	300	420	—
1716P Y	—	110	220	340	475	—
1717P Y	—	100	200	300	420	—
1718P Y	—	110	220	340	500	—

Date	Mintage	Good	VG	F	VF	XF
1719P Y	—	110	220	340	500	—
1720P Y	—	110	220	340	500	—
1721P Y	—	110	220	340	500	—
1722P Y	—	110	220	340	500	—
1723P Y	—	125	250	375	525	—
1724P Y	—	125	250	375	525	—
1728P M	—	100	200	300	420	—

KM# 35 8 REALES

27.0730 g., 0.9170 Silver .7982 oz. ASW **Ruler:** Luis I **Obv:** Cross of Jerusalem, lions and castles in quarters **Obv. Legend:** LVIS PR **Rev:** Crowned pillars of Hercules and waves, value at top center

Date	Mintage	Good	VG	F	VF	XF
ND(1725-27)P Date off flan	—	150	275	375	500	—
1725P Y	—	250	750	1,500	2,500	—
1726P Y	—	220	575	750	1,250	—
1727P Y LUIS PRI.	—	220	575	750	1,500	—

KM# 31a 8 REALES

27.0674 g., 0.9170 Silver .7980 oz. ASW **Ruler:** Philip V **Obv:** Cross of Jerusalem, lions and castles in quarters **Obv. Legend:** PHILIPPVS V D.G.... **Rev:** Pillars of Hercules and waves, value at top center **Rev. Legend:** POTOSI ANO (date) EL PERV

Date	Mintage	Good	VG	F	VF	XF
ND(1729-47)P Date off flan	—	75.00	125	175	225	—
1729P M	—	100	200	325	475	—
1730P M	—	100	200	325	475	—
1732P M	—	100	200	325	475	—
1731P M	—	100	200	325	475	—
1732P YA	—	175	275	500	750	—
1733P YA	—	175	275	500	750	—
1733P E	—	110	220	340	500	—
1734P E	—	100	200	325	475	—
1735P E	—	100	200	325	475	—
1736P E	—	100	200	325	475	—
1737/5P E Rare	—	—	—	—	—	—
1737P E Rare	—	—	—	—	—	—
1737P M/E Rare	—	—	—	—	—	—
1737P M	—	100	200	325	475	—
1738P M	—	100	200	325	475	—
1739P M	—	100	200	325	475	—
1740P M	—	100	200	325	475	—
1740P P	—	110	220	340	500	—
1741P P	—	100	200	325	475	—
1742P P	—	100	200	325	475	—
1742P C/P Rare	—	—	—	—	—	—
1742P C	—	100	200	325	475	—
1743P C	—	100	200	325	475	—
1744P C	—	100	200	325	475	—
1744P q	—	100	200	325	475	—
1745P q	—	100	200	325	475	—
1746P q	—	100	200	325	475	—
1747P q	—	100	200	325	475	—

KM# 40 8 REALES

27.0730 g., 0.9170 Silver .7982 oz. ASW **Ruler:** Ferdinand VI **Obv:** Cross of Jerusalem, lions and castles in quarters **Obv. Legend:** FERDINANDVS VI **Rev:** Pillars of Hercules and waves, value at top center **Rev. Legend:** POTOSI....

Date	Mintage	Good	VG	F	VF	XF
ND(1747-60)P Date off flan	—	60.00	90.00	130	200	—
1747P q Rare	—	—	—	—	—	—
1748P q	—	100	200	325	475	—
1749/8P q Rare	—	—	—	—	—	—
1749P q	—	100	200	325	475	—
1750P q	—	100	200	325	475	—
1750P E	—	100	200	325	475	—
1750P E/q Rare	—	—	—	—	—	—
1751P q	—	100	200	325	475	—
1751P q Rare	—	—	—	—	—	—
Note: Mint mark and assayer's initial transposed						
1751P E	—	110	220	375	575	—
1751P q/E Rare	—	—	—	—	—	—
1752P q	—	100	200	325	475	—
1753/2P q Rare	—	—	—	—	—	—
1753P q	—	100	200	325	475	—
1753P C/q Rare	—	—	—	—	—	—
1753P C	—	100	200	325	475	—
1754P q	—	100	200	325	475	—
1754P q/C Rare	—	—	—	—	—	—
1754P C, q	—	175	275	375	575	—
1754P C	—	110	220	340	475	—
1755P q	—	90.00	175	275	400	—
1756/5P q Rare	—	—	—	—	—	—
1756P q	—	100	200	300	400	—
1757P q	—	90.00	175	275	400	—
1758P q	—	90.00	175	275	400	—
1759/8P q Rare	—	—	—	—	—	—
1759P q	—	90.00	175	275	400	—
1760P q	—	110	220	375	525	—
1760P q, Y Rare	—	—	—	—	—	—
1760P V, Y Rare	—	—	—	—	—	—

KM# 45 8 REALES

27.0730 g., 0.9170 Silver .7982 oz. ASW **Ruler:** Charles III **Obv:** Cross of Jerusalem, lions and castles in quarters **Obv. Legend:** CAROLVS TERTIVS **Rev:** Pillars of Hercules and waves, value at top center

Date	Mintage	Good	VG	F	VF	XF
ND(1760-78)P Date off flan	—	60.00	90.00	130	200	—
1760P Y, V Rare	—	—	—	—	—	—
1760P V, Y	—	110	220	340	500	—
1761P V,Y	—	90.00	175	275	385	—
1762P V, Y	—	90.00	175	275	385	—
1763P V, Y	—	90.00	175	275	385	—
1764P V, Y	—	90.00	175	275	385	—
1765P V, Y	—	90.00	175	275	385	—
1766P V, Y	—	90.00	175	275	385	—
1767P V, Y	—	90.00	175	275	385	—
1768/7P V, Y Rare	—	—	—	—	—	—
1768P V, Y	—	90.00	175	275	385	—
1769/8P V, Y Rare	—	—	—	—	—	—
1769P V, Y	—	90.00	175	275	385	—
1770/69P V, Y Rare	—	—	—	—	—	—
1770P V, Y	—	90.00	175	275	385	—
1770P V, J Rare	—	—	—	—	—	—
1771/0P V, Y Rare	—	—	—	—	—	—

Date	Mintage	Good	VG	F	VF	XF
1771P V, Y	—	90.00	175	275	385	—
1772/1P V, Y	—	90.00	175	275	385	—
1772P V, Y	—	90.00	175	275	385	—
1773/2P V, Y Rare	—	—	—	—	—	—
1773P V, Y	—	110	225	375	575	—
1778P Error; one known	—	—	—	—	—	—

ROYAL COINAGE

Struck on specially prepared round planchets using well centered dies in excellent condition to prove the quality of the minting to the Viceroy or even to the King

KM# R27 1/2 REAL

1.6917 g., 0.9310 Silver .0506 oz. ASW **Ruler:** Philip V **Obv:** Cross of Jerusalem, lions and castles in quarters **Rev:** PHILIPPVS monogram, date below

Date	Mintage	Good	VG	F	VF	XF
1713P	—	—	250	500	750	1,000
1719P	—	—	250	500	750	1,000

KM# R27a 1/2 REAL

1.6917 g., 0.9170 Silver .0498 oz. ASW **Ruler:** Philip V **Obv:** Cross of Jerusalem, lions and castles in quarters **Rev:** PHILIPPVS monogram, date below

Date	Mintage	Good	VG	F	VF	XF
1736P	—	—	250	500	750	1,000

KM# R36 1/2 REAL

1.6921 g., 0.9170 Silver .0498 oz. ASW **Ruler:** Ferdinand VI **Obv:** Cross of Jerusalem, lions and castles in quarters **Rev:** FERDINANDVS monogram, date below

Date	Mintage	Good	VG	F	VF	XF
1759P	—	—	250	500	750	1,000

KM# R28 REAL

3.3834 g., 0.9310 Silver .1013 oz. ASW **Ruler:** Philip V **Obv:** Cross of Jerusalem, castles and lions in quarters **Obv. Legend:** PHILIPVS V **Rev:** Pillars of Hercules and waves, value at top center

Date	Mintage	Good	VG	F	VF	XF
1702P Y	—	—	500	750	1,000	1,500
1708P Y	—	—	500	750	1,000	1,500
1710P Y	—	—	500	750	1,000	1,500
1715P Y	—	—	500	750	1,000	1,500
1723P Y	—	—	500	750	1,000	1,500

KM# R28a REAL

3.3834 g., 0.9170 Silver .0997 oz. ASW **Ruler:** Philip V **Obv:** Cross of Jerusalem, castles and lions in quarters **Obv. Legend:** PHILIPVS V **Rev:** Pillars of Hercules and waves, value at top center

Date	Mintage	Good	VG	F	VF	XF
1733P YA	—	—	500	750	1,000	1,500
1735P E	—	—	500	750	1,000	1,500
1739P M	—	—	500	750	1,000	1,500
1745P q	—	—	500	750	1,000	1,500

KM# R33 REAL

3.3834 g., 0.9170 Silver .0997 oz. ASW **Ruler:** Philip V **Obv. Legend:** LVIS PR

Date	Mintage	Good	VG	F	VF	XF
1726P Y	—	—	500	750	1,000	1,500

KM# R37 REAL

3.3834 g., 0.9170 Silver .0997 oz. ASW **Ruler:** Ferdinand VI **Obv. Legend:** FERNANDVS VI

Date	Mintage	Good	VG	F	VF	XF
1751P q	—	—	500	750	1,000	1,500

KM# R29 2 REALES

6.7668 g., 0.9310 Silver .2026 oz. ASW **Ruler:** Philip V **Obv:** Cross of Jerusalem, lions and castles in quarters **Obv. Legend:** PHILIPVS V D.G... **Rev:** Pillars of Hercules and waves, value at top center

Date	Mintage	Good	VG	F	VF	XF
1702P Y	—	—	750	1,250	1,750	2,500
1715P Y	—	—	750	1,250	1,750	2,500
1716P Y	—	—	750	1,250	1,750	2,500
1721P Y	—	—	750	1,250	1,750	2,500
1722P Y	—	—	750	1,250	1,750	2,500

KM# R29a 2 REALES

6.7668 g., 0.9170 Silver .1995 oz. ASW **Ruler:** Philip V **Obv:** Cross of Jerusalem, lions and castles in quarters **Obv. Legend:** PHILIPVS V D.G... **Rev:** Pillars of Hercules and waves, value at top center

Date	Mintage	Good	VG	F	VF	XF
1729P M	—	—	750	1,250	1,750	2,500
1742P C	—	—	750	1,250	1,750	2,500
1746P q	—	—	750	1,250	1,750	2,500
1747P q	—	—	750	1,250	1,750	2,500

KM# R34 2 REALES

6.7668 g., 0.9170 Silver .1995 oz. ASW **Ruler:** Philip V **Obv. Legend:** LVIS PR

Date	Mintage	Good	VG	F	VF	XF
1725P Y	—	—	750	1,250	1,750	2,500

KM# R38 2 REALES

6.7668 g., 0.9170 Silver .1995 oz. ASW **Ruler:** Ferdinand VI **Obv:** Cross of Jerusalem, lions and castles in quarters **Obv. Legend:** FERNANDVS VI **Rev:** Pillars of Hercules and waves, value at top center

Date	Mintage	Good	VG	F	VF	XF
1748P q	—	—	750	1,250	1,750	2,500
1749P q	—	—	750	1,250	1,750	2,500

KM# R30 4 REALES

13.5337 g., 0.9310 Silver .4051 oz. ASW **Ruler:** Philip V **Obv. Legend:** PHILIPPVS V

Date	Mintage	Good	VG	F	VF	XF
1709P Y	—	—	1,500	2,500	3,500	5,000
1714P Y	—	—	1,500	2,500	3,500	5,000

KM# R30a 4 REALES

13.5337 g., 0.9170 Silver .3990 oz. ASW **Ruler:** Philip V **Obv:** Cross of Jerusalem, lions and castles in quarters **Obv. Legend:** PHILIPPVS V **Rev:** Pillars of Hercules and waves, value at top center

Date	Mintage	Good	VG	F	VF	XF
1731P M	—	—	1,500	2,500	3,500	5,000
1738P M	—	—	1,500	2,500	3,500	5,000

KM# R-A35 4 REALES

0.9310 g., Silver **Ruler:** Philip V **Obv:** Cross of Jerusalem, castles and lions in quarters **Obv. Legend:** LVIS PR... HISPA **Rev:** Crowned pillars and waves, inscriptions PLV-SVL-TRA **Rev. Legend:** POTOSI ANO...

Date	Mintage	Good	VG	F	VF	XF
1727/6P Y	—	—	1,500	2,500	3,500	5,000
1727P Y	—	—	1,500	2,500	3,500	5,000

KM# R26 8 REALES

27.0674 g., 0.9310 Silver .8102 oz. ASW **Ruler:** Charles II **Obv:** Cross of Jerusalem, lions and castles in quarters **Obv. Legend:** CAROLVS II D.G. HISPANIA **Rev:** Pillars of Hercules and waves, value at top center

Date	Mintage	Good	VG	F	VF	XF
1701P F	—	—	800	1,800	2,400	3,000

KM# R31 8 REALES

27.0674 g., 0.9130 Silver .8102 oz. ASW **Ruler:** Philip V **Obv:** Cross of Jerusalem, lions and castles in quarters **Obv. Legend:** PHILIPPVS V D.G... **Rev:** Pillars of Hercules and waves, value at top center **Rev. Legend:** POTOSI ANO (date) EL PERV

Date	Mintage	Good	VG	F	VF	XF
1702P Y	—	—	900	1,900	2,700	3,500
1703P Y	—	—	1,500	3,000	5,000	7,500
1704P Y	—	—	1,000	2,000	3,000	4,000
1705P Y	—	—	900	1,900	2,700	3,500
1706P Y	—	—	1,000	2,000	3,000	4,000
1707P Y	—	—	1,100	2,200	3,300	5,000
1708P Y	—	—	900	1,900	2,700	3,500
1709P Y	—	—	800	1,800	2,400	3,000
1710P Y	—	—	2,200	4,300	6,500	9,000
1711P Y	—	—	2,200	4,300	6,500	9,000
1712P Y	—	—	1,100	2,200	3,300	5,000
1713P Y	—	—	1,500	3,000	5,000	7,500
1714P Y	—	—	1,500	3,000	5,000	7,500
1715P Y	—	—	800	1,800	2,400	3,000
1716P Y	—	—	1,500	3,000	5,000	7,500
1717P Y	—	—	1,100	2,200	3,300	5,000
1718P Y	—	—	1,500	3,000	5,000	7,500
1719P Y	—	—	1,100	2,200	3,300	5,000
1720P Y	—	—	1,000	2,000	3,000	4,000
1721P Y	—	—	900	1,900	2,700	3,500
1722P Y	—	—	900	1,900	2,700	3,500
1723P Y	—	—	1,000	2,000	3,000	4,000
1724P Y	—	—	2,500	5,000	7,500	10,000
1728P M	—	—	1,500	3,000	5,000	7,500

KM# R31a 8 REALES

27.0674 g., 0.9170 Silver .7980 oz. ASW **Ruler:** Philip V **Obv:** Cross of Jerusalem, lions and castles in quarters **Obv. Legend:** PHILIPPVS V D.G... **Rev:** Pillars of Hercules and waves, value at top center **Rev. Legend:** POTOSI ANO (date) EL PERV

Date	Mintage	Good	VG	F	VF	XF
1729P M	—	—	900	1,900	2,700	3,500
1730P M	—	—	2,200	4,300	6,500	9,000
1731P M	—	—	800	1,800	2,400	3,000
1733P YA	—	—	1,500	3,000	5,000	7,500
1734P E	—	—	1,500	3,000	5,000	7,500
1735P E	—	—	800	1,800	2,400	3,000
1736P E	—	—	1,000	2,000	3,000	4,000
1737P E	—	—	800	1,800	2,400	3,000
1737P M/E	—	—	800	1,800	2,400	3,000
1737P M	—	—	800	1,800	2,400	3,000
1738P M	—	—	900	1,900	2,700	3,500
1739P M	—	—	800	1,800	2,400	3,000
1740P M	—	—	800	1,800	2,400	3,000
1740P P/M	—	—	1,500	3,000	5,000	7,500
1741P P	—	—	1,500	3,000	5,000	7,500
1742P P	—	—	1,300	2,600	4,500	6,000
1742P C	—	—	1,300	2,600	4,500	6,000
1743P C	—	—	1,300	2,600	4,500	6,000
1744P C	—	—	1,300	2,600	4,500	6,000
1744P q	—	—	1,300	2,600	4,500	6,000
1745P q	—	—	1,300	2,600	4,500	6,000
1746P q	—	—	900	1,900	2,700	3,500
1747P q One known	—	—	—	—	—	—

KM# R35 8 REALES

27.0674 g., 0.9170 Silver .7980 oz. ASW **Ruler:** Philip V **Obv:** Cross of Jerusalem, lions and castles in quarters **Obv. Legend:** LVIS PR **Rev:** Pillars of Hercules and waves, value at top center

Date	Mintage	Good	VG	F	VF	XF
1725P Y LVIS PRIMERO	—	—	5,000	7,500	10,000	15,000
1725P Y LVIS PR	—	—	15,000	20,000	20,000	25,000
1726+25P Y LVIS PRIMERO	—	—	7,500	11,250	15,000	20,000
1726P Y LVIS PRIMERO	—	—	2,500	5,000	7,500	10,000
1726P Y LVIS PR	—	—	3,250	6,250	8,750	12,500
1727P Y LVIS PR	—	—	3,250	6,250	8,750	12,500

KM# R40 8 REALES

27.0674 g., 0.9170 Silver .7980 oz. ASW **Ruler:** Ferdinand VI **Obv:** Cross of Jerusalem, lions and castles in quarters **Obv. Legend:** FERDINANDVS VI **Rev:** Pillars of Hercules and waves, value at top center **Rev. Legend:** POTOSI...

Date	Mintage	Good	VG	F	VF	XF
1748P q	—	—	2,500	5,000	7,500	10,000
1749P q	—	—	2,500	5,000	7,500	10,000
1750P E	—	—	2,500	5,000	7,500	10,000
1751P E	—	—	2,500	5,000	7,500	10,000
1753P C One known	—	—	—	—	—	—
1755P q Pomegranate flan; One known	—	—	—	—	—	—
1756P q	—	—	5,000	7,500	10,000	15,000
1759P q	—	—	6,250	9,500	125,000	17,500
1761P V , Y One known	—	—	—	—	—	—

MILLED COINAGE

KM# 82 1/4 REAL

0.8458 g., 0.8960 Silver .0244 oz. ASW **Ruler:** Charles IIII **Obv:** Castle **Rev:** Rampant lion left **Note:** There is a variety of 1802 with base of 2 not struck up and frequently miscataloged as 1809.

Date	Mintage	VG	F	VF	XF	Unc
1796PTS	—	10.00	25.00	45.00	90.00	—
1797PTS	—	10.00	25.00	45.00	90.00	—
1798PTS	—	10.00	25.00	45.00	90.00	—
1799PTS	—	10.00	25.00	45.00	90.00	—
1800PTS	—	13.50	35.00	60.00	125	—

KM# 46 1/2 REAL

1.6917 g., 0.9170 Silver .0498 oz. ASW **Ruler:** Charles III **Obv:** Crowned arms **Obv. Legend:** CAR • III • D • G • HISP • ET • IND • R • **Rev:** Crowned globes **Rev. Legend:** VTRA QVE VNUM **Note:** Mint mark in monogram.

Date	Mintage	VG	F	VF	XF	Unc
1767PTS JR	48,000	25.00	50.00	75.00	130	—
1767PTS J.R Rare	Inc. above	—	—	—	—	—
1768PTS JR	71,000	15.00	30.00	50.00	100	—
1769PTS JR	92,000	15.00	30.00	50.00	80.00	—
1769PTS JR Rounded 9; Rare	Inc. above	—	—	—	—	—
1770PTS JR	201,000	15.00	30.00	50.00	80.00	—
1770PTS JR Rare	Inc. above	—	—	—	—	—

Note: Dot above mint mark

KM# 51 1/2 REAL

1.6917 g., 0.9030 Silver .0491 oz. ASW **Ruler:** Charles III **Obv:** Bust right **Obv. Legend:** CAROLUS III • DEI • GRATIA • **Rev:** Crowned arms between pillars **Rev. Legend:** • HISPAN • ET IND • REX • **Note:** Mint mark in monogram.

Date	Mintage	VG	F	VF	XF	Unc
1773PTS JR	—	16.50	32.50	55.00	90.00	—
1774PTS JR	—	13.50	27.50	45.00	75.00	—
1775PTS JR	—	10.00	20.00	35.00	60.00	—
1776PTS JR	—	25.00	50.00	85.00	140	—
1776PTS PR	—	16.50	32.50	55.00	90.00	—
1777PTS PR	—	13.50	27.50	45.00	75.00	—
1778/7PTS	—	17.50	35.00	60.00	100	—
1778PTS PR	—	17.50	35.00	60.00	100	—
1778PTS PR Error CROLUS	—	100	200	350	—	—
1779/7PTS PR	—	13.50	27.50	45.00	75.00	—
1779/8PTS PR	—	13.50	27.50	45.00	75.00	—
1779PTS PR	—	17.50	35.00	60.00	100	—
1780PTS PR	—	10.00	20.00	35.00	60.00	—
1781PTS PR	—	10.00	20.00	35.00	60.00	—
1782/1PTS PR	—	10.00	20.00	35.00	60.00	—
1782PTS PR	—	10.00	20.00	35.00	60.00	—
1783/2PTS PR	—	10.00	20.00	35.00	60.00	—
1783PTS PR	—	10.00	20.00	35.00	60.00	—
1784PTS PR	—	10.00	20.00	35.00	60.00	—
1785PTS PR	—	10.00	20.00	35.00	60.00	—

KM# 51a 1/2 REAL

1.6917 g., 0.8960 Silver .0487 oz. ASW **Ruler:** Charles III **Obv:** Bust right **Rev:** Crowned arms between pillars **Note:** Mint mark in monogram.

Date	Mintage	VG	F	VF	XF	Unc
1786PTS PR	—	10.00	20.00	35.00	60.00	—
1787/6PTS PR	—	13.50	27.50	45.00	75.00	—
1787PTS PR	—	13.50	27.50	45.00	75.00	—
1788PTS PR	—	17.50	35.00	60.00	100	—
1789PTS PR	—	13.50	27.50	45.00	75.00	—

KM# 60 1/2 REAL

1.6921 g., 0.8960 Silver .0487 oz. ASW **Ruler:** Charles IIII **Obv:** Bust right **Obv. Legend:** CAROLUS IV... **Note:** Mintmark in monogram.

Date	Mintage	VG	F	VF	XF	Unc
1789PTS PR	—	20.00	40.00	65.00	110	—
1790PTS PR	—	16.50	32.50	55.00	90.00	—
1791PTS PR	—	16.50	32.50	55.00	90.00	—

KM# 69 1/2 REAL

1.6917 g., 0.8960 Silver .0487 oz. ASW **Ruler:** Charles IIII **Obv:** Laureate bust right **Obv. Legend:** CAROLUS • IIII • DEI • GRATIA • **Rev:** Crowned arms between pillars **Note:** Mint mark in monogram.

Date	Mintage	VG	F	VF	XF	Unc
1791PTS PR large bust	—	17.50	35.00	60.00	100	—
1792PTS PR	—	17.50	35.00	60.00	100	—
1793PTS PR	—	17.50	35.00	60.00	100	—
1794PTS PR	—	17.50	35.00	60.00	100	—
1795PTS PR	—	27.50	55.00	90.00	150	—
1795PTS PP	—	10.00	20.00	40.00	70.00	—
1796PTS PP	—	10.00	20.00	40.00	70.00	—
1797PTS PP	—	10.00	20.00	40.00	70.00	—
1798PTS PP	—	10.00	20.00	40.00	70.00	—
1799PTS PP	—	10.00	20.00	40.00	70.00	—
1800PTS PP	—	10.00	20.00	40.00	70.00	—
1808PTS PI	—	12.50	25.00	45.00	75.00	300

Note: Assayer error with PI

KM# 47 REAL

3.3834 g., 0.9170 Silver .0997 oz. ASW **Ruler:** Charles III **Obv:** Crowned arms **Obv. Legend:** CAR • III • D • G • HISP • ET • IND • R • **Rev:** Crowned globes **Rev. Legend:** VTRA QVE VNUM **Note:** Mint mark in monogram.

Date	Mintage	VG	F	VF	XF	Unc
1767PTS JR	61,000	30.00	60.00	100	175	—
1768PTS JR	96,000	21.50	42.50	70.00	135	—
1769PTS JR Fancy 9	99,000	21.50	42.50	70.00	135	—
1769PTS JR Rounded 9; Rare	Inc. above	—	—	—	—	—
1770PTS JR	212,000	18.50	37.50	62.50	120	—
1770PTS	—	—	—	—	—	—

Note: Mint mark on both sides of date, no assayer's initial

KM# 52 REAL

3.3834 g., 0.9030 Silver .0982 oz. ASW **Ruler:** Charles III **Obv:** Laureate bust right **Obv. Legend:** CAROLUS • III • DEI • GRATIA • **Rev:** Crowned arms between pillars **Rev. Legend:** HISPAN • ET • IND • REX • **Note:** Mint mark in monogram.

Date	Mintage	VG	F	VF	XF	Unc
1773PTS JR	—	16.50	32.50	55.00	85.00	—
1774PTS JR	—	15.00	30.00	50.00	75.00	—
1775PTS JR	—	15.00	30.00	50.00	75.00	—
1776PTS JR	—	25.00	50.00	85.00	140	—
1776PTS PR	—	15.00	30.00	50.00	75.00	—
1776PTS PR/JR	—	25.00	50.00	85.00	140	—
1777PTS PR	—	15.00	30.00	50.00	75.00	—
1778/6PTS PR	—	15.00	30.00	50.00	75.00	—
1778/7PTS PR	—	15.00	30.00	50.00	75.00	—
1778PTS PR	—	15.00	30.00	50.00	75.00	—
1779/8PTS PR	—	15.00	30.00	50.00	75.00	—
1779PTS PR	—	15.00	30.00	50.00	75.00	—
1780/79PTS PR	—	22.50	45.00	75.00	125	—
1780PTS PR	—	15.00	30.00	50.00	75.00	—
1781PTS PR	—	15.00	30.00	50.00	75.00	—
1782/1PTS PR	—	15.00	30.00	50.00	75.00	—
1782PTS PR	—	15.00	30.00	50.00	75.00	—
1783/2PTS PR	—	15.00	30.00	50.00	75.00	—
1783PTS PR	—	15.00	30.00	50.00	75.00	—
1784/3PTS PR	—	15.00	30.00	50.00	75.00	—
1784PTS PR	—	15.00	30.00	50.00	75.00	—
1785PTS PR	—	18.50	37.50	60.00	100	—

KM# 52a REAL

3.3834 g., 0.8960 Silver .0975 oz. ASW **Ruler:** Charles III **Obv:** Laureate bust right **Rev:** Crowned arms between pillars **Note:** Mint mark in monogram.

Date	Mintage	VG	F	VF	XF	Unc
1786/5PTS PR	—	15.00	30.00	50.00	75.00	—

Date	Mintage	VG	F	VF	XF	Unc
1786PTS PR	—	15.00	30.00	50.00	75.00	—
1787PTS PR	—	15.00	30.00	50.00	75.00	—
1788PTS PR	—	15.00	30.00	50.00	75.00	—
1789PTS PR	—	22.50	45.00	75.00	125	—

KM# 61 REAL

3.3841 g., 0.8960 Silver .0975 oz. ASW **Ruler:** Charles IIII **Obv:** Laureate bust right **Obv. Legend:** CAROLUS • IV • DEI • GRATIA • **Rev:** Crowned arms between pillars **Note:** Mint mark in monogram.

Date	Mintage	VG	F	VF	XF	Unc
1789PTS PR	—	17.50	35.00	60.00	100	—
1790/89PTS PR	—	15.00	30.00	50.00	85.00	—
1790PTS PR	—	15.00	30.00	50.00	85.00	—
1791/81PTS PR	—	13.50	27.50	45.00	75.00	—
1791PTS PR	—	17.50	35.00	60.00	100	—

KM# 70 REAL

3.3834 g., 0.8960 Silver .0975 oz. ASW **Ruler:** Charles IIII **Obv:** Laureate bust right **Obv. Legend:** CAROLUS • IIII • DEI • GRATIA • **Rev:** Crowned arms between pillars **Rev. Legend:** HISPAN • ET • IND • REX ... **Note:** Mint mark in monogram.

Date	Mintage	VG	F	VF	XF	Unc
1791PTS PR	—	12.50	25.00	42.50	70.00	325
1792/1PTS PR	—	8.50	17.50	35.00	60.00	—
1792PTS PR	—	8.50	17.50	30.00	50.00	—
1793PTS PR	—	8.50	17.50	35.00	60.00	—
1794PTS PR	—	12.50	25.00	45.00	90.00	—
1795PTS PR	—	22.50	45.00	75.00	150	—
1795PTS PP	—	13.50	27.50	47.50	90.00	—
1796PTS PP	—	14.00	28.50	55.00	95.00	—
1797PTS PP	—	8.50	17.50	35.00	60.00	—
1798PTS PP	—	8.50	17.50	35.00	60.00	—
1799PTS PP	—	14.00	28.50	55.00	95.00	—
1800PTS PP	—	12.50	25.00	45.00	85.00	—

KM# 48 2 REALES

6.7668 g., 0.9170 Silver .1995 oz. ASW **Ruler:** Charles III **Obv:** Crowned arms **Obv. Legend:** CAR • III • D • G • HISP • ET • IND • R • **Rev:** Crowned globes between pillars **Rev. Legend:** VTRA QVE VNUM **Note:** Mint mark in monogram.

Date	Mintage	VG	F	VF	XF	Unc
1767PTS JR	—	55.00	100	150	270	—
1767PTS JR Rare	—	—	—	—	—	—
Note: No dot over mint mark						
1768PTS JR	—	47.50	90.00	130	240	—
1768PTS JR Rare	—	—	—	—	—	—
Note: Dot over mint mark						
1769/8PTS JR Fancy 9; Rare	—	—	—	—	—	—
1769PTS JR Fancy 9	—	47.50	90.00	130	240	—
1769PTS JR Rounded 9; Rare	—	—	—	—	—	—
1770PTS JR	—	40.00	75.00	110	200	—
1770PTS JR Rare	—	—	—	—	—	—
Note: No dot over mint mark						

KM# 53 2 REALES

6.7668 g., 0.9030 Silver .1965 oz. ASW **Ruler:** Charles III **Obv:** Bust right **Obv. Legend:** CAROLUS • III • DEI • GRATIA • **Rev:** Crowned arms between pillars **Rev. Legend:** • HISPAN • ETINDREX • ... **Note:** Mint mark in monogram.

Date	Mintage	VG	F	VF	XF	Unc
1773PTS JR	—	40.00	100	140	200	—
1773PTS JR GRATA (sic)	—	—	—	—	—	—
1774PTS JR	—	37.50	90.00	125	180	—
1775/3PTS JR	—	—	—	—	—	—
1775PTS JR	—	22.50	60.00	85.00	120	—
1776PTS JR	—	37.50	90.00	125	180	—
1776PTS PR	—	16.50	42.50	60.00	87.50	—
1777PTS PR	—	16.50	42.50	60.00	87.50	—
1778PTS PR	—	16.50	42.50	60.00	87.50	—
1779/8PTS PR	—	—	—	—	—	—
1779PTS PR	—	22.50	60.00	85.00	120	—
1780/79PTS PR	—	13.50	35.00	50.00	75.00	—
1780PTS PR	—	16.50	42.50	60.00	87.50	—
1781PTS PR	—	16.50	42.50	60.00	87.50	—
1782/1PTS PR	—	27.50	70.00	100	140	—
1782PTS PR	—	15.00	37.50	55.00	80.00	—
1783PTS PR	—	15.00	37.50	55.00	80.00	—
1784/3PTS PR	—	27.50	70.00	100	150	—
1784PTS PR	—	15.00	37.50	55.00	80.00	—
1785/3PTS PR	—	—	—	—	—	—
1785/4PTS PR	—	17.50	45.00	62.50	90.00	—
1785PTS PR	—	15.00	37.50	55.00	80.00	—
1786/1PTS PR	—	—	—	—	—	—
1786/4PTS PR	—	—	—	—	—	—
1786PTS PR	—	15.00	37.50	55.00	80.00	—
1787PTS PR	—	15.00	37.50	55.00	80.00	—
1788PTS PR	—	15.00	37.50	55.00	80.00	—
1789P PR	—	25.00	55.00	100	185	—

KM# 62 2 REALES

6.7668 g., 0.8960 Silver .1949 oz. ASW **Ruler:** Charles IIII **Obv:** Bust right **Obv. Legend:** CAROLUS IV•DEI•GRATIA• **Rev:** Crowned arms between pillars **Rev. Legend:** HISPAN•ET IND•REX• **Note:** Mint mark in monogram.

Date	Mintage	VG	F	VF	XF	Unc
1789PTS PR	—	35.00	87.50	125	175	—
1790/89PTS PR	—	35.00	87.50	125	175	—
1790PTS PR	—	35.00	87.50	125	175	—

KM# 71 2 REALES

6.7668 g., 0.8960 Silver .1949 oz. ASW **Ruler:** Charles IIII **Obv:** Bust right **Obv. Legend:** CAROLUS • IIII • DEI • GRATIA • **Rev:** Crowned arms between pillars **Rev. Legend:** HISPAN • ET IND • REX • **Note:** Mint mark in monogram.

Date	Mintage	VG	F	VF	XF	Unc
1791PTS PR	—	22.50	57.50	95.00	185	—
1792PTS PR	—	16.50	42.50	75.00	125	—
1793PTS PR	—	13.50	33.50	70.00	115	—
1794PTS PR	—	13.50	32.50	65.00	110	—
1795PTS PR	—	30.00	75.00	125	200	—
1795PTS PP	—	12.50	30.00	60.00	100	—
1795PTS PP/R	—	30.00	75.00	125	200	—
1796PTS PP	—	12.50	30.00	60.00	100	—
1797PTS PP	—	12.50	30.00	60.00	100	—
1798PTS PP	—	12.50	30.00	60.00	100	—
1799PTS PP	—	12.50	30.00	60.00	100	—
1800PTS PP	—	12.50	30.00	60.00	100	—

KM# 49 4 REALES

13.5365 g., 0.9170 Silver .3990 oz. ASW **Ruler:** Charles III **Obv:** Crowned arms **Obv. Legend:** CAROLUS • III • D • G • HISPAN • ET • IND • REX • **Rev:** Crowned globes between pillars **Rev. Legend:** VTRA QVE VNUM **Note:** Mint mark in monogram.

Date	Mintage	VG	F	VF	XF	Unc
1767PTS JR	—	150	250	400	800	—
1768/7PTS JR	—	125	210	350	600	—
1768PTS JR	—	100	175	300	400	—
1769/8PTS JR fancy 9	—	125	200	325	450	—
1769PTS JR fancy 9	—	100	175	300	400	—
1770/69PTS JR	—	—	—	—	—	—
1770PTS JR large	—	100	175	225	350	—
1770PTS JR small	—	100	175	225	350	—

KM# 54 4 REALES

13.5337 g., 0.9030 Silver .3929 oz. ASW **Ruler:** Charles III **Obv:** Laureate bust right **Obv. Legend:** CAROLUS • III • DEI • GRATIA • **Rev:** Crowned arms between pillars **Rev. Legend:** HISPAN • ETIND • REX • **Note:** Mint mark in monogram.

Date	Mintage	VG	F	VF	XF	Unc
1773PTS JR	—	50.00	82.50	135	275	—
1774PTS JR	—	32.50	55.00	90.00	180	—
1775PTS JR	—	32.50	55.00	90.00	180	—
1776PTS JR	—	35.00	60.00	100	200	—
1776PTS PR	—	40.00	67.50	110	225	—
1777PTS PR	—	32.50	55.00	90.00	180	—
1778PTS JR NEX Error	—	175	300	600	1,200	—
1778/7PTS PR	—	35.00	60.00	100	200	—
1778PTS PR	—	32.50	55.00	90.00	180	—
1779/7PTS PR	—	37.50	62.50	105	210	—
1779PTS PR	—	32.50	55.00	90.00	180	—
1780PTS PR	—	32.50	55.00	90.00	180	—
1781PTS PR	—	32.50	55.00	90.00	180	—
1782/1PTS PR	—	32.50	55.00	90.00	180	—
1782PTS PR	—	32.50	55.00	90.00	180	—
1783PTS PR	—	32.50	55.00	90.00	180	—
1784/3PTS PR	—	35.00	60.00	100	200	—
1784PTS PR	—	35.00	60.00	100	200	—
1785/4PTS PR	—	45.00	75.00	125	250	—
1785PTS PR	—	40.00	67.50	110	225	—
1786/4PTS PR	—	45.00	75.00	125	250	—
1786PTS PR	—	40.00	67.50	110	225	—
1787PTS PR	—	35.00	60.00	100	200	—
1788PTS PR	—	35.00	60.00	100	200	—
1789PTS PR	—	125	250	400	650	—

KM# 63 4 REALES

13.5337 g., 0.8960 Silver .3899 oz. ASW **Ruler:** Charles IIII **Obv:** Laureate bust right **Obv. Legend:** CAROLUS IV • DEI • GRATIA • **Rev:** Crowned arms between pillars **Rev. Legend:** HISPAN • ET IND • REX • **Note:** Mint mark in monogram.

Date	Mintage	VG	F	VF	XF	Unc
1789PTS PR	—	42.50	87.50	175	350	—
1790/89PTS PR	—	35.00	82.50	165	325	—
1790PTS PR	—	35.00	82.50	165	325	—

KM# 72 4 REALES

13.5337 g., 0.8960 Silver .3899 oz. ASW **Ruler:** Charles IIII **Obv:** Laureate bust right **Obv. Legend:** CAROLUS • IIII • DEI • GRATIA • **Rev:** Crowned arms between pillars **Rev. Legend:** HISPAN • ET IND • REX • **Note:** Mint mark in monogram.

Date	Mintage	VG	F	VF	XF	Unc
1791PTS PR	—	32.50	67.50	175	350	—
1792/1PTS PR	—	30.00	62.50	150	325	—
1792PTS PR	—	30.00	62.50	150	325	—
1793PTS PR	—	30.00	62.50	150	325	—
1794PTS PR	—	32.50	67.50	175	350	—
1795/4PTS PR	—	37.50	75.00	190	365	—
1795PTS PR	—	32.50	67.50	175	350	—
1795PTS PP	—	40.00	80.00	195	375	—
1796PTS PP	—	30.00	60.00	175	350	—
1797PTS PP	—	30.00	60.00	175	350	—
1798PTS PP	—	30.00	60.00	175	350	—
1799PTS PP	—	30.00	60.00	175	350	—
1800PTS PP	—	30.00	60.00	175	350	—

KM# 50 8 REALES

27.0674 g., 0.9170 Silver .7980 oz. ASW **Ruler:** Charles III **Obv:** Crowned arms **Obv. Legend:** CAROLUS III • D • G • HISPAN • ET IND • REX • **Rev:** Crowned globes between pillars **Rev. Legend:** VTRA QVE VNUM **Note:** Mint mark in monogram.

Date	Mintage	VG	F	VF	XF	Unc
1767PTS JR	—	650	1,250	2,500	5,500	—
Note: 6-petalled rosette below shield						
1767PTS JR	—	650	1,250	2,500	5,500	—
Note: 4-petalled rosette below shield						
1768PTS JR VRTA 4 known	—	3,500	4,500	7,500	—	—
Note: Error in legend, 6-petalled rosette below shield						
1768PTS JR	—	150	275	400	850	—
Note: 6-petalled rosette bleow shield						
1768PTS JR	—	150	275	400	950	—
Note: 4-petalled rosette below shield						
1769PTS JR Fancy 9	—	150	275	400	850	—
Note: Dot after "CAROLUS"						
1769PTS JR Round 9 over fancy 9	—	150	275	375	600	—
Note: No dot after "CAROLUS"						
1769PTS JR Rounded 9	—	125	250	350	500	—
Note: No dot after "CAROLUS"						
1770/69PTS JR	—	—	250	350	500	—
Note: JR dot after "CAROLUS"						
1770PTS JR	—	60.00	120	220	400	—
Note: JR dot after "CAROLUS"						
1770PTS JR	—	75.00	150	250	450	—
Note: Without dot after "CAROLUS"						

KM# 55 8 REALES

27.0674 g., 0.9030 Silver .7858 oz. ASW **Ruler:** Charles III **Obv:** Laureate bust right **Obv. Legend:** CAROLUS • III • DEI • GRATIA • **Rev:** Crowned arms between pillars **Rev. Legend:** HISPAN • ET IND • REX • **Note:** Mint mark in monogram.

Date	Mintage	VG	F	VF	XF	Unc
1773PTS JR	—	80.00	135	225	375	—
1774PTS JR	—	45.00	72.50	120	200	—
1775PTS JR	—	35.00	60.00	100	165	—
1776PTS JR	—	75.00	125	210	350	—
1776PTS PR	—	45.00	72.50	120	200	—
1777PTS PR	—	35.00	60.00	100	175	—
1778PTS PR	—	35.00	60.00	100	175	—
1779PTS PR	—	55.00	90.00	150	250	—
1780/79PTS PR	—	115	190	315	525	—
1780PTS PR	—	35.00	60.00	100	175	—
1781/0PTS PR	—	35.00	60.00	100	175	—
1781PTS PR	—	35.00	60.00	100	175	—
1782/1PTS PR	—	45.00	72.50	120	200	—
1782PTS PR inverted A's	—	47.50	80.00	135	225	—
1782PTS PR	—	47.50	80.00	135	225	—
1783/1PTS PR	—	65.00	110	180	300	—
1783/78PTS PR	—	65.00	110	180	300	—
1783/2PTS PR	—	65.00	110	180	300	—
1783PTS PR	—	47.50	80.00	135	225	—
1784PTS PR	—	75.00	125	210	350	—
1785/4PTS PR	—	47.50	80.00	135	225	—
1785PTS PR	—	47.50	80.00	135	225	—
1786/5PTS PR	—	45.00	72.50	120	200	—
1786PTS PR	—	35.00	60.00	100	175	—
1787PTS PR	—	35.00	60.00	100	175	—
1788/7PTS PR	—	35.00	60.00	100	175	—
1788PTS PR	—	35.00	60.00	100	175	—
1789PTS PR	—	115	190	315	525	—

KM# 64 8 REALES

27.0674 g., 0.8960 Silver .7797 oz. ASW **Ruler:** Charles IIII **Obv:** Laureate bust right **Obv. Legend:** CAROLUS • IV • DEI • GRATIA • **Rev:** Crowned arms between pillars **Rev. Legend:** HISPAN • ET IND • REX • **Note:** Mint mark in monogram.

Date	Mintage	VG	F	VF	XF	Unc
1789PTS PR	—	47.50	80.00	135	225	—
1790PTS PR	—	45.00	72.50	120	200	—

KM# 73 8 REALES

27.0674 g., 0.8960 Silver .7797 oz. ASW **Ruler:** Charles III **Obv:** Laureate bust right **Obv. Legend:** CAROLUS • IIII • DEI • GRATIA • **Rev:** Crowned arms between pillars **Rev. Legend:** HISPAN • ET IND • REX • **Note:** Mint mark in monogram. Prev. KM#73.1.

Date	Mintage	VG	F	VF	XF	Unc
1791PTS PR	—	47.50	80.00	135	245	—
1792PTS PR	—	42.50	72.50	120	225	—
1793PTS PR	—	32.50	55.00	95.00	185	—
1794PTS PR	—	32.50	55.00	95.00	185	—
1794PTS PR Without periods; Rare	—	—	—	—	—	—
1794PTS PP Without periods; Rare	—	—	—	—	—	—
1795/4PTS PR	—	60.00	100	165	275	—
1795PTS PR	—	65.00	110	180	300	—
1795PTS PP	—	32.50	55.00	95.00	185	—
1796PTS PP	—	32.50	55.00	95.00	185	—
1797PTS PP	—	32.50	55.00	95.00	185	—
1798PTS PP	—	32.50	55.00	95.00	185	—
1799PTS PP	—	32.50	55.00	95.00	185	—
1800PTS PP	—	32.50	55.00	95.00	185	850

KM# 56 ESCUDO

3.3834 g., 0.9040 Gold .0984 oz. AGW **Ruler:** Charles III **Obv:** Armored bust right **Obv. Legend:** CAROL • III • D • G • HISP • ET IND • R • **Rev:** Crowned arms in order chain **Rev. Legend:** IN • UTROQ • FELIX • A • D • **Note:** Mint mark in monogram.

Date	Mintage	VG	F	VF	XF	Unc
1778PTS PR	—	175	225	350	700	—
1779PTS PR Rare	—	—	—	—	—	—
1780PTS PR	—	175	225	350	700	—
1781PTS PR	—	175	225	350	700	—
1782PTS PR	—	175	225	350	700	—
1783PTS PR	—	175	225	350	700	—
1784PTS PR	—	150	200	285	500	—
1785PTS PR	—	150	200	285	500	—
1786PTS PR	—	150	200	285	500	—
1787PTS PR	—	150	200	285	500	—
1788PTS PR Rare	—	—	—	—	—	—

KM# 65 ESCUDO

3.3834 g., 0.8750 Gold .0952 oz. AGW **Ruler:** Charles IIII **Obv:** Bust right **Obv. Legend:** CAROLUS•IV•D•G•HISP•ET IND•R• **Note:** Mint mark in monogram.

Date	Mintage	VG	F	VF	XF	Unc
1789PTS PR	—	175	250	450	800	—
1790PTS PR	—	175	225	350	750	—

KM# 78 ESCUDO

3.3834 g., 0.8750 Gold .0952 oz. AGW **Ruler:** Charles IIII **Obv:** Armored bust right **Obv. Legend:** CAROL • IIII • D • G • HISP • ET IND • R • **Rev:** Crowned arms within order chain **Note:** Mint mark in monogram.

Date	Mintage	VG	F	VF	XF	Unc
1791PTS PR	—	175	225	300	525	—
1792PTS PR	—	175	225	300	525	—
1793PTS PR	—	175	225	300	475	—
1794PTS PR	—	175	225	300	600	—
1795PTS PP	—	175	225	300	475	—
1796PTS PP	—	175	225	300	475	—
1797PTS PP	—	175	225	300	475	—
1798PTS PP	—	175	225	300	475	—
1799PTS PP	—	150	200	275	475	—
1800PTS PP	—	150	200	275	475	—

KM# 74 ESCUDO

3.3834 g., 0.8750 Gold .0952 oz. AGW **Ruler:** Charles IIII **Obv:** Laureate bust **Obv. Legend:** CAROL IIII... **Note:** Mint mark in monogram

Date	Mintage	VG	F	VF	XF	Unc
1791PTS PR	—	400	700	1,350	2,500	—

KM# 57 2 ESCUDOS

6.7668 g., 0.9040 Gold .1967 oz. AGW **Ruler:** Charles III **Obv:** Armored bust right **Obv. Legend:** CAROL III • D • G • HISP • ET IND • R • **Rev:** Crowned arms in order chain **Rev. Legend:** IN • UTROQ • FELIX • AUSPICE • DEO • **Note:** Mint mark in monogram.

Date	Mintage	VG	F	VF	XF	Unc
1778PTS PR Rare	—	—	—	—	—	—
1779PTS PR	—	550	800	1,300	2,250	—
1780PTS PR	—	550	800	1,200	2,150	—
1781/0PTS PR	—	550	800	1,300	2,250	—
1781PTS PR	—	475	725	1,150	2,150	—
1782PTS PR	—	800	1,200	1,750	2,500	—
1783PTS PR	—	250	400	850	1,500	—
1784PTS PR	—	250	350	600	1,450	—
1785PTS PR	—	325	475	875	1,600	—
1786PTS PR	—	350	525	900	1,650	—
1787PTS PR	—	550	800	1,250	2,500	—
1788PTS PR	—	475	725	1,200	2,500	—

KM# 66 2 ESCUDOS

6.7668 g., 0.8750 Gold .1904 oz. AGW **Ruler:** Charles IIII **Obv:** Bust right **Obv. Legend:** CAROL IV•D•G•HISP•ET IND•R• **Note:** Mint mark in monogram.

Date	Mintage	VG	F	VF	XF	Unc
1789PTS PR	—	475	675	1,100	2,200	—
1790PTS PR	—	550	800	1,250	2,500	—

KM# 75 2 ESCUDOS

6.7668 g., 0.8750 Gold .1904 oz. AGW **Ruler:** Charles IIII **Obv:** Laureate armored bust right **Obv. Legend:** CAROL • IIII • D • G • HISP • ET IND • R • **Rev:** Crowned arms within order chain **Rev. Legend:** IN • UTROQ • FELIX • AUSPICE • DEO • **Note:** Mint mark in monogram.

Date	Mintage	VG	F	VF	XF	Unc
1791PTS PR	—	800	1,500	2,500	4,750	—

KM# 79 2 ESCUDOS

6.7668 g., 0.8750 Gold .1904 oz. AGW **Ruler:** Charles IIII **Obv:** Armored bust right **Obv. Legend:** CAROLUS • IIII • D • G • HISP • ET IND • R • **Rev:** Crowned arms within order chain **Rev. Legend:** IN • UTROQ • FELIX • AUSPICE • DEO • **Note:** Mint mark in monogram.

Date	Mintage	VG	F	VF	XF	Unc
1793PTS PR	—	400	550	800	1,200	—
1794PTS PR	—	325	525	650	1,200	—
1795PTS PP	—	250	350	800	1,500	—
1796PTS PP	—	400	550	800	1,500	—
1797PTS PP	—	400	550	700	1,300	—
1798PTS PP	—	400	550	700	1,300	—
1799PTS PP	—	325	475	600	1,200	—
1800PTS PP	—	250	350	525	850	—

KM# 58 4 ESCUDOS

13.5337 g., 0.9040 Gold .3934 oz. AGW **Ruler:** Charles III **Obv:** Bust right **Obv. Legend:** CAROL•III•D•G•HISP•ET IND•R• **Rev:** Crowned arms in order chain **Rev. Legend:** IN•UTROQ•FELIX• AUSPICE•DEO **Note:** Mint mark in monogram.

Date	Mintage	VG	F	VF	XF	Unc
1778PTS PR	—	725	1,000	1,850	3,750	—
1779PTS PR	—	725	1,000	1,650	3,250	—
1780PTS PR	—	725	1,000	1,650	3,250	—
1781PTS PR	—	550	850	1,450	3,000	—
1782PTS PR	—	550	850	1,450	3,000	—
1783PTS PR	—	550	850	1,450	3,000	—
1784/3PTS PR	—	550	850	1,450	3,000	—
1784PTS PR	—	550	850	1,450	3,000	—
1785PTS PR	—	550	850	1,450	3,000	—
1786PTS PR	—	550	850	1,450	3,000	—
1787PTS PR	—	550	850	1,450	3,000	—
1788PTS PR	—	550	850	1,450	3,000	—

KM# 67 4 ESCUDOS

13.5337 g., 0.8750 Gold .3808 oz. AGW **Ruler:** Charles IIII **Obv:** Armored bust right **Obv. Legend:** CAROL • IV • D • G • HISP • ET IND • R • **Rev:** Crowned arms within order chain **Rev. Legend:** IN • UTROQ • FELIX • AUSPICE • DEO • **Note:** Mint mark in monogram

Date	Mintage	VG	F	VF	XF	Unc
1789PTS PR Rare	—	—	—	—	—	—
Note: Sotheby's Geneva 5-90 almost VF realized $18,480						
1790PTS PR Rare	—	—	—	—	—	—

KM# 76 4 ESCUDOS

13.5337 g., 0.8750 Gold .3808 oz. AGW **Ruler:** Charles IIII **Obv:** Laureate armored bust right **Obv. Legend:** CAROL • IIII • D • G • HISP • ET IND • R • **Rev:** Crowned arms within order chain **Rev. Inscription:** IN • UTROQ • FELIX • AUSPICE • DEO • **Note:** Mint mark in monogram.

Date	Mintage	VG	F	VF	XF	Unc
1791PTS PR	—	800	1,250	2,450	4,500	—

KM# 80 4 ESCUDOS

13.5337 g., 0.8750 Gold .3807 oz. AGW **Ruler:** Charles IIII **Obv:** Armored bust right **Obv. Legend:** CAROL • IIII • D • G • HISP • ET IND • R • **Rev:** Crowned arms within order chain **Rev. Legend:** IN • UTROQ • FELIX • AUSPICE • DEO • **Note:** Mint mark in monogram.

Date	Mintage	VG	F	VF	XF	Unc
1791PTS PR Large bust	—	475	675	1,250	2,750	—
1792PTS PR Large bust	—	475	675	1,250	2,750	—
1793PTS PR	—	475	675	1,250	2,750	—
1794PTS PR	—	550	750	1,350	2,850	—
1795PTS PR	—	550	750	1,350	2,850	—
1795PTS PP	—	475	750	1,100	2,500	—
1796PTS PP	—	475	600	1,100	2,500	—
1797PTS PP	—	400	550	950	2,450	—
1798PTS PP	—	400	550	950	2,450	—
1799PTS PP	—	400	550	950	2,450	—
1800PTS PP	—	400	550	950	2,450	—

KM# 59 8 ESCUDOS

27.0674 g., 0.9040 Gold .7869 oz. AGW **Ruler:** Charles III **Obv:** Laureate armored bust right **Obv. Legend:** CAROL • III • D • G • HISP • ET IND • R • **Rev:** Crowned arms in Order chain **Rev. Legend:** IN • UTROQ • FELIX • AUSPICE • DEO • **Note:** Mint mark in monogram.

Date	Mintage	VG	F	VF	XF	Unc
1778PTS PR	—	500	700	1,650	2,750	—
1779PTS PR	—	450	600	900	1,850	—
1780PTS PR	—	400	500	750	1,450	—
1781PTS PR	—	400	500	750	1,450	—
1782PTS PR	—	450	600	900	1,600	—
1783PTS PR	—	450	600	900	1,600	—
1784/3PTS PR	—	450	600	900	1,600	—
1784PTS PR	—	450	600	900	1,600	—
1785PTS PR	—	400	500	750	1,600	—
1786/5PTS PR	—	450	600	900	1,600	—
1786PTS PR	—	450	600	900	1,600	—
1787/6PTS PR	—	450	600	900	1,600	—
1787PTS PR	—	450	600	900	1,600	—
1788PTS	—	450	600	900	1,450	—

KM# 68 8 ESCUDOS

27.0674 g., 0.8750 Gold .7615 oz. AGW **Obv:** Armored bust right **Obv. Legend:** CAROL • IV • D • G • HISP • ET IND • R • **Rev:** Crowned arms within order chain **Note:** On 1789 and 1790/89 dates, IV can be seen re-engraved over III. Mint mark in monogram.

Date	Mintage	VG	F	VF	XF	Unc
1789PTS PR	—	500	700	1,000	1,750	—
1790/89PTS PR	—	450	600	900	1,650	—
1790PTS PR	—	400	500	750	1,450	—

KM# 77 8 ESCUDOS

27.0674 g., 0.8750 Gold .7615 oz. AGW **Ruler:** Charles IIII **Obv:** Laureate armored bust right **Obv. Legend:** CAROL • IIII • D • G • HISP • ET IND • R • **Rev:** Crowned arms within order chain **Rev. Legend:** IN • UTROQ • FELIX • AUSPICE • DEO • **Note:** Mint mark in monogram.

Date	Mintage	VG	F	VF	XF	Unc
1791PTS PR	—	1,250	2,000	3,500	6,500	—

KM# 81 8 ESCUDOS

27.0674 g., 0.8750 Gold .7615 oz. AGW **Ruler:** Charles IIII **Obv:** Armored bust right **Obv. Legend:** CAROL • IIII • D • G • HISP • ET IND • R • **Rev:** Crowned arms within order chain **Note:** Mint mark in monogram.

Date	Mintage	VG	F	VF	XF	Unc
1791PTS PR	—	500	750	1,250	2,000	—
1792/1PTS PR	—	375	425	675	1,000	—
1792PTS PR	—	375	425	650	950	—
1793PTS PR	—	375	425	650	950	—
1794PTS PR	—	375	425	650	950	—
1795PTS PP	—	375	425	650	950	—
1796PTS PP	—	375	425	650	950	—
1797PTS PP	—	375	425	650	950	—
1798PTS PP	—	375	425	650	950	—
1799PTS PP	—	375	425	650	950	—
1800PTS PP	—	375	425	650	950	—

The Federative Republic of Brazil, which comprises half the continent of South America and is the only Latin American country deriving its culture and language from Portugal, has an area of 3,286,488 sq. mi. (8,511,965 sq. km.) and a population of *169.2 million. Capital: Brasilia. The economy of Brazil is as varied and complex as any in the developing world. Agriculture is a mainstay of the economy, while only 4 percent of the area is under cultivation. Known mineral resources are almost unlimited in variety and size of reserves. A large, relatively sophisticated industry ranges from basic steel and chemical production to finished consumer goods. Coffee, cotton, iron ore and cocoa are the chief exports.

Brazil was discovered and claimed for Portugal by Admiral Pedro Alvares Cabral in 1500. Portugal established a settlement in 1532 and proclaimed the area a royal colony in 1549. During the Napoleonic Wars, Dom Joao VI established the seat of Portuguese government in Rio de Janeiro. When he returned to Portugal, his son Dom Pedro I declared Brazil's independence on Sept. 7, 1822, and became emperor of Brazil. The Empire of Brazil was maintained until 1889 when the federal republic was established. The Federative Republic was established in 1946 by terms of a constitution drawn up by a constituent assembly. Following a coup in 1964 the armed forces retained overall control under a dictatorship until civilian government was restored on March 15, 1985. The current constitution was adopted in 1988.

RULERS

Portuguese
Pedro,
 As Pedro II, 1683-1706
Joao VI, 1706-1750
Jose I, 1750-1777
Maria I and Pedro III, 1777-1786
Maria I, widow, 1786-1816
Joao, Prince Regent, 1799-1818

MINT MARKS

B - Bahia
R - Rio de Janeiro
W/o mint mark - Lisbon 1715-1805

MONETARY SYSTEM

(Until 1833)
120 Reis = 1 Real
6400 Reis 1 Peca (Dobra = Johannes (Joe) = 4 Escudos

PORTUGUESE COLONY

MILLED COINAGE

KM# 159 5 REIS

Copper **Ruler:** Joao VI **Obv:** Crowned value above date in inner circle **Obv. Legend:** JOHANNSS. V. D. G. P. ET. BRASIL. REX **Rev:** Globe **Note:** Struck at Lisbon for Maranhao.

Date	Mintage	VG	F	VF	XF	Unc
1749	—	10.00	20.00	40.00	75.00	—

KM# 173.1 5 REIS

Copper **Ruler:** Jose I **Obv. Legend:** IOSEPHUS. I. D. G.. **Rev:** Thin parallels on globe **Note:** Struck at Lisbon but without mint mark.

Date	Mintage	VG	F	VF	XF	Unc
1752	—	50.00	90.00	175	450	—
1753	418,000	3.50	6.00	18.00	35.00	—

KM# 188 5 REIS

Copper **Ruler:** Jose I **Obv:** Crowned value above date, beaded circle surrounds **Obv. Legend:** JOSEPHUS • I • D • G • ... **Rev:** Thick parallels on globe

Date	Mintage	VG	F	VF	XF	Unc
1762B	—	2.50	5.50	10.00	27.00	—
1763B	—	3.00	7.00	13.00	35.00	—
1764B	—	2.00	4.50	8.00	22.00	—
1766B	—	2.00	4.50	8.00	22.00	—
1767B	—	2.00	4.50	8.00	22.00	—
1768B	—	2.00	4.50	8.00	22.00	—
1769B	—	2.00	4.50	8.00	22.00	—

KM# 173.2 5 REIS

Copper **Ruler:** Jose I **Obv:** Crowned value above date, beaded circle surrounds **Obv. Legend:** JOSEPHUS • I • D • G • .... **Rev:** Thin parallels on globe

Date	Mintage	VG	F	VF	XF	Unc
1765R	—	2.50	5.50	15.00	32.00	—
1766R	—	2.50	5.50	15.00	32.00	—
1767R	69,000	6.00	14.00	35.00	90.00	—
1768R	7,702	60.00	120	200	350	—
1772R	47,000	4.00	9.00	25.00	55.00	—
1773R	69,000	3.00	7.00	18.00	45.00	—
1774R	125,000	2.50	5.50	15.00	40.00	—
1775R	78,000	2.50	5.50	15.00	40.00	—
1776R	78,000	6.00	14.00	35.00	90.00	—
1777R	62,000	6.00	14.00	35.00	90.00	—

KM# 173.3 5 REIS

Copper **Ruler:** Jose I **Note:** Struck at Lisbon without mint mark.

Date	Mintage	VG	F	VF	XF	Unc
1768 PECUNIA	—	1.00	2.50	9.00	25.00	—
1768 PECUNIA	—	2.00	3.50	10.00	30.00	—
1773	660,000	1.00	2.50	9.00	25.00	—
1774	1,800,000	1.00	2.50	9.00	25.00	—

KM# 200 5 REIS

Copper **Ruler:** Maria I and Pedro III **Obv. Legend:** MARIA. I. E. PETRUS. III. D. G. P. E. **Rev:** Globe **Rev. Legend:** PECUNIA. TOTUM. CIRCUMIT...

Date	Mintage	VG	F	VF	XF	Unc
1778B	575,000	3.00	7.00	18.00	45.00	—
1781B	192,000	2.00	6.00	12.00	30.00	—
1782B	200,000	2.00	5.00	10.00	25.00	—
1784B	389,000	2.00	5.00	10.00	25.00	—
1785B	389,000	2.00	5.00	10.00	25.00	—

KM# 214.1 5 REIS

Copper **Ruler:** Maria I Widow **Obv. Legend:** MARIA. I. D. G. P. ET. BRASILIAE...

Date	Mintage	VG	F	VF	XF	Unc
1786B	395,000	3.00	8.00	20.00	50.00	—
1787B	270,000	3.00	8.00	20.00	50.00	—
1790B	283,000	3.00	8.00	20.00	50.00	—
1791B	402,000	3.00	8.00	20.00	50.00	—
1797B	160,000	15.00	25.00	45.00	90.00	—

KM# 214.2 5 REIS

Copper **Ruler:** Maria I Widow **Obv:** High full arch crown above V

Date	Mintage	VG	F	VF	XF	Unc
1786B	Inc. above	3.00	8.00	20.00	50.00	—
1787B	Inc. above	3.00	8.00	20.00	50.00	—
1790B	Inc. above	3.00	8.00	20.00	50.00	—
1791B	Inc. above	8.00	16.00	35.00	75.00	—

KM# 227 5 REIS

Copper **Ruler:** Joao Prince Regent **Note:** Reduced size.

Date	Mintage	VG	F	VF	XF	Unc
1799B	—	50.00	90.00	175	300	—

KM# 107 10 REIS

Copper **Ruler:** Joao VI **Obv:** Crowned value in inner circle **Obv. Legend:** JOHANNES. V. D. G. P. ET. BRASIL. REX. **Rev:** Globe

Date	Mintage	VG	F	VF	XF	Unc
ND	—	65.00	125	200	350	—

KM# 108 10 REIS

Copper **Ruler:** Joao VI **Obv:** Crowned value and date in inner circle

Date	Mintage	VG	F	VF	XF	Unc
1715	—	4.00	8.00	15.00	45.00	—
1718	—	4.00	8.00	15.00	45.00	—
1719	—	4.00	8.00	15.00	45.00	—
1720	—	4.50	9.00	18.00	50.00	—

KM# 142.1 10 REIS

Copper **Ruler:** Joao VI **Rev:** Globe **Rev. Legend:** PECVNIA

Date	Mintage	VG	F	VF	XF	Unc
1729B	—	5.00	7.00	12.00	35.00	—
1730B	—	5.00	7.00	12.00	35.00	—
1731B Rare	—	—	—	—	—	—
1747B	—	20.00	35.00	75.00	150	—
1748B	—	50.00	75.00	100	200	—

KM# 142.2 10 REIS

Copper **Ruler:** Joao VI **Rev. Legend:** PECUNIA

Date	Mintage	VG	F	VF	XF	Unc
1730B	—	6.00	9.00	22.00	45.00	—
1731B	—	5.00	7.00	12.00	35.00	—
1732B	—	5.00	7.00	12.00	35.00	—

KM# 142.3 10 REIS

Copper **Ruler:** Joao VI **Obv:** Crowned value and date between dots in inner circle **Rev:** Globe

Date	Mintage	VG	F	VF	XF	Unc
1735	—	7.00	12.00	30.00	60.00	—
1736	—	12.00	28.00	60.00	110	—
1746	—	15.00	32.00	70.00	135	—

KM# 142.4 10 REIS

Copper **Ruler:** Joao VI **Obv:** Wthout dots at sides of date

Date	Mintage	VG	F	VF	XF	Unc
1746	—	18.00	35.00	75.00	150	—

KM# 142.5 10 REIS

Copper **Ruler:** Joao VI **Obv:** Crowned value and date in inner circle **Note:** Struck at Lisbon for Maranhao.

Date	Mintage	VG	F	VF	XF	Unc
1749	—	12.00	28.00	60.00	110	—

KM# 165.1 10 REIS

Copper **Ruler:** Jose I **Obv. Legend:** JOSEPHUS. I. D. G.. **Rev:** Thick parallels on globe **Note:** Struck at Rio de Janeiro without mint mark.

Date	Mintage	VG	F	VF	XF	Unc
1751 BRASI	—	50.00	100	200	400	—
1751 BRAS	—	50.00	100	200	400	—

KM# 174.1 10 REIS

Copper **Ruler:** Jose I **Obv. Legend:** JOSEPHUS I. D. G.. **Rev:** Thin parallels on globe **Note:** Struck at Lisbon Mint without mint mark.

Date	Mintage	VG	F	VF	XF	Unc
1752	—	10.00	25.00	60.00	120	—
1753	700,000	6.00	15.00	28.00	60.00	—

KM# 165.2 10 REIS

Copper **Ruler:** Jose I **Obv. Legend:** JOSEPHUS. I. D. G.. **Rev:** Thick parallels on globe

Date	Mintage	VG	F	VF	XF	Unc
1762B	—	8.00	15.00	30.00	60.00	—

KM# 174.2 10 REIS

Copper **Ruler:** Jose I **Rev:** Thin parallels on globe

Date	Mintage	VG	F	VF	XF	Unc
1773	2,021,000	5.00	12.00	22.00	50.00	—
1774	Inc. above	3.00	7.50	15.00	35.00	—
1775	934,000	3.00	7.50	15.00	35.00	—
1776	608,000	3.00	7.50	15.00	35.00	—

KM# 201 10 REIS

Copper **Ruler:** Maria I and Pedro III **Obv. Legend:** MARIA. I. E. PETRUS III... **Rev:** Globe **Rev. Legend:** PECUNIA. TOTUM. CIRCUM. IT..

Date	Mintage	VG	F	VF	XF	Unc
1778	767,000	3.00	5.00	10.00	25.00	—
1781	312,000	5.00	8.00	12.50	30.00	—
1782	295,000	5.00	8.00	12.50	30.00	—
1784	189,000	10.00	14.00	20.00	45.00	—
1785	405,000	10.00	14.00	25.00	55.00	—

KM# 215.1 10 REIS

Copper **Ruler:** Joao Prince Regent **Obv:** Low flat arch crown above "x" **Obv. Legend:** MARIA. I. D. G. P. ET. BRASILIAE...

Date	Mintage	VG	F	VF	XF	Unc
1786	425,000	5.00	9.00	15.00	35.00	—
1787	314,000	5.00	9.00	15.00	35.00	—
1790	379,000	12.00	22.50	35.00	65.00	—
1796	260,000	15.00	30.00	60.00	120	—

KM# 215.2 10 REIS

Copper **Ruler:** Maria I Widow **Obv:** High full arch crown above "x"

Date	Mintage	VG	F	VF	XF	Unc
1786	Inc. above	5.00	9.00	15.00	35.00	—
1787	Inc. above	10.00	20.00	40.00	80.00	—
1790	Inc. above	10.00	20.00	40.00	80.00	—

KM# 228 10 REIS

Copper **Note:** Reduced size.

Date	Mintage	VG	F	VF	XF	Unc
1799	—	5.00	7.50	12.50	35.00	—

KM# 85.2 20 REIS

Silver **Ruler:** Pedro As Pedro II **Obv:** Crowned arms **Rev:** Globe on cross, rosettes in angles

Date	Mintage	VG	F	VF	XF	Unc
ND(1700-1702) P	—	40.00	100	200	350	—

KM# 109 20 REIS

Copper **Ruler:** Joao VI **Obv:** Crowned value and date in inner circle **Obv. Legend:** JOHANNES. V. D. G. P. ET. BRASIL. REX **Rev:** Globe

Date	Mintage	VG	F	VF	XF	Unc
1715	—	8.00	16.00	35.00	60.00	—
1718	—	8.00	16.00	35.00	60.00	—
1719	—	5.00	10.00	20.00	35.00	—
1729	—	8.00	16.00	35.00	60.00	—

KM# 110 20 REIS

Copper **Ruler:** Joao VI **Obv:** Crowned arms. **Rev:** Value in wreath, date at top **Note:** Struck at Lisbon for Minas Gerais.

Date	Mintage	VG	F	VF	XF	Unc
1722	—	6.00	12.00	25.00	45.00	—

KM# 143.1 20 REIS

Copper **Ruler:** Joao VI **Obv:** Crowned value and date in inner circle **Rev:** Globe **Rev. Legend:** PECVNIA

Date	Mintage	VG	F	VF	XF	Unc
1729B	—	6.00	12.00	25.00	45.00	—
1730B	—	6.00	12.00	25.00	45.00	—
1731B	—	6.00	12.00	25.00	45.00	—
1748B	—	70.00	150	250	400	—

KM# 143.2 20 REIS

Copper **Ruler:** Joao VI **Rev. Legend:** PECUNIA

Date	Mintage	VG	F	VF	XF	Unc
1729B	—	6.00	12.00	25.00	45.00	—
1730B	—	6.00	12.00	25.00	45.00	—
1731B	—	7.00	14.00	28.00	55.00	—

KM# 143.3 20 REIS

Copper **Ruler:** Joao VI **Obv:** Crowned value and date between dots in inner circle **Rev:** Globe

Date	Mintage	VG	F	VF	XF	Unc
1735	—	5.00	10.00	20.00	40.00	—
1736	—	5.00	10.00	20.00	40.00	—

KM# 143.4 20 REIS

Copper **Ruler:** Joao VI **Obv:** Crowned value and date between crosses in inner circle

Date	Mintage	VG	F	VF	XF	Unc
1735	—	5.00	10.00	20.00	40.00	—
1736	—	5.00	10.00	20.00	40.00	—
1746	—	6.00	12.00	25.00	50.00	—

KM# 143.5 20 REIS

Copper **Ruler:** Joao VI **Obv:** Crowned value above date in inner circle **Note:** Struck at Lisbon for Maranhao.

Date	Mintage	VG	F	VF	XF	Unc
1749	—	6.00	12.00	25.00	50.00	—

KM# 166.1 20 REIS

Copper **Ruler:** Jose I **Obv. Legend:** JOSEPHUS. I. D. G.. **Rev:** Thick parallels on globe **Note:** Struck at Rio de Janeiro without mint mark.

Date	Mintage	VG	F	VF	XF	Unc
1751	—	45.00	90.00	175	350	—
1752	—	45.00	90.00	175	350	—

KM# 175.1 20 REIS

Copper **Ruler:** Jose I **Obv. Legend:** IOSEPHUS. I. D. G.. **Rev:** Thin parallels on globe **Note:** Struck at Lisbon without mint mark.

Date	Mintage	VG	F	VF	XF	Unc
1752	—	6.00	12.00	20.00	50.00	—
1753	403,000	3.50	6.00	12.00	30.00	—

KM# 166.2 20 REIS

Copper **Ruler:** Jose I **Obv. Legend:** JOSEPHUS. I. D. G.. **Rev:** Thick parallels on globe

Date	Mintage	VG	F	VF	XF	Unc
1761B	—	25.00	55.00	120	200	—

KM# 175.2 20 REIS

Copper **Ruler:** Jose I **Rev:** Thin parallels on globe

Date	Mintage	VG	F	VF	XF	Unc
1773	1,594,000	2.50	5.00	10.00	25.00	—
1774	Inc. above	2.50	5.00	10.00	25.00	—
1775	995,000	2.50	5.00	10.00	25.00	—
1776	607,000	2.50	5.00	10.00	25.00	—

KM# 202 20 REIS

Copper **Ruler:** Maria I and Pedro III **Obv. Legend:** MARIA. I. E. PETRUS. III... **Rev:** Globe **Rev. Legend:** PECUNIA. TOTUM. CIRCUMIT...

Date	Mintage	VG	F	VF	XF	Unc
1778	567,000	3.50	6.00	12.00	30.00	—
1781	55,000	7.50	12.50	22.00	52.00	—
1782	371,000	2.50	5.00	9.00	22.00	—
1784	423,000	2.50	5.00	9.00	22.00	—

KM# 216.1 20 REIS

Copper **Ruler:** Maria I Widow **Obv:** Low flat arch above "XX" **Obv. Legend:** MARIA. I. D. G. P. ET. BRASILIAE...

Date	Mintage	VG	F	VF	XF	Unc
1786	301,000	2.50	5.00	10.00	25.00	—
1787	254,000	2.50	1.00	10.00	25.00	—
1790	348,000	20.00	40.00	90.00	175	—
1796	126,000	50.00	85.00	175	350	—
1799	198,000	50.00	85.00	175	350	—

KM# 216.2 20 REIS

Copper **Ruler:** Maria I Widow **Obv:** High full arch crown above "XX"

Date	Mintage	VG	F	VF	XF	Unc
1786	Inc. above	3.50	6.00	12.00	30.00	—
1787	Inc. above	3.50	6.00	12.00	30.00	—
1790	Inc. above	35.00	65.00	125	250	—
1799	Inc. above	100	200	350	500	—

KM# 229 20 REIS

Copper **Note:** Reduced size

Date	Mintage	VG	F	VF	XF	Unc
1799	—	5.00	7.50	12.00	30.00	—

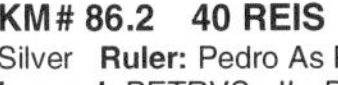

KM# 86.2 40 REIS

Silver **Ruler:** Pedro As Pedro II **Obv:** Crowned arms **Obv. Legend:** PETRVS • II • D • G • P • R • E • B • D • **Rev:** Sash crosses globe on cross, thin straight parallels **Rev. Legend:** SIGN NATA STAB SVBQ **Note:** Varieties exist.

Date	Mintage	Good	VG	F	VF	XF
ND(1700-02)P	—	50.00	80.00	150	250	—

KM# 111 40 REIS

Copper **Obv:** Crowned arms **Obv. Legend:** JOHANNES. V. D. G. P. ET . BRASIL. REX.. **Rev:** Value in wreath, date at top **Note:** Struck at Lisbon for Minas Gerais.

Date	Mintage	VG	F	VF	XF	Unc
1722	—	6.00	12.00	25.00	45.00	—

KM# 184.1 40 REIS

Copper **Ruler:** Jose I **Obv. Legend:** IOSEPHUS. I. D. G.. **Rev:** Thin parallels on globe **Note:** Struck at Lisbon without mint mark. Varieties exist.

Date	Mintage	VG	F	VF	XF	Unc
1753	121,000	3.00	6.00	12.00	25.00	—
1760	216,000	5.00	10.00	20.00	40.00	—

KM# 184.2 40 REIS

Copper **Ruler:** Jose I **Obv. Legend:** JOSEPHUS. I. D. G.. **Rev:** Thin parallels on globe **Note:** Struck at Lisbon without mint mark.

Date	Mintage	VG	F	VF	XF	Unc
1774	231,000	7.00	15.00	30.00	50.00	—

KM# 189 40 REIS

Copper **Ruler:** Jose I **Obv. Legend:** JOSEPHUS. I. D. G.. **Rev:** Thick parallels on globe **Note:** Varieties exist.

Date	Mintage	VG	F	VF	XF	Unc
1762B	—	7.00	15.00	30.00	50.00	—

KM# 203 40 REIS

Copper **Ruler:** Maria I and Pedro III **Obv:** Crowned XL **Obv. Legend:** MARIA. I. E. PETRUS. III.. **Rev:** Globe **Rev. Legend:** PECUNIA. TOTUM. CIRCUMIT..

Date	Mintage	VG	F	VF	XF	Unc
1778	183,000	10.00	20.00	40.00	70.00	—
1781	92,000	10.00	20.00	40.00	70.00	—
1784	90,000	10.00	22.00	45.00	80.00	—

KM# 217.1 40 REIS

Copper **Ruler:** Maria I Widow **Obv:** Low flat arch crown above "XL" **Obv. Legend:** MARIA. I. D. G..

Date	Mintage	VG	F	VF	XF	Unc
1786	100,000	10.00	20.00	40.00	70.00	—
1790	140,000	20.00	40.00	100	200	—
1791	53,000	25.00	50.00	120	250	—
1796	101,000	20.00	40.00	100	200	—

KM# 217.2 40 REIS

Copper **Ruler:** Maria I Widow **Obv:** High full arch crown above "XL"

Date	Mintage	VG	F	VF	XF	Unc
1786	Inc. above	15.00	30.00	50.00	90.00	—
1787	79,000	10.00	20.00	40.00	70.00	—
1790	Inc. above	50.00	100	200	450	—
1791	Inc. above	75.00	150	300	550	—

KM# 230 40 REIS

Copper **Note:** Reduced size

Date	Mintage	VG	F	VF	XF	Unc
1799	—	6.00	12.00	25.00	45.00	—

KM# 176.1 75 REIS

2.2648 g., 0.9170 Silver .0667 oz. ASW **Ruler:** Jose I **Obv:** Crowned "J", florals at right, value at left **Rev:** Globe on cross with "B" at center **Rev. Legend:** SIGN NATA STAB SVBQ

Date	Mintage	Good	VG	F	VF	XF
1752B	—	150	300	500	850	—
1753B	—	50.00	90.00	185	350	—
1754B	—	50.00	90.00	185	350	—

KM# 176.2 75 REIS

2.2648 g., 0.9170 Silver .0667 oz. ASW **Ruler:** Jose I **Obv:** Crowned "J", florals at right, value at left **Rev:** Globe on cross with "R" at center **Rev. Legend:** SIGN • NATA • STAB • SVBQ

Date	Mintage	Good	VG	F	VF	XF
1754R	—	25.00	40.00	75.00	150	—
1755R	—	25.00	40.00	75.00	150	—
1760R	—	60.00	100	200	400	—

KM# 87.2 80 REIS

2.2400 g., 0.9170 Silver .0660 oz. ASW **Ruler:** Pedro As Pedro II **Obv:** Crowned arms **Obv. Legend:** PETRVS • II • D • G • ... **Rev:** Globe on cross with "P" at center **Rev. Legend:** SIGN NATA STAB SVBQ **Note:** Varieties exist.

Date	Mintage	Good	VG	F	VF	XF
1700P	—	35.00	70.00	140	300	—
1701P	—	35.00	70.00	140	300	—

KM# 160 80 REIS

2.2400 g., 0.9170 Silver .0660 oz. ASW **Ruler:** Joao VI **Obv. Legend:** JOHANNES. V. D. G. PORT. REX. E. B. D **Note:** Struck at Lisbon for Maranhao.

Date	Mintage	VG	F	VF	XF	Unc
1749	—	7.50	15.00	30.00	60.00	—

KM# 167 80 REIS

2.4158 g., 0.9170 Silver .0712 oz. ASW **Ruler:** Jose I **Obv. Legend:** JOSEPHUS. I. D. G.. **Rev. Legend:** STAB. SUBQ..

Date	Mintage	VG	F	VF	XF	Unc
1751R	—	7.50	15.00	30.00	60.00	—

KM# 190.1 80 REIS

2.2254 g., 0.9170 Silver .0656 oz. ASW **Ruler:** Jose I **Rev. Legend:** STAB. SVBG... **Note:** Struck at Lisbon without mint mark.

Date	Mintage	VG	F	VF	XF	Unc
1768	100,000	12.00	25.00	45.00	85.00	—
1771	202,000	7.00	15.00	25.00	50.00	—

Note: 1771 has reverse legend starting at 4 o'clock instead of the normal 10 o'clock

KM# 190.2 80 REIS

2.2254 g., 0.9170 Silver .0656 oz. ASW **Ruler:** Jose I **Rev. Legend:** STAB. SUBG..

Date	Mintage	VG	F	VF	XF	Unc
1768	Inc. above	3.75	7.50	12.50	25.00	—
1770	25,000	3.75	7.50	12.50	25.00	—
1771	Inc. above	3.75	7.50	12.50	25.00	—

KM# 204 80 REIS

2.2254 g., 0.9170 Silver .0656 oz. ASW **Ruler:** Maria I and Pedro III **Obv:** Crowned arms **Obv. Legend:** MARIA. I. E. PETRUS. III **Rev:** Globe **Rev. Legend:** SUBG. SIGN. NATA. STAB..

Date	Mintage	VG	F	VF	XF	Unc
1778	12,000	5.00	10.00	20.00	45.00	—
1779	25,000	3.50	6.50	12.50	30.00	—
1780	30,000	3.50	6.50	12.50	30.00	—
1781	29,000	4.00	7.50	15.00	30.00	—
1782	52,000	4.00	7.50	15.00	30.00	—
1785	20,000	5.00	10.00	20.00	45.00	—
1786	24,000	4.00	7.50	15.00	30.00	—

KM# 219.1 80 REIS

2.2254 g., 0.9170 Silver .0656 oz. ASW **Ruler:** Maria I Widow **Obv:** Crowned arms divide crosses at right from value at left **Obv. Legend:** MARIA • I • D • G • PORT • REGINA • ... **Rev:** Globe on cross **Rev. Legend:** SIGN • NATA • STAB • SVBQ •

Date	Mintage	VG	F	VF	XF	Unc
1787	21,000	3.00	7.00	12.00	25.00	—
1788	45,000	4.00	8.00	15.00	30.00	—
1790	92,000	5.00	10.00	17.50	30.00	—
1796	73,000	3.00	7.00	12.00	25.00	—

KM# 219.2 80 REIS

2.2254 g., 0.9170 Silver .0656 oz. ASW **Ruler:** Maria I Widow **Obv:** High crown **Rev:** Globe on cross

Date	Mintage	VG	F	VF	XF	Unc
1787	—	4.00	7.50	15.00	30.00	—
1788	—	5.00	10.00	20.00	45.00	—
1790	—	3.00	7.00	12.00	25.00	—

KM# 177 150 REIS

4.5296 g., 0.9170 Silver .1335 oz. ASW **Ruler:** Jose I **Obv:** Crown above "J", crosses at left, value at right **Rev:** Globe on cross, "B" at center **Rev. Legend:** SIGN • NATA STAB • SVBQ

Date	Mintage	VG	F	VF	XF	Unc
1752B	—	250	400	750	1,200	—
1753B	—	40.00	65.00	100	175	—
1754B	—	35.00	55.00	85.00	140	—
1756B	—	125	225	350	600	—
1768B Rare	—	—	—	—	—	—

KM# 185 150 REIS

4.5296 g., 0.9170 Silver .1335 oz. ASW **Ruler:** Jose I **Obv:**

Crown above "J", florals at right, value at left **Rev:** Curved parallels on globe **Rev. Legend:** SIGN • NATA STAB • SVBQ

Date	Mintage	VG	F	VF	XF	Unc
1754R	—	30.00	50.00	75.00	125	—
1754R	—	35.00	55.00	85.00	140	—
Note: Reverse ATAN NGIS						
1755R	—	35.00	55.00	85.00	140	—
1758R	—	35.00	55.00	85.00	140	—
1760R	—	60.00	120	180	300	—

KM# 195 150 REIS

4.5296 g., 0.9170 Silver .1335 oz. ASW **Ruler:** Jose I **Rev:** Straight parallels on globe

Date	Mintage	VG	F	VF	XF	Unc
1771R	3,468	40.00	70.00	125	200	—

KM# 88.2 160 REIS

Silver **Ruler:** Pedro As Pedro II **Obv:** Crowned arms divide value at left from crosses at right **Obv. Legend:** PETRVS • II • D • G • P • R • E .... **Rev:** Globe on cross with "P" at center **Rev. Legend:** SIGN NATA STAB SVBQ **Note:** Varieties exist.

Date	Mintage	Good	VG	F	VF	XF
1701P	—	5.00	8.00	15.00	35.00	—
1702P Rare	—	—	—	—	—	—

KM# 156.1 160 REIS

4.8315 g., 0.9170 Silver .1424 oz. ASW **Ruler:** Joao VI **Obv:** Crowned arms divide date, value at left **Obv. Legend:** JOANNES. V. D. G. P. REX. E. BRAS. D **Rev:** Round globe on cross

Date	Mintage	VG	F	VF	XF	Unc
1748R	—	5.00	8.00	15.00	35.00	—

KM# 156.2 160 REIS

4.8315 g., 0.9170 Silver .1424 oz. ASW **Ruler:** Joao VI **Rev:** Oval globe on cross

Date	Mintage	VG	F	VF	XF	Unc
1748R	—	5.00	8.00	15.00	35.00	—
1749R	—	6.00	12.00	30.00	60.00	—

KM# 156.5 160 REIS

4.8315 g., 0.9170 Silver .1424 oz. ASW **Ruler:** Joao VI **Note:** Struck at Lisbon for Maranhao.

Date	Mintage	VG	F	VF	XF	Unc
1749	—	5.00	8.00	15.00	35.00	—

KM# 156.3 160 REIS

4.8315 g., 0.9170 Silver .1424 oz. ASW **Rev:** Small globe on cross

Date	Mintage	VG	F	VF	XF	Unc
1750R	—	6.00	12.00	30.00	60.00	—

KM# 156.4 160 REIS

4.8315 g., 0.9170 Silver .1424 oz. ASW **Ruler:** Jose I **Rev:** Large globe on cross

Date	Mintage	VG	F	VF	XF	Unc
1750R	—	5.00	10.00	20.00	40.00	—

KM# 168.1 160 REIS

4.8315 g., 0.9170 Silver .1424 oz. ASW **Obv. Legend:** JOSEPHUS. I. D. G.. **Rev. Legend:** STAB. SUBG..

Date	Mintage	VG	F	VF	XF	Unc
1751R	—	7.50	15.00	25.00	50.00	—

KM# 168.2 160 REIS

4.8315 g., 0.9170 Silver .1424 oz. ASW **Ruler:** Jose I **Obv. Legend:** IOSEPHUS I. D. G.. **Note:** Struck at Lisbon without mint mark.

Date	Mintage	VG	F	VF	XF	Unc
1752 PORT. REX	—	4.50	6.50	20.00	50.00	—
1756 P. REX	—	35.00	70.00	200	400	—

KM# 168.3 160 REIS

4.8315 g., 0.9170 Silver .1424 oz. ASW **Ruler:** Jose I **Rev. Legend:** STAB. SVGQ

Date	Mintage	VG	F	VF	XF	Unc
1757B Rare	—	—	—	—	—	—

KM# 168.4 160 REIS

4.8315 g., 0.9170 Silver .1424 oz. ASW **Ruler:** Jose I **Obv. Legend:** JOSEPHUS. I. D. G..

Date	Mintage	VG	F	VF	XF	Unc
1758B	—	6.00	10.00	17.50	35.00	—

KM# 191.1 160 REIS

4.8315 g., 0.9170 Silver .1424 oz. ASW **Ruler:** Jose I **Note:** Struck at Lisbon without mint mark.

Date	Mintage	VG	F	VF	XF	Unc
1768	94,000	4.50	6.50	12.00	25.00	—

KM# 191.2 160 REIS

4.8315 g., 0.9170 Silver .1424 oz. ASW **Ruler:** Jose I **Rev. Legend:** STAB. SUBQ.. **Note:** Struck at Lisbon Mint without mint mark.

Date	Mintage	VG	F	VF	XF	Unc
1768	Inc. above	4.50	6.50	12.00	25.00	—
1771	47,000	4.50	6.50	12.00	25.00	—
1773	101,000	4.50	6.50	12.00	25.00	—
1776	17,000	5.00	10.00	20.00	40.00	—

KM# 205 160 REIS

4.8315 g., 0.9170 Silver .1424 oz. ASW **Ruler:** Maria I and Pedro III **Obv. Legend:** MARIA. I. E. PETRUS. III.. **Rev. Legend:** SUBQ. SIGN. NATA. STAB..

Date	Mintage	VG	F	VF	XF	Unc
1778	9,007	4.50	6.50	12.00	25.00	—
1779	25,000	4.50	6.50	12.00	25.00	—
1780	26,000	4.50	6.50	12.00	25.00	—
1781	41,000	5.00	7.50	15.00	30.00	—
1783	37,000	6.50	12.50	20.00	35.00	—
1784	21,000	6.00	12.00	18.00	30.00	—
1785	36,000	25.00	50.00	100	200	—
1786	24,000	9.00	18.00	35.00	75.00	—

KM# 220.1 160 REIS

4.8315 g., 0.9170 Silver .1424 oz. ASW **Ruler:** Maria I Widow **Obv. Legend:** MARIA. I. D. G. PORT. REGINA..

Date	Mintage	VG	F	VF	XF	Unc
1787	66,000	4.50	6.50	12.00	25.00	—
1790	62,000	4.50	6.50	12.00	25.00	—
1795	29,000	4.50	6.50	12.00	25.00	—
1797	13,000	6.00	12.00	25.00	50.00	—

KM# 220.2 160 REIS

4.8315 g., 0.9170 Silver .1424 oz. ASW **Ruler:** Maria I Widow **Obv:** High crown

Date	Mintage	VG	F	VF	XF	Unc
1787	—	4.50	6.50	12.00	25.00	—
1788 Rare	—	—	—	—	—	—
1790	—	4.50	6.50	12.00	25.00	—

KM# 178 300 REIS

9.0591 g., 0.9170 Silver .2670 oz. ASW **Ruler:** Jose I **Rev:** Curved parallels on globe

Date	Mintage	VG	F	VF	XF	Unc
1752B	—	45.00	90.00	150	300	—
1753B	—	30.00	60.00	100	200	—
1754B	—	30.00	60.00	100	200	—
1756B	—	45.00	80.00	135	275	—
1757B	—	60.00	115	125	350	—
1758B Rare	—	—	—	—	—	—

KM# 186 300 REIS

9.0591 g., 0.9170 Silver .2670 oz. ASW **Ruler:** Jose I **Rev:** Curved parallels on globe

Date	Mintage	VG	F	VF	XF	Unc
1754R	—	20.00	35.00	50.00	100	—
1755R	—	20.00	35.00	55.00	110	—
1756R	—	22.50	40.00	55.00	100	—
1757R	—	22.50	40.00	65.00	135	—
1758R	—	22.50	40.00	65.00	135	—
1764R	—	20.00	35.00	55.00	110	—

KM# 196 300 REIS

9.0591 g., 0.9170 Silver .2670 oz. ASW **Ruler:** Jose I **Rev:** Straight parallels on globe

Date	Mintage	VG	F	VF	XF	Unc
1771R	26,000	27.50	45.00	75.00	145	—

KM# 89.2 320 REIS

8.9600 g., 0.9170 Silver .2640 oz. ASW **Ruler:** Pedro As Pedro II **Obv:** Crowned arms divide date, value at left **Obv. Legend:** PETRVS • II • D • G • PORT • .... **Rev:** Round globe on cross **Rev. Legend:** SIGN • NATA STAB • SVBQ

Date	Mintage	VG	F	VF	XF	Unc
1701P	—	10.00	15.00	30.00	75.00	—
1702P	—	90.00	175	350	650	—

KM# 157.1 320 REIS

9.6631 g., 0.9170 Silver .2848 oz. ASW **Ruler:** Joao VI **Obv. Legend:** JOHANNES. V. D. G. PORT. REX. E. BRAS. D. **Note:** Varieties exist.

Date	Mintage	VG	F	VF	XF	Unc
1748R	—	10.00	20.00	35.00	80.00	—
1749R	—	6.00	12.00	25.00	45.00	—
1750R	—	6.00	12.00	25.00	45.00	—

KM# 157.2 320 REIS

9.6631 g., 0.9170 Silver .2848 oz. ASW **Ruler:** Joao VI **Note:** Struck at Lisbon for Maranhao.

Date	Mintage	VG	F	VF	XF	Unc
1749	—	6.00	12.00	25.00	45.00	—

KM# 169.1 320 REIS

9.6631 g., 0.9170 Silver .2848 oz. ASW **Ruler:** Jose I **Obv. Legend:** JOSEPHUS. I. D. G.. **Rev. Legend:** STAB. SUBQ.. **Note:** There are several varieties of abbreviations for "BRASIL".

Date	Mintage	VG	F	VF	XF	Unc
1751R	—	8.00	15.00	30.00	65.00	—
1753R	—	8.00	15.00	30.00	65.00	—
1755R	—	10.00	20.00	40.00	85.00	—

KM# 169.2 320 REIS

9.6631 g., 0.9170 Silver .2848 oz. ASW **Ruler:** Jose I **Obv. Legend:** IOSEPHUS. E. D. G... **Rev. Legend:** STAB. SVBQ... **Note:** Struck at Lisbon without mint mark.

Date	Mintage	VG	F	VF	XF	Unc
1752	—	60.00	120	250	450	—
1756	—	8.00	15.00	30.00	65.00	—

KM# 169.3 320 REIS

9.6631 g., 0.9170 Silver .2848 oz. ASW **Ruler:** Jose I **Obv. Legend:** JOSEPHUS. I. D. G..

Date	Mintage	VG	F	VF	XF	Unc
1757B	—	35.00	70.00	150	300	—
1758/7B	—	15.00	30.00	65.00	125	—

KM# 192.2 320 REIS

8.9018 g., 0.9170 Silver .2623 oz. ASW **Ruler:** Jose I **Obv:** Crowned arms divide value at left from florals at right and date above **Obv. Legend:** JOSEPHUS • I • D • G • PORT • REX • ... **Rev. Legend:** SIGN • NATA • STAB • SVBQ •

Date	Mintage	VG	F	VF	XF	Unc
1768	Inc. above	8.00	12.00	20.00	40.00	—
1771 Rare	23,000	—	—	—	—	—
1773	75,000	8.00	12.00	20.00	40.00	—
1776	16,000	10.00	20.00	40.00	75.00	—

KM# 192.1 320 REIS

8.9018 g., 0.9170 Silver .2623 oz. ASW **Ruler:** Jose I **Note:** Struck at Lisbon without mint mark.

Date	Mintage	VG	F	VF	XF	Unc
1768	47,000	65.00	125	275	500	—

KM# 206 320 REIS

8.9018 g., 0.9170 Silver .2623 oz. ASW **Ruler:** Maria I and Pedro III **Obv:** Crowned arms divides date **Obv. Legend:** MARIA • I • E • PETRUS • III • D • G • PORT • .... **Rev:** Globe on cross **Rev. Legend:** SIGN • NATA • STAB • SVBQ •

Date	Mintage	VG	F	VF	XF	Unc
1778	14,000	9.00	15.00	20.00	38.00	—
1779	19,000	9.00	15.00	20.00	38.00	—
1780	63,000	9.00	15.00	20.00	38.00	—
1782	16,000	9.00	15.00	20.00	38.00	—
1783	37,000	9.00	15.00	20.00	38.00	—
1784	23,000	9.00	15.00	20.00	38.00	—
1785	34,000	9.00	15.00	20.00	38.00	—
1786	19,000	9.00	15.00	22.00	45.00	—

KM# 221.1 320 REIS

8.9018 g., 0.9170 Silver .2623 oz. ASW **Ruler:** Maria I Widow **Obv:** High crown **Obv. Legend:** MARIA • I • D • G • PORT • REGINA • ... **Rev:** Globe on cross **Rev. Legend:** SIGN • NATA • STAB • SVBQ •

Date	Mintage	VG	F	VF	XF	Unc
1787	43,000	10.00	17.50	25.00	50.00	—
1788	19,000	10.00	17.50	27.50	55.00	—
1790	37,000	17.50	35.00	45.00	75.00	—
1793	31,000	10.00	17.50	25.00	50.00	—
1797	10,000	10.00	17.50	30.00	60.00	—

KM# 221.2 320 REIS

8.9018 g., 0.9170 Silver .2623 oz. ASW **Ruler:** Maria I Widow **Obv:** Low crown **Rev:** Globe on cross

Date	Mintage	VG	F	VF	XF	Unc
1787	—	10.00	17.50	25.00	50.00	—
1790	—	10.00	17.50	30.00	60.00	—
1793	—	10.00	17.50	27.50	55.00	—

KM# 118 400 REIS
0.8938 g., 0.9170 Gold .0263 oz. AGW **Ruler:** Joao VI **Obv:** Crown above name, value below **Obv. Legend:** IOAN V **Rev:** Maltese cross with "M" at angles

Date	Mintage	VG	F	VF	XF	Unc
1725M	—	175	325	600	1,000	—
1726M	—	225	425	700	1,200	—

KM# 144 400 REIS
0.8938 g., 0.9170 Gold .0263 oz. AGW **Ruler:** Joao VI **Rev:** Cross with "R" in angles, date above

Date	Mintage	VG	F	VF	XF	Unc
1730R	—	400	800	1,500	2,500	—

KM# 145 400 REIS
0.8938 g., 0.9170 Gold .0263 oz. AGW **Ruler:** Joao VI **Obv:** Laureate head right **Rev:** Crown above date **Rev. Legend:** IOAN • V • DE • REX

Date	Mintage	VG	F	VF	XF	Unc
1730M	—	50.00	100	175	250	—
1732M	—	50.00	100	175	250	—
1733M	—	50.00	100	175	250	—
1734M	—	50.00	100	175	250	—

KM# 152 400 REIS
0.8938 g., 0.9170 Gold .0263 oz. AGW **Ruler:** Joao VI

Date	Mintage	VG	F	VF	XF	Unc
1734R	—	50.00	100	175	250	—

KM# 179 600 REIS
18.1183 g., 0.9170 Silver .5340 oz. ASW **Ruler:** Jose I **Obv:** Crown above "J", florals at right, value at left, date below **Rev:** Curved parallels on globe **Rev. Legend:** SIGN • NATA • STAB • SVBQ

Date	Mintage	VG	F	VF	XF	Unc
1752B	—	200	400	650	1,350	—
1754/3B	—	85.00	125	200	375	—
1756B	—	50.00	85.00	165	325	—
1757B	—	75.00	150	300	350	—
1758B	—	35.00	60.00	125	250	—
1760B	—	150	250	450	1,150	—
1768B Rare	—	—	—	—	—	—

KM# 187 600 REIS
18.1183 g., 0.9170 Silver .5340 oz. ASW **Ruler:** Jose I **Obv:** Crown above "J", florals at right, value at left, date below **Rev:** Curved parallels on globe **Rev. Legend:** SIGN • NATA • STAB • SVBQ

Date	Mintage	VG	F	VF	XF	Unc
1754/8R	—	45.00	65.00	125	300	—
1754R	—	35.00	50.00	100	225	—
1755R	—	35.00	50.00	100	225	—
1756/5R	—	35.00	50.00	100	225	—
1756R	—	35.00	50.00	100	225	—
1758R	—	35.00	50.00	100	225	—
1760/58R Rare	—	—	—	—	—	—
1764/54R	—	35.00	50.00	100	225	—
1764R	—	35.00	50.00	100	225	—
1765R	—	85.00	165	300	550	—
1770R	13,000	45.00	65.00	125	300	—

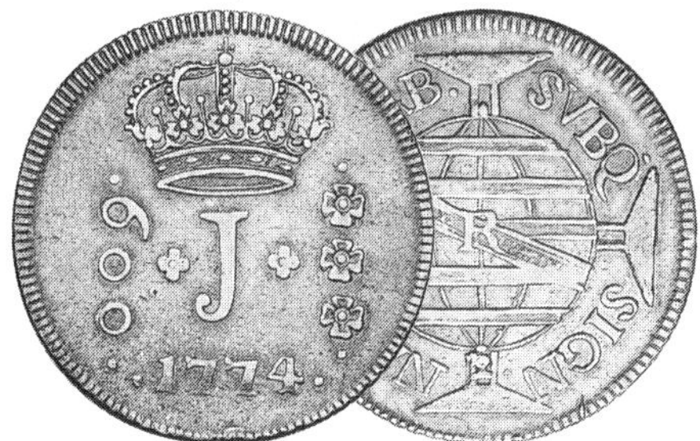

KM# 194 600 REIS
18.1183 g., 0.9170 Silver .5340 oz. ASW **Ruler:** Jose I **Obv:** Crown above "J", florals at right, value at left, date below **Rev:** Straight parallels on globe **Rev. Legend:** SIGN • NATA • STAB • SVBQ

Date	Mintage	VG	F	VF	XF	Unc
1770R	Inc. above	50.00	100	200	375	—
1771R	12,000	40.00	60.00	110	250	—
1774R	19,000	40.00	60.00	110	250	—
1774R Rare	Inc. above	—	—	—	—	—

Note: Retrograde N's on reverse

KM# 90.2 640 REIS
17.9200 g., 0.9170 Silver .5280 oz. ASW **Ruler:** Pedro As Pedro II **Obv:** Crowned arms divide date above and value at left from florals at right **Obv. Legend:** PETRVS • II • D • G • PORT • REX ... **Rev:** Globe on cross, thick, curved parallels **Rev. Legend:** SIGN • NATA • STAB • SVBQ

Date	Mintage	VG	F	VF	XF	Unc
1701P	—	18.50	25.00	40.00	80.00	—
1702P	—	120	200	325	500	—

KM# 158.1 640 REIS
19.3262 g., 0.9170 Silver .5696 oz. ASW **Ruler:** Joao VI **Obv:** Crowned arms divide date, value at left **Obv. Legend:** JOHANNES. V. D. G. PORT. REX. E. BRAS. D **Rev:** Oval globe on cross

Date	Mintage	VG	F	VF	XF	Unc
1748R	—	20.00	35.00	65.00	125	—

KM# 158.2 640 REIS
19.3262 g., 0.9170 Silver .5696 oz. ASW **Ruler:** Joao VI **Obv:** Crowned arms divide date above and value at left from florals at right **Obv. Legend:** IOANNES • V • D • G • PORT • REX .... **Rev:** Round globe on cross **Rev. Legend:** SIGN • NATA • STAB • SVBQ

Date	Mintage	VG	F	VF	XF	Unc
1748R	—	20.00	35.00	65.00	125	—
1749R	—	20.00	35.00	65.00	125	—
1750R	—	25.00	40.00	70.00	150	—

KM# 158.3 640 REIS
19.3262 g., 0.9170 Silver .5696 oz. ASW **Ruler:** Joao VI **Obv:** Crowned arms divide date above and value at left from florals at right **Rev:** Globe on cross **Note:** Struck at Lisbon for Maranhao.

Date	Mintage	VG	F	VF	XF	Unc
1749	—	35.00	70.00	140	275	—

KM# 170.1 640 REIS
19.3262 g., 0.9170 Silver .5696 oz. ASW **Ruler:** Jose I **Obv:** Crowned arms divide date above and value at left from florals at right **Obv. Legend:** JOSEPHUS • I • D • G • P REX • ... **Rev:** Globe on cross, thick curved parallels **Rev. Legend:** SIGN • NATA • STAB • SVBQ

Date	Mintage	VG	F	VF	XF	Unc
1751R BRAS.	—	20.00	30.00	50.00	100	—
1751R BRA.	—	30.00	45.00	70.00	135	—
1752R	—	35.00	45.00	90.00	175	—
1753R	—	75.00	150	300	550	—
1755R	—	60.00	100	200	400	—
1755 Without "R"	—	80.00	120	220	450	—

KM# 170.2 640 REIS
19.3262 g., 0.9170 Silver .5696 oz. ASW **Ruler:** Jose I **Obv:** Crowned arms divide date above and value at left from florals at right **Obv. Legend:** IOSEPHUS. I. D. G.. **Rev:** Globe on cross **Rev. Legend:** STAB. SVBQ.. **Note:** Struck at Lisbon without mint mark.

Date	Mintage	VG	F	VF	XF	Unc
1752	—	55.00	100	200	375	—
1756	—	55.00	100	200	375	—

KM# 170.3 640 REIS
19.3262 g., 0.9170 Silver .5696 oz. ASW **Ruler:** Jose I **Obv:** Crowned arms divide date above and value at left from florals at right **Obv. Legend:** IOSEPHUS • D • G • PORT • REX • ET • BRAS • D • **Rev:** Globe on cross, thick curved parallels **Rev. Legend:** SIGN • NATA • STAB • SVBQ

Date	Mintage	VG	F	VF	XF	Unc
1757B	—	30.00	50.00	100	200	—
1758B	—	40.00	75.00	150	300	—

KM# 170.4 640 REIS
19.3262 g., 0.9170 Silver .5696 oz. ASW **Ruler:** Jose I **Obv. Legend:** JOSEPHUS. I. D. G..

Date	Mintage	VG	F	VF	XF	Unc
1758B	—	45.00	85.00	185	350	—

KM# 193.1 640 REIS
17.8035 g., 0.9170 Silver .5247 oz. ASW **Ruler:** Jose I **Rev. Legend:** NATA. STAB. SVBQ.. **Note:** Struck at Lisbon without mint mark.

Date	Mintage	VG	F	VF	XF	Unc
1768	63,000	20.00	30.00	40.00	80.00	—
1771	110,000	18.50	25.00	35.00	75.00	—

KM# 193.2 640 REIS
17.8035 g., 0.9170 Silver .5247 oz. ASW **Ruler:** Jose I **Obv:** Crowned arms divide date above and value at left from florals at right **Obv. Legend:** JOSEPHUS • I • D • G • PORT • REX • ET • BRAS • D • **Rev:** Globe on cross, thin straight parallels **Rev. Legend:** SIGN • NATA • STAB • SVBQ •

Date	Mintage	VG	F	VF	XF	Unc
1768	Inc. above	20.00	30.00	40.00	80.00	—
1771	Inc. above	18.50	25.00	35.00	75.00	—

KM# 207.1 640 REIS
17.7600 g., 0.9170 Silver .5233 oz. ASW **Ruler:** Maria I and Pedro III **Obv:** Crowned arms divide date above and value at left from florals at right **Obv. Legend:** MARIA • I • ET • PETRUS • III • D • G • PORT • ... **Rev:** Globe on cross, thin straight parallels **Rev. Legend:** SIGN • NATA • STAB • SVBQ

Date	Mintage	VG	F	VF	XF	Unc
1778	19,750	22.50	30.00	40.00	75.00	—
1779	18,750	22.50	30.00	40.00	75.00	—
1780	39,000	22.50	30.00	40.00	75.00	—
1781	31,000	22.50	30.00	40.00	75.00	—
1782	16,250	35.00	65.00	185	250	—
1783	31,000	22.50	30.00	40.00	75.00	—

KM# 207.2 640 REIS

17.7600 g., 0.9170 Silver .5233 oz. ASW **Ruler:** Maria I and Pedro III **Obv:** High crown **Rev:** Globe on cross

Date	Mintage	VG	F	VF	XF	Unc
1780	—	25.00	45.00	90.00	175	—
1781	—	22.50	35.00	60.00	125	—
1783	—	22.50	35.00	60.00	125	—
1784	25,000	22.50	35.00	60.00	125	—
1785	33,750	35.00	65.00	125	250	—
1786	18,750	35.00	65.00	125	250	—

KM# 222.1 640 REIS

17.7600 g., 0.9170 Silver .5233 oz. ASW **Ruler:** Maria I Widow **Obv:** Crowned arms divide date above and value at left from florals at right **Obv. Legend:** MARIA • I • D • G • PORT • REGINA • ... **Rev:** Globe on cross, thin straight parallels **Rev. Legend:** SIGN • NATA • STAB • SVBQ

Date	Mintage	VG	F	VF	XF	Unc
1787	62,000	22.50	35.00	60.00	125	—
1790	19,000	135	275	500	900	—
1792	6,250	135	275	500	900	—
1793	6,250	30.00	50.00	70.00	135	—

KM# 222.3 640 REIS

17.7600 g., 0.9170 Silver .5233 oz. ASW **Ruler:** Maria I Widow **Obv:** High crown

Date	Mintage	VG	F	VF	XF	Unc
1787	—	20.00	40.00	80.00	150	—
1790	—	200	400	750	1,250	—
1795	22,000	225	450	800	1,350	—

KM# 222.2 640 REIS

17.7600 g., 0.9170 Silver .5233 oz. ASW **Ruler:** Maria I Widow **Obv:** High crown above arms **Obv. Legend:** MARIA • I • D • G • PORT • REGINA • ET • BRAS • D • **Rev:** Sash with initial crosses globe within cross **Rev. Legend:** SIGN • NATA • STAB • SVBQ

Date	Mintage	VG	F	VF	XF	Unc
1791R Rare	—	—	—	—	—	—
1792R	3,484,000	120	250	450	800	—
1793R	19,495,000	22.50	45.00	70.00	135	—
1794R	—	18.50	25.00	45.00	90.00	—
1795R	—	150	300	550	950	—
1800R	34,431,000	18.00	25.00	45.00	90.00	—

KM# 231.1 640 REIS

17.7600 g., 0.9170 Silver .5233 oz. ASW **Ruler:** Maria I Widow **Rev. Legend:** SVBQ..

Date	Mintage	VG	F	VF	XF	Unc
1799B	—	200	300	600	1,200	—

KM# 231.2 640 REIS

17.7600 g., 0.9170 Silver .5233 oz. ASW **Ruler:** Maria I Widow **Obv:** Crowned arms divide date above and value at left from florals at right **Obv. Legend:** MARIA • I • D • G • PORT • REGINA • ET • BRAS • D • **Rev:** Sash with initial "B" crosses globe within cross **Rev. Legend:** SIGN • NATA • STAB • SVBQ •

Date	Mintage	VG	F	VF	XF	Unc
1799B	—	25.00	35.00	50.00	90.00	—
1800B	—	25.00	35.00	50.00	90.00	—
1800B	—	18.50	25.00	40.00	75.00	—

KM# 119 800 REIS

1.7930 g., 0.9170 Gold .0528 oz. AGW **Ruler:** Joao VI **Obv:** Head right, date and mint mark below **Obv. Legend:** IOANNES • V • D • G • PORT • ... **Rev:** First variety of crowned arms

Date	Mintage	VG	F	VF	XF	Unc
1727B	—	145	285	475	1,000	—
1729B	—	150	290	480	1,000	—
1731B	—	160	300	490	1,000	—

KM# 120 800 REIS

1.7930 g., 0.9170 Gold .0528 oz. AGW **Ruler:** Joao VI **Obv:** Head right **Obv. Legend:** IOANNESS • V • D • G • PORT • ... **Rev:** Crowned arms within cartouche

Date	Mintage	VG	F	VF	XF	Unc
1727M	—	65.00	125	210	400	—
1728M	—	65.00	125	210	400	—
1729M	—	65.00	125	210	400	—
1730M	—	40.00	110	160	200	—
1731M	—	40.00	110	160	200	—
1732M	—	40.00	110	160	200	—
1733M	—	40.00	110	160	200	—
1734M	—	40.00	110	160	200	—

KM# 121 800 REIS

1.7930 g., 0.9170 Gold .0528 oz. AGW **Ruler:** Joao VI **Obv:** Laureate head right **Obv. Legend:** IOANNES • V • D • G • PORT • ... **Rev:** Crowned arms within cartouche

Date	Mintage	VG	F	VF	XF	Unc
1727R	—	90.00	180	300	675	—
1730R	—	90.00	180	400	900	—

KM# 122 800 REIS

1.7930 g., 0.9170 Gold .0528 oz. AGW **Ruler:** Joao VI **Obv:** Laureate head right **Rev:** Second variety of crowned arms

Date	Mintage	VG	F	VF	XF	Unc
1727B	—	240	400	650	1,500	—
1729B	—	300	550	960	2,000	—

KM# 123 800 REIS

1.7930 g., 0.9170 Gold .0528 oz. AGW **Ruler:** Joao VI **Obv:** Laureate head right **Obv. Legend:** IOANNES • V • D • G • PORT • ... **Rev:** Fourth variety of crowned arms

Date	Mintage	VG	F	VF	XF	Unc
1727B	—	165	325	550	900	—
1732B	—	165	325	550	900	—
1736B	—	165	325	550	900	—
1740B	—	165	325	550	900	—
1743B	—	165	325	550	900	—
1744B	—	165	325	550	900	—
1747B	—	165	325	550	900	—
1749B	—	165	325	550	900	—
1750B	—	165	325	550	900	—

KM# 153 800 REIS

1.7930 g., 0.9170 Gold .0528 oz. AGW **Ruler:** Joao VI **Obv:** Laureate head right **Obv. Legend:** IOANNES • V • D • G • PORT • ... **Rev:** Different crowned arms

Date	Mintage	VG	F	VF	XF	Unc
1734R	—	85.00	165	275	400	—
1736R	—	85.00	165	275	400	—
1749R	—	85.00	165	275	400	—

KM# 180.1 800 REIS

1.7930 g., 0.9170 Gold .0528 oz. AGW **Ruler:** Jose I **Obv:** Date and mint mark below head **Obv. Legend:** JOSEPHUS • I • D • G • PORT • .... **Rev:** Crowned arms

Date	Mintage	F	VF	XF	Unc	BU
1752B	—	225	425	700	1,000	—
1754B	—	125	250	425	600	—
1756B	—	125	250	425	600	—
1757B	—	150	300	500	700	—
1758B	—	125	250	425	600	—
1759B	—	125	250	425	600	—
1763B	—	125	250	600	800	—
1764B	—	125	250	425	600	—
1765B	—	125	250	425	600	—
1766B	—	125	250	425	600	—
1767B	—	125	250	425	600	—
1768B	—	225	425	700	1,000	—
1777B	—	225	425	700	1,000	—

KM# 180.2 800 REIS

1.7930 g., 0.9170 Gold .0528 oz. AGW **Ruler:** Jose I **Obv:** Head right **Obv. Legend:** JOSEPHUS • I • D • G • PORT • ... **Rev:** Crowned ornate arms

Date	Mintage	F	VF	XF	Unc	BU
1752R	—	190	375	600	1,000	—
1763R	—	150	300	500	850	—

KM# 213 800 REIS

1.7930 g., 0.9170 Gold .0528 oz. AGW **Ruler:** Maria I and Pedro III **Obv:** Conjoined busts **Obv. Legend:** MARIA. I. ET. PETRUS. III **Rev:** Stylized arms

Date	Mintage	F	VF	XF	Unc	BU
1782B	—	625	1,250	2,100	3,000	—
1786B	—	625	1,250	2,100	3,000	—

KM# 103 1000 REIS

2.6800 g., 0.9170 Gold .0790 oz. AGW **Ruler:** Joao VI **Obv:** Crowned arms divide crosses at right from value at left **Obv. Legend:** IOANNES • V • D • G • PORT • ... **Rev:** Cross with "R" in angles, date above **Rev. Legend:** IN HOC SIGNO VINCES

Date	Mintage	VG	F	VF	XF	Unc
1708R	—	50.00	100	200	400	—
1726R	—	50.00	100	200	400	—

KM# 104 1000 REIS

2.6800 g., 0.9170 Gold .0790 oz. AGW **Ruler:** Joao VI **Obv:** Crowned arms divide crosses at right from value at left **Obv. Legend:** IOANNES • V • D • G • P • .... **Rev:** Cross with "B" in angles, date above **Rev. Legend:** IN HOC SIGNO VINCES

Date	Mintage	VG	F	VF	XF	Unc
1714B	—	125	250	500	900	—
1715B	—	90.00	180	300	600	—
1716B	—	90.00	200	500	900	—
1717B	—	125	250	500	900	—
1718B	—	90.00	200	400	800	—
1719B	—	90.00	180	300	600	—
1720B	—	90.00	200	400	800	—
1721B	—	90.00	200	400	800	—
1722B	—	90.00	180	300	600	—
1723B	—	90.00	180	300	600	—
1724B	—	90.00	180	300	600	—
1725B	—	90.00	180	300	600	—
1726B	—	90.00	180	300	600	—

KM# 113 1000 REIS

2.6800 g., 0.9170 Gold .0790 oz. AGW **Ruler:** Joao VI **Obv:** Crowned arms divide crosses at right from value at left **Obv. Legend:** IOANNES • V • D • G • P • ... **Rev:** Cross with "M" in angles, date above **Rev. Legend:** IN HOC SIGNO VINCES

Date	Mintage	VG	F	VF	XF	Unc
1724M	—	625	1,250	2,100	3,000	—
1725M	—	165	325	600	1,000	—
1726M	—	165	325	600	1,000	—
1727M	—	215	425	700	1,000	—

KM# 162.4 1000 REIS

2.0100 g., 0.9170 Gold .0592 oz. AGW **Ruler:** Joao VI **Rev. Legend:** DONINVS..

Date	Mintage	F	VF	XF	Unc	BU
1749	—	60.00	100	150	230	—

KM# 161 1000 REIS

2.0100 g., 0.9170 Gold .0592 oz. AGW **Ruler:** Joao VI **Obv:** Crowned arms divide crosses at right from value at left **Obv. Legend:** IOSEPHUS • I • D • G • PORT • REX • **Rev:** Cross within ornamented outline, lined circle surrounds all **Rev. Legend:** ET • BRASILIÆ • DOMINUS • ANNO • **Note:** Struck at Lisbon without mint mark.

Date	Mintage	F	VF	XF	Unc	BU
1749	—	50.00	100	190	300	—
Note: Obverse reversed "D" in "D. G."						
1749	—	50.00	100	190	300	—
Note: Obverse normal "D" in "D. G."						

KM# 162.1 1000 REIS

2.0100 g., 0.9170 Gold .0592 oz. AGW **Ruler:** Jose I **Obv:** Crowned arms divide florals at right from value at left **Obv. Legend:** IOSEPUS • I • D • G • PORT • REX • **Rev:** Cross within ornamented outline, lined circle surrounds all **Rev. Legend:** ET • BRASILIÆ • DOMINUS • ANNO •

Date	Mintage	F	VF	XF	Unc	BU
1752	11,000	50.00	70.00	100	150	—
1771	23,000	50.00	70.00	100	150	—

KM# 162.3 1000 REIS

2.0100 g., 0.9170 Gold .0592 oz. AGW **Ruler:** Jose I **Obv:** Crowned arms divide crosses at right from value at left **Obv. Legend:** JOSEPHUS. I. D. G.. **Rev:** Cross within ornamented circle, lined circle surrounds all **Rev. Legend:** DOMINUS. ANNO..

Date	Mintage	F	VF	XF	Unc	BU
1771	Inc. above	50.00	70.00	100	150	—
1774	Inc. above	50.00	70.00	100	150	—

KM# 162.2 1000 REIS

2.0100 g., 0.9170 Gold .0592 oz. AGW, 16 mm. **Ruler:** Jose I **Obv:** Crowned arms divide florals at right from value at left **Obv. Legend:** JOSEPHUS • I • D • G • PORTUG • REX • **Rev:** Cross within ornamented outline, lined circle surrounds all **Rev. Legend:** ET • BRASILIÆ • DOMINVS • ANNO • **Note:** Reduced size.

Date	Mintage	F	VF	XF	Unc	BU
1771	Inc. above	50.00	70.00	100	150	—
1774	21,000	50.00	70.00	100	150	—

KM# 208 1000 REIS

2.0100 g., 0.9170 Gold .0592 oz. AGW **Ruler:** Maria I and Pedro III **Obv:** Crowned arms divide crosses at right from value at left **Obv. Legend:** MARIA • I • ET • PETRUS • III • D • G • PORTUG • REGES • **Rev:** Cross within ornamented outline, lined circle surrounds all **Rev. Legend:** ET • BRASILIÆ • DOMINI • ANNO • **Note:** Struck in Lisbon without mint mark.

Date	Mintage	F	VF	XF	Unc	BU
1778	2,816	60.00	100	160	250	—
1779	3,000	60.00	100	160	250	—
1781	5,800	60.00	100	160	250	—
1782	—	120	250	500	700	—

KM# 223 1000 REIS

2.0100 g., 0.9170 Gold .0592 oz. AGW **Ruler:** Maria I Widow **Obv:** Crowned arms divide florals at right from value at left **Obv. Legend:** MARIA • I • D • G • PORTUG • REGINA **Rev:** Cross within ornamented outline, lined circle surrounds all **Rev. Legend:** ET • BRASILIÆ • DOMINIA • ANNO • **Note:** Struck at Lisbon without mint mark.

Date	Mintage	F	VF	XF	Unc	BU
1787	6,000	75.00	150	260	375	—

KM# 124 1600 REIS

3.5800 g., 0.9170 Gold .1055 oz. AGW **Ruler:** Joao VI **Obv:** Head right, date and mint mark below **Rev:** First variety of crowned arms

Date	Mintage	VG	F	VF	XF	Unc
1727B	—	225	500	1,000	2,000	—
1729B	—	200	400	800	1,500	—

KM# 125 1600 REIS

3.5800 g., 0.9170 Gold .1055 oz. AGW **Ruler:** Joao VI **Obv:** Head right **Obv. Legend:** IOANNES • V • D • G • PORT • ... **Rev:** Crowned ornate arms

Date	Mintage	VG	F	VF	XF	Unc
1727M	—	700	1,200	2,000	4,000	—
1728M	—	220	500	1,000	2,200	—
1729M	—	220	500	1,000	2,200	—
1730M	—	200	450	900	2,000	—
1731M	—	200	450	900	2,000	—
1732M	—	200	450	900	2,000	—
1733M	—	200	450	900	2,000	—

KM# 126 1600 REIS

3.5800 g., 0.9170 Gold .1055 oz. AGW **Ruler:** Joao VI **Obv:** Laureate head right **Obv. Legend:** IOANNES • V • D • G • PORT • ... **Rev:** Crowned arms within cartouche

Date	Mintage	VG	F	VF	XF	Unc
1727R	—	180	400	900	1,800	—
1728R	—	180	400	900	1,800	—
1729R	—	180	400	900	1,800	—
1730R	—	180	400	900	1,800	—

KM# 127 1600 REIS

3.5800 g., 0.9170 Gold .1055 oz. AGW **Ruler:** Joao VI **Rev:** Second variety of crowned arms

Date	Mintage	VG	F	VF	XF	Unc
1727B	—	250	500	1,000	2,000	—
1729B	—	250	450	900	1,800	—

KM# 128 1600 REIS

3.5800 g., 0.9170 Gold .1055 oz. AGW **Ruler:** Joao VI **Obv:** Laureate head right **Obv. Legend:** IOANNES • V • D • G • PORT • ... **Rev:** Fourth variety of crowned arms

Date	Mintage	VG	F	VF	XF	Unc
1727B	—	250	500	800	1,300	—
1732B	—	150	300	500	1,000	—
1736B	—	225	425	700	1,200	—
1740B	—	200	375	600	1,200	—
1741B Unique	—	—	—	—	—	—
1743B	—	250	450	900	2,000	—
1744B	—	250	450	900	2,000	—
1747B	—	250	450	900	2,000	—
1749B	—	250	450	900	2,000	—
1750B	—	250	450	900	2,000	—

KM# 154 1600 REIS

3.5800 g., 0.9170 Gold .1055 oz. AGW **Ruler:** Joao VI **Obv:** Laureate head right **Obv. Legend:** IOANNES • V • D • G • PORT • ... **Rev:** Different crowned arms, ornate

Date	Mintage	VG	F	VF	XF	Unc
1736R	—	400	800	1,600	2,600	—

KM# 181.1 1600 REIS

3.5800 g., 0.9170 Gold .1055 oz. AGW **Ruler:** Jose I **Obv:** Head right **Obv. Legend:** JOSEPHUS • I • D • G • PORT • ... **Rev:** Crowned ornate arms

Date	Mintage	F	VF	XF	Unc	BU
1752B Rare	—	—	—	—	—	—
1754B	—	225	450	900	1,800	—
1756B	—	225	450	900	1,800	—
1757B	—	225	450	900	1,800	—
1758B	—	225	450	900	1,800	—
1759B	—	225	450	900	1,800	—
1760B	—	225	450	900	1,800	—
1764B	—	225	450	900	1,800	—
1765B	—	225	450	900	1,800	—
1766B	—	225	450	900	1,800	—
1767B	—	225	450	900	1,800	—
1768B	—	225	450	900	1,800	—
1772B	—	225	450	900	1,800	—
1774B	—	225	450	900	1,800	—
1.777B	—	225	450	900	1,800	—

KM# 181.2 1600 REIS

3.5800 g., 0.9170 Gold .1055 oz. AGW **Ruler:** Jose I **Obv:** Head right **Obv. Legend:** JOSEPHUS • I • D • G • PORT • .... **Rev:** Crowned ornate arms

Date	Mintage	F	VF	XF	Unc	BU
1752R	—	200	390	780	1,500	—
1763R	—	180	360	700	1,300	—
1772R	1,732	190	380	760	1,400	—

KM# 211 1600 REIS

3.5800 g., 0.9170 Gold .1055 oz. AGW **Ruler:** Maria I and Pedro III **Obv:** Conjoined busts right **Obv. Legend:** MARIA • I • E • PETRUS • III • D • G • PORT • ... **Rev:** Crowned arms within cartouche **Note:** Varieties exist with mint mark following date or below busts.

Date	Mintage	F	VF	XF	Unc	BU
1780B	—	625	1,250	2,100	3,000	—
1781B	—	625	1,250	2,400	3,800	—
1782B	—	625	1,250	2,400	3,800	—
1784B	—	675	1,350	2,550	4,200	—

KM# 100 2000 REIS

5.3700 g., 0.9170 Gold .1583 oz. AGW **Ruler:** Pedro As Pedro II **Obv:** Crowned arms, value at side **Rev:** Cross with "R" in angles, date above

Date	Mintage	VG	F	VF	XF	Unc
1703R	—	300	600	1,000	2,000	—

KM# 105 2000 REIS

5.3700 g., 0.9170 Gold .1583 oz. AGW **Ruler:** Joao VI **Obv:** Crowned arms divide florals at right from value at left **Obv. Legend:** IOANNES • V • D • G • PORT • ... **Rev:** Cross with "B" in angles, date at top **Rev. Legend:** IN HOC SIGNO VINCES

Date	Mintage	VG	F	VF	XF	Unc
1714B	—	100	200	350	700	—
1715B	—	100	200	350	700	—
1716B	—	100	200	350	700	—
1720B	—	100	200	350	800	—
1722B	—	125	225	375	900	—
1723B	—	100	200	350	800	—
1725B	—	125	225	375	900	—

KM# 112 2000 REIS

5.3700 g., 0.9170 Gold .1583 oz. AGW **Ruler:** Joao VI **Obv:** Crowned arms divide florals at right from value at left **Obv. Legend:** IOANNES • V • D • G • PORT • ... **Rev:** Cross with "R" in angles, date above **Rev. Legend:** IN HOC SIGNO VINCES

Date	Mintage	VG	F	VF	XF	Unc
1723R	—	100	200	400	800	—
1725R	—	90.00	180	300	500	—
1726R	—	90.00	180	300	500	—

KM# 114 2000 REIS

5.3700 g., 0.9170 Gold .1583 oz. AGW **Ruler:** Joao VI **Obv:** Crowned arms divide florals at right from value at left **Obv. Legend:** IOANNES • V • D • G • PORT • ... **Rev:** Cross with "M" in angles, date above **Rev. Legend:** IN HOC SIGNO VINCES

Date	Mintage	VG	F	VF	XF	Unc
1724M	—	700	1,500	2,800	4,500	—
1725M	—	400	1,200	1,800	2,800	—
1726M	—	400	1,200	1,800	2,800	—
1727M	—	500	1,600	2,500	4,000	—

KM# 163 2000 REIS

4.0342 g., 0.9170 Gold .1189 oz. AGW **Ruler:** Joao VI **Obv:** Crowned arms divide florals at right from value at left **Obv. Legend:** IOANNES • V • D • G • PORTVG • REX • **Rev:** Cross within ornamented outline, lined circle surrounds all **Rev. Legend:** ET • BRASILIÆ • DOMINVS • ANNO • **Note:** Struck at Lisbon without mint mark.

Date	Mintage	VG	F	VF	XF	Unc
1749	—	100	175	325	500	—

KM# 182.1 2000 REIS

4.0342 g., 0.9170 Gold .1189 oz. AGW **Ruler:** Jose I **Obv:** Crowned arms divide florals at right from value at left **Obv. Legend:** IOSEPHUS • I • D • G PORTUG • REX • **Rev:** Cross within ornamented outline, lined circle surrounds all **Rev. Legend:** ET • BRASILIÆ • DOMINUS • ANNO •

Date	Mintage	F	VF	XF	Unc	BU
1752	12,000	65.00	110	175	300	—
1754	1,000	65.00	110	175	300	—
1771	47,000	65.00	110	175	300	—

KM# 182.2 2000 REIS

4.0342 g., 0.9170 Gold .1189 oz. AGW **Ruler:** Jose I **Obv:** Crowned arms divide florals at right from value at left **Obv. Legend:** JOSEPHUS • I • D • G • PORTUG • REX • **Rev:** Cross within ornamented outline, lined circle surrounds all **Rev. Legend:** ET • BRASILIÆ • DOMINUS • ANNO •

Date	Mintage	F	VF	XF	Unc	BU
1771	Inc. above	75.00	120	200	300	—

KM# 198 2000 REIS

4.0342 g., 0.9170 Gold .1189 oz. AGW, 19-20 mm. **Ruler:** Jose I **Obv:** Crowned arms divide florals at right from value at left **Obv. Legend:** JOSEPHUS • I • D • G • PORTUG • REX • **Rev:** Cross within ornamented outline, lined circle surrounds all **Rev. Legend:** ET • BRASILIÆ • DOMINUS • ANNO • **Note:** Reduced size, size varies.

Date	Mintage	F	VF	XF	Unc	BU
1771	Inc. above	75.00	120	200	300	—
1773	14,000	75.00	120	200	300	—

KM# 209 2000 REIS

4.0342 g., 0.9170 Gold .1189 oz. AGW **Ruler:** Maria I and Pedro III **Obv:** Crowned arms divide florals at right from value at left **Obv. Legend:** MARIA • I • ET • PETRUS • III • D • G • PORTUG • REGES **Rev:** Cross witihin ornamented outline, lined circle surrounds all **Rev. Legend:** ET • BRASILIÆ • DOMINI • ANNO • **Note:** Struck at Lisbon and Rio de Janeiro without mint mark.

Date	Mintage	F	VF	XF	Unc	BU
1778	7,800	100	200	400	650	—
1781	3,500	150	300	650	950	—
1782	—	140	280	550	900	—
1783	1,500	165	325	700	1,000	—

KM# 224 2000 REIS

4.0342 g., 0.9170 Gold .1189 oz. AGW **Ruler:** Maria I Widow **Obv:** Crowned arms divide florals at right from value at left **Obv. Legend:** • MARIA • I • D • G • PORTUG • REGINA **Rev:** Cross within ornamented outline, lined circle surrounds all **Rev. Legend:** ET • BRASILIÆ • DOMINA • ANNO • **Note:** Struck at Rio de Janeiro without mint mark.

Date	Mintage	F	VF	XF	Unc	BU
1787	1,500	150	300	600	1,000	—
1792	2,251	250	500	800	1,200	—
1793	1,500	250	500	800	1,200	—

KM# 129 3200 REIS

7.1718 g., 0.9170 Gold .2115 oz. AGW **Ruler:** Joao VI **Obv:** Laureate head right, date and mint mark below **Rev:** First variety of crowned arms

Date	Mintage	VG	F	VF	XF	Unc
1727B	—	600	1,400	3,000	6,000	—
1732B	—	600	1,400	3,000	6,000	—

KM# 130 3200 REIS

7.1718 g., 0.9170 Gold .2115 oz. AGW **Ruler:** Joao VI **Obv:** Laureate head right **Obv. Legend:** IOANNES • V • D • G • PORT • ET • ALG • REX • **Rev:** Crowned arms within cartouche

Date	Mintage	VG	F	VF	XF	Unc
1727M Unique	—	—	—	—	—	—
1728M	—	800	1,700	3,500	5,000	—
1729M	—	800	1,700	3,500	5,000	—
1730M	—	800	1,700	3,500	5,000	—
1731M	—	800	1,700	3,500	5,000	—
1732M	—	800	1,700	3,500	5,000	—
1733M	—	800	1,700	3,500	5,000	—

KM# 131 3200 REIS

7.1718 g., 0.9170 Gold .2115 oz. AGW **Ruler:** Joao VI **Obv:** Laureate head right **Obv. Legend:** IOANNES • V • D • G • PORT • ET • ALG • REX • **Rev:** Crowned arms within cartouche

Date	Mintage	VG	F	VF	XF	Unc
1727R	—	500	1,100	2,000	3,500	—
1729R	—	500	1,100	2,000	3,500	—

KM# 132 3200 REIS

7.1718 g., 0.9170 Gold .2115 oz. AGW **Ruler:** Joao VI **Rev:** Second variety of crowned arms

Date	Mintage	VG	F	VF	XF	Unc
1727B	—	800	2,000	3,800	6,000	—
1729B	—	800	2,000	3,800	6,000	—

KM# 133 3200 REIS

7.1718 g., 0.9170 Gold .2115 oz. AGW **Ruler:** Joao VI **Rev:** Fourth variety of crowned arms

Date	Mintage	VG	F	VF	XF	Unc
1727B	—	700	1,500	3,000	4,500	—
1729B	—	700	1,500	3,000	4,500	—
1740B	—	700	1,500	3,000	4,500	—
1744B	—	700	1,500	3,000	4,500	—
1747B	—	700	1,500	3,000	4,500	—
1749B	—	700	1,500	3,000	4,500	—
1750B	—	700	1,500	3,000	4,500	—

KM# 155 3200 REIS

7.1718 g., 0.9170 Gold .2115 oz. AGW **Ruler:** Joao VI **Obv:** Laureate head right **Obv. Legend:** IOANNES • V • D • G • PORT • ET • ALG • REX • **Rev:** Different crowned arms

Date	Mintage	VG	F	VF	XF	Unc
1739R	—	400	700	1,500	3,000	—
1741R	—	400	700	1,500	3,000	—
1749R	—	400	700	1,500	3,000	—

KM# 183.1 3200 REIS

7.1718 g., 0.9170 Gold .2115 oz. AGW **Ruler:** Jose I **Obv:** Laureate head right **Obv. Legend:** JOSEPHUS • I • D • G • PORT • ET • ALG • REX **Rev:** Arms on crowned ornate shield

Date	Mintage	F	VF	XF	Unc	BU
1752B	—	2,000	3,500	5,000	7,000	—
1754B	—	2,000	3,500	5,000	7,000	—
1757B	—	2,000	3,500	5,000	7,000	—
1758B Rare	—	—	—	—	—	—
1759B Rare	—	—	—	—	—	—
1760B Unique	—	—	—	—	—	—
1761B Rare	—	—	—	—	—	—
1763B	—	2,000	3,500	5,000	7,000	—
1764B	—	2,000	3,500	5,000	7,000	—
1765B	—	2,000	3,500	5,000	7,000	—
1766B	—	2,000	3,500	5,000	7,000	—
1767B	—	2,000	3,500	5,000	7,000	—
1768B	—	2,000	3,500	5,000	7,000	—
1773B	—	2,000	3,500	5,000	7,000	—
1775B	—	2,000	3,500	5,000	7,000	—
1777B Rare	—	—	—	—	—	—

KM# 183.2 3200 REIS

7.1718 g., 0.9170 Gold .2115 oz. AGW **Ruler:** Jose I **Obv:** Laureate head right **Obv. Legend:** JOSEPHUS • I • D • G • PORT • ET • ALG • REX **Rev:** Crowned arms within cartouche

Date	Mintage	F	VF	XF	Unc	BU
1755R	—	1,500	2,700	5,000	7,000	—
1756R	—	500	800	1,700	3,000	—
1760R	—	500	800	1,700	3,000	—
1766R	—	500	800	1,700	3,000	—
1772R	1,554	500	800	1,700	3,000	—
1773R	—	1,500	2,700	5,000	7,000	—

KM# 150 3200 REIS
7.1718 g., 0.9170 Gold .2115 oz. AGW **Ruler:** Maria I and Pedro III **Obv:** Conjoined busts right **Obv. Legend:** MARIA • I • ET • PETRUS • III • D • G • PORT • ET • ALG • REGES **Rev:** Crowned ornate arms **Note:** 2 varieties exist with mint mark following date or below busts.

Date	Mintage	F	VF	XF	Unc	BU
1780B	—	700	1,500	3,000	4,000	—
1781B	—	500	1,100	2,200	3,000	—
1782B	—	700	1,500	3,000	4,000	—
1783B	—	500	1,100	2,200	3,000	—
1784B	—	700	1,500	3,000	4,000	—
1785B	—	700	1,500	3,200	4,500	—
1786B	—	1,000	2,250	4,500	8,000	—

KM# 99 4000 REIS
10.7500 g., 0.9170 Gold .3170 oz. AGW **Ruler:** Pedro As Pedro II **Rev:** Cross in quatrefoil, P's in angles, date at top

Date	Mintage	VG	F	VF	XF	Unc
1702P	—	375	725	2,000	2,800	—

KM# 101 4000 REIS
10.7500 g., 0.9170 Gold .3170 oz. AGW **Ruler:** Pedro As Pedro II **Obv:** Crowned arms divide florals at right from value at left **Obv. Legend:** PETRVS • II • D • G • PORT • ET • ALG • REX **Rev:** Cross with R's in angles **Rev. Legend:** IN HOC SIGNO VINCES

Date	Mintage	VG	F	VF	XF	Unc
1703R	—	300	650	1,350	2,150	—
1704R	—	300	600	1,300	2,000	—
1705R	—	300	600	1,300	2,000	—
1706R	—	300	600	1,300	2,000	—
1707R	—	300	700	1,500	2,400	—

KM# 102 4000 REIS
10.7500 g., 0.9170 Gold .3170 oz. AGW **Ruler:** Joao VI **Obv:** Crowned arms divide florals at right from value at left **Obv. Legend:** IOANNES • V • D • G • PORT • ET • ALG • REX **Rev:** Cross with R's in angle **Rev. Legend:** IN HOC SIGNO VINCES

Date	Mintage	VG	F	VF	XF	Unc
1707R Rare	—	—	—	—	—	—
1708R	—	250	500	1,200	2,000	—
1709R	—	250	500	900	1,400	—
1710R	—	250	500	900	1,400	—
1711R	—	250	500	900	1,400	—
1712R	—	200	380	650	900	—
1713R	—	150	300	525	750	—
1714R	—	150	300	525	700	—
1715R	—	150	300	525	700	—
1716R	—	150	300	525	700	—
1717R	—	150	300	525	700	—
1718R	—	150	300	525	700	—
1719R	—	150	300	525	700	—
1720R	—	150	300	525	700	—
1721R	—	150	300	525	700	—
1722R	—	150	300	525	700	—
1723R	—	150	300	525	700	—
1724R	—	150	300	525	700	—
1725R	—	150	300	525	700	—
1726R	—	150	300	525	700	—
1727R	—	150	300	600	800	—

KM# 106 4000 REIS
10.7500 g., 0.9170 Gold .3170 oz. AGW **Ruler:** Joao VI **Obv:** Crowned arms divide florals at right from value at left **Obv. Legend:** IOANNES • V • D • G • PORT • ET • ALG • REX • **Rev:** Cross with B's in angles **Rev. Legend:** IN HOC SIGNO VINCES

Date	Mintage	VG	F	VF	XF	Unc
1714B Rare	—	—	—	—	—	—
1715B	—	900	2,000	3,000	5,000	—
1716B	—	200	375	575	1,000	—
1717B	—	200	375	575	900	—
1718B	—	200	375	575	900	—
1719B	—	200	375	575	900	—
1720B	—	200	375	575	900	—
1721B	—	140	275	500	800	—
1722B	—	140	275	500	800	—
1723B	—	140	275	500	800	—
1724B	—	140	275	500	800	—
1725B	—	140	275	500	800	—
1726B	—	140	275	475	700	—
1727B	—	200	400	800	1,200	—

KM# 115 4000 REIS
10.7500 g., 0.9170 Gold .3170 oz. AGW **Ruler:** Joao VI **Obv:** Crowned arms divide florals at right from value at left **Obv. Legend:** IOANNES • V • D • G • PORT • ET • ALG • REX • **Rev:** Cross with M's in angles **Rev. Legend:** IN HOC SIGNO VINCES

Date	Mintage	VG	F	VF	XF	Unc
1724M Rare	—	—	—	—	—	—
1725M	—	300	1,000	2,000	3,000	—
1726M	—	300	1,000	2,000	3,000	—
1727M	—	325	1,200	2,600	5,000	—

KM# 164 4000 REIS
8.0683 g., 0.9170 Gold .2378 oz. AGW **Ruler:** Joao VI **Obv:** Crowned arms divide florals at right from value at left **Obv. Legend:** IOANNES • V • D • G • PORTVG • ET • ALG • REX **Rev:** Cross within ornamented outline, lined circle surrounds all **Rev. Legend:** ET • BRASILIÆ • DOMINVS • ANNO • **Note:** Struck at Lisbon without mint mark.

Date	Mintage	VG	F	VF	XF	Unc
1749	—	165	325	550	800	—

KM# 171.1 4000 REIS
8.0683 g., 0.9170 Gold .2378 oz. AGW **Ruler:** Jose I **Obv:** Crowned arms divide florals at right from value at left **Obv. Legend:** IOSEPHUS • I • D • G • PORTUG • REX • **Rev:** Cross within ornamented outline, lined circle surrounds all **Rev. Legend:** ET • BRASILIÆ • DOMINVS • ANNO •

Date	Mintage	F	VF	XF	Unc	BU
1751	—	125	225	400	600	—
1752	4,000	125	225	400	600	—
1753	22,000	150	300	500	650	—
1754/3	Inc. above	150	300	500	650	—
1754	6,248	150	300	500	650	—

Date	Mintage	F	VF	XF	Unc	BU
1774	38,000	150	300	500	650	—
1775	56,000	150	300	500	650	—

KM# 171.2 4000 REIS
8.0683 g., 0.9170 Gold .2378 oz. AGW **Ruler:** Jose I **Obv:** Crowned arms divide florals at right from value at left **Obv. Legend:** JOSEPHUS • I • D • G • PORTUG • REX • **Rev:** Cross within ornamented outline, lined circle surrounds all **Rev. Legend:** ET • BRASILIÆ • DOMINVS • ANNO •

Date	Mintage	F	VF	XF	Unc	BU
1751	—	125	200	325	500	—
1753	Inc. above	125	200	325	500	—
1756/5	—	150	250	375	525	—
1756	7,081	125	200	325	500	—
1758	—	125	200	325	500	—
1759	—	125	200	325	500	—
1760	—	125	200	325	500	—
1761	—	125	200	325	500	—
1762	—	125	200	325	500	—
1763	—	125	200	325	500	—
1764	—	125	200	325	500	—
1767	1,029	125	200	325	500	—
1769	24,000	125	200	325	500	—
1771	Inc. above	125	200	325	500	—
1773	25,000	125	200	325	500	—
1774	Inc. above	125	200	325	500	—
1775	Inc. above	125	200	325	500	—
1776	26,000	125	200	325	500	—

KM# 171.3 4000 REIS
8.0683 g., 0.9170 Gold .2378 oz. AGW **Ruler:** Jose I **Obv:** Crowned arms divide florals at right from value at left **Obv. Legend:** IOSEPHUS • I • D • G • PORTUG • REX • **Rev:** Cross within ornamented outline, lined circle surrounds all **Rev. Legend:** ET • BRASILIÆ • DOMINUS • ANNO •

Date	Mintage	F	VF	XF	Unc	BU
1753	Inc. above	125	200	325	500	—
1771	18,000	125	200	325	500	—

KM# 171.4 4000 REIS
8.0683 g., 0.9170 Gold .2378 oz. AGW **Ruler:** Jose I **Obv:** Crowned arms divide florals at right from value at left **Obv. Legend:** JOSEPHUS • I • DG • PORTUG • REX • **Rev:** Cross within ornamented outline, lined circle surrounds all **Rev. Legend:** ET • BRASILIÆ • DOMINVS • ANNO •

Date	Mintage	F	VF	XF	Unc	BU
1763	—	125	200	325	500	—
1771	Inc. above	125	200	325	500	—
1772	4,000	125	200	325	500	—
1774	Inc. above	125	200	325	475	—
1775	Inc. above	125	200	325	475	—
1775 BRASILIE	Inc. above	125	200	325	475	—
1776	Inc. above	125	200	325	475	—
1777	54,000	125	200	325	475	—

KM# 210 4000 REIS

8.0683 g., 0.9170 Gold .2378 oz. AGW **Ruler:** Maria I and Pedro III **Obv:** Crowned arms divide florals at right from value at left **Obv. Legend:** MARIA • I • ET • PETRUS • III • D • G • PORTUG • REGES **Rev:** Cross within ornamented outline, lined circle surrounds all **Rev. Legend:** ET • BRASILIÆ • DOMINI • ANNO • **Note:** Struck at Lisbon and Rio de Janeiro without mint mark.

Date	Mintage	F	VF	XF	Unc	BU
1778	2,741	175	350	650	900	—
1779	5,150	200	375	650	900	—
1781	4,250	180	350	650	900	—
1783	2,000	180	350	650	900	—
1786	3,000	180	350	650	900	—

KM# 225.1 4000 REIS

8.0683 g., 0.9170 Gold .2378 oz. AGW **Ruler:** Maria I Widow **Obv:** Crowned arms divide florals at right from value at left **Obv. Legend:** MARIA I • D • G • PORTUG • REGINA • **Rev:** Cross within ornamented outline, lined circle surrounds **Rev. Legend:** ET • BRASILIÆ • DOMINI • ANNO • **Note:** Struck at Lisbon and Rio de Janeiro without mint mark.

Date	Mintage	F	VF	XF	Unc	BU
1787	2,000	220	350	600	800	—
1790	1,250	180	280	500	900	—
1792	2,050	180	280	500	900	—

KM# 134 6400 REIS

14.3436 g., 0.9170 Gold .4229 oz. AGW **Ruler:** Joao VI **Obv:** Laureate head right **Obv. Legend:** IOANNES • V • D • G • PORT • ET • ALG • REX • **Rev:** First variety of crowned arms

Date	Mintage	VG	F	VF	XF	Unc
1727B Rare	—	—	—	—	—	—
1728B Rare	—	—	—	—	—	—
1729B Rare	—	—	—	—	—	—
1730B Rare	—	—	—	—	—	—

KM# 135 6400 REIS

14.3436 g., 0.9170 Gold .4229 oz. AGW **Ruler:** Joao VI **Obv:** Laureate head right, date and mint mark below **Rev:** Crowned arms

Date	Mintage	VG	F	VF	XF	Unc
1727M Rare	—	—	—	—	—	—
1731M Unique	—	—	—	—	—	—
1732M Rare	—	—	—	—	—	—
1733M Rare	—	—	—	—	—	—
1734M Rare	—	—	—	—	—	—

KM# 136 6400 REIS

14.3436 g., 0.9170 Gold .4229 oz. AGW **Ruler:** Joao VI **Obv:** Laureate head right **Obv. Legend:** IOANNES • V • D • G • PORT • ET • ALG • REX • **Rev:** Crowned ornate arms

Date	Mintage	VG	F	VF	XF	Unc
1727R Rare	—	—	—	—	—	—
1728R Rare	—	—	—	—	—	—
1729R Rare	—	—	—	—	—	—

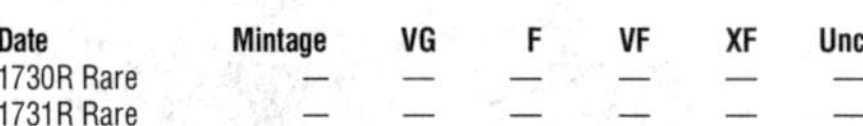

Date	Mintage	VG	F	VF	XF	Unc
1730R Rare	—	—	—	—	—	—
1731R Rare	—	—	—	—	—	—

KM# 137 6400 REIS

14.3436 g., 0.9170 Gold .4229 oz. AGW **Ruler:** Joao VI **Rev:** Second variety of crowned arms

Date	Mintage	VG	F	VF	XF	Unc
1727B Rare	—	—	—	—	—	—
1731B Rare	—	—	—	—	—	—
1732B Rare	—	—	—	—	—	—
1734B Rare	—	—	—	—	—	—

KM# 146 6400 REIS

14.3436 g., 0.9170 Gold .4229 oz. AGW **Ruler:** Joao VI **Rev:** Third variety of crowned arms

Date	Mintage	VG	F	VF	XF	Unc
1729B Rare	—	—	—	—	—	—
1730B Rare	—	—	—	—	—	—
1731B Rare	—	—	—	—	—	—
1732B Unique	—	—	—	—	—	—

KM# 149 6400 REIS

14.3436 g., 0.9170 Gold .4229 oz. AGW **Ruler:** Joao VI **Obv:** Head right **Obv. Legend:** JOANNES • V • D • G • PORT • ET • ALG • REX • **Rev:** Arms within crowned ornate frame

Date	Mintage	VG	F	VF	XF	Unc
1731R Unique	—	—	—	—	—	—
1732R	—	250	500	2,000	3,000	—
1733R	—	250	500	1,500	2,800	—
1734R	—	250	500	1,500	2,800	—
1735R	—	250	500	1,500	2,800	—
1736R	—	250	500	1,500	2,800	—
1737R	—	200	300	525	750	—
1738R	—	200	300	525	750	—
1739R	—	250	350	600	800	—
1740R	—	200	300	525	750	—
1741R	—	200	300	525	750	—
1742R	—	200	300	525	750	—
1743R	—	200	300	525	750	—
1744R	—	200	300	525	750	—
1745R	—	200	300	525	750	—
1746R	—	200	300	525	750	—
1747R	—	200	300	525	750	—
1748R	—	200	300	525	750	—
1749R	—	200	300	525	750	—
1750R	—	200	300	550	900	—

KM# 151 6400 REIS

14.3436 g., 0.9170 Gold .4229 oz. AGW **Ruler:** Joao VI **Obv:** Head right, mint mark and date below head **Obv. Legend:** IOANNES • V • D • G • PORT • ET • ALG • REX • **Rev:** Fourth variety of crowned arms

Date	Mintage	VG	F	VF	XF	Unc
1732B Rare	—	—	—	—	—	—
1734B Rare	—	—	—	—	—	—
1735B	—	500	1,400	2,500	4,000	—
1736B	—	500	1,400	2,500	4,000	—
1737B	—	200	350	600	1,000	—
1738B	—	200	350	600	1,000	—
1739B	—	200	350	600	1,000	—
1740B	—	200	350	600	1,000	—
1741B	—	200	350	600	1,000	—
1742B	—	200	325	550	800	—
1743B	—	200	325	550	800	—
1744B	—	200	325	550	800	—
1745B	—	200	325	550	800	—
1746B	—	200	325	550	800	—
1747B	—	200	325	550	800	—
1748B	—	250	325	550	800	—
1749B	—	200	325	550	800	—
1750B	—	200	325	550	800	—

KM# 172.1 6400 REIS

14.3436 g., 0.9170 Gold .4229 oz. AGW **Ruler:** Jose I **Obv:** Head right, date and mint mark below **Obv. Legend:** JOSEPHUS • I • D • G • PORT • ET • ALG • REX • **Rev:** Arms within crowned ornate shield

Date	Mintage	F	VF	XF	Unc	BU
1751B	—	300	400	700	1,000	—
1751B/R	—	300	400	700	1,000	—
1752/1B	—	300	400	700	1,000	—
1752B/R	—	300	400	700	1,000	—
1753B	—	280	350	500	700	—
1754B	—	280	350	500	700	—
1755B	—	280	350	500	700	—
1756B	—	260	320	450	650	—
1757B	—	260	320	450	650	—
1758B	—	260	320	450	650	—
1759B	—	260	320	450	650	—
1760B	—	260	320	450	650	—
1761B	—	260	320	450	650	—
1762B	—	260	320	450	650	—
1763/2B	—	260	320	450	650	—
1763B	—	260	320	450	650	—
1764B	—	260	320	450	650	—
1765/4B	—	260	320	450	650	—
1765B	—	260	320	450	650	—
1766B	—	260	320	450	650	—
1767B	—	260	320	450	650	—
1768B	—	260	320	450	650	—
1769B	—	260	320	450	650	—
1770B	—	260	320	450	650	—
1771/0B	—	260	320	450	650	—
1771B	—	260	320	450	650	—
1772B	—	260	320	450	650	—
1773B	—	260	320	450	650	—
1774B	—	260	320	450	650	—
1775B	—	260	320	450	650	—
1776B	—	260	320	450	650	—
1777B	—	260	320	450	650	—

KM# 172.2 6400 REIS

14.3436 g., 0.9170 Gold .4229 oz. AGW **Ruler:** Jose I **Obv:** Laureate head right, mint mark and date below **Obv. Legend:** JOSEPHUS • I • D • G • PORT • ET • ALG • REX • **Rev:** Arms on crowned ornate shield

Date	Mintage	F	VF	XF	Unc	BU
1751R	610,000	300	400	700	1,100	—
1752R	567,000	300	400	700	1,100	—
1753/2R	—	300	400	700	1,000	—
1753R	475,000	300	400	700	1,000	—
1754R	326,000	300	400	700	1,000	—
1755R	757,000	260	350	500	750	—
1756R	—	260	350	500	750	—
1757R	495,000	260	350	500	750	—
1758R	309,000	260	350	500	750	—
1759R	355,000	260	350	500	650	—
1760R	586,000	260	350	500	650	—
1761R	563,000	260	350	500	650	—
1762/1R	—	260	350	500	650	—
1762R	475,000	260	350	500	650	—
1763R	418,000	260	350	450	600	—
1764R	367,000	260	350	450	600	—
1765R	330,000	250	320	450	600	—
1766R	572,000	250	320	450	600	—
1767R	476,000	250	320	450	600	—
1768R	424,000	250	320	450	600	—
1769R	368,000	250	320	450	600	—
1770R	365,000	250	320	450	600	—
1771R	404,000	250	320	450	600	—
1772R	378,000	250	320	450	600	—
1773R	404,000	250	320	450	600	—
1774R	363,000	250	320	400	600	—
1775R	338,000	250	320	400	600	—
1776R	390,000	250	320	400	600	—
1777R	347,000	250	320	400	600	—

KM# 199.2 6400 REIS

14.3436 g., 0.9170 Gold .4229 oz. AGW **Ruler:** Maria I and Pedro III **Obv:** Conjoined busts right **Obv. Legend:** MARIA • I • ET • PETRUS • III • D • G • PORT • ET • ALG • REGES **Rev:** Arms within crowned ornate shield

Date	Mintage	F	VF	XF	Unc	BU
1777R Rare	—	—	—	—	—	—
1778R	378,000	250	300	450	650	—
1779R	408,000	250	300	450	650	—
1780R	343,000	250	300	450	650	—
1781R	375,000	250	300	450	650	—
1782R	324,000	250	300	450	650	—
1783R	322,000	250	300	450	650	—
1784R	327,000	250	300	450	650	—
1785R	282,000	250	300	450	650	—
1786R	294,000	250	300	450	650	—

KM# 199.1 6400 REIS

14.3436 g., 0.9170 Gold .4229 oz. AGW **Ruler:** Maria I and Pedro III **Obv:** Conjoined busts right **Obv. Legend:** MARIA • I • ET • PETRUS • III • D • G • PORT • ET • ALG • REGES **Rev:** Arms within crowned ornate shield **Note:** 2 varieties exist with mint mark following date or below busts.

Date	Mintage	F	VF	XF	Unc	BU
1777B Rare	—	—	—	—	—	—
1778B	—	260	450	600	750	—
1778B '...PORT. ALG...'	—	260	450	600	750	—
1779B	—	260	450	600	750	—
1780B	19,000	260	450	600	750	—
1781B	34,000	260	450	600	750	—
1782B	60,000	260	450	600	750	—
1783B	30,000	260	450	600	750	—
1784B	24,000	260	450	600	750	—
1785B	23,000	260	450	600	750	—
1786B	20,000	260	450	600	750	—

KM# 218.1 6400 REIS

14.3436 g., 0.9170 Gold .4229 oz. AGW **Ruler:** Maria I Widow **Obv:** Veiled bust right **Obv. Legend:** MARIA • I • D • G • PORT • ET • ALG • REGINA • **Rev:** Arms within crowned ornate shield

Date	Mintage	F	VF	XF	Unc	BU
1786R	Inc. above	300	500	800	1,000	—
1787R	276,000	250	320	450	750	—
1788/7R	—	250	320	450	750	—
1788R	263,000	250	320	450	750	—
1789R	247,000	250	320	450	750	—

KM# 218.2 6400 REIS

14.3436 g., 0.9170 Gold .4229 oz. AGW **Ruler:** Maria I Widow **Obv:** Veiled bust right **Rev:** Arms within crowned ornate shield

Date	Mintage	F	VF	XF	Unc	BU
1787B	16,000	260	350	550	900	—
1788B	14,000	260	350	550	900	—
1789B	21,000	260	350	550	900	—
1790B	12,000	450	900	1,500	2,000	—

KM# 226.1 6400 REIS

14.3436 g., 0.9170 Gold .4229 oz. AGW **Ruler:** Maria I Widow **Obv:** Bust right with bejeweled headdress **Obv. Legend:** MARIA • I • D • G • PORT • ET • ALG • REGINA • **Rev:** Crowned ornate arms

Date	Mintage	F	VF	XF	Unc	BU
1789R	Inc. above	285	345	450	750	—
1790R	211,000	285	345	450	750	—
1791R	231,000	285	345	450	750	—
1792R	230,000	285	345	450	750	—
1793R	237,000	285	345	450	750	—
1794R	246,000	285	345	450	750	—
1795R	226,000	285	345	450	750	—
1796R	219,000	285	345	450	750	—
1797R	214,000	285	345	450	750	—
1798R	204,000	285	345	450	750	—
1799R	189,000	285	345	450	750	—
1800R	214,000	285	345	450	750	1,250

KM# 226.2 6400 REIS

14.3436 g., 0.9170 Gold .4229 oz. AGW **Ruler:** Maria I Widow **Obv:** Bust right with jeweled headdress **Obv. Legend:** MARIA • I • D • G • PORT • ET • ALG • REGINA • **Rev:** Crowned ornate arms

Date	Mintage	F	VF	XF	Unc	BU
1790B	Inc. above	325	450	900	1,600	—
1791/0B	15,000	295	375	550	850	—
1791B	Inc. above	295	375	550	850	—
1792B	24,000	295	375	550	850	—
1793B	15,000	295	375	550	850	—
1794B	14,000	295	375	550	850	—
1795B	16,000	295	375	550	850	—
1796B	11,000	295	375	550	850	—
1797B	9,775	295	375	550	850	—
1798B	7,864	295	375	550	850	—
1799B	12,000	295	375	550	850	—
1800B	9,567	295	375	550	850	1,850

KM# 116 10000 REIS

26.8900 g., 0.9170 Gold .7928 oz. AGW **Ruler:** Joao VI **Obv:** Crowned arms divide floral chain at right from value at left **Obv. Legend:** IOANNES • V • D • G • PORT • ET • ALG • REX **Rev:** Maltese cross with "M" at angles **Rev. Legend:** IN HOC SIGNO VINCES

Date	Mintage	VG	F	VF	XF	Unc
1724 Rare	—	—	—	—	—	—
1725	—	1,000	1,600	2,000	3,000	—
1726	—	1,200	1,800	2,300	3,000	—
1727	—	1,700	2,500	3,000	3,500	—

KM# 138 12800 REIS

28.6800 g., 0.9170 Gold .8456 oz. AGW **Ruler:** Joao VI **Obv:** Laureate head right, date and mint mark below **Rev:** First variety of crowned arms

Date	Mintage	VG	F	VF	XF	Unc
1727B Rare	—	—	—	—	—	—
1728B Rare	—	—	—	—	—	—
1729B Rare	—	—	—	—	—	—

KM# 139 12800 REIS

28.6800 g., 0.9170 Gold .8456 oz. AGW **Ruler:** Joao VI **Obv:** Laureate head right **Obv. Legend:** IOANNES • V • D • G • PORT • ET • ALG • REX **Rev:** Arms on crowned ornate shield

Date	Mintage	VG	F	VF	XF	Unc
1727M	—	1,200	2,500	3,000	5,000	—
1728M	—	1,000	2,200	2,800	3,400	—
1729M	—	1,000	2,000	2,500	3,000	—
1730M	—	1,000	2,000	2,500	3,000	—
1731/0M	—	1,000	2,000	2,500	3,000	—
1731M	—	1,000	2,000	2,500	3,000	—
1732M	—	1,000	2,000	2,500	3,000	—
1733M	—	1,000	2,000	2,500	3,000	—

KM# 140 12800 REIS

28.6800 g., 0.9170 Gold .8456 oz. AGW **Ruler:** Joao VI

Date	Mintage	VG	F	VF	XF	Unc
1727R	—	700	1,300	2,900	5,000	—
1728R	—	600	1,100	2,200	3,600	—
1729R	—	600	1,100	2,200	3,600	—
1730R	—	600	1,100	2,200	3,600	—
1731R	—	600	1,100	2,200	3,600	—

KM# 141 12800 REIS

28.6800 g., 0.9170 Gold .8456 oz. AGW **Ruler:** Joao VI **Rev:** Second variety of crowned arms

Date	Mintage	VG	F	VF	XF	Unc
1727B Rare	—	—	—	—	—	—
1729B Rare	—	—	—	—	—	—
1730B Rare	—	—	—	—	—	—

KM# 147 12800 REIS

28.6800 g., 0.9170 Gold .8456 oz. AGW **Ruler:** Joao VI **Rev:** Third variety of crowned arms

Date	Mintage	VG	F	VF	XF	Unc
1730B Rare	—	—	—	—	—	—

KM# A148 12800 REIS

28.6800 g., 0.9170 Gold .8456 oz. AGW **Ruler:** Joao VI **Rev:** Fourth variety of crowned arms

Date	Mintage	VG	F	VF	XF	Unc
1730B Rare	—	—	—	—	—	—
1732B Rare	—	—	—	—	—	—

KM# 148 12800 REIS
28.6800 g., 0.9170 Gold .8456 oz. AGW **Ruler:** Joao VI **Rev:** Different crowned arms **Note:** Coins with cord edge command a premium.

Date	Mintage	VG	F	VF	XF	Unc
1731R	—	500	1,400	2,200	3,500	—
1732R	—	500	1,400	2,200	3,500	—
1733R Unique	—	—	—	—	—	—

KM# 117 20000 REIS
53.7800 g., 0.9170 Gold 1.5857 oz. AGW **Ruler:** Joao VI **Obv:** Crowned shield **Obv. Legend:** IOANNES • V • D • G • PORT • ET • ALG • REX **Rev:** M's at angles **Rev. Legend:** IN HOC SIGNO VINCES

Date	Mintage	VG	F	VF	XF	Unc
1724M	—	1,250	2,500	5,000	7,000	—
1725M	—	900	1,200	2,100	3,450	—
1726M	—	900	1,200	2,100	3,450	—
1727M	—	900	1,200	2,500	4,000	—

GOLD BARS

Cuiaba

KM# GB1 NON-DENOMINATED
Gold **Counterstamp:** CUYABA below crown in branches **Note:** Known dates: 1821, 1822. Actual bar size: 89x18mm.

Date	Mintage	Good	VG	F	VF	XF
(1821-22)	—	—	—	—	—	—

Goias

KM# GB2 NON-DENOMINATED
Gold **Counterstamp:** GOIAS in an incuse rectangle **Note:** Known dates: 1790, 1801, 1813, 1814, 1817, 1819, 1820, 1821, 1822, 1823. Actual bar size: 112x18mm.

Date	Mintage	Good	VG	F	VF	XF
(1790-1823)	—	—	—	—	—	—

Mato Grasso

KM# GB3 NON-DENOMINATED
Gold **Counterstamp:** MATO GROSSO above crown in branches **Note:** Known dates: 1784, 1800, 1811, 1812, 1813, 1815, 1816, 1817, 1818, 1819, 1820. Actual bar size: 83x17mm.

Date	Mintage	Good	VG	F	VF	XF
(1784-1820)	—	—	—	—	—	—

Rio Das Mortes

KM# Gb4 NON-DENOMINATED
Gold, 64x16 mm. **Counterstamp:** RIO DAS M. below crowned arms in branches **Note:** Known dates: 1796, 1800, 1804, 1817, 1818. Illustration reduced.

Date	Mintage	Good	VG	F	VF	XF
(1796-1818)	—	—	—	—	—	—

Sabara

KM# Gb5 NON-DENOMINATED
Gold, 78x20 mm. **Counterstamp:** "SABARA" or "V.DO SABARA" below or "V.DO-SAB" above crowned arms **Note:** Known dates: 1778, 1792, 1794, 1796, 1801, 1804-06, 1808-19, 1828, 1832, 1833.

Date	Mintage	Good	VG	F	VF	XF
(1778-1833)	—	—	—	—	—	—

Note: American Numismatic Rarities Eliasberg sale, 4-05, 1805 Sabara, EF realized $77,625. UBS auction 48, 1-00, 1815 Sabara, XF $34,430

Serro Frio

KM# Gb6 NON-DENOMINATED
Gold, 80x17 mm. **Counterstamp:** "S.-F." above or "SERRO FRIO" below crowned arms and AAB monogram in beaded circle **Note:** Known dates: 1809-14, 1816, 1818, 1820, 1829, 1830-32.

Date	Mintage	Good	VG	F	VF	XF
(1809-1832)	—	—	—	—	—	—

Vila Rica

KM# Gb7 NON-DENOMINATED
Gold, 107x17 mm. **Countermark:** Script VCR monogram **Counterstamp:** Crowned arms or crowned arms with "V.-R." above **Note:** Known dates: 1786, 1796, 1799, 1802, 1804, 1807-18, 1828. Illustration reduced.

Date	Mintage	Good	VG	F	VF	XF
	—	—	—	—	—	—

Note: American Numismatic Rarities Eliasberg sale, 4-05, 1809 Villa Rica, EF realized $48,300; 1812 Villa Rica, EF realized $29,900; 1816 Villa Rica, EF realized $29,900. UBS Auction 48, 1-00, 1811 Vila Rica, XF realized $41,750

GOLD BAR RECEIPT

KM# GBR1 NON-DENOMINATED
Gold **Note:** Typical receipt for a gold bar.

Date	Mintage	Good	VG	F	VF	XF
ND	—	—	—	—	—	—

PATTERNS

Including off metal strikes

KM#	Date	Mintage	Identification	Mkt Val
PnA1	1722	—	4000 Reis. Copper. KM#106.	400
PnB1	1727	—	6400 Reis. Silver. KM#134.	—
PnC1	1728	—	6400 Reis. Copper. KM#134.	2,500
PnD1	1747	—	6400 Reis. Silver. KM#149.	2,250
PnE1	1747	—	6400 Reis. Bronze. KM#149.	1,500
Pn1	1753	—	6400 Reis. Silver. KM#172.2	2,000
Pn2	1771	—	6400 Reis. Copper. KM#172.2	1,400
Pn4	1772	—	6400 Reis. Copper. KM#172.2	1,500
Pn3	1772	—	6400 Reis. Silver. Arms of Maria; KM#172.2.	2,250
Pn6	1780	—	6400 Reis. Copper.	1,400
Pn7	1781	—	6400 Reis. Silver.	2,000
PnA8	1786	—	6400 Reis. Copper. KM#218.1	1,500
PnB8	1796	—	6400 Reis. Copper. KM#226.1	1,500

TRIAL STRIKES

KM#	Date	Mintage	Identification	Mkt Val
TS2	1772	—	6400 Reis. Copper. Uniface.	900
TS1	1772	—	6400 Reis. Silver. Uniface.	1,500

BRITISH VIRGIN ISLANDS

The Colony of the Virgin Islands, a British colony situated in the Caribbean Sea northeast of Puerto Rico and west of the Leeward Islands, has an area of 59 sq. mi. (155 sq. km.) and a population of 13,000. Capital: Road Town. The principal islands of the 36-island group are Tortola, Virgin Gorda, Anegada, and Jost Van Dyke. The chief industries are fishing and stock raising. Fish, livestock and bananas are exported.

The Virgin Islands were discovered by Columbus in 1493, and named by him, Las Virgienes, in honor of St. Ursula and her companions. The British Virgin Islands were formerly part of the administration of the Leeward Islands.

TORTOLA

Tortola, which has an area of about 24 sq. mi. (62 sq. km.), is the largest of 36 islands which comprise the British Virgin Islands. It was settled by the Dutch in 1648 and was occupied by the British in 1666. They have held it ever since.

MONETARY SYSTEM
8 Shillings, 3 Pence = 11 Bits = 8 Reales

LEEWARD ISLANDS ADMINISTRATION

PRIVATE COUNTERMARKED COINAGE

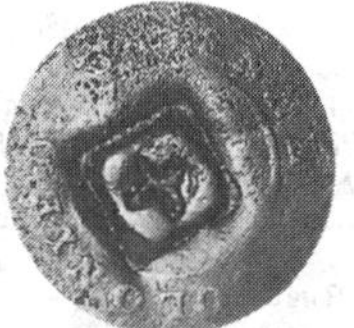

KM# 11 1-1/2 PENCE (Black Dog)
Billon **Countermark:** Small 3 millimeter incuse H **Note:** Countermark in square indent on French and French Guiana, Colony of Cayenne 2 Sous.

Date	Mintage	Good	VG	F	VF	XF
ND	—	—	12.50	25.00	40.00	85.00

KM# 12 1-1/2 PENCE (Black Dog)
Billon **Countermark:** Large 5mm incuse "H" **Note:** Countermark in square indent on French and French Guiana, Colony of Cayenne 2 Sous.

Date	Mintage	Good	VG	F	VF	XF
ND	—	12.00	22.50	37.50	75.00	—

BURMA

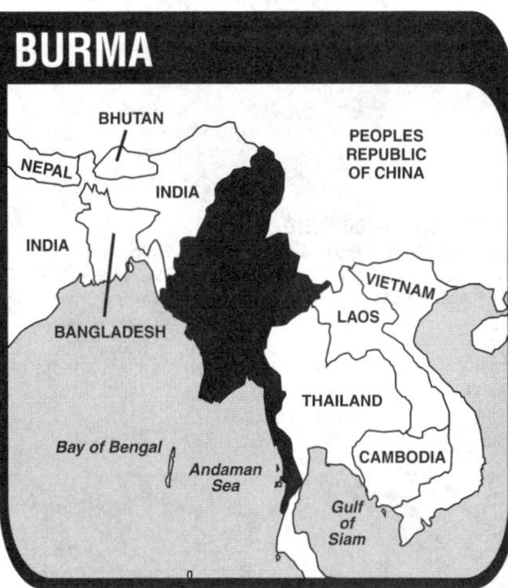

Burma, a country of Southeast Asia fronting on the Bay of Bengal and the Andaman Sea, had an area of 261,218 sq. mi. (678,500 sq. km.).

The first European to reach Burma, in about 1435, was Nicolo Di Conti, a Venetian merchant. During the beginning of the reign of Bodawpaya (1781-1819AD) the kingdom comprised most of the same area as it does today including Arakan which was taken over in 1784-85. The British East India Company, while unsuccessful in its 1612 effort to establish posts along the Bay of Bengal, was enabled by the Anglo-Burmese Wars of 1824-

86 to expand to the whole of Burma and to secure its annexation to British India.

The coins issued by kings Mindon and Thibaw between 1852 and 1885 circulated in Upper Burma. Indian coins were current in Lower Burma, which was annexed in 1852. Burmese coins are frequently known by the equivalent Indian denominations, although their values are inscribed in Burmese units. Upper Burma was annexed in 1885 and the Burmese coinage remained in circulation until 1889, when Indian coins became current throughout Burma. The Chula-Sakarat (CS) dating is sometimes referred to as BE-Burmese Era and began in 638AD.

RULERS

Arakanese
Sanda Thuriya, BE1093-96/1731-34AD
Narapawara, BE1097-98/1735-36AD
Sanda Wizala, BE1098-99/1736-37AD
Madarit Raza, BE1099-1104/1737-42AD
Nara Apaya, BE1104-23/1742-61AD
Sanda Parama, BE1123-26/1761-64AD
Apaya Maha Raza, BE1126-35/1764-73AD
Sanda Thumana, BE1135-39/1773-77AD
Sanda Wimala, BE1139/1777AD
Thaditha Dhammarit, BE1139-44/1777-82AD
Maha Thamada, BE1144-46/1782-84AD
Amarapura Lord, Bodawpaya, BE1146/1784AD

Burmese
Bodawpaya, CS1143-1181/1782-1819AD

MONETARY SYSTEM

Indian Equivalents
1 Silver Kyat = 1 Rupee = 16 Annas
1 Gold Kyat = 1 Mohur = 16 Rupees

STANDARD COINAGE

KM# A1 1/2 PYA (1/2 Pice)
Copper **Obv:** 2 fish **Rev:** Unread inscription

Date	Mintage	Good	VG	F	VF	XF
ND	—	—	—	—	—	—

KM# 1 1/2 PYA (1/2 Pice)
Copper **Obv:** 2 fish **Rev:** Burmese legends

Date	Mintage	Good	VG	F	VF	XF
CS1143 (1781)	—	100	150	250	—	—

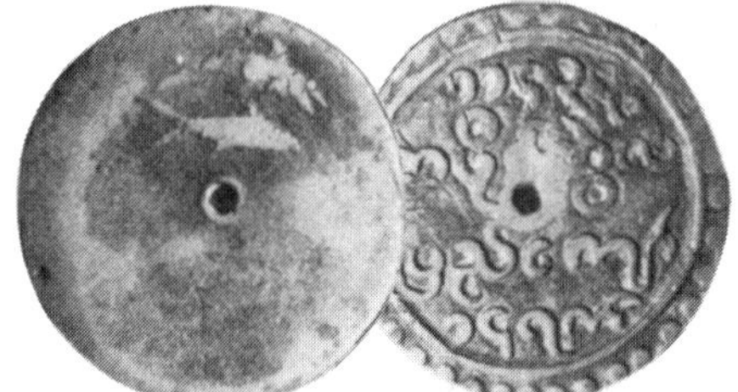

KM# 2.1 1/4 PE (Pice)
Copper, 31-32 mm. **Obv:** Two fish **Rev:** Burmese legend **Note:** Center hole.

Date	Mintage	Good	VG	F	VF	XF
CS1143 (1781)	—	50.00	85.00	145	—	—

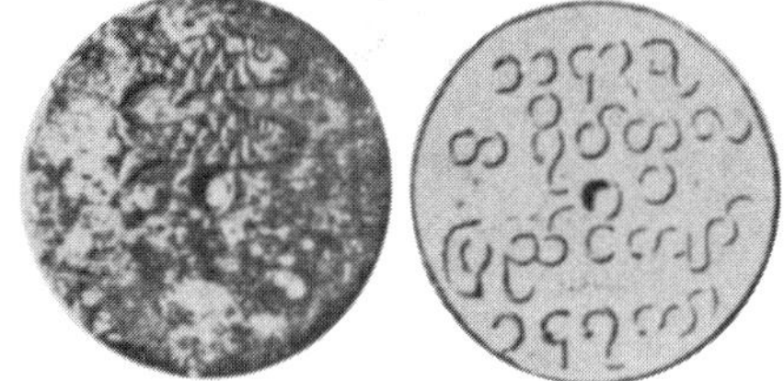

KM# 3.1 1/4 PE (Pice)
Copper, 27-28 mm. **Obv:** Two fish **Rev:** Burmese legend **Note:** Center hole.

Date	Mintage	Good	VG	F	VF	XF
CS1143 (1781)	—	50.00	85.00	145		

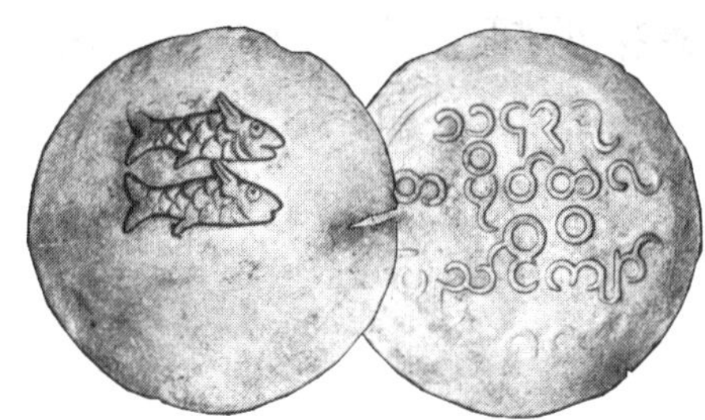

KM# 2.2 1/4 PE (Pice)
Copper **Obv:** Two fish **Rev:** Burmese legend **Note:** Without hole.

Date	Mintage	Good	VG	F	VF	XF
CS1143 (1781)	—	50.00	85.00	145	325	650

KM# 3.2 1/4 PE (Pice)
Copper **Obv:** Two fish **Rev:** Burmese legend **Note:** Without hole.

Date	Mintage	Good	VG	F	VF	XF
CS1143 (1781)	—	25.00	40.00	60.00	90.00	—

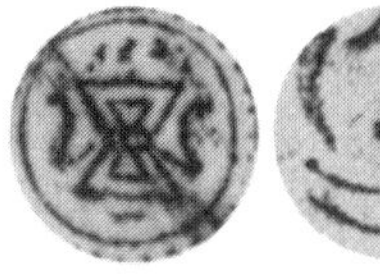

KM# 4 MAT
3.4500 g., Silver

Date	Mintage	Good	VG	F	VF	XF
ND (1781)	—	45.00	75.00	125	225	—

KM# 5 KYAT (Rupee)
9.9800 g., Silver

Date	Mintage	Good	VG	F	VF	XF
ND (1781)	—	65.00	125	175	250	—

CENTRAL ASIA

In the several centuries prior to 1500 which witnessed the breakup of the Mongol Empire and the subsequent rise of smaller successor states, no single power or dynasty was able to control the vast expanses of Western and Central Asia. The region known previously as Transoxiana, the land beyond the Oxus River (modern Amu Darya), became the domain of the Shaybanids, then the Janids. The territory ruled by these dynasties had no set borders, which rather expanded and contracted as the fortunes of the rulers ebbed and flowed. At their greatest extent, the khanate took in parts of what are now northern Iran and Afghanistan, as well as part or all of modern Turkmenistan, Uzbekistan, Kazakhstan, Tadzhikistan and Kyrgyzstan. Coins are known to have been struck by virtually every ruler, but some are quite scarce owing to short reigns or the ever-changing political and economic situation.

MINTS

ابي ورد ابيورد باورد
Abivard

اخشي اخشيكات
Akhshi/Akhshikath

اندجان اندگان
Andigan/Andijan

اسفراين
Asfarayin/Isfarayin

استراباد
Astarabad

اوبه
Awbah

بدخشان
Badakhshan

بلخ
Balkh

بسطام
Bistam

بخارا
Bukhara

دامغان
Damghan

هراة هرات
Herat

حصر
Hisar

كرمين
Karmin

كش
Kish

كوفن كوفين
Kufan/Kufin

لنگر
Langar

Marw

مشهد
Mashhad

نسف
Nasaf

نمرز نيمروز
Nimruz

نسا
Nisa

قرشي
Qarshi (copper only)

قاين
Qayin

قندوز
Qunduz

سبزوار
Sabzavar

سمرقند
Samarqand

تشكند
Tashkand (Tashkent)

ترمز
Termez

تون
Tun

Turbat تربت

Urdu (camp mint) اردو

Yazur يازر

BUKHARA

Bukhara, a city and former emirate in southern Russian Turkestan, formed part (Sogdiana) of the Seleucid empire after the conquest of Alexander the Great and remained an important regional center, sometimes city state, until the 19th century.

The Manghits of Bukhara were successors to the Janids in Bukhara and Samarqand, with a sole mint at Bukhara. Except for some of the issues of Haidar Tora, Manghit coins lack the name of the current ruler, but cite a deceased hero of earlier times. Most issues can by assigned to a ruler only by date. Coins were usually dated on both obverse and reverse, so mismatched dates are very plentiful and common. All coins bear the mint name Bukhara. The gold and silver were generally well-struck until the AH1260s/1840s AD, but were gradually less carefully made, especially the silver coins after the AH1290s/1870s AD. Most copper coins were poorly made and rarely well-preserved.

The gold tilla weighed 4.6 grams and the silver tenga 3.2 grams throughout this coinage. The copper pul used a standard of 4.6 grams un AH1286/1869AD, but individual examples often weigh much less. After copper minting resumed in AH1319/1901AD, the pul weighed 2.6 grams. All the silver and gold coins from the reign of Nasrullah onwards were issued in the name of Amir Ma'sum and are only distinguished from issues prior to AH1242/1826AD by date and style. The later copper coins are always anonymous.

Bukhara became virtually a Russian vassal state in AH1284/1867AD as a consequence of the Czarist invasion of 1866, following which it gradually became a part of Russian Turkestan and then part of Uzbekistan S.S.R., now Uzbekistan, which see.

NOTE: The numerals '0' and '5' have variant forms on the coins of Bukhara, Khiva and Khoqand.

RULERS

Shah Murad, AH1200-15/1785-1800AD
Haidar Tora, AH1215-42/1800-26AD

KHANATE

HAMMERED COINAGE

KM# 22 TENGA

Silver **Ruler:** Shah Murad AH1200-1215/1785-1800AD

Date	Mintage	VG	F	VF	XF	Unc
AH1204	—	—	—	—	—	—
AH1207/1206	—	—	—	—	—	—
AH1214	—	—	—	—	—	—

KM# 10 TILLA

Gold, 22-24 mm. **Ruler:** Abu'l Ghazi AH1171-1200/1758-1758 AD **Note:** Struck posthumously in the name of the Janid ruler. Size varies.

Date	Mintage	VG	F	VF	XF	Unc
AH1201	—	100	125	185	250	—
AH1202	—	100	125	185	250	—
ND	—	100	125	185	250	—

KM# 26 TILLA

Gold **Ruler:** Shah Murad AH1200-1215/1785-1800AD **Obv. Inscription:** "Amir Dauiyal"

Date	Mintage	VG	F	VF	XF	Unc
AH1214	—	—	—	—	—	—

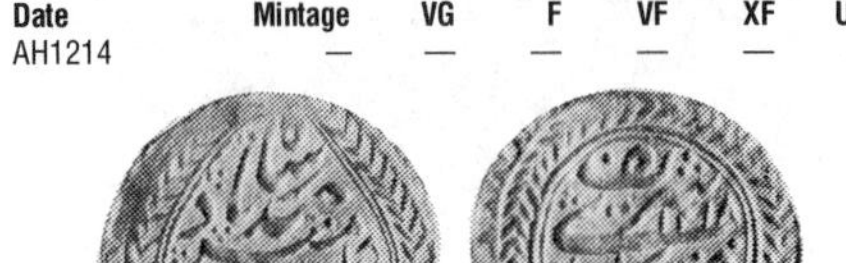

KM# 27 TILLA

Gold **Ruler:** Haidar Tora AH1215-1242/1800-1826 AD **Obv:** Teardrop **Rev:** Circle

Date	Mintage	Good	VG	F	VF	XF
AH1215	—	—	85.00	110	160	220
AH1217//1216	—	—	95.00	120	175	250
AH1218	—	—	85.00	110	160	220
AH1219//1218	—	95.00	120	175	250	—
AH1219	—	—	85.00	110	160	220
AH1220//1216	—	—	95.00	120	175	250

JANID KHANATE

The Janids were the successors to the Shaybanid dynasty and they maintained coinage traditions similar to those of their predecessors. Janid silver coins are almost invariably poorly struck, rarely showing either mint or date. After about AH1090/1679AD, the alloy became increasingly debased and was mostly copper after the early AH1100s/1670s AD. By contrast, the gold coins of the Janids are found to be of high quality and alloy. The original silver tanka conformed to the 4.7 gram weight inherited from the Shaybanids, but sank to below 4 grams by the end of the dynasty. Mint names, when they are visible on the silver coins, have only been recorded for Balkh, Bukhara and Samarqand.

The dates of rule given for the Janid khans are rather tentative. The standard lists in the genealogical references to not agree with the dates found on the coins in all cases.

During the rule of the last Janid, Abu'l-Ghazi Khan in the late 13th/18th century, the territory was split into three smaller principalities: Bukhara, Khiva and Khoqand, which see.

RULERS

Subhan Quli Khan, AH1091-1114/1680-1702AD
'Ubayd Allah Khan I, AH1114-17/1702-05AD
Abu'l-Fayz Khan, AH1117-60/1705-47AD
'Abd al-Mu'min Khan, AH1160-64/1747-51AD
Muhammad Rahim, AH1167-71/1753-58AD
'Abu'l-Ghazi Khan, AH1171-1200/1758-85AD

KHANATE

HAMMERED COINAGE

KM# 26 TANKA

4.2500 g., Billon **Ruler:** 'Ubayd Allah Khan I AH1114-1117

Date	Mintage	Good	VG	F	VF	XF
ND No Mint	—	50.00	85.00	150	250	—

KM# 31 TANKA

4.2500 g., Billon **Ruler:** Abu'l-Fayz Khan AH1117-1160

Date	Mintage	Good	VG	F	VF	XF
ND Rare	—	—	—	—	—	—

KM# 39 TANKA

2.7500 g., Silver **Ruler:** Abu'l-Ghazi Khan AH1171-1200 **Obv:** Ruler's name and titles **Rev:** Mint and date **Note:** Previous Bukhara KM# 21.

Date	Mintage	VG	F	VF	XF	Unc
AH1194 No Mint	—	70.00	115	165	225	—
AH1200 Bukhara	—	60.00	100	150	200	—

KM# 28 TILLA

4.6000 g., Gold **Ruler:** 'Ubayd Allah Khan I AH1114-1117

Date	Mintage	VG	F	VF	XF	Unc
AH1114 Bukhara	—	225	325	500	750	—

KM# 33 TILLA

4.6000 g., Gold **Ruler:** Abu'l-Fayz Khan AH1117-1160 **Obv:** Ruler's names and titles in double circle **Rev:** Kalima in double circle with circle of pellets between **Note:** Normally undated, examples with dates are very rare.

Date	Mintage	VG	F	VF	XF	Unc
AH1125	—	150	225	375	500	—
AH1131 No Mint	—	150	225	375	500	—
ND No Mint	—	100	175	250	350	—

KM# 35 TILLA

4.6000 g., Gold **Ruler:** 'Abd al-Mu'min Khan AH1160-1164 **Obv:** Ruler's names and titles in scalloped boarder **Rev:** Kalima in large cartouche **Note:** Always undated.

Date	Mintage	VG	F	VF	XF	Unc
ND No Mint	—	175	300	450	650	—

KM# 37 TILLA

4.6000 g., Gold **Ruler:** Muhammad Rahim AH1167-1171

Date	Mintage	VG	F	VF	XF	Unc
ND No Mint	—	175	300	450	650	—

KM# 42 TILLA

4.6000 g., Gold, 22 mm. **Ruler:** Abu'l-Ghazi Khan AH1171-1200 **Obv:** Ruler's name, titles and date in ornamented circle **Rev:** Kalima in circle of pellets within two plain circles **Note:** Previous Bukhara KM# 10.

Date	Mintage	VG	F	VF	XF	Unc
AH1181 No Mint	—	200	325	425	600	—
AH1200 Bukhara	—	100	125	185	250	—

CEYLON

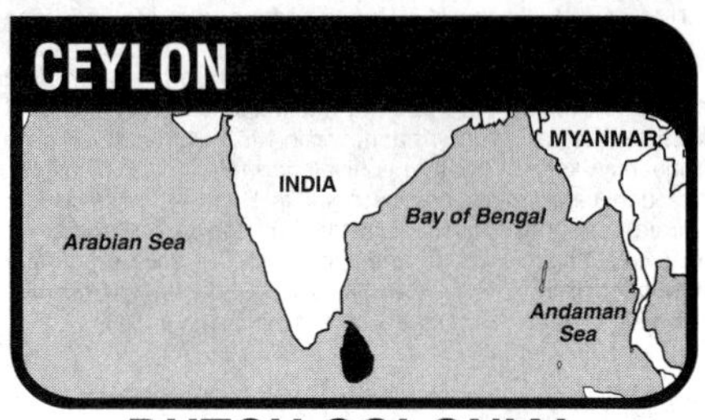

DUTCH COLONIAL

The Dutch first sighted Ceylon in 1602. They made a treaty with the king of Kandy for trading rights and the Dutch would have to expel the Portuguese. Between 1638 and 1658 the Dutch had accomplished their purpose. The Portuguese were gone from Ceylon.

As the Dutch trade with Ceylon prospered the coins in use were local coins and countermarked coins of the Portuguese colonies. It was not until sometime after 1660 that the Dutch began striking anonymous copper coins.

In the second third of the 1700's, copper duits of the Netherlands provinces were sent to the Dutch and used widely there. The VOC monogram on these coins became a familiar sight to the merchants of the sub-continent and the East Indies.

Local coinage started again in 1783.

Netherlands United East India Company

MONETARY SYSTEM

4 Duiten = 1 Stuiver
4 Stuivers = 1 Fanam
4-1/2 Stuivers = 1 Shahi
9-1/2 Stuivers = 1 Larin

OCCUPATION COINAGE

KM# 23 1/8 DUIT

Tin **Obverse:** 17/47 around central depression **Reverse:** Value

Date	Mintage	VG	F	VF	XF	Unc
1747 Rare	—	—	—	—	—	—

KM# 24.1 DUIT

Tin **Obverse:** "C" above "VOC" monogram and date **Reverse:** Bird on tree divides value, 1 D **Note:** Weight varies: 15-16g.

Date	Mintage	Good	VG	F	VF	XF
1782	—	60.00	125	175	275	—

KM# 24.2 DUIT

Tin **Note:** Reduced weight 9.00-11.00 grams.

Date	Mintage	Good	VG	F	VF	XF
1785	—	50.00	90.00	150	225	—
1786	—	50.00	90.00	150	225	—

KM# 33.1 DUIT

Lead **Obverse:** "C" above "VOC" monogram **Reverse:** Value 1 DT and date

Date	Mintage	Good	VG	F	VF	XF
1789	—	20.00	40.00	65.00	100	—
1790	—	35.00	60.00	100	150	—
1791 Rare	—	—	—	—	—	—

KM# 33.2 DUIT

Lead **Reverse:** Value **Rev. Legend:** 1 DUIT

Date	Mintage	Good	VG	F	VF	XF
1792	—	35.00	60.00	100	150	—
1793	—	45.00	80.00	150	250	—

KM# 16 1/8 STUIVER

Copper **Mint:** Jafna **Obverse:** Value in wreath **Reverse:** Value in wreath

Date	Mintage	Good	VG	F	VF	XF
ND(1660-1720)	—	25.00	35.00	60.00	100	—

KM# 17 1/4 STUIVER

Copper **Mint:** Jafna **Obverse:** Value in wreath **Reverse:** Value in wreath

Date	Mintage	Good	VG	F	VF	XF
ND(1660-1720)	—	20.00	25.00	45.00	70.00	—

KM# 25 1/4 STUIVER

Copper **Mint:** Jafna **Obverse:** "C" above "VOC" monogram **Reverse:** Value

Date	Mintage	Good	VG	F	VF	XF
ND(1783)	—	30.00	45.00	70.00	100	—

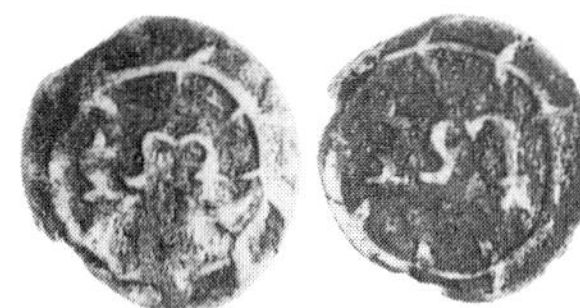

KM# 18.2 1/2 STUIVER

Copper **Mint:** Jafna **Obverse:** Small value in wreath **Reverse:** Small value in wreath

Date	Mintage	Good	VG	F	VF	XF
ND(1660-1720)	—	12.00	22.00	38.00	55.00	—

KM# 18.1 1/2 STUIVER

Copper **Mint:** Jafna **Obverse:** Value in wreath **Reverse:** Value in wreath

Date	Mintage	Good	VG	F	VF	XF
ND(1660-1720)	—	12.00	22.00	38.00	55.00	—

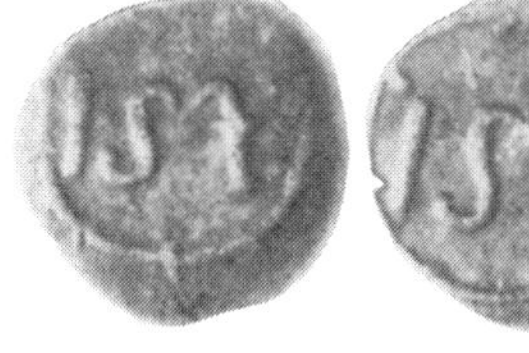

KM# 19.3 STUIVER

Copper **Mint:** Jafna **Obverse:** Value "1 St" in wreath of small leaves (thorns) **Reverse:** Value "1 St" in wreath of small leaves (thorns)

Date	Mintage	Good	VG	F	VF	XF
ND(1660-1720)	—	20.00	35.00	60.00	80.00	—

KM# 19.1 STUIVER

Copper **Mint:** Colombo **Obverse:** Value "1 St" in wreath of leaves **Reverse:** Value "1 St" in wreath of leaves

Date	Mintage	Good	VG	F	VF	XF
ND(ca. 1712)	—	20.00	30.00	55.00	75.00	—

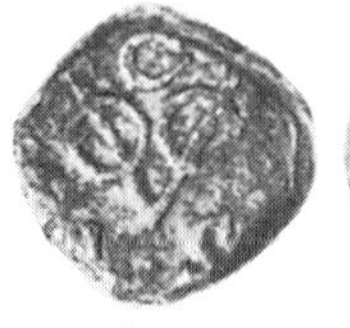

KM# 28 STUIVER

Copper **Mint:** Galle **Obverse:** "G" above "VOC" monogram **Reverse:** Value in Sinhalese **Note:** Struck at Galle Mint.

Date	Mintage	Good	VG	F	VF	XF
1783	—	25.00	40.00	70.00	125	—
1787	—	25.00	40.00	70.00	125	—
1788	—	25.00	40.00	70.00	125	—
1789	—	25.00	40.00	70.00	125	—
1790	—	25.00	40.00	70.00	125	—
1792	—	25.00	40.00	70.00	125	—
1793	—	25.00	40.00	70.00	125	—

KM# 26 STUIVER

Copper **Mint:** Colombo **Obverse:** "C" above "VOC" monogram

Date	Mintage	Good	VG	F	VF	XF
1783	—	10.00	15.00	25.00	50.00	—
1784	—	12.00	18.00	30.00	60.00	—
1785	—	10.00	15.00	25.00	50.00	—
1786	—	10.00	15.00	25.00	50.00	—
1787	—	10.00	15.00	25.00	50.00	—
1788	—	12.00	18.00	30.00	60.00	—
1789	—	10.00	15.00	25.00	50.00	—
1790	—	10.00	15.00	25.00	50.00	—
1791	—	10.00	15.00	25.00	50.00	—
1792	—	9.00	15.00	25.00	50.00	—
1793	—	12.00	18.00	30.00	60.00	—
1794	—	10.00	15.00	25.00	50.00	—

Date	Mintage	Good	VG	F	VF	XF
1795	—	12.00	18.00	30.00	60.00	—

KM# 27 STUIVER

Copper **Mint:** Jafna **Obverse:** "I" (J) above "VOC" monogram and value **Reverse:** Date, value in Tamil

Date	Mintage	Good	VG	F	VF	XF
1783	—	15.00	30.00	50.00	85.00	—
1786 Rare	—	—	—	—	—	—
1788	—	15.00	30.00	50.00	85.00	—
1790	—	15.00	30.00	50.00	85.00	—
1791	—	15.00	30.00	50.00	85.00	—
1792	—	15.00	30.00	50.00	85.00	—
1793	—	—	—	—	—	—

Note: Reported, not confirmed

KM# 34 STUIVER

Copper **Mint:** Trincomalee **Obverse:** "T" above "VOC" monogram **Reverse:** Value and date

Date	Mintage	Good	VG	F	VF	XF
1789	—	15.00	25.00	40.00	75.00	—
1790	—	15.00	25.00	40.00	75.00	—
1791	—	15.00	25.00	40.00	75.00	—
1792	—	15.00	25.00	40.00	75.00	—
1793	—	15.00	25.00	40.00	75.00	—

KM# 20 2 STUIVER

Copper **Mint:** Colombo **Obverse:** Value "11 St" in wreath **Reverse:** Value "11 St" in wreath

Date	Mintage	Good	VG	F	VF	XF
ND(1660-1720)	—	12.50	17.50	25.00	35.00	—

KM# 29a 2 STUIVER

Tin **Mint:** Jafna

Date	Mintage	Good	VG	F	VF	XF
1783 Rare	—	—	—	—	—	—

KM# 29 2 STUIVER

Copper **Mint:** Jafna **Obverse:** "I" (J) above "VOC" monogram and value **Reverse:** Date, value in Tamil **Note:** Varieties exist

Date	Mintage	Good	VG	F	VF	XF
1783	—	30.00	60.00	100	150	—
1784	—	40.00	80.00	140	200	—
1786/3 Rare	—	—	—	—	—	—
1787 Rare	—	—	—	—	—	—
1788	—	30.00	60.00	100	150	—
1789 Rare	—	—	—	—	—	—
1792	—	30.00	60.00	100	150	—
1793	—	40.00	80.00	140	200	—

KM# 30 2 STUIVER

Copper **Mint:** Galle **Obverse:** "G" above "VOC" monogram **Note:** Varieties exist.

Date	Mintage	Good	VG	F	VF	XF
1783	—	20.00	35.00	65.00	125	—
1787	—	20.00	35.00	65.00	125	—
1788	—	20.00	35.00	65.00	125	—
1789	—	20.00	35.00	65.00	125	—
1790	—	25.00	40.00	70.00	130	—
1791	—	25.00	40.00	70.00	130	—
1792	—	25.00	40.00	70.00	130	—

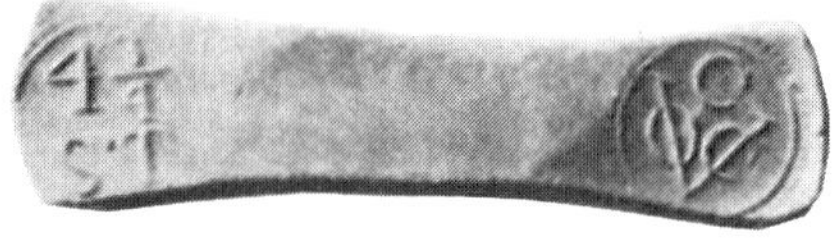

KM# 32 4-3/4 STUIVERS

Copper **Countermark:** "4-3/4 ST" and "C" above "VOC" monogram in stamps at end **Note:** Bonk (bar), length varies; 18 x 85mm to 58 to 105mm. Illustration reduced.

Date	Mintage	Good	VG	F	VF	XF
ND(1785)	—	150	200	300	450	—

KM# 21 6 STUIVERS

Copper **Mint:** Colombo **Countermark:** "VI" in wreath at one end, "St" in wreath at other end, repeated on both sides **Note:** Bonk (bar)varies in size: 98-127mm in length

Date	Mintage	Good	VG	F	VF	XF
ND(c1712)	—	—	—	—	—	—

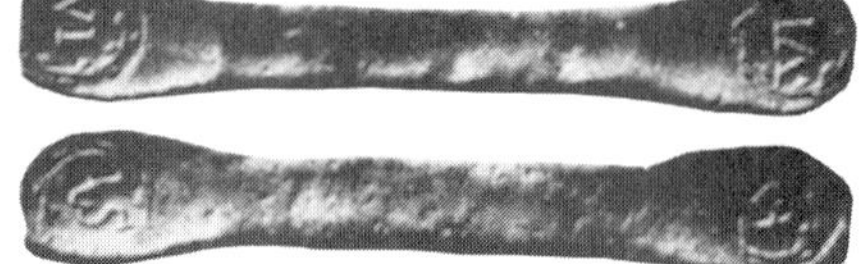

KM# 22 6 STUIVERS

Copper **Countermark:** "VI" in wreath at both ends on one side, "ST" in wreath at both ends on other side **Note:** Illustration reduced.

Date	Mintage	Good	VG	F	VF	XF
ND(1712)	—	—	—	—	—	—

KM# 31.1 RUPEE

Silver **Mint:** Colombo **Obverse:** Corrupted Arabic-Malay legend **Reverse:** Same with date

Date	Mintage	Good	VG	F	VF	XF
1784	122,000	175	250	400	600	—
1786	1,636	175	250	400	600	—
1787	20,000	175	250	400	600	—

KM# 31.2 RUPEE

Silver **Mint:** Tuticorin

Date	Mintage	Good	VG	F	VF	XF
1788	66,000	175	250	400	600	—
1789	37,000	175	250	400	600	—

PATTERNS

Including off metal strikes

KM#	Date	Mintage	Identification	Mkt Val
Pn1	1794	—	1/48 Rupee. Bronze. .	1,000
Pn2	1797	—	1/48 Rupee. Bronze. .	1,000

The Republic of Chile, a ribbon-like country on the Pacific coast of southern South America, has an area of 292,135 sq. mi. (756,950 sq. km.) and a population of *15.21 million. Capital: Santiago. Historically, the economic base of Chile has been the rich mineral deposits of its northern provinces. Copper has accounted for more than 75 percent of Chile's export earnings in recent years. Other important mineral exports are iron ore, iodine and nitrate of soda. Fresh fruits and vegetables, as well as wine are increasingly significant in inter-hemispheric trade.

Diego de Almargo was the first Spaniard to attempt to wrest Chile from the Incas and Araucanian tribes in 1536. He failed, and was followed by Pedro de Valdivia, a favorite of Pizarro, who founded Santiago in 1541. When the Napoleonic Wars involved Spain, leaving the constituent parts of the Spanish Empire to their own devices, Chilean patriots formed a national government and proclaimed the country's independence, Sept. 18, 1810. Independence however, was not secured until Feb. 12, 1818, after a bitter struggle led by Bernardo O'Higgins and San Martin. Despite a long steady history of monetary devaluation, reflected in declining weight and fineness in its currency, Chile developed a strong democracy. This was displaced when rampant inflation characterized chaotic and subsequently repressive governments in the mid to late 20th century.

RULER

Spanish until 1818

MINT MARK

So - Santiago

MINTMASTERS' INITIALS

A	1768-1801	Agustin de Infante y Prado
D	1773-99	Domingo Eizaguirre
DA	1772-99	Domingo Eizaguirre and Agustin de Infante y Prado
J	1749-67	Jose Larrañeta

MONETARY SYSTEM

16 Reales = 1 Escudo

COLONIAL

MILLED COINAGE

KM# 43 1/4 REAL

0.8458 g., 0.8960 Silver .244 oz. ASW **Ruler:** Carlos IV **Obv:** Head right **Obv. Legend:** CAROL IV **Rev:** Cross with castles and lions at quarters **Note:** Mint mark So.

Date	Mintage	VG	F	VF	XF	Unc
1790	322,000	25.00	40.00	85.00	165	—
1791/0	253,000	25.00	40.00	85.00	165	—
1791	Inc. above	20.00	35.00	75.00	150	—

KM# 46 1/4 REAL

0.8458 g., 0.8960 Silver .0244 oz. ASW **Ruler:** Carlos IV **Obv:** Head right **Obv. Legend:** CAROL IIII... **Rev:** Cross with lions and castles at quarters **Note:** Mint mark So.

Date	Mintage	VG	F	VF	XF	Unc
1791	Inc. above	22.00	38.00	80.00	160	—
1792	229,000	20.00	35.00	75.00	150	—

KM# 55 1/4 REAL

0.8458 g., 0.8960 Silver .0244 oz. ASW **Ruler:** Carlos IV **Obv:** Head right **Obv. Legend:** CAROL IIII... **Note:** Mint mark So.

Date	Mintage	VG	F	VF	XF	Unc
1792	Inc. above	45.00	75.00	120	225	—

KM# 56 1/4 REAL

0.8458 g., 0.8960 Silver .0244 oz. ASW **Ruler:** Carlos IV **Obv:** Rampant lion left **Rev:** Castle above date **Note:** Without mint mark.

Date	Mintage	VG	F	VF	XF	Unc
1793	240,000	20.00	35.00	75.00	155	—

KM# 63 1/4 REAL

0.8458 g., 0.8960 Silver .0244 oz. ASW, 12 mm. **Ruler:** Carlos IV **Obv:** Rampant lion left **Rev:** Castle between denomination at right and mint mark at left, date below **Note:** Mint mark So.

Date	Mintage	VG	F	VF	XF	Unc
1796So	63,000	10.00	25.00	60.00	100	—
1797So	66,000	10.00	25.00	60.00	100	—
1798So	50,000	10.00	25.00	65.00	110	—
1799So	42,000	10.00	25.00	65.00	110	—
1800So	72,000	10.00	25.00	60.00	100	—

KM# 6 1/2 REAL

1.6917 g., 0.9170 Silver .0498 oz. ASW **Ruler:** Fernando VI **Obv:** Arms **Obv. Legend:** FRD VI D.G. HISP ETIND.R **Rev:** Pillars, date below **Note:** Mint mark So.

Date	Mintage	VG	F	VF	XF	Unc
1756 J Rare	—	—	—	—	—	—

KM# 15 1/2 REAL

1.6917 g., 0.9170 Silver .0498 oz. ASW **Ruler:** Carlos III **Obv:** Arms **Obv. Legend:** CLR III D.G.... **Rev:** Pillars, date below **Note:** Mint mark So.

Date	Mintage	VG	F	VF	XF	Unc
1760 J Rare	—	—	—	—	—	—

KM# 28 1/2 REAL

1.6917 g., 0.9030 Silver .0491 oz. ASW **Ruler:** Carlos III **Obv:** Bust **Obv. Legend:** CAROLUS III... **Rev:** Arms, pillars **Note:** Mint mark So.

Date	Mintage	VG	F	VF	XF	Unc
1773 DA	9,000	30.00	60.00	175	350	—
1775 DA	65,000	20.00	35.00	75.00	250	—
1776/5 DA	20,000	20.00	40.00	80.00	265	—
1776 DA	Inc. above	20.00	40.00	80.00	265	—
1777 DA	20,000	20.00	40.00	80.00	265	—
1778/6 DA	—	20.00	35.00	75.00	250	—
1778/7 DA	150,000	20.00	35.00	75.00	250	—
1778 DA	Inc. above	20.00	35.00	75.00	250	—
1779/8 DA	—	20.00	35.00	75.00	250	—
1779 DA	49,000	20.00	35.00	75.00	250	—
1780/79 DA	—	20.00	35.00	75.00	250	—
1780/79/8 DA	—	20.00	35.00	75.00	250	—
1780 DA	61,000	20.00	35.00	75.00	250	—
1781 DA	71,000	20.00	35.00	75.00	250	—
1782 DA	54,000	20.00	35.00	75.00	250	—
1783 DA	54,000	20.00	35.00	75.00	250	—
1784/2 DA	—	20.00	35.00	75.00	250	—
1784 DA	109,000	20.00	35.00	75.00	250	—
1785/4 DA	—	20.00	35.00	75.00	250	—
1785/80 DA	—	20.00	35.00	75.00	250	—
1785 DA	80,000	15.00	30.00	65.00	200	—
1786 DA	125,000	15.00	30.00	65.00	200	—
1787/6 DA	79,000	25.00	50.00	100	285	—
1787 DA	Inc. above	20.00	35.00	75.00	250	—
1788/7 DA	—	15.00	30.00	60.00	125	—
1788 DA	175,000	15.00	30.00	60.00	125	—
1789 DA	186,000	15.00	30.00	60.00	125	—

KM# 35 1/2 REAL

1.6917 g., 0.8960 Silver .0487 oz. ASW **Ruler:** Carlos IV **Obv:** Head right **Obv. Legend:** CAROLUS IV **Note:** Mint mark So.

Date	Mintage	VG	F	VF	XF	Unc
1789 DA	Inc. above	10.00	20.00	50.00	110	—
1790 DA	110,000	10.00	20.00	50.00	110	—
1791/0 DA	—	12.00	35.00	70.00	140	—
1791 DA	139,000	10.00	20.00	50.00	110	—

KM# 47 1/2 REAL

1.6917 g., 0.8960 Silver .0487 oz. ASW **Ruler:** Carlos IV **Obv:** Head right **Obv. Legend:** CAROLUS IIII... **Note:** Mint mark So.

Date	Mintage	VG	F	VF	XF	Unc
1791 DA	Inc. above	15.00	30.00	60.00	125	—

KM# 57 1/2 REAL

1.6917 g., 0.8960 Silver .0487 oz. ASW, 17 mm. **Ruler:** Carlos IV **Obv:** Laureate bust right **Obv. Legend:** CAROLUS IIII **Rev:** Crowned arms between columns **Note:** Mint mark So.

Date	Mintage	VG	F	VF	XF	Unc
1792 DA	74,000	8.00	18.00	45.00	100	—
1793 DA	163,000	8.00	18.00	45.00	100	—
1794/3 DA	207,000	8.00	20.00	60.00	120	—
1794 DA	Inc. above	8.00	18.00	45.00	100	—
1795/4 DA	—	15.00	30.00	70.00	140	—
1795 DA	94,000	15.00	30.00	70.00	140	—
1795 DA	—	15.00	30.00	70.00	140	—
Note: Inverted mint mark						
1796/5 DA	126,000	8.00	20.00	60.00	120	—
1796 DA	Inc. above	8.00	20.00	55.00	110	—
1797 DA	125,000	25.00	50.00	100	200	—
1797 DA Error: CAOLUS	—	20.00	40.00	85.00	190	—
1798 DA	109,000	8.00	20.00	45.00	100	—
1799 CA	61,000	8.00	20.00	45.00	100	—
1800 AJ	75,000	8.00	20.00	45.00	100	—

KM# 7 REAL

3.3834 g., 0.9170 Silver .0997 oz. ASW **Obv:** ARMS **Obv. Legend:** FERD VI DG HISPET IND **Rev:** Pillars, date below **Note:** Mint mark So.

Date	Mintage	VG	F	VF	XF	Unc
1758 Rare	—	—	—	—	—	—

KM# 29 REAL

3.3834 g., 0.9030 Silver .0997 oz. ASW **Ruler:** Carlos III **Obv:** Bust **Obv. Legend:** CAROLUS III... **Rev:** Arms, pillars **Note:** Mint mark So.

Date	Mintage	VG	F	VF	XF	Unc
1773 DA	14,000	30.00	70.00	150	375	—
1775 DA	27,000	35.00	75.00	160	400	—
1776/5 DA	—	45.00	85.00	170	425	—
1776 DA	10,000	45.00	85.00	170	425	—
1777 DA	20,000	30.00	70.00	150	375	—
1778/7 DA	95,000	22.00	55.00	120	250	—
1778 DA	Inc. above	22.00	55.00	120	250	—
1779 DA	42,000	28.00	65.00	135	300	—
1780 DA	31,000	28.00	65.00	135	300	—
1781 DA	68,000	25.00	60.00	130	285	—
1782 DA	32,000	28.00	65.00	135	300	—
1783 DA	27,000	28.00	65.00	135	300	—
1784 DA	54,000	25.00	60.00	130	285	—
1785/4 DA	—	25.00	60.00	125	225	—
1785 DA	48,000	25.00	60.00	125	225	—
1786/5 DA	102,000	25.00	60.00	125	225	—
1786 DA	Inc. above	25.00	60.00	125	225	—
1787 DA	60,000	25.00	60.00	125	225	—
1788/7 DA	112,000	25.00	60.00	125	225	—
1788 DA	Inc. above	20.00	50.00	110	200	—
1789 DA	109,000	25.00	60.00	125	225	—

KM# 36 REAL

3.3834 g., 0.8960 Silver .0975 oz. ASW **Ruler:** Carlos IV **Obv:** Bust **Obv. Legend:** CAROLUS IV... **Note:** Mint mark So.

Date	Mintage	VG	F	VF	XF	Unc
1789 DA	Inc. above	25.00	60.00	125	275	—
1790 DA	39,000	22.00	55.00	120	270	—
1791 DA	20,000	22.00	55.00	120	270	—

KM# 48 REAL

3.3834 g., 0.8960 Silver .0975 oz. ASW **Ruler:** Carlos IV **Obv:** Bust **Obv. Legend:** CAROLUS IIII... **Note:** Mint mark So.

Date	Mintage	VG	F	VF	XF	Unc
1791 DA	Inc. above	22.00	55.00	120	270	—

KM# 58 REAL

3.3834 g., 0.8960 Silver .0975 oz. ASW, 21 mm. **Ruler:** Carlos IV **Obv:** Laureate bust right **Obv. Legend:** CAROLUS IIII... **Rev:** Crowned arms between columns **Note:** Mint mark So.

Date	Mintage	VG	F	VF	XF	Unc
1792 DA	24,000	10.00	35.00	65.00	125	—
1793/2 DA	—	12.00	40.00	75.00	150	—
1793 DA	77,000	10.00	35.00	65.00	125	—
1794 DA	54,000	10.00	35.00	65.00	125	—
1795 DA	89,000	25.00	50.00	100	150	—
1796/4 DA	—	—	—	—	—	—
1796/5 DA	64,000	—	—	—	—	—
1796 DA	Inc. above	10.00	35.00	65.00	125	—
1797 DA	85,000	10.00	35.00	65.00	125	—
1798/6 DA	—	12.00	40.00	75.00	150	—
1798 DA	34,000	10.00	35.00	65.00	125	—
1799 DA	48,000	10.00	35.00	65.00	125	—
1800 AJ	48,000	10.00	35.00	65.00	125	—

KM# 8 2 REALES

6.7668 g., 0.9170 Silver .1995 oz. ASW **Ruler:** Fernando VI **Obv:** Arms **Obv. Legend:** FRD VI D. G. HISP ET IND REX **Rev:** Pillars, date below **Note:** Mint mark So.

Date	Mintage	VG	F	VF	XF	Unc
1758 J Rare	—	—	—	—	—	—

KM# 16 2 REALES

6.7682 g., 0.9170 Silver .1995 oz. ASW **Ruler:** Carlos III **Obv:** Arms **Rev:** Pillars, date below **Note:** Mint mark So.

Date	Mintage	VG	F	VF	XF	Unc
1760 J Rare	—	—	—	—	—	—

KM# 30 2 REALES

6.7668 g., 0.9030 Silver .1964 oz. ASW **Ruler:** Carlos III **Obv:** Bust **Obv. Legend:** CAROLUS III... **Rev:** Arms, pillars **Note:** Mint mark So.

Date	Mintage	VG	F	VF	XF	Unc
1773 DA	14,000	75.00	150	300	500	—
1775 DA	34,000	50.00	100	200	400	—
1776 DA	7,000	60.00	110	225	450	—
1777 DA	7,000	60.00	110	225	450	—
1778/6 DA	68,000	50.00	100	200	400	—
1778 DA	Inc. above	45.00	90.00	185	375	—

Date	Mintage	VG	F	VF	XF	Unc
1779 DA	48,000	40.00	85.00	175	350	—
1780 DA	34,000	40.00	85.00	175	350	—
1781 DA	44,000	40.00	85.00	175	350	—
1782 DA	21,000	50.00	100	200	400	—
1783/2 DA	34,000	45.00	90.00	185	375	—
1783 DA	Inc. above	45.00	90.00	185	375	—
1784/1 DA	—	50.00	100	200	400	—
1784 DA	54,000	40.00	85.00	175	350	—
1785/4 DA	—	30.00	75.00	150	300	—
1785 DA	27,000	30.00	75.00	150	300	—
1786 DA	51,000	30.00	75.00	150	300	—
1787 DA	31,000	30.00	75.00	150	300	—
1788 DA	66,000	30.00	75.00	150	300	—
1789 DA	67,000	30.00	75.00	150	300	—

KM# 37 2 REALES

6.7668 g., 0.8960 Silver .1949 oz. ASW **Ruler:** Carlos IV **Obv:** Bust **Obv. Legend:** CAROLUS IV **Note:** Mint mark So.

Date	Mintage	VG	F	VF	XF	Unc
1789 DA	Inc. above	35.00	80.00	175	350	—
1790 DA	47,000	35.00	80.00	175	350	—
1791 DA	54,000	35.00	80.00	175	350	—

KM# 49 2 REALES

6.7668 g., 0.8960 Silver .1949 oz. ASW **Ruler:** Carlos IV **Obv:** Bust **Obv. Legend:** CAROLUS IIII **Note:** Mint mark So.

Date	Mintage	VG	F	VF	XF	Unc
1791 DA	Inc. above	40.00	85.00	185	365	—
1792 DA	14,000	40.00	85.00	185	365	—

KM# 59 2 REALES

6.7668 g., 0.8960 Silver .1949 oz. ASW, 28.5 mm. **Ruler:** Carlos IV **Obv:** Laureate bust right **Obv. Legend:** CAROLUS • IIII • DEI • GRATIA • **Rev:** Crowned arms between pillars **Rev. Legend:** HISPAN * ET • IND • REX • .... **Note:** Mint mark So.

Date	Mintage	VG	F	VF	XF	Unc
1792 DA	Inc. above	18.00	55.00	110	220	—
1793 DA	53,000	16.00	50.00	100	200	—
1794 DA	58,000	16.00	50.00	100	200	—
1795 DA	58,000	16.00	50.00	100	200	—
1796/5 DA	—	18.00	55.00	110	220	—
1796 DA	66,000	16.00	50.00	100	200	—
1797 DA	49,000	16.00	50.00	100	200	—
1798/7 DA	30,000	18.00	55.00	110	220	—
1798 DA	Inc. above	16.00	50.00	100	200	—
1799 DA	41,000	16.00	50.00	100	200	—
1799 DA	Inc. above	16.00	50.00	100	200	—

Note: Inverted mint mark

Date	Mintage	VG	F	VF	XF	Unc
1800 AJ	34,000	16.00	50.00	100	200	—

KM# 9 4 REALES

13.5337 g., 0.9170 Silver .3990 oz. ASW **Ruler:** Fernando VI **Obv:** Arms **Obv. Legend:** FERDINANDUS VI D. G. HISPAN ET IND REX **Rev:** Pillars, date below

Date	Mintage	VG	F	VF	XF	Unc
1758 J Rare	—	—	—	—	—	—

KM# 17 4 REALES

13.5337 g., 0.9170 Silver .3990 oz. ASW **Ruler:** Carlos III **Obv:** Arms **Obv. Legend:** CAROLUS III... **Rev:** Pillars, date below **Note:** Mint mark So.

Date	Mintage	VG	F	VF	XF	Unc
1760 2 known; Rare	—	—	—	—	—	—

Note: Renaissance Auction 12-00 XF realized $54,000

KM# 34 4 REALES

13.5337 g., 0.9030 Silver .3929 oz. ASW **Ruler:** Carlos III **Obv:** Bust **Obv. Legend:** CAROLUS III... **Rev:** Arms, pillars **Note:** Mint mark So.

Date	Mintage	VG	F	VF	XF	Unc
1775 DA	3,000	350	500	650	1,450	—
1776 DA	3,000	350	500	650	1,450	—
1777 DA	3,000	350	500	650	1,450	—
1778 DA	15,000	300	400	500	1,250	—
1779 DA	10,000	300	400	500	1,250	—
1780 DA	9,000	300	400	500	1,250	—
1781 DA	14,000	300	400	500	1,250	—
1782 DA	7,000	300	400	500	1,250	—
1783 DA	10,000	300	400	500	1,250	—
1784 DA	40,000	300	400	500	1,250	—
1785 DA	30,000	300	400	500	950	—
1786 DA	36,000	300	400	500	950	—
1787 DA	25,000	300	400	500	950	—
1788 DA	41,000	300	400	500	950	—
1789/8 DA	45,000	300	400	500	950	—
1789 DA	Inc. above	300	400	500	950	—

KM# 38 4 REALES

13.5337 g., 0.8960 Silver .3899 oz. ASW **Ruler:** Carlos IV **Obv:** Bust right **Obv. Legend:** CAROLUS • IV • DEI • GRATIA • **Rev:** Crowned arms between pillars **Rev. Legend:** HISPAN • ET • IND • REX • ... **Note:** Mint mark So.

Date	Mintage	VG	F	VF	XF	Unc
1789 DA	Inc. above	300	400	500	950	—
1790 DA	9,000	300	400	500	900	—
1791/0 DA	—	325	450	550	1,250	—
1791 DA	6,000	325	450	550	1,250	—

KM# 50 4 REALES

13.5337 g., 0.8960 Silver .3899 oz. ASW **Ruler:** Carlos IV **Obv:** Bust right **Obv. Legend:** CAROLUS IIII... **Note:** Mint mark So.

Date	Mintage	VG	F	VF	XF	Unc
1791 DA	Inc. above	300	400	550	1,000	—
1792 DA	4,000,000	300	400	525	950	—

KM# 60 4 REALES

13.5337 g., 0.8960 Silver .3899 oz. ASW, 35 mm. **Ruler:** Carlos IV **Obv:** Laureate bust right **Obv. Legend:** CAROLUS • IIII • DEI • GRATIA • **Rev:** Crowned arms between columns **Rev. Legend:** HISPAN • ET • IND • REX • ... **Note:** Mint mark So.

Date	Mintage	VG	F	VF	XF	Unc
1792 DA	Inc. above	65.00	115	175	375	—
1793 DA	15,000	60.00	100	150	325	—
1794 DA	17,000	60.00	100	150	325	—
1795 DA	11,000	60.00	100	150	325	—
1796/5 DA	—	60.00	110	160	345	—
1796 DA	11,000	60.00	100	150	325	—
1797 DA	12,000	60.00	100	150	325	—
1798 DA	3,000	70.00	120	185	400	—
1799 DA	8,000	65.00	115	175	375	—
1800 AJ	5,000	65.00	115	175	375	—

KM# 5 8 REALES

27.0674 g., 0.9170 Silver .7980 oz. ASW **Ruler:** Fernando VI **Obv:** Crowned arms, ornaments at right and left **Obv. Legend:** FERDINANDUS • VI • D • G • HISPAN • ET IND • REX **Rev:** Crowned globes between crowned pillars **Rev. Legend:** ...QUE VNUM **Note:** Mint mark So.

Date	Mintage	VG	F	VF	XF	Unc
1751 J Unique	—	—	—	—	—	—

Note: Ponterio Amat Sale 3-91, Poor realized $5,500

Date	Mintage	VG	F	VF	XF	Unc
1753 J Rare	—	—	—	—	—	—
1755/1 J Rare	—	—	—	—	—	—
1757 J Rare	—	—	—	—	—	—
1758 J Rare	—	—	—	—	—	—

Note: Superior December Sale 12-90, VF realized $44,000

KM# 18 8 REALES

27.0674 g., 0.9170 Silver .7980 oz. ASW **Ruler:** Carlos III **Obv:** Crowned arms **Obv. Legend:** CAROLUS • III • D • G • HISPAN • ETIND • REX **Rev:** Crowned globes between crowned pillars **Rev. Legend:** ...VNUM **Note:** Mint mark So.

Date	Mintage	VG	F	VF	XF	Unc
1760 J Rare	—	—	—	—	—	—
1762 J Rare	—	—	—	—	—	—

Note: 1762 J has a cross above the crown on pillar

Date	Mintage	VG	F	VF	XF	Unc
1764 J Rare	—	—	—	—	—	—
1765 J Rare	—	—	—	—	—	—
1767 J	—	3,500	9,000	—	—	—
1768 A	—	3,500	9,000	—	—	—

Note: Ponterio Amat Sale 3-91, VF/XF realized $27,500. Bonhams Patterson sale 7-96, fine cleaned realized $3,300

Date	Mintage	VG	F	VF	XF	Unc
1769 A Rare	—	—	—	—	—	—
1770/69 A Rare	—	—	—	—	—	—

KM# 31 8 REALES

27.0674 g., 0.9030 Silver .7858 oz. ASW **Ruler:** Carlos III **Obv:** Bust **Obv. Legend:** CAROLUS • III • DEI • GRATIA • **Rev:** Crowned arms between pillars **Rev. Legend:** • HISPAN • ET IND • REX • ... **Note:** Mint mark So.

Date	Mintage	VG	F	VF	XF	Unc
1773 DA Rare	27,000	—	—	—	—	—
1775 DA Rare	8,500	—	—	—	—	—

Note: Ponterio Amat Sale 3-91, VF (only known example) realized $13,750

Date	Mintage	VG	F	VF	XF	Unc
1776/5 DA Rare	18,000	—	—	—	—	—
1777 DA	26,000	1,500	3,000	7,500	10,000	—
1778 DA Rare	74,000	—	—	—	—	—
1779/8 DA	99,000	1,500	3,000	4,500	8,000	—
1779 DA	Inc. above	1,500	3,000	4,500	8,000	—
1780 DA	75,000	1,500	3,000	4,500	8,000	—
1781 DA	105,000	1,500	3,000	4,500	8,000	—
1782 DA	60,000	1,500	3,000	4,500	8,000	—
1783/2 DA	74,000	1,500	3,000	4,500	8,000	—
1784 DA	128,000	500	1,250	2,000	3,500	—

Note: Small mint mark

Date	Mintage	VG	F	VF	XF	Unc
1784 DA	Inc. above	500	1,250	2,000	3,500	—

Note: Large mint mark

Date	Mintage	VG	F	VF	XF	Unc
1785/4 DA	130,000	500	1,250	2,000	3,500	—
1785 DA	Inc. above	500	1,250	2,000	3,500	—
1786 DA	149,000	500	1,250	2,000	3,500	—
1787 DA	183,000	500	1,250	2,000	3,500	—
1788 DA	187,000	400	1,000	1,600	2,750	—
1789/8 DA 3 known; Rare						

KM# 39 8 REALES3

27.0674 g., 0.9030 Silver .7858 oz. ASW **Ruler:** Carlos IV **Obv:** Bust right **Obv. Legend:** CAROLUS IV... **Note:** Mint mark So.

Date	Mintage	VG	F	VF	XF	Unc
1789 DA	Inc. above	350	600	1,450	2,350	—
1790 DA	147,000	350	600	1,350	2,150	—
1791 DA	167,000	350	600	1,450	2,350	—

KM# 51 8 REALES

27.0674 g., 0.8960 Silver .7797 oz. ASW, 40 mm. **Ruler:** Carlos IV **Obv:** Laureate bust right **Obv. Legend:** CAROLUS • IIII • DEI • GRATIA • **Rev:** Crowned arms between columns **Rev. Legend:** • HISPAN • ET IND • REX • ... **Note:** Mint mark So.

Date	Mintage	VG	F	VF	XF	Unc
1791 DA	Inc. above	500	850	1,500	2,250	—
1792 DA	161,000	450	800	1,450	2,150	—
1793 DA	206,000	150	200	300	600	—
1794 DA	161,000	150	200	300	600	—
1795 DA	200,000	150	200	300	600	—
1796/5 DA	199,000	150	200	300	600	—
1796 DA C/RAROLUS	—	500	1,000	2,000	3,000	—
1796 DA	Inc. above	150	200	300	600	—
1797/6 DA	—	250	300	400	750	—
1797 DA	195,000	125	175	275	550	—
1798 DA	174,000	125	175	275	550	—
1799 DA	170,000	125	175	275	550	—
1800 AJ CROLUS (error)	—	—	3,000	5,500	—	—
1800 AJ	184,000	125	175	275	550	—

KM# A6 ESCUDO

3.3834 g., 0.9170 Gold .0997 oz. AGW **Ruler:** Fernando VI **Obv:** Large head right **Obv. Legend:** FERDINANDUS VI and date **Rev:** Arms **Rev. Legend:** NOMINA MAGNA SEQUOR **Note:** Mint mark So.

Date	Mintage	VG	F	VF	XF	Unc
1754 J Rare	—	—	—	—	—	—

KM# 10 ESCUDO

3.3834 g., 0.9170 Gold .0997 oz. AGW **Ruler:** Fernando VI **Obv:** Small armored bust **Rev:** Arms **Rev. Legend:** NOMINA MAGNA SEQUOR **Note:** Mint mark So.

Date	Mintage	VG	F	VF	XF	Unc
1758 J	—	1,000	2,000	3,000	5,500	—
1759 J	—	1,000	2,000	3,000	5,500	—

KM# 19 ESCUDO

3.3834 g., 0.9170 Gold .0997 oz. AGW **Ruler:** Carlos III **Obv:** Bust right **Obv. Legend:** CRL • III • D • G • HISP • ... **Rev:** 4-fold arms **Rev. Legend:** NOMINA MAGNA SEQUOR **Note:** Mint mark So.

Date	Mintage	VG	F	VF	XF	Unc
1761 J	—	200	425	750	1,600	—
1762 J	968	200	425	750	1,600	—

KM# 22 ESCUDO

3.3834 g., 0.9170 Gold .0997 oz. AGW **Ruler:** Carlos III **Obv:** Young bust **Obv. Legend:** CAR. III... **Rev. Legend:** IN VTROQ FELIX **Note:** Mint mark So.

Date	Mintage	VG	F	VF	XF	Unc
1763 J	540	200	400	700	1,500	—
1764 J	—	200	400	700	1,500	—
1766 J	—	200	400	700	1,500	—

KM# 26 ESCUDO

3.3834 g., 0.9010 Gold .0980 oz. AGW **Ruler:** Carlos III **Obv:** Standard bust **Obv. Legend:** CAROL III... **Rev:** Arms, Order chain **Note:** Mint mark So.

Date	Mintage	VG	F	VF	XF	Unc
1772 DA	384	250	400	700	1,100	—
1773 DA	3,400	150	225	400	750	—
1774 DA	4,488	150	225	400	750	—
1775 DA	3,128	175	250	450	800	—
1776 DA	5,372	150	225	400	750	—
1777 DA	5,780	150	225	400	750	—
1778 DA	5,508	150	225	400	750	—
1779 DA	6,324	150	225	400	750	—
1780 DA	4,080	150	225	400	750	—
1781 DA	3,332	150	225	400	750	—
1782 DA	3,332	150	225	400	750	—
1783 DA	2,584	150	225	400	750	—
1784 DA	3,264	150	225	400	750	—
1785 DA	2,448	150	225	400	750	—
1786 DA	2,652	150	225	400	750	—
1787 DA	3,060	150	225	400	750	—
1788 DA	3,672	175	250	450	850	—

KM# 45 ESCUDO

3.3834 g., 0.9010 Gold .0980 oz. AGW **Ruler:** Carlos IV **Obv:** Bust right **Obv. Legend:** CAROL • IV • D • G • ... **Rev:** Arms in Order chain, crown above **Rev. Legend:** IN • UTROQ • FELIX • ... **Note:** Mint mark So.

Date	Mintage	VG	F	VF	XF	Unc
1789 DA	—	450	750	1,150	1,750	—
1790/89 DA	—	250	450	800	1,450	—
1790 DA	3,772	200	400	700	1,350	—

KM# 52 ESCUDO

3.3834 g., 0.9010 Gold .0980 oz. AGW **Ruler:** Carlos IV **Obv:** Bust **Obv. Legend:** CAROL IV... **Rev:** Arms in Order chain **Note:** Mint mark So.

Date	Mintage	VG	F	VF	XF	Unc
1791 DA	16,000	450	750	1,150	1,750	—

KM# 61 ESCUDO

3.3834 g., 0.8750 Gold .0952 oz. AGW, 19 mm. **Ruler:** Carlos IV **Obv:** Laureate bust right **Obv. Legend:** CAROL IIII... **Rev:** Crowned arms in order chain **Note:** Mint mark So.

Date	Mintage	VG	F	VF	XF	Unc
1792 DA	27,000	175	300	350	750	—
1793 DA	14,000	175	300	350	750	—
1794 DA	21,000	175	300	350	750	—
1795 DA	21,000	200	325	375	800	—
1796 DA	15,000	200	325	375	800	—
1797 DA	23,000	175	300	350	750	—
1798 DA	15,000	175	300	350	750	—
1799 DA	6,596	200	325	375	800	—
1800 DA	1,836	225	375	450	1,000	—
1800 AJ	—	—	—	—	—	—

KM# 11 2 ESCUDOS

6.7668 g., 0.9170 Gold .1995 oz. AGW **Ruler:** Fernando VI **Obv:** Bust right **Obv. Legend:** FERDINANDUS • VI • D • G • HISP • REX **Rev:** Crowned arms **Rev. Legend:** NOMINA MAGNA SEQUOR **Note:** Mint mark So.

Date	Mintage	VG	F	VF	XF	Unc
1758 J Rare	—	—	—	—	—	—

Note: Spink America Norweb Sale 3-97, holed, bent, VF realized $1,760

KM# 32 2 ESCUDOS

6.7682 g., 0.9040 Gold .1967 oz. AGW **Ruler:** Carlos III **Obv:** Bust **Obv. Legend:** CAROL. III. D. G.... **Rev:** Arms, Order chain **Note:** Mint mark So.

Date	Mintage	VG	F	VF	XF	Unc
1773 DA	850	350	550	750	1,350	—
1774 DA	3,026	300	450	600	1,000	—
1782 DA	1,632	300	450	650	1,100	—
1783 DA	1,292	500	900	1,200	2,000	—
1786 DA	1,394	300	450	600	1,000	—
1787 DA	1,768	300	450	600	1,000	—
1789 DA	2,380	500	900	1,200	2,000	—

KM# 40 2 ESCUDOS

6.7668 g., 0.8750 Gold .1904 oz. AGW **Ruler:** Carlos IV **Obv:** Bust **Obv. Legend:** CAROL. IV... **Rev:** Arms **Note:** Mint mark So.

Date	Mintage	VG	F	VF	XF	Unc
1789 DA	1,632	500	900	1,200	2,000	—
1790 DA	5,508	400	650	900	1,500	—

KM# 53 2 ESCUDOS

6.7668 g., 0.8750 Gold .1904 oz. AGW, 23 mm. **Ruler:** Carlos IV **Obv:** Laureate bust right **Obv. Legend:** CAROL. IIII... **Rev:** Crowned arms **Note:** Mint mark So.

Date	Mintage	VG	F	VF	XF	Unc
1791 DA	6,698	425	650	900	1,500	—
1792 DA	7,760	425	650	900	1,500	—
1793 DA	7,820	425	650	900	1,500	—
1794 DA	7,832	425	650	900	1,500	—
1795 DA	10,000	425	650	900	1,500	—
1796 DA	14,000	425	650	900	1,500	—
1797 DA	11,000	425	650	900	1,500	—
1798 DA	8,500	425	650	900	1,500	—
1799 DA	4,148	425	650	900	1,500	—
1800 AJ	986	450	700	1,000	1,650	—

KM# 2 4 ESCUDOS

13.5337 g., 0.9170 Gold .3990 oz. AGW **Ruler:** Fernando VI **Obv:** Bust right **Obv. Legend:** * FERDINANDUS • VI • D • G • HISP • REX * **Rev:** Crowned arms **Rev. Legend:** * NOMINA MAGNA SEQUOR * **Note:** Mint mark So.

Date	Mintage	VG	F	VF	XF	Unc
1749 J	—	400	600	1,000	1,500	—
1750/5 J	—	400	600	1,000	1,500	—
1750 J	—	400	600	1,000	1,500	—
1751 J	—	650	1,100	1,400	2,500	—
1752 J	—	650	1,100	1,400	2,500	—
1756 J	—	650	1,100	1,400	2,500	—
1757 J	—	650	1,100	1,400	2,500	—
1758 J	—	900	1,750	3,250	6,000	—

KM# 21 4 ESCUDOS

13.5337 g., 0.9170 Gold .3990 oz. AGW **Ruler:** Carlos III **Obv:** Bust **Obv. Legend:** CAROLUS III... **Note:** Mint mark So.

Date	Mintage	VG	F	VF	XF	Unc
1762 J	—	950	1,850	3,000	5,500	—
1763 J	—	900	1,750	2,750	5,000	—

KM# 23 4 ESCUDOS

13.5337 g., 0.9170 Gold .3990 oz. AGW **Ruler:** Carlos III **Obv:** Young bust right **Obv. Legend:** CAROLUS • III • D • G • HISP • ETIND • REX **Rev:** Crowned arms within Order chain **Rev. Legend:** IN • UTROQ • FELIX • AUSPICE • ... **Note:** Mint mark So.

Date	Mintage	VG	F	VF	XF	Unc
1763 J	—	900	1,750	3,000	5,500	—
1764 J	372	850	1,600	2,650	5,000	—
1765 J	11,000	800	1,500	2,500	4,750	—

KM# 33 4 ESCUDOS

13.5337 g., 0.9010 Gold .3920 oz. AGW **Ruler:** Carlos III **Obv:** Standard bust **Obv. Legend:** CAROL • III • D • G • HISP • ET IND • R • **Rev:** Arms in Order chain **Rev. Legend:** IN • UTROQ • FELIX • AUSPICE • DEO • .. **Note:** Mint mark So.

Date	Mintage	VG	F	VF	XF	Unc
1773 DA	170	400	750	1,200	1,900	—
1776 DA	1,615	400	750	1,100	1,750	—
1781 DA	850	400	750	1,150	1,850	—
1782 DA	901	400	750	1,150	1,850	—
1783 DA	612	400	750	1,150	1,850	—
1784 DA	816	350	550	900	1,450	—
1785 DA	816	350	550	900	1,450	—
1786 DA	697	350	550	900	1,450	—
1787 DA	952	350	550	900	1,450	—
1788 DA	1,020	425	800	1,200	1,900	—

KM# 41.1 4 ESCUDOS

13.5337 g., 0.8750 Gold .3807 oz. AGW **Ruler:** Carlos IV **Obv:** Uniformed bust right **Obv. Legend:** CAROL • IV • D • G • HISP • ETIND • R • **Rev:** Arms in Order chain **Rev. Legend:** IN • UTROQ • FELIX • AUSPICE • DEO • .. **Note:** Mint mark So.

Date	Mintage	VG	F	VF	XF	Unc
1789 DA	Inc. above	400	750	1,100	1,750	—
1790 DA	3,332	400	750	1,100	1,750	—
1791 DA	4,879	650	1,100	1,400	2,500	—

KM# 41.2 4 ESCUDOS

13.5337 g., 0.8750 Gold .3807 oz. AGW **Ruler:** Carlos IV **Obv:** Armored bust right **Obv. Legend:** CAROL • IIII • D • G • HISP • ETIND • R • **Rev:** Arms in Order chain **Rev. Legend:** IN • UTROQ • FELIX • AUSPICE • DEO • .. **Note:** Mint mark So.

Date	Mintage	VG	F	VF	XF	Unc
1791 DA	Inc. above	575	1,000	1,300	2,250	—

KM# 62 4 ESCUDOS

13.5337 g., 0.8750 Gold .3807 oz. AGW, 30.5 mm. **Ruler:** Carlos IV **Obv:** Laureate bust right **Obv. Legend:** CAROL • IIII • D • G • HISP • ET IND • R • **Rev:** Crowned arms in order chain **Rev. Legend:** IN • UTROQ • FELIX • AUSPICE • DEO • **Note:** Mint mark So.

Date	Mintage	VG	F	VF	XF	Unc
1792 DA	4,680	700	1,150	1,500	2,750	—
1793 DA	6,238	550	800	1,200	2,000	—
1794 DA	7,140	550	800	1,200	2,000	—
1795 DA	6,808	550	800	1,200	2,000	—
1796 DA	6,970	550	800	1,200	2,000	—
1797 DA	5,950	550	800	1,200	2,000	—
1798 DA	4,471	550	800	1,200	2,000	—
1799 DA	2,754	550	800	1,200	2,000	—
1800 DA	—	750	1,200	1,600	3,000	—
1800 AJ	646	625	1,100	1,400	2,500	—

KM# 1 8 ESCUDOS

27.0730 g., 0.9170 Gold 0.7982 oz. AGW **Obv:** Bust left **Obv. Legend:** PHILIPV D.G. HISPAN ET IND REX **Rev:** Arms, legend around

Date	Mintage	VG	F	VF	XF	Unc
1744 6 known	—	—	—	—	—	—

KM# 3 8 ESCUDOS

27.0674 g., 0.9170 Gold .7980 oz. AGW **Ruler:** Fernando VI **Obv:** Bust right **Obv. Legend:** FERDINANDUS • VI • D • G • HISP • REX **Rev:** Arms, Order chain, fleece above cross **Rev. Legend:** NOMINA MAGNA SEQUOR **Note:** Mint mark So.

Date	Mintage	VG	F	VF	XF	Unc
1750 J	—	350	600	1,100	1,850	—
1751/0 J	—	350	600	1,000	1,750	—
1751 J	—	350	600	950	1,600	—
1752 J	—	1,000	1,750	2,500	3,750	—
1753 J	—	1,000	1,750	2,500	3,750	—
1754 J	—	1,000	1,750	2,500	3,750	—
1755 J	—	1,000	1,750	2,500	3,750	—
1756/5 J	—	1,000	1,800	2,600	3,850	—
1756 J	—	1,000	1,750	2,500	3,750	—
1757 J	—	1,000	1,750	2,500	3,750	—
1758/7 J	—	1,500	2,500	3,500	5,750	—
1758 J	—	1,500	2,500	3,500	5,750	—

KM# 12 8 ESCUDOS

27.0674 g., 0.9170 Gold .7980 oz. AGW **Ruler:** Fernando VI **Obv:** Armored bust right **Obv. Legend:** FERDINANDUS • VI • D • G • HISP • REX **Rev:** Arms, Order chain, fleece below cross **Rev. Legend:** NOMINA MAGNA SEQUOR **Note:** Mint mark So.

Date	Mintage	VG	F	VF	XF	Unc
1758 J	—	1,000	1,750	2,500	3,750	—
1759 J	—	1,000	1,750	2,500	3,750	—

KM# 13 8 ESCUDOS

27.0730 g., 0.9170 Gold .7982 oz. AGW **Ruler:** Fernando VI **Obv:** Large bust, date **Obv. Legend:** FERDIND. VI. D. G. HISPAN ET IND REX **Note:** Mint mark So.

Date	Mintage	VG	F	VF	XF	Unc
1759 J	—	2,000	3,500	5,250	8,000	—
1760/59 J	—	900	1,650	2,400	3,500	—
1760 J	—	900	1,650	2,400	3,500	—

KM# 20 8 ESCUDOS

27.0674 g., 0.9170 Gold .7980 oz. AGW **Ruler:** Carlos III **Obv:** Bust right **Obv. Legend:** CAROLUS • III • D • G • HISPAN • ETIND • REX **Rev:** Arms in Order chain **Rev. Legend:** NOMINA MAGNA SEQUOR **Note:** Mint mark So.

Date	Mintage	VG	F	VF	XF	Unc
1760 J	—	1,500	3,000	4,500	7,500	—
1761 J	—	800	1,500	2,250	3,350	—
1762 J	32,000	800	1,500	2,250	3,350	—
1763/2 J	41,000	800	1,550	2,350	3,450	—
1763 J	Inc. above	800	1,500	2,250	3,350	—

KM# 25 8 ESCUDOS

27.0674 g., 0.9170 Gold .7980 oz. AGW **Ruler:** Carlos III **Obv:** Young bust right **Obv. Legend:** CAROLUS • III • D • G • HISP • ET • IND • REX • **Rev:** Arms in Order chain **Rev. Legend:** IN • UTROQ • FELIX • AUSPICE • DEO • **Note:** Mint mark So.

Date	Mintage	VG	F	VF	XF	Unc
1764 J	36,000	1,200	2,000	3,000	4,500	—
1765 J	35,000	1,200	2,000	3,000	4,500	—
1766 J	23,000	1,200	2,000	3,000	4,500	—
1767 J	—	1,200	2,000	3,000	4,500	—
1767 Inverted A	—	1,500	3,000	4,500	7,500	—
1768 A	—	1,200	2,000	3,000	4,500	—
1768 Inverted A	—	1,250	2,100	3,150	4,650	—
1769 A	—	1,200	2,000	3,000	4,500	—
1770 A	—	1,350	2,250	3,250	5,500	—
1771 A	—	1,200	2,000	3,000	4,500	—
1772/1 A	17,000	1,350	2,250	3,250	5,500	—
1772 A	Inc. above	1,500	3,000	4,500	7,000	—

KM# 27 8 ESCUDOS

27.0674 g., 0.9010 Gold .7841 oz. AGW **Ruler:** Carlos III **Obv:** Bust right **Obv. Legend:** CAROL • III • D • G • HISP • ET IND • R • **Rev:** Arms in Order chain **Rev. Legend:** IN • UTROQ • FELIX • AUSPICE • DEO • **Note:** Mint mark So.

Date	Mintage	VG	F	VF	XF	Unc
1772 DA	Inc. above	375	425	750	1,400	—
1773 DA	33,000	375	425	750	1,250	—
1774 DA	42,000	375	425	750	1,250	—
1775 DA	36,000	375	425	750	1,250	—
1776/3 DA	41,000	375	425	800	1,450	—
1776 DA	Inc. above	375	425	750	1,250	—
1777/6 DA	41,000	375	425	750	1,250	—
1777 DA	Inc. above	375	425	750	1,250	—
1778 DA	42,000	375	425	750	1,150	—
1778 DA ET in legend reversed	Inc. above	425	600	1,000	2,250	—
1779 DA	44,000	375	500	850	1,850	—
1780 DA	42,000	375	425	750	1,150	—
1781/79 DA	43,000	400	500	950	2,150	—
1781 DA	Inc. above	375	425	750	1,150	—
1782/71 DA	—	400	500	950	2,150	—
1782 DA	40,000	375	425	750	1,150	—
1783 DA	34,000	375	425	750	1,150	—
1784/3 DA	37,000	400	500	900	2,000	—
1784 DA	Inc. above	375	450	800	1,750	—
1785/4 DA	34,000	400	500	900	2,000	—
1785 DA	Inc. above	375	425	750	1,150	—
1786 DA	34,000	500	800	1,150	2,500	—
1787 DA	37,000	375	425	750	1,100	—
1788 DA	42,000	375	425	750	1,100	—
1789 DA	41,000	425	600	1,000	2,250	—

KM# 42 8 ESCUDOS

27.0674 g., 0.9010 Gold .7841 oz. AGW **Ruler:** Carlos IV **Obv:** Bust right **Obv. Legend:** CAROL • IV • D • G • HISP • ETIND • R • **Rev:** Arms in Order chain **Note:** Mint mark So.

Date	Mintage	VG	F	VF	XF	Unc
1789 DA	Inc. above	400	600	800	1,200	—
1790 DA	42,000	400	600	800	1,200	—
1790 DA	Inc. above	600	900	1,200	1,800	—
Note: Retrograde "E" in "DEO"						
1791/0 DA	42,000	500	900	2,000	4,000	—
1791 DA	Inc. above	500	900	2,000	4,000	—

KM# 54 8 ESCUDOS

27.0674 g., 0.8750 Gold .7615 oz. AGW, 37.5 mm. **Ruler:** Carlos IV **Obv:** Laureate bust right **Obv. Legend:** CAROL. IIII... **Rev:** Crowned arms in order chain **Rev. Legend:** IN UTROQ FELIX AUSPICE DEO **Note:** Mint mark So.

Date	Mintage	VG	F	VF	XF	Unc
1791 DA	Inc. above	550	725	950	1,350	—
1792 DA	38,000	525	650	800	1,100	—
1793 DA	34,000	525	650	800	1,100	—
1794 DA	40,000	525	650	800	1,100	—
1795 DA	43,000	525	650	800	1,100	—
1796 DA	44,000	525	650	800	1,100	—
1797 DA	43,000	525	650	800	1,100	—
1797 DA HSID in legend	Inc. above	550	725	900	1,350	—
1798 DA	43,000	525	650	800	1,100	—
1799 DA	41,000	525	650	800	1,100	—
1800 DA	54,000	525	675	900	1,600	—
1800 JA	Inc. above	525	675	800	1,350	—

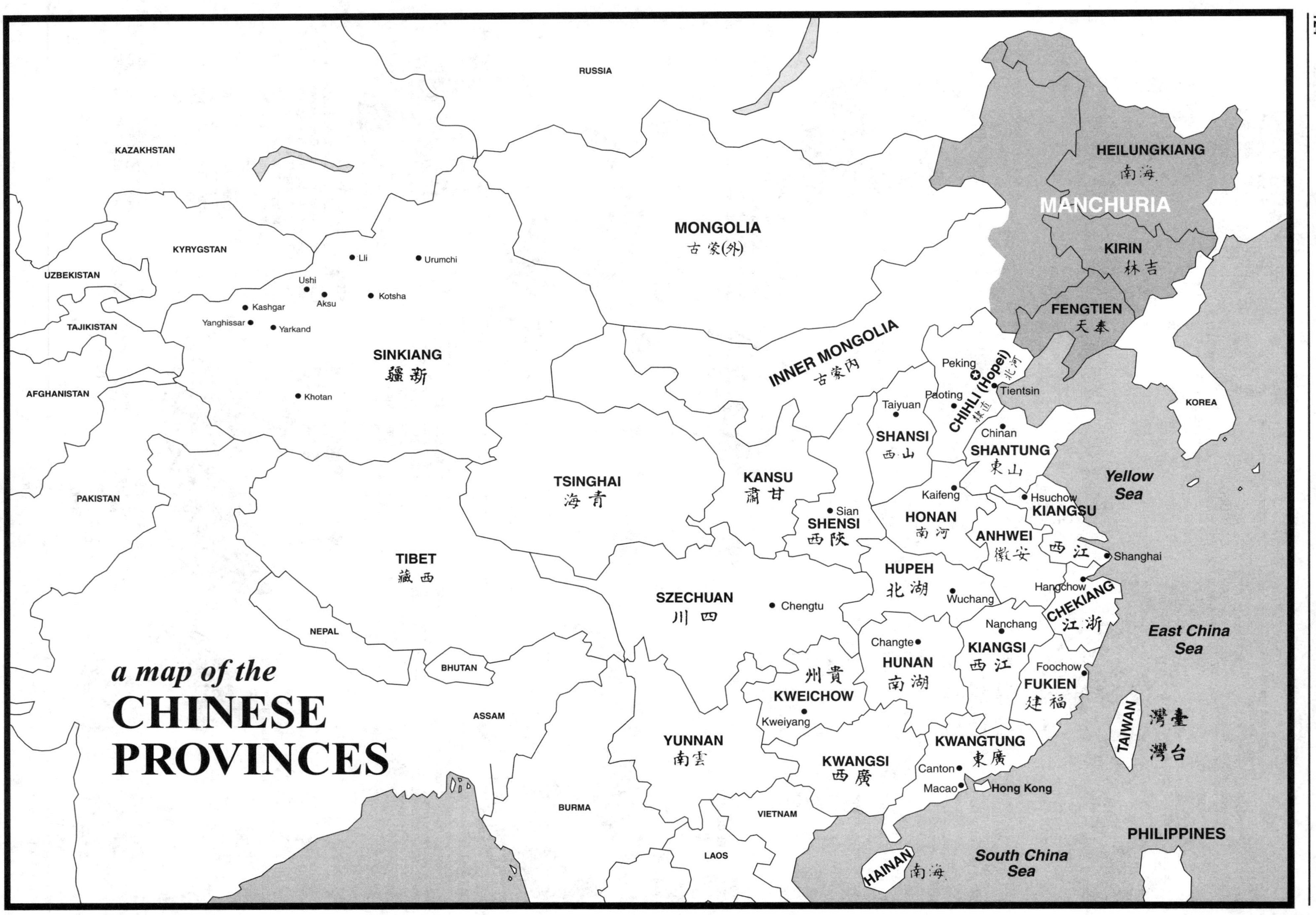
RUSSIA
KAZAKHSTAN
KYRYGSTAN
UZBEKISTAN
TAJIKISTAN
AFGHANISTAN
PAKISTAN
MONGOLIA
INNER MONGOLIA
MANCHURIA
HEILUNGKIANG
KIRIN
FENGTIEN
KOREA
SINKIANG
Lli
Urumchi
Ushi
Aksu
Kotsha
Kashgar
Yanghissar
Yarkand
Khotan
TSINGHAI
TIBET
NEPAL
BHUTAN
ASSAM
BURMA
VIETNAM
LAOS
KANSU
SHANSI
Taiyuan
CHIHLI (Hopei)
Peking
Paoting
Tientsin
SHANTUNG
Chinan
Yellow Sea
SHENSI
Sian
HONAN
Kaifeng
KIANGSU
Hsuchow
ANHWEI
Shanghai
HUPEH
Wuchang
SZECHUAN
Chengtu
Hangchow
CHEKIANG
Nanchang
KIANGSI
Changte
HUNAN
KWEICHOW
Kweiyang
Foochow
FUKIEN
East China Sea
TAIWAN
YUNNAN
KWANGSI
KWANGTUNG
Canton
Macao
Hong Kong
HAINAN
South China Sea
PHILIPPINES
a map of the
CHINESE
PROVINCES

CHINA

EMPIRE

Before 1912, China was ruled by an imperial government. The republican administration which replaced it was itself supplanted on the Chinese mainland by a communist government in 1949, but it has remained in control of Taiwan and other offshore islands in the China Sea with a land area of approximately 14,000 square miles and a population of more than 14 million. The People's Republic of China administers some 3.7 million square miles and an estimated 1.19 billion people. This communist government, officially established on October 1, 1949, was admitted to the United Nations, replacing its nationalist predecessor, the Republic of China, in 1971.

Cast coins in base metals were used in China many centuries before the Christian era, but locally struck coinages of the western type in gold, silver, copper and other metals did not appear until 1888.In spite of the relatively short time that modern coins have been in use, the number of varieties is exceptionally large.

Both Nationalist and Communist China, as well as the prerevolutionary Imperial government and numerous provincial or other agencies, including some foreign-administered agencies and governments, have issued coins in China. Most of these have been in dollar (yuan) or dollar-fraction denominations, based on the internationally used dollar system, but coins in tael denominations were issued in the 1920's and earlier. The striking of coins nearly ceased in the late 1930's through the 1940's due to the war effort and a period of uncontrollable inflation while vast amounts of paper currency were issued by the Nationalist, Communist and Japanese occupation institutions.

EMPERORS

Obverse Types

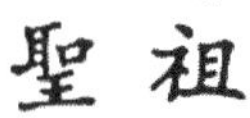

SHENG TSU
1662-1722

Type A

康熙

Reign title: K'ang-Hsi (Kangxi)

康熙通寶

K'ang-hsi T'ung-pao

世宗

SHIH TSUNG
1723-1735

Type A

雍正

Reign title: Yung-chêng (Yongzheng)

雍正通寶

Yung-chêng T'ung-pao

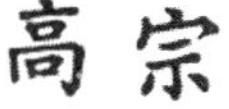

KAO TSUNG
1736-1795

Type A-1

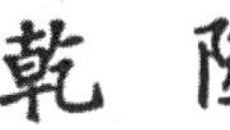

Reign title: Ch'ien-lung (Qianlong)

乾隆通寶

Ch'ien-lung T'ung-pao

Ch'ien-lung - One of the longest ruling and most brilliant emperors in China's entire history. Born on September15, 1711, he ascended the throne on October 18, 1735, at age 24. He fathered 17 sons and 10 daughters by his concubines. Under Ch'ien-lung, China reached its widest limits, but bad management, extravagance and corruption marked the last two decades of Ch'ien-lung's reign and weakened the empire for some time to come. The role of Ch'ien-lung in the arts and letters of his time was a considerable one. He himself wrote prose as well as verse. In 1772 he ordered the making of the "Complete Library in the Four Branches of Literature." Seven handwritten series of the 36,275 volumes were distributed among palaces and libraries between 1782 and 1787. Architecture. painting, porcelain, and particularly jade and ivory-work flourished. After having reigned for 60 years, Ch'ien-lung, out of respect for K'ang-hsi, his near predecessor whose reign had lasted 61 years, announced on October 15, 1795, that he was designating his fifth son, Yung-yen, to succeed him. The aged emperor died February 7, 1799.

Type A-2

This variety of Ch'ien-lung issue has the bottom character written in a different style. This is commonly referred to as a "Shan Lung" commemorative issue. The term "Shan Lung" refers to the special form of the character "lung" appearing in these commemoratives.

Regular form	"Shan Lung"	Shan
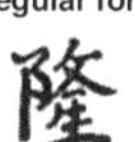		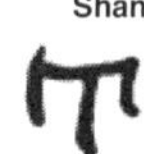

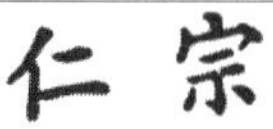

JEN TSUNG
1796-1820

Type A

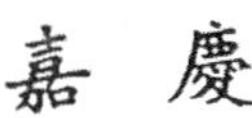

Reign title: Chia-ch'ing (Jiaqing)

嘉慶通寶

Chia-ch'ing T'ung-pao

Chia-ch'ing - Born November 13, 1760 in Peking. He was proclaimed emperor and assumed the reign title in 1796. The White Lotus Rebellion, 1796-1804, broke out in central and western China. Capable generals were appointed to quell the rebellion, but it took the depleted Ch'ing armies five years to put it down. Chia-ch'ing made efforts to restore the finances of the imperial treasury but corruption may have increased as a result of the practice of selling high office as a means of collecting more revenue. Chia-ch'ing died on September 2, 1820, as one of the most unpopular emperors of the Ch'ing dynasty.

ADDITIONAL CHARACTERS

The additional characters illustrated and defined below are found on the reverse of cast bronze cash coins, usually above the square center hole. In the period covered by this catalog the following mints produced cash coins with these additional marks: Board of Revenue and Board of Works in Peking, Kweichow, Aksu and Ili in Sinkiang, Shantung, Szechuan, and all three mints listed in Yunnan.

CHARACTERS

一	I, YI	十一	Shih I	心	Hsin
二	Erh	合	Ho	宇	Yu
三	San	工	Kung	宙	Chou
四	Szu	主	Chu	來	Lai
五	Wu	川	Ch'uan	往	Wang
六	Liu	之	Chih	晋	Chin
七	Ch'i	正	Cheng	村	Ts'un
八	Pa	又	Yu	日	Jih
九	Chiu	山	Shan	列	Lieh
十	Shih	大	Ta	仁	Jen
主	Chung	中	Feng	丰	Shang
順	Shun	云	Yun	手	Shou
天	T'ien	利	Li	穴	Kung
分	Fen				

MINT MARK IDENTIFIER

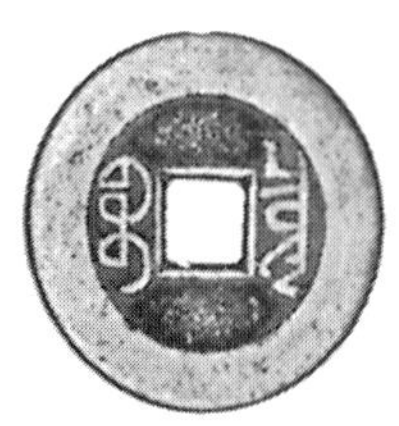

Boo-Clowan (Peking)
Hu-PU BOARD OF REVENUE

Boo-Yuwan (Peking)
Kung-Pu BOARD OZ PUBLIC WORKS

Boo-an
An Mint
ANHWEI

Boo-De
Teh Mint
Chengte
CHIHLI

Boo-U
Wu Mint
Wuch'ang
HUPEH

Boo-San
Shan Mint
Sian
SHENSI

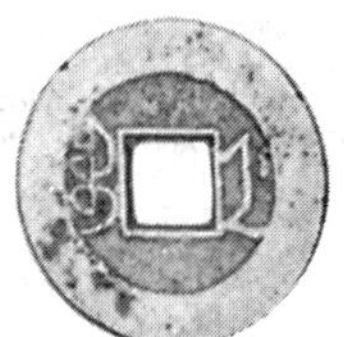

Boo-Je
Chê Mint
Hangchow
CHEKIANG

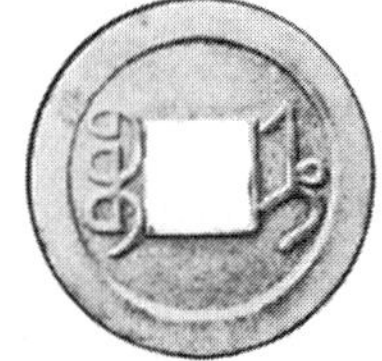
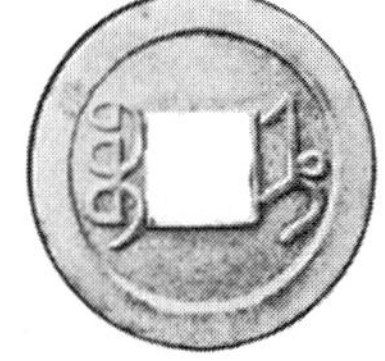

Boo-Ji
Chih Mint
Paoting
CHIHLI

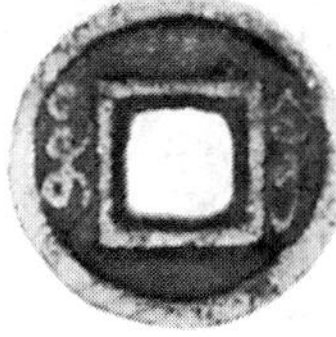

Boo-Gung
Kung Mint
Kungchang
KANSU

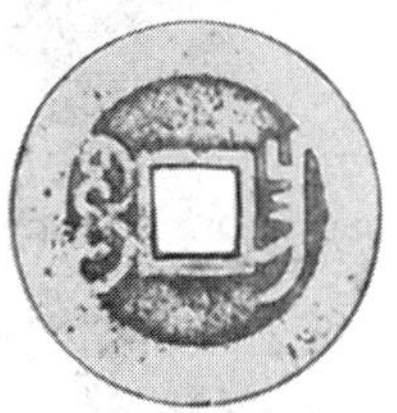

Boo-ch'ang
Ch'ang Mint
Nanchang
KIANGSI

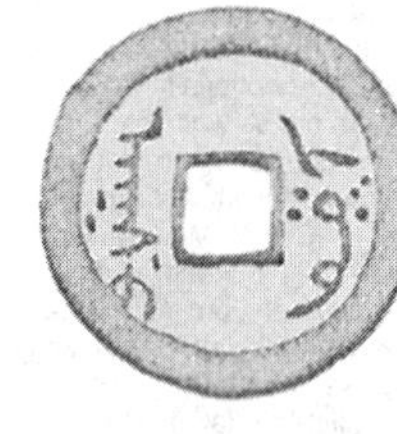

Aksu (Hocheng)
SINKIANG

Boo-Yi
Ili (Hweiyuan)
SINKIANG

Boo-GI
Chi Mint
Chichow
CHIHLI

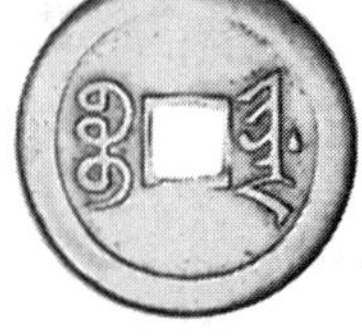

Boo-Jiyen
Ching Mint
Tientsin
CHIHLI

(Through Hsien-Feng era)

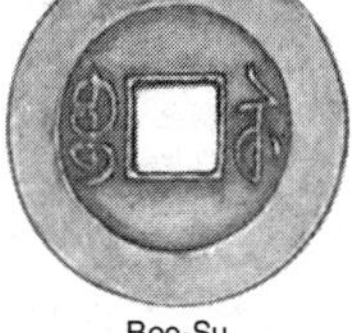

Boo-Su
Su Mint
Soohow
KIANGSU

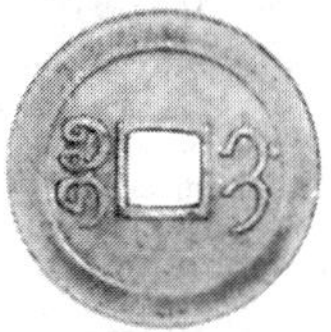

Boo-Gi
Chi Mint
KIRIN

(Kuang-hsu Era)

Kotsha (Kuche)
SINKIANG

Boo-Fung
Fung Mint
FENGTIEN

Boo-Fu
Fu Mint
Fuchou
FUKIEN

Boo-Gui
Kue Mint
Kuelin
KWANGSI

Boo-Guwang
Kuang Mint
Canton
KWANGTUNG

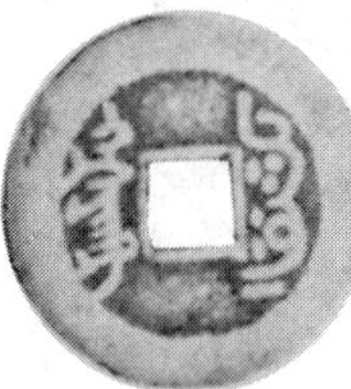

Kashgar (Shufu)
SINKIANG

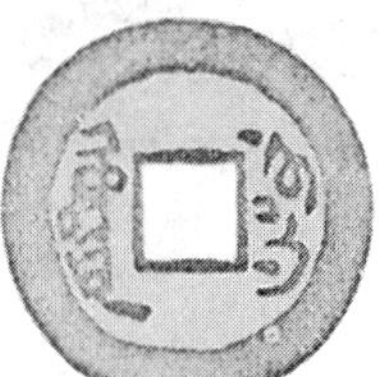

Khotan (Hotien)
SINKIANG

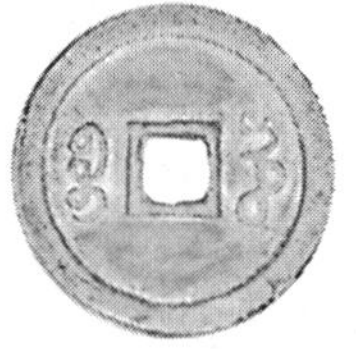

Boo-Ho
Ho Mint
K'aifeng
HONAN

Boo-Giyan
Kwei Mint
Kweiyang
KWEICHOW

Boo-Jin
Chin Mint
Taiyuan
SHANSI

Boo-Di
Di Mint
Urumchi (Tihwa)
SINKIANG

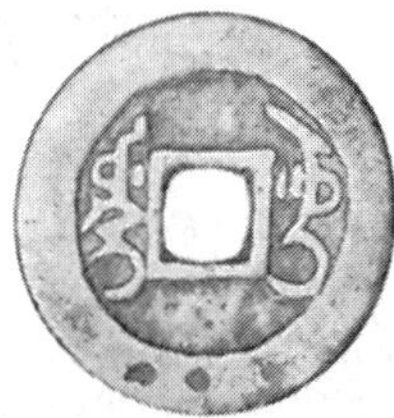

Ushi (Wushih)
SINKIANG

Boo-Nan
Nan Mint
Ch'ang-sha
HUNAN

Boo-Ji
Chi Mint
Chinan
SHANTUNG

Boo-Cuwan
Chuan Mint
Chengtu
SZECHUAN

Yarkand (Soche)
SINKIANG

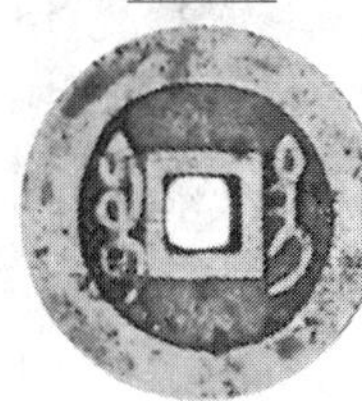

Boo-Tai
Tai Mint
TAIWAN

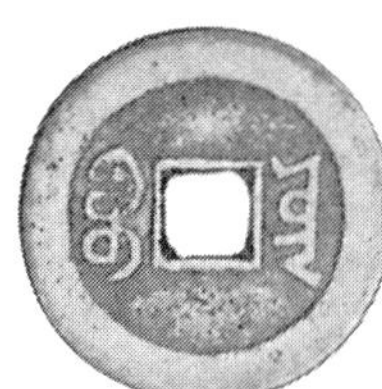

Boo-Yôn
Yûn Mint
Yûnnan Fu
YUNNAN

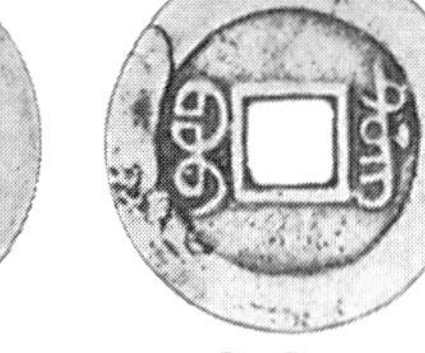

Boo-Dong
Tung Mint
Tungch'uan
YUNNAN

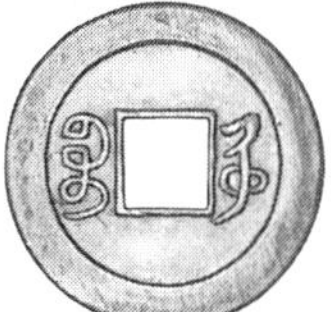

Boo-Gu
Ku Mint
Taku Arsenal
TIENTSIN, CHIHLI

Boo-Fu
Fu Mint
Fuchow
YUNNAN

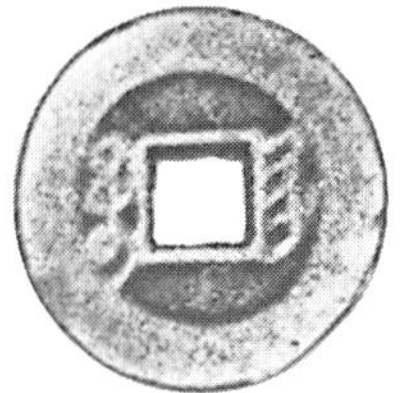

Boo-Jing
Ching Mint
Chingchow Fu
HUPEH

SYCEE (INGOTS)

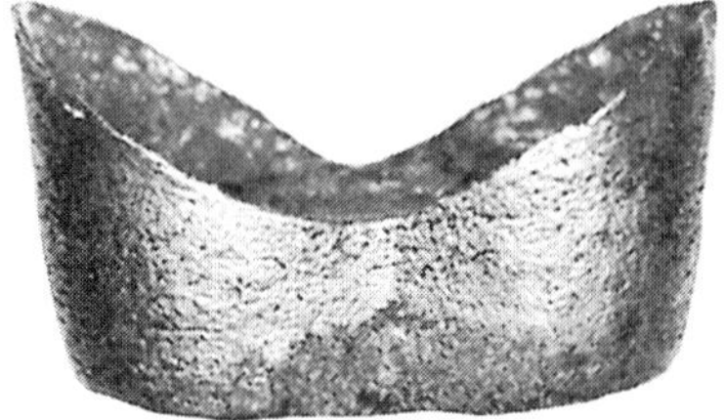

Prior to 1889 the general coinage issued by the Chinese government was the copper-alloy cash coin. Despite occasional shortlived experiments with silver and gold coinage, and disregarding paper money which tended to be unreliable, the government expected the people to get by solely with cash coins. This system worked well for individuals making purchases for themselves, but was unsatisfactory for trade and large business transactions, since a dollar's worth of cash coins weighed about four pounds. As a result, a private currency consisting of silver ingots, usually stamped by the firm which made them, came into use. These were the sycee ingots.

It is not known when these ingots first came into use. Some sources date them to the Yuan (Mongol) dynasty but they are certainly much older. Examples are known from as far back as the Han dynasty (206 BC - 220 AD) but prior to the Sung era (960 - 1280AD) they were used mainly for hoarding wealth. The development of commerce by the Sung dynasty, however, required the use of silver or gold to pay for large purchases. By the Mongol period (1280-1368) silver ingots and paper money had become the dominant currencies, especially for trade. The western explorers who traveled to China during this period (such as Marco Polo) mention both paper money and sycee but not a single one refers to cash coins.

During the Ming dynasty (1368-1644) trade fell off and the use of silver decreased. But toward the end of that dynasty, Dutch and British ships began a new China trade and sycee once again became common. During the 19th and early 20th centuries, the trade in sycee became enormous. Most of the sycee around today are from this period. In 1935 the Chinese government and in 1939 Sinkiang banned the use of sycee and it soon disappeared.

The word sycee (pronounced "sigh - see") is a western corruption of the Chinese word hsi-szu ("fine silk") or hsi yin ("fine silver") and is first known to have appeared in the English language in the late 1600's. By the early 1700's the word appeared regularly in the records of the British East India Company. Westerners also called these ingots "boat money" or "shoe money" owing to the fact that the most common type of ingot resembles a Chinese shoe. The Chinese, however, called the ingots by a variety of names, the most common of which were yuan pao, wen -yin (fine silver) and yin-ting (silver ingot).

The ingots were cast in molds (giving them their characteristic shapes) and while the metal was still semi-liquid, the inscription was impressed. It was due to this procedure that the sides of some sycee are higher than the center. The manufacturers were usually silver firms, often referred to as lu fang's, and after the sycee was finished it was occasionally tested and marked by the kung ku (public assayer).

Sycee were not circulated as we understand it. One didn't usually carry a sycee to market and spend it. Usually the ingots were used as a means of carrying a large amount of money on trips (as we would carry $100 bills instead of $5 bills) or for storing wealth. Large transactions between merchants or banks were paid by means of crates of sycee - each containing 60 fifty tael ingots.

Sycee are known in a variety of shapes the most common of which are the shoe or boat shaped, drum shaped, and loaf shaped (rectangular or hourglass-shaped, with a generally flat surface). Other shapes include one that resembles a double headed axe (this is the oldest type known), one that is square and flat, and others that are "fancy" (in the form of fish, butterflies, leaves, etc.).

Sycee have no denominations as they were simply ingots that passed by weight. Most are in more or less standard weights, however, the most common being 1, 5, 10 and 50 taels. Other weights known include 1/10, 1/5, 1/4, 1/3, 1/2, 2/3, 72/100 (this is the weight of a dollar), 3/4, 2, 3, 4, 6, 7, 8 and 25 taels. Most of the pieces weighing less than 5 taels were used as gifts or souvenirs.

The actual weight of any given value of sycee varied considerably due to the fact that the tael was not a single weight but a general term for a wide range of local weight standards. The weight of the tael varied depending upon location and type of tael in question. For example in one town, the weight of a tael of rice, of silver and of stones may each be different. In addition, the fineness of silver also varied depending upon location and type of tael in question. It was not true, as westerners often wrote, that sycee were made of pure silver. For most purposes, a weight of 37 grams may be used for the tael.

Weights and Current Market Value of Sycee
(Weights are approximate)

1/2 Tael	17-19 grams	26.00
72/100 Tael	25-27 grams	36.00
1 Tael	35-38 grams	46.00
2 Taels	70-75 grams	70.00
3 Taels	100-140 grams	85.00
5 Taels	175-190 grams	110.00
7 Taels	240-260 grams	125.00
10 Taels	350-380 grams	250.00
25 Taels	895-925 grams	3500.00
50 Taels	1790-1850 grams	2000.00
50 Taels, square	1790-1850 grams	1600.00

REFERENCE

Catalog reference Schjöth #: Chinese Currency by Fredrik Schjöth c.1965 by Virgil Hancock, published by Krause Publications, Iola, Wisconsin, U.S.A.

CH'ING DYNASTY
Manchu, 1644 - 1911

K'ang-hsi
1662-1722, Kangxi

CAST COINAGE

KM# 311.1 CASH

Cast Bronze, 25-27 mm. **Obv. Inscription:** "K'ang-hsi T'ung-pao" with open "hsi" **Reverse:** Manchu "Boo-ciowan". **Mint:** Hu-pu Board of Revenue **Note:** Size varies. Schjöth #1419.

Date	Mintage	Good	VG	F	VF	XF
ND(1662-1722)	—	0.50	0.70	1.00	1.50	—

KM# 311.1a CASH

Cast Bronze, 25-27 mm. **Obverse:** Wide rims **Obv. Inscription:** "K'ang-hsi T'ung-pao" with open "hsi" **Reverse:** Manchu "Boo-ciowan" **Mint:** Hu-pu Board of Revenue **Note:** Size varies. Schjöth #1419. Prev. KM#311.1s.

Date	Mintage	Good	VG	F	VF	XF
ND(1662-1722)	—	0.50	0.70	1.00	1.50	—

KM# 311.1b CASH

Cast Bronze, 24 mm. **Obv. Inscription:** K'ang-hsi T'ung-pao. **Reverse:** Manchu "Boo-ciowan". **Mint:** Hu-pu Board of Revenue **Note:** Wide rims. Prev. KM#311.2s.

Date	Mintage	Good	VG	F	VF	XF
ND(1662-1722)	—	0.50	0.70	1.00	1.50	—

KM# 311.2 CASH

Cast Bronze **Obv. Inscription:** K'ang-hsi T'ung-pao **Reverse:** Manchu "Boo-ciowan" with dot above **Mint:** Hu-pu Board of Revenue **Note:** Schjöth #1420.

Date	Mintage	Good	VG	F	VF	XF
ND(1662-1722)	—	14.00	20.00	28.50	40.00	—

KM# 312.1 CASH

Cast Bronze, 25-26 mm. **Obverse:** One dot "T'ung" at right **Obv. Inscription:** K'ang-hsi T'ung-pao **Reverse:** Manchu "Boo-Yuwan" **Mint:** Kung-pu Board of Public Works **Note:** Size varies. Narrow rims. Schjöth #1421.

Date	Mintage	Good	VG	F	VF	XF
ND(1662-1722)	—	0.20	0.50	0.80	2.00	—

KM# 312.2 CASH

Cast Bronze, 25-26 mm. **Obverse:** 2 dot "T'ung" at right **Obv. Inscription:** K'ang-hsi T'ung-pao **Reverse:** Manchu "Boo-Yuwan" **Mint:** Kung-pu Board of Public Works **Note:** Size varies. Wide rims.

Date	Mintage	Good	VG	F	VF	XF
ND(1662-1722)	—	0.20	0.50	0.80	1.50	—

KM# 312a CASH

Cast Bronze, 23-25 mm. **Obv. Inscription:** K'ang-hsi T'ung-pao **Mint:** Kung-pu Board of Public Works **Note:** Reduced size. Schjöth #1422. Prev. KM#313.

Date	Mintage	Good	VG	F	VF	XF
ND(1662-1722)	—	0.50	0.70	1.00	1.50	—

KM# 314 CASH

Cast Bronze, 25 mm. **Obv. Inscription:** K'ang-hsi T'ung-pao **Reverse:** Manchu "Boo" at left, Chinese "Ho" (Honan) at right **Mint:** Honan

Date	Mintage	Good	VG	F	VF	XF
ND(1662-1722)	—	5.00	7.00	10.00	15.00	—

同

KM# 318 CASH

Cast Bronze **Series:** Talisman (Poem Cash) **Obv. Inscription:** K'ang-hsi T'ung-pao **Reverse:** Manchu "Tung" at left, Chinese "T'ung at right **Mint:** Tat'ung **Note:** Schjöth #1423.

Date	Mintage	Good	VG	F	VF	XF
ND(1662-1722)	—	1.50	2.25	3.50	5.00	—

福

KM# 319 CASH

Cast Bronze **Series:** Talisman (Poem Cash) **Obv. Inscription:** K'ang-hsi T'ung-pao **Reverse:** Manchu "Fu" at left, Chinese "Fu" at right **Mint:** Fuchou **Note:** Schjöth #1424.

Date	Mintage	Good	VG	F	VF	XF
ND(1662-1722)	—	1.50	2.25	3.50	5.00	—

KM# 320.1 CASH

Cast Bronze **Series:** Talisman (Poem Cash) **Obv. Inscription:** K'ang-hsi T'ung-pao **Reverse:** Manchu "Lin" at left, Chinese "Lin" at right **Mint:** Linch'ing **Note:** Schjöth #1425.

Date	Mintage	Good	VG	F	VF	XF
ND(1662-1722)	—	1.50	2.25	3.50	5.00	—

KM# 320.2 CASH

Cast Bronze **Series:** Talisman (Poem Cash) **Obv. Inscription:** K'ang-hsi T'ung-pao **Reverse:** Manchu "Lin" at left, Chinese "Lin" at right deviating in style **Mint:** Linch'ing

Date	Mintage	Good	VG	F	VF	XF
ND(1662-1722)	—	1.50	2.25	3.50	5.00	—

東

KM# 321 CASH

Cast Bronze **Series:** Talisman (Poem Cash) **Obv. Inscription:** K'ang-hsi T'ung-pao **Reverse:** Manchu "Dung" at left, Chinese "Tung" at right **Mint:** Shantung **Note:** Schjöth #1426.

Date	Mintage	Good	VG	F	VF	XF
ND(1662-1722)	—	1.50	2.25	3.50	5.00	—

江

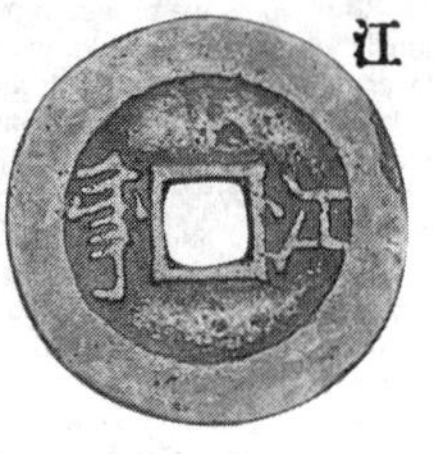

KM# 322 CASH

Cast Bronze **Series:** Talisman (Poem Cash) **Obv. Inscription:** K'ang-hsi T'ung-pao **Reverse:** Manchu "Giyang" at left, Chinese "Chiang" at right **Mint:** Chiangning **Note:** Schjöth #1427.

Date	Mintage	Good	VG	F	VF	XF
ND(1622-1722)	—	1.50	2.25	3.50	5.00	—

宣

KM# 323 CASH

Cast Bronze **Series:** Talisman (Poem Cash) **Obv. Inscription:** K'ang-hsi T'ung-pao **Reverse:** Manchu "Siowan" at left, Chinese "Hsüan" at right **Mint:** Hsüanhua **Note:** Schjöth #1428.

Date	Mintage	Good	VG	F	VF	XF
ND(1622-1722)	—	1.50	2.25	3.50	5.00	—

原

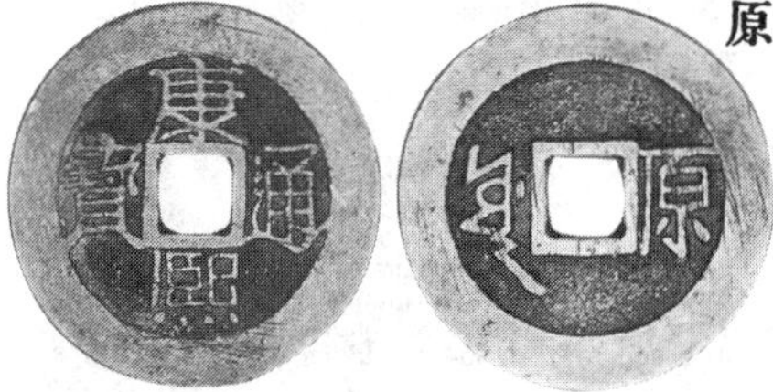

KM# 324 CASH

Cast Bronze **Series:** Talisman (Poem Cash) **Obv. Inscription:** K'ang-hsi T'ung-pao **Reverse:** Manchu "Yuwan" at left, Chinese "Yuan" at right **Mint:** T'aiyüan Fu **Note:** Schjöth #1429.

Date	Mintage	Good	VG	F	VF	XF
ND(1662-1722)	—	1.50	2.25	3.50	5.00	—

蘇

KM# 325 CASH

Cast Bronze **Series:** Talisman (Poem Cash) **Obv. Inscription:** K'ang-hsi T'ung-pao **Reverse:** Manchu "Su" at left, Chinese "Su" at right **Mint:** Soochou **Note:** Schjöth #1430.

Date	Mintage	Good	VG	F	VF	XF
ND(1662-1722)	—	1.50	2.25	3.50	5.00	—

薊

KM# 326 CASH

Cast Bronze **Series:** Talisman (Poem Cash) **Obv. Inscription:** K'ang-hsi T'ung-pao **Reverse:** Manchu "Gi" at left, Chinese "Chi" at right **Mint:** Chichou **Note:** Schjöth #1431.

Date	Mintage	Good	VG	F	VF	XF
ND(1662-1722)	—	1.50	2.25	3.50	5.00	—

昌

KM# 327 CASH

Cast Bronze **Series:** Talisman (Poem Cash) **Obv. Inscription:** K'ang-hsi T'ung-pao **Reverse:** Manchu "Cang" at left, Chinese "Ch'ang" at right **Mint:** Wuch'ang **Note:** Schjöth #1432.

Date	Mintage	Good	VG	F	VF	XF
ND(1662-1722)	—	1.50	2.25	3.50	5.00	—

寧

KM# 328 CASH

Cast Bronze **Series:** Talisman (Poem Cash) **Obv. Inscription:** K'ang-hsi T'ung-pao **Reverse:** Manchu "Ning" at left, Chinese "Ning" at right **Mint:** Ningpo **Note:** Schjöth #1433.

Date	Mintage	Good	VG	F	VF	XF
ND(1662-1722)	—	1.50	2.25	3.50	5.00	—

河

KM# 329 CASH

Cast Bronze **Series:** Talisman (Poem Cash) **Obv. Inscription:** K'ang-hsi T'ung-pao **Reverse:** Manchu "Ho" at left, Chinese "Ho" at right **Mint:** K'aifeng **Note:** Schjöth #1434.

Date	Mintage	Good	VG	F	VF	XF
ND(1662-1722)	—	1.50	2.25	3.50	5.50	—

KM# 330.1 CASH

Cast Bronze, 27 mm. **Series:** Talisman (Poem Cash) **Obv. Inscription:** K'ang-hsi T'ung-pao **Reverse:** Manchu "Nan" at left, Chinese "Nan" at right **Mint:** Ch'angsha **Note:** Schjöth #1435.

Date	Mintage	Good	VG	F	VF	XF
ND(1662-1722)	—	12.50	17.50	25.00	35.00	—

KM# 330.2 CASH

Cast Bronze, 25 mm. **Series:** Talisman (Poem Cash) **Obv. Inscription:** "K'ang-hsi T'ung-pao" **Reverse:** Manchu "Nan" at left, Chinese "Nan" at right **Mint:** Ch'angsha

Date	Mintage	Good	VG	F	VF	XF
ND(1662-1722)	—	3.00	5.00	7.00	10.00	—

Note: The larger 27mm examples were cast during later reigns

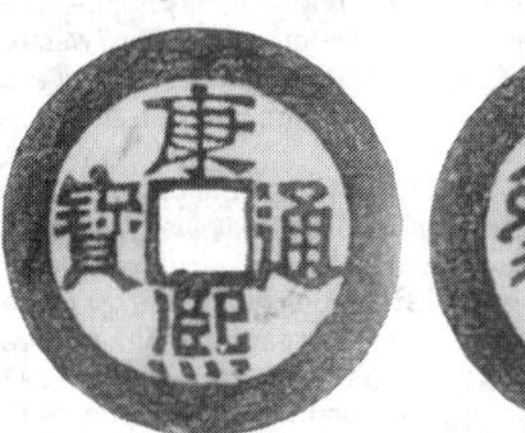

KM# 331.1 CASH

Cast Bronze, 24 mm. **Series:** Talisman (Poem Cash) **Obv. Inscription:** K'ang-hsi T'ung-pao **Reverse:** Manchu "Guwang" at left, Chinese "Kuang" at right **Mint:** Kuangchou **Note:** Schjöth #1436.

Date	Mintage	Good	VG	F	VF	XF
ND(1662-1722)	—	0.70	1.00	1.40	2.00	—

KM# 331.2 CASH

Cast Bronze, 27 mm. **Series:** Talisman (Poem Cash) **Obv. Inscription:** K'ang-hsi T'ung-pao **Reverse:** Large Manchu "Guwang" at left, Chinese "Kuang" at right **Mint:** Kuangchou **Note:** Schjöth #1436.

Date	Mintage	Good	VG	F	VF	XF
ND(1662-1722)	—	70.00	100	140	200	—

Note: The larger 27mm examples were cast during later reigns

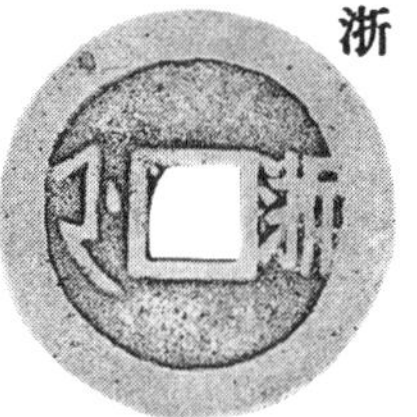

KM# 332 CASH

Cast Bronze, 25 mm. **Series:** Talisman (Poem Cash) **Obv. Inscription:** K'ang-hsi T'ung-pao. **Reverse:** Manchu "Je" at left, Chinese "Chê" at right **Mint:** Chêkiang **Note:** Schjöth #1437.

Date	Mintage	Good	VG	F	VF	XF
ND(1662-1722)	—	1.50	2.25	3.50	5.00	—

KM# 332a CASH

Cast Bronze, 22 mm. **Series:** Talisman (Poem Cash) **Obv. Inscription:** K'ang-hsi T'ung-pao **Reverse:** Small Manchu "Je" at left, Chinese "Chê" at right **Mint:** Chêkiang **Note:** Schjöth #1437.

Date	Mintage	Good	VG	F	VF	XF
ND(1696-1699)	—	1.50	2.25	3.50	5.00	—

KM# 333.1 CASH

Cast Bronze, 24 mm. **Series:** Talisman (Poem Cash) **Obv. Inscription:** "K'ang-hsi T'ung-pao" **Reverse:** Manchu "Tai" at left, Chinese "Tai" at right **Mint:** T'aiwan **Note:** Schjöth #1438.

Date	Mintage	Good	VG	F	VF	XF
ND(1662-1722)	—	5.00	7.00	10.00	15.00	—

KM# 333.2 CASH

Cast Bronze, 27 mm. **Series:** Talisman (Poem Cash) **Obv. Inscription:** "K'ang-hsi T'ung-pao" **Reverse:** Manchu "Tai" at left, Chinese "Tai" at right **Mint:** T'aiwan **Note:** Schjöth #1438. Varieties exist.

Date	Mintage	Good	VG	F	VF	XF
ND(1662-1722)	—	20.00	50.00	80.00	100	—

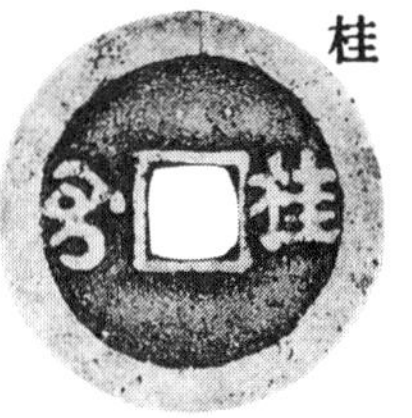

KM# 334 CASH

Cast Bronze **Series:** Talisman (Poem Cash) **Obv. Inscription:** K'ang-hsi T'ung-pao **Reverse:** Manchu "Guway" at left, Chinese "Kuei" at right **Mint:** Kuelin **Note:** Schjöth #1439.

Date	Mintage	Good	VG	F	VF	XF
ND(1662-1722)	—	3.00	5.00	7.00	10.00	—

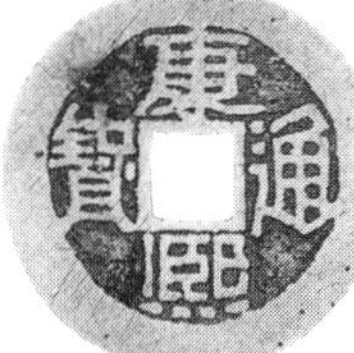

KM# 335.1 CASH

Cast Bronze, 27 mm. **Series:** Talisman (Poem Cash) **Obv. Inscription:** K'ang-hsi T'ung-pao with open "hsi" **Reverse:** Manchu "San" at left, Chinese "Shan" at right **Mint:** Sian **Note:** Schjöth #1440.

Date	Mintage	Good	VG	F	VF	XF
ND(1662-1722)	—	1.50	2.25	3.50	5.00	—

KM# 335.2 CASH

Cast Bronze, 27 mm. **Series:** Talisman (Poem Cash) **Obv. Inscription:** K'ang-hsi T'ung-pao **Reverse:** Manchu "San" at left with extra dot, Chinese "Shan" at right **Mint:** Sian **Note:** Schjöth #1440.

Date	Mintage	Good	VG	F	VF	XF
ND(1662-1722)	—	1.50	2.25	3.50	5.00	—

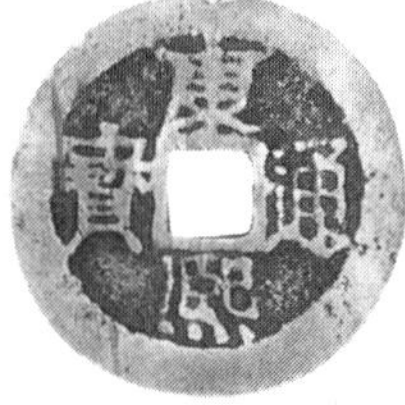

KM# 336 CASH

Cast Bronze, 27 mm. **Series:** Talisman (Poem Cash) **Obv. Inscription:** "K'ang-hsi T'ung-pao" **Reverse:** Manchu "Yôn" at left, Chinese "Yün" at right **Mint:** Yünnan Fu **Note:** Schjöth #1441.

Date	Mintage	Good	VG	F	VF	XF
ND(1662-1722)	—	1.50	2.25	3.50	5.00	—

KM# 337 CASH

Cast Bronze **Series:** Talisman (Poem Cash) **Obv. Inscription:** "K'ang-hsi T'ung-pao" **Reverse:** Manchu "Jiyang" (?) at left, Chinese "Chang" at right **Mint:** Changchou **Note:** Schjöth #1442. See also KM#342.

Date	Mintage	Good	VG	F	VF	XF
ND(1662-1722)	—	1.50	2.25	3.50	5.00	—

KM# A338 CASH

Cast Bronze **Series:** Talisman (Poem Cash) **Obv. Inscription:** K'ang-hsi T'ung-pao **Reverse:** Manchu "Tung" at left, Chinese "T'ung" at right **Mint:** T'ung **Note:** Schjöth #1423.

Date	Mintage	Good	VG	F	VF	XF
ND(1662-1722)	—	0.70	1.00	1.40	2.00	—

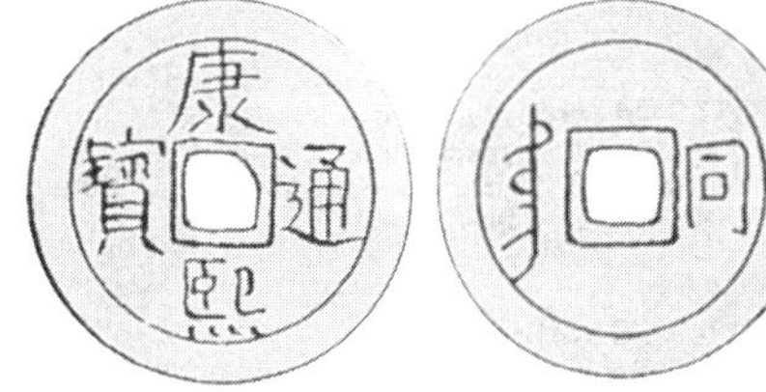

KM# 338 CASH

Cast Bronze **Series:** "Lo han" **Obv. Inscription:** K'ang hsi T'ung-pao **Reverse:** Manchu "Tung" at left, Chinese "T'ung" at right **Mint:** T'ung **Note:** Similar to KM#318. Schjöth #1444.

Date	Mintage	Good	VG	F	VF	XF
ND(1662-1722)	—	5.00	7.00	10.00	15.00	—

KM# 339 CASH

Cast Bronze **Series:** "Lo-han" **Obv. Inscription:** K'ang-hsi T'ung-pao **Reverse:** Manchu "Fu" at left, Chinese "Fu" at right **Mint:** Fuchou **Note:** Similar to KM#319.

Date	Mintage	Good	VG	F	VF	XF
ND(1662-1722)	—	5.00	7.00	10.00	15.00	—

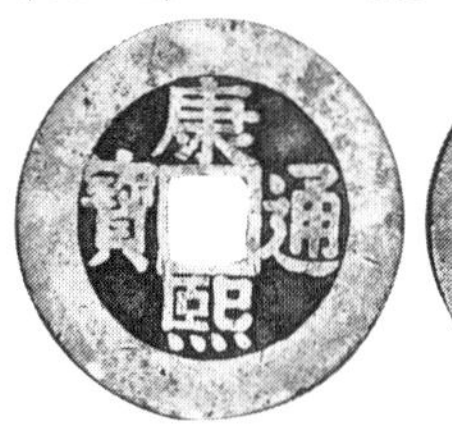

KM# 340 CASH

Cast Brass **Series:** Lo-han **Obv. Inscription:** "K'ang-hsi T'ung-pao" with closed "hsi" **Reverse:** Manchu "Boo-ciowan" **Mint:** Hu-pu Board of Revenue **Note:** Schjöth #1443.

Date	Mintage	Good	VG	F	VF	XF
ND(1662-1722)	—	5.00	7.00	10.00	15.00	—

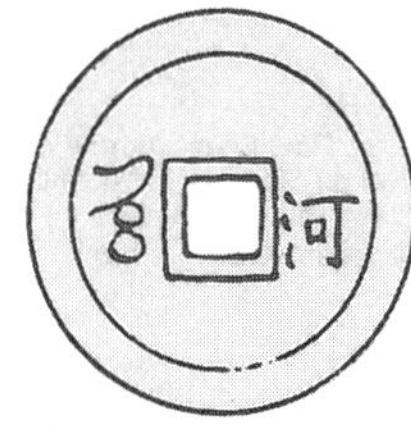

KM# 341 CASH

Cast Brass **Series:** Talisman (Poem Cash) **Obv. Inscription:** "K'ang-hsi T'ung-pao" with closed "hsi" **Reverse:** Manchu "Ho" at left, Chinese "Ho" at right **Mint:** Honan **Note:** Schjöth #1444.

Date	Mintage	Good	VG	F	VF	XF
ND(1662-1722)	—	5.00	7.00	10.00	15.00	—

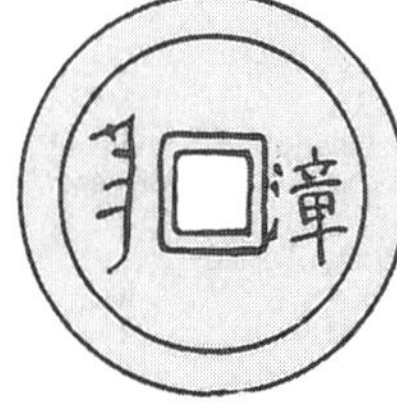

KM# 342 CASH

Cast Brass **Series:** Lo-han **Obv. Inscription:** "K'ang-hsi T'ung-pao" with closed "hsi" **Reverse:** Manchu "Jiyang Chang" at left, Chinese "Chang" at right **Mint:** Changchou **Note:** Schjöth #1445. See also KM#337.

Date	Mintage	Good	VG	F	VF	XF
ND(1662-1722)	—	5.00	7.00	10.00	15.00	—

KM# 345 CASH

Cast Bronze, 28 mm. **Obv. Inscription:** K'ang-hsi T'ung-pao with open hsi **Reverse:** Manchu "Nan" at left, Chinese "Nan" at right **Mint:** Hunan

Date	Mintage	Good	VG	F	VF	XF
ND(1662-1722)	—	85.00	150	220	300	—

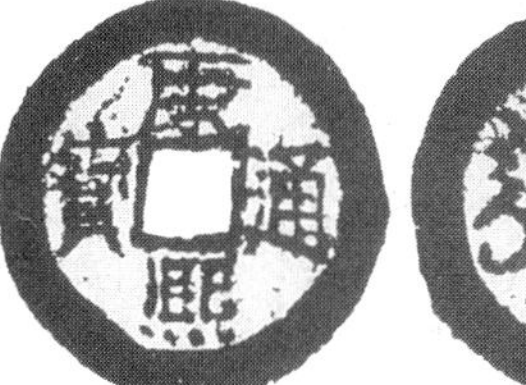

KM# 346 CASH

Cast Bronze **Obv. Inscription:** K'ang-hsi T'ung-pao with open "hsi" **Reverse:** Manchu "Si" at left, Chinese "Hsi" at right **Mint:** Jungho

Date	Mintage	Good	VG	F	VF	XF
ND(1662-1722)	—	300	600	900	1,200	—

KM# 347 CASH

Cast Bronze, 27 mm. **Subject:** K'ang-hsi's 60th Birthday **Obv. Inscription:** K'ang-hsi T'ung-pao with open "hsi" **Reverse:** Chinese "ching" at left, "Ta" at right **Mint:** Fuchou

Date	Mintage	Good	VG	F	VF	XF
ND(1662-1722)	—	65.00	100	140	200	—

KM# 348.1 CASH

Cast Bronze, 26 mm. **Obv. Inscription:** K'ang-hsi T'ung-pao with open "hsi" **Reverse:** Manchu "Fu" at left, Chinese "Fu" at right, "Tzu" (first) above **Mint:** Fuchou

Date	Mintage	Good	VG	F	VF	XF
ND(1662-1722)	—	200	400	600	800	—

KM# 348.2 CASH

Cast Bronze **Obv. Inscription:** K'ang-hsi T'ung-pao with open "hsi" **Reverse:** Manchu "Fu" at left, Chinese "Fu" at right, "Chou" (2nd) above **Mint:** Fuchou

Date	Mintage	Good	VG	F	VF	XF
ND(1662-1722)	—	200	400	600	800	—

KM# 348.3 CASH

Cast Bronze **Obv. Inscription:** K'ang-hsi T'ung-pao with open "hsi" **Reverse:** Manchu "Fu" at left, Chinese "Yin" (3rd) above **Mint:** Fuchou

Date	Mintage	Good	VG	F	VF	XF
ND(1662-1722)	—	200	400	600	800	—

KM# 348.4 CASH

Cast Bronze **Obv. Inscription:** K'ang-hsi T'ung-pao with open "hsi" **Reverse:** Manchu "Fu" at left, Chinese "Si" (6th) above **Mint:** Fuchou

Date	Mintage	Good	VG	F	VF	XF
ND(1662-1722)	—	200	400	600	800	—

KM# 348.7 CASH

Cast Bronze **Obv. Inscription:** K'ang-hsi T'ung-pao with open "hsi" **Reverse:** Manchu "Fu" at left, Chinese "Shen" (9th) above **Mint:** Fuchou

Date	Mintage	Good	VG	F	VF	XF
ND(1662-1722)	—	200	400	600	800	—

KM# 348.8 CASH

Cast Bronze **Obv. Inscription:** K'ang-hsi T'ung-pao with open "hsi" **Reverse:** Manchu "Fu" at left, Chinese "Yu" (10th) above **Mint:** Fuchou

Date	Mintage	Good	VG	F	VF	XF
ND(1662-1722)	—	200	400	600	800	—

KM# 348.9 CASH

Cast Bronze **Obv. Inscription:** K'ang-hsi T'ung-pao with open "hsi" **Reverse:** Manchu "Fu" at left, Chinese "Hai" (12th) above **Mint:** Fuchou

Date	Mintage	Good	VG	F	VF	XF
ND(1662-1722)	—	250	500	750	1,000	—

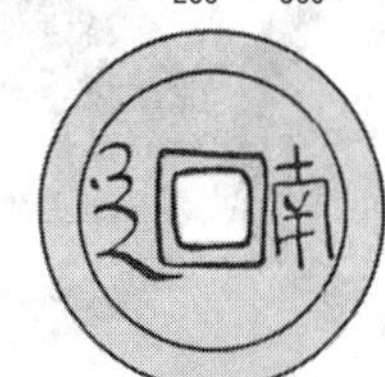

KM# 351 CASH

Cast Red Copper, 23-24 mm. **Series:** Talisman (Poem Cash) **Obv. Inscription:** "K'ang-hsi T'ung-pao" with open "hsi" **Reverse:** Manchu "Nan" at left, Chinese "Nan" at right **Mint:** Ch'angsha **Note:** Size varies. Schjöth #1446.

Date	Mintage	Good	VG	F	VF	XF
ND(1662-1722)	—	12.50	17.50	25.00	35.00	—

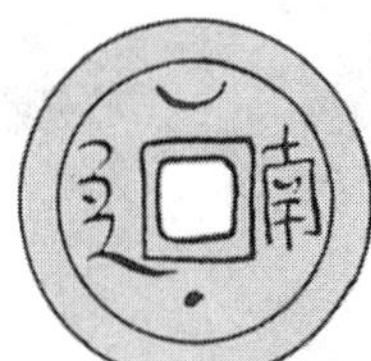

KM# 352 CASH

Cast Red Copper **Obv. Inscription:** "K'ang-hsi T'ung-pao" with open "hsi" **Reverse:** Manchu "Nan" at left, Chinese "Nan" at right, crescent above, dot below **Mint:** Ch'angsha **Note:** Schjöth #1447.

Date	Mintage	Good	VG	F	VF	XF
ND(1662-1722)	—	42.50	70.00	100	150	—

KM# 353 CASH

Cast Red Copper **Obv. Inscription:** "K'ang-hsi T'ung-pao" with open "hsi" **Reverse:** Manchu "Cang" at left, Chinese "Ch'ang" at right. **Mint:** Wuch'ang **Note:** Schjöth #1448.

Date	Mintage	Good	VG	F	VF	XF
ND(1662-1722)	—	1.50	2.25	3.50	5.00	—

廣

KM# 354 CASH

Cast Red Copper **Obv. Inscription:** "K'ang-hsi T'ung-pao" with open "hsi" **Reverse:** Rotated reverse; Manchu "Guwang" at left, Chinese "Kuang" at right **Mint:** Kuangtung **Note:** Schjöth #1449.

Date	Mintage	Good	VG	F	VF	XF
ND(1662-1722)	—	1.50	2.25	3.50	5.00	—

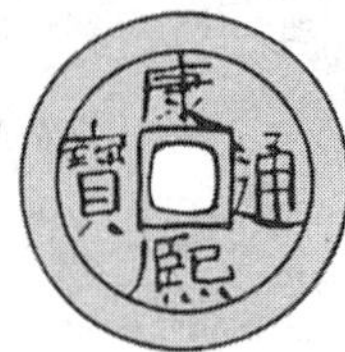

KM# 355 CASH

Cast Red Copper **Obv. Inscription:** "K'ang-hsi T'ung-pao" with open "si" **Rev. Inscription:** "K'ang-hsi T'ung-pao" **Note:** Muling. Schjöth #1450.

Date	Mintage	Good	VG	F	VF	XF
ND(1662-1722)	—	17.50	25.00	35.00	50.00	—

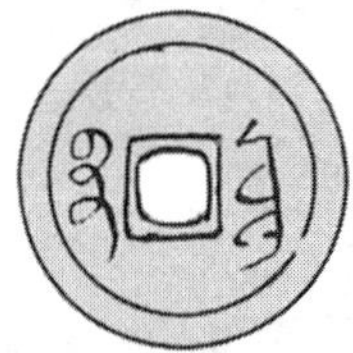

KM# 356 CASH

Cast Red Copper **Obv. Inscription:** "K'ang-hsi T'ung-pao" with open "hsi" **Reverse:** Manchu "Boo-yuwan" **Mint:** Kung-pu Board of Public Works **Note:** Schjöth #1451.

Date	Mintage	Good	VG	F	VF	XF
ND(1662-1722)	—	1.50	2.25	3.50	5.00	—

KM# 357 CASH

Cast Red Copper **Obv. Inscription:** K'ang-hsi T'ung-pao with open "hsi" **Reverse:** Manchu "Boo-kuei" **Mint:** Kueilin **Note:** Reduced size, 19mm. Schjöth #1451.

Date	Mintage	Good	VG	F	VF	XF
ND(1662-1722)	—	1.50	2.25	3.50	5.00	—

KM# A340 CASH

Cast Bronze **Series:** "Lo-han" **Obv. Inscription:** K'ang-hsi T'ung-pao **Reverse:** Manchu "Yuwan" at left, Chinese "Yüan" at right **Mint:** T'aiyüan-fu **Note:** Similar to KM#324.

Date	Mintage	Good	VG	F	VF	XF
ND(1662-1722)	—	5.00	7.00	10.00	15.00	—

KM# B340 CASH

Cast Bronze **Series:** "Lo-han" **Obv. Inscription:** K'ang-hsi T'ung-pao **Reverse:** Manchu "Su" at left, Chinese "Su" at right **Mint:** Soochou **Note:** Similar to KM#325.

Date	Mintage	Good	VG	F	VF	XF
ND(1662-1722)	—	5.00	7.00	10.00	15.00	—

KM# C340 CASH

Cast Bronze **Series:** "Lo-han" **Obv. Inscription:** K'ang-hsi T'ung-pao **Reverse:** Manchu "Gi" at left, chinese "Chi" at right **Mint:** Chichou **Note:** Similar to KM#326.

Date	Mintage	Good	VG	F	VF	XF
ND(1662-1722)	—	5.00	7.00	10.00	15.00	—

KM# D340 CASH

Cast Bronze **Series:** "Lo-han" **Obv. Inscription:** K'ang-hsi T'ung-pao **Reverse:** Manchu "Ning" at left, Chinese "Ning" at right **Mint:** Ningpo **Note:** Similar to KM#328.

Date	Mintage	Good	VG	F	VF	XF
ND(1662-1722)	—	5.00	7.00	10.00	15.00	—

KM# E340 CASH

Cast Bronze **Series:** "Lo-han" **Obv. Inscription:** K'ang-hsi T'ung-pao **Reverse:** Manchu "Nan" at left, Chinese "Nan" at right **Mint:** Ch'angsha **Note:** Similar to KM#330.

Date	Mintage	Good	VG	F	VF	XF
ND(1662-1722)	—	5.00	7.00	10.00	15.00	—

KM# F340 CASH

Cast Bronze **Series:** "Lo-han" **Obv. Inscription:** K'ang-hsi T'ung-pao **Reverse:** Manchu "Guwang" at left, Chinese "Kuang" at right **Mint:** Kuangchou **Note:** Similar to KM#331.

Date	Mintage	Good	VG	F	VF	XF
ND(1662-1722)	—	1.00	1.40	2.00	3.00	—

KM# 312.1a CASH

Cast Bronze **Obverse:** One dot "T'ung" at right **Rev. Inscription:** Manchu Boo-Yuwan **Mint:** Kung-pu Board of Public Works **Note:** Reduced size, corrupt mint product.

Date	Mintage	Good	VG	F	VF	XF
ND(1662-1722)	—	0.15	0.35	0.55	1.00	—

KM# 312.2a CASH

Cast Bronze **Obverse:** 2 dot "T'ung" at right **Rev. Inscription:** Manchu Boo-Yuwan **Mint:** Kung-pu Board of Public Works **Note:** Reduced size, corrupt mint product.

Date	Mintage	Good	VG	F	VF	XF
ND(1662-1722)	—	0.15	0.35	0.55	1.00	—

KM# 312.3 CASH

Cast Bronze, 26 mm. **Obv. Inscription:** "K'ang-hsi Tung-pao" with one dot T'ung **Reverse:** Manchu "Boo-Yuwan" **Note:** Wide rims.

Date	Mintage	Good	VG	F	VF	XF
ND(1662-1722)	—	3.00	6.00	10.00	17.50	—

Yung-chên
Yongzheng
1723-1735

CAST COINAGE

KM# 377 CASH

Cast Brass Or Copper, 27 mm. **Reverse:** Manchu "Boo-cuwan" **Mint:** Chengtu

Date	Mintage	Good	VG	F	VF	XF
ND(1723-35)	—	10.00	22.50	40.00	60.00	—

KM# 366 CASH

Cast Bronze **Obv. Inscription:** Yung-cheng T'ung-pao **Reverse:** Manchu "Boo-cang" **Mint:** Nanch'ang

Date	Mintage	Good	VG	F	VF	XF
ND(1723-1735)	—	4.00	6.00	12.00	20.00	—

KM# 367 CASH

Cast Bronze **Obv. Inscription:** Yung-cheng T'ung-pao **Reverse:** Manchu "Boo-jin" **Mint:** T'aiyüan

Date	Mintage	Good	VG	F	VF	XF
ND(1723-1735)	—	5.00	8.00	15.00	25.00	—

KM# 368 CASH

Cast Bronze, 26.5 mm. **Obv. Inscription:** Yung-cheng T'ung-pao **Reverse:** Manchu "Boo-nan" **Mint:** Ch'angsha

Date	Mintage	Good	VG	F	VF	XF
ND(1723-1735)	—	9.00	15.00	21.00	30.00	—

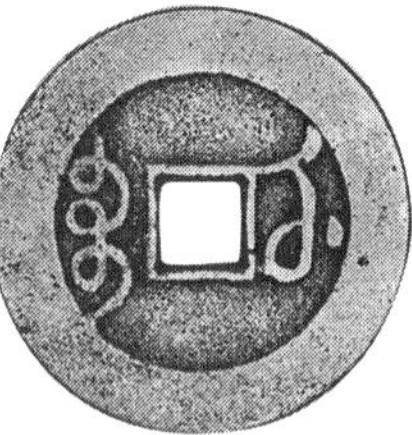

KM# 369 CASH

Cast Bronze **Obv. Inscription:** Yung-cheng T'ung-pao **Reverse:** Manchu "Boo-u" **Mint:** Wuch'ang

Date	Mintage	Good	VG	F	VF	XF
ND(1723-1735)	—	4.00	7.00	10.00	15.00	—

KM# 370 CASH

Cast Bronze **Obv. Inscription:** Yung-cheng T'ung-pao **Reverse:** Manchu "Boo-j'i" **Mint:** Chinan-fu

Date	Mintage	Good	VG	F	VF	XF
ND(1723-1735)	—	5.00	10.00	15.00	30.00	—

KM# 371 CASH

Cast Bronze **Obv. Inscription:** Yung-cheng T'ung-pao **Reverse:** Manchu "Boo-gung" **Mint:** Kungch'ang

Date	Mintage	Good	VG	F	VF	XF
ND(1723-1735)	—	4.00	7.00	10.00	15.00	—

KM# 372 CASH

Cast Bronze **Obv. Inscription:** Yung-cheng T'ung-pao **Reverse:** "Boo-ho" **Mint:** K'aifeng

Date	Mintage	Good	VG	F	VF	XF
ND(1723-1735)	—	5.00	10.00	18.00	35.00	—

KM# 362 CASH

Cast Bronze **Obv. Inscription:** Yung-cheng T'ung-pao **Reverse:** Manchu "Boo-yuwan" **Mint:** Kungpu **Note:** Schjöth #1454.

Date	Mintage	Good	VG	F	VF	XF
ND(1723-1735)	—	1.00	2.00	5.00	10.00	—

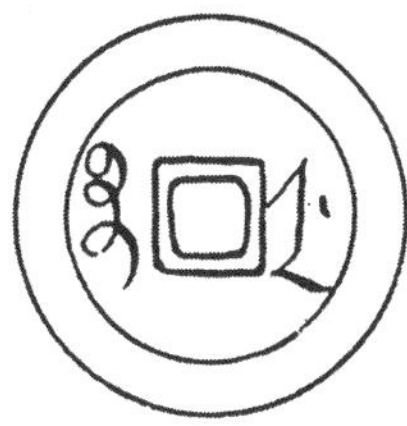

KM# 363 CASH

Cast Bronze, 27 mm. **Obv. Inscription:** Yung-cheng T'ung-pao **Reverse:** Manchu "Boo-je" **Mint:** Hangchou **Note:** Schjöth #1455.

Date	Mintage	Good	VG	F	VF	XF
ND(1723-1735)	—	3.00	5.00	7.00	10.00	—

KM# 364 CASH

Cast Bronze **Obv. Inscription:** Yung-cheng T'ung-pao **Reverse:** Manchu "Boo-yôn" **Mint:** Yünnan-fu **Note:** Schjöth #1456.

Date	Mintage	Good	VG	F	VF	XF
ND(1723-1735)	—	1.25	2.50	4.00	10.00	—

KM# 365 CASH

Cast Bronze **Obv. Inscription:** Yung-cheng T'ung-pao **Reverse:** Manchu "Boo-su" **Mint:** Soochou **Note:** Schjöth #1457.

Date	Mintage	Good	VG	F	VF	XF
ND(1723-1735)	—	3.00	5.00	7.00	10.00	—

KM# 373 CASH

Cast Bronze **Obv. Inscription:** Yung-cheng T'ung-pao **Reverse:** Manchu "Boo-an" **Mint:** Anhui **Note:** Schjöth #1458.

Date	Mintage	Good	VG	F	VF	XF
ND(1723-1735)	—	3.00	5.00	7.00	15.00	—

KM# 375 CASH

Cast Bronze **Obv. Inscription:** Yung-cheng T'ung-pao **Reverse:** Manchu "Boo-kiyan" **Mint:** Kueiyang **Note:** Schjöth #1460.

Date	Mintage	Good	VG	F	VF	XF
ND(1723-1735)	—	2.00	3.50	5.50	10.00	—

KM# 361 CASH

Cast Bronze, 25-27 mm. **Obv. Inscription:** Yung-cheng T'ung-pao **Reverse:** Manchu "Boo-ciowan" **Mint:** Hupu **Note:** Size varies. Schjöth #1453.

Date	Mintage	Good	VG	F	VF	XF
ND(1723-1735)	—	1.00	2.00	3.50	10.00	—

Chien-lung

Qianlong

1736-1795

CAST COINAGE

KM# 389a CASH

Cast Brass Or Copper, 28-30 mm. **Subject:** Shan-lung Commemorative **Obverse:** Type A-2 **Obv. Inscription:** Ch'ien-lung T'ung-pao **Reverse:** Manchu "Boo-ciowan" **Mint:** Hupu **Note:** Size varies. Posthumous issue.

Date	Mintage	Good	VG	F	VF	XF
ND(1736-95)	—	12.50	20.00	28.50	40.00	—

KM# 391 CASH

Cast Brass Or Copper **Subject:** Shan Lung Commemorative **Obverse:** Type A-2 **Obv. Inscription:** Ch'ien-lung T'ung-pao **Reverse:** Manchu "Boo-yuwan" **Mint:** Kungpu

Date	Mintage	Good	VG	F	VF	XF
ND(1736-1795)	—	1.75	3.00	4.25	6.00	—

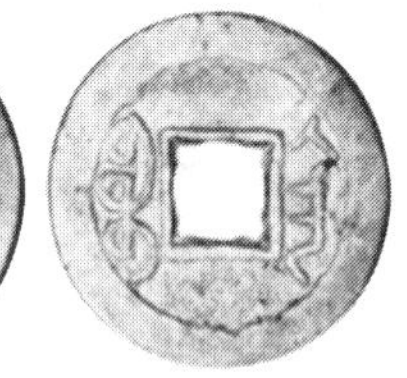

KM# 397 CASH

Cast Brass Or Copper **Obv. Inscription:** Ch'ien-lung T'ung-pao **Reverse:** Type 2 mint mark **Mint:** Sian

Date	Mintage	Good	VG	F	VF	XF
ND(1736-1795)	—	1.25	2.00	2.75	4.00	—

KM# 398 CASH

Cast Brass Or Copper **Obv. Inscription:** Ch'ien-lung T'ung-pao **Reverse:** Type 3 mint mark **Mint:** Sian

Date	Mintage	Good	VG	F	VF	XF
ND(1736-1795)	—	0.85	1.35	2.00	3.00	—

KM# 400a CASH

Lead **Obv. Inscription:** Ch'ien-lung T'ung-pao **Reverse:** Manchu "Boo-fu" **Mint:** Fuchou

Date	Mintage	Good	VG	F	VF	XF
ND(1736-1795)	—	15.00	25.00	35.00	50.00	—

KM# 403 CASH

Cast Brass Or Copper **Obv. Inscription:** Ch'ien-lung T'ung-pao **Reverse:** Manchu "Boo-je", mint mark written differently **Mint:** Hangchou

Date	Mintage	Good	VG	F	VF	XF
ND(1736-1795)	—	0.50	1.00	2.00	3.00	—

KM# 407.3 CASH

Cast Brass Or Copper **Obv. Inscription:** Ch'ien-lung T'ung-pao **Reverse:** Manchu "Boo-u with dot above **Mint:** Wuch'ang

Date	Mintage	Good	VG	F	VF	XF
ND(1736-1795)	—	2.25	3.75	5.50	8.00	—

KM# 407.4 CASH

Cast Brass Or Copper **Obv. Inscription:** Ch'ien-lung T'ung-pao **Reverse:** Manchu "Boo-u" with crescent below **Mint:** Wuch'ang

Date	Mintage	Good	VG	F	VF	XF
ND(1736-1795)	—	3.00	5.00	7.00	10.00	—

KM# 407.5 CASH

Cast Brass Or Copper **Obv. Inscription:** Ch'ien-lung T'ung-pao **Reverse:** Manchu "Boo-u" with solid triangle above **Mint:** Wuch'ang

Date	Mintage	Good	VG	F	VF	XF
ND(1736-1795)	—	—	—	—	—	—

KM# 418 CASH

Cast Brass **Subject:** Shan Lung Commemorative **Obverse:** Type A-2 **Obv. Inscription:** Ch'ien-lung T'ung-pao **Reverse:** Manchu "Boo-kiyan" **Mint:** Kweiyang

Date	Mintage	Good	VG	F	VF	XF
ND(1736-1795)	—	6.00	10.00	14.00	20.00	—

KM# 389 CASH

Cast Brass Or Copper, 24-25 mm. **Subject:** Shan-lung Commemorative **Obverse:** Type A-2 **Obv. Inscription:** Ch'ien-lung T'ung-pao **Reverse:** Manchu "Boo-ciowan" **Mint:** Hupu **Note:** Schjöth #1463. Size varies.

Date	Mintage	Good	VG	F	VF	XF
ND(1736-95)	—	1.50	2.50	3.50	5.00	—
ND(1736-95)	—	1.50	2.50	3.50	5.00	—

KM# 387.1 CASH

Cast Brass Or Copper **Obv. Inscription:** Ch'ien-lung T'ung-pao **Reverse:** Manchu "Boo-ciowan" **Mint:** Hupu **Note:** Schjöth #1464.

Date	Mintage	Good	VG	F	VF	XF
ND(1736-1795)	—	0.15	0.25	0.35	0.50	—

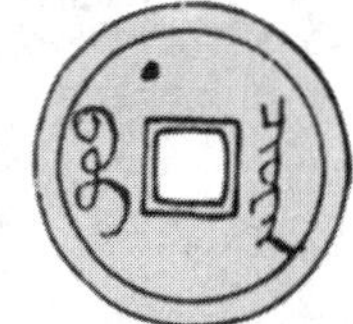

KM# 387.2 CASH

Cast Brass Or Copper **Obv. Inscription:** Ch'ien-lung T'ung-pao **Reverse:** Manchu "Boo-ciowan", dot at upper left **Mint:** Hupu **Note:** Schjöth #1465.

Date	Mintage	Good	VG	F	VF	XF
ND(1736-1795)	—	1.50	2.50	3.50	5.00	—

KM# 394 CASH

Cast Brass Or Copper **Obverse:** Type A-1 **Obv. Inscription:** Ch'ien-lung T'ung-pao **Reverse:** Manchu "Boo-j'i" **Mint:** Paoting **Note:** Schjöth #1467.

Date	Mintage	Good	VG	F	VF	XF
ND(1736-1795)	—	0.50	0.90	1.35	2.00	—

KM# 396 CASH

Cast Brass Or Copper **Obverse:** Type A-1 **Obv. Inscription:** Ch'ien-lung T'ung-pao **Reverse:** Type 1 mint mark, Manchu "Boo-san" **Mint:** Sian **Note:** Schjöth #1468.

Date	Mintage	Good	VG	F	VF	XF
ND(1736-1795)	—	0.85	1.35	2.00	3.00	—

KM# 400 CASH

Cast Brass Or Copper **Obv. Inscription:** Ch'ien-lung T'ung-pao **Reverse:** Manchu "Boo-fu" **Mint:** Fuchou **Note:** Schjöth #1469.

Date	Mintage	Good	VG	F	VF	XF
ND(1736-1795)	—	0.85	1.35	2.00	3.00	—

KM# 402 CASH

Cast Brass Or Copper **Obv. Inscription:** Ch'ien-lung T'ung-pao **Reverse:** Manchu "Boo-je" **Mint:** Hangchou **Note:** Schjöth #1470.

Date	Mintage	Good	VG	F	VF	XF
ND(1736-1795)	—	0.50	0.85	1.35	2.00	—

KM# 405 CASH

Cast Brass Or Copper **Obv. Inscription:** Ch'ien-lung T'ung-pao **Reverse:** Manchu "Boo-su" **Mint:** Kiangsu **Note:** Schjöth #1471. Minor varieties of this mint mark exist.

Date	Mintage	Good	VG	F	VF	XF
ND(1736-1795)	—	0.85	1.35	2.00	3.00	—

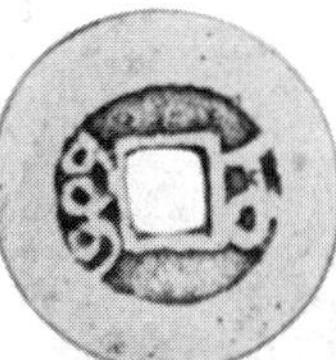

KM# 407.1 CASH

Cast Brass Or Copper **Obverse:** Type A-1 **Obv. Inscription:** Ch'ien-lung T'ung-pao **Reverse:** Manchu "Boo-u" **Mint:** Wuch'ang **Note:** Schjöth #1472-73. Minor varieties of this mint mark exist.

Date	Mintage	Good	VG	F	VF	XF
ND(1736-1795)	—	0.30	0.50	0.70	1.00	—

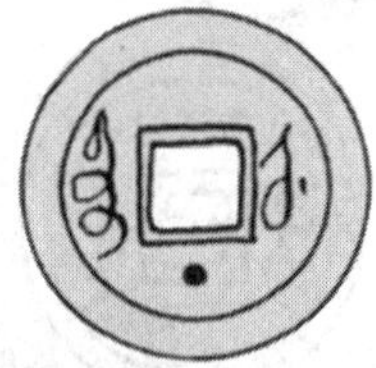

KM# 407.2 CASH

Cast Brass Or Copper **Obv. Inscription:** Ch'ien-lung T'ung-pao **Reverse:** Manchu "Boo-u" with large dot below **Mint:** Wuch'ang **Note:** Schjöth #1474.

Date	Mintage	Good	VG	F	VF	XF
ND(1736-1795)	—	2.25	3.75	5.50	8.00	—

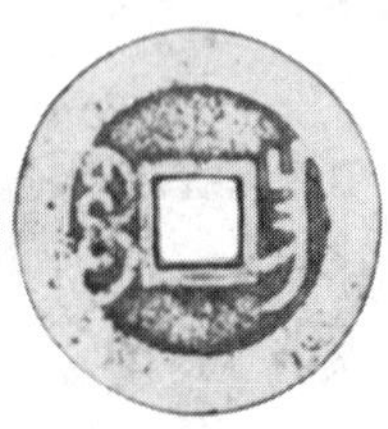

KM# 409 CASH

Cast Brass Or Copper **Obv. Inscription:** Ch'ien-lung T'ung-pao **Reverse:** Manchu "Boo-cang" **Mint:** Nanch'ang **Note:** Schjöth #1475.

Date	Mintage	Good	VG	F	VF	XF
ND(1736-1795)	—	0.50	0.90	1.35	2.00	—

KM# 411 CASH

Cast Brass Or Copper **Obv. Inscription:** Ch'ien-lung T'ung-pao **Reverse:** Manchu "Boo-gui" **Mint:** Kuelin **Note:** Schjöth #1476.

Date	Mintage	Good	VG	F	VF	XF
ND(1736-1795)	—	0.40	0.70	1.00	1.50	—

KM# 413 CASH

Cast Brass Or Copper **Obv. Inscription:** Ch'ien-lung T'ung-pao **Reverse:** Manchu "Boo-guang" **Mint:** Kuangtung **Note:** Schjöth #1477.

Date	Mintage	Good	VG	F	VF	XF
ND(1736-1795)	—	0.85	1.35	2.00	3.00	—

KM# 415 CASH

Cast Brass Or Copper **Obv. Inscription:** Ch'ien-lung T'ung-pao **Reverse:** Manchu "Boo-kian" **Mint:** Kweiyang **Note:** Schjöth #1478.

Date	Mintage	Good	VG	F	VF	XF
ND(1736-1795)	—	0.65	1.10	1.65	2.50	—

KM# 420 CASH

Cast Brass **Obv. Inscription:** Ch'ien-lung T'ung-pao **Reverse:** Manchu "Boo-yôn" **Mint:** Yünnan-fu **Note:** Schjöth #1480.

Date	Mintage	Good	VG	F	VF	XF
ND(1736-1795)	—	0.40	0.70	1.00	1.50	—

KM# 422 CASH

Cast Brass **Obverse:** Type A-1 **Obv. Inscription:** Ch'ien-lung T'ung-pao **Reverse:** Manchu "Boo-nan" **Mint:** Ch'angsha **Note:** Schjöth #1481.

Date	Mintage	Good	VG	F	VF	XF
ND(1736-1795)	—	0.85	1.35	2.00	3.00	—

KM# 423 CASH

Cast Brass **Obv. Inscription:** Ch'ien-lung T'ung-pao **Reverse:** Manchu "Boo" at left, long thin Manchu "nan" at right **Mint:** Ch'angsha **Note:** Schjöth #1482.

Date	Mintage	Good	VG	F	VF	XF
ND(1736-1795)	—	0.85	1.35	2.00	3.00	—

KM# 424 CASH

Cast Brass, 24 mm. **Obv. Inscription:** Ch'ien-lung T'ung-pao **Reverse:** Manchu "Boo" at left, Manchu "nan" at right **Mint:** Ch'angsha **Note:** Schjöth #1483.

Date	Mintage	Good	VG	F	VF	XF
ND(1736-1795)	—	0.85	1.35	2.00	3.00	—

KM# 427 CASH

Cast Brass **Obv. Inscription:** Ch'ien-lung T'ung-pao **Reverse:** Manchu "Boo-cuwan" **Mint:** Chengtu **Note:** Schjöth #1484.

Date	Mintage	Good	VG	F	VF	XF
ND(1736-1795)	—	0.40	0.70	1.00	1.50	—

KM# 430 CASH

Cast Brass **Obv. Inscription:** Ch'ien-lung T'ung-pao **Reverse:** Manchu "Boo-jin" **Mint:** T'aiyüan-fu **Note:** Schjöth #1485.

Date	Mintage	Good	VG	F	VF	XF
ND(1736-1795)	—	0.85	1.35	2.00	3.00	—

KM# 433 CASH

Cast Brass **Obv. Inscription:** Ch'ien-lung T'ung-pao **Reverse:** Manchu "Boo-j'i" **Mint:** Chinan-fu **Note:** Schjöth #1486.

Date	Mintage	Good	VG	F	VF	XF
ND(1736-1795)	—	7.50	12.50	17.50	25.00	—

KM# 388 CASH

Cast Brass Or Copper, 28-30 mm. **Obv. Inscription:** Ch'ien-lung T'ung-pao **Reverse:** Manchu "Boo-ciowan" **Mint:** Hupu **Note:** Size varies.

Date	Mintage	Good	VG	F	VF	XF
ND(1736-1795)	—	12.00	20.00	28.00	40.00	—

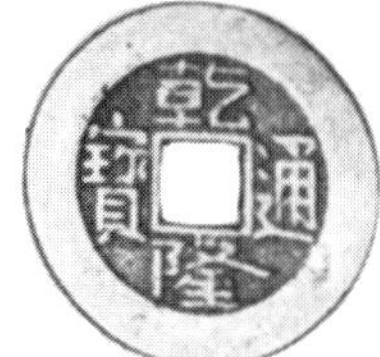

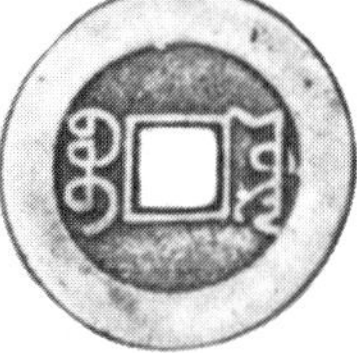

KM# 390 CASH

Cast Brass Or Copper, 21-27 mm. **Obverse:** Type A-1 **Obv. Inscription:** Ch'ien-lung T'ung-pao **Reverse:** Manchu "Boo-yuwan" **Mint:** Kungpu **Note:** Size varies. Schjöth #1466.

Date	Mintage	Good	VG	F	VF	XF
ND(1736-1795)	—	0.15	0.25	0.35	0.50	—

KM# 435 CASH

Cast Brass **Obv. Inscription:** Ch'ien-lung T'ung-pao **Reverse:** Manchu "Boo-tai" **Mint:** T'aiwan **Note:** Schjöth #1487. Mintage of 10 million cast at Fuchow for army pay on Taiwan.

Date	Mintage	Good	VG	F	VF	XF
ND(1739-1740)	—	10.00	20.00	40.00	60.00	—

Chia-ch'ing
1796-1820
CAST COINAGE

KM# 440.4 CASH

Cast Brass **Obv. Inscription:** Chia-ch'ing T'ung-pao **Reverse:** Manchu inscription with dot above **Rev. Inscription:** Boo-ciowan **Mint:** Board of Revenue

Date	Mintage	Good	VG	F	VF	XF
ND(1796-1820)	—	2.00	3.00	4.00	5.00	6.00

KM# 470.4 CASH

Cast Brass, 21.2 mm. **Obv. Inscription:** Chia-ch'ing T'ung-pao **Reverse:** Manchu "Boo-je" **Mint:** Hangchow **Note:** Normal rims.

Date	Mintage	Good	VG	F	VF	XF
ND(1796-1820)	—	0.50	0.90	1.35	2.00	—

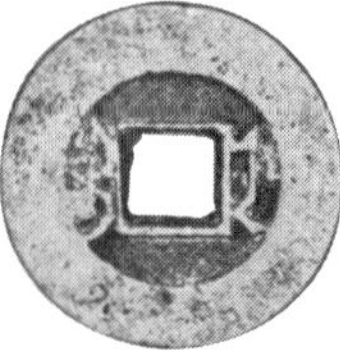

KM# 470.3 CASH

Cast Brass, 23.5 mm. **Obv. Inscription:** Chia-ch'ing T'ung-pao **Reverse:** Small mint mark, Manchu "Boo-je" **Mint:** Hangchow **Note:** Wide rims.

Date	Mintage	Good	VG	F	VF	XF
ND(1796-1820)	—	1.00	1.75	2.75	4.00	—

KM# 440.1 CASH

Cast Brass **Obv. Inscription:** Chia-ch'ing T'ung-pao **Reverse:** Manchu "Boo-ciowan" **Mint:** Hu-pu Board of Revenue

Date	Mintage	Good	VG	F	VF	XF
ND(1796-1820)	—	0.20	0.35	0.50	0.75	—

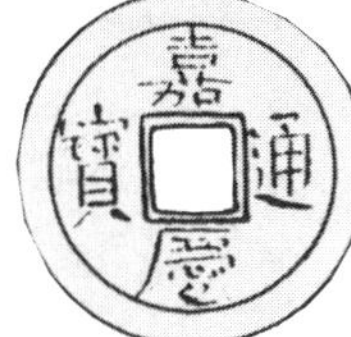

KM# 440.2 CASH

Cast Brass **Obv. Inscription:** Chia-ch'ing T'ung-pao **Reverse:** Manchu Boo-ciowan" with dot at upper left **Mint:** Hupu **Note:** Schjöth #1489.

Date	Mintage	Good	VG	F	VF	XF
ND(1796-1820)	—	2.00	3.00	4.00	5.00	6.00

KM# 440.3 CASH

Cast Brass **Obv. Inscription:** Chia-ch'ing T'ung-pao **Reverse:** Manchu "Boo-ciowan" with dot below **Mint:** Hu-pu Board of Revenue

Date	Mintage	Good	VG	F	VF	XF
ND(1796-1820)	—	2.00	3.00	4.00	5.00	6.00

KM# 441 CASH

Cast Brass, 28-30 mm. **Obv. Inscription:** Chia-ch'ing T'ung-pao **Reverse:** Manchu "Boo-ciowan" **Mint:** Hu-pu Board of Revenue **Note:** Size varies.

Date	Mintage	Good	VG	F	VF	XF
ND(1796-1820)	—	10.00	15.00	20.00	30.00	40.00

KM# 442.1 CASH

Cast Brass **Obv. Inscription:** Chia-ch'ing T'ung-pao **Reverse:** Manchu "Boo-yuwan" **Mint:** Kungpu **Note:** Schjöth #1490.

Date	Mintage	Good	VG	F	VF	XF
ND(1796-1820)	—	0.20	0.30	0.50	0.75	1.00

KM# 442.2 CASH

Cast Brass, 24 mm. **Obv. Inscription:** Chia-ch'ing T'ung-pao **Reverse:** Manchu "Boo-yuwan" with dot above **Mint:** Kungpu **Note:** Schjöth #1489.

Date	Mintage	Good	VG	F	VF	XF
ND(1796-1820)	—	2.00	3.00	4.00	5.00	6.00

KM# 442.3 CASH

Cast Brass **Obv. Inscription:** Chia-ch'ing T'ung-pao **Reverse:** Manchu "Boo-yuwan" with dot below **Mint:** Kungpu **Note:** Schjöth #1491.

Date	Mintage	Good	VG	F	VF	XF
ND(1796-1820)	—	2.00	3.00	4.00	5.00	6.00

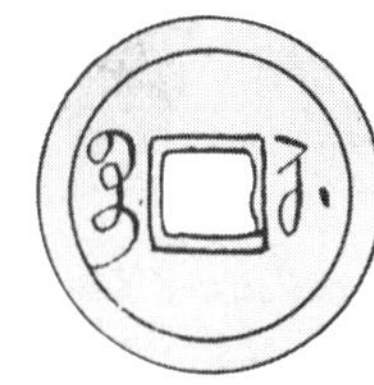

KM# 446 CASH

Cast Brass **Obv. Inscription:** Chia-ch'ing T'ung-pao **Reverse:** Manchu "Boo-su" **Mint:** Soochow **Note:** Schjöth #1492.

Date	Mintage	Good	VG	F	VF	XF
ND(1796-1820)	—	0.85	1.35	2.00	3.00	—

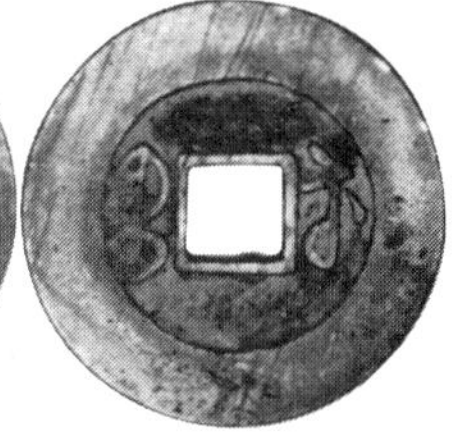

KM# 447a CASH

Cast Brass, 29 mm. **Obv. Inscription:** Chia-ch'ing T'ung-pao **Note:** Wide rims.

Date	Mintage	Good	VG	F	VF	XF
ND(1796-1820)	—	35.00	60.00	85.00	120	—

KM# 449 CASH

Cast Brass **Obv. Inscription:** Chia-ch'ing T'ung-pao **Reverse:** Manchu "Boo-guwang" **Mint:** Kuangtung **Note:** Schjöth #1493.

Date	Mintage	Good	VG	F	VF	XF
ND(1796-1820)	—	0.85	1.35	2.00	3.00	—

KM# 449a CASH

Cast Iron **Obv. Inscription:** Chia-ch'ing T'ung-pao **Reverse:** Manchu "Boo-guwang" **Mint:** Kuang

Date	Mintage	Good	VG	F	VF	XF
ND(1796-1820) Rare	—	—	—	—	—	—

KM# 451 CASH

Cast Brass **Obv. Inscription:** Chia-ch'ing T'ung-pao **Reverse:** Manchu "Boo-nan" **Mint:** Ch'angsha **Note:** Schjöth #1494.

Date	Mintage	Good	VG	F	VF	XF
ND(1796-1820)	—	1.50	2.50	3.50	5.00	—

KM# 453.1 CASH

Cast Brass **Obverse:** Type A **Obv. Inscription:** Chia-ch'ing T'ung-pao **Reverse:** Manchu "Boo-yôn" **Mint:** Yünnan-fu **Note:** Schjöth #1495.

Date	Mintage	Good	VG	F	VF	XF
ND(1796-1820)	—	0.40	0.70	1.00	1.50	—

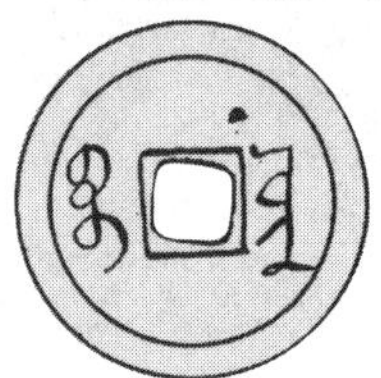

KM# 453.2 CASH

Cast Brass **Obv. Inscription:** Chia-ch'ing T'ung-pao **Reverse:** Manchu "Boo-yôn" with dot at upper right **Mint:** Yünnan-fu **Note:** Schjöth #1496.

Date	Mintage	Good	VG	F	VF	XF
ND(1796-1820)	—	1.25	2.00	2.75	4.00	—

KM# 453.3 CASH

Cast Brass **Obv. Inscription:** Chia-ch'ing T'ung-pao **Reverse:** Manchu "Boo-yôn" with crescent above **Mint:** Yünnan-fu **Note:** Schjöth #1497.

Date	Mintage	Good	VG	F	VF	XF
ND(1796-1820)	—	1.75	3.00	4.25	6.00	—

KM# 455 CASH

Cast Brass **Obverse:** Type A-1 **Obv. Inscription:** Chia-ch'ing T'ung-pao **Reverse:** Type 1 mint mark, Manchu "Boo-dung" **Mint:** Tungch'uan **Note:** Schjöth #1498.

Date	Mintage	Good	VG	F	VF	XF
ND(1796-1820)	—	1.75	3.00	4.25	6.00	—

KM# 456 CASH

Cast Brass **Obv. Inscription:** Chia-ch'ing T'ung-pao **Reverse:** Type 2 mint mark, Manchu "Boo-dung" **Mint:** Tungch'uan

Date	Mintage	Good	VG	F	VF	XF
ND(1796-1820)	—	10.00	17.50	25.00	35.00	—

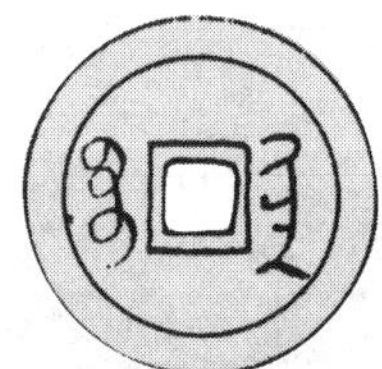

KM# 458.1 CASH

Cast Brass **Obv. Inscription:** Chia-ch'ing T'ung-pao **Reverse:** Manchu "Boo-kiyan" **Mint:** Kweiyang **Note:** Schjöth #1499.

Date	Mintage	Good	VG	F	VF	XF
ND(1796-1820)	—	1.25	2.00	2.75	4.00	—

KM# 458.2 CASH

Cast Brass **Obv. Inscription:** Chia-ch'ing T'ung-pao **Reverse:** Manchu "Boo-kiyan" with dot above **Mint:** Kweiyang

Date	Mintage	Good	VG	F	VF	XF
ND(1796-1820)	—	1.50	2.50	3.50	5.00	—

KM# 460 CASH

Cast Brass **Obv. Inscription:** Chia-ch'ing T'ung-pao **Reverse:** Manchu "Boo-kiyan" with Chinese "Êrh" **Mint:** Kweiyang

Date	Mintage	Good	VG	F	VF	XF
ND(1796-1820)	—	7.50	12.50	17.50	25.00	—

KM# 462 CASH

Cast Brass **Obv. Inscription:** Chia-ch'ing T'ung-pao **Reverse:** Wide Manchu "Boo-fu" **Mint:** Foochou **Note:** Schjöth #1500.

Date	Mintage	Good	VG	F	VF	XF
ND(1796-1820)	—	0.85	1.35	2.00	3.00	—

KM# 463 CASH

Cast Brass **Obv. Inscription:** Chia-ch'ing T'ung-pao **Reverse:** Thin Manchu "Boo-fu" at right **Mint:** Fuchou

Date	Mintage	Good	VG	F	VF	XF
ND(1796-1820)	—	1.75	3.00	4.25	6.00	—

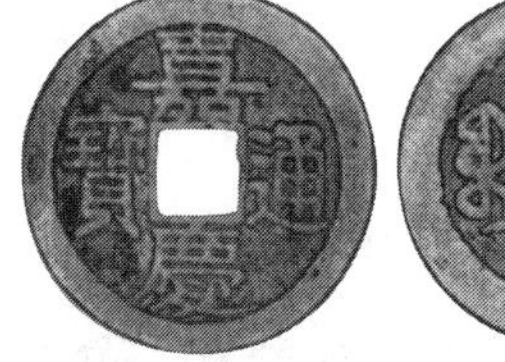

KM# 464 CASH

Cast Brass **Obv. Inscription:** Chia-ch'ing T'ung-pao **Reverse:** Different Manchu "Boo-fu" at right **Mint:** Fuchou

Date	Mintage	Good	VG	F	VF	XF
ND(1796-1820)	—	1.50	2.50	3.50	5.00	—

KM# 465 CASH

Cast Brass, 25-26 mm. **Obverse:** Type A **Obv. Inscription:** Chia-ch'ing T'ung-pao **Reverse:** Manchu Boo-jiyen **Mint:** Chih **Note:** Size varies. Schjöth #1501.

Date	Mintage	Good	VG	F	VF	XF
ND(1796-1820)	—	0.85	1.35	2.00	3.00	—

KM# 466 CASH

Cast Brass, 31 mm. **Obv. Inscription:** Chia-ch'ing T'ung-pao **Reverse:** Manchu "Boo-j'i" **Mint:** Chihli

Date	Mintage	Good	VG	F	VF	XF
ND(1796-1820)	—	60.00	100	140	200	—

KM# 468 CASH

Cast Brass **Obverse:** Type A **Obv. Inscription:** Chia-ch'ing T'ung-pao **Reverse:** Manchu "Boo-san" **Mint:** Sian **Note:** Schjöth #1502.

Date	Mintage	Good	VG	F	VF	XF
ND(1796-1820)	—	2.25	3.75	5.50	8.00	—

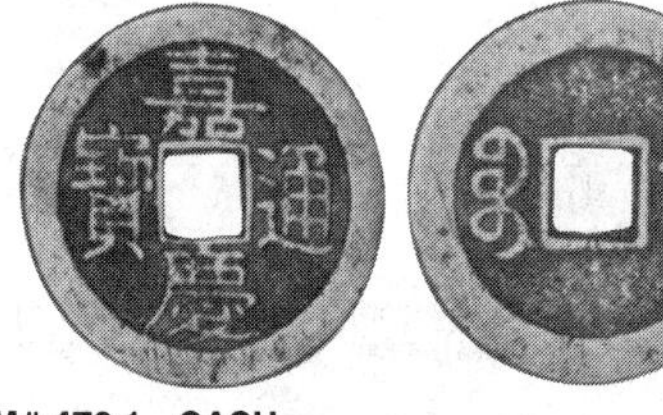

KM# 470.1 CASH

Cast Brass, 25 mm. **Obv. Inscription:** Chia-ch'ing T'ung-pao **Reverse:** Large mint mark, Manchu "Boo-je" **Mint:** Hangchow **Note:** Schjöth #1503.

Date	Mintage	Good	VG	F	VF	XF
ND(1796-1820)	—	0.50	0.90	1.35	2.00	—

KM# 470.2 CASH

Cast Brass **Obv. Inscription:** Chia-ch'ing T'ung-pao **Reverse:** Manchu "Boo-je" with dot at bottom **Mint:** Hangchow

Date	Mintage	Good	VG	F	VF	XF
ND(1796-1820)	—	3.50	6.00	8.50	12.00	—

KM# 470a CASH

Cast Iron **Obv. Inscription:** Chia-ch'ing T'ung-pao **Reverse:** Manchu "Boo-je" **Mint:** Hangchow

Date	Mintage	Good	VG	F	VF	XF
ND(1796-1820) Rare	—	—	—	—	—	—

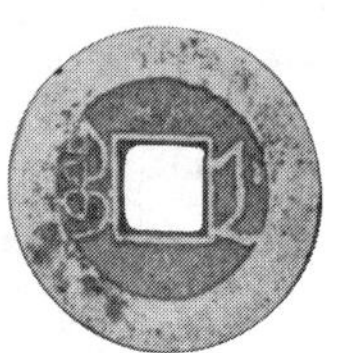

KM# 471 CASH

Cast Brass **Obv. Inscription:** Chia-ch'ing T'ung-pao **Reverse:** Manchu "Boo-je" with small mint mark and wide rims **Mint:** Hangchow

Date	Mintage	Good	VG	F	VF	XF
ND(1796-1820)	—	0.50	0.90	1.35	2.00	—

KM# 474.1 CASH

Cast Brass **Obv. Inscription:** Chia-ch'ing T'ung-pao **Reverse:** Manchu "Boo-u" **Mint:** Wuch'ang **Note:** Schjöth #1504.

Date	Mintage	Good	VG	F	VF	XF
ND(1796-1820)	—	1.75	3.00	4.25	6.00	—

KM# 474.2 CASH

Cast Brass **Obv. Inscription:** Chia-ch'ing T'ung-pao **Reverse:** Manchu "Wu" with circle above **Mint:** Wuch'ang **Note:** Schjöth #1505.

Date	Mintage	Good	VG	F	VF	XF
ND(1796-1820)	—	4.00	6.50	9.00	12.00	—

KM# 474.3 CASH

Cast Brass **Obv. Inscription:** Chia-ch'ing T'ung-pao **Reverse:** Manchu "Boo-u" with crescent above, dot below **Mint:** Wuch'ang **Note:** Schjöth #1506.

Date	Mintage	Good	VG	F	VF	XF
ND(1796-1820)	—	4.00	7.00	10.00	15.00	—

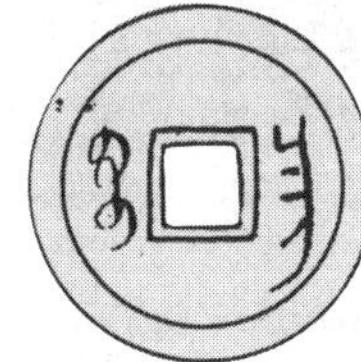

KM# 476.1 CASH

Cast Brass **Obv. Inscription:** Chia-ch'ing T'ung-pao **Reverse:** Manchu "Boo-cang" **Mint:** Nanch'ang **Note:** Schjöth #1507.

Date	Mintage	Good	VG	F	VF	XF
ND(1796-1820)	—	0.50	0.90	1.35	2.00	—

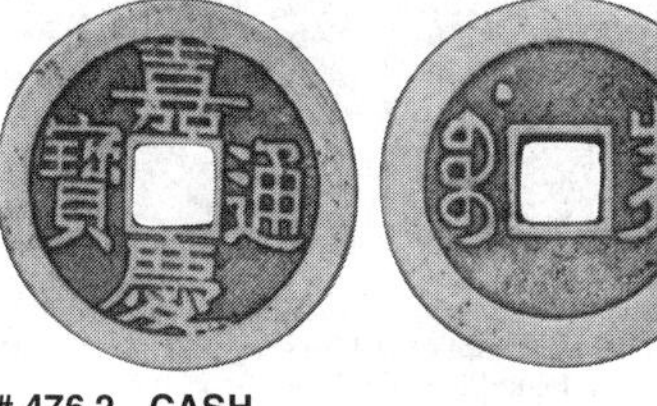

KM# 476.2 CASH

Cast Brass **Obv. Inscription:** Chia-ch'ing T'ung-pao **Reverse:** Manchu "Boo-cang" with dot in upper left corner **Mint:** Nanch'ang **Note:** Schjöth #1508 variation.

Date	Mintage	Good	VG	F	VF	XF
ND(1796-1820)	—	3.00	5.00	7.00	10.00	—

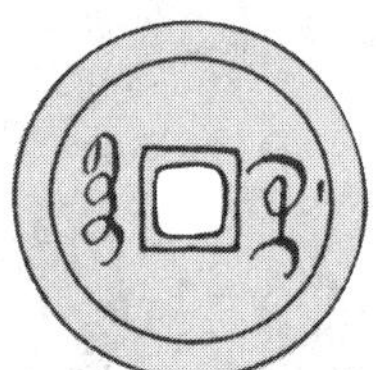

KM# 478 CASH

Cast Brass **Obv. Inscription:** Chia-ch'ing T'ung-pao **Reverse:** Manchu "Boo-qui" **Mint:** Kuelin **Note:** Schjöth #1509.

Date	Mintage	Good	VG	F	VF	XF
ND(1796-1820)	—	0.75	1.00	1.75	3.00	—

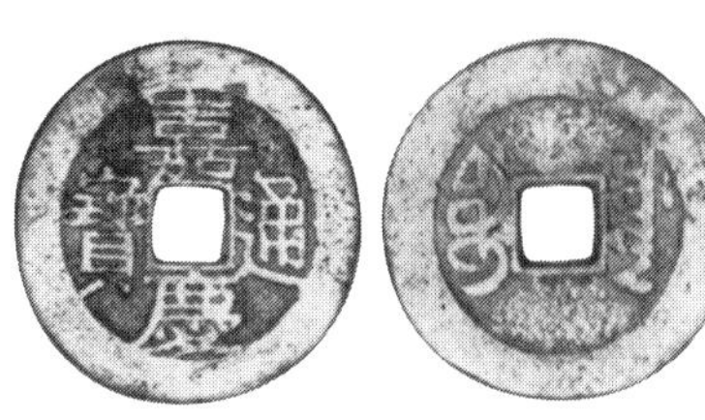

KM# 480 CASH

Cast Brass **Obv. Inscription:** Chia-ch'ing T'ung-pao **Reverse:** Manchu "Boo-cuwan" **Mint:** Chengtu **Note:** Schjöth #1510.

Date	Mintage	Good	VG	F	VF	XF
ND(1796-1820)	—	1.00	1.75	3.00	4.00	—

KM# 482 CASH

Cast Brass **Obv. Inscription:** Chia-ch'ing T'ung-pao **Reverse:** Manchu "Boo-jin" **Mint:** T'aiyüan **Note:** Schjöth #1511.

Date	Mintage	Good	VG	F	VF	XF
ND(1796-1820)	—	1.25	2.00	2.75	4.00	—

PATTERNS

Including off metal castings

KM#	Date	Mintage	Identification	Mkt Val

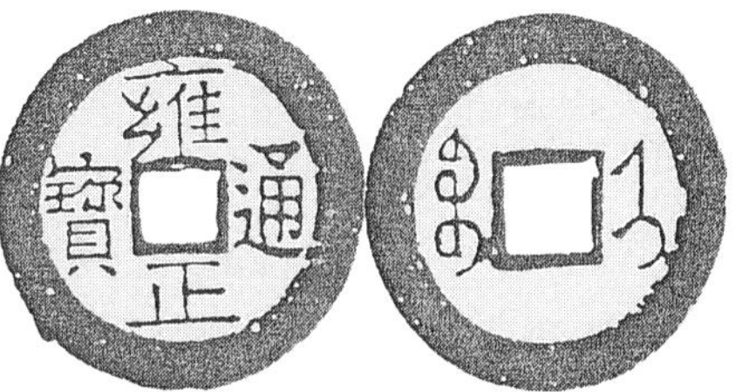

Pn16	ND(1723)	—	Cash. Cast Bronze. "Boo-ji".	300

Pn17	ND(1723)	—	Cash. Cast Bronze. Manchu and Chinese "Ning".	400

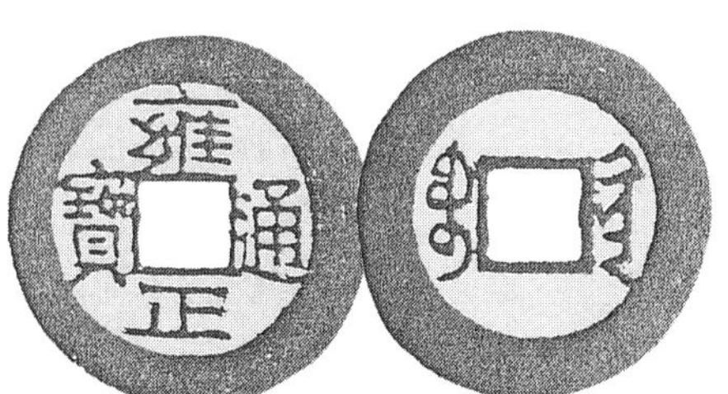

Pn18	ND(1723)	—	2 Cash. Cast Bronze. "Boo-giyan".	500

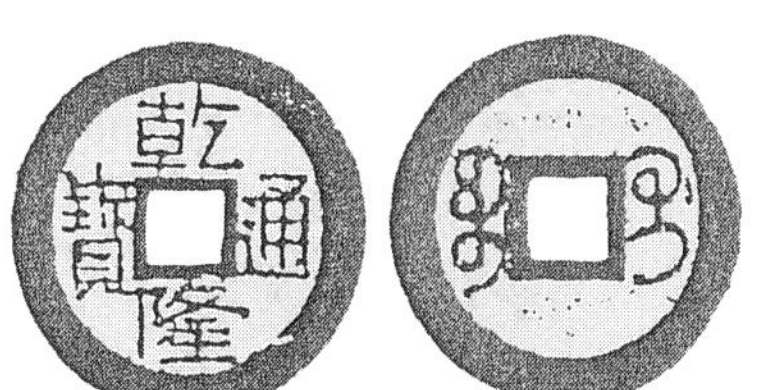

Pn20	ND(1736)	—	Cash. Cast Bronze. "Boo-gui".	80.00

KM#	Date	Mintage	Identification	Mkt Val

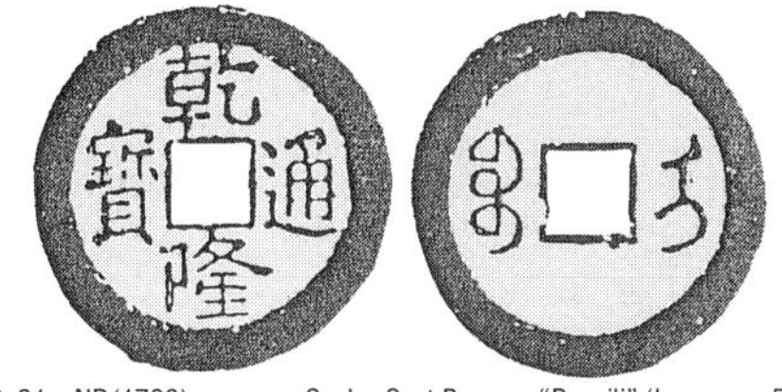

Pn21	ND(1736)	—	Cash. Cast Bronze. "Boo-ili" (by Hu-pu).	500

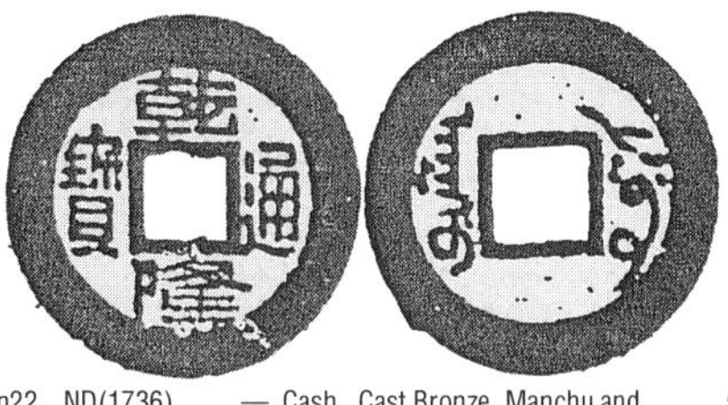

Pn22	ND(1736)	—	Cash. Cast Bronze. Manchu and Turki "Aksu" (by Hu-pu).	500

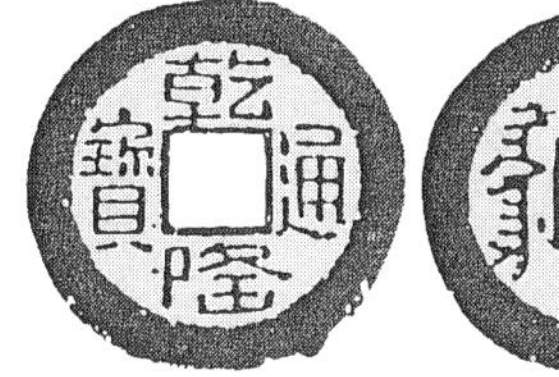

Pn23	ND(1736)	—	Cash. Cast Bronze. Manchu and Turki "Kashgar" (by Hu-pu). Cr#32-1.	1,000

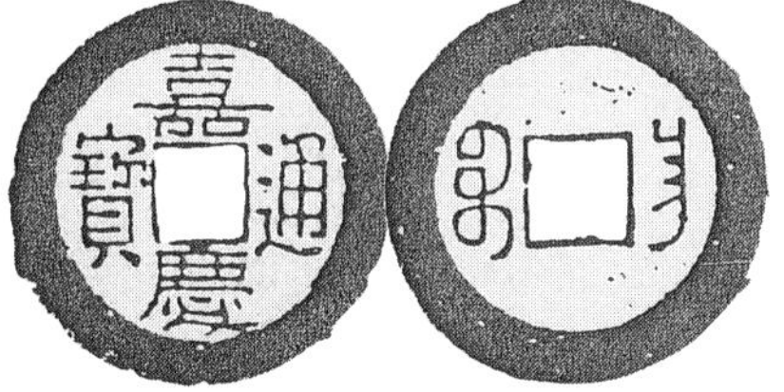

Pn26	ND(1796)	—	Cash. Cast Bronze. "Boo-ch'ang".	160

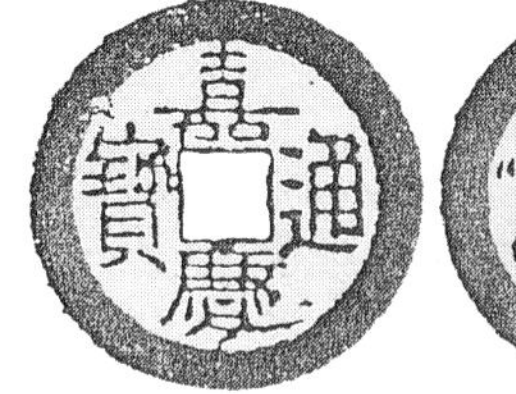 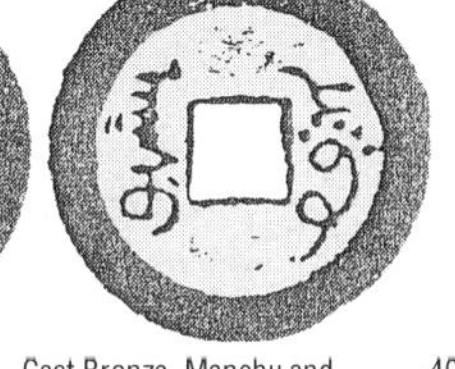

Pn27	ND(1796)	—	Cash. Cast Bronze. Manchu and Turki "Aksu" (by Hu-pu).	400

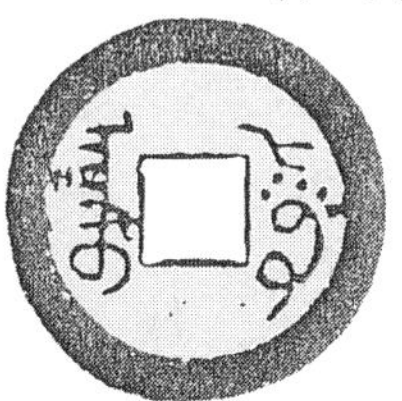

Pn28	ND(1796)	—	Cash. Cast Bronze. Manchu and Turki "Aksu".	200

SINKIANG PROVINCE

Hsinkiang, Xinjiang
"New Dominion"

An autonomous region in western China, often referred to as Chinese Turkestan. High mountains surround 2000 ft. tableland on three sides with a large desert in center of this province. Many salt lakes, mining and some farming and oil. Inhabited by early man and was referred to as the "Silk Route" to the West. Sinkiang (Xinjiang) has been historically under the control of many factions, including Genghis Khan. It became a province in 1884. China has made claim to Sinkiang (Xinjiang) for many, many years. This rule has been more nominal than actual. Sinkiang (Xinjiang) had eight imperial mints, only three of which were in operation toward the end of the reign of Kuang Hsü. Only two mints operated during the early years of the republic. In 1949, due to a drastic coin shortage and lack of confidence in the inflated paper money, it was planned to mint some dollars in Sinkiang (Xinjiang). These did not see much circulation, however, due to the defeat of the nationalists, though they have recently appeared in considerable numbers in today's market.

PATTERNS

NOTE: A number of previously listed cast coins of Sinkiang Province are now known to be patterns - "mother" cash or "seed" cash for which no circulating issues are known. The following coins are, therefore, no longer listed. Most were probably manufactured in Beijing. They are generally made of brass rather than the purer copper usual to Sinkiang. The following coins are, therefore, no longer listed here: Craig #30-9, 30-11a, 30-12a, 30-14, 30-15a, 30-16, 30-17, 28-4.1, 28-8a, 28-9a, 28-9c, 28-10, 31-1a, 31-1v, 31-2, 32-4, 32-5, 33-12, 33-21, 34-2, 34-3, 35-5a and 35-6.

MONETARY SYSTEM

2 Pul = 1 Cash
2 Cash = 5 Li
4 Cash = 10 Li = 1 Fen
25 Cash = 10 Fen = 1 Miscal = 1 Ch'ien, Mace, Tanga
10 Miscals (Mace) = 1 Liang (Tael or Sar)
20 Miscals (Tangas) = 1 Tilla

LOCAL MINT NAMES AND MARKS

Mint	Chinese	Uyghur	Manchu
Aksu	城阿	اقصو	
Ili, now Yining	犁伊	الي	
Kashgar, now Kashi	什喀	كشقر	
Khotan, now Hotan	闐和	ختن	
Kuche, now Kuqa	車庫	كوچا	
Urumchi, now Urumqi	什烏	اورمچي	
Ushi, now Wushi (Uqturpan)	羌爾葉	اوش	
Yangihissar, now Yengisar		ينگى حصار	
Yarkand, now Shache (Yarkant)		ياركند	

EMPIRE

Tsewang Arabtan

1697-1727

CAST TRIBAL COINAGE

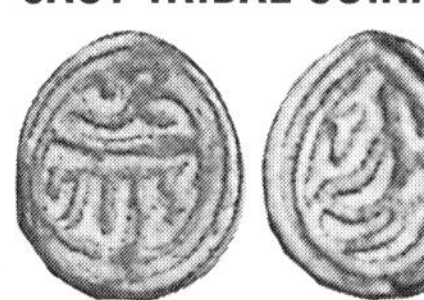

KM# 360 PUL

Cast Copper **Obv. Inscription:** *Tsewang* **Rev. Inscription:** *Zarb Yarkand* **Mint:** Yarkand **Note:** Turki inscriptions. Prev. C36-7.1.

Date	Mintage	Good	VG	F	VF	XF
ND(1697-1727)	—	30.00	50.00	80.00	125	—

Khardan Chirin

1727-1745

CAST TRIBAL COINAGE

KM# 382 PUL

3.1000 g., Silver, 16 mm. **Obv. Inscription:** *Khardan Chirin* **Rev. Inscription:** *Zarb Yarkand* **Mint:** Yarkand **Note:** Turki inscriptions. Prev. C36-9.

Date	Mintage	Good	VG	F	VF	XF
ND(1727-45)	—	100	140	200	275	—

KM# 380 PUL

Cast Copper **Obv. Inscription:** *Khardan Chirin* **Rev. Inscription:** *Zarb Yarkand* **Mint:** Yarkand **Note:** Turki inscriptions. Prev. C36-7.2.

Date	Mintage	Good	VG	F	VF	XF
ND(1727-45)	—	10.00	15.00	25.00	40.00	—

Ch'ien-lung

1736-1795
Kao-tsung

LOCAL CAST COINAGE

C# 34-1a CASH

6.0000 g., Cast Copper, 25.2 mm. **Obverse:** Type A-1 **Obv. Inscription:** "Ch'ien-lung T'ung-pao. **Reverse:** Manchu mint mark at left, Turki at right. **Mint:** Ushi

Date	Mintage	Good	VG	F	VF	XF
ND(1736-95)	—	5.00	7.00	10.00	15.00	—

C# 31-1 CASH

Cast Copper **Subject:** Shan Lung Commemorative **Obv. Inscription:** Ch'ien-lung Tung-pao **Reverse:** Manchu mint mark at left, Turki at right **Mint:** Khotan

Date	Mintage	Good	VG	F	VF	XF
ND(1736-95) Ch'ien-lung Rare	—	—	—	—	—	—

C# 34-1b CASH

Cast Copper, 24.5-25.2 mm. **Obverse:** Type A-2 **Obv. Inscription:** "Ch'ien-lung T'ung-pao **Reverse:** Manchu mint mark at left, Turki at right **Mint:** Ushi **Note:** Weight varies: 3.60-5.20g. Size varies.

Date	Mintage	Good	VG	F	VF	XF
ND(1736-95)	—	1.50	2.25	3.50	5.00	—

C# 30-1.1 CASH

Cast Copper **Obverse:** Type A-1 **Obv. Inscription:** Ch'ien-lung T'ung-pao **Reverse:** Manchu mint mark at left, Turki at right **Mint:** Aksu

Date	Mintage	Good	VG	F	VF	XF
ND(1736-95)	—	1.00	3.00	5.00	10.00	—

C# 30-1.2 CASH

Cast Copper **Obv. Inscription:** Ch'ien-lung T'ung-pao **Reverse:** Turki mint mark at right different **Mint:** Aksu

Date	Mintage	Good	VG	F	VF	XF
ND(1736-95)	—	1.00	3.00	5.00	10.00	—

C# 30-1.3 CASH

Cast Copper **Obv. Inscription:** Ch'ien-lung T'ung-pao **Reverse:** Circle (sun) above **Mint:** Aksu

Date	Mintage	Good	VG	F	VF	XF
ND(1736-95)	—	3.00	5.00	7.50	15.00	—

C# 28-1 CASH

Cast Copper **Obverse:** Type A-1 **Obv. Inscription:** Ch'ien-lung T'ung-pao **Reverse:** Manchu "Boo-yi" **Mint:** Ili

Date	Mintage	Good	VG	F	VF	XF
ND(1736-95)	—	7.50	15.00	22.50	30.00	—

C# 28-1.1 CASH

Cast Copper **Obv. Inscription:** Ch'ien-lung T'ung-pao **Reverse:** Manchu "Boo-yi" with dot above **Mint:** Ili

Date	Mintage	Good	VG	F	VF	XF
ND(1736-95)	—	18.50	37.50	55.00	75.00	—

C# 30-1.4 CASH

Cast Copper **Subject:** Shan-lung Commemorative **Obverse:** Type A-2 **Obv. Inscription:** Ch'ien-lung T'ung-pao **Mint:** Aksu **Note:** Cast during the ninth year of the reign of Kuang-hsü (1883).

Date	Mintage	Good	VG	F	VF	XF
ND(1736-95)	—	4.00	6.00	8.00	16.00	—

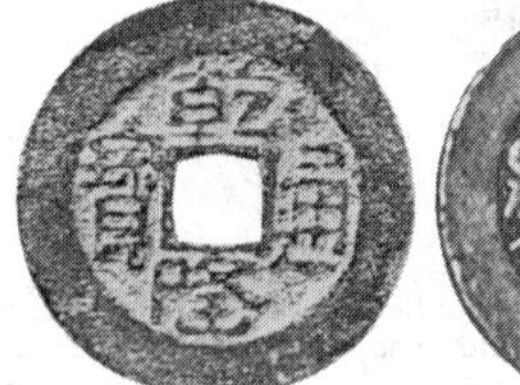

C# 34-1 CASH

7.2000 g., Cast Copper, 26-28 mm. **Obverse:** Type A-2 **Obv. Inscription:** "Ch'ien-lung T'ung-pao **Reverse:** Manchu mint mark at left, Turki at right **Mint:** Ushi **Note:** Size varies. Weight varies: 6.70-7.40g.

Date	Mintage	Good	VG	F	VF	XF
ND(1736-95)	—	10.00	15.00	21.50	30.00	—

C# 33-1 CASH

Cast Copper **Obv. Inscription:** Ch'ien-lung T'ung-pao **Reverse:** Manchu mint mark at left, Turki at right **Mint:** Kuche **Note:** This coin was cast during a later reign.

Date	Mintage	Good	VG	F	VF	XF
ND(1736-95)	—	5.00	7.50	10.00	17.50	—

C# 35-1 CASH

Cast Copper **Rev. Legend:** MANCHU YERKIM **Mint:** Yarkand

Date	Mintage	Good	VG	F	VF	XF
ND(1759-61)	—	11.00	18.00	30.00	42.50	—

C# 35-2 CASH

Cast Brass **Obv. Inscription:** "Ch'ien-lung T'ung-pao **Rev. Legend:** Manchu Yerkiyang at left, Turki at right **Mint:** Yarkand

Date	Mintage	Good	VG	F	VF	XF
ND(1761-95)	—	11.00	18.00	30.00	42.50	—

C# 34-2 10 CASH

Cast Copper **Obv. Inscription:** "Ch'ien-lung T'ung-pao **Reverse:** Manchu mint mark at left, Turki at right, Chinese "Shih"(ten) above **Mint:** Ushi

Date	Mintage	Good	VG	F	VF	XF
ND(1736-95)	—	14.00	20.00	28.50	40.00	—

KM# 2 10 CASH

Cast Copper **Obv. Inscription:** "Ch'ien-lung T'ung-pao. **Reverse:** Manchu "Boo-yuan" with Chinese "K'u" (for Kuche) above.

Date	Mintage	Good	VG	F	VF	XF
ND(1736-95)	—	10.00	20.00	40.00	60.00	—

C# 30-2.1 10 CASH

Cast Copper **Obverse:** Type A-1 **Obv. Inscription:** "Ch'ien-lung T'ung-pao. **Reverse:** Manchu mint mark at left, Turki at right. "Tang" above, "Shih"(ten) below. **Mint:** Aksu **Note:** Cast during the reign of Kuang-hsü (1875-1908).

Date	Mintage	Good	VG	F	VF	XF
ND(1736-95)	—	7.00	10.00	15.00	25.00	—

C# 30-2.2 10 CASH

Cast Copper **Obv. Inscription:** "Ch'ien-lung T'ung-pao. **Reverse:** Chinese "K'a" (Kashgar) above, "Shih"(ten) below. **Mint:** Aksu **Note:** Cast during the reign of Kuang-hsü (1875-1908).

Date	Mintage	Good	VG	F	VF	XF
ND(1736-95)	—	1.75	3.50	4.50	9.00	—

C# 30-3 10 CASH

Cast Copper **Obv. Inscription:** "Ch'ien-lung T'ung-pao. **Reverse:** Chinese "A" (for Aksu) above, "Shih"(ten) below. **Mint:** Aksu **Note:** Cast during the reign of Kuang-hsü (1875-1908).

Date	Mintage	Good	VG	F	VF	XF
ND(1736-95)	—	1.25	3.00	4.50	7.00	—

C# 33-2 10 CASH

Cast Copper **Obv. Inscription:** "Ch'ien-lung T'ung-pao. **Mint:** Kashgar **Note:** This coin was cast during a later reign. 4 varieties are reported.

Date	Mintage	Good	VG	F	VF	XF
ND(1736-95)	—	7.50	10.00	15.00	25.00	—

Atalyq Ghazi

1757

CAST TRIBAL COINAGE

KM# 437 PUL

Cast Copper **Obv. Inscription:** Atalyq Ghazi. **Rev. Inscription:** Zarb Yarkand. **Mint:** Yarkand **Note:** Turki inscriptions. Prev. C#36-11.

Date	Mintage	Good	VG	F	VF	XF
ND(ca.1757)	—	30.00	50.00	80.00	125	—

Chia-ch'ing

1796-1820

LOCAL CAST COINAGE

C# 30-5 CASH

Cast Copper **Obverse:** Type A **Obv. Inscription:** Chia-ch'ing T'ung-pao **Mint:** Aksu

Date	Mintage	Good	VG	F	VF	XF
ND(1796-1820)	—	1.75	4.25	8.00	10.00	—

C# 28-2 CASH

Cast Copper **Obv. Inscription:** Chia-ch'ing T'ung-pao **Reverse:** Manchu inscription **Mint:** Ili

Date	Mintage	Good	VG	F	VF	XF
ND(1796-1820)	—	15.00	30.00	55.00	100	—

C# 28-2.1 CASH

Cast Copper **Obv. Inscription:** Chia-ch'ing T'ung-pao **Reverse:** Vertical line above and below **Mint:** Ili

Date	Mintage	Good	VG	F	VF	XF
ND(1796-1820)	—	30.00	50.00	85.00	125	—

C# 28-2.2 CASH

Cast Copper **Obv. Inscription:** Chia-ch'ing T'ung-pao **Reverse:** Vertical line above **Mint:** Ili

Date	Mintage	Good	VG	F	VF	XF
ND(1796-1820)	—	7.50	15.00	30.00	60.00	—

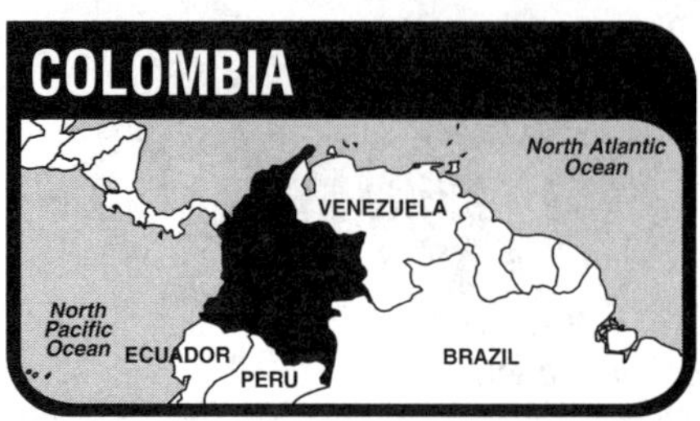

The Republic of Colombia, in the northwestern corner of South America, has an area of 440,831 sq. mi. (1,138,910 sq. km.) and a population of*42.3 million. Capital: Bogota. The economy is primarily agricultural with a mild, rich coffee being the chief crop. Colombia has the world's largest platinum deposits and important reserves of coal, iron ore, petroleum and limestone; other precious metals and emeralds are also mined. Coffee, crude oil, bananas, sugar and emeralds are exported.

The northern coast of present Colombia was one of the first parts of the American continent to be visited by Spanish navigators. At Darien in Panama is the site of the first permanent European settlement on the American mainland in 1510. New Granada, as Colombia was known until 1861, stemmed from the settlement of Santa Marta in 1525. New Granada was established as a Spanish colony in 1549. Independence was declared in 1810, and secured in 1819 when Simon Bolivar united Colombia, Venezuela, Panama and Ecuador as the Republic of Gran Colombia. Venezuela withdrew from the Republic in 1829; Ecuador in 1830; and Panama in 1903.

RULER

Spanish, until 1819

MINT MARKS

C, NER, NR, NRE, RN, S - Cartagena
B, F, FS, N, NR, S, SF - Nuevo Reino (Bogota)
A, M - Medellin (capital), Antioquia (state)
(m) - Medellin, w/o mint mark
P, PN, Pn - Popayan

ASSAYERS' INITIALS

Bogota Mint

Initial	Date	Name
A, ARC, ARCE, VA	1692-1721	Buena Ventura de Arce
J	1757-58	Joaquin de Burgos
J	1758-80	Juan de Chavez
J	1774-1800	Juan Rodriguez Uzguiano
J	1780-1803, 1810-22	Juan Jose Truxillo y Mutienx
M	1732-44	Miguel Molano
S, SAN	1722-32	Jose Sanchez de la Torre
S, SR	1744-57	Sebastian de Rivera (gold only)
V	1758-74	Victoriano del Valle

MONETARY SYSTEM

16 Reales = 1 Escudo

COLONIAL

COB COINAGE

Note: Values given for dated cobs are representative of average strikes with the last two digits of the date discernible. The esthetic appearance, quality of strike, and presence of date, mint mark and assayer initials all have an effect on the value of cobs.

Note: Colombian cob 1/4 Reales, which are all very rare, did not bear dates in their design, but can be dated at least approximately by virtue of the fact that the castle on the obverse and the lion on the reverse match exactly with the castles and lions in the shield of the 8 Reales struck in the same year or period.

NOTE: The cob 1/2 Reales of Colombia are distinguishable from other mints cob 1/2 Reales by virtue of the fact that the P and the S of the PHILIPPVS monogram touch at the top

KM# B7 1/4 REAL

0.8600 g., 0.9310 Silver **Ruler:** Philip V **Obv:** Castle **Rev:** Lion

Date	Mintage	Good	VG	F	VF	XF
ND(1702)	—	200	250	400	650	—

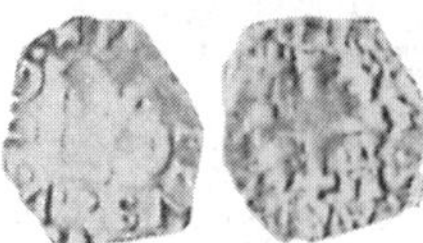

KM# B8 1/2 REAL

1.6917 g., 0.9310 Silver .0506 oz. ASW **Ruler:** Philip V **Obv:** Legend of Philip

Date	Mintage	Good	VG	F	VF	XF
ND(1702-26) Date off flan	—	80.00	140	220	350	—

Date	Mintage	Good	VG	F	VF	XF
1702 Rare	—	—	—	—	—	—
1726 Rare	—	—	—	—	—	—

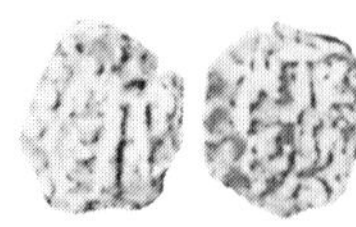

KM# C8 1/2 REAL

1.6917 g., 0.9310 Silver .0506 oz. ASW **Ruler:** Ferdinand VI **Obv:** Legend of Ferdinand VI

Date	Mintage	Good	VG	F	VF	XF
ND(1748) MP Unique	—	—	—	—	—	—

KM# 15 REAL

3.3834 g., 0.9310 Silver .1013 oz. ASW **Obv:** Lions and castles **Rev:** Pillars

Date	Mintage	Good	VG	F	VF	XF
ND(1662-1722) Date off flan; Rare	—	—	—	—	—	—
ND(1692-1722) VA Rare	—	—	—	—	—	—

KM# B15 REAL

3.3834 g., 0.9310 Silver .1013 oz. ASW **Ruler:** Philip V **Obv:** Half shield **Rev:** Letters between pillars of Hercules

Date	Mintage	Good	VG	F	VF	XF
1722 A Unique	—	—	—	—	—	—

KM# C15 REAL

3.3834 g., 0.9170 Silver .0997 oz. ASW **Obv:** Full quartered shield **Rev:** Letters between pillars of Hercules

Date	Mintage	Good	VG	F	VF	XF
ND M Unique	—	—	—	—	—	—

KM# 19 2 REALES

6.7668 g., 0.9310 Silver .2026 oz. ASW **Ruler:** Philip V **Obv:** Legend of Philip V, crowned arms **Rev:** Pillars and waves, mint mark within

Date	Mintage	Good	VG	F	VF	XF
ND(1722-25) Date off flan	—	250	350	475	1,000	—
1722 (ARCE) Rare	—	—	—	—	—	—
1725/4 FS Rare	—	—	—	—	—	—

KM# 20 4 REALES

13.5337 g., 0.9310 Silver .4051 oz. ASW **Ruler:** Philip V **Obv:** Arms **Obv. Legend:** PHILIPVS V D.G **Rev:** Pillars and waves, "PLVS VLTRA" within

Date	Mintage	Good	VG	F	VF	XF
1721 ARC Unique	—	—	—	—	—	—
1722 SAN at left Unique	—	—	—	—	—	—
1722 SAN at right Unique	—	—	—	—	—	—

KM# 12 8 REALES

27.0674 g., 0.9310 Silver .8102 oz. ASW **Ruler:** Philip V **Obv:** Arms within beaded circle, legend of Charles II **Rev:** Pillars, "PLVS VLTRA" and "MM" between

Date	Mintage	Good	VG	F	VF	XF
1702 VA Rare	—	—	—	—	—	—
1703 ARCE Rare	—	—	—	—	—	—

KM# 18 8 REALES

0.9310 Silver **Ruler:** Philip V **Obv:** Arms **Obv. Legend:** PHILIPPVS V DG **Rev:** Pillars, PLVS VLTRA within

Date	Mintage	Good	VG	F	VF	XF
1721 ARC Rare	—	—	—	—	—	—
1722 SAN Rare	—	—	—	—	—	—

KM# 18a 8 REALES

27.0674 g., 0.9170 Silver .7980 oz. ASW **Note:** Struck at the Bogota Mint.

Date	Mintage	Good	VG	F	VF	XF
1742 M Rare	—	—	—	—	—	—

KM# 13 ESCUDO

3.3834 g., 0.9170 Gold .0997 oz. AGW **Ruler:** Philip V **Obv:** Arms **Rev:** Cross of Jerusalem

Date	Mintage	F	VF	XF	Unc	BU
ND(1672-1708) Date off flan	—	1,750	2,000	—	—	—
1708 (ARCE) Rare	—	—	—	—	—	—

KM# 22 ESCUDO

3.3834 g., 0.9170 Gold .0997 oz. AGW **Ruler:** Philip V **Obv:** Arms **Rev:** Cross of Jerusalem

Date	Mintage	F	VF	XF	Unc	BU
ND(1715-46) Date off flan	—	1,500	1,950	—	—	—
1715 (ARCE) Rare	—	—	—	—	—	—
1722 S Rare	—	—	—	—	—	—
1736 M Rare	—	—	—	—	—	—
1741 M Rare	—	—	—	—	—	—
1746 S Rare	—	—	—	—	—	—

KM# A28 ESCUDO

3.3834 g., 0.9170 Gold .0997 oz. AGW **Ruler:** Luis I **Obv:** Arms **Rev:** Cross of Jerusalem

Date	Mintage	Good	VG	F	VF	XF
ND(1724-25) S Rare	—	—	—	—	—	—

KM# 28 ESCUDO

3.3834 g., 0.9170 Gold .0997 oz. AGW **Ruler:** Ferdinand VI **Obv:** Arms **Rev:** Cross of Jerusalem

Date	Mintage	F	VF	XF	Unc	BU
ND(1751-55) Date off flan	—	1,000	1,400	2,000	—	—
1751 S Rare	—	—	—	—	—	—
1754 S Rare	—	—	—	—	—	—
1755 S Rare	—	—	—	—	—	—

KM# 14.2 2 ESCUDOS

6.7682 g., 0.9170 Gold .1995 oz. AGW **Ruler:** Philip V **Note:** No mint mark.

Date	Mintage	F	VF	XF	Unc	BU
ND(1694-1713) Date off flan	—	1,000	1,200	1,500	—	—
1701 ARCE	—	1,400	1,800	2,200	—	—
1702 VA	—	1,400	1,800	2,200	—	—
1703	—	1,400	1,800	2,200	—	—
1704	—	1,400	1,800	2,200	—	—
1705	—	1,400	1,800	2,200	—	—
1706	—	1,400	1,800	2,200	—	—
1707	—	1,400	1,800	2,200	—	—
1708	—	1,400	1,800	2,200	—	—
1709	—	1,400	1,800	2,200	—	—
1710	—	1,400	1,800	2,200	—	—
1711	—	1,400	1,800	2,200	—	—
1712	—	1,400	1,800	2,200	—	—
1713	—	1,400	1,800	2,200	—	—

KM# 17.1 2 ESCUDOS

6.7668 g., 0.9170 Gold .1995 oz. AGW **Ruler:** Philip V **Obv:** Arms **Rev:** Cross within ornamented double outline

Date	Mintage	F	VF	XF	Unc	BU
ND(1714-1716) Date off flan	—	900	1,000	1,200	—	—
1714	—	1,400	1,800	2,200	—	—
1715	—	1,400	1,800	2,500	—	—
1716 Rare	—	—	—	—	—	—

KM# 17.2 2 ESCUDOS

6.7668 g., 0.9170 Gold .1995 oz. AGW **Ruler:** Philip V **Obv:** Arms **Rev:** Cross within ornamented double outline **Note:** Mint mark: F, S

Date	Mintage	F	VF	XF	Unc	BU
ND(1717-46) Date off flan	—	900	1,000	1,300	—	—
1717 Rare	—	—	—	—	—	—
1718 Rare	—	—	—	—	—	—
1719 Rare	—	—	—	—	—	—
1720 Rare	—	—	—	—	—	—
1721 Rare	—	—	—	—	—	—
1722 Rare	—	—	—	—	—	—
1723 S Rare	—	—	—	—	—	—
1724 S Rare	—	—	—	—	—	—
1726 S Rare	—	—	—	—	—	—
1727 S Rare	—	—	—	—	—	—
1728/7 S Rare	—	—	—	—	—	—
1728 S Rare	—	—	—	—	—	—
1729 S Rare	—	—	—	—	—	—
1730 S Rare	—	—	—	—	—	—
1731 S Rare	—	—	—	—	—	—
1732 S Rare	—	—	—	—	—	—
1732 M	—	1,400	1,800	2,200	—	—
1733 M	—	1,400	1,800	2,200	—	—
1734 M	—	1,400	1,800	2,200	—	—
1735 M	—	1,400	1,800	2,200	—	—
1736 M	—	1,400	1,800	2,200	—	—
1737 M	—	1,400	1,800	2,200	—	—
1738 M	—	1,400	1,800	2,200	—	—
1739 M	—	1,400	1,800	2,200	—	—
1740 M	—	1,400	1,800	2,200	—	—
1741 M	—	1,400	1,800	2,200	—	—
1742 M	—	1,400	1,800	2,200	—	—
1743 M	—	1,400	1,800	2,200	—	—
1744 M	—	1,400	1,800	2,200	—	—
1744 S	—	1,400	1,800	2,200	—	—
1745 S	—	1,400	1,800	2,200	—	—
1746 S	—	1,400	1,800	2,200	—	—

KM# A25 2 ESCUDOS

6.7668 g., 0.9170 Gold .1995 oz. AGW **Ruler:** Luis I

Date	Mintage	F	VF	XF	Unc	BU
1724 (S) Rare	—	—	—	—	—	—
1725 (S) Rare	—	—	—	—	—	—

KM# 25 2 ESCUDOS

6.7668 g., 0.9170 Gold .1995 oz. AGW **Ruler:** Ferdinand VI **Obv:** Arms **Rev:** Cross of Jerusalem

Date	Mintage	F	VF	XF	Unc	BU
ND(1747-56) Date off flan	—	900	1,000	1,500	—	—
1747 S	—	1,300	1,600	1,900	—	—
1748 S	—	1,400	1,800	2,200	—	—
1749 S	—	1,400	1,800	2,200	—	—
1750 S	—	1,400	1,800	2,200	—	—
1751 S	—	1,400	1,800	2,200	—	—
1752 S	—	1,400	1,800	2,200	—	—
1753 S	—	1,400	1,800	2,200	—	—
1754 S	—	1,400	1,800	2,200	—	—
1755 S	—	1,400	1,800	2,200	—	—
1756 S	—	1,400	1,800	2,200	—	—

KM# 23 4 ESCUDOS

13.5337 g., 0.9170 Gold .3990 oz. AGW **Ruler:** Philip V **Obv:** Arms **Rev:** Cross of Jerusalem **Note:** Mint mark: F, S

Date	Mintage	F	VF	XF	Unc	BU
ND(1740-46) Date off flan	—	3,000	3,500	4,500	—	—
1740 M Rare	—	—	—	—	—	—
1741 M Rare	—	—	—	—	—	—
1744 S Rare	—	—	—	—	—	—
1745 S Rare	—	—	—	—	—	—
1746 S Rare	—	—	—	—	—	—

KM# 27 4 ESCUDOS

13.5337 g., 0.9170 Gold .3990 oz. AGW **Ruler:** Ferdinand VI **Obv:** Arms **Rev:** Cross of Jerusalem

Date	Mintage	F	VF	XF	Unc	BU
ND(1747-56) Date off flan	—	2,500	3,500	4,500	—	—
1747 S Rare	—	—	—	—	—	—
1748 S Rare	—	—	—	—	—	—
1749 S Rare	—	—	—	—	—	—
1750 S Rare	—	—	—	—	—	—
1751 S Rare	—	—	—	—	—	—
1752 S Rare	—	—	—	—	—	—
1753 S Rare	—	—	—	—	—	—
1754 S Rare	—	—	—	—	—	—
1755 S Rare	—	—	—	—	—	—
1756 S Rare	—	—	—	—	—	—

KM# 24 8 ESCUDOS

27.0674 g., 0.9170 Gold .7980 oz. AGW **Ruler:** Philip V **Obv:** Arms **Rev:** Cross of Jerusalem **Note:** Mint mark: F, S

Date	Mintage	F	VF	XF	Unc	BU
ND(1736-46) Date off flan	—	3,500	4,000	5,000	—	—
1736 M Rare	—	—	—	—	—	—
1743 M Rare	—	—	—	—	—	—
1744 M Rare	—	—	—	—	—	—
1745 S Rare	—	—	—	—	—	—
1746 S Rare	—	—	—	—	—	—

KM# 26 8 ESCUDOS

27.0674 g., 0.9170 Gold .7981 oz. AGW **Ruler:** Ferdinand VI **Obv:** Crowned arms **Obv. Legend:** Ferdnd VI D. G.. **Rev:** Cross within ornamented double outline **Note:** Mint mark: F, S

Date	Mintage	F	VF	XF	Unc	BU
ND(1747-56) Date off flan	—	3,500	4,000	5,000	—	—
1747 S Rare	—	—	—	—	—	—
1748 S Rare	—	—	—	—	—	—
1749 S Rare	—	—	—	—	—	—
1750 S Rare	—	—	—	—	—	—
1751 S Rare	—	—	—	—	—	—
1752 S Rare	—	—	—	—	—	—
1753 S Rare	—	—	—	—	—	—
1754 S Rare	—	—	—	—	—	—
1755 S Rare	—	—	—	—	—	—
1756 S Rare	—	—	—	—	—	—

MILLED COINAGE

KM# 63 1/4 REAL

0.8458 g., 0.8960 Silver .0244 oz. ASW **Obv:** Castle **Rev:** Lion

Date	Mintage	VG	F	VF	XF	Unc
1796NR	—	22.50	45.00	90.00	175	—
1797/6NR	—	25.00	60.00	120	250	—
1797NR	—	15.00	30.00	60.00	125	—
1798/7NR	—	20.00	40.00	75.00	150	—
1798NR	—	20.00	40.00	75.00	150	—
1799/8NR	—	20.00	40.00	75.00	150	—
1799NR	—	15.00	30.00	60.00	100	—
1800/799NR	—	15.00	30.00	60.00	100	—
1800NR	—	20.00	40.00	75.00	150	—

KM# A45 1/2 REAL

1.6917 g., 0.9030 Silver .0491 oz. ASW **Obv:** Crowned arms **Obv. Legend:** CRS • III • D • G • HISP • ET IND R • **Rev:** Pillars and worlds, mint mark, date **Rev. Legend:** VTRA QUE VNVM

Date	Mintage	VG	F	VF	XF	Unc
1760NR JV Rare	—	—	—	—	—	—

KM# 45.1 1/2 REAL

1.6917 g., 0.9030 Silver .0491 oz. ASW **Ruler:** Charles III **Obv:** Bust right **Obv. Legend:** CAROLUS • III • DEI • GRATIA • **Rev:** Arms between pillars

Date	Mintage	VG	F	VF	XF	Unc
1772NR VJ	—	100	150	275	575	—
1773NR VJ	—	80.00	125	250	525	—
1775NR JJ	—	175	350	—	—	—
1776NR JJ	—	65.00	100	175	300	—
1777NR JJ	—	50.00	85.00	150	250	—
1781NR JJ	—	110	175	300	575	—
1784NR JJ	—	110	175	300	575	—

KM# 45.2 1/2 REAL

1.6917 g., 0.9030 Silver .0491 oz. ASW **Ruler:** Charles III **Obv:** Bust right **Rev:** Arms between pillars

Date	Mintage	VG	F	VF	XF	Unc
1772P JS	—	—	—	—	—	—
1774P JS	—	100	175	300	600	—

KM# 57 1/2 REAL

1.6917 g., 0.8960 Silver .0487 oz. ASW **Ruler:** Charles IV **Obv:** Bust right **Obv. Legend:** CAROLUS • IIII • DEI • GRATIA • **Rev:** Crowned arms between pillars

Date	Mintage	VG	F	VF	XF	Unc
1792NR JJ	—	40.00	75.00	150	250	—
1793NR JJ	—	125	250	400	500	—
1794NR JJ	—	75.00	125	200	300	—
1795NR JJ	—	40.00	75.00	150	250	—
1796NR JJ	—	70.00	100	175	275	—
1799NR JJ	—	40.00	75.00	150	250	—

KM# 34 REAL

3.3834 g., 0.9170 Silver .0997 oz. ASW **Ruler:** Charles III **Obv:** Crowned arms **Obv. Legend:** CRS • III • D • G • HISP • ETIND • R • **Rev:** Pillars and worlds, mint mark and date **Rev. Legend:** VTRA QUE VNUM

Date	Mintage	VG	F	VF	XF	Unc
1760NR JV	—	1,200	2,200	4,250	6,500	—

KM# 46.1 REAL

3.3834 g., 0.9030 Silver .0982 oz. ASW **Ruler:** Charles III **Obv:** Bust right **Rev:** Crowned arms between pillars

Date	Mintage	VG	F	VF	XF	Unc
1772NR VJ	—	100	150	350	500	—
1773NR VJ	—	40.00	75.00	150	300	—
1775NR JJ	—	60.00	100	250	450	—
1776NR JJ	—	60.00	100	250	450	—
1777NR JJ	—	60.00	100	250	450	—
1781NR JJ	—	90.00	150	400	650	—
1784NR JJ	—	60.00	100	250	450	—

KM# 46.2 REAL

3.3834 g., 0.9030 Silver .0982 oz. ASW **Ruler:** Charles III **Obv:** Bust right **Obv. Legend:** CAROLUS • III • DEI • GRATIA • **Rev:** Crowned arms between pillars

Date	Mintage	VG	F	VF	XF	Unc
1772P JS	—	50.00	125	250	500	—

KM# 58 REAL

3.3834 g., 0.8960 Silver .0975 oz. ASW **Ruler:** Charles IV **Obv:** Bust right **Obv. Legend:** CAROLUS • IIII • DEI • GRATIA • **Rev:** Crowned arms between pillars **Rev. Legend:** HISPAN • ET • IND • REX • ...

Date	Mintage	VG	F	VF	XF	Unc
1792NR JJ	—	25.00	50.00	125	250	—
1793NR JJ	—	50.00	100	250	450	—
1794/3NR JJ	—	60.00	120	350	450	—
1795NR JJ	—	25.00	50.00	125	250	—
1796NR JJ	—	25.00	65.00	150	325	—
1797NR JJ	—	25.00	50.00	125	250	—
1798NR JJ	—	40.00	80.00	165	350	—
1799NR JJ	—	30.00	60.00	150	300	—
1800NR JJ	—	20.00	40.00	120	250	—

KM# 47 2 REALES

6.7668 g., 0.9030 Silver .1964 oz. ASW **Ruler:** Charles III **Obv:** Bust right **Obv. Legend:** CAROLUS • III • DEI • GRATIA • **Rev:** Crowned arms between pillars **Rev. Legend:** ...HISPAN • ET IND • REX •

Date	Mintage	VG	F	VF	XF	Unc
1772NR VJ	—	90.00	150	350	—	—
1773NR VJ	—	90.00	150	350	—	—
1775NR JJ	—	300	500	1,250	—	—
1777NR JJ	—	225	375	900	—	—
1784NR JJ	—	225	375	900	—	—

KM# 59 2 REALES

6.7668 g., 0.8960 Silver .1949 oz. ASW **Ruler:** Charles IV **Obv:** Bust right

Date	Mintage	VG	F	VF	XF	Unc
1792NR JJ	—	100	185	285	—	—
1793NR JJ	—	60.00	100	200	—	—
1794NR JJ	—	100	185	325	—	—
1795NR JJ	—	150	225	400	—	—
1796NR JJ	—	165	265	425	—	—
1798/7NR JJ	—	90.00	175	300	—	—
1798NR JJ	—	90.00	175	300	—	—

KM# 33 8 REALES

27.0674 g., 0.9170 Silver .7980 oz. ASW **Ruler:** Ferdinand VI **Obv:** Crowned arms **Obv. Legend:** FERDND • VI • D • G • HISPAN • ET IND • REX **Rev:** Crowned globes between crowned pillars **Rev. Legend:** VTRA QUE VNUM

Date	Mintage	VG	F	VF	XF	Unc
1759NR JV Rare	—	—	—	—	—	—

KM# 39 8 REALES

27.0674 g., 0.9170 Silver .7980 oz. ASW **Ruler:** Charles III **Obv:** Crowned arms **Obv. Legend:** CAROLUS III.. **Rev:** 2 Crowned hemispheres between pillars

Date	Mintage	VG	F	VF	XF	Unc
1762NR JV Rare	—	—	—	—	—	—

KM# 29.1 ESCUDO

3.3834 g., 0.9170 Gold .0997 oz. AGW **Ruler:** Ferdinand VI **Obv:** Bust right **Rev:** Crowned arms

Date	Mintage	VG	F	VF	XF	Unc
1756NR S	—	150	300	575	875	—
1757NR J	—	150	300	575	875	—
1758NR J	—	225	450	900	1,500	—
1759NR JV	—	150	300	575	875	—

KM# 29.2 ESCUDO

3.3834 g., 0.9170 Gold .0997 oz. AGW **Ruler:** Ferdinand VI **Obv:** Bust right **Rev:** Crowned arms **Note:** Mint mark: P, PN

Date	Mintage	VG	F	VF	XF	Unc
1758 J	—	100	200	375	575	—
1759 J	—	100	200	375	575	—

KM# 35 ESCUDO

3.3834 g., 0.9170 Gold .0997 oz. AGW **Ruler:** Charles III **Obv:** Bust right **Obv. Legend:** CAROLS • III • D • G • HISP • ET IND • REX • **Rev:** Crowned arms **Rev. Legend:** NOMINA MAGNA SEQUOR

Date	Mintage	VG	F	VF	XF	Unc
1760PN J	—	100	150	250	400	—
1762PN J	—	100	150	250	400	—
1767PN J	—	100	150	250	400	—
1769/7PN J	—	100	150	250	400	—

KM# 42 ESCUDO

3.3834 g., 0.9170 Gold .0997 oz. AGW **Ruler:** Charles III **Obv:** Young bust

Date	Mintage	VG	F	VF	XF	Unc
1763NR JV	—	300	600	900	1,500	—
1767NR JV	—	300	600	900	1,500	—
1771NR VJ	—	300	600	900	1,500	—

KM# 40.1 ESCUDO

3.3834 g., 0.9170 Gold .0997 oz. AGW **Ruler:** Charles III **Obv:** Bust right **Obv. Legend:** CAROL • III • D • G • HISP • ET IND • R • **Rev:** Arms within Order chain **Rev. Legend:** IN • UTROQ • FELIX • ...

Date	Mintage	VG	F	VF	XF	Unc
1772NR VJ	—	75.00	110	140	225	—
1773NR VJ	—	75.00	110	140	225	—
1774NR VJ	—	75.00	110	140	225	—
1774NR JJ	—	75.00	110	140	225	—
1775NR JJ	—	75.00	110	140	225	—
1776NR JJ	—	75.00	110	140	225	—
1777NR JJ	—	75.00	110	140	220	—
1778/7NR JJ	—	75.00	110	140	220	—
1779NR JJ	—	75.00	110	140	220	—
1780NR JJ	—	100	175	275	525	—
1781NR JJ	—	75.00	110	140	220	—
1782NR JJ	—	85.00	135	200	300	—
1783NR JJ	—	85.00	135	200	300	—
1784/3NR JJ	—	85.00	135	200	300	—
1784NR JJ	—	85.00	135	200	300	—

KM# 48.2 ESCUDO

3.3834 g., 0.9010 Gold .0997 oz. AGW **Ruler:** Charles III **Obv:** Bust right **Obv. Legend:** CAROL • III • D • G • HISP • ET IND • R • **Rev:** Arms within Order chain **Rev. Legend:** IN • UTROQ • FELIX • A • D •

Date	Mintage	VG	F	VF	XF	Unc
1772P JS	—	60.00	90.00	125	200	—
1774P JS	—	65.00	100	145	225	—
1776P SF	—	65.00	100	145	225	—
1777P SF	—	65.00	100	145	230	—
1778P SF	—	65.00	100	145	230	—
1779P SF	—	65.00	100	145	230	—
1780P SF	—	65.00	100	145	230	—
1781P SF	—	65.00	100	145	230	—
1782P SF	—	65.00	100	145	230	—
1783P SF	—	65.00	100	145	230	—
1784P SF	—	65.00	100	145	230	—

KM# 48.2a ESCUDO

3.3834 g., 0.8750 Gold .0952 oz. AGW **Ruler:** Charles III **Obv:** Bust right **Rev:** Arms within Order chain

Date	Mintage	VG	F	VF	XF	Unc
1785P SF	—	65.00	100	145	230	—
1786P SF	—	65.00	100	145	230	—
1787P SF	—	65.00	100	145	230	—
1788P SF	—	65.00	100	145	230	—
1789/8P SF	—	65.00	100	145	230	—

KM# 48.1a ESCUDO

3.3834 g., 0.8750 Gold .0952 oz. AGW **Ruler:** Charles III **Obv:** Bust right **Rev:** Arms within Order chain

Date	Mintage	VG	F	VF	XF	Unc
1785NR JJ	—	85.00	135	200	300	—
1786NR JJ	—	85.00	135	200	300	—
1787NR JJ	—	85.00	135	200	300	—
1788NR JJ	—	85.00	135	200	300	—

KM# 54.1 ESCUDO

3.3834 g., 0.8750 Gold .0952 oz. AGW **Ruler:** Charles IV **Obv:** Bust of Charles III right **Obv. Legend:** CAROL IV.. **Rev:** Arms within Order chain

Date	Mintage	VG	F	VF	XF	Unc
1789NR JJ	—	80.00	125	200	300	—
1790NR JJ	—	80.00	125	200	300	—
1791NR JJ	—	80.00	125	200	300	—

KM# 54.2 ESCUDO

3.3834 g., 0.8750 Gold .0952 oz. AGW **Ruler:** Charles IV **Obv:** Bust of Charles III right **Obv. Legend:** CAROL IV.. **Rev:** Arms within Order chain

Date	Mintage	VG	F	VF	XF	Unc
1789/8P SF	—	60.00	100	175	265	—
1790P SF	—	60.00	100	175	265	—

KM# 56.1 ESCUDO

3.3834 g., 0.8750 Gold .0952 oz. AGW **Ruler:** Charles IV **Obv:** Uniformed bust right **Rev:** Crowned arms within Order chain

Date	Mintage	VG	F	VF	XF	Unc
1792NR JJ	—	75.00	135	195	285	—
1793NR JJ	—	75.00	135	195	285	—
1794NR JJ	—	80.00	145	210	310	—
1795NR JJ	—	65.00	110	160	230	—
1796NR JJ	—	65.00	110	160	230	—
1797/6NR JJ	—	65.00	110	160	230	—
1797NR JJ	—	65.00	110	160	230	—
1798NR JJ	—	65.00	110	160	230	—
1799/8NR JJ	—	65.00	110	160	230	—
1799NR JJ	—	65.00	110	160	230	—
1800NR JJ	—	75.00	135	195	285	—

KM# 56.2 ESCUDO

3.3834 g., 0.8750 Gold .0952 oz. AGW **Ruler:** Charles IV **Obv:** Uniformed bust right **Obv. Legend:** CAROL • IIII • D • G • HISP • ... **Rev:** Crowned arms within Order chain **Rev. Legend:** IN • UTROQ • FELIX • A • D •

Date	Mintage	VG	F	VF	XF	Unc
1792P JF	—	75.00	110	160	245	—
1793P JF	—	75.00	110	160	245	—
1794/3P JF	—	75.00	110	160	245	—
1794P JF	—	75.00	110	160	245	—
1795P JF	—	75.00	110	160	245	—
1796P JF	—	75.00	110	160	245	—
1797P JF	—	75.00	110	160	245	—
1797P JJ	—	75.00	110	160	245	—
1798P JF	—	75.00	110	160	245	—
1799P JF	—	75.00	110	160	245	—
1800P JF	—	75.00	110	160	245	—

KM# 30.1 2 ESCUDOS

6.7668 g., 0.9170 Gold .1995 oz. AGW **Ruler:** Ferdinand VI **Obv:** Bust right, date below **Obv. Legend:** FERDND • VI • D • G • HISPAN • ET IND • R • **Rev:** Crowned arms **Rev. Legend:** NOMINA MAGNA SEQUOR

Date	Mintage	VG	F	VF	XF	Unc
1756NR S	—	175	300	500	800	—
1757NR 3	—	175	300	500	000	—
1757NR SJ	—	175	300	500	800	—
1757NR J	—	250	400	600	900	—
1758NR J	—	175	300	500	800	—
1759/8NR J	—	175	300	500	800	—
1759NR J	—	175	300	500	800	—
1760NR JV	—	175	300	500	800	—

KM# 30.2 2 ESCUDOS

6.7668 g., 0.9170 Gold .1995 oz. AGW **Ruler:** Ferdinand VI **Obv:** Bust right, date below **Obv. Legend:** FERDND • VI • D • G • HISPAN • ET IND • REX • **Rev:** Crowned arms **Rev. Legend:** NOMINA MAGNA SEQUOR **Note:** Mint mark: P, PN.

Date	Mintage	VG	F	VF	XF	Unc
1758 J	—	175	300	400	625	—
1759 J	—	175	300	400	625	—
1760 J	—	175	300	400	625	—

KM# 36.1 2 ESCUDOS

6.7668 g., 0.9170 Gold .1995 oz. AGW **Ruler:** Charles III **Obv:** Bust of Ferdinand VI right **Obv. Legend:** CAROLS • III • D • G • HISPAN • ET IND • REX • **Rev:** Crowned arms **Rev. Legend:** NOMINA MAGNA SEQUOR

Date	Mintage	VG	F	VF	XF	Unc
1760NR J	—	225	375	550	950	—
1760NR JV	—	200	350	475	750	—
1761NR JV	—	200	350	475	750	—
1762NR JV	—	200	350	475	750	—

KM# 36.2 2 ESCUDOS

6.7668 g., 0.9170 Gold .1995 oz. AGW **Ruler:** Charles III **Obv:** Bust of Ferdinand VI right **Obv. Legend:** CAROLS • III • D • G • HISP • ET IND • REX • **Rev:** Crowned arms **Rev. Legend:** NOMINA MAGNA SEQUOR

Date	Mintage	VG	F	VF	XF	Unc
1760PN J	—	125	225	400	600	—
1761PN J	—	125	225	400	600	—
1762PN J	—	175	250	400	600	—
1763PN J	—	175	250	400	600	—
1767PN J	—	125	200	350	500	—
1768/7PN J	—	125	200	350	500	—
1768PN J	—	125	200	350	500	—
1769/7PN J	—	125	200	350	500	—
1769PN J	—	125	200	350	500	—
1770PN J	—	125	200	350	500	—
1771/0PN J	—	125	200	350	500	—
1771PN J	—	125	200	350	500	—

KM# 40 2 ESCUDOS

6.7668 g., 0.9170 Gold .1995 oz. AGW **Ruler:** Charles III **Obv:** Young bust right **Obv. Legend:** CAROLUS • III • D • G • HISP • ET IND • REX • **Rev:** Crowned arms **Rev. Legend:** IN • UTROQ • FELIX • AUSPICE • DEO •

Date	Mintage	VG	F	VF	XF	Unc
1762NR JV	—	200	350	500	750	—
1763NR JV	—	200	350	500	750	—
1764/3NR JV	—	200	350	500	700	—
1764NR JV	—	200	350	500	700	—
1765NR JV	—	200	350	500	700	—
1766/5NR JV	—	200	350	500	700	—
1766NR JV	—	200	350	500	700	—
1767NR JV	—	200	350	500	700	—
1768NR JV	—	200	350	500	700	—
1760NR V	—	300	525	750	1,000	—
1770NR VJ	—	200	350	500	700	—

Date	Mintage	VG	F	VF	XF	Unc
1771NR VJ	—	200	350	500	700	—

KM# 49.1 2 ESCUDOS

6.7668 g., 0.9010 Gold .1960 oz. AGW **Ruler:** Charles III **Obv:** Normal bust right **Obv. Legend:** CAROL • III • D • G • HISP • ET IND • R • **Rev:** Arms, Order chain **Rev. Legend:** IN • UTROQ • FELIX • AUSPICE • DEO •

Date	Mintage	VG	F	VF	XF	Unc
1772NR VJ	—	125	175	225	300	—
1773/2NR VJ	—	100	150	225	300	—
1773NR VJ	—	100	150	225	300	—
1774NR VJ	—	125	200	300	400	—
1774NR JJ	—	100	150	225	300	—
1775/4NR JJ	—	100	150	225	300	—
1775NR JJ	—	100	150	225	300	—
1776NR JJ	—	100	150	225	300	—
1777/6NR JJ	—	100	150	225	300	—
1777NR JJ	—	100	150	225	300	—
1778NR JJ	—	100	150	225	300	—
1779NR JJ	—	100	150	225	300	—
1780/79NR JJ	—	125	200	300	400	—
1780NR JJ	—	100	150	225	300	—
1781NR JJ	—	100	150	225	300	—
1782NR JJ	—	100	150	225	300	—
1783/2NR JJ	—	100	150	225	300	—
1783NR JJ	—	100	150	225	300	—
1784NR JJ	—	100	150	225	300	—

KM# 49.2 2 ESCUDOS

6.7668 g., 0.9010 Gold .1960 oz. AGW **Ruler:** Charles III **Obv:** Normal bust right **Obv. Legend:** CAROL • III • D • G • HISP • ET IND • R • **Rev:** Arms, Order chain **Rev. Legend:** IN • UTROQ • FELIX • AUSPICE • DEO •

Date	Mintage	VG	F	VF	XF	Unc
1772P JS	—	100	150	225	300	—
1773/2P JS	—	100	150	225	300	—
1773P JS	—	100	150	225	300	—
1774P JS	—	100	150	225	300	—
1775P JS	—	100	150	225	300	—
1776P SF	—	100	150	225	300	—
1777P SF	—	100	150	225	300	—
1779P SF	—	100	150	225	300	—
1780P SF	—	100	150	225	300	—
1781/0P SF	—	100	150	225	300	—
1781P SF	—	100	150	225	300	—
1782P SF	—	100	150	225	300	—
1783P SF	—	100	150	225	300	—
1784P SF	—	100	150	225	300	—

KM# 49.2a 2 ESCUDOS

6.7668 g., 0.8750 Gold .1904 oz. AGW **Ruler:** Charles III **Obv:** Normal bust right **Obv. Legend:** CAROL.III.. **Rev:** Arms, IN UTROQ...AD, Order chain

Date	Mintage	VG	F	VF	XF	Unc
1785/4P SF	—	100	150	225	300	—
1786P SF	—	100	150	250	350	—
1787P SF	—	100	150	225	300	—
1788P SF	—	100	150	225	300	—

KM# 49.1a 2 ESCUDOS

6.7668 g., 0.8750 Gold .1904 oz. AGW **Ruler:** Charles III **Obv:** Normal bust right **Obv. Legend:** CAROL.III.. **Rev:** Arms, IN UTROQ...AD, Order chain

Date	Mintage	VG	F	VF	XF	Unc
1785/4NR JJ	—	100	150	225	300	—
1785NR JJ	—	100	150	225	300	—
1786NR JJ	—	100	150	250	350	—
1787NR JJ	—	100	150	225	300	—
1788NR JJ	—	100	150	225	300	—
1789NR JJ	—	100	150	250	350	—

KM# 51.1 2 ESCUDOS

6.7668 g., 0.8750 Gold .1904 oz. AGW **Ruler:** Charles IV **Obv:** Bust of Charles III right **Obv. Legend:** CAROL IV.. **Rev:** Arms, IN UTROQ...AD, Order chain

Date	Mintage	VG	F	VF	XF	Unc
1789NR JJ	—	175	250	325	425	—
1790/89NR JJ	—	175	250	350	450	—
1790NR JJ	—	175	250	350	450	—
1791NR JJ	—	175	250	350	450	—

KM# 51.2 2 ESCUDOS

6.7668 g., 0.8750 Gold .1904 oz. AGW **Ruler:** Charles IV **Obv:** Bust right **Obv. Legend:** CAROL • IV • D • G • HISP • ET IND • R • **Rev:** Arms, Order chain **Rev. Legend:** IN • UTROQ • FELIX • AUSPICE • DEO •

Date	Mintage	VG	F	VF	XF	Unc
1789P SF	—	200	275	375	500	—
1790/89P SF	—	125	200	300	425	—
1790P SF	—	125	200	300	425	—
1791P SF	—	200	275	375	500	—

KM# 60.1 2 ESCUDOS

6.7668 g., 0.8750 Gold .1904 oz. AGW **Ruler:** Charles IV **Obv:** Uniformed bust right **Rev:** Crowned arms within Order chain

Date	Mintage	VG	F	VF	XF	Unc
1791NR JJ	—	150	185	275	400	—
1792NR JJ	—	150	175	250	325	—
1793NR JJ	—	200	275	375	500	—
1794NR JJ	—	175	200	300	375	—
1795NR JJ	—	150	175	250	325	—
1796NR JJ	—	250	325	450	600	—
1797/6NR JJ	—	150	185	275	400	—
1797NR JJ	—	175	200	300	375	—
1798NR JJ	—	175	200	300	375	—
1799NR JJ	—	150	175	250	325	—
1800NR JJ	—	200	275	375	500	—

KM# 60.2 2 ESCUDOS

6.7668 g., 0.8750 Gold .1904 oz. AGW **Ruler:** Charles IV **Obv:** Uniformed bust right **Obv. Legend:** CAROL • IIII • D • G • HISP • ET IND • R • **Rev:** Crowned arms within Order chain **Rev. Legend:** IN • UTROQ • FELIX • AUSPICE • DEO •

Date	Mintage	VG	F	VF	XF	Unc
1791P SF	—	150	200	350	600	—
1793P JF	—	145	185	250	375	—
1795P JF	—	300	450	600	850	—
1796P JF	—	145	185	250	375	—
1797P SF	—	145	185	250	375	—
1798P JF	—	145	185	275	400	—
1799P JF	—	145	185	250	375	—

KM# 31.1 4 ESCUDOS

13.5337 g., 0.9710 Gold .3990 oz. AGW **Ruler:** Ferdinand VI **Obv:** Uniformed bust right **Obv. Legend:** FERDND VI D.G. HISPAN ET IND REX **Rev:** Crowned arms

Date	Mintage	VG	F	VF	XF	Unc
1756 S	—	800	1,500	2,500	4,000	—
1757 S	—	700	1,200	2,250	3,750	—
1757 SJ	—	600	1,000	2,000	3,500	—
1757 JS	—	900	1,650	2,750	5,000	—
1758 J	—	600	1,000	2,000	3,500	—
1759 J	—	700	1,500	2,500	4,500	—

KM# 31.2 4 ESCUDOS

13.5337 g., 0.9710 Gold .3990 oz. AGW **Ruler:** Ferdinand VI **Obv:** Uniformed bust right **Obv. Legend:** FERDND • VI • D • G • HISPAN • ET IND • REX **Rev:** Crowned arms **Rev. Legend:** NOMINA MAGNA SEQUOR

Date	Mintage	VG	F	VF	XF	Unc
1758PN J	—	300	625	1,250	1,750	—
1759PN J	—	300	625	1,150	1,650	—
1760PN J	—	300	625	1,150	1,650	—

KM# 37 4 ESCUDOS

13.5337 g., 0.9710 Gold .3990 oz. AGW **Ruler:** Charles III **Obv:** Bust of Ferdinand VI **Obv. Legend:** CAROLS • III • D • G • HISP • ET IND • REX **Rev:** Crowned arms **Rev. Legend:** NOMINA MAGNA SEQUOR

Date	Mintage	VG	F	VF	XF	Unc
1760PN J	—	400	700	1,400	1,850	—
1761PN J	—	350	650	1,150	1,650	—
1762PN J	—	300	600	1,000	1,350	—
1769PN J	—	300	600	1,000	1,350	—

KM# 43.1 4 ESCUDOS

13.5337 g., 0.9710 Gold .3990 oz. AGW **Ruler:** Charles III **Obv:** Young bust right **Obv. Legend:** CAROLUS • III • D • G • HISP • ET IND • REX **Rev:** Crowned arms within Order chain **Rev. Legend:** IN • UTROQ • FELIX • AUSPICE • DEO •

Date	Mintage	VG	F	VF	XF	Unc
1769NR VJ	—	900	1,500	2,250	3,500	—
1770NR VJ	—	1,000	1,750	2,500	3,500	—
1771/0NR VJ	—	1,250	2,000	3,000	5,000	—
1771NR VJ	—	1,000	1,750	2,500	3,500	—

KM# 44 4 ESCUDOS

13.5337 g., 0.9010 Gold .3920 oz. AGW **Ruler:** Charles III **Rev. Legend:** IN UTROQ...A.D

Date	Mintage	VG	F	VF	XF	Unc
1773P JS	—	250	450	650	1,200	—
1776P SF	—	275	475	700	1,350	—
1778P SF	—	225	425	625	1,200	—
1779P SF	—	225	425	625	1,200	—
1780P SF	—	225	425	625	1,200	—
1782/1P SF	—	225	425	625	1,200	—
1782P SF	—	225	400	600	1,000	—
1783P SF	—	225	425	625	1,200	—

KM# 43.2 4 ESCUDOS

13.5337 g., 0.9010 Gold .3920 oz. AGW **Ruler:** Charles III **Obv:** Normal bust right **Obv. Legend:** CAROL • III • D • G • HISP • ET IND • R • **Rev:** Crowned arms within Order chain **Rev. Legend:** IN • UTROQ • FELIX • AUSPICE • DEO •

Date	Mintage	VG	F	VF	XF	Unc
1775NR JJ	—	275	475	700	1,250	—
1776NR JJ	—	225	425	650	1,200	—
1779NR JJ	—	300	500	750	1,300	—

KM# 44a 4 ESCUDOS

13.5337 g., 0.8750 Gold .3807 oz. AGW **Ruler:** Charles III **Rev. Legend:** IN UTROQ...A.D

Date	Mintage	VG	F	VF	XF	Unc
1786P SF	—	225	400	550	900	—

KM# 43.2a 4 ESCUDOS

13.5337 g., 0.8750 Gold .3807 oz. AGW **Ruler:** Charles III **Obv:** Normal bust right **Obv. Legend:** CAROL III.. **Rev:** Crowned arms within Order chain **Rev. Legend:** IN UTROQ...DEO

Date	Mintage	VG	F	VF	XF	Unc
1787NR JJ	—	350	600	850	1,500	—

KM# 52.1 4 ESCUDOS

13.5337 g., 0.8750 Gold .3807 oz. AGW **Ruler:** Charles IV **Obv:** Bust of Charles III **Obv. Legend:** CAROL IV.. **Rev:** Crowned arms within Order chain

Date	Mintage	VG	F	VF	XF	Unc
1789NR JJ	—	450	800	1,350	2,000	—
1790NR JJ	—	300	550	850	1,600	—

KM# 52.2 4 ESCUDOS

13.5337 g., 0.8750 Gold .3807 oz. AGW **Ruler:** Charles IV **Obv:** Bust of Charles III **Obv. Legend:** CAROL • IV • D • G • HISP • ET IND • R • **Rev:** Crowned arms within Order chain **Rev. Legend:** IN • UTROQ • FELIX • AUSPICE • DEO •

Date	Mintage	VG	F	VF	XF	Unc
1790P SF	—	300	550	850	1,600	—

KM# 61.1 4 ESCUDOS

13.5337 g., 0.8750 Gold .3807 oz. AGW **Ruler:** Charles IV **Obv:** Uniformed bust right **Obv. Legend:** CAROL • IIII • D • G • HISP • ET IND • R • **Rev:** Crowned arms within Order chain **Rev. Legend:** IN • UTROQ • FELIX • AUSPICE • DEO •

Date	Mintage	VG	F	VF	XF	Unc
1792NR JJ	—	300	450	650	1,250	—
1793NR JJ	—	300	450	650	1,250	—
1794NR JJ	—	325	550	700	1,300	—
1797NR JJ	—	300	450	600	1,200	—
1798NR JJ	—	325	550	700	1,350	—

KM# 61.2 4 ESCUDOS

13.5337 g., 0.8750 Gold .3807 oz. AGW **Ruler:** Charles IV **Obv:** Uniformed bust right **Obv. Legend:** CAROL • IIII • D • G • HISP • ET IND • R • **Rev:** Crowned arms within Order chain **Rev. Legend:** IN • UTROQ • FELIX • AUSPICE • DEO •

Date	Mintage	VG	F	VF	XF	Unc
1792P JF	—	275	400	600	1,000	—
1793P JF	—	275	400	600	1,000	—
1796/3P JF	—	325	550	750	1,500	—
1796P JF	—	275	400	675	1,400	—
1797P JF	—	300	500	700	1,450	—
1798/7P JF	—	300	500	700	1,450	—
1798P JF	—	300	500	700	1,450	—

KM# 32.1 8 ESCUDOS

27.0674 g., 0.9170 Gold .7980 oz. AGW **Ruler:** Ferdinand VI **Obv:** Bust right **Obv. Legend:** FERDND • VI • D • G • HISPAN • ET IND • REX **Rev:** Crowned arms, legend around **Rev. Legend:** NOMINA MAGNA SEQUOR

Date	Mintage	VG	F	VF	XF	Unc
1756NR S	—	1,000	2,000	4,000	6,500	—
1757NR S	—	700	1,500	3,000	4,500	—
1757NR SJ	—	600	1,250	2,250	3,250	—
1757NR J	—	600	1,250	2,250	3,250	—
1758NR J	—	600	1,250	2,250	3,250	—
1759NR J	—	1,000	2,000	3,500	5,000	—
1759NR JV	—	600	1,250	2,250	3,250	—
1760NR JV	—	600	1,250	2,250	3,250	—

KM# 32.2 8 ESCUDOS

27.0674 g., 0.9170 Gold .7980 oz. AGW **Ruler:** Ferdinand VI **Obv:** Bust right **Obv. Legend:** FERDND VI D.G. HISPAN ET. IND REX **Rev:** Crowned arms, legend around

Date	Mintage	VG	F	VF	XF	Unc
1758PN J	—	600	1,250	1,750	2,500	—
1759PN J	—	600	1,250	1,750	2,500	—
1760PN J	—	700	1,500	2,500	3,500	—

KM# 38.1 8 ESCUDOS

27.0674 g., 0.9170 Gold .7980 oz. AGW **Ruler:** Charles III **Obv:** Bust of Ferdinand VI **Obv. Legend:** CAROLS III.. **Rev:** Arms within Order chain

Date	Mintage	VG	F	VF	XF	Unc
1760NR JV	—	650	1,350	2,000	2,750	—
1761NR JV	—	650	1,350	2,000	2,750	—
1762NR JV	—	800	1,700	3,000	4,000	—

KM# 38.2 8 ESCUDOS

27.0674 g., 0.9170 Gold .7980 oz. AGW **Ruler:** Charles III **Obv:** Bust of Ferdinand VI **Obv. Legend:** CAROLS • III • D • G • HISPAN • ET IND • REX **Rev:** Arms within Order chain **Rev. Legend:** NOMINA MAGNA SEQUOR

Date	Mintage	VG	F	VF	XF	Unc
1760PN J	—	600	1,250	2,000	2,750	—
1761/0PN J	—	600	1,250	2,000	2,750	—
1761PN J	—	600	1,250	2,000	2,750	—
1762PN J	—	600	1,250	2,000	2,750	—
1763/2PN J	—	700	1,500	3,000	4,000	—
1767PN J	—	600	1,250	2,000	2,750	—
1768/7PN J	—	700	1,500	3,000	4,000	—
1769/7PN J	—	600	1,200	1,700	2,500	—
1769PN J	—	600	1,200	1,700	2,500	—
1770PN J	—	600	1,200	1,700	2,500	—
1771PN J	—	600	1,200	1,700	2,500	—

KM# 41 8 ESCUDOS

27.0674 g., 0.9170 Gold .7980 oz. AGW **Ruler:** Charles III **Obv:** Uniformed bust right **Obv. Legend:** CAROLUS • III • D • G • HISP • ET IND • REX **Rev:** Arms within Order chain **Rev. Legend:** IN • UTROQ • FELIX • AUSPICE • DEO • **Note:** Many punctuation varieties exist within the assayer initials.

Date	Mintage	VG	F	VF	XF	Unc
1762NR JV	—	1,200	2,500	4,000	6,000	—
1763NR JV	—	800	1,750	3,000	4,000	—
1764NR JV	—	800	1,750	3,000	4,000	—
1765NR JV	—	800	1,750	3,000	4,000	—
1766NR JV	—	800	1,750	3,000	4,000	—
1767NR JV	—	800	1,750	3,000	4,000	—
1768NR JV	—	800	1,750	3,000	4,000	—
1769NR JV	—	1,750	3,500	6,000	8,500	—
1769NR V	—	1,200	2,500	3,500	5,000	—
1770/69NR VJ	—	1,000	2,000	3,500	5,000	—
1770NR VJ	—	1,000	2,000	3,500	5,000	—
1771NR VJ	—	1,000	2,000	3,500	5,000	—

KM# 50.1 8 ESCUDOS

27.0674 g., 0.9010 Gold .7841 oz. AGW **Ruler:** Charles III **Obv:** Normal bust right **Obv. Legend:** CAROL • III • D • G • HISP • ET IND • R • **Rev:** Crowned arms within Order chain **Rev. Legend:** IN • ITROQ • FELIX • AUSPICE • DEO •

Date	Mintage	VG	F	VF	XF	Unc
1772NR VJ	—	375	550	750	950	—
1773NR VJ	—	375	550	750	950	—
1774NR JJ/VJ	—	400	700	1,200	1,600	—
1774NR VJ	—	375	550	750	950	—
1774NR JJ	—	375	550	750	950	—
1775NR JJ	—	375	550	750	950	—
1776NR JJ	—	375	550	750	950	—
1777/6NR JJ	—	375	550	750	950	—
1777NR JJ	—	375	550	750	950	—
1778/7NR JJ	—	375	550	750	950	—
1778NR JJ	—	375	550	750	950	—
1779NR JJ	—	375	550	750	950	—
1780/79NR JJ	—	375	550	750	950	—
1780NR JJ	—	375	550	750	950	—
1781/0NR JJ	—	375	550	750	950	—
1781NR JJ	—	375	550	750	950	—
1782NR JJ	—	375	550	750	950	—
1783/2NR JJ	—	375	550	750	950	—
1783NR JJ	—	375	550	750	950	—
1784NR JJ	—	375	550	750	950	—

KM# 50.2 8 ESCUDOS

27.0674 g., 0.9010 Gold .7841 oz. AGW **Ruler:** Charles III **Obv:** Normal bust right **Obv. Legend:** CAROL • III • D • G • HISP • ET IND • R • **Rev:** Crowned arms within Order chain **Rev. Legend:** IN • ITROQ • FELIX • AUSPICE • DEO •

Date	Mintage	VG	F	VF	XF	Unc
1772P JS	—	375	550	750	950	—
1773P JS	—	375	550	750	950	—
1774P JS	—	375	550	750	950	—
1775/4P JS	—	375	550	750	950	—
1775P JS	—	375	550	750	950	—
1776P JS	—	550	1,000	1,500	2,500	—
1776P SF	—	375	550	750	950	—
1777P SF	—	375	550	750	950	—
1778P SF	—	375	550	750	950	—
1779P SF	—	375	550	750	950	—
1780P SF	—	375	550	750	950	—
1781P SF	—	375	550	750	950	—
1781P SF	—	375	550	750	950	—
1783P SF	—	375	550	750	950	—
1784P SF	—	375	550	750	950	—

KM# 50.2a 8 ESCUDOS

27.0674 g., 0.8750 Gold .7615 oz. AGW **Ruler:** Charles III **Obv:** Normal bust right **Obv. Legend:** CAROL III.. **Rev:** Crowned arms within Order chain

Date	Mintage	VG	F	VF	XF	Unc
1785P SF	—	375	550	750	950	—
1786P SF	—	375	550	750	950	—
1787P SF	—	375	550	750	950	—
1788P SF	—	375	550	750	950	—
1789/8P SF	—	500	825	1,150	1,500	—

KM# 50.1a 8 ESCUDOS

27.0674 g., 0.8750 Gold .7615 oz. AGW **Ruler:** Charles IV **Obv:** Normal bust of Charles III **Obv. Legend:** CAROL III..

Date	Mintage	VG	F	VF	XF	Unc
1785NR JJ	—	375	550	750	950	—
1786NR JJ	—	375	550	750	950	—
1787NR JJ	—	375	550	750	950	—
1787NR JJ	—	375	550	750	950	—
1788NR JJ	—	375	550	750	950	—
1789NR JJ	—	375	550	750	950	—

KM# 53.1 8 ESCUDOS

27.0674 g., 0.8750 Gold .7615 oz. AGW **Ruler:** Charles IV **Obv:** Bust right **Obv. Legend:** CAROL • VI • D • G • HISP • ET IND • R • **Rev:** Crowned arms within Order chain **Rev. Legend:** IN • ITROQ • FELIX • AUSPICE • DEO •

Date	Mintage	VG	F	VF	XF	Unc
1789NR JJ	—	375	575	775	1,000	—
1790NR JJ	—	375	575	775	1,000	—
1791NR JJ	—	375	575	775	1,000	—

KM# 53.2 8 ESCUDOS

27.0674 g., 0.8750 Gold .7615 oz. AGW **Ruler:** Charles IV **Obv:** Bust of Charles III **Obv. Legend:** CAROL VI.. **Rev:** Crowned arms within Order chain

Date	Mintage	VG	F	VF	XF	Unc
1789P SF	—	350	575	775	1,000	—
1790P SF	—	375	575	775	1,000	—
1791P SF	—	425	650	950	1,200	—

KM# 62.1 8 ESCUDOS

27.0674 g., 0.8750 Gold .7615 oz. AGW **Ruler:** Charles IV **Obv:** Uniformed bust right **Obv. Legend:** CAROL • IIII • D • G • HISP • ET IND • R • **Rev:** Crowned arms within Order chain **Rev. Legend:** IN • ITROQ • FELIX • AUSPICE • DEO •

Date	Mintage	VG	F	VF	XF	Unc
1791NR JJ	—	550	750	900	1,500	—
1792/1NR JJ	—	550	750	900	1,500	—
1792NR JJ	—	550	750	900	1,500	—
1793NR JJ	—	550	750	900	1,500	—
1793NR JJ ET ND	—	625	850	1,150	1,750	—
1794NR JJ	—	550	750	900	1,500	—
1795NR JJ	—	550	750	900	1,500	—
1796NR JJ	—	550	750	900	1,500	—
1797NR JJ	—	550	750	900	1,500	—
1798NR JJ	—	550	750	900	1,500	—
1799NR JJ	—	550	750	900	1,500	—
1800/799NR JJ	—	550	750	900	1,500	—
1800NR JJ	—	550	750	900	1,500	—

KM# 62.2 8 ESCUDOS

27.0674 g., 0.8750 Gold .7615 oz. AGW **Ruler:** Charles IV **Obv:** Uniformed bust right **Obv. Legend:** CAROL • IIII • D • G • HISP • ET ... **Rev:** Crowned arms within Order chain **Rev. Legend:** IN • UTROQ • FELIX • AUSPICE • DEO •

Date	Mintage	VG	F	VF	XF	Unc
1791P SF	—	600	800	1,000	1,650	—
1792P JF	—	550	750	900	1,500	—
1793P JF	—	550	750	900	1,500	—
1794P JF	—	550	750	900	1,500	—
1795/4P JF	—	600	800	1,000	1,650	—
1795P JF	—	550	750	900	1,500	—
1796P JF	—	550	750	900	1,500	—
1797P JF	—	550	750	900	1,500	—
1798P JF	—	550	750	900	1,500	—
1799P JF	—	550	750	900	1,500	—
1800P JF	—	550	750	900	1,500	—

COURLAND

The people of Courland are of Aryan descent primarily from the German Order of Livonian Knights. They were nomadic tribesmen who settled along the Baltic prior to the 13th century. Ideally situated as a trade route and lacking a central government, they were conquered in 1561 by Poland and Sweden.

When the Livonian Order was dissolved in 1561 the then Master of the Order, Gotthard Kettler was made Duke of Courland. During the 17th century, Courland remained part of Poland, but went under Russia after Poland's division. When the Kettler line became extinct in 1737 Courland was awarded to Ernst Johann Biron, chief advisor and lover of Empress Anna of Russia. After her death he was exiled but returned in 1763. He abdicated in favor of his son Peter in 1769.

RULERS

Carl of Saxony, Poland, 1758-1763
Ernst Johann Biron, 1737-1740,1762-1769
Peter Biron, 1769-1795

MINTMASTERS' INITIALS

Initials	Date	Name
ICS	1764-65	Justin Carl Schroder
IFS	1764-65	John Frederic Schmickert

DUCHY

STANDARD COINAGE

KM# 20 SOLIDUS

1.3000 g., Copper **Ruler:** Carl of Saxony, Poland **Obv:** Bust right **Obv. Legend:** D • G • CAROL.... **Rev:** 2 crowned shields of arms

Date	Mintage	VG	F	VF	XF	Unc
1762	—	15.00	25.00	40.00	65.00	—

KM# 23 SOLIDUS

1.3000 g., Copper **Ruler:** Ernst Johann Biron **Subject:** Ernst Johann Biron **Obv:** Crowned "E J" monogram

Date	Mintage	VG	F	VF	XF	Unc
1763	—	10.00	15.00	25.00	40.00	—

KM# 28 SOLIDUS

1.3000 g., Copper **Ruler:** Ernst Johann Biron **Obv:** Bust right **Obv. Legend:** D • G • ERNEST • IOH • DVX • **Rev:** Two crowned shields of arms **Rev. Legend:** IN • LIV • CVRL • ...

Date	Mintage	VG	F	VF	XF	Unc
1764	—	15.00	25.00	40.00	65.00	—
1764 ICS	—	16.50	28.50	50.00	75.00	—
1764 IFS	—	15.00	25.00	40.00	65.00	—

KM# 21 GROSSUS (Grosz)

3.4000 g., Billon, 22 mm. **Ruler:** Carl of Saxony, Poland **Obv:** Bust right **Rev:** 2 crowned shields of arms

Date	Mintage	VG	F	VF	XF	Unc
1762	—	20.00	35.00	55.00	100	—
1763	—	20.00	35.00	55.00	100	—

KM# 24.1 GROSSUS (Grosz)

1.3000 g., Billon, 17 mm. **Ruler:** Ernst Johann Biron **Obv:** Crowned "E J" monogram **Rev:** Two crowned shields of arms **Rev. Legend:** MON. ARGENT. DVC. CVRLAND

Date	Mintage	VG	F	VF	XF	Unc
1763	—	15.00	30.00	50.00	85.00	—
1763 ICS	—	15.00	30.00	50.00	85.00	—
1764 ICS	—	15.00	30.00	50.00	85.00	—

KM# 24.2 GROSSUS (Grosz)

1.3000 g., Billon **Ruler:** Ernst Johann Biron **Rev. Legend:** MON. ARGENTEA. DVC.CVRLAND

Date	Mintage	VG	F	VF	XF	Unc
1763 ICS	—	15.00	30.00	50.00	85.00	—
1764 ICS	—	15.00	30.00	50.00	85.00	—
1765	—	15.00	30.00	50.00	85.00	—

KM# 26 3 GROSZY

2.0000 g., Billon, 21 mm. **Ruler:** Ernst Johann Biron **Obv:** Bust right **Obv. Legend:** D • G • ERNEST • IOH • IN • .... **Rev:** 2 crowned shields of arms **Note:** Varieties exist.

Date	Mintage	VG	F	VF	XF	Unc
1763	—	22.50	37.50	60.00	110	—
1764 ICS	—	22.50	37.50	60.00	110	—

Date	Mintage	VG	F	VF	XF	Unc
1764 IFS	—	22.50	37.50	60.00	110	—
1765 ICS	—	22.50	37.50	60.00	110	—

KM# 22 6 GROSZY

3.7000 g., Billon, 24 mm. **Ruler:** Carl of Saxony, Poland **Obv:** Bust right **Obv. Legend:** D • G • CAROL.... **Rev:** Two crowned shields of arms

Date	Mintage	VG	F	VF	XF	Unc
1762	—	30.00	50.00	85.00	150	—

KM# 27 6 GROSZY

Billon **Ruler:** Ernst Johann Biron **Obv:** Uniformed bust right **Obv. Legend:** D • G • ERNEST • IOH • IN • LIV • ... **Rev:** Two crowned shields of arms **Rev. Legend:** MONETA • ARGENT • DVC • ... **Note:** Varieties exist.

Date	Mintage	VG	F	VF	XF	Unc
1763 ICS	—	27.50	45.00	65.00	120	—
1764 ICS	—	27.50	45.00	65.00	120	—
1765	—	27.50	45.00	65.00	120	—

KM# 29 ORT (18 Grozy - 1 Timf)

6.1000 g., Billon, 28 mm. **Ruler:** Ernst Johann Biron **Obv:** Uniformed bust right **Obv. Legend:** D G ERNEST IOH IN LIV ... **Rev:** Two crowned shields of arms **Rev. Legend:** MONETA • ARGENT • DVC : CVRLAND •

Date	Mintage	VG	F	VF	XF	Unc
1764 ICS Rare	—	—	—	—	—	—

KM# 32 THALER

28.3000 g., Silver **Ruler:** Peter Biron **Subject:** Peter Biron **Obv:** Head right **Obv. Legend:** D • G • PETRUS IN LIV • CURL • ET SEMGAL • DUX **Rev:** Two crowned shields of arms **Rev. Legend:** MON • NOVA • ARG • DUC • CURL • ... **Note:** Dav. #1624.

Date	Mintage	VG	F	VF	XF	Unc
1780	—	65.00	125	250	450	700

TRADE COINAGE

KM# 30 DUCAT

3.5000 g., 0.9860 Gold .1109 oz. AGW **Ruler:** Ernst Johann Biron **Obv:** Small bust right **Rev:** 2 Crowned shields of arms

Date	Mintage	VG	F	VF	XF	Unc
1764 ICS	—	225	425	950	1,600	—

KM# 31 DUCAT

3.5000 g., 0.9860 Gold .1109 oz. AGW **Ruler:** Ernst Johann Biron **Obv:** Large bust right

Date	Mintage	VG	F	VF	XF	Unc
1764 ICS	—	275	475	1,000	1,750	—

KM# 33 DUCAT

3.5000 g., 0.9860 Gold .1109 oz. AGW **Ruler:** Peter Biron **Obv:** Head right **Obv. Legend:** D • G • PETRUS IN LIV • CURL • ... **Rev:** Two crowned shields of arms **Rev. Legend:** MON • AUR • EA • DUC • CURL • ....

Date	Mintage	VG	F	VF	XF	Unc
1780	—	200	400	800	1,350	2,000

KM# 34 2 DUCAT

7.0000 g., 0.9860 Gold .2219 oz. AGW **Ruler:** Ernst Johann Biron

Date	Mintage	VG	F	VF	XF	Unc
1764 Rare	—	—	—	—	—	—

PATTERNS

Including off metal strikes

KM#	Date	Mintage	Identification	Mkt Val
Pn1	1764 ICS	—	3 Groszy. Gold. Uniformed bust right. Two crowned shields of arms.	—

TRIAL STRIKES

KM#	Date	Mintage	Identification	Mkt Val
TS1	ND(1764)	—	6 Groszy. Silver.	—
TS2	1764	—	Ort. Silver.	—

CRIMEA (KRIM)

The Crimea (ancient Tauris or Tauric Chersonese, Turkish Kirim or Krim, Russian Krym) is a peninsula of southern Russia extending into the Black Sea southwest of the Sea of Azov.

In ancient times, the Crimea was inhabited by the Gothsand Scythians, was colonized by the Greeks, and ranked, in part, as a tributary state of Rome. During the succeeding centuries, the Goths, Huns, Khazars, Byzantine Greeks, Kipchak Turks, and the Tatars of Batu Khan who founded the Tatar Khanate in Russia known as the Empire of the Golden Horde overran the Crimea. After the destruction of the Golden Horde by Tamerlane (Timur) in 1395, the Crimean Taters founded an independent khanate under Haji Ghirai which reigned first at Solkhat (Eski Kirim or Stary Krym). The Crimean khans ruled as tributary princes of the Ottoman empire from 1478 to 1777, when they became dependent upon Russia.

Catherine II annexed the Crimea to Russia on April 26,1783, and after a period as the Tavrida province, it was made an autonomous republic of the Russian federation in1921. The Tatars, however, remained fiercely nationalistic and during World War II collaborated with the German-Rumanian occupation force. Upon Russian re-conquest of the Crimea in May, 1944, the entire Tatar population was deported to Russia and Siberia. The autonomous Crimean republic was dissolved and reconstituted as a region of the Russian Soviet Federated Socialist Republic. On Feb. 14, 1954, this region was transferred to the Ukranian Soviet Socialist Republic, becoming its southernmost province.

KHANATE

RULERS

Giray bin Daulat, AH1171-1177/1758-1764AD
Sahib Geray II bin Ahmad Giray, AH1185-1189/1772-1775AD
Shahin Giray bin Ahmad Giray, AH1191-1197/1777-1783AD

MINT MARKS

باغجه سراي

Bagchih-Serai

كفه

Kaffa

MONETARY SYSTEM

3 Manghir (Agcheh, Asper) – 1 Para
2 Para = 1 Ikilik
2-1/2 Ikilik = 1 Beshlik
2 Beshlik = 1 Onlik
2 Onlik = 1 Yirmilik = 1/2 Kurus
2 Yirmilik = 1 Kurus
1-1/2 Kurus = 1 Altmishlik

Russian Names	Turkish Names
2 Polushka = 1 Denga	= 2 Akche
2 Denga = 1 Kopek	= 3 Akche
5 Kopecks = 1 Kyrmis	= 15 Akche
2 Kyrmis = 1 Ishal (Tschal)	= 25 Akche

From AH1017-1169/1608-1756AD silver coins (akeches) and copper coins were struck in the names of 24 Khanate rulers. They are all very similar to the coin illustrated as C#125, usually with the obverse showing the ruler's and his father's names and the reverse with a toughra above *duribe* and the mintname.

STANDARD COINAGE

KM# 10 MANGHIR

Copper **Ruler:** Sahib Geray II bin Ahmad Giray

Date	Mintage	Good	VG	F	VF	XF
AH1185 (1771)	—	30.00	50.00	75.00	135	—

KM# 12 MANGHIR

0.2000 g., Billon **Ruler:** Shahin Giray bin Ahmad Giray **Obv:** Similar to 1 Para, KM#14 **Rev:** Similar to 1 Para, KM#14

Date	Mintage	Good	VG	F	VF	XF
AH1191//2 (1777)	—	30.00	50.00	75.00	135	—

KM# 14 PARA

0.6000 g., Billon **Ruler:** Shahin Giray bin Ahmad Giray

Date	Mintage	Good	VG	F	VF	XF
AH1191//1 (1777)	—	30.00	50.00	75.00	135	—
AH1191//2 (1777)	—	30.00	50.00	75.00	135	—
AH1191//3 (1777)	—	30.00	50.00	75.00	135	—

KM# 16 IKILIK (2 Akche)

Billon, 11 mm. **Ruler:** Shahin Giray bin Ahmad Giray **Obv:** Similar to Yirmilik, C#165 **Rev:** Similar to Yirmilik, C#165 **Note:** Weight varies 1.30-1.55 grams.

Date	Mintage	Good	VG	F	VF	XF
AH1191//4 (1777)	—	50.00	75.00	125	235	—
AH1191//5 (1777)	—	50.00	75.00	125	235	—

KM# 18 BESHLIK

Billon **Ruler:** Shahin Giray bin Ahmad Giray **Obv:** Similar to Polushka, KM#22 **Rev:** Similar to Polushka, KM#22

Date	Mintage	Good	VG	F	VF	XF
AH1191//3 (1777)	—	50.00	75.00	125	235	—
AH1191//4 (1777)	—	50.00	75.00	125	235	—

KM# 20 ONLIK

3.0500 g., Silver **Ruler:** Shahin Giray bin Ahmad Giray

Date	Mintage	Good	VG	F	VF	XF
AH1191//3 (1777)	—	150	300	500	800	—

KM# 22 POLUSHKA (1 Akche)

Copper **Ruler:** Shahin Giray bin Ahmad Giray

Date	Mintage	Good	VG	F	VF	XF
AH1191//2 (1777)	—	30.00	60.00	120	185	—

KM# 24 DENGA (2 Akche)

Copper **Ruler:** Shahin Giray bin Ahmad Giray

Date	Mintage	Good	VG	F	VF	XF
AH1191//3 (1777)	—	35.00	70.00	140	220	—

KM# 26 DENGA (2 Akche)

Copper **Ruler:** Shahin Giray bin Ahmad Giray

Date	Mintage	Good	VG	F	VF	XF
AH1191//4 (1777)	—	35.00	70.00	140	220	—
AH1191//5 (1777)	—	35.00	70.00	140	220	—
AH1191//6 (1777)	—	35.00	70.00	140	220	—

KM# 28 KOPEK (3 Akche)

9.5000 g., Copper **Ruler:** Shahin Giray bin Ahmad Giray

Date	Mintage	Good	VG	F	VF	XF
AH1191//4 (1777) Arabic	—	25.00	45.00	75.00	135	—

KM# 30 KOPEK (3 Akche)

9.5000 g., Copper **Ruler:** Shahin Giray bin Ahmad Giray

Date	Mintage	Good	VG	F	VF	XF
AH1191//4 (1777) Persian	—	25.00	45.00	75.00	135	—

KM# 32 KOPEK (3 Akche)

9.5000 g., Copper **Ruler:** Shahin Giray bin Ahmad Giray **Rev:** Thinner wreath around legend

Date	Mintage	Good	VG	F	VF	XF
AH1191//5 (1777)	—	25.00	45.00	75.00	135	—
AH1191//6 (1777)	—	25.00	45.00	75.00	135	—

KM# 34 KYRMIS (15 Akche)

16.0000 g., Copper **Ruler:** Shahin Giray bin Ahmad Giray **Obv:** Similar to KM#32

Date	Mintage	Good	VG	F	VF	XF
AH1191//4 (1777) Persian	—	70.00	125	225	350	—

KM# 36 KYRMIS (15 Akche)

16.0000 g., Copper **Ruler:** Shahin Giray bin Ahmad Giray

Date	Mintage	Good	VG	F	VF	XF
AH1191//5 (1777)	—	70.00	125	225	350	—
AH1191//6 (1777)	—	70.00	125	225	350	—

KM# 38 KYRMIS (15 Akche)

16.0000 g., Copper **Ruler:** Shahin Giray bin Ahmad Giray

Date	Mintage	Good	VG	F	VF	XF
AH1191//5 (1777)	—	70.00	125	225	350	—

KM# 40 YIRMILIK

8.0000 g., Silver **Ruler:** Shahin Giray bin Ahmad Giray

Date	Mintage	VG	F	VF	XF	Unc
AH1191//4 (1777)	—	125	250	500	1,000	—
AH1191//5 (1777)	—	125	250	500	1,000	—

KM# 42 KURUS

14.4000 g., Silver, 34 mm. **Ruler:** Shahin Giray bin Ahmad Giray

Date	Mintage	VG	F	VF	XF	Unc
AH1191//4 (1777)	—	200	300	600	1,200	—

KM# 44 KURUS

16.0000 g., Silver, 35 mm. **Ruler:** Shahin Giray bin Ahmad Giray

Date	Mintage	VG	F	VF	XF	Unc
AH1191//5 (1777)	—	200	300	600	1,200	—

KM# 46 ALTMISHLIK

Silver **Ruler:** Shahin Giray bin Ahmad Giray **Note:** Weight varies 19.80-22.80 grams.

Date	Mintage	VG	F	VF	XF	Unc
AH1191//2 (1777)	—	250	400	800	1,500	—
AH1191//4 (1777)	—	250	400	800	1,500	—
AH1191//5 (1777)	—	250	400	800	1,500	—
AH1191//6 (1777)	—	250	400	800	1,500	—

KM# 48 ALTILIK ALTIN

21.2000 g., Gold **Ruler:** Shahin Giray bin Ahmad Giray **Obv:** Toughra and flower **Rev:** Mintname within Seal of Solomon

Date	Mintage	VG	F	VF	XF	Unc
AH1191//6 Rare	—	—	—	—	—	—

KM# 50.1 ISCHAL (25 Akche)

75.0000 g., Copper **Ruler:** Shahin Giray bin Ahmad Giray **Rev:** Similar to KM#50.2

Date	Mintage	VG	F	VF	XF	Unc
AH1191//5 (1777)	—	300	600	1,000	1,800	—

KM# 50.2 ISCHAL (25 Akche)

75.0000 g., Copper **Ruler:** Shahin Giray bin Ahmad Giray **Obv:** Modified design

Date	Mintage	VG	F	VF	XF	Unc
AH1191//5 (1777)	—	300	600	1,000	1,800	—

KM# 52 ISCHAL (30 Akche)

84.0000 g., Copper **Ruler:** Shahin Giray bin Ahmad Giray **Obv:** Flowers added

Date	Mintage	VG	F	VF	XF	Unc
AH1191//6 (1777)	—	300	600	1,000	1,800	—

KM# 54 BESHLIK ALTIN

16.0000 g., Gold **Ruler:** Shahin Giray bin Ahmad Giray **Obv:** Toughra and flower **Rev:** Mint name within Seal of Solomon

Date	Mintage	VG	F	VF	XF	Unc
AH1191//6 Rare	—	—	—	—	—	—

EMPIRE

RULER

Catherine II, 1783-1796

MINT MARK

TM – Feodosia Mint

MILLED COINAGE

KM# 56 2 KOPEKS

Silver **Ruler:** Catherine II **Obv:** Crowned EII monogram **Rev:** Value, with two dots

Date	Mintage	F	VF	XF	Unc	BU
	—	—	—	—	—	—
1787TM Rare	—	—	—	—	—	—

KM# 58 5 KOPEKS

Silver **Ruler:** Catherine II **Obv:** Crowned "EII" monogram **Rev:** Value, with five dots

Date	Mintage	F	VF	XF	Unc	BU
1787TM Rare	—	—	—	—	—	—

KM# 60.1 10 KOPEKS

Silver **Ruler:** Catherine II **Obv:** Crowned "EII" monogram **Rev:** Close 10, with ten dots

Date	Mintage	F	VF	XF	Unc	BU
1787TM	—	175	350	550	950	—

KM# 60.2 10 KOPEKS

Silver **Ruler:** Catherine II **Obv:** Crowned "EII" monogram **Rev:** Wide 10, with ten dots

Date	Mintage	F	VF	XF	Unc	BU
1787TM	—	175	350	550	950	—

KM# 62 20 KOPEKS

Silver **Ruler:** Catherine II **Obv:** Crowned "EII" monogram **Rev:** Value with twenty dots

Date	Mintage	F	VF	XF	Unc	BU
1787TM	—	100	200	300	600	—

NOVODELS

KM#	Date	Mintage	Identification	Mkt Val
N2	1787TM	—	20 Kopeks. KM#62.	—

Note: Restruck among other coins as Siberian coppers at St. Petersburg Mint for the All-Russian Fair at Nizhni Novgorod; Inward curl on upper stem of numeral 2

CUBA

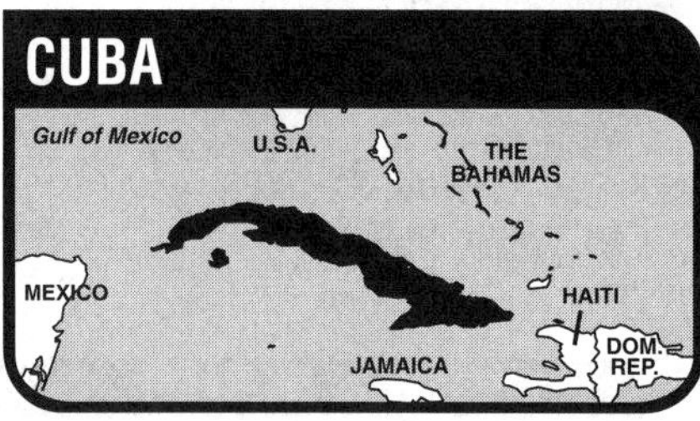

The Republic of Cuba, situated at the northern edge of the Caribbean Sea about 90 miles (145 km.) south of Florida, has an area of 42,804 sq. mi. (110,860 sq. km.) and a population of *11.2 million. Capital: Havana. The Cuban economy is based on the cultivation and refining of sugar, which provides 80 percent of export earnings.

Discovered by Columbus in 1492 and settled by Diego Velasquez in the early 1500s, Cuba remained a Spanish possession until 1898, except for a brief British occupancy of Havana in 1762-63. Cuban attempts to gain freedom were crushed, even while Spain was granting independence to its other American possessions. Ten years of warfare, 1868-78, between Spanish troops and Cuban rebels exacted guarantees of rights which were never implemented. The final revolt, begun in 1895, evoked American sympathy, and with the aid of U.S. troops independence was proclaimed on May 20, 1902. Fulgencio Batista seized the government in 1952 and established a dictatorship. Opposition to Batista, led by Fidel Castro, drove him into exile on Jan. 1, 1959. A communist-type, 25-member collective leadership headed by Castro was inaugurated in March, 1962.

RULER

Spanish, until 1898

VICE-ROYALTY OF NEW SPAIN

Isla de Cuba

SIEGE COINAGE

KM# A1 8 C(UARTOS)

Copper **Obv:** Crowned lion arms divide "F.C/V8" **Rev:** Crowned castle arms divide date

Date	Mintage	Good	VG	F	VF	XF
1741 Rare	—	—	—	—	—	—

Note: Struck at Santiago de Cuba while under blockade of Admiral Vernon's ships

CURACAO

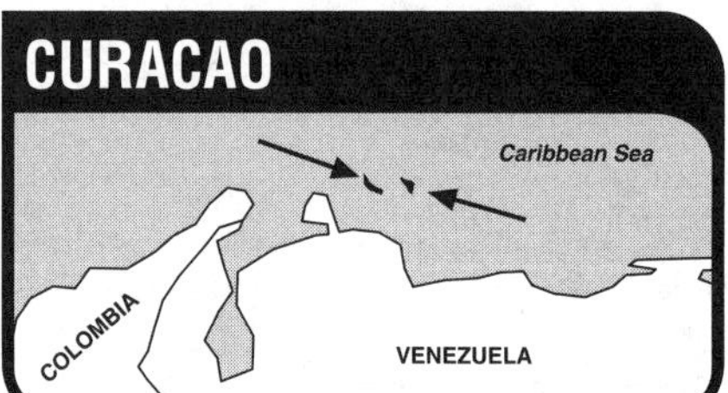

The island of Curacao, the largest of the Netherlands Antilles, which is an autonomous part of the Kingdom of the Netherlands located in the Caribbean Sea 40 miles off the coast of Venezuela

Curacao was discovered by Spanish navigator Alonso de Ojeda in 1499 and was settled by Spain in 1527. The Dutch West India Company took the island from Spain in 1634 and administered it until 1787, when it was surrendered to the United Netherlands. The Dutch held it thereafter except for two periods during the Napoleonic Wars, 1800-1803 and 1807-16, when it was occupied by the British. During World War II, Curacao refined 60 percent of the oil used by the Allies; the refineries were protected by U.S. troops after Germany invaded the Netherlands in 1940.

During the second occupation of the Napoleonic period, the British created an emergency coinage for Curacao by cutting the Spanish dollar into 5 equal segments and countermarking each piece with a rosette indent.

MONETARY SYSTEM

1 Cent (U.S.) = 2-1/2 Stuivers
6 Stuivers = 1 Reaal
8 Realen = 1 Peso, 1793-1801
7-1/2 Pesos = 1 Johannes (unmarked), 1793-99
6 Pesos = 1 Johannes (unmarked), 1799-1815
8 Pesos = 1 Johannes (c/m), 1799-1815

BATAVIAN REPUBLIC

COUNTERMARKED COINAGE

KM# 2 7 STUIVERS

Silver **Countermark:** 7 **Note:** 2.00-2.35 g; countermark in oval indent on French Livre.

CM Date	Host Date	Good	VG	F	VF	XF
ND	ND	75.00	100	145	200	250

KM# 3 7 STUIVERS

Silver **Countermark:** 7 **Note:** 2.00-2.35 g; countermark in oval indent on Spanich Colonial 1 Real.

CM Date	Host Date	Good	VG	F	VF	XF
ND	ND	100	135	185	245	300

KM# 1 CENT

Copper **Note:** Countermark circular CURACAO on U.S. large cent.

CM Date	Host Date	Good	VG	F	VF	XF
ND	ND	225	275	325	450	550

KM# 8 8 PESOS

Gold **Countermark:** W **Obv:** Countermark GI, L, MH and B at edges on a false Brazil 6400 Reis type of KM#172.2 **Rev:** Countermark

CM Date	Host Date	Good	VG	F	VF	XF
ND(1799)	ND Unique	—	—	—	—	—

Note: A multiple island countermark example is known on Brazil KM#218

DANISH WEST INDIES

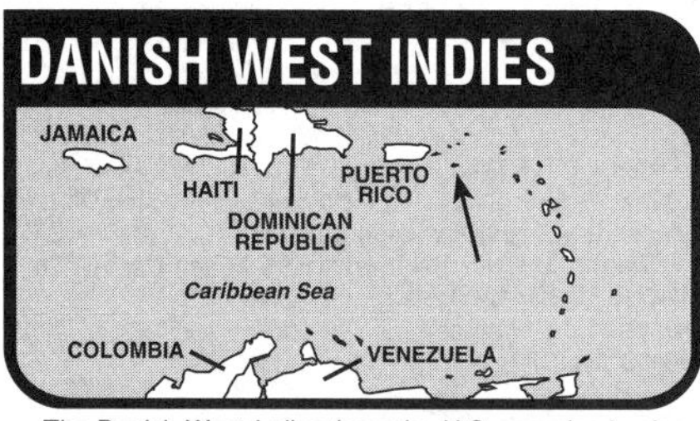

The Danish West Indies (now the U.S. organized unincorporated territory of the Virgin Islands of the United States) consisted of the islands of St. Thomas, St. John, St. Croix, and 62 islets in the Caribbean Sea roughly 40 miles (64 km.) east of Puerto Rico. The islands have a combined area of 133 sq. mi. (352 sq. km.) and a population of *106,000. Capital: Charlotte Amalie. Tourism is the principal industry. Watch movements, costume jewelry, pharmaceuticals, and rum are exported.

The Virgin Islands were discovered by Columbus in 1493, during his second voyage to America. During the 17th century, individual islands, actually the peaks of a submerged mountain range, were held by Spain, Holland, England, France and Denmark. These islands were also the favorite resorts of the buccaneers operating in the Caribbean and the coastal waters of eastern North America. Control of most of the 100-island group finally passed to Denmark, with England securing the easterly remainder. The Danish islands had their own coinage from the early 18th century, based on but unequal to, Denmark's homeland system. In the late 18th and early 19th centuries, Danish silver coinage augmented the islands currency. The Danish islands were purchased by the United States in 1917 for $25 million, mainly to forestall their acquisition by Germany and because they command the Anegada Passage into the Caribbean Sea, a strategic point on the defense perimeter of the Panama Canal.

RULER

Danish, until 1917

MINT MARKS

Three mints were used for coinage of the eighteenth century.

Mint mark	Mint	Description
(a)	Altona	Tall, widely spaced crown
(c)	Copenhagen	Symetrical crown
	Copenhagen	No mint marks but different crowns on 1767 coins
(k)	Kongsberg	Boxy crown

MONETARY SYSTEM

(Until 1849)

96 Skilling = 1 Daler

NOTE: Skilling denominated issues through 1799 are found on a broad range of planchet sizes and alloys, sometimes even for the same date(s). These "contemporary counterfeits" look to be either silvered copper, copper and are not uncommon. It has been reported that some of the 6, 12 and 24 Skillings, dated 1767, were struck in 1782, 1790, 1791, 1795, and 1800. 2 Skillings, Danish coins exported to the Danish West Indies, were minted in 1805.

NOTE: KM#1, 7 and 8 (Ducats) have been moved to Denmark.

DANISH COLONY

The following listings are all believed to be spurious countermarks on a variety of host coins. The few genuine countermarked pieces are currently listed in the *Standard Catalog of World Coins, 1801-1900*.

COLONIAL COINAGE

KM# 2 SKILLING

Copper **Obv:** Crowned double "C6" monogram **Obv. Inscription:** DAN • NORV • VANG • D • G • REX • **Rev:** Value, DANSKE, date within inner circle **Rev. Legend:** DE • DANSK • AMERIC • ....

Date	Mintage	VG	F	VF	XF	Unc
1740 C(h)W	24,000	350	700	1,500	2,700	—

KM# 3 2 SKILLING

Copper **Obv:** Crowned double "C6" monogram **Obv. Legend:** DAN • NORV • VANG • D • G • REX • **Rev:** Value, DANSKE, date within inner circle **Rev. Legend:** DE DANSK AMERIC .... **Note:** Varieties exist.

Date	Mintage	VG	F	VF	XF	Unc
1740	12,000	225	475	1,200	2,400	—

KM# 11 6 SKILLING

1.6240 g., 0.5000 Silver .0261 oz. ASW **Obv:** Crowned C7 monogram **Rev:** Ship within inner circle **Note:** Struck in 1782; fixed date of 1767.

Date	Mintage	VG	F	VF	XF	Unc
1767 Danske	192,000	65.00	150	325	600	—
1767 Daske (error)	Inc. above	75.00	165	350	650	—

KM# 4 12 SKILLING

3.2480 g., 0.5000 Silver .0522 oz. ASW **Obv:** Crowned double C6 monogram **Rev:** Ship within inner circle **Note:** Varieties exist.

Date	Mintage	VG	F	VF	XF	Unc
1740	82,000	45.00	90.00	250	500	—

KM# 5 12 SKILLING

3.2480 g., 0.5000 Silver .0522 oz. ASW **Obv:** Laureate head right **Obv. Legend:** FRIDERICVS • V • D • G • REX • DAN • NOR • V • G • **Rev:** Ship within inner circle

Date	Mintage	VG	F	VF	XF	Unc
1748	51,000	50.00	100	265	525	—

KM# 6.1 12 SKILLING

3.2480 g., 0.5000 Silver .0522 oz. ASW **Obv:** Monogram **Rev:** Ship within inner circle **Rev. Legend:** ...DANSK AMERIC INSULER

Date	Mintage	VG	F	VF	XF	Unc
1748	51,000	50.00	100	265	525	—

KM# 6.2 12 SKILLING

3.2480 g., 0.5000 Silver .0522 oz. ASW **Obv:** Monogram **Obv. Legend:** D • G • DAN • NOR • VAN • GOT • REX • **Rev:** Ship within inner circle **Rev. Legend:** AMERICANSK • M • XXII • SKILL • DANSKE •

Date	Mintage	VG	F	VF	XF	Unc
1757	81,000	10.00	25.00	75.00	185	—
1763	160,000	12.50	30.00	85.00	200	—
1764	199,000	10.00	25.00	75.00	185	—
1765	46,000	20.00	50.00	100	250	—

KM# 12 12 SKILLING

3.2480 g., 0.5000 Silver .0522 oz. ASW **Obv:** Crowned monogram **Obv. Legend:** D • G • DAN • NOR • VAN • GOT • REX • **Rev:** Ship within inner circle **Rev. Legend:** AMERICANSK • M • XXII • SKILL • DANSKE •

Date	Mintage	VG	F	VF	XF	Unc
1767(a)	390,000	10.00	25.00	75.00	185	—
Note: Struck in 1795 and 1800						
1767(c)	80,000	12.50	30.00	100	225	—
Note: Struck in 1782						
1767(k)	240,000	10.00	25.00	75.00	185	—
Note: Struck in 1790 and 1791						

KM# 9 24 SKILLING

6.4960 g., 0.5000 Silver .1044 oz. ASW **Obv:** Crowned monogram **Obv. Legend:** D • G • DAN • NOR • VAN • GOT • REX • **Rev:** Ship within inner circle **Rev. Legend:** AMERICANSK • M • XXIIII • SKILL • DANSKE •

Date	Mintage	VG	F	VF	XF	Unc
1763	64,000	13.50	30.00	85.00	225	—
1764	136,000	10.00	25.00	75.00	210	—
1765	31,000	20.00	65.00	140	375	—

KM# 10 24 SKILLING

6.4960 g., 0.5000 Silver .1044 oz. ASW **Obv:** Crowned monogram **Obv. Legend:** D • G • DAN • NOR • VAN • GOT • REX • **Rev:** Ship within inner circle **Rev. Legend:** AMERICANSK • M • XXIIII • SKILL • DANSKE •

Date	Mintage	VG	F	VF	XF	Unc
1766	57,000	25.00	60.00	130	350	—
1767(a)	75,000	17.50	55.00	120	325	—
Note: Struck in 1800; fixed date 1767						
1767(c)	12,000	27.50	65.00	145	385	—

PATTERNS

Including off metal strikes

KM#	Date	Mintage	Identification	Mkt Val
Pn1	1740 C(h)W	—	Skilling. Gold. KM#2	—
Pn2	1740	—	2 Skilling. Gold.	—
Pn3	1740	—	12 Skilling. Gold. KM#4	—

DANZIG

Danzig is an important seaport on the northern coast of Poland with access to the Baltic Sea. It has at different times belonged to the Teutonic Knights, Pomerania, Russia, and Prussia. It was part of the Polish Kingdom from 1587-1772.

Danzig (Gdansk) was a free city from 1919 to 1939 during which most of its modern coinage was made.

RULERS

August II (of Saxony), 1697-1733
August III (of Poland), 1733-1763
Stanislaus Augustus (of Poland), 1764-1772
Friedrich Wilhelm II (of Prussia), 1786-1797
Friedrich Wilhelm III (of Prussia), 1797-1840

MINT MARKS

A - Berlin

MINT OFFICIALS' INITIALS

Initials	Date	Name
CHS	1759-60	Conrad Heinrich Schwerdtner
III, JJJ	1755-68	Johan Jost Jaster
IS	1753, 1758-59	Johann Sievert
REOE	1754-67	Rudolph Ernst Oeckermann
WR	1753-54	Wilhelm Raths

MONETARY SYSTEM

3 Schilling (Szelag) = 1 Groschen (Grosz)

KINGDOM

STANDARD COINAGE

KM# 87 SOLIDUS

Copper **Ruler:** August II of Saxony **Obv:** Crowned monogram **Rev:** Legend, shield below

Date	Mintage	VG	F	VF	XF	Unc
1715	—	—	—	—	—	—

KM# 100 SOLIDUS

Copper **Ruler:** August III of Poland

Date	Mintage	VG	F	VF	XF	Unc
1753 IS	1,369,000	20.00	30.00	50.00	100	—
1753 WR	Inc. above	5.00	10.00	20.00	35.00	—
1753	Inc. above	10.00	15.00	25.00	50.00	—
1754 WR	Inc. above	7.00	12.00	22.00	45.00	—
1757 WR	Inc. above	7.00	12.00	22.00	45.00	—
1760 WR	Inc. above	7.00	12.00	22.00	45.00	—
1761 REOE	Inc. above	5.00	10.00	15.00	30.00	—
1763 REOE	Inc. above	10.00	20.00	35.00	65.00	—

KM# 116 SOLIDUS

Copper **Ruler:** August III of Poland **Note:** Klippe.

Date	Mintage	VG	F	VF	XF	Unc
1761 REOE	—	60.00	100	175	250	—

KM# 122 SOLIDUS

Copper **Ruler:** Stanislaus Augustus of Poland **Obv:** Crowned "SAR" monogram

Date	Mintage	VG	F	VF	XF	Unc
1765 REOE	—	10.00	15.00	25.00	40.00	—
1766 FLS	—	10.00	15.00	25.00	40.00	—

KM# 130 SOLIDUS

Copper **Ruler:** Friedrich Wilhelm II of Prussia

Date	Mintage	VG	F	VF	XF	Unc
1793 CLM Rare	—	—	—	—	—	—

KM# 90 SZELAG (12 Danarii)

Silver **Ruler:** August II of Saxony **Obv:** Crowned "AR" monogram

Date	Mintage	VG	F	VF	XF	Unc
1715	—	80.00	160	220	—	—

KM# 101 3 GROSZE

Billon **Ruler:** August III of Poland **Obv:** Crowned "A3R" monogram

Date	Mintage	VG	F	VF	XF	Unc
1755	—	15.00	30.00	50.00	100	—

KM# 102 3 GROSZE

Billon **Ruler:** August III of Poland **Note:** Similar to KM#101 but "III" below arms.

Date	Mintage	VG	F	VF	XF	Unc
1755	1,500,000	17.50	35.00	55.00	110	—

KM# 103 3 GROSZE

Silver **Ruler:** August III of Poland **Note:** Klippe.

Date	Mintage	VG	F	VF	XF	Unc
1755 Rare	—	—	—	—	—	—

KM# 104 3 GROSZE
Billon **Ruler:** August III of Poland

Date	Mintage	VG	F	VF	XF	Unc
1758	—	15.00	30.00	50.00	100	—
1760 REOE	5,500,000	15.00	30.00	50.00	100	—
1763 REOE	Inc. above	15.00	30.00	50.00	100	—

KM# 111 3 GROSZE
Silver **Ruler:** August III of Poland **Note:** Octagonal klippe.

Date	Mintage	VG	F	VF	XF	Unc
1760 REOE Rare	—	—	—	—	—	—
1763 REOE Rare	1,000,000	—	—	—	—	—

KM# 110 3 GROSZE
Silver **Ruler:** August III of Poland **Note:** Square klippe.

Date	Mintage	VG	F	VF	XF	Unc
1760 REOE Rare	—	—	—	—	—	—

KM# 123 3 GROSZE
Billon **Ruler:** Stanislaus Augustus of Poland

Date	Mintage	VG	F	VF	XF	Unc
1765 REOE	—	12.50	25.00	35.00	50.00	—
1766 FLS	—	12.50	25.00	35.00	50.00	—

KM# 112 6 GROSZY
Billon **Ruler:** August III of Poland **Obv:** With inner circle

Date	Mintage	VG	F	VF	XF	Unc
1760 REOE	8,000,000	20.00	35.00	65.00	100	—

KM# 113 6 GROSZY
Billon **Ruler:** August III of Poland **Note:** Klippe.

Date	Mintage	VG	F	VF	XF	Unc
1760 REOE	—	50.00	100	250	700	—
1761 REOE	—	50.00	100	250	700	—

KM# 117 6 GROSZY
Billon **Ruler:** August III of Poland **Obv:** Without inner circle

Date	Mintage	VG	F	VF	XF	Unc
1761 REOE	Inc. above	20.00	35.00	65.00	100	—
1762 REOE	Inc. above	20.00	35.00	65.00	100	—
1763 REOE	Inc. above	20.00	35.00	65.00	100	—

KM# 120 6 GROSZY
Billon **Ruler:** Stanislaus Augustus of Poland

Date	Mintage	VG	F	VF	XF	Unc
1764 REOE	—	20.00	40.00	80.00	145	—
1765 REOE	—	20.00	40.00	80.00	145	—

KM# 105 18 GROSZY
6.1000 g., Silver **Ruler:** August III of Poland

Date	Mintage	VG	F	VF	XF	Unc
1758	—	35.00	55.00	90.00	150	—
1759	—	35.00	55.00	90.00	150	—
1759 CHS	—	35.00	55.00	90.00	150	—
1759 REOE	—	35.00	55.00	90.00	150	—
1760 REOE	—	35.00	55.00	90.00	150	—

KM# 114 18 GROSZY
6.1000 g., Silver **Ruler:** August III of Poland **Note:** Klippe.

Date	Mintage	VG	F	VF	XF	Unc
1760 REOE	—	45.00	75.00	125	220	—

KM# 118 30 GROSZY
9.8500 g., Silver **Ruler:** August III of Poland

Date	Mintage	VG	F	VF	XF	Unc
1762 REOE	—	30.00	100	150	225	—

KM# 119 30 GROSZY
9.8500 g., Silver **Ruler:** August III of Poland

Date	Mintage	VG	F	VF	XF	Unc
1763 REOE	—	30.00	100	150	225	—

KM# 119a 30 GROSZY
0.9600 Silver **Ruler:** August III of Poland

Date	Mintage	VG	F	VF	XF	Unc
1763 REOE	—	—	—	—	—	—

KM# 121 60 GROSZY
13.7600 g., Silver **Ruler:** Stanislaus Augustus of Poland **Obv:** Crowned bust right **Rev:** Supported arms above value

Date	Mintage	VG	F	VF	XF	Unc
1767	—	—	—	—	—	—

KM# 115 2 ZLOTE
Silver **Ruler:** August III of Poland **Obv:** Crowned bust of August III right **Rev:** Supported arms, value below

Date	Mintage	VG	F	VF	XF	Unc
1760 REOE	200,000	125	175	275	425	—
1760 REOE Restrike	—	—	—	—	—	—

TRADE COINAGE

KM# 95 DUCAT
3.5000 g., 0.9860 Gold .1109 oz. AGW **Ruler:** August III of Poland

Date	Mintage	VG	F	VF	XF	Unc
1734	—	400	750	1,500	2,500	—

KM# 124 DUCAT
3.5000 g., 0.9860 Gold .1109 oz. AGW **Ruler:** Stanislaus Augustus of Poland **Obv:** Crowned bust right **Rev:** Supported arms

Date	Mintage	VG	F	VF	XF	Unc
1765 Rare	—	—	—	—	—	—

PATTERNS

Including off metal strikes

KM#	Date	Mintage	Identification	Mkt Val
Pn9	1753 WR	—	Solidus. Silver. KM100.	—

KM#	Date	Mintage	Identification	Mkt Val
Pn10	1753 WR	—	Solidus. Gold. KM100.	—
Pn11	1754 WR	—	Solidus. Silver. KM100.	300
Pn12	1754 WR	—	Solidus. Gold. KM#100.	—
Pn13	1755	—	3 Grosze. Gold. KM#102.	—
Pn14	1755	—	3 Grosze. Lead. KM103.	—
Pn15	1757 WR	—	Solidus. Gold. KM100.	—
Pn16	1758	—	3 Grosze. Silver. KM104.	75.00
Pn17	1760 REOE	—	3 Grosze. Gold. KM104.	—

KM#	Date	Mintage	Identification	Mkt Val
PnA18	1760 REOE	—	6 Groszy. Gold. KM112.	—
Pn18	1760 REOE	—	18 Groszy. Gold. KM105.	—
Pn19	1760 REOE	—	2 Zlote. Lead. KM115.	850
Pn20	1761 WR	—	Solidus. Silver. KM100.	—

KM#	Date	Mintage	Identification	Mkt Val
Pn21	1761 WR	—	Solidus. Gold. KM100.	—
Pn22	1761 REOE	—	6 Groszy. Gold. KM117.	—
PnA23	1762	—	Talar.	—
Pn24	1763 WR	—	Solidus. Silver. KM100.	—
PnA25	1763 REOE	—	Solidus. Silver. KM104.	75.00
Pn25	1763 REOE	—	3 Grosze. Gold. KM104.	—
Pn26	1763 REOE	—	6 Groszy. Silver. KM117.	100
Pn27	1763 REOE	—	6 Groszy. Gold. KM117.	—
Pn28	1763 REOE	—	18 Groszy. Gold. KM105.	—
PnA29	1763 REOE	—	30 Groszy. Gold. KM199.	—
Pn29	1764 REOE	—	6 Groszy. Silver. KM120.	1,350
Pn30	1765 REOE	—	6 Groszy. Gold. KM120.	—
Pn32	1766 360	—	3 Grosze. Gold. KM123.	1,350
Pn31	1766 FLS	—	Solidus. Gold. KM122.	—
Pn23	1767 REOE	—	30 Groszy. Gold. KM118.	—
Pn33	1793 CLM	—	Solidus. Silver. KM130.	375

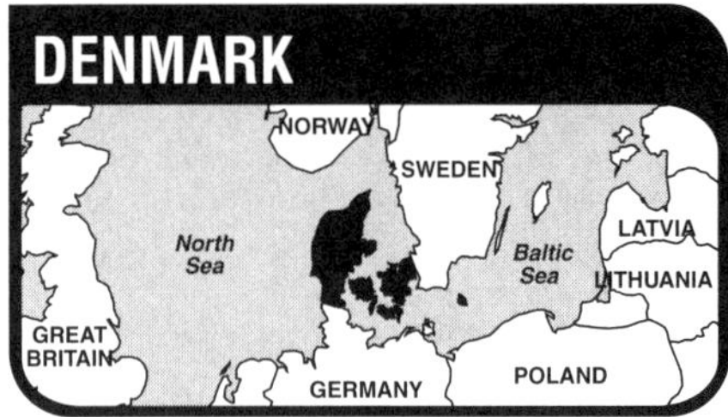

The Kingdom of Denmark (Danmark), a constitutional monarchy located at the mouth of the Baltic Sea, has an area of 16,639 sq. mi. (43,070 sq. km.) and a population of 5.2 million. Capital: Copenhagen. Most of the country is arable. Agriculture, is conducted by large farms served by cooperatives. The largest industries are food processing, iron and metal, and shipping. Machinery, meats (chiefly bacon), dairy products and chemicals are exported.

Denmark, a great power during the Viking period of the 9th-11th centuries, conducted raids on western Europe and England, and in the 11th century united England, Denmark and Norway under the rule of King Canute. Despite a struggle between the crown and the nobility (13th-14th centuries) which forced the King to grant a written constitution, Queen Margaret (Margrethe) (1387-1412) succeeded in uniting Denmark, Norway, Sweden, Finland and Greenland under the Danish crown, placing all of the Nordic countries under the rule of Denmark. An unwise alliance with Napoleon caused the loss of Norway to Sweden in 1814. In the following years a liberal movement was fostered, which succeeded in making Denmark a constitutional monarchy in 1849.

In 1864, Denmark lost Schleswig and Holstein to Prussia. In 1920, Denmark regained North-Schleswig by plebiscite.

The present decimal system of currency was introduced in 1874. As a result of a referendum held September 28, 2000, the currency of the European Monetary Union, the Euro, will not be introduced in Denmark in the foreseeable future.

RULERS

Frederik IV, 1699-1730
Christian VI, 1730-1746
Frederik V, 1746-1766
Christian VII, 1766-1808

MINT MARKS

Mark	Mint	Dates
	Copenhagen	No mint mark 1701-1800
	Altona	1771-1863, no mint mark 1771-1800
Nettle leaf	Gluckstadt	1623-1716, mint mark 1702-16
S	Rendsborg	1716-20, no mintmark
	Rethwisch	1768-69, no mint mark

MINTMASTERS' INITIALS

Altona

Initial	Date	Name
CHL	1771-84	Casper Henrik Lyng
DCL	1784-86	Didrik Christian Liebst
MF	1786-1816	Michael Flor

Copenhagen

Initials	Date	Name
CW, (heart), C(heart)W	1700-46	Christian Wineke, Jr.
	1746-49	Ingeborg Maria Wineke, widow of Christian
PNVH, VH	1749-61	Peter Nicholai van Haven
GWW, W	1761-64	Georg Wilhelm Wahl
K, HSK	1761-84	Hans Schierven Knoph
CHL	1784-97	Caspar Henrik Lyng
HIAB	1797-1810	Hans Jacob Arnold Branth

Glückstadt

Initials	Date	Name
CW	1680-1716	Christian Woltereck

Rethwisch

Initials	Date	Name
KSK	1768-69	Hans Schierven Knoph

Rendsborg

Initials	Date	Name
BH	1716-1720	Bastian Hille

DIECUTTERS' INITIALS

Altona

Initials	Dates	Name
M	1788-91	Mahrenz
PG	1787-88	Peter Leonard Gianelli
A, DIA	1787-88	Daniel Jensen Adzer
DI	1787-88	David Ahron Jacobsen
M	1799	John Milton, London
K	Ca.1800	Conrad Heinrich Küchler

Copenhagen

Initials	Date	Name
W	(1731)-1749-61	Georg Wilhelm Wahl
A, AB, ARBIEN	1744-60	Magnus Gustavus Arbien
W, CW, PCW	1745-57	Peter Christian Winsløw
DIA, A	1764-65	Daniel Jensen Adzer
B	1763-99	Johan Ephraim Bauert
IHW, W, I, H, WOLFF, F	1760-88	Johan Henrik Wolff, engraver
PG	1800-1807	Peter Leonard Gianelli

MONETARY SYSTEM

(Until 1813)
4 Penning = 1 Huid = 1/4 Skilling
6 Penning = 1 Sosling = 1/2 Skilling
16 Skillings = 1 Mark
64 Skilling Danske = 4 Mark = 1 Krone
96 Skilling Danske = 6 Mark = 1 Daler Specie
12 Mark = 1 Ducat

KINGDOM

STANDARD COINAGE

Through 1813

KM# 512.1 1/2 SKILLING

3.6540 g., Copper **Ruler:** Frederik IV **Obv:** Crowned double "F4" monogram in branches **Rev:** Value and date, large lettering

Date	Mintage	VG	F	VF	XF	Unc
1719 CW	—	10.00	30.00	75.00	175	—

KM# 512.2 1/2 SKILLING

3.6400 g., Copper **Ruler:** Frederik IV **Obv:** Crowned double F4 monogram in branches **Rev:** Small lettering

Date	Mintage	VG	F	VF	XF	Unc
1719 CW Rare	—	—	—	—	—	—

KM# 545 1/2 SKILLING

Copper **Ruler:** Christian VI **Obv:** Crowned double "C6" monogram **Rev:** Value, "DANSKE", date

Date	Mintage	VG	F	VF	XF	Unc
1745 CW	—	15.00	25.00	75.00	150	—

KM# 577.1 1/2 SKILLING

Copper **Ruler:** Frederik V **Obv:** Crowned "F5" monogram **Rev:** Value above date

Date	Mintage	VG	F	VF	XF	Unc
1751 PNVH	—	10.00	15.00	65.00	125	—
1755 PNVH	—	7.00	15.00	65.00	125	—

KM# 577.2 1/2 SKILLING

Copper **Ruler:** Frederik V **Obv:** Crowned "F5" monogram **Rev:** Value above date

Date	Mintage	VG	F	VF	XF	Unc
1762 W	—	7.00	15.00	65.00	125	—

KM# 615.1 1/2 SKILLING

Copper **Ruler:** Christian VII **Obv:** Crowned "C7" monogram **Rev:** Value, "DANSKE K.M.", date **Note:** "C" in momogram 15mm high, "7" in monogram 10mm high, thick cross bar.

Date	Mintage	VG	F	VF	XF	Unc
1771	235,776	10.00	25.00	75.00	150	—

KM# 615.2 1/2 SKILLING

Copper **Ruler:** Christian VII **Note:** C in monogram 16mm high, 7 in monogram 9mm high, thin corssbar

Date	Mintage	VG	F	VF	XF	Unc
1771 (1773)	625,920	7.00	15.00	30.00	125	—

KM# 615.3 1/2 SKILLING

Copper **Ruler:** Christian VII **Note:** C in monogram 17mm high, 7 in monogram 12mm high

Date	Mintage	VG	F	VF	XF	Unc
1771 (1784)	1,894,272	5.00	10.00	25.00	125	—

KM# 501 SKILLING

0.9210 g., 0.1560 Silver 0.0046 oz. ASW **Ruler:** Frederik IV **Obv:** Crowned double 4F monogram **Rev:** Value, DANSKE, date

Date	Mintage	VG	F	VF	XF	Unc
1711 CW	—	25.00	40.00	75.00	175	—
1712 CW	—	20.00	35.00	65.00	175	—
1713 CW	—	10.00	20.00	30.00	110	—
1715 CW	—	10.00	20.00	30.00	110	—
1716 CW	—	25.00	50.00	100	200	—
1719 CW	—	10.00	15.00	30.00	110	—

KM# 520 SKILLING

0.9210 g., 0.1560 Silver 0.0046 oz. ASW **Ruler:** Frederik IV **Rev:** Crown shield divides value and date

Date	Mintage	VG	F	VF	XF	Unc
1720 CW	—	4.00	10.00	25.00	60.00	—
1721 CW	—	4.00	10.00	25.00	60.00	—
1722 CW	—	4.00	10.00	25.00	60.00	—
1723 CW	—	10.00	20.00	50.00	150	—

KM# 541 SKILLING

0.9210 g., 0.1560 Silver 0.0046 oz. ASW **Ruler:** Christian VI **Obv:** Crowned double "C6" monogram **Rev:** Value, "DANSKE", date

Date	Mintage	VG	F	VF	XF	Unc
1735 CW	—	15.00	30.00	55.00	150	—
1746 CW	—	20.00	40.00	75.00	175	—

KM# 578.1 SKILLING

0.7680 g., 0.1870 Silver 0.0046 oz. ASW **Ruler:** Frederik V **Obv:** Crowned arms **Rev:** Value above date

Date	Mintage	VG	F	VF	XF	Unc
1751 VH	—	7.00	15.00	35.00	75.00	—
1755 VH	—	4.00	10.00	30.00	70.00	—

KM# 578.2 SKILLING

0.7680 g., 0.1870 Silver 0.0046 oz. ASW **Ruler:** Frederik V **Obv:** Crowned arms **Rev:** Value above date

Date	Mintage	VG	F	VF	XF	Unc
1761 W	—	3.00	5.00	15.00	75.00	—
1762 W	—	3.00	5.00	20.00	85.00	—
1763 W	—	3.00	5.00	20.00	90.00	—
1764 W	—	3.00	5.00	20.00	90.00	—

KM# 616.1 SKILLING

Copper, 29 mm. **Ruler:** Christian VII **Obv:** Crowned double "C7" monogram **Rev:** Value, "DANSKE", date **Note:** Varieties in size of crown exist 27.05-31.45mm; weight varies 8.83-14.1 grams. Struck at Copenhagen, Altona and Køngberg. This type was struck during the period of 1771-85 with a frozen date and in large quantities. For further studies, the book "1 Skilling 1771" by Frank Pedersen, published by Numismatisk Forening in 1991 - Danish.

Date	Mintage	Good	VG	F	VF	XF
1771	54,757,104	3.00	6.00	15.00	40.00	150

KM# 616.2 SKILLING

Copper, 29 mm. **Ruler:** Christian VII **Obv:** Serif top "C"s **Rev:** Value, "DANSKE", date

Date	Mintage	Good	VG	F	VF	XF
1771	Inc. above	10.00	20.00	30.00	100	250

KM# 616.3 SKILLING

Copper, 29 mm. **Ruler:** Christian VII **Obv:** Large, thick "C"s **Rev:** Value, "DANSKE", date

Date	Mintage	Good	VG	F	VF	XF
1771	Inc. above	15.00	30.00	40.00	100	250

KM# 616.4 SKILLING

Copper, 27.05-31.45 mm. **Ruler:** Christian VII **Obv:** Crowned double "C7" monogram **Rev:** "DANKSE" instead of "DANSKE" **Note:** Size varies. Weight varies 8.83-14.1 grams. Struck at Copenhagen, Altona and Kongsberg.

Date	Mintage	Good	VG	F	VF	XF
1771	Inc. above	50.00	100	200	300	700

KM# 616.5 SKILLING

Copper, 27.05-31.45 mm. **Ruler:** Christian VII **Obv:** Crowned double "C7" monogram **Rev:** "DANAKE" instead of "DANSKE" **Note:** Size varies. Weight varies 8.83-14.1 grams. Struck at Copenhagen, Altona and Kongsberg.

Date	Mintage	Good	VG	F	VF	XF
1771	Inc. above	75.00	150	350	550	—

KM# 616.6 SKILLING

Copper, 27.05-31.45 mm. **Ruler:** Christian VII **Obv:** Crowned double "C7" monogram **Rev:** "DNASKE" instead of "DANSKE" **Note:** Size varies. Weight varies 8.83-14.1g. Struck at Copenhagen, Altona and Kongsberg.

Date	Mintage	Good	VG	F	VF	XF
1771	Inc. above	85.00	175	400	750	—

KM# 616.7 SKILLING

Copper, 27.05-31.45 mm. **Ruler:** Christian VII **Obv:** Crowned double "C7" monogram **Rev:** "SKILLING DANSKE M.K." instead of "SKILLING DANSKE K.M." **Note:** Size varies. Weight varies 8.83-14.1g.

Date	Mintage	Good	VG	F	VF	XF
1771	—	60.00	125	225	500	—

KM# 616.8 SKILLING

Copper, 27.05-31.45 mm. **Ruler:** Christian VII **Obv:** Crowned double "C7" monogram **Note:** Size varies. Weight varies 8.83-14.1g. Struck at Copenhagen, Altona and Kongsberg.

Date	Mintage	Good	VG	F	VF	XF
1779 (error for 1771)	Inc. above	175	350	600	900	—

KM# 636 SKILLING

0.7680 g., 0.1870 Silver 0.0046 oz. ASW, 16 mm. **Ruler:** Christian VII **Obv:** Crowned "C7" monogram **Rev:** Value, "DANSKE H.S.K.", date

Date	Mintage	VG	F	VF	XF	Unc
1779 HSK	—	3.00	10.00	25.00	45.00	—
1782 HSK	—	10.00	20.00	35.00	85.00	—

KM# 502 2 SKILLING

1.2990 g., 0.2810 Silver 0.0117 oz. ASW **Ruler:** Frederik IV **Obv:** Crowned double "4F" monogram **Rev:** Value, "DANSKE", date

Date	Mintage	VG	F	VF	XF	Unc
1711 CW	—	20.00	35.00	65.00	150	—
1712 CW	—	10.00	20.00	40.00	100	—
1713 CW	—	15.00	30.00	45.00	100	—
1714 CW	—	20.00	45.00	60.00	175	—
1715 CW	—	15.00	30.00	55.00	125	—
1716 CW	—	20.00	35.00	60.00	125	—
1718 CW	—	50.00	125	225	—	—
1719 CW	—	25.00	45.00	100	—	—
1726 CW Unique	—	—	—	—	—	—

KM# 579.1 2 SKILLING
1.2180 g., 0.3430 Silver 0.0134 oz. ASW **Ruler:** Frederik V **Obv:** Crowned double "F5" monogram **Rev:** Value

Date	Mintage	VG	F	VF	XF	Unc
1750 PNVH	—	10.00	20.00	35.00	95.00	—
1756 PNVH	—	8.00	48.00	35.00	95.00	—

KM# 579.2 2 SKILLING
1.2180 g., 0.3430 Silver 0.0134 oz. ASW **Ruler:** Frederik V **Obv:** Crowned double "F5" monogram **Rev:** Value

Date	Mintage	VG	F	VF	XF	Unc
1761 HSK	—	8.00	18.00	35.00	95.00	—

KM# 579.3 2 SKILLING
1.2180 g., 0.3430 Silver 0.0134 oz. ASW **Ruler:** Frederik V **Obv:** Crowned double "F5" monogram **Rev:** Value

Date	Mintage	VG	F	VF	XF	Unc
1761 GWW	—	8.00	18.00	35.00	95.00	—

KM# 631.1 2 SKILLING
1.1810 g., 0.3430 Silver 0.0130 oz. ASW **Ruler:** Christian VII **Obv:** Crowned "C7" monogram within legend **Rev:** Crowned arms dividing date, value as legend

Date	Mintage	VG	F	VF	XF	Unc
1776 Rare	—	—	—	—	—	—

KM# 631.2 2 SKILLING
1.1810 g., 0.3430 Silver 0.0130 oz. ASW **Ruler:** Christian VII **Obv:** Crowned "C7" monogram within legend **Rev:** Crowned arms dividing date, value as legend

Date	Mintage	VG	F	VF	XF	Unc
1778 HSK	—	3.00	8.00	18.00	35.00	—
1782 HSK	—	3.00	8.00	18.00	35.00	—

KM# 631.3 2 SKILLING
1.1810 g., 0.3430 Silver 0.0130 oz. ASW **Ruler:** Christian VII **Obv:** Crowned "C7" monogram within legend **Obv. Legend:** D • G • DAN • NOR • VAN • GOT • REX • **Rev:** Crowned arms dividing date, value as legend

Date	Mintage	VG	F	VF	XF	Unc
1778 CHL	—	3.00	7.00	15.00	35.00	—
1779 CHL	—	3.00	7.00	15.00	35.00	—
1781 CHL	—	3.00	7.00	15.00	35.00	—
1782 CHL	—	3.00	7.00	15.00	35.00	—
1783 CHL	—	3.00	7.00	14.00	30.00	—
1784 CHL Rare	—	—	—	—	—	—

KM# 631.4 2 SKILLING
1.1810 g., 0.3430 Silver 0.0130 oz. ASW **Ruler:** Christian VII **Obv:** Crowned "C7" monogram within legend **Rev:** Crowned arms dividing date, value as legend

Date	Mintage	VG	F	VF	XF	Unc
1784 DCL	—	3.00	7.00	15.00	35.00	—
1785 DCL	—	3.00	7.00	15.00	35.00	—

KM# 526 4 SKILLING
2.7510 g., 0.3120 Silver 0.0276 oz. ASW **Ruler:** Frederik IV **Obv:** Crowned double "F4" monogram, legend around **Rev:** Value, "DANSKE", date

Date	Mintage	VG	F	VF	XF	Unc
1727 CW	—	5.00	10.00	20.00	40.00	—
1728 CW	—	5.00	10.00	20.00	40.00	—
1729 CW	—	7.00	14.00	20.00	45.00	—
1730 CW	—	5.00	11.00	20.00	40.00	—

KM# 598 4 SKILLING
2.7500 g., 0.3120 Silver 0.0276 oz. ASW **Ruler:** Frederik V **Obv:** Crowned "FV" monogram **Obv. Legend:** PRUDENTIA • E • T CONSTANTIA • **Rev:** Value above date

Date	Mintage	VG	F	VF	XF	Unc
1764 HSK	—	10.00	18.00	35.00	65.00	—

KM# 644 4 SKILLING
2.7500 g., 0.3120 Silver 0.0276 oz. ASW **Ruler:** Christian VII **Obv:** Crowned "C VII" monogram **Rev:** "III SKILLING", date

Date	Mintage	VG	F	VF	XF	Unc
1783	—	7.00	14.00	35.00	85.00	—

KM# 470 8 SKILLING
3.0570 g., 0.5620 Silver 0.0552 oz. ASW **Ruler:** Frederik IV **Obv:** Armored bust right **Obv. Legend:** FERD • IIII • DEI • GRATIA • **Rev:** Large crown divides value, heart divides date in legend below **Rev. Legend:** DAN • NOR • VAN • GOT • REX •

Date	Mintage	VG	F	VF	XF	Unc
1700	—	11.00	22.00	50.00	100	—
1701	—	14.00	29.00	65.00	125	—
1702	—	15.00	30.00	65.00	125	—
1703	—	18.00	35.00	75.00	150	—
1704	—	14.00	29.00	65.00	100	—
1705	—	55.00	125	20.00	—	—

KM# 527 8 SKILLING
3.0570 g., 0.5620 Silver 0.0552 oz. ASW **Ruler:** Frederik IV **Obv:** Crowned double "F4" monogram, legend around **Rev:** Value, "DANSKE", date

Date	Mintage	VG	F	VF	XF	Unc
1728 CW	—	85.00	175	350	600	—

KM# 528 8 SKILLING
3.0570 g., 0.5620 Silver 0.0552 oz. ASW **Ruler:** Frederik IV **Obv:** Armored bust right

Date	Mintage	VG	F	VF	XF	Unc
1729 CW	—	14.00	29.00	55.00	100	—
1730 CW	—	17.00	35.00	75.00	100	—

KM# 595 8 SKILLING
3.0570 g., 0.5620 Silver 0.0552 oz. ASW **Ruler:** Frederik V **Obv:** Crowned double "F5" monogram **Rev:** Value above date

Date	Mintage	VG	F	VF	XF	Unc
1763 HSK	—	40.00	100	200	400	—

KM# 596 8 SKILLING
3.0570 g., 0.5620 Silver 0.0552 oz. ASW **Ruler:** Frederik V **Obv:** Crowned single "F5" monogram **Note:** C8a.

Date	Mintage	VG	F	VF	XF	Unc
1763	—	100	225	500	—	—

KM# 597 8 SKILLING
3.0570 g., 0.5620 Silver 0.0552 oz. ASW **Ruler:** Frederik V **Obv:** Crowned "FV" monogram **Note:** C8b.

Date	Mintage	VG	F	VF	XF	Unc
1763	—	55.00	125	250	450	—

KM# 626 8 SKILLING
3.0570 g., 0.5620 Silver 0.0552 oz. ASW **Ruler:** Christian VII **Obv:** Crowned "C7" monogram **Rev:** "VIII SKILLING", date

Date	Mintage	VG	F	VF	XF	Unc
1773 HSK	—	18.00	35.00	75.00	150	—
1783 HSK	—	10.00	25.00	50.00	100	—

KM# 642 8 SKILLING
3.0570 g., 0.5620 Silver 0.0552 oz. ASW **Ruler:** Christian VII **Obv:** Crowned monogram **Obv. Legend:** D • G • DAN • NOR • VAN • GOT • REX • **Rev:** Crowned oval arms

Date	Mintage	VG	F	VF	XF	Unc
1782 HSK Rare	—	—	—	—	—	—

KM# 495 12 SKILLING
3.8980 g., 0.5620 Silver 0.0704 oz. ASW **Ruler:** Frederik IV **Obv:** Crowned double "F4" monogram **Rev:** TOLF/SKILLING/DANSKE/date

Date	Mintage	VG	F	VF	XF	Unc
1710 CW	—	18.00	35.00	65.00	125	—
1711 CW	—	17.00	28.00	55.00	100	—

KM# 504 12 SKILLING
3.8980 g., 0.5620 Silver 0.0704 oz. ASW **Ruler:** Frederik IV **Rev:** XII/SKILLING

Date	Mintage	VG	F	VF	XF	Unc
1712 CW	—	17.00	42.50	85.00	—	—
1713 CW	—	10.00	17.00	40.00	100	—
1714/3 CW	—	12.00	22.50	52.50	115	—
1714 CW	—	10.00	18.00	40.00	100	—
1715 CW	—	17.00	42.50	95.00	—	—
1716 CW	—	10.00	18.00	40.00	100	—
1717 CW	—	10.00	18.00	40.00	100	—
1718 CW	—	10.00	18.00	40.00	100	—
1719 CW	—	40.00	100	225	—	—

KM# 513 12 SKILLING
3.8980 g., 0.5620 Silver 0.0704 oz. ASW **Ruler:** Frederik IV **Rev:** Crowned rectangular shield, date in legend

Date	Mintage	VG	F	VF	XF	Unc
1719 CW	—	100	175	350	—	—

KM# 521 12 SKILLING
3.8980 g., 0.5620 Silver 0.0704 oz. ASW **Ruler:** Frederik IV **Obv:** Crowned double monogram **Obv. Legend:** DOMINUS * MIHI * ADIUTOR • **Rev:** Crowned shield, date in legend

Date	Mintage	VG	F	VF	XF	Unc
1720 CW	—	10.00	21.00	35.00	75.00	—
1721 CW	—	10.00	21.00	35.00	75.00	—
1722 CW	—	14.00	25.00	40.00	85.00	—

KM# 522 12 SKILLING
3.8980 g., 0.5620 Silver 0.0704 oz. ASW **Ruler:** Frederik IV **Obv:** Portrait right **Rev:** Crowned shield, date in legend

Date	Mintage	VG	F	VF	XF	Unc
1721 CW Rare	—	—	—	—	—	—

KM# 505 16 SKILLING
5.1970 g., 0.6250 Silver 0.1044 oz. ASW **Ruler:** Frederik IV **Obv:** Bust right **Rev:** Value, "DANSKE", date **Note:** Coins dated 1717, 1718 and 1719 are contemporary counterfeits originating in Holland.

Date	Mintage	VG	F	VF	XF	Unc
1713 CW	—	35.00	70.00	150	—	—
1714 CW	—	19.00	30.00	75.00	150	—
1715 CW	—	19.00	30.00	75.00	150	—
1716 CW	—	18.00	35.00	85.00	200	—

KM# 506 MARK (16 Skilling)
5.1970 g., 0.6250 Silver 0.1044 oz. ASW **Ruler:** Frederik IV **Obv:** Bust right **Rev:** Value, "DANSKE", date

Date	Mintage	VG	F	VF	XF	Unc
1713 CW Rare	—	—	—	—	—	—

KM# 536 24 SKILLING
9.1710 g., 0.5620 Silver 0.1657 oz. ASW **Ruler:** Christian VI **Obv:** Bust right **Obv. Legend:** CHRIST • VI • D • G • REX • DAN • .... **Rev:** Crowned arms divide date, value in legend right of crown

Date	Mintage	VG	F	VF	XF	Unc
1731 CW Heart on crossbar	—	70.00	125	225	350	—
1731 CW Without heart	—	35.00	70.00	150	250	—
1732 CW Without heart	—	35.00	35.00	125	200	—

KM# 538 24 SKILLING
9.1710 g., 0.5620 Silver 0.1657 oz. ASW **Ruler:** Christian VI **Obv:** Crowned double C6 monogram **Rev:** Crowned arms divided date, value in legend right of crown

Date	Mintage	VG	F	VF	XF	Unc
1732 CW	—	50.00	70.00	125	200	—
Note: Legend reads counter-clockwise.						
1732 CW	—	29.00	60.00	100	135	—
1733 CW	—	21.00	50.00	85.00	150	—
1734 CW	—	21.00	50.00	85.00	150	—
1735 CW	—	30.00	85.00	125	250	—
1736 CW	—	21.00	55.00	100	175	—
1737 CW Rare	—	—	—	—	—	—
1740 CW	—	29.00	55.00	125	200	—
1741 CW	—	21.00	45.00	95.00	150	—
1742 CW	—	21.00	50.00	100	150	—
1743 CW	—	30.00	55.00	100	150	—

KM# 580 24 SKILLING
9.1710 g., 0.5620 Silver 0.1657 oz. ASW **Ruler:** Frederik V **Obv:** Head right **Rev:** Crowned arms divide date

Date	Mintage	VG	F	VF	XF	Unc
1750 PNVH	—	85.00	200	350	650	—
1751 PNVH	—	125	225	400	700	—

KM# 582.1 24 SKILLING
9.1710 g., 0.5620 Silver 0.1657 oz. ASW **Ruler:** Frederik V **Obv:** Crowned double "F5" monogram **Rev:** Crowned arms

Date	Mintage	VG	F	VF	XF	Unc
1750 PNVH	—	29.00	50.00	100	175	—
1753 PNVH	—	30.00	55.00	100	175	—
1756 PNVH	—	30.00	55.00	100	175	—
1757 PNVH	—	28.00	45.00	90.00	150	—
1758 PNVH	—	28.00	45.00	90.00	150	—
1759 PNVH	—	28.00	45.00	90.00	150	—

KM# 581 24 SKILLING
9.1710 g., 0.5620 Silver 0.1657 oz. ASW **Ruler:** Frederik V **Obv:** Armored bust right

Date	Mintage	VG	F	VF	XF	Unc
1751	—	75.00	175	350	650	—

KM# 582.2 24 SKILLING
9.1710 g., 0.5620 Silver 0.1657 oz. ASW **Ruler:** Frederik V

Date	Mintage	VG	F	VF	XF	Unc
1762 HSK	—	28.00	45.00	85.00	150	—
1763 HSK	—	24.00	35.00	70.00	125	—
1764 HSK	—	29.00	55.00	100	150	—

KM# 602 24 SKILLING
9.1710 g., 0.5620 Silver 0.1657 oz. ASW **Ruler:** Christian VII **Obv:** Crowned "C VII" monogram **Rev:** Crowned, round draped arms

Date	Mintage	VG	F	VF	XF	Unc
1767 HSK	—	250	450	800	1,400	—

KM# 635.1 24 SKILLING
9.1710 g., 0.5620 Silver 0.1657 oz. ASW **Ruler:** Christian VII **Obv:** Crowned "C7" monogram **Note:** Struck at Altona. Mintmasters' initials: CHL.

Date	Mintage	VG	F	VF	XF	Unc
1778	—	250	350	600	1,000	—
1782	—	125	225	450	650	—
1783	—	100	175	350	650	—

KM# 635.2 24 SKILLING
9.1710 g., 0.5620 Silver 0.1657 oz. ASW **Ruler:** Christian VII

Date	Mintage	VG	F	VF	XF	Unc
1779 HSK	—	125	250	450	650	—

KM# 643 24 SKILLING
9.1710 g., 0.5620 Silver 0.1657 oz. ASW **Ruler:** Christian VII **Rev:** Crowned oval arms, without drape

Date	Mintage	VG	F	VF	XF	Unc
1782	—	200	450	900	—	—

KM# 627 32 SKILLING
12.2280 g., 0.5620 Silver 0.2209 oz. ASW **Ruler:** Christian VII **Obv:** Bust right **Rev:** Arms

Date	Mintage	VG	F	VF	XF	Unc
1775 HSK	—	—	—	2,100	3,500	—

KM# 628 32 SKILLING
12.2280 g., 0.5620 Silver 0.2209 oz. ASW **Ruler:** Christian VII **Obv:** Bust left **Obv. Legend:** CHRISTIANVS • VII • D • G • DAN • NORV • G • REX • **Rev:** Crowned arms

Date	Mintage	VG	F	VF	XF	Unc
1775	—	—	—	2,500	4,000	—

KM# 507 MARK
248.0000 g., Copper **Ruler:** Frederik IV **Shape:** Square **Note:** Plate Money. Five stamps: Four cyphers in corners, value and date in center.

Date	Mintage	VG	F	VF	XF	Unc
1714 CW Unique	—	—	—	—	—	—

KM# 479.1 6 MARK (Reise)
26.9830 g., 0.8330 Silver 0.7226 oz. ASW **Ruler:** Frederik IV **Obv:** Armored bust right **Obv. Legend:** FRID • IIII • D • G • REX • DAN • NOR • ... **Rev:** Norwegian arms dividing "6-M", date below in inner circle **Note:** Dav. #1289.

Date	Mintage	VG	F	VF	XF	Unc
1704	—	400	800	1,800	3,000	—

KM# 479.2 6 MARK (Reise)
26.9830 g., 0.8330 Silver 0.7226 oz. ASW **Ruler:** Frederik IV **Obv:** Armored bust right **Rev:** Norwegian arms dividing "6-M", date below in inner circle

Date	Mintage	Good	VG	F	VF	XF
1704	—	—	400	800	2,100	3,000

KM# 539 6 MARK (Reise)
26.9830 g., 0.8330 Silver 0.7226 oz. ASW **Ruler:** Christian VI **Obv:** Armored bust right **Obv. Legend:** CHRIST • VI • D • G • REX • DAN • NOR ... **Rev:** Crowned shield with Norwegian arms separating "6-M", date below **Note:** Dav. #1295.

Date	Mintage	VG	F	VF	XF	Unc
1732 Rare	4,534	—	—	—	—	—
1733	5,000	—	1,000	2,000	3,000	—

KM# 575 6 MARK (Reise)
28.8930 g., 0.8750 Silver 0.8128 oz. ASW **Ruler:** Frederik V **Subject:** 300th Anniversary - Reign of House of Oldenburg in Denmark **Obv:** Laureate armored bust right **Obv. Legend:** FRIDERICUS • V • D • G • REX • DAN • NOR • V • G • **Note:** Dav. #1301.

Date	Mintage	VG	F	VF	XF	Unc
1749 PCW	5,008	250	650	1,300	2,500	—
1749 W	Inc. above	200	450	1,100	2,100	—

KM# 621 1/2 KRONE
8.9940 g., 0.8330 Silver 0.2409 oz. ASW **Ruler:** Christian VII **Subject:** Anniversary - Birth of Christian VII **Obv:** Bust right **Obv. Legend:** CHRIST • VII • D • G • REX • DAN • NOR • V • G • **Rev:** "DEN 29 JANUARII" within wreath **Rev. Inscription:** GLORIA • EX AMORE • PATRIAE •

Date	Mintage	VG	F	VF	XF	Unc
1771 K	—	200	300	600	1,250	—

KM# 448 KRONE (4 Mark)
17.9980 g., 0.8330 Silver 0.4820 oz. ASW **Ruler:** Frederik IV **Obv:** Bust right **Obv. Legend:** FRID • IIII • D • G • DAN • NOR • VA • GO • RE... **Rev:** Three crowned double "F4" monograms, arms between **Rev. Legend:** DOMINUS • MI HI • ADIUTOR • **Note:** Dav. #A1287.

Date	Mintage	VG	F	VF	XF	Unc
1699	—	300	550	1,000	1,325	—
1700	—	120	250	700	1,100	—
1701	—	300	550	1,000	1,400	—
1702	—	125	300	800	1,100	—

KM# 503 KRONE (4 Mark)
22.2720 g., 0.6710 Silver 0.4805 oz. ASW **Ruler:** Frederik IV **Obv:** Horseman to right **Obv. Legend:** FRIDERICVS • IIII • D • G • REX • DAN • NOR • ... **Rev:** Small crowned arms in double order chain with divided date below **Rev. Legend:** DOMINUS MI HI ADIUTOR • **Note:** Dav. #A1290.

Date	Mintage	VG	F	VF	XF	Unc
1711 CW	7,905	125	200	450	650	—

KM# 523 KRONE (4 Mark)
22.2720 g., 0.6710 Silver 0.4805 oz. ASW **Ruler:** Frederik IV **Obv:** Horseman right **Obv. Legend:** FRIDERICUS • IIII • D • G • REX • DAN • NOR • V • G • **Rev:** Large crowned arms in double order chain **Rev. Legend:** DOMINUS • MI HI • ADIUTOR • **Note:** Dav. #A1290A.

Date	Mintage	VG	F	VF	XF	Unc
1723 CW	—	500	900	1,500	2,400	—

KM# 524 KRONE (4 Mark)
22.2720 g., 0.6710 Silver 0.4805 oz. ASW **Ruler:** Frederik IV **Obv:** Crowned "F4" monograms **Obv. Legend:** DOMINUS • MIHI • ADIUTOR • **Rev:** Crown in circle **Note:** Dav. #A1291.

Date	Mintage	VG	F	VF	XF	Unc
1724 CW	3,040	200	400	700	1,100	—
1726 CW	4,526	225	450	900	1,200	—

KM# 537 KRONE (4 Mark)
22.2720 g., 0.6710 Silver 0.4805 oz. ASW **Ruler:** Christian VI **Obv:** Armored bust right **Obv. Legend:** CHRIST • VI • D • G • REX • DAN • NORV • V • G • **Rev:** Crown above DEO ET POPVLO within circle **Note:** Dav. #A1294.

Date	Mintage	VG	F	VF	XF	Unc
1731 CW Small crown	90,000	150	350	650	1,000	—
1731 CW Large crown	Inc. above	100	225	400	700	—
1732 CW	9,836	150	350	600	900	—

KM# 560 KRONE (4 Mark)
17.9980 g., 0.8330 Silver 0.4820 oz. ASW **Ruler:** Frederik V **Obv:** Modified bust **Obv. Legend:** FRIDERICVS • V • DEI • GRATIA • **Rev:** Crown, small heart divides date below **Rev. Legend:** DAN • NOR • VAN • GOT • REX **Edge:** Plain

Date	Mintage	VG	F	VF	XF	Unc
1747 A	—	200	300	600	850	—

KM# 559 KRONE (4 Mark)
17.9980 g., 0.8330 Silver 0.4820 oz. ASW **Ruler:** Frederik V **Obv:** Head right **Obv. Legend:** FRIDERICUS V DEI GRATIA • **Rev:** Crown, small heart divides date below **Rev. Legend:** DAN • NOR • VAN • GOT • REX **Edge:** Lettered **Note:** Dav. #1300A.

Date	Mintage	VG	F	VF	XF	Unc
1747 W	—	175	300	650	950	—

KM# 571 KRONE (4 Mark)
17.9980 g., 0.8330 Silver 0.4820 oz. ASW **Ruler:** Frederik V **Obv:** Laureate head right **Obv. Legend:** FRIDERICUS V DEI GRATIA • **Rev:** Crowned arms in sprays **Rev. Legend:** DAN NORV VAN GOTH REX

Date	Mintage	VG	F	VF	XF	Unc
1748 W	—	125	250	500	700	—

KM# 572 KRONE (4 Mark)
17.9980 g., 0.8330 Silver 0.4820 oz. ASW **Ruler:** Frederik V **Obv:** Head right **Obv. Legend:** FRIDERICUS V DEI GRATIA **Rev:** Modified sprays with horizontal lines in ribbon sash below crowned arms **Rev. Legend:** DAN NORV VAN GOTH REX

Date	Mintage	VG	F	VF	XF	Unc
1748	—	275	450	750	1,250	—

KM# 622 KRONE (4 Mark)
17.9980 g., 0.8330 Silver 0.4820 oz. ASW **Ruler:** Christian VII **Obv:** Bust right **Obv. Legend:** CHRIST • VII • D • G • REX • DAN • NOR • VAN • GOT • **Rev:** "DEN 29 IANUARII" within wreath **Rev. Legend:** ... • AMORE • PATRIÆ •

Date	Mintage	VG	F	VF	XF	Unc
1771 K	—	275	350	850	1,500	—

KM# 477 2 KRONE
35.9760 g., 0.8330 Silver 0.9635 oz. ASW **Ruler:** Frederik IV **Obv:** Bust right **Obv. Legend:** FRID • IIII • D • G • DAN • NOR • VA • GO • REX • **Rev:** Crowned "F4" monograms with arms between **Note:** Dav. #1287.

Date	Mintage	VG	F	VF	XF	Unc
1702 Unique	—	—	—	—	—	—

KM# 561 2 KRONE
35.9760 g., 0.8330 Silver 0.9635 oz. ASW **Ruler:** Frederik V **Obv:** Head right **Obv. Legend:** FRIDERICUS V DEI GRATIA • **Rev:** Crown with PRUDENTIA ET CONSTANTIA below **Rev. Legend:** DAN • NOR • VAN • GOT • REX **Note:** Dav. #1300.

Date	Mintage	VG	F	VF	XF	Unc
1747	—	350	600	1,100	1,700	—

KM# 525 3 KRONE
45.2870 g., 0.9930 Silver 1.4458 oz. ASW **Ruler:** Frederik IV **Obv:** Armored bust right **Obv. Legend:** FRIDER • IIII • D • G • REX • DAN • NOR • V • GO • **Rev:** Three arms crowned in order collar within circle of 15 shields, date below **Rev. Legend:** DITM • COM • OLD • .... **Note:** Dav. #1293.

Date	Mintage	VG	F	VF	XF	Unc
1726	86	—	—	6,500	11,000	—

KM# 546 3 KRONE
45.2870 g., 0.9930 Silver 1.4458 oz. ASW **Ruler:** Frederik V **Subject:** Death of Christian VI and Accession of Frederik V **Obv:** Frederik V **Obv. Legend:** FRIDERICUS • V • D • G • REX • DAN • NORV • V • G • **Rev:** Christian VI **Rev. Legend:** CHRISTIANUS • VI • D • G • REX • DAN • NOR • V • G • **Note:** Dav. #1297.

Date	Mintage	VG	F	VF	XF	Unc
ND(1747)	—	325	650	1,000	1,650	—
ND (1747)	500	400	850	1,300	2,100	—

KM# 652 1/15 SPECIE DALER

3.3700 g., 0.5000 Silver 0.0542 oz. ASW **Ruler:** Christian VII
Obv: Crowned arms **Rev:** Value

Date	Mintage	VG	F	VF	XF	Unc
1796 MF	—	18.00	35.00	85.00	175	—
1797 MF	—	15.00	30.00	85.00	175	—
1799 MF	—	15.00	30.00	85.00	175	—

KM# 604 1/4 SPECIEDALER

7.2240 g., 0.8750 Silver 0.2032 oz. ASW **Ruler:** Christian VII
Obv: Crowned double "C7" monogram **Obv. Legend:** D • G • DAN • NOR • VAN • GOT • REX • **Rev:** Crowned round arms within ribbon **Rev. Legend:** GLORIA • EX • AMORE • PATRIÆ • **Note:** Struck at Rethwisch.

Date	Mintage	Good	VG	F	VF	XF
1769 HSK	—	175	225	350	600	1,100

KM# 653 1/3 SPECIEDALER

9.6310 g., 0.8750 Silver 0.2709 oz. ASW **Ruler:** Christian VII

Date	Mintage	Good	VG	F	VF	XF
1798 HIAB Rare	—	—	—	—	—	—

KM# 606 1/2 SPECIEDALER

14.4470 g., 0.8750 Silver 0.4064 oz. ASW **Ruler:** Frederik III
Obv: Crowned double "C7" monogram dividing value

Date	Mintage	Good	VG	F	VF	XF
1769	—	150	200	300	750	1,700

KM# 605 1/2 SPECIEDALER

14.4470 g., 0.8750 Silver 0.4064 oz. ASW **Ruler:** Christian VII
Obv: Crowned double "C7" monogram **Rev:** Crowned round arms within ribbons **Note:** Struck at Rethwisch.

Date	Mintage	Good	VG	F	VF	XF
1769 HSK	—	230	320	500	825	2,000

KM# 633.1 1/2 SPECIEDALER

14.4470 g., 0.8750 Silver 0.4064 oz. ASW **Ruler:** Christian VII
Obv: Crowned oval arms between branches value

Date	Mintage	Good	VG	F	VF	XF
1777 Unique	—	—	—	—	—	—

KM# 633.2 1/2 SPECIEDALER

14.4470 g., 0.8750 Silver 0.4064 oz. ASW **Ruler:** Christian VII

Date	Mintage	Good	VG	F	VF	XF
1786 DCL	—	150	250	375	875	2,000

KM# 480.1 SPECIEDALER

28.8930 g., 0.8750 Silver 0.8128 oz. ASW **Ruler:** Frederik IV
Obv: Armored bust right **Obv. Legend:** FRID • IIII • D • G • DAN • NOR • VAN • GOT • REX • **Rev:** Crowned arms in double chain within legend **Edge Lettering:** DOMINUS MIHI ADIVTOR ANNO REGNI QUINTO **Note:** Dav. #1288.

Date	Mintage	VG	F	VF	XF	Unc
1704	300	—	1,400	3,000	4,000	—

KM# 480.2 SPECIEDALER

28.8930 g., 0.8750 Silver 0.8128 oz. ASW **Ruler:** Frederik IV
Obv: Armored bust right **Rev:** Crowned arms in double chain within legend **Note:** No edge inscription.

Date	Mintage	Good	VG	F	VF	XF
1704 Rare	Inc. above	—	—	—	—	—

KM# 562 SPECIEDALER

28.8930 g., 0.8750 Silver 0.8128 oz. ASW **Ruler:** Frederik V
Subject: Coronation of King Frederick V **Obv:** Crowned, robed king standing below canopy **Obv. Legend:** FRIDERICUS V • D • G • REX • DAN • NOR • **Rev:** Crowned arms supported by wildmen **Rev. Legend:** PRUDENTIA ET CONSTANTIA • **Note:** Dav. #1299.

Date	Mintage	VG	F	VF	XF	Unc
1747 A	—	400	550	1,100	1,600	—

KM# 599 SPECIEDALER

28.8930 g., 0.8750 Silver 0.8128 oz. ASW **Ruler:** Frederik V
Obv: Laureate head right **Obv. Legend:** FRIDERICUS • V • D • G • DAN • NOR • V • G • REX • **Rev:** Crowned , oval arms in order chain within sprigs **Rev. Legend:** PRUDENTIA ET CONSTANTIA **Note:** Dav. #1302.

Date	Mintage	VG	F	VF	XF	Unc
1764 H • S • K • ; B			400	900	1,500	
1765 H • S • K • ; B Rare	—	—	—	—	—	—

KM# 600 SPECIEDALER

28.8930 g., 0.8750 Silver 0.8128 oz. ASW **Ruler:** Frederik V
Obv: Laureate head right **Obv. Legend:** FRIDERICUS • V • D • G • DAN • NOR • VAN • GOT • REX • **Rev:** Crowned arms in Order chain and wreath **Rev. Legend:** PRUDENTIA ET CONSTANTIA **Note:** Dav. #1302A.

Date	Mintage	VG	F	VF	XF	Unc
1764 DIA/DIA	—	—	600	1,300	1,900	—
1764 DIA/- Rare	—	—	—	—	—	—
1764 DIA/IHW Rare	Inc. above	—	—	—	—	—

KM# 601 SPECIEDALER

28.8930 g., 0.8750 Silver 0.8128 oz. ASW **Ruler:** Frederik V
Obv: Laureate head right **Obv. Legend:** FRIDERICUS V D • G • REX • DAN • NORV • VAND • G • **Rev:** Crowned arms within Order chain **Rev. Legend:** PRUDENTIA ET CONSTANTIA **Note:** Dav. #1302B.

Date	Mintage	VG	F	VF	XF	Unc
1764 IHW/IW	—	—	550	1,300	1,800	—
1765 IHW/- Rare	—	—	—	—	—	—

KM# 603 SPECIEDALER

28.8930 g., 0.8750 Silver 0.8128 oz. ASW **Ruler:** Christian VII
Obv: Crowned "C7" monograms **Obv. Legend:** D • G • DAN • NOR • VAN • GOT • REX • **Rev:** Crowned Norwegian arms, date below **Rev. Legend:** GLORIA • EX • AMORE • PATRIÆ • **Note:** Dav. #1304. Struck at Rethwisch.

Date	Mintage	VG	F	VF	XF	Unc
1768 HSK	—	650	850	1,500	2,600	—
1769 HSK Rare	—	—	—	—	—	—

KM# 607 SPECIEDALER

28.8930 g., 0.8750 Silver 0.8128 oz. ASW **Ruler:** Christian VII
Obv: Armored bust right **Obv. Legend:** CHRIST • VII • D • G • REX • DAN • NOR • VAN • GOT • **Rev:** Crowned round arms within ribbon **Rev. Legend:** GLORIA • EX AMORE • PATRIÆ : **Note:** Dav. #1305.

Date	Mintage	VG	F	VF	XF	Unc
1769 HSK; B	51	—	750	1,550	2,750	—

KM# 608 SPECIEDALER
28.8930 g., 0.8750 Silver 0.8128 oz. ASW **Ruler:** Christian VII **Obv:** Crowned double "C7" monogram **Obv. Legend:** D • G • DAN • NOR • VAN • GOT • REX • **Rev:** Crowned round arms within ribbon **Rev. Legend:** GLORIA • EX AMORE • PATRIÆ • **Note:** Dav. #1306. Struck at Rethwisch.

Date	Mintage	VG	F	VF	XF	Unc
1769 HSK	—	85.00	150	350	750	—

KM# 623 SPECIEDALER
28.8930 g., 0.8750 Silver 0.8128 oz. ASW **Ruler:** Christian VII **Obv:** Smaller crown and thinner "C's" **Rev:** Smaller crown and sprays instead of ribbons **Note:** Dav. #1307.

Date	Mintage	VG	F	VF	XF	Unc
1771 HSK	—	125	250	450	700	—

KM# 632.1 SPECIEDALER
28.8930 g., 0.8750 Silver 0.8128 oz. ASW **Ruler:** Frederik V **Obv:** Smaller crown, taller monogram **Obv. Legend:** D • G • DAN • NORV • VAND • GOTH • REX • **Rev:** Crowned oval arms between branches **Rev. Legend:** GLORIA • EX AMORE • PATRIÆ • **Note:** Dav. #1308.

Date	Mintage	VG	F	VF	XF	Unc
1776HSK	—	200	350	500	750	—
1780HSK	—	200	350	500	750	—

KM# 632.2 SPECIEDALER
28.8930 g., 0.8750 Silver 0.8128 oz. ASW **Ruler:** Christian VII

Date	Mintage	VG	F	VF	XF	Unc
1776 CHL	—	80.00	150	300	600	—

KM# 634 SPECIEDALER
28.8930 g., 0.8750 Silver 0.8128 oz. ASW **Ruler:** Christian VII **Obv:** Crowned C7 monogram **Obv. Legend:** D • G • REX • DAN • NOR • VAN • GO • DVX ... **Rev:** crowned, oval arms within sprigs **Rev. Legend:** GLORIA EX AMORE PATRIÆ • **Note:** Dav. #1309.

Date	Mintage	VG	F	VF	XF	Unc
1777	—	80.00	175	400	600	—

KM# 651.1 SPECIEDALER
28.8930 g., 0.8750 Silver 0.8128 oz. ASW **Ruler:** Christian VII **Obv:** Head right **Obv. Legend:** CHRISTIANUS • VII • D • G • DAN • NORV • V • G • REX • **Rev:** Crowned oval arms **Note:** Dav. #1313.

Date	Mintage	VG	F	VF	XF	Unc
1795 MF; B	—	100	200	350	550	—
1797 MF; B	—	70.00	125	225	350	—
1801 MF; B	—	175	300	550	1,000	—

KM# 651.2 SPECIEDALER
28.8930 g., 0.8750 Silver 0.8128 oz. ASW **Ruler:** Christian VII

Date	Mintage	VG	F	VF	XF	Unc
1796 CHL; B	—	100	200	300	450	—
1797 CHL; B	—	250	400	550	700	—

KM# 651.3 SPECIEDALER
28.8930 g., 0.8750 Silver 0.8128 oz. ASW **Ruler:** Christian VII

Date	Mintage	VG	F	VF	XF	Unc
1798 HIAB; B	—	100	200	300	450	—
1799 HIAB; B	—	100	200	300	450	—

KM# 654 SPECIEDALER
28.8930 g., 0.8750 Silver 0.8128 oz. ASW **Ruler:** Christian VII **Obv:** Head right **Obv. Legend:** CHRISTIANUS • VII • D • G • DAN • NORV • V • G • REX • **Rev:** Crowned oval arms **Note:** Dav. 1315.

Date	Mintage	VG	F	VF	XF	Unc
1799 HIAB; PG	—	125	250	400	650	—

KM# 640.1 SPECIEDALER (Albertdaler)
28.0630 g., 0.8680 Silver 0.7831 oz. ASW **Ruler:** Christian VII **Obv:** Wildman standing behind crowned arms **Rev:** Large crowned arms **Note:** Dav. #1310. 1786 date struck at Poppelbüttel, others struck at Altona.

Date	Mintage	VG	F	VF	XF	Unc
1781 Unique	—	—	—	—	—	—
Note: Club in left hand						
1781	—	600	800	1,200	2,100	—
1784	—	600	800	1,200	2,100	—
1786	10,601	700	900	1,300	2,300	—

KM# 640.2 SPECIEDALER (Albertdaler)
28.0630 g., 0.8680 Silver 0.7831 oz. ASW **Obv:** Wildman standing behind crowned arms **Rev:** Small crowned arms **Note:** Dav. #1310.

Date	Mintage	VG	F	VF	XF	Unc
1796	—	600	750	1,100	1,900	—

KM# 645 SPECIEDALER (Rigsdaler Courant)
23.5820 g., 0.8750 Silver 0.6634 oz. ASW **Ruler:** Christian VII **Obv:** Uniformed bust right **Obv. Legend:** CHRISTIAN DEN VII • DANMARKS OG NORGES KONGE **Rev:** Norwegian arms **Note:** Dav. #1312.

Date	Mintage	VG	F	VF	XF	Unc
1788	—	400	750	1,500	2,800	—

KM# 563 2 SPECIEDALER
57.7860 g., 0.8750 Silver 1.6256 oz. ASW **Ruler:** Frederik V **Subject:** Coronation of Frederik V **Obv:** Crowned, robed King standing under canopy **Obv. Legend:** FRIDERICVS • V • D • G • REX • DAN • NOR • **Rev:** Crowned arms supported by wildmen **Rev. Legend:** PRVDENTIA ET CONSTANTIA • **Note:** Dav. #1298

Date	Mintage	VG	F	VF	XF	Unc
1747 A	—	—	850	1,700	2,700	—

TRADE COINAGE

Danish East India Co.

D.O.C. - Dansk Ostindisk Compagni

Originally formed in 1616 to develop trade and colonization in Asia and the East Indies under the protection of Christian IV. It was dissolved in 1634 and later reorganized in 1670 lasting until 1729 when it was closed due to its debts.

A few years later the company reorganized under the name, Danish Asiatic Company - D.A.C. Coins bearing these initials can be found listed under Tranquebar.

KM# 637 PIASTRE
26.9820 g., 0.9020 Silver 0.7824 oz. ASW **Ruler:** Christian VII **Issuer:** Danish Asiatic Company (Danish East India Co. until 1729), Founded in 1732 to promote trade in Bengal India. The company handed over its property rights to the Danish government in 1777 but continued its trading activities until 1839 **Obv:** Large crowned arms

Obv. Legend: CHRISTIANVS • VII • D • G • DAN • NOR • VAN • GOT • REX • **Rev:** Large crown above circular arms between pillars **Rev. Legend:** GLORIA • EX AMORE • PATRIÆ • **Note:** Five examples known to exist. Dav. #411.

Date	Mintage	VG	F	VF	XF	Unc
1771 Rare	543	—	—	—	—	—

Note: Peters sale 12-82 EF-AU realized $25,250; Peters I.N.S. sale 1-84 VF-XF realized $15,750

KM# 638 PIASTRE

26.9820 g., 0.9020 Silver 0.7824 oz. ASW **Ruler:** Christian VII **Issuer:** Danish Asiatic Co.(Danish East India Co. until 1729), Founded in 1732 to promote trade in Bengal India. The company handed over its property rights to the Danish government in 1777 but continued its trading activities until 1839 **Obv:** Small crowned arms **Obv. Legend:** CHRISTIANVS • VII • D • G • DAN • NOR • VAN • GOT • REX • **Rev:** Small crown above circular arms between pillars **Rev. Legend:** GLORIA • EX • AMORE • PATRIÆ **Note:** Twenty examples known to exist. Dav. #411A.

Date	Mintage	VG	F	VF	XF	Unc
1771(1774) Rare	45,000	—	—	—	—	—

Note: Rasmussen/Ahlstrom Hede sale 9-88 VF realized $17,650; Ponterio C.I.C.F. 1990 sale 3-90 XF (ex. Hede) realized $16,500

KM# 639.2 PIASTRE

26.9820 g., 0.9020 Silver 0.7824 oz. ASW **Ruler:** Christian VII **Issuer:** Danish Asiatic Company **Obv:** Crowned arms **Rev:** ISLAN in ribbon **Note:** 21 examples known to exist. Dav. #412A.

Date	Mintage	VG	F	VF	XF	Unc
1777 Rare	Inc. above	—	—	—	—	—

Note: Spink & Son Zurich Salvesen sale 10-88 XF realized $21,450

KM# 639.1 PIASTRE

26.9820 g., 0.9020 Silver 0.7824 oz. ASW **Ruler:** Christian VII **Issuer:** Danish Asiatic Company **Obv:** Crowned arms **Rev:** "ISLAND" in ribbon **Note:** Struck at Kongsberg. Three examples known to exist. Dav. #412.1.

Date	Mintage	VG	F	VF	XF	Unc
1777 Rare	50,000	—	—	—	—	—

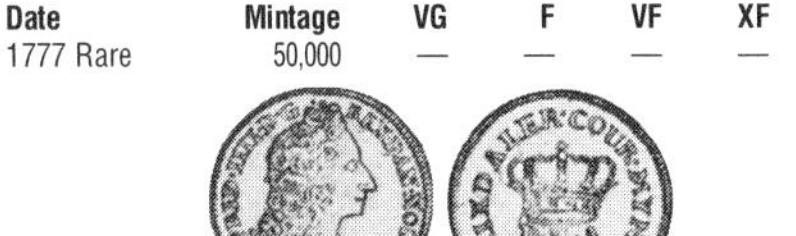

KM# 510 1/2 DUCAT COURANT

1.4350 g., 0.8750 Gold 0.0404 oz. AGW **Ruler:** Frederik IV **Obv:** Bust right **Obv. Legend:** FRID • IIII • D • G • REX • DAN • NOR • V • G • **Rev:** Crown above date **Rev. Legend:** ...RINDALER • COUR • MYNT •

Date	Mintage	VG	F	VF	XF	Unc
1715	598	450	550	1,000	1,400	—

KM# 585 12 MARK (Ducat Courant)

3.1180 g., 0.8750 Gold 0.0877 oz. AGW **Ruler:** Frederik V **Obv:** Helmeted head right **Obv. Legend:** FRIDERISVS • V • D • G • DAN • NOR • V • G • REX • **Rev:** Large crown, value and date below **Rev. Legend:** PRUDENTIA ET CONSTANTIA

Date	Mintage	VG	F	VF	XF	Unc
1757 VH	—	150	250	450	800	—
1758	—	150	250	500	850	—

KM# 586.1 12 MARK (Ducat Courant)

3.1180 g., 0.8750 Gold 0.0877 oz. AGW **Ruler:** Frederik V **Obv:** Crowned "F's" and "V" in triangle **Obv. Legend:** D • G • DAN • NOR • VAN • GOT • REX • **Rev:** Crown, value and date below **Rev. Legend:** PRUDENTIA ET CONSTANTIA •

Date	Mintage	VG	F	VF	XF	Unc
1757 VH	—	150	200	400	750	—

Note: Two varieties known, with mintmaster initials "VH" dividing the date or placed below the date

KM# 586.2 12 MARK (Ducat Courant)

3.1180 g., 0.8750 Gold 0.0877 oz. AGW **Ruler:** Frederik V **Obv:** Crowned "F's" and "V" in triangle

Date	Mintage	VG	F	VF	XF	Unc
1763 K	—	175	300	500	800	—

KM# 587.1 12 MARK (Ducat Courant)

3.1180 g., 0.8750 Gold 0.0877 oz. AGW **Ruler:** Frederik V **Obv:** Bare head right, curl below **Obv. Legend:** FRIDERICVS • V • D • G • DAN • NOR • V • G • REX • **Rev:** Crown above value and date **Rev. Legend:** PRUDENTIA ET CONSTANTIA •

Date	Mintage	VG	F	VF	XF	Unc
1757 VH; AB Unique	—	—	—	—	—	—
1758 VH; AB	—	450	750	1,000	1,300	—

KM# 587.2 12 MARK (Ducat Courant)

3.1180 g., 0.8750 Gold 0.0877 oz. AGW **Ruler:** Frederik V **Obv:** Bare head right, curl below **Rev:** Crown above date

Date	Mintage	VG	F	VF	XF	Unc
1758 VH; A	—	200	325	550	950	—

KM# 587.3 12 MARK (Ducat Courant)

3.1180 g., 0.8750 Gold 0.0877 oz. AGW **Ruler:** Frederik V **Obv:** Bare head right, curl below **Rev:** Crown above value and date **Note:** 1759 date known without curl below.

Date	Mintage	VG	F	VF	XF	Unc
1758 VH; W	—	90.00	125	225	350	—
1759 VH; W	—	90.00	125	225	300	—
1760 VH; W	—	90.00	125	225	300	—
1761 VH; W	—	90.00	125	225	300	—

KM# 587.4 12 MARK (Ducat Courant)

3.1180 g., 0.8750 Gold 0.0877 oz. AGW **Ruler:** Frederik V **Obv:** Bare head right, curl below **Rev:** Crown above value and date

Date	Mintage	VG	F	VF	XF	Unc
1761 W; W	—	90.00	125	225	300	—

KM# 587.5 12 MARK (Ducat Courant)

3.1180 g., 0.8750 Gold 0.0877 oz. AGW **Ruler:** Frederik V **Obv:** Bare head right, curl below **Rev:** Crown above value and date

Date	Mintage	VG	F	VF	XF	Unc
1761 K; W	—	90.00	125	225	300	—
1762 K; W	—	90.00	125	225	300	—
1763 K; W	—	100	150	250	350	—

KM# 587.6 12 MARK (Ducat Courant)

3.1180 g., 0.8750 Gold 0.0877 oz. AGW **Ruler:** Frederik V **Obv:** Bare head right, curl below **Rev:** Crown above value and date

Date	Mintage	VG	F	VF	XF	Unc
1763 K; A	—	150	175	250	400	—

KM# 587.7 12 MARK (Ducat Courant)

3.1180 g., 0.8750 Gold 0.0877 oz. AGW **Ruler:** Frederik V **Obv:** Bare head right, curl below **Rev:** Crown above value and date

Date	Mintage	VG	F	VF	XF	Unc
1765 HSK; DIA	—	750	1,100	1,800	2,500	—

KM# 624 12 MARK (Ducat Courant)

3.1180 g., 0.8750 Gold 0.0877 oz. AGW **Ruler:** Christian VII **Obv:** Bust right **Rev:** "DEN 29 JANUARII" within wreath

Date	Mintage	VG	F	VF	XF	Unc
1771 K	—	650	1,300	2,600	4,500	—

KM# 641.1 12 MARK (Ducat Courant)

3.1180 g., 0.8750 Gold 0.0877 oz. AGW **Ruler:** Christian VII **Obv:** Moneyer's initial W below bust **Obv. Legend:** CHRISTIANUS • VII • D • G • REX • DAN • NOR • V • G • **Rev:** Crown above value **Rev. Legend:** GLORIA EX AMORE PATRIÆ •

Date	Mintage	F	VF	XF	Unc	BU
1781 CHL	—	350	650	1,000	1,400	—
1782 CHL	—	250	550	1,000	1,300	—
1783 CHL	—	300	600	1,000	1,300	—

KM# 641.2 12 MARK (Ducat Courant)

3.1180 g., 0.8750 Gold 0.0877 oz. AGW **Ruler:** Christian VII **Obv:** Moneyer's initial B below bust **Rev:** Crown above value

Date	Mintage	F	VF	XF	Unc	BU
1783 CHL	—	300	600	1,000	1,300	—

KM# 641.3 12 MARK (Ducat Courant)

3.1180 g., 0.8750 Gold 0.0877 oz. AGW **Ruler:** Christian VII **Obv:** Moneyer's initial B below bust **Rev:** Crown above value

Date	Mintage	F	VF	XF	Unc	BU
1783 HSK	—	350	700	1,100	1,500	—

KM# 641.4 12 MARK (Ducat Courant)

3.1180 g., 0.8750 Gold 0.0877 oz. AGW **Ruler:** Christian VII **Obv:** Moneyer's initial W below bust **Rev:** Crown above value

Date	Mintage	F	VF	XF	Unc	BU
1785 DCL	—	250	550	1,000	1,300	—

KM# 508 DUCAT COURANT

2.8700 g., 0.8750 Gold 0.0807 oz. AGW **Ruler:** Frederik IV **Obv:** Bust right **Obv. Legend:** FRID • IIII • D • G • REX • DAN • NOR • V • G • **Rev:** Crown above date **Rev. Legend:** RIXDALER • COUR • MYNT •

Date	Mintage	VG	F	VF	XF	Unc
1714	—	400	750	1,200	1,700	—
1715 CW	—	350	550	900	1,300	—
1716 CW	—	250	400	750	1,100	—

KM# 509 2 DUCAT COURANT

5.7400 g., 0.8750 Gold 0.1615 oz. AGW **Ruler:** Frederik IV **Obv:** Bust right **Rev:** Large crown above date

Date	Mintage	VG	F	VF	XF	Unc
1714 Unique	—	—	—	—	—	—

KM# 474 DUCAT

3.4900 g., 0.9790 Gold 0.1098 oz. AGW **Ruler:** Frederik IV **Rev:** Three-masted ship in harbor of Christiansborg fortress

Date	Mintage	VG	F	VF	XF	Unc
1701	—	1,300	2,000	2,700	3,500	—

KM# 478 DUCAT

3.4900 g., 0.9790 Gold 0.1098 oz. AGW **Ruler:** Frederik IV **Obv:** Figure left on rearing horse **Rev:** Three crowned arms and three crowned "F4" monograms alternate in circle

Date	Mintage	VG	F	VF	XF	Unc
1702	—	2,000	3,000	—	—	—
ND	—	700	1,100	1,800	2,400	—

KM# 481 DUCAT

3.4900 g., 0.9790 Gold 0.1098 oz. AGW **Ruler:** Frederik IV **Obv:** Large of bust right **Obv. Legend:** FRID • IIII • D • G • DAN • NOVG • REX • **Rev:** Christiansborg fortress in inner circle, "IN GUINEA" in exergue **Rev. Legend:** CHRISTIANSBORG • I • GUINEA •

Date	Mintage	VG	F	VF	XF	Unc
1704	—	800	1,400	2,000	—	—
ND Rare	—	—	—	—	—	—

KM# 484 DUCAT

3.4900 g., 0.9790 Gold 0.1098 oz. AGW **Ruler:** Frederik IV **Obv:** Small bust right **Obv. Legend:** FRID • IIII • D • G • REX • DAN • NOR • V • G • **Rev:** Christiansborg fortress in inner circle, date in exergue **Rev. Legend:** CHRISTIANSBORG • I • GUINEA •

Date	Mintage	VG	F	VF	XF	Unc
1708	—	800	1,400	1,900	2,800	—
1725	—	750	1,300	1,900	2,700	—

KM# 485 DUCAT

3.4900 g., 0.9790 Gold 0.1098 oz. AGW **Ruler:** Frederik IV **Obv:** Bust right with date below **Rev:** Three crowned arms and three crowned "F4" monograms alternate in circle

Date	Mintage	VG	F	VF	XF	Unc
1708	—	900	1,500	2,400	4,000	—
1709 Rare	—	—	—	—	—	—

KM# 487 DUCAT

3.4900 g., 0.9790 Gold 0.1098 oz. AGW **Ruler:** Frederik IV **Obv:** Armored bust right **Obv. Legend:** FRID • IIII • D • G • REX • DANNOR • VG • **Rev:** Crowned arms in double Order collar **Rev. Legend:** DOMINUS • MI HI • ADIUTOR •

Date	Mintage	VG	F	VF	XF	Unc
1709	—	500	900	1,300	2,100	—
1723	—	500	850	1,200	2,100	—
1726	—	400	750	1,200	2,100	—

KM# 496 DUCAT

3.4900 g., 0.9790 Gold 0.1098 oz. AGW **Ruler:** Frederik IV **Obv:** Figure right on prancing horse, date in exergue **Obv. Legend:** FRID • IIII • D • G • REX • DAN • NOR • V • G • **Rev:** Crowned arms within double Order chain **Rev. Legend:** DOMINUS • MI HI • ADIUTOR •

Date	Mintage	VG	F	VF	XF	Unc
1710 Unique	—	—	—	—	—	—
1711	—	650	1,100	1,500	3,000	—

KM# 497 DUCAT

3.4900 g., 0.9790 Gold 0.1098 oz. AGW **Ruler:** Frederik IV **Obv:** Figure left on rearing horse **Rev:** Crowned double F4 monogram

Date	Mintage	VG	F	VF	XF	Unc
ND Rare	—	—	—	—	—	—

KM# 535 DUCAT

3.4900 g., 0.9790 Gold 0.1098 oz. AGW **Ruler:** Christian VI **Obv:** Crowned double "C6" monogram **Obv. Legend:** D • G • REX • DAN • NOR • VAN • GO • **Rev:** Fortress of Christiansborg in inner circle, two-line date in exergue **Rev. Legend:** CHRISTIANSBORG • I • GUINEA •

Date	Mintage	VG	F	VF	XF	Unc
1730	—	600	1,000	1,400	2,300	—

KM# 540 DUCAT

3.4900 g., 0.9790 Gold 0.1098 oz. AGW **Ruler:** Christian VI **Obv:** Uniformed bust right **Obv. Legend:** CHRIST • VI • D • G • REX • DAN • NORV • V • G • **Rev:** Christiansborg fortress **Rev. Legend:** DEO ET POPVIC

Date	Mintage	VG	F	VF	XF	Unc
1732	—	750	1,300	2,300	3,500	—

KM# 542 DUCAT

3.4900 g., 0.9790 Gold 0.1098 oz. AGW **Ruler:** Christian VI **Obv:** Crowned double C6 monogram **Obv. Legend:** D • G • REX • DAN • NORV • VAN • G • **Rev:** Fortress of Christiansborg in inner circle, date in exergue **Rev. Legend:** CHRISTIANSBORG • I • GUINEA •

Date	Mintage	VG	F	VF	XF	Unc
1738	—	450	850	1,500	2,300	—
1740	—	400	750	1,400	2,000	—

KM# 547 DUCAT

3.4900 g., 0.9790 Gold 0.1098 oz. AGW **Ruler:** Frederik V **Subject:** Death of Christian VI and Accession of Frederik V **Obv:** Bust of Frederik V right **Obv. Legend:** FRIDERICVS • V • D • G • REX • DAN • NOR • V • G • **Rev:** Bust of Christian VI right **Rev. Legend:** CHRISTIANVS • VI • D • G • REX • DAN • NOR • V • G •

Date	Mintage	VG	F	VF	XF	Unc
ND A-A	—	850	1,400	2,000	3,000	—

KM# 548 DUCAT

3.4900 g., 0.9790 Gold 0.1098 oz. AGW **Ruler:** Frederik V **Obv:** Armored bust right **Obv. Legend:** FRIDERICVS • V • D • G • REX • DAN • NOR • V • G • **Rev:** Crowned arms with "EX AURO SINICO" in exergue

Date	Mintage	VG	F	VF	XF	Unc
1746 A	—	1,000	2,100	3,500	5,500	—

KM# 549 DUCAT

3.4900 g., 0.9790 Gold 0.1098 oz. AGW **Ruler:** Frederik V **Obv:** Uniformed bust right **Obv. Legend:** FRIDERICVS • V • D • G • REX • DAN • NOR • V • G • **Rev:** Galley wtih "EX AURO SINICO" in exergue

Date	Mintage	VG	F	VF	XF	Unc
1746 A	—	750	1,650	2,900	4,500	—

KM# 550 DUCAT

3.4900 g., 0.9790 Gold 0.1098 oz. AGW **Ruler:** Frederik V **Obv:** Head right **Obv. Legend:** FRIDERICVS • V • D • G • REX • DAN • NOR • V • G • **Rev:** Crowned arms with "EX AURO SINICO" in exergue

Date	Mintage	VG	F	VF	XF	Unc
1746	—	450	1,200	1,800	3,000	—

KM# 551 DUCAT

3.4900 g., 0.9790 Gold 0.1098 oz. AGW **Ruler:** Frederik V **Obv:** Head right **Rev:** Galley with "EX AURO SINICO" in exergue **Note:** EX AURO SINICO indicates "of Chinese gold" obtained by the Danish-Asiatic Trading Co.

Date	Mintage	VG	F	VF	XF	Unc
1746 Rare	—	—	—	—	—	—

KM# 552 DUCAT

3.4900 g., 0.9790 Gold 0.1098 oz. AGW **Ruler:** Frederik V **Obv:** Head right **Obv. Legend:** FRIDERICVS • V • D • G • REX • DAN • NOR • V • G • **Rev:** Christiansborg Fort (in Guinea) and ship **Note:** Made of gold from Guinea in Africa.

Date	Mintage	VG	F	VF	XF	Unc
1746	—	550	1,100	2,900	4,000	—

KM# 564 DUCAT

3.4900 g., 0.9790 Gold 0.1098 oz. AGW **Ruler:** Frederik V **Obv:** Bust right **Obv. Legend:** FRIDERICVS • V • D • G • REX • DAN • NORV • G • **Rev:** Crowned oval arms; date in exergue **Rev. Legend:** PRUDENTIA ET CONSTANTIA

Date	Mintage	VG	F	VF	XF	Unc
1747	—	500	1,200	1,800	2,700	—

KM# 565 DUCAT

3.4900 g., 0.9790 Gold 0.1098 oz. AGW **Ruler:** Frederik V **Obv:** Crowned, robed King standing looking right **Obv. Legend:** FRIDERICVS • V • D • G • REX • DAN • NOR • V • G • **Rev:** Crowned draped oval arms **Rev. Legend:** PRUDENTIA ET CONSTANTIA

Date	Mintage	VG	F	VF	XF	Unc
1747	—	500	1,200	1,800	2,700	—

KM# 566 DUCAT

3.4900 g., 0.9790 Gold 0.1098 oz. AGW **Ruler:** Frederik V **Obv:** Crowned, robed King standing looking right **Obv. Legend:** FRIDERICVS • V • D • G • REX • DAN • NOR • V • G • **Rev:** Fortress of Christiansborg in Guinea **Rev. Legend:** • CHRISTIANSBORG I GUINEA • **Note:** Made of gold from Guinea in Africa.

Date	Mintage	VG	F	VF	XF	Unc
1747	—	500	1,000	1,500	2,400	—

KM# 573 DUCAT

3.4900 g., 0.9790 Gold 0.1098 oz. AGW **Ruler:** Frederik V **Obv:** King on horseback right **Rev:** Crowned double "F5" monogram **Note:** Reduced diameter, greater thickness.

Date	Mintage	VG	F	VF	XF	Unc
1748	—	225	350	1,000	1,800	—

KM# 577 DUCAT

3.5000 g., 0.9860 Gold 0.1109 oz. AGW **Ruler:** Frederik V

Date	Mintage	VG	F	VF	XF	Unc
1749 VH	—	—	550	1,400	2,600	—

KM# 583 DUCAT

3.4900 g., 0.9790 Gold 0.1098 oz. AGW **Ruler:** Frederik V **Obv:** Head right **Obv. Legend:** FRIDERICVS • V • D • G • REX • DAN • NOR • V • G • **Rev:** Three-masted ship left

Date	Mintage	VG	F	VF	XF	Unc
1753	—	300	550	1,600	2,900	—
1754	—	250	450	1,200	1,900	—
1756	—	300	450	1,200	2,300	—

KM# 588 DUCAT

3.4900 g., 0.9790 Gold 0.1098 oz. AGW **Ruler:** Frederik V **Obv:** Bust right **Obv. Legend:** FRIDERICVS • V • D • G • DAN • NORV • V • G • REX • **Rev:** Crowned arms with garland, "EBENEZER" below, date in exergue

Date	Mintage	VG	F	VF	XF	Unc
1758	—	500	950	1,700	2,600	—

KM# 625 DUCAT SPECIE

3.4900 g., 0.9790 Gold 0.1098 oz. AGW **Ruler:** Christian VII **Obv:** Wild man standing with shield **Rev:** Four-line legend in square tablet

Date	Mintage	F	VF	XF	Unc	BU
1771	341	6,500	11,000	12,000	17,000	—

KM# 650 DUCAT SPECIE

3.4900 g., 0.9790 Gold 0.1098 oz. AGW **Ruler:** Christian VII **Obv:** Standing wildman with shield and staff divides date **Obv. Legend:** MONETA AVREA DANICA • **Rev:** Five-line legend in square tablet

Date	Mintage	F	VF	XF	Unc	BU
1791	—	450	800	1,400	2,400	—
1792	—	450	800	1,400	2,400	—
1794	—	500	850	1,400	2,400	—
1802	—	400	850	1,600	1,900	—

KM# 475 2 DUCAT

6.9810 g., 0.9790 Gold 0.2197 oz. AGW **Ruler:** Frederik IV **Obv:** Armored bust right, date below **Obv. Legend:** FRID • IIII • D • G • DAN • NO • V • G • REX • **Rev:** Crowned double "F4" monograms

Date	Mintage	VG	F	VF	XF	Unc
1701 Rare	—	—	—	—	—	—
1704 Rare	—	—	—	—	—	—

KM# 476 2 DUCAT

6.9810 g., 0.9790 Gold 0.2197 oz. AGW **Ruler:** Frederik IV **Obv:** Armored bust right **Obv. Legend:** FRID • IIII • D • G • REX • DAN • NO • V • GOT • **Rev:** Fortress of Christiansborg in Guinea **Rev. Legend:** CHRISTIANS • BORG •

Date	Mintage	VG	F	VF	XF	Unc
1701	—	900	1,600	2,300	4,000	—
1704	—	800	1,500	2,200	4,000	—

KM# 486 2 DUCAT

6.9810 g., 0.9790 Gold 0.2197 oz. AGW **Ruler:** Frederik IV **Obv:** Bust right with date below **Rev:** Three crowned arms and three crowned "F4" monograms alternate in circle

Date	Mintage	VG	F	VF	XF	Unc
1708 Rare	—	—	—	—	—	—
1709 Unique	—	—	—	—	—	—

KM# A488 2 DUCAT

6.9810 g., 0.9790 Gold 0.2197 oz. AGW **Ruler:** Frederik IV **Rev:** "SOC. IND. OCC" in exergue below ship

Date	Mintage	VG	F	VF	XF	Unc
1708	—	—	—	4,750	7,650	—

KM# 488 2 DUCAT

6.9810 g., 0.9790 Gold 0.2197 oz. AGW **Ruler:** Frederik IV **Rev:** Crowned arms in double Order collar

Date	Mintage	VG	F	VF	XF	Unc
1709 Rare	—	—	—	—	—	—

KM# 498 2 DUCAT

6.9810 g., 0.9790 Gold 0.2197 oz. AGW **Ruler:** Frederik IV **Obv:** Figure right on prancing horse, date in exergue

Date	Mintage	VG	F	VF	XF	Unc
1710 Rare	—	—	—	—	—	—
1711 Rare	—	—	—	—	—	—

KM# 499 2 DUCAT

6.9810 g., 0.9790 Gold 0.2197 oz. AGW **Ruler:** Frederik IV **Obv:** Figure on rearing horse facing left **Rev:** Crowned double "F4" monogram

Date	Mintage	VG	F	VF	XF	Unc
ND Rare	—	—	—	—	—	—

KM# 500 2 DUCAT

6.9810 g., 0.9790 Gold 0.2197 oz. AGW **Ruler:** Frederik IV **Obv:** Figure on rearing horse facing left **Rev:** Three crowned arms and three crowned "F4" monograms alternate in circle

Date	Mintage	VG	F	VF	XF	Unc
ND Unique	—	—	—	—	—	—

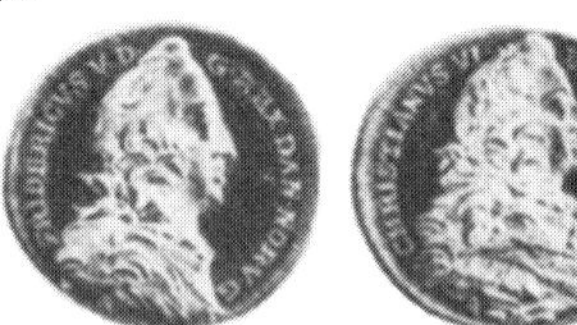

KM# 553 2 DUCAT

6.9810 g., 0.9790 Gold 0.2197 oz. AGW **Ruler:** Frederik V **Subject:** Death of Christian VI and Accession of Frederik V **Obv:** Bust of Frederik V **Obv. Legend:** FRIDERICVS • V • D • G • REX • DAN • NORV • G • **Rev:** Bust of Christian VI **Rev. Legend:** CHRISTIANVS • VI • D • G • REX • DAN • NORV •

Date	Mintage	VG	F	VF	XF	Unc
ND(1746) A-A	—	1,500	3,000	5,000	8,500	—

KM# 554 2 DUCAT

6.9810 g., 0.9790 Gold 0.2197 oz. AGW **Ruler:** Frederik V **Obv:** Head of Frederik V **Rev:** Bust of Christian VI

Date	Mintage	VG	F	VF	XF	Unc
ND (1746) Unique	—	—	—	—	—	—

KM# 555 2 DUCAT

6.9810 g., 0.9790 Gold 0.2197 oz. AGW **Ruler:** Frederik V **Obv:** Armored bust right **Rev:** Crowned arms with "EX AURO SINICO" in exergue

Date	Mintage	VG	F	VF	XF	Unc
1746	—	1,800	3,500	6,000	8,000	—

KM# 556 2 DUCAT

6.9810 g., 0.9790 Gold 0.2197 oz. AGW **Rev:** Galley with "EX AURO SINICO" in exergue **Note:** "EX AURO SINICO" indicated "of Chinese gold" obtained by the Danish-Asiatic Trading Co.

Date	Mintage	VG	F	VF	XF	Unc
1746	—	1,400	2,500	4,000	5,500	—

KM# 557 2 DUCAT

6.9810 g., 0.9790 Gold 0.2197 oz. AGW **Ruler:** Frederik V **Obv:** Head right **Obv. Legend:** FRIDERICVS • V • D • G • REX • DAN • NOR • V • G • **Rev:** Crowned arms with "EX AURO SINICO" in exergue

Date	Mintage	VG	F	VF	XF	Unc
1746 Unique	—	—	—	—	—	—

KM# 558 2 DUCAT

6.9810 g., 0.9790 Gold 0.2197 oz. AGW **Rev:** View of Christiansborg Fort (in Guinea) and ship at sea

Date	Mintage	VG	F	VF	XF	Unc
1746 Rare	—	—	—	—	—	—

KM# 567 2 DUCAT

6.9810 g., 0.9790 Gold 0.2197 oz. AGW **Ruler:** Frederik V **Obv:** Bust right **Rev:** Crowned oval arms, date in exergue

Date	Mintage	VG	F	VF	XF	Unc
1747 Rare	—	—	—	—	—	—

KM# 568.1 2 DUCAT

6.9810 g., 0.9790 Gold 0.2197 oz. AGW **Ruler:** Frederik V **Obv:** Head right **Rev:** Wings on left side of arms

Date	Mintage	VG	F	VF	XF	Unc
1747	—	950	2,000	3,000	5,000	—

KM# 568.2 2 DUCAT

6.9810 g., 0.9790 Gold 0.2197 oz. AGW **Obv:** Head of Frederik V right **Rev:** Without wings on left side of arms

Date	Mintage	VG	F	VF	XF	Unc
1747	—	950	2,000	3,000	5,000	—

KM# 569 2 DUCAT

6.9810 g., 0.9790 Gold 0.2197 oz. AGW **Ruler:** Frederik V **Obv:** Crowned and robed King holding scepter, right **Rev:** Crowned arms, date in exergue

Date	Mintage	VG	F	VF	XF	Unc
1747	—	950	2,000	3,000	5,000	—
1747 Unique; Date on obverse	—	—	—	—	—	—

KM# 570 2 DUCAT

6.9810 g., 0.9790 Gold 0.2197 oz. AGW **Ruler:** Frederik V **Obv:** Crowned and robed King holding scepter, right **Rev:** Christiansberg Castle in Guinea

Date	Mintage	VG	F	VF	XF	Unc
1747	—	1,000	2,100	3,500	5,000	—

KM# 574 2 DUCAT

6.9810 g., 0.9790 Gold 0.2197 oz. AGW **Ruler:** Frederik V **Obv:** King on horseback right **Rev:** Crowned double "F5" monogram

Date	Mintage	VG	F	VF	XF	Unc
1748 Rare	—	—	—	—	—	—

KM# 576 2 DUCAT

Gold **Ruler:** Frederik V **Rev:** Crowned ornate arms with "DWC" on ribbon **Note:** Struck in Copenhagen for the Danish West Indies Company.

Date	Mintage	VG	F	VF	XF	Unc
1749 VH	—	—	—	4,500	6,750	—

KM# 584 2 DUCAT

6.9810 g., 0.9790 Gold 0.2197 oz. AGW **Ruler:** Frederik V **Obv:** Head right **Rev:** Three-masted ship left

Date	Mintage	VG	F	VF	XF	Unc
1753 Unique	—	—	—	—	—	—

KM# 482 5 DUCAT

17.4520 g., 0.9790 Gold 0.5493 oz. AGW **Ruler:** Frederik IV **Obv:** Bust right **Obv. Legend:** FRIDERICVS • IIII • D • G • REX • DAN • NOR • VAN • GOT • **Rev:** Ship

Date	Mintage	VG	F	VF	XF	Unc
1704 Rare	261	—	—	—	—	—

Note: 133 10-Ducat pieces were struck with these dies but none survived

KM# 629 CHR(ISTIANS) D'OR

6.6810 g., 0.9030 Gold 0.1940 oz. AGW **Ruler:** Christian VII **Obv:** Head right, date below **Obv. Legend:** CHRIST • VII • D • G • REX • DAN • NORV • V • G • **Rev:** 3 crowned double "C7" monograms **Rev. Legend:** GLORIA EX AMORE PATRIÆ •

Date	Mintage	F	VF	XF	Unc	BU
ND(1771) W	207	1,500	2,800	4,000	7,000	—
1775 W	23,000	1,200	2,100	3,000	4,000	—

KM# 630 CHR(ISTIANS) D'OR

6.6810 g., 0.9030 Gold 0.1940 oz. AGW **Obv:** Head right, date below **Rev:** Crowned double "C7" monograms

Date	Mintage	VG	F	VF	XF	Unc
1775	23,000		900	2,000	3,500	5,500

PATTERNS

Including off metal strikes

KM#	Date	Mintage	Identification	Mkt Val
Pn42	1701	—	Ducat. Silver. KM#474	—
Pn43	1708	—	Ducat. Silver. KM#481	—
Pn44	1708	—	Ducat. Silver. KM#485	—
Pn45	1709	—	Ducat. Silver. KM#487	—
Pn46	1714	—	2 Ducat Courant. Silver. KM#509	—
PnA46	1747	—	Krone. Silver.	—
Pn47	1781	—	Daler. Silver. KM#640	—

GLUCKSTADT

DUCHY

STANDARD COINAGE

KM# 4 2 SKILLING

1.1060 g., 0.3290 Silver 0.0117 oz. ASW **Ruler:** Frederik IV

Date	Mintage	Good	VG	F	VF	XF
1714 CW	—	—	21.00	40.00	70.00	—
1715 CW	—	—	3.50	7.00	18.00	35.00
Note: Due to a damaged die, some 1715 coins may appear to be dated 1713, though none of this date exist						
1716 CW	—	—	5.00	12.00	24.00	40.00

KM# 1 8 SKILLING

3.0570 g., 0.5620 Silver 0.0552 oz. ASW **Ruler:** Frederik IV

Date	Mintage	Good	VG	F	VF	XF
1702	—	—	10.00	21.00	50.00	95.00
1703	—	—	10.00	21.00	50.00	95.00
1704	—	—	10.00	18.00	45.00	95.00
1704 Error FRID VI	—	—	40.00	175	300	—
1705 Rare	—	—	—	—	—	—

KM# 3 8 SKILLING

3.0570 g., 0.5620 Silver 0.0552 oz. ASW **Ruler:** Frederik IV

Date	Mintage	Good	VG	F	VF	XF
1711	—	—	11.00	21.00	65.00	125
1712	—	—	25.00	50.00	85.00	150
1713	—	—	29.00	55.00	100	—

TRADE COINAGE

KM# 2.1 DUCAT

3.4900 g., 0.9790 Gold 0.1098 oz. AGW **Ruler:** Frederik IV **Rev:** Date

Date	Mintage	VG	F	VF	XF	Unc
1705 Rare	—	—	—	—	—	—

KM# 2.2 DUCAT

3.4900 g., 0.9790 Gold 0.1098 oz. AGW **Ruler:** Frederik IV **Obv:** Date

Date	Mintage	VG	F	VF	XF	Unc
1705 Rare	—	—	—	—	—	—
1706 Rare	—	—	—	—	—	—

HOLSTEIN-GOTTORP-RENDSBORG

DUCHY

STANDARD COINAGE

KM# 5 SKILLING

0.7690 g., 0.1870 Silver 0.0046 oz. ASW

Date	Mintage	VG	F	VF	XF	Unc
1719 BH	—	2.00	4.00	12.00	29.00	—
Note: Small monogram						
1719 BH	—	4.50	10.00	21.00	35.00	—
Note: Large monogram						
1720 BH	—	3.50	8.50	15.00	30.00	—
Note: Small monogram						
1720 BH	—	3.50	14.00	29.00	50.00	—
Note: Large monogram						

KM# 6 12 SKILLING

3.8980 g., 0.5620 Silver 0.0704 oz. ASW

Date	Mintage	VG	F	VF	XF	Unc
1716 BH	—	10.00	18.00	35.00	65.00	—
1717 BH	—	10.00	18.00	35.00	65.00	—
1718 BH	—	10.00	18.00	35.00	65.00	—
1719 BH	—	10.00	18.00	35.00	65.00	—
1720 BH	—	19.00	35.00	70.00	125	—

TRADE COINAGE

KM# 7 1/2 DUCAT

1.7450 g., 0.9790 Gold 0.0549 oz. AGW

Date	Mintage	VG	F	VF	XF	Unc
1719 BH	—	500	1,000	1,500	2,400	—

KM# 8 DUCAT

3.4900 g., 0.9790 Gold 0.1098 oz. AGW

Date	Mintage	VG	F	VF	XF	Unc
1718 BH Rare	—	—	—	—	—	—
1719 BH	—	1,300	2,600	3,500	6,500	—

DOMINICA

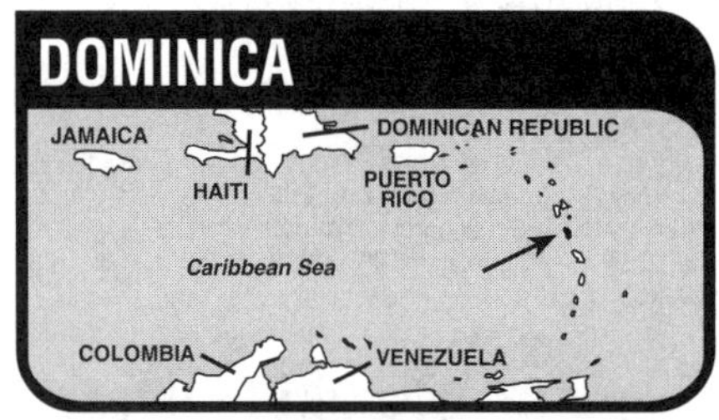

The Commonwealth of Dominica, situated in the Lesser Antilles midway between Guadeloupe to the north and Martinique to the south, has an area of 290 sq. mi. (750 sq. km.) and a population of 82,608. Capital: Roseau. Agriculture is the chief economic activity of the mountainous island. Bananas are the chief export.

Columbus discovered and named the island on Nov. 3, 1493. Spain neglected it and it was finally colonized by the French in 1632. The British drove the French from the island in 1756. Thereafter it changed hands between the French and British a dozen or more times before becoming permanently British in 1805. Around 1761, pierced or mutilated silver from Martinique was used on the island. A council in 1798 acknowledged and established value for these mutilated coins and ordered other cut and countermarked to be made in Dominica. These remained in use until 1862, when they were demonetized and sterling became the standard. Throughout the greater part of its British history, Dominica was a presidency of the Leeward Islands. In 1940 its administration was transferred to the Windward Islands and it was established as a separate colony with considerable local autonomy. From 1955, Dominica was a member of the currency board of the British Caribbean Territories (Eastern Group), which issued its own coins until 1965. Dominica became a West Indies associated state with a built in option for independence in 1967. Full independence was attained on Nov. 3, 1978. Dominica, which has a republican form of government, is a member of the Commonwealth of Nations.

RULER

British, until 1978

MONETARY SYSTEM

(Until 1798)

10 Bits = 7 Shillings 6 Pence = 1 Dollar

(From 1798 until 1813)

11 Bits = 8 Shillings 3 Pence = 1 Dollar

BRITISH COLONY

COUNTERMARKED COINAGE

1813

KM# 1 1-1/2 BITS (Moco)

Silver **Countermark:** Script "D" with rays and small star in the loop of the letter overstruck on crenated circular center plug of Spanish or Spanish Colonial 8 Reales **Note:** Varieties exist in the shape of the letter and the size and position of the star. Contemporary imitations and modern copies exist.

CM Date	Host Date	Good	VG	F	VF	XF
ND(1798)	ND(1772-89)	25.00	45.00	75.00	150	250

KM# 3.1 11 BITS

Silver **Obv:** Hole at center of laureate bust right **Rev:** Center hole between pillars, crown above **Note:** Crenated center hole in Mexico City 8 Reales, KM#106.

CM Date	Host Date	Good	VG	F	VF	XF
ND(1798)	ND(1772-1789)	200	400	800	1,500	—

KM# 3.2 11 BITS

Silver **Obv:** Hole at center of laureate bust right **Rev:** Center hole between pillars, crown above **Note:** Crenated center hole in Mexico City 8 Reales, KM#107.

CM Date	Host Date	Good	VG	F	VF	XF
ND(1798)	ND(1789-1790)	225	425	850	1,600	—

KM# 3.3 11 BITS

Silver **Obv:** Hole at center of laureate bust right **Rev:** Center hole between pillars, crown above **Note:** Crenated center hole in Mexico City 8 Reales, KM#109.

CM Date	Host Date	Good	VG	F	VF	XF
ND(1798)	ND(1781-1808)	225	425	850	1,600	—

KM# 3.4 11 BITS

Silver **Obv:** Hole at center of laureate bust right **Rev:** Center hole between pillars, crown above **Note:** Crenated center hole in Peru 8 Reales, KM#97. The center plug was used for the 1 1/2 Bits, KM#1.

CM Date	Host Date	Good	VG	F	VF	XF
ND(1798)	ND(1791-1800)	225	425	850	1,600	—

EGYPT

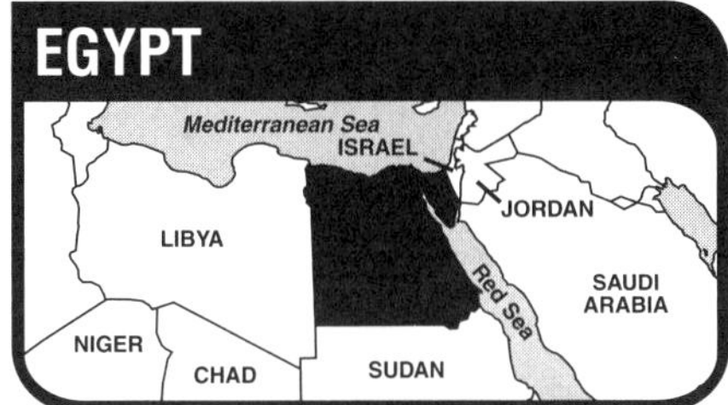

The Arab Republic of Egypt, located on the northeastern corner of Africa, has an area of 385,229 sq. mi. (1,1001,450 sq. km.) and a population of 62.4 million. Capital: Cairo. Although Egypt is an almost rainless expanse of desert, its economy is predominantly agricultural. Cotton, rice and petroleum are exported. Other main sources of income are revenues from the Suez Canal, remittances of Egyptian workers abroad and tourism.

Egyptian history dates back to about 3000 B.C. when the empire was established by uniting the upper and lower kingdoms. Following its 'Golden Age' (16th to 13th centuries B.C.), Egypt was conquered by Persia (525 B.C.) and Alexander the Great (332 B.C.). The Ptolemies, descended from one of Alexander's generals, ruled until the suicide of Cleopatra (30 B.C.) when Egypt became the private domain of the Roman emperor, and subsequently part of the Byzantine world. Various Muslim dynasties ruled Egypt from 641 on, including Ayyubid Sultans to 1250 and Mamluks to 1517, when it was conquered by the Ottoman Turks, interrupted by the occupation of Napoleon (1798-1801). A semi-independent dynasty was founded by Muhammad Ali in 1805 which lasted until 1952. Turkish rule became increasingly casual, permitting Great Britain to inject its influence by purchasing shares in the Suez Canal. British troops occupied Egypt in 1882, becoming the de facto rulers. On Dec. 14, 1914, Egypt was made a protectorate of Britain. British occupation ended on Feb. 28, 1922, when Egypt became a sovereign, independent kingdom. The monarchy was abolished and a republic proclaimed on June 18, 1953.

On Feb. 1, 1958, Egypt and Syria formed the United Arab Republic. Yemen joined on March 8 in an association known as the United Arab States. Syria withdrew from the United Arab Republic on Sept. 29, 1961, and on Dec. 26 Egypt dissolved its ties with Yemen in the United Arab States. On Sept. 2, 1971, Egypt finally shed the name United Arab Republic in favor of the Arab Republic of Egypt.

RULERS

Ottoman, until 1882
Ali Bey, rebel,
AH1183-1186, 1769-1772AD

MONETARY SYSTEM

40 Paras = 1 Qirsh (Piastre)

MINT MARKS

Egyptian coins issued prior to the advent of the British Protectorate series of Sultan Hussein Kamil introduced in 1916 were very similar to Turkish coins of the same period. They can best be distinguished by the presence of the Arabic word *Misr* Egypt) on the reverse, which generally appears immediately above the Muslim accession date of the ruler, which is presented in Arabic numerals. Each coin is individually dated according to the regnal years.

INITIAL LETTERS

Letters, symbols and numerals were placed on coins during the reigns of Mustafa II (1695) until Selim III (1789). They have been observed in various positions but the most common position being over *bin* in the third row of the obverse. In Egypt these letters and others used on the Paras (Medins) above the word *duribe* on the reverse during this period.

INITIAL LETTERS, NUMERALS

Alif	ba	ha	ha	dal
ا	ب	ح	ح	د
i	ii	iii	iv	v
ra	sin	sad	(?) sm	ta
ر	س	ص	صم	ط
vi	vii	viii	ix	x
tha	'ain	(hamza)	kaf	mim
ظ	ع	ء	ق	م
xi	xii	xiii	xiv	xv
noon	noon w/o dot	ha	(?) ra	ah
ن	ں	هو	ر	اح
xvi	xvii	xviii	xix	xx
es	ba	bkr	ha	raa
اس	با	بكر	حا	را
xxi	xxii	xxiii	xxiv	xxv
ragib	sma	msi	'aa	gha
راغب	سا	مصي	عا	غا
xxvi	xxvii	xxviii	xxvix	xxx
'ab	'abd	'ad	'an	md
عب	عبد	عد	عن	مد
xxxi	xxxii	xxxiii	xxxiv	xxxv
mr	mk	mdm	mha	ha
مر	مط	مصم	مها	ه
xxxvi	xxxvii	xxxviii	xxxix	xl
ya	42a	md6	6md	6mdm
يا	١٢٤	مد٦	٦مد	٦مصم
xli	xlii	xliii	xliv	xlv

REGNAL YEAR IDENTIFICATION

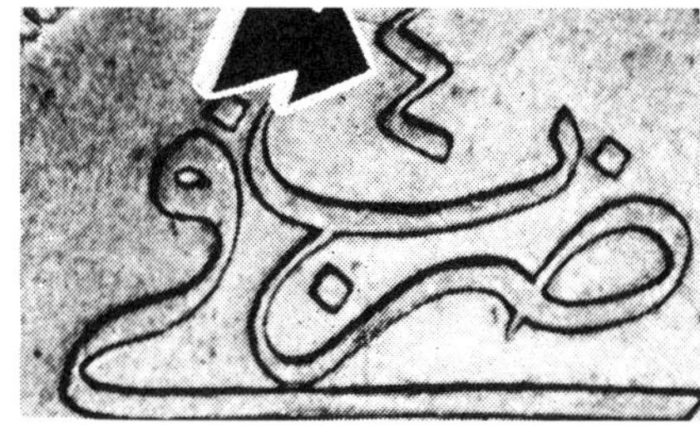

4
Duriba fi

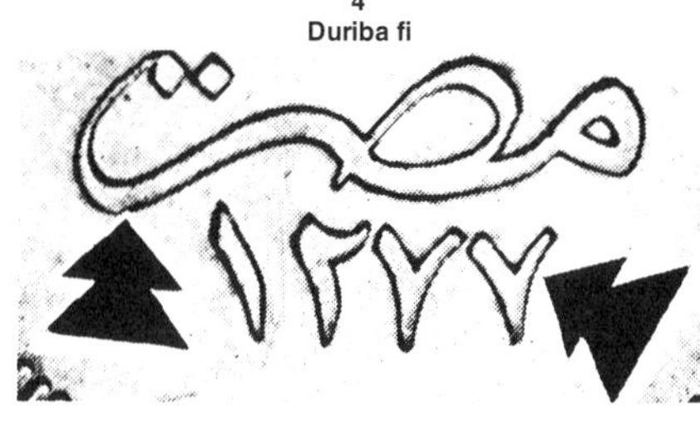

Misr — Accession Date

DENOMINATIONS

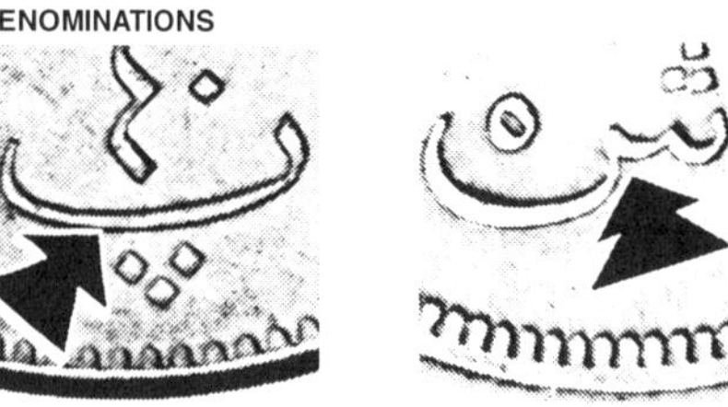

Para — Qirsh

NOTE: The unit of value on coins of this period is generally presented on the obverse immediately below the toughra, as shown in the illustrations above.

OTTOMAN EMPIRE

1595 - 1914AD

Mustafa II

AH1106-15/1695-1703AD

HAMMERED COINAGE

KM# 62 SHERIFI ALTIN

3.2000 g., Gold **Mint:** Misr

Date	Mintage	VG	F	VF	XF	Unc
AH1106	—	100	200	300	450	—

KM# 63 JEDID ESHREFI ALTIN

3.2500 g., Gold, 17-20 mm. **Obverse:** Tughra **Reverse:** Mint name **Mint:** Misr

Date	Mintage	VG	F	VF	XF	Unc
AH1109	—	75.00	100	150	250	—
AH1113	—	100	250	350	600	—

Ahmed III

AH1115-1143/1703-1730AD

HAMMERED COINAGE

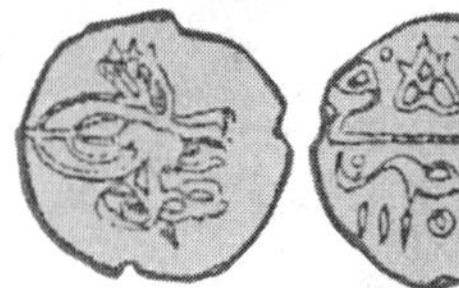

KM# 65 JEDID

3.1500 g., Copper Or Bronze, 17-20 mm. **Obverse:** Toughra **Reverse:** Mint name **Mint:** Misr **Note:** Varieties exist.

Date	Mintage	VG	F	VF	XF	Unc
AH1115	—	10.00	20.00	30.00	50.00	—

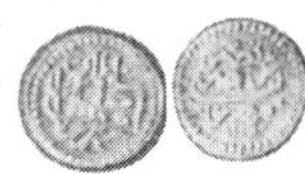

KM# 66 AKCE

Silver **Mint:** Misr **Note:** Weight varies 0.14-.016 grams.

Date	Mintage	VG	F	VF	XF	Unc
AH1115	—	6.00	12.00	20.00	40.00	—

KM# 68 PARA

0.4500 g., Silver **Obverse:** Legends **Reverse:** Legends **Mint:** Misr

Date	Mintage	VG	F	VF	XF	Unc
AH1115	—	8.00	15.00	25.00	45.00	—

KM# 69 PARA

0.6800 g., Silver **Obverse:** Toughra **Reverse:** Legends **Mint:** Misr

Date	Mintage	VG	F	VF	XF	Unc
AH1115	—	10.00	15.00	20.00	25.00	—

KM# 70 BESLIK

2.9600 g., Silver, 24 mm. **Obverse:** Toughra **Reverse:** Mint name **Mint:** Misr

Date	Mintage	VG	F	VF	XF	Unc
AH1115 Rare	—	—	—	—	—	—

KM# 71 1/2 ALTIN

1.7000 g., Gold **Obverse:** Toughra **Reverse:** Legend **Mint:** Misr **Note:** Similar to 1-1/2 Altin, KM#75.

Date	Mintage	VG	F	VF	XF	Unc
AH1115 Rare	—	—	—	—	—	—
ND iii (twice) Rare	—	—	—	—	—	—
ND xxxvi (twice) Rare	—	—	—	—	—	—

KM# 72 ESHREFI ALTIN

Gold **Obverse:** Mint name below toughra **Reverse:** Legend **Mint:** Misr **Note:** Weight varies: 3.30-3.45g.

Date	Mintage	VG	F	VF	XF	Unc
AH1115	—	100	150	200	300	—
ND xiv	—	100	150	200	300	—
ND xv	—	100	150	200	300	—
ND xviii	—	100	150	200	300	—
ND xxviii	—	100	150	200	300	—

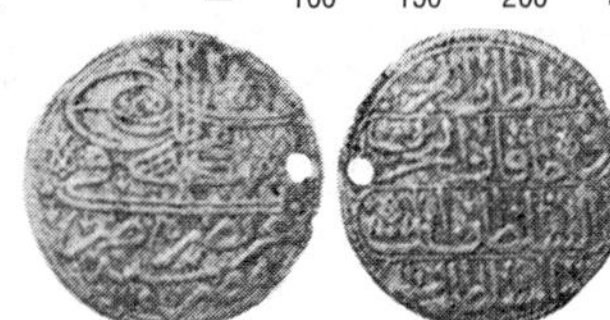

KM# 75 1-1/2 ALTIN

5.0900 g., Gold **Obverse:** Toughra **Reverse:** Legends **Mint:** Misr **Note:** Weight varies, 4.87-5.09 grams

Date	Mintage	VG	F	VF	XF	Unc
AH1115	—	375	500	850	1,200	—
ND xxxvi (twice)	—	375	500	850	1,200	—

KM# 78 2 ALTIN

5.0900 g., Gold, 34 mm. **Obverse:** Toughra above legends within inner circle **Reverse:** Legend within inner circle **Mint:** Misr

Date	Mintage	VG	F	VF	XF	Unc
AH1115 Rare	—	—	—	—	—	—

KM# 77 2 ALTIN

5.0900 g., Gold, 28 mm. **Obverse:** Toughra within beaded circle **Reverse:** Legend, mint name and date within beaded circle **Mint:** Misr

Date	Mintage	VG	F	VF	XF	Unc
AH1115 Rare	—	—	—	—	—	—
ND xiv	—	—	—	—	—	—

Mahmud I

AH1143-1168/1730-1754AD

HAMMERED COINAGE

KM# 81 JEDID

2.0000 g., Copper Or Bronze, 16.7 mm. **Obverse:** Legend **Rev. Legend:** Without Sanat

Date	Mintage	Good	VG	F	VF	XF
AH1143	—	15.00	30.00	50.00	75.00	—

KM# 80 JEDID

2.3000 g., Copper Or Bronze, 15.7-17 mm. **Obverse:** Toughra **Rev. Legend:** With "SANAT" **Note:** Weight varies: 1.90-2.30g.

Date	Mintage	Good	VG	F	VF	XF
AH1143	—	15.00	30.00	50.00	75.00	—
AH1143 v	—	15.00	30.00	50.00	75.00	—

KM# 82.1 MEDIN

0.5000 g., Silver **Obverse:** Toughra **Reverse:** Legend **Note:** With initial letters. Varieties exist.

Date	Mintage	VG	F	VF	XF	Unc
AH1143	—	5.00	10.00	15.00	28.00	—
AH1143 v	—	5.00	10.00	15.00	28.00	—
AH1143 vii	—	5.00	10.00	15.00	28.00	—
AH1143 xii	—	5.00	10.00	15.00	28.00	—
AH1143 xv	—	5.00	10.00	15.00	28.00	—
AH1143 xxxii	—	5.00	10.00	15.00	28.00	—

KM# 82.2 MEDIN

0.5000 g., Silver **Obverse:** Toughra **Reverse:** Legend **Note:** Without initial letters. Varieties exist.

Date	Mintage	VG	F	VF	XF	Unc
AH1143	—	5.00	10.00	15.00	28.00	—

KM# 83 ZERI MAHBUB NISFIYE

1.2500 g., Gold **Obverse:** Toughra **Reverse:** Legend

Date	Mintage	VG	F	VF	XF	Unc
AH1143	—	50.00	100	180	250	—
AH1143 xii	—	50.00	100	180	250	—
AH1143 xxv	—	50.00	100	180	250	—

KM# 84 ZERI MAHBUB NISFIYE

1.2500 g., Gold **Obverse:** Legend with "Nisfiye" at lower right near toughra **Reverse:** Legend

Date	Mintage	VG	F	VF	XF	Unc
AH1143	—	100	200	300	450	—
AH1143 xv and vii	—	100	200	300	450	—
AH1143 xx and xli	—	100	200	300	450	—

KM# 85 YARIM ZINJIRLI ALTIN

Gold, 14 mm. **Obverse:** Toughra **Reverse:** Legend **Note:** Weight varies 1.65-1.70 grams.

Date	Mintage	VG	F	VF	XF	Unc
AH1143	—	50.00	85.00	130	225	—
AH1143 vii and xvi	—	50.00	85.00	130	225	—

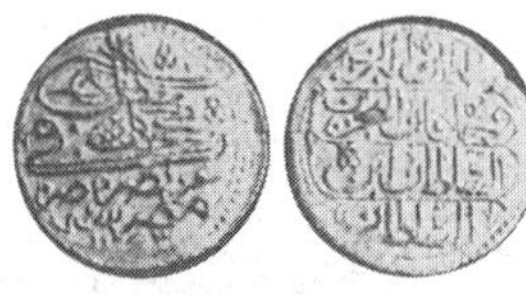

KM# A86 1/2 ZERI MAHBUB

Gold, 15-20 mm. **Obverse:** Toughra above legend **Reverse:** Legend **Note:** Weight varies 0.93-1.26 grams. Size varies.

Date	Mintage	VG	F	VF	XF	Unc
AH1143	—	35.00	65.00	90.00	150	—

KM# 89.1 ZERI MAHBUB

Gold **Obverse:** Grape between two arrows at right of toughra **Reverse:** Legend **Note:** Similar to KM#88 without initial letter.

Date	Mintage	VG	F	VF	XF	Unc
AH1143	—	45.00	75.00	125	175	—

KM# 89.2 ZERI MAHBUB

Gold **Obverse:** Toughra **Reverse:** Legend **Note:** Similar to KM#88 with initial letter.

Date	Mintage	VG	F	VF	XF	Unc
AH1143	—	60.00	90.00	125	200	—
AH1143 xi	—	60.00	90.00	125	200	—

KM# 90 ZERI MAHBUB

Gold **Obverse:** Rose between 2 arrows **Reverse:** Legend **Note:** Varieties exist.

Date	Mintage	VG	F	VF	XF	Unc
AH1143	—	60.00	90.00	130	200	—
AH1143 xxiv	—	60.00	90.00	130	200	—
AH1143 xxix	—	60.00	90.00	130	200	—

KM# 86 ZERI MAHBUB

Gold **Obverse:** Small lotus at right of toughra **Reverse:** Legend **Note:** Weight varies 2.50-2.60 grams. Variety with wider rim exists.

Date	Mintage	VG	F	VF	XF	Unc
AH1143	—	60.00	90.00	125	200	—
AH1143 vii	—	60.00	90.00	125	200	—
AH1143 xii Large	—	60.00	90.00	125	200	—
AH1143 xii Small	—	60.00	90.00	125	200	—
AH1143 xxv	—	60.00	90.00	125	200	—
AH1143 xxv + xii	—	60.00	90.00	125	200	—
AH1143 xxv + v Small	—	60.00	90.00	125	200	—
AH1143 xxv + v Large	—	60.00	90.00	125	200	—
AH1143 xxv + xvi	—	60.00	90.00	125	200	—

KM# 87 ZERI MAHBUB

Gold **Obverse:** Rose branch at right of toughra **Reverse:** Legend

Date	Mintage	VG	F	VF	XF	Unc
AH1143	—	60.00	90.00	125	200	—
AH1143 xv	—	60.00	90.00	125	200	—
AH1143 xv + v	—	60.00	90.00	125	200	—
AH1143 xii + xxv	—	60.00	90.00	125	200	—
AH1143 xii - xxv + xi	—	60.00	90.00	125	200	—

KM# 88 ZERI MAHBUB

Gold **Obverse:** Grape between 2 arrows at right of toughra **Reverse:** Legend "Rayheb" as initials

Date	Mintage	VG	F	VF	XF	Unc
AH1143	—	60.00	90.00	125	200	—
AH1143 xxvi	—	60.00	90.00	125	200	—

KM# 91 ZINJIRLI ALTIN

3.4500 g., Gold, 18 mm. **Obverse:** Toughra **Reverse:** Legend **Mint:** Misr **Note:** Varieties exist.

Date	Mintage	VG	F	VF	XF	Unc
AH1143	—	60.00	90.00	150	240	—
AH1143 iii	—	60.00	90.00	150	240	—
AH1143 iii - xvi	—	60.00	90.00	150	240	—
AH1143 xvii	—	60.00	90.00	150	240	—

KM# 92 BIRBUCHUK TUGHRALI ALTIN

Gold **Obverse:** Toughra above legend within inner circle, ornamental border **Reverse:** Legend within inner circle, ornamental border **Note:** Weight varies 4.87-5.15 grams.

Date	Mintage	VG	F	VF	XF	Unc
AH1143	—	150	450	900	1,500	—

KM# 93 CHIFTE ZERI MAHBUB

5.0000 g., Gold, 33 mm.

Date	Mintage	VG	F	VF	XF	Unc
AH1143	—	150	350	600	1,150	—
AH1143 XXV	—	150	350	600	1,150	—
AH1143 v	—	150	350	600	1,150	—

Osman III

AH1168-1171/1754-1757AD

HAMMERED COINAGE

KM# 94 JEDID

0.8000 g., Copper, 15 mm. **Obverse:** Toughra **Reverse:** Legend

Date	Mintage	Good	VG	F	VF	XF
AH1168	—	27.50	55.00	75.00	100	—

KM# 95 PARA

0.5000 g., Billon, 15-16 mm. **Obverse:** Toughra **Reverse:** Legend **Note:** Weight varies 0.37-0.50 grams. Size varies.

Date	Mintage	Good	VG	F	VF	XF
AH1168 xii	—	6.00	12.50	25.00	40.00	—
AH1168 vii	—	6.00	12.50	25.00	40.00	—
AH1168 viii	—	6.00	12.50	25.00	40.00	—

KM# 96 1/2 ZERI MAHBUB

1.0500 g., Gold, 17-20 mm. **Obverse:** Toughra above legend **Reverse:** Legend **Note:** Weight varies 0.93-1.20 grams. Size varies. Similar to 1 Zeri Mahbub, KM#97.

Date	Mintage	VG	F	VF	XF	Unc
AH1168 vii	—	175	235	340	480	—
AH1168 viii	—	175	235	340	480	—

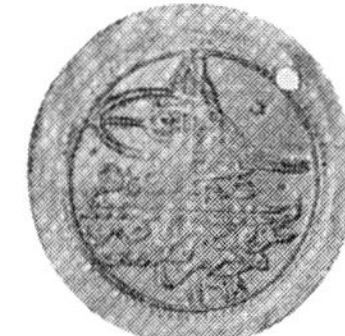

KM# 98 ZERI MAHBUB

Gold, 20-25 mm. **Obverse:** Toughra above legend **Reverse:** Legend **Note:** Weight varies 2.20-3.70 grams. Variety with wide rim exists. Size varies.

Date	Mintage	VG	F	VF	XF	Unc
AH1168 xii - viii	—	175	235	300	375	—

KM# 97 ZERI MAHBUB

Gold **Obverse:** Toughra above legend **Reverse:** Legend **Note:** Weight varies 2.20-2.60 grams.

Date	Mintage	VG	F	VF	XF	Unc
AH1168 xii - viii	—	75.00	150	220	300	—
AH1168 vii	—	75.00	150	220	300	—

KM# A99 1-1/2 ZERI MAHBUB

3.7500 g., Gold

Date	Mintage	VG	F	VF	XF	Unc
AH1168	—	350	500	700	1,000	—

KM# 99 2 ZERI MAHBUB

5.3000 g., Gold, 35 mm.

Date	Mintage	VG	F	VF	XF	Unc
AH1168 iii and viii	—	400	600	800	1,100	—

Mustafa III

AH1171-1187/1757-1774AD

HAMMERED COINAGE

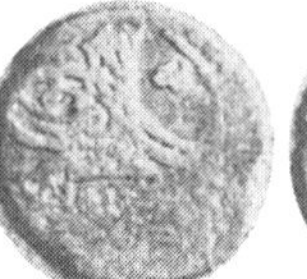
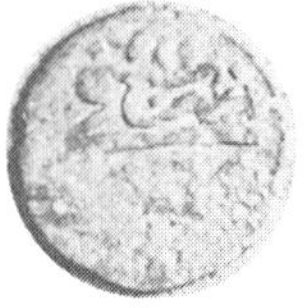

KM# 100 JEDID

Copper, 17-18 mm. **Obverse:** Toughra **Reverse:** Legend **Note:** Weight varies: 1.40-2.0g.

Date	Mintage	Good	VG	F	VF	XF
AH1171//81	—	20.00	32.50	50.00	75.00	—
AH1171//82	—	20.00	32.50	50.00	75.00	—
AH1171//83	—	20.00	32.50	50.00	75.00	—

KM# 101 PARA

Billon, 14-16 mm. **Obverse:** Toughra **Reverse:** Legend, value **Note:** Weight varies 0.32-0.50 grams. Size varies.

Date	Mintage	Good	VG	F	VF	XF
AH1171//1	—	2.00	4.00	8.00	12.00	—
AH1171 vii	—	2.00	4.00	8.00	12.00	—
AH1171 xxiv	—	2.00	4.00	8.00	12.00	—
AH1171 "mk"	—	2.00	4.00	8.00	12.00	—
AH1171 xxxviii	—	2.00	4.00	8.00	12.00	—
AH1171 i	—	2.00	4.00	8.00	12.00	—
AH1171 xliii	—	2.00	4.00	8.00	12.00	—
AH1171 xlvi	—	2.00	4.00	8.00	12.00	—
AH1171//4	—	2.00	4.00	8.00	12.00	—
AH1171//6	—	2.00	4.00	8.00	12.00	—
AH1171//8	—	2.00	4.00	8.00	12.00	—
AH1171//82	—	2.00	4.00	8.00	12.00	—
AH1171//86	—	2.00	4.00	8.00	12.00	—
AH1171//87	—	2.00	4.00	8.00	12.00	—

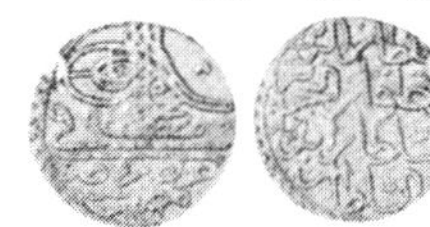

KM# 102 1/4 ZERI MAHBUB

0.6500 g., Gold, 13 mm. **Obverse:** Toughra above legend **Reverse:** Legend **Note:** Weight varies 0.62-0.65 grams.

Date	Mintage	VG	F	VF	XF	Unc
AH1171 xliv	—	110	160	200	265	—

KM# 103 1/2 ZERI MAHBUB

1.2400 g., Gold, 17-18 mm. **Obverse:** Toughra above legend **Reverse:** Legend **Note:** Size varies.

Date	Mintage	VG	F	VF	XF	Unc
AH1171 xxxviii	—	100	150	300	500	—

KM# 105.2 ZERI MAHBUB

2.5700 g., Gold **Obverse:** Arabic "4" **Reverse:** "Nun"

Date	Mintage	VG	F	VF	XF	Unc
AH1171 xvi	—	60.00	100	125	185	—

KM# 105.1 ZERI MAHBUB

2.6000 g., Gold **Obverse:** Toughra above legend **Reverse:** Legend

Date	Mintage	VG	F	VF	XF	Unc
AH1171 vii	—	60.00	100	125	185	—
AH1171 viii	—	60.00	100	125	185	—
AH1171 xlii	—	60.00	100	125	185	—
AH1171 xlii-xvi	—	60.00	100	125	185	—
AH1171 xliv Toughra I	—	60.00	100	125	185	—
AH1171 xliv Toughra II	—	60.00	100	125	185	—
AH1171 xiv (Twice)	—	60.00	100	125	185	—

KM# 106 ZERI MAHBUB

2.6000 g., Gold **Obverse:** Toughra above legend **Reverse:** Legend

Date	Mintage	VG	F	VF	XF	Unc
AH1171	—	110	160	200	265	—

KM# 107 ZERI MAHBUB

Gold, 21 mm. **Obverse:** Legend **Reverse:** Legend **Note:** Weight varies 2.40-2.59 grams.

Date	Mintage	VG	F	VF	XF	Unc
AH1171//9	—	80.00	120	180	300	—
AH1171/83	—	80.00	120	180	300	—
AH1171//86	—	80.00	120	180	300	—

KM# 108 ASHRAFI

Gold, 19 mm. **Obverse:** Toughra **Reverse:** Mint name above date **Note:** Weight varies: 3.44-3.45g.

Date	Mintage	VG	F	VF	XF	Unc
AH1171//81	—	400	600	1,200	1,800	—
AH1171//82	—	400	600	1,200	1,800	—
AH1171//83	—	400	600	1,200	1,800	—

KM# 111 2 ZERI MAHBUB

5.0900 g., Gold **Obverse:** Toughra, legend **Reverse:** Legend

Date	Mintage	VG	F	VF	XF	Unc
AH1171	—	500	750	1,200	2,000	—

KM# 109 2 ZERI MAHBUB

Gold, 29-32 mm. **Note:** Similar to Zeri Mahbub, KM#105. Weight varies: 4.90-5.15g. Size varies.

Date	Mintage	VG	F	VF	XF	Unc
AH1171 xviii	—	500	750	1,200	2,000	—
AH1171 xlx	—	500	750	1,200	2,000	—

KM# 110 2 ZERI MAHBUB

5.2000 g., Gold, 34 mm. **Obverse:** Legend is 3 lines **Reverse:** Legend is 3 lines

Date	Mintage	VG	F	VF	XF	Unc
AH1171/9	—	500	750	1,200	2,000	—
AH1171//86	—	500	750	1,200	2,000	—

Ali Bey

AH1183-1185/1769-1771AD

NOTE: KM#112-113 and 118-119 have Mustafa's accession date AH1171 while KM#114-117 have Ali's accession date AH1183. All coins have toughra or name of Mustafa III, and all but KM#112 also have Ali's initial.

HAMMERED COINAGE

KM# 112 JEDID

0.8200 g., Copper, 18-19 mm. **Obverse:** Toughra **Note:** Similar to Para, KM#101.

Date	Mintage	Good	VG	F	VF	XF
AH1171//87	—	30.00	40.00	50.00	75.00	—

KM# 113 PARA

Billon **Obverse:** Toughra **Reverse:** Legend **Note:** Similar to Para, KM#101 but with "A(li) Misr..." above date.

Date	Mintage	Good	VG	F	VF	XF
AH1171 (sic) xxix	—	10.00	15.00	25.00	40.00	—

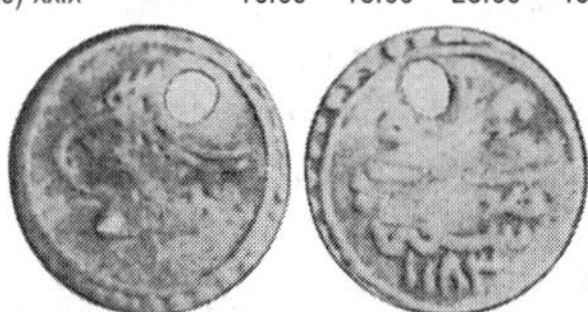

KM# 114 5 PARA

Silver, 18-20 mm. **Obverse:** Toughra **Reverse:** Legend **Note:** Weight varies: 1.60-2.10g.

Date	Mintage	Good	VG	F	VF	XF
AH1183 xxix	—	140	200	300	500	—

KM# 115 10 PARA

4.1500 g., Silver, 24 mm. **Obverse:** Toughra **Reverse:** Legend **Note:** Similar to 1 Para, KM#113.

Date	Mintage	Good	VG	F	VF	XF
AH1183 xxix	—	150	250	500	1,000	—

KM# 116 20 PARA

Silver, 29-30 mm. **Obverse:** Toughra **Reverse:** Legend **Note:** Weight varies: 6.80-7.80g.

Date	Mintage	Good	VG	F	VF	XF
AH1171//85	—	170	270	400	800	—
AH1183//85	—	170	270	400	800	—
AH1183 xxix	—	170	270	400	800	—
ND	—	170	270	400	800	—

KM# 117 PIASTRE

Silver, 35.5-37 mm. **Obverse:** Toughra **Reverse:** Legend **Note:** Weight varies: 11.50-16.5g.

Date	Mintage	Good	VG	F	VF	XF
AH1171//85	—	350	500	650	1,200	—
AH1183//85	—	350	500	650	1,200	—
AH1183 xxix	—	350	500	650	1,200	—
ND	—	—	—	—	—	—

Note: Reported, not confirmed

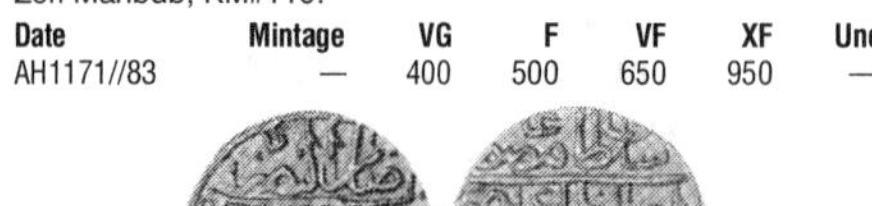

KM# 118 1/2 ZERI MAHBUB

Gold **Obverse:** Legend **Reverse:** Legend **Note:** Similar to 1 Zeri Mahbub, KM#119.

Date	Mintage	VG	F	VF	XF	Unc
AH1171//83	—	400	500	650	950	—

KM# 104 1/2 ZERI MAHBUB

Gold **Obverse:** Legend **Reverse:** Legend **Note:** Weight varies 1.10-1.30 grams.

Date	Mintage	VG	F	VF	XF	Unc
AH1171//(11)81	—	100	150	300	500	—
AH1171//(118)8	—	100	150	300	500	—
AH1171//(11)81	—	100	150	300	500	—
AH1171//(11)87	—	100	150	300	500	—
AH1171//(11)87	—	100	150	300	500	—
AH1171//(118)8	—	100	150	300	500	—

KM# 119 ZERI MAHBUB

Gold **Obverse:** Legend **Reverse:** Legend **Note:** Weight varies 2.20-2.60 grams.

Date	Mintage	VG	F	VF	XF	Unc
AH1171//80	—	150	320	550	900	—
AH1171//82	—	150	320	550	800	—
AH1171//83	—	100	250	450	600	—

Abdul Hamid I

AH1187-1203/1774-89AD

HAMMERED COINAGE

KM# A120 JEDID

Copper, 18 mm. **Obverse:** Toughra **Reverse:** Ornament

Date	Mintage	Good	VG	F	VF	XF
AH1187/1	—	30.00	50.00	75.00	100	—

KM# 120 PARA

Billon, 15 mm. **Obverse:** First Toughra inscribed "Abdul Hamid Shah bin Ahmad al Muzaffer da'ima" **Reverse:** Legend **Note:** Weight varies 0.30-0.40 grams.

Date	Mintage	Good	VG	F	VF	XF
AH1187//1	—	15.00	22.50	32.50	50.00	—

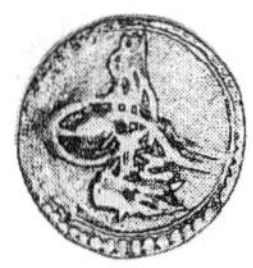 

KM# 121 PARA

Billon, 15-16 mm. **Obverse:** Second Toughra inscribed "Han Abdul Hamid bin Ahamad" al Muzaffer da'ima **Reverse:** Legend **Note:** Weight varies: 0.30-0.40g. Size varies.

Date	Mintage	Good	VG	F	VF	XF
AH1187//(118)8	—	2.00	4.00	8.00	12.00	—
AH1187//(1190)	—	2.00	4.00	8.00	12.00	—
AH1187//(119)1	—	2.00	4.00	8.00	12.00	—
AH1187//(119)2	—	2.00	4.00	8.00	12.00	—
AH1187//(119)3	—	2.00	4.00	8.00	12.00	—
AH1187//(119)4	—	2.00	4.00	8.00	12.00	—
AH1187//(119)5	—	2.00	4.00	8.00	12.00	—
AH1187//(119)6	—	2.00	4.00	8.00	12.00	—
AH1187//(119)7	—	2.00	4.00	8.00	12.00	—
AH1187//(1)200	—	2.00	4.00	8.00	12.00	—
AH1187//(1)201	—	—	—	—	—	—
AH1187//(1)201	—	4.00	8.00	12.00	16.00	—

KM# 122 5 PARA

1.4500 g., Billon

Date	Mintage	Good	VG	F	VF	XF
AH1187//(119)1	—	—	—	—	—	—

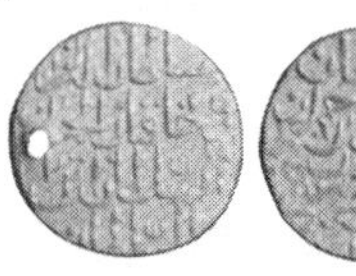

KM# 123 1/4 ZERI MAHBUB (Rubiya)

0.8600 g., Gold, 14 mm. **Obverse:** Legend **Reverse:** Legend

Date	Mintage	VG	F	VF	XF	Unc
AH1187//(118)9	—	100	200	340	580	—
AH1187//(119)2	—	100	200	340	580	—

KM# 124.1 1/2 ZERI MAHBUB

1.2500 g., Gold **Obverse:** Toughra, legend **Reverse:** Legend **Note:** First toughra inscribed. Prev. KM#124.

Date	Mintage	VG	F	VF	XF	Unc
AH1187 xxxii	—	100	150	300	450	—

KM# 124.2 1/2 ZERI MAHBUB

1.2500 g., Gold **Obverse:** Toughra, legend **Reverse:** Legend **Note:** Second Toughra inscribed.

Date	Mintage	VG	F	VF	XF	Unc
AH1187//(119)1-2	—	175	300	450	650	—
AH1187//(119)1-2 xxxii	—	120	200	400	550	—

KM# 125 1/2 ZERI MAHBUB

1.3000 g., Gold, 17-22 mm. **Obverse:** Legend **Reverse:** Legend **Note:** Size varies.

Date	Mintage	VG	F	VF	XF	Unc
AH1187//(118)8	—	100	150	200	300	—
AH1187//(119)2	—	60.00	100	150	225	—
AH1187//(119)3	—	60.00	100	150	225	—
AH1187//(119)7	—	60.00	100	150	225	—
AH1187//119(8)	—	120	170	250	400	—
AH1187//(119)9	—	120	170	250	400	—

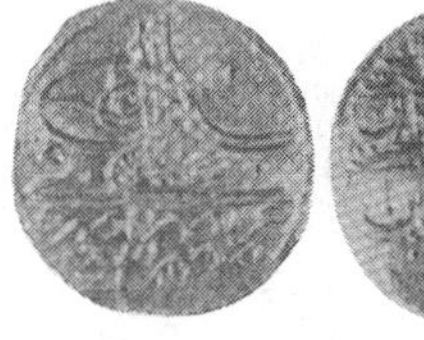

KM# 126.1 ZERI MAHBUB

Gold **Obverse:** Toughra, legend **Reverse:** Legend **Note:** Weight varies 2.20-2.50 grams. First toughra inscribed as above.

Date	Mintage	VG	F	VF	XF	Unc
AH1187//(119)1	—	500	750	1,100	1,500	—

KM# 126.2 ZERI MAHBUB

Gold **Obverse:** Toughra, legend **Reverse:** Legend

Date	Mintage	VG	F	VF	XF	Unc
AH1187//(119)2	—	70.00	90.00	135	200	—
AH1187//(119)15 xxxii	—	70.00	90.00	150	250	—

KM# 127 ZERI MAHBUB

Gold **Obverse:** Legend **Reverse:** Legend

Date	Mintage	VG	F	VF	XF	Unc
AH1187//(119)2	—	70.00	90.00	135	200	—
AH1187//(119)7	—	100	150	250	400	—
AH1187//(119)8	—	70.00	100	150	250	—

KM# 128 ZERI MAHBUB

Gold **Obverse:** Legend **Reverse:** Legend **Note:** Initial letter "bkr".

Date	Mintage	VG	F	VF	XF	Unc
AH1187//(119)2	—	175	235	300	400	—

KM# 129.1 ASHRAFI

3.4500 g., Gold **Obverse:** Toughra **Reverse:** Ornaments

Date	Mintage	VG	F	VF	XF	Unc
AH1187//(119)9	—	275	400	650	950	—

KM# 129.2 ASHRAFI

3.4500 g., Gold **Obverse:** Toughra **Reverse:** Without ornaments

Date	Mintage	VG	F	VF	XF	Unc
AH1187//(119)9	—	320	500	750	1,100	—

KM# 131 2 ZERI MAHBUB

4.9600 g., Gold, 39 mm. **Obverse:** Legend is 4 lines **Reverse:** Legend is 4 lines

Date	Mintage	VG	F	VF	XF	Unc
AH1187//(119)2	—	—	—	—	—	—
AH1187//(119)3	—	350	700	1,250	1,750	—

KM# 130 2 ZERI MAHBUB

Gold **Obverse:** Toughra, legend within inner circle **Reverse:** Legend within inner circle **Note:** Weight varies 4.90-5.10 grams.

Date	Mintage	VG	F	VF	XF	Unc
AH1187//(119)2	—	275	600	1,000	1,550	—
AH1187//(119)4	—	275	600	1,000	1,550	—

KM# 132 2 ZERI MAHBUB

4.8500 g., Gold, 31 mm. **Note:** Similar to Ashrafi, KM#129.

Date	Mintage	VG	F	VF	XF	Unc
AH1187//(119)7	—	350	700	1,250	1,750	—

KM# A130 ALTIN

3.8200 g., Gold **Obverse:** Toughra within inner circle, wreath surrounds **Reverse:** Legend within inner circle, wreath surrounds

Date	Mintage	VG	F	VF	XF	Unc
AH1187/1 Rare	—	—	—	—	—	—
AH1187/1 Rare	—	—	—	—	—	—

KM# B130 1-1/2 FINDIK

5.0200 g., Gold, 35 mm.

Date	Mintage	VG	F	VF	XF	Unc
AH1187/7	—	200	300	400	500	—

Selim III

First Reign AH1203-1212/1789-1798AD; Second Reign AH1216-1222/1801-1807AD

FIRST TOUGHRA SERIES

Heavy coinage based on a Piastre weighing approximately 19.20 g with first Toughra.

The first Toughra inscribed: *Han Selim bin-Mustafa al-Muzaffer Dai'ma.*

SECOND TOUGHRA SERIES

Light coinage based on a Piastre weighing approximately 12.80 g with second Toughra.

The second Toughra inscribed: *Selim Han bin-Mustafa al-Muzaffer Dai'ma.*

HAMMERED COINAGE

KM# 133 AKCE

0.1500 g., Billon

Date	Mintage	Good	VG	F	VF	XF
AH1203//1	—	—	—	—	—	—
AH1203//5	—	—	—	—	—	—
Note: Reported, not confirmed						
AH1203//9	—	—	—	—	—	—
Note: Reported, not confirmed						
AH1203//10	—	—	—	—	—	—
AH1203//11	—	—	—	—	—	—
AH1203//15	—	—	—	—	—	—
Note: Reported, not confirmed						
AH1203//16	—	—	—	—	—	—
Note: Reported, not confirmed						

KM# 134 PARA

0.3500 g., Billon **Obverse:** Toughra **Reverse:** Legend **Note:** For similar coins with regnal year 13 refer to French Occupation.

Date	Mintage	Good	VG	F	VF	XF
AH1203//1	—	5.00	7.50	12.50	20.00	—
AH1203//2	—	5.00	7.50	12.50	20.00	—
AH1203//3	—	5.00	7.50	12.50	20.00	—
AH1203//4	—	5.00	7.50	12.50	20.00	—
AH1203//5	—	5.00	7.50	12.50	20.00	—
AH1203//6	—	5.00	7.50	12.50	20.00	—
AH1203//7	—	5.00	7.50	12.50	20.00	—
AH1203//8	—	5.00	7.50	12.50	20.00	—
AH1203//9	—	5.00	7.50	12.50	20.00	—
AH1203//10	—	5.00	7.50	12.50	20.00	—
AH1203//11	—	5.00	7.50	12.50	20.00	—
AH1203//12	—	5.00	7.50	12.50	20.00	—
AH1203//15	—	5.00	7.50	12.50	20.00	—
AH1203//16	—	5.00	7.50	12.50	20.00	—
AH1203//17	—	5.00	7.50	12.50	20.00	—
AH1203//18	—	5.00	7.50	12.50	20.00	—
AH1203//19	—	5.00	7.50	12.50	20.00	—

KM# A134 PARA

0.3500 g., Billon **Note:** First Toughra.

Date	Mintage	Good	VG	F	VF	XF
AH1203//1 (1789)	—	5.00	8.00	15.00	30.00	—

KM# 135 5 PARA

1.6000 g., Billon **Obverse:** Toughra **Reverse:** Legend **Note:** For similar coins with regnal year 13, refer to French Occupation.

Date	Mintage	Good	VG	F	VF	XF
AH1203//12	—	—	—	—	—	—
AH1203//16	—	50.00	100	200	300	—

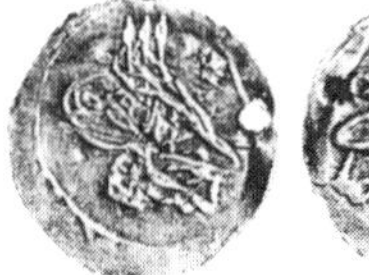

KM# 139 1/4 ZERI MAHBUB (Rubiya)

Gold, 16 mm. **Obverse:** Toughra **Reverse:** Legend **Note:** Weight varies: .50-0.90 grams.

Date	Mintage	Good	VG	F	VF	XF
ND	—	60.00	100	180	250	—
AH1203//3	—	60.00	100	180	250	—
AH1203//7	—	60.00	100	180	250	—

KM# 140 1/2 ZERI MAHBUB

Gold **Obverse:** Toughra **Reverse:** Legend **Note:** Weight varies: .95-1.30 grams.

Date	Mintage	VG	F	VF	XF	Unc
AH1203//2	—	50.00	100	200	400	—
AH1203//4	—	50.00	100	200	400	—
AH1203//5	—	50.00	100	200	400	—
AH1203//20	—	50.00	100	200	400	—
AH1203//21	—	50.00	100	200	400	—

KM# 141 ZERI MAHBUB

Gold **Obverse:** Toughra **Reverse:** Legend **Note:** Weight varies: 2.50-2.60 grams.

Date	Mintage	VG	F	VF	XF	Unc
AH1203//1	—	70.00	120	200	275	—
AH1203 I and VII	—	70.00	120	200	275	—
AH1203 VIII	—	70.00	120	200	275	—
AH1203//15	—	70.00	120	200	275	—
AH1203//16	—	70.00	120	200	275	—

KM# 142 2 ZERI MAHBUB
Gold **Obverse:** Toughra **Reverse:** Legend **Note:** Weight varies: 3.76-5.00 grams.

Date	Mintage	VG	F	VF	XF	Unc
AH1203 i and vii	—	160	240	420	600	—

FRENCH OCCUPATION
AH1212-1216 / 1798-1801AD
OCCUPATION COINAGE

KM# 146 5 PARA
Billon **Obverse:** Toughra **Reverse:** Legend

Date	Mintage	VG	F	VF	XF	Unc
AH1203//13	—	275	375	500	600	—

KM# 147 10 PARA
3.5000 g., Billon, 20 mm.

Date	Mintage	VG	F	VF	XF	Unc
AH1203//13	—	300	600	1,000	1,400	—

KM# 148 20 PARA
6.1580 g., Billon, 28 mm. **Obverse:** Toughra **Reverse:** Legend

Date	Mintage	VG	F	VF	XF	Unc
AH1203//13	90,000	325	450	600	750	—
AH1203//14	—	325	450	600	750	—

KM# 149 PIASTRE
12.3160 g., Billon **Obverse:** Toughra **Reverse:** Legend **Note:** Varieties exist with ornaments.

Date	Mintage	VG	F	VF	XF	Unc
AH1203//13	31,000	400	800	1,250	1,700	—

KM# 150 1/4 ZERI MAHBUB
0.6480 g., 0.6850 Gold 0.0143 oz. AGW, 17 mm. **Obverse:** Toughra **Reverse:** Legend **Note:** Initial letter was for Bonaparte.

Date	Mintage	VG	F	VF	XF	Unc
AH1203//13	—	100	150	200	250	—
AH1203 ii	—	150	250	325	400	—
AH1203//14	—	—	—	—	—	—

KM# 151 1/2 ZERI MAHBUB
1.2960 g., 0.6850 Gold 0.0285 oz. AGW, 19 mm. **Obverse:** Toughra **Reverse:** Legend **Note:** Initial letter was for Bonaparte.

Date	Mintage	VG	F	VF	XF	Unc
AH1203//13	—	275	350	425	500	—
AH1203 ii	—	350	425	500	575	—
AH1203//14	—	800	1,000	1,200	1,500	—

KM# 152 ZERI MAHBUB
2.5920 g., 0.6850 Gold 0.0571 oz. AGW **Obverse:** Toughra **Reverse:** Legend **Note:** Initial letter was for Bonaparte.

Date	Mintage	VG	F	VF	XF	Unc
AH1203 ii	—	175	250	325	400	—
AH1203//13	—	100	150	200	250	—
AH1203//14	—	200	300	450	600	—
AH1203//15	—	200	300	450	600	—

PATTERNS
Including off metal strikes

KM#	Date	Mintage	Identification	Mkt Val
Pn1	AH(1788)	—	Para. Billon.	—

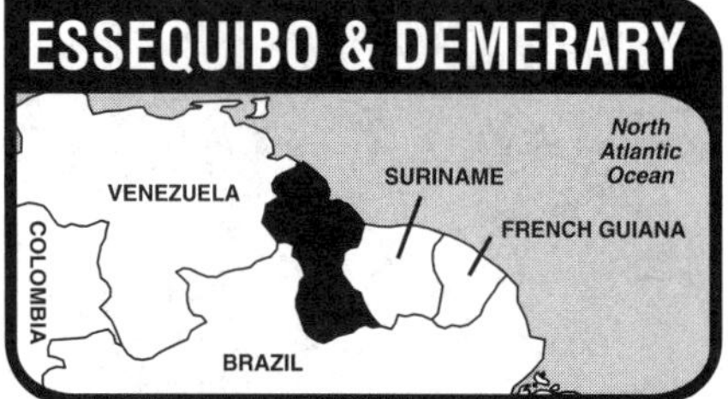

The original area of Essequibo and Demerary, which included present-day Suriname, French Guiana, and parts of Brazil and Venezuela was sighted by Columbus in 1498.The first European settlement was made late in the 16th century by the Dutch, however, the region was claimed for the British by Sir Walter Raleigh during the reign of Elizabeth I. For the next 150 years, possession alternated between the Dutch and the British, with a short interval of French control. The British exercised de facto control after 1796, although the area, which included the Dutch colonies of Essequibo, Demerary and Berbice, was not ceded to them by the Dutch until 1814. From 1803 to 1831, Essequibo and Demerary were administered separately from Berbice. The three colonies were united in the British Crown Colony of British Guiana in 1831. British Guiana won internal self-government in 1952 and full independence, under the traditional name of Guyana, on May 26,1966. Guyana became a republic on Feb. 23, 1970. It is a member of the Commonwealth of Nations. The president is the Chief of State. The prime minister is the Head of Government.

MONETARY SYSTEM

(Until 1839)
20 Stiver = 1 Guilder (Gulden)
3 Guilders = 12 Bits = 5 Shillings = 1 Dollar
(Commencing 1839)
3-1/8 Guilders = 50 Pence

ESSEQUIBO AND DEMERARY
COUNTERMARKED COINAGE
1798-1799 Gold Control Coinage

As a measure for reducing the large number of false and underweight gold coins in circulation, usually of Portugal or Brazil 6400 Reis type, coins of less than 10.76 grams were countermarked for removal.

These coins were granted full legal status for one year and circulated during that time alongside full weight gold coins before being withdrawn in August 1799. Further difficulties dictated that all mutilated, plugged, and defective gold coins were withdrawn in 1808.

KM# 3 22 GUILDER
Gold **Note:** 'ED' Countermark in oval on false Brazil 6400 Reis, type of KM#172.2. 10.24-10.67 grams.

CM Date	Host Date	Good	VG	F	VF	XF
ND	ND(1798-99) 3 known	—	—	—	—	—

Note: NFA Bank Leu Garrett sale 5-84 VF realized $5,250

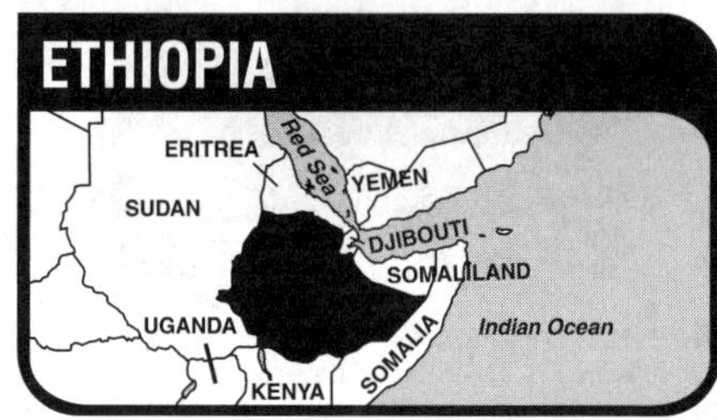

The People's Federal Republic of Ethiopia (formerly the Peoples Democratic Republic and the Empire of Ethiopia), Africa's oldest independent nation, faces the Red Sea in East-Central Africa. The country has an area of 424,214 sq. mi. (1,004,390 sq. km.) and a population of 56 million people who are divided among 40 tribes that speak some 270 languages and dialects. Capital: Addis Ababa. The economy is predominantly agricultural and pastoral. Gold and platinum are mined and petroleum fields are being developed. Coffee, oilseeds, hides and cereals are exported.

Legend claims that Menelik I, the son born to Solomon, King of Israel, by the Queen of Sheba, settled in Axum in North Ethiopia to establish the dynasty, which reigned with only brief interruptions until 1974. Modern Ethiopian history began with the reign of Emperor Menelik II (1889-1913) under whose guidance the country emerged from medieval isolation. Progress continued throughout the reigns of Menelik's daughter, Empress Zauditu, and her successor Emperor Haile Selassie I who was coronated in 1930. Ethiopia was invaded by Italy in 1935, and together with Italian Somaliland and Eritrea became part of Italian East Africa. Victor Emmanuel III, as declared by Mussolini, would be Ethiopia's emperor as well as a king of Italy. Liberated by British and Ethiopian troops in 1941, Ethiopia reinstated Haile Selassie I to the throne. The 225th consecutive Solomonic ruler was deposed by a military committee on Sept 12, 1974. In July 1976 Ethiopia's military provisional government referred to the country as Socialist Ethiopia. After establishing a new regime in 1991, Ethiopia became a federated state and is now the Federal Republic of Ethiopia. Following 2 years of provisional government, the province of Eritrea held a referendum on independence in May 1993 leading to the proclamation of its independence on May 24.

No coins, patterns or presentation pieces are known bearing Emperor Lij Yasu's likeness or titles. Coins of Menelik II were struck during this period with dates frozen.

HARAR

Harar, a province and city located in eastern Ethiopia, was founded by Arab immigrants from Yemen in the 7th century. The sultanate conquered Ethiopia in the mid-16th century, and was in turn conquered by Egypt in 1875 and by Ethiopia in 1887.

TITLE

al-Harar

RULERS
Abd al-Shakur,
AH1197-1209/AD1783-1794
Ahmad II,
AH1209-1236/AD1794-1821

MONETARY SYSTEM

Not known; 22 Mahallak were said to be equal to one Ashrafi. In the late 18th and the 19th century the Ashrafi in Harar was a fictitious medium used in accounts, which varied in value against the Maria Theresa Dollar. In the 1st half of the 19th century, 3 Ashrafi were thought to be one Maria Theresa Dollar.

The brass coins are of various sizes, but were probably all called Mahallak'. The denominations of the billon and silver are unknown.

SULTANATE
BILLON COINAGE

KM# 1 MAHALLAK
Billon, 11-12 mm. **Ruler:** Abd al-Shakur AD1783-94 **Note:** Anonymous. Approx. 2.15-2.50g.

Date	Mintage	Good	VG	F	VF	XF
AH1197	—	10.00	15.00	30.00	110	—
AH1202	—	10.00	15.00	30.00	110	—
AH1204	—	10.00	15.00	30.00	110	—

KM# 2 MAHALLAK
Billon, 11-14 mm. **Ruler:** Abd al-Shakur AD1783-94 **Note:** Weight varies: 1.30-2.80g.

Date	Mintage	Good	VG	F	VF	XF
AH1203	—	12.00	20.00	40.00	125	—
AH1204	—	7.00	12.00	30.00	110	—
AH1205	—	10.00	15.00	30.00	110	—
AH1214	—	15.00	30.00	60.00	215	—

FRANCE

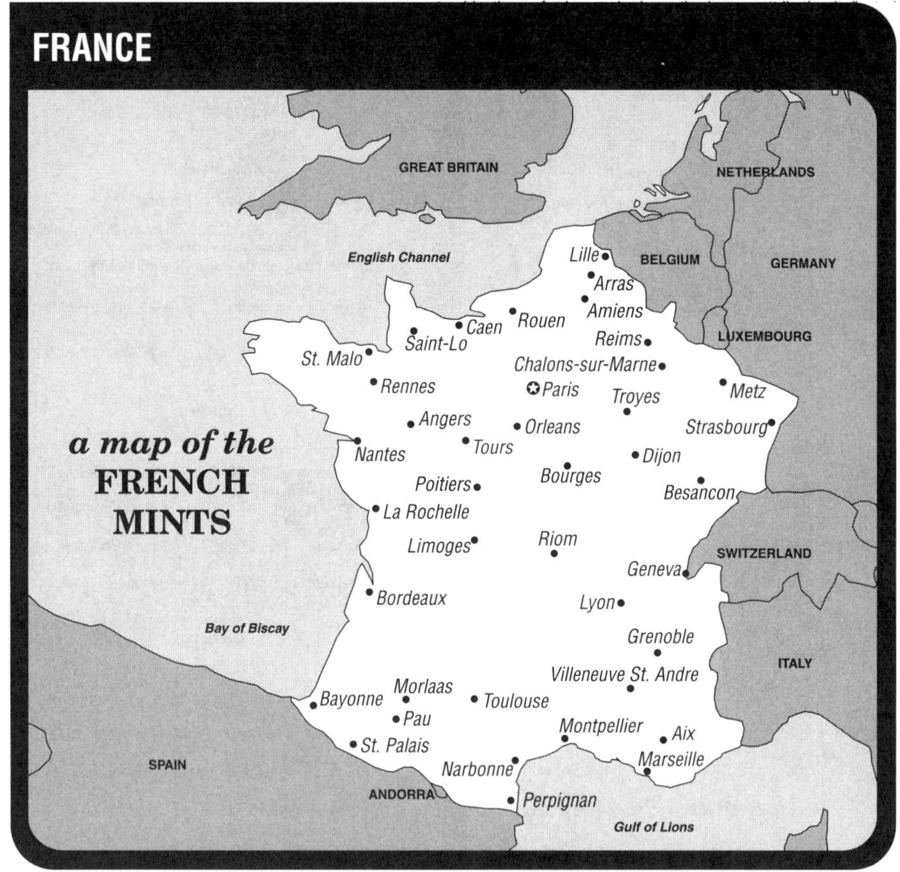

France, the Gaul of ancient times, emerged from the Renaissance as a modern centralized national state which reached its zenith during the reign of Louis XIV (1643-1715) when it became an absolute monarchy and the foremost power in Europe. Although his reign marks the golden age of French culture, the domestic abuses and extravagance of Louis XIV plunged France into a series of costly wars. This, along with a system of special privileges granted the nobility and other favored groups, weakened the monarchy and brought France to bankruptcy. This laid the way for the French Revolution of 1789-99 that shook Europe and affected the whole world.

The monarchy was abolished and the First Republic formed in 1793. The new government fell in 1799 to a coup led by Napoleon Bonaparte who, after declaring himself First Consul for life, in 1804 had himself proclaimed Emperor of France and King of Italy.

RULERS

Louis XIV, 1643-1715
Louis XV, 1715-1774
Louis XVI, 1774-1790
First Republic
Constituency, 1791-1792
Convention, 1793-1795
Directory, 1795-1799, L'an 4-7
Consulate, 1799-1803, L'an 8-11
Napoleon as First Consul, 1799-1804

MINT MARKS AND PRIVY MARKS

In addition to the date and mint mark which are customary on western civilization coinage, most coins manufactured by the French Mints contain two or three small 'Marks or Differents' as the French call them. These privy marks represent the men responsible for the dies which struck the coins. One privy mark is sometimes for the Engraver General (since 1880 the title is Chief Engraver). The other privy mark is the signature of the Mint Director of each mint; another one is the different' of the local engraver. Three other marks appeared at the end of Louis XIV's reign: one for the Director General of Mints, one for the General Engineer of Mechanical edge-marking, one identifying over struck coins in 1690-1705 and in 1715-1723. Equally amazing and unique is that sometimes the local assayer's or Judge-custody's 'different' or 'secret pellet' appears. Since 1880 this privy mark has represented the office rather than the personage of both the Administration of Coins & Medals and the Mint Director, and a standard privy mark has been used (cornucopia).

For most dates these privy marks are important though minor features for advanced collectors or local researchers. During some issue dates, however, the marks changed. To be even more accurate sometimes the marks changed when the date didn't, even though it should have. These coins can be attributed to the proper mintage report only by considering the privy marks. Previous references (before G. Sobin and F. Droulers) have by and large ignored these privy marks. It is entirely possible that unattributed varieties may exist for any privy mark transition. All transition years which may have two or three varieties or com-

MONETARY SYSTEM

1726-1794

6 Livres = 1 Ecu
1 Louis d'or = 24 Livres
4 Ecus = 1 Louis d'or
Permanent Equivalence Table
1 Livre = 20 Sols
1 Sol = 12 Deniers
1 Liard = 3 Deniers

ENGRAVER GENERALS' PRIVY MARKS

Mark	Desc.	Date	Name
	Sun (usually) or none	1682-1703	Joseph Roettiers
	Sun (usually) or none	1704-15	Norbert Roettiers
	None	1768-72	Charles Norbert Roettiers
	None	1774-91	Benjamin Duvivier
	Dupre or Dupree	1791-93	Augustus Dupre
	Bow shooting Artemise	1795-1803	Augustus Dupre

LOCAL ENGRAVERS' PRIVY MARKS

Engraver Generals' and local engravers' privy marks may appear on coins of mints which are dated as follows:

A – Paris

Mark	Desc.	Date	Name
		1694-1703	Joseph Roettiers
		1702	Unknown
	Flower	1704-48	George Roettiers
	Rowel	1726	
	Tower	1740-86	
	Scallop	1740-93	
	Lion's head	1742-88	
	Flower	1749-59	Joseph Roettiers de la Bertaiche
	Ermine	1750	
	Cross	1748-59	Joseph-Charles Roettiers de la Bertaiche
	Fleur-de-lised Cross	1760-72	Charles Norbert Roettiers
	Star	1772-73	Laurent Leonard
	Lyre	1774-93	Francois Bernier

AA – Metz

Mark	Desc.	Date	Name
	Bordered triangle	1701-03	Unknown
	Rowel	1704-05	Charles-Louis Durand
	Hermine	1705-13	Isaac Pantaleon
	Hermine	1716-20	Pierre Pantaleon
	Hermine	1720-49	Jean Pantaleon
	Hermine	1749-93	Charles-Augustus Pantaleon
	Hermine	ANII	Herbelet

B – Rouen

Mark	Desc.	Date	Name
	Root	1701-04	Pierre Racine de Boscherville
	Swan	1704-43	Pierre Racine de Boscherville
	Swan	1744-57	Alexander Racine de Boscherville
	Goat	1758-83	Nicolas Belin ?
	Scallop	1788-92	Jean-Jacques_Claude Jacques
		1792-94	Jacques, Jr.

BB – Strasbourg

Mark	Desc.	Date	Name
	Rowel	1701-04	Charles-Louis Durand
	Star	1716-17	Pierre de la Hay II
	Rowel	1717-60	Pierre l'Ecrivain
	Rowel	1760-86	Jean Guerin
	Rowel	1789-94	Christopher Guerin

C – Caen

Mark	Desc.	Date	Name
		1693-1703	Thomas Bernard III
	Chessboard rock	1709-11	Olivier-Laurent Rocque
		1711-15	Jean Pierrot
	Barred anchor	1716-40	Claude Rocque
	Triangle	1741	Jean Pierrot
		1742-53	Claude Rocque
	Barred chess-rock	1753-61	Thomas Bernard
	Hermine	1761-71	Fransoies Hue Du Noyer

D – Lyon

Mark	Desc.	Date	Name
	Eagle's head	1675-1709	Clair Jacquemin I
	Eagle's head	1709-42	Bertrand Jacquemin
	Eagle's head	1743-59	Clair Jacquemin III
	Eagle's head	1759-60	Clair Jacquemin IV
	Eagle's head	1760-82	Jean Hubert Bernavon

E - Tours

Mark	Desc.	Date	Name
	Cross	1699-1722	Charles Thomas II
	Open star	1722-32	Martin Petit
	Open star	1734-57	Francois Crette
	Star	1760-67	Jacques-Nicolaus Petit
	Star	1767-71	Jacques Petit

G – Poitiers

Mark	Desc.	Date	Name
	G or none	1705	Jean Grillaud
	Clover	1709-11	Jean Grillaud ?
	Stretched open hand	1711-15	Jean Grillaud
	Latin cross	1716-32	Jean Grillaud
	Pomegranate	1733-44	Pierre Grillet
	Heart	1744-61	Jean Ambroise Antoine Grillaud
	Pomegranate	1762-71	Pierre Grillet

H – La Rochelle

Mark	Desc.	Date	Name
	Acorn	1697-1704	Jacques Biollay
	Acorn	1718-23	Suidre
	Acorn	1729-33	Pierre
		1737-86	Gilles Nassivet
	Pitcher	1786-93	J. Jacques Biollay

I – Limoges

Mark	Desc.	Date	Name
	Latin cross	1693-1725	Francois Ponroy
	Pinpoint Latin cross	1725	Jean-Baptiste Daniel la Valee
	Pinpoint cross	1725-57	Marc David la Valee
	Cross	1760-74	Alard-Francois-Joseph Gamot
	Cross	1775-93	Jean Baptiste Daniel la Valee

K - Bordeaux

Mark	Desc.	Date	Name
	Tower	1708-09	Unknown
	Fleur-de-lis	1696-1715	Jacques Petit I
	Fleur-de-lis	1715-43	Jacques Petit II
	Fleur-de-lis	1743-58	Jacques Petit III
	Millwheel	1758-90	Jean Moulinier
	Mirror	1790-92	Antoine-Fransois Charpentior

Crowned L - Lille

L - Bayonne

Mark	Desc.	Date	Name
	Natural rose	1695-1735	Leon Mousset
	Rosette	1735-43	Philippe Ninon
	Rosette	1736-70	Christophe Rossy
	Flower	1770-91	Jean Baptiste Rossy

M - Toulouse

Mark	Desc.	Date	Name
	Scallop	1726-92	L.P. Jacques Pouzeau

Crowned M - Metz

N - Montpellier

Mark	Desc.	Date	Name
	Campanula	1701-02	
	Castle tower	1709-15	Louis Brodu I
	Dove	1716-17	Louis Brodu
	Hat	1718-19	Louis Brodu
	Crown	1726-27	Paul Thubert
		1728-64	Jean Andre Brondes
		1768-75	Jean Louis Meileer
	Tree of May	1776-93	Jean Bongues

O - Riom

Mark	Desc.	Date	Name
	Clover	1697-1744	Jean Villa
	Clover	1744-47	Jean Dapsol

P - Dijon

Mark	Desc.	Date	Name
	Clover	1637-1736	Guillaume Desvarennes
		1691-1738	Simon Roger
	Triangle	1761-72	Jean-Francois Durand

Q – Narbonne

Q – Perpignan

Mark	Desc.	Date	Name
	Bee	1711-17	Etienne Theverin
	Heart	1717-20	Pierre Daquinot
	Star	1721-22	Jean Jacques Pouzrux
	Hat	1724-40	Louis Brodu
	Dove	1741-59	C.P. Barthelemy
	Heart	1772-81	Nicolas Vial
	Mortar	1781-85	Francois Lilach & Joseph Grahes & Thomas Deyt
	Bomb	1785-87	
	Flat cup	1787-90	Nicolas-Francois Bompart

R – Villeneuve St. André

R - Orleáns

Mark	Desc.	Date	Name
	Lion's head	1726-35	Jean Louis Guiquero
	Lion's head	1738-42	Marc Amy Guiquero
	Lion's head	1739-51	Francois Dupeis
	Lion's head	1757-81	Marc-Amy Guiquero
	Star	1784-83	Joseph Amy Guiquero

Crowned S - Troyes

S - Reims

Mark	Desc.	Date	Name
	Square	1693-1701	Pierre Delahaye
	Triple bordered diamond	1704	Pierre Delahaye
	Triple bordered diamond	1709-18	Pierre Delahaye
	Hermine	1723-26	Jean-Louis Guiquero
	Pear	1726-61	Alexis Etienne Rousselet
	Gosling (dope)	1762-72	Jerome Savoye

T - Nantes

Mark	Desc.	Date	Name
	Cross	1698-1709	Jean Beranger
	Griffin	1713-28	Mathieu Georges Pinot
	Crowned animal	1749-53	Olivier Laurent Cos
	Rampant lion	1755-74	Jean Le Beau
	Pear	1779-93	Louis Salomon Poirier

V - Troyes

Mark	Desc.	Date	Name
	Double ring	1690-1710	Paul Rondot
	Double circle	1710-26	Nicolas Rondot
		1726-39	Guillaume Fagnier
	Eagle w/wings spread out	1739-60	Edme Alexandre
	Cross	1760-72	Jacques Rondot

W - Lille

Mark	Desc.	Date	Name
	Duckling	1700-02	Claude Hardy
	Heart	1702-08	Claude Francois Hardy
	Diamond	1713-22	Claude Francois Hardy
	Diamond	1732-44	Hugues-Joseph Gamot
	Half fleur-de-lis	1775-93	A.F.J. Gamot

X - Amiens

Mark	Desc.	Date	Name
	Star	1699-1703	Pierre-Gabriel Lemoyne
	Flower bud	1704-06	Pierre Gabriel Lemoyne
	Heart	1712-49	Charles Spens I
	Heart	1750-65	Firmin de Ribeaucourt

Y - Bourges

Mark	Desc.	Date	Name
	Paddle-wheel (2 in 1703-05)	1692-1704	Francois Delobel
	Diamond	1709-13	Claude Francois Hardy
	Crescent	1713-57	Pierre Boucault
	Crescent	1760-71	Jacques Julien

Z – Grenoble

Mark	Desc.	Date	Name
	Flying bird	1702-06	Charles herve
	Blacksmith's apron	1709-10	Claude Herve
	Turned over crown	1712-36	Francois Jaley
	Turned over crown	1737-71	Pierre Chabert

(2 inverted C's) - Besancon

Mark	Desc.	Date	Name
	Swan	1699-1704	Bon-Anatole Nicole
	Moor's head	1705-07	Antoine Messot
	Moor's head	1704-18	Hughes Morand
	Star	1726-35	Antoine Messot
	Cut-off clover	1736-42	C.L. Aime Couche
	Clover	1748-50	Toussaint Viotte
	Firebrand	1750-65	Toussaint Viotte
	Leaf	1765-72	Unknown

Marseille

Mark	Desc.	Date	Name
	Crow	1787-94	Charles Honore Graille

& - Aix

Mark	Desc.	Date	Name
	Small Diamond	1664-1708	Jean Joseph Cabassol
	Diamond	1709-36	Esprit C.M. Cabossal
	Diamond	1737-67	Joseph Charles Cabossal
	Diamond	1767-74	E.C.M.J. Cabossal
	Edged disc	1775-76	Etienne Borelly

9 – Rennes

Mark	Desc.	Date	Name
	Heart	1692-1704	Rene Mathias
	Duckling	1704-19	Jean Pierrot de Clernay
	Duckling	1719-33	Jean-Francois Pierrot de LaMasionneuve
	Duckling	1734-59	Charles-Marie Pierrot de Clunay
	Duckling	1759-71	Charles-Henri Pierrot de Clunay

Legend DD or/and (cow) - Pau

Mark	Desc	Date	Name
	Heart	1696-1702	Jacques de Soubiran
	Malta Cross	1704-15	Pierre de Loyard
	Cross	1727-40	Pierre Duvive - Dufour ?
	Sheaf of wheat	1746-59	Jean Antoine Duvinet
	Sheaf of wheat	1759-94	Pierre Joseph Duvivet

Mint Directors' Privy Marks

A – Paris, Central Mint

Some modern coins struck from dies produced at the Paris Mint have the A mint mark. In the absence of a mint mark, the cornucopia privy mark serves to attribute a coin to Paris design.

Mark	Desc.	Date	Name
	Scallop	1701-03	Louis Euldes
	Star	1709-11	Louis Euldes
	Clover	1711-17	Jean Faubert des Figires
	Clover	1717-19	Pierre La Tourdes Essarts
	Fox	1720-38	Mathieu Renard de Tasta
	Fox & Diamond	1738-57	M. Renard de Petiton
	Linden tree	1791-93	Jean Dupeyron de la Coste
	Heron	1766-83	Jean Dupeyron de la Coste I
	Heron	1784-91	Jean Dupeyron de la Coste II
	Leopard	1791-93	Alexandre Roettiers de Montaleau
	Level	1797	Jean-Jacques Anfrye
	Cornucopia	L'AN 4-5 (1795-96)	

AA - Metz

Mark	Desc.	Date	Name
	Greek cross	1701-05	Jean Sauvayre
	Greek cross	1705-07	Jean Debrye
	Bomb	1709-13	Jean Roncourt
	Knight's banner	1716-23	Laurent Barot
	Millstone	1724-38	Laurent Barot
	Rose	1738-64	Nicolas Blaize
	Star	1764-69	Etienne Taizon
	Crescent	1769-83	Francois-Etienne Barbe
	Bomb	1784-94	J. Fr. Leclerc

(b) - Brussels

B - Dieppe

B - Rouen

Mark	Desc	Date	Name
		1701-04	Jean Robillard ?
	Cat & bird	1709-13	
	Bordered circle	1716-23	Michel Abraham Cottard
	Spade	1725-49	Dominique de Peinturier de Guillerville
	Spade	1744-80	Guillaume Pantin
	Lamb with flag	1786-L'AN 2	Joseph Lambert

BB - Strasbourg

Mark	Desc.	Date	Name
	Double diamond	1701-04	Francois Fodere
	Anchor	1707	
	Heart	1718-34	Jean Valentin Begerie
	Heart with pellets flanking	1738-40	
	Heart	1743-92	
	Heart	1792-L'AN 2	

BD - Pau

C - Caen

Mark	Desc.	Date	Name
	Rowel	1709-37	P.J. de Goupilliere de St. Hilaine
	Rowel	1738-66	Antoine Goupilliere de St. Hilaine

CH - Chalons

D - Lyon

Mark	Desc.	Date	Name
	Brand-fire	1701-23	Mathurin Laisne
	Brand-fire	1723-30	Antoine Laisne
		1726-30	Antoine Laisne
	Small sunburst	1730-47	Jean Louis Loir
	Sun	1747-48	Leonard Brudique
	4 screws around frame	1748-52	Jean Carra
	Kite hawk	1752-84	Charles or Jean Millanois
	Bee	1785-93	Jean-Claude Gabet
	Sheaf	L'AN 2	Jean-Francois Poret

E - Tours

Mark	Desc.	Date	Name
	Heart	1702-03	
	Clover	1709-19	
	Crescent	1721-28	Leonard Rolland
	Triple circle	1731-33	Francois Rolland
	Heart	1736-51	Pierre Petiteau
	Tower	1764	
	Heart	1768	

G - Poitiers

Mark	Desc.	Date	Name
	Latin cross	1692-1706	Gaspard Perrin
	Heart	1709-29	Gaspard Perrin
	2 poppies w/stem	1730-67	Huques Saillard I
	Crowned double heart	1770-71	Hugues Salliard II

H – La Rochelle

Mark	Desc.	Date	Name
	Arrow	1697-1723	Jean Donat
	Star	1724-25	Guichot
	Griffin	1725-37	Etienne-Bernard de la Molere
	Wheat-ear	1737-38	Michel Dergny
	Star or Rowel	1738-54	Robert de Verigny
	Swan	1755-64	Charles Mesnard de la Garde
	Acorn	1764-84	Augustin Mathieu Beaupied de Clermont
	Anchor	1785-L'AN 2	Francois Seguy

I - Limoges

Mark	Desc.	Date	Name
	Harp	1698-1725	Pierre David de la Vergne
	Harp	1725-65	Bernard David de la Vergne
	Fasces of 5 arrows	1766-91	Louis Naurissart de Forest
	Fasces of 3 arrows	1791-L'AN 2	Francois Allnaud

K - Bordeaux

Mark	Desc.	Date	Name
	None	1697-1705	Bernard la Molire
	Millstone	1705-12	Bernard Sibirol and Bernard la Molere
	Crescent	1709-10	Bernard la Molere
	Millstone	1711-46	Bernard la Molere de Siberol
	Double intertwined chevron	1747-55	Blaise Jeandeau
	Temple portal	1780-89	Antoine du Temple
	Caduceus	1788-L'AN 2	Laurent Bruno Lhoste

L - Bayonne

Mark	Desc.	Date	Name
	Pink (none in 1691-1703)	1691-1710	Michel Porchery
	Diamond	1710-31	Jean de Lacroix de Ravignon
	Heraldic blackbird	1731-35	Claude Esmonin
	Greyhound	1735-59	Pierre Arnaud de Lissaque
	Pellets flanking 2 tulips in sattire	1759-77	Pierre d'Arippe
	Pellets flanking 2 tulips on 1 stem	1777-79	Jean d'Arripe de Cazaux
	Pellets flanking 2 tulips on 1 stem	1780-86	Pierre d'Arripe de Lannecaude

M - Toulouse

Mark	Desc.	Date	Name
	Castle tower	1701-14	Cr. Marchand de la Tournelle
	Flower	1716-17	
	Castle tower	1724-37	
	Circle in star	1740-60	
	Bird in flight	1764-73	
	Crown	1766-92	
	Cow's head	1792-L'AN 2	

N - Montpellier

Mark	Desc.	Date	Name
	Sinople tree	1701-03	Jean Canelaux
	Star	1704-24	Jean Guillot
	Rooster	1724-27	Jean-Pierre Gailhac
	Pellets flanking carpenter's square	1730-36	Gustave-Adolphe Perricard
	Ancient anchor	1737-66	Antoine de Larroque
	Stretched "M"	1766-91	Etienne Bernard
	Rook	1791-94 L'AN 2	Paul-David Bazille, (1791-93);
	Rook	1793-AN II	Marc-David Bazille

O - Clermont

O - Riom

Mark	Desc.	Date	Name
		1701-05	Nicolas Carlet
	Diamond	1710-16	
	Flower	1717	
	Maple leaf	1724-61	J.F. Coste Dumesnil
		1761-65	Claude-Charles Legat

P - Dijon

Mark	Desc.	Date	Name
	Dagger	1711-14	Louis Jacquine
	Holy Spirit dove	1715-22	

Desc.	Date	Name
Tree of May	1722-28	Louis Verdet
Anchor	1728-64	Pierre Nardot
Ignited torch	1767-72	Michel Belot

P - Semur

Q - Perpignan

Mark	Desc.	Date	Name
	Top & bottom of scallop shell	1716-28	Christophe Bourdeau de Bruch
	Scallop shell	1729-43	Christophe Bordeau de Bruch
	Scallop shell	1743-59	Jean Bordeaude Bruch
	Scallop shell	1763-70	Jean Bordeau de Bruch Castera
	Triangle in circle	1770-77	Pierre-Martin-Charles-
	Fireworks grenade	1777-79	Pierre-Etienne Bezombes
	Cannon	1781-91	Jean Ribes
	Cannon	1791-92	Joseph Dastros
	Anchor	1792-93	Jean-Jacques Anfrye
	Grapes	L'AN 5-1795-96	Joseph Dastros

R - Orleáns

Mark	Desc.	Date	Name
	Garden Lily	1718-24	Jacques-Joseph Benoist
	Axe head	1720-24	Jean-Baptiste de Voulges
	Star	1740-45	Pierre-Antoine Masson
	Pellets flanking star	1742-50	Louis-Nicolas Ternision
	Dog running right	1751-69	Jean-Baptiste Arnault
	Dog running right	1769-73	Gabriel Porcher des Rolands
	Dog running right	1773-77	Noell-Ythier Porcher des Rolands
	Dog walking left	1780-82	Mathieu-Pierre Combret
	Greyhound running left	1783-88	Mathieu-Pierre Combret
	Bordered triangle	1788-91	Louis Boyan Petit-Bois
	Dividers	1792-L'AN II	Charles-Pierre Delespine

S - Reims

Mark	Desc.	Date	Name
	Acorn	1696-1705	Jacques Lagoille
	Acorn inverted	1705-36	Jacques Lagoille
	Key	1740-43	Pierre-Etienne Clay de Coincy
	Poppy in full bloom	1743-72	Jean Baptiste Cliquot

T - Nantes

Mark	Desc.	Date	Name
	Sacred heart	1700-06	Pierre Manuez
	Sacred heart	1701-02	Monet
	Sacred heart	1702-06	Rene Griquet de la Lorgbine
	Heart	1707-12	Denis-Franson's Menard
	Heart	1712-27	Thomas Fachu
	Inverted garden lily	1727-39	Claude Chalumeau
	Tower	1739-52	Jacques Mathieu
	Tower	1752-82	Le Blond de Tour
	Greyhound seated	1782-L'AN 2	Marie-Joseph Francois

U - Turin

Mark	Desc.	Date	Name

V – Troyes
(See also S)

Mark	Desc.	Date	Name
	Scallop	1701-05	Jean Baptiste de Mallerois
	Clover	1723-38	Matthieu Renard de Petition
	Tower	1738-39	J.M. le Blond de la Tour
	Linden tree	1739-55	Mathieu Tillet
	Dove	1767-72	Michel Grasson

W - Lille

Mark	Desc.	Date	Name
	None or barred cross	1701-05	Jean Simon
	Oblique bar	1706-23	Jean Baptiste de la Tour
	Bar	1724-34	P.F. Baret de Ferrand
	Bar	1735-47	Jean Baptiste Luc Baret d'Urchial
	Heron	1741-54	Jean Dupeyron de LaCoste
	Chevron	1755-73	David Francois Lepage
	Chevron	1773-84	Louis-Theophile Francois Lepage
	Star	1785-92	Louis-Theophile Francois
	Level	1793-L'AN 2	Pierre-Claude Chesnel

X - Amiens

Mark	Desc.	Date	Name
	Clover	1709-16	Martin Julliot
	Laid ear of wheat staff	1727-77	Nicolas Julli0ot
	Cut-off garden lily	1727-39	Francois Robert Lepicie
	Cut-off garden lily	1739-65	Nicolas Jacques Pirlot
	Quickset hedge	1775	Charles-Nicolas La Haye

Y - Bourges

Mark	Desc.	Date	Name
	Gauntlet	1701-05	Francois Caron
	Elephant	1710-12	Pierre-Francois Baret de Ferrand
	She-duckling right	1726-30	Hugues Saillard
	Bird left	1730-71	Claude Nicolas Bertrand

Z - Grenoble

Mark	Desc.	Date	Name
	Pellets flanking dolphin	1702-10	Jean-Pierre Legay
	Double dolphin	1710-19	Raymond Amar
	Double dolphin	1719-51	Antoine Amar
	Dolphin	1757-60	Jean Amar
	Dolphin	1760-68	Jean-Baptiste Carny
	Dolphin	1757-60	Bruno Micou
	Dolphin	1770-71	Jacques Falquet du Planta

9 - Rennes

Mark	Desc.	Date	Name
	Lion rampant	1693-1709	Jean-Jacques Baraly
	Sheaf	1710-23	Gilles Gardin de Boishamont
	Axe	1724	Guy-Jacques L's Hermitte de la Feillaye
	Sheaf	1724-45	G. Gardin de Boishamont
	Hermine	1745-58	Joseph-Jacques Sebashien Garzon
	Lion rampant	1758-77	Joseph Leon

& - Aix

Mark	Desc.	Date	Name
	None	1692-1703	Marc Pielat du Pignet
	Heart	1704-36	Marc Pielat Du Pignet
	Anchor	1736-58	Gustave-Adolphe Perricard
	Lion left	1759-63	A.B. Tabaries de Granseignes

Desc.	Date	Name
Heart	1763-75	Cyprien Sabatier
Horizontal bow	1775-77	Bernard Bernard

2 back to back C's - Besancon

Mark	Desc.	Date	Name
	Uprooted conifers	1701-02	Jean-Baptiste's Bonhomme
	Uprooted conifers	1703-12	Claude-Francois Arbilleur
	Lighted torch	1712-31	Jean Louis Loir
	Griffin?	1731-38	Francois Lawtal
	Eagle's head	1738-42	Francois Gallevier de Mierry
	Cock	1748-51	Jean Canbet
	Flying dove w/olive sprig in beak	1764-72	Jean-Charles Noe Fleur

M (MA) Monogram - Marseille

Mark	Desc.	Date	Name
	Star	AN II-1787-90	Jean-Baptiste-Casimer Prou Gaillard
	Star	1791	Cyprian Prou Gaillard
	Star	1792	Callonbou

Legend ending NARE and/or Cow - Pau

Mark	Desc.	Date	Name
	Hunting dog right	1709	Martin Courant
	Hunting dog right	1701-09	Jacques de Monaix
	Lion rampant right	1710-15	Jean de Monaix
	Lion rampant right	1716-23	Jean Jacques de Monaix
	Pellets flanking fleur-de-lis	1724-33	Roussel d'Inval de La Mothe Bussy
	Garden lily	1734-45	Francois de Vicq
	Tulip flanked by 2 pellets	1745-89	Pierre-Pascal d'Arripe de Sadiras
	Hand of Justice	1777-89	Michel Soulon
	Star	1789-L'an II	Jean Baptiste Souton

KINGDOM

MILLED COINAGE

KM# 284.22 LIARD

Copper **Ruler:** Louis XIV **Mint:** Lille **Note:** Mint mark: Crowned L.

Date	Mintage	VG	F	VF	XF	Unc
1701	—	17.00	40.00	100	350	—
1702	140,000	20.00	50.00	125	400	—

KM# 284.1 LIARD

Copper **Ruler:** Louis XIV **Mint:** Paris **Obverse:** Older mailed bust right

Date	Mintage	VG	F	VF	XF	Unc
1701A	—	18.00	40.00	110	350	—

KM# 284.17 LIARD

Copper **Ruler:** Louis XIV **Mint:** Lille

Date	Mintage	VG	F	VF	XF	Unc
1707W	203,000	20.00	50.00	125	400	—

KM# 407 LIARD

Copper **Ruler:** Louis XIV **Mint:** Lille **Obverse:** Head right

Date	Mintage	VG	F	VF	XF	Unc
1713W	—	25.00	60.00	145	500	—
1714W	1,300,000	25.00	60.00	145	500	—
1715W	1,320,000	25.00	60.00	145	500	—

KM# 450.1 LIARD

Copper **Ruler:** Louis XV **Mint:** Paris **Obverse:** Boy head of Louis XV right **Reverse:** Crowned square arms with date above

Date	Mintage	VG	F	VF	XF	Unc
1720A	—	4.00	7.00	20.00	85.00	—
1721A	—	5.00	9.00	25.00	100	—

KM# 450.2 LIARD

Copper **Ruler:** Louis XV **Mint:** Metz **Obverse:** Boy head of Louis XV right **Reverse:** Crowned square arms with date above

Date	Mintage	VG	F	VF	XF	Unc
1720AA	—	5.00	9.00	25.00	100	—

KM# 450.3 LIARD

Copper **Ruler:** Louis XV **Mint:** Strasbourg **Obverse:** Boy head of Louis XV right **Reverse:** Crowned square arms with date above

Date	Mintage	VG	F	VF	XF	Unc
1720BB	—	3.00	5.00	14.00	75.00	—
1721BB	—	5.00	9.00	25.00	100	—

KM# 450.6 LIARD

Copper **Ruler:** Louis XV **Mint:** Besancon **Obverse:** Boy head of Louis XV right **Reverse:** Crowned square arms with date above **Note:** Mint mark: Back to back C's.

Date	Mintage	VG	F	VF	XF	Unc
1720	—	4.00	7.00	20.00	85.00	—
1721	—	5.00	9.00	25.00	100	—

KM# 450.4 LIARD

Copper **Ruler:** Louis XV **Mint:** Reims **Obverse:** Boy head of Louis XV right **Reverse:** Crowned square arms with date above

Date	Mintage	VG	F	VF	XF	Unc
1721S	3,150,000	3.00	5.00	14.00	75.00	—

KM# 450.5 LIARD

Copper **Ruler:** Louis XV **Mint:** Troyes **Obverse:** Boy head of Louis XV right **Reverse:** Crowned square arms with date above

Date	Mintage	VG	F	VF	XF	Unc
1721V	—	5.00	9.00	25.00	100	—

KM# 540 LIARD

Copper **Ruler:** Louis XV **Mint:** Aix **Obverse:** Older head of Louis XV right **Reverse:** Crowned arms with rounded bottom, date above **Note:** Mark mark: &.

Date	Mintage	VG	F	VF	XF	Unc
1767	—	5.00	12.00	30.00	130	—
1768	—	4.00	10.00	25.00	110	—
1769	—	4.00	10.00	25.00	110	—
1771	—	5.00	12.00	13.00	130	—

KM# 543.1 LIARD

Copper **Ruler:** Louis XV **Mint:** Paris **Obverse:** Old head of Louis XV right **Reverse:** Crowned square arms with date above

Date	Mintage	VG	F	VF	XF	Unc
1768A	—	3.00	7.00	18.00	75.00	—
1769A	—	3.00	7.00	18.00	75.00	—
1770A	—	3.00	7.00	18.00	75.00	—
1772A	—	3.00	7.00	18.00	75.00	—

KM# 543.2 LIARD

Copper **Ruler:** Louis XV **Mint:** Metz **Obverse:** Older head of Louis XV right **Reverse:** Crowned square arms with date above

Date	Mintage	VG	F	VF	XF	Unc
1769AA	—	4.00	10.00	25.00	85.00	—
1770AA	—	3.00	7.00	18.00	75.00	—
1772AA	—	3.00	7.00	18.00	75.00	—
1774AA	—	3.00	7.00	18.00	75.00	—

KM# 543.11 LIARD

Copper **Ruler:** Louis XV **Mint:** Lille **Obverse:** Older head of Louis XV right **Reverse:** Crowned square arms with date above

Date	Mintage	VG	F	VF	XF	Unc
1769W	—	3.00	7.00	18.00	75.00	—
1770W	—	2.50	5.00	15.00	65.00	—
1771W	—	2.50	5.00	15.00	65.00	—
1773W	—	2.50	5.00	15.00	65.00	—
1774W	30,000	4.00	8.00	20.00	85.00	—

KM# 543.9 LIARD

Copper **Ruler:** Louis XV **Mint:** Reims **Obverse:** Older head of Louis XV right **Reverse:** Crowned square arms with date above

Date	Mintage	VG	F	VF	XF	Unc
1769S	—	2.50	5.00	15.00	65.00	—
1770S	—	2.50	5.00	15.00	65.00	—
1771S	—	3.00	7.00	18.00	75.00	—
1772S	—	3.00	7.00	18.00	75.00	—
1773S	—	3.00	7.00	18.00	75.00	—

KM# 543.12 LIARD

Copper **Ruler:** Louis XV **Mint:** Besancon **Obverse:** Older head of Louis XV right **Reverse:** Crowned square arms with date above **Note:** Mint mark: Back to back C's.

Date	Mintage	VG	F	VF	XF	Unc
1769	—	3.00	7.00	18.00	75.00	—
1770	—	3.00	7.00	18.00	75.00	—
1771	—	3.00	7.00	18.00	75.00	—
1772	—	3.00	7.00	18.00	75.00	—

KM# 543.10 LIARD

Copper **Ruler:** Louis XV **Mint:** Troyes **Obverse:** Older head of Louis XV right **Reverse:** Crowned square arms with date above

Date	Mintage	VG	F	VF	XF	Unc
1770V	—	3.00	7.00	18.00	75.00	—
1771V	268,000	3.00	7.00	18.00	75.00	—
1772V	—	3.00	7.00	18.00	75.00	—

KM# 543.7 LIARD

Copper **Ruler:** Louis XV **Mint:** Toulouse **Obverse:** Older head of Louis XV right **Reverse:** Crowned square arms with date above

Date	Mintage	VG	F	VF	XF	Unc
1770M	—	6.00	12.00	35.00	135	—
1773M	288,000	6.00	12.00	35.00	135	—
1777M	—	4.00	8.00	20.00	85.00	—

KM# 543.8 LIARD

Copper **Ruler:** Louis XV **Mint:** Montpellier **Obverse:** Older head of Louis XV right **Reverse:** Crowned square arms with date above

Date	Mintage	VG	F	VF	XF	Unc
1770N	—	4.00	8.00	20.00	85.00	—
1771N	—	4.00	8.00	20.00	85.00	—
1772N	—	4.00	8.00	20.00	85.00	—

KM# 543.3 LIARD

Copper **Ruler:** Louis XV **Mint:** Strasbourg **Obverse:** Older head of Louis XV right **Reverse:** Crowned square arms with date above

Date	Mintage	VG	F	VF	XF	Unc
1770BB	—	3.00	7.00	18.00	75.00	—
1771BB	—	5.00	9.00	20.00	80.00	—
1773BB	—	5.00	9.00	20.00	80.00	—

KM# 543.4 LIARD

Copper **Ruler:** Louis XV **Mint:** Lyon **Obverse:** Older head of Louis XV right **Reverse:** Crwoned square arms with date above

Date	Mintage	VG	F	VF	XF	Unc
1770D	—	4.00	8.00	20.00	85.00	—
1771D	—	4.00	8.00	20.00	85.00	—
1772D	—	4.00	8.00	20.00	85.00	—

KM# 543.5 LIARD

Copper **Ruler:** Louis XV **Mint:** La Rochelle **Obverse:** Older head of Louis XV right **Reverse:** Crowned square arms with date above

Date	Mintage	VG	F	VF	XF	Unc
1771H	—	35.00	65.00	125	200	—
1774H	—	4.00	8.00	20.00	85.00	—

KM# 543.6 LIARD

Copper **Ruler:** Louis XV **Mint:** Limoges **Obverse:** Older head of Louis XV right **Reverse:** Crowned square arms with date above

Date	Mintage	VG	F	VF	XF	Unc
1773I	659,000	6.00	12.00	35.00	135	—
1774I	—	4.00	8.00	20.00	85.00	—

KM# 585.6 LIARD

Copper **Ruler:** Louis XVI **Mint:** La Rochelle **Obverse:** Head left **Obv. Legend:** LUDOV • XVI • D • GRATIA • **Reverse:** Crowned arms of France **Rev. Legend:** FRANC • ET NAVAR • REX •

Date	Mintage	VG	F	VF	XF	Unc
1777H	1,407,000	2.00	4.00	10.00	40.00	—
1779H	655,000	2.50	5.00	12.00	45.00	—
1781H	819,000	2.50	5.00	12.00	45.00	—
1782H	899,000	2.50	5.00	12.00	45.00	—
1791H	615,000	2.50	5.00	12.00	45.00	—

KM# 585.14 LIARD

Copper **Ruler:** Louis XVI **Mint:** Lille **Obverse:** Head left **Reverse:** Crowned arms of France

Date	Mintage	VG	F	VF	XF	Unc
1777W	1,501,000	2.00	4.00	12.00	45.00	—
1778W	1,557,000	2.00	4.00	10.00	40.00	—
1779W	1,803,000	2.00	4.00	10.00	40.00	—
1781W	3,191,000	2.00	4.00	10.00	40.00	—
1782W	2,555,000	2.00	4.00	10.00	40.00	—
1783W	2,802,000	2.00	4.00	10.00	40.00	—
1785W	2,115,000	2.00	4.00	10.00	40.00	—
1786W	—	2.00	4.00	10.00	40.00	—
1788W	202,000	2.00	4.00	10.00	40.00	—
1789W	—	2.00	4.00	10.00	40.00	—
1790W	—	2.00	4.00	10.00	40.00	—

KM# 585.15 LIARD

Copper **Ruler:** Louis XVI **Mint:** Aix **Obverse:** Head left **Reverse:** Crowned arms of France **Note:** Mint mark: &. The dot appears below the third letter of the monarch's name and denotes second semester coinage.

Date	Mintage	VG	F	VF	XF	Unc
1778	2,678,000	2.00	4.00	10.00	40.00	—
1780	2,765,000	—	—	—	—	—
1782	567,000	2.00	4.00	10.00	40.00	—
1784	566,000	2.00	4.00	10.00	40.00	—
1786	200,000	—	—	—	—	—

Note: Reported, not confirmed

KM# 585.1 LIARD

Copper **Ruler:** Louis XVI **Mint:** Paris **Obverse:** Head left **Reverse:** Crowned arms of France

Date	Mintage	VG	F	VF	XF	Unc
1780A	164,000	3.00	6.00	20.00	50.00	—

KM# 585.2 LIARD

Copper **Ruler:** Louis XVI **Mint:** Metz **Obverse:** Head left **Reverse:** Crowned arms of France

Date	Mintage	VG	F	VF	XF	Unc
1782AA	1,317,000	2.00	4.00	10.00	40.00	—
1785AA	1,000,000	—	—	—	—	—
Note: Reported, not confirmed						
1786AA	—	2.00	4.00	10.00	40.00	—
1789AA	—	2.00	4.00	12.00	45.00	—

KM# 585.13 LIARD

Copper **Ruler:** Louis XVI **Mint:** Nantes **Obverse:** Head left **Reverse:** Crowned arms of France

Date	Mintage	VG	F	VF	XF	Unc
1784T	1,427,000	2.50	5.00	12.00	45.00	—
1785T	592,000	2.50	5.00	12.00	45.00	—
1786T	—	2.00	4.00	10.00	40.00	—
1787T	—	2.00	4.00	10.00	40.00	—
1789T	1,000,000	2.00	4.00	10.00	40.00	—
1790T	—	2.00	4.00	10.00	40.00	—
1791T	579,000	2.00	4.00	10.00	40.00	—

KM# 585.11 LIARD

Copper **Ruler:** Louis XVI **Mint:** Montpellier **Obverse:** Head left **Reverse:** Crowned arms of France

Date	Mintage	VG	F	VF	XF	Unc
1784N	955,000	2.50	5.00	12.00	45.00	—
1785N	280,000	2.50	5.00	15.00	50.00	—
1789N	2,667,000	2.00	4.00	10.00	40.00	—
1790N	—	2.00	4.00	10.00	40.00	—
1791N	—	2.00	4.00	10.00	40.00	—

KM# 585.7 LIARD

Copper **Ruler:** Louis XVI **Mint:** Limoges **Obverse:** Head left **Reverse:** Crowned arms of France

Date	Mintage	VG	F	VF	XF	Unc
1784I	781,000	2.50	5.00	12.00	45.00	—
1791I	1,202,000	2.00	4.00	10.00	40.00	—

KM# 585.9 LIARD

Copper **Ruler:** Louis XVI **Mint:** Bayonne **Obverse:** Head left **Reverse:** Crowned arms of France

Date	Mintage	VG	F	VF	XF	Unc
1784L	8,614,000	2.00	4.00	10.00	40.00	—
1785L	1,244,000	2.00	4.00	10.00	40.00	—

KM# 585.4 LIARD

Copper **Ruler:** Louis XVI **Mint:** Strasbourg **Obverse:** Head left **Reverse:** Crowned arms of France

Date	Mintage	VG	F	VF	XF	Unc
1784BB	1,333,000	—	—	—	—	—
Note: Reported, not confirmed						
1785BB	96,000	5.00	12.00	35.00	80.00	—

KM# 585.5 LIARD

Copper **Ruler:** Louis XVI **Mint:** Lyon **Obverse:** Head left **Reverse:** Crowned arms of France

Date	Mintage	VG	F	VF	XF	Unc
1784D	133,000	—	—	—	—	—
Note: Reported, not confirmed						
1786D	2,000,000	—	—	—	—	—
Note: Reported, not confirmed						
1788D	666,000	2.00	4.00	10.00	40.00	—
1790D	2,000,000	2.00	4.00	10.00	40.00	—
1791D	16,995,000	2.00	4.00	10.00	40.00	—

KM# 588 LIARD

Copper **Ruler:** Louis XVI **Mint:** Pau **Rev. Legend:** ....RE.BD (ligate BD). **Note:** Issued for Province of Bearn. Mint mark: Cow.

Date	Mintage	VG	F	VF	XF	Unc
1785	193,000	5.00	10.00	25.00	80.00	—

KM# 585.3 LIARD

Copper **Ruler:** Louis XVI **Mint:** Rouen **Obverse:** Head left **Reverse:** Crowned arms of France

Date	Mintage	VG	F	VF	XF	Unc
1785B	1,333,000	—	—	—	—	—
Note: Reported, not confirmed						
1788B	—	2.00	4.00	10.00	40.00	—
1790B	2,000,000	2.00	4.00	10.00	40.00	—
1791B	—	5.00	8.00	15.00	50.00	—

KM# 585.12 LIARD

Copper **Ruler:** Louis XVI **Mint:** Orléans **Obverse:** Head left **Reverse:** Crowned arms of France

Date	Mintage	VG	F	VF	XF	Unc
1789R	—	2.00	4.00	10.00	40.00	—

KM# 585.10 LIARD

Copper **Ruler:** Louis XVI **Mint:** Toulouse **Obverse:** Head left **Reverse:** Crowned arms of France

Date	Mintage	VG	F	VF	XF	Unc
1789M	2,667,000	2.00	4.00	10.00	40.00	—
1790M	—	2.00	4.00	10.00	40.00	—

KM# 585.8 LIARD

Copper **Ruler:** Louis XVI **Mint:** Bordeaux **Obverse:** Head left **Reverse:** Crowned arms of France

Date	Mintage	VG	F	VF	XF	Unc
1791K	3,683,000	2.00	4.00	10.00	40.00	—

KM# 309 2 DENIERS

Copper **Ruler:** Louis XIV **Mint:** Strasbourg **Reverse:** Crown above 3 fleur-de-lis

Date	Mintage	VG	F	VF	XF	Unc
1707BB	—	12.00	30.00	60.00	175	—
1708BB	—	8.00	20.00	40.00	125	—

KM# 608.1 3 DENIERS (Liard)

Bronze **Mint:** Lyon **Obverse:** LOUIS XVI ROI DES FRANCOIS **Reverse:** Liberty cap above column dividing value, oak wreath in background **Rev. Legend:** LANATIONLA LOILEROI

Date	Mintage	VG	F	VF	XF	Unc
1792D	—	10.00	20.00	50.00	140	—

KM# 609 3 DENIERS (Liard)
Bronze **Mint:** Strasbourg **Obverse:** Head of Louis XVI left **Obv. Legend:** LOUIS XVI ROI DES FRANCAIS **Reverse:** Liberty cap above column dividing value, oak wreath in background **Rev. Legend:** LANATION LA LOILE ROI *

Date	Mintage	VG	F	VF	XF	Unc
1792BB	—	10.00	25.00	70.00	160	—

KM# 310 4 DENIERS
Copper **Ruler:** Louis XIV **Mint:** Strasbourg **Obverse:** Armored bust right **Reverse:** Crown above 3 fleur-de-lis

Date	Mintage	VG	F	VF	XF	Unc
1704BB	—	15.00	35.00	80.00	230	—
1705BB	—	15.00	35.00	85.00	245	—
1707BB	—	8.00	20.00	55.00	145	—
1708BB	418,000	8.00	20.00	55.00	145	—

KM# 400.1 6 DENIERS
Copper **Ruler:** Louis XIV **Mint:** La Rochelle **Obverse:** 3 crowned double L's forming triangle, mint mark at center **Reverse:** Filigree cross with fleur-de-lis at ends

Date	Mintage	VG	F	VF	XF	Unc
1710H	—	18.00	35.00	70.00	200	—
1711H	—	18.00	35.00	70.00	200	—

KM# 400.2 6 DENIERS
Copper **Ruler:** Louis XIV **Mint:** Montpellier

Date	Mintage	VG	F	VF	XF	Unc
1710N	2,026,000	15.00	28.00	60.00	160	—
1711N	8,652,000	12.00	25.00	50.00	150	—
1712N	8,219,000	12.00	25.00	50.00	150	—

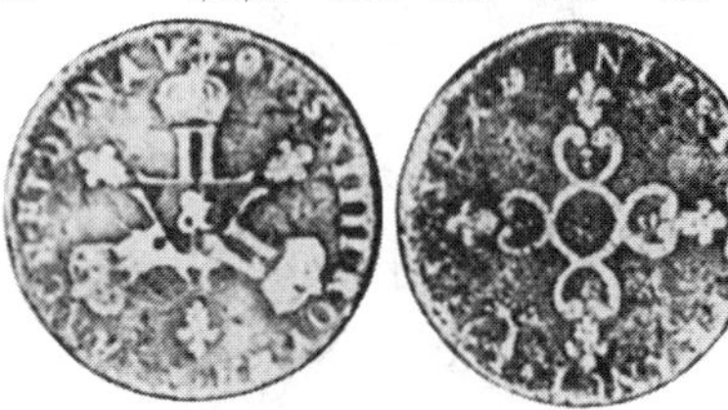

KM# 400.3 6 DENIERS
Copper **Ruler:** Louis XIV **Mint:** Aix **Obverse:** Crowned monograms form triangle, mint mark at center, fleur-de-lis at corners **Reverse:** Filigree cross with fleur-de-lis at ends **Note:** Mint mark: &.

Date	Mintage	VG	F	VF	XF	Unc
1710	—	15.00	30.00	60.00	180	—
1711	—	15.00	30.00	60.00	180	—
1712	—	15.00	30.00	60.00	180	—

KM# 610.1 6 DENIERS
Bronze **Mint:** Lyon **Obverse:** LOUIS XVI ROI DES FRANCOIS **Reverse:** Liberty cap above column dividing value, oak wreath in background **Rev. Legend:** LANATION LA LOI LE ROI **Note:** Similar to KM#611.

Date	Mintage	VG	F	VF	XF	Unc
1792D	—	10.00	30.00	80.00	200	—

KM# 611 6 DENIERS
Bronze **Mint:** Strasbourg **Obverse:** LOUIS XVI ROI DES FRANCAIS **Reverse:** Liberty cap above column dividing value, oak wreath in background **Rev. Legend:** LANATION LA LOI LE ROI

Date	Mintage	VG	F	VF	XF	Unc
1792BB	—	10.00	25.00	65.00	175	—
1793BB	—	20.00	50.00	140	300	—

KM# 600.1 12 DENIERS
Bronze **Mint:** Paris **Obverse:** LOUIS XVI ROI DES FRANCOIS **Reverse:** Liberty cap above column dividing value, wreath surrounds **Rev. Legend:** LANATION LALOI LE ROI ; • 3• DELALIB•, below

Date	Mintage	VG	F	VF	XF	Unc
1791A	—	2.50	5.00	20.00	120	—
1792A	—	2.50	5.00	20.00	120	—
1793A	—	4.00	10.00	30.00	150	—

KM# 600.11 12 DENIERS
Bronze, 31.1 mm. **Mint:** Marseille **Obverse:** Bust of Louis XVI left **Obv. Legend:** LOUIS XVI ROI DES FRANCOIS **Reverse:** Liberty cap above column dividing value, wreath surrounds **Rev. Legend:** LANATION LA LOILE ROI

Date	Mintage	VG	F	VF	XF	Unc
1791MA	—	5.00	12.00	35.00	125	—
1792MA	—	4.00	10.00	30.00	135	—
1793MA	—	7.00	16.00	50.00	150	—

KM# 601 12 DENIERS
Bronze **Mint:** Strasbourg **Obverse:** LOUIS XVI ROI DES FRANCAIS • **Reverse:** Liberty cap above column dividing value, wreath surrounds **Rev. Legend:** LANATION LA LOI LE ROI *

Date	Mintage	VG	F	VF	XF	Unc
1791BB	—	7.00	16.00	50.00	175	—
1792BB	—	5.00	12.00	35.00	125	—
1793BB	—	7.00	16.00	50.00	175	—

KM# 285.3 15 DENIERS
Billon **Ruler:** Louis XIV **Mint:** Rouen

Date	Mintage	VG	F	VF	XF	Unc
1692B	—	9.00	22.00	45.00	135	—
1693B	—	9.00	22.00	45.00	135	—
1695B	—	—	—	—	—	—
1696B	—	—	—	—	—	—
1698B	—	—	—	—	—	—
1700B	—	—	—	—	—	—
1701B	—	—	—	—	—	—
1703B	—	—	—	—	—	—

KM# 285.11 15 DENIERS
Billon **Ruler:** Louis XIV **Mint:** Toulouse

Date	Mintage	VG	F	VF	XF	Unc
1701M	—	—	—	—	—	—

KM# 285.19 15 DENIERS
Billon **Ruler:** Louis XIV **Mint:** Bourges

Date	Mintage	VG	F	VF	XF	Unc
1701Y	—	—	—	—	—	—

KM# 285.15 15 DENIERS
Billon **Ruler:** Louis XIV **Mint:** Reims

Date	Mintage	VG	F	VF	XF	Unc
1701S	—	—	—	—	—	—
1702S	—	—	—	—	—	—

KM# 285.22 15 DENIERS
Billon **Ruler:** Louis XIV **Mint:** Lille **Obverse:** Crowned double monograms form cross with fleur-de-lis at angles **Reverse:** Crowned shield **Note:** Mint mark: Crowned L.

Date	Mintage	VG	F	VF	XF	Unc
1701	—	15.00	35.00	75.00	220	—
1705	—	20.00	40.00	100	285	—

KM# 401 15 DENIERS
Billon **Ruler:** Louis XIV **Mint:** Metz **Obverse:** Crowned double L **Reverse:** Outlined cross with fleur-de-lis in angles

Date	Mintage	VG	F	VF	XF	Unc
1710AA	—	20.00	50.00	100	250	—
1711AA	—	20.00	50.00	100	250	—
1712AA	—	20.00	50.00	100	250	—
1713AA	Est. 1,706,000	20.00	50.00	100	250	—

KM# 311 16 DENIERS
Billon **Ruler:** Louis XIV **Mint:** Strasbourg **Obverse:** Crowned shield of France dividing value **Reverse:** Fleur-de-lis at ends of outlined cross

Date	Mintage	VG	F	VF	XF	Unc
1701BB	797,000	10.00	25.00	50.00	160	—
1702BB	762,000	10.00	25.00	50.00	160	—
1703BB	333,000	12.00	30.00	60.00	185	—
1704BB	349,000	12.00	30.00	60.00	185	—
1705BB	384,000	12.00	30.00	60.00	185	—
1706BB	—	12.00	30.00	60.00	185	—
1707BB	340,000	12.00	30.00	60.00	185	—
1708BB	215,000	12.00	30.00	60.00	185	—
1710BB	65,000	15.00	40.00	80.00	225	—
1711BB	—	15.00	40.00	80.00	225	—
1712BB	—	15.00	40.00	80.00	225	—
1715BB	—	40.00	95.00	200	475	—

KM# 378.1 30 DENIERS
Billon **Ruler:** Louis XIV **Mint:** Metz **Obverse:** Crowned double monogram, three fleur-de-lis **Obv. Legend:** LVD • XIIII • FR • ET • NAV • REX • 1711 **Reverse:** Outlined cross with fleur-de-lis at each angle

Date	Mintage	VG	F	VF	XF	Unc
1709AA	465,000	20.00	50.00	100	275	—
1710AA	13,270,000	18.00	45.00	90.00	250	—
1711AA	17,612,000	18.00	45.00	90.00	250	—
1712AA	13,455,000	18.00	45.00	90.00	250	—
1713AA	10,360,000	18.00	45.00	90.00	250	—

KM# 378.2 30 DENIERS
Billon **Ruler:** Louis XIV **Mint:** Lyon

Date	Mintage	VG	F	VF	XF	Unc
1710D	16,664,000	18.00	45.00	90.00	250	—
1711D	13,807,000	18.00	45.00	90.00	250	—
1712D	26,720,000	16.00	40.00	80.00	225	—
1713D	10,381,000	18.00	45.00	90.00	250	—

KM# 451.2 1/2 SOL
Copper **Ruler:** Louis XV **Mint:** Metz

Date	Mintage	VG	F	VF	XF	Unc
1719AA	—	5.00	15.00	45.00	135	—
1720AA	—	3.00	6.00	16.00	65.00	—

KM# 451.3 1/2 SOL
Copper **Ruler:** Louis XV **Mint:** Strasbourg

Date	Mintage	VG	F	VF	XF	Unc
1719BB	—	3.00	6.00	16.00	65.00	—
1720BB	—	3.00	6.00	16.00	65.00	—

KM# 451.8 1/2 SOL
Copper **Ruler:** Louis XV **Mint:** Reims

Date	Mintage	VG	F	VF	XF	Unc
1720S	—	3.00	6.00	16.00	65.00	—
1721S	3,881,000	4.00	8.00	18.00	75.00	—

KM# 451.1 1/2 SOL
Copper **Ruler:** Louis XV **Mint:** Paris **Obverse:** Boy head of Louis XV right **Obv. Legend:** LUDOVICUS • XV • DEI • GRATIA • **Reverse:** Crowned square arms with date above

Date	Mintage	VG	F	VF	XF	Unc
1720A	—	2.00	5.00	15.00	60.00	—
1721A	—	2.00	5.00	15.00	60.00	—

KM# 451.5 1/2 SOL
Copper **Ruler:** Louis XV **Mint:** Bordeaux **Obverse:** Boy head of Louis XV right **Reverse:** Crowned square arms with date above

Date	Mintage	VG	F	VF	XF	Unc
1722K	—	4.00	8.00	20.00	80.00	—

KM# 451.4 1/2 SOL
Copper **Ruler:** Louis XV **Mint:** La Rochelle **Obverse:** Boy head of Louis XV right **Reverse:** Crowned square arms with date above

Date	Mintage	VG	F	VF	XF	Unc
1723H	—	6.00	20.00	60.00	145	—

KM# 451.7 1/2 SOL
Copper **Ruler:** Louis XV **Mint:** Perpignan **Obverse:** Boy head of Louis XV right **Reverse:** Crowned square arms with date above

Date	Mintage	VG	F	VF	XF	Unc
1723Q	—	4.00	8.00	20.00	80.00	—
1724Q Unique	—	—	—	—	—	—

KM# 451.6 1/2 SOL
Copper **Ruler:** Louis XV **Mint:** Montpellier **Obverse:** Boy head of Louis XV right **Reverse:** Crowned square arms with date above

Date	Mintage	VG	F	VF	XF	Unc
1724N Unique	—	—	—	—	—	—

KM# 541 1/2 SOL

Copper **Ruler:** Louis XV **Mint:** Aix **Obverse:** Older head of Louis XV right **Reverse:** Crowned arms with rounded bottom, date below **Note:** Mint mark: &.

Date	Mintage	VG	F	VF	XF	Unc
1767	—	3.00	7.00	25.00	90.00	—
1768	—	3.00	7.00	25.00	90.00	—
1770	—	5.00	10.00	40.00	125	—
1771	—	5.00	10.00	40.00	125	—
1773	—	5.00	10.00	40.00	125	—

KM# 544.1 1/2 SOL

Copper **Ruler:** Louis XV **Mint:** Paris **Obverse:** Older head right **Reverse:** Crowned square arms with date below

Date	Mintage	VG	F	VF	XF	Unc
1768A	—	3.00	6.00	20.00	80.00	—
1769A	—	3.00	6.00	20.00	80.00	—
1770A	—	6.00	15.00	40.00	135	—
1773A	—	4.00	8.00	25.00	90.00	—
1774A	70,000	4.00	8.00	25.00	90.00	—

KM# 544.4 1/2 SOL

Copper **Ruler:** Louis XV **Mint:** Lyon **Obverse:** Older head right **Reverse:** Crowned square arms with date below

Date	Mintage	VG	F	VF	XF	Unc
1769D	—	3.00	6.00	20.00	80.00	—
1770D	—	3.00	6.00	20.00	80.00	—
1771D	—	4.00	8.00	25.00	90.00	—
1774D	—	4.00	8.00	25.00	90.00	—

KM# 544.7 1/2 SOL

Copper **Ruler:** Louis XV **Mint:** Toulouse **Obverse:** Older head right **Reverse:** Crowned square arms with date below

Date	Mintage	VG	F	VF	XF	Unc
1769M	—	4.00	8.00	25.00	95.00	—
1770M	—	4.00	8.00	25.00	95.00	—

KM# 544.9 1/2 SOL

Copper **Ruler:** Louis XV **Mint:** Reims **Obverse:** Older head right **Reverse:** Crowned square arms with date below

Date	Mintage	VG	F	VF	XF	Unc
1769S	—	3.00	6.00	20.00	80.00	—
1770S	—	4.00	8.00	30.00	95.00	—
1771S	—	4.00	8.00	25.00	90.00	—
1772S	—	4.00	8.00	25.00	90.00	—

KM# 544.11 1/2 SOL

Copper **Ruler:** Louis XV **Mint:** Lille **Obverse:** Older head right **Reverse:** Crowned square arms with date below

Date	Mintage	VG	F	VF	XF	Unc
1769W	—	4.00	8.00	25.00	90.00	—
1770W	—	4.00	8.00	25.00	90.00	—
1771W	—	4.00	10.00	35.00	110	—
1772W	—	10.00	20.00	50.00	150	—

KM# 544.12 1/2 SOL

Copper **Ruler:** Louis XV **Mint:** Besancon **Obverse:** Older head right **Reverse:** Crowned square arms with date below **Note:** Mint mark: Back to back C's.

Date	Mintage	VG	F	VF	XF	Unc
1769	—	3.00	6.00	20.00	80.00	—
1770	—	3.00	6.00	20.00	80.00	—
1771	—	4.00	8.00	25.00	90.00	—
1772	—	4.00	8.00	25.00	90.00	—

KM# 544.10 1/2 SOL

Copper **Ruler:** Louis XV **Mint:** Troyes **Obverse:** Older head right **Reverse:** Crowned square arms with date below

Date	Mintage	VG	F	VF	XF	Unc
1770V		4.00	8.00	26.00	90.00	—
1771V	195,000	4.00	8.00	25.00	90.00	—

KM# 544.8 1/2 SOL

Copper **Ruler:** Louis XV **Mint:** Montpellier **Obverse:** Older head right **Reverse:** Crowned square arms with date below

Date	Mintage	VG	F	VF	XF	Unc
1770N	—	6.00	15.00	40.00	135	—
1771N	—	3.00	6.00	20.00	80.00	—
1773N	—	4.00	8.00	25.00	90.00	—

KM# 544.2 1/2 SOL

Copper **Ruler:** Louis XV **Mint:** Metz **Obverse:** Older head right **Reverse:** Crowned square arms with date below

Date	Mintage	VG	F	VF	XF	Unc
1770AA	—	5.00	12.00	30.00	110	—

KM# 544.3 1/2 SOL

Copper **Ruler:** Louis XV **Mint:** Strasbourg **Obverse:** Older head right **Reverse:** Crowned square arms with date below

Date	Mintage	VG	F	VF	XF	Unc
1770BB	—	3.00	6.00	20.00	80.00	—
1771BB	—	3.00	6.00	20.00	80.00	—
1773BB	—	3.00	8.00	25.00	90.00	—

KM# 544.6 1/2 SOL

Copper **Ruler:** Louis XV **Mint:** Limoges **Obverse:** Older head right **Reverse:** Crowned square arms with date below

Date	Mintage	VG	F	VF	XF	Unc
1773I	803,000	3.00	6.00	20.00	80.00	—
1774I	—	3.00	6.00	20.00	80.00	—

KM# 544.5 1/2 SOL

Copper **Ruler:** Louis XV **Mint:** La Rochelle **Obverse:** Older head right **Reverse:** Crowned square arms with date below

Date	Mintage	VG	F	VF	XF	Unc
1774H	—	4.00	8.00	25.00	90.00	—

KM# 586.15 1/2 SOL

Copper **Ruler:** Louis XVI **Mint:** Lille **Obverse:** Head left **Reverse:** Crowned arms of France

Date	Mintage	VG	F	VF	XF	Unc
1777W	—	3.00	6.00	18.00	65.00	—
Note: Mintage included in KM#585.14						
1778W	—	3.00	6.00	18.00	65.00	—
Note: Mintage included in KM#585.14						
1781W	—	4.00	8.00	20.00	80.00	—
Note: Mintage included in KM#585.14						
1788W	—	4.00	8.00	20.00	80.00	—
Note: Mintage included in KM#585.14						
1789W	—	3.00	6.00	18.00	65.00	—
1790W	—	4.00	8.00	20.00	80.00	—
1791W	—	4.00	8.00	20.00	80.00	—

KM# 586.12 1/2 SOL

Copper **Ruler:** Louis XVI **Mint:** Montpellier **Obverse:** Head left **Reverse:** Crowned arms of France

Date	Mintage	VG	F	VF	XF	Unc
1778/7N	—	5.00	10.00	25.00	100	—
1779N	1,232,000	3.00	6.00	18.00	65.00	—
1780/79N	Inc. above	5.00	10.00	25.00	100	—
1780N	187,000	5.00	10.00	25.00	100	—
1782N	—	4.00	8.00	20.00	80.00	—
1787N	—	3.00	6.00	18.00	65.00	—
1789N	1,333,000	3.00	6.00	18.00	65.00	—
1790N	—	4.00	8.00	20.00	80.00	—

KM# 586.6 1/2 SOL

Copper **Ruler:** Louis XVI **Mint:** La Rochelle **Obverse:** Head left **Reverse:** Crowned arms of France

Date	Mintage	VG	F	VF	XF	Unc
1778H	—	3.00	6.00	18.00	65.00	—
1780H	773,000	3.00	6.00	18.00	65.00	—
1782H	—	4.00	8.00	20.00	80.00	—
1791H	—	4.00	8.00	20.00	80.00	—
Note: Mintage included In KM#585						

KM# 586.7 1/2 SOL

Copper **Ruler:** Louis XVI **Mint:** Limoges **Obverse:** Head left **Reverse:** Crowned arms of France

Date	Mintage	VG	F	VF	XF	Unc
1778I	—	3.00	8.00	20.00	70.00	—
1791I	—	3.00	6.00	18.00	65.00	—
Note: Mintage included In KM#585.7						

KM# 586.16 1/2 SOL

Copper **Ruler:** Louis XVI **Mint:** Aix **Obverse:** Head left **Reverse:** Crowned arms of France **Note:** Mint mark: Ampersand. The "dot" appears below the third letter of the monarch's name and denotes second semester coinage.

Date	Mintage	VG	F	VF	XF	Unc
1778	—	3.00	6.00	18.00	65.00	—
Note: Mintage included in KM#585.15						
1779	1,271,000	3.00	6.00	18.00	65.00	—
1780	—	3.00	6.00	18.00	65.00	—
Note: Mintage included in KM#585.15						
1781	636,000	4.00	8.00	20.00	80.00	—
1782	—	4.00	8.00	20.00	80.00	—
Note: Mintage included in KM#585.15						
1783	52,000	10.00	25.00	75.00	200	—
1784	500,000	—	—	—	—	—
Note: Reported, not confirmed						
1785	320,000	5.00	10.00	35.00	125	—
1786	500,000	4.00	8.00	20.00	80.00	—
1787	—	—	—	—	—	—
Note: Reported, not confirmed						

KM# 586.5 1/2 SOL

Copper **Ruler:** Louis XVI **Mint:** Lyon **Obverse:** Head left **Reverse:** Crowned arms of France

Date	Mintage	VG	F	VF	XF	Unc
1779D	4,196,000	—	—	—	—	—
1784D	667,000	—	—	—	—	—
Note: Reported, not confirmed						
1786D	500,000	—	—	—	—	—
Note: Reported, not confirmed						
1788D	—	4.00	8.00	20.00	80.00	—
Note: Mintage included in KM#585.5						
1790D	1,000,000	—	—	—	—	—
Note: Reported, not confirmed						

KM# 586.1 1/2 SOL

Copper **Ruler:** Louis XVI **Mint:** Paris **Obverse:** Head left **Obv. Legend:** LUDOV • XVI • D • GRATIA • **Reverse:** Crowned arms of France **Rev. Legend:** FRANCIÆ ET NAVARRÆ • REX •

Date	Mintage	VG	F	VF	XF	Unc
1780	—	4.00	8.00	20.00	80.00	—
Note: Mintage included in KM#585.1						
1781	164,000	6.00	12.00	40.00	135	—
1782	168,000	6.00	12.00	40.00	135	—
1783	124,000	7.00	15.00	50.00	175	—
1784/3	—	7.00	15.00	50.00	175	—
1784	97,000	8.00	20.00	60.00	195	—
1785	328,000	5.00	10.00	25.00	100	—
1789	—	3.00	6.00	18.00	65.00	—

KM# 586.2 1/2 SOL

Copper **Ruler:** Louis XVI **Mint:** Metz **Obverse:** Head left **Reverse:** Crowned arms of France

Date	Mintage	VG	F	VF	XF	Unc
1781AA	1,042,000	3.00	6.00	18.00	65.00	—
1782AA	—	3.00	6.00	18.00	65.00	—
Note: Mintage included in KM#585						
1785AA	1,000,000	—	—	—	—	—
Note: Reported, not confirmed						
1786AA	—	3.00	6.00	18.00	65.00	—
1787AA	—	3.00	6.00	18.00	65.00	—
1788AA	291,000	5.00	10.00	25.00	100	—
1791AA	4,105,000	3.00	6.00	18.00	65.00	—

KM# 586.10 1/2 SOL

Copper **Ruler:** Louis XVI **Mint:** Toulouse **Obverse:** Head left **Reverse:** Crowned arms of France

Date	Mintage	VG	F	VF	XF	Unc
1783M	1,175,000	3.00	6.00	18.00	65.00	—
1784M	799,000	5.00	9.00	20.00	80.00	—
1789M	1,333,000	3.00	6.00	18.00	65.00	—

KM# 586.4 1/2 SOL

Copper **Ruler:** Louis XVI **Mint:** Strasbourg **Obverse:** Head left **Reverse:** Crowned arms of France

Date	Mintage	VG	F	VF	XF	Unc
1784BB	667,000	4.00	8.00	20.00	80.00	—
1785BB	480,000	4.00	8.00	20.00	80.00	—

KM# 586.3 1/2 SOL

Copper **Ruler:** Louis XVI **Mint:** Rouen **Obverse:** Head left **Reverse:** Crowned arms of France

Date	Mintage	VG	F	VF	XF	Unc
1785B	673,000	4.00	8.00	20.00	80.00	—
1788B	800,000	—	—	—	—	—
Note: Reported, not confirmed						
1790B	1,000,000	—	—	—	—	—
Note: Reported, not confirmed						
1791B	16,995,000	2.00	5.00	12.00	60.00	—

KM# 586.9 1/2 SOL

Copper **Ruler:** Louis XVI **Mint:** Bayonne **Obverse:** Head left **Reverse:** Crowned arms of France

Date	Mintage	VG	F	VF	XF	Unc
1785L	—	3.00	6.00	18.00	65.00	—
Note: Mintage included in KM#585.9						
1786L	—	3.00	6.00	18.00	65.00	—

KM# 589 1/2 SOL

Copper **Ruler:** Louis XVI **Mint:** Pau **Rev. Legend:** ....RE.BD (ligate BD). **Note:** Issued for Province of Bearn. Mint mark: Cow.

Date	Mintage	VG	F	VF	XF	Unc
1785	—	8.00	15.00	35.00	150	—
1786		8.00	15.00	35.00	150	

KM# 586.14 1/2 SOL

Copper **Ruler:** Louis XVI **Mint:** Nantes **Obverse:** Head left **Reverse:** Crowned arms of France

Date	Mintage	VG	F	VF	XF	Unc
1785T	—	4.00	8.00	20.00	80.00	—
Note: Mintage included in KM#585.11						
1786T	—	3.00	6.00	18.00	65.00	—
1787T	—	3.00	6.00	18.00	65.00	—
1788T	460,000	4.00	8.00	20.00	80.00	—
1789T	500,000	4.00	8.00	20.00	80.00	—
1790T	—	4.00	8.00	20.00	80.00	—
1791T	—	—	—	—	—	—

KM# 586.11 1/2 SOL

Copper **Ruler:** Louis XVI **Mint:** Marseille **Obverse:** Head left **Reverse:** Crowned arms of France

Date	Mintage	VG	F	VF	XF	Unc
1788MA	1,375,000	3.00	6.00	18.00	65.00	—
1789MA	—	3.00	6.00	18.00	65.00	—
1791MA	2,121,000	3.00	6.00	18.00	65.00	—

KM# 586.13 1/2 SOL

Copper **Ruler:** Louis XVI **Mint:** Orléans **Obverse:** Head left **Reverse:** Crowned arms of France

Date	Mintage	VG	F	VF	XF	Unc
1789R	—	3.00	6.00	18.00	65.00	—

KM# 586.8 1/2 SOL

Copper **Ruler:** Louis XVI **Mint:** Bordeaux **Obverse:** Head left **Reverse:** Crowned arms of France

Date	Mintage	VG	F	VF	XF	Unc
1791K	—	3.00	6.00	18.00	65.00	—
Note: Mintage included in KM#585.8						
1791K	176,000	5.00	10.00	25.00	100	—

KM# 439.1 SOL

Copper **Ruler:** Louis XV **Mint:** Paris **Obverse:** Boy head of Louis XV right **Reverse:** Crowned square arms with date above

Date	Mintage	VG	F	VF	XF	Unc
1719A	—	4.00	10.00	25.00	90.00	—

KM# 439.2 SOL

Copper **Ruler:** Louis XV **Mint:** Metz **Obverse:** Boy head of Louis XV right **Reverse:** Crowned square arms with date above

Date	Mintage	VG	F	VF	XF	Unc
1719AA	—	4.00	10.00	25.00	90.00	—
1720AA	—	4.00	10.00	30.00	100	—

KM# 439.3 SOL

Copper **Ruler:** Louis XV **Mint:** Rouen **Obverse:** Boy head of Louis XV right **Reverse:** Crowned square arms with date above

Date	Mintage	VG	F	VF	XF	Unc
1719B	—	4.00	10.00	25.00	90.00	—
1720B	—	4.00	10.00	30.00	100	—

KM# 439.4 SOL

Copper **Ruler:** Louis XV **Mint:** Strasbourg **Obverse:** Boy head of Louis XV right **Reverse:** Crowned square arms with date above

Date	Mintage	VG	F	VF	XF	Unc
1719BB	—	4.00	10.00	25.00	90.00	—
1720BB	—	4.00	10.00	30.00	100	—

KM# 439.7 SOL

Copper **Ruler:** Louis XV **Mint:** Reims **Obverse:** Boy head of Louis XV right **Reverse:** Crowned square arms with date above

Date	Mintage	VG	F	VF	XF	Unc
1719S	1,743,000	4.00	10.00	25.00	90.00	—
1720S	—	4.00	10.00	25.00	90.00	—

KM# 439.8 SOL

Copper **Ruler:** Louis XV **Mint:** Troyes **Obverse:** Boy head of Louis XV right **Reverse:** Crowned square arms with date above

Date	Mintage	VG	F	VF	XF	Unc
1721V	—	4.00	10.00	30.00	100	—

KM# 462 SOL

Copper **Ruler:** Louis XV **Mint:** Pau **Obverse:** Crowned double L's form triangle; fleur-de-lis at angles **Reverse:** PRODUIT/DES MINES/DE/FRANCE in ornamental cartouche; date below **Note:** Mining Sol issued for Province of Bearn. Mint mark: Cow.

Date	Mintage	VG	F	VF	XF	Unc
1721	—	20.00	60.00	175	450	—
1723	—	10.00	20.00	50.00	175	—
1724	—	8.00	16.00	45.00	160	—
1727	—	7.50	15.00	40.00	150	—
1728	—	12.50	25.00	70.00	200	—

KM# 439.5 SOL

Copper **Ruler:** Louis XV **Mint:** La Rochelle **Obverse:** Boy head of Louis XV right **Reverse:** Crowned square arms with date above

Date	Mintage	VG	F	VF	XF	Unc
1722H	—	4.00	10.00	30.00	100	—

KM# 439.6 SOL

Copper **Ruler:** Louis XV **Mint:** Perpignan **Obverse:** Boy head of Louis XV right **Reverse:** Crowned square arms with date above

Date	Mintage	VG	F	VF	XF	Unc
1722Q	—	4.00	10.00	25.00	90.00	—
1723Q	—	4.00	10.00	30.00	100	—
1724Q	—	5.00	12.00	40.00	140	—

KM# 501.1 SOL

Billon **Ruler:** Louis XV **Mint:** Paris **Obverse:** Crowned L amid 3 fleur-de-lis **Reverse:** Crowned floral double L monogram; date below

Date	Mintage	VG	F	VF	XF	Unc
1739A	—	5.00	12.00	35.00	125	—
1740A	—	4.00	8.00	25.00	85.00	—
1746A	—	5.00	12.00	35.00	125	—
1748A	—	6.00	15.00	40.00	160	—

KM# 501.4 SOL

Billon **Ruler:** Louis XV **Mint:** Caen **Obverse:** Crowned L amid 3 fleur-de-lis **Reverse:** Crowned floral double L monogram, date below

Date	Mintage	VG	F	VF	XF	Unc
1739C	19,000	5.00	12.00	35.00	125	—

KM# 501.7 SOL

Billon **Ruler:** Louis XV **Mint:** Limoges **Obverse:** Crowned L amid 3 fleur-de-lis **Reverse:** Crowned floral double L monogram, date below

Date	Mintage	VG	F	VF	XF	Unc
1739I	—	5.00	12.00	30.00	110	—
1740I	159,000	4.00	8.00	20.00	80.00	—

KM# 501.9 SOL

Billon **Ruler:** Louis XV **Mint:** Dijon **Obverse:** Crowned L amid 3 fleur-de-lis **Reverse:** Crowned floral double L monogram, date below

Date	Mintage	VG	F	VF	XF	Unc
1739P	64,000	4.00	8.00	20.00	80.00	—
1740P	64,000	4.00	8.00	20.00	80.00	—

KM# 501.14 SOL

Billon **Ruler:** Louis XV **Mint:** Besancon **Obverse:** Crowned L amid 3 fleur-de-lis **Reverse:** Crowned floral double L monogram, date below **Note:** Mint mark: Back to back C's.

Date	Mintage	VG	F	VF	XF	Unc
1739	15,000	5.00	12.00	35.00	125	—

KM# 501.10 SOL

Billon **Ruler:** Louis XV **Mint:** Nantes **Obverse:** Crowned L amid 3 fleur-de-lis **Reverse:** Crowned floral double L monogram, date below

Date	Mintage	VG	F	VF	XF	Unc
1740T	—	4.00	8.00	20.00	80.00	—

KM# 501.11 SOL

Billon **Ruler:** Louis XV **Mint:** Troyes **Obverse:** Crowned L amid 3 fleur-de-lis **Reverse:** Crowned floral double L monogram, date below

Date	Mintage	VG	F	VF	XF	Unc
1740V	12,000	8.00	20.00	45.00	160	—

KM# 501.12 SOL

Billon **Ruler:** Louis XV **Mint:** Lille **Obverse:** Crowned L amid 3 fleur-de-lis **Reverse:** Crowned floral double L monogram, date below

Date	Mintage	VG	F	VF	XF	Unc
1740W	—	4.00	8.00	20.00	80.00	—

KM# 501.13 SOL

Billon **Ruler:** Louis XV **Mint:** Amiens **Obverse:** Crowned L amid 3 fleur-de-lis **Reverse:** Crowned floral double L monogram, date below

Date	Mintage	VG	F	VF	XF	Unc
1740X	32,000	4.00	8.00	20.00	80.00	—

KM# 501.8 SOL

Billon **Ruler:** Louis XV **Mint:** Riom **Obverse:** Crowned L amid 3 fleur-de-lis **Reverse:** Crowned floral double L monogram, date below

Date	Mintage	VG	F	VF	XF	Unc
1740O	66,000	6.00	12.00	25.00	90.00	—

KM# 501.5 SOL

Billon **Ruler:** Louis XV **Mint:** Lyon **Obverse:** Crowned L amid 3 fleur-de-lis **Reverse:** Crowned floral double L monogram, date below

Date	Mintage	VG	F	VF	XF	Unc
1740D	715,000	4.00	8.00	20.00	80.00	—

KM# 501.6 SOL

Billon **Ruler:** Louis XV **Mint:** Poitiers **Obverse:** Crowned L amid 3 fleur-de-lis **Reverse:** Crowned floral double L monogram, date below

Date	Mintage	VG	F	VF	XF	Unc
1740G	86,000	6.00	12.00	25.00	90.00	—

KM# 501.2 SOL

Billon **Ruler:** Louis XV **Mint:** Metz **Obverse:** Crowned L amid 3 fleur-de-lis **Reverse:** Crowned floral double L monogram, date below

Date	Mintage	VG	F	VF	XF	Unc
1740AA	—	4.00	8.00	20.00	80.00	—

KM# 501.3 SOL

Billon **Ruler:** Louis XV **Mint:** Strasbourg **Obverse:** Crowned L amid 3 fleur-de-lis **Reverse:** Crowned floral double L monogram, date below

Date	Mintage	VG	F	VF	XF	Unc
1740BB	—	4.00	8.00	20.00	80.00	—
1746BB	—	5.00	12.00	30.00	110	—

KM# 542 SOL

Copper **Ruler:** Louis XV **Mint:** Aix **Obverse:** Older head right **Obv. Legend:** LUDOV • XV • D • GRATIA • **Reverse:** Crowned arms with round bottom, date above **Note:** Mint mark: &.

Date	Mintage	VG	F	VF	XF	Unc
1767	—	4.00	10.00	30.00	120	—
1768	—	3.00	9.00	25.00	110	—
1770	—	4.00	10.00	30.00	120	—
1771	—	4.00	10.00	30.00	120	—
1772	—	7.00	15.00	35.00	140	—
1773	—	7.00	15.00	35.00	140	—

KM# 545.1 SOL

Copper **Ruler:** Louis XV **Mint:** Paris **Obverse:** Old head right **Obv. Legend:** LUDOV • XV • D • GRATIA • **Reverse:** Crowned square arms with date above

Date	Mintage	VG	F	VF	XF	Unc
1768A	—	3.00	6.00	18.00	85.00	—
1770A	—	3.00	6.00	18.00	85.00	—
1771A	—	3.00	6.00	18.00	85.00	—
1772A	—	3.00	6.00	18.00	85.00	—
1773A	43,000	5.00	10.00	25.00	100	—

KM# 545.10 SOL

Copper **Ruler:** Louis XV **Mint:** Reims **Obverse:** Older head right **Reverse:** Crowned square arms with date above

Date	Mintage	VG	F	VF	XF	Unc
1769S	—	5.00	8.00	20.00	90.00	—
1770S	—	3.00	6.00	16.00	80.00	—
1771S	787,000	3.00	6.00	16.00	80.00	—
1772S	—	3.00	6.00	16.00	80.00	—
1773S	137,000	3.00	6.00	16.00	80.00	—

KM# 545.12 SOL

Copper **Ruler:** Louis XV **Mint:** Lille **Obverse:** Older head right **Reverse:** Crowned square arms with date above

Date	Mintage	VG	F	VF	XF	Unc
1769W	—	5.00	8.00	20.00	90.00	—
1770W	—	3.00	6.00	16.00	80.00	—
1771W	—	3.00	6.00	16.00	80.00	—
1772W	—	3.00	6.00	16.00	80.00	—
1773W	323,000	3.00	6.00	16.00	80.00	—
1774W	2,339,000	3.00	6.00	12.00	60.00	—

KM# 545.13 SOL

Copper **Ruler:** Louis XV **Mint:** Besancon **Obverse:** Older head right **Reverse:** Crowned square arms with date above **Note:** Mint mark: Back to back C's.

Date	Mintage	VG	F	VF	XF	Unc
1769	—	5.00	8.00	20.00	90.00	—
1770	—	3.00	6.00	16.00	80.00	—
1771	—	3.00	6.00	16.00	80.00	—
1772	—	3.00	6.00	16.00	80.00	—

KM# 545.9 SOL

Copper **Ruler:** Louis XV **Mint:** Montpellier **Obverse:** Older head right **Reverse:** Crowned square arms with date above

Date	Mintage	VG	F	VF	XF	Unc
1770N	—	3.00	6.00	16.00	80.00	—
1771N	—	3.00	6.00	16.00	80.00	—
1772N	—	3.00	6.00	16.00	80.00	—
1773N	286,000	3.00	6.00	16.00	80.00	—

KM# 545.11 SOL

Copper **Ruler:** Louis XV **Mint:** Troyes **Obverse:** Older head right **Reverse:** Crowned square arms with date above

Date	Mintage	VG	F	VF	XF	Unc
1770V	—	3.00	6.00	16.00	80.00	—
1771V	—	3.00	6.00	16.00	80.00	—
1772V	560,000	3.00	6.00	16.00	80.00	—

KM# 545.3 SOL

Copper **Ruler:** Louis XV **Mint:** Rouen **Obverse:** Older head right **Reverse:** Crowned square arms with date above

Date	Mintage	VG	F	VF	XF	Unc
1770B	—	3.00	6.00	20.00	90.00	—

KM# 545.5 SOL

Copper **Ruler:** Louis XV **Mint:** Lyon **Obverse:** Older head right **Reverse:** Crowned square arms with date above

Date	Mintage	VG	F	VF	XF	Unc
1770D	—	3.00	6.00	16.00	80.00	—
1771D	—	3.00	6.00	16.00	80.00	—
1772D	—	3.00	6.00	16.00	85.00	—
1773D	—	5.00	10.00	25.00	100	—
1774D	1,700,000	3.00	6.00	12.00	65.00	—

KM# 545.4 SOL

Copper **Ruler:** Louis XV **Mint:** Strasbourg **Obverse:** Older head right **Reverse:** Crowned square arms with date above

Date	Mintage	VG	F	VF	XF	Unc
1771BB	—	3.00	6.00	14.00	70.00	—
1772BB	—	3.00	6.00	14.00	75.00	—
1773BB	—	5.00	10.00	25.00	100	—
1774BB	1,351,000	3.00	6.00	14.00	70.00	—

KM# 545.2 SOL

Copper **Ruler:** Louis XV **Mint:** Metz **Obverse:** Older head right **Reverse:** Crowned square arms with date above

Date	Mintage	VG	F	VF	XF	Unc
1771AA	—	3.00	6.00	16.00	80.00	—
1772AA	—	3.00	6.00	16.00	80.00	—
1774AA	585,000	3.00	6.00	16.00	80.00	—

KM# 545.7 SOL

Copper **Ruler:** Louis XV **Mint:** Limoges **Obverse:** Older head right **Reverse:** Crowned square arms with date above

Date	Mintage	VG	F	VF	XF	Unc
1772I	—	3.00	6.00	16.00	80.00	—
1773I	916,000	3.00	6.00	12.00	65.00	—
1773I FRANCAE (Error)	—	3.00	6.00	12.00	65.00	—
1774I	1,068,000	3.00	6.00	12.00	65.00	—

KM# 545.8 SOL

Copper **Ruler:** Louis XV **Mint:** Toulouse **Obverse:** Older head right **Reverse:** Crowned square arms with date above

Date	Mintage	VG	F	VF	XF	Unc
1774M	864,000	3.00	6.00	14.00	70.00	—

KM# 545.6 SOL

Copper **Ruler:** Louis XV **Mint:** La Rochelle **Obverse:** Older head right **Reverse:** Crowned square arms with date above

Date	Mintage	VG	F	VF	XF	Unc
1774H	1,828,000	3.00	6.00	14.00	70.00	—

KM# 578.6 SOL

Copper **Ruler:** Louis XVI **Mint:** La Rochelle **Obverse:** Head left **Reverse:** Crowned arms of France

Date	Mintage	VG	F	VF	XF	Unc
1777H	—	4.00	8.00	20.00	80.00	—
Note: Mintage included in KM#585.6						
1778H	89,000	—	—	—	—	—
1779H	—	4.00	8.00	20.00	80.00	—
Note: Mintage included in KM#585.6						
1780H	—	2.50	5.00	13.00	60.00	—
1781H	—	4.00	8.00	20.00	80.00	—
Note: Mintage included in KM#585.6						
1783H	84,000	4.00	8.00	20.00	80.00	—
1784H	533,000	2.50	5.00	13.00	60.00	—
1785H	—	2.50	5.00	13.00	60.00	—
1786H	—	2.50	5.00	13.00	60.00	—
1787H	—	2.50	5.00	13.00	60.00	—
1788H	42,000	—	—	—	—	—
1789H	—	2.50	5.00	13.00	60.00	—
1791H	—	2.50	5.00	13.00	60.00	—
Note: Mintage included in KM#585.6						

KM# 578.12 SOL

Copper **Ruler:** Louis XVI **Mint:** Montpellier **Obverse:** Head left **Reverse:** Crowned arms of France

Date	Mintage	VG	F	VF	XF	Unc
1777N	127,000	—	—	—	—	—
1778N	—	4.00	8.00	20.00	80.00	—
1779N	—	2.50	5.00	13.00	60.00	—
Note: Mintage included in KM#586.12						
1780N	—	4.00	8.00	20.00	80.00	—
Note: Mintage included in KM#586.11						
1783N	855,000	2.50	5.00	13.00	60.00	—
1784N	—	2.50	5.00	13.00	60.00	—
Note: Mintage included in KM#585.11						
1785N	—	2.50	5.00	13.00	60.00	—
Note: Mintage included in KM#585.11						
1789N	667,000	2.50	5.00	13.00	60.00	—
1790N	—	2.50	5.00	13.00	60.00	—
1791N	1,101,000	2.50	5.00	13.00	60.00	—

KM# 578.14 SOL

Copper **Ruler:** Louis XVI **Mint:** Orléans **Obverse:** Head left **Reverse:** Crowned arms of France

Date	Mintage	VG	F	VF	XF	Unc
1777R	400,000	—	—	—	—	—
Note: Reported, not confirmed						
1782R	181,000	4.00	8.00	20.00	80.00	—
1783R	61,000	5.00	10.00	25.00	100	—
1784R	155,000	4.00	8.00	20.00	80.00	—
1785R	73,000	4.00	8.00	20.00	80.00	—
1786R	—	2.50	5.00	13.00	60.00	—
1787R	—	2.50	5.00	13.00	60.00	—
1788R	9,480	10.00	20.00	50.00	165	—
1789R	—	2.50	5.00	13.00	60.00	—
1790R	—	2.50	5.00	13.00	60.00	—
1791R	5,039,000	2.00	4.00	10.00	50.00	—
1791R	Inc. above	2.00	4.00	10.00	50.00	—
1791R LUDOV XIV (Error)	—	7.00	15.00	35.00	100	—

KM# 578.16 SOL

Copper **Ruler:** Louis XVI **Mint:** Lille **Obverse:** Head left **Reverse:** Crowned arms of France

Date	Mintage	VG	F	VF	XF	Unc
1777W	—	2.50	5.00	13.00	60.00	—
Note: Mintage included in KM#585.14						
1778W	—	2.50	5.00	13.00	60.00	—
Note: Mintage included in KM#585.14						
1779W	—	2.50	5.00	13.00	60.00	—
Note: Mintage included in KM#585.14						
1780W	1,426,000	2.50	5.00	13.00	60.00	—
1781W	—	2.50	5.00	13.00	60.00	—
Note: Mintage included in KM#585.14						
1782W	—	2.50	5.00	13.00	60.00	—
Note: Mintage included in KM#585.14						
1783W	—	2.50	5.00	13.00	60.00	—
Note: Mintage included in KM#585.14						
1784W	2,424,000	2.50	5.00	13.00	60.00	—
1785W	—	2.50	5.00	13.00	60.00	—
Note: Mintage included in KM#585.14						
1786W	—	2.50	5.00	13.00	60.00	—
1787W	—	2.50	5.00	13.00	60.00	—
1788W	—	4.00	8.00	20.00	80.00	—
1789W	—	2.50	5.00	13.00	60.00	—
1790W	—	2.50	5.00	13.00	60.00	—
1791W	451,000	2.50	5.00	13.00	60.00	—
1791W	Inc. above	2.50	5.00	13.00	60.00	—

KM# 578.17 SOL

Copper **Ruler:** Louis XVI **Mint:** Aix **Obverse:** Head left **Reverse:** Crowned arms of France **Note:** Mint mark: &.

Date	Mintage	VG	F	VF	XF	Unc
1778	—	2.50	5.00	13.00	60.00	—
Note: Mintage included in KM#585.15						
1779	—	2.50	5.00	13.00	60.00	—
Note: Mintage included in KM#586.16						
1780	—	2.50	5.00	13.00	60.00	—
Note: Mintage included in KM#585.15						
1781	—	4.00	8.00	20.00	80.00	—
Note: Mintage included in KM#585.16						
1782	—	4.00	8.00	20.00	80.00	—
Note: Mintage included in KM#585.15						
1783	—	—	—	—	—	—
Note: Mintage included in KM#586.16						
1783	—	—	—	—	—	—
Note: Mintage included in KM#585.15						
1785	—	4.00	8.00	20.00	80.00	—
Note: Mintage included in KM#586.16						
1786	250,000	2.50	5.00	13.00	60.00	—

KM# 578.7 SOL

Copper **Ruler:** Louis XVI **Mint:** Limoges **Obverse:** Head left **Reverse:** Crowned arms of France

Date	Mintage	VG	F	VF	XF	Unc
1778I	—	—	—	—	—	—
1779I	764,000	2.50	5.00	13.00	60.00	—
1780I	1,024,000	2.50	5.00	13.00	60.00	—
1783I	205,000	2.50	5.00	13.00	60.00	—
1784I	—	2.50	5.00	13.00	60.00	—
Note: Mintage included in KM#585.7						
1785I	757,000	2.50	5.00	13.00	60.00	—
1787I	—	2.50	5.00	13.00	60.00	—
1791I	—	3.00	8.00	16.00	70.00	—
Note: Mintage included in KM#585.7						

KM# 578.1 SOL

Copper **Ruler:** Louis XVI **Mint:** Paris **Obverse:** Head left **Obv. Legend:** LUDOV • XVI • D • GRATIA **Reverse:** Crowned arms of France **Rev. Legend:** FRANCIÆ ET NAVARRÆ • REX •

Date	Mintage	VG	F	VF	XF	Unc
1779A	51,000	—	—	—	—	—
1781A	—	4.00	8.00	20.00	80.00	—
Note: Mintage included in KM#586.1						
1783A	—	4.00	8.00	20.00	80.00	—
Note: Mintage included in KM#586.1						
1784A	—	4.00	8.00	20.00	80.00	—
Note: Mintage included in KM#586.1						
1785A	—	4.00	8.00	20.00	80.00	—
Note: Mintage included in KM#586.1						
1786A	—	2.50	5.00	15.00	65.00	—
1788A	349,000	—	—	—	—	—
1789A	—	2.50	5.00	15.00	65.00	—
1791A (he)	—	2.50	5.00	15.00	65.00	—
1791A (he)	—	2.50	5.00	15.00	65.00	—
1791A (l)	—	2.50	5.00	15.00	65.00	—
1791A (L)	—	2.50	5.00	15.00	65.00	—
1791A GRTIA (Error)	—	6.00	12.00	30.00	90.00	—

KM# 578.5 SOL

Copper **Ruler:** Louis XVI **Mint:** Lyon **Obverse:** Head left **Reverse:** Crowned arms of France

Date	Mintage	VG	F	VF	XF	Unc
1779D	—	2.50	5.00	13.00	60.00	—
Note: Mintage included in KM#586.5						
1784D	1,712,000	2.50	5.00	13.00	60.00	—
1785D	—	2.50	5.00	13.00	60.00	—
1786D	250,000	2.50	5.00	13.00	60.00	—
1787D	—	2.50	5.00	13.00	60.00	—
1788D	—	—	—	—	—	—
1790D	3,000,000	2.50	5.00	13.00	60.00	—
1791D	—	2.50	5.00	13.00	60.00	—
1791D	—	2.50	5.00	13.00	60.00	—

KM# 579 SOL

Copper **Ruler:** Louis XVI **Mint:** Pau **Reverse:** Legend ends: ...RE: BD (ligate BD) **Note:** Mint mark: Cow. Issued for Province of Bearn.

Date	Mintage	VG	F	VF	XF	Unc
1779	3,214,000	2.50	5.00	13.00	60.00	—
1780	2,923,000	2.50	5.00	13.00	60.00	—
1783	162,000	4.00	8.00	20.00	80.00	—
1784	412,000	4.00	8.00	20.00	80.00	—
1785	573,000	4.00	8.00	20.00	80.00	—
1788	817,000	4.00	8.00	20.00	80.00	—

KM# 578.2 SOL

Copper **Ruler:** Louis XVI **Mint:** Metz **Obverse:** Head left **Reverse:** Crowned arms of France

Date	Mintage	VG	F	VF	XF	Unc
1780AA	497,000	2.50	7.00	15.00	65.00	—
1781AA	—	—	—	—	—	—
1782AA	—	2.50	5.00	13.00	60.00	—
Note: Mintage included in KM#585.2						
1783AA	165,000	4.00	8.00	20.00	80.00	—
1784AA	1,252,000	2.50	5.00	13.00	60.00	—
1785AA	892,000	2.50	5.00	13.00	60.00	—
1786AA	—	2.50	5.00	13.00	60.00	—
1788AA	—	4.00	8.00	20.00	80.00	—
Note: Mintage included in KM#586.2						
1790AA	—	2.50	5.00	13.00	60.00	—
1791AA	—	2.00	4.00	10.00	50.00	—
Note: Mintage included in KM#586.2						

KM# 578.8 SOL

Copper **Ruler:** Louis XVI **Mint:** Bordeaux **Obverse:** Head left **Reverse:** Crowned arms of France

Date	Mintage	VG	F	VF	XF	Unc
1783K	396,000	2.50	5.00	13.00	60.00	—
1784K	1,108,000	2.50	5.00	13.00	60.00	—
1785K	79,000	4.00	8.00	20.00	80.00	—
1786K	—	2.50	5.00	13.00	60.00	—
1787K	—	2.50	5.00	13.00	60.00	—
1788K	—	2.50	5.00	13.00	60.00	—
1789K	—	2.50	5.00	13.00	60.00	—
1790K	120,000	4.00	8.00	20.00	80.00	—
1791K	—	2.50	5.00	13.00	60.00	—
Note: Mintage included in KM#585.8						
1791K	—	2.50	5.00	13.00	60.00	—
Note: Mintage included in KM#585.8						

KM# 578.9 SOL

Copper **Ruler:** Louis XVI **Mint:** Bayonne **Obverse:** Head left **Reverse:** Crowned arms of France

Date	Mintage	VG	F	VF	XF	Unc
1783L	1,000,000	—	—	—	—	—
1784L Rare	1,000,000	—	—	—	—	—
1785L	—	5.00	10.00	25.00	80.00	—

KM# 578.10 SOL

Copper **Ruler:** Louis XVI **Mint:** Toulouse **Obverse:** Head left **Reverse:** Crowned arms of France

Date	Mintage	VG	F	VF	XF	Unc
1783M	—	2.50	5.00	13.00	60.00	—
Note: Mintage included in KM#586,10						
1784M	—	2.50	5.00	13.00	60.00	—
Note: Mintage included in KM#586.10						
1789M	667,000	2.50	5.00	13.00	60.00	—
1790M	—	2.50	5.00	13.00	60.00	—
1791M	2,192,000	2.50	5.00	13.00	60.00	—

KM# 578.4 SOL

Copper **Ruler:** Louis XVI **Mint:** Strasbourg **Obverse:** Head left **Reverse:** Crowned arms of France

Date	Mintage	VG	F	VF	XF	Unc
1783BB	—	2.50	5.00	13.00	60.00	—
1784BB	—	2.50	5.00	13.00	60.00	—
Note: Mintage included in KM#586.4						
1785BB	720,000	2.50	5.00	13.00	60.00	—
1791BB	—	2.50	5.00	13.00	60.00	—
1791BB	—	2.50	5.00	13.00	60.00	—

KM# 578.15 SOL

Copper **Ruler:** Louis XVI **Mint:** Nantes **Obverse:** Head left **Reverse:** Crowned arms of France

Date	Mintage	VG	F	VF	XF	Unc
1784T Rare	2,000,000	—	—	—	—	—
1785T	—	3.00	9.00	20.00	70.00	—
Note: Mintage included in KM#585.13						
1786T	—	3.00	9.00	20.00	70.00	—
1787T	—	3.00	9.00	20.00	70.00	—
1788T	—	4.00	10.00	22.00	80.00	—
Note: Mintage included in KM#586.14						
1789T	500,000	—	—	—	—	—
Note: Reported, not confirmed						
1791T	—	2.50	5.00	13.00	60.00	—
Note: Mintage included in KM#585.13						

KM# 578.3 SOL

Copper **Ruler:** Louis XVI **Mint:** Rouen **Obverse:** Head left **Reverse:** Crowned arms of France

Date	Mintage	VG	F	VF	XF	Unc
1785B	—	2.50	5.00	13.00	60.00	—
Note: Mintage included in KM#586.3						
1787B	1,600,000	—	—	—	—	—
Note: Reported, not confirmed						
1788B	—	2.50	5.00	13.00	60.00	—
1789B	—	2.50	5.00	13.00	60.00	—
1790B	3,000,000	2.50	5.00	13.00	60.00	—
1791B	—	2.00	4.00	10.00	50.00	—
Note: Mintage included in KM#586.3						
1791B	—	2.00	4.00	10.00	50.00	—
Note: Mintage included in KM#586.3						

KM# 578.11 SOL

Copper **Ruler:** Louis XVI **Mint:** Marseille **Obverse:** Head left **Reverse:** Crowned arms of France

Date	Mintage	VG	F	VF	XF	Unc
1787MA	—	2.50	5.00	13.00	60.00	—
1788MA	—	2.50	5.00	13.00	60.00	—
Note: Mintage included in KM#586.11						
1789MA	—	2.50	5.00	13.00	60.00	—
1791MA	—	2.50	5.00	13.00	60.00	—
Note: Mintage included in KM#586.11						

KM# 602.2 SOL

Copper **Ruler:** Louis XVI **Mint:** Lyon

Date	Mintage	VG	F	VF	XF	Unc
1791D	—	4.00	8.00	20.00	80.00	—

KM# 578.13 SOL

Copper **Ruler:** Louis XVI **Mint:** Perpignan **Obverse:** Head left **Reverse:** Crowned arms of France

Date	Mintage	VG	F	VF	XF	Unc
1791Q	Inc. above	4.00	8.00	15.00	65.00	—

KM# 602.1 SOL

Copper **Ruler:** Louis XVI **Mint:** Metz **Note:** The "dot" appears below the third letter of the monarch's name and denotes second semester coinage.

Date	Mintage	VG	F	VF	XF	Unc
1791AA	—	4.00	8.00	20.00	80.00	—

Note: Mintage included in KM#586.2

KM# 602.3 SOL

Copper **Ruler:** Louis XVI **Mint:** Limoges **Note:** The "dot" appears below the third letter of the monarch's name and denotes second semester coinage.

Date	Mintage	VG	F	VF	XF	Unc
1791I	—	6.00	10.00	24.00	90.00	—

Note: Mintage included in KM#586.2

KM# 602.4 SOL

Copper **Ruler:** Louis XVI **Mint:** Perpignan **Note:** The "dot" appears below the third letter of the monarch's name and denotes second semester coinage.

Date	Mintage	VG	F	VF	XF	Unc
1791Q	—	4.00	8.00	20.00	80.00	—

Note: Mintage included in KM#578.13

KM# 500.7 2 SOLS

Billon **Ruler:** Louis XV **Mint:** Tours

Date	Mintage	VG	F	VF	XF	Unc
1738E	21,000	4.00	7.00	20.00	55.00	—
1739E	1,029,000	2.00	4.00	12.00	30.00	—
1740E	511,000	3.00	5.00	14.00	35.00	—
1741E	210,000	3.00	5.00	14.00	35.00	—
1742E	88,000	4.00	7.00	16.00	45.00	—
1743E	62,000	4.00	7.00	16.00	45.00	—
1744E	63,000	4.00	7.00	16.00	45.00	—
1745E	26,000	5.00	9.00	18.00	55.00	—
1746E	54,000	4.00	7.00	16.00	45.00	—

KM# 500.8 2 SOLS

Billon **Ruler:** Louis XV **Mint:** Poitiers

Date	Mintage	VG	F	VF	XF	Unc
1738G	115,000	3.00	5.00	14.00	35.00	—
1739G	581,000	3.00	5.00	14.00	35.00	—
1740G	170,000	3.00	5.00	14.00	35.00	—
1741G	—	3.00	5.00	14.00	35.00	—
1742G	76,000	4.00	7.00	16.00	45.00	—

KM# 500.1 2 SOLS

Billon **Ruler:** Louis XV **Mint:** Paris **Obverse:** Crowned L with 3 fleur-de-lis **Obv. Legend:** LUD • XV • D • G • FR • ET NAV • REX **Reverse:** Crowned floral double L monogram, date above **Rev. Legend:** SIT NOM • DOM • H BENEDICTUM

Date	Mintage	VG	F	VF	XF	Unc
1738A	2,771,000	2.00	4.00	12.00	30.00	—
1739A	8,069,000	2.00	4.00	10.00	25.00	—
1740A	1,090,000	2.00	4.00	12.00	30.00	—
1741A	—	3.00	5.00	14.00	35.00	—
1742A	—	3.00	5.00	14.00	35.00	—
1743A	436,000	3.00	5.00	14.00	35.00	—
1744A	—	3.00	5.00	14.00	35.00	—
1745A	293,000	3.00	5.00	14.00	35.00	—
1746A	467,000	3.00	5.00	14.00	35.00	—
1747A	327,000	3.00	5.00	14.00	35.00	—
1748A	—	3.00	5.00	14.00	35.00	—
1749A	—	3.00	5.00	14.00	35.00	—
1750A	266,000	3.00	5.00	14.00	35.00	—
1751A	234,000	2.00	4.00	12.00	30.00	—
1752A	92,000	3.00	5.00	14.00	35.00	—
1753A	115,000	3.00	5.00	14.00	35.00	—
1754A	—	3.00	5.00	14.00	35.00	—
1755A	—	3.00	5.00	14.00	35.00	—
1756A	129,000	3.00	5.00	14.00	35.00	—
1757A	—	3.00	5.00	14.00	35.00	—
1758A	—	3.00	5.00	14.00	35.00	—
1759A	—	3.00	5.00	14.00	35.00	—
1760A	—	3.00	5.00	14.00	35.00	—
1761A	—	3.00	5.00	14.00	35.00	—
1762A	—	3.00	5.00	14.00	35.00	—
1763A	—	3.00	5.00	14.00	35.00	—
1764A	—	2.00	4.00	12.00	30.00	—

KM# 500.2 2 SOLS

Billon **Ruler:** Louis XV **Mint:** Metz **Obverse:** Crowned L with 3 fleur-de-lis **Reverse:** Crowned floral double L monogram, date above

Date	Mintage	VG	F	VF	XF	Unc
1738AA	—	3.00	5.00	14.00	35.00	—
1739AA	1,787,000	2.00	4.00	12.00	30.00	—
1740AA	—	3.00	5.00	14.00	35.00	—
1741AA	—	3.00	5.00	14.00	35.00	—
1742AA	—	3.00	5.00	14.00	35.00	—
1743AA	—	3.00	5.00	14.00	35.00	—
1744AA	—	3.00	5.00	14.00	35.00	—
1745AA	—	3.00	5.00	14.00	35.00	—
1746AA	—	2.00	4.00	12.00	30.00	—
1747AA	—	3.00	5.00	14.00	35.00	—
1748AA	—	3.00	5.00	14.00	35.00	—
1749AA	—	3.00	5.00	14.00	35.00	—
1750AA	—	3.00	5.00	14.00	35.00	—
1762AA	—	4.00	7.00	16.00	45.00	—

KM# 500.3 2 SOLS

Billon **Ruler:** Louis XV **Mint:** Rouen **Obverse:** Crowned L with 3 fleur-de-lis **Reverse:** Crowned floral double L monogram, date above

Date	Mintage	VG	F	VF	XF	Unc
1738B	367,000	3.00	5.00	14.00	35.00	—
1739B	2,462,000	2.00	4.00	12.00	30.00	—
1740B	—	3.00	5.00	14.00	35.00	—
1741B	—	3.00	5.00	14.00	35.00	—
1742B	80,000	4.00	7.00	16.00	45.00	—

KM# 500.4 2 SOLS

Billon **Ruler:** Louis XV **Mint:** Strasbourg **Obverse:** Crowned L with 3 fleur-de-lis **Reverse:** Crowned floral double L monogram, date above

Date	Mintage	VG	F	VF	XF	Unc
1738BB	442,000	2.00	4.00	12.00	30.00	—
1739BB	911,000	2.00	4.00	12.00	30.00	—
1740BB	198,000	2.00	4.00	12.00	30.00	—
1741BB	—	2.00	4.00	12.00	30.00	—
1742BB	—	2.00	4.00	12.00	30.00	—
1743BB	—	2.00	4.00	12.00	30.00	—
1744BB	327,000	2.00	4.00	12.00	30.00	—
1745BB	—	2.00	4.00	12.00	30.00	—
1746BB	—	2.00	4.00	12.00	30.00	—
1747BB	—	2.00	4.00	12.00	30.00	—
1748BB	—	2.00	4.00	12.00	30.00	—
1749BB	—	2.00	4.00	12.00	30.00	—
1750BB	—	2.00	4.00	12.00	30.00	—
1756BB	47,000	3.00	6.00	15.00	40.00	—
1757BB	—	2.00	4.00	12.00	30.00	—
1758BB	—	2.00	4.00	12.00	30.00	—
1759BB	—	2.00	4.00	12.00	30.00	—
1760BB	—	2.00	4.00	12.00	30.00	—
1761BB	—	2.00	4.00	12.00	30.00	—
1762BB	—	2.00	4.00	10.00	25.00	—

KM# 500.16 2 SOLS

Billon **Ruler:** Louis XV **Mint:** Dijon **Obverse:** Crowned L with 3 fleur-de-lis **Reverse:** Crwoned floral double L monogram, date above

Date	Mintage	VG	F	VF	XF	Unc
1738P	212,000	3.00	5.00	14.00	35.00	—
1739P	1,383,000	2.00	4.00	12.00	30.00	—
1740P	326,000	3.00	5.00	14.00	35.00	—
1741P	—	3.00	5.00	14.00	35.00	—
1742P	130,000	3.00	5.00	14.00	35.00	—
1743P	163,000	3.00	5.00	14.00	35.00	—
1744P	168,000	3.00	5.00	14.00	35.00	—

KM# 500.18 2 SOLS

Billon **Ruler:** Louis XV **Mint:** Orléans **Obverse:** Crowned L with 3 fleur-de-lis **Reverse:** Crowned floral double L monogram, date above

Date	Mintage	VG	F	VF	XF	Unc
1738R	22,000	4.00	7.00	16.00	45.00	—
1739R	875,000	3.00	5.00	14.00	35.00	—
1740R	—	3.00	5.00	14.00	35.00	—
1741R	—	3.00	5.00	14.00	35.00	—

KM# 500.19 2 SOLS

Billon **Ruler:** Louis XV **Mint:** Reims **Obverse:** Crowned L with 3 fleur-de-lis **Reverse:** Crowned floral double L monogram, date above

Date	Mintage	VG	F	VF	XF	Unc
1738S	285,000	3.00	5.00	14.00	35.00	—
1739S	1,681,000	2.00	4.00	12.00	30.00	—
1740S	408,000	3.00	5.00	14.00	35.00	—

KM# 500.21 2 SOLS

Billon **Ruler:** Louis XV **Mint:** Troyes **Obverse:** Crowned L with 3 fleur-de-lis **Reverse:** Crowned floral double L monogram, date above

Date	Mintage	VG	F	VF	XF	Unc
1738V	122,000	3.00	5.00	14.00	35.00	—
1739V	987,000	3.00	5.00	14.00	35.00	—
1740V	240,000	3.00	5.00	14.00	35.00	—
1741V	92,000	4.00	7.00	16.00	45.00	—
1742V	32,000	4.00	7.00	16.00	45.00	—
1755V	—	4.00	7.00	16.00	45.00	—

KM# 500.22 2 SOLS

Billon **Ruler:** Louis XV **Mint:** Lille **Obverse:** Crowned L with 3 fleur-de-lis **Reverse:** Crowned floral double L monogram, date above

Date	Mintage	VG	F	VF	XF	Unc
1738W	340,000	3.00	5.00	14.00	35.00	—
1739W	6,475,000	1.50	3.00	8.00	22.00	—
1740W	405,000	3.00	5.00	14.00	35.00	—
1741W	—	3.00	5.00	14.00	35.00	—
1742W	—	3.00	5.00	14.00	35.00	—
1743W	175,000	3.00	5.00	14.00	35.00	—
1744W	354,000	3.00	5.00	14.00	35.00	—
1745W	152,000	3.00	5.00	14.00	35.00	—
1746W	119,000	3.00	5.00	14.00	35.00	—
1747W	169,000	3.00	5.00	14.00	35.00	—
1748W	—	3.00	5.00	14.00	35.00	—
1749W	—	3.00	5.00	14.00	35.00	—

KM# 500.23 2 SOLS

Billon **Ruler:** Louis XV **Mint:** Amiens **Obverse:** Crowned L with 3 fleur-de-lis **Reverse:** Crowned floral double L monogram, date above

Date	Mintage	VG	F	VF	XF	Unc
1738X	172,000	3.00	5.00	14.00	35.00	—
1739X	1,742,000	2.00	4.00	12.00	30.00	—

KM# 500.24 2 SOLS

Billon **Ruler:** Louis XV **Mint:** Bourges **Obverse:** Crowned L with 3 fleur-de-lis **Reverse:** Crowned floral double L monogram, date above

Date	Mintage	VG	F	VF	XF	Unc
1739Y	685,000	3.00	5.00	14.00	35.00	—
1740Y	231,000	3.00	5.00	14.00	35.00	—

KM# 500.25 2 SOLS

Billon **Ruler:** Louis XV **Mint:** Grenoble **Obverse:** Crowned L with 3 fleur-de-lis **Reverse:** Crowned floral double L monogram, date above

Date	Mintage	VG	F	VF	XF	Unc
1739Z	269,000	4.00	7.00	16.00	45.00	—
1740Z	149,000	4.00	7.00	16.00	45.00	—

KM# 500.27 2 SOLS

Billon **Ruler:** Louis XV **Mint:** Aix **Obverse:** Crowned L with 3 fleur-de-lis **Reverse:** Crowned floral double L monogram, date above **Note:** Mint mark: &.

Date	Mintage	VG	F	VF	XF	Unc
1739	—	3.00	5.00	14.00	35.00	—

KM# 500.26 2 SOLS

Billon **Ruler:** Louis XV **Mint:** Rennes **Obverse:** Crowned L with 3 fleur-de-lis **Reverse:** Crowned floral double L monogram, date above **Note:** Mint mark: 9.

Date	Mintage	VG	F	VF	XF	Unc
1739	607,000	3.00	5.00	14.00	35.00	—
1740	801,000	3.00	5.00	14.00	35.00	—
1741	—	3.00	5.00	14.00	35.00	—
1742	109,000	3.00	5.00	14.00	35.00	—

KM# 500.28 2 SOLS

Billon **Ruler:** Louis XV **Mint:** Besancon **Obverse:** Crowned L with 3 fleur-de-lis **Reverse:** Crowned floral double L monogram, date above **Note:** Mint mark: Back to back C's.

Date	Mintage	VG	F	VF	XF	Unc
1739	1,761,000	2.00	4.00	10.00	25.00	—
1740	213,000	3.00	5.00	14.00	35.00	—
1741	—	3.00	5.00	14.00	35.00	—

KM# 500.20 2 SOLS

Billon **Ruler:** Louis XV **Mint:** Nantes **Obverse:** Crowned L with 3 fleur-de-lis **Reverse:** Crowned floral double L monogram, date above

Date	Mintage	VG	F	VF	XF	Unc
1739T	442,000	3.00	5.00	14.00	35.00	—
1740T	—	3.00	5.00	14.00	35.00	—
1743T	—	3.00	5.00	14.00	35.00	—

KM# 500.17 2 SOLS

Billon **Ruler:** Louis XV **Mint:** Perpignan **Obverse:** Crowned L with 3 fleur-de-lis **Reverse:** Crowned floral double L monogram, date above

Date	Mintage	VG	F	VF	XF	Unc
1739Q	—	4.00	7.00	16.00	45.00	—
1740Q	329,000	3.00	5.00	14.00	35.00	—
1744Q	—	6.00	12.00	40.00	95.00	—

KM# 500.5 2 SOLS

Billon **Ruler:** Louis XV **Mint:** Caen **Obverse:** Crowned L with 3 fleur-de-lis **Reverse:** Crowned floral double L monogram, date above

Date	Mintage	VG	F	VF	XF	Unc
1739C	1,581,000	2.00	4.00	12.00	30.00	—
1740C	598,000	2.00	4.00	12.00	30.00	—
1741C	310,000	2.00	4.00	12.00	30.00	—
1742C	195,000	2.00	4.00	12.00	30.00	—
1743C	168,000	2.00	4.00	12.00	30.00	—
1744C	116,000	2.00	4.00	12.00	30.00	—
1745C	100,000	3.00	6.00	15.00	40.00	—
1746C	98,000	3.00	6.00	15.00	40.00	—
1747C	71,000	3.00	6.00	15.00	40.00	—
1748C	79,000	3.00	6.00	15.00	40.00	—
1749C	68,000	3.00	6.00	15.00	40.00	—
1750C	82,000	3.00	6.00	15.00	40.00	—
1751C	59,000	3.00	6.00	15.00	40.00	—

KM# 500.6 2 SOLS

Billon **Ruler:** Louis XV **Mint:** Lyon **Obverse:** Crowned L with 3 fleur-de-lis **Reverse:** Crowned floral double L monogram, date above

Date	Mintage	VG	F	VF	XF	Unc
1739D	2,771,000	2.00	4.00	12.00	30.00	—
1740D	678,000	3.00	5.00	14.00	35.00	—
1741D	394,000	3.00	5.00	14.00	35.00	—

KM# 500.9 2 SOLS

Billon **Ruler:** Louis XV **Mint:** La Rochelle **Obverse:** Crowned L with 3 fleur-de-lis **Reverse:** Crowned floral double L monogram, date above

Date	Mintage	VG	F	VF	XF	Unc
1739H	668,000	3.00	5.00	14.00	35.00	—
1740H	218,000	3.00	5.00	14.00	35.00	—
1741H	—	3.00	5.00	14.00	35.00	—
1742H	26,000	5.00	9.00	18.00	55.00	—
1743H	26,000	5.00	9.00	18.00	55.00	—
1744H	23,000	5.00	9.00	18.00	55.00	—
1745H	23,000	5.00	9.00	18.00	55.00	—
1746H	28,000	5.00	9.00	18.00	55.00	—
1747H	67,000	4.00	7.00	16.00	45.00	—
1748H	—	3.00	5.00	14.00	35.00	—
1749H	—	3.00	5.00	14.00	35.00	—
1750H	—	3.00	5.00	14.00	35.00	—
1751H	63,000	4.00	7.00	16.00	45.00	—

KM# 500.10 2 SOLS

Billon **Ruler:** Louis XV **Mint:** Limoges **Obverse:** Crowned L with 3 fleur-de-lis **Reverse:** Crowned floral double L monogram, date above

Date	Mintage	VG	F	VF	XF	Unc
1739I	631,000	3.00	5.00	14.00	35.00	—
1740I	602,000	3.00	5.00	14.00	35.00	—
1741I	—	3.00	5.00	14.00	35.00	—
1742I	104,000	3.00	5.00	14.00	35.00	—

KM# 500.11 2 SOLS

Billon **Ruler:** Louis XV **Mint:** Bordeaux **Obverse:** Crowned L with 3 fleur-de-lis **Reverse:** Crowned floral double L monogram, date above

Date	Mintage	VG	F	VF	XF	Unc
1739K	1,283,000	2.00	4.00	12.00	30.00	—
1740K	522,000	3.00	5.00	14.00	35.00	—
1741K	—	3.00	5.00	14.00	35.00	—
1742K	—	3.00	5.00	14.00	35.00	—
1743K	87,000	4.00	7.00	16.00	45.00	—
1744K	143,000	3.00	5.00	14.00	35.00	—

KM# 500.12 2 SOLS

Billon **Ruler:** Louis XV **Mint:** Bayonne **Obverse:** Crowned L with 3 fleur-de-lis **Reverse:** Crowned floral double L monogram, date above

Date	Mintage	VG	F	VF	XF	Unc
1739L	—	3.00	5.00	14.00	35.00	—
1740L	129,000	3.00	5.00	14.00	35.00	—
1741L	75,000	4.00	7.00	16.00	45.00	—
1742L	17,000	5.00	9.00	18.00	55.00	—
1743L	—	3.00	5.00	14.00	35.00	—
1744L	—	3.00	5.00	14.00	35.00	—
1745L	—	3.00	5.00	14.00	35.00	—
1746L	—	3.00	5.00	14.00	35.00	—
1747L	—	3.00	5.00	14.00	35.00	—
1748L	—	3.00	5.00	14.00	35.00	—
1749L	—	3.00	5.00	14.00	35.00	—
1750L	—	3.00	5.00	14.00	35.00	—
1751L	—	4.00	7.00	16.00	45.00	—

KM# 500.13 2 SOLS

Billon **Ruler:** Louis XV **Mint:** Toulouse **Obverse:** Crowned L with 3 fleur-de-lis **Reverse:** Crowned floral double L monogram, date above

Date	Mintage	VG	F	VF	XF	Unc
1739M	2,005,000	2.00	4.00	10.00	25.00	—
1740M	665,000	3.00	5.00	14.00	35.00	—
1741M	292,000	3.00	5.00	14.00	35.00	—
1742M	246,000	3.00	5.00	14.00	35.00	—

KM# 500.14 2 SOLS

Billon **Ruler:** Louis XV **Mint:** Montpellier **Obverse:** Crowned L with 3 fleur-de-lis **Reverse:** Crowned floral double L monogram, date above

Date	Mintage	VG	F	VF	XF	Unc
1739N	1,091,000	2.00	4.00	12.00	30.00	—
1740N	401,000	3.00	5.00	14.00	35.00	—
1741N	103,000	3.00	5.00	14.00	35.00	—
1742N	—	3.00	5.00	14.00	35.00	—

KM# 500.15 2 SOLS

Billon **Ruler:** Louis XV **Mint:** Riom **Obverse:** Crowned L with 3 fleur-de-lis **Reverse:** Crowned floral double L monogram, date above

Date	Mintage	VG	F	VF	XF	Unc
1739O	1,756,000	2.00	4.00	12.00	30.00	—
1740O	419,000	3.00	5.00	14.00	35.00	—
1743O	136,000	3.00	5.00	14.00	35.00	—

KM# 500.29 2 SOLS

Billon **Ruler:** Louis XV **Mint:** Pau **Obverse:** Crowned L with 3 fleur-de-lis **Reverse:** Crowned floral double L monogram, date above **Note:** Mint mark: Cow.

Date	Mintage	VG	F	VF	XF	Unc
1743	20,000	5.00	10.00	30.00	90.00	—

KM# 603.1 2 SOLS

Bronze **Mint:** Paris **Obverse:** Bust left **Obv. Legend:** LOUIS XVI ROI DES FRANCOIS • **Reverse:** Liberty cap above fasces, oak wreath in background **Rev. Legend:** LANATION LA LOI LE ROI • 3 DE LA LIBERTE, below

Date	Mintage	VG	F	VF	XF	Unc
1791A	—	3.00	7.00	25.00	100	—
1792A	—	3.00	7.00	25.00	100	—
1793A	—	6.00	14.00	40.00	150	—

KM# 337.1 5 SOLS (1/16 ECU)

1.6960 g., 0.7980 Silver 0.0435 oz. ASW **Ruler:** Louis XIV **Mint:** Paris **Obverse:** Draped bust right **Reverse:** Crown above, crossed scepter and hand of Justice, fleur-de-lis in angles

Date	Mintage	VG	F	VF	XF	Unc
1702A	17,926	4.00	10.00	20.00	50.00	—
1703A	1,903,000	—	—	40.00	95.00	—

KM# 337.2 5 SOLS (1/16 ECU)

1.6960 g., 0.7980 Silver 0.0435 oz. ASW **Ruler:** Louis XIV **Mint:** Metz **Obverse:** Draped bust right **Reverse:** Crown above crossed sceptre, hand of Justice and 3 fleur-de-lis

Date	Mintage	VG	F	VF	XF	Unc
1702AA	889,000	—	—	—	—	—

KM# 337.3 5 SOLS (1/16 ECU)

1.6960 g., 0.7980 Silver 0.0435 oz. ASW **Ruler:** Louis XIV **Mint:** Rouen **Obverse:** Draped bust right **Reverse:** Crown above, crossed sceptre and hand of Justice, fleur-de-lis in angles

Date	Mintage	VG	F	VF	XF	Unc
1702B	4,727,000	5.00	12.00	25.00	65.00	—

KM# 337.4 5 SOLS (1/16 ECU)

1.6960 g., 0.7980 Silver 0.0435 oz. ASW **Ruler:** Louis XIV **Mint:** Strasbourg **Obverse:** Draped bust right **Reverse:** Crown above, crossed sceptre and hand of Justice, fleur-de-lis in angles

Date	Mintage	VG	F	VF	XF	Unc
1702BB	1,544,000	5.00	12.00	25.00	65.00	—
1703BB	—	4.00	10.00	20.00	50.00	—
1704BB	—	4.00	10.00	20.00	50.00	—

KM# 337.5 5 SOLS (1/16 ECU)

1.6960 g., 0.7980 Silver 0.0435 oz. ASW **Ruler:** Louis XIV **Mint:** Caen **Obverse:** Draped bust right **Reverse:** Crown above, crossed sceptre and hand of Justice, fleur-de-lis in angles

Date	Mintage	VG	F	VF	XF	Unc
1702C	2,832,000	6.00	15.00	30.00	75.00	—

KM# 337.6 5 SOLS (1/16 ECU)

1.6960 g., 0.7980 Silver 0.0435 oz. ASW **Ruler:** Louis XIV **Mint:** Lyon **Obverse:** Draped bust right **Reverse:** Crown above, crossed sceptre and hand of Justice, fleur-de-lis in angles

Date	Mintage	VG	F	VF	XF	Unc
1702D	3,642,000	5.00	12.00	25.00	65.00	—
1703D	—	6.00	15.00	30.00	75.00	—

KM# 337.7 5 SOLS (1/16 ECU)

1.6960 g., 0.7980 Silver 0.0435 oz. ASW **Ruler:** Louis XIV **Mint:** Tours **Obverse:** Draped bust right **Reverse:** Crown above, crossed sceptre and hand of Justice, fleur-de-lis in angles

Date	Mintage	VG	F	VF	XF	Unc
1702E	1,697,000	5.00	12.00	25.00	65.00	—
1703E	—	6.00	15.00	30.00	75.00	—

KM# 337.8 5 SOLS (1/16 ECU)

1.6960 g., 0.7980 Silver 0.0435 oz. ASW **Ruler:** Louis XIV **Mint:** Poitiers **Obverse:** Draped bust right **Reverse:** Crown above, crossed sceptre and hand of Justice, fleur-de-lis in angles

Date	Mintage	VG	F	VF	XF	Unc
1702G	979,000	7.00	16.00	32.00	80.00	—

KM# 337.9 5 SOLS (1/16 ECU)

1.6960 g., 0.7980 Silver 0.0435 oz. ASW **Ruler:** Louis XIV **Mint:** La Rochelle **Obverse:** Draped bust right **Reverse:** Crown above, crossed sceptre and hand of Justice, fleur-de-lis in angles

Date	Mintage	VG	F	VF	XF	Unc
1702H	1,281,000	5.00	12.00	25.00	65.00	—

KM# 337.10 5 SOLS (1/16 ECU)

1.6960 g., 0.7980 Silver 0.0435 oz. ASW **Ruler:** Louis XIV **Mint:** Limoges **Obverse:** Draped bust right **Reverse:** Crown above, crossed sceptre and hand of Justice, fleur-de-lis in angles

Date	Mintage	VG	F	VF	XF	Unc
1702I	1,023,000	—	—	—	—	—

KM# 337.11 5 SOLS (1/16 ECU)

1.6960 g., 0.7980 Silver 0.0435 oz. ASW **Ruler:** Louis XIV **Mint:** Bordeaux **Obverse:** Draped bust right **Reverse:** Crown above, crossed sceptre and hand of Justice, fleur-de-lis in angles

Date	Mintage	VG	F	VF	XF	Unc
1702K	1,435,000	6.00	15.00	30.00	75.00	—

KM# 337.12 5 SOLS (1/16 ECU)

1.6960 g., 0.7980 Silver 0.0435 oz. ASW **Ruler:** Louis XIV **Mint:** Bayonne **Obverse:** Draped bust right **Reverse:** Crown above, crossed sceptre and hand of Justice, fleur-de-lis in angles

Date	Mintage	VG	F	VF	XF	Unc
1702L	162,000	—	—	—	—	—

KM# 337.13 5 SOLS (1/16 ECU)

1.6960 g., 0.7980 Silver 0.0435 oz. ASW **Ruler:** Louis XIV **Mint:** Toulouse **Obverse:** Draped bust right **Reverse:** Crown above, crossed sceptre and hand of Justice, fleur-de-lis in angles

Date	Mintage	VG	F	VF	XF	Unc
1702M	2,574,000	5.00	12.00	25.00	65.00	—
1703M	—	6.00	15.00	30.00	75.00	—

KM# 337.14 5 SOLS (1/16 ECU)

1.6960 g., 0.7980 Silver 0.0435 oz. ASW **Ruler:** Louis XIV **Mint:** Montpellier **Obverse:** Draped bust right **Reverse:** Crown above, crossed sceptre and hand of Justice, fleur-de-lis in angles

Date	Mintage	VG	F	VF	XF	Unc
1702N	1,754,000	5.00	12.00	25.00	65.00	—
1703N	152,000	—	—	—	—	—

KM# 337.15 5 SOLS (1/16 ECU)

1.6960 g., 0.7980 Silver 0.0435 oz. ASW **Ruler:** Louis XIV **Mint:** Riom **Obverse:** Draped bust right **Reverse:** Crown above, crossed sceptre and hand of Justice, fleur-de-lis in angles

Date	Mintage	VG	F	VF	XF	Unc
1702O	1,431,000	10.00	20.00	45.00	85.00	—

KM# 337.16 5 SOLS (1/16 ECU)

1.6960 g., 0.7980 Silver 0.0435 oz. ASW **Ruler:** Louis XIV **Mint:** Dijon **Obverse:** Draped bust right **Reverse:** Crown above, crossed sceptre and hand of Justice, fleur-de-lis in angles

Date	Mintage	VG	F	VF	XF	Unc
1702P	1,446,000	6.00	14.00	28.00	70.00	—

KM# 337.17 5 SOLS (1/16 ECU)

1.6960 g., 0.7980 Silver 0.0435 oz. ASW **Ruler:** Louis XIV **Mint:** Troyes **Obverse:** Draped bust right **Reverse:** Crown above, crossed sceptre and hand of Justice, fleur-de-lis in angles

Date	Mintage	VG	F	VF	XF	Unc
1702S	1,203,000	—	—	—	—	—

KM# 337.18 5 SOLS (1/16 ECU)

1.6960 g., 0.7980 Silver 0.0435 oz. ASW **Ruler:** Louis XIV **Mint:** Nantes **Obverse:** Draped bust right **Reverse:** Crown above, crossed sceptre and hand of Justice, fleur-de-lis in angles

Date	Mintage	VG	F	VF	XF	Unc
1702T	1,660,000	6.00	14.00	28.00	70.00	—

KM# 337.19 5 SOLS (1/16 ECU)

1.6960 g., 0.7980 Silver 0.0435 oz. ASW **Ruler:** Louis XIV **Mint:** Troyes **Obverse:** Draped bust right **Reverse:** Crown above, crossed sceptre and hand of Justice, fleur-de-lis in angles

Date	Mintage	VG	F	VF	XF	Unc
1702V	781,000	—	—	—	—	—

KM# 337.20 5 SOLS (1/16 ECU)

1.6960 g., 0.7980 Silver 0.0435 oz. ASW **Ruler:** Louis XIV **Mint:** Lille **Obverse:** Draped bust right **Reverse:** Crown above, crossed sceptre and hand of Justice, fleur-de-lis in angles

Date	Mintage	VG	F	VF	XF	Unc
1702W	4,019,000	6.00	14.00	28.00	70.00	—
1703W	56,000	—	—	—	—	—

KM# 337.21 5 SOLS (1/16 ECU)

1.6960 g., 0.7980 Silver 0.0435 oz. ASW **Ruler:** Louis XIV **Mint:** Amiens **Obverse:** Draped bust right **Reverse:** Crown above, crossed sceptre and hand of Justice, fleur-de-lis in angles

Date	Mintage	VG	F	VF	XF	Unc
1702X	1,140,000	—	—	—	—	—

KM# 337.22 5 SOLS (1/16 ECU)

1.6960 g., 0.7980 Silver 0.0435 oz. ASW **Ruler:** Louis XIV **Mint:** Bourges **Obverse:** Draped bust right **Reverse:** Crown above, crossed sceptre and hand of Justice, fleur-de-lis in angles

Date	Mintage	VG	F	VF	XF	Unc
1702Y	795,000	—	—	—	—	—

KM# 337.23 5 SOLS (1/16 ECU)

1.6960 g., 0.7980 Silver 0.0435 oz. ASW **Ruler:** Louis XIV **Mint:** Grenoble **Obverse:** Draped bust right **Reverse:** Crown above, crossed sceptre and hand of Justice, fleur-de-lis in angles

Date	Mintage	VG	F	VF	XF	Unc
1702Z	339,000	—	—	—	—	—

KM# 337.24 5 SOLS (1/16 ECU)

1.6960 g., 0.7980 Silver 0.0435 oz. ASW **Ruler:** Louis XIV **Mint:** Aix **Obverse:** Draped bust right **Reverse:** Crown above, crossed sceptre and hand of Justice, fleur-de-lis in angles **Note:** Mint mark: &.

Date	Mintage	VG	F	VF	XF	Unc
1702	1,754,000	6.00	14.00	28.00	70.00	—

KM# 337.25 5 SOLS (1/16 ECU)

1.6960 g., 0.7980 Silver 0.0435 oz. ASW **Ruler:** Louis XIV **Mint:** Rennes **Obverse:** Draped bust right **Reverse:** Crown above, crossed sceptre and hand of Justice, fleur-de-lis in angles **Note:** Mint mark: 9.

Date	Mintage	VG	F	VF	XF	Unc
1702	3,467,000	6.00	14.00	28.00	70.00	—

KM# 337.26 5 SOLS (1/16 ECU)

1.6960 g., 0.7980 Silver 0.0435 oz. ASW **Ruler:** Louis XIV **Mint:** Besancon **Obverse:** Draped bust right **Reverse:** Crown above, crossed sceptre and hand of Justice, fleur-de-lis in angles **Note:** Mint mark: Back to back C's.

Date	Mintage	VG	F	VF	XF	Unc
1702	1,088,000	7.00	16.00	32.00	80.00	—

KM# 337.27 5 SOLS (1/16 ECU)

1.6960 g., 0.7980 Silver 0.0435 oz. ASW **Ruler:** Louis XIV **Mint:** Pau **Obverse:** Draped bust right **Reverse:** Crown above, crossed sceptre and hand of Justice, fleur-de-lis in angles **Note:** Mint mark: Cow.

Date	Mintage	VG	F	VF	XF	Unc
1702	65,000	50.00	95.00	190	480	—

KM# 416.1 6 SOLS (1/20 ECU)

1.5290 g., 0.9170 Silver 0.0451 oz. ASW **Ruler:** Louis XV **Mint:** Paris **Obverse:** Young bust of Louis XV right **Reverse:** Crowned circular arms

Date	Mintage	VG	F	VF	XF	Unc
1716A	—	60.00	110	450	1,000	—

KM# 416.2 6 SOLS (1/20 ECU)

1.5290 g., 0.9170 Silver 0.0451 oz. ASW **Ruler:** Louis XV **Mint:** Bordeaux **Obverse:** Young bust of Louis XV right **Reverse:** Crowned circular arms

Date	Mintage	VG	F	VF	XF	Unc
1716K	—	75.00	150	475	1,000	—

KM# 416.3 6 SOLS (1/20 ECU)

1.5290 g., 0.9170 Silver 0.0451 oz. ASW **Ruler:** Louis XV **Mint:** Lille **Obverse:** Young bust of Louis XV right **Reverse:** Crowned circular arms

Date	Mintage	VG	F	VF	XF	Unc
1716W	—	75.00	150	475	1,000	—

KM# 417 6 SOLS (1/20 ECU)

1.5290 g., 0.9170 Silver 0.0451 oz. ASW **Ruler:** Louis XV **Mint:** Pau **Obverse:** Young bust of Louis XV right, legend ends with ligate BD **Reverse:** Crowned circular arms **Note:** Issued for Province of Bearn. Mint mark: Cow.

Date	Mintage	VG	F	VF	XF	Unc
1716	—	75.00	150	500	1,250	—

KM# 416.4 6 SOLS (1/20 ECU)

1.5290 g., 0.9170 Silver 0.0451 oz. ASW **Ruler:** Louis XV **Mint:** Rennes **Obverse:** Young bust of Louis XV right **Reverse:** Crowned circular arms **Note:** Mint mark: 9.

Date	Mintage	VG	F	VF	XF	Unc
1717	—	75.00	150	475	1,000	—

KM# 480.1 6 SOLS (1/20 ECU)

1.4740 g., 0.9170 Silver 0.0435 oz. ASW **Ruler:** Louis XV **Mint:** Paris **Obverse:** Young bust left **Obv. Legend:** LUD • XV • D • G • FR • ET • NAV • REX • **Reverse:** Crowned oval arms within wreath **Rev. Legend:** SIT NOMEN DOMINI BENEDICTUM

Date	Mintage	VG	F	VF	XF	Unc
1726A	—	6.00	15.00	35.00	90.00	—
1727A	—	6.00	15.00	35.00	90.00	—
1729A	—	6.00	15.00	35.00	90.00	—
1730A	—	6.00	15.00	35.00	90.00	—
1732A	—	6.00	15.00	35.00	90.00	—
1736A	—	6.00	15.00	35.00	90.00	—
1737A	—	10.00	25.00	60.00	150	—

KM# 480.2 6 SOLS (1/20 ECU)

1.4740 g., 0.9170 Silver 0.0435 oz. ASW **Ruler:** Louis XV **Mint:** Metz **Obverse:** Young bust left **Reverse:** Crowned oval arms within wreath

Date	Mintage	VG	F	VF	XF	Unc
1727AA	—	6.00	15.00	38.00	95.00	—

KM# 480.3 6 SOLS (1/20 ECU)

1.4740 g., 0.9170 Silver 0.0435 oz. ASW **Ruler:** Louis XV **Mint:** Rouen **Obverse:** Young bust left **Reverse:** Crowned oval arms within wreath

Date	Mintage	VG	F	VF	XF	Unc
1727B	—	8.00	20.00	45.00	110	—

KM# 480.4 6 SOLS (1/20 ECU)

1.4740 g., 0.9170 Silver 0.0435 oz. ASW **Ruler:** Louis XV **Mint:** Strasbourg **Obverse:** Young bust left **Reverse:** Crowned oval arms within wreath

Date	Mintage	VG	F	VF	XF	Unc
1727BB	—	6.00	15.00	35.00	90.00	—
1729BB	—	8.00	20.00	45.00	110	—
1730BB	—	8.00	20.00	45.00	110	—

KM# 480.5 6 SOLS (1/20 ECU)

1.4740 g., 0.9170 Silver 0.0435 oz. ASW **Ruler:** Louis XV **Mint:** Caen **Obverse:** Young bust left **Reverse:** Crowned oval arms within wreath

Date	Mintage	VG	F	VF	XF	Unc
1727C	44,000	8.00	20.00	45.00	110	—
1729C	226,000	6.00	15.00	35.00	90.00	—

KM# 480.6 6 SOLS (1/20 ECU)

1.4740 g., 0.9170 Silver 0.0435 oz. ASW **Ruler:** Louis XV **Mint:** Lyon **Obverse:** Young bust left **Reverse:** Crowned oval arms within wreath

Date	Mintage	VG	F	VF	XF	Unc
1727D	—	6.00	15.00	35.00	90.00	—
1728D	—	6.00	15.00	35.00	90.00	—

KM# 480.7 6 SOLS (1/20 ECU)

1.4740 g., 0.9170 Silver 0.0435 oz. ASW **Ruler:** Louis XV **Mint:** Tours **Obverse:** Young bust left **Reverse:** Crowned oval arms within wreath

Date	Mintage	VG	F	VF	XF	Unc
1727E	—	6.00	15.00	35.00	90.00	—

KM# 480.8 6 SOLS (1/20 ECU)

1.4740 g., 0.9170 Silver 0.0435 oz. ASW **Ruler:** Louis XV **Mint:** Poitiers **Obverse:** Young bust right **Reverse:** Crowned oval arms within wreath

Date	Mintage	VG	F	VF	XF	Unc
1727G	—	8.00	20.00	45.00	110	—
1729G	—	8.00	20.00	45.00	110	—

KM# 480.13 6 SOLS (1/20 ECU)

1.4740 g., 0.9170 Silver 0.0435 oz. ASW **Ruler:** Louis XV **Mint:** Montpellier **Obverse:** Young bust left **Reverse:** Crowned oval arms within wreath

Date	Mintage	VG	F	VF	XF	Unc
1727N	47,000	8.00	20.00	45.00	110	—
1740N	—	8.00	20.00	50.00	130	—

KM# 480.17 6 SOLS (1/20 ECU)

1.4740 g., 0.9170 Silver 0.0435 oz. ASW **Ruler:** Louis XV **Mint:** Orléans **Obverse:** Young bust left **Reverse:** Crowned oval arms within wreath

Date	Mintage	VG	F	VF	XF	Unc
1727R	44,000	8.00	20.00	45.00	110	—

KM# 480.18 6 SOLS (1/20 ECU)

1.4740 g., 0.9170 Silver 0.0435 oz. ASW **Ruler:** Louis XV **Mint:** Reims **Obverse:** Young bust left **Reverse:** Crowned oval arms within wreath

Date	Mintage	VG	F	VF	XF	Unc
1727S	—	8.00	20.00	50.00	130	—

KM# 480.19 6 SOLS (1/20 ECU)

1.4740 g., 0.9170 Silver 0.0435 oz. ASW **Ruler:** Louis XV **Mint:** Nantes **Obverse:** Young bust left **Reverse:** Crowned oval arms within wreath

Date	Mintage	VG	F	VF	XF	Unc
1727T	—	6.00	15.00	35.00	90.00	—
1729T	—	6.00	15.00	35.00	90.00	—
1733T	—	10.00	25.00	65.00	160	—
1737T	—	8.00	20.00	45.00	120	—

KM# 480.21 6 SOLS (1/20 ECU)

1.4740 g., 0.9170 Silver 0.0435 oz. ASW **Ruler:** Louis XV **Mint:** Lille **Obverse:** Young bust left **Reverse:** Crowned oval arms within wreath

Date	Mintage	VG	F	VF	XF	Unc
1727W	—	6.00	15.00	35.00	90.00	—
1728W	90,000	8.00	20.00	45.00	110	—
1730W	138,000	8.00	20.00	45.00	110	—

KM# 480.22 6 SOLS (1/20 ECU)

1.4740 g., 0.9170 Silver 0.0435 oz. ASW **Ruler:** Louis XV **Mint:** Amiens **Obverse:** Young bust left **Reverse:** Crowned oval arms within wreath

Date	Mintage	VG	F	VF	XF	Unc
1727X	—	6.00	15.00	35.00	90.00	—
1728X	—	8.00	20.00	45.00	110	—

KM# 480.23 6 SOLS (1/20 ECU)

1.4740 g., 0.9170 Silver 0.0435 oz. ASW **Ruler:** Louis XV **Mint:** Bourges **Obverse:** Young bust left **Reverse:** Crowned oval arms within wreath

Date	Mintage	VG	F	VF	XF	Unc
1727Y	—	6.00	15.00	35.00	90.00	—
1729Y	—	6.00	15.00	35.00	90.00	—

KM# 480.24 6 SOLS (1/20 ECU)

1.4740 g., 0.9170 Silver 0.0435 oz. ASW **Ruler:** Louis XV **Mint:** Grenoble **Obverse:** Young bust left **Reverse:** Crowned oval arms within wreath

Date	Mintage	VG	F	VF	XF	Unc
1727Z	—	6.00	15.00	35.00	90.00	—

KM# 480.20 6 SOLS (1/20 ECU)

1.4740 g., 0.9170 Silver 0.0435 oz. ASW **Ruler:** Louis XV **Mint:** Troyes **Obverse:** Young bust left **Reverse:** Crowned oval arms within wreath

Date	Mintage	VG	F	VF	XF	Unc
1728V	15,000	8.00	20.00	50.00	130	—
1730V	—	8.00	20.00	50.00	130	—

KM# 480.14 6 SOLS (1/20 ECU)

1.4740 g., 0.9170 Silver 0.0435 oz. ASW **Ruler:** Louis XV **Mint:** Riom **Obverse:** Young bust left **Reverse:** Crowned oval arms within wreath

Date	Mintage	VG	F	VF	XF	Unc
1728O	—	8.00	20.00	45.00	110	—
1740O	—	15.00	35.00	90.00	220	—

KM# 480.10 6 SOLS (1/20 ECU)

1.4740 g., 0.9170 Silver 0.0435 oz. ASW **Ruler:** Louis XV **Mint:** Bordeaux **Obverse:** Young bust left **Reverse:** Crowned oval arms within wreath

Date	Mintage	VG	F	VF	XF	Unc
1728K	890,000	6.00	15.00	35.00	90.00	—

KM# 480.11 6 SOLS (1/20 ECU)

1.4740 g., 0.9170 Silver 0.0435 oz. ASW **Ruler:** Louis XV **Mint:** Bayonne **Obverse:** Young bust left **Obv. Legend:** LVD • XV • D • G • FR • ET • NAV • REX • **Reverse:** Crowned oval arms within wreath **Rev. Legend:** SIT NOMEN DOMINI BENEDICTUM

Date	Mintage	VG	F	VF	XF	Unc
1728L	—	6.00	15.00	35.00	90.00	—
1730L	—	6.00	15.00	35.00	90.00	—
1736L	—	15.00	35.00	100	240	—

KM# 480.25 6 SOLS (1/20 ECU)

1.4740 g., 0.9170 Silver 0.0435 oz. ASW **Ruler:** Louis XV **Mint:** Rennes **Obverse:** Young bust left **Reverse:** Crowned oval arms within wreath **Note:** Mint mark: 9.

Date	Mintage	VG	F	VF	XF	Unc
1728	—	12.00	30.00	75.00	195	—
1729	—	8.00	20.00	45.00	110	—
1730	—	8.00	20.00	50.00	130	—
1731	—	8.00	20.00	45.00	110	—
1732	—	15.00	35.00	85.00	200	—

KM# 480.26 6 SOLS (1/20 ECU)

1.4740 g., 0.9170 Silver 0.0435 oz. ASW **Ruler:** Louis XV **Mint:** Besancon **Obverse:** Young bust left **Reverse:** Crowned oval arms within wreath **Note:** Mint mark: Back to back C's.

Date	Mintage	VG	F	VF	XF	Unc
1728	—	8.00	20.00	45.00	110	—

KM# 480.9 6 SOLS (1/20 ECU)

1.4740 g., 0.9170 Silver 0.0435 oz. ASW **Ruler:** Louis XV **Mint:** Limoges **Obverse:** Young bust left **Reverse:** Crowned oval arms within wreath

Date	Mintage	VG	F	VF	XF	Unc
1729I	—	6.00	15.00	35.00	90.00	—
1730I	—	8.00	20.00	45.00	110	—
1731I	—	6.00	15.00	35.00	90.00	—

KM# 480.12 6 SOLS (1/20 ECU)

1.4740 g., 0.9170 Silver 0.0435 oz. ASW **Ruler:** Louis XV **Mint:** Toulouse **Obverse:** Young bust left **Reverse:** Crowned oval arms within wreath

Date	Mintage	VG	F	VF	XF	Unc
1730M	—	6.00	15.00	35.00	90.00	—
1740M	—	8.00	20.00	55.00	140	—

KM# 480.16 6 SOLS (1/20 ECU)

1.4740 g., 0.9170 Silver 0.0435 oz. ASW **Ruler:** Louis XV **Mint:** Perpignan **Obverse:** Young bust left **Reverse:** Crowned oval arms within wreath

Date	Mintage	VG	F	VF	XF	Unc
1733Q	—	6.00	15.00	35.00	90.00	—

KM# 510.1 6 SOLS (1/20 ECU)

1.4740 g., 0.9170 Silver 0.0435 oz. ASW **Ruler:** Louis XV **Mint:** Paris **Obverse:** Mature bust left **Obv. Legend:** LUD • XV • D • G • FR • ET • NAV • REX **Reverse:** Crowned oval arms within wreath **Rev. Legend:** SIT NOMEN DOMINI BENEDICTUM

Date	Mintage	VG	F	VF	XF	Unc
1740A	26,000	6.00	15.00	35.00	100	—
1740A Proof	—	Value: 425				
1741A	—	5.00	12.00	30.00	80.00	—
1743A	31,000	5.00	12.00	30.00	80.00	—
1744A	70,000	5.00	12.00	30.00	80.00	—
1746A	9,540	6.00	15.00	40.00	100	—
1747A	9,240	6.00	15.00	40.00	100	—
1749A	4,520	10.00	20.00	45.00	120	—
1750A	12,000	6.00	15.00	35.00	100	—
1752A	4,117	10.00	20.00	45.00	120	—
1756A	8,578	10.00	20.00	45.00	120	—
1759A	—	6.00	15.00	35.00	100	—
1760A	—	5.00	12.00	30.00	80.00	—
1765A	—	5.00	12.00	30.00	80.00	—
1766A	—	5.00	12.00	30.00	80.00	—

KM# 510.9 6 SOLS (1/20 ECU)

1.4740 g., 0.9170 Silver 0.0435 oz. ASW **Ruler:** Louis XV **Mint:** Montpellier **Obverse:** Mature bust left **Reverse:** Crowned oval arms within wreath

Date	Mintage	VG	F	VF	XF	Unc
1740N	—	6.00	15.00	35.00	100	—
1748N	—	6.00	15.00	35.00	100	—
1769N	—	5.00	12.00	30.00	80.00	—

KM# 510.12 6 SOLS (1/20 ECU)

1.4740 g., 0.9170 Silver 0.0435 oz. ASW **Ruler:** Louis XV **Mint:** Orléans **Obverse:** Mature bust left **Reverse:** Crowned oval arms within wreath

Date	Mintage	VG	F	VF	XF	Unc
1740R	11,000	6.00	15.00	35.00	100	—
1749R	—	6.00	15.00	35.00	100	—

KM# 510.13 6 SOLS (1/20 ECU)

1.4740 g., 0.9170 Silver 0.0435 oz. ASW **Ruler:** Louis XV **Mint:** Reims **Obverse:** Mature bust left **Reverse:** Crowned oval arms within wreath

Date	Mintage	VG	F	VF	XF	Unc
1740S	—	6.00	15.00	35.00	100	—
1741S	—	6.00	15.00	35.00	100	—
1744S	—	8.00	17.00	45.00	125	—
1752S	44,000	6.00	15.00	35.00	100	—

KM# 480.15 6 SOLS (1/20 ECU)
1.4740 g., 0.9170 Silver 0.0435 oz. ASW **Ruler:** Louis XV **Mint:** Dijon

Date	Mintage	VG	F	VF	XF	Unc
1740P	5,789	15.00	35.00	80.00	200	—

KM# 510.17 6 SOLS (1/20 ECU)
1.4740 g., 0.9170 Silver 0.0435 oz. ASW **Ruler:** Louis XV **Mint:** Amiens **Obverse:** Mature bust left **Reverse:** Crowned oval arms within wreath

Date	Mintage	VG	F	VF	XF	Unc
1740X	8,508	10.00	30.00	55.00	125	—

KM# 510.11 6 SOLS (1/20 ECU)
1.4740 g., 0.9170 Silver 0.0435 oz. ASW **Ruler:** Louis XV **Mint:** Dijon **Obverse:** Mature bust left **Reverse:** Crowned oval arms within wreath

Date	Mintage	VG	F	VF	XF	Unc
1741P	—	5.00	12.00	30.00	80.00	—

KM# 510.16 6 SOLS (1/20 ECU)
1.4740 g., 0.9170 Silver 0.0435 oz. ASW **Ruler:** Louis XV **Mint:** Lille **Obverse:** Mature bust left **Reverse:** Crowned oval arms within wreath

Date	Mintage	VG	F	VF	XF	Unc
1741W	—	5.00	12.00	30.00	80.00	—
1743W	—	5.00	12.00	30.00	80.00	—
1744W	—	5.00	12.00	30.00	80.00	—
1745W	13,000	6.00	15.00	40.00	100	—
1747W	170,000	5.00	12.00	30.00	80.00	—
1748W	142,000	5.00	12.00	30.00	80.00	—
1749W	71,000	5.00	12.00	30.00	80.00	—
1750W	42,000	6.00	15.00	35.00	100	—
1753W	22,000	6.00	15.00	35.00	100	—

KM# 510.14 6 SOLS (1/20 ECU)
1.4740 g., 0.9170 Silver 0.0435 oz. ASW **Ruler:** Louis XV **Mint:** Nantes **Obverse:** Mature bust left **Reverse:** Crowned oval arms within wreath

Date	Mintage	VG	F	VF	XF	Unc
1741T	—	5.00	12.00	30.00	80.00	—

KM# 510.7 6 SOLS (1/20 ECU)
1.4740 g., 0.9170 Silver 0.0435 oz. ASW **Ruler:** Louis XV **Mint:** La Rochelle **Obverse:** Mature bust left **Reverse:** Crowned oval arms within wreath

Date	Mintage	VG	F	VF	XF	Unc
1741H	—	6.00	15.00	35.00	100	—

KM# 510.8 6 SOLS (1/20 ECU)
1.4740 g., 0.9170 Silver 0.0435 oz. ASW **Ruler:** Louis XV **Mint:** Bayonne **Obverse:** Mature bust left **Reverse:** Crowned oval arms within wreath

Date	Mintage	VG	F	VF	XF	Unc
1743L	—	5.00	12.00	30.00	80.00	—
1766L	—	5.00	12.00	30.00	80.00	—
1769L	—	5.00	12.00	30.00	80.00	—

KM# 510.10 6 SOLS (1/20 ECU)
1.4740 g., 0.9170 Silver 0.0435 oz. ASW **Ruler:** Louis XV **Mint:** Riom **Obverse:** Head left **Obv. Legend:** LUD • XV • D • G • FR • ET NAV • REX • **Reverse:** Crowned oval arms within wreath **Rev. Legend:** SIT NOMEN DOMINI BENEDICTUM

Date	Mintage	VG	F	VF	XF	Unc
1743O	—	10.00	20.00	40.00	120	—
1748O	—	18.00	45.00	150	400	—

KM# 510.15 6 SOLS (1/20 ECU)
1.4740 g., 0.9170 Silver 0.0435 oz. ASW **Ruler:** Louis XV **Mint:** Troyes **Obverse:** Head left **Reverse:** Crowned oval arms within wreath

Date	Mintage	VG	F	VF	XF	Unc
1743V	12,000	6.00	15.00	35.00	100	—
1744V	10,000	6.00	15.00	35.00	100	—
1752V	—	6.00	15.00	35.00	100	—

KM# 510.6 6 SOLS (1/20 ECU)
1.4740 g., 0.9170 Silver 0.0435 oz. ASW **Ruler:** Louis XV **Mint:** Riom **Obverse:** Head left **Reverse:** Crowned oval arms within wreath

Date	Mintage	VG	F	VF	XF	Unc
1743O	90,000	5.00	12.00	30.00	80.00	—
1747O	49,000	5.00	12.00	30.00	80.00	—
1748O	201,000	5.00	12.00	30.00	80.00	—

KM# 510.3 6 SOLS (1/20 ECU)
1.4740 g., 0.9170 Silver 0.0435 oz. ASW **Ruler:** Louis XV **Mint:** Strasbourg **Obverse:** Head left **Reverse:** Crowned oval arms within wreath

Date	Mintage	VG	F	VF	XF	Unc
1743BB	—	5.00	12.00	30.00	80.00	—

KM# 510.4 6 SOLS (1/20 ECU)
1.4740 g., 0.9170 Silver 0.0435 oz. ASW **Ruler:** Louis XV **Mint:** Caen **Obverse:** Head left **Reverse:** Crowned oval arms within wreath

Date	Mintage	VG	F	VF	XF	Unc
1743C	87,000	5.00	12.00	30.00	80.00	—

KM# 510.2 6 SOLS (1/20 ECU)
1.4740 g., 0.9170 Silver 0.0435 oz. ASW **Ruler:** Louis XV **Mint:** Metz **Obverse:** Head left **Reverse:** Crowned oval arms within wreath

Date	Mintage	VG	F	VF	XF	Unc
1744AA	—	15.00	35.00	80.00	200	—
1748AA	—	6.00	15.00	35.00	100	—
1760AA	—	5.00	12.00	30.00	80.00	—
1769AA	—	5.00	10.00	30.00	70.00	—

KM# 510.5 6 SOLS (1/20 ECU)
1.4740 g., 0.9170 Silver 0.0435 oz. ASW **Ruler:** Louis XV **Mint:** Lyon **Obverse:** Head left **Reverse:** Crowned oval arms within wreath

Date	Mintage	VG	F	VF	XF	Unc
1750D	—	6.00	18.00	45.00	100	—

KM# 531 6 SOLS (1/20 ECU)
1.4740 g., 0.9170 Silver 0.0435 oz. ASW **Ruler:** Louis XV **Mint:** Pau **Obverse:** Similar to KM#510.1 but legend ends with ligate BD **Obv. Legend:** LUDXV DG FR ET NA BD **Reverse:** Crowned oval arms within wreath **Rev. Legend:** SIT NOMEN DOMINI BENEDICTUM **Note:** Mint mark: Cow. Issued for Province of Bearn.

Date	Mintage	VG	F	VF	XF	Unc
1754	15,000	8.00	15.00	40.00	120	—
1762	30,000	8.00	15.00	35.00	110	—
1764	58,000	8.00	15.00	35.00	110	—
1766	84,000	8.00	15.00	35.00	110	—
1770	24,000	8.00	15.00	35.00	110	—

KM# 552.1 6 SOLS (1/20 ECU)
1.4740 g., 0.9170 Silver 0.0435 oz. ASW **Ruler:** Louis XV **Mint:** Paris **Obverse:** Old laureate head left **Obv. Legend:** LUD • XV • D • G • FR • ET NAV • REX • **Reverse:** Crowned oval arms within wreath **Rev. Legend:** SIT NOMEN DOMINI BENEDICTUM **Note:** Posthumous issue.

Date	Mintage	VG	F	VF	XF	Unc
1771A	—	12.00	30.00	70.00	175	—
1773A	—	12.00	30.00	70.00	175	—
1779A	176,000	5.00	11.00	30.00	60.00	—

KM# 552.2 6 SOLS (1/20 ECU)
1.4740 g., 0.9170 Silver 0.0435 oz. ASW **Ruler:** Louis XV **Mint:** Strasbourg **Obverse:** Old laureate head left **Reverse:** Crowned oval arms within wreath

Date	Mintage	VG	F	VF	XF	Unc
1773BB	—	12.00	30.00	70.00	175	—

KM# 552.3 6 SOLS (1/20 ECU)
1.4740 g., 0.9170 Silver 0.0435 oz. ASW **Ruler:** Louis XV **Mint:** Limoges **Obverse:** Old laureate head left **Reverse:** Crowned oval arms within wreath

Date	Mintage	VG	F	VF	XF	Unc
1773I	—	15.00	35.00	75.00	180	—
1774I	—	15.00	35.00	75.00	180	—

KM# 552.4 6 SOLS (1/20 ECU)
1.4740 g., 0.9170 Silver 0.0435 oz. ASW **Ruler:** Louis XV **Mint:** Bayonne **Obverse:** Old laureate head left **Reverse:** Crowned oval arms within wreath

Date	Mintage	VG	F	VF	XF	Unc
1773L	—	12.00	30.00	70.00	175	—

KM# 552.5 6 SOLS (1/20 ECU)
1.4740 g., 0.9170 Silver 0.0435 oz. ASW **Ruler:** Louis XV **Mint:** Pau **Obverse:** Old laureate head left **Reverse:** Crowned oval arms within wreath **Note:** Mint mark: Cow.

Date	Mintage	VG	F	VF	XF	Unc
1773	—	20.00	50.00	120	300	—

KM# 587 6 SOLS (1/20 ECU)
1.4740 g., 0.9170 Silver 0.0435 oz. ASW **Ruler:** Louis XV **Mint:** Paris **Obverse:** Bust left **Obv. Legend:** LUD • XVI • D • G • FR • ETN • REX • **Reverse:** Crowned oval arms within oak leaf wreath **Rev. Legend:** SIT NOMEN DOMINI BENEDICTUM **Note:** The "dot" appears below the third letter of the monarch's name and denotes second semester coinage.

Date	Mintage	VG	F	VF	XF	Unc
1782/79A Without dot	—	12.00	30.00	60.00	150	—
1782A	22,000	15.00	35.00	75.00	175	—
1783A	53,000	10.00	20.00	50.00	125	—

KM# 348.2 10 SOLS-1/8 ECU
3.3920 g., 0.7980 Silver 0.0870 oz. ASW **Ruler:** Louis XIV **Mint:** Strasbourg **Obverse:** Draped bust right **Reverse:** 4 Crowns and 3 fleur-de-lis at center

Date	Mintage	VG	F	VF	XF	Unc
1702BB	—	15.00	35.00	75.00	220	—
1703BB	—	12.00	30.00	65.00	200	—
1704BB	—	12.00	30.00	65.00	200	—
1705BB	—	15.00	35.00	75.00	220	—
1706BB	—	15.00	35.00	75.00	220	—

KM# 349.1 10 SOLS-1/8 ECU
3.2630 g., 0.7980 Silver 0.0837 oz. ASW **Ruler:** Louis XIV **Mint:** Paris **Obverse:** Draped bust right **Obv. Legend:** LVD • XIIII • D • G • FR • ET • NAV • REX • **Reverse:** Crown above crossed scepter and hand of Justice, 3 fleur-de-lis in angles **Rev. Legend:** DOMINE SALVVM FAC REGEM

Date	Mintage	VG	F	VF	XF	Unc
1703A	—	9.00	22.00	45.00	120	—
1704A	—	9.00	22.00	45.00	120	—
1705A	—	9.00	22.00	45.00	120	—
1706A	—	9.00	22.00	45.00	120	—
1707A	—	9.00	22.00	45.00	120	—

KM# 349.2 10 SOLS-1/8 ECU
3.2630 g., 0.7980 Silver 0.0837 oz. ASW **Ruler:** Louis XIV **Mint:** Rouen **Obverse:** Draped bust right **Reverse:** Crown above crossed sceptre and hand of Justice, 3 fleur-de-lis in angles

Date	Mintage	VG	F	VF	XF	Unc
1703B	—	12.00	30.00	60.00	150	—
1704B	—	15.00	35.00	65.00	160	—
1705B	—	15.00	35.00	65.00	160	—
1706B	—	20.00	45.00	95.00	175	—
1707B	—	12.00	30.00	60.00	150	—

KM# 349.3 10 SOLS-1/8 ECU
3.2630 g., 0.7980 Silver 0.0837 oz. ASW **Ruler:** Louis XIV **Mint:** Lyon **Obverse:** Draped bust right **Obv. Legend:** LVD • XIIII • D • G • FR • ET • NAV • REX • **Reverse:** Crown above crossed sceptre and hand of Justice, 3 fleur-de-lis in angles **Rev. Legend:** DOMINE • SALVVM * FAC • REGEM •

Date	Mintage	VG	F	VF	XF	Unc
1703D	—	15.00	35.00	65.00	160	—
1704D	—	9.00	22.00	45.00	120	—
1705D	—	9.00	22.00	45.00	120	—
1706D	—	9.00	22.00	45.00	120	—
1707D	—	9.00	22.00	45.00	120	—

KM# 349.4 10 SOLS-1/8 ECU
3.2630 g., 0.7980 Silver 0.0837 oz. ASW **Ruler:** Louis XIV **Mint:** La Rochelle **Obverse:** Draped bust right **Reverse:** Crown above crossed sceptre and hand of Justice, 3 fleur-de-lis in angles

Date	Mintage	VG	F	VF	XF	Unc
1703H	—	12.00	30.00	60.00	150	—
1704H	—	10.00	25.00	50.00	135	—
1705H	—	—	—	—	—	—
1706H	—	10.00	25.00	50.00	135	—
1707H	—	9.00	22.00	45.00	120	—

KM# 349.5 10 SOLS-1/8 ECU
3.2630 g., 0.7980 Silver 0.0837 oz. ASW **Ruler:** Louis XIV **Mint:** Bordeaux **Obverse:** Draped bust right **Reverse:** Crown above crossed sceptre and hand of Justice, 3 fleur-de-lis in angles

Date	Mintage	VG	F	VF	XF	Unc
1703K	—	12.00	30.00	60.00	150	—
1704K	—	10.00	22.00	50.00	135	—
1705K	—	17.00	40.00	75.00	185	—
1706K	—	12.00	30.00	60.00	150	—
1707K	—	9.00	22.00	45.00	120	—

KM# 349.13 10 SOLS-1/8 ECU
3.2630 g., 0.7980 Silver 0.0837 oz. ASW **Ruler:** Louis XIV **Mint:** Aix **Obverse:** Draped bust right **Reverse:** Crown above crossed sceptre and hand of Justice, 3 fleur-de-lis in angles **Note:** Mint mark: &.

Date	Mintage	VG	F	VF	XF	Unc
1703	—	—	—	—	—	—
1706	—	20.00	45.00	85.00	200	—
1707	—	10.00	20.00	50.00	135	—

KM# 349.12 10 SOLS-1/8 ECU

3.2630 g., 0.7980 Silver 0.0837 oz. ASW **Ruler:** Louis XIV **Mint:** Rennes **Obverse:** Draped bust right **Reverse:** Crown above crossed sceptre and hand of Justice, 3 fleur-de-lis in angles **Note:** Mint mark: 9.

Date	Mintage	VG	F	VF	XF	Unc
1703	—	10.00	20.00	60.00	150	—
1704	—	10.00	20.00	50.00	135	—
1705	—	8.00	20.00	40.00	100	—
1706	—	8.00	20.00	40.00	100	—
1707	—	8.00	20.00	40.00	100	—
1708	—	—	—	—	—	—

KM# 349.7 10 SOLS-1/8 ECU

3.2630 g., 0.7980 Silver 0.0837 oz. ASW **Ruler:** Louis XIV **Mint:** Toulouse **Obverse:** Draped bust right **Reverse:** Crown above crossed sceptre and hand of Justice, 3 fleur-de-lis in angles

Date	Mintage	VG	F	VF	XF	Unc
1704M	—	10.00	22.00	50.00	135	—
1705M	—	—	—	—	—	—
1706M	—	—	—	—	—	—
1707M	—	—	—	—	—	—
1708M	—	—	—	—	—	—

KM# 348.1 10 SOLS-1/8 ECU

3.3920 g., 0.7980 Silver 0.0870 oz. ASW **Ruler:** Louis XIV **Mint:** Metz **Obverse:** Draped bust right **Reverse:** 4 crowns and 3 fleur-de-lis at center **Rev. Legend:** DOMINE • SALVVM • FAC • REGEM •

Date	Mintage	VG	F	VF	XF	Unc
1704AA	—	—	—	—	—	—
1705AA	—	10.00	20.00	50.00	145	—
1706AA	—	10.00	20.00	50.00	145	—
1707AA	—	10.00	20.00	50.00	145	—

KM# 349.9 10 SOLS-1/8 ECU

3.2630 g., 0.7980 Silver 0.0837 oz. ASW **Ruler:** Louis XIV **Mint:** Nantes **Obverse:** Draped bust right **Reverse:** Crown above crossed sceptre and hand of Justice, 3 fleur-de-lis in angles

Date	Mintage	VG	F	VF	XF	Unc
1705T	—	—	—	—	—	—
1706T	—	9.00	22.00	45.00	120	—
1707T	—	9.00	22.00	45.00	120	—

KM# 349.10 10 SOLS-1/8 ECU

3.2630 g., 0.7980 Silver 0.0837 oz. ASW **Ruler:** Louis XIV **Mint:** Troyes **Obverse:** Draped bust right **Reverse:** Crown above crossed sceptre and hand of Justice, 3 fleur-de-lis in angles

Date	Mintage	VG	F	VF	XF	Unc
1705V	—	—	—	—	—	—
1707V	—	15.00	35.00	65.00	160	—

KM# 349.11 10 SOLS-1/8 ECU

3.2630 g., 0.7980 Silver 0.0837 oz. ASW **Ruler:** Louis XIV **Mint:** Lille **Obverse:** Draped bust right **Reverse:** Crown above crossed sceptre and hand of Justice, 3 fleur-de-lis in angles

Date	Mintage	VG	F	VF	XF	Unc
1706W	—	20.00	45.00	85.00	200	—
1707W	—	—	—	—	—	—

KM# 349.8 10 SOLS-1/8 ECU

3.2630 g., 0.7980 Silver 0.0837 oz. ASW **Ruler:** Louis XIV **Mint:** Reims **Obverse:** Draped bust right **Reverse:** Crown above crossed sceptre and hand of Justice, 3 fleur-de-lis in angles

Date	Mintage	VG	F	VF	XF	Unc
1706S	—	—	—	—	—	—

KM# 349.6 10 SOLS-1/8 ECU

3.2630 g., 0.7980 Silver 0.0837 oz. ASW **Ruler:** Louis XIV **Mint:** Bayonne **Obverse:** Draped bust right **Reverse:** Crown above crossed sceptre and hand of Justice, 3 fleur-de-lis in angles

Date	Mintage	VG	F	VF	XF	Unc
1707L	—	9.00	22.00	45.00	120	—

KM# 349.14 10 SOLS-1/8 ECU

3.2630 g., 0.7980 Silver 0.0837 oz. ASW **Ruler:** Louis XIV **Mint:** Besancon **Obverse:** Draped bust right **Reverse:** Crown above crossed sceptre and hand of Justice, 3 fleur-de-lis in angles **Note:** Mint mark: Back to back C's.

Date	Mintage	VG	F	VF	XF	Unc
1707	—	—	—	—	—	—

KM# 375 10 SOLS-1/8 ECU

3.2630 g., 0.7980 Silver 0.0837 oz. ASW **Ruler:** Louis XIV **Mint:** Pau **Note:** Mint mark: Cow.

Date	Mintage	VG	F	VF	XF	Unc
1707	—	20.00	45.00	85.00	200	—

KM# 402 10 SOLS-1/8 ECU

3.0980 g., 0.7980 Silver 0.0795 oz. ASW **Ruler:** Louis XIV **Mint:** Strasbourg **Obverse:** Mailed bust right **Obv. Legend:** LVD • XIIII • D • G • FR • ET • NAV • REX • **Reverse:** Crowned shield of France dividing date **Rev. Legend:** ARGENTINENSIS MONETA NOVA

Date	Mintage	VG	F	VF	XF	Unc
1710BB	—	25.00	65.00	135	280	—
1711BB	—	30.00	75.00	150	350	—
1712BB	—	50.00	135	275	650	—

KM# 442 10 SOLS-1/8 ECU

2.0400 g., 0.9170 Silver 0.0601 oz. ASW **Ruler:** Louis XV **Mint:** Pau **Note:** Mint mark: Cow. Issued for Province of Bearn. Similar to KM#441.1 but obverse legend ends with ligate BD.

Date	Mintage	VG	F	VF	XF	Unc
1718	—	10.00	20.00	55.00	135	—

KM# 441.17 10 SOLS-1/8 ECU

2.0400 g., 0.9170 Silver 0.0601 oz. ASW **Ruler:** Louis XV **Mint:** Besancon **Obverse:** Laureate bust right **Reverse:** Crowned quartered arms divide value **Note:** Mint mark: Back to back C's.

Date	Mintage	VG	F	VF	XF	Unc
1719	—	5.00	10.00	35.00	75.00	—

KM# 441.16 10 SOLS-1/8 ECU

2.0400 g., 0.9170 Silver 0.0601 oz. ASW **Ruler:** Louis XV **Mint:** Rennes **Obverse:** Laureate bust right **Reverse:** Crowned quartered arms divide value **Note:** Mint mark: 9.

Date	Mintage	VG	F	VF	XF	Unc
1719	732,000	5.00	10.00	35.00	75.00	—

KM# 441.1 10 SOLS-1/8 ECU

2.0400 g., 0.9170 Silver 0.0601 oz. ASW **Ruler:** Louis XV **Mint:** Paris **Obverse:** Young bust of Louis XV right **Reverse:** Crowned arms of France and Navarre quartered divide value (X-S)

Date	Mintage	VG	F	VF	XF	Unc
1719A	—	5.00	10.00	30.00	60.00	—

KM# 441.2 10 SOLS-1/8 ECU

2.0400 g., 0.9170 Silver 0.0601 oz. ASW **Ruler:** Louis XV **Mint:** Metz

Date	Mintage	VG	F	VF	XF	Unc
1719AA	—	5.00	10.00	35.00	75.00	—

KM# 441.3 10 SOLS-1/8 ECU

2.0400 g., 0.9170 Silver 0.0601 oz. ASW **Ruler:** Louis XV **Mint:** Rouen

Date	Mintage	VG	F	VF	XF	Unc
1719B	560,000	5.00	10.00	35.00	75.00	—

KM# 441.4 10 SOLS-1/8 ECU

2.0400 g., 0.9170 Silver 0.0601 oz. ASW **Ruler:** Louis XV **Mint:** Caen

Date	Mintage	VG	F	VF	XF	Unc
1719C	167,000	5.00	10.00	35.00	75.00	—

KM# 441.5 10 SOLS-1/8 ECU

2.0400 g., 0.9170 Silver 0.0601 oz. ASW **Ruler:** Louis XV **Mint:** Lyon

Date	Mintage	VG	F	VF	XF	Unc
1719D	—	5.00	10.00	35.00	75.00	—

KM# 441.6 10 SOLS-1/8 ECU

2.0400 g., 0.9170 Silver 0.0601 oz. ASW **Ruler:** Louis XV **Mint:** Poitiers

Date	Mintage	VG	F	VF	XF	Unc
1719G	341,000	5.00	10.00	35.00	75.00	—

KM# 441.7 10 SOLS-1/8 ECU

2.0400 g., 0.9170 Silver 0.0601 oz. ASW **Ruler:** Louis XV **Mint:** La Rochelle

Date	Mintage	VG	F	VF	XF	Unc
1719H	117,000	5.00	10.00	35.00	75.00	—

KM# 441.8 10 SOLS-1/8 ECU

2.0400 g., 0.9170 Silver 0.0601 oz. ASW **Ruler:** Louis XV **Mint:** Montpellier

Date	Mintage	VG	F	VF	XF	Unc
1719N	—	10.00	20.00	50.00	110	—

KM# 441.9 10 SOLS-1/8 ECU

2.0400 g., 0.9170 Silver 0.0601 oz. ASW **Ruler:** Louis XV **Mint:** Riom

Date	Mintage	VG	F	VF	XF	Unc
1719O	—	8.00	18.00	45.00	100	—

KM# 441.10 10 SOLS-1/8 ECU

2.0400 g., 0.9170 Silver 0.0601 oz. ASW **Ruler:** Louis XV **Mint:** Dijon

Date	Mintage	VG	F	VF	XF	Unc
1719P	—	8.00	18.00	45.00	100	—

KM# 441.11 10 SOLS-1/8 ECU

2.0400 g., 0.9170 Silver 0.0601 oz. ASW **Ruler:** Louis XV **Mint:** Perpignan

Date	Mintage	VG	F	VF	XF	Unc
1719Q	—	10.00	20.00	50.00	110	—

KM# 441.12 10 SOLS-1/8 ECU

2.0400 g., 0.9170 Silver 0.0601 oz. ASW **Ruler:** Louis XV **Mint:** Orléans

Date	Mintage	VG	F	VF	XF	Unc
1719R	250,000	5.00	10.00	35.00	75.00	—

KM# 441.13 10 SOLS-1/8 ECU

2.0400 g., 0.9170 Silver 0.0601 oz. ASW **Ruler:** Louis XV **Mint:** Troyes

Date	Mintage	VG	F	VF	XF	Unc
1719V	390,000	5.00	10.00	35.00	75.00	—

KM# 441.14 10 SOLS-1/8 ECU

2.0400 g., 0.9170 Silver 0.0601 oz. ASW **Ruler:** Louis XV **Mint:** Lille **Obverse:** Laureate bust right **Obv. Legend:** LUD • XV • D • G • FR • ET • NA • REX • **Reverse:** Crowned quartered arms divide value **Rev. Legend:** SIT NOMEN DOMINI BENEDICTVM

Date	Mintage	VG	F	VF	XF	Unc
1719W	631,000	5.00	10.00	35.00	75.00	—

KM# 441.15 10 SOLS-1/8 ECU

2.0400 g., 0.9170 Silver 0.0601 oz. ASW **Ruler:** Louis XV **Mint:** Bourges **Obverse:** Laureate bust right **Reverse:** Crowned quartered arms divide value

Date	Mintage	VG	F	VF	XF	Unc
1719Y	528,000	8.00	12.00	40.00	80.00	—

KM# 418.1 12 SOLS (1/10 ECU)

3.0590 g., 0.9170 Silver 0.0902 oz. ASW **Ruler:** Louis XV **Mint:** Paris **Obverse:** Young bust of Louis XV right **Reverse:** Crowned circular arms

Date	Mintage	VG	F	VF	XF	Unc
1716A	—	5.00	10.00	30.00	90.00	—

KM# 418.2 12 SOLS (1/10 ECU)

3.0590 g., 0.9170 Silver 0.0902 oz. ASW **Ruler:** Louis XV **Mint:** Strasbourg **Obverse:** Young bust of Louis XV right **Reverse:** Crowned circular arms

Date	Mintage	VG	F	VF	XF	Unc
1716BB	1,299,000	5.00	10.00	30.00	90.00	—
1718BB	—	5.00	10.00	30.00	90.00	—

KM# 418.3 12 SOLS (1/10 ECU)

3.0590 g., 0.9170 Silver 0.0902 oz. ASW **Ruler:** Louis XV **Mint:** Caen **Obverse:** Young bust right **Reverse:** Crowned circular arms

Date	Mintage	VG	F	VF	XF	Unc
1716C	—	7.00	15.00	45.00	140	—

KM# 418.4 12 SOLS (1/10 ECU)

3.0590 g., 0.9170 Silver 0.0902 oz. ASW **Ruler:** Louis XV **Mint:** Lyon **Obverse:** Young bust of Louis XV right **Reverse:** Crowned circular arms

Date	Mintage	VG	F	VF	XF	Unc
1716D	531,000	6.00	13.00	40.00	120	—
1717D	91,000	7.00	15.00	45.00	140	—

KM# 418.5 12 SOLS (1/10 ECU)

3.0590 g., 0.9170 Silver 0.0902 oz. ASW **Ruler:** Louis XV **Mint:** Tours **Obverse:** Young bust of Louis XV right **Reverse:** Crowned circular arms

Date	Mintage	VG	F	VF	XF	Unc
1716E	—	7.00	15.00	45.00	140	—

KM# 418.6 12 SOLS (1/10 ECU)

3.0590 g., 0.9170 Silver 0.0902 oz. ASW **Ruler:** Louis XV **Mint:** Poitiers **Obverse:** Young bust of Louis XV right **Reverse:** Crowned circular arms

Date	Mintage	VG	F	VF	XF	Unc
1716G	—	8.00	18.00	45.00	140	—
1717G	99,000	8.00	18.00	45.00	140	—

KM# 418.7 12 SOLS (1/10 ECU)

3.0590 g., 0.9170 Silver 0.0902 oz. ASW **Ruler:** Louis XV **Mint:** La Rochelle **Obverse:** Young bust of Louis XV right **Reverse:** Crowned circular arms

Date	Mintage	VG	F	VF	XF	Unc
1716H	—	7.00	15.00	45.00	140	—

KM# 418.8 12 SOLS (1/10 ECU)

3.0590 g., 0.9170 Silver 0.0902 oz. ASW **Ruler:** Louis XV **Mint:** Limoges **Obverse:** Young bust of Louis XV right **Reverse:** Crowned circular arms

Date	Mintage	VG	F	VF	XF	Unc
1716I	—	7.00	15.00	45.00	140	—

KM# 418.9 12 SOLS (1/10 ECU)

3.0590 g., 0.9170 Silver 0.0902 oz. ASW **Ruler:** Louis XV **Mint:** Bordeaux **Obverse:** Young bust of Louis XV right **Reverse:** Crowned circular arms

Date	Mintage	VG	F	VF	XF	Unc
1716K	—	10.00	30.00	70.00	200	—

KM# 418.10 12 SOLS (1/10 ECU)

3.0590 g., 0.9170 Silver 0.0902 oz. ASW **Ruler:** Louis XV **Mint:** Toulouse **Obverse:** Young bust of Louis XV right **Reverse:** Crowned circular arms

Date	Mintage	VG	F	VF	XF	Unc
1716M	—	6.00	12.00	35.00	100	—
1717M	—	7.00	15.00	45.00	140	—

KM# 418.11 12 SOLS (1/10 ECU)

3.0590 g., 0.9170 Silver 0.0902 oz. ASW **Ruler:** Louis XV **Mint:** Montpellier **Obverse:** Young bust of Louis XV right **Reverse:** Crowned circular arms

Date	Mintage	VG	F	VF	XF	Unc
1716N	—	7.00	15.00	45.00	140	—

KM# 418.12 12 SOLS (1/10 ECU)

3.0590 g., 0.9170 Silver 0.0902 oz. ASW **Ruler:** Louis XV **Mint:** Dijon **Obverse:** Young bust of Louis XV right **Reverse:** Crowned circular arms

Date	Mintage	VG	F	VF	XF	Unc
1716P	—	5.00	10.00	30.00	90.00	—

KM# 418.20 12 SOLS (1/10 ECU)
3.0590 g., 0.9170 Silver 0.0902 oz. ASW **Ruler:** Louis XV **Mint:** Grenoble **Obverse:** Young bust of Louis XV right **Reverse:** Crowned circular arms

Date	Mintage	VG	F	VF	XF	Unc
1716Z	65,000	7.00	15.00	45.00	140	—

KM# 418.14 12 SOLS (1/10 ECU)
3.0590 g., 0.9170 Silver 0.0902 oz. ASW **Ruler:** Louis XV **Mint:** Reims **Obverse:** Young bust of Louis XV right **Reverse:** Crowned circular arms

Date	Mintage	VG	F	VF	XF	Unc
1716S	—	7.00	15.00	45.00	140	—

KM# 418.15 12 SOLS (1/10 ECU)
3.0590 g., 0.9170 Silver 0.0902 oz. ASW **Ruler:** Louis XV **Mint:** Nantes **Obverse:** Young bust of Louis XV right **Reverse:** Crowned circular arms

Date	Mintage	VG	F	VF	XF	Unc
1716T	—	7.00	15.00	45.00	140	—

KM# 418.16 12 SOLS (1/10 ECU)
3.0590 g., 0.9170 Silver 0.0902 oz. ASW **Ruler:** Louis XV **Mint:** Troyes **Obverse:** Young bust of Louis XV right **Reverse:** Crowned circular arms

Date	Mintage	VG	F	VF	XF	Unc
1716V	—	7.00	15.00	45.00	140	—

KM# 418.17 12 SOLS (1/10 ECU)
3.0590 g., 0.9170 Silver 0.0902 oz. ASW **Ruler:** Louis XV **Mint:** Lille **Obverse:** Young bust of Louis XV right **Reverse:** Crowned circular arms

Date	Mintage	VG	F	VF	XF	Unc
1716W	—	5.00	10.00	30.00	100	—
1717W	—	5.00	10.00	35.00	110	—
1718W	—	7.00	15.00	45.00	140	—

KM# 418.18 12 SOLS (1/10 ECU)
3.0590 g., 0.9170 Silver 0.0902 oz. ASW **Ruler:** Louis XV **Mint:** Amiens **Obverse:** Young bust of Louis XV right **Reverse:** Crowned circular arms

Date	Mintage	VG	F	VF	XF	Unc
1716X	—	7.00	15.00	45.00	140	—
1717X	—	7.00	15.00	45.00	140	—

KM# 418.22 12 SOLS (1/10 ECU)
3.0590 g., 0.9170 Silver 0.0902 oz. ASW **Ruler:** Louis XV **Mint:** Aix **Obverse:** Young bust of Louis XV right **Reverse:** Crowned circular arms **Note:** Mint mark: &.

Date	Mintage	VG	F	VF	XF	Unc
1716	—	5.00	10.00	30.00	90.00	—

KM# 418.21 12 SOLS (1/10 ECU)
3.0590 g., 0.9170 Silver 0.0902 oz. ASW **Ruler:** Louis XV **Mint:** Rennes **Obverse:** Young bust of Louis XV right **Reverse:** Crowned circular arms **Note:** Mint mark: 9.

Date	Mintage	VG	F	VF	XF	Unc
1716	—	7.00	15.00	45.00	140	—

KM# 418.23 12 SOLS (1/10 ECU)
3.0590 g., 0.9170 Silver 0.0902 oz. ASW **Ruler:** Louis XV **Mint:** Besancon **Obverse:** Young bust of Louis XV right **Reverse:** Crowned circular arms **Note:** Mint mark: Back to back C's.

Date	Mintage	VG	F	VF	XF	Unc
1716	—	10.00	30.00	70.00	200	—
1718	—	7.00	15.00	45.00	140	—

KM# 418.19 12 SOLS (1/10 ECU)
3.0590 g., 0.9170 Silver 0.0902 oz. ASW **Ruler:** Louis XV **Mint:** Bourges **Obverse:** Young bust of Louis XV right **Reverse:** Crowned circular arms

Date	Mintage	VG	F	VF	XF	Unc
1717Y	—	10.00	18.00	48.00	145	—

KM# 418.13 12 SOLS (1/10 ECU)
3.0590 g., 0.9170 Silver 0.0902 oz. ASW **Ruler:** Louis XV **Mint:** Perpignan **Obverse:** Young bust of Louis XV right **Obv. Legend:** LVD • XV • D • G • FR • ET • NAV • REX • **Reverse:** Crowned circular arms **Rev. Legend:** SIT NOMEN DOMINI BENEDICTVM

Date	Mintage	VG	F	VF	XF	Unc
1717Q	—	40.00	85.00	250	600	—

KM# 432.2 12 SOLS (1/10 ECU)
2.4470 g., 0.9170 Silver 0.0721 oz. ASW **Ruler:** Louis XV **Mint:** Metz

Date	Mintage	VG	F	VF	XF	Unc
1718AA	—	10.00	30.00	80.00	220	—

KM# 432.3 12 SOLS (1/10 ECU)
2.4470 g., 0.9170 Silver 0.0721 oz. ASW **Ruler:** Louis XV **Mint:** Strasbourg

Date	Mintage	VG	F	VF	XF	Unc
1718BB	—	9.00	22.00	48.00	125	—
1719BB	155,000	9.00	22.00	48.00	125	—

KM# 432.4 12 SOLS (1/10 ECU)
2.4470 g., 0.9170 Silver 0.0721 oz. ASW **Ruler:** Louis XV **Mint:** Lyon

Date	Mintage	VG	F	VF	XF	Unc
1718D	392,000	7.00	18.00	45.00	120	—

KM# 432.5 12 SOLS (1/10 ECU)
2.4470 g., 0.9170 Silver 0.0721 oz. ASW **Ruler:** Louis XV **Mint:** Montpellier

Date	Mintage	VG	F	VF	XF	Unc
1718N	—	10.00	30.00	85.00	220	—

KM# 432.6 12 SOLS (1/10 ECU)
2.4470 g., 0.9170 Silver 0.0721 oz. ASW **Ruler:** Louis XV **Mint:** Nantes

Date	Mintage	VG	F	VF	XF	Unc
1718T	—	8.00	25.00	65.00	180	—

KM# 432.7 12 SOLS (1/10 ECU)
2.4470 g., 0.9170 Silver 0.0721 oz. ASW **Ruler:** Louis XV **Mint:** Amiens

Date	Mintage	VG	F	VF	XF	Unc
1718X	—	15.00	45.00	120	275	—

KM# 432.8 12 SOLS (1/10 ECU)
2.4470 g., 0.9170 Silver 0.0721 oz. ASW **Ruler:** Louis XV **Mint:** Grenoble **Obverse:** Laureate bust right **Obv. Legend:** LVDXV • D • G • FR • ET • NAV • REX **Reverse:** Crowned quartered arms **Rev. Legend:** SIT • NOMEN • DOMINI • BENEDICTVM

Date	Mintage	VG	F	VF	XF	Unc
1718Z	99,000	8.00	25.00	65.00	180	—
1719Z	—	8.00	25.00	65.00	180	—

KM# 432.1 12 SOLS (1/10 ECU)
2.4470 g., 0.9170 Silver 0.0721 oz. ASW **Ruler:** Louis XV **Mint:** Paris **Note:** Issued for Navarre. Similar to 10 Sols, KM#441.1, but without value.

Date	Mintage	VG	F	VF	XF	Unc
1718A	—	10.00	30.00	80.00	220	—

KM# 431 12 SOLS (1/10 ECU)
3.0590 g., 0.9170 Silver 0.0902 oz. ASW **Ruler:** Louis XV **Mint:** Pau **Note:** Mint mark: Cow. Similar to KM#418.1 but obverse legend with ligate BD.

Date	Mintage	VG	F	VF	XF	Unc
1718	—	10.00	30.00	70.00	200	—

KM# 432.9 12 SOLS (1/10 ECU)
2.4470 g., 0.9170 Silver 0.0721 oz. ASW **Ruler:** Louis XV **Mint:** Rennes **Note:** Mint mark: 9.

Date	Mintage	VG	F	VF	XF	Unc
1719	21,000	10.00	30.00	80.00	220	—

KM# 481.25 12 SOLS (1/10 ECU)
2.9480 g., 0.9170 Silver 0.0869 oz. ASW **Ruler:** Louis XV **Mint:** Aix **Note:** Mint mark: &.

Date	Mintage	VG	F	VF	XF	Unc
1726	—	6.00	12.00	35.00	100	—
1729	148,000	6.00	12.00	35.00	100	—
1731	—	6.00	12.00	35.00	100	—

KM# 481.1 12 SOLS (1/10 ECU)
2.9480 g., 0.9170 Silver 0.0869 oz. ASW **Ruler:** Louis XV **Mint:** Paris **Obverse:** Young bust left **Obv. Legend:** LUD • XV • D • G • FR • ET NAV • REX • **Reverse:** Crowned oval arms within wreath **Rev. Legend:** SIT NOMEN DOMINI BENEDICTUM

Date	Mintage	VG	F	VF	XF	Unc
1726A	—	5.00	10.00	25.00	75.00	—
1728A	—	5.00	10.00	25.00	75.00	—
1729A	—	6.00	12.00	35.00	100	—
1730A	—	6.00	12.00	35.00	100	—
1731A	—	5.00	10.00	25.00	75.00	—
1732A	—	5.00	10.00	25.00	75.00	—
1733A	—	6.00	12.00	35.00	100	—
1734A	—	5.00	10.00	30.00	85.00	—

KM# 481.13 12 SOLS (1/10 ECU)
2.9480 g., 0.9170 Silver 0.0869 oz. ASW **Ruler:** Louis XV **Mint:** Toulouse **Obverse:** Young bust left **Reverse:** Crowned oval arms within wreath

Date	Mintage	VG	F	VF	XF	Unc
1726M	—	12.00	35.00	100	300	—
1730M	—	12.00	35.00	100	300	—
1740M	—	7.00	14.00	40.00	130	—

KM# 481.14 12 SOLS (1/10 ECU)
2.9480 g., 0.9170 Silver 0.0869 oz. ASW **Ruler:** Louis XV **Mint:** Montpellier **Obverse:** Young bust left **Reverse:** Crowned oval arms within wreath

Date	Mintage	VG	F	VF	XF	Unc
1726N	331,000	8.00	16.00	45.00	140	—
1727N	41,000	7.00	14.00	40.00	120	—
1730N	—	6.00	12.00	35.00	100	—
1740N	—	7.00	14.00	40.00	130	—

KM# 481.15 12 SOLS (1/10 ECU)
2.9480 g., 0.9170 Silver 0.0869 oz. ASW **Ruler:** Louis XV **Mint:** Dijon **Obverse:** Young bust left **Reverse:** Crowned oval arms within wreath

Date	Mintage	VG	F	VF	XF	Unc
1726P	—	10.00	30.00	85.00	225	—
1731P	—	6.00	12.00	35.00	100	—
1732P	—	8.00	18.00	55.00	160	—
1740P	—	10.00	30.00	85.00	225	—

KM# 481.16 12 SOLS (1/10 ECU)
2.9480 g., 0.9170 Silver 0.0869 oz. ASW **Ruler:** Louis XV **Mint:** Perpignan **Obverse:** Young bust left **Reverse:** Crowned oval arms within wreath

Date	Mintage	VG	F	VF	XF	Unc
1726Q	—	6.00	12.00	35.00	100	—
1728Q	—	12.00	35.00	100	300	—
1730Q	—	7.00	15.00	45.00	135	—
1740Q	—	15.00	40.00	125	400	—

KM# 481.17 12 SOLS (1/10 ECU)
2.9480 g., 0.9170 Silver 0.0869 oz. ASW **Ruler:** Louis XV **Mint:** Orléans **Obverse:** Young bust left **Reverse:** Crowned oval arms within wreath

Date	Mintage	VG	F	VF	XF	Unc
1726R	940,000	7.00	14.00	40.00	130	—

KM# 481.18 12 SOLS (1/10 ECU)
2.9480 g., 0.9170 Silver 0.0869 oz. ASW **Ruler:** Louis XV **Mint:** Reims **Obverse:** Young bust left **Reverse:** Crowned oval arms within wreath

Date	Mintage	VG	F	VF	XF	Unc
1726S	91,000	6.00	12.00	35.00	100	—
1728S	51,000	6.00	12.00	35.00	100	—
1731S	—	7.00	15.00	45.00	135	—

KM# 481.19 12 SOLS (1/10 ECU)
2.9480 g., 0.9170 Silver 0.0869 oz. ASW **Ruler:** Louis XV **Mint:** Nantes **Obverse:** Young bust left **Reverse:** Crowned oval arms within wreath

Date	Mintage	VG	F	VF	XF	Unc
1726T	—	5.00	10.00	25.00	75.00	—
1728T	—	5.00	10.00	25.00	75.00	—
1729T	—	6.00	12.00	35.00	100	—
1731T	—	6.00	12.00	35.00	100	—
1732T	—	6.00	12.00	35.00	100	—
1733T	—	6.00	12.00	35.00	100	—
1736T	—	6.00	12.00	35.00	100	—

KM# 481.20 12 SOLS (1/10 ECU)
2.9480 g., 0.9170 Silver 0.0869 oz. ASW **Ruler:** Louis XV **Mint:** Troyes **Obverse:** Young bust left **Reverse:** Crowned oval arms within wreath

Date	Mintage	VG	F	VF	XF	Unc
1726V	119,000	6.00	12.00	35.00	100	—

KM# 481.21 12 SOLS (1/10 ECU)
2.9480 g., 0.9170 Silver 0.0869 oz. ASW **Ruler:** Louis XV **Mint:** Lille **Obverse:** Young bust left **Reverse:** Crowned oval arms within wreath

Date	Mintage	VG	F	VF	XF	Unc
1726W	—	6.00	12.00	35.00	100	—
1729W	75,000	6.00	12.00	35.00	100	—

KM# 481.22 12 SOLS (1/10 ECU)
2.9480 g., 0.9170 Silver 0.0869 oz. ASW **Ruler:** Louis XV **Mint:** Bourges **Obverse:** Young bust left **Reverse:** Crowned oval arms within wreath

Date	Mintage	VG	F	VF	XF	Unc
1726Y	—	7.00	14.00	40.00	130	—
1727Y		7.00	14.00	40.00	130	

KM# 481.23 12 SOLS (1/10 ECU)
2.9480 g., 0.9170 Silver 0.0869 oz. ASW **Ruler:** Louis XV **Mint:** Grenoble **Obverse:** Young bust left **Reverse:** Crowned oval arms within wreath

Date	Mintage	VG	F	VF	XF	Unc
1726Z	47,000	7.00	14.00	40.00	130	—

KM# 481.6 12 SOLS (1/10 ECU)
2.9480 g., 0.9170 Silver 0.0869 oz. ASW **Ruler:** Louis XV **Mint:** Lyon **Obverse:** Young bust left **Reverse:** Crowned oval arms within wreath

Date	Mintage	VG	F	VF	XF	Unc
1726D	—	5.00	10.00	25.00	75.00	—
1727D	—	5.00	10.00	25.00	75.00	—
1728D	—	6.00	12.00	35.00	100	—
1730D	—	6.00	12.00	35.00	100	—
1738D	—	6.00	12.00	35.00	100	—

KM# 481.7 12 SOLS (1/10 ECU)
2.9480 g., 0.9170 Silver 0.0869 oz. ASW **Ruler:** Louis XV **Mint:** Tours **Obverse:** Young bust left **Reverse:** Crowned oval arms within wreath

Date	Mintage	VG	F	VF	XF	Unc
1726E	250,000	6.00	12.00	35.00	100	—
1727E	66,000	6.00	12.00	35.00	100	—

KM# 481.8 12 SOLS (1/10 ECU)
2.9480 g., 0.9170 Silver 0.0869 oz. ASW **Ruler:** Louis XV **Mint:** Poitiers **Obverse:** Young bust left **Reverse:** Crowned oval arms within wreath

Date	Mintage	VG	F	VF	XF	Unc
1726G	—	6.00	12.00	35.00	100	—
1727G	—	6.00	12.00	35.00	100	—
1731G	—	7.00	15.00	55.00	160	—

KM# 481.3 12 SOLS (1/10 ECU)
2.9480 g., 0.9170 Silver 0.0869 oz. ASW **Ruler:** Louis XV **Mint:** Rouen **Obverse:** Young bust left **Reverse:** Crowned oval arms within wreath

Date	Mintage	VG	F	VF	XF	Unc
1726B	—	5.00	10.00	25.00	75.00	—

KM# 481.4 12 SOLS (1/10 ECU)
2.9480 g., 0.9170 Silver 0.0869 oz. ASW **Ruler:** Louis XV **Mint:** Strasbourg **Obverse:** Young bust left **Reverse:** Crowned oval arms within wreath

Date	Mintage	VG	F	VF	XF	Unc
1726BB	—	5.00	10.00	25.00	75.00	—
1727BB	—	6.00	12.00	35.00	100	—

KM# 481.5 12 SOLS (1/10 ECU)
2.9480 g., 0.9170 Silver 0.0869 oz. ASW **Ruler:** Louis XV **Mint:** Caen **Obverse:** Young bust left **Reverse:** Crowned oval arms within wreath

Date	Mintage	VG	F	VF	XF	Unc
1727C	78,000	7.00	14.00	40.00	120	—

KM# 481.26 12 SOLS (1/10 ECU)
2.9480 g., 0.9170 Silver 0.0869 oz. ASW **Ruler:** Louis XV **Mint:** Besancon **Obverse:** Young bust left **Reverse:** Crowned oval arms within wreath **Note:** Mint mark: Back to back C's.

Date	Mintage	VG	F	VF	XF	Unc
1727	—	10.00	25.00	75.00	200	—
1728	—	6.00	12.00	35.00	100	—
1729	—	6.00	12.00	35.00	100	—
1730	—	6.00	12.00	35.00	100	—

KM# 481.2 12 SOLS (1/10 ECU)
2.9480 g., 0.9170 Silver 0.0869 oz. ASW **Ruler:** Louis XV **Mint:** Metz **Obverse:** Young bust left **Reverse:** Crowned oval arms within wreath

Date	Mintage	VG	F	VF	XF	Unc
1728AA	—	5.00	10.00	25.00	75.00	—
1729AA	—	6.00	12.00	35.00	100	—
1730AA	—	6.00	12.00	35.00	100	—

KM# 481.11 12 SOLS (1/10 ECU)
2.9480 g., 0.9170 Silver 0.0869 oz. ASW **Ruler:** Louis XV **Mint:** Bordeaux **Obverse:** Young bust left **Reverse:** Crowned oval arms within wreath

Date	Mintage	VG	F	VF	XF	Unc
1729K	—	6.00	12.00	35.00	100	—

KM# 481.24 12 SOLS (1/10 ECU)
2.9480 g., 0.9170 Silver 0.0869 oz. ASW **Ruler:** Louis XV **Mint:** Rennes **Obverse:** Young bust left **Reverse:** Crowned oval arms within wreath **Note:** Mint mark: 9.

Date	Mintage	VG	F	VF	XF	Unc
1729	—	6.00	12.00	35.00	100	—
1730	—	8.00	16.00	45.00	140	—
1731	—	8.00	16.00	45.00	140	—
1733	—	8.00	18.00	55.00	160	—

KM# 481.12 12 SOLS (1/10 ECU)
2.9480 g., 0.9170 Silver 0.0869 oz. ASW **Ruler:** Louis XV **Mint:** Bayonne **Obverse:** Young bust left **Reverse:** Crowned oval arms within wreath

Date	Mintage	VG	F	VF	XF	Unc
1730L	—	6.00	12.00	35.00	100	—

KM# 481.9 12 SOLS (1/10 ECU)
2.9480 g., 0.9170 Silver 0.0869 oz. ASW **Ruler:** Louis XV **Mint:** La Rochelle **Obverse:** Young bust left **Reverse:** Crowned oval arms within wreath

Date	Mintage	VG	F	VF	XF	Unc
1730H	—	6.00	12.00	35.00	100	—

KM# 481.10 12 SOLS (1/10 ECU)
2.9480 g., 0.9170 Silver 0.0869 oz. ASW **Ruler:** Louis XV **Mint:** Limoges **Obverse:** Young bust left **Reverse:** Crowned oval arms within wreath

Date	Mintage	VG	F	VF	XF	Unc
1730I	—	10.00	25.00	60.00	175	—

KM# 511.8 12 SOLS (1/10 ECU)
2.9480 g., 0.9170 Silver 0.0869 oz. ASW **Ruler:** Louis XV **Mint:** Poitiers

Date	Mintage	VG	F	VF	XF	Unc
1740G	190,000	5.00	9.00	25.00	70.00	—
1741G	59,000	6.00	11.00	30.00	80.00	—
1745G	—	7.00	13.00	38.00	95.00	—
1749G	163,000	5.00	9.00	25.00	70.00	—
1750G	103,000	5.00	9.00	25.00	70.00	—
1754G	—	6.00	11.00	30.00	80.00	—

KM# 511.9 12 SOLS (1/10 ECU)
2.9480 g., 0.9170 Silver 0.0869 oz. ASW **Ruler:** Louis XV **Mint:** La Rochelle

Date	Mintage	VG	F	VF	XF	Unc
1740H	—	7.00	13.00	35.00	100	—
1743H	12,000	8.00	15.00	40.00	120	—
1769H	—	7.00	13.00	35.00	100	—
1770H	—	7.00	13.00	35.00	100	—

KM# 511.14 12 SOLS (1/10 ECU)
2.9480 g., 0.9170 Silver 0.0869 oz. ASW **Ruler:** Louis XV **Mint:** Montpellier

Date	Mintage	VG	F	VF	XF	Unc
1740N	—	7.00	13.00	35.00	100	—
1741N	—	6.00	11.00	30.00	80.00	—
1745N	—	5.00	9.00	25.00	70.00	—
1746N	—	8.00	15.00	40.00	120	—
1748N	—	5.00	9.00	25.00	70.00	—
1753N	—	5.00	9.00	25.00	70.00	—
1759N	—	6.00	11.00	30.00	80.00	—
1761N	—	7.00	13.00	35.00	100	—
1763N	—	7.00	13.00	35.00	100	—
1764N	—	6.00	11.00	30.00	80.00	—
1765N	—	6.00	11.00	30.00	80.00	—
1766N	—	5.00	9.00	25.00	70.00	—
1768N	—	6.00	11.00	30.00	80.00	—
1769N	—	6.00	11.00	30.00	80.00	—

KM# 511.15 12 SOLS (1/10 ECU)
2.9480 g., 0.9170 Silver 0.0869 oz. ASW **Ruler:** Louis XV **Mint:** Riom

Date	Mintage	VG	F	VF	XF	Unc
1740O	18,000	7.00	13.00	35.00	100	—
1741O	—	6.00	11.00	30.00	80.00	—
1747O	—	5.00	9.00	25.00	70.00	—

KM# 511.6 12 SOLS (1/10 ECU)
2.9480 g., 0.9170 Silver 0.0869 oz. ASW **Ruler:** Louis XV **Mint:** Lyon

Date	Mintage	VG	F	VF	XF	Unc
1740D	87,000	5.00	9.00	25.00	70.00	—
1741D	101,000	5.00	9.00	25.00	70.00	—
1744D	48,000	6.00	11.00	30.00	80.00	—
1746D	113,000	5.00	9.00	25.00	70.00	—
1755D	—	7.00	13.00	35.00	100	—
1756D	—	5.00	9.00	25.00	70.00	—
1757D	—	5.00	9.00	25.00	70.00	—
1758D	—	6.00	11.00	30.00	80.00	—
1765D	—	5.00	9.00	25.00	70.00	—
1767D	—	5.00	9.00	25.00	70.00	—
1768D	—	5.00	9.00	25.00	70.00	—
1769D	—	8.00	15.00	40.00	120	—

KM# 511.18 12 SOLS (1/10 ECU)
2.9480 g., 0.9170 Silver 0.0869 oz. ASW **Ruler:** Louis XV **Mint:** Orléans

Date	Mintage	VG	F	VF	XF	Unc
1740R	31,000	7.00	13.00	35.00	100	—
1756R	8,190	9.00	17.00	55.00	145	—
1762R	—	6.00	11.00	30.00	80.00	—
1763R	—	6.00	11.00	30.00	85.00	—
1766R	—	7.00	13.00	35.00	100	—
1767R	—	9.00	17.00	55.00	145	—

KM# 511.1 12 SOLS (1/10 ECU)
2.9480 g., 0.9170 Silver 0.0869 oz. ASW **Ruler:** Louis XV **Mint:** Paris **Obverse:** Mature head with head band left **Obv. Legend:** LUD • XV • D • G • FR • ET NAV • REX **Reverse:** Crowned oval arms within wreath **Rev. Legend:** SIT NOMEN DOMINI BENEDICTUM

Date	Mintage	VG	F	VF	XF	Unc
1740A	91,000	5.00	9.00	25.00	70.00	—
1740A Proof	—	Value: 525				
1741A	—	5.00	9.00	25.00	70.00	—
1743A	125,000	5.00	9.00	25.00	70.00	—
1744A	447,000	5.00	9.00	25.00	70.00	—
1745A	519,000	5.00	9.00	25.00	70.00	—
1746A	456,000	5.00	9.00	25.00	70.00	—
1747A	435,000	5.00	9.00	25.00	70.00	—
1748A	315,000	5.00	9.00	25.00	70.00	—
1749A	350,000	5.00	9.00	25.00	70.00	—
1750A	—	5.00	9.00	25.00	70.00	—
1751A	—	5.00	9.00	25.00	70.00	—
1752A	—	5.00	9.00	25.00	70.00	—
1753A	—	7.00	13.00	35.00	100	—
1756A	145,000	5.00	9.00	25.00	70.00	—
1758A	—	5.00	9.00	25.00	70.00	—
1761A	—	6.00	11.00	30.00	80.00	—
1764A	—	6.00	11.00	30.00	80.00	—
1765A	—	5.00	9.00	25.00	70.00	—
1766A	—	5.00	9.00	25.00	70.00	—
1767A	—	5.00	9.00	25.00	70.00	—
1768A	—	5.00	9.00	25.00	70.00	—
1769A	—	5.00	9.00	25.00	70.00	—
1770A	—	5.00	9.00	25.00	70.00	—

KM# 511.27 12 SOLS (1/10 ECU)
2.9480 g., 0.9170 Silver 0.0869 oz. ASW **Ruler:** Louis XV **Mint:** Besancon **Obverse:** Mature head with headband left **Reverse:** Crowned oval arms within wreath **Note:** Mint mark: Back to back C's.

Date	Mintage	VG	F	VF	XF	Unc
1740	43,000	6.00	11.00	30.00	80.00	—
1743	—	6.00	11.00	30.00	80.00	—
1771	—	8.00	15.00	40.00	120	—

KM# 481.27 12 SOLS (1/10 ECU)
2.9480 g., 0.9170 Silver 0.0869 oz. ASW **Ruler:** Louis XV **Mint:** Pau **Note:** Mint mark: Cow.

Date	Mintage	VG	F	VF	XF	Unc
1740	—	35.00	100	285	650	—

KM# 511.25 12 SOLS (1/10 ECU)
2.9480 g., 0.9170 Silver 0.0869 oz. ASW **Ruler:** Louis XV **Mint:** Rennes **Obverse:** Mature head with headband left **Reverse:** Crowned oval arms within wreath **Note:** Mint mark: 9.

Date	Mintage	VG	F	VF	XF	Unc
1741	196,000	5.00	9.00	25.00	70.00	—

KM# 511.26 12 SOLS (1/10 ECU)
2.9480 g., 0.9170 Silver 0.0869 oz. ASW **Ruler:** Louis XV **Mint:** Aix **Obverse:** Mature head with headband left **Reverse:** Crowned oval arms within wreath **Note:** Mint mark: &.

Date	Mintage	VG	F	VF	XF	Unc
1741	—	6.00	11.00	30.00	80.00	—
1750	—	8.00	15.00	40.00	120	—
1755	—	6.00	11.00	30.00	80.00	—

Date	Mintage	VG	F	VF	XF	Unc
1760	—	7.00	13.00	35.00	100	—
1764	—	6.00	11.00	30.00	80.00	—
1765	—	6.00	11.00	30.00	80.00	—

KM# 511.20 12 SOLS (1/10 ECU)
2.9480 g., 0.9170 Silver 0.0869 oz. ASW **Ruler:** Louis XV **Mint:** Nantes **Obverse:** Mature head with headband left **Reverse:** Crowned oval arms within wreath

Date	Mintage	VG	F	VF	XF	Unc
1741T	—	5.00	9.00	25.00	70.00	—
1743T	25,000	7.00	13.00	35.00	100	—
1745T	21,000	7.00	13.00	35.00	100	—
1746T	68,000	6.00	11.00	30.00	80.00	—
1764T	—	6.00	11.00	30.00	80.00	—

KM# 511.2 12 SOLS (1/10 ECU)
2.9480 g., 0.9170 Silver 0.0869 oz. ASW **Ruler:** Louis XV **Mint:** Metz **Obverse:** Mature head with headband left **Reverse:** Crowned oval arms within wreath

Date	Mintage	VG	F	VF	XF	Unc
1741AA	—	5.00	9.00	25.00	70.00	—
1748AA	—	5.00	9.00	25.00	70.00	—
1749AA	—	6.00	11.00	30.00	80.00	—
1750AA	—	7.00	13.00	35.00	100	—
1769AA	—	5.00	9.00	25.00	70.00	—

KM# 511.3 12 SOLS (1/10 ECU)
2.9480 g., 0.9170 Silver 0.0869 oz. ASW **Ruler:** Louis XV **Mint:** Rouen **Obverse:** Mature head with headband left **Reverse:** Crowned oval arms within wreath

Date	Mintage	VG	F	VF	XF	Unc
1741B	—	5.00	9.00	25.00	70.00	—
1742B	102,000	6.00	11.00	30.00	80.00	—

KM# 511.4 12 SOLS (1/10 ECU)
2.9480 g., 0.9170 Silver 0.0869 oz. ASW **Ruler:** Louis XV **Mint:** Strasbourg **Obverse:** Mature head with headband left **Reverse:** Crowned oval arms within wreath

Date	Mintage	VG	F	VF	XF	Unc
1741BB	—	5.00	9.00	25.00	70.00	—

KM# 511.5 12 SOLS (1/10 ECU)
2.9480 g., 0.9170 Silver 0.0869 oz. ASW **Ruler:** Louis XV **Mint:** Caen **Obverse:** Mature head with headband left **Reverse:** Crowned oval arms within wreath

Date	Mintage	VG	F	VF	XF	Unc
1741C	126,000	5.00	9.00	25.00	70.00	—
1743C	211,000	5.00	9.00	25.00	70.00	—

KM# 511.7 12 SOLS (1/10 ECU)
2.9480 g., 0.9170 Silver 0.0869 oz. ASW **Ruler:** Louis XV **Mint:** Tours **Obverse:** Mature head with headband left **Reverse:** Crowned oval arms within wreath

Date	Mintage	VG	F	VF	XF	Unc
1741E	—	7.00	13.00	38.00	95.00	—

KM# 511.16 12 SOLS (1/10 ECU)
2.9480 g., 0.9170 Silver 0.0869 oz. ASW **Ruler:** Louis XV **Mint:** Dijon **Obverse:** Mature head with headband left **Reverse:** Crowned oval arms within wreath

Date	Mintage	VG	F	VF	XF	Unc
1741P	—	5.00	9.00	25.00	70.00	—
1743P	15,000	7.00	13.00	35.00	100	—
1744P	28,000	7.00	13.00	35.00	100	—
1746P	20,000	7.00	13.00	35.00	100	—
1747P	36,000	7.00	13.00	35.00	100	—
1748P	48,000	6.00	11.00	30.00	80.00	—
1750P	12,000	8.00	15.00	40.00	120	—
1753P	13,000	8.00	15.00	40.00	120	—
1756P	26,000	7.00	13.00	35.00	100	—
1758P	—	6.00	11.00	30.00	80.00	—
1764P	—	8.00	15.00	40.00	120	—

KM# 511.23 12 SOLS (1/10 ECU)
2.9480 g., 0.9170 Silver 0.0869 oz. ASW **Ruler:** Louis XV **Mint:** Amiens **Obverse:** Mature head with headband left **Reverse:** Crowned oval arms within wreath

Date	Mintage	VG	F	VF	XF	Unc
1741X	—	5.00	9.00	25.00	70.00	—

KM# 511.10 12 SOLS (1/10 ECU)
2.9480 g., 0.9170 Silver 0.0869 oz. ASW **Ruler:** Louis XV **Mint:** Limoges **Obverse:** Mature head with headband left **Reverse:** Crowned oval arms within wreath

Date	Mintage	VG	F	VF	XF	Unc
1741I	—	6.00	11.00	30.00	80.00	—

KM# 511.11 12 SOLS (1/10 ECU)
2.9480 g., 0.9170 Silver 0.0869 oz. ASW **Ruler:** Louis XV **Mint:** Bordeaux **Obverse:** Mature head with headband left **Reverse:** Crowned oval arms within wreath

Date	Mintage	VG	F	VF	XF	Unc
1741K	—	5.00	9.00	25.00	70.00	—

KM# 511.12 12 SOLS (1/10 ECU)
2.9480 g., 0.9170 Silver 0.0869 oz. ASW **Ruler:** Louis XV **Mint:** Bayonne **Obverse:** Mature head with headband left **Reverse:** Crowned oval arms within wreath

Date	Mintage	VG	F	VF	XF	Unc
1741L	—	7.00	11.00	30.00	80.00	—
1750L	—	5.00	9.00	25.00	70.00	—
1766L	—	5.00	9.00	25.00	70.00	—
1769L	—	5.00	9.00	25.00	70.00	—

KM# 511.13 12 SOLS (1/10 ECU)
2.9480 g., 0.9170 Silver 0.0869 oz. ASW **Ruler:** Louis XV **Mint:** Toulouse **Obverse:** Mature head with headband left **Reverse:** Crowned oval arms within wreath

Date	Mintage	VG	F	VF	XF	Unc
1741M	143,000	5.00	9.00	25.00	70.00	—

Date	Mintage	VG	F	VF	XF	Unc
1745M	42,000	6.00	11.00	30.00	80.00	—
1747M	38,000	7.00	13.00	35.00	100	—
1754M	36,000	7.00	13.00	35.00	100	—
1759M	—	5.00	9.00	25.00	70.00	—
1760M	—	5.00	9.00	25.00	70.00	—
1764M	—	6.00	11.00	30.00	80.00	—
1767M	—	6.00	11.00	30.00	80.00	—
1769M	—	5.00	9.00	25.00	70.00	—

KM# 520 12 SOLS (1/10 ECU)

2.9480 g., 0.9170 Silver 0.0869 oz. ASW **Ruler:** Louis XV **Mint:** Pau **Obverse:** Head with headband left **Obv. Legend:** LUD • XV • D • G • FR • ET NA • .. **Reverse:** Crowned oval arms within wreath **Rev. Legend:** SIT NOMEN DOMINI BENEDICTUM **Note:** Mint mark: Cow. Issued for Province of Bearn. Similar to KM#511.1 but obverse legend ends with ligate BD.

Date	Mintage	VG	F	VF	XF	Unc
1743	46,000	7.00	13.00	35.00	100	—
1746	44,000	7.00	13.00	35.00	100	—
1756	24,000	9.00	17.00	45.00	135	—
1760	33,000	7.00	13.00	35.00	100	—
1764	24,000	8.00	15.00	40.00	120	—
1767	25,000	8.00	15.00	40.00	120	—

KM# 511.22 12 SOLS (1/10 ECU)

2.9480 g., 0.9170 Silver 0.0869 oz. ASW **Ruler:** Louis XV **Mint:** Lille **Obverse:** Mature head with headband left **Reverse:** Crowned oval arms within wreath

Date	Mintage	VG	F	VF	XF	Unc
1743W	28,000	7.00	13.00	35.00	100	—
1746W	64,000	6.00	11.00	30.00	80.00	—
1747W	89,000	6.00	11.00	30.00	80.00	—
1748W	75,000	6.00	11.00	30.00	80.00	—
1749W	32,000	7.00	13.00	35.00	100	—
1750W	71,000	5.00	9.00	25.00	70.00	—
1753W	30,000	7.00	13.00	35.00	100	—
1758W	—	5.00	9.00	25.00	70.00	—

KM# 511.17 12 SOLS (1/10 ECU)

2.9480 g., 0.9170 Silver 0.0869 oz. ASW **Ruler:** Louis XV **Mint:** Perpignan **Obverse:** Mature head with headband left **Reverse:** Crowned oval arms within wreath

Date	Mintage	VG	F	VF	XF	Unc
1744Q	—	5.00	9.00	25.00	70.00	—
1771Q	—	8.00	15.00	40.00	120	—

KM# 511.24 12 SOLS (1/10 ECU)

2.9480 g., 0.9170 Silver 0.0869 oz. ASW **Ruler:** Louis XV **Mint:** Grenoble **Obverse:** Mature head with headband left **Reverse:** Crowned oval arms within wreath

Date	Mintage	VG	F	VF	XF	Unc
1747Z	29,000	7.00	13.00	35.00	100	—
1749Z	—	10.00	25.00	65.00	185	—
1754Z	18,000	8.00	15.00	40.00	120	—
1756Z	38,000	7.00	13.00	35.00	100	—
1759Z	18,000	—	—	—	—	—
1762Z	12,000	8.00	15.00	40.00	120	—

KM# 511.19 12 SOLS (1/10 ECU)

2.9480 g., 0.9170 Silver 0.0869 oz. ASW **Ruler:** Louis XV **Mint:** Reims **Obverse:** Mature head with headband left **Reverse:** Crowned oval arms within wreath

Date	Mintage	VG	F	VF	XF	Unc
1748S	40,000	6.00	11.00	30.00	80.00	—
1761S	—	6.00	11.00	30.00	80.00	—
1764S	—	6.00	11.00	30.00	80.00	—
1767S	—	7.00	13.00	35.00	100	—

KM# 511.21 12 SOLS (1/10 ECU)

2.9480 g., 0.9170 Silver 0.0869 oz. ASW **Ruler:** Louis XV **Mint:** Troyes **Obverse:** Mature head with headband left **Reverse:** Crowned oval arms within wreath

Date	Mintage	VG	F	VF	XF	Unc
1757V	—	6.00	11.00	30.00	80.00	—

KM# 550.1 12 SOLS (1/10 ECU)

2.9480 g., 0.9170 Silver 0.0869 oz. ASW **Ruler:** Louis XV **Mint:** Paris **Obverse:** Laureate head left **Obv. Legend:** LUD XV D G FR ET NAV REX **Reverse:** Crowned oval arms within oak leaf wreath **Rev. Legend:** SIT NOMEN DOMINI BENEDICTUM •

Date	Mintage	VG	F	VF	XF	Unc
1770/69A	—	10.00	30.00	90.00	230	—
1771A	—	10.00	30.00	85.00	210	—
1772A	—	10.00	30.00	85.00	210	—
1773A	—	10.00	30.00	85.00	210	—

KM# 550.4 12 SOLS (1/10 ECU)

2.9480 g., 0.9170 Silver 0.0869 oz. ASW **Ruler:** Louis XV **Mint:** Limoges **Obverse:** Laureate head left **Reverse:** Crowned oval arms within oak leaf wreath

Date	Mintage	VG	F	VF	XF	Unc
1772I	—	10.00	30.00	90.00	230	—
1773I	—	10.00	30.00	85.00	210	—

KM# 550.5 12 SOLS (1/10 ECU)

2.9480 g., 0.9170 Silver 0.0869 oz. ASW **Ruler:** Louis XV **Mint:** Bayonne **Obverse:** Laureate head left **Reverse:** Crowned oval arms within oak leaf wreath

Date	Mintage	VG	F	VF	XF	Unc
1772L	—	10.00	30.00	90.00	230	—

KM# 550.6 12 SOLS (1/10 ECU)

2.9480 g., 0.9170 Silver 0.0869 oz. ASW **Ruler:** Louis XV **Mint:** Perpignan **Obverse:** Laureate head left **Reverse:** Crowned oval arms within oak leaf wreath

Date	Mintage	VG	F	VF	XF	Unc
1772Q	—	10.00	30.00	90.00	230	—

KM# 550.2 12 SOLS (1/10 ECU)

2.9480 g., 0.9170 Silver 0.0869 oz. ASW **Ruler:** Louis XV **Mint:** Metz **Obverse:** Laureate head left **Reverse:** Crowned oval arms within oak leaf wreath

Date	Mintage	VG	F	VF	XF	Unc
1773AA	—	12.00	40.00	100	260	—

KM# 550.3 12 SOLS (1/10 ECU)

2.9480 g., 0.9170 Silver 0.0869 oz. ASW **Ruler:** Louis XV **Mint:** Strasbourg **Obverse:** Laureate head left **Reverse:** Crowned oval arms within oak leaf wreath

Date	Mintage	VG	F	VF	XF	Unc
1773BB	—	10.00	30.00	90.00	230	—

KM# 550.7 12 SOLS (1/10 ECU)

2.9480 g., 0.9170 Silver 0.0869 oz. ASW **Ruler:** Louis XV **Mint:** Pau **Obverse:** Laureate head left **Reverse:** Crowned oval arms within oak leaf wreath **Note:** Mint mark: Cow.

Date	Mintage	VG	F	VF	XF	Unc
1773	—	12.00	40.00	100	250	—

KM# 568.9 12 SOLS (1/10 ECU)

2.9480 g., 0.9170 Silver 0.0869 oz. ASW **Ruler:** Louis XVI **Mint:** Montpellier **Obverse:** Bust left **Reverse:** Crowned arms of France within branches

Date	Mintage	VG	F	VF	XF	Unc
1775N	19,000	8.00	20.00	55.00	140	—
1777N	36,000	5.00	15.00	40.00	100	—
1782N	16,000	5.00	15.00	40.00	100	—
1788N	13,000	5.00	15.00	40.00	100	—
1789N	—	5.00	15.00	40.00	100	—

KM# 568.5 12 SOLS (1/10 ECU)

2.9480 g., 0.9170 Silver 0.0869 oz. ASW **Ruler:** Louis XVI **Mint:** Limoges **Obverse:** Bust left **Reverse:** Crowned arms of France within branches

Date	Mintage	VG	F	VF	XF	Unc
1775I	42,000	5.00	15.00	40.00	100	—
1778I	124,000	4.00	10.00	25.00	70.00	—
1779I	57,000	8.00	20.00	55.00	140	—
1780I	115,000	8.00	20.00	55.00	140	—
1781I	32,000	10.00	25.00	60.00	150	—
1784I	70,000	4.00	10.00	25.00	70.00	—
1785I	50,000	4.00	12.00	35.00	80.00	—
1788I	32,000	5.00	15.00	40.00	100	—

KM# 568.12 12 SOLS (1/10 ECU)

2.9480 g., 0.9170 Silver 0.0869 oz. ASW **Ruler:** Louis XVI **Mint:** Aix **Obverse:** Bust left **Reverse:** Crowned arms of France within branches **Note:** Mint mark: &. The "dot" appears below the third letters of the monarch's name and denotes second semester coinage.

Date	Mintage	VG	F	VF	XF	Unc
1775	14,000	—	—	—	—	—
1776	7,934	—	—	—	—	—

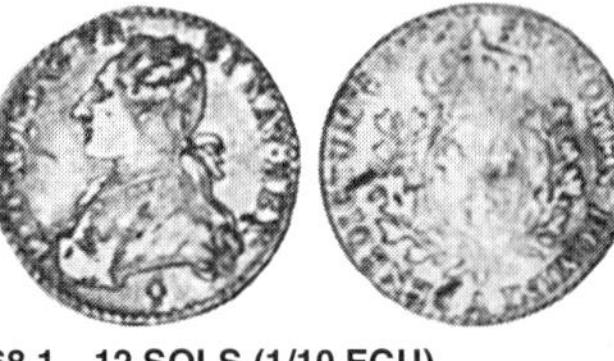

KM# 568.1 12 SOLS (1/10 ECU)

2.9480 g., 0.9170 Silver 0.0869 oz. ASW **Ruler:** Louis XVI **Mint:** Paris **Obverse:** Bust left **Obv. Legend:** LUD • XVI • D • G • FR • ETNAV • REX • **Reverse:** Crowned arms of France within branches **Rev. Legend:** SIT NOMEN DOMINI BENEDICTUM

Date	Mintage	VG	F	VF	XF	Unc
1775A	16,000	5.00	15.00	40.00	110	—
1776A	35,000	5.00	15.00	40.00	110	—
1777A	12,000	5.00	15.00	40.00	110	—
1778/7A	111,000	4.00	10.00	25.00	70.00	—
1778A	Inc. above	4.00	10.00	25.00	70.00	—
1778A	Inc. above	4.00	10.00	25.00	70.00	—
1779A	111,000	4.00	10.00	25.00	70.00	—
1780A	33,000	5.00	15.00	40.00	110	—
1780A	Inc. above	5.00	15.00	40.00	110	—
1781A	33,000	5.00	15.00	40.00	110	—
1782A	117,000	4.00	10.00	25.00	70.00	—
1783A	70,000	4.00	12.00	35.00	85.00	—
1784A	47,000	4.00	12.00	35.00	85.00	—
1784A LVD. XV (error)	—	8.00	20.00	55.00	150	—
1785A	90,000	4.00	10.00	25.00	70.00	—
1785/4A LVD. XV (error)	—	8.00	20.00	55.00	150	—
1786A	—	4.00	10.00	25.00	70.00	—
1786A LVD. XV (error)	—	8.00	20.00	65.00	175	—
1787A	—	—	—	—	—	—
Note: Reported, not confirmed						
1788A	—	—	—	—	—	—
Note: Reported, not confirmed						
1789A	—	4.00	10.00	30.00	85.00	—
1790A	—	—	—	—	—	—
Note: Reported, not confirmed						

KM# 568.6 12 SOLS (1/10 ECU)

2.9480 g., 0.9170 Silver 0.0869 oz. ASW **Ruler:** Louis XVI **Mint:** Bayonne **Obverse:** Bust left **Reverse:** Crowned arms of France within branches

Date	Mintage	VG	F	VF	XF	Unc
1777L	29,000	8.00	20.00	55.00	140	—
1780L	14,000	8.00	20.00	55.00	140	—
1783L	16,000	5.00	15.00	40.00	100	—
1790L	—	5.00	15.00	40.00	100	—

KM# 568.10 12 SOLS (1/10 ECU)

2.9480 g., 0.9170 Silver 0.0869 oz. ASW **Ruler:** Louis XVI **Mint:** Perpignan **Obverse:** Bust left **Reverse:** Crowned arms of France within branches

Date	Mintage	VG	F	VF	XF	Unc
1777Q	22,000	8.00	20.00	55.00	140	—
1779Q	35,000	5.00	15.00	40.00	100	—
1780Q	28,000	5.00	15.00	40.00	100	—
1785Q	20,000	5.00	15.00	40.00	100	—
1786Q	26,000	5.00	15.00	40.00	100	—

KM# 576 12 SOLS (1/10 ECU)

2.9480 g., 0.9170 Silver 0.0869 oz. ASW **Ruler:** Louis XVI **Mint:** Pau **Obv. Legend:** ....RE.BD (ligate BD). **Note:** Mint mark: Cow. Issued for Province of Bearn.

Date	Mintage	VG	F	VF	XF	Unc
1777	12,000	12.00	25.00	75.00	175	—

KM# 568.7 12 SOLS (1/10 ECU)

2.9480 g., 0.9170 Silver 0.0869 oz. ASW **Ruler:** Louis XVI **Mint:** Toulouse **Obverse:** Bust left **Reverse:** Crowned arms of France within branches

Date	Mintage	VG	F	VF	XF	Unc
1778M	25,000	5.00	15.00	40.00	100	—
1779M	51,000	4.00	10.00	25.00	75.00	—
1789M	200,000	3.00	6.00	20.00	60.00	—

KM# 568.2 12 SOLS (1/10 ECU)

2.9480 g., 0.9170 Silver 0.0869 oz. ASW **Ruler:** Louis XVI **Mint:** Metz **Obverse:** Bust left **Reverse:** Crowned arms of France within branches

Date	Mintage	VG	F	VF	XF	Unc
1779AA	40,000	5.00	15.00	40.00	100	—
1782AA	15,000	5.00	15.00	40.00	100	—
1784AA	38,000	5.00	15.00	40.00	100	—

KM# 568.3 12 SOLS (1/10 ECU)

2.9480 g., 0.9170 Silver 0.0869 oz. ASW **Ruler:** Louis XVI **Mint:** Lyon **Obverse:** Bust left **Reverse:** Crowned arms of France within branches

Date	Mintage	VG	F	VF	XF	Unc
1780D	38,000	5.00	15.00	40.00	100	—
1787D	17,000	5.00	15.00	40.00	100	—
1788D	—	5.00	15.00	40.00	100	—

KM# 568.11 12 SOLS (1/10 ECU)

2.9480 g., 0.9170 Silver 0.0869 oz. ASW **Ruler:** Louis XVI **Mint:** Orléans **Obverse:** Bust left **Reverse:** Crowned arms of France within branches

Date	Mintage	VG	F	VF	XF	Unc
1784R	13,000	5.00	15.00	40.00	100	—
1786R	21,000	5.00	15.00	40.00	100	—
1787R	375,000	3.00	6.00	20.00	60.00	—

KM# 568.8 12 SOLS (1/10 ECU)

2.9480 g., 0.9170 Silver 0.0869 oz. ASW **Ruler:** Louis XVI **Mint:** Marseille **Obverse:** Bust left **Reverse:** Crowned arms of France within branches

Date	Mintage	VG	F	VF	XF	Unc
1788MA	92,000	4.00	12.00	35.00	80.00	—

KM# 568.4 12 SOLS (1/10 ECU)

2.9480 g., 0.9170 Silver 0.0869 oz. ASW **Ruler:** Louis XVI **Mint:** La Rochelle **Obverse:** Bust left **Reverse:** Crowned arms of France within branches

Date	Mintage	VG	F	VF	XF	Unc
1788H	11,000	9.00	20.00	50.00	125	—

KM# 475.4 15 SOLS (1/8 ECU)

2.9480 g., 0.9170 Silver 0.0869 oz. ASW **Ruler:** Louis XV **Mint:** Tours

Date	Mintage	VG	F	VF	XF	Unc
1725E	8,066	50.00	100	320	700	—

KM# 475.5 15 SOLS (1/8 ECU)

2.9480 g., 0.9170 Silver 0.0869 oz. ASW **Ruler:** Louis XV **Mint:** Montpellier

Date	Mintage	VG	F	VF	XF	Unc
1725N	261,000	25.00	70.00	200	450	—

KM# 475.6 15 SOLS (1/8 ECU)

2.9480 g., 0.9170 Silver 0.0869 oz. ASW **Ruler:** Louis XV **Mint:** Reims

Date	Mintage	VG	F	VF	XF	Unc
1725S	—	30.00	80.00	225	550	—

KM# 475.7 15 SOLS (1/8 ECU)

2.9480 g., 0.9170 Silver 0.0869 oz. ASW **Ruler:** Louis XV **Mint:** Troyes

Date	Mintage	VG	F	VF	XF	Unc
1725V	21,000	30.00	80.00	225	550	—

KM# 475.1 15 SOLS (1/8 ECU)

2.9480 g., 0.9170 Silver 0.0869 oz. ASW **Ruler:** Louis XV **Mint:** Paris **Obverse:** Laureate armored bust right **Obv. Legend:** LUD • XV • D • G • FR • ET NAV • REX • **Reverse:** 4 Fleur-de-lis form square at center, 4 crowns divided by back to back L's surround **Rev. Legend:** SIT NOMEN DOMINI BENEDICT • 1723 *

Date	Mintage	VG	F	VF	XF	Unc
1725A	—	25.00	70.00	200	450	—

KM# 475.2 15 SOLS (1/8 ECU)

2.9480 g., 0.9170 Silver 0.0869 oz. ASW **Ruler:** Louis XV **Mint:** Strasbourg **Obverse:** Laureate armored bust right **Reverse:** 4 Fleur-de-lis form square at center, 4 crowns divided by back to back L's surround

Date	Mintage	VG	F	VF	XF	Unc
1725BB	—	25.00	70.00	200	450	—

KM# 475.3 15 SOLS (1/8 ECU)

2.9480 g., 0.9170 Silver 0.0869 oz. ASW **Ruler:** Louis XV **Mint:** Caen **Obverse:** Laureate armored bust right **Reverse:** 4 Fleur-de-lis form square at center, 4 crowns divided by back to back L's surround

Date	Mintage	VG	F	VF	XF	Unc
1725C	14,000	30.00	80.00	225	550	—

KM# 475.8 15 SOLS (1/8 ECU)

2.9480 g., 0.9170 Silver 0.0869 oz. ASW **Ruler:** Louis XV **Mint:** Aix **Note:** Mint mark: &.

Date	Mintage	VG	F	VF	XF	Unc
1725	—	30.00	80.00	225	550	—

KM# 475.9 15 SOLS (1/8 ECU)

2.9480 g., 0.9170 Silver 0.0869 oz. ASW **Ruler:** Louis XV **Mint:** Besancon **Note:** Mint mark: Back to back C's.

Date	Mintage	VG	F	VF	XF	Unc
1725	—	30.00	80.00	225	550	—

KM# 604.1 15 SOLS (1/8 ECU)

5.0000 g., 0.6660 Silver 0.1071 oz. ASW **Mint:** Paris **Obverse:** Head of Louis XVI left **Obv. Legend:** LOUIS XVI ROI DES FRANCOIS **Reverse:** Standing Genius writing the Constitution **Rev. Legend:** REGNE DE LALOI •

Date	Mintage	VG	F	VF	XF	Unc
1791A	494,000	6.00	18.00	50.00	140	—
1792A	—	6.00	18.00	50.00	140	—

KM# 605.1 15 SOLS (1/8 ECU)

5.0000 g., 0.6660 Silver 0.1071 oz. ASW **Mint:** Metz **Obverse:** Legend ends: ...FRANCAIS

Date	Mintage	VG	F	VF	XF	Unc
1791AA	206,000	15.00	40.00	100	300	—

KM# 440.5 20 SOLS (1/6 ECU)

4.0790 g., 0.9170 Silver 0.1203 oz. ASW **Ruler:** Louis XV **Mint:** Caen

Date	Mintage	VG	F	VF	XF	Unc
1719C	418,000	12.00	25.00	45.00	135	—
1720C	997,000	10.00	20.00	35.00	100	—

KM# 440.6 20 SOLS (1/6 ECU)

4.0790 g., 0.9170 Silver 0.1203 oz. ASW **Ruler:** Louis XV **Mint:** Lyon

Date	Mintage	VG	F	VF	XF	Unc
1719D	—	10.00	20.00	35.00	100	—
1720D	—	10.00	20.00	35.00	100	—

KM# 440.7 20 SOLS (1/6 ECU)

4.0790 g., 0.9170 Silver 0.1203 oz. ASW **Ruler:** Louis XV **Mint:** Tours

Date	Mintage	VG	F	VF	XF	Unc
1719E	—	10.00	20.00	35.00	100	—
1720E	426,000	10.00	20.00	35.00	100	—

KM# 440.8 20 SOLS (1/6 ECU)

4.0790 g., 0.9170 Silver 0.1203 oz. ASW **Ruler:** Louis XV **Mint:** Poitiers

Date	Mintage	VG	F	VF	XF	Unc
1719G	586,000	10.00	20.00	35.00	100	—

KM# 440.9 20 SOLS (1/6 ECU)

4.0790 g., 0.9170 Silver 0.1203 oz. ASW **Ruler:** Louis XV **Mint:** La Rochelle

Date	Mintage	VG	F	VF	XF	Unc
1719H	—	10.00	20.00	35.00	110	—
1720H	736,000	10.00	20.00	35.00	100	—

KM# 440.10 20 SOLS (1/6 ECU)

4.0790 g., 0.9170 Silver 0.1203 oz. ASW **Ruler:** Louis XV **Mint:** Limoges

Date	Mintage	VG	F	VF	XF	Unc
1719I	—	20.00	60.00	150	375	—

KM# 440.11 20 SOLS (1/6 ECU)

4.0790 g., 0.9170 Silver 0.1203 oz. ASW **Ruler:** Louis XV **Mint:** Bordeaux

Date	Mintage	VG	F	VF	XF	Unc
1719K	—	10.00	20.00	35.00	100	—
1720K	—	10.00	20.00	35.00	100	—

KM# 440.12 20 SOLS (1/6 ECU)

4.0790 g., 0.9170 Silver 0.1203 oz. ASW **Ruler:** Louis XV **Mint:** Bayonne

Date	Mintage	VG	F	VF	XF	Unc
1719	—	10.00	20.00	35.00	100	—
1720	—	10.00	20.00	35.00	100	—

KM# 440.13 20 SOLS (1/6 ECU)

4.0790 g., 0.9170 Silver 0.1203 oz. ASW **Ruler:** Louis XV **Mint:** Montpellier

Date	Mintage	VG	F	VF	XF	Unc
1719N	394,000	10.00	20.00	35.00	100	—
1720N	17,000	12.00	25.00	50.00	150	—

KM# 440.15 20 SOLS (1/6 ECU)

4.0790 g., 0.9170 Silver 0.1203 oz. ASW **Ruler:** Louis XV **Mint:** Dijon **Obverse:** Young bust right **Obv. Legend:** LVD • XV • D • G • FR • ET • NAV • REX **Reverse:** Crowned arms of France and Navarre quartered divide value **Rev. Legend:** SIT • NOMEN • DOMINI BENEDICTVM •

Date	Mintage	VG	F	VF	XF	Unc
1719P	—	10.00	20.00	35.00	100	—
1720P	—	15.00	45.00	110	275	—

KM# 440.16 20 SOLS (1/6 ECU)

4.0790 g., 0.9170 Silver 0.1203 oz. ASW **Ruler:** Louis XV **Mint:** Perpignan **Obverse:** Young bust right **Reverse:** Crowned arms of France and Navarre quartered divide value

Date	Mintage	VG	F	VF	XF	Unc
1719Q	—	10.00	20.00	35.00	100	—

KM# 440.17 20 SOLS (1/6 ECU)

4.0790 g., 0.9170 Silver 0.1203 oz. ASW **Ruler:** Louis XV **Mint:** Orléans **Obverse:** Young bust right **Reverse:** Crowned arms of France and Navarre quartered divide value

Date	Mintage	VG	F	VF	XF	Unc
1719R	—	10.00	20.00	35.00	100	—
1720R	719,000	10.00	20.00	35.00	100	—

KM# 440.18 20 SOLS (1/6 ECU)

4.0790 g., 0.9170 Silver 0.1203 oz. ASW **Ruler:** Louis XV **Mint:** Reims **Obverse:** Young bust right **Reverse:** Crowned arms of France and Navarre quartered divide value

Date	Mintage	VG	F	VF	XF	Unc
1719S	1,187,000	10.00	20.00	35.00	100	—
1720S	404,000	10.00	20.00	35.00	100	—

KM# 440.19 20 SOLS (1/6 ECU)

4.0790 g., 0.9170 Silver 0.1203 oz. ASW **Ruler:** Louis XV **Mint:** Nantes **Obverse:** Young bust right **Reverse:** Crowned arms of France and Navarre quartered divide value

Date	Mintage	VG	F	VF	XF	Unc
1719T	—	10.00	20.00	35.00	100	—
1720T	368,000	10.00	20.00	35.00	100	—

KM# 440.20 20 SOLS (1/6 ECU)

4.0790 g., 0.9170 Silver 0.1203 oz. ASW **Ruler:** Louis XV **Mint:** Troyes **Obverse:** Young bust right **Reverse:** Crowned arms of France and Navarre quartered divide value

Date	Mintage	VG	F	VF	XF	Unc
1719V	97,000	10.00	30.00	70.00	175	—

KM# 440.21 20 SOLS (1/6 ECU)

4.0790 g., 0.9170 Silver 0.1203 oz. ASW **Ruler:** Louis XV **Mint:** Lille **Obverse:** Young bust right **Reverse:** Crowned arms of France and Navarre quartered divide value

Date	Mintage	VG	F	VF	XF	Unc
1719W	810,000	10.00	20.00	35.00	100	—
1720W	679,000	10.00	20.00	35.00	100	—

KM# 440.22 20 SOLS (1/6 ECU)

4.0790 g., 0.9170 Silver 0.1203 oz. ASW **Ruler:** Louis XV **Mint:** Amiens **Obverse:** Young bust right **Reverse:** Crowned arms of France and Navarre quartered divide value

Date	Mintage	VG	F	VF	XF	Unc
1719X	—	10.00	20.00	35.00	100	—
1720X	380,000	10.00	20.00	35.00	100	—

KM# 440.23 20 SOLS (1/6 ECU)

4.0790 g., 0.9170 Silver 0.1203 oz. ASW **Ruler:** Louis XV **Mint:** Bourges **Obverse:** Young bust right **Reverse:** Crowned arms of France and Navarre quartered divide value

Date	Mintage	VG	F	VF	XF	Unc
1719Y	—	10.00	20.00	35.00	100	—

KM# 440.1 20 SOLS (1/6 ECU)

4.0790 g., 0.9170 Silver 0.1203 oz. ASW **Ruler:** Louis XV **Mint:** Paris **Obverse:** Young bust right **Obv. Legend:** LVD XV D G FR ET NAV REX **Reverse:** Crowned arms of France and Navarre quartered divide value **Rev. Legend:** SIT NOMEN DOMINI BENEDICTUM

Date	Mintage	VG	F	VF	XF	Unc
1719A	—	10.00	20.00	35.00	100	—

KM# 440.2 20 SOLS (1/6 ECU)

4.0790 g., 0.9170 Silver 0.1203 oz. ASW **Ruler:** Louis XV **Mint:** Metz **Obverse:** Young bust right **Reverse:** Crowned arms of France and Navarre quartered divide value

Date	Mintage	VG	F	VF	XF	Unc
1719AA	237,000	10.00	20.00	35.00	100	—
1720AA	—	12.00	25.00	55.00	150	—

KM# 440.3 20 SOLS (1/6 ECU)

4.0790 g., 0.9170 Silver 0.1203 oz. ASW **Ruler:** Louis XV **Mint:** Rouen **Obverse:** Young bust right **Reverse:** Crowned arms of France and Navarre quartered divide value

Date	Mintage	VG	F	VF	XF	Unc
1719B	—	10.00	20.00	35.00	100	—
1720B	1,798,000	10.00	20.00	35.00	100	—

KM# 440.25 20 SOLS (1/6 ECU)

4.0790 g., 0.9170 Silver 0.1203 oz. ASW **Ruler:** Louis XV **Mint:** Aix **Obverse:** Young bust right **Reverse:** Crowned arms of France and Navarre quartered divide value **Note:** Mint mark: &.

Date	Mintage	VG	F	VF	XF	Unc
1719	—	12.00	25.00	45.00	135	—
1720	—	12.00	25.00	45.00	135	—

KM# 440.26 20 SOLS (1/6 ECU)

4.0790 g., 0.9170 Silver 0.1203 oz. ASW **Ruler:** Louis XV **Mint:** Besancon **Obverse:** Young bust right **Reverse:** Crowned arms of France and Navarre quartered divide value **Note:** Mint mark:)(.

Date	Mintage	VG	F	VF	XF	Unc
1719	—	10.00	20.00	35.00	100	—
1720	—	10.00	20.00	35.00	100	—

KM# 454.20 20 SOLS (1/6 ECU)

4.0790 g., 0.9170 Silver 0.1203 oz. ASW **Ruler:** Louis XV **Mint:** Lille

Date	Mintage	VG	F	VF	XF	Unc
1720W	—	8.00	16.00	40.00	110	—
1721W	—	7.00	15.00	35.00	100	—

KM# 454.21 20 SOLS (1/6 ECU)

4.0790 g., 0.9170 Silver 0.1203 oz. ASW **Ruler:** Louis XV **Mint:** Amiens

Date	Mintage	VG	F	VF	XF	Unc
1720X	—	8.00	16.00	40.00	110	—
1721X	—	8.00	16.00	40.00	110	—
1722X	—	10.00	18.00	55.00	140	—

KM# 454.22 20 SOLS (1/6 ECU)

4.0790 g., 0.9170 Silver 0.1203 oz. ASW **Ruler:** Louis XV **Mint:** Bourges

Date	Mintage	VG	F	VF	XF	Unc
1720Y	—	8.00	16.00	40.00	110	—
1721Y	—	8.00	16.00	40.00	110	—
1722Y	—	8.00	16.00	40.00	110	—

KM# 454.27 20 SOLS (1/6 ECU)

4.0790 g., 0.9170 Silver 0.1203 oz. ASW **Ruler:** Louis XV **Mint:** Pau **Note:** Mint mark: Cow.

Date	Mintage	VG	F	VF	XF	Unc
1720	—	12.00	25.00	65.00	160	—

KM# 452 20 SOLS (1/6 ECU)
4.0790 g., 0.9170 Silver 0.1203 oz. ASW **Ruler:** Louis XV **Mint:** Pau **Note:** Mint mark: Cow. Issued for Province of Bearn. Similar to KM#440.1 but obverse legend ends with ligate BD.

Date	Mintage	VG	F	VF	XF	Unc
1720	—	15.00	35.00	80.00	190	—

KM# 453 20 SOLS (1/6 ECU)
Silver **Ruler:** Louis XV **Mint:** Paris **Obverse:** Young bust right **Obv. Legend:** LUD • XV • D • G • FR • ET • NAV • REX • **Reverse:** Crowned double L monogram **Rev. Legend:** SIT NOMEN DOMINI BENEDICTUM **Note:** Livre de la Compagnie des Indes.

Date	Mintage	VG	F	VF	XF	Unc
1720A	6,919,000	20.00	60.00	145	250	—

KM# 440.4 20 SOLS (1/6 ECU)
4.0790 g., 0.9170 Silver 0.1203 oz. ASW **Ruler:** Louis XV **Mint:** Strasbourg

Date	Mintage	VG	F	VF	XF	Unc
1720BB	433,000	10.00	20.00	35.00	100	—

KM# 454.6 20 SOLS (1/6 ECU)
4.0790 g., 0.9170 Silver 0.1203 oz. ASW **Ruler:** Louis XV **Mint:** Lyon

Date	Mintage	VG	F	VF	XF	Unc
1720D	449,000	8.00	16.00	40.00	110	—
1721D	1,190,000	7.00	15.00	35.00	100	—
1722D	400,000	8.00	16.00	40.00	110	—
1723D	—	10.00	18.00	55.00	140	—

KM# 454.8 20 SOLS (1/6 ECU)
4.0790 g., 0.9170 Silver 0.1203 oz. ASW **Ruler:** Louis XV **Mint:** Poitiers

Date	Mintage	VG	F	VF	XF	Unc
1720G	—	8.00	16.00	40.00	110	—
1721G	—	8.00	16.00	40.00	110	—
1723G	—	12.00	25.00	65.00	160	—

KM# 454.10 20 SOLS (1/6 ECU)
4.0790 g., 0.9170 Silver 0.1203 oz. ASW **Ruler:** Louis XV **Mint:** Limoges

Date	Mintage	VG	F	VF	XF	Unc
1720I	—	8.00	16.00	40.00	110	—
1721I	—	8.00	16.00	40.00	110	—

KM# 454.15 20 SOLS (1/6 ECU)
4.0790 g., 0.9170 Silver 0.1203 oz. ASW **Ruler:** Louis XV **Mint:** Dijon

Date	Mintage	VG	F	VF	XF	Unc
1720P	—	8.00	16.00	40.00	110	—
1721P	—	8.00	16.00	40.00	110	—

KM# 454.16 20 SOLS (1/6 ECU)
4.0790 g., 0.9170 Silver 0.1203 oz. ASW **Ruler:** Louis XV **Mint:** Orléans

Date	Mintage	VG	F	VF	XF	Unc
1720R	162,000	8.00	16.00	40.00	110	—
1721R	635,000	8.00	16.00	40.00	110	—
1722R	—	8.00	16.00	40.00	110	—

KM# 454.17 20 SOLS (1/6 ECU)
4.0790 g., 0.9170 Silver 0.1203 oz. ASW **Ruler:** Louis XV **Mint:** Reims

Date	Mintage	VG	F	VF	XF	Unc
1720S	—	8.00	16.00	40.00	110	—
1721S	—	8.00	16.00	40.00	110	—

KM# 454.18 20 SOLS (1/6 ECU)
4.0790 g., 0.9170 Silver 0.1203 oz. ASW **Ruler:** Louis XV **Mint:** Nantes

Date	Mintage	VG	F	VF	XF	Unc
1720T	—	8.00	16.00	40.00	110	—
1721T	—	8.00	16.00	40.00	110	—
1722T	—	8.00	16.00	40.00	110	—

KM# 440.24 20 SOLS (1/6 ECU)
4.0790 g., 0.9170 Silver 0.1203 oz. ASW **Ruler:** Louis XV **Mint:** Grenoble

Date	Mintage	VG	F	VF	XF	Unc
1720Z	90,000	10.00	30.00	75.00	175	—

KM# 454.1 20 SOLS (1/6 ECU)
4.0790 g., 0.9170 Silver 0.1203 oz. ASW **Ruler:** Louis XV **Obverse:** Young laureate bust right **Obv. Legend:** LUD • XV • D • G • FR • ET • NAV • REX • **Reverse:** Crowned arms of France **Rev. Legend:** SIT NOMEN DOMINI BENEDICTUM

Date	Mintage	VG	F	VF	XF	Unc
1720	—	8.00	16.00	40.00	110	—
1721	—	8.00	16.00	40.00	110	—

KM# 440.14 20 SOLS (1/6 ECU)
4.0790 g., 0.9170 Silver 0.1203 oz. ASW **Ruler:** Louis XV **Mint:** Riom

Date	Mintage	VG	F	VF	XF	Unc
1720O	140,000	10.00	20.00	35.00	100	—

KM# 454.2 20 SOLS (1/6 ECU)
4.0790 g., 0.9170 Silver 0.1203 oz. ASW **Ruler:** Louis XV **Mint:** Metz **Obverse:** Young laureate bust right **Reverse:** Crowned arms of France

Date	Mintage	VG	F	VF	XF	Unc
1721AA	—	8.00	16.00	40.00	110	—
1722AA	—	8.00	16.00	40.00	110	—

KM# 454.3 20 SOLS (1/6 ECU)
4.0790 g., 0.9170 Silver 0.1203 oz. ASW **Ruler:** Louis XV **Mint:** Rouen **Obverse:** Young laureate bust right **Reverse:** Crowned arms of France

Date	Mintage	VG	F	VF	XF	Unc
1721B	—	8.00	16.00	40.00	110	—
1722B	—	8.00	16.00	40.00	110	—
1723B	—	10.00	18.00	55.00	140	—

KM# 454.4 20 SOLS (1/6 ECU)
4.0790 g., 0.9170 Silver 0.1203 oz. ASW **Ruler:** Louis XV **Mint:** Strasbourg **Obverse:** Young laureate bust right **Reverse:** Crowned arms of France

Date	Mintage	VG	F	VF	XF	Unc
1721BB	—	12.00	25.00	65.00	160	—

KM# 454.5 20 SOLS (1/6 ECU)
4.0790 g., 0.9170 Silver 0.1203 oz. ASW **Ruler:** Louis XV **Mint:** Caen **Obverse:** Young laureate bust right **Reverse:** Crowned arms of France

Date	Mintage	VG	F	VF	XF	Unc
1721C	—	10.00	18.00	55.00	140	—

KM# 454.11 20 SOLS (1/6 ECU)
4.0790 g., 0.9170 Silver 0.1203 oz. ASW **Ruler:** Louis XV **Mint:** Bordeaux **Obverse:** Young laureate bust right **Reverse:** Crowned arms of France

Date	Mintage	VG	F	VF	XF	Unc
1721K	903,000	8.00	16.00	40.00	110	—

KM# 454.12 20 SOLS (1/6 ECU)
4.0790 g., 0.9170 Silver 0.1203 oz. ASW **Ruler:** Louis XV **Mint:** Toulouse **Obverse:** Young laureate bust right **Reverse:** Crowned arms of France

Date	Mintage	VG	F	VF	XF	Unc
1721M	—	8.00	16.00	40.00	110	—

KM# 454.13 20 SOLS (1/6 ECU)
4.0790 g., 0.9170 Silver 0.1203 oz. ASW **Ruler:** Louis XV **Mint:** Montpellier **Obverse:** Young laureate bust right **Reverse:** Crowned arms of France

Date	Mintage	VG	F	VF	XF	Unc
1721N	—	8.00	16.00	40.00	110	—
1722N	—	8.00	16.00	40.00	110	—

KM# 454.14 20 SOLS (1/6 ECU)
4.0790 g., 0.9170 Silver 0.1203 oz. ASW **Ruler:** Louis XV **Mint:** Riom **Obverse:** Young laureate bust right **Reverse:** Crowned arms of France

Date	Mintage	VG	F	VF	XF	Unc
1721O	—	12.00	25.00	75.00	175	—
1722O	—	10.00	18.00	60.00	140	—

KM# 454.9 20 SOLS (1/6 ECU)
4.0790 g., 0.9170 Silver 0.1203 oz. ASW **Ruler:** Louis XV **Mint:** La Rochelle **Obverse:** Young laureate bust right **Reverse:** Crowned arms of France

Date	Mintage	VG	F	VF	XF	Unc
1721H	—	8.00	16.00	40.00	110	—

KM# 454.7 20 SOLS (1/6 ECU)
4.0790 g., 0.9170 Silver 0.1203 oz. ASW **Ruler:** Louis XV **Mint:** Tours **Obverse:** Young laureate bust right **Reverse:** Crowned arms of France

Date	Mintage	VG	F	VF	XF	Unc
1721E	—	8.00	16.00	40.00	110	—
1722E	142,000	8.00	16.00	40.00	110	—

KM# 454.23 20 SOLS (1/6 ECU)
4.0790 g., 0.9170 Silver 0.1203 oz. ASW **Ruler:** Louis XV **Mint:** Grenoble **Obverse:** Young laureate bust right **Reverse:** Crowned arms of France

Date	Mintage	VG	F	VF	XF	Unc
1721Z	261,000	10.00	18.00	55.00	140	—
1722Z	70,000	12.00	25.00	65.00	160	—

KM# 454.24 20 SOLS (1/6 ECU)
4.0790 g., 0.9170 Silver 0.1203 oz. ASW **Ruler:** Louis XV **Mint:** Rennes **Obverse:** Young laureate bust right **Reverse:** Crowned arms of France **Note:** Mint mark: 9.

Date	Mintage	VG	F	VF	XF	Unc
1721	—	8.00	16.00	40.00	110	—

KM# 454.26 20 SOLS (1/6 ECU)
4.0790 g., 0.9170 Silver 0.1203 oz. ASW **Ruler:** Louis XV **Mint:** Besancon **Obverse:** Young laureate bust right **Reverse:** Crowned arms of France **Note:** Mint mark: Back to back C's.

Date	Mintage	VG	F	VF	XF	Unc
1721	—	10.00	18.00	55.00	140	—
1722	—	12.00	25.00	65.00	160	—

KM# 454.19 20 SOLS (1/6 ECU)
4.0790 g., 0.9170 Silver 0.1203 oz. ASW **Ruler:** Louis XV **Mint:** Troyes **Obverse:** Young laureate bust right **Reverse:** Crowned arms of France

Date	Mintage	VG	F	VF	XF	Unc
1722V	—	10.00	18.00	55.00	140	—

KM# 454.25 20 SOLS (1/6 ECU)
4.0790 g., 0.9170 Silver 0.1203 oz. ASW, 24 mm. **Ruler:** Louis XV **Mint:** Aix **Obverse:** Young laureate bust right **Reverse:** Crowned arms of France **Note:** Mint mark: &.

Date	Mintage	VG	F	VF	XF	Unc
1723	—	8.00	18.00	43.00	115	—

KM# 482.1 24 SOLS (1/5 ECU)
5.5850 g., 0.9170 Silver 0.1647 oz. ASW **Ruler:** Louis XV **Mint:** Paris **Obverse:** Bust left **Obv. Legend:** LUD • XV • D • G • FR • ET • NAV • REX **Reverse:** Crowned arms of France within wreath **Rev. Legend:** SIT NOMEN DOMINI BENEDICTUM

Date	Mintage	VG	F	VF	XF	Unc
1726A	—	7.00	15.00	45.00	145	—
1727A	—	7.00	15.00	45.00	145	—
1728A	—	10.00	25.00	80.00	225	—
1729A	—	8.00	17.00	50.00	165	—
1730A	—	8.00	17.00	50.00	165	—
1731A	—	8.00	17.00	50.00	165	—
1737A	—	10.00	22.00	70.00	210	—

KM# 482.4 24 SOLS (1/5 ECU)
5.5850 g., 0.9170 Silver 0.1647 oz. ASW **Ruler:** Louis XV **Mint:** Strasbourg **Obverse:** Bust left **Reverse:** Crowned arms of France within wreath

Date	Mintage	VG	F	VF	XF	Unc
1726BB	—	8.00	17.00	50.00	165	—
1729BB	—	8.00	17.00	50.00	165	—

KM# 482.5 24 SOLS (1/5 ECU)
5.5850 g., 0.9170 Silver 0.1647 oz. ASW **Ruler:** Louis XV **Mint:** Lyon **Obverse:** Bust right **Reverse:** Crowned arms of France within wreath

Date	Mintage	VG	F	VF	XF	Unc
1726D	200,000	8.00	17.00	50.00	165	—
1727D	403,000	7.00	15.00	45.00	145	—
1728D	520,000	7.00	15.00	45.00	145	—
1729D	63,000	10.00	22.00	70.00	210	—
1730D	—	10.00	22.00	70.00	210	—

KM# 482.9 24 SOLS (1/5 ECU)
5.5850 g., 0.9170 Silver 0.1647 oz. ASW **Ruler:** Louis XV **Mint:** Bordeaux **Obverse:** Bust left **Reverse:** Crowned arms of France within wreath

Date	Mintage	VG	F	VF	XF	Unc
1726K	—	7.00	15.00	45.00	145	—
1727K	—	10.00	22.00	70.00	210	—

KM# 482.10 24 SOLS (1/5 ECU)
5.5850 g., 0.9170 Silver 0.1647 oz. ASW **Ruler:** Louis XV **Mint:** Bayonne **Obverse:** Bust left **Reverse:** Crowned arms of France within wreath

Date	Mintage	VG	F	VF	XF	Unc
1726L	—	8.00	17.00	50.00	165	—
1728L	—	7.00	15.00	45.00	145	—
1729L	149,000	8.00	17.00	50.00	165	—

KM# 482.11 24 SOLS (1/5 ECU)
5.5850 g., 0.9170 Silver 0.1647 oz. ASW **Ruler:** Louis XV **Mint:** Toulouse **Obverse:** Bust left **Reverse:** Crowned arms of France within wreath

Date	Mintage	VG	F	VF	XF	Unc
1726M	—	10.00	22.00	70.00	210	—
1728M	—	10.00	22.00	70.00	210	—
1729M	57,000	10.00	22.00	70.00	210	—

KM# 482.12 24 SOLS (1/5 ECU)
5.5850 g., 0.9170 Silver 0.1647 oz. ASW **Ruler:** Louis XV **Mint:** Montpellier **Obverse:** Bust left **Reverse:** Crowned arms of France within wreath

Date	Mintage	VG	F	VF	XF	Unc
1726N	228,000	7.00	15.00	45.00	145	—
1728N	183,000	8.00	17.00	50.00	165	—

KM# 482.13 24 SOLS (1/5 ECU)
5.5850 g., 0.9170 Silver 0.1647 oz. ASW **Ruler:** Louis XV **Mint:** Dijon **Obverse:** Bust left **Reverse:** Crowned arms of France within wreath

Date	Mintage	VG	F	VF	XF	Unc
1726P	—	8.00	17.00	50.00	165	—
1727P	—	12.00	30.00	90.00	270	—

KM# 482.15 24 SOLS (1/5 ECU)
5.5850 g., 0.9170 Silver 0.1647 oz. ASW **Ruler:** Louis XV **Mint:** Orléans **Obverse:** Bust left **Reverse:** Crowned arms of France within wreath

Date	Mintage	VG	F	VF	XF	Unc
1726R	—	10.00	22.00	70.00	210	—
1727R	39,000	8.00	17.00	50.00	165	—

KM# 482.16 24 SOLS (1/5 ECU)
5.5850 g., 0.9170 Silver 0.1647 oz. ASW **Ruler:** Louis XV **Mint:** Reims **Obverse:** Bust left **Reverse:** Crowned arms of France within wreath

Date	Mintage	VG	F	VF	XF	Unc
1726S	26,000	12.00	30.00	100	290	—
1727S	—	12.00	30.00	100	290	—
1729S	—	12.00	30.00	100	290	—

KM# 482.17 24 SOLS (1/5 ECU)
5.5850 g., 0.9170 Silver 0.1647 oz. ASW **Ruler:** Louis XV **Mint:** Nantes **Obverse:** Bust left **Reverse:** Crowned arms of France within wreath

Date	Mintage	VG	F	VF	XF	Unc
1726T	—	7.00	15.00	45.00	145	—
1727T	—	8.00	17.00	50.00	165	—
1728T	25,000	10.00	22.00	70.00	210	—

KM# 482.18 24 SOLS (1/5 ECU)
5.5850 g., 0.9170 Silver 0.1647 oz. ASW **Ruler:** Louis XV **Mint:** Troyes **Obverse:** Bust left **Reverse:** Crowned arms of France within wreath

Date	Mintage	VG	F	VF	XF	Unc
1726V	16,000	10.00	22.00	70.00	210	—
1729V	—	10.00	22.00	70.00	210	—

KM# 482.19 24 SOLS (1/5 ECU)
5.5850 g., 0.9170 Silver 0.1647 oz. ASW **Ruler:** Louis XV **Mint:** Lille **Obverse:** Bust left **Reverse:** Crowned arms of France within wreath

Date	Mintage	VG	F	VF	XF	Unc
1726W	—	7.00	15.00	45.00	145	—
1727W	—	8.00	17.00	50.00	165	—
1728W	21,000	10.00	22.00	70.00	210	—
1730W	—	10.00	22.00	70.00	210	—

KM# 482.20 24 SOLS (1/5 ECU)
5.5850 g., 0.9170 Silver 0.1647 oz. ASW **Ruler:** Louis XV **Mint:** Amiens **Obverse:** Bust left **Obv. Legend:** LUD XV D G FR ET NAV REX **Reverse:** Crowned arms of France within wreath **Rev. Legend:** SIT NOMEN DOMINI BENEDICTUM

Date	Mintage	VG	F	VF	XF	Unc
1726X	—	8.00	17.00	50.00	165	—
1727X	—	18.00	35.00	100	325	—
1730X	—	10.00	22.00	70.00	210	—

KM# 482.21 24 SOLS (1/5 ECU)
5.5850 g., 0.9170 Silver 0.1647 oz. ASW **Ruler:** Louis XV **Mint:** Bourges **Obverse:** Bust left **Reverse:** Crowned arms of France within wreath

Date	Mintage	VG	F	VF	XF	Unc
1726Y	—	8.00	17.00	50.00	165	—
1727Y	—	10.00	22.00	70.00	210	—

KM# 482.24 24 SOLS (1/5 ECU)
5.5850 g., 0.9170 Silver 0.1647 oz. ASW **Ruler:** Louis XV **Mint:** Aix **Obverse:** Bust left **Reverse:** Crowned arms of France within wreath **Note:** Mint mark: &.

Date	Mintage	VG	F	VF	XF	Unc
1726	—	7.00	15.00	45.00	145	—
1728	—	7.00	15.00	45.00	145	—

KM# 482.23 24 SOLS (1/5 ECU)
5.5850 g., 0.9170 Silver 0.1647 oz. ASW **Ruler:** Louis XV **Mint:** Rennes **Obverse:** Bust left **Reverse:** Crowned arms of France within wreath **Note:** Mint mark: 9.

Date	Mintage	VG	F	VF	XF	Unc
1726	—	10.00	22.00	70.00	210	—
1728	120,000	8.00	17.00	50.00	165	—
1729	—	10.00	22.00	70.00	210	—
1730	—	10.00	22.00	70.00	210	—
1732	—	10.00	22.00	70.00	210	—

KM# 483 24 SOLS (1/5 ECU)
5.5850 g., 0.9170 Silver 0.1647 oz. ASW **Ruler:** Louis XV **Mint:** Pau **Note:** Mint mark: Cow. Issued for Province of Bearn. Similar to KM#482.1 but obverse legend ends with ligate BD.

Date	Mintage	VG	F	VF	XF	Unc
1726	—	14.00	35.00	100	300	—
1729	—	14.00	35.00	100	300	—

KM# 482.22 24 SOLS (1/5 ECU)
5.5850 g., 0.9170 Silver 0.1647 oz. ASW **Ruler:** Louis XV **Mint:** Grenoble **Obverse:** Bust left **Reverse:** Crowned arms of France within wreath

Date	Mintage	VG	F	VF	XF	Unc
1727Z	—	8.00	17.00	50.00	165	—
1728Z	—	10.00	22.00	70.00	210	—

KM# 482.2 24 SOLS (1/5 ECU)
5.5850 g., 0.9170 Silver 0.1647 oz. ASW **Ruler:** Louis XV **Mint:** Metz **Obverse:** Bust left **Reverse:** Crowned arms of France within wreath

Date	Mintage	VG	F	VF	XF	Unc
1727AA	—	10.00	22.00	70.00	210	—
1728AA	—	10.00	22.00	70.00	210	—

KM# 482.3 24 SOLS (1/5 ECU)
5.5850 g., 0.9170 Silver 0.1647 oz. ASW **Ruler:** Louis XV **Mint:** Rouen **Obverse:** Bust left **Reverse:** Crowned arms of France within wreath

Date	Mintage	VG	F	VF	XF	Unc
1727B	—	8.00	17.00	50.00	165	—
1728B	—	20.00	45.00	125	300	—
1729B	—	15.00	35.00	95.00	250	—
1730B	—	10.00	22.00	70.00	210	—

KM# 482.7 24 SOLS (1/5 ECU)
5.5850 g., 0.9170 Silver 0.1647 oz. ASW **Ruler:** Louis XV **Mint:** La Rochelle **Obverse:** Bust left **Reverse:** Crowned arms of France within wreath

Date	Mintage	VG	F	VF	XF	Unc
1727H	—	8.00	17.00	50.00	165	—
1729H	—	8.00	17.00	50.00	165	—

KM# 482.8 24 SOLS (1/5 ECU)
5.5850 g., 0.9170 Silver 0.1647 oz. ASW **Ruler:** Louis XV **Mint:** Limoges **Obverse:** Bust left **Reverse:** Crowned arms of France within wreath

Date	Mintage	VG	F	VF	XF	Unc
1727I	—	8.00	17.00	50.00	165	—

KM# 482.6 24 SOLS (1/5 ECU)
5.5850 g., 0.9170 Silver 0.1647 oz. ASW **Ruler:** Louis XV **Mint:** Tours **Obverse:** Bust left **Reverse:** Crowned arms of France within wreath

Date	Mintage	VG	F	VF	XF	Unc
1728E	90,000	10.00	19.00	55.00	175	—

KM# 482.14 24 SOLS (1/5 ECU)
5.5850 g., 0.9170 Silver 0.1647 oz. ASW **Ruler:** Louis XV **Mint:** Perpignan **Obverse:** Bust left **Reverse:** Crowned arms of France within wreath

Date	Mintage	VG	F	VF	XF	Unc
1728Q	—	—	—	—	—	—

KM# 482.25 24 SOLS (1/5 ECU)
5.5850 g., 0.9170 Silver 0.1647 oz. ASW **Ruler:** Louis XV **Mint:** Besancon **Note:** Mint mark: Back to back C's.

Date	Mintage	VG	F	VF	XF	Unc
1729	—	10.00	22.00	70.00	210	—

KM# 515.21 24 SOLS (1/5 ECU)
5.5850 g., 0.9170 Silver 0.1647 oz. ASW **Ruler:** Louis XV **Mint:** Rennes **Obverse:** Head left **Reverse:** Crowned arms of France within wreath **Note:** Mint mark: 9.

Date	Mintage	VG	F	VF	XF	Unc
1741	26,000	9.00	18.00	60.00	200	—
1742	6,377	15.00	32.00	110	300	—

KM# 515.1 24 SOLS (1/5 ECU)
5.5850 g., 0.9170 Silver 0.1647 oz. ASW **Ruler:** Louis XV **Mint:** Paris **Obverse:** Head left **Obv. Legend:** LUD • XV • D • G • FR • ET • NAV • REX • **Reverse:** Crowned arms of France within wreath **Rev. Legend:** SIT • NOMEN • DOMINI • BENEDICTUM *

Date	Mintage	VG	F	VF	XF	Unc
1741A	—	8.00	15.00	40.00	160	—
1750A	—	—	—	—	—	—
1753A	—	9.00	18.00	45.00	190	—
1757A	—	9.00	18.00	45.00	190	—
1763A	—	9.00	18.00	45.00	190	—
1764A	—	9.00	18.00	45.00	190	—
1765A	—	9.00	18.00	45.00	190	—
1766A	—	9.00	18.00	45.00	190	—
1768A	—	9.00	18.00	45.00	190	—
1770A	—	—	—	—	—	—

KM# 515.2 24 SOLS (1/5 ECU)
5.5850 g., 0.9170 Silver 0.1647 oz. ASW **Ruler:** Louis XV **Mint:** Metz **Obverse:** Head left **Reverse:** Crowned arms of France within wreath

Date	Mintage	VG	F	VF	XF	Unc
1741AA	—	14.00	30.00	100	315	—

KM# 515.3 24 SOLS (1/5 ECU)
5.5850 g., 0.9170 Silver 0.1647 oz. ASW **Ruler:** Louis XV **Mint:** Rouen **Obverse:** Head left **Reverse:** Crowned arms of France within wreath

Date	Mintage	VG	F	VF	XF	Unc
1741B	—	9.00	18.00	60.00	200	—
1742B	98,000	9.00	18.00	60.00	200	—

KM# 515.4 24 SOLS (1/5 ECU)
5.5850 g., 0.9170 Silver 0.1647 oz. ASW **Ruler:** Louis XV **Mint:** Strasbourg **Obverse:** Head left **Reverse:** Crowned arms of France within wreath

Date	Mintage	VG	F	VF	XF	Unc
1741BB	135,000	9.00	18.00	60.00	200	—

KM# 515.5 24 SOLS (1/5 ECU)
5.5850 g., 0.9170 Silver 0.1647 oz. ASW **Ruler:** Louis XV **Mint:** Caen **Obverse:** Head left **Reverse:** Crowned arms of France within wreath

Date	Mintage	VG	F	VF	XF	Unc
1741C	36,000	15.00	30.00	100	280	—

KM# 515.8 24 SOLS (1/5 ECU)
5.5850 g., 0.9170 Silver 0.1647 oz. ASW **Ruler:** Louis XV **Mint:** Bordeaux **Obverse:** Head left **Reverse:** Crowned arms of France within wreath

Date	Mintage	VG	F	VF	XF	Unc
1741K	—	9.00	18.00	60.00	200	—
1755K	—	10.00	20.00	75.00	250	—

KM# 515.15 24 SOLS (1/5 ECU)
5.5850 g., 0.9170 Silver 0.1647 oz. ASW **Ruler:** Louis XV **Mint:** Orléans **Obverse:** Head left **Reverse:** Crowned arms of France within wreath

Date	Mintage	VG	F	VF	XF	Unc
1741R	—	9.00	18.00	60.00	200	—
1753R	6,314	10.00	20.00	75.00	260	—
1759R	—	10.00	20.00	75.00	250	—
1760R	—	9.00	18.00	60.00	200	—
1764R	—	10.00	20.00	75.00	250	—
1766R	—	9.00	18.00	60.00	200	—

KM# 515.16 24 SOLS (1/5 ECU)
5.5850 g., 0.9170 Silver 0.1647 oz. ASW **Ruler:** Louis XV **Mint:** Reims **Obverse:** Head left **Reverse:** Crowned arms of France within wreath

Date	Mintage	VG	F	VF	XF	Unc
1741S	—	9.00	18.00	60.00	200	—
1750S	35,000	9.00	18.00	60.00	200	—
1759S	—	10.00	20.00	75.00	250	—

KM# 515.17 24 SOLS (1/5 ECU)
5.5850 g., 0.9170 Silver 0.1647 oz. ASW **Ruler:** Louis XV **Mint:** Nantes **Obverse:** Head left **Reverse:** Crowned arms of France within wreath

Date	Mintage	VG	F	VF	XF	Unc
1741T	—	9.00	18.00	60.00	200	—

KM# 515.18 24 SOLS (1/5 ECU)
5.5850 g., 0.9170 Silver 0.1647 oz. ASW **Ruler:** Louis XV **Mint:** Troyes **Obverse:** Head left **Reverse:** Crowned arms of France within wreath

Date	Mintage	VG	F	VF	XF	Unc
1741V	19,000	9.00	18.00	60.00	200	—

KM# 515.19 24 SOLS (1/5 ECU)
5.5850 g., 0.9170 Silver 0.1647 oz. ASW **Ruler:** Louis XV **Mint:** Lille **Obverse:** Head left **Reverse:** Crowned arms of France within wreath

Date	Mintage	VG	F	VF	XF	Unc
1741W	17,000	9.00	18.00	60.00	200	—

KM# 515.12 24 SOLS (1/5 ECU)
5.5850 g., 0.9170 Silver 0.1647 oz. ASW **Ruler:** Louis XV **Mint:** Dijon **Obverse:** Head left **Reverse:** Crowned arms of France within wreath

Date	Mintage	VG	F	VF	XF	Unc
1741P	—	10.00	20.00	75.00	250	—
1758P	—	10.00	20.00	75.00	250	—

KM# 515.13 24 SOLS (1/5 ECU)
5.5850 g., 0.9170 Silver 0.1647 oz. ASW **Ruler:** Louis XV **Mint:** Riom **Obverse:** Head left **Reverse:** Crowned arms of France within wreath

Date	Mintage	VG	F	VF	XF	Unc
1741O	—	20.00	45.00	145	375	—

KM# 515.14 24 SOLS (1/5 ECU)
5.5850 g., 0.9170 Silver 0.1647 oz. ASW **Ruler:** Louis XV **Mint:** Perpignan **Obverse:** Head left **Reverse:** Crowned arms of France within wreath

Date	Mintage	VG	F	VF	XF	Unc
1744Q	—	9.00	18.00	60.00	200	—
1764Q	—	10.00	20.00	75.00	250	—

KM# 515.6 24 SOLS (1/5 ECU)
5.5850 g., 0.9170 Silver 0.1647 oz. ASW **Ruler:** Louis XV **Mint:** Lyon **Obverse:** Head left **Reverse:** Crowned arms of France within wreath

Date	Mintage	VG	F	VF	XF	Unc
1749D	—	10.00	20.00	75.00	250	—
1756D	—	12.00	25.00	90.00	270	—

KM# 530 24 SOLS (1/5 ECU)
5.5850 g., 0.9170 Silver 0.1647 oz. ASW **Ruler:** Louis XV **Mint:** Pau **Obverse:** Head left **Obv. Legend:** LUD • XV • D • G • FR • ET • NA • RE • .. **Reverse:** Crowned arms of France within wreath **Rev. Legend:** SIT NOMEN DOMINI BENEDICTUM **Note:** Mint mark: Cow. Issued for Province of Bearn. Similar to KM#515.1. Obverse legend ends with ligate BD.

Date	Mintage	VG	F	VF	XF	Unc
1750	—	12.00	25.00	85.00	280	—
1752	1,405	25.00	45.00	120	375	—
1759	18,000	12.00	25.00	85.00	280	—
1766	43,000	10.00	20.00	75.00	200	—
1767	27,000	12.00	25.00	85.00	280	—
1770	13,000	12.00	25.00	85.00	280	—

KM# 515.23 24 SOLS (1/5 ECU)
5.5850 g., 0.9170 Silver 0.1647 oz. ASW **Ruler:** Louis XV **Mint:** Besancon **Obverse:** Head left **Reverse:** Crowned arms of France within wreath **Note:** Mint mark: Back to back C's.

Date	Mintage	VG	F	VF	XF	Unc
1756	15,000	12.00	25.00	85.00	280	—
1759	—	12.00	25.00	85.00	280	—
1770	—	12.00	25.00	85.00	280	—

KM# 515.11 24 SOLS (1/5 ECU)
5.5850 g., 0.9170 Silver 0.1647 oz. ASW **Ruler:** Louis XV **Mint:** Montpellier **Obverse:** Head left **Reverse:** Crowned arms of France within wreath

Date	Mintage	VG	F	VF	XF	Unc
1759N	—	10.00	20.00	75.00	250	—

KM# 515.9 24 SOLS (1/5 ECU)
5.5850 g., 0.9170 Silver 0.1647 oz. ASW **Ruler:** Louis XV **Mint:** Bayonne **Obverse:** Head left **Reverse:** Crowned arms of France within wreath

Date	Mintage	VG	F	VF	XF	Unc
1759L	—	10.00	20.00	75.00	250	—
1762L	—	9.00	18.00	60.00	200	—
1766L	—	9.00	18.00	60.00	200	—
1769L	—	9.00	18.00	60.00	200	—

KM# 515.20 24 SOLS (1/5 ECU)
5.5850 g., 0.9170 Silver 0.1647 oz. ASW **Ruler:** Louis XV **Mint:** Grenoble **Obverse:** Head left **Reverse:** Crowned arms of France within wreath

Date	Mintage	VG	F	VF	XF	Unc
1760Z	—	12.00	25.00	85.00	280	—
1762Z	—	12.00	25.00	85.00	280	—

KM# 515.10 24 SOLS (1/5 ECU)
5.5850 g., 0.9170 Silver 0.1647 oz. ASW **Ruler:** Louis XV **Mint:** Toulouse **Obverse:** Head left **Reverse:** Crowned arms of France within wreath

Date	Mintage	VG	F	VF	XF	Unc
1766M	—	15.00	35.00	110	300	—

KM# 515.22 24 SOLS (1/5 ECU)
5.5850 g., 0.9170 Silver 0.1647 oz. ASW **Ruler:** Louis XV **Mint:** Aix **Obverse:** Head left **Reverse:** Crowned arms of France within wreath **Note:** Mint mark: &.

Date	Mintage	VG	F	VF	XF	Unc
1766	—	12.00	25.00	85.00	280	—

KM# 515.7 24 SOLS (1/5 ECU)
5.5850 g., 0.9170 Silver 0.1647 oz. ASW **Ruler:** Louis XV **Mint:** La Rochelle **Obverse:** Head left **Reverse:** Crowned arms of France within wreath

Date	Mintage	VG	F	VF	XF	Unc
1769H	—	9.00	18.00	60.00	200	—
1770H	—	9.00	18.00	60.00	200	—

KM# 553.1 24 SOLS (1/5 ECU)
5.5850 g., 0.9170 Silver 0.1647 oz. ASW **Ruler:** Louis XV **Mint:** Paris **Obverse:** Laureate head left **Obv. Legend:** LUD • XV • D • G • FR • ET • NAV • REX • **Reverse:** Crowned arms of France within wreath **Rev. Legend:** SIT NOMEN DOMINI BENEDICTUM **Note:** Similar to 12 Sols, KM#550.1.

Date	Mintage	VG	F	VF	XF	Unc
1771A	—	40.00	80.00	200	525	—
1772A	—	40.00	80.00	200	525	—
1773A	—	40.00	80.00	200	525	—

KM# 553.3 24 SOLS (1/5 ECU)
5.5850 g., 0.9170 Silver 0.1647 oz. ASW **Ruler:** Louis XV **Mint:** Bayonne **Obverse:** Laureate head left **Reverse:** Crowned arms of France within wreath

Date	Mintage	VG	F	VF	XF	Unc
1772L	—	30.00	60.00	150	400	—

KM# 560 24 SOLS (1/5 ECU)
5.5850 g., 0.9170 Silver 0.1647 oz. ASW **Ruler:** Louis XV **Mint:** Pau **Obverse:** Legend ends with ligate BD **Obv. Legend:** LUD • XV • D • G • FR • ET • NA • RE • ... **Reverse:** Crowned arms of France within wreath **Rev. Legend:** SIT NOMEN DOMINI BENEDICTUM **Note:** Mint mark: Cow. Issued for Province of Bearn.

Date	Mintage	VG	F	VF	XF	Unc
1773	—	40.00	80.00	200	525	—

KM# 553.2 24 SOLS (1/5 ECU)
5.5850 g., 0.9170 Silver 0.1647 oz. ASW **Ruler:** Louis XV **Mint:** Strasbourg **Obverse:** Laureate head left **Reverse:** Crowned arms of France within wreath

Date	Mintage	VG	F	VF	XF	Unc
1774BB	—	30.00	60.00	150	400	—

KM# 569.1 24 SOLS (1/5 ECU)
5.8350 g., 0.9170 Silver 0.1720 oz. ASW **Ruler:** Louis XVI **Mint:** Paris **Obverse:** Bust left **Obv. Legend:** LVD • XVI • D • G • FR • ET NAV • REX • **Reverse:** Crowned arms of France within branches **Rev. Legend:** SIT NOMEN DOMINI H BENEDICTUM

Date	Mintage	VG	F	VF	XF	Unc
1775A	11,000	10.00	30.00	80.00	180	—
1776A	7,515	12.00	35.00	85.00	190	—
1777A	5,010	—	—	—	—	—
1778A	36,000	7.00	20.00	70.00	160	—
1778A	Inc. above	7.00	20.00	70.00	160	—
1779A	—	—	—	—	—	—
Note: Reported, not confirmed						
1780A	8,270	—	—	—	—	—
1781A	8,880	10.00	30.00	80.00	180	—
1782A	60,000	7.00	15.00	60.00	140	—
1783A	28,000	7.00	20.00	70.00	160	—
1784A	13,000	7.00	20.00	70.00	160	—
1785A	26,000	7.00	20.00	70.00	160	—
1786A	—	7.00	15.00	60.00	140	—
1789A	—	7.00	15.00	30.00	100	—
1790A	—	7.00	20.00	70.00	160	—

KM# 570 24 SOLS (1/5 ECU)
5.8350 g., 0.9170 Silver 0.1720 oz. ASW **Ruler:** Louis XVI **Mint:** Pau **Obv. Legend:** ....RE.BD (ligate BD). **Note:** Mint mark: Cow. Issued for Province of Bearn.

Date	Mintage	VG	F	VF	XF	Unc
1775	14,000	15.00	40.00	90.00	200	—
1777	32,000	10.00	30.00	80.00	180	—

KM# 569.14 24 SOLS (1/5 ECU)
5.8350 g., 0.9170 Silver 0.1720 oz. ASW **Ruler:** Louis XVI **Mint:** Aix **Obverse:** Bust left **Reverse:** Crowned arms of France within branches **Note:** Mint mark: &. The "dot" appears below the third letter of the monarch's name and denotes second semester coinage.

Date	Mintage	VG	F	VF	XF	Unc
1775	24,000	7.00	20.00	70.00	160	—
1776	7,119	15.00	40.00	90.00	200	—
1782	6,609	15.00	40.00	90.00	200	—

KM# 569.7 24 SOLS (1/5 ECU)
5.8350 g., 0.9170 Silver 0.1720 oz. ASW **Ruler:** Louis XVI **Mint:** Bayonne **Obverse:** Bust left **Reverse:** Crowned arms of France within branches

Date	Mintage	VG	F	VF	XF	Unc
1775L	17,000	7.00	20.00	70.00	160	—
1777L	21,000	7.00	20.00	70.00	160	—
1780L	13,000	7.00	20.00	70.00	160	—
1783L	7,645	—	—	—	—	—
1790L	—	7.00	20.00	70.00	160	—

KM# 569.5 24 SOLS (1/5 ECU)
5.8350 g., 0.9170 Silver 0.1720 oz. ASW **Ruler:** Louis XVI **Mint:** Limoges **Obverse:** Bust left **Reverse:** Crowned arms of France within branches

Date	Mintage	VG	F	VF	XF	Unc
1776I	16,000	7.00	20.00	70.00	160	—
1780I	20,000	—	—	—	—	—
1781I	15,000	—	—	—	—	—
1784I	36,000	—	—	—	—	—
1785I	29,000	7.00	20.00	70.00	160	—
1788I	18,000	7.00	20.00	70.00	160	—

KM# 569.10 24 SOLS (1/5 ECU)
5.8350 g., 0.9170 Silver 0.1720 oz. ASW **Ruler:** Louis XVI **Mint:** Montpellier **Obverse:** Bust left **Reverse:** Crowned arms of France within branches

Date	Mintage	VG	F	VF	XF	Unc
1776N	25,000	7.00	20.00	70.00	160	—
1782N	4,790,000	—	—	—	—	—
1786N	15,000	—	—	—	—	—
1787N	—	7.00	20.00	70.00	160	—

KM# 569.8 24 SOLS (1/5 ECU)
5.8350 g., 0.9170 Silver 0.1720 oz. ASW **Ruler:** Louis XVI **Mint:** Toulouse **Obverse:** Bust left **Reverse:** Crowned arms of France within branches

Date	Mintage	VG	F	VF	XF	Unc
1778M	46,000	7.00	20.00	70.00	160	—
1788M	13,000	7.00	20.00	70.00	160	—

KM# 569.2 24 SOLS (1/5 ECU)
5.8350 g., 0.9170 Silver 0.1720 oz. ASW **Ruler:** Louis XVI **Mint:** Metz **Obverse:** Bust left **Reverse:** Crowned arms of France within branches

Date	Mintage	VG	F	VF	XF	Unc
1779AA	—	7.00	20.00	70.00	160	—

KM# 569.11 24 SOLS (1/5 ECU)
5.8350 g., 0.9170 Silver 0.1720 oz. ASW **Ruler:** Louis XVI **Mint:** Perpignan **Obverse:** Bust left **Reverse:** Crowned arms of France within branches

Date	Mintage	VG	F	VF	XF	Unc
1780Q	8,800	—	—	—	—	—
1785Q	32,000	7.00	20.00	70.00	160	—
1786Q	29,000	7.00	20.00	70.00	160	—

KM# 569.6 24 SOLS (1/5 ECU)
5.8350 g., 0.9170 Silver 0.1720 oz. ASW **Ruler:** Louis XVI **Mint:** Bordeaux **Obverse:** Bust left **Reverse:** Crowned arms of France within branches

Date	Mintage	VG	F	VF	XF	Unc
1781K	4,600	15.00	40.00	90.00	200	—

KM# 569.12 24 SOLS (1/5 ECU)
5.8350 g., 0.9170 Silver 0.1720 oz. ASW **Ruler:** Louis XVI **Mint:** Orléans **Obverse:** Bust left **Obv. Legend:** LUD • XVI • D • G • FR • ET NAV • REX • **Reverse:** Crowned arms of France within branches **Rev. Legend:** SIT NOMEN DOMINI BENEDICTUM *

Date	Mintage	VG	F	VF	XF	Unc
1784R	30,000	7.00	20.00	70.00	160	—
1786R	87,000	7.00	15.00	30.00	100	—
1787R	26,000	7.00	20.00	70.00	160	—

KM# 569.4 24 SOLS (1/5 ECU)
5.8350 g., 0.9170 Silver 0.1720 oz. ASW **Ruler:** Louis XVI **Mint:** La Rochelle **Obverse:** Bust left **Reverse:** Crowned arms of France within branches

Date	Mintage	VG	F	VF	XF	Unc
1786H	—	—	—	—	—	—
Note: Reported, not confirmed						
1788H	21,000	7.00	20.00	70.00	160	—

KM# 569.3 24 SOLS (1/5 ECU)
5.8350 g., 0.9170 Silver 0.1720 oz. ASW **Ruler:** Louis XVI **Mint:** Lyon **Obverse:** Bust left **Reverse:** Crowned arms of France within branches

Date	Mintage	VG	F	VF	XF	Unc
1787D	7,398	10.00	30.00	80.00	180	—

KM# 569.13 24 SOLS (1/5 ECU)
5.8350 g., 0.9170 Silver 0.1720 oz. ASW **Ruler:** Louis XVI **Mint:** Lille **Obverse:** Bust left **Reverse:** Crowned arms of France within branches

Date	Mintage	VG	F	VF	XF	Unc
1788W	27,000	7.00	20.00	70.00	160	—
1789W	—	7.00	15.00	60.00	140	—

KM# 569.9 24 SOLS (1/5 ECU)
5.8350 g., 0.9170 Silver 0.1720 oz. ASW **Ruler:** Louis XVI **Mint:** Marseille **Obverse:** Bust left **Reverse:** Crowned arms of France within branches

Date	Mintage	VG	F	VF	XF	Unc
1788MA	32,000	7.00	20.00	70.00	160	—

KM# 410.1 30 SOLS (1/4 ECU)
7.6480 g., 0.9170 Silver 0.2255 oz. ASW **Ruler:** Louis XV **Mint:** Paris **Obverse:** Young bust of Louis XV right **Reverse:** 3 crowns from triangle with fleur-de-lis in angles

Date	Mintage	VG	F	VF	XF	Unc
1715A Rare	3,620	—	—	—	—	—

KM# 410.2 30 SOLS (1/4 ECU)
7.6480 g., 0.9170 Silver 0.2255 oz. ASW **Ruler:** Louis XVI **Mint:** Aix **Note:** Mint mark: &.

Date	Mintage	VG	F	VF	XF	Unc
1715 Rare	—	—	—	—	—	—

KM# 419.23 30 SOLS (1/4 ECU)
7.6480 g., 0.9170 Silver 0.2255 oz. ASW **Ruler:** Louis XV **Mint:** Aix **Note:** Mint mark: &.

Date	Mintage	VG	F	VF	XF	Unc
1716	—	20.00	60.00	120	325	—
1717	—	25.00	85.00	170	400	—

KM# 419.22 30 SOLS (1/4 ECU)
7.6480 g., 0.9170 Silver 0.2255 oz. ASW **Ruler:** Louis XV **Mint:** Rennes **Note:** Mint mark: 9.

Date	Mintage	VG	F	VF	XF	Unc
1716	—	20.00	60.00	120	325	—
1717	—	20.00	60.00	120	325	—

KM# 419.1 30 SOLS (1/4 ECU)
7.6480 g., 0.9170 Silver 0.2255 oz. ASW **Ruler:** Louis XV **Mint:** Paris **Obverse:** Young bust right **Obv. Legend:** LUD • XV • D • G • FR • ET • NAV • REX • **Reverse:** Crowned circular arms **Rev. Legend:** SIT NOMEN • DOMINI • BENEDICTUM

Date	Mintage	VG	F	VF	XF	Unc
1716A	—	15.00	50.00	100	275	—

KM# 419.2 30 SOLS (1/4 ECU)
7.6480 g., 0.9170 Silver 0.2255 oz. ASW **Ruler:** Louis XV **Mint:** Metz **Obverse:** Young bust of Louis XV right **Reverse:** Crowned circular arms

Date	Mintage	VG	F	VF	XF	Unc
1716AA	—	20.00	60.00	120	325	—

KM# 419.3 30 SOLS (1/4 ECU)
7.6480 g., 0.9170 Silver 0.2255 oz. ASW **Ruler:** Louis XV **Mint:** Rouen **Obverse:** Young bust of Louis XV right **Reverse:** Crowned circular arms

Date	Mintage	VG	F	VF	XF	Unc
1716B	—	20.00	60.00	120	325	—

KM# 419.4 30 SOLS (1/4 ECU)
7.6480 g., 0.9170 Silver 0.2255 oz. ASW **Ruler:** Louis XV **Mint:** Caen **Obverse:** Young bust of Louis XV right **Reverse:** Crowned circular arms

Date	Mintage	VG	F	VF	XF	Unc
1716C	—	25.00	85.00	170	400	—
1717C	—	25.00	85.00	170	400	—

KM# 419.5 30 SOLS (1/4 ECU)
7.6480 g., 0.9170 Silver 0.2255 oz. ASW **Ruler:** Louis XV **Mint:** Lyon **Obverse:** Young bust of Louis XV right **Reverse:** Crowned circular arms

Date	Mintage	VG	F	VF	XF	Unc
1716D	345,000	20.00	60.00	120	325	—

KM# 419.6 30 SOLS (1/4 ECU)
7.6480 g., 0.9170 Silver 0.2255 oz. ASW **Ruler:** Louis XV **Mint:** Tours **Obverse:** Young bust of Louis XV right **Reverse:** Crowned circular arms

Date	Mintage	VG	F	VF	XF	Unc
1716E	—	20.00	60.00	120	325	—
1717E	80,000	25.00	85.00	170	400	—

KM# 419.7 30 SOLS (1/4 ECU)
7.6480 g., 0.9170 Silver 0.2255 oz. ASW **Ruler:** Louis XV **Mint:** Poitiers **Obverse:** Young bust of Louis XV right **Reverse:** Crowned circular arms

Date	Mintage	VG	F	VF	XF	Unc
1716G	—	25.00	85.00	170	400	—
1717G	—	25.00	85.00	170	400	—

KM# 419.8 30 SOLS (1/4 ECU)
7.6480 g., 0.9170 Silver 0.2255 oz. ASW **Ruler:** Louis XV **Mint:** La Rochelle **Obverse:** Young bust of Louis XV right **Reverse:** Crowned circular arms

Date	Mintage	VG	F	VF	XF	Unc
1716H	—	20.00	60.00	120	325	—

KM# 419.9 30 SOLS (1/4 ECU)
7.6480 g., 0.9170 Silver 0.2255 oz. ASW **Ruler:** Louis XV **Mint:** Limoges **Obverse:** Young bust of Louis XV right **Reverse:** Crowned circular arms

Date	Mintage	VG	F	VF	XF	Unc
1716I	—	20.00	60.00	120	325	—

KM# 419.10 30 SOLS (1/4 ECU)
7.6480 g., 0.9170 Silver 0.2255 oz. ASW **Ruler:** Louis XV **Mint:** Bordeaux **Obverse:** Young bust of Louis XV right **Reverse:** Crowned circular arms

Date	Mintage	VG	F	VF	XF	Unc
1716K	—	20.00	60.00	120	325	—
1717K	144,000	20.00	60.00	120	325	—

KM# 419.11 30 SOLS (1/4 ECU)
7.6480 g., 0.9170 Silver 0.2255 oz. ASW **Ruler:** Louis XV **Mint:** Toulouse **Obverse:** Young bust of Louis XV right **Reverse:** Crowned circular arms

Date	Mintage	VG	F	VF	XF	Unc
1716M	—	20.00	60.00	120	325	—

KM# 419.12 30 SOLS (1/4 ECU)
7.6480 g., 0.9170 Silver 0.2255 oz. ASW **Ruler:** Louis XV **Mint:** Montpellier **Obverse:** Young bust of Louis XV right **Reverse:** Crowned circular arms

Date	Mintage	VG	F	VF	XF	Unc
1716N	—	20.00	60.00	120	325	—
1718N	—	25.00	85.00	170	400	—

KM# 419.13 30 SOLS (1/4 ECU)
7.6480 g., 0.9170 Silver 0.2255 oz. ASW **Ruler:** Louis XV **Mint:** Riom **Obverse:** Young bust of Louis XV right **Reverse:** Crowned circular arms

Date	Mintage	VG	F	VF	XF	Unc
1716O	—	20.00	60.00	120	325	—

KM# 419.14 30 SOLS (1/4 ECU)
7.6480 g., 0.9170 Silver 0.2255 oz. ASW **Ruler:** Louis XV **Mint:** Dijon **Obverse:** Young bust of Louis XV right **Reverse:** Crowned circular arms

Date	Mintage	VG	F	VF	XF	Unc
1716P	—	20.00	60.00	120	325	—
1717P	—	25.00	85.00	170	400	—

KM# 419.15 30 SOLS (1/4 ECU)
7.6480 g., 0.9170 Silver 0.2255 oz. ASW **Ruler:** Louis XV **Mint:** Reims **Obverse:** Young bust of Louis XV right **Reverse:** Crowned circular arms

Date	Mintage	VG	F	VF	XF	Unc
1716S	—	20.00	60.00	120	325	—

KM# 419.16 30 SOLS (1/4 ECU)
7.6480 g., 0.9170 Silver 0.2255 oz. ASW **Ruler:** Louis XV **Mint:** Nantes **Obverse:** Young bust of Louis XV right **Reverse:** Crowned circular arms

Date	Mintage	VG	F	VF	XF	Unc
1716T	—	20.00	60.00	120	325	—
1718T	—	25.00	85.00	170	400	—

KM# 419.17 30 SOLS (1/4 ECU)
7.6480 g., 0.9170 Silver 0.2255 oz. ASW **Ruler:** Louis XV **Mint:** Troyes **Obverse:** Young bust of Louis XV right **Reverse:** Crowned circular arms

Date	Mintage	VG	F	VF	XF	Unc
1716V	—	20.00	60.00	120	325	—

KM# 419.18 30 SOLS (1/4 ECU)
7.6480 g., 0.9170 Silver 0.2255 oz. ASW **Ruler:** Louis XV **Mint:** Lille **Obverse:** Young bust of Louis XV right **Reverse:** Crowned circular arms

Date	Mintage	VG	F	VF	XF	Unc
1716W	—	20.00	60.00	120	325	—
1717W	—	20.00	60.00	120	325	—

KM# 419.19 30 SOLS (1/4 ECU)
7.6480 g., 0.9170 Silver 0.2255 oz. ASW **Ruler:** Louis XV **Mint:** Amiens **Obverse:** Young bust of Louis XV right **Reverse:** Crowned circular arms

Date	Mintage	VG	F	VF	XF	Unc
1716X	—	20.00	60.00	120	325	—

KM# 419.20 30 SOLS (1/4 ECU)
7.6480 g., 0.9170 Silver 0.2255 oz. ASW **Ruler:** Louis XV **Mint:** Bourges **Obverse:** Young bust of Louis XV right **Reverse:** Crowned circular arms

Date	Mintage	VG	F	VF	XF	Unc
1716Y	—	20.00	60.00	120	325	—

KM# 419.21 30 SOLS (1/4 ECU)
7.6480 g., 0.9170 Silver 0.2255 oz. ASW **Ruler:** Louis XV **Mint:** Grenoble **Obverse:** Young bust right **Obv. Legend:** LVD • XV • D • G • FR • ET • NAV • REX **Reverse:** Crowned circular arms **Rev. Legend:** SIT NOMEN • DOMINI • BENEDICTVM

Date	Mintage	VG	F	VF	XF	Unc
1716Z	77,000	20.00	60.00	120	325	—

KM# 433.2 30 SOLS (1/4 ECU)
6.1180 g., 0.9170 Silver 0.1804 oz. ASW **Ruler:** Louis XV **Mint:** Metz

Date	Mintage	VG	F	VF	XF	Unc
1718AA	—	35.00	80.00	200	500	—

KM# 433.3 30 SOLS (1/4 ECU)
6.1180 g., 0.9170 Silver 0.1804 oz. ASW **Ruler:** Louis XV **Mint:** Rouen

Date	Mintage	VG	F	VF	XF	Unc
1718B	48,000	35.00	80.00	200	500	—
1719B	—	40.00	95.00	225	600	—

KM# 433.4 30 SOLS (1/4 ECU)
6.1180 g., 0.9170 Silver 0.1804 oz. ASW **Ruler:** Louis XV **Mint:** Strasbourg

Date	Mintage	VG	F	VF	XF	Unc
1718BB	—	35.00	80.00	200	500	—

KM# 433.5 30 SOLS (1/4 ECU)
6.1180 g., 0.9170 Silver 0.1804 oz. ASW **Ruler:** Louis XV **Mint:** Lyon

Date	Mintage	VG	F	VF	XF	Unc
1718D	—	35.00	80.00	200	500	—
1719D	—	40.00	95.00	225	600	—

KM# 433.6 30 SOLS (1/4 ECU)
6.1180 g., 0.9170 Silver 0.1804 oz. ASW **Ruler:** Louis XV **Mint:** Poitiers

Date	Mintage	VG	F	VF	XF	Unc
1718G	—	40.00	95.00	225	600	—

KM# 433.7 30 SOLS (1/4 ECU)
6.1180 g., 0.9170 Silver 0.1804 oz. ASW **Ruler:** Louis XV **Mint:** La Rochelle

Date	Mintage	VG	F	VF	XF	Unc
1718H	—	35.00	80.00	200	500	—

KM# 433.8 30 SOLS (1/4 ECU)
6.1180 g., 0.9170 Silver 0.1804 oz. ASW **Ruler:** Louis XV **Mint:** Reims

Date	Mintage	VG	F	VF	XF	Unc
1718S	—	35.00	80.00	200	500	—

KM# 433.9 30 SOLS (1/4 ECU)
6.1180 g., 0.9170 Silver 0.1804 oz. ASW **Ruler:** Louis XV **Mint:** Nantes

Date	Mintage	VG	F	VF	XF	Unc
1718T	—	35.00	80.00	200	500	—

KM# 433.10 30 SOLS (1/4 ECU)
6.1180 g., 0.9170 Silver 0.1804 oz. ASW **Ruler:** Louis XV **Mint:** Troyes **Obverse:** Young bust right **Obv. Legend:** LVD • XV • D • G • FR • ET • NAV • REX **Reverse:** Crowned arms of France and Navarre quartered **Rev. Legend:** SIT NOMEN DOMINI BENEDICTVM

Date	Mintage	VG	F	VF	XF	Unc
1718V	229,000	35.00	80.00	200	500	—

KM# 433.11 30 SOLS (1/4 ECU)
6.1180 g., 0.9170 Silver 0.1804 oz. ASW **Ruler:** Louis XV **Mint:** Lille **Obverse:** Young bust of Louis XV right **Reverse:** Crowned arms of France and Navarre quartered

Date	Mintage	VG	F	VF	XF	Unc
1718W	—	35.00	80.00	200	500	—

KM# 433.12 30 SOLS (1/4 ECU)
6.1180 g., 0.9170 Silver 0.1804 oz. ASW **Ruler:** Louis XV **Mint:** Amiens **Obverse:** Young bust of Louis XV right **Reverse:** Crowned arms of France and Navarre quartered

Date	Mintage	VG	F	VF	XF	Unc
1718X	—	35.00	80.00	200	500	—

KM# 433.13 30 SOLS (1/4 ECU)
6.1180 g., 0.9170 Silver 0.1804 oz. ASW **Ruler:** Louis XV **Mint:** Grenoble **Obverse:** Young bust of Louis XV right **Reverse:** Crowned arms of France and Navarre quartered

Date	Mintage	VG	F	VF	XF	Unc
1718Z	30,000	40.00	95.00	225	600	—

KM# 433.14 30 SOLS (1/4 ECU)
6.1180 g., 0.9170 Silver 0.1804 oz. ASW **Ruler:** Louis XV **Mint:** Besancon **Obverse:** Young bust of Louis XV right **Reverse:** Crowned arms of France and Navarre quartered **Note:** Mint mark: Back to back C's.

Date	Mintage	VG	F	VF	XF	Unc
1718	—	40.00	95.00	225	600	—

KM# 433.1 30 SOLS (1/4 ECU)
6.1180 g., 0.9170 Silver 0.1804 oz. ASW **Ruler:** Louis XV **Mint:** Paris **Obverse:** Young laureate armored bust right **Obv. Legend:** LUD • XV • D • G • FR • ET • NAV • REX • **Reverse:** Crowned arms of France and Navarre quartered **Rev. Legend:** SIT NOMEN • DOMINI • BENEDICTVM **Note:** Issued for Navarre.

Date	Mintage	VG	F	VF	XF	Unc
1718A	—	35.00	80.00	200	500	—

KM# 476.1 30 SOLS (1/4 ECU)
5.8950 g., 0.9170 Silver 0.1738 oz. ASW **Ruler:** Louis XV **Mint:** Paris **Obverse:** Young armored bust of Louis XV right **Reverse:** 8 L's cruciform with crowns in angles

Date	Mintage	VG	F	VF	XF	Unc
1725A	—	40.00	100	250	600	—

KM# 476.2 30 SOLS (1/4 ECU)
5.8950 g., 0.9170 Silver 0.1738 oz. ASW **Ruler:** Louis XV **Mint:** Metz **Obverse:** Young armored bust of Louis XV right **Reverse:** 8 L's cruciform with crowns in angles

Date	Mintage	VG	F	VF	XF	Unc
1725AA	—	45.00	110	275	675	—

KM# 476.3 30 SOLS (1/4 ECU)
5.8950 g., 0.9170 Silver 0.1738 oz. ASW **Ruler:** Louis XV **Mint:** Rouen **Obverse:** Young armored bust of Louis XV right **Reverse:** 8 L's cruciform with crowns in angles

Date	Mintage	VG	F	VF	XF	Unc
1725B	—	45.00	110	275	675	—

KM# 476.4 30 SOLS (1/4 ECU)

5.8950 g., 0.9170 Silver 0.1738 oz. ASW **Ruler:** Louis XV **Mint:** Strasbourg **Obverse:** Young armored bust of Louis XV right **Reverse:** 8 L's cruciform with crowns in angles

Date	Mintage	VG	F	VF	XF	Unc
1725BB	—	45.00	110	275	675	—

KM# 476.5 30 SOLS (1/4 ECU)

5.8950 g., 0.9170 Silver 0.1738 oz. ASW **Ruler:** Louis XV **Mint:** Lyon **Obverse:** Young armored bust of Louis XV right **Reverse:** 8 L's cruciform with crowns in angles

Date	Mintage	VG	F	VF	XF	Unc
1725D	251,000	45.00	110	275	675	—

KM# 476.6 30 SOLS (1/4 ECU)

5.8950 g., 0.9170 Silver 0.1738 oz. ASW **Ruler:** Louis XV **Mint:** Poitiers **Obverse:** Young armored bust of Louis XV right **Reverse:** 8 L's cruciform with crowns in angles

Date	Mintage	VG	F	VF	XF	Unc
1725G	42,000	45.00	110	275	675	—

KM# 476.7 30 SOLS (1/4 ECU)

5.8950 g., 0.9170 Silver 0.1738 oz. ASW **Ruler:** Louis XV **Mint:** Montpellier **Obverse:** Young armored bust of Louis XV right

Date	Mintage	VG	F	VF	XF	Unc
1725N	544,000	40.00	100	250	600	—

KM# 476.8 30 SOLS (1/4 ECU)

5.8950 g., 0.9170 Silver 0.1738 oz. ASW **Ruler:** Louis XV **Mint:** Lille **Obverse:** Young armored bust of Louis XV right **Reverse:** 8 L's cruciform with crowns in angles

Date	Mintage	VG	F	VF	XF	Unc
1725W	—	45.00	110	275	675	—

KM# 476.9 30 SOLS (1/4 ECU)

5.8950 g., 0.9170 Silver 0.1738 oz. ASW **Ruler:** Louis XV **Mint:** Amiens **Obverse:** Young armored bust of Louis XV right **Reverse:** 8 L's cruciform with crowns in angles

Date	Mintage	VG	F	VF	XF	Unc
1725X	—	45.00	110	275	675	—

KM# 606.1 30 SOLS

10.0000 g., 0.6660 Silver 0.2141 oz. ASW **Mint:** Paris **Obverse:** Head left **Obv. Legend:** LOUIS XVI ROI DES FRANCOIS **Reverse:** Standing Genius writing the Constitution **Rev. Legend:** REGNE DE LALOI •

Date	Mintage	VG	F	VF	XF	Unc
1791A	1,125,000	10.00	25.00	75.00	175	—
1792A	—	10.00	25.00	75.00	175	—

KM# 607.1 30 SOLS

10.0000 g., 0.6660 Silver 0.2141 oz. ASW **Mint:** Strasbourg **Obverse:** Legend ends: FRANCAIS

Date	Mintage	VG	F	VF	XF	Unc
1791BB	18,000	30.00	80.00	200	400	—
1792BB	—	25.00	60.00	150	350	—
1793BB	—	30.00	80.00	200	400	—

KM# 371 33 SOLS

9.2950 g., 0.8330 Silver 0.2489 oz. ASW **Ruler:** Louis XIV **Mint:** Strasbourg **Obverse:** Sceptre with hand of Justice crosses sword, 3 fleur-de-lis, crown in angles **Obv. Legend:** ARGENTINENSIS MONETA NOVA **Reverse:** Crowned circular shield of France, palms at side **Rev. Legend:** BENEDICTUM 1705 SIT • NOMEN • DOMINI

Date	Mintage	VG	F	VF	XF	Unc
1705BB	—	40.00	90.00	185	275	—
1706BB	—	55.00	125	250	400	—
1707BB	—	45.00	100	200	300	—
1708BB	—	65.00	160	325	500	—

KM# 408.3 1/20 ECU

1.5240 g., 0.9170 Silver 0.0449 oz. ASW **Ruler:** Louis XIV **Mint:** Lyon **Obverse:** Mailed bust right **Reverse:** 3 Crowns, 3 fleur-de-lis, mint mark at center

Date	Mintage	VG	F	VF	XF	Unc
1710D	—	125	275	450	900	—
1711D	—	175	350	600	1,200	—

KM# 408.8 1/20 ECU

1.5240 g., 0.9170 Silver 0.0449 oz. ASW **Ruler:** Louis XIV **Mint:** Toulouse **Obverse:** Mailed bust right **Reverse:** 3 Crowns, 3 fleur-de-lis, mint mark at center

Date	Mintage	VG	F	VF	XF	Unc
1710M	—	—	—	—	—	—
1712M	—	125	275	450	900	—
1713M	—	150	300	500	950	—

KM# 408.9 1/20 ECU

1.5240 g., 0.9170 Silver 0.0449 oz. ASW **Ruler:** Louis XIV **Mint:** Montpellier **Obverse:** Mailed bust right **Reverse:** 3 Crowns, 3 fleur-de-lis, mint mark at center

Date	Mintage	VG	F	VF	XF	Unc
1710N	—	125	275	450	900	—
1711N	—	150	300	500	950	—

KM# 408.4 1/20 ECU

1.5240 g., 0.9170 Silver 0.0449 oz. ASW **Ruler:** Louis XIV **Mint:** Tours **Obverse:** Mailed bust right **Reverse:** 3 Crowns, 3 fleur-de-lis, mint mark at center

Date	Mintage	VG	F	VF	XF	Unc
1711E	—	175	350	575	1,150	—
1712E	—	—	—	—	—	—
1713E	—	—	—	—	—	—

KM# 408.5 1/20 ECU

1.5240 g., 0.9170 Silver 0.0449 oz. ASW **Ruler:** Louis XIV **Mint:** Poitiers **Obverse:** Mailed bust right **Reverse:** 3 Crowns, 3 fleur-de-lis, mint mark at center

Date	Mintage	VG	F	VF	XF	Unc
1711G	—	150	300	500	950	—

KM# 408.11 1/20 ECU

1.5240 g., 0.9170 Silver 0.0449 oz. ASW **Ruler:** Louis XIV **Mint:** Aix **Obverse:** Mailed bust right **Reverse:** 3 Crowns, 3 fleur-de-lis, mint mark at center **Note:** Mint mark: &.

Date	Mintage	VG	F	VF	XF	Unc
1711	—	175	350	575	1,150	—

KM# 408.12 1/20 ECU

1.5240 g., 0.9170 Silver 0.0449 oz. ASW **Ruler:** Louis XIV **Mint:** Rennes **Obverse:** Mailed bust right **Reverse:** 3 Crowns, 3 fleur-de-lis, mint mark at center **Note:** Mint mark: 9.

Date	Mintage	VG	F	VF	XF	Unc
1711	—	125	275	450	900	—
1713	—	—	—	—	—	—
1715	—	—	—	—	—	—

KM# 408.13 1/20 ECU

1.5240 g., 0.9170 Silver 0.0449 oz. ASW **Ruler:** Louis XIV **Mint:** Pau **Obverse:** Mailed bust right **Reverse:** 3 Crowns, 3 fleur-de-lis, mint mark at center **Note:** Mint mark: Cow.

Date	Mintage	VG	F	VF	XF	Unc
1711	—	250	500	900	1,800	—

KM# 408.7 1/20 ECU

1.5240 g., 0.9170 Silver 0.0449 oz. ASW **Ruler:** Louis XIV **Mint:** Limoges **Obverse:** Mailed bust right **Reverse:** 3 Crowns, 3 fleur-de-lis, mint mark at center

Date	Mintage	VG	F	VF	XF	Unc
1711I	—	175	350	575	1,150	—

KM# 408.10 1/20 ECU

1.5240 g., 0.9170 Silver 0.0449 oz. ASW **Ruler:** Louis XIV **Mint:** Nantes **Obverse:** Mailed bust right **Reverse:** 3 Crowns, 3 fleur-de-lis, mint mark at center

Date	Mintage	VG	F	VF	XF	Unc
1712T	—	125	275	450	900	—

KM# 408.2 1/20 ECU

1.5240 g., 0.9170 Silver 0.0449 oz. ASW **Ruler:** Louis XIV **Mint:** Rouen **Obverse:** Mailed bust right **Reverse:** 3 Crowns, 3 fleur-de-lis, mint mark at center

Date	Mintage	VG	F	VF	XF	Unc
1712B	—	125	275	450	900	—

KM# 408.1 1/20 ECU

1.5240 g., 0.9170 Silver 0.0449 oz. ASW **Ruler:** Louis XIV **Mint:** Paris **Obverse:** Mailed bust right **Reverse:** 3 crowns, 3 fleur-de-lis, mint mark at center

Date	Mintage	VG	F	VF	XF	Unc
1713A	—	150	300	500	950	—

KM# 408.6 1/20 ECU

1.5240 g., 0.9170 Silver 0.0449 oz. ASW **Ruler:** Louis XIV **Mint:** La Rochelle **Obverse:** Mailed bust right **Reverse:** 3 Crowns, 3 fleur-de-lis, mint mark at center

Date	Mintage	VG	F	VF	XF	Unc
1715H	—	225	450	750	1,500	—

KM# 320 1/16 ECU

1.4740 g., 0.9170 Silver 0.0435 oz. ASW **Ruler:** Louis XIV **Reverse:** Crowned quartered shield, crossed scepters, hand of Justice behind

Date	Mintage	VG	F	VF	XF	Unc
1701	—	200	400	800	1,750	—
1702	—	—	—	—	—	—
1703	—	—	—	—	—	—

KM# 372.1 1/16 ECU

1.4740 g., 0.9170 Silver 0.0435 oz. ASW **Ruler:** Louis XIV **Mint:** Bayonne **Obverse:** Mailed bust right

Date	Mintage	VG	F	VF	XF	Unc
1705L	—	225	425	850	1,850	—

KM# 372.2 1/16 ECU

1.4740 g., 0.9170 Silver 0.0435 oz. ASW **Ruler:** Louis XIV **Mint:** Lille

Date	Mintage	VG	F	VF	XF	Unc
1705W	—	225	425	850	1,850	—

KM# 477.1 1/16 ECU

1.4740 g., 0.9170 Silver 0.0435 oz. ASW **Ruler:** Louis XV **Mint:** Paris **Obverse:** Young armored bust of Louis XV right **Reverse:** 8 L's cruciform with crowns in angles

Date	Mintage	VG	F	VF	XF	Unc
1725A	—	35.00	100	250	600	—

KM# 477.2 1/16 ECU

1.4740 g., 0.9170 Silver 0.0435 oz. ASW **Ruler:** Louis XV **Mint:** Metz **Obverse:** Laureate bust right **Obv. Legend:** LUD • XV • D • G • FR • ET • NAV • REX • **Reverse:** 4 Fleur-de-lis form square at center, 4 crowns separated by back to back L's surround **Rev. Legend:** SIT NOMEN DOMINI BENEDICT •

Date	Mintage	VG	F	VF	XF	Unc
1725AA	—	50.00	175	425	900	—

KM# 477.3 1/16 ECU

1.4740 g., 0.9170 Silver 0.0435 oz. ASW **Ruler:** Louis XV **Mint:** Caen **Obverse:** Laureate bust right **Reverse:** 4 Fleur-de-lis form square at center, 4 crowns separated by back to back L's surround

Date	Mintage	VG	F	VF	XF	Unc
1725C	23,000	35.00	100	250	600	—

KM# 477.4 1/16 ECU

1.4740 g., 0.9170 Silver 0.0435 oz. ASW **Ruler:** Louis XV **Mint:** Montpellier **Obverse:** Laureate bust right **Reverse:** 4 Fleur-de-lis form square at center, 4 crowns separated by back to back L's surround

Date	Mintage	VG	F	VF	XF	Unc
1725N	—	35.00	100	250	600	—

KM# 477.5 1/16 ECU

1.4740 g., 0.9170 Silver 0.0435 oz. ASW **Ruler:** Louis XV **Mint:** Orléans **Obverse:** Laureate bust right **Reverse:** 4 Fleur-de-lis form square at center, 4 crowns separated by back to back L's surround

Date	Mintage	VG	F	VF	XF	Unc
1725R	15,000	40.00	125	325	700	—

KM# 477.6 1/16 ECU

1.4740 g., 0.9170 Silver 0.0435 oz. ASW **Ruler:** Louis XV **Mint:** Besancon **Obverse:** Laureate bust right **Reverse:** 4 Fleur-de-lis form square at center, 4 crowns separated by back to back L's surround **Note:** Mint mark: Back to back C's.

Date	Mintage	VG	F	VF	XF	Unc
1725	—	25.00	80.00	225	500	—

KM# 290.19 1/12 ECU (10 Sols)

2.2610 g., 0.9170 Silver 0.0667 oz. ASW **Ruler:** Louis XIV **Mint:** Besancon **Obverse:** Mailed bust right **Reverse:** Palm branches below crowned circular shield of France **Note:** Mint mark: Back-to-back C's.

Date	Mintage	VG	F	VF	XF	Unc
1694	11,000	—	—	—	—	—
1695	5,187	—	—	—	—	—
1696	—	60.00	140	275	575	—
1697	3,516	—	—	—	—	—
1698	1,083	—	—	—	—	—
1699	759	—	—	—	—	—
1701	—	100	200	400	850	—

KM# 322 1/12 ECU (10 Sols)

2.2610 g., 0.9170 Silver 0.0667 oz. ASW **Ruler:** Louis XIV **Mint:** Pau **Reverse:** Crowned circular shield of France, Navarre and Bearn crossed scepters and hand of Justice behind **Note:** Mint mark: Cow.

Date	Mintage	VG	F	VF	XF	Unc
1701 Rare	—	—	—	—	—	—

KM# 321.1 1/12 ECU (10 Sols)

2.2610 g., 0.9170 Silver 0.0667 oz. ASW **Ruler:** Louis XIV **Mint:** Paris **Obverse:** Mailed bust right **Reverse:** Crowned circular shield of France, crossed scepters and hand of Justice behind

Date	Mintage	VG	F	VF	XF	Unc
1701A	—	45.00	110	225	575	—
1702A	—	—	—	175	—	—
1703A	—	45.00	110	225	575	—

KM# 321.2 1/12 ECU (10 Sols)

2.2610 g., 0.9170 Silver 0.0667 oz. ASW **Ruler:** Louis XIV **Mint:** Metz **Obverse:** Mailed bust right **Reverse:** Crowned circular shield of France, crossed sceptres and hand of Justice behind

Date	Mintage	VG	F	VF	XF	Unc
1702AA	—	50.00	125	260	750	—

KM# 321.3 1/12 ECU (10 Sols)

2.2610 g., 0.9170 Silver 0.0667 oz. ASW **Ruler:** Louis XIV **Mint:** Rouen **Obverse:** Mailed bust right **Reverse:** Crowned circular shield of France, crossed sceptres and hand of Justice behind

Date	Mintage	VG	F	VF	XF	Unc
1702B	—	45.00	110	225	575	—

KM# 321.4 1/12 ECU (10 Sols)

2.2610 g., 0.9170 Silver 0.0667 oz. ASW **Ruler:** Louis XIV **Mint:** Caen **Obverse:** Mailed bust right **Reverse:** Crowned circular shield of France, crossed sceptres and hand of Justice behind

Date	Mintage	VG	F	VF	XF	Unc
1702C	—	45.00	110	225	575	—

KM# 321.5 1/12 ECU (10 Sols)

2.2610 g., 0.9170 Silver 0.0667 oz. ASW **Ruler:** Louis XIV **Mint:** Lyon **Obverse:** Mailed bust right **Reverse:** Crowned circular shield of France, crossed sceptres and hand of Justice behind

Date	Mintage	VG	F	VF	XF	Unc
1702D	—	40.00	100	200	500	—
1703D	—	50.00	125	250	625	—
1704D	—	75.00	185	375	900	—

KM# 321.6 1/12 ECU (10 Sols)

2.2610 g., 0.9170 Silver 0.0667 oz. ASW **Ruler:** Louis XIV **Mint:** Tours **Obverse:** Mailed bust right **Reverse:** Crowned circular shield of France, crossed sceptres and hand of Justice behind

Date	Mintage	VG	F	VF	XF	Unc
1702E	—	45.00	110	225	575	—
1703E	—	60.00	150	300	750	—

KM# 321.11 1/12 ECU (10 Sols)

2.2610 g., 0.9170 Silver 0.0667 oz. ASW **Ruler:** Louis XIV **Mint:** Montpellier **Obverse:** Mailed bust right **Reverse:** Crowned circular shield of France, crossed sceptres and hand of Justice behind

Date	Mintage	VG	F	VF	XF	Unc
1702N	204,000	45.00	110	225	575	—
1703N	20,000	—	—	—	—	—

KM# 321.12 1/12 ECU (10 Sols)

2.2610 g., 0.9170 Silver 0.0667 oz. ASW **Ruler:** Louis XIV **Mint:** Dijon **Obverse:** Mailed bust right **Reverse:** Crowned circular shield of France, crossed sceptres and hand of Justice behind

Date	Mintage	VG	F	VF	XF	Unc
1702P	—	40.00	100	200	500	—

KM# 321.13 1/12 ECU (10 Sols)

2.2610 g., 0.9170 Silver 0.0667 oz. ASW **Ruler:** Louis XIV **Mint:** Troyes **Obverse:** Mailed bust right **Reverse:** Crowned circular shield of France, crossed sceptres and hand of Justice behind

Date	Mintage	VG	F	VF	XF	Unc
1702S	—	50.00	125	250	625	—

KM# 321.14 1/12 ECU (10 Sols)

2.2610 g., 0.9170 Silver 0.0667 oz. ASW **Ruler:** Louis XIV **Mint:** Nantes **Obverse:** Mailed bust right **Reverse:** Crowned circular shield of France, crossed sceptres and hand of Justice behind

Date	Mintage	VG	F	VF	XF	Unc
1702T	—	50.00	125	250	625	—

KM# 321.15 1/12 ECU (10 Sols)

2.2610 g., 0.9170 Silver 0.0667 oz. ASW **Ruler:** Louis XIV **Mint:** Troyes **Obverse:** Mailed bust right **Reverse:** Crowned circular shield of France, crossed sceptres and hand of Justice behind

Date	Mintage	VG	F	VF	XF	Unc
1702V	91,000	50.00	125	250	625	—
1703V	910,000	—	—	—	—	—

KM# 321.16 1/12 ECU (10 Sols)

2.2610 g., 0.9170 Silver 0.0667 oz. ASW **Ruler:** Louis XIV **Mint:** Lille **Obverse:** Mailed bust right **Reverse:** Crowned circular shield of France, crossed sceptres and hand of Justice behind

Date	Mintage	VG	F	VF	XF	Unc
1702W	481,000	40.00	100	200	500	—
1703W	17,000	—	—	—	—	—

KM# 321.17 1/12 ECU (10 Sols)

2.2610 g., 0.9170 Silver 0.0667 oz. ASW **Ruler:** Louis XIV **Mint:** Amiens **Obverse:** Mailed bust right **Reverse:** Crowned circular shield of France, crossed sceptres and hand of Justice behind

Date	Mintage	VG	F	VF	XF	Unc
1702X	—	60.00	150	300	750	—
1703X	—	75.00	185	375	900	—

KM# 321.18 1/12 ECU (10 Sols)

2.2610 g., 0.9170 Silver 0.0667 oz. ASW **Ruler:** Louis XIV **Mint:** Bourges **Obverse:** Mailed bust right **Reverse:** Crowned circular shield of France, crossed sceptres and hand of Justice behind

Date	Mintage	VG	F	VF	XF	Unc
1702Y	—	60.00	150	300	750	—

KM# 339 1/12 ECU (10 Sols)

2.2610 g., 0.9170 Silver 0.0667 oz. ASW **Ruler:** Louis XIV **Mint:** Grenoble **Reverse:** Crowned circular shield of Dauphine

Date	Mintage	VG	F	VF	XF	Unc
1702Z	—	1,000	2,000	3,500	5,000	—
1703Z	—	1,200	2,200	4,000	6,000	—

KM# 321.19 1/12 ECU (10 Sols)

2.2610 g., 0.9170 Silver 0.0667 oz. ASW **Ruler:** Louis XIV **Mint:** Rennes **Obverse:** Mailed bust right **Reverse:** Crowned circular shield of France, crossed sceptres and hand of Justice behind **Note:** Mint mark: 9.

Date	Mintage	VG	F	VF	XF	Unc
1702	—	50.00	125	250	625	—

KM# 321.20 1/12 ECU (10 Sols)

2.2610 g., 0.9170 Silver 0.0667 oz. ASW **Ruler:** Louis XIV **Mint:** Aix **Note:** Mint mark: &.

Date	Mintage	VG	F	VF	XF	Unc
1702	—	50.00	125	250	625	—

KM# 321.8 1/12 ECU (10 Sols)

2.2610 g., 0.9170 Silver 0.0667 oz. ASW **Ruler:** Louis XIV **Mint:** La Rochelle **Obverse:** Mailed bust right **Reverse:** Crowned circular shield of France, crossed sceptres and hand of Justice behind

Date	Mintage	VG	F	VF	XF	Unc
1702H	—	50.00	125	250	625	—

KM# 321.9 1/12 ECU (10 Sols)

2.2610 g., 0.9170 Silver 0.0667 oz. ASW **Ruler:** Louis XIV **Mint:** Limoges **Obverse:** Mailed bust right **Reverse:** Crowned circular shield of France, crossed sceptres and hand of Justice behind

Date	Mintage	VG	F	VF	XF	Unc
1702I	—	50.00	125	250	625	—

KM# 321.21 1/12 ECU (10 Sols)

2.2610 g., 0.9170 Silver 0.0667 oz. ASW **Ruler:** Louis XIV **Mint:** Besancon **Obverse:** Mailed bust right **Reverse:** Crowned circular shield of France, crossed sceptres and hand of Justice behind **Note:** Mint mark: Back to back C's.

Date	Mintage	VG	F	VF	XF	Unc
1702	—	60.00	150	300	750	—

KM# 321.10 1/12 ECU (10 Sols)

2.2610 g., 0.9170 Silver 0.0667 oz. ASW **Ruler:** Louis XIV **Mint:** Toulouse **Obverse:** Mailed bust right **Reverse:** Crowned circular shield of France, crossed sceptres and hand of Justice behind

Date	Mintage	VG	F	VF	XF	Unc
1703M	—	75.00	185	375	900	—

KM# 321.7 1/12 ECU (10 Sols)

2.2610 g., 0.9170 Silver 0.0667 oz. ASW **Ruler:** Louis XIV **Mint:** Poitiers **Obverse:** Mailed bust right **Obv. Legend:** LVD • XIIII • D • G • FR • ET • NAV • REX • **Reverse:** Crowned circular shield of France, crossed sceptres and hand of Justice behind **Rev. Legend:** BENEDICTVM SIT NOMEN DOMINI

Date	Mintage	VG	F	VF	XF	Unc
1703G	—	50.00	125	250	625	—

KM# 350.12 1/12 ECU (10 Sols)

2.2610 g., 0.9170 Silver 0.0667 oz. ASW **Ruler:** Louis XIV **Mint:** Troyes **Obverse:** Armored bust right **Reverse:** 8 Crowned L's cruciform, fleur-de-lis in angles

Date	Mintage	VG	F	VF	XF	Unc
1704S	—	80.00	200	425	950	—
1705S	—	—	—	—	—	—

KM# 350.13 1/12 ECU (10 Sols)

2.2610 g., 0.9170 Silver 0.0667 oz. ASW **Ruler:** Louis XIV **Mint:** Nantes **Obverse:** Armored bust right **Reverse:** 8 Crowned L's cruciform, fleur-de-lis in angles

Date	Mintage	VG	F	VF	XF	Unc
1704T	—	—	—	—	—	—
1705T	—	100	220	450	1,000	—

KM# 350.14 1/12 ECU (10 Sols)

2.2610 g., 0.9170 Silver 0.0667 oz. ASW **Ruler:** Louis XIV **Mint:** Troyes **Obverse:** Armored bust right **Reverse:** 8 Crowned L's cruciform, fleur-de-lis in angles

Date	Mintage	VG	F	VF	XF	Unc
1704V	89,000	—	—	—	—	—
1705V	89,000	—	—	—	—	—

KM# 350.15 1/12 ECU (10 Sols)

2.2610 g., 0.9170 Silver 0.0667 oz. ASW **Ruler:** Louis XIV **Mint:** Lille **Obverse:** Armored bust right **Reverse:** 8 Crowned L's cruciform, fleur-de-lis in angles

Date	Mintage	VG	F	VF	XF	Unc
1704W	420,000	75.00	185	400	900	—
1705W	—	—	—	—	—	—

KM# 350.16 1/12 ECU (10 Sols)

2.2610 g., 0.9170 Silver 0.0667 oz. ASW **Ruler:** Louis XIV **Mint:** Amiens **Obverse:** Armored bust right **Reverse:** 8 Crowned L's cruciform, fleur-de-lis in angles

Date	Mintage	VG	F	VF	XF	Unc
1704X	—	80.00	200	425	950	—

KM# 350.18 1/12 ECU (10 Sols)

2.2610 g., 0.9170 Silver 0.0667 oz. ASW **Ruler:** Louis XIV **Mint:** Grenoble **Obverse:** Armored bust right **Reverse:** 8 Crowned L's cruciform, fleur-de-lis in angles

Date	Mintage	VG	F	VF	XF	Unc
1704Z	—	80.00	200	425	950	—

KM# 351 1/12 ECU (10 Sols)

2.2610 g., 0.9170 Silver 0.0667 oz. ASW **Ruler:** Louis XIV **Mint:** Amiens **Obverse:** Laureate head right

Date	Mintage	VG	F	VF	XF	Unc
1704X	—	250	500	1,000	—	—
1705X	—	250	500	1,000	—	—

KM# 350.1 1/12 ECU (10 Sols)

2.2610 g., 0.9170 Silver 0.0667 oz. ASW **Ruler:** Louis XIV **Mint:** Paris **Obverse:** Armored bust right **Reverse:** 8 crowned L's cruciform, fleur-de-lis in angles

Date	Mintage	VG	F	VF	XF	Unc
1704A	1,647,000	50.00	135	300	750	—
1705A	—	50.00	135	300	750	—

KM# 350.2 1/12 ECU (10 Sols)

2.2610 g., 0.9170 Silver 0.0667 oz. ASW **Ruler:** Louis XIV **Mint:** Rouen **Obverse:** Armored bust right **Reverse:** 8 Crowned L's cruciform, fleur-de-lis in angles

Date	Mintage	VG	F	VF	XF	Unc
1704B	—	80.00	200	425	950	—

KM# 350.3 1/12 ECU (10 Sols)

2.2610 g., 0.9170 Silver 0.0667 oz. ASW **Ruler:** Louis XIV **Mint:** Caen **Obverse:** Armored bust right **Reverse:** 8 Crowned L's cruciform, fleur-de-lis in angles

Date	Mintage	VG	F	VF	XF	Unc
1704C	—	80.00	200	425	950	—
1705C	—	80.00	200	425	950	—

KM# 350.4 1/12 ECU (10 Sols)

2.2610 g., 0.9170 Silver 0.0667 oz. ASW **Ruler:** Louis XIV **Mint:** Lyon **Obverse:** Armored bust right **Reverse:** 8 Crowned L's cruciform, fleur-de-lis in angles

Date	Mintage	VG	F	VF	XF	Unc
1704D	83,000	80.00	200	425	950	—
1705D	18,000	—	—	—	—	—

KM# 350.5 1/12 ECU (10 Sols)

2.2610 g., 0.9170 Silver 0.0667 oz. ASW **Ruler:** Louis XIV **Mint:** La Rochelle **Obverse:** Armored bust right **Reverse:** 8 Crowned L's cruciform, fleur-de-lis in angles

Date	Mintage	VG	F	VF	XF	Unc
1704H	—	80.00	200	425	950	—

KM# 350.6 1/12 ECU (10 Sols)

2.2610 g., 0.9170 Silver 0.0667 oz. ASW **Ruler:** Louis XIV **Mint:** Limoges **Obverse:** Armored bust right **Reverse:** 8 Crowned L's cruciform, fleur-de-lis in angles

Date	Mintage	VG	F	VF	XF	Unc
1704I	—	80.00	200	425	950	—

KM# 350.7 1/12 ECU (10 Sols)

2.2610 g., 0.9170 Silver 0.0667 oz. ASW **Ruler:** Louis XIV **Mint:** Bordeaux **Obverse:** Armored bust right **Reverse:** 8 Crowned L's cruciform, fleur-de-lis in angles

Date	Mintage	VG	F	VF	XF	Unc
1704K	—	—	—	—	—	—
1705K	—	80.00	200	425	950	—

KM# 350.8 1/12 ECU (10 Sols)

2.2610 g., 0.9170 Silver 0.0667 oz. ASW **Ruler:** Louis XIV **Mint:** Toulouse **Obverse:** Armored bust right **Reverse:** 8 Crowned L's cruciform, fleur-de-lis in angles

Date	Mintage	VG	F	VF	XF	Unc
1704M	—	80.00	200	425	950	—
1705M	—	100	220	450	1,000	—

KM# 350.9 1/12 ECU (10 Sols)

2.2610 g., 0.9170 Silver 0.0667 oz. ASW **Ruler:** Louis XIV **Mint:** Montpellier **Obverse:** Armored right **Reverse:** 8 Crowned L's cruciform, fleur-de-lis in angles

Date	Mintage	VG	F	VF	XF	Unc
1704N	27,000	—	—	—	—	—
1705N	59,000	—	—	—	—	—

KM# 350.10 1/12 ECU (10 Sols)

2.2610 g., 0.9170 Silver 0.0667 oz. ASW **Ruler:** Louis XIV **Mint:** Dijon **Obverse:** Armored bust right **Reverse:** 8 Crowned L's cruciform, fleur-de-lis in angles

Date	Mintage	VG	F	VF	XF	Unc
1704P	—	80.00	200	425	950	—

KM# 350.19 1/12 ECU (10 Sols)

2.2610 g., 0.9170 Silver 0.0667 oz. ASW **Ruler:** Louis XIV **Mint:** Aix **Obverse:** Armored bust right **Reverse:** 8 Crowned L's cruciform, fleur-de-lis in angles **Note:** Mint mark: &.

Date	Mintage	VG	F	VF	XF	Unc
1704	—	—	—	—	—	—
1705	—	—	—	—	—	—

KM# 350.20 1/12 ECU (10 Sols)

2.2610 g., 0.9170 Silver 0.0667 oz. ASW **Ruler:** Louis XIV **Mint:** Rennes **Obverse:** Armored bust right **Reverse:** 8 Crowned L's cruciform, fleur-de-lis in angles **Note:** Mint mark: 9.

Date	Mintage	VG	F	VF	XF	Unc
1704	—	80.00	200	425	950	—
1705	—	100	220	500	1,000	—

KM# 350.11 1/12 ECU (10 Sols)

2.2610 g., 0.9170 Silver 0.0667 oz. ASW **Ruler:** Louis XIV **Mint:** Riom **Obverse:** Armored bust right **Reverse:** 8 Crowned L's cruciform, fleur-de-lis in angles

Date	Mintage	VG	F	VF	XF	Unc
1705O	—	100	200	450	1,000	—

KM# 350.17 1/12 ECU (10 Sols)

2.2610 g., 0.9170 Silver 0.0667 oz. ASW **Ruler:** Louis XIV **Mint:** Bourges **Obverse:** Armored bust right **Reverse:** 8 Crowned L's cruciform, fleur-de-lis in angles

Date	Mintage	VG	F	VF	XF	Unc
1705Y	—	80.00	200	425	950	—

KM# 463.3 1/12 ECU (10 Sols)

2.2610 g., 0.9170 Silver 0.0667 oz. ASW **Ruler:** Louis XV **Mint:** Caen

Date	Mintage	VG	F	VF	XF	Unc
1720C	92,000	6.00	14.00	40.00	100	—
1721C	6,676,000	4.00	7.00	25.00	65.00	—

KM# 463.17 1/12 ECU (10 Sols)

2.2610 g., 0.9170 Silver 0.0667 oz. ASW **Ruler:** Louis XV **Mint:** Bourges **Obverse:** Young laureate bust right **Reverse:** Crowned arms of France

Date	Mintage	VG	F	VF	XF	Unc
1720Y	—	6.00	14.00	40.00	100	—
1721Y	—	6.00	14.00	40.00	100	—

KM# 463.10 1/12 ECU (10 Sols)

2.2610 g., 0.9170 Silver 0.0667 oz. ASW **Ruler:** Louis XV **Mint:** Perpignan

Date	Mintage	VG	F	VF	XF	Unc
1720Q	—	6.00	14.00	40.00	100	—

KM# 463.11 1/12 ECU (10 Sols)
2.2610 g., 0.9170 Silver 0.0667 oz. ASW **Ruler:** Louis XV **Mint:** Orléans **Obverse:** Young laureate bust right **Obv. Legend:** LUD • XV • D • G • FR • ET • NAV • REX • **Reverse:** Crowned arms of France **Rev. Legend:** SIT NOMEN DOMINI BENEDICTUM

Date	Mintage	VG	F	VF	XF	Unc
1720R	18,000	8.00	20.00	55.00	140	—
1721R	128,000	6.00	14.00	40.00	100	—

KM# 463.12 1/12 ECU (10 Sols)
2.2610 g., 0.9170 Silver 0.0667 oz. ASW **Ruler:** Louis XV **Mint:** Reims **Obverse:** Young laureate bust right **Reverse:** Crowned arms of France

Date	Mintage	VG	F	VF	XF	Unc
1721S	—	6.00	14.00	40.00	100	—
1722S	—	6.00	14.00	40.00	100	—

KM# 463.13 1/12 ECU (10 Sols)
2.2610 g., 0.9170 Silver 0.0667 oz. ASW **Ruler:** Louis XV **Mint:** Nantes **Obverse:** Young laureate bust right **Reverse:** Crowned arms of France

Date	Mintage	VG	F	VF	XF	Unc
1721T	—	6.00	16.00	42.00	100	—

KM# 463.14 1/12 ECU (10 Sols)
2.2610 g., 0.9170 Silver 0.0667 oz. ASW **Ruler:** Louis XV **Mint:** Troyes **Obverse:** Young laureate bust right **Reverse:** Crowned arms of France

Date	Mintage	VG	F	VF	XF	Unc
1721V	—	6.00	14.00	40.00	100	—
1722V	—	6.00	14.00	40.00	100	—

KM# 463.15 1/12 ECU (10 Sols)
2.2610 g., 0.9170 Silver 0.0667 oz. ASW **Ruler:** Louis XV **Mint:** Lille **Obverse:** Young laureate bust right **Reverse:** Crowned arms of France

Date	Mintage	VG	F	VF	XF	Unc
1721W	—	6.00	14.00	40.00	100	—
1722W	—	6.00	14.00	40.00	100	—

KM# 463.16 1/12 ECU (10 Sols)
2.2610 g., 0.9170 Silver 0.0667 oz. ASW **Ruler:** Louis XV **Mint:** Amiens **Obverse:** Young laureate bust right **Reverse:** Crowned arms of France

Date	Mintage	VG	F	VF	XF	Unc
1721X	—	6.00	14.00	40.00	100	—

KM# 463.7 1/12 ECU (10 Sols)
2.2610 g., 0.9170 Silver 0.0667 oz. ASW **Ruler:** Louis XV **Mint:** Limoges **Obverse:** Young laureate bust right **Reverse:** Crowned arms of France

Date	Mintage	VG	F	VF	XF	Unc
1721I	—	9.00	20.00	55.00	120	—

KM# 463.9 1/12 ECU (10 Sols)
2.2610 g., 0.9170 Silver 0.0667 oz. ASW **Ruler:** Louis XV **Mint:** Dijon **Obverse:** Young laureate bust right **Reverse:** Crowned arms of France

Date	Mintage	VG	F	VF	XF	Unc
1721P	—	8.00	16.00	42.00	100	—

KM# 463.18 1/12 ECU (10 Sols)
2.2610 g., 0.9170 Silver 0.0667 oz. ASW **Ruler:** Louis XV **Mint:** Rennes **Obverse:** Young laureate bust right **Reverse:** Crowned arms of France **Note:** Mint mark: 9.

Date	Mintage	VG	F	VF	XF	Unc
1721	—	6.00	14.00	40.00	100	—
1723	—	6.00	14.00	40.00	100	—

KM# 464 1/12 ECU (10 Sols)
2.2610 g., 0.9170 Silver 0.0667 oz. ASW **Ruler:** Louis XV **Mint:** Pau **Note:** Mint mark: Cow. Similar to KM#463.3 but obverse legend ends with ligate BD.

Date	Mintage	VG	F	VF	XF	Unc
1721	—	10.00	30.00	75.00	170	—

KM# 463.1 1/12 ECU (10 Sols)
2.2610 g., 0.9170 Silver 0.0667 oz. ASW **Ruler:** Louis XV **Mint:** Paris **Obverse:** Young laureate bust right **Reverse:** Crowned arms in square shield

Date	Mintage	VG	F	VF	XF	Unc
1721A	—	4.00	7.00	25.00	65.00	—
1722A	—	6.00	14.00	40.00	100	—

KM# 463.2 1/12 ECU (10 Sols)
2.2610 g., 0.9170 Silver 0.0667 oz. ASW **Ruler:** Louis XV **Mint:** Rouen **Obverse:** Young laureate bust right **Reverse:** Crowned arms of France

Date	Mintage	VG	F	VF	XF	Unc
1721B	—	6.00	14.00	40.00	100	—
1722B	—	6.00	14.00	40.00	100	—

KM# 463.4 1/12 ECU (10 Sols)
2.2610 g., 0.9170 Silver 0.0667 oz. ASW **Ruler:** Louis XV **Mint:** Lyon **Obverse:** Young laureate bust right **Reverse:** Crowned arms of France

Date	Mintage	VG	F	VF	XF	Unc
1722D	105,000	6.00	14.00	40.00	100	—

KM# 463.5 1/12 ECU (10 Sols)
2.2610 g., 0.9170 Silver 0.0667 oz. ASW **Ruler:** Louis XV **Mint:** Tours **Obverse:** Young laureate bust right **Reverse:** Crowned arms of France

Date	Mintage	VG	F	VF	XF	Unc
1722E	—	6.00	14.00	40.00	100	—

KM# 463.6 1/12 ECU (10 Sols)
2.2610 g., 0.9170 Silver 0.0667 oz. ASW **Ruler:** Louis XV **Mint:** Poitiers **Obverse:** Young laureate bust right **Reverse:** Crowned arms of France

Date	Mintage	VG	F	VF	XF	Unc
1722G	—	6.00	14.00	40.00	100	—

KM# 463.8 1/12 ECU (10 Sols)
2.2610 g., 0.9170 Silver 0.0667 oz. ASW **Ruler:** Louis XV **Mint:** Bayonne **Obverse:** Young laureate bust right **Reverse:** Crowned arms of France

Date	Mintage	VG	F	VF	XF	Unc
1723L	—	6.00	14.00	40.00	100	—

KM# 379.1 1/10 ECU
3.0490 g., 0.9170 Silver 0.0899 oz. ASW **Ruler:** Louis XIV **Mint:** Paris **Obverse:** Mailed bust right **Reverse:** 3 Crowns and 3 fleur-de-lis in angles

Date	Mintage	VG	F	VF	XF	Unc
1709A	—	12.00	30.00	65.00	150	—
1710A	—	12.00	30.00	65.00	150	—
1711A	—	12.50	32.00	70.00	165	—
1712A	—	12.50	32.00	70.00	165	—
1713A	—	12.00	30.00	65.00	150	—
1715A	—	—	—	—	—	—

KM# 379.16 1/10 ECU
3.0490 g., 0.9170 Silver 0.0899 oz. ASW **Ruler:** Louis XIV **Mint:** Troyes **Obverse:** Mailed bust right **Reverse:** 3 Crowns and 3 fleur-de-lis in angles

Date	Mintage	VG	F	VF	XF	Unc
1709S	—	15.00	35.00	80.00	175	—
1710S	—	12.50	32.00	75.00	170	—
1711S	—	12.50	32.00	75.00	170	—
1715S	—	27.00	60.00	135	300	—

KM# 379.17 1/10 ECU
3.0490 g., 0.9170 Silver 0.0899 oz. ASW **Ruler:** Louis XIV **Mint:** Nantes **Obverse:** Mailed bust right **Reverse:** 3 Crowns and 3 fleur-de-lis in angles

Date	Mintage	VG	F	VF	XF	Unc
1710T	—	12.50	32.00	70.00	160	—
1711T	—	12.00	30.00	65.00	145	—
1712T	—	12.00	30.00	65.00	145	—
1713T	—	—	—	—	—	—
1714T	—	30.00	65.00	150	350	—
1715T	—	27.00	60.00	135	300	—

KM# 379.18 1/10 ECU
3.0490 g., 0.9170 Silver 0.0899 oz. ASW **Ruler:** Louis XIV **Mint:** Troyes **Obverse:** Mailed bust right **Reverse:** 3 Crowns and 3 fleur-de-lis in angles

Date	Mintage	VG	F	VF	XF	Unc
1710V	—	—	—	—	—	—
1711V	—	20.00	45.00	100	225	—
1713V	—	—	—	—	—	—
1715V	—	—	—	—	—	—

KM# 379.11 1/10 ECU
3.0490 g., 0.9170 Silver 0.0899 oz. ASW **Ruler:** Louis XIV **Mint:** Toulouse **Obverse:** Mailed bust right **Reverse:** 3 Crowns and 3 fleur-de-lis in angles

Date	Mintage	VG	F	VF	XF	Unc
1710M	—	—	—	—	—	—
1711M	—	12.50	32.00	70.00	165	—
1712M	—	—	—	—	—	—
1714M	—	—	—	—	—	—
1715M	—	—	—	—	—	—

KM# 379.12 1/10 ECU
3.0490 g., 0.9170 Silver 0.0899 oz. ASW **Ruler:** Louis XIV **Mint:** Montpellier **Obverse:** Mailed bust right **Reverse:** 3 Crowns and 3 fleur-de-lis in angles

Date	Mintage	VG	F	VF	XF	Unc
1710N	—	20.00	45.00	100	225	—
1711N	—	12.50	32.00	70.00	160	—
1712N	—	20.00	45.00	100	225	—
1713N	—	12.50	32.00	70.00	160	—
1715N	—	—	—	—	—	—

KM# 379.14 1/10 ECU
3.0490 g., 0.9170 Silver 0.0899 oz. ASW **Ruler:** Louis XIV **Mint:** Dijon **Obverse:** Mailed bust right **Reverse:** 3 Crowns and 3 fleur-de-lis in angles

Date	Mintage	VG	F	VF	XF	Unc
1710P	—	12.00	30.00	65.00	145	—
1711P	—	15.00	35.00	80.00	175	—

KM# 379.2 1/10 ECU
3.0490 g., 0.9170 Silver 0.0899 oz. ASW **Ruler:** Louis XIV **Mint:** Rouen **Obverse:** Mailed bust right **Reverse:** 3 Crowns and 3 fleur-de-lis in angles

Date	Mintage	VG	F	VF	XF	Unc
1710B	—	15.00	35.00	80.00	175	—
1711B	—	12.50	32.00	75.00	170	—
1712B	—	—	—	—	—	—
1713B	—	40.00	85.00	165	375	—
1715B	—	—	—	—	—	—

KM# 379.3 1/10 ECU
3.0490 g., 0.9170 Silver 0.0899 oz. ASW **Ruler:** Louis XIV **Mint:** Caen **Obverse:** Mailed bust right **Reverse:** 3 Crowns and 3 fleur-de-lis in angles

Date	Mintage	VG	F	VF	XF	Unc
1710C	—	15.00	35.00	80.00	175	—
1711C	—	12.00	30.00	65.00	145	—
1712C	—	—	—	—	—	—
1713C	—	—	—	—	—	—
1715C	—	—	—	—	—	—

KM# 379.4 1/10 ECU
3.0490 g., 0.9170 Silver 0.0899 oz. ASW **Ruler:** Louis XIV **Mint:** Lyon **Obverse:** Mailed bust right **Reverse:** 3 Crowns and 3 fleur-de-lis in angles

Date	Mintage	VG	F	VF	XF	Unc
1710D	—	12.50	32.00	70.00	160	—
1711D	—	12.00	30.00	65.00	145	—
1715D	—	—	—	—	—	—

KM# 379.5 1/10 ECU
3.0490 g., 0.9170 Silver 0.0899 oz. ASW **Ruler:** Louis XIV **Mint:** Tours **Obverse:** Mailed bust right **Reverse:** 3 Crowns and 3 fleur-de-lis in angles

Date	Mintage	VG	F	VF	XF	Unc
1710E	—	—	—	—	—	—
1711E	—	20.00	45.00	100	225	—
1712E	—	—	—	—	—	—
1713E	—	—	—	—	—	—
1714E	—	—	—	—	—	—
1715E	—	15.00	35.00	80.00	175	—

KM# 379.6 1/10 ECU
3.0490 g., 0.9170 Silver 0.0899 oz. ASW **Ruler:** Louis XIV **Mint:** Poitiers **Obverse:** Mailed bust right **Reverse:** 3 Crowns and 3 fleur-de-lis in angles

Date	Mintage	VG	F	VF	XF	Unc
1710G	—	27.00	60.00	135	300	—
1711G	—	12.50	32.00	75.00	170	—
1712G	—	30.00	65.00	150	325	—
1713G	—	20.00	45.00	100	225	—
1714G	—	27.00	60.00	135	300	—
1715G	—	15.00	35.00	80.00	175	—

KM# 379.7 1/10 ECU
3.0490 g., 0.9170 Silver 0.0899 oz. ASW **Ruler:** Louis XIV **Mint:** La Rochelle **Obverse:** Mailed bust right **Reverse:** 3 Crowns and 3 fleur-de-lis in angles

Date	Mintage	VG	F	VF	XF	Unc
1710H	—	—	—	—	—	—
1711H	—	12.50	32.00	75.00	170	—
1715H	—	27.00	60.00	135	300	—

KM# 379.8 1/10 ECU
3.0490 g., 0.9170 Silver 0.0899 oz. ASW **Ruler:** Louis XIV **Mint:** Limoges **Obverse:** Mailed bust right **Reverse:** 3 Crowns and 3 fleur-de-lis in angles

Date	Mintage	VG	F	VF	XF	Unc
1710I	—	—	—	—	—	—
1711I	—	30.00	65.00	150	325	—
1712I	—	—	—	—	—	—

KM# 379.9 1/10 ECU
3.0490 g., 0.9170 Silver 0.0899 oz. ASW **Ruler:** Louis XIV **Mint:** Bordeaux **Obverse:** Mailed bust right **Reverse:** 3 Crowns and 3 fleur-de-lis in angles

Date	Mintage	VG	F	VF	XF	Unc
1710K	—	20.00	45.00	100	225	—
1711K	—	12.00	30.00	65.00	145	—
1712K	—	12.50	32.00	70.00	160	—
1713K	—	15.00	35.00	80.00	175	—
1714K	—	20.00	45.00	100	225	—
1715K	—	12.50	32.00	70.00	160	—

KM# 379.24 1/10 ECU
3.0490 g., 0.9170 Silver 0.0899 oz. ASW **Ruler:** Louis XIV **Mint:** Aix **Obverse:** Mailed bust right **Reverse:** 3 Crowns and 3 fleur-de-lis in angles **Note:** Mint mark: &.

Date	Mintage	VG	F	VF	XF	Unc
1710	—	15.00	35.00	80.00	175	—
1711	—	15.00	35.00	80.00	175	—
1712	—	40.00	90.00	200	450	—
1714	—	40.00	90.00	200	450	—

KM# 379.23 1/10 ECU
3.0490 g., 0.9170 Silver 0.0899 oz. ASW **Ruler:** Louis XIV **Mint:** Rennes **Obverse:** Mailed bust right **Reverse:** 3 Crowns and 3 fleur-de-lis in angles **Note:** Mint mark: 9.

Date	Mintage	VG	F	VF	XF	Unc
1710	—	12.00	30.00	65.00	145	—
1711	—	12.00	30.00	65.00	145	—
1712	—	12.00	30.00	65.00	145	—
1713	—	27.00	60.00	135	300	—
1714	—	20.00	45.00	100	225	—
1715	—	40.00	85.00	165	375	—

KM# 379.25 1/10 ECU
3.0490 g., 0.9170 Silver 0.0899 oz. ASW **Ruler:** Louis XIV **Mint:** Besancon **Obverse:** Mailed bust right **Reverse:** 3 Crowns and 3 fleur-de-lis in angles **Note:** Mint mark: Back to back C's.

Date	Mintage	VG	F	VF	XF	Unc
1710	Est. 120,000	15.00	35.00	80.00	175	—
1711	276,000	12.50	32.00	70.00	160	—
1712	64,000	—	—	—	—	—
1713	166,000	—	—	—	—	—
1715	50,000	27.00	60.00	135	300	—

KM# 379.26 1/10 ECU
3.0490 g., 0.9170 Silver 0.0899 oz. ASW **Ruler:** Louis XIV **Mint:** Pau **Obverse:** Mailed bust right **Reverse:** 3 Crowns and 3 fleur-de-lis in angles **Note:** Mint mark: Cow.

Date	Mintage	VG	F	VF	XF	Unc
1710	—	27.00	60.00	135	300	—
1711	—	27.00	60.00	135	300	—
1712	—	27.00	60.00	135	300	—
1713	—	27.00	60.00	135	300	—
1714	—	30.00	65.00	145	350	—
1715	—	27.00	60.00	135	300	—

KM# 379.20 1/10 ECU
3.0490 g., 0.9170 Silver 0.0899 oz. ASW **Ruler:** Louis XIV **Mint:** Amiens **Obverse:** Mailed bust right **Reverse:** 3 Crowns and 3 fleur-de-lis in angles

Date	Mintage	VG	F	VF	XF	Unc
1710X	—	20.00	45.00	100	225	—
1711X	—	12.00	30.00	65.00	145	—
1712X	—	12.50	32.00	70.00	160	—
1713X	—	15.00	35.00	80.00	175	—
1714X	—	15.00	35.00	80.00	175	—
1715X	—	—	—	—	—	—

KM# 379.21 1/10 ECU
3.0490 g., 0.9170 Silver 0.0899 oz. ASW **Ruler:** Louis XIV **Mint:** Bourges **Obverse:** Mailed bust right **Obv. Legend:** LVD • XIIII • D • G • FR • ET • NAV • REX • **Reverse:** 3 Crowns and 3 fleur-de-lis in angles **Rev. Legend:** BENEDICTVM 1715 SIT • NOMEN • DOMINI

Date	Mintage	VG	F	VF	XF	Unc
1711Y	—	20.00	45.00	100	225	—
1712Y	—	20.00	45.00	100	225	—
1713Y	—	—	—	—	—	—
1715Y	—	15.00	35.00	80.00	175	—

KM# 379.22 1/10 ECU
3.0490 g., 0.9170 Silver 0.0899 oz. ASW **Ruler:** Louis XIV **Mint:** Grenoble **Obverse:** Mailed bust right **Reverse:** 3 Crowns and 3 fleur-de-lis in angles

Date	Mintage	VG	F	VF	XF	Unc
1711Z	—	20.00	45.00	100	225	—
1712Z	—	40.00	90.00	200	450	—
1712Z	—	40.00	90.00	200	450	—
1713Z	—	—	—	—	—	—
1715Z	—	—	—	—	—	—

KM# 379.10 1/10 ECU
3.0490 g., 0.9170 Silver 0.0899 oz. ASW **Ruler:** Louis XIV **Mint:** Bayonne **Obverse:** Mailed bust right **Reverse:** 3 Crowns and 3 fleur-de-lis in angles

Date	Mintage	VG	F	VF	XF	Unc
1711L	—	12.50	32.00	75.00	170	—
1714L	—	20.00	45.00	100	225	—
1715L	—	27.00	60.00	135	300	—

KM# 379.15 1/10 ECU
3.0490 g., 0.9170 Silver 0.0899 oz. ASW **Ruler:** Louis XIV **Mint:** Perpignan **Obverse:** Mailed bust right **Reverse:** 3 Crowns and 3 fleur-de-lis in angles

Date	Mintage	VG	F	VF	XF	Unc
1711Q	—	35.00	75.00	175	400	—
1713Q	—	65.00	145	325	750	—

KM# 379.13 1/10 ECU
3.0490 g., 0.9170 Silver 0.0899 oz. ASW **Ruler:** Louis XIV **Mint:** Riom **Obverse:** Mailed bust right **Reverse:** 3 Crowns and 3 fleur-de-lis in angles

Date	Mintage	VG	F	VF	XF	Unc
1711O	—	—	—	—	—	—

KM# 379.19 1/10 ECU
3.0490 g., 0.9170 Silver 0.0899 oz. ASW **Ruler:** Louis XIV **Mint:** Lille **Obverse:** Mailed bust right **Reverse:** 3 Crowns and 3 fleur-de-lis in angles

Date	Mintage	VG	F	VF	XF	Unc
1713W	—	15.00	35.00	80.00	175	—
1715W	—	10.00	27.00	60.00	135	—

KM# 373.2 1/8 ECU
4.7000 g., 0.8570 Silver 0.1295 oz. ASW **Ruler:** Louis XIV **Mint:** Lille **Obverse:** Draped bust right **Reverse:** Crowned circular shield, crossed sceptres and hand of Justice behind

Date	Mintage	VG	F	VF	XF	Unc
1701W	—	275	600	1,350	2,750	—
1702W	—	275	600	1,350	2,750	—
1705W	—	—	—	—	—	—

KM# 373.1 1/8 ECU
4.7000 g., 0.8570 Silver 0.1295 oz. ASW **Ruler:** Louis XIV **Mint:** Bayonne **Obverse:** Draped bust right **Reverse:** Crowned circular shield, crossed scepters and hand of Justice behind

Date	Mintage	VG	F	VF	XF	Unc
1705L	—	—	—	—	—	—

KM# 324.1 1/4 ECU
6.7460 g., 0.9170 Silver 0.1989 oz. ASW **Ruler:** Louis XIV **Mint:** Paris **Obverse:** Mailed bust right **Reverse:** Crowned circular shield of France, crossed scepters and hand of Justice behind

Date	Mintage	VG	F	VF	XF	Unc
1701A	—	85.00	165	360	600	—
1702A	—	75.00	150	310	540	—

KM# 324.2 1/4 ECU
6.7460 g., 0.9170 Silver 0.1989 oz. ASW **Ruler:** Louis XIV **Mint:** Rouen **Obverse:** Mailed bust right **Reverse:** Crowned circular shield of France, crossed sceptres and hand of Justice behind

Date	Mintage	VG	F	VF	XF	Unc
1701B	—	100	200	400	700	—
1702B	—	100	200	400	700	—

KM# 324.8 1/4 ECU
6.7460 g., 0.9170 Silver 0.1989 oz. ASW **Ruler:** Louis XIV **Mint:** Bayonne **Obverse:** Mailed bust right **Reverse:** Crowned circular shield of France, crossed sceptres and hand of Justice behind

Date	Mintage	VG	F	VF	XF	Unc
1701L	Est. 2,448	—	—	—	—	—
1702L	—	110	215	425	745	—

KM# 324.9 1/4 ECU
6.7460 g., 0.9170 Silver 0.1989 oz. ASW **Ruler:** Louis XIV **Mint:** Montpellier **Obverse:** Mailed bust right **Reverse:** Crowned circular shield of France, crossed sceptres and hand of Justice behind

Date	Mintage	VG	F	VF	XF	Unc
1701N	28,000	—	—	—	—	—
1702N	177,000	85.00	165	330	580	—
1703N	12,000	—	—	—	—	—

KM# 324.10 1/4 ECU
6.7460 g., 0.9170 Silver 0.1989 oz. ASW **Ruler:** Louis XIV **Mint:** Riom **Obverse:** Mailed bust right **Reverse:** Crowned circular shield of France, crossed sceptres and hand of Justice behind

Date	Mintage	VG	F	VF	XF	Unc
1701O	—	110	215	425	745	—

KM# 340.2 1/4 ECU
6.7460 g., 0.9170 Silver 0.1989 oz. ASW **Ruler:** Louis XIV **Mint:** Lille

Date	Mintage	VG	F	VF	XF	Unc
1701W	—	90.00	180	360	630	—
1702W	120,000	85.00	165	330	580	—
1703W	860	—	—	—	—	—

KM# 342 1/4 ECU
9.4800 g., 0.8570 Silver 0.2612 oz. ASW **Ruler:** Louis XIV **Mint:** Lille **Reverse:** Crowned circular shield of France, Navarre, Old and New Burgundy with crossed scepters and hand of Justice behind

Date	Mintage	VG	F	VF	XF	Unc
1701W	—	425	850	1,650	2,800	—
1702W Rare	—	—	—	—	—	—
1703W Rare	—	—	—	—	—	—

KM# 324.13 1/4 ECU
6.7460 g., 0.9170 Silver 0.1989 oz. ASW **Ruler:** Louis XIV **Mint:** Troyes **Obverse:** Mailed bust right **Reverse:** Crowned circular shield of France, crossed sceptres and hand of Justice behind

Date	Mintage	VG	F	VF	XF	Unc
1701V	—	110	215	425	745	—
1702V	Est. 90,000	—	—	—	—	—
1703V	—	—	—	—	—	—

KM# 324.17 1/4 ECU
6.7460 g., 0.9170 Silver 0.1989 oz. ASW **Ruler:** Louis XIV **Mint:** Aix **Obverse:** Mailed bust right **Reverse:** Crowned circular shield of France, crossed sceptres and hand of Justice behind **Note:** Mint mark: &.

Date	Mintage	VG	F	VF	XF	Unc
1701	—	90.00	180	360	630	—
1702	—	90.00	180	360	630	—

KM# 324.16 1/4 ECU
6.7460 g., 0.9170 Silver 0.1989 oz. ASW **Ruler:** Louis XIV **Mint:** Rennes **Obverse:** Mailed bust right **Obv. Legend:** LVD • XIIII • D • G • FR • ET • NAV • REX • **Reverse:** Sceptre with hand of Justice crosses sword, fleur-de-lis at angles, crown above **Rev. Legend:** DOMINE • SALVVM • FAC • REGEM • **Note:** Mint mark: 9.

Date	Mintage	VG	F	VF	XF	Unc
1701	—	90.00	180	360	630	—
1702	—	85.00	165	330	580	—

KM# 341 1/4 ECU
6.7460 g., 0.9170 Silver 0.1989 oz. ASW **Ruler:** Louis XIV **Mint:** Pau **Obverse:** Mailed bust right **Reverse:** Crowned circular shield of France, Navarre and Bearn, crossed scepters and hand of Justice behind **Note:** Mint mark: Cow.

Date	Mintage	VG	F	VF	XF	Unc
1701	—	750	1,500	3,000	5,000	—
1702	—	750	1,500	3,000	5,000	—

KM# 324.18 1/4 ECU
6.7460 g., 0.9170 Silver 0.1989 oz. ASW **Ruler:** Louis XIV **Mint:** Besancon **Note:** Mint mark: Back to back C's.

Date	Mintage	VG	F	VF	XF	Unc
1701	—	100	200	400	700	—
1702	—	110	215	425	745	—

KM# 340.1 1/4 ECU
6.7460 g., 0.9170 Silver 0.1989 oz. ASW **Ruler:** Louis XIV **Mint:** Lyon **Obverse:** Mailed bust right

Date	Mintage	VG	F	VF	XF	Unc
1702D	—	90.00	180	360	630	—

KM# 324.14 1/4 ECU
6.7460 g., 0.9170 Silver 0.1989 oz. ASW **Ruler:** Louis XIV **Mint:** Amiens

Date	Mintage	VG	F	VF	XF	Unc
1702X	—	90.00	180	360	630	—

KM# 343 1/4 ECU
6.7460 g., 0.9170 Silver 0.1989 oz. ASW **Ruler:** Louis XIV **Mint:** Grenoble **Reverse:** Round circular shield of Dauphine, crossed scepters and hand of Justice behind

Date	Mintage	VG	F	VF	XF	Unc
1702Z Rare	—	—	—	—	—	—

KM# 344 1/4 ECU
6.7460 g., 0.9170 Silver 0.1989 oz. ASW **Ruler:** Louis XIV **Mint:** Strasbourg **Obverse:** Large fleur-de-lis **Reverse:** Crowned circular shield of France, crossed scepters and hand of Justice behind

Date	Mintage	VG	F	VF	XF	Unc
1702BB	—	425	850	1,650	2,800	—

KM# 324.11 1/4 ECU
6.7460 g., 0.9170 Silver 0.1989 oz. ASW **Ruler:** Louis XIV **Mint:** Dijon **Obverse:** Mailed bust right **Obv. Legend:** LVD • XIIII • D • G • FR • ET • NAV • REX • **Reverse:** Crowned circular shield of France with crossed sceptre and hand of Justice behind **Rev. Legend:** BENEDICTVM • SIT • NOMEN • DOMINI

Date	Mintage	VG	F	VF	XF	Unc
1702P	—	90.00	180	360	630	—

KM# 324.12 1/4 ECU
6.7460 g., 0.9170 Silver 0.1989 oz. ASW **Ruler:** Louis XIV **Mint:** Nantes

Date	Mintage	VG	F	VF	XF	Unc
1702T	—	90.00	180	360	630	—

KM# 324.3 1/4 ECU
6.7460 g., 0.9170 Silver 0.1989 oz. ASW **Ruler:** Louis XIV **Mint:** Caen

Date	Mintage	VG	F	VF	XF	Unc
1702C	—	100	200	400	700	—

KM# 324.4 1/4 ECU
6.7460 g., 0.9170 Silver 0.1989 oz. ASW **Ruler:** Louis XIV **Mint:** Lyon

Date	Mintage	VG	F	VF	XF	Unc
1702D	—	100	200	400	700	—

KM# 324.5 1/4 ECU
6.7460 g., 0.9170 Silver 0.1989 oz. ASW **Ruler:** Louis XIV **Mint:** Tours

Date	Mintage	VG	F	VF	XF	Unc
1702E	—	110	215	425	745	—

KM# 324.6 1/4 ECU
6.7460 g., 0.9170 Silver 0.1989 oz. ASW **Ruler:** Louis XIV **Mint:** Poitiers

Date	Mintage	VG	F	VF	XF	Unc
1702G	—	100	200	400	700	—

KM# 324.7 1/4 ECU
6.7460 g., 0.9170 Silver 0.1989 oz. ASW **Ruler:** Louis XIV **Mint:** Bordeaux

Date	Mintage	VG	F	VF	XF	Unc
1702K	—	90.00	180	360	630	—
1703K	280,000	—	—	—	—	—

KM# 324.15 1/4 ECU
6.7460 g., 0.9170 Silver 0.1989 oz. ASW **Ruler:** Louis XIV **Mint:** Bourges

Date	Mintage	VG	F	VF	XF	Unc
1703Y	—	110	215	425	745	—

KM# 352.7 1/4 ECU
6.7460 g., 0.9170 Silver 0.1989 oz. ASW **Ruler:** Louis XIV **Mint:** Bordeaux **Obverse:** Mailed bust right **Reverse:** 8 Crowned L's back to back, shield of France at center

Date	Mintage	VG	F	VF	XF	Unc
1704K	—	100	200	400	700	—

KM# 352.8 1/4 ECU

6.7460 g., 0.9170 Silver 0.1989 oz. ASW **Ruler:** Louis XIV **Mint:** Toulouse **Obverse:** Mailed bust right **Reverse:** 8 Crowned L's back to back, shield of France at center

Date	Mintage	VG	F	VF	XF	Unc
1704M	—	100	200	400	700	—

KM# 352.9 1/4 ECU

6.7460 g., 0.9170 Silver 0.1989 oz. ASW **Ruler:** Louis XIV **Mint:** Montpellier **Obverse:** Mailed bust right **Reverse:** 8 Crowned L's back to back, shield of France at center

Date	Mintage	VG	F	VF	XF	Unc
1704N	74,000	—	—	—	—	—
1705N	41,000	—	—	—	—	—

KM# 352.10 1/4 ECU

6.7460 g., 0.9170 Silver 0.1989 oz. ASW **Ruler:** Louis XIV **Mint:** Riom **Obverse:** Mailed bust right **Reverse:** 8 Crowned L's back to back, shield of France at center

Date	Mintage	VG	F	VF	XF	Unc
1704O	—	100	200	400	700	—

KM# 352.11 1/4 ECU

6.7460 g., 0.9170 Silver 0.1989 oz. ASW **Ruler:** Louis XIV **Mint:** Nantes **Obverse:** Mailed bust right **Reverse:** 8 Crowned L's back to back, shield of France at center

Date	Mintage	VG	F	VF	XF	Unc
1704T	89,000	—	—	—	—	—
1705T	43,000	100	200	400	700	—

KM# 352.12 1/4 ECU

6.7460 g., 0.9170 Silver 0.1989 oz. ASW **Ruler:** Louis XIV **Mint:** Troyes **Obverse:** Mailed bust right **Reverse:** 8 Crowned L's back to back, shield of France at center

Date	Mintage	VG	F	VF	XF	Unc
1704V	77,000	100	200	400	700	—
1705V	—	100	200	400	700	—

KM# 352.13 1/4 ECU

6.7460 g., 0.9170 Silver 0.1989 oz. ASW **Ruler:** Louis XIV **Mint:** Amiens **Obverse:** Mailed bust right **Reverse:** 8 Crowned L's back to back, shield of France at center

Date	Mintage	VG	F	VF	XF	Unc
1704X	—	100	200	400	700	—

KM# 352.16 1/4 ECU

6.7460 g., 0.9170 Silver 0.1989 oz. ASW **Ruler:** Louis XIV **Mint:** Rennes **Obverse:** Mailed bust right **Reverse:** 8 Crowned L's back to back, shield of France at center **Note:** Mint mark: 9.

Date	Mintage	VG	F	VF	XF	Unc
1704	—	100	200	400	700	—
1705	—	—	—	400	—	—
1709	20,000	140	280	550	900	—

KM# 352.17 1/4 ECU

6.7460 g., 0.9170 Silver 0.1989 oz. ASW **Ruler:** Louis XIV **Mint:** Aix **Obverse:** Mailed bust right **Reverse:** 8 Crowned L's back to back, shield of France at center **Note:** Mint mark: &.

Date	Mintage	VG	F	VF	XF	Unc
1704	—	100	200	400	700	—

KM# 352.1 1/4 ECU

6.7460 g., 0.9170 Silver 0.1989 oz. ASW **Ruler:** Louis XIV **Mint:** Paris **Obverse:** Mailed bust right **Reverse:** 8 Crowned L's back to back, shield of France at center

Date	Mintage	VG	F	VF	XF	Unc
1704A	1,536,000	—	—	—	—	—

KM# 352.2 1/4 ECU

6.7460 g., 0.9170 Silver 0.1989 oz. ASW **Ruler:** Louis XIV **Mint:** Rouen **Obverse:** Mailed bust right **Reverse:** 8 Crowned L's back to back, shield of France at center

Date	Mintage	VG	F	VF	XF	Unc
1704B	—	100	200	400	700	—
1705B	—	100	200	400	700	—

KM# 352.3 1/4 ECU

6.7460 g., 0.9170 Silver 0.1989 oz. ASW **Ruler:** Louis XIV **Mint:** Caen **Obverse:** Mailed bust right **Reverse:** 8 Crowned L's back to back, shield of France at center

Date	Mintage	VG	F	VF	XF	Unc
1704C	—	—	—	—	—	—

KM# 352.4 1/4 ECU

6.7460 g., 0.9170 Silver 0.1989 oz. ASW **Ruler:** Louis XIV **Mint:** Tours **Obverse:** Mailed bust right **Reverse:** 8 Crowned L's back to back, shield of France at center

Date	Mintage	VG	F	VF	XF	Unc
1704E	—	—	—	—	—	—
1705E	—	100	200	400	700	—

KM# 352.5 1/4 ECU

6.7460 g., 0.9170 Silver 0.1989 oz. ASW **Ruler:** Louis XIV **Mint:** La Rochelle **Obverse:** Mailed bust right **Reverse:** 8 Crowned L's back to back, shield of France at center

Date	Mintage	VG	F	VF	XF	Unc
1704H	—	85.00	165	330	580	—

KM# 352.15 1/4 ECU

6.7460 g., 0.9170 Silver 0.1989 oz. ASW **Ruler:** Louis XIV **Mint:** Grenoble **Obverse:** Mailed bust right **Reverse:** 8 Crowned L's back to back, shield of France at center

Date	Mintage	VG	F	VF	XF	Unc
1704Z	—	—	—	—	—	—

KM# 353.1 1/4 ECU

6.7460 g., 0.9170 Silver 0.1989 oz. ASW **Ruler:** Louis XIV **Mint:** Lyon **Obverse:** Bust right **Reverse:** 8 Crowned L's back to back, fleur-de-lis at angles

Date	Mintage	VG	F	VF	XF	Unc
1704D	—	85.00	165	330	580	—
1705D	19,000	110	215	425	745	—

KM# 353.2 1/4 ECU

6.7460 g., 0.9170 Silver 0.1989 oz. ASW **Ruler:** Louis XIV **Mint:** Lille **Obverse:** Bust right **Reverse:** 8 Crowned L"s back to back, fleur-de-lis at angles

Date	Mintage	VG	F	VF	XF	Unc
1704W	122,000	85.00	165	330	580	—
1705W	—	110	215	425	745	—

KM# 354 1/4 ECU

6.7460 g., 0.9170 Silver 0.1989 oz. ASW **Ruler:** Louis XIV **Mint:** Pau **Obverse:** Mailed bust right **Reverse:** 8 crowned L's back to back, shield of France, Navarre and Bearn at center **Note:** Mint mark: Cow.

Date	Mintage	VG	F	VF	XF	Unc
1704	—	1,100	2,200	4,200	7,000	—

KM# 374 1/4 ECU

6.7460 g., 0.9170 Silver 0.1989 oz. ASW **Ruler:** Louis XIV **Mint:** Lille **Reverse:** Crossed scepters

Date	Mintage	VG	F	VF	XF	Unc
1705W	—	700	1,400	2,800	4,650	—

KM# 352.6 1/4 ECU

6.7460 g., 0.9170 Silver 0.1989 oz. ASW **Ruler:** Louis XIV **Mint:** Limoges **Obverse:** Mailed bust right **Reverse:** 8 Crowned L's back to back, shield of France at center

Date	Mintage	VG	F	VF	XF	Unc
1705I	—	75.00	150	250	500	—

KM# 352.14 1/4 ECU

6.7460 g., 0.9170 Silver 0.1989 oz. ASW **Ruler:** Louis XIV **Mint:** Bourges **Obverse:** Mailed bust right **Reverse:** 8 Crowned L's back to back, shield of France at center

Date	Mintage	VG	F	VF	XF	Unc
1705Y	—	—	—	—	—	—

KM# 376.11 1/4 ECU

6.1960 g., 0.7980 Silver 0.1590 oz. ASW **Ruler:** Louis XIV **Mint:** Aix **Obverse:** Mailed bust right **Reverse:** Crown above crossed sceptres, 3 fleur-de-lis in angles **Note:** Mint mark: &.

Date	Mintage	VG	F	VF	XF	Unc
1707	—	—	—	—	—	—
1708	—	—	—	—	—	—

KM# 376.10 1/4 ECU

6.1960 g., 0.7980 Silver 0.1590 oz. ASW **Ruler:** Louis XIV **Mint:** Rennes **Obverse:** Mailed bust right **Reverse:** Crown above crossed sceptres, 3 fleur-de-lis in angles **Note:** Mint mark: 9.

Date	Mintage	VG	F	VF	XF	Unc
1707	—	18.00	35.00	70.00	125	—
1709	—	18.00	35.00	70.00	125	—

KM# 376.1 1/4 ECU

6.1960 g., 0.7980 Silver 0.1590 oz. ASW **Ruler:** Louis XIV **Mint:** Paris **Obverse:** Mailed bust right **Reverse:** Crown above crossed scepters, 3 fleur-de-lis in angles

Date	Mintage	VG	F	VF	XF	Unc
1707A	—	16.00	32.00	65.00	115	—
1708A	—	16.00	32.00	65.00	115	—

KM# 376.2 1/4 ECU

6.1960 g., 0.7980 Silver 0.1590 oz. ASW **Ruler:** Louis XIV **Mint:** Rouen **Obverse:** Mailed bust right **Reverse:** Crown above crossed sceptres, 3 fleur-de-lis in angles

Date	Mintage	VG	F	VF	XF	Unc
1707B	—	18.00	35.00	70.00	125	—
1708B	—	18.00	35.00	75.00	135	—

KM# 376.3 1/4 ECU

6.1960 g., 0.7980 Silver 0.1590 oz. ASW **Ruler:** Louis XIV **Mint:** Lyon **Obverse:** Mailed bust right **Reverse:** Crown above crossed sceptres, 3 fleur-de-lis in angles

Date	Mintage	VG	F	VF	XF	Unc
1707D	—	25.00	50.00	100	175	—
1708D	—	16.00	32.00	65.00	115	—

KM# 376.4 1/4 ECU

6.1960 g., 0.7980 Silver 0.1590 oz. ASW **Ruler:** Louis XIV **Mint:** La Rochelle **Obverse:** Mailed bust right **Reverse:** Crown above crossed sceptres, 3 fleur-de-lis in angles

Date	Mintage	VG	F	VF	XF	Unc
1707H	—	28.00	55.00	110	185	—
1708H	—	16.00	32.00	70.00	125	—

KM# 376.5 1/4 ECU

6.1960 g., 0.7980 Silver 0.1590 oz. ASW **Ruler:** Louis XIV **Mint:** Bordeaux **Obverse:** Mailed bust right **Reverse:** Crown above crossed sceptres, 3 fleur-de-lis in angles

Date	Mintage	VG	F	VF	XF	Unc
1707K	—	25.00	50.00	100	175	—
1708K	—	25.00	50.00	100	175	—

KM# 376.6 1/4 ECU

6.1960 g., 0.7980 Silver 0.1590 oz. ASW **Ruler:** Louis XIV **Mint:** Bayonne **Obverse:** Mailed bust right **Reverse:** Crown above crossed sceptres, 3 fleur-de-lis in angles

Date	Mintage	VG	F	VF	XF	Unc
1707L	—	—	—	—	—	—
1708L	—	35.00	75.00	150	250	—

KM# 376.7 1/4 ECU

6.1960 g., 0.7980 Silver 0.1590 oz. ASW **Ruler:** Louis XIV **Mint:** Toulouse **Obverse:** Mailed bust right **Reverse:** Crown above crossed sceptres, 3 fleur-de-lis in angles

Date	Mintage	VG	F	VF	XF	Unc
1707M	—	—	—	—	—	—
1708M	—	—	—	—	—	—

KM# 376.8 1/4 ECU

6.1960 g., 0.7980 Silver 0.1590 oz. ASW **Ruler:** Louis XIV **Mint:** Nantes **Obverse:** Mailed bust right **Reverse:** Crown above crossed sceptres, 3 fleur-de-lis in angles

Date	Mintage	VG	F	VF	XF	Unc
1707T	—	20.00	40.00	80.00	140	—
1708T	—	16.00	32.00	70.00	125	—

KM# 376.9 1/4 ECU

6.1960 g., 0.7980 Silver 0.1590 oz. ASW **Ruler:** Louis XIV **Mint:** Lille **Obverse:** Mailed bust right **Reverse:** Crown above crossed sceptres, 3 fleur-de-lis in angles

Date	Mintage	VG	F	VF	XF	Unc
1707W	—	—	—	—	—	—
1708W	—	—	—	—	—	—

KM# 376.12 1/4 ECU

6.1960 g., 0.7980 Silver 0.1590 oz. ASW **Ruler:** Louis XIV **Mint:** Amiens **Obverse:** Mailed bust right **Reverse:** Crown above crossed sceptres, 3 fleur-de-lis in angles

Date	Mintage	VG	F	VF	XF	Unc
1707X	—	20.00	40.00	80.00	140	—
1708X	—	—	—	—	—	—

KM# 377 1/4 ECU

6.1960 g., 0.7980 Silver 0.1590 oz. ASW **Ruler:** Louis XIV **Mint:** Pau **Note:** Mint mark: Cow.

Date	Mintage	VG	F	VF	XF	Unc
1707	—	35.00	75.00	150	250	—
1708	—	—	—	—	—	—

KM# 380.26 1/4 ECU

7.5950 g., 0.9170 Silver 0.2239 oz. ASW **Ruler:** Louis XIV **Mint:** Pau **Obverse:** Mailed bust right **Reverse:** 3 Crowns, fleur-de-lis in openings **Note:** Mint mark: Cow.

Date	Mintage	VG	F	VF	XF	Unc
1709	—	—	—	—	—	—
1710	—	—	—	—	—	—
1711	—	110	225	450	750	—
1712	—	—	—	—	—	—
1715	—	—	—	—	—	—

KM# 380.25 1/4 ECU

7.5950 g., 0.9170 Silver 0.2239 oz. ASW **Ruler:** Louis XIV **Mint:** Besancon **Obverse:** Mailed bust right **Reverse:** 3 Crowns, fleur-de-lis in openings **Note:** Mint mark: Back to back C's.

Date	Mintage	VG	F	VF	XF	Unc
1709	—	—	—	—	—	—
1710	—	65.00	135	270	450	—
1711	—	—	—	—	—	—

KM# 380.1 1/4 ECU

7.5950 g., 0.9170 Silver 0.2239 oz. ASW **Ruler:** Louis XIV **Mint:** Paris **Obverse:** Mailed bust right **Reverse:** 3 Crowns, fleur-de-lis in openings

Date	Mintage	VG	F	VF	XF	Unc
1709A	—	60.00	125	250	400	—
1710A	—	60.00	125	250	400	—
1711A	—	40.00	80.00	165	275	—
1712A	—	50.00	100	200	350	—
1714A	—	70.00	140	280	450	—
1715A	—	90.00	190	375	625	—

KM# 380.2 1/4 ECU

7.5950 g., 0.9170 Silver 0.2239 oz. ASW **Ruler:** Louis XIV **Mint:** Rouen **Obverse:** Mailed bust right **Obv. Legend:** LVD • XIIII • D • G • FR • ET • NAV • REX • **Reverse:** 3 Crowns, fleur-de-lis in openings **Rev. Legend:** BENEDICTVM 1710 SIT • NOMEN • DOMINI

Date	Mintage	VG	F	VF	XF	Unc
1709B	—	85.00	165	330	580	—
1710B	—	85.00	165	330	580	—
1711B	—	75.00	150	300	525	—
1712B	—	—	—	—	—	—
1713B	—	—	—	—	—	—
1714B	—	—	—	—	—	—
1715B	—	70.00	140	280	450	—

KM# 380.3 1/4 ECU

7.5950 g., 0.9170 Silver 0.2239 oz. ASW **Ruler:** Louis XIV **Mint:** Caen **Obverse:** Mailed bust right **Reverse:** 3 Crowns, fleur-de-lis in openings

Date	Mintage	VG	F	VF	XF	Unc
1709C	—	—	—	—	—	—
1710C	—	—	—	—	—	—
1711C	—	—	—	—	—	—
1712C	—	—	—	—	—	—
1713C	—	—	—	—	—	—
1715C	—	—	—	—	—	—

KM# 380.4 1/4 ECU

7.5950 g., 0.9170 Silver 0.2239 oz. ASW **Ruler:** Louis XIV **Mint:** Lyon **Obverse:** Mailed bust right **Reverse:** 3 Crowns, fleur-de-lis in openings

Date	Mintage	VG	F	VF	XF	Unc
1709D	—	45.00	90.00	180	300	—
1710D	—	60.00	125	250	400	—
1711D	—	45.00	90.00	180	300	—
1712D	—	60.00	125	250	400	—

KM# 380.5 1/4 ECU

7.5950 g., 0.9170 Silver 0.2239 oz. ASW **Ruler:** Louis XIV **Mint:** Tours **Obverse:** Mailed bust right **Reverse:** 3 Crowns, fleur-de-lis in openings

Date	Mintage	VG	F	VF	XF	Unc
1709E	—	—	—	—	—	—
1710E	—	—	—	—	—	—
1711E	—	—	—	—	—	—
1712E	—	—	—	—	—	—
1713E	—	—	—	—	—	—
1714E	—	—	—	—	—	—
1715E	—	75.00	150	300	525	—

KM# 380.23 1/4 ECU

7.5950 g., 0.9170 Silver 0.2239 oz. ASW **Ruler:** Louis XIV **Mint:** Rennes **Obverse:** Mailed bust right **Reverse:** 3 Crowns, fleur-de-lis in openings **Note:** Mint mark: 9.

Date	Mintage	VG	F	VF	XF	Unc
1709	—	—	—	—	—	—
1710	—	65.00	135	270	450	—
1711	—	60.00	125	250	400	—
1712	—	—	—	—	—	—
1713	—	—	—	—	—	—
1714	—	65.00	135	270	450	—
1715	—	—	—	—	—	—

KM# 380.20 1/4 ECU

7.5950 g., 0.9170 Silver 0.2239 oz. ASW **Ruler:** Louis XIV **Mint:** Amiens **Obverse:** Mailed bust right **Reverse:** 3 Crowns, fleur-de-lis in openings

Date	Mintage	VG	F	VF	XF	Unc
1709X	—	90.00	180	360	630	—
1710X	—	75.00	150	300	525	—
1711X	—	60.00	125	250	400	—
1712X	—	65.00	135	270	450	—
1713X	—	75.00	150	300	525	—
1714X	—	—	—	—	—	—
1715X	—	85.00	165	330	580	—

KM# 380.16 1/4 ECU

7.5950 g., 0.9170 Silver 0.2239 oz. ASW **Ruler:** Louis XIV **Mint:** Troyes **Obverse:** Mailed bust right **Reverse:** 3 Crowns, fleur-de-lis in openings

Date	Mintage	VG	F	VF	XF	Unc
1709S	—	75.00	150	300	525	—
1710S	—	—	—	—	—	—
1711S	—	65.00	135	270	450	—
1715S	—	—	—	—	—	—

KM# 380.17 1/4 ECU

7.5950 g., 0.9170 Silver 0.2239 oz. ASW **Ruler:** Louis XIV **Mint:** Nantes **Obverse:** Mailed bust right **Reverse:** 3 Crowns, fleur-de-lis in openings

Date	Mintage	VG	F	VF	XF	Unc
1709T	—	75.00	150	300	525	—
1710T	—	—	—	—	—	—
1711T	—	—	—	—	—	—
1712T	—	—	—	—	—	—
1715T	—	—	—	—	—	—

KM# 380.8 1/4 ECU

7.5950 g., 0.9170 Silver 0.2239 oz. ASW **Ruler:** Louis XIV **Mint:** Limoges **Obverse:** Mailed bust right **Reverse:** 3 Crowns, fleur-de-lis in openings

Date	Mintage	VG	F	VF	XF	Unc
1709I	—	—	—	—	—	—
1710I	—	—	—	—	—	—
1711I	—	—	—	—	—	—
1712I	—	—	—	—	—	—
1713I	—	—	—	—	—	—
1714I	—	—	—	—	—	—
1715I	—	—	—	—	—	—

KM# 380.11 1/4 ECU

7.5950 g., 0.9170 Silver 0.2239 oz. ASW **Ruler:** Louis XIV **Mint:** Toulouse **Obverse:** Mailed bust right **Reverse:** 3 Crowns, fleur-de-lis in openings

Date	Mintage	VG	F	VF	XF	Unc
1709M	—	—	—	—	—	—
1710M	—	—	—	—	—	—
1711M	—	—	—	—	—	—
1712M	—	75.00	150	300	525	—
1713M	—	—	—	—	—	—
1715M	—	—	—	—	—	—

KM# 380.12 1/4 ECU

7.5950 g., 0.9170 Silver 0.2239 oz. ASW **Ruler:** Louis XIV **Mint:** Montpellier **Obverse:** Mailed bust right **Reverse:** 3 Crowns, fleur-de-lis in openings

Date	Mintage	VG	F	VF	XF	Unc
1709N	—	—	—	—	—	—
1710N	—	—	—	—	—	—
1711N	—	65.00	135	270	450	—
1712N	—	75.00	150	300	525	—
1713N	—	—	—	—	—	—
1715N	—	—	—	—	—	—

KM# 380.14 1/4 ECU

7.5950 g., 0.9170 Silver 0.2239 oz. ASW **Ruler:** Louis XIV **Mint:** Dijon **Obverse:** Mailed bust right **Reverse:** 3 Crowns, fleur-de-lis in openings

Date	Mintage	VG	F	VF	XF	Unc
1709P	—	—	—	—	—	—
1710P	—	40.00	80.00	165	275	—
1711P	—	65.00	135	270	450	—
1712P	—	—	—	—	—	—

KM# 380.13 1/4 ECU

7.5950 g., 0.9170 Silver 0.2239 oz. ASW **Ruler:** Louis XIV **Mint:** Riom **Obverse:** Mailed bust right **Reverse:** 3 Crowns, fleur-de-lis in openings

Date	Mintage	VG	F	VF	XF	Unc
1710O	—	—	—	—	—	—
1711O	—	—	—	—	—	—
1715O	—	—	—	—	—	—

KM# 380.9 1/4 ECU

7.5950 g., 0.9170 Silver 0.2239 oz. ASW **Ruler:** Louis XIV **Mint:** Bordeaux **Obverse:** Mailed bust right **Reverse:** 3 Crowns, fleur-de-lis in openings

Date	Mintage	VG	F	VF	XF	Unc
1710K	—	—	—	—	—	—
1711K	—	85.00	165	330	580	—
1712K	—	—	—	—	—	—
1713K	—	85.00	165	330	580	—

KM# 380.10 1/4 ECU

7.5950 g., 0.9170 Silver 0.2239 oz. ASW **Ruler:** Louis XIV **Mint:** Bayonne **Obverse:** Mailed bust right **Reverse:** 3 Crowns, fleur-de-lis in openings

Date	Mintage	VG	F	VF	XF	Unc
1710L	—	65.00	135	270	450	—
1711L	—	65.00	135	270	450	—
1715L	—	85.00	165	330	580	—

KM# 380.18 1/4 ECU

7.5950 g., 0.9170 Silver 0.2239 oz. ASW **Ruler:** Louis XIV **Mint:** Troyes **Obverse:** Mailed bust right **Reverse:** 3 Crowns, fleur-de-lis in openings

Date	Mintage	VG	F	VF	XF	Unc
1710V	—	75.00	150	300	525	—
1711V	—	65.00	135	270	450	—
1712V	—	85.00	165	330	580	—
1713V	—	—	—	—	—	—

KM# 380.21 1/4 ECU

7.5950 g., 0.9170 Silver 0.2239 oz. ASW **Ruler:** Louis XIV **Mint:** Bourges **Obverse:** Mailed bust right **Reverse:** 3 Crowns, fleur-de-lis in openings

Date	Mintage	VG	F	VF	XF	Unc
1710Y	—	90.00	180	360	630	—
1711Y	—	90.00	180	360	630	—
1715Y	—	85.00	165	330	580	—

KM# 404 1/4 ECU

6.1960 g., 0.8330 Silver 0.1659 oz. ASW **Ruler:** Louis XIV **Mint:** Strasbourg **Reverse:** Crowned shield of France

Date	Mintage	VG	F	VF	XF	Unc
1710BB	—	45.00	90.00	180	300	—
1711BB	—	50.00	100	200	350	—
1712BB	—	60.00	125	250	400	—

KM# 380.24 1/4 ECU

7.5950 g., 0.9170 Silver 0.2239 oz. ASW **Ruler:** Louis XIV **Mint:** Aix **Obverse:** Mailed bust right **Reverse:** 3 Crowns, fleur-de-lis in openings **Note:** Mint mark: &.

Date	Mintage	VG	F	VF	XF	Unc
1710	—	65.00	135	270	450	—
1712	—	65.00	135	270	450	—

KM# 380.6 1/4 ECU

7.5950 g., 0.9170 Silver 0.2239 oz. ASW **Ruler:** Louis XIV **Mint:** Poitiers **Obverse:** Mailed bust right **Reverse:** 3 Crowns, fleur-de-lis in openings

Date	Mintage	VG	F	VF	XF	Unc
1710G	—	—	—	—	—	—
1711G	—	75.00	150	300	525	—
1712G	—	60.00	125	250	400	—
1713G	—	—	—	—	—	—
1714G	—	—	—	—	—	—
1715G	—	—	—	—	—	—

KM# 380.7 1/4 ECU

7.5950 g., 0.9170 Silver 0.2239 oz. ASW **Ruler:** Louis XIV **Mint:** La Rochelle **Obverse:** Mailed bust right **Reverse:** 3 Crowns, fleur-de-lis in openings

Date	Mintage	VG	F	VF	XF	Unc
1710H	—	—	—	—	—	—
1711H	—	90.00	180	360	630	—
1715H	—	—	—	—	—	—

KM# 380.22 1/4 ECU

7.5950 g., 0.9170 Silver 0.2239 oz. ASW **Ruler:** Louis XIV **Mint:** Grenoble **Obverse:** Mailed bust right **Reverse:** 3 Crowns, fleur-de-lis in openings

Date	Mintage	VG	F	VF	XF	Unc
1711Z	—	—	—	—	—	—
1712Z	—	—	—	—	—	—
1713Z	—	—	—	—	—	—

KM# 380.15 1/4 ECU

7.5950 g., 0.9170 Silver 0.2239 oz. ASW **Ruler:** Louis XIV **Mint:** Perpignan **Obverse:** Mailed bust right **Reverse:** 3 Crowns, fleur-de-lis in openings

Date	Mintage	VG	F	VF	XF	Unc
1711Q	—	—	—	—	—	—
1712Q	—	—	—	—	—	—

KM# 380.19 1/4 ECU

7.5950 g., 0.9170 Silver 0.2239 oz. ASW **Ruler:** Louis XIV **Mint:** Lille **Obverse:** Mailed bust right **Reverse:** 3 Crowns, fleur-de-lis in openings

Date	Mintage	VG	F	VF	XF	Unc
1713W	—	85.00	165	330	580	—
1715W	—	90.00	180	360	630	—

KM# 455.1 1/3 ECU

8.1580 g., 0.9170 Silver 0.2405 oz. ASW **Ruler:** Louis XV **Mint:** Paris **Obverse:** Young laureate bust right **Obv. Legend:** LUD • XV • D • G • FR • ET • NAV • REX • **Reverse:** Crowned back to back L's in cruciform, fleur-de-lis at angles **Rev. Legend:** CHRS • REGN • VINC • IMP *

Date	Mintage	VG	F	VF	XF	Unc
1720A	11,031,000	10.00	15.00	45.00	140	—

KM# 455.2 1/3 ECU

8.1580 g., 0.9170 Silver 0.2405 oz. ASW **Ruler:** Louis XV **Mint:** Metz **Obverse:** Young laureate bust right **Reverse:** Crowned back to back L's in cruciform, fleur-de-lis at angles

Date	Mintage	VG	F	VF	XF	Unc
1720AA	188,000	12.00	25.00	70.00	185	—

KM# 455.3 1/3 ECU

8.1580 g., 0.9170 Silver 0.2405 oz. ASW **Ruler:** Louis XV **Mint:** Rouen **Obverse:** Young laureate bust right **Reverse:** Crowned back to back L's in cruciform, fleur-de-lis at angles

Date	Mintage	VG	F	VF	XF	Unc
1720B	3,363,000	10.00	15.00	55.00	160	—

KM# 455.4 1/3 ECU

8.1580 g., 0.9170 Silver 0.2405 oz. ASW **Ruler:** Louis XV **Mint:** Strasbourg **Obverse:** Young laureate bust right **Reverse:** Crowned back to back L's in cruciform, fleur-de-lis at angles

Date	Mintage	VG	F	VF	XF	Unc
1720BB	837,000	10.00	15.00	55.00	160	—

KM# 455.5 1/3 ECU

8.1580 g., 0.9170 Silver 0.2405 oz. ASW **Ruler:** Louis XV **Mint:** Caen **Obverse:** Young laureate bust right **Reverse:** Crowned back to back L's in cruciform, fleur-de-lis at angles

Date	Mintage	VG	F	VF	XF	Unc
1720C	930,000	10.00	15.00	55.00	160	—

KM# 455.6 1/3 ECU

8.1580 g., 0.9170 Silver 0.2405 oz. ASW **Ruler:** Louis XV **Mint:** Lyon **Obverse:** Young laureate bust right **Reverse:** Crowned back to back L's in cruciform, fleur-de-lis at angles

Date	Mintage	VG	F	VF	XF	Unc
1720D	409,000	10.00	15.00	55.00	160	—

KM# 455.7 1/3 ECU

8.1580 g., 0.9170 Silver 0.2405 oz. ASW **Ruler:** Louis XV **Mint:** Poitiers **Obverse:** Young laureate bust right **Reverse:** Crowned back to back L's in cruciform, fleur-de-lis at angles

Date	Mintage	VG	F	VF	XF	Unc
1720G	596,000	10.00	20.00	65.00	180	—

KM# 455.8 1/3 ECU

8.1580 g., 0.9170 Silver 0.2405 oz. ASW **Ruler:** Louis XV **Mint:** La Rochelle **Obverse:** Young laureate bust right **Reverse:** Crowned back to back L's in cruciform, fleur-de-lis at angles

Date	Mintage	VG	F	VF	XF	Unc
1720H	752,000	10.00	20.00	65.00	180	—

KM# 455.9 1/3 ECU

8.1580 g., 0.9170 Silver 0.2405 oz. ASW **Ruler:** Louis XV **Mint:** Limoges **Obverse:** Young laureate bust right **Reverse:** Crowned back to back L's in cruciform, fleur-de-lis at angles

Date	Mintage	VG	F	VF	XF	Unc
1720I	506,000	10.00	15.00	55.00	160	—

KM# 455.10 1/3 ECU

8.1580 g., 0.9170 Silver 0.2405 oz. ASW **Ruler:** Louis XV **Mint:** Bordeaux **Obverse:** Young laureate bust right **Reverse:** Crowned back to back L's in cruciform, fleur-de-lis at angles

Date	Mintage	VG	F	VF	XF	Unc
1720K	2,733,000	10.00	15.00	55.00	160	—

KM# 455.11 1/3 ECU

8.1580 g., 0.9170 Silver 0.2405 oz. ASW **Ruler:** Louis XV **Mint:** Toulouse **Obverse:** Young laureate bust right **Obv. Legend:** LVD • XV • D • G • FR • ET • NAU • REX • **Reverse:** Crowned back to back L's in cruciform, fleur-de-lis at angles **Rev. Legend:** CHRS • REGN • VINC • IMP *

Date	Mintage	VG	F	VF	XF	Unc
1720M	—	20.00	30.00	75.00	190	—

KM# 455.12 1/3 ECU

8.1580 g., 0.9170 Silver 0.2405 oz. ASW **Ruler:** Louis XV **Mint:** Montpellier **Obverse:** Young laureate bust right **Reverse:** Crowned back to back L's in cruciform, fleur-de-lis at angles

Date	Mintage	VG	F	VF	XF	Unc
1720N	1,076,000	10.00	15.00	55.00	160	—

KM# 455.13 1/3 ECU

8.1580 g., 0.9170 Silver 0.2405 oz. ASW **Ruler:** Louis XV **Mint:** Riom **Obverse:** Young laureate bust right **Reverse:** Crowned back to back L's in cruciform, fleur-de-lis at angles

Date	Mintage	VG	F	VF	XF	Unc
1720O	—	30.00	60.00	125	375	—

KM# 455.14 1/3 ECU

8.1580 g., 0.9170 Silver 0.2405 oz. ASW **Ruler:** Louis XV **Mint:** Orléans **Obverse:** Young laureate bust right **Reverse:** Crowned back to back L's in cruciform, fleur-de-lis at angles

Date	Mintage	VG	F	VF	XF	Unc
1720R	477,000	10.00	20.00	65.00	180	—

KM# 455.15 1/3 ECU

8.1580 g., 0.9170 Silver 0.2405 oz. ASW **Ruler:** Louis XV **Mint:** Reims **Obverse:** Young laureate bust right **Reverse:** Crowned back to back L's in cruciform, fleur-de-lis at angles

Date	Mintage	VG	F	VF	XF	Unc
1720S	—	18.00	30.00	75.00	190	—

KM# 455.16 1/3 ECU

8.1580 g., 0.9170 Silver 0.2405 oz. ASW **Ruler:** Louis XV **Mint:** Nantes **Obverse:** Young laureate bust right **Reverse:** Crowned back to back L's in cruciform, fleur-de-lis at angles

Date	Mintage	VG	F	VF	XF	Unc
1720T	1,556,000	10.00	15.00	55.00	160	—

KM# 455.17 1/3 ECU

8.1580 g., 0.9170 Silver 0.2405 oz. ASW **Ruler:** Louis XV **Mint:** Troyes **Obverse:** Young laureate bust right **Reverse:** Crowned back to back L's in cruciform, fleur-de-lis at angles

Date	Mintage	VG	F	VF	XF	Unc
1720V	89,000	18.00	32.00	80.00	200	—

KM# 455.18 1/3 ECU

8.1580 g., 0.9170 Silver 0.2405 oz. ASW **Ruler:** Louis XV **Mint:** Lille **Obverse:** Young laureate bust right **Reverse:** Crowned back to back L's in cruciform, fleur-de-lis at angles

Date	Mintage	VG	F	VF	XF	Unc
1720W	816,000	10.00	15.00	55.00	160	—
1720W REGNA	—	10.00	15.00	55.00	160	—

KM# 455.19 1/3 ECU

8.1580 g., 0.9170 Silver 0.2405 oz. ASW **Ruler:** Louis XV **Mint:** Amiens **Obverse:** Young laureate bust right **Reverse:** Crowned back to back L's in cruciform, fleur-de-lis at angles

Date	Mintage	VG	F	VF	XF	Unc
1720X	669,000	10.00	15.00	55.00	160	—

KM# 455.20 1/3 ECU

8.1580 g., 0.9170 Silver 0.2405 oz. ASW **Ruler:** Louis XV **Mint:** Bourges **Obverse:** Young laureate bust right **Reverse:** Crowned back to back L's in cruciform, fleur-de-lis at angles

Date	Mintage	VG	F	VF	XF	Unc
1720Y	610,000	10.00	20.00	65.00	180	—

KM# 455.21 1/3 ECU

8.1580 g., 0.9170 Silver 0.2405 oz. ASW **Ruler:** Louis XV **Mint:** Grenoble **Obverse:** Young laureate bust right **Reverse:** Crowned back to back L's in cruciform, fleur-de-lis at angles

Date	Mintage	VG	F	VF	XF	Unc
1720Z	98,000	15.00	30.00	80.00	200	—

KM# 457.1 1/3 ECU

8.1580 g., 0.9170 Silver 0.2405 oz. ASW **Ruler:** Louis XV **Mint:** Paris **Obverse:** Young laureate bust right **Obv. Legend:** LUD • XV • D • G • FR • ET • NAV • REX • **Reverse:** Crowned arms of France **Rev. Legend:** SIT NOMEN DOMINI BENEDICTUM *

Date	Mintage	VG	F	VF	XF	Unc
1720A	8,374,000	8.00	15.00	50.00	150	—
1721A	7,299,000	8.00	15.00	45.00	125	—
1722A	—	8.00	20.00	60.00	180	—
1723A	—	8.00	25.00	75.00	225	—

KM# 457.2 1/3 ECU

8.1580 g., 0.9170 Silver 0.2405 oz. ASW **Ruler:** Louis XV **Mint:** Metz **Obverse:** Young laureate bust right **Reverse:** Crowned arms of France

Date	Mintage	VG	F	VF	XF	Unc
1720AA	—	10.00	25.00	75.00	225	—
1722AA	—	10.00	25.00	75.00	225	—

KM# 457.3 1/3 ECU

8.1580 g., 0.9170 Silver 0.2405 oz. ASW **Ruler:** Louis XV **Mint:** Rouen **Obverse:** Young laureate bust right **Reverse:** Crowned arms of France

Date	Mintage	VG	F	VF	XF	Unc
1720B	294,000	10.00	20.00	60.00	180	—
1721B	1,879,000	10.00	20.00	60.00	180	—
1722B	—	10.00	25.00	75.00	225	—
1723B	—	15.00	30.00	90.00	275	—

KM# 457.6 1/3 ECU

8.1580 g., 0.9170 Silver 0.2405 oz. ASW **Ruler:** Louis XV **Mint:** Lyon **Obverse:** Young laureate bust right **Reverse:** Crowned arms of France

Date	Mintage	VG	F	VF	XF	Unc
1720D	72,000	15.00	30.00	90.00	275	—
1721D	520,000	8.00	20.00	60.00	180	—
1722D	528,000	8.00	25.00	75.00	225	—
1723D	49,000	15.00	30.00	90.00	275	—

KM# 457.7 1/3 ECU

8.1580 g., 0.9170 Silver 0.2405 oz. ASW **Ruler:** Louis XV **Mint:** Tours **Obverse:** Young laureate bust right **Reverse:** Crowned arms of France

Date	Mintage	VG	F	VF	XF	Unc
1720E	47,000	15.00	30.00	90.00	275	—
1721E	129,000	10.00	20.00	60.00	180	—
1722E	63,000	15.00	30.00	90.00	275	—
1723E	—	10.00	25.00	75.00	225	—

KM# 457.8 1/3 ECU

8.1580 g., 0.9170 Silver 0.2405 oz. ASW **Ruler:** Louis XV **Mint:** Poitiers **Obverse:** Young laureate bust right **Reverse:** Crowned arms of France

Date	Mintage	VG	F	VF	XF	Unc
1720G	88,000	10.00	25.00	75.00	225	—
1721G	375,000	10.00	20.00	60.00	180	—
1722G	266,000	10.00	25.00	75.00	225	—
1723G	121,000	10.00	25.00	75.00	225	—

KM# 457.9 1/3 ECU

8.1580 g., 0.9170 Silver 0.2405 oz. ASW **Ruler:** Louis XV **Mint:** La Rochelle **Obverse:** Young laureate bust right **Reverse:** Crowned arms of France

Date	Mintage	VG	F	VF	XF	Unc
1720H	84,000	10.00	25.00	75.00	225	—
1721H	698,000	10.00	20.00	60.00	180	—
1722H	—	10.00	25.00	75.00	225	—
1723H	—	15.00	30.00	90.00	275	—

KM# 457.10 1/3 ECU

8.1580 g., 0.9170 Silver 0.2405 oz. ASW **Ruler:** Louis XV **Mint:** Limoges **Obverse:** Young laureate bust right **Reverse:** Crowned arms of France

Date	Mintage	VG	F	VF	XF	Unc
1720I	78,000	10.00	25.00	75.00	225	—
1722I	—	15.00	35.00	100	300	—

KM# 457.11 1/3 ECU

8.1580 g., 0.9170 Silver 0.2405 oz. ASW **Ruler:** Louis XV **Mint:** Bordeaux **Obverse:** Young laureate bust right **Reverse:** Crowned arms of France

Date	Mintage	VG	F	VF	XF	Unc
1720K	388,000	10.00	20.00	60.00	180	—
1721K	904,000	10.00	20.00	60.00	180	—
1722K	—	10.00	20.00	60.00	180	—

KM# 457.14 1/3 ECU

8.1580 g., 0.9170 Silver 0.2405 oz. ASW **Ruler:** Louis XV **Mint:** Montpellier **Obverse:** Young laureate bust right **Reverse:** Crowned arms of France

Date	Mintage	VG	F	VF	XF	Unc
1720N	106,000	10.00	25.00	75.00	225	—

KM# 457.15 1/3 ECU

8.1580 g., 0.9170 Silver 0.2405 oz. ASW **Ruler:** Louis XV **Mint:** Riom **Obverse:** Young laureate bust right **Reverse:** Crowned arms of France

Date	Mintage	VG	F	VF	XF	Unc
1720O	—	15.00	30.00	90.00	275	—
1721O	469,000	10.00	20.00	60.00	180	—
1722O	263,000	10.00	25.00	75.00	225	—

KM# 457.16 1/3 ECU

8.1580 g., 0.9170 Silver 0.2405 oz. ASW **Ruler:** Louis XV **Mint:** Dijon **Obverse:** Young laureate bust right **Reverse:** Crowned arms of France

Date	Mintage	VG	F	VF	XF	Unc
1720P	68,000	15.00	30.00	90.00	275	—
1721P	287,000	10.00	25.00	75.00	225	—
1722P	—	10.00	20.00	60.00	180	—

KM# 457.17 1/3 ECU

8.1580 g., 0.9170 Silver 0.2405 oz. ASW **Ruler:** Louis XV **Mint:** Perpignan **Obverse:** Young laureate bust right **Reverse:** Crowned arms of France

Date	Mintage	VG	F	VF	XF	Unc
1720Q	—	10.00	25.00	75.00	225	—
1722Q	—	10.00	25.00	75.00	225	—
1723Q	—	10.00	25.00	75.00	225	—

KM# 457.18 1/3 ECU

8.1580 g., 0.9170 Silver 0.2405 oz. ASW **Ruler:** Louis XV **Mint:** Orléans **Obverse:** Young laureate bust right **Reverse:** Crowned arms of France

Date	Mintage	VG	F	VF	XF	Unc
1720R	202,000	10.00	20.00	60.00	180	—
1721R	672,000	10.00	20.00	60.00	180	—
1722R	407,000	10.00	25.00	75.00	225	—

KM# 457.19 1/3 ECU

8.1580 g., 0.9170 Silver 0.2405 oz. ASW **Ruler:** Louis XV **Mint:** Reims **Obverse:** Young laureate bust right **Reverse:** Crowned arms of France

Date	Mintage	VG	F	VF	XF	Unc
1720S	—	10.00	20.00	60.00	180	—
1721S	435,000	8.00	20.00	60.00	180	—
1722S	—	15.00	30.00	90.00	275	—
1723S	—	15.00	30.00	90.00	275	—

KM# 457.20 1/3 ECU

8.1580 g., 0.9170 Silver 0.2405 oz. ASW **Ruler:** Louis XV **Mint:** Nantes **Obverse:** Young laureate bust right **Obv. Legend:** LUD • XV • D • G • FR • ET • NAV • REX • **Reverse:** Crowned arms of France **Rev. Legend:** SIT NOMEN DOMINI BENEDICTUM

Date	Mintage	VG	F	VF	XF	Unc
1720T	268,000	10.00	20.00	60.00	180	—
1721T	1,144,000	8.00	20.00	60.00	180	—
1722T	—	10.00	20.00	60.00	180	—
1723T	—	10.00	15.00	50.00	150	—

KM# 457.21 1/3 ECU

8.1580 g., 0.9170 Silver 0.2405 oz. ASW **Ruler:** Louis XV **Mint:** Troyes **Obverse:** Young laureate bust right **Reverse:** Crowned arms of France

Date	Mintage	VG	F	VF	XF	Unc
1720V	257,000	8.00	20.00	60.00	180	—
1722V	—	15.00	30.00	90.00	275	—

KM# 457.22 1/3 ECU

8.1580 g., 0.9170 Silver 0.2405 oz. ASW **Ruler:** Louis XV **Mint:** Lille **Obverse:** Young laureate bust right **Reverse:** Crowned arms of France

Date	Mintage	VG	F	VF	XF	Unc
1720W	—	10.00	20.00	60.00	180	—
1721W	742,000	8.00	20.00	60.00	180	—
1722W	133,000	10.00	25.00	75.00	225	—

KM# 457.23 1/3 ECU

8.1580 g., 0.9170 Silver 0.2405 oz. ASW **Ruler:** Louis XV **Mint:** Amiens **Obverse:** Young laureate bust right **Reverse:** Crowned arms of France

Date	Mintage	VG	F	VF	XF	Unc
1720X	82,000	15.00	30.00	90.00	275	—
1721X	536,000	8.00	20.00	60.00	180	—
1722X	—	10.00	20.00	60.00	180	—

KM# 457.24 1/3 ECU

8.1580 g., 0.9170 Silver 0.2405 oz. ASW **Ruler:** Louis XV **Mint:** Bourges **Obverse:** Young laureate bust right **Reverse:** Crowned arms of France

Date	Mintage	VG	F	VF	XF	Unc
1720Y	44,000	15.00	30.00	90.00	275	—
1721Y	271,000	10.00	25.00	75.00	225	—
1722Y	—	10.00	25.00	75.00	225	—

KM# 457.25 1/3 ECU

8.1580 g., 0.9170 Silver 0.2405 oz. ASW **Ruler:** Louis XV **Mint:** Grenoble **Obverse:** Young laureate bust right **Reverse:** Crowned arms of France

Date	Mintage	VG	F	VF	XF	Unc
1720Z	61,000	15.00	30.00	90.00	275	—
1721Z	140,000	10.00	25.00	75.00	225	—
1722Z	31,000	15.00	30.00	90.00	275	—

KM# 455.23 1/3 ECU

8.1580 g., 0.9170 Silver 0.2405 oz. ASW **Ruler:** Louis XV **Mint:** Aix **Note:** Mint mark: &.

Date	Mintage	VG	F	VF	XF	Unc
1720	—	15.00	30.00	80.00	200	—

KM# 455.22 1/3 ECU

8.1580 g., 0.9170 Silver 0.2405 oz. ASW **Ruler:** Louis XV **Mint:** Rennes **Note:** Mint mark: 9.

Date	Mintage	VG	F	VF	XF	Unc
1720	422,000	10.00	15.00	55.00	160	—

KM# 457.26 1/3 ECU

8.1580 g., 0.9170 Silver 0.2405 oz. ASW **Ruler:** Louis XV **Mint:** Rennes **Obverse:** Young laureate bust right **Reverse:** Crowned arms of France **Note:** Mint mark: 9.

Date	Mintage	VG	F	VF	XF	Unc
1720	1,703,000	8.00	20.00	60.00	180	—
1721	2,958,000	8.00	15.00	50.00	150	—
1722	2,495,000	8.00	15.00	50.00	150	—
1723	1,990,000	8.00	20.00	60.00	180	—

KM# 455.24 1/3 ECU

8.1580 g., 0.9170 Silver 0.2405 oz. ASW **Ruler:** Louis XV **Mint:** Besancon **Note:** Mint mark: Back to back C's.

Date	Mintage	VG	F	VF	XF	Unc
1720	138,000	10.00	20.00	65.00	180	—

KM# 456 1/3 ECU

8.1580 g., 0.9170 Silver 0.2405 oz. ASW **Ruler:** Louis XV **Mint:** Pau **Obv. Legend:** ....RE.BD (ligate BD). **Note:** Mint mark: Cow. Issued for Province of Bearn.

Date	Mintage	VG	F	VF	XF	Unc
1720	—	20.00	45.00	140	325	—

KM# 458 1/3 ECU

8.1580 g., 0.9170 Silver 0.2405 oz. ASW **Ruler:** Louis XV **Mint:** Pau **Obv. Legend:** ....RE.BD (ligate BD). **Note:** Mint mark: Cow. Issued for Province of Bearn.

Date	Mintage	VG	F	VF	XF	Unc
1720	—	15.00	30.00	90.00	275	—
1721	185,000	15.00	30.00	90.00	275	—
1722	82,000	15.00	35.00	100	300	—

KM# 457.27 1/3 ECU

8.1580 g., 0.9170 Silver 0.2405 oz. ASW **Ruler:** Louis XV **Mint:** Aix **Obverse:** Young laureate bust right **Reverse:** Crowned arms of France **Note:** Mint mark: &.

Date	Mintage	VG	F	VF	XF	Unc
1721	—	10.00	25.00	75.00	225	—
1722	—	15.00	35.00	110	325	—

KM# 457.28 1/3 ECU

8.1580 g., 0.9170 Silver 0.2405 oz. ASW **Ruler:** Louis XV **Mint:** Besancon **Obverse:** Young laureate bust right **Reverse:** Crowned arms of France **Note:** Mint mark: ....RE.BD (ligate BD).

Date	Mintage	VG	F	VF	XF	Unc
1721	157,000	10.00	25.00	75.00	225	—
1722	—	15.00	35.00	100	300	—

KM# 457.12 1/3 ECU

8.1580 g., 0.9170 Silver 0.2405 oz. ASW **Ruler:** Louis XV **Mint:** Bayonne **Obverse:** Young laureate bust right **Reverse:** Crowned arms of France

Date	Mintage	VG	F	VF	XF	Unc
1721L	—	10.00	25.00	75.00	225	—
1722L	—	10.00	25.00	75.00	225	—

KM# 457.13 1/3 ECU

8.1580 g., 0.9170 Silver 0.2405 oz. ASW **Ruler:** Louis XV **Mint:** Toulouse **Obverse:** Young laureate bust right **Reverse:** Crowned arms of France

Date	Mintage	VG	F	VF	XF	Unc
1721M	—	10.00	20.00	60.00	180	—

KM# 457.4 1/3 ECU

8.1580 g., 0.9170 Silver 0.2405 oz. ASW **Ruler:** Louis XV **Mint:** Strasbourg **Obverse:** Young laureate bust right **Reverse:** Crowned arms of France

Date	Mintage	VG	F	VF	XF	Unc
1721BB	187,000	10.00	20.00	60.00	180	—
1722BB	—	10.00	25.00	75.00	225	—
1723BB	—	15.00	35.00	110	325	—

KM# 457.5 1/3 ECU

8.1580 g., 0.9170 Silver 0.2405 oz. ASW **Ruler:** Louis XV **Mint:** Caen **Obverse:** Young laureate bust right **Reverse:** Crowned arms of France

Date	Mintage	VG	F	VF	XF	Unc
1721C	694,000	10.00	20.00	60.00	180	—
1722C	561,000	8.00	20.00	60.00	180	—
1723C	173,000	10.00	25.00	75.00	225	—

KM# 308 1/2 ECU

15.3340 g., 0.8330 Silver 0.4107 oz. ASW **Ruler:** Louis XIV **Mint:** Strasbourg **Obverse:** Large fleur-de-lis **Reverse:** Crowned quartered shield of France

Date	Mintage	VG	F	VF	XF	Unc
1694BB	—	65.00	130	325	550	—
1695BB	—	80.00	160	400	700	—
1696BB	—	85.00	175	425	750	—
1697BB	—	100	220	490	850	—
1701BB	—	100	225	625	1,000	—
1702BB	—	120	250	700	1,200	—

KM# 357 1/2 ECU (40 Sols)

13.5440 g., 0.9170 Silver 0.3993 oz. ASW **Ruler:** Louis XIV **Mint:** Pau **Obverse:** Armored bust right **Reverse:** 8 L's back to back, shield of France, Navarre and Bearn at center **Note:** Mint mark: Cow.

Date	Mintage	VG	F	VF	XF	Unc
1704	—	850	1,750	3,450	5,750	—

KM# 325.1 1/2 ECU (43 Sols)

13.5440 g., 0.9170 Silver 0.3993 oz. ASW **Ruler:** Louis XIV **Mint:** Paris **Obverse:** Mailed bust right **Reverse:** Crowned circular shield of France, crossed scepters and hand of Justice behind **Edge Lettering:** DOMINE SALVUM FAC REGEM

Date	Mintage	VG	F	VF	XF	Unc
1701A	—	50.00	100	250	435	—
1702A	—	—	—	—	—	—
1703A	—	55.00	110	275	490	—

KM# 325.3 1/2 ECU (43 Sols)

13.5440 g., 0.9170 Silver 0.3993 oz. ASW **Ruler:** Louis XIV **Mint:** Rouen **Obverse:** Mailed bust right **Reverse:** Crowned circular shield of France, crossed sceptres and hand of Justice behind

Date	Mintage	VG	F	VF	XF	Unc
1701B	—	55.00	110	275	480	—
1703B	—	65.00	135	330	575	—

KM# 325.4 1/2 ECU (43 Sols)

13.5440 g., 0.9170 Silver 0.3993 oz. ASW **Ruler:** Louis XIV **Mint:** Caen **Obverse:** Mailed bust right **Reverse:** Crowned circular shield of France, crossed sceptres and hand of Justice behind

Date	Mintage	VG	F	VF	XF	Unc
1701C	—	—	—	275	480	—
1702C	—	65.00	135	330	575	—

KM# 325.6 1/2 ECU (43 Sols)

13.5440 g., 0.9170 Silver 0.3993 oz. ASW **Ruler:** Louis XIV **Mint:** Tours **Obverse:** Mailed bust right **Reverse:** Crowned circular shield of France, crossed sceptres and hand of Justice behind

Date	Mintage	VG	F	VF	XF	Unc
1701E	—	65.00	135	330	575	—
1702E	—	55.00	110	275	480	—

KM# 325.13 1/2 ECU (43 Sols)

13.5440 g., 0.9170 Silver 0.3993 oz. ASW **Ruler:** Louis XIV **Mint:** Montpellier **Obverse:** Mailed bust right **Reverse:** Crowned circular shield of France, crossed sceptres and hand of Justice behind

Date	Mintage	VG	F	VF	XF	Unc
1701N	—	—	—	—	—	—
1702N	529,000	55.00	110	275	480	—
1703N	38,000	—	—	—	—	—

KM# 325.14 1/2 ECU (43 Sols)

13.5440 g., 0.9170 Silver 0.3993 oz. ASW **Ruler:** Louis XIV **Mint:** Riom **Obverse:** Mailed bust right **Reverse:** Crowned circular shield of France, crossed sceptres and hand of Justice behind

Date	Mintage	VG	F	VF	XF	Unc
1701O	—	65.00	135	330	575	—
1702O	—	65.00	135	330	575	—

KM# 325.15 1/2 ECU (43 Sols)

13.5440 g., 0.9170 Silver 0.3993 oz. ASW **Ruler:** Louis XIV **Mint:** Dijon **Obverse:** Mailed bust right **Reverse:** Crowned circular shield of France, crossed sceptres and hand of Justice behind

Date	Mintage	VG	F	VF	XF	Unc
1701P	—	65.00	135	330	575	—
1702P	—	65.00	135	330	575	—
1703P	—	65.00	135	330	575	—

KM# 325.16 1/2 ECU (43 Sols)

13.5440 g., 0.9170 Silver 0.3993 oz. ASW **Ruler:** Louis XIV **Mint:** Perpignan **Obverse:** Mailed bust right **Reverse:** Crowned circular shield of France, crossed sceptres and hand of Justice behind

Date	Mintage	VG	F	VF	XF	Unc
1701Q	—	65.00	135	330	575	—

KM# 325.17 1/2 ECU (43 Sols)

13.5440 g., 0.9170 Silver 0.3993 oz. ASW **Ruler:** Louis XIV **Mint:** Troyes **Obverse:** Mailed bust right **Reverse:** Crowned circular shield of France, crossed sceptres and hand of Justice behind

Date	Mintage	VG	F	VF	XF	Unc
1701S	—	65.00	135	330	575	—
1702S	—	65.00	135	330	575	—

KM# 325.10 1/2 ECU (43 Sols)

13.5440 g., 0.9170 Silver 0.3993 oz. ASW **Ruler:** Louis XIV **Mint:** Bordeaux **Obverse:** Mailed bust right **Reverse:** Crowned circular shield of France, crossed sceptres and hand of Justice behind

Date	Mintage	VG	F	VF	XF	Unc
1701K	—	65.00	135	330	575	—
1702K	—	65.00	135	330	575	—
1703K	—	65.00	135	330	575	—

KM# 325.11 1/2 ECU (43 Sols)

13.5440 g., 0.9170 Silver 0.3993 oz. ASW **Ruler:** Louis XIV **Mint:** Bayonne **Obverse:** Mailed bust right **Reverse:** Crowned circular shield of France, crossed sceptres and hand of Justice behind

Date	Mintage	VG	F	VF	XF	Unc
1701L	—	135	275	675	1,200	—
1702L	—	65.00	135	330	575	—
1703L	57,000	—	—	—	—	—

KM# 325.19 1/2 ECU (43 Sols)

13.5440 g., 0.9170 Silver 0.3993 oz. ASW **Ruler:** Louis XIV **Mint:** Troyes **Obverse:** Mailed bust right **Reverse:** Crowned circular shield of France, crossed sceptres and hand of Justice behind

Date	Mintage	VG	F	VF	XF	Unc
1701V	—	65.00	135	330	575	—
1702V	298,000	65.00	135	330	575	—
1703V	—	—	—	—	—	—

KM# 326.1 1/2 ECU (43 Sols)

13.5440 g., 0.9170 Silver 0.3993 oz. ASW **Ruler:** Louis XIV **Mint:** Lyon **Obverse:** Bust right **Reverse:** Crowned circular shield of France, crossed scepters, hand of Justice behind **Edge Lettering:** DOMINE SALVUM FAC REGEM

Date	Mintage	VG	F	VF	XF	Unc
1701D	—	60.00	115	285	500	—
1702D	—	60.00	115	285	500	—

KM# 326.2 1/2 ECU (43 Sols)

13.5440 g., 0.9170 Silver 0.3993 oz. ASW **Ruler:** Louis XIV **Mint:** Lille

Date	Mintage	VG	F	VF	XF	Unc
1701W	—	60.00	115	285	500	—
1702W	—	60.00	115	285	500	—
1703W	—	—	—	—	—	—
1704W	—	—	—	—	—	—

KM# 325.23 1/2 ECU (43 Sols)

13.5440 g., 0.9170 Silver 0.3993 oz. ASW **Ruler:** Louis XIV **Mint:** Aix **Obverse:** Mailed bust right **Reverse:** Crowned circular shield of France, crossed sceptres and hand of Justice behind **Note:** Mint mark: &.

Date	Mintage	VG	F	VF	XF	Unc
1701	—	65.00	135	330	575	—
1702	—	65.00	135	330	575	—

KM# 325.22 1/2 ECU (43 Sols)

13.5440 g., 0.9170 Silver 0.3993 oz. ASW **Ruler:** Louis XIV **Mint:** Rennes **Obverse:** Mailed bust right **Reverse:** Crowned circular shield of France, crossed sceptres and hand of Justice behind **Note:** Mint mark: 9.

Date	Mintage	VG	F	VF	XF	Unc
1701	—	60.00	115	285	500	—
1702	—	—	—	285	500	—
1703	—	65.00	135	330	575	—

KM# 327 1/2 ECU (43 Sols)

13.5440 g., 0.9170 Silver 0.3993 oz. ASW **Ruler:** Louis XIV **Mint:** Pau **Obverse:** Mailed bust right **Reverse:** Crowned circular shield of France, Navarre and Bearn, crossed scepters, hand of Justice behind **Note:** Mint mark: Cow.

Date	Mintage	VG	F	VF	XF	Unc
1701	—	725	1,450	2,850	4,750	—
1702	—	725	1,450	3,000	5,000	—
1703	—	—	—	—	—	—

KM# 325.20 1/2 ECU (43 Sols)

13.5440 g., 0.9170 Silver 0.3993 oz. ASW **Ruler:** Louis XIV **Mint:** Amiens **Obverse:** Mailed bust right **Reverse:** Crowned circular shield of France, crossed sceptres and hand of Justice behind

Date	Mintage	VG	F	VF	XF	Unc
1702X	—	—	—	—	—	—

KM# 325.21 1/2 ECU (43 Sols)

13.5440 g., 0.9170 Silver 0.3993 oz. ASW **Ruler:** Louis XIV **Mint:** Bourges **Obverse:** Mailed bust right **Reverse:** Crowned circular shield of France, crossed sceptres and hand of Justice behind

Date	Mintage	VG	F	VF	XF	Unc
1702Y	—	65.00	135	330	575	—

KM# 325.12 1/2 ECU (43 Sols)

13.5440 g., 0.9170 Silver 0.3993 oz. ASW **Ruler:** Louis XIV **Mint:** Toulouse **Obverse:** Mailed bust right **Reverse:** Crowned circular shield of France, crossed sceptres and hand of Justice behind

Date	Mintage	VG	F	VF	XF	Unc
1702M	—	65.00	135	330	575	—

KM# 325.18 1/2 ECU (43 Sols)

13.5440 g., 0.9170 Silver 0.3993 oz. ASW **Ruler:** Louis XIV **Mint:** Nantes **Obverse:** Mailed bust right **Reverse:** Crowned circular shield of France, crossed sceptres and hand of Justice behind

Date	Mintage	VG	F	VF	XF	Unc
1702T	—	65.00	135	330	575	—

KM# 325.7 1/2 ECU (43 Sols)

13.5440 g., 0.9170 Silver 0.3993 oz. ASW **Ruler:** Louis XIV **Mint:** Poitiers **Obverse:** Mailed bust right **Reverse:** Crowned circular shield of France, crossed sceptres and hand of Justice behind

Date	Mintage	VG	F	VF	XF	Unc
1702G	—	65.00	135	330	575	—

KM# 325.8 1/2 ECU (43 Sols)

13.5440 g., 0.9170 Silver 0.3993 oz. ASW **Ruler:** Louis XIV **Mint:** La Rochelle **Obverse:** Mailed bust right **Reverse:** Crowned circular shield of France, crossed sceptres and hand of Justice behind

Date	Mintage	VG	F	VF	XF	Unc
1702H	—	65.00	135	330	575	—

KM# 325.9 1/2 ECU (43 Sols)

13.5440 g., 0.9170 Silver 0.3993 oz. ASW **Ruler:** Louis XIV **Mint:** Limoges **Obverse:** Mailed bust right **Reverse:** Crowned circular shield of France, crossed sceptres and hand of Justice behind

Date	Mintage	VG	F	VF	XF	Unc
1702I	—	65.00	135	330	575	—

KM# 325.5 1/2 ECU (43 Sols)

13.5440 g., 0.9170 Silver 0.3993 oz. ASW **Ruler:** Louis XIV **Mint:** Lyon **Obverse:** Mailed bust right **Reverse:** Crowned circular shield of France, crossed sceptres and hand of Justice behind

Date	Mintage	VG	F	VF	XF	Unc
1702D	—	55.00	110	275	480	—

KM# 325.2 1/2 ECU (43 Sols)
13.5440 g., 0.9170 Silver 0.3993 oz. ASW **Ruler:** Louis XIV **Mint:** Metz **Obverse:** Mailed bust right **Reverse:** Crowned circular shield of France, crossed sceptres and hand of Justice behind

Date	Mintage	VG	F	VF	XF	Unc
1702AA	—	65.00	135	330	575	—

KM# 409.2 1/2 ECU (44 Sols)
12.3920 g., 0.8330 Silver 0.3319 oz. ASW **Ruler:** Louis XIV **Mint:** Strasbourg **Obverse:** Mailed bust right **Obv. Legend:** LVD • XIIII • D • G • FR • ET • NAV • REX • **Reverse:** Crowned shield of France divides date **Rev. Legend:** ARGENTINENSIS MONETA NOVA

Date	Mintage	VG	F	VF	XF	Unc
1709BB	—	55.00	115	280	500	—
1710BB	—	65.00	135	330	575	—
1711BB	—	80.00	170	425	750	—
1712BB	—	80.00	170	425	750	—
1713BB	—	95.00	190	475	825	—
1714BB	—	110	220	530	925	—

KM# 409.1 1/2 ECU (44 Sols)
12.3920 g., 0.8330 Silver 0.3319 oz. ASW **Ruler:** Louis XIV **Mint:** Paris **Obverse:** Mailed bust right **Reverse:** Crowned shield of France divides date

Date	Mintage	VG	F	VF	XF	Unc
1713A	—	65.00	135	350	650	—
1714A	—	—	—	—	—	—

KM# 411 1/2 ECU (44 Sols)
15.2960 g., 0.9170 Silver 0.4509 oz. ASW **Ruler:** Louis XV **Mint:** Paris **Obverse:** Young bust of Louis XV right **Reverse:** 3 Crowns form triangle with fleur-de-lis in angles

Date	Mintage	VG	F	VF	XF	Unc
1715A Rare	—	—	—	—	—	—

KM# 420.1 1/2 ECU (44 Sols)
15.2960 g., 0.9170 Silver 0.4509 oz. ASW **Ruler:** Louis XV **Obverse:** Young bust right **Obv. Legend:** LVD • XV • D • G • FΠ • ET • NAV • REX • **Reverse:** Crowned round arms of France **Rev. Legend:** SIT • NOMEN • DOMINI • BENEDICTUM

Date	Mintage	VG	F	VF	XF	Unc
1716	—	20.00	45.00	125	300	—
1717	—	20.00	50.00	140	325	—

KM# 420.2 1/2 ECU (44 Sols)
15.2960 g., 0.9170 Silver 0.4509 oz. ASW **Ruler:** Louis XV **Mint:** Rouen **Obverse:** Young bust right **Reverse:** Crowned round arms of France

Date	Mintage	VG	F	VF	XF	Unc
1716B	—	30.00	70.00	160	375	—

KM# 420.3 1/2 ECU (44 Sols)
15.2960 g., 0.9170 Silver 0.4509 oz. ASW **Ruler:** Louis XV **Mint:** Strasbourg **Obverse:** Young bust right **Reverse:** Crowned round arms of France

Date	Mintage	VG	F	VF	XF	Unc
1716BB	—	30.00	70.00	160	375	—

KM# 420.4 1/2 ECU (44 Sols)
15.2960 g., 0.9170 Silver 0.4509 oz. ASW **Ruler:** Louis XV **Mint:** Caen **Obverse:** Young bust right **Reverse:** Crowned round arms of France

Date	Mintage	VG	F	VF	XF	Unc
1716C	—	30.00	70.00	160	375	—
1718C	—	30.00	80.00	180	400	—

KM# 420.5 1/2 ECU (44 Sols)
15.2960 g., 0.9170 Silver 0.4509 oz. ASW **Ruler:** Louis XV **Mint:** Lyon **Obverse:** Young bust right **Reverse:** Crowned round arms of France

Date	Mintage	VG	F	VF	XF	Unc
1716D	493,000	30.00	70.00	160	375	—

KM# 420.6 1/2 ECU (44 Sols)
15.2960 g., 0.9170 Silver 0.4509 oz. ASW **Ruler:** Louis XV **Mint:** Tours **Obverse:** Young bust right **Reverse:** Crowned round arms of France

Date	Mintage	VG	F	VF	XF	Unc
1716E	352,000	30.00	70.00	160	375	—

KM# 420.7 1/2 ECU (44 Sols)
15.2960 g., 0.9170 Silver 0.4509 oz. ASW **Ruler:** Louis XV **Mint:** Poitiers **Obverse:** Young bust right **Reverse:** Crowned round arms of France

Date	Mintage	VG	F	VF	XF	Unc
1716G	—	30.00	70.00	160	375	—

KM# 420.8 1/2 ECU (44 Sols)
15.2960 g., 0.9170 Silver 0.4509 oz. ASW **Ruler:** Louis XV **Mint:** La Rochelle **Obverse:** Young bust right **Reverse:** Crowned round arms of France

Date	Mintage	VG	F	VF	XF	Unc
1716H	289,000	30.00	70.00	160	375	—
1718H	—	50.00	150	350	575	—

KM# 420.9 1/2 ECU (44 Sols)
15.2960 g., 0.9170 Silver 0.4509 oz. ASW **Ruler:** Louis XV **Mint:** Limoges **Obverse:** Young bust right **Reverse:** Crowned round arms of France

Date	Mintage	VG	F	VF	XF	Unc
1716I	—	30.00	70.00	160	375	—

KM# 420.10 1/2 ECU (44 Sols)
15.2960 g., 0.9170 Silver 0.4509 oz. ASW **Ruler:** Louis XV **Mint:** Bordeaux **Obverse:** Young bust right **Reverse:** Crowned round arms of France

Date	Mintage	VG	F	VF	XF	Unc
1716K	—	30.00	70.00	160	375	—

KM# 420.11 1/2 ECU (44 Sols)
15.2960 g., 0.9170 Silver 0.4509 oz. ASW **Ruler:** Louis XV **Mint:** Bayonne **Obverse:** Young bust right **Reverse:** Crowned round arms of France

Date	Mintage	VG	F	VF	XF	Unc
1716L	—	30.00	70.00	160	375	—

KM# 420.12 1/2 ECU (44 Sols)
15.2960 g., 0.9170 Silver 0.4509 oz. ASW **Ruler:** Louis XV **Mint:** Toulouse **Obverse:** Young bust right **Reverse:** Crowned round arms of France

Date	Mintage	VG	F	VF	XF	Unc
1716M	—	30.00	70.00	160	375	—

KM# 420.13 1/2 ECU (44 Sols)
15.2960 g., 0.9170 Silver 0.4509 oz. ASW **Ruler:** Louis XV **Mint:** Montpellier **Obverse:** Young bust right **Reverse:** Crowned round arms of France

Date	Mintage	VG	F	VF	XF	Unc
1716N	—	30.00	70.00	160	375	—

KM# 420.14 1/2 ECU (44 Sols)
15.2960 g., 0.9170 Silver 0.4509 oz. ASW **Ruler:** Louis XV **Mint:** Riom **Obverse:** Young bust right **Reverse:** Crowned round arms of France

Date	Mintage	VG	F	VF	XF	Unc
1716O	—	40.00	100	200	525	—

KM# 420.15 1/2 ECU (44 Sols)
15.2960 g., 0.9170 Silver 0.4509 oz. ASW **Ruler:** Louis XV **Mint:** Dijon **Obverse:** Young bust right **Reverse:** Crowned round arms of France

Date	Mintage	VG	F	VF	XF	Unc
1716P	—	30.00	70.00	160	375	—

KM# 420.16 1/2 ECU (44 Sols)
15.2960 g., 0.9170 Silver 0.4509 oz. ASW **Ruler:** Louis XV **Mint:** Reims **Obverse:** Young bust right **Reverse:** Crowned round arms of France

Date	Mintage	VG	F	VF	XF	Unc
1716S	—	30.00	70.00	160	375	—
1718S	—	30.00	80.00	180	400	—

KM# 420.17 1/2 ECU (44 Sols)
15.2960 g., 0.9170 Silver 0.4509 oz. ASW **Ruler:** Louis XV **Mint:** Nantes **Obverse:** Young bust right **Reverse:** Crowned round arms of France

Date	Mintage	VG	F	VF	XF	Unc
1716T	—	30.00	70.00	160	375	—
1717T	—	20.00	50.00	140	325	—

KM# 420.18 1/2 ECU (44 Sols)
15.2960 g., 0.9170 Silver 0.4509 oz. ASW **Ruler:** Louis XV **Mint:** Troyes **Obverse:** Young bust right **Reverse:** Crowned round arms of France

Date	Mintage	VG	F	VF	XF	Unc
1716V	—	30.00	70.00	160	375	—
1717V	—	30.00	70.00	160	375	—

KM# 420.19 1/2 ECU (44 Sols)
15.2960 g., 0.9170 Silver 0.4509 oz. ASW **Ruler:** Louis XV **Mint:** Lille **Obverse:** Young bust right **Reverse:** Crowned round arms of France

Date	Mintage	VG	F	VF	XF	Unc
1716W	—	30.00	70.00	160	375	—

KM# 420.20 1/2 ECU (44 Sols)
15.2960 g., 0.9170 Silver 0.4509 oz. ASW **Ruler:** Louis XV **Mint:** Amiens **Obverse:** Young bust right **Reverse:** Crowned round arms of France

Date	Mintage	VG	F	VF	XF	Unc
1716X	—	30.00	70.00	160	375	—
1717X	—	30.00	80.00	180	400	—

KM# 420.21 1/2 ECU (44 Sols)
15.2960 g., 0.9170 Silver 0.4509 oz. ASW **Ruler:** Louis XV **Mint:** Bourges **Obverse:** Young bust right **Reverse:** Crowned round arms of France

Date	Mintage	VG	F	VF	XF	Unc
1716Y	—	30.00	70.00	160	375	—
1717Y	—	30.00	70.00	160	375	—

KM# 422 1/2 ECU (44 Sols)
12.3920 g., 0.8330 Silver 0.3319 oz. ASW **Ruler:** Louis XV **Mint:** Strasbourg **Reverse:** Crowned arms divide date

Date	Mintage	VG	F	VF	XF	Unc
1716BB	—	45.00	90.00	180	400	—
1718BB Rare	—	—	—	—	—	—

KM# 420.23 1/2 ECU (44 Sols)
15.2960 g., 0.9170 Silver 0.4509 oz. ASW **Ruler:** Louis XV **Mint:** Aix **Obverse:** Young bust right **Reverse:** Crowned round arms of France **Note:** Mint mark: &.

Date	Mintage	VG	F	VF	XF	Unc
1716	—	30.00	70.00	160	375	—

KM# 420.22 1/2 ECU (44 Sols)
15.2960 g., 0.9170 Silver 0.4509 oz. ASW **Ruler:** Louis XV **Mint:** Rennes **Obverse:** Young bust right **Reverse:** Crowned round arms of France **Note:** Mint mark: 9.

Date	Mintage	VG	F	VF	XF	Unc
1716	—	30.00	70.00	160	375	—

KM# 420.24 1/2 ECU (44 Sols)
15.2960 g., 0.9170 Silver 0.4509 oz. ASW **Ruler:** Louis XV **Mint:** Besancon **Obverse:** Young bust right **Reverse:** Crowned round arms of France **Note:** Mint mark: Back to back C's.

Date	Mintage	VG	F	VF	XF	Unc
1716	—	20.00	45.00	125	275	—
1717	—	30.00	80.00	180	400	—

KM# 421 1/2 ECU (44 Sols)
15.2960 g., 0.9170 Silver 0.4509 oz. ASW **Ruler:** Louis XV **Mint:** Pau **Obverse:** Legend ends with ligate BD **Note:** Mint mark: Cow.

Date	Mintage	VG	F	VF	XF	Unc
1716	—	40.00	100	200	500	—

KM# 434.1 1/2 ECU (44 Sols)
12.2370 g., 0.9170 Silver 0.3608 oz. ASW **Ruler:** Louis XV **Mint:** Metz **Obverse:** Laureate, draped young bust right **Obv. Legend:** LVD • XV • D • G • FR • ET • NAV • REX **Reverse:** Crowned arms of France and Navarre quartered **Rev. Legend:** SIT • NOMEN • DOMINI • BENEDICTUM

Date	Mintage	VG	F	VF	XF	Unc
1718AA	23,000	80.00	150	400	900	—

KM# 434.2 1/2 ECU (44 Sols)
12.2370 g., 0.9170 Silver 0.3608 oz. ASW **Ruler:** Louis XV **Mint:** Lyon **Obverse:** Laureate, draped young bust right **Reverse:** Crowned, quartered arms of France and Navarre

Date	Mintage	VG	F	VF	XF	Unc
1718D	411,000	80.00	150	400	900	—
1719D	—	80.00	150	400	900	—

KM# 434.5 1/2 ECU (44 Sols)
12.2370 g., 0.9170 Silver 0.3608 oz. ASW **Ruler:** Louis XV **Mint:** Montpellier **Obverse:** Laureate, draped young bust right **Reverse:** Crowned, quartered arms of France and Navarre

Date	Mintage	VG	F	VF	XF	Unc
1718N	—	80.00	150	400	900	—

KM# 434.9 1/2 ECU (44 Sols)
12.2370 g., 0.9170 Silver 0.3608 oz. ASW **Ruler:** Louis XV **Mint:** Troyes **Obverse:** Laureate, draped young bust right **Reverse:** Crowned, quartered arms of France and Navarre

Date	Mintage	VG	F	VF	XF	Unc
1718V	—	80.00	150	400	900	—

KM# 434.10 1/2 ECU (44 Sols)
12.2370 g., 0.9170 Silver 0.3608 oz. ASW **Ruler:** Louis XV **Mint:** Lille **Obverse:** Laureate, draped young bust right **Reverse:** Crowned, quartered arms of France and Navarre

Date	Mintage	VG	F	VF	XF	Unc
1718W	—	80.00	150	400	900	—
1719W	—	80.00	150	400	900	—

KM# 434.11 1/2 ECU (44 Sols)
12.2370 g., 0.9170 Silver 0.3608 oz. ASW **Ruler:** Louis XV **Mint:** Amiens **Obverse:** Laureate, draped young bust right **Reverse:** Crowned, quartered arms of France and Navarre

Date	Mintage	VG	F	VF	XF	Unc
1718X	—	80.00	150	400	900	—
1719X	—	80.00	150	400	900	—

KM# 434.12 1/2 ECU (44 Sols)
12.2370 g., 0.9170 Silver 0.3608 oz. ASW **Ruler:** Louis XV **Mint:** Grenoble **Obverse:** Laureate, draped young bust right **Reverse:** Crowned, quartered arms of France and Navarre

Date	Mintage	VG	F	VF	XF	Unc
1718Z	80,000	80.00	150	400	900	—

KM# 434.6 1/2 ECU (44 Sols)
12.2370 g., 0.9170 Silver 0.3608 oz. ASW **Ruler:** Louis XV **Mint:** Perpignan **Obverse:** Laureate, draped young bust right **Reverse:** Crowned, quartered arms of France and Navarre

Date	Mintage	VG	F	VF	XF	Unc
1719Q	—	80.00	150	400	900	—

KM# 434.7 1/2 ECU (44 Sols)
12.2370 g., 0.9170 Silver 0.3608 oz. ASW **Ruler:** Louis XV **Mint:** Orléans **Obverse:** Laureate, draped young bust right **Reverse:** Crowned, quartered arms of France and Navarre

Date	Mintage	VG	F	VF	XF	Unc
1719R	—	80.00	150	400	900	—

KM# 434.8 1/2 ECU (44 Sols)
12.2370 g., 0.9170 Silver 0.3608 oz. ASW **Ruler:** Louis XV **Mint:** Reims **Obverse:** Laureate, draped young bust right **Reverse:** Crowned, quartered arms of France and Navarre

Date	Mintage	VG	F	VF	XF	Unc
1719S	183,000	80.00	150	400	900	—

KM# 434.3 1/2 ECU (44 Sols)
12.2370 g., 0.9170 Silver 0.3608 oz. ASW **Ruler:** Louis XV **Mint:** La Rochelle **Obverse:** Laureate, draped young bust right **Reverse:** Crowned, quartered arms of France and Navarre

Date	Mintage	VG	F	VF	XF	Unc
1719H	—	80.00	150	400	900	—

KM# 434.4 1/2 ECU (44 Sols)
12.2370 g., 0.9170 Silver 0.3608 oz. ASW **Ruler:** Louis XV **Mint:** Bordeaux **Obverse:** Laureate, draped young bust right **Reverse:** Crowned, quartered arms of France and Navarre

Date	Mintage	VG	F	VF	XF	Unc
1719K	—	80.00	150	400	900	—

KM# 434.13 1/2 ECU (44 Sols)
12.2370 g., 0.9170 Silver 0.3608 oz. ASW **Ruler:** Louis XV **Mint:** Rennes **Obverse:** Laureate, draped young bust right **Reverse:** Crowned, quartered arms of France and Navarre **Note:** Mint mark: 9.

Date	Mintage	VG	F	VF	XF	Unc
1719	—	80.00	150	400	900	—

KM# 434.14 1/2 ECU (44 Sols)
12.2370 g., 0.9170 Silver 0.3608 oz. ASW **Ruler:** Louis XV **Mint:** Aix **Obverse:** Laureate, draped young bust right **Reverse:** Crowned, quartered arms of France and Navarre **Note:** Mint mark: &.

Date	Mintage	VG	F	VF	XF	Unc
1719	—	80.00	150	400	900	—

KM# 465.13 1/2 ECU (44 Sols)
12.2370 g., 0.9170 Silver 0.3608 oz. ASW **Ruler:** Louis XV **Mint:** Lille

Date	Mintage	VG	F	VF	XF	Unc
1720W	—	100	250	650	1,250	—
1721W	—	100	200	500	950	—
1722W	—	100	200	525	1,000	—

KM# 465.1 1/2 ECU (44 Sols)
12.2370 g., 0.9170 Silver 0.3608 oz. ASW **Ruler:** Louis XV **Mint:** Paris **Reverse:** Crowned arms in square shield

Date	Mintage	VG	F	VF	XF	Unc
1721A	—	100	200	500	1,200	—
1722A	—	100	250	650	1,500	—

KM# 465.5 1/2 ECU (44 Sols)
12.2370 g., 0.9170 Silver 0.3608 oz. ASW **Ruler:** Louis XV **Mint:** Bordeaux

Date	Mintage	VG	F	VF	XF	Unc
1721K	44,000	100	200	500	1,200	—

KM# 465.6 1/2 ECU (44 Sols)
12.2370 g., 0.9170 Silver 0.3608 oz. ASW **Ruler:** Louis XV **Mint:** Toulouse

Date	Mintage	VG	F	VF	XF	Unc
1721M	—	100	200	500	1,200	—

KM# 465.7 1/2 ECU (44 Sols)
12.2370 g., 0.9170 Silver 0.3608 oz. ASW **Ruler:** Louis XV **Mint:** Montpellier

Date	Mintage	VG	F	VF	XF	Unc
1721N	—	100	200	500	1,200	—
1723N	—	100	200	500	1,200	—

KM# 465.8 1/2 ECU (44 Sols)
12.2370 g., 0.9170 Silver 0.3608 oz. ASW **Ruler:** Louis XV **Mint:** Riom

Date	Mintage	VG	F	VF	XF	Unc
1721O	—	100	250	650	1,500	—

KM# 465.9 1/2 ECU (44 Sols)
12.2370 g., 0.9170 Silver 0.3608 oz. ASW **Ruler:** Louis XV **Mint:** Orléans

Date	Mintage	VG	F	VF	XF	Unc
1721R	40,000	100	300	700	1,600	—
1723R	—	100	250	550	1,250	—

KM# 465.3 1/2 ECU (44 Sols)
12.2370 g., 0.9170 Silver 0.3608 oz. ASW **Ruler:** Louis XV **Mint:** Caen

Date	Mintage	VG	F	VF	XF	Unc
1721C	—	100	250	650	1,500	—

KM# 465.11 1/2 ECU (44 Sols)
12.2370 g., 0.9170 Silver 0.3608 oz. ASW **Ruler:** Louis XV **Mint:** Nantes

Date	Mintage	VG	F	VF	XF	Unc
1721T	—	100	200	500	1,200	—

KM# 465.12 1/2 ECU (44 Sols)
12.2370 g., 0.9170 Silver 0.3608 oz. ASW **Ruler:** Louis XV **Mint:** Troyes

Date	Mintage	VG	F	VF	XF	Unc
1721V	—	100	200	500	1,200	—

KM# 465.14 1/2 ECU (44 Sols)
12.2370 g., 0.9170 Silver 0.3608 oz. ASW **Ruler:** Louis XV **Mint:** Rennes **Note:** Mint mark: 9.

Date	Mintage	VG	F	VF	XF	Unc
1721	—	100	200	500	1,200	—

KM# 465.2 1/2 ECU (44 Sols)
12.2370 g., 0.9170 Silver 0.3608 oz. ASW **Ruler:** Louis XV **Mint:** Rouen

Date	Mintage	VG	F	VF	XF	Unc
1722B	—	100	200	500	1,200	—

KM# 465.4 1/2 ECU (44 Sols)
12.2370 g., 0.9170 Silver 0.3608 oz. ASW **Ruler:** Louis XV **Mint:** Lyon

Date	Mintage	VG	F	VF	XF	Unc
1723D	—	100	200	500	1,200	—

KM# 465.10 1/2 ECU (44 Sols)
12.2370 g., 0.9170 Silver 0.3608 oz. ASW **Ruler:** Louis XV **Mint:** Reims

Date	Mintage	VG	F	VF	XF	Unc
1724S	—	150	300	750	1,750	—

KM# 478.1 1/2 ECU (44 Sols)
11.7900 g., 0.9170 Silver 0.3476 oz. ASW **Ruler:** Louis XV **Mint:** Paris **Obverse:** Laureate armored bust right **Obv. Legend:** LUD • XV • D • G • FR • ET • NAV • REX • **Reverse:** 4 Fleur-de-lis form square at center, 4 crowns separated by back to back L's surround **Rev. Legend:** SIT • NOMEN • DOMINI • BENEDICTUM

Date	Mintage	VG	F	VF	XF	Unc
1725A	—	100	250	600	1,200	—

KM# 478.2 1/2 ECU (44 Sols)
11.7900 g., 0.9170 Silver 0.3476 oz. ASW **Ruler:** Louis XV **Mint:** Metz **Obverse:** Laureate armored bust right **Reverse:** 4 Fleur-de-lis form square at center, 4 crowns separated by back to back L's surround

Date	Mintage	VG	F	VF	XF	Unc
1725AA	—	100	250	600	1,200	—

KM# 478.3 1/2 ECU (44 Sols)
11.7900 g., 0.9170 Silver 0.3476 oz. ASW **Ruler:** Louis XV **Mint:** Rouen **Obverse:** Laureate armored bust right **Reverse:** 4 Fleur-de-lis form square at center, 4 crowns separated by back to back L's surround

Date	Mintage	VG	F	VF	XF	Unc
1725B	—	100	250	600	1,200	—

KM# 478.4 1/2 ECU (44 Sols)
11.7900 g., 0.9170 Silver 0.3476 oz. ASW **Ruler:** Louis XV **Mint:** Lyon **Obverse:** Laureate armored bust right **Reverse:** 4 Fleur-de-lis form square at center, 4 crowns separated by back to back L's surround

Date	Mintage	VG	F	VF	XF	Unc
1725D	—	100	250	600	1,200	—

KM# 478.5 1/2 ECU (44 Sols)
11.7900 g., 0.9170 Silver 0.3476 oz. ASW **Ruler:** Louis XV **Mint:** Poitiers **Obverse:** Laureate armored bust right **Reverse:** 4 Fleur-de-lis form square at center, 4 crowns separated by back to back L's surround

Date	Mintage	VG	F	VF	XF	Unc
1725G	—	100	250	600	1,200	—

KM# 478.6 1/2 ECU (44 Sols)
11.7900 g., 0.9170 Silver 0.3476 oz. ASW **Ruler:** Louis XV **Mint:** Montpellier **Obverse:** Laureate armored bust right **Reverse:** 4 Fleur-de-lis form square at center, 4 crowns separated by back to back L's surround

Date	Mintage	VG	F	VF	XF	Unc
1725N	362,000	100	250	600	1,200	—

KM# 478.7 1/2 ECU (44 Sols)
11.7900 g., 0.9170 Silver 0.3476 oz. ASW **Ruler:** Louis XV **Mint:** Dijon **Obverse:** Laureate armored bust right **Reverse:** 4 Fleur-de-lis form square at center, 4 crowns separated by back to back L's surround

Date	Mintage	VG	F	VF	XF	Unc
1725P	—	100	250	600	1,200	—

KM# 478.8 1/2 ECU (44 Sols)
11.7900 g., 0.9170 Silver 0.3476 oz. ASW **Ruler:** Louis XV **Mint:** Orléans **Obverse:** Laureate armored bust right **Reverse:** 4 Fleur-de-lis form square at center, 4 crowns separated by back to back L's surround

Date	Mintage	VG	F	VF	XF	Unc
1725R	—	100	250	600	1,200	—

KM# 478.9 1/2 ECU (44 Sols)
11.7900 g., 0.9170 Silver 0.3476 oz. ASW **Ruler:** Louis XV **Mint:** Reims **Obverse:** Laureate armored bust right **Reverse:** 4 Fleur-de-lis form square at center, 4 crowns separated by back to back L's surround

Date	Mintage	VG	F	VF	XF	Unc
1725S	—	100	250	600	1,200	—

KM# 478.10 1/2 ECU (44 Sols)
11.7900 g., 0.9170 Silver 0.3476 oz. ASW **Ruler:** Louis XV **Mint:** Lille **Obverse:** Laureate armored bust right **Reverse:** 4 Fleur-de-lis form square at center, 4 crowns separated by back to back L's surround

Date	Mintage	VG	F	VF	XF	Unc
1725W	—	100	250	600	1,200	—

KM# 478.11 1/2 ECU (44 Sols)
11.7900 g., 0.9170 Silver 0.3476 oz. ASW **Ruler:** Louis XV **Mint:** Amiens **Obverse:** Laureate armored bust right **Reverse:** 4 Fleur-de-lis form square at center, 4 crowns separated by back to back L's surround

Date	Mintage	VG	F	VF	XF	Unc
1725X	—	100	250	600	1,200	—

KM# 478.12 1/2 ECU (44 Sols)
11.7900 g., 0.9170 Silver 0.3476 oz. ASW **Ruler:** Louis XV **Mint:** Rennes **Obverse:** Laureate armored bust right **Reverse:** 4 Fleur-de-lis form square at center, 4 crowns separated by back to back L's surround **Note:** Mint mark: 9.

Date	Mintage	VG	F	VF	XF	Unc
1725	78,000	100	250	600	1,200	—

KM# 478.13 1/2 ECU (44 Sols)
11.7900 g., 0.9170 Silver 0.3476 oz. ASW **Ruler:** Louis XV **Mint:** Besancon **Obverse:** Laureate armored bust right **Reverse:** 4 Fleur-de-lis form square at center, 4 crowns separated by back to back L's surround **Note:** Mint mark: Back to back C's.

Date	Mintage	VG	F	VF	XF	Unc
1725	—	100	250	600	1,200	—

KM# 484.27 1/2 ECU (44 Sols)
14.7440 g., 0.9170 Silver 0.4347 oz. ASW **Ruler:** Louis XV **Mint:** Besancon **Note:** Mint mark: Back to back C's.

Date	Mintage	VG	F	VF	XF	Unc
1726	—	15.00	30.00	100	300	—
1727	—	15.00	30.00	100	300	—
1728	—	15.00	30.00	100	300	—

KM# 485 1/2 ECU (44 Sols)
14.7440 g., 0.9170 Silver 0.4347 oz. ASW **Ruler:** Louis XV **Mint:** Pau **Obv. Legend:** ....RE.BD (ligate BD). **Note:** Mint mark: Cow. Issued for Province of Bearn.

Date	Mintage	VG	F	VF	XF	Unc
1726	47,000	15.00	30.00	110	350	—
1727	36,000	15.00	30.00	110	350	—
1730	86,000	25.00	60.00	200	500	—
1735	70,000	15.00	30.00	110	350	—
1736	37,000	15.00	30.00	110	350	—
1738	68,000	15.00	30.00	110	350	—
1739	—	15.00	30.00	110	350	—

KM# 484.26 1/2 ECU (44 Sols)
14.7440 g., 0.9170 Silver 0.4347 oz. ASW **Ruler:** Louis XV **Mint:** Aix **Note:** Mint mark: &.

Date	Mintage	VG	F	VF	XF	Unc
1726	—	10.00	20.00	50.00	175	—
1727	—	10.00	20.00	50.00	175	—
1728	—	15.00	25.00	75.00	250	—
1729	519,000	10.00	20.00	50.00	175	—
1730	—	10.00	20.00	50.00	175	—
1731	—	10.00	20.00	50.00	175	—
1733	—	10.00	20.00	50.00	175	—
1735	—	15.00	25.00	75.00	250	—

KM# 484.24 1/2 ECU (44 Sols)
14.7440 g., 0.9170 Silver 0.4347 oz. ASW **Ruler:** Louis XV **Mint:** Grenoble **Obverse:** Young bust left **Obv. Legend:** LUD • XV • D • G • FR • ET • NAV • REX • **Reverse:** Crowned oval arms of France within wreath **Rev. Legend:** SIT NOMEN DOMINI BENEDICTUM

Date	Mintage	VG	F	VF	XF	Unc
1726Z	53,000	15.00	30.00	100	300	—
1727Z	—	15.00	30.00	100	300	—
1728Z	—	15.00	30.00	100	300	—

KM# 484.1 1/2 ECU (44 Sols)
14.7440 g., 0.9170 Silver 0.4347 oz. ASW **Ruler:** Louis XV **Mint:** Paris **Obverse:** Young bust left **Obv. Legend:** LUD • XV • D • G • FR • ET • NAV • REX • **Reverse:** Crowned oval arms of France within wreath **Rev. Legend:** SIT NOMEN DOMINI BENEDICTUM

Date	Mintage	VG	F	VF	XF	Unc
1726A	—	10.00	20.00	50.00	175	—
1728A	—	10.00	20.00	50.00	175	—
1730A	—	10.00	20.00	50.00	175	—

KM# 484.2 1/2 ECU (44 Sols)
14.7440 g., 0.9170 Silver 0.4347 oz. ASW **Ruler:** Louis XV
Mint: Metz **Obverse:** Young bust left **Reverse:** Crowned oval arms of France within wreath

Date	Mintage	VG	F	VF	XF	Unc
1726AA	—	15.00	25.00	75.00	250	—
1728AA	—	10.00	20.00	50.00	175	—

KM# 484.3 1/2 ECU (44 Sols)
14.7440 g., 0.9170 Silver 0.4347 oz. ASW **Ruler:** Louis XV
Mint: Rouen **Obverse:** Young bust left **Reverse:** Crowned oval arms of France within wreath

Date	Mintage	VG	F	VF	XF	Unc
1726B	—	10.00	20.00	50.00	175	—
1728B	—	15.00	25.00	75.00	250	—
1729B	—	10.00	20.00	50.00	175	—
1730B	—	15.00	25.00	75.00	250	—
1731B	—	15.00	25.00	75.00	250	—
1732B	—	15.00	25.00	75.00	250	—
1739B	—	15.00	25.00	75.00	250	—
1740B	—	15.00	30.00	100	325	—

KM# 484.4 1/2 ECU (44 Sols)
14.7440 g., 0.9170 Silver 0.4347 oz. ASW **Ruler:** Louis XV
Mint: Strasbourg **Obverse:** Young bust left **Reverse:** Crowned oval arms of France within wreath

Date	Mintage	VG	F	VF	XF	Unc
1726BB	—	15.00	25.00	75.00	250	—
1727BB	—	15.00	25.00	75.00	250	—
1728BB	603,000	10.00	20.00	50.00	175	—
1729BB	—	15.00	25.00	75.00	250	—
1731BB	—	15.00	25.00	75.00	250	—
1733BB	—	15.00	30.00	100	325	—
1738BB	194,000	10.00	20.00	50.00	175	—
1739BB	31,000	15.00	30.00	100	325	—
1740BB	201,000	15.00	25.00	75.00	250	—

KM# 484.5 1/2 ECU (44 Sols)
14.7440 g., 0.9170 Silver 0.4347 oz. ASW **Ruler:** Louis XV
Mint: Caen **Obverse:** Young bust left **Reverse:** Crowned oval arms of France within wreath

Date	Mintage	VG	F	VF	XF	Unc
1726C	134,000	15.00	25.00	75.00	250	—
1728C	105,000	10.00	20.00	50.00	175	—
1729C	262,000	10.00	20.00	50.00	175	—
1730C	241,000	10.00	20.00	50.00	175	—
1731C	278,000	10.00	20.00	50.00	175	—
1733C	219,000	10.00	20.00	50.00	175	—
1734C	147,000	10.00	20.00	50.00	175	—
1735C	—	12.00	25.00	60.00	190	—
1736C	169,000	10.00	20.00	50.00	175	—
1737C	156,000	10.00	20.00	50.00	175	—

KM# 484.6 1/2 ECU (44 Sols)
14.7440 g., 0.9170 Silver 0.4347 oz. ASW **Ruler:** Louis XV
Mint: Lyon **Obverse:** Young bust left **Reverse:** Crowned oval arms of France within wreath

Date	Mintage	VG	F	VF	XF	Unc
1726D	1,255,000	10.00	20.00	50.00	175	—
1727D	368,000	10.00	20.00	50.00	175	—
1728D	373,000	10.00	20.00	50.00	175	—
1729D	190,000	10.00	20.00	50.00	175	—

KM# 484.7 1/2 ECU (44 Sols)
14.7440 g., 0.9170 Silver 0.4347 oz. ASW **Ruler:** Louis XV
Mint: Tours **Obverse:** Young bust left **Reverse:** Crowned oval arms of France within wreath

Date	Mintage	VG	F	VF	XF	Unc
1726E	191,000	15.00	25.00	75.00	250	—
1728E	164,000	10.00	20.00	50.00	175	—
1729E	529,000	10.00	20.00	50.00	175	—
1730E	431,000	10.00	20.00	50.00	175	—
1731E	150,000	10.00	20.00	50.00	175	—

KM# 484.8 1/2 ECU (44 Sols)
14.7440 g., 0.9170 Silver 0.4347 oz. ASW **Ruler:** Louis XV
Mint: Poitiers **Obverse:** Young bust left **Reverse:** Crowned oval arms of France within wreath

Date	Mintage	VG	F	VF	XF	Unc
1726G	—	15.00	30.00	100	325	—
1729G	—	15.00	30.00	100	325	—
1730G	—	15.00	30.00	100	325	—
1731G	—	15.00	25.00	80.00	265	—

KM# 484.9 1/2 ECU (44 Sols)
14.7440 g., 0.9170 Silver 0.4347 oz. ASW **Ruler:** Louis XV
Mint: La Rochelle **Obverse:** Young bust left **Reverse:** Crowned oval arms of France within wreath

Date	Mintage	VG	F	VF	XF	Unc
1726H	—	15.00	25.00	75.00	250	—
1727H	—	15.00	25.00	75.00	250	—
1728H	—	15.00	25.00	75.00	250	—

KM# 484.11 1/2 ECU (44 Sols)
14.7440 g., 0.9170 Silver 0.4347 oz. ASW **Ruler:** Louis XV
Mint: Bayonne **Obverse:** Young bust left **Reverse:** Crowned oval arms of France within wreath

Date	Mintage	VG	F	VF	XF	Unc
1726L	—	15.00	25.00	75.00	250	—
1729L	786,000	10.00	20.00	50.00	175	—
1730L	—	10.00	20.00	50.00	175	—
1733L	—	15.00	30.00	100	325	—
1735L	—	15.00	25.00	75.00	250	—
1738L	71,000	15.00	30.00	85.00	300	—
1739L	—	15.00	30.00	100	325	—

KM# 484.12 1/2 ECU (44 Sols)
14.7440 g., 0.9170 Silver 0.4347 oz. ASW **Ruler:** Louis XV
Mint: Toulouse **Obverse:** Young bust left **Reverse:** Crowned oval arms of France within wreath

Date	Mintage	VG	F	VF	XF	Unc
1726M	—	10.00	20.00	50.00	175	—
1728M	—	15.00	30.00	100	325	—
1729M	532,000	10.00	20.00	50.00	175	—
1730M	—	10.00	20.00	50.00	175	—

KM# 484.13 1/2 ECU (44 Sols)
14.7440 g., 0.9170 Silver 0.4347 oz. ASW **Ruler:** Louis XV
Mint: Montpellier **Obverse:** Young bust left **Reverse:** Crowned oval arms of France within wreath

Date	Mintage	VG	F	VF	XF	Unc
1726N	548,000	10.00	20.00	50.00	175	—
1727N	31,000	15.00	30.00	100	325	—
1729N	256,000	10.00	20.00	50.00	175	—
1730N	57,000	15.00	30.00	100	325	—

KM# 484.14 1/2 ECU (44 Sols)
14.7440 g., 0.9170 Silver 0.4347 oz. ASW **Ruler:** Louis XV
Mint: Riom **Obverse:** Young bust left **Reverse:** Crowned oval arms of France within wreath

Date	Mintage	VG	F	VF	XF	Unc
1726O	—	15.00	25.00	75.00	250	—
1728O	—	15.00	25.00	75.00	250	—
1729O	299,000	10.00	20.00	50.00	175	—
1730O	169,000	10.00	20.00	50.00	175	—
1731O	78,000	15.00	30.00	100	325	—

KM# 484.15 1/2 ECU (44 Sols)
14.7440 g., 0.9170 Silver 0.4347 oz. ASW **Ruler:** Louis XV
Mint: Dijon **Obverse:** Young bust left **Reverse:** Crowned oval arms of France within wreath

Date	Mintage	VG	F	VF	XF	Unc
1726P	—	15.00	25.00	75.00	250	—
1727P	—	15.00	25.00	75.00	250	—
1730P	—	15.00	30.00	100	325	—
1731P	—	15.00	25.00	75.00	250	—

KM# 484.16 1/2 ECU (44 Sols)
14.7440 g., 0.9170 Silver 0.4347 oz. ASW **Ruler:** Louis XV
Mint: Perpignan **Obverse:** Young bust left **Reverse:** Crowned oval arms of France within wreath

Date	Mintage	VG	F	VF	XF	Unc
1726Q	—	15.00	25.00	75.00	250	—

KM# 484.17 1/2 ECU (44 Sols)
14.7440 g., 0.9170 Silver 0.4347 oz. ASW **Ruler:** Louis XV
Mint: Orléans **Obverse:** Young bust left **Reverse:** Crowned oval arms of France within wreath

Date	Mintage	VG	F	VF	XF	Unc
1726R	—	15.00	25.00	75.00	250	—
1728R	—	15.00	25.00	75.00	250	—
1729R	—	15.00	30.00	100	325	—
1730R	—	15.00	30.00	100	325	—

KM# 484.18 1/2 ECU (44 Sols)
14.7440 g., 0.9170 Silver 0.4347 oz. ASW **Ruler:** Louis XV
Mint: Reims **Obverse:** Young bust left **Reverse:** Crowned oval arms of France within wreath

Date	Mintage	VG	F	VF	XF	Unc
1726S	—	15.00	30.00	100	325	—
1728S	—	15.00	30.00	100	325	—

KM# 484.19 1/2 ECU (44 Sols)
14.7440 g., 0.9170 Silver 0.4347 oz. ASW **Ruler:** Louis XV
Mint: Nantes **Obverse:** Young bust left **Reverse:** Crowned oval arms of France within wreath

Date	Mintage	VG	F	VF	XF	Unc
1726T	—	15.00	25.00	75.00	250	—
1727T	—	15.00	25.00	75.00	250	—
1728T	—	15.00	25.00	75.00	250	—
1730T	—	15.00	25.00	75.00	250	—
1732T	—	15.00	25.00	75.00	250	—
1733T	—	15.00	25.00	75.00	250	—
1735T	—	15.00	25.00	75.00	250	—

KM# 484.20 1/2 ECU (44 Sols)
14.7440 g., 0.9170 Silver 0.4347 oz. ASW **Ruler:** Louis XV
Mint: Troyes **Obverse:** Young bust left **Reverse:** Crowned oval arms of France within wreath

Date	Mintage	VG	F	VF	XF	Unc
1726V	141,000	15.00	25.00	75.00	250	—
1727V	—	15.00	25.00	75.00	250	—
1728V	16,000	20.00	40.00	125	400	—
1730V	52,000	15.00	30.00	100	325	—
1732V	26,000	15.00	30.00	100	325	—
1734V	11,000	20.00	40.00	150	425	—

KM# 484.21 1/2 ECU (44 Sols)
14.7440 g., 0.9170 Silver 0.4347 oz. ASW **Ruler:** Louis XV
Mint: Lille **Obverse:** Young bust left **Reverse:** Crowned oval arms of France within wreath

Date	Mintage	VG	F	VF	XF	Unc
1726W	—	10.00	20.00	50.00	175	—
1728W	203,000	10.00	20.00	50.00	175	—
1729W	160,000	10.00	20.00	50.00	175	—

KM# 484.22 1/2 ECU (44 Sols)
14.7440 g., 0.9170 Silver 0.4347 oz. ASW **Ruler:** Louis XV
Mint: Amiens **Obverse:** Young bust left **Reverse:** Crowned oval arms of France within wreath

Date	Mintage	VG	F	VF	XF	Unc
1726X	—	15.00	25.00	75.00	250	—
1727X	—	15.00	25.00	75.00	250	—
1728X	—	15.00	30.00	100	325	—
1729X	—	15.00	25.00	75.00	250	—
1730X	—	15.00	30.00	100	325	—
1740X	7,451	20.00	40.00	150	425	—

KM# 484.23 1/2 ECU (44 Sols)
14.7440 g., 0.9170 Silver 0.4347 oz. ASW **Ruler:** Louis XV
Mint: Bourges **Obverse:** Young bust left **Reverse:** Crowned oval arms of France within wreath

Date	Mintage	VG	F	VF	XF	Unc
1727Y	—	15.00	25.00	75.00	250	—
1728Y	120,000	15.00	25.00	75.00	250	—
1729Y	—	15.00	25.00	75.00	250	—
1730Y	71,000	15.00	30.00	100	325	—

KM# 484.25 1/2 ECU (44 Sols)
14.7440 g., 0.9170 Silver 0.4347 oz. ASW **Ruler:** Louis XV
Mint: Rennes **Obverse:** Young bust left **Reverse:** Crowned oval arms of France within wreath **Note:** Mint mark: 9.

Date	Mintage	VG	F	VF	XF	Unc
1727	—	15.00	25.00	75.00	250	—
1728	673,000	10.00	20.00	50.00	175	—
1729	—	15.00	25.00	75.00	250	—
1731	—	15.00	30.00	100	325	—
1732	—	10.00	20.00	50.00	175	—

KM# 484.10 1/2 ECU (44 Sols)
14.7440 g., 0.9170 Silver 0.4347 oz. ASW **Ruler:** Louis XV
Mint: Bordeaux

Date	Mintage	VG	F	VF	XF	Unc
1728K	134,000	15.00	25.00	75.00	250	—
1729K	—	15.00	25.00	75.00	250	—
1730K	—	15.00	25.00	75.00	250	—

KM# 516.3 1/2 ECU (44 Sols)
14.7440 g., 0.9170 Silver 0.4347 oz. ASW **Ruler:** Louis XV
Mint: Rouen

Date	Mintage	VG	F	VF	XF	Unc
1741B	—	10.00	25.00	100	300	—
1742B	97,000	10.00	25.00	100	300	—

KM# 516.4 1/2 ECU (44 Sols)
14.7440 g., 0.9170 Silver 0.4347 oz. ASW **Ruler:** Louis XV
Mint: Strasbourg

Date	Mintage	VG	F	VF	XF	Unc
1741BB	—	10.00	20.00	60.00	200	—
1742BB	60,000	15.00	30.00	125	350	—
1757BB	—	20.00	40.00	140	400	—

KM# 516.5 1/2 ECU (44 Sols)
14.7440 g., 0.9170 Silver 0.4347 oz. ASW **Ruler:** Louis XV
Mint: Caen

Date	Mintage	VG	F	VF	XF	Unc
1741C	56,000	15.00	30.00	125	350	—

KM# 516.6 1/2 ECU (44 Sols)
14.7440 g., 0.9170 Silver 0.4347 oz. ASW **Ruler:** Louis XV
Mint: Lyon

Date	Mintage	VG	F	VF	XF	Unc
1741D	53,000	15.00	30.00	125	350	—
1745D	44,000	15.00	30.00	125	350	—
1747D	51,000	15.00	30.00	125	350	—
1767D	—	15.00	30.00	125	350	—

KM# 516.7 1/2 ECU (44 Sols)
14.7440 g., 0.9170 Silver 0.4347 oz. ASW **Ruler:** Louis XV
Mint: Tours

Date	Mintage	VG	F	VF	XF	Unc
1741E	—	15.00	30.00	125	350	—
1742E	15,000	15.00	30.00	125	350	—

KM# 516.8 1/2 ECU (44 Sols)
14.7440 g., 0.9170 Silver 0.4347 oz. ASW **Ruler:** Louis XV
Mint: Poitiers

Date	Mintage	VG	F	VF	XF	Unc
1741G	—	15.00	30.00	125	350	—
1750G	—	15.00	30.00	125	350	—
1767G	—	20.00	40.00	140	400	—

KM# 516.9 1/2 ECU (44 Sols)
14.7440 g., 0.9170 Silver 0.4347 oz. ASW **Ruler:** Louis XV
Mint: La Rochelle

Date	Mintage	VG	F	VF	XF	Unc
1741H	—	10.00	25.00	100	300	—
1751H	—	25.00	50.00	150	450	—
1758H	—	15.00	30.00	125	350	—
1760H	—	20.00	40.00	140	400	—
1762H	—	15.00	30.00	125	350	—
1763H	—	15.00	30.00	125	350	—
1764H	—	15.00	30.00	125	350	—
1765H	—	15.00	30.00	125	350	—
1766H	—	15.00	30.00	125	350	—
1770H	—	20.00	40.00	140	400	—
1772H	—	20.00	45.00	150	450	—

KM# 516.25 1/2 ECU (44 Sols)
14.7440 g., 0.9170 Silver 0.4347 oz. ASW **Ruler:** Louis XV
Mint: Besancon **Note:** Mint mark: Back to back C's.

Date	Mintage	VG	F	VF	XF	Unc
1741	—	50.00	120	300	800	—
1755	—	15.00	30.00	125	350	—
1765	—	15.00	30.00	125	350	—

KM# 516.1 1/2 ECU (44 Sols)
14.7440 g., 0.9170 Silver 0.4347 oz. ASW **Ruler:** Louis XV
Mint: Paris **Obverse:** Laureate head left **Obv. Legend:** LUD • XV • D • G • FR • ET • NAV • REX • **Reverse:** Crowned oval arms of France within wreath **Rev. Legend:** SIT NOMEN DOMINI BENEDICTUM

Date	Mintage	VG	F	VF	XF	Unc
1741A	—	10.00	25.00	100	300	—
1741A Proof	—	Value: 2,000				
1744A	8,568	20.00	40.00	140	400	—
1756A	—	10.00	25.00	100	300	—
1759A	—	15.00	30.00	125	350	—
1761A	—	15.00	30.00	125	350	—
1763A	—	15.00	30.00	125	350	—
1765A	—	15.00	30.00	125	350	—
1766A	—	15.00	30.00	125	350	—
1767A	—	15.00	30.00	125	350	—
1768A	—	10.00	25.00	100	300	—

KM# 516.19 1/2 ECU (44 Sols)
14.7440 g., 0.9170 Silver 0.4347 oz. ASW **Ruler:** Louis XV
Mint: Nantes **Obverse:** Head with headband left **Reverse:** Crowned oval arms of France within wreath

Date	Mintage	VG	F	VF	XF	Unc
1741T	—	12.00	25.00	100	300	—
1742T	48,000	12.00	25.00	100	300	—
1765T	—	20.00	40.00	140	400	—
1766T	—	20.00	45.00	150	450	—
1768T	—	15.00	30.00	125	350	—
1770T	—	20.00	40.00	140	400	—
1772T	—	—	—	—	—	—

KM# 516.20 1/2 ECU (44 Sols)
14.7440 g., 0.9170 Silver 0.4347 oz. ASW **Ruler:** Louis XV
Mint: Troyes **Obverse:** Head with headband left **Reverse:** Crowned oval arms of France within wreath

Date	Mintage	VG	F	VF	XF	Unc
1741V	8,724	20.00	40.00	140	400	—

KM# 516.21 1/2 ECU (44 Sols)
14.7440 g., 0.9170 Silver 0.4347 oz. ASW **Ruler:** Louis XV
Mint: Lille **Obverse:** Head with headband left **Reverse:** Crowned oval arms of France within wreath

Date	Mintage	VG	F	VF	XF	Unc
1741W	58,000	10.00	25.00	100	300	—
1742W	126,000	10.00	20.00	80.00	250	—
1743W	419,000	10.00	20.00	80.00	250	—
1744W	12,000	15.00	30.00	125	350	—
1745W	20,000	15.00	30.00	125	350	—
1746W	453,000	10.00	20.00	80.00	250	—
1747W	369,000	10.00	20.00	80.00	250	—
1748W	492,000	10.00	20.00	80.00	250	—
1749W	146,000	10.00	25.00	90.00	275	—
1750W	52,000	12.00	25.00	100	300	—
1751W	21,000	15.00	30.00	125	350	—
1754W	26,000	15.00	30.00	125	350	—
1755W	37,000	15.00	30.00	125	350	—
1756W	22,000	15.00	30.00	125	350	—
1757W	42,000	15.00	30.00	125	350	—
1759W	156,000	10.00	25.00	90.00	275	—
1760W	7,138	20.00	40.00	140	400	—
1761W	12,000	15.00	35.00	130	360	—
1762W	5,644	20.00	40.00	140	400	—
1763W	7,334	20.00	40.00	140	400	—
1766W	16,000	15.00	30.00	125	350	—
1774W	66,000	20.00	40.00	140	400	—

KM# 516.22 1/2 ECU (44 Sols)
14.7440 g., 0.9170 Silver 0.4347 oz. ASW **Ruler:** Louis XV
Mint: Amiens **Obverse:** Head with headband left **Reverse:** Crowned oval arms of France within wreath

Date	Mintage	VG	F	VF	XF	Unc
1741X	—	15.00	30.00	125	350	—
1742X	8,020	20.00	40.00	140	400	—
1744X	40,000	15.00	30.00	125	350	—
1755X	—	20.00	40.00	140	400	—

KM# 516.17 1/2 ECU (44 Sols)
14.7440 g., 0.9170 Silver 0.4347 oz. ASW **Ruler:** Louis XV
Mint: Orléans **Obverse:** Head with headband left **Obv. Legend:** LUD • XV • D • G • FR • ET • NAV • REX • **Reverse:** Crowned oval arms of France within wreath **Rev. Legend:** SIT NOMEN DOMINI BENEDICTUM

Date	Mintage	VG	F	VF	XF	Unc
1741R	—	15.00	30.00	125	350	—
1743R	6,998	20.00	40.00	140	400	—
1758R	—	20.00	40.00	140	400	—
1761R	—	30.00	70.00	250	675	—

KM# 516.24 1/2 ECU (44 Sols)
14.7440 g., 0.9170 Silver 0.4347 oz. ASW **Ruler:** Louis XV
Mint: Grenoble

Date	Mintage	VG	F	VF	XF	Unc
1741Z	10,000	20.00	40.00	150	450	—

KM# 516.2 1/2 ECU (44 Sols)
14.7440 g., 0.9170 Silver 0.4347 oz. ASW **Ruler:** Louis XV
Mint: Metz **Obverse:** Head with headband left **Reverse:** Crowned oval arms of France within wreath

Date	Mintage	VG	F	VF	XF	Unc
1742AA	17,000	20.00	40.00	140	400	—

KM# 516.11 1/2 ECU (44 Sols)
14.7440 g., 0.9170 Silver 0.4347 oz. ASW **Ruler:** Louis XV
Mint: Bayonne **Obverse:** Head with headband left **Reverse:** Crowned oval arms of France within wreath

Date	Mintage	VG	F	VF	XF	Unc
1742L	—	15.00	30.00	125	350	—
1750L	—	15.00	30.00	125	350	—
1751L	—	15.00	30.00	125	350	—
1756L	—	10.00	25.00	100	300	—
1757L	—	15.00	30.00	125	350	—
1761L	—	15.00	30.00	125	350	—
1763L	—	15.00	30.00	125	350	—
1764L	—	15.00	30.00	125	350	—
1765L	—	15.00	30.00	125	350	—
1766L	—	15.00	30.00	125	350	—
1767L	—	15.00	30.00	125	350	—

KM# 516.13 1/2 ECU (44 Sols)
14.7440 g., 0.9170 Silver 0.4347 oz. ASW **Ruler:** Louis XV
Mint: Montpellier **Obverse:** Head with headband left **Reverse:** Crowned oval arms of France within wreath

Date	Mintage	VG	F	VF	XF	Unc
1742N	—	15.00	30.00	125	350	—
1749N	—	15.00	30.00	125	350	—
1750N	—	20.00	40.00	140	400	—
1756N	—	15.00	30.00	125	350	—

KM# 516.14 1/2 ECU (44 Sols)
14.7440 g., 0.9170 Silver 0.4347 oz. ASW **Ruler:** Louis XV
Mint: Riom **Obverse:** Head with headband left **Reverse:** Crowned oval arms of France within wreath

Date	Mintage	VG	F	VF	XF	Unc
1744O	27,000	15.00	30.00	125	350	—
1745O	—	15.00	30.00	125	350	—
1748O	25,000	15.00	30.00	125	350	—
1749O	25,000	15.00	30.00	125	350	—
1750O	23,000	15.00	30.00	125	350	—
1753O	24,000	15.00	30.00	125	350	—
1754O	9,486	20.00	40.00	150	425	—

KM# 516.16 1/2 ECU (44 Sols)
14.7440 g., 0.9170 Silver 0.4347 oz. ASW **Ruler:** Louis XV
Mint: Perpignan **Obverse:** Head with headband left **Reverse:** Crowned oval arms of France within wreath

Date	Mintage	VG	F	VF	XF	Unc
1744Q	—	15.00	30.00	125	350	—
1753Q	—	15.00	30.00	125	350	—
1754Q	—	15.00	30.00	125	350	—
1765Q	—	15.00	30.00	125	350	—
1772Q	—	20.00	45.00	150	450	—

KM# 516.18 1/2 ECU (44 Sols)
14.7440 g., 0.9170 Silver 0.4347 oz. ASW **Ruler:** Louis XV
Mint: Reims **Obverse:** Head with headband left **Reverse:** Crowned oval arms of France within wreath

Date	Mintage	VG	F	VF	XF	Unc
1744S	39,000	15.00	30.00	125	350	—
1747S	21,000	15.00	30.00	125	350	—
1748S	12,000	15.00	30.00	125	350	—
1753S	9,430	20.00	40.00	150	460	—
1756S	15,000	15.00	30.00	125	350	—
1762S	—	15.00	30.00	125	350	—

KM# 516.10 1/2 ECU (44 Sols)
14.7440 g., 0.9170 Silver 0.4347 oz. ASW **Ruler:** Louis XV
Mint: Limoges **Obverse:** Head with headband left **Reverse:** Crowned oval arms of France within wreath

Date	Mintage	VG	F	VF	XF	Unc
1744I	8,046	20.00	40.00	140	400	—
1745I	7,306	20.00	40.00	140	400	—
1746I	7,120	20.00	40.00	140	400	—
1747I	9,284	20.00	40.00	140	400	—
1763I	—	35.00	75.00	225	675	—
1768I	—	20.00	40.00	140	400	—

KM# 521 1/2 ECU (44 Sols)
14.7440 g., 0.9170 Silver 0.4347 oz. ASW **Ruler:** Louis XV
Mint: Pau **Obv. Legend:** ....RE.BD (ligate BD). **Note:** Mint mark: Cow. Issued for Province of Bearn.

Date	Mintage	VG	F	VF	XF	Unc
1745	37,000	15.00	30.00	125	350	—
1746	52,000	15.00	30.00	125	350	—
1750	—	15.00	30.00	125	350	—
1751	3,758	25.00	50.00	175	500	—
1752	5,499	25.00	50.00	175	500	—
1753	13,000	25.00	50.00	175	500	—
1754	23,000	20.00	40.00	140	400	—
1755	12,000	20.00	40.00	140	400	—
1756	46,000	15.00	30.00	125	350	—
1761	18,000	20.00	40.00	140	400	—
1766	30,000	25.00	50.00	175	500	—
1767	25,000	20.00	40.00	140	400	—
1769	59,000	40.00	100	250	750	—

KM# 516.12 1/2 ECU (44 Sols)
14.7440 g., 0.9170 Silver 0.4347 oz. ASW **Ruler:** Louis XV
Mint: Toulouse **Obverse:** Head with headband left **Reverse:** Crowned oval arms of France within wreath

Date	Mintage	VG	F	VF	XF	Unc
1746M	67,000	15.00	30.00	125	350	—

KM# 516.23 1/2 ECU (44 Sols)
14.7440 g., 0.9170 Silver 0.4347 oz. ASW **Ruler:** Louis XV
Mint: Bourges **Obverse:** Head with headband left **Reverse:** Crowned oval arms of France within wreath

Date	Mintage	VG	F	VF	XF	Unc
1750Y	—	20.00	40.00	140	400	—

KM# 516.15 1/2 ECU (44 Sols)
14.7440 g., 0.9170 Silver 0.4347 oz. ASW **Ruler:** Louis XV
Mint: Dijon **Obverse:** Head with headband left **Reverse:** Crowned oval arms of France within wreath

Date	Mintage	VG	F	VF	XF	Unc
1751P	13,000	15.00	30.00	125	350	—
1759P	—	25.00	50.00	150	450	—
1761P	—	15.00	30.00	125	350	—
1763P	—	20.00	40.00	140	400	—
1767P	—	20.00	40.00	140	400	—
1768P	—	20.00	40.00	140	400	—
1769P	—	20.00	40.00	140	400	—
1770P	—	20.00	40.00	140	400	—

KM# 554.1 1/2 ECU (44 Sols)
14.7440 g., 0.9170 Silver 0.4347 oz. ASW **Ruler:** Louis XV
Mint: Paris

Date	Mintage	VG	F	VF	XF	Unc
1771A	—	125	300	850	1,400	—
1771A Proof	—	Value: 3,000				
1772A	—	125	300	850	1,400	—

KM# 554.3 1/2 ECU (44 Sols)
14.7440 g., 0.9170 Silver 0.4347 oz. ASW **Ruler:** Louis XV
Mint: Limoges

Date	Mintage	VG	F	VF	XF	Unc
1772I	—	125	325	950	1,600	—
1773I	—	125	325	950	1,600	—

KM# 554.4 1/2 ECU (44 Sols)
14.7440 g., 0.9170 Silver 0.4347 oz. ASW **Ruler:** Louis XV
Mint: Bayonne

Date	Mintage	VG	F	VF	XF	Unc
1772L	—	125	325	950	1,600	—
1774L	6,873	125	325	950	1,600	—

KM# 554.5 1/2 ECU (44 Sols)
14.7440 g., 0.9170 Silver 0.4347 oz. ASW **Ruler:** Louis XV
Mint: Perpignan

Date	Mintage	VG	F	VF	XF	Unc
1772Q	—	125	325	950	1,600	—
1773Q	—	125	325	950	1,600	—

KM# 554.6 1/2 ECU (44 Sols)
14.7440 g., 0.9170 Silver 0.4347 oz. ASW **Ruler:** Louis XV
Mint: Nantes

Date	Mintage	VG	F	VF	XF	Unc
1772/1T	—	125	300	850	1,400	—
1772T	—	125	300	850	1,400	—
1773T	—	125	300	850	1,400	—
1774T	2,888	150	400	1,100	1,800	—

KM# 554.2 1/2 ECU (44 Sols)
14.7440 g., 0.9170 Silver 0.4347 oz. ASW **Ruler:** Louis XV
Mint: La Rochelle

Date	Mintage	VG	F	VF	XF	Unc
1773H	—	150	400	1,100	1,800	—

KM# 562.1 1/2 ECU (44 Sols)

14.7440 g., 0.9170 Silver 0.4347 oz. ASW **Ruler:** Louis XVI **Mint:** Paris **Obverse:** Uniformed bust left **Obv. Legend:** LUD • XVI • D • G • FR • ET NAV • REX • **Reverse:** Crowned arms of France within branches **Rev. Legend:** SIT NOMEN DOMINI BENEDICTUM

Date	Mintage	VG	F	VF	XF	Unc
1774A	5,102	50.00	125	250	600	—
1775A	18,000	30.00	70.00	140	350	—
1776A	10,000	30.00	70.00	140	350	—
1777A	2,970	—	—	—	—	—
1778A	2,724	—	—	—	—	—
1779A	10,000	—	—	—	—	—
1780A	8,202	30.00	70.00	140	350	—
1781A	10,000	30.00	70.00	140	350	—
1782A	15,000	30.00	70.00	140	350	—
1783A	123,000	15.00	40.00	80.00	200	—
1784A	402,000	15.00	40.00	80.00	200	—
1784A	Inc. above	15.00	40.00	80.00	200	—
1785A	29,000	25.00	50.00	120	300	—
1788A	—	25.00	50.00	120	300	—
1789A	7,789	30.00	70.00	140	350	—
1790A	—	15.00	35.00	70.00	175	—
1790A	—	15.00	35.00	70.00	175	—
1791A (he)	778,000	12.50	30.00	60.00	150	—
1791A (he)	Inc. above	12.50	30.00	60.00	150	—
1791A (l)	Inc. above	12.50	30.00	60.00	150	—
1791A (.L)	Inc. above	12.50	30.00	60.00	150	—
1792A	—	30.00	70.00	140	350	—

KM# 561 1/2 ECU (44 Sols)

14.7440 g., 0.9170 Silver 0.4347 oz. ASW **Ruler:** Louis XV **Mint:** Pau **Obv. Legend:** ....RE.BD (ligate BD). **Note:** Mint mark: Cow. Issued for Province of Bearn.

Date	Mintage	VG	F	VF	XF	Unc
1774	4,563	150	400	1,100	1,800	—

KM# 571 1/2 ECU (44 Sols)

14.7440 g., 0.9170 Silver 0.4347 oz. ASW **Ruler:** Louis XVI **Mint:** Pau **Obverse:** Uniformed bust left **Obv. Legend:** ....RE.BD. (ligate BD). **Reverse:** Crowned arms of France within branches **Rev. Legend:** SIT NOMEN DOMINI BENEDICTUM **Note:** Mint mark: Cow. Province of Bearn.

Date	Mintage	VG	F	VF	XF	Unc
1775	4,681	—	—	—	—	—
1785	5,436	40.00	100	200	500	—

KM# 562.12 1/2 ECU (44 Sols)

14.7440 g., 0.9170 Silver 0.4347 oz. ASW **Ruler:** Louis XVI **Mint:** Nantes **Obverse:** Uniformed bust left **Reverse:** Crowned arms of France within branches

Date	Mintage	VG	F	VF	XF	Unc
1775T	1,644	—	—	—	—	—
1777T	9,145	30.00	70.00	140	350	—
1778T	3,189	—	—	—	—	—
1779T	1,688	—	—	—	—	—
1780T	1,637	—	—	—	—	—
1781T	1,363	—	—	—	—	—
1782T	2,237	—	—	—	—	—
1783T	1,641	40.00	100	200	500	—
1784T	5,037	30.00	70.00	140	350	—
1785T	2,194	—	—	—	—	—
1787T	1,924	35.00	90.00	180	450	—
1789T	—	30.00	70.00	140	350	—
1790T	—	30.00	70.00	140	350	—
1791T	4,217	30.00	70.00	140	350	—

KM# 562.3 1/2 ECU (44 Sols)

14.7440 g., 0.9170 Silver 0.4347 oz. ASW **Ruler:** Louis XVI **Mint:** Strasbourg **Obverse:** Uniformed bust left **Reverse:** Crowned arms of France within branches

Date	Mintage	VG	F	VF	XF	Unc
1775BB	7,018	—	—	—	—	—
1779BB	4,783	—	—	—	—	—
1780BB	3,789	30.00	80.00	160	400	—
1781BB	4,706	—	—	—	—	—
1790DD	—	30.00	80.00	100	400	—

KM# 562.4 1/2 ECU (44 Sols)

14.7440 g., 0.9170 Silver 0.4347 oz. ASW **Ruler:** Louis XVI **Mint:** La Rochelle **Obverse:** Uniformed bust left **Reverse:** Crowned arms of France within branches

Date	Mintage	VG	F	VF	XF	Unc
1775H	1,922	40.00	100	200	500	—
1776H	780	60.00	160	330	750	—
1777H	834	60.00	160	330	750	—
1778H	1,940	40.00	100	200	500	—
1779H	2,632	35.00	90.00	180	450	—
1780H	2,370	35.00	90.00	180	450	—
1781H	1,952	40.00	100	200	500	—
1782H	3,164	30.00	80.00	160	400	—
1783H	724	60.00	150	320	750	—
1784H	—	50.00	125	210	550	—
1790H	—	35.00	90.00	180	450	—

KM# 562.5 1/2 ECU (44 Sols)

14.7440 g., 0.9170 Silver 0.4347 oz. ASW **Ruler:** Louis XVI **Mint:** Limoges **Obverse:** Uniformed bust left **Reverse:** Crowned arms of France within branches

Date	Mintage	VG	F	VF	XF	Unc
1775I	20,000	30.00	65.00	125	350	—
1780I	12,000	30.00	70.00	140	350	—
1781I	8,430	—	—	—	—	—

KM# 562.14 1/2 ECU (44 Sols)

14.7440 g., 0.9170 Silver 0.4347 oz. ASW **Ruler:** Louis XVI **Mint:** Aix **Obverse:** Uniformed bust left **Reverse:** Crowned arms of France within branches **Note:** Mint mark: &. The "dot" appears below the third letter of the monarch's name and denotes second semester coinage.

Date	Mintage	VG	F	VF	XF	Unc
1775	18,000	30.00	70.00	140	350	—
1776	19,000	—	—	—	—	—
1777	35,000	25.00	60.00	120	300	—
1778	3,993	—	—	—	—	—

KM# 562.7 1/2 ECU (44 Sols)

14.7440 g., 0.9170 Silver 0.4347 oz. ASW **Ruler:** Louis XVI **Mint:** Bayonne **Obverse:** Uniformed bust left **Reverse:** Crowned arms of France within branches

Date	Mintage	VG	F	VF	XF	Unc
1775L	7,415	—	—	—	—	—
1776L	6,782	—	—	—	—	—
1777L	20,000	—	—	—	—	—
1778L	4,799	35.00	80.00	160	400	—
1779L	2,927	—	—	—	—	—
1780L	7,280	30.00	70.00	140	350	—
1781L	9,433	—	—	—	—	—
1782L	50,000	25.00	60.00	120	300	—
1783L	34,000	25.00	60.00	120	300	—
1786L	5,395	—	—	—	—	—
1788L	7,789	—	—	—	—	—
1789L	—	30.00	70.00	140	350	—

KM# 562.9 1/2 ECU (44 Sols)

14.7440 g., 0.9170 Silver 0.4347 oz. ASW **Ruler:** Louis XVI **Mint:** Montpellier **Obverse:** Uniformed bust left **Reverse:** Crowned arms of France within branches

Date	Mintage	VG	F	VF	XF	Unc
1775N	6,512	30.00	80.00	160	400	—

KM# 562.10 1/2 ECU (44 Sols)

14.7440 g., 0.9170 Silver 0.4347 oz. ASW **Ruler:** Louis XVI **Mint:** Perpignan **Obverse:** Uniformed bust left **Reverse:** Crowned arms of France within branches

Date	Mintage	VG	F	VF	XF	Unc
1775Q	10,000	—	—	—	—	—
1776Q	13,000	30.00	70.00	140	350	—
1778Q	21,000	—	—	—	—	—
1779Q	21,000	25.00	60.00	140	350	—
1781Q	10,000	—	—	—	—	—
1782Q	11,000	—	—	—	—	—
1784Q	17,000	—	—	—	—	—
1785Q	20,000	30.00	70.00	140	350	—
1786Q	41,000	25.00	60.00	120	300	—
1787Q	16,000	30.00	70.00	140	350	—
1790Q	5,050	—	—	—	—	—

KM# 562.13 1/2 ECU (44 Sols)

14.7440 g., 0.9170 Silver 0.4347 oz. ASW **Ruler:** Louis XVI **Mint:** Lille **Obverse:** Uniformed bust left **Reverse:** Crowned arms of France within branches

Date	Mintage	VG	F	VF	XF	Unc
1779W	155,000	15.00	40.00	80.00	200	—
1780W	147,000	15.00	40.00	80.00	200	—
1787W	2,822	—	—	—	—	—
1791W	117,000	—	—	—	—	—

KM# 562.11 1/2 ECU (44 Sols)

14.7440 g., 0.9170 Silver 0.4347 oz. ASW **Ruler:** Louis XVI **Mint:** Orléans **Obverse:** Uniformed bust left **Reverse:** Crowned arms of France within branches

Date	Mintage	VG	F	VF	XF	Unc
1780R	548	—	—	—	—	—
1781R	484	—	—	—	—	—
1783R	5,212	—	—	—	—	—
1784R	20,000	—	—	—	—	—

KM# 562.6 1/2 ECU (44 Sols)

14.7440 g., 0.9170 Silver 0.4347 oz. ASW **Ruler:** Louis XVI **Mint:** Bordeaux **Obverse:** Uniformed bust left **Reverse:** Crowned arms of France within branches

Date	Mintage	VG	F	VF	XF	Unc
1781K	1,952	—	—	—	—	—

KM# 562.2 1/2 ECU (44 Sols)

14.7440 g., 0.9170 Silver 0.4347 oz. ASW **Ruler:** Louis XVI **Mint:** Metz **Obverse:** Uniformed bust left **Reverse:** Crowned arms of France within branches

Date	Mintage	VG	F	VF	XF	Unc
1790AA	—	30.00	70.00	140	350	—

KM# 562.8 1/2 ECU (44 Sols)

14.7440 g., 0.9170 Silver 0.4347 oz. ASW **Ruler:** Louis XVI **Mint:** Marseille **Obverse:** Uniformed bust left **Reverse:** Crowned arms of France within branches

Date	Mintage	VG	F	VF	XF	Unc
1790MA	—	40.00	100	200	500	—

KM# 346 1/2 ECU (45 Sols)

15.3340 g., 0.8330 Silver 0.4107 oz. ASW **Ruler:** Louis XIV **Mint:** Strasbourg **Obverse:** Fleur-de-lis fleuree **Reverse:** Crowned circular shield of France, crossed scepters behind

Date	Mintage	VG	F	VF	XF	Unc
1701BB	—	1,100	2,250	4,200	7,000	—
1702BB	—	1,100	2,250	4,200	7,000	—
1703BB	—	1,600	3,150	5,800	9,500	—

KM# 328 1/2 ECU (45 Sols)

18.8200 g., 0.8570 Silver 0.5185 oz. ASW **Ruler:** Louis XIV **Mint:** Lille **Reverse:** Crowned circular shield of France, Navarre, Old and New Burgundy with crossed scepters and hand of Justice behind

Date	Mintage	VG	F	VF	XF	Unc
1701W	—	550	1,100	2,200	3,750	—
1702W	—	625	1,250	2,500	4,250	—

KM# 345 1/2 ECU (45 Sols)

13.5440 g., 0.9170 Silver 0.3993 oz. ASW **Ruler:** Louis XIV **Mint:** Grenoble **Reverse:** Crowned circular shield of Dauphine

Date	Mintage	VG	F	VF	XF	Unc
1702Z	—	3,500	6,000	10,000	17,500	—

KM# 355.1 1/2 ECU (45 Sols)

13.5440 g., 0.9170 Silver 0.3993 oz. ASW **Ruler:** Louis XIV **Mint:** Paris **Obverse:** Mailed bust right **Reverse:** 8 L's back to back, ends crowned, fleur-de-lis in angles

Date	Mintage	VG	F	VF	XF	Unc
1704A	8,670,000	60.00	115	285	500	—
1705A	—	65.00	135	330	575	—

KM# 355.2 1/2 ECU (45 Sols)

13.5440 g., 0.9170 Silver 0.3993 oz. ASW **Ruler:** Louis XIV **Mint:** Rouen **Obverse:** Mailed bust right **Reverse:** 8 L's back to back, ends crowned, fleur-de-lis in angles

Date	Mintage	VG	F	VF	XF	Unc
1704B	—	85.00	175	425	750	—

KM# 355.3 1/2 ECU (45 Sols)

13.5440 g., 0.9170 Silver 0.3993 oz. ASW **Ruler:** Louis XIV **Mint:** Caen **Obverse:** Mailed bust right **Reverse:** 8 L's back to back, ends crowned, fleur-de-lis in angles

Date	Mintage	VG	F	VF	XF	Unc
1704C	—	85.00	175	425	750	—
1705C	—	85.00	175	425	750	—

KM# 355.4 1/2 ECU (45 Sols)

13.5440 g., 0.9170 Silver 0.3993 oz. ASW **Ruler:** Louis XIV **Mint:** Lyon **Obverse:** Mailed bust right **Reverse:** 8 L's back to back, ends crowned, fleur-de-lis in angles

Date	Mintage	VG	F	VF	XF	Unc
1704D	—	75.00	150	380	670	—

KM# 355.5 1/2 ECU (45 Sols)

13.5440 g., 0.9170 Silver 0.3993 oz. ASW **Ruler:** Louis XIV **Mint:** Tours **Obverse:** Mailed bust right **Obv. Legend:** LVD • XIIII • D • G • FR • ET • NAV • REX • **Reverse:** 8 L's back to back, ends crowned, fleur-de-lis in angles **Rev. Legend:** BENEDICTUM SIT NOMEN DOMINI

Date	Mintage	VG	F	VF	XF	Unc
1704E	—	85.00	175	425	750	—
1705E	—	85.00	175	425	750	—

KM# 355.6 1/2 ECU (45 Sols)

13.5440 g., 0.9170 Silver 0.3993 oz. ASW **Ruler:** Louis XIV **Mint:** La Rochelle **Obverse:** Mailed bust right **Reverse:** 8 L's back to back, ends crowned, fleur-de-lis in angles

Date	Mintage	VG	F	VF	XF	Unc
1704H	—	85.00	175	425	750	—

KM# 355.7 1/2 ECU (45 Sols)

13.5440 g., 0.9170 Silver 0.3993 oz. ASW **Ruler:** Louis XIV **Mint:** Limoges **Obverse:** Mailed bust right **Reverse:** 8 L's back to back, ends crowned, fleur-de-lis in angles

Date	Mintage	VG	F	VF	XF	Unc
1704I	—	65.00	135	330	575	—

KM# 355.8 1/2 ECU (45 Sols)

13.5440 g., 0.9170 Silver 0.3993 oz. ASW **Ruler:** Louis XIV **Mint:** Bayonne **Obverse:** Mailed bust right **Reverse:** 8 L's back to back, ends crowned, fleur-de-lis in angles

Date	Mintage	VG	F	VF	XF	Unc
1704L	—	—	—	—	—	—

KM# 355.9 1/2 ECU (45 Sols)

13.5440 g., 0.9170 Silver 0.3993 oz. ASW **Ruler:** Louis XIV **Mint:** Toulouse **Obverse:** Mailed bust right **Reverse:** 8 L's back to back, ends crowned, fleur-de-lis in angles

Date	Mintage	VG	F	VF	XF	Unc
1704M	—	85.00	175	425	750	—

KM# 355.10 1/2 ECU (45 Sols)

13.5440 g., 0.9170 Silver 0.3993 oz. ASW **Ruler:** Louis XIV **Mint:** Montpellier **Obverse:** Mailed bust right **Reverse:** 8 L's back to back, ends crowned, fleur-de-lis in angles

Date	Mintage	VG	F	VF	XF	Unc
1704N	345,000	65.00	135	330	575	—
1705N	138,000	—	—	—	—	—

KM# 355.11 1/2 ECU (45 Sols)

13.5440 g., 0.9170 Silver 0.3993 oz. ASW **Ruler:** Louis XIV **Mint:** Riom **Obverse:** Mailed bust right **Reverse:** 8 L's back to back, ends crowned, fleur-de-lis in angles

Date	Mintage	VG	F	VF	XF	Unc
1704O	—	85.00	175	425	750	—

KM# 355.12 1/2 ECU (45 Sols)

13.5440 g., 0.9170 Silver 0.3993 oz. ASW **Ruler:** Louis XIV **Mint:** Dijon **Obverse:** Mailed bust right **Reverse:** 8 L's back to back, ends crowned, fleur-de-lis in angles

Date	Mintage	VG	F	VF	XF	Unc
1704P	—	75.00	150	380	670	—

KM# 355.13 1/2 ECU (45 Sols)

13.5440 g., 0.9170 Silver 0.3993 oz. ASW **Ruler:** Louis XIV **Mint:** Troyes **Obverse:** Mailed bust right **Reverse:** 8 L's back to back, ends crowned, fleur-de-lis in angles

Date	Mintage	VG	F	VF	XF	Unc
1704S	—	—	—	—	—	—

KM# 355.14 1/2 ECU (45 Sols)

13.5440 g., 0.9170 Silver 0.3993 oz. ASW **Ruler:** Louis XIV **Mint:** Nantes **Obverse:** Mailed bust right **Reverse:** 8 L's back to back, ends crowned, fleur-de-lis in angles

Date	Mintage	VG	F	VF	XF	Unc
1704T	433,000	75.00	150	380	670	—
1705T	154,000	—	—	—	—	—

KM# 355.15 1/2 ECU (45 Sols)

13.5440 g., 0.9170 Silver 0.3993 oz. ASW **Ruler:** Louis XIV **Mint:** Troyes **Obverse:** Mailed bust right **Reverse:** 8 L's back to back, ends crowned, fleur-de-lis in angles

Date	Mintage	VG	F	VF	XF	Unc
1704V	274,000	—	—	—	—	—
1705V	—	—	—	—	—	—

KM# 355.16 1/2 ECU (45 Sols)

13.5440 g., 0.9170 Silver 0.3993 oz. ASW **Ruler:** Louis XIV **Mint:** Amiens **Obverse:** Mailed bust right **Reverse:** 8 L's back to back, ends crowned, fleur-de-lis in angles

Date	Mintage	VG	F	VF	XF	Unc
1704X	—	75.00	150	380	670	—

KM# 355.17 1/2 ECU (45 Sols)

13.5440 g., 0.9170 Silver 0.3993 oz. ASW **Ruler:** Louis XIV **Mint:** Bourges **Obverse:** Mailed bust right **Reverse:** 8 L's back to back, ends crowned, fleur-de-lis in angles

Date	Mintage	VG	F	VF	XF	Unc
1704Y	—	75.00	150	380	670	—
1707Y	—	100	200	500	875	—

KM# 355.18 1/2 ECU (45 Sols)

13.5440 g., 0.9170 Silver 0.3993 oz. ASW **Ruler:** Louis XIV **Mint:** Grenoble **Obverse:** Mailed bust right **Reverse:** 8 L's back to back, ends crowned, fleur-de-lis in angles

Date	Mintage	VG	F	VF	XF	Unc
1704Z	—	95.00	190	475	825	—

KM# 356.1 1/2 ECU (45 Sols)

13.5440 g., 0.9170 Silver 0.3993 oz. ASW **Ruler:** Louis XIV **Mint:** Lyon **Obverse:** Bust right

Date	Mintage	VG	F	VF	XF	Unc
1704D	1,201,000	65.00	135	330	575	—
1705D	913,000	85.00	175	425	750	—

KM# 356.2 1/2 ECU (45 Sols)

13.5440 g., 0.9170 Silver 0.3993 oz. ASW **Ruler:** Louis XIV **Mint:** Lille

Date	Mintage	VG	F	VF	XF	Unc
1704W	127,000	65.00	135	330	575	—
1705W	—	95.00	190	475	825	—

KM# 355.20 1/2 ECU (45 Sols)

13.5440 g., 0.9170 Silver 0.3993 oz. ASW **Ruler:** Louis XIV **Mint:** Aix **Obverse:** Mailed bust right **Reverse:** 8 L's back to back, ends crowned, fleur-de-lis in angles **Note:** Mint mark: &.

Date	Mintage	VG	F	VF	XF	Unc
1704	—	75.00	150	380	670	—

KM# 355.19 1/2 ECU (45 Sols)

13.5440 g., 0.9170 Silver 0.3993 oz. ASW **Ruler:** Louis XIV **Mint:** Rennes **Obverse:** Mailed bust right **Reverse:** 8 L's back to back, ends crowned, fleur-de-lis in angles **Note:** Mint mark: 9.

Date	Mintage	VG	F	VF	XF	Unc
1704	29,000	70.00	140	350	620	—
1705	—	95.00	190	475	825	—
1708	—	95.00	190	475	825	—
1709	49,000	165	325	825	1,450	—

KM# 355.21 1/2 ECU (45 Sols)

13.5440 g., 0.9170 Silver 0.3993 oz. ASW **Ruler:** Louis XIV **Mint:** Besancon **Obverse:** Mailed bust right **Reverse:** 8 L's back to back, ends crowned, fleur-de-lis in angles **Note:** Mint mark: Back to back C's.

Date	Mintage	VG	F	VF	XF	Unc
1704	—	85.00	175	425	750	—

KM# 358 1/2 ECU (51 Sols = 4 Deniers)

18.8200 g., 0.8570 Silver 0.5185 oz. ASW **Ruler:** Louis XIV **Mint:** Lille **Obverse:** Mailed bust right **Reverse:** Crowned flat top quartered shield of France, Old and New Burgundy, crossed sceptres behind

Date	Mintage	VG	F	VF	XF	Unc
1704W	6,000	1,600	3,100	6,000	9,750	—
1705W	—	1,700	3,350	6,500	11,000	—

KM# 359 1/2 ECU (36 Sols = 6 Deniers)

15.3340 g., 0.8330 Silver 0.4107 oz. ASW **Ruler:** Louis XIV **Mint:** Strasbourg **Obverse:** Large fleur-de-lis **Reverse:** 8 L's back to back, crowned ends, fleur-de-lis in angles

Date	Mintage	VG	F	VF	XF	Unc
1704BB	—	900	1,800	3,500	5,800	—

KM# 382.1 1/2 ECU (36 Sols = 6 Deniers)

15.2440 g., 0.9170 Silver 0.4494 oz. ASW **Ruler:** Louis XIV **Mint:** Paris **Obverse:** Mailed bust right **Obv. Legend:** LVD • XIIII • D • G • FR • ET • NAV • REX • **Reverse:** 3 Crowns, fleur-de-lis in angles **Rev. Legend:** BENEDICTVM SIT NOMEN DOMINI

Date	Mintage	VG	F	VF	XF	Unc
1709A	—	42.00	85.00	215	375	—
1710A	—	32.00	65.00	165	285	—
1711A	—	40.00	80.00	200	350	—
1712A	—	40.00	80.00	200	350	—
1713A	—	42.00	85.00	215	375	—
1714A	—	42.00	85.00	215	375	—
1715A	—	75.00	145	365	640	—

KM# 382.2 1/2 ECU (36 Sols = 6 Deniers)

15.2440 g., 0.9170 Silver 0.4494 oz. ASW **Ruler:** Louis XIV **Mint:** Rouen **Obverse:** Mailed bust right **Reverse:** 3 Crowns, fleur-de-lis in angles

Date	Mintage	VG	F	VF	XF	Unc
1709B	—	55.00	115	280	500	—
1710B	—	—	—	—	—	—
1711B	—	75.00	145	365	640	—
1712B	—	—	—	—	—	—
1714B	—	—	—	—	—	—

KM# 382.3 1/2 ECU (36 Sols = 6 Deniers)

15.2440 g., 0.9170 Silver 0.4494 oz. ASW **Ruler:** Louis XIV **Mint:** Caen **Obverse:** Mailed bust right **Reverse:** 3 Crowns, fleur-de-lis in angles

Date	Mintage	VG	F	VF	XF	Unc
1709C	—	55.00	115	280	500	—
1710C	—	65.00	135	330	575	—
1711C	—	—	—	—	—	—
1712C	—	65.00	135	330	575	—
1713C	—	75.00	145	365	640	—

KM# 382.4 1/2 ECU (36 Sols = 6 Deniers)

15.2440 g., 0.9170 Silver 0.4494 oz. ASW **Ruler:** Louis XIV **Mint:** Lyon **Obverse:** Mailed bust right **Reverse:** 3 Crowns, fleur-de-lis in angles

Date	Mintage	VG	F	VF	XF	Unc
1709D	—	40.00	80.00	200	350	—
1710D	—	—	—	—	—	—
1712D	—	65.00	135	330	575	—

KM# 382.5 1/2 ECU (36 Sols = 6 Deniers)

15.2440 g., 0.9170 Silver 0.4494 oz. ASW **Ruler:** Louis XIV **Mint:** Tours **Obverse:** Mailed bust right **Reverse:** 3 Crowns, fleur-de-lis in angles

Date	Mintage	VG	F	VF	XF	Unc
1709E	—	65.00	135	330	575	—
1710E	—	75.00	145	365	640	—
1711E	—	—	—	—	—	—
1712E	—	85.00	175	435	765	—
1713E	—	—	—	—	—	—
1714E	—	—	—	—	—	—
1715E	—	—	—	—	—	—

KM# 382.6 1/2 ECU (36 Sols = 6 Deniers)

15.2440 g., 0.9170 Silver 0.4494 oz. ASW **Ruler:** Louis XIV **Mint:** Poitiers **Obverse:** Mailed bust right **Reverse:** 3 Crowns, fleur-de-lis in angles

Date	Mintage	VG	F	VF	XF	Unc
1709G	—	—	—	—	—	—
1710G	—	—	—	—	—	—
1711G	—	—	—	—	—	—
1712G	—	—	—	—	—	—
1713G	—	—	—	—	—	—
1714G	—	—	—	—	—	—

KM# 382.7 1/2 ECU (36 Sols = 6 Deniers)

15.2440 g., 0.9170 Silver 0.4494 oz. ASW **Ruler:** Louis XIV **Mint:** La Rochelle **Obverse:** Mailed bust right **Reverse:** 3 Crowns, fleur-de-lis in angles

Date	Mintage	VG	F	VF	XF	Unc
1709H	—	—	—	—	—	—
1710H	—	—	—	—	—	—
1711H	—	75.00	145	365	640	—
1714H	—	—	—	—	—	—
1715H	—	—	—	—	—	—

KM# 382.8 1/2 ECU (36 Sols = 6 Deniers)

15.2440 g., 0.9170 Silver 0.4494 oz. ASW **Ruler:** Louis XIV **Mint:** Limoges **Obverse:** Mailed bust right **Reverse:** 3 Crowns, fleur-de-lis in angles

Date	Mintage	VG	F	VF	XF	Unc
1709I	—	—	—	—	—	—
1710I	—	—	—	—	—	—
1711I	—	—	—	—	—	—
1712I	—	—	—	—	—	—
1713I	—	—	—	—	—	—
1714I	—	—	—	—	—	—

KM# 382.9 1/2 ECU (36 Sols = 6 Deniers)

15.2440 g., 0.9170 Silver 0.4494 oz. ASW **Ruler:** Louis XIV **Mint:** Bordeaux **Obverse:** Mailed bust right **Reverse:** 3 Crowns, fleur-de-lis in angles

Date	Mintage	VG	F	VF	XF	Unc
1709K	—	—	—	—	—	—
1710K	—	55.00	115	280	500	—
1711K	—	—	—	—	—	—

KM# 382.11 1/2 ECU (36 Sols = 6 Deniers)

15.2440 g., 0.9170 Silver 0.4494 oz. ASW **Ruler:** Louis XIV **Mint:** Toulouse **Obverse:** Mailed bust right **Reverse:** 3 Crowns, fleur-de-lis in angles

Date	Mintage	VG	F	VF	XF	Unc
1709M	—	75.00	145	365	640	—
1710M	—	—	—	—	—	—
1711M	—	65.00	135	330	575	—
1712M	—	65.00	135	330	575	—
1713M	—	—	—	—	—	—

KM# 382.12 1/2 ECU (36 Sols = 6 Deniers)

15.2440 g., 0.9170 Silver 0.4494 oz. ASW **Ruler:** Louis XIV **Mint:** Montpellier **Obverse:** Mailed bust right **Reverse:** 3 Crowns, fleur-de-lis in angles

Date	Mintage	VG	F	VF	XF	Unc
1709N	—	—	—	—	—	—
1710N	—	65.00	135	330	575	—
1711N	—	—	—	—	—	—
1712N	—	65.00	135	330	575	—
1713N	—	65.00	135	330	575	—
1714N	—	—	—	—	—	—

KM# 382.14 1/2 ECU (36 Sols = 6 Deniers)

15.2440 g., 0.9170 Silver 0.4494 oz. ASW **Ruler:** Louis XIV **Mint:** Dijon **Obverse:** Mailed bust right **Reverse:** 3 Crowns, fleur-de-lis in angles

Date	Mintage	VG	F	VF	XF	Unc
1709P	—	75.00	145	365	640	—
1710P	—	42.00	85.00	215	375	—
1711P	—	50.00	100	250	435	—
1712P	—	—	—	—	—	—
1713P	—	—	—	—	—	—
1714P	—	—	—	—	—	—

KM# 382.16 1/2 ECU (36 Sols = 6 Deniers)

15.2440 g., 0.9170 Silver 0.4494 oz. ASW **Ruler:** Louis XIV **Mint:** Reims **Obverse:** Mailed bust right **Reverse:** 3 Crowns, fleur-de-lis in angles

Date	Mintage	VG	F	VF	XF	Unc
1709S	—	50.00	100	250	435	—
1710S	—	—	—	—	—	—
1711S	—	50.00	100	250	435	—

KM# 382.17 1/2 ECU (36 Sols = 6 Deniers)

15.2440 g., 0.9170 Silver 0.4494 oz. ASW **Ruler:** Louis XIV **Mint:** Nantes **Obverse:** Mailed bust right **Reverse:** 3 Crowns, fleur-de-lis in angles

Date	Mintage	VG	F	VF	XF	Unc
1709T	—	55.00	115	280	500	—
1710T	—	—	—	—	—	—
1711T	—	55.00	115	280	500	—
1712T	—	75.00	145	365	640	—
1713T	—	75.00	145	365	640	—
1715T	—	—	—	—	—	—

KM# 382.18 1/2 ECU (36 Sols = 6 Deniers)
15.2440 g., 0.9170 Silver 0.4494 oz. ASW **Ruler:** Louis XIV **Mint:** Troyes **Obverse:** Mailed bust right **Obv. Legend:** LVD • XIIII • D • G • FR • ET • NAV • REX • **Reverse:** 3 Crowns, fleur-de-lis in angles **Rev. Legend:** BENEDICTUM SIT NOMEN DOMINI

Date	Mintage	VG	F	VF	XF	Unc
1709V	—	75.00	145	365	640	—
1710V	—	—	—	—	—	—
1711V	—	50.00	100	250	435	—
1712V	—	55.00	115	280	500	—
1713V	—	75.00	145	365	640	—
1714V	—	—	—	—	—	—
1715V	—	—	—	—	—	—

KM# 382.24 1/2 ECU (36 Sols = 6 Deniers)
15.2440 g., 0.9170 Silver 0.4494 oz. ASW **Ruler:** Louis XIV **Mint:** Aix **Obverse:** Mailed bust right **Reverse:** 3 Crowns, fleur-de-lis in angles **Note:** Mint mark: &.

Date	Mintage	VG	F	VF	XF	Unc
1709	—	55.00	115	280	500	—
1710	—	42.00	85.00	215	375	—
1711	—	55.00	115	280	500	—
1712	—	55.00	115	280	500	—

KM# 382.23 1/2 ECU (36 Sols = 6 Deniers)
15.2440 g., 0.9170 Silver 0.4494 oz. ASW **Ruler:** Louis XIV **Mint:** Rennes **Obverse:** Mailed bust right **Reverse:** 3 Crowns, fleur-de-lis in angles **Note:** Mint mark: 9.

Date	Mintage	VG	F	VF	XF	Unc
1709	—	50.00	100	250	435	—
1710	—	42.00	85.00	215	375	—
1711	—	42.00	85.00	215	375	—
1712	—	—	—	—	—	—
1713	—	—	—	—	—	—

KM# 382.25 1/2 ECU (36 Sols = 6 Deniers)
15.2440 g., 0.9170 Silver 0.4494 oz. ASW **Ruler:** Louis XIV **Mint:** Besancon **Obverse:** Mailed bust right **Reverse:** 3 Crowns, fleur-de-lis in angles **Note:** Mint mark: Back to back C's.

Date	Mintage	VG	F	VF	XF	Unc
1709	—	65.00	135	330	575	—
1710	—	—	—	—	—	—
1711	—	65.00	135	330	575	—
1713	—	—	—	—	—	—
1715	—	—	—	—	—	—

KM# 382.26 1/2 ECU (36 Sols = 6 Deniers)
15.2440 g., 0.9170 Silver 0.4494 oz. ASW **Ruler:** Louis XIV **Mint:** Pau **Obverse:** Mailed bust right **Reverse:** 3 Crowns, fleur-de-lis in angles **Note:** Mint mark: Cow.

Date	Mintage	VG	F	VF	XF	Unc
1709	—	—	—	—	—	—
1710	—	55.00	115	280	500	—
1711	—	—	—	—	—	—
1712	—	55.00	115	280	500	—
1713	—	—	—	—	—	—

KM# 382.20 1/2 ECU (36 Sols = 6 Deniers)
15.2440 g., 0.9170 Silver 0.4494 oz. ASW **Ruler:** Louis XIV **Mint:** Amiens **Obverse:** Mailed bust right **Reverse:** 3 Crowns, fleur-de-lis in angles

Date	Mintage	VG	F	VF	XF	Unc
1709X	—	55.00	115	280	500	—
1710X	—	75.00	145	365	640	—
1711X	—	50.00	100	250	435	—
1712X	—	55.00	115	280	500	—
1713X	—	75.00	145	365	640	—
1714X	—	65.00	135	330	575	—
1715X	—	80.00	170	425	750	—

KM# 382.22 1/2 ECU (36 Sols = 6 Deniers)
15.2440 g., 0.9170 Silver 0.4494 oz. ASW **Ruler:** Louis XIV **Mint:** Grenoble **Obverse:** Mailed bust right **Reverse:** 3 Crowns, fleur-de-lis in angles

Date	Mintage	VG	F	VF	XF	Unc
1710Z	—	65.00	135	330	575	—
1711Z	—	—	—	—	—	—
1712Z	—	—	—	—	—	—
1713Z	—	—	—	—	—	—

KM# 382.13 1/2 ECU (36 Sols = 6 Deniers)
15.2440 g., 0.9170 Silver 0.4494 oz. ASW **Ruler:** Louis XIV **Mint:** Riom **Obverse:** Mailed bust right **Reverse:** 3 Crowns, fleur-de-lis in angles

Date	Mintage	VG	F	VF	XF	Unc
17100	—	65.00	135	330	575	—
17110	—	65.00	135	330	575	—
17120	—	—	—	—	—	—
17130	—	—	—	—	—	—
17140	—	—	—	—	—	—

KM# 382.10 1/2 ECU (36 Sols = 6 Deniers)
15.2440 g., 0.9170 Silver 0.4494 oz. ASW **Ruler:** Louis XIV **Mint:** Bayonne **Obverse:** Mailed bust right **Reverse:** 3 Crowns, fleur-de-lis in angles

Date	Mintage	VG	F	VF	XF	Unc
1710L	—	55.00	115	280	500	—

KM# 382.15 1/2 ECU (36 Sols = 6 Deniers)
15.2440 g., 0.9170 Silver 0.4494 oz. ASW **Ruler:** Louis XIV **Mint:** Perpignan **Obverse:** Mailed bust right **Reverse:** 3 Crowns, fleur-de-lis in angles

Date	Mintage	VG	F	VF	XF	Unc
1711Q	—	—	—	—	—	—
1712Q	—	—	—	—	—	—

KM# 382.21 1/2 ECU (36 Sols = 6 Deniers)
15.2440 g., 0.9170 Silver 0.4494 oz. ASW **Ruler:** Louis XIV **Mint:** Bourges **Obverse:** Mailed bust right **Reverse:** 3 Crowns, fleur-de-lis in angles

Date	Mintage	VG	F	VF	XF	Unc
1711Y	—	—	—	—	—	—
1712Y	—	—	—	—	—	—
1713Y	—	—	—	—	—	—

KM# 382.19 1/2 ECU (36 Sols = 6 Deniers)
15.2440 g., 0.9170 Silver 0.4494 oz. ASW **Ruler:** Louis XIV **Mint:** Lille **Obverse:** Mailed bust right **Reverse:** 3 Crowns, fleur-de-lis in angles

Date	Mintage	VG	F	VF	XF	Unc
1713W	—	55.00	115	280	500	—
1714W	—	50.00	100	250	435	—

KM# 613.1 1/2 ECU (3 Livres)
15.0000 g., 0.9170 Silver 0.4422 oz. ASW **Mint:** Paris **Obverse:** Head left **Obv. Legend:** LOUIS XVI ROI DES FRANCOIS • **Reverse:** Standing Genius writing the Constitution **Rev. Legend:** REGNE DE LALOI •

Date	Mintage	VG	F	VF	XF	Unc
1792A	—	75.00	185	350	700	—
1793A	—	90.00	210	400	800	—

KM# 614 1/2 ECU (3 Livres)
15.0000 g., 0.9170 Silver 0.4422 oz. ASW **Mint:** Strasbourg **Obverse:** Head left **Obv. Legend:** LOUIS XVI ROI DES FRANCAIS • **Reverse:** Standing Genius writing the Constitution **Rev. Legend:** REGNE DE LA LOI •

Date	Mintage	VG	F	VF	XF	Unc
1792BB	—	275	600	1,200	2,500	—

KM# 298.1 ECU
Silver **Ruler:** Louis XIV **Mint:** Paris **Obverse:** Bust with square neckline **Reverse:** Crowned round arms in palm sprays **Note:** Values given for the KM#298 issues are for examples struck over recalled ECU. Clear examples struck on new planchets command an average 20-30% premium. Dav. #3813.

Date	Mintage	VG	F	VF	XF	Unc
1701A	—	—	—	—	—	—
1701A	—	—	—	—	—	—

KM# 329.1 ECU
Silver **Ruler:** Louis XIV **Mint:** Paris **Obverse:** Armored bust right **Obv. Legend:** LVD • XIIII • D • G • FR • ET • NAV • REX • **Reverse:** Crowned arms of France with sceptre and hand of Justice behind **Rev. Legend:** BENEDICTVS • SIT • NOMEN • DOMINI • **Note:** Dav. #1316.

Date	Mintage	VG	F	VF	XF	Unc
1701A	—	60.00	120	240	425	—
1702A	—	60.00	120	240	425	—
1703A	—	60.00	120	240	425	—
1704A	—	70.00	150	300	550	—

KM# 330 ECU
Silver **Ruler:** Louis XIV **Mint:** Toulouse **Obverse:** Smaller bust **Reverse:** Crowned 4-part round arms of France, Old and New Burgundy and Navarre on crossed sceptres **Note:** Dav. #1317.

Date	Mintage	VG	F	VF	XF	Unc
1701M	—	1,650	3,000	5,000	8,000	—
1702M	—	2,000	3,500	6,000	9,500	—
1703M	—	—	—	—	—	—

KM# 331 ECU
Silver **Ruler:** Louis XIV **Mint:** Pau **Obverse:** Taller bust **Obv. Legend:** LVD • XIIII • D • G • FR • ET .. **Reverse:** Crowned 3-part round arms of France, Navarre and Bearn on crossed scepters **Rev. Legend:** BENEDICTVS SIT • NOMEN • DOMINI • **Note:** Issued for Provinces of Navarre and Bearn. Dav. #1318. Mint mark: Cow.

Date	Mintage	VG	F	VF	XF	Unc
1701	—	1,200	2,200	4,000	6,500	—
1702	—	1,200	2,200	4,000	6,500	—
1703	—	1,350	2,500	4,500	7,500	—

KM# 329.24 ECU
Silver **Ruler:** Louis XIV **Mint:** Besancon **Obverse:** Armored bust right **Reverse:** Crowned arms of France with sceptre and hand of Justice behind **Note:** Mint mark: &.

Date	Mintage	VG	F	VF	XF	Unc
1701	—	75.00	160	325	600	—
1702	—	65.00	135	275	475	—
1703	—	110	220	460	785	—

KM# 329.23 ECU
Silver **Ruler:** Louis XIV **Mint:** Rennes **Obverse:** Armored bust right **Reverse:** Crowned arms of France with sceptre and hand of Justice behind **Note:** Mint mark: 9.

Date	Mintage	VG	F	VF	XF	Unc
1701	—	60.00	120	240	425	—
1702	—	60.00	120	240	425	—
1703	—	75.00	160	325	600	—

KM# 329.2 ECU

Silver **Ruler:** Louis XIV **Mint:** Metz **Obverse:** Armored bust right **Reverse:** Crowned arms of France with sceptre and hand of Justice behind

Date	Mintage	VG	F	VF	XF	Unc
1701AA	—	70.00	150	300	550	—
1702AA	—	120	180	350	650	—
1703AA	—	—	—	—	—	—

KM# 329.3 ECU

Silver **Ruler:** Louis XIV **Mint:** Rouen **Obverse:** Armored bust right **Reverse:** Crowned arms of France with sceptre and hand of Justice behind

Date	Mintage	VG	F	VF	XF	Unc
1701B	—	65.00	135	275	475	—
1702B	—	75.00	160	325	600	—
1703B	—	110	225	465	850	—

KM# 329.4 ECU

Silver **Ruler:** Louis XIV **Mint:** Strasbourg **Obverse:** Armored bust right **Reverse:** Crowned arms of France with sceptre and hand of Justice behind

Date	Mintage	VG	F	VF	XF	Unc
1701BB	—	65.00	135	275	475	—
1702BB	—	90.00	180	350	650	—

KM# 329.5 ECU

Silver **Ruler:** Louis XIV **Mint:** Caen **Obverse:** Armored bust right **Reverse:** Crowned arms of France with sceptre and hand of Justice behind

Date	Mintage	VG	F	VF	XF	Unc
1701C	—	70.00	150	300	550	—
1702C	—	75.00	160	325	600	—

KM# 329.6 ECU

Silver **Ruler:** Louis XIV **Mint:** Lyon **Obverse:** Armored bust right **Reverse:** Crowned arms of France with sceptre and hand of Justice behind

Date	Mintage	VG	F	VF	XF	Unc
1701D	—	60.00	120	240	425	—
1702D	—	75.00	160	325	600	—
1703D	—	110	225	465	850	—

KM# 329.7 ECU

Silver **Ruler:** Louis XIV **Mint:** Tours **Obverse:** Armored bust right **Reverse:** Crowned arms of France with sceptre and hand of Justice behind

Date	Mintage	VG	F	VF	XF	Unc
1701E	—	70.00	150	300	550	—
1702E	—	70.00	150	300	550	—
1703E	—	110	225	465	850	—

KM# 329.8 ECU

Silver **Ruler:** Louis XIV **Mint:** Poitiers **Obverse:** Armored bust right **Reverse:** Crowned arms of France with sceptre and hand of Justice behind

Date	Mintage	VG	F	VF	XF	Unc
1701G	—	75.00	160	325	600	—
1702G	—	90.00	180	350	650	—
1703G	—	110	225	465	850	—

KM# 329.9 ECU

Silver **Ruler:** Louis XIV **Mint:** La Rochelle **Obverse:** Armored bust right **Reverse:** Crowned arms of France with sceptre and hand of Justice behind

Date	Mintage	VG	F	VF	XF	Unc
1701H	—	90.00	180	350	650	—
1702H	—	70.00	150	300	550	—
1703H	—	65.00	135	275	475	—

KM# 329.10 ECU

Silver **Ruler:** Louis XIV **Mint:** Limoges **Obverse:** Armored bust right **Reverse:** Crowned arms of France with sceptre and hand of Justice behind

Date	Mintage	VG	F	VF	XF	Unc
1701I	—	65.00	135	275	475	—
1702I	—	90.00	180	350	650	—
1703I	—	110	225	465	850	—

KM# 329.11 ECU

Silver **Ruler:** Louis XIV **Mint:** Bordeaux **Obverse:** Armored bust right **Reverse:** Crowned arms of France with sceptre and hand of Justice behind

Date	Mintage	VG	F	VF	XF	Unc
1701K	—	70.00	150	300	550	—
1702K	—	90.00	180	350	650	—
1703K	—	—	—	—	—	—

KM# 329.12 ECU

Silver **Ruler:** Louis XIV **Mint:** Bayonne **Obverse:** Armored bust right **Reverse:** Crowned arms of France with sceptre and hand of Justice behind

Date	Mintage	VG	F	VF	XF	Unc
1701L	—	75.00	160	325	600	—
1702L	—	65.00	135	275	475	—
1703L	—	—	—	—	—	—
1704L	—	—	—	—	—	—

KM# 329.13 ECU

Silver **Ruler:** Louis XIV **Mint:** Toulouse **Obverse:** Armored bust right **Reverse:** Crowned arms of France with sceptre and hand of Justice behind

Date	Mintage	VG	F	VF	XF	Unc
1701M	—	60.00	120	240	425	—
1702M	—	60.00	120	240	425	—
1703M	—	90.00	180	350	650	—

KM# 329.14 ECU

Silver **Ruler:** Louis XIV **Mint:** Montpellier **Obverse:** Armored bust right **Reverse:** Crowned arms of France with sceptre and hand of Justice behind

Date	Mintage	VG	F	VF	XF	Unc
1701N	—	60.00	120	240	425	—
1702N	—	70.00	150	300	550	—
1703N	—	—	—	—	—	—

KM# 329.15 ECU

Silver **Ruler:** Louis XIV **Mint:** Riom **Obverse:** Armored bust right **Reverse:** Crowned arms of France with sceptre and hand of Justice behind

Date	Mintage	VG	F	VF	XF	Unc
1701O	—	90.00	180	350	650	—
1702O	—	75.00	160	325	600	—
1703O	—	125	275	500	900	—

KM# 329.16 ECU

Silver **Ruler:** Louis XIV **Mint:** Dijon **Obverse:** Armored bust right **Reverse:** Crowned arms of France with sceptre and hand of Justice behind

Date	Mintage	VG	F	VF	XF	Unc
1701P	—	60.00	120	240	425	—
1702P	—	65.00	135	275	475	—
1703P	—	90.00	180	350	650	—

KM# 329.17 ECU

Silver **Ruler:** Louis XIV **Mint:** Troyes **Obverse:** Armored bust right **Reverse:** Crowned arms of France with sceptre and hand of Justice behind

Date	Mintage	VG	F	VF	XF	Unc
1701S	—	70.00	150	300	550	—
1702S	—	110	220	460	785	—
1703S	—	90.00	180	350	650	—

KM# 329.18 ECU

Silver **Ruler:** Louis XIV **Mint:** Nantes **Obverse:** Armored bust right **Obv. Legend:** LVD • XIIII • D • G • FR • ET • NAV • REX **Reverse:** Crowned arms of France with sceptre and hand of Justice behind **Rev. Legend:** BENEDICTUM SIT NOMEN DOMINI

Date	Mintage	VG	F	VF	XF	Unc
1701T	—	75.00	160	325	600	—
1702T	—	65.00	135	275	475	—
1703T	—	70.00	150	300	550	—

KM# 329.19 ECU

Silver **Ruler:** Louis XIV **Mint:** Troyes **Obverse:** Armored bust right **Reverse:** Crowned arms of France with sceptre and hand of Justice behind

Date	Mintage	VG	F	VF	XF	Unc
1701V	—	65.00	135	275	475	—
1702V	—	90.00	180	350	650	—
1703V Reported, not confirmed	—	—	—	—	—	—

KM# 329.20 ECU

Silver **Ruler:** Louis XIV **Mint:** Lille **Obverse:** Armored bust right **Reverse:** Crowned arms of France with sceptre and hand of Justice behind

Date	Mintage	VG	F	VF	XF	Unc
1701W	—	60.00	120	240	425	—
1702W	—	60.00	120	240	425	—
1703W	—	110	225	465	850	—

KM# 329.21 ECU

Silver **Ruler:** Louis XIV **Mint:** Amiens **Obverse:** Armored bust right **Reverse:** Crowned arms of France with sceptre and hand of Justice behind

Date	Mintage	VG	F	VF	XF	Unc
1701X	—	90.00	180	350	650	—
1702X	—	90.00	180	350	650	—
1703X	—	—	—	—	—	—

KM# 329.22 ECU

Silver **Ruler:** Louis XIV **Mint:** Bourges **Obverse:** Armored bust right **Reverse:** Crowned arms of France with sceptre and hand of Justice behind

Date	Mintage	VG	F	VF	XF	Unc
1701Y	—	90.00	180	350	650	—
1702Y	—	90.00	180	350	650	—
1703Y	—	90.00	180	350	650	—

KM# 329.25 ECU

Silver **Ruler:** Louis XIV **Mint:** Besancon **Obverse:** Armored bust right **Reverse:** Crowned arms of France with sceptre and hand of Justice behind

Date	Mintage	VG	F	VF	XF	Unc
1701	—	65.00	135	275	475	—
1702	—	—	—	—	—	—
1703	—	90.00	180	350	650	—

KM# 347 ECU

Silver **Ruler:** Louis XIV **Mint:** Grenoble **Reverse:** Crowned arms of France and Dauphine **Note:** Issued for Province of Dauphine. Dav. #1319.

Date	Mintage	VG	F	VF	XF	Unc
1702Z Rare	—	—	—	—	—	—

KM# 360.17 ECU

Silver **Ruler:** Louis XIV **Mint:** Troyes **Obverse:** Armored bust right **Reverse:** Crowned double L's in cruciform, fleur-de-lis in angles, arms of France in center **Note:** Mint mark: Crowned S.

Date	Mintage	VG	F	VF	XF	Unc
1704	—	90.00	185	375	650	—
1705	—	100	225	425	750	—

KM# 360.26 ECU

Silver **Ruler:** Louis XIV **Mint:** Besancon **Obverse:** Armored bust right **Reverse:** Crowned double L's in cruciform, fleur-de-lis in angles, arms of France in center **Note:** Mint mark: Back to back C's.

Date	Mintage	VG	F	VF	XF	Unc
1704	—	125	250	450	800	—
1705	—	100	225	425	750	—
1708	—	—	—	—	—	—
1709	—	—	—	—	—	—

KM# 361 ECU

Silver **Ruler:** Louis XIV **Mint:** Pau **Obverse:** Armored bust right **Obv. Legend:** LVD XIV BENEDICRVM ... **Reverse:** 3-part arms of France, Navarre and Bearn in center of crowned L's **Rev. Legend:** BENEDICTVM SIT NOMEN DOMINI **Note:** Mint mark: Cow. Dav. #1321.

Date	Mintage	VG	F	VF	XF	Unc
1704	—	1,000	2,000	3,500	5,500	—
1705	—	1,350	2,500	4,500	7,500	—
1706	—	—	—	—	—	—
1707	—	—	—	—	—	—
1708	—	—	—	—	—	—
1709	—	1,650	3,000	5,000	8,000	—

KM# 360.24 ECU

Silver **Ruler:** Louis XIV **Mint:** Rennes **Obverse:** Armored bust right **Reverse:** Crowned double L's in cruciform, fleur-de-lis in angles, arms of France in center **Note:** Mint mark: 9.

Date	Mintage	VG	F	VF	XF	Unc
1704	—	75.00	150	300	550	—
1705	—	60.00	125	260	475	—
1707	—	75.00	150	300	550	—
1708	—	90.00	185	375	650	—
1709	—	125	250	450	800	—

KM# 360.25 ECU

Silver **Ruler:** Louis XIV **Mint:** Aix **Obverse:** Armored bust right **Reverse:** Crowned double L's in cruciform, fleur-de-lis in angles, arms of France in center **Note:** Mint mark: &.

Date	Mintage	VG	F	VF	XF	Unc
1704	—	90.00	185	375	650	—
1705	—	90.00	185	375	650	—
1706	—	100	225	425	750	—
1707	—	175	325	550	900	—
1708	—	175	325	550	900	—
1709	—	—	—	—	—	—

KM# 360.1 ECU

Silver **Ruler:** Louis XIV **Mint:** Paris **Obverse:** Armored bust right **Obv. Legend:** LVD•XIIII•D•G•FR•ET•NAV•REX• **Reverse:** Crowned double L's in cruciform, fleur-de-lis in angles, arms of France in center **Rev. Legend:** BENEDICTVM SIT NOMEN DOMINI **Note:** Dav. #1320.

Date	Mintage	VG	F	VF	XF	Unc
1704A	—	50.00	100	200	350	—
1705A	—	60.00	125	250	450	—
1707A	—	100	225	425	750	—
1708A	—	90.00	190	385	700	—
1709A	—	125	250	450	800	—

KM# 362.1 ECU

Silver **Ruler:** Louis XIV **Mint:** Paris **Obverse:** Draped bust right **Obv. Legend:** LVD•XIIII•D•G•FR•ET•NAV•REX• **Reverse:** Crowned back to back L"s form center square holding round arms of France **Rev. Legend:** BENEDICTVM SIT•NOMEN DOMINI **Note:** Dav. #1322.

Date	Mintage	VG	F	VF	XF	Unc
1704A	—	475	950	1,750	3,000	—
1705A	—	500	1,000	2,000	3,500	—
1706A	—	850	1,650	3,000	5,000	—
1708A	—	—	—	—	—	—

KM# 360.2 ECU

Silver **Ruler:** Louis XIV **Mint:** Metz **Obverse:** Armored bust right **Reverse:** Crowned double L's in cruciform, fleur-de-lis in angles, arms of France in center

Date	Mintage	VG	F	VF	XF	Unc
1704AA	—	100	225	425	750	—
1705AA	—	—	—	—	—	—

KM# 360.3 ECU

Silver **Ruler:** Louis XIV **Mint:** Rouen **Obverse:** Armored bust right **Reverse:** Crowned double L's in cruciform, fleur-de-lis in angles, arms of France in center

Date	Mintage	VG	F	VF	XF	Unc
1704B	—	90.00	190	385	700	—
1705B	—	100	225	425	750	—
1708B	—	—	—	—	—	—

KM# 360.4 ECU

Silver **Ruler:** Louis XIV **Mint:** Strasbourg **Obverse:** Armored bust right **Reverse:** Crowned double L's in cruciform, fleur-de-lis in angles, arms of France in center

Date	Mintage	VG	F	VF	XF	Unc
1704BB	—	100	225	425	750	—

KM# 360.5 ECU

Silver **Ruler:** Louis XIV **Mint:** Caen **Obverse:** Armored bust right **Reverse:** Crowned double L's in cruciform, fleur-de-lis in angles, arms of France in center

Date	Mintage	VG	F	VF	XF	Unc
1704C	—	100	225	425	750	—
1705C	—	90.00	185	375	650	—

KM# 360.6 ECU

Silver **Ruler:** Louis XIV **Mint:** Lyon **Obverse:** Armored bust right **Reverse:** Crowned double L's in cruciform, fleur-de-lis in angles, arms of France in center

Date	Mintage	VG	F	VF	XF	Unc
1704D	—	75.00	150	300	550	—
1705D	—	90.00	185	375	650	—
1706D	—	65.00	135	275	500	—
1707D	—	100	225	425	750	—
1708D	—	90.00	185	375	650	—
1709D	—	100	225	425	750	—

KM# 360.7 ECU

Silver **Ruler:** Louis XIV **Mint:** Tours **Obverse:** Armored bust right **Reverse:** Crowned double L's in cruciform, fleur-de-lis in angles, arms of France in center

Date	Mintage	VG	F	VF	XF	Unc
1704E	—	90.00	185	375	650	—
1705E	—	100	225	425	750	—
1707E	—	—	—	—	—	—

Note: Reported, not confirmed

KM# 360.9 ECU

Silver **Ruler:** Louis XIV **Mint:** La Rochelle **Obverse:** Armored bust right **Reverse:** Crowned double L's in cruciform, fleur-de-lis in angles, arms of France in center

Date	Mintage	VG	F	VF	XF	Unc
1704H	—	100	225	425	750	—
1705H	—	90.00	185	375	650	—
1706H	—	90.00	185	375	650	—
1707H	—	175	325	550	900	—
1708H	—	90.00	185	375	650	—
1709H	—	—	—	—	—	—

KM# 360.10 ECU

Silver **Ruler:** Louis XIV **Mint:** Limoges **Obverse:** Armored bust right **Reverse:** Crowned double L's in cruciform, fleur-de-lis in angles, arms of France in center

Date	Mintage	VG	F	VF	XF	Unc
1704I	—	90.00	190	385	700	—
1705I	—	90.00	190	385	700	—

KM# 360.11 ECU

Silver **Ruler:** Louis XIV **Mint:** Bordeaux **Obverse:** Armored bust right **Reverse:** Crowned double L's in cruciform, fleur-de-lis in angles, arms of France in center

Date	Mintage	VG	F	VF	XF	Unc
1704K	—	90.00	185	375	650	—
1705K	—	125	250	450	800	—
1708K	—	90.00	185	375	650	—
1709K	—	125	250	450	800	—

KM# 360.12 ECU

Silver **Ruler:** Louis XIV **Mint:** Bayonne **Obverse:** Armored bust right **Reverse:** Crowned double L's in cruciform, fleur-de-lis in angles, arms of France in center

Date	Mintage	VG	F	VF	XF	Unc
1704L	—	125	250	450	800	—
1705L	—	—	—	—	—	—
1708L	—	90.00	185	375	650	—

KM# 360.13 ECU

Silver **Ruler:** Louis XIV **Mint:** Toulouse **Obverse:** Armored bust right **Reverse:** Crowned double L's in cruciform, fleur-de-lis in angles, arms of France in center

Date	Mintage	VG	F	VF	XF	Unc
1704M	—	90.00	190	385	700	—
1707M	—	175	325	550	900	—

KM# 360.14 ECU

Silver **Ruler:** Louis XIV **Mint:** Montpellier **Obverse:** Armored bust right **Reverse:** Crowned double L's in cruciform, fleur-de-lis in angles, arms of France in center

Date	Mintage	VG	F	VF	XF	Unc
1704N	—	65.00	135	275	500	—
1705N	—	90.00	185	375	650	—
1709N	—	—	—	—	—	—

KM# 360.15 ECU

Silver **Ruler:** Louis XIV **Mint:** Riom **Obverse:** Armored bust right **Reverse:** Crowned double L's in cruciform, fleur-de-lis in angles, arms of France in center

Date	Mintage	VG	F	VF	XF	Unc
1704O	—	90.00	185	375	650	—
1705O	—	100	225	425	750	—

KM# 360.16 ECU

Silver **Ruler:** Louis XIV **Mint:** Dijon **Obverse:** Armored bust right **Reverse:** Crowned double L's in cruciform, fleur-de-lis in angles, arms of France in center

Date	Mintage	VG	F	VF	XF	Unc
1704P	—	90.00	185	375	650	—
1705P	—	100	225	425	750	—
1706P	—	175	325	550	900	—
1707P	—	—	—	—	—	—

KM# 360.18 ECU

Silver **Ruler:** Louis XIV **Mint:** Nantes **Obverse:** Armored bust right **Reverse:** Crowned double L's in cruciform, fleur-de-lis in angles, arms of France in center

Date	Mintage	VG	F	VF	XF	Unc
1704T	—	75.00	150	300	550	—
1705T	—	90.00	185	375	650	—
1708T	—	175	325	550	900	—
1709T	—	—	—	—	—	—

KM# 360.19 ECU

Silver **Ruler:** Louis XIV **Mint:** Troyes **Obverse:** Armored bust right **Reverse:** Crowned double L's in cruciform, fleur-de-lis in angles, arms of France in center

Date	Mintage	VG	F	VF	XF	Unc
1704V	—	90.00	185	375	650	—

KM# 360.20 ECU

Silver **Ruler:** Louis XIV **Mint:** Lille **Obverse:** Armored bust right **Reverse:** Crowned double L's in cruciform, fleur-de-lis in angles, arms of France in center

Date	Mintage	VG	F	VF	XF	Unc
1704W	—	60.00	125	250	450	—
1705W	—	90.00	185	375	650	—

KM# 360.21 ECU

Silver **Ruler:** Louis XIV **Mint:** Amiens **Obverse:** Armored bust right **Reverse:** Crowned double L's in cruciform, fleur-de-lis in angles, arms of France in center

Date	Mintage	VG	F	VF	XF	Unc
1704X	—	75.00	150	300	550	—
1705X	—	100	225	425	750	—
1706X	—	100	225	425	750	—

KM# 360.22 ECU

Silver **Ruler:** Louis XIV **Mint:** Bourges **Obverse:** Armored bust right **Reverse:** Crowned double L's in cruciform, fleur-de-lis in angles, arms of France in center

Date	Mintage	VG	F	VF	XF	Unc
1704Y	—	90.00	190	385	700	—

KM# 360.23 ECU

Silver **Ruler:** Louis XIV **Mint:** Grenoble **Obverse:** Armored bust right **Reverse:** Crowned double L's in cruciform, fleur-de-lis in angles, arms of France in center

Date	Mintage	VG	F	VF	XF	Unc
1704Z	—	100	225	425	750	—
1705Z	—	175	325	550	900	—

KM# 360.8 ECU

Silver **Ruler:** Louis XIV **Mint:** Poitiers **Obverse:** Armored bust right **Reverse:** Crowned double L's in cruciform, fleur-de-lis in angles, arms of France in center

Date	Mintage	VG	F	VF	XF	Unc
1705G	—	100	225	425	750	—
1706G	—	—	—	—	—	—

KM# 385 ECU

Silver **Ruler:** Louis XIV **Mint:** Lille **Obverse:** Bust right **Reverse:** Crowned square shield with arms of France and Old and New Burgundy **Note:** Issued for Province Flanders. Dav. #1323.

Date	Mintage	VG	F	VF	XF	Unc
1705W Rare	—	—	—	—	—	—

KM# 362.2 ECU

Silver **Ruler:** Louis XIV **Mint:** Nantes **Obverse:** Draped bust right **Reverse:** Crowned back to back L"s form center square holding round arms of France

Date	Mintage	VG	F	VF	XF	Unc
1708/7T	—	750	1,500	2,750	4,500	—

KM# 384.2 ECU

Silver **Ruler:** Louis XIV **Mint:** Limoges **Obverse:** Armored bust right **Reverse:** Crowned back to back L"s form center square holding round arms of France

Date	Mintage	VG	F	VF	XF	Unc
1709I	—	—	—	—	—	—

Note: Reported, not confirmed

KM# 384.3 ECU

Silver **Ruler:** Louis XIV **Mint:** Bayonne **Obverse:** Armored bust right **Reverse:** Crowned back to back L"s form center square holding round arms of France

Date	Mintage	VG	F	VF	XF	Unc
1709L Rare	—	—	—	—	—	—

KM# 386.2 ECU

Silver **Ruler:** Louis XIV **Mint:** Rouen **Obverse:** Armored bust right **Reverse:** 3 Crowns, fleur-de-lis in angles

Date	Mintage	VG	F	VF	XF	Unc
1709B	—	50.00	95.00	200	350	—
1710B	—	55.00	100	210	385	—
1711B	—	60.00	120	240	425	—
1712B	—	120	270	500	900	—
1713B	—	80.00	160	330	600	—
1714B	—	120	270	500	900	—
1715B	—	—	—	—	—	—

KM# 386.3 ECU

Silver **Ruler:** Louis XIV **Mint:** Caen **Obverse:** Armored bust right **Reverse:** 3 Crowns, fleur-de-lis in angles

Date	Mintage	VG	F	VF	XF	Unc
1709C	—	65.00	135	270	475	—
1710C	—	80.00	160	330	600	—
1711C	—	65.00	135	270	475	—
1712C	—	110	220	450	775	—
1713C	—	120	270	500	900	—
1714C	—	—	—	—	—	—

KM# 386.4 ECU

Silver **Ruler:** Louis XIV **Mint:** Lyon **Obverse:** Armored bust right **Reverse:** 3 Crowns, fleur-de-lis in angles

Date	Mintage	VG	F	VF	XF	Unc
1709D	—	80.00	160	330	600	—
1710D	—	50.00	95.00	200	350	—
1711D	—	65.00	135	270	475	—
1712D	—	70.00	150	300	550	—
1713D	—	90.00	180	350	650	—
1714D	—	150	300	550	950	—
1715D	—	65.00	135	270	475	—

KM# 386.5 ECU

Silver **Ruler:** Louis XIV **Mint:** Tours **Obverse:** Armored bust right **Reverse:** 3 Crowns, fleur-de-lis in angles

Date	Mintage	VG	F	VF	XF	Unc
1709E	—	65.00	135	270	475	—
1710E	—	110	220	450	775	—
1711E	—	110	220	450	775	—
1712E	—	90.00	180	350	650	—
1713E	—	110	220	450	775	—
1714E	—	110	220	450	775	—
1715E	—	120	270	500	900	—

KM# 386.6 ECU

Silver **Ruler:** Louis XIV **Mint:** Poitiers **Obverse:** Armored bust right **Reverse:** 3 Crowns, fleur-de-lis in angles

Date	Mintage	VG	F	VF	XF	Unc
1709G	—	90.00	180	350	650	—
1710G	—	—	—	—	—	—
1711G	—	—	—	—	—	—
1712G	—	120	270	500	900	—
1713G	—	200	400	650	1,100	—
1714G	—	—	—	—	—	—

KM# 386.7 ECU

Silver **Ruler:** Louis XIV **Mint:** La Rochelle **Obverse:** Armored bust right **Reverse:** 3 Crowns, fleur-de-lis in angles

Date	Mintage	VG	F	VF	XF	Unc
1709H	—	90.00	180	350	650	—
1710H	—	50.00	95.00	200	350	—
1711H	—	60.00	120	240	425	—
1712H	—	75.00	160	330	600	—
1713H	—	90.00	180	350	650	—
1714H	—	—	—	—	—	—
1715H	—	110	220	450	775	—

KM# 386.8 ECU

Silver **Ruler:** Louis XIV **Mint:** Limoges **Obverse:** Armored bust right **Reverse:** 3 Crowns, fleur-de-lis in angles

Date	Mintage	VG	F	VF	XF	Unc
1709I	—	150	300	550	1,000	—
1710I	—	120	270	500	900	—
1711I	—	120	270	500	900	—
1712I	—	110	220	450	775	—
1713I	—	120	270	500	900	—
1714I	—	120	270	500	900	—

KM# 386.9 ECU

Silver **Ruler:** Louis XIV **Mint:** Bordeaux **Obverse:** Armored bust right **Reverse:** 3 Crowns, fleur-de-lis in angles

Date	Mintage	VG	F	VF	XF	Unc
1709K	—	60.00	120	240	425	—
1710K	—	55.00	100	200	400	—
1711K	—	65.00	135	270	475	—
1712K	—	90.00	180	350	650	—
1713K	—	90.00	180	350	650	—
1714K	—	120	270	500	900	—
1715K	—	—	—	—	—	—

KM# 386.10 ECU

Silver **Ruler:** Louis XIV **Mint:** Bayonne **Obverse:** Armored bust right **Reverse:** 3 Crowns, fleur-de-lis in angles

Date	Mintage	VG	F	VF	XF	Unc
1709L	—	65.00	135	270	475	—
1710L	—	75.00	160	330	600	—
1711L	—	75.00	160	330	600	—
1712L	—	110	220	450	775	—
1713L	—	110	220	450	775	—
1715L	—	120	270	500	900	—

KM# 386.11 ECU

Silver **Ruler:** Louis XIV **Mint:** Toulouse **Obverse:** Armored bust right **Reverse:** 3 Crowns, fleur-de-lis in angles

Date	Mintage	VG	F	VF	XF	Unc
1709M	—	65.00	135	270	475	—
1710M	—	110	220	450	775	—
1711M	—	90.00	180	350	650	—
1712M	—	120	270	500	900	—
1713M	—	—	—	—	—	—
1714M	—	120	270	500	900	—
1715M	—	—	—	—	—	—

KM# 386.12 ECU

Silver **Ruler:** Louis XIV **Mint:** Montpellier **Obverse:** Armored bust right **Reverse:** 3 Crowns, fleur-de-lis in angles

Date	Mintage	VG	F	VF	XF	Unc
1709N	—	65.00	135	270	475	—
1710N	—	70.00	150	300	550	—
1711N	—	90.00	180	350	650	—
1712N Reported, not confirmed	—	—	—	—	—	—

KM# 386.13 ECU

Silver **Ruler:** Louis XIV **Mint:** Riom **Obverse:** Armored bust right **Reverse:** 3 Crowns, fleur-de-lis in angles

Date	Mintage	VG	F	VF	XF	Unc
1709O	—	120	270	500	900	—
1710O	—	90.00	180	350	650	—
1711O	—	120	270	500	900	—
1712O	—	160	325	660	1,200	—
1713O	—	215	400	250	1,450	—

KM# 386.14 ECU

Silver **Ruler:** Louis XIV **Mint:** Dijon **Obverse:** Armored bust right **Reverse:** 3 Crowns, fleur-de-lis in angles

Date	Mintage	VG	F	VF	XF	Unc
1709P	—	65.00	135	270	475	—
1710P	—	75.00	160	330	600	—
1713P	—	200	375	650	1,100	—
1714P	—	—	—	—	—	—
1715P	—	—	—	—	—	—

KM# 386.20 ECU

Silver **Ruler:** Louis XIV **Mint:** Amiens **Obverse:** Armored bust right **Reverse:** 3 Crowns, fleur-de-lis in angles

Date	Mintage	VG	F	VF	XF	Unc
1709X	—	50.00	95.00	200	350	—
1710X	—	60.00	120	240	425	—
1711X	—	60.00	120	240	425	—
1712X	—	110	220	450	775	—
1713X	—	90.00	180	350	650	—
1714X	—	110	220	450	775	—
1715X	—	120	270	500	900	—

KM# 386.21 ECU

Silver **Ruler:** Louis XIV **Mint:** Bourges **Obverse:** Armored bust right **Reverse:** 3 Crowns, fleur-de-lis in angles

Date	Mintage	VG	F	VF	XF	Unc
1709Y	—	—	—	—	—	—
1710Y	—	80.00	160	330	600	—
1711Y	—	110	220	450	775	—
1712Y	—	120	270	500	900	—
1713Y	—	120	270	500	900	—
1714Y	—	—	—	—	—	—

KM# 386.22 ECU

Silver **Ruler:** Louis XIV **Mint:** Grenoble **Obverse:** Armored bust right **Reverse:** 3 Crowns, fleur-de-lis in angles

Date	Mintage	VG	F	VF	XF	Unc
1709Z	—	185	375	675	1,200	—
1710Z	—	150	335	635	1,150	—
1711Z	—	—	—	—	—	—
1712Z	—	270	400	935	1,850	—
1713Z	—	—	—	—	—	—
1714Z	—	—	—	—	—	—

KM# 386.16 ECU

Silver **Ruler:** Louis XIV **Mint:** Reims **Obverse:** Armored bust right **Reverse:** 3 Crowns, fleur-de-lis in angles

Date	Mintage	VG	F	VF	XF	Unc
1709S	—	50.00	95.00	200	350	—
1710S	—	55.00	100	210	385	—
1711S	—	70.00	150	300	550	—
1712S	—	—	—	—	—	—
1713S	—	—	—	—	—	—

KM# 386.17 ECU

Silver **Ruler:** Louis XIV **Mint:** Nantes **Obverse:** Armored bust right **Reverse:** 3 Crowns, fleur-de-lis in angles

Date	Mintage	VG	F	VF	XF	Unc
1709T	—	55.00	95.00	210	390	—
1710T	—	60.00	120	240	425	—
1711T	—	65.00	135	270	475	—
1712T	—	50.00	95.00	200	350	—
1713T	—	65.00	135	270	475	—
1714T	—	110	220	450	775	—
1715T	—	90.00	180	350	650	—

KM# 386.18 ECU

Silver **Ruler:** Louis XIV **Mint:** Troyes **Obverse:** Armored bust right **Reverse:** 3 Crowns, fleur-de-lis in angles

Date	Mintage	VG	F	VF	XF	Unc
1709V	—	70.00	150	300	550	—
1710V	—	90.00	180	350	650	—
1711V	—	120	270	500	900	—
1713V	—	—	—	—	—	—

KM# 387 ECU

Silver **Ruler:** Louis XIV **Mint:** Pau **Obverse:** Bust right **Obv. Legend:** LVD • XIIII • D • G • FR • ET • NA • RE • B • **Reverse:** 3 Crowns, fleur-de-lis in angles **Rev. Legend:** BENEDICTVS SIT • NOMEN • DOMINI • **Note:** Mint mark: Cow. Issued for Province of Bearn. Dav. #A1324.

Date	Mintage	VG	F	VF	XF	Unc
1709	—	120	240	475	850	—
1710	—	120	240	475	850	—
1711	—	125	300	550	975	—
1712	—	125	300	550	975	—

KM# 386.25 ECU

Silver **Ruler:** Louis XIV **Mint:** Besancon **Obverse:** Armored bust right **Reverse:** 3 Crowns, fleur-de-lis in angles **Note:** Mint mark:)(.

Date	Mintage	VG	F	VF	XF	Unc
1709	—	80.00	160	330	600	—
1710	—	80.00	160	330	600	—
1711	—	110	220	450	775	—
1712	—	150	300	550	950	—
1713	—	210	400	650	1,100	—
1714	—	—	—	—	—	—

KM# 384.1 ECU

Silver **Ruler:** Louis XIV **Mint:** Paris **Obverse:** Armored bust right **Obv. Legend:** LVD • XIIII • D • G • FR • ET • NAV • REX • **Reverse:** Crowned back to back L"s form center square holding round arms of France **Rev. Legend:** BENEDICTUS SIT • NOMEN • DOMINI **Note:** Dav. #1322A.

Date	Mintage	VG	F	VF	XF	Unc
1709A Rare	—	—	—	—	—	—

KM# 386.1 ECU

Silver **Ruler:** Louis XIV **Mint:** Paris **Obverse:** Armored bust right **Obv. Legend:** LVD • XIIII • D • G • FR • ET • NAV • REX • **Reverse:** 3 Crowns, fleur-de-lis in angles **Rev. Legend:** BENEDICTVS SIT • NOMEN • DOMINI **Note:** Dav. #1324.

Date	Mintage	VG	F	VF	XF	Unc
1709A	—	45.00	90.00	180	325	—
1710A	—	50.00	95.00	200	350	—
1711A	—	50.00	95.00	200	350	—
1712A	—	50.00	95.00	200	350	—
1713A	—	50.00	95.00	200	350	—
1714A	—	90.00	180	350	650	—
1715A	—	60.00	120	240	425	—

KM# 386.24 ECU

Silver **Ruler:** Louis XIV **Mint:** Aix **Obverse:** Armored bust right **Reverse:** 3 Crowns, fleur-de-lis in angles **Note:** Mint mark: &.

Date	Mintage	VG	F	VF	XF	Unc
1709	—	90.00	180	350	650	—
1710	—	80.00	160	330	600	—
1712	—	120	270	500	900	—
1713	—	120	270	500	900	—

KM# 386.23 ECU

Silver **Ruler:** Louis XIV **Mint:** Rennes **Obverse:** Armored bust right **Reverse:** 3 Crowns, fleur-de-lis in angles **Note:** Mint mark: 9.

Date	Mintage	VG	F	VF	XF	Unc
1709	—	50.00	95.00	200	350	—
1710	—	50.00	95.00	200	350	—
1711	—	50.00	95.00	200	350	—
1712	—	50.00	95.00	200	350	—
1713	—	65.00	135	270	475	—
1714	—	80.00	160	330	600	—
1715	—	50.00	95.00	200	350	—

KM# 386.15 ECU

Silver **Ruler:** Louis XIV **Mint:** Perpignan **Obverse:** Armored bust right **Reverse:** 3 Crowns, fleur-de-lis in angles

Date	Mintage	VG	F	VF	XF	Unc
1712Q	—	150	300	550	950	—
1713Q	—	—	—	—	—	—
1714Q	—	—	—	—	—	—

KM# 386.19 ECU

Silver **Ruler:** Louis XIV **Mint:** Lille **Obverse:** Armored bust right **Reverse:** 3 Crowns, fleur-de-lis in angles

Date	Mintage	VG	F	VF	XF	Unc
1713W	—	110	220	450	775	—

KM# 412.2 ECU

30.5990 g., 0.9170 Silver 0.9021 oz. ASW **Ruler:** Louis XV **Mint:** La Rochelle

Date	Mintage	VG	F	VF	XF	Unc
1715H Rare	—	—	—	—	—	—

KM# 412.4 ECU

30.5990 g., 0.9170 Silver 0.9021 oz. ASW **Ruler:** Louis XV **Mint:** Lille **Obv. Legend:** LUD

Date	Mintage	VG	F	VF	XF	Unc
1715W	27,000	2,500	5,000	9,000	15,000	—

KM# 412.3 ECU

30.5990 g., 0.9170 Silver 0.9021 oz. ASW **Ruler:** Louis XV **Mint:** Rennes **Note:** Mint mark: 9.

Date	Mintage	VG	F	VF	XF	Unc
1715 Rare	—	—	—	—	—	—

KM# 412.1 ECU

30.5990 g., 0.9170 Silver 0.9021 oz. ASW **Ruler:** Louis XV **Mint:** Paris **Obverse:** Young draped bust right **Reverse:** 3 crowns form triangle, fleur-de-lis in angles **Note:** Dav. #1325.

Date	Mintage	VG	F	VF	XF	Unc
1715A	—	2,500	5,000	9,000	15,000	—

KM# 414.1 ECU

30.5990 g., 0.9170 Silver 0.9021 oz. ASW **Ruler:** Louis XV **Mint:** Paris **Obverse:** Draped young bust right **Obv. Legend:** LVD • XV • D • G • FR • ET • NAV • REX * **Reverse:** Crowned round arms of France **Rev. Legend:** SIT NOMEN DOMINI BENEDICTUM **Note:** Dav. #1326.

Date	Mintage	VG	F	VF	XF	Unc
1715A	107,000	50.00	100	300	600	—
1716A	4,235,000	40.00	80.00	200	400	—
1717A	525,000	40.00	80.00	650	400	—
1718A	—	40.00	80.00	200	400	—

KM# 414.25 ECU

30.5990 g., 0.9170 Silver 0.9021 oz. ASW **Ruler:** Louis XV **Mint:** Rennes **Obverse:** Draped young bust right **Reverse:** Crowned round arms of France **Note:** Mint mark: 9.

Date	Mintage	VG	F	VF	XF	Unc
1716	2,024,000	50.00	200	500	900	—
1717	1,296,000	50.00	200	500	900	—
1718	871,000	50.00	200	500	900	—

KM# 414.26 ECU

30.5990 g., 0.9170 Silver 0.9021 oz. ASW **Ruler:** Louis XV **Mint:** Aix **Obverse:** Draped young bust right **Reverse:** Crowned round arms of France **Note:** Mint mark: &.

Date	Mintage	VG	F	VF	XF	Unc
1716	—	85.00	175	525	1,150	—
1717	—	85.00	175	435	875	—
1718	—	175	350	875	1,750	—

KM# 414.27 ECU

30.5990 g., 0.9170 Silver 0.9021 oz. ASW **Ruler:** Louis XV **Mint:** Besancon **Obverse:** Draped young bust right **Reverse:** Crowned round arms of France **Note:** Mint mark: Back to back C's. Varieties exist.

Date	Mintage	VG	F	VF	XF	Unc
1716	—	85.00	175	525	1,150	—
1717	86,000	130	265	700	1,575	—
1718	—	265	525	1,225	3,000	—

KM# 423 ECU

30.5990 g., 0.9170 Silver 0.9021 oz. ASW **Ruler:** Louis XV **Mint:** Pau **Obv. Legend:** ....RE.BD (ligate BD). **Note:** Mint mark: Cow. Issued for Province of Bearn. Dav. #A1326.

Date	Mintage	VG	F	VF	XF	Unc
1716	—	265	525	1,225	2,750	—
1717	20,000	265	525	1,225	2,750	—

KM# 414.2 ECU

30.5990 g., 0.9170 Silver 0.9021 oz. ASW **Ruler:** Louis XV **Mint:** Metz **Obverse:** Draped young bust right **Reverse:** Crowned round arms of France

Date	Mintage	VG	F	VF	XF	Unc
1716AA	—	85.00	175	525	1,225	—

KM# 414.3 ECU

30.5990 g., 0.9170 Silver 0.9021 oz. ASW **Ruler:** Louis XV **Mint:** Rouen **Obverse:** Draped young bust right **Reverse:** Crowned round arms of France

Date	Mintage	VG	F	VF	XF	Unc
1716B	600,000	85.00	175	525	1,225	—
1717B	196,000	85.00	175	525	1,225	—
1718B	86,000	130	265	700	1,575	—

KM# 414.4 ECU

30.5990 g., 0.9170 Silver 0.9021 oz. ASW **Ruler:** Louis XV **Mint:** Strasbourg **Obverse:** Draped young bust right **Reverse:** Crowned round arms of France

Date	Mintage	VG	F	VF	XF	Unc
1716BB	—	130	265	620	1,320	—
1718BB	—	220	435	1,150	2,350	—

KM# 414.5 ECU

30.5990 g., 0.9170 Silver 0.9021 oz. ASW **Ruler:** Louis XV **Mint:** Caen **Obverse:** Draped young bust right **Reverse:** Crowned round arms of France

Date	Mintage	VG	F	VF	XF	Unc
1716C	188,000	85.00	175	525	1,150	—
1717C	98,000	130	265	700	1,575	—

KM# 414.6 ECU

30.5990 g., 0.9170 Silver 0.9021 oz. ASW **Ruler:** Louis XV **Mint:** Lyon **Obverse:** Draped young bust right **Reverse:** Crowned round arms of France

Date	Mintage	VG	F	VF	XF	Unc
1716D	1,496,000	130	265	620	1,320	—
1717D	91,000	130	265	700	1,575	—

KM# 414.7 ECU

30.5990 g., 0.9170 Silver 0.9021 oz. ASW **Ruler:** Louis XV **Mint:** Tours **Obverse:** Draped young bust right **Reverse:** Crowned round arms of France

Date	Mintage	VG	F	VF	XF	Unc
1716E	852,000	85.00	175	525	1,150	—
1717E	—	85.00	175	525	1,150	—
1718E	925,000	85.00	175	525	1,150	—

KM# 414.8 ECU

30.5990 g., 0.9170 Silver 0.9021 oz. ASW **Ruler:** Louis XV **Mint:** Poitiers **Obverse:** Draped young bust right **Reverse:** Crowned round arms of France

Date	Mintage	VG	F	VF	XF	Unc
1716G	—	85.00	175	525	1,150	—
1717G	—	85.00	175	525	1,150	—

KM# 414.9 ECU

30.5990 g., 0.9170 Silver 0.9021 oz. ASW **Ruler:** Louis XV **Mint:** La Rochelle **Obverse:** Draped young bust right **Reverse:** Crowned round arms of France

Date	Mintage	VG	F	VF	XF	Unc
1716H	312,000	130	265	620	1,320	—
1717H	—	130	265	620	1,320	—

KM# 414.10 ECU

30.5990 g., 0.9170 Silver 0.9021 oz. ASW **Ruler:** Louis XV **Mint:** Limoges **Obverse:** Draped young bust right **Reverse:** Crowned round arms of France

Date	Mintage	VG	F	VF	XF	Unc
1716I	—	84.00	175	525	1,150	—
1718I	—	130	265	700	1,575	—

KM# 414.11 ECU

30.5990 g., 0.9170 Silver 0.9021 oz. ASW **Ruler:** Louis XV **Mint:** Bordeaux **Obverse:** Draped young bust right **Reverse:** Crowned round arms of France

Date	Mintage	VG	F	VF	XF	Unc
1716K	—	85.00	175	435	875	—
1717K	—	85.00	175	435	875	—

KM# 414.12 ECU

30.5990 g., 0.9170 Silver 0.9021 oz. ASW **Ruler:** Louis XV **Mint:** Bayonne **Obverse:** Draped young bust right **Reverse:** Crowned round arms of France

Date	Mintage	VG	F	VF	XF	Unc
1716L	—	85.00	175	435	875	—
1717L	—	85.00	175	435	875	—

KM# 414.13 ECU

30.5990 g., 0.9170 Silver 0.9021 oz. ASW **Ruler:** Louis XV **Mint:** Toulouse **Obverse:** Draped young bust right **Reverse:** Crowned round arms of France

Date	Mintage	VG	F	VF	XF	Unc
1716M	89,000	85.00	175	525	1,150	—
1717M	—	85.00	175	525	1,150	—

KM# 414.14 ECU

30.5990 g., 0.9170 Silver 0.9021 oz. ASW **Ruler:** Louis XV **Mint:** Montpellier **Obverse:** Draped young bust right **Reverse:** Crowned round arms of France

Date	Mintage	VG	F	VF	XF	Unc
1716N	124,000	85.00	175	350	700	—
1717N	69,000	85.00	175	350	700	—
1718N	18,000	175	350	875	1,750	—

KM# 414.15 ECU

30.5990 g., 0.9170 Silver 0.9021 oz. ASW **Ruler:** Louis XV **Mint:** Riom **Obverse:** Draped young bust right **Reverse:** Crowned round arms of France

Date	Mintage	VG	F	VF	XF	Unc
1716O	—	85.00	175	435	875	—
1717O	—	85.00	175	435	875	—
1718O	—	130	265	700	1,575	—

KM# 414.16 ECU

30.5990 g., 0.9170 Silver 0.9021 oz. ASW **Ruler:** Louis XV **Mint:** Dijon **Obverse:** Draped young bust right **Reverse:** Crowned round arms of France

Date	Mintage	VG	F	VF	XF	Unc
1716P	—	85.00	175	435	875	—
1717P	20,000	115	300	700	1,250	—

KM# 414.17 ECU

30.5990 g., 0.9170 Silver 0.9021 oz. ASW **Ruler:** Louis XV **Mint:** Perpignan **Obverse:** Draped young bust right **Reverse:** Crowned round arms of France

Date	Mintage	VG	F	VF	XF	Unc
1716Q	—	85.00	175	435	875	—
1717Q	—	85.00	175	525	1,150	—
1718Q	—	85.00	175	435	875	—

KM# 414.18 ECU

30.5990 g., 0.9170 Silver 0.9021 oz. ASW **Ruler:** Louis XV **Mint:** Reims **Obverse:** Draped young bust right **Reverse:** Crowned round arms of France

Date	Mintage	VG	F	VF	XF	Unc
1716S	—	130	265	650	1,575	—
1717S	36,000	175	350	875	1,950	—
1718S	—	175	350	875	1,950	—

KM# 414.19 ECU

30.5990 g., 0.9170 Silver 0.9021 oz. ASW **Ruler:** Louis XV **Mint:** Nantes **Obverse:** Draped young bust right **Reverse:** Crowned round arms of France

Date	Mintage	VG	F	VF	XF	Unc
1716T	—	85.00	175	525	1,150	—
1717T	218,000	85.00	175	525	1,150	—
1718T	—	175	350	875	1,950	—

KM# 414.20 ECU

30.5990 g., 0.9170 Silver 0.9021 oz. ASW **Ruler:** Louis XV **Mint:** Troyes **Obverse:** Draped young bust right **Reverse:** Crowned round arms of France

Date	Mintage	VG	F	VF	XF	Unc
1716V	85,000	175	350	700	1,750	—
1717V	—	175	350	700	1,750	—

KM# 414.21 ECU

30.5990 g., 0.9170 Silver 0.9021 oz. ASW **Ruler:** Louis XV **Mint:** Lille **Obverse:** Draped young bust right **Reverse:** Crowned round arms of France

Date	Mintage	VG	F	VF	XF	Unc
1716W	439,000	85.00	175	525	1,150	—
1717W	140,000	85.00	175	525	1,150	—
1718W	—	130	265	600	1,400	—

KM# 414.22 ECU

30.5990 g., 0.9170 Silver 0.9021 oz. ASW **Ruler:** Louis XV **Mint:** Amiens **Obverse:** Draped young bust right **Reverse:** Crowned round arms of France

Date	Mintage	VG	F	VF	XF	Unc
1716X	—	175	350	875	1,850	—
1717X	61,000	175	350	875	1,850	—
1718X	—	175	350	875	1,850	—

KM# 414.23 ECU

30.5990 g., 0.9170 Silver 0.9021 oz. ASW **Ruler:** Louis XV **Mint:** Bourges **Obverse:** Draped young bust right **Reverse:** Crowned round arms of France

Date	Mintage	VG	F	VF	XF	Unc
1716Y	9,908	130	265	700	1,575	—
1717Y	39,000	130	265	700	1,575	—
1718Y	—	130	265	700	1,575	—

KM# 414.24 ECU

30.5990 g., 0.9170 Silver 0.9021 oz. ASW **Ruler:** Louis XV **Mint:** Grenoble **Obverse:** Draped young bust right **Reverse:** Crowned round arms of France

Date	Mintage	VG	F	VF	XF	Unc
1716Z	192,000	220	435	965	2,650	—
1717Z	16,000	265	525	1,225	2,850	—

KM# 435.2 ECU

24.4750 g., 0.9170 Silver 0.7215 oz. ASW **Ruler:** Louis XV **Mint:** Metz

Date	Mintage	VG	F	VF	XF	Unc
1718AA	—	50.00	125	300	700	—

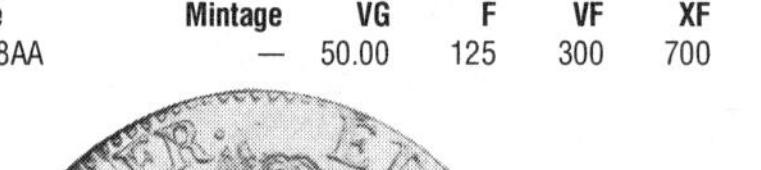

KM# 435.3 ECU

24.4750 g., 0.9170 Silver 0.7215 oz. ASW **Ruler:** Louis XV **Mint:** Rouen

Date	Mintage	VG	F	VF	XF	Unc
1718B	1,513,000	35.00	85.00	250	650	—
1719B	—	50.00	125	300	750	—

KM# 435.4 ECU

24.4750 g., 0.9170 Silver 0.7215 oz. ASW **Ruler:** Louis XV **Mint:** Strasbourg

Date	Mintage	VG	F	VF	XF	Unc
1718BB	—	80.00	200	400	900	—

KM# 435.5 ECU

24.4750 g., 0.9170 Silver 0.7215 oz. ASW **Ruler:** Louis XV **Mint:** Caen

Date	Mintage	VG	F	VF	XF	Unc
1718C	—	50.00	125	300	800	—
1719C	591,000	50.00	125	300	800	—

KM# 435.6 ECU

24.4750 g., 0.9170 Silver 0.7215 oz. ASW **Ruler:** Louis XV **Mint:** Lyon

Date	Mintage	VG	F	VF	XF	Unc
1718D	1,760,000	30.00	75.00	225	550	—
1719D	—	35.00	85.00	250	600	—

KM# 435.7 ECU

24.4750 g., 0.9170 Silver 0.7215 oz. ASW **Ruler:** Louis XV **Mint:** Tours

Date	Mintage	VG	F	VF	XF	Unc
1718E	88,000	50.00	125	300	800	—
1719E	614,000	30.00	75.00	175	500	—

KM# 435.8 ECU

24.4750 g., 0.9170 Silver 0.7215 oz. ASW **Ruler:** Louis XV **Mint:** Poitiers

Date	Mintage	VG	F	VF	XF	Unc
1718G	177,000	45.00	85.00	250	600	—
1719G	69,000	80.00	200	400	900	—

KM# 435.9 ECU

24.4750 g., 0.9170 Silver 0.7215 oz. ASW **Ruler:** Louis XV **Mint:** La Rochelle

Date	Mintage	VG	F	VF	XF	Unc
1718H	—	75.00	175	450	1,200	—
1719H	—	50.00	125	300	800	—

KM# 435.10 ECU

24.4750 g., 0.9170 Silver 0.7215 oz. ASW **Ruler:** Louis XV **Mint:** Limoges

Date	Mintage	VG	F	VF	XF	Unc
1718I	—	50.00	125	300	800	—
1719I	—	80.00	200	400	900	—

KM# 435.11 ECU

24.4750 g., 0.9170 Silver 0.7215 oz. ASW **Ruler:** Louis XV **Mint:** Bordeaux

Date	Mintage	VG	F	VF	XF	Unc
1718K	—	30.00	75.00	175	500	—
1719K	—	35.00	85.00	250	600	—

KM# 435.12 ECU

24.4750 g., 0.9170 Silver 0.7215 oz. ASW **Ruler:** Louis XV **Mint:** Bayonne

Date	Mintage	VG	F	VF	XF	Unc
1718L	—	35.00	85.00	250	650	—

KM# 435.13 ECU

24.4750 g., 0.9170 Silver 0.7215 oz. ASW **Ruler:** Louis XV **Mint:** Toulouse

Date	Mintage	VG	F	VF	XF	Unc
1718M	—	50.00	125	300	725	—
1719M	—	50.00	125	300	725	—

KM# 435.14 ECU

24.4750 g., 0.9170 Silver 0.7215 oz. ASW **Ruler:** Louis XV **Mint:** Montpellier

Date	Mintage	VG	F	VF	XF	Unc
1718N	902,000	35.00	85.00	250	600	—
1719N	567,000	35.00	85.00	250	600	—

KM# 435.16 ECU

24.4750 g., 0.9170 Silver 0.7215 oz. ASW **Ruler:** Louis XV **Mint:** Dijon

Date	Mintage	VG	F	VF	XF	Unc
1718P	—	50.00	125	300	800	—
1719P	—	50.00	125	300	800	—

KM# 435.17 ECU

24.4750 g., 0.9170 Silver 0.7215 oz. ASW **Ruler:** Louis XV **Mint:** Perpignan

Date	Mintage	VG	F	VF	XF	Unc
1718Q	—	35.00	85.00	250	600	—
1719Q	—	50.00	125	300	700	—

KM# 435.18 ECU

24.4750 g., 0.9170 Silver 0.7215 oz. ASW **Ruler:** Louis XV **Mint:** Orléans

Date	Mintage	VG	F	VF	XF	Unc
1718R	—	50.00	125	300	800	—
1719R	—	50.00	125	300	800	—

KM# 435.19 ECU

24.4750 g., 0.9170 Silver 0.7215 oz. ASW **Ruler:** Louis XV **Mint:** Reims

Date	Mintage	VG	F	VF	XF	Unc
1718S	—	35.00	85.00	250	650	—
1719S	—	35.00	85.00	250	650	—

KM# 435.20 ECU

24.4750 g., 0.9170 Silver 0.7215 oz. ASW **Ruler:** Louis XV **Mint:** Nantes

Date	Mintage	VG	F	VF	XF	Unc
1718T	—	35.00	85.00	250	650	—
1719T	—	35.00	85.00	300	700	—

KM# 435.21 ECU

24.4750 g., 0.9170 Silver 0.7215 oz. ASW **Ruler:** Louis XV **Mint:** Troyes

Date	Mintage	VG	F	VF	XF	Unc
1718V	—	35.00	85.00	250	600	—
1719V	—	35.00	85.00	250	650	—

KM# 435.22 ECU

24.4750 g., 0.9170 Silver 0.7215 oz. ASW **Ruler:** Louis XV **Mint:** Lille

Date	Mintage	VG	F	VF	XF	Unc
1718W	—	30.00	75.00	225	550	—
1719W	26,000	80.00	200	400	900	—

KM# 435.23 ECU

24.4750 g., 0.9170 Silver 0.7215 oz. ASW **Ruler:** Louis XV **Mint:** Amiens

Date	Mintage	VG	F	VF	XF	Unc
1718X	—	30.00	75.00	175	500	—
1719X	—	30.00	75.00	175	525	—

KM# 435.24 ECU

24.4750 g., 0.9170 Silver 0.7215 oz. ASW **Ruler:** Louis XV **Mint:** Bourges

Date	Mintage	VG	F	VF	XF	Unc
1718Y	—	50.00	125	300	800	—

KM# 435.25 ECU

24.4750 g., 0.9170 Silver 0.7215 oz. ASW **Ruler:** Louis XV **Mint:** Grenoble

Date	Mintage	VG	F	VF	XF	Unc
1718Z	233,000	35.00	85.00	250	650	—

KM# 436 ECU

24.4750 g., 0.9170 Silver 0.7215 oz. ASW **Ruler:** Louis XV **Mint:** Pau **Obverse:** Legend ends: ...RE. BD. (ligate BD) **Obv. Legend:** ....RE.BD (ligate BD). **Note:** Mint mark: Cow. Issued for Province of Bearn.

Date	Mintage	VG	F	VF	XF	Unc
1718	—	90.00	200	400	1,000	—
1719	—	90.00	200	400	1,000	—

KM# 435.28 ECU

24.4750 g., 0.9170 Silver 0.7215 oz. ASW **Ruler:** Louis XV **Mint:** Besancon **Obverse:** Laureate armored young bust right **Reverse:** Crowned quartered arms of France and Navarre **Note:** Mint mark: Back to back C's.

Date	Mintage	VG	F	VF	XF	Unc
1718	—	35.00	85.00	250	650	—

KM# 435.27 ECU

24.4750 g., 0.9170 Silver 0.7215 oz. ASW **Ruler:** Louis XV **Mint:** Aix **Obverse:** Laureate armored young bust right **Reverse:** Crowned quartered arms of France and Navarre **Note:** Mint mark: &.

Date	Mintage	VG	F	VF	XF	Unc
1718	—	35.00	85.00	250	650	—
1719	—	35.00	85.00	250	650	—

KM# 435.26 ECU

24.4750 g., 0.9170 Silver 0.7215 oz. ASW **Ruler:** Louis XV **Mint:** Rennes **Obverse:** Laureate armored young bust right **Reverse:** Crowned quartered arms of France and Navarre **Note:** Mint mark: 9.

Date	Mintage	VG	F	VF	XF	Unc
1718	1,772,000	30.00	75.00	200	500	—
1719	1,794,000	30.00	75.00	200	500	—

KM# 435.1 ECU

24.4750 g., 0.9170 Silver 0.7215 oz. ASW **Ruler:** Louis XV **Mint:** Paris **Obverse:** Laureate armored young bust right **Obv. Legend:** LVD • XV • D • G • FR • ET • NAV • REX **Reverse:** Crowned quartered arms of France and Navarre **Rev. Legend:** SIT • NOMEN • DOMINI • BENEDICTUM **Note:** Dav. #1327. Issued for Province of Navarre.

Date	Mintage	VG	F	VF	XF	Unc
1718A	7,443,000	30.00	75.00	175	500	—
1719A	—	30.00	75.00	175	550	—

KM# 435.15 ECU

24.4750 g., 0.9170 Silver 0.7215 oz. ASW **Ruler:** Louis XV **Mint:** Riom **Obverse:** Laureate armored young bust right **Reverse:** Crowned quartered arms of France and Navarre

Date	Mintage	VG	F	VF	XF	Unc
1719O	—	50.00	125	300	700	—

KM# 459.1 ECU

24.4750 g., 0.9170 Silver 0.7215 oz. ASW **Ruler:** Louis XV **Mint:** Paris **Obverse:** Draped laureate young bust right **Obv. Legend:** LUD • XV • D • G • FR • ET • NAV • REX **Reverse:** Crowned arms of France **Rev. Legend:** SIT NOMEN DOMINI • BENEDICTUM

Date	Mintage	VG	F	VF	XF	Unc
1720A	—	60.00	175	400	875	—
1721A	—	60.00	175	450	975	—
1722A	—	70.00	220	525	1,200	—
1723A	—	90.00	265	625	1,350	—
1724A	—	70.00	220	525	1,150	—

KM# 459.2 ECU

24.4750 g., 0.9170 Silver 0.7215 oz. ASW **Ruler:** Louis XV **Mint:** Metz **Obverse:** Draped laureate young bust right **Reverse:** Crowned arms of France

Date	Mintage	VG	F	VF	XF	Unc
1720AA	—	70.00	220	525	1,100	—
1721AA	—	90.00	265	625	1,300	—
1722AA	—	70.00	220	525	1,100	—
1723AA	—	160	450	750	1,750	—

KM# 459.3 ECU

24.4750 g., 0.9170 Silver 0.7215 oz. ASW **Ruler:** Louis XV **Mint:** Rouen **Obverse:** Draped laureate young bust right **Reverse:** Crowned arms of France

Date	Mintage	VG	F	VF	XF	Unc
1720B	—	130	400	800	1,600	—
1721B	—	90.00	265	625	1,300	—
1722B	—	90.00	265	625	1,300	—
1723B	—	165	475	975	1,950	—
1724B	—	90.00	265	625	1,300	—

KM# 459.9 ECU

24.4750 g., 0.9170 Silver 0.7215 oz. ASW **Ruler:** Louis XV **Mint:** La Rochelle **Obverse:** Draped laureate young bust right **Reverse:** Crowned arms of France

Date	Mintage	VG	F	VF	XF	Unc
1720H	—	90.00	265	625	1,300	—
1721H	—	130	400	800	1,600	—
1723H	—	130	400	800	1,600	—
1724H	—	90.00	265	625	1,300	—

KM# 459.10 ECU

24.4750 g., 0.9170 Silver 0.7215 oz. ASW **Ruler:** Louis XV **Mint:** Limoges **Obverse:** Draped laureate young bust right **Reverse:** Crowned arms of France

Date	Mintage	VG	F	VF	XF	Unc
1720I	—	90.00	265	625	1,300	—
1721I	—	90.00	265	625	1,300	—

KM# 459.13 ECU

24.4750 g., 0.9170 Silver 0.7215 oz. ASW **Ruler:** Louis XV **Mint:** Montpellier **Obverse:** Draped laureate young bust right **Reverse:** Crowned arms of France

Date	Mintage	VG	F	VF	XF	Unc
1720N	—	70.00	220	525	1,150	—
1721N	—	70.00	220	525	1,150	—
1722N	—	70.00	220	525	1,150	—
1724N	35,000	160	450	750	1,750	—

KM# 459.14 ECU

24.4750 g., 0.9170 Silver 0.7215 oz. ASW **Ruler:** Louis XV **Mint:** Riom **Obverse:** Draped laureate young bust right **Reverse:** Crowned arms of France

Date	Mintage	VG	F	VF	XF	Unc
1720O	—	90.00	265	625	1,300	—
1721O	—	90.00	265	625	1,300	—
1723O	17,000	160	450	750	1,750	—

KM# 459.6 ECU

24.4750 g., 0.9170 Silver 0.7215 oz. ASW **Ruler:** Louis XV **Mint:** Lyon **Obverse:** Draped laureate young bust right **Reverse:** Crowned arms of France

Date	Mintage	VG	F	VF	XF	Unc
1720D	—	70.00	220	525	1,150	—
1721D	250,000	70.00	220	525	1,150	—
1722D	123,000	90.00	265	625	1,300	—
1723D	—	90.00	265	625	1,300	—

KM# 459.7 ECU

24.4750 g., 0.9170 Silver 0.7215 oz. ASW **Ruler:** Louis XV **Mint:** Tours **Obverse:** Draped laureate young bust right **Reverse:** Crowned arms of France

Date	Mintage	VG	F	VF	XF	Unc
1720E	—	70.00	220	525	1,150	—
1721E	—	90.00	265	625	1,300	—
1722E	81,000	125	350	700	1,400	—

KM# 459.17 ECU

24.4750 g., 0.9170 Silver 0.7215 oz. ASW **Ruler:** Louis XV **Mint:** Orléans **Obverse:** Draped laureate young bust right **Reverse:** Crowned arms of France

Date	Mintage	VG	F	VF	XF	Unc
1720R	22,000	90.00	265	625	1,300	—
1721R	159,000	90.00	265	625	1,300	—
1722R	—	90.00	265	625	1,300	—
1724R	—	90.00	265	625	1,300	—

KM# 459.21 ECU

24.4750 g., 0.9170 Silver 0.7215 oz. ASW **Ruler:** Louis XV **Mint:** Lille **Obverse:** Draped laureate young bust right **Reverse:** Crowned arms of France

Date	Mintage	VG	F	VF	XF	Unc
1720W	85,000	70.00	220	525	1,150	—
1721W	189,000	70.00	220	525	1,150	—
1722W	—	60.00	175	400	875	—
1723W	15,000	160	450	750	1,750	—
1724W	—	70.00	220	525	1,150	—

KM# 459.22 ECU

24.4750 g., 0.9170 Silver 0.7215 oz. ASW **Ruler:** Louis XV **Mint:** Amiens **Obverse:** Draped laureate young bust right **Reverse:** Crowned arms of France

Date	Mintage	VG	F	VF	XF	Unc
1720X	—	70.00	220	525	1,150	—
1721X	—	60.00	175	400	875	—
1722X	—	175	350	1,050	2,100	—
1723X	—	160	450	750	1,750	—
1724X	—	125	350	700	1,400	—

KM# 459.24 ECU

24.4750 g., 0.9170 Silver 0.7215 oz. ASW **Ruler:** Louis XV **Mint:** Grenoble **Obverse:** Draped laureate young bust right **Reverse:** Crowned arms of France

Date	Mintage	VG	F	VF	XF	Unc
1720Z	408,000	60.00	175	400	875	—
1721Z	79,000	90.00	265	625	1,300	
1722Z	26,000	220	625	1,600	3,000	—

KM# 459.25 ECU

24.4750 g., 0.9170 Silver 0.7215 oz. ASW **Ruler:** Louis XV **Mint:** Rennes **Obverse:** Draped laureate young bust right **Reverse:** Crowned arms of France **Note:** Mint mark: 9.

Date	Mintage	VG	F	VF	XF	Unc
1720	554,000	70.00	220	525	1,150	—
1721	—	60.00	175	400	875	—
1723	127,000	70.00	220	475	975	—
1724	728,000	70.00	220	525	1,150	—

KM# 459.26 ECU

24.4750 g., 0.9170 Silver 0.7215 oz. ASW **Ruler:** Louis XV **Mint:** Aix **Obverse:** Draped laureate young bust right **Reverse:** Crowned arms of France **Note:** Mint mark: &.

Date	Mintage	VG	F	VF	XF	Unc
1721	—	125	350	700	1,600	—
1722	—	125	350	700	1,600	—
1723	—	125	350	700	1,600	—

KM# 459.27 ECU

24.4750 g., 0.9170 Silver 0.7215 oz. ASW **Ruler:** Louis XV **Mint:** Besancon **Obverse:** Draped laureate young bust right **Reverse:** Crowned arms of France **Note:** Mint mark: Back to back C's.

Date	Mintage	VG	F	VF	XF	Unc
1721	—	90.00	265	625	1,300	—
1723	—	—	—	—	—	—

KM# 459.5 ECU

24.4750 g., 0.9170 Silver 0.7215 oz. ASW **Ruler:** Louis XV **Mint:** Caen **Obverse:** Draped laureate young bust right **Reverse:** Crowned arms of France

Date	Mintage	VG	F	VF	XF	Unc
1721/0	—	90.00	265	625	1,300	—
1721	756,000	60.00	220	525	875	—
1722	187,000	90.00	265	625	1,300	—
1723	63,000	90.00	265	625	1,300	—

KM# 459.23 ECU

24.4750 g., 0.9170 Silver 0.7215 oz. ASW **Ruler:** Louis XV **Mint:** Bourges **Obverse:** Draped laureate young bust right **Reverse:** Crowned arms of France

Date	Mintage	VG	F	VF	XF	Unc
1721Y	—	160	450	875	1,950	—

KM# 459.19 ECU

24.4750 g., 0.9170 Silver 0.7215 oz. ASW **Ruler:** Louis XV **Mint:** Nantes **Obverse:** Draped laureate young bust right **Reverse:** Crowned arms of France

Date	Mintage	VG	F	VF	XF	Unc
1721T	—	70.00	220	525	1,150	—
1723T	—	90.00	265	625	1,300	—
1724T	—	90.00	265	625	1,300	—

KM# 459.20 ECU

24.4750 g., 0.9170 Silver 0.7215 oz. ASW **Ruler:** Louis XV **Mint:** Troyes **Obverse:** Draped laureate young bust right **Reverse:** Crowned arms of France

Date	Mintage	VG	F	VF	XF	Unc
1721V	—	90.00	265	625	1,300	—
1723V	64,000	160	450	875	1,950	—
1724V	61,000	160	450	875	1,950	—

KM# 459.8 ECU

24.4750 g., 0.9170 Silver 0.7215 oz. ASW **Ruler:** Louis XV **Mint:** Poitiers **Obverse:** Draped laureate young bust right **Reverse:** Crowned arms of France

Date	Mintage	VG	F	VF	XF	Unc
1721G	—	90.00	265	625	1,300	—
1722G		90.00	265	625	1,300	—

KM# 459.15 ECU

24.4750 g., 0.9170 Silver 0.7215 oz. ASW **Ruler:** Louis XV **Mint:** Dijon **Obverse:** Draped laureate young bust right **Reverse:** Crowned arms of France

Date	Mintage	VG	F	VF	XF	Unc
1721P	—	90.00	265	625	1,300	—
1722P	—	90.00	265	625	1,300	—
1723P	73,000	90.00	265	625	1,300	—
1724P	—	90.00	265	625	1,300	—

KM# 459.16 ECU

24.4750 g., 0.9170 Silver 0.7215 oz. ASW **Ruler:** Louis XV **Mint:** Perpignan **Obverse:** Draped laureate young bust right **Reverse:** Crowned arms of France

Date	Mintage	VG	F	VF	XF	Unc
1721Q	—	90.00	265	625	1,300	—
1722Q	—	90.00	265	625	1,300	—

KM# 459.11 ECU

24.4750 g., 0.9170 Silver 0.7215 oz. ASW **Ruler:** Louis XV **Mint:** Bordeaux **Obverse:** Draped laureate young bust right **Reverse:** Crowned arms of France

Date	Mintage	VG	F	VF	XF	Unc
1721K	267,000	70.00	220	525	1,150	—

KM# 459.12 ECU

24.4750 g., 0.9170 Silver 0.7215 oz. ASW **Ruler:** Louis XV **Mint:** Toulouse **Obverse:** Draped laureate young bust right **Reverse:** Crowned arms of France

Date	Mintage	VG	F	VF	XF	Unc
1721M	—	90.00	265	625	1,300	—
1722M	—	70.00	220	525	1,150	—
1724M	—	160	450	875	1,950	—

KM# 459.4 ECU
24.4750 g., 0.9170 Silver 0.7215 oz. ASW **Ruler:** Louis XV **Mint:** Strasbourg **Obverse:** Draped laureate young bust right **Reverse:** Crowned arms of France

Date	Mintage	VG	F	VF	XF	Unc
1722BB	—	125	350	700	1,600	—
1723BB	—	125	350	700	1,600	—
1724BB	—	125	350	700	1,600	—

KM# 459.18 ECU
24.4750 g., 0.9170 Silver 0.7215 oz. ASW **Ruler:** Louis XV **Mint:** Reims **Obverse:** Draped laureate young bust right **Reverse:** Crowned arms of France

Date	Mintage	VG	F	VF	XF	Unc
1723/2S	—	70.00	220	525	1,150	—
1723S	—	160	450	750	1,750	—

KM# 467 ECU
24.4750 g., 0.9170 Silver 0.7215 oz. ASW **Ruler:** Louis XV **Mint:** Pau **Obv. Legend:** ....RE.BD (ligate BD). **Note:** Mint mark: Cow. Issued for Province of Bearn.

Date	Mintage	VG	F	VF	XF	Unc
1723 Rare	9,046	—	—	—	—	—

KM# 472.28 ECU
23.5900 g., 0.9170 Silver 0.6955 oz. ASW **Ruler:** Louis XV **Mint:** Besancon **Note:** Mint mark: Back to back C's.

Date	Mintage	VG	F	VF	XF	Unc
1724	—	135	350	600	1,300	—
1725	—	135	350	600	1,300	—

KM# 472.27 ECU
23.5900 g., 0.9170 Silver 0.6955 oz. ASW **Ruler:** Louis XV **Mint:** Aix **Note:** Mint mark: &.

Date	Mintage	VG	F	VF	XF	Unc
1724	—	135	350	600	1,300	—
1725	—	110	265	500	1,150	—

KM# 472.26 ECU
23.5900 g., 0.9170 Silver 0.6955 oz. ASW **Ruler:** Louis XV **Mint:** Rennes **Note:** Mint mark: 9.

Date	Mintage	VG	F	VF	XF	Unc
1724	311,000	135	350	600	1,300	—
1725	2,431,000	110	265	500	1,150	—

KM# 472.1 ECU
23.5900 g., 0.9170 Silver 0.6955 oz. ASW **Ruler:** Louis XV **Mint:** Paris **Obverse:** Laureate armored bust right **Obv. Legend:** LUD • XV D • G • FR • ET NAV • REX • **Reverse:** 4 Fleur-de-lis form square at center, 4 crowns separated by back to back L's surround **Rev. Legend:** SIT NOMEN DOM • BENEDICTUM **Note:** Dav. #1329.

Date	Mintage	VG	F	VF	XF	Unc
1724A	—	135	350	600	1,350	—
1725A	—	135	350	600	1,350	—

KM# 472.2 ECU
23.5900 g., 0.9170 Silver 0.6955 oz. ASW **Ruler:** Louis XV **Mint:** Metz **Obverse:** Laureate armored bust right **Reverse:** 4 Fleur-de-lis form square at center, 4 crowns separated by back to back L's surround

Date	Mintage	VG	F	VF	XF	Unc
1724AA	27,000	135	350	600	1,350	—
1725AA	181,000	135	350	600	1,350	—

KM# 472.3 ECU
23.5900 g., 0.9170 Silver 0.6955 oz. ASW **Ruler:** Louis XV **Mint:** Rouen **Obverse:** Laureate armored bust right **Reverse:** 4 Fleur-de-lis form square at center, 4 crowns separated by back to back L's surround

Date	Mintage	VG	F	VF	XF	Unc
1724B	—	135	350	600	1,350	—
1725B	—	110	265	500	1,150	—

KM# 472.5 ECU
23.5900 g., 0.9170 Silver 0.6955 oz. ASW **Ruler:** Louis XV **Mint:** Caen

Date	Mintage	VG	F	VF	XF	Unc
1724C	102,000	135	350	600	1,350	—
1725C	—	110	265	500	1,150	—

KM# 472.6 ECU
23.5900 g., 0.9170 Silver 0.6955 oz. ASW **Ruler:** Louis XV **Mint:** Lyon

Date	Mintage	VG	F	VF	XF	Unc
1724D	313,000	135	350	525	1,300	—
1725D	839,000	135	350	525	1,300	—

KM# 472.7 ECU
23.5900 g., 0.9170 Silver 0.6955 oz. ASW **Ruler:** Louis XV **Mint:** Tours

Date	Mintage	VG	F	VF	XF	Unc
1724E	—	190	450	825	1,800	—
1725E	882,000	190	450	825	1,800	—

KM# 472.8 ECU
23.5900 g., 0.9170 Silver 0.6955 oz. ASW **Ruler:** Louis XV **Mint:** Poitiers

Date	Mintage	VG	F	VF	XF	Unc
1724G	18,000	190	450	825	1,800	—
1725G	228,000	135	350	525	1,300	—

KM# 472.9 ECU
23.5900 g., 0.9170 Silver 0.6955 oz. ASW **Ruler:** Louis XV **Mint:** La Rochelle

Date	Mintage	VG	F	VF	XF	Unc
1724H	—	90.00	225	425	975	—
1725H	—	190	525	975	2,100	—

KM# 472.10 ECU
23.5900 g., 0.9170 Silver 0.6955 oz. ASW **Ruler:** Louis XV **Mint:** Limoges

Date	Mintage	VG	F	VF	XF	Unc
1724I	—	135	350	600	1,350	—
1725I	—	90.00	225	425	975	—

KM# 472.11 ECU
23.5900 g., 0.9170 Silver 0.6955 oz. ASW **Ruler:** Louis XV **Mint:** Bordeaux **Obverse:** Laureate armored bust right **Obv. Legend:** LUD • XV D • G • FR • ET NAV • REX • **Reverse:** 4 Fleur-de-lis form square at center, 4 crowns separated by back to back L's surround **Rev. Legend:** SITNOMENDOM • BENEDICTUM

Date	Mintage	VG	F	VF	XF	Unc
1724K	—	150	375	675	1,500	—
1725K	—	150	375	675	1,500	—

KM# 472.14 ECU
23.5900 g., 0.9170 Silver 0.6955 oz. ASW **Ruler:** Louis XV **Mint:** Montpellier **Obverse:** Laureate armored bust right **Reverse:** 4 Fleur-de-lis form square at center, 4 crowns separated by back to back L's surround

Date	Mintage	VG	F	VF	XF	Unc
1724N	304,000	135	350	600	1,350	—
1725N	477,000	110	200	500	1,150	—

KM# 472.15 ECU
23.5900 g., 0.9170 Silver 0.6955 oz. ASW **Ruler:** Louis XV **Mint:** Riom **Obverse:** Laureate armored bust right **Reverse:** 4 Fleur-de-lis form square at center, 4 crowns separated by back to back L's surround

Date	Mintage	VG	F	VF	XF	Unc
1724O	42,000	150	375	675	1,500	—
1725O	415,000	130	300	575	1,450	—

KM# 472.16 ECU
23.5900 g., 0.9170 Silver 0.6955 oz. ASW **Ruler:** Louis XV **Mint:** Dijon **Obverse:** Laureate armored bust right **Reverse:** 4 Fleur-de-lis form square at center, 4 crowns separated by back to back L's surround

Date	Mintage	VG	F	VF	XF	Unc
1724P	—	135	350	600	1,350	—

KM# 472.19 ECU
23.5900 g., 0.9170 Silver 0.6955 oz. ASW **Ruler:** Louis XV **Mint:** Reims **Obverse:** Laureate armored bust right **Reverse:** 4 Fleur-de-lis form square at center, 4 crowns separated by back to back L's surround

Date	Mintage	VG	F	VF	XF	Unc
1724S	—	135	350	525	1,300	—
1725S	—	135	350	525	1,300	—

KM# 472.20 ECU
23.5900 g., 0.9170 Silver 0.6955 oz. ASW **Ruler:** Louis XV **Mint:** Nantes **Obverse:** Laureate armored bust right **Reverse:** 4 Fleur-de-lis form square at center, 4 crowns separated by back to back L's surround

Date	Mintage	VG	F	VF	XF	Unc
1724T	—	135	350	525	1,300	—
1725T	—	190	450	825	1,800	—

KM# 472.22 ECU
23.5900 g., 0.9170 Silver 0.6955 oz. ASW **Ruler:** Louis XV **Mint:** Lille **Obverse:** Laureate armored bust right **Reverse:** 4 Fleur-de-lis form square at center, 4 crowns separated by back to back L's surround

Date	Mintage	VG	F	VF	XF	Unc
1724W	—	135	350	600	1,350	—
1725W	—	150	375	675	1,500	—

KM# 472.23 ECU
23.5900 g., 0.9170 Silver 0.6955 oz. ASW **Ruler:** Louis XV **Mint:** Amiens **Obverse:** Laureate armored bust right **Reverse:** 4 Fleur-de-lis form square at center, 4 crowns separated by back to back L's surround

Date	Mintage	VG	F	VF	XF	Unc
1724X	—	135	350	600	1,350	—
1725X	—	110	265	500	1,150	—

KM# 472.25 ECU
23.5900 g., 0.9170 Silver 0.6955 oz. ASW **Ruler:** Louis XV **Mint:** Grenoble **Obverse:** Laureate armored bust right **Reverse:** 4 Fleur-de-lis form square at center, 4 crowns separated by back to back L's surround

Date	Mintage	VG	F	VF	XF	Unc
1724Z	51,000	135	350	525	1,300	—
1725Z	258,000	110	265	500	1,300	—

KM# 472.24 ECU
23.5900 g., 0.9170 Silver 0.6955 oz. ASW **Ruler:** Louis XV **Mint:** Bourges **Obverse:** Laureate armored bust right **Reverse:** 4 Fleur-de-lis form square at center, 4 crowns separated by back to back L's surround

Date	Mintage	VG	F	VF	XF	Unc
1725Y	—	135	350	600	1,350	—

KM# 472.21 ECU
23.5900 g., 0.9170 Silver 0.6955 oz. ASW **Ruler:** Louis XV **Mint:** Troyes **Obverse:** Laureate armored bust right **Reverse:** 4 Fleur-de-lis form square at center, 4 crowns separated by back to back L's surround

Date	Mintage	VG	F	VF	XF	Unc
1725V	319,000	135	350	525	1,300	—

KM# 472.17 ECU
23.5900 g., 0.9170 Silver 0.6955 oz. ASW **Ruler:** Louis XV **Mint:** Perpignan **Obverse:** Laureate armored bust right **Reverse:** 4 Fleur-de-lis form square at center, 4 crowns separated by back to back L's surround

Date	Mintage	VG	F	VF	XF	Unc
1725Q	—	135	350	600	1,350	—

KM# 472.18 ECU
23.5900 g., 0.9170 Silver 0.6955 oz. ASW **Ruler:** Louis XV **Mint:** Orléans **Obverse:** Laureate armored bust right **Reverse:** 4 Fleur-de-lis form square at center, 4 crowns separated by back to back L's surround

Date	Mintage	VG	F	VF	XF	Unc
1725R	—	135	350	600	1,350	—

KM# 472.12 ECU
23.5900 g., 0.9170 Silver 0.6955 oz. ASW **Ruler:** Louis XV **Mint:** Bayonne **Obverse:** Laureate armored bust right **Reverse:** 4 Fleur-de-lis form square at center, 4 crowns separated by back to back L's surround

Date	Mintage	VG	F	VF	XF	Unc
1725L	—	135	350	575	1,300	—

KM# 472.13 ECU
23.5900 g., 0.9170 Silver 0.6955 oz. ASW **Ruler:** Louis XV **Mint:** Toulouse **Obverse:** Laureate armored bust right **Reverse:** 4 Fleur-de-lis form square at center, 4 crowns separated by back to back L's surround

Date	Mintage	VG	F	VF	XF	Unc
1725M	—	135	350	575	1,300	—

KM# 472.4 ECU
23.5900 g., 0.9170 Silver 0.6955 oz. ASW **Ruler:** Louis XV **Mint:** Strasbourg **Obverse:** Laureate armored bust right **Reverse:** 4 Fleur-de-lis form square at center, 4 crowns separated by back to back L's surround

Date	Mintage	VG	F	VF	XF	Unc
1725BB	—	150	375	675	1,500	—

KM# 479 ECU
23.5900 g., 0.9170 Silver 0.6955 oz. ASW **Ruler:** Louis XV **Mint:** Pau **Obv. Legend:** ....RE.BD (ligate BD). **Note:** Mint mark: Cow. Issued for Province of Bearn.

Date	Mintage	VG	F	VF	XF	Unc
1725	364,000	125	300	450	1,000	—

KM# 487 ECU

29.4880 g., 0.9170 Silver 0.8693 oz. ASW **Ruler:** Louis XV **Mint:** Pau **Obv. Legend:** ....RE.BD (ligate BD). **Note:** Mint mark: Cow. Issued for Province of Bearn. Dav. #A1330.

Date	Mintage	VG	F	VF	XF	Unc
1726	424,000	25.00	35.00	55.00	160	—
1727	187,000	25.00	45.00	75.00	200	—
1728	—	25.00	45.00	75.00	200	—
1729	301,000	25.00	45.00	75.00	200	—
1730	416,000	25.00	35.00	55.00	160	—
1731	—	40.00	75.00	150	400	—
1732	446,000	25.00	45.00	75.00	200	—
1733	246,000	25.00	45.00	75.00	200	—
1734	—	25.00	45.00	75.00	200	—
1735	304,000	25.00	45.00	75.00	200	—
1736	158,000	25.00	45.00	75.00	200	—
1738	246,000	25.00	45.00	75.00	200	—
1739	—	30.00	50.00	100	300	—
1740	78,000	40.00	75.00	160	450	—

KM# 486.28 ECU

29.4880 g., 0.9170 Silver 0.8693 oz. ASW **Ruler:** Louis XV **Mint:** Besancon **Note:** Mint mark: Back to back C's.

Date	Mintage	VG	F	VF	XF	Unc
1726	—	30.00	45.00	75.00	200	—
1727	—	30.00	45.00	75.00	200	—
1731	—	30.00	45.00	75.00	200	—
1732	—	30.00	45.00	75.00	200	—
1733	—	30.00	45.00	75.00	200	—
1735	—	30.00	45.00	75.00	200	—
1736	—	30.00	50.00	100	300	—
1737	—	50.00	90.00	200	500	—

KM# 486.1 ECU

29.4880 g., 0.9170 Silver 0.8693 oz. ASW **Ruler:** Louis XV **Mint:** Paris **Obverse:** Bust left **Obv. Legend:** LUD • XV • D • G • FR • ET • NAV • REX • **Reverse:** Crowned round arms of France within sprays **Rev. Legend:** SIT NOMEN DOMINI BENEDICTUM **Note:** Dav. #1330.

Date	Mintage	VG	F	VF	XF	Unc
1726A	—	25.00	35.00	45.00	140	—
1727A	—	25.00	35.00	45.00	140	—
1728A	—	25.00	35.00	45.00	140	—
1729A	—	25.00	35.00	45.00	140	—
1730/29A	—	25.00	35.00	45.00	140	—
1730A	—	25.00	35.00	45.00	150	—
1731A	—	30.00	45.00	85.00	225	—
1732A	398,000	25.00	35.00	45.00	150	—
1733A	—	25.00	35.00	45.00	150	—
1734A	—	25.00	35.00	45.00	150	—
1735A	—	25.00	35.00	45.00	140	—
1736A	—	25.00	35.00	45.00	150	—
1737A	—	25.00	35.00	45.00	150	—
1738A	307,000	25.00	35.00	45.00	150	—
1739A	145,000	30.00	45.00	80.00	225	—

KM# 486.26 ECU

29.4880 g., 0.9170 Silver 0.8693 oz. ASW **Ruler:** Louis XV **Mint:** Rennes **Note:** Mint mark: 9.

Date	Mintage	VG	F	VF	XF	Unc
1726	2,630,000	25.00	35.00	45.00	140	—
1727	—	25.00	35.00	45.00	140	—
1728	727,000	25.00	35.00	55.00	160	—
1729	—	25.00	35.00	55.00	160	—
1730	—	25.00	35.00	45.00	140	—
1731	—	30.00	45.00	75.00	200	—
1732	—	25.00	35.00	55.00	160	—
1733	—	30.00	45.00	75.00	200	—
1734	—	25.00	35.00	45.00	140	—
1735	—	25.00	35.00	55.00	160	—
1736	—	25.00	45.00	75.00	200	—
1737	—	25.00	45.00	75.00	200	—
1738	164,000	25.00	35.00	55.00	160	—
1739	89,000	30.00	50.00	100	300	—
1740	81,000	30.00	50.00	100	300	—

KM# 486.27 ECU

29.4880 g., 0.9170 Silver 0.8693 oz. ASW **Ruler:** Louis XV **Mint:** Aix **Note:** Mint mark: &.

Date	Mintage	VG	F	VF	XF	Unc
1726	—	25.00	35.00	55.00	150	—
1727	191,000	25.00	35.00	55.00	150	—
1728	156,000	30.00	45.00	75.00	200	—
1729	215,000	30.00	45.00	75.00	200	—
1730	—	30.00	45.00	75.00	200	—
1731	—	30.00	45.00	75.00	200	—
1732	—	25.00	35.00	55.00	150	—
1733	—	25.00	35.00	55.00	150	—
1734	—	25.00	35.00	55.00	150	—
1735	—	25.00	35.00	55.00	150	—
1736	—	30.00	50.00	100	300	—
1737	—	25.00	45.00	75.00	200	—
1738/7	—	25.00	35.00	45.00	140	—
1738	—	25.00	35.00	45.00	140	—
1739	—	25.00	45.00	75.00	200	—
1740/39	—	25.00	45.00	75.00	200	—
1740	63,000	25.00	45.00	75.00	200	—
1740	—	25.00	45.00	75.00	200	—
1741	—	40.00	75.00	150	400	—

KM# 486.2 ECU

29.4880 g., 0.9170 Silver 0.8693 oz. ASW **Ruler:** Louis XV **Mint:** Metz

Date	Mintage	VG	F	VF	XF	Unc
1726AA	—	25.00	35.00	55.00	140	—
1727AA	—	25.00	35.00	55.00	140	—
1728AA	45,000	30.00	50.00	100	300	—
1729AA	—	25.00	45.00	75.00	200	—
1730/29AA	—	25.00	35.00	55.00	140	—
1730AA	—	25.00	45.00	75.00	200	—
1731AA	—	25.00	45.00	75.00	200	—
1732AA	—	25.00	45.00	75.00	200	—
1733AA	—	25.00	45.00	75.00	200	—
1734AA	—	25.00	45.00	75.00	200	—
1735/4AA	—	30.00	50.00	100	300	—
1735AA	—	30.00	50.00	100	300	—
1736AA	—	25.00	45.00	75.00	200	—
1737AA	—	25.00	45.00	75.00	200	—
1739AA	—	25.00	45.00	75.00	200	—

KM# 486.3 ECU

29.4880 g., 0.9170 Silver 0.8693 oz. ASW **Ruler:** Louis XV **Mint:** Rouen

Date	Mintage	VG	F	VF	XF	Unc
1726B	477,000	25.00	35.00	45.00	140	—
1727B	—	25.00	35.00	55.00	150	—
1728B	676,000	25.00	35.00	55.00	150	—
1732B	—	30.00	45.00	75.00	200	—
1733B	—	30.00	45.00	75.00	200	—
1734B	—	25.00	45.00	75.00	200	—
1735B	—	25.00	35.00	55.00	150	—
1736B	—	25.00	45.00	75.00	200	—
1737B	—	25.00	45.00	75.00	200	—
1738B	429,000	25.00	35.00	55.00	150	—
1739B	170,000	25.00	35.00	55.00	160	—
1740B	122,000	25.00	45.00	75.00	200	—

KM# 486.4 ECU

29.4880 g., 0.9170 Silver 0.8693 oz. ASW **Ruler:** Louis XV **Mint:** Strasbourg

Date	Mintage	VG	F	VF	XF	Unc
1726BB	—	25.00	35.00	55.00	150	—
1727BB	—	30.00	45.00	75.00	200	—
1728BB	—	30.00	45.00	75.00	200	—
1729BB	—	30.00	45.00	75.00	200	—
1730BB	—	30.00	45.00	75.00	200	—
1732BB	—	30.00	45.00	75.00	200	—
1733BB	—	30.00	45.00	75.00	200	—
1737BB	—	25.00	35.00	55.00	150	—
1738BB	518,000	25.00	35.00	55.00	150	—
1739BB	238,000	25.00	35.00	55.00	150	—
1740BB	81,000	30.00	45.00	75.00	200	—

KM# 486.5 ECU

29.4880 g., 0.9170 Silver 0.8693 oz. ASW **Ruler:** Louis XV **Mint:** Caen

Date	Mintage	VG	F	VF	XF	Unc
1726C	1,277,000	30.00	50.00	100	300	—
1727C	—	35.00	55.00	125	350	—
1728C	252,000	30.00	50.00	100	300	—
1738C	—	25.00	35.00	55.00	150	—
1740C	—	40.00	75.00	150	400	—

KM# 486.6 ECU

29.4880 g., 0.9170 Silver 0.8693 oz. ASW **Ruler:** Louis XV **Mint:** Lyon

Date	Mintage	VG	F	VF	XF	Unc
1726D	—	25.00	35.00	45.00	140	—
1727D	—	25.00	35.00	45.00	140	—
1728/7D	—	25.00	35.00	55.00	150	—
1728D	—	25.00	35.00	55.00	150	—
1729D	577,000	25.00	35.00	45.00	140	—
1730D	—	30.00	45.00	75.00	200	—
1731D	76,000	30.00	45.00	75.00	200	—
1732D	—	25.00	35.00	55.00	150	—
1733/2D	—	30.00	45.00	75.00	200	—
1733D	—	30.00	45.00	75.00	200	—
1734D	—	30.00	45.00	75.00	200	—
1736D	133,000	30.00	45.00	75.00	200	—
1737D	186,000	30.00	45.00	75.00	200	—
1738D	301,000	25.00	35.00	55.00	150	—
1739D	31,000	30.00	50.00	100	300	—
1740D	33,000	30.00	50.00	100	300	—

KM# 486.7 ECU

29.4880 g., 0.9170 Silver 0.8693 oz. ASW **Ruler:** Louis XV **Mint:** Tours

Date	Mintage	VG	F	VF	XF	Unc
1726E	834,000	30.00	45.00	75.00	200	—
1727E	476,000	30.00	45.00	75.00	200	—
1728E	263,000	30.00	45.00	75.00	200	—
1731E	15,000	30.00	45.00	75.00	200	—
1732E	153,000	30.00	50.00	100	300	—
1733E	145,000	30.00	50.00	100	300	—
1734E	113,000	30.00	50.00	100	300	—
1735E	135,000	30.00	50.00	100	300	—
1736/5E	—	30.00	50.00	100	300	—
1736E	109,000	30.00	50.00	100	300	—
1737E	80,000	30.00	50.00	100	300	—
1738E	213,000	25.00	35.00	55.00	150	—
1739E	—	30.00	50.00	100	300	—
1740E	75,000	30.00	45.00	75.00	200	—

KM# 486.8 ECU

29.4880 g., 0.9170 Silver 0.8693 oz. ASW **Ruler:** Louis XV **Mint:** Poitiers

Date	Mintage	VG	F	VF	XF	Unc
1726G	427,000	25.00	35.00	55.00	150	—
1727G	—	30.00	50.00	100	300	—
1728G	47,000	30.00	45.00	75.00	200	—
1736G	—	30.00	45.00	75.00	200	—
1737G	—	30.00	45.00	75.00	200	—
1738G	23,000	30.00	50.00	100	300	—
1739G	29,000	30.00	50.00	100	300	—
1740G	12,000	30.00	55.00	125	350	—

KM# 486.9 ECU

29.4880 g., 0.9170 Silver 0.8693 oz. ASW **Ruler:** Louis XV **Mint:** La Rochelle

Date	Mintage	VG	F	VF	XF	Unc
1726H	—	30.00	45.00	75.00	200	—
1727H	—	30.00	45.00	75.00	200	—
1728H	—	30.00	45.00	75.00	200	—
1729H	—	30.00	45.00	75.00	200	—
1730H	—	30.00	45.00	75.00	200	—
1731H	—	30.00	45.00	75.00	200	—
1732H	150,000	30.00	45.00	75.00	200	—
1733H	—	30.00	45.00	75.00	200	—
1734H	—	30.00	45.00	75.00	200	—
1735H	—	30.00	45.00	75.00	200	—
1736H	—	35.00	55.00	125	350	—
1737H	—	35.00	55.00	125	350	—
1738H	205,000	30.00	45.00	75.00	200	—
1739H	85,000	30.00	45.00	75.00	200	—
1740H	88,000	30.00	45.00	75.00	200	—

KM# 486.10 ECU

29.4880 g., 0.9170 Silver 0.8693 oz. ASW **Ruler:** Louis XV **Mint:** Limoges

Date	Mintage	VG	F	VF	XF	Unc
1726I	—	25.00	35.00	55.00	150	—
1727I	—	30.00	45.00	75.00	200	—
1728I	—	30.00	45.00	75.00	200	—
1729I	—	30.00	45.00	75.00	200	—
1730I	—	30.00	45.00	75.00	200	—
1731I	—	30.00	45.00	75.00	200	—
1732I	—	30.00	45.00	75.00	200	—
1733I	—	30.00	45.00	75.00	200	—
1734I	—	30.00	45.00	75.00	200	—
1735I	—	30.00	45.00	75.00	200	—
1736I	—	30.00	45.00	75.00	200	—
1737I	—	30.00	45.00	75.00	200	—
1738I	—	30.00	45.00	75.00	200	—
1739I	—	30.00	50.00	100	300	—
1740I	—	30.00	45.00	75.00	200	—

KM# 486.11 ECU

29.4880 g., 0.9170 Silver 0.8693 oz. ASW **Ruler:** Louis XV **Mint:** Bordeaux

Date	Mintage	VG	F	VF	XF	Unc
1726K	—	25.00	35.00	45.00	140	—
1727K	—	25.00	35.00	55.00	150	—
1728K	693,000	25.00	35.00	55.00	150	—
1729K	—	30.00	45.00	75.00	200	—
1730K	—	30.00	45.00	75.00	200	—
1731K	—	30.00	45.00	75.00	200	—
1732K	337,000	30.00	45.00	75.00	200	—
1733K	—	30.00	45.00	75.00	200	—
1734K	—	25.00	35.00	45.00	140	—
1735K	—	25.00	35.00	55.00	150	—
1737K	—	25.00	35.00	55.00	150	—
1738K	130,000	30.00	45.00	75.00	200	—
1739K	77,000	30.00	45.00	75.00	200	—
1740K	90,000	30.00	45.00	75.00	200	—

KM# 486.12 ECU

29.4880 g., 0.9170 Silver 0.8693 oz. ASW **Ruler:** Louis XV **Mint:** Bayonne

Date	Mintage	VG	F	VF	XF	Unc
1726L	—	25.00	35.00	45.00	140	—
1727L	—	30.00	45.00	75.00	200	—
1728L	—	25.00	35.00	55.00	150	—
1731L	—	25.00	35.00	55.00	150	—
1732L	—	25.00	35.00	55.00	150	—
1733L	—	25.00	35.00	55.00	150	—
1734L	—	25.00	35.00	55.00	150	—
1735L	—	25.00	35.00	55.00	150	—
1736L	—	25.00	35.00	55.00	150	—

Date	Mintage	VG	F	VF	XF	Unc
1737L	—	25.00	35.00	55.00	150	—
1738L	—	25.00	35.00	55.00	150	—
1739L	469,000	25.00	35.00	55.00	150	—
1740L	441,000	30.00	45.00	75.00	200	—
1741/0L	—	30.00	50.00	100	300	—
1741L	—	30.00	50.00	100	300	—

KM# 486.13 ECU

29.4880 g., 0.9170 Silver 0.8693 oz. ASW **Ruler:** Louis XV
Mint: Toulouse

Date	Mintage	VG	F	VF	XF	Unc
1726M	—	25.00	35.00	55.00	150	—
1727M	—	25.00	35.00	55.00	150	—
1728M	—	30.00	45.00	75.00	200	—
1731M	—	30.00	45.00	75.00	200	—
1732M	—	25.00	35.00	55.00	150	—
1733M	—	30.00	45.00	75.00	200	—
1734M	86,000	30.00	45.00	75.00	200	—
1735M	—	30.00	45.00	75.00	200	—
1736M	—	30.00	45.00	75.00	200	—
1737M	—	30.00	50.00	100	300	—
1738M	54,000	30.00	45.00	75.00	200	—
1739M	44,000	30.00	45.00	75.00	200	—
1740M	48,000	30.00	45.00	75.00	200	—

KM# 486.14 ECU

29.4880 g., 0.9170 Silver 0.8693 oz. ASW **Ruler:** Louis XV
Mint: Montpellier

Date	Mintage	VG	F	VF	XF	Unc
1726N	679,000	25.00	35.00	55.00	140	—
1727N	143,000	25.00	35.00	55.00	150	—
1728N	157,000	30.00	45.00	75.00	200	—
1730N	50,000	30.00	45.00	75.00	200	—
1732N	—	25.00	35.00	55.00	150	—
1733N	—	30.00	45.00	75.00	200	—
1734N	131,000	25.00	35.00	55.00	150	—
1735/4N	—	25.00	35.00	55.00	150	—
1735N	—	25.00	35.00	55.00	150	—
1736N	—	30.00	45.00	75.00	200	—
1737N	—	30.00	45.00	75.00	200	—
1738N	—	25.00	35.00	55.00	150	—
1739N	17,000	35.00	55.00	125	350	—
1740/39N	—	35.00	55.00	125	350	—
1740N	15,000	35.00	55.00	125	350	—

KM# 486.15 ECU

29.4880 g., 0.9170 Silver 0.8693 oz. ASW **Ruler:** Louis XV
Mint: Riom

Date	Mintage	VG	F	VF	XF	Unc
1726O	—	25.00	35.00	55.00	150	—
1727O	—	30.00	45.00	75.00	200	—
1728O	—	25.00	35.00	55.00	150	—
1730O	—	25.00	35.00	55.00	150	—
1731O	77,000	30.00	45.00	75.00	200	—
1732O	88,000	30.00	45.00	75.00	200	—
1733/2O	—	30.00	45.00	75.00	200	—
1733O	—	25.00	35.00	55.00	150	—
1734O	59,000	30.00	45.00	75.00	200	—
1735O	60,000	30.00	45.00	75.00	200	—
1736O	—	30.00	45.00	75.00	200	—
1737O	44,000	30.00	50.00	100	300	—
1739O	28,000	30.00	50.00	100	300	—
1740O	33,000	30.00	50.00	100	300	—

KM# 486.16 ECU

29.4880 g., 0.9170 Silver 0.8693 oz. ASW **Ruler:** Louis XV
Mint: Dijon

Date	Mintage	VG	F	VF	XF	Unc
1726P	—	25.00	35.00	55.00	150	—
1727P	—	25.00	35.00	55.00	150	—
1728P	—	30.00	45.00	75.00	200	—
1729P	—	30.00	50.00	100	300	—
1730P	—	30.00	45.00	75.00	200	—
1731P	—	30.00	45.00	75.00	200	—
1732P	—	25.00	35.00	55.00	150	—
1733P	—	30.00	50.00	100	300	—
1735P	—	30.00	45.00	75.00	200	—
1736P	—	35.00	60.00	125	375	—
1737P	—	30.00	45.00	75.00	200	—
1738P	15,000	30.00	45.00	75.00	200	—

KM# 486.17 ECU

29.4880 g., 0.9170 Silver 0.8693 oz. ASW **Ruler:** Louis XV
Mint: Perpignan

Date	Mintage	VG	F	VF	XF	Unc
1726Q	—	25.00	35.00	55.00	150	—
1727Q	—	30.00	45.00	75.00	200	—
1728Q	—	30.00	45.00	75.00	200	—
1729Q	89,000	25.00	35.00	55.00	150	—
1730Q	—	30.00	45.00	75.00	200	—
1731Q	—	30.00	50.00	100	300	—
1732Q	—	30.00	45.00	75.00	200	—
1733Q	—	30.00	45.00	75.00	200	—
1734Q	—	30.00	45.00	75.00	200	—
1735Q	—	25.00	35.00	45.00	140	—
1736Q	—	30.00	45.00	75.00	200	—
1737Q	—	30.00	45.00	75.00	200	—
1738Q	—	30.00	50.00	100	300	—
1739Q	4,917	55.00	125	375	650	—
1740Q	11,000	40.00	75.00	150	400	—

KM# 486.18 ECU

29.4880 g., 0.9170 Silver 0.8693 oz. ASW **Ruler:** Louis XV
Mint: Orléans

Date	Mintage	VG	F	VF	XF	Unc
1726R	—	25.00	35.00	55.00	150	—
1727R	—	30.00	45.00	75.00	200	—
1728R	—	25.00	35.00	55.00	150	—
1730R	—	30.00	45.00	75.00	200	—
1731R	—	30.00	45.00	75.00	200	—
1732R	88,000	30.00	45.00	75.00	200	—
1733R	—	30.00	45.00	75.00	200	—
1734R	—	30.00	45.00	75.00	200	—
1735R	—	30.00	45.00	75.00	200	—
1736R	—	30.00	45.00	75.00	200	—
1737R	—	30.00	45.00	75.00	200	—
1738R	45,000	30.00	45.00	75.00	200	—
1739R	40,000	30.00	45.00	75.00	200	—

KM# 486.19 ECU

29.4880 g., 0.9170 Silver 0.8693 oz. ASW **Ruler:** Louis XV
Mint: Reims

Date	Mintage	VG	F	VF	XF	Unc
1726S	—	30.00	50.00	100	300	—
1727S	—	25.00	35.00	55.00	150	—
1728S	—	30.00	45.00	75.00	200	—
1729S	—	25.00	35.00	55.00	150	—
1730S	—	25.00	35.00	55.00	150	—
1731/0S	—	30.00	45.00	75.00	200	—
1731S	—	30.00	45.00	75.00	200	—
1732S	—	30.00	45.00	75.00	200	—
1733/2S	—	30.00	45.00	75.00	200	—
1733S	—	30.00	45.00	75.00	200	—
1735S	—	30.00	45.00	75.00	200	—
1736S	—	30.00	50.00	100	300	—
1737S	—	30.00	45.00	75.00	200	—
1739S	16,000	30.00	50.00	100	300	—
1741S	—	40.00	75.00	150	400	—

KM# 486.20 ECU

29.4880 g., 0.9170 Silver 0.8693 oz. ASW **Ruler:** Louis XV
Mint: Nantes

Date	Mintage	VG	F	VF	XF	Unc
1726T	—	25.00	35.00	45.00	140	—
1727T	—	25.00	35.00	55.00	150	—
1728/7T	—	25.00	35.00	55.00	150	—
1728T	—	30.00	45.00	75.00	200	—
1729/8T	—	30.00	45.00	75.00	200	—
1729T	—	30.00	45.00	75.00	200	—
1730T	—	25.00	35.00	55.00	150	—
1731T	—	25.00	35.00	55.00	150	—
1732T	—	25.00	35.00	55.00	150	—
1733T	—	30.00	45.00	75.00	200	—
1734T	—	25.00	35.00	55.00	150	—
1735T	—	25.00	35.00	55.00	150	—
1736T	—	25.00	35.00	55.00	150	—
1737T	—	30.00	45.00	75.00	200	—
1738T	—	30.00	45.00	75.00	200	—
1739T	101,000	30.00	45.00	75.00	200	—
1740T	106,000	25.00	35.00	45.00	140	—

KM# 486.21 ECU

29.4880 g., 0.9170 Silver 0.8693 oz. ASW **Ruler:** Louis XV
Mint: Troyes

Date	Mintage	VG	F	VF	XF	Unc
1726V	596,000	25.00	35.00	55.00	150	—
1727V	194,000	30.00	45.00	75.00	200	—
1728V	137,000	30.00	45.00	75.00	215	—
1729V	64,000	30.00	50.00	100	300	—
1730V	54,000	30.00	50.00	100	300	—
1731V	22,000	30.00	50.00	100	300	—
1732/1V	—	30.00	45.00	75.00	200	—
1732V	35,000	30.00	50.00	100	300	—
1734V	33,000	40.00	75.00	150	400	—
1735V	36,000	40.00	75.00	150	400	—
1736V	34,000	40.00	75.00	150	400	—
1738V	19,000	40.00	75.00	150	400	—
1739V	17,000	30.00	50.00	100	300	—
1740V	22,000	35.00	55.00	125	350	—

KM# 486.22 ECU

29.4880 g., 0.9170 Silver 0.8693 oz. ASW **Ruler:** Louis XV
Mint: Lille

Date	Mintage	VG	F	VF	XF	Unc
1726W	—	25.00	35.00	55.00	150	—
1727W	567,000	25.00	35.00	55.00	150	—
1728W	126,000	25.00	35.00	55.00	150	—
1729W	77,000	30.00	45.00	75.00	200	—
1730W	88,000	30.00	45.00	75.00	200	—
1731W	82,000	30.00	45.00	75.00	200	—
1733W	42,000	30.00	45.00	75.00	200	—
1734W	31,000	30.00	45.00	75.00	200	—
1735W	82,000	30.00	45.00	75.00	200	—
1736W	25,000	30.00	45.00	75.00	200	—
1737W	34,000	30.00	45.00	75.00	200	—
1738W	64,000	30.00	45.00	75.00	200	—
1739W	17,000	30.00	50.00	100	300	—
1740W	28,000	30.00	50.00	100	300	—

KM# 486.23 ECU

29.4880 g., 0.9170 Silver 0.8693 oz. ASW **Ruler:** Louis XV
Mint: Amiens

Date	Mintage	VG	F	VF	XF	Unc
1726X	—	30.00	45.00	75.00	200	—
1727X	—	30.00	45.00	75.00	200	—
1728X	—	30.00	45.00	75.00	200	—
1729X	—	30.00	45.00	75.00	200	—
1730X	—	30.00	45.00	75.00	200	—
1731X	—	30.00	45.00	75.00	200	—
1732X	119,000	30.00	50.00	100	300	—
1733X	—	30.00	50.00	75.00	200	—
1734X	—	30.00	50.00	75.00	200	—
1735X	—	30.00	50.00	75.00	200	—
1736X	—	30.00	50.00	75.00	200	—
1737X	—	30.00	50.00	100	300	—
1738X	60,000	30.00	45.00	75.00	200	—
1739X	39,000	30.00	50.00	100	300	—

KM# 486.24 ECU

29.4880 g., 0.9170 Silver 0.8693 oz. ASW **Ruler:** Louis XV
Mint: Bourges

Date	Mintage	VG	F	VF	XF	Unc
1726Y	—	25.00	35.00	55.00	150	—
1727Y	—	30.00	45.00	75.00	200	—
1730/28Y	—	30.00	50.00	100	300	—
1730Y	27,000	30.00	50.00	100	300	—
1731Y	—	30.00	50.00	100	300	—
1732Y	27,000	30.00	50.00	100	300	—
1733Y	—	30.00	45.00	75.00	200	—
1734Y	—	30.00	45.00	75.00	200	—
1735Y	—	30.00	45.00	75.00	200	—
1737Y	—	30.00	45.00	75.00	200	—
1738Y	21,000	35.00	55.00	125	350	—
1739Y	20,000	35.00	55.00	125	350	—
1740Y	20,000	35.00	55.00	125	350	—

KM# 486.25 ECU

29.4880 g., 0.9170 Silver 0.8693 oz. ASW **Ruler:** Louis XV
Mint: Grenoble

Date	Mintage	VG	F	VF	XF	Unc
1726Z	721,000	30.00	45.00	75.00	200	—
1727Z	—	30.00	45.00	75.00	200	—
1728Z	—	40.00	75.00	150	400	—
1729Z	52,000	30.00	45.00	75.00	200	—
1730Z	—	30.00	45.00	75.00	200	—
1731Z	—	30.00	45.00	75.00	200	—
1732Z	30,000	30.00	45.00	75.00	200	—
1733Z	35,000	30.00	45.00	75.00	200	—
1734Z	106,000	30.00	45.00	75.00	200	—
1735Z	27,000	30.00	50.00	100	300	—
1736/5Z	—	35.00	55.00	125	350	—
1736Z	28,000	35.00	55.00	125	350	—
1737Z	22,000	35.00	55.00	125	350	—
1738Z	25,000	40.00	75.00	150	400	—
1739Z	46,000	30.00	50.00	100	300	—
1740Z	—	40.00	75.00	150	400	—
1741Z	—	40.00	75.00	150	400	—

KM# 512.1 ECU

29.4880 g., 0.9170 Silver 0.8693 oz. ASW **Ruler:** Louis XV
Mint: Paris **Obverse:** Head with headband left **Obv. Legend:** LUD • XV • D • G • FR • ET NAV • REX **Reverse:** Crowned round arms of France within sprays **Rev. Legend:** SIT NOMEN DOMINI BENEDICTUM **Note:** Dav. #1331.

Date	Mintage	VG	F	VF	XF	Unc
1740A	153,000	35.00	55.00	125	400	—
1740A	—	Value: 1,750				
1741A	—	25.00	35.00	75.00	200	—
1742A	115,000	25.00	35.00	75.00	200	—
1743/2A	—	25.00	35.00	75.00	200	—
1743A	122,000	25.00	35.00	75.00	200	—
1744A	103,000	30.00	45.00	100	300	—
1745/4A	—	30.00	45.00	100	300	—
1745A	76,000	30.00	45.00	100	300	—
1746/5A	—	25.00	35.00	75.00	200	—
1746A	390,000	25.00	35.00	75.00	200	—
1747/6A	—	30.00	45.00	100	300	—
1747A	50,000	30.00	45.00	100	300	—
1748A	55,000	30.00	45.00	100	300	—
1750/48A	—	35.00	55.00	125	400	—
1750A	55,000	30.00	45.00	100	300	—
1751A	—	30.00	45.00	100	300	—
1752A	39,000	30.00	45.00	100	300	—
1753A	41,000	30.00	45.00	100	300	—
1754A	—	30.00	45.00	100	300	—
1755A	—	30.00	45.00	100	300	—
1756A	180,000	25.00	35.00	75.00	200	—
1757A	—	25.00	35.00	75.00	200	—

Date	Mintage	VG	F	VF	XF	Unc
1758A	—	25.00	35.00	75.00	200	—
1759A	—	25.00	35.00	75.00	200	—
1760A	—	25.00	35.00	75.00	200	—
1761/0A	—	25.00	35.00	75.00	200	—
1761A	—	25.00	35.00	75.00	200	—
1762A	—	25.00	35.00	75.00	200	—
1763A	—	25.00	35.00	75.00	200	—
1764A	—	25.00	35.00	75.00	200	—
1765A	—	25.00	35.00	75.00	200	—
1766A	—	25.00	35.00	75.00	200	—
1767A	—	25.00	35.00	75.00	200	—
1768A	—	25.00	35.00	75.00	200	—
1769A	—	25.00	35.00	75.00	200	—
1770A	—	25.00	35.00	75.00	200	—
1772A	—	25.00	45.00	100	300	—

KM# 512.12 ECU

29.4880 g., 0.9170 Silver 0.8693 oz. ASW **Ruler:** Louis XV
Mint: Bayonne **Obverse:** Head with headband left **Reverse:** Crowned round arms of France within sprays

Date	Mintage	VG	F	VF	XF	Unc
1741L	—	25.00	35.00	75.00	200	—
1742L	316,000	25.00	35.00	75.00	200	—
1743L	538,000	25.00	35.00	75.00	200	—
1744L	—	25.00	35.00	75.00	200	—
1745L	—	25.00	35.00	75.00	200	—
1746L	342,000	25.00	35.00	75.00	200	—
1748L	—	30.00	45.00	100	300	—
1749L	100,000	25.00	35.00	75.00	200	—
1750L	—	25.00	35.00	75.00	200	—
1751L	—	25.00	35.00	75.00	200	—
1752L	—	25.00	35.00	75.00	200	—
1753L	—	30.00	45.00	100	300	—
1754L	118,000	25.00	35.00	75.00	200	—
1755L	—	30.00	45.00	100	300	—
1756L	—	25.00	35.00	75.00	200	—
1757/6L	—	25.00	35.00	75.00	200	—
1757L	—	25.00	35.00	75.00	200	—
1758L	—	30.00	45.00	100	300	—
1759L	—	30.00	45.00	100	300	—
1760L	—	30.00	45.00	100	300	—
1761L	—	25.00	35.00	75.00	200	—
1762L	—	25.00	35.00	75.00	200	—
1763/2L	—	25.00	35.00	75.00	200	—
1763L	—	25.00	35.00	75.00	200	—
1764L	—	25.00	35.00	55.00	150	—
1765L	—	25.00	35.00	55.00	150	—
1766L	—	25.00	35.00	55.00	150	—
1767L	—	25.00	35.00	75.00	200	—
1768L	—	25.00	35.00	55.00	150	—
1769L	—	25.00	35.00	55.00	150	—
1770L	—	25.00	35.00	75.00	200	—
1771L	—	25.00	35.00	55.00	150	—

KM# 512.13 ECU

29.4880 g., 0.9170 Silver 0.8693 oz. ASW **Ruler:** Louis XV
Mint: Toulouse **Obverse:** Head with headband left **Reverse:** Crowned round arms of France within sprays

Date	Mintage	VG	F	VF	XF	Unc
1741M	16,000	35.00	55.00	125	400	—
1742M	32,000	35.00	55.00	125	400	—
1744M	51,000	35.00	55.00	125	400	—
1745M	30,000	35.00	55.00	125	400	—
1747M	159,000	30.00	45.00	100	300	—
1748M	27,000	35.00	55.00	125	400	—
1750M	27,000	35.00	55.00	125	400	—
1751M	19,000	35.00	55.00	125	400	—
1752M	33,000	35.00	55.00	125	400	—
1754/3M	—	35.00	55.00	125	400	—
1754M	61,000	30.00	45.00	100	300	—
1755M	55,000	30.00	45.00	100	300	—
1756M	337,000	30.00	45.00	100	300	—
1757M	—	30.00	45.00	100	300	—
1758M	—	30.00	45.00	100	300	—
1759M	—	30.00	45.00	100	300	—
1760M	—	30.00	45.00	100	300	—
1762/0M	—	35.00	55.00	125	400	—
1763M	—	30.00	45.00	100	300	—
1764M	—	30.00	45.00	100	300	—
1765/4M	—	30.00	45.00	100	300	—
1765M	—	30.00	45.00	100	300	—
1766M	—	30.00	45.00	100	300	—
1767M	—	25.00	35.00	75.00	200	—
1768M	—	30.00	45.00	100	300	—
1769M	—	30.00	45.00	100	300	—
1770M	—	30.00	45.00	100	300	—

KM# 512.26 ECU

29.4880 g., 0.9170 Silver 0.8693 oz. ASW **Ruler:** Louis XV
Mint: Aix **Obverse:** Head with headband left **Reverse:** Crowned round arms of France within sprays **Note:** Mint mark: &.

Date	Mintage	VG	F	VF	XF	Unc
1741	18,000	45.00	75.00	175	500	—
1742	82,000	35.00	55.00	125	400	—
1743	82,000	35.00	55.00	125	400	—
1744	—	25.00	45.00	100	300	—
1745	—	25.00	35.00	75.00	200	—
1746/5	—	25.00	35.00	75.00	200	—
1746	—	25.00	35.00	75.00	200	—
1747	310,000	30.00	45.00	100	300	—
1748	—	30.00	45.00	100	300	—
1751	—	30.00	45.00	100	300	—
1753	—	35.00	55.00	125	400	—
1754	—	30.00	45.00	100	300	—
1755	—	30.00	45.00	100	300	—
1756	—	25.00	35.00	75.00	200	—
1759	—	35.00	55.00	125	400	—
1760	—	30.00	45.00	100	300	—
1761	—	35.00	55.00	125	400	—
1764	—	25.00	35.00	75.00	200	—
1765	—	30.00	45.00	100	300	—
1766	—	25.00	35.00	75.00	200	—
1767	—	25.00	35.00	75.00	200	—
1768	—	25.00	35.00	75.00	200	—
1769	—	25.00	35.00	75.00	200	—
1770	—	25.00	35.00	75.00	200	—
1771	—	25.00	35.00	75.00	200	—
1772	—	65.00	125	300	750	—

KM# 512.3 ECU

29.4880 g., 0.9170 Silver 0.8693 oz. ASW **Ruler:** Louis XV
Mint: Rouen **Obverse:** Head with headband left **Reverse:** Crowned round arms of France within sprays

Date	Mintage	VG	F	VF	XF	Unc
1741B	—	35.00	55.00	125	400	—
1742B	123,000	30.00	45.00	100	300	—
1743B	190,000	25.00	35.00	75.00	200	—
1744B	100,000	30.00	45.00	100	300	—
1747B	27,000	35.00	55.00	125	400	—
1748B	41,000	35.00	55.00	125	400	—
1749B	25,000	35.00	55.00	125	400	—
1750/48B	—	35.00	55.00	125	400	—
1750B	28,000	35.00	55.00	125	400	—
1751B	65,000	30.00	45.00	100	300	—
1752B	12,000	35.00	55.00	125	400	—
1753B	—	30.00	45.00	100	300	—
1754B	—	35.00	55.00	125	400	—
1756B	18,000	35.00	55.00	125	400	—
1759B	—	30.00	45.00	100	300	—
1760B	—	45.00	75.00	175	400	—
1763B	—	30.00	45.00	100	300	—
1764B	—	30.00	45.00	100	300	—
1767B	—	30.00	45.00	100	300	—
1769B	—	30.00	45.00	100	300	—
1770B	—	30.00	45.00	100	300	—
1771B	—	30.00	45.00	100	300	—

KM# 512.4 ECU

29.4880 g., 0.9170 Silver 0.8693 oz. ASW **Ruler:** Louis XV
Mint: Strasbourg **Obverse:** Head with headband left **Reverse:** Crowned round arms of France within sprays

Date	Mintage	VG	F	VF	XF	Unc
1741BB	—	35.00	55.00	125	400	—
1742BB	28,000	35.00	55.00	125	400	—
1743BB	22,000	35.00	55.00	125	400	—
1744BB	22,000	35.00	55.00	125	400	—
1745BB	47,000	35.00	55.00	125	400	—
1746BB	21,000	35.00	55.00	125	400	—
1748BB	41,000	35.00	55.00	125	400	—
1750BB	8,589	50.00	85.00	220	560	—
1753BB	5,710	45.00	75.00	175	500	—
1754BB	—	30.00	45.00	100	300	—
1757BB	—	30.00	45.00	100	300	—
1758BB	—	30.00	45.00	100	300	—
1759BB	—	25.00	35.00	75.00	200	—
1762BB	—	30.00	45.00	100	300	—
1767BB	—	30.00	45.00	100	300	—
1770BB	—	30.00	45.00	100	300	—
1772BB	—	45.00	75.00	175	500	—

KM# 512.7 ECU

29.4880 g., 0.9170 Silver 0.8693 oz. ASW **Ruler:** Louis XV
Mint: Tours **Obverse:** Head with headband left **Reverse:** Crowned round arms of France within sprays

Date	Mintage	VG	F	VF	XF	Unc
1741E	15,000	45.00	75.00	175	500	—
1742E	38,000	35.00	55.00	125	400	—
1743E	43,000	30.00	45.00	100	300	—
1744E	37,000	45.00	75.00	175	500	—
1745E	41,000	30.00	45.00	100	300	—
1746E	—	45.00	75.00	190	525	—
1747E	32,000	35.00	55.00	125	400	—
1748E	37,000	35.00	55.00	125	400	—
1749E	18,000	35.00	55.00	125	400	—
1750E	18,000	35.00	55.00	125	400	—
1751E	15,000	45.00	75.00	175	500	—
1753E	12,000	45.00	75.00	175	500	—
1754E	9,492	45.00	75.00	175	500	—
1757E	5,212	45.00	75.00	175	500	—
1760E	28,000	35.00	55.00	125	400	—
1763E	—	35.00	55.00	125	400	—
1764E	—	35.00	55.00	125	400	—
1768E	—	35.00	55.00	125	400	—

KM# 512.9 ECU

29.4880 g., 0.9170 Silver 0.8693 oz. ASW **Ruler:** Louis XV
Mint: La Rochelle **Obverse:** Head with headband left **Reverse:** Crowned round arms of France within sprays

Date	Mintage	VG	F	VF	XF	Unc
1741H	—	30.00	45.00	100	300	—
1742H	370,000	25.00	35.00	55.00	150	—
1743H	312,000	25.00	35.00	75.00	200	—
1744H	46,000	30.00	45.00	100	300	—
1745H	35,000	30.00	45.00	100	300	—
1746H	111,000	30.00	45.00	100	300	—
1747H	70,000	30.00	45.00	100	300	—
1748H	68,000	30.00	45.00	100	300	—
1749H	103,000	30.00	45.00	100	300	—
1750H	—	30.00	45.00	100	300	—
1752H	29,000	30.00	45.00	100	300	—
1754H	—	30.00	45.00	100	300	—
1755H	—	30.00	45.00	100	300	—
1756H	—	30.00	45.00	100	300	—
1757H	—	30.00	45.00	100	300	—
1759H	—	30.00	45.00	100	300	—
1760H	—	30.00	45.00	100	300	—
1761H	—	30.00	45.00	100	300	—
1763H	—	30.00	45.00	100	300	—
1764H	—	30.00	45.00	100	300	—
1765H	—	30.00	45.00	100	300	—
1766H	—	30.00	45.00	100	300	—
1767H	—	30.00	45.00	100	300	—
1769H	—	30.00	45.00	100	300	—
1770H	—	30.00	45.00	100	300	—

KM# 512.10 ECU

29.4880 g., 0.9170 Silver 0.8693 oz. ASW **Ruler:** Louis XV
Mint: Limoges **Obverse:** Head with headband left **Reverse:** Crowned round arms of France within sprays

Date	Mintage	VG	F	VF	XF	Unc
1741I	—	35.00	55.00	125	400	—
1742I	8,556	35.00	55.00	125	400	—
1743I	13,000	35.00	55.00	125	400	—
1744I	16,000	35.00	55.00	125	400	—
1745I	19,000	35.00	55.00	125	400	—
1746I	13,000	35.00	55.00	125	400	—
1747I	14,000	35.00	55.00	125	400	—
1749I	4,450	45.00	75.00	175	500	—
1750I	—	35.00	55.00	125	400	—
1754I	—	35.00	55.00	125	400	—
1755I	—	35.00	55.00	125	400	—
1757I	—	35.00	55.00	125	400	—
1758I	—	35.00	55.00	125	400	—
1761I	—	35.00	55.00	125	400	—
1762I	—	35.00	55.00	125	400	—
1763I	—	35.00	55.00	125	400	—
1764I	—	30.00	45.00	100	300	—
1765I	—	30.00	45.00	100	300	—
1767I	—	25.00	35.00	75.00	200	—
1768I	—	30.00	45.00	100	300	—
1769I	—	30.00	45.00	100	300	—
1770I	—	25.00	35.00	75.00	200	—

KM# 512.17 ECU

29.4880 g., 0.9170 Silver 0.8693 oz. ASW **Ruler:** Louis XV
Mint: Perpignan **Obverse:** Head with headband left **Reverse:** Crowned round arms of France within sprays

Date	Mintage	VG	F	VF	XF	Unc
1741Q	8,305	45.00	75.00	175	500	—
1742Q	14,000	35.00	55.00	125	400	—
1743Q	32,000	35.00	55.00	125	400	—
1745Q	—	35.00	55.00	125	400	—
1746Q	64,000	30.00	45.00	100	300	—
1747Q	—	30.00	45.00	100	300	—
1748Q	—	30.00	45.00	100	300	—
1750Q	—	30.00	45.00	100	300	—
1751Q	—	—	—	—	—	—

Date	Mintage	VG	F	VF	XF	Unc
1752Q	—	—	—	—	—	—
1753Q	—	30.00	45.00	100	300	—
1754Q	—	30.00	45.00	100	300	—
1755Q	—	30.00	45.00	100	300	—
1756Q	—	30.00	45.00	100	300	—
1757Q	—	30.00	45.00	100	300	—
1758Q	—	30.00	45.00	100	300	—
1759Q	—	30.00	45.00	100	300	—
1763Q	—	25.00	35.00	75.00	200	—
1764Q	—	25.00	35.00	75.00	200	—
1766/5Q	—	25.00	35.00	75.00	200	—
1766Q	—	30.00	45.00	100	300	—
1767Q	—	30.00	45.00	100	300	—
1768Q	—	25.00	35.00	75.00	200	—
1769Q	—	25.00	35.00	75.00	200	—
1770Q	—	30.00	45.00	100	300	—
1771Q	—	30.00	45.00	100	300	—

KM# 523.18 ECU

29.4880 g., 0.9170 Silver 0.8693 oz. ASW **Ruler:** Louis XV
Mint: Orléans

Date	Mintage	VG	F	VF	XF	Unc
1741/0R	—	40.00	65.00	150	450	—
1742/1R	—	30.00	45.00	100	300	—
1742R	26,000	35.00	55.00	125	400	—
1743R	31,000	35.00	55.00	125	400	—
1746R	12,000	35.00	55.00	125	400	—
1748R	17,000	35.00	55.00	125	400	—
1751R	4,214	45.00	75.00	175	500	—
1755R	—	35.00	55.00	125	400	—
1756R	232,000	25.00	35.00	75.00	200	—
1757R	—	35.00	55.00	125	400	—
1758R	—	35.00	55.00	125	400	—
1759R	—	25.00	35.00	75.00	200	—
1760R	—	30.00	45.00	100	300	—
1761R	—	30.00	45.00	100	300	—
1762R	—	30.00	45.00	100	300	—
1763R	—	25.00	35.00	55.00	150	—
1764R	—	30.00	45.00	100	300	—
1765R	—	25.00	35.00	75.00	200	—
1766R	—	25.00	35.00	75.00	200	—
1767R	—	30.00	45.00	100	300	—
1768/7R	—	30.00	45.00	100	300	—
1768R	—	35.00	55.00	125	400	—
1769R	—	30.00	45.00	100	300	—
1770R	—	45.00	70.00	165	475	—
1773R Rare	—	—	—	—	—	—

KM# 512.19 ECU

29.4880 g., 0.9170 Silver 0.8693 oz. ASW **Ruler:** Louis XV
Mint: Reims **Obverse:** Head with headband left **Reverse:** Crowned round arms of France within sprays

Date	Mintage	VG	F	VF	XF	Unc
1741S	—	35.00	55.00	125	400	—
1742S	—	55.00	100	275	650	—
1743S	10,000	35.00	55.00	125	400	—
1745S	—	25.00	35.00	75.00	200	—
1754S	—	45.00	75.00	175	500	—
1754/49S	—	65.00	125	300	750	—
1755S	—	45.00	75.00	175	500	—
1760S	—	30.00	45.00	100	300	—
1763S	—	45.00	75.00	175	500	—
1768/7S	—	75.00	145	350	825	—

KM# 512.20 ECU

29.4880 g., 0.9170 Silver 0.8693 oz. ASW **Ruler:** Louis XV
Mint: Nantes **Obverse:** Head with headband left **Reverse:** Crowned round arms of France within sprays

Date	Mintage	VG	F	VF	XF	Unc
1741T	—	25.00	35.00	75.00	200	—
1742T	302,000	25.00	35.00	75.00	200	—
1743T	172,000	25.00	35.00	75.00	200	—
1744T	431,000	25.00	35.00	75.00	200	—
1745T	229,000	30.00	45.00	100	300	—
1746T	105,000	25.00	35.00	75.00	200	—
1747T	69,000	40.00	60.00	125	400	—
1748T	46,000	40.00	60.00	125	400	—
1749T	117,000	30.00	45.00	100	300	—
1750T	156,000	30.00	45.00	100	300	—
1751T	125,000	30.00	45.00	100	300	—
1753T	26,000	45.00	75.00	175	500	—
1755T	—	25.00	35.00	75.00	200	—
1756T	26,000	40.00	60.00	125	400	—
1757T	—	30.00	55.00	110	320	—
1758/6T	—	30.00	55.00	110	320	—
1758T	—	30.00	55.00	110	320	—
1760T	—	30.00	55.00	110	320	—
1761T	—	30.00	55.00	110	320	—
1763T	—	30.00	55.00	110	320	—
1764T	—	30.00	55.00	110	320	—
1765T	—	30.00	55.00	110	320	—
1766T	—	30.00	55.00	110	320	—
1767T	—	30.00	55.00	110	320	—
1768/7T	—	30.00	55.00	110	320	—
1768T	—	30.00	55.00	110	320	—
1769T	—	30.00	55.00	110	320	—

KM# 512.21 ECU

29.4880 g., 0.9170 Silver 0.8693 oz. ASW **Ruler:** Louis XV
Mint: Troyes

Date	Mintage	VG	F	VF	XF	Unc
1742V	8,311	65.00	125	300	750	—
1746V	12,000	65.00	125	300	750	—
1747V	11,000	45.00	75.00	175	500	—
1748V	7,156	65.00	125	300	750	—
1753V	3,998	65.00	125	300	750	—
1754V	4,069	65.00	125	300	750	—
1755V	2,592	65.00	125	300	750	—
1756V	11,000	65.00	125	300	750	—
1758V	2,744	45.00	75.00	175	500	—
1759V	2,025	65.00	125	300	750	—
1760V	13,000	35.00	55.00	125	400	—
1763V	4,061	55.00	100	225	625	—
1767V	5,373	45.00	75.00	175	500	—

KM# 512.22 ECU

29.4880 g., 0.9170 Silver 0.8693 oz. ASW **Ruler:** Louis XV
Mint: Lille

Date	Mintage	VG	F	VF	XF	Unc
1742W	23,000	30.00	45.00	100	300	—
1743W	15,000	35.00	55.00	125	400	—
1745W	—	35.00	55.00	125	400	—
1746W	70,000	30.00	45.00	100	300	—
1748W	204,000	25.00	35.00	75.00	200	—
1749W	59,000	35.00	55.00	125	400	—
1759W	105,000	35.00	55.00	125	400	—
1760W	154,000	30.00	45.00	100	300	—
1761W	42,000	35.00	55.00	125	400	—
1762W	33,000	45.00	75.00	175	500	—
1763W	25,000	45.00	75.00	175	500	—
1764W	13,000	45.00	75.00	175	500	—
1765W	20,000	45.00	75.00	175	500	—
1767W	8,383	45.00	75.00	175	500	—
1768W	11,000	45.00	75.00	175	500	—
1770/69W	—	45.00	75.00	175	500	—
1770W	9,299	45.00	75.00	175	500	—
1772W	21,000	55.00	100	225	625	—

KM# 512.23 ECU

29.4880 g., 0.9170 Silver 0.8693 oz. ASW **Ruler:** Louis XV
Mint: Amiens **Obverse:** Head left **Obv. Legend:** LUD • XV • D • G • FR • ET • NAV • REX • **Reverse:** Crowned round arms of France within branches **Rev. Legend:** SIT NOMEN DOMINI BENEDICTUM

Date	Mintage	VG	F	VF	XF	Unc
1742X	7,336	55.00	100	225	625	—
1745X	32,000	45.00	75.00	175	500	—
1746X	—	45.00	75.00	175	500	—
1747X	—	35.00	55.00	125	400	—
1748/7X	—	35.00	55.00	125	400	—
1748X	—	35.00	55.00	125	400	—
1749X	—	30.00	45.00	100	300	—
1751X	18,000	35.00	55.00	125	400	—
1752X	18,000	35.00	55.00	125	400	—
1753X	11,000	35.00	55.00	125	400	—
1755X	—	75.00	150	375	850	—
1756X	17,000	35.00	55.00	125	400	—
1760X	—	30.00	45.00	100	300	—
1765X	—	35.00	55.00	125	400	—
1765X BENEDITUM	—	65.00	125	320	775	—
1767X	—	45.00	75.00	175	500	—
1770X	—	45.00	75.00	175	500	—

KM# 512.24 ECU

29.4880 g., 0.9170 Silver 0.8693 oz. ASW **Ruler:** Louis XV
Mint: Bourges **Obverse:** Head left **Reverse:** Crowned round arms of France within branches

Date	Mintage	VG	F	VF	XF	Unc
1742Y	18,000	45.00	75.00	175	500	—
1743Y	12,000	45.00	75.00	175	500	—
1744Y	19,000	45.00	75.00	175	500	—
1745Y	13,000	45.00	75.00	175	500	—
1746Y	11,000	45.00	75.00	175	500	—
1747Y	15,000	45.00	75.00	175	500	—
1749Y	12,000	45.00	75.00	175	500	—
1750Y	12,000	45.00	75.00	175	500	—
1751/0Y	—	45.00	75.00	175	500	—
1751Y	12,000	45.00	75.00	175	500	—
1752Y	—	35.00	55.00	125	400	—
1753Y	5,701	45.00	75.00	175	500	—
1754Y	—	45.00	75.00	175	500	—
1755Y	—	45.00	75.00	175	500	—
1756Y	—	30.00	45.00	100	300	—
1757Y	—	45.00	75.00	175	500	—
1760Y	—	35.00	55.00	125	400	—
1763Y	—	45.00	75.00	175	500	—
1766/5Y	—	75.00	145	350	800	—
1767Y	—	45.00	75.00	175	500	—

KM# 512.25 ECU

29.4880 g., 0.9170 Silver 0.8693 oz. ASW **Ruler:** Louis XV
Mint: Grenoble **Obverse:** Head left **Reverse:** Crowned round arms of France within branches

Date	Mintage	VG	F	VF	XF	Unc
1742Z	13,000	55.00	100	225	625	—
1743Z	4,666	55.00	100	225	625	—
1744Z	43,000	55.00	100	225	625	—
1745Z	43,000	55.00	100	225	625	—
1746Z	13,000	55.00	100	225	625	—
1748Z	2,230	65.00	125	300	750	—
1749Z	4,481	55.00	100	225	625	—
1760Z	28,000	55.00	100	225	625	—
1762Z	1,686	65.00	125	300	750	—
1765Z	2,471	55.00	100	225	625	—
1767Z	—	55.00	100	225	625	—

KM# 512.11 ECU

29.4880 g., 0.9170 Silver 0.8693 oz. ASW **Ruler:** Louis XV
Mint: Bordeaux **Obverse:** Head left **Reverse:** Crowned round arms of France within branches

Date	Mintage	VG	F	VF	XF	Unc
1742K	168,000	30.00	45.00	100	300	—
1743K	85,000	35.00	55.00	125	400	—
1744K	69,000	35.00	55.00	125	400	—
1745K	54,000	35.00	55.00	125	400	—
1746K	53,000	35.00	55.00	125	400	—
1748K	57,000	35.00	55.00	125	400	—
1749K	99,000	35.00	55.00	125	400	—
1750K	136,000	30.00	45.00	100	300	—
1751K	106,000	30.00	45.00	100	300	—
1752K	33,000	30.00	45.00	100	300	—
1753K	37,000	35.00	55.00	125	400	—
1754K	—	35.00	55.00	125	400	—
1755/4K	—	30.00	45.00	100	300	—
1755K	—	30.00	45.00	100	300	—
1757K	—	45.00	75.00	175	500	—
1758K	—	35.00	55.00	125	400	—
1759K	—	35.00	55.00	125	400	—
1761/0K	—	35.00	55.00	125	400	—
1761K	—	35.00	55.00	125	400	—
1763K	—	25.00	35.00	75.00	200	—
1764K	—	25.00	35.00	75.00	200	—
1765/4K	—	25.00	35.00	75.00	200	—
1765K	—	25.00	35.00	75.00	200	—
1766K	—	25.00	35.00	75.00	200	—
1767K	—	25.00	35.00	75.00	200	—
1768K	—	25.00	35.00	75.00	200	—
1769K	—	25.00	35.00	75.00	200	—
1770K	—	25.00	35.00	75.00	200	—

KM# 512.8 ECU

29.4880 g., 0.9170 Silver 0.8693 oz. ASW **Ruler:** Louis XV
Mint: Poitiers **Obverse:** Head left **Reverse:** Crowned round arms of France within branches

Date	Mintage	VG	F	VF	XF	Unc
1742G	3,351	45.00	75.00	175	500	—
1744G	4,078	35.00	55.00	125	400	—
1745G	13,000	35.00	55.00	125	400	—
1746G	2,937	35.00	55.00	125	400	—
1747G	2,505	35.00	55.00	125	400	—
1748G	2,832	55.00	100	225	625	—
1749G	—	65.00	135	300	800	—
1750G	—	35.00	55.00	125	400	—
1751G	1,765	55.00	100	225	625	—
1754G	—	35.00	55.00	125	400	—
1757G	—	35.00	55.00	125	400	—
1760G	—	35.00	55.00	125	400	—
1762G	—	35.00	55.00	125	400	—

Date	Mintage	VG	F	VF	XF	Unc
1765G	—	35.00	55.00	125	400	—
1771G	—	65.00	135	300	800	—

KM# 512.5 ECU

29.4880 g., 0.9170 Silver 0.8693 oz. ASW **Ruler:** Louis XV **Mint:** Caen

Date	Mintage	VG	F	VF	XF	Unc
1742C	23,000	35.00	55.00	125	400	—
1743C	21,000	35.00	55.00	125	400	—
1744C	46,000	35.00	55.00	125	400	—
1745C	34,000	35.00	55.00	125	400	—
1746C	32,000	35.00	55.00	125	400	—
1748C	34,000	35.00	55.00	125	400	—
1749C	23,000	35.00	55.00	125	400	—
1750C	26,000	35.00	55.00	125	400	—
1751C	16,000	35.00	55.00	125	400	—
1753C	15,000	35.00	55.00	125	400	—
1754C	15,000	35.00	55.00	125	400	—
1757C	11,000	35.00	55.00	125	400	—
1760C	90,000	25.00	40.00	85.00	300	—
1761C	10,000	35.00	55.00	125	400	—
1762C	11,000	35.00	55.00	125	400	—
1763C	11,000	35.00	55.00	125	400	—
1766C	6,514	45.00	75.00	175	500	—
1768/7C	—	65.00	125	300	750	—
1768C	6,008	55.00	100	225	625	—
1770C	6,256	55.00	100	225	625	—
1772C	—	65.00	125	300	750	—

KM# 512.27 ECU

29.4880 g., 0.9170 Silver 0.8693 oz. ASW **Ruler:** Louis XV **Mint:** Rennes **Obverse:** Head with headband left **Reverse:** Crowned round arms of France within sprays **Note:** Mint mark: 9.

Date	Mintage	VG	F	VF	XF	Unc
1742	89,000	35.00	55.00	125	400	—
1743	77,000	45.00	75.00	175	500	—
1744	—	30.00	45.00	100	300	—
1746	—	25.00	35.00	75.00	200	—
1747	—	30.00	45.00	100	300	—
1749	24,000	35.00	55.00	125	400	—
1751	27,000	35.00	55.00	125	400	—
1753/1	—	35.00	55.00	125	400	—
1753	19,000	35.00	55.00	125	400	—
1754	—	35.00	55.00	125	400	—
1755	—	35.00	55.00	125	400	—
1756	—	30.00	45.00	100	300	—
1757	—	30.00	45.00	100	300	—
1759	—	35.00	55.00	125	400	—
1762	—	35.00	55.00	125	400	—
1763	—	35.00	55.00	125	400	—
1764	—	35.00	55.00	125	400	—
1765	—	35.00	55.00	125	400	—
1766	—	35.00	55.00	125	400	—
1769	—	35.00	55.00	125	400	—

KM# 512.14 ECU

29.4880 g., 0.9170 Silver 0.8693 oz. ASW **Ruler:** Louis XV **Mint:** Montpellier **Obverse:** Head left **Reverse:** Crowned round arms of France within branches

Date	Mintage	VG	F	VF	XF	Unc
1742N	—	45.00	75.00	175	500	—
1743N	11,000	45.00	75.00	175	500	—
1744N	—	25.00	35.00	75.00	200	—
1747N	—	25.00	35.00	75.00	200	—
1748/7N	—	25.00	35.00	75.00	200	—
1748N	—	25.00	35.00	75.00	200	—
1752/48N	—	30.00	45.00	100	300	—
1752N	—	35.00	55.00	125	400	—
1753/48N	—	30.00	45.00	100	300	—
1753N	—	35.00	55.00	125	400	—
1759N	—	35.00	55.00	125	400	—
1763N	—	30.00	45.00	100	300	—
1764N	—	25.00	35.00	75.00	200	—
1765N	—	30.00	45.00	100	300	—
1766/5N	—	25.00	35.00	75.00	200	—
1766N	—	30.00	45.00	100	300	—
1767N	—	30.00	45.00	100	300	—
1768N	—	25.00	35.00	75.00	200	—
1769N	—	25.00	35.00	75.00	200	—
1770N	—	25.00	35.00	75.00	200	—

KM# 512.28 ECU

29.4880 g., 0.9170 Silver 0.8693 oz. ASW **Ruler:** Louis XV **Mint:** Besancon **Obverse:** Head with headband left **Reverse:** Crowned round arms of France within sprays **Note:** Mint mark: Back to back C's.

Date	Mintage	VG	F	VF	XF	Unc
1742	3,167	65.00	125	300	750	—
1752	2,565	65.00	125	300	750	—
1760	—	55.00	100	225	625	—
1765/4	—	55.00	100	225	625	—
1765	—	55.00	100	225	625	—

KM# 518 ECU

29.4880 g., 0.9170 Silver 0.8693 oz. ASW **Ruler:** Louis XV **Mint:** Pau **Obverse:** Head left **Obv. Legend:** ....RE.BD (ligate BD). **Reverse:** Crowned round arms of France within branches **Rev. Legend:** SIT NOMEN DOMINI BENEDICTUM **Note:** Mint mark: Cow. Issued for Province of Bearn. Dav. #A1331.

Date	Mintage	VG	F	VF	XF	Unc
1742	130,000	25.00	45.00	85.00	300	—
1745	40,000	35.00	65.00	175	500	—
1746	237,000	25.00	45.00	85.00	300	—
1747	147,000	25.00	45.00	85.00	300	—
1748	194,000	25.00	45.00	85.00	300	—
1749	139,000	25.00	45.00	85.00	300	—
1750	99,000	30.00	55.00	150	425	—
1751	—	30.00	55.00	150	425	—
1752	65,000	30.00	55.00	150	425	—
1753	115,000	25.00	45.00	85.00	300	—
1754	202,000	25.00	35.00	75.00	250	—
1755	207,000	—	—	—	—	—
1756	749,000	25.00	35.00	75.00	250	—
1757	454,000	25.00	35.00	75.00	250	—
1758/7	—	25.00	35.00	75.00	250	—
1758	317,000	25.00	35.00	75.00	250	—
1759	295,000	—	—	—	—	—
1760	299,000	25.00	35.00	75.00	250	—
1761	1,219,000	25.00	35.00	55.00	200	—
1762	1,139,000	25.00	35.00	55.00	200	—
1763	1,298,000	25.00	35.00	55.00	200	—
1764	1,724,000	25.00	35.00	55.00	200	—
1765	2,819,000	25.00	35.00	50.00	150	—
1766	1,560,000	25.00	35.00	55.00	200	—
1767	1,927,000	25.00	35.00	55.00	200	—
1768	1,388,000	25.00	35.00	55.00	200	—
1769	—	25.00	35.00	55.00	200	—
1770	1,122,000	25.00	35.00	55.00	200	—
1771	821,000	25.00	35.00	65.00	225	—

KM# 512.2 ECU

29.4880 g., 0.9170 Silver 0.8693 oz. ASW **Ruler:** Louis XV **Mint:** Metz

Date	Mintage	VG	F	VF	XF	Unc
1742/0AA	—	35.00	55.00	125	400	—
1742AA	—	35.00	55.00	125	400	—
1743AA	—	35.00	55.00	125	400	—
1750AA	—	35.00	55.00	125	400	—
1751AA	—	35.00	55.00	125	400	—
1752AA	—	35.00	55.00	125	400	—
1753AA	—	35.00	55.00	125	400	—
1754AA	—	35.00	55.00	125	400	—
1756AA	9,262	35.00	55.00	125	400	—
1759AA	—	35.00	55.00	125	400	—
1760AA	—	35.00	55.00	125	400	—
1762AA	—	35.00	55.00	125	400	—
1764AA	—	35.00	55.00	125	400	—
1765AA	—	35.00	55.00	125	400	—
1766AA	—	35.00	55.00	125	400	—
1767AA	—	35.00	55.00	125	400	—
1769AA	—	35.00	55.00	125	400	—

KM# 512.15 ECU

29.4880 g., 0.9170 Silver 0.8693 oz. ASW **Ruler:** Louis XV **Mint:** Riom **Obverse:** Head left **Reverse:** Crowned round arms of France within branches

Date	Mintage	VG	F	VF	XF	Unc
1743O	23,000	55.00	100	225	625	—
1746O	18,000	65.00	125	300	750	—
1747O	16,000	55.00	100	225	625	—
1760O	—	65.00	125	300	750	—

Date	Mintage	VG	F	VF	XF	Unc
1762O	—	55.00	100	225	625	—
1763O	—	45.00	75.00	175	500	—
1764O	—	45.00	75.00	175	500	—

KM# 512.16 ECU

29.4880 g., 0.9170 Silver 0.8693 oz. ASW **Ruler:** Louis XV **Mint:** Dijon **Obverse:** Head left **Reverse:** Crowned round arms of France within branches

Date	Mintage	VG	F	VF	XF	Unc
1743P	18,000	55.00	100	225	625	—
1746P	9,077	55.00	100	225	625	—
1749P	—	60.00	125	300	750	—
1752P	3,527	65.00	125	300	750	—
1760P	—	45.00	75.00	175	500	—

KM# 512.6 ECU

29.4880 g., 0.9170 Silver 0.8693 oz. ASW **Ruler:** Louis XV **Mint:** Lyon **Obverse:** Head left **Reverse:** Crowned round arms of France within branches

Date	Mintage	VG	F	VF	XF	Unc
1744D	17,000	35.00	55.00	125	400	—
1745D	5,795	45.00	75.00	175	500	—
1746D	—	30.00	45.00	100	300	—
1748D	31,000	30.00	45.00	100	300	—
1752D	98,000	30.00	45.00	100	300	—
1753D	17,000	35.00	55.00	125	400	—
1754D	163,000	25.00	35.00	75.00	200	—
1755D	47,000	35.00	55.00	125	400	—
1756D	—	25.00	35.00	75.00	200	—
1757D	—	35.00	55.00	125	400	—
1758D	—	35.00	55.00	125	400	—
1759D	—	25.00	35.00	75.00	200	—
1760D	—	35.00	55.00	125	400	—
1762D	—	35.00	55.00	125	400	—
1763D	—	25.00	35.00	75.00	200	—
1764D	—	25.00	35.00	75.00	200	—
1765D	—	25.00	35.00	75.00	200	—
1766D	—	25.00	35.00	75.00	200	—
1767D	—	30.00	45.00	100	300	—
1768D	—	35.00	55.00	125	400	—
1769D	—	25.00	35.00	75.00	200	—
1770D	—	35.00	55.00	125	400	—

KM# 551.1 ECU

29.4880 g., 0.9170 Silver 0.8693 oz. ASW **Ruler:** Louis XV **Mint:** Paris **Obverse:** Laureate head left **Obv. Legend:** LUD • XV • D • G • FR • ET • NAV • REX • **Reverse:** Crowned round arms of France within branches **Rev. Legend:** SIT NOMEN DOMINI BENEDICTUM **Note:** Dav. #1332.

Date	Mintage	VG	F	VF	XF	Unc
1770A	—	40.00	70.00	250	600	—
1770A Proof	—	Value: 2,500				
1771A	—	25.00	35.00	125	400	—
1771A Proof	—	Value: 3,000				
1772A	—	25.00	35.00	125	400	—

Date	Mintage	VG	F	VF	XF	Unc
1773A	37,000	30.00	50.00	175	500	—
1774A	1,740,000	25.00	35.00	125	400	—

KM# 551.18 ECU

29.4880 g., 0.9170 Silver 0.8693 oz. ASW **Ruler:** Louis XV **Mint:** Rennes **Obverse:** Laureate head left **Reverse:** Crowned round arms of France within branches **Note:** Mint mark: 9.

Date	Mintage	VG	F	VF	XF	Unc
1771	—	40.00	70.00	250	600	—

KM# 551.2 ECU

29.4880 g., 0.9170 Silver 0.8693 oz. ASW **Ruler:** Louis XV **Mint:** Metz **Obverse:** Laureate head left **Reverse:** Crowned round arms of France within branches

Date	Mintage	VG	F	VF	XF	Unc
1771AA	—	40.00	70.00	250	600	—
1773AA	—	45.00	85.00	300	800	—

KM# 551.4 ECU

29.4880 g., 0.9170 Silver 0.8693 oz. ASW **Ruler:** Louis XV **Mint:** Caen **Obverse:** Laureate head left **Reverse:** Crowned round arms of France within branches

Date	Mintage	VG	F	VF	XF	Unc
1771C	—	40.00	70.00	250	600	—

KM# 551.5 ECU

29.4880 g., 0.9170 Silver 0.8693 oz. ASW **Ruler:** Louis XV **Mint:** Lyon **Obverse:** Laureate head left **Reverse:** Crowned round arms of France within branches

Date	Mintage	VG	F	VF	XF	Unc
1771D	—	30.00	50.00	175	500	—
1772D	—	45.00	85.00	300	800	—
1773D	91,000	30.00	50.00	175	500	—
1774D	260,000	25.00	35.00	125	400	—

KM# 551.6 ECU

29.4880 g., 0.9170 Silver 0.8693 oz. ASW **Ruler:** Louis XV **Mint:** La Rochelle **Obverse:** Laureate head left **Reverse:** Crowned round arms of France within branches

Date	Mintage	VG	F	VF	XF	Unc
1771H	—	40.00	70.00	250	600	—
1772H	—	40.00	70.00	250	600	—
1773H	—	30.00	50.00	175	500	—

KM# 551.7 ECU

29.4880 g., 0.9170 Silver 0.8693 oz. ASW **Ruler:** Louis XV **Mint:** Limoges **Obverse:** Laureate head left **Reverse:** Crowned round arms of France within branches

Date	Mintage	VG	F	VF	XF	Unc
1771I	—	25.00	35.00	125	400	—
1772I	—	30.00	50.00	175	500	—
1773I	—	30.00	50.00	175	500	—
1774I	224,000	25.00	35.00	125	400	—

KM# 551.8 ECU

29.4880 g., 0.9170 Silver 0.8693 oz. ASW **Ruler:** Louis XV **Mint:** Bordeaux **Obverse:** Laureate head left **Reverse:** Crowned round arms of France within branches

Date	Mintage	VG	F	VF	XF	Unc
1771K	—	25.00	35.00	125	400	—
1772K	—	30.00	50.00	175	500	—
1773K	88,000	30.00	50.00	175	500	—
1774K	27,000	40.00	70.00	250	600	—

KM# 551.9 ECU

29.4880 g., 0.9170 Silver 0.8693 oz. ASW **Ruler:** Louis XV **Mint:** Bayonne **Obverse:** Laureate head left **Reverse:** Crowned round arms of France within branches

Date	Mintage	VG	F	VF	XF	Unc
1771L	—	30.00	50.00	175	500	—
1772L	—	30.00	50.00	175	500	—
1773L	—	25.00	35.00	125	400	—
1774L	2,428,000	25.00	35.00	125	400	—

KM# 551.10 ECU

29.4880 g., 0.9170 Silver 0.8693 oz. ASW **Ruler:** Louis XV **Mint:** Toulouse **Obverse:** Laureate head left **Reverse:** Crowned round arms of France within branches

Date	Mintage	VG	F	VF	XF	Unc
1771M	—	45.00	85.00	300	800	—
1772M	—	30.00	50.00	175	500	—
1773M	77,000	45.00	85.00	300	800	—
1774M	99,000	30.00	50.00	175	500	—

KM# 551.11 ECU

29.4880 g., 0.9170 Silver 0.8693 oz. ASW **Ruler:** Louis XV **Mint:** Montpellier **Obverse:** Laureate head left **Reverse:** Crowned round arms of France within branches

Date	Mintage	VG	F	VF	XF	Unc
1771N	—	30.00	50.00	175	500	—
1772N	—	40.00	80.00	275	700	—
1773N	—	30.00	50.00	175	500	—
1774N	49,000	40.00	70.00	250	600	—

KM# 551.15 ECU

29.4880 g., 0.9170 Silver 0.8693 oz. ASW **Ruler:** Louis XV **Mint:** Reims **Obverse:** Laureate head left **Reverse:** Crowned round arms of France within branches

Date	Mintage	VG	F	VF	XF	Unc
1771S	—	45.00	85.00	300	800	—
1772S	—	45.00	85.00	300	800	—

KM# 551.16 ECU

29.4880 g., 0.9170 Silver 0.8693 oz. ASW **Ruler:** Louis XV **Mint:** Nantes **Obverse:** Laureate head left **Reverse:** Crowned round arms of France within branches

Date	Mintage	VG	F	VF	XF	Unc
1771/69T	—	25.00	35.00	125	400	—
1771T	—	25.00	35.00	125	400	—
1772T	—	25.00	35.00	125	400	—
1773T	—	25.00	35.00	125	400	—
1774T	12,000	30.00	50.00	175	500	—

KM# 551.17 ECU

29.4880 g., 0.9170 Silver 0.8693 oz. ASW **Ruler:** Louis XV **Mint:** Lille **Obverse:** Laureate head left **Reverse:** Crowned round arms of France within branches

Date	Mintage	VG	F	VF	XF	Unc
1771W	—	40.00	70.00	250	600	—
1772W	21,000	30.00	50.00	175	500	—
1773W	—	30.00	50.00	175	500	—
1774W	388,000	25.00	35.00	125	400	—

KM# 555 ECU

29.4880 g., 0.9170 Silver 0.8693 oz. ASW **Ruler:** Louis XV **Mint:** Pau **Obverse:** Legend ends: ...RE. BD. (ligate BD) **Note:** Mint mark: Cow. Issued for Province of Bearn. Dav. #A1332.

Date	Mintage	VG	F	VF	XF	Unc
1771	—	30.00	50.00	175	500	—
1772	1,311,000	30.00	50.00	175	500	—
1773	529,000	30.00	50.00	175	500	—
1774	601,000	30.00	50.00	175	500	—

KM# 551.13 ECU

29.4880 g., 0.9170 Silver 0.8693 oz. ASW **Ruler:** Louis XV **Mint:** Perpignan **Obverse:** Laureate head left **Obv. Legend:** LUD • XV • D • G • FR • ET • NAV • REX • **Reverse:** Crowned round arms of France within branches **Rev. Legend:** SIT • NOMEN • DOMINI BENEDICTUM

Date	Mintage	VG	F	VF	XF	Unc
1771Q	—	40.00	70.00	250	600	—
1772Q	—	30.00	50.00	175	500	—
1773Q	—	30.00	50.00	175	500	—
1774Q	506,000	25.00	35.00	125	400	—

KM# 551.12 ECU

29.4880 g., 0.9170 Silver 0.8693 oz. ASW **Ruler:** Louis XV **Mint:** Dijon **Obverse:** Laureate head left **Reverse:** Crowned round arms of France within branches

Date	Mintage	VG	F	VF	XF	Unc
1772P	—	45.00	85.00	300	800	—

KM# 551.3 ECU

29.4880 g., 0.9170 Silver 0.8693 oz. ASW **Ruler:** Louis XV **Mint:** Rouen **Obverse:** Laureate head left **Reverse:** Crowned round arms of France within branches

Date	Mintage	VG	F	VF	XF	Unc
1772B	—	40.00	70.00	250	600	—
1773B	—	30.00	50.00	175	500	—
1774B	51,000	30.00	50.00	175	500	—

KM# 551.19 ECU

29.4880 g., 0.9170 Silver 0.8693 oz. ASW **Ruler:** Louis XV **Mint:** Aix **Obverse:** Laureate head left **Reverse:** Crowned round arms of France within branches **Note:** Mint mark: &.

Date	Mintage	VG	F	VF	XF	Unc
1772	—	30.00	50.00	175	500	—
1773	—	40.00	70.00	250	600	—
1774	581,000	30.00	50.00	175	500	—

KM# 564.1 ECU

29.4880 g., 0.9170 Silver 0.8693 oz. ASW **Ruler:** Louis XVI **Obverse:** Ornamental stitching on uniform **Obv. Legend:** LUD • XVI • D • G • FR • ET NAV REX **Reverse:** Crowned arms of France within branches **Rev. Legend:** SIT NOMEN DOMINI A BENEDICTUM

Date	Mintage	VG	F	VF	XF	Unc
1774 Proof	—	Value: 4,000				
1775	365,000	30.00	50.00	110	240	—
1775	Inc. above	30.00	50.00	110	240	—
1776	513,000	30.00	50.00	110	240	—
1776	Inc. above	30.00	50.00	110	240	—
1777	239,000	36.00	55.00	125	275	—
1778	4,464	—	—	—	—	—
1779	30,000	42.00	70.00	170	350	—
1780	15,000	55.00	95.00	210	425	—
1781	200,000	30.00	50.00	120	270	—
1781	Inc. above	30.00	50.00	120	270	—
1782	369,000	30.00	48.00	110	240	—
1782	Inc. above	30.00	48.00	110	240	—
1783	2,889,000	30.00	45.00	65.00	180	—
1783	Inc. above	30.00	45.00	65.00	180	—
1784/74	4,791,000	65.00	120	180	350	—
1784	Inc. above	30.00	45.00	65.00	180	—
1784	Inc. above	30.00	45.00	65.00	180	—
1785	571,000	30.00	45.00	110	240	—
1786	5,797	—	—	—	—	—
1787	11,000	48.00	80.00	210	425	—
1788	439,000	30.00	45.00	110	240	—
1789	—	36.00	55.00	120	240	—
1789	Inc. above	36.00	55.00	120	240	—
1790	3,086,000	30.00	45.00	65.00	180	—
1790	Inc. above	30.00	45.00	65.00	180	—
1791 (he)	1,756,000	30.00	50.00	120	250	—
1791 (he)	Inc. above	30.00	45.00	110	240	—
1791 (I)	Inc. above	100	200	450	1,200	—
1792	—	150	375	700	1,500	—

KM# 551.14 ECU

29.4880 g., 0.9170 Silver 0.8693 oz. ASW **Ruler:** Louis XV **Mint:** Orléans **Obverse:** Laureate head left **Reverse:** Crowned round arms of France within branches

Date	Mintage	VG	F	VF	XF	Unc
1774R	3,188	85.00	200	450	1,200	—

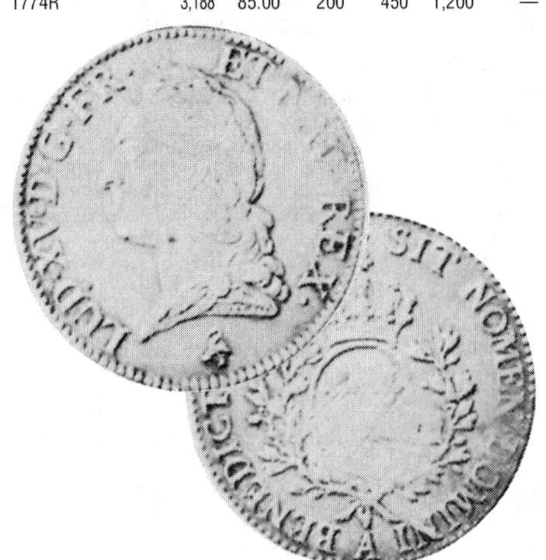

KM# 563 ECU

29.4880 g., 0.9170 Silver 0.8693 oz. ASW **Ruler:** Louis XVI **Mint:** Paris **Obverse:** Head left **Obv. Legend:** LUD • XV • D • G • FR • ET NAV REX • **Reverse:** Crowned arms of France within branches **Rev. Legend:** SIT NOMEN DOMINI A BENEDICTUM **Note:** Posthumous Issue. Louis XV died on May 1, 1774, consequently any second semester issues are posthumous.

Date	Mintage	VG	F	VF	XF	Unc
1774A	—	55.00	100	275	625	—

KM# 572 ECU

29.4880 g., 0.9170 Silver 0.8693 oz. ASW **Ruler:** Louis XVI **Mint:** Pau **Obverse:** Uniformed bust left **Obv. Legend:** ....RE.BD. (ligate BD). **Reverse:** Crowned arms of France within branches **Rev. Legend:** SIT NOMEN DOMINI BENEDICTUM **Note:** Mint mark: Cow. Issued for Province of Bearn. Dav. #1334.

Date	Mintage	VG	F	VF	XF	Unc
1775 (p)	184,000	25.00	40.00	100	225	—
1776 (p)	136,000	30.00	45.00	100	250	—
1777 (p)	241,000	25.00	40.00	100	225	—
1778 (p)	708,000	25.00	35.00	75.00	175	—
1779 (p)	1,948,000	20.00	30.00	50.00	140	—
1780 (p)	1,557,000	20.00	30.00	50.00	140	—
1781 (p)	1,141,000	20.00	30.00	50.00	140	—
1782 (p)	694,000	20.00	30.00	50.00	140	—
1783 (p)	811,000	20.00	30.00	50.00	140	—
1784 (p)	1,530,000	20.00	30.00	50.00	140	—
1785 (p)	1,857,000	20.00	30.00	50.00	140	—
1786 (p)	2,254,000	20.00	30.00	50.00	125	—
1787 (p)	646,000	20.00	30.00	60.00	150	—
1788 (p)	682,000	20.00	30.00	60.00	150	—
1789 (p)	3,122	55.00	95.00	225	475	—
1790 (p)	5,339	55.00	95.00	225	475	—
1791 (p)	1,690	80.00	125	300	650	—

KM# 564.2 ECU

29.4880 g., 0.9170 Silver 0.8693 oz. ASW **Ruler:** Louis XVI **Mint:** Metz

Date	Mintage	VG	F	VF	XF	Unc
1775AA	10,000	50.00	100	210	425	—
1776AA	7,246	50.00	100	210	425	—
1777AA	3,118	—	—	—	—	—
1778AA	3,652	60.00	110	240	550	—
1780AA	2,501	65.00	130	300	600	—
1781AA	4,639	60.00	110	240	475	—
1782AA	3,142	—	—	—	—	—
1785AA	5,491	55.00	110	240	550	—
1789AA	83,000	30.00	60.00	180	350	—
1790AA	—	30.00	50.00	120	270	—
Note: Mintage include in C#77.13						
1791AA	39,000	48.00	90.00	180	350	—

KM# 564.3 ECU

29.4880 g., 0.9170 Silver 0.8693 oz. ASW **Ruler:** Louis XVI **Mint:** Rouen **Obverse:** Uniformed bust left **Reverse:** Crowned arms of France within branches

Date	Mintage	VG	F	VF	XF	Unc
1775B	16,000	—	—	—	—	—
1776B	8,602	50.00	100	210	425	—
1777B	8,525	50.00	100	210	425	—
1778B	7,135	—	—	—	—	—
1779B	4,532	60.00	110	240	475	—
1780B	10,000	45.00	95.00	210	425	—
1781B	2,680	—	—	—	—	—
1783B	55,000	30.00	65.00	170	325	—
1784B	13,000	—	—	—	—	—
1785B	9,379	50.00	100	210	425	—
1786B	3,823	60.00	110	240	550	—
1787B	7,821	50.00	100	210	425	—
1788B	73,000	30.00	65.00	150	325	—
1789B	235,000	30.00	50.00	120	270	—
1790B	139,000	30.00	50.00	120	270	—
1791B	1,736	80.00	150	400	900	—

KM# 564.4 ECU

29.4880 g., 0.9170 Silver 0.8693 oz. ASW **Ruler:** Louis XVI **Mint:** Strasbourg **Obverse:** Uniformed bust left **Obv. Legend:** LUD • XVI • D • G • FR • ET NAV • REX **Reverse:** Crowned arms of France within branches **Rev. Legend:** SIT NOMEN DOMINI BENEDICTUM

Date	Mintage	VG	F	VF	XF	Unc
1775BB	3,347	60.00	110	240	475	—
1778BB	3,009	65.00	120	270	550	—
1779BB	4,783	60.00	110	240	475	—
1784BB	—	—	—	—	—	—
Note: Reported, not confirmed						
1790BB	65,000	36.00	65.00	180	325	—
1791BB	23,000	48.00	90.00	180	350	—

KM# 564.5 ECU

29.4880 g., 0.9170 Silver 0.8693 oz. ASW **Ruler:** Louis XVI **Mint:** Lyon **Obverse:** Uniformed bust left **Reverse:** Crowned arms of France within branches

Date	Mintage	VG	F	VF	XF	Unc
1775D	171,000	30.00	50.00	120	270	—
1776D	5,165	55.00	110	240	475	—
1777D	33,000	42.00	65.00	150	325	—
1778D	63,000	36.00	55.00	130	300	—
1782D	36,000	42.00	65.00	150	325	—
1789D	40,000	42.00	65.00	150	325	—
1790D	96,000	42.00	65.00	150	325	—
1791D	3,208	60.00	110	270	575	—

KM# 564.6 ECU

29.4880 g., 0.9170 Silver 0.8693 oz. ASW **Ruler:** Louis XVI **Mint:** La Rochelle **Obverse:** Uniformed bust left **Reverse:** Crowned arms of France within branches

Date	Mintage	VG	F	VF	XF	Unc
1775H	7,261	48.00	100	210	425	—
1776H	6,763	50.00	110	240	450	—
1777H	5,627	—	—	—	—	—
1778H	3,950	60.00	110	240	550	—
1779H	5,172	55.00	110	240	475	—
1780H	4,659	—	—	—	—	—
1781H	4,206	60.00	110	240	550	—
1782H	7,936	48.00	100	210	425	—
1783H	3,481	—	—	—	—	—
1784H	13,000	45.00	95.00	210	400	—
1785H	4,969	60.00	110	240	550	—
1786H	2,148	70.00	130	300	600	—
1787H	5,562	55.00	110	240	475	—
1788H	1,411	80.00	150	325	650	—
1789H	15,000	50.00	110	240	450	—
1790H	—	45.00	95.00	210	425	—

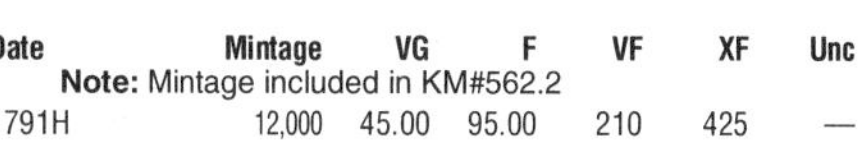

Date	Mintage	VG	F	VF	XF	Unc
Note: Mintage included in KM#562.2						
1791H	12,000	45.00	95.00	210	425	—

KM# 564.7 ECU

29.4880 g., 0.9170 Silver 0.8693 oz. ASW **Ruler:** Louis XVI **Mint:** Limoges **Obverse:** Uniformed bust left **Reverse:** Crowned arms of France within branches

Date	Mintage	VG	F	VF	XF	Unc
1775I	265,000	30.00	48.00	120	270	—
1776I	109,000	30.00	48.00	120	270	—
1777I	89,000	36.00	55.00	130	300	—
1778I	18,000	42.00	90.00	210	425	—
1779I	172,000	30.00	48.00	120	270	—
1780I	81,000	36.00	55.00	130	300	—
1781I	54,000	42.00	65.00	150	325	—
1782I	149,000	30.00	48.00	120	270	—
1783I	257,000	30.00	48.00	120	270	—
1784I	3,012,000	30.00	42.00	70.00	180	—
1785I	1,255,000	30.00	42.00	90.00	210	—
1786I	124,000	30.00	48.00	120	270	—
1787I	123,000	30.00	48.00	120	270	—
1788I	499,000	30.00	42.00	110	240	—
1789I	15,000	42.00	95.00	210	425	—
1790I	2,430,000	30.00	42.00	80.00	210	—
1791I	1,629,000	36.00	48.00	85.00	210	—

KM# 564.8 ECU

29.4880 g., 0.9170 Silver 0.8693 oz. ASW **Ruler:** Louis XVI **Mint:** Bordeaux **Obverse:** Uniformed bust left **Reverse:** Crowned arms of France within branches

Date	Mintage	VG	F	VF	XF	Unc
1775K	613,000	30.00	42.00	95.00	210	—
1776K	692,000	30.00	42.00	95.00	210	—
1777K	447,000	30.00	42.00	110	240	—
1778K	59,000	42.00	65.00	150	325	—
1779K	8,064	48.00	100	210	425	—
1780K	5,315	55.00	110	240	475	—
1781K	34,000	42.00	65.00	180	325	—
1782K	16,000	42.00	95.00	210	425	—
1783K	99,000	36.00	55.00	130	300	—
1784K	304,000	30.00	42.00	110	240	—
1784K Reversed K	Inc. above	60.00	110	240	550	—
1785K	185,000	30.00	48.00	120	270	—
1787K	4,195	48.00	110	240	475	—
1788K	—	42.00	90.00	180	400	—
1789K	42,000	42.00	65.00	150	325	—
1790K	105,000	30.00	48.00	120	270	—
1791K	3,652	60.00	110	260	550	—

KM# 564.9 ECU

29.4880 g., 0.9170 Silver 0.8693 oz. ASW **Ruler:** Louis XVI **Mint:** Bayonne **Obverse:** Uniformed bust left **Reverse:** Crowned arms of France within branches

Date	Mintage	VG	F	VF	XF	Unc
1775L	833,000	30.00	42.00	95.00	210	—
1776L	1,039,000	30.00	42.00	90.00	210	—
1777/6L	944,000	30.00	48.00	110	210	—
1777L	Inc. above	30.00	42.00	95.00	210	—
1778L	287,000	30.00	48.00	120	270	—
1779L	760,000	30.00	42.00	100	210	—
1780L	368,000	30.00	42.00	110	240	—
1781L	178,000	30.00	48.00	120	300	—
1782L	419,000	30.00	42.00	110	240	—
1783L	963,000	30.00	42.00	100	210	—
1784L	1,906,000	30.00	42.00	80.00	180	—
1785L	2,005,000	30.00	42.00	80.00	180	—
1786L	2,314,000	30.00	42.00	80.00	180	—
1787L	1,211,000	30.00	42.00	90.00	210	—
1788L	2,038,000	30.00	42.00	80.00	180	—
1789L	—	30.00	42.00	100	210	—
1790L	500,000	30.00	42.00	110	240	—
1791L	11,000	48.00	100	210	425	—

KM# 564.10 ECU

29.4880 g., 0.9170 Silver 0.8693 oz. ASW **Ruler:** Louis XVI **Mint:** Toulouse **Obverse:** Uniformed bust left **Reverse:** Crowned arms of France within branches

Date	Mintage	VG	F	VF	XF	Unc
1775M	132,000	30.00	48.00	120	300	—
1776M	88,000	36.00	55.00	130	300	—

Date	Mintage	VG	F	VF	XF	Unc
1777M	355,000	30.00	42.00	110	240	—
1778M	289,000	30.00	48.00	120	300	—
1779M	334,000	30.00	42.00	110	240	—
1780M	326,000	30.00	42.00	110	240	—
1781M	264,000	30.00	48.00	120	300	—
1782M	203,000	30.00	48.00	120	300	—
1783M	260,000	30.00	48.00	120	300	—
1784M	614,000	30.00	42.00	100	210	—
1785M	1,205,000	30.00	42.00	90.00	210	—
1786M	1,715,000	30.00	42.00	80.00	180	—
1787M	539,000	30.00	42.00	110	240	—
1788M	1,343,000	30.00	42.00	90.00	210	—
1789M	1,200,000	30.00	42.00	90.00	210	—
1790M	147,000	30.00	48.00	120	300	—
1791M	35,000	42.00	90.00	180	350	—
1792M	—	165	345	850	2,000	—

KM# 564.17 ECU

29.4880 g., 0.9170 Silver 0.8693 oz. ASW **Ruler:** Louis XVI **Mint:** Aix **Note:** Mint mark: &. The "dot" appears below the third letter of the monarch's name and denotes second semester coinage.

Date	Mintage	VG	F	VF	XF	Unc
1775	480,000	30.00	45.00	110	240	—
1776	5,951	—	—	—	—	—
1777	137,000	30.00	50.00	125	270	—
1778	5,685	—	—	—	—	—
1779	6,018	—	—	—	—	—
1780	5,327	—	—	—	—	—
1783	5,128	—	—	—	—	—
1784	3,181	—	—	—	—	—

KM# 564.12 ECU

29.4880 g., 0.9170 Silver 0.8693 oz. ASW **Ruler:** Louis XVI **Mint:** Montpellier

Date	Mintage	VG	F	VF	XF	Unc
1775N	190,000	30.00	48.00	120	300	—
1775N Inverted N	Inc. above	30.00	48.00	120	300	—
1776N	42,000	42.00	65.00	180	325	—
1777N	20,000	—	—	—	—	—
1778N	25,000	—	—	—	—	—
1779N	30,000	42.00	70.00	180	325	—
1780N	81,000	36.00	55.00	130	300	—
1781N	20,000	—	—	—	—	—
1782N	2,362	65.00	130	270	575	—
1783N	3,996	60.00	110	240	475	—
1784N	62,000	42.00	65.00	150	325	—
1785N	7,231	—	—	—	—	—
1787N	3,739	—	—	—	—	—
1789N	—	55.00	110	240	475	—
1790N	223,000	30.00	48.00	120	270	—
1791N	27,000	42.00	90.00	180	400	—

KM# 564.13 ECU

29.4880 g., 0.9170 Silver 0.8693 oz. ASW **Ruler:** Louis XVI **Mint:** Perpignan

Date	Mintage	VG	F	VF	XF	Unc
1775Q	429,000	30.00	45.00	110	240	—
1776Q	533,000	30.00	42.00	100	210	—
1777Q	262,000	30.00	48.00	120	270	—
1778Q	346,000	30.00	45.00	110	240	—
1779Q	108,000	30.00	48.00	120	270	—
1780Q	6,244	48.00	100	210	425	—
1781Q	1,006,999	30.00	42.00	95.00	210	—
1782Q	843,000	30.00	42.00	95.00	210	—
1783Q	495,000	30.00	42.00	95.00	240	—
1784Q	748,000	30.00	42.00	95.00	210	—
1785Q	963,000	30.00	42.00	95.00	210	—
1786Q	779,000	30.00	42.00	95.00	210	—
1786Q LUD. XI. (Error)	—	90.00	180	325	600	—
1787Q	415,000	30.00	45.00	110	240	—
1788Q	672,000	30.00	45.00	110	240	—
1789Q	905,000	30.00	42.00	95.00	210	—
1790Q	166,000	30.00	48.00	120	270	—
1791Q	5,050	60.00	130	240	475	—

KM# 564.14 ECU

29.4880 g., 0.9170 Silver 0.8693 oz. ASW **Ruler:** Louis XVI **Mint:** Orléans

Date	Mintage	VG	F	VF	XF	Unc
1775R	1,301	—	—	—	—	—
1776R	2,086	—	—	—	—	—
1777R	789	—	—	—	—	—
1780R	3,564	60.00	120	270	550	—
1781R	2,322	—	—	—	—	—
1782R	2,693	—	—	—	—	—
1783R	212,000	30.00	48.00	120	270	—
1784R	478,000	30.00	45.00	110	240	—
1785R	1,742,000	30.00	42.00	80.00	210	—
1786R	306,000	30.00	45.00	110	240	—
1787R	842,000	30.00	42.00	95.00	210	—
1788R	7,715	—	—	—	—	—
1789R	596,000	30.00	45.00	110	240	—
1790R	58,000	42.00	65.00	150	350	—
1791R	8,740	55.00	110	240	475	—

KM# 564.15 ECU

29.4880 g., 0.9170 Silver 0.8693 oz. ASW **Ruler:** Louis XVI **Mint:** Nantes

Date	Mintage	VG	F	VF	XF	Unc
1775T	15,000	42.00	90.00	180	400	—
1776T	12,000	—	—	—	—	—
1777T	18,000	42.00	90.00	180	400	—
1778T	10,000	—	—	—	—	—
1779T	10,000	42.00	95.00	210	425	—
1780T	7,752	48.00	100	210	425	—
1781T	11,000	42.00	95.00	180	400	—
1782T	16,000	42.00	95.00	180	400	—
1783T	15,000	42.00	95.00	180	400	—
1784T	20,000	42.00	95.00	180	400	—
1785T	7,992	48.00	110	240	475	—
1787T	18,000	42.00	95.00	180	400	—
1788T	5,729	—	—	—	—	—
1789T	—	42.00	95.00	180	400	—
1790T	—	42.00	65.00	150	325	—
1791T	19,000	42.00	95.00	180	400	—

KM# 564.16 ECU

29.4880 g., 0.9170 Silver 0.8693 oz. ASW **Ruler:** Louis XVI **Mint:** Lille

Date	Mintage	VG	F	VF	XF	Unc
1775W	1,336,000	30.00	42.00	90.00	210	—
1775W Inverted W	Inc. above	30.00	42.00	90.00	210	—
1776W	450,000	30.00	42.00	110	240	—
1777W	261,000	30.00	48.00	130	270	—
1778W	60,000	42.00	55.00	130	300	—
1779W	40,000	42.00	65.00	150	325	—
1780W	8,715	—	—	—	—	—
1781W	12,000	42.00	95.00	210	425	—
1782W	2,822	—	—	—	—	—
1783W	114,000	30.00	48.00	120	270	—
1784W	8,051	48.00	100	210	425	—
1785W	2,739	65.00	130	270	575	—
1786W	—	42.00	90.00	180	400	—
1787W	2,822	65.00	130	270	575	—
1788W	203,000	30.00	48.00	120	270	—
1789W	—	36.00	60.00	150	325	—
1790W	104,000	30.00	48.00	120	270	—
1791W	26,000	42.00	90.00	180	400	—

KM# 564.11 ECU

29.4880 g., 0.9170 Silver 0.8693 oz. ASW **Ruler:** Louis XVI **Mint:** Marseille **Obverse:** Uniformed bust left **Reverse:** Crowned arms of France within branches

Date	Mintage	VG	F	VF	XF	Unc
1787MA	—	—	—	—	—	—
Note: Reported, not confirmed						
1788MA	30,000	—	—	—	—	—
1789MA	—	60.00	110	240	550	—
1790MA	243,000	36.00	80.00	150	400	—
1791MA	40,000	60.00	110	240	550	—

KM# 615.1 ECU (6 Livres)

30.0000 g., 0.9170 Silver 0.8844 oz. ASW **Mint:** Paris **Obverse:** Head left **Obv. Legend:** LOUIS XVI ROI DES FRANCOIS • **Reverse:** Standing Genius writing the Constitution **Rev. Legend:** REGNE DE LALOI • **Note:** Dav. #1335.

Date	Mintage	VG	F	VF	XF	Unc
1792A	—	35.00	75.00	125	250	—
1793A	—	35.00	75.00	125	250	—

KM# 616 ECU (6 Livres)

30.0000 g., 0.9170 Silver 0.8844 oz. ASW **Mint:** Strasbourg **Obverse:** Legend ends: ...FRANCAIS **Note:** Weak strikes and adjustment filing marks are quite common for this series. Specimens fully struck without adjustment marks command a premium. Dav. #1335A.

Date	Mintage	VG	F	VF	XF	Unc
1792BB	—	175	325	725	1,750	—
1793BB	—	200	425	900	2,250	—

KM# 332.7 1/2 LOUIS D'OR

3.3500 g., 0.9170 Gold 0.0988 oz. AGW **Ruler:** Louis XIV **Mint:** Montpellier

Date	Mintage	VG	F	VF	XF	Unc
1701N	—	240	425	675	1,150	—
1702N Rare	—	—	—	—	—	—
1703N Rare	—	—	—	—	—	—

KM# 332.8 1/2 LOUIS D'OR

3.3500 g., 0.9170 Gold 0.0988 oz. AGW **Ruler:** Louis XIV **Mint:** Riom

Date	Mintage	VG	F	VF	XF	Unc
17010	—	350	475	775	1,400	—
17020	—	270	450	650	1,200	—

KM# 332.1 1/2 LOUIS D'OR

3.3500 g., 0.9170 Gold 0.0988 oz. AGW **Ruler:** Louis XIV **Mint:** Paris **Obverse:** Laureate head of Louis XIV **Reverse:** 8 "L's" cruciform with crown at end of each arm; batons in angles, mint mark at center

Date	Mintage	VG	F	VF	XF	Unc
1701A	—	240	425	600	1,150	—
1702A	—	240	425	600	1,100	—
1704A	—	300	550	775	1,300	—

KM# 332.5 1/2 LOUIS D'OR

3.3500 g., 0.9170 Gold 0.0988 oz. AGW **Ruler:** Louis XIV **Mint:** Bordeaux

Date	Mintage	VG	F	VF	XF	Unc
1701K	—	240	425	600	1,100	—

KM# 332.16 1/2 LOUIS D'OR

3.3500 g., 0.9170 Gold 0.0988 oz. AGW **Ruler:** Louis XIV **Mint:** Aix **Note:** Mint mark: &.

Date	Mintage	VG	F	VF	XF	Unc
1701	—	240	425	600	1,100	—

KM# 332.15 1/2 LOUIS D'OR

3.3500 g., 0.9170 Gold 0.0988 oz. AGW **Ruler:** Louis XIV **Mint:** Rennes **Note:** Mint mark: 9.

Date	Mintage	VG	F	VF	XF	Unc
1701	—	240	425	600	1,100	—

KM# 332.17 1/2 LOUIS D'OR

3.3500 g., 0.9170 Gold 0.0988 oz. AGW **Ruler:** Louis XIV **Mint:** Besancon **Note:** Mint mark: Back to back C's.

Date	Mintage	VG	F	VF	XF	Unc
1701	—	240	425	600	1,100	—

KM# 333 1/2 LOUIS D'OR

3.3500 g., 0.9170 Gold 0.0988 oz. AGW **Ruler:** Louis XIV **Mint:** Pau **Obv. Legend:** ....RE.BD (ligate BD). **Note:** Mint mark: Cow. Issued for Province of Bearn.

Date	Mintage	VG	F	VF	XF	Unc
1701	—	240	425	600	1,100	—

KM# 332.6 1/2 LOUIS D'OR

3.3500 g., 0.9170 Gold 0.0988 oz. AGW **Ruler:** Louis XIV **Mint:** Toulouse

Date	Mintage	VG	F	VF	XF	Unc
1702M	—	240	425	600	1,100	—

KM# 332.2 1/2 LOUIS D'OR

3.3500 g., 0.9170 Gold 0.0988 oz. AGW **Ruler:** Louis XIV **Mint:** Rouen

Date	Mintage	VG	F	VF	XF	Unc
1702B	—	240	425	600	1,100	—

KM# 332.3 1/2 LOUIS D'OR

3.3500 g., 0.9170 Gold 0.0988 oz. AGW **Ruler:** Louis XIV **Mint:** Caen

Date	Mintage	VG	F	VF	XF	Unc
1702C	—	240	425	600	1,100	—

KM# 332.4 1/2 LOUIS D'OR

3.3500 g., 0.9170 Gold 0.0988 oz. AGW **Ruler:** Louis XIV **Mint:** Lyon

Date	Mintage	VG	F	VF	XF	Unc
1702D	—	240	425	600	1,100	—

KM# 332.9 1/2 LOUIS D'OR

3.3500 g., 0.9170 Gold 0.0988 oz. AGW **Ruler:** Louis XIV **Mint:** Dijon

Date	Mintage	VG	F	VF	XF	Unc
1702P	—	240	425	600	1,100	—

KM# 332.10 1/2 LOUIS D'OR

3.3500 g., 0.9170 Gold 0.0988 oz. AGW **Ruler:** Louis XIV **Mint:** Nantes

Date	Mintage	VG	F	VF	XF	Unc
1702T	—	240	425	600	1,100	—
1704T Rare	—	—	—	—	—	—

KM# 332.11 1/2 LOUIS D'OR

3.3500 g., 0.9170 Gold 0.0988 oz. AGW **Ruler:** Louis XIV **Mint:** Troyes

Date	Mintage	VG	F	VF	XF	Unc
1702V Rare	—	—	—	—	—	—
1703V Rare	—	—	—	—	—	—

KM# 332.12 1/2 LOUIS D'OR
3.3500 g., 0.9170 Gold 0.0988 oz. AGW **Ruler:** Louis XIV **Mint:** Lille

Date	Mintage	VG	F	VF	XF	Unc
1702W Rare	—	—	—	—	—	—
1703W Rare	—	—	—	—	—	—

KM# 332.13 1/2 LOUIS D'OR
3.3500 g., 0.9170 Gold 0.0988 oz. AGW **Ruler:** Louis XIV **Mint:** Amiens

Date	Mintage	VG	F	VF	XF	Unc
1702X	—	240	425	600	1,100	—

KM# 332.14 1/2 LOUIS D'OR
3.3500 g., 0.9170 Gold 0.0988 oz. AGW **Ruler:** Louis XIV **Mint:** Bourges

Date	Mintage	VG	F	VF	XF	Unc
1702Y	—	270	450	650	1,200	—

KM# 363.1 1/2 LOUIS D'OR
3.3500 g., 0.9170 Gold 0.0988 oz. AGW **Ruler:** Louis XIV **Mint:** Paris **Reverse:** Alternate batons and crowned fleur-de-lis, mm at center

Date	Mintage	VG	F	VF	XF	Unc
1704A	—	400	725	950	1,700	—
1705A	—	400	725	950	1,700	—
1709A Rare	—	—	—	—	—	—

KM# 363.2 1/2 LOUIS D'OR
3.3500 g., 0.9170 Gold 0.0988 oz. AGW **Ruler:** Louis XIV **Mint:** Metz

Date	Mintage	VG	F	VF	XF	Unc
1704AA	—	475	850	1,100	1,750	—

KM# 363.3 1/2 LOUIS D'OR
3.3500 g., 0.9170 Gold 0.0988 oz. AGW **Ruler:** Louis XIV **Mint:** Rouen

Date	Mintage	VG	F	VF	XF	Unc
1704B	—	475	850	900	1,750	—
1705B	—	475	850	900	1,750	—

KM# 363.4 1/2 LOUIS D'OR
3.3500 g., 0.9170 Gold 0.0988 oz. AGW **Ruler:** Louis XIV **Mint:** Strasbourg

Date	Mintage	VG	F	VF	XF	Unc
1704BB	—	475	850	1,100	1,800	—

KM# 363.5 1/2 LOUIS D'OR
3.3500 g., 0.9170 Gold 0.0988 oz. AGW **Ruler:** Louis XIV **Mint:** Caen

Date	Mintage	VG	F	VF	XF	Unc
1704C	—	475	850	1,100	1,750	—

KM# 363.6 1/2 LOUIS D'OR
3.3500 g., 0.9170 Gold 0.0988 oz. AGW **Ruler:** Louis XIV **Mint:** Lyon

Date	Mintage	VG	F	VF	XF	Unc
1704D Rare	—	—	—	—	—	—

KM# 363.8 1/2 LOUIS D'OR
3.3500 g., 0.9170 Gold 0.0988 oz. AGW **Ruler:** Louis XIV **Mint:** La Rochelle

Date	Mintage	VG	F	VF	XF	Unc
1704H	—	475	850	1,100	1,750	—
1705H	—	475	850	1,100	1,750	—

KM# 363.9 1/2 LOUIS D'OR
3.3500 g., 0.9170 Gold 0.0988 oz. AGW **Ruler:** Louis XIV **Mint:** Bayonne

Date	Mintage	VG	F	VF	XF	Unc
1704L	—	—	—	—	—	—

Note: Reported, not confirmed

KM# 363.10 1/2 LOUIS D'OR
3.3500 g., 0.9170 Gold 0.0988 oz. AGW **Ruler:** Louis XIV **Mint:** Toulouse

Date	Mintage	VG	F	VF	XF	Unc
1704M	—	475	850	1,100	1,750	—

KM# 363.11 1/2 LOUIS D'OR
3.3500 g., 0.9170 Gold 0.0988 oz. AGW **Ruler:** Louis XIV **Mint:** Montpellier

Date	Mintage	VG	F	VF	XF	Unc
1704N Rare	—	—	—	—	—	—
1705N Rare	—	—	—	—	—	—

KM# 363.12 1/2 LOUIS D'OR
3.3500 g., 0.9170 Gold 0.0988 oz. AGW **Ruler:** Louis XIV **Mint:** Riom

Date	Mintage	VG	F	VF	XF	Unc
1704O	—	475	850	1,100	1,800	—

KM# 363.13 1/2 LOUIS D'OR
3.3500 g., 0.9170 Gold 0.0988 oz. AGW **Ruler:** Louis XIV **Mint:** Troyes

Date	Mintage	VG	F	VF	XF	Unc
1704S	—	475	850	1,100	1,800	—

KM# 363.14 1/2 LOUIS D'OR
3.3500 g., 0.9170 Gold 0.0988 oz. AGW **Ruler:** Louis XIV **Mint:** Nantes

Date	Mintage	VG	F	VF	XF	Unc
1704T Rare	—	—	—	—	—	—
1705T Rare	—	—	—	—	—	—

KM# 363.15 1/2 LOUIS D'OR
3.3500 g., 0.9170 Gold 0.0988 oz. AGW **Ruler:** Louis XIV **Mint:** Troyes

Date	Mintage	VG	F	VF	XF	Unc
1704V Rare	—	—	—	—	—	—
1705V Rare	—	—	—	—	—	—

KM# 363.16 1/2 LOUIS D'OR
3.3500 g., 0.9170 Gold 0.0988 oz. AGW **Ruler:** Louis XIV **Mint:** Lille

Date	Mintage	VG	F	VF	XF	Unc
1704W Rare	—	—	—	—	—	—
1705W	—	—	—	—	—	—

Note: Reported, not confirmed

KM# 363.17 1/2 LOUIS D'OR
3.3500 g., 0.9170 Gold 0.0988 oz. AGW **Ruler:** Louis XIV **Mint:** Bourges

Date	Mintage	VG	F	VF	XF	Unc
1704Y	—	475	850	1,100	1,750	—

KM# 363.18 1/2 LOUIS D'OR
3.3500 g., 0.9170 Gold 0.0988 oz. AGW **Ruler:** Louis XIV **Mint:** Grenoble

Date	Mintage	VG	F	VF	XF	Unc
1704Z	—	—	—	—	—	—

Note: Reported, not confirmed

KM# 364 1/2 LOUIS D'OR
3.3500 g., 0.9170 Gold 0.0988 oz. AGW **Ruler:** Louis XIV **Mint:** Pau **Obverse:** Laureate head right **Obv. Legend:** LVD • XIIII • D • G • FR • ET • NA • RE • B • **Reverse:** Crossed hand of Justice and sceptre with crowned fleur-de-lis at angles **Rev. Legend:** CHRS • REGN • VINC • IMP **Note:** Mint mark: Cow. Issued for Province of Bearn.

Date	Mintage	VG	F	VF	XF	Unc
1704	—	475	850	1,100	1,750	—
1705	—	475	850	1,100	1,750	—

KM# 363.20 1/2 LOUIS D'OR
3.3500 g., 0.9170 Gold 0.0988 oz. AGW **Ruler:** Louis XIV **Mint:** Besancon **Note:** Mint mark: Back to back C's.

Date	Mintage	VG	F	VF	XF	Unc
1704	—	475	850	1,100	1,750	—

KM# 363.19 1/2 LOUIS D'OR
3.3500 g., 0.9170 Gold 0.0988 oz. AGW **Ruler:** Louis XIV **Mint:** Rennes **Note:** Mint mark: 9.

Date	Mintage	VG	F	VF	XF	Unc
1704	—	475	850	1,100	1,750	—
1705	—	475	850	1,100	1,750	—

KM# 363.7 1/2 LOUIS D'OR
3.3500 g., 0.9170 Gold 0.0988 oz. AGW **Ruler:** Louis XIV **Mint:** Poitiers

Date	Mintage	VG	F	VF	XF	Unc
1706G	—	475	850	1,100	1,750	—

KM# 388.1 1/2 LOUIS D'OR
3.3500 g., 0.9170 Gold 0.0988 oz. AGW **Ruler:** Louis XIV **Mint:** Paris **Obverse:** Date and mint mark below head **Obv. Legend:** LVD • XIIII • D • G • ... **Reverse:** Crowned back to back "L's" in cruciform, fleur-de-lis at angles **Rev. Legend:** CHRS • REGN • VINC • IMP

Date	Mintage	VG	F	VF	XF	Unc
1709A	—	475	850	1,200	1,900	—
1710A	—	550	950	1,300	2,150	—
1711A	—	550	950	1,300	2,150	—
1712A Rare	—	—	—	—	—	—
1713A Rare	—	—	—	—	—	—
1715A Rare	—	—	—	—	—	—

KM# 388.4 1/2 LOUIS D'OR
3.3500 g., 0.9170 Gold 0.0988 oz. AGW **Ruler:** Louis XIV **Mint:** Lyon **Obverse:** Laureate head right **Reverse:** Crowned back to back L"s in cruciform, fleur-de-lis at angles

Date	Mintage	VG	F	VF	XF	Unc
1709D	—	550	950	1,300	2,150	—
1710D	—	550	950	1,300	2,150	—
1711D	—	475	850	1,200	1,900	—
1713D	—	550	950	1,300	2,150	—

KM# 388.5 1/2 LOUIS D'OR
3.3500 g., 0.9170 Gold 0.0988 oz. AGW **Ruler:** Louis XIV **Mint:** Tours **Obverse:** Laureate head right **Reverse:** Crowned back to back L"s in cruciform, fleur-de-lis at angles

Date	Mintage	VG	F	VF	XF	Unc
1709E Rare	—	—	—	—	—	—
1710E Rare	—	—	—	—	—	—
1711E Rare	—	—	—	—	—	—
1712E Rare	—	—	—	—	—	—

KM# 388.8 1/2 LOUIS D'OR
3.3500 g., 0.9170 Gold 0.0988 oz. AGW **Ruler:** Louis XIV **Mint:** Limoges **Obverse:** Laureate head right **Reverse:** Crowned back to back L"s in cruciform, fleur-de-lis at angles

Date	Mintage	VG	F	VF	XF	Unc
1709I Rare	—	—	—	—	—	—
1711I Rare	—	—	—	—	—	—
1712I Rare	—	—	—	—	—	—

KM# 388.9 1/2 LOUIS D'OR
3.3500 g., 0.9170 Gold 0.0988 oz. AGW **Ruler:** Louis XIV **Mint:** Bordeaux **Obverse:** Laureate head right **Reverse:** Crowned back to back L"s in cruciform, fleur-de-lis at angles

Date	Mintage	VG	F	VF	XF	Unc
1709K	—	550	1,100	1,450	2,750	—
1710K Rare	—	—	—	—	—	—

KM# 388.10 1/2 LOUIS D'OR
3.3500 g., 0.9170 Gold 0.0988 oz. AGW **Ruler:** Louis XIV **Mint:** Toulouse **Obverse:** Laureate head right **Reverse:** Crowned back to back L"s in cruciform, fleur-de-lis at angles

Date	Mintage	VG	F	VF	XF	Unc
1709M	—	475	950	1,300	2,150	—
1710M	—	475	950	1,300	2,150	—
1711M Rare	—	—	—	—	—	—
1712M Rare	—	—	—	—	—	—

KM# 388.11 1/2 LOUIS D'OR
3.3500 g., 0.9170 Gold 0.0988 oz. AGW **Ruler:** Louis XIV **Mint:** Montpellier **Obverse:** Laureate head right **Reverse:** Crowned back to back L"s in cruciform, fleur-de-lis at angles

Date	Mintage	VG	F	VF	XF	Unc
1709N Rare	—	—	—	—	—	—
1710N Rare	—	—	—	—	—	—
1711N	320,000	475	950	1,300	2,150	—
1712N	—	475	950	1,300	2,150	—
1713N	—	475	950	1,300	2,150	—

KM# 388.22 1/2 LOUIS D'OR
3.3500 g., 0.9170 Gold 0.0988 oz. AGW **Ruler:** Louis XIV **Mint:** Besancon **Obverse:** Laureate head right **Reverse:** Crowned back to back L"s in cruciform, fleur-de-lis at angles **Note:** Mint mark: Back to back C's.

Date	Mintage	VG	F	VF	XF	Unc
1709	—	475	950	1,300	2,150	—
1710 Rare	—	—	—	—	—	—
1711	—	475	950	1,300	2,150	—

KM# 389 1/2 LOUIS D'OR
3.3500 g., 0.9170 Gold 0.0988 oz. AGW **Ruler:** Louis XIV **Mint:** Pau **Obv. Legend:** ....RE.BD (ligate BD). **Note:** Mint mark: Cow. Issued for Province of Bearn.

Date	Mintage	VG	F	VF	XF	Unc
1709	—	475	1,100	1,800	2,700	—

KM# 388.21 1/2 LOUIS D'OR
3.3500 g., 0.9170 Gold 0.0988 oz. AGW **Ruler:** Louis XIV **Mint:** Aix **Obverse:** Laureate head right **Reverse:** Crowned back to back L"s in cruciform, fleur-de-lis at angles **Note:** Mint mark: &.

Date	Mintage	VG	F	VF	XF	Unc
1709	—	475	950	1,300	2,150	—
1710	662	475	950	1,300	2,150	—
1711	—	475	950	1,300	2,150	—
1712 Rare	—	—	—	—	—	—

KM# 388.20 1/2 LOUIS D'OR
3.3500 g., 0.9170 Gold 0.0988 oz. AGW **Ruler:** Louis XIV **Mint:** Rennes **Obverse:** Laureate head right **Reverse:** Crowned back to back L"s in cruciform, fleur-de-lis at angles **Note:** Mint mark: 9.

Date	Mintage	VG	F	VF	XF	Unc
1710 Rare	—	—	—	—	—	—

KM# 388.13 1/2 LOUIS D'OR
3.3500 g., 0.9170 Gold 0.0988 oz. AGW **Ruler:** Louis XIV **Mint:** Dijon **Obverse:** Laureate head right **Reverse:** Crowned back to back L"s in cruciform, fleur-de-lis at angles

Date	Mintage	VG	F	VF	XF	Unc
1710P	—	475	950	1,300	2,150	—
1711P	—	475	950	1,300	2,150	—
1712P Rare	—	—	—	—	—	—

KM# 388.2 1/2 LOUIS D'OR
3.3500 g., 0.9170 Gold 0.0988 oz. AGW **Ruler:** Louis XIV **Mint:** Rouen **Obverse:** Laureate head right **Reverse:** Crowned back to back L"s in cruciform, fleur-de-lis at angles

Date	Mintage	VG	F	VF	XF	Unc
1710B	—	550	950	1,300	2,150	—
1711B Rare	—	—	—	—	—	—

KM# 388.3 1/2 LOUIS D'OR
3.3500 g., 0.9170 Gold 0.0988 oz. AGW **Ruler:** Louis XIV **Mint:** Caen **Obverse:** Laureate head right **Reverse:** Crowned back to back L"s in cruciform, fleur-de-lis at angles

Date	Mintage	VG	F	VF	XF	Unc
1710C Rare	—	—	—	—	—	—
1711C Rare	—	—	—	—	—	—
1712C Rare	—	—	—	—	—	—

KM# 388.17 1/2 LOUIS D'OR
3.3500 g., 0.9170 Gold 0.0988 oz. AGW **Ruler:** Louis XIV **Mint:** Troyes **Obverse:** Laureate head right **Reverse:** Crowned back to back L"s in cruciform, fleur-de-lis at angles

Date	Mintage	VG	F	VF	XF	Unc
1710V Rare	—	—	—	—	—	—
1712V	—	475	950	1,300	2,150	—

KM# 388.18 1/2 LOUIS D'OR
3.3500 g., 0.9170 Gold 0.0988 oz. AGW **Ruler:** Louis XIV **Mint:** Amiens **Obverse:** Laureate head right **Reverse:** Crowned back to back L"s in cruciform, fleur-de-lis at angles

Date	Mintage	VG	F	VF	XF	Unc
1710X	—	550	1,100	1,450	2,750	—

Date	Mintage	VG	F	VF	XF	Unc
1711X	—	475	1,000	1,400	2,200	—
1712X Rare	—	—	—	—	—	—

KM# 388.7 1/2 LOUIS D'OR

3.3500 g., 0.9170 Gold 0.0988 oz. AGW **Ruler:** Louis XIV **Mint:** La Rochelle **Obverse:** Laureate head right **Reverse:** Crowned back to back L"s in cruciform, fleur-de-lis at angles

Date	Mintage	VG	F	VF	XF	Unc
1710H Rare	—	—	—	—	—	—
1711H Rare	—	—	—	—	—	—
1712H Rare	—	—	—	—	—	—

KM# 388.19 1/2 LOUIS D'OR

3.3500 g., 0.9170 Gold 0.0988 oz. AGW **Ruler:** Louis XIV **Mint:** Grenoble

Date	Mintage	VG	F	VF	XF	Unc
1711Z Rare	—	—	—	—	—	—
1712Z Rare	—	—	—	—	—	—
1713Z Rare	—	—	—	—	—	—

KM# 388.14 1/2 LOUIS D'OR

3.3500 g., 0.9170 Gold 0.0988 oz. AGW **Ruler:** Louis XIV **Mint:** Perpignan **Obverse:** Laureate head right **Reverse:** Crowned back to back L"s in cruciform, fleur-de-lis at angles

Date	Mintage	VG	F	VF	XF	Unc
1711Q Rare	—	—	—	—	—	—

KM# 388.15 1/2 LOUIS D'OR

3.3500 g., 0.9170 Gold 0.0988 oz. AGW **Ruler:** Louis XIV **Mint:** Troyes **Obverse:** Laureate head right **Reverse:** Crowned back to back L"s in cruciform, fleur-de-lis at angles

Date	Mintage	VG	F	VF	XF	Unc
1711S	—	475	950	1,300	2,150	—

KM# 388.6 1/2 LOUIS D'OR

3.3500 g., 0.9170 Gold 0.0988 oz. AGW **Ruler:** Louis XIV **Mint:** Poitiers **Obverse:** Laureate head right **Reverse:** Crowned back to back L"s in cruciform, fleur-de-lis at angles

Date	Mintage	VG	F	VF	XF	Unc
1711G Rare	—	—	—	—	—	—
1712G Rare	—	—	—	—	—	—

KM# 388.12 1/2 LOUIS D'OR

3.3500 g., 0.9170 Gold 0.0988 oz. AGW **Ruler:** Louis XIV **Mint:** Riom **Obverse:** Laureate head right **Reverse:** Crowned back to back L"s in cruciform, fleur-de-lis at angles

Date	Mintage	VG	F	VF	XF	Unc
1712O	—	550	1,100	1,450	2,750	—

KM# 388.16 1/2 LOUIS D'OR

3.3500 g., 0.9170 Gold 0.0988 oz. AGW **Ruler:** Louis XIV **Mint:** Nantes **Obverse:** Laureate head right **Reverse:** Crowned back to back L"s in cruciform, fleur-de-lis at angles

Date	Mintage	VG	F	VF	XF	Unc
1715T	—	550	1,100	1,450	2,750	—

KM# 424.2 1/2 LOUIS D'OR

4.0790 g., 0.9170 Gold 0.1203 oz. AGW **Ruler:** Louis XV **Mint:** Caen

Date	Mintage	VG	F	VF	XF	Unc
1716C	—	1,000	2,250	3,250	6,000	—

KM# 424.3 1/2 LOUIS D'OR

4.0790 g., 0.9170 Gold 0.1203 oz. AGW **Ruler:** Louis XV **Mint:** Tours

Date	Mintage	VG	F	VF	XF	Unc
1716E	5,994	1,000	2,250	3,250	6,000	—

KM# 424.4 1/2 LOUIS D'OR

4.0790 g., 0.9170 Gold 0.1203 oz. AGW **Ruler:** Louis XV **Mint:** La Rochelle

Date	Mintage	VG	F	VF	XF	Unc
1716H	—	1,000	2,250	3,250	6,000	—

KM# 424.5 1/2 LOUIS D'OR

4.0790 g., 0.9170 Gold 0.1203 oz. AGW **Ruler:** Louis XV **Mint:** Montpellier

Date	Mintage	VG	F	VF	XF	Unc
1716N	—	1,000	2,250	3,250	6,000	—

KM# 424.6 1/2 LOUIS D'OR

4.0790 g., 0.9170 Gold 0.1203 oz. AGW **Ruler:** Louis XV **Mint:** Reims

Date	Mintage	VG	F	VF	XF	Unc
1716S	—	1,000	2,250	3,250	6,000	—

KM# 424.7 1/2 LOUIS D'OR

4.0790 g., 0.9170 Gold 0.1203 oz. AGW **Ruler:** Louis XV **Mint:** Nantes

Date	Mintage	VG	F	VF	XF	Unc
1716T	—	1,000	2,250	3,250	6,000	—

KM# 424.8 1/2 LOUIS D'OR

4.0790 g., 0.9170 Gold 0.1203 oz. AGW **Ruler:** Louis XV **Mint:** Troyes

Date	Mintage	VG	F	VF	XF	Unc
1716V	4,374	1,000	2,250	3,250	6,000	—

KM# 424.9 1/2 LOUIS D'OR

4.0790 g., 0.9170 Gold 0.1203 oz. AGW **Ruler:** Louis XV **Mint:** Lille

Date	Mintage	VG	F	VF	XF	Unc
1716W	—	1,000	2,250	3,250	6,000	—

KM# 424.10 1/2 LOUIS D'OR

4.0790 g., 0.9170 Gold 0.1203 oz. AGW **Ruler:** Louis XV **Mint:** Grenoble

Date	Mintage	VG	F	VF	XF	Unc
1716Z	5,025	1,000	2,250	3,250	6,000	—

KM# 424.11 1/2 LOUIS D'OR

4.0790 g., 0.9170 Gold 0.1203 oz. AGW **Ruler:** Louis XV **Mint:** Besancon **Note:** Mint mark: Back to back C's.

Date	Mintage	VG	F	VF	XF	Unc
1716	—	1,000	2,250	3,250	6,000	—

KM# 424.1 1/2 LOUIS D'OR

4.0790 g., 0.9170 Gold 0.1203 oz. AGW **Ruler:** Louis XV **Mint:** Metz **Note:** Similar to 1 Louis D'or KM#425.

Date	Mintage	VG	F	VF	XF	Unc
1716AA	—	1,000	2,250	3,250	6,000	—

KM# 429.1 1/2 LOUIS D'OR

3.0590 g., 0.9170 Gold 0.0902 oz. AGW **Ruler:** Louis XV **Mint:** Paris **Note:** Similar to 1 Louis D'or, KM#430.1.

Date	Mintage	VG	F	VF	XF	Unc
1717A	70,000	900	2,000	3,000	5,500	—

KM# 437.1 1/2 LOUIS D'OR

4.8350 g., 0.9170 Gold 0.1425 oz. AGW **Ruler:** Louis XV **Mint:** Paris **Note:** Similar to 1 Louis D'or, KM#438.1.

Date	Mintage	VG	F	VF	XF	Unc
1718A	—	1,250	2,500	4,250	7,500	—
1719A	—	1,250	2,500	4,250	7,500	—

KM# 429.2 1/2 LOUIS D'OR

3.0590 g., 0.9170 Gold 0.0902 oz. AGW **Ruler:** Louis XV **Mint:** Rouen

Date	Mintage	VG	F	VF	XF	Unc
1718B Rare	—	—	—	—	—	—

KM# 437.3 1/2 LOUIS D'OR

4.8350 g., 0.9170 Gold 0.1425 oz. AGW **Ruler:** Louis XV **Mint:** Lyon

Date	Mintage	VG	F	VF	XF	Unc
1718D	—	1,250	2,500	4,250	7,500	—
1719D	—	—	—	—	—	—

KM# 437.4 1/2 LOUIS D'OR

4.8350 g., 0.9170 Gold 0.1425 oz. AGW **Ruler:** Louis XV **Mint:** Montpellier

Date	Mintage	VG	F	VF	XF	Unc
1719N	—	1,250	2,500	4,250	7,500	—

KM# 437.2 1/2 LOUIS D'OR

4.8350 g., 0.9170 Gold 0.1425 oz. AGW **Ruler:** Louis XV **Mint:** Strasbourg

Date	Mintage	VG	F	VF	XF	Unc
1719BB	49,000	1,250	2,500	4,250	7,500	—

KM# 437.6 1/2 LOUIS D'OR

4.8350 g., 0.9170 Gold 0.1425 oz. AGW **Ruler:** Louis XV **Mint:** Aix **Note:** Mint mark: &.

Date	Mintage	VG	F	VF	XF	Unc
1719	—	1,250	2,500	4,250	7,500	—

KM# 460.1 1/2 LOUIS D'OR

4.8950 g., 0.9170 Gold 0.1443 oz. AGW **Ruler:** Louis XV **Mint:** Paris **Note:** Similar to 1 Louis D'or, KM#461.1.

Date	Mintage	VG	F	VF	XF	Unc
1720A	11,000	900	1,650	2,850	5,250	—
1721A	5,530	1,000	1,900	3,500	6,000	—
1722A	15,000	1,000	1,800	3,200	5,750	—
1723A Rare	21,000	—	—	—	—	—

KM# 460.11 1/2 LOUIS D'OR

4.8950 g., 0.9170 Gold 0.1443 oz. AGW **Ruler:** Louis XV **Mint:** Rennes **Note:** Mint mark: 9.

Date	Mintage	VG	F	VF	XF	Unc
1720 Rare	—	—	—	—	—	—

KM# 437.5 1/2 LOUIS D'OR

4.8350 g., 0.9170 Gold 0.1425 oz. AGW **Ruler:** Louis XV **Mint:** Lille

Date	Mintage	VG	F	VF	XF	Unc
1720W	7,880	1,250	2,500	4,250	7,500	—

KM# 437.7 1/2 LOUIS D'OR

4.8350 g., 0.9170 Gold 0.1425 oz. AGW **Ruler:** Louis XV **Mint:** Grenoble

Date	Mintage	VG	F	VF	XF	Unc
1720Z Rare	—	—	—	—	—	—

KM# 460.3 1/2 LOUIS D'OR

4.8950 g., 0.9170 Gold 0.1443 oz. AGW **Ruler:** Louis XV **Mint:** Lyon

Date	Mintage	VG	F	VF	XF	Unc
1721D	5,843	950	1,750	3,000	5,500	—
1722D	—	950	1,750	3,000	5,500	—
1723D	1,036	1,000	1,850	3,500	6,250	—

KM# 460.4 1/2 LOUIS D'OR

4.8950 g., 0.9170 Gold 0.1443 oz. AGW **Ruler:** Louis XV **Mint:** Bordeaux

Date	Mintage	VG	F	VF	XF	Unc
1721K Rare	426	—	—	—	—	—
1722K	—	950	1,750	3,000	5,500	—

KM# 460.10 1/2 LOUIS D'OR

4.8950 g., 0.9170 Gold 0.1443 oz. AGW **Ruler:** Louis XV **Mint:** Grenoble

Date	Mintage	VG	F	VF	XF	Unc
1721Z Rare	225	—	—	—	—	—
1722Z Rare	193	—	—	—	—	—
1723Z Rare	85	—	—	—	—	—

KM# 460.9 1/2 LOUIS D'OR

4.8950 g., 0.9170 Gold 0.1443 oz. AGW **Ruler:** Louis XV **Mint:** Orléans

Date	Mintage	VG	F	VF	XF	Unc
1721R Rare	159	—	—	—	—	—

KM# 460.8 1/2 LOUIS D'OR

4.8950 g., 0.9170 Gold 0.1443 oz. AGW **Ruler:** Louis XV **Mint:** Bayonne

Date	Mintage	VG	F	VF	XF	Unc
1722L	—	1,000	1,850	3,500	6,250	—

KM# 460.7 1/2 LOUIS D'OR

4.8950 g., 0.9170 Gold 0.1443 oz. AGW **Ruler:** Louis XV **Mint:** Caen

Date	Mintage	VG	F	VF	XF	Unc
1722C Rare	608	—	—	—	—	—
1723C Rare	—	—	—	—	—	—

KM# 460.2 1/2 LOUIS D'OR

4.8950 g., 0.9170 Gold 0.1443 oz. AGW **Ruler:** Louis XV **Mint:** Strasbourg

Date	Mintage	VG	F	VF	XF	Unc
1723BB	800	950	1,750	3,000	5,500	—

KM# 473.1 1/2 LOUIS D'OR

3.2630 g., 0.9170 Gold 0.0962 oz. AGW **Ruler:** Louis XV **Mint:** Paris

Date	Mintage	VG	F	VF	XF	Unc
1723A Rare	—	—	—	—	—	—
1724A	—	2,000	3,500	4,750	8,000	—
1725A	—	2,000	3,500	4,750	8,000	—

KM# 460.5 1/2 LOUIS D'OR

4.8950 g., 0.9170 Gold 0.1443 oz. AGW **Ruler:** Louis XV **Mint:** Lille

Date	Mintage	VG	F	VF	XF	Unc
1723W	—	950	1,750	3,000	5,500	—

KM# 460.6 1/2 LOUIS D'OR

4.8950 g., 0.9170 Gold 0.1443 oz. AGW **Ruler:** Louis XV **Mint:** Amiens

Date	Mintage	VG	F	VF	XF	Unc
1723X	—	950	1,750	3,000	5,500	—

KM# 473.2 1/2 LOUIS D'OR

3.2630 g., 0.9170 Gold 0.0962 oz. AGW **Ruler:** Louis XV **Mint:** Lyon

Date	Mintage	VG	F	VF	XF	Unc
1724D Rare	—	—	—	—	—	—

KM# 488.1 1/2 LOUIS D'OR

4.0790 g., 0.9170 Gold 0.1203 oz. AGW **Ruler:** Louis XV **Mint:** Paris **Obverse:** Draped bust left **Obv. Legend:** LUD • XV • D • G • FR • ET • NAV • REX • **Reverse:** Crown above two oval arms **Rev. Legend:** CHRS • REGN • VINC • IMPER

Date	Mintage	VG	F	VF	XF	Unc
1726A	—	125	200	300	600	—
1728A	—	150	225	350	700	—
1729A	—	125	200	300	600	—
1730A	—	125	200	300	600	—
1731A	—	125	200	300	600	—
1732A	—	125	200	300	600	—
1733A	—	150	225	350	700	—
1736A	—	150	225	350	—	—
1737A	—	150	225	350	700	—
1739A	—	150	225	350	700	—

KM# 488.3 1/2 LOUIS D'OR

4.0790 g., 0.9170 Gold 0.1203 oz. AGW **Ruler:** Louis XV **Mint:** Strasbourg **Obverse:** Draped bust left **Reverse:** Crown above two oval arms

Date	Mintage	VG	F	VF	XF	Unc
1726BB	—	125	200	300	600	—
1730BB	—	150	225	350	700	—
1734BB	—	150	225	350	700	—

KM# 488.4 1/2 LOUIS D'OR

4.0790 g., 0.9170 Gold 0.1203 oz. AGW **Ruler:** Louis XV **Mint:** Caen **Obverse:** Draped bust left **Reverse:** Crown above two oval arms

Date	Mintage	VG	F	VF	XF	Unc
1726C	1,429	150	225	350	700	—
1730C	6,078	150	225	350	700	—
1731C	—	150	225	350	700	—

KM# 488.5 1/2 LOUIS D'OR

4.0790 g., 0.9170 Gold 0.1203 oz. AGW **Ruler:** Louis XV **Mint:** Poitiers **Obverse:** Draped bust left **Reverse:** Crown above two oval arms

Date	Mintage	VG	F	VF	XF	Unc
1726G	—	150	225	350	700	—
1727G	—	125	200	300	600	—

KM# 488.9 1/2 LOUIS D'OR

4.0790 g., 0.9170 Gold 0.1203 oz. AGW **Ruler:** Louis XV **Mint:** Montpellier **Obverse:** Draped bust left **Reverse:** Crown above two oval arms

Date	Mintage	VG	F	VF	XF	Unc
1726N	22,000	150	225	350	700	—

KM# 488.10 1/2 LOUIS D'OR

4.0790 g., 0.9170 Gold 0.1203 oz. AGW **Ruler:** Louis XV **Mint:** Riom **Obverse:** Draped bust left **Reverse:** Crown above two oval arms

Date	Mintage	VG	F	VF	XF	Unc
17260	—	150	225	350	700	—
17290	—	150	225	350	700	—
17300	—	175	275	400	875	—

KM# 488.11 1/2 LOUIS D'OR

4.0790 g., 0.9170 Gold 0.1203 oz. AGW **Ruler:** Louis XV **Mint:** Dijon **Obverse:** Draped bust left **Reverse:** Crown above two oval arms

Date	Mintage	VG	F	VF	XF	Unc
1726P	—	150	225	350	700	—
1731P	—	150	225	350	700	—

KM# 488.12 1/2 LOUIS D'OR

4.0790 g., 0.9170 Gold 0.1203 oz. AGW **Ruler:** Louis XV **Mint:** Reims **Obverse:** Draped bust left **Reverse:** Crown above two oval arms

Date	Mintage	VG	F	VF	XF	Unc
1726S	—	150	225	350	700	—
1727S	—	150	225	350	700	—

KM# 488.13 1/2 LOUIS D'OR

4.0790 g., 0.9170 Gold 0.1203 oz. AGW **Ruler:** Louis XV **Mint:** Lille **Obverse:** Draped bust left **Reverse:** Crown above two oval arms

Date	Mintage	VG	F	VF	XF	Unc
1726W	—	125	200	300	600	—

KM# 488.7 1/2 LOUIS D'OR

4.0790 g., 0.9170 Gold 0.1203 oz. AGW **Ruler:** Louis XV **Mint:** Bayonne **Obverse:** Draped bust left **Reverse:** Crown above two oval arms

Date	Mintage	VG	F	VF	XF	Unc
1726L	—	150	225	350	700	—
1727L	—	150	225	350	700	—
1728L	—	150	225	350	700	—
1730L	—	150	225	350	700	—
1735L	—	175	275	400	875	—

KM# 488.15 1/2 LOUIS D'OR

4.0790 g., 0.9170 Gold 0.1203 oz. AGW **Ruler:** Louis XV **Mint:** Rennes **Obverse:** Draped bust left **Reverse:** Crown above two oval arms **Note:** Mint mark: 9.

Date	Mintage	VG	F	VF	XF	Unc
1726	3,156	150	225	375	750	—
1727	—	150	225	375	750	—
1729	—	150	225	375	750	—
1730	—	150	225	375	750	—
1731	—	150	225	375	750	—
1732	—	150	225	375	750	—
1733	—	175	275	425	875	—
1734	—	150	225	375	750	—

KM# 488.16 1/2 LOUIS D'OR

4.0790 g., 0.9170 Gold 0.1203 oz. AGW **Ruler:** Louis XV **Mint:** Besancon **Obverse:** Draped bust left **Reverse:** Crown above two oval arms **Note:** Mint mark: Back to back C's.

Date	Mintage	VG	F	VF	XF	Unc
1727	—	150	225	300	600	—
1728	—	150	225	300	600	—
1729	—	150	225	300	600	—

KM# 488.2 1/2 LOUIS D'OR

4.0790 g., 0.9170 Gold 0.1203 oz. AGW **Ruler:** Louis XV **Mint:** Rouen **Obverse:** Draped bust left **Reverse:** Crown above two oval arms

Date	Mintage	VG	F	VF	XF	Unc
1727B	—	125	200	300	600	—
1730B	—	150	225	350	700	—

KM# 488.14 1/2 LOUIS D'OR

4.0790 g., 0.9170 Gold 0.1203 oz. AGW **Ruler:** Louis XV **Mint:** Amiens **Obverse:** Draped bust left **Reverse:** Crown above two oval arms

Date	Mintage	VG	F	VF	XF	Unc
1728X	—	150	225	350	700	—
1729X	—	150	225	350	700	—
1730X	—	150	225	350	700	—

KM# 488.6 1/2 LOUIS D'OR

4.0790 g., 0.9170 Gold 0.1203 oz. AGW **Ruler:** Louis XV **Mint:** Limoges **Obverse:** Draped bust left **Reverse:** Crown above two oval arms

Date	Mintage	VG	F	VF	XF	Unc
1729I	34,000	125	200	300	600	—
1730I	—	125	200	300	600	—
1731I	—	150	225	350	700	—
1732I	—	150	225	350	700	—
1733I	1,926	150	225	350	700	—

KM# 488.8 1/2 LOUIS D'OR

4.0790 g., 0.9170 Gold 0.1203 oz. AGW **Ruler:** Louis XV **Mint:** Toulouse **Obverse:** Draped bust left **Reverse:** Crown above two oval arms

Date	Mintage	VG	F	VF	XF	Unc
1730M	—	125	200	300	600	—

KM# 517.11 1/2 LOUIS D'OR

4.0790 g., 0.9170 Gold 0.1203 oz. AGW **Ruler:** Louis XV **Mint:** Aix **Note:** Mint mark: &.

Date	Mintage	VG	F	VF	XF	Unc
1741	—	225	450	650	1,150	—
1742	4,340	200	400	600	1,100	—

KM# 517.1 1/2 LOUIS D'OR

4.0790 g., 0.9170 Gold 0.1203 oz. AGW **Ruler:** Louis XV **Mint:** Paris **Obverse:** Head left **Obv. Legend:** LUD • XV • D • G • FR • ET • NAV • REX • **Reverse:** Crown above arms of France and Navarre **Rev. Legend:** CHRS • REGN • VINC • IMPER

Date	Mintage	VG	F	VF	XF	Unc
1741A	—	200	400	600	1,100	—
1742A	—	200	400	600	1,100	—
1743A	2,231	200	400	600	1,100	—
1744A	300	250	550	900	1,650	—
1745A	1,739	200	400	600	1,100	—
1746A	—	200	400	600	1,100	—
1747A	878	275	500	800	1,400	—
1749A	1,130	200	400	600	1,100	—
1750A	—	200	400	600	1,100	—
1751A	—	200	400	600	1,100	—
1753A	—	200	400	600	1,100	—
1755A	—	200	400	600	1,100	—
1768A	—	200	400	600	1,100	—
1769A	—	225	450	650	1,150	—

KM# 517.3 1/2 LOUIS D'OR

4.0790 g., 0.9170 Gold 0.1203 oz. AGW **Ruler:** Louis XV **Mint:** Bayonne **Obverse:** Head left **Reverse:** Crown above arms of France and Navarre

Date	Mintage	VG	F	VF	XF	Unc
1742L	4,904	200	375	600	1,100	—

KM# 517.6 1/2 LOUIS D'OR

4.0790 g., 0.9170 Gold 0.1203 oz. AGW **Ruler:** Louis XV **Mint:** Riom **Obverse:** Head left **Reverse:** Crown above arms of France and Navarre

Date	Mintage	VG	F	VF	XF	Unc
17420	1,495	200	400	600	1,100	—

KM# 517.9 1/2 LOUIS D'OR

4.0790 g., 0.9170 Gold 0.1203 oz. AGW **Ruler:** Louis XV **Mint:** Lille **Obverse:** Head left **Reverse:** Crown above arms of France and Navarre

Date	Mintage	VG	F	VF	XF	Unc
1743W	2,660	200	400	600	1,100	—
1754W	—	200	400	600	1,100	—

KM# 517.7 1/2 LOUIS D'OR

4.0790 g., 0.9170 Gold 0.1203 oz. AGW **Ruler:** Louis XV **Mint:** Reims **Obverse:** Head left **Reverse:** Crown above arms of France and Navarre

Date	Mintage	VG	F	VF	XF	Unc
1746S	5,940	200	400	600	1,100	—
1752S	2,810	200	400	600	1,100	—
1753S	3,735	200	400	600	1,100	—
1755S	3,136	200	400	600	1,100	—
1763S	1,186	200	400	600	1,100	—
1766S	—	225	450	650	1,150	—
1768S	2,454	200	400	600	1,100	—

KM# 517.8 1/2 LOUIS D'OR

4.0790 g., 0.9170 Gold 0.1203 oz. AGW **Ruler:** Louis XV **Mint:** Troyes **Obverse:** Head left **Reverse:** Crown above arms of France and Navarre

Date	Mintage	VG	F	VF	XF	Unc
1752V	1,936	200	400	600	1,100	—

KM# 517.2 1/2 LOUIS D'OR

4.0790 g., 0.9170 Gold 0.1203 oz. AGW **Ruler:** Louis XV **Mint:** Limoges **Obverse:** Head left **Reverse:** Crown above arms of France and Navarre

Date	Mintage	VG	F	VF	XF	Unc
1753I	—	200	400	600	1,100	—

KM# 517.4 1/2 LOUIS D'OR

4.0790 g., 0.9170 Gold 0.1203 oz. AGW **Ruler:** Louis XV **Mint:** Toulouse **Obverse:** Head left **Reverse:** Crown above arms of France and Navarre

Date	Mintage	VG	F	VF	XF	Unc
1755M	—	225	400	650	1,150	—

KM# 517.5 1/2 LOUIS D'OR

4.0790 g., 0.9170 Gold 0.1203 oz. AGW **Ruler:** Louis XV **Mint:** Montpellier **Obverse:** Head left **Reverse:** Crown above arms of France and Navarre

Date	Mintage	VG	F	VF	XF	Unc
1755N	30,000	200	400	600	1,100	—

KM# 517.10 1/2 LOUIS D'OR

4.0790 g., 0.9170 Gold 0.1203 oz. AGW **Ruler:** Louis XV **Mint:** Rennes **Obverse:** Head left **Reverse:** Crown above arms of France and Navarre **Note:** Mint mark: 9.

Date	Mintage	VG	F	VF	XF	Unc
1763	7,640	200	400	600	1,100	—

KM# 558 1/2 LOUIS D'OR

4.0790 g., 0.9170 Gold 0.1203 oz. AGW **Ruler:** Louis XV **Mint:** Paris **Obverse:** Old head of Louis XV left

Date	Mintage	VG	F	VF	XF	Unc
1772A	—	3,000	4,500	7,500	—	—

KM# 573.1 1/2 LOUIS D'OR

4.0790 g., 0.9170 Gold 0.1203 oz. AGW **Ruler:** Louis XVI **Mint:** Paris **Obverse:** Uniformed bust left **Obv. Legend:** LUD • XVI • D • G • FR • ET NAV • REX • **Reverse:** Crowned arms of France and Navarre in ovals **Rev. Legend:** CHRS • REGN • VINC • IMPER *

Date	Mintage	VG	F	VF	XF	Unc
1775A	585	900	1,700	3,250	6,500	—
1777A	—	1,000	2,000	3,750	7,500	—
1784A	766	900	1,700	3,250	6,500	—

KM# 573.3 1/2 LOUIS D'OR

4.0790 g., 0.9170 Gold 0.1203 oz. AGW **Ruler:** Louis XVI **Mint:** Bayonne **Obverse:** Uniformed bust left **Reverse:** Crowned arms of France and Navarre in ovals

Date	Mintage	VG	F	VF	XF	Unc
1776L	683	900	1,600	3,250	6,500	—

KM# 573.2 1/2 LOUIS D'OR

4.0790 g., 0.9170 Gold 0.1203 oz. AGW **Ruler:** Louis XVI **Mint:** Limoges **Obverse:** Uniformed bust left **Reverse:** Crowned arms of France and Navarre in ovals

Date	Mintage	VG	F	VF	XF	Unc
1777I	2,241	600	1,100	2,750	6,000	—

KM# 567.16 LOUIS D'OR

8.1580 g., 0.9170 Gold 0.2405 oz. AGW **Ruler:** Louis XVI **Mint:** Aix **Note:** Mint mark: &.

Date	Mintage	VG	F	VF	XF	Unc
1784	274	—	—	—	—	—
1775	37,000	450	950	1,600	3,500	—
1776	19,000	550	1,100	2,000	4,000	—
1777	13,000	550	1,100	2,000	4,000	—
1778	8,255	—	—	—	—	—
1779	3,352	—	—	—	—	—
1780	1,266	—	—	—	—	—
1781	517	900	1,700	3,250	6,500	—
1782	1,272	—	—	—	—	—
1783	2,802	—	—	—	—	—
1784	—	—	—	—	—	—

KM# 302.24 LOUIS D'OR

6.6900 g., 0.9170 Gold 0.1972 oz. AGW **Ruler:** Louis XIV **Mint:** Rennes **Note:** Mint mark: 9.

Date	Mintage	VG	F	VF	XF	Unc
1693	—	240	350	600	1,200	—
1694	—	240	350	600	1,200	—
1695	—	240	350	600	1,200	—
1696	—	300	475	725	1,300	—
1697	—	300	475	725	1,300	—
1700	—	240	350	600	1,200	—
1701	—	240	350	600	1,200	—
1701	—	240	350	600	1,200	—

KM# 302.6 LOUIS D'OR

6.6900 g., 0.9170 Gold 0.1972 oz. AGW **Ruler:** Louis XIV **Mint:** Lyon

Date	Mintage	VG	F	VF	XF	Unc
1693D	—	300	475	725	1,300	—
1694D	—	240	350	600	1,200	—
1695D	—	240	350	600	1,200	—
1696D	—	240	350	600	1,200	—
1697D	—	240	350	600	1,200	—
1698D Rare	—	—	—	—	—	—
1699D Rare	—	—	—	—	—	—
1700D	—	240	350	600	1,200	—
1701D Rare	—	—	—	—	—	—
1701D Rare	—	—	—	—	—	—

KM# 302.9 LOUIS D'OR

6.6900 g., 0.9170 Gold 0.1972 oz. AGW **Ruler:** Louis XIV **Mint:** La Rochelle

Date	Mintage	VG	F	VF	XF	Unc
1693H Rare	—	—	—	—	—	—

Date	Mintage	VG	F	VF	XF	Unc
1694H	—	240	350	600	1,200	—
1695H	—	240	350	600	1,200	—
1698H	—	300	475	725	1,300	—
1699H	—	240	350	600	1,200	—
1700H Rare	—	—	—	—	—	—
1701H Rare	—	—	—	—	—	—
1701H Rare	—	—	—	—	—	—

KM# 302.11 LOUIS D'OR

6.6900 g., 0.9170 Gold 0.1972 oz. AGW **Ruler:** Louis XIV **Mint:** Bordeaux

Date	Mintage	VG	F	VF	XF	Unc
1693K	—	240	350	600	1,200	—
1694K Rare	—	—	—	—	—	—
1695K	—	240	350	600	1,200	—
1696K	—	240	350	600	1,200	—
1698K Rare	—	—	—	—	—	—
1699K Rare	—	—	—	—	—	—
1700K Rare	—	—	—	—	—	—
1701K Rare	—	—	—	—	—	—
1701K Rare	—	—	—	—	—	—

KM# 302.12 LOUIS D'OR

6.6900 g., 0.9170 Gold 0.1972 oz. AGW **Ruler:** Louis XIV **Mint:** Bayonne

Date	Mintage	VG	F	VF	XF	Unc
1693L Rare	—	—	—	—	—	—
1694L	—	240	350	600	1,200	—
1696L	—	240	350	600	1,200	—
1700L Rare	—	—	—	—	—	—
1701L Rare	—	—	—	—	—	—
1701L Rare	—	—	—	—	—	—

KM# 302.17 LOUIS D'OR

6.6900 g., 0.9170 Gold 0.1972 oz. AGW **Ruler:** Louis XIV **Mint:** Reims

Date	Mintage	VG	F	VF	XF	Unc
1693S	—	250	400	600	1,100	—
1695S	—	200	300	500	1,000	—
1696S	—	200	300	500	1,000	—
1697S Rare	—	—	—	—	—	—
1699S Rare	—	—	—	—	—	—
1700S Rare	—	—	—	—	—	—
1701S Rare	—	—	—	—	—	—
1701S Rare	—	—	—	—	—	—

KM# 302.20 LOUIS D'OR

6.6900 g., 0.9170 Gold 0.1972 oz. AGW **Ruler:** Louis XIV **Mint:** Lille

Date	Mintage	VG	F	VF	XF	Unc
1693W	—	240	350	600	1,200	—
1694W	—	240	350	600	1,200	—
1695W	—	240	350	600	1,200	—
1696W	—	240	350	600	1,200	—
1697W Rare	—	—	—	—	—	—
1698W Rare	—	—	—	—	—	—
1699W	—	240	350	600	1,200	—
1700W	—	240	350	600	1,200	—
1701W Rare	—	—	—	—	—	—
1701W Rare	—	—	—	—	—	—

KM# 302.4 LOUIS D'OR

6.6900 g., 0.9170 Gold 0.1972 oz. AGW **Ruler:** Louis XIV **Mint:** Strasbourg **Obverse:** Older laureate head of Lois XIV **Reverse:** 4 L's around mint mark

Date	Mintage	VG	F	VF	XF	Unc
1694BB	—	240	350	600	1,200	—
1695BB	—	240	350	600	1,200	—
1696BB	—	240	350	600	1,200	—
1697BB	—	240	350	600	1,200	—
1700BB Rare	—	—	—	—	—	—
1701BB Rare	—	—	—	—	—	—
1701BB Rare	—	—	—	—	—	—

KM# 334.1 LOUIS D'OR

6.6900 g., 0.9170 Gold 0.1972 oz. AGW **Ruler:** Louis XIV **Mint:** Paris **Obverse:** Laureate head right **Obv. Legend:** LVD • XIIII • D • G FR • ET • NAV • REX • **Reverse:** Crowned back to back L's, Hand of Justice and sceptre cross at center **Rev. Legend:** CHRS • REGN • VINC • IMP

Date	Mintage	VG	F	VF	XF	Unc
1700A	—	240	400	550	1,150	—
1701A	—	240	400	550	1,150	—
1701A	—	240	400	550	1,150	—
1702A	—	240	400	550	1,150	—
1703A	—	240	400	550	1,150	—
1704A Rare	—	—	—	—	—	—

KM# 334.2 LOUIS D'OR

6.6900 g., 0.9170 Gold 0.1972 oz. AGW **Ruler:** Louis XIV **Mint:** Metz

Date	Mintage	VG	F	VF	XF	Unc
1701AA	—	475	650	1,200	1,800	—

KM# 334.3 LOUIS D'OR

6.6900 g., 0.9170 Gold 0.1972 oz. AGW **Ruler:** Louis XIV **Mint:** Rouen

Date	Mintage	VG	F	VF	XF	Unc
1701B	—	240	425	575	1,200	—
1702B	—	240	400	475	1,000	—
1703B	—	240	425	575	1,200	—

KM# 334.4 LOUIS D'OR

6.6900 g., 0.9170 Gold 0.1972 oz. AGW **Ruler:** Louis XIV **Mint:** Strasbourg

Date	Mintage	VG	F	VF	XF	Unc
1701BB	—	240	350	475	1,000	—
1702BB	—	240	350	475	1,000	—

KM# 334.11 LOUIS D'OR

6.6900 g., 0.9170 Gold 0.1972 oz. AGW **Ruler:** Louis XIV **Mint:** Bordeaux

Date	Mintage	VG	F	VF	XF	Unc
1701K	—	240	400	550	1,100	—
1702K	—	240	400	550	1,100	—
1703K	—	240	400	550	1,100	—

KM# 334.12 LOUIS D'OR

6.6900 g., 0.9170 Gold 0.1972 oz. AGW **Ruler:** Louis XIV **Mint:** Bayonne

Date	Mintage	VG	F	VF	XF	Unc
1701L	—	240	400	550	1,100	—
1703L Rare	—	—	—	—	—	—
1704L Rare	—	—	—	—	—	—

KM# 334.13 LOUIS D'OR

6.6900 g., 0.9170 Gold 0.1972 oz. AGW **Ruler:** Louis XIV **Mint:** Toulouse

Date	Mintage	VG	F	VF	XF	Unc
1701M	—	240	350	475	1,000	—
1702M	—	350	550	950	1,500	—

KM# 334.14 LOUIS D'OR

6.6900 g., 0.9170 Gold 0.1972 oz. AGW **Ruler:** Louis XIV **Mint:** Montpellier

Date	Mintage	VG	F	VF	XF	Unc
1701N	—	240	350	475	1,000	—
1702N	—	240	350	475	1,000	—
1703N Rare	—	—	—	—	—	—

KM# 334.15 LOUIS D'OR

6.6900 g., 0.9170 Gold 0.1972 oz. AGW **Ruler:** Louis XIV **Mint:** Riom

Date	Mintage	VG	F	VF	XF	Unc
1701O	—	240	350	475	1,000	—
1702O	—	240	350	475	1,000	—

KM# 334.16 LOUIS D'OR

6.6900 g., 0.9170 Gold 0.1972 oz. AGW **Ruler:** Louis XIV **Mint:** Dijon

Date	Mintage	VG	F	VF	XF	Unc
1701P	—	240	350	475	1,000	—
1702P	—	240	350	475	1,000	—
1703P	—	240	400	550	1,100	—

KM# 334.17 LOUIS D'OR

6.6900 g., 0.9170 Gold 0.1972 oz. AGW **Ruler:** Louis XIV **Mint:** Villeneuve St. André

Date	Mintage	VG	F	VF	XF	Unc
1701R Rare	—	—	—	—	—	—

KM# 334.18 LOUIS D'OR

6.6900 g., 0.9170 Gold 0.1972 oz. AGW **Ruler:** Louis XIV **Mint:** Reims

Date	Mintage	VG	F	VF	XF	Unc
1701S Rare	—	—	—	—	—	—
1702S	—	240	350	475	1,000	—

KM# 334.6 LOUIS D'OR

6.6900 g., 0.9170 Gold 0.1972 oz. AGW **Ruler:** Louis XIV **Mint:** Lyon

Date	Mintage	VG	F	VF	XF	Unc
1701D	—	240	350	475	1,000	—
1702D	—	240	350	475	1,000	—
1703D Rare	—	—	—	—	—	—

KM# 334.7 LOUIS D'OR

6.6900 g., 0.9170 Gold 0.1972 oz. AGW **Ruler:** Louis XIV **Mint:** Tours

Date	Mintage	VG	F	VF	XF	Unc
1701E	—	240	350	475	1,000	—
1702E Rare	—	—	—	—	—	—
1703E	—	240	400	575	1,150	—

KM# 334.9 LOUIS D'OR

6.6900 g., 0.9170 Gold 0.1972 oz. AGW **Ruler:** Louis XIV **Mint:** La Rochelle

Date	Mintage	VG	F	VF	XF	Unc
1701H	—	240	350	475	1,000	—
1702H	—	240	350	475	1,000	—
1703H	—	240	400	550	1,100	—

KM# 334.21 LOUIS D'OR

6.6900 g., 0.9170 Gold 0.1972 oz. AGW **Ruler:** Louis XIV **Mint:** Lille

Date	Mintage	VG	F	VF	XF	Unc
1701W	—	240	400	600	1,300	—
1702W	—	240	350	550	1,200	—
1703W Rare	—	—	—	—	—	—

KM# 334.22 LOUIS D'OR

6.6900 g., 0.9170 Gold 0.1972 oz. AGW **Ruler:** Louis XIV **Mint:** Amiens

Date	Mintage	VG	F	VF	XF	Unc
1701X	—	240	400	600	1,300	—
1702X	—	240	350	550	1,200	—

KM# 334.26 LOUIS D'OR

6.6900 g., 0.9170 Gold 0.1972 oz. AGW **Ruler:** Louis XIV **Mint:** Aix **Note:** Mint mark: &.

Date	Mintage	VG	F	VF	XF	Unc
1701	—	240	350	475	1,000	—
1702	—	240	400	575	1,200	—
1703 Rare	—	—	—	—	—	—

KM# 334.25 LOUIS D'OR

6.6900 g., 0.9170 Gold 0.1972 oz. AGW **Ruler:** Louis XIV **Mint:** Rennes **Note:** Mint mark: 9.

Date	Mintage	VG	F	VF	XF	Unc
1701	—	240	350	475	1,000	—
1702	—	240	350	475	1,000	—

KM# 334.27 LOUIS D'OR

6.6900 g., 0.9170 Gold 0.1972 oz. AGW **Ruler:** Louis XIV **Mint:** Besancon **Note:** Mint mark: Back to back C's.

Date	Mintage	VG	F	VF	XF	Unc
1701	—	240	425	650	1,200	—
1702 Rare	—	—	—	—	—	—

KM# 334.23 LOUIS D'OR

6.6900 g., 0.9170 Gold 0.1972 oz. AGW **Ruler:** Louis XIV **Mint:** Bourges

Date	Mintage	VG	F	VF	XF	Unc
1702Y	—	240	350	475	1,000	—

KM# 334.10 LOUIS D'OR

6.6900 g., 0.9170 Gold 0.1972 oz. AGW **Ruler:** Louis XIV **Mint:** Limoges

Date	Mintage	VG	F	VF	XF	Unc
1702I	—	240	425	575	1,200	—
1703I Rare	—	—	—	—	—	—

KM# 334.8 LOUIS D'OR

6.6900 g., 0.9170 Gold 0.1972 oz. AGW **Ruler:** Louis XIV **Mint:** Poitiers

Date	Mintage	VG	F	VF	XF	Unc
1702G	—	240	350	475	1,000	—

KM# 334.19 LOUIS D'OR

6.6900 g., 0.9170 Gold 0.1972 oz. AGW **Ruler:** Louis XIV **Mint:** Nantes

Date	Mintage	VG	F	VF	XF	Unc
1702T	—	200	300	400	825	—
1704T Rare	—	—	—	—	—	—

KM# 334.20 LOUIS D'OR

6.6900 g., 0.9170 Gold 0.1972 oz. AGW **Ruler:** Louis XIV **Mint:** Troyes

Date	Mintage	VG	F	VF	XF	Unc
1702V	—	240	350	475	1,000	—

KM# 334.5 LOUIS D'OR
6.6900 g., 0.9170 Gold 0.1972 oz. AGW **Ruler:** Louis XIV **Mint:** Caen

Date	Mintage	VG	F	VF	XF	Unc
1702C	—	240	350	475	1,000	—
1703C	—	240	400	575	1,200	—

KM# 334.24 LOUIS D'OR
6.6900 g., 0.9170 Gold 0.1972 oz. AGW **Ruler:** Louis XIV **Mint:** Grenoble

Date	Mintage	VG	F	VF	XF	Unc
1703Z Rare	—	—	—	—	—	—

KM# 365.1 LOUIS D'OR
6.6900 g., 0.9170 Gold 0.1972 oz. AGW **Ruler:** Louis XIV **Mint:** Paris **Obverse:** Laureate head right **Obv. Legend:** LVD • XIIII • D • G • ... **Reverse:** Crossed sceptres with crowned fleur-de-lis at angles, circle at center **Rev. Legend:** CHRS • REGN • VINC • IMP

Date	Mintage	VG	F	VF	XF	Unc
1704A	—	175	250	400	1,000	—
1705A	—	200	275	425	1,000	—
1706A	—	200	300	450	1,000	—
1707A	—	200	300	450	1,000	—
1708A Rare	—	—	—	—	—	—
1709A Rare	—	—	—	—	—	—

KM# 365.2 LOUIS D'OR
6.6900 g., 0.9170 Gold 0.1972 oz. AGW **Ruler:** Louis XIV **Mint:** Rouen **Obverse:** Laureate head right **Reverse:** Crossed sceptres with crowned fleur-de-lis at angles, circle at center

Date	Mintage	VG	F	VF	XF	Unc
1704B	—	200	300	450	1,000	—
1705B	—	200	300	450	1,000	—
1706B Rare	—	—	—	—	—	—

KM# 365.3 LOUIS D'OR
6.6900 g., 0.9170 Gold 0.1972 oz. AGW **Ruler:** Louis XIV **Mint:** Strasbourg **Obverse:** Laureate head right **Reverse:** Crossed sceptres with crowned fleur-de-lis at angles, circle at center

Date	Mintage	VG	F	VF	XF	Unc
1704BB	—	225	350	500	1,100	—
1705BB Rare	—	—	—	—	—	—
1706BB	—	225	350	500	1,100	—

KM# 365.4 LOUIS D'OR
6.6900 g., 0.9170 Gold 0.1972 oz. AGW **Ruler:** Louis XIV **Mint:** Caen **Obverse:** Laureate head right **Reverse:** Crossed sceptres with crowned fleur-de-lis at angles, circle at center

Date	Mintage	VG	F	VF	XF	Unc
1704C	—	200	300	450	1,000	—

KM# 365.5 LOUIS D'OR
6.6900 g., 0.9170 Gold 0.1972 oz. AGW **Ruler:** Louis XIV **Mint:** Lyon **Obverse:** Laureate head right **Reverse:** Crossed sceptres with crowned fleur-de-lis at angles, circle at center

Date	Mintage	VG	F	VF	XF	Unc
1704D	—	200	300	450	1,000	—
1705D		225	350	500	1,100	
1706D Rare	—	—	—	—	—	—

KM# 365.6 LOUIS D'OR
6.6900 g., 0.9170 Gold 0.1972 oz. AGW **Ruler:** Louis XIV **Mint:** Tours **Obverse:** Laureate head right **Reverse:** Crossed sceptres with crowned fleur-de-lis at angles, circle at center

Date	Mintage	VG	F	VF	XF	Unc
1704E	—	225	350	500	1,100	—
1705E Rare	—	—	—	—	—	—
1709E Rare	—	—	—	—	—	—

KM# 365.7 LOUIS D'OR
6.6900 g., 0.9170 Gold 0.1972 oz. AGW **Ruler:** Louis XIV **Mint:** Poitiers **Obverse:** Laureate head right **Reverse:** Crossed sceptres with crowned fleur-de-lis at angles, circle at center

Date	Mintage	VG	F	VF	XF	Unc
1704G	—	225	350	500	1,100	—

KM# 365.8 LOUIS D'OR
6.6900 g., 0.9170 Gold 0.1972 oz. AGW **Ruler:** Louis XIV **Mint:** La Rochelle **Obverse:** Laureate head right **Reverse:** Crossed sceptres with crowned fleur-de-lis at angles, circle at center

Date	Mintage	VG	F	VF	XF	Unc
1704H	—	200	300	450	1,000	—

KM# 365.9 LOUIS D'OR
6.6900 g., 0.9170 Gold 0.1972 oz. AGW **Ruler:** Louis XIV **Mint:** Limoges **Obverse:** Laureate head right **Reverse:** Crossed sceptres with crowned fleur-de-lis at angles, circle at center

Date	Mintage	VG	F	VF	XF	Unc
1704I	—	200	300	450	1,000	—
1705I Rare	—	—	—	—	—	—

KM# 365.10 LOUIS D'OR
6.6900 g., 0.9170 Gold 0.1972 oz. AGW **Ruler:** Louis XIV **Mint:** Bordeaux **Obverse:** Laureate head right **Reverse:** Crossed sceptres with crowned fleur-de-lis at angles, circle at center

Date	Mintage	VG	F	VF	XF	Unc
1704K	—	200	275	400	1,000	—
1705K	—	200	300	450	1,000	—

KM# 365.11 LOUIS D'OR
6.6900 g., 0.9170 Gold 0.1972 oz. AGW **Ruler:** Louis XIV **Mint:** Bayonne **Obverse:** Laureate head right **Reverse:** Crossed sceptres with crowned fleur-de-lis at angles, circle at center

Date	Mintage	VG	F	VF	XF	Unc
1704L	—	200	300	500	1,100	—
1705L Rare	—	—	—	—	—	—

KM# 365.12 LOUIS D'OR
6.6900 g., 0.9170 Gold 0.1972 oz. AGW **Ruler:** Louis XIV **Mint:** Toulouse **Obverse:** Laureate head right **Reverse:** Crossed sceptres with crowned fleur-de-lis at angles, circle at center

Date	Mintage	VG	F	VF	XF	Unc
1704M	—	225	350	500	1,100	—
1707M Rare	—	—	—	—	—	—

KM# 365.13 LOUIS D'OR
6.6900 g., 0.9170 Gold 0.1972 oz. AGW **Ruler:** Louis XIV **Mint:** Montpellier **Obverse:** Laureate head right **Reverse:** Crossed sceptres with crowned fleur-de-lis at angles, circle at center

Date	Mintage	VG	F	VF	XF	Unc
1704N	—	200	300	450	1,000	—
1705N Rare	—	—	—	—	—	—
1706N	—	200	300	450	1,000	—

KM# 365.14 LOUIS D'OR
6.6900 g., 0.9170 Gold 0.1972 oz. AGW **Ruler:** Louis XIV **Mint:** Riom **Obverse:** Laureate head right **Reverse:** Crossed sceptres with crowned fleur-de-lis at angles, circle at center

Date	Mintage	VG	F	VF	XF	Unc
1704O	—	200	300	450	1,000	—
1705O Rare	—	—	—	—	—	—

KM# 365.15 LOUIS D'OR
6.6900 g., 0.9170 Gold 0.1972 oz. AGW **Ruler:** Louis XIV **Mint:** Dijon **Obverse:** Laureate head right **Reverse:** Crossed sceptres with crowned fleur-de-lis at angles, circle at center

Date	Mintage	VG	F	VF	XF	Unc
1704P	—	200	300	450	1,000	—
1705P	—	200	300	450	1,000	—
1708P	—	200	300	450	1,000	—

KM# 365.16 LOUIS D'OR
6.6900 g., 0.9170 Gold 0.1972 oz. AGW **Ruler:** Louis XIV **Mint:** Villeneuve St. André **Obverse:** Laureate head right **Reverse:** Crossed sceptres with crowned fleur-de-lis at angles, circle at center

Date	Mintage	VG	F	VF	XF	Unc
1704R	—	250	500	750	1,250	—
1705R	—	250	500	750	1,250	—

KM# 365.18 LOUIS D'OR
6.6900 g., 0.9170 Gold 0.1972 oz. AGW **Ruler:** Louis XIV **Mint:** Nantes **Obverse:** Laureate head right **Reverse:** Crossed sceptres with crowned fleur-de-lis at angles, circle at center

Date	Mintage	VG	F	VF	XF	Unc
1704T	—	200	300	450	1,000	—
1705T Rare	—	—	—	—	—	—
1709T Rare	—	—	—	—	—	—

KM# 365.19 LOUIS D'OR
6.6900 g., 0.9170 Gold 0.1972 oz. AGW **Ruler:** Louis XIV **Mint:** Troyes **Obverse:** Laureate head right **Reverse:** Crossed sceptres with crowned fleur-de-lis at angles, circle at center

Date	Mintage	VG	F	VF	XF	Unc
1704V Rare	—	—	—	—	—	—
1705V Rare	—	—	—	—	—	—

KM# 365.20 LOUIS D'OR
6.6900 g., 0.9170 Gold 0.1972 oz. AGW **Ruler:** Louis XIV **Mint:** Lille **Obverse:** Laureate head right **Reverse:** Crossed sceptres with crowned fleur-de-lis at angles, circle at center

Date	Mintage	VG	F	VF	XF	Unc
1704W	—	225	350	500	1,100	—
1705W	—	200	300	450	1,000	—
1706W Rare	—	—	—	—	—	—

KM# 365.21 LOUIS D'OR
6.6900 g., 0.9170 Gold 0.1972 oz. AGW **Ruler:** Louis XIV **Mint:** Amiens **Obverse:** Laureate head right **Reverse:** Crossed sceptres with crowned fleur-de-lis at angles, circle at center

Date	Mintage	VG	F	VF	XF	Unc
1704X	—	225	350	500	1,100	—
1705X	—	250	450	700	1,200	—

KM# 365.22 LOUIS D'OR
6.6900 g., 0.9170 Gold 0.1972 oz. AGW **Ruler:** Louis XIV **Mint:** Bourges **Obverse:** Laureate head right **Reverse:** Crossed sceptres with crowned fleur-de-lis at angles, circle at center

Date	Mintage	VG	F	VF	XF	Unc
1704Y	—	200	300	450	1,000	—
1705Y Rare	—	—	—	—	—	—

KM# 365.23 LOUIS D'OR
6.6900 g., 0.9170 Gold 0.1972 oz. AGW **Ruler:** Louis XIV **Mint:** Grenoble **Obverse:** Laureate head right **Reverse:** Crossed sceptres with crowned fleur-de-lis at angles, circle at center

Date	Mintage	VG	F	VF	XF	Unc
1704Z	—	225	350	500	1,100	—
1709Z Rare	—	—	—	—	—	—

KM# 367 LOUIS D'OR
6.6900 g., 0.9170 Gold 0.1972 oz. AGW **Ruler:** Louis XIV **Mint:** Paris **Obverse:** Laureate bust with longer hair right **Obv. Legend:** LVD • XIIII • D • G • FR • ET • NAV • REX • **Reverse:** Crossed sceptres with crowned fleur-de-lis at angles, circle at center **Rev. Legend:** CHRS REGN VINC IMP

Date	Mintage	VG	F	VF	XF	Unc
1704A	—	250	600	900	1,500	—
1705A	—	250	600	900	1,500	—
1707A	—	250	600	900	1,500	—
1709A	—	250	600	900	1,500	—

KM# 365.26 LOUIS D'OR
6.6900 g., 0.9170 Gold 0.1972 oz. AGW **Ruler:** Louis XIV **Mint:** Besancon **Note:** Mint mark: Back to back C's.

Date	Mintage	VG	F	VF	XF	Unc
1704	—	200	300	450	1,000	—

KM# 365.17 LOUIS D'OR
6.6900 g., 0.9170 Gold 0.1972 oz. AGW **Ruler:** Louis XIV **Mint:** Troyes **Note:** Mint mark: Crowned S.

Date	Mintage	VG	F	VF	XF	Unc
1704	—	200	300	450	1,000	—
1705 Rare	—	—	—	—	—	—

KM# 365.25 LOUIS D'OR
6.6900 g., 0.9170 Gold 0.1972 oz. AGW **Ruler:** Louis XIV **Mint:** Rennes **Note:** Mint mark: 9.

Date	Mintage	VG	F	VF	XF	Unc
1704	—	200	300	450	1,000	—
1707	—	200	300	450	1,000	—
1708 Rare	—	—	—	—	—	—
1709 Rare	—	—	—	—	—	—

KM# 366 LOUIS D'OR
6.6900 g., 0.9170 Gold 0.1972 oz. AGW **Ruler:** Louis XIV **Mint:** Pau **Obverse:** Laureate head right **Obv. Legend:** ....RE.BD (ligate BD). **Reverse:** Crossed sceptres with crowned fleur-de-lis at angles, circle at center **Rev. Legend:** CHRS REGN VINC IMP **Note:** Mint mark: Cow. Issued for Province of Bearn.

Date	Mintage	VG	F	VF	XF	Unc
1704	—	220	500	850	1,500	—
1705 Rare	—	—	—	—	—	—

KM# 365.24 LOUIS D'OR
6.6900 g., 0.9170 Gold 0.1972 oz. AGW **Ruler:** Louis XIV **Mint:** Aix **Note:** Mint mark: &.

Date	Mintage	VG	F	VF	XF	Unc
1704	—	200	275	425	1,000	—
1705	—	200	300	450	1,000	—
1707	—	200	300	450	1,000	—

KM# 390.25 LOUIS D'OR
8.1300 g., 0.9170 Gold 0.2397 oz. AGW **Ruler:** Louis XIV **Mint:** Aix **Note:** Mint mark: &.

Date	Mintage	VG	F	VF	XF	Unc
1709	—	200	400	600	1,200	—
1710	—	250	450	750	1,500	—

KM# 391 LOUIS D'OR
8.1300 g., 0.9170 Gold 0.2397 oz. AGW **Ruler:** Louis XIV **Mint:** Pau **Obverse:** Legend ends: ...RE. BD. (ligate BD) **Note:** Mint mark: Cow. Issued for Province of Bearn.

Date	Mintage	VG	F	VF	XF	Unc
1709	—	200	400	600	1,200	—
1710	—	250	450	750	1,500	—
1711	—	250	450	750	1,500	—
1712	—	200	400	600	1,200	—
1713	—	250	450	750	1,500	—
1714	—	300	575	900	1,800	—
1715	—	250	450	775	1,650	—

KM# 390.24 LOUIS D'OR
8.1300 g., 0.9170 Gold 0.2397 oz. AGW **Ruler:** Louis XIV **Mint:** Rennes **Note:** Mint mark: 9.

Date	Mintage	VG	F	VF	XF	Unc
1709	—	250	450	750	1,500	—
1710	—	250	450	750	1,500	—
1711 Rare	—	—	—	—	—	—
1712 Rare	—	—	—	—	—	—
1713	—	250	450	850	1,650	—
1714 Rare	—	—	—	—	—	—
1715 Rare	—	—	—	—	—	—

KM# 390.17 LOUIS D'OR

8.1300 g., 0.9170 Gold 0.2397 oz. AGW **Ruler:** Louis XIV **Mint:** Troyes **Note:** Mint mark: Crowned S.

Date	Mintage	VG	F	VF	XF	Unc
1709	—	200	400	600	1,200	—
1710	560,000	200	400	600	1,200	—
1711	—	200	400	600	1,200	—
1712 Rare	—	—	—	—	—	—
1713 Rare	—	—	—	—	—	—
1715 Rare	—	—	—	—	—	—

KM# 390.26 LOUIS D'OR

8.1300 g., 0.9170 Gold 0.2397 oz. AGW **Ruler:** Louis XIV **Mint:** Besancon **Note:** Mint mark: Back to back C's.

Date	Mintage	VG	F	VF	XF	Unc
1709	—	200	400	600	1,200	—
1710	—	200	400	600	1,200	—
1711 Rare	—	—	—	—	—	—
1712	—	300	500	900	1,700	—
1713 Rare	—	—	—	—	—	—
1714 Rare	—	—	—	—	—	—
1715 Rare	—	—	—	—	—	—

KM# 390.1 LOUIS D'OR

8.1300 g., 0.9170 Gold 0.2397 oz. AGW **Ruler:** Louis XIV **Mint:** Paris **Obverse:** Laureate head right **Obv. Legend:** LVD • XIIII • D • G • FR • ET • NAV • REX **Reverse:** Crowned back to back L's with flower in center square, fleur-de-lis at angles **Rev. Legend:** CHRS • REGN • VINC • IMP

Date	Mintage	VG	F	VF	XF	Unc
1709A	—	200	400	600	1,200	—
1710A	—	200	400	600	1,200	—
1711A	—	200	400	600	1,200	—
1712A	—	200	400	600	1,200	—
1713A	—	200	400	600	1,200	—
1714A	—	250	450	750	1,500	—
1715A	—	300	500	900	1,700	—

KM# 390.2 LOUIS D'OR

8.1300 g., 0.9170 Gold 0.2397 oz. AGW **Ruler:** Louis XIV **Mint:** Rouen **Obverse:** Laureate head right **Reverse:** Crowned back to back L's with flower in center square, fleur-de-lis at angles

Date	Mintage	VG	F	VF	XF	Unc
1709B	—	200	400	600	1,200	—
1710B	—	250	450	750	1,500	—
1711B	—	250	450	750	1,500	—
1712B Rare	—	—	—	—	—	—
1713B	—	250	450	750	1,500	—
1714B	—	200	400	600	1,200	—
1715B	—	250	450	750	1,500	—

KM# 390.3 LOUIS D'OR

8.1300 g., 0.9170 Gold 0.2397 oz. AGW **Ruler:** Louis XIV **Mint:** Caen **Obverse:** Laureate head right **Reverse:** Crowned back to back L's with flower in center square, fleur-de-lis at angles

Date	Mintage	VG	F	VF	XF	Unc
1709C Rare	—	—	—	—	—	—
1710C Rare	—	—	—	—	—	—
1711C Rare	—	—	—	—	—	—
1712C Rare	—	—	—	—	—	—
1713C Rare	—	—	—	—	—	—
1714C Rare	—	—	—	—	—	—
1715C Rare	—	—	—	—	—	—

KM# 390.4 LOUIS D'OR

8.1300 g., 0.9170 Gold 0.2397 oz. AGW **Ruler:** Louis XIV **Mint:** Lyon **Obverse:** Laureate head right **Reverse:** Crowned back to back L's with flower in center square, fleur-de-lis at angles

Date	Mintage	VG	F	VF	XF	Unc
1709D	—	200	400	600	1,200	—
1710D	—	200	400	600	1,200	—
1711D	—	200	400	600	1,200	—
1712D Rare	—	—	—	—	—	—
1713D	—	250	450	750	1,500	—
1714D	—	250	450	750	1,500	—
dD Rare	—	—	—	—	—	—

KM# 390.5 LOUIS D'OR

8.1300 g., 0.9170 Gold 0.2397 oz. AGW **Ruler:** Louis XIV **Mint:** Tours **Obverse:** Laureate head right **Reverse:** Crowned back to back L's with flower in center square, fleur-de-lis at angles

Date	Mintage	VG	F	VF	XF	Unc
1709E Rare	—	—	—	—	—	—
1710E Rare	—	—	—	—	—	—
1711E	—	250	450	900	1,700	—
1712E Rare	—	—	—	—	—	—
1713E Rare	—	—	—	—	—	—
1714E Rare	—	—	—	—	—	—
1715E Rare	—	—	—	—	—	—

KM# 390.6 LOUIS D'OR

8.1300 g., 0.9170 Gold 0.2397 oz. AGW **Ruler:** Louis XIV **Mint:** Poitiers **Obverse:** Laureate head right **Reverse:** Crowned back to back L's with flower in center square, fleur-de-lis at angles

Date	Mintage	VG	F	VF	XF	Unc
1709G Rare	—	—	—	—	—	—
1710G Rare	—	—	—	—	—	—
1711G Rare	—	—	—	—	—	—
1712G Rare	—	—	—	—	—	—
1713G	—	300	500	900	1,700	—
1714G Rare	—	—	—	—	—	—
1715G Rare	—	—	—	—	—	—

KM# 390.7 LOUIS D'OR

8.1300 g., 0.9170 Gold 0.2397 oz. AGW **Ruler:** Louis XIV **Mint:** La Rochelle **Obverse:** Laureate head right **Reverse:** Crowned back to back L's with flower in center square, fleur-de-lis at angles

Date	Mintage	VG	F	VF	XF	Unc
1709H	—	250	450	750	1,500	—
1710H	—	250	450	750	1,500	—
1711H	—	250	450	750	1,500	—
1712H Rare	—	—	—	—	—	—
1713H Rare	—	—	—	—	—	—
1714H	—	300	500	900	1,700	—

KM# 390.8 LOUIS D'OR

8.1300 g., 0.9170 Gold 0.2397 oz. AGW **Ruler:** Louis XIV **Mint:** Limoges **Obverse:** Laureate head right **Reverse:** Crowned back to back L's with flower in center square, fleur-de-lis at angles

Date	Mintage	VG	F	VF	XF	Unc
1709I Rare	—	—	—	—	—	—
1710I Rare	—	—	—	—	—	—
1711I Rare	—	—	—	—	—	—
1712I Rare	—	—	—	—	—	—
1713I	—	300	500	900	1,700	—
1714I Rare	—	—	—	—	—	—
1715I Rare	—	—	—	—	—	—

KM# 390.9 LOUIS D'OR

8.1300 g., 0.9170 Gold 0.2397 oz. AGW **Ruler:** Louis XIV **Mint:** Bordeaux **Obverse:** Laureate head right **Reverse:** Crowned back to back L's with flower in center square, fleur-de-lis at angles

Date	Mintage	VG	F	VF	XF	Unc
1709K Rare	—	—	—	—	—	—
1710K	—	200	400	600	1,200	—
1711K	340,000	200	400	600	1,200	—

KM# 390.10 LOUIS D'OR

8.1300 g., 0.9170 Gold 0.2397 oz. AGW **Ruler:** Louis XIV **Mint:** Bayonne **Obverse:** Laureate head right **Reverse:** Crowned back to back L's with flower in center square, fleur-de-lis at angles

Date	Mintage	VG	F	VF	XF	Unc
1709L	—	300	500	900	1,750	—
1710L	—	200	400	600	1,200	—

KM# 390.11 LOUIS D'OR

8.1300 g., 0.9170 Gold 0.2397 oz. AGW **Ruler:** Louis XIV **Mint:** Toulouse **Obverse:** Laureate head right **Reverse:** Crowned back to back L's with flower in center square, fleur-de-lis at angles

Date	Mintage	VG	F	VF	XF	Unc
1709M	—	200	400	600	1,200	—
1710M	—	250	450	750	1,500	—
1711M Rare	—	—	—	—	—	—
1712M Rare	—	—	—	—	—	—
1713M Rare	—	—	—	—	—	—
1714M Rare	—	—	—	—	—	—
1715M Rare	—	—	—	—	—	—

KM# 390.12 LOUIS D'OR

8.1300 g., 0.9170 Gold 0.2397 oz. AGW **Ruler:** Louis XIV **Mint:** Montpellier **Obverse:** Laureate head right

Date	Mintage	VG	F	VF	XF	Unc
1709N Rare	—	—	—	—	—	—
1710N	—	200	400	600	1,200	—
1711N Rare	—	—	—	—	—	—
1712N	—	300	500	900	1,800	—
1713N Rare	—	—	—	—	—	—
1715N	—	250	450	750	1,500	—

KM# 390.13 LOUIS D'OR

8.1300 g., 0.9170 Gold 0.2397 oz. AGW **Ruler:** Louis XIV **Mint:** Riom **Obverse:** Laureate head right **Reverse:** Crowned back to back L's with flower in center square, fleur-de-lis at angles

Date	Mintage	VG	F	VF	XF	Unc
1709O Rare	—	—	—	—	—	—
1710O Rare	—	—	—	—	—	—
1711O Rare	—	—	—	—	—	—
1712O Rare	—	—	—	—	—	—
1713O Rare	—	—	—	—	—	—
1714O Rare	—	—	—	—	—	—
1715O Rare	—	—	—	—	—	—

KM# 390.14 LOUIS D'OR

8.1300 g., 0.9170 Gold 0.2397 oz. AGW **Ruler:** Louis XIV **Mint:** Dijon **Obverse:** Laureate head right **Reverse:** Crowned back to back L's with flower in center square, fleur-de-lis at angles

Date	Mintage	VG	F	VF	XF	Unc
1709P	—	250	450	750	1,500	—
1710P	—	250	450	750	1,500	—
1711P	—	250	450	750	1,500	—
1712P Rare	—	—	—	—	—	—
1713P Rare	—	—	—	—	—	—

KM# 390.21 LOUIS D'OR

8.1300 g., 0.9170 Gold 0.2397 oz. AGW **Ruler:** Louis XIV **Mint:** Amiens

Date	Mintage	VG	F	VF	XF	Unc
1709X	—	250	450	750	1,500	—
1710X	—	200	400	600	1,200	—
1711X	—	200	400	600	1,200	—
1712X	—	300	500	900	1,700	—
1713X Rare	—	—	—	—	—	—
1714X Rare	—	—	—	—	—	—
1715X Rare	—	—	—	—	—	—

KM# 390.22 LOUIS D'OR

8.1300 g., 0.9170 Gold 0.2397 oz. AGW **Ruler:** Louis XIV **Mint:** Bourges

Date	Mintage	VG	F	VF	XF	Unc
1709Y	—	300	500	1,000	1,800	—
1710Y	—	200	400	700	1,100	—
1711Y Rare	—	—	—	—	—	—
1712Y Rare	—	—	—	—	—	—
1713Y Rare	—	—	—	—	—	—
1714Y Rare	—	—	—	—	—	—
1715Y Rare	—	—	—	—	—	—

KM# 390.23 LOUIS D'OR

8.1300 g., 0.9170 Gold 0.2397 oz. AGW **Ruler:** Louis XIV **Mint:** Grenoble

Date	Mintage	VG	F	VF	XF	Unc
1709Z Rare	—	—	—	—	—	—
1710Z Rare	—	—	—	—	—	—
1711Z Rare	—	—	—	—	—	—
1712Z Rare	—	—	—	—	—	—
1713Z Rare	—	—	—	—	—	—
1714Z Rare	—	—	—	—	—	—
1715Z Rare	—	—	—	—	—	—

KM# 390.16 LOUIS D'OR

8.1300 g., 0.9170 Gold 0.2397 oz. AGW **Ruler:** Louis XIV **Mint:** Villeneuve St. André

Date	Mintage	VG	F	VF	XF	Unc
1709R Rare	—	—	—	—	—	—

KM# 390.18 LOUIS D'OR

8.1300 g., 0.9170 Gold 0.2397 oz. AGW **Ruler:** Louis XIV **Mint:** Nantes

Date	Mintage	VG	F	VF	XF	Unc
1709T Rare	—	—	—	—	—	—
1710T Rare	—	—	—	—	—	—
1711T Rare	—	—	—	—	—	—
1712T	—	250	450	750	1,500	—
1713T Rare	—	—	—	—	—	—
1714T Rare	—	—	—	—	—	—
1715T	—	250	450	750	1,500	—

KM# 390.19 LOUIS D'OR

8.1300 g., 0.9170 Gold 0.2397 oz. AGW **Ruler:** Louis XIV **Mint:** Troyes

Date	Mintage	VG	F	VF	XF	Unc
1709V	—	250	450	750	1,500	—
1710V Rare	—	—	—	—	—	—
1711V Rare	—	—	—	—	—	—
1712V Rare	—	—	—	—	—	—
1713V Rare	—	—	—	—	—	—
1714V Rare	—	—	—	—	—	—
1715V Rare	—	—	—	—	—	—

KM# 390.20 LOUIS D'OR

8.1300 g., 0.9170 Gold 0.2397 oz. AGW **Ruler:** Louis XIV **Mint:** Lille **Obverse:** Laureate head right **Reverse:** Crowned back to back L's with flower in center square, fleur-de-lis at angles

Date	Mintage	VG	F	VF	XF	Unc
1711W	—	250	450	750	1,500	—
1713W Rare	—	—	—	—	—	—
1714W Rare	—	—	—	—	—	—
1715W Rare	—	—	—	—	—	—

KM# 390.15 LOUIS D'OR

8.1300 g., 0.9170 Gold 0.2397 oz. AGW **Ruler:** Louis XIV **Mint:** Perpignan **Obverse:** Laureate head right **Reverse:** Crowned back to back L's with flower in center square, fleur-de-lis at angles

Date	Mintage	VG	F	VF	XF	Unc
1711Q	—	250	450	750	1,500	—
1712Q	—	300	500	1,000	1,800	—

KM# 415.1 LOUIS D'OR

8.1580 g., 0.9170 Gold 0.2405 oz. AGW **Ruler:** Louis XV **Mint:** Montpellier **Obverse:** Boy head of Louis XV right; date and mint mark below **Reverse:** Crowned double L's cruciform with fleur-de-lis in angles

Date	Mintage	VG	F	VF	XF	Unc
1715N	3,265	2,750	6,500	9,000	15,000	—
1715N	3,265	2,750	6,500	9,000	15,000	—

KM# 415.2 LOUIS D'OR

8.1580 g., 0.9170 Gold 0.2405 oz. AGW **Ruler:** Louis XV **Mint:** Aix **Note:** Mint mark: &.

Date	Mintage	VG	F	VF	XF	Unc
1715	—	3,250	7,500	10,000	16,000	—

KM# 425.19 LOUIS D'OR

8.1580 g., 0.9170 Gold 0.2405 oz. AGW **Ruler:** Louis XV **Mint:** Aix **Note:** Mint mark: &.

Date	Mintage	VG	F	VF	XF	Unc
1716	—	725	2,200	3,200	6,500	—

KM# 425.18 LOUIS D'OR

8.1580 g., 0.9170 Gold 0.2405 oz. AGW **Ruler:** Louis XV **Mint:** Rennes **Note:** Mint mark: 9.

Date	Mintage	VG	F	VF	XF	Unc
1716	—	775	2,400	3,400	7,000	—

KM# 425.1 LOUIS D'OR

8.1580 g., 0.9170 Gold 0.2405 oz. AGW **Ruler:** Louis XV **Mint:** Paris **Obverse:** Young head right **Obv. Legend:** LVD • XV • D • G • FR • ET • NAV • REX • **Reverse:** Crowned arms of France **Rev. Legend:** CHRS • REGN • N • VINC IMP *

Date	Mintage	VG	F	VF	XF	Unc
1716A	—	650	2,000	3,000	6,000	—

KM# 425.2 LOUIS D'OR

8.1580 g., 0.9170 Gold 0.2405 oz. AGW **Ruler:** Louis XV **Mint:** Rouen **Obverse:** Young head right **Reverse:** Crowned arms of France

Date	Mintage	VG	F	VF	XF	Unc
1716B	—	725	2,200	3,200	6,500	—

KM# 425.3 LOUIS D'OR

8.1580 g., 0.9170 Gold 0.2405 oz. AGW **Ruler:** Louis XV **Mint:** Lyon **Obverse:** Young head right **Reverse:** Crowned arms of France

Date	Mintage	VG	F	VF	XF	Unc
1716D	25,000	725	2,200	3,200	6,500	—

KM# 425.4 LOUIS D'OR

8.1580 g., 0.9170 Gold 0.2405 oz. AGW **Ruler:** Louis XV **Mint:** Tours **Obverse:** Young head right **Reverse:** Crowned arms of France

Date	Mintage	VG	F	VF	XF	Unc
1716E	—	650	2,000	3,000	6,000	—

KM# 425.5 LOUIS D'OR

8.1580 g., 0.9170 Gold 0.2405 oz. AGW **Ruler:** Louis XV **Mint:** Poitiers **Obverse:** Young head right **Reverse:** Crowned arms of France

Date	Mintage	VG	F	VF	XF	Unc
1716G	—	725	2,200	3,200	6,500	—

KM# 425.6 LOUIS D'OR

8.1580 g., 0.9170 Gold 0.2405 oz. AGW **Ruler:** Louis XV **Mint:** La Rochelle **Obverse:** Young head right **Reverse:** Crowned arms of France

Date	Mintage	VG	F	VF	XF	Unc
1716H	—	725	2,200	3,200	6,500	—

KM# 425.7 LOUIS D'OR

8.1580 g., 0.9170 Gold 0.2405 oz. AGW **Ruler:** Louis XV **Mint:** Bordeaux **Obverse:** Young head right **Reverse:** Crowned arms of France

Date	Mintage	VG	F	VF	XF	Unc
1716K	—	975	3,000	4,500	9,000	—

KM# 425.8 LOUIS D'OR

8.1580 g., 0.9170 Gold 0.2405 oz. AGW **Ruler:** Louis XV **Mint:** Bayonne **Obverse:** Young head right **Reverse:** Crowned arms of France

Date	Mintage	VG	F	VF	XF	Unc
1716L	—	725	2,200	3,200	6,500	—

KM# 425.9 LOUIS D'OR

8.1580 g., 0.9170 Gold 0.2405 oz. AGW **Ruler:** Louis XV **Mint:** Toulouse **Obverse:** Young head right **Reverse:** Crowned arms of France

Date	Mintage	VG	F	VF	XF	Unc
1716M	28,000	725	2,200	3,200	6,500	—

KM# 425.10 LOUIS D'OR

8.1580 g., 0.9170 Gold 0.2405 oz. AGW **Ruler:** Louis XV **Mint:** Montpellier **Obverse:** Young head right **Reverse:** Crowned arms of France

Date	Mintage	VG	F	VF	XF	Unc
1716N	72,000	975	3,000	4,500	9,000	—

KM# 425.11 LOUIS D'OR

8.1580 g., 0.9170 Gold 0.2405 oz. AGW **Ruler:** Louis XV **Mint:** Perpignan **Obverse:** Young head right **Reverse:** Crowned arms of France

Date	Mintage	VG	F	VF	XF	Unc
1716Q	—	975	3,000	4,500	9,000	—

KM# 425.12 LOUIS D'OR

8.1580 g., 0.9170 Gold 0.2405 oz. AGW **Ruler:** Louis XV **Mint:** Reims **Obverse:** Young head right **Reverse:** Crowned arms of France

Date	Mintage	VG	F	VF	XF	Unc
1716S	—	725	2,200	3,200	6,500	—

KM# 425.13 LOUIS D'OR

8.1580 g., 0.9170 Gold 0.2405 oz. AGW **Ruler:** Louis XV **Mint:** Nantes **Obverse:** Young head right **Reverse:** Crowned arms of France

Date	Mintage	VG	F	VF	XF	Unc
1716T	—	725	2,200	3,200	6,500	—

KM# 425.14 LOUIS D'OR

8.1580 g., 0.9170 Gold 0.2405 oz. AGW **Ruler:** Louis XV **Mint:** Troyes **Obverse:** Young head right **Reverse:** Crowned arms of France

Date	Mintage	VG	F	VF	XF	Unc
1716V	—	725	2,200	3,200	6,500	—

KM# 425.15 LOUIS D'OR

8.1580 g., 0.9170 Gold 0.2405 oz. AGW **Ruler:** Louis XV **Mint:** Lille **Obverse:** Young head right **Reverse:** Crowned arms of France

Date	Mintage	VG	F	VF	XF	Unc
1716W	—	775	2,400	3,500	7,000	—

KM# 425.16 LOUIS D'OR

8.1580 g., 0.9170 Gold 0.2405 oz. AGW **Ruler:** Louis XV **Mint:** Amiens **Obverse:** Young head right **Reverse:** Crowned arms of France

Date	Mintage	VG	F	VF	XF	Unc
1716X	3,649	725	2,200	3,200	6,500	—

KM# 425.17 LOUIS D'OR

8.1580 g., 0.9170 Gold 0.2405 oz. AGW **Ruler:** Louis XV **Mint:** Grenoble **Obverse:** Young head right **Reverse:** Crowned arms of France

Date	Mintage	VG	F	VF	XF	Unc
1716Z	13,000	725	2,200	3,200	6,500	—

KM# 430.2 LOUIS D'OR

6.1180 g., 0.9170 Gold 0.1804 oz. AGW **Ruler:** Louis XV **Mint:** Metz

Date	Mintage	VG	F	VF	XF	Unc
1717AA	4,000	—	—	—	—	—

Note: Reported, not confirmed

KM# 430.1 LOUIS D'OR

6.1180 g., 0.9170 Gold 0.1804 oz. AGW **Ruler:** Louis XV **Mint:** Paris **Obverse:** Crowned head left **Obv. Legend:** LVD • XV • D • G • FR • ET • NAV • REX • **Reverse:** Crowned arms of France and Navarre in cruciform, fleur-de-lis at angles **Rev. Legend:** CHRS • REGN • VINC • IMP • **Note:** Issued for Noailles.

Date	Mintage	VG	F	VF	XF	Unc
1717A	447,000	1,000	1,750	2,500	3,500	5,000

KM# 438.24 LOUIS D'OR

9.7900 g., 0.9170 Gold 0.2886 oz. AGW **Ruler:** Louis XV **Mint:** Besancon **Note:** Mint mark:Back to back C's.

Date	Mintage	VG	F	VF	XF	Unc
1718	—	300	650	1,100	2,150	—

KM# 438.23 LOUIS D'OR

9.7900 g., 0.9170 Gold 0.2886 oz. AGW **Ruler:** Louis XV **Mint:** Aix **Note:** Mint mark: &.

Date	Mintage	VG	F	VF	XF	Unc
1718	—	375	750	1,250	2,550	—
1719	—	425	900	1,600	2,900	—

KM# 438.1 LOUIS D'OR

9.7900 g., 0.9170 Gold 0.2886 oz. AGW **Ruler:** Louis XV **Mint:** Paris **Obverse:** Young laureate bust right **Obv. Legend:** LVD • XV • D • G • FR • ST • NAV • REX • **Reverse:** Round arms of France at center of 8-pointed cross **Rev. Legend:** CHRISTVS REGNAT VINCIT IMPERAT

Date	Mintage	VG	F	VF	XF	Unc
1718A	—	250	450	700	1,500	—
1719A	—	275	525	800	1,700	—

KM# 438.2 LOUIS D'OR

9.7900 g., 0.9170 Gold 0.2886 oz. AGW **Ruler:** Louis XV **Mint:** Motz **Obvorco:** Young lauroato hoad right **Rovorco:** Round armc of France at center of 8-pointed cross

Date	Mintage	VG	F	VF	XF	Unc
1718AA	—	300	650	1,100	2,150	—

KM# 438.3 LOUIS D'OR

9.7900 g., 0.9170 Gold 0.2886 oz. AGW **Ruler:** Louis XV **Mint:** Rouen **Obverse:** Young laureate head right **Reverse:** Round arms of France at center of 8-pointed cross

Date	Mintage	VG	F	VF	XF	Unc
1718B	23,000	300	650	1,100	2,150	—

KM# 438.4 LOUIS D'OR

9.7900 g., 0.9170 Gold 0.2886 oz. AGW **Ruler:** Louis XV **Mint:** Strasbourg **Obverse:** Young laureate head right **Reverse:** Round arms of France at center of 8-pointed cross

Date	Mintage	VG	F	VF	XF	Unc
1718BB	—	300	650	1,100	2,150	—

KM# 438.5 LOUIS D'OR

9.7900 g., 0.9170 Gold 0.2886 oz. AGW **Ruler:** Louis XV **Mint:** Caen **Obverse:** Young laureate head right **Reverse:** Round arms of France at center of 8-pointed cross

Date	Mintage	VG	F	VF	XF	Unc
1718C	—	300	650	1,100	2,150	—
1719C	16,000	300	650	1,100	2,150	—

KM# 438.6 LOUIS D'OR

9.7900 g., 0.9170 Gold 0.2886 oz. AGW **Ruler:** Louis XV **Mint:** Lyon **Obverse:** Young laureate head right **Reverse:** Round arms of France at center of 8-pointed cross

Date	Mintage	VG	F	VF	XF	Unc
1718D	—	300	650	1,100	2,150	—
1719D	—	375	750	1,250	2,550	—

KM# 438.7 LOUIS D'OR

9.7900 g., 0.9170 Gold 0.2886 oz. AGW **Ruler:** Louis XV **Mint:** Tours **Obverse:** Young laureate head right **Reverse:** Round arms of France at center of 8-pointed cross

Date	Mintage	VG	F	VF	XF	Unc
1718E	7,338	300	650	1,100	2,150	—
1719E	14,000	300	650	1,100	2,150	—

KM# 438.8 LOUIS D'OR

9.7900 g., 0.9170 Gold 0.2886 oz. AGW **Ruler:** Louis XV **Mint:** Bordeaux **Obverse:** Young laureate head right **Reverse:** Round arms of France at center of 8-pointed cross

Date	Mintage	VG	F	VF	XF	Unc
1718K	32,000	300	650	1,100	2,150	—

KM# 438.9 LOUIS D'OR

9.7900 g., 0.9170 Gold 0.2886 oz. AGW **Ruler:** Louis XV **Mint:** Bayonne **Obverse:** Young laureate head right **Reverse:** Round arms of France at center of 8-pointed cross

Date	Mintage	VG	F	VF	XF	Unc
1718L	—	300	650	1,100	2,150	—
1719L	—	375	750	1,250	2,550	—

KM# 438.10 LOUIS D'OR

9.7900 g., 0.9170 Gold 0.2886 oz. AGW **Ruler:** Louis XV **Mint:** Toulouse **Obverse:** Young laureate head right **Reverse:** Round arms of France at center of 8-pointed cross

Date	Mintage	VG	F	VF	XF	Unc
1718M	—	300	650	1,100	2,150	—
1719M	—	375	750	1,250	2,550	—

KM# 438.11 LOUIS D'OR

9.7900 g., 0.9170 Gold 0.2886 oz. AGW **Ruler:** Louis XV **Mint:** Montpellier **Obverse:** Young laureate head right **Reverse:** Round arms of France at center of 8-pointed cross

Date	Mintage	VG	F	VF	XF	Unc
1718N	41,000	300	650	1,100	2,150	—
1719N	57,000	300	650	1,100	2,150	—

KM# 438.12 LOUIS D'OR

9.7900 g., 0.9170 Gold 0.2886 oz. AGW **Ruler:** Louis XV **Mint:** Riom **Obverse:** Young laureate head right **Reverse:** Round arms of France at center of 8-pointed cross

Date	Mintage	VG	F	VF	XF	Unc
1718O	—	375	750	1,250	2,550	—

KM# 438.13 LOUIS D'OR

9.7900 g., 0.9170 Gold 0.2886 oz. AGW **Ruler:** Louis XV **Mint:** Dijon **Obverse:** Young laureate head right **Reverse:** Round arms of France at center of 8-pointed cross

Date	Mintage	VG	F	VF	XF	Unc
1718P	—	300	650	1,100	2,150	—
1719P	—	375	750	1,250	2,550	—

KM# 438.14 LOUIS D'OR

9.7900 g., 0.9170 Gold 0.2886 oz. AGW **Ruler:** Louis XV **Mint:** Perpignan **Obverse:** Young laureate head right **Reverse:** Round arms of France at center of 8-pointed cross

Date	Mintage	VG	F	VF	XF	Unc
1718Q	—	300	650	1,100	2,150	—
1719Q	—	375	750	1,250	2,550	—

KM# 438.15 LOUIS D'OR

9.7900 g., 0.9170 Gold 0.2886 oz. AGW **Ruler:** Louis XV **Mint:** Reims **Obverse:** Young laureate head right **Reverse:** Round arms of France at center of 8-pointed cross

Date	Mintage	VG	F	VF	XF	Unc
1718S	—	300	650	1,100	2,150	—

KM# 438.16 LOUIS D'OR

9.7900 g., 0.9170 Gold 0.2886 oz. AGW **Ruler:** Louis XV **Mint:** Nantes **Obverse:** Young laureate head right **Reverse:** Round arms of France at center of 8-pointed cross

Date	Mintage	VG	F	VF	XF	Unc
1718T	—	300	650	1,100	2,150	—
1719T	—	300	650	1,100	2,150	—

KM# 438.17 LOUIS D'OR

9.7900 g., 0.9170 Gold 0.2886 oz. AGW **Ruler:** Louis XV **Mint:** Troyes **Obverse:** Young laureate head right **Reverse:** Round arms of France at center of 8-pointed cross

Date	Mintage	VG	F	VF	XF	Unc
1718V	—	300	650	1,100	2,150	—
1719V	—	300	650	1,100	2,150	—

KM# 438.18 LOUIS D'OR

9.7900 g., 0.9170 Gold 0.2886 oz. AGW **Ruler:** Louis XV **Mint:** Lille **Obverse:** Young laureate head right **Reverse:** Round arms of France at center of 8-pointed cross

Date	Mintage	VG	F	VF	XF	Unc
1718W	—	300	650	1,100	2,150	—
1719W	—	300	650	1,100	2,150	—

KM# 438.19 LOUIS D'OR

9.7900 g., 0.9170 Gold 0.2886 oz. AGW **Ruler:** Louis XV **Mint:** Amiens **Obverse:** Young laureate head right **Reverse:** Round arms of France at center of 8-pointed cross

Date	Mintage	VG	F	VF	XF	Unc
1718X	—	300	650	1,100	2,150	—
1719X	—	300	650	1,100	2,150	—

KM# 438.20 LOUIS D'OR

9.7900 g., 0.9170 Gold 0.2886 oz. AGW **Ruler:** Louis XV **Mint:** Bourges **Obverse:** Young laureate head right **Reverse:** Round arms of France at center of 8-pointed cross

Date	Mintage	VG	F	VF	XF	Unc
1718Y	—	375	750	1,250	2,550	—

KM# 438.21 LOUIS D'OR

9.7900 g., 0.9170 Gold 0.2886 oz. AGW **Ruler:** Louis XV **Mint:** Grenoble **Obverse:** Young laureate head right **Reverse:** Round arms of France at center of 8-pointed cross

Date	Mintage	VG	F	VF	XF	Unc
1718Z	49,000	375	750	1,250	2,550	—
1719Z	7,593	375	750	1,250	2,550	—

KM# 438.22 LOUIS D'OR

9.7900 g., 0.9170 Gold 0.2886 oz. AGW **Ruler:** Louis XV **Mint:** Rennes **Obverse:** Young laureate head right **Reverse:** Round arms of France at center of 8-pointed cross **Note:** Mint mark: 9.

Date	Mintage	VG	F	VF	XF	Unc
1719	—	—	—	—	—	—

KM# 461.1 LOUIS D'OR

9.7900 g., 0.9170 Gold 0.2886 oz. AGW **Ruler:** Louis XV **Mint:** Paris **Obverse:** Laureate head right **Obv. Legend:** LUD • XV • D • G • FR • ET • NAV • REX • **Reverse:** Crowned double L monogram with 3 fleur-de-lis **Rev. Legend:** CHRISTUS REGNAT VINCIT IMPERAT

Date	Mintage	VG	F	VF	XF	Unc
1720A	—	300	600	1,000	1,950	—
1721A	—	300	600	1,000	1,950	—
1722A	—	300	600	1,000	1,950	—
1723A	—	300	600	1,000	1,950	—

KM# 461.4 LOUIS D'OR

9.7900 g., 0.9170 Gold 0.2886 oz. AGW **Ruler:** Louis XV **Mint:** Strasbourg **Obverse:** Laureate head right **Reverse:** Crowned double L monogram with 3 fleur-de-lis

Date	Mintage	VG	F	VF	XF	Unc
1720BB	667	600	1,250	2,600	4,500	—
1721BB	55,000	300	600	1,000	1,950	—
1722BB	—	300	600	1,000	1,950	—

KM# 461.6 LOUIS D'OR

9.7900 g., 0.9170 Gold 0.2886 oz. AGW **Ruler:** Louis XV **Mint:** Lyon **Obverse:** Laureate head right **Reverse:** Crowned double L monogram with 3 fleur-de-lis

Date	Mintage	VG	F	VF	XF	Unc
1720D	29,000	300	600	1,000	1,950	—
1721D	—	300	600	1,000	1,950	—

KM# 461.9 LOUIS D'OR

9.7900 g., 0.9170 Gold 0.2886 oz. AGW **Ruler:** Louis XV **Mint:** La Rochelle **Obverse:** Laureate head right **Reverse:** Crowned double L monogram with 3 fleur-de-lis

Date	Mintage	VG	F	VF	XF	Unc
1720H	23,000	300	600	1,000	1,950	—
1721H	37,000	300	600	1,000	1,950	—
1723H	—	400	700	1,250	2,450	—

KM# 461.10 LOUIS D'OR

9.7900 g., 0.9170 Gold 0.2886 oz. AGW **Ruler:** Louis XV **Mint:** Limoges **Obverse:** Laureate head right **Reverse:** Crowned double L monogram with 3 fleur-de-lis

Date	Mintage	VG	F	VF	XF	Unc
1720I	3,620	300	600	1,000	1,950	—

KM# 461.11 LOUIS D'OR

9.7900 g., 0.9170 Gold 0.2886 oz. AGW **Ruler:** Louis XV **Mint:** Bayonne **Obverse:** Laureate head right **Reverse:** Crowned double L monogram with 3 fleur-de-lis

Date	Mintage	VG	F	VF	XF	Unc
1720L	803	500	1,150	2,400	4,350	—
1721L	—	300	600	1,000	1,950	—
1722L	—	300	600	1,000	1,950	—

KM# 461.15 LOUIS D'OR

9.7900 g., 0.9170 Gold 0.2886 oz. AGW **Ruler:** Louis XV **Mint:** Nantes **Obverse:** Laureate head right **Reverse:** Crowned double L monogram with 3 fleur-de-lis

Date	Mintage	VG	F	VF	XF	Unc
1720T	500	500	1,000	2,000	4,000	—

KM# 461.16 LOUIS D'OR

9.7900 g., 0.9170 Gold 0.2886 oz. AGW **Ruler:** Louis XV **Mint:** Troyes **Obverse:** Laureate head right **Reverse:** Crowned double L monogram with 3 fleur-de-lis

Date	Mintage	VG	F	VF	XF	Unc
1720V	—	300	600	1,000	1,950	—

KM# 461.17 LOUIS D'OR

9.7900 g., 0.9170 Gold 0.2886 oz. AGW **Ruler:** Louis XV **Mint:** Lille **Obverse:** Laureate head right **Reverse:** Crowned double L monogram with 3 fleur-de-lis

Date	Mintage	VG	F	VF	XF	Unc
1720W	19,000	300	600	1,000	1,950	—
1721W	139,000	300	600	1,000	1,950	—
1722W	51,000	300	600	1,000	1,950	—

KM# 461.18 LOUIS D'OR

9.7900 g., 0.9170 Gold 0.2886 oz. AGW **Ruler:** Louis XV **Mint:** Amiens **Obverse:** Laureate head right **Reverse:** Crowned double L monogram with 3 fleur-de-lis

Date	Mintage	VG	F	VF	XF	Unc
1721X	9,621	300	600	1,000	1,950	—

KM# 461.12 LOUIS D'OR

9.7900 g., 0.9170 Gold 0.2886 oz. AGW **Ruler:** Louis XV **Mint:** Toulouse **Obverse:** Laureate head right **Reverse:** Crowned double L monogram with 3 fleur-de-lis

Date	Mintage	VG	F	VF	XF	Unc
1721M	—	300	600	1,000	1,950	—

KM# 461.13 LOUIS D'OR

9.7900 g., 0.9170 Gold 0.2886 oz. AGW **Ruler:** Louis XV **Mint:** Montpellier **Obverse:** Laureate head right **Reverse:** Crowned double L monogram with 3 fleur-de-lis

Date	Mintage	VG	F	VF	XF	Unc
1721N	31,000	300	600	1,000	1,950	—
1722N	15,000	400	800	1,300	2,450	—

KM# 461.5 LOUIS D'OR

9.7900 g., 0.9170 Gold 0.2886 oz. AGW **Ruler:** Louis XV **Mint:** Caen **Obverse:** Laureate head right **Reverse:** Crowned double L monogram with 3 fleur-de-lis

Date	Mintage	VG	F	VF	XF	Unc
1721C	6,128	300	600	1,000	1,950	—

KM# 461.2 LOUIS D'OR

9.7900 g., 0.9170 Gold 0.2886 oz. AGW **Ruler:** Louis XV **Mint:** Metz **Obverse:** Laureate head right **Reverse:** Crowned double L monogram with 3 fleur-de-lis

Date	Mintage	VG	F	VF	XF	Unc
1721AA	—	300	600	1,000	1,950	—

KM# 461.3 LOUIS D'OR

9.7900 g., 0.9170 Gold 0.2886 oz. AGW **Ruler:** Louis XV **Mint:** Rouen **Obverse:** Laureate head right **Reverse:** Crowned double L monogram with 3 fleur-de-lis

Date	Mintage	VG	F	VF	XF	Unc
1721B	20,000	300	600	1,000	1,950	—

KM# 461.20 LOUIS D'OR

9.7900 g., 0.9170 Gold 0.2886 oz. AGW **Ruler:** Louis XV **Mint:** Rennes **Obverse:** Laureate head right **Reverse:** Crowned double L monogram with 3 fleur-de-lis **Note:** Mint mark: 9.

Date	Mintage	VG	F	VF	XF	Unc
1721	45,000	300	600	1,000	1,950	—
1722	69,000	300	600	1,000	1,950	—
1723	—	300	600	1,000	1,950	—

KM# 461.21 LOUIS D'OR

9.7900 g., 0.9170 Gold 0.2886 oz. AGW **Ruler:** Louis XV **Mint:** Aix **Obverse:** Laureate head right **Reverse:** Crowned double L monogram with 3 fleur-de-lis **Note:** Mint mark: &.

Date	Mintage	VG	F	VF	XF	Unc
1721	—	400	800	1,300	2,450	—

KM# 466 LOUIS D'OR

9.7900 g., 0.9170 Gold 0.2886 oz. AGW **Ruler:** Louis XV **Mint:** Pau **Obv. Legend:** ....RE.BD (ligate BD). **Note:** Mint mark: Cow. Issued for Province of Bearn.

Date	Mintage	VG	F	VF	XF	Unc
1722	65,000	500	1,000	2,000	3,750	—
1723	—	600	1,200	2,500	5,000	—

KM# 461.7 LOUIS D'OR

9.7900 g., 0.9170 Gold 0.2886 oz. AGW **Ruler:** Louis XV **Mint:** Tours **Obverse:** Laureate head right **Reverse:** Crowned double L monogram with 3 fleur-de-lis

Date	Mintage	VG	F	VF	XF	Unc
1722E	4,261	350	700	1,250	2,450	—

KM# 461.8 LOUIS D'OR

9.7900 g., 0.9170 Gold 0.2886 oz. AGW **Ruler:** Louis XV **Mint:** Poitiers **Obverse:** Laureate head right **Reverse:** Crowned double L monogram with 3 fleur-de-lis

Date	Mintage	VG	F	VF	XF	Unc
1722G	4,115	300	600	1,000	1,950	—

KM# 461.19 LOUIS D'OR

9.7900 g., 0.9170 Gold 0.2886 oz. AGW **Ruler:** Louis XV **Mint:** Bourges **Obverse:** Laureate head right **Reverse:** Crowned double L monogram with 3 fleur-de-lis

Date	Mintage	VG	F	VF	XF	Unc
1722Y	3,346	300	600	1,000	1,950	—

KM# 468.1 LOUIS D'OR

6.5250 g., 0.9170 Gold 0.1924 oz. AGW **Ruler:** Louis XV **Mint:** Paris **Obverse:** Laureate head right **Obv. Legend:** LUD • XV • D • G • FR • ET • NAV • REX **Reverse:** Crowned double L monogram within palms **Rev. Legend:** CHRS • REGN • VINC • IMP •

Date	Mintage	VG	F	VF	XF	Unc
1723A	—	200	350	500	950	—

KM# 468.2 LOUIS D'OR

6.5250 g., 0.9170 Gold 0.1924 oz. AGW **Ruler:** Louis XV **Mint:** Rouen **Obverse:** Laureate head right **Reverse:** Crowned double L monogram within palms

Date	Mintage	VG	F	VF	XF	Unc
1723B	—	200	400	600	1,000	—

KM# 468.3 LOUIS D'OR

6.5250 g., 0.9170 Gold 0.1924 oz. AGW **Ruler:** Louis XV **Mint:** Strasbourg **Obverse:** Laureate head right **Reverse:** Crowned double L monogram within palms

Date	Mintage	VG	F	VF	XF	Unc
1723BB	—	250	500	800	1,400	—

KM# 468.4 LOUIS D'OR

6.5250 g., 0.9170 Gold 0.1924 oz. AGW **Ruler:** Louis XV **Mint:** Caen **Obverse:** Laureate head right **Reverse:** Crowned double L monogram within palms

Date	Mintage	VG	F	VF	XF	Unc
1723C	—	225	400	650	1,250	—

KM# 468.5 LOUIS D'OR

6.5250 g., 0.9170 Gold 0.1924 oz. AGW **Ruler:** Louis XV **Mint:** Lyon **Obverse:** Laureate head right **Reverse:** Crowned double L monogram within palms

Date	Mintage	VG	F	VF	XF	Unc
1723D	2,980	250	500	850	1,600	—

KM# 468.6 LOUIS D'OR

6.5250 g., 0.9170 Gold 0.1924 oz. AGW **Ruler:** Louis XV **Mint:** Toulouse **Obverse:** Laureate head right **Reverse:** Crowned double L monogram within palms

Date	Mintage	VG	F	VF	XF	Unc
1723M	43,000	225	400	650	1,250	—

KM# 468.7 LOUIS D'OR

6.5250 g., 0.9170 Gold 0.1924 oz. AGW **Ruler:** Louis XV **Mint:** La Rochelle **Obverse:** Laureate head right **Reverse:** Crowned double L monogram within palms

Date	Mintage	VG	F	VF	XF	Unc
1723H	—	225	400	650	1,250	—

KM# 468.8 LOUIS D'OR

6.5250 g., 0.9170 Gold 0.1924 oz. AGW **Ruler:** Louis XV **Mint:** Bordeaux **Obverse:** Laureate head right **Reverse:** Crowned double L monogram within palms

Date	Mintage	VG	F	VF	XF	Unc
1723K	—	250	500	800	1,400	—

KM# 468.9 LOUIS D'OR

6.5250 g., 0.9170 Gold 0.1924 oz. AGW **Ruler:** Louis XV **Mint:** Bayonne **Obverse:** Laureate head right **Reverse:** Crowned double L monogram within palms

Date	Mintage	VG	F	VF	XF	Unc
1723L	—	225	400	650	1,250	—

KM# 468.10 LOUIS D'OR

6.5250 g., 0.9170 Gold 0.1924 oz. AGW **Ruler:** Louis XV **Mint:** Toulouse **Obverse:** Laureate head right **Reverse:** Crowned double L monogram within palms

Date	Mintage	VG	F	VF	XF	Unc
1723M	—	225	400	650	1,250	—

KM# 468.11 LOUIS D'OR

6.5250 g., 0.9170 Gold 0.1924 oz. AGW **Ruler:** Louis XV **Mint:** Montpellier **Obverse:** Laureate head right **Reverse:** Crowned double L monogram within palms

Date	Mintage	VG	F	VF	XF	Unc
1723N	179,000	225	400	700	1,325	—

KM# 468.12 LOUIS D'OR

6.5250 g., 0.9170 Gold 0.1924 oz. AGW **Ruler:** Louis XV **Mint:** Dijon **Obverse:** Laureate head right **Reverse:** Crowned double L monogram within palms

Date	Mintage	VG	F	VF	XF	Unc
1723P	—	225	400	650	1,250	—

KM# 468.13 LOUIS D'OR

6.5250 g., 0.9170 Gold 0.1924 oz. AGW **Ruler:** Louis XV **Mint:** Perpignan **Obverse:** Laureate head right **Reverse:** Crowned double L monogram within palms

Date	Mintage	VG	F	VF	XF	Unc
1723Q	—	225	400	650	1,250	—

KM# 468.14 LOUIS D'OR

6.5250 g., 0.9170 Gold 0.1924 oz. AGW **Ruler:** Louis XV **Mint:** Orléans **Obverse:** Laureate head right **Reverse:** Crowned double L monogram within palms

Date	Mintage	VG	F	VF	XF	Unc
1723R	70,000	225	400	650	1,250	—

KM# 468.15 LOUIS D'OR

6.5250 g., 0.9170 Gold 0.1924 oz. AGW **Ruler:** Louis XV **Mint:** Reims **Obverse:** Laureate head right **Reverse:** Crowned double L monogram within palms

Date	Mintage	VG	F	VF	XF	Unc
1723S	—	250	500	800	1,400	—

KM# 468.16 LOUIS D'OR

6.5250 g., 0.9170 Gold 0.1924 oz. AGW **Ruler:** Louis XV **Mint:** Nantes **Obverse:** Laureate head right **Reverse:** Crowned double L monogram within palms

Date	Mintage	VG	F	VF	XF	Unc
1723T	—	225	400	650	1,250	—

KM# 468.17 LOUIS D'OR

6.5250 g., 0.9170 Gold 0.1924 oz. AGW **Ruler:** Louis XV **Mint:** Troyes **Obverse:** Laureate head right **Reverse:** Crowned double L monogram within palms

Date	Mintage	VG	F	VF	XF	Unc
1723V	52,000	225	400	650	1,250	—

KM# 468.18 LOUIS D'OR

6.5250 g., 0.9170 Gold 0.1924 oz. AGW **Ruler:** Louis XV **Mint:** Lille **Obverse:** Laureate head right **Reverse:** Crowned double L monogram within palms

Date	Mintage	VG	F	VF	XF	Unc
1723W	59,000	225	400	650	1,250	—

KM# 468.19 LOUIS D'OR

6.5250 g., 0.9170 Gold 0.1924 oz. AGW **Ruler:** Louis XV **Mint:** Amiens **Obverse:** Laureate head right **Reverse:** Crowned double L monogram within palms

Date	Mintage	VG	F	VF	XF	Unc
1723X	—	225	400	650	1,250	—

KM# 470.1 LOUIS D'OR

6.5250 g., 0.9170 Gold 0.1924 oz. AGW **Ruler:** Louis XV **Mint:** Paris **Obverse:** Young laureate head right **Obv. Legend:** LUD • XV • D • G • FR • ET • NAV • REX **Reverse:** Crowned double L monogram within palms **Rev. Legend:** CHRS • REGN • VINC • IMP •

Date	Mintage	VG	F	VF	XF	Unc
1723A	—	250	500	800	1,250	—
1724A	—	200	450	700	1,000	—
1725A	—	200	450	700	1,000	—

KM# 461.14 LOUIS D'OR

9.7900 g., 0.9170 Gold 0.2886 oz. AGW **Ruler:** Louis XV **Mint:** Reims **Obverse:** Laureate head right **Reverse:** Crowned double L monogram with 3 fleur-de-lis

Date	Mintage	VG	F	VF	XF	Unc
1723S	—	500	1,000	2,000	4,000	—

KM# 469 LOUIS D'OR

6.5250 g., 0.9170 Gold 0.1924 oz. AGW **Ruler:** Louis XV **Mint:** Pau **Obv. Legend:** ....RE.BD (ligate BD). **Note:** Mint mark: Cow. Issued for Province of Bearn.

Date	Mintage	VG	F	VF	XF	Unc
1723	27,000	250	500	800	1,450	—

KM# 468.20 LOUIS D'OR

6.5250 g., 0.9170 Gold 0.1924 oz. AGW **Ruler:** Louis XV **Mint:** Rennes **Note:** Mint mark: 9.

Date	Mintage	VG	F	VF	XF	Unc
1723	—	225	400	650	1,250	—

KM# 468.21 LOUIS D'OR

6.5250 g., 0.9170 Gold 0.1924 oz. AGW **Ruler:** Louis XV **Mint:** Aix **Note:** Mint mark: &.

Date	Mintage	VG	F	VF	XF	Unc
1723	—	225	400	650	1,250	—

KM# 470.8 LOUIS D'OR

6.5250 g., 0.9170 Gold 0.1924 oz. AGW **Ruler:** Louis XV **Mint:** La Rochelle

Date	Mintage	VG	F	VF	XF	Unc
1723H	—	300	600	1,000	1,750	—
1724H	—	250	500	800	1,250	—
1725H	—	250	500	800	1,250	—

KM# 470.9 LOUIS D'OR

6.5250 g., 0.9170 Gold 0.1924 oz. AGW **Ruler:** Louis XV **Mint:** Limoges **Reverse:** Crowned double L monogram within palms

Date	Mintage	VG	F	VF	XF	Unc
1724I	—	250	500	800	1,250	—
1725I	—	250	500	800	1,250	—

KM# 470.10 LOUIS D'OR

6.5250 g., 0.9170 Gold 0.1924 oz. AGW **Ruler:** Louis XV **Mint:** Bordeaux **Obverse:** Young laureate head right **Reverse:** Crowned double L monogram within palms

Date	Mintage	VG	F	VF	XF	Unc
1724K	—	200	450	700	1,000	—
1725K	—	250	500	800	1,250	—

KM# 470.11 LOUIS D'OR

6.5250 g., 0.9170 Gold 0.1924 oz. AGW **Ruler:** Louis XV **Mint:** Bayonne **Obverse:** Young laureate head right **Reverse:** Crowned double L monogram within palms

Date	Mintage	VG	F	VF	XF	Unc
1724L	—	250	500	800	1,250	—
1725L	—	250	500	800	1,250	—

KM# 470.12 LOUIS D'OR

6.5250 g., 0.9170 Gold 0.1924 oz. AGW **Ruler:** Louis XV **Mint:** Toulouse **Obverse:** Young laureate head right **Reverse:** Crowned double L monogram within palms

Date	Mintage	VG	F	VF	XF	Unc
1724M	—	250	500	800	1,250	—

KM# 470.13 LOUIS D'OR

6.5250 g., 0.9170 Gold 0.1924 oz. AGW **Ruler:** Louis XV **Mint:** Montpellier **Obverse:** Young laureate head right **Reverse:** Crowned double L monogram within palms

Date	Mintage	VG	F	VF	XF	Unc
1724N	253,000	200	450	700	1,000	—
1725N	185,000	200	450	700	1,000	—

KM# 470.14 LOUIS D'OR

6.5250 g., 0.9170 Gold 0.1924 oz. AGW **Ruler:** Louis XV **Mint:** Riom **Obverse:** Young laureate head right **Reverse:** Crowned double L monogram within palms

Date	Mintage	VG	F	VF	XF	Unc
1724O	101,000	250	500	800	1,250	—
1725O	36,000	250	500	800	1,250	—

KM# 470.15 LOUIS D'OR

6.5250 g., 0.9170 Gold 0.1924 oz. AGW **Ruler:** Louis XV **Mint:** Dijon **Obverse:** Young laureate head right **Reverse:** Crowned double L monogram within palms

Date	Mintage	VG	F	VF	XF	Unc
1724P	—	250	500	800	1,250	—

KM# 470.16 LOUIS D'OR

6.5250 g., 0.9170 Gold 0.1924 oz. AGW **Ruler:** Louis XV **Mint:** Perpignan **Obverse:** Young laureate head right **Reverse:** Crowned double L monogram within palms

Date	Mintage	VG	F	VF	XF	Unc
1724Q	—	250	500	800	1,250	—
1725Q	—	300	600	1,000	1,750	—

KM# 470.17 LOUIS D'OR

6.5250 g., 0.9170 Gold 0.1924 oz. AGW **Ruler:** Louis XV **Mint:** Orléans **Obverse:** Young laureate head right **Reverse:** Crowned double L monogram within palms

Date	Mintage	VG	F	VF	XF	Unc
1724R	125,000	250	500	800	1,250	—

KM# 470.18 LOUIS D'OR

6.5250 g., 0.9170 Gold 0.1924 oz. AGW **Ruler:** Louis XV **Mint:** Reims **Obverse:** Young laureate head right **Reverse:** Crowned double L monogram within palms

Date	Mintage	VG	F	VF	XF	Unc
1724S	36,000	250	500	800	1,250	—
1725S	—	250	500	800	1,250	—

KM# 470.19 LOUIS D'OR

6.5250 g., 0.9170 Gold 0.1924 oz. AGW **Ruler:** Louis XV **Mint:** Nantes **Obverse:** Young laureate head right **Reverse:** Crowned double L monogram within palms

Date	Mintage	VG	F	VF	XF	Unc
1724T	—	250	500	800	1,250	—

KM# 470.26 LOUIS D'OR

6.5250 g., 0.9170 Gold 0.1924 oz. AGW **Ruler:** Louis XV **Mint:** Aix **Obverse:** Young laureate head right **Reverse:** Crowned double L monogram within palms **Note:** Mint mark: &.

Date	Mintage	VG	F	VF	XF	Unc
1724	—	250	500	800	1,350	—

KM# 470.25 LOUIS D'OR

6.5250 g., 0.9170 Gold 0.1924 oz. AGW **Ruler:** Louis XV **Mint:** Rennes **Obverse:** Young laureate head right **Reverse:** Crowned double L monogram within palms **Note:** Mint mark: 9.

Date	Mintage	VG	F	VF	XF	Unc
1724	233,000	200	400	600	1,000	—

KM# 474 LOUIS D'OR

6.5250 g., 0.9170 Gold 0.1924 oz. AGW **Ruler:** Louis XV **Mint:** Pau **Obv. Legend:** ....RE.BD (ligate BD). **Note:** Mint mark: Cow. Issued for Province of Bearn.

Date	Mintage	VG	F	VF	XF	Unc
1724	—	300	600	1,000	1,400	—
1725	51,000	300	600	1,000	1,400	—

KM# 470.2 LOUIS D'OR

6.5250 g., 0.9170 Gold 0.1924 oz. AGW **Ruler:** Louis XV **Mint:** Rouen **Obverse:** Young laureate head right **Reverse:** Crowned double L monogram within palms

Date	Mintage	VG	F	VF	XF	Unc
1724B	27,000	250	500	800	1,250	—

KM# 470.3 LOUIS D'OR

6.5250 g., 0.9170 Gold 0.1924 oz. AGW **Ruler:** Louis XV **Mint:** Strasbourg **Obverse:** Young laureate head right **Reverse:** Crowned double L monogram within palms

Date	Mintage	VG	F	VF	XF	Unc
1724BB	—	300	600	1,000	1,500	—

KM# 470.4 LOUIS D'OR

6.5250 g., 0.9170 Gold 0.1924 oz. AGW **Ruler:** Louis XV **Mint:** Caen **Obverse:** Young laureate head right **Reverse:** Crowned double L monogram within palms

Date	Mintage	VG	F	VF	XF	Unc
1724C	100,000	250	500	800	1,250	—
1725C	35,000	250	300	800	1,250	—

KM# 470.5 LOUIS D'OR

6.5250 g., 0.9170 Gold 0.1924 oz. AGW **Ruler:** Louis XV **Mint:** Lyon **Obverse:** Young laureate head right **Reverse:** Crowned double L monogram within palms

Date	Mintage	VG	F	VF	XF	Unc
1724D	8,229	300	600	1,000	1,750	—

KM# 470.6 LOUIS D'OR

6.5250 g., 0.9170 Gold 0.1924 oz. AGW **Ruler:** Louis XV **Mint:** Tours **Obverse:** Young laureate head right **Reverse:** Crowned double L monogram within palms

Date	Mintage	VG	F	VF	XF	Unc
1724E	62,000	250	500	800	1,250	—

KM# 470.7 LOUIS D'OR

6.5250 g., 0.9170 Gold 0.1924 oz. AGW **Ruler:** Louis XV **Mint:** Poitiers **Obverse:** Young laureate head right **Reverse:** Crowned double L monogram within palms

Date	Mintage	VG	F	VF	XF	Unc
1724G	45,000	250	500	800	1,250	—

KM# 470.21 LOUIS D'OR

6.5250 g., 0.9170 Gold 0.1924 oz. AGW **Ruler:** Louis XV **Mint:** Lille **Obverse:** Young laureate head right **Reverse:** Crowned double L monogram within palms

Date	Mintage	VG	F	VF	XF	Unc
1724W	—	250	500	800	1,250	—
1725W	—	250	500	800	1,250	—

KM# 470.22 LOUIS D'OR

6.5250 g., 0.9170 Gold 0.1924 oz. AGW **Ruler:** Louis XV **Mint:** Amiens **Obverse:** Young laureate head right **Reverse:** Crowned double L monogram within palms

Date	Mintage	VG	F	VF	XF	Unc
1724X	—	250	500	800	1,250	—
1725X	—	250	500	800	1,250	—

KM# 470.23 LOUIS D'OR

6.5250 g., 0.9170 Gold 0.1924 oz. AGW **Ruler:** Louis XV **Mint:** Bourges **Obverse:** Young laureate head right **Reverse:** Crowned double L monogram within palms

Date	Mintage	VG	F	VF	XF	Unc
1724Y	—	250	500	800	1,250	—

KM# 470.24 LOUIS D'OR

6.5250 g., 0.9170 Gold 0.1924 oz. AGW **Ruler:** Louis XV **Mint:** Grenoble **Obverse:** Young laureate head right **Reverse:** Crowned double L monogram within palms

Date	Mintage	VG	F	VF	XF	Unc
1724Z	97,000	250	500	800	1,250	—
1725Z	22,000	250	500	800	1,250	—

KM# 470.20 LOUIS D'OR

6.5250 g., 0.9170 Gold 0.1924 oz. AGW **Ruler:** Louis XV **Mint:** Troyes **Obverse:** Young laureate head right **Reverse:** Crowned double L monogram within palms

Date	Mintage	VG	F	VF	XF	Unc
1725V	21,000	250	500	800	1,250	—

KM# 489.27 LOUIS D'OR

8.1580 g., 0.9170 Gold 0.2405 oz. AGW **Ruler:** Louis XV **Mint:** Aix **Obverse:** Draped bust left **Reverse:** Crown above arms of France and Navarre **Note:** Mint mark: &.

Date	Mintage	VG	F	VF	XF	Unc
1726	285,000	175	275	315	500	—
1727	105,000	175	275	315	500	—
1728	59,000	175	275	335	575	—
1729	57,000	175	275	315	500	—
1730	35,000	175	275	335	575	—
1731	24,000	175	275	335	575	—
1732	24,000	175	275	335	575	—
1733	26,000	175	275	335	575	—
1734	18,000	175	275	335	575	—
1735	22,000	175	275	335	575	—
1736	18,000	175	275	335	575	—
1737	41,000	175	275	335	575	—
1738	45,000	175	275	335	575	—
1739	36,000	175	275	335	575	—

KM# 490 LOUIS D'OR

8.1580 g., 0.9170 Gold 0.2405 oz. AGW **Ruler:** Louis XV **Mint:** Pau **Note:** Mint mark: Cow. Issued for Province of Bearn.

Date	Mintage	VG	F	VF	XF	Unc
1726	45,000	200	300	385	675	—
1727	28,000	200	300	385	675	—
1728	37,000	200	300	385	675	—
1729	14,000	200	300	400	825	—
1730	9,303	200	300	400	825	—
1733	5,643	225	325	450	900	—
1734	—	225	325	450	900	—
1735	4,903	225	325	450	900	—

KM# 489.26 LOUIS D'OR

8.1580 g., 0.9170 Gold 0.2405 oz. AGW **Ruler:** Louis XV **Mint:** Rennes **Obverse:** Draped bust left **Reverse:** Crown above arms of France and Navarre **Note:** Mint mark: 9.

Date	Mintage	VG	F	VF	XF	Unc
1726	117,000	175	275	315	500	—
1727	—	175	275	335	575	—
1728	61,000	175	275	335	575	—
1729	—	175	275	335	575	—
1730	24,000	175	275	335	575	—
1731	—	175	275	335	575	—
1732	36,000	175	275	335	575	—
1733	—	175	275	335	575	—
1734	32,000	175	275	335	575	—
1735	23,000	175	275	335	575	—
1736	27,000	175	275	335	575	—
1737	18,000	175	275	335	575	—
1738	16,000	175	275	335	575	—

KM# 489.28 LOUIS D'OR

8.1580 g., 0.9170 Gold 0.2405 oz. AGW **Ruler:** Louis XV **Mint:** Besancon **Obverse:** Draped bust left **Reverse:** Crown above arms of France and Navarre **Note:** Mint mark: Back to back C's.

Date	Mintage	VG	F	VF	XF	Unc
1726	—	175	275	335	575	—
1727	—	175	275	335	575	—
1728	15,000	175	275	335	575	—
1730	11,000	175	275	335	575	—
1731	2,914	200	300	385	675	—
1733	4,323	200	300	385	675	—
1734	2,858	200	300	385	675	—

KM# 489.1 LOUIS D'OR

8.1580 g., 0.9170 Gold 0.2405 oz. AGW **Ruler:** Louis XV **Mint:** Paris **Obverse:** Draped bust left **Obv. Legend:** LUD • XV • D • G • FR • ET • NAV • REX • **Reverse:** Crown above arms of France and Navarre **Rev. Inscription:** CHRS • REGN • VINC • IMPER •

Date	Mintage	VG	F	VF	XF	Unc
1726A	—	175	275	315	500	—
1727A	—	175	275	315	500	—
1728A	—	175	275	315	500	—
1729A	—	175	275	315	500	—
1730A	—	175	275	315	500	—
1731A	—	175	275	315	500	—
1732A	180,000	175	275	315	500	—
1733A	—	175	275	315	500	—
1734A	—	175	275	315	500	—
1735A	—	175	275	335	600	—
1736A	—	175	275	335	600	—
1737A	—	175	275	335	600	—
1738A	90,000	175	275	335	600	—
1739A	74,000	175	275	375	700	—

KM# 489.2 LOUIS D'OR

8.1580 g., 0.9170 Gold 0.2405 oz. AGW **Ruler:** Louis XV **Mint:** Metz **Obverse:** Draped bust left **Reverse:** Crown above arms of France and Navarre

Date	Mintage	VG	F	VF	XF	Unc
1726AA	—	175	275	335	575	—
1727AA	—	175	275	335	575	—
1728AA	—	175	275	335	575	—
1729AA	—	175	275	335	575	—
1731AA	20,000	175	275	335	575	—
1734AA	—	175	275	365	675	—
1737AA	—	225	375	500	900	—

KM# 489.3 LOUIS D'OR

8.1580 g., 0.9170 Gold 0.2405 oz. AGW **Ruler:** Louis XV **Mint:** Rouen **Obverse:** Draped bust left **Reverse:** Crown above arms of France and Navarre

Date	Mintage	VG	F	VF	XF	Unc
1726B	—	175	275	365	585	—
1727B	—	175	275	365	585	—
1728B	80,000	175	275	365	585	—
1729B	65,000	175	275	365	585	—
1730B	53,000	175	275	365	585	—
1731B	48,000	175	275	365	585	—
1732B	37,000	175	275	365	585	—
1733B	34,000	175	275	365	585	—
1734B	27,000	175	275	365	585	—
1735B	31,000	175	275	365	585	—
1736B	23,000	175	275	365	585	—
1737B	22,000	175	275	365	585	—
1738B	20,000	175	275	365	585	—
1739B	14,000	175	275	365	585	—
1740B	7,350	200	300	450	800	—

KM# 489.4 LOUIS D'OR

8.1580 g., 0.9170 Gold 0.2405 oz. AGW **Ruler:** Louis XV **Mint:** Strasbourg **Obverse:** Draped bust left **Reverse:** Crown above arms of France and Navarre

Date	Mintage	VG	F	VF	XF	Unc
1726BB	—	175	275	335	575	—
1727BB	—	175	275	335	575	—
1729BB	—	175	275	335	575	—
1730BB	—	175	275	335	575	—
1734BB	—	200	300	385	675	—
1737BB	9,968	200	300	385	675	—
1740BB	2,061	200	300	400	700	—

KM# 489.5 LOUIS D'OR

8.1580 g., 0.9170 Gold 0.2405 oz. AGW **Ruler:** Louis XV **Mint:** Caen **Obverse:** Draped bust left **Reverse:** Crown above arms of France and Navarre

Date	Mintage	VG	F	VF	XF	Unc
1726C	122,000	175	275	315	500	—
1727C	54,000	175	275	335	575	—
1728C	29,000	175	275	335	575	—
1729C	27,000	175	275	335	575	—
1730C	20,000	175	275	335	575	—
1731C	22,000	175	275	335	575	—
1732C	16,000	175	275	335	575	—
1733C	15,000	175	275	335	575	—
1734C	8,764	200	300	385	675	—
1735C	13,000	175	275	335	575	—
1736C	12,000	175	275	335	575	—
1737C	10,000	175	275	335	575	—
1738C	9,840	200	300	385	675	—

KM# 489.6 LOUIS D'OR

8.1580 g., 0.9170 Gold 0.2405 oz. AGW **Ruler:** Louis XV **Mint:** Lyon **Obverse:** Draped bust left **Reverse:** Crown above arms of France and Navarre

Date	Mintage	VG	F	VF	XF	Unc
1726D	480,000	175	275	315	500	—
1727D	115,000	175	275	335	575	—
1728D	51,000	175	275	335	575	—
1729D	42,000	175	275	315	500	—
1730D	35,000	175	275	335	575	—
1731D	28,000	175	275	335	575	—
1732D	23,000	175	275	335	575	—
1733D	24,000	175	275	335	575	—
1734D	20,000	175	275	335	575	—
1736D	17,000	175	275	335	575	—
1737D	17,000	175	275	335	575	—
1738D	27,000	175	275	335	575	—
1739D	11,000	175	275	335	575	—

KM# 489.7 LOUIS D'OR

8.1580 g., 0.9170 Gold 0.2405 oz. AGW **Ruler:** Louis XV **Mint:** Tours **Obverse:** Draped bust left **Reverse:** Crown above arms of France and Navarre

Date	Mintage	VG	F	VF	XF	Unc
1726E	114,000	175	275	315	500	—
1727E	50,000	175	275	335	575	—
1728E	37,000	175	275	335	575	—
1729E	29,000	175	275	335	575	—
1730E	24,000	175	275	335	575	—
1731E	26,000	175	275	335	575	—
1732E	19,000	175	275	335	575	—
1733E	18,000	175	275	335	575	—
1734E	17,000	175	275	335	575	—
1735E	19,000	175	275	335	575	—
1736E	12,000	175	275	335	575	—
1737E	13,000	175	275	335	575	—
1738E	23,000	175	275	335	575	—
1739E	10,000	175	275	335	575	—
1740E	3,397	200	300	400	700	—

KM# 489.8 LOUIS D'OR

8.1580 g., 0.9170 Gold 0.2405 oz. AGW **Ruler:** Louis XV **Mint:** Poitiers **Obverse:** Draped bust left **Reverse:** Crown above arms of France and Navarre

Date	Mintage	VG	F	VF	XF	Unc
1726G	—	175	275	335	575	—
1728G	12,000	175	275	335	575	—
1729G	7,842	200	300	385	675	—
1730G	4,976	200	300	385	675	—
1731G	9,336	200	300	385	675	—

KM# 489.9 LOUIS D'OR

8.1580 g., 0.9170 Gold 0.2405 oz. AGW **Ruler:** Louis XV **Mint:** La Rochelle **Obverse:** Draped bust left **Reverse:** Crown above arms of France and Navarre

Date	Mintage	VG	F	VF	XF	Unc
1726H	—	175	275	335	575	—
1727H	—	175	275	335	575	—
1728H	37,000	175	275	335	575	—
1730H	29,000	175	275	335	575	—
1731H	27,000	175	275	335	575	—
1732H	22,000	175	275	335	575	—
1734H	17,000	175	275	335	575	—
1735H	21,000	175	275	335	575	—
1736H	22,000	175	275	335	575	—

Date	Mintage	VG	F	VF	XF	Unc
1737H	22,000	175	275	335	575	—
1738H	16,000	175	275	335	575	—

KM# 489.10 LOUIS D'OR

8.1580 g., 0.9170 Gold 0.2405 oz. AGW **Ruler:** Louis XV **Mint:** Limoges **Obverse:** Draped bust right **Reverse:** Crown above arms of France and Navarre

Date	Mintage	VG	F	VF	XF	Unc
1726I	—	175	275	335	575	—
1727I	—	175	275	335	575	—
1730I	16,000	175	275	335	575	—
1734I	10,000	175	275	335	575	—
1736I	9,308	200	300	385	675	—
1739I	6,717	200	300	385	675	—

KM# 489.11 LOUIS D'OR

8.1580 g., 0.9170 Gold 0.2405 oz. AGW **Ruler:** Louis XV **Mint:** Bordeaux **Obverse:** Draped bust left **Reverse:** Crown above arms of France and Navarre

Date	Mintage	VG	F	VF	XF	Unc
1726K	—	175	275	335	575	—
1727K	—	175	275	335	575	—
1728K	64,000	175	275	335	575	—
1729K	49,000	175	275	335	575	—
1730K	42,000	175	275	335	575	—
1731K	36,000	175	275	335	575	—
1732K	31,000	175	275	335	575	—
1733K	27,000	175	275	335	575	—
1735K	20,663	175	275	335	575	—
1736K	20,000	175	275	335	575	—
1738K	25,000	175	275	335	575	—
1740K	3,420	200	300	385	675	—

KM# 489.12 LOUIS D'OR

8.1580 g., 0.9170 Gold 0.2405 oz. AGW **Ruler:** Louis XV **Mint:** Bayonne **Obverse:** Draped bust left **Obv. Legend:** LUD • XV • D • G • FR • ET • NAV • REX • **Reverse:** Crown above arms of France and Navarre **Rev. Legend:** CHRS • REGN • VINC • IMPER •

Date	Mintage	VG	F	VF	XF	Unc
1726L	—	175	275	335	575	—
1727L	—	175	275	335	575	—
1728L	—	175	275	335	575	—
1729L	17,000	175	275	335	575	—
1730L	—	175	275	335	575	—
1731L	—	200	300	385	675	—
1732L	—	200	300	385	675	—
1733L	—	175	275	335	575	—
1735L	—	200	300	385	675	—
1738L	20,000	175	275	335	575	—

KM# 489.13 LOUIS D'OR

8.1580 g., 0.9170 Gold 0.2405 oz. AGW **Ruler:** Louis XV **Mint:** Toulouse **Obverse:** Draped bust left **Reverse:** Crown above arms of France and Navarre

Date	Mintage	VG	F	VF	XF	Unc
1726M	193,000	175	275	315	500	—
1727M	101,000	175	275	335	575	—
1728M	71,000	175	275	335	575	—
1729M	43,000	175	275	335	575	—
1730M	37,000	175	275	335	575	—
1731M	27,000	175	275	335	575	—
1732M	21,000	175	275	335	575	—
1733M	18,000	175	275	335	575	—
1734M	17,000	175	275	335	575	—
1735M	16,000	175	275	335	575	—
1738M	13,000	175	275	335	575	—
1739M	10,000	175	275	335	575	—
1740M	4,218	200	300	385	675	—

KM# 489.14 LOUIS D'OR

8.1580 g., 0.9170 Gold 0.2405 oz. AGW **Ruler:** Louis XV **Mint:** Montpellier **Obverse:** Draped bust left **Reverse:** Crown above arms of France and Navarre

Date	Mintage	VG	F	VF	XF	Unc
1726N	305,000	175	275	315	500	—
1727N	86,000	175	275	335	575	—
1728N	49,000	175	275	335	575	—
1729N	28,000	175	275	335	575	—
1730N	21,000	175	275	335	575	—
1731N	18,000	175	275	335	575	—
1732N	14,000	175	275	335	575	—
1733N	13,000	175	275	335	575	—
1734N	12,000	175	275	335	575	—
1735N	12,000	175	275	335	575	—
1738N	7,815	200	300	385	675	—

KM# 489.15 LOUIS D'OR

8.1580 g., 0.9170 Gold 0.2405 oz. AGW **Ruler:** Louis XV **Mint:** Riom **Obverse:** Draped bust left **Reverse:** Crown above arms of France and Navarre

Date	Mintage	VG	F	VF	XF	Unc
1726O	115,000	175	275	315	500	—
1727O	49,000	175	275	335	575	—
1728O	36,000	175	275	335	575	—
1729O	25,000	175	275	335	575	—
1730O	25,000	175	275	335	575	—
1731O	18,000	175	275	335	575	—
1732O	16,000	175	275	335	575	—
1733O	14,000	175	275	335	575	—
1734O	11,000	175	275	335	575	—
1735O	13,000	175	275	335	575	—
1740O	1,839	250	375	500	850	—

KM# 489.16 LOUIS D'OR

8.1580 g., 0.9170 Gold 0.2405 oz. AGW **Ruler:** Louis XV **Mint:** Dijon **Obverse:** Draped bust left **Reverse:** Crown above arms of France and Navarre

Date	Mintage	VG	F	VF	XF	Unc
1726P	—	175	275	335	575	—
1727P	—	175	275	335	575	—
1730P	—	175	275	335	575	—
1731P	6,730	175	275	385	675	—
1732P	16,000	175	275	335	575	—
1733P	8,519	175	275	385	675	—
1734P	6,334	175	275	385	675	—
1738P	4,725	200	300	385	675	—
1739P	4,072	200	300	385	675	—
1740P	916	300	400	650	1,350	—

KM# 489.17 LOUIS D'OR

8.1580 g., 0.9170 Gold 0.2405 oz. AGW **Ruler:** Louis XV **Mint:** Perpignan **Obverse:** Draped bust left **Reverse:** Crown above arms of France and Navarre

Date	Mintage	VG	F	VF	XF	Unc
1726Q	38,000	175	275	335	575	—
1727Q	13,000	175	275	335	575	—
1728Q	7,680	200	300	385	675	—
1730Q	4,028	200	300	385	675	—
1731Q	3,139	200	300	385	675	—
1733Q	1,995	250	375	500	900	—
1734Q	3,008	200	300	385	675	—
1737Q	2,910	200	300	385	675	—
1738Q	13,000	175	275	335	575	—
1739Q	5,954	200	300	385	675	—
1740Q	1,967	250	375	500	900	—

KM# 489.18 LOUIS D'OR

8.1580 g., 0.9170 Gold 0.2405 oz. AGW **Ruler:** Louis XV **Mint:** Orléans **Obverse:** Draped bust left **Reverse:** Crown above arms of France and Navarre

Date	Mintage	VG	F	VF	XF	Unc
1726R	116,000	175	275	315	500	—
1727R	50,000	175	275	335	575	—
1728R	36,000	175	275	335	575	—
1729R	27,000	175	275	335	575	—
1730R	27,000	175	275	335	575	—
1732R	15,000	175	275	335	575	—
1733R	12,000	175	275	335	575	—
1736R	9,323	200	300	385	675	—
1739R	7,408	200	300	385	675	—

KM# 489.19 LOUIS D'OR

8.1580 g., 0.9170 Gold 0.2405 oz. AGW **Ruler:** Louis XV **Mint:** Reims **Obverse:** Draped bust left **Reverse:** Crown above arms of France and Navarre

Date	Mintage	VG	F	VF	XF	Unc
1726S	—	175	275	335	575	—
1727S	—	175	275	335	575	—
1728S	40,000	175	275	335	575	—
1729S	24,000	175	275	335	575	—
1730S	20,000	175	275	335	575	—
1731S	18,000	175	275	335	575	—
1732S	16,000	175	275	335	575	—
1733S	13,000	175	275	335	575	—
1737S	5,693	200	300	385	675	—

KM# 489.20 LOUIS D'OR

8.1580 g., 0.9170 Gold 0.2405 oz. AGW **Ruler:** Louis XV **Mint:** Nantes **Obverse:** Draped bust left **Reverse:** Crown above arms of France and Navarre

Date	Mintage	VG	F	VF	XF	Unc
1726T	91,000	175	275	335	575	—
1727T	58,000	175	275	335	575	—
1728T	55,000	175	275	335	575	—
1729T	49,000	175	275	335	575	—
1730T	47,000	175	275	335	575	—
1731T	43,000	175	275	335	575	—
1732T	48,000	175	275	335	575	—
1733T	46,000	175	275	335	575	—
1734T	42,000	175	275	335	575	—
1735T	52,000	175	275	335	575	—
1736T	48,000	175	275	335	575	—
1737T	41,000	175	275	335	575	—
1738T	31,000	175	275	335	575	—
1739T	22,000	175	275	335	575	—
1740T	2,649	250	400	500	900	—

KM# 489.21 LOUIS D'OR

8.1580 g., 0.9170 Gold 0.2405 oz. AGW **Ruler:** Louis XV **Mint:** Troyes **Obverse:** Draped bust left **Reverse:** Crown above arms of France and Navarre

Date	Mintage	VG	F	VF	XF	Unc
1726V	91,000	175	275	335	575	—
1727V	41,000	175	275	335	575	—
1728V	25,000	175	275	335	575	—
1730V	16,000	175	275	335	575	—
1731V	9,900	200	300	385	675	—
1732V	8,735	200	300	385	675	—
1733V	8,708	200	300	385	675	—
1734V	4,575	200	300	385	675	—
1736V	5,614	200	300	385	675	—

KM# 489.22 LOUIS D'OR

8.1580 g., 0.9170 Gold 0.2405 oz. AGW **Ruler:** Louis XV **Mint:** Lille **Obverse:** Draped bust left **Reverse:** Crown above arms of France and Navarre

Date	Mintage	VG	F	VF	XF	Unc
1726W	—	175	275	315	500	—
1727W	113,000	175	275	315	500	—
1728W	63,000	175	275	335	575	—
1729W	40,000	175	275	315	500	—
1730W	1,368	250	375	550	950	—
1731W	19,000	175	275	335	575	—
1733W	7,484	200	300	385	675	—
1734W	6,786	200	300	385	675	—
1736W	4,973	200	300	385	675	—
1737W	23,000	175	275	335	575	—
1738W	20,000	175	275	335	575	—
1739W	2,339	200	300	385	675	—

KM# 489.23 LOUIS D'OR

8.1580 g., 0.9170 Gold 0.2405 oz. AGW **Ruler:** Louis XV **Mint:** Amiens **Obverse:** Draped bust left **Reverse:** Crown above arms of France and Navarre

Date	Mintage	VG	F	VF	XF	Unc
1726X	—	175	275	315	500	—
1727X	—	175	275	335	575	—
1728X	35,000	175	275	335	575	—
1729X	32,000	175	275	335	575	—
1731X	15,000	175	275	335	575	—
1732X	12,000	175	275	335	575	—
1733X	10,000	175	275	335	575	—
1734X	8,284	200	300	385	675	—
1735X	9,364	200	300	385	675	—
1738X	5,847	200	300	385	675	—
1740X	—	200	300	385	675	—

KM# 489.24 LOUIS D'OR

8.1580 g., 0.9170 Gold 0.2405 oz. AGW **Ruler:** Louis XV **Mint:** Bourges **Obverse:** Draped bust left **Reverse:** Crown above arms of France and Navarre

Date	Mintage	VG	F	VF	XF	Unc
1726Y	7,328	200	300	385	675	—
1727Y	20,000	175	275	335	575	—
1728Y	1,911	250	375	500	900	—
1730Y	—	250	375	500	900	—
1732Y	7,958	200	300	385	675	—
1733Y	8,982	200	300	385	675	—

KM# 489.25 LOUIS D'OR

8.1580 g., 0.9170 Gold 0.2405 oz. AGW **Ruler:** Louis XV **Mint:** Grenoble **Obverse:** Draped bust left **Reverse:** Crown above arms of France and Navarre

Date	Mintage	VG	F	VF	XF	Unc
1726Z	91,000	175	275	335	575	—
1727Z	30,000	175	275	335	575	—
1728Z	14,000	175	275	335	575	—
1729Z	14,000	175	275	335	575	—
1730Z	12,000	175	275	335	575	—
1731Z	8,794	200	300	385	675	—
1732Z	7,119	175	275	335	575	—
1734Z	4,980	175	275	335	575	—
1736Z	5,839	175	275	335	575	—
1737Z	5,016	175	275	335	575	—
1738Z	4,231	175	275	335	575	—
1739Z	3,833	175	275	335	575	—

KM# 513.1 LOUIS D'OR

8.1580 g., 0.9170 Gold 0.2405 oz. AGW **Ruler:** Louis XV **Mint:** Paris **Obverse:** Head left **Obv. Legend:** LUD • XV • D • G • FR • ETNAV • REX • **Reverse:** Crown above arms of France and Navarre **Rev. Legend:** CHRS • REGN • VINC • IMPER

Date	Mintage	VG	F	VF	XF	Unc
1740A	104,000	175	250	325	500	—
1741A	—	175	250	325	500	—
1742A	66,000	175	250	325	500	—
1743A	75,000	175	250	325	500	—
1744A	14,000	200	300	400	650	—
1745A	13,000	200	300	400	650	—
1746A	21,000	200	300	400	650	—
1747A	32,000	200	300	400	650	—
1748A	26,000	200	300	400	650	—
1749A	27,000	200	300	400	650	—
1750A	—	200	300	400	650	—
1751A	—	200	300	400	650	—
1752A	20,000	200	300	400	650	—
1753A	—	175	250	325	500	—
1754A	50,000	175	250	325	500	—
1755A	77,000	175	250	325	500	—
1756A	27,000	200	300	400	650	—
1758A	47,000	175	250	325	500	—
1759A	29,000	200	300	400	650	—
1761A	—	200	300	400	650	—
1766A	17,000	200	300	400	650	—
1768A	—	200	300	400	650	—
1769A	—	200	300	400	650	—
1770A	—	200	300	400	650	—

KM# 513.26 LOUIS D'OR

8.1580 g., 0.9170 Gold 0.2405 oz. AGW **Ruler:** Louis XV **Mint:** Rennes **Note:** Mint mark: 9.

Date	Mintage	VG	F	VF	XF	Unc
1740	8,202	200	300	425	650	—
1741	21,000	200	300	425	650	—
1744	—	175	250	325	500	—

KM# 514 LOUIS D'OR

8.1580 g., 0.9170 Gold 0.2405 oz. AGW **Ruler:** Louis XV **Mint:** Pau **Obv. Legend:** ....RE.BD (ligate BD). **Note:** Mint mark: Cow. Issued for Province of Bearn.

Date	Mintage	VG	F	VF	XF	Unc
1740	21,000	200	300	500	800	—
1746	2,978	225	375	550	1,000	—
1750	1,846	225	375	550	950	—
1753	—	225	375	550	950	—
1754	691	225	375	550	950	—
1755	1,292	225	375	550	950	—
1756	708,000	225	375	550	950	—
1763	165,000	200	300	475	750	—
1764	45,000	200	300	475	750	—
1766	90,000	200	300	475	750	—
1767	160,000	200	300	475	750	—
1768	129,000	200	300	475	750	—
1769	—	200	300	475	750	—
1770	67,000	200	300	475	750	—

KM# 513.27 LOUIS D'OR

8.1580 g., 0.9170 Gold 0.2405 oz. AGW **Ruler:** Louis XV **Mint:** Aix **Obverse:** Head left **Reverse:** Crown above arms of France and Navarre **Note:** Mint mark: &.

Date	Mintage	VG	F	VF	XF	Unc
1740	—	—	—	—	—	—
1741	—	200	350	550	1,000	—
1742	69,000	175	250	325	500	—
1743	161,000	175	250	325	500	—
1744	—	175	250	325	500	—
1745	65,000	175	250	325	500	—
1746	30,000	185	275	400	600	—
1747	18,000	185	275	400	600	—
1748	5,940	185	275	400	600	—
1751	4,257	200	300	425	650	—
1752	—	200	300	425	650	—
1753	9,229	200	300	425	650	—
1755	14,000	200	350	550	1,000	—
1756	59,000	175	250	325	500	—
1757	7,069	200	300	425	650	—
1767	3,090	200	325	475	800	—

KM# 513.3 LOUIS D'OR

8.1580 g., 0.9170 Gold 0.2405 oz. AGW **Ruler:** Louis XV **Mint:** Rouen **Obverse:** Head left **Reverse:** Crown above arms of France and Navarre

Date	Mintage	VG	F	VF	XF	Unc
1740B	5,904	200	300	425	650	—
1741B	—	175	250	325	500	—
1742B	3,102	200	300	425	650	—
1743B	2,190	200	300	425	650	—
1761B	1,099	200	300	425	650	—

KM# 513.4 LOUIS D'OR

8.1580 g., 0.9170 Gold 0.2405 oz. AGW **Ruler:** Louis XV **Mint:** Strasbourg **Obverse:** Head left **Reverse:** Crown above arms of France and Navarre

Date	Mintage	VG	F	VF	XF	Unc
1740BB	6,795	200	325	475	800	—
1742BB	4,540	200	300	425	650	—
1744BB	30,000	200	300	425	650	—
1745BB	11,000	200	300	425	650	—
1746BB	33,000	200	300	425	650	—
1747BB	50,000	175	250	325	500	—
1750BB	2,606	200	350	475	800	—
1751BB	—	200	300	425	650	—
1752BB	4,180	200	300	425	650	—
1753BB	3,693	200	300	425	650	—
1754BB	—	200	300	425	650	—
1755BB	—	200	300	425	650	—
1761BB	315,000	175	250	325	500	—
1762BB	—	175	250	325	500	—

KM# 513.7 LOUIS D'OR

8.1580 g., 0.9170 Gold 0.2405 oz. AGW **Ruler:** Louis XV **Mint:** Tours **Obverse:** Head left **Reverse:** Crown above arms of France and Navarre

Date	Mintage	VG	F	VF	XF	Unc
1740E	5,517	200	325	475	800	—
1741E	9,563	200	300	425	650	—
1746E	2,780	200	325	500	925	—

KM# 513.12 LOUIS D'OR

8.1580 g., 0.9170 Gold 0.2405 oz. AGW **Ruler:** Louis XV **Mint:** Bayonne **Obverse:** Head left **Reverse:** Crown above arms of France and Navarre

Date	Mintage	VG	F	VF	XF	Unc
1740L	42,000	175	250	325	500	—
1741L	76,000	175	250	325	500	—
1742L	39,000	175	250	325	500	—
1770L	—	200	300	425	600	—

KM# 513.14 LOUIS D'OR

8.1580 g., 0.9170 Gold 0.2405 oz. AGW **Ruler:** Louis XV **Mint:** Montpellier **Obverse:** Head left **Reverse:** Crown above arms of France and Navarre

Date	Mintage	VG	F	VF	XF	Unc
1740N	9,007	200	300	425	650	—
1743N	16,000	200	300	425	650	—
1744N	—	200	300	425	650	—
1747N	—	200	300	425	650	—
1757N	—	200	300	425	650	—
1758N	8,464	200	300	425	650	—
1759N	3,226	200	300	425	650	—

KM# 513.17 LOUIS D'OR

8.1580 g., 0.9170 Gold 0.2405 oz. AGW **Ruler:** Louis XV **Mint:** Perpignan **Obverse:** Head left **Reverse:** Crown above arms of France and Navarre

Date	Mintage	VG	F	VF	XF	Unc
1740Q	4,408	200	325	475	800	—
1741Q	4,300	200	300	425	650	—
1742Q	12,000	200	300	425	650	—
1743Q	2,699	200	325	500	925	—

KM# 513.20 LOUIS D'OR

8.1580 g., 0.9170 Gold 0.2405 oz. AGW **Ruler:** Louis XV **Mint:** Nantes **Obverse:** Head left **Reverse:** Crown above arms of France and Navarre

Date	Mintage	VG	F	VF	XF	Unc
1740T	36,000	175	250	325	500	—
1741T	51,000	175	250	325	500	—
1742T	24,000	175	250	325	500	—

KM# 513.22 LOUIS D'OR

8.1580 g., 0.9170 Gold 0.2405 oz. AGW **Ruler:** Louis XV **Mint:** Lille **Obverse:** Head left **Obv. Legend:** LUD • XV • D • G • FR • ETNAV • REX • **Reverse:** Crown above arms of France and Navarre **Rev. Legend:** CHRS • REGN • VINC • IMPER •

Date	Mintage	VG	F	VF	XF	Unc
1740W	6,401	200	300	425	650	—
1741W	23,000	200	300	425	650	—
1742W	70,000	175	250	325	500	—
1743W	1,306	200	325	475	800	—
1744W	375,000	175	250	325	500	—
1745W	296,000	175	250	325	500	—
1746W	474,000	175	250	325	500	—
1747W	327,000	175	250	325	500	—
1748W	210,000	175	250	325	500	—
1749W	171,000	175	250	325	500	—
1750W	12,000	200	300	425	650	—
1751W	4,065	200	300	425	650	—
1753W	4,875	200	300	425	650	—
1755W	3,780	200	325	500	850	—
1770W	75,000	175	250	325	500	—
1771W	—	200	300	425	650	—

KM# 513.23 LOUIS D'OR

8.1580 g., 0.9170 Gold 0.2405 oz. AGW **Ruler:** Louis XV **Mint:** Amiens

Date	Mintage	VG	F	VF	XF	Unc
1740X	—	200	325	475	800	—
1741X	16,000	200	300	425	650	—
1742X	62,000	175	250	325	500	—
1747X	45,000	175	250	325	500	—
1748X	25,000	200	300	425	650	—
1757X	1,365	225	350	550	900	—

KM# 513.21 LOUIS D'OR

8.1580 g., 0.9170 Gold 0.2405 oz. AGW **Ruler:** Louis XV **Mint:** Troyes **Obverse:** Head left **Reverse:** Crown above arms of France and Navarre

Date	Mintage	VG	F	VF	XF	Unc
1741V	3,450	200	325	475	800	—
1742V	2,329	200	325	475	800	—
1744V	1,650	200	325	475	800	—
1751V	1,112	200	325	500	850	—

KM# 513.15 LOUIS D'OR

8.1580 g., 0.9170 Gold 0.2405 oz. AGW **Ruler:** Louis XV **Mint:** Riom **Obverse:** Head left **Reverse:** Crown above arms of France and Navarre

Date	Mintage	VG	F	VF	XF	Unc
1741O	7,215	200	300	425	650	—
1743O	2,150	200	325	500	850	—
1749O	3,766	200	300	425	650	—
1750O	4,864	200	300	425	650	—
1751O	2,944	200	325	500	850	—

KM# 513.9 LOUIS D'OR

8.1580 g., 0.9170 Gold 0.2405 oz. AGW **Ruler:** Louis XV **Mint:** La Rochelle **Obverse:** Head left **Reverse:** Crown above arms of France and Navarre

Date	Mintage	VG	F	VF	XF	Unc
1741H	14,000	200	300	425	650	—
1742H	14,000	200	300	425	650	—
1743H	8,213	200	300	425	650	—
1747H	6,998	200	300	425	650	—
1751H	9,900	200	300	425	650	—
1752H	6,361	200	300	425	650	—
1757H	3,582	200	300	425	650	—
1761H	3,577	200	300	425	650	—
1763H	3,972	200	300	425	650	—
1764H	6,132	200	300	425	650	—
1765H	3,413	200	300	425	650	—

KM# 513.6 LOUIS D'OR
8.1580 g., 0.9170 Gold 0.2405 oz. AGW **Ruler:** Louis XV **Mint:** Lyon **Obverse:** Head left **Reverse:** Crown above arms of France and Navarre

Date	Mintage	VG	F	VF	XF	Unc
1741D	24,000	200	300	425	650	—
1742D	9,368	200	300	425	650	—
1743D	13,000	200	300	425	650	—
1747D	9,102	200	300	425	650	—
1750D	4,052	200	300	425	650	—
1753D	412	400	650	1,000	1,600	—
1754D	26,000	200	300	425	650	—
1758D	11,000	200	300	425	650	—
1766D	7,609	200	300	425	650	—

KM# 513.19 LOUIS D'OR
8.1580 g., 0.9170 Gold 0.2405 oz. AGW **Ruler:** Louis XV **Mint:** Reims **Obverse:** Head left **Reverse:** Crown above arms of France and Navarre

Date	Mintage	VG	F	VF	XF	Unc
1741S	4,541	200	300	425	650	—
1744S	4,639	200	300	425	650	—
1747S	6,468	200	300	425	650	—
1749S	6,552	200	300	425	650	—
1756S	1,304	200	325	500	925	—
1770S	615	250	450	600	1,100	—

KM# 513.5 LOUIS D'OR
8.1580 g., 0.9170 Gold 0.2405 oz. AGW **Ruler:** Louis XV **Mint:** Caen **Obverse:** Head left **Reverse:** Crown above arms of France and Navarre

Date	Mintage	VG	F	VF	XF	Unc
1742C	4,406	200	300	425	650	—
1744C	5,659	200	300	425	650	—
1750C	3,183	200	300	425	650	—
1763C	1,370	200	300	500	850	—

KM# 513.10 LOUIS D'OR
8.1580 g., 0.9170 Gold 0.2405 oz. AGW **Ruler:** Louis XV **Mint:** Limoges **Obverse:** Head left **Reverse:** Crown above arms of France and Navarre

Date	Mintage	VG	F	VF	XF	Unc
1742I	6,799	200	300	425	650	—
1743I	3,217	200	325	500	850	—

KM# 513.11 LOUIS D'OR
8.1580 g., 0.9170 Gold 0.2405 oz. AGW **Ruler:** Louis XV **Mint:** Bordeaux **Obverse:** Head left **Reverse:** Crown above arms of France and Navarre

Date	Mintage	VG	F	VF	XF	Unc
1742K	20,000	200	300	425	650	—
1747K	—	200	300	425	650	—
1749K	4,830	200	300	425	650	—
1755K	—	200	300	425	650	—

KM# 513.13 LOUIS D'OR
8.1580 g., 0.9170 Gold 0.2405 oz. AGW **Ruler:** Louis XV **Mint:** Toulouse **Obverse:** Head left **Reverse:** Crown above arms of France and Navarre

Date	Mintage	VG	F	VF	XF	Unc
1742M	4,335	200	300	425	650	—
1751M	1,639	200	325	500	850	—

KM# 513.18 LOUIS D'OR
8.1580 g., 0.9170 Gold 0.2405 oz. AGW **Ruler:** Louis XV **Mint:** Orléans **Obverse:** Head left **Reverse:** Crown above arms of France and Navarre

Date	Mintage	VG	F	VF	XF	Unc
1742R	5,456	200	300	425	650	—
1743R	2,950	200	325	475	800	—
1745R	1,334	200	325	475	800	—
1766R	—	200	300	425	650	—
1767R	—	200	300	425	650	—
1768R	—	200	300	425	650	—

KM# 513.25 LOUIS D'OR
8.1580 g., 0.9170 Gold 0.2405 oz. AGW **Ruler:** Louis XV **Mint:** Grenoble **Obverse:** Head left **Reverse:** Crown above arms of France and Navarre

Date	Mintage	VG	F	VF	XF	Unc
1742Z	—	200	300	475	800	—
1743Z	7,175	200	300	475	800	—

KM# 513.8 LOUIS D'OR
8.1580 g., 0.9170 Gold 0.2405 oz. AGW **Ruler:** Louis XV **Mint:** Poitiers **Obverse:** Head left **Reverse:** Crown above arms of France and Navarre

Date	Mintage	VG	F	VF	XF	Unc
1743G	6,019	200	300	425	650	—
1747G	4,421	200	300	425	650	—
1760G	1,204	200	325	500	850	—
1765G	1,159	200	325	500	850	—

KM# 513.2 LOUIS D'OR
8.1580 g., 0.9170 Gold 0.2405 oz. AGW **Ruler:** Louis XV **Mint:** Metz **Obverse:** Head left **Reverse:** Crown above arms of France and Navarre

Date	Mintage	VG	F	VF	XF	Unc
1744AA	—	200	310	435	675	—
1748AA	—	200	300	425	650	—

KM# 513.16 LOUIS D'OR
8.1580 g., 0.9170 Gold 0.2405 oz. AGW **Ruler:** Louis XV **Mint:** Dijon **Obverse:** Head left **Reverse:** Crown above arms of France and Navarre

Date	Mintage	VG	F	VF	XF	Unc
1745P	4,343	200	300	425	650	—
1746P	6,181	200	300	425	650	—
1747P	5,491	200	300	425	650	—
1748P	1,738	200	325	500	850	—

KM# 513.24 LOUIS D'OR
8.1580 g., 0.9170 Gold 0.2405 oz. AGW **Ruler:** Louis XV **Mint:** Bourges **Obverse:** Head left **Reverse:** Crown above arms of France and Navarre

Date	Mintage	VG	F	VF	XF	Unc
1746Y	3,314	200	325	475	800	—
1747Y	2,001	200	325	475	800	—
1748Y	2,916	200	325	475	800	—
1751Y	3,577	200	300	425	650	—
1769Y	304	400	700	1,400	2,500	—

KM# 513.28 LOUIS D'OR
8.1580 g., 0.9170 Gold 0.2405 oz. AGW **Ruler:** Louis XV **Mint:** Besancon **Obverse:** Head left **Reverse:** Crown above arms of France and Navarre **Note:** Mint mark: Back to back C's.

Date	Mintage	VG	F	VF	XF	Unc
1749	2,169	200	325	475	800	—
1756	5,372	200	300	425	650	—

KM# 556.1 LOUIS D'OR
8.1580 g., 0.9170 Gold 0.2405 oz. AGW **Ruler:** Louis XV **Mint:** Paris

Date	Mintage	VG	F	VF	XF	Unc
1771A	—	600	1,300	1,900	2,800	—
1772A	—	600	1,300	1,900	2,800	—
1773A	—	600	1,300	1,900	2,800	—
1774A	—	600	1,300	1,900	2,800	—

KM# 556.4 LOUIS D'OR
8.1580 g., 0.9170 Gold 0.2405 oz. AGW **Ruler:** Louis XV **Mint:** Aix **Note:** Mint mark: &.

Date	Mintage	VG	F	VF	XF	Unc
1772	12,000	600	1,350	1,900	2,850	—

KM# 556.3 LOUIS D'OR
8.1580 g., 0.9170 Gold 0.2405 oz. AGW **Ruler:** Louis XV **Mint:** Montpellier

Date	Mintage	VG	F	VF	XF	Unc
1773N	1,701	675	1,450	2,200	4,000	—
1774N	5,767	675	1,450	2,200	4,000	—

KM# 565 LOUIS D'OR
8.1580 g., 0.9170 Gold 0.2405 oz. AGW **Ruler:** Louis XVI **Mint:** Paris **Obverse:** Uniformed bust left **Obv. Legend:** LUD • XVI • D • G • FR • ET NAV • REX • **Reverse:** Crowned arms of France within branches **Rev. Legend:** CHRS • REGN • VINC • IMPER

Date	Mintage	VG	F	VF	XF	Unc
1774A	—	850	1,650	3,000	5,000	—

KM# 566 LOUIS D'OR
8.1580 g., 0.9170 Gold 0.2405 oz. AGW **Ruler:** Louis XVI **Reverse:** Date above crown

Date	Mintage	VG	F	VF	XF	Unc
1774	—	—	—	5,500	10,000	—

KM# 567.1 LOUIS D'OR
8.1580 g., 0.9170 Gold 0.2405 oz. AGW **Ruler:** Louis XVI **Mint:** Paris **Obverse:** Uniformed bust left **Obv. Legend:** LUD • XVI • D • G • FR • ET NAV • REX • **Reverse:** Crowned arms of France and Navarre in ovals **Rev. Legend:** CHRS • REGN • VINC • IMPER

Date	Mintage	VG	F	VF	XF	Unc
1774	490,000	300	650	1,000	2,200	—
1775	221,000	300	650	1,000	2,200	—
1776	133,000	300	650	1,000	2,200	—
1777	104,000	300	650	1,000	2,200	—
1778	48,000	300	650	1,000	2,200	—
1779	6,899	550	1,100	2,000	4,500	—
1780	2,895	650	1,300	2,250	5,000	—
1781	6,333	550	1,100	2,000	4,500	—
1782	255,000	300	650	1,000	2,200	—
1783	90,000	300	650	1,000	2,200	—
1783	Inc. above	300	650	1,000	2,200	—
1784	16,000	300	650	1,000	2,200	—

KM# 556.2 LOUIS D'OR
8.1580 g., 0.9170 Gold 0.2405 oz. AGW **Ruler:** Louis XV **Mint:** La Rochelle

Date	Mintage	VG	F	VF	XF	Unc
1774H	2,887	675	1,450	2,200	4,000	—

KM# 567.3 LOUIS D'OR
8.1580 g., 0.9170 Gold 0.2405 oz. AGW **Ruler:** Louis XVI **Mint:** Strasbourg **Obverse:** Uniformed bust left **Reverse:** Crowned arms of France and Navarre in ovals

Date	Mintage	VG	F	VF	XF	Unc
1775BB	604	750	1,500	2,600	5,000	—
1780BB	391	—	—	—	—	—
1781BB	394	950	1,750	2,750	5,750	—
1785BB	541	1,000	1,900	3,200	6,000	—

KM# 567.4 LOUIS D'OR
8.1580 g., 0.9170 Gold 0.2405 oz. AGW **Ruler:** Louis XVI **Mint:** Lyon **Obverse:** Uniformed bust left **Reverse:** Crowned arms of France and Navarre in ovals

Date	Mintage	VG	F	VF	XF	Unc
1775D	13,000	550	1,100	2,000	4,000	—

KM# 567.5 LOUIS D'OR
8.1580 g., 0.9170 Gold 0.2405 oz. AGW **Ruler:** Louis XVI **Mint:** La Rochelle **Obverse:** Uniformed bust left **Reverse:** Crowned arms of France and Navarre in ovals

Date	Mintage	VG	F	VF	XF	Unc
1775H	5,315	450	1,000	2,000	4,000	—
1776H	2,443	450	1,000	2,000	4,000	—
1777H	3,156	450	1,000	2,000	4,000	—
1778H	2,680	450	1,000	2,000	4,000	—
1779H	4,880	450	1,000	2,000	4,000	—
1780H	2,779	450	1,000	2,000	4,000	—
1781H	2,325	—	—	—	—	—
1782H	3,863	450	1,000	2,000	4,000	—
1783H	3,061	450	1,000	2,000	4,000	—
1784H	1,166	—	—	—	—	—
1785H	747	—	—	—	—	—

KM# 567.6 LOUIS D'OR
8.1580 g., 0.9170 Gold 0.2405 oz. AGW **Ruler:** Louis XVI **Mint:** Limoges **Obverse:** Uniformed bust left **Reverse:** Crowned arms of France and Navarre in ovals

Date	Mintage	VG	F	VF	XF	Unc
1775I	2,397	450	1,000	2,000	4,000	—

KM# 567.7 LOUIS D'OR
8.1580 g., 0.9170 Gold 0.2405 oz. AGW **Ruler:** Louis XVI **Mint:** Bordeaux **Obverse:** Uniformed bust left **Reverse:** Crowned arms of France and Navarre in ovals

Date	Mintage	VG	F	VF	XF	Unc
1775K	934	—	—	—	—	—
1780K	—	650	1,300	2,250	4,500	—

KM# 567.8 LOUIS D'OR
8.1580 g., 0.9170 Gold 0.2405 oz. AGW **Ruler:** Louis XVI **Mint:** Bayonne **Obverse:** Uniformed bust left **Reverse:** Crowned arms of France and Navarre in ovals

Date	Mintage	VG	F	VF	XF	Unc
1775L	24,000	—	—	—	—	—
1776L	11,000	—	—	—	—	—
1777L	813	—	—	—	—	—

KM# 567.9 LOUIS D'OR
8.1580 g., 0.9170 Gold 0.2405 oz. AGW **Ruler:** Louis XVI **Mint:** Toulouse **Obverse:** Uniformed bust left **Reverse:** Crowned arms of France and Navarre in ovals

Date	Mintage	VG	F	VF	XF	Unc
1775M	8,491	550	1,100	2,000	4,000	—
1783M	1,173	—	—	—	—	—
1784M	1,525	—	—	—	—	—

KM# 567.10 LOUIS D'OR
8.1580 g., 0.9170 Gold 0.2405 oz. AGW **Ruler:** Louis XVI **Mint:** Montpellier **Obverse:** Uniformed bust left **Reverse:** Crowned arms of France and Navarre in ovals

Date	Mintage	VG	F	VF	XF	Unc
1775N	19,000	550	1,100	2,000	4,000	—
1776N	13,000	550	1,100	2,000	4,000	—
1778N	2,664	650	1,300	2,250	4,500	—
1779N	2,208	650	1,300	2,250	4,500	—
1780N	340	—	—	—	—	—
1781N	1,116	—	—	—	—	—
1782N	1,897	—	—	—	—	—
1783N	1,746	—	—	—	—	—
1784N	354	—	—	—	—	—
1785N	414	—	—	—	—	—

KM# 567.11 LOUIS D'OR
8.1580 g., 0.9170 Gold 0.2405 oz. AGW **Ruler:** Louis XVI **Mint:** Perpignan **Obverse:** Uniformed bust left **Reverse:** Crowned arms of France and Navarre in ovals

Date	Mintage	VG	F	VF	XF	Unc
1775Q	1,220	—	—	—	—	—

KM# 567.15 LOUIS D'OR
8.1580 g., 0.9170 Gold 0.2405 oz. AGW **Ruler:** Louis XVI **Mint:** Lille **Obverse:** Uniformed bust left **Reverse:** Crowned arms of France and Navarre in ovals

Date	Mintage	VG	F	VF	XF	Unc
1775W	91,000	450	850	1,500	3,000	—

KM# 574 LOUIS D'OR
8.1580 g., 0.9170 Gold 0.2405 oz. AGW **Ruler:** Louis XVI **Mint:** Pau **Obv. Legend:** ....RE.BD. (ligate BD). **Note:** Mint mark: Cow. Issued for Province of Bearn.

Date	Mintage	VG	F	VF	XF	Unc
1775 (p)	15,000	550	1,100	2,000	4,000	—
1776 (p)	13,000	550	1,100	2,000	4,000	—
1777 (p)	11,000	550	1,100	2,000	4,000	—

KM# 567.12 LOUIS D'OR
8.1580 g., 0.9170 Gold 0.2405 oz. AGW **Ruler:** Louis XVI **Mint:** Orléans **Obverse:** Uniformed bust left **Reverse:** Crowned arms of France and Navarre in ovals

Date	Mintage	VG	F	VF	XF	Unc
1776R	431	—	—	—	—	—
1780R Reported, not confirmed	—	—	—	—	—	—
1782R	226	—	—	—	—	—

KM# 567.14 LOUIS D'OR

8.1580 g., 0.9170 Gold 0.2405 oz. AGW **Ruler:** Louis XVI **Mint:** Nantes **Obverse:** Uniformed bust left **Reverse:** Crowned arms of France and Navarre in ovals

Date	Mintage	VG	F	VF	XF	Unc
1779T	—	650	1,300	2,250	4,500	—

KM# 590 LOUIS D'OR

7.6490 g., 0.9170 Gold 0.2255 oz. AGW **Ruler:** Louis XVI **Mint:** Paris **Obverse:** Head of Louis XVI left

Date	Mintage	VG	F	VF	XF	Unc
1785A Rare	7	—	—	—	—	—

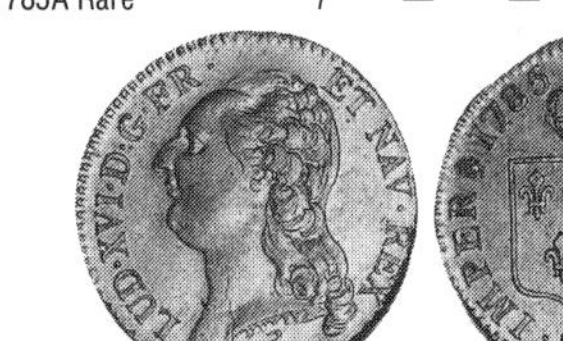

KM# 591.1 LOUIS D'OR

7.6490 g., 0.9170 Gold 0.2255 oz. AGW **Ruler:** Louis XVI **Mint:** Paris **Obverse:** Head left **Obv. Legend:** LUD • XVI • D • G • FR • ET NAV • REX • **Reverse:** Crowned arms of France and Navarre in shields **Rev. Legend:** CHRS • REGN • VINC • IMPER

Date	Mintage	VG	F	VF	XF	Unc
1785A	50,000	200	275	350	675	—
1786A	5,370,000	150	200	250	350	—
1786A	Inc. above	150	200	250	350	—
1787A	1,927,000	150	200	250	350	—
1787A	Inc. above	150	200	250	350	—
1788A	837,000	150	200	250	350	—
1789A	—	150	200	250	350	—
1790A	164,000	175	225	300	450	—
1792A	—	275	425	550	800	—

KM# 591.2 LOUIS D'OR

7.6490 g., 0.9170 Gold 0.2255 oz. AGW **Ruler:** Louis XVI **Mint:** Metz **Obverse:** Head left **Reverse:** Crowned arms of France and Navarre in shields

Date	Mintage	VG	F	VF	XF	Unc
1785AA	597,000	225	325	425	675	—
1786AA	Inc. above	150	200	250	400	—
1787AA	193,000	150	200	300	450	—
1788AA	73,000	175	225	350	475	—
1789AA Reported, not confirmed	—	—	—	—	—	—
1790AA	13,000	225	325	425	700	—

KM# 591.5 LOUIS D'OR

7.6490 g., 0.9170 Gold 0.2255 oz. AGW **Ruler:** Louis XVI **Mint:** Lyon **Obverse:** Head left **Reverse:** Crowned arms of France and Navarre in shields

Date	Mintage	VG	F	VF	XF	Unc
1785D	58,000	175	250	325	600	—
1786D	899,000	150	200	250	400	—
1786D	Inc. above	150	200	250	400	—
1787D	424,000	150	200	250	400	—
1787D	Inc. above	150	200	250	400	—
1788/7D	—	150	200	250	400	—
1788D	256,000	150	200	250	400	—
1789D	89,000	150	225	300	475	—
1790D	41,000	175	275	360	525	—
1791D	—	250	375	525	950	—
1792D	—	275	475	675	1,200	—

KM# 591.7 LOUIS D'OR

7.6490 g., 0.9170 Gold 0.2255 oz. AGW **Ruler:** Louis XVI **Mint:** Limoges **Obverse:** Head left **Reverse:** Crowned arms of France and Navarre in shields

Date	Mintage	VG	F	VF	XF	Unc
1785I	751,000	225	325	425	650	—
1786I	Inc. above	150	200	250	400	—
1786I	Inc. above	150	200	250	400	—
1787I	109,000	150	200	250	400	—
1788I	36,000	175	250	325	525	—
1788I	Inc. above	175	250	325	525	—
1789I	22,000	175	250	325	525	—
1790I	7,622	275	425	500	800	—
1791I	—	225	425	500	800	—

KM# 591.8 LOUIS D'OR

7.6490 g., 0.9170 Gold 0.2255 oz. AGW **Ruler:** Louis XVI **Mint:** Bordeaux **Obverse:** Head left **Reverse:** Crowned arms of France and Navarre in shields

Date	Mintage	VG	F	VF	XF	Unc
1785K	38,000	175	250	350	650	—
1786K	504,000	150	200	250	400	—
1787K	19,000	—	—	—	—	—
1789K	—	175	250	300	475	—

KM# 591.14 LOUIS D'OR

7.6490 g., 0.9170 Gold 0.2255 oz. AGW **Ruler:** Louis XVI **Mint:** Nantes **Obverse:** Head left **Reverse:** Crowned arms of France and Navarre in shields

Date	Mintage	VG	F	VF	XF	Unc
1785T	—	225	325	450	800	—
1786T	830,000	150	200	250	400	—
1786T	Inc. above	150	200	250	400	—
Note: The "dot" appears below the third letter of the monarch's name and denotes second semester coinage						
1787T	221,000	150	200	250	400	—
1788T	50,000	175	250	325	475	—
1789T	59,000	—	—	—	—	—
1790T	22,000	—	—	—	—	—

KM# 591.15 LOUIS D'OR

7.6490 g., 0.9170 Gold 0.2255 oz. AGW **Ruler:** Louis XVI **Mint:** Lille **Obverse:** Head left **Reverse:** Crowned arms of France and Navarre in shields

Date	Mintage	VG	F	VF	XF	Unc
1785W	1,299,000	200	275	350	650	—
1786W	Inc. above	150	200	250	425	—
1786W	Inc. above	150	200	250	425	—
Note: The "dot" appears below the third letter of the monarch's name and denotes second semester coinage						
1787W	304,000	150	200	250	425	—
1788W	174,000	150	200	250	425	—
Note: The "dot" appears below the third letter of the monarch's name and denotes second semester coinage						
1789W	104,000	150	200	250	450	—
1790W	133,000	—	—	—	—	—
1791W	2,562	225	425	600	1,000	—
1792W	1,983	—	—	—	—	—

KM# 567.2 LOUIS D'OR

8.1580 g., 0.9170 Gold 0.2405 oz. AGW **Ruler:** Louis XVI **Mint:** Rouen

Date	Mintage	VG	F	VF	XF	Unc
1785B	13,000	—	—	—	—	—

KM# 591.11 LOUIS D'OR

7.6490 g., 0.9170 Gold 0.2255 oz. AGW **Ruler:** Louis XVI **Mint:** Montpellier **Obverse:** Head left **Reverse:** Crowned arms of France and Navarre in shields

Date	Mintage	VG	F	VF	XF	Unc
1786N	284,000	150	200	250	400	—
1786N	Inc. above	150	200	250	400	—
1787N	44,000	175	250	350	500	—
1788N	29,000	175	250	350	500	—
1789N	17,000	175	250	360	525	—
1790N	9,683	—	—	—	—	—
1791N	1,389	275	425	625	1,150	—

KM# 591.6 LOUIS D'OR

7.6490 g., 0.9170 Gold 0.2255 oz. AGW **Ruler:** Louis XVI **Mint:** La Rochelle **Obverse:** Head left **Reverse:** Crowned arms of France and Navarre in shields

Date	Mintage	VG	F	VF	XF	Unc
1786H	367,000	150	200	250	400	—
1786H	Inc. above	150	200	250	400	—
1787H	65,000	175	250	350	550	—
1788H	23,000	175	250	350	550	—
1789H	17,000	175	250	350	550	—
1790H	7,530	250	350	450	725	—
1791H	3,113	250	350	500	900	—

KM# 591.3 LOUIS D'OR

7.6490 g., 0.9170 Gold 0.2255 oz. AGW **Ruler:** Louis XVI **Mint:** Rouen **Obverse:** Head left **Reverse:** Crowned arms of France and Navarre in shields

Date	Mintage	VG	F	VF	XF	Unc
1786B	419,000	150	200	300	450	—
1787B	99,000	175	200	300	450	—
1788B	30,000	175	225	350	500	—
1789B	—	225	325	350	500	—
1790B	24,000	175	225	400	600	—

KM# 591.4 LOUIS D'OR

7.6490 g., 0.9170 Gold 0.2255 oz. AGW **Ruler:** Louis XVI **Mint:** Strasbourg **Obverse:** Head left **Reverse:** Crowned arms of France and Navarre in shields

Date	Mintage	VG	F	VF	XF	Unc
1786BB	248,000	175	250	350	650	—
1786BB	—	325	625	1,000	1,500	—
Note: Horn on head						

KM# 591.10 LOUIS D'OR

7.6490 g., 0.9170 Gold 0.2255 oz. AGW **Ruler:** Louis XVI **Mint:** Marseille **Obverse:** Head left **Reverse:** Crowned arms of France and Navarre in shields

Date	Mintage	VG	F	VF	XF	Unc
1787MA	—	200	300	450	700	—
1789MA	—	200	300	450	700	—
1790MA	13,000	—	—	—	—	—
1791MA	2,073	275	425	600	1,100	—

KM# 591.13 LOUIS D'OR

7.6490 g., 0.9170 Gold 0.2255 oz. AGW **Ruler:** Louis XVI **Mint:** Orléans **Obverse:** Head left **Reverse:** Crowned arms of France and Navarre in shields

Date	Mintage	VG	F	VF	XF	Unc
1787R	—	200	300	450	700	—
1789R	10,000	200	300	450	700	—
1790R	6,819	200	300	450	750	—
1791R	4,359	—	—	—	—	—

KM# 591.12 LOUIS D'OR

7.6490 g., 0.9170 Gold 0.2255 oz. AGW **Ruler:** Louis XVI **Mint:** Perpignan **Obverse:** Head left **Reverse:** Crowned arms of France and Navarre in shields

Date	Mintage	VG	F	VF	XF	Unc
1789Q	20,000	—	—	—	—	—

KM# 591.9 LOUIS D'OR

7.6490 g., 0.9170 Gold 0.2255 oz. AGW **Ruler:** Louis XVI **Mint:** Toulouse **Obverse:** Head left **Reverse:** Crowned arms of France and Navarre in shields

Date	Mintage	VG	F	VF	XF	Unc
1789M	19,000	200	300	450	650	—
1792M	—	225	425	650	1,000	—

KM# 617.1 LOUIS D'OR

7.6000 g., 0.9000 Gold 0.2199 oz. AGW **Ruler:** Louis XVI **Mint:** Paris **Obverse:** Head left **Obv. Legend:** LOUIS XVI ROI DES FRANCOIS **Reverse:** Standing Genius writing the Constitution **Rev. Legend:** REGNE DE LA LOI •

Date	Mintage	VG	F	VF	XF	Unc
1792A	—	600	1,250	2,750	4,500	—
1793A	—	800	1,750	3,250	5,000	—

KM# 617.2 LOUIS D'OR

7.6000 g., 0.9000 Gold 0.2199 oz. AGW **Ruler:** Louis XVI **Mint:** Toulouse **Obverse:** Head left **Reverse:** Standing Genius writing the Constitution

Date	Mintage	VG	F	VF	XF	Unc
1793M	—	1,250	2,500	4,000	6,500	—

KM# 335.1 2 LOUIS D'OR

13.3900 g., 0.9170 Gold 0.3948 oz. AGW **Ruler:** Louis XIV **Mint:** Paris **Obverse:** Laureate head right **Obv. Legend:** LVD • XIIII • D • G FR • ET • NAV • REX **Reverse:** Crowned back to back L's with sceptre and hand of Justice crossed at center behind circle **Rev. Legend:** CHRS REGN VINC IMP

Date	Mintage	VG	F	VF	XF	Unc
1700A	—	550	1,000	2,150	3,700	—
1701A	—	550	1,000	2,150	3,700	—
1701A	—	550	1,000	2,150	3,700	—
1702A	—	550	1,000	2,150	3,700	—
1703A	—	550	1,000	2,150	3,700	—
1704A Rare	—	—	—	—	—	—

KM# 335.10 2 LOUIS D'OR

13.3900 g., 0.9170 Gold 0.3948 oz. AGW **Ruler:** Louis XIV **Mint:** Toulouse

Date	Mintage	VG	F	VF	XF	Unc
1701M	—	650	1,300	2,800	4,550	—
1702M	—	550	1,100	2,150	3,400	—
1703M	—	550	1,100	2,150	3,400	—

KM# 335.4 2 LOUIS D'OR

13.3900 g., 0.9170 Gold 0.3948 oz. AGW **Ruler:** Louis XIV **Mint:** Strasbourg

Date	Mintage	VG	F	VF	XF	Unc
1701BB	—	550	1,100	2,200	3,550	—
1702BB	—	550	1,100	2,200	3,550	—
1704BB Rare	—	—	—	—	—	—

KM# 335.5 2 LOUIS D'OR

13.3900 g., 0.9170 Gold 0.3948 oz. AGW **Ruler:** Louis XIV **Mint:** Lyon

Date	Mintage	VG	F	VF	XF	Unc
1701D	—	550	1,100	2,150	3,400	—
1702D	—	550	1,100	2,150	3,400	—
1703D Rare	—	—	—	—	—	—

KM# 335.6 2 LOUIS D'OR

13.3900 g., 0.9170 Gold 0.3948 oz. AGW **Ruler:** Louis XIV **Mint:** La Rochelle

Date	Mintage	VG	F	VF	XF	Unc
1701H	—	600	1,200	2,500	4,300	—
1702H	—	550	1,100	2,150	3,400	—
1703H	—	600	1,200	2,500	4,300	—
1704H Rare	—	—	—	—	—	—

KM# 335.21 2 LOUIS D'OR

13.3900 g., 0.9170 Gold 0.3948 oz. AGW **Ruler:** Louis XIV **Mint:** Aix **Obverse:** Laureate head right **Reverse:** Crowned back to back L's with sceptre and hand of Justice crossed at center behind circle **Note:** Mint mark: &.

Date	Mintage	VG	F	VF	XF	Unc
1701	—	550	1,100	2,150	3,400	—
1703 Rare	—	—	—	—	—	—

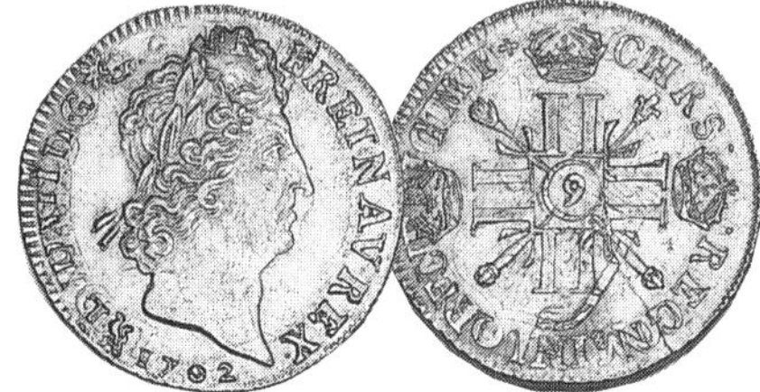

KM# 335.20 2 LOUIS D'OR

13.3900 g., 0.9170 Gold 0.3948 oz. AGW **Ruler:** Louis XIV **Mint:** Rennes **Obverse:** Larueate head right **Reverse:** Crowned back to back L's with sceptre and hand of Justice crossed at center behind circle **Note:** Mint mark: 9.

Date	Mintage	VG	F	VF	XF	Unc
1701	—	550	1,100	2,150	3,400	—
1702	—	550	1,100	2,150	3,400	—
1703 Rare	—	—	—	—	—	—
1704 Rare	—	—	—	—	—	—

KM# 335.22 2 LOUIS D'OR

13.3900 g., 0.9170 Gold 0.3948 oz. AGW **Ruler:** Louis XIV **Mint:** Besancon **Obverse:** Laureate head right **Reverse:** Crowned back to back L's with sceptre and hand of Justice crossed at center behind circle **Note:** Mint mark: Back to back C's.

Date	Mintage	VG	F	VF	XF	Unc
1701	—	550	1,100	2,150	3,400	—
1702	—	550	1,100	2,150	3,400	—
1703 Rare	—	—	—	—	—	—

KM# 336 2 LOUIS D'OR

13.3900 g., 0.9170 Gold 0.3948 oz. AGW **Ruler:** Louis XIV **Mint:** Pau **Obverse:** Legend ends: ...RE. BD. (ligate BD) **Note:** Mint mark: Cow. Issued for Province of Bearn.

Date	Mintage	VG	F	VF	XF	Unc
1701	—	600	1,200	2,650	4,550	—
1703	—	600	1,200	2,650	4,550	—

KM# 335.7 2 LOUIS D'OR

13.3900 g., 0.9170 Gold 0.3948 oz. AGW **Ruler:** Louis XIV **Mint:** Limoges **Obverse:** Laureate head right **Reverse:** Crowned back to back L's with sceptre and hand of Justice crossed at center behind circle

Date	Mintage	VG	F	VF	XF	Unc
1702I	—	650	1,300	2,800	4,550	—
1703I	—	550	1,100	2,150	3,400	—

KM# 335.8 2 LOUIS D'OR

13.3900 g., 0.9170 Gold 0.3948 oz. AGW **Ruler:** Louis XIV **Mint:** Bordeaux **Obverse:** Larueate head right **Reverse:** Crowned back to back L's with sceptre and hand of Justice crossed at center behind circle

Date	Mintage	VG	F	VF	XF	Unc
1702K	—	550	1,100	2,150	3,400	—
1703K	—	550	1,100	2,150	3,400	—

KM# 335.9 2 LOUIS D'OR

13.3900 g., 0.9170 Gold 0.3948 oz. AGW **Ruler:** Louis XIV **Mint:** Bayonne **Obverse:** Laureate head right **Reverse:** Crowned back to back L's with sceptre and hand of Justice crossed at center behind circle

Date	Mintage	VG	F	VF	XF	Unc
1702L	—	600	1,200	2,400	3,700	—

KM# 335.19 2 LOUIS D'OR

13.3900 g., 0.9170 Gold 0.3948 oz. AGW **Ruler:** Louis XIV **Mint:** Grenoble **Obverse:** Laureate head right **Reverse:** Crowned back to back L's with sceptre and hand of Justice crossed at center behind circle

Date	Mintage	VG	F	VF	XF	Unc
1702Z	—	550	1,100	2,300	3,550	—
1703Z	—	600	1,200	2,500	4,300	—

KM# 335.11 2 LOUIS D'OR

13.3900 g., 0.9170 Gold 0.3948 oz. AGW **Ruler:** Louis XIV **Mint:** Montpellier **Obverse:** Laureate head right **Reverse:** Crowned back to back L's with sceptre and hand of Justice crossed at center behind circle

Date	Mintage	VG	F	VF	XF	Unc
1702N	—	550	1,100	2,150	3,400	—
1703N Rare	—	—	—	—	—	—
1704N Rare	—	—	—	—	—	—

KM# 335.12 2 LOUIS D'OR

13.3900 g., 0.9170 Gold 0.3948 oz. AGW **Ruler:** Louis XIV **Mint:** Riom **Obverse:** Laureate head right **Reverse:** Crowned back to back L's with sceptre and hand of Justice crossed at center behind circle

Date	Mintage	VG	F	VF	XF	Unc
1702O Rare	—	—	—	—	—	—

KM# 335.13 2 LOUIS D'OR

13.3900 g., 0.9170 Gold 0.3948 oz. AGW **Ruler:** Louis XIV **Mint:** Dijon **Obverse:** Laureate head right **Reverse:** Crowned back to back L's with sceptre and hand of Justice crossed at center behind circle

Date	Mintage	VG	F	VF	XF	Unc
1702P	—	550	1,100	2,150	3,400	—
1703P Rare	—	—	—	—	—	—

KM# 335.14 2 LOUIS D'OR

13.3900 g., 0.9170 Gold 0.3948 oz. AGW **Ruler:** Louis XIV **Mint:** Reims **Obverse:** Laureate head right **Reverse:** Crowned back to back L's with sceptre and hand of Justice crossed at center behind circle

Date	Mintage	VG	F	VF	XF	Unc
1702S	—	550	1,100	2,150	3,400	—

KM# 335.15 2 LOUIS D'OR

13.3900 g., 0.9170 Gold 0.3948 oz. AGW **Ruler:** Louis XIV **Mint:** Nantes **Obverse:** Laureate head right **Reverse:** Crowned back to back L's with sceptre and hand of Justice crossed at center behind circle

Date	Mintage	VG	F	VF	XF	Unc
1702T Rare	—	—	—	—	—	—
1704T Rare	—	—	—	—	—	—

KM# 335.16 2 LOUIS D'OR

13.3900 g., 0.9170 Gold 0.3948 oz. AGW **Ruler:** Louis XIV **Mint:** Troyes **Obverse:** Laureate head right **Reverse:** Crowned back to back L's with sceptre and hand of Justice crossed at center behind circle

Date	Mintage	VG	F	VF	XF	Unc
1702V	—	600	1,200	2,500	4,300	—

KM# 335.17 2 LOUIS D'OR

13.3900 g., 0.9170 Gold 0.3948 oz. AGW **Ruler:** Louis XIV **Mint:** Lille **Obverse:** Laureate head right **Reverse:** Crowned back to back L's with sceptre and hand of Justice crossed at center behind circle

Date	Mintage	VG	F	VF	XF	Unc
1702W	—	600	1,200	2,500	4,300	—
1703W Rare	—	—	—	—	—	—

KM# 335.2 2 LOUIS D'OR

13.3900 g., 0.9170 Gold 0.3948 oz. AGW **Ruler:** Louis XIV **Mint:** Metz **Obverse:** Laureate head right **Reverse:** Crowned back to back L's with sceptre and hand of Justice crossed at center behind circle

Date	Mintage	VG	F	VF	XF	Unc
1702AA Rare	—	—	—	—	—	—
1703AA Rare	—	—	—	—	—	—

KM# 335.3 2 LOUIS D'OR

13.3900 g., 0.9170 Gold 0.3948 oz. AGW **Ruler:** Louis XIV **Mint:** Rouen **Obverse:** Laureate head right **Reverse:** Crowned back to back L's with sceptre and hand of Justice crossed at center behind circle

Date	Mintage	VG	F	VF	XF	Unc
1702B	—	550	1,100	2,150	3,400	—

KM# 335.18 2 LOUIS D'OR

13.3900 g., 0.9170 Gold 0.3948 oz. AGW **Ruler:** Louis XIV **Mint:** Amiens **Obverse:** Laureate head right **Reverse:** Crowned back to back L's with sceptre and hand of Justice crossed at center behind circle

Date	Mintage	VG	F	VF	XF	Unc
1703X	—	550	1,100	2,300	3,550	—

KM# 368.1 2 LOUIS D'OR

13.3900 g., 0.9170 Gold 0.3948 oz. AGW **Ruler:** Louis XIV **Mint:** Paris **Obverse:** Laureate head right **Obv. Legend:** LVD • XIIII • D • G • FR • ET • NAV • REX **Reverse:** Sceptre and hand of Justice crossed back of center circle, crowned fleur-de-lis at angles **Rev. Legend:** CHRS • REGN • VINC • IMP

Date	Mintage	VG	F	VF	XF	Unc
1704A	—	550	1,100	2,400	4,200	—
1705A	—	550	1,100	2,400	4,200	—
1706A	—	550	1,100	2,650	4,450	—
1707A Rare	—	—	—	—	—	—

KM# 368.2 2 LOUIS D'OR

13.3900 g., 0.9170 Gold 0.3948 oz. AGW **Ruler:** Louis XIV **Mint:** Metz **Obverse:** Laureate head right **Reverse:** Sceptre and hand of Justice crossed back of center circle, crowned fleur-de-lis at angles

Date	Mintage	VG	F	VF	XF	Unc
1704AA Rare	—	—	—	—	—	—
1705AA	—	550	1,100	2,650	4,450	—

KM# 368.3 2 LOUIS D'OR

13.3900 g., 0.9170 Gold 0.3948 oz. AGW **Ruler:** Louis XIV **Mint:** Strasbourg **Obverse:** Laureate head right **Reverse:** Sceptre and hand of Justice crossed back of center circle, crowned fleur-de-lis at angles

Date	Mintage	VG	F	VF	XF	Unc
1704BB	—	550	1,200	2,900	4,700	—

KM# 368.5 2 LOUIS D'OR

13.3900 g., 0.9170 Gold 0.3948 oz. AGW **Ruler:** Louis XIV **Mint:** Lyon **Obverse:** Laureate head right **Reverse:** Sceptre and hand of Justice crossed back of center circle, crowned fleur-de-lis at angles

Date	Mintage	VG	F	VF	XF	Unc
1704D	—	550	1,100	2,650	4,450	—
1705D	—	550	1,100	2,650	4,450	—
1707D Rare	—	—	—	—	—	—
1708D Rare	—	—	—	—	—	—

KM# 368.6 2 LOUIS D'OR

13.3900 g., 0.9170 Gold 0.3948 oz. AGW **Ruler:** Louis XIV **Mint:** Poitiers **Obverse:** Laureate head right **Reverse:** Sceptre and hand of Justice crossed back of center circle, crowned fleur-de-lis at angles

Date	Mintage	VG	F	VF	XF	Unc
1704G	—	550	1,100	2,650	4,450	—
1705G Rare	—	—	—	—	—	—

KM# 368.7 2 LOUIS D'OR

13.3900 g., 0.9170 Gold 0.3948 oz. AGW **Ruler:** Louis XIV **Mint:** La Rochelle **Obverse:** Laureate head right **Reverse:** Sceptre and hand of Justice crossed back of center circle, crowned fleur-de-lis at angles

Date	Mintage	VG	F	VF	XF	Unc
1704H Rare	—	—	—	—	—	—
1705H Rare	—	—	—	—	—	—
1706H	—	550	1,100	2,650	4,450	—
1707H Rare	—	—	—	—	—	—
1708H Rare	—	—	—	—	—	—
1709H Rare	—	—	—	—	—	—

KM# 368.8 2 LOUIS D'OR

13.3900 g., 0.9170 Gold 0.3948 oz. AGW **Ruler:** Louis XIV **Mint:** Bordeaux **Obverse:** Laureate head right **Reverse:** Sceptre and hand of Justice crossed back of center circle, crowned fleur-de-lis at angles

Date	Mintage	VG	F	VF	XF	Unc
1704K Rare	—	—	—	—	—	—
1705K Rare						
1706K Rare	—	—	—	—	—	—

Date	Mintage	VG	F	VF	XF	Unc
1707K Rare	—	—	—	—	—	—
1708K Rare	—	—	—	—	—	—
1709K Rare	—	—	—	—	—	—

KM# 368.9 2 LOUIS D'OR

13.3900 g., 0.9170 Gold 0.3948 oz. AGW **Ruler:** Louis XIV **Mint:** Bayonne **Obverse:** Laureate head right **Reverse:** Sceptre and hand of Justice crossed back of center circle, crowned fleur-de-lis at angles

Date	Mintage	VG	F	VF	XF	Unc
1704L	—	550	1,100	2,650	4,450	—
1705L	—	550	1,100	2,650	4,450	—
1706L	19	1,200	2,400	4,800	8,400	—
1707L Rare	—	—	—	—	—	—
1708L	—	600	1,200	3,000	5,400	—

KM# 368.10 2 LOUIS D'OR

13.3900 g., 0.9170 Gold 0.3948 oz. AGW **Ruler:** Louis XIV **Mint:** Toulouse **Obverse:** Laureate head right **Reverse:** Sceptre and hand of Justice crossed back of center circle, crowned fleur-de-lis at angles

Date	Mintage	VG	F	VF	XF	Unc
1704M	—	550	1,100	2,650	4,450	—
1705M	—	600	1,200	3,000	5,400	—

KM# 368.11 2 LOUIS D'OR

13.3900 g., 0.9170 Gold 0.3948 oz. AGW **Ruler:** Louis XIV **Mint:** Montpellier **Obverse:** Laureate head right **Reverse:** Sceptre and hand of Justice crossed back of center circle, crowned fleur-de-lis at angles

Date	Mintage	VG	F	VF	XF	Unc
1704N	—	550	1,100	2,650	4,450	—
1705N Rare	—	—	—	—	—	—

KM# 368.13 2 LOUIS D'OR

13.3900 g., 0.9170 Gold 0.3948 oz. AGW **Ruler:** Louis XIV **Mint:** Dijon **Obverse:** Laureate head right **Reverse:** Sceptre and hand of Justice crossed back of center circle, crowned fleur-de-lis at angles

Date	Mintage	VG	F	VF	XF	Unc
1704P	—	725	1,450	3,600	6,600	—
1705P Rare	—	—	—	—	—	—
1706P Rare	—	—	—	—	—	—

KM# 368.15 2 LOUIS D'OR

13.3900 g., 0.9170 Gold 0.3948 oz. AGW **Ruler:** Louis XIV **Mint:** Nantes **Obverse:** Laureate head right **Reverse:** Sceptre and hand of Justice crossed back of center circle, crowned fleur-de-lis at angles

Date	Mintage	VG	F	VF	XF	Unc
1704T Rare	—	—	—	—	—	—
1705T Rare	—	—	—	—	—	—

KM# 368.16 2 LOUIS D'OR

13.3900 g., 0.9170 Gold 0.3948 oz. AGW **Ruler:** Louis XIV **Mint:** Lille **Obverse:** Laureate head right **Reverse:** Sceptre and hand of Justice crossed back of center circle, crowned fleur-de-lis at angles

Date	Mintage	VG	F	VF	XF	Unc
1704W Rare	—	—	—	—	—	—
1707W Rare	—	—	—	—	—	—

KM# 368.17 2 LOUIS D'OR

13.3900 g., 0.9170 Gold 0.3948 oz. AGW **Ruler:** Louis XIV **Mint:** Grenoble **Obverse:** Laureate head right **Reverse:** Sceptre and hand of Justice crossed back of center circle, crowned fleur-de-lis at angles

Date	Mintage	VG	F	VF	XF	Unc
1704Z Rare	—	—	—	—	—	—
1705Z Rare	—	—	—	—	—	—
1706Z Rare	—	—	—	—	—	—
1707Z Rare	—	—	—	—	—	—
1709Z Rare	—	—	—	—	—	—

KM# 370 2 LOUIS D'OR

13.3900 g., 0.9170 Gold 0.3948 oz. AGW **Ruler:** Louis XIV **Mint:** Paris **Obverse:** Laureate head with longer hair right

Date	Mintage	VG	F	VF	XF	Unc
1704A Rare	—	—	—	—	—	—
1705A	—	550	1,100	2,650	4,450	—
1706A	—	550	1,100	2,650	4,450	—
1707A	—	550	1,200	3,000	4,800	—

KM# 369 2 LOUIS D'OR

13.3900 g., 0.9170 Gold 0.3948 oz. AGW **Ruler:** Louis XIV **Mint:** Pau **Obverse:** Laureate head right **Obv. Legend:** ....RE.BD (ligate BD). **Reverse:** Sceptre and hand of Justice crossed back of center circle, crowned fleur-de-lis at angles **Rev. Legend:** CHRS REGN VINC IMP **Note:** Mint mark: Cow. Issued for Province of Bearn.

Date	Mintage	VG	F	VF	XF	Unc
1704	—	725	1,300	3,250	5,700	—
1705	—	725	1,300	2,900	5,400	—
1706 Rare	—	—	—	—	—	—
1707 Rare	—	—	—	—	—	—
1708 Rare	—	—	—	—	—	—
1709 Rare	—	—	—	—	—	—

KM# 368.14 2 LOUIS D'OR

13.3900 g., 0.9170 Gold 0.3948 oz. AGW **Ruler:** Louis XIV **Mint:** Troyes **Obverse:** Laureate head right **Reverse:** Sceptre and hand of Justice crossed back of center circle, crowned fleur-de-lis at angles **Note:** Mint mark: Crowned S.

Date	Mintage	VG	F	VF	XF	Unc
1704	—	550	1,100	2,650	4,450	—

KM# 368.18 2 LOUIS D'OR

13.3900 g., 0.9170 Gold 0.3948 oz. AGW **Ruler:** Louis XIV **Mint:** Rennes **Obverse:** Laureate head right **Reverse:** Sceptre and hand of Justice crossed back of center circle, crowned fleur-de-lis at angles **Note:** Mint mark: 9.

Date	Mintage	VG	F	VF	XF	Unc
1704	—	600	1,200	3,000	5,400	—
1705 Rare	—	—	—	—	—	—
1706 Rare	—	—	—	—	—	—
1707 Rare	—	—	—	—	—	—
1709	—	725	1,450	3,600	6,600	—

KM# 368.19 2 LOUIS D'OR

13.3900 g., 0.9170 Gold 0.3948 oz. AGW **Ruler:** Louis XIV **Mint:** Aix **Obverse:** Laureate head right **Reverse:** Sceptre and hand of Justice crossed back of center circle, crowned fleur-de-lis at angles **Note:** Mint mark: &.

Date	Mintage	VG	F	VF	XF	Unc
1704	—	600	1,200	3,000	5,400	—
1705 Rare	—	—	—	—	—	—
1706	—	600	1,200	3,000	5,400	—

KM# 368.20 2 LOUIS D'OR

13.3900 g., 0.9170 Gold 0.3948 oz. AGW **Ruler:** Louis XIV **Mint:** Besancon **Obverse:** Laureate head right **Reverse:** Sceptre and hand of Justice crossed back of center circle, crowned fleur-de-lis at angles **Note:** Mint mark: Back to back C'S.

Date	Mintage	VG	F	VF	XF	Unc
1705 Rare	—	—	—	—	—	—
1706 Rare	—	—	—	—	—	—

KM# 368.12 2 LOUIS D'OR

13.3900 g., 0.9170 Gold 0.3948 oz. AGW **Ruler:** Louis XIV **Mint:** Riom **Obverse:** Laureate head right **Reverse:** Sceptre and hand of Justice crossed back of center circle, crowned fleur-de-lis at angles

Date	Mintage	VG	F	VF	XF	Unc
1705O	—	550	1,100	2,650	4,450	—

KM# 368.4 2 LOUIS D'OR

13.3900 g., 0.9170 Gold 0.3948 oz. AGW **Ruler:** Louis XIV **Mint:** Caen **Obverse:** Laureate head right **Reverse:** Sceptre and hand of Justice crossed back of center circle, crowned fleur-de-lis at angles

Date	Mintage	VG	F	VF	XF	Unc
1705C	—	600	1,200	3,000	5,400	—

KM# 405.2 2 LOUIS D'OR

16.2500 g., 0.9170 Gold 0.4791 oz. AGW **Ruler:** Louis XIV **Mint:** Rouen

Date	Mintage	VG	F	VF	XF	Unc
1709B	—	1,150	2,250	4,750	7,200	—
1710B Rare	14,000	—	—	—	—	—
1711B	13,000	1,150	2,250	4,750	7,200	—

KM# 405.3 2 LOUIS D'OR

16.2500 g., 0.9170 Gold 0.4791 oz. AGW **Ruler:** Louis XIV **Mint:** Caen

Date	Mintage	VG	F	VF	XF	Unc
1710C	3,828	1,150	2,250	4,750	7,200	—
1711C Rare	8,377	—	—	—	—	—
1712C	2,444	1,150	2,250	4,750	7,200	—
1713C Rare	4,218	—	—	—	—	—

KM# 405.4 2 LOUIS D'OR

16.2500 g., 0.9170 Gold 0.4791 oz. AGW **Ruler:** Louis XIV **Mint:** Lyon

Date	Mintage	VG	F	VF	XF	Unc
1710D	147,000	775	1,950	4,250	6,500	—
1715D Rare	16,000	—	—	—	—	—

KM# 405.6 2 LOUIS D'OR

16.2500 g., 0.9170 Gold 0.4791 oz. AGW **Ruler:** Louis XIV **Mint:** La Rochelle

Date	Mintage	VG	F	VF	XF	Unc
1710H Rare	4,770	—	—	—	—	—
1711H	5,218	1,300	2,600	5,200	10,000	—
1712H Rare	4,159	—	—	—	—	—
1713H Rare	4,458	—	—	—	—	—

KM# 405.8 2 LOUIS D'OR

16.2500 g., 0.9170 Gold 0.4791 oz. AGW **Ruler:** Louis XIV **Mint:** Bayonne

Date	Mintage	VG	F	VF	XF	Unc
1710L	—	1,150	2,250	4,750	7,200	—
1710L	—	1,150	2,250	4,750	7,200	—
1712L	—	1,150	2,250	4,750	7,200	—

KM# 405.9 2 LOUIS D'OR

16.2500 g., 0.9170 Gold 0.4791 oz. AGW **Ruler:** Louis XIV **Mint:** Toulouse

Date	Mintage	VG	F	VF	XF	Unc
1710M	16,000	1,150	2,250	4,750	7,200	—
1711M	11,000	1,150	2,250	4,750	7,200	—
1712M Rare	10,000	—	—	—	—	—
1713M Rare	10,000	—	—	—	—	—
1715M Rare	4,628	—	—	—	—	—

KM# 405.10 2 LOUIS D'OR

16.2500 g., 0.9170 Gold 0.4791 oz. AGW **Ruler:** Louis XIV **Mint:** Montpellier

Date	Mintage	VG	F	VF	XF	Unc
1710N	20,000	1,150	2,250	4,750	7,200	—
1711N Rare	6,005	—	—	—	—	—
1712N Rare	8,227	—	—	—	—	—
1713N Rare	4,432	—	—	—	—	—
1714N Rare	1,015	—	—	—	—	—
1715N Rare	3,324	—	—	—	—	—

KM# 405.12 2 LOUIS D'OR

16.2500 g., 0.9170 Gold 0.4791 oz. AGW **Ruler:** Louis XIV **Mint:** Dijon

Date	Mintage	VG	F	VF	XF	Unc
1710P	9,025	1,150	2,250	4,750	7,200	—

KM# 405.16 2 LOUIS D'OR

16.2500 g., 0.9170 Gold 0.4791 oz. AGW **Ruler:** Louis XIV **Mint:** Troyes

Date	Mintage	VG	F	VF	XF	Unc
1710V	—	1,150	2,250	4,750	7,200	—

KM# 405.18 2 LOUIS D'OR

16.2500 g., 0.9170 Gold 0.4791 oz. AGW **Ruler:** Louis XIV **Mint:** Amiens

Date	Mintage	VG	F	VF	XF	Unc
1710X Rare	—	—	—	—	—	—

KM# 405.22 2 LOUIS D'OR

16.2500 g., 0.9170 Gold 0.4791 oz. AGW **Ruler:** Louis XIV **Mint:** Besancon **Note:** Mint mark: Back to back C's.

Date	Mintage	VG	F	VF	XF	Unc
1710	8,610	1,150	2,250	4,750	7,200	—
1711	21,000	1,150	2,250	4,750	7,200	—
1713 Rare	—	—	—	—	—	—

KM# 405.20 2 LOUIS D'OR

16.2500 g., 0.9170 Gold 0.4791 oz. AGW **Ruler:** Louis XIV **Mint:** Rennes **Note:** Mint mark: 9.

Date	Mintage	VG	F	VF	XF	Unc
1710 Rare	2,935	—	—	—	—	—
1711 Rare	2,299	—	—	—	—	—
1712 Rare	6,440	—	—	—	—	—
1713 Rare	4,170	—	—	—	—	—
1715 Rare	1,247	—	—	—	—	—

KM# 405.14 2 LOUIS D'OR

16.2500 g., 0.9170 Gold 0.4791 oz. AGW **Ruler:** Louis XIV **Mint:** Troyes **Note:** Mint mark: Crowned S.

Date	Mintage	VG	F	VF	XF	Unc
1710	91,000	775	1,950	4,250	6,500	—

KM# 406 2 LOUIS D'OR

16.2500 g., 0.9170 Gold 0.4791 oz. AGW **Ruler:** Louis XIV **Mint:** Pau **Obv. Legend:** ....RE.BD (ligate BD). **Note:** Mint mark: Cow. Issued for Province of Bearn.

Date	Mintage	VG	F	VF	XF	Unc
1711 Rare	—	—	—	—	—	—
1712 Rare	—	—	—	—	—	—
1713 Rare	—	—	—	—	—	—
1714 Rare	—	—	—	—	—	—

KM# 405.21 2 LOUIS D'OR

16.2500 g., 0.9170 Gold 0.4791 oz. AGW **Ruler:** Louis XIV **Mint:** Aix **Note:** Mint mark: &.

Date	Mintage	VG	F	VF	XF	Unc
1711	—	1,150	2,250	4,750	7,200	—

KM# 405.19 2 LOUIS D'OR

16.2500 g., 0.9170 Gold 0.4791 oz. AGW **Ruler:** Louis XIV **Mint:** Grenoble

Date	Mintage	VG	F	VF	XF	Unc
1711Z Rare	—	—	—	—	—	—
1712Z Rare	244	—	—	—	—	—
1713Z Rare	501	—	—	—	—	—

KM# 405.13 2 LOUIS D'OR

16.2500 g., 0.9170 Gold 0.4791 oz. AGW **Ruler:** Louis XIV **Mint:** Perpignan

Date	Mintage	VG	F	VF	XF	Unc
1711Q Rare	28,000	—	—	—	—	—
1712Q	17,000	1,150	2,250	4,750	7,200	—
1713Q Rare	14,000	—	—	—	—	—
1714Q Rare	3,413	—	—	—	—	—

KM# 405.11 2 LOUIS D'OR

16.2500 g., 0.9170 Gold 0.4791 oz. AGW **Ruler:** Louis XIV **Mint:** Riom

Date	Mintage	VG	F	VF	XF	Unc
1711O Rare	862	—	—	—	—	—

KM# 405.7 2 LOUIS D'OR

16.2500 g., 0.9170 Gold 0.4791 oz. AGW **Ruler:** Louis XIV **Mint:** Bordeaux

Date	Mintage	VG	F	VF	XF	Unc
1712K	8,212	1,150	2,250	4,750	7,200	—
1713K	24,000	1,150	2,250	4,750	7,200	—
1714K Rare	4,515	—	—	—	—	—
1715K Rare	18,000	—	—	—	—	—

KM# 405.1 2 LOUIS D'OR

16.2500 g., 0.9170 Gold 0.4791 oz. AGW **Ruler:** Louis XIV **Obverse:** Laureate head right **Obv. Legend:** LVD • XIIII • D • G • FR • ET • NAV • REX • **Reverse:** Crowned back to back L's, fleur-de-lis at angles **Rev. Legend:** CHRS • REGN • VINC • IMP

Date	Mintage	VG	F	VF	XF	Unc
1712	144,000	775	1,950	4,250	6,600	—
1713 Rare	12,000	—	—	—	—	—
1715 Rare	1,179	—	—	—	—	—

KM# 405.5 2 LOUIS D'OR

16.2500 g., 0.9170 Gold 0.4791 oz. AGW **Ruler:** Louis XIV **Mint:** Tours **Obverse:** Laureate head right **Reverse:** Crowned back to back L's, fleur-de-lis at angles

Date	Mintage	VG	F	VF	XF	Unc
1713E Rare	3,908	—	—	—	—	—
1714E Rare	3,724	—	—	—	—	—
1715E Rare	2,368	—	—	—	—	—

KM# 405.15 2 LOUIS D'OR

16.2500 g., 0.9170 Gold 0.4791 oz. AGW **Ruler:** Louis XIV **Mint:** Nantes **Obverse:** Laureate head right **Reverse:** Crowned back to back L's, fleur-de-lis at angles

Date	Mintage	VG	F	VF	XF	Unc
1713T	7,194	1,150	2,250	4,750	7,200	—
1714T Rare	1,313	—	—	—	—	—
1715T	765	1,300	2,600	5,200	10,000	—

KM# 405.17 2 LOUIS D'OR

16.2500 g., 0.9170 Gold 0.4791 oz. AGW **Ruler:** Louis XIV **Mint:** Lille **Obverse:** Laureate head right **Reverse:** Crowned back to back L's, fleur-de-lis at angles

Date	Mintage	VG	F	VF	XF	Unc
1714W Rare	—	—	—	—	—	—

KM# 426.2 2 LOUIS D'OR

16.3160 g., 0.9170 Gold 0.4810 oz. AGW **Ruler:** Louis XV **Mint:** Metz

Date	Mintage	VG	F	VF	XF	Unc
1716AA	—	1,750	4,400	9,600	14,500	—

KM# 426.3 2 LOUIS D'OR

16.3160 g., 0.9170 Gold 0.4810 oz. AGW **Ruler:** Louis XV **Mint:** Strasbourg

Date	Mintage	VG	F	VF	XF	Unc
1716BB	—	1,750	4,400	9,600	14,500	—

KM# 426.4 2 LOUIS D'OR

16.3160 g., 0.9170 Gold 0.4810 oz. AGW **Ruler:** Louis XV **Mint:** Caen

Date	Mintage	VG	F	VF	XF	Unc
1716C	—	1,750	4,400	9,600	14,500	—

KM# 426.5 2 LOUIS D'OR

16.3160 g., 0.9170 Gold 0.4810 oz. AGW **Ruler:** Louis XV **Mint:** Lyon

Date	Mintage	VG	F	VF	XF	Unc
1716D	—	1,750	4,400	9,600	14,500	—

KM# 426.6 2 LOUIS D'OR

16.3160 g., 0.9170 Gold 0.4810 oz. AGW **Ruler:** Louis XV **Mint:** Limoges

Date	Mintage	VG	F	VF	XF	Unc
1716I	1,887	1,750	4,400	9,600	14,500	—

KM# 426.7 2 LOUIS D'OR

16.3160 g., 0.9170 Gold 0.4810 oz. AGW **Ruler:** Louis XV **Mint:** Bordeaux

Date	Mintage	VG	F	VF	XF	Unc
1716K	—	1,750	4,400	9,600	14,500	—

KM# 426.8 2 LOUIS D'OR

16.3160 g., 0.9170 Gold 0.4810 oz. AGW **Ruler:** Louis XV **Mint:** Bayonne

Date	Mintage	VG	F	VF	XF	Unc
1716L	—	1,750	4,400	9,600	14,500	—

KM# 426.9 2 LOUIS D'OR

16.3160 g., 0.9170 Gold 0.4810 oz. AGW **Ruler:** Louis XV **Mint:** Perpignan

Date	Mintage	VG	F	VF	XF	Unc
1716Q	—	1,750	4,400	9,600	14,500	—

KM# 426.10 2 LOUIS D'OR

16.3160 g., 0.9170 Gold 0.4810 oz. AGW **Ruler:** Louis XV **Mint:** Troyes

Date	Mintage	VG	F	VF	XF	Unc
1716S	—	1,750	4,400	9,600	14,500	—

KM# 426.11 2 LOUIS D'OR

16.3160 g., 0.9170 Gold 0.4810 oz. AGW **Ruler:** Louis XV **Mint:** Nantes

Date	Mintage	VG	F	VF	XF	Unc
1716T	—	1,750	4,400	9,600	14,500	—

KM# 428.1 2 LOUIS D'OR

12.2350 g., 0.9170 Gold 0.3607 oz. AGW **Ruler:** Louis XV **Mint:** Paris **Obverse:** Crowned young head left **Obv. Legend:** LVD • XV • D • G • FR • ET • NAV • REX **Reverse:** Crowned arms of France and Navarre in cruciform with fleur-de-lis at angles **Rev. Legend:** CHRS • REGN • VINC • IMP •

Date	Mintage	VG	F	VF	XF	Unc
1716A	—	850	1,500	2,750	5,000	—
1717A	376,000	450	900	2,000	3,600	—
1718/7A	—	550	1,100	2,450	4,500	—
1718A	—	550	1,100	2,450	4,500	—

KM# 426.12 2 LOUIS D'OR

16.3160 g., 0.9170 Gold 0.4810 oz. AGW **Ruler:** Louis XV **Mint:** Besancon **Note:** Mint mark: Back to back C's.

Date	Mintage	VG	F	VF	XF	Unc
1716	—	1,750	4,400	9,600	14,500	—

KM# 427 2 LOUIS D'OR

16.3160 g., 0.9170 Gold 0.4810 oz. AGW **Ruler:** Louis XV **Mint:** Pau **Obv. Legend:** ....RE. BD. (ligate BD) **Note:** Mint mark: Cow. Issued for Province of Bearn.

Date	Mintage	VG	F	VF	XF	Unc
1716	—	3,000	6,000	10,000	15,000	—

KM# 426.1 2 LOUIS D'OR

16.3160 g., 0.9170 Gold 0.4810 oz. AGW **Ruler:** Louis XV **Mint:** Paris **Note:** Similar to 1 Louis D'or, KM#425.

Date	Mintage	VG	F	VF	XF	Unc
1716A	—	1,400	3,500	7,900	12,500	—

KM# 428.2 2 LOUIS D'OR

12.2350 g., 0.9170 Gold 0.3607 oz. AGW **Ruler:** Louis XV **Mint:** Strasbourg **Obverse:** Crowned young head left **Reverse:** Crowned arms of France and Navarre in cruciform with fleur-de-lis at angles

Date	Mintage	VG	F	VF	XF	Unc
1718BB	—	550	1,100	2,450	4,500	—

KM# 428.3 2 LOUIS D'OR

12.2350 g., 0.9170 Gold 0.3607 oz. AGW **Ruler:** Louis XV **Mint:** Lyon **Obverse:** Crowned young head left **Reverse:** Crowned arms of France and Navarre in cruciform with fleur-de-lis at angles

Date	Mintage	VG	F	VF	XF	Unc
1718D	—	550	1,100	2,450	4,500	—

KM# 428.4 2 LOUIS D'OR

12.2350 g., 0.9170 Gold 0.3607 oz. AGW **Ruler:** Louis XV **Mint:** Villeneuve St. André **Obverse:** Crowned young head left **Reverse:** Crowned arms of France and Navarre in cruciform with fleur-de-lis at angles

Date	Mintage	VG	F	VF	XF	Unc
1718R	—	550	1,100	2,450	4,500	—

KM# 428.5 2 LOUIS D'OR

12.2350 g., 0.9170 Gold 0.3607 oz. AGW **Ruler:** Louis XV **Mint:** Troyes **Obverse:** Crowned young head left **Reverse:** Crowned arms of France and Navarre in cruciform with fleur-de-lis at angles

Date	Mintage	VG	F	VF	XF	Unc
1718S	—	550	1,100	2,450	4,500	—

KM# 428.6 2 LOUIS D'OR

12.2350 g., 0.9170 Gold 0.3607 oz. AGW **Ruler:** Louis XV **Mint:** Lille **Obverse:** Crowned young head left **Reverse:** Crowned arms of France and Navarre in cruciform with fleur-de-lis at angles

Date	Mintage	VG	F	VF	XF	Unc
1718W	30,000	550	1,100	2,450	4,500	—

KM# 471 2 LOUIS D'OR

13.0500 g., 0.9170 Gold 0.3847 oz. AGW **Ruler:** Louis XV **Mint:** Paris **Note:** Similar to 1 Louis D'or, KM#468.1.

Date	Mintage	VG	F	VF	XF	Unc
1723A	—	1,750	3,250	5,750	9,000	—
1724A	—	1,500	2,750	5,250	8,250	—

KM# 519.22 2 LOUIS D'OR

16.3160 g., 0.9170 Gold 0.4810 oz. AGW **Ruler:** Louis XV **Mint:** Aix **Obverse:** Head left **Obv. Legend:** LUD • XV • D • G • FR • ETNAV • REX • **Reverse:** Crown above arms of France and Navarre **Rev. Legend:** CHRS • REGN • VINC • IMPE • **Note:** Mint mark: &.

Date	Mintage	VG	F	VF	XF	Unc
1742	35,000	250	400	750	1,250	—
1743	—	250	450	1,000	1,700	—
1744	—	250	400	750	1,250	—

KM# 519.3 2 LOUIS D'OR

16.3160 g., 0.9170 Gold 0.4810 oz. AGW **Ruler:** Louis XV **Mint:** Rouen **Obverse:** Head with headband left **Reverse:** Crown above arms of France and Navarre

Date	Mintage	VG	F	VF	XF	Unc
1742B	2,630	250	450	1,000	1,700	—
1743B	3,485	250	450	1,000	1,700	—
1744B	1,093	300	600	1,350	2,250	—
1745B	2,619	250	450	1,000	1,700	—
1746B	1,552	300	600	1,350	2,250	—
1747B	1,097	300	600	1,350	2,250	—
1748B	2,613	250	450	1,000	1,700	—
1750B	1,812	250	450	1,000	1,700	—
1751B	2,214	250	450	1,000	1,700	—
1756B	1,419	300	000	1,350	2,250	—
1757B	1,250	300	600	1,350	2,250	—

Date	Mintage	VG	F	VF	XF	Unc
1768B	827	325	700	1,500	3,000	—
1773B	1,496	300	600	1,350	2,500	—
1774B	244	400	750	1,575	3,150	—

KM# 519.10 2 LOUIS D'OR

16.3160 g., 0.9170 Gold 0.4810 oz. AGW **Ruler:** Louis XV **Mint:** Bayonne **Obverse:** Head with headband left **Reverse:** Crown above arms of France and Navarre

Date	Mintage	VG	F	VF	XF	Unc
1742L	23,000	250	400	750	1,250	—
1743L	35,000	250	400	750	1,250	—
1745L	18,000	250	400	750	1,250	—
1754L	9,399	250	450	1,000	1,700	—
1755L	15,000	250	400	750	1,250	—
1756L	14,000	250	400	750	1,250	—
1757L	15,000	250	400	750	1,250	—
1758L	19,000	250	400	750	1,250	—
1763L	56,000	250	400	750	1,250	—

KM# 519.12 2 LOUIS D'OR

16.3160 g., 0.9170 Gold 0.4810 oz. AGW **Ruler:** Louis XV **Mint:** Montpellier **Obverse:** Head with headband left **Reverse:** Crown above arms of France and Navarre

Date	Mintage	VG	F	VF	XF	Unc
1742N	2,687	250	450	1,000	1,700	—
1743N	18,000	250	400	750	1,250	—
1746N	—	250	450	1,000	1,700	—
1747N	3,270	250	450	1,000	1,700	—
1749N	—	250	450	1,000	1,700	—
1750N	1,446	300	600	1,350	2,250	—
1755N	2,075	250	450	1,000	1,700	—

KM# 519.13 2 LOUIS D'OR

16.3160 g., 0.9170 Gold 0.4810 oz. AGW **Ruler:** Louis XV **Mint:** Riom **Obverse:** Head with headband left **Reverse:** Crown above arms of France and Navarre

Date	Mintage	VG	F	VF	XF	Unc
1742O	1,527	300	600	1,350	2,250	—
1743O	1,369	300	600	1,350	2,250	—

KM# 519.15 2 LOUIS D'OR

16.3160 g., 0.9170 Gold 0.4810 oz. AGW **Ruler:** Louis XV **Mint:** Orléans **Obverse:** Head with headband left **Reverse:** Crown above arms of France and Navarre

Date	Mintage	VG	F	VF	XF	Unc
1742R	1,381	300	600	1,350	2,250	—
1743R	1,258	300	600	1,350	2,250	—
1766R	59,000	250	450	750	1,250	—
1767R	93,000	250	450	750	1,250	—
1768R	40,000	250	450	750	1,250	—

KM# 519.16 2 LOUIS D'OR

16.3160 g., 0.9170 Gold 0.4810 oz. AGW **Ruler:** Louis XV **Mint:** Nantes **Obverse:** Head with headband left **Reverse:** Crown above arms of France and Navarre

Date	Mintage	VG	F	VF	XF	Unc
1742T	6,086	250	450	1,000	1,700	—
1743T	20,000	250	400	750	1,250	—
1744T	31,000	250	400	750	1,250	—
1745T	10,000	250	450	1,000	1,700	—
1747T	8,600	250	450	1,000	1,700	—
1749T	4,165	250	450	1,000	1,700	—
1751T	9,471	250	450	1,000	1,700	—
1753T	9,333	250	450	1,000	1,700	—
1755T	2,948	250	450	1,000	1,700	—
1756T	1,580	250	450	1,125	1,900	—
1759T	21,000	250	400	750	1,250	—
1760T	2,474	250	450	1,000	1,700	—
1770T	797	310	525	1,300	2,400	—

KM# 519.18 2 LOUIS D'OR

16.3160 g., 0.9170 Gold 0.4810 oz. AGW **Ruler:** Louis XV **Mint:** Lille **Obverse:** Head with headband left **Reverse:** Crown above arms of France and Navarre

Date	Mintage	VG	F	VF	XF	Unc
1742W	1,754	250	450	1,125	1,900	—
1744W	24,000	250	400	750	1,250	—
1745W	1,755	250	450	1,125	1,900	—

KM# 519.20 2 LOUIS D'OR

16.3160 g., 0.9170 Gold 0.4810 oz. AGW **Ruler:** Louis XV **Mint:** Grenoble **Obverse:** Head with headband left **Reverse:** Crown above arms of France and Navarre

Date	Mintage	VG	F	VF	XF	Unc
1742Z	20,000	250	400	750	1,250	—
1743Z	41,000	250	400	750	1,250	—
1744Z	29,000	250	400	750	1,250	—
1746Z	1,568	250	450	1,125	1,900	—

KM# 519.1 2 LOUIS D'OR

16.3160 g., 0.9170 Gold 0.4810 oz. AGW **Ruler:** Louis XV **Mint:** Paris **Obverse:** Head with headband left **Obv. Legend:** LUD • XV • D • G • FR • ET • NAV • REX **Reverse:** Crown above arms of France and Navarre **Rev. Legend:** CHRS • REGN • VINC • IMPE •

Date	Mintage	VG	F	VF	XF	Unc
1742	16,000	250	400	750	1,250	—
1743	5,946	250	450	1,000	1,700	—
1744	21,000	250	400	750	1,250	—
1745	—	250	400	750	1,250	—
1751	—	250	450	1,000	1,700	—
1768	—	250	450	1,000	1,700	—
1769	—	250	400	750	1,250	—
1770	—	250	400	750	1,250	—

KM# 519.6 2 LOUIS D'OR

16.3160 g., 0.9170 Gold 0.4810 oz. AGW **Ruler:** Louis XV **Mint:** Tours **Obverse:** Head with headband left **Reverse:** Crown above arms of France and Navarre

Date	Mintage	VG	F	VF	XF	Unc
1742E	1,770	250	450	1,000	1,800	—
1743E	4,683	250	450	1,000	1,800	—
1744E	3,874	250	450	1,000	1,800	—
1745E	2,294	250	450	1,000	1,800	—
1747E	1,890	250	450	1,000	1,800	—
1750E	1,372	300	600	1,350	2,250	—
1751E	1,278	300	600	1,350	2,250	—
1753E	1,809	250	450	1,000	1,800	—

KM# 519.7 2 LOUIS D'OR

16.3160 g., 0.9170 Gold 0.4810 oz. AGW **Ruler:** Louis XV **Mint:** La Rochelle **Obverse:** Head with headband left **Reverse:** Crown above arms of France and Navarre

Date	Mintage	VG	F	VF	XF	Unc
1743H	3,298	250	450	1,000	1,700	—
1748H	—	250	450	1,000	1,700	—
1759H	10,000	250	450	1,000	1,700	—

KM# 519.19 2 LOUIS D'OR

16.3160 g., 0.9170 Gold 0.4810 oz. AGW **Ruler:** Louis XV **Mint:** Amiens **Obverse:** Head with headband left **Reverse:** Crown above arms of France and Navarre

Date	Mintage	VG	F	VF	XF	Unc
1743X	2,318	250	450	1,000	1,700	—
1744X	12,000	250	450	1,000	1,700	—
1745X	12,000	250	450	1,000	1,700	—
1746X	1,250	300	600	1,350	2,250	—

KM# 519.17 2 LOUIS D'OR

16.3160 g., 0.9170 Gold 0.4810 oz. AGW **Ruler:** Louis XV **Mint:** Troyes **Obverse:** Head with headband left **Reverse:** Crown above arms of France and Navarre

Date	Mintage	VG	F	VF	XF	Unc
1743V	767	400	650	1,575	2,750	—
1747V	1,187	300	550	1,300	2,000	—

KM# 519.14 2 LOUIS D'OR

16.3160 g., 0.9170 Gold 0.4810 oz. AGW **Ruler:** Louis XV **Mint:** Perpignan **Obverse:** Head with headband left **Reverse:** Crown above arms of France and Navarre

Date	Mintage	VG	F	VF	XF	Unc
1743Q	7,665	250	450	1,000	1,700	—
1744Q	11,000	250	450	1,000	1,700	—
1745Q	11,000	250	450	1,000	1,700	—
1746Q	5,268	250	450	1,000	1,700	—
1747Q	3,495	250	450	1,000	1,700	—
1748Q	3,038	250	450	1,000	1,700	—
1750Q	2,029	250	450	1,000	1,700	—
1751Q	3,199	250	450	1,000	1,700	—
1752Q	2,183	250	450	1,000	1,700	—
1754Q	4,252	250	450	1,000	1,700	—
1756Q	22,000	250	400	750	1,250	—
1763Q	8,018	250	450	1,000	1,700	—
1767Q	1,140	300	600	1,350	2,500	—
1768Q	1,653	250	450	1,125	1,900	—

KM# 519.11 2 LOUIS D'OR

16.3160 g., 0.9170 Gold 0.4810 oz. AGW **Ruler:** Louis XV **Mint:** Toulouse **Obverse:** Head with headband left **Reverse:** Crown above arms of France and Navarre

Date	Mintage	VG	F	VF	XF	Unc
1743M	7,034	250	450	1,000	1,700	—
1745M	6,357	250	450	1,000	1,700	—
1749M	1,842	250	450	1,125	1,900	—
1753M	5,012	250	450	1,000	1,700	—
1755M	7,609	250	450	1,000	1,700	—
1756M	10,022	250	450	1,000	1,700	—
1759M	5,241	250	450	1,000	1,700	—
1760M	6,863	250	450	1,000	1,700	—
1763M	2,869	250	450	1,000	1,700	—
1765M	4,665	250	450	1,000	1,700	—
1767M	8,342	250	450	1,000	1,700	—
1773M	8,595	250	450	1,000	1,700	—
1774M	—	250	450	1,000	1,700	—

KM# 519.4 2 LOUIS D'OR

16.3160 g., 0.9170 Gold 0.4810 oz. AGW **Ruler:** Louis XV **Mint:** Strasbourg **Obverse:** Head with headband left **Reverse:** Crown above arms of France and Navarre

Date	Mintage	VG	F	VF	XF	Unc
1743BB	80,000	250	400	750	1,250	—
1744BB	93,000	250	400	750	1,250	—
1745BB	183,000	250	350	675	1,125	—
1746BB	93,000	250	400	750	1,250	—
1747BB	181,000	250	350	675	1,125	—
1748BB	180,000	250	350	675	1,125	—
1749BB	60,000	250	400	750	1,250	—
1751BB	—	250	400	750	1,250	—
1756BB	68,000	250	400	750	1,250	—
1757BB	29,000	250	400	750	1,250	—
1758BB	407,000	250	350	675	1,125	—
1759BB	343,000	250	350	675	1,125	—
1760BB	200,000	250	350	675	1,125	—
1761BB	—	250	400	750	1,250	—
1762BB	22,000	250	400	750	1,250	—

KM# 519.5 2 LOUIS D'OR

16.3160 g., 0.9170 Gold 0.4810 oz. AGW **Ruler:** Louis XV **Mint:** Lyon **Obverse:** Head with headband left **Reverse:** Crown above arms of France and Navarre

Date	Mintage	VG	F	VF	XF	Unc
1743D	7,828	250	450	1,000	1,700	—
1744D	4,893	250	450	1,000	1,700	—
1745D	2,437	250	450	1,000	1,700	—
1753D	206	650	1,100	2,800	5,000	—
1755D	6,960	250	450	1,000	1,700	—
1756D	78,000	250	400	750	1,250	—
1757D	13,000	250	450	1,000	1,700	—
1759D	608	400	650	1,750	3,200	—
1761D	4,461	250	450	1,000	1,700	—
1770D	2,419	250	450	1,000	1,750	—

KM# 519.21 2 LOUIS D'OR

16.3160 g., 0.9170 Gold 0.4810 oz. AGW **Ruler:** Louis XV **Mint:** Rennes **Obverse:** Head with headband left **Reverse:** Crown above arms of France and Navarre **Note:** Mint mark: 9.

Date	Mintage	VG	F	VF	XF	Unc
1743	8,964	250	450	1,000	1,700	—
1744	4,043	250	450	1,000	1,700	—
1746	7,514	250	450	1,000	1,700	—
1748	3,546	250	450	1,000	1,700	—
1760	33,000	250	400	750	1,250	—
1765	1,367	300	600	1,350	2,250	—

KM# 519.8 2 LOUIS D'OR

16.3160 g., 0.9170 Gold 0.4810 oz. AGW **Ruler:** Louis XV **Mint:** Limoges **Obverse:** Head with headband left **Reverse:** Crown above arms of France and Navarre

Date	Mintage	VG	F	VF	XF	Unc
1744I	2,680	250	450	1,000	1,700	—
1745I	2,537	250	450	1,000	1,700	—
1749I	2,256	250	450	1,000	1,700	—
1754I	1,439	300	600	1,350	2,250	—
1756I	1,080	300	600	1,350	2,250	—
1763I	940	315	620	1,450	2,600	—
1769I	9,014	250	450	1,000	1,700	—

KM# 519.9 2 LOUIS D'OR

16.3160 g., 0.9170 Gold 0.4810 oz. AGW **Ruler:** Louis XV **Mint:** Bordeaux **Obverse:** Head with headband left **Reverse:** Crown above arms of France and Navarre

Date	Mintage	VG	F	VF	XF	Unc
1744K	8,940	250	450	1,000	1,700	—
1745K	6,585	250	450	1,000	1,700	—
1747K	8,595	250	450	1,000	1,700	—
1748K	5,970	250	450	1,000	1,700	—
1750K	8,670	250	450	1,000	1,700	—
1751K	5,730	250	450	1,000	1,700	—
1752K	3,990	250	450	1,000	1,700	—
1753K	44,000	250	400	750	1,250	—
1754K	20,000	250	400	750	1,250	—
1757K	3,885	250	450	1,000	1,700	—
1758K	2,659	250	450	1,000	1,700	—
1760K	5,782	250	450	1,000	1,700	—
1762K	5,250	250	450	1,000	1,700	—
1764K	11,000	250	450	1,000	1,700	—
1766K	32,000	250	400	750	1,250	—
1767K	38,000	250	400	750	1,250	—
1768K	6,272	250	450	1,000	1,700	—

KM# 519.2 2 LOUIS D'OR

16.3160 g., 0.9170 Gold 0.4810 oz. AGW **Ruler:** Louis XV **Mint:** Metz **Obverse:** Head with headband left **Reverse:** Crown above arms of France and Navarre

Date	Mintage	VG	F	VF	XF	Unc
1744AA	—	250	450	1,000	1,700	—
1751AA	—	250	450	1,000	1,700	—
1752AA	—	250	450	1,000	1,700	—
1753AA	—	250	400	750	1,250	—
1754AA	—	250	400	750	1,250	—
1755AA	—	250	400	750	1,250	—
1756AA	60,000	250	400	750	1,250	—
1757AA	—	250	400	750	1,250	—

KM# 522 2 LOUIS D'OR

16.3160 g., 0.9170 Gold 0.4810 oz. AGW **Ruler:** Louis XV **Mint:** Pau **Obv. Legend:** ....RE.BD (ligate BD). **Note:** Mint mark: Cow. Issued for Province of Bearn.

Date	Mintage	VG	F	VF	XF	Unc
1745	258	450	750	1,700	3,000	—
1751	2,350	250	450	1,000	1,800	—
1752	2,417	250	450	1,000	1,800	—
1753	9,181	250	450	950	1,650	—
1754	12,000	250	450	950	1,650	—
1755	8,746	250	450	950	1,650	—
1756	22,000	250	400	725	1,200	—
1757	8,275	250	450	950	1,650	—
1758	14,000	250	450	950	1,650	—
1759	51,000	250	400	725	1,200	—
1760	77,000	250	400	725	1,200	—
1761	71,000	250	400	725	1,200	—
1762	29,000	250	400	725	1,200	—
1763	69,000	250	400	725	1,200	—
1764	123,000	250	400	725	1,200	—
1765	74,000	250	400	725	1,200	—
1766	32,000	250	400	750	1,200	—
1767	17,000	250	400	750	1,200	—
1769	—	250	450	950	1,650	—

KM# 557.1 2 LOUIS D'OR

16.3160 g., 0.9170 Gold 0.4810 oz. AGW **Ruler:** Louis XV **Mint:** Paris **Obverse:** Laureate head left **Obv. Legend:** LUD • XV • D • G • FR • ET NAV • REX • **Reverse:** Crown above arms of France and Navarre **Rev. Legend:** CHRS • REGN • VINC • IMPE

Date	Mintage	VG	F	VF	XF	Unc
1771A	—	650	1,300	3,250	4,900	—

KM# 557.3 2 LOUIS D'OR

16.3160 g., 0.9170 Gold 0.4810 oz. AGW **Ruler:** Louis XV **Mint:** Limoges

Date	Mintage	VG	F	VF	XF	Unc
1771I	38,000	575	1,300	3,250	4,900	—
1772I	34,000	575	1,300	3,250	4,900	—

Date	Mintage	VG	F	VF	XF	Unc
1773I	4,604	650	1,550	3,900	5,900	—
1774I	484	775	1,950	4,950	7,500	—

KM# 557.8 2 LOUIS D'OR

16.3160 g., 0.9170 Gold 0.4810 oz. AGW **Ruler:** Louis XV **Mint:** Lille

Date	Mintage	VG	F	VF	XF	Unc
1771W	30,000	575	1,300	3,250	4,900	—
1772W	90,000	575	1,300	3,250	4,900	—
1773W	—	575	1,300	3,250	4,900	—
1774W	34,000	575	1,300	3,250	4,900	—

KM# 557.4 2 LOUIS D'OR

16.3160 g., 0.9170 Gold 0.4810 oz. AGW **Ruler:** Louis XV **Mint:** Bordeaux **Obverse:** Laureate head left **Reverse:** Crown above arms of France and Navarre

Date	Mintage	VG	F	VF	XF	Unc
1772K	—	575	1,300	3,600	5,200	—
1773K	13,000	575	1,300	3,600	5,200	—

KM# 557.7 2 LOUIS D'OR

16.3160 g., 0.9170 Gold 0.4810 oz. AGW **Ruler:** Louis XV **Mint:** Nantes **Obverse:** Laureate head left **Reverse:** Crown above arms of France and Navarre

Date	Mintage	VG	F	VF	XF	Unc
1772T	—	775	1,950	4,900	7,200	—
1773T	1,575	725	1,650	4,550	6,800	—
1775T	—	775	1,950	4,900	7,200	—

Note: Coins dated 1775 are engraver's errors

KM# 557.2 2 LOUIS D'OR

16.3160 g., 0.9170 Gold 0.4810 oz. AGW **Ruler:** Louis XV **Mint:** Lyon **Obverse:** Laureate head left **Reverse:** Crown above arms of France and Navarre

Date	Mintage	VG	F	VF	XF	Unc
1772D	13,000	575	1,300	3,600	5,200	—
1773D	9,595	575	1,300	3,600	5,200	—
1774D	13,000	575	1,300	3,600	5,200	—

KM# 559 2 LOUIS D'OR

16.3160 g., 0.9170 Gold 0.4810 oz. AGW **Ruler:** Louis XV **Mint:** Pau **Obv. Legend:** ....RE.BD (ligate BD). **Note:** Mint mark: Cow. Issued for Province of Bearn.

Date	Mintage	VG	F	VF	XF	Unc
1772	3,897	725	1,650	4,550	6,800	—
1774	2,796	775	1,950	4,900	7,200	—

KM# 557.6 2 LOUIS D'OR

16.3160 g., 0.9170 Gold 0.4810 oz. AGW **Ruler:** Louis XV **Mint:** Toulouse **Obverse:** Laureate head left **Reverse:** Crown above arms of France and Navarre

Date	Mintage	VG	F	VF	XF	Unc
1773M	—	575	1,300	3,600	5,200	—

KM# 557.5 2 LOUIS D'OR

16.3160 g., 0.9170 Gold 0.4810 oz. AGW **Ruler:** Louis XV **Mint:** Bayonne **Obverse:** Laureate head left **Reverse:** Crown above arms of France and Navarre

Date	Mintage	VG	F	VF	XF	Unc
1774L	39,000	575	1,300	3,250	4,900	—

KM# 575.1 2 LOUIS D'OR

16.3160 g., 0.9170 Gold 0.4810 oz. AGW **Ruler:** Louis XVI **Mint:** Paris **Obverse:** Uniformed bust left **Obv. Legend:** LUD • XVI • D • G • FR • ET NAV • REX • **Reverse:** Crowned arms of France and Navarre in ovals **Rev. Legend:** CHRS • REGN • VINC • IMPER

Date	Mintage	VG	F	VF	XF	Unc
1775A	10,000	450	1,000	2,250	3,850	—
1776A	9,662	450	1,000	2,250	3,850	—
1777A	275	—	—	—	—	—
1783A	1,870	—	—	—	—	—
1784A	623	—	—	—	—	—

KM# 575.2 2 LOUIS D'OR

16.3160 g., 0.9170 Gold 0.4810 oz. AGW **Ruler:** Louis XVI **Mint:** Metz **Obverse:** Uniformed bust left **Reverse:** Crowned arms of France and Navarre in ovals

Date	Mintage	VG	F	VF	XF	Unc
1775AA	678	—	—	—	—	—
1776AA	269	—	—	—	—	—
1777AA	525	—	—	—	—	—
1778AA	259	—	—	—	—	—
1779AA	307	—	—	—	—	—
1781AA	487	—	—	—	—	—
1782AA	123	—	—	—	—	—
1783AA	279	—	—	—	—	—
1784AA	324	—	—	—	—	—
1785AA	324	—	—	—	—	—

KM# 575.3 2 LOUIS D'OR

16.3160 g., 0.9170 Gold 0.4810 oz. AGW **Ruler:** Louis XVI **Mint:** Rouen **Obverse:** Uniformed bust left **Reverse:** Crowned arms of France and Navarre in ovals

Date	Mintage	VG	F	VF	XF	Unc
1775B	4,853	500	1,100	2,500	4,500	—
1776B	5,724	—	—	—	—	—
1777B	6,828	500	1,100	2,500	4,500	—
1778B	2,902	—	—	—	—	—
1779B	682	—	—	—	—	—
1780B	443	—	—	—	—	—
1781B	130	950	1,975	3,900	6,000	—
1783B	1,956	—	—	—	—	—
1784B	1,444	—	—	—	—	—
1785B	280	—	—	—	—	—

KM# 575.4 2 LOUIS D'OR

16.3160 g., 0.9170 Gold 0.4810 oz. AGW **Ruler:** Louis XVI **Mint:** Strasbourg **Obverse:** Uniformed bust left **Reverse:** Crowned arms of France and Navarre in ovals

Date	Mintage	VG	F	VF	XF	Unc
1775BB	5,378	—	—	—	—	—
1776BB	4,423	—	—	—	—	—
1777BB	2,498	—	—	—	—	—
1779BB	179	—	—	—	—	—

KM# 575.5 2 LOUIS D'OR

16.3160 g., 0.9170 Gold 0.4810 oz. AGW **Ruler:** Louis XVI **Mint:** Lyon **Obverse:** Uniformed bust left **Reverse:** Crowned arms of France and Navarre in ovals

Date	Mintage	VG	F	VF	XF	Unc
1775D	64,000	300	700	1,625	2,700	—
1776D	79,000	300	700	1,625	2,700	—
1777D	53,000	300	700	1,625	2,700	—
1778D	19,000	300	700	1,625	2,700	—

KM# 575.7 2 LOUIS D'OR

16.3160 g., 0.9170 Gold 0.4810 oz. AGW **Ruler:** Louis XVI **Mint:** Limoges **Obverse:** Uniformed bust left **Reverse:** Crowned arms of France and Navarre in ovals

Date	Mintage	VG	F	VF	XF	Unc
1775I	39,000	300	700	1,625	2,700	—
1776I	35,000	300	700	1,625	2,700	—
1777I	32,000	300	700	1,625	2,700	—
1778I	1,960	500	1,250	2,700	4,500	—
1779I	—	500	1,250	2,700	4,500	—
1780I	841	500	1,250	2,700	4,500	—
1781I	261	—	—	—	—	—

KM# 575.8 2 LOUIS D'OR

16.3160 g., 0.9170 Gold 0.4810 oz. AGW **Ruler:** Louis XVI **Mint:** Bordeaux **Obverse:** Uniformed bust left **Reverse:** Crowned arms of France and Navarre in ovals

Date	Mintage	VG	F	VF	XF	Unc
1775K	38,000	300	700	1,625	2,700	—
1776K	73,000	300	700	1,625	2,700	—
1777K	39,000	300	700	1,625	2,700	—
1778K	1,850	—	—	—	—	—
1779K	779	—	—	—	—	—
1781K	404	—	—	—	—	—
1782K	910	600	1,400	2,950	5,000	—
1783K	1,006	600	1,400	2,950	5,000	—
1784K	234	—	—	—	—	—

KM# 575.9 2 LOUIS D'OR

16.3160 g., 0.9170 Gold 0.4810 oz. AGW **Ruler:** Louis XVI **Mint:** Bayonne **Obverse:** Uniformed bust left **Reverse:** Crowned arms of France and Navarre in ovals

Date	Mintage	VG	F	VF	XF	Unc
1775L	18,000	300	750	1,800	3,150	—
1776L	15,000	300	750	1,800	3,150	—

KM# 575.10 2 LOUIS D'OR

16.3160 g., 0.9170 Gold 0.4810 oz. AGW **Ruler:** Louis XVI **Mint:** Toulouse **Obverse:** Uniformed bust left **Reverse:** Crowned arms of France and Navarre in ovals

Date	Mintage	VG	F	VF	XF	Unc
1775M	1,328	500	1,250	2,700	4,500	—
1776M	4,332	400	1,100	2,350	4,000	—
1777M	4,560	—	—	—	—	—
1778M	6,273	400	1,100	2,350	4,000	—
1779M	3,225	400	1,100	2,350	4,000	—
1780M	233	—	—	—	—	—
1781M	770	—	—	—	—	—
1782M	499	—	—	—	—	—
1783M	499	—	—	—	—	—

KM# 575.12 2 LOUIS D'OR

16.3160 g., 0.9170 Gold 0.4810 oz. AGW **Ruler:** Louis XVI **Mint:** Perpignan **Obverse:** Uniformed bust left **Reverse:** Crowned arms of France and Navarre in ovals

Date	Mintage	VG	F	VF	XF	Unc
1775Q	1,220	—	—	—	—	—
1776Q	14,000	—	—	—	—	—
1777Q	3,586	—	—	—	—	—
1778Q	1,074	—	—	—	—	—
1784Q	368	—	—	—	—	—

KM# 575.13 2 LOUIS D'OR

16.3160 g., 0.9170 Gold 0.4810 oz. AGW **Ruler:** Louis XVI **Mint:** Nantes **Obverse:** Uniformed bust left **Reverse:** Crowned arms of France and Navarre in ovals

Date	Mintage	VG	F	VF	XF	Unc
1775T	12,000	400	900	2,000	3,350	—
1776T	7,737	400	900	2,000	3,350	—
1777T	9,890	400	900	2,000	3,350	—
1778T	8,749	400	900	2,000	3,350	—
1779T	2,849	500	1,100	2,700	4,500	—
1780T	2,660	—	—	—	—	—
1781T	1,637	—	—	—	—	—
1782T	5,644	400	900	2,000	3,350	—
1783T	5,683	—	—	—	—	—
1784T	4,536	—	—	—	—	—

KM# 575.14 2 LOUIS D'OR

16.3160 g., 0.9170 Gold 0.4810 oz. AGW **Ruler:** Louis XVI **Mint:** Lille **Obverse:** Uniformed bust left **Reverse:** Crowned arms of France and Navarre in ovals

Date	Mintage	VG	F	VF	XF	Unc
1775W	68,000	300	700	1,650	2,750	—
1776W	49,000	300	700	1,650	2,750	—
1777W	96,000	300	700	1,650	2,750	—
1778W	42,000	300	700	1,650	2,750	—
1779W	13,000	400	900	2,000	3,350	—
1780W	9,240	400	900	2,000	3,350	—
1781W	8,100	400	900	2,000	3,350	—
1782W	24,000	—	—	—	—	—
1783W	27,000	300	700	1,650	2,750	—
1784W	13,000	400	900	2,000	3,350	—

KM# 575.15 2 LOUIS D'OR

16.3160 g., 0.9170 Gold 0.4810 oz. AGW **Ruler:** Louis XVI **Mint:** Aix **Obverse:** Uniformed bust left **Reverse:** Crowned arms of France and Navarre in ovals **Note:** Mint mark: &.

Date	Mintage	VG	F	VF	XF	Unc
1775	67,000	300	800	1,800	3,150	—
1776	29,000	—	—	—	—	—
1777	14,000	400	1,000	2,100	3,650	—
1778	5,905	—	—	—	—	—

KM# 575.11 2 LOUIS D'OR

16.3160 g., 0.9170 Gold 0.4810 oz. AGW **Ruler:** Louis XVI **Mint:** Montpellier **Obverse:** Uniformed bust left **Reverse:** Crowned arms of France and Navarre in ovals

Date	Mintage	VG	F	VF	XF	Unc
1776N	5,027	500	1,250	2,700	4,500	—
1777N	5,347	500	1,250	2,700	4,500	—

KM# 577 2 LOUIS D'OR

16.3160 g., 0.9170 Gold 0.4810 oz. AGW **Ruler:** Louis XVI **Mint:** Pau **Obverse:** Uniformed bust left **Obv. Legend:** ....RE.BD. (ligate BD). **Reverse:** Crowned arms of France and Navarre in ovals **Rev. Legend:** CHRS • REGN • VINC • IMPER **Note:** Mint mark: Cow. Issued for Province of Bearn.

Date	Mintage	VG	F	VF	XF	Unc
1777 (p)	21,000	400	1,100	2,350	4,000	—
1778 (p)	25,000	400	1,100	2,350	4,000	—
1781 (p)	1,054	—	—	—	—	—
1782 Rare	544	—	—	—	—	—

KM# 575.6 2 LOUIS D'OR

16.3160 g., 0.9170 Gold 0.4810 oz. AGW **Ruler:** Louis XVI **Mint:** La Rochelle **Obverse:** Uniformed bust left **Reverse:** Crowned arms of France and Navarre in ovals

Date	Mintage	VG	F	VF	XF	Unc
1778H	4,154	—	—	—	—	—

KM# 592.1 2 LOUIS D'OR

15.2970 g., 0.9170 Gold 0.4510 oz. AGW **Ruler:** Louis XVI **Mint:** Paris **Obverse:** Head left **Obv. Legend:** LUD • XVI • D • G • FR • ET NAV • REX • **Reverse:** Crowned arms of France and Navarre in shields **Rev. Legend:** CHRS • REGN • VINC • IMP ...

Date	Mintage	VG	F	VF	XF	Unc
1785A	27,000	250	400	850	1,750	—
1786A	2,350,000	225	315	525	950	—
1787A	—	250	350	625	1,100	—
1788A	—	250	350	625	1,100	—
1790A	—	250	350	625	1,100	—
1791A	34,000	250	350	625	1,100	—
1791A	Inc. above	250	350	625	1,100	—

Note: The "dot" appears below the third letter of the monarch's name and denotes second semester coinage

Date	Mintage	VG	F	VF	XF	Unc
1792A	—	300	450	925	1,550	—
1792A	—	300	500	1,200	2,200	—

Note: The "dot" appears below the third letter of the monarch's name and denotes second semester coinage

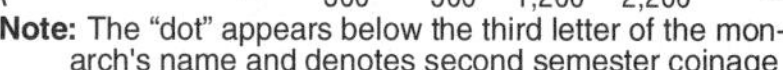

KM# 592.5 2 LOUIS D'OR

15.2970 g., 0.9170 Gold 0.4510 oz. AGW **Ruler:** Louis XVI **Mint:** Lyon **Obverse:** Head left **Reverse:** Crowned arms of France and Navarre in shields

Date	Mintage	VG	F	VF	XF	Unc
1785D	—	300	450	925	2,000	—
1786D	1,072,000	225	315	525	950	—
1786D	Inc. above	225	315	525	950	—

Note: The "dot" appears below the third letter of the monarch's name and denotes second semester coinage

Date	Mintage	VG	F	VF	XF	Unc
1787D	109,000	225	315	525	950	—
1788D	—	250	350	625	1,000	—

KM# 592.7 2 LOUIS D'OR

15.2970 g., 0.9170 Gold 0.4510 oz. AGW **Ruler:** Louis XVI **Mint:** Limoges **Obverse:** Head left **Reverse:** Crowned arms of France and Navarre in shields

Date	Mintage	VG	F	VF	XF	Unc
1785I	—	300	450	925	2,000	—
1786I	208,000	250	350	525	950	—
1787I	10,000	250	350	525	950	—

KM# 592.14 2 LOUIS D'OR

15.2970 g., 0.9170 Gold 0.4510 oz. AGW **Ruler:** Louis XVI **Mint:** Nantes **Obverse:** Head left **Reverse:** Crowned arms of France and Navarre in shields

Date	Mintage	VG	F	VF	XF	Unc
1785T	650	360	750	1,750	3,400	—
1786T	396,000	225	315	525	950	—
1786T	Inc. above	225	315	525	950	—

Note: The "dot" appears below the third letter of the monarch's name and denotes second semester coinage

Date	Mintage	VG	F	VF	XF	Unc
1787T	3,073	250	400	850	1,525	—
1788T	7,233	250	400	850	1,525	—
1789T	—	225	315	525	950	—
1790T	667	350	600	1,450	2,600	—
1791T	667	350	600	1,450	2,750	—

KM# 592.15 2 LOUIS D'OR

15.2970 g., 0.9170 Gold 0.4510 oz. AGW **Ruler:** Louis XVI **Mint:** Lille **Obverse:** Head left **Reverse:** Crowned arms of France and Navarre in shields

Date	Mintage	VG	F	VF	XF	Unc
1785W	3,960	300	500	1,100	2,150	—
1786W	239,000	225	315	525	850	—
1786W	Inc. above	225	315	525	850	—

Note: The "dot" appears below the third letter of the monarch's name and denotes second semester coinage

Date	Mintage	VG	F	VF	XF	Unc
1787W	—	250	350	625	1,000	—
1788W	—	250	350	625	1,000	—
1789W	—	260	360	645	1,100	—
1790W	—	250	400	850	1,525	—
1791W	7,959	250	400	750	1,450	—

KM# 592.11 2 LOUIS D'OR

15.2970 g., 0.9170 Gold 0.4510 oz. AGW **Ruler:** Louis XVI **Mint:** Montpellier **Obverse:** Head left **Reverse:** Crowned arms of France and Navarre in shields

Date	Mintage	VG	F	VF	XF	Unc
1786N	217,000	225	315	525	850	—
1787N	27,000	250	350	625	1,000	—

KM# 592.8 2 LOUIS D'OR

15.2970 g., 0.9170 Gold 0.4510 oz. AGW **Ruler:** Louis XVI **Mint:** Bordeaux **Obverse:** Head left **Reverse:** Crowned arms of France and Navarre in shields

Date	Mintage	VG	F	VF	XF	Unc
1786K	492,000	225	315	525	850	—
1786K	Inc. above	225	315	525	850	—

Note: The "dot" appears below the third letter of the monarch's name and denotes second semester coinage

Date	Mintage	VG	F	VF	XF	Unc
1787K	42,000	225	315	525	850	—
1788K	18,000	260	260	645	1,100	—
1789K	23,000	250	350	625	1,000	—
1790K	7,381	250	400	850	1,525	—
1791K	903	250	400	850	1,700	—

KM# 592.6 2 LOUIS D'OR

15.2970 g., 0.9170 Gold 0.4510 oz. AGW **Ruler:** Louis XVI **Mint:** La Rochelle **Obverse:** Head left **Reverse:** Crowned arms of France and Navarre in shields

Date	Mintage	VG	F	VF	XF	Unc
1786H	43,000	250	350	625	1,000	—
1787H	12,000	250	400	850	1,525	—

KM# 592.2 2 LOUIS D'OR

15.2970 g., 0.9170 Gold 0.4510 oz. AGW **Ruler:** Louis XVI **Mint:** Metz **Obverse:** Head left **Reverse:** Crowned arms of France and Navarre in shields

Date	Mintage	VG	F	VF	XF	Unc
1786AA	307,000	225	315	525	950	—
1786AA	Inc. above	225	315	525	950	—

Note: The "dot" appears below the third letter of the monarch's name and denotes second semester coinage

Date	Mintage	VG	F	VF	XF	Unc
1787AA	155,000	225	315	525	950	—
1788AA	153,000	225	315	525	950	—
1789AA	—	250	350	625	1,100	—
1790AA	—	250	350	625	1,100	—
1791AA	1,150	—	—	—	—	—

KM# 592.3 2 LOUIS D'OR

15.2970 g., 0.9170 Gold 0.4510 oz. AGW **Ruler:** Louis XVI **Mint:** Rouen **Obverse:** Head left **Reverse:** Crowned arms of France and Navarre in shields

Date	Mintage	VG	F	VF	XF	Unc
1786B	251,000	225	315	525	950	—
1787B	87,000	225	315	525	950	—
1788B	19,000	—	—	—	—	—
1789B	—	250	350	625	1,100	—
1790B	—	250	400	850	1,700	—
1791B	1,072	—	—	—	—	—

KM# 592.4 2 LOUIS D'OR

15.2970 g., 0.9170 Gold 0.4510 oz. AGW **Ruler:** Louis XVI **Mint:** Strasbourg **Obverse:** Head left **Reverse:** Crowned arms of France and Navarre in shields

Date	Mintage	VG	F	VF	XF	Unc
1786BB	139,000	250	350	750	1,150	—
1790BB	—	250	400	850	1,525	—
1791BB	4,230	250	400	850	1,525	—
1792BB	—	300	550	1,200	2,200	—

KM# 592.13 2 LOUIS D'OR

15.2970 g., 0.9170 Gold 0.4510 oz. AGW **Ruler:** Louis XVI **Mint:** Orléans **Obverse:** Head left **Reverse:** Crowned arms of France and Navarre in shields

Date	Mintage	VG	F	VF	XF	Unc
1787R	—	250	400	850	1,525	—

KM# 592.10 2 LOUIS D'OR

15.2970 g., 0.9170 Gold 0.4510 oz. AGW **Ruler:** Louis XVI **Mint:** Marseille **Obverse:** Head left **Reverse:** Crowned arms of France and Navarre in shields

Date	Mintage	VG	F	VF	XF	Unc
1789MA	—	250	400	850	1,525	—
1790MA	—	250	400	850	1,525	—

KM# 592.12 2 LOUIS D'OR

15.2970 g., 0.9170 Gold 0.4510 oz. AGW **Ruler:** Louis XVI **Mint:** Perpignan **Obverse:** Head left **Reverse:** Crowned arms of France and Navarre in shields

Date	Mintage	VG	F	VF	XF	Unc
1789Q	—	250	350	625	1,000	—
1790Q	2,944	—	—	—	—	—

KM# 592.9 2 LOUIS D'OR

15.2970 g., 0.9170 Gold 0.4510 oz. AGW **Ruler:** Louis XVI **Mint:** Toulouse **Obverse:** Head left **Reverse:** Crowned arms of France and Navarre in shields

Date	Mintage	VG	F	VF	XF	Unc
1790M	—	250	350	625	1,000	—
1791M	8,921	250	400	850	1,525	—
1791M	Inc. above	250	400	850	1,525	—

Note: The "dot" appears below the third letter of the monarch's name and denotes second semester coinage

FIRST REPUBLIC

1793-1794, L'An 2

ECU COINAGE

KM# 608.2 3 DENIERS (Liard)

Bronze **Mint:** Limoges **Obverse:** Head of Louis XVI left **Reverse:** Liberty cap above column dividing value, oak wreath in background

Date	Mintage	VG	F	VF	XF	Unc
1792I	—	10.00	25.00	70.00	175	—
1792I Bell metal	—	10.00	20.00	50.00	150	—

KM# 610.2 6 DENIERS

Bronze **Mint:** Limoges **Obverse:** Head of Louis XVI left **Reverse:** Liberty cap above column dividing value, oak wreath in background

Date	Mintage	VG	F	VF	XF	Unc
1792I	—	10.00	20.00	60.00	160	—

KM# 610.4 6 DENIERS

Bronze **Mint:** Marseille **Obverse:** Head of Louis XVI left **Reverse:** Liberty cap above column dividing value, oak wreath in background

Date	Mintage	VG	F	VF	XF	Unc
1792MA	—	20.00	45.00	110	275	—

KM# 610.5 6 DENIERS

Bronze **Mint:** Nantes **Obverse:** Head of Louis XVI left **Reverse:** Liberty cap above column dividing value, oak wreath in background

Date	Mintage	VG	F	VF	XF	Unc
1792T	—	10.00	20.00	60.00	150	—
1793T	—	10.00	30.00	80.00	200	—

KM# 610.3 6 DENIERS

Bronze **Mint:** Bordeaux **Obverse:** Head of Louis XVI left **Reverse:** Liberty cap above column dividing value, oak wreath in background

Date	Mintage	VG	F	VF	XF	Unc
1793K	—	20.00	45.00	110	275	—

KM# 600.7 12 DENIERS

Bronze **Mint:** Limoges

Date	Mintage	VG	F	VF	XF	Unc
1791I	—	5.00	12.00	40.00	125	—
1792I	—	4.00	10.00	30.00	100	—

KM# 600.8 12 DENIERS

Bronze **Mint:** Bordeaux

Date	Mintage	VG	F	VF	XF	Unc
1791K	—	4.00	10.00	30.00	100	—

Date	Mintage	VG	F	VF	XF	Unc
1792K	—	4.00	10.00	30.00	100	—
1793K	—	4.00	10.00	40.00	150	—

KM# 600.9 12 DENIERS

Bronze **Mint:** Bayonne

Date	Mintage	VG	F	VF	XF	Unc
1791L	—	5.00	12.00	35.00	135	—
1792L	—	4.00	10.00	30.00	115	—
1793L	—	5.00	12.00	35.00	135	—

KM# 600.10 12 DENIERS

Bronze **Mint:** Toulouse

Date	Mintage	VG	F	VF	XF	Unc
1791M	—	5.00	12.00	35.00	115	—
1792M	—	4.00	10.00	30.00	100	—
1793M	—	5.00	12.00	35.00	125	—

KM# 600.12 12 DENIERS

Bronze **Mint:** Montpellier **Obverse:** Bust of Louis XVI left **Reverse:** Liberty cap above column dividing value, wreath surrounds

Date	Mintage	VG	F	VF	XF	Unc
1791N	—	5.00	12.00	35.00	100	—
1792N	—	5.00	12.00	35.00	115	—
1793N	—	5.00	12.00	35.00	125	—

KM# 600.13 12 DENIERS

Bronze **Mint:** Perpignan **Obverse:** Bust of Louis XVI left **Reverse:** Liberty cap above column dividing value, wreath surrounds

Date	Mintage	VG	F	VF	XF	Unc
1791Q	—	5.00	12.00	50.00	200	—
1792Q	—	5.00	12.00	35.00	150	—

KM# 600.14 12 DENIERS

Bronze **Mint:** Orléans **Obverse:** Bust of Louis XVI left **Reverse:** Liberty cap above column dividing value, wreath surrounds

Date	Mintage	VG	F	VF	XF	Unc
1791R	—	4.00	10.00	30.00	100	—
1792R	—	4.00	10.00	30.00	100	—
1793R	—	10.00	25.00	60.00	200	—

KM# 600.15 12 DENIERS

Bronze **Mint:** Nantes **Obverse:** Bust of Louis XVI left **Reverse:** Liberty cap above column dividing value, wreath surrounds

Date	Mintage	VG	F	VF	XF	Unc
1791T	—	5.00	12.00	35.00	125	—
1792T	—	4.00	10.00	30.00	110	—
1793T	—	4.00	10.00	30.00	110	—

KM# 600.2 12 DENIERS

Bronze **Mint:** Metz **Obverse:** Bust of Louis XVI left **Reverse:** Liberty cap above column dividing value, wreath surrounds

Date	Mintage	VG	F	VF	XF	Unc
1791AA	—	4.00	10.00	30.00	120	—
1792AA	—	5.00	12.00	35.00	115	—

KM# 600.3 12 DENIERS

Bronze **Mint:** Rouen **Obverse:** Bust of Louis XVI left **Reverse:** Liberty cap above column dividing value, wreath surrounds

Date	Mintage	VG	F	VF	XF	Unc
1791B	—	2.50	5.00	20.00	120	—
1792B	—	4.00	10.00	30.00	135	—
1793B	—	5.00	12.00	40.00	160	—

KM# 600.4 12 DENIERS

Bronze **Mint:** Strasbourg **Obverse:** Bust of Louis XVI left **Reverse:** Liberty cap above column dividing value, wreath surrounds

Date	Mintage	VG	F	VF	XF	Unc
1791BB	—	7.00	16.00	50.00	200	—
1792BB	—	2.50	5.00	25.00	120	—

KM# 600.5 12 DENIERS

Bronze **Mint:** Lyon **Obverse:** Bust of Louis XVI left **Reverse:** Liberty cap above column dividing value, wreath surrounds

Date	Mintage	VG	F	VF	XF	Unc
1791	—	5.00	12.00	35.00	140	—
1792D	—	6.00	15.00	45.00	150	—
1792D .	—	6.00	15.00	45.00	150	—
1793D	—	8.00	18.00	50.00	165	—
1793D .	—	8.00	18.00	50.00	165	—

KM# 600.6 12 DENIERS

Bronze **Mint:** La Rochelle **Obverse:** Bust of Louis XVI left **Reverse:** Liberty cap above column dividing value, wreath surrounds

Date	Mintage	VG	F	VF	XF	Unc
1792H	—	8.00	18.00	50.00	165	—

KM# 600.16 12 DENIERS

Bronze **Mint:** Lille **Obverse:** Bust of Lois XVI left **Reverse:** Liberty cap above column dividing value, wreath surrounds

Date	Mintage	VG	F	VF	XF	Unc
1792W	—	5.00	12.00	40.00	135	—
1793W	—	5.00	12.00	35.00	125	—

KM# 600.17 12 DENIERS

Bronze **Mint:** Pau **Obverse:** Bust of Louis XVI left **Reverse:** Liberty cap above column dividing value, wreath surrounds **Note:** Mint mark: Cow.

Date	Mintage	VG	F	VF	XF	Unc
1792	—	10.00	20.00	65.00	225	—
1793	—	12.00	25.00	75.00	250	—

KM# 618.1 1/2 SOL

Bronze **Mint:** La Rochelle

Date	Mintage	VG	F	VF	XF	Unc
LAN II//1793H Restrike	—	40.00	125	300	700	—
LAN II// 1793H	—	35.00	100	250	600	—

KM# 618.2 1/2 SOL

Bronze **Mint:** Limoges

Date	Mintage	VG	F	VF	XF	Unc
LAN II//1793I Rare	—	—	—	—	—	—

KM# 619.1 SOL

Bronze **Mint:** Paris **Obverse:** Inscription within rectangle **Reverse:** Wreath hung around liberty cap at center of scales

Date	Mintage	VG	F	VF	XF	Unc
LAN II//1793A	—	20.00	50.00	130	450	—

KM# 619.2 SOL

Bronze **Mint:** Metz **Obverse:** Inscription on rectangle **Reverse:** Wreath hung around liberty cap at center of scales

Date	Mintage	VG	F	VF	XF	Unc
LAN II//1793AA	—	10.00	30.00	100	260	—

KM# 619.3 SOL

Bronze **Mint:** Rouen **Obverse:** Inscription within rectangle **Reverse:** Wreath hung around liberty cap at center of scales

Date	Mintage	VG	F	VF	XF	Unc
LAN II//1793B	—	15.00	50.00	150	400	—

KM# 619.4 SOL

Bronze **Mint:** Strasbourg **Obverse:** Inscription within rectangle **Reverse:** Wreath hung around liberty cap at center of scales

Date	Mintage	VG	F	VF	XF	Unc
LAN II//1793BB	—	12.00	32.50	110	275	—

KM# 619.5 SOL

Bronze **Mint:** Lyon **Obverse:** Inscription within rectangle **Reverse:** Wreath hung around liberty cap at center of scales

Date	Mintage	VG	F	VF	XF	Unc
LAN II//1793D	—	15.00	35.00	110	275	—
LAN II//1793D	—	20.00	40.00	125	300	—

Note: Eagle's head left

KM# 619.6 SOL

Bronze **Mint:** La Rochelle **Obverse:** Inscription within rectangle **Reverse:** Wreath hung around liberty cap at center of scales

Date	Mintage	VG	F	VF	XF	Unc
LAN II//1793H	—	20.00	50.00	125	375	—

KM# 619.7 SOL

Bronze **Mint:** Limoges **Obverse:** Inscription within rectangle **Reverse:** Wreath hung around liberty cap at center of scales

Date	Mintage	VG	F	VF	XF	Unc
LAN II//1793I	—	15.00	35.00	120	300	—

KM# 619.8 SOL

Bronze **Mint:** Bayonne **Obverse:** Inscriptions within rectangle **Reverse:** Wreath hung around liberty cap at center of scales

Date	Mintage	VG	F	VF	XF	Unc
LAN II//1793L	—	12.00	32.50	110	275	—

KM# 619.9 SOL

Bronze **Mint:** Marseille **Obverse:** Inscription within rectangle **Reverse:** Wreath hung around liberty cap at center of scales

Date	Mintage	VG	F	VF	XF	Unc
LAN II//1793MA	20,000	25.00	60.00	175	460	—

KM# 619.10 SOL

Bronze **Mint:** Montpellier **Obverse:** Inscription within rectangle **Reverse:** Wreath hung around liberty cap at center of scales

Date	Mintage	VG	F	VF	XF	Unc
LAN II//1793N	—	15.00	35.00	110	300	—

KM# 619.11 SOL

Bronze **Mint:** Nantes **Obverse:** Inscription within rectangle **Reverse:** Wreath hung around liberty cap at center of scales

Date	Mintage	VG	F	VF	XF	Unc
LAN II//1793T	200,000	12.00	32.50	110	275	—

KM# 619.12 SOL

Bronze **Mint:** Lille **Obverse:** Inscription within rectangle **Reverse:** Wreath hung around liberty cap at center of scales

Date	Mintage	VG	F	VF	XF	Unc
LAN II//1793W	—	12.00	32.50	110	275	—

KM# 620.1 SOL

Bronze **Mint:** Metz **Obverse:** Inscription within rectangle **Obv. Legend:** REPUBLIQUE FRANCIOSE **Reverse:** Wreath hung around liberty cap at center of scales **Rev. Legend:** LIBERTE E'GALITE **Note:** Without A.D. date.

Date	Mintage	VG	F	VF	XF	Unc
LAN II (1793-94)AA	—	20.00	50.00	150	375	—

KM# 620.2 SOL

Bronze **Mint:** Rouen **Obverse:** Inscription within rectangle **Reverse:** Wreath hung around liberty cap at center of scales **Note:** Without A.D. date.

Date	Mintage	VG	F	VF	XF	Unc
LAN II (1793-94)B Reported, not confirmed	—	—	—	—	—	—

KM# 620.3 SOL

Bronze **Mint:** Strasbourg **Obverse:** Inscription within rectangle **Reverse:** Wreath hung around liberty cap at center of scales **Note:** Without A.D. date.

Date	Mintage	VG	F	VF	XF	Unc
LAN II (1793-94)BB	—	20.00	60.00	175	400	—

KM# 620.4 SOL

Bronze **Mint:** Lyon **Obverse:** Inscription within rectangle **Reverse:** Wreath hung around liberty cap at center of scales **Note:** Without A.D. date.

Date	Mintage	VG	F	VF	XF	Unc
LAN II (1793-94)D Rare	—	—	—	—	—	—

KM# 620.5 SOL

Bronze **Mint:** Limoges **Obverse:** Inscription within rectangle **Reverse:** Wreath hung around liberty cap at center of scales **Note:** Without A.D. date.

Date	Mintage	VG	F	VF	XF	Unc
LAN II (1793-94)I	—	20.00	60.00	175	400	—

KM# 620.6 SOL

Bronze **Mint:** Marseille **Obverse:** Inscription within rectangle **Reverse:** Wreath hung around liberty cap at center of scales **Note:** Without A.D. date.

Date	Mintage	VG	F	VF	XF	Unc
LAN II (1793-94)MA	—	30.00	80.00	225	500	—

KM# 620.7 SOL

Bronze **Mint:** Montpellier **Obverse:** Inscription within rectangle **Reverse:** Wreath hung around liberty cap at center of scales **Note:** Without A.D. date.

Date	Mintage	VG	F	VF	XF	Unc
LAN II (1793-94)N	—	30.00	80.00	225	500	—

KM# 620.8 SOL

Bronze **Mint:** Pau **Obverse:** Inscription within rectangle **Reverse:** Wreath hung around liberty cap at center of scales **Note:** Without A.D. date. Mint mark: Cow.

Date	Mintage	VG	F	VF	XF	Unc
LAN II (1793-94)	—	35.00	90.00	275	650	—

KM# 603.14 2 SOLS

Bronze **Mint:** Orléans

Date	Mintage	VG	F	VF	XF	Unc
1791R	—	7.00	18.00	50.00	185	—
1792R	—	6.00	14.00	40.00	150	—
1793R	—	7.00	18.00	50.00	175	—

KM# 603.15 2 SOLS

Bronze **Mint:** Nantes

Date	Mintage	VG	F	VF	XF	Unc
1791T	—	8.00	20.00	60.00	210	—
1792T	—	4.00	10.00	35.00	125	—
1793T	—	6.00	14.00	40.00	150	—

KM# 603.16 2 SOLS

Bronze **Mint:** Lille

Date	Mintage	VG	F	VF	XF	Unc
1791W	—	8.00	20.00	60.00	200	—
1792W	—	6.00	14.00	40.00	150	—
1793W	—	6.00	14.00	40.00	150	—

KM# 603.2 2 SOLS

Bronze **Mint:** Metz **Obverse:** Bust of Louis XVI left **Reverse:** Liberty cap above fasces, oak wreath in background

Date	Mintage	VG	F	VF	XF	Unc
1791AA	—	4.00	10.00	35.00	125	—
1792AA	—	4.00	10.00	35.00	125	—
1793AA	—	7.00	18.00	50.00	175	—

KM# 603.3 2 SOLS

Bronze **Mint:** Rouen **Obverse:** Bust of Louis XVI left **Reverse:** Liberty cap above fasces, oak wreath in background

Date	Mintage	VG	F	VF	XF	Unc
1791B	—	4.00	10.00	35.00	125	—
1792B	—	6.00	14.00	40.00	150	—
1793B	—	6.00	14.00	40.00	150	—

KM# 603.4 2 SOLS

Bronze **Mint:** Strasbourg **Obverse:** Bust of Louis XVI left **Reverse:** Liberty cap above fasces, oak wreath in background

Date	Mintage	VG	F	VF	XF	Unc
1791BB	—	7.00	18.00	50.00	175	—
1792BB	—	6.00	14.00	40.00	150	—
1793BB	—	7.00	18.00	50.00	175	—

KM# 603.8 2 SOLS

Bronze **Mint:** Bordeaux **Obverse:** Bust of Louis XVI left **Reverse:** Liberty cap above fasces, oak wreath in background

Date	Mintage	VG	F	VF	XF	Unc
1791K	—	6.00	14.00	40.00	150	—
1792K	—	7.00	18.00	50.00	175	—

KM# 603.9 2 SOLS

Bronze **Mint:** Bayonne **Obverse:** Bust of Louis XVI left **Reverse:** Liberty cap above fasces, oak wreath in background

Date	Mintage	VG	F	VF	XF	Unc
1791L	—	7.00	18.00	50.00	175	—
1792L	—	7.00	18.00	50.00	175	—
1793L	—	7.00	18.00	50.00	175	—

KM# 603.10 2 SOLS

Bronze **Mint:** Toulouse **Obverse:** Bust of Louis XVI left **Reverse:** Liberty cap above fasces, oak wreath in background

Date	Mintage	VG	F	VF	XF	Unc
1791M	—	6.00	14.00	40.00	150	—
1792M	—	6.00	14.00	40.00	150	—

KM# 603.6 2 SOLS

Bronze **Mint:** La Rochelle **Obverse:** Bust of Louis XVI left **Reverse:** Liberty cap above fasces, oak wreath in background

Date	Mintage	VG	F	VF	XF	Unc
1791H	—	6.00	14.00	40.00	150	—
1792H	—	6.00	14.00	40.00	150	—

KM# 603.7 2 SOLS

Bronze **Mint:** Limoges **Obverse:** Bust of Louis XVI left **Reverse:** Liberty cap above fasces, oak wreath in background

Date	Mintage	VG	F	VF	XF	Unc
1792I	—	6.00	14.00	40.00	150	—

KM# 603.11 2 SOLS

Bronze **Mint:** Marseille **Obverse:** Bust of Louis XVI left **Reverse:** Liberty cap above fasces, oak wreath in background

Date	Mintage	VG	F	VF	XF	Unc
1792MA	—	6.00	14.00	40.00	150	—
1793MA	—	6.00	14.00	40.00	150	—

KM# 603.12 2 SOLS

Bronze **Mint:** Montpellier **Obverse:** Bust of Louis XVI left **Reverse:** Liberty cap above fasces, oak wreath in background

Date	Mintage	VG	F	VF	XF	Unc
1792N	—	6.00	14.00	40.00	150	—
1793N	—	7.00	18.00	50.00	175	—

KM# 603.13 2 SOLS

Bronze **Mint:** Perpignan **Obverse:** Bust of Louis XVI left **Reverse:** Liberty cap above fasces, oak wreath in background

Date	Mintage	VG	F	VF	XF	Unc
1792Q	—	6.00	14.00	40.00	150	—
1793Q	—	8.00	20.00	60.00	200	—

KM# 603.5 2 SOLS

Bronze **Mint:** Lyon **Obverse:** Bust of Louis XVI left **Reverse:** Liberty cap above fasces, oak wreath in background

Date	Mintage	VG	F	VF	XF	Unc
1792D	—	6.00	14.00	40.00	150	—
1793D	—	7.00	18.00	50.00	175	—

KM# 603.17 2 SOLS

Bronze **Mint:** Pau **Obverse:** Bust of Louis XVI left **Reverse:** Liberty cap above fasces, oak wreath in background **Note:** Mint mark: Cow.

Date	Mintage	VG	F	VF	XF	Unc
1792	—	10.00	35.00	75.00	225	—
1793	—	10.00	35.00	75.00	225	—

KM# 612 2 SOLS

Bronze **Mint:** Strasbourg **Obverse:** Bust left **Obv. Legend:** LOUIS XIV ROI DES FRANCAIS • **Reverse:** Liberty cap above fasces, oak wreath surrounds **Rev. Legend:** LANATION LA LOI LE ROI • * DE LA LIBERTE, below

Date	Mintage	VG	F	VF	XF	Unc
1792//LAN 4BB	—	10.00	20.00	60.00	225	—
1793//LAN 4BB	—	15.00	30.00	80.00	265	—
1793//LAN 5BB	—	15.00	30.00	80.00	265	—

KM# 621.1 2 SOLS

Bronze **Mint:** Paris **Obverse:** Inscription within rectangle **Reverse:** Wreath hung around liberty cap at center of scales **Rev. Legend:** LIBERTE E'GALITE •

Date	Mintage	VG	F	VF	XF	Unc
1793//LAN IIA	—	—	—	—	—	—

Note: Reported, not confirmed

KM# 621.2 2 SOLS

Bronze **Mint:** Metz **Obverse:** Inscription within rectangle **Reverse:** Wreath hung around liberty cap at center of scales

Date	Mintage	VG	F	VF	XF	Unc
1793//LAN IIAA	—	15.00	40.00	100	325	—

KM# 621.3 2 SOLS

Bronze **Mint:** Rouen **Obverse:** Inscription within rectangle **Reverse:** Wreath hung around liberty cap at center of scales

Date	Mintage	VG	F	VF	XF	Unc
1793//LAN IIB	—	15.00	45.00	120	350	—
1793//LAN IIB Restrike	—	—	—	—	525	—

KM# 621.4 2 SOLS

Bronze **Mint:** Strasbourg **Obverse:** Inscription within rectangle **Reverse:** Wreath hung around liberty cap at center of scales

Date	Mintage	VG	F	VF	XF	Unc
1793//LAN IIBB	—	15.00	40.00	110	325	—

KM# 621.5 2 SOLS

Bronze **Mint:** Lyon **Obverse:** Inscription within rectangle **Reverse:** Wreath hung around liberty cap at center of scales

Date	Mintage	VG	F	VF	XF	Unc
1793//LAN IID Rare	—	—	—	—	—	—

KM# 621.6 2 SOLS

Bronze **Mint:** La Rochelle **Obverse:** Inscription within rectangle **Reverse:** Wreath hung around liberty cap at center of scales

Date	Mintage	VG	F	VF	XF	Unc
1793//LAN IIH	—	20.00	60.00	150	425	—

KM# 621.7 2 SOLS

Bronze **Mint:** Limoges **Obverse:** Inscription within rectangle **Reverse:** Wreath hung around liberty cap at center of scales

Date	Mintage	VG	F	VF	XF	Unc
1793//LAN III	—	20.00	60.00	150	400	—

KM# 621.8 2 SOLS

Bronze **Mint:** Bayonne **Obverse:** Inscription within rectangle **Reverse:** Wreath hung around liberty cap at center of scales

Date	Mintage	VG	F	VF	XF	Unc
1793//LAN IIL	—	20.00	60.00	150	400	—

KM# 621.9 2 SOLS

Bronze **Mint:** Marseille **Obverse:** Inscription within rectangle **Reverse:** Wreath hung around liberty cap at center of scales

Date	Mintage	VG	F	VF	XF	Unc
1793//LAN IIMA	—	20.00	60.00	150	425	—

KM# 621.10 2 SOLS

Bronze **Mint:** Montpellier **Obverse:** Inscription within rectangle **Reverse:** Wreath hung around liberty cap at center of scales

Date	Mintage	VG	F	VF	XF	Unc
1793//LAN IIN	—	15.00	45.00	120	350	—

KM# 621.11 2 SOLS

Bronze **Mint:** Orléans **Obverse:** Inscription within rectangle **Reverse:** Wreath hung around liberty cap at center of scales

Date	Mintage	VG	F	VF	XF	Unc
1793//LAN IIR	—	20.00	50.00	125	350	—

KM# 621.12 2 SOLS

Bronze **Mint:** Nantes **Obverse:** Inscription within rectangle **Reverse:** Wreath hung around liberty cap at center of scales

Date	Mintage	VG	F	VF	XF	Unc
1793//LAN IIT	70,000	25.00	70.00	175	500	—

KM# 621.13 2 SOLS

Bronze **Mint:** Lille **Obverse:** Inscription within rectangle **Reverse:** Wreath hung around liberty cap at center of scales

Date	Mintage	VG	F	VF	XF	Unc
1793//LAN IIW	—	25.00	70.00	160	450	—

KM# 622 2 SOLS

Bronze **Mint:** Rouen **Edge Lettering:** BON. POUR. BORD. MARSEILLE. LYON. ROUEN. NANT. ET. STRSB

Date	Mintage	VG	F	VF	XF	Unc
1793B	—	—	—	—	—	—

KM# 621.14 2 SOLS

Bronze **Mint:** Pau **Obverse:** Inscription within rectangle **Reverse:** Wreath hung around liberty cap at center of scales **Note:** Mint mark: Cow.

Date	Mintage	VG	F	VF	XF	Unc
1793//LAN II	—	35.00	85.00	225	600	—

KM# 623.1 2 SOLS

Bronze **Mint:** Strasbourg **Obverse:** Inscription within rectangle **Obv. Legend:** REPUBLIQUE FRANCOISE • **Reverse:** Wreath hung around liberty cap at center of scales **Rev. Legend:** LIBERTE E'GALITE • **Note:** Without A.D. date.

Date	Mintage	VG	F	VF	XF	Unc
LAN II (1793-94)BB	—	30.00	100	250	650	—

KM# 623.2 2 SOLS

Bronze **Mint:** Limoges **Obverse:** Inscription within rectangle **Reverse:** Wreath hung around liberty cap at center of scales **Note:** Without A.D. date.

Date	Mintage	VG	F	VF	XF	Unc
LAN II (1793-94)I	—	25.00	90.00	225	600	—

KM# 623.3 2 SOLS

Bronze **Mint:** Montpellier **Obverse:** Inscription within rectangle **Reverse:** Wreath hung around liberty cap at center of scales **Note:** Without A.D. date.

Date	Mintage	VG	F	VF	XF	Unc
LAN II (1793-94)N	—	35.00	140	300	700	—

KM# 623.4 2 SOLS

Bronze **Mint:** Orléans **Obverse:** Inscription within rectangle **Reverse:** Wreath hung around liberty cap at center of scales **Note:** Without A.D. date.

Date	Mintage	VG	F	VF	XF	Unc
LAN II (1793-94)R	—	30.00	100	250	650	—

KM# 623.5 2 SOLS

Bronze **Mint:** Lille **Obverse:** Inscription within rectangle **Reverse:** Wreath hung around liberty cap at center of scales **Note:** Without A.D. date.

Date	Mintage	VG	F	VF	XF	Unc
LAN II (1793-94)W	—	35.00	120	275	675	—

KM# 623.6 2 SOLS

Bronze **Mint:** Pau **Obverse:** Inscription within rectangle **Reverse:** Wreath hung around liberty cap at center of scales **Note:** Without A.D. date. Mint mark: Cow.

Date	Mintage	VG	F	VF	XF	Unc
LAN II (1793-94)	—	40.00	150	320	750	—

KM# 604.8 15 SOLS (1/8 ECU)

5.0000 g., 0.6660 Silver 0.1071 oz. ASW **Mint:** Toulouse

Date	Mintage	VG	F	VF	XF	Unc
1791M	193,000	10.00	30.00	70.00	175	—
1792M	—	10.00	30.00	70.00	175	—

KM# 604.9 15 SOLS (1/8 ECU)

5.0000 g., 0.6660 Silver 0.1071 oz. ASW **Mint:** Marseille

Date	Mintage	VG	F	VF	XF	Unc
1791MA	63,000	15.00	50.00	120	300	—
1792MA	—	10.00	30.00	70.00	175	—

KM# 604.10 15 SOLS (1/8 ECU)

5.0000 g., 0.6660 Silver 0.1071 oz. ASW **Mint:** Montpellier

Date	Mintage	VG	F	VF	XF	Unc
1791N	157,000	10.00	30.00	70.00	175	—
1792N	—	10.00	30.00	70.00	175	—

KM# 604.11 15 SOLS (1/8 ECU)

5.0000 g., 0.6660 Silver 0.1071 oz. ASW **Mint:** Perpignan

Date	Mintage	VG	F	VF	XF	Unc
1791Q	—	25.00	75.00	175	400	—
1792Q	—	10.00	30.00	70.00	175	—

KM# 604.12 15 SOLS (1/8 ECU)

5.0000 g., 0.6660 Silver 0.1071 oz. ASW **Mint:** Orléans

Date	Mintage	VG	F	VF	XF	Unc
1791R	157,000	10.00	30.00	70.00	175	—
1792R	—	10.00	30.00	70.00	175	—

KM# 604.13 15 SOLS (1/8 ECU)

5.0000 g., 0.6660 Silver 0.1071 oz. ASW **Mint:** Nantes

Date	Mintage	VG	F	VF	XF	Unc
1791T	25,000	12.00	40.00	95.00	240	—
1792T	—	12.00	40.00	95.00	240	—

KM# 604.14 15 SOLS (1/8 ECU)

5.0000 g., 0.6660 Silver 0.1071 oz. ASW **Mint:** Lille

Date	Mintage	VG	F	VF	XF	Unc
1791W	169,000	6.00	18.00	50.00	140	—
1792W	—	6.00	18.00	50.00	140	—

KM# 605.2 15 SOLS (1/8 ECU)

5.0000 g., 0.6660 Silver 0.1071 oz. ASW **Mint:** Strasbourg

Date	Mintage	VG	F	VF	XF	Unc
1791BB	88,000	15.00	50.00	120	350	—
1792BB	—	10.00	30.00	80.00	250	—

KM# 605.3 15 SOLS (1/8 ECU)

5.0000 g., 0.6660 Silver 0.1071 oz. ASW **Mint:** Lyon

Date	Mintage	VG	F	VF	XF	Unc
1791D	—	10.00	30.00	80.00	250	—
1792D	—	10.00	30.00	80.00	250	—

KM# 605.4 15 SOLS (1/8 ECU)

5.0000 g., 0.6660 Silver 0.1071 oz. ASW **Mint:** Bordeaux

Date	Mintage	VG	F	VF	XF	Unc
1791K	—	15.00	50.00	120	350	—
1792K	—	15.00	50.00	120	350	—

KM# 605.5 15 SOLS (1/8 ECU)

5.0000 g., 0.6660 Silver 0.1071 oz. ASW **Mint:** Marseille

Date	Mintage	VG	F	VF	XF	Unc
1791MA	—	15.00	50.00	120	350	—
1792MA	—	12.00	35.00	100	250	—

KM# 604.15 15 SOLS (1/8 ECU)

5.0000 g., 0.6660 Silver 0.1071 oz. ASW **Mint:** Pau **Note:** Mint mark: Cow.

Date	Mintage	VG	F	VF	XF	Unc
1791	24,000	12.00	40.00	95.00	240	—
1792	—	15.00	50.00	125	300	—
1793	—	20.00	75.00	175	475	—

KM# 604.2 15 SOLS (1/8 ECU)

5.0000 g., 0.6660 Silver 0.1071 oz. ASW **Mint:** Rouen **Obverse:** Head of Louis XVI left **Reverse:** Standing Genius writing the Constitution

Date	Mintage	VG	F	VF	XF	Unc
1791B	23,000	15.00	50.00	125	300	—
1792B	—	10.00	30.00	70.00	200	—

KM# 604.3 15 SOLS (1/8 ECU)

5.0000 g., 0.6660 Silver 0.1071 oz. ASW **Mint:** Lyon **Obverse:** Head of Louis XVI left **Reverse:** Standing Genius writing the Constitution

Date	Mintage	VG	F	VF	XF	Unc
1791D	272,000	6.00	18.00	50.00	140	—

KM# 604.4 15 SOLS (1/8 ECU)

5.0000 g., 0.6660 Silver 0.1071 oz. ASW **Mint:** La Rochelle
Obverse: Head of Louis XVI left **Reverse:** Standing Genius writing the Constitution

Date	Mintage	VG	F	VF	XF	Unc
1791H	90,000	10.00	30.00	70.00	200	—
1792H	—	6.00	18.00	50.00	140	—

KM# 604.5 15 SOLS (1/8 ECU)

5.0000 g., 0.6660 Silver 0.1071 oz. ASW **Mint:** Limoges
Obverse: Head of Louis XVI left **Obv. Legend:** LOUIS XVI ROI DES FRANCOIS **Reverse:** Standing Genius writing the Constitution **Rev. Legend:** REGNE DE LA LOI

Date	Mintage	VG	F	VF	XF	Unc
1791I	4,000,000	4.00	12.00	35.00	85.00	—
1792I	—	5.00	15.00	40.00	100	—

KM# 604.6 15 SOLS (1/8 ECU)

5.0000 g., 0.6660 Silver 0.1071 oz. ASW **Mint:** Bordeaux
Obverse: Head of Louis XVI left **Reverse:** Standing Genius writing the Constitution

Date	Mintage	VG	F	VF	XF	Unc
1791K	29,000	15.00	50.00	125	300	—
1792K	—	10.00	30.00	70.00	200	—

KM# 604.7 15 SOLS (1/8 ECU)

5.0000 g., 0.6660 Silver 0.1071 oz. ASW **Mint:** Bayonne
Obverse: Head of Louis XVI left **Reverse:** Standing Genius writing the Constitution

Date	Mintage	VG	F	VF	XF	Unc
1792L	—	12.00	40.00	100	250	—

KM# 606.4 30 SOLS

10.0000 g., 0.6660 Silver 0.2141 oz. ASW **Mint:** Strasbourg

Date	Mintage	VG	F	VF	XF	Unc
1791BB	18,000	15.00	40.00	100	275	—
1792BB	—	15.00	35.00	90.00	225	—

KM# 606.5 30 SOLS

10.0000 g., 0.6660 Silver 0.2141 oz. ASW **Mint:** Lyon

Date	Mintage	VG	F	VF	XF	Unc
1791D	—	15.00	35.00	90.00	225	—
1792D	—	15.00	35.00	90.00	225	—
1793D	—	15.00	35.00	95.00	250	—

KM# 606.6 30 SOLS

10.0000 g., 0.6660 Silver 0.2141 oz. ASW **Mint:** La Rochelle

Date	Mintage	VG	F	VF	XF	Unc
1791H	—	15.00	35.00	90.00	225	—
1792H	—	15.00	35.00	90.00	225	—

KM# 606.7 30 SOLS

10.0000 g., 0.6660 Silver 0.2141 oz. ASW **Mint:** Limoges

Date	Mintage	VG	F	VF	XF	Unc
1791I	1,711,000	10.00	25.00	75.00	175	—
1792I	—	10.00	25.00	75.00	175	—

KM# 606.8 30 SOLS

10.0000 g., 0.6660 Silver 0.2141 oz. ASW **Mint:** Bordeaux

Date	Mintage	VG	F	VF	XF	Unc
1791K	19,000	15.00	40.00	100	275	—
1792K	—	15.00	40.00	100	275	—
1793K	—	20.00	50.00	140	325	—

KM# 606.12 30 SOLS

10.0000 g., 0.6660 Silver 0.2141 oz. ASW **Mint:** Montpellier
Obverse: Head of Louis XVI left **Reverse:** Standing Genius writing the Constitution

Date	Mintage	VG	F	VF	XF	Unc
1791N	1,253	40.00	100	250	600	—
1792N	—	15.00	40.00	100	275	—
1793N	—	30.00	80.00	200	500	—

KM# 606.15 30 SOLS

10.0000 g., 0.6660 Silver 0.2141 oz. ASW **Mint:** Nantes
Obverse: Head of Louis XVI left **Reverse:** Standing Genius writing the Constitution

Date	Mintage	VG	F	VF	XF	Unc
1791T	29,000	15.00	40.00	100	275	—
1792T	—	15.00	40.00	100	275	—

KM# 606.16 30 SOLS

10.0000 g., 0.6660 Silver 0.2141 oz. ASW **Mint:** Lille **Obverse:** Head of Louis XVI left **Reverse:** Standing Genius writing the Constitution

Date	Mintage	VG	F	VF	XF	Unc
1791W	117,000	15.00	35.00	90.00	225	—
1792W	—	15.00	35.00	90.00	225	—
1793W	—	15.00	35.00	95.00	250	—

KM# 606.17 30 SOLS

10.0000 g., 0.6660 Silver 0.2141 oz. ASW **Mint:** Pau **Obverse:** Head of Louis XVI left **Reverse:** Standing Genius writing the Constitution **Note:** Mint mark: Cow.

Date	Mintage	VG	F	VF	XF	Unc
1791	—	—	—	—	—	—
1792	—	20.00	50.00	125	300	—
1793	—	20.00	50.00	135	345	—

KM# 606.11 30 SOLS

10.0000 g., 0.6660 Silver 0.2141 oz. ASW **Mint:** Marseille
Obverse: Head of Louis XVI left **Reverse:** Standing Genius writing the Constitution

Date	Mintage	VG	F	VF	XF	Unc
1792MA	—	15.00	40.00	100	275	—
1793MA	—	15.00	40.00	100	285	—

KM# 607.2 30 SOLS

10.0000 g., 0.6660 Silver 0.2141 oz. ASW **Mint:** Marseille

Date	Mintage	VG	F	VF	XF	Unc
1792MA	—	40.00	100	225	500	—

KM# 606.13 30 SOLS

10.0000 g., 0.6660 Silver 0.2141 oz. ASW **Mint:** Perpignan
Obverse: Head of Louis XVI left **Reverse:** Standing Genius writing the Constitution

Date	Mintage	VG	F	VF	XF	Unc
1792Q	—	15.00	35.00	90.00	225	—
1793Q	—	15.00	35.00	90.00	235	—

KM# 606.14 30 SOLS

10.0000 g., 0.6660 Silver 0.2141 oz. ASW **Mint:** Orléans
Obverse: Head of Louis XVI left **Reverse:** Standing Genius writing the Constitution

Date	Mintage	VG	F	VF	XF	Unc
1792R	—	20.00	50.00	125	300	—

KM# 606.2 30 SOLS

10.0000 g., 0.6660 Silver 0.2141 oz. ASW **Mint:** Metz **Obverse:** Head of Louis XVI left **Reverse:** Standing Genius writing the Constitution

Date	Mintage	VG	F	VF	XF	Unc
1792AA	—	15.00	35.00	90.00	225	—

KM# 606.3 30 SOLS

10.0000 g., 0.6660 Silver 0.2141 oz. ASW **Mint:** Rouen
Obverse: Head of Louis XVI left **Reverse:** Standing Genius writing the Constitution

Date	Mintage	VG	F	VF	XF	Unc
1792B	—	15.00	35.00	90.00	225	—

KM# 606.9 30 SOLS

10.0000 g., 0.6660 Silver 0.2141 oz. ASW **Mint:** Bayonne
Obverse: Head of Louis XVI left **Obv. Legend:** • LOUIS XVI ROI DES FRANCOIS • **Reverse:** Standing Genius writing the Constitution **Rev. Legend:** REGNE DE LA LOI •

Date	Mintage	VG	F	VF	XF	Unc
1792L	—	30.00	80.00	200	500	—

KM# 606.10 30 SOLS

10.0000 g., 0.6660 Silver 0.2141 oz. ASW **Mint:** Toulouse
Obverse: Head of Louis XVI left **Reverse:** Standing Genius writing the Constitution

Date	Mintage	VG	F	VF	XF	Unc
1793M		20.00	50.00	135	325	

KM# 613.2 1/2 ECU (3 Livres)

15.0000 g., 0.9170 Silver 0.4422 oz. ASW **Mint:** Bordeaux
Obverse: Head left **Reverse:** Standing Genius writing the Constitution

Date	Mintage	VG	F	VF	XF	Unc
1792K	—	150	300	700	1,500	—

KM# 613.3 1/2 ECU (3 Livres)

15.0000 g., 0.9170 Silver 0.4422 oz. ASW **Mint:** Montpellier
Obverse: Head left **Reverse:** Standing Genius writing the Constitution

Date	Mintage	VG	F	VF	XF	Unc
1792N	—	125	250	500	1,200	—

KM# 613.4 1/2 ECU (3 Livres)

15.0000 g., 0.9170 Silver 0.4422 oz. ASW **Mint:** Nantes **Obverse:** Head left **Reverse:** Standing Genius writing the Constitution

Date	Mintage	VG	F	VF	XF	Unc
1792T	—	150	300	700	1,500	—

KM# 615.2 ECU (6 Livres)

30.0000 g., 0.9170 Silver 0.8844 oz. ASW **Mint:** Metz

Date	Mintage	VG	F	VF	XF	Unc
1792AA	—	75.00	200	400	775	—
1793AA	—	65.00	150	325	650	—

KM# 615.3 ECU (6 Livres)

30.0000 g., 0.9170 Silver 0.8844 oz. ASW **Mint:** Rouen

Date	Mintage	VG	F	VF	XF	Unc
1792B	—	40.00	90.00	175	425	—
1793B	—	65.00	150	325	675	—

KM# 615.4 ECU (6 Livres)

30.0000 g., 0.9170 Silver 0.8844 oz. ASW **Mint:** Lyon

Date	Mintage	VG	F	VF	XF	Unc
1792D	—	65.00	150	325	650	—
1793D	—	65.00	150	275	650	—

KM# 615.5 ECU (6 Livres)

30.0000 g., 0.9170 Silver 0.8844 oz. ASW **Mint:** La Rochelle

Date	Mintage	VG	F	VF	XF	Unc
1792H	—	50.00	150	300	650	—

KM# 615.6 ECU (6 Livres)

30.0000 g., 0.9170 Silver 0.8844 oz. ASW **Mint:** Limoges

Date	Mintage	VG	F	VF	XF	Unc
1792I	—	35.00	75.00	125	250	—
1792I FARNCOIS (Error)	—	70.00	140	260	630	—
1793I	—	90.00	225	350	850	—

KM# 615.7 ECU (6 Livres)

30.0000 g., 0.9170 Silver 0.8844 oz. ASW **Mint:** Bordeaux

Date	Mintage	VG	F	VF	XF	Unc
1792K	—	50.00	125	250	600	—
1793K	—	50.00	125	225	675	—

KM# 615.8 ECU (6 Livres)

30.0000 g., 0.9170 Silver 0.8844 oz. ASW **Mint:** Bayonne

Date	Mintage	VG	F	VF	XF	Unc
1792L	—	75.00	200	400	850	—
1793L	—	40.00	100	200	475	—

KM# 615.9 ECU (6 Livres)

30.0000 g., 0.9170 Silver 0.8844 oz. ASW **Mint:** Toulouse

Date	Mintage	VG	F	VF	XF	Unc
1792M	—	50.00	125	225	550	—
1793M	—	40.00	100	185	475	—

KM# 615.10 ECU (6 Livres)

30.0000 g., 0.9170 Silver 0.8844 oz. ASW **Mint:** Marseille

Date	Mintage	VG	F	VF	XF	Unc
1792MA	—	80.00	200	350	750	—
1793MA	—	50.00	125	250	750	—

KM# 615.11 ECU (6 Livres)

30.0000 g., 0.9170 Silver 0.8844 oz. ASW **Mint:** Montpellier

Date	Mintage	VG	F	VF	XF	Unc
1792N	—	75.00	175	350	750	—
1793N	—	65.00	150	275	675	—

KM# 615.12 ECU (6 Livres)

30.0000 g., 0.9170 Silver 0.8844 oz. ASW **Mint:** Orléans

Date	Mintage	VG	F	VF	XF	Unc
1792R	—	50.00	125	250	600	—
1793R	—	50.00	125	200	550	—

KM# 615.13 ECU (6 Livres)

30.0000 g., 0.9170 Silver 0.8844 oz. ASW **Mint:** Nantes

Date	Mintage	VG	F	VF	XF	Unc
1792T	—	80.00	200	350	750	—
1793T	—	80.00	200	425	900	—

KM# 615.14 ECU (6 Livres)

30.0000 g., 0.9170 Silver 0.8844 oz. ASW **Mint:** Lille

Date	Mintage	VG	F	VF	XF	Unc
1792W	—	50.00	125	225	550	—
1793W	—	65.00	150	275	700	—

KM# 624.2 6 LIVRES

30.0000 g., 0.9170 Silver 0.8844 oz. ASW **Mint:** Metz

Date	Mintage	VG	F	VF	XF	Unc
1793//LAN IIAA	—	75.00	200	425	975	—

KM# 624.3 6 LIVRES

30.0000 g., 0.9170 Silver 0.8844 oz. ASW **Mint:** Rouen

Date	Mintage	VG	F	VF	XF	Unc
1793//LAN IIB	—	125	300	450	1,350	—

KM# 624.4 6 LIVRES

30.0000 g., 0.9170 Silver 0.8844 oz. ASW **Mint:** Strasbourg

Date	Mintage	VG	F	VF	XF	Unc
1793//LAN IIBB	—	125	300	450	1,350	—

KM# 624.5 6 LIVRES

30.0000 g., 0.9170 Silver 0.8844 oz. ASW **Mint:** Rouen

Date	Mintage	VG	F	VF	XF	Unc
1793//LAN II	—	75.00	200	350	850	—

KM# 624.6 6 LIVRES

30.0000 g., 0.9170 Silver 0.8844 oz. ASW **Mint:** Bayonne

Date	Mintage	VG	F	VF	XF	Unc
1793//LAN IIL	—	75.00	200	400	900	—

KM# 624.7 6 LIVRES

30.0000 g., 0.9170 Silver 0.8844 oz. ASW **Mint:** Marseille

Date	Mintage	VG	F	VF	XF	Unc
1793//LAN IIMA	—	100	250	450	1,100	—

KM# 624.8 6 LIVRES

30.0000 g., 0.9170 Silver 0.8844 oz. ASW **Mint:** Montpellier

Date	Mintage	VG	F	VF	XF	Unc
1793//LAN IIN	—	125	300	450	1,200	—

KM# 624.9 6 LIVRES

30.0000 g., 0.9170 Silver 0.8844 oz. ASW **Mint:** Nantes

Date	Mintage	VG	F	VF	XF	Unc
1793//LAN IIT	—	150	350	650	1,500	—

KM# 624.10 6 LIVRES

30.0000 g., 0.9170 Silver 0.8844 oz. ASW **Mint:** Lille

Date	Mintage	VG	F	VF	XF	Unc
1793//LAN IIW	—	75.00	200	375	800	—

KM# 625.2 6 LIVRES

30.0000 g., 0.9170 Silver 0.8844 oz. ASW **Mint:** Strasbourg

Date	Mintage	VG	F	VF	XF	Unc
LAN IIBB	—	250	700	1,200	3,500	—

KM# 625.3 6 LIVRES

30.0000 g., 0.9170 Silver 0.8844 oz. ASW **Mint:** Marseille

Date	Mintage	VG	F	VF	XF	Unc
LAN IIMA	—	300	800	1,400	4,000	—

KM# 625.4 6 LIVRES

30.0000 g., 0.9170 Silver 0.8844 oz. ASW **Mint:** Lille

Date	Mintage	VG	F	VF	XF	Unc
LAN IIW	—	200	500	1,000	2,500	—

KM# 624.1 6 LIVRES

30.0000 g., 0.9170 Silver 0.8844 oz. ASW **Mint:** Paris **Obverse:** With A.D. date **Note:** Dav. #1336.

Date	Mintage	VG	F	VF	XF	Unc
1793//LAN IIA	—	50.00	100	175	465	—

KM# 625.1 6 LIVRES

30.0000 g., 0.9170 Silver 0.8844 oz. ASW **Mint:** Rouen **Obverse:** Without AD date **Obv. Legend:** REGNE DE LA LOI **Reverse:** Value within wreath **Rev. Legend:** • REPUBLIQUE FRANCOISE • **Note:** Dav. #1336A.

Date	Mintage	VG	F	VF	XF	Unc
LAN IIB	—	200	500	1,000	2,500	—

KM# 626.1 24 LIVRES

7.6000 g., 0.9000 Gold 0.2199 oz. AGW **Mint:** Paris **Obverse:** Standing Genius writing the Constitution **Obv. Legend:** • REGNE DE LA LOI • **Reverse:** Value within wreath **Rev. Legend:** • REPUBLIQUE FRANCOISE •

Date	Mintage	VG	F	VF	XF	Unc
1793A	—	500	1,000	2,500	4,500	—

KM# 626.2 24 LIVRES

7.6000 g., 0.9000 Gold 0.2199 oz. AGW **Mint:** Strasbourg **Obverse:** Standing Genius writing the Constitution **Reverse:** Value within wreath

Date	Mintage	VG	F	VF	XF	Unc
1793BB	—	1,000	2,000	4,000	7,000	—

KM# 626.3 24 LIVRES

7.6000 g., 0.9000 Gold 0.2199 oz. AGW **Mint:** Rouen **Obverse:** Standing Genius writing the Constitution **Reverse:** Value within wreath

Date	Mintage	VG	F	VF	XF	Unc
1793	—	600	1,250	2,750	5,250	—

KM# 626.4 24 LIVRES

7.6000 g., 0.9000 Gold 0.2199 oz. AGW **Mint:** Montpellier **Obverse:** Standing Genius writing the Constitution **Reverse:** Value within wreath

Date	Mintage	VG	F	VF	XF	Unc
1793N	—	—	—	—	8,500	—

KM# 626.5 24 LIVRES

7.6000 g., 0.9000 Gold 0.2199 oz. AGW **Mint:** Lille **Obverse:** Standing Genius writing the Constitution **Reverse:** Value within wreath

Date	Mintage	VG	F	VF	XF	Unc
1793W	—	600	1,250	2,650	4,750	—

DECIMAL COINAGE

KM# 646 CENTIME

2.0000 g., Bronze, 18 mm. **Mint:** Paris **Obverse:** Liberty head left **Obv. Legend:** REPUBLIQUE FRANCAISE • **Reverse:** Value within beaded circle

Date	Mintage	VG	F	VF	XF	Unc
LAN 6 (1797-98)A	100,083,000	2.00	5.00	20.00	90.00	—
LAN 7 (1798-99)A	Inc. above	3.00	6.00	25.00	100	—
LAN 8 (1799-1800)A	Inc. above	20.00	40.00	65.00	175	—

KM# 635.1 5 CENTIMES

5.0000 g., Bronze, 23 mm. **Mint:** Paris **Obverse:** Liberty head left **Obv. Legend:** REPUBLIQUE FRANCAISE • **Reverse:** Value

Date	Mintage	VG	F	VF	XF	Unc
LAN 4/3 (1795)A	12,308,000	5.00	10.00	20.00	70.00	—
LAN 4 (1795-96)A	Inc. above	5.00	10.00	20.00	70.00	—
LAN 5 (1796)A	Inc. above	15.00	30.00	75.00	185	—

KM# 635.2 5 CENTIMES

5.0000 g., Bronze **Mint:** Limoges **Obverse:** Liberty head left **Reverse:** Value

Date	Mintage	VG	F	VF	XF	Unc
LAN 4 (1795-96)I	780,000	8.00	20.00	50.00	135	—
LAN 5 (1796)I	Inc. above	35.00	75.00	150	350	—

KM# 635.3 5 CENTIMES

5.0000 g., Bronze **Mint:** Nantes **Obverse:** Liberty head left **Reverse:** Value

Date	Mintage	VG	F	VF	XF	Unc
LAN 4 (1795-96)T	—	15.00	40.00	80.00	250	—
LAN 5 (1796)T	Inc. above	45.00	100	175	375	—

KM# 635.4 5 CENTIMES

5.0000 g., Bronze **Mint:** Lille **Obverse:** Liberty head left **Reverse:** Value

Date	Mintage	VG	F	VF	XF	Unc
LAN 4 (1795-96)W	Inc. above	45.00	100	175	375	—
LAN 5 (1796)W	Inc. above	45.00	100	175	375	—

KM# 640.1 5 CENTIMES

10.0000 g., Bronze **Mint:** Paris **Obverse:** Liberty head left **Obv. Legend:** REPUBLIQUE FRANCAISE • * **Reverse:** Value within oak wreath

Date	Mintage	VG	F	VF	XF	Unc
LAN 5 (1796-97)A	26,880,000	3.00	6.00	15.00	65.00	—
LAN 5 (1796-97)A CNIQ (error)	Inc. above	35.00	75.00	150	275	—
LAN 6 (1797-98)A	Inc. above	7.00	20.00	40.00	150	—
LAN 7/5 (1798-99)A	Inc. above	4.00	8.00	20.00	85.00	—
LAN 7/5 A/R (1798-99)A	Inc. above	4.00	8.00	20.00	85.00	—
LAN 7/6 (1798-99)A	Inc. above	4.00	8.00	20.00	85.00	—
LAN 7 (1798-99)A	Inc. above	4.00	8.00	20.00	85.00	—
LAN 8/5 (1799-1800)A	37,323,000	5.00	10.00	30.00	100	—
LAN 8/7 (1799-1800)A	Inc. above	4.00	8.00	20.00	85.00	—
LAN 8/7 A/R (1799-1800)A	Inc. above	3.00	6.00	17.50	110	—
LAN 8 (1799-1800)A	Inc. above	3.00	6.00	15.00	60.00	—
LAN 9 (1800-01)A	Inc. above	6.00	15.00	35.00	135	—

KM# 640.2 5 CENTIMES

10.0000 g., Bronze **Mint:** Metz **Obverse:** Liberty head left **Reverse:** Value within oak wreath

Date	Mintage	VG	F	VF	XF	Unc
LAN 5 (1796-97)AA	2,230,000	4.00	8.00	20.00	100	—
LAN 6 (1797-98)AA	Inc. above	15.00	35.00	75.00	200	—
LAN 8/6 (1799-1800)AA	20,002,000	4.00	8.00	20.00	100	—
LAN 8 (1799-1800)AA	Inc. above	3.00	6.00	15.00	85.00	—
LAN 9 (1800-01)AA	Inc. above	15.00	35.00	75.00	250	—

KM# 640.3 5 CENTIMES

10.0000 g., Bronze **Mint:** Rouen **Obverse:** Liberty head left **Reverse:** Value within oak wreath

Date	Mintage	VG	F	VF	XF	Unc
LAN 5 (1796-97)B	3,026,000	4.00	8.00	25.00	125	—
LAN 6 (1797-98)B	Inc. above	15.00	45.00	100	250	—

KM# 640.4 5 CENTIMES

10.0000 g., Bronze **Mint:** Strasbourg **Obverse:** Liberty head left **Reverse:** Value within oak wreath

Date	Mintage	VG	F	VF	XF	Unc
LAN 5 (1796-97)BB	3,660,000	4.00	8.00	20.00	100	—
LAN 6/5 (1797-98)BB	Inc. above	15.00	40.00	70.00	225	—
LAN 6 (1797-98)BB	Inc. above	12.50	32.50	60.00	200	—
LAN 7/5 (1798-99)BB	Inc. above	4.00	8.00	20.00	100	—
LAN 7 (1798-99)BB	Inc. above	4.00	8.00	20.00	100	—
LAN 8/7 (1799-1800)BB	7,984,000	4.00	8.00	20.00	100	—
LAN 8 (1799-1800)BB CNIQ (error)	Inc. above	50.00	100	200	350	—
LAN 8 (1799-1800)BB	Inc. above	4.00	8.00	20.00	100	—
LAN 9 (1800-01)BB	Inc. above	6.00	15.00	35.00	135	—

KM# 640.5 5 CENTIMES

10.0000 g., Bronze **Mint:** Lyon **Obverse:** Liberty head left **Reverse:** Value within oak wreath

Date	Mintage	VG	F	VF	XF	Unc
LAN 5 (1796-97)D	1,475,000	6.00	15.00	35.00	150	—
LAN 6 (1797-98)D	Inc. above	20.00	50.00	100	225	—
LAN 7 (1798-99)D	Inc. above	15.00	30.00	90.00	200	—
LAN 8 (1799-1800)D	691,000	20.00	50.00	115	225	—
LAN 9 (1800-01)D	Inc. above	15.00	40.00	100	225	—

KM# 642.2 5 CENTIMES

10.0000 g., Bronze **Mint:** Metz

Date	Mintage	Good	VG	F	VF	XF
LAN 5 (1796-97)AA	Inc. above	12.00	30.00	80.00	200	—
LAN 6 (1797-98)AA	Inc. above	—	—	—	—	—

Note: Reported, not confirmed

KM# 642.3 5 CENTIMES

10.0000 g., Bronze **Mint:** Rouen

Date	Mintage	Good	VG	F	VF	XF
LAN 5 (1796-97)B	Inc. above	13.50	32.00	85.00	220	—
LAN 6 (1797-98)B	Inc. above	—	—	—	—	—

Note: Reported, not confirmed

KM# 642.4 5 CENTIMES

10.0000 g., Bronze **Mint:** Strasbourg

Date	Mintage	Good	VG	F	VF	XF
LAN 5 (1796-97)BB	Inc. above	—	—	—	—	—

Note: Reported, not confirmed

KM# 642.5 5 CENTIMES

10.0000 g., Bronze **Mint:** Lyon

Date	Mintage	Good	VG	F	VF	XF
LAN 5 (1796-97)D	Inc. above	13.50	32.00	85.00	220	—
LAN 6 (1797-98)D	Inc. above	—	—	—	—	—

Note: Reported, not confirmed

KM# 642.6 5 CENTIMES

10.0000 g., Bronze **Mint:** Limoges **Obverse:** Liberty head left **Reverse:** Value within oak wreath

Date	Mintage	Good	VG	F	VF	XF
LAN 5 (1796-97)I	Inc. above	13.50	32.00	85.00	220	—
LAN 6 (1797-98)I	Inc. above	—	—	—	—	—
Note: Reported, not confirmed						
LAN 8 (1799-1800)I	Inc. above	—	—	—	—	—
Note: Reported, not confirmed						

KM# 642.7 5 CENTIMES

10.0000 g., Bronze **Mint:** Orléans

Date	Mintage	Good	VG	F	VF	XF
LAN 5 (1797-97)R	—	—	—	—	—	—
Note: Reported, not confirmed						

KM# 642.8 5 CENTIMES

10.0000 g., Bronze **Mint:** Nantes

Date	Mintage	Good	VG	F	VF	XF
LAN 5 (1796-97)T	—	—	—	—	—	—
Note: Reported, not confirmed						

KM# 642.9 5 CENTIMES

10.0000 g., Bronze **Mint:** Lille

Date	Mintage	Good	VG	F	VF	XF
LAN 5 (1796-97)W	—	—	—	—	—	—
Note: Reported, not confirmed						
LAN 6 (1797-98)W	—	16.00	40.00	100	250	—
LAN 7 (1798-99)W	—	—	—	—	—	—
LAN 8 (1799-1800)W	—	—	—	—	—	—

KM# 640.7 5 CENTIMES

10.0000 g., Bronze **Mint:** Limoges **Obverse:** Liberty head left **Reverse:** Value within oak wreath

Date	Mintage	VG	F	VF	XF	Unc
LAN 5 (1796-97)I	9,608,000	4.00	8.00	20.00	100	—
LAN 5 (1796-97)I CNIQ (error)	Inc. above	35.00	75.00	150	275	—
LAN 6 (1797-98)I	Inc. above	15.00	40.00	90.00	200	—
LAN 8 (1799-1800)I	4,582,000	4.00	8.00	25.00	125	—
LAN 8 (1799-1800)I CNIQ (error)	Inc. above	50.00	100	200	350	—
LAN 9 (1800-01)I	Inc. above	10.00	30.00	60.00	175	—

KM# 640.8 5 CENTIMES

10.0000 g., Bronze **Mint:** Bordeaux **Obverse:** Liberty head left **Reverse:** Value within oak wreath

Date	Mintage	VG	F	VF	XF	Unc
LAN 5 (1796-97)K	1,997,000	—	—	—	—	—
Note: Reported, not confirmed						
LAN 6 (1797-98)K	Inc. above	15.00	40.00	90.00	200	—
LAN 7 (1798-99)K	Inc. above	6.00	15.00	35.00	125	—
LAN 8 (1799-1800)K	4,639,000	4.00	8.00	25.00	125	—
LAN 9 (1800-01)K	Inc. above	10.00	25.00	50.00	175	—

KM# 640.9 5 CENTIMES

10.0000 g., Bronze **Mint:** Orléans **Obverse:** Liberty head left **Reverse:** Value within oak wreath

Date	Mintage	VG	F	VF	XF	Unc
LAN 5 (1796-97)R	5,667,000	5.00	10.00	25.00	125	—

KM# 640.10 5 CENTIMES

10.0000 g., Bronze **Mint:** Nantes **Obverse:** Liberty head left **Reverse:** Value within oak wreath

Date	Mintage	VG	F	VF	XF	Unc
LAN 5 (1796-97)T	18,000	40.00	80.00	150	325	—

KM# 640.11 5 CENTIMES

10.0000 g., Bronze **Mint:** Lille **Obverse:** Liberty head left **Obv. Legend:** REPUBLIQUE FRANCAISE • * **Reverse:** Value within oak wreath

Date	Mintage	VG	F	VF	XF	Unc
LAN 5 (1796-97)W	2,743,000	4.00	8.00	20.00	100	—
LAN 6 (1797-98)W	Inc. above	15.00	40.00	90.00	200	—
LAN 7/5 (1798-99)W	Inc. above	5.00	10.00	20.00	100	—
LAN 7 (1798-99)W	Inc. above	5.00	10.00	20.00	100	—
LAN 8/5 (1799-1800)W	12,738,000	—	—	—	—	—
LAN 8 (1799-1800)W	12,738,000	4.00	8.00	20.00	100	—
LAN 9 (1800-01)W	Inc. above	10.00	25.00	50.00	150	—

KM# 642.1 5 CENTIMES

10.0000 g., Bronze **Mint:** Paris **Obverse:** Liberty head left **Obv. Legend:** REPUBLIQUE FRANCAISE • * **Reverse:** Value within oak wreath **Note:** KM#640 struck over Un Decime, KM#630.

Date	Mintage	Good	VG	F	VF	XF
LAN 5 (1796-97)A	Inc. above	—	—	—	—	—

Date	Mintage	Good	VG	F	VF	XF
Note: Reported, not confirmed						
LAN 6 (1797-98)A	Inc. above	12.00	30.00	80.00	200	—
LAN 7 (1798-99)A	Inc. above	12.00	30.00	80.00	200	—
LAN 8 (1799-1800A	Inc. above	—	—	—	—	—
Note: Reported, not confirmed						

KM# 642.6a 5 CENTIMES

Bell Metal **Mint:** Limoges **Obverse:** Liberty head left **Reverse:** Value within oak wreath

Date	Mintage	Good	VG	F	VF	XF
LAN 8 (1799-1800)I	—	—	—	—	—	—

KM# 640.6 5 CENTIMES

10.0000 g., Bronze **Mint:** Poitiers

Date	Mintage	VG	F	VF	XF	Unc
LAN 8 (1799-1800)G	2,005,000	10.00	20.00	50.00	150	—
LAN 9 (1800-01)G	Inc. above	15.00	35.00	60.00	160	—

KM# 645.6 DECIME

20.0000 g., Bronze **Mint:** Limoges

Date	Mintage	Good	VG	F	VF	XF
LAN 4 (1795-96)I	—	12.00	30.00	80.00	200	—
LAN 5 (1796-97)I	—	16.00	40.00	100	250	—
LAN 6 (1797-98)I	—	—	—	—	—	—
Note: Reported, not confirmed						
LAN 7 (1799-1800)I	—	—	—	—	—	—
Note: Reported, not confirmed						

KM# 645.1 DECIME

20.0000 g., Bronze, 31 mm. **Mint:** Paris **Obverse:** Liberty head left **Obv. Legend:** REPUBLIQUE FRANCAISE • * **Reverse:** Value within oak wreath **Note:** KM#644 overstruck on 2 Decimes, KM#638.

Date	Mintage	Good	VG	F	VF	XF
LAN 4 (1795-96)A	—	10.00	25.00	60.00	150	—
LAN 5 (1796-97)A	—	12.00	30.00	80.00	200	—
LAN 6 (1797-98)A	—	12.00	30.00	80.00	200	—
LAN 8 (1799-1800)A	—	16.00	40.00	100	250	—

KM# 636.1 DECIME

10.0000 g., Bronze, 28 mm. **Mint:** Paris **Obverse:** Liberty head left **Obv. Legend:** REPUBLIQUE FRANCAISE • * **Reverse:** Value within oak wreath **Rev. Legend:** DECIME

Date	Mintage	VG	F	VF	XF	Unc
LAN 4 (1795-96)A	3,606,000	15.00	25.00	80.00	195	—
LAN 5 (1796)A	Inc. above	30.00	75.00	150	300	—

KM# 636.2 DECIME

10.0000 g., Bronze **Mint:** Lyon **Obverse:** Liberty head left **Reverse:** Value within oak wreath

Date	Mintage	VG	F	VF	XF	Unc
LAN 4 (1795-96)D	255,000	30.00	75.00	150	300	—
LAN 5 (1796)D	Inc. above	40.00	80.00	175	375	—

KM# 636.3 DECIME

10.0000 g., Bronze **Mint:** Limoges **Obverse:** Liberty head left **Reverse:** Value within oak wreath

Date	Mintage	VG	F	VF	XF	Unc
LAN 4 (1795-96)I	694,000	20.00	60.00	150	300	—
LAN 5 (1796)I	Inc. above	65.00	160	275	650	—

KM# 636.4 DECIME

10.0000 g., Bronze **Mint:** Bordeaux **Obverse:** Liberty head left **Reverse:** Value within oak wreath

Date	Mintage	VG	F	VF	XF	Unc
LAN 4 (1795-96)K Rare	—	—	—	—	—	—

KM# 637.2 DECIME

20.0000 g., Bronze **Mint:** Lyon

Date	Mintage	VG	F	VF	XF	Unc
LAN 4 (1795-96)D	—	—	—	—	—	—
Note: Reported, not confirmed						

KM# 637.3 DECIME

20.0000 g., Bronze **Mint:** Limoges

Date	Mintage	VG	F	VF	XF	Unc
LAN 4 (1795-96)I	—	20.00	50.00	150	400	—

KM# 637.1 DECIME

20.0000 g., Bronze, 31 mm. **Mint:** Paris **Obverse:** Liberty head left **Obv. Legend:** REPUBLIQUE FRANCAISE • * **Reverse:** Value within oak wreath **Note:** UN countermarked over obliterated 2 and 5 obliterated from DECIMES, KM#638.

Date	Mintage	VG	F	VF	XF	Unc
LAN 4 (1795-96)A	—	12.50	25.00	75.00	200	—
LAN 5 (1796-97)A	—	30.00	75.00	150	400	—

KM# 644.7 DECIME

20.0000 g., Bronze **Mint:** Limoges **Obverse:** Liberty head left **Reverse:** Value within oak wreath

Date	Mintage	VG	F	VF	XF	Unc
LAN 5 (1796-97)I	3,800,000	7.50	15.00	35.00	150	—
LAN 6 (1797-98)I	Inc. above	15.00	40.00	100	250	—
LAN 8 (1799-1800)I	3,424,000	7.50	15.00	35.00	140	—
LAN 9 (1800-01)I	Inc. above	10.00	20.00	50.00	150	—

KM# 644.9 DECIME

20.0000 g., Bronze **Mint:** Orléans **Obverse:** Liberty head left **Reverse:** Value within oak wreath

Date	Mintage	VG	F	VF	XF	Unc
LAN 5 (1796-97)R	1,980,000	10.00	20.00	50.00	175	—

KM# 644.10 DECIME

20.0000 g., Bronze **Mint:** Nantes **Obverse:** Liberty head left **Reverse:** Value within oak wreath

Date	Mintage	VG	F	VF	XF	Unc
LAN 5 (1796-97)T	84,000	50.00	100	250	625	—

KM# 644.11 DECIME

20.0000 g., Bronze **Mint:** Lille **Obverse:** Liberty head left **Reverse:** Value within oak wreath

Date	Mintage	VG	F	VF	XF	Unc
LAN 5 (1796-97)W	3,948,000	7.50	15.00	35.00	150	—
LAN 6 (1797-98)W	Inc. above	40.00	100	215	600	—
LAN 7 (1798-99)W	Inc. below	5.00	10.00	30.00	125	—
LAN 8 (1799-1800)W	6,004,000	5.00	10.00	30.00	135	—
LAN 9 (1800-01)W	Inc. above	10.00	20.00	50.00	175	—

KM# 637.4 DECIME

20.0000 g., Bronze **Mint:** Lyon **Obverse:** Liberty head left **Reverse:** Value within oak wreath **Rev. Legend:** UN DECIME

Date	Mintage	VG	F	VF	XF	Unc
LAN 5 (1796-97)D	—	—	—	—	—	—
Note: Reported, not confirmed						

KM# 637.5 DECIME

20.0000 g., Bronze **Mint:** Limoges **Obverse:** Liberty head left **Reverse:** Value within oak wreath

Date	Mintage	VG	F	VF	XF	Unc
LAN 5 (1796-97)I Rare	—	—	—	—	—	—

KM# 644.1 DECIME

20.0000 g., Bronze, 32 mm. **Mint:** Paris **Obverse:** Liberty head left **Obv. Legend:** REPUBLIQUE FRANCAISE • * **Reverse:** Value within oak wreath

Date	Mintage	VG	F	VF	XF	Unc
LAN 5 (1796-97)A	46,581,000	5.00	10.00	25.00	100	—
LAN 6 (1797-98)A	Inc. above	15.00	30.00	75.00	175	—
LAN 7/5 (1798-99)A	Inc. below	5.00	10.00	25.00	100	—
LAN 7 (1798-99)A	Inc. below	5.00	10.00	25.00	100	—
LAN 8 (1799-1800)A	22,951,000	5.00	10.00	25.00	100	—
LAN 9 (1800-01)A	—	7.50	15.00	30.00	125	—

KM# 644.2 DECIME
20.0000 g., Bronze **Mint:** Metz **Obverse:** Liberty head left **Reverse:** Value within oak wreath

Date	Mintage	VG	F	VF	XF	Unc
LAN 5 (1796-97)AA	224,000	15.00	40.00	100	250	—
LAN 6 (1797-98)AA	Inc. above	20.00	50.00	150	350	—
LAN 7 (1798-99)AA	—	10.00	20.00	50.00	150	—
LAN 8 (1799-1800)AA	9,996,000	5.00	10.00	25.00	100	—
LAN 8/5AA	—	—	30.00	—	—	—

KM# 644.3 DECIME
20.0000 g., Bronze **Mint:** Rouen **Obverse:** Liberty head left **Reverse:** Value within oak wreath

Date	Mintage	VG	F	VF	XF	Unc
LAN 5 (1796-97)B	2,041,000	10.00	20.00	50.00	150	—
LAN 6 (1797-98)B	567,000	15.00	40.00	100	250	—

KM# 644.4 DECIME
20.0000 g., Bronze **Mint:** Strasbourg **Obverse:** Liberty head left **Reverse:** Value within oak wreath

Date	Mintage	VG	F	VF	XF	Unc
LAN 5 (1796-97)BB	418,000	15.00	30.00	75.00	200	—
LAN 6 (1797-98)BB	Inc. above	20.00	50.00	125	250	—
LAN 7 (1798-99)BB	Inc. below	10.00	20.00	50.00	150	—
LAN 8 (1799-1800)BB	3,786,000	7.50	15.00	35.00	175	—
LAN 9 (1800-01)BB	Inc. above	10.00	20.00	50.00	150	—

KM# 644.5 DECIME
20.0000 g., Bronze **Mint:** Lyon **Obverse:** Liberty head left **Reverse:** Value within oak wreath

Date	Mintage	VG	F	VF	XF	Unc
LAN 5 (1796-97)D	4,826,000	7.50	15.00	35.00	150	—
LAN 6 (1797-98)D	255,000	25.00	50.00	125	325	—
LAN 7 (1798-99)D	Inc. below	15.00	30.00	75.00	200	—
LAN 8 (1799-1800)D	1,676,000	10.00	20.00	55.00	175	—
LAN 9 (1800-01)D	Inc. above	15.00	30.00	75.00	200	—

KM# 645.7 DECIME
20.0000 g., Bronze **Mint:** Orléans

Date	Mintage	Good	VG	F	VF	XF
LAN 5 (1796-97)R	—	16.00	40.00	100	250	—

KM# 645.8 DECIME
20.0000 g., Bronze **Mint:** Nantes

Date	Mintage	Good	VG	F	VF	XF
LAN 5 (1796-97)T	—	16.00	40.00	100	250	—

KM# 645.9 DECIME
20.0000 g., Bronze **Mint:** Lille

Date	Mintage	Good	VG	F	VF	XF
LAN 5 (1796-97)W	—	16.00	40.00	100	250	—
LAN 6 (1797-98)W	—	—	—	—	—	—
Note: Reported, not confirmed						
LAN 7 (1798-99)W	—	16.00	40.00	100	250	—

KM# 645.2 DECIME
20.0000 g., Bronze **Mint:** Metz

Date	Mintage	Good	VG	F	VF	XF
LAN 5 (1796-97)AA	—	12.00	30.00	80.00	200	—
LAN 6 (1797-98)AA	—	—	—	—	—	—
Note: Reported, not confirmed						
LAN 8 (1799-1800)AA	—	16.00	40.00	100	250	—

KM# 645.3 DECIME
20.0000 g., Bronze **Mint:** Rouen

Date	Mintage	Good	VG	F	VF	XF
LAN 5 (1796-97)B	—	14.00	35.00	900	225	—
LAN 6 (1797-98)B	—	—	—	—	—	—
Note: Reported, not confirmed						

KM# 645.4 DECIME
20.0000 g., Bronze **Mint:** Strasbourg

Date	Mintage	Good	VG	F	VF	XF
LAN 5 (1796-97)BB	—	—	—	—	—	—
Note: Reported, not confirmed						

KM# 645.5 DECIME
20.0000 g., Bronze **Mint:** Lyon

Date	Mintage	Good	VG	F	VF	XF
LAN 5 (1796-97)D	—	16.00	40.00	100	250	—
LAN 6 (1797-98)D	—	—	—	—	—	—
Note: Reported, not confirmed						

KM# 644.8 DECIME
20.0000 g., Bronze **Mint:** Bordeaux **Obverse:** Liberty head left **Reverse:** Value within oak wreath

Date	Mintage	VG	F	VF	XF	Unc
LAN 7 (1798-99)K	Inc. below	10.00	20.00	50.00	175	—
LAN 8 (1799-1800)K	3,816,000	7.50	15.00	35.00	150	—
LAN 9 (1800-01)K	Inc. above	10.00	20.00	50.00	175	—

KM# 644.6 DECIME
20.0000 g., Bronze **Mint:** Poitiers **Obverse:** Liberty head left **Reverse:** Value within oak wreath

Date	Mintage	VG	F	VF	XF	Unc
LAN 8 (1799-1800)G	1,000,000	25.00	50.00	100	225	—
LAN 9 (1800-01)G	Inc. above	15.00	30.00	75.00	150	—

KM# 638.1 2 DECIMES
20.0000 g., Bronze, 31 mm. **Mint:** Paris **Obverse:** Liberty head left **Obv. Legend:** REPUBLIQUE FRANCAISE • * **Reverse:** Value within oak wreath

Date	Mintage	VG	F	VF	XF	Unc
LAN 4 (1795-96)A	15,166,000	25.00	65.00	150	300	—
LAN 5 (1796-97)A	Inc. above	50.00	125	200	400	—

KM# 638.2 2 DECIMES
20.0000 g., Bronze **Mint:** Lyon **Obverse:** Liberty head left **Reverse:** Value within oak wreath

Date	Mintage	VG	F	VF	XF	Unc
LAN 4 (1795-96)D	—	175	425	650	1,200	—
LAN 5 (1796-97)D	2,428	100	225	425	800	—

KM# 638.3 2 DECIMES
20.0000 g., Bronze **Mint:** Limoges **Obverse:** Liberty head left **Reverse:** Value within oak wreath

Date	Mintage	VG	F	VF	XF	Unc
LAN 4 (1795-96)I	1,209,000	40.00	110	200	425	—
LAN 5 (1796-97)I	Inc. above	65.00	160	360	600	—

KM# 638.4 2 DECIMES
20.0000 g., Bronze **Mint:** Bordeaux **Obverse:** Liberty head left **Reverse:** Value within oak wreath

Date	Mintage	VG	F	VF	XF	Unc
LAN 4 (1795-96)K	—	200	500	900	1,800	—

KM# 639.2 5 FRANCS
25.0000 g., 0.9000 Silver 0.7234 oz. ASW **Mint:** Strasbourg **Obverse:** Hercules group **Reverse:** Value within oak wreath

Date	Mintage	VG	F	VF	XF	Unc
LAN 5 (1796-97)BB	25,000	60.00	125	475	1,400	—
LAN 6 (1797-98)BB	65,000	50.00	100	325	1,200	—
LAN 7 (1798-99)BB	7,306	75.00	125	425	2,150	—
LAN 8 (1799-1800)BB	3,603	—	—	—	—	—
Note: Reported, not confirmed						
LAN 9 (1800-01)BB	1,086	—	—	—	—	—
Note: Reported, not confirmed						

KM# 639.10 5 FRANCS
25.0000 g., 0.9000 Silver 0.7234 oz. ASW **Mint:** Lille **Obverse:** Hercules group **Reverse:** Value within oak wreath

Date	Mintage	VG	F	VF	XF	Unc
LAN 6 (1797-98)W	70,000	50.00	100	275	1,000	—
LAN 8 (1799-1800)W	9,884	75.00	135	375	1,500	—

KM# 639.3 5 FRANCS
25.0000 g., 0.9000 Silver 0.7234 oz. ASW **Mint:** Lyon **Obverse:** Hercules group **Reverse:** Value within oak wreath

Date	Mintage	VG	F	VF	XF	Unc
LAN 8 (1799-1800)D	3,049	—	—	—	—	—
Note: Reported, not confirmed						
LAN 9 (1800-01)D	24,000	60.00	125	350	1,250	—

TOKEN ISSUES

KM# Tn4 18 DENIERS
Billon **Issuer:** Caisse Metallique, Paris **Obverse:** Liberty cap on pole above crossed fasces **Reverse:** 4-line inscription; date in exergue

Date	Mintage	VG	F	VF	XF	Unc
1792	—	10.00	20.00	40.00	90.00	—

KM# Tn4a 18 DENIERS
Copper **Issuer:** Caisse Metallique, Paris

Date	Mintage	VG	F	VF	XF	Unc
1792	—	10.00	20.00	40.00	90.00	—

KM# Tn5 18 DENIERS
Billon **Issuer:** Caisse Metallique, Paris **Obverse:** Epee and branch replace crossed fasces

Date	Mintage	VG	F	VF	XF	Unc
1792	—	10.00	25.00	50.00	90.00	—

KM# Tn5a 18 DENIERS
Silver **Issuer:** Caisse Metallique, Paris

Date	Mintage	VG	F	VF	XF	Unc
1792 Rare	—	—	—	—	—	—

KM# Tn6 18 DENIERS
Billon **Issuer:** Caisse Populaire, Paris **Obverse:** Liberty cap on pole above crossed fasces in outside legend **Reverse:** 5-line inscription in circle; legend around border

Date	Mintage	VG	F	VF	XF	Unc
1792	—	15.00	40.00	75.00	125	—

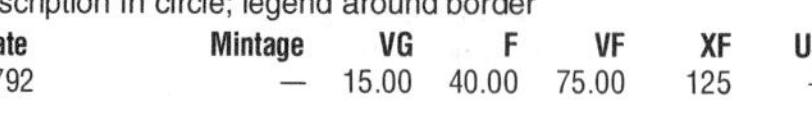

KM# Tn22 SOL
Bronze **Issuer:** Monneron Freres, Paris **Obverse:** Hercules **Obv. Legend:** LES FRANCAIS UNIS SONT INVINCIBLES **Reverse:** Inscription within inner circle **Rev. Legend:** REVOLUTION FRANCAISE **Note:** Hercules. No original strikings exist. Probably struck in the 1850s.

Date	Mintage	VG	F	VF	XF	Unc
1792	—	—	40.00	75.00	125	—

KM# Tn1 1 SOL 6 DENIERS
Billon **Issuer:** Boyere, Paris **Obverse:** Liberty cap on pole above crossed fasces **Reverse:** 6-line inscription date in outside legend

Date	Mintage	VG	F	VF	XF	Unc
1792	—	180	300	500	750	—

KM# Tn23 2 SOLS
Bronze **Issuer:** Monneron Freres, Paris **Obverse:** Figure seated left **Obv. Legend:** LIBERTE SOUS LA LOI **Reverse:** Six line inscription and date within inner circle **Rev. Legend:** ...MONNERON FRERES NEGOCIANS

Date	Mintage	VG	F	VF	XF	Unc
1791	—	5.00	10.00	20.00	50.00	—

KM# Tn23a 2 SOLS
Silver **Issuer:** Monneron Freres, Paris

Date	Mintage	VG	F	VF	XF	Unc
1791	—	—	400	750	1,250	—

KM# Tn24 2 SOLS
Bronze **Issuer:** Monneron Freres, Paris **Obverse:** High relief M.B. at base of column

Date	Mintage	VG	F	VF	XF	Unc
1791	—	—	—	500	800	—

KM# Tn25 2 SOLS
Bronze **Issuer:** Monneron Freres, Paris **Obverse:** Figure seated left **Obv. Legend:** LIBERTE SOUS LA LOI **Reverse:** Six line inscription within inner circle **Rev. Legend:** REVOLUTION FRANCAISE

Date	Mintage	VG	F	VF	XF	Unc
1792	—	5.00	10.00	20.00	50.00	—

KM# Tn25a 2 SOLS
Silver **Issuer:** Monneron Freres, Paris

Date	Mintage	VG	F	VF	XF	Unc
1792	—	—	—	—	—	—

KM# Tn26 2 SOLS
Bronze **Issuer:** Monneron Freres, Paris **Reverse:** No brackets on PATENTE

Date	Mintage	VG	F	VF	XF	Unc
1792	—	2.50	5.00	17.50	50.00	—

KM# Tn36 2 SOLS
Silver **Issuer:** Monnoye D'Urgence **Obverse:** 7-line inscription **Reverse:** Outer legend around circle

Date	Mintage	VG	F	VF	XF	Unc
1792	—	200	350	750	1,250	—

KM# Tn27 2 SOLS
Bronze **Issuer:** Monneron Freres, Paris **Obverse:** Hercules **Obv. Legend:** LE SAGE SSE GUIDE SA FORCE **Reverse:** Six line inscription within inner circle **Rev. Legend:** REVOLUTION FRANCAISE **Note:** Hercules. No original strikings exist. Probably struck in the 1850s.

Date	Mintage	VG	F	VF	XF	Unc
1792	—	—	40.00	90.00	150	—

KM# Tn7 2 SOLS
Copper **Issuer:** Clemanson, et Comp., Lyon **Obverse:** Fasces topped by liberty cap in circle, no flags, legend around border **Reverse:** 9-line inscription in circle; legend around border

Date	Mintage	VG	F	VF	XF	Unc
1792	—	300	500	750	1,250	—

KM# Tn8 2 SOLS
Copper **Issuer:** Clemanson, et Comp., Lyon **Obverse:** With flags **Reverse:** Inscription within inner circle

Date	Mintage	VG	F	VF	XF	Unc
1792	—	10.00	20.00	40.00	100	—

KM# Tn37 2 SOLS 6 DENIERS
Copper **Issuer:** Caisse de Bonne Foy, Paris **Obverse:** Legend reads small NGE in EXCHANGE **Obv. Legend:** PAYABLEENECHANGE D'ASSIGNATS **Reverse:** Hands holding pole with liberty cap at top

Date	Mintage	VG	F	VF	XF	Unc
1791	—	12.50	20.00	40.00	75.00	—

KM# Tn38 2 SOLS 6 DENIERS
Copper **Issuer:** Caisse de Bonne Foy, Paris **Obverse:** Legend is uniform size letters in EXCHANGE **Reverse:** Inscription

Date	Mintage	VG	F	VF	XF	Unc
1791	—	200	350	750	1,250	—

KM# Tn44 3 SOLS
Bronze **Issuer:** Caisse de Bonne Foy, Paris **Obverse:** Figure facing **Obv. Legend:** PAYABLE ENE CHANGE D'ASSIGNATS **Reverse:** Hands holding pole with liberty cap at top

Date	Mintage	VG	F	VF	XF	Unc
LAN III (1791)	—	30.00	60.00	100	150	—

KM# Tn44a 3 SOLS
Silver **Issuer:** Caisse de Bonne Foy, Paris

Date	Mintage	VG	F	VF	XF	Unc
LAN III (1791)	—	—	—	—	—	—

Note: Reported, not confirmed

KM# Tn29 5 SOLS
Bronze **Issuer:** Monneron Freres, Paris **Reverse:** 6-line inscription in circle, without date in outer legend

Date	Mintage	VG	F	VF	XF	Unc
1791	—	10.00	25.00	50.00	125	—

KM# Tn12 5 SOLS
Copper **Issuer:** V. Givry **Obverse:** Lis in circle; outer legend **Reverse:** 4-line inscription

Date	Mintage	VG	F	VF	XF	Unc
ND(1791)	—	200	450	750	1,350	—

KM# Tn15 5 SOLS
Silver **Issuer:** Lefevre, Lesage et Comp., Paris **Obverse:** Liberty cap at top of pole within wreath **Reverse:** Large 5 in 50

Date	Mintage	VG	F	VF	XF	Unc
1792	—	15.00	30.00	50.00	75.00	—

KM# Tn16 5 SOLS
Silver **Issuer:** Lefevre, Lesage et Comp., Paris **Obverse:** Liberty cap at top of pole within wreath **Reverse:** Small 5 in 50

Date	Mintage	VG	F	VF	XF	Unc
1792	—	15.00	25.00	40.00	75.00	—

KM# Tn17 5 SOLS
Silver **Issuer:** Lefevre, Lesage et Comp., Paris **Reverse:** Without space after 50

Date	Mintage	VG	F	VF	XF	Unc
1792	—	15.00	30.00	50.00	75.00	—

KM# Tn28 5 SOLS
Bronze **Issuer:** Monneron Freres, Paris **Obverse:** Allegiance scene; Roman numeral date in exergue **Reverse:** 6-line legend and date in exergue; legend around border

Date	Mintage	VG	F	VF	XF	Unc
1792	—	10.00	25.00	50.00	125	—

KM# Tn30 5 SOLS
Bronze **Issuer:** Monneron Freres, Paris **Obverse:** Allegiance scene; Arabic date in exergue **Reverse:** 7-line inscription; LAN III in inner circle; legend around border

Date	Mintage	VG	F	VF	XF	Unc
1792//LAN III	—	7.50	15.00	50.00	100	—

KM# Tn30a 5 SOLS
Silver **Issuer:** Monneron Freres, Paris

Date	Mintage	VG	F	VF	XF	Unc
1792//LAN III	—	—	—	900	1,500	—

KM# Tn31 5 SOLS
Bronze **Issuer:** Monneron Freres, Paris **Obverse:** Allegiance scene **Obv. Legend:** VIVRE LIBRAS OU MOURIR **Reverse:** LAN IV is date in inner circle **Rev. Legend:** ...NAGOCIANS A PARIS •

Date	Mintage	VG	F	VF	XF	Unc
1792	—	5.00	10.00	20.00	50.00	—

KM# Tn35 5 SOLS
Bronze **Issuer:** Monneron Freres, Paris **Obverse:** Hercules **Obv. Legend:** LES FRANCAIS UNIS SONT INVINCIBLES **Reverse:** Inscription within inner circle **Rev. Legend:** REVOLUTION FRANCAISE •

Date	Mintage	VG	F	VF	XF	Unc
1792	—	30.00	50.00	85.00	150	—

KM# Tn35a 5 SOLS
Silver **Issuer:** Monneron Freres, Paris

Date	Mintage	VG	F	VF	XF	Unc
1792 Rare	—	—	—	—	—	—

KM# Tn32 5 SOLS
Silver **Issuer:** Potter, Paris

Date	Mintage	VG	F	VF	XF	Unc
1792	—	15.00	35.00	75.00	125	—

KM# Tn39 5 SOLS
Silver **Issuer:** Potter, Paris **Obverse:** 5-line legend within outside legend

Date	Mintage	VG	F	VF	XF	Unc
1792	—	15.00	30.00	45.00	85.00	—

KM# Tn34 5 SOLS
Bronze **Issuer:** Monneron Freres, Paris **Note:** Edge legend ends: ...DEPARTEMENS.

Date	Mintage	VG	F	VF	XF	Unc
1792	—	—	—	40.00	75.00	—

KM# Tn33 5 SOLS

Bronze **Issuer:** Monneron Freres, Paris **Reverse:** Inscription within circle **Rev. Legend:** REVOLUTION FRANCAISE **Note:** Edge legend ends: ...DEPARTEMENTS.

Date	Mintage	VG	F	VF	XF	Unc
1792	—	—	20.00	50.00	100	—

KM# Tn40 7 SOLS

Silver **Issuer:** Potter, Paris **Obverse:** 8-line inscription **Reverse:** 6-line inscription

Date	Mintage	VG	F	VF	XF	Unc
1792	—	20.00	40.00	75.00	125	—

KM# Tn9 10 SOLS

Bell Metal **Issuer:** Dairolant **Obverse:** Bust of Mirabeau left within legend **Reverse:** 8-line inscription within ornamented border

Date	Mintage	VG	F	VF	XF	Unc
1792	—	300	500	750	1,250	—

KM# Tn13 10 SOLS

Silver **Issuer:** Le Clech et Comp., Clermont **Obverse:** 5-line inscription in wreath; legend around border **Reverse:** 6-line inscription, legend around border

Date	Mintage	VG	F	VF	XF	Unc
1792	—	50.00	100	400	700	—

KM# Tn14 10 SOLS

Silver **Issuer:** Le Clech et Comp., Clermont **Reverse:** Value in center of outside legend

Date	Mintage	VG	F	VF	XF	Unc
LAN 4 (1792)	—	50.00	100	400	700	—

KM# Tn18 10 SOLS

Silver **Issuer:** Lefevre, Lesage et Comp., Paris **Obverse:** Standing figure **Reverse:** Inscription, legend around outer rim

Date	Mintage	VG	F	VF	XF	Unc
1792	—	15.00	25.00	50.00	75.00	—

KM# Tn41 10 SOLS

Silver **Issuer:** Potter, Paris **Obverse:** 8-line inscription **Reverse:** 6-line inscription **Rev. Legend:** 10 SOLS...

Date	Mintage	VG	F	VF	XF	Unc
1792	—	15.00	30.00	60.00	100	—

KM# Tn42 10 SOLS

Silver **Issuer:** Potter, Paris **Reverse:** 6-line inscription **Rev. Legend:** B. P. 10 SOLS... **Note:** Values given here are for later strikings from the 19th Century. Original strikings are very rare.

Date	Mintage	VG	F	VF	XF	Unc
1792	—	15.00	30.00	60.00	100	—

KM# Tn19 10 SOLS

Silver **Issuer:** Lefevre, Lesage et Comp., Paris **Obverse:** Seated figure **Reverse:** Inscription, legend around outer rim

Date	Mintage	VG	F	VF	XF	Unc
1792	—	15.00	25.00	50.00	75.00	—

KM# Tn3 15 SOLS

Billon **Issuer:** Brun **Obverse:** 4-line inscription above branches **Reverse:** 2-line inscription within outside legend

Date	Mintage	VG	F	VF	XF	Unc
AN 4 (1795)	—	200	350	600	850	—

KM# Tn2 18 SOLS

Billon **Issuer:** Brun **Obverse:** Rooster left below banner **Reverse:** 7-line inscription within outside legend

Date	Mintage	VG	F	VF	XF	Unc
ND(1792)	—	200	350	600	850	—

KM# Tn20 20 SOLS

Silver **Issuer:** Lefevre, Lesage et Comp., Paris **Obverse:** Seated figure **Reverse:** Inscription, legend around outer rim

Date	Mintage	VG	F	VF	XF	Unc
1792	—	20.00	30.00	65.00	100	—

KM# Tn43 20 SOLS

Silver **Issuer:** Potter, Paris **Obverse:** Inscription, legend around outer rim **Reverse:** Inscription within inner circle, legend around outer rim

Date	Mintage	VG	F	VF	XF	Unc
1792	—	20.00	30.00	50.00	80.00	—

KM# Tn43a 20 SOLS

Silver **Issuer:** Potter, Paris

Date	Mintage	VG	F	VF	XF	Unc
1972 Error	—	35.00	60.00	100	175	—

KM# Tn21 20 SOLS

Silver **Issuer:** Lefevre, Lesage et Comp., Paris **Obverse:** Seated figure **Reverse:** Inscription within inner circle, legend around outer rim

Date	Mintage	VG	F	VF	XF	Unc
1792	—	20.00	30.00	65.00	100	—

KM# Tn11 5 CENTIMES

Copper **Issuer:** Fabrique du Vast, Cherbourg **Reverse:** Value

Date	Mintage	VG	F	VF	XF	Unc
ND(1794)	—	15.00	20.00	30.00	50.00	—

KM# Tn45 10 CENTIMES

Copper **Issuer:** Fabrique du Vast, Cherbourg

Date	Mintage	VG	F	VF	XF	Unc
ND(1794)	—	15.00	25.00	35.00	65.00	—

CONSULSHIP

Napoleon as First Consul

DECIMAL COINAGE

KM# 639.1 5 FRANCS

25.0000 g., 0.9000 Silver 0.7234 oz. ASW **Mint:** Paris **Obverse:** Hercules group **Obv. Legend:** UNION ET FORCE • * **Reverse:** Value within oak wreath **Rev. Legend:** REPUBLIQUE FRANCAISE **Edge Lettering:** GARANTIE NATIONALE **Note:** Dav. #1337.

Date	Mintage	VG	F	VF	XF	Unc
LAN 4 (1795-96)A	7,471,000	25.00	50.00	125	375	—
LAN 5/4 (1796)A	Inc. above	40.00	75.00	175	425	—
LAN 5 (1796-97)A	Inc. above	22.00	45.00	100	350	—
LAN 6 (1797-98)A	1,452,000	22.00	45.00	100	400	—
LAN 7 (1798-99)A	2,656,000	15.00	40.00	100	350	—
LAN 8 (1799-1800)A	1,079,000	25.00	45.00	125	450	—
LAN 9 (1800-01)A	196,000	22.00	45.00	120	500	—
LAN 10 (1801-02)A	561,000	35.00	75.00	175	550	—
LAN 11 (1802-03)A	1,558,000	25.00	60.00	150	450	—

KM# 639.5 5 FRANCS

25.0000 g., 0.9000 Silver 0.7234 oz. ASW **Mint:** Bordeaux **Obverse:** Hercules group **Reverse:** Value within oak wreath

Date	Mintage	VG	F	VF	XF	Unc
LAN 5 (1796-97)K	228,000	30.00	80.00	220	550	—
LAN 6 (1797-98)K	89,000	30.00	80.00	220	850	—
LAN 7 (1798-99)K	64,000	40.00	100	250	900	—
LAN 8 (1799-1800)K	74,000	50.00	120	280	975	—
LAN 9 (1800-01)K	28,000	50.00	120	280	975	—
LAN 10 (1801-02)K	60,000	40.00	100	250	600	900
LAN 11 (1802-03)K	29,000	60.00	100	250	600	900

KM# 639.6 5 FRANCS

25.0000 g., 0.9000 Silver 0.7234 oz. ASW **Mint:** Bayonne **Obverse:** Hercules group **Obv. Legend:** UNION ET FORCE **Reverse:** Value within oak wreath **Rev. Legend:** REPUBLIQUE FRANCAISE

Date	Mintage	VG	F	VF	XF	Unc
LAN 5 (1796-97)L	—	100	275	550	2,000	—
LAN 6 (1797-98)L	181,000	35.00	90.00	275	750	—
LAN 7 (1798-99)L	419,000	20.00	60.00	175	500	—
LAN 8 (1799-1800)L	395,000	20.00	60.00	175	500	—
LAN 9 (1800-01)L	311,000	20.00	60.00	175	485	—
LAN 10 (1801-02)L	165,000	35.00	90.00	225	550	—
LAN 11 (1802-03)L	170,000	35.00	90.00	225	550	—

KM# 639.8 5 FRANCS

25.0000 g., 0.9000 Silver 0.7234 oz. ASW **Mint:** Perpignan **Obverse:** Hercules group **Reverse:** Value within oak wreath

Date	Mintage	VG	F	VF	XF	Unc
LAN 5 (1796-97)Q	537,000	20.00	40.00	110	500	—
LAN 6 (1797-98)Q	478,000	30.00	60.00	135	475	—
LAN 7 (1798-99)Q	616,000	20.00	40.00	125	450	—
LAN 8 (1799-1800)Q	1,160,000	15.00	30.00	100	425	—
LAN 9 (1800-01)Q	174,000	35.00	90.00	225	550	—
LAN 10 (1801-02)Q	134,000	35.00	90.00	225	550	—
LAN 11 (1802-03)Q	360,000	30.00	80.00	200	500	—

KM# 639.9 5 FRANCS

25.0000 g., 0.9000 Silver 0.7234 oz. ASW **Mint:** Nantes **Obverse:** Hercules group **Reverse:** Value within oak wreath

Date	Mintage	VG	F	VF	XF	Unc
LAN 5 (1796-97)T	19,000	60.00	125	350	1,250	—
LAN 6 (1797-98)T	49,000	50.00	120	300	1,150	—
LAN 7 (1798-99)T	35,000	50.00	120	300	1,150	—
LAN 8 (1799-1800)T	47,000	50.00	120	300	1,150	—
LAN 9 (1800-01)T	20,000	60.00	135	350	1,200	—
LAN 10 (1801-02)T Reported, not confirmed	5,232	—	—	—	—	—
LAN 11 (1802-03)T	9,950	70.00	165	400	1,350	—

KM# 639.4 5 FRANCS

25.0000 g., 0.9000 Silver 0.7234 oz. ASW **Mint:** Poitiers **Obverse:** Hercules group **Reverse:** Value within oak wreath

Date	Mintage	VG	F	VF	XF	Unc
LAN 9 (1799-1800)G	6,985	100	250	500	2,000	—
LAN 10 (1801-02)G	4,447	125	300	600	22.00	—

KM# 639.7 5 FRANCS
25.0000 g., 0.9000 Silver 0.7234 oz. ASW **Mint:** Marseille **Obverse:** Hercules group **Reverse:** Value within oak wreath

Date	Mintage	VG	F	VF	XF	Unc
LAN 9 (1800-01)MA	2,201	—	—	—	—	—
LAN 10 (1801-02)MA	39,000	50.00	125	300	1,150	—
LAN 11 (1802-03)MA	160,000	35.00	90.00	225	550	—

ESSAIS

Standard metals unless otherwise noted

KM#	Date	Mintage	Identification	Mkt Val
E3	1740	—	Ecu. Gold. KM#512.1.	9,000
E4	1741	—	1/2 Ecu. Silver. KM#516.1.	—

PATTERNS

Including off metal strikes

KM#	Date	Mintage	Identification	Mkt Val
Pn12	1740A	—	1/20 Ecu. 6 Sols.	—
Pn13	1740A	—	1/10 Ecu.	—
Pn14	1740A	—	Ecu. au Bandeau.	—
Pn15	1740A	—	Ecu. Gold. au Bandeau.	—
Pn16	1741A	—	1/2 Ecu.	—
Pn17	1770A	—	Ecu.	—
Pn18	1771A	—	1/2 Ecu.	—
Pn19	1771A	—	Ecu.	—

KM#	Date	Mintage	Identification	Mkt Val
PnB20	1793//LAN 5	—	24 Livres. Copper.	1,250

PIEFORTS WITH ESSAI

Double thickness; standard metals unless otherwise noted

KM#	Date	Mintage	Identification	Mkt Val
P80	1710	—	6 Deniers. Lettered edge, DENIER FORT.	—

TRIAL STRIKES

KM#	Date	Mintage	Identification	Mkt Val
TS1	(1796-87)	—	Ecu. Uniface.	—

FRENCH STATES

AIRE

(Aire-sur-la-lys, Artois)

A town in north France on the Lys, lies in a low and marshy area at the junction of 3. canals

In the middle ages, Aire belonged to the counts of Flanders and a charter of 1188 is still extant. It was given to France by the Peace of Utrecht in 1713. In World War I, it was one of the headquarters of the British Army Expeditionary Forces.

NOTE: See also Spanish Netherlands-Artois.

COUNTY

SIEGE COINAGE

1710

Issued by the governor, M. de Goesbriant under Allied siege

KM# 15.1 25 SOLS
Silver **Obv:** Crowned circular shield, date below **Note:** Uniface diamond klippe.

Date	Mintage	VG	F	VF	XF	Unc
1710	—	60.00	120	250	450	—

KM# 15.2 25 SOLS
Silver **Obv:** Crowned circular shield, date below **Note:** Uniface octagonal klippe.

Date	Mintage	VG	F	VF	XF	Unc
1710	—	50.00	100	200	300	—

KM# 16 50 SOLS
Silver **Obv:** Crowned circular shield divides date **Note:** Uniface octagonal klippe.

Date	Mintage	VG	F	VF	XF	Unc
1710	—	75.00	150	350	500	—

LILLE

A city located 130 miles northeast of Paris with a population of 190,546. Manufactures textiles, iron, steel, machinery and chemicals and operates sugar refineries, breweries and distilleries.

Founded ca.1030, the city was the medieval capital of Flanders but was a possession of Austria and Spain until it was recaptured by Louis XIV. Lille was captured in 1708 and coins were struck while the city was beseiged. It was later restored to France in 1713.

The Germans occupied the city from 1914-1918 and it was an important link in the Hindenburg Line during WWI. In 1940 the Germans once again occupied the city and remained until towards the end of WWII in 1944.

CITY

SIEGE COINAGE

Issued under the Authority of Marshal Louis Francois Boofllers during a three month resistance of the allied English forces under Marlborough and Austrian under Eugene.

KM# 5 5 SOLS
Copper **Obv:** Crowned circular shield, crossed sceptres behind **Rev:** Inscription

Date	Mintage	VG	F	VF	XF	Unc
1708	—	15.00	25.00	50.00	75.00	—

KM# 6 10 SOLS
Copper **Obv:** Similar to 5 Sols, KM#5 **Rev:** Similar to 20 Sols, KM#7

Date	Mintage	VG	F	VF	XF	Unc
1708	—	20.00	30.00	50.00	85.00	—

KM# 7 20 SOLS
Copper **Obv:** Crowned circular shield on crossed pikes, Order chain in background **Rev:** Inscription

Date	Mintage	VG	F	VF	XF	Unc
1708	—	20.00	35.00	65.00	110	—

ORANGE

Principality in south-central France, with the town of Orange being 18 miles north of Avignon. Originally became of importance during the time of Charlemagne. Passed through the houses of Baux and Chalon. William III (1650-1702) was the last ruler of Orange. William's attention was drawn to the Netherlands and in 1672 the troops of Louis XIV occupied Orange and it was incorporated into France (though actual title did not pass until 1713). William became King of England in 1689.

RULERS
Philip William, 1584-1618
Maurice, 1618-1625
Frederick Henry, 1625-1647
William IX of Nassau, 1647-1650
William Henry of Nassau, 1650-1702

MONETARY SYSTEM
3 Deniers = 1 Liard
4 Liards = 1 Sol
20 Sols = 1 Livre
6 Livres = 1 Ecu
4 Ecus = 1 D'or

PRINCIPALITY

STANDARD COINAGE

KM# 109 DENIER TOURNOIS
Copper **Obv:** Similar to KM#107 **Rev:** Cornet and three lis

Date	Mintage	VG	F	VF	XF	Unc
ND(1650-1702)	—	12.50	25.00	50.00	100	—

KM# 111 DENIER TOURNOIS
Copper **Obv:** Later bust

Date	Mintage	VG	F	VF	XF	Unc
ND(1650-1702)	—	12.50	25.00	50.00	100	—

TRADE COINAGE

KM# 125 ZECCHINO
3.5000 g., 0.9860 Gold 0.1109 oz. AGW **Obv:** Prince kneeling before Christ **Rev:** Madonna in oval shield

Date	Mintage	VG	F	VF	XF	Unc
ND(1650-1702)	—	350	800	1,300	2,000	—

The coins catalogued under this heading were not issued for use in any particular colony but were intended for general use in the West Indies, particularly Martinique, Guadeloupe, and Saint-Dominique (western Hispaniola) until it attained independence as Haiti in 1804.

RULER
French

MINT MARKS
A - Paris
H – LaRochelle

MONETARY SYSTEM
100 Centimes = 1 Franc

COLONIAL

MILLED COINAGE

KM# 3 6 DENIERS
Bronze **Obverse:** Head right **Obv. Legend:** LVD • XV • D • G • ... **Reverse:** Value, date

Date	Mintage	Good	VG	F	VF	XF
1717Q Rare	—	—	—	—	—	—

KM# 8 6 DENIERS (2 Sols)
1.9000 g., Billon **Obverse:** Double L monogram **Reverse:** Value within decorative circle **Note:** Similar to 3 Sous, KM#9.

Date	Mintage	VG	F	VF	XF	Unc
1786A	—	30.00	60.00	120	325	—

KM# 5.1 9 DENIERS

Copper **Obverse:** Crowned monogram **Obv. Legend:** SIT • NOMEN • DOMINI • BENEDICTUM • **Reverse:** Value, date **Rev. Legend:** COLONIES FRANCOISES

Date	Mintage	Good	VG	F	VF	XF
1721B	—	15.00	30.00	100	200	—
1722B	—	8.00	15.00	60.00	125	—

KM# 5.2 9 DENIERS

Copper **Mint:** La Rochelle **Obverse:** Crowned monogram **Reverse:** Value, date

Date	Mintage	Good	VG	F	VF	XF
1721H	—	10.00	25.00	75.00	175	—
1722/1H	—	15.00	35.00	95.00	195	—
1722H	—	10.00	25.00	75.00	175	—

KM# 4 12 DENIERS (Sol)

Bronze **Obverse:** Young bust of Louis XV right **Reverse:** Value and date

Date	Mintage	Good	VG	F	VF	XF
1717Q Rare	—	—	—	—	—	—

Note: Heritage ANA sale 8-90, F-15 realized $29,000

KM# 6 12 DENIERS (Sol)

Bronze **Mint:** Paris **Obverse:** Arms of France within crowned wreath **Obv. Legend:** SIT NOMEN DOMINI BENEDICTUM **Reverse:** Crossed sceptres divide monogram **Rev. Legend:** COLONIES FRANCOISES

Date	Mintage	Good	VG	F	VF	XF
1767A	—	18.00	40.00	90.00	285	—

KM# 7 3 SOLS (Trois Sous)

1.9000 g., Billon **Mint:** Paris **Obverse:** Crowned Lis within legend **Reverse:** Value and date within legend

Date	Mintage	VG	F	VF	XF	Unc
1781A	—	10.00	20.00	50.00	100	—

KM# 9 3 SOLS (Trois Sous)

1.9000 g., Billon **Obverse:** Double L monogram **Obv. Legend:** LUD • XVI • D • G • FR • ET NAV • REX • **Reverse:** Value and date within decorative circle

Date	Mintage	VG	F	VF	XF	Unc
1787I	—	20.00	50.00	100	300	—

COUNTERMARKED COINAGE

1763

KM# 1.1 STAMPEE

Billon **Countermark:** Large (12mm) crowned C. **Note:** Countermark on France 2 Sols, KM#500.1.

CM Date	Host Date	Good	VG	F	VF	XF
ND(1763)	ND	5.00	10.00	20.00	45.00	—

KM# 1.2 STAMPEE

Billon **Countermark:** Small (7mm) crowned C. **Note:** Countermark on France 2 Sols, KM#500.1.

CM Date	Host Date	Good	VG	F	VF	XF
ND(1763)	ND	5.00	12.50	30.00	65.00	—

COUNTERSTAMPED COINAGE

1779

KM# 2 STAMPEE

Billon **Counterstamp:** Large (12mm) crowned C **Note:** Counterstamp on blank planchet.

CS Date	Host Date	Good	VG	F	VF	XF
ND(1779)	ND	5.00	10.00	17.50	40.00	—

ESSAIS

Standard metals unless otherwise noted

KM#	Date	Mintage	Identification	Mkt Val
E1	1781A	—	3 Sols. Silver. . Denomination.	425
E2	1781R	—	3 Sols. Billon. . Monogram Ls.	500

The French Overseas Department of Guiana, located on the northeast coast of South America, bordered by Surinam and Brazil, has an area of 33,399 sq. mi. (91,000 sq. km.). Capital: Cayenne. Placer gold mining and shrimp processing are the chief industries. Shrimp, lumber, gold, cocoa, and bananas are exported.

The coast of Guiana was sighted by Columbus in 1498 and explored by Amerigo Vespucci in 1499. The French established the first successful trading stations and settlements, and placed the area under direct control of the French Crown in 1674. Portuguese and British forces occupied French Guiana for five years during the Napoleonic Wars. Devil's Island, the notorious penal colony in French Guiana where Capt. Alfred Dreyfus was imprisoned, was established in 1852 and finally closed in 1947. When France adopted a new constitution in 1946, French Guiana voted to remain within the French Union as an Overseas Department. It now hosts some of the French and Common Market space and satellite stations.

In the late 18th century, a series of 2 sous coins was struck for the colony. It is probable that contemporary imitations of these issues, many emanating from Birmingham, England, outnumber the originals. These, both genuine and bogus, host coins for many West Indies counterstamps. As an Overseas Department, Guiana now uses the coins of metropolitan France, however, the franc used in the former colony was always distinct in value from that of the homeland as well as that used in the islands of the French West Indies.

RULER

French

MINT MARK

A – Paris

MONETARY SYSTEM

(Commencing 1794)

100 Centimes = 10 Decimes = 1 Franc

COLONY OF CAYENNE

COLONIAL COINAGE

KM# 1 2 SOUS

Billon, Copper, Or Bronze, 23 mm. **Obv:** Flat base crown **Note:** Coins dated 1780, 1781, 1783 and 1786 are regarded by many authorities as spurious. Coins with curved base crown are contemporary forgeries, mostly of brass and originating in Birmingham. Many die varieties exist, notably with Roman and Arabic 1's for the first numeral in the date and in numerous metals.

Date	Mintage	VG	F	VF	XF	Unc
1780A	—	5.00	12.50	35.00	110	—
1781A	—	8.00	22.00	60.00	125	—
1782A	—	5.00	10.00	30.00	95.00	—
1783A	—	10.00	25.00	65.00	145	—
1786A	—	10.00	25.00	65.00	145	—
1787A	—	10.00	25.00	65.00	145	—
1788A	—	12.00	30.00	75.00	165	—
1789A	—	2.00	5.00	12.50	35.00	—
1790A	—	15.00	35.00	85.00	225	—

KM# 1a 2 SOUS

Silver

Date	Mintage	VG	F	VF	XF	Unc
1789	—	30.00	60.00	150	325	—

KM# 2a 3 SOUS

Copper

Date	Mintage	VG	F	VF	XF	Unc
1781	—	—	—	—	—	—

Note: Reported, not confirmed

PIEFORTS

KM#	Date	Mintage	Identification	Mkt Val
P1	1789A	—	10 Centimes.	500

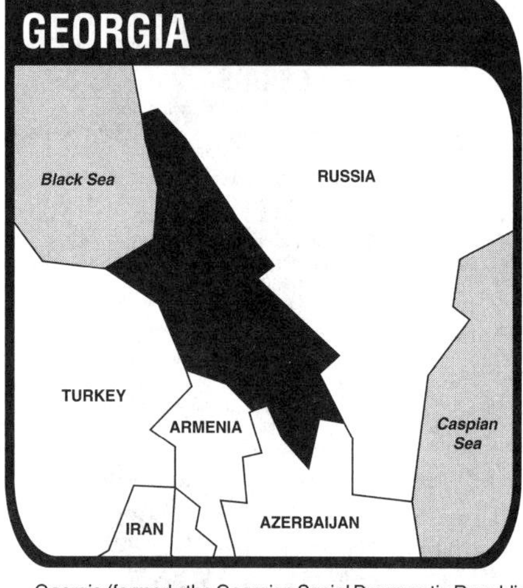

Georgia (formerly the Georgian Social Democratic Republic under the U.S.S.R.), is bounded by the Black Sea to the west and by Turkey, Armenia and Azerbaijan. It occupies the western part of Transcaucasia covering an area of 26,900 sq. mi. (69,700 sq. km.) and a population of 5.7 million. Capitol: Tbilisi. Hydro-electricity, minerals, forestry and agriculture are the chief industries.

The Georgian dynasty first emerged after the Macedonian victory over the Achaemenid Persian Empire in the 4th century B.C. Roman "friendship" was imposed in 65 B.C. after Pompey's victory over Mithradates. The Georgians embraced Christianity in the 4th century A.D. During the next three centuries Georgia was involved in the ongoing conflicts between the Byzantine and Persian empires. The latter developed control until Georgia regained its independence in 450-503 A.D. but then it reverted to a Persian province in 533 A.D., then restored as a kingdom by the Byzantines in 562 A.D. It was established as an Arab emirate in the 8th century. The Seljuk Turks invaded but the crusades thwarted their interests. Over the following centuries, Turkish and Persian rivalries along with civil strife divided the area under the two influences.

Through significant contributions of Georgian kings (King David the Builder 1089-1124 and King Tamara 1136-1224), Georgia reached its peak of political, economic, and military development from the XI - to the XIII century. During these centuries the significant architectural and literary masterpieces that had won international recognition were created. Georgia had also regained territories that had been invaded by Islamic countries.

Czarist Russian interests increased and a treaty of alliance was signed on July 24, 1773 whereby Russia guaranteed Georgian independence and it acknowledged Russian suzerainty. Persia invaded again in 1795 leaving Tiflis in ruins. Russia slowly took over annexing piece-by-piece and soon developed total domination. After the Russian Revolution the Georgians, Armenians, and Azerbaijanis formed the short-lived Transcaucasian Federal Republic on Sept. 20, 1917, which broke up into three independent republics on May 26, 1918. A Germano-- Georgian treaty was signed on May 28, 1918, followed by a Turko-Georgian peace treaty on June 4. The end of WW I and the collapse of the central powers allowed free elections.

On May 20, 1920, Soviet Russia concluded a peace treaty, recognizing its independence, but later invaded on Feb. 11, 1921 and a soviet republic was proclaimed. On March 12, 1922 Stalin included Georgia in a newly formed Transcaucasian Soviet Federated Socialist Republic. On Dec. 5, 1936 the T.S.F.S.R. was dissolved and Georgia became a direct member of the U.S.S.R. The collapse of the U.S.S.R. allowed full transition to independence and on April 9, 1991 a unanimous vote declared the republic an independent state based on its original treaty of independence of May 1918.

RULERS

Ottoman

Ahmad III, AH1115-1143/1703-1730AD

Mahmud II, AH1143-1148/1730-1735AD

Iranian

T'eimuraz II, Alone, AH1157-1166/1744-1752AD

With Erekle II, AH1166-1176/1752-1762AD

Erekle II, AH1176-1213/1762-1798AD

Local

Giorgi XII, AH1213-1215/1798-1800AD

MINT NAME

تفليس

Tiflis

MONETARY SYSTEM

5 Dinar = 1 Puli (Kazbegi)

4 Puli = 1 Bisti

2-1/2 Bisti = 1 Shahi

1/4 Abazi (Abassi) = 4 Para

1/2 Abazi = 8 Para

8 Para = 1 Beslik
4 Shahi = 1 Abazi
1 Abazi = 16 Para
16 Para = 1 Onluk
5 Abazi = 1 Rouble

KINGDOM

OTTOMAN COINAGE

KM# 15.2 FALUS

Copper **Ruler:** Ahmad III **Obv:** Peacock left

Date	Mintage	Good	VG	F	VF	XF
AH1130	—	—	—	—	—	—

KM# 15.1 FALUS

Copper **Ruler:** Ahmad III **Obv:** Peacock right

Date	Mintage	Good	VG	F	VF	XF
AH1130	—	15.00	25.00	40.00	65.00	—
AH1131	—	15.00	25.00	40.00	65.00	—

KM# 5 1/4 ABBASI

Silver **Ruler:** Ahmad III **Obv:** Toughra **Note:** Weight varies 1.18-1.31 grams. 15-16mm.

Date	Mintage	Good	VG	F	VF	XF
AH1115	—	—	—	—	—	—

KM# 20 1/4 ABBASI

1.3000 g., Silver, 13 mm. **Ruler:** Mahmud I **Obv:** Toughra

Date	Mintage	Good	VG	F	VF	XF
AH1143	—	250	400	600	800	—

KM# 6 1/2 ABBASI

Silver, 16-20 mm. **Ruler:** Ahmad III **Obv:** Toughra **Rev:** Inscription **Note:** Weight varies: 2.20-2.65g. Size varies.

Date	Mintage	Good	VG	F	VF	XF
AH1115	—	150	200	400	500	—

KM# 21 1/2 ABBASI

2.5000 g., Silver, 16 mm. **Ruler:** Mahmud I **Obv:** Toughra

Date	Mintage	Good	VG	F	VF	XF
AH1143	—	200	300	450	600	—

KM# 7 ABBASI

Silver, 23-26 mm. **Ruler:** Ahmad III **Obv:** Toughra **Rev:** Inscription **Note:** Weight varies: 4.49-5.32g. Size varies.

Date	Mintage	Good	VG	F	VF	XF
AH1115	—	15.00	30.00	50.00	80.00	—

Note: Overstrikes on Safavid Abbasis exist.

KM# 8 CEDID CINCIRLI

Gold, 18-19 mm. **Ruler:** Ahmad III **Obv:** Toughra **Rev:** Inscription **Note:** Weight varies: 3.30-3.47g. Size varies.

Date	Mintage	Good	VG	F	VF	XF
AH1115	—	—	750	1,250	1,850	—

KM# 9 TEK ESHREFI

3.0600 g., Gold, 29-30 mm. **Ruler:** Ahmad III **Obv:** Toughra **Note:** Size varies.

Date	Mintage	Good	VG	F	VF	XF
AH1115 Rare	—	—	—	—	—	—

KM# 10 ALTUN

Gold **Ruler:** Ahmad III **Obv:** Toughra **Rev:** Inscription **Note:** Weight varies 6.08-6.75 grams. Size varies 31-32mm.

Date	Mintage	Good	VG	F	VF	XF
AH1115	—	500	750	1,000	1,100	—

KM# 22 ONLUK (Abbasi = 16 Para)

5.2800 g., Silver, 21-22 mm. **Ruler:** Mahmud I **Obv:** Toughra **Rev:** Arabic legend, "Duriba Fi Tiflis" **Note:** Weight varies: 5.05-5.44g. Size varies.

Date	Mintage	Good	VG	F	VF	XF
AH1143	—	150	200	350	500	—

Note: Overstrikes on Safavid Abbasis exist

LOCAL COINAGE

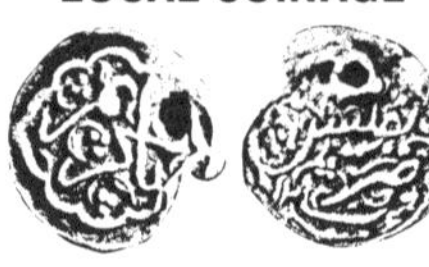

KM# 46 1/2 ABAZI

1.5000 g., Silver **Ruler:** Erekle (Heracles) II **Obv:** Legend **Rev:** Legend **Note:** Anonymous issues.

Date	Mintage	VG	F	VF	XF	Unc
AH1183	—	18.50	30.00	50.00	90.00	—
AH1206	—	18.50	30.00	50.00	90.00	—
AH1211	—	18.50	30.00	50.00	90.00	—

KM# 17 ABAZI

3.0200 g., Silver **Ruler:** T'eimuraz II, with Erekle II **Obv:** Legend **Rev:** Legend **Note:** Anonymous issue.

Date	Mintage	Good	VG	F	VF	XF
AH1166	—	20.00	35.00	60.00	100	—

KM# 33 ABAZI

3.1000 g., Silver **Ruler:** T'eimuraz II, with Erekle II **Note:** Anonymous issue.

Date	Mintage	VG	F	VF	XF	Unc
AH1168	—	20.00	35.00	60.00	100	—

KM# 39 ABAZI

3.1000 g., Silver **Ruler:** Erekle (Heracles) II **Obv:** Legend **Rev:** Legend **Note:** Anonymous issues.

Date	Mintage	VG	F	VF	XF	Unc
AH1179	—	20.00	30.00	45.00	60.00	—
AH1180	—	20.00	30.00	45.00	60.00	—
AH1182	—	20.00	30.00	45.00	60.00	—
AH1183	—	20.00	30.00	45.00	60.00	—
AH1184	—	20.00	30.00	45.00	60.00	—
AH1190	—	20.00	30.00	45.00	60.00	—
AH1192	—	20.00	30.00	45.00	60.00	—
AH1193	—	20.00	30.00	45.00	60.00	—
AH1194	—	20.00	30.00	45.00	60.00	—
AH1195	—	20.00	30.00	45.00	60.00	—
AH1196	—	20.00	30.00	45.00	60.00	—
AH1197	—	20.00	30.00	45.00	60.00	—
AH1198	—	20.00	30.00	45.00	60.00	—
AH1166	—	20.00	30.00	45.00	60.00	—

Note: With inverted 9's (error)

Date	Mintage	VG	F	VF	XF	Unc
AH1201	—	20.00	30.00	45.00	60.00	—
AH1202	—	20.00	30.00	45.00	60.00	—
AH1203	—	20.00	30.00	45.00	60.00	—
AH1204	—	20.00	30.00	45.00	60.00	—
AH1205	—	20.00	30.00	45.00	60.00	—
AH1206	—	20.00	30.00	45.00	60.00	—
AH1207	—	20.00	30.00	45.00	60.00	—
AH1208	—	20.00	30.00	45.00	60.00	—
AH1209	—	20.00	30.00	45.00	60.00	—
AH1210	—	20.00	30.00	45.00	60.00	—
AH1211	—	20.00	30.00	45.00	60.00	—

KM# 67 ABAZI

2.9500 g., Silver **Ruler:** Giorgi XII **Obv:** Legend **Rev:** Legend **Note:** Anonymous issues.

Date	Mintage	Good	VG	F	VF	XF
AH1213	—	25.00	45.00	75.00	125	—

KM# 45 3 ABAZI

8.9000 g., Silver **Ruler:** Erekle (Heracles) II **Note:** Anonymous issues. Similar to Abazi, KM#39.

Date	Mintage	VG	F	VF	XF	Unc
AH1182	—	—	—	—	—	—

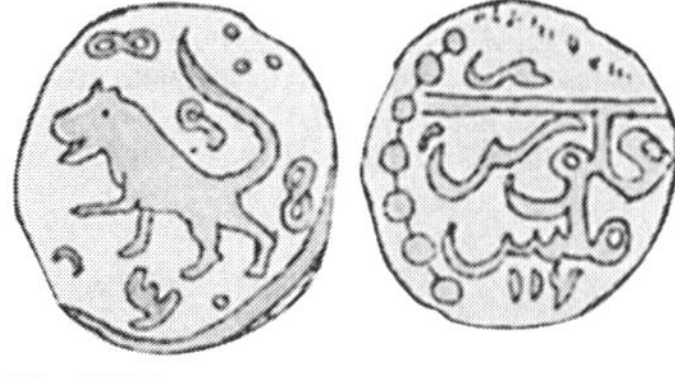

KM# 25 PULI

4.2700 g., Copper **Ruler:** T'eimuraz II, alone **Obv:** Lion left **Rev:** Legend

Date	Mintage	Good	VG	F	VF	XF
AH1160	—	15.00	25.00	40.00	65.00	—
AH1162	—	15.00	25.00	40.00	65.00	—
AH1163	—	15.00	25.00	40.00	65.00	—

KM# 35 PULI

4.7600 g., Copper **Ruler:** Erekle (Heracles) II **Obv:** Crowned scales over orb between swords **Rev:** 3 Georgian letters in cartouche mint name below

Date	Mintage	Good	VG	F	VF	XF
AH1178	—	11.50	18.50	30.00	50.00	—
AH1179	—	11.50	18.50	30.00	50.00	—

KM# 50 PULI

Copper **Ruler:** Erekle (Heracles) II **Obv:** Fish between floral designs **Rev:** Legend **Note:** Weight varies 5.90-5.94 grams.

Date	Mintage	Good	VG	F	VF	XF
AH1190	—	11.50	18.50	30.00	50.00	—
AH1195	—	11.50	18.50	30.00	50.00	—

KM# 55 PULI

4.5000 g., Copper **Ruler:** Erekle (Heracles) II **Note:** Similar to Bisti, KM#47.

Date	Mintage	Good	VG	F	VF	XF
AH1201 (1787)	—	—	—	—	—	—

KM# 63 PULI

4.4000 g., Copper **Ruler:** Giorgi XII **Obv:** Fish between floral designs **Rev:** Legends **Note:** Similar to 2 Puli, KM#64.

Date	Mintage	Good	VG	F	VF	XF
AH1213	—	15.00	25.00	40.00	65.00	—

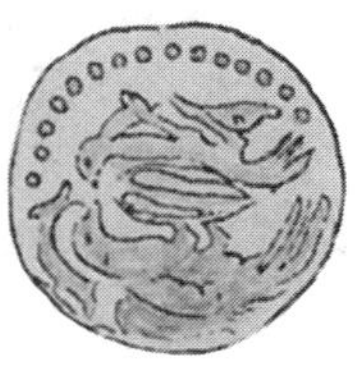

KM# 32 2 PULI

Copper **Ruler:** T'eimuraz II, with Erekle II **Obv:** Falcon striking heron **Rev:** Legend

Date	Mintage	Good	VG	F	VF	XF
AH1165	—	15.00	25.00	40.00	65.00	—
AH1166	—	15.00	25.00	40.00	65.00	—
AH1169	—	15.00	25.00	40.00	65.00	—

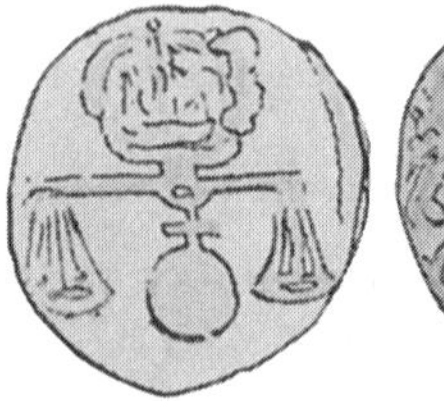

KM# 36 2 PULI

Copper **Ruler:** Erekle (Heracles) II **Obv:** Crown above orb at center of sscales **Rev:** 3 Letters within design **Note:** Weight varies 8.00-9.00 grams.

Date	Mintage	Good	VG	F	VF	XF
AH1178	—	15.00	28.00	50.00	70.00	—
AH1179	—	15.00	28.00	50.00	70.00	—

KM# 51 2 PULI

11.0000 g., Copper **Ruler:** Erekle (Heracles) II **Obv:** Fish between floral designs **Rev:** Legend

Date	Mintage	Good	VG	F	VF	XF
AH1190	—	15.00	28.00	50.00	70.00	—
AH1195	—	15.00	28.00	50.00	70.00	—

KM# 56 2 PULI

Copper **Ruler:** Erekle (Heracles) II **Obv:** Double-headed eagle **Rev:** Legend **Note:** Weight varies 8.00-9.00 grams.

Date	Mintage	Good	VG	F	VF	XF
AH1201 (1787) Error 1787	—	15.00	28.00	50.00	70.00	—

KM# 64 2 PULI

Copper **Ruler:** Giorgi XII **Obv:** Fish between floral designs **Rev:** Legends **Note:** Weight varies 9.00-10.00 grams.

Date	Mintage	Good	VG	F	VF	XF
AH1213	—	15.00	28.00	45.00	70.00	—
AH1215	—	15.00	28.00	45.00	70.00	—

KM# 66 SHAHI

0.7400 g., Billon **Ruler:** Giorgi XII **Obv:** Legend **Rev:** Legend **Note:** Anonymous issues. Some authorities believe this coin to possibly be a counterfeit 1/2 Abazi.

Date	Mintage	Good	VG	F	VF	XF
AH1213	—	—	—	—	—	—

KM# 60 BISTI

Copper **Ruler:** Erekle (Heracles) II **Obv:** Eagle with orb and sword divides date below **Rev:** Legend within beaded circle **Note:** Weight varies 19.00-22.00 grams.

Date	Mintage	Good	VG	F	VF	XF
AH1201 (1786)	—	15.00	25.00	40.00	65.00	—
AH1210 (1796)	—	15.00	25.00	40.00	65.00	—

KM# 57 BISTI

16.6000 g., Copper **Ruler:** Erekle (Heracles) II **Obv:** Double-headed eagle **Rev:** Legend

Date	Mintage	Good	VG	F	VF	XF
AH1201 (1787) Error	—	50.00	70.00	100	140	—
AH1202 (1788)	—	11.50	18.50	30.00	50.00	—

KM# 68 BISTI

Copper **Ruler:** David, as Regent **Obv:** Peacock **Rev. Legend:** "TPLS" (TIFLIS)

Date	Mintage	Good	VG	F	VF	XF
AH1215 Rare	—	—	—	—	—	—

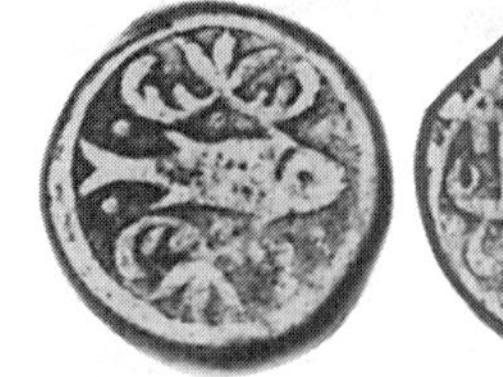

KM# 65 BISTI (4 Puli)

19.4400 g., Copper **Ruler:** Giorgi XII **Obv:** Fish between floral designs **Rev:** Legend **Note:** Anonymous issues.

Date	Mintage	Good	VG	F	VF	XF
AH1213 Rare	—	—	—	—	—	—

KM# 62 BISTI (4 Puli)

19.4400 g., Copper **Ruler:** Erekle (Heracles) II **Obv:** Fish between floral designs **Rev:** Legend

Date	Mintage	Good	VG	F	VF	XF
AH1213 (1798)	—	—	—	—	—	—

COUNTERMARKED COINAGE

Countermark: Monogram of Erekle II in square

KM# 37 PULI

4.7600 g., Copper **Ruler:** Erekle (Heracles) II **Countermark:** Monogram of Erekle II in square; monogram of Puli, KM#35

CM Date	Host Date	Good	VG	F	VF	XF
ND(1796-98)	AH1178	15.00	25.00	40.00	65.00	—
ND(1796-98)	AH1179	15.00	25.00	40.00	65.00	—

KM# 38 2 PULI

Copper **Ruler:** Erekle (Heracles) II **Countermark:** Monogram on 2 Puli, KM#36 **Note:** Weight varies 8.00-9.00 grams.

CM Date	Host Date	Good	VG	F	VF	XF
ND(1796-98)	AH1178	18.00	28.00	45.00	70.00	—
ND(1796-98)	AH1179	18.00	28.00	45.00	70.00	—

KM# 58 BISTI

16.6000 g., Copper **Ruler:** Erekle (Heracles) II **Countermark:** Monogram on Bisti, KM#57

CM Date	Host Date	Good	VG	F	VF	XF
ND(1796-98)	AH1201	15.00	25.00	40.00	65.00	—
ND(1796-98)	AH1202	15.00	25.00	40.00	65.00	—

KM# 61 BISTI

Copper **Ruler:** Erekle (Heracles) II **Countermark:** Monogram on Bisti, KM#60 **Note:** Weight varies 19.00-22.00 grams.

CM Date	Host Date	Good	VG	F	VF	XF
ND(1796-98)	AH1210	12.00	20.00	35.00	60.00	—

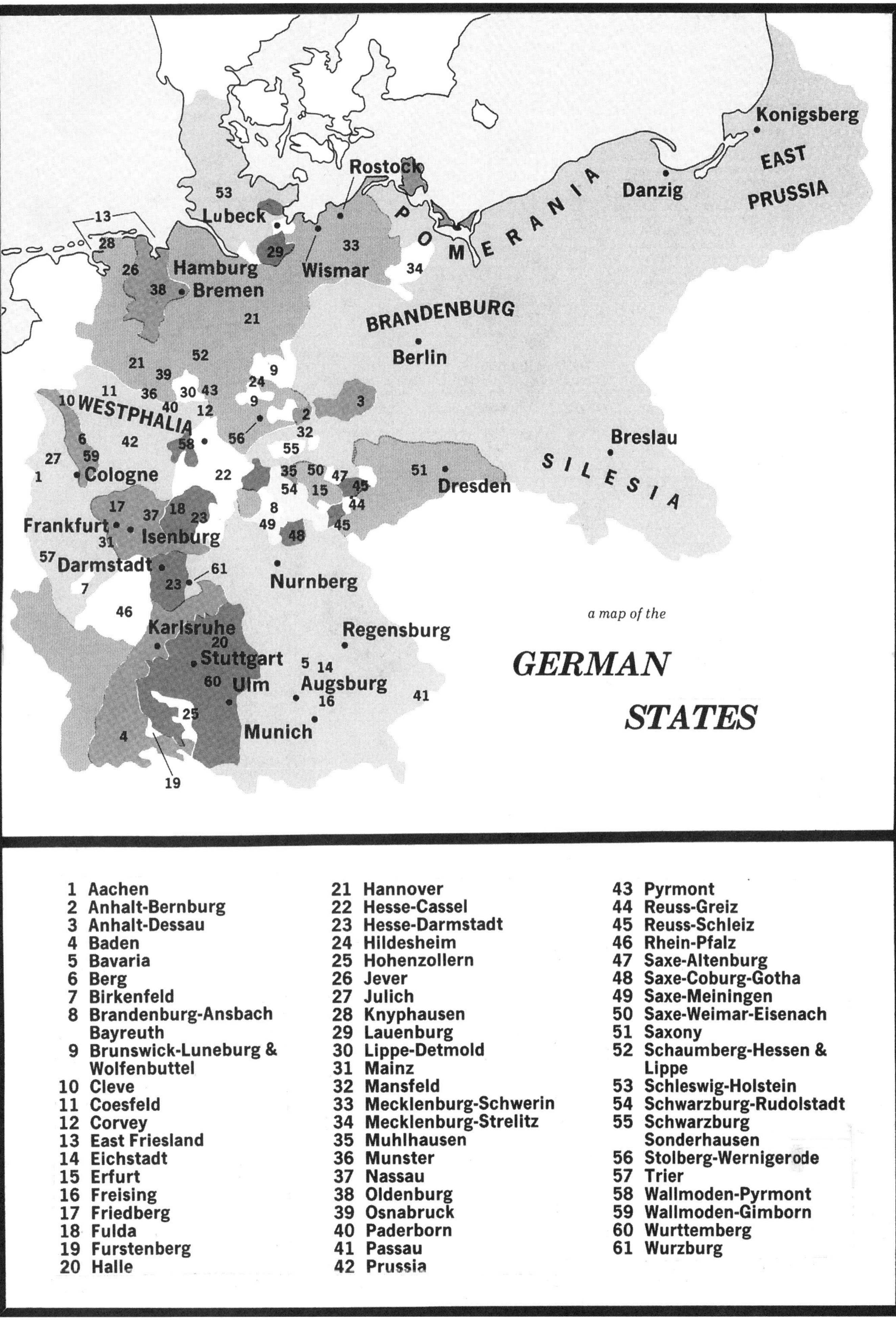

a map of the

GERMAN STATES

1 Aachen
2 Anhalt-Bernburg
3 Anhalt-Dessau
4 Baden
5 Bavaria
6 Berg
7 Birkenfeld
8 Brandenburg-Ansbach Bayreuth
9 Brunswick-Luneburg & Wolfenbuttel
10 Cleve
11 Coesfeld
12 Corvey
13 East Friesland
14 Eichstadt
15 Erfurt
16 Freising
17 Friedberg
18 Fulda
19 Furstenberg
20 Halle
21 Hannover
22 Hesse-Cassel
23 Hesse-Darmstadt
24 Hildesheim
25 Hohenzollern
26 Jever
27 Julich
28 Knyphausen
29 Lauenburg
30 Lippe-Detmold
31 Mainz
32 Mansfeld
33 Mecklenburg-Schwerin
34 Mecklenburg-Strelitz
35 Muhlhausen
36 Munster
37 Nassau
38 Oldenburg
39 Osnabruck
40 Paderborn
41 Passau
42 Prussia
43 Pyrmont
44 Reuss-Greiz
45 Reuss-Schleiz
46 Rhein-Pfalz
47 Saxe-Altenburg
48 Saxe-Coburg-Gotha
49 Saxe-Meiningen
50 Saxe-Weimar-Eisenach
51 Saxony
52 Schaumberg-Hessen & Lippe
53 Schleswig-Holstein
54 Schwarzburg-Rudolstadt
55 Schwarzburg Sonderhausen
56 Stolberg-Wernigerode
57 Trier
58 Wallmoden-Pyrmont
59 Wallmoden-Gimborn
60 Wurttemberg
61 Wurzburg

GERMAN STATES

Although the origin of the German Empire can be traced to the Treaty of Verdun that ceded Charlemagne's lands east of the Rhine to German Prince Louis, it was for centuries little more than a geographic expression, consisting of hundreds of effectively autonomous big and little states. Nominally the states owed their allegiance to the Holy Roman Emperor, who was also a German king, but as the Emperors exhibited less and less concern for Germany the actual power devolved on the lords of the individual states. The fragmentation of the empire climaxed with the tragic denouement of the Thirty Years War, 1618-48, which devastated much of Germany, destroyed its agriculture and medieval commercial eminence and ended the attempt of the Hapsburgs to unify Germany. Deprived of administrative capacity by a lack of resources, the imperial authority became utterly powerless. At this time Germany contained an estimated 1,800 individual states, some with a population of as little as 300. The German Empire of recent history (the creation of Bismarck) was formed on April 14, 1871, when the king of Prussia became German Emperor William I. The new empire comprised 4 kingdoms, 6 grand duchies, 12 duchies and principalities, 3 free cities and the non-autonomous province of Alsace-Lorraine. The states had the right to issue gold and silver coins of higher value than 1 Mark; coins of 1 Mark and under were general issues of the empire.

MINT MARKS

A - Amberg (Bavaria), 1763-1794
B - Bayreuth, Franconia (Prussia), 1796-1804
B - Breslau (Prussia, Silesia), 1750-1826
C - Dresden (Saxony), 1779-1804
D - Aurich (East Friesland under Prussia), 1750-1806
G - Stettin In Pomerania (Prussia), 1750-1806
P.R. - Dusseldorf (Julich-Berg), 1783-1804

MONETARY SYSTEM

Until 1871 the Mark (Marck) was a measure of weight.

North German States until 1837

2 Heller = 1 Pfennig
8 Pfennige = 1 Mariengroschen
12 Pfennige = 1 Groschen
24 Groschen = 1 Thaler
2 Gulden = 1-1/3 Reichsthaler
1 Speciesthaler (before 1753)
1 Convention Thaler (after 1753)

South German States until 1837

8 Heller = 4 Pfennige = 1 Kreuzer
24 Kreuzer Landmunze = 20 Kreuzer Convention Munze
120 Convention Kreuzer = 2 Convention Gulden = 1 Convention Thaler

AACHEN

(Achen, Urbs Aquensis, Aquis Grani)

FREE CITY

(Achen, Urbs Aquensis, Aquis Grani)

This city, at the meeting point of Germany, Belgium and the Netherlands, 39 miles (65 Kilometers) west-southwest of Cologne, was founded by the Romans. It is the traditional birthplace of Charlemagne and served as the site for imperial coronations from his time until the early part of the 16th century. An imperial mint was established in Aachen in 1166 and continued in use until the early 14th century, at which time the city was raised to tree status and began producing its own coinage. The city coinage came to an end in 1798, just prior to French annexation in 1801. Prussia gained control of Aachen at the end of the Napoleonic Wars and made it part of its western provinces in 1815.

ARMS: Crowned eagle.

CROSS REFERENCES:

M = Julius Menadier, ***Die Aachener Münzen***, Berlin, 1913.
F = Gisela Förschner, ***Deutsche Münzen Mittelalter bis Neuzeit***, v. 1 – ***Aachen bis Augsburg***, Melsungen, 1984.

Mint Officials' Initials

Initials	Date	Name
GS	1797-99?	Godefried Stanislaus
IK	1764-67, 1790?	Johann Kohl
MR	1758-61	Rensonet

MONETARY SYSTEM

24 Heller = 1 Marck
48 Marck = 1 Reichsthaler

STANDARD COINAGE

KM# 31 4 HELLER

Copper **Obverse:** Arms divide date **Reverse:** Legend above value **Rev. Legend:** REICHS/STAT.ACH/IIII

Date	Mintage	VG	F	VF	XF	Unc
1713	40,000	4.00	9.00	16.00	35.00	—
1713	40,000	4.00	9.00	16.00	35.00	—
1715	50,000	4.00	9.00	16.00	35.00	—
1716	200,000	4.00	9.00	16.00	35.00	—
1732	20,000	4.00	9.00	16.00	35.00	—
1734	150,000	4.00	9.00	16.00	35.00	—
1737	300,000	4.00	9.00	16.00	35.00	—
1738	350,000	4.00	9.00	16.00	35.00	—
1741	120,000	4.00	9.00	16.00	35.00	—
1742	120,000	4.00	9.00	16.00	35.00	—
1743	800,000	4.00	9.00	16.00	35.00	—
1744	800,000	4.00	9.00	16.00	35.00	—
1745	600,000	4.00	9.00	16.00	35.00	—
1751	800,000	4.00	9.00	16.00	35.00	—
1752	200,000	4.00	9.00	16.00	35.00	—
1753	200,000	4.00	9.00	16.00	35.00	—
1754	500,000	4.00	9.00	16.00	35.00	—
1757	300,000	4.00	9.00	16.00	35.00	—
1758	300,000	4.00	9.00	16.00	35.00	—
1759	150,000	4.00	9.00	16.00	35.00	—

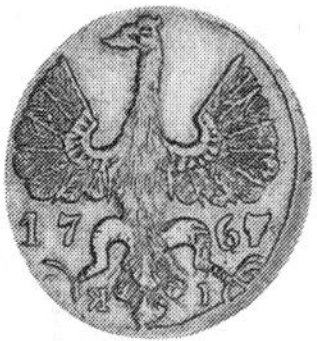

KM# 52 4 HELLER

Copper **Obverse:** Arms divide date **Reverse:** Value above legend **Rev. Legend:** IIII REICHS STAT.ACH

Date	Mintage	VG	F	VF	XF	Unc
1763	—	4.00	7.00	12.00	25.00	—
1765 IK	185,000	4.00	7.00	12.00	25.00	—
1767 IK Upside down	460,000	4.00	7.00	12.00	25.00	—
1790	—	4.00	7.00	12.00	25.00	—
1791	—	4.00	7.00	12.00	25.00	—
1792	400,000	4.00	7.00	12.00	25.00	—
1793	600,000	4.00	7.00	12.00	25.00	—
1795	—	4.00	7.00	12.00	25.00	—
1798	—	15.00	25.00	35.00	55.00	—

KM# 51 12 HELLER

Copper **Obverse:** Arms divide date **Reverse:** Value above legend **Note:** Many varieties exist.

Date	Mintage	VG	F	VF	XF	Unc
1757	—	5.00	8.00	12.00	22.00	—
1758	1,874,000	5.00	8.00	12.00	22.00	—
1758 MR	Inc. above	5.00	8.00	12.00	22.00	—
1759	1,713,000	5.00	8.00	12.00	22.00	—
1759 MR	Inc. above	5.00	8.00	12.00	22.00	—
1760	1,900,000	5.00	8.00	12.00	22.00	—
1760 MR	Inc. above	5.00	8.00	12.00	22.00	—
1761 MR	300,000	5.00	8.00	12.00	22.00	—
1764 IK	150,000	5.00	8.00	12.00	22.00	—
1765 IK	1,200,000	5.00	8.00	12.00	22.00	—
1767 IK	1,248,000	5.00	8.00	12.00	22.00	—
1790	1,400,000	5.00	8.00	12.00	22.00	—
1791 IK	Inc. above	5.00	8.00	12.00	22.00	—
1791 IK Upside down	Inc. above	5.00	8.00	12.00	22.00	—
1791	—	5.00	8.00	12.00	22.00	—
1792	1,750,000	5.00	8.00	12.00	22.00	—
1793	350,000	5.00	8.00	12.00	22.00	—
1794	1,260,000	5.00	8.00	12.00	22.00	—
1797	408,000	5.00	8.00	12.00	22.00	—
1797 GS	Inc. above	5.00	8.00	12.00	22.00	—
1798	—	15.00	25.00	35.00	55.00	—

KM# 32 MARCK

Silver **Obverse:** Value **Obv. Legend:** I/MARCK/ACH **Reverse:** Charlemagne above arms, date

Date	Mintage	VG	F	VF	XF	Unc
(17)07	—	25.00	40.00	75.00	140	—

KM# 38 MARCK

Silver **Obverse:** Without date **Reverse:** Date in center, titles of Karl VI

Date	Mintage	VG	F	VF	XF	Unc
1727	—	15.00	35.00	60.00	125	—
1728	—	15.00	35.00	60.00	125	—

KM# 47 MARCK

Silver **Obverse:** Titles of Francis I

Date	Mintage	VG	F	VF	XF	Unc
1753	—	10.00	20.00	40.00	125	—

KM# 33 2 MARCK

Silver **Obverse:** Titles of Joseph I **Reverse:** Charlemagne above arms

Date	Mintage	VG	F	VF	XF	Unc
(17)07	—	15.00	22.00	40.00	80.00	—

KM# 39 2 MARCK

Silver **Obverse:** Titles of Karl VI

Date	Mintage	VG	F	VF	XF	Unc
1727	—	6.00	12.00	25.00	60.00	—
1728	—	6.00	12.00	25.00	60.00	—

KM# 48 2 MARCK

Silver **Obverse:** Titles of Francis I **Reverse:** Charlemagne and shield within inner circle

Date	Mintage	VG	F	VF	XF	Unc
1753	—	10.00	20.00	40.00	100	—

KM# 34 3 MARCK

Silver **Obverse:** Value, titles of Joseph I **Obv. Legend:** III/MARCK/ACH **Reverse:** 1/2 length figure of Charlemagne, date

Date	Mintage	VG	F	VF	XF	Unc
(17)07	—	30.00	45.00	75.00	140	—

KM# 41 3 MARCK

Silver **Obverse:** Titles of Karl VI

Date	Mintage	VG	F	VF	XF	Unc
1728	—	15.00	22.00	40.00	80.00	—

KM# 50 3 MARCK

Silver **Obverse:** Titles of Francis I **Reverse:** Charlemagne and shield within inner circle

Date	Mintage	VG	F	VF	XF	Unc
1754	—	25.00	60.00	125	250	—

KM# 35 8 MARCK

Silver **Obverse:** Eagle with 8 on breast, double legends **Reverse:** Woman with wine ladle divides date **Note:** Varieties exist.

Date	Mintage	VG	F	VF	XF	Unc
1708	—	40.00	65.00	100	175	—

KM# 42 8 MARCK

Silver **Obverse:** Eagle with 8 on breast, double legends **Reverse:** Imperial crown above date within inner circle, legend surrounds

Date	Mintage	VG	F	VF	XF	Unc
1752	—	50.00	100	200	400	—
1753	—	50.00	100	200	400	—

KM# 36 16 MARCK

Silver **Obverse:** Eagle with 16 on breast, double legends **Reverse:** Woman with wine ladle divides date

Date	Mintage	VG	F	VF	XF	Unc
(1708)	—	60.00	100	150	250	—

KM# 37 16 MARCK

Silver **Reverse:** Imperial crown, double legends, date in chronogram

Date	Mintage	VG	F	VF	XF	Unc
1711	—	45.00	75.00	115	200	—

KM# 43 16 MARCK

Silver **Obverse:** Eagle with 16 on breast, double legends **Reverse:** Imperial crown above date within inner circle, legend surrounds

Date	Mintage	VG	F	VF	XF	Unc
1752	—	50.00	100	200	400	—
1756	—	50.00	100	200	400	—

KM# 44 32 MARCK

Silver **Obverse:** 32 within small center circle, double legends **Reverse:** Crossed sword and sceptre divide imperial crown above from frame below

Date	Mintage	VG	F	VF	XF	Unc
ND(1752-56)	—	100	200	350	750	—
1755	—	100	200	350	750	—

TRADE COINAGE

KM# 55 DUCAT

3.5000 g., 0.9860 Gold 0.1109 oz. AGW **Obverse:** Uniformed bust right **Reverse:** Justice seated right

Date	Mintage	VG	F	VF	XF	Unc
1748	—	300	500	900	2,250	—

KM# 49 DUCAT

3.5000 g., 0.9860 Gold 0.1109 oz. AGW **Obverse:** Crowned standing figure 1/4 right **Reverse:** Inscription within square, wreath surrounds **Note:** Fr. #11.

Date	Mintage	VG	F	VF	XF	Unc
1753	—	300	450	800	2,150	—

PATTERNS

Including off metal strikes

KM#	Date	Mintage	Identification	Mkt Val
Pn1	(17)07	—	Marck. Gold. KM#32.	800
Pn2	1711	—	16 Marck. Gold. KM#37.	—
Pn3	1713	—	4 Heller. Gold. KM#31.	—
Pn4	1728	—	Marck. Gold. Klippe, KM#38.	—
Pn5	1728	—	2 Marck. Gold. KM#39.	—
Pn6	1738	—	4 Heller. Silver. KM#31.	—
Pn7	1741	—	4 Heller. Silver. KM#31.	—
Pn8	1742	—	4 Heller. Silver. KM#31.	—
Pn9	1743	—	4 Heller. Silver. KM#31.	—
PnA10	1748	—	Ducat. Silver. KM#55.	250
Pn10	1751	—	4 Heller. Silver. KM#31.	—
Pn11	1752	—	8 Marck. Gold. KM#42.	—
Pn12	1753	—	Ducat. Silver. KM#49.	250
Pn13	1754	—	3 Marck. Gold. KM#50.	—
Pn14	1758	—	12 Heller. Silver. KM#51.	—

TRIAL STRIKES

KM#	Date	Mintage	Identification	Mkt Val
TS1	1751	—	4 Heller. Copper. Large flan.	—
TS2	1753	—	4 Heller. Copper. Large flan.	—
TS3	1765	—	4 Heller. Copper. Large flan.	—
TS4	1767	—	4 Heller. Copper. Uniface, reverse.	—
TS5	1793	—	4 Heller. Copper. Large flan.	—

AALEN

A town on the Kocher River, ten miles south of Ellwangen in Swabia, joining other Swabian towns and cities in 1423 to form a local monetary union, but only an issue of the 17th century is known.

TOWN

REGULAR COINAGE

KM# 1 PFENNIG

Copper **Note:** Uniface; Crowned eel in shield (arms) below I-P, Legend: AALEN S M.

Date	Mintage	Good	VG	F	VF	XF
ND17?? Rare	—	—	—	—	—	—

ANHALT-BERNBURG

Located in north-central Germany. Appeared as part of the patrimony of Albrecht the Bear of Brandenburg in 1170. Bracteates were first made in the 12th century. It was originally in the inheritance of Heinrich the Fat in 1252 and became extinct in 1468. The division of 1603, among the sons of Joachim Ernst, revitalized Anhalt-Bernburg. Bernburg passed to Dessau after the death of Alexander Carl in 1863.

RULERS

Viktor I Amadeus, 1656-1718
Karl Friedrich, 1718-1721
Viktor II Friedrich, 1721-1765
Friedrich Albrecht, 1765-1796
Alexius Friedrich Christian, 1796-1834

MINT OFFICIALS' INITIALS

Initials	Date	Name
HCAS, HSS, S	1767-94	Heinrich Christian, Andreas Siegel
HCRF	1744-49	Heinrich Christian, Rudolf Friese
HS	1795-1821	Hans Schluter
IGS	1753-67	Johann Gottfried Siegel
HS, IHA	1744-53	Johann Heinrich Siegel
IIG	1727-28, 1747	Johann Jeremias Grundler

DUCHY

REGULAR COINAGE

KM# 12 PFENNIG

Billon **Ruler:** Viktor II Friedrich **Obverse:** VF monogram **Reverse:** Value

Date	Mintage	VG	F	VF	XF	Unc
1744 IHS	—	12.50	25.00	45.00	90.00	—
1745 IHS	—	12.50	25.00	45.00	90.00	—

KM# 25.1 PFENNIG

Copper **Ruler:** Viktor II Friedrich **Obverse:** Crowned bear walking left on wall **Reverse:** Value above legend and date **Rev. Legend:** •I•/PFENNING/SCHEIDE MVNZE

Date	Mintage	VG	F	VF	XF	Unc
1746 HCRF	—	3.00	5.00	10.00	20.00	—
1748 HCRF	—	3.00	5.00	10.00	20.00	—
1748 IHS	—	3.00	5.00	10.00	20.00	—
1750 IHS	—	3.00	5.00	10.00	20.00	—
1751 IHS	—	3.00	5.00	10.00	20.00	—
1752 IHS	—	3.00	5.00	10.00	20.00	—
1753 IHS	—	3.00	5.00	10.00	20.00	—
1754	—	3.00	5.00	10.00	20.00	—
1755	—	3.00	5.00	10.00	20.00	—
1757	—	3.00	5.00	10.00	20.00	—

KM# 25.2 PFENNIG

Copper **Ruler:** Viktor II Friedrich **Obverse:** Bear on wall **Reverse:** Value above legend and date **Rev. Legend:** I/PFENNIG

Date	Mintage	VG	F	VF	XF	Unc
1757	—	3.00	5.00	10.00	20.00	—
1758	—	3.00	5.00	10.00	20.00	—
1760	—	3.00	5.00	10.00	20.00	—

KM# 55 PFENNIG

Copper **Ruler:** Friedrich Albrecht **Obverse:** Crowned bear left walking on wall **Reverse:** Value above date **Note:** Varieties exist.

Date	Mintage	VG	F	VF	XF	Unc
1776 S	—	4.00	7.00	15.00	25.00	—
1777 S	—	4.00	7.00	15.00	25.00	—
1793	—	4.00	7.00	17.50	30.00	—
1794	—	4.00	7.00	17.50	30.00	—
1795	—	4.00	7.00	17.50	30.00	—

KM# 61 PFENNIG

Copper **Ruler:** Alexius Friedrich Christian **Obverse:** Crowned AFC monogram **Rev. Inscription:** Value and date in five lines

Date	Mintage	F	VF	XF	Unc
1796	—	8.00	15.00	25.00	135
1797	—	8.00	15.00	25.00	135

KM# 62.1 PFENNIG

Copper **Ruler:** Alexius Friedrich Christian **Obverse:** Crowned bear walking on wall **Reverse:** Value and date **Rev. Legend:** PFENN

Date	Mintage	F	VF	XF	Unc
1796	—	8.00	15.00	20.00	125

KM# 62.2 PFENNIG

Copper **Ruler:** Alexius Friedrich Christian **Rev. Legend:** I/PFENNIG/SCHEIDE/MÜNZE

Date	Mintage	F	VF	XF	Unc
1796	—	6.00	10.00	18.00	60.00

KM# 62.3 PFENNIG

Copper **Ruler:** Alexius Friedrich Christian **Obverse:** Crowned bear walking left on wall **Reverse:** Value above legend and date **Rev. Legend:** SCHEIDE/MUNTZ

Date	Mintage	F	VF	XF	Unc
1797	—	6.00	10.00	18.00	60.00
1799	—	6.00	10.00	18.00	60.00

KM# 62.4 PFENNIG

Copper **Ruler:** Alexius Friedrich Christian **Obverse:** Crowned bear on wall **Reverse:** Value, legend and date **Rev. Legend:** SCHEIDE/MUNTZ

Date	Mintage	F	VF	XF	Unc
1797	—	6.00	10.00	18.00	60.00

KM# 32 1-1/2 PFENNIG

Copper **Ruler:** Viktor II Friedrich **Obverse:** Crowned bear walking on wall **Rev. Legend:** 1 1/2/PFENNIG/F•A•B•S•M

Date	Mintage	VG	F	VF	XF	Unc
1747 HCRF	—	4.50	8.50	17.50	35.00	—

KM# 56 1-1/2 PFENNIG

Copper **Ruler:** Friedrich Albrecht **Obverse:** Crowned bear walking left on wall **Reverse:** Value, date and legend within scalloped circle **Rev. Legend:** 1 1/2/PFENNIG/F • A • B • S • M

Date	Mintage	VG	F	VF	XF	Unc
1776 S	—	10.00	20.00	35.00	75.00	—

KM# 13 2 PFENNIG

Billon **Ruler:** Viktor II Friedrich **Obverse:** VF monogram **Reverse:** Value

Date	Mintage	VG	F	VF	XF	Unc
1744 IHS	—	15.00	30.00	50.00	90.00	—
1745	—	15.00	30.00	50.00	90.00	—

KM# 14 3 PFENNIG

Billon **Ruler:** Viktor II Friedrich **Obverse:** VF monogram **Reverse:** Value

Date	Mintage	VG	F	VF	XF	Unc
1744 IHS	—	7.50	15.00	25.00	50.00	—
1744 HS	—	7.50	15.00	25.00	50.00	—
1745 IHS	—	7.50	15.00	25.00	50.00	—

KM# 35 3 PFENNIG

Billon **Ruler:** Viktor II Friedrich **Obverse:** Crowned bear walking left on wall **Reverse:** Value and date **Rev. Legend:** *3*/GUTE/PFENN

Date	Mintage	VG	F	VF	XF	Unc
1749 IHS	—	6.00	12.00	20.00	45.00	—

KM# 38.1 3 PFENNIG

Copper **Ruler:** Viktor II Friedrich **Obverse:** Crowned bear walking left on wall **Obv. Legend:** PERRVMPENDVM **Reverse:** Value, date and legend **Rev. Legend:** *3*/PFENNIG/F • A • B • L • M

Date	Mintage	VG	F	VF	XF	Unc
1753	—	4.50	7.50	15.00	30.00	—

KM# 38.2 3 PFENNIG

Copper **Ruler:** Viktor II Friedrich **Obverse:** Crowned bear on wall **Reverse:** Value, date and legend **Rev. Legend:** 3/PFENNIG

Date	Mintage	VG	F	VF	XF	Unc
1760	—	4.50	7.50	15.00	30.00	—

KM# 15 4 PFENNIG

Billon **Ruler:** Viktor II Friedrich **Obverse:** VF monogram **Reverse:** Value

Date	Mintage	VG	F	VF	XF	Unc
1744 HS	—	7.50	15.00	27.50	55.00	—
1745 HS	—	7.50	15.00	27.50	55.00	—

KM# 26 4 PFENNIG

Billon **Ruler:** Viktor II Friedrich **Obverse:** Crowned bear walking on wall **Rev. Inscription:** IIII/PFENNING

Date	Mintage	VG	F	VF	XF	Unc
1746 HSRF	—	7.50	15.00	25.00	50.00	—

KM# 33 4 PFENNIG

Billon **Ruler:** Viktor II Friedrich **Rev. Inscription:** 4/PFENNING

Date	Mintage	VG	F	VF	XF	Unc
1747 HCRF	—	7.50	15.00	27.50	55.00	—
1748 HCRF	—	7.50	15.00	27.50	55.00	—
1749 IHS	—	7.50	15.00	27.50	55.00	—

KM# 16 6 PFENNIG

Billon **Ruler:** Viktor II Friedrich **Obverse:** Crowned bear walking on wall **Reverse:** Value

Date	Mintage	VG	F	VF	XF	Unc
1744 HS	—	7.50	15.00	30.00	60.00	—
1745 HS	—	7.50	15.00	30.00	60.00	—
1746 HCRF	—	7.50	15.00	30.00	60.00	—
1747 HCRF	—	7.50	15.00	30.00	60.00	—
1749 HCRF	—	7.50	15.00	30.00	60.00	—
1749 IHS	—	7.50	15.00	30.00	60.00	—
1750 IHS	—	7.50	15.00	30.00	60.00	—
1751 IHS	—	7.50	15.00	30.00	60.00	—
1752 IHS	—	7.50	15.00	30.00	60.00	—
1753 IHS	—	7.50	15.00	30.00	60.00	—
1753	—	7.50	15.00	30.00	60.00	—
1754 IHS	—	7.50	15.00	30.00	60.00	—
1755	—	7.50	15.00	30.00	60.00	—
1756	—	7.50	15.00	30.00	60.00	—
1757	—	7.50	15.00	30.00	60.00	—
1758	—	7.50	15.00	30.00	60.00	—

KM# 17 MARIENGROSCHEN

Billon **Ruler:** Viktor II Friedrich **Obverse:** Crowned bear walking left on wall **Rev. Legend:** FURSTL. ANHALT BERNB. LAND MUNTZ **Rev. Inscription:** *I*/MARIEN/GROS:

Date	Mintage	VG	F	VF	XF	Unc
1744 HS	—	6.50	13.50	27.50	55.00	—
1744 IHS	—	6.50	13.50	27.50	55.00	—
1746 HCRF	—	6.50	13.50	27.50	55.00	—
1749 IHS	—	6.50	13.50	27.50	55.00	—
1750 IHS	—	6.50	13.50	27.50	55.00	—
1761	—	6.50	13.50	27.50	55.00	—

KM# 5 6 MARIENGROSCHEN

Silver **Ruler:** Viktor II Friedrich **Obverse:** Crowned bear walking on wall **Reverse:** Value

Date	Mintage	VG	F	VF	XF	Unc
1727 IIG	—	35.00	75.00	120	180	—

KM# 6 12 MARIENGROSCHEN

Silver **Ruler:** Viktor II Friedrich **Obverse:** Crowned bear walking on wall **Rev. Inscription:** XII/MARIENGROS

Date	Mintage	VG	F	VF	XF	Unc
1727 IIG	—	25.00	60.00	100	175	—

KM# 7 24 MARIENGROSCHEN (2/3 Thaler)

Silver **Ruler:** Viktor II Friedrich **Obverse:** Value and inscription within inner circle, legend surrounds **Obv. Legend:** VICTOR • FRIDERICUS • D • G • P • A • DVX... **Reverse:** Crowned bear walking left on wall **Rev. Legend:** PERRUMPENDUM

Date	Mintage	VG	F	VF	XF	Unc
1727 IIG	—	50.00	100	175	250	—

KM# 63 24 MARIENGROSCHEN (2/3 Thaler)

13.0800 g., 0.9860 Silver 0.4146 oz. ASW **Ruler:** Alexius Friedrich Christian **Obverse:** Value, date and inscription **Obv. Legend:** ALEXIUS FRIEDRICH CHRISTIAN... **Reverse:** Crowned bear walking left on wall

Date	Mintage	F	VF	XF	Unc
1796 HS	—	30.00	50.00	75.00	150
1797 HS	—	30.00	50.00	75.00	150

KM# 64 24 MARIENGROSCHEN (2/3 Thaler)

13.0800 g., 0.9860 Silver 0.4146 oz. ASW **Ruler:** Alexius Friedrich Christian **Obverse:** Value, date within beaded inner circle, legend surrounds **Reverse:** Crowned bear walking left on wall

Date	Mintage	F	VF	XF	Unc
1796 HS	—	40.00	100	175	300

KM# 65 24 MARIENGROSCHEN (2/3 Thaler)

13.0800 g., 0.9860 Silver 0.4146 oz. ASW **Ruler:** Alexius Friedrich Christian **Obv. Inscription:** XXIIII/MARIENGROSCHEN

Date	Mintage	F	VF	XF	Unc
1796 HS	—	30.00	55.00	85.00	175

KM# 66 24 MARIENGROSCHEN (2/3 Thaler)

13.0800 g., 0.9860 Silver 0.4146 oz. ASW **Ruler:** Alexius Friedrich Christian **Obverse:** 2/3 in oval within gate of wall

Date	Mintage	F	VF	XF	Unc
1796 HS	—	75.00	125	225	425

KM# 42.1 8 GUTE GROSCHEN

Silver **Ruler:** Viktor II Friedrich **Obverse:** Head right **Obv. Legend:** V.FRID.D.G.P.A.DVX.S.A.&.W.CA... **Reverse:** Value and date **Rev. Legend:** Small GUTE

Date	Mintage	VG	F	VF	XF	Unc
1758	—	30.00	50.00	80.00	150	—
1759	—	30.00	50.00	80.00	150	—

KM# 42.2 8 GUTE GROSCHEN

Silver **Ruler:** Viktor II Friedrich **Obverse:** Head right **Reverse:** Value and date **Rev. Inscription:** Large GUTE

Date	Mintage	VG	F	VF	XF	Unc
1758	—	30.00	50.00	80.00	150	—

KM# 50 8 GUTE GROSCHEN

Silver **Ruler:** Viktor II Friedrich **Obverse:** Crowned VF monogram **Reverse:** Value **Rev. Legend:** 60 EINE FEINE MARK

Date	Mintage	VG	F	VF	XF	Unc
1760	—	35.00	55.00	90.00	160	—

KM# 51 8 GUTE GROSCHEN

Silver **Ruler:** Viktor II Friedrich **Reverse:** Crowned arms, value **Rev. Legend:** 60 EINE FEINE MARK; 8 GUTE GROSCHEN

Date	Mintage	VG	F	VF	XF	Unc
1760	—	35.00	55.00	90.00	160	—

KM# 52 1/48 THALER

Billon **Ruler:** Viktor II Friedrich **Obverse:** *48*/EINEN/THALER **Reverse:** Crowned bear walking left on wall

Date	Mintage	VG	F	VF	XF	Unc
1760	—	6.00	12.00	20.00	40.00	—
1761	—	6.00	12.00	20.00	40.00	—

KM# 57 1/48 THALER

0.9700 g., 0.2500 Silver 0.0078 oz. ASW **Ruler:** Friedrich Albrecht **Obverse:** Crowned FA monogram **Reverse:** 48/EINEN/THALER/date **Note:** Varieties exist.

Date	Mintage	VG	F	VF	XF	Unc
1793	—	4.00	8.00	15.00	30.00	—
1794	—	4.00	8.00	15.00	30.00	—
1795	—	4.00	8.00	15.00	30.00	—
1796	—	4.00	8.00	15.00	30.00	—

KM# A60 1/48 THALER

Billon **Ruler:** Friedrich Albrecht **Obverse:** Crowned FA (block letters) monogram **Rev. Inscription:** 48 / EINEN / THALER

Date	Mintage	VG	F	VF	XF	Unc
1794	—	4.00	10.00	18.00	30.00	—

KM# 18 1/24 THALER

Billon **Ruler:** Viktor II Friedrich **Obverse:** Crowned bear walking on wall **Reverse:** Value **Rev. Legend:** NACH DEM..

Date	Mintage	VG	F	VF	XF	Unc
1744 HS	—	7.50	15.00	30.00	60.00	—
1746 HCRF	—	7.50	15.00	30.00	60.00	—
1750 IHS	—	7.50	15.00	30.00	60.00	—

KM# 40 1/24 THALER

Billon **Ruler:** Viktor II Friedrich **Obv. Legend:** FVRSTL. ANHALT. BERNVBRG. LANDMVNTZ

Date	Mintage	VG	F	VF	XF	Unc
1757 IGS	—	5.00	10.00	20.00	40.00	—

KM# 43 1/24 THALER

Billon **Ruler:** Viktor II Friedrich **Obverse:** Crown above VF monogram

Date	Mintage	VG	F	VF	XF	Unc
1758	—	12.50	25.00	45.00	90.00	—

KM# 48 1/24 THALER

Billon **Ruler:** Viktor II Friedrich **Obv. Inscription:** *24*/EINEN/THALER/date **Reverse:** Crowned bear walking left on wall

Date	Mintage	VG	F	VF	XF	Unc
1759	—	6.00	12.50	25.00	50.00	—
1760	—	6.00	12.50	25.00	50.00	—
1761	—	6.00	12.50	25.00	50.00	—

KM# 19 1/12 THALER

Billon **Ruler:** Viktor II Friedrich **Obverse:** Crowned bear walking on wall **Obv. Legend:** PERRVMPENDVM **Reverse:** Value **Rev. Legend:** NACH DEM..

Date	Mintage	VG	F	VF	XF	Unc
1744 HS	—	12.50	25.00	40.00	80.00	—
1746 HCRF	—	12.50	25.00	40.00	80.00	—
1750 IHS	—	12.50	25.00	40.00	80.00	—
1750	—	10.00	20.00	40.00	80.00	—

KM# 41 1/12 THALER

Billon **Ruler:** Viktor II Friedrich **Obv. Legend:** FVRSTL. ANHALT. BERNVRG. LANDMVNTZ

Date	Mintage	VG	F	VF	XF	Unc
1757 IGS	—	6.00	12.50	30.00	60.00	—

KM# 53 1/12 THALER

Billon **Ruler:** Viktor II Friedrich **Reverse:** Value

Date	Mintage	VG	F	VF	XF	Unc
1760	—	15.00	30.00	50.00	100	—

KM# 68 1/12 THALER

Billon **Ruler:** Alexius Friedrich Christian **Obverse:** Value and date within inner circle, legend surrounds **Reverse:** Crowned bear walking left on wall

Date	Mintage	F	VF	XF	Unc
1799 HS	—	15.00	30.00	60.00	120

KM# 8 1/6 THALER

Silver **Ruler:** Viktor II Friedrich **Obverse:** Crowned arms with value "1/6" at bottom **Obv. Legend:** VICTOR • FRIEDERICUS • D • G • P ... **Reverse:** Crowned bear walking left on wall **Rev. Legend:** PERRUMPENDUM

Date	Mintage	VG	F	VF	XF	Unc
1727 IIG	—	15.00	30.00	55.00	120	—
1730 IIG	—	15.00	30.00	55.00	120	—
1733 IIG	—	15.00	30.00	55.00	120	—
1742 IIG	—	15.00	30.00	55.00	120	—
1744 HS	—	15.00	30.00	55.00	120	—
1744 IHS	—	15.00	30.00	55.00	120	—

KM# 27 1/6 THALER

Silver **Ruler:** Viktor II Friedrich **Obv. Legend:** NACH DEN LIEPZ. FVS

Date	Mintage	VG	F	VF	XF	Unc
1746 HCRF	—	15.00	30.00	55.00	125	—
1750 IHS	—	15.00	30.00	55.00	125	—
1752 IHS	—	15.00	30.00	55.00	125	—

KM# 39 1/6 THALER

Silver **Ruler:** Viktor II Friedrich **Obverse:** Head right **Obv. Legend:** V. FRID D G. ... **Reverse:** *VI*/EINEN/THALER

Date	Mintage	VG	F	VF	XF	Unc
1754	—	7.50	15.00	30.00	60.00	—
1758	—	7.50	15.00	30.00	60.00	—
1760	—	7.50	15.00	30.00	60.00	—

KM# 44 1/6 THALER

Silver **Ruler:** Viktor II Friedrich **Subject:** Birthday of Friedrich Albrecht **Rev. Legend:** FR. ALBR. P. A. B. NAT..

Date	Mintage	VG	F	VF	XF	Unc
1758	—	—	—	—	—	—

KM# 45 1/6 THALER

Silver **Ruler:** Viktor II Friedrich **Obverse:** Crowned VF monogram **Reverse:** Value

Date	Mintage	VG	F	VF	XF	Unc
1758	—	20.00	40.00	80.00	160	—
1759	—	20.00	40.00	80.00	160	—

KM# 46 1/6 THALER

Silver **Ruler:** Viktor II Friedrich **Obverse:** Head right **Reverse:** Value

Date	Mintage	VG	F	VF	XF	Unc
1758	—	10.00	20.00	40.00	80.00	—
1759	—	10.00	20.00	40.00	80.00	—

KM# 69 1/6 THALER

5.4000 g., 0.5410 Silver 0.0939 oz. ASW **Ruler:** Alexius Friedrich Christian **Obverse:** Crowned bear walking left on wall **Reverse:** Value and date within inner circle **Rev. Legend:** •VI•/EINEN/THALER

Date	Mintage	F	VF	XF	Unc
1799 HS	—	10.00	20.00	40.00	80.00

KM# 9 1/3 THALER

Silver **Ruler:** Viktor II Friedrich **Obverse:** Crowned shield with value below divides date **Obv. Legend:** VICT FRID • DG P ANH DUX... **Reverse:** Crowned bear walking left on wall **Rev. Legend:** PERRVMPENDVM

Date	Mintage	VG	F	VF	XF	Unc
1727 IIG	—	20.00	50.00	100	200	—
1730 IIG	—	20.00	50.00	100	200	—
1733 IIG	—	20.00	50.00	100	200	—
1742 IIG	—	20.00	50.00	100	200	—
1747 HCRF	—	20.00	50.00	100	200	—
1750 IHS	—	20.00	50.00	100	200	—

KM# 20 1/3 THALER

Silver **Ruler:** Viktor II Friedrich **Obverse:** Bust **Reverse:** Arms

Date	Mintage	VG	F	VF	XF	Unc
1744 HS	—	40.00	80.00	160	350	—
1750 IHS	—	40.00	80.00	160	350	—

KM# 28 1/3 THALER

Silver **Ruler:** Viktor II Friedrich **Obverse:** Crowned bear walking on wall **Rev. Legend:** NACH DEN LIEPZ. FUS

Date	Mintage	VG	F	VF	XF	Unc
1746 HCRF	—	20.00	40.00	100	200	—

KM# 36 1/3 THALER

Silver **Ruler:** Viktor II Friedrich **Obverse:** Bust **Obv. Legend:** NACH DEN LIEPZ. FUS

Date	Mintage	VG	F	VF	XF	Unc
1750 IHS	—	20.00	40.00	100	200	—

KM# 47 1/3 THALER

Silver **Ruler:** Viktor II Friedrich **Subject:** Birthday of Prince **Obverse:** Crowned VF monogram **Obv. Legend:** NATUS 20 • SEPT • 1700... **Reverse:** Crowned bear walking on wall **Rev. Legend:** PERRVMPENDVM

Date	Mintage	VG	F	VF	XF	Unc
1758	—	40.00	80.00	160	350	—

KM# 49 1/3 THALER

Silver **Ruler:** Viktor II Friedrich **Obverse:** Bust right **Reverse:** Value

Date	Mintage	VG	F	VF	XF	Unc
1759	—	30.00	60.00	100	200	—

KM# 70 1/3 THALER

7.0200 g., 0.8330 Silver 0.1880 oz. ASW **Ruler:** Alexius Friedrich Christian **Obverse:** Value and date within inner circle **Obv. Legend:** ALEXIUS FRIEDR... **Reverse:** Crowned bear walking left on wall

Date	Mintage	F	VF	XF	Unc
1799	—	45.00	90.00	180	350
1799 HS	—	45.00	90.00	180	350

KM# 10.1 2/3 THALER

Silver **Ruler:** Viktor II Friedrich **Obverse:** Crowned shield with value below divides date **Obv. Legend:** VICTOR FRIDERICVS D • G • P • A •... **Reverse:** Crowned bear walking left on wall with archway **Rev. Legend:** PERRVMPENDVM

Date	Mintage	VG	F	VF	XF	Unc
1727 IIG	—	50.00	100	150	200	—
1729 IIG	—	50.00	100	150	200	—
1730 IIG	—	75.00	175	225	300	—
1733 IIG	—	50.00	125	250	400	—
1742 IIG	—	50.00	100	150	200	—
1744 HS	—	50.00	100	150	200	—
1747 HCRF	—	50.00	120	175	250	—
1750 IHS	—	50.00	100	150	200	—

KM# 10.2 2/3 THALER

Silver **Ruler:** Viktor II Friedrich **Obverse:** Crowned shield with value below divides date **Obv. Legend:** * VICTOR • FRIDERICUS • D • G • P • A... **Reverse:** Crowned bear walking left on wall without archway **Rev. Legend:** PERRUMPENDUM

Date	Mintage	VG	F	VF	XF	Unc
1727 IIG	—	50.00	100	150	200	—

KM# 21 2/3 THALER

Silver **Ruler:** Viktor II Friedrich **Obverse:** Crowned shield with value below divides date **Obv. Legend:** VICT • FRID • D G P ANH DUX... **Reverse:** Bear walking left on wall

Date	Mintage	VG	F	VF	XF	Unc
1744 HS	—	50.00	120	200	300	—
1750 IHS	—	50.00	120	200	300	—

KM# 29 2/3 THALER

Silver **Ruler:** Viktor II Friedrich

Date	Mintage	VG	F	VF	XF	Unc
1746 HCRF	—	50.00	100	150	200	—

KM# 58.1 2/3 THALER

14.0300 g., 0.8330 Silver 0.3757 oz. ASW **Ruler:** Friedrich Albrecht **Obverse:** Crowned bear walking left on wall **Obv. Legend:** (rosette) ANHALT (rosette) BERNB: (rosette) CONV:M.... **Reverse:** XX/EINE FEINE/MARK in sprays

Date	Mintage	VG	F	VF	XF	Unc
1793	—	50.00	100	150	200	—

KM# 58.2 2/3 THALER

14.0300 g., 0.8330 Silver 0.3757 oz. ASW **Ruler:** Friedrich Albrecht **Obverse:** Crowned bear walking left on wall **Obv. Legend:** FURSTL (rosette) ANHALT (rosette)BERNB•... **Reverse:** XX/EINEFEINE/MARCK within sprays

Date	Mintage	VG	F	VF	XF	Unc
1793	—	50.00	100	150	200	—

KM# 71 2/3 THALER

14.0300 g., 0.8330 Silver 0.3757 oz. ASW **Ruler:** Alexius Friedrich Christian **Obverse:** Value and date, legend surrounds **Obv. Legend:** ALEXIUS FRIEDRICH CHRISTIAN... **Reverse:** Crowned bear walking left on wall

Date	Mintage	F	VF	XF	Unc
1799 HS	—	50.00	120	175	250

KM# 3 THALER

Silver **Ruler:** Viktor I Amadeus **Obverse:** 16-line inscription, date in Roman numerals **Reverse:** Crowned bear leaning on tree, counting house in background **Note:** Dav. #2921. Mining Thaler.

Date	Mintage	VG	F	VF	XF	Unc
1711	—	750	1,200	2,000	4,000	—

KM# 4 THALER

Silver **Ruler:** Viktor I Amadeus **Reverse:** Miner standing with pick and ore trough, date **Note:** Dav. #2992.

Date	Mintage	VG	F	VF	XF	Unc
1711	—	750	1,200	2,000	4,000	—

KM# 22 THALER

Silver **Ruler:** Viktor II Friedrich **Obverse:** Bust left **Obv. Legend:** VICT • FRID • D.G.P.ANH... **Reverse:** Crowned arms **Rev. Legend:** NACH REICHS SCHROT VND KORN **Note:** Dav. #1901.

Date	Mintage	VG	F	VF	XF	Unc
1744 HS Rare	—	—	—	—	—	—

KM# 30 THALER

Silver **Ruler:** Viktor II Friedrich **Obverse:** Crowned bear walking left on wall **Obv. Legend:** PERRVMPENDVM **Reverse:** Crowned shield **Rev. Legend:** VICT.FRID.D:G.P.ANH... **Note:** Dav. #1902.

Date	Mintage	VG	F	VF	XF	Unc
1746 HCRF Rare	—	—	—	—	—	—

KM# 34 THALER

Silver **Ruler:** Viktor II Friedrich **Obverse:** Crowned arms supported by bears **Obv. Legend:** VICT•FRID•D•G•P•ANH... **Reverse:** Mining scene **Note:** Dav. #1903. Mining Thaler.

Date	Mintage	VG	F	VF	XF	Unc
1747 HCRF	—	400	950	1,750	2,750	—

KM# 37 THALER

Silver **Ruler:** Viktor II Friedrich **Obverse:** Armored bust left **Obv. Legend:** VICT • FRID • D • G • P • ANH • DVX • S • A • & W • C • ASC. D • B • & S • **Reverse:** Crowned arms **Rev. Legend:** NACH DEM REICHS SHROT VND KORN **Note:** Dav. #1904.

Date	Mintage	VG	F	VF	XF	Unc
1750 IHS	—	300	800	1,500	2,500	—

KM# 59 THALER

28.0600 g., 0.8330 Silver 0.7515 oz. ASW **Ruler:** Friedrich Albrecht **Obverse:** Bust left with medal on chest **Obv. Legend:** FRIED: ALBRECHT FURST ZU ANHALT BERNB: **Reverse:** Crowned circular arms in order chain **Rev. Legend:** X EINE FEINE MARK **Note:** Convention Thaler. Dav. #1905.

Date	Mintage	F	VF	XF	Unc
1793	—	200	350	675	1,500
1794	—	250	400	725	1,600

KM# 60 THALER

28.0600 g., 0.8330 Silver 0.7515 oz. ASW **Ruler:** Friedrich Albrecht **Obverse:** Bust left with medal on chest **Obv. Legend:** FRIED • ALBRECHT • FURST • ZU • ANHALT • BERNB • **Reverse:** Crowned oval arms in sprays **Rev. Legend:** X EINE FEINE MARCK **Note:** Dav. #1906.

Date	Mintage	F	VF	XF	Unc
1795 HS	—	200	350	650	1,500
1796 HS	—	200	350	650	1,500

KM# 23 2-1/2 THALER

3.3200 g., 0.9000 Gold 0.0961 oz. AGW **Ruler:** Viktor II Friedrich **Obverse:** Bust right **Reverse:** Crowned arms **Note:** Fr.#22.

Date	Mintage	VG	F	VF	XF	Unc
1744 HS	—	750	1,500	2,750	4,500	—

KM# 24 5 THALER

6.6500 g., 0.9000 Gold 0.1924 oz. AGW **Ruler:** Viktor II Friedrich **Obverse:** Bust right **Reverse:** Crowned arms **Note:** Fr#21.

Date	Mintage	VG	F	VF	XF	Unc
1744 HS	—	1,000	2,000	3,250	5,500	—

KM# 67 5 THALER

6.6500 g., 0.9000 Gold 0.1924 oz. AGW **Ruler:** Alexius Friedrich Christian **Obverse:** Armored bust left **Reverse:** Crowned arms within palms **Rev. Legend:** H - S/5. THALER/1796 **Note:** Fr.#24.

Date	Mintage	F	VF	XF	Unc
1796 HS	—	600	1,200	2,000	3,500

TRADE COINAGE

KM# 11 DUCAT

3.5000 g., 0.9860 Gold 0.1109 oz. AGW **Ruler:** Viktor II Friedrich **Obverse:** Crowned arms **Obv. Legend:** VICTOR FRID DG... **Reverse:** Crowned bear walking left on wall **Rev. Legend:** PERRVMPNDVM **Note:** Fr.#20.

Date	Mintage	VG	F	VF	XF	Unc
1730 IIG	—	250	450	900	1,700	—
1733 IIG	—	250	450	900	1,700	—
1741 IIG	—	250	450	900	1,700	—
1744 HS	—	250	450	900	1,700	—
1750 IHS	—	250	450	900	1,700	—
1761 IGS	—	250	450	900	1,700	—

KM# 31 DUCAT

3.5000 g., 0.9860 Gold 0.1109 oz. AGW **Ruler:** Viktor II Friedrich **Rev. Legend:** PERRVMPENDVM (on banner)

Date	Mintage	VG	F	VF	XF	Unc
1746 HCRF	—	350	550	1,200	1,850	—
1747 HCRF	—	350	550	1,200	1,850	—

KM# 54 DUCAT

3.5000 g., 0.9860 Gold 0.1109 oz. AGW **Ruler:** Viktor II Friedrich **Obverse:** Legend around arms **Obv. Legend:** SENIOR DOMVS **Reverse:** PERRVMPENDVM (on banner)

Date	Mintage	VG	F	VF	XF	Unc
1761 IGS	—	350	550	1,200	1,850	—

PATTERNS

Including off metal strikes

KM#	Date	Mintage	Identification	Mkt Val
Pn1	1744	—	Ducat. Silver. KM#11.	—
Pn2	1747	—	Ducat. Copper. .KM#31.	—
Pn3	1758	—	1/6 Thaler. Gold. KM#44.	—
Pn4	1758	—	1/3 Thaler. Gold. KM#47.	—

ANHALT-BERNBURG-SCHAUMBURG-HOYM

The title to Schaumburg was inherited through marriage by a branch of Anhalt-Bernburg in 1692. The separate line of Anhalt-Bernburg-Schaumburg-Hoym was founded in 1707 and became extinct in 1812, the title then falling to Austria by marriage.

RULERS

Lebrecht, 1707-1727
Victor Amadeus Adolph, 1727-1772
Karl Ludwig, 1772-1806

MINT OFFICIALS' INITIALS

Initials	Date	Name
B(F)N	1764-90	Philipp Christian Bunsen, in Frankfurt am Main and
	1763-77	Georg Neumeister, warden in Frankfurt
S	1767-94	Heinrich Christian Andreas Siegel in Bernburg

DUCHY

REGULAR COINAGE

KM# 1 1/2 THALER (Convention)
11.7700 g., 0.9860 Silver 0.3731 oz. ASW **Ruler:** Karl Ludwig **Obverse:** Inscription within inner circle, legend surrounds **Obv. Legend:** * CARL LUDWIG FURST ZU ANHALT SCHAUMBURG **Obv. Inscription:** GOTT/ SEGNE FERNER/ DAS HOLZAPPELER/ BERGWERCK/ FEIN SILBER/ 1774/ .B.(F).N. **Reverse:** Sun above mining camp and hills **Rev. Legend:** AN GOTTES SEGEN...

Date	Mintage	F	VF	XF	Unc
1774 B(F)N/S	—	500	700	1,000	1,650

KM# 2 THALER (Convention)
23.5500 g., 0.9860 Silver 0.7465 oz. ASW **Ruler:** Karl Ludwig **Obverse:** Inscription within inner circle, legend surrounds **Obv. Legend:** CARL LUDWIG FURST ZU ANHALT SCHAUMBURG * **Obv. Inscription:** GOTT/SEGNE FERNER/DAS HOLZAPPELER/BERGWERCK/FEIN SILBER/1774/.B.(F).N. **Reverse:** Sun above mining camp and hills **Rev. Legend:** AN GOTTES SEGEN * 1ST ALLES GELEGEN * **Note:** Dav. #1907.

Date	Mintage	F	VF	XF	Unc
1774 B(F)N/S	—	225	500	1,150	1,850

ANHALT-KOTHEN

Köthen has a checkered history after the patrimony of Heinrich the Fat in 1252. It was often ruled with other segments of the House of Anhalt. Founded as a separate line in 1603, became extinct in 1665 and passed to Plötzkau which changed the name to Köthen. It passed to Dessau after the death of Heinrich in 1847.

RULERS
Emanuel Lebrecht, 1671-1704
Leopold, 1704-1728
August Ludwig, 1728-1755

MINT OFFICIALS' INITIALS

Initials	Date	Name
AW	1750-51	Alexius Wegelin
CW	1688-1739	Christian Wermuth, die-cutter in Gotha

DUCHY

REGULAR COINAGE

KM# 30 3 PFENNIG
Billon **Ruler:** August Ludwig **Obverse:** Arms **Reverse:** 3 in orb

Date	Mintage	VG	F	VF	XF	Unc
1751 AW	—	15.00	30.00	65.00	110	—

KM# 31 4 PFENNIG
Billon **Ruler:** August Ludwig **Obverse:** Arms **Reverse:** Value

Date	Mintage	VG	F	VF	XF	Unc
1751 AW	—	7.50	15.00	35.00	60.00	—

KM# 32 6 PFENNIG
Billon **Ruler:** August Ludwig **Obverse:** Arms **Reverse:** Value

Date	Mintage	VG	F	VF	XF	Unc
1751 AW	—	8.50	17.50	40.00	65.00	—

KM# 33 1/24 THALER
Billon **Ruler:** August Ludwig **Obverse:** Crowned AL monogram **Reverse:** Value in wreath

Date	Mintage	VG	F	VF	XF	Unc
1751 AW	—	20.00	40.00	75.00	150	—

KM# 34 1/24 THALER
Billon **Ruler:** August Ludwig **Rev. Legend:** NACH DEM LEIPZIGER FVS

Date	Mintage	VG	F	VF	XF	Unc
1751 AW	—	10.00	10.00	40.00	70.00	—

KM# 35 1/12 THALER
Billon **Ruler:** August Ludwig **Obverse:** Crowned AL monogram **Reverse:** Value in wreath

Date	Mintage	VG	F	VF	XF	Unc
1751 AW	—	25.00	40.00	80.00	150	—

KM# 36 1/12 THALER
Billon **Ruler:** August Ludwig **Rev. Legend:** NACH DEM LEIPZIGER FUS

Date	Mintage	VG	F	VF	XF	Unc
1751 AW	—	10.00	17.50	35.00	65.00	—

KM# 28 1/3 THALER
Silver **Ruler:** August Ludwig **Obverse:** Crowned shield above value **Obv. Legend:** D • G • AVGVST • LVDOVIC • P • ANH... **Reverse:** Crowned bear walking left on wall **Rev. Legend:** INVIA NVLLA •

Date	Mintage	VG	F	VF	XF	Unc
1750 AW	—	40.00	90.00	175	275	—

KM# 24 2/3 THALER
Silver **Ruler:** August Ludwig **Obverse:** Crowned shield with bear supporters, value below **Obv. Legend:** D.G. AVGVSTVS LVDOVICVS PRINCEPS AMHALT * **Reverse:** Bear holding shield at left

Date	Mintage	VG	F	VF	XF	Unc
1747 IIG	—	65.00	150	275	550	—
1750 AW	—	60.00	145	265	530	—

KM# 23 THALER
Silver **Ruler:** August Ludwig **Subject:** Death of Emanuel Lebrecht **Obverse:** Bust right, date **Reverse:** Helmeted arms, VT FERT...

Date	Mintage	VG	F	VF	XF	Unc
1704 CW Rare	—	—	—	—	—	—

KM# 37 THALER (Reichsthaler)
Silver **Ruler:** August Ludwig **Obverse:** Bust right **Reverse:** Bear holding shield **Note:** Dav. #1910.

Date	Mintage	VG	F	VF	XF	Unc
1751 AW	—	200	400	750	1,700	—

KM# 25 4/3 REICHSTHALER
Silver **Ruler:** August Ludwig **Obverse:** Crowned arms supported by bears **Obv. Legend:** D • G • AUGUSTUS LUDOVICUS PRINCEPS ANHALT **Reverse:** Bear holding shield **Rev. Legend:** DVX SAX • ANGR • ET WESTPH... **Note:** Dav. #1908.

Date	Mintage	VG	F	VF	XF	Unc
1747 AW	—	200	400	750	1,650	—

KM# 26 1-1/3 REICHSTHALER
Silver **Ruler:** August Ludwig **Obverse:** Armored bust right **Obv. Legend:** D • G • AVGVSTVS LVDOVICVS PRINCEPS ANHALT **Reverse:** Bear holding shield **Rev. Legend:** DVX SAX • ANGR • ET WESTPH • COM • ASCAN • DOM • B • E T S * **Note:** Dav. #1909.

Date	Mintage	VG	F	VF	XF	Unc
1747 AW	—	150	300	600	1,350	—

TRADE COINAGE

KM# 27.1 DUCAT
3.5000 g., 0.9860 Gold 0.1109 oz. AGW **Ruler:** August Ludwig **Obverse:** Crowned arms supported by bears **Obv. Legend:** D G • AVGVSTVS LVDOVICVS PRINCEPS ANHALT **Reverse:** Bear holding shield **Note:** Fr.#26.

Date	Mintage	VG	F	VF	XF	Unc
1747 IIG	—	300	600	1,250	2,250	—
1751 AW	—	300	600	1,250	2,250	—

KM# 27.2 DUCAT
3.5000 g., 0.9860 Gold 0.1109 oz. AGW **Ruler:** August Ludwig **Obverse:** Crowned arms with bear supporters **Reverse:** Date in Roman numerals

Date	Mintage	VG	F	VF	XF	Unc
1747 IIG	—	350	650	1,350	2,500	—

KM# 38 DUCAT
3.5000 g., 0.9860 Gold 0.1109 oz. AGW **Ruler:** August Ludwig **Obverse:** Head right **Reverse:** Bear holding shield **Note:** Fr.#27.

Date	Mintage	VG	F	VF	XF	Unc
1751 AW	—	400	900	1,650	3,000	—

TRIAL STRIKES

KM#	Date	Mintage	Identification	Mkt Val
TS1	1750	—	Ducat. Copper. Script AL monogram. Bear walking on wall. RECTO GRADU.	—

ANHALT-ZERBST

Zerbst was one of the major parts of the division of 1252. It was divided into Zerbst and Dessau in 1396 and absorbed Bernburg in 1486. Zerbst ceded to Dessau in 1508 and was given to the 4th son of Joachim Ernst in the division of 1603. It became extinct in 1793 and was divided between Dessau, Bernburg and Köthen.

RULERS
Carl Wilhelm, 1667-1718
Johann August, 1718-1742
Johann Ludwig and Christian August, 1742-1746
Christian August, alone, 1746-1747
Johanna Elisabeth von Holstein-Gottorp, Dowager Princess Regent, 1747-1752, died 1760
Friedrich August, 1747-1793

MINT OFFICIALS' INITIALS

Initials	Date	Name
GW	1701	
HCRF	1744-53	Heinrich Christian Rudolf Friese
HS, IHS	1744-53	Johann Heinrich Siegel in Harzgerode
IGS	1753-67	Johann Gottfried Siegel in Harzgerode
IIG, JJG	1727-28, 1747	Johann Jeremias Grundler in Stolberg

DUCHY

REGULAR COINAGE

KM# 49 HELLER
Copper **Ruler:** Friedrich August **Obverse:** Bust right **Obv. Legend:** D • G • F • - A • P • A • **Reverse:** Arms divide date, value below **Rev. Legend:** F • A • Z • L • M •, below; I. PFENNING

Date	Mintage	VG	F	VF	XF	Unc
1766	—	8.00	12.50	20.00	38.00	—

KM# 50 PFENNING

Copper, 24 mm. **Ruler:** Friedrich August **Obverse:** Armored bust right **Obv. Legend:** D • G • F • - A • P • A • **Reverse:** Arms divide date, value below **Rev. Legend:** F • A • Z • L • M •, below; I • PFENNING

Date	Mintage	VG	F	VF	XF	Unc
1766	—	8.00	12.50	20.00	38.00	—

KM# 51 PFENNING

Copper, 20 mm. **Ruler:** Friedrich August **Obverse:** Armored bust right **Obv. Legend:** D • G • F • - A • P • A • **Reverse:** Arms divide date, value below **Rev. Legend:** F • A • Z • L • M •, below; I • PFENNING

Date	Mintage	VG	F	VF	XF	Unc
1766	—	8.00	12.50	20.00	38.00	—

KM# 38 4 PFENNIG

1.5200 g., 0.1600 Silver 0.0078 oz. ASW **Ruler:** Johanna Elisabeth von Holstein-Gottorp, Dowager Princess Regent Died 1760 **Obverse:** Crowned IEFA monogram **Reverse:** Value, F. A. Z. L. M

Date	Mintage	VG	F	VF	XF	Unc
1749 HCRF	—	12.00	25.00	50.00	75.00	—
1749	—	12.00	25.00	50.00	75.00	—

KM# 53 4 PFENNIG

1.5200 g., 0.1600 Silver 0.0078 oz. ASW **Ruler:** Friedrich August **Obverse:** Arms **Reverse:** Value and date in circle, F. A. Z. L. M. across center

Date	Mintage	VG	F	VF	XF	Unc
1767	—	18.00	32.00	55.00	75.00	—

KM# 54 4 PFENNIG

1.5200 g., 0.1600 Silver 0.0078 oz. ASW **Ruler:** Friedrich August **Reverse:** Without F. A. Z. L. M

Date	Mintage	VG	F	VF	XF	Unc
1767	—	20.00	35.00	60.00	80.00	—

KM# 39 6 PFENNIG (Sechser)

Billon **Ruler:** Friedrich August **Obverse:** Crowned IEFA monogram **Reverse:** Value, F. A. Z. L. M

Date	Mintage	VG	F	VF	XF	Unc
1749 HCRF	—	9.00	18.00	35.00	60.00	—
1749	—	9.00	18.00	35.00	60.00	—

KM# 46 16 PFENNIGE (4 Groschen)

2.4100 g., 0.4100 Silver 0.0318 oz. ASW **Ruler:** Friedrich August **Obverse:** Armored bust right within wreath of laurel and palm **Reverse:** Arms within sprays

Date	Mintage	VG	F	VF	XF	Unc
1764	—	40.00	65.00	85.00	150	—

KM# 55 16 PFENNIGE (4 Groschen)

2.4100 g., 0.4100 Silver 0.0318 oz. ASW **Ruler:** Friedrich August **Obverse:** Arms **Reverse:** Value and date in circle, value in Roman numerals

Date	Mintage	VG	F	VF	XF	Unc
1767	—	32.50	50.00	80.00	130	—

KM# 47 32 PFENNIGE (10 Kreuzer)

3.9000 g., 0.5000 Silver 0.0627 oz. ASW **Ruler:** Friedrich August **Obverse:** Bust right, date below **Reverse:** Arms and value

Date	Mintage	Good	VG	F	VF	XF
1764	—	40.00	65.00	85.00	150	—

KM# 56.1 4 GROSCHEN

5.4000 g., 0.5410 Silver 0.0939 oz. ASW **Ruler:** Friedrich August **Obv. Inscription:** IV/ GROSCHEN/ F • A • Z • L • M **Reverse:** Legend **Rev. Inscription:** LXXX/ E • F • MARCK/ AD • NORMAM/ CONVENTIO/ NIS

Date	Mintage	F	VF	XF	Unc
1767	—	10.00	35.00	75.00	185

KM# 56.2 4 GROSCHEN

5.4000 g., 0.5410 Silver 0.0939 oz. ASW **Ruler:** Friedrich August **Obverse:** Legend and date **Obv. Legend:** F • A • F • Z • A • /IV/GROSCHEN/F • A • Z • L • M **Reverse:** Legend **Rev. Legend:** E• F• MARCK/AD• NORMAM/CONVENTI/ONIS

Date	Mintage	F	VF	XF	Unc
1767	—	10.00	35.00	75.00	185

KM# 41 8 GUTE GROSCHEN

Silver **Ruler:** Friedrich August **Obverse:** Head right **Reverse:** Value and date

Date	Mintage	VG	F	VF	XF	Unc
1758	—	10.00	20.00	45.00	80.00	—

KM# 36 GULDEN (2/3 Thaler)

Silver **Ruler:** Johann Ludwig and Christian August **Subject:** Death of Johann Ludwig

Date	Mintage	VG	F	VF	XF	Unc
1746	—	50.00	100	200	300	—

KM# 37 GULDEN (2/3 Thaler)

Silver **Ruler:** Christian August alone **Subject:** Death of Friedrich August's Father

Date	Mintage	VG	F	VF	XF	Unc
1747	—	50.00	100	200	300	—

KM# 44 GULDEN (2/3 Thaler)

Silver **Ruler:** Friedrich August **Subject:** Death of Johanna Eliszbeth **Obverse:** Bust right **Reverse:** 7-line inscription

Date	Mintage	VG	F	VF	XF	Unc
1760	—	50.00	100	200	300	—

KM# 42 1/48 THALER

Billon **Ruler:** Friedrich August **Obverse:** Crowned FA monogram **Reverse:** Value

Date	Mintage	VG	F	VF	XF	Unc
1758	—	10.00	20.00	30.00	55.00	—

KM# 40 1/24 THALER (Groschen)

Billon **Ruler:** Friedrich August **Obverse:** Crowned IEFA monogram **Reverse:** Value, F. A. Z. L. M

Date	Mintage	VG	F	VF	XF	Unc
1749 HCRF	—	10.00	22.00	45.00	80.00	—
1749	—	10.00	22.00	45.00	80.00	—

KM# 43 1/12 THALER (Doppelgroschen)

Billon **Ruler:** Friedrich August

Date	Mintage	VG	F	VF	XF	Unc
1758	—	12.00	25.00	50.00	85.00	—

KM# 52 1/6 THALER

Silver **Ruler:** Friedrich August **Obverse:** Crowned monogram within branches **Obv. Legend:** AD. NORMAM - CONVENTIONIS **Reverse:** Value and date within beaded circle, legend surrounds

Date	Mintage	F	VF	XF	Unc
1766	—	45.00	75.00	135	300

KM# 31 2/3 THALER

Silver **Ruler:** Johann August **Obverse:** Crowned monogram **Reverse:** Crowned arms

Date	Mintage	VG	F	VF	XF	Unc
1728 JJG	—	90.00	150	250	450	—

KM# 32 2/3 THALER

Silver **Ruler:** Johann August **Obverse:** Conjoined busts ofJohann Ludwig and Christian August right **Obv. Legend:** D • G • IOH • LVD • & CHR • AVG • ANH • D • S • A • & W • C • A • D •... **Reverse:** Crowned arms divide date

Date	Mintage	VG	F	VF	XF	Unc
1742	—	75.00	125	200	375	—

KM# 34 2/3 THALER

Silver **Ruler:** Johann Ludwig and Christian August **Subject:** Marriage of Johann Ludwig and Sophie Augustas **Obverse:** Conjoined busts right **Obv. Legend:** D • G • IOAN • LVD • & • CHR • AVG • PR • ANH • D • SAX • CONCORDIA • **Reverse:** Date in chronogram

Date	Mintage	VG	F	VF	XF	Unc
1745	—	150	275	450	750	—

KM# 45.1 2/3 THALER

12.1000 g., 0.8750 Silver 0.3404 oz. ASW **Ruler:** Friedrich August **Obverse:** Armored bust right **Reverse:** Date in Roman numerals

Date	Mintage	F	VF	XF	Unc
1763	—	200	325	500	1,250

KM# 45.2 2/3 THALER

12.1000 g., 0.8750 Silver 0.3404 oz. ASW **Ruler:** Friedrich August **Obverse:** Armored bust right **Reverse:** Date in Arabic numerals **Note:** Varieties exist.

Date	Mintage	F	VF	XF	Unc
1767	—	200	325	500	1,250

KM# 58 THALER
Silver **Ruler:** Carl Wilhelm **Obverse:** Bust right **Reverse:** Helmeted arms, date in Roman numerals **Note:** Varieties exist.

Date	Mintage	VG	F	VF	XF	Unc
1701	—	1,200	2,000	3,000	4,500	—
1701 GW	—	1,200	2,000	3,000	4,500	—

KM# 57 THALER
28.0600 g., 0.8330 Silver 0.7515 oz. ASW **Ruler:** Friedrich August **Obverse:** Armored bust right **Obv. Legend:** D • G • FRID • AUGUST • P • ANHALT • D • S • A • & • W • C • A • D • S • V • I • & • D • **Reverse:** Helmeted arms with supporters **Rev. Legend:** * DOMINI • GRATIA • SIT • NOBISCUM *, below arms; X • E • F • M • S • * F • A • Z • L • M • 1767 AD • NORMAM • CONVENTIONIS • **Note:** Dav. #1913.

Date	Mintage	VG	F	VF	XF	Unc
1767	—	1,500	3,000	5,000	—	—

KM# 30 2 THALER
Silver **Ruler:** Carl Wilhelm **Obverse:** Bust right **Reverse:** Helmeted arms, date in Roman numerals **Note:** Dav. #1911.

Date	Mintage	VG	F	VF	XF	Unc
1701	—	2,250	4,000	6,000	9,000	—

TRADE COINAGE

KM# 21 1/2 DUCAT
1.7500 g., 0.9860 Gold 0.0555 oz. AGW **Ruler:** Carl Wilhelm **Obverse:** Head right **Reverse:** Crowned monogram

Date	Mintage	VG	F	VF	XF	Unc
ND	—	300	700	1,500	2,800	—

KM# 33 DUCAT
3.5000 g., 0.9860 Gold 0.1109 oz. AGW **Ruler:** Johann Ludwig and Christian August **Obverse:** Conjoined busts of Johann Ludwig and Christian August right **Reverse:** Crowned arms divide date

Date	Mintage	VG	F	VF	XF	Unc
1742	—	200	400	1,000	1,750	—

KM# 35 DUCAT
3.5000 g., 0.9860 Gold 0.1109 oz. AGW **Ruler:** Johann Ludwig and Christian August **Subject:** Wedding of Sophia Augusta Frederika and Karl Peter Ulric **Obverse:** Wedding inscription

Date	Mintage	VG	F	VF	XF	Unc
1745	—	450	900	1,500	2,000	—

KM# 48 DUCAT
3.5000 g., 0.9860 Gold 0.1109 oz. AGW **Ruler:** Friedrich August **Obverse:** Bust right **Reverse:** Arms and date

Date	Mintage	F	VF	XF	Unc
1764	—	700	1,500	2,250	3,500
1767	—	600	1,250	2,000	3,250

PATTERNS

Including off metal strikes

KM#	Date	Mintage	Identification	Mkt Val
Pn4	1745	—	2/3 Thaler. Gold. KM#34.	—
Pn6	1767	—	4 Groschen. Copper. KM#56.1.	—
Pn7	1767	—	Thaler. Copper. KM#57.	—
Pn5	1767	—	16 Pfennige. Copper. KM#55.	125

ARENBERG

A small principality with lands between the present-day Belgian border and the Rhine, west of Koblenz. The earliest lords of Arenberg are mentioned in the 12th century. The title and lands passed in marriage to the countship of Mark from where a new line of Arenberg lords began in the 14th century. At the end of the 15th century branch lines were founded in Sedan, Lumain and Rochefort. The male line of Arenberg became extinct in 1541 and passed by marriage to Ligne-Barbancon in 1547. The new line was raised to the rank of count in 1549, to prince in 1576 and to that of duke in 1644. The right to mint coins was granted in 1570. Philipp Franz issued Arenberg's only 17th century thaler. The lands on the left bank of the Rhine were lost to France in 1801 and the remaining possessions were mediatized in 1810.

RULERS
Leopold Philipp Karl, 1691-1754
Under regency of Maria Henrietta, 1691-1706
Alone, 1706-1754
Karl Leopold, 1754-1778
Ludwig Engelbert, 1778-1803

PRINCIPALITY

REGULAR COINAGE

KM# 7 THALER
Silver **Ruler:** Ludwig Engelbert **Obverse:** Bust right **Reverse:** Crowned, mantled and supported arms, date below **Note:** Dav. #1914. Convention Thaler.

Date	Mintage	VG	F	VF	XF	Unc
1783	—	1,500	3,000	5,000	8,000	—

KM# 9 THALER
Silver **Ruler:** Ludwig Engelbert **Obverse:** Bust right **Obv. Legend:** LVD • ENG • D • G • DVX • ARENBERGAE • S • R • I • P • **Reverse:** Crowned and mantled arms **Rev. Legend:** X • EINE * MARCK • F • **Note:** Dav. #1915.

Date	Mintage	VG	F	VF	XF	Unc
1785	—	500	700	1,150	1,850	—

TRADE COINAGE

KM# 8 DUCAT
3.5000 g., 0.9860 Gold 0.1109 oz. AGW **Ruler:** Ludwig Engelbert **Obverse:** Bust right **Obv. Legend:** SVD • ENG • D • G • DVX • ARENBERGAE • S • R • I • P • **Reverse:** Crowned and mantled arms **Note:** Fr. #39.

Date	Mintage	VG	F	VF	XF	Unc
1783	—	1,650	3,000	5,000	8,000	—

PATTERNS

Including off metal strikes

KM#	Date	Mintage	Identification	Mkt Val
Pn1	1783	—	Ducat. Bronze. KM#8.	—

AUGSBURG

BISHOPRIC

Founded in the late 9th century in the city of Augsburg, the bishopric eventually extended as far as the Bavarian frontier on the north and east, to Tyrol on the south and to Upper Swabia on the west. The earliest episcopal coinage dates from the mid-10th century and issues continued through each of the next eight and one-half centuries. The bishopric was secularized in 1803 and was absorbed by Bavaria.

RULERS
Alexander Sigismund von Pfalz-Neuburg, 1690-1737
Johann Franz von Stauffenberg, 1737-1740
Josef von Hessen-Darmstadt, 1740-1768
Clemens Wenzel, Prince of Poland and Saxony, Bishop, 1768-1803

MINT OFFICIALS' INITIALS

Initials	Date	Name
M	1717-41	Christian Ernst Muller
PHM	d.1718	Philipp Heinrich Muller, die-cutter and medailleur

Reference:
F = Gisela Förschner, Deutsche Münzen Mittelalter bis Neuzeit, v. 1 – Aachen bis Augsburg, Melsungen, 1984.

REGULAR COINAGE

KM# 21 HELLER
Copper **Ruler:** Clemens Wenzel Prince of Poland and Saxony **Obverse:** Crowned arms **Reverse:** Value and date

Date	Mintage	VG	F	VF	XF	Unc
1773	—	4.00	8.00	20.00	40.00	—

KM# 22 1/4 KREUTZER
Copper **Ruler:** Clemens Wenzel Prince of Poland and Saxony **Obverse:** Crowned arms, legend around border **Reverse:** Value and date

Date	Mintage	VG	F	VF	XF	Unc
1773	—	4.00	8.00	20.00	40.00	—

KM# 23 1/2 KREUTZER
Copper **Ruler:** Clemens Wenzel Prince of Poland and Saxony **Obverse:** Crowned arms, legend around border **Reverse:** Value and date

Date	Mintage	VG	F	VF	XF	Unc
1773	—	4.00	8.00	20.00	40.00	—

KM# 24 KREUTZER
Copper **Ruler:** Clemens Wenzel Prince of Poland and Saxony **Obverse:** Crowned arms, legend around border **Reverse:** Value and date

Date	Mintage	VG	F	VF	XF	Unc
1773	—	5.00	10.00	20.00	40.00	—
1774	—	5.00	10.00	20.00	40.00	—
1775	—	5.00	10.00	20.00	40.00	—

KM# 25 10 KREUTZER
Silver **Ruler:** Clemens Wenzel Prince of Poland and Saxony **Obverse:** Bust right **Reverse:** Crowned arms

Date	Mintage	VG	F	VF	XF	Unc
1773	—	10.00	22.00	45.00	90.00	—
1774	—	10.00	22.00	45.00	90.00	—
1775	—	10.00	22.00	45.00	90.00	—

KM# 26 20 KREUTZER
Silver **Ruler:** Clemens Wenzel Prince of Poland and Saxony

Date	Mintage	VG	F	VF	XF	Unc
1773	—	10.00	30.00	70.00	150	—

KM# 27 1/48 THALER (2-1/2 Kreutzer)
Silver **Ruler:** Clemens Wenzel Prince of Poland and Saxony **Obverse:** Crowned arms, legend around border **Reverse:** Value and date

Date	Mintage	VG	F	VF	XF	Unc
1773	—	6.00	10.00	25.00	50.00	—

KM# 28 1/24 THALER (5 Kreutzer)
Silver **Ruler:** Clemens Wenzel Prince of Poland and Saxony **Obverse:** Crowned arms, legend around border **Reverse:** Value and date

Date	Mintage	VG	F	VF	XF	Unc
1773	—	8.00	15.00	40.00	75.00	—

KM# 17 1/4 THALER

Silver **Ruler:** Josef von Hesse-Darmstadt **Obverse:** Bust right with cross on chest **Reverse:** Mitre divides two crowned shields **Note:** Species.

Date	Mintage	VG	F	VF	XF	Unc
1744 M	—	60.00	150	300	500	—

KM# 18 1/2 THALER

Silver **Ruler:** Josef von Hesse-Darmstadt **Obverse:** Bust right with cross on chest **Obv. Legend:** IOSEPH•D•G•EP•AUGUST • S • R • I • PR • LANDG • HASS • **Reverse:** Mitre divides two crowned shields **Note:** Species.

Date	Mintage	VG	F	VF	XF	Unc
1744 M	—	50.00	150	300	500	—

KM# 19 THALER

Silver **Ruler:** Josef von Hesse-Darmstadt **Obverse:** Bust right with cross on chest **Obv. Legend:** IOSEPH•D•G•EP•AUGUST S • R • I • PR • LANDGR • HASS • **Reverse:** Mitre divides two crowned shields **Rev. Legend:** AUGUSTANO SACERDOTIO ORNATO ET AUCTO **Note:** Species. Dav. #1916.

Date	Mintage	VG	F	VF	XF	Unc
1744 M	—	100	250	450	800	—

TRADE COINAGE

KM# 15 DUCAT

3.5000 g., 0.9860 Gold 0.1109 oz. AGW **Ruler:** Alexander Sigismund von Pfalz-Neuberg **Obverse:** Head right, date below **Reverse:** Two crowned shields

Date	Mintage	VG	F	VF	XF	Unc
1708	—	600	1,250	2,750	3,750	—

KM# 20 DUCAT

3.5000 g., 0.9860 Gold 0.1109 oz. AGW **Ruler:** Josef von Hesse-Darmstadt **Obverse:** Bust right with cross on chest **Reverse:** Mitre divides two crowned shields, date below

Date	Mintage	VG	F	VF	XF	Unc
1744	—	450	1,000	2,250	3,500	—

KM# 16 2 DUCAT

7.0000 g., 0.9860 Gold 0.2219 oz. AGW **Ruler:** Alexander Sigismund von Pfalz-Neuberg **Obverse:** Head right **Obv. Legend:** ALEX • SIG • D • G • EPISC • AVG • **Reverse:** Crown above two shields

Date	Mintage	VG	F	VF	XF	Unc
1708	—	2,000	4,500	6,500	9,000	—

FREE CITY

Founded by the Romans about 15B.C. and named Augusta Vindelicorum in honor of the Emperor Augustus, the city was the site of a German imperial mint for several centuries from about the year 1000. In 1276, Augsburg was made a free imperial city, but did not receive the right to strike its own coins until 1521. Earlier date issues were produced under the office of the Imperial Chamberlain. Augsburg's coinage came to an end in 1805 and the city followed the bishopric into Bavarian envelopment in the following year.

MINT OFFICIALS' INITIALS

Initials	Date	Name
B	1731-56	Konrad Borer, die-cutter
CM, M	1714-41	Christian Ernst Müller, die-cutter
FH, F(A)H	1761-66	Frings, mint warden and Johann Christian Holeisen
FT	1758	Frings, mint warden and Thiebaud, die-cutter
PHM, M or *	1677-1718	Philipp Heinrich Müller, die-cutter
T, IT	1740-69	Jonas Peter Thiebaud, die-cutter
* or **	1775-82	Peter Neuss

Reference:

F = Albert von Forster, ***Die Erzeugnisse der Stempelschneidekunst in Augsburg und Ph. H. Müller's nach meiner Sammlung beschrieben Und die Augsburger Stadtmünzen,*** Leipzig, 1910.

REGULAR COINAGE

KM# 128 HELLER

Copper **Obverse:** Pine cone divides date **Reverse:** Eight-armed cross with rosette in center **Note:** Struck on octagonal flan. Varieties exist.

Date	Mintage	VG	F	VF	XF	Unc
1715	—	3.00	6.00	12.00	28.00	—
1718	—	3.00	6.00	12.00	28.00	—
1719	—	3.00	6.00	12.00	28.00	—
1721	—	3.00	6.00	12.00	28.00	—
1722	—	3.00	6.00	12.00	28.00	—
1723	—	3.00	6.00	12.00	28.00	—
1726	—	3.00	6.00	12.00	28.00	—
1728	—	3.00	6.00	12.00	28.00	—
1729	—	3.00	6.00	12.00	28.00	—
1730	—	3.00	6.00	12.00	28.00	—
1731	—	3.00	6.00	12.00	28.00	—
1733	—	3.00	6.00	12.00	28.00	—
1734	—	3.00	6.00	12.00	28.00	—
1735	—	3.00	6.00	12.00	28.00	—
1736	—	3.00	6.00	12.00	28.00	—
1737	—	3.00	6.00	12.00	28.00	—
1738	—	3.00	6.00	12.00	28.00	—
1739	—	3.00	6.00	12.00	28.00	—
1740	—	3.00	6.00	12.00	28.00	—

KM# 144 HELLER

Copper **Obverse:** Pine cone in cartouche divides date **Reverse:** Maltese cross in cartouche **Note:** Struck on octagonal flan. Varieties exist.

Date	Mintage	VG	F	VF	XF	Unc
1740	—	3.00	7.00	16.00	35.00	—
1741	—	3.00	7.00	16.00	35.00	—
1742	—	3.00	7.00	16.00	35.00	—
1743	—	3.00	7.00	16.00	35.00	—

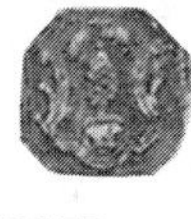

KM# 150 HELLER

Copper **Obverse:** Small pine cone in cartouche **Reverse:** Cross divides date

Date	Mintage	VG	F	VF	XF	Unc
1744	—	3.00	6.00	12.00	30.00	—
1745	—	3.00	6.00	12.00	30.00	—
1746	—	3.00	6.00	12.00	30.00	—
1747	—	3.00	6.00	12.00	30.00	—

KM# 151 HELLER

Copper **Obverse:** Larger pine cone in branches **Reverse:** Cross divides date

Date	Mintage	VG	F	VF	XF	Unc
1744	—	3.00	6.00	12.00	30.00	—
1745	—	3.00	6.00	12.00	30.00	—
1747	—	3.00	6.00	12.00	30.00	—
1748	—	3.00	6.00	12.00	30.00	—
1749	—	3.00	6.00	12.00	30.00	—
1750	—	3.00	6.00	12.00	30.00	—
1751	—	3.00	6.00	12.00	30.00	—
1752	—	3.00	6.00	12.00	30.00	—
1753	—	3.00	6.00	12.00	30.00	—
1754	—	3.00	6.00	12.00	30.00	—
1755	—	3.00	6.00	12.00	30.00	—
1757	—	3.00	6.00	12.00	30.00	—
1758	—	3.00	6.00	12.00	30.00	—
1759	—	3.00	6.00	12.00	30.00	—
1775	—	3.00	6.00	12.00	30.00	—
1776	—	3.00	6.00	12.00	30.00	—

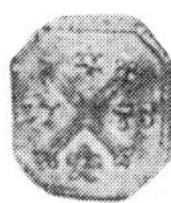

KM# 170 HELLER

Copper **Obverse:** Pine cone in cartouche **Reverse:** Cross divides date

Date	Mintage	VG	F	VF	XF	Unc
1760	—	3.00	6.00	12.00	30.00	—
1761	—	3.00	6.00	12.00	30.00	—
1763	—	3.00	6.00	12.00	30.00	—
1764	—	3.00	6.00	12.00	30.00	—
1765	—	3.00	6.00	12.00	30.00	—
1766	—	3.00	6.00	12.00	30.00	—
1769	—	3.00	6.00	12.00	30.00	—
1770	—	3.00	6.00	12.00	30.00	—
1771	—	3.00	6.00	12.00	30.00	—
1772	—	3.00	6.00	12.00	30.00	—
1773	—	3.00	6.00	12.00	30.00	—
1774	—	3.00	6.00	12.00	30.00	—
1775	—	3.00	6.00	12.00	30.00	—

KM# 188 HELLER

Copper **Obverse:** Crowned arms **Reverse:** Value, date

Date	Mintage	VG	F	VF	XF	Unc
1780	—	2.00	5.00	10.00	28.00	—
1782	—	2.00	5.00	10.00	28.00	—
1786	—	2.00	5.00	10.00	28.00	—
1788	—	2.00	5.00	10.00	28.00	—
1793	—	2.00	5.00	10.00	28.00	—
1796	—	2.00	5.00	10.00	28.00	—
1797	—	2.00	5.00	10.00	28.00	—
1798	—	2.00	5.00	10.00	28.00	—
1801	—	2.00	5.00	10.00	28.00	—

KM# 129 PFENNING

Copper **Obverse:** Pine cone in circle **Reverse:** I/PFENNING/STATT/MYNZ/ date

Date	Mintage	Good	VG	F	VF	XF
1715	—	6.00	10.00	16.00	28.00	—

KM# 164 PFENNING

Copper **Obverse:** Pine cone in branches **Reverse:** Value and date

Date	Mintage	VG	F	VF	XF	Unc
1758 FT	—	5.00	9.00	18.00	40.00	—

KM# 168 PFENNING

Copper **Obverse:** Pine cone within cartouche **Reverse:** Value and date

Date	Mintage	VG	F	VF	XF	Unc
1759	—	4.00	8.00	15.00	35.00	—
1761	—	4.00	8.00	15.00	35.00	—
1762	—	4.00	8.00	15.00	35.00	—
1763	—	4.00	8.00	15.00	35.00	—
1780	—	4.00	8.00	15.00	35.00	—

KM# 181 PFENNING

Copper **Reverse:** Legend without STADTMYNZ

Date	Mintage	VG	F	VF	XF	Unc
1764	—	4.00	8.00	15.00	35.00	—
1765	—	4.00	8.00	15.00	35.00	—
1766	—	4.00	8.00	15.00	35.00	—

KM# 189 PFENNING

Copper **Obverse:** Pine cone within shield **Reverse:** Value, inscription and date **Rev. Inscription:** STADTMYNZ

Date	Mintage	VG	F	VF	XF	Unc
1780	—	3.00	6.00	12.00	32.00	—
1781	—	3.00	6.00	12.00	32.00	—
1782	—	3.00	6.00	12.00	32.00	—
1786	—	3.00	6.00	12.00	32.00	—
1789	—	3.00	6.00	12.00	32.00	—
1796	—	3.00	6.00	12.00	32.00	—
1797	—	3.00	6.00	12.00	32.00	—
1798	—	3.00	6.00	12.00	32.00	—
1799	—	3.00	6.00	12.00	32.00	—
1800	—	3.00	6.00	12.00	32.00	—
1801	—	3.00	6.00	12.00	32.00	—
1802	—	3.00	6.00	12.00	32.00	—
1803	—	3.00	6.00	12.00	32.00	—

KM# 135 2 PFENNIG

Copper **Obverse:** Pine cone within branches **Reverse:** II/PFENNIG/STADTMUNTZ/date

Date	Mintage	Good	VG	F	VF	XF
1725	—	6.00	10.00	16.00	30.00	—

KM# 165 2 PFENNIG

Copper **Obverse:** Pine cone within branches **Reverse:** Value, inscription and date

Date	Mintage	VG	F	VF	XF	Unc
1758 FT	—	3.00	6.00	12.00	30.00	—
1759	—	3.00	6.00	12.00	30.00	—

KM# 169 2 PFENNIG

Copper **Obverse:** Pine cone within cartouche **Reverse:** Value and date

Date	Mintage	VG	F	VF	XF	Unc
1759	—	4.00	8.00	16.00	35.00	—
1762	—	4.00	8.00	16.00	35.00	—
1763	—	4.00	8.00	16.00	35.00	—
1764	—	4.00	8.00	16.00	35.00	—
1765	—	4.00	8.00	16.00	35.00	—
1780 Star	—	4.00	8.00	16.00	35.00	—

KM# 182 2 PFENNIG

Copper **Reverse:** Legend without STADMYNZ

Date	Mintage	VG	F	VF	XF	Unc
1764	—	4.00	8.00	16.00	35.00	—
1765	—	4.00	8.00	16.00	35.00	—
1766	—	4.00	8.00	16.00	35.00	—
1769	—	4.00	8.00	16.00	35.00	—

KM# 109 KREUTZER

Silver **Obverse:** Crowned imperial eagle with 1 in orb circle, titles of Leopold **Reverse:** Pine cone divides date within circle **Note:** Varieties exist.

Date	Mintage	VG	F	VF	XF	Unc
1702	—	8.00	15.00	27.00	55.00	—
1703	—	8.00	15.00	27.00	55.00	—

KM# 116 KREUTZER

Silver **Obverse:** Titles of Josef I

Date	Mintage	VG	F	VF	XF	Unc
1706	—	—	—	—	—	—

KM# 137 KREUTZER

Silver **Obverse:** Titles of Karl VI **Reverse:** Pine cone on pedestal divides date **Note:** Varieties exist.

Date	Mintage	VG	F	VF	XF	Unc
1726	—	5.00	10.00	18.00	38.00	—

KM# 185 KREUTZER

Billon **Obverse:** Value in orb on breast of crowned double eagle **Reverse:** Pine cone in pot divides date

Date	Mintage	VG	F	VF	XF	Unc
1766 FH	—	15.00	30.00	50.00	100	—

KM# 166 2-1/2 KREUTZER

Billon **Obverse:** Pine cone in pot divides date **Reverse:** Crowned double-headed imperial eagle, value below

Date	Mintage	VG	F	VF	XF	Unc
1758	—	20.00	45.00	90.00	175	—

KM# 167 5 KREUTZER

Billon **Obverse:** Pine cone on pedestal divides date and SW **Reverse:** Crowned double-headed imperial eagle, value below

Date	Mintage	VG	F	VF	XF	Unc
1758	—	20.00	40.00	70.00	125	—
1759	—	20.00	40.00	70.00	125	—

KM# 186 5 KREUTZER

Billon

Date	Mintage	VG	F	VF	XF	Unc
1766 FH	—	17.50	35.00	60.00	100	—

KM# 171 10 KREUTZER

Billon **Obverse:** Imperial eagle **Reverse:** Pine cone on pedestal

Date	Mintage	VG	F	VF	XF	Unc
1760 T	—	12.50	25.00	50.00	100	—

KM# 176 10 KREUTZER

Billon **Obverse:** Crowned double-headed imperial eagle with shield on breast **Reverse:** Pine cone on pedestal within branches

Date	Mintage	VG	F	VF	XF	Unc
1761 T-F(A)H	—	7.50	15.00	30.00	60.00	—
1763 T-F(A)H	—	7.50	15.00	30.00	60.00	—
1764 T-F(A)H	—	7.50	15.00	30.00	60.00	—
1765 T-F(A)H	—	7.50	15.00	30.00	60.00	—

KM# 172 20 KREUTZER

Billon **Obverse:** Imperial eagle **Reverse:** Pine cone on pedestal

Date	Mintage	VG	F	VF	XF	Unc
1760 T	—	15.00	30.00	70.00	150	—

KM# 177 20 KREUTZER

Billon **Obverse:** Pine cone on pedestal within branches **Reverse:** Crowned double-headed imperial eagle with shield on breast

Date	Mintage	VG	F	VF	XF	Unc
1761 T-F(A)H	—	12.50	25.00	55.00	100	—
1763 T-F(A)H	—	12.50	25.00	55.00	100	—
1764 T-F(A)H	—	12.50	25.00	55.00	100	—
1765 T-F(A)H	—	12.50	25.00	55.00	100	—

KM# 130 1/32 THALER

Silver **Obverse:** Crowned imperial eagle **Reverse:** Pine cone divides date within circle, XXXII EINEN...

Date	Mintage	VG	F	VF	XF	Unc
1715	—	50.00	90.00	135	200	—

KM# 131 1/16 THALER

Silver **Obverse:** Crowned imperial eagle **Reverse:** Pine cone divides date within circle, XVI EINEN...

Date	Mintage	VG	F	VF	XF	Unc
1715	—	60.00	100	150	225	—

KM# 117 1/8 THALER

Silver **Obverse:** Bust of Josef I right **Reverse:** Pine cone between two river gods, crowned imperial eagle above, date below

Date	Mintage	VG	F	VF	XF	Unc
1708	—	—	—	—	—	—

KM# 125 1/8 THALER

Silver **Obverse:** Bust of Karl VI right **Reverse:** Pine cone between two branches, date above, 1/8 below

Date	Mintage	VG	F	VF	XF	Unc
1713	—	—	—	—	—	—

KM# 136 1/8 THALER

Silver **Obverse:** Crowned imperial eagle, orb with 1/8 on breast **Reverse:** Pine cone between two branches, date above

Date	Mintage	VG	F	VF	XF	Unc
1725	—	—	—	—	—	—

KM# 118 1/4 THALER

Silver **Obverse:** Bust and titles of Josef I **Reverse:** Pine cone on pedestal between two river gods, date below

Date	Mintage	VG	F	VF	XF	Unc
1708	—	—	—	—	—	—

KM# 126 1/4 THALER

Silver **Obverse:** Bust of Karl VI right **Reverse:** Crowned imperial eagle with pine cone in oval shield on breast, 1/4 below, date above

Date	Mintage	VG	F	VF	XF	Unc
1713	—	—	—	—	—	—

KM# 154 1/4 THALER

Silver **Obverse:** City view **Reverse:** Armored bust of Francis I right

Date	Mintage	VG	F	VF	XF	Unc
1745 T	—	80.00	220	450	750	—

KM# 155 1/4 THALER

Silver **Obverse:** Armored bust of Francis I right **Obv. Legend:** FRANCISCUS • I • - D • G • ROM • IMP • S • A • **Reverse:** Arms within cartouche

Date	Mintage	VG	F	VF	XF	Unc
1745 T	—	75.00	200	400	650	—

KM# 119 1/2 THALER

Silver **Obverse:** Bust of Josef I right **Reverse:** Crowned imperial eagle above pine cone supported by two river gods, date below

Date	Mintage	VG	F	VF	XF	Unc
1708	—	550	1,000	1,750	2,800	—

KM# 127 1/2 THALER

Silver **Obverse:** Bust of Karl VI right

Date	Mintage	VG	F	VF	XF	Unc
1713	—	—	—	—	—	—
1725	—	—	—	—	—	—

KM# 156 1/2 THALER

Silver **Obverse:** Crown above pine cone on pedestal **Reverse:** Crowned double-headed imperial eagle with sword and orb

Date	Mintage	VG	F	VF	XF	Unc
1745 T	—	75.00	150	350	650	—

KM# 173 1/2 THALER

Silver **Subject:** Francis I **Obverse:** Pine cone on pedestal within crowned cartouche **Reverse:** Head right **Rev. Legend:** FRANCISCVS I • D • G • I • S • A • GER • IER • REX • L • B • M • H • D •

Date	Mintage	VG	F	VF	XF	Unc
1760 T	—	65.00	125	250	400	—

KM# 179 1/2 THALER

Silver **Subject:** Peace of Hubertusburg **Obverse:** Standing figure left of arms on pedestal **Reverse:** Head of Francis I right

Date	Mintage	VG	F	VF	XF	Unc
1763	—	125	250	450	800	—

KM# 120 THALER

Silver **Obverse:** Crowned imperial eagle above pine cone supported by two river gods, date below **Reverse:** Bust of Josef I right **Note:** Dav. #1917.

Date	Mintage	VG	F	VF	XF	Unc
1708	—	700	1,200	2,000	3,500	—

KM# 122.1 THALER

Silver **Obverse:** Without orb on eagle's breast **Reverse:** Karl VI **Note:** Dav. #1918.

Date	Mintage	VG	F	VF	XF	Unc
1711	—	700	1,200	2,000	3,500	—

KM# 122.2 THALER

Silver **Obverse:** Orb on eagle's breast **Obv. Legend:** AVGVSTA VIN - DELICORVM **Reverse:** Bust of Karl VI right **Rev. Legend:** CAROL • VI • D • G • R • - I • S • A • G • H • H • B • REX • **Note:** Dav. #1919.

Date	Mintage	VG	F	VF	XF	Unc
1725	—	200	350	600	1,000	—

Note: Coin illustrated is inserted in a jewelry bezel

KM# 145 THALER

Silver **Obverse:** City view with arms and river gods in foreground **Obv. Legend:** AUGUSTA VINDELICORUM **Reverse:** Armored laureate bust of Karl VI right **Rev. Legend:** CAROLUS VI • D • G • - R • I • S • A • G • H • H • B • REX • **Note:** Dav. #1921.

Date	Mintage	F	VF	XF	Unc
1740 IT	—	750	1,250	2,500	4,000

KM# 148 THALER

Silver **Subject:** Karl VII **Obverse:** Crowned double-headed imperial eagle with arms on breast **Obv. Legend:** AUGUSTA • VIN • DELICORUM • **Reverse:** Armored laureate bust right **Rev. Legend:** CAROLUS VII • D • - G • ROM • IMP • S • A • * **Note:** Dav. #1922.

Date	Mintage	F	VF	XF	Unc
1743 IT	—	500	850	1,350	2,250

KM# 152 THALER

Silver **Obverse:** City view beneath "all seeing eye of God" **Obv. Legend:** AUGUSTA VINDELICORUM **Reverse:** Armored laureate bust of Karl VII right **Rev. Legend:** CAROLUS VII • D • - G • ROM • IMP • S • A • * **Note:** Dav. #1924.

Date	Mintage	F	VF	XF	Unc
MDCCXLIV (1744) IT	—	400	750	1,250	2,200

KM# 157 THALER

Silver **Subject:** Franz I **Obverse:** Seated figure with pine cone left **Obv. Legend:** AUGUSTA - VINDELIC • **Reverse:** Laureate bust right **Rev. Legend:** FRANCISCUS • I • D • - G • ROM • IMP • SEMP • AUG • **Note:** Dav. #1925.

Date	Mintage	VG	F	VF	XF	Unc
1745 IT	—	200	400	700	1,100	—
1745 T	—	200	400	700	1,100	—

KM# 174 THALER

Silver **Obverse:** Crowned double-headed imperial eagle with arms on breast **Obv. Legend:** FRANCISCUS I • D • - G • ROM • IMP • SEMP • AUG • **Reverse:** Draped laureate bust of Franz I right **Rev. Legend:** AUGUSTA VINDELIC • - AD NORM • CONVENT • **Note:** Dav. #1926.

Date	Mintage	VG	F	VF	XF	Unc
1760	—	100	125	175	300	—

KM# 175 THALER

Silver **Reverse:** Pine cone and river gods **Note:** Dav. #1927.

Date	Mintage	VG	F	VF	XF	Unc
1760	—	150	225	350	700	—

KM# 180 THALER

Silver **Obverse:** Imperial eagle above city arms on pedestal with river gods at sides **Obv. Legend:** AUGUST: VIND • - AD NORM: CONV • **Reverse:** Armored bust of IFranz I right **Rev. Legend:** FRANCISCUS I • D: G • - ROM • IMP • SEMP • AUG * **Note:** Dav. #1928.

Date	Mintage	VG	F	VF	XF	Unc
1763 F(A)H	—	100	150	200	500	—

KM# 183 THALER

Silver **Obverse:** Armored laureate bust of Franz I right **Obv. Legend:** AUGUSTA VINDELICOR: - AD NORM: CONVENTIO: **Reverse:** Armored laureate bust of Franz I right **Rev. Legend:** FRANCISCUS I • D: G • - ROM • IMP • SEMP • AUG * **Note:** Dav. #1929.

Date	Mintage	VG	F	VF	XF	Unc
1764 T-F(A)H	—	75.00	100	150	225	—

KM# 184 THALER

Silver **Obverse:** Crowned arms within branches **Obv. Legend:** AUGUSTA VINDELICOR • AD NORM • CONVENT • , X. EINE FEINE MARCK below **Reverse:** Laureate head of Franz I right **Rev. Legend:** FRANCISCUS I • D • G • ROM • IMP • SEM • AUG • **Note:** Dav. #1930.

Date	Mintage	VG	F	VF	XF	Unc
1765 IT-F(A)H	—	75.00	100	150	225	—

KM# 146 2 THALER

Silver **Obverse:** Crowned arms in branches with river gods at sides **Obv. Legend:** LIB: S: R: I: CIVIT: AUGUSTA VINDEL: **Reverse:** Titles of Karl VI **Rev. Legend:** D: G: CAROLUS VI: - ROM: IMP: S: AUGUSTUS • **Note:** Dav. #1920.

Date	Mintage	VG	F	VF	XF	Unc
1740 IT	—	1,450	2,250	3,500	5,000	—

KM# 153 2 THALER

Silver **Obverse:** City view **Reverse:** Crowned arms in branches with river gods at sides **Note:** Similar to 1 Thaler, KM#152. Dav. #1920.

Date	Mintage	VG	F	VF	XF	Unc
1744 IT Rare	—	—	—	—	—	—

TRADE COINAGE

KM# 132 1/2 DUCAT

1.7500 g., 0.9860 Gold 0.0555 oz. AGW **Obverse:** Laureate head of Karl VI right **Reverse:** Seated female figure next to pine cone on pedestal

Date	Mintage	VG	F	VF	XF	Unc
1717	—	400	650	950	1,750	—

KM# 163 1/2 DUCAT

1.7500 g., 0.9860 Gold 0.0555 oz. AGW **Subject:** Celebrating the Middle of the Eighteenth Century **Obverse:** Bust of Janus on pedestal within which is a pine cone **Reverse:** Two oval arms in baroque frame, date in Roman numerals above

Date	Mintage	VG	F	VF	XF	Unc
1750	—	150	300	550	950	—

KM# 110 DUCAT

3.5000 g., 0.9860 Gold 0.1109 oz. AGW **Obverse:** Pine cone between river gods **Reverse:** Bust of Leopold right

Date	Mintage	VG	F	VF	XF	Unc
1701	—	250	350	600	1,250	—

KM# 114 DUCAT

3.5000 g., 0.9860 Gold 0.1109 oz. AGW **Subject:** Leopold **Obverse:** Figure seated left holding pine cone **Reverse:** Laureate bust right

Date	Mintage	VG	F	VF	XF	Unc
1701	—	300	500	800	1,500	—
1702	—	300	500	800	1,500	—

KM# 115 DUCAT

3.5000 g., 0.9860 Gold 0.1109 oz. AGW **Subject:** Josef I **Obverse:** Figure seated left holding pine cone **Reverse:** Armored bust right

Date	Mintage	VG	F	VF	XF	Unc
MDCCV (1705)	—	300	500	800	1,500	—
MDCCVII (1707)	—	300	500	800	1,500	—

KM# 121 DUCAT

3.5000 g., 0.9860 Gold 0.1109 oz. AGW **Reverse:** Pine cone between river gods, date in exergue

Date	Mintage	VG	F	VF	XF	Unc
1708	—	250	350	600	1,250	—
1711	—	250	350	600	1,250	—

KM# 123 DUCAT

3.5000 g., 0.9860 Gold 0.1109 oz. AGW **Subject:** Karl VI **Obverse:** Crowned imperial eagle above arms with supporters **Obv. Legend:** AVGVSTA VIN - DELICORVM **Reverse:** Armored laureate bust right **Rev. Legend:** CAR • VI • D • G • R • I • - S • A • G • H • H • & • B • RX •

Date	Mintage	VG	F	VF	XF	Unc
1711	—	250	350	600	1,250	—
1714	—	250	350	600	1,250	—
1715	—	250	350	600	1,250	—

KM# 124 DUCAT

3.5000 g., 0.9860 Gold 0.1109 oz. AGW **Subject:** Coronation of Emperor Karl VI **Obverse:** Bust right **Reverse:** Crowned eagle flying to left towards sun above, date below

Date	Mintage	VG	F	VF	XF	Unc
1711	—	—	900	1,400	2,800	—

KM# 138 DUCAT

3.5000 g., 0.9860 Gold 0.1109 oz. AGW **Obverse:** Arms left of standing figure, date divided below **Obv. Legend:** AVGVSTA VINDELICORVN • **Reverse:** Bust of Karl VI right **Rev. Legend:** CAROL • V I• - D • G • ROM • IMP • S • A •

Date	Mintage	VG	F	VF	XF	Unc
1726 B	—	250	350	600	1,250	—

KM# 139 DUCAT

3.5000 g., 0.9860 Gold 0.1109 oz. AGW **Subject:** 200th Anniversary of Augsburg Confession **Obverse:** Harbor scene **Reverse:** Date in chronogram

Date	Mintage	VG	F	VF	XF	Unc
1730	—	—	250	500	1,150	—

KM# 140 DUCAT

3.5000 g., 0.9860 Gold 0.1109 oz. AGW **Obverse:** Book on table, figure at each side, pine cone at lower left, date below **Reverse:** Six-line inscription

Date	Mintage	VG	F	VF	XF	Unc
1730	—	—	200	400	850	—

KM# 141 DUCAT

3.5000 g., 0.9860 Gold 0.1109 oz. AGW **Obverse:** Inscription beneath arabesque design **Reverse:** Opened book with date on pages in front of menorah, pine cone below

Date	Mintage	VG	F	VF	XF	Unc
1730	—	—	250	500	1,000	—

KM# 142 DUCAT

3.5000 g., 0.9860 Gold 0.1109 oz. AGW **Obverse:** Pine cone between river gods, date divided below **Obv. Legend:** AVGVSTA VINDELIC **Reverse:** Bust of Karl VI right **Rev. Legend:** CAROL • VI • D • - G • ROM • IMP • S • A •

Date	Mintage	VG	F	VF	XF	Unc
1737 M	—	300	500	800	1,500	—
1737 B	—	300	500	800	1,500	—
1738 B	—	300	500	800	1,500	—

KM# 147 DUCAT

3.5000 g., 0.9860 Gold 0.1109 oz. AGW **Subject:** Karl VII **Obverse:** Seated figure holding pine cone left **Obv. Legend:** AUGUSTA - VINDELIC • **Reverse:** Laureate bust right **Rev. Legend:** CAROLUS • VII • - D • G • ROM • IMP • S • A •

Date	Mintage	VG	F	VF	XF	Unc
1742 IT	—	250	350	600	1,250	—

KM# 149 DUCAT

3.5000 g., 0.9860 Gold 0.1109 oz. AGW **Obverse:** Castles above arms within cartouche **Obv. Legend:** CAROLUS VII • - D • G • ROM • IMP • S • A • **Reverse:** Armored bust of Karl VII right **Rev. Legend:** CAROLUS VII • - D • G • ROM • IMP • S • A •

Date	Mintage	VG	F	VF	XF	Unc
1743 IT	—	300	550	1,000	1,750	—

KM# 158 DUCAT

3.5000 g., 0.9860 Gold 0.1109 oz. AGW **Subject:** Franz I **Obverse:** Crowned double-headed imperial eagle above city arms on pedestal flanked by river gods **Obv. Legend:** AUGUSTA • VIN - DELICORUM • **Reverse:** Laureate bust right **Rev. Legend:** FRANCISCUS I • - D • G • ROM • IMP • SEM • AV •

Date	Mintage	VG	F	VF	XF	Unc
1745 T	—	400	800	1,300	2,000	—

KM# 178 DUCAT

3.5000 g., 0.9860 Gold 0.1109 oz. AGW **Obverse:** Pine cone on pedestal, branch curling around top **Obv. Legend:** AVGVSTA VIN - DELICORVM * **Reverse:** Head of Franz I right **Rev. Legend:** FRANC•I•D•G•R•I•S•A•GER•IER•REX•L•B•M•H•D•

Date	Mintage	VG	F	VF	XF	Unc
1762 T-F(A)H	—	600	1,250	2,250	3,250	—
1763 T-F(A)H	—	500	1,100	2,000	3,000	—

KM# 187 DUCAT

3.5000 g., 0.9860 Gold 0.1109 oz. AGW **Subject:** Josef II **Obverse:** Crowned arms within ornate frame **Obv. Legend:** AUGUSTA VINDELIC • **Reverse:** Armored bust right **Rev. Legend:** IOSEPHUS II • - D • G • RO • IMP • S • A •

Date	Mintage	F	VF	XF	Unc
1767 T	—	600	1,000	1,800	2,750

KM# 143 2 DUCAT

7.0000 g., 0.9860 Gold 0.2219 oz. AGW **Obverse:** Laureate bust of Karl VI right **Reverse:** Pine cone between river gods, date in exergue

Date	Mintage	VG	F	VF	XF	Unc
1738 B	—	500	1,250	2,250	3,750	—

KM# A158 2 DUCAT

7.0000 g., 0.9860 Gold 0.2219 oz. AGW **Note:** Struck with 1/4 Thaler dies, KM#154.

Date	Mintage	VG	F	VF	XF	Unc
1745 T	—	2,000	4,000	6,500	10,000	—

KM# B158 2 DUCAT

7.0000 g., 0.9860 Gold 0.2219 oz. AGW **Note:** Struck with 1/4 Thaler dies, KM#155.

Date	Mintage	VG	F	VF	XF	Unc
1745 T	—	2,000	4,000	6,500	10,000	—

KM# C158 3 DUCAT

10.5000 g., 0.9860 Gold . 0.3328 oz. AGW

Date	Mintage	VG	F	VF	XF	Unc
1745 T	—	3,000	5,500	9,500	14,500	—

Note: Struck with 1/4 Thaler dies, KM#154

KM# D158 3 DUCAT

10.5000 g., 0.9860 Gold . 0.3328 oz. AGW **Note:** Struck with 1/4 Thaler dies, KM#155.

Date	Mintage	VG	F	VF	XF	Unc
1745 T	—	3,000	5,500	9,500	14,500	—

KM# A176 6 DUCAT

21.0000 g., 0.9860 Gold . 0.6657 oz. AGW **Note:** Struck with 1/2 Thaler dies, KM#173.

Date	Mintage	VG	F	VF	XF	Unc
1760 T Rare	—	—	—	—	—	—

KM# A181 6 DUCAT

21.0000 g., 0.9860 Gold . 0.6657 oz. AGW **Note:** Struck with 1/2 Thaler dies, KM#179.

Date	Mintage	VG	F	VF	XF	Unc
1763 T	—	—	—	—	—	—

KM# A149 10 DUCAT

35.0000 g., 0.9860 Gold 1.1095 oz. AGW **Note:** Struck with 1 Thaler dies, KM#148.

Date	Mintage	VG	F	VF	XF	Unc
1743 IT Rare	—	—	—	—	—	—

KM# A154 10 DUCAT

35.0000 g., 0.9860 Gold 1.1095 oz. AGW **Obverse:** City view **Reverse:** Laureate bust of Karl VII **Note:** Struck with 1 Thaler dies, KM#152.

Date	Mintage	VG	F	VF	XF	Unc
1744 IT Rare	—	—	—	—	—	—

KM# A147 12 DUCAT

42.0000 g., 0.9860 Gold 1.3314 oz. AGW **Note:** Struck with 1 Thaler dies, KM#145.

Date	Mintage	VG	F	VF	XF	Unc
1740 IT Rare	—	—	—	—	—	—

KM# E158 12 DUCAT

42.0000 g., 0.9860 Gold 1.3314 oz. AGW **Note:** Struck with 1 Thaler dies, KM#157.

Date	Mintage	VG	F	VF	XF	Unc
1745 T Rare	—	—	—	—	—	—

PATTERNS

Including off metal strikes

KM#	Date	Mintage	Identification	Mkt Val
Pn1	1708	—	2 Ducat. Silver. KM#16	150
Pn8	1702	—	Heller. Silver. KM#23	75.00
Pn9	1707	—	Heller. Gold. KM#23	500
Pn10	1717	—	Ducat. Silver. KM#133	100
Pn11	1717	—	Ducat. Silver. KM#134	85.00
Pn12	1730	—	Ducat. Silver. KM#139	150
Pn13	1730	—	Ducat. Silver. KM#140	85.00
Pn14	1730	—	Ducat. Silver. KM#141	85.00
Pn15	1731	—	Heller. Silver. KM#128	90.00
Pn16	1731	—	Heller. Gold. KM#128	650
Pn17	1734	—	Heller. Gold. KM#128	650
Pn18	1735	—	Heller. Silver. KM#128	90.00
Pn19	1736	—	Heller. Silver. KM#128	90.00
Pn20	1736	—	Heller. Gold. KM#128	650
Pn21	1737	—	Heller. Silver. KM#128	90.00
Pn22	1737	—	Heller. Gold. KM#128	650
Pn23	1738	—	Heller. Silver. KM#128	90.00
Pn24	1738	—	Heller. Gold. KM#128	650
Pn25	1739	—	Heller. Silver. KM#128	90.00
Pn26	1739	—	Heller. Gold. KM#128	650
Pn27	1740	—	Heller. Silver. KM#128	90.00

KM#	Date	Mintage	Identification	Mkt Val
Pn28	1740	—	Heller. Silver. . KM#144	75.00
Pn30	1742	—	Heller. Silver. . KM#144	75.00
Pn31	1742	—	Heller. Gold. . KM#144	650
Pn32	1743	—	Heller. Silver. . KM#144	75.00
Pn33	1743	—	Heller. Gold. . KM#144	650
Pn34	1744	—	Heller. Silver. . KM#150	—
Pn35	1744	—	Heller. Gold. . KM#150	—
Pn36	1744	—	Heller. Silver. . KM#151	—
Pn37	1744	—	Thaler. Gold. . KM#152	—
Pn38	1745	—	Heller. Gold. . KM#150	—
Pn39	1745	—	Heller. Silver. . KM#151	—
Pn45	1749	—	Heller. Silver. . KM#151	—
Pn46	1749	—	Heller. Gold. . KM#151	—
Pn47	1750	—	1/2 Ducat. Silver. . KM#163	—
Pn48	1752	—	Heller. Silver. . KM#151	—
Pn49	1752	—	Heller. Gold. . KM#151	—
Pn50	1753	—	Heller. Gold. . KM#151	—
Pn51	1754	—	Heller. Silver. . KM#151	—
Pn52	1756	—	Heller. Silver. . KM#151	—
Pn53	1756	—	Heller. Gold. . KM#151	—
Pn54	1757	—	Heller. Gold. . KM#151	—
Pn55	1759	—	Pfenning. Silver. . KM#168	—
Pn56	1760	—	Heller. Silver. . KM#170	—
Pn59	1764	—	Heller. Gold. . KM#170	—
Pn60	1775	—	Heller. Gold. . KM#151	—
Pn61	1775	—	Heller. Gold. . KM#170	—
Pn62	1776	—	Heller. Gold. . KM#151	—
Pn63	1786	—	Heller. Silver. . KM#188	—
Pn64	1796	—	Heller. Silver. . KM#188	—

BADEN

The earliest rulers of Baden, in the southwestern part of Germany along the Rhine, descended from the dukes of Zähringen in the late 11th century. The first division of the territory occurred in 1190, when separate lines of margraves were established in Baden and in Hachberg. Immediately prior to its extinction in 1418, Hachberg was sold back to Baden, which underwent several minor divisions itself during the next century. Baden acquired most of the Countship of Sponheim from Electoral Pfalz near the end of the 15th century. In 1515, the most significant division of the patrimony took place, in which the Baden-Baden and Baden-(Pforzheim) Durlach lines were established.

BADEN-BADEN LINE

RULERS

Ludwig Wilhelm, 1677-1707
Ludwig Georg, 1707-1761
Under Regency of his Mother, Francisca Sibylla until 1727
August Georg, 1761-1771

ARMS

Baden – diagonal bar from upper left to lower right
The usual arrangement is shield of 4-fold arms of Baden quartered with Sponheim

MINT OFFICIALS' INITIALS

Initials	Date	Name
IPB	Ca.1704	Johann Peter Bischof in Würzburg

REGULAR COINAGE

KM# 18 60 KREUZER (Gulden)

Silver **Ruler:** Ludwig Wilhelm **Obverse:** Bust right, value 60 (kreuzer) below **Reverse:** Crowned arms, date left, initials right, surrounded by Order of the Golden Fleece

Date	Mintage	VG	F	VF	XF	Unc
1704 IPB	—	200	400	650	1,000	—

TRADE COINAGE

KM# 19 DUCAT

3.5000 g., 0.9860 Gold 0.1109 oz. AGW **Ruler:** Ludwig Georg Under Regency **Subject:** Peace of Rastatt **Obverse:** Conjoined busts of Francisca Sibylla and Ludwig Georg right

Date	Mintage	VG	F	VF	XF	Unc
1714	—	400	800	1,400	2,000	—

KM# 20 2 DUCAT

7.0000 g., 0.9860 Gold 0.2219 oz. AGW **Ruler:** Ludwig Georg Under Regency **Subject:** Marriage of Ludwig Georg to Marianne von Schwarzenberg **Obverse:** Two oval arms in cartouche **Reverse:** Nine-line inscription, date in Roman numerals

Date	Mintage	VG	F	VF	XF	Unc
1721 Rare	—	—	—	—	—	—

BADEN-DURLACH LINE

Grand Duchy

Although Baden-Durlach was founded upon the division of Baden in 1515, the youngest son of Christoph I did not begin ruling in his own right until the demise of his father. This part of Baden was called Pforzheim until 1565, when the margrave moved his seat from the former to Durlach, located to the west and nearer the Rhine. After the male line of Baden-Baden failed in 1771 and the two parts of Baden were reunited, the fortunes of the margraviate continued to grow. Karlsruhe, near Durlach, was developed into a well-planned capital city. The ruler was given the rank of elector in 1803, only to be raised to grand duke three years later. The monarchy came to an end in 1918, but had by this time become one of the largest states in Germany.

RULERS

Friedrich VII Magnus, 1677-1709
Karl IV Wilhelm, 1709-1738
Karl Friedrich, 1738-1811, under guardianship of grandmother Magdalena
Wilhelmine and uncle Karl August, 1738-1745
Margrave in all Baden, 1771-1803

MINT OFFICIALS' INITIALS

Initials	Date	Name
B	1778-1808	Johann Martin Buckle
B, HB	1790-1812	Johann Heinrich Boltschauser, die-cutter and mint warden
BC, CC, CBC BG	1742-51	Carl Benedikt von Carben
BIB	1707-33	Balthasar Johann Bethmann in Darmstadt
CS, S	1761-1811	Ernst Christoph Steinhauser, mint warden
GW, W	1760-79	Johann Georg Worscheler
H	1740-69	Johann Jakob Handmann, die-cutter
Gm HG	1769-79	Johann Jakob Hauter
IT	1740-69	Jonas Thiebaud (Thibaud), die-cutter in Augsburg
MS	1740-?	Martin Sorberg
S	1744-99	Anton Schaeffer
S	1763-70	Johann Christoph Schepp, die-cutter and engraver

REGULAR COINAGE

KM# 112 1/4 KREUZER

Copper **Obverse:** Crowned arms **Reverse:** Value and date within cartouche

Date	Mintage	VG	F	VF	XF	Unc
1766 S-W	—	10.00	20.00	40.00	80.00	—

KM# 70 1/2 KREUZER

Silver **Ruler:** Karl IV Wilhelm **Note:** Uniface. Crowned arms between two branches, value divides date below.

Date	Mintage	VG	F	VF	XF	Unc
1733	87,000	25.00	50.00	100	200	—

KM# 87 1/2 KREUZER

Silver **Note:** Crowned oval arms in ornate frame divides date.

Date	Mintage	VG	F	VF	XF	Unc
1741 Rare	228,000	—	—	—	—	—

KM# 97 1/2 KREUZER

Billon **Ruler:** Karl Friedrich Margrave in Durlach **Note:** Uniface. Value in branches; date below.

Date	Mintage	VG	F	VF	XF	Unc
1749	60,000	3.00	8.00	20.00	65.00	—
1750	452,000	3.00	8.00	20.00	65.00	—

KM# 113 1/2 KREUZER

Copper **Ruler:** Karl Friedrich Margrave in Durlach **Obverse:** Crowned arms between two branches **Reverse:** Value and date within cartouche

Date	Mintage	VG	F	VF	XF	Unc
ND	—	3.00	8.00	20.00	60.00	—
1766 S W	—	3.00	8.00	20.00	60.00	—

KM# 124 1/2 KREUZER

Copper **Obverse:** Crowned arms between two branches **Reverse:** Value within cartouche

Date	Mintage	VG	F	VF	XF	Unc
1772 S H	—	3.00	8.00	20.00	60.00	—

KM# 65 KREUZER

Silver **Ruler:** Karl IV Wilhelm **Obverse:** Crowned arms between two branches **Reverse:** Crowned double-C monogram divides value I-K, date below **Note:** Varieties exist.

Date	Mintage	VG	F	VF	XF	Unc
1732	—	12.00	25.00	45.00	80.00	—
1733	1,871,000	12.00	25.00	45.00	80.00	—
1734	25,000	12.00	25.00	45.00	80.00	—

KM# 78 KREUZER

Silver **Ruler:** Karl IV Wilhelm **Obverse:** Crowned and mantled three-fold oval arms **Reverse:** I/KREU/TZER/date in wreath

Date	Mintage	VG	F	VF	XF	Unc
1736	1,389,000	6.00	12.00	25.00	65.00	—

KM# 98 KREUZER

Billon **Ruler:** Karl Friedrich Margrave in Durlach **Obverse:** Crowned arms within cartouche **Reverse:** Value and date within cartouche

Date	Mintage	VG	F	VF	XF	Unc
1749 BC Rare	34,000	—	—	—	—	—

KM# 101 KREUZER

Billon **Ruler:** Karl Friedrich Margrave in Durlach **Obverse:** Crowned monogram **Reverse:** Value and date within cartouche

Date	Mintage	VG	F	VF	XF	Unc
1751 BC	1,235,000	6.00	12.00	25.00	65.00	—

KM# 114 KREUZER

Copper **Ruler:** Karl Friedrich Margrave in Durlach **Obverse:** Crowned arms between branches **Reverse:** Value and date within cartouche

Date	Mintage	VG	F	VF	XF	Unc
1766 W	—	3.00	8.00	20.00	60.00	—

KM# 125 KREUZER

Copper **Obverse:** Crowned arms between two branches **Reverse:** Value and date within cartouche

Date	Mintage	VG	F	VF	XF	Unc
1772 H	—	3.00	8.00	20.00	60.00	—

KM# 99 ALBUS (2 Kreuzer)

Billon **Ruler:** Karl Friedrich Margrave in Durlach **Subject:** The County of Sponheim **Obverse:** Crowned monogram **Reverse:** Value and date within cartouche

Date	Mintage	VG	F	VF	XF	Unc
1749 BC	1,484,000	5.00	10.00	15.00	40.00	—
1750 BC	2,633,000	5.00	10.00	15.00	40.00	—
1751 BC	583,000	5.00	10.00	15.00	40.00	—
1751 BG	Inc. above	5.00	10.00	15.00	40.00	—

KM# 80 2 KREUZER (1/2 Batzen)

Silver **Ruler:** Karl IV Wilhelm **Obverse:** Crowned arms **Reverse:** Value and date within wreath

Date	Mintage	VG	F	VF	XF	Unc
1737	2,324,000	15.00	28.00	55.00	90.00	—

KM# 81 2 KREUZER (1/2 Batzen)

Silver **Ruler:** Karl IV Wilhelm **Obverse:** Crowned and mantled oval arms in cartouche **Reverse:** 2/KREU/ZER/date in cartouche

Date	Mintage	VG	F	VF	XF	Unc
1737	Inc. above	15.00	28.00	55.00	90.00	—

KM# 88 2 KREUZER (1/2 Batzen)

Silver **Obverse:** Arms within crowned mantle **Reverse:** Value and date within cartouche

Date	Mintage	VG	F	VF	XF	Unc
1742	—	—	—	—	—	—
1742 BC	224,000	6.00	20.00	30.00	60.00	—
1743 BC	1,232,000	6.00	20.00	30.00	60.00	—

KM# 71 2-1/2 KREUZER

Silver **Ruler:** Karl IV Wilhelm **Obverse:** Crowned monogram divides value **Reverse:** Crowned arms within cartouche **Note:** Similar to 5 Kreuzer, KM#66 but value: 2-1/2 KR.

Date	Mintage	VG	F	VF	XF	Unc
1733	57,000	—	—	—	—	—

KM# 121 2-1/2 KREUZER

Billon **Ruler:** Karl Friedrich Margrave in Durlach **Obverse:** Crowned arms within branches **Reverse:** BADEN/DURLACH and date within palms

Date	Mintage	VG	F	VF	XF	Unc
1768 W	255,000	8.00	17.00	35.00	75.00	—

KM# 106 3 KREUZER (1 Groschen)

Billon **Ruler:** Karl Friedrich Margrave in Durlach **Obverse:** Crowned arms within cartouche **Reverse:** Value and date within cartouche

Date	Mintage	VG	F	VF	XF	Unc
1764 GW	—	5.00	10.00	20.00	40.00	—

KM# 66 5 KREUZER

Silver **Ruler:** Karl IV Wilhelm **Obverse:** Crowned monogram within inner circle **Reverse:** Crowned arms within cartouche

Date	Mintage	VG	F	VF	XF	Unc
1732	107,000	15.00	32.00	60.00	100	—
1733	464,000	15.00	32.00	60.00	100	—
1734	234,000	15.00	32.00	60.00	100	—
1735	120,000	15.00	32.00	60.00	100	—

KM# 77 5 KREUZER

Silver **Ruler:** Karl IV Wilhelm **Obverse:** Crowned and mantled three-fold arms **Reverse:** Value, date in five lines within wreath

Date	Mintage	VG	F	VF	XF	Unc
1735	Inc. above	15.00	32.00	60.00	100	—
1736	106,000	15.00	32.00	60.00	100	—

KM# 109 5 KREUZER

Billon **Ruler:** Karl Friedrich Margrave in Durlach **Obverse:** Head without armor right **Reverse:** Crowned arms in branches

Date	Mintage	F	VF	XF	Unc
1765 S W	170,000	20.00	40.00	90.00	200
1766 S W	—	20.00	40.00	90.00	200

KM# 118 5 KREUZER

Billon **Ruler:** Karl Friedrich Margrave in Durlach **Obverse:** Head with armor right **Reverse:** Crowned three-fold arms within branches

Date	Mintage	F	VF	XF	Unc
1767 S	174,000	12.00	30.00	90.00	175
1768 S	—	12.00	30.00	90.00	175
1768 S H	188,000	12.00	30.00	90.00	175
1772 S H	196,000	12.00	30.00	90.00	175
1775 S H	97,000	12.00	30.00	90.00	175

KM# 67 10 KREUZER (Zehner)

Silver **Ruler:** Karl IV Wilhelm **Obverse:** Crowned eight-fold arms **Reverse:** Value, date in four lines wtihin circle **Note:** Varieties exist.

Date	Mintage	VG	F	VF	XF	Unc
1732	17,000	—	—	—	—	—

KM# 72 10 KREUZER (Zehner)

Silver **Ruler:** Karl IV Wilhelm **Reverse:** In cartouche

Date	Mintage	VG	F	VF	XF	Unc
1733	7,770	—	—	—	—	—

KM# 110 10 KREUZER (Zehner)

Silver **Ruler:** Karl Friedrich Margrave in Durlach **Obverse:** Head without armor right **Reverse:** Crowned three-part arms in branches

Date	Mintage	VG	F	VF	XF	Unc
1765 S W	296,000	15.00	35.00	80.00	160	—

KM# 119 10 KREUZER (Zehner)

Silver **Ruler:** Karl Friedrich Margrave in Durlach **Obverse:** Head with armor right **Reverse:** Crowned three-fold arms within branches

Date	Mintage	VG	F	VF	XF	Unc
1767 S W	105,000	10.00	30.00	70.00	140	—
1767 H W	Inc. above	10.00	30.00	70.00	140	—
1768 H W	56,000	10.00	30.00	70.00	140	—

KM# 122 10 KREUZER (Zehner)

Silver **Ruler:** Karl Friedrich Margrave in Durlach **Obverse:** Small head with armor right **Reverse:** Crowned three-fold arms within branches

Date	Mintage	VG	F	VF	XF	Unc
1769 H W	—	10.00	25.00	55.00	115	—
1770 H W	—	10.00	25.00	55.00	115	—
1772 H W	37,000	10.00	25.00	55.00	115	—
1774 H W	34,000	10.00	25.00	55.00	115	—
1775 H W	49,000	10.00	25.00	55.00	115	—

KM# 90 12 KREUZER (3 Batzen)

Silver **Obverse:** Crowned three-fold arms within Order chain **Reverse:** Value, legend and date within cartouche

Date	Mintage	F	VF	XF	Unc
1745 CBC	—	45.00	80.00	190	375
1745 BC	Inc. above	45.00	80.00	190	375

KM# 91 12 KREUZER (3 Batzen)

Silver **Ruler:** Karl Friedrich Margrave in Durlach **Obverse:** Crowned three-fold arms **Reverse:** Value and date within cartouche

Date	Mintage	F	VF	XF	Unc
1746 CBC	236,000	35.00	65.00	130	275

KM# 92 12 KREUZER (3 Batzen)

Silver **Ruler:** Karl Friedrich Margrave in Durlach **Obverse:** Crowned three-fold arms within mantle **Reverse:** Value, legend and date within cartouche

Date	Mintage	F	VF	XF	Unc
1747 CBC	978,000	35.00	65.00	140	300
1747 BC	Inc. above	35.00	65.00	140	300
1748 BC	1,061,000	35.00	65.00	130	275
1750 BC	374,000	35.00	65.00	130	275

KM# 100 12 KREUZER (3 Batzen)

Silver **Ruler:** Karl Friedrich Margrave in Durlach **Obverse:** Crowned shield of multiple arms **Reverse:** Value, legend and date within cartouche

Date	Mintage	F	VF	XF	Unc
1750 BC Rare	Inc. above	—	—	—	—

KM# 89 12 KREUZER (Kipper)

Silver **Obverse:** Arms within crowned mantle **Reverse:** Value, legend and date within ornate circle

Date	Mintage	F	VF	XF	Unc
ND1745 CC-MS	60,000	100	170	300	600

KM# 68 20 KREUZER

Silver **Obverse:** Crowned oval three-fold arms in baroque frame **Reverse:** Value, date in five lines within cartouche

Date	Mintage	VG	F	VF	XF	Unc
1732	18,000	20.00	40.00	90.00	150	—

KM# 103 20 KREUZER

Silver **Ruler:** Karl Friedrich Margrave in Durlach **Obverse:** Head right **Obv. Legend:** CAROLUS FRID: D.G. MARCHIO BAD & H. **Reverse:** Crowned arms on pedestal with value **Rev. Legend:** LX EINE FEINE - MARCK

Date	Mintage	VG	F	VF	XF	Unc
1763 S W	74,000	25.00	50.00	100	175	—

KM# 107 20 KREUZER

Silver **Ruler:** Karl Friedrich Margrave in Durlach **Obverse:** Head right **Reverse:** Crowned arms on pedestal with value

Date	Mintage	VG	F	VF	XF	Unc
1764 S W	—	25.00	50.00	95.00	165	—

KM# 123 20 KREUZER

Silver **Ruler:** Karl Friedrich Margrave in Durlach **Obverse:** Head right **Obv. Legend:** CAROLUS FRID: D • G • MARCHIO BAD & H • **Reverse:** Crowned three-fold arms within branches, value below **Rev. Inscription:** LX EINE FEINE MARCK

Date	Mintage	VG	F	VF	XF	Unc
1771 H W	43,000	20.00	40.00	75.00	140	—
1773 H W	167,000	20.00	40.00	75.00	140	—
1774 H W	37,000	30.00	60.00	110	200	—

KM# 130 20 KREUZER

Silver **Ruler:** Karl Friedrich Margrave in Durlach **Obverse:** Head right **Obv. Legend:** CAROLUS FR: D • G•MARCHIO BAD & H • **Reverse:** Crowned three-fold arms within branches, value below **Rev. Legend:** LX EINE FEINE MARCK

Date	Mintage	VG	F	VF	XF	Unc
1779 H S	14,000	30.00	60.00	110	200	—

KM# 69 30 KREUZER (1/2 Gulden)

Silver **Ruler:** Karl IV Wilhelm **Obverse:** Head right **Reverse:** Crowned and mantled three-fold oval arms, value around, date divided below

Date	Mintage	VG	F	VF	XF	Unc
1733	4,440	45.00	80.00	140	200	—
1734	39,000	45.00	80.00	140	200	—
1735	446,000	45.00	80.00	140	200	—
1736	750,000	45.00	80.00	140	200	—

KM# 73 60 KREUZER

Silver **Ruler:** Karl IV Wilhelm **Obverse:** Bust right **Reverse:** Crowned oval eight-fold arms in baroque frame, date below

Date	Mintage	VG	F	VF	XF	Unc
1733	—	—	—	—	—	—

KM# 86 60 KREUZER (Gulden)

Silver **Ruler:** Karl Friedrich Under guardianship **Obverse:** Crowned and mantled arms **Reverse:** Crowned 8-pointed cross with linked C's at angles

Date	Mintage	F	VF	XF	Unc
1740 H	6,432	175	250	350	800

KM# 93 1/2 THALER

Silver **Ruler:** Karl Friedrich Margrave in Durlach **Obverse:** Armored bust right **Obv. Legend:** CAR • FRID • D: G • MARCH • BAAD & H • **Reverse:** Crowned and mantled arms

Date	Mintage	F	VF	XF	Unc
1747 S BC	5,496	150	350	625	1,200

KM# 115 1/2 THALER (1 Gulden)

14.0300 g., 0.8330 Silver 0.3757 oz. ASW **Ruler:** Karl Friedrich Margrave in Durlach **Obverse:** Armored bust right **Obv. Legend:** CAROLUS FRID: D.G. MARCHIO BAD & H. **Reverse:** Crowned arms with griffin supporters **Rev. Legend:** ADNORMAM CONVENTIONIS •

Date	Mintage	VG	F	VF	XF	Unc
1766 S W	14,000	80.00	110	200	375	—

KM# 116 1/2 THALER (1 Gulden)

14.0300 g., 0.8330 Silver 0.3757 oz. ASW **Ruler:** Karl Friedrich Margrave in Durlach **Reverse:** Crowned arms with griffin supporters

Date	Mintage	VG	F	VF	XF	Unc
1766 S W	Inc. above	75.00	100	150	300	—
1767 S W	18,000	75.00	100	150	300	—
1768 S W	9,439	75.00	100	150	300	—

KM# 126 1/2 THALER (1 Gulden)

14.0300 g., 0.8330 Silver 0.3757 oz. ASW **Ruler:** Karl Friedrich Margrave in all Baden **Obverse:** Head right **Obv. Legend:** CAROLUS FRID • D: G • MARCHIO BAD • & H • **Reverse:** Crowned arms within branches

Date	Mintage	VG	F	VF	XF	Unc
1774 H W	—	75.00	125	240	400	—
1778 H W	5,209	75.00	125	240	400	—
1779 S W	697	75.00	125	240	400	—

KM# 104 THALER (Convention)

28.6000 g., 0.8330 Silver 0.7659 oz. ASW **Ruler:** Karl Friedrich Margrave in Durlach **Obverse:** Head right **Obv. Legend:** CAROLUS FRID: D.G. MARCHIO BAD & HOCH: **Reverse:** Crowned three-fold arms **Rev. Legend:** AD NORMAM • CONVENTIONIS •, X.EINE FEINE MARCK. below **Note:** Dav. #1931.

Date	Mintage	VG	F	VF	XF	Unc
1763 S GW	4,659	100	150	225	400	—

KM# 105 THALER (Convention)

28.6000 g., 0.8330 Silver 0.7659 oz. ASW **Ruler:** Karl Friedrich Margrave in Durlach **Obverse:** Head right **Obv. Legend:** CAROLUS FRIDERICUS • D.G. MARCHIO BAD & HOCHB • **Reverse:** Crowned arms within branches **Note:** Dav. #1932.

Date	Mintage	VG	F	VF	XF	Unc
1763	Inc. above	125	175	300	550	—

KM# 108 THALER (Convention)

28.6000 g., 0.8330 Silver 0.7659 oz. ASW **Ruler:** Karl Friedrich Margrave in Durlach **Obverse:** Armored bust right **Obv. Legend:** CAROLUS FRID: D.G. MARCHIO BAD • ET H. **Reverse:** Crowned arms with griffin supporters **Rev. Legend:** AD NORMAM CONVENTIONIS **Note:** Dav. #1933.

Date	Mintage	VG	F	VF	XF	Unc
1764 S W	17,000	90.00	135	225	450	—
1765 S W	520,000	90.00	135	225	450	—
1766 S W	367,000	90.00	135	225	450	—

KM# 117 THALER (Convention)

28.6000 g., 0.8330 Silver 0.7659 oz. ASW **Ruler:** Karl Friedrich Margrave in Durlach **Obverse:** Armored bust right **Obv. Legend:** CAROLUS FRID: D • G • MARCHIO BAD • ET • H • **Reverse:** Crowned arms with griffin supporters **Rev. Legend:** AD NORMAM - CONVENTIONIS, • X • EINE F • MARCK • **Note:** Dav. #1934.

Date	Mintage	VG	F	VF	XF	Unc
1766 S W	Inc. above	70.00	110	175	400	—
1767 S W	219,000	70.00	110	175	400	—
1768/7 S W	31,000	70.00	110	175	400	
1768 H W	Inc. above	70.00	110	175	400	—
1772 H W	7,680	70.00	110	175	400	—

KM# 129.1 THALER (Convention)

28.6000 g., 0.8330 Silver 0.7659 oz. ASW **Ruler:** Karl Friedrich Margrave in all Baden **Obverse:** Head right **Obv. Legend:** CAROLUS FRID • D: G • MARCHIO BAD • & H • **Reverse:** S below shield **Rev. Legend:** X EINE FEINE MARCK **Note:** Dav. #1935.

Date	Mintage	VG	F	VF	XF	Unc
1778 H/ /W	7,921	125	200	300	500	—
1778 IH/ / W	14,000	125	200	300	500	—
1779 H/ /S	2,677	125	200	300	500	—

KM# 129.2 THALER (Convention)

28.6000 g., 0.8330 Silver 0.7659 oz. ASW **Ruler:** Karl Friedrich Margrave in all Baden **Obverse:** Head right **Obv. Legend:** CAROLUS FRID • D • G • MARCHIO BAD • & H • **Reverse:** W below shield **Rev. Legend:** X EINE FEINE MARCK

Date	Mintage	VG	F	VF	XF	Unc
1778 IH/ / W	—	125	200	300	500	—

TRADE COINAGE

KM# 75 1/2 CAROLIN

4.8500 g., 0.7700 Gold 0.1201 oz. AGW **Ruler:** Karl IV Wilhelm **Obverse:** Armored bust right **Reverse:** Four shields cruciform with linked C's in angles and Baden shield at center

Date	Mintage	VG	F	VF	XF	Unc
1734	708	650	1,200	2,500	4,500	—

KM# 74 CAROLIN

9.7000 g., 0.7700 Gold 0.2401 oz. AGW **Ruler:** Karl IV Wilhelm **Obverse:** Armored bust right **Reverse:** Four shields cruciform with linked C's in angles and Baden shield at center

Date	Mintage	VG	F	VF	XF	Unc
1733	—	400	750	1,850	3,000	—
1734	—	400	750	1,850	3,000	—

KM# 76 CAROLIN

9.7000 g., 0.7700 Gold 0.2401 oz. AGW **Ruler:** Karl IV Wilhelm **Obverse:** Large armored bust right **Reverse:** Crowned and mantled round arms, date below

Date	Mintage	VG	F	VF	XF	Unc
1734	—	400	750	1,850	3,000	—
1735	3,776	400	750	1,850	3,000	—

KM# 94 1/4 DUCAT

0.8750 g., 0.9860 Gold 0.0277 oz. AGW **Ruler:** Karl Friedrich Margrave in Durlach **Obverse:** Crowned arms

Date	Mintage	VG	F	VF	XF	Unc
1747	—	150	300	525	875	—

KM# 63 1/2 DUCAT

1.7500 g., 0.9860 Gold 0.0555 oz. AGW **Ruler:** Karl IV Wilhelm **Obverse:** Armored bust right **Reverse:** Crowned arms with griffin supporters, date below

Date	Mintage	VG	F	VF	XF	Unc
1721 BIB	—	300	550	1,000	1,550	—

KM# 82 1/2 DUCAT

1.7500 g., 0.9860 Gold 0.0555 oz. AGW **Ruler:** Karl IV Wilhelm **Obverse:** Crowned arms with griffin supporters **Reverse:** Value and date in cartouche

Date	Mintage	VG	F	VF	XF	Unc
1737	—	250	500	900	1,450	—

KM# 95 1/2 DUCAT

1.7500 g., 0.9860 Gold 0.0555 oz. AGW **Ruler:** Karl Friedrich Margrave in Durlach **Obverse:** Armored bust right **Reverse:** Crowned three-fold arms

Date	Mintage	VG	F	VF	XF	Unc
1747 BC	—	200	425	800	1,350	—

KM# 64 DUCAT

3.5000 g., 0.9860 Gold 0.1109 oz. AGW **Ruler:** Karl IV Wilhelm **Obverse:** Armored bust right **Reverse:** Crowned arms with griffin supporters, date below

Date	Mintage	VG	F	VF	XF	Unc
1721 BIB	300	450	900	1,900	2,850	—

KM# 79 DUCAT

3.5000 g., 0.9860 Gold 0.1109 oz. AGW **Ruler:** Karl IV Wilhelm **Reverse:** Crowned and mantled arms, date below

Date	Mintage	VG	F	VF	XF	Unc
1736 Rare	—	—	—	—	—	—

KM# 83 DUCAT

3.5000 g., 0.9860 Gold 0.1109 oz. AGW **Ruler:** Karl IV Wilhelm **Obverse:** Value and date in circle wtih garlands in border **Reverse:** Crowned arms with griffin supporters

Date	Mintage	VG	F	VF	XF	Unc
1737 IT	12,000	350	750	1,650	2,500	—

KM# 85 DUCAT

3.5000 g., 0.9860 Gold 0.1109 oz. AGW **Obverse:** Crowned arms with griffin supporters **Reverse:** Value and date in cartouche

Date	Mintage	VG	F	VF	XF	Unc
1738	177	300	675	1,150	1,850	—

KM# 96 DUCAT

3.5000 g., 0.9860 Gold 0.1109 oz. AGW **Ruler:** Karl Friedrich Margrave in Durlach **Obverse:** Armored bust right **Reverse:** Crowned and mantled arms

Date	Mintage	VG	F	VF	XF	Unc
1747 BC	—	325	700	1,250	2,000	—

KM# 102 DUCAT

3.5000 g., 0.9860 Gold 0.1109 oz. AGW **Ruler:** Karl Friedrich Margrave in Durlach **Obverse:** Armored bust right **Reverse:** Crowned and mantled arms within Order chain

Date	Mintage	VG	F	VF	XF	Unc
1751 S-BC	500	500	1,000	1,750	2,950	—

KM# 111 DUCAT

3.5000 g., 0.9860 Gold 0.1109 oz. AGW **Ruler:** Karl Friedrich Margrave in Durlach **Obverse:** Bust right **Reverse:** Crowned arms with griffin supporters

Date	Mintage	VG	F	VF	XF	Unc
1765 S-W	1,406	500	1,000	1,700	2,850	—

KM# 120 DUCAT

3.5000 g., 0.9860 Gold 0.1109 oz. AGW **Ruler:** Karl Friedrich Margrave in Durlach **Obverse:** Head right **Reverse:** Crowned arms with griffin supporters

Date	Mintage	VG	F	VF	XF	Unc
1767 W	—	500	1,000	1,700	2,850	—
1768 W	—	500	1,000	1,700	2,850	—

KM# 127 DUCAT

3.6500 g., 0.9350 Gold 0.1097 oz. AGW **Ruler:** Karl Friedrich Margrave in all Baden **Subject:** Birth of Twin Princesses **Obverse:** Amalie Frederika of Hesse right **Obv. Legend:** AMAL • FRID • PRINC • HER • BAD • H • L • HASS • **Reverse:** Crown above two shields of arms

Date	Mintage	F	VF	XF	Unc
1776	—	500	1,000	1,650	2,750

KM# 128 DUCAT

3.6500 g., 0.9350 Gold 0.1097 oz. AGW **Ruler:** Karl Friedrich Margrave in all Baden **Subject:** Birth of Twin Princesses **Obverse:** Heads facing each other **Reverse:** Inscription

Date	Mintage	F	VF	XF	Unc
1776	—	450	900	1,500	2,500

KM# 131 DUCAT

3.6500 g., 0.9350 Gold 0.1097 oz. AGW **Ruler:** Karl Friedrich Margrave in all Baden **Subject:** Birth of Prince Charles **Obverse:** Bust right **Obv. Legend:** CAR • FRID • D • G • MARCH • BAD • **Reverse:** Crowned and mantled arms

Date	Mintage	F	VF	XF	Unc
1786 CS-B	—	500	950	1,600	2,650

KM# 84 2 DUCAT

7.0000 g., 0.9860 Gold 0.2219 oz. AGW **Ruler:** Karl IV Wilhelm **Obverse:** Value and date in ornamental tablet **Reverse:** Crowned and mantled arms

Date	Mintage	VG	F	VF	XF	Unc
1737	—	1,000	1,850	3,200	5,000	—

PATTERNS

Including off metal strikes

KM#	Date	Mintage	Identification	Mkt Val
Pn3	1704	—	60 Kreuzer. Tin. KM#18.	—
Pn4	1714	—	Ducat. Silver. KM#19.	150
Pn5	1721	—	2 Ducat. Silver. KM#20.	185
PnA5	1732	—	Kreuzer. Gold. KM#65.	—
Pn6	1736	—	Kreuzer. Copper. KM#78.	—
Pn7	1737	—	2 Kreuzer. Copper. KM#80.	—
Pn8	1738	—	Ducat. Silver. KM#85.	—
Pn9	1740	—	Gulden. Lead. KM#86.	—
Pn10	1742	—	2 Kreuzer. Copper. KM#88.	—
Pn11	1747	—	Gulden. Lead. KM#93.	—
Pn12	1751	—	Albus. Copper. KM#99.	—
Pn13	1751	—	Thaler. Lead. KM#104.	—
Pn14	1763	—	Thaler. Lead. KM#105.	—
Pn15	1765	—	Thaler. Lead. KM#108.	—
Pn16	1766	—	Thaler. Lead. KM#117.	—
Pn17	1772	—	Thaler. Lead. KM#117.	—
Pn18	1776	—	Ducat. Silver. KM#127.	—
Pn19	1778	—	Thaler. Lead. KM#129.1.	—
Pn20	1786	—	Ducat. Silver. KM#131.	—

TRIAL STRIKES

Durlach Line

KM#	Date	Mintage	Identification	Mkt Val
TS1	1784	—	Ducat. Copper. Crowned and mantled arms.	—
TS2	(1784)	—	Ducat. Copper. Crowned arms in baroque frame.	—

BAMBERG

BISHOPRIC

The bishopric was founded in 1007 by Emperor Heinrich II (1002-24) in the town of Bamberg, 32 miles (53 kilometers) north-northwest of Nürnberg. The bishops began issuing their own coinage almost from the beginning and were given the rank of Prince of the Empire by the emperor about 1250. The bishopric was secularized in 1801 and was incorporated into Bavaria the following year.

RULERS

Lothar Franz, Freiherr von Schönborn, 1693-1729
Friedrich Karl, Graf von Schönborn, 1729-1746
Johann Philipp Anton, Freiherr von Frankenstein, 1746-1753
Franz Konrad, Graf von Stadion, 1753-1757
Adam Friedrich, Graf von Seinsheim, 1757-1779
Franz Ludwig, Freiherr von Erthal, 1779-1795
Christoph Franz, Freiherr von Buseck, 1795-1801 (d. 1807)

ARMS: Lion rampant left over which superimposed a diagonal band from upper left to lower right.

MINT MARKS

B - Bamberg Mint
F - Fürth Mint

MINT OFFICIALS' INITIALS

Initials	Date	Name
CGL	1746-55	Carl Gottlieb Laufer
F	1755-64	Johann martin Forster
F(N)S	1760-64	Johann Martin Forster and Siegmund Scholz
GFN or +	1682-1724	Georg Friedrich Nurnberger, die-cutter and mintmaster in Nurnberg
GN	1754-62	Georg Neumeister, warden
ILO, OE	1740-87	Johann Leonhard Oexlein, die-cutter
MP	1762-90	Johann Nikolaus Martihengo and Franz Hermann Pranghe, warden
PPW	1771	Peter Paul Werner, die-cutter
R	1764-93	George Nikolaus Riedner
S(N)R	1760-74	Siegmund Scholz, warden and G.N. Riedner
VBW	1685, 1695-1729	Ulrich Buckhard Wildering in Mainz

REGULAR COINAGE

KM# 127 HELLER

Copper **Ruler:** Adam Friedrich **Obverse:** Arms **Reverse:** Value and date

Date	Mintage	VG	F	VF	XF	Unc
1761	—	4.00	7.00	13.50	25.00	—
1762	—	4.00	7.00	13.50	25.00	—

KM# 133 HELLER

Copper **Ruler:** Adam Friedrich **Obverse:** Arms **Reverse:** Value "I HELLER" and date

Date	Mintage	VG	F	VF	XF	Unc
1772	—	4.00	7.00	13.50	25.00	—
1780	—	4.00	7.00	13.50	25.00	—
1786	—	4.00	7.00	13.50	25.00	—

KM# 97 PFENNIG

Silver **Ruler:** Luther Franz **Obverse:** Three shields of arms, lower one divides date, value 1 above **Note:** Uniface.

Date	Mintage	VG	F	VF	XF	Unc
1700	—	7.00	15.00	25.00	40.00	—
1710	—	7.00	15.00	25.00	40.00	—
1712	—	7.00	15.00	25.00	40.00	—
1713	—	7.00	15.00	25.00	40.00	—
1717	—	7.00	15.00	25.00	40.00	—

KM# 128 PFENNIG

Copper **Ruler:** Adam Friedrich **Obverse:** Arms **Reverse:** Value and date

Date	Mintage	VG	F	VF	XF	Unc
1761	—	5.00	10.00	15.00	30.00	—

KM# 129 1/2 KREUZER
Copper **Ruler:** Adam Friedrich **Obverse:** Arms **Reverse:** Value and date

Date	Mintage	VG	F	VF	XF	Unc
1762	—	7.00	12.00	20.00	40.00	—
1763	—	7.00	12.00	20.00	40.00	—

KM# A131 KREUZER
Billon **Ruler:** Adam Friedrich **Obverse:** Arms **Reverse:** Value and date

Date	Mintage	VG	F	VF	XF	Unc
1763 F	—	10.00	20.00	30.00	50.00	—
1765 MP	—	10.00	20.00	30.00	50.00	—
1766 R	—	10.00	20.00	30.00	50.00	—

KM# 142 KREUZER
Billon **Ruler:** Franz Ludwig **Obverse:** Arms **Reverse:** Value above date

Date	Mintage	VG	F	VF	XF	Unc
1786	—	10.00	20.00	30.00	50.00	—

KM# 131 2-1/2 KREUZER
Billon **Ruler:** Adam Friedrich **Obverse:** Crowned half-figure facing with cross and staff **Reverse:** Value and date within scalloped circle **Note:** Similar to 5 Kreuzer, KM#132.

Date	Mintage	VG	F	VF	XF	Unc
1766 S(N)R	—	10.00	20.00	40.00	75.00	—

KM# 98 3 KREUZER
Silver **Ruler:** Friederich Karl **Subject:** Death of Lothar Franz **Obverse:** Crowned and mantled oval arms **Reverse:** Ten-line inscription with date, imperial orb with 3 below

Date	Mintage	VG	F	VF	XF	Unc
1729	—	25.00	40.00	75.00	125	—

KM# 118 3 KREUZER
Silver **Ruler:** Franz Conrad **Subject:** Death of Johann Philipp Anton **Obverse:** Helmeted arms **Reverse:** Inscription

Date	Mintage	VG	F	VF	XF	Unc
1753	—	15.00	30.00	60.00	120	—

KM# 120 3 KREUZER
Silver **Ruler:** Adam Friedrich **Subject:** Death of Franz Conrad **Obverse:** Helmeted arms **Obv. Legend:** FRANCISCUS CONRADUS... **Reverse:** Inscription

Date	Mintage	VG	F	VF	XF	Unc
1757	—	15.00	30.00	60.00	120	—

KM# 134 3 KREUZER
Billon **Ruler:** Franz Ludwig **Subject:** Death of Adam Friedrich **Obverse:** Helmeted arms **Reverse:** Inscription

Date	Mintage	VG	F	VF	XF	Unc
1779	—	18.50	27.50	50.00	90.00	—

KM# 144 3 KREUZER
Silver **Ruler:** Christoph Franz **Subject:** Death of Franz Ludwig **Obverse:** Helmeted arms **Reverse:** Nine-line inscription

Date	Mintage	VG	F	VF	XF	Unc
1795	—	15.00	30.00	60.00	125	—

KM# 85 4 KREUZER (Batzen)
Silver **Ruler:** Luther Franz **Reverse:** St. Heinrich

Date	Mintage	VG	F	VF	XF	Unc
1700 GFN	1,093,000	12.00	25.00	40.00	80.00	—
1716 GFN	—	12.00	25.00	40.00	80.00	—

KM# 132 5 KREUZER
Billon **Ruler:** Adam Friedrich **Obverse:** Crowned arms within crowned mantle **Reverse:** Value and date within scalloped circle

Date	Mintage	VG	F	VF	XF	Unc
1766 S(N)R	—	8.00	18.00	30.00	50.00	—

KM# 143 20 KREUZER
Silver **Ruler:** Franz Ludwig **Obverse:** Bust right **Reverse:** Quartered arms

Date	Mintage	F	VF	XF	Unc
1788 MF	—	20.00	45.00	90.00	180

Note: Refer also to Wurzburg listings

KM# 148 20 KREUZER
Silver **Ruler:** Christoph Franz **Obverse:** Crowned arms within crowned mantle **Reverse:** Value within Order chain dividing date, legend below **Note:** Convention 20 Kreuzer.

Date	Mintage	F	VF	XF	Unc
1800	—	20.00	40.00	80.00	200

KM# 149 1/2 THALER
Silver **Ruler:** Christoph Franz **Subject:** Christoph Franz **Obverse:** Bust right **Obv. Legend:** CHRISTOPH FRANZ B: ZU • BAMB: D • H • R • R • FURST **Reverse:** Value within oval above city scene, date below **Rev. Legend:** NACH DEM CONVENTIONSFUSE; XX EINEFEINE MARK in wreath

Date	Mintage	F	VF	XF	Unc
1800	—	125	250	400	600

KM# 150 1/2 THALER
Silver **Ruler:** Christoph Franz **Obverse:** Fuller bust right **Obv. Legend:** CHRISTOPH FRANZ B: ZU BAMB: D • H • R • R • FURST **Reverse:** Value within oval above city scene **Rev. Legend:** NACH DEM CONVENTIONSFUSE; XX EINEFEINE MARK in wreath

Date	Mintage	F	VF	XF	Unc
1800	—	100	150	250	500

KM# 116 THALER
Silver **Ruler:** Johann Philip Anton **Obverse:** Bust with cross on chest right **Obv. Legend:** IOANN • PHILIPP • ANTON • D • G • EPISCOP • BAMB • S • R • I • PRINCEPS • **Reverse:** Helmeted arms with cross, sword and mace behind **Rev. Legend:** INVIOLATA FIDES PAX ET CONCORDIA FIRMANT **Note:** Dav. #1937.

Date	Mintage	VG	F	VF	XF	Unc
1750 CGL	—	200	350	600	1,150	—

KM# 146 THALER
Silver **Ruler:** Franz Ludwig **Obverse:** Crowned arms within crowned mantle **Obv. Legend:** FRANZ • LUDWIG • B • ZU • BAMBERG • U • WURZB • D • H • R • R • FURST • HERZOG • Z • FRANKEN • **Reverse:** Legend within wreath, date divided **Rev. Legend:** ZUM BESTEN DES VATERLANDS in wreath, BAM - BERG above, ZEHN EINE FEINE MARK below **Note:** Contribution Thaler. Dav. #1939.

Date	Mintage	VG	F	VF	XF	Unc
1795	—	90.00	125	160	275	—

Note: Made from the silver service of the Bishop

KM# 151 THALER
Silver **Ruler:** Christoph Franz **Obverse:** Crowned arms with large mantle, divided date in lower field **Obv. Legend:** CHRISTOPH FRANZ BISCHOF ZU BAMBERG DES • H • R • R • FÜRST **Reverse:** Value within oval above city scene **Rev. Legend:** NACH DEM CONVENTIONSFUSE; X EINEFEINE MARK in oval; BAMBERG in exergue **Note:** Dav. #1940.

Date	Mintage	F	VF	XF	Unc
1800	—	175	300	600	1,200

KM# 152 THALER
Silver **Ruler:** Christoph Franz **Obverse:** Crowned arms with small mantle, divided date in upper field **Obv. Legend:** CHRISTOPH FRANZ BISCHOF ZU BAMBERG DES • G • R• FÜRST **Reverse:** Value within oval above city scene **Rev. Legend:** NACH DEM CONVENTIONSFUSE; X EINEFEINE MARK in oval; BAMBERG in frame below **Note:** Dav. #1941.

Date	Mintage	F	VF	XF	Unc
1800	—	125	250	450	1,000

KM# 153 THALER

Silver **Ruler:** Christoph Franz **Obverse:** Crowned arms within small crowned mantle **Obv. Legend:** CHRISTOPH FRANZ BISCHOF ZU BAMBERG DES • H • R • R • FURST • **Reverse:** Value within oval above city scene **Rev. Legend:** NACH DEM BONVENTIONSFUSE; X EINEFEINE MARK in oval; BAMBERG in exergue below **Note:** Mule. Dav. #1941A.

Date	Mintage	F	VF	XF	Unc
1800	—	125	250	450	1,000

KM# 108.1 2-1/2 GULDEN (1/4 Carolin)

Gold **Ruler:** Friederich Karl **Obverse:** Bust right **Reverse:** Crowned and mantled arms, date above, value 2 1/2 Gul below

Date	Mintage	VG	F	VF	XF	Unc
1735	—	650	1,150	2,000	3,500	—

KM# 109.1 2-1/2 GULDEN (1/4 Carolin)

Gold **Ruler:** Friederich Karl **Reverse:** Crowned and mantled shield with CF monogram, date above, value 2 1/2 Gul below

Date	Mintage	VG	F	VF	XF	Unc
1735	—	650	1,150	2,000	3,500	—

KM# 108.2 2-1/2 GULDEN (1/4 Carolin)

Gold **Ruler:** Friederich Karl **Reverse:** Value 2 1/2 G

Date	Mintage	VG	F	VF	XF	Unc
1736	—	650	1,150	2,000	3,500	—

KM# 109.2 2-1/2 GULDEN (1/4 Carolin)

Gold **Ruler:** Friederich Karl **Reverse:** Value 2 1/2 G

Date	Mintage	VG	F	VF	XF	Unc
1736	—	650	1,150	2,000	3,500	—

KM# 110 5 GULDEN (1/2 Carolin)

Gold **Ruler:** Friederich Karl **Obverse:** Bust right **Reverse:** Crowned and mantled arms, date above, value 5 G below

Date	Mintage	VG	F	VF	XF	Unc
1735	—	1,000	1,750	3,250	5,000	—

KM# 111 5 GULDEN (1/2 Carolin)

Gold **Ruler:** Friederich Karl **Reverse:** Crowned and mantled shield with CF monogram, date above, value 5 Gul below

Date	Mintage	VG	F	VF	XF	Unc
1735	—	1,000	1,750	3,250	5,000	—
1736	—	1,000	1,750	3,250	5,000	—

KM# 113.1 10 GULDEN (Carolin)

Gold **Ruler:** Friederich Karl **Reverse:** Crowned and mantled shield with CF monogram, date above, value 10 Gl below

Date	Mintage	VG	F	VF	XF	Unc
1730	—	1,350	2,500	3,750	5,500	—
1735	—	1,350	2,500	3,750	5,500	—

KM# 113.2 10 GULDEN (Carolin)

Gold **Ruler:** Friederich Karl **Reverse:** Value 10 Gul

Date	Mintage	VG	F	VF	XF	Unc
1735	—	1,350	2,500	3,750	5,500	—
1736	—	1,350	2,500	3,750	5,500	—

KM# 112.1 10 GULDEN (Carolin)

Gold **Ruler:** Friederich Karl **Obverse:** Bust right **Reverse:** Crowned and mantled arms, date above, value 10 Guld below

Date	Mintage	VG	F	VF	XF	Unc
1735	—	1,350	2,500	3,750	5,500	—

KM# 112.2 10 GULDEN (Carolin)

Gold **Ruler:** Friederich Karl **Reverse:** Value 10 Gul

Date	Mintage	VG	F	VF	XF	Unc
1735	—	1,350	2,500	3,750	5,500	—
1736	—	1,350	2,500	3,750	5,500	—

KM# 113.3 10 GULDEN (Carolin)

Gold **Ruler:** Friederich Karl **Reverse:** Value 10 GULD

Date	Mintage	VG	F	VF	XF	Unc
1736	—	1,350	2,500	3,750	5,500	—

TRADE COINAGE

KM# 100 1/2 DUCAT

1.7500 g., 0.9860 Gold 0.0555 oz. AGW **Ruler:** Friederich Karl **Obverse:** Crowned oval arms in cartouche **Reverse:** Crowned and mantled oval shield with FC monogram, date below

Date	Mintage	VG	F	VF	XF	Unc
1729	—	600	1,000	1,750	2,750	—
ND	—	—	—	—	—	—

KM# 101 DUCAT

3.5000 g., 0.9860 Gold 0.1109 oz. AGW **Ruler:** Friederich Karl **Obverse:** Crowned oval arms supported by two lions **Reverse:** Crowned and mantled oval shield with FC monogram, date below

Date	Mintage	VG	F	VF	XF	Unc
1729	—	700	1,150	2,000	3,500	—
1730	—	700	1,150	2,000	3,500	—
1731	—	700	1,150	2,000	3,500	—

KM# 102 DUCAT

3.5000 g., 0.9860 Gold 0.1109 oz. AGW **Ruler:** Friederich Karl **Obverse:** Bust right

Date	Mintage	VG	F	VF	XF	Unc
1729	—	700	1,150	2,000	3,500	—

KM# 103 DUCAT

3.5000 g., 0.9860 Gold 0.1109 oz. AGW **Reverse:** Crowned and helmeted arms, supported by two lions, date

Date	Mintage	VG	F	VF	XF	Unc
1729	—	700	1,150	2,000	3,500	—

KM# 107 DUCAT

3.5000 g., 0.9860 Gold 0.1109 oz. AGW **Ruler:** Friederich Karl **Reverse:** Crowned and mantled arms, date above **Note:** Varieties exist.

Date	Mintage	VG	F	VF	XF	Unc
1731	—	700	1,150	2,000	3,500	—
1732	—	700	1,150	2,000	3,500	—
1733	—	700	1,150	2,000	3,500	—
1734	—	700	1,150	2,000	3,500	—

KM# 114 DUCAT

3.5000 g., 0.9860 Gold 0.1109 oz. AGW **Subject:** Homage of the City of Bamberg **Obverse:** Five helmets, crown and cross above complex arms **Reverse:** Knight standing holding banner and shield

Date	Mintage	F	VF	XF	Unc
1746	—	450	950	2,150	3,250

KM# 117 DUCAT

3.5000 g., 0.9860 Gold 0.1109 oz. AGW **Ruler:** Johann Philip Anton **Obverse:** Bust right **Reverse:** Crowned arms

Date	Mintage	F	VF	XF	Unc
1750 CGL	—	500	1,000	2,200	3,500

KM# 119 DUCAT

3.5000 g., 0.9860 Gold 0.1109 oz. AGW **Ruler:** Franz Conrad **Subject:** Homage of the City of Bamberg **Obverse:** Bust left **Reverse:** Helmeted arms, date in choronogram

Date	Mintage	F	VF	XF	Unc
1753 PPW/CGL	—	450	950	2,150	3,250

KM# 121 DUCAT

3.5000 g., 0.9860 Gold 0.1109 oz. AGW **Subject:** Homage of Bamberg **Obverse:** Bust right above inscription **Reverse:** Standing knight with shield and banner

Date	Mintage	F	VF	XF	Unc
1757	—	450	950	2,150	3,250

KM# 135 DUCAT

3.5000 g., 0.9860 Gold 0.1109 oz. AGW **Subject:** Homage of Bamberg **Obverse:** Bust right above inscription **Reverse:** Figure with shield right of triangular design

Date	Mintage	F	VF	XF	Unc
1779	—	400	800	1,650	2,600

KM# 147 DUCAT

3.5000 g., 0.9860 Gold 0.1109 oz. AGW **Subject:** Homage of Bamberg **Obverse:** Bust left **Reverse:** Figure with shield standing left of crowned stone at right

Date	Mintage	F	VF	XF	Unc
1795	—	400	700	1,150	1,850

KM# 104 2 DUCAT

7.0000 g., 0.9860 Gold 0.2219 oz. AGW **Ruler:** Friederich Karl **Obverse:** Bust right **Reverse:** Crowned and helmeted arms supported by two lions, date

Date	Mintage	F	VF	XF	Unc
1729 Rare	—	—	—	—	—
1730 Rare	—	—	—	—	—
1731 Rare	—	—	—	—	—

KM# 105 4 DUCAT

14.0000 g., 0.9860 Gold 0.4438 oz. AGW **Obverse:** Bust right **Reverse:** Crowned and helmeted arms supported by two lions, date

Date	Mintage	F	VF	XF	Unc
ND Rare	—	—	—	—	—

KM# 106 7-1/2 DUCAT

0.9890 g., Gold **Ruler:** Luther Franz **Obverse:** Bust right **Reverse:** Crowned and helmeted arms supported by 2 lions, date

Date	Mintage	Good	VG	F	VF	XF
ND Rare	—	—	—	—	—	—

PATTERNS

Including off metal strikes

KM#	Date	Mintage	Identification	Mkt Val
Pn4	ND(1729)	—	7-1/2 Ducat. Silver. KM#106	—
Pn5	ND(1729)	—	7-1/2 Ducat. Copper. KM#106	—
Pn6	ND1746	—	Ducat. Silver. 3.9000 g. KM#114	—
Pn7	ND1746	—	Ducat. Silver. 7.8000 g. KM#114	—
Pn8	ND1753	—	Ducat. Silver. 2.9300 g. KM#119	—
Pn9	ND1779	—	Ducat. Silver. KM#135	100
Pn10	ND1795	—	Ducat. Silver. 3.9000 g. KM#147	—

BAVARIA

(Bayern)

One of the largest states in Germany, Bavaria was a duchy from earliest times, ruled by the Agilholfingen dynasty from 553 until it was suppressed by Charlemagne in 788. Bavaria remained a territory of the Carolingian Empire from that time until 911, when the son of the Count of Scheyern was made duke and began a new line of rulers there. A number of dukes during the next century and a half were elected emperor, but when the mail line became extinct, Empress Agnes gave Bavaria to the Counts of Nordheim in 1061. His descendant, Heinrich XII the Lion, fell out of favor with the emperor and was deposed. The duchy was then entrusted to Otto VI von Wittelsbach, Count of Scheyern and descendant of the counts who had ruled from the early 10th century. Duke Otto I, as he was known from 1180 on, was the ancestor of the dynasty which ruled in Bavaria until 1918 and, from the late 13th century, in the Rhine Palatinate as well (see Electoral Pfalz). The first of several divisions took place in 1255 when lines in Upper and Lower Bavaria were established. The line in Lower Bavaria became extinct in 1340 and the territory reverted to Upper Bavaria. Meanwhile, the division of Upper Bavaria and the Palatinate took place and was confirmed by treaty in 1329, although the electoral vote residing with the Wittelsbachs was to be held jointly by the two branches. In 1347, Bavaria and all other holdings of the family in Brandenburg, the Tyrol and Holland were divided among six brothers. Munich had become the chief city of the duchy by this time. In 1475, Duke Stephen I, who had reunited most of the family's holdings in Bavaria, died and left three sons who promptly divided their patrimony once again. The lines of Ingolstadt, Landshut and Munich were founded, but as the other lines died out, the one seated in Munich regained control of all of Bavaria. Duke Albrecht IV instituted primogeniture in 1506 and from that time on, Bavaria remained united. When Elector Friedrich V of the Palatinate (Pfalz) was elected King of Bohemia in 1618, an event which helped precipitate the Thirty Years' War, Duke Maximilian I of Bavaria sided with the emperor against his kinsman. The electoral dignity had been given to the Pfalz branch of the Wittelsbachs by the Golden Bull of 1356, a fact which was a source of contention with the Bavarian branch of the family. With the ouster of Friedrich V, Maximilian I obtained the electoral right and control of the Palatinate in 1623, then also ruled over the Upper Palatinate (Oberpfalz) from 1628 until the conclusion of the war and the Peace of Westphalia. The Bavarian Wittelsbachs became extinct in 1777 and the line in Electoral Pfalz acquired Bavaria, thus uniting the two main territories of the dynasty under a single ruler for the first time since the early 14th century. When Napoleon abolished the Holy Roman Empire in 1806, bringing an end to the electoral system, the ruler of Bavaria was raised to the rank of king. The 19th century saw tragedy upon tragedy visit the royal family. Because of his opposition to the parliamentary reform movement, Ludwig I was forced to abdicate in 1848. His grandson, Ludwig II, inspired by his upbringing to spend his fortune building the fairy tale castle of Neuschwanstein, was forcibly removed by court nobles and died under mysterious circumstances in 1886. His younger brother, Otto, was declared insane and the kingdom was ruled by his uncle, the beloved Prince Luitpold, as prince regent. Ludwig II, the last King of Bavaria, was forced to abdicate at the end of World War I.

RULERS

Maximilian II Emanuel, 1679-1726
Karl Albrecht, 1726-1745
Maximilian III Josef, 1745-1777
Karl Theodor, 1777-1799
Maximilian IV Josef, Elector 1799-1806

MINT OFFICIALS' INITIALS

Amberg Mint

Initials	Date	Name
	1763	Johann Michael Beutelhauser, mint director
	1763	Johann König, mint contractor
	1763-80	Johann Dominikus Kimprunn, mintmaster
	Ca.1763-94	Karl Jacob Pucher, warden
	1763-80	Johann Georg Wissger, die-cutter
	1766-69	Johann Joseph Promoli, warden

Mannheim Mint

Initials	Date	Name
AS	1778-95	Anton Schaeffer

Munich Mint

Initials	Date	Name
	1701-05	Friedrich Canzler, warden
	1705-14	Moritz Angermayr, mintmaster
	1705	Johann Gregor Faeschler, warden
	Ca.1705	Adam Kolb, die-cutter
	1719	Franz Ferdinand Müller, warden
	1719-38	Franz Moritz Angermayr, warden
	1724	Franz Heinrich Schrettinger, die-cutter
	1725	Franz Ferdinand Müllere, mintmaster
	1726-45	Kaspar Zaller, die-cutter
	1737-45	Maximilian Rigart, warden
FAS	1738-87	Franz Andreas Schega, die-cutter and medailleur
	1745-66	Andreas Cammerloher, warden
	1748	Kaspar Gregor Lachenmayr, mint director
	1748-52	Franz Michael Grimm, warden
	1751-93	Sigmund Graf von Haimhausen, mintmaster
	1753	Georg Friedrich Jaster, mintmaster
	1761-85	Joseph Oecker, warden
	1763-94	Karl Jakob Pucker, warden
	1764	Michael Hammer, die-cutter
ST, HST	Ca.1767-82	Heinrich Straub, die-cutter and medailleur
IS, IIS, ISF	1768-1804	Joseph Ignatz Schäufel, die-cutter (d.1812)
	1769-?	Johann Joseph Promoli, warden
	1775	Michael Dimler, die-cutter
CD, CDF	1784-1804	Cajetan Destouches, die-cutter
	1787-93	Joseph Heinrich Le Prieur
	1793-1837	Joseph Heinrich Le Prieur, mint director

ARMS: Wittelsbach and Bavaria – field of lozenges (diamond shapes); Pfalz – rampant lion, usually to the left

MINT MARKS

A – Amberg, 1763-95
M - Munich

DUCHY

REGULAR COINAGE

KM# 324 NON-DENOMINATED

14.0300 g., 0.8330 Silver 0.3757 oz. ASW **Ruler:** Maximilian IV, Josef as Elector **Obverse:** Uniformed bust right **Reverse:** Text within wreath **Note:** School prize without denomination.

Date	Mintage	F	VF	XF	Unc
ND(1799-1805)	—	150	250	400	750

KM# 236 HELLER

Copper **Ruler:** Maximilian III, Josef **Obverse:** Arms divide date in legend **Reverse:** Value in diamond

Date	Mintage	VG	F	VF	XF	Unc
1761	—	8.00	12.00	25.00	50.00	—
1765	—	8.00	12.00	25.00	50.00	—

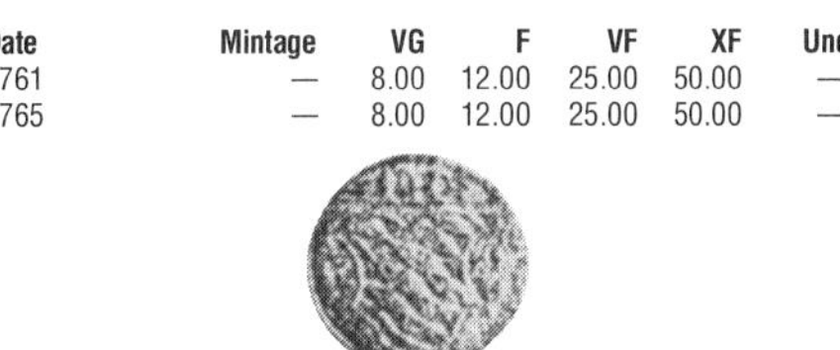

KM# 235 HELLER

Copper **Ruler:** Maximilian III, Josef **Mint:** Munich **Obverse:** Arms divide date, 1H **Note:** Uniface

Date	Mintage	VG	F	VF	XF	Unc
1761	—	40.00	90.00	150	250	—

KM# 242 HELLER

Copper **Ruler:** Maximilian III, Josef **Mint:** Amberg **Obverse:** Arms divide C-B, date above **Reverse:** Value and date **Note:** Uniface

Date	Mintage	VG	F	VF	XF	Unc
1765A	—	9.00	15.00	30.00	60.00	—

KM# 243 HELLER

Copper **Ruler:** Maximilian III, Josef **Obverse:** Arms divide CB, date above **Reverse:** Value and date

Date	Mintage	VG	F	VF	XF	Unc
1765 A	—	6.00	12.00	25.00	50.00	—

KM# 266 HELLER

Copper **Ruler:** Karl Theodor **Obverse:** Arms divide date **Reverse:** Value within diamond

Date	Mintage	VG	F	VF	XF	Unc
1780	—	5.00	10.00	18.00	35.00	—
1781	—	5.00	10.00	18.00	35.00	—
1782	—	5.00	10.00	18.00	35.00	—
1783	—	5.00	10.00	18.00	35.00	—
1785	—	5.00	10.00	18.00	35.00	—
1786	—	5.00	10.00	18.00	35.00	—
1787	—	5.00	10.00	18.00	35.00	—
1788	—	5.00	10.00	18.00	35.00	—
1789	—	5.00	10.00	18.00	35.00	—
1790	—	5.00	10.00	18.00	35.00	—
1791	—	5.00	10.00	18.00	35.00	—
1792	—	5.00	10.00	18.00	35.00	—
1793	—	5.00	10.00	18.00	35.00	—
1795	—	5.00	10.00	18.00	35.00	—
1796	—	5.00	10.00	18.00	35.00	—
1798	—	5.00	10.00	18.00	35.00	—
1799	—	5.00	10.00	18.00	35.00	—

KM# 267 HELLER

Copper **Ruler:** Maximilian IV, Josef as Elector **Obverse:** Diamond shield dividing date **Reverse:** Value

Date	Mintage	VG	F	VF	XF	Unc
1780A	—	5.00	10.00	18.00	35.00	—
1783A	—	5.00	10.00	18.00	35.00	—

KM# 287 HELLER

Copper **Ruler:** Maximilian IV, Josef as Elector **Obverse:** Crowned arms within branches, date divided above **Reverse:** Value within diamond

Date	Mintage	VG	F	VF	XF	Unc
1793A	—	15.00	30.00	60.00	120	—
1794A	—	15.00	30.00	60.00	120	—

KM# 305 HELLER

Copper **Ruler:** Maximilian IV, Josef as Elector **Obverse:** Shield and date in diamond **Reverse:** Value: 1/HEL/LER in diamond

Date	Mintage	F	VF	XF	Unc
1799	—	15.00	35.00	100	175
1800	—	15.00	35.00	100	175

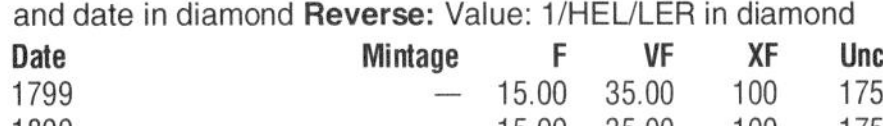

KM# 112 PFENNIG

Billon **Ruler:** Maximilian II, Emanuel **Obverse:** C divides date above Bavarian arms in branches **Note:** Uniface.

Date	Mintage	VG	F	VF	XF	Unc
1700	—	5.00	10.00	20.00	40.00	—
1701	—	5.00	10.00	20.00	40.00	—
1702	—	5.00	10.00	20.00	40.00	—
1703	—	5.00	10.00	20.00	40.00	—
1704	—	5.00	10.00	20.00	40.00	—
1705	—	5.00	10.00	20.00	40.00	—

KM# 136 PFENNIG

Billon **Ruler:** Maximilian II, Emanuel **Obverse:** Crowned imperial eagle wtih value on breast, date below **Note:** Uniface. Austrian Administration.

Date	Mintage	VG	F	VF	XF	Unc
1705	—	5.00	10.00	20.00	40.00	—
1706	—	5.00	10.00	20.00	40.00	—
1707	—	5.00	10.00	20.00	40.00	—
1708	—	5.00	10.00	20.00	40.00	—
1709	—	5.00	10.00	20.00	40.00	—
1710	—	5.00	10.00	20.00	40.00	—
1711	—	5.00	10.00	20.00	40.00	—
1712	—	5.00	10.00	20.00	40.00	—
1713	—	5.00	10.00	20.00	40.00	—
1714	—	5.00	10.00	20.00	40.00	—

KM# 147 PFENNIG

Billon **Ruler:** Maximilian II, Emanuel **Note:** Second reign of Maximilian II Emanuel.

Date	Mintage	VG	F	VF	XF	Unc
1715	—	5.00	10.00	20.00	40.00	—
1717	—	5.00	10.00	20.00	40.00	—
1718	—	5.00	10.00	20.00	40.00	—
1719	—	5.00	10.00	20.00	40.00	—
1720	—	5.00	10.00	20.00	40.00	—
1721	—	5.00	10.00	20.00	40.00	—
1722	—	5.00	10.00	20.00	40.00	—
1723	—	5.00	10.00	20.00	40.00	—
1724	—	5.00	10.00	20.00	40.00	—
1725	—	5.00	10.00	20.00	40.00	—
1726	—	5.00	10.00	20.00	40.00	—

KM# 165 PFENNIG

Billon **Ruler:** Karl Albrecht **Note:** Karl Albrecht as Elector. C divides date above Bavarian arms.

Date	Mintage	VG	F	VF	XF	Unc
1726	—	5.00	10.00	20.00	40.00	—
1727	—	5.00	10.00	20.00	40.00	—
1728	—	5.00	10.00	20.00	40.00	—
1730	—	5.00	10.00	20.00	40.00	—
1732	—	5.00	10.00	20.00	40.00	—
1733	—	5.00	10.00	20.00	40.00	—
1734	—	5.00	10.00	20.00	40.00	—
1735	—	5.00	10.00	20.00	40.00	—
1736	—	5.00	10.00	20.00	40.00	—
1737	—	5.00	10.00	20.00	40.00	—
1738	—	5.00	10.00	20.00	40.00	—
1739	—	5.00	10.00	20.00	40.00	—
1740	—	5.00	10.00	20.00	40.00	—
1741	—	5.00	10.00	20.00	40.00	—

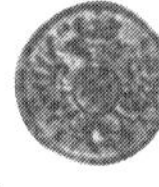

KM# 199 PFENNIG

Billon **Ruler:** Karl Albrecht **Obverse:** Crowned imperial eagle, date below **Note:** Uniface. Karl Albrecht as Emperor Charles VII.

Date	Mintage	VG	F	VF	XF	Unc
1744	—	5.00	12.00	25.00	60.00	—

KM# 205 PFENNIG

Silver **Ruler:** Maximilian III, Josef **Mint:** Munich **Note:** Uniface

Date	Mintage	VG	F	VF	XF	Unc
1745	—	5.00	10.00	20.00	40.00	—
1746	—	5.00	10.00	20.00	40.00	—
1748	—	5.00	10.00	20.00	40.00	—
1749	—	5.00	10.00	20.00	40.00	—
1751	—	5.00	10.00	20.00	40.00	—
1752	—	5.00	10.00	20.00	40.00	—
1753	—	5.00	10.00	20.00	40.00	—
1754	—	5.00	10.00	20.00	40.00	—
1755	—	5.00	10.00	20.00	40.00	—
1757	—	5.00	10.00	20.00	40.00	—
1758	—	5.00	10.00	20.00	40.00	—
1762	—	5.00	10.00	20.00	40.00	—
1763	—	5.00	10.00	20.00	40.00	—
1764	—	5.00	10.00	20.00	40.00	—
1765	—	5.00	10.00	20.00	40.00	—

KM# 232 PFENNIG

Silver **Ruler:** Maximilian III, Josef **Obverse:** C divides date above Bavarian arms **Reverse:** Value within wreath

Date	Mintage	VG	F	VF	XF	Unc
1759	—	5.00	10.00	20.00	40.00	—
1760	—	5.00	10.00	20.00	40.00	—
1761	—	5.00	10.00	20.00	40.00	—

KM# 237 PFENNIG

Copper **Ruler:** Maximilian III, Josef **Obverse:** Lozenge shield of arms **Reverse:** Value above date

Date	Mintage	VG	F	VF	XF	Unc
1761	—	2.50	5.00	10.00	20.00	—
1762	—	2.50	5.00	10.00	20.00	—
1763	—	2.50	5.00	10.00	20.00	—
1763A	—	10.00	35.00	75.00	150	—
1764	—	2.50	5.00	10.00	20.00	—
1764A	—	10.00	35.00	75.00	150	—
1765	—	2.50	5.00	10.00	20.00	—
1765A	—	10.00	35.00	75.00	150	—
1766	—	2.50	5.00	10.00	20.00	—
1766A	—	10.00	35.00	75.00	150	—
1767	—	2.50	5.00	10.00	20.00	—
1767A	—	10.00	35.00	75.00	150	—
1768	—	2.50	5.00	10.00	20.00	—
1768A	—	10.00	35.00	75.00	150	—
1769	—	2.50	5.00	10.00	20.00	—
1769A	—	10.00	35.00	75.00	150	—
1770	—	2.50	5.00	10.00	20.00	—
1770A	—	10.00	35.00	75.00	150	—
1771	—	2.50	5.00	10.00	20.00	—
1772	—	2.50	5.00	10.00	20.00	—
1773	—	2.50	5.00	10.00	20.00	—
1776	—	2.50	5.00	10.00	20.00	—
1777	—	2.50	5.00	10.00	20.00	—
1782	—	1.00	2.00	5.00	15.00	—
1782A	—	10.00	35.00	75.00	150	—
1783	—	1.00	2.00	5.00	15.00	—
1783A	—	10.00	35.00	75.00	150	—
1784	—	1.00	2.00	5.00	15.00	—
1785	—	1.00	2.00	5.00	15.00	—
1786	—	1.00	2.00	5.00	15.00	—
1787	—	1.00	2.00	5.00	15.00	—
1788	—	1.00	2.00	5.00	15.00	—
1789	—	1.00	2.00	5.00	15.00	—
1790	—	1.00	2.00	5.00	15.00	—
1792	—	1.00	2.00	5.00	15.00	—
1793	—	1.00	2.00	5.00	15.00	—
1793A	—	10.00	35.00	75.00	150	—
1794	—	1.00	2.00	5.00	15.00	—
1795	—	1.00	2.00	5.00	15.00	—
1796	—	1.00	2.00	5.00	15.00	—
1797	—	1.00	2.00	5.00	15.00	—
1798	—	1.00	2.00	5.00	15.00	—
1799	—	1.00	2.00	5.00	15.00	—

KM# 288 PFENNIG

Copper **Ruler:** Karl Theodor **Obverse:** Crowned three-fold arms in spray

Date	Mintage	VG	F	VF	XF	Unc
1793A	—	15.00	30.00	60.00	120	—
1794A	—	15.00	30.00	60.00	120	—

KM# 289 PFENNIG

Copper **Ruler:** Karl Theodor **Obverse:** Arms in Order chain

Date	Mintage	VG	F	VF	XF	Unc
1793A	—	15.00	30.00	60.00	120	—
1794A	—	15.00	30.00	60.00	120	—

KM# 306 PFENNIG

Copper **Ruler:** Maximilian IV, Josef as Elector **Obverse:** Bavarian shield in ornamental cartouche **Reverse:** Value above date

Date	Mintage	F	VF	XF	Unc
1799	—	15.00	30.00	75.00	150
1800	—	15.00	30.00	75.00	150

KM# 245 2 PFENNIG

Copper **Ruler:** Maximilian III, Josef **Obverse:** Arms divide CB **Reverse:** Value and date

Date	Mintage	VG	F	VF	XF	Unc
1766	—	3.00	7.00	15.00	30.00	—
1766 A	—	20.00	75.00	150	250	—
1767	—	5.00	12.00	25.00	60.00	—

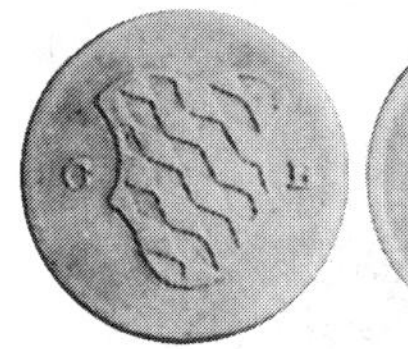

KM# 269 2 PFENNIG

Copper **Ruler:** Karl Theodor **Obverse:** Arms divide CB **Reverse:** Value and date

Date	Mintage	VG	F	VF	XF	Unc
1786	—	1.00	5.00	10.00	25.00	—
1790	—	1.00	5.00	10.00	25.00	—
1793	—	1.00	5.00	10.00	25.00	—
1795	—	1.00	5.00	10.00	25.00	—
1796	—	1.00	5.00	10.00	25.00	—

KM# 290 2 PFENNIG

Copper **Ruler:** Karl Theodor **Obverse:** Crowned three-fold arms in spray

Date	Mintage	VG	F	VF	XF	Unc
1793A	—	25.00	45.00	75.00	130	—

KM# 307 2 PFENNIG

Copper **Ruler:** Maximilian IV, Josef as Elector **Obverse:** Bavarian shield **Reverse:** Denomination

Date	Mintage	F	VF	XF	Unc
1799	—	35.00	75.00	150	250
1800	—	35.00	75.00	150	250

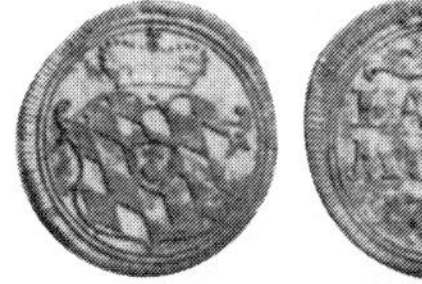

KM# 225 10 PFENNIG (2-1/2 Kreuzer)

Silver **Ruler:** Maximilian III, Josef **Obverse:** Crowned arms **Reverse:** Value and date

Date	Mintage	VG	F	VF	XF	Unc
1754	—	20.00	40.00	80.00	150	—

KM# 141 1/2 KREUZER

Silver **Subject:** Austrian Administration **Note:** Uniface. Crowned imperial eagle with value on breast, date below.

Date	Mintage	VG	F	VF	XF	Unc
1707	—	5.00	7.50	15.00	30.00	—
1709	—	5.00	7.50	15.00	30.00	—

KM# 159 1/2 KREUZER

Silver **Ruler:** Maximilian II, Emanuel **Note:** Uniface. Second reign of Maximilian II Emanuel.

Date	Mintage	VG	F	VF	XF	Unc
1725	—	7.00	15.00	30.00	60.00	—

KM# 185 1/2 KREUZER

Billon **Ruler:** Karl Albrecht **Note:** Bavarian arms divide C-B, date at top, value at bottom.

Date	Mintage	VG	F	VF	XF	Unc
1740	—	5.00	10.00	20.00	40.00	—

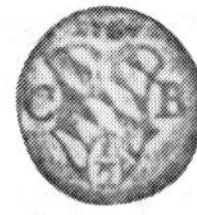

KM# 213 1/2 KREUZER

Billon **Ruler:** Maximilian III, Josef **Obverse:** Bavarian arms divide C-B, date at top, value at bottom. **Note:** Uniface.

Date	Mintage	VG	F	VF	XF	Unc
1746	—	3.00	6.00	12.00	25.00	—
1753	—	3.00	6.00	12.00	25.00	—
1755	—	3.00	6.00	12.00	25.00	—
1757	—	3.00	6.00	12.00	25.00	—
1758	—	3.00	6.00	12.00	25.00	—
1761	—	3.00	6.00	12.00	25.00	—
1762	—	3.00	6.00	12.00	25.00	—
1763	—	3.00	6.00	12.00	25.00	—
1764	—	3.00	6.00	12.00	25.00	—
1764A	—	8.00	25.00	45.00	90.00	—
1765	—	3.00	6.00	12.00	25.00	—
1765A	—	8.00	25.00	45.00	90.00	—
1767	—	3.00	6.00	12.00	25.00	—

KM# 246 1/2 KREUZER

Copper **Ruler:** Maximilian III, Josef **Obverse:** Bavarian arms divide C-B **Reverse:** Value and date

Date	Mintage	VG	F	VF	XF	Unc
1766	—	3.00	6.00	12.00	25.00	—
1766A	—	3.00	6.00	12.00	25.00	—
1767	—	3.00	6.00	12.00	25.00	—

KM# 120 KREUZER

Silver **Ruler:** Maximilian II, Emanuel **Obverse:** Head right **Reverse:** Crowned double-headed imperial eagle with arms on breast **Note:** First reign.

Date	Mintage	VG	F	VF	XF	Unc
1692	—	8.00	15.00	28.00	40.00	—
1695	—	8.00	15.00	28.00	40.00	—
1696	—	8.00	15.00	28.00	40.00	—
1697	—	8.00	15.00	28.00	40.00	—
1698	—	8.00	15.00	28.00	40.00	—
1699	—	8.00	15.00	28.00	40.00	—
1700	—	8.00	15.00	28.00	40.00	—
1701	—	8.00	15.00	28.00	40.00	—
1702	—	8.00	15.00	28.00	40.00	—
1703	—	—	—	—	—	—

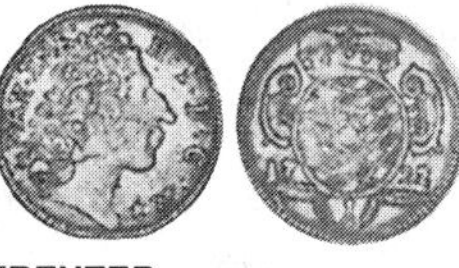

KM# 148 KREUZER

Silver **Ruler:** Maximilian II, Emanuel **Obverse:** Head right **Reverse:** Crowned arms divide date, value below **Note:** Second reign of Maximilian II Emanuel.

Date	Mintage	VG	F	VF	XF	Unc
1715	—	6.00	10.00	20.00	40.00	—
1717	—	6.00	10.00	20.00	40.00	—
1718	—	6.00	10.00	20.00	40.00	—
1719	—	6.00	10.00	20.00	40.00	—
1720	—	6.00	10.00	20.00	40.00	—
1721	—	6.00	10.00	20.00	40.00	—
1722	—	6.00	10.00	20.00	40.00	—
1723	—	6.00	10.00	20.00	40.00	—
1724	—	6.00	10.00	20.00	40.00	—

KM# 166 KREUZER

Silver **Ruler:** Karl Albrecht **Obverse:** Head right **Reverse:** Crowned arms **Note:** Karl Albrecht as Elector

Date	Mintage	VG	F	VF	XF	Unc
1726	—	5.00	10.00	20.00	40.00	—
1727	—	5.00	10.00	20.00	40.00	—
1731	—	5.00	10.00	20.00	40.00	—
1732	—	5.00	10.00	20.00	40.00	—
1734	—	5.00	10.00	20.00	40.00	—
1735	—	5.00	10.00	20.00	40.00	—
1736	—	5.00	10.00	20.00	40.00	—
1737	—	5.00	10.00	20.00	40.00	—

KM# 173 KREUZER

Silver **Ruler:** Karl Albrecht **Obverse:** Bust right

Date	Mintage	VG	F	VF	XF	Unc
1732	—	3.00	7.00	15.00	25.00	—

KM# 200 KREUZER

Silver **Ruler:** Karl Albrecht **Obverse:** Laureate head right **Reverse:** Crowned imperial eagle, value divides date at bottom **Note:** Karl Albrecht as Emperor Karl VII.

Date	Mintage	VG	F	VF	XF	Unc
1744	—	4.00	10.00	20.00	40.00	—
1745	—	4.00	10.00	20.00	40.00	—

KM# 207 KREUZER

Silver **Ruler:** Maximilian III, Josef **Obverse:** Head right **Reverse:** Crowned arms within cartouche

Date	Mintage	VG	F	VF	XF	Unc
1745	—	3.00	7.00	15.00	30.00	—
1746	—	3.00	7.00	15.00	30.00	—

Date	Mintage	VG	F	VF	XF	Unc
1747	—	3.00	7.00	15.00	30.00	—
1748	—	3.00	7.00	15.00	30.00	—
1749	—	3.00	7.00	15.00	30.00	—
1751	—	3.00	7.00	15.00	30.00	—
1752	—	3.00	7.00	15.00	30.00	—
1753	—	3.00	7.00	15.00	30.00	—
1754	—	3.00	7.00	15.00	30.00	—
1755	—	3.00	7.00	15.00	30.00	—
1756	—	3.00	7.00	15.00	30.00	—
1757	—	3.00	7.00	15.00	30.00	—
1758	—	3.00	7.00	15.00	30.00	—
1759	—	3.00	7.00	15.00	30.00	—
1760	—	3.00	7.00	15.00	30.00	—
1761	—	3.00	7.00	15.00	30.00	—
1762	—	3.00	7.00	15.00	30.00	—
1763	—	3.00	7.00	15.00	30.00	—
1763A	—	20.00	35.00	90.00	125	—
1764	—	3.00	7.00	15.00	30.00	—
1764A	—	320	35.00	90.00	125	—
1765	—	3.00	7.00	15.00	30.00	—
1765A	—	20.00	35.00	90.00	125	—
1766	—	3.00	7.00	15.00	30.00	—
1766A	—	20.00	35.00	90.00	125	—
1767	—	3.00	7.00	15.00	30.00	—
1768A	—	20.00	35.00	90.00	125	—
1769	—	3.00	7.00	15.00	30.00	—

KM# 206 KREUZER

Silver **Ruler:** Maximilian III, Josef **Note:** Vicariat issue.

Date	Mintage	VG	F	VF	XF	Unc
1745	—	—	—	—	—	—

KM# 294 KREUZER

0.7700 g., 0.1870 Silver 0.0046 oz. ASW **Ruler:** Karl Theodor **Obverse:** Head right **Reverse:** Crowned round arms, value numeral divides date

Date	Mintage	VG	F	VF	XF	Unc
1794	—	4.00	10.00	20.00	40.00	—
1798	—	4.00	10.00	20.00	40.00	—

KM# 298 KREUZER

0.7700 g., 0.1870 Silver 0.0046 oz. ASW **Ruler:** Karl Theodor **Obverse:** Head right **Reverse:** Crowned arms and date

Date	Mintage	VG	F	VF	XF	Unc
1795	—	4.00	10.00	20.00	40.00	—
1796	—	4.00	10.00	20.00	40.00	—
1797	—	4.00	10.00	20.00	40.00	—

KM# 308 KREUZER

0.7700 g., 0.1870 Silver 0.0046 oz. ASW **Ruler:** Maximilian IV, Josef as Elector **Obverse:** Head right, MAX. IOS. **Reverse:** Crowned shield within palm branches

Date	Mintage	F	VF	XF	Unc
1799	—	25.00	100	150	300
1800	—	25.00	100	150	300
1802	—	25.00	100	150	300
1803	—	25.00	100	150	300

KM# 315 KREUZER

0.7700 g., 0.1870 Silver 0.0046 oz. ASW **Ruler:** Maximilian IV, Josef as Elector **Obv. Legend:** MAX. IOS. H. I. B. C. **Reverse:** Without numeric value

Date	Mintage	F	VF	XF	Unc
1800	—	25.00	100	150	300
1801	—	25.00	100	150	300
1802	—	25.00	100	150	300
1803	—	25.00	100	150	300
1806/0	—	25.00	110	160	325

KM# 220 2 KREUZER (1/2 Batzen)

Silver **Ruler:** Maximilian III, Josef **Mint:** Munich

Date	Mintage	VG	F	VF	XF	Unc
1753	—	10.00	20.00	50.00	100	—
1754	—	10.00	20.00	50.00	100	—

KM# 132 3 KREUZER (Groschen)

Silver **Ruler:** Maximilian II, Emanuel **Obverse:** Larger bust right **Reverse:** Crowned divided arms within circle, value below

Date	Mintage	VG	F	VF	XF	Unc
1701		9.00	18.00	38.00	70.00	
1702	—	9.00	18.00	38.00	70.00	—
1705		9.00	18.00	38.00	70.00	—

KM# 138 3 KREUZER (Groschen)

Silver **Ruler:** Maximilian II, Emanuel **Subject:** Austrian occupation **Obverse:** Bust of Josef I right **Reverse:** Crowned double-headed imperial eagle with crowned divided arms on breast

Date	Mintage	Good	VG	F	VF	XF
1705	—	—	10.00	20.00	40.00	80.00
1706	—	—	10.00	20.00	40.00	80.00
1707	—	—	10.00	20.00	40.00	80.00
1708	—	—	10.00	20.00	40.00	80.00
1709	—	—	10.00	20.00	40.00	80.00
1710	—	—	10.00	20.00	40.00	80.00
1711	—	—	10.00	20.00	40.00	80.00

KM# 143 3 KREUZER (Groschen)

Silver **Ruler:** Maximilian II, Emanuel **Obverse:** Karl VI **Reverse:** Crowned double-headed imperial eagle

Date	Mintage	Good	VG	F	VF	XF
1712	—	—	12.00	25.00	50.00	100
1713	—	—	12.00	25.00	50.00	100
1714	—	—	12.00	25.00	50.00	100

KM# 149 3 KREUZER (Groschen)

Silver **Ruler:** Maximilian II, Emanuel **Obverse:** Maximilian II Emanuel **Reverse:** Divided arms within cartouche **Note:** Second reign.

Date	Mintage	VG	F	VF	XF	Unc
1715	—	5.00	12.00	25.00	50.00	—
1716	—	5.00	12.00	25.00	50.00	—
1717	—	5.00	12.00	25.00	50.00	—
1718	—	5.00	12.00	25.00	50.00	—
1719	—	5.00	12.00	25.00	50.00	—
1720	—	5.00	12.00	25.00	50.00	—
1721	—	5.00	12.00	25.00	50.00	—
1722	—	5.00	12.00	25.00	50.00	—
1723	—	5.00	12.00	25.00	50.00	—
1724	—	5.00	12.00	25.00	50.00	—
1725	—	5.00	12.00	25.00	50.00	—
1726	—	5.00	12.00	25.00	50.00	—

KM# 167 3 KREUZER (Groschen)

Silver **Ruler:** Karl Albrecht **Obverse:** Head right **Reverse:** Crowned divided arms

Date	Mintage	VG	F	VF	XF	Unc
1726	—	10.00	25.00	50.00	100	—
1727	—	10.00	25.00	50.00	100	—
1728	—	10.00	25.00	50.00	100	—
1730	—	10.00	25.00	50.00	100	—
1731	—	10.00	25.00	50.00	100	—
1732	—	10.00	25.00	50.00	100	—
1733	—	10.00	25.00	50.00	100	—

KM# 179 3 KREUZER (Groschen)

Silver **Ruler:** Karl Albrecht **Obverse:** Bust right **Reverse:** Crowned arms within Order chain

Date	Mintage	VG	F	VF	XF	Unc
1733	—	10.00	20.00	40.00	60.00	—
1734	—	10.00	20.00	40.00	60.00	—
1736	—	10.00	20.00	40.00	60.00	—
1737	—	10.00	20.00	40.00	60.00	—

KM# 180 3 KREUZER (Groschen)

Silver **Ruler:** Karl Albrecht **Obverse:** Head right **Reverse:** Crown above divided arms within Order chain

Date	Mintage	VG	F	VF	XF	Unc
1733	—	10.00	20.00	40.00	60.00	—
1736	—	10.00	20.00	40.00	60.00	—

KM# 186 3 KREUZER (Groschen)

Silver **Ruler:** Karl Albrecht **Obverse:** Bust right **Reverse:** Crowned double-headed eagle with crowned divided arms on breast **Note:** Vicariat issue.

Date	Mintage	VG	F	VF	XF	Unc
1740	—	15.00	30.00	60.00	125	—

KM# 201 3 KREUZER (Groschen)

Silver **Ruler:** Karl Albrecht **Obverse:** Head right **Reverse:** Crowned double-headed eagle with crowned divided shield on breast **Note:** Karl Albrecht as Emperor Karl VII.

Date	Mintage	VG	F	VF	XF	Unc
1744	—	25.00	50.00	100	200	—
1745	—	25.00	50.00	100	200	—

KM# 209 3 KREUZER (Groschen)

Silver **Ruler:** Maximilian III, Josef **Obverse:** Head right **Reverse:** Divided arms within crowned Order chain **Note:** Maximilian III Joseph.

Date	Mintage	VG	F	VF	XF	Unc
1745	—	3.00	8.00	15.00	30.00	—
1747	—	3.00	8.00	15.00	30.00	—
1748	—	3.00	8.00	15.00	30.00	—
1751	—	3.00	8.00	15.00	30.00	—
1752	—	3.00	8.00	15.00	30.00	—
1754	—	3.00	8.00	15.00	30.00	—
1763	—	3.00	8.00	15.00	30.00	—
1764	—	3.00	8.00	15.00	30.00	—
1765	—	3.00	8.00	15.00	30.00	—
1766	—	3.00	8.00	15.00	30.00	—
1767	—	3.00	8.00	15.00	30.00	—

KM# 208 3 KREUZER (Groschen)

Silver **Ruler:** Maximilian III, Josef **Obverse:** Head right **Note:** Vicariat issue.

Date	Mintage	VG	F	VF	XF	Unc
1745	—	20.00	45.00	90.00	175	—

KM# 238 3 KREUZER (Groschen)

Silver **Ruler:** Maximilian III, Josef **Mint:** Amberg **Obverse:** Head right **Reverse:** Divided arms within Order chain

Date	Mintage	VG	F	VF	XF	Unc
1763A	—	5.00	15.00	30.00	60.00	—
1764A	—	5.00	15.00	30.00	60.00	—
1765A	—	5.00	15.00	30.00	60.00	—
1766A	—	5.00	15.00	30.00	60.00	—
1767A	—	5.00	15.00	30.00	60.00	—

KM# 295 3 KREUZER (Groschen)
1.3500 g., 0.3330 Silver 0.0145 oz. ASW **Ruler:** Karl Theodor **Obverse:** Head right **Reverse:** Crowned arms, date below

Date	Mintage	VG	F	VF	XF	Unc
1794	—	7.00	18.00	35.00	65.00	—
1795	—	7.00	18.00	35.00	65.00	—
1796	—	7.00	18.00	35.00	65.00	—
1797	—	7.00	18.00	35.00	65.00	—
1798	—	7.00	18.00	35.00	65.00	—

KM# 309 3 KREUZER (Groschen)
1.3500 g., 0.3330 Silver 0.0145 oz. ASW **Ruler:** Maximilian IV, Josef as Elector **Obverse:** Head right, legend **Obv. Legend:** MAX. IOS. P. B. **Reverse:** Crowned oval arms separating value

Date	Mintage	F	VF	XF	Unc
1799	—	40.00	60.00	175	375
1800	—	40.00	60.00	175	375

KM# 187 6 KREUZER
Silver **Ruler:** Karl Albrecht **Obverse:** Bust right **Reverse:** Double-headed eagle with crowned arms on breast **Note:** Vicariat issue.

Date	Mintage	VG	F	VF	XF	Unc
1740	—	20.00	40.00	85.00	175	—

KM# 197 6 KREUZER
Silver **Ruler:** Karl Albrecht **Obverse:** Laureate head right **Reverse:** Crowned double-headed imperial eagle with crowned arms on breast **Note:** Karl Allbrecht as Emperor Karl VII

Date	Mintage	VG	F	VF	XF	Unc
1742	—	25.00	50.00	100	200	—
1744	—	25.00	50.00	100	200	—
1745	—	25.00	50.00	100	200	—

KM# 210 6 KREUZER
Silver **Ruler:** Maximilian III, Josef **Mint:** Munich **Obverse:** Head right **Reverse:** Double-headed eagle with arms on breast **Note:** Vicariat issue

Date	Mintage	VG	F	VF	XF	Unc
1745	—	15.00	35.00	75.00	150	—

KM# 211 6 KREUZER
Silver **Ruler:** Maximilian III, Josef **Obverse:** Bust right

Date	Mintage	VG	F	VF	XF	Unc
1745	—	8.00	15.00	30.00	60.00	—
1746	—	8.00	15.00	30.00	60.00	—
1747	—	8.00	15.00	30.00	60.00	—
1748	—	8.00	15.00	30.00	60.00	—
1749	—	8.00	15.00	30.00	60.00	—
1750	—	8.00	15.00	30.00	60.00	—
1751	—	8.00	15.00	30.00	60.00	—
1752	—	8.00	15.00	30.00	60.00	—

KM# 247 6 KREUZER
Silver **Ruler:** Maximilian III, Josef **Mint:** Amberg **Obverse:** Bust right **Reverse:** Crowned divided arms within Order chain

Date	Mintage	VG	F	VF	XF	Unc
1766	—	12.00	35.00	75.00	150	—
1767	—	12.00	35.00	75.00	150	—

KM# 296 6 KREUZER
2.7000 g., 0.3330 Silver 0.0289 oz. ASW **Ruler:** Karl Theodor **Obverse:** Head right **Reverse:** Crowned arms, date below

Date	Mintage	VG	F	VF	XF	Unc
1794	—	12.00	35.00	75.00	150	—
1795	—	12.00	35.00	75.00	150	—
1796	—	12.00	35.00	75.00	150	—
1797	—	12.00	35.00	75.00	150	—
1798	—	12.00	35.00	75.00	150	—

KM# 310 6 KREUZER
2.7000 g., 0.3330 Silver 0.0289 oz. ASW **Ruler:** Maximilian IV, Josef as Elector **Obverse:** Head right **Obv. Legend:** MAX. IOS. P. B. **Reverse:** Crowned arms, date below

Date	Mintage	F	VF	XF	Unc
1799	—	25.00	120	250	400
1800	—	25.00	120	250	400

KM# 226 10 KREUZER
Silver **Ruler:** Maximilian III, Josef **Obverse:** Bust right within wreath **Reverse:** Madonna and child on pedestal with value, branches flank

Date	Mintage	VG	F	VF	XF	Unc
1754	—	15.00	40.00	90.00	175	—
1755	—	15.00	40.00	90.00	175	—
1756	—	15.00	40.00	90.00	175	—
1757	—	15.00	40.00	90.00	175	—
1758	—	15.00	40.00	90.00	175	—

KM# 239 10 KREUZER
Silver **Ruler:** Maximilian III, Josef **Obverse:** Bust right within wreath **Reverse:** Crowned divided arms within Order chain, pedestal below holds value, branches flank

Date	Mintage	VG	F	VF	XF	Unc
1763A	—	10.00	20.00	45.00	90.00	—
1764	—	5.00	10.00	20.00	40.00	—
1764A	—	10.00	20.00	45.00	90.00	—
1766	—	5.00	10.00	20.00	40.00	—
1767	—	5.00	10.00	20.00	40.00	—
1767A	—	10.00	20.00	45.00	90.00	—
1768	—	5.00	10.00	20.00	40.00	—
1768A	—	10.00	20.00	45.00	90.00	—
1769	—	5.00	10.00	20.00	40.00	—
1769A	—	10.00	20.00	45.00	90.00	—
1770	—	5.00	10.00	20.00	40.00	—
1770A	—	10.00	20.00	45.00	90.00	—
1771	—	5.00	10.00	20.00	40.00	—
1772	—	5.00	10.00	20.00	40.00	—
1773	—	5.00	10.00	20.00	40.00	—
1774	—	5.00	10.00	20.00	40.00	—
1775	—	5.00	10.00	20.00	40.00	—
1776	—	5.00	10.00	20.00	40.00	—
1777	—	5.00	10.00	20.00	40.00	—

KM# 255 10 KREUZER (Convention)
Silver **Ruler:** Karl Theodor **Obverse:** Bust right in wreath **Reverse:** Madonna and child above pedestal with value, branches flank

Date	Mintage	F	VF	XF	Unc
1778	—	20.00	40.00	60.00	150
1779	—	20.00	40.00	60.00	150
1780	—	20.00	40.00	60.00	150
1781	—	20.00	40.00	60.00	150
1781A	—	25.00	50.00	125	175
1782	—	20.00	40.00	60.00	150
1782A	—	25.00	50.00	125	175
1783	—	20.00	40.00	60.00	150
1783A	—	25.00	50.00	125	175
1784	—	20.00	40.00	60.00	150
1785	—	20.00	40.00	60.00	150
1786	—	20.00	40.00	60.00	150
1787	—	20.00	40.00	60.00	150
1788	—	20.00	40.00	60.00	150
1789	—	20.00	40.00	60.00	150
1790	—	20.00	40.00	60.00	150
1791	—	20.00	40.00	60.00	150
1792	—	20.00	40.00	60.00	150
1793	—	20.00	40.00	60.00	150
1794	—	20.00	40.00	60.00	150
1795	—	20.00	40.00	60.00	150
1796	—	20.00	40.00	60.00	150
1797	—	20.00	40.00	60.00	150
1798	—	20.00	40.00	60.00	150

KM# 272 10 KREUZER (Convention)
Silver **Ruler:** Karl Theodor **Obverse:** Head right **Reverse:** Double-headed eagle with arms on breast, value below **Note:** Vicariat issue.

Date	Mintage	F	VF	XF	Unc
1790	—	35.00	60.00	125	250

KM# 282 10 KREUZER (Convention)
Silver **Ruler:** Karl Theodor **Obverse:** Head right **Reverse:** Double-headed eagle with crowned arms on breast **Note:** Vicariat issue.

Date	Mintage	F	VF	XF	Unc
1792	—	35.00	60.00	125	250

KM# 316 10 KREUZER (Convention)
3.9000 g., 0.5000 Silver 0.0627 oz. ASW **Ruler:** Maximilian IV, Josef as Elector **Obverse:** Head right within wreath **Reverse:** Crowned three-fold oval arms

Date	Mintage	F	VF	XF	Unc
1800	—	100	200	400	750
1801 Rare	—	—	—	—	—

KM# 215 12 KREUZER (4 Groschen)
Silver **Ruler:** Maximilian III, Josef **Mint:** Munich **Obverse:** Head right **Obv. Legend:** MAX • IOX • - H • I • B • C • & • **Reverse:** Crown above arms within Order chain, date and value divided below **Rev. Legend:** LAND - MUNZ

Date	Mintage	VG	F	VF	XF	Unc
1747	—	6.00	12.00	25.00	50.00	—
1748	—	6.00	12.00	25.00	50.00	—
1749	—	6.00	12.00	25.00	50.00	—

Date	Mintage	VG	F	VF	XF	Unc
1750	—	6.00	12.00	25.00	50.00	—
1751	—	6.00	12.00	25.00	50.00	—
1752	—	6.00	12.00	25.00	50.00	—
1763	—	6.00	12.00	25.00	50.00	—
1763A	—	12.00	25.00	50.00	100	—
1764	—	6.00	12.00	25.00	50.00	—
1764A	—	12.00	25.00	50.00	100	—
1765	—	6.00	12.00	25.00	50.00	—

KM# 129.2 15 KREUZER

Silver **Ruler:** Maximilian II, Emanuel **Obverse:** Bust right within beaded circle **Reverse:** Crowned arms within beaded circle, value below

Date	Mintage	VG	F	VF	XF	Unc
1700	—	22.00	40.00	80.00	170	—
1701	—	22.00	40.00	80.00	170	—
1702	—	22.00	40.00	80.00	170	—
1703	—	22.00	40.00	80.00	170	—

KM# 129.3 15 KREUZER

Silver **Ruler:** Maximilian II, Emanuel **Mint:** Augsburg **Obverse:** Pine cone on bust

Date	Mintage	VG	F	VF	XF	Unc
1704	—	20.00	35.00	70.00	150	—

KM# 150 15 KREUZER

Silver **Ruler:** Maximilian II, Emanuel **Obverse:** Draped bust right **Obv. Legend:** MAX • BMA • - H • I • B • C • & • **Reverse:** Rampant lion holding sword and capped arms, value divides date below **Rev. Legend:** LAND - MINZ **Note:** Second riegn of Maximiliam II Emanuel.

Date	Mintage	VG	F	VF	XF	Unc
1715	—	15.00	30.00	60.00	120	—
1717	—	15.00	30.00	60.00	120	—
1718	—	15.00	30.00	60.00	120	—

KM# 172 15 KREUZER

Silver **Ruler:** Karl Albrecht **Obverse:** Head right **Reverse:** Rampant lion left with sword, crowned arms at left, value divides date below

Date	Mintage	VG	F	VF	XF	Unc
1727	—	35.00	65.00	130	255	—
1729	—	35.00	65.00	130	255	—
1731	—	35.00	65.00	130	255	—

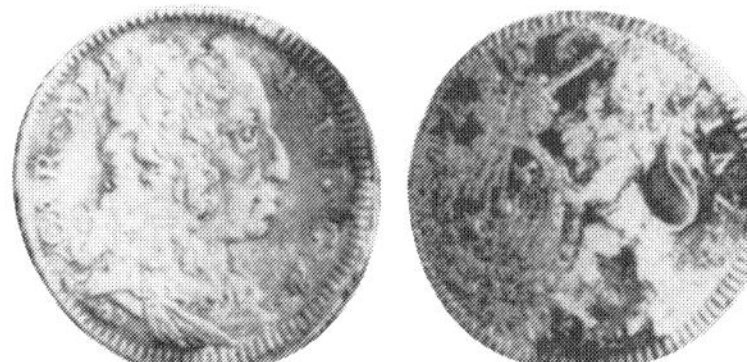

KM# 174 15 KREUZER

Silver **Ruler:** Karl Albrecht **Obverse:** Draped bust right **Reverse:** Rampant lion left with sword, crowned arms at left, value divides date below

Date	Mintage	VG	F	VF	XF	Unc
1732	—	50.00	80.00	160	300	—

KM# 221 20 KREUZER

Silver **Ruler:** Maximilian III, Josef **Mint:** Munich **Obverse:** Bust right within wreath **Reverse:** Crowned divided arms within Order chain, pedestal holds value below, branches flank **Note:** Without mintmark.

Date	Mintage	VG	F	VF	XF	Unc
1753	—	20.00	40.00	85.00	165	—
1754	—	20.00	40.00	85.00	165	—
1755	—	20.00	40.00	85.00	165	—
1756	—	20.00	40.00	85.00	165	—
1757	—	20.00	40.00	85.00	165	—
1758	—	20.00	40.00	85.00	165	—
1763	—	20.00	40.00	85.00	165	—
1774A	—	30.00	60.00	120	250	—

KM# 240 20 KREUZER

Silver **Ruler:** Maximilian III, Josef **Obverse:** Bust right within wreath **Obv. Legend:** D • G • MAX • IOS • U • B • & • P • - S • D • C • P • R • S • R • I • A • & • E • L • L • **Reverse:** Crowned arms within Order chain, pedestal below holds value and divides date **Rev. Legend:** IN DEO - CONSILIUM

Date	Mintage	VG	F	VF	XF	Unc
1763	—	5.00	10.00	20.00	40.00	—
1763A	—	10.00	20.00	45.00	90.00	—
1764	—	5.00	10.00	20.00	40.00	—
1764A	—	10.00	20.00	45.00	90.00	—
1765A	—	10.00	20.00	45.00	90.00	—
1766	—	5.00	10.00	20.00	40.00	—
1766A	—	10.00	20.00	45.00	90.00	—
1767	—	5.00	10.00	20.00	40.00	—
1767A	—	10.00	20.00	45.00	90.00	—
1768	—	5.00	10.00	20.00	40.00	—
1768A	—	10.00	20.00	45.00	90.00	—
1769	—	5.00	10.00	20.00	40.00	—
1769A	—	10.00	20.00	45.00	90.00	—
1770	—	5.00	10.00	20.00	40.00	—
1770A	—	10.00	20.00	45.00	90.00	—
1771	—	5.00	10.00	20.00	40.00	—
1772	—	5.00	10.00	20.00	40.00	—
1773	—	5.00	10.00	20.00	40.00	—
1774	—	5.00	10.00	20.00	40.00	—
1774A	—	10.00	20.00	45.00	90.00	—
1776	—	5.00	10.00	20.00	40.00	—
1776A	—	10.00	20.00	45.00	90.00	—
1777	—	5.00	10.00	20.00	40.00	—

KM# 250 20 KREUZER

Silver **Ruler:** Maximilian III, Josef **Obverse:** Bust right above value within diamond **Reverse:** Madonna and child within diamond

Date	Mintage	VG	F	VF	XF	Unc
1770	—	15.00	30.00	75.00	150	—
1772A	—	15.00	30.00	75.00	150	—
1773	—	15.00	30.00	75.00	150	—
1776A	—	15.00	30.00	75.00	150	—

KM# 251 20 KREUZER

Silver **Ruler:** Maximilian III, Josef **Obverse:** Bust right above value within diamond **Reverse:** Crowned arms within Order chain with griffin supporters, diamond surrounds

Date	Mintage	VG	F	VF	XF	Unc
1770	—	60.00	120	250	500	—
1772	—	60.00	120	250	500	—
1773	—	60.00	120	250	500	—
1776	—	60.00	120	250	500	—
1777	—	60.00	120	250	500	—

KM# 273 20 KREUZER

Silver **Ruler:** Karl Theodor **Obverse:** Bust right **Reverse:** Arms of Baden superimposed on double-headed eagle **Note:** Vicariat issue.

Date	Mintage	VG	F	VF	XF	Unc
1790	—	40.00	75.00	150	300	—

KM# 283 20 KREUZER

Silver **Ruler:** Karl Theodor **Obverse:** Bust right **Reverse:** Eagle with arms on breast

Date	Mintage	VG	F	VF	XF	Unc
1792	—	45.00	80.00	160	320	—

KM# 291 20 KREUZER

Silver **Ruler:** Karl Theodor **Obverse:** Bust in wreath **Reverse:** Three-fold oval arms

Date	Mintage	VG	F	VF	XF	Unc
1793A	—	60.00	120	250	500	—
1794A	—	60.00	120	250	500	—

KM# 311 20 KREUZER

6.6800 g., 0.5830 Silver 0.1252 oz. ASW **Ruler:** Maximilian IV, Josef as Elector **Obverse:** Bust right within wreath **Obv. Legend:** D • G • MAX • IOS • C • P • R • V • B • D • S • R • I • A • & • EL • D • I • C • & • M • **Reverse:** Crowned arms within crossed branches, date and value below **Rev. Legend:** PRO DEO - ET POPULO

Date	Mintage	F	VF	XF	Unc
1799	—	65.00	120	275	500
1800	—	65.00	120	275	500

KM# 256 20 KREUZER (Convention)

Silver **Ruler:** Karl Theodor **Obverse:** Bust right within wreath **Obv. Legend:** CAR • THEOD • D • G • C • P • R • - U • B • D • S • R • I • A • & • EL • D • I • C • M • **Reverse:** Madonna and child above pedestal holding value and dividing date

Date	Mintage	F	VF	XF	Unc
1778	—	10.00	22.50	45.00	90.00
1778A	—	15.00	25.00	60.00	175
1779	—	10.00	22.50	45.00	90.00
1779A	—	15.00	25.00	60.00	175
1780	—	10.00	22.50	45.00	90.00
1780A	—	15.00	25.00	60.00	175
1781	—	10.00	22.50	45.00	90.00
1781A	—	15.00	25.00	60.00	175
1782	—	10.00	22.50	45.00	90.00
1782A	—	15.00	25.00	60.00	175
1783	—	10.00	22.50	45.00	90.00
1783A	—	15.00	25.00	60.00	175
1784	—	10.00	22.50	45.00	90.00
1785	—	10.00	22.50	45.00	90.00
1786	—	10.00	22.50	45.00	90.00
1787	—	10.00	22.50	45.00	90.00
1788	—	10.00	22.50	45.00	90.00
1789	—	10.00	22.50	45.00	90.00
1790	—	10.00	22.50	45.00	90.00
1791	—	10.00	22.50	45.00	90.00

Date	Mintage	F	VF	XF	Unc
1792	—	10.00	22.50	45.00	90.00
1793	—	10.00	22.50	45.00	90.00
1794	—	10.00	22.50	45.00	90.00
1795	—	10.00	22.50	45.00	90.00
1796	—	10.00	22.50	45.00	90.00
1797	—	10.00	22.50	45.00	90.00
1798	—	10.00	22.50	45.00	90.00
1799	—	10.00	22.50	45.00	90.00

KM# 216 24 KREUZER

Silver **Ruler:** Maximilian III, Josef **Mint:** Munich **Obverse:** Maximilian III Josef **Reverse:** Crowned arms within Order chains

Date	Mintage	VG	F	VF	XF	Unc
1747	—	100	220	450	700	—

KM# 151 30 KREUZER

Silver **Ruler:** Maximilian II, Emanuel **Obverse:** Head right **Reverse:** Rampant lion left with sword, crowned arms at left, value divides date below **Note:** Second reign of Maximilian II Emanuel.

Date	Mintage	VG	F	VF	XF	Unc
1715	—	20.00	40.00	85.00	160	—
1718	—	20.00	40.00	85.00	160	—
1719	—	20.00	40.00	85.00	160	—

KM# 156 30 KREUZER

Silver **Ruler:** Maximilian II, Emanuel **Obverse:** Smaller head right **Reverse:** Rampant lion left with sword, crowned arms at left, value divides date below

Date	Mintage	VG	F	VF	XF	Unc
1720	—	20.00	40.00	85.00	160	—
1721	—	20.00	40.00	85.00	160	—
1724	—	20.00	40.00	85.00	160	—
1726	—	20.00	40.00	85.00	160	—

KM# 168 30 KREUZER

Silver **Ruler:** Karl Albrecht **Obverse:** Six-pointed star below bust **Obv. Legend:** CAR • ALB • - H • I • B • C • & • **Reverse:** Rampant lion left with sword, crowned arms at left, value divides date below **Rev. Legend:** LAND - MUNZ •

Date	Mintage	VG	F	VF	XF	Unc
1726	—	15.00	30.00	60.00	140	—
1727	—	15.00	30.00	60.00	140	—
1728	—	15.00	30.00	60.00	140	—
1729	—	15.00	30.00	60.00	140	—
1730	—	15.00	30.00	60.00	140	—
1731	—	15.00	30.00	60.00	140	—
1732	—	15.00	30.00	60.00	140	—

KM# 175.1 30 KREUZER

Silver **Ruler:** Karl Albrecht **Obverse:** Bust right, no star below **Obv. Legend:** CAR • ALB • - H • I • B • C • & • **Reverse:** Rampant lion left with sword, crowned arms at left, value divides date below **Rev. Legend:** LAND - MINZ **Note:** Large date.

Date	Mintage	VG	F	VF	XF	Unc
1732	—	15.00	30.00	60.00	140	—

KM# 175.2 30 KREUZER

Silver **Ruler:** Karl Albrecht **Obverse:** No star below bust **Obv. Legend:** CAR • ALB • - H • I • B • C • & • **Reverse:** Rampant lion left with sword, crowned arms at left, value divides date below **Rev. Legend:** LAND - MINZ **Note:** Small dates.

Date	Mintage	VG	F	VF	XF	Unc
1733	—	15.00	30.00	60.00	140	—
1734	—	15.00	30.00	60.00	140	—
1735	—	15.00	30.00	60.00	140	—

KM# 214 30 KREUZER

Silver **Ruler:** Maximilian III, Josef **Mint:** Munich **Obverse:** Draped bust right **Reverse:** Crowned arms in double Order collar, date divided below, value divided at sides

Date	Mintage	VG	F	VF	XF	Unc
1746	—	25.00	50.00	100	225	—

KM# 227 30 KREUZER

Silver **Ruler:** Maximilian III, Josef **Obverse:** Bust right above value, diamond surrounds **Reverse:** Madonna and child within diamond

Date	Mintage	VG	F	VF	XF	Unc
1754	—	75.00	150	300	550	—
1756	—	75.00	150	300	550	—

KM# 248 4 GROSCHEN

Silver **Ruler:** Maximilian III, Josef **Obverse:** Crowned arms within order chain with supporters **Obv. Legend:** LAND - MUNZ **Reverse:** Value and date within wreath **Rev. Legend:** * 4 */GROSCHEN/date

Date	Mintage	VG	F	VF	XF	Unc
1766	—	20.00	50.00	125	225	—
1767	—	20.00	50.00	125	225	—

KM# 188 1/4 THALER

Silver **Ruler:** Karl Albrecht **Obverse:** Conjoined busts of Karl Albrecht and Karl III Philipp **Reverse:** Imperial eagle with arms of Bavaria and Pfalz on breast **Note:** Vicariat issue.

Date	Mintage	VG	F	VF	XF	Unc
1740	—	150	300	450	800	—

KM# 144 1/2 THALER

Silver **Ruler:** Maximilian II, Emanuel **Mint:** Augsburg **Obverse:** Portrait of Karl VI **Reverse:** Austrian double eagle

Date	Mintage	Good	VG	F	VF	XF
1713A	—	—	—	—	—	—

KM# 189 1/2 THALER

Silver **Ruler:** Karl Albrecht **Mint:** Munich **Obverse:** Conjoined busts of Karl Albrecht and Karl III Philipp of Pfalz **Reverse:** Imperial eagle with arms of Bavaria and Pfalz on breast

Date	Mintage	VG	F	VF	XF	Unc
1740	—	250	500	900	1,400	—

KM# 222 1/2 THALER

Silver **Ruler:** Maximilian III, Josef **Subject:** Maximilian III Josef **Obverse:** Armored bust right **Reverse:** Madonna and child

Date	Mintage	VG	F	VF	XF	Unc
1753	—	25.00	50.00	100	225	—
1754	—	25.00	50.00	100	225	—
1759	—	25.00	50.00	100	225	—
1761	—	25.00	50.00	100	225	—
1762	—	25.00	50.00	100	225	—
1765	—	25.00	50.00	100	225	—
1768	—	25.00	50.00	100	225	—
1769	—	25.00	50.00	100	225	—
1770	—	25.00	50.00	100	225	—
1772	—	25.00	50.00	100	225	—
1773	—	25.00	50.00	100	225	—
1774	—	25.00	50.00	100	225	—
1775	—	25.00	50.00	100	225	—
1777	—	25.00	50.00	100	225	—

KM# 241 1/2 THALER

Silver **Ruler:** Maximilian III, Josef **Mint:** Amberg **Obverse:** Armored bust right **Obv. Legend:** D • G • MAX • IOS • U • B • - D • S • R • I • A • & EL • L • L • **Reverse:** Madonna and child **Rev. Legend:** PATRONA - BAVARIAE •

Date	Mintage	VG	F	VF	XF	Unc
1763A	—	45.00	75.00	150	300	—
1764A	—	45.00	75.00	150	300	—
1768A	—	45.00	75.00	150	300	—
1774A	—	45.00	75.00	150	300	—

KM# 253 1/2 THALER

14.0300 g., 0.8330 Silver 0.3757 oz. ASW **Ruler:** Maximilian III, Josef **Obverse:** Head right **Reverse:** Crowned arms within palms, date below

Date	Mintage	VG	F	VF	XF	Unc
1775	—	50.00	80.00	185	375	—

KM# 257 1/2 THALER

14.0300 g., 0.8330 Silver 0.3757 oz. ASW **Obverse:** Bust of Karl Theodor right **Reverse:** Crowned arms within branches

Date	Mintage	VG	F	VF	XF	Unc
1778	—	45.00	100	200	400	—
1779	—	45.00	100	200	400	—
1780	—	45.00	100	200	400	—
1781	—	45.00	100	200	400	—
1784	—	45.00	100	200	400	—
1786	—	45.00	100	200	400	—
1787	—	45.00	100	200	400	—
1788	—	45.00	100	200	400	—
1789	—	45.00	100	200	400	—
1790	—	45.00	100	200	400	—
1791	—	45.00	100	200	400	—
1792	—	45.00	100	200	400	—
1793	—	45.00	100	200	400	—
1794	—	45.00	100	200	400	—
1795	—	45.00	100	200	400	—
1796	—	45.00	100	200	400	—
1797	—	45.00	100	200	400	—
1798	—	45.00	100	200	400	—

KM# 262 1/2 THALER

14.0300 g., 0.8330 Silver 0.3757 oz. ASW **Ruler:** Karl Theodor **Reverse:** Madonna

Date	Mintage	VG	F	VF	XF	Unc
1779	—	175	350	750	1,500	—
1782	—	175	350	750	1,500	—

KM# 274 1/2 THALER

14.0300 g., 0.8330 Silver 0.3757 oz. ASW **Ruler:** Karl Theodor **Obverse:** Armored bust right **Reverse:** Double-headed eagle with crowned arms in Order chain on breast **Note:** Vicariat issue.

Date	Mintage	VG	F	VF	XF	Unc
1790	—	100	200	350	600	—

KM# 284 1/2 THALER

14.0300 g., 0.8330 Silver 0.3757 oz. ASW **Ruler:** Karl Theodor **Obverse:** Head right **Reverse:** Double-headed eagle with complex arms on breast **Note:** Vicariat issue.

Date	Mintage	VG	F	VF	XF	Unc
1792	—	100	225	375	650	—

KM# 312 1/2 THALER

14.0300 g., 0.8330 Silver 0.3757 oz. ASW **Ruler:** Maximilian IV, Josef as Elector **Obverse:** Head right **Reverse:** Crowned three-fold arms within branches

Date	Mintage	F	VF	XF	Unc
1799	—	500	1,000	2,000	3,500
1800	—	500	1,000	2,000	3,500

KM# 252 1/2 THALER (Convention)

14.0300 g., 0.8330 Silver 0.3757 oz. ASW **Ruler:** Maximilian III, Josef

Date	Mintage	VG	F	VF	XF	Unc
1774	—	50.00	80.00	185	375	—

KM# A190 THALER

Silver **Ruler:** Karl Albrecht **Obverse:** Bust right, legend not continuous at top **Reverse:** Madonna and child beside arms **Note:** Dav. #1942.

Date	Mintage	VG	F	VF	XF	Unc
1738	—	1,000	1,750	3,000	5,000	—

KM# 191 THALER

Silver **Ruler:** Karl Albrecht **Obverse:** Bust right **Obv. Legend:** D: G: CAR: ALB: S: & INF: BAV: AC SUP: PAL: DUX CO: PAL: R: S: R: I: A: & EL: **Reverse:** Double-headed eagle with crowned arms on breast **Rev. Legend:** EIUSQUE IN P: RH: SUEV: ET FR: IUR: CONPROV: ET VICARIUS L: L: **Note:** Vicariat issue. Dav. #1943.

Date	Mintage	VG	F	VF	XF	Unc
1740	—	200	450	900	2,100	—

KM# 190 THALER

Silver **Ruler:** Karl Albrecht **Mint:** Munich **Obverse:** Karl Albrecht and Karl III Philipp of Pfalz **Obv. Legend:** D: G: CAR: ALB: & CAR: PHIL: S: R: I: ELECTORES EIUSQ: **Reverse:** Double-headed eagle with two crowned arms on breast **Rev. Legend:** IN PART: RHENI SUEV: ET IUR: FRANCON: VICARIORUM **Note:** Vicariat issue. Dav. #1945.

Date	Mintage	VG	F	VF	XF	Unc
1740	—	200	450	800	1,800	—

KM# 192 THALER

Silver **Ruler:** Karl Albrecht **Mint:** Mannheim **Obverse:** Karl Albrecht and Karl III Philipp of Pfalz **Reverse:** Double-headed eagle with two crowned arms on breast **Note:** Vicariat issue. Dav. #1946.

Date	Mintage	VG	F	VF	XF	Unc
1740	—	200	450	900	1,500	—

KM# 198 THALER

Silver **Ruler:** Karl Albrecht **Mint:** Munich **Subject:** Karl Albrecht as Emperor Karl VII **Obverse:** Armored laureate bust right **Obv. Legend:** CAR • VII • D • G • R • I • S • A • - GERM • ET • BOH • REX **Reverse:** Crowned double-headed imperial eagle with arms on breast **Rev. Legend:** UTR: BAV: ET PAL: SUP: DUX COM: - PAL: RH: ARCHID: AUST: S: R: I: E: L • L • **Note:** Dav. #1947.

Date	Mintage	VG	F	VF	XF	Unc
1743	—	200	450	800	1,800	—

KM# 224 THALER

Silver **Ruler:** Maximilian III, Josef **Obverse:** Bust right **Obv. Legend:** D • G • MAX • IOS • U • B • & P • S • D • C • P • R • S • R • I • A • & EL • L • L • **Reverse:** Crowned arms with lion supporters **Note:** Dav. #1948.

Date	Mintage	VG	F	VF	XF	Unc
1753	—	15.00	30.00	75.00	150	—
1754	—	15.00	30.00	75.00	150	—
1755	—	15.00	30.00	75.00	150	—
1756	—	15.00	30.00	75.00	150	—
1757	—	15.00	30.00	75.00	150	—
1758	—	15.00	30.00	75.00	150	—
1759	—	15.00	30.00	75.00	150	—

KM# 223.2 THALER

Silver **Ruler:** Maximilian III, Josef **Obverse:** Bust right **Obv. Legend:** D • G • MAX • IOS • U • B • & P • S • D • C • P • R • S • R • I • A • & EL • L • L • **Reverse:** Madonna and child with rays around **Rev. Legend:** PATRONA BAVARIAE **Note:** Dav.#1952.

Date	Mintage	VG	F	VF	XF	Unc
1754	—	15.00	30.00	75.00	150	—
1755	—	15.00	30.00	75.00	150	—
1756	—	15.00	30.00	75.00	150	—
1757	—	15.00	30.00	75.00	150	—
1758	—	15.00	30.00	75.00	150	—
1759	—	15.00	30.00	75.00	150	—

KM# 233.1 THALER

Silver **Ruler:** Maximilian III, Josef **Obverse:** Legend divided at top **Obv. Legend:** D • G • MAX • IOS • U • B • - D • S • R • I • A • & EL • L • L • **Reverse:** Crowned quartered arms within Order chain with lion supporters **Note:** Dav. #1949.

Date	Mintage	VG	F	VF	XF	Unc
1759	—	15.00	30.00	50.00	100	—
1760	—	15.00	30.00	50.00	100	—
1761	—	15.00	30.00	50.00	100	—
1763	—	15.00	30.00	50.00	100	—
1768	—	15.00	30.00	50.00	100	—

KM# 234.1 THALER

Silver **Ruler:** Maximilian III, Josef **Obverse:** Bust right **Obv. Legend:** D • G • MAX • IOS • U • - B • D • S • R • I • A • & EL • L • L • **Reverse:** Radiant Madonna and child **Rev. Legend:** PATRONA - BAVARIAE **Note:** Dav. #1953.

Date	Mintage	VG	F	VF	XF	Unc
1760	—	15.00	30.00	50.00	100	—
1761	—	15.00	30.00	50.00	100	—
1762	—	15.00	30.00	50.00	100	—
1763	—	15.00	30.00	50.00	100	—
1764	—	15.00	30.00	50.00	100	—
1765	—	15.00	30.00	50.00	100	—
1766	—	15.00	30.00	50.00	100	—
1767	—	15.00	30.00	50.00	100	—
1768	—	15.00	30.00	50.00	100	—
1769	—	15.00	30.00	50.00	100	—
1770	—	15.00	30.00	50.00	100	—
1771	—	15.00	30.00	50.00	100	—
1772	—	15.00	25.00	50.00	100	—
1773	—	15.00	25.00	50.00	100	—
1774	—	15.00	25.00	50.00	100	—
1775	—	15.00	25.00	50.00	100	—
1776	—	15.00	25.00	50.00	100	—
1777	—	15.00	25.00	50.00	100	—

KM# 234.2 THALER

Silver **Ruler:** Maximilian III, Josef **Mint:** Amberg **Obverse:** "A" below bust **Obv. Legend:** D • G • MAX • IOS • U • B • - D • S • R • I • A • & EL • L • L • **Reverse:** Radiant Madonna and child **Rev. Legend:** PATRONA - BAVARIAE **Note:** Dav. #1954.

Date	Mintage	VG	F	VF	XF	Unc
1763A	—	15.00	30.00	50.00	100	—
1764A	—	15.00	30.00	50.00	100	—
1765A	—	15.00	30.00	50.00	100	—
1766A	—	15.00	30.00	50.00	100	—
1767A	—	15.00	30.00	50.00	100	—
1768A	—	15.00	30.00	50.00	100	—
1769A	—	15.00	30.00	50.00	100	—

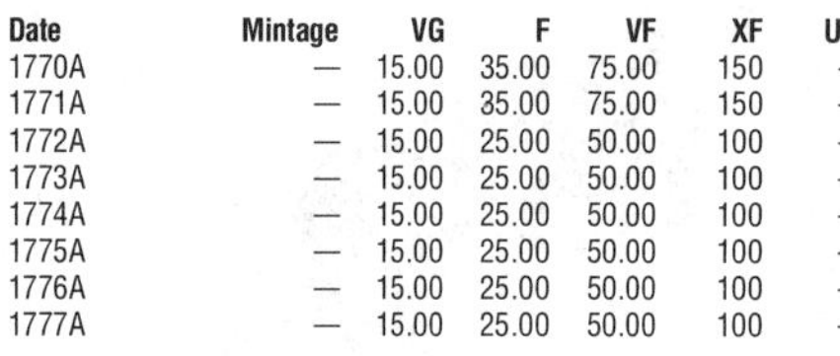

Date	Mintage	VG	F	VF	XF	Unc
1770A	—	15.00	35.00	75.00	150	—
1771A	—	15.00	35.00	75.00	150	—
1772A	—	15.00	25.00	50.00	100	—
1773A	—	15.00	25.00	50.00	100	—
1774A	—	15.00	25.00	50.00	100	—
1775A	—	15.00	25.00	50.00	100	—
1776A	—	15.00	25.00	50.00	100	—
1777A	—	15.00	25.00	50.00	100	—

KM# 233.2 THALER

Silver **Ruler:** Maximilian III, Josef **Mint:** Amberg **Obverse:** "A" below bust **Obv. Legend:** D • G • MAX • IOS • U • B • - D • S • R • I • A • & • EL • L • L • **Reverse:** Crowned quartered arms with lion supporters, leafy spray below **Note:** Dav. #1950

Date	Mintage	VG	F	VF	XF	Unc
1763A	—	75.00	150	350	700	—
1767A	—	50.00	100	200	500	—
1768A	—	50.00	100	200	500	—

KM# 233.3 THALER

Silver **Ruler:** Maximilian III, Josef **Obverse:** Bust right **Reverse:** Smaller supported coat of arms **Note:** Dav. #1951.

Date	Mintage	VG	F	VF	XF	Unc
1768A	—	50.00	100	200	500	—

KM# 244 THALER

Silver **Ruler:** Maximilian III, Josef **Subject:** Levant Trade **Obverse:** Bust right **Obv. Legend:** D • G • MAX • IOS • U • B • - D • S • R • I • A • & • EL • L • L • **Reverse:** Rampant lion left with shield, date below **Note:** Dav. #1955.

Date	Mintage	VG	F	VF	XF	Unc
1765	—	200	500	1,500	2,500	—

KM# 249 THALER

Silver **Ruler:** Maximilian III, Josef **Mint:** Amberg **Obverse:** Rampant lion holding sword left with crowned shield **Obv. Legend:** D • G • MAX • IOS • UT • BAV • & P • S • D • CO • PA • R • **Reverse:** Inscription within wreath of palm and laurel **Rev. Legend:** SAC • ROM • IMP • ARCHID • & ELECT • LAND • LEUCHT •, *AD NORMAM CONVENT. 1768. A in wreath **Note:** Dav. #1956.

Date	Mintage	VG	F	VF	XF	Unc
1768A	—	200	450	900	1,700	—

KM# 260.1 THALER

28.0600 g., 0.8330 Silver 0.7515 oz. ASW **Ruler:** Karl Theodor **Obverse:** H. ST. on shoulder **Obv. Legend:** CAR • TH • D • G • C • P • R • V • - B • D • S • R • I • A • & EL • D • I • C • M • **Reverse:** Radiant Madonna and child **Rev. Legend:** PATRONA - BAVARIAE **Note:** Dav. #1964.

Date	Mintage	F	VF	XF	Unc
1778	—	50.00	110	180	800
1779	—	50.00	110	180	800
1780	—	50.00	110	180	800
1781	—	50.00	110	180	800
1782	—	50.00	110	180	800
1783	—	55.00	115	190	825

KM# 260.3 THALER

28.0600 g., 0.8330 Silver 0.7515 oz. ASW **Ruler:** Karl Theodor **Obverse:** I. SCH. on shoulder **Obv. Legend:** CAR • TH • D • G • C • P • R • V • - B • D • S • R • I • A • & EL • D • I • C • M • **Reverse:** Radiant Madonna and child **Rev. Legend:** PATRONA - BAVARIAE **Note:** Dav. #1965.

Date	Mintage	F	VF	XF	Unc
1778	—	40.00	80.00	160	850
1779	—	40.00	80.00	160	850
1780	—	40.00	80.00	160	850
1781	—	40.00	80.00	160	850
1782	—	40.00	80.00	160	850
1783	—	40.00	80.00	160	850
1784	—	40.00	80.00	160	850
1786	—	40.00	80.00	160	850
1787	—	40.00	80.00	160	850
1788	—	40.00	80.00	160	850
1789	—	40.00	80.00	160	850
1790	—	40.00	80.00	160	850
1791	—	40.00	80.00	160	850
1792	—	40.00	80.00	160	850
1793	—	40.00	80.00	160	850
1794	—	40.00	80.00	160	850

KM# 260.2 THALER

28.0600 g., 0.8330 Silver 0.7515 oz. ASW **Ruler:** Karl Theodor **Obverse:** "A" below bust **Reverse:** Radiant Madonna and child **Note:** Dav. #1967.

Date	Mintage	F	VF	XF	Unc
1778A	—	75.00	155	250	1,150
1779A	—	80.00	165	275	1,250

KM# 258.1 THALER

28.0600 g., 0.8330 Silver 0.7515 oz. ASW **Ruler:** Karl Theodor **Obverse:** Bust right, H. S. on truncation **Obv. Legend:** CAR • THEODOR • D • G • C • P • R • UTR • BAV • DUX • **Reverse:** Crowned two-fold arms within sprays **Rev. Legend:** S • R • I • ARCHID • & - EL • DUX I • C • & M • **Note:** Dav. #1957.

Date	Mintage	F	VF	XF	Unc
1778	—	400	675	1,150	1,850
1779	—	400	675	1,150	1,850
1780	—	400	675	1,150	1,850
1781	—	400	675	1,150	1,850

KM# 258.2 THALER

28.0600 g., 0.8330 Silver 0.7515 oz. ASW **Ruler:** Maximilian IV, Josef as Elector **Obverse:** ST below head **Reverse:** Crowned arms within branches **Rev. Legend:** Ends: ... ELECTOR. D. I. C. M. **Note:** Dav. #1958.

Date	Mintage	F	VF	XF	Unc
1780	—	500	850	1,400	2,350
1781	—	500	850	1,400	2,350

KM# 258.3 THALER

28.0600 g., 0.8330 Silver 0.7515 oz. ASW **Ruler:** Karl Theodor **Obverse:** Hair tied behind neck **Obv. Legend:** CAR • THEODOR • D • G • C • P • R • V • B • D • S • R • I • A • D • & EL • **Reverse:** AS below crossed laurel branches **Rev. Legend:** AD NORMAM - CONVENTION **Note:** Varieties exist. Dav. #1959

Date	Mintage	F	VF	XF	Unc
1778 AS	—	175	350	700	1,250
1779 AS	—	175	350	700	1,250
1780 AS	—	175	350	700	1,250
1781 AS	—	175	350	700	1,250
1782 AS	—	175	350	700	1,250
1783 AS	—	175	350	700	1,250
1784 AS	—	175	350	700	1,250
1785 AS	—	175	350	700	1,250
1786 AS	—	175	350	700	1,250
1787 AS	—	175	350	700	1,250
1788 AS	—	175	350	700	1,250
1789 AS	—	175	350	700	1,250
1790 AS	—	175	350	700	1,250
1791 AS	—	175	350	700	1,250
1792 AS	—	175	350	700	1,250
1793 AS	—	175	350	700	1,250
1794 AS	—	175	350	700	1,250
1795 AS	—	175	350	700	1,250

KM# 258.4 THALER

28.0600 g., 0.8330 Silver 0.7515 oz. ASW **Ruler:** Maximilian IV, Josef as Elector **Mint:** Mannheim **Obverse:** Hair loose **Reverse:** Crowned arms within branches **Note:** Dav. #1961

Date	Mintage	F	VF	XF	Unc
1790	—	200	385	775	1,350
1791	—	200	385	775	1,350
1792	—	200	385	775	1,350
1793	—	200	385	775	1,350

KM# 259 THALER

28.0600 g., 0.8330 Silver 0.7515 oz. ASW **Ruler:** Karl Theodor **Obverse:** Small bust right, hair tied behind neck, H. ST. on shoulder **Reverse:** Madonna and child **Note:** Dav. #1963.

Date	Mintage	F	VF	XF	Unc
1778	—	60.00	120	200	875
1779	—	60.00	120	200	875
1780	—	60.00	120	200	875
1781	—	60.00	120	200	875

KM# 275 THALER

28.0600 g., 0.8330 Silver 0.7515 oz. ASW **Ruler:** Maximilian IV, Josef as Elector **Obverse:** Armored bust right with script C.D. below **Obv. Legend:** CAR• TH • D • G • C • P • R • V • B • D • S • R • I • A • & • E • & • I • P • RH • SVEV • & • I • FRANC • PROV • & • VIC • **Reverse:** Eagle with three-fold arms on breast **Rev. Legend:** IVL • CL • & • MONT • D • L • L • P • M • M • M • A • Z • C • V • S • M • & • R • D • I • R • **Note:** Vicariat issue. Dav. #1969.

Date	Mintage	F	VF	XF	Unc
1790	—	225	375	650	1,200

KM# 276 THALER

28.0600 g., 0.8330 Silver 0.7515 oz. ASW **Ruler:** Karl Theodor **Obverse:** Draped bust right, with script C. D. below **Note:** Vicariat issue. Dav. #1970.

Date	Mintage	F	VF	XF	Unc
1790	—	350	600	1,000	1,850

KM# 277 THALER

28.0600 g., 0.8330 Silver 0.7515 oz. ASW **Ruler:** Karl Theodor **Obverse:** Harnessed bust **Rev. Legend:** Ends: ... CONVENTION **Note:** Dav. #1960.

Date	Mintage	F	VF	XF	Unc
1781	—	175	350	700	1,250

KM# A292 THALER

28.0600 g., 0.8330 Silver 0.7515 oz. ASW **Ruler:** Karl Theodor **Obverse:** Armored bust left **Note:** Vicariat issue. Dav. #1971.

Date	Mintage	F	VF	XF	Unc
1790 Rare	—	—	—	—	—

KM# A285 THALER

28.0600 g., 0.8330 Silver 0.7515 oz. ASW **Ruler:** Karl Theodor **Obverse:** Bust right, AS below **Obv. Legend:** CAR • THEODOR • D: G • C • P • R • V • B • D • S • R • I • A • D • & EL • PROV • & VICAR • **Reverse:** Imperial eagle with 9-part shield in Order chains on breast **Rev. Legend:** * IN • PART • RHENI • SVEV • ET • IVR • FRANCON * **Note:** Vicariat issue. Dav. #1972.

Date	Mintage	F	VF	XF	Unc
1790	—	250	450	800	1,350

KM# 281.1 THALER

28.0600 g., 0.8330 Silver 0.7515 oz. ASW **Ruler:** Karl Theodor **Obverse:** Older bust, continuous legend **Reverse:** Radiant Madonna and child **Note:** Dav. #1966.

Date	Mintage	F	VF	XF	Unc
1791	—	45.00	65.00	200	1,000
1792	—	45.00	65.00	200	1,000
1793	—	45.00	65.00	200	1,000
1794	—	45.00	65.00	200	1,000

KM# 285 THALER

28.0600 g., 0.8330 Silver 0.7515 oz. ASW **Ruler:** Karl Theodor **Obverse:** CD on truncation **Obv. Legend:** C • TH • D • G • C • P • R • V • B • D • S • R • I • A • & • E • & • I • P • RH • SVEV • & • I • FR • PROV • & • VIC • **Reverse:** Imperial eagle with 9-part shield in Order chains on breast **Rev. Legend:** IVL • CL • & • M • D • L • L • P • M • M • M • A • Z • C • V • S • M • & • R • D • I • R • **Note:** Vicariat issue. Dav. #1973.

Date	Mintage	F	VF	XF	Unc
1792 CD	—	250	425	700	1,150

KM# 292 THALER

28.0600 g., 0.8330 Silver 0.7515 oz. ASW **Ruler:** Karl Theodor **Obverse:** Large bust right, AS below **Obv. Legend:** CAR • THEOD • D: G • C • P • R • V • B • D • S • R • I • A • D • & EL • PROV • & VICAR **Reverse:** Round three-part arms on breast of eagle **Rev. Legend:** IN • PART • RHENI • SVEV • ET • IVR • FRANCON • **Note:** Dav. #1974.

Date	Mintage	F	VF	XF	Unc
1792	—	250	425	700	1,150

KM# 293 THALER

28.0600 g., 0.8330 Silver 0.7515 oz. ASW **Ruler:** Karl Theodor **Mint:** Amberg **Obverse:** Armored bust right with "A" beneath **Reverse:** Crowned three-fold arms in spray, date below **Note:** Dav. #1962.

Date	Mintage	VG	F	VF	XF	Unc
1794A	—	100	250	350	500	—

KM# 281.2 THALER

28.0600 g., 0.8330 Silver 0.7515 oz. ASW **Ruler:** Karl Theodor **Obverse:** Bust right **Obv. Legend:** CAR • TH • D • G • C • P • R • V • B • D • S • R • I • A • & • EL • D • I • C • & • M • **Reverse:** Ligate AE in legend **Rev. Legend:** PATRONA - BAVARIÆ **Note:** Dav. #1966A.

Date	Mintage	F	VF	XF	Unc
1795	—	45.00	65.00	200	1,000
1796	—	45.00	65.00	200	1,000
1797	—	45.00	65.00	200	1,000
1798	—	45.00	65.00	200	1,000
1799	—	45.00	65.00	200	1,000

KM# 299 THALER

28.0600 g., 0.8330 Silver 0.7515 oz. ASW **Ruler:** Karl Theodor **Issuer:** Abbott of St. Emmeram Monastery **Obverse:** Bust right, three-line inscription around border **Reverse:** Madonna and child **Note:** Dav. #1968.

Date	Mintage	VG	F	VF	XF	Unc
1796 Rare	—	—	—	—	—	—

KM# 313 THALER

28.0000 g., 0.8330 Silver 0.7499 oz. ASW **Ruler:** Maximilian IV, Josef as Elector **Obverse:** Head right **Obv. Legend:** D • G • MAX • IOS • C • P • R • V • B • D • S • R • I • A • & • L • D • I • C • & • M • **Reverse:** Crowned three-fold arms within branches **Rev. Legend:** PRO DEO ET POPULO **Note:** Dav. #1975.

Date	Mintage	F	VF	XF	Unc
1799	—	80.00	130	275	500
1800	—	80.00	130	275	500
1801	—	80.00	130	275	500
1802	—	95.00	140	300	700

KM# 223.1 THALER (Convention)

Silver **Ruler:** Maximilian III, Josef **Mint:** Munich **Obverse:** Draped bust right **Obv. Legend:** D • G • MAX • IOS • U • B • & P • S • D • C • P • R • S • R • I • A • & EL • L • L • **Reverse:** Madonna and child without rays around **Rev. Legend:** PATRONA BAVARIAE **Note:** Dav. #A1952.

Date	Mintage	VG	F	VF	XF	Unc
1753	—	15.00	30.00	75.00	150	—

KM# 193 2 THALER

Silver **Ruler:** Karl Albrecht **Obverse:** Armored bust right **Reverse:** Imperial eagle with crowned arms in Order collar on breast, date in legend **Note:** Vicariat issue. Dav. #1944.

Date	Mintage	VG	F	VF	XF	Unc
1740 Rare	—	—	—	—	—	—

TRADE COINAGE

KM# 119 GOLDGULDEN

3.5000 g., 0.9860 Gold 0.1109 oz. AGW **Ruler:** Maximilian III, Josef **Obverse:** Draped bust right **Reverse:** Date divided by Madonna and child above and arms below **Note:** First reign. Fr. #219/220.

Date	Mintage	VG	F	VF	XF	Unc
1700	—	200	400	600	950	—
1701	—	200	400	600	950	—
1702	—	200	400	600	950	—
1703	—	200	400	600	950	—
1704	—	200	400	600	950	—
1715	—	200	400	600	950	—

KM# 135 GOLDGULDEN

3.5000 g., 0.9860 Gold 0.1109 oz. AGW **Ruler:** Maximilian II, Emanuel **Subject:** Occupation of Augsburg **Obverse:** Pine cone below bust **Reverse:** Date divided by Madonna and child above and arms below

Date	Mintage	VG	F	VF	XF	Unc
1704	—	400	800	1,350	2,500	—

KM# 194 GOLDGULDEN

3.5000 g., 0.9860 Gold 0.1109 oz. AGW **Ruler:** Karl Albrecht **Obverse:** Head right **Reverse:** Double-headed imperial eagle with crowned arms on breast **Note:** Vicariat issue. Fr. #239.

Date	Mintage	VG	F	VF	XF	Unc
1740	—	300	600	1,150	2,250	—

KM# 195 2 GOLDGULDEN

7.0000 g., 0.9860 Gold 0.2219 oz. AGW **Ruler:** Karl Albrecht **Obverse:** Head right **Reverse:** Imperial eagle with Bavarian arms on breast, date in legend **Note:** Vicariat issue. Fr. #238.

Date	Mintage	VG	F	VF	XF	Unc
1740	—	2,000	4,000	7,500	11,500	—

KM# 169 1/4 CAROLIN

2.4250 g., 0.7700 Gold 0.0600 oz. AGW **Ruler:** Karl Albrecht **Mint:** Munich **Obverse:** Young head right **Reverse:** Madonna and child with arms below **Note:** Fr.#231.

Date	Mintage	VG	F	VF	XF	Unc
1726	—	200	500	800	1,250	—
1727	—	150	300	500	900	—
1728	—	150	300	500	900	—
1729	—	150	300	500	900	—
1730	—	150	300	500	900	—
1731	—	150	300	500	900	—

KM# 176 1/4 CAROLIN

2.4250 g., 0.7700 Gold 0.0600 oz. AGW **Ruler:** Karl Albrecht **Obverse:** Older head right **Reverse:** Madonna and child with arms below **Note:** Fr.#234.

Date	Mintage	VG	F	VF	XF	Unc
1732	—	200	400	750	1,200	—
1733	—	200	400	750	1,200	—
1734	—	200	400	750	1,200	—
1735	—	200	400	750	1,200	—

KM# 170 1/2 CAROLIN

4.8500 g., 0.7700 Gold 0.1201 oz. AGW **Ruler:** Karl Albrecht **Mint:** Munich **Obverse:** Young head right **Reverse:** Madonna and child with arms below **Note:** Fr.#230.

Date	Mintage	VG	F	VF	XF	Unc
1726	—	175	325	600	950	—
1727	—	175	325	600	950	—
1728/7	—	250	500	1,000	1,500	—
1728	—	175	325	600	950	—
1729	—	175	325	600	950	—
1730	—	175	325	600	950	—
1731	—	175	325	600	950	—

KM# 177 1/2 CAROLIN

4.8500 g., 0.7700 Gold 0.1201 oz. AGW **Ruler:** Karl Albrecht **Obverse:** Older head right **Reverse:** Madonna and child with arms below **Note:** Fr.#233.

Date	Mintage	VG	F	VF	XF	Unc
1732	—	175	325	600	950	—
1733	—	175	325	600	950	—
1735	—	175	325	600	950	—
1736	—	175	325	600	950	—

KM# 181 1/2 CAROLIN

4.8500 g., 0.7700 Gold 0.1201 oz. AGW **Ruler:** Karl Albrecht **Obverse:** Cuirassed bust right **Note:** Fr.#233.

Date	Mintage	VG	F	VF	XF	Unc
1734	—	250	450	750	1,250	—
1737	—	250	450	750	1,250	—

KM# 171 CAROLIN

9.7000 g., 0.7700 Gold 0.2401 oz. AGW **Ruler:** Karl Albrecht **Mint:** Munich **Obverse:** Young head of Karl Albrecht **Reverse:** Madonna and child with arms below **Note:** Fr.#229.

Date	Mintage	VG	F	VF	XF	Unc
1726	—	250	500	900	1,350	—
1727	—	250	500	900	1,350	—
1728	—	250	500	900	1,350	—
1729	—	250	500	900	1,350	—
1730	—	250	500	900	1,350	—
1731	—	250	500	900	1,350	—
1732	—	250	500	900	1,350	—

KM# 178 CAROLIN

9.7000 g., 0.7700 Gold 0.2401 oz. AGW **Ruler:** Karl Albrecht **Obverse:** Draped bust right **Reverse:** Madonna and child with arms below **Note:** Fr.#232.

Date	Mintage	VG	F	VF	XF	Unc
1732	—	300	600	1,000	1,500	—
1733	—	300	600	1,000	1,500	—
1734	—	300	600	1,000	1,500	—
1735	—	300	600	1,000	1,500	—

KM# 182 CAROLIN

9.7000 g., 0.7700 Gold 0.2401 oz. AGW **Ruler:** Karl Albrecht **Obverse:** Cuirassed bust right **Reverse:** Madonna and child with arms below **Note:** Fr.#232.

Date	Mintage	VG	F	VF	XF	Unc
1734	—	300	600	1,000	1,500	—
1737	—	300	600	1,000	1,500	—

KM# 140 DUCAT

3.4900 g., 0.9860 Gold 0.1106 oz. AGW **Ruler:** Maximilian II, Emanuel **Subject:** Austrian Administration **Obverse:** Armored and laureate bust of Josef I right **Reverse:** Crowned Imperial eagle with oval arms on breast, crown divides date

Date	Mintage	VG	F	VF	XF	Unc
1705	—	400	900	1,600	2,500	—
1706	—	400	900	1,600	2,500	—
1707	—	400	900	1,600	2,500	—
1708	—	400	900	1,600	2,500	—
1709	—	400	900	1,600	2,500	—
1710	—	400	900	1,600	2,500	—

KM# 146 DUCAT

3.4900 g., 0.9860 Gold 0.1106 oz. AGW **Ruler:** Maximilian II, Emanuel **Reverse:** Heart shaped arms on breast

Date	Mintage	VG	F	VF	XF	Unc
1712 Rare	—	—	—	—	—	—

KM# 157 DUCAT

3.4900 g., 0.9860 Gold 0.1106 oz. AGW **Ruler:** Maximilian II, Emanuel **Subject:** Wedding of Karl Albrecht **Obverse:** AB monogram **Reverse:** Wedding inscription **Note:** Fr. #241.

Date	Mintage	VG	F	VF	XF	Unc
1722	—	400	900	1,600	2,500	—

KM# 183 DUCAT

3.4900 g., 0.9860 Gold 0.1106 oz. AGW **Ruler:** Karl Albrecht **Obverse:** Armored bust right **Reverse:** Crowned arms in Order collar with lion supporters, date in exergue **Note:** Only dies are known to exist, not any coins.

Date	Mintage	VG	F	VF	XF	Unc
1737	—	—	—	—	—	—

KM# 184 DUCAT

3.4900 g., 0.9860 Gold 0.1106 oz. AGW **Ruler:** Karl Albrecht **Obverse:** Crowned arms with lion supporters, crown divides date **Reverse:** Radiant Madonna and child **Note:** Fr. #236.

Date	Mintage	VG	F	VF	XF	Unc
1737	—	400	800	1,500	2,800	—
1739	—	400	800	1,500	2,800	—

KM# 196 DUCAT

3.4900 g., 0.9860 Gold 0.1106 oz. AGW **Ruler:** Karl Albrecht **Obverse:** Head right **Reverse:** Imperial eagle with Bavarian arms on breast, date in legend **Note:** Vicariat issue. Fr. #240.

Date	Mintage	VG	F	VF	XF	Unc
1740	—	850	1,650	3,500	6,500	—

KM# 212 DUCAT

3.4900 g., 0.9860 Gold 0.1106 oz. AGW **Ruler:** Maximilian III, Josef **Mint:** Munich **Obverse:** Head right **Reverse:** Double-headed imperial eagle with crowned arms in Order chain on breast **Note:** Vicariat issue.

Date	Mintage	VG	F	VF	XF	Unc
1745	—	900	1,750	3,650	6,750	—

KM# 217 DUCAT

3.4900 g., 0.9860 Gold 0.1106 oz. AGW **Ruler:** Maximilian III, Josef **Subject:** Marriage of Maximilian and Marie Anne **Obverse:** Conjoined busts of Maximilian III Josef and Marie Anne right **Note:** Fr. #243.

Date	Mintage	VG	F	VF	XF	Unc
1747	—	200	500	1,000	1,650	—

KM# 228 DUCAT

3.4900 g., 0.9860 Gold 0.1106 oz. AGW **Ruler:** Maximilian III, Josef **Obverse:** Bust right **Reverse:** Crowned arms in Order chain with lion supporters **Note:** Fr. #249.

Date	Mintage	VG	F	VF	XF	Unc
1755	—	400	900	1,800	3,000	—
1756	—	150	400	800	1,250	—
1757	—	150	400	800	1,250	—
1758	—	150	400	800	1,250	—
1759	—	150	400	800	1,250	—
1760	—	150	400	800	1,250	—
1761	—	150	400	800	1,250	—
1762	—	150	400	800	1,250	—
1763	—	150	400	800	1,250	—
1764	—	250	600	1,250	2,250	—
1765	—	250	600	1,250	2,250	—
1766	—	150	400	800	1,250	—
1767	—	250	600	1,250	2,250	—
1768	—	150	400	800	1,250	—
1769	—	150	400	800	1,250	—
1770	—	150	400	800	1,250	—
1771	—	150	400	800	1,250	—
1772	—	150	400	800	1,250	—
1773	—	150	400	800	1,250	—
1774	—	150	400	800	1,250	—
1775	—	200	600	1,200	2,200	—

KM# 229 DUCAT

3.4900 g., 0.9860 Gold 0.1106 oz. AGW **Ruler:** Maximilian III, Josef **Obverse:** Bust right **Reverse:** Danube river god **Note:** Struck with gold from Danube River area. Fr. #246.

Date	Mintage	VG	F	VF	XF	Unc
MDCCLVI (1756)	—	850	1,650	4,250	8,500	—
MDCCLX (1760)	—	850	1,650	4,250	8,500	—
MDCCLXII (1762)	—	850	1,650	4,250	8,500	—

KM# 231 DUCAT

3.4900 g., 0.9860 Gold 0.1106 oz. AGW **Ruler:** Maximilian III, Josef **Obverse:** Bust right **Reverse:** Inn river god seated right **Note:** Struck with gold from Inn River area. Fr. #247.

Date	Mintage	VG	F	VF	XF	Unc
MDCCLVI (1756)	—	900	1,750	4,500	9,000	—
MDCCLX (1760)	—	900	1,750	4,500	9,000	—
MDCCLXII (1762)	—	900	1,750	4,500	9,000	—

KM# 230 DUCAT

3.4900 g., 0.9860 Gold 0.1106 oz. AGW **Ruler:** Maximilian III, Josef **Obverse:** Bust right **Reverse:** Isar river god **Note:** Struck with gold from Isar River area. Fr. #248.

Date	Mintage	VG	F	VF	XF	Unc
MDCCLVI (1756)	—	850	1,650	4,250	8,500	—
MDCCLX (1760)	—	850	1,650	4,250	8,500	—
MDCCLXII (1762)	—	850	1,650	4,250	8,500	—

KM# 261 DUCAT

3.4900 g., 0.9860 Gold 0.1106 oz. AGW **Ruler:** Karl Theodor **Obverse:** Head right **Reverse:** Crowned three-fold arms within branches **Note:** Fr. #255.

Date	Mintage	F	VF	XF	Unc
1778	—	450	850	1,500	2,500
1779	—	450	850	1,500	2,500
1780	—	450	850	1,500	2,500
1781	—	450	850	1,500	2,500
1782	—	450	850	1,500	2,500
1784	—	450	850	1,500	2,500
1786	—	450	850	1,500	2,500
1787	—	450	850	1,500	2,500
1788	—	450	850	1,500	2,500
1789	—	450	850	1,500	2,500
1791	—	450	850	1,500	2,500
1792	—	450	850	1,500	2,500
1793	—	450	850	1,500	2,500

KM# 263 DUCAT

3.4900 g., 0.9370 Gold 0.1051 oz. AGW **Ruler:** Karl Theodor **Subject:** Danube River **Obverse:** Head right **Reverse:** River god seated left **Note:** Fr. #250.

Date	Mintage	F	VF	XF	Unc
MDCCLXXIX (1779)	—	850	1,650	4,250	8,500
MDCCLXXX (1780)	—	850	1,650	4,250	8,500
MDCCXCIII (1793)	—	850	1,650	4,250	8,500

KM# 264 DUCAT

3.4900 g., 0.9370 Gold 0.1051 oz. AGW **Ruler:** Karl Theodor **Subject:** Inn River **Obverse:** Head right **Reverse:** River god seated right **Note:** Fr. #251.

Date	Mintage	F	VF	XF	Unc
MDCCLXXIX (1779)	—	900	1,750	4,500	9,000
MDCCLXXX (1780)	—	900	1,750	4,500	9,000
MDCCXCIII (1793)	—	900	1,750	4,500	9,000
MDCCXCVIII (1798)	—	900	1,750	4,500	9,000

KM# 265 DUCAT

3.4900 g., 0.9370 Gold 0.1051 oz. AGW **Ruler:** Karl Theodor **Subject:** Isar River **Obverse:** Head right **Reverse:** Isar river god with water jug **Note:** Fr. #252.

Date	Mintage	F	VF	XF	Unc
MDCCLXXIX (1779)	—	850	1,650	4,250	8,500
MDCCLXXX (1780)	—	850	1,650	4,250	8,500
MDCCXCIII (1793)	—	850	1,650	4,250	8,500
MDCCXCVIII (1798)	—	850	1,650	4,250	8,500

KM# 278 DUCAT

3.4900 g., 0.9370 Gold 0.1051 oz. AGW **Ruler:** Karl Theodor **Obverse:** Large head right **Reverse:** Double-headed eagle with crowned arms in Order chain on breast **Note:** Vicariat issue. Fr. #258.

Date	Mintage	F	VF	XF	Unc
1790	—	900	1,750	4,500	9,000
1792	—	950	1,800	4,700	9,500

KM# 286 DUCAT

3.4900 g., 0.9370 Gold 0.1051 oz. AGW **Ruler:** Karl Theodor **Obverse:** Small head **Note:** Fr. #261.

Date	Mintage	F	VF	XF	Unc
1792	—	950	1,800	4,700	9,500

KM# 297 DUCAT
3.4900 g., 0.9370 Gold 0.1051 oz. AGW **Ruler:** Karl Theodor **Obverse:** Head right **Reverse:** Crowned three-fold arms within branches

Date	Mintage	F	VF	XF	Unc
1794	—	450	850	1,500	2,500
1795	—	450	850	1,500	2,500
1796	—	450	850	1,500	2,500
1797	—	450	850	1,500	2,500
1798	—	450	850	1,500	2,500

KM# 314.2 DUCAT
3.4900 g., 0.9370 Gold 0.1051 oz. AGW **Ruler:** Maximilian IV, Josef as Elector **Obverse:** Head right **Obv. Legend:** D • G • MAXIM • IOSEPH • C • P • R • V • B • D • S • R • I • A • & • EL • **Reverse:** Crowned three-fold arms within branches **Rev. Legend:** PRO DEO ET POPULO

Date	Mintage	F	VF	XF	Unc
1799	—	1,000	1,500	2,500	3,000
1800	—	1,000	1,500	2,500	3,000
1801	—	1,000	1,500	2,500	3,000
1802	—	1,000	1,500	2,500	3,000
1803	—	1,100	1,600	2,650	3,500

KM# 314.1 DUCAT
3.4900 g., 0.9370 Gold 0.1051 oz. AGW **Ruler:** Maximilian IV, Josef as Elector **Obverse:** Head right **Obv. Legend:** D • G • MAX • IOS • C • P • R • V • B • D • S • R • I • A • & • EL • D • I • C • & • M • **Reverse:** Crowned three-fold arms within branches **Rev. Legend:** PRO DEO ET POPULO **Note:** Fr. #262.

Date	Mintage	F	VF	XF	Unc
1799	—	1,250	1,750	2,750	3,350
1800	—	750	1,250	2,250	2,850
1801	—	750	1,250	2,250	2,850
1802	—	1,000	1,500	2,500	3,200

KM# 270 2 DUCAT
7.0000 g., 0.9860 Gold 0.2219 oz. AGW **Ruler:** Karl Theodor **Obverse:** Head right **Reverse:** Crowned three-fold arms in spray, date below **Note:** Fr. #254.

Date	Mintage	F	VF	XF	Unc
1787	—	3,500	5,500	8,000	13,500

KM# 279 2 DUCAT
7.0000 g., 0.9860 Gold 0.2219 oz. AGW **Ruler:** Karl Theodor **Reverse:** Eagle with three-fold arms on breast, value below **Note:** Vacariat issue. Fr. #257/260.

Date	Mintage	F	VF	XF	Unc
1790	—	2,500	5,000	7,500	12,500
1792	—	2,500	5,000	7,500	12,500

KM# 271 3 DUCAT
10.5000 g., 0.9860 Gold 0.3328 oz. AGW **Ruler:** Karl Theodor **Obverse:** Head right **Obv. Legend:** CAR • THEOD • D • G • C • P • R • VTR • B • D • **Reverse:** Crowned three-fold arms within branches, value below **Rev. Legend:** S • R • I • ARCH • & EL • DVX • I • CL • & • M • **Note:** Fr. #253.

Date	Mintage	F	VF	XF	Unc
1787	—	4,000	6,500	10,000	15,000

KM# 280 3 DUCAT
10.5000 g., 0.9860 Gold 0.3328 oz. AGW **Ruler:** Karl Theodor **Obverse:** Head right **Obv. Legend:** C • TH • D • G • C • P • R • V • B • D • S • R • I • A • & • E • & • I • P• R • S • & I • F • PRO • & • VIC * **Reverse:** Double-headed eagle with crowned complex arms on breast **Note:** Vacariat issue. Fr. #256.

Date	Mintage	F	VF	XF	Unc
1790	—	4,500	7,500	11,500	17,500
1792	—	5,000	8,000	13,500	18,500

KM# 218 5 DUCAT
17.5000 g., 0.9860 Gold 0.5547 oz. AGW **Ruler:** Maximilian III, Josef **Subject:** Marriage of Maximilian III Josef and Marie Anne **Obverse:** Conjoined busts right **Reverse:** Inscription on large stone at right, figure at left **Note:** Fr. #245.

Date	Mintage	VG	F	VF	XF	Unc
1747	—	—	2,200	4,250	7,000	—

KM# 153 1/2 MAXIMILIAN D'OR
3.3200 g., 0.9000 Gold 0.0961 oz. AGW **Ruler:** Maximilian II, Emanuel **Mint:** Munich **Obverse:** Head right **Reverse:** Madonna and child with arms below **Note:** Fr. #227.

Date	Mintage	VG	F	VF	XF	Unc
1715	—	150	300	500	900	—
1716	—	150	300	500	900	—
1717	—	150	300	500	900	—
1718	—	150	300	500	900	—
1719	—	150	300	500	900	—
1720	—	150	300	500	900	—
1721	—	150	300	500	900	—
1722	—	150	300	500	900	—
1723	—	150	300	500	900	—
1724	—	150	300	500	900	—
1725	—	150	300	500	900	—

KM# 158 1/2 MAXIMILIAN D'OR
3.3200 g., 0.9000 Gold 0.0961 oz. AGW **Ruler:** Maximilian II, Emanuel **Obverse:** Draped bust right **Reverse:** Madonna and child with arms below

Date	Mintage	VG	F	VF	XF	Unc
1722	—	150	300	525	950	—
1723	—	150	300	525	950	—

KM# 154 MAXIMILIAN D'OR
6.6500 g., 0.9000 Gold 0.1924 oz. AGW **Ruler:** Maximilian II, Emanuel **Mint:** Munich **Obverse:** Head right **Reverse:** Madonna and child with arms below **Note:** Fr. #226.

Date	Mintage	VG	F	VF	XF	Unc
1715	—	175	325	550	1,000	—
1716	—	175	325	550	1,000	—
1717	—	175	325	550	1,000	—
1718	—	175	325	550	1,000	—
1719	—	175	325	550	1,000	—
1720	—	175	325	550	1,000	—
1721	—	175	325	550	1,000	—
1722	—	175	325	550	1,000	—
1723	—	175	325	550	1,000	—
1724	—	175	325	550	1,000	—
1725	—	175	325	550	1,000	—
1726	—	175	325	550	1,000	—

KM# 219 MAXIMILIAN D'OR
6.6500 g., 0.9000 Gold 0.1924 oz. AGW **Ruler:** Maximilian III, Josef **Obverse:** Head right **Reverse:** Madonna and child with arms below **Note:** Fr. #242.

Date	Mintage	VG	F	VF	XF	Unc
1747	—	200	550	1,150	2,000	—
1751	—	200	550	1,150	2,000	—
1752	—	200	550	1,150	2,000	—
1767	—	300	650	1,450	2,250	—

KM# 155 2 MAXIMILIAN D'OR
13.3000 g., 0.9000 Gold 0.3848 oz. AGW **Ruler:** Maximilian II, Emanuel **Mint:** Munich **Obverse:** Head right **Reverse:** Madonna and child, shield of arms at lower right **Note:** Fr. #225.

Date	Mintage	VG	F	VF	XF	Unc
1717	—	1,200	2,500	4,000	7,000	—

PATTERNS

Including off metal strikes

KM#	Date	Mintage	Identification	Mkt Val
Pn1	1742	—	2 Ducat.	—
PnA2	1747	—	Ducat. Silver. KM#217	—

BENTHEIM-TECKLENBURG-RHEDA

The county of Tecklenburg was located about halfway between the cities of Münster and Osnabrück in Westphalia and was acquired by Bentheim through marriage during the first half of the 13th century and the separate line of Bentheim-Tecklenburg was founded in 1269. The lordship of Rheda, to the southeast of Tecklenburg, was acquired by marriage in the mid-14th century. After the reunification of the 16th century, a new line of Bentheim-Tecklenburg-Rheda was founded in 1606. The county of Tecklenburg was lost to Solms in 1696, then sold to Prussia in 1707. Rheda was mediatized in 1805.

RULERS

Johann Adolf, 1674-1701
Friedrich Moritz, 1701-1710
Moritz Kasimir I, 1710-1768
Moritz Kasimir II, 1768-1805

MINT OFFICIALS' INITIALS

Initials	Date	Name
ILC		Johann Schitzkey of Liegnitz, die-cutter for Cologne, initials read Johann Liegnitz Coloniensis
IS, JS		Johann (Wilhelm) Salter

COUNTY / LORDSHIP

REGULAR COINAGE

KM# 151 PFENNING
Copper **Obverse:** Crowned MC monogram **Reverse:** G. B. T. RHEDA...,value, date **Note:** Varieties exist.

Date	Mintage	VG	F	VF	XF	Unc
1760	—	10.00	20.00	30.00	50.00	—

KM# 152 3 PFENNING (Dreier)

Copper **Ruler:** Moritz Kasimir I **Obverse:** Crowned script MC monogram **Reverse:** 3-Line inscription with value and date in circle **Rev. Inscription:** III/PFENNING/1760 **Note:** Varieties exist.

Date	Mintage	VG	F	VF	XF	Unc
1760	—	10.00	20.00	30.00	50.00	—

KM# 153 6 PFENNING (1/42 Thaler)

Copper **Ruler:** Moritz Kasimir I **Obverse:** Crowned MC monogram **Reverse:** G. B. T. RHEDA...,value, date **Note:** Varieties exist.

Date	Mintage	VG	F	VF	XF	Unc
1760 IS	—	10.00	20.00	30.00	55.00	—
1760	—	10.00	20.00	30.00	55.00	—
1761 IS	—	10.00	20.00	30.00	55.00	—
1761	—	10.00	20.00	30.00	55.00	—

BIBERACH

Located in Württemberg 22 miles to the southwest of Ulm, Biberach became a free imperial city in 1312. The city came under the control of Baden in 1803 and then of Württemberg in 1806.

MINT OFFICIALS' INITIALS

Initials	Date	Name
IB	1730	Johann Bohringer, die-cutter
S	1730-57	Johann Christoph Schaupp, die-cutter

FREE CITY

REGULAR COINAGE

KM# 15 GROSCHEN

Silver **Subject:** 200th Anniversary of the Augsburg Confession **Obverse:** Temple on rock, lightning from clouds above **Reverse:** Six-line inscription with date

Date	Mintage	VG	F	VF	XF	Unc
1730 S	—	25.00	45.00	85.00	160	—

TRADE COINAGE

KM# 10 DUCAT

3.5000 g., 0.9860 Gold 0.1109 oz. AGW **Subject:** 200th Anniversary of the Reformation **Obverse:** Bible on table, dove above, BIBERACH/date below **Reverse:** Flying angel with trumpet and snake in shape of ring

Date	Mintage	VG	F	VF	XF	Unc
1717	—	—	2,000	3,500	6,000	—

KM# 16 DUCAT

3.5000 g., 0.9860 Gold 0.1109 oz. AGW **Subject:** 200th Anniversary of the Augsburg Confession **Obverse:** Church on rock divides date, lightning from clouds above **Reverse:** Seven-line inscription

Date	Mintage	VG	F	VF	XF	Unc
1730 IB	—	—	2,500	4,000	7,000	—

PATTERNS

Including off metal strikes

KM#	Date	Mintage	Identification	Mkt Val
Pn1	1717	—	Ducat. Silver. . KM#10	160
Pn2	1730	—	Ducat. Silver. . KM#16	200

BOCHOLT

This provincial town in the bishopric of Munster is located near the Dutch border. It had a local copper coinage from 1615-1762. Bocholt passed to Salm-Salm in 1803 and later went to Prussia.

MONETARY SYSTEM

21 Heller = 6 Pfennig = 1/60 Thaler

PROVINCIAL TOWN

REGULAR COINAGE

KM# 26.1 10-1/2 HELLER

Copper **Obverse:** Uprooted beechtree with beam across trunk, STADT BOCHOLT..., date **Reverse:** Value XH

Date	Mintage	VG	F	VF	XF	Unc
1762	—	12.00	20.00	40.00	80.00	—

KM# 26.2 10-1/2 HELLER

Copper **Obverse:** Uprooted beech tree with beam across trunk within shield **Reverse:** Value X

Date	Mintage	VG	F	VF	XF	Unc
1762	—	12.00	20.00	40.00	80.00	—

KM# 25 21 HELLER

Copper **Obverse:** Uprooted beech tree with beam across trunk within circle **Reverse:** Value XXI within circle

Date	Mintage	VG	F	VF	XF	Unc
1761	—	10.00	20.00	35.00	60.00	—
1762	—	10.00	20.00	35.00	60.00	—

BRANDENBURG-ANSBACH

Located in northern Bavaria. The first coins appeared ca. 1150. This area was given and sold to many individuals, usually with some relationship to the elector of Brandenburg. It was sold to Prussia in 1791 and was ceded to Bavaria in 1806.

RULERS

Georg Friedrich II, 1692-1703
Wilhelm Friedrich, 1703-1723
Karl Wilhelm Friedrich, 1723-1757
under regency of his mother
Christine Charlotte until 1729
Alexander, 1757-1791

MINT MARKS

(c) - Crailsheim, pot hook
(d) - Dachsbach, lily
F - Furth
(f) - Furth, cloverleaf
(k) - Kitzingen, crenellated tower top
O - Onolzbach (Ansbach)
(r) - Roth, rosette
R - Roth
(s) - Schwabach, four-petaled flower
S - Schwabach

MINT OFFICIALS' INITIALS

Initials	Date	Name
AV, V	d.1754	Andreas Vestner, die-cutter in Nurnberg
G, IGS	1750-91	Johann Samuel Gotzinger, die-cutter
G		Unknown, but not Gotzinger
GH	1683-1711	Georg Hautsch, die-cutter in Nurnberg
ICE	1765-68	Johann Christian E. Berhard
K-E	1748-65	Johann Bernhard Kern, warden and Johann Jacob Ebenauer, mintmaster in Schwabach
PG		Unknown
PHM-(*)	d.1718	Philipp Heinrich Muller, medailleur in Nurnberg & Augsburg
PPW	d.1771	Peter Paul Werner, die-cutter in Nurnberg
V	d.1740	Georg Wilhelm Vestner, die-cutter in Nurnberg
W-E	1769-81	Westphal and Ebenauer
W-K	1768-81	Westphal and Kern
WH		Unknown

DUCHY

Margraviate

REGULAR COINAGE

KM# 130 HELLER

Copper **Ruler:** Georg Friedrich II **Obverse:** Crowned arms **Reverse:** 1/HEL/LER/date

Date	Mintage	VG	F	VF	XF	Unc
1699	—	7.00	12.00	20.00	35.00	—
1700	—	7.00	12.00	20.00	35.00	—
1701	—	7.00	12.00	20.00	35.00	—

KM# 140 HELLER

Copper **Ruler:** Wilhelm Friedrich **Obverse:** Crowned arms **Reverse:** Value and date **Note:** Similar to KM#130.

Date	Mintage	VG	F	VF	XF	Unc
1710	—	7.00	12.00	20.00	35.00	—
1711	—	7.00	12.00	20.00	35.00	—
1712	—	7.00	12.00	20.00	35.00	—
1713	—	7.00	12.00	20.00	35.00	—
1714	—	7.00	12.00	20.00	35.00	—
1715	—	7.00	12.00	20.00	35.00	—
1716	—	7.00	12.00	20.00	35.00	—

KM# 210 HELLER

Copper **Ruler:** Karl Wilhelm Friedrich under Regency of his mother Christine Charlotte until 1729 **Obverse:** Crowned oval arms **Reverse:** 1/HELLER/date

Date	Mintage	VG	F	VF	XF	Unc
1751	—	8.00	15.00	30.00	55.00	—

KM# 135 PFENNING

Billon **Ruler:** Wilhelm Friedrich **Obverse:** Two oval arms, value 1 divides date above **Note:** Uniface. Varieties exist.

Date	Mintage	VG	F	VF	XF	Unc
1703	—	6.00	10.00	20.00	35.00	—
1704	—	6.00	10.00	20.00	35.00	—
1705	—	6.00	10.00	20.00	35.00	—
1707	—	6.00	10.00	20.00	35.00	—
1708	—	6.00	10.00	20.00	35.00	—
1709	—	6.00	10.00	20.00	35.00	—
1710	—	6.00	10.00	20.00	35.00	—
1711	—	6.00	10.00	20.00	35.00	—
1712	—	6.00	10.00	20.00	35.00	—
1713	—	6.00	10.00	20.00	35.00	—
1714	—	6.00	10.00	20.00	35.00	—
1715	—	6.00	10.00	20.00	35.00	—
1716	—	6.00	10.00	20.00	35.00	—
1717	—	6.00	10.00	20.00	35.00	—
1718	—	6.00	10.00	20.00	35.00	—
1719	—	6.00	10.00	20.00	35.00	—
1722	—	6.00	10.00	20.00	35.00	—

KM# 160 PFENNING

Billon **Ruler:** Karl Wilhelm Friedrich under Regency of his mother Christine Charlotte until 1729

Date	Mintage	VG	F	VF	XF	Unc
1729	—	6.00	10.00	20.00	35.00	—
1730	—	6.00	10.00	20.00	35.00	—
1731	—	6.00	10.00	20.00	35.00	—
1732	—	6.00	10.00	20.00	35.00	—
1733	—	6.00	10.00	20.00	35.00	—
1734	—	6.00	10.00	20.00	35.00	—
1735	—	6.00	10.00	20.00	35.00	—
1736	—	6.00	10.00	20.00	35.00	—
1737	—	6.00	10.00	20.00	35.00	—
1739	—	6.00	10.00	20.00	35.00	—
1740	—	6.00	10.00	20.00	35.00	—
1741	—	6.00	10.00	20.00	35.00	—
1742	—	6.00	10.00	20.00	35.00	—
1743	—	6.00	10.00	20.00	35.00	—
1744	—	6.00	10.00	20.00	35.00	—
1745	—	6.00	10.00	20.00	35.00	—
1746	—	6.00	10.00	20.00	35.00	—
1747	—	6.00	10.00	20.00	35.00	—
1748	—	6.00	10.00	20.00	35.00	—
1749	—	6.00	10.00	20.00	35.00	—
1750	—	6.00	10.00	20.00	35.00	—
1751	—	6.00	10.00	20.00	35.00	—
1752	—	6.00	10.00	20.00	35.00	—
1753	—	6.00	10.00	20.00	35.00	—

KM# 180 PFENNING

Billon **Ruler:** Karl Wilhelm Friedrich under Regency of his mother Christine Charlotte until 1729 **Obverse:** Two shields, Brandenburg eagle on left, Hohenzollern arms on right, date above

Date	Mintage	VG	F	VF	XF	Unc
1731	—	6.00	10.00	20.00	35.00	—
1733	—	6.00	10.00	20.00	35.00	—

KM# 211 PFENNING

Copper **Ruler:** Karl Wilhelm Friedrich under Regency of his mother Christine Charlotte until 1729 **Obverse:** Crowned Brandenburg eagle with Hohenzollern arms on breast, B-O at top **Reverse:** Value and date

Date	Mintage	VG	F	VF	XF	Unc
1752	—	5.00	10.00	20.00	30.00	—
1753	—	5.00	10.00	20.00	30.00	—

KM# 221 PFENNING

Billon **Ruler:** Karl Wilhelm Friedrich under Regency of his mother Christine Charlotte until 1729 **Obverse:** Two oval arms in cartouche, date above

Date	Mintage	VG	F	VF	XF	Unc
1754	—	8.00	15.00	25.00	50.00	—
1756	—	8.00	15.00	25.00	50.00	—
1757	—	8.00	15.00	25.00	50.00	—

KM# 232 PFENNING

Copper **Obverse:** Crowned arms **Reverse:** Value in cartouche

Date	Mintage	VG	F	VF	XF	Unc
1757	—	3.00	5.00	10.00	20.00	—

KM# 257 PFENNING
Billon **Ruler:** Alexander **Obverse:** Two shields of arms, date above **Reverse:** Blank

Date	Mintage	VG	F	VF	XF	Unc
1763	—	3.00	5.00	10.00	20.00	—

KM# 272 PFENNING
Copper **Ruler:** Alexander **Obverse:** Arms above branches, S below **Reverse:** Value and date

Date	Mintage	VG	F	VF	XF	Unc
1766	—	3.00	5.00	10.00	20.00	—

KM# 290 PFENNING
Billon **Ruler:** Alexander **Obverse:** Arms **Reverse:** Value above date

Date	Mintage	VG	F	VF	XF	Unc
1770-90	—	3.00	5.00	10.00	20.00	—

KM# 327 PFENNING
Billon **Ruler:** Alexander **Obverse:** Hohenzollern arms **Reverse:** Eagle dividing value

Date	Mintage	VG	F	VF	XF	Unc
1781	—	3.00	5.00	10.00	20.00	—

KM# 340 PFENNING
Billon **Ruler:** Alexander **Reverse:** Value on eagle's breast

Date	Mintage	VG	F	VF	XF	Unc
1791	—	3.00	5.00	10.00	20.00	—

KM# 212 1-1/2 PFENNING
Copper **Ruler:** Karl Wilhelm Friedrich under Regency of his mother Christine Charlotte until 1729 **Obverse:** Crowned Brandenburg eagle with Hohenzollern arms on breast, B-O at top **Reverse:** Value, date in cartouche

Date	Mintage	VG	F	VF	XF	Unc
1752	—	7.50	15.00	30.00	45.00	—

KM# 213 2 PFENNING
Copper **Ruler:** Karl Wilhelm Friedrich under Regency of his mother Christine Charlotte until 1729 **Obverse:** Crowned Brandenburg eagle with Hohenzollern arms on breast, B-O at top **Reverse:** Value, date in cartouche

Date	Mintage	VG	F	VF	XF	Unc
1752	—	5.00	10.00	25.00	50.00	—

KM# 233 2 PFENNING
Copper **Obverse:** Crowned arms **Reverse:** Value in cartouche

Date	Mintage	VG	F	VF	XF	Unc
1757	—	3.00	7.00	15.00	30.00	—

KM# 214 4 PFENNING
Copper, 26 mm. **Ruler:** Karl Wilhelm Friedrich under Regency of his mother Christine Charlotte until 1729 **Obverse:** Crowned Brandenburg eagle with Hohenzollern arms on breast, B-O at top **Reverse:** Value, date in cartouche

Date	Mintage	VG	F	VF	XF	Unc
1752	—	10.00	20.00	30.00	50.00	—

KM# 273 4 PFENNING
Billon **Ruler:** Alexander **Obverse:** Arms **Reverse:** Value and date

Date	Mintage	VG	F	VF	XF	Unc
1764	—	5.00	10.00	20.00	35.00	—
1766	—	5.00	10.00	20.00	35.00	—
1768	—	5.00	10.00	20.00	35.00	—
1774	—	5.00	10.00	20.00	35.00	—
1775	—	5.00	10.00	20.00	35.00	—
1777	—	5.00	10.00	20.00	35.00	—
1778	—	5.00	10.00	20.00	35.00	—
1779	—	5.00	10.00	20.00	35.00	—
1780	—	5.00	10.00	20.00	35.00	—
1781	—	5.00	10.00	20.00	35.00	—
1782	—	5.00	10.00	20.00	35.00	—
1783	—	5.00	10.00	20.00	35.00	—
1789	—	5.00	10.00	20.00	35.00	—

KM# 116 KREUZER (4 Pfennig)
Silver **Ruler:** Georg Friedrich II **Obverse:** Bust right **Reverse:** Crowned eagle with I on breast, date divided above **Note:** Similar to KM#136.

Date	Mintage	VG	F	VF	XF	Unc
1700	—	8.00	15.00	28.00	45.00	—
1701	—	8.00	15.00	28.00	45.00	—
1702	—	8.00	15.00	28.00	45.00	—

KM# 136 KREUZER (4 Pfennig)
Silver **Ruler:** Wilhelm Friedrich **Obverse:** Armored bust right **Reverse:** Crowned eagle with shield on breast within circle **Note:** Varieties exist.

Date	Mintage	VG	F	VF	XF	Unc
1703	—	7.00	12.00	22.00	40.00	—
1704	—	7.00	12.00	22.00	40.00	—
1707	—	7.00	12.00	22.00	40.00	—
1708	—	7.00	12.00	22.00	40.00	—
1709	—	7.00	12.00	22.00	40.00	—
1710	—	7.00	12.00	22.00	40.00	—
1711	—	7.00	12.00	22.00	40.00	—
1714	—	7.00	12.00	22.00	40.00	—
1715	—	7.00	12.00	22.00	40.00	—
1716	—	7.00	12.00	22.00	40.00	—
1717	—	7.00	12.00	22.00	40.00	—
1719	—	7.00	12.00	22.00	40.00	—
1720	—	7.00	12.00	22.00	40.00	—
1721	—	7.00	12.00	22.00	40.00	—
1722	—	7.00	12.00	22.00	40.00	—

KM# 154 KREUZER (4 Pfennig)
Silver **Ruler:** Karl Wilhelm Friedrich under Regency of his mother Christine Charlotte until 1729 **Obverse:** Crowned double-C monogram divides date **Reverse:** Eagle with Hohenzollern arms on breast, value I below

Date	Mintage	VG	F	VF	XF	Unc
1726	—	20.00	30.00	60.00	95.00	—

KM# 181 KREUZER (4 Pfennig)
Billon **Ruler:** Karl Wilhelm Friedrich under Regency of his mother Christine Charlotte until 1729 **Obverse:** Bust **Obv. Legend:** CAR. WILH. FR... **Reverse:** Eagle, 1 on breast

Date	Mintage	VG	F	VF	XF	Unc
1732	—	5.00	10.00	20.00	40.00	—
1733	—	5.00	10.00	20.00	40.00	—
1734	—	5.00	10.00	20.00	40.00	—
1735	—	5.00	10.00	20.00	40.00	—
1736	—	5.00	10.00	20.00	40.00	—
1737	—	5.00	10.00	20.00	40.00	—
1740	—	5.00	10.00	20.00	40.00	—
1741	—	5.00	10.00	20.00	40.00	—
1742	—	5.00	10.00	20.00	40.00	—
1743	—	5.00	10.00	20.00	40.00	—
1744	—	5.00	10.00	20.00	40.00	—
1745	—	5.00	10.00	20.00	40.00	—

KM# 222 KREUZER (4 Pfennig)
Silver **Ruler:** Karl Wilhelm Friedrich under Regency of his mother Christine Charlotte until 1729 **Obverse:** Bust right **Reverse:** Crowned eagle with value 1 on breast

Date	Mintage	VG	F	VF	XF	Unc
1754	—	7.00	12.00	25.00	45.00	—

KM# 254 KREUZER (4 Pfennig)
Billon **Ruler:** Alexander **Obverse:** Head right **Reverse:** Crowned eagle divides date, value on breast

Date	Mintage	VG	F	VF	XF	Unc
1759	—	3.00	6.00	12.00	28.00	—
1760	—	3.00	6.00	12.00	28.00	—
1761	—	3.00	6.00	12.00	28.00	—
1763	—	3.00	6.00	12.00	28.00	—
ND	—	3.00	6.00	12.00	28.00	—

KM# 263 KREUZER (4 Pfennig)
Billon **Ruler:** Alexander **Obverse:** Eagle in diamond **Reverse:** Value and date in diamond

Date	Mintage	VG	F	VF	XF	Unc
1765S	—	3.00	6.00	12.00	28.00	—

KM# 325 KREUZER (4 Pfennig)
Billon **Ruler:** Alexander **Obverse:** Crowned arms **Reverse:** Value above date

Date	Mintage	VG	F	VF	XF	Unc
1780	—	2.00	5.00	10.00	25.00	—
1784	—	2.00	5.00	10.00	25.00	—

KM# 330 KREUZER (4 Pfennig)
Billon **Ruler:** Alexander **Obverse:** Crowned and mantled arms **Reverse:** Value and date within cartouche

Date	Mintage	VG	F	VF	XF	Unc
1780	—	2.00	5.00	10.00	25.00	—
1784	—	2.00	5.00	10.00	25.00	—
1785	—	2.00	5.00	10.00	25.00	—
1786	—	2.00	5.00	10.00	25.00	—
1787	—	2.00	5.00	10.00	25.00	—
1788	—	2.00	5.00	10.00	25.00	—
1789	—	2.00	5.00	10.00	25.00	—
1790	—	2.00	5.00	10.00	25.00	—
1791	—	2.00	5.00	10.00	25.00	—

KM# 250 2 KREUZER (1/2 Batzen)
Billon **Ruler:** Alexander **Obverse:** Arms **Reverse:** Eagle

Date	Mintage	VG	F	VF	XF	Unc
1760	—	10.00	20.00	30.00	75.00	—

KM# 277 2-1/2 KREUZER
Billon **Ruler:** Alexander **Obverse:** Crowned round arms **Reverse:** Value and date **Note:** Convention 2-1/2 Kreuzer

Date	Mintage	VG	F	VF	XF	Unc
1767-79	—	5.00	10.00	20.00	40.00	—

KM# 309 2-1/2 KREUZER
Billon **Ruler:** Alexander **Obverse:** Armored bust right **Reverse:** Crowned eagled with shield on breast

Date	Mintage	VG	F	VF	XF	Unc
1779	—	10.00	18.00	35.00	70.00	—
1785	—	10.00	18.00	35.00	70.00	—

KM# 333 2-1/2 KREUZER
Billon **Ruler:** Alexander **Obverse:** Armored bust right **Reverse:** Crowned eagle with shield on breast

Date	Mintage	VG	F	VF	XF	Unc
1786	—	10.00	15.00	30.00	60.00	—

KM# 192 3 KREUZER (Groschen)
Silver **Ruler:** Karl Wilhelm Friedrich under Regency of his mother Christine Charlotte until 1729 **Obverse:** Bust right **Reverse:** Crowned oval arms in baroque frame, value (3) divides date below

Date	Mintage	VG	F	VF	XF	Unc
1735	—	10.00	20.00	35.00	65.00	—

KM# 141 4 KREUZER (Batzen)
Silver **Ruler:** Wilhelm Friedrich **Obverse:** Two oval arms in baroque frame **Reverse:** Crowned eagle, value 4 on breast, date divided above

Date	Mintage	VG	F	VF	XF	Unc
1715	—	12.00	25.00	60.00	100	—

KM# 251 4 KREUZER (Batzen)
Billon **Ruler:** Alexander **Obverse:** Arms **Reverse:** Hohenzollern arms

Date	Mintage	VG	F	VF	XF	Unc
1760	—	12.00	25.00	50.00	100	—

KM# 202 6 KREUZER
Silver **Ruler:** Karl Wilhelm Friedrich under Regency of his mother Christine Charlotte until 1729 **Obverse:** Armored bust right **Reverse:** Crowned arms in baroque frame, value 6 divides date at bottom

Date	Mintage	VG	F	VF	XF	Unc
1745	—	6.00	12.00	25.00	50.00	—
1746	—	7.00	14.00	30.00	60.00	—
1747	—	7.00	14.00	30.00	60.00	—
1748	—	6.00	12.00	25.00	50.00	—
1749	—	6.00	12.00	25.00	50.00	—
1750	—	6.00	12.00	25.00	50.00	—
1751	—	6.00	12.00	25.00	50.00	—
1752	—	7.00	14.00	30.00	60.00	—
1753	—	7.00	14.00	30.00	60.00	—

KM# 223 6 KREUZER
Silver **Ruler:** Karl Wilhelm Friedrich under Regency of his mother Christine Charlotte until 1729 **Reverse:** Crowned arms in smaller, less ornate shield separates date, value VI. KR. below

Date	Mintage	VG	F	VF	XF	Unc
1754	—	6.00	12.00	25.00	50.00	—

KM# 243 6 KREUZER

Silver **Ruler:** Alexander **Obverse:** Armored bust right **Reverse:** Crowned arms within baroque frame

Date	Mintage	VG	F	VF	XF	Unc
1758	—	10.00	25.00	50.00	100	—

KM# 274 6 KREUZER

Billon **Ruler:** Alexander **Obverse:** Shield on pedestal **Reverse:** Value, date

Date	Mintage	VG	F	VF	XF	Unc
1766	—	15.00	30.00	60.00	125	—
1784	—	15.00	30.00	60.00	125	—

KM# 328 6 KREUZER

Billon **Ruler:** Alexander **Obverse:** Bust in wreath **Reverse:** Crowned arms on pedestal, value below

Date	Mintage	VG	F	VF	XF	Unc
1781	—	15.00	30.00	60.00	125	—

KM# 264 10 KREUZER

Silver **Ruler:** Alexander **Obverse:** Head right in sprays **Reverse:** Crowned arms on pedestal, date below **Note:** Convention 10 Kreuzer.

Date	Mintage	VG	F	VF	XF	Unc
1765	—	10.00	20.00	40.00	100	—
1780	—	10.00	20.00	40.00	100	—

KM# 186 15 KREUZER

Silver **Ruler:** Karl Wilhelm Friedrich under Regency of his mother Christine Charlotte until 1729 **Obverse:** Bust right **Reverse:** Crowned oval arms in baroque frame, value (15) divides date below

Date	Mintage	VG	F	VF	XF	Unc
1734	—	20.00	35.00	65.00	110	—
1735	—	20.00	35.00	65.00	110	—

KM# 230 20 KREUZER

Silver **Ruler:** Karl Wilhelm Friedrich under Regency of his mother Christine Charlotte until 1729 **Obverse:** Bust right **Reverse:** Crowned eagle on pedestal with value between two branches, date below

Date	Mintage	VG	F	VF	XF	Unc
1756	—	15.00	35.00	65.00	120	—

KM# 246 20 KREUZER

Silver **Ruler:** Alexander

Date	Mintage	VG	F	VF	XF	Unc
1759	—	6.00	12.00	20.00	50.00	—
1760	—	6.00	12.00	20.00	50.00	—
1761	—	6.00	12.00	20.00	50.00	—
1762	—	6.00	12.00	20.00	50.00	—

KM# 255.2 20 KREUZER

Silver **Ruler:** Alexander **Obverse:** Smaller head right within wreath **Reverse:** Arms in baroque frame, value within pedestal below flanked by branches

Date	Mintage	VG	F	VF	XF	Unc
1764S	—	7.00	14.00	30.00	60.00	—

KM# 331 20 KREUZER

Silver **Ruler:** Alexander **Obverse:** Head right within wreath **Obv. Legend:** ALEXANDER • D • G • - MARCH: BRAND: **Reverse:** Crowned arms on pedestal holding value, branches flank **Rev. Legend:** LX • ST • EINE - FEINE • MARK

Date	Mintage	VG	F	VF	XF	Unc
1765	—	6.00	12.00	20.00	50.00	—
1784 WK	—	6.00	12.00	20.00	50.00	—
1785 WK	—	6.00	12.00	20.00	50.00	—

KM# 255.1 20 KREUZER

Silver **Ruler:** Alexander **Obverse:** Head right within wreath **Reverse:** Arms in baroque frame, value within pedestal below flanked by branches **Note:** Convention 20 Kreuzer. Varieties exist.

Date	Mintage	VG	F	VF	XF	Unc
1765S	—	7.00	14.00	30.00	60.00	—
1773S	—	7.00	14.00	30.00	60.00	—
1774S	—	7.00	14.00	30.00	60.00	—
1775S	—	7.00	14.00	30.00	60.00	—
1781S	—	7.00	14.00	30.00	60.00	—
1783S	—	7.00	14.00	30.00	60.00	—
1784S WK	—	7.00	14.00	30.00	60.00	—
1785S WK	—	7.00	14.00	30.00	60.00	—
1787S WK	—	7.00	14.00	30.00	60.00	—

KM# 289 20 KREUZER

Silver **Ruler:** Alexander **Obverse:** Head right, 's' below, all within rhombus **Obv. Legend:** ALEXANDER - MARCH: - BRAND: - DVX BOR: **Reverse:** Crowned quartered arms with eagle supporters, value below, all within rhombus

Date	Mintage	VG	F	VF	XF	Unc
1772S	—	10.00	25.00	50.00	100	—

KM# 310 20 KREUZER

Silver **Ruler:** Alexander **Obverse:** Bust right **Reverse:** Quartered arms supported

Date	Mintage	VG	F	VF	XF	Unc
1779	—	15.00	35.00	75.00	100	—

KM# 311 20 KREUZER

Silver **Ruler:** Alexander **Obverse:** Head right, value below, rhombus surrounds **Reverse:** Eagle shield on Hohenzollern shield on imperial eagle, rhombus surrounds

Date	Mintage	VG	F	VF	XF	Unc
1779	—	15.00	35.00	75.00	100	—

KM# 312 20 KREUZER

Silver **Ruler:** Alexander **Reverse:** Eagle shield on imperial eagle

Date	Mintage	VG	F	VF	XF	Unc
1779	—	12.50	30.00	60.00	125	—

KM# 322 20 KREUZER

Silver **Ruler:** Karl Wilhelm Friedrich under Regency of his mother Christine Charlotte until 1729 **Obverse:** Bust right, value below, rhombus surrounds **Obv. Legend:** ALEXANDER • D • G • MARCH • BRAND • **Reverse:** Hohenzollem shield on imperial eagle, rhombus surrounds **Rev. Legend:** ZEHEN EINE - FEINE • MARK

Date	Mintage	VG	F	VF	XF	Unc
1780	—	25.00	50.00	100	200	—

KM# 190 30 KREUZER

Silver **Ruler:** Karl Wilhelm Friedrich under Regency of his mother Christine Charlotte until 1729 **Obverse:** Bust **Reverse:** Arms

Date	Mintage	VG	F	VF	XF	Unc
1735	—	12.50	25.00	45.00	75.00	—
1735G	—	12.50	25.00	45.00	75.00	—

KM# 191 30 KREUZER

Silver **Ruler:** Karl Wilhelm Friedrich under Regency of his mother Christine Charlotte until 1729 **Obverse:** Bust right **Reverse:** Crowned oval arms and eagle in Order chain, date below

Date	Mintage	VG	F	VF	XF	Unc
1735	—	15.00	30.00	60.00	120	—
1735 WH	—	15.00	30.00	60.00	120	—
1736	—	—	—	—	—	—

KM# 224 30 KREUZER

Silver **Ruler:** Karl Wilhelm Friedrich under Regency of his mother Christine Charlotte until 1729 **Obverse:** Bust right **Reverse:** Eagle in rhombus

Date	Mintage	VG	F	VF	XF	Unc
1754 S	—	15.00	30.00	100	175	—

KM# 150 GROSCHEN (1/24 Thaler)

Silver **Ruler:** Karl Wilhelm Friedrich under Regency of his mother Christine Charlotte until 1729 **Subject:** Death of Wilhelm Friedrich **Obverse:** Bust right **Reverse:** Inscription with date

Date	Mintage	VG	F	VF	XF	Unc
1723	—	40.00	85.00	125	200	—

KM# 161 GROSCHEN (1/24 Thaler)

Billon **Ruler:** Karl Wilhelm Friedrich under Regency of his mother Christine Charlotte until 1729 **Subject:** Accession Commemorative **Obverse:** Bust **Reverse:** SIS/FELIX in wreath

Date	Mintage	VG	F	VF	XF	Unc
1729	—	5.00	10.00	20.00	40.00	—

KM# 194 GROSCHEN (1/24 Thaler)

Billon **Ruler:** Karl Wilhelm Friedrich under Regency of his mother Christine Charlotte until 1729 **Subject:** School Prize **Obverse:** Eagle with Hohenzollern arms **Reverse:** Inscription

Date	Mintage	VG	F	VF	XF	Unc
1737	—	6.00	12.00	30.00	60.00	—

KM# 216 GROSCHEN (1/24 Thaler)

Billon **Ruler:** Karl Wilhelm Friedrich under Regency of his mother Christine Charlotte until 1729 **Obverse:** Eagle with arms on breast **Reverse:** Imperial orb

Date	Mintage	VG	F	VF	XF	Unc
1753	—	5.00	10.00	20.00	40.00	—

KM# 225 GROSCHEN (1/24 Thaler)

Billon **Ruler:** Karl Wilhelm Friedrich under Regency of his mother Christine Charlotte until 1729 **Obverse:** Bust **Reverse:** Eagle with arms on breast

Date	Mintage	VG	F	VF	XF	Unc
1754	—	5.00	10.00	20.00	40.00	—

KM# 234 GROSCHEN (1/24 Thaler)

Billon **Obverse:** Crowned eagle, arms in baroque frame, date below **Reverse:** Value

Date	Mintage	VG	F	VF	XF	Unc
1757 S	—	10.00	20.00	40.00	80.00	—

KM# 162 2 GROSCHEN (1/12 Thaler)

Silver **Ruler:** Karl Wilhelm Friedrich under Regency of his mother Christine Charlotte until 1729 **Subject:** Accession Commemorative **Obverse:** Armored bust right **Reverse:** Inscription within wreath

Date	Mintage	VG	F	VF	XF	Unc
1729	—	10.00	20.00	40.00	70.00	—

KM# 229 1/12 THALER (Doppelgroschen)

Silver **Ruler:** Karl Wilhelm Friedrich under Regency of his mother Christine Charlotte until 1729 **Obverse:** Bust right **Reverse:** Inscription and value

Date	Mintage	VG	F	VF	XF	Unc
ND	—	7.00	15.00	30.00	60.00	—
1755 S	—	7.00	15.00	30.00	60.00	—
1756 S	—	7.00	15.00	30.00	60.00	—
ND	—	7.00	15.00	30.00	60.00	—

KM# 235 1/12 THALER (Doppelgroschen)
Silver **Obverse:** Crowned arms within baroque frame **Reverse:** Value

Date	Mintage	VG	F	VF	XF	Unc
1757 S	—	8.00	16.00	32.00	65.00	—

KM# 151 1/6 THALER (1/4 Gulden)
Silver **Obverse:** Bust **Obv. Legend:** C. W. PRIDERIC M. B. D... **Reverse:** Value

Date	Mintage	VG	F	VF	XF	Unc
ND	—	10.00	20.00	40.00	60.00	—

KM# 231 1/6 THALER (1/4 Gulden)
Silver **Ruler:** Karl Wilhelm Friedrich under Regency of his mother Christine Charlotte until 1729 **Subject:** Seven Year War **Obverse:** Bust **Reverse:** Value

Date	Mintage	VG	F	VF	XF	Unc
1755 S	—	15.00	30.00	60.00	120	—
1756 S	—	15.00	30.00	60.00	120	—

KM# 236 1/6 THALER (1/4 Gulden)
Silver **Ruler:** Karl Wilhelm Friedrich under Regency of his mother Christine Charlotte until 1729 **Subject:** Death of Ruler **Obverse:** Armored bust right **Reverse:** 9-Line inscription

Date	Mintage	VG	F	VF	XF	Unc
1757	—	15.00	35.00	75.00	150	—

KM# 237 1/6 THALER (1/4 Gulden)
Silver **Obverse:** Crowned CFCA monogram **Rev. Inscription:** * VI * / EINEN / THALER / B.O.S.L.M.

Date	Mintage	VG	F	VF	XF	Unc
1757	—	15.00	35.00	75.00	150	—

KM# 158 1/4 THALER
Silver **Ruler:** Karl Wilhelm Friedrich under Regency of his mother Christine Charlotte until 1729 **Obverse:** Bust of Christine Charlotte left **Reverse:** Entwined crowned C's in cruciform **Note:** Similar to 1/2 Thaler, KM#155.

Date	Mintage	VG	F	VF	XF	Unc
1727	—	60.00	100	180	275	—

KM# 163 1/4 THALER
Silver **Ruler:** Karl Wilhelm Friedrich under Regency of his mother Christine Charlotte until 1729 **Subject:** Accession Commemorative **Obverse:** Armored bust left **Reverse:** Crowned arms within cartouche

Date	Mintage	VG	F	VF	XF	Unc
1729	—	50.00	100	300	600	—

KM# 164 1/4 THALER
Silver **Ruler:** Karl Wilhelm Friedrich under Regency of his mother Christine Charlotte until 1729 **Obverse:** Bust right

Date	Mintage	VG	F	VF	XF	Unc
1729	—	50.00	100	300	600	—

KM# 182 1/4 THALER
Silver **Ruler:** Karl Wilhelm Friedrich under Regency of his mother Christine Charlotte until 1729 **Obverse:** Bust right **Reverse:** Crowned arms in baroque frame, date below

Date	Mintage	VG	F	VF	XF	Unc
1732	—	50.00	100	300	600	—

KM# 193 1/4 THALER
Silver **Ruler:** Karl Wilhelm Friedrich under Regency of his mother Christine Charlotte until 1729 **Subject:** Inauguration of New Anhalt Gymnasium **Obverse:** Armored bust right **Reverse:** Gymnasium above inscription

Date	Mintage	VG	F	VF	XF	Unc
1736	—	20.00	40.00	75.00	150	—

KM# 195 1/4 THALER
Silver **Ruler:** Karl Wilhelm Friedrich under Regency of his mother Christine Charlotte until 1729 **Subject:** Death of Wilhelmine Karoline, Daughter of Johann Friedrich **Obverse:** Bust left, four-line inscription below **Reverse:** Eighteen-line inscription with date

Date	Mintage	VG	F	VF	XF	Unc
1737 Rare	—	—	—	—	—	—

KM# 252 1/4 THALER
Silver **Ruler:** Alexander **Note:** Convention 1/4 Thaler.

Date	Mintage	F	VF	XF	Unc
1760	—	35.00	50.00	125	200
1763	—	35.00	50.00	125	200

KM# 265 1/4 THALER
Silver **Ruler:** Alexander **Obverse:** Margrave on horseback, roman date below **Reverse:** Eagle with lion shield, flags at left and right

Date	Mintage	F	VF	XF	Unc
1765	—	100	165	275	475

KM# 278 1/4 THALER
Silver **Ruler:** Alexander **Obverse:** Armored bust right **Reverse:** Three buildings in horseshoe form

Date	Mintage	F	VF	XF	Unc
1767	—	150	225	425	700

KM# 281 1/4 THALER
Silver **Ruler:** Alexander **Subject:** Acquisition of Bayreuth **Obverse:** Busts facing above inscription **Reverse:** Shielded arms flank podium with open book

Date	Mintage	F	VF	XF	Unc
1769	—	130	200	350	600

KM# 298 1/4 THALER
Silver **Ruler:** Alexander **Obverse:** Bust right **Reverse:** Arms

Date	Mintage	VG	F	VF	XF	Unc
1775	—	45.00	80.00	150	300	—

KM# 313 1/4 THALER
Silver **Ruler:** Alexander **Subject:** Peace of Teschen **Obverse:** Sun rays above figure standing left of shield of arms and podium **Reverse:** Inscription within wreath

Date	Mintage	VG	F	VF	XF	Unc
1779	—	35.00	65.00	125	275	—

KM# 334 1/4 THALER
Silver **Ruler:** Alexander **Subject:** 100th Anniversary of Neustadt-Erlangen **Obverse:** City view above inscription **Reverse:** Inscription

Date	Mintage	VG	F	VF	XF	Unc
1786	—	15.00	35.00	75.00	150	—

KM# 155 1/2 THALER
Silver **Ruler:** Karl Wilhelm Friedrich under Regency of his mother Christine Charlotte until 1729 **Obverse:** Bust of Christine Charlotte left **Reverse:** Entwined crowned C's in cruciform

Date	Mintage	VG	F	VF	XF	Unc
1726	—	150	275	550	1,100	—

KM# 165 1/2 THALER
Silver **Ruler:** Karl Wilhelm Friedrich under Regency of his mother Christine Charlotte until 1729 **Subject:** Wedding of Karl Wilhelm Friedrich and Frederika Louise **Obverse:** Busts facing each other **Reverse:** Plumes top ribboned pillar

Date	Mintage	VG	F	VF	XF	Unc
1729 V	—	100	250	500	1,000	—
1729 WH	—	100	250	500	1,000	—

KM# 166 1/2 THALER
Silver **Ruler:** Karl Wilhelm Friedrich under Regency of his mother Christine Charlotte until 1729 **Subject:** Accession Commemorative **Obverse:** Armored bust left **Reverse:** Crowned arms within cartouche **Note:** Similar to 1/4 Thaler, KM#163.

Date	Mintage	VG	F	VF	XF	Unc
1729 V	—	75.00	200	400	600	—

KM# 175.2 1/2 THALER
Silver **Ruler:** Karl Wilhelm Friedrich under Regency of his mother Christine Charlotte until 1729 **Obverse:** Armored bust right **Reverse:** Justice seated **Note:** Double thick flan.

Date	Mintage	VG	F	VF	XF	Unc
1730 V	—	500	900	1,500	2,500	—

KM# 175.1 1/2 THALER

Silver **Ruler:** Karl Wilhelm Friedrich under Regency of his mother Christine Charlotte until 1729 **Subject:** Consecration of New Ansbach Justice Board **Obverse:** Armored bust right **Reverse:** Justice seated

Date	Mintage	VG	F	VF	XF	Unc
1730 V	—	200	400	800	1,200	—

KM# 183 1/2 THALER

Silver **Ruler:** Karl Wilhelm Friedrich under Regency of his mother Christine Charlotte until 1729 **Obverse:** Bust right **Reverse:** Crowned and mantled oval arms, without inscription, date below

Date	Mintage	VG	F	VF	XF	Unc
1732	—	100	250	400	600	—

KM# 196 1/2 THALER

Silver **Ruler:** Karl Wilhelm Friedrich under Regency of his mother Christine Charlotte until 1729 **Subject:** Death of Wilhelmine Karoline, Daughter of Johann Friedrich **Obverse:** Bust left, four-line inscription below **Reverse:** Eighteen-line inscription with date

Date	Mintage	VG	F	VF	XF	Unc
1737 Rare	—	—	—	—	—	—

KM# 203.1 1/2 THALER

Silver **Ruler:** Karl Wilhelm Friedrich under Regency of his mother Christine Charlotte until 1729 **Obverse:** Armored bust right **Reverse:** Crowned complex arms within mantle

Date	Mintage	VG	F	VF	XF	Unc
1746 PPW	—	100	200	400	900	—
1747 PPW	—	100	200	400	900	—

KM# 203.2 1/2 THALER

Silver **Ruler:** Karl Wilhelm Friedrich under Regency of his mother Christine Charlotte until 1729 **Obverse:** Legend without D. G. **Reverse:** Crowned complex arms within mantle

Date	Mintage	VG	F	VF	XF	Unc
1746 PPW	—	100	200	400	900	—

KM# 253 1/2 THALER

Silver **Ruler:** Alexander **Obverse:** Draped bust right **Obv. Legend:** ALEXANDER • M • B • D • B • **Reverse:** Crowned A's in cruciform, arms at center **Note:** Convention 1/2 Thaler.

Date	Mintage	F	VF	XF	Unc
1760 G	—	85.00	150	300	600

KM# 266.1 1/2 THALER

14.1400 g., 0.8330 Silver 0.3787 oz. ASW, 35.6 mm. **Ruler:** Alexander **Mint:** Schwabach **Obverse:** Bust right without Order cross below **Reverse:** Three coats of arms below crown **Edge:** Ornamented

Date	Mintage	F	VF	XF	Unc
1761G-KES one known	—	—	—	—	—

KM# 266.2 1/2 THALER

Silver **Obverse:** Bust of Alexander right with Order cross below **Reverse:** Three shields of arms

Date	Mintage	F	VF	XF	Unc
1765	—	90.00	150	250	400

KM# 261 1/2 THALER

Silver **Ruler:** Alexander

Date	Mintage	F	VF	XF	Unc
1764	—	50.00	100	200	400

KM# 267 1/2 THALER

Silver **Ruler:** Alexander **Obverse:** Margrave on horseback **Reverse:** Eagle with lion shield

Date	Mintage	F	VF	XF	Unc
1765	—	155	250	350	725

KM# 279 1/2 THALER

Silver **Ruler:** Alexander **Obverse:** Armored bust right **Obv. Legend:** ALEXANDER • D • G • MARCH: BRAND • D • B • & • S • **Reverse:** Three buildings in horseshoe form

Date	Mintage	F	VF	XF	Unc
1767	—	65.00	120	200	400

KM# 299 1/2 THALER

Silver **Ruler:** Alexander **Obverse:** Armored bust right **Obv. Legend:** ALEXANDER • D • G • MARCH • BRAND • **Reverse:** Crowned quartered arms with eagle supporters

Date	Mintage	F	VF	XF	Unc
1775 G//S-WK	—	75.00	150	300	600

KM# 341 2/3 THALER

12.5100 g., Silver, 35.3 mm. **Ruler:** Alexander **Mint:** Schwabach **Obverse:** Bust right Legend begins "ALEXANDER" **Reverse:** Crowned arms between two eagles and above value divided date **Edge:** Ornamented **Note:** Dav. #314.

Date	Mintage	F	VF	XF	Unc
1757 G	—	185	350	—	—

KM# 342 2/3 THALER

Silver **Ruler:** Alexander **Mint:** Schwabach **Obverse:** Bust right, legend begins "C.F.C." **Reverse:** Crowned arms same as KM#341 **Edge:** Ornamented **Note:** Dav. #315.

Date	Mintage	F	VF	XF	Unc
1757 G(s)	—	35.00	70.00	150	300

KM# 217 2/3 THALER (Gulden)

Silver **Ruler:** Karl Wilhelm Friedrich under Regency of his mother Christine Charlotte until 1729 **Obverse:** Armored bust right **Obv. Legend:** CAROLUS WILH • FRID • D • G • M • B • D • P • & • S • B • N • C • S • **Reverse:** Value divides date in exergue **Note:** Varieties exist.

Date	Mintage	F	VF	XF	Unc
1752	—	35.00	70.00	150	300
1753	—	35.00	70.00	150	300
1753 G	—	35.00	70.00	150	300
1753 ISG	—	35.00	70.00	150	300

KM# 218 2/3 THALER (Gulden)

Silver **Ruler:** Karl Wilhelm Friedrich under Regency of his mother Christine Charlotte until 1729 **Obverse:** Armored bust right **Reverse:** Value divides date within scrollwork **Note:** Varieties exist.

Date	Mintage	F	VF	XF	Unc
1753	—	35.00	70.00	150	300
1753 G	—	35.00	70.00	150	300
1753 ISG	—	35.00	70.00	150	300

KM# 142 THALER

Silver **Ruler:** Wilhelm Friedrich **Obverse:** Armored bust right **Obv. Legend:** WILHELMVS FRID: D: G: MARCH: BRAND: **Reverse:** Helmeted complex arms, ornaments flank **Rev. Legend:** RECTE FACIENDO - NEMINEM TIMEAS **Note:** Dav. #1976.

Date	Mintage	VG	F	VF	XF	Unc
1715	—	175	350	700	1,400	—
1715(r)	—	175	350	700	1,400	—

KM# 156 THALER

Silver **Ruler:** Karl Wilhelm Friedrich under Regency of his mother Christine Charlotte until 1729 **Obverse:** Bust of Christine Charlotte left **Reverse:** Entwined crowned C's in cruciform **Note:** Similar to 1/2 Thaler KM#155 but struck on thick flan.

Date	Mintage	VG	F	VF	XF	Unc
1726 Rare	—	—	—	—	—	—

KM# 159 THALER

Silver **Ruler:** Karl Wilhelm Friedrich under Regency of his mother Christine Charlotte until 1729 **Obverse:** Bust of Christine Charlotte left **Obv. Legend:** CHRIST: CAR: TVTRIX: REG: BRAND: ONOLD: **Reverse:** Arms of Brandenburg and Wurttemberg-Oels **Note:** Dav. #1977.

Date	Mintage	F	VF	XF	Unc
1727 V	—	200	400	800	1,500

KM# 167 THALER

Silver **Ruler:** Karl Wilhelm Friedrich under Regency of his mother Christine Charlotte until 1729 **Subject:** Wedding of Karl Wilhelm Friedrich and Frederika Louise **Obverse:** Busts facing each other **Obv. Legend:** CARL • WILH • FRID • MARCH • BR * FRID • LVDOVICA • PR • BOR •; SAC • NVPT • CELEB • BEROL • /A • CIOIOCCXXVIIII/V • **Reverse:** A smoking altar **Rev. Legend:** PERPETVO •; VOTA PVBLICA • below **Note:** Dav. #1978.

Date	Mintage	F	VF	XF	Unc
1729 V	—	300	600	1,200	2,000

KM# 168 THALER

Silver **Ruler:** Karl Wilhelm Friedrich under Regency of his mother Christine Charlotte until 1729 **Subject:** Accession Commemorative **Obverse:** Bust left **Reverse:** Crowned and mantled arms **Note:** Dav. #1979.

Date	Mintage	F	VF	XF	Unc
1729 V	—	350	700	1,500	2,750

KM# 176 THALER

Silver **Ruler:** Karl Wilhelm Friedrich under Regency of his mother Christine Charlotte until 1729 **Subject:** 200th Anniversary of Augsburg Confession **Obverse:** Armored bust right **Obv. Legend:** CAROLVS WILH: FR: - M. BR: D. BOR: B: BOR.; below AVGVST • CONF • SVSTINET •/MDCCXXX. **Reverse:** Armored bust of George IV right **Rev. Legend:** GEORGIVS • MARCH • - BRAND • ONOLDINVS •; below AVGVST CONF • EXHIBET •/MDXXX **Note:** Dav. #1980.

Date	Mintage	F	VF	XF	Unc
1730 V	—	300	600	1,200	2,000

KM# 177 THALER

Silver **Ruler:** Karl Wilhelm Friedrich under Regency of his mother Christine Charlotte until 1729 **Subject:** 200th Anniversary of Augsburg Confession **Obverse:** Armored bust right **Obv. Legend:** CAROLVS WILH: FR: - M. BR: D. BOR: B. NOR.; below AVGVST• CONF•SVSTINET•/MDCCXXX **Reverse:** Figure with cross seated left **Rev. Legend:** ILLAE SUNT QVAE TESTIFICANTUR DE ME; in exergue FELICITAS• SEC•II•/AVG•CONF•/V• **Note:** Dav. #1981.

Date	Mintage	F	VF	XF	Unc
1730 V	—	350	675	1,350	2,500

KM# 178 THALER

Silver **Ruler:** Karl Wilhelm Friedrich under Regency of his mother Christine Charlotte until 1729 **Note:** Mule. Reverses of KM#176 and 177. Dav. #1981A.

Date	Mintage	F	VF	XF	Unc
ND(1730) Rare	—	—	—	—	—

KM# 184 THALER

Silver **Ruler:** Karl Wilhelm Friedrich under Regency of his mother Christine Charlotte until 1729 **Obverse:** Armored bust right **Obv. Legend:** CAR. WILH. - FRID. M. B. D. P. **Reverse:** Nine helmets above shield **Rev. Legend:** SALVS PVBLICA - SALVS MEA • **Note:** Dav. #1982.

Date	Mintage	F	VF	XF	Unc
1732	—	700	1,500	2,500	—
1732 V	—	700	1,500	2,500	—

KM# 204 THALER

Silver **Ruler:** Karl Wilhelm Friedrich under Regency of his mother Christine Charlotte until 1729 **Obverse:** Armored bust right **Obv. Legend:** CAR • GVILH • FRID • M • BR • P • S • D • B • N • **Reverse:** Thirteen helmets above shield **Rev. Legend:** SALVS PVBLICA SALVS MEA **Note:** Dav. #1983.

Date	Mintage	F	VF	XF	Unc
ND1746 P P WERNER	—	275	600	1,000	1,750

KM# 215 THALER

Silver **Ruler:** Karl Wilhelm Friedrich under Regency of his mother Christine Charlotte until 1729 **Obverse:** Armored bust right **Obv. Legend:** CAROLUS WILH • FRID • D • G • M • B • D • P • & S • B • N • C • S • **Reverse:** Arms within crowned mantle **Rev. Legend:** EIN REICHS - THALER **Note:** Reichs Thaler. Dav. #1984.

Date	Mintage	F	VF	XF	Unc
1752 G	—	275	600	1,100	—
1752 ISG	—	275	600	1,100	—

KM# 226 THALER

Silver **Ruler:** Karl Wilhelm Friedrich under Regency of his mother Christine Charlotte until 1729 **Obverse:** Armored bust right **Obv. Legend:** CAR • WILH • FRID • D • G • M • B • D • P • & • S • B • N • C • S • **Reverse:** Eagle with shield on breast divides date **Rev. Legend:** ZEHEN EINE - FEINE MARK; SCHWABACH/K. & E. below **Note:** Convention Thaler. Dav. #1985.

Date	Mintage	F	VF	XF	Unc
1754	—	100	225	450	1,000
1754 ISG//K-E	—	100	225	450	1,000
1754 PPW//K-E	—	100	225	450	1,000

KM# 240 THALER

Silver **Ruler:** Karl Wilhelm Friedrich under Regency of his mother Christine Charlotte until 1729 **Subject:** Falcon Hunting **Obverse:** Armored bust right **Obv. Legend:** CAROLUS WILH • FRID • D • G • M • E • D • F • & • S • B • N • C • S • **Reverse:** Falcon sitting with falcon flying above **Note:** Dav. #2926.

Date	Mintage	F	VF	XF	Unc
ND	—	725	1,250	2,000	3,500

KM# 238 THALER

Silver **Obverse:** Bust right **Reverse:** Crowned arms supported by lions, date below **Note:** Dav. #1987.

Date	Mintage	F	VF	XF	Unc
1757 PPW	—	125	275	600	1,200

KM# 239 THALER

Silver **Ruler:** Karl Wilhelm Friedrich under Regency of his mother Christine Charlotte until 1729 **Subject:** Death of Ruler **Obverse:** Armored bust right **Obv. Legend:** CAR • WILH • FRID • D • G • M • BR • D • PR • & S • B • N • COM • SAYN • **Reverse:** Inscription in 9 lines **Rev. Inscription:** NATUS/ XII. MAY. MDCCXII./ DESPONSATUS/ XXX.MAY MDCCXXIX/ DENATUS/ III.AUG.MDCCLVII./ ANN/ REGIM:XXIIX./ AET: XLV. **Note:** Dav. #1988.

Date	Mintage	F	VF	XF	Unc
1757 PPW	—	500	1,000	1,750	3,000

KM# 241 THALER

Silver **Ruler:** Alexander **Obverse:** Small armored bust right **Obv. Legend:** C • F • C • ALEXANDER • D • G • M • B • D • & • S • L • N • C • S • **Reverse:** Crowned and mantled arms with Order chain **Rev. Legend:** EIN REICHS - THALER **Note:** Dav. #1989.

Date	Mintage	F	VF	XF	Unc
1757 G	—	100	200	400	800

KM# 244 THALER

Silver, 42 mm. **Ruler:** Alexander **Obverse:** Cloaked armored bust right **Obv. Legend:** C•F•C•ALEXANDER•D•G•M•B•D•B• & •S•B•N•C•S• **Reverse:** Crowned supported arms **Note:** Dav. #1990.

Date	Mintage	F	VF	XF	Unc
1758 G//KE Rare	—	—	—	—	—

KM# 245 THALER

Silver **Ruler:** Karl Wilhelm Friedrich under Regency of his mother Christine Charlotte until 1729 **Obverse:** Large bust with Order right **Reverse:** Crowned supported arms **Note:** Dav. #1991.

Date	Mintage	F	VF	XF	Unc
1758 G//K-E Rare	—	—	—	—	—
1759 G//K-E Rare	—	—	—	—	—
1760 G//K-E Rare	—	—	—	—	—

KM# 258 THALER

Silver **Ruler:** Alexander **Obverse:** Cloaked bust right **Obv. Legend:** ALEXANDER. D. G. M. B. D. B. &. S. B. N. **Reverse:** Crowned complex arms with lion supporters and Order chain **Rev. Legend:** ZEHEN EINE FEINE MARK **Note:** Dav. #1992.

Date	Mintage	F	VF	XF	Unc
1763 ISG//K-E	—	300	700	1,250	—

KM# 262 THALER

Silver **Ruler:** Alexander **Obverse:** Armored cloaked bust right **Obv. Legend:** ALEXANDER • D • G • M • B • D • B • & • S • B • N • **Reverse:** Crowned complex arms with lion supporters **Rev. Legend:** ZEHEN EINE FEINE MARK **Note:** Dav. #1993.

Date	Mintage	F	VF	XF	Unc
1764 S-K-E	—	75.00	150	300	700

KM# 268 THALER

Silver **Ruler:** Alexander **Obverse:** Large bust right **Note:** Dav. #1994.

Date	Mintage	F	VF	XF	Unc
1765 G//S-K-F	—	450	900	1,500	—

KM# 270 THALER

Silver **Ruler:** Alexander **Obverse:** Margrave on horseback left **Obv. Legend:** ALEXANDER. D. G. M. B. D. B. &. S. B. N. CIRC: FRANC: CAPITANEUS.; MDCCLXV/SCHWABACH below **Reverse:** Eagle with lion shield, flags at left and right **Note:** Dav. #1996.

Date	Mintage	F	VF	XF	Unc
1765 KK	—	175	325	650	1,100

KM# 269 THALER

Silver **Ruler:** Alexander **Obverse:** Smaller bust right with Order cross below **Obv. Legend:** ALEXANDER. D. G. MARCH: BRAND: D. B. &. S. **Reverse:** Three shields of arms within crowned cartouche with lion supporters **Rev. Legend:** ZEHEN EINE FEINE MARK; K-K below **Note:** Varieties exist with lions looking to outer edges. Dav. #1995.

Date	Mintage	F	VF	XF	Unc
1765 G//S-K-E	—	100	200	400	800
1766 G//S-KK	—	100	200	400	800

KM# 275 THALER

Silver **Ruler:** Alexander **Obverse:** Large bust right without Order cross extending below truncation **Note:** Dav. #1997.

Date	Mintage	F	VF	XF	Unc
1766 G//S-KK	—	125	250	500	900

KM# 280.1 THALER

27.8500 g., Silver **Ruler:** Alexander **Obverse:** Curl below sharp pointed bust truncation **Obv. Legend:** ALEXANDER • D • G • MARCH: BRAND: D. B. &. S. **Rev. Legend:** ZEHEN EINE FEINE MARK **Note:** Dav. #1998.

Date	Mintage	F	VF	XF	Unc
1767 G//S-KK	—	100	200	400	800
1768. G//S-KK	—	100	200	400	800

KM# 280.2 THALER

27.7200 g., Silver **Ruler:** Alexander **Mint:** Schwabach **Obverse:** Hanging curl below bust with notched truncation **Reverse:** Lions tails end before and after the legend ends

Date	Mintage	F	VF	XF	Unc
1768 G//S-KKS	—	100	200	400	800

KM# 284.1 THALER

Silver **Ruler:** Alexander **Obverse:** Large head right **Obv. Legend:** ALEXANDER • D • G • MARGH: BRAND: D • B • & • S: B: N: **Reverse:** Crowned complex arms with supporters, flags and cannons below **Rev. Legend:** ZEHEN EINE FEINE MARK **Note:** Dav. #A2001.

Date	Mintage	F	VF	XF	Unc
1769 G//S-WK	—	125	250	450	825

KM# 282 THALER

Silver **Ruler:** Alexander **Subject:** Acquisition of Bayreuth **Obverse:** Two facing busts with MDLVII and MDCCLXIX beneath them **Obv. Legend:** GEORG: FRID: & ALEXANDER • MARCH: BRAND: **Obv. Inscription:** BURGGRAVII NORIMBERG:/ SVPERIORIS & INFERIORIS/ PRINCIPATVS • S **Reverse:** Open book on altar with shields at right and left **Rev. Legend:** PROVIDENTIA ET PACTIS. **Rev. Inscription:** IN MEMORIAM CONIVNCTIONIS/ VTRIVSQUE BURGGRAVIATVS/ NORICI/ D XX IAN MDCCLXIX **Note:** Dav. #1999.

Date	Mintage	F	VF	XF	Unc
MDCCLXIX (1769) S//G	—	200	350	650	1,250

KM# 283 THALER

Silver **Ruler:** Alexander **Subject:** Acquisition of Bayreuth **Obverse:** Head right **Obv. Legend:** ALEXANDER • D • G • MARCH: BRAND: D • B • & • S • B • N • **Reverse:** Inscription within circle of ribbon, shields at left and right, eagle above **Rev. Legend:** FELIX CONIUNCTION , M/DCC/LXIX in ribbon **Note:** Dav. #2000.

Date	Mintage	F	VF	XF	Unc
MDCCLXIX (1769) G//S	—	200	350	600	1,100

KM# 284.2 THALER

Silver **Ruler:** Alexander **Obverse:** Small head right **Obv. Legend:** ALEXANDER • D • G • MARCH: BRAND: D • B • & • S • B • N • **Reverse:** Crowned complex arms with supporters, flags and cannons below **Rev. Legend:** ZEHEN EINE FEINE MARK **Note:** Dav. #2001.

Date	Mintage	F	VF	XF	Unc
1771 G//S-WK	—	145	275	475	875

KM# 284.3 THALER

Silver **Ruler:** Alexander **Obverse:** Small head right **Obv. Legend:** ALEXANDER • D: G: MARCH: BR: D: B: & S: B: N: **Reverse:** Crowned complex arms with supporters, flags and cannons below **Rev. Legend:** ZEHEN EINE FEINE MARK **Note:** Dav. #2001A.

Date	Mintage	F	VF	XF	Unc
1771 G//S-WK	—	125	250	450	825

KM# 291 THALER

Silver **Ruler:** Alexander **Obverse:** Head right **Obv. Legend:** ALEXANDER • D: G: MARCH: BRAND: **Reverse:** Rampant lion left with shield **Rev. Legend:** ZEHEN EINE FEINE MARK; in exergue SCHWABACH 1773 **Note:** Dav. #2003.

Date	Mintage	F	VF	XF	Unc
1773 G//WK	—	125	250	450	825

KM# 293 THALER

Silver **Ruler:** Alexander **Obverse:** Armored bust right **Note:** Dav. #2004.

Date	Mintage	F	VF	XF	Unc
1773 G//WK	—	125	250	450	850

KM# 292 THALER

Silver **Ruler:** Alexander **Obverse:** Head right **Obv. Legend:** ALEXANDER • D: G: MARCH: BRAND: **Reverse:** Eagle holding crowned arms **Rev. Legend:** ZEHEN EINE FEINE MARK; in exergue SCHWABACH 1773 **Note:** Dav. #2005.

Date	Mintage	F	VF	XF	Unc
1773 G//WK	—	225	425	775	1,400

KM# 297 THALER

Silver **Ruler:** Alexander **Obverse:** Armored bust right with Order cross below **Obv. Legend:** ALEXANDER • D: G: MARCH: BRAND: **Reverse:** Large fir tree at center, small trees in fenced background **Rev. Legend:** SYLVARVM CVL - TVRAE PRAEMIVM **Note:** Forestry Prize Thaler. Dav. #2009.

Date	Mintage	F	VF	XF	Unc
1774 G	—	650	1,000	1,750	3,000

KM# 294 THALER

Silver **Ruler:** Alexander **Obverse:** Head right **Obv. Legend:** ALEXANDER • D: G: MARCH: BRAND: **Reverse:** Hohenzollern arms, lion at right **Rev. Legend:** ZEHEN EINE FEINE MARK; in exergue SCHWABACH 1774 **Note:** Dav. #2006.

Date	Mintage	F	VF	XF	Unc
1774 G//WK	—	100	200	400	750

KM# 295 THALER

Silver **Ruler:** Alexander **Obverse:** Head right **Reverse:** Lion holds crowned shield of four coats of arms on military trophies **Note:** Dav. #2007.

Date	Mintage	F	VF	XF	Unc
1774 G//WK	—	125	250	475	850

KM# 296 THALER

Silver **Ruler:** Alexander **Obverse:** Armored bust right, Order chain below **Obv. Legend:** ALEXANDER • D: G: MARCH: BRAND: **Reverse:** Lion holding crowned shield of arms, flags and cannons below **Rev. Legend:** ZEHEN EINE FEINE MARK; in exergue SCHWABACH 1774 **Note:** Dav. #2008.

Date	Mintage	F	VF	XF	Unc
1774 G//WK	—	100	200	375	675

KM# 303 THALER

Silver **Ruler:** Alexander **Obverse:** Head right **Reverse:** Crowned quartered arms with eagle supporters **Note:** Dav. #2012.

Date	Mintage	F	VF	XF	Unc
1775 G//S	—	90.00	175	325	550

KM# 300 THALER

Silver **Ruler:** Alexander **Obverse:** Armored bust right with Order cross below **Obv. Legend:** ALEXANDER • D: G: MARCH: BRAND: **Reverse:** Inscription and date **Rev. Inscription:** BELOHNUNG/ WEGEN DES/ FLEISIG GETRIBENEN/ KLEE•BAVES/ 1775 **Note:** Clover Cultivation Prize Thaler. Dav. #2010.

Date	Mintage	F	VF	XF	Unc
1775 G	—	775	1,250	2,000	3,200

KM# 301 THALER

Silver **Ruler:** Alexander **Obverse:** Similar to KM#296 with Order star below bust **Obv. Legend:** ALEXANDER • D: G: MARCH: BRAND: **Reverse:** Crowned quartered arms with eagle supporters **Rev. Legend:** ZEHEN EINE FEINE MARK **Note:** Varieties exist. Dav. #2011.

Date	Mintage	F	VF	XF	Unc
1775 G//S	—	125	225	425	800

KM# 302 THALER

Silver **Ruler:** Alexander **Obverse:** Without Order star below bust **Reverse:** Shield without support **Note:** Varieties exist. Dav. #2013.

Date	Mintage	F	VF	XF	Unc
1775 G//S-WK	—	75.00	145	245	450
1776 G//S-WK	—	75.00	145	245	450

KM# 304.2 THALER

Silver **Ruler:** Alexander **Obverse:** Bust of Alexander right, order in front of shoulder **Obv. Legend:** ALEXANDER • D:G: MARCH: ERAND: **Reverse:** 15 helmeted coats of arms in order chain **Note:** Dav. #2014.

Date	Mintage	VG	F	VF	XF	Unc
1777G	—	80.00	165	300	500	—

KM# 304.1 THALER

Silver **Ruler:** Alexander **Obverse:** Bust right, order below **Obv. Legend:** ALEXANDER • D: G: MARCH: BRAND: **Reverse:** Multiple helmets above many divided shield in Order chain **Rev. Legend:** ZEHEN - EINE FEINE - MARK. **Note:** Dav. #2014.

Date	Mintage	F	VF	XF	Unc
1777 G	—	80.00	165	300	500

KM# 306 THALER

Silver **Ruler:** Alexander **Reverse:** Crowned shield of arms in double Order chain **Note:** Dav. #2015.

Date	Mintage	F	VF	XF	Unc
1778 G//WK	—	125	225	450	1,000

KM# 307 THALER

Silver **Ruler:** Alexander **Obverse:** Armored bust right **Obv. Legend:** ALEXANDER • D • G • MARCH: BRAND: **Reverse:** Crowned quartered arms with eagle supporters, double Order chain below **Note:** Dav. #2016.

Date	Mintage	F	VF	XF	Unc
1778 G//WK	—	90.00	175	325	550

KM# 308 THALER

Silver **Ruler:** Alexander **Obverse:** Armored bust right with Order cross below **Obv. Legend:** ALEXANDER • D: G: MARCH: BRAND: **Reverse:** Crowned arms on war trophies **Rev. Legend:** AD NORMAM CONVENTIONIS; in exergue X • EINE FEINE MARK/SCHWABACH/1776 **Note:** Dav. #2017.

Date	Mintage	F	VF	XF	Unc
1778 G//WK	—	125	250	400	800

KM# 314 THALER

Silver **Ruler:** Alexander **Subject:** Revival of the Order of the Red Eagle **Obverse:** Armored draped bust right **Obv. Legend:** ALEXANDER • D • G • MARCH: BRAND: **Reverse:** Eagle and motto at center of radiant star within crowned circle, Order chain surrounds **Note:** Dav. #2018.

Date	Mintage	F	VF	XF	Unc
1779 G	—	145	275	450	850

KM# 315 THALER

Silver **Ruler:** Alexander **Obverse:** Armored bust right with Order cross below **Obv. Legend:** ALEXANDER • D • G • MARCH • BRAND • **Reverse:** Eagle with arms divides date within two rings of 32 shields **Note:** Dav. #2019.

Date	Mintage	F	VF	XF	Unc
1779 G	—	145	275	450	850

KM# 316 THALER

Silver **Ruler:** Alexander **Obverse:** Armored bust right **Obv. Legend:** ALEXANDER • D: G: MARCH: BRAND: **Reverse:** SCHWABACH and date in exergue **Rev. Legend:** ZEHEN EINE FEINE MARK; SCHWABACH and W 1779 E below **Note:** Dav. #2021.

Date	Mintage	F	VF	XF	Unc
1779 G//WK	—	350	675	1,150	1,650

KM# 317 THALER

Silver **Ruler:** Alexander **Subject:** Peace of Teschen **Obverse:** Inscription in 9 lines **Obv. Inscription:** DOM/ PRO INSTAVRATA/ GERMANIAE PACE/ CHRIST. FRIED. CAROL. / ALEXANDER./ MARCHIO BRANDENBVRG / GRATIARVM MONVMENTVM / FIERI FECIT./ MDCCLXXVIIII. **Reverse:** Standing female with shield below **Rev. Legend:** VIRTVTE ET AEQVITATE PACATA GERMANIA; in exergue TESCHINAE and G. **Note:** Dav. #2022.

Date	Mintage	F	VF	XF	Unc
1779 G	—	325	475	700	1,250

KM# 318 THALER

Silver **Ruler:** Alexander **Subject:** Peace of Teschen **Obverse:** Standing female left of shield and altar **Obv. Legend:** DEO CONSERVATORI PACIS; in exergue GERMANIA VOTI COMPOS /MDCCLXXVIIII/D.XIII. MAY. **Reverse:** Inscription within wreath **Rev. Inscription:** IN MEMORIAM PACIS TESCHINENSIS **Note:** Dav. #2023.

Date	Mintage	F	VF	XF	Unc
1779	—	425	650	1,000	1,250

KM# 326 THALER

Silver **Ruler:** Alexander **Obverse:** Armored bust right **Obv. Legend:** ALEXANDER • D • G • MARCH • BRAND • **Reverse:** Crowned and mantled arms, S below, date at sides **Rev. Legend:** ZEHEN EINE FEINE MARK **Note:** Dav. #2024.

Date	Mintage	F	VF	XF	Unc
1780 G//S-WK	—	125	250	450	800

KM# 329 THALER

Silver **Ruler:** Alexander **Obverse:** Head right with G below **Obv. Legend:** ALEXANDER • D • G • MARCH • BRAND • **Reverse:** Arms within crowned mantle **Rev. Legend:** ZEHEN EINE FEINE MARK **Note:** Dav. #2026.

Date	Mintage	F	VF	XF	Unc
1784 G//S-WK	—	175	300	500	1,200

KM# 332 THALER

Silver **Ruler:** Alexander **Obverse:** Larger head with G below **Obv. Legend:** ALEXANDER • D • G • MARCH • BRAND • **Reverse:** Arms within crowned mantle **Rev. Legend:** ZEHEN EINE - FEINE • MARK **Note:** Dav. #2027.

Date	Mintage	F	VF	XF	Unc
1785 G//S-WK	—	225	350	650	1,300

TRADE COINAGE

KM# 187 1/2 CAROLIN

4.8500 g., 0.7700 Gold 0.1201 oz. AGW **Ruler:** Karl Wilhelm Friedrich under Regency of his mother Christine Charlotte until 1729 **Obverse:** Armored bust right **Obv. Legend:** CAR • WILH • - FRID • M • B • D • P • **Reverse:** Crowned arms **Rev. Legend:** SALVS PVBLICA - SALVS MEA •

Date	Mintage	F	VF	XF	Unc
1734	—	400	1,000	1,650	2,650
1735	—	400	1,000	1,650	2,650

KM# 188 CAROLIN

9.7000 g., 0.7700 Gold 0.2401 oz. AGW **Ruler:** Karl Wilhelm Friedrich under Regency of his mother Christine Charlotte until 1729 **Obverse:** Armored bust right **Obv. Legend:** CAR • WILH • - FRID • M • B • D • P • **Reverse:** Crowned arms within Order chain, date divided below **Rev. Legend:** SALVS PVBLICA - SALVS MEA •

Date	Mintage	F	VF	XF	Unc
1734	—	500	1,250	2,150	3,250
1735	—	500	1,250	2,150	3,250

KM# 276 CAROLIN

9.7000 g., 0.7700 Gold 0.2401 oz. AGW **Ruler:** Alexander **Obverse:** Bust right

Date	Mintage	F	VF	XF	Unc
1766	—	450	1,000	2,000	3,000

KM# 144 1/4 DUCAT

0.8750 g., 0.9860 Gold 0.0277 oz. AGW **Ruler:** Wilhelm Friedrich **Obverse:** Bust right **Reverse:** Two crowned shields of arms

Date	Mintage	VG	F	VF	XF	Unc
1717	—	150	300	600	900	—
1718	—	150	300	600	900	—

KM# 143 DUCAT

3.5000 g., 0.9860 Gold 0.1109 oz. AGW **Ruler:** Wilhelm Friedrich **Obverse:** Armored bust right **Reverse:** Crowned complex arms

Date	Mintage	VG	F	VF	XF	Unc
1715	—	350	700	1,350	2,150	—

KM# 145 DUCAT

3.5000 g., 0.9860 Gold 0.1109 oz. AGW **Ruler:** Wilhelm Friedrich **Obverse:** Bust right **Reverse:** Two crowned and mantled oval arms, date divided above

Date	Mintage	VG	F	VF	XF	Unc
1718	—	—	1,500	2,350	3,500	—

KM# 152 DUCAT

3.5000 g., 0.9860 Gold 0.1109 oz. AGW **Ruler:** Karl Wilhelm Friedrich under Regency of his mother Christine Charlotte until 1729 **Subject:** Death of Wilhelm Friedrich **Obverse:** Bust right **Reverse:** Eight-line inscription with date

Date	Mintage	VG	F	VF	XF	Unc
1723	—	—	—	—	—	—

KM# 157 DUCAT

3.5000 g., 0.9860 Gold 0.1109 oz. AGW **Ruler:** Karl Wilhelm Friedrich under Regency of his mother Christine Charlotte until 1729 **Obverse:** Bust of Christine Charlotte left **Obv. Legend:** CHRIST: CAR: TVTRIX: REG: BR: ON: **Reverse:** Crowned monogram above date **Rev. Legend:** GLORIA • DEI - CVRA • MEA •

Date	Mintage	VG	F	VF	XF	Unc
1726	—	300	650	1,250	2,000	—

KM# 169 DUCAT

3.5000 g., 0.9860 Gold 0.1109 oz. AGW **Ruler:** Karl Wilhelm Friedrich under Regency of his mother Christine Charlotte until 1729 **Obverse:** Bust right **Reverse:** Displayed eagle with arms on breast

Date	Mintage	VG	F	VF	XF	Unc
1729	—	300	650	1,250	2,000	—

KM# 179 DUCAT

3.5000 g., 0.9860 Gold 0.1109 oz. AGW **Ruler:** Karl Wilhelm Friedrich under Regency of his mother Christine Charlotte until 1729 **Subject:** 200th Anniversary of Augsburg Confession **Obverse:** Bust right **Reverse:** Confession on altar, date

Date	Mintage	VG	F	VF	XF	Unc
1730 Rare	—	—	—	—	—	—

KM# 189 DUCAT

3.5000 g., 0.9860 Gold 0.1109 oz. AGW **Ruler:** Karl Wilhelm Friedrich under Regency of his mother Christine Charlotte until 1729 **Obverse:** Bust right **Reverse:** Crowned manifold arms, date

Date	Mintage	VG	F	VF	XF	Unc
1734	—	350	750	1,500	2,750	—

KM# 200 DUCAT

3.5000 g., 0.9860 Gold 0.1109 oz. AGW **Ruler:** Karl Wilhelm Friedrich under Regency of his mother Christine Charlotte until 1729 **Reverse:** Two crowned shields of arms

Date	Mintage	VG	F	VF	XF	Unc
1740	—	250	650	1,250	2,000	—
1747	—	250	650	1,250	2,000	—
1750	—	250	650	1,250	2,000	—

KM# 201 DUCAT

3.5000 g., 0.9860 Gold 0.1109 oz. AGW **Ruler:** Karl Wilhelm Friedrich under Regency of his mother Christine Charlotte until 1729 **Reverse:** Eagle holding shield of arms

Date	Mintage	VG	F	VF	XF	Unc
1744	—	250	650	1,250	2,000	—

KM# 219 DUCAT

3.5000 g., 0.9860 Gold 0.1109 oz. AGW **Ruler:** Karl Wilhelm Friedrich under Regency of his mother Christine Charlotte until 1729 **Obverse:** Armored bust right **Obv. Legend:** FRIEDR. WILHELM II KOENIG VON PREUSSEN **Reverse:** Eagle above arms **Rev. Legend:** ZEHN EINE FEINE MARK

Date	Mintage	VG	F	VF	XF	Unc
1753	—	350	900	1,800	3,000	—

KM# 220 DUCAT

3.5000 g., 0.9860 Gold 0.1109 oz. AGW **Obverse:** Hunting scene with horseman, attacking falcon above **Reverse:** Hooded falcon in landscape with dove flying above

Date	Mintage	VG	F	VF	XF	Unc
ND	—	300	800	1,600	2,800	—

KM# 227 DUCAT

3.5000 g., 0.9860 Gold 0.1109 oz. AGW **Ruler:** Karl Wilhelm Friedrich under Regency of his mother Christine Charlotte until 1729 **Subject:** Wedding of Alexander **Obverse:** Two shields of arms **Reverse:** Four-line inscription

Date	Mintage	VG	F	VF	XF	Unc
1754	—	100	300	600	900	—

KM# 242 DUCAT

3.5000 g., 0.9860 Gold 0.1109 oz. AGW **Ruler:** Alexander **Obverse:** Armored bust right **Reverse:** Brandenburg eagle in arms

Date	Mintage	VG	F	VF	XF	Unc
1757	—	250	400	900	1,650	—

KM# 256 DUCAT

3.5000 g., 0.9860 Gold 0.1109 oz. AGW **Ruler:** Alexander **Obverse:** Armored bust right **Reverse:** Arms

Date	Mintage	F	VF	XF	Unc
1762	—	350	800	1,500	2,500

KM# 260 DUCAT

3.5000 g., 0.9860 Gold 0.1109 oz. AGW **Ruler:** Alexander **Obverse:** Armored bust right **Reverse:** Three shields of arms within cartouche

Date	Mintage	F	VF	XF	Unc
1763 S	—	350	800	1,500	2,500

KM# 271 DUCAT

3.5000 g., 0.9860 Gold 0.1109 oz. AGW **Ruler:** Alexander **Obverse:** Margrave on horseback left **Reverse:** Eagle with lion shield

Date	Mintage	F	VF	XF	Unc
1765	—	500	1,250	2,250	3,250

KM# 285 DUCAT

3.5000 g., 0.9860 Gold 0.1109 oz. AGW **Ruler:** Alexander **Subject:** Acquisition of Bayreuth **Obverse:** Head right **Reverse:** Date within ribbon, shields at right and left, eagle above

Date	Mintage	F	VF	XF	Unc
1769 G//S	—	500	1,250	2,250	3,250

KM# 286 DUCAT

3.5000 g., 0.9860 Gold 0.1109 oz. AGW **Subject:** Acquisition of Bayreuth **Obverse:** Facing busts of Georg Friedrich and Alexander **Reverse:** Altar with book on top and crowned shield on each side

Date	Mintage	F	VF	XF	Unc
1769	—	350	800	1,750	2,750

KM# 287 DUCAT

3.5000 g., 0.9860 Gold 0.1109 oz. AGW **Ruler:** Alexander **Obverse:** Armored figure right of altar **Reverse:** Inscription

Date	Mintage	F	VF	XF	Unc
1769	—	250	650	1,250	2,250

KM# 305 DUCAT

3.5000 g., 0.9860 Gold 0.1109 oz. AGW **Ruler:** Alexander **Obverse:** Bust right **Reverse:** Crown above three shields of arms, value below, date at sides

Date	Mintage	F	VF	XF	Unc
1777	—	450	900	2,000	3,000

KM# 319 DUCAT

3.5000 g., 0.9860 Gold 0.1109 oz. AGW **Ruler:** Alexander **Subject:** Revival of the Order of the Red Eagle **Reverse:** Crowned Order star in collar of the Order, date below

Date	Mintage	F	VF	XF	Unc
1779 G	—	600	1,250	2,250	3,000

KM# 153 2 DUCAT

7.0000 g., 0.9860 Gold 0.2219 oz. AGW **Ruler:** Karl Wilhelm Friedrich under Regency of his mother Christine Charlotte until 1729 **Subject:** Death of Wilhelm Friedrich **Obverse:** Bust right **Reverse:** Eight-line inscription with date

Date	Mintage	VG	F	VF	XF	Unc
1723	—	—	525	800	1,350	—

KM# 170.1 2 DUCAT

7.0000 g., 0.9860 Gold 0.2219 oz. AGW **Ruler:** Karl Wilhelm Friedrich under Regency of his mother Christine Charlotte until 1729 **Obverse:** Bust right **Reverse:** Displayed eagle with arms on breast

Date	Mintage	VG	F	VF	XF	Unc
1729	—	500	1,000	2,000	3,250	—

KM# 170.2 2 DUCAT

7.0000 g., 0.9860 Gold 0.2219 oz. AGW **Ruler:** Karl Wilhelm Friedrich under Regency of his mother Christine Charlotte until 1729 **Obverse:** Armored bust right **Reverse:** Eagle with arms on breast **Note:** Double thick flan.

Date	Mintage	VG	F	VF	XF	Unc
1729	—	500	1,000	2,000	3,250	—

KM# 185 2 DUCAT

7.0000 g., 0.9860 Gold 0.2219 oz. AGW **Ruler:** Karl Wilhelm Friedrich under Regency of his mother Christine Charlotte until 1729 **Subject:** Passage of Salzburg Emigrants **Obverse:** Bust right **Reverse:** Three-line inscription between branches, SALIZB. EMIGR/ date below

Date	Mintage	VG	F	VF	XF	Unc
1732 Rare	—	—	—	—	—	—

KM# 197 2 DUCAT

7.0000 g., 0.9860 Gold 0.2219 oz. AGW **Ruler:** Karl Wilhelm Friedrich under Regency of his mother Christine Charlotte until 1729 **Obverse:** Bust right **Reverse:** Open book, ORA LABORA SPERA, date around

Date	Mintage	VG	F	VF	XF	Unc
1737 Rare	—	—	—	—	—	—

KM# 228 2 DUCAT

7.0000 g., 0.9860 Gold 0.2219 oz. AGW **Ruler:** Karl Wilhelm Friedrich under Regency of his mother Christine Charlotte until 1729 **Subject:** Wedding of Alexander **Obverse:** Cherubs above two shielded arms **Reverse:** Inscription with date below

Date	Mintage	VG	F	VF	XF	Unc
1754	—	400	850	1,800	2,850	—

KM# A179 4 DUCAT

14.0000 g., 0.9860 Gold 0.4438 oz. AGW **Ruler:** Karl Wilhelm Friedrich under Regency of his mother Christine Charlotte until 1729 **Obverse:** Bust left **Reverse:** Crowned and mantled arms **Note:** Similar to 1 Thaler, KM#168.

Date	Mintage	VG	F	VF	XF	Unc
1729 Rare	—	—	—	—	—	—

KM# A180 4 DUCAT

14.0000 g., 0.9860 Gold 0.4438 oz. AGW **Ruler:** Karl Wilhelm Friedrich under Regency of his mother Christine Charlotte until 1729 **Obverse:** Bust right **Reverse:** Confession on altar, date **Note:** Similar to 1 Ducat, KM#179.

Date	Mintage	VG	F	VF	XF	Unc
1730 Rare	—	—	—	—	—	—

KM# B179 6 DUCAT

21.0000 g., 0.9860 Gold 0.6657 oz. AGW **Ruler:** Karl Wilhelm Friedrich under Regency of his mother Christine Charlotte until 1729

Date	Mintage	VG	F	VF	XF	Unc
1729 Rare	—	—	—	—	—	—

KM# B180 10 DUCAT (Portugalöser)

35.0000 g., 0.9860 Gold 1.1095 oz. AGW **Subject:** 200th Anniversary of Augsburg Confession **Note:** Struck with 1 Thaler dies, KM#176.

Date	Mintage	VG	F	VF	XF	Unc
1730 V Rare	—	—	—	—	—	—

KM# C179 12 DUCAT

42.0000 g., 0.9860 Gold 1.3314 oz. AGW **Note:** Struck with 1 Thaler dies, KM#168.

Date	Mintage	VG	F	VF	XF	Unc
1729 Rare	—	—	—	—	—	—

PATTERNS

Including off metal strikes

KM#	Date	Mintage	Identification	Mkt Val
Pn2	1717	—	Kreuzer. Gold. . KM#136	450
Pn3	1723	—	6 Kreuzer. Copper. . KM#202	—
Pn4	1723	—	Ducat. Silver. . KM#152	125
Pn5	1723	—	2 Ducat. Silver. . KM#153	150
Pn6	1730	—	Ducat. Silver. . KM#179	125
Pn7	1732	—	2 Ducat. Silver. . KM#185	225
Pn8	1736	—	1/4 Thaler. Gold. . KM#193	—
Pn9	1737	—	2 Ducat. Silver. . KM#197	125

BRANDENBURG-ANSBACH-BAYREUTH

Held by Prussia from 1791 to 1805 and then given to Bavaria.

RULERS

Friedrich Wilhelm II of Prussia, 1791-1797
Friedrich Wilhelm III of Prussia, 1797-1805

MARGRAVIATE

REGULAR COINAGE

KM# 5 PFENNIG

0.2000 g., 0.1180 Silver 0.0008 oz. ASW **Ruler:** Friedrich Wilhelm II of Prussia **Obverse:** Crowned Prussian eagle **Reverse:** Crown above monogram divides date

Date	Mintage	VG	F	VF	XF	Unc
1792S	—	3.00	7.00	10.00	20.00	—
1793S	—	3.00	7.00	10.00	20.00	—
1794S	—	3.00	7.00	10.00	20.00	—
1795S	—	3.00	7.00	10.00	20.00	—
1796B	—	3.00	7.00	10.00	20.00	—

KM# 12 PFENNIG

0.2600 g., 0.1110 Silver 0.0009 oz. ASW **Ruler:** Friedrich Wilhelm II of Prussia **Obverse:** Crown above monogram divides date **Reverse:** Value

Date	Mintage	VG	F	VF	XF	Unc
1796B	—	3.00	5.00	7.00	15.00	—
1797B	—	3.00	5.00	7.00	15.00	—

KM# 17 PFENNIG

0.2600 g., 0.1110 Silver 0.0009 oz. ASW **Ruler:** Friedrich Wilhelm III of Prussia **Obverse:** Crowned FWR monogram **Reverse:** Denomination

Date	Mintage	F	VF	XF	Unc
1799B	534,000	12.00	25.00	55.00	120
1801B	616,000	12.00	25.00	55.00	150
1803B	984,000	15.00	30.00	65.00	150

KM# 6 KREUZER

0.7600 g., 0.1630 Silver 0.0040 oz. ASW **Ruler:** Friedrich Wilhelm II of Prussia **Obverse:** Crowned eagle with monogram on breast **Reverse:** Value and date within cartouche

Date	Mintage	VG	F	VF	XF	Unc
1792S	—	3.00	5.00	7.00	15.00	—
1793S	—	3.00	5.00	7.00	15.00	—
1794S	—	3.00	5.00	7.00	15.00	—
1796B	—	3.00	5.00	7.00	15.00	—
1797B	—	3.00	5.00	7.00	15.00	—

KM# 14 KREUZER

0.7600 g., 0.1630 Silver 0.0040 oz. ASW **Ruler:** Friedrich Wilhelm III of Prussia **Obverse:** Crowned Prussian eagle **Reverse:** Value and date within cartouche

Date	Mintage	F	VF	XF	Unc
1798B	310,000	4.00	8.00	22.00	60.00
1799B	415,000	4.00	8.00	22.00	60.00
1800B	533,000	4.00	8.00	22.00	60.00

KM# 10 3 KREUZER

1.1300 g., 0.3430 Silver 0.0125 oz. ASW **Ruler:** Friedrich Wilhelm II of Prussia **Obverse:** Crowned Prussian eagle above date **Reverse:** Value

Date	Mintage	VG	F	VF	XF	Unc
1794S	—	3.00	7.00	15.00	30.00	—
1795S	—	3.00	7.00	15.00	30.00	—

KM# 10a 3 KREUZER

1.0500 g., 0.3360 Silver 0.0113 oz. ASW **Ruler:** Friedrich Wilhelm II of Prussia **Obverse:** Crowned Prussian eagle **Reverse:** Value **Note:** Varieties exist.

Date	Mintage	VG	F	VF	XF	Unc
1796B	—	3.00	7.00	15.00	30.00	—
1797B	—	3.00	7.00	15.00	30.00	—

KM# 15 3 KREUZER

1.0500 g., 0.3360 Silver 0.0113 oz. ASW **Ruler:** Friedrich Wilhelm III of Prussia **Obverse:** Crowned Prussian eagle **Reverse:** Value above spray

Date	Mintage	F	VF	XF	Unc
1798B	559,000	9.00	22.00	40.00	125
1799B	1,114,000	8.00	20.00	32.00	115
1800B	1,076,000	8.00	20.00	32.00	115
1801B	1,335,000	8.00	20.00	32.00	115
1802B	1,330,000	5.00	18.00	30.00	110

KM# 13 6 KREUZER

2.4400 g., 0.3750 Silver 0.0294 oz. ASW **Obverse:** Crowned Prussian eagle within oval, branches surround **Reverse:** Value and date

Date	Mintage	VG	F	VF	XF	Unc
1797B	—	5.00	10.00	15.00	40.00	—

KM# 16 6 KREUZER

2.4400 g., 0.3750 Silver 0.0294 oz. ASW **Ruler:** Friedrich Wilhelm III of Prussia **Obverse:** Crowned Prussian eagle within oval, wreath surrounds **Reverse:** Value

Date	Mintage	F	VF	XF	Unc
1798B	759,000	15.00	35.00	55.00	95.00
1799B	537,000	15.00	35.00	55.00	95.00
1800B	383,000	20.00	40.00	65.00	110
1801B	340,000	20.00	40.00	65.00	110
1802B	249,000	20.00	40.00	80.00	125

KM# 7 GULDEN

14.8500 g., 0.7500 Silver 0.3581 oz. ASW **Ruler:** Friedrich Wilhelm II of Prussia **Obverse:** Large bust right **Obv. Legend:** FRIED • WILHELM KOENIG VON PREUSSEN **Reverse:** Short and stocky eagle in arms with supporters

Date	Mintage	VG	F	VF	XF	Unc
1792S	—	40.00	60.00	100	250	—
1794S	—	40.00	60.00	100	250	—

KM# 8 GULDEN

14.8500 g., 0.7500 Silver 0.3581 oz. ASW **Ruler:** Friedrich Wilhelm II of Prussia **Obverse:** Smaller bust **Obv. Legend:** FRIED • WILHELM • KOENIG VON • PREUSSEN • **Reverse:** Eagle in arms is tall and thin

Date	Mintage	VG	F	VF	XF	Unc
1792S	—	40.00	60.00	100	250	—

KM# 9 GULDEN

14.8500 g., 0.7500 Silver 0.3581 oz. ASW **Ruler:** Friedrich Wilhelm II of Prussia **Obverse:** Medium bust

Date	Mintage	VG	F	VF	XF	Unc
1792S	—	40.00	60.00	100	250	—

KM# 11 THALER

28.0600 g., 0.8330 Silver 0.7515 oz. ASW **Ruler:** Friedrich Wilhelm II of Prussia **Obverse:** Armored bust right with Order cross below **Obv. Legend:** FRIEDR. WILHELM II KOENIG VON PREUSSEN **Reverse:** Crowned arms within branches **Rev. Legend:** ZEHN EINE FEINE MARK **Note:** Convention Thaler. Dav. #2600.

Date	Mintage	VG	F	VF	XF	Unc
1794	—	100	150	300	500	—
1795	—	100	150	300	500	—
1796	—	100	150	300	500	—

BRANDENBURG-BAYREUTH

Located in northern Bavaria. Became the property of the first Hohenzollern Elector of Brandenburg, Friedrich I. Bayreuth, passed to several individuals and became extinct in 1769 with the lands passing to Ansbach.

RULERS

Christian Ernst, 1655-1712
Georg Wilhelm, 1712-1726
Georg Friedrich Karl, 1726-1735
Friedrich, 1735-1763
Friedrich Christian, 1763-69
Christian Friedrich Karl Alexander, 1769-1791

MINT MARKS
B - Bayersdorf
(b) - Bayreuth
C,(c), (cu) - heart, (K) - Kulmbach
(cr) urn - Creussen
(d) bee - Dachsbach
(e) half-moon - Erlangen
F - Furth

MINT OFFICIALS' INITIALS

Initials	Date	Name
CLR	1742-68	Christoph Lorenz Ruckdeschel
ES	1765-66	Eberhard & Schmiedhammer
G	1750-95	Johann Samuel Gotzinger (Ansbach)
GFN	1682-1724	Georg Friedrich Nurnberger, die-cutter and mintmaster in Nüremberg
GFN	1682-1710	Georg Friedrich Nurnberger, mintmaster of the Franconian Circle
H, IAH	-1776	Johann Adam Hanf, die-cutter in Bayreuth
HZ		Unknown
IAP		Unknown
ICE		Unknown
ILR, LR	1726-40	Johann Lorenz Ruckdeschel
OEXLEIN	1740-87	Johann Leonhard Oexlein, die-cutter in Nurnberg
PPW	-1771	Peter Paul Werner, die-cutter in Nurnberg
RE	1766-68	Ruckdeschel & Eberhard
SK		Unknown

DUCHY
Margraviate
REGULAR COINAGE

KM# 109 HELLER
Copper **Obverse:** Crowned oval Hohenzollern arms in baroque frame **Reverse:** 1/HEL/LER/date

Date	Mintage	VG	F	VF	XF	Unc
1698	—	7.00	12.00	25.00	45.00	—
1699	—	7.00	12.00	25.00	45.00	—
1700	—	7.00	12.00	25.00	45.00	—
1701	—	7.00	12.00	25.00	45.00	—
1702	—	7.00	12.00	25.00	45.00	—
1703	—	7.00	12.00	25.00	45.00	—
1704	—	7.00	12.00	25.00	45.00	—
1705	—	7.00	12.00	25.00	45.00	—
1706	—	7.00	12.00	25.00	45.00	—
1707	—	7.00	12.00	25.00	45.00	—
1710	—	7.00	12.00	25.00	45.00	—
1711	—	7.00	12.00	25.00	45.00	—
1712	—	7.00	12.00	25.00	45.00	—
ND	—	7.00	12.00	25.00	45.00	—

KM# 120 HELLER
Copper **Ruler:** George Wilhelm **Obverse:** Crowned Hohenzollern arms

Date	Mintage	VG	F	VF	XF	Unc
1712	—	8.00	15.00	30.00	55.00	—
1716	—	8.00	15.00	30.00	55.00	—

KM# 144 HELLER
Copper **Ruler:** George Wilhelm **Obverse:** Crowned GW monogram **Reverse:** Value

Date	Mintage	VG	F	VF	XF	Unc
1722	—	6.00	10.00	16.00	30.00	—
1723	—	6.00	10.00	16.00	30.00	—
1724	—	6.00	10.00	16.00	30.00	—

KM# 170 HELLER
Copper **Ruler:** Georg Friedrich Karl **Obverse:** Crowned GFC monogram between two palm branches **Reverse:** 1/BAYREV/THER/HELLER/date

Date	Mintage	VG	F	VF	XF	Unc
1730	—	20.00	40.00	65.00	95.00	—

KM# 184 HELLER
Copper **Ruler:** Friedrich **Obverse:** Crowned F monogram with star **Reverse:** Value and date

Date	Mintage	VG	F	VF	XF	Unc
1738	—	4.00	8.00	15.00	30.00	—
1739	—	4.00	8.00	15.00	30.00	—
1740	—	4.00	8.00	15.00	30.00	—
1742	—	4.00	8.00	15.00	30.00	—
1743	—	4.00	8.00	15.00	30.00	—
1744	—	4.00	8.00	15.00	30.00	—
1745	—	4.00	8.00	15.00	30.00	—

KM# 205 HELLER
Copper **Ruler:** Friedrich **Obverse:** Crowned F monogram with star **Reverse:** Value and date **Note:** Exists without star on reverse.

Date	Mintage	VG	F	VF	XF	Unc
1749	—	4.00	8.00	15.00	30.00	—
1750	—	4.00	8.00	15.00	30.00	—
1751	—	4.00	8.00	15.00	30.00	—
1752	—	4.00	8.00	15.00	30.00	—
1753	—	4.00	8.00	15.00	30.00	—
1755	—	4.00	8.00	15.00	30.00	—
1758	—	4.00	8.00	15.00	30.00	—

KM# 253 HELLER
Copper **Ruler:** Frederich Christian **Obverse:** FC script monogram **Reverse:** Three-line value and date

Date	Mintage	VG	F	VF	XF	Unc
1767	—	3.00	5.00	7.00	20.00	—

KM# 254 HELLER
Copper **Ruler:** Frederich Christian **Obverse:** Crowned FC monogram **Reverse:** Value and date

Date	Mintage	VG	F	VF	XF	Unc
1767	—	5.00	8.00	15.00	30.00	—

KM# 122 PFENNIG
Billon **Obverse:** Crowned two oval arms in baroque frame **Reverse:** Crowned eagle divides date

Date	Mintage	VG	F	VF	XF	Unc
1704	—	5.00	10.00	20.00	35.00	—
1712	—	5.00	10.00	20.00	35.00	—
1713	—	5.00	10.00	20.00	35.00	—
1714	—	5.00	10.00	20.00	35.00	—
1715	—	5.00	10.00	20.00	35.00	—
1716	—	5.00	10.00	20.00	35.00	—
1717	—	5.00	10.00	20.00	35.00	—
1718	—	5.00	10.00	20.00	35.00	—
1719	—	5.00	10.00	20.00	35.00	—
1720	—	5.00	10.00	20.00	35.00	—
1721	—	5.00	10.00	20.00	35.00	—
1722	—	5.00	10.00	20.00	35.00	—
1723	—	5.00	10.00	20.00	35.00	—
1724	—	5.00	10.00	20.00	35.00	—
1725	—	5.00	10.00	20.00	35.00	—
1726	—	5.00	10.00	20.00	35.00	—

KM# 161 PFENNIG
Billon **Ruler:** Georg Friedrich Karl **Obverse:** Crowned two oval arms in baroque frame **Reverse:** Crowned eagle divides date **Note:** Similar to KM#122.

Date	Mintage	VG	F	VF	XF	Unc
1727 ILR	—	4.00	8.00	16.00	32.00	—
1728 ILR	—	4.00	8.00	16.00	32.00	—
1729 ILR	—	4.00	8.00	16.00	32.00	—
1730 ILR	—	4.00	8.00	16.00	32.00	—
1731 ILR	—	4.00	8.00	16.00	32.00	—
1732 ILR	—	4.00	8.00	16.00	32.00	—
1733 ILR	—	4.00	8.00	16.00	32.00	—
1734 ILR	—	4.00	8.00	16.00	32.00	—
1735 ILR	—	4.00	8.00	16.00	32.00	—

KM# 180 PFENNIG
Billon **Ruler:** Friedrich **Obverse:** Two oval arms in crowned baroque frame **Reverse:** Orb with value divides date

Date	Mintage	VG	F	VF	XF	Unc
1735 ILR	—	3.50	7.00	14.00	30.00	—
1736 ILR	—	3.50	7.00	14.00	30.00	—
1737 ILR	—	3.50	7.00	14.00	30.00	—
1738 ILR	—	3.50	7.00	14.00	30.00	—
1739 ILR	—	3.50	7.00	14.00	30.00	—
1740 ILR	—	3.50	7.00	14.00	30.00	—
1741	—	3.50	7.00	14.00	30.00	—
1742 CLR	—	3.50	7.00	14.00	30.00	—
1743 CLR	—	3.50	7.00	14.00	30.00	—
1744 CLR	—	3.50	7.00	14.00	30.00	—
1745 CLR	—	3.50	7.00	14.00	30.00	—
1746 CLR	—	3.50	7.00	14.00	30.00	—
1747 CLR	—	3.50	7.00	14.00	30.00	—
1748 CLR	—	3.50	7.00	14.00	30.00	—
1749 CLR	—	3.50	7.00	14.00	30.00	—
1750 CLR	—	3.50	7.00	14.00	30.00	—

KM# 198 PFENNIG
Billon **Ruler:** Friedrich **Note:** Uniface.

Date	Mintage	VG	F	VF	XF	Unc
1747	—	3.00	7.00	14.00	30.00	—
1748	—	3.00	7.00	14.00	30.00	—
1749	—	3.00	7.00	14.00	30.00	—
1750	—	3.00	7.00	14.00	30.00	—
1751	—	3.00	7.00	14.00	30.00	—
1752	—	3.00	7.00	14.00	30.00	—
1753	—	3.00	7.00	14.00	30.00	—
1754	—	3.00	7.00	14.00	30.00	—

KM# 206 PFENNIG
Billon **Ruler:** Friedrich **Obverse:** Crowned eagle divides date **Reverse:** Crowned and mantled arms above value

Date	Mintage	VG	F	VF	XF	Unc
1751 CLR	—	8.00	14.00	20.00	40.00	—
1752 CLR	—	8.00	14.00	20.00	40.00	—
1753 CLR	—	8.00	14.00	20.00	40.00	—
1758 CLR	—	8.00	14.00	20.00	40.00	—
1759 CLR	—	8.00	14.00	20.00	40.00	—
1763 CLR	—	8.00	14.00	20.00	40.00	—

KM# 230 PFENNIG
Billon **Ruler:** Frederich Christian **Obverse:** Two shields and date **Note:** Uniface

Date	Mintage	VG	F	VF	XF	Unc
1763	—	3.00	7.00	14.00	30.00	—
1764	—	3.00	7.00	14.00	30.00	—
1765	—	3.00	7.00	14.00	30.00	—
1766	—	3.00	7.00	14.00	30.00	—
1767	—	3.00	7.00	14.00	30.00	—

KM# 244 PFENNIG
Billon **Ruler:** Frederich Christian **Obverse:** Crowned eagle **Reverse:** Crowned and mantled arms

Date	Mintage	VG	F	VF	XF	Unc
1764	—	3.00	7.00	14.00	30.00	—

KM# 265 PFENNIG
Billon **Ruler:** Alexander **Obverse:** Hohenzollern arms **Reverse:** Value with B and date below

Date	Mintage	VG	F	VF	XF	Unc
1780	—	3.00	7.00	14.00	30.00	—
1781	—	3.00	7.00	14.00	30.00	—
1782	—	3.00	7.00	14.00	30.00	—
1783	—	3.00	7.00	14.00	30.00	—

KM# 207 2 PFENNIG
Billon **Ruler:** Friedrich **Obverse:** Crowned eagle **Reverse:** Value and date

Date	Mintage	VG	F	VF	XF	Unc
1751 CLR	—	3.00	7.00	14.00	30.00	—
1752 CLR	—	3.00	7.00	14.00	30.00	—

KM# 171 3 PFENNIG (Dreier)
Silver **Ruler:** Georg Friedrich Karl **Obverse:** Crowned eagle divides date **Reverse:** Crowned and mantled Hohenzollern arms, value 3 below

Date	Mintage	VG	F	VF	XF	Unc
1732 ILR	—	8.00	15.00	30.00	65.00	—

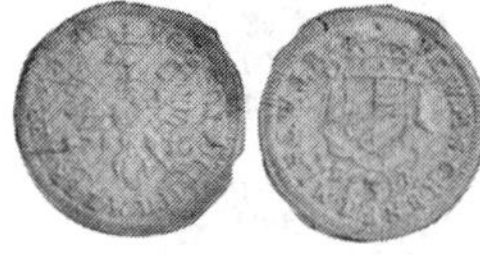

KM# 181 3 PFENNIG (Dreier)
Billon **Ruler:** Friedrich **Obverse:** Crowned eagle **Reverse:** Arms

Date	Mintage	VG	F	VF	XF	Unc
1736 ILR	—	5.00	10.00	25.00	50.00	—
1737 ILR	—	5.00	10.00	25.00	50.00	—
1741	—	5.00	10.00	25.00	50.00	—
1749 CLR	—	5.00	10.00	25.00	50.00	—

KM# 191 3 PFENNIG (Dreier)
Billon **Ruler:** Friedrich **Obverse:** Crowned arms **Reverse:** Value: 3 GUTE PFEN..., date

Date	Mintage	VG	F	VF	XF	Unc
1745 CLR	—	5.00	10.00	25.00	50.00	—

KM# 260 4 PFENNIG

Billon **Ruler:** Alexander **Obverse:** Eagle and B **Reverse:** Value and date

Date	Mintage	VG	F	VF	XF	Unc
1778	—	8.00	15.00	30.00	60.00	—
1779	—	8.00	15.00	30.00	60.00	—

KM# 266 4 PFENNIG

Billon **Ruler:** Alexander **Obverse:** Hohenzollern arms **Reverse:** Value with B and date below

Date	Mintage	VG	F	VF	XF	Unc
1780	—	8.00	15.00	30.00	60.00	—

KM# 116 6 PFENNIG

Silver **Ruler:** Christian Ernst **Obverse:** Crowned oval arms between branches divide date **Reverse:** Eagle, value 6 on breast

Date	Mintage	VG	F	VF	XF	Unc
1702 IAP	—	15.00	32.00	65.00	100	—
1703 IAP	—	15.00	32.00	65.00	100	—
1704 IAP	—	15.00	32.00	65.00	100	—

KM# 174 6 PFENNIG

Billon **Obverse:** Crowned eagle **Reverse:** Value and B above sprays

Date	Mintage	VG	F	VF	XF	Unc
ND	—	4.00	8.00	18.00	30.00	—

KM# 208 1/2 KREUZER

Copper **Ruler:** Friedrich **Obverse:** Crowned F monogram, date below **Reverse:** Value above inscription

Date	Mintage	VG	F	VF	XF	Unc
1752	—	7.00	15.00	30.00	60.00	—

KM# 115 KREUZER

Silver **Ruler:** Christian Ernst **Obverse:** Bust right **Obv. Legend:** EINEN CREVZER **Reverse:** Crowned eagle, Hohenzollern arms on breast, date in legend

Date	Mintage	VG	F	VF	XF	Unc
1697	—	12.00	20.00	40.00	80.00	—
1700	—	10.00	18.00	35.00	70.00	—
1701	—	10.00	18.00	35.00	70.00	—
1702 IAP	—	10.00	18.00	35.00	70.00	—
1704 IAP	—	10.00	18.00	35.00	70.00	—
1705 IAP	—	10.00	18.00	35.00	70.00	—
1706 IAP	—	10.00	18.00	35.00	70.00	—
1707 IAP	—	10.00	18.00	35.00	70.00	—
1708 IAP	—	10.00	18.00	35.00	70.00	—
1709 IAP	—	10.00	18.00	35.00	70.00	—
1710 IAP	—	10.00	18.00	35.00	70.00	—

KM# 121 KREUZER

Silver **Ruler:** Christian Ernst **Obverse:** Bust right **Reverse:** Crowned eagle, value 1 on breast, date in legend

Date	Mintage	VG	F	VF	XF	Unc
1711	—	10.00	18.00	35.00	70.00	—
1712	—	10.00	18.00	35.00	70.00	—

KM# 123 KREUZER

Silver **Ruler:** George Wilhelm **Reverse:** Crowned eagle with value on breast

Date	Mintage	VG	F	VF	XF	Unc
1712 IAP	—	10.00	20.00	38.00	75.00	—
1713 IAP	—	10.00	20.00	38.00	75.00	—
1714 IAP	—	10.00	20.00	38.00	75.00	—
1715 IAP	—	10.00	20.00	38.00	75.00	—
1716 IAP	—	10.00	20.00	38.00	75.00	—
1717 IAP	—	10.00	20.00	38.00	75.00	—
1718 IAP	—	10.00	20.00	38.00	75.00	—
1719 IAP	—	10.00	20.00	38.00	75.00	—
1720 IAP	—	10.00	20.00	38.00	75.00	—
1721 IAP	—	10.00	20.00	38.00	75.00	—
1722 IAP	—	10.00	20.00	38.00	75.00	—
1723 IAP	—	10.00	20.00	38.00	75.00	—
1724 IAP	—	10.00	20.00	38.00	75.00	—

KM# 172 KREUZER

Silver **Ruler:** Georg Friedrich Karl **Obverse:** Crowned eagle divides date **Reverse:** Crowned and mantled Hohenzollern arms, value below

Date	Mintage	VG	F	VF	XF	Unc
1732 ILR	—	12.00	25.00	45.00	85.00	—

KM# 190 KREUZER

Billon **Ruler:** Friedrich

Date	Mintage	VG	F	VF	XF	Unc
1741	—	4.00	8.00	15.00	30.00	—
1742 CLR	—	4.00	8.00	15.00	30.00	—
1743 CLR	—	4.00	8.00	15.00	30.00	—
1744 CLR	—	4.00	8.00	15.00	30.00	—

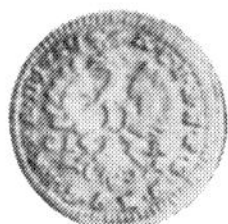

KM# 192 KREUZER

Billon **Ruler:** Friedrich **Obverse:** Armored bust right **Reverse:** Crowned eagle with value on breast

Date	Mintage	VG	F	VF	XF	Unc
1745 CLR	—	3.00	6.00	12.00	25.00	—
1746 CLR	—	3.00	6.00	12.00	25.00	—
1747 CLR	—	3.50	7.00	14.00	30.00	—
1748 CLR	—	3.50	7.00	14.00	30.00	—
1749 CLR	—	3.50	7.00	14.00	30.00	—
1750 CLR	—	3.50	7.00	14.00	30.00	—
1751 CLR	—	3.00	6.00	12.00	25.00	—
1752 CLR	—	3.00	6.00	12.00	25.00	—
1753 CLR	—	3.00	6.00	12.00	25.00	—

KM# 194 KREUZER

Billon **Ruler:** Friedrich **Obverse:** Arms **Reverse:** 1 in imperial orb, date

Date	Mintage	VG	F	VF	XF	Unc
1746 CLR	—	4.00	8.00	15.00	30.00	—

KM# 209 KREUZER

Copper **Ruler:** Friedrich **Obverse:** Crowned F monogram, date below **Reverse:** Value above inscription

Date	Mintage	VG	F	VF	XF	Unc
1752	—	15.00	35.00	75.00	150	—

KM# 228 KREUZER

Copper **Ruler:** Friedrich **Obverse:** Armored bust right **Reverse:** Crowned eagle with value on breast **Note:** Similar to KM#192.

Date	Mintage	VG	F	VF	XF	Unc
1762	—	5.00	10.00	20.00	35.00	—

KM# 245 KREUZER

Billon **Ruler:** Frederich Christian **Obverse:** Bust right **Reverse:** Value on eagle

Date	Mintage	VG	F	VF	XF	Unc
1764	—	5.00	10.00	20.00	40.00	—
1765 CLR	—	5.00	10.00	20.00	40.00	—
1766	—	5.00	10.00	20.00	40.00	—
1767	—	5.00	10.00	20.00	40.00	—

KM# 271 KREUZER

Billon **Ruler:** Alexander **Obverse:** Hohenzollern arms **Reverse:** Value with B and date below

Date	Mintage	VG	F	VF	XF	Unc
1785B	—	5.00	10.00	25.00	50.00	—
1786B	—	5.00	10.00	25.00	50.00	—

KM# 275 KREUZER

Billon **Ruler:** Alexander **Obverse:** Crowned shield **Reverse:** Value and date within cartouche

Date	Mintage	VG	F	VF	XF	Unc
1789S	—	7.00	15.00	30.00	60.00	—

KM# 193 2 KREUZER (1/2 Batzen)

Silver **Ruler:** Friedrich **Obverse:** Bust right **Reverse:** Crowned eagle, value 2 on breast, date in legend

Date	Mintage	VG	F	VF	XF	Unc
1745 CLR	—	7.00	12.00	25.00	45.00	—

KM# 247 2-1/2 KREUZER

Billon **Ruler:** Frederich Christian **Obverse:** FC monogram **Reverse:** Crowned arms **Note:** Convention 2-1/2 Kreuzer.

Date	Mintage	VG	F	VF	XF	Unc
1765	—	5.00	10.00	20.00	40.00	—
1766	—	5.00	10.00	20.00	40.00	—
1767	—	5.00	10.00	20.00	40.00	—
1768	—	5.00	10.00	20.00	40.00	—

KM# 261 2-1/2 KREUZER

Billon **Ruler:** Frederich Christian **Obverse:** Bust right **Reverse:** Eagle

Date	Mintage	VG	F	VF	XF	Unc
1779	—	5.00	10.00	15.00	30.00	—

KM# 267 2-1/2 KREUZER

Billon **Ruler:** Alexander **Obverse:** Arms **Reverse:** Three-line inscription with date below

Date	Mintage	VG	F	VF	XF	Unc
1779	—	3.00	6.00	12.00	20.00	—
1780	—	3.00	6.00	12.00	20.00	—
1781	—	3.00	6.00	12.00	20.00	—
1783	—	3.00	6.00	12.00	20.00	—
1785	—	3.00	6.00	12.00	20.00	—
1786	—	3.00	6.00	12.00	20.00	—

KM# 117 4 KREUZER (Batzen)

Silver **Ruler:** Christian Ernst **Obverse:** Eagle, Hohenzollern arms on breast, tail divides date **Reverse:** Imperial orb with value 4

Date	Mintage	VG	F	VF	XF	Unc
1704 GFN	—	28.00	50.00	80.00	125	—

KM# 229 4 KREUZER (Batzen)

Billon **Ruler:** Friedrich

Date	Mintage	VG	F	VF	XF	Unc
1762	—	—	—	—	—	—
1763	—	10.00	20.00	30.00	40.00	—

KM# 231 4 KREUZER (Batzen)

Billon **Obverse:** Crowned eagle shield on pedestal **Reverse:** Value and date

Date	Mintage	VG	F	VF	XF	Unc
1763	—	5.00	10.00	15.00	30.00	—

KM# 232 5 KREUZER

Billon **Ruler:** Frederich Christian **Note:** Convention 5 Kreuzer.

Date	Mintage	VG	F	VF	XF	Unc
1763	—	6.00	12.00	25.00	50.00	—
1764	—	6.00	12.00	25.00	50.00	—
1765	—	6.00	12.00	25.00	50.00	—
1766	—	6.00	12.00	25.00	50.00	—
1767	—	6.00	12.00	25.00	50.00	—
1768	—	6.00	12.00	25.00	50.00	—

KM# 233 10 KREUZER

Silver **Ruler:** Frederich Christian **Obverse:** Bust right in wreath **Reverse:** Crowned eagle on pedestal showing value **Note:** Convention 10 Kreuzer.

Date	Mintage	VG	F	VF	XF	Unc
1763	—	8.00	16.00	32.00	70.00	—
1765	—	8.00	16.00	32.00	70.00	—

KM# 249 10 KREUZER

Silver **Ruler:** Frederich Christian **Obverse:** Head right within branches **Reverse:** Eagle arms on pedestal showing value

Date	Mintage	VG	F	VF	XF	Unc
1765 ES	—	8.00	16.00	32.00	70.00	—
1766 ES	—	8.00	16.00	32.00	70.00	—
1768 CLR	—	8.00	16.00	32.00	70.00	—

KM# 268 10 KREUZER

Silver **Ruler:** Alexander **Obverse:** Bust right **Reverse:** Eagle shield on pedestal

Date	Mintage	F	VF	XF	Unc
1780	—	28.50	45.00	75.00	135

KM# 107 15 KREUZER

Silver **Ruler:** Alexander **Obverse:** Bust right, value XV below **Reverse:** Crowned eagle, Hohenzollern arms on breast, neck divides date

Date	Mintage	VG	F	VF	XF	Unc
1696	—	—	—	—	—	—
1702 IAP	—	—	—	—	—	—

KM# 124 15 KREUZER

Silver **Ruler:** George Wilhelm **Subject:** Death of Christian Ernst **Obverse:** Bust right **Reverse:** Eight-line inscription with date, value XV below

Date	Mintage	VG	F	VF	XF	Unc
1712	—	80.00	140	200	300	—

KM# 132 15 KREUZER

Silver **Ruler:** George Wilhelm **Subject:** 200th Anniversary of Reformation **Obverse:** Bust right, value XV below **Reverse:** Altar with open Bible divides date, sun shining down through clouds

Date	Mintage	VG	F	VF	XF	Unc
1717 SK	—	70.00	130	180	260	—

KM# 133 15 KREUZER

Silver **Ruler:** George Wilhelm **Obverse:** Without indication of value

Date	Mintage	VG	F	VF	XF	Unc
1717 SK	—	70.00	130	180	260	—

KM# 234 15 KREUZER

Silver **Note:** Convention 15 Kreuzer.

Date	Mintage	VG	F	VF	XF	Unc
1763	—	35.00	90.00	140	250	—

KM# 225 20 KREUZER

Silver **Ruler:** Friedrich **Obverse:** Head right within wreath **Reverse:** Eagle arms on pedestal showing value

Date	Mintage	VG	F	VF	XF	Unc
1760 CLR	—	8.00	15.00	30.00	60.00	—
1761 CLR	—	8.00	15.00	30.00	60.00	—
1762 CLR	—	8.00	15.00	30.00	60.00	—
1763	—	8.00	15.00	30.00	60.00	—

KM# 236 20 KREUZER

Silver **Ruler:** Frederich Christian **Obverse:** Bust right within wreath **Reverse:** Eagle arms on pedestal showing value

Date	Mintage	VG	F	VF	XF	Unc
1763 CLR	—	9.00	18.00	35.00	75.00	—
1764 CLR	—	9.00	18.00	35.00	75.00	—
1765 CLR	—	9.00	18.00	35.00	75.00	—

KM# 235 20 KREUZER

Silver **Ruler:** Frederich Christian **Subject:** Death of Friedrich **Obverse:** Bust **Reverse:** Date after legend **Rev. Legend:** NATVS... **Note:** Convention 20 Kreuzer.

Date	Mintage	VG	F	VF	XF	Unc
1763 CLR	—	15.00	30.00	75.00	150	—

KM# 250 20 KREUZER

Silver **Ruler:** Frederich Christian **Obverse:** Head right within wreath **Reverse:** Crowned arms within branches on pedestal showing value and dividing date

Date	Mintage	VG	F	VF	XF	Unc
1766 ES	—	9.00	18.00	35.00	75.00	—
1766 CLR	—	9.00	18.00	35.00	75.00	—
1768 CLR	—	9.00	18.00	35.00	75.00	—

KM# 269 20 KREUZER

Silver **Ruler:** Alexander **Obverse:** Head right **Reverse:** Crowned arms within branches on pedestal showing value and dividing date

Date	Mintage	F	VF	XF	Unc
1780	—	20.00	40.00	80.00	150
1782	—	20.00	40.00	80.00	150

KM# 272.1 20 KREUZER

Silver **Ruler:** Alexander **Obverse:** Wreath without ribbon below bust **Reverse:** Crowned arms within branches on pedestal showing value and dividing date

Date	Mintage	F	VF	XF	Unc
1784 EB	—	20.00	40.00	80.00	150

KM# 272.2 20 KREUZER

Silver **Ruler:** Alexander **Obverse:** Wreath with ribbon below bust **Reverse:** Crowned arms within branches on pedestal showing value and dividing date

Date	Mintage	F	VF	XF	Unc
1785 EB	—	30.00	60.00	100	185

KM# 274 20 KREUZER

Silver **Ruler:** Frederich Christian **Obverse:** Head right within wreath **Reverse:** Crowned arms on pedestal within branches showing value and dividing date

Date	Mintage	F	VF	XF	Unc
1787	—	40.00	80.00	125	225

KM# 175 30 KREUZER

Silver **Ruler:** Friedrich **Obverse:** Armored bust right **Reverse:** Crowned arms within ornate shield, cross below

Date	Mintage	VG	F	VF	XF	Unc
1735	—	10.00	20.00	50.00	100	—
1736	—	12.00	25.00	60.00	120	—
1737	—	12.00	25.00	60.00	120	—

KM# 255 30 KREUZER

Silver **Ruler:** Frederich Christian **Note:** Convention 30 Kreuzer.

Date	Mintage	F	VF	XF	Unc
1767	—	75.00	120	200	325

KM# 134 GROSCHEN (1/24 Thaler)

Silver **Ruler:** George Wilhelm **Subject:** 200th Anniversary of Reformation **Obverse:** Two oval arms in crowned cartouche **Reverse:** Six-line inscription, date in chronogram, value below

Date	Mintage	VG	F	VF	XF	Unc
1717 SK	—	15.00	30.00	60.00	95.00	—

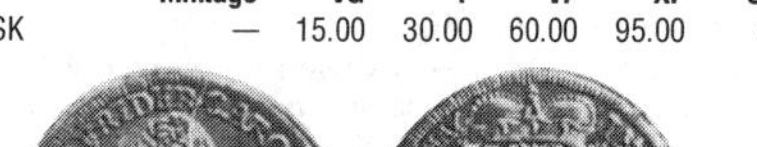

KM# 162 GROSCHEN (1/24 Thaler)

Silver **Ruler:** Georg Friedrich Karl **Subject:** Accession of Georg Friedrich Karl **Obverse:** Bust right **Reverse:** Crowned complex arms

Date	Mintage	VG	F	VF	XF	Unc
1727	—	50.00	90.00	140	225	—

KM# 248 GROSCHEN (1/24 Thaler)

Billon **Ruler:** Frederich Christian **Obverse:** Bust right **Reverse:** Legend

Date	Mintage	VG	F	VF	XF	Unc
1765	—	35.00	60.00	100	165	—

KM# 173 1/48 THALER

Silver **Ruler:** Georg Friedrich Karl **Obverse:** Crowned eagle divides date **Reverse:** Crowned and mantled Hohenzollern arms, value below

Date	Mintage	VG	F	VF	XF	Unc
1732 ILR	—	8.00	15.00	30.00	60.00	—

KM# 182 1/48 THALER

Billon **Ruler:** Friedrich **Obverse:** Eagle **Reverse:** Hohenzollern arms, value below

Date	Mintage	VG	F	VF	XF	Unc
1736 ILR	—	5.00	10.00	20.00	45.00	—
1737 ILR	—	5.00	10.00	20.00	45.00	—
1738 ILR	—	5.00	10.00	20.00	45.00	—
1739 ILR	—	5.00	10.00	20.00	45.00	—
1740 ILR	—	5.00	10.00	20.00	45.00	—
1741	—	5.00	10.00	20.00	45.00	—
1744 CLR	—	5.00	10.00	20.00	45.00	—
1745 CLR	—	5.00	10.00	20.00	45.00	—
1746 CLR	—	5.00	10.00	20.00	45.00	—

KM# 200 1/48 THALER

Billon **Ruler:** Friedrich **Obverse:** Eagle with Hohenzollern arms on breast **Reverse:** Value

Date	Mintage	VG	F	VF	XF	Unc
1748 CLR	—	5.00	10.00	20.00	45.00	—
1750 CLR	—	5.00	10.00	20.00	45.00	—
1751 CLR	—	5.00	10.00	20.00	45.00	—

KM# 90 1/24 THALER (Groschen)

Silver **Ruler:** Alexander **Obverse:** Orb with value within inner circle, legend surrounds **Reverse:** Eagle with shield on breast within inner circle **Note:** Similar to KM#125.

Date	Mintage	VG	F	VF	XF	Unc
1680	—	10.00	20.00	40.00	80.00	—
1684	—	10.00	20.00	40.00	80.00	—
1695	—	10.00	20.00	40.00	80.00	—
1696	—	10.00	20.00	40.00	80.00	—
1702 IAP	—	10.00	20.00	40.00	80.00	—
1703 IAP	—	10.00	20.00	40.00	80.00	—
1704 IAP	—	10.00	20.00	40.00	80.00	—
1705 IAP	—	10.00	20.00	40.00	80.00	—
1706 IAP	—	10.00	20.00	40.00	80.00	—
1707 IAP	—	10.00	20.00	40.00	80.00	—
1708 IAP	—	10.00	20.00	40.00	80.00	—
1709 IAP	—	10.00	20.00	40.00	80.00	—
1710 IAP	—	10.00	20.00	40.00	80.00	—
1711 IAP	—	10.00	20.00	40.00	80.00	—

KM# 125 1/24 THALER (Groschen)

Silver **Ruler:** George Wilhelm **Obverse:** Orb with value within inner circle, legend surrounds **Reverse:** Eagle with shield on breast within inner circle

Date	Mintage	VG	F	VF	XF	Unc
1712 IAP	—	8.00	16.00	32.00	65.00	—
1713 IAP	—	8.00	16.00	32.00	65.00	—
1714 IAP	—	8.00	16.00	32.00	65.00	—
1715 IAP	—	8.00	16.00	32.00	65.00	—
1716 IAP	—	8.00	16.00	32.00	65.00	—
1717 IAP	—	8.00	16.00	32.00	65.00	—
1718 IAP	—	8.00	16.00	32.00	65.00	—
1719 IAP	—	8.00	16.00	32.00	65.00	—
1720 IAP	—	8.00	16.00	32.00	65.00	—
1721 IAP	—	8.00	16.00	32.00	65.00	—
1722 IAP	—	8.00	16.00	32.00	65.00	—
1723 IAP	—	8.00	16.00	32.00	65.00	—
1724 IAP	—	8.00	16.00	32.00	65.00	—
1725 IAP	—	8.00	16.00	32.00	65.00	—
1726 IAP	—	8.00	16.00	32.00	65.00	—

KM# 152 1/24 THALER (Groschen)

Silver **Ruler:** Georg Friedrich Karl **Subject:** Death of Georg Wilhelm **Obverse:** Armored bust right **Reverse:** Value 24 below inscription

Date	Mintage	VG	F	VF	XF	Unc
1726 LR	—	20.00	40.00	75.00	125	—

KM# 153 1/24 THALER (Groschen)

Silver **Ruler:** Georg Friedrich Karl **Reverse:** Without indication of value

Date	Mintage	VG	F	VF	XF	Unc
1726 ILR	—	20.00	40.00	75.00	125	—

KM# 163 1/24 THALER (Groschen)

Silver **Ruler:** Georg Friedrich Karl

Date	Mintage	VG	F	VF	XF	Unc
1727 ILR	—	8.00	15.00	25.00	50.00	—
1728 ILR	—	8.00	15.00	25.00	50.00	—
1729 ILR	—	8.00	15.00	25.00	50.00	—
1730 ILR	—	8.00	15.00	25.00	50.00	—
1731 ILR	—	8.00	15.00	25.00	50.00	—
1732 ILR	—	8.00	15.00	25.00	50.00	—
1733 ILR	—	8.00	15.00	25.00	50.00	—
1734 ILR	—	8.00	15.00	25.00	50.00	—

KM# 176 1/24 THALER (Groschen)

Silver **Ruler:** Friedrich **Subject:** Death of Georg Friedrich Karl **Obverse:** Armored bust right **Reverse:** Seven-line inscription, value 24 below

Date	Mintage	VG	F	VF	XF	Unc
1735 ILR	—	20.00	35.00	50.00	90.00	—

KM# 177 1/24 THALER (Groschen)

Billon **Subject:** Accession Commemorative **Obverse:** Bust right **Reverse:** Arms **Rev. Legend:** IN MEMOR...

Date	Mintage	VG	F	VF	XF	Unc
1735 ILR	—	8.00	17.00	35.00	70.00	—

KM# 183 1/24 THALER (Groschen)

Billon **Ruler:** Friedrich **Obverse:** Orb with value **Reverse:** Eagle with arms on breast divides date

Date	Mintage	VG	F	VF	XF	Unc
1735 ILR	—	5.00	10.00	20.00	45.00	—
1736 ILR	—	5.00	10.00	20.00	45.00	—
1737 ILR	—	5.00	10.00	20.00	45.00	—

KM# 185 1/24 THALER (Groschen)

Billon **Ruler:** Friedrich **Obverse:** Eagle with arms on breast divides date **Reverse:** Orb with value **Note:** Similar to KM#183.

Date	Mintage	VG	F	VF	XF	Unc
1738 ILR	—	5.00	10.00	20.00	45.00	—
1740 ILR	—	5.00	10.00	20.00	45.00	—

KM# 210 1/24 THALER (Groschen)

Billon **Ruler:** Friedrich **Obverse:** Bust right **Reverse:** Value: 24 EINEN REICHS THALER

Date	Mintage	VG	F	VF	XF	Unc
1752	—	5.00	10.00	20.00	45.00	—

KM# 211 1/24 THALER (Groschen)

Billon **Ruler:** Friedrich **Obverse:** Crowned eagle with arms on breast divides date **Reverse:** Orb with value

Date	Mintage	VG	F	VF	XF	Unc
1752 CLR	—	5.00	10.00	20.00	45.00	—
1753 CLR	—	5.00	10.00	20.00	45.00	—

KM# 218 1/24 THALER (Groschen)

Billon **Ruler:** Friedrich **Obverse:** Similar to KM#211 but legend complete **Reverse:** Orb with value

Date	Mintage	VG	F	VF	XF	Unc
1756 CLR	—	5.00	10.00	20.00	45.00	—
1758 CLR	—	5.00	10.00	20.00	45.00	—
1759 CLR	—	5.00	10.00	20.00	45.00	—
1760 CLR	—	5.00	10.00	20.00	45.00	—
1763 CLR	—	5.00	10.00	20.00	45.00	—

KM# 226 1/24 THALER (Groschen)

Billon **Ruler:** Friedrich **Obverse:** Crowned legend with name of ruler **Reverse:** Value

Date	Mintage	VG	F	VF	XF	Unc
1760	—	5.00	10.00	20.00	45.00	—

KM# 103 1/12 THALER (2 Groschen)

Silver **Ruler:** Christian Ernst **Obverse:** Crowned two oval arms in baroque frame **Reverse:** 12/EINEN/THAL/ date

Date	Mintage	VG	F	VF	XF	Unc
1695	—	12.00	25.00	45.00	80.00	—
1696	—	12.00	25.00	45.00	80.00	—
1702 IAP	—	12.00	25.00	45.00	80.00	—
1706 IAP	—	12.00	25.00	45.00	80.00	—
1707 IAP	—	12.00	25.00	45.00	80.00	—
1710 IAP	—	12.00	25.00	45.00	80.00	—
1711 IAP	—	12.00	25.00	45.00	80.00	—
1712 IAP	—	12.00	25.00	45.00	80.00	—

KM# 126 1/12 THALER (2 Groschen)

Silver **Ruler:** George Wilhelm **Subject:** Death of Christian Ernst **Obverse:** Altar with orb on top **Reverse:** Insctription

Date	Mintage	VG	F	VF	XF	Unc
1712	—	50.00	80.00	125	175	—

KM# 127 1/12 THALER (2 Groschen)

Silver **Ruler:** George Wilhelm **Obverse:** Crowned two oval arms in baroque frame **Reverse:** 12/EINEN/THAL/ date

Date	Mintage	VG	F	VF	XF	Unc
1712 IAP	—	10.00	20.00	35.00	55.00	—
1714 IAP	—	10.00	20.00	35.00	55.00	—
1719 IAP	—	10.00	20.00	35.00	55.00	—
1719 SR	—	10.00	20.00	35.00	55.00	—
1720 IAP	—	10.00	20.00	35.00	55.00	—

KM# 135 1/12 THALER (2 Groschen)

Silver **Ruler:** George Wilhelm **Subject:** 200th Anniversary of Reformation **Obverse:** Bust right **Reverse:** Five-line inscription, date in chronogram, value below

Date	Mintage	VG	F	VF	XF	Unc
1717	—	20.00	45.00	75.00	120	—

KM# 136 1/12 THALER (2 Groschen)

Silver **Ruler:** George Wilhelm **Reverse:** Six-line inscription

Date	Mintage	VG	F	VF	XF	Unc
1717 SK	—	20.00	45.00	75.00	120	—

KM# 154 1/12 THALER (2 Groschen)

Silver **Ruler:** Georg Friedrich Karl **Subject:** Death of Georg Wilhelm **Obverse:** Seven-line inscription with date, value 12 below **Reverse:** Orange tree in tub

Date	Mintage	VG	F	VF	XF	Unc
1726 ILR	—	25.00	50.00	90.00	150	—

KM# 155 1/12 THALER (2 Groschen)

Silver **Obverse:** Without indication of value

Date	Mintage	VG	F	VF	XF	Unc
1726 ILR	—	25.00	50.00	90.00	150	—

KM# 178 1/12 THALER (2 Groschen)

Silver **Ruler:** Friedrich **Subject:** Death of Georg Friedrich Karl **Obverse:** Inscription **Reverse:** Dove flying towards sun at left, globe at right

Date	Mintage	VG	F	VF	XF	Unc
1735 ILR	—	25.00	50.00	85.00	140	—

KM# 195 1/12 THALER (2 Groschen)

Silver **Ruler:** Friedrich **Note:** Reichs 1/12 Thaler.

Date	Mintage	VG	F	VF	XF	Unc
1746 CLR	—	10.00	20.00	30.00	50.00	—
1747 CLR	—	10.00	20.00	30.00	50.00	—
1753 CLR	—	10.00	20.00	30.00	50.00	—

KM# 199 1/12 THALER (2 Groschen)
Silver **Ruler:** Friedrich **Obverse:** Bust right **Reverse:** LAND MUNZ, value, date

Date	Mintage	VG	F	VF	XF	Unc
1747 CLR	—	10.00	20.00	45.00	90.00	—
1752 CLR	—	10.00	20.00	45.00	90.00	—
1753 CLR	—	10.00	20.00	45.00	90.00	—
1756 CLR	—	10.00	20.00	45.00	90.00	—
1757 CLR	—	10.00	20.00	45.00	90.00	—
1758 CLR	—	10.00	20.00	45.00	90.00	—
1759 CLR	—	10.00	20.00	45.00	90.00	—

KM# 237 1/12 THALER (2 Groschen)
Silver

Date	Mintage	VG	F	VF	XF	Unc
1763 CLR	—	32.50	50.00	100	200	—

KM# 212 1/6 THALER
Silver **Ruler:** Friedrich **Obverse:** Head right **Obv. Legend:** 72 EINE FEINE MARCK **Reverse:** Date in center **Rev. Legend:** VI EINEN REICHS CONSTITUTIONS MAESIGEN THALER, 63 EINEN 14 LOTHIGE MARCK in margin

Date	Mintage	VG	F	VF	XF	Unc
1752	—	280	400	575	850	—

KM# 213 1/6 THALER
Silver **Ruler:** Friedrich **Obverse:** Bust right **Reverse:** Value and date **Note:** Reichs 1/6 Thaler.

Date	Mintage	VG	F	VF	XF	Unc
1752	—	—	—	—	—	—
Note: Reported, not confirmed						
1757 B	—	10.00	20.00	40.00	80.00	—
1759 B	—	10.00	20.00	40.00	80.00	—

KM# 219 1/6 THALER
Silver **Obverse:** Monogram **Reverse:** Value

Date	Mintage	VG	F	VF	XF	Unc
1758	—	15.00	25.00	45.00	90.00	—

KM# 238 1/6 THALER
Silver **Ruler:** Frederich Christian **Obverse:** Bust right **Reverse:** Value and date

Date	Mintage	VG	F	VF	XF	Unc
1763	—	30.00	50.00	85.00	175	—

KM# 156 1/4 THALER
Silver **Subject:** Bird Shooting Commemorative **Obverse:** Eagle standing on column base, wreath in beak, date below **Reverse:** Shooting scene on lake **Shape:** Square **Note:** Klippe.

Date	Mintage	VG	F	VF	XF	Unc
1726	—	—	325	500	1,000	—

KM# 128 1/2 THALER
Silver **Ruler:** George Wilhelm **Subject:** Death of Christian Ernst **Reverse:** Inscription

Date	Mintage	VG	F	VF	XF	Unc
1712	—	150	280	400	650	—

KM# 137 1/2 THALER
Silver **Ruler:** George Wilhelm **Subject:** Bird Shooting Commemorative **Obverse:** Crowned oval arms (eagle wtih Hohenzollern arms on breast), GW monogram at each corner **Reverse:** Bird stand, GW monogram in corner, bottom one divides date **Note:** Klippe.

Date	Mintage	VG	F	VF	XF	Unc
1718	—	—	325	475	750	—
1720	—	—	325	475	750	—
1721	—	—	325	475	750	—

KM# 145 1/2 THALER
Silver **Ruler:** George Wilhelm **Obverse:** Crowned monogram, ornaments in corners **Reverse:** Shooting plaza, date below

Date	Mintage	VG	F	VF	XF	Unc
1722	—	—	475	800	1,400	—

KM# 146 1/2 THALER
Silver **Ruler:** George Wilhelm **Obverse:** Suspended Order above two arms connected by branches **Reverse:** Shooting scene on lake, date below

Date	Mintage	VG	F	VF	XF	Unc
1723	—	—	475	800	1,400	—

KM# 147 1/2 THALER
Silver **Ruler:** George Wilhelm **Subject:** Target Shooting Commemorative **Obverse:** Crowned monogram within two branches, date below **Reverse:** Eagle holding wreath in beak and rifle in claw **Shape:** Square **Note:** Klippe.

Date	Mintage	VG	F	VF	XF	Unc
1724	—	—	600	1,000	1,750	—

KM# 148 1/2 THALER
Silver **Ruler:** George Wilhelm **Subject:** Bird Shooting Commemorative **Obverse:** Monogram within branches, crowned Order below **Reverse:** Shooting scene, date **Note:** Klippe.

Date	Mintage	VG	F	VF	XF	Unc
1724	—	—	325	475	750	—

KM# 150 1/2 THALER
Silver **Ruler:** George Wilhelm **Obverse:** Palm tree with monogram on trunk, date along one side **Reverse:** Bird stand, inscription along four sides

Date	Mintage	VG	F	VF	XF	Unc
1725	—	—	450	725	1,250	—

KM# 157.2 1/2 THALER
Silver **Note:** Struck on normal size flan.

Date	Mintage	VG	F	VF	XF	Unc
1726	—	—	375	575	900	—

KM# 157.1 1/2 THALER
Silver **Obverse:** Eagle standing on column base, wreath in beak, date below **Reverse:** Shooting scene on lake **Note:** Struck on thick flan.

Date	Mintage	VG	F	VF	XF	Unc
1726	—	—	325	600	1,200	—

KM# 215 1/2 THALER
Silver **Ruler:** Friedrich **Obverse:** Bust **Reverse:** Arms, value ZWANZIG EINE... **Note:** Convention 1/4 Thaler.

Date	Mintage	VG	F	VF	XF	Unc
1754 IAH	—	25.00	50.00	125	250	—
1755	—	—	—	—	—	—

KM# 227 1/2 THALER
Silver **Ruler:** Friedrich **Reverse:** Value: XX EINE...

Date	Mintage	VG	F	VF	XF	Unc
1760	—	—	—	—	—	—

KM# 239 1/2 THALER
Silver **Ruler:** Frederich Christian **Subject:** Death of Friedrich **Obverse:** Armored bust right **Reverse:** Inscription

Date	Mintage	VG	F	VF	XF	Unc
1763 CLR	—	100	200	400	600	—
1763 OEXLEIN-CLR	—	100	200	400	600	—

KM# 240 1/2 THALER
Silver **Ruler:** Frederich Christian **Obverse:** Armored bust right **Reverse:** Crowned arms

Date	Mintage	F	VF	XF	Unc
1763	—	125	250	375	650
1766	—	125	225	350	600
1767	—	125	225	350	600

KM# 220 2/3 THALER (Gulden)
Silver **Ruler:** Friedrich **Obverse:** Armored bust right **Reverse:** Crowned complex arms with supporters

Date	Mintage	VG	F	VF	XF	Unc
1758	—	30.00	60.00	125	250	—

KM# 118 THALER
Silver **Ruler:** Christian Ernst **Obverse:** Bust right **Reverse:** Arms **Note:** Dav. #2029.

Date	Mintage	VG	F	VF	XF	Unc
1704 GFN	—	300	600	1,250	2,500	—

KM# 129 THALER
Silver **Ruler:** George Wilhelm **Subject:** Death of Christian Ernst **Obverse:** Bust right **Reverse:** Eleven-line inscription with date **Note:** Dav. #2030.

Date	Mintage	VG	F	VF	XF	Unc
1712	—	175	350	750	1,500	—

KM# 130 THALER
Silver **Reverse:** Twelve-line inscription with date **Note:** Dav. #2030A.

Date	Mintage	VG	F	VF	XF	Unc
1712	—	175	350	750	1,500	—

KM# 131 THALER

Silver **Ruler:** George Wilhelm **Subject:** Accession of Georg Wilhelm **Obverse:** Armored bust right **Obv. Legend:** GEORGIVS GVILELMVS. D.G. MARG. BRAND. B.M.ST.P.M.&c: DVX. **Reverse:** Helmeted ornate complex arms **Rev. Legend:** IN MEM: REGIMI: D • X • MAII • MDCCXII • - SVSCEPTI • QVOD • FELIX • FAVSTVMQ • SIT * **Note:** Dav. #2031.

Date	Mintage	VG	F	VF	XF	Unc
1712 PPW-SR Rare	—	—	—	—	—	—

KM# 142 THALER

Silver **Ruler:** George Wilhelm **Subject:** Bird Shooting Commemorative **Obverse:** Crowned oval arms (eagle with Hohenzollern arms on breast), GW monogram in each corner **Reverse:** Bird stand, GW monogram in each corner, bottom one divides date **Note:** Klippe. Dav. #2927.

Date	Mintage	VG	F	VF	XF	Unc
1718	—	175	350	700	1,400	—
1721	—	175	350	700	1,400	—
1722	—	175	350	700	1,400	—
1723	—	175	350	700	1,400	—
1724	—	175	350	700	1,400	—

KM# 149 THALER

Silver **Ruler:** George Wilhelm **Obverse:** Monogram within branches, crowned order below **Reverse:** Shooting scene, date **Note:** Dav. #2927.

Date	Mintage	VG	F	VF	XF	Unc
1724	—	175	350	700	1,400	—

KM# 151 THALER

Silver **Ruler:** George Wilhelm **Obverse:** Palm tree with monogram on trunk, date along one side **Reverse:** Bird stand, inscription on four sides **Note:** Struck on thick flan. Dav. #2927.

Date	Mintage	VG	F	VF	XF	Unc
1725	—	300	500	950	1,750	—

KM# 158 THALER

Silver **Obverse:** Eagle standing on column base, wreath in beak, date below **Reverse:** Shooting scene on lake **Note:** Struck on thick flan. Dav. #2927.

Date	Mintage	VG	F	VF	XF	Unc
1726	—	300	500	950	1,750	—

KM# 214.1 THALER

Silver **Ruler:** Friedrich **Obverse:** Armored bust right **Obv. Legend:** FRIDERICVS. D. G. M. B. D. P. ET S. B. N. **Reverse:** Eagle above arms, flags at left and right **Rev. Legend:** EIN REICHS THALER **Note:** Reichs Thaler. Dav. #2032.

Date	Mintage	VG	F	VF	XF	Unc
1752 PPW-CLR	—	40.00	85.00	175	350	—
1752 IAH-CLR	—	40.00	85.00	175	350	—
1752 H-CLR	—	40.00	85.00	175	350	—
1752 CLR	—	40.00	85.00	175	350	—

KM# 216.1 THALER

Silver **Ruler:** Friedrich **Reverse:** Arms, branches with flags and cannons, date and BAYREUTH below **Note:** Convention Thaler. Dav. #2033.

Date	Mintage	VG	F	VF	XF	Unc
1754 IAH	—	150	300	650	1,250	—
1755 IAH	—	150	300	650	1,250	—

KM# 216.2 THALER

Silver **Ruler:** Friedrich **Reverse:** Hatted arms in branches, flags and cannons dividing date, BAYREUTH and CLR below **Note:** Dav. #2034.

Date	Mintage	VG	F	VF	XF	Unc
1755 H//CLR	—	85.00	175	350	800	—

KM# 217.1 THALER

Silver **Ruler:** Friedrich **Obverse:** Bust right, E below **Reverse:** Crowned arms supported by lions, date below **Note:** Dav. #2035.

Date	Mintage	VG	F	VF	XF	Unc
1755 E-CLR	—	75.00	150	300	750	—

KM# 214.2 THALER

Silver, 16 mm. **Ruler:** Friedrich **Note:** Smaller size. Dav. #2036.

Date	Mintage	VG	F	VF	XF	Unc
1757 CLR	—	40.00	85.00	175	350	—

KM# 216.3 THALER

Silver **Ruler:** Friedrich **Obverse:** Armored bust right **Obv. Legend:** FRIDERICVS D • G • M • B • D • P • ET S • B • N • **Reverse:** Crowned complex arms, flags and cannons below **Rev. Legend:** ZEHEN EINE - FEINE MARCK, BAYREUTH/ C•L•R• below **Note:** Dav. #2037.

Date	Mintage	VG	F	VF	XF	Unc
1760 CLR	—	75.00	150	300	750	—

KM# 216.4 THALER

Silver **Ruler:** Friedrich **Obverse:** OEXLEIN below bust **Reverse:** Crowned complex arms, flags and cannons below **Note:** Dav. #2037A.

Date	Mintage	VG	F	VF	XF	Unc
1760 OEXLEIN-CLR Rare	—	—	—	—	—	—

KM# 217.2 THALER

Silver **Ruler:** Friedrich **Obverse:** Without E below bust **Reverse:** Crowned arms with lion supporters **Note:** Dav. #2038.

Date	Mintage	VG	F	VF	XF	Unc
1760 CLR	—	150	300	650	1,500	—

KM# 241 THALER

Silver **Ruler:** Frederich Christian **Subject:** Death of Friedrich **Obverse:** Armored bust right **Obv. Legend:** FRIDERICVS D • G • M • B: D • P • ET S • B • N • **Reverse:** Inscription **Rev. Inscription:** PRINCEPS/ PIVS SAPIENS/ MAGNANIMVS CLEMENS/ LIBERALIS STATOR LITTERARVM/ NATUS/ WEVERLINGAE D.XC. MAY MDCCXI/ PRIMIS NUPTIIS ADPARATIS/ BEROLINI D. XX.NOV.MDCCXXX/ GVBERNACVLA SVSCEPIT/ BARVT **Note:** Dav. #2039.

Date	Mintage	VG	F	VF	XF	Unc
1763 CLR	—	150	300	500	1,000	—

KM# 242 THALER

Silver **Ruler:** Frederich Christian **Obverse:** Armored bust right **Obv. Legend:** FRID • CHRIST • D • G • M • B • D • P • ET S • B • N • **Reverse:** Crowned complex arms divide date below **Rev. Legend:** ZEHEN EINE - FEINE MARK, BAYREUTH/C•L•R• below **Note:** Dav. #2040.

Date	Mintage	F	VF	XF	Unc
1763 CLR	—	100	150	250	500

KM# 251 THALER

Silver **Ruler:** Frederich Christian **Obverse:** Armored bust right **Obv. Legend:** FRID • CHRIST • D • G • M • B • D • P • ET S • B • N • **Reverse:** Crowned complex arms divide date below **Rev. Legend:** ZEHEN EINE - FEINE MARK, BAYREUTH/E*S below **Note:** Dav. #2041.

Date	Mintage	F	VF	XF	Unc
1766 ES	—	100	150	250	500

KM# 252 THALER

Silver **Ruler:** Frederich Christian **Obverse:** Armored bust right **Obv. Legend:** FRID • CHRIST • D • G • M • B • D • P • ET S • B • N • **Reverse:** B in cartouche below arms dividing date and E - S **Rev. Legend:** ZEHEN EINE - FEINE MARK **Note:** Dav. #2042.

Date	Mintage	F	VF	XF	Unc
1766 ES	—	75.00	125	200	450
1768 RE	—	100	175	250	550

KM# 257 THALER

Silver **Ruler:** Frederich Christian **Subject:** Friedrich Christian **Obverse:** Armored bust right **Obv. Legend:** FRID: CHRISTIAN • MARCH: BRAND: D • B • & S • **Reverse:** Inscription **Rev. Inscription:** PRINCEPS/PIVS. IVSTVS. CLEMENS./ NATVS./ 17. IVL. 1708./OBIT./20. JAN. 1769./AETATIS./LX./S. **Note:** Dav. #2043.

Date	Mintage	F	VF	XF	Unc
1769 G//S	—	175	275	450	800

KM# 262 THALER

Silver **Ruler:** Alexander **Obverse:** Armored bust right **Obv. Legend:** ALEXANDER • D • G • MARCH: BRAND: **Reverse:** Lion holding arms at left **Rev. Legend:** ZEHEN EINE FEINE MARK, BAY - REUTH./17 - 79 below **Note:** Dav. #2020.

Date	Mintage	F	VF	XF	Unc
1779	—	140	200	400	800
1779 ICE	—	140	200	400	800
1779 W//ED	—	140	200	400	800

KM# 264 THALER

Silver **Ruler:** Alexander **Obverse:** Armored bust right **Obv. Legend:** ALEXANDER. D.G. MARCH. BRAND. **Reverse:** Lion holding arms within Order chain **Rev. Legend:** ZEHEN EINE FEINE MARK •, BAY - REUTH below **Note:** Dav. #2025.

Date	Mintage	F	VF	XF	Unc
1782 ED	—	125	175	350	700
1783 EP	—	125	175	350	700

KM# 273 THALER

Silver **Ruler:** Alexander **Obverse:** Bust right **Reverse:** Crowned and mantled arms, with supporters, divided date with B in circle and E-B below **Note:** Dav. #2028.

Date	Mintage	F	VF	XF	Unc
1786	—	150	250	425	800

KM# 196 5 THALER

6.6500 g., 0.9000 Gold 0.1924 oz. AGW **Ruler:** Friedrich **Obverse:** Bust **Reverse:** Arms, monogram

Date	Mintage	F	VF	XF	Unc
1746	—	1,000	2,000	3,500	5,500

TRADE COINAGE

KM# 143 1/2 DUCAT

1.7500 g., 0.9860 Gold 0.0555 oz. AGW **Ruler:** George Wilhelm **Obverse:** Bust right **Reverse:** Crowned cross of Order, date in legend

Date	Mintage	VG	F	VF	XF	Unc
1721	—	900	1,800	3,000	5,000	—

KM# 72 DUCAT

3.5000 g., 0.9860 Gold 0.1109 oz. AGW **Ruler:** Christian Ernst **Obverse:** Bust right **Reverse:** Arms in inner circle

Date	Mintage	VG	F	VF	XF	Unc
1659	—	200	450	900	1,500	—
1662	—	200	450	900	1,500	—
1677	—	200	450	900	1,500	—
1694	—	200	450	900	1,500	—
1708	—	200	450	900	1,500	—
ND	—	200	450	900	1,500	—

KM# 140 DUCAT

3.5000 g., 0.9860 Gold 0.1109 oz. AGW **Ruler:** George Wilhelm **Obverse:** Bust right

Date	Mintage	VG	F	VF	XF	Unc
1720	—	300	600	1,200	2,000	—
1721	—	300	600	1,200	2,000	—
1722	—	300	600	1,200	2,000	—

KM# 159 DUCAT

3.5000 g., 0.9860 Gold 0.1109 oz. AGW **Ruler:** Georg Friedrich Karl **Subject:** Death of Georg Wilhelm **Reverse:** Six-line inscription

Date	Mintage	VG	F	VF	XF	Unc
1726	—	—	—	1,350	2,250	—

KM# 164 DUCAT

3.5000 g., 0.9860 Gold 0.1109 oz. AGW **Ruler:** Georg Friedrich Karl **Obverse:** Swan before tree **Reverse:** 11-line inscription

Date	Mintage	VG	F	VF	XF	Unc
1727	—	250	500	950	1,650	—

KM# 179 DUCAT

3.5000 g., 0.9860 Gold 0.1109 oz. AGW **Ruler:** Friedrich **Obverse:** Bust right **Reverse:** Crowned and mantled arms

Date	Mintage	F	VF	XF	Unc
1735	—	500	1,200	2,000	3,000
1746	—	500	1,200	2,000	3,000

KM# 197 DUCAT

3.5000 g., 0.9860 Gold 0.1109 oz. AGW **Ruler:** Friedrich **Obverse:** Equestrian figure left, date below **Reverse:** Order star

Date	Mintage	F	VF	XF	Unc
1746	—	500	1,200	2,000	3,000

KM# 243 DUCAT

3.5000 g., 0.9860 Gold 0.1109 oz. AGW **Ruler:** Frederich Christian **Obverse:** Bust right

Date	Mintage	F	VF	XF	Unc
1763	—	500	950	1,500	2,200

KM# 246 DUCAT

3.5000 g., 0.9860 Gold 0.1109 oz. AGW **Ruler:** Frederich Christian **Subject:** Birthday of Friedrich Christian **Obverse:** Bust right **Reverse:** Crowned Bible, sword and scales

Date	Mintage	F	VF	XF	Unc
1764	—	600	1,100	1,600	2,500

KM# 256 DUCAT

3.5000 g., 0.9860 Gold 0.1109 oz. AGW **Ruler:** Frederich Christian **Obverse:** Man on horse rearing right, date below **Reverse:** Crowned Order star

Date	Mintage	F	VF	XF	Unc
1767	—	500	950	1,500	2,200

KM# 141 2 DUCAT

7.0000 g., 0.9860 Gold 0.2219 oz. AGW **Ruler:** George Wilhelm **Obverse:** Bust right **Reverse:** Arms in inner circle

Date	Mintage	VG	F	VF	XF	Unc
1720	—	900	2,000	4,200	6,500	—

KM# 160 2 DUCAT

7.0000 g., 0.9860 Gold 0.2219 oz. AGW **Ruler:** Georg Friedrich Karl **Subject:** Death of Georg Wilhelm **Reverse:** Six-line inscription

Date	Mintage	VG	F	VF	XF	Unc
1726	—	650	1,100	2,200	3,500	—

KM# A119 10 DUCAT (Portugalöser)

35.0000 g., 0.9860 Gold 1.1095 oz. AGW **Ruler:** Christian Ernst **Note:** Struck with 1 Thaler dies, KM#118.

Date	Mintage	VG	F	VF	XF	Unc
1704 GFN Rare	—	—	—	—	—	—

PATTERNS

Including off metal strikes

KM#	Date	Mintage	Identification	Mkt Val
Pn4	1702	—	1/24 Thaler. Copper. . KM#90	—
Pn5	1704	—	4 Kreuzer. Copper. . KM#117	—
Pn6	1704	—	Thaler. Gold. . KM#118	—
Pn7	1715	—	1/24 Thaler. Copper. . KM#125	100
Pn8	1717	—	1/24 Thaler. Copper. . KM#125	100
Pn9	1719	—	1/24 Thaler. Copper. . KM#125	100
Pn10	1721	—	1/2 Ducat. Silver. . KM#143	—
Pn11	1722	—	1/24 Thaler. Copper. . KM#125	100
Pn12	1726	—	1/24 Thaler. Gold. . KM#153	2,250
Pn13	1727	—	Groschen. Gold. . KM#162	—
Pn14	1727	—	Ducat. Silver. . KM#164	—
Pn15	1745	—	Pfennig. Copper. . KM#180	—

BRAUNAU

A city on the Inn River (in Austria), on the border of present-day Germany, about halfway between Munich and Enns, Austria. The Austrian army besieged Bavarian forces under the command of Duke Ludwig Friedrich of Saxe-Hildburghausen, there in 1743 during which time siege coinage was issued.

AUSTRIAN MILITARY OCCUPATION

SIEGE COINAGE

1743

KM# 1 KREUZER

Lead/Tin **Obverse:** Crowned oval Saxon arms between two palm branches, BRAVNAV above, date divided below by 1 **Shape:** Octagonal **Note:** Uniface

Date	Mintage	Good	VG	F	VF	XF
1743	—	25.00	65.00	100	175	—

KM# 2 3 KREUZER

Lead/Tin **Obverse:** Crowned oval Saxon arms between two palm branches, 3 below, date divided above, BRAVNAV at left, LFH at right **Shape:** Octagonal **Note:** Uniface

Date	Mintage	Good	VG	F	VF	XF
1743	—	35.00	75.00	135	250	—

KM# 3 15 KREUZER (1/4 Gulden)

Lead/Tin **Obverse:** 15 below arms divides IM-VF. **Shape:** Octagonal **Note:** Uniface

Date	Mintage	Good	VG	F	VF	XF
1743	—	50.00	150	200	300	—

KM# 4 30 KREUZER (1/2 Gulden)

Lead/Tin **Obverse:** Crowned oval Saxon arms between two palm branches, 30 below divides IM-VF, BRAVNAV above date **Shape:** Octagonal **Note:** Uniface

Date	Mintage	Good	VG	F	VF	XF
1743	—	80.00	150	275	375	—

KM# 5 GULDEN (60 Kreuzer)

Lead/Tin **Obverse:** 1 below arms divides IM-VF **Shape:** Octagonal **Note:** Uniface

Date	Mintage	Good	VG	F	VF	XF
1743	—	175	300	750	1,250	—

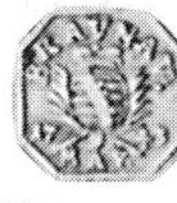

KM# 6 1/16 THALER

Silver **Obverse:** Crowned oval Saxon arms between two palm branches, BRAVNAV above, date divided by 9/MAY **Shape:** Octagonal **Note:** Uniface

Date	Mintage	VG	F	VF	XF	Unc
1743	—	200	325	500	900	—

KM# 7 1/8 THALER

Silver **Obverse:** Crowned oval Saxon arms between two palm branches, 9/MAY below, date divided above, BRAVNAV at left, LFHZS at right **Shape:** Octagonal **Note:** Uniface

Date	Mintage	VG	F	VF	XF	Unc
1743	—	300	525	800	1,350	—

KM# 8 1/4 THALER

Silver **Obverse:** 9/MAY divides IM-VF below arms **Shape:** Octagonal **Note:** Uniface

Date	Mintage	VG	F	VF	XF	Unc
1743	—	400	725	1,000	1,850	—

KM# 9 1/2 THALER

Silver **Obverse:** Crowned oval Saxon arms between two palm branches, 9/MAY divides IM-VF below, BRAVNAV above **Shape:** Octagonal **Note:** Uniface

Date	Mintage	VG	F	VF	XF	Unc
1743	—	500	900	1,250	2,250	—

TRADE COINAGE

KM# 10 1/2 DUCAT

1.7500 g., 0.9860 Gold 0.0555 oz. AGW **Obverse:** Crowned Saxon arms in palm branches, date divided near bottom **Shape:** Octagonal **Note:** Uniface

Date	Mintage	VG	F	VF	XF	Unc
1743	—	—	—	2,500	4,000	—

KM# 11 DUCAT

3.5000 g., 0.9860 Gold 0.1109 oz. AGW **Obverse:** Crowned Saxon arms in palm branches, crown divides date **Shape:** Octagonal **Note:** Uniface

Date	Mintage	VG	F	VF	XF	Unc
1743	—	—	—	4,000	6,500	—

KM# 12 2 DUCAT

7.0000 g., 0.9860 Gold 0.2219 oz. AGW **Obverse:** Crowned Saxon arms in palm branches, crown divides date **Shape:** Octagonal **Note:** Uniface

Date	Mintage	VG	F	VF	XF	Unc
1743	—	—	—	7,000	10,000	—

BREMEN

Established at about the same time as the bishopric in 787, Bremen was under the control of the bishops and archbishops until joining the Hanseatic League in 1276. Archbishop Albrecht II granted the mint right to the city in 1369, but this was not formalized by imperial decree until 1541. In 1646, Bremen was raised to free imperial status and continued to strike its own coins into the early 20th century. The city lost its free imperial status in 1803 and was controlled by France from 1806 until 1813. Regaining it independence in 1815, Bremen joined the North German Confederation in 1867 and the German Empire in 1871.

MINT OFFICIALS' INITIALS

Initials	Date	Name
	1720	Johann Grevenstein, mintmaster
	1723	Heinrich Christoph Hille, mintmaster
	1737-43	Matthias Meyer, warden
	1743-56	Matthias Meyer, mintmaster
	1742-?	Johann Stadtlander, die-cutter
	1743-47	Martin Fischer, die-cutter
	1744	Christoph Hoffmann, die-cutter
	1745-46	Paul Gödeke, die-cutter
JGB, IGB	1747-61	Johann Gottlieb Bringmann (Brinkmann), die-cutter and mintmaster
	1780-1811	Eberhard Christian Poppe, warden

ARMS:

Key, often in shield

FREE CITY

REGULAR COINAGE

KM# 155 SCHWAREN

Billon **Obverse:** Key with date in legend **Reverse:** St. Peter in circle

Date	Mintage	VG	F	VF	XF	Unc
1687	144,000	8.00	15.00	28.00	55.00	—
1690	—	8.00	15.00	28.00	55.00	—
1697	180,000	8.00	15.00	28.00	55.00	—
1708	—	8.00	15.00	28.00	55.00	—

KM# 166 SCHWAREN

Copper **Obverse:** Key divides date **Reverse:** Value with ornaments

Date	Mintage	VG	F	VF	XF	Unc
1719	—	2.50	5.00	10.00	22.00	—
1720	155,000	2.50	5.00	10.00	22.00	—
1726	105,000	2.50	5.00	10.00	22.00	—
1730	217,000	2.50	5.00	10.00	22.00	—
1731	78,000	2.50	5.00	10.00	22.00	—
1732	65,000	2.50	5.00	10.00	22.00	—
1740	155,000	2.50	5.00	10.00	22.00	—
1741	Inc. above	2.50	5.00	10.00	22.00	—
1768 DB	193,000	2.50	5.00	10.00	22.00	—
1781 DB	219,000	2.00	4.00	8.00	18.00	—
1797 DB	220,000	2.00	4.00	8.00	18.00	—

KM# 215 SCHWAREN

Copper **Obverse:** Key divides date **Reverse:** Value with ornaments **Note:** Klippe.

Date	Mintage	VG	F	VF	XF	Unc
1781 DB	—	—	—	—	—	—

KM# 220 2-1/2 SCHWAREN

Copper **Reverse:** D. B. in exergue

Date	Mintage	F	VF	XF	Unc
1797	154,000	5.00	12.00	25.00	50.00
1802	196,000	5.00	12.00	25.00	50.00

KM# 100.1 1/2 GROTE

Billon **Obverse:** Key divides date in circle **Reverse:** Cross in circle **Note:** Varieties exist.

Date	Mintage	VG	F	VF	XF	Unc
1640	90,000	8.00	15.00	25.00	45.00	—
1659	17,000	8.00	15.00	25.00	45.00	—
1672	—	8.00	15.00	25.00	45.00	—
1688	—	8.00	15.00	25.00	45.00	—
1708 R	—	8.00	15.00	25.00	45.00	—
1731 IP	31,000	8.00	15.00	25.00	45.00	—
1732 IP	48,000	8.00	15.00	25.00	45.00	—
1733 IP	—	8.00	15.00	25.00	45.00	—

KM# 100.2 1/2 GROTE

Billon **Obverse:** Without circles **Reverse:** Without circles

Date	Mintage	VG	F	VF	XF	Unc
1741 GLC	—	8.00	15.00	25.00	45.00	—
1742 GLC	—	8.00	15.00	25.00	45.00	—
1750	316,000	8.00	15.00	25.00	45.00	—
1752	—	8.00	15.00	25.00	45.00	—

KM# 208 1/2 GROTE

Billon **Obverse:** Crowned key divides date **Reverse:** Legend in quatrefoil

Date	Mintage	VG	F	VF	XF	Unc
1765 RDDB	287,000	5.00	10.00	20.00	30.00	—

KM# 209 1/2 GROTE

Billon **Reverse:** Legend in palm wreath

Date	Mintage	VG	F	VF	XF	Unc
1768 DB	85,000	8.00	15.00	25.00	45.00	—

KM# 210 1/2 GROTE

Copper **Reverse:** Legend in laurel wreath

Date	Mintage	VG	F	VF	XF	Unc
1771 DB	139,000	6.00	12.00	22.00	35.00	—
1772 DB	91,000	8.00	15.00	25.00	45.00	—

KM# 211 1/2 GROTE

Copper **Note:** Klippe.

Date	Mintage	VG	F	VF	XF	Unc
1771 DB	—	—	—	—	—	—

KM# 216 1/2 GROTE

0.7300 g., 0.1660 Silver 0.0039 oz. ASW **Obverse:** Crowned key **Reverse:** Value and date

Date	Mintage	VG	F	VF	XF	Unc
1781 OHK	288,000	2.00	5.00	10.00	30.00	—

KM# 217 1/2 GROTE

Billon **Obverse:** Key divides date **Reverse:** Value

Date	Mintage	VG	F	VF	XF	Unc
1789 DB	182,000	2.00	5.00	10.00	30.00	—

KM# 160 GROTEN

Silver **Obverse:** Key within shield **Reverse:** Titles of Joseph I

Date	Mintage	VG	F	VF	XF	Unc
1708	413,000	8.00	15.00	25.00	45.00	—
1709	Inc. above	8.00	15.00	25.00	45.00	—

KM# 175 GROTEN

Silver **Obverse:** Key within shield **Reverse:** Titles of Charles VI

Date	Mintage	VG	F	VF	XF	Unc
1733 IP	—	10.00	20.00	35.00	65.00	—
1734 IP	—	10.00	20.00	35.00	65.00	—

KM# 176 GROTEN

Silver **Obverse:** Key within shield **Reverse:** Without circles, 1 in oval on eagle's breast

Date	Mintage	VG	F	VF	XF	Unc
1737 GL	578,000	8.00	15.00	30.00	55.00	—
1738 GLC	Inc. above	8.00	15.00	30.00	55.00	—
1739 GLC	—	8.00	15.00	30.00	55.00	—
1740 GLC	413,000	8.00	15.00	30.00	55.00	—

KM# 180 GROTEN

Silver **Obverse:** Key within shield **Reverse:** Titles of Charles VII

Date	Mintage	VG	F	VF	XF	Unc
1742 GLC	1,105,000	5.00	10.00	20.00	40.00	—

KM# 196 GROTEN

Silver **Obverse:** Key within shield

Date	Mintage	VG	F	VF	XF	Unc
1743	1,393,000	5.00	10.00	20.00	40.00	—

KM# 197 GROTEN

Silver **Obverse:** Key within shield

Date	Mintage	VG	F	VF	XF	Unc
1743	—	—	—	—	—	—
1744	1,500,000	5.00	10.00	20.00	40.00	—

KM# 198 GROTEN

Silver **Obverse:** Key within shield **Reverse:** Spanish shield ornamented on top and sides

Date	Mintage	VG	F	VF	XF	Unc
1743	Inc. above	5.00	10.00	20.00	40.00	—
1744	Inc. above	5.00	10.00	20.00	40.00	—

KM# 199 GROTEN

Silver **Obverse:** Key within shield **Reverse:** Crowned imperial eagle

Date	Mintage	VG	F	VF	XF	Unc
1745	2,146,000	3.50	7.00	15.00	30.00	—

KM# 188 GROTEN

Silver **Reverse:** Oval ornamented shield

Date	Mintage	VG	F	VF	XF	Unc
1745	Inc. above	2.50	5.00	10.00	20.00	—

KM# 201 GROTEN

Silver **Note:** Varieties exist.

Date	Mintage	VG	F	VF	XF	Unc
1745	Inc. above	2.50	5.00	10.00	20.00	—

KM# 202 GROTEN

Silver **Obverse:** Plain shield **Reverse:** Crowned double-headed eagle with value on breast

Date	Mintage	VG	F	VF	XF	Unc
1746	2,456,000	2.50	5.00	10.00	20.00	—
1747	2,621,000	2.50	5.00	10.00	20.00	—
1748	2,447,000	2.50	5.00	10.00	20.00	—
1752	2,696,000	2.50	5.00	10.00	20.00	—

KM# 203 GROTEN

Silver **Obverse:** Key within ornate shield

Date	Mintage	VG	F	VF	XF	Unc
1746	Inc. above	2.50	5.00	10.00	20.00	—

KM# 212 GROTEN

Silver **Obverse:** Key within ornate shield

Date	Mintage	VG	F	VF	XF	Unc
1746	Inc. above	2.50	5.00	10.00	20.00	—
1753	2,588,000	2.50	5.00	10.00	20.00	—

KM# 213 GROTEN

Silver **Reverse:** Spanish shield

Date	Mintage	VG	F	VF	XF	Unc
1747	Inc. above	—	—	—	—	—
1748	Inc. above	—	—	—	—	—
1752	Inc. above	—	—	—	—	—
1754	2,938,000	2.50	5.00	10.00	20.00	—
1755	1,915,000	2.50	5.00	10.00	20.00	—
1763	1,275,000	—	—	—	—	—

KM# 214 GROTEN

Silver **Obverse:** Ornamentation on top

Date	Mintage	VG	F	VF	XF	Unc
1749	2,350,000	2.50	5.00	10.00	20.00	—

KM# 218 GROTEN

Silver **Obverse:** More ornamentation at top **Reverse:** Double-headed eagle with value on breast

Date	Mintage	VG	F	VF	XF	Unc
1750	2,382,000	2.50	5.00	10.00	20.00	—
1751	2,575,000	2.50	5.00	10.00	20.00	—

KM# 219 GROTEN

Silver **Obverse:** Key on shield with crosses at top and sides **Reverse:** Crowned imperial eagle, titles of Francis I

Date	Mintage	VG	F	VF	XF	Unc
1763	—	2.50	5.00	10.00	20.00	—

KM# 222 GROTEN

Silver **Obverse:** Shield with divides initials, crown above, crosses at sides

Date	Mintage	VG	F	VF	XF	Unc
1763 RDDB	1,275,000	2.50	5.00	10.00	20.00	—

KM# 223 GROTEN

Silver **Obverse:** Star above Key on open shield

Date	Mintage	VG	F	VF	XF	Unc
1763	Inc. above	2.50	5.00	10.00	20.00	—

KM# 224 GROTEN

Silver **Obverse:** Key within wreath of oak and laurel, crown above

Date	Mintage	VG	F	VF	XF	Unc
1763	Inc. above	2.50	5.00	10.00	20.00	—
1764	Inc. above	2.50	5.00	10.00	20.00	—
1764 RDDB	203,000	2.50	5.00	10.00	20.00	—

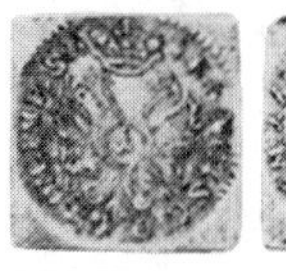

KM# 204 GROTEN

Silver **Obverse:** Crowned key within wreath **Reverse:** Crowned double-headed imperial eagle with value on breast **Note:** Klippe.

Date	Mintage	VG	F	VF	XF	Unc
1764	—	—	—	—	—	—

Note: Multiple legend and punctuation varieties exist for each date and type

KM# 161 2 GROTE / 1/36 THALER

Silver **Obverse:** Oval arms in ornamented shield, date in legend **Reverse:** Titles of Joseph I

Date	Mintage	VG	F	VF	XF	Unc
1709	711,000	9.00	15.00	30.00	55.00	—

KM# 177 2 GROTE / 1/36 THALER

Silver **Obverse:** Arms in oval baroque frame, 36 above, date in legend **Reverse:** Crowned double-headed imperial eagle, titles of Charles VI

Date	Mintage	VG	F	VF	XF	Unc
1738 GLC	578,000	9.00	18.00	32.00	65.00	—
1739 GLC	Est. 1	9.00	18.00	32.00	65.00	—

KM# 205 6 GROTE / 1/12 THALER

Silver **Obverse:** Crowned key in baroque frame, date below legend **Obv. Inscription:** N.D.R.FUS **Reverse:** Crowned double-headed imperial eagle, value

Date	Mintage	VG	F	VF	XF	Unc
1763	61,000	5.00	12.00	25.00	50.00	—
1764	—	7.00	15.00	30.00	60.00	—

KM# 206 6 GROTE / 1/12 THALER

Silver **Obverse:** Key within crowned ornate shield **Reverse:** Crowned double-headed imperial eagle with value on breast **Note:** Klippe.

Date	Mintage	VG	F	VF	XF	Unc
1764	—	—	—	—	—	—

KM# 207 6 GROTE / 1/12 THALER

Silver **Obverse:** Without N. D. R., date in legend **Reverse:** Crowned double-headed imperial eagle **Note:** Similar to KM#205.

Date	Mintage	VG	F	VF	XF	Unc
1764 RDDB	—	5.00	12.00	25.00	50.00	—
1764 DB	—	5.00	12.00	25.00	50.00	—
1764 RDBD Error	—	5.00	12.00	25.00	50.00	—

KM# 195 24 GROTE (1/3 Thaler)

Silver **Obverse:** Crowned shielded arms **Reverse:** Crowned double-headed imperial eagle, titles of Francis I

Date	Mintage	VG	F	VF	XF	Unc
1749	1,890	25.00	50.00	100	200	—

KM# 200 48 GROTE (2/3 Thaler)

Silver **Obverse:** Crowned and supported arms **Reverse:** Crowned double-headed imperial eagle, titles of Francis I

Date	Mintage	VG	F	VF	XF	Unc
1753	1,242	25.00	75.00	150	285	—

KM# 191 1/2 THALER

Silver **Obverse:** Crowned and supported arms **Reverse:** Crowned double-headed imperial eagle, titles of Francis I

Date	Mintage	F	VF	XF	Unc
1747 MF	—	100	150	200	450
1748	1,190	100	150	200	450

KM# 192 1/2 THALER

Silver **Obverse:** Similar to KM#191 but arms rest on ornate pedestal **Reverse:** Crowned double-headed imperial eagle

Date	Mintage	F	VF	XF	Unc
1748	Inc. above	100	150	200	450

KM# 193 1/2 THALER

Silver **Obverse:** Crowned and supported arms on ornate pedestal **Reverse:** Crowned double-headed imperial eagle **Note:** Similar to KM#192 but with thicker planchet.

Date	Mintage	F	VF	XF	Unc
1748	50	—	—	3,500	6,000

KM# 170 THALER

Silver **Obverse:** Crowned and supported arms, Roman numeral date below **Obv. Legend:** MONETA NOVA REIPUB: BREMENSIS * **Reverse:** Crowned imperial eagle, large orb on breast, titles of Charles VI **Rev. Legend:** CAROL. VI. D. G. ROM. IMP. SEMP. AUG. HISP. HUNG. & BOH. REX **Note:** Dav. #2045.

Date	Mintage	F	VF	XF	Unc
MDCCXXIII (1723)	—	275	550	1,100	1,850

KM# 181 THALER

Silver **Obverse:** Crowned and supported oval arms, Roman numeral date below **Reverse:** Crowned imperial eagle, titles of Charles VII and date in legend **Note:** Dav. #2047.

Date	Mintage	F	VF	XF	Unc
MDCCXLII (1742) GLC	783	800	1,200	1,750	2,800

KM# 183 THALER

Silver **Obverse:** Crowned arms with supporters **Obv. Legend:** MONETA•NOVA•REIPUBL: BREMENSIS• **Reverse:** Crowned double-headed imperial eagle with orb on breast **Rev. Legend:** CAROL: VII • D • G • ROM: IMP: SEMP: AUG • 1743 **Note:** Dav. #2049.

Date	Mintage	F	VF	XF	Unc
1743 MF	Inc. above	250	500	900	1,650

KM# 185 THALER

Silver **Obverse:** Crowned and supported oval arms, date in panel below **Obv. Legend:** MON • LIB • REIP • BREMENS •, M.F. at bottom **Reverse:** Crowned double-headed imperial eagle, titles of Charles VII **Rev. Legend:** CAROLUS • VI • - D • G • ROM • IMP • S • A • **Note:** Dav. #2051.

Date	Mintage	F	VF	XF	Unc
1744 MF	109	400	700	1,200	2,500

KM# 186 THALER

Silver **Obverse:** Crowned and supported oval arms, date in panel below **Reverse:** Crowned imperial eagle holds orb and scepter, titles of Charles VII **Note:** Klippe. Dav. #2051A.

Date	Mintage	F	VF	XF	Unc
1744 MF Rare	—	—	—	—	—

KM# 194 THALER

Silver **Obverse:** Crowned and supported oval arms **Reverse:** Crowned imperial eagle **Note:** Struck from 1/2 Thaler dies. Thick flan. Dav. #2052.

Date	Mintage	F	VF	XF	Unc
1748	50	1,200	2,000	3,000	4,500

KM# 171 2 THALER

Silver **Obverse:** Crowned supported shield, date in Roman numerals **Obv. Legend:** MONETA NOVA REIPUB: BREMENSIS * **Reverse:** Crowned imperial eagle, titles of Charles VI **Rev. Legend:** CAROL. VI. D. G. ROM. IMP. SEMP. AUG. HISP. HUNG. & BOH. REX **Note:** Dav. #2044.

Date	Mintage	VG	F	VF	XF	Unc
MDCCXXIII (1723) Rare	—	—	—	—	—	—

KM# 182 2 THALER

Silver **Obverse:** Crowned and supported oval arms in legend **Reverse:** Crowned imperial eagle, titles of Charles VII and date in legend **Note:** Dav. #2046.

Date	Mintage	VG	F	VF	XF	Unc
1742 GLC Rare	51	—	—	—	—	—

KM# 184 2 THALER

Silver **Obverse:** Crowned supported arms **Obv. Legend:** MONETA. NOVA. REIPUBL: BREMENSIS. **Reverse:** Crowned imperial eagle, titles of Charles VII **Rev. Legend:** CAROLUS. VII. - D.G. ROM. IMP. S. A. **Note:** Dav. #2048.

Date	Mintage	VG	F	VF	XF	Unc
1743 MF	Inc. above	600	1,200	2,000	3,500	—

KM# 187 2 THALER

Silver **Obverse:** Crowned and supported oval arms, date in panel below **Reverse:** Crowned double-headed imperial eagle holds scepter and orb **Note:** Dav. #2050.

Date	Mintage	VG	F	VF	XF	Unc
1744 MF	78	1,200	2,000	3,000	5,000	—

TRADE COINAGE

KM# 165 DUCAT

3.5000 g., 0.9860 Gold 0.1109 oz. AGW **Obverse:** Crowned arms with lion supporters in inner circle, date in legend **Reverse:** Crowned imperial eagle in inner circle, titles of Josef I

Date	Mintage	VG	F	VF	XF	Unc
1710 GCR	—	900	2,000	3,250	5,000	—

KM# 172 DUCAT

3.5000 g., 0.9860 Gold 0.1109 oz. AGW **Obverse:** Crowned arms with lion supporters, Roman numeral date below **Obv. Legend:** MONETA NOVA REIPUB: BREMENSIS **Reverse:** Crowned double-headed imperial eagle in inner circle, itles of Karl VI **Rev. Legend:** CAROL. VI. D.G. ROM. IMP. SEMP. AUG. HISP. HUNG. ET. BOH. REX

Date	Mintage	VG	F	VF	XF	Unc
MDCCXXIII (1723)	470	350	750	1,500	2,500	—

KM# 189 DUCAT

3.5000 g., 0.9860 Gold 0.1109 oz. AGW **Obverse:** Crowned arms with lion supporters **Obv. Legend:** MONETA AUG • LIB • REIPUBL • BREMENSIS **Reverse:** Imperial double eagle, titles of Francis I **Rev. Legend:** FRANCISCUS • D • G • - ROM • IMPERAT • S • A •

Date	Mintage	VG	F	VF	XF	Unc
1745	141	500	1,000	1,750	2,750	—
1746	823	300	600	1,200	2,200	—

KM# 190 2 DUCAT

7.0000 g., 0.9860 Gold 0.2219 oz. AGW **Obverse:** Crowned arms with lion supporters in inner circle **Obv. Legend:** • MONETA AUG • LIB • REIPUBL • BREMENSIS • **Reverse:** Crowned imperial eagle, titles of Francis I **Rev. Legend:** FRANCISCUS • D • G • - ROM • IMPERAT • S • A •

Date	Mintage	VG	F	VF	XF	Unc
1746	—	1,000	2,000	3,500	5,500	—

PATTERNS

Including off metal strikes

KM#	Date	Mintage	Identification	Mkt Val
Pn13	1708	—	Schwaren. Gold. . KM#155	1,000
Pn14	1708	—	Groten. Gold. . KM#160	—
Pn15	1730	—	Schwaren. Silver. . KM#166	200
Pn16	1731	—	Schwaren. Gold. . KM#166	—
Pn17	1733	—	Schwaren. Gold. . KM#175	—
Pn18	1742	—	Thaler. Gold. . KM#181	—
Pn19	1743	—	Groten. Gold. . KM#180	—
Pn20	1744	—	Thaler. Gold. . KM#185	—
Pn21	1747	—	1/12 Thaler. Gold. . KM#191	—
Pn22	1748	—	1/12 Thaler. Gold. . KM#191	—
Pn23	1748	—	1/12 Thaler. Gold. . KM#192	—
Pn24	1763	—	6 Grote / 1/12 Thaler. Gold. . KM#205	—
Pn25	1764	—	Groten. Gold. . KM#188	650
Pn26	1764	—	6 Grote / 1/12 Thaler. Gold. . KM#207	—
Pn27	1765	—	1/2 Groten. Gold. . KM#208	—
Pn28	1768	—	Schwaren. Silver. . KM#166	200
Pn29	1768	—	1/2 Grote. Gold. . KM#209	—
Pn30	1771	—	1/2 Grote. Gold. . KM#210	—
PnA31	1781	—	Schwaren. Gold. . KM#166	—
Pn31	1781	—	Schwaren. Silver. . KM#166	175
Pn32	1781	—	Schwaren. Silver. Klippe; KM#215	—
Pn33	1781	24	1/2 Grote. Gold. KM#216	—
Pn34	1782	—	Schwaren. Silver. KM#166	—
Pn35	1789	—	1/2 Grote. Silver. KM#167; thick flan.	—
PnA36	1789	—	1/2 Grote. Gold. KM#217; weight of 1 Ducat.	—
PnB36	1797	—	Schwaren. Silver. KM#166; 25 milimeter flan	175
PnC36	1797	—	Schwaren. Gold. KM#166	—
Pn36	1789	—	1/2 Grote. Gold. KM#217; weight of 1/2 Ducat.	325
PnA37	1789	—	1/2 Grote. Gold. KM#217, weight of 1 Ducat.	—
PnB37	1781	—	Schwaren. Copper. KM166.	—
Pn37	1797	—	2-1/2 Schwaren. Silver. KM#220	200

BRESLAU

BISHOPRIC

One of the chief cities of Silesia, Breslau is the present day Wroclaw in Poland, 135 miles (225 kilometers) east of Dresden and 200 miles (330 kilometers) southwest of Warsaw. The site was settled in the early 10th century and a bishopric was soon established in close proximity to the town. The bishop was made a Prince of the Empire in 1290 and he obtained the right to coin money at the same time. The fortunes of the bishopric closely followed those of the city. The portion of territory which came into the possession of Prussia was secularized in 1810.

RULERS

Franz Ludwig, Pfalzgraf von Neuburg, 1683-1732
Philipp Ludwig, Graf von Sinzendorf, 1732-47
Philipp Gotthard, Graf von Schaffgotsch, 1747-95
Josef Christian, Fürst von Hohenlohe-Waldenburg-Bartenstein, 1795-1810 (1823)

MINT OFFICIALS' INITIALS

Initials	Date	Name
LPH/(backwards R)H	1678-1701	Leonhard Paul Haller, warden and mintmaster
SS	1701-17	Siegmund Strasser, warden
B	1702-43	Philipp Christoph Becker, die-cutter in Vienna
DG	1714-44	Antonio DeGennaro, die-cutter in Vienna
D/ID	1776-1803	Ignaz Donner, die-cutter in Vienna
K	1776-1805	Anton Friedrich König, die-cutter in Breslau

ARMS

Breslau/Neisse – one to six lilies
Austria – horizontal shaded bar across middle of shield
Silesia – eagle, crescent moon on breast

NOTE: The arms of Neisse, a principality acquired by the bishops, are usually found on the episcopal coinage of Breslau, being practically identical, one with the other.

REGULAR COINAGE

C# 1 1/2 THALER

Silver **Ruler:** Philipp Gotthard **Obverse:** Bust right **Reverse:** Crowned and mantled arms

Date	Mintage	Good	VG	F	VF	XF
1754 D	—	—	75.00	175	350	500
1770	—	—	75.00	175	350	500
1777	—	—	75.00	175	350	500

C# 5 1/2 THALER

Silver **Ruler:** Joseph Christian **Obverse:** Bust right **Obv. Legend:** * IOSEPH . D.G. PRIN. AB HOHENLOHE WALD. BART. **Reverse:** Cardinals hat above crowned and mantled arms with supporters **Note:** Convention 1/2 Thaler.

Date	Mintage	Good	VG	F	VF	XF
1796 K	—	—	75.00	175	250	450

C# 5a 1/2 THALER

Silver **Ruler:** Joseph Christian **Obverse:** Bust right **Reverse:** Cardinals hat above crowned and mantled arms with supporters **Note:** Square klippe. Convention 1/2 Thaler.

Date	Mintage	Good	VG	F	VF	XF
1796 K	—	—	—	—	—	750

C# 5b 1/2 THALER

Silver **Ruler:** Joseph Christian **Obverse:** Bust right **Reverse:** Cardinals hat above crowned and mantled arms with supporters **Note:** Octagonal klippe. Convention 1/2 Thaler.

Date	Mintage	Good	VG	F	VF	XF
1796 K	—	—	—	—	—	750

C# 2 THALER

Silver **Ruler:** Philipp Gotthard **Obverse:** Bust right **Obv. Legend:** PHIL • GOTTHARD • D • G • PR • DE • SCHAFFGOTSCH • **Rev. Legend:** EPISC: WRATISL: PR: NISS: - ET • DUX • GROTTKOV • **Note:** Convention Thaler. Dav. #2053.

Date	Mintage	Good	VG	F	VF	XF
1753 D	—	—	200	450	750	1,200
1770 D	—	—	175	350	500	900
1773 D	—	—	175	350	500	900
1777	—	—	175	350	500	900

TRADE COINAGE

FR# 583 DUCAT

3.5000 g., 0.9860 Gold 0.1109 oz. AGW **Ruler:** Franz Ludwig von Neuberg **Obverse:** Bust right **Reverse:** Elaborate arms topped by mitre dividing date

Date	Mintage	VG	F	VF	XF	Unc
1702	—	200	450	750	1,300	—
1707	—	200	450	750	1,300	—
1711	—	200	450	750	1,300	—
1715	—	200	450	750	1,300	—
1720	—	200	450	750	1,300	—
1723	—	200	450	750	1,300	—
1726	—	200	450	750	1,300	—
1727	—	200	450	750	1,300	—
1730	—	200	450	750	1,300	—
1731	—	200	450	750	1,300	—
1732	—	200	450	750	1,300	—

FR# 587 DUCAT

Ruler: Philip Ludwig von Sinzendorf **Obverse:** Bust right **Reverse:** Cardinals hat above arms

Date	Mintage	VG	F	VF	XF	Unc
1738	—	200	450	750	1,300	—

FR# 528 DUCAT

3.5000 g., 0.9860 Gold 0.1109 oz. AGW **Subject:** Philip Ludwig

Date	Mintage	VG	F	VF	XF	Unc
1738	—	200	450	700	1,250	—

C# 3.1 DUCAT

3.5000 g., 0.9860 Gold 0.1109 oz. AGW **Ruler:** Philipp Gotthard **Obverse:** Bust right **Reverse:** Helmeted arms with Order chain below within crowned mantle

Date	Mintage	VG	F	VF	XF	Unc
1748	—	350	500	800	1,750	—
1752 D	—	350	500	800	1,750	—
1753	—	350	500	800	1,750	—

C# 3.2 DUCAT

3.5000 g., 0.9860 Gold 0.1109 oz. AGW **Ruler:** Philipp Gotthard **Obverse:** Bust right **Reverse:** Helmeted arms with Order chain below within crowned mantle

Date	Mintage	VG	F	VF	XF	Unc
1770	—	350	500	800	1,750	—
1777	—	350	500	800	1,750	—

C# 6 DUCAT

3.5000 g., 0.9860 Gold 0.1109 oz. AGW **Ruler:** Joseph Christian **Note:** Similar to C#3.

Date	Mintage	VG	F	VF	XF	Unc
1796	—	450	650	1,250	2,500	—

C# 4 5 DUCAT (1/2 Portugalöser)

17.5000 g., 0.9860 Gold 0.5547 oz. AGW **Ruler:** Philipp Gotthard **Obverse:** Bust right **Reverse:** Helmeted arms with Order chain below within crowned mantle **Note:** Similar to Ducat C#3.

Date	Mintage	VG	F	VF	XF	Unc
1748 Rare	—	—	—	—	—	—

FR# 521 6 DUCAT

21.0000 g., 0.9860 Gold 0.6657 oz. AGW **Obverse:** Bust of Franz Ludwig right **Reverse:** Arms

Date	Mintage	VG	F	VF	XF	Unc
1730 Rare	—	—	—	—	—	—

FR# 519 10 DUCAT (Portugalöser)

35.0000 g., 0.9860 Gold 1.1095 oz. AGW **Obverse:** Bust of Franz Ludwig right **Reverse:** Arms

Date	Mintage	VG	F	VF	XF	Unc
1701 Rare	—	—	—	—	—	—

BRETZENHEIM

Located in the Rhineland. Purchased by Carl Theodor of Pfalz-Sulzbach in 1790. The principality was mediatized in 1803. Karl August was the only one to issue coins for Bretzenheim.

RULERS

Karl August, 1790-1803

PRINCIPALITY

REGULAR COINAGE

KM# 1 10 KREUZER

Silver **Ruler:** Karl August **Obverse:** Draped bust right **Obv. Legend:** CAR • AVG • D • G • S • R • I • PRINC • DE • BREZENHEIM • **Reverse:** Crowned arms on 8-pointed cross within Order chain, value divides date below **Rev. Legend:** AD • NORMAM CONVENTIONIS **Note:** Convention 10 Kreuzer

Date	Mintage	VG	F	VF	XF	Unc
1790	—	160	275	450	750	—

KM# 2 20 KREUZER

Silver **Ruler:** Karl August **Obverse:** Draped bust right **Obv. Legend:** CAR • AVG • D • G • S • R • I • PRINC • DE • BREZENHEIM • **Reverse:** Crowned arms on 8-pointed cross within Order chain, value divides date below **Rev. Legend:** AD NORMAM CONVENTIONIS **Note:** Convention 20 Kreuzer

Date	Mintage	VG	F	VF	XF	Unc
1790	—	145	225	375	650	—

KM# 3 1/2 THALER

Silver **Ruler:** Karl August **Obverse:** Draped bust right **Obv. Legend:** CAR • AVG • D • G • S • R • I • PRINC • DE • BREZENHEIM • **Reverse:** Crowned arms on 8-pointed cross within Order chain, date below **Rev. Legend:** AD NORMAM CONVENTIONIS **Note:** Convention 1/2 Thaler.

Date	Mintage	VG	F	VF	XF	Unc
1790 A.S.	—	225	375	600	1,100	—

KM# 4 THALER

Silver **Ruler:** Karl August **Obverse:** Draped bust right **Obv. Legend:** CAR • AVGVST • D: G • S • R • I • PRINCEPS • D • E • BREZENHEIM • **Reverse:** Crowned arms on 8-pointed cross within Order chain, Ostrich supporters **Rev. Legend:** AD NORMAM CONVENTIONIS **Note:** Convention Thaler. Dav. #2055.

Date	Mintage	VG	F	VF	XF	Unc
1790 A.S.	—	300	525	900	1,650	—

TRADE COINAGE

KM# 5 DUCAT

3.5000 g., 0.9860 Gold 0.1109 oz. AGW **Ruler:** Karl August **Obverse:** Head right **Obv. Legend:** CAR • AVG • D • G • S • R • I • PRINC • DE • BREZENHEIM • **Reverse:** Crowned arms on 8-pointed cross within Order chain, crown divides date above

Date	Mintage	F	VF	XF	Unc
1790	—	1,500	2,500	4,000	6,500

BRUNSWICK-BLANKENBURG

A county located in the Harz Mountains to the southwest of Halberstadt, Blankenburg was established in the late 11th century. The line was divided into Blankenburg and Regenstein in 1162 and, when Blankenburg became extinct in 1368, its lands and titles reverted to Regenstein. In 1599, Regenstein itself became extinct and both titles fell to Brunswick. A short-lived separate line for Blankenburg was established from Brunswick-Wolfenbüttel in the early 18th century for which coins were issued.

RULERS

Ludwig Rudolf, 1714-1731

MINT OFFICIALS' INITIALS

Initials	Date	Name
CPS	1725-53	Christian Philipp Spangenberg in Clausthal
HCH	1669-1729	Heinrich Christoph Hille in Brunswick
W	1688-1739	Christian Wermuth, die-cutter in Gotha

COUNTY

REGULAR COINAGE

KM# 22 PFENNIG

Copper **Ruler:** Ludwig Rudolf **Obverse:** Crowned LR monogram **Reverse:** Value, date in seven lines **Note:** Mining Pfennig.

Date	Mintage	VG	F	VF	XF	Unc
1722 W	—	20.00	40.00	75.00	125	—

KM# 23 3 PFENNIG

Copper **Ruler:** Ludwig Rudolf **Obverse:** Crowned LR monogram **Reverse:** Value, date in seven lines **Note:** Mining 3 Pfennig.

Date	Mintage	VG	F	VF	XF	Unc
1722 W	—	25.00	45.00	85.00	140	—

KM# 5 12 MARIENGROSCHEN

Silver **Ruler:** Ludwig Rudolf **Obverse:** Value in three lines **Reverse:** Leaping horse left, date below in Roman numerals

Date	Mintage	VG	F	VF	XF	Unc
1715 HCH	—	40.00	80.00	150	275	—
1718 HCH	—	40.00	80.00	150	275	—
1720 HCH	—	40.00	80.00	150	275	—

KM# 6 24 MARIENGROSCHEN

Silver **Ruler:** Ludwig Rudolf **Obverse:** Value in three lines **Reverse:** Leaping horse left, date below in Roman numerals

Date	Mintage	VG	F	VF	XF	Unc
1715 HCH	—	50.00	100	200	350	—
1720 HCH	—	50.00	100	200	350	—
1724 HCH	—	50.00	100	200	350	—

KM# 7 THALER

Silver **Ruler:** Ludwig Rudolf **Obverse:** Armored bust right **Obv. Legend:** LUD: RUD: D.G. DUX BRUNS. ET LUN. **Reverse:** Horse running left, Roman daate below **Note:** Dav. #2133.

Date	Mintage	VG	F	VF	XF	Unc
1715 HCH	—	250	500	900	1,600	—
1716 HCH	—	250	500	900	1,600	—
1718 HCH	—	250	500	900	1,600	—
1719 HCH	—	250	500	900	1,600	—
1720 HCH	—	250	500	900	1,600	—
1722 HCH	—	250	500	900	1,600	—
1724 HCH	—	250	500	900	1,600	—
1725 HCH	—	250	500	900	1,600	—
1727 HCH	—	250	500	900	1,600	—

KM# 25 THALER

Silver **Ruler:** Ludwig Rudolf **Obverse:** Bust right **Reverse:** Wildman, tree on right, date below in Roman numerals **Note:** Dav. #2134.

Date	Mintage	VG	F	VF	XF	Unc
1726 HCH	—	350	650	1,200	2,000	—

KM# 33 THALER

Silver **Ruler:** Ludwig Rudolf **Obverse:** Armored bust right **Obv. Legend:** LVDOVIC9 RVDOLPH9 D • G • DVX BR • ET • LVNEB •, S•L• on arm **Reverse:** Wildman with crowned shield on left, tree on right **Rev. Legend:** EX ADVERSO DECVS - MDCCXXVII **Note:** Dav. #2135.

Date	Mintage	VG	F	VF	XF	Unc
1727 HCH	—	350	650	1,200	2,000	—

KM# 36 THALER

Silver **Ruler:** Ludwig Rudolf **Obverse:** Armored bust right **Obv. Legend:** LVDOVIC9 RVDOLPH9 D • G • DVX BR • ET • LVNEB • **Reverse:** Larger crowned arms in round shield, smaller wildman **Rev. Legend:** EX - ADVERSO DECVS MDCCXXIX **Note:** Dav. #2136.

Date	Mintage	VG	F	VF	XF	Unc
1729 CPS	—	350	650	1,200	2,000	—

TRADE COINAGE

KM# 10 1/4 DUCAT

0.8750 g., 0.9860 Gold 0.0277 oz. AGW **Ruler:** Ludwig Rudolf **Obverse:** Crowned LR monogram **Reverse:** Rearing horse left, date in exergue

Date	Mintage	VG	F	VF	XF	Unc
1717 HCH	—	100	200	400	650	—
1719 HCH	—	100	200	400	650	—
1720 HCH	—	100	200	400	650	—
1722 HCH	—	100	200	400	650	—
1723 HCH	—	100	200	400	650	—
1725 HCH	—	100	200	400	650	—
ND	—	100	200	400	650	—

KM# 34 1/4 DUCAT

0.8750 g., 0.9860 Gold 0.0277 oz. AGW **Ruler:** Ludwig Rudolf **Obverse:** Crowned monogram **Reverse:** Leaping horse, date below

Date	Mintage	VG	F	VF	XF	Unc
1727	—	100	200	400	650	—

KM# 35 1/4 DUCAT

0.8750 g., 0.9860 Gold 0.0277 oz. AGW **Ruler:** Ludwig Rudolf **Reverse:** Wildman holding tree dividing date

Date	Mintage	VG	F	VF	XF	Unc
1728 HCH	—	100	200	400	650	—
ND	—	100	200	400	650	—

KM# 8 1/2 DUCAT

1.7500 g., 0.9860 Gold 0.0555 oz. AGW **Ruler:** Ludwig Rudolf **Obverse:** Crowned LR monogram **Reverse:** Rearing horse, date in exergue

Date	Mintage	VG	F	VF	XF	Unc
1715	—	200	400	750	1,150	—
1726	—	200	400	750	1,150	—

KM# 13 1/2 DUCAT

1.7500 g., 0.9860 Gold 0.0555 oz. AGW **Ruler:** Ludwig Rudolf **Reverse:** Wildman holding tree dividing date

Date	Mintage	VG	F	VF	XF	Unc
1718 HCH	—	125	250	450	850	—
1719 HCH	—	125	250	450	850	—
1720 HCH	—	125	250	450	850	—
1721 HCH	—	125	250	450	850	—
1723 HCH	—	125	250	450	850	—
1725 HCH	—	125	250	450	850	—
1726 HCH	—	125	250	450	850	—
1727 HCH	—	125	250	450	850	—
1728 HCH	—	125	250	450	850	—

KM# 26 1/2 DUCAT

1.7500 g., 0.9860 Gold 0.0555 oz. AGW **Ruler:** Ludwig Rudolf **Reverse:** Helmet with plumes and horse divides date

Date	Mintage	VG	F	VF	XF	Unc
1726 HCH	—	150	350	600	1,000	—
1727 HCH	—	150	350	600	1,000	—

KM# 14 1/2 DUCAT

1.7500 g., 0.9860 Gold 0.0555 oz. AGW **Ruler:** Ludwig Rudolf **Note:** Klippe.

Date	Mintage	VG	F	VF	XF	Unc
ND	—	175	375	650	1,000	—

KM# 27 1/2 DUCAT

1.7500 g., 0.9860 Gold 0.0555 oz. AGW **Ruler:** Ludwig Rudolf **Obverse:** Monogram **Reverse:** Leaping horse left **Note:** Klippe.

Date	Mintage	VG	F	VF	XF	Unc
ND	—	—	—	1,000	2,000	—

KM# 9 DUCAT

3.5000 g., 0.9860 Gold 0.1109 oz. AGW **Ruler:** Ludwig Rudolf **Obverse:** Crowned monogram **Reverse:** Rearing horse left

Date	Mintage	VG	F	VF	XF	Unc
MDCCXV (1715) HCH	—	300	650	1,150	1,850	—
MDCCXVIII (1718) HCH	—	300	650	1,150	1,850	—
MDCCXXIII (1723) HCH	—	300	650	1,150	1,850	—

KM# 11 DUCAT

3.5000 g., 0.9860 Gold 0.1109 oz. AGW **Ruler:** Ludwig Rudolf **Subject:** Bicentennial of Reformation **Obverse:** Armored bust right **Reverse:** View of Blankenburg with angel flying above

Date	Mintage	VG	F	VF	XF	Unc
1717	—	300	700	1,400	2,000	—

KM# 12 DUCAT

3.5000 g., 0.9860 Gold 0.1109 oz. AGW **Ruler:** Ludwig Rudolf **Obverse:** Crowned arms within Order chain **Reverse:** Wildman with tree at right

Date	Mintage	VG	F	VF	XF	Unc
1717 HCH	—	200	400	800	1,550	—
1719 HCH	—	200	400	800	1,550	—
1720 HCH	—	200	400	800	1,550	—
1721 HCH	—	200	400	800	1,550	—
1723 HCH	—	200	400	800	1,550	—
1726 HCH	—	200	400	800	1,550	—

KM# 20 DUCAT

3.5000 g., 0.9860 Gold 0.1109 oz. AGW **Ruler:** Ludwig Rudolf **Obverse:** Head right **Reverse:** View of Blankenburg with horse above

Date	Mintage	VG	F	VF	XF	Unc
1720	—	400	900	1,600	2,500	—

KM# 21 DUCAT

3.5000 g., 0.9860 Gold 0.1109 oz. AGW **Ruler:** Ludwig Rudolf **Obverse:** Crowned LR monogram **Reverse:** Wildman holding tree dividing date

Date	Mintage	VG	F	VF	XF	Unc
1720 HCH	—	300	650	1,150	1,850	—

KM# 24 DUCAT

3.5000 g., 0.9860 Gold 0.1109 oz. AGW **Ruler:** Ludwig Rudolf **Obverse:** Bust right **Reverse:** Leaping horse left, date below in Roman numerals

Date	Mintage	VG	F	VF	XF	Unc
1722 HCH	—	450	950	1,750	2,750	—
1725 HCH	—	450	950	1,750	2,750	—

KM# 29 DUCAT

3.5000 g., 0.9860 Gold 0.1109 oz. AGW **Ruler:** Ludwig Rudolf **Reverse:** Starburst in circle of clouds, date in exergue

Date	Mintage	VG	F	VF	XF	Unc
1726	—	400	900	1,600	2,500	—
1730	—	400	900	1,600	2,500	—

KM# 30 DUCAT

3.5000 g., 0.9860 Gold 0.1109 oz. AGW **Ruler:** Ludwig Rudolf **Obverse:** Crowned LR monogram **Reverse:** Rearing horse, date in exergue **Note:** Mining Ducat.

Date	Mintage	VG	F	VF	XF	Unc
1726	—	450	950	1,750	2,750	—

KM# 31 DUCAT

3.5000 g., 0.9860 Gold 0.1109 oz. AGW **Ruler:** Ludwig Rudolf **Obverse:** Bust right **Reverse:** Leaping horse above mining district, date below **Note:** Mining Ducat.

Date	Mintage	VG	F	VF	XF	Unc
1726 HCH	—	600	1,150	2,000	3,250	—

KM# 32 DUCAT

3.5000 g., 0.9860 Gold 0.1109 oz. AGW **Ruler:** Ludwig Rudolf **Obverse:** Crowned arms within Order chain **Reverse:** Date below legend **Rev. Legend:** EX ADVERSO DECVS **Note:** Similar to KM#12.

Date	Mintage	VG	F	VF	XF	Unc
1726 HCH	—	275	450	900	1,650	—
1727 HCH	—	275	450	900	1,650	—

KM# 28 DUCAT

3.5000 g., 0.9860 Gold 0.1109 oz. AGW **Ruler:** Ludwig Rudolf **Obverse:** Head right **Reverse:** Horse left within crowned shield

Date	Mintage	VG	F	VF	XF	Unc
1726	—	250	450	900	1,600	—
1727	—	250	450	900	1,600	—
1728	—	250	450	900	1,600	—
1730	—	250	450	900	1,600	—

KM# A10 12 DUCAT

42.0000 g., 0.9860 Gold 1.3314 oz. AGW **Ruler:** Ludwig Rudolf **Note:** Struck with 1 Thaler dies, KM#7.

Date	Mintage	VG	F	VF	XF	Unc
1715 HCH Rare	—	—	—	—	—	—

BRUNSWICK-LUNEBURG-CALENBERG-HANNOVER

Located in north-central Germany. The first duke began his rule in 1235. The first coinage appeared c. 1175. There was considerable shuffling of territory until 1692 when Ernst August became the elector of Hannover. George Ludwig became George I of England in 1714. There was separate coinage for Lüneburg until during the reign of George III. The name was changed to Hannover in 1814.

RULERS

George Ludwig (George I of England), 1698-1727
George II August (George II of England), 1727-1760
George III, (King of Great Britain), 1760-1814
After 1814 see Kingdom of Hannover

MINT OFFICIALS' INITIALS

Celle Mint

Initials	Date	Name
III	1687-1705	Jobst Jakob Janisch

Clausthal Mint

Initials	Date	Name
C	1751-53, 1790-92, 1800-02	Commission
CPS, S	1725-53	Christian Philipp Spangenberg
HB	1675-1711	Heinrich Bonhorst
IWS, S	1753-90	Johann Wilhelm Schlemm
PLM	1792-1800	Philipp Ludwig Magius

Hannover Mint

Initials	Date	Name
Star, C, star	1763-68	Commission
IAS	1748-64	Johann anton Schrodor
IHZ	1769-82	Julius Heinrich Zwilgmeier

Zellerfeld Mint

Initials	Date	Name
B, HCB	1711-25	Heinrich Christian Bonhorst
C	1719-23, 31, 1778-79, 1786-91	Commission
CS, CES	1779-86	Christoph Engelhard Seidensticker
EPH	1723-31	Ernst Peter Hecht
HH	1712-19	Heinrich Horst
IAB	1731-39	Johann Albrecht Brauns
IAP	1763-73	Johann Anton Pfeffer
IBH	1739-63	Johann Benjamin Hecht
LCR	1773-78	Ludwig Christian Ruperti
RB	1676-1711	Rudolf Bornemann
***	1698-1715	Used instead of initials during this period

NOTE: From 1715 on, the titles are changed on the coinage to reflect the ruler's elevation to "King of Great Britain, France and Ireland" as well as elector and duke of Brunswick and Lüneburg.

ELECTORATE

REGULAR COINAGE

KM# 5 PFENNING

Silver **Ruler:** George Ludwig **Obverse:** Horse leaping left, date below **Note:** Uniface. Hohlpfennig type.

Date	Mintage	VG	F	VF	XF	Unc
1698	—	3.00	6.00	10.00	20.00	—
1700	—	3.00	6.00	10.00	20.00	—
1704	—	3.00	6.00	10.00	20.00	—
1712	—	3.00	6.00	10.00	20.00	—

KM# 24 PFENNING

Copper **Ruler:** George Ludwig **Obverse:** Crowned GLC monogram **Reverse:** Value, date

Date	Mintage	VG	F	VF	XF	Unc
1699	—	7.00	12.00	22.00	40.00	—
1709	—	7.00	12.00	22.00	40.00	—

KM# 30 PFENNING

Silver **Ruler:** George Ludwig **Obverse:** Crowned monogram, date **Note:** Uniface. Hohlpfennig type.

Date	Mintage	VG	F	VF	XF	Unc
1700 RB	—	4.00	8.00	15.00	30.00	—
1704 RB	—	4.00	8.00	15.00	30.00	—
1705 RB	—	4.00	8.00	15.00	30.00	—
1706 RB	—	4.00	8.00	15.00	30.00	—
1707 RB	—	4.00	8.00	15.00	30.00	—
1708 RB	—	4.00	8.00	15.00	30.00	—
1710 RB	—	4.00	8.00	15.00	30.00	—
1712 HH	—	4.00	8.00	15.00	30.00	—
1713 HH	—	4.00	8.00	15.00	30.00	—
1715 HH	—	4.00	8.00	15.00	30.00	—

KM# 104.1 PFENNING

Silver **Ruler:** George Ludwig **Obverse:** Crowned GR monogram divides date **Note:** Hohlpfennig type

Date	Mintage	VG	F	VF	XF	Unc
1716 HH	—	6.00	10.00	20.00	40.00	—
1717 HH	—	6.00	10.00	20.00	40.00	—
1718 HH	—	6.00	10.00	20.00	40.00	—
1723	—	6.00	10.00	20.00	40.00	—

KM# 104.2 PFENNING

Silver **Ruler:** George Ludwig **Note:** With halbert.

Date	Mintage	VG	F	VF	XF	Unc
1717 HH	—	6.00	10.00	18.00	35.00	—
1718 HH	—	6.00	10.00	18.00	35.00	—

KM# 116 PFENNING

Copper **Ruler:** George Ludwig **Obverse:** Crowned GR monogram **Reverse:** Value, date

Date	Mintage	VG	F	VF	XF	Unc
1717	—	6.00	10.00	18.00	35.00	—
1718	—	6.00	10.00	18.00	35.00	—
1719	—	6.00	10.00	18.00	35.00	—
1721	—	6.00	10.00	18.00	35.00	—
1722	—	6.00	10.00	18.00	35.00	—
1723 HCB	—	6.00	10.00	18.00	35.00	—
1726 CPS	—	6.00	10.00	18.00	35.00	—

KM# 161 PFENNING

Silver **Ruler:** George Ludwig **Obverse:** Crowned GR monogram, date below **Note:** Uniface. Hohlpfennig type

Date	Mintage	VG	F	VF	XF	Unc
1723	—	6.00	10.00	18.00	35.00	—

KM# 164 PFENNING

Copper **Ruler:** George Ludwig **Obverse:** Wildman, tree in right hand **Reverse:** Value, date

Date	Mintage	VG	F	VF	XF	Unc
1724 EPH	—	3.00	6.00	12.00	30.00	—
1725 EPH	—	3.00	6.00	12.00	30.00	—
1726 EPH	—	3.00	6.00	12.00	30.00	—

KM# 167 PFENNING

Copper **Ruler:** George Ludwig **Obverse:** St. Andrew with cross **Reverse:** Value, date

Date	Mintage	VG	F	VF	XF	Unc
1725	—	4.00	8.00	15.00	35.00	—
1726	—	4.00	8.00	15.00	35.00	—

KM# 204.1 PFENNING

Copper **Ruler:** George II August **Obverse:** Crowned GR monogram, mintmaster's initials below **Reverse:** Value, date

Date	Mintage	VG	F	VF	XF	Unc
1729 CPS	—	4.00	8.00	15.00	30.00	—
1734 CPS	—	4.00	8.00	15.00	30.00	—
1736 CPS	—	4.00	8.00	15.00	30.00	—
1737 CPS	—	4.00	8.00	15.00	30.00	—
1739 CPS	—	4.00	8.00	15.00	30.00	—
1740 CPS	—	4.00	8.00	15.00	30.00	—
1741 CPS	—	4.00	8.00	15.00	30.00	—
1742 S	—	4.00	8.00	15.00	30.00	—
1744 CPS	—	4.00	8.00	15.00	30.00	—
1745 CPS	—	4.00	8.00	15.00	30.00	—
1746 CPS	—	4.00	8.00	15.00	30.00	—
1747 CPS	—	4.00	8.00	15.00	30.00	—
1749 CPS	—	4.00	8.00	15.00	30.00	—
1750 CPS	—	4.00	8.00	15.00	30.00	—
1752 S	—	4.00	8.00	15.00	30.00	—
1752 C	—	4.00	8.00	15.00	30.00	—
1753 IWS	—	4.00	8.00	15.00	30.00	—
1753 S	—	4.00	8.00	15.00	30.00	—
1754 IWS	—	4.00	8.00	15.00	30.00	—
1754 S	—	4.00	8.00	15.00	30.00	—
1755 IWS	—	4.00	8.00	15.00	30.00	—
1756 IWS	—	4.00	8.00	15.00	30.00	—
1757 IWS	—	4.00	8.00	15.00	30.00	—
1758 IWS	—	4.00	8.00	15.00	30.00	—
1759 IWS	—	4.00	8.00	15.00	30.00	—

KM# 204.2 PFENNING

Copper **Ruler:** George II August **Obverse:** Crowned GR monogram **Reverse:** Value, date **Note:** Similar to KM#204.1 but without mintmaster's initials.

Date	Mintage	VG	F	VF	XF	Unc
1729	—	4.00	8.00	15.00	30.00	—
1732	—	4.00	8.00	15.00	30.00	—
1733	—	4.00	8.00	15.00	30.00	—
1734	—	4.00	8.00	15.00	30.00	—
1739	—	4.00	8.00	15.00	30.00	—
1740	—	4.00	8.00	15.00	30.00	—
1741	—	4.00	8.00	15.00	30.00	—
1742	—	4.00	8.00	15.00	30.00	—
1743	—	4.00	8.00	15.00	30.00	—
1744	—	4.00	8.00	15.00	30.00	—
1745	—	4.00	8.00	15.00	30.00	—
1746	—	4.00	8.00	15.00	30.00	—
1748	—	4.00	8.00	15.00	30.00	—
1749	—	4.00	8.00	15.00	30.00	—
1750	—	4.00	8.00	15.00	30.00	—
1753	—	4.00	8.00	15.00	30.00	—
1755	—	4.00	8.00	15.00	30.00	—

KM# 205 PFENNING

Copper **Ruler:** George II August **Obverse:** St. Andrew with cross **Reverse:** Value, date

Date	Mintage	VG	F	VF	XF	Unc
1729	—	4.00	8.00	16.00	32.00	—
1732	—	4.00	8.00	16.00	32.00	—
1734	—	4.00	8.00	16.00	32.00	—
1736	—	4.00	8.00	16.00	32.00	—
1739	—	4.00	8.00	16.00	32.00	—

KM# 215.1 PFENNING

Copper **Ruler:** George II August **Obverse:** Wildman with tree in right hand **Reverse:** Value, date

Date	Mintage	VG	F	VF	XF	Unc
1730 EPH	—	4.00	8.00	15.00	30.00	—
1732 IAB	—	4.00	8.00	15.00	30.00	—
1737 IAB	—	4.00	8.00	15.00	30.00	—
1737 CPS	—	4.00	8.00	15.00	30.00	—

KM# 215.3 PFENNING

Copper **Ruler:** George II August **Obverse:** Wildman holding tree in his right hand with forest in background **Reverse:** Large letters, "MUNTZ" **Edge:** Plain

Date	Mintage	F	VF	XF	Unc
1737 IAB	—	8.00	15.00	30.00	—

KM# 215.2 PFENNING

Copper **Ruler:** George II August **Obverse:** Wildman holding tree in his right hand, forest in background **Reverse:** Large letters in value, "MVNTZ"

Date	Mintage	VG	F	VF	XF	Unc
1741 IBH	—	4.00	8.00	15.00	30.00	—
1742 IBH	—	4.00	8.00	15.00	30.00	—
1743 IBH	—	4.00	8.00	15.00	30.00	—
1745 IBH	—	4.00	8.00	15.00	30.00	—
1747 IBH	—	4.00	8.00	15.00	30.00	—
1749 IBH	—	4.00	8.00	15.00	30.00	—
1750 IBH	—	4.00	8.00	15.00	30.00	—
1752 IBH	—	4.00	8.00	15.00	30.00	—
1753 IBH	—	4.00	8.00	15.00	30.00	—
1754 IBH	—	4.00	8.00	15.00	30.00	—
1755 IBH	—	4.00	8.00	15.00	30.00	—
1756 IBH	—	4.00	8.00	15.00	30.00	—
1758 IBH	—	4.00	8.00	15.00	30.00	—
1758/5 IBH	—	4.00	8.00	15.00	30.00	—
1759 IBH	—	4.00	8.00	15.00	30.00	—
1760 IBH	—	4.00	8.00	15.00	30.00	—

KM# 330.1 PFENNING

Copper **Ruler:** George III **Obverse:** Wildman holding tree with branches on left side, trees in background **Reverse:** Denomination lines close together

Date	Mintage	F	VF	XF	Unc
1760 IBH	—	10.00	20.00	40.00	80.00
1762 IBH	—	10.00	20.00	40.00	80.00
1763 IAP	—	10.00	20.00	40.00	80.00
1764 IAP	—	10.00	20.00	40.00	80.00
1765 IAP	—	10.00	20.00	40.00	80.00
1766 IAP	—	10.00	20.00	40.00	80.00
1768 IAP	—	10.00	20.00	40.00	80.00
1769 IAP	—	10.00	20.00	40.00	80.00
1770 IAP	—	10.00	20.00	40.00	80.00
1772 IAP	—	10.00	20.00	40.00	80.00
1774 LCR	—	10.00	20.00	40.00	80.00
1776 LCR	—	10.00	20.00	40.00	80.00
1777 LCR	—	10.00	20.00	40.00	80.00
1778 LCR	—	10.00	20.00	40.00	80.00

KM# 337 PFENNING

Copper **Ruler:** George III **Obverse:** Crowned GR monogram, initials below **Reverse:** Value, date **Note:** Similar to KM#360 but denomination PFENNING.

Date	Mintage	F	VF	XF	Unc
1761 IWS	—	4.00	7.00	12.00	40.00
1762 IWS	—	4.00	7.00	12.00	40.00
1763 IWS	—	4.00	7.00	12.00	40.00
1764 IWS	—	4.00	7.00	12.00	40.00
1765 IWS	—	4.00	7.00	12.00	40.00
1767 IWS	—	4.00	7.00	12.00	40.00
1768 IWS	—	4.00	7.00	12.00	40.00

KM# 355 PFENNING

Billon **Ruler:** George III **Obverse:** Crowned GR monogram divides date **Reverse:** Blank

Date	Mintage	F	VF	XF	Unc
1761	—	5.00	10.00	20.00	85.00

KM# 360.1 PFENNING

Copper **Ruler:** George III **Obverse:** Crowned GR monogram **Reverse:** Denomination, PFENN

Date	Mintage	F	VF	XF	Unc
1768 IWS	—	7.00	15.00	35.00	65.00
1769 IWS	—	7.00	15.00	35.00	65.00
1770 IWS	—	7.00	15.00	35.00	65.00
1771 IWS	—	7.00	15.00	35.00	65.00
1772 IWS	—	7.00	15.00	35.00	65.00
1773 IWS	—	7.00	15.00	35.00	65.00
1774 IWS	—	7.00	15.00	35.00	65.00
1775 IWS	—	7.00	15.00	35.00	65.00
1776 IWS	—	7.00	15.00	35.00	65.00
1777 IWS	—	7.00	15.00	35.00	65.00
1778 IWS	—	7.00	15.00	35.00	65.00
1779 IWS	—	7.00	15.00	35.00	65.00
1780 IWS	—	7.00	15.00	35.00	65.00
1781 IWS	—	7.00	15.00	35.00	65.00
1782 IWS	—	7.00	15.00	35.00	65.00
1783 IWS	—	7.00	15.00	35.00	65.00
1784 IWS	—	7.00	15.00	35.00	65.00
1785 IWS	—	7.00	15.00	35.00	65.00
1786 IWS	—	7.00	15.00	35.00	65.00
1787 IWS	—	7.00	15.00	35.00	65.00
1788 IWS	—	7.00	15.00	35.00	65.00
1789 IWS	—	7.00	15.00	35.00	65.00
1790 IWS	—	7.00	15.00	35.00	65.00
1790 .C.	—	7.00	15.00	35.00	65.00
1791 .C.	—	7.00	15.00	35.00	65.00
1792 .C.	—	7.00	15.00	35.00	65.00
1793 PLM	—	7.00	15.00	35.00	65.00
1794 PLM	—	7.00	15.00	35.00	65.00
1795 PLM	—	7.00	15.00	35.00	65.00
1796 PLM	—	7.00	15.00	35.00	65.00
1797 PLM	—	7.00	15.00	35.00	65.00
1798 PLM	—	7.00	15.00	35.00	65.00
1799 PLM	—	7.00	15.00	35.00	65.00
1800/700 PLM	—	8.00	16.00	40.00	75.00
1800 PLM	—	7.00	15.00	35.00	65.00
1801 .C.	—	7.00	15.00	35.00	65.00

KM# 380 PFENNING

Copper **Ruler:** George III **Obverse:** Standing St. Andrew facing, cross **Reverse:** Value, date

Date	Mintage	F	VF	XF	Unc
1780 IWS	—	8.00	20.00	50.00	75.00
1781 IWS	—	8.00	20.00	50.00	75.00
1782 IWS	—	8.00	20.00	50.00	75.00
1782 C	—	8.00	20.00	50.00	75.00
1783 IWS	—	8.00	20.00	50.00	75.00
1784 IWS	—	8.00	20.00	50.00	75.00
1785 IWS	—	8.00	20.00	50.00	75.00
1786 IWS	—	8.00	20.00	50.00	75.00
1787 IWS	—	8.00	20.00	50.00	75.00
1788 IWS	—	8.00	20.00	50.00	75.00
1789 IWS	—	8.00	20.00	50.00	75.00
1793 PLM	—	8.00	20.00	50.00	75.00
1801 C	—	8.00	20.00	50.00	75.00
1802 C	—	8.00	20.00	50.00	75.00

KM# 330.2 PFENNING

Copper **Ruler:** George III **Obverse:** Without small pine trees on flat ground **Reverse:** Value, date

Date	Mintage	F	VF	XF	Unc
1780 CES	—	10.00	20.00	40.00	80.00
1781 CES	—	10.00	20.00	40.00	80.00
1783 CES	—	10.00	20.00	40.00	80.00
1784 CES	—	10.00	20.00	40.00	80.00
1785 CES	—	10.00	20.00	40.00	80.00
1788 .C.	—	10.00	20.00	40.00	80.00

KM# 330.3 PFENNING

Copper **Ruler:** George III **Obverse:** Small hill and tiny trees **Reverse:** Value, date

Date	Mintage	F	VF	XF	Unc
1794 PLM	—	10.00	20.00	40.00	80.00
1795 PLM	—	10.00	20.00	40.00	80.00
1796 PLM	—	10.00	20.00	40.00	80.00

KM# 381 PFENNING

Copper **Ruler:** George III **Obverse:** Cross below St. Andrew's right arm

Date	Mintage	F	VF	XF	Unc
1782 S	—	7.50	15.00	22.00	65.00

KM# 136 1-1/2 PFENNING

Copper **Ruler:** George Ludwig **Obverse:** Crowned GR monogram **Reverse:** Value, date

Date	Mintage	VG	F	VF	XF	Unc
1718	—	9.00	16.00	32.00	60.00	—
1721	—	9.00	16.00	32.00	60.00	—
1722	—	9.00	16.00	32.00	60.00	—

KM# 310 1-1/2 PFENNING

Copper **Ruler:** George II August **Obverse:** Crowned GR monogram **Reverse:** Value, date

Date	Mintage	VG	F	VF	XF	Unc
1750 S	—	5.00	9.00	18.00	35.00	—

KM# 397 1-1/2 PFENNING

Copper **Ruler:** George III **Obverse:** Crowned GR monogram **Reverse:** Value, date

Date	Mintage	F	VF	XF	Unc
1792 .C.	—	8.00	16.00	32.00	70.00
1792 PLM	—	8.00	16.00	32.00	70.00

KM# 268 2 PFENNING

Copper **Ruler:** George III **Obverse:** Horse left **Reverse:** Value, date

Date	Mintage	F	VF	XF	Unc
1735 Rare	—	—	—	—	—

KM# 402 2 PFENNING

Copper **Ruler:** George III **Obverse:** Crowned monogram **Reverse:** Denomination, date

Date	Mintage	F	VF	XF	Unc
1794 PLM	—	5.00	15.00	35.00	75.00
1795 PLM	—	5.00	15.00	35.00	75.00
1796 PLM	—	5.00	15.00	35.00	75.00
1797 PLM	—	5.00	15.00	35.00	75.00
1798 PLM	—	5.00	15.00	35.00	75.00
1799 PLM	—	5.00	15.00	35.00	75.00
1800 PLM	—	5.00	15.00	35.00	75.00

KM# 44 3 PFENNING (Dreier)

Billon **Ruler:** George Ludwig **Obverse:** Crowned GL monogram **Reverse:** Imperial orb with 3 divides date

Date	Mintage	VG	F	VF	XF	Unc
1704 RB	—	6.00	12.00	25.00	40.00	—
1705 RB	—	6.00	12.00	25.00	40.00	—
1706 RB	—	6.00	12.00	25.00	40.00	—
1707 RB	—	6.00	12.00	25.00	40.00	—
1708 RB	—	6.00	12.00	25.00	40.00	—
1710 RB	—	6.00	12.00	25.00	40.00	—
1712 HH	—	6.00	12.00	25.00	40.00	—
1713 HH	—	6.00	12.00	25.00	40.00	—

KM# 105 3 PFENNING (Dreier)

Billon **Ruler:** George Ludwig **Obverse:** Crowned GR monogram

Date	Mintage	VG	F	VF	XF	Unc
1716 HH	—	6.00	12.00	20.00	35.00	—
1717 HH	—	6.00	12.00	20.00	35.00	—
1717 HCB	—	6.00	12.00	20.00	35.00	—
1718 HCB	—	6.00	12.00	20.00	35.00	—
1719 HCB	—	6.00	12.00	20.00	35.00	—
1721 HCB	—	6.00	12.00	20.00	35.00	—
1723 HCB	—	6.00	12.00	20.00	35.00	—
1724 EPH	—	6.00	12.00	20.00	35.00	—

KM# 117 3 PFENNING (Dreier)

Billon **Ruler:** George Ludwig **Obverse:** Crowned GR monogram **Reverse:** Value, date in 4 lines

Date	Mintage	VG	F	VF	XF	Unc
1717 HCB	—	9.00	20.00	32.00	55.00	—

KM# 162 3 PFENNING (Dreier)

Billon **Ruler:** George Ludwig **Obverse:** 3 also near monogram

Date	Mintage	VG	F	VF	XF	Unc
1723 HCB	—	6.00	12.00	25.00	50.00	—
1724	—	6.00	12.00	25.00	50.00	—

KM# 239 3 PFENNING (Dreier)

Billon **Ruler:** George II August **Reverse:** Imperial orb with 3 **Rev. Legend:** NACH DEM

Date	Mintage	VG	F	VF	XF	Unc
1731 C	—	5.00	12.00	25.00	50.00	—
1733 CPS	—	5.00	12.00	25.00	50.00	—
1740 CPS	—	5.00	12.00	25.00	50.00	—
1741 CPS	—	5.00	12.00	25.00	50.00	—
1742 CPS	—	5.00	12.00	25.00	50.00	—
1743 CPS	—	5.00	12.00	25.00	50.00	—
1744 CPS	—	5.00	12.00	25.00	50.00	—
1751 C	—	5.00	12.00	25.00	50.00	—

KM# 242 3 PFENNING (Dreier)

Billon **Ruler:** George II August **Reverse:** Imperial orb with 3

Date	Mintage	VG	F	VF	XF	Unc
1732 CPS	—	5.00	12.00	25.00	50.00	—
1733 CPS	—	5.00	12.00	25.00	50.00	—

KM# 25 4 PFENNING

Billon **Ruler:** George Ludwig **Obverse:** Horse leaping left **Reverse:** Value, date **Note:** Varieties exist.

Date	Mintage	VG	F	VF	XF	Unc
1699	—	8.00	15.00	25.00	40.00	—
1700 HB	—	8.00	15.00	25.00	40.00	—
1701 HB	—	8.00	15.00	25.00	40.00	—
1702 HB	—	8.00	15.00	25.00	40.00	—
1704 HB	—	8.00	15.00	25.00	40.00	—
1705 HB	—	8.00	15.00	25.00	40.00	—
1706 HB	—	8.00	15.00	25.00	40.00	—
1707 HB	—	8.00	15.00	25.00	40.00	—
1708 HB	—	8.00	15.00	25.00	40.00	—
1709 HB	—	8.00	15.00	25.00	40.00	—
1710 HB	—	8.00	15.00	25.00	40.00	—
1711 HB	—	8.00	15.00	25.00	40.00	—
1712 HCB	—	8.00	15.00	25.00	40.00	—
1713 HCB	—	8.00	15.00	25.00	40.00	—
1714 HCB	—	8.00	15.00	25.00	40.00	—
1715 HCB	—	8.00	15.00	25.00	40.00	—

KM# 36 4 PFENNING

Billon **Ruler:** George Ludwig **Obverse:** Crowned GL monogram **Reverse:** Value, with GVTE..., date in 4 lines **Note:** Gute 4 Pfenning.

Date	Mintage	VG	F	VF	XF	Unc
1702	—	—	—	—	—	—

KM# 45 4 PFENNING

Billon **Ruler:** George Ludwig **Reverse:** Value with LAND MUNTZ

Date	Mintage	VG	F	VF	XF	Unc
1704 RB	—	8.00	15.00	25.00	40.00	—
1705 RB	—	8.00	15.00	25.00	40.00	—
1706 RB	—	8.00	15.00	25.00	40.00	—
1707 RB	—	8.00	15.00	25.00	40.00	—
1710 RB	—	8.00	15.00	25.00	40.00	—
1711 RB	—	8.00	15.00	25.00	40.00	—
1713 HH	—	8.00	15.00	25.00	40.00	—

KM# 118 4 PFENNING

Billon **Ruler:** George Ludwig **Obverse:** Crowned GR monogram **Reverse:** Value, date

Date	Mintage	VG	F	VF	XF	Unc
1717 HCB	—	10.00	20.00	35.00	55.00	—
1717 HH	—	10.00	20.00	35.00	55.00	—
1718 HH	—	10.00	20.00	35.00	55.00	—
1718 HCB	—	10.00	20.00	35.00	55.00	—
1719 HCB	—	10.00	20.00	35.00	55.00	—
1720 HCB	—	10.00	20.00	35.00	55.00	—
1723 HCB	—	10.00	20.00	35.00	55.00	—
1726 HCB	—	10.00	20.00	35.00	55.00	—
1727 CPS	—	10.00	20.00	35.00	55.00	—

KM# 206 4 PFENNING

Billon **Ruler:** George II August **Obverse:** Crowned GR monogram **Reverse:** Value, date

Date	Mintage	VG	F	VF	XF	Unc
1729	—	5.00	10.00	20.00	40.00	—
1729 EPH	—	5.00	10.00	20.00	40.00	—
1729 CPS	—	5.00	10.00	20.00	40.00	—
1731 CPS	—	5.00	10.00	20.00	40.00	—
1732 CPS	—	5.00	10.00	20.00	40.00	—
1733 CPS	—	5.00	10.00	20.00	40.00	—
1733 IAB	—	5.00	10.00	20.00	40.00	—
1735 CPS	—	5.00	10.00	20.00	40.00	—
1735 IAB	—	5.00	10.00	20.00	40.00	—
1738 CPS	—	5.00	10.00	20.00	40.00	—
1739 IBH	—	5.00	10.00	20.00	40.00	—
1744 IBH	—	5.00	10.00	20.00	40.00	—
1745 IBH	—	5.00	10.00	20.00	40.00	—
1746 IBH	—	5.00	10.00	20.00	40.00	—
1750 IBH	—	5.00	10.00	20.00	40.00	—
1752 IBH	—	5.00	10.00	20.00	40.00	—
1753 IBH	—	5.00	10.00	20.00	40.00	—
1754 IBH	—	5.00	10.00	20.00	40.00	—
1755 IBH	—	5.00	10.00	20.00	40.00	—
1756 IBH	—	5.00	10.00	20.00	40.00	—
1759 IBH	—	5.00	10.00	20.00	40.00	—
1760 IBH	—	5.00	10.00	20.00	40.00	—

KM# 265 4 PFENNING

Billon **Ruler:** George II August **Obverse:** Crowned monogram **Reverse:** Value, date

Date	Mintage	VG	F	VF	XF	Unc
1739 CPS	—	5.00	10.00	20.00	40.00	—
1740 CPS	—	5.00	10.00	20.00	40.00	—
1741 CPS	—	5.00	10.00	20.00	40.00	—
1742 CPS	—	5.00	10.00	20.00	40.00	—
1743 CPS	—	5.00	10.00	20.00	40.00	—
1744 CPS	—	5.00	10.00	20.00	40.00	—
1745 CPS	—	5.00	10.00	20.00	40.00	—
1754 IWS	—	5.00	10.00	20.00	40.00	—
1755 IWS	—	5.00	10.00	20.00	40.00	—
1759 IWS	—	5.00	10.00	20.00	40.00	—

KM# 331 4 PFENNING

Billon **Ruler:** George III **Reverse:** K. GR. BR.., value

Date	Mintage	F	VF	XF	Unc
1760 IBH	—	3.00	7.00	15.00	40.00
1762 IBH	—	3.00	7.00	15.00	40.00
1763 IAP	—	3.00	7.00	15.00	40.00
1765 IAP	—	3.00	7.00	15.00	40.00
1766 IAP	—	3.00	7.00	15.00	40.00
1768 IAP	—	3.00	7.00	15.00	40.00
1770 IAP	—	3.00	7.00	15.00	40.00
1771 IAP	—	3.00	7.00	15.00	40.00
1772 IAP	—	3.00	7.00	15.00	40.00
1775 LCR	—	3.00	7.00	15.00	40.00
1777 LCR	—	3.00	7.00	15.00	40.00
1779 .C.	—	3.00	7.00	15.00	40.00

KM# 338 4 PFENNING

Billon **Ruler:** George III **Obverse:** Crowned GR monogram **Reverse:** Value **Rev. Legend:** NACH DEM LEIPZIGER FUS

Date	Mintage	F	VF	XF	Unc
1761 IWS	—	10.00	20.00	40.00	75.00

KM# 344 4 PFENNING

Billon **Ruler:** George III **Obverse:** Crowned GR monogram **Reverse:** Value, date

Date	Mintage	F	VF	XF	Unc
1762 IWS	—	10.00	20.00	40.00	70.00
1763 IWS	—	10.00	20.00	40.00	70.00
1764 IWS	—	10.00	20.00	40.00	70.00
1765 IWS	—	10.00	20.00	40.00	70.00
1767 IWS	—	10.00	20.00	40.00	70.00
1769 IWS	—	10.00	20.00	40.00	70.00
1771 IWS	—	10.00	20.00	40.00	70.00
1772 IWS	—	10.00	20.00	40.00	70.00
1774 IWS	—	10.00	20.00	40.00	70.00
1776 IWS	—	10.00	20.00	40.00	70.00
1777 IWS	—	10.00	20.00	40.00	70.00
1779 IWS	—	10.00	20.00	40.00	70.00
1780 IWS	—	10.00	20.00	40.00	70.00
1781 IWS	—	10.00	20.00	40.00	70.00
1782 IWS	—	10.00	20.00	40.00	70.00
1783 IWS	—	10.00	20.00	40.00	70.00
1784 IWS	—	10.00	20.00	40.00	70.00
1785 IWS	—	10.00	20.00	40.00	70.00
1787 IWS	—	10.00	20.00	40.00	70.00
1788 IWS	—	10.00	20.00	40.00	70.00
1791 .C.	—	10.00	20.00	40.00	70.00
1792 .C.	—	10.00	20.00	40.00	70.00
1793 PLM	—	10.00	20.00	40.00	70.00
1795 PLM	—	10.00	20.00	40.00	70.00
1797 PLM	—	10.00	20.00	40.00	70.00

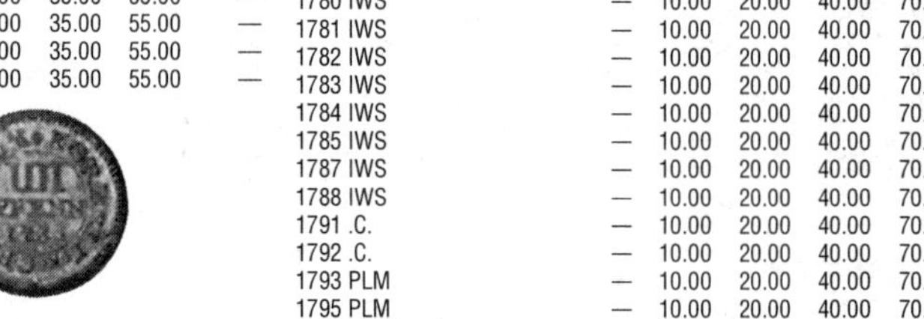

Date	Mintage	F	VF	XF	Unc
1799 PLM	—	10.00	20.00	40.00	70.00
1802 .C.	—	10.00	20.00	40.00	70.00
1804 GFM	—	7.00	15.00	30.00	60.00

KM# 398 4 PFENNING

Copper **Ruler:** George III **Obverse:** Standing St. Andrew, cross **Reverse:** Value, date

Date	Mintage	F	VF	XF	Unc
1792 .C.	—	10.00	20.00	40.00	100
1794 PLM	—	10.00	20.00	40.00	100

KM# 403 4 PFENNING

Copper **Ruler:** George III **Reverse:** Value, date

Date	Mintage	F	VF	XF	Unc
1794 PLM	—	6.00	10.00	30.00	100
1795 PLM	—	6.00	10.00	30.00	100
1796 PLM	—	6.00	10.00	30.00	100

KM# 40 4-1/2 PFENNIG

Billon **Ruler:** George Ludwig **Obverse:** Crowned GL monogram **Reverse:** Value, date in 3 lines in circle

Date	Mintage	VG	F	VF	XF	Unc
1703	—	20.00	40.00	75.00	150	—

KM# 39 4-1/2 PFENNIG

Billon **Ruler:** George Ludwig **Obverse:** Crowned GL monogram **Reverse:** Value, date in 4 lines **Note:** Gute 4-1/2 Pfennig.

Date	Mintage	VG	F	VF	XF	Unc
1703	—	20.00	40.00	75.00	150	—
1703 RB	—	20.00	40.00	75.00	150	—

KM# 119 6 PFENNIG

Billon **Ruler:** George Ludwig **Obverse:** Crowned GR monogram **Reverse:** Value, date in 4 lines

Date	Mintage	VG	F	VF	XF	Unc
1717 HCB	—	15.00	25.00	45.00	80.00	—

KM# 120 6 PFENNIG

Billon **Ruler:** George Ludwig **Reverse:** Imperial orb with VI divides date

Date	Mintage	VG	F	VF	XF	Unc
1717 HCB	—	10.00	20.00	40.00	75.00	—
1718 HCB	—	10.00	20.00	40.00	75.00	—
1719 HCB	—	10.00	20.00	40.00	75.00	—
1721 HCB	—	10.00	20.00	40.00	75.00	—
1722 HCB	—	10.00	20.00	40.00	75.00	—

KM# 137 6 PFENNIG

Billon **Ruler:** George Ludwig **Reverse:** Value 6

Date	Mintage	VG	F	VF	XF	Unc
1718 HCB	—	15.00	25.00	45.00	80.00	—
1719 HCB	—	15.00	25.00	45.00	80.00	—

KM# 249 6 PFENNIG

Billon **Ruler:** George II August **Reverse:** Imperial orb with VI

Date	Mintage	VG	F	VF	XF	Unc
1733 CPS	—	8.00	15.00	30.00	60.00	—
1735 CPS	—	8.00	15.00	30.00	60.00	—

KM# 270 6 PFENNIG

Billon **Ruler:** George II August **Rev. Legend:** NACH DEM

Date	Mintage	VG	F	VF	XF	Unc
1740 CPS	—	8.00	15.00	30.00	60.00	—
1751 C	—	8.00	15.00	30.00	60.00	—

KM# 350 6 PFENNIG

Billon **Ruler:** George III **Obverse:** Crowned GR monogram **Reverse:** VI in orb

Date	Mintage	F	VF	XF	Unc
1763 IWS	—	10.00	30.00	60.00	125
1764 IWC		7.00	25.00	60.00	100

KM# 26 MARIENGROSCHEN

Silver **Ruler:** George Ludwig **Obverse:** Value, date in 4 lines **Reverse:** Madonna and child

Date	Mintage	VG	F	VF	XF	Unc
1699 HB	—	5.00	10.00	15.00	30.00	—
1700 HB	—	5.00	10.00	15.00	30.00	—
1701 HB	—	5.00	10.00	15.00	30.00	—
1702 HB	—	5.00	10.00	15.00	30.00	—
1703 HB	—	5.00	10.00	15.00	30.00	—
1703 III	—	5.00	10.00	15.00	30.00	—
1704 HB	—	5.00	10.00	15.00	30.00	—
1705 HB	—	5.00	10.00	15.00	30.00	—
1706 HB	—	5.00	10.00	15.00	30.00	—
1706 RB	—	5.00	10.00	15.00	30.00	—
1707 HB	—	5.00	10.00	15.00	30.00	—
1707 RB	—	5.00	10.00	15.00	30.00	—
1708 HB	—	5.00	10.00	15.00	30.00	—
1708 ***	—	5.00	10.00	15.00	30.00	—
1709 HB	—	5.00	10.00	15.00	30.00	—
1709 RB	—	5.00	10.00	15.00	30.00	—
1710 HB	—	5.00	10.00	15.00	30.00	—
1710 RB	—	5.00	10.00	15.00	30.00	—
1711 HB	—	5.00	10.00	15.00	30.00	—
1712 HCB	—	5.00	10.00	15.00	30.00	—
1712 HH	—	5.00	10.00	15.00	30.00	—
1713 HCB	—	5.00	10.00	15.00	30.00	—
1713 HH	—	5.00	10.00	15.00	30.00	—
1714 HCB	—	5.00	10.00	15.00	30.00	—
1714 HH	—	5.00	10.00	15.00	30.00	—
1715 HCB	—	5.00	10.00	15.00	30.00	—

KM# 106 MARIENGROSCHEN

Silver **Ruler:** George Ludwig **Obverse:** Crowned GR monogram **Reverse:** Value, date in 4 lines

Date	Mintage	VG	F	VF	XF	Unc
1716 HCB	—	7.00	15.00	30.00	50.00	—
1717 HCB	—	7.00	15.00	30.00	50.00	—
1718 HCB	—	7.00	15.00	30.00	50.00	—
1719 HCB	—	7.00	15.00	30.00	50.00	—
1720 HCB	—	7.00	15.00	30.00	50.00	—
1721 HCB	—	7.00	15.00	30.00	50.00	—
1722 HCB	—	7.00	15.00	30.00	50.00	—
1724	—	7.00	15.00	30.00	50.00	—
1724 EPH	—	7.00	15.00	30.00	50.00	—
1727 CPS	—	7.00	15.00	30.00	50.00	—

KM# 121 MARIENGROSCHEN

Silver **Ruler:** George Ludwig **Reverse:** Without MARIEN

Date	Mintage	VG	F	VF	XF	Unc
1717 HCB	—	10.00	20.00	35.00	65.00	—

KM# 172 MARIENGROSCHEN

Billon **Ruler:** George II August **Obverse:** Crowned monogram **Reverse:** With MARIEN

Date	Mintage	VG	F	VF	XF	Unc
1727 CPS	—	5.00	10.00	18.00	36.00	—
1729 CPS	—	5.00	10.00	18.00	36.00	—
1730 CPS	—	5.00	10.00	18.00	36.00	—
1731 CPS	—	5.00	10.00	18.00	36.00	—
1733 CPS	—	5.00	10.00	18.00	36.00	—
1734 CPS	—	5.00	10.00	18.00	36.00	—
1735 CPS	—	5.00	10.00	18.00	36.00	—
1735 IAB	—	5.00	10.00	18.00	36.00	—
1736 CPS	—	5.00	10.00	18.00	36.00	—
1741 IBH	—	5.00	10.00	18.00	36.00	—
1744 IBH	—	5.00	10.00	18.00	36.00	—
1746 IBH	—	5.00	10.00	18.00	36.00	—
1747 IBH	—	5.00	10.00	18.00	36.00	—
1748 IBH	—	5.00	10.00	18.00	36.00	—
1749 IBH	—	5.00	10.00	18.00	36.00	—
1751 IBH	—	5.00	10.00	18.00	36.00	—
1752 IBH	—	5.00	10.00	18.00	36.00	—
1753 IBH	—	5.00	10.00	18.00	36.00	—
1754 IBH	—	5.00	10.00	18.00	36.00	—
1760 IBH	—	5.00	10.00	18.00	36.00	—

KM# 260 MARIENGROSCHEN

Billon **Ruler:** George II August **Reverse:** Date in field **Rev. Legend:** NACH DEM

Date	Mintage	VG	F	VF	XF	Unc
1738 CPS	—	5.00	10.00	18.00	36.00	—
1739 CPS	—	5.00	10.00	18.00	36.00	—
1740 CPS	—	5.00	10.00	18.00	36.00	—
1741 CPS	—	5.00	10.00	18.00	36.00	—
1742 CPS	—	5.00	10.00	18.00	36.00	—
1751 C	—	5.00	10.00	18.00	36.00	—
1753 C	—	5.00	10.00	18.00	36.00	—
1753 IWS	—	5.00	10.00	18.00	36.00	—
1755 IWS	—	5.00	10.00	18.00	36.00	—
1758 IWS	—	5.00	10.00	18.00	36.00	—

KM# 278 MARIENGROSCHEN

Billon **Ruler:** George II August **Note:** Similar to KM#260 but date in legend.

Date	Mintage	VG	F	VF	XF	Unc
1741 CPS	—	5.00	10.00	18.00	36.00	—
1742 CPS	—	5.00	10.00	18.00	36.00	—
1743 CPS	—	5.00	10.00	18.00	36.00	—
1744 CPS	—	5.00	10.00	18.00	36.00	—
1745 CPS	—	5.00	10.00	18.00	36.00	—
1747 CPS	—	5.00	10.00	18.00	36.00	—

KM# 339 MARIENGROSCHEN

Billon **Ruler:** George III **Obverse:** Crowned GR monogram **Reverse:** Value **Rev. Legend:** NACH DEM LEIPZIGER FUS

Date	Mintage	F	VF	XF	Unc
1761 IWS Rare	—	—	—	—	—

KM# 345 MARIENGROSCHEN

Billon **Ruler:** George III **Obverse:** Crowned GR monogram **Reverse:** Value, date

Date	Mintage	F	VF	XF	Unc
1762 IWS	—	10.00	25.00	40.00	65.00
1763 IWS	—	10.00	25.00	40.00	65.00
1765 IWS	—	10.00	25.00	40.00	65.00
1766 IWS	—	10.00	25.00	40.00	65.00
1767 IWS	—	10.00	25.00	40.00	65.00
1768 IWS	—	10.00	25.00	40.00	65.00
1769 IWS	—	10.00	25.00	40.00	65.00
1770 IWS	—	10.00	25.00	40.00	65.00
1771 IWS	—	10.00	25.00	40.00	65.00
1773 IWS	—	10.00	25.00	40.00	65.00
1774 IWS	—	10.00	25.00	40.00	65.00
1775 IWS	—	10.00	25.00	40.00	65.00
1776 IWS	—	10.00	25.00	40.00	65.00
1777 IWS	—	10.00	25.00	40.00	65.00
1778 IWS	—	10.00	25.00	40.00	65.00
1779 IWS	—	10.00	25.00	40.00	65.00
1781 IWS	—	10.00	25.00	40.00	65.00
1782 IWS	—	10.00	25.00	40.00	65.00
1783 IWS	—	10.00	25.00	40.00	65.00
1784 IWS	—	10.00	25.00	40.00	65.00
1785 IWS	—	10.00	25.00	40.00	65.00
1787 IWS	—	10.00	25.00	40.00	65.00
1790 .C.	—	10.00	25.00	40.00	65.00
1791 .C.	—	10.00	25.00	40.00	65.00
1793 PLM	—	10.00	25.00	40.00	65.00
1797 PLM	—	10.00	25.00	40.00	65.00
1799 PLM	—	10.00	25.00	40.00	65.00
1802 .C.	—	10.00	25.00	40.00	65.00
1803 GFM	—	10.00	25.00	40.00	95.00
1804 GFM	—	10.00	25.00	40.00	95.00

KM# 351 MARIENGROSCHEN

Billon **Ruler:** George III **Reverse:** Value, K. GR. BR

Date	Mintage	F	VF	XF	Unc
1763 IAP	—	5.00	12.00	25.00	50.00
1764 IAP	—	5.00	12.00	25.00	50.00
1765 IAP	—	5.00	12.00	25.00	50.00
1766 IAP	—	5.00	12.00	25.00	50.00
1768 IAP	—	5.00	12.00	25.00	50.00
1769 IWS	—	5.00	12.00	25.00	50.00
1770 IAP	—	5.00	12.00	25.00	50.00
1771 IAP	—	5.00	12.00	25.00	50.00
1775 LCR	—	5.00	12.00	25.00	50.00
1776 LCR	—	5.00	12.00	25.00	50.00

KM# 6 2 MARIENGROSCHEN

Silver **Ruler:** George Ludwig **Obverse:** Value in 3 lines, date in legend **Reverse:** Wildman, tree in right hand

Date	Mintage	VG	F	VF	XF	Unc
1698 ***	—	5.00	10.00	16.00	35.00	—
1700 ***	—	5.00	10.00	16.00	35.00	—
1701 ***	—	5.00	10.00	16.00	35.00	—
1702 ***	—	5.00	10.00	16.00	35.00	—
1703 ***	—	5.00	10.00	16.00	35.00	—
1704 ***	—	5.00	10.00	16.00	35.00	—
1707 ***	—	5.00	10.00	16.00	35.00	—
1708 ***	—	5.00	10.00	16.00	35.00	—
1709 ***	—	5.00	10.00	16.00	35.00	—
1710 ***	—	5.00	10.00	16.00	35.00	—
1711 C	—	5.00	10.00	16.00	35.00	—

KM# 31 2 MARIENGROSCHEN

Silver **Ruler:** George Ludwig **Obverse:** Value and date within inner circle **Reverse:** Horse leaping left within inner circle

Date	Mintage	VG	F	VF	XF	Unc
1700	—	5.00	9.00	18.00	35.00	—
1702	—	5.00	9.00	18.00	35.00	—
1704	—	5.00	9.00	18.00	35.00	—
1705 HB	—	5.00	9.00	18.00	35.00	—

KM# 52 2 MARIENGROSCHEN

Silver **Ruler:** George Ludwig **Obverse:** Value, date **Reverse:** St. Andrew **Note:** Varieties exist.

Date	Mintage	VG	F	VF	XF	Unc
1706 HB	—	6.00	12.00	20.00	40.00	—
1708 HB	—	6.00	12.00	20.00	40.00	—

Date	Mintage	VG	F	VF	XF	Unc
ND	—	6.00	12.00	20.00	40.00	—

KM# 84 2 MARIENGROSCHEN

Silver **Ruler:** George Ludwig **Obverse:** Value, date in 4 lines **Reverse:** Wildman, tree in right hand

Date	Mintage	VG	F	VF	XF	Unc
1712 HH	—	7.00	15.00	30.00	55.00	—
1713 HH	—	7.00	15.00	30.00	55.00	—
1714 HH	—	7.00	15.00	30.00	55.00	—
1715 HH	—	7.00	15.00	30.00	55.00	—

KM# 85 2 MARIENGROSCHEN

Silver **Ruler:** George Ludwig **Obverse:** 6 lines with FEIN SILB

Date	Mintage	VG	F	VF	XF	Unc
1713 HH	—	5.00	10.00	16.00	35.00	—
1714 HH	—	5.00	10.00	16.00	35.00	—
1715 HH	—	5.00	10.00	16.00	35.00	—

KM# 83 2 MARIENGROSCHEN

Silver **Ruler:** George Ludwig **Obverse:** Value, date **Reverse:** Horse leaping left

Date	Mintage	VG	F	VF	XF	Unc
1713 HCB	—	5.00	9.00	18.00	35.00	—
1714 HCB	—	5.00	9.00	18.00	35.00	—

KM# 122 2 MARIENGROSCHEN

Silver **Ruler:** George Ludwig **Obverse:** Crowned GR monogram **Reverse:** Value, date in 4 lines **Rev. Legend:** LAND MUNTZ

Date	Mintage	VG	F	VF	XF	Unc
1717 HCB	—	9.00	18.00	35.00	65.00	—
1718 HCB	—	9.00	18.00	35.00	65.00	—
1719 HCB	—	9.00	18.00	35.00	65.00	—
1720 HCB	—	9.00	18.00	35.00	65.00	—
1725 HCB	—	9.00	18.00	35.00	65.00	—
1727 CPS	—	9.00	18.00	35.00	65.00	—

KM# 123 2 MARIENGROSCHEN

Silver **Ruler:** George Ludwig **Reverse:** Value, date in 4 lines, without legend

Date	Mintage	VG	F	VF	XF	Unc
1717 HCB	—	10.00	25.00	40.00	65.00	—

KM# 124 2 MARIENGROSCHEN

Silver **Ruler:** George Ludwig **Obverse:** Crowned GR monogram **Reverse:** Value, date **Rev. Legend:** VON FEINEM SILBER

Date	Mintage	VG	F	VF	XF	Unc
1717 HCB	—	18.00	40.00	75.00	120	—
1717 HH	—	18.00	40.00	75.00	120	—
1719 C	—	18.00	40.00	75.00	120	—
1720 C	—	18.00	40.00	75.00	120	—
1723	—	15.00	30.00	55.00	90.00	—
1724	—	15.00	30.00	55.00	90.00	—
1725 EPH	—	18.00	40.00	75.00	120	—
1726 EPH	—	18.00	40.00	75.00	120	—

KM# 168 2 MARIENGROSCHEN

Silver **Ruler:** George Ludwig **Obverse:** Date below monogram **Reverse:** Value in 3 lines

Date	Mintage	VG	F	VF	XF	Unc
1725	—	—	—	—	—	—

KM# 169 2 MARIENGROSCHEN

Silver **Ruler:** George Ludwig **Obverse:** 2 in field

Date	Mintage	VG	F	VF	XF	Unc
1726 EPH	—	15.00	30.00	55.00	90.00	—

KM# 173 2 MARIENGROSCHEN

Silver **Ruler:** George II August **Obverse:** Crowned GR monogram **Reverse:** Value, date

Date	Mintage	F	VF	XF	Unc
1727 CPS	—	10.00	20.00	40.00	75.00
1729 CPS	—	10.00	20.00	40.00	75.00
1731 CPS	—	10.00	20.00	40.00	75.00
1732 CPS	—	10.00	20.00	40.00	75.00
1734 CPS	—	10.00	20.00	40.00	75.00
1735 CPS	—	10.00	20.00	40.00	75.00
1737 CPS	—	10.00	20.00	40.00	75.00
1740 CPS	—	10.00	20.00	40.00	75.00

KM# 216 2 MARIENGROSCHEN

Silver **Ruler:** George II August **Obverse:** Value, date **Reverse:** Wildman

Date	Mintage	F	VF	XF	Unc
1730 EPH	—	12.00	25.00	50.00	100
1731 IAB	—	12.00	25.00	50.00	100
1732 IAB	—	12.00	25.00	50.00	100
1733 IAB	—	12.00	25.00	50.00	100
1734 IAB	—	12.00	25.00	50.00	100
1735 IAB	—	12.00	25.00	50.00	100
1736 IAB	—	12.00	25.00	50.00	100
1737 IAB	—	12.00	25.00	50.00	100
1738 IAB	—	12.00	25.00	50.00	100
1739 IAB	—	12.00	25.00	50.00	100
1739 C	—	12.00	25.00	50.00	100
1739 IBH	—	12.00	25.00	50.00	100
1740 IBH	—	12.00	25.00	50.00	100
1741 IBH	—	12.00	25.00	50.00	100
1742 IBH	—	12.00	25.00	50.00	100
1743 IBH	—	12.00	25.00	50.00	100
1745 IBH	—	12.00	25.00	50.00	100
1746 IBH	—	12.00	25.00	50.00	100
1748 IBH	—	12.00	25.00	50.00	100
1750 IBH	—	12.00	25.00	50.00	100
1751 IBH	—	12.00	25.00	50.00	100
1753 IBH	—	12.00	25.00	50.00	100
1756 IBH	—	12.00	25.00	50.00	100
1758 IBH	—	12.00	25.00	50.00	100
1759 IBH	—	12.00	25.00	50.00	100
1760 IBH	—	12.00	25.00	50.00	100

KM# 271 2 MARIENGROSCHEN

Silver **Ruler:** George II August **Obverse:** Crowned GR monogram **Reverse:** Value, date

Date	Mintage	F	VF	XF	Unc
1740 CPS	—	10.00	20.00	40.00	75.00
1741 CPS	—	10.00	20.00	40.00	75.00
1742 CPS	—	10.00	20.00	40.00	75.00
1744 CPS	—	10.00	20.00	40.00	75.00
1745 CPS	—	10.00	20.00	40.00	75.00
1747 CPS	—	10.00	20.00	40.00	75.00
1752 C	—	10.00	20.00	40.00	75.00
1753 IWS	—	10.00	20.00	40.00	75.00

KM# 279 2 MARIENGROSCHEN

Silver **Ruler:** George II August **Reverse:** Date in field **Rev. Legend:** NACH DEM

Date	Mintage	F	VF	XF	Unc
1741 CPS	—	10.00	20.00	40.00	75.00
1743 CPS	—	10.00	20.00	40.00	75.00
1748 CPS	—	10.00	20.00	40.00	75.00
1749 CPS	—	10.00	20.00	40.00	75.00
1750 CPS	—	10.00	20.00	40.00	75.00
1751 C	—	10.00	20.00	40.00	75.00
1757 IWS	—	10.00	20.00	40.00	75.00
1759 IWS	—	10.00	20.00	40.00	75.00
1760 IWS	—	10.00	20.00	40.00	75.00

KM# 332 2 MARIENGROSCHEN

Billon **Ruler:** George III **Obverse:** Crowned GR monogram **Reverse:** Value

Date	Mintage	F	VF	XF	Unc
1760 IWS	—	10.00	30.00	60.00	100
1762 IWS	—	10.00	30.00	60.00	100

KM# 352 2 MARIENGROSCHEN

0.9930 Silver **Ruler:** George III **Obverse:** Value **Reverse:** Wildman

Date	Mintage	F	VF	XF	Unc
1763 IAP	—	10.00	20.00	40.00	75.00
1766 IAP	—	10.00	20.00	40.00	75.00
1768 IAP	—	10.00	20.00	40.00	75.00
1769 IAP	—	10.00	20.00	40.00	75.00
1770 IAP	—	10.00	20.00	40.00	75.00
1771 IAP	—	10.00	20.00	40.00	75.00
1772 IAP	—	10.00	20.00	40.00	75.00
1773 IAP	—	10.00	20.00	40.00	75.00
1774 LCR	—	10.00	20.00	40.00	75.00
1775 LCR	—	10.00	20.00	40.00	75.00
1776 LCR	—	10.00	20.00	40.00	75.00
1778 LCR	—	10.00	20.00	40.00	75.00
1779 .C.	—	10.00	20.00	40.00	75.00
1780 CES	—	10.00	20.00	40.00	75.00
1781 CES	—	10.00	20.00	40.00	75.00
1782 CES	—	10.00	20.00	40.00	75.00
1783 CES	—	10.00	20.00	40.00	75.00
1785 CES	—	10.00	20.00	40.00	75.00

KM# 384 2 MARIENGROSCHEN

0.9930 Silver **Ruler:** George III **Reverse:** Date in center legend

Date	Mintage	F	VF	XF	Unc
1785 CES	—	10.00	20.00	40.00	75.00

KM# 125 3 MARIENGROSCHEN

Silver **Ruler:** George Ludwig **Obverse:** Crowned 4-fold arms **Reverse:** Value, date in 4 lines

Date	Mintage	VG	F	VF	XF	Unc
1717 HCB	—	12.00	25.00	45.00	70.00	—

KM# 126 3 MARIENGROSCHEN

Silver **Ruler:** George Ludwig **Obverse:** Horse leaping left

Date	Mintage	VG	F	VF	XF	Unc
1717 HCB	—	12.00	25.00	45.00	70.00	—

KM# 127 3 MARIENGROSCHEN

Silver **Ruler:** George Ludwig **Obverse:** Crowned GR monogram

Date	Mintage	VG	F	VF	XF	Unc
1717 HCB	—	10.00	20.00	40.00	65.00	—

KM# 32 4 MARIENGROSCHEN

Silver **Ruler:** George Ludwig **Obverse:** Value in 3 lines, date in legend **Reverse:** Wildman, tree in right hand

Date	Mintage	VG	F	VF	XF	Unc
1700 ***	—	6.00	12.00	25.00	45.00	—
1701 ***	—	6.00	12.00	25.00	45.00	—
1702 ***	—	6.00	12.00	25.00	45.00	—
1703 ***	—	6.00	12.00	25.00	45.00	—
1708 ***	—	6.00	12.00	25.00	45.00	—
1710 ***	—	6.00	12.00	25.00	45.00	—

KM# 33 4 MARIENGROSCHEN

Silver **Ruler:** George Ludwig **Obverse:** Value in 4 lines **Reverse:** Horse leaping left, date below **Note:** Varieties exist.

Date	Mintage	VG	F	VF	XF	Unc
1700	—	6.00	12.00	25.00	45.00	—
1703 HB	—	6.00	12.00	25.00	45.00	—
1704 HB	—	6.00	12.00	25.00	45.00	—
1705 HB	—	6.00	12.00	25.00	45.00	—
1712 HCB	—	5.00	10.00	20.00	40.00	—
1713 HCB	—	5.00	10.00	20.00	40.00	—
1714 HCB	—	5.00	10.00	20.00	40.00	—

KM# 53 4 MARIENGROSCHEN

Silver **Ruler:** George Ludwig **Obverse:** Value, date **Reverse:** St. Andrew

Date	Mintage	VG	F	VF	XF	Unc
1706 HB	—	7.00	15.00	30.00	55.00	—
1707 HB	—	7.00	15.00	30.00	55.00	—
1708 HB	—	7.00	15.00	30.00	55.00	—

KM# 62 4 MARIENGROSCHEN

Silver **Ruler:** George Ludwig **Obverse:** Value, date **Reverse:** Wildman **Note:** Varieties exist.

Date	Mintage	VG	F	VF	XF	Unc
1711 HH	—	10.00	20.00	35.00	65.00	—
1712 HH	—	7.00	15.00	25.00	50.00	—
1714 HH	—	7.00	15.00	25.00	50.00	—

KM# 107 4 MARIENGROSCHEN

Silver **Ruler:** George Ludwig **Obverse:** Crowned GR monogram **Reverse:** Value, date in 4 lines **Rev. Legend:** VON FEINEM SILBER

Date	Mintage	VG	F	VF	XF	Unc
1716 HCB	—	20.00	35.00	65.00	120	—
1717 HCB	—	20.00	35.00	65.00	120	—
1717 HH	—	20.00	35.00	65.00	120	—
1719 C	—	20.00	35.00	65.00	120	—
1721 C	—	20.00	35.00	65.00	120	—
1725 EPH	—	20.00	35.00	65.00	120	—

KM# 128 4 MARIENGROSCHEN (1/9 Thaler)

Silver **Ruler:** George Ludwig **Obverse:** 4 crowned arms in cruciform, 1/9 in center **Reverse:** Value IIII, date in 4 lines

Date	Mintage	VG	F	VF	XF	Unc
1717 HCB	—	14.00	28.00	50.00	85.00	—

KM# 129 4 MARIENGROSCHEN (1/9 Thaler)

Silver **Ruler:** George Ludwig **Obverse:** Crowned GR monogram **Reverse:** Value, date in 4 lines **Rev. Legend:** LAND MUNTZ

Date	Mintage	VG	F	VF	XF	Unc
1717 HCB	—	15.00	30.00	60.00	120	—

KM# 138 4 MARIENGROSCHEN (1/9 Thaler)
Silver **Ruler:** George Ludwig **Obverse:** Crowned arms **Reverse:** Value, date

Date	Mintage	VG	F	VF	XF	Unc
1718 HCB	—	12.00	25.00	45.00	75.00	—
1719 HCB	—	12.00	25.00	45.00	75.00	—

KM# 155 4 MARIENGROSCHEN (1/9 Thaler)
Silver **Ruler:** George Ludwig **Reverse:** Value, date in 4 lines

Date	Mintage	VG	F	VF	XF	Unc
1720 HCB	—	10.00	20.00	35.00	60.00	—
1721 HCB	—	10.00	20.00	35.00	60.00	—
1722 HCB	—	10.00	20.00	35.00	60.00	—
1723 HCB	—	10.00	20.00	35.00	60.00	—
1724 HCB	—	10.00	20.00	35.00	60.00	—
1726 CPS	—	10.00	20.00	35.00	60.00	—
1727 CPS	—	10.00	20.00	35.00	60.00	—

KM# 174 4 MARIENGROSCHEN (1/9 Thaler)
Silver **Ruler:** George II August **Reverse:** Value, date

Date	Mintage	F	VF	XF	Unc
1727 CPS	—	12.00	25.00	50.00	125
1728 CPS	—	12.00	25.00	50.00	125
1729 CPS	—	12.00	25.00	50.00	125
1730 CPS	—	12.00	25.00	50.00	125
1731 CPS	—	12.00	25.00	50.00	125
1733 CPS	—	12.00	25.00	50.00	125
1734 CPS	—	12.00	25.00	50.00	125
1735 CPS	—	12.00	25.00	50.00	125

KM# 175 4 MARIENGROSCHEN (1/9 Thaler)
Silver **Ruler:** George II August **Obverse:** Crowned GR monogram **Reverse:** Value, IIII

Date	Mintage	F	VF	XF	Unc
1727 EPH	—	—	—	—	—
1729 EPH	—	—	—	—	—

KM# 217 4 MARIENGROSCHEN (1/9 Thaler)
Silver **Ruler:** George II August **Obverse:** Value, date **Reverse:** Wildman

Date	Mintage	F	VF	XF	Unc
1730 EPH	—	10.00	20.00	40.00	100
1731 IAB	—	10.00	20.00	40.00	100
1732 IAB	—	10.00	20.00	40.00	100
1733 IAB	—	10.00	20.00	40.00	100
1734 IAB	—	10.00	20.00	40.00	100
1735 IAB	—	10.00	20.00	40.00	100
1736 IAB	—	10.00	20.00	40.00	100
1737 IAD	—	10.00	20.00	40.00	100
1738 IAB	—	10.00	20.00	40.00	100
1739 IAB	—	10.00	20.00	40.00	100
1739 C	—	10.00	20.00	40.00	100
1739 IBH	—	10.00	20.00	40.00	100
1740 IBH	—	10.00	20.00	40.00	100
1741 IBH	—	10.00	20.00	40.00	100
1742 IBH	—	10.00	20.00	40.00	100
1743 IBH	—	10.00	20.00	40.00	100
1744 IBH	—	10.00	20.00	40.00	100
1745 IBH	—	10.00	20.00	40.00	100
1746 IBH	—	10.00	20.00	40.00	100
1747 IBH	—	10.00	20.00	40.00	100
1748 IBH	—	10.00	20.00	40.00	100
1749 IBH	—	10.00	20.00	40.00	100
1750 IBH	—	10.00	20.00	40.00	100
1751 IBH	—	10.00	20.00	40.00	100
1753 IBH	—	10.00	20.00	40.00	100
1754 IBH	—	10.00	20.00	40.00	100
1755 IBH	—	10.00	20.00	40.00	100
1756 IBH	—	10.00	20.00	40.00	100
1758 IBH	—	10.00	20.00	40.00	100
1759 IBH	—	10.00	20.00	40.00	100
1760 IBH	—	10.00	20.00	40.00	100

KM# 261 4 MARIENGROSCHEN (1/9 Thaler)
Silver **Ruler:** George II August **Obverse:** Crowned quartered arms **Obv. Legend:** N.D. LEIPZ. FVS

Date	Mintage	F	VF	XF	Unc
1738 CPS	—	12.00	30.00	60.00	125

KM# 296 4 MARIENGROSCHEN (1/9 Thaler)
Silver **Ruler:** George II August **Rev. Legend:** NACH. DEM

Date	Mintage	F	VF	XF	Unc
1746 CPS	—	20.00	50.00	100	200
1752 C	—	20.00	50.00	100	200

KM# 346 4 MARIENGROSCHEN (1/9 Thaler)
Silver **Ruler:** George III **Obverse:** Value **Reverse:** Wildman

Date	Mintage	F	VF	XF	Unc
1762 IBH	—	5.00	10.00	20.00	65.00
1763 IAP	—	5.00	10.00	20.00	65.00
1764 IAP	—	5.00	10.00	20.00	65.00
1766 IAP	—	5.00	10.00	20.00	65.00
1767 IAP	—	5.00	10.00	20.00	65.00
1768 IAP	—	5.00	10.00	20.00	65.00
1769 IAP	—	5.00	10.00	20.00	65.00
1770 IAP	—	5.00	10.00	20.00	65.00
1771 IAP	—	5.00	10.00	20.00	65.00
1772 IAP	—	5.00	10.00	20.00	65.00
1773 LCR	—	5.00	10.00	20.00	65.00
1774 LCR	—	5.00	10.00	20.00	65.00
1775 LCR	—	5.00	10.00	20.00	65.00
1776 LCR	—	5.00	10.00	20.00	65.00
1777 LCR	—	5.00	10.00	20.00	65.00
1778 LCR	—	5.00	10.00	20.00	65.00
1779 .C.	—	5.00	10.00	20.00	65.00
1780 CES	—	5.00	10.00	20.00	65.00
1781 CES	—	5.00	10.00	20.00	65.00
1782 CES	—	5.00	10.00	20.00	65.00
1783 CES	—	5.00	10.00	20.00	65.00
1784 CES	—	5.00	10.00	20.00	65.00
1785 CES	—	5.00	10.00	20.00	65.00
1786 .C.	—	5.00	10.00	20.00	65.00

KM# 390 4 MARIENGROSCHEN (1/9 Thaler)
Silver **Ruler:** George III **Reverse:** Date in center legend

Date	Mintage	F	VF	XF	Unc
1787 .C.	—	5.00	10.00	20.00	65.00
1788 .C.	—	5.00	10.00	20.00	65.00

KM# 11 6 MARIENGROSCHEN
Silver **Ruler:** George Ludwig **Obverse:** Value, date **Reverse:** Wildman, tree in right hand

Date	Mintage	VG	F	VF	XF	Unc
1699 ***	—	10.00	20.00	35.00	65.00	—
1700 ***	—	10.00	20.00	35.00	65.00	—
1701 ***	—	10.00	20.00	35.00	65.00	—
1702 ***	—	10.00	20.00	35.00	65.00	—
1703 ***	—	10.00	20.00	35.00	65.00	—
1704 ***	—	10.00	20.00	35.00	65.00	—
1705 ***	—	10.00	20.00	35.00	65.00	—
1706 ***	—	10.00	20.00	35.00	65.00	—
1707 ***	—	10.00	20.00	35.00	65.00	—
1708 ***	—	10.00	20.00	35.00	65.00	—
1709 ***	—	10.00	20.00	35.00	65.00	—
1710 ***	—	10.00	20.00	35.00	65.00	—
1711 ***	—	10.00	20.00	35.00	65.00	—

KM# 12 6 MARIENGROSCHEN (1/6 Thaler)
Silver **Ruler:** George Ludwig **Obverse:** Value VI..., date in circle **Reverse:** Horse leaping left, value Y6 below in circle

Date	Mintage	VG	F	VF	XF	Unc
1698 HB	—	10.00	22.00	40.00	70.00	—
1700 HB	—	10.00	22.00	40.00	70.00	—
1701 HB	—	10.00	22.00	40.00	70.00	—
1702 HB	—	10.00	22.00	40.00	70.00	—
1704 HB	—	10.00	22.00	40.00	70.00	—
1705 HB	—	10.00	22.00	40.00	70.00	—
1706 HB	—	10.00	22.00	40.00	70.00	—
1707 HB	—	10.00	22.00	40.00	70.00	—

KM# 54 6 MARIENGROSCHEN (1/6 Thaler)
Silver **Ruler:** George Ludwig **Note:** Similar to KM#12 but without circle.

Date	Mintage	VG	F	VF	XF	Unc
1707	—	20.00	35.00	60.00	95.00	—

KM# 56 6 MARIENGROSCHEN (1/6 Thaler)
Silver **Ruler:** George Ludwig **Obverse:** Value, date **Reverse:** St. Andrew

Date	Mintage	VG	F	VF	XF	Unc
1708 HB	—	20.00	35.00	60.00	100	—
1709 HB	—	20.00	35.00	60.00	100	—

KM# 60 6 MARIENGROSCHEN (1/6 Thaler)
Silver **Ruler:** George Ludwig **Obverse:** Date in legend **Reverse:** St. Andrew

Date	Mintage	VG	F	VF	XF	Unc
1710 HB	—	20.00	35.00	60.00	100	—
1711 HB	—	20.00	35.00	60.00	100	—

KM# 63 6 MARIENGROSCHEN (1/6 Thaler)
Silver **Ruler:** George Ludwig **Obverse:** Additional title of AR. TH. (Imperial Treasurer) **Reverse:** St. Andrew

Date	Mintage	VG	F	VF	XF	Unc
1711 HCB	—	50.00	95.00	125	200	—
1712 HCB	—	50.00	95.00	125	200	—
1713 HCB	—	50.00	95.00	125	200	—

KM# 71 6 MARIENGROSCHEN (1/6 Thaler)
Silver **Ruler:** George Ludwig **Obverse:** Value, date in 5 lines **Reverse:** Similar to KM#11 but 6 to lower right

Date	Mintage	VG	F	VF	XF	Unc
1712 HH	—	8.00	16.00	30.00	60.00	—
1713 HH	—	8.00	16.00	30.00	60.00	—
1714 HH	—	8.00	16.00	30.00	60.00	—
1715 HH	—	8.00	16.00	30.00	60.00	—

KM# 86 6 MARIENGROSCHEN (1/6 Thaler)
Silver **Ruler:** George Ludwig **Reverse:** Horse leaping left

Date	Mintage	VG	F	VF	XF	Unc
1713 HCB	—	9.00	20.00	35.00	65.00	—

KM# 91 6 MARIENGROSCHEN (1/6 Thaler)
Silver **Ruler:** George Ludwig **Obverse:** Value, date **Obv. Legend:** * GEORG: LUD: D • G • D • B • & • L • S • R • I • AR • TH • & • EL **Reverse:** Horse leaping left **Rev. Legend:** IN RECTO DECVS

Date	Mintage	VG	F	VF	XF	Unc
1714 HCB	—	25.00	65.00	100	175	—
1715 HCB	—	25.00	65.00	100	175	—

KM# 99 6 MARIENGROSCHEN (1/6 Thaler)
Silver **Ruler:** George Ludwig **Obverse:** Value, date in legend

Date	Mintage	VG	F	VF	XF	Unc
1715 HH	—	9.00	18.00	30.00	60.00	—

KM# 284 8 GUTE GROSCHEN
Silver **Ruler:** George II August **Obverse:** Bust **Reverse:** Value

Date	Mintage	F	VF	XF	Unc
1742	—	15.00	30.00	60.00	120

KM# 285 8 GUTE GROSCHEN
Silver **Ruler:** George II August **Obverse:** Value, date in 5 lines **Reverse:** Horse left

Date	Mintage	F	VF	XF	Unc
1742 CPS	—	15.00	30.00	60.00	120

KM# 34 12 MARIENGROSCHEN

Silver **Ruler:** George Ludwig **Obverse:** Value XII... in 3 lines, date in legend **Obv. Legend:** * GEORG: LUD: D: G: D: BR: & L: S: R: I: EL: **Reverse:** Wildman, tree in right hand, 12 to right **Rev. Legend:** IN RECTO DECUS.

Date	Mintage	VG	F	VF	XF	Unc
1700 ***	—	12.00	25.00	45.00	85.00	—
1702 ***	—	12.00	25.00	45.00	85.00	—
1703 ***	—	12.00	25.00	45.00	85.00	—
1704 ***	—	12.00	25.00	45.00	85.00	—
1705 ***	—	12.00	25.00	45.00	85.00	—
1706 ***	—	12.00	25.00	45.00	85.00	—
1707 ***	—	12.00	25.00	45.00	85.00	—
1708 ***	—	12.00	25.00	45.00	85.00	—
1709 ***	—	12.00	25.00	45.00	85.00	—
1710 ***	—	12.00	25.00	45.00	85.00	—
1711 HH	—	12.00	25.00	45.00	85.00	—

KM# 37 12 MARIENGROSCHEN

Silver **Ruler:** George Ludwig **Obverse:** Value, date **Obv. Legend:** GEORG: LVD • D • G • D • BR • & LUN: S • R • I • E • * **Reverse:** Saint carrying cross **Rev. Legend:** SANCT. ANDREAS - REVIVISOENS

Date	Mintage	VG	F	VF	XF	Unc
1702 HB	—	40.00	85.00	120	200	—
1703 HB	—	40.00	85.00	120	200	—
1704 HB	—	40.00	85.00	120	200	—
1705 HB	—	40.00	85.00	120	200	—

KM# 64 12 MARIENGROSCHEN

Silver **Ruler:** George Ludwig **Obverse:** Value, date **Reverse:** Wildman, tree in right hand **Note:** Similar to KM#34, but V. FEIN. SILB added to value.

Date	Mintage	VG	F	VF	XF	Unc
1711 HH	—	15.00	30.00	50.00	100	—

KM# 72 12 MARIENGROSCHEN

Silver **Ruler:** George Ludwig **Obverse:** Title of Imperial Treasurer added **Obv. Legend:** GEORG • LVD • D • G • D • BR • & S • R • I • AR • TH • & I • E • **Reverse:** Wildman, tree in right hand, 12 at right **Rev. Legend:** IN RECTO DECUS

Date	Mintage	VG	F	VF	XF	Unc
1712 HH	—	12.00	25.00	45.00	85.00	—
1713 HH	—	12.00	25.00	45.00	85.00	—
1714 HH	—	12.00	25.00	45.00	85.00	—
1715 HH	—	12.00	25.00	45.00	85.00	—

KM# 92 12 MARIENGROSCHEN

Silver **Ruler:** George Ludwig **Reverse:** Without V. FEIN. SILB

Date	Mintage	VG	F	VF	XF	Unc
1714 HH	—	35.00	70.00	110	165	—

KM# 272 16 GUTE GROSCHEN (Gulden)

Silver **Ruler:** George II August **Obverse:** Value **Reverse:** Horse leaping left

Date	Mintage	F	VF	XF	Unc
1740 CPS	—	50.00	100	150	275
1741 CPS	—	50.00	100	150	275
1742 CPS	—	50.00	100	150	275
1743 CPS	—	50.00	100	150	275
1752 C	—	50.00	100	150	275
1756 IWS	—	50.00	100	150	275

KM# 280 16 GUTE GROSCHEN (Gulden)

Silver **Ruler:** George II August **Obverse:** Laureate bust left

Date	Mintage	F	VF	XF	Unc
1741 CPS	—	50.00	100	150	275
1742 CPS	—	50.00	100	150	275
1743 CPS	—	50.00	100	150	275
1756 IWS	—	50.00	100	150	275

KM# 281 16 GUTE GROSCHEN (Gulden)

Silver **Ruler:** George II August **Obverse:** Crowned quartered arms **Reverse:** Similar to KM#272 obverse

Date	Mintage	F	VF	XF	Unc
1741 Rare	—	—	—	—	—
1742 Rare	—	—	—	—	—

KM# 340 16 GUTE GROSCHEN (Gulden)

Silver **Ruler:** George III **Obverse:** Arms **Reverse:** Value

Date	Mintage	F	VF	XF	Unc
1761 IWS Rare	—	—	—	—	—
1763 IWS Rare	—	—	—	—	—

KM# 15 24 MARIENGROSCHEN (Gulden)

Silver **Ruler:** George Ludwig **Obverse:** Value, date in legend **Obv. Legend:** GEORG: LUD: D: G: D: BR: & L: S: R: I: ELECT: **Reverse:** Wildman with tree in right hand, 24 at right **Rev. Legend:** IN RECTO DECUS

Date	Mintage	VG	F	VF	XF	Unc
1698 ***	—	25.00	40.00	65.00	100	—
1699 ***	—	25.00	40.00	65.00	100	—
1700 ***	—	25.00	40.00	65.00	100	—
1701 ***	—	25.00	40.00	65.00	100	—
1702 ***	—	25.00	40.00	65.00	100	—
1703 ***	—	25.00	40.00	65.00	100	—
1704 ***	—	25.00	40.00	65.00	100	—
1705 ***	—	25.00	40.00	65.00	100	—
1706 ***	—	25.00	40.00	65.00	100	—
1707 ***	—	25.00	40.00	65.00	100	—
1708 ***	—	25.00	40.00	65.00	100	—
1709 ***	—	25.00	40.00	65.00	100	—
1710 ***	—	25.00	40.00	65.00	100	—
1711 ***	—	25.00	40.00	65.00	100	—
1711 C	—	25.00	40.00	65.00	100	—
1711 HH	—	25.00	40.00	65.00	100	—

KM# 73 24 MARIENGROSCHEN (Gulden)

Silver **Ruler:** George Ludwig **Obverse:** Title of Imperial Treasurer added **Reverse:** Wildman with tree in right hand, 24 at right

Date	Mintage	VG	F	VF	XF	Unc
1712 HH	—	25.00	40.00	65.00	100	—
1713 HH	—	25.00	40.00	65.00	100	—
1714 HH	—	25.00	40.00	65.00	100	—
1715 HH	—	25.00	40.00	65.00	100	—

KM# 311 24 MARIENGROSCHEN (Gulden)

Silver **Ruler:** George II August **Obverse:** Value XXIV GVTE **Reverse:** Horse left

Date	Mintage	F	VF	XF	Unc
1750	—	60.00	120	200	300

KM# 341 24 MARIENGROSCHEN (Gulden)

Silver **Ruler:** George III **Obverse:** Crowned arms above 2/3 in oval **Reverse:** Value above date

Date	Mintage	F	VF	XF	Unc
1761 IWS	—	30.00	50.00	85.00	140
1762 IWS	—	30.00	50.00	85.00	140
1763 IWS	—	30.00	50.00	85.00	140
1764 IWS	—	30.00	50.00	85.00	140
1765 IWS	—	30.00	50.00	85.00	140
1766 IWS	—	30.00	50.00	85.00	140
1767 IWS	—	30.00	50.00	85.00	140
1768 IWS	—	30.00	50.00	85.00	140
1769 IWS	—	30.00	50.00	85.00	140
1770 IWS	—	30.00	50.00	85.00	140
1771 IWS	—	30.00	50.00	85.00	140
1772 IWS	—	30.00	50.00	85.00	140
1773 IWS	—	30.00	50.00	85.00	140
1774 IWS	—	30.00	50.00	85.00	140
1775 IWS	—	30.00	50.00	85.00	140
1776 IWS	—	30.00	50.00	85.00	140
1777 IWS	—	30.00	50.00	85.00	140
1778 IWS	—	30.00	50.00	85.00	140
1779 IWS	—	30.00	50.00	85.00	140
1780 IWS	—	30.00	50.00	85.00	140
1781 IWS	—	30.00	50.00	85.00	140
1782 IWS	—	30.00	50.00	85.00	140
1783 IWS	—	30.00	50.00	85.00	140
1784 IWS	—	30.00	50.00	85.00	140
1785 IWS	—	30.00	50.00	85.00	140
1786 IWS	—	30.00	50.00	85.00	140
1787 IWS	—	30.00	50.00	85.00	140
1788 IWS	—	30.00	50.00	85.00	140
1789 IWS	—	30.00	50.00	85.00	140
1790 IWS	—	30.00	50.00	85.00	140
1790 .C.	—	30.00	50.00	85.00	140
1791 .C.	—	30.00	50.00	85.00	140
1792 .C.	—	30.00	50.00	85.00	140
1792 PLM	—	30.00	50.00	85.00	140
1793 PLM	—	30.00	50.00	85.00	140
1794 PLM	—	30.00	50.00	85.00	140
1795 PLM	—	30.00	50.00	85.00	140
1796 PLM	—	30.00	50.00	85.00	140
1797 PLM	—	30.00	50.00	85.00	140
1798 PLM	—	30.00	50.00	85.00	140
1799 PLM	—	30.00	50.00	85.00	140
1800 PLM	—	20.00	40.00	85.00	140
1800 .C.	—	20.00	40.00	85.00	140
1800 EC	—	20.00	40.00	85.00	140
1801 PLM	—	20.00	40.00	85.00	140

KM# 347 24 MARIENGROSCHEN (Gulden)

Silver **Ruler:** George III **Obverse:** Crowned quartered arms, value below **Reverse:** Wildman with tree in right hand, 24 at right

Date	Mintage	F	VF	XF	Unc
1762 IBH	—	40.00	75.00	150	300
1763 IAP	—	40.00	75.00	150	300
1764 IAP	—	40.00	75.00	150	300
1765 IAP	—	40.00	75.00	150	300
1766 IAP	—	40.00	75.00	150	300
1767 IAP	—	40.00	75.00	150	300
1768 IAP	—	40.00	75.00	150	300
1769 IAP	—	40.00	75.00	150	300
1770 IAP	—	40.00	75.00	150	300
1771 IAP	—	40.00	75.00	150	300
1772 IAP	—	40.00	75.00	150	300
1773 IAP	—	40.00	75.00	150	300
1774 LCR	—	40.00	75.00	150	300
1775 LCR	—	40.00	75.00	150	300
1776 LCR	—	40.00	75.00	150	300
1777 LCR	—	40.00	75.00	150	300
1778 LCR	—	40.00	75.00	150	300
1779 .C.	—	40.00	75.00	150	300
1780 CES	—	40.00	75.00	150	300
1781 CES	—	40.00	75.00	150	300
1782 CES	—	40.00	75.00	150	300
1783 CES	—	40.00	75.00	150	300
1784 CES	—	40.00	75.00	150	300

KM# 385 24 MARIENGROSCHEN (Gulden)

Silver **Ruler:** George III **Obverse:** Plain arms divide date, value below

Date	Mintage	F	VF	XF	Unc
1785 CES	—	40.00	70.00	120	200
1786 .C.	—	40.00	70.00	120	200
1787 .C.	—	40.00	70.00	120	200
1788 .C.	—	40.00	70.00	120	200
1789 .C.	—	40.00	70.00	120	200

KM# 130 1/24 THALER (Groschen)

Silver **Ruler:** George Ludwig **Obverse:** Crowned GR monogram **Reverse:** Value, date in 4 lines

Date	Mintage	VG	F	VF	XF	Unc
1717 HCB	—	15.00	30.00	50.00	90.00	—
1718 HCB	—	15.00	30.00	50.00	90.00	—
1719 HCB	—	15.00	30.00	50.00	90.00	—
1721 HCB	—	15.00	30.00	50.00	90.00	—
1722 HCB	—	15.00	30.00	50.00	90.00	—

KM# 250 1/24 THALER (Groschen)

Billon **Ruler:** George II August **Obverse:** Horse left **Reverse:** Value, date

Date	Mintage	F	VF	XF	Unc
1733 CPS	—	10.00	20.00	40.00	80.00
1735 CPS	—	10.00	20.00	40.00	80.00

KM# 252 1/24 THALER (Groschen)

Billon **Ruler:** George II August **Obverse:** Crowned GR monogram **Reverse:** Value, date

Date	Mintage	F	VF	XF	Unc
1735 CPS	—	10.00	20.00	40.00	80.00

KM# 282 1/24 THALER (Groschen)

Billon **Ruler:** George II August **Obverse:** Crowned monogram **Reverse:** Value

Date	Mintage	F	VF	XF	Unc
1741 CPS	—	10.00	20.00	40.00	80.00
1746 CPOS	—	10.00	20.00	40.00	80.00
1748 CPS	—	10.00	20.00	40.00	80.00

KM# 314 1/24 THALER (Groschen)

Billon **Ruler:** George II August **Obverse:** Horse leaping left **Reverse:** Value **Rev. Legend:** NACH DEM....

Date	Mintage	F	VF	XF	Unc
1751 C	—	10.00	20.00	40.00	80.00
1752 C	—	10.00	20.00	40.00	80.00
1754 IWS	—	10.00	20.00	40.00	80.00
1756 IWS	—	10.00	20.00	40.00	80.00

KM# 333 1/24 THALER (Groschen)

Billon **Ruler:** George III **Rev. Legend:** NACH DEM REICHS FUS

Date	Mintage	F	VF	XF	Unc
1760 IWS	—	5.00	10.00	20.00	65.00
1760 IAS	—	5.00	10.00	20.00	65.00
1761 IAS	—	5.00	10.00	20.00	65.00
1762 IAS	—	5.00	10.00	20.00	65.00
1762 IWS	—	5.00	10.00	20.00	65.00
1764 IWS	—	5.00	10.00	20.00	65.00
1764 .C.	—	5.00	10.00	20.00	65.00
1768 .C.	—	5.00	10.00	20.00	65.00
1769 IHZ	—	5.00	10.00	20.00	65.00

KM# 334 1/24 THALER (Groschen)

Billon **Ruler:** George III **Reverse:** Value **Rev. Legend:** NACH DEM LEIPZIGER FUS

Date	Mintage	F	VF	XF	Unc
1760 IWS Rare	—	—	—	—	—

KM# 131 1/12 THALER (2 Groschen)

Silver **Ruler:** George Ludwig **Obverse:** Value, date **Reverse:** Horse leaping left **Note:** Varieties exist.

Date	Mintage	VG	F	VF	XF	Unc
1717 HCB	—	10.00	20.00	35.00	60.00	—
1719 HCB	—	10.00	20.00	35.00	60.00	—
1721 HCB	—	10.00	20.00	35.00	60.00	—

KM# 243 1/12 THALER (2 Groschen)

Silver **Ruler:** George II August **Obverse:** Horse left **Reverse:** Value, date

Date	Mintage	F	VF	XF	Unc
1732 CPS	—	15.00	40.00	80.00	150
1734 CPS	—	15.00	40.00	80.00	150
1735 CPS	—	15.00	40.00	80.00	150
1736 CPS	—	15.00	40.00	80.00	150

KM# 262 1/12 THALER (2 Groschen)

Silver **Ruler:** George II August **Obv. Legend:** N.D. LEIPZ. FVS

Date	Mintage	F	VF	XF	Unc
1738 CPS	—	15.00	40.00	80.00	150
1739 CPS	—	15.00	40.00	80.00	150
1740 CPS	—	15.00	40.00	80.00	150

KM# 283 1/12 THALER (2 Groschen)

Silver **Ruler:** George II August **Obverse:** Horse leaping left **Reverse:** Value, date

Date	Mintage	F	VF	XF	Unc
1741 CPS	—	15.00	40.00	80.00	150
1742 CPS	—	15.00	40.00	80.00	150
1743 CPS	—	15.00	40.00	80.00	150
1744 CPS	—	15.00	40.00	80.00	150
1745 CPS	—	15.00	40.00	80.00	150
1746 CPS		15.00	40.00	80.00	150
1747 CPS	—	15.00	40.00	80.00	150
1748 CPS	—	15.00	40.00	80.00	150
1749 CPS	—	15.00	40.00	80.00	150
1750 CPS	—	15.00	40.00	80.00	150
1751 C	—	15.00	40.00	80.00	150
1752 C	—	15.00	40.00	80.00	150
1757 IWS	—	15.00	40.00	80.00	150

KM# 335 1/12 THALER (2 Groschen)

Billon **Ruler:** George III **Obverse:** Horse **Reverse:** Value **Rev. Legend:** NACH DEM LEIPZIGER FUS

Date	Mintage	F	VF	XF	Unc
1760 IWS	—	4.00	7.00	20.00	75.00

KM# 336 1/12 THALER (2 Groschen)

Silver **Ruler:** George III **Obverse:** Horse left **Reverse:** Denomination

Date	Mintage	F	VF	XF	Unc
1760 IAS	—	4.00	10.00	20.00	65.00
1760 IWS	—	4.00	10.00	20.00	65.00
1761 IAS	—	4.00	10.00	20.00	65.00
1761 IWS	—	4.00	10.00	20.00	65.00
1762 IAS	—	4.00	10.00	20.00	65.00
1762 IWS	—	4.00	10.00	20.00	65.00
1763 IAS	—	4.00	10.00	20.00	65.00
1763 IWS	—	4.00	10.00	20.00	65.00
1763 .C.	—	4.00	10.00	20.00	65.00
1764 IWS	—	4.00	10.00	20.00	65.00
1764 .C.	—	4.00	10.00	20.00	65.00
1765 .C.	—	4.00	10.00	20.00	65.00
1767 .C.	—	4.00	10.00	20.00	65.00
1768 IWS	—	4.00	10.00	20.00	65.00
1768 .C.	—	4.00	10.00	20.00	65.00
1769 IWS	—	4.00	10.00	20.00	65.00
1769 IHZ	—	4.00	10.00	20.00	65.00
1770 IWS	—	4.00	10.00	20.00	65.00
1771 IWS	—	4.00	10.00	20.00	65.00
1772 IWS	—	4.00	10.00	20.00	65.00
1772 IHZ	—	4.00	10.00	20.00	65.00
1773 IWS	—	4.00	10.00	20.00	65.00
1774 IWS	—	4.00	10.00	20.00	65.00
1775 IWS	—	4.00	10.00	20.00	65.00
1776 IWS	—	4.00	10.00	20.00	65.00
1777 IWS	—	4.00	10.00	20.00	65.00
1778 IWS	—	4.00	10.00	20.00	65.00
1779 IWS	—	4.00	10.00	20.00	65.00
1780 IWS	—	4.00	10.00	20.00	65.00
1781 IWS	—	4.00	10.00	20.00	65.00
1782 IWS	—	4.00	10.00	20.00	65.00
1783 IWS	—	4.00	10.00	20.00	65.00
1784 IWS	—	4.00	10.00	20.00	65.00
1785 IWS	—	4.00	10.00	20.00	65.00
1786 IWS	—	4.00	10.00	20.00	65.00
1787 IWS	—	4.00	10.00	20.00	65.00
1788 IWS	—	4.00	10.00	20.00	65.00
1789 IWS	—	4.00	10.00	20.00	65.00
1790 .C.	—	4.00	10.00	20.00	65.00
1791 .C.	—	4.00	10.00	20.00	65.00
1792 .C.	—	4.00	10.00	20.00	65.00
1792 PLM	—	4.00	10.00	20.00	65.00
1793 PLM	—	4.00	10.00	20.00	65.00
1794 PLM	—	4.00	10.00	20.00	65.00
1795 PLM	—	4.00	10.00	20.00	65.00
1796 PLM	—	4.00	10.00	20.00	65.00
1797 PLM	—	4.00	10.00	20.00	65.00
1798 PLM	—	4.00	10.00	20.00	65.00
1799 PLM	—	4.00	10.00	20.00	65.00
1800 PLM	—	4.00	8.00	20.00	50.00
1801 PLM	—	4.00	8.00	20.00	50.00
1801 EC	—	5.00	10.00	25.00	60.00
1801 .C.	8,780	4.00	8.00	25.00	60.00
1801 GFM	—	4.00	10.00	20.00	65.00
1802 .C.	—	5.00	10.00	25.00	60.00
1802 GFM	—	6.00	15.00	30.00	65.00
1803 GFM	—	8.00	20.00	35.00	70.00
1804 GFM	—	5.00	15.00	25.00	50.00
1805 GFM	—	5.00	10.00	20.00	45.00
1806 GFM	—	5.00	15.00	25.00	50.00
1807 GFM	—	5.00	15.00	25.00	50.00

KM# 41 1/8 THALER

Silver **Ruler:** George Ludwig **Note:** Similar to 2/3 Thaler, KM#17 but R. 1/8T below horse.

Date	Mintage	VG	F	VF	XF	Unc
1703 HB	—	30.00	65.00	100	200	—
1704 HB	—	30.00	65.00	100	200	—

KM# 93 1/8 THALER

Silver **Ruler:** George Ludwig **Note:** Death of Sophia von der Pfalz Mother of George I Ludwig.

Date	Mintage	VG	F	VF	XF	Unc
1714	—	40.00	75.00	120	200	—

KM# 139 1/8 THALER

Silver **Ruler:** George Ludwig **Obverse:** 4 crowned arms in cruciform **Reverse:** Horse leaping left, date in legend

Date	Mintage	VG	F	VF	XF	Unc
1718 HCB	—	25.00	50.00	100	200	—

KM# 156 1/8 THALER

Silver **Ruler:** George Ludwig **Note:** Similar to 1/4 Thaler, KM#157 but R. 1/8 T below.

Date	Mintage	VG	F	VF	XF	Unc
1720 HCB	—	25.00	50.00	100	200	—
1726 CPS	—	25.00	50.00	100	200	—

KM# 176 1/8 THALER

Silver **Ruler:** George Ludwig **Subject:** Death of George I Ludwig **Obverse:** Bust right **Reverse:** 10-line inscription with date

Date	Mintage	VG	F	VF	XF	Unc
1727 CPS	—	25.00	50.00	80.00	150	—

KM# 201 1/8 THALER

Silver **Ruler:** George II August **Obverse:** Bust left, value below **Reverse:** Crowned shields in cruciform

Date	Mintage	F	VF	XF	Unc
1728 CPS	—	75.00	125	250	500

KM# 218 1/8 THALER

Silver **Ruler:** George II August **Obverse:** Crowned quartered arms **Reverse:** Horse left, value below

Date	Mintage	F	VF	XF	Unc
1730 CPS	—	75.00	150	300	550

KM# 244 1/8 THALER

Silver **Ruler:** George II August **Reverse:** Crowned quartered arms

Date	Mintage	F	VF	XF	Unc
1732 CPS	—	75.00	150	300	550

KM# 108 1/6 THALER

Silver **Ruler:** George Ludwig **Subject:** George Ludwig **Obverse:** Bust right **Reverse:** Crowned shields in cruciform

Date	Mintage	VG	F	VF	XF	Unc
1716 B	—	12.00	25.00	50.00	100	—
1717 B	—	12.00	25.00	50.00	100	—
1718 B	—	12.00	25.00	50.00	100	—
1720 B	—	12.00	25.00	50.00	100	—
1721 B	—	12.00	25.00	50.00	100	—
1722 B	—	12.00	25.00	50.00	100	—
1723 B	—	12.00	25.00	50.00	100	—
1724 B	—	12.00	25.00	50.00	100	—
1726 CPS	—	12.00	25.00	50.00	100	—

KM# 109 1/6 THALER

Silver **Ruler:** George Ludwig **Obverse:** Crowned shields in cruciform **Reverse:** Wildman, tree in right hand, date in legend

Date	Mintage	VG	F	VF	XF	Unc
1716 B	—	20.00	45.00	75.00	125	—
1720 C	—	20.00	45.00	75.00	125	—
1721 C	—	20.00	45.00	75.00	125	—
1722 C	—	20.00	45.00	75.00	125	—
1723 EPH	—	20.00	45.00	75.00	125	—
1724 EPH	—	20.00	45.00	75.00	125	—
1725 EPH	—	20.00	45.00	75.00	125	—

KM# 143 1/6 THALER

Silver **Ruler:** George Ludwig **Obverse:** Crowned shields in cruciform **Reverse:** Horse leaping left

Date	Mintage	VG	F	VF	XF	Unc
1719 HCB	—	18.00	35.00	60.00	100	—
1720 HCB	—	18.00	35.00	60.00	100	—
1721 HCB	—	18.00	35.00	60.00	100	—
1722 HCB	—	18.00	35.00	60.00	100	—
1724 HCB	—	18.00	35.00	60.00	100	—
1727 CPS	—	18.00	35.00	60.00	100	—

KM# 144 1/6 THALER

Silver **Ruler:** George Ludwig **Reverse:** St. Andrew with cross, date in legend

Date	Mintage	VG	F	VF	XF	Unc
1719 B	—	18.00	35.00	60.00	100	—
1719 HCB	—	18.00	35.00	60.00	100	—
1721 HCB	—	18.00	35.00	60.00	100	—
1722 HCB	—	18.00	35.00	60.00	100	—
1724 HCB	—	18.00	35.00	60.00	100	—
1726 EPH	—	18.00	35.00	60.00	100	—

KM# 170 1/6 THALER

Silver **Ruler:** George Ludwig **Reverse:** Wildman, tree in right hand, date in legend, 6 (mariengroschen) added in field

Date	Mintage	VG	F	VF	XF	Unc
1726 EPH	—	25.00	50.00	90.00	150	—

KM# 177 1/6 THALER

Silver **Ruler:** George II August **Obverse:** Bust left, value below **Reverse:** 4 crowned shields in cruciform, date

Date	Mintage	F	VF	XF	Unc
1727 CPS	—	50.00	120	200	325
1758	—	—	—	—	—

Note: Reported, not confirmed

KM# 178 1/6 THALER

Silver **Ruler:** George II August **Obverse:** 4 crowned shields in cruciform **Reverse:** Horse left

Date	Mintage	F	VF	XF	Unc
1727 CPS	—	50.00	100	150	250
1729	—	40.00	75.00	140	225

KM# 179 1/6 THALER

Silver **Ruler:** George II August **Reverse:** Wildman with tree in right hand

Date	Mintage	F	VF	XF	Unc
1727 EPH Rare	—	—	—	—	—

KM# 180 1/6 THALER

Silver **Ruler:** George II August **Obverse:** Crowned quartered arms **Obv. Legend:** FEIN SILB **Reverse:** Wildman with tree in right hand, 6 at right

Date	Mintage	F	VF	XF	Unc
1727 EPH	—	35.00	70.00	130	235
1730 EPH	—	35.00	70.00	130	235
1731 C	—	35.00	70.00	130	235
1731 IAB	—	35.00	70.00	130	235
1732 IAB	—	35.00	70.00	130	235
1733 IAB	—	35.00	70.00	130	235
1734 IAB	—	35.00	70.00	130	235
1735 IAB	—	35.00	70.00	130	235
1736 IAB	—	35.00	70.00	130	235
1737 IAB	—	35.00	70.00	130	235
1738 IAB	—	35.00	70.00	130	235
1739 IAB	—	35.00	70.00	130	235
1739 C	—	35.00	70.00	130	235
1739 IBH	—	35.00	70.00	130	235
1740 IBH	—	35.00	70.00	130	235
1741 IBH	—	35.00	70.00	130	235
1742 IBH	—	35.00	70.00	130	235
1743 IBH	—	35.00	70.00	130	235
1744 IBH	—	35.00	70.00	130	235
1745 IBH	—	35.00	70.00	130	235
1746 IBH	—	35.00	70.00	130	235
1747 IBH	—	35.00	70.00	130	235
1748 IBH	—	35.00	70.00	130	235
1749 IBH	—	35.00	70.00	130	235
1750 IBH	—	35.00	70.00	130	235
1751 IBH	—	35.00	70.00	130	235
1753 IBH	—	35.00	70.00	130	235
1756 IBH	—	35.00	70.00	130	235
1757 IBH	—	35.00	70.00	130	235
1758 IBH	—	35.00	70.00	130	235
1759 IBH	—	35.00	70.00	130	235
1760 IBH	—	35.00	70.00	130	235

KM# 207 1/6 THALER

Silver **Ruler:** George II August **Obverse:** Crowned shields in cruciform **Reverse:** St. Andrew

Date	Mintage	F	VF	XF	Unc
1729 CPS	—	25.00	50.00	100	200

KM# 219 1/6 THALER

Silver **Ruler:** George II August

Date	Mintage	F	VF	XF	Unc
1730 CPS	—	50.00	120	200	325
1734 CPS	—	50.00	120	200	325
1736 CPS	—	50.00	120	200	325

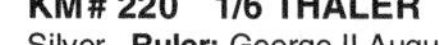

KM# 220 1/6 THALER

Silver **Ruler:** George II August **Obverse:** Crowned quartered arms **Reverse:** Horse left

Date	Mintage	F	VF	XF	Unc
1730 CPS	—	20.00	40.00	85.00	170
1732 CPS	—	20.00	40.00	85.00	170

KM# 221 1/6 THALER

Silver **Ruler:** George II August **Obverse:** Crowned quartered arms **Reverse:** St. Andrew

Date	Mintage	F	VF	XF	Unc
1730 CPS	—	25.00	50.00	100	200
1731 CPS	—	25.00	50.00	100	200
1732 CPS	—	25.00	50.00	100	200

KM# 266 1/6 THALER

Silver **Ruler:** George II August **Obverse:** Armored bust left **Obv. Legend:** GEORGE II AUGUST LEIPZIGER FUSS **Reverse:** Crowned quartered arms

Date	Mintage	F	VF	XF	Unc
1739 CPS	—	50.00	100	200	350
1740 CPS	—	50.00	100	200	350

KM# 267 1/6 THALER

Silver **Ruler:** George II August **Obverse:** Bust left **Reverse:** Horse left

Date	Mintage	F	VF	XF	Unc
1739 CPS Rare	—	—	—	—	—

KM# 297 1/6 THALER

Silver **Ruler:** George II August **Obverse:** Bust left **Obv. Legend:** REICHS FUSS **Reverse:** Crowned quartered arms

Date	Mintage	F	VF	XF	Unc
1746 CPS	—	50.00	120	175	300

KM# 298 1/6 THALER

Silver **Ruler:** George II August **Obverse:** Crowned quartered arms **Obv. Legend:** REICHS FUSS **Reverse:** St. Andrew

Date	Mintage	F	VF	XF	Unc
1746 CPS	—	25.00	50.00	100	200
1753 IWS	—	25.00	50.00	100	200
1756 IWS	—	25.00	50.00	100	200
1757 IWS	—	25.00	50.00	100	200
1759 IWS	—	25.00	50.00	100	200

KM# 342 1/6 THALER

Silver **Ruler:** George III **Obverse:** Crowned arms, value below **Reverse:** St. Andrew

Date	Mintage	F	VF	XF	Unc
1761 IWS	—	20.00	50.00	100	200
1762 IWS	—	20.00	50.00	100	200
1764 IWS	—	20.00	50.00	100	200
1768 IWS	—	20.00	50.00	100	200
1769 IWS	—	20.00	50.00	100	200
1771 IWS	—	20.00	50.00	100	200
1780 IWS	—	20.00	50.00	100	200
1782 IWS	—	20.00	50.00	100	200
1785 IWS	—	20.00	50.00	100	200
1786 IWS	—	20.00	50.00	100	200
1789 IWS	—	20.00	50.00	100	200
1790 IWS	—	20.00	50.00	100	200
1790 .C.	—	20.00	50.00	100	200

KM# 348 1/6 THALER

Silver **Ruler:** George III **Obverse:** Crowned quartered arms, value below **Reverse:** Wildman with tree in right hand, 6 at right

Date	Mintage	F	VF	XF	Unc
1762 IBH	—	12.00	25.00	50.00	125
1763 IAP	—	12.00	25.00	50.00	125
1764 IAP	—	12.00	25.00	50.00	125
1765/4 IAP	—	20.00	35.00	75.00	150
1765 IAP	—	12.00	25.00	50.00	125
1766 IAP	—	12.00	25.00	50.00	125
1767 IAP	—	12.00	25.00	50.00	125
1768 IAP	—	12.00	25.00	50.00	125
1769 IAP	—	12.00	25.00	50.00	125
1770 IAP	—	12.00	25.00	50.00	125
1771 IAP	—	12.00	25.00	50.00	125
1772 IAP	—	12.00	25.00	50.00	125
1773 IAP	—	12.00	25.00	50.00	125
1773 LCR	—	12.00	25.00	50.00	125
1774 LCR	—	12.00	25.00	50.00	125
1775 LCR	—	12.00	25.00	50.00	125
1776 LCR	—	12.00	25.00	50.00	125
1778 LCR	—	12.00	25.00	50.00	125
1779 .C.	—	12.00	25.00	50.00	125
1780 CES	—	12.00	25.00	50.00	125
1781 CES	—	12.00	25.00	50.00	125
1782 CES	—	12.00	25.00	50.00	125
1783 CES	—	12.00	25.00	50.00	125
1784 CES	—	12.00	25.00	50.00	125

KM# 366 1/6 THALER

Silver **Ruler:** George III **Obverse:** Head right **Reverse:** Baroque arms

Date	Mintage	F	VF	XF	Unc
1773 IWS	—	15.00	30.00	60.00	185
1780 IWS	—	15.00	30.00	60.00	185
1782 IWS	—	15.00	30.00	60.00	185

KM# 370 1/6 THALER

Silver **Ruler:** George III **Obverse:** Mailed bust

Date	Mintage	F	VF	XF	Unc
1776 IWS	—	20.00	40.00	80.00	200
1778 IWS	—	20.00	40.00	80.00	200
1779 IWS	—	20.00	40.00	80.00	200

KM# 382 1/6 THALER

Silver **Ruler:** George III **Obverse:** Head **Reverse:** Plain arms

Date	Mintage	F	VF	XF	Unc
1783 IWS	—	20.00	50.00	100	225
1784 IWS	—	20.00	50.00	100	225

KM# 386 1/6 THALER

Silver **Ruler:** George III **Obverse:** Arms divide date **Reverse:** Wildman

Date	Mintage	F	VF	XF	Unc
1785 CES	—	10.00	20.00	40.00	150
1786 .C.	—	10.00	20.00	40.00	150
1787 .C.	—	10.00	20.00	40.00	150
1788 .C.	—	10.00	20.00	40.00	150
1789 .C.	—	10.00	20.00	40.00	150
1790 .C.	—	10.00	20.00	40.00	150
1791 .C.	—	10.00	20.00	40.00	150

KM# 389 1/6 THALER

Silver **Ruler:** George III **Obverse:** Head right **Reverse:** Arms within Order garter, crown above

Date	Mintage	F	VF	XF	Unc
1786 IWS	—	15.00	25.00	50.00	150
1787 IWS	—	15.00	25.00	50.00	150
1789 IWS	—	15.00	25.00	50.00	150

KM# 395 1/6 THALER

Silver **Ruler:** George III **Obverse:** Crowned quartered arms, value below **Obv. Legend:** N.D.R.F. added **Reverse:** Wildman with tree in right hand, 6 at right

Date	Mintage	F	VF	XF	Unc
1790 C.	—	12.00	30.00	60.00	150
1791 C.	—	12.00	30.00	60.00	150

KM# 400 1/6 THALER

Silver **Ruler:** George III **Obverse:** Head right **Reverse:** Crowned square quartered arms, value below

Date	Mintage	F	VF	XF	Unc
1792 .C.	—	15.00	25.00	50.00	135
1794 PLM	—	15.00	25.00	50.00	135
1795/94 PLM	—	15.00	25.00	50.00	135
1795 PLM	—	15.00	25.00	50.00	135
1796 PLM	—	15.00	25.00	50.00	135
1797 PLM	—	15.00	25.00	50.00	135

KM# 401 1/6 THALER

Silver **Ruler:** George III **Obverse:** Date in circular legend **Reverse:** Wildman with tree in right hand, 6 at right

Date	Mintage	F	VF	XF	Unc
1793 PLM	—	10.00	25.00	50.00	125
1794 PLM	—	10.00	25.00	50.00	125
1795 PLM	—	10.00	25.00	50.00	125
1797 PLM	—	10.00	25.00	50.00	125
1798 PL[M	—	10.00	25.00	50.00	125
1799 PLM	—	10.00	25.00	50.00	125
1800 PLM	—	10.00	25.00	50.00	125

KM# 404 1/6 THALER

Silver **Ruler:** George III **Obverse:** Small head right **Reverse:** Crowned quartered arms, value below

Date	Mintage	F	VF	XF	Unc
1796 PLM	—	15.00	25.00	50.00	150
1798 PLM	—	15.00	25.00	50.00	150
1799 PLM	—	15.00	25.00	50.00	150
1800 .C.	—	15.00	25.00	50.00	150

KM# 42 1/4 THALER

Silver **Ruler:** George Ludwig **Obverse:** Crowned arms divide date **Reverse:** Horse leaping left, 1/4 below

Date	Mintage	VG	F	VF	XF	Unc
1703 HB	—	35.00	75.00	125	250	—

KM# 55 1/4 THALER

Silver **Ruler:** George Ludwig **Obverse:** Date in legend

Date	Mintage	VG	F	VF	XF	Unc
1707 HB	—	55.00	120	200	325	—

KM# 94 1/4 THALER

Silver **Ruler:** George Ludwig **Subject:** Death of Sophia von der Pfalz, Mother of George I Ludwig **Obverse:** Veiled bust right **Reverse:** Inscription

Date	Mintage	VG	F	VF	XF	Unc
1714	—	25.00	65.00	125	250	—

KM# 140 1/4 THALER

Silver **Ruler:** George Ludwig **Obverse:** Crowned shields in cruciform **Reverse:** Horse leaping left, 1/4 below, date in legend

Date	Mintage	VG	F	VF	XF	Unc
1718 HCB	—	35.00	75.00	110	185	—

KM# 157 1/4 THALER

Silver **Ruler:** George Ludwig **Subject:** George Ludwig **Obverse:** Bust right, value below **Reverse:** Crowned shields in cruciform

Date	Mintage	VG	F	VF	XF	Unc
1720 HCB	—	35.00	75.00	110	185	—
1726 CPS	—	35.00	75.00	110	185	—

KM# 158 1/4 THALER

Silver **Ruler:** George Ludwig **Obverse:** Without stated value

Date	Mintage	VG	F	VF	XF	Unc
1720 HCB Rare	—	—	—	—	—	—

KM# 159 1/4 THALER

Silver **Ruler:** George Ludwig **Obverse:** Similar to reverse of 1/6 Thaler, KM#108, without value stated **Reverse:** Wildman, tree in right hand, date in legend

Date	Mintage	VG	F	VF	XF	Unc
1720 C	—	35.00	75.00	110	185	—

KM# 160 1/4 THALER

Silver **Ruler:** George Ludwig **Obverse:** Crowned and supported 4-fold arms in Order of the Garter **Reverse:** Wildman, tree in right hand, value R. 1/4T. in field, date in legend

Date	Mintage	VG	F	VF	XF	Unc
1722 C Rare	—	—	—	—	—	—
1723 EPH Rare	—	—	—	—	—	—
1724 EPH Rare	—	—	—	—	—	—
1726 EPH	—	175	325	450	750	—

KM# 181 1/4 THALER

Silver **Ruler:** George II August **Subject:** Death of George I Ludwig **Obverse:** Laureate draped bust right **Reverse:** Inscription

Date	Mintage	VG	F	VF	XF	Unc
1727 CPS	—	45.00	100	200	400	—

KM# 202 1/4 THALER

Silver **Ruler:** George II August **Obverse:** Bust left, value below **Reverse:** 4 crowned shields in cruciform, date

Date	Mintage	F	VF	XF	Unc
1728	—	25.00	50.00	100	200

KM# 222 1/4 THALER

Silver **Ruler:** George II August **Obverse:** Crowned quartered arms, crown divides date **Reverse:** Wildman with tree in right hand

Date	Mintage	F	VF	XF	Unc
1730 EPH	—	250	500	1,000	1,600
1734 IAB	—	50.00	100	200	325
1739 IBH	—	50.00	100	200	325
1754 IBH	—	50.00	100	200	325

KM# 245 1/4 THALER

Silver **Ruler:** George II August **Obverse:** Bust left, value below **Reverse:** Crowned quartered arms

Date	Mintage	F	VF	XF	Unc
1732 CPS	—	25.00	50.00	100	200

KM# 246 1/4 THALER

Silver **Ruler:** George II August **Obverse:** Crowned quartered arms **Reverse:** Horse left

Date	Mintage	F	VF	XF	Unc
1732 CPS	—	50.00	100	200	325
1739 CPS	—	50.00	100	200	325

KM# 254 1/4 THALER

Silver **Ruler:** George II August **Subject:** Death of Wilhelmine Caroline **Obverse:** Bust left, legend in 4 lines below **Reverse:** 18-line inscription

Date	Mintage	F	VF	XF	Unc
1737	—	60.00	125	250	400

KM# 38 1/3 THALER

Silver **Ruler:** George Ludwig **Obverse:** Date divided just below ground under horse **Reverse:** St. Andrew with cross

Date	Mintage	VG	F	VF	XF	Unc
1702 HB	—	35.00	80.00	110	200	—

KM# 46 1/3 THALER

Silver **Ruler:** George Ludwig **Obverse:** Crowned complex arms divide date at top and initials below **Reverse:** St. Andrew with cross

Date	Mintage	VG	F	VF	XF	Unc
1705 HB	—	20.00	50.00	80.00	160	—

KM# 47 1/3 THALER

Silver **Ruler:** George Ludwig **Obverse:** Date in legend **Reverse:** St. Andrew with cross

Date	Mintage	VG	F	VF	XF	Unc
1705 HB	—	15.00	30.00	60.00	125	—
1706 HB	—	15.00	30.00	60.00	125	—
1707 HB	—	15.00	30.00	60.00	125	—
1708 HB	—	15.00	30.00	60.00	125	—
1709 HB	—	15.00	30.00	60.00	125	—
1710 HB	—	15.00	30.00	60.00	125	—
1711 HB	—	15.00	30.00	60.00	125	—

KM# 65 1/3 THALER

Silver **Ruler:** George Ludwig **Obverse:** Title of Imperial Treasurer added **Reverse:** St. Andrew with cross

Date	Mintage	VG	F	VF	XF	Unc
1711 HB	—	25.00	60.00	85.00	165	—
1711 HCB	—	25.00	60.00	85.00	165	—

KM# 66 1/3 THALER

Silver **Ruler:** George Ludwig **Obverse:** Imperial crown in central shield of arms

Date	Mintage	VG	F	VF	XF	Unc
1711 HCB	—	30.00	65.00	100	185	—
1712 HCB	—	30.00	65.00	100	185	—
1713 HCB	—	30.00	65.00	100	185	—

KM# 74 1/3 THALER

Silver **Ruler:** George Ludwig **Obverse:** Draped bust right **Reverse:** Crowned complex arms **Note:** Similar to 2/3 Thaler, KM#76.

Date	Mintage	VG	F	VF	XF	Unc
1712 HCB	—	20.00	45.00	75.00	140	—
1713 HCB	—	20.00	45.00	75.00	140	—
1714 HCB	—	20.00	45.00	75.00	140	—
1715 HCB	—	20.00	45.00	75.00	140	—

KM# 110 1/3 THALER

Silver **Ruler:** George Ludwig **Subject:** George Ludwig **Obverse:** Bust right **Reverse:** Crowned shields in cruciform

Date	Mintage	VG	F	VF	XF	Unc
1716 HCB	—	75.00	140	200	285	—
1717 HCB	—	75.00	140	200	285	—
1718 HCB	—	75.00	140	200	285	—
1720 HCB	—	75.00	140	200	285	—
1721 HCB	—	75.00	140	200	285	—
1722 HCB	—	75.00	140	200	285	—
1724 HCB	—	75.00	140	200	285	—
1725 HCB	—	75.00	140	200	285	—
1726 CPS	—	75.00	140	200	285	—
1727 CPS	—	75.00	140	200	285	—

KM# 111 1/3 THALER

Silver **Ruler:** George Ludwig **Obverse:** Similar to reverse of KM#108, but value 1/3 **Reverse:** Wildman, tree in right hand, date in legend

Date	Mintage	VG	F	VF	XF	Unc
1716 HH	—	20.00	40.00	75.00	115	—
1718 HH	—	20.00	40.00	75.00	115	—
1719 HH	—	20.00	40.00	75.00	115	—
1720 C	—	20.00	40.00	75.00	115	—
1721 C	—	20.00	40.00	75.00	115	—
1722 C	—	20.00	40.00	75.00	115	—
1723 EPH	—	20.00	40.00	75.00	115	—

KM# 145 1/3 THALER

Silver **Ruler:** George Ludwig **Obverse:** Crowned shields in cruciform **Reverse:** St. Andrew

Date	Mintage	VG	F	VF	XF	Unc
1719 HCB	—	18.00	35.00	60.00	100	—
1721 HCB	—	18.00	35.00	60.00	100	—
1722 HCB	—	18.00	35.00	60.00	100	—
1724 HCB	—	18.00	35.00	60.00	100	—
1727 CPS	—	18.00	35.00	60.00	100	—

KM# 146 1/3 THALER

Silver **Ruler:** George Ludwig **Obverse:** Similar to reverse of KM#108, but value 1/3 **Reverse:** Horse leaping left, date in legend

Date	Mintage	VG	F	VF	XF	Unc
1719 HCB	—	18.00	35.00	60.00	100	—
1720 HCB	—	18.00	35.00	60.00	100	—
1721 HCB	—	18.00	35.00	60.00	100	—
1723 HCB	—	18.00	35.00	60.00	100	—
1725 HCB	—	18.00	35.00	60.00	100	—

KM# 163 1/3 THALER

Silver **Ruler:** George Ludwig **Obverse:** Crowned shields in cruciform **Reverse:** Wildman with tree in right hand, 12 at right **Note:** Similar to 2/3 Thaler, KM#112.2 but 12 (mariengroschen) added in field.

Date	Mintage	VG	F	VF	XF	Unc
1723 EPH	—	20.00	40.00	75.00	115	—
1724 EPH	—	20.00	40.00	75.00	115	—
1725 EPH	—	20.00	40.00	75.00	115	—
1726 EPH	—	20.00	40.00	75.00	115	—
1727 EPH	—	20.00	40.00	75.00	115	—

KM# 182 1/3 THALER

Silver **Ruler:** George II August **Obverse:** Bust left, value below **Reverse:** 4 crowned shields in cruciform, date

Date	Mintage	F	VF	XF	Unc
1727 CPS	—	50.00	100	200	425
1728 CPS	—	50.00	100	200	425
1729 CPS	—	200	400	600	1,000

KM# 208 1/3 THALER

Silver **Ruler:** George II August **Obverse:** 4 crowned shields in cruciform **Reverse:** St. Andrew with cross

Date	Mintage	F	VF	XF	Unc
1729 CPS	—	—	—	—	—

KM# 223 1/3 THALER

Silver **Ruler:** George II August **Subject:** George II August **Obverse:** Bust left **Reverse:** Crowned quartered arms

Date	Mintage	F	VF	XF	Unc
1730 CPS	—	100	200	350	500
1736 CPS	—	100	200	350	500

KM# 224 1/3 THALER

Silver **Ruler:** George II August **Obverse:** Bust left **Reverse:** Horse left

Date	Mintage	F	VF	XF	Unc
1730 CPS Rare	—	—	—	—	—
1736 CPS Rare	—	—	—	—	—

KM# 225 1/3 THALER

Silver **Ruler:** George II August **Obverse:** Crowned quartered arms **Reverse:** Wildman with tree in right hand

Date	Mintage	F	VF	XF	Unc
1730 EPH	—	50.00	130	200	300
1731 C	—	35.00	100	150	250
1733 IAB	—	35.00	100	150	250
1734 IAB	—	35.00	100	150	250
1735 IAB	—	35.00	100	150	250

Date	Mintage	F	VF	XF	Unc
1736 IAB	—	35.00	100	150	250
1752/42	—	35.00	100	150	250

KM# 240 1/3 THALER

Silver **Ruler:** George II August **Obverse:** Crowned quartered arms, value below **Reverse:** St. Andrew

Date	Mintage	F	VF	XF	Unc
1731 CPS	—	50.00	125	235	350
1732 CPS	—	50.00	125	235	350
1734 CPS	—	50.00	125	235	350

KM# 247 1/3 THALER

Silver **Ruler:** George II August **Obverse:** Crowned quartered arms **Reverse:** Horse left

Date	Mintage	F	VF	XF	Unc
1732 CPS	—	100	250	500	900
1734 CPS	—	100	250	500	900
1736 CPS	—	100	250	500	900

KM# 255 1/3 THALER

Silver **Ruler:** George II August **Obverse:** Crowned quartered arms **Reverse:** Wildman with tree in right hand, 12 at right

Date	Mintage	F	VF	XF	Unc
1737 IAB	—	35.00	100	150	250
1738 IAB	—	35.00	100	150	250
1739 C	—	50.00	140	200	300
1740 IBH	—	35.00	100	150	250
1741 IBH	—	35.00	100	150	250
1742 IBH	—	35.00	100	150	250
1743 IBH	—	35.00	100	150	250
1744 IBH	—	35.00	100	150	250
1746 IBH	—	35.00	100	150	250
1747 IBH	—	35.00	100	150	250
1748 IBH	—	35.00	100	150	250
1749 IBH	—	35.00	100	150	250
1750 IBH	—	35.00	100	150	250
1751 IBH	—	35.00	100	150	250
1752 IBH	—	35.00	100	150	250
1754 IBH	—	35.00	100	150	250
1755 IBH	—	35.00	100	150	250
1756 IBH	—	35.00	100	150	250
1758 IBH	—	35.00	100	150	250
1759 IBH	—	35.00	100	150	250
1760 IBH	—	35.00	100	150	250

KM# 273 1/3 THALER

Silver **Ruler:** George II August **Obv. Legend:** N. D. LEIPZ. F **Reverse:** St. Andrew with cross

Date	Mintage	F	VF	XF	Unc
1740 CPS	—	—	—	—	—

KM# 274 1/3 THALER

Silver **Ruler:** George II August **Obverse:** Crowned quartered arms, value below **Obv. Legend:** N. D. REICHS. F. (1/3) FEIN SILB **Reverse:** St. Andrew with cross

Date	Mintage	F	VF	XF	Unc
1740 CPS	—	50.00	150	200	285
1743 CPS	—	50.00	150	200	285
1746 CPS	—	50.00	150	200	285
1749 CPS	—	25.00	50.00	100	200
1751 C	—	50.00	150	200	285

KM# 323 1/3 THALER

Silver **Ruler:** George II August **Obv. Legend:** N. D. REICHS **Reverse:** Horse left

Date	Mintage	F	VF	XF	Unc
1754 IWS	—	—	—	—	—

KM# 326 1/3 THALER

Silver **Ruler:** George II August **Obv. Legend:** ... (1/3) FEIN SILBER **Reverse:** St. Andrew with cross

Date	Mintage	F	VF	XF	Unc
1758 IWS	—	50.00	150	200	285

KM# 349 1/3 THALER

Silver **Ruler:** George III **Obverse:** Crowned quartered arms, value below **Reverse:** Wildman with tree in right hand, 12 at right

Date	Mintage	F	VF	XF	Unc
1762 IBH	—	30.00	50.00	100	200
1764 IAP	—	30.00	50.00	100	200
1765 IAP	—	30.00	50.00	100	200
1766 IAP	—	30.00	50.00	100	200
1767 IAP	—	30.00	50.00	100	200
1768 IAP	—	30.00	50.00	100	200
1769 IAP	—	30.00	50.00	100	200
1770 IAP	—	30.00	50.00	100	200
1771 IAP	—	30.00	50.00	100	200
1772 LCR	—	30.00	50.00	100	200
1772 LCR	—	30.00	50.00	100	200
1773 LCR	—	30.00	50.00	100	200
1774 LCR	—	30.00	50.00	100	200
1775 LCR	—	30.00	50.00	100	200
1776 LCR	—	30.00	50.00	100	200
1777 LCR	—	30.00	50.00	100	200
1778 LCR	—	30.00	50.00	100	200
1779 .C.	—	30.00	50.00	100	200
1780 CES	—	30.00	50.00	100	200
1781 CES	—	30.00	50.00	100	200
1782 CES	—	30.00	50.00	100	200
1783 CES	—	30.00	50.00	100	200
1784 CES	—	30.00	50.00	100	200

KM# 356 1/3 THALER

Silver **Ruler:** George III **Obverse:** Crowned quartered arms **Reverse:** St. Andrew

Date	Mintage	F	VF	XF	Unc
1764 IWS	—	40.00	75.00	125	325
1766 IWS	—	40.00	75.00	125	325
1770 IWS	—	40.00	75.00	125	325

KM# 358 1/3 THALER

Silver **Ruler:** George III **Obverse:** Arms **Reverse:** Horse

Date	Mintage	F	VF	XF	Unc
1767 .C.	—	50.00	100	200	400

KM# 368 1/3 THALER

Silver **Ruler:** George III **Subject:** George III **Obverse:** Head right **Reverse:** Crowned quartered arms within ornate frame

Date	Mintage	F	VF	XF	Unc
1774 IWS	—	40.00	75.00	175	350
1777 IWS	—	40.00	75.00	175	350

KM# 373 1/3 THALER

Silver **Ruler:** George III **Obverse:** Head right **Reverse:** Crowned quartered arms with supporters

Date	Mintage	F	VF	XF	Unc
1778 IWS	—	40.00	65.00	150	325
1779 IWS	—	40.00	65.00	150	325

KM# 374 1/3 THALER

Silver **Ruler:** George III **Obverse:** Crowned quartered arms on ornate shield, value below **Reverse:** St. Andrew

Date	Mintage	F	VF	XF	Unc
1779 IWS	—	30.00	50.00	75.00	225
1781 IWS	—	30.00	50.00	75.00	225
1783 IWS	—	30.00	50.00	75.00	225
1784 IWS	—	30.00	50.00	75.00	225
1788 IWS	—	30.00	50.00	75.00	225
1790 .C.	—	30.00	50.00	75.00	225
1793 PLM	—	30.00	50.00	75.00	225

KM# 387 1/3 THALER

Silver **Ruler:** George III **Obverse:** Crowned quartered arms divide date, value below **Reverse:** Wildman with tree in right hand

Date	Mintage	F	VF	XF	Unc
1781	—	30.00	45.00	75.00	200
1785 CES	—	30.00	45.00	75.00	200
1785 .C.	—	30.00	45.00	75.00	200
1786 .C.	—	30.00	45.00	75.00	200
1787 .C.	—	30.00	45.00	75.00	200
1788 .C.	—	30.00	45.00	75.00	200
1789 .C.	—	30.00	45.00	75.00	200

KM# 388 1/3 THALER

Silver **Ruler:** George III **Obverse:** Head right **Reverse:** Crowned quartered arms, value below, date above

Date	Mintage	F	VF	XF	Unc
1785 IWS	—	30.00	50.00	100	225
1786 IWS	—	30.00	50.00	100	225
1787 IWS	—	30.00	50.00	100	225
1788 IWS	—	30.00	50.00	100	225
1789 IWS	—	30.00	50.00	100	225
1790 IWS	—	30.00	50.00	100	225

KM# 391.1 1/3 THALER

Silver **Ruler:** George III **Obverse:** Head right **Reverse:** Crowned quartered arms, value below

Date	Mintage	F	VF	XF	Unc
1789 IWS	—	30.00	50.00	100	225
1790 .C.	—	30.00	50.00	100	225
1791 .C.	—	30.00	50.00	100	225
1800 .C.	—	30.00	50.00	100	225

KM# 391.2 1/3 THALER
Silver **Ruler:** George III **Obverse:** PLM below bust **Reverse:** Crowned quartered arms, value below, crown divides date above

Date	Mintage	F	VF	XF	Unc
1793 PLM	—	30.00	50.00	100	225
1794 PLM	—	30.00	50.00	100	225
1795 PLM	—	30.00	50.00	100	225
1796 PLM	—	30.00	50.00	100	225
1797 PLM	—	30.00	50.00	100	225
1798 PLM	—	30.00	50.00	100	225
1799 PLM	—	30.00	50.00	100	225
1800 PLM	—	30.00	50.00	100	225

KM# 43 1/2 THALER
Silver **Ruler:** George Ludwig **Obverse:** Crowned complex arms divide date **Reverse:** Horse leaping left **Note:** Similar to 2/3 Thaler, KM#17, but value 1/2.

Date	Mintage	VG	F	VF	XF	Unc
1703 HB	—	65.00	125	225	375	—

KM# 75 1/2 THALER
Silver **Ruler:** George Ludwig **Obverse:** Imperial crown in central shield, date in legend

Date	Mintage	VG	F	VF	XF	Unc
1712 HCB	—	60.00	150	300	600	—

KM# 87 1/2 THALER
Silver **Ruler:** George Ludwig **Reverse:** Wildman, tree in right hand, without value shown

Date	Mintage	VG	F	VF	XF	Unc
1712	—	—	—	—	—	—
1713 HH	—	75.00	140	275	450	—

KM# 95 1/2 THALER
Silver **Ruler:** George Ludwig **Obverse:** Imperial crown in central shield, date below **Reverse:** Horse leaping left

Date	Mintage	VG	F	VF	XF	Unc
1714 HCB	—	40.00	90.00	125	225	—

KM# 96 1/2 THALER
Silver **Ruler:** George Ludwig **Subject:** Death of Sophia von der Pfalz, Mother of George I Ludwig **Obverse:** Bust right **Reverse:** 12-line inscription with date

Date	Mintage	VG	F	VF	XF	Unc
1714	—	75.00	150	300	600	—

KM# 141 1/2 THALER
Silver, 38 mm. **Ruler:** George Ludwig **Obverse:** Crowned and supported 4-fold arms in Order of the Garter, date divided at top **Reverse:** Horse leaping left, without indication of value

Date	Mintage	VG	F	VF	XF	Unc
1718 hh	—	35.00	80.00	125	225	—

KM# 147 1/2 THALER
Silver, 38 mm. **Ruler:** George Ludwig **Reverse:** Wildman, tree in right hand, without indication of value

Date	Mintage	VG	F	VF	XF	Unc
1718	—	—	—	—	—	—
1719	—	50.00	100	200	400	—
1723 EPH	—	50.00	100	—	400	—
1724 EPH	—	50.00	100	200	400	—
1727 EPH	—	50.00	100	200	400	—

KM# 184 1/2 THALER
Silver **Ruler:** George Ludwig **Subject:** Death of George I Ludwig **Obverse:** Armored bust right **Reverse:** Inscription

Date	Mintage	VG	F	VF	XF	Unc
1727 CPS	—	100	200	400	600	—

KM# 183 1/2 THALER
Silver **Ruler:** George Ludwig **Obverse:** Bust right **Reverse:** Crowned shields in cruciform **Note:** Similar to 1/4 Thaler, KM#157, but value 1/2 below.

Date	Mintage	VG	F	VF	XF	Unc
1727 CPS	—	40.00	80.00	140	250	—

KM# 241 1/2 THALER
Silver **Ruler:** George II August **Obverse:** Crowned quartered arms **Reverse:** Wildman with tree in right hand, 1/2 at lower right

Date	Mintage	F	VF	XF	Unc
1731 C Rare	—	—	—	—	—
1735 IAB Rare	—	—	—	—	—

KM# 248 1/2 THALER
Silver **Ruler:** George II August **Obverse:** Bust left, value below **Reverse:** Crowned quartered arms

Date	Mintage	F	VF	XF	Unc
1732 CPS Rare	—	—	—	—	—

KM# 256 1/2 THALER
Silver **Ruler:** George II August **Subject:** Death of Wilhelmine Caroline **Obverse:** Bust left, 4-line legend below **Reverse:** 8-line inscription

Date	Mintage	F	VF	XF	Unc
1737 Rare	—	—	—	—	—

KM# 275 1/2 THALER
Silver **Ruler:** George II August **Obverse:** Crowned quartered arms **Reverse:** Horse left

Date	Mintage	F	VF	XF	Unc
1740 CPS	—	50.00	100	200	400

KM# A17 2/3 THALER (Gulden)
Silver **Ruler:** Ernst August **Obverse:** Bust right **Reverse:** Leaping horse left, value divides date below **Note:** Prev. Bruns.-Lune-Calenberg 2/3 Thaler, KM#381.

Date	Mintage	VG	F	VF	XF	Unc
1721	—	30.00	60.00	125	225	—

Note: Later restrike in low grade silver

KM# 17 2/3 THALER (Gulden)
Silver **Ruler:** George Ludwig **Obverse:** Crowned complex arms divide date **Reverse:** Horse leaping left, value below

Date	Mintage	VG	F	VF	XF	Unc
1700 HB	—	25.00	60.00	90.00	135	—
1701 HB	—	25.00	60.00	90.00	135	—
1702 HB	—	25.00	60.00	90.00	135	—
1703 HB	—	25.00	60.00	90.00	135	—
1704 HB	—	25.00	60.00	90.00	135	—
1705 HB	—	25.00	60.00	90.00	135	—

KM# 48 2/3 THALER (Gulden)
Silver **Ruler:** George Ludwig **Obverse:** Crowned complex arms **Obv. Legend:** GEORG: LUD: D • G • D • BR • & • LUN: S • R • I • ELECT: **Reverse:** Horse leaping left, value below **Rev. Legend:** IN RECTO DECUS

Date	Mintage	VG	F	VF	XF	Unc
1705 HB	—	30.00	65.00	100	150	—
1706 HB	—	30.00	65.00	100	150	—
1707 HB	—	30.00	65.00	100	150	—
1708 HB	—	30.00	65.00	100	150	—
1709 HB	—	30.00	65.00	100	150	—
1710 HB	—	30.00	65.00	100	150	—
1711 HB	—	30.00	65.00	100	150	—
1711 HCB	—	30.00	65.00	100	150	—

KM# 67 2/3 THALER (Gulden)
Silver **Ruler:** George Ludwig **Obverse:** Crowned complex arms divide initials **Reverse:** Horse leaping left

Date	Mintage	VG	F	VF	XF	Unc
1711 hb	—	35.00	80.00	130	225	—

KM# 68 2/3 THALER (Gulden)
Silver **Ruler:** George Ludwig **Obverse:** Imperial crown in central shield of arms **Reverse:** Horse leaping left

Date	Mintage	VG	F	VF	XF	Unc
1711 HCB	—	35.00	80.00	130	225	—
1712 HCB	—	35.00	80.00	130	225	—
1713 HCB	—	35.00	80.00	130	225	—
1714 HCB	—	35.00	80.00	130	225	—
1715 HCB	—	35.00	80.00	130	225	—

KM# 76 2/3 THALER (Gulden)
Silver **Ruler:** George Ludwig **Subject:** George Ludwig **Obverse:** Armored bust right **Reverse:** Crowned complex arms

Date	Mintage	VG	F	VF	XF	Unc
1712 HCB	—	35.00	75.00	115	200	—
1713 HCB	—	35.00	75.00	115	200	—

KM# 100 2/3 THALER (Gulden)
Silver **Ruler:** George Ludwig **Obverse:** Head right **Obv. Legend:** GEORGIVS • D • G • MAG • BRIT • FR • & HIB • REX • F • D • **Reverse:** Crowned shield in cruciform, value at center

Date	Mintage	VG	F	VF	XF	Unc
1715 HCB	—	40.00	90.00	120	225	—
1716 HCB	—	40.00	90.00	120	225	—
1717 HCB	—	40.00	90.00	120	225	—
1718 HCB	—	40.00	90.00	120	225	—
1719 HCB	—	40.00	90.00	120	225	—
1720 HCB	—	40.00	90.00	120	225	—
1721 HCB	—	40.00	90.00	120	225	—
1722 HCB	—	40.00	90.00	120	225	—
1723 HCB	—	40.00	90.00	120	225	—
1724 HCB	—	40.00	90.00	120	225	—
1725 HCB	—	40.00	90.00	120	225	—
1726 CPS	—	40.00	90.00	120	225	—
1727 CPS	—	40.00	90.00	120	225	—

KM# 112.1 2/3 THALER (Gulden)

Silver **Ruler:** George Ludwig **Obverse:** With 24 in field **Reverse:** Horse leaping left

Date	Mintage	VG	F	VF	XF	Unc
1716 HH	—	20.00	45.00	80.00	125	—
1717 HH	—	20.00	45.00	80.00	125	—
1718 HH	—	20.00	45.00	80.00	125	—
1719 HH	—	20.00	45.00	80.00	125	—
1719 HH-C	—	20.00	45.00	80.00	125	—
1719 C	—	20.00	45.00	80.00	125	—
1720 C	—	20.00	45.00	80.00	125	—
1721 C	—	20.00	45.00	80.00	125	—

KM# 148 2/3 THALER (Gulden)

Silver **Ruler:** George Ludwig **Obverse:** Crowned shields in cruciform, value at center **Obv. Legend:** GEORGIVS - D • G • M • BR • II - FR • DT • HIB • - REX • F • D • - **Reverse:** Horse leaping left

Date	Mintage	VG	F	VF	XF	Unc
1719 HCB	—	18.00	40.00	75.00	110	—
1720 HCB	—	18.00	40.00	75.00	110	—
1721 HCB	—	18.00	40.00	75.00	110	—
1722 HCB	—	18.00	40.00	75.00	110	—
1723 HCB	—	18.00	40.00	75.00	110	—
1724 HCB	—	18.00	40.00	75.00	110	—
1725 HCB	—	18.00	40.00	75.00	110	—
1726 CPS	—	18.00	40.00	75.00	110	—
1727 CPS	—	18.00	40.00	75.00	110	—

KM# 112.2 2/3 THALER (Gulden)

Silver **Ruler:** George Ludwig **Obverse:** Without 24 in field **Reverse:** Horse leaping left

Date	Mintage	VG	F	VF	XF	Unc
1722 C	—	20.00	45.00	80.00	125	—
1723 C	—	20.00	45.00	80.00	125	—
1723 EPH	—	20.00	45.00	80.00	125	—
1724 EPH	—	20.00	45.00	80.00	125	—
1725 EPH	—	20.00	45.00	80.00	125	—
1726 EPH	—	20.00	45.00	80.00	125	—
1727 EPH	—	20.00	45.00	80.00	125	—

KM# 185 2/3 THALER (Gulden)

Silver **Ruler:** George II August **Subject:** George II August **Obverse:** Laureate draped bust left **Obv. Legend:** GEORG • II • D • G • M • BRIT • FR • ET • HIB • REX • F • D • **Reverse:** Crowned shields in cruciform, value at center

Date	Mintage	F	VF	XF	Unc
1727 CPS	—	100	250	500	1,000
1728 CPS	—	100	250	500	1,000
1729 CPS	—	100	250	500	1,000

KM# 186 2/3 THALER (Gulden)

Silver **Ruler:** George II August **Obverse:** Crowned shields in cruciform, value at center **Reverse:** Horse leaping left **Rev. Legend:** NEC ASPERA TERRENI

Date	Mintage	F	VF	XF	Unc
1727 CPS	—	50.00	150	250	500
1728 CPS	—	50.00	150	250	500
1729 CPS	—	50.00	150	250	500

KM# 187 2/3 THALER (Gulden)

Silver **Ruler:** George II August **Obverse:** 4 crowned shields in cruciform, 2/3 in center **Reverse:** Wildman with tree in right hand, 24 at lower right

Date	Mintage	F	VF	XF	Unc
1727 EPH	—	50.00	125	250	500
1728 EPH	—	50.00	125	250	500
1729 EPH	—	50.00	125	250	500

KM# 226 2/3 THALER (Gulden)

Silver **Ruler:** George II August **Obverse:** Bust left **Reverse:** Crowned quartered arms

Date	Mintage	F	VF	XF	Unc
1730 CPS	—	150	350	700	1,400
1731 CPS	—	150	350	700	1,400
1732 CPS	—	150	350	700	1,400
1736 CPS	—	150	350	700	1,400
1740 CPS	—	150	350	700	1,400

KM# 227 2/3 THALER (Gulden)

Silver **Ruler:** George II August **Obverse:** Crowned quartered arms, value **Reverse:** Horse left

Date	Mintage	F	VF	XF	Unc
1730 CPS	—	50.00	150	250	500
1731 CPS	—	50.00	150	250	500
1732 CPS	—	50.00	150	250	500
1733 CPS	—	50.00	150	250	500
1734 CPS	—	50.00	150	250	500
1735 CPS	—	50.00	150	250	500
1736 CPS	—	50.00	150	250	500
1737 CPS	—	50.00	150	250	500

KM# 228 2/3 THALER (Gulden)

Silver **Ruler:** George II August **Reverse:** Horse left, value

Date	Mintage	F	VF	XF	Unc
1730 EPH	—	100	300	600	1,200
1731 IAB	—	100	300	600	1,200
1732 IAB	—	100	300	600	1,200
1733 IAB	—	100	300	600	1,200
1735 IAB	—	100	300	600	1,200
1736 IAB	—	100	300	600	1,200
1737 IAB	—	100	300	600	1,200
1738 IAB	—	100	300	600	1,200
1740 IBH	—	100	300	600	1,200
1741 IBH	—	100	300	600	1,200
1742 IBH	—	100	300	600	1,200
1743 IBH	—	100	300	600	1,200
1749 IBH	—	100	300	600	1,200

KM# 229 2/3 THALER (Gulden)

Silver **Ruler:** George II August **Obverse:** Crowned quartered arms, value below **Reverse:** Wildman with tree in right hand

Date	Mintage	F	VF	XF	Unc
1730 EPH	—	35.00	75.00	140	300
1731 IAB	—	35.00	75.00	140	300
1732 IAB	—	35.00	75.00	140	300
1733 IAB	—	35.00	75.00	140	300
1734 IAB	—	35.00	75.00	140	300
1735 IAB	—	35.00	75.00	140	300
1736 IAB	—	35.00	75.00	140	300
1737 IAB	—	35.00	75.00	140	300
1738 IAB	—	35.00	75.00	140	300
1739 C	—	35.00	75.00	140	300
1739 IBH	—	35.00	75.00	140	300
1740 IBH	—	35.00	75.00	140	300
1741 IBH	—	35.00	75.00	140	300
1742 IBH	—	35.00	75.00	140	300
1743 IBH	—	35.00	75.00	140	300

KM# 263 2/3 THALER (Gulden)

Silver **Ruler:** George II August **Obverse:** Bust left **Obv. Legend:** LEIPZIGER FUSS **Reverse:** Crowned cruciform

Date	Mintage	F	VF	XF	Unc
1738 CPS	—	200	450	900	1,800
1739 CPS	—	200	450	900	1,800

KM# 264 2/3 THALER (Gulden)

Silver **Ruler:** George II August **Obverse:** Crowned quartered arms **Obv. Legend:** N. D. LEIPZ. F **Reverse:** Horse left, value

Date	Mintage	F	VF	XF	Unc
1738 CPS	—	100	300	600	1,200
1739 CPS	—	100	300	600	1,200
1740 CPS	—	100	300	600	1,200

KM# 277 2/3 THALER (Gulden)

Silver **Ruler:** George II August **Obverse:** Crowned quartered arms, value below **Obv. Legend:** GEORG • II • D • G • M • B • F & H • REX • - F • D • B • & L • DVX • S • B • I • A • T • & EL •, N. D. REICHS. F below arms **Reverse:** Horse leaping left **Rev. Legend:** NEC ASPERA TERRENI

Date	Mintage	F	VF	XF	Unc
1740 CPS	—	50.00	140	300	600
1741 CPS	—	50.00	140	300	600
1742 CPS	—	50.00	140	300	600
1743 CPS	—	50.00	140	300	600
1744 CPS	—	50.00	140	300	600
1745 CPS	—	50.00	140	300	600
1746 CPS	—	50.00	140	300	600
1747 CPS	—	50.00	140	300	600
1748 CPS	—	50.00	140	300	600
1749 CPS	—	50.00	140	300	600
1750 CPS	—	50.00	140	300	600
1751 C	—	50.00	140	300	600
1752 C	—	50.00	140	300	600
1753 IWS	—	50.00	140	300	600
1754 IWS	—	50.00	140	300	600
1755 IWS	—	50.00	140	300	600
1757 IWS	—	50.00	140	300	600
1758 IWS	—	50.00	140	300	600
1759 IWS	—	50.00	140	300	600
1760 IWS	—	50.00	140	300	600

KM# 276 2/3 THALER (Gulden)

Silver **Ruler:** George II August **Obverse:** Bust left **Obv. Legend:** REICHS FUSS **Note:** Crowned cruciform.

Date	Mintage	F	VF	XF	Unc
1740 CPS	—	100	250	500	1,000
1741 CPS	—	100	250	500	1,000
1742 CPS	—	100	250	500	1,000
1743 CPS	—	100	250	500	1,000
1744 CPS	—	100	250	500	1,000
1746 CPS	—	100	250	500	1,000
1751 C	—	100	250	500	1,000
1752 C	—	100	250	500	1,000

KM# 286 2/3 THALER (Gulden)

Silver **Ruler:** George II August **Obverse:** Crowned quartered arms on ornate shield, value below **Reverse:** Wildman with tree in right hand

Date	Mintage	F	VF	XF	Unc
1743 IBH	—	35.00	75.00	150	350
1744 IBH	—	35.00	75.00	150	350
1745 IBH	—	35.00	75.00	150	350
1746 IBH	—	35.00	75.00	150	350
1747 IBH	—	35.00	75.00	150	350
1748 IBH	—	35.00	75.00	150	350
1749 IBH	—	35.00	75.00	150	350
1750 IBH	—	35.00	75.00	150	350
1751 IBH	—	35.00	75.00	150	350

Date	Mintage	F	VF	XF	Unc
1752 IBH	—	35.00	75.00	150	350
1753 IBH	—	35.00	75.00	150	350
1754 IBH	—	35.00	75.00	150	350
1755 IBH	—	35.00	75.00	150	350
1756 IBH	—	35.00	75.00	150	350
1757 IBH	—	35.00	75.00	150	350
1758 IBH	—	35.00	75.00	150	350
1759 IBH	—	35.00	75.00	150	350
1760 IBH	—	35.00	75.00	150	350

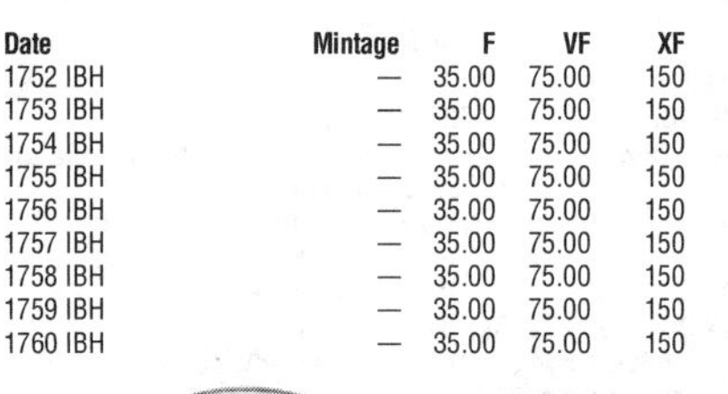

KM# 290 2/3 THALER (Gulden)

Silver **Ruler:** George II August **Obverse:** Crowned quartered arms in baroque shield **Reverse:** Horse left

Date	Mintage	F	VF	XF	Unc
1744 IBH	—	40.00	100	200	400
1745 IBH	—	40.00	100	200	400
1746 IBH	—	40.00	100	200	400
1747 IBH	—	40.00	100	200	400
1748 IBH	—	40.00	100	200	400
1749 IBH	—	40.00	100	200	400
1752 IBH	—	40.00	100	200	400
1753 IBH	—	40.00	100	200	400
1755 IBH	—	40.00	100	200	400
1758 IBH	—	40.00	100	200	400
1759 IBH	—	40.00	100	200	400
1760 IBH	—	40.00	100	200	400

KM# 319 2/3 THALER (Gulden)

Silver **Ruler:** George II August **Obverse:** Armored bust left **Reverse:** Crowned quartered arms within ornate frame, value below

Date	Mintage	F	VF	XF	Unc
1752 IAS	—	200	600	1,200	2,400
1754 IAS	—	200	600	1,200	2,400
1754 IWS	—	200	600	1,200	2,400

KM# 365 2/3 THALER (Gulden)

Silver **Ruler:** George III **Subject:** George III **Obverse:** Head left **Obv. Legend:** GEORG • III • D • G • M • BRIT • FR • & • HIB • REX • FD • **Reverse:** Crowned quartered arms on ornate shield, value below

Date	Mintage	F	VF	XF	Unc
1772 IWS	—	40.00	75.00	150	375
1773 IWS	—	40.00	75.00	150	375
1774 IWS	—	40.00	75.00	150	375
1775 IWS	—	40.00	75.00	150	375
1776 IWS	—	40.00	75.00	150	375
1777 IWS	—	40.00	75.00	150	375
1779 IWS	—	40.00	75.00	150	375
1780 IWS	—	40.00	75.00	150	375
1781 IWS	—	40.00	75.00	150	375
1782 IWS	—	40.00	75.00	150	375
1783 IWS	—	40.00	75.00	150	375
1784 IWS	—	40.00	75.00	150	375
1785 IWS	—	40.00	75.00	150	375
1786 IWS	—	40.00	75.00	150	375
1787 IWS	—	40.00	75.00	150	375
1788 IWS	—	40.00	75.00	150	375
1789 IWS	—	40.00	75.00	150	375
1790 .C.	—	40.00	75.00	150	375
1791/0 .C.	—	70.00	135	225	400
1791 .C.	—	40.00	75.00	150	375
1792 PLM	—	40.00	75.00	150	375
1793 PLM	—	40.00	75.00	150	375
1794 PLM	—	40.00	75.00	150	375
1795 PLM	—	40.00	75.00	150	375
1796 PLM	—	40.00	75.00	150	375
1797 PLM	—	40.00	75.00	150	375
1798 PLM	—	40.00	75.00	150	375
1799 PLM	—	40.00	75.00	150	375
1800 PLM	—	40.00	75.00	150	375
1800 .C.	—	40.00	75.00	150	375

KM# 371 2/3 THALER (Gulden)

Silver **Ruler:** George III **Obverse:** Head right **Obv. Legend:** GEORG • III • D • G • M • BRIT • FR • & • HIB • REX • FD • **Reverse:** Crowned quartered arms within Order chain with supporters

Date	Mintage	F	VF	XF	Unc
1776 IWS	—	60.00	125	250	500
1778 IWS	—	60.00	125	250	500
1781 IWS	—	60.00	125	250	500

KM# 19 THALER

Silver **Ruler:** George Ludwig **Note:** Dav. #6654 and #2057.

Date	Mintage	F	VF	XF	Unc
1700 HB	—	125	225	350	—
1701 HB	—	90.00	165	300	675
1702 HB	—	90.00	165	300	675
1703 HB	—	90.00	165	300	675
1704 HB	—	90.00	165	300	675
1705 HB	—	90.00	165	300	675

KM# 20 THALER

Silver **Ruler:** George Ludwig **Note:** Dav. #6655 and #2061.

Date	Mintage	F	VF	XF	Unc
1700 HB	—	125	225	350	—
1701 HB	—	100	175	325	750
1702 HB	—	100	175	325	750
1703 HB	—	100	175	325	750
1704 HB	—	100	175	325	750
1705 HB	—	100	175	325	750

KM# 35 THALER

Silver **Ruler:** George Ludwig **Obverse:** Crowned complex arms within ornate frame **Obv. Legend:** GEORG: LUD: D: G: D: BR: & L: S: R: I: EL **Reverse:** Wildman with tree in right hand, RB at right **Rev. Legend:** IN RECTO DECUS **Note:** Dav. #6653 and #2065.

Date	Mintage	F	VF	XF	Unc
1700 RB	—	80.00	150	250	650
1701 RB	—	80.00	150	250	650
1702 RB	—	80.00	150	250	650
1703 RB	—	80.00	150	250	650
1704 RB	—	80.00	150	250	650
1705 RB	—	80.00	150	250	650
1706 RB	—	80.00	150	250	650
1707 RB	—	80.00	150	250	650
1708 RB	—	80.00	150	250	650
1709 RB	—	80.00	150	250	650
1710 RB	—	80.00	150	250	650
1711 RB	—	80.00	150	250	650

KM# 50 THALER

Silver **Ruler:** George Ludwig **Obverse:** Date in legend, small crown **Reverse:** St. Andrew

Date	Mintage	F	VF	XF	Unc
1705 HB Rare	—	—	—	—	—

KM# 49 THALER

Silver **Ruler:** George Ludwig **Obverse:** Crowned complex arms, date above **Obv. Legend:** GEORG: LUD: D • G • D • BR • & • LUN: S • R • I • ELECT: **Reverse:** Horse leaping left **Rev. Legend:** IN RECTO DECUS **Note:** Dav. #2058.

Date	Mintage	F	VF	XF	Unc
1705 HB	—	90.00	165	300	675
1706 HB	—	90.00	165	300	675
1707 HB	—	90.00	165	300	675
1708 HB	—	90.00	165	300	675
1709 HB	—	90.00	165	300	675
1710 HB	—	90.00	165	300	675

KM# 51 THALER

Silver **Ruler:** George Ludwig **Obverse:** Date in legend, large crown **Obv. Legend:** • * • GEORG: LUD: D • G • D • BR • ET LUN: S • R • I • ELECT: **Reverse:** St. Andrew **Rev. Legend:** SANCTVS * ANDREAS * REVIVISCENS **Note:** Dav. #2062.

Date	Mintage	F	VF	XF	Unc
1705 HB	—	70.00	125	225	550
1706 HB	—	70.00	125	225	550
1707 HB	—	70.00	125	225	550
1708 HB	—	70.00	125	225	550
1709 HB	—	70.00	125	225	550
1710 HB	—	70.00	125	225	550

KM# 69 THALER

Silver **Ruler:** George Ludwig **Note:** Similar to KM#19 but title of Imperial Treasurer added. Dav. #2059.

Date	Mintage	F	VF	XF	Unc
1711 HB	—	90.00	165	300	675
1711 HCB	—	90.00	165	300	675
1712 HCB	—	90.00	165	300	675

KM# 70 THALER

Silver **Ruler:** George Ludwig **Note:** Similar to KM#20, but title of Imperial Treasurer added. Dav. #2063.

Date	Mintage	F	VF	XF	Unc
1711 HB	—	90.00	125	225	550

KM# 78.1 THALER

Silver **Ruler:** George Ludwig **Note:** Similar to KM#70, but with initials HCB added. Dav. #2063A.

Date	Mintage	F	VF	XF	Unc
1712 HB	—	90.00	125	225	550
1712 HCB	—	90.00	125	225	550
1713 HCB	—	90.00	125	225	550

KM# 77 THALER

Silver **Ruler:** George Ludwig **Obverse:** Crowned complex arms within ornate frame **Obv. Legend:** GEORG: LVD: D • G • D • BR • & L • S • R• I • A • THES • & EL • **Reverse:** Wildman with tree in right hand **Rev. Legend:** IN RECTO DECUS, R•B at right **Note:** Dav. #2066.

Date	Mintage	F	VF	XF	Unc
1712 HH	—	80.00	150	250	650
1713 HH	—	80.00	150	250	650
1714 HH	—	80.00	150	250	650
1715 HH	—	80.00	150	250	650

KM# 79 THALER

Silver **Ruler:** George Ludwig **Obverse:** Armored draped bust right **Obv. Legend:** GEORGE: LUD: D • G • D • B • & • L • S • R • I • AR • TH • & • EL • **Reverse:** Crowned arms encircled by Order of the Garter, date in legend **Rev. Legend:** IN RECTO DECUS **Note:** Dav. #2067. 1711 of this type is a pattern.

Date	Mintage	F	VF	XF	Unc
1712 HCB	—	200	350	650	1,200
1714 HCB	—	200	350	650	1,200

KM# 80 THALER

Silver **Ruler:** George Ludwig **Reverse:** Without Order of the Garter **Note:** Dav. #2068.

Date	Mintage	F	VF	XF	Unc
1712 HCB	—	350	600	1,000	1,650
1713 HCB	—	350	600	1,000	1,650
1714 HCB	—	350	600	1,000	1,650

KM# 88.1 THALER

Silver **Ruler:** George Ludwig **Obverse:** Crowned complex arms **Obv. Legend:** GEORG: LUD: D • G • D • BR • & LUN: S • R • I • AR • TH • & EL • **Reverse:** Horse leaping left **Rev. Legend:** IN RECTO DECUS **Note:** Similar to KM#19 but imperial crown in central shield of arms. Dav. #2060.

Date	Mintage	F	VF	XF	Unc
1713 HCB	—	90.00	165	300	675
1714 HCB	—	90.00	165	300	675
1715 HCB	—	90.00	165	300	675

KM# 97 THALER

Silver **Ruler:** George Ludwig **Subject:** Death of Sophia von der Pfalz, Mother of George I Ludwig **Obverse:** Veiled bust right **Obv. Legend:** * SOPHIA • D • G • EX • STIRTE • EL • PAL • ELECT • VID • BR • ET • LVN • MAG • BRIT • HAERES * **Reverse:** Inscription **Rev. Inscription:** NATA/XIII. OCT. MDCXXX./NVPTA MENSE SEPT:/MDCLVIII./AD SVCCESSIONEM. M. BRIT/NOMINATA. MDCCI./SVB VESPERAM. VIII. IVNII./MDCCXIV. IN HORTIS/ HERRENHAUSANIS ADHVC/VEGETO ET FIRMO PASSV/DE AMBVLANS SVBITA/ET PLACIDA MORTE/EREPTA * **Note:** Dav. #2069.

Date	Mintage	F	VF	XF	Unc
1714	—	200	350	650	1,150

KM# 78.2 THALER

Silver **Ruler:** George Ludwig **Obverse:** Crowned complex arms, date above **Obv. Legend:** GEORG: LUD: D • G • D • BR • & LUN: S • R • I • AR • TH • & EL • **Reverse:** St. Andrew with cross behind **Rev. Legend:** SANCTVS * ANDREAS * REVIVISCENS **Note:** Dav. #2064.

Date	Mintage	F	VF	XF	Unc
1714 HCB	—	90.00	125	225	550
1715 HCB	—	90.00	125	225	550

KM# 88.2 THALER

Silver **Ruler:** George Ludwig **Obverse:** Crowned complex arms **Obv. Legend:** GEORG: LUD: D • G • D • BR • & LUN: S • R • I • AR • TH • & EL • **Reverse:** Mintmaster's initials below horse **Rev. Legend:** IN RECTO DECUS **Note:** Dav. #2060A,

Date	Mintage	F	VF	XF	Unc
1715 HCB	—	—	—	—	—

KM# 101.1 THALER

Silver **Ruler:** George Ludwig **Obverse:** Laureate head right **Obv. Legend:** GEORGIUS • D • G • MAG • BRIT • FR • ET • HIB • REX • F • D • **Reverse:** Arms within Order garter, supporters left and right, crown above **Rev. Legend:** BRUN • ET • LUN • DUX • S • R • I • A • THES • ET • HIB • REX • F • D • **Note:** Dav. #2078.

Date	Mintage	F	VF	XF	Unc
1715 HCB	—	125	225	400	850
1716 HCB	—	125	225	400	850
1717 HCB	—	125	225	400	850

KM# 114 THALER

Silver **Ruler:** George Ludwig **Obverse:** Arms within Order garter, supporters left and right, crown above **Obv. Legend:**

GEORGIUS • D • G • MAG • BRIT • FRANC • ET • HIB • REX • FID • D • **Reverse:** Wildman with tree in right hand **Rev. Legend:** BRUN • & • LUN • DUX • S • R • I • A • R • THES • & EL • **Note:** Dav. #2076.

Date	Mintage	F	VF	XF	Unc
1716 HH	—	90.00	165	300	650
1717 HH	—	90.00	165	300	650
1718 HH	—	90.00	165	300	650
1719 HH	—	90.00	165	300	650
1720 C	—	90.00	165	300	650
1721 C	—	90.00	165	300	650
1722 C	—	90.00	165	300	650
1723 C	—	90.00	165	300	650
1723 EPH	—	90.00	165	300	650
1724 EPH	—	90.00	165	300	650
1725 EPH	—	90.00	165	300	650
1726 EPH	—	90.00	165	300	650
1727 EPH	—	90.00	165	300	650

KM# 113.1 THALER

Silver **Ruler:** George Ludwig **Note:** Dav. #2070.

Date	Mintage	F	VF	XF	Unc
1716 HCB	—	150	300	600	1,250
1717 HCB	—	150	300	600	1,250
1718 HCB	—	90.00	165	320	725

KM# 132 THALER

Silver **Ruler:** George Ludwig **Obverse:** 4 crowned arms in cruciform, date in legend **Reverse:** Horse leaping left **Note:** Dav. #2071.

Date	Mintage	F	VF	XF	Unc
1717 HCB	—	—	400	700	1,300

KM# 133.1 THALER

Silver **Ruler:** George Ludwig **Obverse:** Arms within Order garter, supporters left and right, crown above **Reverse:** St. Andrew **Note:** Dav. #2074.

Date	Mintage	F	VF	XF	Unc
1717 HCB	—	90.00	165	300	700

KM# 134 THALER

Silver **Ruler:** George Ludwig **Obverse:** Crowned shields in cruciform **Obv. Legend:** GEORGIUS - D • G • MAG • BR • - FR • ET • HIB • - REX • FID • D • **Reverse:** Wildman with tree in right hand **Rev. Legend:** BRUN • & • LUN • DUX • S • R • I • A • R • THES • & EL • **Note:** Dav. #2077.

Date	Mintage	F	VF	XF	Unc
1717 HH	—	90.00	165	300	650
1718 HH	—	90.00	165	300	650
1719 HH	—	90.00	165	300	650
1719 HH-C	—	90.00	165	300	650
1719 C	—	90.00	165	300	650
1720 C	—	90.00	165	300	650
1721 C	—	90.00	165	300	650
1722 C	—	90.00	165	300	650
1723 C	—	90.00	165	300	650
1723 EPH	—	90.00	165	300	650
1724 EPH	—	90.00	165	300	650
1725 EPH	—	90.00	165	300	650
1726 EPH	—	90.00	165	300	650
1727 EPH	—	90.00	165	300	650

KM# 135 THALER

Silver **Ruler:** George Ludwig **Obverse:** Bust right **Reverse:** 4 crowned arms in cruciform, date in legend **Note:** Dav. #2079.

Date	Mintage	F	VF	XF	Unc
1717 HCB	—	125	225	400	850

KM# 101.2 THALER

Silver **Ruler:** George Ludwig **Obverse:** Laureate head right **Reverse:** Arms within Order garter, supporters left and right, crown above **Note:** Dav. #2080.

Date	Mintage	F	VF	XF	Unc
1718 HCB	—	125	225	400	850

KM# 133.2 THALER

Silver **Ruler:** George Ludwig **Obverse:** Arms within Order garter, supporters left and right, crown above **Obv. Legend:** GEORGIVS • D • G • M • BRIT • FR • ET HIB • REX F • D • **Reverse:** St. Andrew **Rev. Legend:** BRUN • ET • LUN • DUX • S • R • I • A • THES • ET • EL • **Note:** Dav. #2075.

Date	Mintage	F	VF	XF	Unc
1718 HCB	—	90.00	165	300	700
1719 HCB	—	90.00	165	300	700
1720 HCB	—	90.00	165	300	700
1721 HCB	—	90.00	165	300	700
1722 HCB	—	90.00	165	300	700
1723 HCB	—	90.00	165	300	700
1724 HCB	—	90.00	165	300	700
1725 HCB	—	90.00	165	300	700
1726 CPS	—	90.00	165	300	700
1727 CPS	—	90.00	165	300	700

KM# 113.3 THALER

Silver **Ruler:** George Ludwig **Obverse:** Arms within Order garter, supporters left and right, crown above **Reverse:** Horse leaping left **Note:** Dav. #2073. Varieties exist.

Date	Mintage	F	VF	XF	Unc
1725 HCB	—	90.00	165	320	725
1726 CPS	—	90.00	165	320	725
1727 CPS	—	90.00	165	320	725

KM# 113.2 THALER

Silver **Ruler:** George Ludwig **Obverse:** Arms within Order garter, supporters left and right, crown above **Obv. Legend:** GEORGIVS • D • G • MAG • BRIT • FR • ET • HIB • REX • F • D • **Reverse:** Horse leaping left **Rev. Legend:** BRVNS • ET • LVN • DVX • S • R • I • A • THES • ET • EL(ECT) * **Note:** Dav. #2072.

Date	Mintage	F	VF	XF	Unc
1718 HCB	—	90.00	165	320	725
1719 HCB	—	90.00	165	320	725
1720 HCB	—	90.00	165	320	725
1721 HCB	—	90.00	165	320	725
1722 HCB	—	90.00	165	320	725
1723 HCB	—	90.00	165	320	725
1724 HCB	—	90.00	165	320	725

KM# 101.3 THALER

Silver **Ruler:** George Ludwig **Obverse:** Armored bust right **Obv. Legend:** GEORGIVS • D • G • MAG • BRIT • FR • ET • HIB • REX • F • D • **Reverse:** Arms within Order garter, supporters left and right, crown above **Rev. Legend:** BRVN • ET • LVN • DVX • S • R • I • A • TH(ES) • ET • EL • **Note:** Dav. #2081.

Date	Mintage	F	VF	XF	Unc
1719 HCB	—	90.00	165	350	750
1720 HCB	—	90.00	165	350	750
1721 HCB	—	90.00	165	350	750
1722 HCB	—	90.00	165	350	750
1723 HCB	—	90.00	165	350	750
1724 HCB	—	90.00	165	350	750
1725 HCB	—	90.00	165	350	750
1726 CPS	—	90.00	165	350	750
1727 CPS	—	90.00	165	350	750

KM# 188 THALER

Silver **Ruler:** George Ludwig **Subject:** Death of George I Ludwig **Obverse:** Cloaked laureate bust right **Obv. Legend:** GEORGIVS • I • D • G • M • BRIT • FR • ET • HIB • REX • F • D • BR • ET • LVN • DVX • S • R • I • A • TH • ET • EL * **Reverse:** Inscription **Rev. Inscription:** NAT • HANOVER • / VIII • IVN • MDCLX • SN •/ SVSCEPIT REGIMEN/ ELECTORATVS • IV • FEB •/ MDCXCIIX • INTRODVCTCS/ IN COLLEG • ELECTORALE/ VII • SEPT • MDCCIIX • REX • M •/ BRIT • XII • AUG • MDCCXIV •/ **Note:** Dav. #2082.

Date	Mintage	F	VF	XF	Unc
1727 CPS	—	150	275	500	1,000

KM# 190 THALER

Silver **Ruler:** George II August **Obverse:** 4 crowned shields in cruciform, star in center **Reverse:** Horse left, date in Arabic numerals **Note:** Dav. #2083.

Date	Mintage	F	VF	XF	Unc
1727 EPH	—	135	250	450	1,000

KM# 191 THALER

Silver **Ruler:** George II August **Reverse:** Date in Roman numerals **Note:** Dav. #2084.

Date	Mintage	F	VF	XF	Unc
1727 EPH	—	135	250	450	1,000
1729 EPH	—	135	250	450	1,000

KM# 193 THALER

Silver **Ruler:** George II August **Obverse:** Crowned arms supported by lion and unicorn within Order chain **Reverse:** Horse left, date below **Note:** Dav. #2085.

Date	Mintage	F	VF	XF	Unc
1727 CPS	—	135	250	450	1,000
1729 CPS	—	135	250	450	1,000

KM# 194.1 THALER

Silver **Ruler:** George II August **Obverse:** Large crowned shield separates legend **Obv. Legend:** GEORG • II • D • G • M • B • R • F • & • H • REX • F • D • BR • & **Reverse:** Arabic date **Rev. Legend:** NEC ASPERA TERRENT **Note:** Dav. #2086.

Date	Mintage	F	VF	XF	Unc
1727 CPS	—	135	250	550	1,200
1730 CPS	—	90.00	165	350	800
1731 CPS	—	90.00	165	350	800
1732 CPS	—	90.00	165	350	800
1733 CPS	—	90.00	165	350	800
1734 CPS	—	90.00	165	350	800
1735 CPS	—	90.00	165	350	800
1736 CPS	—	90.00	165	350	800
1737 CPS	—	90.00	165	350	800
1738 CPS	—	90.00	165	350	800
1739 CPS	—	90.00	165	350	800
1740 CPS	—	90.00	165	350	800
1741 CPS	—	90.00	165	350	800
1742 CPS	—	90.00	165	350	800
1743 CPS	—	90.00	165	350	800
1744 CPS	—	90.00	165	350	800
1745 CPS	—	90.00	165	350	800
1746 CPS	—	90.00	165	350	800
1747 CPS	—	90.00	165	350	800
1748 CPS	—	90.00	165	350	800
1749 CPS	—	90.00	165	350	800

KM# 196 THALER

Silver **Ruler:** George II August **Note:** Dav. #2090.

Date	Mintage	F	VF	XF	Unc
1727 EPH	—	90.00	165	300	700
1728 EPH	—	90.00	165	300	700
1729 EPH	—	90.00	165	300	700

KM# 197 THALER

Silver **Ruler:** George II August **Obverse:** 4 crowned shields in cruciform, crowns break legend, star in center **Note:** Dav. #2091.

Date	Mintage	F	VF	XF	Unc
1727 EPH	—	100	225	450	1,000
1729 EPH	—	100	225	450	1,000

KM# 195 THALER

Silver **Ruler:** George II August **Obverse:** Crowned arms supported by lion and unicorn in Order chain, date **Reverse:** St. Andrew with cross **Note:** Dav. #2088.

Date	Mintage	F	VF	XF	Unc
1727 CPS	—	135	250	450	1,000
1729 CPS	—	135	250	450	1,000

KM# 189 THALER

Silver **Ruler:** George II August **Obverse:** Draped bust left **Obv. Legend:** GEORGIVS • II • D • G • M • BRIT • FR • ET • HIB • REX • F • D • **Reverse:** Arms within Order garter, supporters left and right, crown above **Rev. Legend:** BRVNS • ET • LVN • DVX • S • R • I • A • THES • ET • EL • **Note:** Dav. #2093.

Date	Mintage	F	VF	XF	Unc
1727 CPS	—	275	500	900	1,500
1728 CPS	—	275	500	900	1,500
1729 CPS	—	275	500	900	1,500

KM# 192 THALER

Silver **Ruler:** George II August **Obverse:** Crowns above shields break legend **Note:** Dav. #2094.

Date	Mintage	F	VF	XF	Unc
1727 EPH	—	135	250	450	1,000
1729 EPH	—	135	250	450	1,000

KM# 231.1 THALER

Silver **Ruler:** George II August **Obverse:** Small bust left **Reverse:** Date above crown **Note:** Dav. #2095.

Date	Mintage	F	VF	XF	Unc
1730 CPS	—	200	450	1,000	2,500
1732 CPS	—	200	450	1,000	2,500
1735 CPS	—	200	450	1,000	2,500
1736 CPS	—	200	450	1,000	2,500
1737 CPS	—	200	450	1,000	2,500
1738 CPS	—	200	450	1,000	2,500
1740 CPS	—	200	450	1,000	2,500
1748 CPS	—	200	450	1,000	2,500

KM# 232.1 THALER

Silver **Ruler:** George II August **Obverse:** Crowned quartered arms **Obv. Legend:** GEORGIVS • II • D • G • M • BRIT • F • & H • REX • F • D • **Reverse:** St. Andrew with cross **Rev. Legend:** BR • ET • LVN • DVX • S • R • I • A • TH • ET • EL • **Note:** Dav. #2089.

Date	Mintage	F	VF	XF	Unc
1730 CPS	—	90.00	165	300	700
1734 CPS	—	90.00	165	300	700
1735 CPS	—	90.00	165	300	700
1736 CPS	—	90.00	165	300	700
1737 CPS	—	90.00	165	300	700
1738 CPS	—	90.00	165	300	700
1740 CPS	—	90.00	165	300	700
1743 CPS	—	90.00	165	300	700
1744 CPS	—	90.00	165	300	700
1745 CPS	—	90.00	165	300	700
1746 CPS	—	90.00	165	300	700
1747 CPS	—	90.00	165	300	700
1748 CPS	—	90.00	165	300	700
1749 CPS	—	90.00	165	300	700
1750 CPS	—	90.00	165	300	700
1751 C	—	90.00	165	300	700
1752 C	—	90.00	165	300	700
1752 IWS	—	90.00	165	300	700
1753 IWS	—	90.00	165	300	700
1754 IWS	—	90.00	165	300	700
1755 IWS	—	90.00	165	300	700
1756 IWS	—	90.00	165	300	700
1757 IWS	—	90.00	165	300	700
1758 IWS	—	90.00	165	300	700
1759 IWS	—	90.00	165	300	700
1760 IWS	—	90.00	165	300	700

KM# 233 THALER

Silver **Ruler:** George II August **Obverse:** Shield with plain sides **Obv. Legend:** GEORG • II • D • G • MAG • BR: FR • ET • HIB • REX • F • D • **Reverse:** Wildman with tree in right hand **Rev. Legend:** BRUN • & LUN • DUX • S • R • I • AR • THES • & EL •, E•P•H• in exergue **Note:** Dav. #2092.

Date	Mintage	F	VF	XF	Unc
1730 EPH	—	200	400	750	1,300
1731 C	—	200	400	750	1,300
1731 IAB	—	200	400	750	1,300
1732 IAB	—	200	400	750	1,300
1733 IAB	—	200	400	750	1,300
1734 IAB	—	200	400	750	1,300
1735 IAB	—	200	400	750	1,300
1736 IAB	—	200	400	750	1,300
1737 IAB	—	200	400	750	1,300
1738 IAB	—	200	400	750	1,300
1739 IBH	—	200	400	750	1,300
1740 IBH	—	200	400	750	1,300
1741 IBH	—	200	400	750	1,300
1742 IBH	—	200	400	750	1,300
1743 IBH	—	200	400	750	1,300
1744 IBH	—	200	400	750	1,300

KM# 230 THALER

Silver **Ruler:** George II August **Obverse:** Crowned quartered arms **Obv. Legend:** GEORG • II • D • G • M • BRIT • FR • & H • REX • F • D • BR • & • L • DVX • S • R • I • A • TH • & EL * **Reverse:** Horse leaping left, Roman date **Rev. Legend:** NEC ASPERA TERRENT **Note:** Dav. #2087.

Date	Mintage	F	VF	XF	Unc
1730 EPH	—	135	250	450	1,000
1731 C	—	135	250	450	1,000
1731 IAB	—	135	250	450	1,000
1733 IAB	—	135	250	450	1,000
1734 IAB	—	135	250	450	1,000
1735 IAB	—	135	250	450	1,000
1736 IAB	—	135	250	450	1,000
1737 IAB	—	135	250	450	1,000
1738 IAB	—	135	250	450	1,000
1739 IAB	—	135	250	450	1,000
1739 IBH	—	135	250	450	1,000
1740 IBH	—	135	250	450	1,000
1743 IBH	—	135	250	450	1,000
1745 IBH	—	135	250	450	1,000
1748 IBH	—	135	250	450	1,000
1753 IBH	—	135	250	450	1,000

KM# 251 THALER

Silver **Ruler:** George II August **Obverse:** Crowned arms supported by lion and unicorn within Order chain **Reverse:** Horse left, date in Roman numerals below **Note:** Varieties exist.

Date	Mintage	F	VF	XF	Unc
1733 CPS	—	135	250	450	1,000

KM# 257 THALER

Silver **Ruler:** George II August **Subject:** Death of Wilhelmina Caroline **Obverse:** Bust left, 4-line legend below **Reverse:** 18-line inscription **Note:** Dav. #2096.

Date	Mintage	F	VF	XF	Unc
1737	—	300	750	1,500	2,500

KM# 287 THALER

Silver **Ruler:** George II August **Obverse:** Crowned quartered arms in baroque shield **Reverse:** Horse leaping left

Date	Mintage	F	VF	XF	Unc
1743	—	135	250	450	1,000
1744	—	135	250	450	1,000
1745 IBH	—	135	250	450	1,000
1748 IBH	—	135	250	450	1,000

KM# 288 THALER

Silver **Ruler:** George II August **Obverse:** Shield with baroque frame **Obv. Legend:** GEORG • II • D • G • MAG • BR • FR • ET • HIB • REX • F • D • **Reverse:** Wildman with tree in right hand **Rev. Legend:** BRUN • & LUN • DUX • S • R • I • AR • THES • & EL • **Note:** Dav. #2092A.

Date	Mintage	F	VF	XF	Unc
1743 IBH	—	200	400	750	1,300
1746 IBH	—	200	400	750	1,300
1748 IBH	—	200	400	750	1,300
1749 IBH	—	200	400	750	1,300
1750 IBH	—	200	400	750	1,300
1755 IBH	—	200	400	750	1,300

KM# 291 THALER

Silver **Ruler:** George II August **Subject:** White Swan Mine **Obverse:** Crowned quartered arms in ornate frame **Obv. Legend:** GEORG • II • D • G • M • BRIT • FR • & H • REX • F • D • BR • & L • DVX • S • R • I • A • TH • & EL • * **Reverse:** Swan on lake amid hills, clouds above **Rev. Legend:** CANDIDVS HAEC PROFERT MONTANVS PRAEMIA CYGNVS, below in 5 lines: DIE GRVBE/WEISSER SCHWAN/KAM IN AVSBEVT/IM Q: LVCIAE 1732/I.B.H. **Note:** Mining Thaler. Dav. #2097.

Date	Mintage	F	VF	XF	Unc
1744 IBH	—	135	250	550	1,200
1745 IBH	—	135	250	550	1,200
1748 IBH	—	135	250	550	1,200
1749 IBH	—	135	250	550	1,200
1750 IBH	—	135	250	550	1,200
1752 IBH	—	135	250	550	1,200
1756 IBH	—	135	250	550	1,200

KM# 292 THALER

Silver **Ruler:** George II August **Subject:** Cronenburg's Luck Mine **Obverse:** Crowned quartered arms on ornate shield **Obv. Legend:** GEORG • II • D • G • M • BRIT • FR • & H • REX • F • D • BR • & L • DVX • S • R • I • A • TH • & EL • * **Reverse:** Arm with wreath above mining scene **Rev. Legend:** NON - MARCESCET, below in 5 lines: DIE GRVBE/CRONENBVRGS GLVCK/KAM IN AVSBEVT/IM QV: LVCIAE 1705/I.B.H. **Note:** Dav. #2098.

Date	Mintage	F	VF	XF	Unc
1745 IBH	—	200	450	800	1,500
1749 IBH	—	200	450	800	1,500
1750 IBH	—	200	450	800	1,500
1752 IBH	—	200	450	800	1,500

KM# 293 THALER

Silver **Ruler:** George II August **Subject:** Lautenthal's Luck Mine **Obverse:** Crowned quartered arms on ornate shield **Obv. Legend:** GEORG • II • D • G • M • BRIT • FR • & H • REX • F • D • BR • & L • DVX • S • R • I • A • TH • EL • * **Reverse:** Lute player in front of mining scene **Rev. Legend:** TV QVONDAM ABIECTAM REDDIS DEVS ALME SONORAM, below in 5 lines: DIE GRVBE/LAVTENTHALS GLVCK/KAM IN AVSBEVT/IM QV: REM 1685/I.B.H. **Note:** Dav. #2099.

Date	Mintage	F	VF	XF	Unc
1745 IBH	—	200	450	800	1,500
1749 IBH	—	200	450	800	1,500
1752 IBH	—	200	450	800	1,500
1756 IBH	—	200	450	800	1,500

KM# 294 THALER

Silver **Ruler:** George II August **Subject:** Goodness of the Lord Mine **Obverse:** Crowned quartered arms within ornate shield **Obv. Legend:** GEORG • II • D • G • M • BRIT • FR • & H • REX • F • D • BR • & L • DVX • S • R • I • A • TH • & EL • * **Reverse:** Mining scene with mountains and shining sun **Rev. Legend:** DIE ERDE IST VOLL GVTE DES HERRN, below in 5 lines: DIE GRVBE/GVTE DES HERRN/KAM IN AVSBEVT/IM QV: REM: 1740/I.B.H. **Note:** Dav. #2100.

Date	Mintage	F	VF	XF	Unc
1745 IBH	—	200	450	800	1,500
1749 IBH	—	200	450	800	1,500
1756 IBH	—	200	450	800	1,500

KM# 295 THALER

Silver **Ruler:** George II August **Subject:** Rainbow Mine **Obverse:** Crowned quartered arms within ornate shield **Obv. Legend:** GEORG • II • D • G • M • BRIT • FR • & H • REX • F • D • BR • & L • DVX • S • R • I • A • TH • & EL • * **Reverse:** Rainbow over mining scene **Rev. Legend:** LOBE DEN, DER IHN GEMACHT HAT. SYR. C. 43., below in 5 lines: DIE GRVBE/REGENBOGEN/KAM WIED:IN AVSB:/IM Q: LVCIÆ date/I.B.H. **Note:** Dav. #2101.

Date	Mintage	F	VF	XF	Unc
1745 IBH	—	200	500	900	1,600
1748 IBH	—	200	500	900	1,600
1749 IBH	—	200	500	900	1,600
1752 IBH	—	200	500	900	1,600

KM# 312 THALER

Silver **Ruler:** George II August **Subject:** Bliefeld Mine **Obverse:** Crowned quartered arms on ornate shield **Obv. Legend:** GEORG • II • D • G • M • BRIT • FR • & H • REX • F • D • BR • & L • DVX • S • R • I • A • TH • & EL • * **Reverse:** Clouds above mining scene with column at center **Rev. Legend:** REDEVNT SATVRNIA REGNA, below in 5 lines: DIE GRVBE/H: AVG: FRIED: BLEYFELD:/KAM WIED: IN AVSB:/IM QV: REM: date/I.B.H. **Note:** Dav. #2102.

Date	Mintage	F	VF	XF	Unc
1750 IBH	—	150	275	650	1,200
1752 IBH	—	150	275	650	1,200

KM# 194.2 THALER

Silver **Ruler:** George II August **Obverse:** Smaller crowned shield within continuous legend **Obv. Legend:** GEORG.II.D.G.M.B... **Reverse:** Rosettes at sides of date **Rev. Legend:** NEC ASPERA TERRENT **Note:** Dav. #2086A.

Date	Mintage	F	VF	XF	Unc
1751 C	—	90.00	165	350	800
1752 C	—	90.00	165	350	800
1753 IWS	—	90.00	165	350	800
1754 IWS	—	90.00	165	350	800
1755 IWS	—	90.00	165	350	800
1756 IWS	—	90.00	165	350	800
1757 IWS	—	90.00	165	350	800
1758 IWS	—	90.00	165	350	800
Note: Edge inscription varieties exist					
1758 IWS	—	90.00	165	350	800
Note: Edge inscription varieties exist					
1759 IWS	—	90.00	165	350	800
1760 IWS	—	90.00	165	350	800
Note: Edge inscription varieties exist					

KM# 231.2 THALER

Silver **Ruler:** George II August **Obverse:** Large bust left **Obv. Legend:** GEORG • II • D • G • M • BRIT • FR • ET • H • REX • F • D • **Reverse:** Crown divides date **Rev. Legend:** BRVNS • ET • LVN • DVX • S • R • I • A • TH • ET • EL •

Date	Mintage	F	VF	XF	Unc
1751 C	—	200	450	1,000	2,500

KM# 320 THALER

Silver **Ruler:** George II August **Subject:** King Karl Mine **Reverse:** 2 crowned columns in mining scene **Note:** Dav. #2103.

Date	Mintage	F	VF	XF	Unc
1752 IBH Rare	—	—	—	—	—

KM# 232.2 THALER

Silver **Ruler:** George III **Obverse:** Crowned quartered arms **Obv. Legend:** GEORG • II • D • G • M • BRIT • FR • ET • HIB • REX • F • D • **Reverse:** St. Andrew with cross **Rev. Legend:** BR • & • LUN • DUX • S • - R • - I • A • TH • & EL **Note:** Dav. #2089A.

Date	Mintage	F	VF	XF	Unc
1760 IWS	—	90.00	165	300	700
1761 IWS	—	90.00	165	300	700
1763 IWS	—	90.00	165	300	700

KM# 343 THALER

Silver **Ruler:** George III **Obverse:** Crowned quartered arms **Obv. Legend:** GEORG • III • D • G • M • BRIT • FR • & • HIB • REX • F • D • **Reverse:** St. Andrew with cross **Rev. Legend:** BR • & • LUN • DUX - S • - R • I • - A • TH • & • EL • **Note:** Dav. #2104.

Date	Mintage	F	VF	XF	Unc
1761 IWS	—	90.00	165	325	800
1762 IWS	—	90.00	165	325	800
1763 IWS	—	90.00	165	325	800
1764 IWS	—	90.00	165	325	800
1765 IWS	—	90.00	165	325	800
1766 IWS	—	90.00	165	325	800
1767 IWS	—	90.00	165	325	800
1768 IWS	—	90.00	165	325	800
1769 IWS	—	90.00	165	325	800
1770 IWS	—	90.00	165	325	800
1771 IWS	—	90.00	165	325	800
1772 IWS	—	90.00	165	325	800
1773 IWS	—	90.00	165	325	800

KM# 354 THALER

Silver **Ruler:** George III **Reverse:** Wildman and tree **Note:** Dav. #2105.

Date	Mintage	F	VF	XF	Unc
1763 IAP	—	175	300	700	1,500
1764 IAP	—	175	300	700	1,500
1765 IAP	—	175	300	700	1,500
1770 IAP	—	175	300	700	1,500
1774 LCR	—	175	300	700	1,500
1775 LCR	—	175	300	700	1,500
1776 LCR	—	175	300	700	1,500
1784 CES	—	175	300	700	1,500

KM# 353 THALER

Silver **Ruler:** George III **Subject:** Lautenthal Mine **Obverse:** Crowned quartered arms on ornate shield **Obv. Legend:** GEORG • III • D • G • M • BRIT • FR • & H • REX • S • R • I • A • TH • & EL * **Reverse:** Lute player in front of mines **Rev. Legend:** TV QVONDAM ABIECTAM REDDIS DEVS ALME SONORAM, below in 5 lines: DIE GRVBE/LAVTENTHALS GLVCK/KAM IN AVSBEVT/IM QV: REM: date/ I.A.P. **Note:** Dav. #2108.

Date	Mintage	F	VF	XF	Unc
1763 IAP	—	275	500	750	1,750

KM# 357 THALER

Silver **Ruler:** George III **Subject:** Segen Gottes Mine **Obverse:** Crowned quartered arms on ornate shield **Obv. Legend:** GEORG • III • D • G • M • BRIT • FR • & H • REX • F • D • BR • & L • DVX • S • R • I • A • TH • & EL * **Reverse:** View of mine **Rev. Legend:** AN GOTTES SEGEN IST ALLES GELEGEN, below in 5 lines: DIE GRVBE/SEGEN GOTTES/KAM IN AVSBEVT/IM Q: CRVC: date/I.A.P. **Note:** Dav. #2109.

Date	Mintage	F	VF	XF	Unc
1765 IAP	—	200	350	750	1,500

KM# 367 THALER

Silver **Ruler:** George III **Subject:** George III **Obverse:** Armored bust right **Obv. Legend:** GEORG • III • D • G • M • BR • FR • & • HIB • REX • F • D • **Reverse:** Crowned quartered arms on ornate shield **Rev. Legend:** BRUNS • & • LUN • DUX • S • R • I • A • TH • & • ELECT **Note:** Dav. #2106.

Date	Mintage	F	VF	XF	Unc
1773 IWS	—	375	700	1,250	2,000
1774 IWS	—	375	700	1,250	2,000
1776 IWS	—	375	700	1,250	2,000
1779 IWS	—	375	700	1,250	2,000
1780 IWS	—	375	700	1,250	2,000
1782 IWS	—	375	700	1,250	2,000
1784 IWS	—	375	700	1,250	2,000
1786 IWS	—	375	700	1,250	2,000
1791 .C.	—	375	700	1,250	2,000
1792 PLM	—	375	700	1,250	2,000
1794 PLM	—	375	700	1,250	2,000
1797 PLM	—	375	700	1,250	2,000

KM# 369 THALER

Silver **Ruler:** George III **Obverse:** Supported arms **Reverse:** GUTE DES HERRN Mine **Note:** Dav. #2110.

Date	Mintage	F	VF	XF	Unc
1774 LCR	—	300	600	1,000	2,000

KM# 372 THALER

Silver **Ruler:** George III **Obverse:** Laureate draped bust right **Obv. Legend:** GEORG • III • D • G • M • BRIT • FR • & HIB • REX • F • D • **Reverse:** Crowned arms within Order chain with supporters **Rev. Legend:** BRUNS • & • LUN • DUX • S • R • I • A • TH • & • ELECT **Note:** Dav. #2107.

Date	Mintage	F	VF	XF	Unc
1777 IWS	—	165	325	650	1,350
1778 IWS	—	165	325	650	1,350

KM# 327 5 THALER

6.6500 g., 0.9000 Gold 0.1924 oz. AGW **Ruler:** George II August **Obverse:** Crowned quartered arms on ornate shield **Obv. Legend:** GEORG • II • D • G • M • B • F • ET • H • REX F • D • **Reverse:** Value and date **Rev. Legend:** BRUNS • ET LUN • DUX S • R • I • A • H • ET ELECT • *

Date	Mintage	VG	F	VF	XF	Unc
1758 IAS	—	400	950	1,600	2,500	—

KM# 361 5 THALER

6.6500 g., 0.9000 Gold 0.1924 oz. AGW **Ruler:** George III **Subject:** George III **Obverse:** Head right **Reverse:** Crowned quartered arms on ornate shield

Date	Mintage	F	VF	XF	Unc
1768 .C.	—	1,500	2,750	4,500	6,500

KM# 383 5 THALER

6.6500 g., 0.9000 Gold 0.1924 oz. AGW **Ruler:** George III

Date	Mintage	F	VF	XF	Unc
1783	—	1,750	3,000	5,000	7,500

TRADE COINAGE

KM# 324 1/4 GOLDGULDEN (1/2 Thaler)

0.8750 g., 0.9860 Gold 0.0277 oz. AGW **Ruler:** George II August **Obverse:** Laureate head left **Reverse:** Value inside border legend, date at top

Date	Mintage	VG	F	VF	XF	Unc
1754 S	—	100	150	225	350	—
1756 S	—	100	150	225	350	—
1757 S	—	100	150	225	350	—

KM# 300 1/2 GOLDGULDEN (Thaler)

1.7500 g., 0.9860 Gold 0.0555 oz. AGW **Ruler:** George II August **Obverse:** Laureate head left **Reverse:** Value inside border legend, date at top

Date	Mintage	VG	F	VF	XF	Unc
1749 S	—	125	200	325	550	—
1750 S	—	125	200	325	550	—
1754 S	—	125	200	325	550	—
1754 IAS	—	125	200	325	550	—
1756 S	—	125	200	325	550	—

KM# 301 GOLDGULDEN (2 Thaler)

3.5000 g., 0.9860 Gold 0.1109 oz. AGW **Ruler:** George II August **Obverse:** Head left **Reverse:** Value and date

Date	Mintage	VG	F	VF	XF	Unc
1749 S	—	150	275	450	700	—
1750 S	—	150	275	450	700	—
1750 IAS	—	150	275	450	700	—
1751 S	—	150	275	450	700	—
1751 IAS	—	150	275	450	700	—
1752 S	—	150	275	450	700	—
1753 IAS	—	150	275	450	700	—
1754 IAS	—	150	275	450	700	—

KM# 315 GOLDGULDEN (2 Thaler)

3.5000 g., 0.9860 Gold 0.1109 oz. AGW **Ruler:** George II August **Obverse:** Crowned quartered arms in baroque shield **Reverse:** Value and date

Date	Mintage	VG	F	VF	XF	Unc
1751 S	—	150	275	450	725	—
1752 S	—	150	275	450	725	—
1752 IAS	—	150	275	450	725	—
1753 IAS	—	150	275	450	725	—
1754 S	—	150	275	450	725	—
1754 IAS	—	150	275	450	725	—
1755 S	—	150	275	450	725	—
1755 IAS	—	150	275	450	725	—
1756 IAS	—	150	275	450	725	—

KM# 322 GOLDGULDEN (2 Thaler)

3.5000 g., 0.9860 Gold 0.1109 oz. AGW **Ruler:** George II August **Obverse:** Plainer shield with scalloped sides **Reverse:** Value and date

Date	Mintage	VG	F	VF	XF	Unc
1753	—	125	250	400	600	—
1754 IAS	—	125	250	400	600	—
1755	—	125	250	400	600	—
1756	—	125	250	400	600	—

KM# 302 2 GOLDGULDEN (4 Thaler)

7.0000 g., 0.9860 Gold 0.2219 oz. AGW **Ruler:** George II August **Obverse:** Head left **Reverse:** Value and date

Date	Mintage	VG	F	VF	XF	Unc
1749 S	—	175	300	475	750	—
1750 S	—	175	300	475	750	—
1750 IAS	—	175	300	475	750	—
1751 IAS	—	175	300	475	750	—
1752 IAS	—	175	300	475	750	—
1753 IAS	—	175	300	475	750	—
1754 IAS	—	175	300	475	750	—

KM# 303 2 GOLDGULDEN (4 Thaler)

7.0000 g., 0.9860 Gold 0.2219 oz. AGW **Ruler:** George II August **Obverse:** Crowned quartered arms **Reverse:** Value and date

Date	Mintage	VG	F	VF	XF	Unc
1749 S	—	185	325	500	800	—
1750 S	—	185	325	500	800	—
1750 IAS	—	185	325	500	800	—
1751 IAS	—	185	325	500	800	—
1752 IAS	—	185	325	500	800	—
1753 IAS	—	185	325	500	800	—
1754 IAS	—	185	325	500	800	—
1755 IAS	—	185	325	500	800	—

KM# 304 4 GOLDGULDEN (8 Thaler)

14.0000 g., 0.9860 Gold 0.4438 oz. AGW **Ruler:** George II August **Obverse:** Draped bust left **Reverse:** Value and date

Date	Mintage	VG	F	VF	XF	Unc
1749 IAS	—	500	1,000	1,650	2,200	—
1750 IAS	—	500	1,000	1,650	2,200	—
1751 IAS	—	500	1,000	1,650	2,200	—
1752 IAS	—	500	1,000	1,650	2,200	—

KM# 313 4 GOLDGULDEN (8 Thaler)

14.0000 g., 0.9860 Gold 0.4438 oz. AGW **Ruler:** George II August **Obverse:** Head left **Reverse:** Value and date

Date	Mintage	VG	F	VF	XF	Unc
1750 IAS Rare	—	—	—	—	—	—

KM# 165 1/4 DUCAT

0.8750 g., 0.9860 Gold 0.0277 oz. AGW **Ruler:** George Ludwig **Obverse:** Head right **Reverse:** Horse left

Date	Mintage	VG	F	VF	XF	Unc
1724 B	—	125	225	550	1,200	—

KM# 234 1/4 DUCAT

0.8750 g., 0.9860 Gold 0.0277 oz. AGW **Ruler:** George II August **Obverse:** Crowned monogram **Reverse:** Horse left

Date	Mintage	VG	F	VF	XF	Unc
1730	—	100	200	400	900	—

KM# 258 1/4 DUCAT

0.8750 g., 0.9860 Gold 0.0277 oz. AGW **Ruler:** George II August **Obverse:** Head left **Reverse:** Horse left

Date	Mintage	VG	F	VF	XF	Unc
1737 S	—	100	200	500	1,000	—

KM# 259 1/4 DUCAT

0.8750 g., 0.9860 Gold 0.0277 oz. AGW **Ruler:** George II August **Reverse:** Crowned arms

Date	Mintage	VG	F	VF	XF	Unc
1737	—	100	200	500	1,000	—

KM# 142 1/2 DUCAT

1.7500 g., 0.9860 Gold 0.0555 oz. AGW **Ruler:** George Ludwig **Obverse:** Head right **Reverse:** 4 crowned arms in cruciform, date divided at top

Date	Mintage	VG	F	VF	XF	Unc
1718	—	150	250	475	750	—

KM# 166 1/2 DUCAT

1.7500 g., 0.9860 Gold 0.0555 oz. AGW **Ruler:** George Ludwig **Obverse:** Laureate bust of George I right, Bust of George Wilhelm right

Date	Mintage	VG	F	VF	XF	Unc
1724	—	100	200	350	650	—

KM# 235 1/2 DUCAT

1.7500 g., 0.9860 Gold 0.0555 oz. AGW **Ruler:** George II August **Obverse:** Laureate bust left **Reverse:** Crowned arms, crown divides date

Date	Mintage	VG	F	VF	XF	Unc
1730 S	—	100	150	300	550	—
1734 S	—	100	150	300	550	—
1737	—	100	150	300	550	—

KM# 21 DUCAT

3.5000 g., 0.9860 Gold 0.1109 oz. AGW **Ruler:** George Ludwig **Obverse:** Crowned arms **Reverse:** Horse leaping left

Date	Mintage	VG	F	VF	XF	Unc
1698	—	300	525	1,000	1,750	—
1700	—	300	525	1,000	1,750	—
1701 HB	—	300	525	1,000	1,750	—
1705 HB	—	300	525	1,000	1,750	—
1709	—	300	525	1,000	1,750	—
1712	—	300	525	1,000	1,750	—
1714	—	300	525	1,000	1,750	—

KM# 61 DUCAT

3.5000 g., 0.9860 Gold 0.1109 oz. AGW **Ruler:** George Ludwig **Subject:** Gold from Harz Mines **Obverse:** Crowned arms **Reverse:** AURB HERC added in exergue

Date	Mintage	VG	F	VF	XF	Unc
1710 HB	—	350	650	1,200	2,000	—
1713	—	350	650	1,200	2,000	—
1714	—	350	650	1,200	2,000	—
1715	—	350	650	1,200	2,000	—

KM# 81 DUCAT

3.5000 g., 0.9860 Gold 0.1109 oz. AGW **Ruler:** George Ludwig **Obverse:** Head right **Reverse:** Crowned complex arms

Date	Mintage	VG	F	VF	XF	Unc
1712 HCB	—	300	525	1,000	1,750	—
1714 HCB	—	300	525	1,000	1,750	—
1715 HCB	—	300	525	1,000	1,750	—
1716 HCB	—	300	525	1,000	1,750	—
1717 B	—	300	525	1,000	1,750	—
1721 B	—	300	525	1,000	1,750	—
1723	—	300	525	1,000	1,750	—

KM# 82 DUCAT

3.5000 g., 0.9860 Gold 0.1109 oz. AGW **Ruler:** George Ludwig **Subject:** Gold from Harz Mines **Reverse:** AURB. HERC added to legend

Date	Mintage	VG	F	VF	XF	Unc
1712 HCB	—	350	650	1,200	2,000	—
1713 HCB	—	350	650	1,200	2,000	—
1714 HCB	—	350	650	1,200	2,000	—

KM# 89 DUCAT

3.5000 g., 0.9860 Gold 0.1109 oz. AGW **Ruler:** George Ludwig **Obverse:** Laureate head right

Date	Mintage	VG	F	VF	XF	Unc
1713 HCB	—	300	525	1,000	1,750	—

KM# 98 DUCAT

3.5000 g., 0.9860 Gold 0.1109 oz. AGW **Ruler:** George Ludwig **Obverse:** Crowned arms with imperial crown in central shield **Reverse:** Horse leaping left, date in legend

Date	Mintage	VG	F	VF	XF	Unc
1714 HCB	—	—	—	—	—	—

KM# 102.1 DUCAT

3.5000 g., 0.9860 Gold 0.1109 oz. AGW **Ruler:** George Ludwig **Obverse:** Large bust right **Reverse:** Crowned shields in cruciform, sceptres at angles

Date	Mintage	VG	F	VF	XF	Unc
1715 HCB	—	200	325	650	1,250	—
1716 HCB	—	200	325	650	1,250	—

KM# 103 DUCAT

3.5000 g., 0.9860 Gold 0.1109 oz. AGW **Ruler:** George Ludwig **Subject:** Gold from Harz Mines **Obverse:** AURB. HERC added below bust **Reverse:** Crowned shields in cruciform, sceptres in angles

Date	Mintage	VG	F	VF	XF	Unc
1715 HCB	—	350	650	1,200	2,000	—
1716 HCB	—	350	650	1,200	2,000	—
1717 B	—	350	650	1,200	2,000	—
1723 B	—	350	650	1,200	2,000	—
1727 S	—	350	650	1,200	2,000	—

KM# 102.2 DUCAT

3.5000 g., 0.9860 Gold 0.1109 oz. AGW **Ruler:** George Ludwig **Obverse:** Small bust right **Reverse:** Crowned shields in cruciform, sceptres in angles

Date	Mintage	VG	F	VF	XF	Unc
1717 B	—	200	325	650	1,250	—

Date	Mintage	VG	F	VF	XF	Unc
1720 B	—	200	325	650	1,250	—
1721 B	—	200	325	650	1,250	—
1724 B	—	200	325	650	1,250	—
1727 S	—	200	325	650	1,250	—

KM# 171 DUCAT

3.5000 g., 0.9860 Gold 0.1109 oz. AGW **Ruler:** George Ludwig **Obverse:** Cruciform arms with garter, star in center date divided at top **Reverse:** Wildman with tree

Date	Mintage	VG	F	VF	XF	Unc
1725 EPH	—	350	650	1,200	2,000	—
1726 EPH	—	350	650	1,200	2,000	—

KM# 198 DUCAT

3.5000 g., 0.9860 Gold 0.1109 oz. AGW **Ruler:** George Ludwig **Subject:** Gold from Harz Mines **Obverse:** 4 crowned shields in cruciform, star in center **Reverse:** Rearing horse, AUR. HERC. added to legend

Date	Mintage	VG	F	VF	XF	Unc
1727 S	—	300	550	1,150	2,000	—

KM# 203 DUCAT

3.5000 g., 0.9860 Gold 0.1109 oz. AGW **Ruler:** George II August **Obverse:** 4 crowned shields in cruciform, star in center **Reverse:** Horse left

Date	Mintage	VG	F	VF	XF	Unc
1728 S	—	300	525	1,000	1,750	—
1730 S	—	300	525	1,000	1,750	—

KM# 209 DUCAT

3.5000 g., 0.9860 Gold 0.1109 oz. AGW **Ruler:** George II August **Subject:** Gold from Harz Mines **Obverse:** Laureate bust left, AUR. HERC below **Reverse:** Cruciform arms with scepters in angles, date divided

Date	Mintage	VG	F	VF	XF	Unc
1729 S	—	300	550	1,150	2,000	—

KM# 210 DUCAT

3.5000 g., 0.9860 Gold 0.1109 oz. AGW **Ruler:** George II August **Subject:** Harzgold **Rev. Legend:** EX. AUR. HERC

Date	Mintage	VG	F	VF	XF	Unc
1729 S	—	300	550	1,150	2,000	—

KM# 236 DUCAT

3.5000 g., 0.9860 Gold 0.1109 oz. AGW **Ruler:** George II August **Obverse:** Head left **Reverse:** Crowned quartered arms

Date	Mintage	VG	F	VF	XF	Unc
1730 S	—	300	525	1,000	1,750	—
1732 S	—	300	525	1,000	1,750	—

KM# 237 DUCAT

3.5000 g., 0.9860 Gold 0.1109 oz. AGW **Ruler:** George II August **Obverse:** Crowned quartered arms **Reverse:** Horse left, date below

Date	Mintage	VG	F	VF	XF	Unc
1730 S	—	200	325	650	1,250	—
1732 S	—	200	325	650	1,250	—
1733 S	—	200	325	650	1,250	—
1737 S	—	200	325	650	1,250	—

KM# 238 DUCAT

3.5000 g., 0.9860 Gold 0.1109 oz. AGW **Ruler:** George II August **Subject:** Gold from Harz Mines **Obverse:** Crowned quartered arms **Reverse:** Date in Arabic numerals **Rev. Legend:** AUR. HERC

Date	Mintage	VG	F	VF	XF	Unc
1730 S	—	300	550	1,100	1,850	—
1735 S	—	300	550	1,100	1,850	—
1736 S	—	300	550	1,100	1,850	—
1737 S	—	300	550	1,100	1,850	—
1739 S	—	300	550	1,100	1,850	—
1741 S	—	300	550	1,100	1,850	—
1746 S	—	300	550	1,100	1,850	—
1750 S	—	300	550	1,100	1,850	—
1756 IBH	—	300	550	1,100	1,850	—

KM# 289 DUCAT

3.5000 g., 0.9860 Gold 0.1109 oz. AGW **Ruler:** George II August **Rev. Legend:** EX. AUR. HERC. INF

Date	Mintage	VG	F	VF	XF	Unc
1743 S	—	300	525	1,000	1,750	—
1748 S	—	300	525	1,000	1,750	—

KM# 299 DUCAT

3.5000 g., 0.9860 Gold 0.1109 oz. AGW **Ruler:** George II August **Obverse:** Bust left **Reverse:** Crowned quartered arms, date **Rev. Legend:** AUR. HERC

Date	Mintage	VG	F	VF	XF	Unc
1747 S	—	400	650	1,200	2,000	—

KM# 316 DUCAT

3.5000 g., 0.9860 Gold 0.1109 oz. AGW **Ruler:** George II August **Obverse:** Head left **Reverse:** Value and date

Date	Mintage	VG	F	VF	XF	Unc
1751 IAS	—	250	500	1,000	1,750	—

KM# 317 DUCAT

3.5000 g., 0.9860 Gold 0.1109 oz. AGW **Ruler:** George II August **Obverse:** Horse left **Reverse:** Value, date

Date	Mintage	VG	F	VF	XF	Unc
1751 IAS	—	400	650	1,200	2,000	—

KM# 318 DUCAT

3.5000 g., 0.9860 Gold 0.1109 oz. AGW **Ruler:** George II August **Subject:** Gold from Harz Mines **Obverse:** Legend in exergue **Obv. Legend:** EX AURO HERC

Date	Mintage	VG	F	VF	XF	Unc
1751 IAS	—	400	650	1,200	2,000	—

KM# 325 DUCAT

3.5000 g., 0.9860 Gold 0.1109 oz. AGW **Ruler:** George II August **Subject:** Gold from Harz Mines **Obverse:** Crowned quartered arms **Reverse:** Date in Roman numerals **Rev. Legend:** EX. AUR. HERCIN

Date	Mintage	VG	F	VF	XF	Unc
1755 IBH	—	300	525	1,000	1,750	—

KM# 359 DUCAT

3.5000 g., 0.9860 Gold 0.1109 oz. AGW **Ruler:** George III **Obverse:** Crowned quartered arms **Reverse:** Legend is below horse **Rev. Legend:** EX AURO HERC

Date	Mintage	F	VF	XF	Unc
1767 IAP	—	300	550	1,000	1,650
1774 LCR	—	300	550	1,000	1,650
1776 LCR	—	300	550	1,000	1,650
1780 CES	—	300	550	1,000	1,650
1783 CES	—	300	550	1,000	1,650
1785 CES	—	300	550	1,000	1,650
1789 .C.	—	300	550	1,000	1,650

KM# 396 DUCAT

3.5000 g., 0.9860 Gold 0.1109 oz. AGW **Ruler:** George III **Obverse:** Crowned quartered arms **Reverse:** Horse left

Date	Mintage	F	VF	XF	Unc
1791 .C.	—	300	550	1,000	1,650
1793 PLM	—	300	550	1,000	1,650
1795 PLM	—	300	550	1,000	1,650
1796 PLM	—	300	550	1,000	1,650
1797 PLM	—	200	450	800	1,450
1798 PLM	—	200	450	800	1,450
1799 PLM	—	200	450	800	1,450
1800 PLM	—	200	450	800	1,450

KM# 115 2 DUCAT

7.0000 g., 0.9860 Gold 0.2219 oz. AGW **Ruler:** George Ludwig **Obverse:** Crowned arms **Reverse:** Rearing horse, date in exergue

Date	Mintage	VG	F	VF	XF	Unc
1707 HB	—	400	1,000	2,250	3,500	—

KM# 90 2 DUCAT

7.0000 g., 0.9860 Gold 0.2219 oz. AGW **Ruler:** George Ludwig **Obverse:** Bust right, titles of Imperial Treasurer added **Reverse:** Horse leaping left

Date	Mintage	VG	F	VF	XF	Unc
1713 HCB	—	—	—	—	—	—

KM# 199 2 DUCAT

7.0000 g., 0.9860 Gold 0.2219 oz. AGW **Ruler:** George Ludwig **Subject:** Death of George I Ludwig **Reverse:** 5-line inscription

Date	Mintage	VG	F	VF	XF	Unc
1727 CPS	—	800	1,650	3,000	5,000	—

KM# 200 4 DUCAT

14.0000 g., 0.9860 Gold 0.4438 oz. AGW **Ruler:** George II August **Subject:** Death of George I Ludwig **Obverse:** Laureate bust of George I right **Reverse:** 5-line inscription

Date	Mintage	VG	F	VF	XF	Unc
1727 CPS Rare	—	—	—	—	—	—

PATTERNS

Including off metal strikes

KM#	Date	Mintage	Identification	Mkt Val
Pn1	1726	—	Pfenning. Gold. KM#164.	—
Pn2	1726	—	Pfenning. Gold. KM#167.	—
Pn3	1729	—	Pfenning. Gold. KM#205.	550
Pn4	1730	—	Pfenning. Gold. KM#205.	550

KM#	Date	Mintage	Identification	Mkt Val
Pn5	1732	—	Pfenning. Gold. KM#205.	550
Pn6	1732	—	Pfenning. Gold. KM#215.	500
Pn7	1732	—	Pfenning. Gold. KM#215.	500
Pn8	1734	—	Pfenning. Gold. KM#215.	500
Pn9	1737	—	Pfenning. Gold. KM#205.	550
Pn10		—	Pfenning. Gold. KM#205.	500
Pn11	1737	—	Pfenning. Gold. KM#215.	500
Pn12	1739	—	Pfenning. Gold. KM#215.	500
Pn13	1746	—	Pfenning. Gold. KM#215.	500
Pn14	1750	—	Pfenning. Gold. KM#215.	500
Pn15	1750	—	Pfenning. Gold. KM#215.	500
Pn16		—	Pfenning. Gold. KM#215.	500
Pn17	1753	—	Pfenning. Silver. KM#204.1.	—
Pn18	1753	—	1/2 Thaler. Gold.	—
Pn19		—	2 Goldgulden. Silver. KM#302.	—

BRUNSWICK-LUNEBURG-CELLE

This division of Brunswick-Lüneburg, centered in Celle (Zelle), about 20 miles northeast of the city of Hannover, was founded in 1521. The last duke died in 1705 and Celle passed to Brunswick-Lüneburg-Calenberg-Hannover.

RULERS

Georg II Wilhelm, 1665-1705

MINT MARKS

N - Nienburg Mint

*** - Zellerfeld Mint, 1698-1715

MINT OFFICIALS' INITIALS

Initials	Date	Name
HB	1675-1711	Heinrich Bonhorst in Clausthal
Iii/III/JJJ	1687-1705	Jobst Jakob Janisch in Celle

DUCHY

REGULAR COINAGE

KM# 360 PFENNIG

Copper **Ruler:** Georg II Wilhelm **Obverse:** Horse leaping left in wreath, crowned GW; Similar to KM#318, but crowned GW monogram on horse's flank **Reverse:** Value in 4 lines

Date	Mintage	VG	F	VF	XF	Unc
1701	—	2.50	5.00	10.00	22.00	—
1702	—	2.50	5.00	10.00	22.00	—
1703	—	2.50	5.00	10.00	22.00	—

KM# 361 PFENNIG

Copper **Ruler:** Georg II Wilhelm **Obverse:** Horse left **Reverse:** Date below value

Date	Mintage	VG	F	VF	XF	Unc
1701	—	3.00	6.00	12.00	25.00	—

KM# 363 PFENNIG

Copper **Ruler:** Georg II Wilhelm **Obverse:** Horse leaping left **Reverse:** Horse leaping right, without value **Rev. Legend:** FIDE. PUBLICA..

Date	Mintage	VG	F	VF	XF	Unc
1703	—	3.00	6.00	12.00	25.00	—

KM# 366 PFENNIG

Copper **Ruler:** Georg II Wilhelm **Note:** Similar to KM#318, but value, date in 3 lines.

Date	Mintage	VG	F	VF	XF	Unc
1705	—	4.00	8.00	15.00	30.00	—

KM# 362 1-1/2 PFENNIG

Copper **Ruler:** Georg II Wilhelm **Obverse:** Horse leaping left, G. W. D. G. D. B. & L. above horse **Reverse:** Value

Date	Mintage	VG	F	VF	XF	Unc
1701	—	5.00	10.00	20.00	32.00	—
1702	—	5.00	10.00	20.00	32.00	—
1703	—	5.00	10.00	20.00	32.00	—

KM# 329 3 PFENNIG

Silver **Ruler:** Georg II Wilhelm **Obverse:** Crowned GW monogram divides date **Reverse:** Imperial orb with 3

Date	Mintage	VG	F	VF	XF	Unc
1690 iii	—	8.00	15.00	30.00	50.00	—
1690 III	—	8.00	15.00	30.00	50.00	—
1703 iiii	—	8.00	15.00	30.00	50.00	—

KM# 338.1 MARIENGROSCHEN

Silver **Ruler:** Georg II Wilhelm **Obverse:** Value in 4 lines, date **Obv. Legend:** F: BR: L: LANDTMUNTZ **Reverse:** Madonna and child

Date	Mintage	VG	F	VF	XF	Unc
1691 RD	—	8.00	22.00	40.00	65.00	—
1697 JJJ	—	8.00	22.00	40.00	65.00	—
1703 III	—	8.00	22.00	40.00	65.00	—

KM# 338.2 MARIENGROSCHEN

Silver **Ruler:** Georg II Wilhelm **Obverse:** Value 1/MARIEN/GROS:, date, HB in inner circle **Obv. Legend:** C. F. BR. LUN. LANDTMUNTZ **Reverse:** Madonna and child

Date	Mintage	VG	F	VF	XF	Unc
1706 HB	—	—	—	—	—	—

KM# 322 2 MARIENGROSCHEN

Silver **Ruler:** Georg II Wilhelm **Obverse:** Crowned GW monogram, date in legend **Reverse:** Value in 4 lines

Date	Mintage	VG	F	VF	XF	Unc
1702 JJJ	—	10.00	22.00	40.00	65.00	—
1703 JJJ	—	10.00	22.00	40.00	65.00	—

KM# 364 4 MARIENGROSCHEN

Silver **Ruler:** Georg II Wilhelm **Obverse:** Horse leaping left **Reverse:** Value

Date	Mintage	VG	F	VF	XF	Unc
1703 III	—	25.00	50.00	100	165	—
1703 iii	—	25.00	50.00	100	165	—
1704 III	—	25.00	50.00	100	165	—
1704 iii	—	25.00	50.00	100	165	—
1704 JJJ	—	25.00	50.00	100	165	—

KM# 367 HALB REICHSORT (1/8 Thaler)

Silver **Ruler:** Georg II Wilhelm **Subject:** Death of Georg II Wilhelm **Obverse:** Armored bust right **Obv. Legend:** GEORG: WILH: - D: G: D: BR: ET L: **Reverse:** Inscription in 8 lines

Date	Mintage	VG	F	VF	XF	Unc
1705	—	—	150	250	450	—

KM# 323 1/48 THALER (1/2 Groschen)

Silver **Ruler:** Georg II Wilhelm **Obverse:** Crowned GW monogram **Reverse:** Value, date **Rev. Legend:** F. BR. LANTMUNTZ

Date	Mintage	VG	F	VF	XF	Unc
1703	—	7.00	15.00	30.00	50.00	—
1703 iii	—	7.00	15.00	30.00	50.00	—
1704 iii	—	7.00	15.00	30.00	50.00	—

KM# 356 1/48 THALER (1/2 Groschen)

Silver **Ruler:** Georg II Wilhelm **Obverse:** Monogram of ornate letters **Reverse:** Value within orb

Date	Mintage	VG	F	VF	XF	Unc
1698 III	—	7.00	15.00	30.00	50.00	—
1703	—	7.00	15.00	30.00	50.00	—
1704 iii	—	7.00	15.00	30.00	50.00	—

KM# 365 1/48 THALER (1/2 Groschen)

Silver **Ruler:** Georg II Wilhelm **Obverse:** Crowned GW monogram, date below crown

Date	Mintage	VG	F	VF	XF	Unc
1704	—	9.00	18.00	32.00	55.00	—

KM# 349 1/24 THALER (Groschen)

Silver **Ruler:** Georg II Wilhelm **Obverse:** Latin titles and date below horse **Reverse:** Imperial orb with 24

Date	Mintage	VG	F	VF	XF	Unc
1702 iii	—	6.00	15.00	30.00	60.00	—
1702 JJJ	—	6.00	15.00	30.00	60.00	—
1703 iii	—	6.00	15.00	30.00	60.00	—
1703 JJJ	—	6.00	15.00	30.00	60.00	—

KM# 368 1/4 THALER

Silver **Ruler:** Georg II Wilhelm **Subject:** Death of Georg II Wilhelm **Obverse:** Bust right **Reverse:** 10-line inscription with date

Date	Mintage	VG	F	VF	XF	Unc
1705	—	—	200	300	550	—

KM# 369 1/2 THALER

Silver **Ruler:** Georg II Wilhelm **Subject:** Death of Georg II Wilhelm **Obverse:** Armored bust right **Obv. Legend:** GEORG: WILH: - D: G: D: BR: ET L: **Reverse:** Inscription in 11 lines

Date	Mintage	VG	F	VF	XF	Unc
1705	—	—	300	450	750	—

KM# 370 THALER

Silver **Ruler:** Georg II Wilhelm **Subject:** Death of Georg Wllhelm **Obverse:** Armored bust right **Obv. Legend:** GEORG: WILH: - D: G: D: BR: ET L: **Reverse:** Inscription in 11 lines **Note:** Dav. #2056.

Date	Mintage	VG	F	VF	XF	Unc
1705	—	—	350	550	900	—

BRUNSWICK-WOLFENBUTTEL

(Braunschweig-Wolfenbüttel)

Located in north-central Germany. Wolfenbüttel was annexed to Brunswick in 1257. One of the five surviving sons of Albrecht II founded the first line in Wolfenbüttel in 1318. A further division in Wolfenbüttel and Lüneburg was undertaken in 1373. Another division occurred in 1495, but the Wolfenbüttel duchy survived in the younger line. Heinrich IX was forced out of his territory during the religious wars of the mid-sixteenth century by Duke Johann Friedrich I of Saxony and Landgrave Philipp of Hessen in 1542, but was restored to his possessions in 1547. Duke Friedrich Ulrich was forced to cede the Grubenhagen lands, which had been acquired by Wolfenbüttel in 1596, to Lüneburg in 1617. When the succession died out in 1634, the lands and titles fell to the cadet line in Dannenberg. The line became extinct once again and passed to Brunswick-Bevern in 1735 from which a new succession of Wolfenbüttel dukes descended. The ducal family was beset by continual personal and political tragedy during the nineteenth century. Two of the dukes were killed in battles with Napoleon, the territories were occupied by the French and became part of the Kingdom of Westphalia, another duke was forced out by a revolt in 1823. From 1884 until 1913, Brunswick-Wolfenbüttel was governed by Prussia and then turned over to a younger prince of Brunswick who married a daughter of Kaiser Wilhelm II. His reign was short, however, as he was forced to abdicate at the end of World War I.

RULERS

Rudolf August, 1666-1704
Anton Ulrich, as joint ruler, 1685-1704
alone, 1704-1714
August Wilhelm, 1714-1731
Ludwig Rudolph, 1731-1735
Ferdinand Albrecht II, 1735
Karl I, 1735-1780
Karl Wilhelm Ferdinand, 1780-1806

MINT OFFICIALS' INITIALS

Brunswick Mint

Initials	Date	Name
HCH	1689-1729	Heinrich Christoph Hille, mintmaster
IHT	1729-32	Hohann Heinrich Thiele, mintmaster
Bid, D	1732-42	Bernhard Julius Dedekind, mintmaster
EK	1742-50	Engelhard Johann Krull, mintmaster
M	1742-48	Mahrenholz, die-cutter
E	1750-66	Johann Christoph Ebeling, die-cutter
ACB	1751-59	Andreas Christoph Blechschmidt, mintmaster
IDB	1760-79	Johann David Biller, mintmaster
K	1766-1802	Christian Friedrich Krull, die-cutter
MC	1779-1806, 1820	Münz-Commission

Clausthal Mint

Initials	Date	Name
HB	1675-1711	Heinrich Bonhorst, mintmaster
CPS, S	1725-53	Christian Philipp Spangenberg

Goslar Mint

Initials	Date	Name
RB	1685-1704	Rudolf Bornemann, mintmaster

Zellerfeld Mint

Initials	Date	Name
RB	1676-1711	Rudolf Bornemann, mintmaster
***	1698-1715	Used in place of mintmasters' initials
C, star C star	1711-12, 1719-23, 31	Münz-Commission
HH	1712-19	Heinrich Horst, mintmaster
EPH	1723-31	Ernst Peter Hecht, mintmaster
IAB	1731-39	Johann Albrecht Brauns, mintmaster
IBH	1739-63	Johann Benjamin Hecht, mintmaster
CES, CS	1779-86	Christoph Engelhard Seidensticker, mintmaster

Miscellaneous

Initials	Date	Name
PHM	1650-1718	Philipp Heinrich Müller, goldsmith, die-cutter, medailleur in Nürnberg and Augsburg
GFN	1682-1724	Georg Friedrich Nürnberger, die-cutter, mintmaster in Nürnberg

DUCHY

REGULAR COINAGE

KM# 948 DENIER

Copper **Ruler:** Karl I

Date	Mintage	F	VF	XF	Unc
1758	—	7.00	14.00	28.00	65.00

KM# 891 PFENNIG

Copper **Ruler:** Karl I **Obverse:** Horse rearing left **Reverse:** Value and date

Date	Mintage	F	VF	XF	Unc
ND MC	—	3.50	7.00	15.00	50.00
1736	—	3.50	7.00	15.00	50.00
1737	—	3.50	7.00	15.00	50.00
1738	—	3.50	7.00	15.00	50.00
1739	—	3.50	7.00	15.00	50.00
1741	—	3.50	7.00	15.00	50.00
1742	—	3.50	7.00	15.00	50.00
1743	—	3.50	7.00	15.00	50.00
1744	—	3.50	7.00	15.00	50.00
1745	—	3.50	7.00	15.00	50.00
1746	—	3.50	7.00	15.00	50.00
1747	—	3.50	7.00	15.00	50.00
1748	—	3.50	7.00	15.00	50.00
1749	—	3.50	7.00	15.00	50.00
1750	—	3.50	7.00	15.00	50.00
1751	—	3.50	7.00	15.00	50.00
1752	—	3.50	7.00	15.00	50.00
1753	—	3.50	7.00	15.00	50.00
1754	—	3.50	7.00	15.00	50.00
1755	—	3.50	7.00	15.00	50.00
1756	—	3.50	7.00	15.00	50.00
1757	—	3.50	7.00	15.00	50.00
1758	—	3.50	7.00	15.00	50.00
1759	—	3.50	7.00	15.00	50.00
1760	—	3.50	7.00	15.00	50.00
1761	—	3.50	7.00	15.00	50.00
1762	—	3.50	7.00	15.00	50.00
1763	—	3.50	7.00	15.00	50.00
1764	—	3.50	7.00	15.00	50.00
1765	—	3.50	7.00	15.00	50.00
1766	—	3.50	7.00	15.00	50.00
1767	—	3.50	7.00	15.00	50.00
1768	—	3.50	7.00	15.00	50.00
1769	—	3.50	7.00	15.00	50.00
1770	—	3.50	7.00	15.00	50.00
1771	—	3.50	7.00	15.00	50.00
1772	—	3.50	7.00	15.00	50.00
1773	—	3.50	7.00	15.00	50.00
1776	—	3.50	7.00	15.00	50.00
1777	—	3.50	7.00	15.00	50.00
1778	—	3.50	7.00	15.00	50.00
1779	—	3.50	7.00	15.00	50.00

KM# 691 PFENNIG

Silver **Ruler:** Anton Ulrich as Joint ruler **Obverse:** Horse leaping left, date **Reverse:** Value

Date	Mintage	Good	VG	F	VF	XF
1703	—	—	10.00	25.00	40.00	75.00
1706	—	—	10.00	25.00	40.00	75.00

KM# 642 PFENNIG

Copper **Ruler:** Anton Ulrich Alone **Obverse:** Horse leaping left **Reverse:** Value, date in 5 lines

Date	Mintage	VG	F	VF	XF	Unc
1704	—	5.00	10.00	18.00	35.00	—
1705	—	5.00	10.00	18.00	35.00	—
1706	—	5.00	10.00	18.00	35.00	—
1707	—	5.00	10.00	18.00	35.00	—
1708	—	5.00	10.00	18.00	35.00	—
1709	—	5.00	10.00	18.00	35.00	—
1710	—	5.00	10.00	18.00	35.00	—
1713	—	5.00	10.00	18.00	35.00	—

KM# 643 PFENNIG

Silver **Ruler:** Anton Ulrich Alone **Obverse:** Crowned cursive AU monogram divides date **Note:** Uniface

Date	Mintage	VG	F	VF	XF	Unc
1704 RB	—	8.00	16.00	35.00	55.00	—

KM# 679 PFENNIG

Copper **Ruler:** Anton Ulrich Alone **Obverse:** Crowned cursive AV monogram divides date

Date	Mintage	VG	F	VF	XF	Unc
1705 RB	—	12.00	30.00	66.00	90.00	—
1706 RB	—	12.00	30.00	66.00	90.00	—
1707 RB	—	12.00	30.00	66.00	90.00	—
1708 RB	—	12.00	30.00	66.00	90.00	—
1712 HH	—	12.00	30.00	66.00	90.00	—
1713 HH	—	12.00	30.00	66.00	90.00	—

KM# 725 PFENNIG

Copper **Ruler:** August Wilhelm **Obverse:** Horse leaping left **Reverse:** Value, date in 5 lines

Date	Mintage	VG	F	VF	XF	Unc
1714	—	5.00	10.00	18.00	35.00	—
1717	—	5.00	10.00	18.00	35.00	—
1718	—	5.00	10.00	18.00	35.00	—
1719	—	5.00	10.00	18.00	35.00	—
1722	—	5.00	10.00	18.00	35.00	—
1723	—	5.00	10.00	18.00	35.00	—
1724	—	5.00	10.00	18.00	35.00	—
1725	—	5.00	10.00	18.00	35.00	—
1729	—	5.00	10.00	18.00	35.00	—

KM# 724 PFENNIG

Copper **Ruler:** August Wilhelm **Note:** AW monogram, date.

Date	Mintage	VG	F	VF	XF	Unc
1714 HH	—	8.00	15.00	25.00	45.00	—
1715 HH	—	8.00	15.00	25.00	45.00	—
1716 HH	—	8.00	15.00	25.00	45.00	—
1717 HH	—	8.00	15.00	25.00	45.00	—
1718 HH	—	8.00	15.00	25.00	45.00	—

KM# 778 PFENNIG

Copper **Ruler:** August Wilhelm **Obverse:** Wildman, tree in left hand **Reverse:** Value, date

Date	Mintage	VG	F	VF	XF	Unc
1724 EPH	—	7.00	14.00	25.00	45.00	—
1725 EPH	—	7.00	14.00	25.00	45.00	—
1726 EPH	—	7.00	14.00	25.00	45.00	—
1729 EPH	—	7.00	14.00	25.00	45.00	—
1730 EPH	—	7.00	14.00	25.00	45.00	—

KM# 780 PFENNIG

Copper **Ruler:** August Wilhelm **Obverse:** Horse leaping left in circle **Reverse:** Value, date

Date	Mintage	VG	F	VF	XF	Unc
1725	—	5.00	10.00	18.00	35.00	—
1727	—	5.00	10.00	18.00	35.00	—
1729	—	5.00	10.00	18.00	35.00	—
1730	—	5.00	10.00	18.00	35.00	—
1731	—	5.00	10.00	18.00	35.00	—

KM# 803 PFENNIG

Copper **Ruler:** Ludwig Rudolph **Obverse:** Crowned script LR monogram divides date **Reverse:** Value in 4 lines

Date	Mintage	VG	F	VF	XF	Unc
1731	—	4.00	8.00	15.00	25.00	—
1732	—	4.00	8.00	15.00	25.00	—
1733	—	4.00	8.00	15.00	25.00	—

KM# 829 PFENNIG

Copper **Ruler:** Ludwig Rudolph **Obverse:** Horse leaping left, date below

Date	Mintage	VG	F	VF	XF	Unc
1733	—	5.00	10.00	16.00	30.00	—
1734	—	5.00	10.00	16.00	30.00	—

KM# 830 PFENNIG

Copper **Ruler:** Ludwig Rudolph **Reverse:** Date in legend

Date	Mintage	VG	F	VF	XF	Unc
1733	—	5.00	10.00	16.00	30.00	—
1734	—	5.00	10.00	16.00	30.00	—
1735	—	5.00	10.00	16.00	30.00	—

KM# 847 PFENNIG

Copper **Ruler:** Ludwig Rudolph **Obverse:** Wildman, tree in left hand **Reverse:** Value, date in 5 lines

Date	Mintage	VG	F	VF	XF	Unc
1734 Rare	—	—	—	—	—	—

KM# 851 PFENNIG

Copper **Ruler:** Ludwig Rudolph **Obverse:** Horse leaping left **Reverse:** Value I. . ., date in 5 lines

Date	Mintage	VG	F	VF	XF	Unc
1735	—	4.00	8.00	16.00	30.00	—

KM# 901.1 PFENNIG

Copper **Ruler:** Karl I **Obverse:** Wildman with tree in left hand **Reverse:** Value, date

Date	Mintage	F	VF	XF	Unc
1737 IAB	—	6.00	12.00	25.00	60.00

KM# 901.2 PFENNIG

Copper **Ruler:** Karl I **Obverse:** Wildman with tree in left hand **Reverse:** Value, date

Date	Mintage	F	VF	XF	Unc
1739 IBH	—	6.00	12.00	25.00	60.00
1739/41 IBH	—	6.00	12.00	25.00	60.00
1741 IBH	—	6.00	12.00	25.00	60.00
1742 IBH	—	6.00	12.00	25.00	60.00
1743 IBH	—	6.00	12.00	25.00	60.00
1745 IBH	—	6.00	12.00	25.00	60.00
1746 IBH	—	6.00	12.00	25.00	60.00
1747 IBH	—	6.00	12.00	25.00	60.00
1749 IBH	—	6.00	12.00	25.00	60.00
1750 IBH	—	6.00	12.00	25.00	60.00
1752 IBH	—	6.00	12.00	25.00	60.00
1754 IBH	—	6.00	12.00	25.00	60.00
1755 IBH	—	6.00	12.00	25.00	60.00
1756 IBH	—	6.00	12.00	25.00	60.00
1758 IBH	—	6.00	12.00	25.00	60.00
1759 IBH	—	6.00	12.00	25.00	60.00
1760 IBH	—	6.00	12.00	25.00	60.00
1761 IBH	—	6.00	12.00	25.00	60.00
1762 IBH	—	6.00	12.00	25.00	60.00

KM# 901.3 PFENNIG

Copper **Ruler:** Karl I **Obverse:** Wildman with tree in left hand **Reverse:** Value, date

Date	Mintage	F	VF	XF	Unc
1763 IAP	—	6.00	12.00	25.00	60.00
1765 IAP	—	6.00	12.00	25.00	60.00
1766 IAP	—	6.00	12.00	25.00	60.00
1768 IAP	—	6.00	12.00	25.00	60.00
1769 IAP	—	6.00	12.00	25.00	60.00
1770 IAP	—	6.00	12.00	25.00	60.00
1772 IAP	—	6.00	12.00	25.00	60.00

KM# 901.4 PFENNIG

Copper **Ruler:** Karl I **Obverse:** Wildman with tree **Reverse:** Value, date

Date	Mintage	F	VF	XF	Unc
1774 LCR	—	6.00	12.00	25.00	60.00
1776 LCR	—	6.00	12.00	25.00	60.00
1777 LCR	—	6.00	12.00	25.00	60.00
1778 LCR	—	6.00	12.00	25.00	60.00

KM# 901.5 PFENNIG

Copper **Ruler:** Karl I **Obverse:** Wildman with tree **Reverse:** Value, date

Date	Mintage	F	VF	XF	Unc
1780 CES	—	6.00	12.00	25.00	60.00

KM# 995 PFENNIG

Copper **Ruler:** Karl Wilhelm Ferdinand **Obverse:** Horse running left **Reverse:** Denomination, legend and date

Date	Mintage	F	VF	XF	Unc
1780 MC	—	4.00	8.00	18.00	40.00
1781 MC	—	4.00	8.00	18.00	40.00
1782 MC	—	4.00	8.00	18.00	40.00
1783 MC	—	4.00	8.00	18.00	40.00
1784 MC	—	4.00	8.00	18.00	40.00
1785 MC	—	4.00	8.00	18.00	40.00
1786 MC	—	4.00	8.00	18.00	40.00
1787 MC	—	4.00	8.00	18.00	40.00
1788 MC	—	4.00	8.00	18.00	40.00
1789 MC	—	4.00	8.00	18.00	40.00
1790 MC	—	4.00	8.00	18.00	40.00
1791 MC	—	4.00	8.00	18.00	40.00
1792 MC	—	4.00	8.00	18.00	40.00
1793 MC	—	4.00	8.00	18.00	40.00
1794 MC	—	4.00	8.00	18.00	40.00
1795 MC	—	4.00	8.00	18.00	40.00
1796 MC	—	4.00	8.00	18.00	40.00
1797 MC	—	4.00	8.00	18.00	40.00
1798 MC	—	4.00	8.00	18.00	40.00
1799 MC	—	4.00	8.00	18.00	40.00
1800 MC	—	4.00	8.00	18.00	40.00
1801 MC	—	4.00	8.00	18.00	40.00
1802 MC	—	4.00	8.00	20.00	45.00
1803 MC	—	4.00	8.00	18.00	40.00
1804 MC	—	4.00	8.00	18.00	40.00
1805 MC	—	4.00	8.00	18.00	40.00
1806 MC	—	5.00	10.00	18.00	40.00

KM# 996 PFENNIG

Copper **Ruler:** Karl Wilhelm Ferdinand **Obverse:** Wildman with tree in left hand **Reverse:** Value, date

Date	Mintage	F	VF	XF	Unc
1780 CES	—	4.00	9.00	18.00	45.00
1781 CES	—	4.00	9.00	18.00	45.00
1783 CES	—	4.00	9.00	18.00	45.00
1784 CES	—	4.00	9.00	18.00	45.00
1785 CES	—	4.00	9.00	18.00	45.00
1788 C	—	4.00	9.00	18.00	45.00

KM# 925 1-1/2 PFENNIGE

Copper **Ruler:** Karl I **Obverse:** Horse left **Reverse:** Value, date

Date	Mintage	F	VF	XF	Unc
1747	—	5.00	10.00	20.00	50.00
1767	—	5.00	10.00	20.00	50.00

KM# 644 2 PFENNIGE

Silver **Ruler:** Anton Ulrich Alone **Subject:** Death of Rudolf August **Obverse:** Crowned RA monogram **Reverse:** 6-line inscription with date, value 2/PF below

Date	Mintage	VG	F	VF	XF	Unc
1704 HCH	—	12.50	25.00	50.00	90.00	—

KM# 831 2 PFENNIGE

Silver **Ruler:** Ludwig Rudolph **Obverse:** Crowned script LR monogram **Reverse:** 2/PFEN/date

Date	Mintage	VG	F	VF	XF	Unc
1733	—	10.00	20.00	40.00	80.00	—
1735	—	10.00	20.00	40.00	80.00	—

KM# 852 2 PFENNIGE

Silver **Ruler:** Ludwig Rudolph **Obverse:** Horse leaping left **Reverse:** Value, date

Date	Mintage	VG	F	VF	XF	Unc
1735	—	7.00	15.00	30.00	55.00	—

KM# 892 2 PFENNIGE

Billon **Ruler:** Karl I **Obverse:** Horse leaping left **Reverse:** Value, date

Date	Mintage	F	VF	XF	Unc
1736	—	7.00	15.00	30.00	75.00
1776	—	7.00	15.00	30.00	75.00

KM# 981 2 PFENNIGE

Copper **Ruler:** Karl I **Obverse:** Horse left **Reverse:** Value, date

Date	Mintage	F	VF	XF	Unc
1772	—	5.00	10.00	20.00	65.00

KM# 1040 2-1/2 PFENNIGE

Copper **Ruler:** Karl Wilhelm Ferdinand **Obverse:** Horse leaping left **Reverse:** Value, date

Date	Mintage	F	VF	XF	Unc
1792 M.C.	—	5.00	10.00	25.00	80.00

KM# 557 3 PFENNIG

Silver **Ruler:** Rudolf August **Obverse:** Crowned intertwined cursive RAV **Reverse:** Imperial orb with 3 divides date

Date	Mintage	VG	F	VF	XF	Unc
1685 RB	—	10.00	20.00	35.00	65.00	—
1692 HCH	—	10.00	20.00	35.00	65.00	—
1702 HCH	—	10.00	20.00	35.00	65.00	—

KM# 680 3 PFENNIG

Silver **Ruler:** Anton Ulrich Alone **Obverse:** Crowned AV monogram **Reverse:** Imperial orb with 3 divides date

Date	Mintage	VG	F	VF	XF	Unc
1705 RB	—	18.00	35.00	65.00	100	—
1706 RB	—	18.00	35.00	65.00	100	—
1707 RB	—	18.00	35.00	65.00	100	—
1708 RB	—	18.00	35.00	65.00	100	—
1710 RB	—	18.00	35.00	65.00	100	—
1711 RB	—	18.00	35.00	65.00	100	—
1712 HH	—	18.00	35.00	65.00	100	—
1713 HH	—	18.00	35.00	65.00	100	—

KM# 722 3 PFENNIG

Silver **Ruler:** August Wilhelm **Obverse:** Crowned AW monogram

Date	Mintage	VG	F	VF	XF	Unc
1713 HH	—	8.00	16.00	30.00	55.00	—
1714 HH	—	8.00	16.00	30.00	55.00	—
1715 HH	—	8.00	16.00	30.00	55.00	—
1716 HH	—	8.00	16.00	30.00	55.00	—
1718 HH	—	8.00	16.00	30.00	55.00	—

KM# 963 3 PFENNIG

Billon **Ruler:** Karl I **Obverse:** *B*S.M. **Reverse:** III PFENIG

Date	Mintage	F	VF	XF	Unc
1761	—	—	—	—	—

Note: Reported, not confirmed

KM# 639 4 PFENNIGE

Silver **Ruler:** Anton Ulrich as Joint ruler **Obverse:** Crowned intertwined cursive RAV monogram **Reverse:** Date below value 4

Date	Mintage	VG	F	VF	XF	Unc
1702	—	12.00	25.00	40.00	70.00	—

KM# 645 4 PFENNIGE

Silver **Ruler:** Anton Ulrich Alone **Obverse:** RAU monogram **Reverse:** Value IIII. . . with date

Date	Mintage	VG	F	VF	XF	Unc
1704	—	12.00	25.00	40.00	70.00	—

KM# 646 4 PFENNIGE

Silver **Ruler:** Anton Ulrich Alone **Obverse:** Horse leaping left, date below **Reverse:** Value IIII. . . in 4 lines

Date	Mintage	VG	F	VF	XF	Unc
1704 HCH	—	8.00	16.00	30.00	55.00	—
1705 HCH	—	8.00	16.00	30.00	55.00	—
1706 HCH	—	8.00	16.00	30.00	55.00	—

KM# 701 4 PFENNIGE

Silver **Ruler:** Anton Ulrich Alone **Obverse:** Crowned AV monogram **Reverse:** Value IIII. . ., date in 3 lines

Date	Mintage	VG	F	VF	XF	Unc
1704 RB	—	8.00	16.00	30.00	55.00	—
1705 RB	—	8.00	16.00	30.00	55.00	—
1706 RB	—	8.00	16.00	30.00	55.00	—
1708 RB	—	8.00	16.00	30.00	55.00	—
1709 RB	—	8.00	16.00	30.00	55.00	—
1710 RB	—	8.00	16.00	30.00	55.00	—
1711 RB	—	8.00	16.00	30.00	55.00	—
1712 RB	—	8.00	16.00	30.00	55.00	—
1713 HH	—	8.00	16.00	30.00	55.00	—

KM# 705 4 PFENNIGE

Silver **Ruler:** Anton Ulrich Alone **Reverse:** Date below value

Date	Mintage	VG	F	VF	XF	Unc
1710 HB	—	10.00	20.00	35.00	60.00	—

KM# 726 4 PFENNIGE

Silver **Ruler:** August Wilhelm **Obverse:** Crowned AV monogram **Reverse:** Value IIII. . ., date in 4 lines

Date	Mintage	VG	F	VF	XF	Unc
1714 HH	—	10.00	20.00	35.00	65.00	—
1715 HH	—	10.00	20.00	35.00	65.00	—
1716 HH	—	10.00	20.00	35.00	65.00	—
1717 HH	—	10.00	20.00	35.00	65.00	—
1718 HH	—	10.00	20.00	35.00	65.00	—
1724 EPH	—	10.00	20.00	35.00	65.00	—
1726 EPH	—	10.00	20.00	35.00	65.00	—
1728 EPH	—	10.00	20.00	35.00	65.00	—

KM# 832 4 PFENNIGE

Silver **Ruler:** Ludwig Rudolph **Obverse:** Crowned script LR monogram **Reverse:** Value IIII/PFEN, date

Date	Mintage	VG	F	VF	XF	Unc
1733	—	8.00	16.00	30.00	55.00	—

KM# 853 4 PFENNIGE

Silver **Ruler:** Ferdinand Ulbrecht II **Obverse:** Crowned cursive FA monogram **Reverse:** Value IIII. . ., date in 3 lines

Date	Mintage	VG	F	VF	XF	Unc
1735 IAB	—	10.00	20.00	35.00	65.00	—

KM# 893 4 PFENNIGE

Billon **Ruler:** Karl I **Obverse:** Crowned C monogram **Reverse:** Value, date **Rev. Legend:** F. Br. LVN. . .

Date	Mintage	F	VF	XF	Unc
1736 IAB	—	7.00	15.00	30.00	65.00
1739 IAB	—	7.00	15.00	30.00	65.00
1742 IBH	—	7.00	15.00	30.00	65.00
1744 IBH	—	7.00	15.00	30.00	65.00
1749 IBH	—	7.00	15.00	30.00	65.00
1750 IBH	—	7.00	15.00	30.00	65.00
1751 IBH	—	7.00	15.00	30.00	65.00
1752 IBH	—	7.00	15.00	30.00	65.00
1753 IBH	—	7.00	15.00	30.00	65.00
1755 IBH	—	7.00	15.00	30.00	65.00
1759 IBH	—	7.00	15.00	30.00	65.00
1761 IBH	—	7.00	15.00	30.00	65.00
1762 IBH	—	7.00	15.00	30.00	65.00
1763 IAP	—	7.00	15.00	30.00	65.00
1765 IAP	—	7.00	15.00	30.00	65.00
1766 IAP	—	7.00	15.00	30.00	65.00
1768 IAP	—	7.00	15.00	30.00	65.00
1770 IAP	—	7.00	15.00	30.00	65.00
1771 IAO	—	7.00	15.00	30.00	65.00
1775 LCR	—	7.00	15.00	30.00	65.00
1777 LCR	—	7.00	15.00	30.00	65.00
1779 C	—	7.00	15.00	30.00	65.00

KM# 926 4 PFENNIGE

Billon **Ruler:** Karl I **Obverse:** Horse left **Reverse:** Value, L.M., date

Date	Mintage	F	VF	XF	Unc
1747	—	8.00	20.00	40.00	75.00
1748	—	8.00	20.00	40.00	75.00
1750	—	8.00	20.00	40.00	75.00

KM# 933 4 PFENNIGE

Billon **Ruler:** Karl I **Rev. Legend:** FURSTL. BRAUNS. . .

Date	Mintage	F	VF	XF	Unc
1748	—	7.00	15.00	30.00	65.00
1749	—	7.00	15.00	30.00	65.00
1750	—	7.00	15.00	30.00	65.00
1752	—	7.00	15.00	30.00	65.00
1753	—	7.00	15.00	30.00	65.00
1756	—	7.00	15.00	30.00	65.00
1757	—	7.00	15.00	30.00	65.00

KM# 960 4 PFENNIGE

Billon **Ruler:** Karl I **Obverse:** *B*S.M. **Reverse:** IIII PEFNIG, date

Date	Mintage	F	VF	XF	Unc
1760 IDB	—	7.00	15.00	30.00	65.00
1761 IDB	—	7.00	15.00	30.00	65.00

KM# 965 4 PFENNIGE

Billon **Ruler:** Karl I **Obverse:** Horse left, CAROLVS. . . **Reverse:** Value, date, NACH DEM. . .

Date	Mintage	F	VF	XF	Unc
1762 IDB	—	7.00	15.00	30.00	65.00

KM# 967 4 PFENNIGE

Billon **Ruler:** Karl I **Obverse:** Horse left **Reverse:** Value **Rev. Legend:** MVIII E.F. . .

Date	Mintage	F	VF	XF	Unc
1764 IDB	—	7.00	15.00	30.00	65.00
1772 IDB	—	7.00	15.00	30.00	65.00

KM# 997 4 PFENNIGE

Billon **Ruler:** Karl Wilhelm Ferdinand **Obverse:** Horse **Reverse:** Denomination

Date	Mintage	F	VF	XF	Unc
1780 MC	—	10.00	20.00	30.00	50.00
1787 MC	—	10.00	20.00	30.00	50.00
1788 MC	—	10.00	20.00	30.00	50.00
1790 MC	—	10.00	20.00	30.00	50.00
1792 MC	—	10.00	20.00	30.00	50.00
1793 MC	—	10.00	20.00	30.00	50.00
1795 MC	—	10.00	20.00	30.00	50.00
1796 MC	—	10.00	20.00	30.00	50.00
1797 MC	—	10.00	20.00	30.00	50.00
1798 MC	—	10.00	20.00	30.00	50.00
1799 MC	—	10.00	20.00	30.00	50.00
1800 MC	—	10.00	20.00	30.00	50.00
1801 MC	—	10.00	20.00	30.00	50.00
1802 MC	—	8.00	15.00	30.00	50.00
1803 MC	—	10.00	20.00	35.00	55.00
1804 MC	—	8.00	15.00	25.00	45.00

KM# 638 6 PFENNIGE

Silver **Ruler:** Anton Ulrich as Joint ruler **Obverse:** Horse leaping left **Reverse:** Value VI in orb

Date	Mintage	VG	F	VF	XF	Unc
1701	—	10.00	20.00	35.00	65.00	—
1702	—	10.00	20.00	35.00	65.00	—

KM# 695 6 PFENNIGE

Silver **Ruler:** Anton Ulrich Alone **Note:** Similar to KM#804.

Date	Mintage	VG	F	VF	XF	Unc
1707	—	12.00	25.00	40.00	75.00	—
1708	—	12.00	25.00	40.00	75.00	—
1709	—	12.00	25.00	40.00	75.00	—
1710	—	12.00	25.00	40.00	75.00	—
1711	—	12.00	25.00	40.00	75.00	—
1712	—	12.00	25.00	40.00	75.00	—
1713	—	12.00	25.00	40.00	75.00	—

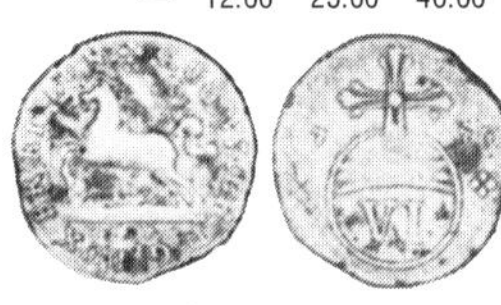

KM# 742 6 PFENNIGE

Silver **Ruler:** August Wilhelm **Obverse:** Horse rearing left **Reverse:** Value within imperial orb

Date	Mintage	VG	F	VF	XF	Unc
1715	—	8.00	15.00	30.00	60.00	—
1720	—	8.00	15.00	30.00	60.00	—
1722	—	8.00	15.00	30.00	60.00	—
1723	—	8.00	15.00	30.00	60.00	—
1724	—	8.00	15.00	30.00	60.00	—
1725	—	8.00	15.00	30.00	60.00	—
1726	—	8.00	15.00	30.00	60.00	—
1727	—	8.00	15.00	30.00	60.00	—
1728	—	8.00	15.00	30.00	60.00	—
1729	—	8.00	15.00	30.00	60.00	—
1730	—	8.00	15.00	30.00	60.00	—

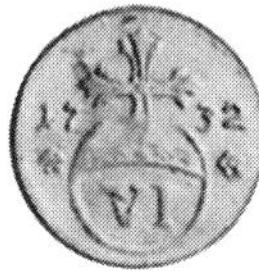

KM# 804 6 PFENNIGE

Silver **Ruler:** Ludwig Rudolph **Obverse:** Horse rearing left **Reverse:** Value within imperial orb

Date	Mintage	VG	F	VF	XF	Unc
1731	—	10.00	20.00	35.00	65.00	—
1732	—	10.00	20.00	35.00	65.00	—
1733	—	10.00	20.00	35.00	65.00	—
1734	—	10.00	20.00	35.00	65.00	—
1735	—	10.00	20.00	35.00	65.00	—

KM# 854 6 PFENNIGE

Silver **Obverse:** Horse rearing left **Reverse:** Value within imperial orb

Date	Mintage	VG	F	VF	XF	Unc
1735	—	10.00	20.00	35.00	65.00	—

KM# 855 6 PFENNIGE

Billon **Ruler:** Karl I **Obverse:** Horse rearing left **Reverse:** Value within imperial orb

Date	Mintage	F	VF	XF	Unc
1735	—	5.00	15.00	30.00	60.00
1736	—	5.00	15.00	30.00	60.00
1737	—	5.00	15.00	30.00	60.00
1738	—	5.00	15.00	30.00	60.00
1739	—	5.00	15.00	30.00	60.00
1741	—	5.00	15.00	30.00	60.00
1742	—	5.00	15.00	30.00	60.00
1743	—	5.00	15.00	30.00	60.00
1744	—	5.00	15.00	30.00	60.00
1745	—	5.00	15.00	30.00	60.00
1746	—	5.00	15.00	30.00	60.00
1747	—	5.00	15.00	30.00	60.00
1748	—	5.00	15.00	30.00	60.00
1749	—	5.00	15.00	30.00	60.00
1750	—	5.00	15.00	30.00	60.00
1751	—	5.00	15.00	30.00	60.00
1752	—	5.00	15.00	30.00	60.00
1753	—	5.00	15.00	30.00	60.00
1755	—	5.00	15.00	30.00	60.00
1756	—	5.00	15.00	30.00	60.00
1759	—	5.00	15.00	30.00	60.00

KM# 968 6 PFENNIGE

Billon **Ruler:** Karl I **Rev. Legend:** DCLXXII E.F. . .

Date	Mintage	F	VF	XF	Unc
1764 IDB	—	8.00	20.00	40.00	80.00
1772 IDB	—	8.00	20.00	40.00	80.00
1775 IDB	—	8.00	20.00	40.00	80.00

KM# 1019 6 PFENNIGE

Billon **Ruler:** Karl Wilhelm Ferdinand **Obverse:** Horse **Reverse:** Denomination

Date	Mintage	F	VF	XF	Unc
1784 MC	—	15.00	35.00	75.00	125
1787 MC	—	15.00	35.00	75.00	125
1788 MC	—	15.00	35.00	75.00	125
1791 MC	—	15.00	35.00	75.00	125
1793 MC	—	15.00	35.00	75.00	125
1800 MC	—	15.00	35.00	75.00	125
1802 MC	—	15.00	35.00	75.00	125
1804 MC	—	15.00	35.00	75.00	125

KM# 763 MARIENGROSCHEN

Silver **Ruler:** August Wilhelm **Obverse:** Crowned AW monogram **Reverse:** Value I. . ., date in 4 lines

Date	Mintage	VG	F	VF	XF	Unc
1717 HH	—	10.00	20.00	42.00	75.00	—
1724 EPH	—	10.00	20.00	42.00	75.00	—
1727 EPH	—	10.00	20.00	42.00	75.00	—
1728 EPH	—	10.00	20.00	42.00	75.00	—
1730 EPH	—	10.00	20.00	42.00	75.00	—

KM# 805 MARIENGROSCHEN

Silver **Ruler:** Ludwig Rudolph **Obverse:** Crowned script LR monogram **Reverse:** Value I. . . in 4 lines

Date	Mintage	VG	F	VF	XF	Unc
1731 IAB	—	10.00	20.00	42.00	75.00	—

KM# 856 MARIENGROSCHEN

Silver **Ruler:** Ferdinand Ulbrecht II **Obverse:** Crowned cursive FA monogram **Reverse:** Value I. . . date in 4 lines

Date	Mintage	VG	F	VF	XF	Unc
1735 IAB	—	10.00	20.00	42.00	75.00	—

KM# 910 MARIENGROSCHEN

Billon **Ruler:** Karl I **Obverse:** Crowned ornate "C" **Reverse:** Value **Rev. Legend:** FVRSTL. BR. LVN. . .

Date	Mintage	F	VF	XF	Unc
1741 IBH	—	8.00	20.00	40.00	80.00
1745 IBH	—	8.00	20.00	40.00	80.00
1749 IBH	—	8.00	20.00	40.00	80.00
1752 IBH	—	8.00	20.00	40.00	80.00
1754 IBH	—	8.00	20.00	40.00	80.00
1756 IBH	—	8.00	20.00	40.00	80.00
1757 IBH	—	8.00	20.00	40.00	80.00
1758 IBH	—	8.00	20.00	40.00	80.00
1760 IBH	—	8.00	20.00	40.00	80.00
1763 IAP	—	8.00	20.00	40.00	80.00
1764 IAP	—	8.00	20.00	40.00	80.00
1765 IAP	—	8.00	20.00	40.00	80.00
1766 IAP	—	8.00	20.00	40.00	80.00
1769 IAP	—	8.00	20.00	40.00	80.00
1770 IAP	—	8.00	20.00	40.00	80.00
1771 IAP	—	8.00	20.00	40.00	80.00
1774 LCR	—	8.00	20.00	40.00	80.00
1775 LCR	—	8.00	20.00	40.00	80.00
1776 LCR	—	8.00	20.00	40.00	80.00

KM# 934 MARIENGROSCHEN

Billon **Ruler:** Karl I **Rev. Legend:** FVRSTL. LUNEB. . .

Date	Mintage	F	VF	XF	Unc
1748 EK	—	8.00	20.00	40.00	80.00
1749 EK	—	8.00	20.00	40.00	80.00
1750 EK	—	8.00	20.00	40.00	80.00
1751	—	8.00	20.00	40.00	80.00
1752	—	8.00	20.00	40.00	80.00
1755 ACB	—	8.00	20.00	40.00	80.00
1757	—	8.00	20.00	40.00	80.00
1758	—	8.00	20.00	40.00	80.00
1759	—	8.00	20.00	40.00	80.00

KM# 982 MARIENGROSCHEN

Billon **Ruler:** Karl I **Obverse:** Value and date in 4 lines **Obv. Legend:** FVRSTL. BR. LVN. LAND. MVNTZ. . . **Reverse:** Crowned C monogram

Date	Mintage	F	VF	XF	Unc
1774 LCR	—	8.00	20.00	40.00	80.00

KM# 1031 MARIENGROSCHEN

Billon **Ruler:** Karl Wilhelm Ferdinand **Obverse:** Horse rearing left **Reverse:** Denomination, date

Date	Mintage	F	VF	XF	Unc
1787 MC	—	12.00	35.00	70.00	145
1788 MC	—	10.00	20.00	45.00	60.00
1789 MC	—	10.00	20.00	45.00	60.00
1790 MC	—	10.00	20.00	45.00	60.00
1791 MC	—	10.00	20.00	45.00	60.00
1792 MC	—	10.00	20.00	45.00	60.00
1793 MC	—	10.00	20.00	45.00	60.00
1799 MC	—	10.00	20.00	45.00	60.00
1800 MC	—	10.00	20.00	45.00	60.00
1802 MC	—	10.00	20.00	45.00	60.00
1803 MC	—	10.00	20.00	45.00	60.00
1804 MC	—	10.00	20.00	55.00	75.00
1805 MC	—	8.00	15.00	25.00	40.00
1806 MC	—	10.00	20.00	40.00	50.00

KM# 647 GROSCHEN (1/24 Thaler)

Silver **Ruler:** Anton Ulrich Alone **Subject:** Death of Rudolf August **Obverse:** Bust right **Reverse:** 6-line legend with date, value 1/GG in oval below

Date	Mintage	VG	F	VF	XF	Unc
1704 HCH	—	18.00	35.00	70.00	110	—

KM# 784 GROSCHEN (1/24 Thaler)

Silver **Ruler:** August Wilhelm **Subject:** 200th Anniversary - Reformation of the City of Brunswick **Obverse:** Horse leaping left **Reverse:** 12-line legend with date, value 1. G. GR. below

Date	Mintage	VG	F	VF	XF	Unc
1728 HCH	—	25.00	50.00	80.00	125	—

KM# 568 2 MARIENGROSCHEN

Silver **Ruler:** Anton Ulrich as Joint ruler **Obverse:** Wildman holding tree with both hands to left **Reverse:** Value II. . . in 3 lines, date in legend

Date	Mintage	VG	F	VF	XF	Unc
1701	—	12.00	25.00	45.00	70.00	—
1702	—	12.00	25.00	45.00	70.00	—

KM# 648 2 MARIENGROSCHEN

Silver **Ruler:** Anton Ulrich Alone **Subject:** Death of Rudolf August **Obverse:** Bust right **Reverse:** 6-line inscription with date

Date	Mintage	VG	F	VF	XF	Unc
1704 HCH	—	20.00	45.00	80.00	125	—

KM# 649 2 MARIENGROSCHEN

Silver **Obverse:** Wildman holding tree with both hands to his left **Reverse:** Value II. . . in 3 lines, date in legend

Date	Mintage	VG	F	VF	XF	Unc
1704 ***	—	10.00	20.00	35.00	65.00	—

KM# 681 2 MARIENGROSCHEN

Silver **Ruler:** Anton Ulrich Alone **Obverse:** Value II. . . in 3 lines, date in legend **Reverse:** Wildman holding tree with both hands to his left

Date	Mintage	VG	F	VF	XF	Unc
1705 ***	—	6.00	10.00	25.00	45.00	—
1706 ***	—	6.00	10.00	25.00	45.00	—
1707 ***	—	6.00	10.00	25.00	45.00	—
1708 ***	—	6.00	10.00	25.00	45.00	—
1709 ***	—	6.00	10.00	25.00	45.00	—
1710 ***	—	6.00	10.00	25.00	45.00	—
1711 ***	—	6.00	10.00	25.00	45.00	—

KM# 712 2 MARIENGROSCHEN

Silver **Ruler:** Anton Ulrich Alone **Obverse:** FEIN. SILB added below value

Date	Mintage	VG	F	VF	XF	Unc
1711 HH	—	7.00	12.00	25.00	50.00	—
1712 HH	—	7.00	12.00	25.00	50.00	—
1713 HH	—	7.00	12.00	25.00	50.00	—
1714 HH	—	7.00	12.00	25.00	50.00	—

KM# 727 2 MARIENGROSCHEN

Silver **Ruler:** August Wilhelm **Obverse:** Value, date **Reverse:** Wildman with tree at right **Note:** Similar to KM#779 without 2 at left of wildman.

Date	Mintage	VG	F	VF	XF	Unc
1714 HH	—	12.00	25.00	40.00	65.00	—
1717 HH	—	12.00	25.00	40.00	65.00	—
1718 HH	—	12.00	25.00	40.00	65.00	—
1719 C	—	12.00	25.00	40.00	65.00	—
1720 C	—	12.00	25.00	40.00	65.00	—
1722 C	—	12.00	25.00	40.00	65.00	—
1723 EPH	—	12.00	25.00	40.00	65.00	—
1724 EPH	—	12.00	25.00	40.00	65.00	—

KM# 752 2 MARIENGROSCHEN

Silver **Ruler:** August Wilhelm **Obverse:** Crowned AW monogram **Reverse:** Horse leaping left, value 2/M.G. dvides date below

Date	Mintage	VG	F	VF	XF	Unc
1716 HH	—	8.00	16.00	30.00	55.00	—
1718 HH	—	8.00	16.00	30.00	55.00	—
1719 HH	—	8.00	16.00	30.00	55.00	—
1719 C	—	8.00	16.00	30.00	55.00	—
1720 C	—	8.00	16.00	30.00	55.00	—
1721 C	—	8.00	16.00	30.00	55.00	—
1723 EPH	—	8.00	16.00	30.00	55.00	—
1724 EPH	—	8.00	16.00	30.00	55.00	—
1725 EPH	—	8.00	16.00	30.00	55.00	—
1727 EPH	—	8.00	16.00	30.00	55.00	—
1728 EPH	—	8.00	16.00	30.00	55.00	—
1730 EPH	—	8.00	16.00	30.00	55.00	—

KM# 779 2 MARIENGROSCHEN

Silver **Ruler:** August Wilhelm **Obverse:** Value, date **Reverse:** Wildman with tree at right, 2 at left

Date	Mintage	VG	F	VF	XF	Unc
1724 EPH	—	12.00	25.00	45.00	70.00	—
1725 EPH	—	12.00	25.00	45.00	70.00	—
1726 EPH	—	12.00	25.00	45.00	70.00	—
1727 EPH	—	12.00	25.00	45.00	70.00	—
1728 EPH	—	12.00	25.00	45.00	70.00	—
1729 EPH	—	12.00	25.00	45.00	70.00	—
1730 EPH	—	12.00	25.00	45.00	70.00	—

KM# 806 2 MARIENGROSCHEN

Silver **Ruler:** Ludwig Rudolph **Obverse:** II/MARIEN/ GROSCH/ FEIN SILB, date in legend **Reverse:** Wildman, tree in left hand, value 2 to left

Date	Mintage	VG	F	VF	XF	Unc
1731 IAB	—	12.00	25.00	40.00	65.00	—
1732 IAB	—	12.00	25.00	40.00	65.00	—
1733 IAB	—	12.00	25.00	40.00	65.00	—
1734 IAB	—	12.00	25.00	40.00	65.00	—

KM# 857 2 MARIENGROSCHEN

Silver **Obverse:** Crowned cursive FA monogram **Reverse:** Horse leaping left, 2 M.G. divides date below

Date	Mintage	VG	F	VF	XF	Unc
1735 IAB	—	12.00	25.00	45.00	70.00	—

KM# 858 2 MARIENGROSCHEN

Silver **Obverse:** Value II etc. in 4 lines, date in legend **Reverse:** Wildman, tree in left hand, 2 on left

Date	Mintage	VG	F	VF	XF	Unc
1735 IAB	—	—	—	—	—	—

KM# 859 2 MARIENGROSCHEN

Silver **Ruler:** Karl I **Obverse:** Crowned ornate "C" **Reverse:** Horse rearing left

Date	Mintage	F	VF	XF	Unc
1735 IAB	—	7.00	14.00	30.00	75.00
1736 IAB	—	7.00	14.00	30.00	75.00
1737 IAB	—	7.00	14.00	30.00	75.00
1738 IAB	—	7.00	14.00	30.00	75.00
1739 IAB	—	7.00	14.00	30.00	75.00
1739 C	—	7.00	14.00	30.00	75.00
1739 IBH	—	7.00	14.00	30.00	75.00
1740 IBH	—	7.00	14.00	30.00	75.00
1741 IBH	—	7.00	14.00	30.00	75.00
1742 IBH	—	7.00	14.00	30.00	75.00
1743 IBH	—	7.00	14.00	30.00	75.00
1745 IBH	—	7.00	14.00	30.00	75.00
1747 IBH	—	7.00	14.00	30.00	75.00
1748 IBH	—	7.00	14.00	30.00	75.00
1750 IBH	—	7.00	14.00	30.00	75.00
1752 IBH	—	7.00	14.00	30.00	75.00
1755 IBH	—	7.00	14.00	30.00	75.00
1756 IBH	—	7.00	14.00	30.00	75.00
1757 IBH	—	7.00	14.00	30.00	75.00
1762 IBH	—	7.00	14.00	30.00	75.00
1765 IAP	—	7.00	14.00	30.00	75.00
1770 IAP	—	7.00	14.00	30.00	75.00
1780 CES	—	7.00	14.00	30.00	75.00

KM# 860 2 MARIENGROSCHEN

Silver **Ruler:** Karl I **Obverse:** Value within circle **Reverse:** Wildman with tree at right

Date	Mintage	F	VF	XF	Unc
1735 IAB	—	7.00	14.00	30.00	75.00
1737 IAB	—	7.00	14.00	30.00	75.00
1739 IBH	—	7.00	14.00	30.00	75.00
1740 IBH	—	7.00	14.00	30.00	75.00
1742 IBH	—	7.00	14.00	30.00	75.00
1744 IBH	—	7.00	14.00	30.00	80.00
1745 IBH	—	7.00	14.00	30.00	80.00
1748 IBH	—	7.00	14.00	30.00	80.00
1749 IBH	—	7.00	14.00	30.00	80.00
1751 IBH	—	7.00	14.00	30.00	80.00
1752 IBH	—	7.00	14.00	30.00	80.00
1753 IBH	—	7.00	14.00	30.00	80.00
1755 IBH	—	7.00	14.00	30.00	80.00
1756 IBH	—	7.00	14.00	30.00	80.00
1757 IBH	—	7.00	14.00	30.00	80.00
1758 IBH	—	7.00	14.00	30.00	80.00
1761 IBH	—	7.00	14.00	30.00	80.00
1763 IAP	—	7.00	14.00	30.00	80.00
1766 IAP	—	7.00	14.00	30.00	80.00
1770 IAP	—	7.00	14.00	30.00	80.00
1771 IAP	—	7.00	14.00	30.00	80.00
1772 IAP	—	7.00	14.00	30.00	80.00
1774 LCR	—	7.00	14.00	30.00	80.00
1776 LCR	—	7.00	14.00	30.00	80.00
1777 LCR	—	7.00	14.00	30.00	80.00
1778 LCR	—	7.00	14.00	30.00	80.00
1780 CES	—	7.00	14.00	30.00	80.00

KM# 927 2 MARIENGROSCHEN

Silver **Ruler:** Karl I **Obverse:** Crowned ornate 'C' monogram **Reverse:** Value within circle

Date	Mintage	F	VF	XF	Unc
1747 EK	—	6.00	12.00	25.00	65.00
1748 EK	—	6.00	12.00	25.00	65.00
1749 EK	—	6.00	12.00	25.00	65.00
1750 EK	—	6.00	12.00	25.00	65.00
1751 EK	—	6.00	12.00	25.00	65.00
1751	—	6.00	12.00	25.00	65.00
1752	—	6.00	12.00	25.00	65.00
1753	—	6.00	12.00	25.00	65.00
1754 ACB	—	6.00	12.00	25.00	65.00
1757 ACB	—	6.00	12.00	25.00	65.00
1758 ACB	—	6.00	12.00	25.00	65.00
1759 ACB	—	6.00	12.00	25.00	65.00

KM# 1004 2 MARIENGROSCHEN

Silver **Ruler:** Karl Wilhelm Ferdinand **Obverse:** Crowned monogram **Reverse:** Horse

Date	Mintage	F	VF	XF	Unc
1781 CES	—	7.00	15.00	35.00	80.00
1783 CES	—	7.00	15.00	35.00	80.00
1784 CRS	—	7.00	15.00	35.00	80.00
1787 C	—	7.00	15.00	35.00	80.00

KM# 1005 2 MARIENGROSCHEN

Silver **Ruler:** Karl Wilhelm Ferdinand **Obverse:** Value **Reverse:** Wildman

Date	Mintage	F	VF	XF	Unc
1781 CES	—	6.00	12.00	25.00	65.00
1782 CES	—	6.00	12.00	25.00	65.00
1783 CES	—	6.00	12.00	25.00	65.00
1784 CES	—	6.00	12.00	25.00	65.00
1786 C	—	6.00	12.00	25.00	65.00
1789 C	—	6.00	12.00	25.00	65.00

KM# 650 2 GUTE GROSCHEN

Silver **Subject:** Death of Rudolf August **Obverse:** Bust right **Reverse:** 6-line legend with date, value 2/GG in oval below

Date	Mintage	VG	F	VF	XF	Unc
1704 HCH	—	25.00	50.00	90.00	150	—

KM# 785 2 GUTE GROSCHEN

Silver **Ruler:** August Wilhelm **Subject:** 200th Anniversary of Reformation in the City of Brunswick **Obverse:** Horse leaping left **Reverse:** 12-line legend with date, value 2. G. GR. below

Date	Mintage	VG	F	VF	XF	Unc
1728 HCH	—	30.00	60.00	100	175	—

KM# 795 2 GUTE GROSCHEN

Silver **Ruler:** August Wilhelm **Subject:** 200th Anniversary of Augsburg Confession **Obverse:** Horse leaping left **Reverse:** 8-line legend with date

Date	Mintage	VG	F	VF	XF	Unc
1730 IHT	—	20.00	45.00	80.00	140	—

KM# 807 2 GUTE GROSCHEN

Silver **Ruler:** Ludwig Rudolph **Subject:** Homage of the City of Brunswick - 20 October 1731 **Obverse:** Crowned LR monogram **Reverse:** Inscription and value

Date	Mintage	VG	F	VF	XF	Unc
1731 IHT	—	20.00	45.00	80.00	140	—

KM# 833 2 GUTE GROSCHEN

Silver **Ruler:** Ludwig Rudolph **Subject:** Marriage of Karl I and Philippine Charlotte of Prussia **Obverse:** Crowned cursive mirror-image P CPC monogram **Reverse:** 6-line legend with Roman numeral date, value II GG below

Date	Mintage	VG	F	VF	XF	Unc
1733 BID	—	30.00	65.00	110	185	—

KM# 834 2 GUTE GROSCHEN

Silver **Ruler:** Ludwig Rudolph **Subject:** Marriage of Karl I's Sister, Elisabeth Christine and Friedrich II of Prussia **Obverse:** Crowned cursive mirror-image C monogram **Reverse:** 9-line legend with Roman numeral date, value II GG below

Date	Mintage	VG	F	VF	XF	Unc
1733 BIC	—	30.00	65.00	110	185	—

KM# 808 3 GROSCHEN

Silver **Ruler:** Ludwig Rudolph **Subject:** Death of August Wilhelm **Obverse:** Bust right **Reverse:** 10-line legend with date

Date	Mintage	VG	F	VF	XF	Unc
1731 IHT	—	30.00	60.00	100	175	—

KM# 651 4 MARIENGROSCHEN

Silver **Obverse:** Wildman holding tree with both hands to left, 4 left of wildman **Reverse:** Value in 3 lines, date in legend

Date	Mintage	VG	F	VF	XF	Unc
1704 ***	—	4.00	10.00	25.00	50.00	—

KM# 652 4 MARIENGROSCHEN

Silver **Ruler:** Anton Ulrich Alone **Obverse:** Horse leaping left, 4 below **Reverse:** Value IIII. . . in 3 lines, date in legend

Date	Mintage	VG	F	VF	XF	Unc
1704 HCH	—	12.00	25.00	45.00	75.00	—
1705 HCH	—	12.00	25.00	45.00	75.00	—

KM# 682 4 MARIENGROSCHEN

Silver **Ruler:** Anton Ulrich Alone **Obverse:** Value III. . . **Reverse:** Wildman holding tree with both hands, 4 to left of wildman

Date	Mintage	VG	F	VF	XF	Unc
1705 ***	—	7.00	15.00	30.00	55.00	—
1706 ***	—	7.00	15.00	30.00	55.00	—
1709 ***	—	7.00	15.00	30.00	55.00	—
1710 ***	—	7.00	15.00	30.00	55.00	—

KM# 713 4 MARIENGROSCHEN

Silver **Ruler:** Anton Ulrich Alone **Obverse:** FEIN. DILB.. added

Date	Mintage	VG	F	VF	XF	Unc
1711 HH	—	8.00	18.00	32.00	60.00	—
1712 HH	—	8.00	18.00	32.00	60.00	—
1713 HH	—	8.00	18.00	32.00	60.00	—

KM# 728 4 MARIENGROSCHEN

Silver **Ruler:** August Wilhelm **Obverse:** Value IIII. . . in 4 lines, date in legend **Reverse:** Wildman, tree in left hand, 4 left of wildman

Date	Mintage	VG	F	VF	XF	Unc
1714 HH	—	10.00	20.00	40.00	70.00	—
1715 HH	—	10.00	20.00	40.00	70.00	—
1717 HH	—	10.00	20.00	40.00	70.00	—
1718 HH	—	10.00	20.00	40.00	70.00	—
1719 C	—	10.00	20.00	40.00	70.00	—
1721 C	—	10.00	20.00	40.00	70.00	—
1723 EPH	—	10.00	20.00	40.00	70.00	—
1724 EPH	—	10.00	20.00	40.00	70.00	—
1725 EPH	—	10.00	20.00	40.00	70.00	—

Date	Mintage	VG	F	VF	XF	Unc
1727 EPH	—	10.00	20.00	40.00	70.00	—
1729 EPH	—	10.00	20.00	40.00	70.00	—
1730 EPH	—	10.00	20.00	40.00	70.00	—
1731 EPH	—	10.00	20.00	40.00	70.00	—
1732 EPH	—	10.00	20.00	40.00	70.00	—

KM# 764 4 MARIENGROSCHEN

Silver **Ruler:** August Wilhelm **Obverse:** Crowned AW monogram **Reverse:** Horse leaping left, value 4/M.G. divides date below

Date	Mintage	VG	F	VF	XF	Unc
1717 HH	—	10.00	20.00	45.00	70.00	—
1719 C	—	10.00	20.00	45.00	70.00	—
1721 C	—	10.00	20.00	45.00	70.00	—
1723 EPH	—	10.00	20.00	45.00	70.00	—

KM# 809 4 MARIENGROSCHEN

Silver **Ruler:** Ludwig Rudolph **Obverse:** IIII/MARIEN/GROSCH/ FEIN SILB, date in legend **Reverse:** Wildman, tree in left hand, value 4 to left

Date	Mintage	VG	F	VF	XF	Unc
1731 IAB	—	25.00	55.00	90.00	165	—
1732 IAB	—	25.00	55.00	90.00	165	—
1733 IAB	—	25.00	55.00	90.00	165	—
1734 IAB	—	25.00	55.00	90.00	165	—
1735 IAB	—	25.00	55.00	90.00	165	—

KM# 861 4 MARIENGROSCHEN

Silver **Ruler:** Ferdinand Ulbrecht II **Obverse:** Crowned cursive FA monogram **Reverse:** Horse leaping left, $.M.G. divides date below

Date	Mintage	VF	F	VF	XF	Unc
1735 IAB	—	15.00	30.00	55.00	95.00	—

KM# 862 4 MARIENGROSCHEN

Silver **Obverse:** Value IIII. . . in 4 lines, date in legend **Reverse:** Wildman, tree in left hand, 4 to left

Date	Mintage	VG	F	VF	XF	Unc
1735 IAB	—	20.00	40.00	75.00	120	—

KM# 863 4 MARIENGROSCHEN

Silver **Obverse:** Value in 4 lines, date in legend **Reverse:** Wildman, tree in right hand (die of George II) **Note:** Mule.

Date	Mintage	VG	F	VF	XF	Unc
1735 IAB Rare	—	—	—	—	—	—

KM# 864 4 MARIENGROSCHEN

Silver **Ruler:** Karl I **Obverse:** Value in 4 lines, date in legend **Reverse:** Wildman with tree in left hand

Date	Mintage	F	VF	XF	Unc
1735 IAB	—	10.00	25.00	50.00	100
1736 IAB		10.00	25.00	50.00	100
1737 IAB	—	10.00	25.00	50.00	100
1738 IAB	—	10.00	25.00	50.00	100
1739 IAB	—	10.00	25.00	50.00	100
1740 IBH	—	10.00	25.00	50.00	100
1741 IBH	—	10.00	25.00	50.00	100
1742 IBH	—	10.00	25.00	50.00	100
1743 IBH	—	10.00	25.00	50.00	100
1745 IBH	—	10.00	25.00	50.00	100
1748 IBH	—	10.00	25.00	50.00	100
1749 IBH	—	10.00	25.00	50.00	100
1750 IBH	—	10.00	25.00	50.00	100
1752 IBH	—	10.00	25.00	50.00	100
1754 IBH	—	10.00	25.00	50.00	100
1756 IBH	—	10.00	25.00	50.00	100
1759 IBH	—	10.00	25.00	50.00	100
1762 IBH	—	10.00	25.00	50.00	100
1763 IAP	—	10.00	25.00	50.00	100
1764 IAP	—	10.00	25.00	50.00	100
1767 IAP	—	10.00	25.00	50.00	100
1768 IAP	—	10.00	25.00	50.00	100
1770 IAP	—	10.00	25.00	50.00	100
1771 IAP	—	10.00	25.00	50.00	100
1772 IAP	—	10.00	25.00	50.00	100
1773 IAP	—	10.00	25.00	50.00	100
1773 LCR	—	10.00	25.00	50.00	100
1775 LCR	—	10.00	25.00	50.00	100
1776 LCR	—	10.00	25.00	50.00	100
1777 LCR	—	10.00	25.00	50.00	100
1778 LCR	—	10.00	25.00	50.00	100
1779 C	—	10.00	25.00	50.00	100
1780 CES	—	10.00	25.00	50.00	100

KM# 894 4 MARIENGROSCHEN

Silver **Ruler:** Karl I **Obverse:** Crowned C monogram **Reverse:** Horse leaping left

Date	Mintage	F	VF	XF	Unc
1736 IAB	—	12.00	30.00	60.00	125
1738 IAB	—	12.00	30.00	60.00	125
1739 IAB	—	12.00	30.00	60.00	125
1739 C	—	12.00	30.00	60.00	125
1739 IBH	—	12.00	30.00	60.00	125
1741 IBH	—	12.00	30.00	60.00	125
1742 IBH	—	12.00	30.00	60.00	125
1743 IBH	—	12.00	30.00	60.00	125
1747 IBH	—	12.00	30.00	60.00	125
1749 IBH	—	12.00	30.00	60.00	125
1751 IBH	—	12.00	30.00	60.00	125
1752 IBH	—	12.00	30.00	60.00	125
1753 IBH	—	12.00	30.00	60.00	125
1755 IBH	—	12.00	30.00	60.00	125
1758 IBH	—	12.00	30.00	60.00	125
1760 IBH	—	12.00	30.00	60.00	125
1762 IBH	—	12.00	30.00	60.00	125
1765 IAP	—	12.00	30.00	60.00	125
1768 IAP	—	12.00	30.00	60.00	125
1769 IAP	—	12.00	30.00	60.00	125
1770 IAP	—	12.00	30.00	60.00	125
1772 IAP	—	12.00	30.00	60.00	125
1774 LCR	—	12.00	30.00	60.00	125
1775 LCR	—	12.00	30.00	60.00	125
1778 LCR	—	12.00	30.00	60.00	125
1780 CES	—	12.00	30.00	60.00	125

KM# 1006 4 MARIENGROSCHEN

Silver **Ruler:** Karl Wilhelm Ferdinand **Obverse:** Crowned CW monogram **Reverse:** Horse leaping left

Date	Mintage	F	VF	XF	Unc
1781 CES	—	8.00	20.00	40.00	80.00
1782 CES	—	8.00	20.00	40.00	80.00
1783 CES	—	8.00	20.00	40.00	80.00
1784 CES	—	8.00	20.00	40.00	80.00

KM# 1007 4 MARIENGROSCHEN

Silver **Ruler:** Karl Wilhelm Ferdinand **Obverse:** Value in 4 lines, date in legend **Reverse:** Wildman with tree in left hand

Date	Mintage	F	VF	XF	Unc
1781 CES	—	6.00	18.00	35.00	65.00
1782 CES	—	6.00	18.00	35.00	65.00
1783 CES	—	6.00	18.00	35.00	65.00
1784 CES	—	6.00	18.00	35.00	65.00
1785 CES	—	6.00	18.00	35.00	65.00
1786 C	—	6.00	18.00	35.00	65.00

KM# 1028 4 MARIENGROSCHEN

Silver **Ruler:** Karl Wilhelm Ferdinand **Obverse:** Date in center legend **Reverse:** Wildman with tree in left hand

Date	Mintage	F	VF	XF	Unc
1787 C	—	8.00	20.00	40.00	80.00
1788 C	—	8.00	20.00	40.00	80.00
1789 C	—	8.00	20.00	40.00	80.00

KM# 653 6 MARIENGROSCHEN (1/6 Thaler)

Silver **Ruler:** Anton Ulrich Alone **Obverse:** Wildman **Reverse:** Value VI. . ., date in 4 lines **Note:** Similar to KM#569.

Date	Mintage	VG	F	VF	XF	Unc
1704 ***	—	15.00	30.00	50.00	85.00	—
1705 ***	—	15.00	30.00	50.00	85.00	—

KM# 683 6 MARIENGROSCHEN (1/6 Thaler)

Silver **Ruler:** Anton Ulrich Alone **Obverse:** Value VI. . . in 3 lines, date in legend **Reverse:** Wildman hodling tree with both hands, 6 to left of wildman

Date	Mintage	VG	F	VF	XF	Unc
1705 ***	—	8.00	18.00	32.00	65.00	—
1706 ***	—	8.00	18.00	32.00	65.00	—
1707 ***	—	8.00	18.00	32.00	65.00	—
1708 ***	—	8.00	18.00	32.00	65.00	—
1709 ***	—	8.00	18.00	32.00	65.00	—
1710 ***	—	8.00	18.00	32.00	65.00	—
1711 ***	—	8.00	18.00	32.00	65.00	—

KM# 714 6 MARIENGROSCHEN (1/6 Thaler)

Silver **Ruler:** Anton Ulrich Alone **Obverse:** FEIN. SILB. added

Date	Mintage	VG	F	VF	XF	Unc
1711 HH	—	10.00	20.00	35.00	65.00	—
1712 HH	—	10.00	20.00	35.00	65.00	—
1713 HH	—	10.00	20.00	35.00	65.00	—
1714 HH	—	10.00	20.00	35.00	65.00	—

KM# 729 6 MARIENGROSCHEN (1/6 Thaler)

Silver **Ruler:** August Wilhelm **Obverse:** Value in 4 lines, date in legend **Reverse:** Wildman with tree in left hand **Note:** Similar to KM#753 but without 6 at left of wildman.

Date	Mintage	VG	F	VF	XF	Unc
1714 HH	—	15.00	30.00	50.00	85.00	—
1715 HH	—	15.00	30.00	50.00	85.00	—

KM# 753 6 MARIENGROSCHEN (1/6 Thaler)

Silver **Ruler:** August Wilhelm **Obverse:** Value in 4 lines, date in legend **Reverse:** Wildman with tree in left hand, 6 at left

Date	Mintage	VG	F	VF	XF	Unc
1716 HH	—	15.00	30.00	50.00	85.00	—
1717 HH	—	15.00	30.00	50.00	85.00	—
1718 HH	—	15.00	30.00	50.00	85.00	—
1719 C	—	15.00	30.00	50.00	85.00	—
1720 C	—	15.00	30.00	50.00	85.00	—
1721 C	—	15.00	30.00	50.00	85.00	—
1722 C	—	15.00	30.00	50.00	85.00	—
1723 EPH	—	15.00	30.00	50.00	85.00	—
1724 EPH	—	15.00	30.00	50.00	85.00	—
1725 EPH	—	15.00	30.00	50.00	85.00	—
1726 EPH	—	15.00	30.00	50.00	85.00	—
1727 EPH	—	15.00	30.00	50.00	85.00	—
1728 EPH	—	15.00	30.00	50.00	85.00	—
1729 EPH	—	15.00	30.00	50.00	85.00	—
1730 EPH	—	15.00	30.00	50.00	85.00	—

KM# 810 6 MARIENGROSCHEN (1/6 Thaler)

Silver **Ruler:** Ludwig Rudolph **Obverse:** Value in 4 lines, date in legend **Reverse:** Wildman with tree in left hand, 6 at left

Date	Mintage	VG	F	VF	XF	Unc
1731 IAB	—	20.00	40.00	75.00	120	—
1732 IAB	—	20.00	40.00	75.00	120	—
1733 IAB	—	20.00	40.00	75.00	120	—
1734 IAB	—	20.00	40.00	75.00	120	—
1735 IAB	—	20.00	40.00	75.00	120	—
1737 IAB	—	20.00	40.00	75.00	120	—

KM# 872 6 MARIENGROSCHEN (1/6 Thaler)

Silver **Ruler:** Karl I **Obverse:** Value in 4 lines, date in legend **Reverse:** Wildman with tree in left hand, 6 at left

Date	Mintage	VG	F	VF	XF	Unc
1735 IAB	—	12.00	25.00	45.00	80.00	—
1736 IAB	—	12.00	25.00	45.00	80.00	—
1737 IAB	—	12.00	25.00	45.00	80.00	—
1738 IAB	—	12.00	25.00	45.00	80.00	—
1739 C	—	12.00	25.00	45.00	80.00	—
1739 IBH	—	12.00	25.00	45.00	80.00	—
1740 IBH	—	12.00	25.00	45.00	80.00	—
1741 IBH	—	12.00	25.00	45.00	80.00	—
1742 IBH	—	12.00	25.00	45.00	80.00	—
1744 IBH	—	12.00	25.00	45.00	80.00	—

Date	Mintage	VG	F	VF	XF	Unc
1746 IBH	—	12.00	25.00	45.00	80.00	—
1748 IBH	—	12.00	25.00	45.00	80.00	—
1749 IBH	—	12.00	25.00	45.00	80.00	—
1750 IBH	—	12.00	25.00	45.00	80.00	—
1751 IBH	—	12.00	25.00	45.00	80.00	—
1753 IBH	—	12.00	25.00	45.00	80.00	—
1754 IBH	—	12.00	25.00	45.00	80.00	—
1755 IBH	—	12.00	25.00	45.00	80.00	—
1756 IBH	—	12.00	25.00	45.00	80.00	—
1757 IBH	—	12.00	25.00	45.00	80.00	—
1761 IBH	—	12.00	25.00	45.00	80.00	—
1763 IAP	—	12.00	25.00	45.00	80.00	—
1764 IAP	—	12.00	25.00	45.00	80.00	—
1765 IAP	—	12.00	25.00	45.00	80.00	—
1767/6 IAP	—	12.00	25.00	45.00	80.00	—
1767 IAP	—	12.00	25.00	45.00	80.00	—
1768 IAP	—	12.00	25.00	45.00	80.00	—
1769 IAP	—	12.00	25.00	45.00	80.00	—
1770 IAP	—	12.00	25.00	45.00	80.00	—
1771 IAP	—	12.00	25.00	45.00	80.00	—
1772 IAP	—	12.00	25.00	45.00	80.00	—
1773 LCR	—	12.00	25.00	45.00	80.00	—
1774 LCR	—	12.00	25.00	45.00	80.00	—
1775 LCR	—	12.00	25.00	45.00	80.00	—
1776 LCR	—	12.00	25.00	45.00	80.00	—
1777 LCR	—	12.00	25.00	45.00	80.00	—
1778 LCR	—	12.00	25.00	45.00	80.00	—
1779 C	—	12.00	25.00	45.00	80.00	—
1780 CES	—	12.00	25.00	45.00	80.00	—

KM# 865 6 MARIENGROSCHEN (1/6 Thaler)

Silver **Ruler:** Ferdinand Ulbrecht II **Note:** Ferdinand Albrecht II.

Date	Mintage	VG	F	VF	XF	Unc
1735 IAB	—	20.00	45.00	80.00	130	—

KM# 1008 6 MARIENGROSCHEN (1/6 Thaler)

Silver **Ruler:** Karl Wilhelm Ferdinand **Obverse:** Value, mint mark **Reverse:** Wildman

Date	Mintage	F	VF	XF	Unc
1781 CES	—	12.00	30.00	60.00	125
1782 CES	—	12.00	30.00	60.00	125
1783 CES	—	12.00	30.00	60.00	125
1784 CES	—	12.00	30.00	60.00	125

KM# 1024 6 MARIENGROSCHEN (1/6 Thaler)

Silver **Ruler:** Karl Wilhelm Ferdinand **Reverse:** Wildman, mint mark

Date	Mintage	F	VF	XF	Unc
1785 CES	—	12.00	30.00	60.00	125
1785 C	—	12.00	30.00	60.00	125
1786 C	—	12.00	30.00	60.00	125
1787 C	—	12.00	30.00	60.00	125
1788 C	—	12.00	30.00	60.00	125

KM# 947 8 GUTE GROSCHEN

Silver **Ruler:** Karl I **Obverse:** Crowned arms **Reverse:** Value, date

Date	Mintage	F	VF	XF	Unc
1756 ACB	—	12.00	30.00	65.00	175
1757 ACB	—	12.00	30.00	65.00	175
1758 ACB	—	12.00	30.00	65.00	175
1759 ACB	—	12.00	30.00	65.00	175

KM# 949 8 GUTE GROSCHEN

Silver **Ruler:** Karl I **Obverse:** Horse left **Reverse:** Value, date

Date	Mintage	F	VF	XF	Unc
1758 ACB	—	10.00	25.00	55.00	150
1759 ACB	—	10.00	25.00	55.00	150
1759 ACB	—	10.00	25.00	55.00	150

KM# 951 8 GUTE GROSCHEN

Silver **Ruler:** Karl I **Obverse:** Crowned ornate monogram **Reverse:** Value, date

Date	Mintage	F	VF	XF	Unc
1759 ACB	—	10.00	30.00	65.00	175
1760 IDB	—	10.00	25.00	55.00	150
1761 IDB	—	10.00	25.00	55.00	150
1762 IDB	—	10.00	25.00	55.00	150

KM# 1017 8 GUTE GROSCHEN

Silver **Ruler:** Karl Wilhelm Ferdinand **Obverse:** Crowned complex arms within ornate shield **Obv. Legend:** CAROLVS GVIL • FERD • D • G • DVX BRVNSV • ET • LVN * **Reverse:** Value, date

Date	Mintage	F	VF	XF	Unc
1783 MC	—	15.00	40.00	85.00	220
1784 MC	—	15.00	40.00	85.00	220

KM# 1026 8 GUTE GROSCHEN

Silver **Ruler:** Karl Wilhelm Ferdinand **Obverse:** Crowned and mantled arms **Reverse:** Denomination, date

Date	Mintage	F	VF	XF	Unc
1786 MC	—	15.00	35.00	80.00	200
1787 MC	—	15.00	35.00	80.00	200
1788 MC	—	15.00	35.00	80.00	200
1791 MC	—	15.00	35.00	80.00	200
1793 MC	—	15.00	35.00	80.00	200
1794 MC	—	15.00	35.00	80.00	200
1796 MC	—	15.00	35.00	80.00	200
1797 MC	—	15.00	35.00	80.00	200
1798 MC	—	15.00	35.00	80.00	200
1799 MC	—	15.00	35.00	80.00	200
1801 MC	—	15.00	35.00	80.00	140
1803 MC	—	15.00	35.00	75.00	130
1804 MC	—	15.00	35.00	80.00	140
1805 MC	—	15.00	35.00	90.00	150

KM# 570 12 MARIENGROSCHEN (1/3 Thaler)

Silver **Ruler:** Anton Ulrich as Joint ruler **Obverse:** Wildman holding tree with two hands at left, 12 at left of wildman **Reverse:** Value XII...in 3 lines, date in legend

Date	Mintage	VG	F	VF	XF	Unc
1700	—	18.00	35.00	55.00	100	—
1701	—	18.00	35.00	55.00	100	—
1702	—	18.00	35.00	55.00	100	—
1703	—	18.00	35.00	55.00	100	—

KM# 654 12 MARIENGROSCHEN (1/3 Thaler)

Silver **Ruler:** Anton Ulrich Alone **Obverse:** Wildman with tree held in both hands at right, value at left **Reverse:** Value, date in legend **Note:** Similar to KM#570.

Date	Mintage	VG	F	VF	XF	Unc
1704 ***	—	18.00	35.00	55.00	100	—
1705	—	18.00	35.00	55.00	100	—

KM# 684 12 MARIENGROSCHEN (1/3 Thaler)

Silver **Ruler:** Anton Ulrich Alone **Obverse:** Value, date in legend **Reverse:** Wildman with tree held in both hands at right, value at left

Date	Mintage	VG	F	VF	XF	Unc
1705 ***	—	15.00	25.00	45.00	85.00	—
1706 ***	—	15.00	25.00	45.00	85.00	—
1707 ***	—	15.00	25.00	45.00	85.00	—
1708 ***	—	15.00	25.00	45.00	85.00	—
1709 ***	—	15.00	25.00	45.00	85.00	—
1710 ***	—	15.00	25.00	45.00	85.00	—
1711 ***	—	15.00	25.00	45.00	85.00	—
1711 *C*	—	15.00	25.00	45.00	85.00	—

KM# 715 12 MARIENGROSCHEN (1/3 Thaler)

Silver **Ruler:** Anton Ulrich Alone **Obverse:** FEIN. SILB. added

Date	Mintage	VG	F	VF	XF	Unc
1711 HH	—	20.00	40.00	60.00	120	—
1712 HH	—	20.00	40.00	60.00	120	—
1713 HH	—	20.00	40.00	60.00	120	—
1714 HH	—	20.00	40.00	60.00	120	—

KM# 730 12 MARIENGROSCHEN (1/3 Thaler)

Silver **Ruler:** August Wilhelm **Obverse:** Value within inner circle, date in legend **Reverse:** Wildman with tree in left hand, value at left

Date	Mintage	VG	F	VF	XF	Unc
1714 HH	—	20.00	45.00	65.00	125	—
1715 HH	—	20.00	45.00	65.00	125	—
1716 HH	—	20.00	45.00	65.00	125	—
1717 HH	—	20.00	45.00	65.00	125	—
1718 HH	—	20.00	45.00	65.00	125	—
1719 HH	—	20.00	45.00	65.00	125	—
1719 C	—	20.00	45.00	65.00	125	—
1720 C	—	20.00	45.00	65.00	125	—
1721 C	—	20.00	45.00	65.00	125	—
1722 C	—	20.00	45.00	65.00	125	—
1723 C	—	20.00	45.00	65.00	125	—
1723 EPH	—	20.00	45.00	65.00	125	—
1724 EPH	—	20.00	45.00	65.00	125	—
1725 EPH	—	20.00	45.00	65.00	125	—
1726 EPH	—	20.00	45.00	65.00	125	—
1727 EPH	—	20.00	45.00	65.00	125	—
1728 EPH	—	20.00	45.00	65.00	125	—
1729 EPH	—	20.00	45.00	65.00	125	—
1731 EPH	—	20.00	45.00	65.00	125	—

KM# 811 12 MARIENGROSCHEN (1/3 Thaler)

Silver **Ruler:** Ludwig Rudolph **Obverse:** Value within inner circle, date in legend **Reverse:** Wildman with tree in left hand, value at left

Date	Mintage	VG	F	VF	XF	Unc
1731 IAB	—	18.00	35.00	55.00	95.00	—
1732 IAB	—	18.00	35.00	55.00	95.00	—
1733 IAB	—	18.00	35.00	55.00	95.00	—
1734 IAB	—	18.00	35.00	55.00	95.00	—
1735 IAB	—	18.00	35.00	55.00	95.00	—

KM# 866 12 MARIENGROSCHEN (1/3 Thaler)

Silver **Ruler:** Ferdinand Ulbrecht II

Date	Mintage	VG	F	VF	XF	Unc
1735 IAB	—	25.00	50.00	100	200	—

KM# 867 12 MARIENGROSCHEN (1/3 Thaler)
Silver **Ruler:** Karl I **Obverse:** Value within inner circle, date in legend **Reverse:** Wildman with tree in left hand

Date	Mintage	F	VF	XF	Unc
1735 IAB	—	10.00	40.00	80.00	175
1736 IAB	—	10.00	40.00	80.00	175
1737 IAB	—	10.00	40.00	80.00	175
1738 IAB	—	10.00	40.00	80.00	175
1739 C	—	10.00	40.00	80.00	175
1739 IBH	—	10.00	40.00	80.00	175
1740 IBH	—	10.00	40.00	80.00	175
1741 IBH	—	10.00	40.00	80.00	175
1742 IBH	—	15.00	50.00	100	200
1743 IBH	—	10.00	40.00	80.00	175
1744 IBH	—	10.00	40.00	80.00	175
1745 IBH	—	10.00	40.00	80.00	175
1746 IBH	—	10.00	40.00	80.00	175
1747 IBH	—	10.00	40.00	80.00	175
1748 IBH	—	10.00	40.00	80.00	175
1749 IBH	—	10.00	40.00	80.00	175
1752 IBH	—	10.00	40.00	80.00	175
1753 IBH	—	15.00	50.00	100	200
1754 IBH	—	10.00	40.00	80.00	175
1755 IBH	—	10.00	40.00	80.00	175
1756 IBH	—	10.00	40.00	80.00	175
1757 IBH	—	10.00	40.00	80.00	175
1758 IBH	—	10.00	40.00	80.00	175
1759 IBH	—	10.00	40.00	80.00	175
1760 IBH	—	10.00	40.00	80.00	175
1761 IBH	—	10.00	40.00	80.00	175
1762 IBH	—	10.00	40.00	80.00	175
1763 IAP	—	10.00	40.00	80.00	175
1764 IAP	—	10.00	40.00	80.00	175
1765 IAP	—	10.00	40.00	80.00	175
1766 IAP	—	10.00	40.00	80.00	175
1768 IAP	—	10.00	40.00	80.00	175
1769 IAP	—	10.00	40.00	80.00	175
1770 IAP	—	10.00	40.00	80.00	175
1771 IAP	—	10.00	40.00	80.00	175
1772 IAP	—	10.00	40.00	80.00	175
1773 IAP	—	10.00	40.00	80.00	175
1773 LCR	—	10.00	40.00	80.00	175
1774 LCR	—	10.00	40.00	80.00	175
1775 LCR	—	10.00	40.00	80.00	175
1776 LCR	—	15.00	50.00	100	200
1777 LCR	—	10.00	40.00	80.00	175
1778 LCR	—	10.00	40.00	80.00	175
1779 C	—	10.00	40.00	80.00	175
1780 CES	—	30.00	80.00	150	300

KM# 1009 12 MARIENGROSCHEN (1/3 Thaler)
Silver **Ruler:** Karl Wilhelm Ferdinand **Obverse:** Value, date in circular legend **Reverse:** Wildman

Date	Mintage	F	VF	XF	Unc
1781 CES	—	20.00	50.00	100	225
1782 CES	—	20.00	50.00	100	225
1783 CES	—	20.00	50.00	100	225
1784 CES	—	20.00	50.00	100	225
1785 CES	—	20.00	50.00	100	225

KM# 1027 12 MARIENGROSCHEN (1/3 Thaler)
Silver **Ruler:** Karl Wilhelm Ferdinand **Obverse:** Date and mint mark in center inscription

Date	Mintage	F	VF	XF	Unc
1786 C	—	20.00	50.00	100	225

KM# 1029 12 MARIENGROSCHEN (1/3 Thaler)
Silver **Ruler:** Karl Wilhelm Ferdinand **Reverse:** Mint mark in exergue

Date	Mintage	F	VF	XF	Unc
1787 C	—	20.00	50.00	100	225
1788 C	—	20.00	50.00	100	225
1789 C	—	20.00	50.00	100	225

KM# 998 16 GUTE GROSCHEN
Silver **Ruler:** Karl Wilhelm Ferdinand **Obverse:** Crowned complex arms **Reverse:** Value, date

Date	Mintage	F	VF	XF	Unc
1780 MC	—	20.00	40.00	100	220
1781 MC	—	20.00	40.00	100	220
1782 MC	—	20.00	40.00	100	220
1783 MC	—	20.00	40.00	100	220
1784 MC	—	20.00	40.00	100	220

KM# 1020 16 GUTE GROSCHEN
Silver **Ruler:** Karl Wilhelm Ferdinand **Obverse:** Arms **Reverse:** Denomination

Date	Mintage	F	VF	XF	Unc
1784 MC	—	18.00	40.00	100	220
1785 MC	—	18.00	40.00	100	220
1786 MC	—	18.00	40.00	100	220
1787 MC	—	18.00	40.00	100	220
1788 MC	—	18.00	40.00	100	220
1789 MC	—	18.00	40.00	100	220
1790 MC	—	18.00	40.00	100	220
1791 MC	—	18.00	40.00	100	220
1792 MC	—	18.00	40.00	100	220
1793 MC	—	18.00	40.00	100	220
1794 MC	—	18.00	40.00	100	220
1795 MC	—	18.00	40.00	100	220
1796 MC	—	18.00	40.00	100	220
1797 MC	—	18.00	40.00	100	220
1798 MC	—	18.00	40.00	100	220
1799 MC	—	18.00	40.00	100	220
1801 MC	—	35.00	85.00	150	220
1802 MC	—	35.00	160	150	220
Note: Removed per Means, 2004					
1803 MC	—	60.00	160	300	425
1804 MC	—	55.00	150	275	400
1805 MC	—	35.00	100	150	250

KM# 559 24 MARIENGROSCHEN (2/3 Thaler)
Silver **Ruler:** Anton Ulrich as Joint ruler **Obverse:** Wildman with tree in both hands at right, value at left **Reverse:** Value within inner circle, date in legend

Date	Mintage	VG	F	VF	XF	Unc
1700	—	25.00	50.00	75.00	150	—
1701	—	25.00	50.00	75.00	150	—
1702	—	25.00	50.00	75.00	150	—
1703	—	25.00	50.00	75.00	150	—
1704	—	25.00	50.00	75.00	150	—

KM# 615 24 MARIENGROSCHEN (2/3 Thaler)
Silver **Ruler:** Anton Ulrich as Joint ruler **Obverse:** Horse leaping left, 2/3 in oval below

Date	Mintage	VG	F	VF	XF	Unc
1700 HCH	—	30.00	65.00	115	200	—
1701 HCH	—	30.00	65.00	115	200	—
1702 HCH	—	30.00	65.00	115	200	—
1703 HCH	—	30.00	65.00	115	200	—
1704 HCH	—	30.00	65.00	115	200	—
1705 HCH	—	30.00	65.00	115	200	—

KM# 655 24 MARIENGROSCHEN (2/3 Thaler)
Silver **Obverse:** Horse leaping left, value 2/3 below **Reverse:** XXIIII. . . in 3 lines, date in legend

Date	Mintage	VG	F	VF	XF	Unc
1704 HCH	—	35.00	75.00	135	225	—

KM# 656 24 MARIENGROSCHEN (2/3 Thaler)
Silver **Ruler:** Anton Ulrich Alone **Obverse:** Wildman holding tree with both hands to his left, 24 on left **Reverse:** 24. . . V. FEIN. SILB., date in legend

Date	Mintage	VG	F	VF	XF	Unc
1704 ***	—	25.00	50.00	75.00	160	—
1705 ***	—	25.00	50.00	75.00	160	—

KM# 685 24 MARIENGROSCHEN (2/3 Thaler)
Silver **Ruler:** Anton Ulrich Alone **Obverse:** Value within inner circle, date in legend **Reverse:** Wildman with tree held in both hands, value at left

Date	Mintage	VG	F	VF	XF	Unc
1705 ***	—	25.00	50.00	75.00	160	—
1706 ***	—	25.00	50.00	75.00	160	—
1707 ***	—	25.00	50.00	75.00	160	—
1708 ***	—	25.00	50.00	75.00	160	—
1709 ***	—	25.00	50.00	75.00	160	—
1710 ***	—	25.00	50.00	75.00	160	—
1711 ***	—	25.00	50.00	75.00	160	—
1711	—	25.00	50.00	75.00	160	—
1711 *C*	—	25.00	50.00	75.00	160	—
1711 HH	—	25.00	50.00	75.00	160	—
1712 HH	—	25.00	50.00	75.00	160	—
1713 HH	—	25.00	50.00	75.00	160	—
1714 HH	—	25.00	50.00	75.00	160	—
Note: Varieties exist						

KM# 731 24 MARIENGROSCHEN (2/3 Thaler)
Silver **Ruler:** August Wilhelm **Obverse:** Value within inner circle, date in legend **Reverse:** Wildman with tree in left hand, value at left

Date	Mintage	VG	F	VF	XF	Unc
1714 HH	—	25.00	50.00	85.00	175	—
1715 HH	—	25.00	50.00	85.00	175	—
1716 HH	—	25.00	50.00	85.00	175	—
1717 HH	—	25.00	50.00	85.00	175	—
1718 HH	—	25.00	50.00	85.00	175	—
1719 C	—	25.00	50.00	85.00	175	—
1720 C	—	25.00	50.00	85.00	175	—
1721 C	—	25.00	50.00	85.00	175	—

Date	Mintage	VG	F	VF	XF	Unc
1722 C	—	25.00	50.00	85.00	175	—
1723 C	—	25.00	50.00	85.00	175	—
1723 EPH	—	25.00	50.00	85.00	175	—
1724 EPH	—	25.00	50.00	85.00	175	—
1725 EPH	—	25.00	50.00	85.00	175	—
1726 EPH	—	25.00	50.00	85.00	175	—
1727 EPH	—	25.00	50.00	85.00	175	—
1728 EPH	—	25.00	50.00	85.00	175	—
1729 EPH	—	25.00	50.00	85.00	175	—
1730 EPH	—	25.00	50.00	85.00	175	—

KM# A812 24 MARIENGROSCHEN (2/3 Thaler)

Silver **Ruler:** August Wilhelm

Date	Mintage	VG	F	VF	XF	Unc
1715 HCH	—	30.00	65.00	120	200	—
1720 HCH	—	30.00	65.00	120	200	—
1724 HCH	—	30.00	65.00	120	200	—

KM# 812 24 MARIENGROSCHEN (2/3 Thaler)

Silver **Ruler:** Ludwig Rudolph **Obverse:** Value within inner circle, date in legend **Reverse:** Wildman with tree in left hand, value at left

Date	Mintage	VG	F	VF	XF	Unc
1731 C	—	25.00	45.00	70.00	150	—
1731 IAB	—	25.00	45.00	70.00	150	—
1732 IAB	—	25.00	45.00	70.00	150	—
1733 IAB	—	25.00	45.00	70.00	150	—
1734 IAB	—	25.00	45.00	70.00	150	—
1735 IAB	—	25.00	45.00	70.00	150	—

KM# 813 24 MARIENGROSCHEN (2/3 Thaler)

Silver **Ruler:** Ludwig Rudolph **Obverse:** Horse leaping left, value in oval below

Date	Mintage	VG	F	VF	XF	Unc
1731 C	—	30.00	65.00	120	200	—
1731 IAB	—	30.00	65.00	120	200	—
1734 IAB	—	30.00	65.00	120	200	—

KM# 869 24 MARIENGROSCHEN (2/3 Thaler)

Silver **Ruler:** Ferdinand Ulbrecht II **Obverse:** Value within inner circle, date in legend **Reverse:** Wildman with tree in left hand, value at left

Date	Mintage	VG	F	VF	XF	Unc
1735 IAB	—	25.00	50.00	85.00	175	—

KM# 868 24 MARIENGROSCHEN (2/3 Thaler)

Silver **Obverse:** Horse leaping left, value in oval below **Note:** Similar to KM#813.

Date	Mintage	VG	F	VF	XF	Unc
1735 IAB	—	40.00	80.00	140	250	—

KM# 870 24 MARIENGROSCHEN (2/3 Thaler)

Silver **Ruler:** Karl I **Obverse:** Value within inner circle, date in legend **Reverse:** Wildman with tree in left hand

Date	Mintage	F	VF	XF	Unc
1735 IAB	—	30.00	60.00	100	200
1736 IAB	—	30.00	60.00	100	200
1737 IAB	—	30.00	60.00	100	200
1738 IAB	—	30.00	60.00	100	200
1739 IAB	—	30.00	60.00	100	200
1739 IBH	—	30.00	60.00	100	200
1739 C	—	30.00	60.00	100	200
1740 IBH	—	30.00	60.00	100	200
1741 IBH	—	30.00	60.00	100	200
1742 IBH	—	30.00	60.00	100	200
1743 IBH	—	30.00	60.00	100	200
1744 IBH	—	30.00	60.00	100	200
1745 IBH	—	30.00	60.00	100	200
1746 IBH	—	30.00	60.00	100	200
1747 IBH	—	30.00	60.00	100	200
1748 IBH	—	30.00	60.00	100	200
1749 IBH	—	30.00	60.00	100	200
1750 IBH	—	30.00	60.00	100	200
1751 IBH	—	40.00	70.00	110	220
1752 IBH	—	30.00	60.00	100	200
1753 IBH	—	30.00	60.00	100	200
1754 IBH	—	30.00	60.00	100	200
1755 IBH	—	30.00	60.00	100	200
1756 IBH	—	30.00	60.00	100	200
1757 IBH	—	30.00	60.00	100	200
1758 IBH	—	30.00	60.00	100	200
1759 IBH	—	30.00	60.00	100	200
1760 IBH	—	30.00	60.00	100	200
1761 IBH	—	30.00	60.00	100	200
1762 IBH	—	30.00	60.00	100	200
1763 IAP	—	30.00	60.00	100	200
1764 IAP	—	30.00	60.00	100	200
1765 IAP	—	45.00	75.00	125	250
1766 IAP	—	30.00	60.00	100	200
1767 IAP	—	30.00	60.00	100	200
1768 IAP	—	30.00	60.00	100	200
1769 IAP	—	30.00	60.00	100	200
1770 IAP	—	30.00	60.00	100	200
1771 IAP	—	45.00	75.00	125	250
1772 IAP	—	30.00	60.00	100	200
1773 IAP	—	30.00	60.00	100	200
1773 LCR	—	30.00	60.00	100	200
1774 LCR	—	30.00	60.00	100	200
1775 LCR	—	30.00	60.00	100	200
1776 LCR	—	30.00	60.00	100	200
1777 LCR	—	30.00	60.00	100	200
1778 LCR	—	30.00	60.00	100	200
1779 C	—	30.00	60.00	100	200
1780 CES	—	30.00	60.00	100	200

KM# 895 24 MARIENGROSCHEN (2/3 Thaler)

Silver **Ruler:** Karl I **Obverse:** Value within inner circle, date in legend

Date	Mintage	F	VF	XF	Unc
1736 IAB	—	40.00	90.00	150	250
1737 IAB	—	40.00	90.00	150	250
1738 IAB	—	40.00	90.00	150	250
1739 IAB	—	40.00	90.00	150	250
1739 C	—	40.00	90.00	150	250
1739 IBH	—	40.00	90.00	150	250
1740 IBH	—	40.00	90.00	150	250
1741 IBH	—	40.00	90.00	150	250
1743 IBH	—	40.00	90.00	150	250
1744 IBH	—	40.00	90.00	150	250
1745 IBH	—	40.00	90.00	150	250
1746 IBH	—	40.00	90.00	150	250
1747 IBH	—	40.00	90.00	150	250
1748 IBH	—	40.00	90.00	150	250
1749 IBH	—	40.00	90.00	150	250
1750 IBH	—	40.00	90.00	150	250
1751 IBH	—	40.00	90.00	150	250
1752 IBH	—	40.00	90.00	150	250
1753 IBH	—	40.00	90.00	150	250
1754 IBH	—	40.00	90.00	150	250
1755 IBH	—	40.00	90.00	150	250
1757 IBH	—	40.00	90.00	150	250
1758 IBH	—	40.00	90.00	150	250
1759 IBH	—	40.00	90.00	150	250
1760 IBH	—	75.00	150	250	400
1761 IBH	—	40.00	90.00	150	250
1762 IBH	—	40.00	90.00	150	250
1763 IDB	—	40.00	100	175	300
1763 IAP	—	40.00	90.00	150	250
1764 IAP	—	40.00	90.00	150	250
1765 IAP	—	40.00	90.00	150	250
1766 IAP	—	40.00	90.00	150	250
1767 IAP	—	40.00	90.00	150	250
1768 IAP	—	40.00	90.00	150	250
1769 IAP	—	40.00	90.00	150	250
1770 IAP	—	40.00	90.00	150	250
1771 IAP	—	40.00	90.00	150	250
1772 IAP	—	40.00	90.00	150	250
1773 IAP	—	40.00	90.00	150	250
1773 LCR	—	40.00	100	175	300
1774 LCR	—	40.00	90.00	150	250
1775 LCR	—	40.00	90.00	150	250
1776 LCR	—	40.00	90.00	150	250
1780 CES	—	40.00	90.00	150	250

KM# 1010 24 MARIENGROSCHEN (2/3 Thaler)

Silver **Ruler:** Karl Wilhelm Ferdinand **Obverse:** Baroque arms **Reverse:** Wildman

Date	Mintage	F	VF	XF	Unc
1781 CES	—	75.00	185	400	750
1782 CES	—	75.00	185	400	750
1783 CES	—	75.00	185	400	750

KM# 1011 24 MARIENGROSCHEN (2/3 Thaler)

Silver **Ruler:** Karl Wilhelm Ferdinand **Obverse:** Date in circular legend **Reverse:** Wildman with tree in left hand, value at left

Date	Mintage	F	VF	XF	Unc
1781 CES	—	45.00	100	225	475
1782 CES	—	45.00	100	225	475
1783 CES	—	45.00	100	225	475
1784 CES	—	45.00	100	225	475
1786 C	—	45.00	100	225	475

KM# 1012 24 MARIENGROSCHEN (2/3 Thaler)

Silver **Ruler:** Karl Wilhelm Ferdinand **Obverse:** Value **Reverse:** Horse

Date	Mintage	F	VF	XF	Unc
1781 CES	—	55.00	115	250	575

KM# 1021 24 MARIENGROSCHEN (2/3 Thaler)

Silver **Ruler:** Karl Wilhelm Ferdinand **Obverse:** Plain arms

Date	Mintage	F	VF	XF	Unc
1784 CES	—	55.00	115	250	575
1786 C	—	55.00	115	250	575

KM# 1022 24 MARIENGROSCHEN (2/3 Thaler)

Silver **Ruler:** Karl Wilhelm Ferdinand **Obverse:** Date below value in center **Reverse:** Wildman with tree in left hand, value at left

Date	Mintage	F	VF	XF	Unc
1784 CES	—	45.00	100	225	475
1785 CES	—	45.00	100	225	475
1786 CES	—	45.00	100	225	475
1786 C	—	45.00	100	225	475
1787 C	—	45.00	100	225	475
1788 C	—	45.00	100	225	475
1789 C	—	45.00	100	225	475

KM# 1033 24 MARIENGROSCHEN (2/3 Thaler)

Silver **Ruler:** Karl Wilhelm Ferdinand **Obverse:** Horse leaping left

Date	Mintage	F	VF	XF	Unc
1789 MC	—	25.00	50.00	125	300
1790 MC	—	25.00	50.00	125	300
1795 MC	—	25.00	50.00	125	300
1796 MC	—	25.00	50.00	125	300
1797 MC	—	25.00	50.00	125	300
1798 MC	—	25.00	50.00	125	300
1799 MC	—	25.00	50.00	125	300
1800 MC	—	25.00	50.00	125	300

Note: Varieties exist

KM# 1034 24 MARIENGROSCHEN (2/3 Thaler)
Silver **Ruler:** Karl Wilhelm Ferdinand

Date	Mintage	F	VF	XF	Unc
1789 MC	—	25.00	60.00	140	325
1790 MC	—	25.00	60.00	140	325
1791 MC	—	25.00	60.00	140	325
1792 MC	—	25.00	60.00	140	325
1793 MC	—	25.00	60.00	140	325
1794 MC	—	25.00	60.00	140	325
1795 MC	—	25.00	60.00	140	325
1796 MC	—	25.00	60.00	140	325
1797 MC	—	25.00	60.00	140	325
1798 MC	—	25.00	60.00	140	325
1799 MC	—	25.00	60.00	140	325
1800 MC	—	25.00	60.00	140	325
1801 MC	—	25.00	65.00	100	240
1802 MC	—	30.00	75.00	155	270
1803 MC	—	25.00	65.00	110	200
1804 MC	—	30.00	75.00	155	270
1805 MC	—	25.00	60.00	125	225
1806 MC	—	25.00	70.00	150	250

KM# 961 1/48 THALER
Billon **Ruler:** Karl I **Obverse:** B at top, S at left, M at right **Reverse:** Value, date

Date	Mintage	F	VF	XF	Unc
1760 IDB	—	5.00	15.00	30.00	60.00
1761 IDB	—	5.00	15.00	30.00	60.00

KM# 657 1/24 THALER (Groschen)
Silver **Ruler:** Anton Ulrich as Joint ruler **Subject:** Death of Anton Ulrich's Wife, Elisabeth Juliane **Obverse:** Head right **Obv. Legend:** ELIS. IVL. . ., value 24 below **Reverse:** 9-line inscrption with Roman numeral date

Date	Mintage	VG	F	VF	XF	Unc
1704 HCH	—	30.00	60.00	90.00	150	—

KM# 765 1/24 THALER (Groschen)
Silver **Ruler:** August Wilhelm **Obverse:** Horse leaping left **Reverse:** Imperial orb with 24 divides date

Date	Mintage	VG	F	VF	XF	Unc
1717 HCH	—	12.00	25.00	40.00	70.00	—

KM# 928 1/24 THALER (Groschen)
Billon **Ruler:** Karl I **Obverse:** Horse left **Obv. Legend:** CAROLUS. . . **Reverse:** Value

Date	Mintage	F	VF	XF	Unc
1747 EK	—	5.00	15.00	30.00	60.00
1748 EK	—	5.00	15.00	30.00	60.00
1751	—	5.00	15.00	30.00	60.00
1753	—	5.00	15.00	30.00	60.00
1755 ACB	—	5.00	15.00	30.00	60.00
1757 ACB	—	5.00	15.00	30.00	60.00

KM# 962 1/24 THALER (Groschen)
Billon **Ruler:** Karl I **Reverse:** Value

Date	Mintage	F	VF	XF	Unc
1760 IDB	—	5.00	15.00	30.00	60.00
1760	—	5.00	15.00	30.00	60.00
1761 IDB	—	5.00	15.00	30.00	60.00
1762 IDB	—	5.00	15.00	30.00	60.00

KM# 969 1/24 THALER (Groschen)
Billon **Ruler:** Karl I **Rev. Legend:** CCCXX. . ., value

Date	Mintage	F	VF	XF	Unc
1764 IDB	—	5.00	15.00	30.00	60.00
1772 IDB	—	5.00	15.00	30.00	60.00
1776 IDB	—	5.00	15.00	30.00	60.00
1777 IDB	—	5.00	15.00	30.00	60.00

KM# 999 1/24 THALER (Groschen)
Billon **Ruler:** Karl Wilhelm Ferdinand **Obverse:** Horse **Reverse:** Denomination

Date	Mintage	F	VF	XF	Unc
1780 MC	—	5.00	15.00	30.00	60.00
1781 MC	—	5.00	15.00	30.00	60.00
1786 MC	—	5.00	15.00	30.00	60.00
1787 MC	—	5.00	15.00	30.00	60.00
1788 MC	—	5.00	15.00	30.00	60.00
1790 MC	—	5.00	15.00	30.00	60.00
1797 MC	—	5.00	15.00	30.00	60.00
1798 MC	—	5.00	15.00	30.00	60.00
1802 MC	—	20.00	50.00	90.00	150

KM# 658 1/18 THALER
Silver **Ruler:** Anton Ulrich as Joint ruler **Subject:** Death of Anton Ulrich's Wife, Elisabeth Julianne **Obverse:** Head right,18 below **Obv. Legend:** ELIS. IVL. . . . **Reverse:** 9-line inscription with Roman numeral date

Date	Mintage	VG	F	VF	XF	Unc
1704 HCH	—	30.00	70.00	110	175	—

KM# 743 1/18 THALER
Silver **Ruler:** August Wilhelm **Obverse:** Crowned AW monogram, date in legend **Reverse:** Horse leaping left, 1/18 in oval below

Date	Mintage	VG	F	VF	XF	Unc
1715 HH	—	12.00	25.00	45.00	75.00	—
1716 HH	—	12.00	25.00	45.00	75.00	—

KM# 616 1/12 THALER (2 Groschen)
Silver **Ruler:** Anton Ulrich as Joint ruler **Obv. Legend:** NACH DEN..., Horse leaping left, date below horse **Reverse:** Value 12. . ., LANDMUNTZ IN 5 lines

Date	Mintage	VG	F	VF	XF	Unc
1694	—	12.00	25.00	50.00	85.00	—
1695	—	12.00	25.00	50.00	85.00	—
1697	—	12.00	25.00	50.00	85.00	—
1703	—	12.00	25.00	50.00	85.00	—
1704	—	12.00	25.00	50.00	85.00	—

Note: Varieties exist

KM# 626 1/12 THALER (2 Groschen)
Silver **Ruler:** Anton Ulrich as Joint ruler **Reverse:** Date below value

Date	Mintage	VG	F	VF	XF	Unc
1699 HCH	—	12.00	25.00	50.00	85.00	—
1700 HCH	—	12.00	25.00	50.00	85.00	—
1701 HCH	—	12.00	25.00	50.00	85.00	—
1702 HCH	—	12.00	25.00	50.00	85.00	—
1703 HCH	—	12.00	25.00	50.00	85.00	—

KM# 659 1/12 THALER (2 Groschen)
Silver **Obverse:** Horse leaping left, date below **Reverse:** Value in 3 lines

Date	Mintage	VG	F	VF	XF	Unc
1704 HCH	—	10.00	20.00	40.00	75.00	—

KM# 660 1/12 THALER (2 Groschen)
Silver **Ruler:** Anton Ulrich Alone **Reverse:** Date in legend

Date	Mintage	VG	F	VF	XF	Unc
1704 HCH	—	10.00	20.00	40.00	75.00	—
1705 HCH	—	10.00	20.00	40.00	75.00	—
1706 HCH	—	10.00	20.00	40.00	75.00	—
1707 HCH	—	10.00	20.00	40.00	75.00	—
1708 HCH	—	10.00	20.00	40.00	75.00	—
1709 HCH	—	10.00	20.00	40.00	75.00	—
1710 HCH	—	10.00	20.00	40.00	75.00	—
1711 HCH	—	10.00	20.00	40.00	75.00	—
1712 HCH	—	10.00	20.00	40.00	75.00	—
1713 HCH	—	10.00	20.00	40.00	75.00	—
1714 HCH	—	10.00	20.00	40.00	75.00	—

KM# 661 1/12 THALER (2 Groschen)
Silver **Ruler:** Anton Ulrich as Joint ruler **Subject:** Death of Anton Ulrich's wife, Elisabeth Juliane **Obv. Legend:** ELIS. IVL. . ., head right, 12 below **Reverse:** 9-line legend with roman numeral date

Date	Mintage	VG	F	VF	XF	Unc
1704 HCH	—	40.00	80.00	115	200	—

KM# 732 1/12 THALER (2 Groschen)
Silver **Ruler:** August Wilhelm **Obverse:** Horse leaping left **Reverse:** 12/EINEN/THALER, date in legend

Date	Mintage	VG	F	VF	XF	Unc
1714 HCH	—	12.00	25.00	50.00	85.00	—
1715 HCH	—	12.00	25.00	50.00	85.00	—
1716 HCH	—	12.00	25.00	50.00	85.00	—
1717 HCH	—	12.00	25.00	50.00	85.00	—
1718 HCH	—	12.00	25.00	50.00	85.00	—
1719 HCH	—	12.00	25.00	50.00	85.00	—
1720 HCH	—	12.00	25.00	50.00	85.00	—
1721 HCH	—	12.00	25.00	50.00	85.00	—
1722 HCH	—	12.00	25.00	50.00	85.00	—
1723 HCH	—	12.00	25.00	50.00	85.00	—
1724 HCH	—	12.00	25.00	50.00	85.00	—
1725 HCH	—	12.00	25.00	50.00	85.00	—
1726 HCH	—	12.00	25.00	50.00	85.00	—
1727 HCH	—	12.00	25.00	50.00	85.00	—
1728 HCH	—	12.00	25.00	50.00	85.00	—
1729 IHT	—	12.00	25.00	50.00	85.00	—
1730 IHT	—	12.00	25.00	50.00	85.00	—
1731 IHT	—	12.00	25.00	50.00	85.00	—

KM# 814 1/12 THALER (2 Groschen)
Silver **Ruler:** Ludwig Rudolph **Reverse:** 12/EINEN/THALER **Rev. Legend:** NACH DEN. . ., date

Date	Mintage	VG	F	VF	XF	Unc
1731 IHT	—	10.00	20.00	35.00	60.00	—
1732 HT	—	10.00	20.00	35.00	60.00	—

KM# 835 1/12 THALER (2 Groschen)
Silver **Ruler:** Ludwig Rudolph **Obverse:** Date below horse

Date	Mintage	VG	F	VF	XF	Unc
1733 BID	—	8.00	15.00	30.00	55.00	—
1734 BID	—	8.00	15.00	30.00	55.00	—

KM# 871 1/12 THALER (2 Groschen)
Silver **Reverse:** Date below value

Date	Mintage	VG	F	VF	XF	Unc
1735 BID	—	20.00	45.00	65.00	110	—

KM# 902 1/12 THALER (2 Groschen)
Silver **Ruler:** Karl I **Obverse:** Horse leaping left **Reverse:** Value, date **Rev. Legend:** NACH DEM. . .

Date	Mintage	F	VF	XF	Unc
1737 BID	—	10.00	20.00	40.00	80.00
1740 BID	—	10.00	20.00	40.00	80.00
1762 IDB	—	10.00	20.00	40.00	80.00
1764 IDB	—	10.00	20.00	40.00	80.00

KM# 929 1/12 THALER (2 Groschen)
Silver **Ruler:** Karl I **Reverse:** Without NACH DEM. . .

Date	Mintage	F	VF	XF	Unc
1747 EK	—	7.50	15.00	30.00	60.00
1748 EK	—	7.50	15.00	30.00	60.00
1749 EK	—	7.50	15.00	30.00	60.00
1750 EK	—	7.50	15.00	30.00	60.00
1751	—	7.50	15.00	30.00	60.00
1752	—	7.50	15.00	30.00	60.00
1753	—	7.50	15.00	30.00	60.00
1754 ACB	—	7.50	15.00	30.00	60.00
1756 ACB	—	7.50	15.00	30.00	60.00
1757 ACB	—	7.50	15.00	30.00	60.00
1758 ACB	—	7.50	15.00	30.00	60.00

KM# 970 1/12 THALER (2 Groschen)
Silver **Ruler:** Karl I **Obverse:** Horse leaping left **Reverse:** Value, date, CLS...

Date	Mintage	F	VF	XF	Unc
1764 IDB	—	7.50	15.00	30.00	60.00
1765 IDB	—	7.50	15.00	30.00	60.00
1766 IDB	—	7.50	15.00	30.00	60.00
1767 IDB	—	7.50	15.00	30.00	60.00
1768 IDB	—	7.50	15.00	30.00	60.00
1769 IDB	—	7.50	15.00	30.00	60.00
1770 IDB	—	7.50	15.00	30.00	60.00
1771 IDB	—	7.50	15.00	30.00	60.00
1772 IDB	—	7.50	15.00	30.00	60.00
1773 IDB	—	7.50	15.00	30.00	60.00
1774 IDB	—	7.50	15.00	30.00	60.00
1775 IDB	—	7.75	15.00	30.00	60.00
1776 IDB	—	7.50	15.00	30.00	60.00
1777 IDB	—	7.50	15.00	30.00	60.00
1778 IDB	—	7.50	15.00	30.00	60.00
1779 IDB	—	7.50	15.00	30.00	60.00
1779 MC	—	7.50	15.00	30.00	60.00
1780 MC	—	7.50	15.00	30.00	60.00

KM# 1000 1/12 THALER (2 Groschen)
Billon **Ruler:** Karl Wilhelm Ferdinand **Obverse:** Rearing horse left **Reverse:** Denomination and date, F.R. below, within circle

Date	Mintage	F	VF	XF	Unc
1780 MC	—	5.00	15.00	60.00	75.00
1781 MC	—	5.00	15.00	60.00	75.00
1782 MC	—	5.00	15.00	60.00	75.00
1783 MC	—	5.00	15.00	60.00	75.00
1784 MC	—	5.00	15.00	60.00	75.00
1787 MC	—	5.00	15.00	60.00	75.00
1788 MC	—	5.00	15.00	60.00	75.00
1789 MC	—	5.00	15.00	60.00	75.00
1790 MC	—	5.00	15.00	60.00	75.00
1791 MC	—	5.00	15.00	60.00	75.00
1792 MC	—	5.00	15.00	60.00	75.00
1793 MC	—	5.00	15.00	60.00	75.00
1794 MC	—	5.00	15.00	60.00	75.00
1795 MC	—	5.00	15.00	60.00	75.00
1796 MC	—	5.00	15.00	60.00	75.00
1797 MC	—	5.00	15.00	60.00	75.00
1798 MC	—	5.00	15.00	60.00	75.00
1799 MC	—	5.00	15.00	60.00	75.00
1800 MC	—	5.00	15.00	60.00	75.00
1801 MC	—	5.00	15.00	60.00	75.00
1802 MC	—	5.00	15.00	60.00	75.00
1803 MC	—	5.00	15.00	60.00	75.00
1804 MC	—	5.00	15.00	60.00	75.00
1805 MC	—	5.00	10.00	50.00	60.00
1806 MC	—	5.00	10.00	30.00	50.00

KM# 744 1/9 THALER
Silver **Ruler:** August Wilhelm **Obverse:** Crowned AW monogram, date in legend **Reverse:** Horse leaping left, value in oval below

Date	Mintage	VG	F	VF	XF	Unc
1715 HH	—	30.00	60.00	100	185	—

KM# 745 1/9 THALER
Silver **Ruler:** August Wilhelm **Reverse:** Date divided by value at bottom

Date	Mintage	VG	F	VF	XF	Unc
1715 HH	—	30.00	60.00	100	185	—

KM# 662 1/8 THALER
Silver **Ruler:** Anton Ulrich Alone **Subject:** Death of Rudolf August **Obverse:** Armored bust right **Reverse:** Inscription

Date	Mintage	VG	F	VF	XF	Unc
1704 HCH	—	25.00	55.00	90.00	175	—

KM# 733 1/8 THALER
Silver **Obverse:** Helmeted 11-fold arms divide date **Reverse:** Wildman holding tree with both hands to his left **Note:** (Species).

Date	Mintage	VG	F	VF	XF	Unc
1714 HH	—	90.00	160	280	425	—

KM# 746 1/8 THALER
Silver **Ruler:** August Wilhelm **Obverse:** Helmeted complex arms **Reverse:** Wildman with tree in left hand

Date	Mintage	VG	F	VF	XF	Unc
1715 HH	—	20.00	45.00	80.00	135	—
1720 C	—	20.00	45.00	80.00	135	—
1723 EPH	—	20.00	45.00	80.00	135	—

KM# 796 1/8 THALER
Silver **Ruler:** August Wilhelm **Subject:** 200th Anniversary of Augsburg Confession **Obverse:** Horse rearing left **Reverse:** Inscription

Date	Mintage	VG	F	VF	XF	Unc
1730 IHT	—	30.00	75.00	140	220	—

KM# 747 1/6 THALER
Silver **Ruler:** August Wilhelm **Obverse:** Crowned AW monogram, date in legend **Reverse:** Horse leaping left, 1/6 below

Date	Mintage	VG	F	VF	XF	Unc
1715 HH	—	25.00	50.00	90.00	145	—
1717 HH	—	25.00	50.00	90.00	145	—

KM# 754 1/6 THALER
Silver **Ruler:** August Wilhelm **Obverse:** Crowned monogram **Reverse:** Date divided by value

Date	Mintage	VG	F	VF	XF	Unc
1716 HH	—	20.00	40.00	75.00	115	—
1717 HH	—	20.00	40.00	75.00	115	—
1719 C	—	20.00	40.00	75.00	115	—
1721 C	—	20.00	40.00	75.00	115	—
1723 EPH	—	20.00	40.00	75.00	115	—
1724 EPH	—	20.00	40.00	75.00	115	—
1725 EPH	—	20.00	40.00	75.00	115	—
1729 EPH	—	20.00	40.00	75.00	115	—

KM# 930 1/6 THALER
Silver **Ruler:** Karl I **Obverse:** Horse rearing left **Reverse:** Value, date

Date	Mintage	F	VF	XF	Unc
1747 EK	—	10.00	20.00	40.00	80.00
1748 EK	—	10.00	20.00	40.00	80.00
1751	—	10.00	20.00	40.00	80.00
1752	—	10.00	20.00	40.00	80.00
1753	—	10.00	20.00	40.00	80.00
1754 ACB	—	10.00	20.00	40.00	80.00
1755 ACB	—	10.00	20.00	40.00	80.00
1755 IDB	—	10.00	20.00	40.00	80.00
1756 ACB	—	10.00	20.00	40.00	80.00
1757 ACB	—	10.00	20.00	40.00	80.00
1758 ACB	—	10.00	20.00	40.00	80.00
1759 ACB	—	10.00	20.00	40.00	80.00

KM# 952 1/6 THALER
Silver **Ruler:** Karl I **Obverse:** Crowned C monogram **Reverse:** Value, date

Date	Mintage	F	VF	XF	Unc
1759 ACB	—	15.00	30.00	50.00	100
1760 IDB	—	15.00	30.00	50.00	100
1761 IDB	—	15.00	30.00	50.00	100
1762 IDB	—	15.00	30.00	50.00	100

KM# 971 1/6 THALER
Silver **Ruler:** Karl I **Obverse:** Horse left **Reverse:** Value date, LXXX. . .

Date	Mintage	F	VF	XF	Unc
1764 IDB	—	10.00	25.00	50.00	100
1765 IDB	—	10.00	25.00	50.00	100
1766 IDB	—	10.00	25.00	50.00	100
1767 IDB	—	10.00	25.00	50.00	100
1768 IDB	—	10.00	25.00	50.00	100
1769 IDB	—	10.00	25.00	50.00	100
1770 IDB	—	10.00	25.00	50.00	100
1771 IDB	—	10.00	25.00	50.00	100
1772 IDB	—	10.00	25.00	50.00	100
1773 IDB	—	10.00	25.00	50.00	100
1774 IDB	—	10.00	25.00	50.00	100
1775 IDB	—	10.00	25.00	50.00	100
1777 IDB	—	10.00	25.00	50.00	100
1778 IDB	—	10.00	25.00	50.00	100
1779 IDB	—	10.00	25.00	50.00	100
1779 MC	—	10.00	25.00	50.00	100
1780 MC	—	10.00	25.00	50.00	100

KM# 1001 1/6 THALER
Silver **Ruler:** Karl Wilhelm Ferdinand **Obverse:** Rearing horse left **Reverse:** Denomination and date within circle

Date	Mintage	F	VF	XF	Unc
1780 MC	—	6.00	15.00	30.00	90.00
1781 MC	—	6.00	15.00	30.00	90.00
1782 MC	—	6.00	15.00	30.00	90.00
1783 MC	—	6.00	15.00	30.00	90.00
1784 MC	—	6.00	15.00	30.00	90.00
1785 MC	—	6.00	15.00	30.00	90.00
1786 MC	—	6.00	15.00	30.00	90.00
1787 MC	—	6.00	15.00	30.00	90.00
1788 MC	—	6.00	15.00	30.00	90.00
1789 MC	—	6.00	15.00	30.00	90.00
1790 MC	—	6.00	15.00	30.00	90.00
1791 MC	—	6.00	15.00	30.00	90.00
1792 MC	—	6.00	15.00	30.00	90.00
1793 MC	—	6.00	15.00	30.00	90.00
1794 MC	—	6.00	15.00	30.00	90.00
1795 MC	—	6.00	15.00	30.00	90.00
1797 MC	—	6.00	15.00	30.00	90.00
1798 MC	—	6.00	15.00	30.00	90.00
1799 MC	—	6.00	15.00	30.00	90.00
1801 MC	—	10.00	25.00	55.00	85.00
1802 MC	—	10.00	25.00	50.00	75.00
1803 MC	—	10.00	25.00	40.00	60.00
1804 MC	—	10.00	25.00	45.00	70.00

KM# 592 1/4 THALER
Silver **Ruler:** Anton Ulrich as Joint ruler **Mint:** Zellerfeld

Date	Mintage	VG	F	VF	XF	Unc
1691 RB	—	30.00	60.00	125	200	—
1702 RB	—	30.00	60.00	125	200	—

KM# 663 1/4 THALER
Silver **Ruler:** Anton Ulrich Alone **Subject:** Death of Rudolf August **Obverse:** Bust right **Reverse:** 14-line inscription with date

Date	Mintage	VG	F	VF	XF	Unc
1704 HCH	—	30.00	65.00	110	220	—

KM# 664 1/4 THALER
Silver **Obverse:** Helmeted 11-fold arms

Date	Mintage	VG	F	VF	XF	Unc
1704 ***	—	30.00	65.00	110	220	—

KM# 723 1/4 THALER
Silver **Ruler:** Anton Ulrich Alone **Obverse:** Helmeted complex arms **Reverse:** Wildman holding tree with both hands at right, value in oval between wildman and tree **Note:** Similar to KM#748 but wildman holding tree with both hands to his left, 1/4 oval between wildman and tree.

Date	Mintage	VG	F	VF	XF	Unc
1713 HH	—	175	300	475	800	—

KM# 748 1/4 THALER
Silver **Ruler:** August Wilhelm **Obverse:** Helmeted complex arms **Reverse:** Wildman with tree in his left hand

Date	Mintage	VG	F	VF	XF	Unc
1715 HH	—	30.00	60.00	100	200	—
1716 HH	—	30.00	60.00	100	200	—
1717 HH	—	30.00	60.00	100	200	—
1719 C-HH	—	30.00	60.00	100	200	—
1719 C	—	30.00	60.00	100	200	—
1721 C	—	30.00	60.00	100	200	—

KM# 776 1/4 THALER
Silver **Ruler:** August Wilhelm **Reverse:** R. T. with value **Note:** Reichs.

Date	Mintage	VG	F	VF	XF	Unc
1723 EPH	—	40.00	80.00	125	250	—
1724 EPH	—	40.00	80.00	125	250	—
1727 EPH	—	40.00	80.00	125	250	—

KM# 826 1/4 THALER
Silver **Ruler:** Ludwig Rudolph **Obverse:** Helmeted 12-fold arms, date in legend **Reverse:** Wildman, tree in left hand, R. 1/4T. to left

Date	Mintage	VG	F	VF	XF	Unc
1732 IAB	—	40.00	80.00	125	250	—
1733 IAB	—	40.00	80.00	125	250	—
1734 IAB	—	40.00	80.00	125	250	—

KM# 873 1/4 THALER
Silver **Ruler:** Ferdinand Ulbrecht II

Date	Mintage	VG	F	VF	XF	Unc
1735 IAB	—	25.00	50.00	80.00	150	—

KM# 896 1/4 THALER
Silver **Ruler:** Karl I **Obverse:** Arms in shield, helmets above **Reverse:** Wildman with tree in left hand, value at lower left

Date	Mintage	F	VF	XF	Unc
1736 IAB	—	25.00	60.00	125	250
1738 IAB	—	25.00	60.00	125	250
1739 IBH	—	25.00	60.00	125	250
1742 IBH	—	25.00	60.00	125	250
1748 IBH	—	25.00	60.00	125	250
1750 IBH	—	25.00	60.00	125	250

KM# 935 1/4 THALER

Silver **Ruler:** Karl I **Obverse:** Crowned arms with crossed sceptres **Reverse:** Rampant lion left within shield **Note:** Albertus.

Date	Mintage	F	VF	XF	Unc
1748 EK	—	70.00	140	250	500

KM# 749 1/3 THALER

Silver **Ruler:** August Wilhelm **Obverse:** Crowned monogram **Obv. Legend:** VON FEINEM SILBER... **Reverse:** Horse leaping left above value

Date	Mintage	VG	F	VF	XF	Unc
1715 HH	—	40.00	80.00	125	225	—
1716 HH	—	40.00	80.00	125	225	—

KM# 755 1/3 THALER

Silver **Ruler:** August Wilhelm **Obverse:** Crowned monogram **Obv. Legend:** D. G. DUX. BRUNSVIG. ET LUNEBURG **Reverse:** Horse leaping left above value

Date	Mintage	VG	F	VF	XF	Unc
1716 HH	—	20.00	45.00	80.00	125	—
1717 HH	—	20.00	45.00	80.00	125	—
1719 HH	—	20.00	45.00	80.00	125	—
1721 C	—	20.00	45.00	80.00	125	—
1723 EPH	—	20.00	45.00	80.00	125	—
1727 EPH	—	20.00	45.00	80.00	125	—
1730 EPH	—	20.00	45.00	80.00	125	—

KM# 972 1/3 THALER

Silver **Ruler:** Karl I **Obverse:** Bust right **Reverse:** Horse leaping left **Note:** Convention 1/3 Thaler.

Date	Mintage	F	VF	XF	Unc
1764 IDB	—	25.00	50.00	80.00	150
1765 IDB	—	25.00	50.00	80.00	150
1765 E/IDB	—	25.00	50.00	80.00	150
1766 IDB	—	25.00	50.00	80.00	150
1768/6 IDB	—	25.00	50.00	80.00	150
1768 IDB	—	30.00	60.00	90.00	200
1770 IDB	—	25.00	50.00	80.00	150

KM# 980 1/3 THALER

Silver **Ruler:** Karl I **Obverse:** Bust right **Reverse:** Horse leaping right

Date	Mintage	F	VF	XF	Unc
1771 E/IDB	—	25.00	50.00	80.00	150
1773 E/IDB	—	25.00	50.00	80.00	150
1775 E/IDB	—	40.00	80.00	120	250
1776 E/IDB	—	30.00	60.00	90.00	200
1777 E/IDB	—	25.00	50.00	80.00	150
1779 K/MC	—	25.00	50.00	80.00	150

KM# 575 1/2 THALER

Silver **Ruler:** Anton Ulrich as Joint ruler **Obverse:** Crowned 11-fold arms, date divided below **Reverse:** 2 wildman holding 2 interwined trees **Note:** Similar to 1 Thaler, KM#571.

Date	Mintage	VG	F	VF	XF	Unc
1687 RB	—	40.00	80.00	125	225	—
1691 RB	—	40.00	80.00	125	225	—
1697 RB	—	40.00	80.00	125	225	—
1702 RB	—	40.00	80.00	125	225	—

KM# 635 1/2 THALER

Silver **Ruler:** Anton Ulrich as Joint ruler **Obverse:** Crowned 11-fold arms **Reverse:** Wildman holding tree with 2 hands to his left, date in legend

Date	Mintage	VG	F	VF	XF	Unc
1700 RB	—	50.00	100	150	245	—
1701 RB	—	50.00	100	150	245	—

KM# 665 1/2 THALER

Silver **Ruler:** Anton Ulrich Alone **Subject:** Death of Rudolf August **Obverse:** Helmeted 11-fold arms **Reverse:** 14-line inscription with date

Date	Mintage	VG	F	VF	XF	Unc
1704 RB	—	150	275	400	750	—

KM# 692 1/2 THALER

Silver **Ruler:** Anton Ulrich Alone **Obverse:** Head right **Reverse:** Helmeted 11-fold arms

Date	Mintage	VG	F	VF	XF	Unc
1706 HCH	—	90.00	160	300	525	—

KM# 734 1/2 THALER

Silver **Obverse:** Helmeted 14-fold arms, date in legend **Reverse:** Wildman holding tree with both hands to his left, 1/2 S.R.T. left **Note:** Species-Reichs 1/2 Thaler.

Date	Mintage	VG	F	VF	XF	Unc
1714 HH	—	125	225	350	575	—

KM# 756 1/2 THALER

Silver **Ruler:** August Wilhelm **Obverse:** Crowned AW monogram **Reverse:** Horse leaping left, Roman numeral date below

Date	Mintage	VG	F	VF	XF	Unc
1716 HH	—	45.00	90.00	150	245	—

KM# 766 1/2 THALER

Silver **Ruler:** August Wilhelm **Subject:** 200th Anniversary of Reformation **Obverse:** Armored bust right **Reverse:** Inscription

Date	Mintage	VG	F	VF	XF	Unc
1717 HCH	—	200	325	550	900	—

Note: Date in ancient Roman numerals

KM# 767 1/2 THALER

Silver **Ruler:** August Wilhelm **Obverse:** Helmeted complex arms **Reverse:** Wildman with tree in left hand **Note:** Similar to 1/4 Thaler, KM#748.

Date	Mintage	VG	F	VF	XF	Unc
1717 HH	—	45.00	90.00	150	245	—
1721 C	—	45.00	90.00	150	245	—

KM# 777 1/2 THALER

Silver **Ruler:** August Wilhelm **Obverse:** Armored draped bust right **Reverse:** Helmeted complex arms with ornaments **Note:** Reichs 1/2 Thaler.

Date	Mintage	VG	F	VF	XF	Unc
1723 EPH	—	50.00	110	185	300	—
1724 EPH	—	50.00	110	185	300	—
1725 EPH	—	50.00	110	185	300	—

KM# 827 1/2 THALER

Silver **Ruler:** Ludwig Rudolph **Obverse:** Helmeted 12-fold arms, date in legend **Reverse:** Wildman, tree in left hand, R. 1/2 T. to left

Date	Mintage	VG	F	VF	XF	Unc
1732 IAB	—	45.00	90.00	150	245	—
1733 IAB	—	45.00	90.00	150	245	—
1735 IAB	—	45.00	90.00	150	245	—

KM# 836 1/2 THALER

Silver **Ruler:** Ludwig Rudolph **Subject:** Marriage of Karl (I) and Philippine Charlotte of Prussia **Obverse:** Crowned cursive mirror-image P CPC monogram **Reverse:** 6-line legend with Roman numeral date, value below

Date	Mintage	VG	F	VF	XF	Unc
1733 BID	—	150	275	400	750	—

KM# 837 1/2 THALER

Silver **Ruler:** Ludwig Rudolph **Subject:** Marraige of Karl (I)'s Sister, Elisabeth Christine and Friedrich (II) of Prussia **Obverse:** Crowned cursive mirror-image EC monogram **Reverse:** 9-line legend with Roman numeral date, value below

Date	Mintage	VG	F	VF	XF	Unc
1733 BID	—	150	275	500	1,000	—

Note: Date in ancient Roman numerals

KM# 874 1/2 THALER

Silver **Ruler:** Ferdinand Ulbrecht II **Obverse:** Helmeted 12-fold arms, date in legend **Reverse:** Wildman, tree in left hand, R 1/2 T to left

Date	Mintage	VG	F	VF	XF	Unc
1735 IAB	—	25.00	50.00	100	200	—

KM# 897 1/2 THALER

Silver **Ruler:** Karl I **Obverse:** Arms in shield, helmets above **Reverse:** Wildman with tree in left hand, value at lower left

Date	Mintage	F	VF	XF	Unc
1736 IAB	—	60.00	150	300	700
1737 IAB	—	60.00	150	300	700

KM# 931 1/2 THALER

Silver **Ruler:** Karl I **Obverse:** Crowned complex arms with crossed sceptres **Reverse:** Rampant lion left within shield **Note:** Albertus.

Date	Mintage	F	VF	XF	Unc
1747 EK	—	100	200	300	500
1748 EK	—	75.00	150	200	350

KM# 985 1/2 THALER

Silver **Ruler:** Karl I **Obverse:** Head **Reverse:** Horse left, XX EINE FEINE. . . below **Note:** Convention 1/2 Thaler.

Date	Mintage	F	VF	XF	Unc
1776 IDB	—	70.00	140	280	500

KM# 983.1 2/3 THALER

Silver **Ruler:** Karl I **Obverse:** Head right **Reverse:** Horse leaping left

Date	Mintage	F	VF	XF	Unc
1775 G/IDB	—	30.00	60.00	125	250
1776 E/IDB	—	30.00	60.00	125	250
1777 K/IDB	—	30.00	60.00	125	250
1779 K/IDB	—	30.00	60.00	125	250
1779 K/MC	—	30.00	60.00	125	250

Date	Mintage	F	VF	XF	Unc
1777 KR/IDB	—	30.00	60.00	125	250
1775 E/IDB	—	30.00	60.00	125	250

KM# 627 2/3 THALER

Silver **Ruler:** Anton Ulrich as Joint ruler **Obverse:** Crowned 14-fold arms divide date **Reverse:** Horse leaping left, value 2/3 below

Date	Mintage	VG	F	VF	XF	Unc
1699 HCH	—	50.00	100	150	250	—
1700 HCH	—	50.00	100	150	250	—
1702 HCH	—	50.00	100	150	250	—

KM# 636 2/3 THALER

Silver **Ruler:** Anton Ulrich as Joint ruler **Reverse:** Date divided by value below horse

Date	Mintage	VG	F	VF	XF	Unc
1700 HCH	—	25.00	55.00	90.00	175	—
1704 HCH	—	25.00	55.00	90.00	175	—
1705 HCH	—	25.00	55.00	90.00	175	—
1706 HCH	—	25.00	55.00	90.00	175	—
1707 HCH	—	25.00	55.00	90.00	175	—
1708 HCH	—	25.00	55.00	90.00	175	—
1709 HCH	—	25.00	55.00	90.00	175	—
1710 HCH	—	25.00	55.00	90.00	175	—
1711 HCH	—	25.00	55.00	90.00	175	—

KM# 666 2/3 THALER

Silver **Obverse:** Crowned complex arms divide date **Reverse:** Horse leaping left, value below **Note:** Similar to KM#627.

Date	Mintage	VG	F	VF	XF	Unc
1704 HCH	—	40.00	70.00	120	215	—

KM# 717 2/3 THALER

Silver **Ruler:** Anton Ulrich Alone **Obverse:** Bust right **Reverse:** Similar to KM#636

Date	Mintage	VG	F	VF	XF	Unc
1711 HCH	—	50.00	100	175	350	—
1712 HCH	—	50.00	100	175	350	—

KM# 735 2/3 THALER

Silver **Ruler:** August Wilhelm **Obverse:** Crowned AW monogram, date in legend **Reverse:** Horse leaping left, value 2/3 below

Date	Mintage	VG	F	VF	XF	Unc
1714 HH	—	60.00	125	225	375	—
1715 HH	—	60.00	125	225	375	—
1716 HH	—	60.00	125	225	375	—

KM# 736 2/3 THALER

Silver **Ruler:** August Wilhelm **Obverse:** Bust right **Reverse:** Horse leaping left, value divides date below

Date	Mintage	VG	F	VF	XF	Unc
1714 HCH	—	20.00	50.00	80.00	165	—
1715 HCH	—	20.00	50.00	80.00	165	—

KM# 757 2/3 THALER

Silver **Ruler:** August Wilhelm **Obverse:** Crowned monogram **Reverse:** Horse leaping left

Date	Mintage	VG	F	VF	XF	Unc
1716 HH	—	30.00	65.00	115	200	—
1717 HH	—	30.00	65.00	115	200	—
1718 HH	—	30.00	65.00	115	200	—
1719 C	—	30.00	65.00	115	200	—
1720 C	—	30.00	65.00	115	200	—
1721 C	—	30.00	65.00	115	200	—
1722 C	—	30.00	65.00	115	200	—
1723 EPH	—	30.00	65.00	115	200	—
1724 EPH	—	30.00	65.00	115	200	—
1725 EPH	—	30.00	65.00	115	200	—
1726 EPH	—	30.00	65.00	115	200	—
1727 EPH	—	30.00	65.00	115	200	—
1728 EPH	—	30.00	65.00	115	200	—
1729 EPH	—	30.00	65.00	115	200	—
1730 EPH	—	30.00	65.00	115	200	—

KM# 768 2/3 THALER

Silver **Ruler:** August Wilhelm **Obverse:** Crowned 14-fold arms

Date	Mintage	VG	F	VF	XF	Unc
1717 HCH	—	35.00	70.00	120	215	—
1720 HCH	—	35.00	70.00	120	215	—
1724 HCH	—	35.00	70.00	120	215	—

KM# 815 2/3 THALER

Silver **Ruler:** Ludwig Rudolph **Obverse:** Bust right **Reverse:** Horse leaping left, Roman numeral date and value below

Date	Mintage	VG	F	VF	XF	Unc
1731 IHT	—	40.00	75.00	125	220	—
1735 BID	—	40.00	75.00	125	220	—

KM# 875 2/3 THALER

Silver **Obverse:** Head right **Reverse:** Without value

Date	Mintage	VG	F	VF	XF	Unc
1735 BID	—	550	1,000	1,350	1,850	—

KM# 876 2/3 THALER

Silver **Reverse:** FEIN SILB:, date and value at bottom

Date	Mintage	VG	F	VF	XF	Unc
1735	—	225	400	650	1,000	—

KM# 877 2/3 THALER

Silver **Obverse:** Bust right **Reverse:** Without value

Date	Mintage	VG	F	VF	XF	Unc
1735	—	125	250	400	650	—

KM# 898 2/3 THALER

Silver **Ruler:** Karl I **Obverse:** Armored bust right **Reverse:** Horse leaping left **Note:** Similar to KM#903 but without 2/3 below horse.

Date	Mintage	F	VF	XF	Unc
1736 BID	—	50.00	120	240	500
1737 BID	—	50.00	120	240	500
1740 BID	—	50.00	120	240	500

KM# 903 2/3 THALER

Silver **Ruler:** Karl I **Obverse:** Armored bust right **Obv. Legend:** CAROLVS D•G•DVX•BRUNS•ET•LVNEB• **Reverse:** Horse leaping left, value below divides date **Rev. Legend:** NVNQNAM RETRORSVM

Date	Mintage	F	VF	XF	Unc
1737 BID	—	50.00	120	240	500
1740 BID	—	50.00	120	240	500

KM# 973.1 2/3 THALER

Silver **Ruler:** Karl I **Obverse:** Armored draped bust right **Obv. Legend:** CAROLVS D•G•DVX BR•ET•LVN• **Reverse:** Horse leaping left, value divides date below **Rev. Legend:** NVNQVAM RETRORSVM **Note:** 2/3 Thaler Convention.

Date	Mintage	F	VF	XF	Unc
1764 IDB	—	30.00	50.00	100	250
1764 E/IDB	—	30.00	50.00	100	250
1765 E/IDB	—	30.00	50.00	100	250
1765 IDB	—	30.00	50.00	100	250
1766 IDB	—	30.00	50.00	100	250
1768 IDB	—	30.00	50.00	100	250
1770 IDB	—	30.00	50.00	100	250
1771 IDB	—	30.00	50.00	100	250
1773 IDB	—	30.00	50.00	100	250
1775 IDB	—	30.00	50.00	100	250
1779 MC	—	30.00	50.00	100	250

KM# 973.2 2/3 THALER

Silver **Ruler:** Karl I **Obverse:** Legend broken by head **Obv. Legend:** CAROLVS - D • G • DVX BR ET LV **Reverse:** Horse leaping left, value divides date below **Rev. Legend:** NVNQNAM RETRORSVM

Date	Mintage	F	VF	XF	Unc
1775 G//IDB	—	30.00	50.00	100	250

KM# 983.2 2/3 THALER

Silver **Ruler:** Karl I **Obverse:** Smaller bust right **Obv. Legend:** CAROLVS D•G•DVX BR•ET LVNEB• **Reverse:** Horse leaping left, value divides date below **Rev. Legend:** NVNQNAM RETRORSVM

Date	Mintage	F	VF	XF	Unc
1779 K/MC	—	30.00	50.00	100	250

KM# 637 THALER

Silver **Ruler:** Anton Ulrich as Joint ruler **Obverse:** Helmeted 11-fold arms, date in legend **Reverse:** Wildman holding tree with both hands to his left **Note:** Dav. #6391.

Date	Mintage	F	VF	XF	Unc
1700 RB	—	110	175	300	625

KM# A577 THALER

Silver **Ruler:** Anton Ulrich as Joint ruler **Obverse:** Bust of 2 Dukes right within inner circle **Note:** Dav. #2111.

Date	Mintage	F	VF	XF	Unc
1701 RB	—	100	200	350	750
1702	—	100	200	350	750
1703	—	100	200	350	750

KM# A637 THALER

Silver **Ruler:** Anton Ulrich as Joint ruler **Obverse:** Helmeted 11-fold arms, date in legend **Reverse:** Wildman holding tree with both hands to his left **Note:** Dav. #2112

Date	Mintage	F	VF	XF	Unc
1701 RB	—	65.00	135	250	575
1702 RB	—	65.00	135	250	575
1703 RB	—	65.00	135	250	575
1704 RB	—	65.00	135	250	575

KM# 640 THALER

Silver **Ruler:** Anton Ulrich as Joint ruler **Subject:** Dissolution of Brotherly Agreement **Obverse:** Horses pulling ball in opposite directions, unicorn and eagle with lightning bolt in background **Obv. Legend:** QVOD VI NON POTVIT **Reverse:** Broken orb with monogram on column, hand above at right, clouds in background **Rev. Legend:** DISIECTVM EST ARTE MINISTRA on band at top, numeral date at bottom **Note:** Dav. #2930.

Date	Mintage	F	VF	XF	Unc
1702	—	1,000	1,600	2,250	3,000

KM# 641 THALER

Silver **Ruler:** Anton Ulrich as Joint ruler **Obverse:** Lightning from cloud instead of eagle, NON-VI in and to either side of cloud **Reverse:** Band: SED ARTE **Note:** Dav. #2931.

Date	Mintage	F	VF	XF	Unc
1702	—	1,000	1,600	2,250	3,000

KM# 667 THALER

Silver **Ruler:** Anton Ulrich Alone **Subject:** Death of August **Obverse:** Armored draped bust right **Obv. Legend:** RUDOLPHUS • AUGUSTUS • D • G • DUX • BR: ET • L: **Reverse:** Inscription **Rev. Inscription:** PRINCEPS/PIVS. IVSTVS. PACIFICVS/CVIVS/ HONOS. NOMEM. LAVDESQVE/PER. OMNE. MANEBVNT. AEVVM/GVBERNACVLVM. SVMSIT. A. MDCLXVI/FRATRE. REGIMINIS. PARTICIPE. FEC:/A. MDCLXXXV/ET SIC/ CVRSV/ QVEM. DEDERAT. FORTVNA/REMIGIO ALTISSIMI/STRENVE. PERACTO/IN AETER **Note:** Dav. #2113.

Date	Mintage	F	VF	XF	Unc
1704 HCH	—	165	335	575	1,000

KM# 668 THALER

Silver **Ruler:** Anton Ulrich Alone **Obverse:** Larger bust **Reverse:** 13-line inscription **Note:** Dav. #2114.

Date	Mintage	F	VF	XF	Unc
1704 RB	—	165	335	575	1,000

KM# 669 THALER

Silver **Ruler:** Anton Ulrich Alone **Obverse:** Helmeted complex arms within ornate frame **Obv. Legend:** D: G: ANTHON ULRICH DUX BR: & LU: **Reverse:** Wildman with tree at right, forest of small trees in background **Rev. Legend:** LABORE ET CONSTANTIA **Note:** Dav. #2115.

Date	Mintage	F	VF	XF	Unc
1704 RB	—	65.00	135	250	575
1705 RB	—	65.00	135	250	575

KM# 670 THALER

Silver **Ruler:** Anton Ulrich Alone **Obverse:** Date in legend **Note:** Dav. #2115A.

Date	Mintage	F	VF	XF	Unc
1704 RB	—	65.00	135	250	575
1705 RB	—	65.00	135	250	575

KM# 671 THALER

Silver **Subject:** Death of Anton Ulrich's Wife, Elisabeth Juliane **Obverse:** Bust of Duchess right, dates below **Obv. Legend:** DIVA ELISAB. IVLIA. D.G. DVC. BRVN. ET LVN, below: .NATA 1634.DENATA 1704. **Reverse:** Figure on cloud above Salzdahlum Palace, crown on cushion **Rev. Legend:** DESERVISSE IVVAT **Note:** Dav. #2122.

Date	Mintage	F	VF	XF	Unc
1704	—	250	450	800	1,550
1704 HCH	—	250	450	800	1,550

KM# 672 THALER

Silver **Obverse:** Dates to right in legend **Obv. Legend:** DIVA • ELIS • IVL • D • G • D • BR • ET - LVN: NATA 1634. DENATA 1704. **Reverse:** Figure on cloud above Salzdahlum Palace, crown on cushion **Rev. Legend:** DESERVISSE IVVAT **Note:** Dav. #2123.

Date	Mintage	F	VF	XF	Unc
1704	—	350	550	900	1,650
1704 HCH	—	350	550	900	1,650

KM# 686.1 THALER

Silver **Ruler:** Anton Ulrich Alone **Obverse:** Helmeted complex arms with ornaments **Obv. Legend:** D: G: ANTHON. ULRICH DUX BR: & LU: **Reverse:** Wildman with tree at right, R.B at left **Rev. Legend:** CONSTANTER **Note:** Dav. #2116

Date	Mintage	F	VF	XF	Unc
1705 RB	—	65.00	135	250	575
1706 RB	—	65.00	135	250	575
1707 RB	—	65.00	135	250	575
1708 RB	—	65.00	135	250	575
1709 RB	—	65.00	135	250	575
1710 RB	—	65.00	135	250	575
1711 RB	—	65.00	135	250	575

KM# 687 THALER

Silver **Ruler:** Anton Ulrich Alone **Subject:** Visit of Anton Ulrich to Zellerfeld Mint **Obverse:** Salzdahlum place, sundial suspended at upper left, sun shinning from upper left **Reverse:** 2 miners in mine, CONSTANTER on ribbon above, date below **Note:** Dav. #2932.

Date	Mintage	F	VF	XF	Unc
1705	—	650	1,100	1,750	—

KM# 693.1 THALER

Silver **Ruler:** Anton Ulrich Alone **Obverse:** Armored draped bust right **Obv. Legend:** ANTONIUS ULRICUS. D: G: DUX BR: ET LUN: **Reverse:** Helmeted complex arms with ornaments **Rev. Legend:** CONSTANTER **Note:** Dav. #2119.

Date	Mintage	F	VF	XF	Unc
1706 HCH	—	350	550	900	1,550

KM# 693.2 THALER

Silver **Ruler:** Anton Ulrich Alone **Obverse:** Armored draped bust right **Obv. Legend:** ANTONIUS ULRIC: - D.G. DUX. BR: ET LUNEB: **Reverse:** Helmeted complex arms with ornaments **Rev. Legend:** CONSTANTER **Note:** Dav. #2120.

Date	Mintage	F	VF	XF	Unc
1710 HCH	—	350	530	900	1,500
1711 HCH	—	350	550	900	1,500
1712 HCH	—	350	550	900	1,500

KM# 706 THALER

Silver **Subject:** Conversion of Anton Ulrich to Catholicism **Obverse:** Bust right **Reverse:** Rock in sea, SEMPER IDEM above, CONSTANTER below **Note:** Dav. #2121.

Date	Mintage	F	VF	XF	Unc
ND	—	400	650	1,200	2,000

KM# 686.2 THALER

Silver **Ruler:** Anton Ulrich Alone **Obverse:** Helmeted complex arms with ornaments **Obv. Legend:** D • G • ANTONI9 ULRIC9 DUX BR • & LUN • **Reverse:** Cruder image of wildman **Rev. Legend:** CONSTANTER **Note:** Dav. #2117.

Date	Mintage	F	VF	XF	Unc
1712 HH	—	65.00	135	250	575

KM# 686.3 THALER

Silver **Ruler:** Anton Ulrich Alone **Obverse:** Helmeted complex arms **Reverse:** Wildman **Note:** Dav. #2118.

Date	Mintage	F	VF	XF	Unc
1713 HH	—	65.00	135	250	575
1714 HH	—	65.00	135	250	575

KM# 737 THALER

Silver **Ruler:** August Wilhelm **Subject:** Death of Anton Ulrich **Obverse:** Bust right **Reverse:** 16-line inscription with Roman numeral date **Note:** Dav. #2124.

Date	Mintage	F	VF	XF	Unc
1714 HCH	—	250	450	800	1,300

KM# 738 THALER

Silver **Ruler:** August Wilhelm **Obverse:** Armored draped bust right **Obv. Legend:** AUGUSTUS WILH. - D.G. DUX. BR. ET. LUN. **Reverse:** Helmeted arms with ornaments **Rev. Legend:** PARTA TUERI **Note:** Dav. #2125.

Date	Mintage	F	VF	XF	Unc
1714 HCH	—	450	750	1,250	2,000

KM# 739 THALER

Silver **Ruler:** August Wilhelm **Obverse:** Helmeted complex arms with ornaments **Obv. Legend:** D.G. AVGVSTVS. WILHELMVS. DVX. BR. & LVN. **Reverse:** Wildman, tree in left hand **Rev. Legend:** PARTA TVERI **Note:** Dav. #2126.

Date	Mintage	F	VF	XF	Unc
1714 HH	—	65.00	135	250	575
1715 HH	—	65.00	135	250	575
1716 HH	—	65.00	135	250	575
1717 HH	—	65.00	135	250	575
1718 HH	—	65.00	135	250	575
1719 HH	—	65.00	135	250	575
1719 C-HH	—	65.00	135	250	575
1720 C	—	65.00	135	250	575
1721 C	—	65.00	135	250	575
1722 C	—	65.00	135	250	575
1723 EPH	—	65.00	135	250	575
1724 EPH	—	65.00	135	250	575
1725 EPH	—	65.00	135	250	575
1726 EPH	—	65.00	135	250	575
1727 EPH	—	65.00	135	250	575
1728 EPH	—	65.00	135	250	575
1729 EPH	—	65.00	135	250	575
1730 EPH	—	65.00	135	250	575

KM# 758 THALER

Silver **Ruler:** August Wilhelm **Obverse:** Crowned AW monogram **Obv. Legend:** D • G • DUX • BRUNSVIC • - ET LUNEBURG • **Reverse:** Horse leaping left **Rev. Legend:** PARTA TVERI **Note:** Dav. #2127.

Date	Mintage	F	VF	XF	Unc
1716 HH	—	100	175	350	750
1717 HH	—	100	175	350	750
1718 HH	—	100	175	350	750
1719 C	—	100	175	350	750
1720 C	—	100	175	350	750
1721 C	—	100	175	350	750
1722 C	—	100	175	350	750
1723 EPH	—	100	175	350	750
1724 EPH	—	100	175	350	750
1725 EPH	—	100	175	350	750
1727 EPH	—	100	175	350	750
1728 EPH	—	100	175	350	750
1729 EPH	—	100	175	350	750
1730 EPH	—	100	175	350	750

KM# 769 THALER

Silver **Ruler:** August Wilhelm **Subject:** 200th Anniversary of Reformation **Obverse:** Armored draped bust right **Obv. Legend:** AUGUSTUS. WILH. - D.G. DUX. BR. ET. LUN. **Reverse:** Inscription **Rev. Inscription:** IN MEMORIAM/IVBILAEI.II/OB/ VER. DOCTRINAM. CHRIST/ANTE. HOS. CC. ANNOS/A. CORRVPTELIS/VANISQ. PONTIFICIOR. COMMENTIS/AVSPICE DEO/VINDICE D. M. LVTHERO/ FELICITER. REPVRGATAM/M D CCXVII/PR. KAL. ET. KAL. NOV./IN. TERRIS. BR. WOLFFEN./ CELEBRATI/ H.C.H. **Note:** Dav.#2128

Date	Mintage	F	VF	XF	Unc
1717 HCH	—	250	450	800	1,450

KM# 838 THALER

Silver **Ruler:** August Wilhelm **Obverse:** Large head right **Reverse:** Wildman, tree in left hand, right hand holding crowned arms **Note:** Dav.#2135.

Date	Mintage	F	VF	XF	Unc
1727 HCH	—	250	450	900	1,500
1729 CPS	—	250	450	900	1,500
1733 D-BID	—	250	450	900	1,500

KM# 786 THALER

Silver **Ruler:** August Wilhelm **Subject:** 200th Anniversary of Reformation in the City of Brunswick **Obverse:** Bust right **Reverse:** 10-line legend with roman numeral date **Note:** Dav.#2129.

Date	Mintage	F	VF	XF	Unc
1728 HCH	—	550	800	1,400	2,250

KM# 798 THALER

Silver **Ruler:** August Wilhelm **Subject:** 200th Anniversary of Augsburg Confession **Obverse:** Armored draped bust right **Obv. Legend:** AUGUSTUS. WILH. - D.G. DUX. BR. ET. LUN. **Reverse:** I.H.T. below palm leaves **Rev. Inscription:** • CHRISTO •/PURIORIS RELIGIONIS/CONSERVATORI/ECCLESIA TERRARUM BRUNSVICO WOLFFENB./DIVINITUS ACCEPTI CC. AB HINC ANNIS/CORROBORATA PER CONFESSIONEM AUGUSTANAM/EVANGELICA DOCTRINA:/BENEFICII MEMOR./DEBITAS PERSOLVIT GRATIAS/M D CCXXX. XXV. IUNII. **Note:** Dav.#2130.

Date	Mintage	F	VF	XF	Unc
1730 IHT	—	400	600	1,000	1,700

KM# 816 THALER

Silver **Subject:** Death of August Wilhelm **Obverse:** Draped bust right **Obv. Legend:** AUGUSTUS. WILH. - D.G. DUX. BR. ET. LUN. **Reverse:** Inscription in 13 lines **Note:** Dav.#2132.

Date	Mintage	F	VF	XF	Unc
1731 IHT	—	250	450	800	1,450

KM# 817 THALER

Silver **Ruler:** Ludwig Rudolph **Obverse:** Helmeted complex arms with ornaments **Obv. Legend:** D • G • LVDOVICVS • RVDOLPHVS • DVX • BR • & LVN • **Reverse:** Wildman with tree in left hand **Rev. Legend:** EX ADVERSO DECVS. **Note:** Dav.#2137.

Date	Mintage	F	VF	XF	Unc
1731 C	—	65.00	135	250	575
1731 IAB	—	65.00	135	250	575
1732 IAB	—	65.00	135	250	575
1733 IAB	—	65.00	135	250	575
1734 IAB	—	65.00	135	250	575

KM# 818 THALER

Silver **Ruler:** Ludwig Rudolph **Reverse:** Horse leaping left **Note:** Dav.#2138.

Date	Mintage	F	VF	XF	Unc
1731 C	—	175	350	700	1,350
1733 IAB	—	175	350	700	1,350
1734 IAB	—	175	350	700	1,350
1735 IAB	—	175	350	700	1,350

KM# 878.1 THALER

Silver **Obverse:** Bust right **Reverse:** Horse leaping left, Roman numeral date below **Note:** Dav.#2139.

Date	Mintage	F	VF	XF	Unc
1735 BID	—	200	400	750	1,400

KM# 878.2 THALER

Silver **Obv. Legend:** LVDOVICVS. RVDOLPHVS. D. G. DVS. BR. ET. LVNEB:. **Note:** Dav.#2140.

Date	Mintage	F	VF	XF	Unc
1735 D-BID	—	200	400	750	1,400

KM# 879 THALER

Silver **Subject:** Death of Ludwig Rudolph **Obverse:** Bust right **Reverse:** 13-line inscription with Roman numeral date **Note:** Dav.#2141.

Date	Mintage	F	VF	XF	Unc
1735	—	400	600	1,000	1,600

KM# 880 THALER

Silver **Obverse:** Helmeted 12-fold arms, date in legend **Reverse:** Horse leaping left **Note:** Dav.#2142.

Date	Mintage	F	VF	XF	Unc
1735 IAB	—	300	500	800	1,500

KM# 881 THALER

Silver **Ruler:** Ferdinand Ulbrecht II **Reverse:** Wildman, tree in left hand **Note:** Dav.#2143

Date	Mintage	F	VF	XF	Unc
1735 IAB	—	450	750	1,250	—

KM# 882 THALER

Silver **Ruler:** Ferdinand Ulbrecht II **Subject:** Death of Ferdinand Albrecht II **Obverse:** Armored bust right **Obv. Legend:** FERDINAND • ALBERT • - D • G • DVX • BR • ET • LVN: **Reverse:** Inscription in 12 lines **Rev. Inscription:** PRINCEPS/IVSTVS CONSTANS/IN BELLO AB IPSO/AETATIS FLORE/ IMPERTERRUTVS/D. XIX MART. M D CLXXX NATVS/ TERRARVM BRVNSV. WOLFENB./GVERNACVLVM VI TANTVM MENSES/GLORIOSE MODERATVS/D. III SEPTEMBR. MDCCXXXV/EX SALINA VALLE/TVTISSIMVM INTRAVIT/PORTVM/*/B.I.D. **Note:** Dav.#2144.

Date	Mintage	F	VF	XF	Unc
1735 BID	—	600	900	1,500	—

KM# 884 THALER

Silver **Ruler:** Karl I **Obverse:** Helmeted complex arms with ornaments **Obv. Legend:** D • G • CAROLVS • DVX • BRVNSVIC • & LVNEBVRG • **Reverse:** Horse leaping left, value below **Rev. Legend:** NVNQNAM RETRORSVM, below: I.A.P. **Note:** Dav.#2146.

Date	Mintage	F	VF	XF	Unc
1735 IAB	—	200	400	800	1,500
1736 IAB	—	175	275	500	1,000
1748 IBH	—	175	275	500	1,000
1750 IBH	—	175	275	500	1,000
1755 IBH	—	175	275	500	1,000
1760 IBH	—	175	275	500	1,000
1763 IAP	—	175	275	500	1,000
1770 IAP	—	175	275	500	1,000

KM# 883 THALER

Silver **Ruler:** Karl I **Obv. Legend:** D • G • CAROLVS • DVX • BRVNSVIC • & LVNEB • **Reverse:** Helmeted complex arms with ornaments **Rev. Legend:** NVNQNAM RETRORSVM **Note:** Dav. #2145.

Date	Mintage	F	VF	XF	Unc
1735 IAB	—	85.00	175	300	625
1736 IAB	—	85.00	175	300	625
1737 IAB	—	85.00	175	300	625
1738 IAB	—	85.00	175	300	625
1739 IBH	—	85.00	175	300	625
1740 IBH	—	85.00	175	300	625
1741 IBH	—	85.00	175	300	625
1742 IBH	—	85.00	175	300	625
1744 IBH	—	85.00	175	300	625
1746 IBH	—	85.00	175	300	625
1748 IBH	—	85.00	175	300	625
1750 IBH	—	100	200	400	625
1755 IBH	—	100	200	400	625
1758 IBH	—	100	200	400	625
1760 IBH	—	100	200	400	625
1763 IBH	—	100	200	400	625
1775 LCR	—	100	200	400	625

KM# 911 THALER

Silver **Ruler:** Karl I **Obverse:** Bust right **Reverse:** Horse left, date below **Note:** Dav.#2147.

Date	Mintage	F	VF	XF	Unc
1742 K Rare	—	—	—	—	—

KM# 920 THALER

Silver **Ruler:** Karl I **Subject:** Goodness of the Lord Mine **Obverse:** Crowned complex arms with wildmen supporters **Obv. Legend:** D • G • CAROLVS - DVX • BRVNSVIC • - LVNEB • **Reverse:** View of the mines **Rev. Legend:** DIE ERDE IST VOLL GVTE DES HERRN, below in 5 lines: DIE GRVBE/GVTE DES HERRN/KAM IN AVSBEVT/IM Q REM: date/I.B.H. **Note:** Mining Thaler. Dav.#2163.

Date	Mintage	F	VF	XF	Unc
1743 IBH	—	300	600	900	2,000
1745 IBH	—	300	600	900	2,000
1747 IBH	—	300	600	900	2,000
1748 IBH	—	300	600	900	2,000

KM# 921 THALER

Silver **Ruler:** Karl I **Subject:** White Swan Mine **Obverse:** Crowned complex arms with wildmen supporters **Obv. Legend:** D • G • CAROLVS - DVX • BRVNSVIC • - LVNEB • **Reverse:** Swan and view of mine **Rev. Inscription:** CANDIDVS HAEC PROFERT MONTANVS PRAEMIA CYGNVS, below in 5 lines: DIE GRVBE/WEISSER SCHWAN/KAM IN AVSBEVT/IM Q: LVCIAE date/I.B.H. **Note:** Dav.#2156.

Date	Mintage	F	VF	XF	Unc
1744 IBH	—	200	400	700	1,500
1745 IBH	—	200	400	700	1,500
1747 IBH	—	200	400	700	1,500
1748 IBH	—	200	400	700	1,500

KM# 922.1 THALER

Silver **Ruler:** Karl I **Subject:** Cronenburg's Luck Mine **Obverse:** Crowned complex arms with wildmen supporters **Reverse:** View of the mine **Note:** Dav.#2158.

Date	Mintage	F	VF	XF	Unc
1744 IBH	—	250	500	800	1,500

KM# 922.2 THALER

Silver **Ruler:** Karl I **Note:** Dav.#2159.

Date	Mintage	F	VF	XF	Unc
1745 IBH	—	250	500	800	1,500
1748 IBH	—	250	500	800	1,500

KM# 923.1 THALER

Silver **Ruler:** Karl I **Subject:** Lautenthal's Luck Mine **Obverse:** Crowned complex arms with wildmen supporters **Obv. Legend:** D.G. CAROLVS - DVX • BRVNSVIC • - LVNEB • **Reverse:** View of the mine **Rev. Legend:** TV QVONDAM ABIECTAM REDDIS DEVS ALME SONORAM, below in 5 lines: DIE GREVBE/ LAVTENTHALS GLVCK/KAM IN AVSBEVT/IM QV: REM: date/I.B.H. **Note:** Dav.#2161.

Date	Mintage	F	VF	XF	Unc
1745 IBH	—	250	500	800	1,500
1748 IBH	—	250	500	800	1,500

KM# 924 THALER

Silver **Ruler:** Karl I **Subject:** Rainbow Mine **Obverse:** Crowned complex arms with wildmen supporters **Reverse:** Mine view **Note:** Dav.#2165.

Date	Mintage	F	VF	XF	Unc
1745 IBH	—	250	500	800	1,500
1746 IBH	—	250	500	800	1,500
1748 IBH	—	250	500	800	1,500

KM# 932 THALER

Silver **Ruler:** Karl I **Obverse:** Crowned arms with Burgundian cross **Reverse:** Arms with rampant lion **Note:** Albertus Thaler. Dav.#2148.

Date	Mintage	F	VF	XF	Unc
1747 EK	—	250	500	700	1,400

KM# 941 THALER

Silver **Ruler:** Karl I **Subject:** Cronenburg's Luck Mine **Obverse:** Crowned complex arms with wildmen supporters **Reverse:** Mine view **Rev. Legend:** NON - MARCESCET., below in 5 lines: DIE GRVBE/CRONENBVRGS GLVCK/KAM IN AVSBEVT/IM QV: LVCIAE date/I.B.H. **Note:** Dav.#2160.

Date	Mintage	F	VF	XF	Unc
1750 IBH	—	250	500	800	1,500
1752 IBH	—	250	500	800	1,500

KM# 940 THALER

Silver **Ruler:** Karl I **Subject:** White Swan Mine **Obverse:** Crowned complex arms with wildmen supporters **Obv. Legend:** D.G. CAROLVS - DVX • BRVNSVIC • - LVNEB • **Reverse:** Swan on lake, clouds above mine scene **Rev. Legend:** CANDIDVS HAEC PROFERT MONTANVS PRAEMIA CYGNVS, below in 5 lines: DIE GRVBE/WEISSER SCHWAN/KAM IN AVSBEVT/IM Q: LVCIAE date/I.B.H. **Note:** Dav.#2157.

Date	Mintage	F	VF	XF	Unc
1750 IBH	—	200	400	700	1,500
1752 IBH	—	200	400	700	1,500

KM# 942 THALER

Silver **Ruler:** Karl I **Subject:** Bleifeld Mine **Obverse:** Crowned complex oval arms with wildmen supporters **Obv. Legend:** D.G. CAROLVS • - DVX • BRVNSVIC • - LVNEB • **Reverse:** Tower and mine view **Rev. Legend:** REDEVNT SATVRNIA REGNA., below in 5 lines: DIE GRVBE/H: AVG: FRIED:BLEYFELD:/KAM WIED: IN AVSB:/IM QV: REM: date/I.B.H. **Note:** Mining Thaler. Dav.#2167.

Date	Mintage	F	VF	XF	Unc
1750 IBH	—	250	500	800	1,500
1752 IBH	—	250	500	800	1,500

KM# 923.2 THALER

Silver **Note:** Dav.#2162.

Date	Mintage	F	VF	XF	Unc
1752 IBH	—	250	500	800	1,500
1761 IBH	—	250	500	800	1,500

KM# 943 THALER

Silver **Ruler:** Karl I **Subject:** Goodness of the Lord Mine **Obverse:** Crowned complex oval arms with wildmen supporters **Obv. Legend:** D.G. CAROLVS • - DVX • BRVNSVIC • - LVNEB • **Reverse:** Mine view **Rev. Legend:** DIE ERDE IST VOLL GVTE DES HERRN, below in 5 lines: DIE GRVBE/GVTE DES HERRN/ KAM IN AVSBEVT/IM Q REM: date/I.B.H. **Note:** Dav.#2164.

Date	Mintage	F	VF	XF	Unc
1752 IBH	—	300	600	1,000	2,000

KM# 945 THALER

Silver **Ruler:** Karl I **Subject:** Rainbow Mine **Obverse:** Crowned complex oval arms with wildmen supporters **Obv. Legend:** D.G. CAROLVS • - DVX • BRVNSVIC • - LVNEB • **Reverse:** Mine view with rainbow **Rev. Inscription:** LOBE DEN, DER IHN GEMACHT HAT. SYR. C. 43., below in 5 lines: DIE GRUBE/REGENBOGEN/ KAM WIED. IN. AVSB:/IM Q: LVCIÆ date/ I.B.H. **Note:** Dav.#2166.

Date	Mintage	F	VF	XF	Unc
1752 IBH	—	250	500	800	1,500

KM# 946 THALER

Silver **Ruler:** Karl I **Subject:** King Karl Mine **Obverse:** Crowned complex oval arms with wildmen supporters **Obv. Legend:** D.G. CAROLVS • - DVX • BRVNSVIC • - LVNEB • **Reverse:** View of the mine **Rev. Legend:** PLVS VLTRA on band, below in 5 lines: DIE GRVBE/KONIG CARL/KAM IN AVSBEVT/IM QV: REM: date/ I.B.H. **Note:** Dav.#2168.

Date	Mintage	F	VF	XF	Unc
1752 IBH	—	250	500	800	1,500

KM# 950 THALER

Silver **Ruler:** Karl I **Obverse:** Bust right **Reverse:** Horse left, date in legend **Note:** Dav.#2149.

Date	Mintage	F	VF	XF	Unc
1758 ACB	—	75.00	150	275	550
1759 ACB	—	75.00	150	275	550

KM# 953 THALER

Silver **Ruler:** Karl I **Obverse:** Crowned ornate 'C' monogram **Reverse:** Value and date within wreath **Rev. Legend:** *I*/THALER/HZ. BR. L.L.M./* 1759 */A.C.B. **Note:** Dav.#2150.

Date	Mintage	F	VF	XF	Unc
1759 ACB	—	100	200	350	750

KM# 964 THALER

Silver **Ruler:** Karl I **Subject:** Blessing of God Mine **Obverse:** Crowned complex oval arms with wildmen supporters **Obv. Legend:** D.G. CAROLVS • DVX • BRVNSVIC • LVNEB • **Reverse:** View of the mine **Rev. Legend:** AN GOTTES SEGEN IST ALLES GELEGEN, below in 6 lines: DIE GRVBE/SEGEN GOTTES/IM IN AVSBEVT/IM Q: CRVC: date/I.A.P. **Note:** Dav.#2169.

Date	Mintage	F	VF	XF	Unc
1761 IBH	—	300	500	800	1,500

KM# 966.1 THALER

Silver **Ruler:** Karl I **Obverse:** Armored bust right **Obv. Legend:** CAROLVS D • G • DVX BRVNSVIC • ET LVNEB • **Reverse:** Horse leaping left **Rev. Legend:** NVNQVAM RETRORSVM • date, below: X• EINE FEINE MARCK/CONVENT• M•/I.D.B. **Note:** Convention Thaler. Dav.#2151.

Date	Mintage	F	VF	XF	Unc
1763 E-IDB	—	50.00	100	250	525
1764 E-IDB	—	50.00	100	250	525
1765 E-IDB	—	50.00	100	250	525

KM# 975.1 THALER

Silver **Ruler:** Karl I **Obverse:** Armored bust right, E below **Obv. Legend:** . . . BRVNS. ET LVN. **Reverse:** Crowned 12-fold arms in baroque frame **Note:** Dav.#2152.

Date	Mintage	F	VF	XF	Unc
1768 E-IDB Rare	—	—	—	—	—

KM# 975.2 THALER

Silver **Ruler:** Karl I **Obverse:** Armored bust right **Obv. Legend:** . . . BRVNSVIC. ET LUNES. **Reverse:** Crowned complex arms in baroque frame **Note:** Dav.#2153.

Date	Mintage	F	VF	XF	Unc
1769 E-IDB Rare	—	—	—	—	—

KM# 966.2 THALER

Silver **Ruler:** Karl I **Obverse:** Draped bust right, E below **Obv. Legend:** . . . BRVNS. ET LVN. **Reverse:** Horse left **Note:** Dav.#2154.

Date	Mintage	F	VF	XF	Unc
1776 E-IDB	—	50.00	100	250	525

KM# 988 THALER

Silver **Ruler:** Karl I **Obverse:** Head right **Obv. Legend:** CAROLVS D • G • DVX BRVNSV • ET LVN • **Reverse:** Horse left **Rev. Legend:** NVNQVAM RETRORSVM • date, below: X.EINE FEINE MARK/CONVENT.M./M.C. **Note:** Dav.#2155.

Date	Mintage	F	VF	XF	Unc
1779 K-MC	—	75.00	125	250	525

KM# 1016 THALER

Silver **Ruler:** Karl Wilhelm Ferdinand **Obverse:** Arms **Reverse:** Value **Note:** Species Thaler. Dav.#2171.

Date	Mintage	F	VF	XF	Unc
1782 MC	—	100	150	275	475
1783 MC	—	100	150	275	475

KM# 1018 THALER

Silver **Ruler:** Karl Wilhelm Ferdinand **Obverse:** Head right, K below **Obv. Legend:** CAROLVS GVIL • FERD • D • G • DVX BR • ET • LVN • **Reverse:** Crowned complex arms within Order chain **Rev. Legend:** X EINE FEINE MARK CONVENTIONS M. 1783 **Note:** Dav.#2172.

Date	Mintage	F	VF	XF	Unc
1783 MC	—	300	600	900	1,500

KM# 1030 THALER

Silver **Ruler:** Karl Wilhelm Ferdinand **Obverse:** Small arms **Obv. Legend:** * CAROLVS GVIL • FERD • D • G • DVX BRVNSV • ET LVN • **Reverse:** Denomination, date **Rev. Legend:** * X EINE FEINE MARK CONVENTIONS M. **Note:** Dav.#2173.

Date	Mintage	F	VF	XF	Unc
1787 MC	—	40.00	75.00	125	250
1788 MC	—	40.00	75.00	125	250
1789 MC	—	40.00	75.00	125	250
1790 MC	—	40.00	75.00	125	250
1792 MC	—	40.00	75.00	125	250
1794 MC	—	40.00	75.00	125	250
1795 MC	—	40.00	75.00	125	250
1796 MC	—	40.00	75.00	125	250
1801 Rare	—	—	—	—	—

KM# 688 1-1/4 THALER

Silver **Ruler:** Anton Ulrich Alone **Subject:** Visit of Anton Ulrich to Zellerfeld Mint **Obverse:** Salzdahlum Palace, sundial suspended at upper left, sun shining from upper left **Reverse:** 2 miners in mine, CONSTANTER on ribbon above, date below **Note:** 1-1/4 Mining Thaler. Dav.#2932.

Date	Mintage	VG	F	VF	XF	Unc
1705	—	750	1,250	1,900	3,250	—

KM# 689 1-1/2 THALER

Silver **Ruler:** Anton Ulrich Alone **Subject:** Visit of Anton Ulrich to Zellerfeld Mint **Obverse:** Salzdahlum Palace, sundial suspended at uppr left, sun shining from upper right **Obv. Legend:** AUGENTER VITA DIESQUE, below: ARDENTIB * VOTIS • **Reverse:** 2 miners in mine, CONSTANTER on ribbon above, date below **Note:** 1-1/2 Mining Thaler. Dav.#A2932.

Date	Mintage	VG	F	VF	XF	Unc
1705	—	—	—	1,200	1,850	—

KM# 707 1-1/2 THALER

43.5000 g., Silver **Subject:** Conversion of Anton Ulrich to Catholicism **Obverse:** Bust right **Reverse:** Rock in sea, SEMPER IDEM above, CONSTANTER below **Note:** Struck from 1 Thaler dies. Dav.#2121A.

Date	Mintage	VG	F	VF	XF	Unc
ND Rare	—	—	—	—	—	—

KM# 787 1-1/2 THALER

43.5000 g., Silver **Ruler:** August Wilhelm **Subject:** 200th Anniversary of Reformation in the City of Brunswick **Obverse:** Bust right **Reverse:** Altar with Bible and date, EX SINCERITATE

Date	Mintage	VG	F	VF	XF	Unc
1728	—	—	—	1,600	2,500	—

KM# 708 2 THALER

Silver **Ruler:** Anton Ulrich Alone **Obverse:** Armored draped bust right **Obv. Legend:** ANTONIUS ULRICUS. D: G: DUX BR: ET LUNEBURG. **Reverse:** Horse leaping left in front of Roman-syle racecourse **Rev. Legend:** ALIORUM. ABSUMOR. IN. USUS

Date	Mintage	VG	F	VF	XF	Unc
ND(ca. 1710)	—	1,000	1,650	2,850	4,750	—

KM# 819 2 THALER

Silver **Ruler:** Ludwig Rudolph **Subject:** Death of August Wilhelm **Obverse:** Bust right **Reverse:** 12-line inscription with Roman numeral date **Note:** Dav.#2131.

Date	Mintage	VG	F	VF	XF	Unc
1731 IHT Rare	—	—	—	—	—	—

KM# A947 2 THALER

57.5300 g., Silver **Note:** 2 Reise Thaler. Similar to 1 Thaler, KM#946. Dav. #6356.

Date	Mintage	VG	F	VF	XF	Unc
ND Rare	—	—	—	—	—	—

KM# 912 2-1/2 THALER

3.3200 g., 0.9000 Gold 0.0961 oz. AGW **Ruler:** Karl I **Obverse:** Bust right **Reverse:** Crowned 12-fold arms

Date	Mintage	F	VF	XF	Unc
1742 EK	—	400	800	1,200	2,000

KM# 913 2-1/2 THALER

3.3200 g., 0.9000 Gold 0.0961 oz. AGW **Ruler:** Karl I **Subject:** Carl **Obverse:** Armored bust with sash crossing chest right **Reverse:** Horse leaping left

Date	Mintage	F	VF	XF	Unc
1742 EK-M	—	200	350	475	850
1743 EK-M	—	200	350	475	850
1744 EK-M	—	200	350	475	850
1746 EK-M	—	200	350	475	850
1747 EK-M	—	200	350	475	850
1748 EK-M	—	200	350	475	850
1749 EK-M	—	200	350	475	850
1750 EK-M	—	200	350	475	850
1751 M	—	200	350	475	850
1754	—	200	350	475	850
1757 E-ACB	—	200	350	475	850
1759 E-ACB	—	200	350	475	850
1760 E-IDB	—	300	500	750	1,200
1761 E-IDB	—	200	350	475	850
1762 E-IDB	—	200	350	475	850
1763 E-IDB	—	200	350	475	850
1764 E-IDB	—	200	350	475	850
1765 E-IDB	—	200	350	475	850
1766 E-IDB	—	200	350	475	850
1767 E-IDB	—	200	350	475	850
1768 E-IDB	—	200	350	475	850
1769 E-IDB	—	400	800	1,200	2,000
1770 E-IDB	—	200	350	475	850
1771	—	200	350	475	850
1773	—	200	350	475	850
1774 E-IDB	—	300	500	750	1,200
1775 E-IDB	—	200	350	475	850

KM# 986 2-1/2 THALER

3.3200 g., 0.9000 Gold 0.0961 oz. AGW **Ruler:** Karl I **Obverse:** Bust right **Reverse:** Running horse left

Date	Mintage	F	VF	XF	Unc
1777 IDB	—	225	450	900	1,500

KM# 1013 2-1/2 THALER

3.3200 g., 0.9000 Gold 0.0961 oz. AGW **Ruler:** Karl Wilhelm Ferdinand **Obverse:** Arms **Reverse:** Value

Date	Mintage	F	VF	XF	Unc
1781 MC	—	250	500	1,000	1,500
1782 MC	—	275	550	1,100	1,650

KM# 1032 2-1/2 THALER

3.3200 g., 0.9000 Gold 0.0961 oz. AGW **Ruler:** Karl Wilhelm Ferdinand **Obverse:** Arms change **Reverse:** Value and date

Date	Mintage	F	VF	XF	Unc
1788 MC	—	275	550	1,100	1,650
1789 MC	—	250	500	1,000	1,500
1791 MC	—	275	550	1,100	1,650
1793 MC	—	275	550	1,100	1,650
1794 MC	—	250	500	1,000	1,500
1796 MC	—	250	500	1,000	1,500
1800 MC	—	250	500	1,000	1,500
1801 MC	—	375	750	1,350	2,000
1801 MC	—	375	750	1,350	2,000
1802 MC	—	300	625	1,150	1,750
1806 MC	—	300	625	1,150	2,000

KM# 709 3 THALER

Silver **Ruler:** Anton Ulrich Alone **Subject:** Conversion of Anton Ulrich to Catholicism **Obverse:** Bust right **Reverse:** Rock in sea, SEMPER IDEM above, CONSTANTER below **Note:** Dav. #2121.

Date	Mintage	VG	F	VF	XF	Unc
ND(1710) Rare	—	—	—	—	—	—

KM# 914 5 THALER

6.6500 g., 0.9000 Gold 0.1924 oz. AGW **Ruler:** Karl I **Obverse:** Armored bust right **Reverse:** Crowned arms with value below, date in legend

Date	Mintage	F	VF	XF	Unc
1742	—	500	1,200	1,750	2,500
1742 EK	—	500	1,200	1,750	2,500

KM# 915 5 THALER

6.6500 g., 0.9000 Gold 0.1924 oz. AGW **Ruler:** Karl I **Obverse:** Armored bust right **Reverse:** Horse leaping left

Date	Mintage	F	VF	XF	Unc
1742 EK-M	—	200	425	850	1,500
1743 EK-M	—	200	425	850	1,500
1744 EK-M	—	200	425	850	1,500
1744 EK	—	200	425	850	1,500
1745 EK-M	—	200	425	850	1,500
1746 EK-M	—	200	425	850	1,500
1747 EK-M	—	200	425	850	1,500
1748 EK-M	—	400	1,200	1,500	2,500
1749 EK-M	—	200	425	850	1,500
1750 EK-M	—	200	425	850	1,500
1751	—	200	425	850	1,500

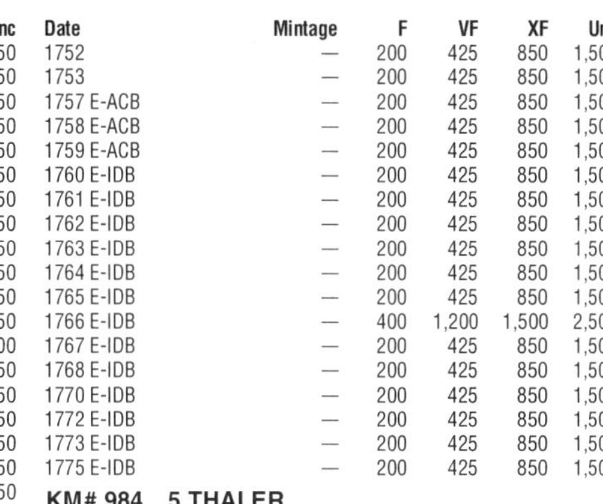

Date	Mintage	F	VF	XF	Unc
1752	—	200	425	850	1,500
1753	—	200	425	850	1,500
1757 E-ACB	—	200	425	850	1,500
1758 E-ACB	—	200	425	850	1,500
1759 E-ACB	—	200	425	850	1,500
1760 E-IDB	—	200	425	850	1,500
1761 E-IDB	—	200	425	850	1,500
1762 E-IDB	—	200	425	850	1,500
1763 E-IDB	—	200	425	850	1,500
1764 E-IDB	—	200	425	850	1,500
1765 E-IDB	—	200	425	850	1,500
1766 E-IDB	—	400	1,200	1,500	2,500
1767 E-IDB	—	200	425	850	1,500
1768 E-IDB	—	200	425	850	1,500
1770 E-IDB	—	200	425	850	1,500
1772 E-IDB	—	200	425	850	1,500
1773 E-IDB	—	200	425	850	1,500
1775 E-IDB	—	200	425	850	1,500

KM# 984 5 THALER

6.6500 g., 0.9000 Gold 0.1924 oz. AGW **Ruler:** Karl I **Obverse:** Head right **Reverse:** Running horse left

Date	Mintage	F	VF	XF	Unc
1775 IDB	—	500	1,350	1,950	2,750
1776 IDB	—	500	1,350	1,950	2,750
1777 IDB	—	500	1,350	1,950	2,750
1778 IDB	—	500	1,350	1,950	2,750

KM# 1002 5 THALER

6.6500 g., 0.9000 Gold 0.1924 oz. AGW **Ruler:** Karl Wilhelm Ferdinand **Obverse:** Arms **Reverse:** Value

Date	Mintage	F	VF	XF	Unc
1780 MC	—	375	675	1,100	1,650
1781 MC	—	375	675	1,100	1,650
1782 MC	—	375	675	1,100	1,650
1783 MC	—	375	675	1,100	1,650

KM# 1025 5 THALER

6.6500 g., 0.9000 Gold 0.1924 oz. AGW **Ruler:** Karl Wilhelm Ferdinand **Obverse:** Crowned arms within Order chain **Obv. Legend:** FERDINANDVS CAROLVS GVILIELMVS **Reverse:** Value, date

Date	Mintage	F	VF	XF	Unc
1785 MC	—	350	650	1,100	1,650
1786 MC	—	350	650	1,100	1,650
1790 MC	—	350	650	1,100	1,650
1795 MC	—	350	650	1,100	1,650
1796 MC	—	350	650	1,100	1,650
1797 MC	—	350	650	1,100	1,650
1798 MC	—	350	650	1,100	1,650
1799 MC	—	350	650	1,100	1,650
1800 MC	—	450	750	1,150	1,850
1801 MC	—	475	875	1,250	2,000
1802 MC	—	325	625	1,000	1,800
1803 MC Rare	—	—	—	—	—
1804 MC	—	475	875	1,250	2,000
1805 MC	—	450	750	1,150	1,850
1806 MC	—	450	750	1,150	1,850

KM# 916 10 THALER

13.3000 g., 0.9000 Gold 0.3848 oz. AGW **Obverse:** Armored bust of Carl right **Reverse:** Crowned arms with value below, date in legend

Date	Mintage	F	VF	XF	Unc
1742	—	750	1,350	2,200	3,500

KM# 917 10 THALER

13.3000 g., 0.9000 Gold 0.3848 oz. AGW **Ruler:** Karl I **Obverse:** Armored bust right **Reverse:** Horse leaping left

Date	Mintage	F	VF	XF	Unc
1742 EK-M	—	450	900	1,500	2,250
1743 EK-M	—	450	900	1,500	2,250
1744 EK-M	—	450	900	1,500	2,250
1745 EK-M	—	450	900	1,500	2,250
1746 EK-M	—	450	900	1,500	2,250
1747 EK-M	—	450	900	1,500	2,250
1748 EK-M	—	450	900	1,500	2,250
1750	—	450	900	1,500	2,250
1753	—	450	900	1,500	2,250
1756	—	450	900	1,500	2,250
1758	—	450	900	1,500	2,250
1760 E-IDB	—	450	900	1,500	2,250
1761 E-IDB	—	450	900	1,500	2,250

Date	Mintage	F	VF	XF	Unc
1762/1 E-IDB	—	450	900	1,500	2,250
1762 E-IDB	—	450	900	1,500	2,250
1763 E-IDB	—	400	800	1,400	2,250
1764 E-IDB	—	400	800	1,400	2,250

KM# 987.1 10 THALER

13.3000 g., 0.9000 Gold 0.3848 oz. AGW **Ruler:** Karl I **Obverse:** Head right **Obv. Legend:** CAROLVS D•G• DVX BR• ET LVN **Reverse:** Horse leaping left

Date	Mintage	F	VF	XF	Unc
1775 IDB	—	—	—	—	—

KM# 987.2 10 THALER

13.3000 g., 0.9000 Gold 0.3848 oz. AGW **Ruler:** Karl I **Obverse:** Head right **Obv. Legend:** CAROLVS D•G• DVX BRVNS• ET LVN• **Reverse:** Horse leaping left

Date	Mintage	F	VF	XF	Unc
1777 IDB	—	750	1,250	1,750	2,750

KM# 1014 10 THALER

13.3000 g., 0.9000 Gold 0.3848 oz. AGW **Ruler:** Karl Wilhelm Ferdinand

Date	Mintage	F	VF	XF	Unc
1781 MC	—	800	1,350	2,000	3,000
1782 MC	—	800	1,350	2,000	3,000
1783 MC	—	800	1,350	2,000	3,000
1784 MC	—	800	1,350	2,000	3,000

KM# 1041 10 THALER

13.3000 g., 0.9000 Gold 0.3848 oz. AGW **Ruler:** Karl Wilhelm Ferdinand **Obverse:** Change in arms **Obv. Legend:** FERDINANDVS CAROLVS GVILIELMVS **Reverse:** Value, date

Date	Mintage	F	VF	XF	Unc
1794 MC	—	800	1,350	2,000	3,000
1795 MC	—	800	1,350	2,000	3,000
1796 MC	—	800	1,350	2,000	3,000
1797 MC	—	800	1,350	2,000	3,000
1799 MC	—	800	1,350	2,000	3,000
1800 MC	—	675	1,150	2,000	3,000
1801 MC	—	675	1,150	2,000	3,000
1804 MC	—	750	1,250	2,000	3,000
1805 MC	—	550	875	1,500	2,500
1806 MC	—	750	1,250	1,850	2,750

TRADE COINAGE

KM# 673 1/4 DUCAT

0.8750 g., 0.9860 Gold 0.0277 oz. AGW **Subject:** Death of Rudolf August **Obverse:** Bust of Rudolf August right **Reverse:** Four-line inscription

Date	Mintage	VG	F	VF	XF	Unc
1704	—	250	400	700	1,200	—

KM# 759 1/4 DUCAT

0.8750 g., 0.9860 Gold 0.0277 oz. AGW **Ruler:** August Wilhelm **Obverse:** Crowned cursive AW monogram **Reverse:** Horse leaping left, Arabic date below

Date	Mintage	VG	F	VF	XF	Unc
1716 HH	—	200	350	550	800	—
1717 HH	—	200	350	550	800	—

KM# 770 1/4 DUCAT

0.8750 g., 0.9860 Gold 0.0277 oz. AGW **Ruler:** August Wilhelm **Obverse:** Crowned AW monogram **Reverse:** Rearing horse, Roman numeral date in exergue

Date	Mintage	VG	F	VF	XF	Unc
1717 HCH	—	100	175	300	500	—
1718 HCH	—	100	175	300	500	—

KM# 850 1/4 DUCAT

0.8750 g., 0.9860 Gold 0.0277 oz. AGW **Ruler:** Ludwig Rudolph **Obverse:** Crowned cursive monogram **Reverse:** Horse rearing left, date below

Date	Mintage	VG	F	VF	XF	Unc
1734	—	150	275	475	750	—

KM# 699 1/2 DUCAT

1.7500 g., 0.9860 Gold 0.0555 oz. AGW **Ruler:** Anton Ulrich Alone **Obverse:** Bust of Anton Ulrich right **Reverse:** Rearing horse, date in exergue

Date	Mintage	VG	F	VF	XF	Unc
1708 HCH	—	100	200	500	900	—
1709 HCH	—	100	200	500	900	—

KM# 700 1/2 DUCAT

1.7500 g., 0.9860 Gold 0.0555 oz. AGW **Ruler:** Anton Ulrich Alone **Obverse:** Crowned ornate monogram **Reverse:** Horse rearing left

Date	Mintage	VG	F	VF	XF	Unc
1708 HCH	—	100	175	350	550	—
1709 HCH	—	100	175	350	550	—

KM# 750 1/2 DUCAT

1.7500 g., 0.9860 Gold 0.0555 oz. AGW **Ruler:** August Wilhelm **Obverse:** Crowned AW monogram **Reverse:** Arabic date

Date	Mintage	VG	F	VF	XF	Unc
1715 HH	—	125	250	550	800	—
1716 HH	—	125	250	550	800	—

KM# 760 1/2 DUCAT

1.7500 g., 0.9860 Gold 0.0555 oz. AGW **Ruler:** August Wilhelm **Reverse:** Roman numeral date

Date	Mintage	VG	F	VF	XF	Unc
1716 HCH	—	275	450	750	1,250	—
1718 HCH	—	275	450	750	1,250	—
1721 HCH	—	275	450	750	1,250	—

KM# 674 3/4 DUCAT

2.6250 g., 0.9860 Gold 0.0832 oz. AGW **Ruler:** Anton Ulrich Alone **Subject:** Death of Rudolf August **Obverse:** Bust of Rudolf August right **Reverse:** Five-line inscription

Date	Mintage	VG	F	VF	XF	Unc
1704	—	175	350	700	1,150	—

KM# 625 DUCAT

3.5000 g., 0.9860 Gold 0.1109 oz. AGW **Ruler:** Anton Ulrich as Joint ruler **Obverse:** Bust of Rudolf August right **Reverse:** Bust of Anton Ulrich right **Note:** Varieties exist.

Date	Mintage	VG	F	VF	XF	Unc
1698 HCH	—	225	500	1,150	2,000	—
1701 HCH	—	225	500	1,150	2,000	—
ND HCH	—	225	500	1,150	2,000	—

KM# 675 DUCAT

3.5000 g., 0.9860 Gold 0.1109 oz. AGW **Ruler:** Anton Ulrich Alone **Subject:** Death of Rudolf August **Reverse:** Eight-line inscription

Date	Mintage	VG	F	VF	XF	Unc
1704 HCH	—	200	500	1,150	2,000	—

KM# 676 DUCAT

3.5000 g., 0.9860 Gold 0.1109 oz. AGW **Subject:** Death of Elisabeth Juliane, Wife of Anton Ulrich **Obverse:** Bust of Elisabeth Juliane right

Date	Mintage	VG	F	VF	XF	Unc
1704 HCH	—	350	650	1,250	2,000	—

KM# 690 DUCAT

3.5000 g., 0.9860 Gold 0.1109 oz. AGW **Ruler:** Anton Ulrich Alone **Obverse:** Bust right **Reverse:** Crowned arms

Date	Mintage	VG	F	VF	XF	Unc
1705	—	200	400	900	1,500	—

KM# 696 DUCAT

3.5000 g., 0.9860 Gold 0.1109 oz. AGW **Ruler:** Anton Ulrich Alone **Obverse:** Bust right **Reverse:** Rearing horse, Arabic date in exergue

Date	Mintage	VG	F	VF	XF	Unc
1707 HCH	—	200	400	900	1,500	—

KM# 697 DUCAT

3.5000 g., 0.9860 Gold 0.1109 oz. AGW **Ruler:** Anton Ulrich Alone **Obverse:** Crowned AU monogram

Date	Mintage	VG	F	VF	XF	Unc
1707 HCH	—	200	400	900	1,500	—

KM# 710 DUCAT

3.5000 g., 0.9860 Gold 0.1109 oz. AGW **Ruler:** Anton Ulrich Alone **Subject:** Gold From Harz Mountains **Obverse:** Head right **Note:** Varieties exist.

Date	Mintage	VG	F	VF	XF	Unc
1710 HCH	—	350	700	1,500	2,500	—

KM# 711 DUCAT

3.5000 g., 0.9860 Gold 0.1109 oz. AGW **Ruler:** Anton Ulrich Alone **Obverse:** Crowned AU monogram

Date	Mintage	VG	F	VF	XF	Unc
1710 HCH	—	300	600	1,200	1,800	—

KM# 718 DUCAT

3.5000 g., 0.9860 Gold 0.1109 oz. AGW **Ruler:** Anton Ulrich Alone **Obverse:** Bust right **Reverse:** Horse leaping left, Roman numeral date below **Note:** Varieties exist.

Date	Mintage	VG	F	VF	XF	Unc
1711 HCH	—	625	925	1,275	1,900	—
1712 HCH	—	625	925	1,275	1,900	—

KM# 719 DUCAT

3.5000 g., 0.9860 Gold 0.1109 oz. AGW **Ruler:** Anton Ulrich Alone **Obverse:** Crowned AU monogram

Date	Mintage	VG	F	VF	XF	Unc
1711 HCH	—	550	800	1,125	1,750	—

KM# 740 DUCAT

3.5000 g., 0.9860 Gold 0.1109 oz. AGW **Ruler:** August Wilhelm **Obverse:** Draped bust right **Reverse:** Horse leaping left **Note:** Varieties exist.

Date	Mintage	VG	F	VF	XF	Unc
1714 HCH	—	150	300	650	1,000	—
1716 HCH	—	150	300	650	1,000	—
1719 HCH	—	150	300	650	1,000	—
1722 HCH	—	150	300	650	1,000	—
1723 HCH	—	150	300	650	1,000	—
1728 HCH	—	150	300	650	1,000	—

KM# 761 DUCAT

3.5000 g., 0.9860 Gold 0.1109 oz. AGW **Ruler:** August Wilhelm **Obverse:** Crowned AW monogram

Date	Mintage	VG	F	VF	XF	Unc
1716	—	225	450	1,000	1,600	—

KM# 771 DUCAT

3.5000 g., 0.9860 Gold 0.1109 oz. AGW **Ruler:** August Wilhelm **Subject:** Bicentennial of the Reformation **Obverse:** Head right **Reverse:** Inscription

Date	Mintage	VG	F	VF	XF	Unc
1717 HCH	—	225	450	1,000	1,600	—

KM# 772 DUCAT

3.5000 g., 0.9860 Gold 0.1109 oz. AGW **Ruler:** August Wilhelm **Subject:** Gold from Harz Mountains

Date	Mintage	VG	F	VF	XF	Unc
1719	—	200	500	1,100	1,750	—
1721	—	200	500	1,100	1,750	—
1728	—	200	500	1,100	1,750	—
1729	—	200	500	1,100	1,750	—
1730	—	200	500	1,100	1,750	—

KM# 782 DUCAT

3.5000 g., 0.9860 Gold 0.1109 oz. AGW **Ruler:** August Wilhelm **Obverse:** Crowned 11-fold arms, date in legend **Reverse:** Wildman, tree in left hand

Date	Mintage	VG	F	VF	XF	Unc
1725 EPH	—	600	875	1,200	1,850	—
1728	—	600	875	1,200	1,850	—

KM# 781 DUCAT

3.5000 g., 0.9860 Gold 0.1109 oz. AGW **Ruler:** August Wilhelm

Date	Mintage	VG	F	VF	XF	Unc
[illegible]	[illegible]	[illegible]	[illegible]	1,000	1,000	

KM# 788 DUCAT

3.5000 g., 0.9860 Gold 0.1109 oz. AGW **Ruler:** August Wilhelm **Subject:** Lower Harz Gold **Obverse:** Helmeted arms **Reverse:** Horse leaping left, Roman numeral date below

Date	Mintage	VG	F	VF	XF	Unc
1729	—	550	800	1,125	1,750	—
1730	—	550	800	1,125	1,750	—

KM# 799 DUCAT

3.5000 g., 0.9860 Gold 0.1109 oz. AGW **Ruler:** August Wilhelm **Subject:** Bicentennial of Augsburg Confession **Obverse:** Bust right **Reverse:** Inscription

Date	Mintage	VG	F	VF	XF	Unc
1730 IHT	—	325	750	1,400	2,250	—

KM# 800 DUCAT

3.5000 g., 0.9860 Gold 0.1109 oz. AGW **Ruler:** August Wilhelm **Subject:** Gold from Harz Mountains **Obverse:** Crowned arms **Reverse:** Rearing horse, date in exergue

Date	Mintage	VG	F	VF	XF	Unc
1730 IHT	—	325	650	1,250	2,000	—

KM# 820 DUCAT

3.5000 g., 0.9860 Gold 0.1109 oz. AGW **Subject:** Death of August Wilhelm **Obverse:** Bust of August Wilhelm right **Reverse:** Five-line inscription

Date	Mintage	VG	F	VF	XF	Unc
1731 IHT	—	225	450	1,000	1,600	—

KM# 821 DUCAT

3.5000 g., 0.9860 Gold 0.1109 oz. AGW **Ruler:** Ludwig Rudolph **Subject:** Gold from Harz Mountains **Obverse:** Head right **Reverse:** Helmet with plumes and horse divides date

Date	Mintage	VG	F	VF	XF	Unc
1731 S	—	350	700	1,500	2,500	—
1732 S	—	350	700	1,500	2,500	—

KM# 822 DUCAT

3.5000 g., 0.9860 Gold 0.1109 oz. AGW **Ruler:** Ludwig Rudolph **Obverse:** Head right **Reverse:** Horse rearing left

Date	Mintage	VG	F	VF	XF	Unc
1731	—	150	300	600	1,000	—
1732	—	150	300	600	1,000	—
1734	—	150	300	600	1,000	—

KM# 823 DUCAT

3.5000 g., 0.9860 Gold 0.1109 oz. AGW **Ruler:** Ludwig Rudolph **Obverse:** Head right **Reverse:** Horse left within crowned shield

Date	Mintage	VG	F	VF	XF	Unc
1731	—	300	650	1,200	2,000	—
1732	—	300	650	1,200	2,000	—
1733	—	300	650	1,200	2,000	—

KM# 828 DUCAT

3.5000 g., 0.9860 Gold 0.1109 oz. AGW **Subject:** Gold from Harz Mountains

Date	Mintage	VG	F	VF	XF	Unc
1732	—	300	650	1,200	2,000	—
1733	—	300	650	1,200	2,000	—
1734	—	300	650	1,200	2,000	—

KM# 839 DUCAT

3.5000 g., 0.9860 Gold 0.1109 oz. AGW **Subject:** Marriage of Karl (I) and Philippine Charlotte of Prussia **Obverse:** Crowned cursive mirror-image 9 PC monogram **Reverse:** Six-line legend with Roman numeral date, value below

Date	Mintage	VG	F	VF	XF	Unc
1733 BIC	—	600	900	1,200	1,850	—

KM# 840 DUCAT

3.5000 g., 0.9860 Gold 0.1109 oz. AGW **Subject:** Marriage of Karl (I)'s Sister, Elisabeth Christine and Friedrich (II) of Prussia **Obverse:** Crowned cursive mirror-image EC monogram **Reverse:** Nine-line inscription with Roman numeral date, value below

Date	Mintage	VG	F	VF	XF	Unc
1733 BIC	—	600	900	1,200	1,850	—

KM# 841 DUCAT

3.5000 g., 0.9860 Gold 0.1109 oz. AGW **Ruler:** Ludwig Rudolph **Obverse:** Head right **Reverse:** Starburst in circle of clouds, date in exergue

Date	Mintage	VG	F	VF	XF	Unc
1733	—	300	700	1,400	2,250	—

KM# 842 DUCAT

3.5000 g., 0.9860 Gold 0.1109 oz. AGW **Obverse:** Rearing horse, date below **Reverse:** Wildman holding tree and arms, date

Date	Mintage	VG	F	VF	XF	Unc
1733	—	200	450	1,000	1,600	—

KM# 843 DUCAT

3.5000 g., 0.9860 Gold 0.1109 oz. AGW **Ruler:** Ludwig Rudolph **Obverse:** Head right **Reverse:** Wildman with tree in left hand and arms in right

Date	Mintage	VG	F	VF	XF	Unc
1733	—	200	300	600	1,000	—

KM# 844 DUCAT

3.5000 g., 0.9860 Gold 0.1109 oz. AGW, 21 mm. **Ruler:** Ludwig Rudolph **Reverse:** Date in legend

Date	Mintage	VG	F	VF	XF	Unc
1733 D-BID	—	200	400	1,000	1,600	—

KM# 845 DUCAT

3.5000 g., 0.9860 Gold 0.1109 oz. AGW **Ruler:** Ludwig Rudolph **Reverse:** Wildman without crowned arms

Date	Mintage	VG	F	VF	XF	Unc
1733	—	200	400	1,000	1,600	—

KM# 885 DUCAT

3.5000 g., 0.9860 Gold 0.1109 oz. AGW **Subject:** Death of Ludwig Rudolf **Obverse:** Head right **Reverse:** Inscription

Date	Mintage	VG	F	VF	XF	Unc
1735 BID	—	200	400	1,000	1,600	—

KM# 886 DUCAT

3.5000 g., 0.9860 Gold 0.1109 oz. AGW **Ruler:** Ferdinand Ulbrecht II **Obverse:** Bust right **Reverse:** Horse leaping left

Date	Mintage	VG	F	VF	XF	Unc
1735 S	—	300	600	1,300	2,200	—

KM# 887 DUCAT

3.5000 g., 0.9860 Gold 0.1109 oz. AGW **Subject:** Gold from Harz Mountains

Date	Mintage	VG	F	VF	XF	Unc
1735	—	300	600	1,300	2,200	—

KM# 888 DUCAT

3.5000 g., 0.9860 Gold 0.1109 oz. AGW **Ruler:** Ferdinand Ulbrecht II **Obverse:** Crowned FA monogram

Date	Mintage	VG	F	VF	XF	Unc
1735 BID	—	300	600	1,300	2,200	—

KM# 889 DUCAT

3.5000 g., 0.9860 Gold 0.1109 oz. AGW **Obverse:** Crowned arms

Date	Mintage	VG	F	VF	XF	Unc
1735	—	300	600	1,300	2,200	—

KM# 890 DUCAT

3.5000 g., 0.9860 Gold 0.1109 oz. AGW **Subject:** Death of Ferdinand Albrecht II **Obverse:** Head of Ferdinand Albrecht II right **Reverse:** Eight-line legend

Date	Mintage	VG	F	VF	XF	Unc
1735 BID	—	300	600	1,300	2,200	—

KM# 899 DUCAT

3.5000 g., 0.9860 Gold 0.1109 oz. AGW **Ruler:** Karl I **Obverse:** Armored bust left **Reverse:** Date below horse in Roman numerals **Rev. Legend:** EX. AVR. HERC. INF.

Date	Mintage	F	VF	XF	Unc
1736 S	—	500	1,200	2,000	3,000

KM# 900 DUCAT

3.5000 g., 0.9860 Gold 0.1109 oz. AGW **Ruler:** Karl I **Obverse:** Armored bust left **Reverse:** Date in Arabic numerals

Date	Mintage	F	VF	XF	Unc
1736 BID	—	200	500	1,200	2,000

KM# 904 DUCAT

3.5000 g., 0.9860 Gold 0.1109 oz. AGW **Ruler:** Karl I **Obverse:** Head right **Reverse:** Horse leaping left

Date	Mintage	F	VF	XF	Unc
1737 BID	—	300	600	1,000	2,000
1738 BID	—	300	600	1,000	2,000
1739 BID	—	300	600	1,000	2,000
1742 BID	—	300	600	1,000	2,000

KM# 905 DUCAT

3.5000 g., 0.9860 Gold 0.1109 oz. AGW **Ruler:** Karl I **Obverse:** Bust right

Date	Mintage	F	VF	XF	Unc
1739 S	—	400	900	2,000	3,000

KM# 918 DUCAT

3.5000 g., 0.9860 Gold 0.1109 oz. AGW **Ruler:** Karl I **Obverse:** Bust right

Date	Mintage	F	VF	XF	Unc
1742 EK Rare	—	—	—	—	—

KM# 919 DUCAT

3.5000 g., 0.9860 Gold 0.1109 oz. AGW **Ruler:** Karl I **Reverse:** Value: DVCAT

Date	Mintage	F	VF	XF	Unc
1742 EK Rare	—	—	—	—	—

KM# 936 DUCAT

3.5000 g., 0.9860 Gold 0.1109 oz. AGW **Ruler:** Karl I **Rev. Legend:** EX AVR. HERC.

Date	Mintage	F	VF	XF	Unc
1749	—	400	900	2,000	3,000

KM# 974 DUCAT

3.5000 g., 0.9860 Gold 0.1109 oz. AGW **Ruler:** Karl I **Obverse:** Unadorned bust right

Date	Mintage	F	VF	XF	Unc
1765 E-IDB	—	—	—	—	—

KM# 1003 DUCAT

3.5000 g., 0.9860 Gold 0.1109 oz. AGW **Obverse:** Crowned complex arms **Reverse:** Value and date

Date	Mintage	F	VF	XF	Unc
1780 MC	—	450	750	1,250	1,500

KM# 1015 DUCAT

3.5000 g., 0.9860 Gold 0.1109 oz. AGW **Ruler:** Karl Wilhelm Ferdinand

Date	Mintage	F	VF	XF	Unc
1781 MC	—	450	750	1,250	1,500
1782 MC	—	450	750	1,250	1,500
1783 MC	—	450	750	1,250	1,500
1784 MC	—	450	750	1,250	1,500

KM# 1023 DUCAT

3.5000 g., 0.9860 Gold 0.1109 oz. AGW **Ruler:** Karl Wilhelm Ferdinand **Obverse:** Crowned arms **Reverse:** Value, date

Date	Mintage	F	VF	XF	Unc
1784 MC	—	450	750	1,250	1,500
1785 MC	—	450	750	1,250	1,500
1786 MC	—	450	750	1,250	1,500
1787 MC	—	450	750	1,250	1,500
1788 MC	—	450	750	1,250	1,500
1789 MC	—	450	750	1,250	1,500
1792 MC	—	450	750	1,250	1,500
1794 MC	—	750	1,000	1,750	2,000
1797 MC	—	450	750	1,250	1,500
1798 MC	—	450	750	1,250	1,500
1800 MC	—	600	1,000	1,650	2,000
1801 MC	—	450	750	1,250	1,600

KM# 677 2 DUCAT

7.0000 g., 0.9860 Gold 0.2219 oz. AGW **Subject:** Death of Anton Ulrich's Wife, Elisabeth Juliane **Obverse:** Bust right **Reverse:** Six-line inscription with Roman numeral date

Date	Mintage	VG	F	VF	XF	Unc
1704 ***	—	750	1,500	3,000	5,500	—

KM# 678 2 DUCAT

7.0000 g., 0.9860 Gold 0.2219 oz. AGW **Subject:** Death of Elisabeth Juliane, Wife of Anton Ulrich **Obverse:** Bust of Elisabeth Juliane right **Reverse:** Salzdahlum Palace with reclining figure above

Date	Mintage	VG	F	VF	XF	Unc
1704 HCH	—	750	1,500	3,000	5,500	—

KM# 698 2 DUCAT

7.0000 g., 0.9860 Gold 0.2219 oz. AGW **Ruler:** Anton Ulrich Alone **Obverse:** Bust right

Date	Mintage	VG	F	VF	XF	Unc
1707 HCH	—	450	1,000	1,800	3,750	—

KM# 720 2 DUCAT

7.0000 g., 0.9860 Gold 0.2219 oz. AGW **Ruler:** Anton Ulrich Alone **Obverse:** Bust right **Reverse:** Horse leaping left, Roman numeral date below

Date	Mintage	VG	F	VF	XF	Unc
1711 HCH	—	550	1,125	2,000	4,000	—

KM# 721 2 DUCAT

7.0000 g., 0.9860 Gold 0.2219 oz. AGW **Ruler:** Anton Ulrich Alone **Subject:** Gold from Harz Mountains

Date	Mintage	VG	F	VF	XF	Unc
1712 HCH	—	850	1,650	3,500	6,000	—

KM# 741 2 DUCAT

7.0000 g., 0.9860 Gold 0.2219 oz. AGW **Ruler:** August Wilhelm **Subject:** Death of Anton Ulrich **Obverse:** Duke in cradle **Reverse:** Inscription with date

Date	Mintage	VG	F	VF	XF	Unc
1714	—	500	1,100	1,850	4,000	—

KM# 762 2 DUCAT

7.0000 g., 0.9860 Gold 0.2219 oz. AGW **Ruler:** August Wilhelm **Obverse:** Crowned arms within Order chain **Reverse:** Value and date **Note:** Varieties exist.

Date	Mintage	VG	F	VF	XF	Unc
1716 HCH	—	300	750	1,500	2,500	—
1718 HCH	—	300	750	1,500	2,500	—
1722 HCH	—	300	750	1,500	2,500	—
1728	—	300	750	1,500	2,500	—

KM# 783 2 DUCAT

7.0000 g., 0.9860 Gold 0.2219 oz. AGW **Ruler:** August Wilhelm **Obverse:** Crowned AW monogram

Date	Mintage	VG	F	VF	XF	Unc
1727 Rare	—	—	—	—	—	—

KM# 801 2 DUCAT

7.0000 g., 0.9860 Gold 0.2219 oz. AGW **Ruler:** August Wilhelm **Obverse:** Bust right **Reverse:** Six-line inscription

Date	Mintage	VG	F	VF	XF	Unc
1730 IHT	—	400	1,000	2,100	3,000	—

KM# 802 2 DUCAT

7.0000 g., 0.9860 Gold 0.2219 oz. AGW **Ruler:** August Wilhelm **Subject:** The Duke's Birthday **Obverse:** Wildman with tree at right and crowned arms at left **Reverse:** Inscription

Date	Mintage	VG	F	VF	XF	Unc
1730 IHT	—	400	1,000	2,100	3,000	—

KM# 824 2 DUCAT

7.0000 g., 0.9860 Gold 0.2219 oz. AGW **Ruler:** Ludwig Rudolph **Obverse:** Head right

Date	Mintage	VG	F	VF	XF	Unc
1732 BID	—	550	1,300	2,850	4,250	—
1733 BID	—	550	1,300	2,850	4,250	—

KM# A679 3 DUCAT

10.5000 g., 0.9860 Gold 0.3328 oz. AGW **Subject:** Death of Elisabeth Juliana **Obverse:** Bust of Elisabeth Juliana **Reverse:** Salzdahlum Castle with reclining figure

Date	Mintage	VG	F	VF	XF	Unc
1704 Rare	—	—	—	—	—	—

KM# A694 6 DUCAT

21.0000 g., 0.9860 Gold 0.6657 oz. AGW **Ruler:** Anton Ulrich Alone **Obverse:** Bust right **Reverse:** Arms

Date	Mintage	VG	F	VF	XF	Unc
1706 Rare	—	—	—	—	—	—

KM# 751 6 DUCAT

21.0000 g., 0.9860 Gold 0.6657 oz. AGW **Ruler:** August Wilhelm **Subject:** 53rd Birthday of August Wilhelm **Obverse:** Bust right **Reverse:** Allegorical figure of Brunswick commonwealth, Roman numeral date below

Date	Mintage	VG	F	VF	XF	Unc
1715 Rare	—	—	—	—	—	—

KM# A676 10 DUCAT (Portugalöser)

35.0000 g., 0.9860 Gold 1.1095 oz. AGW **Ruler:** Anton Ulrich Alone **Subject:** Death of Rudolf August **Reverse:** Multiple line inscription

Date	Mintage	VG	F	VF	XF	Unc
1704 Rare	—	—	—	—	—	—

KM# 694 10 DUCAT (Portugalöser)

35.0000 g., 0.9860 Gold 1.1095 oz. AGW **Ruler:** Anton Ulrich Alone **Obverse:** Bust right **Reverse:** Helmeted 14-fold arms divide date **Note:** Struck with 1 Thaler dies, KM#693.

Date	Mintage	VG	F	VF	XF	Unc
1706 HCH	—	4,500	6,500	8,500	12,500	—

KM# 773 10 DUCAT (Portugalöser)

35.0000 g., 0.9860 Gold 1.1095 oz. AGW **Ruler:** August Wilhelm **Obverse:** Armored bust right **Obv. Legend:** AUGUSTUS. WILH. - D.G. DUX. BR. ET. LUN. **Reverse:** Helmeted arms **Note:** Similar to 1 Thaler, KM#738.

Date	Mintage	VG	F	VF	XF	Unc
1720 HCH	—	4,500	6,500	8,500	12,500	—

PATTERNS

Including off metal strikes

KM#	Date	Mintage	Identification	Mkt Val
Pn6	1702	—	Thaler. Gold. KM#641	12,000
Pn8	1713	—	6 Pfennige. Copper. KM#695	—
Pn10	1726	—	Pfennig. Gold. KM#778	450
Pn11	1728	—	Groschen. Gold. KM#784	—
Pn12	1730	—	Ducat. Copper. KM#788	—
Pn13	1730	—	Ducat. Copper. KM#799	—
Pn14	1732	—	2 Ducat. Copper. KM#824	—
Pn15	1734	—	Pfennig. Gold. KM#803	500
Pn16	1734	—	Pfennig. Gold. .Similar to KM#847.	425
Pn17	1734	—	2 Pfennige. Gold. Horse. Orb.	—
Pn18	1735	—	Pfennig. Gold. . KM#830	450
Pn19	1735	—	2 Pfennige. Gold. KM#852	475
Pn20	1735	—	6 Pfennige. Gold. KM#854	700
Pn21	1736	—	2 Pfennige. Gold. KM#892	—
Pn22	1737	—	Pfennig. Gold. KM#891	—
Pn23	1738	—	6 Pfennige. Gold. KM#855	—
Pn24	1739	—	Pfennig. Gold. KM#901	—
Pn25	1742	—	Pfennig. Gold. KM#901	—
Pn26	1742	—	Thaler. Copper. KM#911	—
Pn27	1743	—	Pfennig. Gold. KM#891	—
Pn28	1746	—	Pfennig. Gold. KM#901	—
Pn29	1749	—	Pfennig. Gold. KM#901	—
Pn30	1750	—	Pfennig. Gold. KM#901	—
Pn31	1752	—	Pfennig. Gold. KM#901	—
Pn32	1752	—	1/12 Thaler. Gold. KM#929	—
Pn33	1754	—	Pfennig. Gold. KM#891	—
Pn34	1754	—	Pfennig. Gold. KM#901	—
Pn35	1758	—	Pfennig. Gold. KM#891	—
Pn36	1758	—	1/6 Thaler. Gold. KM#930	—
Pn37	1758	—	5 Thaler. Silver. KM#915	550
Pn38	1769	—	Pfennig. Gold. KM#901	—
Pn39	1771	—	2/3 Thaler. Copper. KM#973.1	—
Pn40	1772	—	Pfennig. Gold. KM#901	—
Pn41	1776	—	Pfennig. Gold. KM#901	—
Pn42	1779	—	2/3 Thaler. Copper. KM#973.1	—

TRIAL STRIKES

KM#	Date	Mintage	Identification	Mkt Val
TS1	1736	—	6 Pfennige. Uniface.	—
TS2		—	1/24 Thaler. Uniface, KM#928.	—
TS3	(1758)	—	Denier. Uniface.	—

BUCHHORN

Located on the northeast shore of Lake Constance, Buchhorn became the smallest imperial city in 1274. In 1802 it passed to Bavaria, then to Württemberg in 1810. The following year the name of the city was changed to Friedrichshafen, which it has retained until the present time.

FREE CITY

REGULAR COINAGE

KM# 1 PFENNIG

Copper **Obverse:** City arms (beechtree left, hunting horn right) **Note:** Uniface

Date	Mintage	VG	F	VF	XF	Unc
ND(ca.1700)	—	18.00	35.00	60.00	100	—

KM# 2 PFENNIG

Obverse: Vertical line divides beech tree and hunting horn

Date	Mintage	VG	F	VF	XF	Unc
ND(ca.1700)	—	12.00	25.00	45.00	80.00	—

KM# 3 2 PFENNIG (1/2 Kreuzer)

Billon **Obverse:** 3 Shields, 1 at top divides date, 2 at bottom between 2 lower shields **Note:** Uniface

Date	Mintage	VG	F	VF	XF	Unc
1704	—	30.00	55.00	85.00	150	—

KM# 4 KREUZER

Silver **Obverse:** Crowned Imperial eagle with value "1" on breast, titles of Leopold I in legend **Reverse:** City arms in oval, 8-armed cross behind, date in legend **Note:** Varieties exist.

Date	Mintage	VG	F	VF	XF	Unc
1704	—	25.00	45.00	65.00	130	—

KM# 5 ALBUS (2 Kreuzer)

Silver **Obverse:** Crowned Imperial eagle, 2 on breast, titles of Leopold I **Reverse:** Value, date in 3 lines

Date	Mintage	VG	F	VF	XF	Unc
1704	—	35.00	60.00	90.00	165	—

CLEVES

(Cleve, Kleve)

The county, later duchy, of Cleves, located on both sides of the Rhine at the Dutch Border, had its beginnings in the early 11th century. It passed in marriage to the counts of Mark in 1368, who were raised to the rank of duke in 1417. In 1511 Julich, Berg and Ravensburg were obtained by marriage. The last duke died in 1609 without a male heir, causing a great struggle for the various territories between Pfalz-Neuburg, Brandenburg-Prussia and Saxony. (See Jülich-Cleves-Berg for coinage to 1609). Eventually, the first two won out and made a pact to divide the territories between them. Brandenburg Prussia obtained Cleves, Mark and Ravensberg, while Pfalz-Neuburg received Jülich and Berg. Saxony refused to give up its claims and, though never managing to obtain any territory, the dukes continued to place the arms of Cleves on their coinage throughout the rest of the 17th century. The rulers of Brandenburg-Prussia and Pfalz-Neuburg struck a joint coinage in the disputed terri-- tories until the formal division in 1624. The joint coinage struck in Cleves is listed here. That of Jülich-Berg is listed under that name. The special coinage of Brandenburg-Prussia for Mark and Ravensberg are included under those placenames.

RULERS

Friedrich III of Brandenburg-Prussia (I of Prussia), 1688-(1701)-1713

Friedrich Wilhelm I of Prussia, 1713-1740

Friedrich II (The Great) of Prussia, 1740-1786

MINT MARKS

C - Cleves

MINT OFFICIALS' INITIALS

Initials	Date	Name
AGP	1742	Anton Gottfried Pott
GK	1741-55	Georg Kuster
ICM	1741-57	Johann Konrad Marme, die-cutter in Cleves

MONETARY SYSTEM

8 Duit = 1 Stüber

60 Stüber = 1 Reichsthaler

5 Reichsthalers = 1 Friedrich D'or

DUCHY

REGULAR COINAGE

KM# 45 DUIT

Copper **Ruler:** Friedrich II **Obverse:** Crowned arms with supporters **Reverse:** Value, date

Date	Mintage	VG	F	VF	XF	Unc
1749	—	2.50	5.00	15.00	30.00	—
1750	—	2.50	5.00	15.00	30.00	—

KM# 53 DUIT

Copper **Ruler:** Friedrich II **Obverse:** Crowned arms with supporters **Reverse:** Value, date

Date	Mintage	VG	F	VF	XF	Unc
1752	—	2.50	5.00	15.00	30.00	—
1753	—	2.50	5.00	15.00	30.00	—

KM# 55 1/4 STUBER

Copper **Ruler:** Friedrich II **Mint:** Cleves **Obverse:** Crowned arms with supporters, square shield **Reverse:** Value, date

Date	Mintage	VG	F	VF	XF	Unc
1753C	—	3.00	10.00	20.00	40.00	—
1754C	—	3.00	10.00	20.00	40.00	—
1755C	—	3.00	10.00	20.00	40.00	—

KM# 50 STUBER (21 Heller)

Billon **Ruler:** Friedrich II **Mint:** Cleves **Obverse:** Crowned arms within branches **Reverse:** Value, date

Date	Mintage	VG	F	VF	XF	Unc
1751C	—	3.00	10.00	20.00	40.00	—
1752C	—	3.00	10.00	20.00	40.00	—

KM# 60 STUBER (21 Heller)
Billon **Ruler:** Friedrich II **Mint:** Cleves **Obverse:** Crowned monogram divides date **Reverse:** Value above sprays

Date	Mintage	VG	F	VF	XF	Unc
1764C	641,000	3.00	10.00	25.00	50.00	—

KM# 51 2 STUBER
Billon **Ruler:** Friedrich II **Mint:** Cleves **Obverse:** Crowned arms within branches **Reverse:** Value, date

Date	Mintage	VG	F	VF	XF	Unc
1751C	—	2.50	5.00	15.00	30.00	—
1752C	—	2.50	5.00	15.00	30.00	—
1753C	—	2.50	5.00	15.00	30.00	—
1754C	—	2.50	5.00	15.00	30.00	—
1755C	—	2.50	5.00	15.00	30.00	—
1756C	—	2.50	5.00	15.00	30.00	—

KM# 57 4 KREUZER (Batzen)
Silver **Ruler:** Friedrich II **Obverse:** Eagle in crowned cartouche, date divided above **Reverse:** Legend in cartouche **Rev. Legend:** 4/KREU/ZER/C

Date	Mintage	VG	F	VF	XF	Unc
1754	1,718,000	20.00	50.00	100	200	—
1755	Inc. above	20.00	50.00	100	200	—

KM# 61 5 STUBER (1/12 Thaler)
Silver **Ruler:** Friedrich II **Mint:** Cleves **Subject:** Friedrich II **Obverse:** Laureate head right **Reverse:** Value, date

Date	Mintage	VG	F	VF	XF	Unc
1765C	—	5.00	12.00	35.00	75.00	—

KM# 64 5 STUBER (1/12 Thaler)
Silver **Ruler:** Friedrich II **Mint:** Cleves **Obverse:** Laureate head right **Obv. Legend:** FRIDERICUS BORUSSORUM REX **Reverse:** Value, date

Date	Mintage	VG	F	VF	XF	Unc
1766C	—	4.00	10.00	30.00	60.00	—
1767C	—	4.00	10.00	30.00	60.00	—

KM# 62 10 STUBER (1/6 Thaler)
Silver **Ruler:** Friedrich II **Mint:** Cleves **Obverse:** Laureate head right **Obv. Legend:** FRIDERICUS BORUSSORUM REX. **Reverse:** Value, date

Date	Mintage	VG	F	VF	XF	Unc
1765C	—	5.00	15.00	40.00	80.00	—

KM# 63 THALER-60 STüBER (1 Reichsthaler)
Silver **Ruler:** Friedrich II **Mint:** Cleves **Obverse:** Laureate head right **Obv. Legend:** FRIDERICUS BORUSSORUM REX. **Reverse:** Crowned eagle within flags and cannons

Date	Mintage	VG	F	VF	XF	Unc
1765C	—	20.00	60.00	125	250	—

TRADE COINAGE

KM# 56 1/2 FRIEDRICH D'OR
3.3408 g., 0.9030 Gold 0.0970 oz. AGW **Ruler:** Friedrich II **Mint:** Cleves **Subject:** Friedrich II **Obverse:** Armored bust right **Reverse:** Crowned eagle within flags and cannons

Date	Mintage	VG	F	VF	XF	Unc
1753C	—	600	1,250	2,500	4,500	—

KM# 52 FRIEDRICH D'OR
6.6815 g., 0.9030 Gold 0.1940 oz. AGW **Ruler:** Friedrich II **Mint:** Cleves **Subject:** Friedrich II **Obverse:** Armored bust right **Reverse:** Crowned eagle withih flags and cannons

Date	Mintage	VG	F	VF	XF	Unc
1751C	—	1,000	2,000	4,000	6,500	—
1752C	—	1,000	2,000	4,000	6,500	—
1753C	—	1,000	2,000	4,000	6,500	—

KM# 58 FRIEDRICH D'OR
6.6815 g., 0.9030 Gold 0.1940 oz. AGW **Ruler:** Friedrich II **Mint:** Cleves **Obverse:** Head of Friedrich right **Reverse:** Eagle in shield on trophies of arms, date below

Date	Mintage	VG	F	VF	XF	Unc
1754C	—	1,200	2,250	4,500	7,000	—
1755C	—	1,200	2,250	4,500	7,000	—

KM# 54 2 FRIEDRICH D'OR
13.3630 g., 0.9030 Gold 0.3879 oz. AGW **Ruler:** Friedrich II **Mint:** Cleves **Subject:** Friedrich II

Date	Mintage	VG	F	VF	XF	Unc
1752C	—	2,500	4,500	6,500	10,000	—
1753C	—	2,500	4,500	6,500	10,000	—

PATTERNS

Inlcuding off metal strikes

KM#	Date	Mintage	Identification	Mkt Val
Pn1	1751C	—	Friedrich D'Or. Gold.	—
Pn2	1755	—	4 Kreuzer. Copper. KM#57.	—

COESFELD

(Cosveldt)

The town of Coesfeld in Westphalia is located on the Berkel River some 19 miles (32 kilometers) west of Münster. Although Coesfeld belonged to the bishops of Münster, it was permitted to issue a local minor coinage from the late 16th century until 1763. When the bishopric was secularized in 1802, Coesfeld was acquired by the Rhinegraves of Salm. The latter's territories were soon mediatized in 1806 and became a part of Joachim Murat's grand duchy of Berg. Coesfeld finally passed to Prussia along with the rest of Berg at the conclusion of the Napoleonic Wars.

REFERENCE

H = Wolf Holtmann,"Beschreibung der Coesfelder Kupfermün", in ***Geschichtsblätter des Kreises Coesfeld***, 1 (1979)

CITY

REGULAR COINAGE

KM# 11 PFENNIG
Copper **Obverse:** Crowned bull's head within circle **Obv. Legend:** STADT. COSVELT **Reverse:** Value within box **Note:** Varieties exist.

Date	Mintage	VG	F	VF	XF	Unc
1708	—	6.00	12.00	25.00	50.00	—
1708	—	6.00	12.00	25.00	50.00	—
1713	127,000	6.00	12.00	25.00	50.00	—

KM# 5 2 PFENNIG
Copper **Obverse:** Crowned bull's head within shield, circle surrounds **Reverse:** Value within square **Note:** Varieties exist.

Date	Mintage	VG	F	VF	XF	Unc
1713	212,000	7.00	15.00	28.00	55.00	—
1713	212,000	7.00	15.00	28.00	55.00	—

KM# 13 2 PFENNIG
Copper **Obverse:** Crowned bull's head within beaded circle **Obv. Legend:** STADT. COSVELT **Reverse:** Value within square

Date	Mintage	VG	F	VF	XF	Unc
1708	—	7.00	15.00	28.00	55.00	—

KM# 7 4 PFENNIG
Copper **Obverse:** Crowned bull's head within shield, circle surrounds **Reverse:** Value within square **Note:** Varieties exist.

Date	Mintage	VG	F	VF	XF	Unc
1708	—	6.00	12.00	30.00	50.00	—
1708	—	6.00	12.00	30.00	50.00	—
1713	117,000	6.00	12.00	30.00	50.00	—

KM# 14 4 PFENNIG
Copper **Obverse:** Crowned bull's head within shield, circle surrounds **Obv. Legend:** STADT COSVELDT **Reverse:** Value within square

Date	Mintage	VG	F	VF	XF	Unc
1763	—	7.00	12.00	25.00	45.00	—

KM# 9 8 PFENNIG
Copper **Obverse:** Crowned bull's head within shield, circle surrounds **Reverse:** Value within square **Note:** Varieties exist.

Date	Mintage	VG	F	VF	XF	Unc
1713	93,000	7.00	16.00	32.00	60.00	—

COLOGNE

ARCHBISHOPRIC

(Köln)

A bishopric was established in the city of Roman foundation in 313 and transformed into an archbishopric by Charlemagne in 785. Joint issues of coinage by the archbishops and the emperors began in the mid-10th century and the first independent ecclesiastic issues appeared in the late 11th century. Upon the breakup of the old duchy of Saxony in 1180, the archbishop obtained the duchy of Westphalia. The archbishops became Electors of the Empire by the Gold Bull of 1356 and continued to gain power and territory during the ensuing centuries. In 1801, Cologne was secularized and its lands west of the Rhine were taken by France. Several principalities divided Cologne's territories east of the Rhine, the largest portions having been taken by Hesse-Darmstadt and Nassau.

RULERS

Josef Clemens, Herzog von Bayern, 1688-1723
Clemens August, Herzog von Bayern, 1723-1761
Sede Vacante, 1761
Maximilian Friedrich, Graf von Königsegg-Rothenfels, 1761-84
Maximilian Franz von Österreich, 1784-1801

NOTE: For issues struck by electors/archbishops of Cologne as dukes of Westphalia, see Westphalia.

MINT OFFICIALS' INITIALS

Initials	Years	Officials
EG, EGF	1750-75	Elias Gervais, die-cutter in Neuweid and Coblenz
G		
FW	1698-1728	Friedrich Wendeis, in Bonn
ICS	1776-1801	J. Christian Stockicht
IH	1733-38	Johann Hittorff, in Bonn
IK, K	1739-ca.1776	Jacob Kohlhass, in Bonn
M	1735-57	Johann Konrad Marme
NR	1672-1725	Norbert Roettiers, die-cutter in Bruxelles
S	1748-99	Anton Schaffer, in Mannheim
W	1764-66	Eberhard Wyon, die-cutter

ARMS

Archbishopric - cross

REGULAR COINAGE

KM# 80 2 HELLER (Pfennig)

Silver **Ruler:** Josef Clemens von Bayern **Obverse:** Crowned 4-fold arms of Bavaria-Pfalz divide 2-H

Date	Mintage	VG	F	VF	XF	Unc
1698 FW	—	20.00	40.00	70.00	100	—
1717 FW	—	20.00	40.00	70.00	100	—

KM# 123 2 HELLER (Pfennig)

Silver **Ruler:** Clemens August von Bayern **Note:** Without indication of value.

Date	Mintage	VG	F	VF	XF	Unc
1726 FW	—	6.00	12.00	25.00	45.00	—

KM# 83 8 HELLER (4 Pfennig)

Silver **Ruler:** Josef Clemens von Bayern **Obverse:** Arms of Bavaria in circle **Reverse:** Arms of Cologne (cross) in circle, date at top in legend

Date	Mintage	VG	F	VF	XF	Unc
1699 FW	—	7.00	14.00	28.00	45.00	—
1700 FW	—	7.00	14.00	28.00	45.00	—
1701 FW	—	7.00	14.00	28.00	45.00	—

KM# 90 8 HELLER (4 Pfennig)

Silver **Ruler:** Josef Clemens von Bayern **Obverse:** Arms of Cologne (cross) in circle, date in legend at top **Reverse:** Value VIII in center

Date	Mintage	VG	F	VF	XF	Unc
1705	—	10.00	20.00	40.00	65.00	—
1715 FW	—	10.00	20.00	40.00	65.00	—

KM# 91 8 HELLER (4 Pfennig)

Silver **Ruler:** Josef Clemens von Bayern **Obverse:** Crowned arms of Bavaria divide date in circle **Reverse:** Arms of Cologne (cross) in circle

Date	Mintage	VG	F	VF	XF	Unc
1715 FW	—	10.00	20.00	40.00	65.00	—

KM# 92 8 HELLER (4 Pfennig)

Silver **Ruler:** Josef Clemens von Bayern **Obverse:** Arms not in circle **Reverse:** Arms not in circle, date in legend

Date	Mintage	VG	F	VF	XF	Unc
1715 FW	—	10.00	20.00	40.00	60.00	—
1716 FW	—	10.00	20.00	40.00	60.00	—
ND	—	10.00	20.00	40.00	60.00	—

KM# 103 8 HELLER (4 Pfennig)

Silver **Ruler:** Josef Clemens von Bayern **Reverse:** Arms in circle

Date	Mintage	VG	F	VF	XF	Unc
1717 FW	—	10.00	20.00	40.00	60.00	—

KM# 104 8 HELLER (4 Pfennig)

Silver **Ruler:** Josef Clemens von Bayern **Obverse:** Arms in circle **Note:** Varieties exist.

Date	Mintage	VG	F	VF	XF	Unc
1717 FW	—	10.00	20.00	40.00	60.00	—
1722 FW	—	12.00	25.00	45.00	70.00	—

KM# 110 8 HELLER (4 Pfennig)

Silver **Ruler:** Josef Clemens von Bayern **Reverse:** Date divided by shield

Date	Mintage	VG	F	VF	XF	Unc
1719 FW	—	10.00	20.00	40.00	60.00	—

KM# 118 8 HELLER (4 Pfennig)

Silver **Ruler:** Josef Clemens von Bayern **Obverse:** Crowned 4-fold arms of Bavaria-Pfalz in circle **Reverse:** Arms of Cologne (cross) in circle, date in legend

Date	Mintage	VG	F	VF	XF	Unc
1722 FW	—	12.00	25.00	45.00	70.00	—

KM# 122 8 HELLER (4 Pfennig)

Billon **Ruler:** Clemens August von Bayern **Obverse:** Quartered arms of Bavaria and Pfalz **Reverse:** Arms of Cologne, date

Date	Mintage	VG	F	VF	XF	Unc
1724 FW	—	5.00	7.50	15.00	30.00	—
1726 FW	—	5.00	7.50	15.00	30.00	—

KM# 119 1/4 STUBER

Copper **Ruler:** Josef Clemens von Bayern **Obverse:** Crowned cursive JC monogram **Reverse:** Date in legend **Rev. Legend:** 1/4/STUBER

Date	Mintage	VG	F	VF	XF	Unc
1722 FW	—	7.00	15.00	30.00	55.00	—

KM# 135.1 1/4 STUBER

Copper **Ruler:** Clemens August von Bayern **Obverse:** Crowned CAC monogram **Reverse:** Value, date

Date	Mintage	VG	F	VF	XF	Unc
1736	—	2.50	5.00	10.00	20.00	—
1737	225,000	2.50	5.00	10.00	20.00	—
1739	—	2.50	5.00	10.00	20.00	—
1740	—	2.50	5.00	10.00	20.00	—
1741	—	2.50	5.00	10.00	20.00	—
1742	—	2.50	5.00	10.00	20.00	—
1743	—	2.50	5.00	10.00	20.00	—
1745	672,000	2.50	5.00	10.00	20.00	—
1746	Inc. above	2.50	5.00	10.00	20.00	—
1747	Inc. above	2.50	5.00	10.00	20.00	—
1748	—	2.50	5.00	10.00	20.00	—
1749	—	2.50	5.00	10.00	20.00	—
1750	—	2.50	5.00	10.00	20.00	—
1756	—	2.50	5.00	10.00	20.00	—
1759	—	2.50	5.00	10.00	20.00	—
1760	—	2.50	5.00	10.00	20.00	—

KM# 135.2 1/4 STUBER

Copper **Ruler:** Clemens August von Bayern **Obverse:** Crowned CAC monogram **Reverse:** Retrograde 4 in 1/4

Date	Mintage	VG	F	VF	XF	Unc
1759	—	2.50	5.00	10.00	20.00	—

KM# 161 1/4 STUBER

Copper **Ruler:** Maximilian Friedrich, Graf von Königsegg-Rothenfels **Obverse:** Crowned monogram **Reverse:** Value and date within cartouche **Note:** Many major die varieties exist.

Date	Mintage	VG	F	VF	XF	Unc
1763	—	3.50	8.00	15.00	30.00	—
1764	—	3.50	8.00	15.00	30.00	—
1765	—	3.50	8.00	15.00	30.00	—
1765 EG	—	—	—	—	—	—
1766 EG-IK	—	3.50	8.00	15.00	30.00	—
1767 IK	—	5.00	10.00	20.00	40.00	—
1767 EG-IK	—	5.00	10.00	20.00	40.00	—

KM# 175 1/4 STUBER

Billon **Ruler:** Maximilian Friedrich, Graf von Königsegg-Rothenfels **Obverse:** Bust right **Reverse:** Value and date

Date	Mintage	VG	F	VF	XF	Unc
1776 G	—	7.00	15.00	30.00	65.00	—

KM# 138 STUBER

Billon **Ruler:** Clemens August von Bayern **Obverse:** Crowned CA monogram **Reverse:** Value, date

Date	Mintage	VG	F	VF	XF	Unc
1739 IK	—	4.00	9.00	17.50	35.00	—
1741	—	4.00	9.00	17.50	35.00	—
1743	7,680,000	4.00	9.00	17.50	35.00	—
1744	Inc. above	4.00	9.00	17.50	35.00	—
1748 IK	985,000	4.00	9.00	17.50	35.00	—
1749 IK	Inc. above	4.00	9.00	17.50	35.00	—

KM# 176 STUBER

Billon **Ruler:** Maximilian Friedrich, Graf von Königsegg-Rothenfels **Obverse:** Armored bust right **Reverse:** Value, date within circle

Date	Mintage	VG	F	VF	XF	Unc
1776 G	—	5.00	10.00	20.00	40.00	—
1777 G	—	5.00	10.00	20.00	40.00	—

KM# 141 2 STUBER

Billon **Ruler:** Clemens August von Bayern **Obverse:** Crowned CAC monogram **Reverse:** Value II STUBER, date

Date	Mintage	VG	F	VF	XF	Unc
1749 IK	480,000	8.00	18.00	40.00	80.00	—

KM# 142 2 STUBER

Billon **Ruler:** Clemens August von Bayern **Reverse:** Value **Rev. Legend:** 2 STUBER

Date	Mintage	VG	F	VF	XF	Unc
1749 IK	Inc. above	6.00	12.00	30.00	60.00	—

KM# 165 2-1/2 STUBER

Billon **Ruler:** Maximilian Friedrich, Graf von Königsegg-Rothenfels **Obverse:** Cologne cross with Konigsegg arms in center **Reverse:** Value and date

Date	Mintage	VG	F	VF	XF	Unc
1765	—	28.50	45.00	75.00	120	—

KM# 143 3 STUBER

Billon **Ruler:** Clemens August von Bayern **Obverse:** Crowned ornate arms of Bavaria-Pfalz and Cologne **Reverse:** Value, date

Date	Mintage	VG	F	VF	XF	Unc
1749 IK	545,000	6.00	12.00	22.00	45.00	—
1750 IK	Inc. above	6.00	12.00	22.00	45.00	—
1750 K	275,000	6.00	12.00	22.00	45.00	—

KM# 162 6 STUBER

Billon **Ruler:** Maximilian Friedrich, Graf von Königsegg-Rothenfels **Obverse:** Crowned ornate arms **Reverse:** Value, date within circle

Date	Mintage	VG	F	VF	XF	Unc
1764	—	15.00	20.00	40.00	75.00	—
1765 W	—	15.00	20.00	40.00	75.00	—

KM# 166 6 STUBER

Billon **Ruler:** Maximilian Friedrich, Graf von Königsegg-Rothenfels **Obverse:** Crowned oval arms **Reverse:** Value, date within branches of laurel and palm

Date	Mintage	VG	F	VF	XF	Unc
1765 IK	—	15.00	22.00	45.00	85.00	—
1766 EG-IK	—	15.00	22.00	45.00	85.00	—
1766 W-IK	—	20.00	30.00	60.00	100	—

KM# 107 2 ALBUS

Silver **Ruler:** Josef Clemens von Bayern **Obverse:** Arms of Cologne (cross) in circle **Reverse:** Crowned arms of Bavaria in circle, date divided below, 2.ALB at bottoom

Date	Mintage	VG	F	VF	XF	Unc
1718 FW	—	15.00	30.00	50.00	75.00	—
1719 FW	—	15.00	30.00	50.00	75.00	—

KM# 115 2 ALBUS

Silver **Ruler:** Josef Clemens von Bayern **Obverse:** Date divided by arms, without circles

Date	Mintage	VG	F	VF	XF	Unc
1720	—	20.00	35.00	60.00	100	—
1721	—	20.00	35.00	60.00	100	—

KM# 116 2 ALBUS

Silver **Ruler:** Josef Clemens von Bayern **Reverse:** Crowned 4-fold arms of Bavaria-Pfalz

Date	Mintage	VG	F	VF	XF	Unc
1721	—	20.00	35.00	60.00	100	—

KM# 105 4 ALBUS (Blaffert)

Silver **Ruler:** Josef Clemens von Bayern **Obverse:** Crowned oval arms **Reverse:** Date **Rev. Legend:** IIII/ALBVS/COLSCH

Date	Mintage	VG	F	VF	XF	Unc
1717	—	—	—	—	—	—

KM# 108 4 ALBUS (Blaffert)

Silver **Ruler:** Josef Clemens von Bayern **Obverse:** Ornate arms of Cologne (cross) **Reverse:** Crowned 4-fold arms of Bavaria-Pfalz divide date, 4.ALB. below

Date	Mintage	VG	F	VF	XF	Unc
1718 FW	—	12.00	20.00	45.00	90.00	—

KM# 109 4 ALBUS (Blaffert)

Silver **Ruler:** Josef Clemens von Bayern **Obverse:** Ornate arms of Cologne(cross) divide date **Reverse:** Crowned ornate 4-fold arms divide FW

Date	Mintage	VG	F	VF	XF	Unc
1718 FW	—	12.00	20.00	40.00	70.00	—
1719 FW	—	12.00	20.00	40.00	70.00	—
1720 FW	—	12.00	20.00	40.00	70.00	—
1721	—	12.00	20.00	40.00	70.00	—
1721 FW	—	12.00	20.00	40.00	70.00	—
1722 FW	—	10.00	18.00	30.00	60.00	—
1723 FW	—	10.00	18.00	30.00	60.00	—

KM# 124 4 ALBUS (Blaffert)

Billon **Ruler:** Clemens August von Bayern **Obverse:** Quartered arms of Bavaria and Pfalz **Reverse:** Arms of Cologne, date, value 4 ALB

Date	Mintage	VG	F	VF	XF	Unc
1726 FW	—	15.00	30.00	60.00	120	—

KM# 137 4 ALBUS (Blaffert)

Billon **Ruler:** Clemens August von Bayern **Obverse:** Crowned arms of Cologne with quartered arms of Bavaria-Pfalz at center **Reverse:** Value and date **Rev. Legend:** IIII ALBUS

Date	Mintage	VG	F	VF	XF	Unc
1739 IK	—	25.00	45.00	100	200	—

KM# 136 8 ALBUS

Silver **Ruler:** Clemens August von Bayern **Obverse:** Crowned oval arms of Cologne (cross) with central shield of Bavaria-Pfalz all in baroque frame **Reverse:** Date **Rev. Legend:** VIII/ALBUS

Date	Mintage	VG	F	VF	XF	Unc
1737 IH	—	—	—	—	—	—
Note: Reported, not confirmed						
1739 IK Rare	—	—	—	—	—	—

KM# 130 10 KREUZER

Billon **Ruler:** Clemens August von Bayern **Obverse:** 7 crowned arms in oval shields **Reverse:** Value, date within circular ornate frame

Date	Mintage	VG	F	VF	XF	Unc
1735 IH	—	15.00	40.00	90.00	200	—
1736 IH	—	15.00	40.00	90.00	200	—

KM# 134 20 KREUZER

Silver **Ruler:** Clemens August von Bayern **Obverse:** 7 Oval arms within crowned shield **Reverse:** Value, date within ornate circular frame

Date	Mintage	VG	F	VF	XF	Unc
1735 IH	—	20.00	35.00	75.00	150	—
1736 IH	—	20.00	35.00	75.00	150	—

KM# 148 6 MARIENGROSCHEN

Silver **Ruler:** Clemens August von Bayern **Obverse:** Crowned complex arms **Reverse:** Value, daate within circle

Date	Mintage	VG	F	VF	XF	Unc
1754 IK	—	12.00	25.00	50.00	85.00	—

KM# 93 1/12 THALER (2 Groschen)

Silver **Ruler:** Josef Clemens von Bayern **Obverse:** Crowned arms of Cologne (cross) with central shield of Bavaria-Pfalz divides date **Rev. Legend:** 12/EINEN/REICHS/THAL **Note:** Varieties exist.

Date	Mintage	VG	F	VF	XF	Unc
1715 FW	—	10.00	25.00	50.00	85.00	—
1717 FW	—	10.00	25.00	50.00	85.00	—
1718 FW	—	10.00	25.00	50.00	85.00	—
1720 FW	—	10.00	25.00	50.00	85.00	—
1722 FW	—	10.00	25.00	50.00	85.00	—

KM# 106 1/12 THALER (2 Groschen)

Silver **Ruler:** Josef Clemens von Bayern **Reverse:** Oval arms and date below value

Date	Mintage	VG	F	VF	XF	Unc
1717 FW	—	15.00	30.00	60.00	95.00	—

KM# 139 1/12 THALER (2 Groschen)

Billon **Ruler:** Clemens August von Bayern **Obverse:** Crowned ornate arms of Bavaria-Pfalz and Cologne **Reverse:** Value, date **Rev. Legend:** 12 EINEN REICHS THAL

Date	Mintage	VG	F	VF	XF	Unc
1739 IH	—	20.00	40.00	80.00	120	—

KM# 150 1/8 THALER

Silver **Ruler:** Clemens August von Bayern **Obverse:** Crowned monogram **Reverse:** Date above inscription **Note:** Mining 1/8 Thaler.

Date	Mintage	VG	F	VF	XF	Unc
1759	—	150	250	550	1,000	—

KM# 156 1/8 THALER (12 Stüber)

Silver **Ruler:** Clemens August von Bayern **Obverse:** St. Peter above shield **Reverse:** 4-line inscription and date **Note:** Sede vacante issue.

Date	Mintage	VG	F	VF	XF	Unc
1761	—	85.00	165	250	500	—

KM# 163 1/8 THALER (12 Stüber)

Silver **Ruler:** Maximilian Friedrich, Graf von Königsegg-Rothenfels **Obverse:** Complex coat of arms **Reverse:** Weight "80 EINE MARCK FEIN" and date in wreath

Date	Mintage	VG	F	VF	XF	Unc
1764 W-K	—	15.00	25.00	40.00	75.00	—
1764 W-IK	—	20.00	30.00	50.00	95.00	—
1765 W-IK	—	15.00	25.00	40.00	75.00	—
1765 EG-IK	—	20.00	30.00	50.00	95.00	—
1766 EG-IK	—	15.00	25.00	40.00	75.00	—

KM# 94 1/6 THALER (1/4 Gulden)

Silver **Ruler:** Josef Clemens von Bayern **Obverse:** Bust right **Reverse:** Crowned complex arms **Note:** Similar to KM#95 but date in legend and reverse.

Date	Mintage	VG	F	VF	XF	Unc
1715 FW	—	20.00	40.00	80.00	125	—
1715 NR-FW	—	20.00	40.00	80.00	125	—

KM# 95 1/6 THALER (1/4 Gulden)

Silver **Ruler:** Josef Clemens von Bayern **Obverse:** Bust right **Reverse:** Crowned complex arms divides date and FW **Note:** Varieties exist.

Date	Mintage	VG	F	VF	XF	Unc
1715 FW	—	25.00	50.00	100	165	—
1716 FW	—	25.00	50.00	100	165	—
1721 FW	—	25.00	50.00	100	165	—

KM# 149 1/6 THALER (1/4 Gulden)

Silver **Ruler:** Clemens August von Bayern **Obverse:** Crowned complex arms **Reverse:** Value, date within circle

Date	Mintage	VG	F	VF	XF	Unc
1754 IK	—	10.00	20.00	45.00	80.00	—
1755 IK	—	10.00	20.00	45.00	80.00	—
1756 IK	—	10.00	20.00	45.00	80.00	—

KM# 151 1/4 THALER

Silver **Ruler:** Clemens August von Bayern **Obverse:** Crowned complex arms with supporters **Reverse:** Date above legend, mining scene below **Note:** Mining 1/4 Thaler.

Date	Mintage	F	VF	XF	Unc
1759	—	250	450	800	1,250

KM# 158 1/4 THALER (24 Stüber)

Silver **Ruler:** Clemens August von Bayern **Obverse:** St. Peter oval shield **Reverse:** Madonna, child and wise men **Note:** Sede vacante issue.

Date	Mintage	F	VF	XF	Unc
1761	—	300	500	1,000	1,650

KM# 167 1/4 THALER (24 Stüber)

Silver **Ruler:** Maximilian Friedrich, Graf von Königsegg-Rothenfels **Subject:** Maximilian Friedrich

Date	Mintage	F	VF	XF	Unc
1765 W-IK	—	90.00	150	250	425
1765 EG-IK	—	—	—	—	—
1766 EG-IK	—	90.00	150	250	425

KM# 96 1/3 THALER (1/2 Gulden)

Silver **Ruler:** Josef Clemens von Bayern **Obverse:** Bust right **Reverse:** Crowned arms with central shield of Bavaria-Pfalz, 1/3 in oval at bottom, date in legend

Date	Mintage	VG	F	VF	XF	Unc
1715 FW	—	500	750	1,250	2,000	—

KM# 152 1/2 THALER

Silver **Ruler:** Clemens August von Bayern **Obverse:** Bust of archbishop right, date **Reverse:** Mining scene within legend **Note:** Mining 1/2 Thaler.

Date	Mintage	F	VF	XF	Unc
1759	—	300	700	1,200	2,000

KM# 168 1/2 THALER

Silver **Ruler:** Maximilian Friedrich, Graf von Königsegg-Rothenfels **Obverse:** Bust right **Reverse:** Crowned arms with supporters

Date	Mintage	F	VF	XF	Unc
1765 EG-IK	—	175	300	500	1,000

KM# 87 2/3 THALER (Gulden)

Silver **Ruler:** Josef Clemens von Bayern **Obverse:** Bust right **Reverse:** Ornate 12-fold arms arranged differently

Date	Mintage	VG	F	VF	XF	Unc
1701 FW	—	750	1,250	2,000	3,000	—

KM# 88 2/3 THALER (Gulden)

Silver **Ruler:** Josef Clemens von Bayern **Reverse:** Date in legend

Date	Mintage	VG	F	VF	XF	Unc
1701 FW	—	750	1,250	2,000	3,000	—

KM# 97 2/3 THALER (Gulden)

Silver **Ruler:** Josef Clemens von Bayern **Obverse:** Bust right **Reverse:** Crowned II's in cruciform, double C's in angles, round Bavarian arms in center, date in legend

Date	Mintage	VG	F	VF	XF	Unc
1715 NR	—	750	1,250	2,000	3,000	—

KM# 98 2/3 THALER (Gulden)

Silver **Ruler:** Josef Clemens von Bayern **Obverse:** Capped bust right **Reverse:** Similar to KM#76 but 14-fold arms **Rev. Legend:** RECTE.CONSTANTER

Date	Mintage	VG	F	VF	XF	Unc
1715 FW	—	45.00	75.00	165	300	—

KM# 99 2/3 THALER (Gulden)

Silver **Ruler:** Josef Clemens von Bayern **Reverse:** Arms in ornate shield

Date	Mintage	VG	F	VF	XF	Unc
1715 NR-FW	—	45.00	75.00	165	300	—

KM# 100 2/3 THALER (Gulden)

Silver **Ruler:** Josef Clemens von Bayern **Rev. Legend:** MONETA. NOVA

Date	Mintage	VG	F	VF	XF	Unc
1715 FW	—	45.00	75.00	165	300	—

KM# 117 2/3 THALER (Gulden)

Silver **Ruler:** Josef Clemens von Bayern **Reverse:** Ornate arms within Order chain

Date	Mintage	VG	F	VF	XF	Unc
1721	—	50.00	100	250	500	—

KM# 101 THALER

Silver **Ruler:** Josef Clemens von Bayern **Obverse:** Bust right **Reverse:** Crowned II's in cruciform, double C in angles, round Bavarian arms in center, date in legend **Note:** Dav. #2174.

Date	Mintage	F	VF	XF	Unc
1715	—	2,000	4,000	7,000	11,000

KM# 153 THALER

Silver **Ruler:** Clemens August von Bayern **Subject:** Clemens Augustus **Obverse:** Bust right **Obv. Legend:** CLeMens AVgVstVs BaVarIae et. **Reverse:** Mining scene within legend **Rev. Legend:** WestphaLIae DBX IVre InstaVrbat, in exergue: ARGENT.PUR. E. FOD./WESTP. **Note:** Mining Thaler. Dav. #2175.

Date	Mintage	F	VF	XF	Unc
1759 EGF	—	2,000	3,500	6,500	10,000

KM# 159 THALER

Silver **Ruler:** Clemens August von Bayern **Obverse:** Radiant figure with shield facing **Obv. Legend:** CAPIT • ECCLES • METROPOLIT • COLON • SEDE • VACANTE • **Reverse:** Nativity **Rev. Legend:** CASPAR MELCHIOR BALTHASAR 1761 **Note:** Sede vacante issue. Dav. #2176.

Date	Mintage	F	VF	XF	Unc
1761	—	600	1,200	2,500	4,000

KM# 160 THALER

Silver **Ruler:** Maximilian Friedrich, Graf von Königsegg-Rothenfels **Obverse:** Bust left, date below **Reverse:** Crowned and supported arms; value below **Note:** Dav. #2177.

Date	Mintage	F	VF	XF	Unc
1762 EGF	—	1,250	2,000	4,000	—

KM# 164 THALER

Silver **Ruler:** Maximilian Friedrich, Graf von Königsegg-Rothenfels **Obverse:** Bust right **Obv. Legend:** MAX • FRID • D • G • AR • EP & EL • COL • E & P • M • W • & A • D • **Reverse:** Crowned complex arms with supporters **Rev. Legend:** IUSTITIA ET MANSUETUDINE, 10 EINE MARCK FEIN in cartouche below **Note:** Dav. #2178.

Date	Mintage	F	VF	XF	Unc
1764 IK-W	—	1,000	1,750	3,000	5,000
1765 IK-W	—	1,000	1,750	3,000	5,000

KM# 169 THALER

Silver **Ruler:** Maximilian Friedrich, Graf von Königsegg-Rothenfels **Reverse:** Crowned and supported oval arms; value below **Note:** Dav. #2180.

Date	Mintage	F	VF	XF	Unc
1766 IK-EG	—	800	1,250	1,750	2,500

KM# 177 THALER

Silver **Ruler:** Maximilian Friedrich, Graf von Königsegg-Rothenfels **Obverse:** Larger bust right, date below **Obv. Legend:** MAXIMILIAN FRID: D: G: ARCH: EP: & ELECT: COL. **Reverse:** Crowned complex arms with supporters **Rev. Legend:** IUSTITIA ET MANSUETUDINE, X EINE FEINE MARK below **Note:** Dav. #2181.

Date	Mintage	F	VF	XF	Unc
1777 EG-ICS	—	250	400	600	1,500

TRADE COINAGE

KM# 102 DUCAT

3.5000 g., 0.9860 Gold 0.1109 oz. AGW **Ruler:** Josef Clemens von Bayern **Obverse:** Bust right in skull cap **Reverse:** Nativity scene **Note:** Varieties exist.

Date	Mintage	VG	F	VF	XF	Unc
1715 FW	—	450	800	1,500	3,000	—

KM# 120 DUCAT

3.5000 g., 0.9860 Gold 0.1109 oz. AGW **Ruler:** Josef Clemens von Bayern **Obverse:** Capped bust right **Reverse:** Crowned 7-fold ornately-shaped arms with central shield of 4-fold arms of Bavaria-Pfalz surrounded by Order chain divide date

Date	Mintage	VG	F	VF	XF	Unc
1722 FW	—	450	800	1,500	3,000	—

KM# 121 DUCAT

3.5000 g., 0.9860 Gold 0.1109 oz. AGW **Ruler:** Josef Clemens von Bayern **Obverse:** Bust left **Reverse:** Adoration of the Magi, date in Roman numerals

Date	Mintage	VG	F	VF	XF	Unc
1723 FW	—	350	700	1,500	3,000	—

KM# 125 DUCAT

3.5000 g., 0.9860 Gold 0.1109 oz. AGW **Ruler:** Clemens August von Bayern **Obverse:** Bust right **Reverse:** Date in Roman numerals

Date	Mintage	VG	F	VF	XF	Unc
1726 FW	—	400	900	1,700	3,000	—

KM# 140 DUCAT

3.5000 g., 0.9860 Gold 0.1109 oz. AGW **Ruler:** Clemens August von Bayern **Obverse:** Older bust **Reverse:** Date in Arabic numerals

Date	Mintage	VG	F	VF	XF	Unc
1742 IK	—	350	800	1,600	2,800	—
1744 IK	—	350	800	1,600	2,800	—

KM# 145 DUCAT

3.5000 g., 0.9860 Gold 0.1109 oz. AGW **Ruler:** Clemens August von Bayern **Reverse:** Seated Madonna and child with crowned arms at right **Rev. Legend:** TUO PRAESIDIO

Date	Mintage	VG	F	VF	XF	Unc
1750 IK-S	—	300	700	1,200	2,000	—
1750 IK-M	—	300	700	1,200	2,000	—

KM# 146 DUCAT

3.5000 g., 0.9860 Gold 0.1109 oz. AGW **Ruler:** Clemens August von Bayern **Obverse:** Bust 3/4 right **Reverse:** Legend within radiant circle

Date	Mintage	VG	F	VF	XF	Unc
1750 IK-M	—	300	700	1,200	2,000	—

KM# 147 DUCAT

3.5000 g., 0.9860 Gold 0.1109 oz. AGW **Ruler:** Clemens August von Bayern **Obverse:** Bust right **Reverse:** Legend within radiant circle

Date	Mintage	VG	F	VF	XF	Unc
1750 IK-M	—	300	700	1,200	2,000	—
1750 M	—	300	700	1,200	2,000	—

KM# 131 1/2 CAROLIN

4.8500 g., 0.7700 Gold 0.1201 oz. AGW **Ruler:** Clemens August von Bayern **Obverse:** Bust right **Reverse:** Date above 7 shields of arms on crowned mantle

Date	Mintage	VG	F	VF	XF	Unc
1735 IH	—	400	900	1,600	2,700	—
1736 IH	—	400	900	1,600	2,700	—

KM# 132 CAROLIN

9.7000 g., 0.7700 Gold 0.2401 oz. AGW **Ruler:** Clemens August von Bayern **Subject:** Clemens August **Obverse:** Bust right **Reverse:** 7 Oval arms within crowned mantle

Date	Mintage	VG	F	VF	XF	Unc
1735 IH	—	500	1,200	2,100	3,200	—

KM# 133 CAROLIN

9.7000 g., 0.7700 Gold 0.2401 oz. AGW **Ruler:** Clemens August von Bayern **Obverse:** Bust left **Reverse:** Madonna, arms, date below

Date	Mintage	VG	F	VF	XF	Unc
1735 IH	—	500	1,200	2,100	3,200	—

CATHEDRAL CHAPTER

When archbishop-elector Josef Clemens was forced to flee to Liege during the War of the Spanish Succession in 1702, the cathedral chapter assumed the responsibility of minting in his absence until his return in 1715.

REGULAR COINAGE

KM# 204 8 HELLER

Silver **Obverse:** Arms within circle **Reverse:** Value within circle **Note:** Mule.

Date	Mintage	VG	F	VF	XF	Unc
1705/1701	—	20.00	40.00	60.00	100	—
1705/1705	—	20.00	40.00	60.00	100	—

KM# 201 8 HELLER

Silver **Obverse:** Arms within circle **Reverse:** Value within circle **Note:** Varieties exist.

Date	Mintage	VG	F	VF	XF	Unc
1703 FW	—	10.00	20.00	40.00	70.00	—
1704 FW	—	10.00	20.00	40.00	70.00	—
1704/3 FW	—	10.00	20.00	40.00	70.00	—

KM# 203 8 HELLER

Silver **Obverse:** Date above arms **Reverse:** Value within circle

Date	Mintage	VG	F	VF	XF	Unc
1705 FW	—	10.00	20.00	40.00	70.00	—
1711	—	10.00	20.00	40.00	70.00	—
1712 FW	—	10.00	20.00	40.00	70.00	—

KM# 202 1/12 THALER (2 Groschen)

Silver

Date	Mintage	VG	F	VF	XF	Unc
1704 FW	—	20.00	40.00	65.00	110	—
1707 FW	—	20.00	40.00	65.00	110	—
1708 FW	—	20.00	40.00	65.00	110	—
1710 FW	—	20.00	40.00	65.00	110	—
1711 FW	—	20.00	40.00	65.00	110	—

KM# 205 1/12 THALER (2 Groschen)

Silver **Obverse:** Larger arms surrounded by arabesques in circle **Reverse:** Value, date within circle

Date	Mintage	VG	F	VF	XF	Unc
1707 FW	—	20.00	45.00	75.00	120	—

FREE CITY

(Köln)
Free City

One of the oldest cities in Europe, Cologne on the Rhine was founded as the Roman colony of Colonia Agrippinensis in 50 A.D. The town grew in importance after becoming the site of a bishopric and later an archbishopric. For two centuries beginning about the mid-10th century, Cologne contained an imperial mint. The archbishops had nominal control of the city until the 12th century. In 1201, Cologne joined the Hanseatic League and gained the right to govern itself in 1288. As the commercial importance of Cologne rose through membership in the League, it finally gained the mint right in 1474 and was soon striking its own coinage. The city remained in the Catholic fold after the Reformation, but its importance as a commercial center wqned during the next several centuries. The French occupied Cologne in 1794 and annexed it three years later. At the end of the Napoleonic Wars in 1815, it was acquired by Prussia.

RULERS

Josef Clemens von Bayern, 1688-1723
Clemens August von Bayern, 1723-1761
Sede Vacante, 1761
Maximilian Friedrich, Graf von ¬¬Konigsegg-Rothenfels, 1761-1784
Maximilian Franz von Osterreich, ¬¬1784-1801
Anton Victor von Osterreich, 1801

NOTE: For issues struck by electors/archbishops of Cologne as dukes of Westphalia, see Westphalia.

MINT OFFICIALS' INITIALS

LETTER	DATE	NAME
TB	ca.1678-1717	Tobias Bernard, die-cutter in Paris
P	1685-1702	Johann Post, warden
NL	1699-1700	Nikolaus Longerich, mintmaster
IAL	1700-05	Johann Adam Longerich, mintmaster
FHH	1702-19; 1705-13	Franz Hermann Hermanns, warden; mintmaster
LC/LCf	1708-37	Gabriel le Clerc, die-cutter in Berlin
IH/IIH	1713-22?	Johann Josef Hermanns, mintmaster
	1720-52	Johann Jacob Hüls, warden
	1723	Johann Rütgers, mintmaster
HK	1723-35	Heinrich Kippers, mintmaster
VL/V.LON	1726-64	Franz Anton van Loon, die-cutter
GH	1735-65	Gerhard Hüls, mintmaster
WYON	1740-50	Peter Wyon, die-cutter
S	1748-99	Anton Schäffer, die-cutter in Mannheim
	1752-72	Johann Josef Langenberg, warden
W	1764-66	Eberhard Wyon, die-cutter
IGH	1765-97; 1775-97	Johann Gerhard Hüls, mintmaster; warden

ARMS

Divided horizontally, 3 crowns in upper half, lower half shaded, usually with cross-hatching, but sometimes with other devices.

REGULAR COINAGE

KM# 410 HELLER

Silver **Note:** Spikes on crowns tall and thin.

Date	Mintage	VG	F	VF	XF	Unc
ND(1716)	—	6.00	12.00	25.00	45.00	—

KM# 445 HELLER

Silver **Note:** 11 small flames below crowns.

Date	Mintage	VG	F	VF	XF	Unc
ND(1792)	—	4.00	8.00	20.00	40.00	—

KM# 440 4 HELLER

Copper **Obverse:** Crowned double-headed imperial eagle with city arms on breast **Reverse:** Value and date

Date	Mintage	VG	F	VF	XF	Unc
1750	48,000	2.50	5.00	12.00	25.00	—
1760	48,000	2.50	5.00	12.00	25.00	—
1768/6	—	3.00	6.00	15.00	30.00	—
1768/7	—	4.00	8.00	18.00	35.00	—
1768	—	2.50	5.00	12.00	25.00	—
1788	—	2.50	5.00	12.00	25.00	—
1789	—	2.50	5.00	12.00	25.00	—
1792	—	2.50	5.00	12.00	25.00	—

KM# 446 8 HELLER (Fettmännchen)

Copper **Obverse:** Crowned arms and eagle **Reverse:** Value and date

Date	Mintage	VG	F	VF	XF	Unc
1793	—	9.50	25.00	45.00	90.00	—

KM# 416 2 ALBUS

Silver **Obverse:** Crowned imperial eagle with orb on breast, titles of Karl VI **Reverse:** Oval city arms (3 crowns above 11 flames) in baroque frame, date in legend, 2. ALB below arms

Date	Mintage	VG	F	VF	XF	Unc
1717 IH	—	6.00	12.00	25.00	50.00	—
1718 IIH	—	6.00	12.00	25.00	50.00	—
1720 IH	—	6.00	12.00	25.00	50.00	—

KM# 430 4 ALBUS (Blaffert)

Silver **Obverse:** Date in legend **Obv. Legend:** IIII/ALB./COLN **Reverse:** Crowned imperial eagle, city arms on breast, titles of Karl VI

Date	Mintage	VG	F	VF	XF	Unc
1732 HK	—	12.00	20.00	40.00	70.00	—

KM# 431 8 ALBUS

Silver **Obverse:** Crowned imperial eagle, city arms on breast, titles of Karl VI **Reverse:** Date in legend **Rev. Legend:** VIII/ALB. COLN

Date	Mintage	VG	F	VF	XF	Unc
1733 HK	—	15.00	30.00	50.00	90.00	—
1734 HK	—	15.00	30.00	50.00	90.00	—
1735 GH	—	15.00	30.00	50.00	90.00	—

KM# 411 1/6 THALER (1/4 Gulden)

Silver **Obverse:** Crowned double-headed imperial eagle with arms on breast **Reverse:** City arms within ornate frame divide date above, circle surrounds

Date	Mintage	VG	F	VF	XF	Unc
1716 IIH	—	15.00	30.00	50.00	90.00	—
1717 IIH	—	15.00	30.00	50.00	90.00	—
1720 IIH	—	15.00	30.00	50.00	90.00	—
1721 IIH	—	15.00	30.00	50.00	90.00	—
1722 IIH	—	15.00	30.00	50.00	90.00	—

KM# 412 1/3 THALER (1/2 Gulden)

Silver **Obverse:** Crowned double-headed imperial eagle with arms on breast **Reverse:** City arms within ornate frame **Note:** Similar to 1/6 Thaler, KM#411, but value 1/3.

Date	Mintage	VG	F	VF	XF	Unc
1716 IIH	—	65.00	125	250	400	—

KM# 417 1/2 THALER
Silver **Subject:** Homage to Karl VI **Obverse:** Laureate bust right **Reverse:** Sun shining through clouds, crescent moon in lower left, HOMAG COLON/date below

Date	Mintage	VG	F	VF	XF	Unc
1717 IIH	—	750	1,250	2,000	3,000	—

KM# 418 1/2 THALER
Silver **Obverse:** Crowned imperial eagle, orb on breast, titles of Karl VI

Date	Mintage	VG	F	VF	XF	Unc
1717	—	275	500	900	1,450	—

KM# 419 1/2 THALER
Silver **Obverse:** Crown above 2 flagstaffs **Reverse:** Laureate bust right

Date	Mintage	VG	F	VF	XF	Unc
1717 IIH	—	750	1,250	2,000	3,000	—

KM# 413 2/3 THALER (Gulden)
Silver **Obverse:** City arms within ornate frame, value below **Reverse:** Crowned double-headed imperial eagle with orb on breast

Date	Mintage	VG	F	VF	XF	Unc
1716 IIH	—	750	1,250	2,000	3,000	—

KM# 414 2/3 THALER (Gulden)
Silver **Reverse:** Laureate bust right

Date	Mintage	VG	F	VF	XF	Unc
1716 IIH	—	900	1,500	2,500	3,500	—

KM# 398 THALER
Silver **Obverse:** Crowned imperial eagle with orb on breast divide date **Reverse:** Helmeted arms supported by lion and griffin **Note:** Dav. #5173. Varieties exist.

Date	Mintage	F	VF	XF	Unc
1699 NL	—	165	425	950	—
1700 NL	—	165	425	950	—
1700 IAL	—	165	425	950	—
1701 IAL	—	350	700	1,200	2,000
1702 IAL	—	350	700	1,200	2,000

KM# 402 THALER
Silver **Subject:** Homage to Josef I **Obverse:** City view, REICHS 8/9 FVES and divided date **Obv. Legend:** VIDI • LVNAM • ADORARE • ME • **Reverse:** Laureate bust right, titles of Josef I **Rev. Legend:** IOSEPHUS • I • D: G • ROM. - IMPERATOR • SEMP • AVG • **Note:** Dav. #2183.

Date	Mintage	F	VF	XF	Unc
1705	—	1,200	2,000	3,500	5,000
ND	—	1,200	2,000	3,500	5,000

KM# 403 THALER
Silver **Obverse:** Eagle with sword and scepter flying above city view **Obv. Legend:** SOLIS. ALES. ME. PROTEGET. ALIS **Reverse:** Armored bust right **Rev. Legend:** IOSEPHVS. I D.G. - ROM. IMPERATOR. S. A. **Note:** Dav. #2184.

Date	Mintage	F	VF	XF	Unc
1705 FHH	—	750	1,250	1,800	2,500

KM# 420 THALER
Silver **Subject:** Homage to Karl VI **Obverse:** Bust and titles of Karl VI **Reverse:** Date below city view **Rev. Legend:** HOMAG. COLON **Note:** Dav. #2185.

Date	Mintage	F	VF	XF	Unc
1717 TB	—	750	1,250	1,800	2,500

KM# 421 THALER
Silver **Obverse:** Sun shining through clouds, crescent moon in lower left, date below **Obv. Legend:** CONCESSO • LVMINE • FVLGET •, below: HOMAG: COLON: **Reverse:** Armored bust of Karl VI right **Rev. Legend:** CAR • VI • D • G •- ROM • IMP • S • AVG • **Note:** Dav. #2186.

Date	Mintage	F	VF	XF	Unc
1717 IH-LCf	—	850	1,400	2,000	3,000

KM# 426.1 THALER
Silver **Reverse:** Similar to KM#398, but without fraction at bottom, date in legend, BURG. HK. FUES in cartouche **Note:** Dav. #2187.

Date	Mintage	VG	F	VF	XF	Unc
1726 V. LON-HK	—	1,200	1,750	2,750	3,500	—

KM# 426.2 THALER
Silver **Reverse:** HK in cartouche divides BURG. FUES **Note:** Dav. #2188.

Date	Mintage	VG	F	VF	XF	Unc
1727 V. LON-HK	—	850	1,400	2,000	3,250	—

KM# 426.3 THALER
Silver **Obverse:** Larger armored bust breaking the legend **Obv. Legend:** CAROL • VI • D • G • R • I • S • A •- GER • HIS • HUN • BO • REX • **Reverse:** Helmeted arms with lion and griffin supporters **Rev. Legend:** MON. NOvA. LIB. REIPUB: COLONIENSIS. 1727, below: BURG.(HK)FUES. **Note:** Dav. #2188A.

Date	Mintage	VG	F	VF	XF	Unc
1727 V. LON-HK	—	850	1,400	2,000	3,250	—

KM# 426.4 THALER
Silver **Obverse:** Bust right **Obv. Legend:** CAROLUS. VI **Reverse:** Arms with supporters **Note:** Dav. #2188B.

Date	Mintage	VG	F	VF	XF	Unc
1727 V. LON-HK	—	850	1,400	2,000	3,250	—

KM# 426.5 THALER
Silver **Obverse:** Without name below head **Reverse:** Arms with supporters **Note:** Dav. #2188C. Varieties exist.

Date	Mintage	VG	F	VF	XF	Unc
1727 HK	—	850	1,400	2,000	3,250	—

KM# 435 THALER
Silver **Subject:** Homage to Karl VII **Obverse:** Helmeted and supported by lion and griffon, twooval shields of Cologne and Wurzburg **Obv. Legend:** MONETA NOVA LIB •- ET IMPER • CIVIT • COLON • 1742 **Reverse:** Laureate bust right, titles of Karl VII **Rev. Legend:** CAROLVS VII • D • - G • ROM • IMP • SEMP • AVG • **Note:** Dav. #2189.

Date	Mintage	F	VF	XF	Unc
1742 GH-WYON	—	1,000	1,750	2,750	4,250

TOKEN COINAGE

KM# Tn1 BRODT RATION PENNING (Bread)
Copper **Obverse:** Crowned double-headed imperial eagle with city arms on breast **Reverse:** Value divides date

Date	Mintage	VG	F	VF	XF	Unc
1789	—	5.00	13.50	35.00	80.00	—

KM# Tn1a BRODT RATION PENNING (Bread)
Silver **Obverse:** Crowned double-headed imperial eagle with city arms on breast **Reverse:** Value divides date

Date	Mintage	VG	F	VF	XF	Unc
1789	—	125	200	300	400	—

KM# Tn2 BRODT RATION PENNING (Bread)
Copper **Obverse:** Crowned double-headed imperial eagle with city arms on breast **Reverse:** Value

Date	Mintage	VG	F	VF	XF	Unc
ND(1789)	—	3.50	10.00	18.50	35.00	—

TRADE COINAGE

KM# 404 DUCAT
3.5000 g., 0.9860 Gold 0.1109 oz. AGW **Obverse:** Bust right **Reverse:** Helmeted arms with griffon and lion supporters

Date	Mintage	VG	F	VF	XF	Unc
1705	—	300	700	1,500	2,350	—
1708	—	300	700	1,500	2,350	—

KM# 405 DUCAT
3.5000 g., 0.9860 Gold 0.1109 oz. AGW **Obverse:** Imperial eagle

Date	Mintage	VG	F	VF	XF	Unc
1705	—	300	700	1,500	2,350	—

KM# 422 DUCAT
3.5000 g., 0.9860 Gold 0.1109 oz. AGW **Obverse:** Helmeted oval arms in baroque frame, griffin and lion supporters, date at end of legend **Obv. Legend:** DVCATVS. CIVIT. COLON. **Reverse:** Armored laureate bust right, legend begins at upper right **Rev. Legend:** CAR. VI. D.G. R. I. S. — A. HI. HV. BO. REX. **Note:** Variety of Fr# 772.

Date	Mintage	VG	F	VF	XF	Unc
1717 IIH	—	300	600	1,200	2,000	—
1717 IIH-LC	—	400	800	1,400	2,250	—
1718 IIH-LC	—	400	800	1,400	2,250	—

KM# 425 DUCAT
3.5000 g., 0.9860 Gold 0.1109 oz. AGW **Obverse:** Crowned imperial eagle with Cologne arms on breast **Reverse:** Laureate armored bust right

Date	Mintage	VG	F	VF	XF	Unc
1724 HK-LC	—	200	400	800	1,550	—
1724 HK-VL	—	200	400	800	1,550	—

KM# 423.1 DUCAT
3.5000 g., 0.9860 Gold .1109 oz. AGW 0.1109 oz. AGW **Obverse:** Helmeted oval arms in baroque frame, griffin and lion supporters, date at end of legend **Obv. Legend:** DVCAT. CIVIT. — COLONIEN. **Reverse:** Draped laureate bust right, legend begins at lower left **Rev. Legend:** CAROL. VI. D.G. R. I. S. A. GER. HI. HU. BO. REX.

Date	Mintage	VG	F	VF	XF	Unc
1726 HK	—	300	600	1,200	2,000	—

KM# 423.2 DUCAT
3.5000 g., 0.9860 Gold .1109 oz. AGW 0.1109 oz. AGW **Obverse:** Helmeted oval arms in baroque frame, griffin and lion supporters, date divided below **Obv. Legend:** DUCAT. CIVIT. COLON. **Reverse:** Draped bust to right, legend begins at lower left **Rev. Legend:** CAROL. VI. D.G. R. I. S. A. GER. HI. HU. BO. REX. **Note:** Variety of Fr# 772.

Date	Mintage	VG	F	VF	XF	Unc
1727 HK-VL	—	300	650	1,200	1,850	—
1731 HK	—	300	600	1,200	2,000	—

KM# 424.1 DUCAT
3.5000 g., 0.9860 Gold .1109 oz. AGW 0.1109 oz. AGW **Obverse:** Helmeted oval arms in baroque frame, griffin and lion supporters **Obv. Legend:** DUCAT. CIVIT. COLON. **Reverse:** Draped laureate bust to right, legend begins at lower left, date at end **Rev. Legend:** CAROL. VI. D.G. R. I. S. A. GER. HI. HU. BO. REX. **Note:** Variety of Fr# 772.

Date	Mintage	VG	F	VF	XF	Unc
1736 GH	—	400	800	1,400	2,250	—

KM# 424.2 DUCAT
3.5000 g., 0.9860 Gold .1109 oz. AGW 0.1109 oz. AGW **Obverse:** Helmeted oval arms in baroque frame, griffin and lion supporters **Obv. Legend:** DUCAT. CIVIT. COLON. **Reverse:** Draped laureate bust to right, date below shoulder, legend begins at lower left **Rev. Legend:** CAR. VI. D.G. R. I. — S. A. GE. HI. HU. B. REX. **Note:** Variety of Fr# 772.

Date	Mintage	VG	F	VF	XF	Unc
1739 GH	—	300	600	1,200	2,000	—

KM# 428 DUCAT
3.5000 g., 0.9860 Gold 0.1109 oz. AGW **Obverse:** Bust right **Obv. Legend:** CAROL•VI•DG... **Reverse:** Helmeted supported arms

Date	Mintage	VG	F	VF	XF	Unc
ND (ca.1740) GH-W	—	—	—	—	—	—

KM# 436 DUCAT
3.5000 g., 0.9860 Gold 0.1109 oz. AGW **Obverse:** Laureate bust right, titles of Karl VII **Reverse:** 2 oval arms of Cologne and Wurzburg, plumed helmet above, supported by lion and griffin, date below

Date	Mintage	VG	F	VF	XF	Unc
1742 GH-W	—	2,000	3,000	5,000	8,000	—

KM# 441 DUCAT
3.5000 g., 0.9860 Gold 0.1109 oz. AGW **Subject:** Franz I **Reverse:** Bust right **Rev. Legend:** FRANC • D G...

Date	Mintage	VG	F	VF	XF	Unc
1750 GH-S	—	200	350	900	1,600	—
1753 GH-S	—	200	350	900	1,600	—
ND GH-W	—	200	350	900	1,600	—

KM# 442 DUCAT
3.5000 g., 0.9860 Gold 0.1109 oz. AGW **Obverse:** Laureate bust of Josef II right

Date	Mintage	VG	F	VF	XF	Unc
1767 IGH-S	—	400	1,000	2,200	3,500	—

KM# 427 12 DUCAT
42.0000 g., 0.9860 Gold 1.3314 oz. AGW **Obverse:** Crowned imperial eagle, orb on breast **Reverse:** Helmeted arms supported by lion and griffin, date in legend

Date	Mintage	VG	F	VF	XF	Unc
1727 HK-V. LON	—	—	—	—	25,000	—

PATTERNS

Including off metal strikes

KM#	Date	Mintage	Identification	Mkt Val
Pn4	1701	—	8 Heller. Gold. KM#83.	—
Pn21	(1716)	—	Heller. Gold. KM#410.	450
Pn22	1768	—	4 Heller. Silver. KM#440.	120
Pn23	1789	—	4 Heller. Silver. KM#440.	120
Pn24	(1792)	—	Heller. Gold. KM#445.	500
Pn25	1793	—	8 Heller. Silver. **KM#446.**	—

CONSTANCE

BISHOPRIC

(Konstanz, Kostnitz, Costnitz)

This bishopric, which is centered on the city of the same name, was transferred to that location from Vindinissa in Aargau late in the 6th century. The first episcopal coinage was produced at the end of the 9th century and minting continued intermittently during the next 850 years. By the time of the Protestant Reformation, the bishop had become a Prince of the Empire and ruled over a large expanse of territory encompassing much of what is now southwest Germany and northern Switzerland. In 1527, Bishop Hugo refused to submit to the Reformation and was forced to flee the city. He went to Meersburg, across the lake on the north shore, and it became the bishop's residence until the diocese was secularized in 1802. It was acquired by Baden along with the city at that time.

RULERS

Markwart Rudolf von Rodt, 1689-1704
Johann Franz II, Schenk von Staufenberg, 1704-1740
Damian Hugo von Schoenborn, 1740-1743
Casimir Heinrich Anton von Sickingen, 1743-1750
Franz Conrad von Rodt, 1750-1775
Maximillian Christoph von Rodt, 1775-1800

MINT MARKS

G = Günzburg Mint

MINT OFFICIALS' INITIALS

Initials	Date	Name
FH	1760-94	Friedrich Heuglin, warden in Stuttgart

REGULAR COINAGE

KM# 25 1/2 KREUZER
Copper **Ruler:** Franz Conrad von Rodt **Mint:** Gunzburg **Obverse:** Arms **Reverse:** Value above date and mint

Date	Mintage	VG	F	VF	XF	Unc
1772G	—	10.00	18.00	30.00	50.00	—

KM# 26 KREUZER
Copper **Ruler:** Franz Conrad von Rodt **Mint:** Gunzburg **Obverse:** Cardinal's hat and mitre above quartered arms within mantle **Reverse:** Value and date

Date	Mintage	VG	F	VF	XF	Unc
1772G	—	10.00	20.00	35.00	60.00	—

KM# 16 20 KREUZER
Silver **Ruler:** Franz Conrad von Rodt **Obverse:** Bust left **Reverse:** Crowned arms, value below

Date	Mintage	VG	F	VF	XF	Unc
1761 FH	—	20.00	35.00	75.00	150	—

KM# 27 1/48 THALER
Billon **Ruler:** Franz Conrad von Rodt **Obverse:** Arms **Reverse:** Value above date and mint

Date	Mintage	VG	F	VF	XF	Unc
1772	—	10.00	15.00	30.00	60.00	—

KM# 28 1/24 THALER
Billon **Ruler:** Franz Conrad von Rodt **Obverse:** Cardinal's hat and mitre above quartered arms within mantle **Reverse:** Value and date

Date	Mintage	VG	F	VF	XF	Unc
1772	—	15.00	25.00	50.00	100	—

KM# A18 1/4 THALER
Silver **Ruler:** Franz Conrad von Rodt **Obverse:** Bust left **Reverse:** Cardinal's hat and crown above quartered arms within mantle

Date	Mintage	VG	F	VF	XF	Unc
1761 FH	—	40.00	70.00	150	275	—

KM# 17 1/2 THALER
Silver **Ruler:** Franz Conrad von Rodt **Obverse:** Bust left **Reverse:** Cardinal's hat and crown above quartered arms within mantle **Note:** Similar to 1 Thaler, KM#18.

Date	Mintage	VG	F	VF	XF	Unc
1761 FH	—	50.00	90.00	140	275	—

KM# 18 THALER
Silver **Ruler:** Franz Conrad von Rodt **Subject:** Franz Conrad **Obverse:** Bust left **Obv. Legend:** FRAN: CON: TIT: S: MA: DE POP: CARD: DE RODT: EPIS: CONST: S: R: I: PRIN: **Reverse:** Cardinal's hat and crown above quartered arms within mantle **Rev. Legend:** PRO ECCLESIA ET PRO PATRIA. **Note:** Dav. #2190.

Date	Mintage	VG	F	VF	XF	Unc
1761 FH	—	175	275	400	750	—

TRADE COINAGE

KM# 10 DUCAT
3.5000 g., 0.9860 Gold 0.1109 oz. AGW **Ruler:** Johann Franz II, Schenk von Staufenberg **Obverse:** 2 shields of arms topped by mitre and crown, date at bottom **Reverse:** Arms in ornamental cartouche

Date	Mintage	VG	F	VF	XF	Unc
1737	—	750	1,500	3,000	6,000	—

KM# 19 DUCAT
3.5000 g., 0.9860 Gold 0.1109 oz. AGW **Ruler:** Franz Conrad von Rodt **Subject:** Franz Conrad **Obverse:** Bust left **Reverse:** Cardinal's hat and crown above quartered arms within mantle

Date	Mintage	VG	F	VF	XF	Unc
1761	—	350	700	1,350	2,500	—

KM# 11 2 DUCAT
7.0000 g., 0.9860 Gold 0.2219 oz. AGW **Ruler:** Johann Franz II, Schenk von Staufenberg **Obverse:** 2 shields of arms topped by mitre and crown, date at bottom **Reverse:** Arms in ornamental cartouche

Date	Mintage	VG	F	VF	XF	Unc
1737	—	3,000	4,500	6,500	10,000	—

FREE CITY

Located at the western end of the Bodensee (Lake Constance) and on the German-Swiss border, Constance stands on the site of the late Roman fortress of Constantia. When the bishopric in Aargau was transferred to the place shortly before 600, the town began to grow in importance. An Imperial mint was established in Constance at the beginning of the 11th century and it functioned until about 1250. Constance became an imperial free city in either 1192 or 1255, but the bishop controlled most of its affairs at least until the Protestant Reformation. The city joined the League of Schmalkalden in 1530, but was the lone Protestant holdout in the region after 1547. Karl V took Constance in 1548 and incorporated it into his Austrian realm. The city retained its coinage rights, however, and continued minting until about 1733. Constance became part of Baden in 1803.

ARMS

Cross, horizontal bar usually shaded, often a single-headed eagle above.

REGULAR COINAGE

KM# 194 1/4 KREUZER
Billon **Obverse:** Oval city arms in cartouche, date above **Reverse:** C above 1/4

Date	Mintage	VG	F	VF	XF	Unc
1703	—	20.00	40.00	70.00	120	—

KM# 191 1/2 KREUZER
Billon **Obverse:** Oval city arms in cartouche, 1/2 below, date in legend **Note:** Uniface. Varieties exist.

Date	Mintage	VG	F	VF	XF	Unc
1702	—	25.00	50.00	90.00	145	—
1723	—	25.00	50.00	90.00	145	—

KM# 192 KREUZER
Billon **Obverse:** Crowned double-headed imperial eagle **Reverse:** Bishops facing each other, arms below **Note:** Similar to KM#200, but titles of Leopold I.

Date	Mintage	VG	F	VF	XF	Unc
1702	—	6.00	12.00	25.00	50.00	—

KM# 201 KREUZER
Billon **Obverse:** Oval city arms in baroque shield, value 1 below

Date	Mintage	VG	F	VF	XF	Unc
ND(1711-1733)	—	6.00	12.00	22.00	40.00	—

KM# 200 KREUZER
Billon **Obverse:** Titles of Karl VI in legend **Reverse:** Arms at center

Date	Mintage	VG	F	VF	XF	Unc
1715	—	6.00	12.00	22.00	40.00	—
1717	—	6.00	12.00	22.00	40.00	—
1723	—	6.00	12.00	22.00	40.00	—
1724	—	6.00	12.00	22.00	40.00	—

KM# 193 4 KREUZER (1 Batzen)
Silver **Obverse:** Oval city arms in baroque frame, date in legend **Reverse:** Crowned imperial eagle, 4 in orb on breast, titles of Leopold I

Date	Mintage	VG	F	VF	XF	Unc
1702	—	50.00	90.00	175	325	—

KM# 202 15 KREUZER
Silver **Obverse:** Date above saints **Reverse:** Titles of Karl VI in legend

Date	Mintage	VG	F	VF	XF	Unc
1715	—	50.00	90.00	165	250	—

KM# 210 THALER
Silver **Obverse:** City view, CONSTANTIA below **Reverse:** City arms in center with 4 oval arms around divide date, all surrounded by 20 small oval arms **Note:** Regiments Thaler. Dav. #2192.

Date	Mintage	VG	F	VF	XF	Unc
1724	—	1,750	3,000	5,000	8,000	—

KM# 211 2 THALER
Silver **Obverse:** City view, CONSTANTIA below **Reverse:** City arms in center with 4 oval arms around divide date, all surrounded by 20 small oval arms **Note:** Dav. #2191.

Date	Mintage	F	VF	XF	Unc
1724	—	5,500	8,000	12,000	—

COUNTERMARKED COINAGE

1723

KM# 203 15 KREUZER
Silver **Countermark:** Constance City arms **Note:** Countermark on 15 Kreuzer, KM#202.

CM Date	Host Date	Good	VG	F	VF	XF
ND(ca.1716)	1715	—	135	200	275	400

CORVEY

(Corvei-Corbie-Corbey-Curbei)

ABBEY and BISHOPRIC

Located on the Weser River just east of Höxter in Westphalia, the Benedictine abbey of Corvey was founded in 820 at the instigation of Emperor Ludwig the Pious (814-40) by monks from the monastery of Corbei in Picardy. Not long after it was established, the new abbey received the mint right as stated in the surviving document dated 1 June 833. Over the next several decades, Corvey also received the right to mint coins in several nearby towns including Marsberg and Meppen. Except for a long period between about 1370 and 1500, Corvey produced a long series of coinage. In 1793, the abbey was transformed into a bishopric, but did not long remain an independent entity. Corvey was secularized in 1803 and its territory was acquired by Nassau-Dietz the same year. After having been incorporated into the Kingdom of Westphalia (1807-13) during the Napoleonic Wars, Corvey was absorbed by Prussia in 1813. Corvey struck some joint issues with Höxter and these are included here.

RULERS

Florenz von der Velde, 1696-1714
Maximilian von Horrich, 1714-1721
Karl von Plittersdorf, 1722-1737
Kaspar II von Böselager-Hohneburg, 1737-1758
Philip, Freiherr Spiegel von Disenberg, 1758-1776
Theodor von Brabeck, Abbot, 1776-1793
Bishop, 1793-1794
Ferdinand, Freiherr von Lünig, 1794-1803

MINT OFFICIALS' INITIALS

Initials	Date	Name
AP, AGP	1715, 1721, 1725	Anton Gottfried Pott
HCH	1689-1729	Heinrich Christoph Hille in Brunswick
NO, HLO	1698-1706	Heinrich Laurenz Odendahl in Westphalia

ARMS

2-fold divided horizontally, lower half usually shaded by various devices

BENEDICTINE ABBEY

REGULAR COINAGE

KM# 110 PFENNIG (Schwerer - heavy)
Copper **Ruler:** Florenz **Obverse:** Round arms, date in legend **Reverse:** Value: I/SCHWER/PFEN **Rev. Legend:** FURSTL. CORVEY..

Date	Mintage	VG	F	VF	XF	Unc
1703	—	—	—	—	—	—

KM# 111 PFENNIG (Schwerer - heavy)
Copper **Ruler:** Florenz **Obverse:** Round arms, date in legend **Reverse:** Value: II/SCHWER/PFEN **Rev. Legend:** FURSTL. CORVEY..

Date	Mintage	VG	F	VF	XF	Unc
1703	—	—	—	—	—	—

KM# 116 PFENNIG (Schwerer - heavy)
Copper **Ruler:** Florenz **Obverse:** Crowned 4-fold arms **Reverse:** Value within circle **Note:** Similar to 2 Pfennig, KM#117.

Date	Mintage	VG	F	VF	XF	Unc
1704	—	8.00	16.00	35.00	60.00	—

KM# 126 PFENNIG (Schwerer - heavy)
Copper **Ruler:** Maximilian **Obverse:** Crowned oval 4-fold arms **Reverse:** Date in legend

Date	Mintage	VG	F	VF	XF	Unc
1715	—	6.00	12.00	25.00	45.00	—

KM# 117 2 PFENNIG
Copper, 20 mm. **Ruler:** Florenz **Obverse:** Crowned 4-fold arms, date in legend **Reverse:** Value within circle

Date	Mintage	VG	F	VF	XF	Unc
1704	—	6.00	12.00	25.00	45.00	—

KM# 127 2 PFENNIG
Copper **Ruler:** Maximilian **Obverse:** Crowned oval 4-fold arms **Reverse:** Date in legend

Date	Mintage	VG	F	VF	XF	Unc
1715	—	6.00	12.00	25.00	45.00	—
1717	—	10.00	20.00	40.00	65.00	—

KM# 170 2 PFENNIG
Copper **Ruler:** Theodor Abbot **Obverse:** Crowned shielded arms **Reverse:** Value within circle

Date	Mintage	VG	F	VF	XF	Unc
1787	—	4.00	8.00	16.00	35.00	—

KM# 112 4 PFENNIG
Silver **Ruler:** Florenz **Obverse:** Crowned 4-fold arms **Reverse:** Value **Rev. Legend:** IIII/GUTE/PF

Date	Mintage	VG	F	VF	XF	Unc
1703	—	75.00	135	225	350	—

KM# 131 4 PFENNIG
Copper **Ruler:** Maximilian **Note:** Similar to 2 Pfennig KM#117, but reverse value: IIII/PFEN/date.

Date	Mintage	VG	F	VF	XF	Unc
1717	—	6.00	12.00	25.00	45.00	—

KM# 165 4 PFENNIG
Billon **Ruler:** Philip Freiherr Spiegel **Obverse:** Crowned monogram **Reverse:** Value, date

Date	Mintage	VG	F	VF	XF	Unc
1765	—	40.00	80.00	150	250	—

KM# 171 4 PFENNIG
Copper **Ruler:** Theodor Abbot **Obverse:** Crowned arms **Reverse:** Value above date

Date	Mintage	VG	F	VF	XF	Unc
1787	—	5.00	10.00	20.00	40.00	—

KM# 118 6 PFENNIG (Schwerer - heavy)
Silver **Ruler:** Florenz **Obverse:** Crowned double-F monogram divides date **Reverse:** Value **Rev. Legend:** VI/SCHWER/PFEN

Date	Mintage	VG	F	VF	XF	Unc
1706 HLO	—	—	—	—	—	—

KM# 113 MARIENGROSCHEN
Silver **Ruler:** Florenz **Obverse:** Crowned 4-fold arms, date in legend **Rev. Legend:** I.MARIEN/GROS

Date	Mintage	VG	F	VF	XF	Unc
1703	—	45.00	85.00	170	275	—

KM# 128 MARIENGROSCHEN
Silver **Ruler:** Maximilian **Obverse:** Crowned round 4-fold arms, date in legend **Reverse:** Value, date within circle

Date	Mintage	VG	F	VF	XF	Unc
1715	—	65.00	125	250	425	—

KM# 114 24 MARIENGROSCHEN (2/3 Thaler)
Silver **Ruler:** Florenz **Obverse:** Crowned 4-fold arms **Reverse:** Value, date in legend **Rev. Legend:** XXIIII/MARIEN/GROSCH

Date	Mintage	VG	F	VF	XF	Unc
1703 HLO	—	—	—	—	—	—

KM# 155 24 MARIENGROSCHEN (2/3 Thaler)
Silver **Ruler:** Kaspar II **Obverse:** Crowned arms **Obv. Legend:** D. G. CASPAREIUS PRINCEPS.. **Reverse:** St. Vitus standing **Rev. Legend:** POSVIT..

Date	Mintage	VG	F	VF	XF	Unc
1753	—	85.00	175	350	600	—

KM# 156 24 MARIENGROSCHEN (2/3 Thaler)
Silver **Ruler:** Kaspar II **Obverse:** Helmeted arms **Reverse:** St. Vitus standing

Date	Mintage	VG	F	VF	XF	Unc
ND(1753)	—	70.00	150	300	500	—

KM# 157 24 MARIENGROSCHEN (2/3 Thaler)
Silver **Ruler:** Kaspar II **Obverse:** Helmeted arms **Reverse:** St. Vitus standing **Rev. Legend:** DA PACEM DOMINE..

Date	Mintage	VG	F	VF	XF	Unc
ND(1753)	—	60.00	125	250	400	—

KM# 129 1/48 THALER (1/2 Groschen)
Silver **Ruler:** Maximilian **Obverse:** Crowned oval 4-fold arms **Reverse:** Value, date in legend **Rev. Legend:** 48/I/REICHS/TH/AGP

Date	Mintage	VG	F	VF	XF	Unc
1715 AGP	—	45.00	100	200	350	—

KM# 115 1/12 THALER (2 Groschen)
Silver **Ruler:** Florenz **Obverse:** Crowned oval 4-fold arms in cartouche **Reverse:** Value, date in legend **Rev. Legend:** 12/EINEN/REICHS/THAL

Date	Mintage	VG	F	VF	XF	Unc
1703 HLO	—	45.00	80.00	160	275	—
1704 HLO	—	45.00	80.00	160	275	—

KM# 130 1/12 THALER (2 Groschen)
Silver **Ruler:** Maximilian **Obverse:** Crowned 4-fold arms **Reverse:** Value within circle

Date	Mintage	VG	F	VF	XF	Unc
1715	—	30.00	60.00	120	225	—
1715 AGP	—	30.00	60.00	120	225	—

KM# 139 1/12 THALER (2 Groschen)
Silver **Ruler:** Karl **Obverse:** Crowned 4-fold arms on ornate shield **Reverse:** Value, date in legend

Date	Mintage	VG	F	VF	XF	Unc
1725	—	30.00	60.00	120	225	—

KM# 166 1/12 THALER (2 Groschen)
Billon **Ruler:** Philip Freiherr Spiegel **Obverse:** Arms **Obv. Legend:** PHILIPPUS.. **Reverse:** Value, date

Date	Mintage	VG	F	VF	XF	Unc
1765	—	15.00	30.00	60.00	100	—

KM# 167 1/16 THALER
Silver **Ruler:** Philip Freiherr Spiegel **Obverse:** 4-Fold arms within crowned mantle **Reverse:** Value and date within circle

Date	Mintage	VG	F	VF	XF	Unc
1765	—	20.00	45.00	80.00	150	—

KM# 119.1 THALER
Silver **Ruler:** Florenz **Obverse:** Date below helmeted arms **Reverse:** St. Vitus standing **Note:** Dav. #2193.

Date	Mintage	F	VF	XF	Unc
1706 HO	—	400	800	1,500	2,500

KM# 119.2 THALER
Silver **Ruler:** Florenz **Obverse:** Mitre above helmeted 4-fold arms **Obv. Legend:** FLORENTIUS. D:G: ABBAS. CORBEIENSIS. S: R: I: PRINC: **Reverse:** St. Vitus standing, date divided by lion below **Rev. Legend:** SANCTVS VITVS PATRONVS CORBEIENSIS **Note:** Dav. #2194.

Date	Mintage	F	VF	XF	Unc
1709 HCH	—	400	800	1,500	2,500

KM# 125 THALER
Silver **Ruler:** Florenz **Obverse:** Mitre above helmeted 4-fold arms **Obv. Legend:** * SOLEMNI RITU IUBILAEUM CELEBRABAT REV • ET • CELS • PR • D • FLORENT • ABBAS • CORBIENS • S • R • I • PR • XX AP • **Reverse:** 6 crowns with inscriptions and/or dates, date divided near bottom **Rev. Legend:** * AN: QUO PRAESENT • REV • ET CEL • PR • D • FRANC • ARNOL • EP • MON • ET PAD • AC • SER • PR • D • ANT • VLR • D • BR • ET LUN • **Note:** Dav. #2195.

Date	Mintage	F	VF	XF	Unc
1713	—	1,000	1,800	2,750	—

KM# 132 THALER

Silver **Ruler:** Maximilian **Obverse:** Mitre above helmeted 4-fold arms **Obv. Legend:** MAXIMILIANUS D. G. ABBAS CORBEIENSIS S. R. I. PRINCEPS **Reverse:** St. Vitus with lion, falcon and palm branch, Roman numeral date below **Rev. Legend:** SANCTVS VITVS PATRONVS CORBEIENSIS **Note:** Dav. #2196.

Date	Mintage	F	VF	XF	Unc
1717	—	250	550	1,000	1,650
1718	—	250	550	1,000	1,650

KM# 133 THALER

Silver **Ruler:** Maximilian **Reverse:** Arabic date **Note:** Dav. #2196A.

Date	Mintage	F	VF	XF	Unc
1718	—	250	550	1,000	1,650

KM# 135 THALER

Silver **Ruler:** Maximilian **Obverse:** Mitre above helmeted 4-fold arms **Obv. Legend:** MAXIMILIANUS D • G • ABBAS CORBEIENSIS S • R • I • PRINCEPS **Reverse:** Date divided by saint near bottom **Rev. Legend:** SANCTVS VITVS PATRONVS CORBEIENSIS **Note:** Dav. #2197.

Date	Mintage	F	VF	XF	Unc
1721 AP	—	250	550	1,000	1,650

KM# 136 THALER

Silver **Ruler:** Karl **Obverse:** Roman numeral date in legend **Note:** Dav. #2198.

Date	Mintage	F	VF	XF	Unc
1723 Rare	—	—	—	—	—

KM# 137 THALER

Silver **Ruler:** Karl **Obverse:** Mitre above helmeted 4-fold arms **Obv. Legend:** CAROLVS D. G. ABBAS CORBEIENSIS S. R. I. PRINCEPS **Reverse:** Roman numeral date in exergue **Rev. Legend:** SANCTVS VITVS PATRONVVS CORBEIENSIS **Note:** Dav. #2199.

Date	Mintage	F	VF	XF	Unc
MDCCXXIII (1723)	—	300	600	1,100	1,850

KM# 145 THALER

Silver **Ruler:** Kaspar II **Obverse:** Helmeted arms **Obv. Legend:** CASPARUS D. G. ABBAS CORBEIENSIS S. R. I. PRINCEPS. 1739 **Reverse:** St. Vitus standing **Rev. Legend:** SANCTVS VITVS PATRONUS CORBEIENSIS **Note:** Dav. #2200.

Date	Mintage	F	VF	XF	Unc
1739	—	350	750	1,400	2,250
ND	—	350	750	1,400	2,250

KM# 158 THALER

Silver **Ruler:** Kaspar II **Obverse:** Mitre above helmeted 4-fold arms **Obv. Legend:** PHILIPPUS D • G • ABBAS CORBEIENSIS S • R • I • PRINCEPS 1758 **Reverse:** St. Vitus standing **Rev. Legend:** SANCTVS VITVS PATRONVS CORBEIENSIS **Note:** Dav. #2201.

Date	Mintage	F	VF	XF	Unc
1758	—	350	750	1,400	2,250

TRADE COINAGE

KM# 138 DUCAT

3.5000 g., 0.9860 Gold 0.1109 oz. AGW **Ruler:** Karl **Obverse:** St. Vitus standing **Reverse:** Crowned arms **Rev. Legend:** CAROLUS **Note:** Fr. 848.

Date	Mintage	VG	F	VF	XF	Unc
1724	—	900	1,750	3,000	5,000	—
ND	—	900	1,750	3,000	5,000	—

KM# 150 DUCAT

3.5000 g., 0.9860 Gold 0.1109 oz. AGW **Ruler:** Kaspar II **Reverse:** Crowned arms **Rev. Legend:** CASPARUS **Note:** Fr. 849.

Date	Mintage	VG	F	VF	XF	Unc
1743	—	500	1,000	2,000	3,750	—
1748	—	500	1,000	2,000	3,750	—
1753	—	500	1,000	2,000	3,750	—

KM# 159 DUCAT

3.5000 g., 0.9860 Gold 0.1109 oz. AGW **Ruler:** Kaspar II **Obverse:** Crowned arms **Obv. Legend:** PHILIPPUS **Reverse:** St. Vitus standing **Note:** Fr. 850.

Date	Mintage	VG	F	VF	XF	Unc
1758	—	900	1,750	3,000	5,000	—

KM# 160.1 DUCAT

3.5000 g., 0.9860 Gold 0.1109 oz. AGW **Ruler:** Philip Freiherr Spiegel **Obverse:** Bust right **Reverse:** Crowned and mantled arms **Rev. Legend:** IUSTITIA ET PRUDENTIA **Note:** Fr. 850.

Date	Mintage	VG	F	VF	XF	Unc
1759	—	750	1,500	2,500	4,750	—

KM# 160.2 DUCAT

3.5000 g., 0.9860 Gold 0.1109 oz. AGW **Ruler:** Philip Freiherr Spiegel **Obverse:** Bust right **Reverse:** Crowned and mantled arms **Rev. Legend:** IUSTITIA AND PRUDENTIA

Date	Mintage	VG	F	VF	XF	Unc
1759	—	750	1,500	2,500	4,750	—

KM# 168 DUCAT

3.5000 g., 0.9860 Gold 0.1109 oz. AGW **Ruler:** Philip Freiherr Spiegel **Reverse:** Helmeted arms

Date	Mintage	VG	F	VF	XF	Unc
1769 Rare	—	—	—	—	—	—

PATTERNS

Including off metal strikes

KM#	Date	Mintage	Identification	Mkt Val
Pn3	1759	—	Ducat. Silver. KM#160.2.	175

CRAILSHEIM

IMPERIAL BARONY

The barony of Crailsheim was located in Franconia, about mid-way between Hall in Swabia and Ansbach. The family was one of the oldest Franconian noble lines, first mentioned in 1386. They were raised to the rank of imperial baron in 1701 and took part in the governmental and military affairs of Brandenburg-Ansbach. It was absorbed by Württemberg early in the 19th century.

RULER

Albrecht Ernst Friedrich, 1728-1794

REGULAR COINAGE

KM# 1 6 KREUZER

Silver **Ruler:** Albrecht Ernst Friedrich **Obverse:** Bust right **Reverse:** Helmeted arms (crown above bar), order ribbon suspended below. **Rev. Legend:** S: CA & REB: APOST...

Date	Mintage	VG	F	VF	XF	Unc
ND(ca.1759) Rare	—	—	—	—	—	—

DORTMUND

(Tremoniensis)

Dortmund is located in Westphalia, 50 miles east of Düsseldorf. It was the site of an imperial mint from the 10th to early 16th century and later had its own city coinage, dated pieces being known from 1553 to 1760. In 1803 Dortmund was annexed to Nassau-Dillenburg and passed to Prussia in 1815.

MINT OFFICIALS' INITIALS

Initials	Date	Name
GH	1735-65	Gerhard Huls, city of Cologne
HS	1752-58	Heinrich Schwarze
IAL	1705-07	Johann Adam Longerich
IIH	1713-22	Johann Joseph Hermann, city of Cologne
LC, LCf	1708-37	Gabriel LeClerc, die-cutter in Berlin

ARMS

Eagle with wings spread, head usually turned to left.

CITY

REGULAR COINAGE

KM# 105 1/4 STUBER

Copper **Obverse:** Crowned arms within shield **Reverse:** Value, date

Date	Mintage	VG	F	VF	XF	Unc
1752	—	6.00	12.00	25.00	40.00	—
1753 HS	—	5.00	10.00	20.00	35.00	—
1754	—	5.00	10.00	20.00	35.00	—
1754 HS	—	5.00	10.00	20.00	35.00	—
1755 HS	—	5.00	10.00	22.00	38.00	—
1756 HS	—	5.00	10.00	22.00	38.00	—

KM# 109 1/4 STUBER

Copper **Obverse:** Eagle in shield without crown **Reverse:** Value, date within circle

Date	Mintage	VG	F	VF	XF	Unc
1758 HS	—	4.00	8.00	16.00	30.00	—
1759 HS	—	4.00	8.00	16.00	30.00	—
1760 HS	—	4.00	8.00	16.00	30.00	—

KM# 106 6 PFENNING (1/2 Schilling)

Billon **Obverse:** Eagle, DORTMUND in banner below **Reverse:** Imperial orb with value divides date

Date	Mintage	VG	F	VF	XF	Unc
1754 HS	—	6.00	12.00	28.00	55.00	—
1755 HS	—	6.00	12.00	28.00	55.00	—
1756 HS	—	6.00	12.00	28.00	55.00	—

KM# 108 4 KREUZER

Billon **Obverse:** Eagle **Reverse:** Value, date in three lines

Date	Mintage	VG	F	VF	XF	Unc
1757 HS	—	7.00	15.00	30.00	55.00	—

KM# 107 1/24 THALER

Billon **Obverse:** Arms divide HS **Reverse:** Value, date

Date	Mintage	VG	F	VF	XF	Unc
1754 HS	—	35.00	75.00	125	200	—
1756 HS	—	35.00	75.00	125	200	—
1757 HS	—	35.00	75.00	125	200	—
1758 HS	—	35.00	75.00	125	200	—

KM# 110 1/12 THALER

Silver **Obverse:** Arms divide HS **Reverse:** Value, date

Date	Mintage	VG	F	VF	XF	Unc
1758 HS	—	50.00	100	200	300	—
1759 HS	—	50.00	100	200	300	—

KM# 111 1/6 THALER

Silver **Obverse:** Bust of Franz I right **Reverse:** Value, eagle divides date at bottom

Date	Mintage	VG	F	VF	XF	Unc
1758 HS	—	100	250	400	750	—

KM# 80 THALER

Silver **Obverse:** Laureate bust of Josef I right, titles around **Obv. Legend:** IOSEPHVS • I • D: G • ROM • - IMPERATOR• SEMP • AVG • **Reverse:** Eagle, head left, in circle, divides date **Rev. Legend:** * MONETA * NOVA: CIVIT: IMPER: TREMONIENSIS *, in circle: DA * PACEM * D: OMINE **Note:** Dav. #2204.

Date	Mintage	VG	F	VF	XF	Unc
1705 IAL	—	5,000	7,000	9,000	12,000	—

KM# 85 THALER

Silver **Subject:** Homage to Karl VI **Obverse:** Eagle, head left, below DOM. CONS. NOS. **Obv. Legend:** MON: HOMAG: CIVIT: I. TREMON:, in exergue below: DOM•CONS•NOS•IN•/17• PACE•17• **Reverse:** Laureate bust of Karl VI, titles around **Rev. Legend:** CAR•VI•D•G•- ROM•IMP•S•AVG• **Note:** Dav. #2205.

Date	Mintage	VG	F	VF	XF	Unc
1717 LCf-IIH	—	3,250	5,000	7,500	10,000	—

KM# 86 THALER

Silver **Note:** Struck on smaller, thicker flan. Dav. #2205B.

Date	Mintage	VG	F	VF	XF	Unc
1717 LCf-IIH	—	5,000	7,500	9,000	11,000	—

KM# 95 THALER

Silver **Subject:** Homage to Karl VII **Obverse:** Bust and titles of Karl VII **Note:** Dav. #2206.

Date	Mintage	VG	F	VF	XF	Unc
1742 GH	—	800	1,500	2,500	4,000	—

KM# 87 2 THALER

Silver **Obverse:** Laureate bust of Karl VI right, titles around **Reverse:** Eagle, head left, below DOM. CONS. IN. /17. PACE. 17.

Date	Mintage	VG	F	VF	XF	Unc
1717 LCf-IIH Rare	—	—	—	—	—	—

KM# 88 2 THALER

Silver **Note:** Octagonal klippe. Dav. #2205A.

Date	Mintage	VG	F	VF	XF	Unc
1717 LCf-IIH	—	2,000	3,500	6,500	10,000	—

KM# 97 2 THALER

Silver **Note:** Octagonal klippe. Dav. #2206B.

Date	Mintage	VG	F	VF	XF	Unc
1742 GH	—	2,250	4,000	7,500	11,000	—

KM# 96 2 THALER

Silver **Subject:** Homage to Karl VII **Obverse:** Bust and titles of Karl VII **Note:** Klippe. Dav. #2206A.

Date	Mintage	VG	F	VF	XF	Unc
1742 GH	—	2,000	3,500	6,500	10,000	—

TRADE COINAGE

KM# 89 DUCAT

3.5000 g., 0.9860 Gold 0.1109 oz. AGW **Subject:** Homage to Karl VI **Obverse:** Laureate bust of Karl VI right **Reverse:** Displayed eagle, date in legend

Date	Mintage	VG	F	VF	XF	Unc
1717 LC-IIH	—	1,500	2,750	5,000	8,500	—

KM# 98 DUCAT

3.5000 g., 0.9860 Gold 0.1109 oz. AGW **Subject:** Homage to Karl VII **Obverse:** Laureate bust of Karl VII right **Reverse:** Displayed eagle, date in legend

Date	Mintage	VG	F	VF	XF	Unc
1742 GH	—	1,350	2,500	4,750	8,000	—

KM# 99 DUCAT

3.5000 g., 0.9860 Gold 0.1109 oz. AGW **Note:** Klippe.

Date	Mintage	VG	F	VF	XF	Unc
1742 GH	—	1,500	2,750	5,000	8,500	—

KM# 90 2 DUCAT

7.0000 g., 0.9860 Gold 0.2219 oz. AGW **Subject:** Homage to Karl VI **Obverse:** Laureate bust of Karl VI right **Reverse:** Displayed eagle, date in legend **Note:** Klippe. Struck on square flan.

Date	Mintage	VG	F	VF	XF	Unc
1717 LC-IIH	—	4,500	6,500	8,500	12,500	—

KM# 100 2 DUCAT

7.0000 g., 0.9860 Gold 0.2219 oz. AGW **Subject:** Homage to Karl VII **Obverse:** Bust of Karl VII right **Reverse:** Displayed eagle, date in legend **Note:** Klippe.

Date	Mintage	VG	F	VF	XF	Unc
1742 GH	—	4,000	6,000	8,000	12,000	—

PATTERNS

Including off metal strikes

KM#	Date	Mintage	Identification	Mkt Val
Pn1	1752	—	1/4 Stuber. Silver. KM#105	250

EAST FRIESLAND

(Ostfriesland)

The countship, and later principality, of East Friesland was located along the North Sea coast between the Rivers Ems and Weser. By the late 14th and early 15th centuries, several powerful families controlled various areas of what was to become the countship. The Cirksena family of Greetsyl managed to emerge during this period as a leading force in the region through astute marriages and sometimes by armed might. Ulrich I Cirksena was created the first count of East Friesland in 1454. This confirmed his line as the ruling dynasty with the capital at Aurich. In 1654, the count was raised to the rank of prince. In 1744, the Cirksenas became extinct and East Friesland passed to Prussia, which maintained the mint at Aurich for the new province. East Friesland became part of Hannover at the end of the Napoleonic Wars in 1815, but returned to Prussian control when Hannover itself was absorbed by Prussia in 1866.

RULERS

Christian Eberhard, 1665-1708
Georg Albrecht, 1708-1734
Karl Edward, 1734-1744
Friedrich II (The Great) of Prussia, 1740-1786
Friedrich Wilhelm II (of Prussia), 1786-1797
Friedrich Wilhelm III (of Prussia), 1797-1807

MINT MARKS

A - Berlin
B - Breslau
D - Aurich
F - Magdeburg
Star - Dresden

MINT OFFICIALS' INITIALS

Initials	Date	Name
OA	Ca.1713-18	Unknown
K	Ca.1723	Unknown
ICG	1730-46	Johann Christian Gittermann, mintmaster
BID	1747-49	Bernhard Julius Dedekind, mintmaster

ARMS

East Friesland, a combination of the old arms of the two foremost families, the crowned harpy of Cirksena and four 6-pointed stars of Idzinga. The stars are usually placed two on the harpy's shoulders and one each to lower left and right of legs and/or tail. Groningen, horizontal bar across center.

MONETARY SYSTEM

Witte = 4 Hohlpfennig = 1/3 Schilling = 1/20 Schaf = 1/10 Stüber
Ciffert = 6 Witten
Stüber = 10 Witten = 1/30 Reichstaler
Schaf = 20 Witten = 2 Stüber
Flindrich = 3 Stüber
Schilling = 6 Stüber
288 Pfennige = 54 Stüber = 36 Mariengroschen = 1 Reichsthaler

COUNTSHIP

Principality from 1654

REGULAR COINAGE

KM# 148 1/4 STUBER (2-1/2 Witten)

Billon **Obverse:** Titles of Georg Albrecht

Date	Mintage	VG	F	VF	XF	Unc
ND	—	8.00	15.00	30.00	55.00	—

KM# 174 1/4 STUBER (2-1/2 Witten)
Billon **Obverse:** Titles of Charles Edward

Date	Mintage	VG	F	VF	XF	Unc
ND	—	12.00	25.00	50.00	90.00	—

KM# 196 1/4 STUBER (2-1/2 Witten)
Billon **Ruler:** Friedrich II (The Great) of Prussia **Obverse:** Crowned monogram **Reverse:** Value, date

Date	Mintage	VG	F	VF	XF	Unc
1746 ICG	58,000	15.00	35.00	100	200	—

KM# 201 1/4 STUBER (2-1/2 Witten)
Billon **Ruler:** Friedrich II (The Great) of Prussia **Obverse:** Crowned monogram **Reverse:** Value, date

Date	Mintage	VG	F	VF	XF	Unc
1747 BID	97,000	7.50	20.00	50.00	100	—

KM# 212 1/4 STUBER (2-1/2 Witten)
Billon **Ruler:** Friedrich II (The Great) of Prussia **Mint:** Aurich **Obverse:** Crowned floral script FR monogram, date below **Reverse:** Value and mint mark in wreath

Date	Mintage	VG	F	VF	XF	Unc
1752D	—	13.50	30.00	75.00	150	—

KM# 213 1/4 STUBER (2-1/2 Witten)
Billon **Ruler:** Friedrich II (The Great) of Prussia **Mint:** Aurich **Obverse:** Crowned monogram **Reverse:** Value above date

Date	Mintage	VG	F	VF	XF	Unc
1752D	—	13.50	30.00	75.00	150	—

KM# 219 1/4 STUBER (2-1/2 Witten)
Copper **Ruler:** Friedrich II (The Great) of Prussia **Mint:** Aurich **Obverse:** Crowned monogram **Reverse:** Value, date

Date	Mintage	VG	F	VF	XF	Unc
1753D	—	2.00	5.00	15.00	30.00	—
1754D	—	2.00	5.00	15.00	30.00	—

KM# 234 1/4 STUBER (2-1/2 Witten)
Copper **Ruler:** Friedrich II (The Great) of Prussia **Mint:** Aurich **Obverse:** Crowned script FR monogram **Reverse:** Value and date, D below

Date	Mintage	VG	F	VF	XF	Unc
1764D	—	3.00	7.00	20.00	40.00	—
1765D	—	3.00	7.00	20.00	40.00	—
1767D	233,000	3.00	7.00	20.00	40.00	—

KM# 250 1/4 STUBER (2-1/2 Witten)
Copper **Ruler:** Friedrich II (The Great) of Prussia **Mint:** Berlin **Reverse:** A below date

Date	Mintage	VG	F	VF	XF	Unc
1777A	562,000	3.00	7.00	20.00	40.00	—
1778A	Inc. above	3.00	7.00	20.00	40.00	—
1779A	—	3.00	7.00	20.00	40.00	—
1781A	—	3.00	7.00	20.00	40.00	—
1784A	108,000	3.00	7.00	20.00	40.00	—

KM# 261 1/4 STUBER (2-1/2 Witten)
Copper **Ruler:** Friedrich Wilhelm II (of Prussia) **Mint:** Berlin **Obverse:** Crowned monogram **Reverse:** Value, date

Date	Mintage	VG	F	VF	XF	Unc
1787A	86,000	3.00	6.00	15.00	30.00	—

KM# 270 1/4 STUBER (2-1/2 Witten)
Copper **Ruler:** Friedrich Wilhelm II (of Prussia) **Mint:** Berlin **Obverse:** Crowned monogram **Reverse:** Value, date **Note:** Similar to KM#261. Mint mark between asterisks.

Date	Mintage	VG	F	VF	XF	Unc
1792A	120,000	3.00	7.00	20.00	40.00	—

KM# 271 1/4 STUBER (2-1/2 Witten)
Copper **Ruler:** Friedrich Wilhelm II (of Prussia) **Mint:** Berlin **Obverse:** Crowned monogram **Reverse:** Value, date **Note:** Similar to KM#272.

Date	Mintage	VG	F	VF	XF	Unc
1794A	—	3.00	7.00	20.00	40.00	—

KM# 272 1/4 STUBER (2-1/2 Witten)
Copper **Ruler:** Friedrich Wilhelm III (of Prussia) **Mint:** Berlin **Obverse:** Crowned monogram **Reverse:** Value, date

Date	Mintage	F	VF	XF	Unc
1799A	216,000	5.00	15.00	30.00	75.00
1802A	1,296,000	4.00	12.50	25.00	75.00
1803A	Inc. above	4.00	12.50	25.00	75.00
1804A	216,000	4.00	12.50	25.00	75.00

KM# 147 1/2 STUBER
Silver **Ruler:** Christian Eberhard **Obverse:** Helmeted harpy arms divide date **Rev. Legend:** IN DEO SPE MEA

Date	Mintage	VG	F	VF	XF	Unc
1706	—	15.00	30.00	60.00	100	—
1707	—	15.00	30.00	60.00	100	—
ND	—	15.00	30.00	60.00	100	—

KM# 155 1/2 STUBER
Silver **Ruler:** Georg Albrecht

Date	Mintage	VG	F	VF	XF	Unc
1712	—	10.00	20.00	40.00	65.00	—
1713	—	10.00	20.00	40.00	65.00	—
1715	—	10.00	20.00	40.00	65.00	—
1716	—	10.00	20.00	40.00	65.00	—

KM# 156 1/2 STUBER
Silver **Ruler:** Georg Albrecht **Obverse:** Crowned harpy arms **Reverse:** Shield at center of cross with O F H S in angles

Date	Mintage	VG	F	VF	XF	Unc
1713 OA	—	12.00	25.00	50.00	90.00	—
1716 OA	—	12.00	25.00	50.00	90.00	—
1717 OA	—	12.00	25.00	50.00	90.00	—
1718 OA	—	12.00	25.00	50.00	90.00	—

KM# 247 1/2 STUBER
Billon **Ruler:** Friedrich II (The Great) of Prussia **Mint:** Berlin **Obverse:** Crowned script FR monogram, A below **Reverse:** Value and date

Date	Mintage	VG	F	VF	XF	Unc
1772A	—	6.50	15.00	40.00	80.00	—
1781A	108,000	6.50	15.00	40.00	80.00	—

KM# 260 1/2 STUBER
Billon **Ruler:** Friedrich II (The Great) of Prussia **Mint:** Berlin **Obverse:** Crowned arms divide date, in inner circle **Reverse:** Floreated cross with O F H S in angels

Date	Mintage	VG	F	VF	XF	Unc
1781A	54,000	17.50	40.00	100	200	—
1782A	Inc. above	17.50	40.00	100	200	—

KM# A231 3 PFENNIG
4.0000 g., Copper, 26 mm. **Ruler:** Friedrich II (The Great) of Prussia **Mint:** Aurich **Obverse:** Crowned ornate script FR monogram **Reverse:** 4-line inscription of value, date divided by mint mark at bottom **Rev. Inscription:** 3/PFEN:/SCHEIDE/MUNZ. **Note:** Former Prussia KM#291.

Date	Mintage	VG	F	VF	XF	Unc
1763D	—	15.00	25.00	50.00	85.00	—

KM# 195 4 PFENNIG
Billon **Ruler:** Friedrich II (The Great) of Prussia **Obverse:** Crowned monogram **Reverse:** Value, date

Date	Mintage	VG	F	VF	XF	Unc
1746 ICG	12,000	125	250	400	600	—

KM# 200 4 PFENNIG
Billon **Ruler:** Friedrich II (The Great) of Prussia **Obverse:** Crowned monogram **Reverse:** Value, date

Date	Mintage	VG	F	VF	XF	Unc
1747 BID	222,000	28.50	60.00	100	200	—
1748 BID	Inc. above	28.50	60.00	100	200	—

KM# 210 4 PFENNIG
Billon **Ruler:** Friedrich II (The Great) of Prussia **Mint:** Aurich **Obverse:** Crowned script FR monogram in branches **Reverse:** Value, date

Date	Mintage	VG	F	VF	XF	Unc
1752D	—	20.00	35.00	60.00	125	—

KM# 211 4 PFENNIG
Billon **Ruler:** Friedrich II (The Great) of Prussia **Obverse:** Crowned monogram **Reverse:** Value, date

Date	Mintage	VG	F	VF	XF	Unc
1752D	—	20.00	35.00	60.00	125	—
1752F	—	20.00	35.00	60.00	125	—
1753D	—	20.00	35.00	60.00	125	—
1753F	—	20.00	35.00	60.00	125	—

KM# 231 4 PFENNIG
Billon **Ruler:** Friedrich II (The Great) of Prussia **Mint:** Aurich **Obverse:** Crowned script FR monogram **Reverse:** Value, D divides date

Date	Mintage	VG	F	VF	XF	Unc
1764D	1,482,000	8.50	16.50	30.00	65.00	—
1765D	335,000	9.50	18.50	35.00	75.00	—
1766D	539,000	9.00	17.50	32.50	70.00	—
1767D	1,227,000	8.50	16.50	30.00	65.00	—
1768D	22,000	17.50	30.00	55.00	120	—

KM# 232 4 PFENNIG
Billon **Ruler:** Friedrich II (The Great) of Prussia **Reverse:** F below date

Date	Mintage	VG	F	VF	XF	Unc
1764 F	180,000	10.00	20.00	42.50	80.00	—

KM# 233 4 PFENNIG
Billon **Ruler:** Friedrich II (The Great) of Prussia **Mint:** Berlin **Obverse:** Crowned block FR monogram divides date **Reverse:** Value with Arabic 4, A below

Date	Mintage	VG	F	VF	XF	Unc
1764A	1,092,000	5.50	11.00	22.50	42.50	—
1766A	269,000	6.50	13.00	26.50	50.00	—

KM# 249 4 PFENNIG
Billon **Ruler:** Friedrich II (The Great) of Prussia **Mint:** Berlin **Obverse:** Crowned block FR monogram in cartouche **Reverse:** Value with Roman 4, date and A below

Date	Mintage	VG	F	VF	XF	Unc
1774A	—	14.00	27.50	50.00	85.00	—

KM# 245 STUBER
Billon **Ruler:** Friedrich II (The Great) of Prussia **Mint:** Berlin **Obverse:** Laureate head right **Obv. Legend:** FRIDERIC: BORUSS: REX • **Reverse:** Crowned imperial eagle above value and date

Date	Mintage	VG	F	VF	XF	Unc
1771A	3,697,000	6.00	11.50	27.50	50.00	—
1772A	199,000	15.00	30.00	60.00	125	—
1775A	—	6.00	11.50	27.50	50.00	—
1776A	—	6.00	11.50	27.50	50.00	—
1777A	—	6.00	11.50	27.50	50.00	—
1781A	—	6.00	11.50	27.50	50.00	—
1783A Rare	—	—	—	—	—	—

KM# 248 2 STUBER

Billon **Ruler:** Friedrich II (The Great) of Prussia **Mint:** Berlin **Obverse:** Laureate head right **Reverse:** Crowned flying eagle above value, A divides date

Date	Mintage	VG	F	VF	XF	Unc
1772A	—	30.00	75.00	125	200	—
1773A	—	8.50	27.50	65.00	110	—
1775A	—	8.50	27.50	65.00	110	—

KM# 175 MARIENGROSCHEN (1/36 Thaler)

Silver **Ruler:** Georg Albrecht **Obverse:** Crowned GA monogram **Reverse:** Value, date in five lines

Date	Mintage	VG	F	VF	XF	Unc
1730	—	15.00	30.00	50.00	85.00	—
1733	—	15.00	30.00	50.00	85.00	—
1734	—	15.00	30.00	50.00	85.00	—

KM# 183 MARIENGROSCHEN (1/36 Thaler)

Silver **Ruler:** Karl Edward **Obverse:** Crowned script CE monogram **Reverse:** Value in four lines, date in legend

Date	Mintage	VG	F	VF	XF	Unc
1735	—	15.00	30.00	60.00	95.00	—
1736	—	15.00	30.00	60.00	95.00	—
1737	—	15.00	30.00	60.00	95.00	—

KM# 197 MARIENGROSCHEN (1/36 Thaler)

Billon **Ruler:** Friedrich II (The Great) of Prussia **Obverse:** Crowned monogram **Reverse:** Value, date

Date	Mintage	VG	F	VF	XF	Unc
1746 ICG	—	125	250	400	700	—

KM# 202 MARIENGROSCHEN (1/36 Thaler)

Billon **Ruler:** Friedrich II (The Great) of Prussia **Obverse:** Crowned monogram **Reverse:** Value, date

Date	Mintage	VG	F	VF	XF	Unc
1747 BID	139,000	55.00	110	225	450	—
1748 BID	Inc. above	55.00	110	225	450	—

KM# 214 MARIENGROSCHEN (1/36 Thaler)

Billon **Ruler:** Friedrich II (The Great) of Prussia **Mint:** Aurich **Obverse:** Crowned arms, eagle in arms holds sword and scepter **Reverse:** Value, date

Date	Mintage	VG	F	VF	XF	Unc
1752D	—	6.00	12.00	27.50	50.00	—

KM# 215 MARIENGROSCHEN (1/36 Thaler)

Billon **Ruler:** Friedrich II (The Great) of Prussia **Obverse:** Crowned arms, eagle in arms holds scepter and orb **Reverse:** Value, date

Date	Mintage	VG	F	VF	XF	Unc
1752F	—	12.00	25.00	50.00	100	—
1753D	—	6.00	12.00	27.50	50.00	—
1754D	3,800,000	6.00	12.00	27.50	50.00	—
1755D	—	6.00	12.00	27.50	50.00	—
1756D	—	6.00	12.00	27.50	50.00	—

KM# 230 MARIENGROSCHEN (1/36 Thaler)

Billon **Ruler:** Friedrich II (The Great) of Prussia **Mint:** Aurich **Obverse:** Crowned arms within ornate shield **Reverse:** Value, date

Date	Mintage	VG	F	VF	XF	Unc
1761D	—	7.50	15.00	37.50	65.00	—

KM# 235 MARIENGROSCHEN (1/36 Thaler)

Billon **Ruler:** Friedrich II (The Great) of Prussia **Mint:** Magdeburg **Obverse:** Crowned script FR monogram in cartouche **Reverse:** Value above date, F below

Date	Mintage	VG	F	VF	XF	Unc
1764F	426,000	5.00	22.50	50.00	100	—

KM# 237 MARIENGROSCHEN (1/36 Thaler)

Billon **Ruler:** Friedrich II (The Great) of Prussia **Mint:** Aurich **Reverse:** D below date

Date	Mintage	VG	F	VF	XF	Unc
1767D	1,221,000	7.50	13.50	27.50	60.00	—
1768D	Inc. above	7.50	13.50	27.50	60.00	—

KM# 246 MARIENGROSCHEN (1/36 Thaler)

Billon **Ruler:** Friedrich II (The Great) of Prussia **Mint:** Berlin **Reverse:** Value and date, A below

Date	Mintage	VG	F	VF	XF	Unc
1771A	—	11.00	22.50	40.00	80.00	—
1774A	108,000	11.00	22.50	40.00	80.00	—
1775A	Inc. above	11.00	22.50	40.00	80.00	—

KM# 176 2 MARIENGROSCHEN (1/18 Thaler)

Silver **Ruler:** Georg Albrecht **Obverse:** Crowned monogram **Reverse:** Value, date within circle

Date	Mintage	VG	F	VF	XF	Unc
1730	—	30.00	60.00	120	185	—
1731	—	30.00	60.00	120	185	—
1733	—	30.00	60.00	120	185	—
1734	—	30.00	60.00	120	185	—

KM# 184 2 MARIENGROSCHEN (1/18 Thaler)

Silver **Ruler:** Karl Edward **Obverse:** Crowned script CE monogram **Reverse:** Value in four lines, date in legend

Date	Mintage	VG	F	VF	XF	Unc
1735	—	15.00	30.00	60.00	95.00	—
1736	—	15.00	30.00	60.00	95.00	—
1737	—	15.00	30.00	60.00	95.00	—
1738	—	15.00	30.00	60.00	95.00	—

KM# 198 2 MARIENGROSCHEN (1/18 Thaler)

Billon **Ruler:** Friedrich II (The Great) of Prussia **Obverse:** Crowned monogram **Reverse:** Value, date

Date	Mintage	VG	F	VF	XF	Unc
1746 ICG	7,830	40.00	100	200	400	—

KM# 216 2 MARIENGROSCHEN (1/18 Thaler)

Billon **Ruler:** Friedrich II (The Great) of Prussia **Mint:** Aurich **Obverse:** Crowned arms **Reverse:** Value, date

Date	Mintage	VG	F	VF	XF	Unc
1752D	—	200	300	500	750	—

KM# 236 2 MARIENGROSCHEN (1/18 Thaler)

Billon **Ruler:** Friedrich II (The Great) of Prussia **Mint:** Magdeburg **Obverse:** Crowned script FR monogram in cartouche **Reverse:** Value and date, D below

Date	Mintage	VG	F	VF	XF	Unc
1764F	230,000	11.00	22.50	45.00	80.00	—

KM# 221 4 MARIENGROSCHEN

Billon **Ruler:** Friedrich II (The Great) of Prussia **Mint:** Aurich **Obverse:** Crowned arms, no shield **Reverse:** Value, date

Date	Mintage	VG	F	VF	XF	Unc
1756D	—	18.00	35.00	60.00	125	—
1757D	—	18.00	35.00	60.00	125	—

KM# 222 6 MARIENGROSCHEN

Billon **Ruler:** Friedrich II (The Great) of Prussia **Mint:** Dresden **Obverse:** Head right **Reverse:** Value and date within palm branches

Date	Mintage	VG	F	VF	XF	Unc
1758Star	—	15.00	40.00	100	200	—

KM# 223 12 MARIENGROSCHEN

Billon **Ruler:** Friedrich II (The Great) of Prussia **Mint:** Dresden **Obverse:** Head right **Obv. Legend:** FRIDERICUS BORUSSORUM REX **Reverse:** Value and date within palm branches

Date	Mintage	VG	F	VF	XF	Unc
1758Star	—	25.00	50.00	85.00	145	—

KM# A220.1 8 GUTE GROSCHEN

8.6600 g., 0.6250 Silver 0.1740 oz. ASW **Ruler:** Friedrich II (The Great) of Prussia **Mint:** Aurich **Obverse:** Bust to right **Obv. Legend:** FRIDERICUS - BORUSSORUM REX **Reverse:** Crowned eagle with war flags and trophies, 3-line inscription above, date divided by mint mark below **Rev. Inscription:** 8/GUTE/GROSCHEN

Date	Mintage	VG	F	VF	XF	Unc
1754D	56,925	80.00	150	225	375	600

KM# A220.2 8 GUTE GROSCHEN

8.6600 g., 0.6250 Silver 0.1740 oz. ASW **Ruler:** Friedrich II (The Great) of Prussia **Mint:** Aurich **Obverse:** Bust to right **Obv. Legend:** FRIDERICUS BORUSSORUM REX **Reverse:** Crowned eagle with war flags and trophies, 4-line inscription with date above, mint mark below **Rev. Inscription:** 8/GUTE/GROSCHEN/(date)

Date	Mintage	VG	F	VF	XF	Unc
1754D	Inc. above	80.00	150	225	375	600

KM# A220.4 8 GUTE GROSCHEN

8.6600 g., 0.6250 Silver 0.1740 oz. ASW **Ruler:** Friedrich II (The Great) of Prussia **Mint:** Aurich **Obverse:** Bust to right **Obv. Legend:** FRIDERICUS BORUSSORUM REX **Reverse:** 4-line inscription with date above flags, drum and cannon, mint mark below **Rev. Inscription:** 8/GUTE/GROSCHEN/(date)

Date	Mintage	VG	F	VF	XF	Unc
1754D	Inc. above	80.00	150	225	375	600

KM# A220.3 8 GUTE GROSCHEN

8.6600 g., 0.6250 Silver 0.1740 oz. ASW **Ruler:** Friedrich II (The Great) of Prussia **Mint:** Aurich **Obverse:** Bust to right **Obv. Legend:** FRIDERICUS BORUSSORUM REX **Reverse:** 4-line inscription with date and mint mark above crowned eagle with flags and trophies **Rev. Inscription:** 8/GUTE/GROSCHEN/17 D 55

Date	Mintage	VG	F	VF	XF	Unc
1755D	—	80.00	150	225	375	600

KM# A220.5 8 GUTE GROSCHEN
8.6600 g., 0.6250 Silver 0.1740 oz. ASW **Ruler:** Friedrich II (The Great) of Prussia **Mint:** Aurich **Obverse:** Bust to right **Obv. Legend:** FRIDERICUS BORUSSORUM REX **Reverse:** 4-line inscription with date above flags and trophies, mint mark at bottom **Rev. Inscription:** 8/GUTE/GROSCHEN/(date)

Date	Mintage	VG	F	VF	XF	Unc
1756D	—	80.00	150	225	375	600

KM# 199 1/24 THALER
Billon **Ruler:** Friedrich II (The Great) of Prussia **Obverse:** Crowned monogram **Reverse:** Value, date

Date	Mintage	VG	F	VF	XF	Unc
1746 ICG	21,000	27.50	60.00	130	275	—

KM# 203 1/24 THALER
Billon **Ruler:** Friedrich II (The Great) of Prussia **Obverse:** Crowned monogram within cartouche **Reverse:** Value, date

Date	Mintage	VG	F	VF	XF	Unc
1748 BID	71,000	25.00	50.00	100	200	—

KM# 166 1/12 THALER (2 Groschen)
Silver **Obverse:** Crowned GA monogram **Reverse:** Similar to KM#185

Date	Mintage	VG	F	VF	XF	Unc
1729	—	30.00	60.00	100	165	—
1730	—	30.00	60.00	100	165	—
1733	—	30.00	60.00	100	165	—
1734	—	30.00	60.00	100	165	—

KM# 185 1/12 THALER (2 Groschen)
Silver **Ruler:** Karl Edward **Obverse:** Crowned monogram **Reverse:** Value within circle, date in legend

Date	Mintage	VG	F	VF	XF	Unc
1736 ICG	—	25.00	40.00	75.00	125	—
1738 ICG	—	25.00	40.00	75.00	125	—
1739 ICG	—	25.00	40.00	75.00	125	—
1740 ICG	—	25.00	40.00	75.00	125	—
1741 ICG	—	25.00	40.00	75.00	125	—
1742 ICG	—	25.00	40.00	75.00	125	—
1743 ICG	—	25.00	40.00	75.00	125	—
1747 ICG	—	25.00	40.00	75.00	125	—

KM# A237 1/12 THALER (2 Groschen)
3.7100 g., 0.3750 Silver 0.0447 oz. ASW, 22 mm. **Ruler:** Friedrich II (The Great) of Prussia **Mint:** Aurich **Obverse:** Head to right **Obv. Legend:** FRIDERICUS BORUSSORUM REX **Reverse:** 4-line inscription of value, date divided by mint mark at bottom **Rev. Inscription:** 12/EINEN/REICHS/THALER

Date	Mintage	VG	F	VF	XF	Unc
1764D	—	7.00	20.00	35.00	60.00	—

KM# C237 1/12 THALER (2 Groschen)
3.7100 g., 0.3750 Silver 0.0447 oz. ASW, 22 mm. **Ruler:** Friedrich II (The Great) of Prussia **Mint:** Aurich **Obverse:** Head to right of Berlin type **Obv. Legend:** FRIDERICUS BORUSSORUM REX **Reverse:** 4-line inscription of value, dated divided by mint mark below **Rev. Inscription:** 12/EINEN/REICHS/THALER

Date	Mintage	VG	F	VF	XF	Unc
1765D	—	7.00	20.00	35.00	60.00	—
1766D	—	7.00	20.00	35.00	60.00	—
1767D	—	7.00	20.00	35.00	60.00	—
1768D	—	7.00	20.00	35.00	60.00	—

KM# 220 1/9 THALER (4 Mariengroschen)
Billon **Ruler:** Friedrich II (The Great) of Prussia **Mint:** Aurich

Date	Mintage	VG	F	VF	XF	Unc
1755D	—	100	250	400	750	—

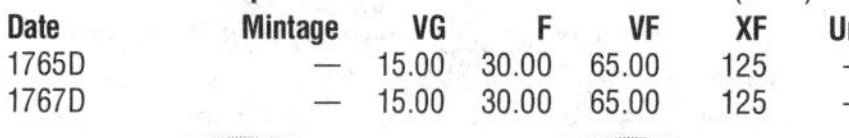

KM# 177 1/6 THALER
Silver **Ruler:** Georg Albrecht **Obverse:** Armored bust right **Reverse:** Crowned 6-fold oval arms within ornate frame

Date	Mintage	VG	F	VF	XF	Unc
1730	—	275	450	800	1,325	—

KM# 186 1/6 THALER
Silver **Ruler:** Karl Edward **Reverse:** Crowned six-fold arms, value 1/6 below divides date

Date	Mintage	VG	F	VF	XF	Unc
1736 ICG	—	125	275	475	850	—
1737 ICG	—	125	275	475	850	—

KM# 217 1/6 THALER
5.4700 g., 0.5000 Silver 0.0879 oz. ASW, 26 mm. **Ruler:** Friedrich II (The Great) of Prussia **Mint:** Aurich **Obverse:** Draped bust right **Obv. Inscription:** FRIDERICUS BORUSSORUM REX **Reverse:** 4-line inscription of value, date divided by mintmark below **Rev. Inscription:** VI/EINEN/REICHS/THALER

Date	Mintage	VG	F	VF	XF	Unc
1752D	—	10.00	20.00	45.00	75.00	—
1753D	—	10.00	20.00	45.00	75.00	—
1754D	—	10.00	20.00	45.00	75.00	—

KM# B237.1 1/6 THALER
5.3400 g., 0.5208 Silver 0.0894 oz. ASW, 27 mm. **Ruler:** Friedrich II (The Great) of Prussia **Mint:** Aurich **Obverse:** Head right **Obv. Legend:** FRIDERICUS BORUSSORUM REX **Reverse:** 5-line inscription of value and date, mint mark below **Rev. Inscription:** 6/EINEN/REICHS/THALER/(date)

Date	Mintage	VG	F	VF	XF	Unc
1764D	—	15.00	30.00	65.00	125	—

KM# B237.2 1/6 THALER
5.3400 g., 0.5208 Silver 0.0894 oz. ASW, 27 mm. **Ruler:** Friedrich II (The Great) of Prussia **Mint:** Aurich **Obverse:** Berlin-type head right **Obv. Legend:** FRIDERICUS BORUSSORUM REX **Reverse:** 5-line inscription of value and date, mint mark below **Rev. Inscription:** 6/EINEN/REICHS/THALER/(date)

Date	Mintage	VG	F	VF	XF	Unc
1765D	—	15.00	30.00	65.00	125	—
1767D	—	15.00	30.00	65.00	125	—

KM# 165 1/3 THALER
Silver **Ruler:** Georg Albrecht **Subject:** Death of Christina Ludovica of Nassau, Wife of Georg Albrecht **Obverse:** Inscription **Reverse:** Grains growing from skull

Date	Mintage	VG	F	VF	XF	Unc
1723 K	—	75.00	125	250	450	—

KM# 178 2/3 THALER (Gulden)
Silver **Ruler:** Georg Albrecht **Obverse:** Bust right **Reverse:** Crowned ornate six-fold arms, date

Date	Mintage	VG	F	VF	XF	Unc
1730 ICG	—	500	1,000	1,600	2,500	—

KM# 180 2/3 THALER (Gulden)
Silver **Obverse:** Armored bust riht **Reverse:** Crowned 6-fold arms

Date	Mintage	VG	F	VF	XF	Unc
1734 ICG	—	350	600	1,000	1,500	—

KM# 188 2/3 THALER (Gulden)
Silver **Ruler:** Karl Edward

Date	Mintage	VG	F	VF	XF	Unc
1738 ICG	—	750	1,000	1,500	2,250	—

KM# 179 THALER
Silver **Ruler:** Georg Albrecht **Obverse:** Bust right **Reverse:** Crowned six-fold arms, date divided below **Note:** Dav. #2506.

Date	Mintage	VG	F	VF	XF	Unc
1730 ICG	—	550	1,250	2,000	3,000	—

KM# 181 THALER
Silver **Ruler:** Georg Albrecht **Obverse:** Armored bust right **Obv. Legend:** GEORGIVS ALBERTVS D.G. PRINC. FRISIAE OR • **Reverse:** Date connected below arms **Rev. Legend:** DOMINVS ESEN • - STEDESD • & WITM • **Note:** Dav. #2507.

Date	Mintage	VG	F	VF	XF	Unc
1734 ICG	—	1,250	2,500	3,500	5,500	—

KM# 182 THALER
Silver **Ruler:** Karl Edward **Obverse:** Bust right **Note:** Dav. #2508.

Date	Mintage	VG	F	VF	XF	Unc
1734	—	1,250	2,500	3,500	5,500	—

KM# D237 THALER
22.2700 g., 0.7500 Silver 0.5370 oz. ASW, 37.5 mm. **Ruler:** Friedrich II (The Great) of Prussia **Mint:** Aurich **Obverse:** Laureate head right **Obv. Legend:** FRIDERICUS BORUSSORUM REX **Reverse:** Crowned eagle with flags and trophies, legend above, date divided by mint mark below **Rev. Legend:** EIN REICHS THALER **Note:** Dav. #2586B

Date	Mintage	VG	F	VF	XF	Unc
1765D	—	200	350	675	1,850	—

TRADE COINAGE

KM# 146 DUCAT
3.5000 g., 0.9860 Gold 0.1109 oz. AGW **Ruler:** Christian Eberhard **Obverse:** Bust right **Reverse:** Crowned arms

Date	Mintage	VG	F	VF	XF	Unc
1702	—	650	1,250	3,000	6,000	—

KM# 157 DUCAT
3.5000 g., 0.9860 Gold 0.1109 oz. AGW **Ruler:** Georg Albrecht **Obverse:** Bust right **Reverse:** Crowned arms

Date	Mintage	VG	F	VF	XF	Unc
1715 OA	—	600	1,200	2,750	5,500	—
1730 ICG	—	600	1,200	2,750	5,500	—
1731 ICG	—	600	1,200	2,750	5,500	—

KM# 187 DUCAT
3.5000 g., 0.9860 Gold 0.1109 oz. AGW **Ruler:** Karl Edward **Obverse:** Bust right **Obv. Legend:** CAROLVS EDZARDVS D. G. PR • FRIS • OR **Reverse:** Crowned arms **Rev. Legend:** DOMINVS ES • ST • ET WITM •

Date	Mintage	VG	F	VF	XF	Unc
1737 ICG	—	500	1,000	2,500	4,500	—

KM# 218 FRIEDRICH D'OR

6.6800 g., 0.9060 Gold 0.1946 oz. AGW **Ruler:** Friedrich II (The Great) of Prussia **Mint:** Aurich

Date	Mintage	VG	F	VF	XF	Unc
1752D	—	2,500	4,500	7,000	10,000	—
1753D	—	2,500	4,500	7,000	10,000	—

PATTERNS

Including off metal strikes

KM#	Date	Mintage	Identification	Mkt Val
Pn4	1723	—	Ciffert. Gold. Klippe. KM#165.	—
Pn5	1755	—	1/9 Thaler. Billon. KM#220.	—
Pn6	1771	—	Mariengroschen. Billon. FR monogram in branches.	25.00
Pn7	1771	—	Mariengroschen. Billon. FR monogram in cartouche.	25.00

EICHSTATT

BISHOPRIC

(Eichstädt)

A Bishopric in central Bavaria, which was founded in 745. The Imperial Mint was founded c.908 and Episcopal coinage began in the 11th century. Eichstätt was secularized in 1802 and given to Salzburg. It passed to Bavaria in 1805.

RULERS

Johann Martin von Eyb, 1697-1704
Johann Anton I Knebel von Katzenellenbogen, 1705-1725
Sede Vacante, April 27-July 3, 1725
Franz Ludwig, Schenk von Castell, 1725-1736
Johann Anton II von Freiberg-Hopferau, 1736-1757
Raimund Anton Graf von Strasoldo, 1757-1781
Sede Vacante, 1781
Johann Anton III, Freiherr von Zehmen, 1781-1790
Sede Vacante, 1790
Josef, Graf von Stubenberg, 1790-1802

MINT OFFICIALS' INITIALS

Initials	Date	Name
(c), GFN	1682-1724	Georg Friedrich Nurnberger, mintmaster and die-cutter in Nüremberg
CD	1784-1807	Cajetan Destouches
F	1755-64	Johann Martin Forster
FSN		Johann Martin Forster, and Siegmund Scholz in Nürnberg
IOS, IS, SCH	1768-1812	Ignaz Joseph Schaufel
KR	1781	Georg Knoll, warden and George Nikolaus Riedner
MF	1755-57	Georg Michael Mann, warden and Johann Martin Forster in Nüremberg
NML	1746-55	Georg Michael Mann in Nürnberg and Carl Gottlieb Laufer
NSR, SRN	1746-55	Siegmund Scholz and George Nikolaus Reidner in Nürnberg
OE, I.L. OEXLEIN	1740-87	Johann Leonhard Oexlein, die-cutter in Nüremberg
R	1764-93	Georg Nikolaus Riedner
S	1760-74	Siegmund Scholz
W	1761-90	Johann Peter Werner

ARMS

A bishop's crozier.

REGULAR COINAGE

KM# 50 1/2 KREUZER

Silver **Ruler:** Johann Martin von Eub **Obverse:** Two oval shields of Eichstatt and Eyb arms, value 1/2 in oval above divides date **Note:** Uniface

Date	Mintage	VG	F	VF	XF	Unc
1701 Two known	—	—	—	—	—	—

KM# 67 KREUZER

Billon **Ruler:** Johann Anton II von Freiberg-Hopferau **Obverse:** Crowned, quartered arms of Eichstätt and Freyburg **Reverse:** Value, date in cartouche

Date	Mintage	VG	F	VF	XF	Unc
1755 NML	—	5.00	10.00	20.00	40.00	—

KM# 80 KREUZER

Billon **Ruler:** Raimund Anton Graf von Strasoldo **Obverse:** Crowned arms

Date	Mintage	VG	F	VF	XF	Unc
1763 Rare	—	—	—	—	—	—

KM# 68 2-1/2 KREUZER

Billon **Ruler:** Johann Anton II von Freiberg-Hopferau **Obverse:** Crowned, quartered arms of Eichstätt and Freyburg **Reverse:** LAND MUNZ, date

Date	Mintage	VG	F	VF	XF	Unc
1755 NML	—	7.00	15.00	30.00	60.00	—

KM# 84 2-1/2 KREUZER

Billon **Ruler:** Raimund Anton Graf von Strasoldo **Obverse:** Two shields of arms **Reverse:** Value and date

Date	Mintage	VG	F	VF	XF	Unc
1764 NSR	—	10.00	20.00	45.00	75.00	—

KM# 65 3 KREUZER (Groschen)

Billon **Ruler:** Johann Anton II von Freiberg-Hopferau **Obverse:** Crowned, quartered arms of Eichstätt and Freyburg divide 3 K **Reverse:** St. Willibald seated on throne

Date	Mintage	VG	F	VF	XF	Unc
ND(1750-55) NML	—	8.00	16.00	35.00	70.00	—

KM# 66 5 KREUZER

Billon **Ruler:** Johann Anton II von Freiberg-Hopferau **Obverse:** Crowned, quartered arms of Eichstätt and Freyburg divide 5 K **Reverse:** St. Willibald seated on throne

Date	Mintage	VG	F	VF	XF	Unc
ND(1750-55)	—	7.50	15.00	40.00	80.00	—

KM# 81 5 KREUZER

Silver **Ruler:** Raimund Anton Graf von Strasoldo **Obverse:** Crowned arms, date below **Reverse:** Value

Date	Mintage	VG	F	VF	XF	Unc
1763 FSN	—	20.00	35.00	70.00	135	—
1765 SRN	—	50.00	80.00	150	250	—

KM# 69 10 KREUZER

Silver **Ruler:** Johann Anton II von Freiberg-Hopferau **Obverse:** Crowned, quartered arms of Eichstatt and Freyburg, 20 KR divided above **Reverse:** Value and date within palm branches

Date	Mintage	VG	F	VF	XF	Unc
1755 NML	—	15.00	30.00	90.00	180	—

KM# 82 10 KREUZER

Silver **Ruler:** Raimund Anton Graf von Strasoldo **Obverse:** Crowned arms, date below **Reverse:** Value

Date	Mintage	VG	F	VF	XF	Unc
1763 FSN	—	12.00	25.00	60.00	125	—
1765 SRN	—	12.00	25.00	60.00	125	—

KM# 70 20 KREUZER

Silver **Ruler:** Johann Anton II von Freiberg-Hopferau **Obverse:** Crowned, quartered arms of Eichstätt and Freyburg, 20 K divided at bottom **Reverse:** 60 EINE...

Date	Mintage	VG	F	VF	XF	Unc
1755 NML	—	10.00	35.00	75.00	145	—

KM# 83 20 KREUZER

Silver **Ruler:** Raimund Anton Graf von Strasoldo **Obverse:** Crowned, quartered arms of Eichstatt and Freyburg **Reverse:** Value within wreath

Date	Mintage	VG	F	VF	XF	Unc
1763 FSN	—	30.00	60.00	90.00	165	—
1765 SRN	—	30.00	60.00	90.00	165	—

KM# 71 30 KREUZER

Silver **Ruler:** Johann Anton II von Freiberg-Hopferau **Obverse:** Bust right above value within rhombus **Reverse:** Crowned, quartered arms of Eichstatt and Freyburg divide date within rhombus

Date	Mintage	VG	F	VF	XF	Unc
1755 OE-NML	—	25.00	65.00	100	175	—

KM# 85 30 KREUZER

Silver **Ruler:** Raimund Anton Graf von Strasoldo **Obverse:** Bust right **Reverse:** Crowned arms, value below; Roman numeral date to right

Date	Mintage	VG	F	VF	XF	Unc
1764 NSR	—	65.00	120	225	375	—

KM# 72 1/2 THALER

Silver **Ruler:** Johann Anton II von Freiberg-Hopferau **Obverse:** Bust right **Reverse:** Crowned arms divide date, 20 EINE... below

Date	Mintage	F	VF	XF	Unc
1755 I.L. OEXLEIN-NML	—	150	265	550	850

KM# 86 1/2 THALER

Silver **Ruler:** Raimund Anton Graf von Strasoldo **Obverse:** Bust right **Reverse:** Quartered arms of Eichstatt and Freyburg, mitre, crown and helmet above

Date	Mintage	F	VF	XF	Unc
1764 NSR	—	150	250	500	800

KM# 91 1/2 THALER

Silver **Note:** Convention 1/2 Thaler.

Date	Mintage	F	VF	XF	Unc
1783 IS	—	65.00	125	225	450

KM# 96 1/2 THALER

Silver **Obverse:** Bust right **Reverse:** Date in chronogram

Date	Mintage	F	VF	XF	Unc
1796 CD	—	65.00	125	225	450

KM# 73 THALER

Silver **Ruler:** Johann Anton II von Freiberg-Hopferau **Obverse:** Bust right **Obv. Legend:** IOANN: ANTON: D: G: EP: EYSTETTENSIS S: R: I: P:, I.L. OXLEIN F. on arm **Reverse:** Crowned arms divide date, 10 EINE... below **Rev. Legend:** 10 EINE FEINE MARCK • below **Note:** Dav. #2207.

Date	Mintage	F	VF	XF	Unc
1755 I.L. OEXLEIN-NML	—	350	600	1,000	2,000

KM# 75 THALER

Silver **Subject:** Sede Vacante Issue **Obverse:** Shield within center, date below, 15 oval arms surround **Obv. Legend:** CAPITULUM REGNANS SEDE VACANTE, in center: FORTIS CONCORDIA NEXUS, 10 EINE FEINE MARCK at bottom **Reverse:** Radiant symbol above figures, shield lower center **Rev. Legend:** HIC PLANTAVIT: DEUS INCREMENTUM DEDIT: HAEC RIGAVIT:, I. L. OEXLEIN fec. at bottom **Note:** Dav. #2208.

Date	Mintage	F	VF	XF	Unc
1757 MF-I.L. OEXLEIN	—	200	300	625	950

KM# 87 THALER

Silver **Ruler:** Raimund Anton Graf von Strasoldo **Subject:** Raimund Anton **Obverse:** Bust right **Obv. Legend:** RAIM • ANTONIUS - D • G • EP • EYST • S • R • I • P • **Reverse:** Crowned, quartered ornate arms **Rev. Legend:** X EINE - FEINE - MARCK - MDCCLXIV, below: INTIMA CANDENT • **Note:** Dav. #2209.

Date	Mintage	F	VF	XF	Unc
1764 NSF	—	125	200	400	800

KM# 90 THALER

Silver **Subject:** Sede Vacante Issue **Obverse:** 13 oval arms form circle with 3 shields of arms and date within ornate frame at center **Obv. Legend:** CAPITULUM REGNANS SEDE VACANTE., 10 EINE FEINE MARCK. below **Reverse:** City view **Rev. Legend:** HAC SUB TUTELA **Note:** Convention Thaler. Dav. #2210.

Date	Mintage	F	VF	XF	Unc
1781 KR/OE	—	200	300	625	950

KM# 92 THALER

Silver **Ruler:** Johann Anton III, Freiherr von Zehmen **Obverse:** Bust right **Obv. Legend:** IOANN • ANTON III • D • G • EP • EYSTETTENSIS S • R • I • P • **Reverse:** Helmeted ornate arms **Rev. Legend:** 10 EINE FEINE MARCK. **Note:** Dav. #2211.

Date	Mintage	F	VF	XF	Unc
1783 IOS SCH	—	150	225	450	850

KM# 97 THALER

Silver **Ruler:** Josef, Graf von Stubenberg **Subject:** Joseph **Obverse:** Bust right **Obv. Legend:** IOSEPHVS • D • G • EPISC • EVSTETTENSIS S • R • I • P • **Reverse:** Date in chronogram **Rev. Legend:** VasCVLIs aVLar argentels patrlae InDIgentI MInIstraVIt aVXILIa. **Note:** Dav. #2213.

Date	Mintage	F	VF	XF	Unc
1796 CD	—	125	200	375	700

KM# 95 2 THALER

Silver **Subject:** Sede Vacante Issue **Obverse:** Saints above vacant throne **Obv. Legend:** CAPITULUM EYSTETTENSE - REGNANS SEDE VACANTE, below: 17.V EINE FEINE MARK. **Reverse:** Tree with 15 shields in branches, one shield below trunk, abbey and lands in background **Rev. Legend:** EX UNO OMNIS NOSTRA SALUS, below: WILIBALDS-BURG. in band **Note:** Convention 2 Thaler. Dav. #2212.

Date	Mintage	F	VF	XF	Unc
1790 W	—	300	550	850	1,500

COUNTERSTAMPED COINAGE

KM# 55 2 THALER

Silver **Counterstamp:** Two shields of Eichstätt and unknown arms **Obverse:** Bust of Leopold I right, two counterstamps, date above and Cathedral chapter arms with CRE above (Capitulum Regnans Eystettense) **Reverse:** Crowned imperial eagle, date 1692 divided above **Note:** Sede vacante issue.

CS Date	Host Date	Good	VG	F	VF	XF
1725	1691 Unique	—	—	—	—	—

TRADE COINAGE

KM# 60 DUCAT

3.4900 g., 0.9860 Gold 0.1106 oz. AGW **Obverse:** St. Willibald **Reverse:** Helmeted and mitred arms

Date	Mintage	VG	F	VF	XF	Unc
1738	—	220	425	900	2,000	—

KM# 61 DUCAT

3.4900 g., 0.9860 Gold 0.1106 oz. AGW **Ruler:** Johann Anton II von Freiberg-Hopferau **Obverse:** Helmeted and mitred arms **Reverse:** St. Walburga

Date	Mintage	VG	F	VF	XF	Unc
1738	—	200	400	850	2,000	—

KM# 74 DUCAT

3.4700 g., 0.9860 Gold 0.1100 oz. AGW **Ruler:** Johann Anton II von Freiberg-Hopferau **Obverse:** Bust right **Reverse:** Crowned arms divide date

Date	Mintage	VG	F	VF	XF	Unc
1755 I.L. OE-MNL	—	700	1,500	3,000	6,000	—

EINBECK

(Eimbeck)

The town of Einbeck, near the confluence of the Leine and Ilme Rivers, 38 miles (65 kilometers) south of Hannover, was associated early on with the nearby monastery of St. Alexander which was founded about 1080. Its first mention as a town came in 1274 and soon thereafter it was the location of a mint for the dukes of Brunswick-Grubenhagen. At some point during the 15th century, Einbeck obtained the mint right and began striking its own local coinage in 1498. By an edict of Johann Friedrich, Duke of Brunswick-Lüneburg-Calenberg (1665-79) in 1674, the minting of silver coinage was halted, but the town continued striking undated copper pfennigs until 1717.

CITY

REGULAR COINAGE

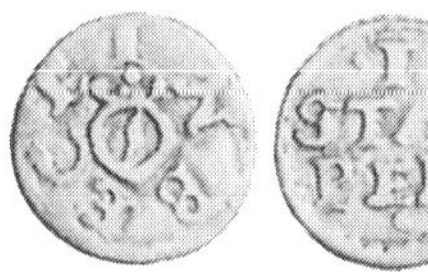

KM# 40 PFENNIG

Copper **Obverse:** EINBECK around **Reverse:** Value **Note:** Varieties exist.

Date	Mintage	VG	F	VF	XF	Unc
ND(1647-1717)	—	10.00	22.00	35.00	60.00	—

KM# 41 PFENNIG

Copper **Obverse:** With rosette **Note:** Varieties exist.

Date	Mintage	VG	F	VF	XF	Unc
ND(1647-1717)	—	10.00	22.00	35.00	60.00	—

ELLWANGEN

Founded as a Benedictine Abbey about 764 but not recognized as a town until about 1229, Ellwangen is located in northern Württemberg about 18 miles northwest of Nordlingen. The Abbey was reorganized as a college in 1460. The mint right was obtained in 1555. The town was mediatized and the properties given to Württemberg in 1803.

RULERS (Provosts)

Franz Ludwig von der Pfalz, 1694-1732
Franz Georg, Graf von Schonborn, 1732-1756
Anton Ignaz, von Fugger-Glott, 1756-1787
Clemens Wenzel, Herzog von Sachsen, 1787-1803

MINT OFFICIALS' INITIALS

Initials	Date	Name
GFN	1682-1704	George Friedrich Nurnberger mintmaster in Nuremberg
GM	1762-94	Gotthard Martinengo mintmaster at Coblenz
CIL	1683-1707	Christoph Jakob Leherr, die-cutter and engraver in Augsburg
EG	1750-75	Elias Gervais engraver at Coblenz

PROVOSTSHIP

Abbey

REGULAR COINAGE

KM# 20 1/2 THALER

Silver **Ruler:** Anton Ignaz **Obverse:** EG below bust **Reverse:** Arms within crowned mantle

Date	Mintage	VG	F	VF	XF	Unc
1765 EG-GM	—	75.00	150	350	700	—

KM# 21 THALER

Silver **Ruler:** Anton Ignaz **Obverse:** EG below bust **Obv. Legend:** ANT • IGN• D: G: S • R • I • PRINCEPS • PRAEP • AC DOM • ELVANCENSIS *1765* **Reverse:** Arms within crowned mantle **Rev. Legend:** AD NORMAM - CONVENTIONIS, below: X EINE MARK FEIN SILBER **Note:** Dav. #2214.

Date	Mintage	VG	F	VF	XF	Unc
1765 EG-GM	—	300	650	1,400	2,250	—

ERBACH

The lords of Erbach, located in the Odenwalde about 20 miles to the southeast of Darmstadt, are known from the early 12th century. Beginning in the early 13th century and lasting until 1806, the rulers of Erbach held the office of hereditary cupbearer to the elector-counts palatine of the Rhine. The rank of count was obtained from the emperor in 1532. The countship was divided by the four sons of Georg IV in 1605, although they struck a joint coinage. The family patrimony was further divided during the later 17th and early 18th centuries. Only some rulers of the several branches struck coins. Erbach was mediatized and its lands went to Hesse-Darmstadt in 1806.

RULERS

Philipp Ludwig, 1693-1720
Friedrich Karl, 1720-1731
Georg Wilhelm, 1731-1757

COUNTY

REGULAR COINAGE

KM# 20 THALER

Silver **Obverse:** Large cloverleaf in foreground of landscape, castle to left, rising sun right, Roman numeral date below **Obv. Legend:** ICH SELBST BELONE AM BESTEN **Rev. Legend:** FUR DIE BEREIT/WILLIGE BEFOLGUNG/GUT GEMEINTER/ LEHREN

Date	Mintage	VG	F	VF	XF	Unc
1793	—	—	—	—	—	—

ERFURT

(Erfordia)

The city of Erfurt is located in northern Thuringia (Thüringen), about 12.5 miles (21 kilometers) west of Weimar. It was a place of some importance as early as 741 when it became a branch bishopric of Mainz. The archbishops of the latter city remained very much involved in the affairs of Erfurt throughout the High Middle Ages and even located one of their mints there from the 11th through the 13th centuries. An imperial mint also produced coinage in Erfurt during the 12th century. By the mid-13th century, however, the town gained enough power to force the archbishop to grant it self-governing rights. Erfurt was given the right to mint its own coins in 1341 and 1354, and a long series of coins began which lasted until the beginning of the 19th century. Having joined the Hanseatic League during the early 15th century, Erfurt was at the height of its power and prestige, but events began to cause the decline of the city. Saxony managed to wrest control of Erfurt away from Mainz in 1483. During the Thirty Years' War, the city was seized and occupied by Swedish forces in 1631. The treaties which ended the war in 1648 gave control of Erfurt back to Mainz, but the good citizens refused to submit. The city held out until 1664 when it was captured by the archbishop's forces. It remained under Mainz until 1803, when the archbishopric was secularized, and then passed to Prussia.

RULERS

Emerich Josef, Freiherr von Brielbach Buresheim, 1763-1774
Friedrich Carl Josef, Freiherr von und zu Erthal, Archbishop, 1774-1802

MINT OFFICIALS' INITIALS

Initials	Date	Name
W	1732-62	Johann Heinrich Werner, die-cutter
A	Ca.1770	Unknown
B	Ca.1770-01	Unknown
D	Ca.1773	Unknown
	1773-76	Johann Zacharias Schröter, mint director
F	1776-?	Jonas Fischer, warden
C	1779-1804	Julianus Eberhard Volkmar Claus, mint director
E	ca.1781-98	Unknown

ARMS

6-spoked wheel of Mainz, sometimes in 2-fold shield, half of which is 3 vertical bars (Capellendorf).

CITY

REGULAR COINAGE

KM# 105 HELLER

Copper **Obverse:** Crowned arms in baroque frame **Reverse:** Value, date **Note:** Prev. KM#95.

Date	Mintage	VG	F	VF	XF	Unc
1756	—	3.00	6.00	10.00	25.00	—
1756 W	—	3.00	6.00	10.00	25.00	—
1757	—	3.00	6.00	10.00	25.00	—
1758	—	3.00	6.00	10.00	25.00	—
1758 W	—	3.00	6.00	10.00	25.00	—
1759	—	3.00	6.00	10.00	25.00	—
1760	—	3.00	6.00	10.00	25.00	—

KM# 106 HELLER

Copper **Reverse:** Date in floral sprays **Note:** Prev. KM#96.

Date	Mintage	VG	F	VF	XF	Unc
1756	—	3.00	6.00	12.00	25.00	—

KM# 107 HELLER

Copper **Reverse:** Value and date in cartouche **Note:** Prev. KM#97.

Date	Mintage	VG	F	VF	XF	Unc
1756	—	3.00	6.00	12.00	25.00	—

KM# 108 HELLER

Copper **Obverse:** Crowned and mantled arms **Reverse:** Value, date **Note:** Prev. KM#98.

Date	Mintage	VG	F	VF	XF	Unc
1759	—	3.00	6.00	12.00	25.00	—

KM# 109 HELLER

Copper **Obverse:** Crowned arms between branches **Note:** Prev. KM#99.

Date	Mintage	VG	F	VF	XF	Unc
1760	—	3.00	6.00	12.00	25.00	—

KM# 104 HELLER

Copper **Ruler:** Emerich Josef, Freiherr von Brielbach Buresheim **Obverse:** EJ monogram above wheel **Reverse:** Value, date

Date	Mintage	VG	F	VF	XF	Unc
1769	—	2.00	4.00	8.00	18.00	—

KM# 113 HELLER

Copper **Ruler:** Emerich Josef, Freiherr von Brielbach Buresheim **Obverse:** Arms in sprays **Reverse:** Value and date **Note:** Prev. KM#103.

Date	Mintage	VG	F	VF	XF	Unc
1769	—	2.00	4.00	9.00	20.00	—

KM# 114 HELLER

Copper **Ruler:** Emerich Josef, Freiherr von Brielbach Buresheim **Obverse:** EJ monogram above wheel **Note:** Prev. KM#104.

Date	Mintage	VG	F	VF	XF	Unc
1769	—	2.00	4.00	8.00	18.00	—

KM# 135 3 PFENNIG (Dreier)

5.5600 g., Copper, 24.6 mm. **Obverse:** Crown above wheel in wreath **Obv. Legend:** "I.F.C.D.G.S.S.M.A.E.--.R.I.P.G.A.C.P.--E.E.W." **Reverse:** "3 PFENNIG / S.M / 1760" in wreath **Note:** This is not Mainz KM-331.

Date	Mintage	F	VF	XF	Unc
1760	—	10.00	20.00	35.00	—

KM# 115 3 PFENNIG (Dreier)
Billon **Ruler:** Emerich Josef, Freiherr von Brielbach Buresheim **Obverse:** Wheel of Mainz within palm branches, crown and E I above **Reverse:** Value, date in cartouche **Note:** Prev. KM#105.

Date	Mintage	F	VF	XF	Unc
1770	—	6.00	12.00	30.00	60.00
1771	—	6.00	12.00	30.00	60.00

KM# 116 1/48 THALER
Billon **Ruler:** Emerich Josef, Freiherr von Brielbach Buresheim **Note:** Prev. KM#106.

Date	Mintage	F	VF	XF	Unc
1770 A	—	10.00	20.00	40.00	70.00
1770 B	—	10.00	20.00	40.00	70.00
1771 B	—	10.00	20.00	40.00	70.00
1773 D	—	10.00	20.00	40.00	70.00

KM# 117 1/48 THALER
Billon **Ruler:** Emerich Josef, Freiherr von Brielbach Buresheim **Obverse:** Oval wheel **Note:** Prev. KM#107.

Date	Mintage	F	VF	XF	Unc
1770 B	—	10.00	20.00	40.00	70.00

KM# 120 1/48 THALER
Billon **Ruler:** Friedrich Carl Josef Archbishop **Note:** Prev. KM#110.

Date	Mintage	F	VF	XF	Unc
1781 E	—	6.00	12.00	30.00	85.00

KM# 121 1/48 THALER
Billon **Ruler:** Friedrich Carl Josef Archbishop **Note:** Prev. KM#111.

Date	Mintage	F	VF	XF	Unc
1784 C	—	6.00	12.00	30.00	85.00

KM# 122 1/48 THALER
Billon **Ruler:** Friedrich Carl Josef Archbishop **Note:** Prev. KM#112.

Date	Mintage	F	VF	XF	Unc
1788 E	—	6.00	12.00	30.00	85.00
1789 E	—	6.00	12.00	30.00	85.00
1790 E	—	6.00	12.00	30.00	85.00
1791 E	—	6.00	12.00	30.00	85.00
1793 E	240,000	6.00	12.00	30.00	85.00
1794 E	—	6.00	12.00	30.00	85.00

KM# 125 1/48 THALER
Billon **Ruler:** Friedrich Carl Josef Archbishop **Note:** Prev. KM#115.

Date	Mintage	F	VF	XF	Unc
1798 E	—	5.00	10.00	25.00	50.00

KM# 130 1/48 THALER
Billon **Ruler:** Friedrich Carl Josef Archbishop **Obverse:** Arms in long shield **Note:** Prev. KM#120.

Date	Mintage	F	VF	XF	Unc
1800 C	—	10.00	20.00	35.00	65.00

KM# 131 1/24 THALER
Billon **Ruler:** Friedrich Carl Josef Archbishop **Obverse:** Arms in long shield **Note:** Prev. KM#121.

Date	Mintage	F	VF	XF	Unc
1800 C	—	10.00	20.00	35.00	70.00

PATTERNS

Including off metal strikes

KM#	Date	Mintage	Identification	Mkt Val
Pn7	1800	—	1/24 Thaler. Gold. KM#191.	500

ESSEN

ABBEY

The city of Essen lies in the Ruhr Valley, about 18 miles (30 kilometers) northeast of Düsseldorf and about the same distance west of Dortmund. A Benedictine abbey for women was founded in the place during the first half of the 9th century and the town of Essen grew up around the religious institution. The earliest coinage was of the imperial type pfennigs dating from the first half of the 11th century. The abbess attained the distinction as a princess of the Empire in 1275 and it is from that time that coinage of the abbesses themselves first dates. In the general secularization of the Empire in 1802-03, Essen was given to Prussia, but passed to Berg in 1806. Prussia regained possession of the monastery and city at the end of the Napoleonic Wars in 1815. There was no coinage during the 16th century.

RULERS
Bernhardine Sophie, Grafin von Ostfriesland-Ritberg, 1691-1726
Francesca Christine, Grafin von Pfalz-Sulzbach, 1726-1776
Maria Kunigunde, Grafin von Sachsen, 1776-1803

CONVENT

TRADE COINAGE

KM# 35 DUCAT
3.5000 g., 0.9860 Gold 0.1109 oz. AGW **Ruler:** Francesca Christine **Obverse:** Crowned arms in cartouche, crossed sword and crozier behind dividing date below **Reverse:** Madonna standing holding Child **Note:** Varieties exist. Fr.933.

Date	Mintage	VG	F	VF	XF	Unc
1753 Rare	—	—	—	—	—	—
1754	—	500	1,000	2,000	4,000	—

ESSLINGEN

FREE CITY

A city located 9 miles southeast of Stüttgart in Württemberg, known to have existed before the end of the 8th century. An imperial mint was established there during the 11th century and it received the status of free imperial city in 1209. The only known modern coinage of Esslingen dates from the first quarter of the 18th century. The city passed to Württemberg in 1802.

REGULAR COINAGE

KM# 5 1/2 THALER
Silver **Subject:** Homage to Josef I **Obverse:** Representation of the Biblical Joseph dreaming **Reverse:** Inscription with date

Date	Mintage	VG	F	VF	XF	Unc
1705	—	125	250	475	800	—

KM# 12 1/2 THALER
Silver **Subject:** 200th Anniversary of the Reformation **Obverse:** Rays from God's eye radiating over city view of Esslingen, date in legend **Reverse:** Bust of Martin Luther 1/2 right, double legends

Date	Mintage	VG	F	VF	XF	Unc
1717	—	100	225	425	700	—

TRADE COINAGE

KM# 13 2 DUCAT
7.0000 g., 0.9860 Gold 0.2219 oz. AGW **Subject:** 200th Anniversary of the Reformation **Note:** Fr.#934. Struck with 1/2 Thaler dies, KM#12.

Date	Mintage	VG	F	VF	XF	Unc
1717	—	500	900	1,750	3,250	—

KM# 14 5 DUCAT (1/2 Portugalöser)
17.5000 g., 0.9860 Gold 0.5547 oz. AGW **Subject:** 200th Anniversary of the Reformation **Note:** Fr. #934a. Struck with 1/2 Thaler dies, KM#12.

Date	Mintage	VG	F	VF	XF	Unc
1717	—	5,000	7,000	10,000	13,500	—

KM# 15 6 DUCAT
21.0000 g., 0.9860 Gold 0.6657 oz. AGW **Subject:** 200th Anniversary of the Reformation **Note:** Fr. #935. Struck with 1/2 Thaler dies, KM#12.

Date	Mintage	VG	F	VF	XF	Unc
1717	—	6,250	8,500	11,000	14,500	—

FRANCONIAN CIRCLE

(Frankischer Kreis)

The Holy Roman Empire was divided into six administrative circles in 1500, the number being raised to ten in 1512. The Franconian Circle was one of these and comprised about the same territory as the ancient division of Franconia, north of Bavaria. Under the imperial coinage reforms of 1559 and 1566, the Franconian Circle was permitted to have only four mints at Nüremberg, Schwabach, Wertheim and Würzburg, although others were opened at various times. During the 17th and 18th centuries a sporadic coinage of the Franconian Circle was produced at one or another of these mints. The circle also counterstamped coins from other territories entering its jurisdiction.

MINT MARKS
F - Furth Mint
N - Nüremberg Mint
S - Schwabach Mint

MINT OFFICIALS' INITIALS

Initials	Date	Name
GFN	1682-1710	Georg Friedrich Nurnberger

NOTE: The usual design of most coins of the Franconian Circle incorporates the four arms of Bamberg, Brandenburg-Ansbach, Brandenburg-Bayreuth and Nuremberg.

IMPERIAL CIRCLE

REGULAR COINAGE

KM# 25 15 KREUZER (1/4 Gulden)
Silver **Obverse:** Legend within laurel branches **Reverse:** Date at center of 4 crowned shields on branches

Date	Mintage	VG	F	VF	XF	Unc
1726N	—	25.00	50.00	85.00	145	—
1726S	—	40.00	80.00	125	185	—

PATTERNS

Including off metal strikes

KM#	Date	Mintage	Identification	Mkt Val
Pn1	1726S	—	15 Kreuzer. Tin. KM#25	55.00

FRANKFURT AM MAIN

One of the largest cities of modern Germany, Frankfurt is located on the north bank of the Main River about 25 miles (42 kilometers) upstream from where it joins the Rhine at Mainz. It was the site of a Roman camp in the first century. Frankfurt was a commercial center from the early Middle Ages and became a favored location for imperial councils during the Carolingian period because of its central location. An imperial mint operated from early times and had a large production during the 12th to 14th centuries. Local issues were produced from at least the mid-14th century, but it was not until 1428 that the city was officially granted the right to coin its own money. In establishing the seven permanent electors of the Empire in 1356, the Golden Bull also made Frankfurt the site of those elections and increased the prestige of the city even further. Frankfurt remained a free city until 1806 and then was the capital of the Grand Duchy of Frankfurt from 1810 until 1814, only to regain its free status in 1815. The city chose the wrong side in the Austro-Prussian War of 1866 and thus was absorbed by victorious Prussia in the latter year.

MINT MARKS
F - Frankfurt

MINT OFFICIALS' INITIALS

Frankfurt Mint

Initials	Date	Name
ARW	1742-84	Adam Rudolf Werner, die-cutter and engraver in Stüttgart
B(F)N	1764-89	Bunsen & Neumeister
BIB	1738-42	Balthasar Johann Bengeradt
EK, EIK	1742	Engelhard Johann Krail
G.B., I.G.B.	1790-1825	Johann Georg Bunsen
GH	1798-1816	Georg Hille, warden
GN	1764-89	Georg Neumeister, warden

H.G.B.H.	1790-98	Hille & Bunsen
IF, IIF	1690-1737	Johann Jeremias Freytag
IH, HH	1790-98	Heinrich Hille
IIE	1740-70	Johann Jacob Enke in Hanau
I.L.OE., OE	1740-87	Johann Leonard Oexlein, die-cutter-medailleur in Nüremberg
IT, IOT	1762-64	Johann Otto Trumer
PB, PCB	1764-90	Philipp Christian Bunsen

Darmstadt Mint

Initials	Date	Name
GCF	1741-48, 1752-66	Georg Conrad Fehr

NOTE: In some instances old dies were used with initials beyond the date range of the man that held the position.

ARMS

Crowned eagle, usually in circle.

FREE CITY

REGULAR COINAGE

KM# 247 HELLER

Copper **Obverse:** Crowned displayed eagle with F on breast **Reverse:** Value above date

Date	Mintage	VG	F	VF	XF	Unc
1767 PCB	—	2.50	5.00	10.00	20.00	—
1773 PCB	—	2.50	5.00	10.00	20.00	—

KM# 252 HELLER

Copper **Obverse:** Crowned displayed eagle; P(F)B below **Reverse:** Value and date

Date	Mintage	VG	F	VF	XF	Unc
1773 Without dot after B	—	3.00	6.00	12.00	30.00	—
1773 Dot after B	—	3.00	6.00	12.00	30.00	—
1782	—	3.00	8.00	20.00	40.00	—

KM# 247a HELLER

Silver **Obverse:** Without F on breast **Reverse:** Value, date

Date	Mintage	VG	F	VF	XF	Unc
1774 PCB	—	12.00	35.00	50.00	100	—

KM# 268 PFENNIG

Copper **Mint:** Frankfurt **Obverse:** Eagle **Reverse:** *1* / PFENNIG / date /* **Note:** Varieties exist.

Date	Mintage	F	VF	XF	Unc
1786F PB	—	2.50	6.00	14.00	30.00
1787F PB	—	2.50	6.00	14.00	30.00
1788F PB	—	2.50	6.00	14.00	30.00
1789F PB	—	2.50	6.00	14.00	30.00
1790F PB	—	2.50	6.00	14.00	30.00
1790F GB	—	2.50	6.00	14.00	30.00
1791F GB	—	2.50	6.00	14.00	30.00
1792F GB	—	2.50	6.00	14.00	30.00
1793F GB	—	2.50	6.00	14.00	30.00
1794F PB	—	2.50	6.00	14.00	30.00
1794F GB	—	2.50	6.00	14.00	30.00
1795F PB	—	2.50	6.00	14.00	30.00
1795F GB	—	2.50	6.00	14.00	30.00
1796F GB	—	2.50	6.00	14.00	30.00
1797F PB	—	2.50	6.00	14.00	30.00
1797F GB	—	2.50	6.00	14.00	30.00
1798F GB	—	2.50	6.00	14.00	30.00
1799F GB	—	2.50	6.00	14.00	30.00
1800F GB	—	2.50	6.00	14.00	30.00
1801F GB	—	3.00	7.00	15.00	30.00
1801F GB	—	3.00	7.00	15.00	30.00
1802F GB	—	3.00	7.00	15.00	30.00
1803F PB	—	3.00	7.00	15.00	30.00
1803F GB	—	3.00	7.00	15.00	30.00
1804F GB	—	3.00	7.00	15.00	30.00
1805F GB	—	4.00	8.00	18.00	35.00
1806F GB	—	4.00	8.00	20.00	40.00

KM# 287 2 PFENNIG

Copper **Obverse:** Crowned displayed eagle **Reverse:** Value above date

Date	Mintage	F	VF	XF	Unc
1795 G(F)B	—	10.00	20.00	40.00	75.00

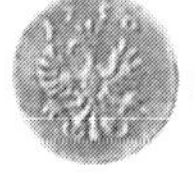

KM# 210 1/4 KREUZER

Copper **Obverse:** Date above crowned eagle **Reverse:** Fraction

Date	Mintage	VG	F	VF	XF	Unc
1750	—	15.00	30.00	80.00	160	—
1751	—	15.00	30.00	80.00	160	—
1752	—	15.00	30.00	80.00	160	—
1754	—	15.00	30.00	80.00	160	—
1756	—	15.00	30.00	80.00	160	—
1758	—	15.00	30.00	80.00	160	—

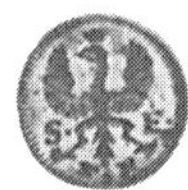

KM# 240 1/4 KREUZER

Copper **Obverse:** Crowned displayed eagle divides S-F **Reverse:** Value above date

Date	Mintage	VG	F	VF	XF	Unc
1765 BN	—	15.00	30.00	60.00	120	—

KM# 223 KREUZER

Billon **Obverse:** Crowned displayed eagle with flowers at side **Obv. Legend:** FRANCFURT **Reverse:** Value above date on ornamental shield

Date	Mintage	VG	F	VF	XF	Unc
1763 OT	—	5.00	15.00	35.00	100	—
1763 IT	—	5.00	15.00	35.00	100	—

KM# 228.1 KREUZER

Billon **Obverse:** Without flowers **Obv. Legend:** FRANCFURT **Reverse:** Value above date in cinquefoil cartouche

Date	Mintage	VG	F	VF	XF	Unc
1764 G*P.C.B*N	—	4.00	12.00	25.00	45.00	—
1765 G PCB N	—	4.00	12.00	25.00	45.00	—
1773 G PCB N	—	4.00	12.00	25.00	45.00	—
1774 G PCB N	—	4.00	12.00	25.00	45.00	—
1775 G PCB N	—	4.00	12.00	25.00	45.00	—
1776 G PCB N	—	4.00	12.00	25.00	45.00	—
1778 G PCB N	—	4.00	12.00	25.00	45.00	—

KM# 253 KREUZER

Billon **Obverse:** Crowned eagle divides value **Reverse:** City view above date

Date	Mintage	VG	F	VF	XF	Unc
1773 BN	—	4.00	12.00	25.00	45.00	—
1773 B.N.	—	4.00	12.00	25.00	45.00	—

KM# 257.1 KREUZER

Billon **Obverse:** 3-line inscription **Obv. Legend:** FRANCFURT **Reverse:** Value and date

Date	Mintage	VG	F	VF	XF	Unc
1778 G PCB N	—	7.50	15.00	30.00	50.00	—
1788 G PCB N	—	7.50	15.00	30.00	50.00	—
1789 G PCB N	—	7.50	15.00	30.00	50.00	—

KM# 228.2 KREUZER

Billon **Obv. Legend:** FRANKFURT **Note:** Varieties of style of eagle exist.

Date	Mintage	VG	F	VF	XF	Unc
1778 G PCB N	—	4.00	12.00	25.00	45.00	—

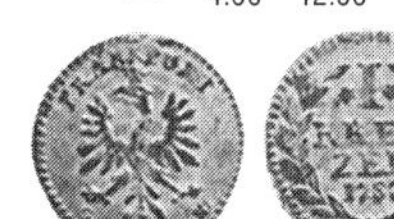

KM# 265.1 KREUZER

Billon **Obverse:** Crowned displayed eagle, FRANKFURT on 1 line **Reverse:** Value and date in wreath

Date	Mintage	VG	F	VF	XF	Unc
1780 G PCB N	—	5.00	15.00	30.00	50.00	—

KM# 265.2 KREUZER

Billon **Obv. Legend:** FRANCKFURT

Date	Mintage	VG	F	VF	XF	Unc
1782 G PCB N	—	5.00	15.00	30.00	50.00	—

KM# 265.3 KREUZER

Billon **Obv. Legend:** FRANCFURT

Date	Mintage	VG	F	VF	XF	Unc
1783 G PCB N	—	5.00	15.00	30.00	50.00	—

KM# 267 KREUZER

Billon **Obverse:** FRANKFURT on two lines **Reverse:** Value and date in wreath

Date	Mintage	VG	F	VF	XF	Unc
1784 G PCB N	—	5.00	15.00	30.00	65.00	—
1786 G PCB N	—	5.00	15.00	30.00	65.00	—
1787 G PCB N	—	5.00	15.00	30.00	65.00	—
1788 G PCB N	—	5.00	15.00	30.00	65.00	—
1789 G PCB N	—	5.00	15.00	30.00	65.00	—

KM# 257.2 KREUZER

Billon **Obv. Legend:** FRANKFURT

Date	Mintage	VG	F	VF	XF	Unc
1788 G PCB N	—	7.50	15.00	30.00	50.00	—

KM# 211 4 KREUZER

Billon **Obverse:** Displayed eagle **Reverse:** Value and date

Date	Mintage	VG	F	VF	XF	Unc
1757 HS Rare	—	—	—	—	—	—

KM# 215 5 KREUZER

Silver **Obverse:** Crowned displayed eagle on pedestal, 240 in pedestal **Reverse:** Cross with arm ends joined in garlands

Date	Mintage	VG	F	VF	XF	Unc
1762 IOT	—	20.00	35.00	65.00	140	—

KM# 241 5 KREUZER

Silver **Obverse:** Crowned displayed eagle in diamond divides S-F **Reverse:** 240 and date in diamond, value at sides

Date	Mintage	VG	F	VF	XF	Unc
1765 G PCB N	—	20.00	40.00	70.00	145	—

KM# 258 5 KREUZER

Silver **Obverse:** Crowned displayed eagle in diamond, date below **Reverse:** Value in wreath, mural crown above

Date	Mintage	VG	F	VF	XF	Unc
1778 G PCB N	—	15.00	30.00	50.00	110	—
1779 G PCB N	—	15.00	30.00	50.00	110	—
1785 G PCB N	—	20.00	40.00	75.00	150	—

KM# 216.1 10 KREUZER

Silver **Obverse:** Crowned displayed eagle on pedestal, 120 in pedestal **Reverse:** Cross with arm ends joined in garland, legend in German

Date	Mintage	VG	F	VF	XF	Unc
1762 IOT	—	35.00	80.00	150	260	—

KM# 216.2 10 KREUZER

Silver **Obverse:** Crowned eagle on pedestal **Reverse:** Cross

Date	Mintage	VG	F	VF	XF	Unc
1762 IOT	—	40.00	90.00	180	300	—

KM# 224 10 KREUZER

Silver **Obverse:** Crowned displayed eagle on pedestal, value 10 in pedestal

Date	Mintage	VG	F	VF	XF	Unc
1763 IOT	—	40.00	90.00	180	300	—

KM# 242 10 KREUZER

Silver **Reverse:** Cross without enclosing circle

Date	Mintage	VG	F	VF	XF	Unc
1765 G PCB N	—	30.00	70.00	120	210	—

KM# 250.1 10 KREUZER

Silver **Obverse:** Eagle with hanging wings **Reverse:** Value within wreath, small towers above

Date	Mintage	VG	F	VF	XF	Unc
1776 G PCB N	—	15.00	40.00	80.00	150	—

KM# 250.2 10 KREUZER

Silver **Obverse:** Displayed eagle **Reverse:** Value within wreath, small towers above

Date	Mintage	VG	F	VF	XF	Unc
1778 G PCB N	—	20.00	45.00	85.00	160	—
1779 G PCB N	—	35.00	75.00	150	300	—

KM# 269.1 10 KREUZER

Silver **Obverse:** Crowned oval arms, denomination in cartouche **Reverse:** 4-line German inscription and date

Date	Mintage	VG	F	VF	XF	Unc
1788 G PCB N	—	14.00	36.00	65.00	120	—

KM# 269.2 10 KREUZER

Silver **Obverse:** Crowned oval arms, value within cartouoche **Reverse:** Inscription in Latin

Date	Mintage	VG	F	VF	XF	Unc
1788 G PCB N	—	13.00	32.00	60.00	100	—

KM# 212 6 ALBUS (12 Kreuzer)

Silver **Obverse:** Crowned displayed eagle, date above **Reverse:** Value in inner circle **Note:** Presumably a private pattern of the mintmaster, Georg Conrad Fehr at Darmstadt.

Date	Mintage	VG	F	VF	XF	Unc
1758 GCF Rare	—	—	—	—	—	—

KM# 217 20 KREUZER

Silver **Obverse:** Crowned displayed eagle on pedestal, 60 in pedestal **Reverse:** Cross with arm ends joined by garlands

Date	Mintage	VG	F	VF	XF	Unc
1762 IOT	—	20.00	40.00	80.00	165	—

KM# 218 20 KREUZER

Silver **Rev. Legend:** NOMEN DOMINI TURRIS FORTISSIMA **Note:** Varieties exist.

Date	Mintage	VG	F	VF	XF	Unc
1762 IOT	—	50.00	130	220	480	—

KM# 226 20 KREUZER

Silver **Obverse:** Displayed eagle on pedestal with value **Reverse:** Ornate cross with joining garlands at angles **Note:** Varieties exist.

Date	Mintage	VG	F	VF	XF	Unc
1763 IOT	—	20.00	40.00	80.00	165	—
1764 IOT	—	20.00	40.00	80.00	165	—

KM# 225 20 KREUZER

Silver **Obverse:** Crowned eagle on pedestal with value **Reverse:** Date and denomination, cross with arm ends joined by garlands **Rev. Legend:** NOMEN DOMINI TURRIS FORTISSIMA

Date	Mintage	VG	F	VF	XF	Unc
1763 IOT	—	20.00	40.00	80.00	165	—

KM# 227 20 KREUZER

Silver **Obverse:** Crowned displayed eagle on pedestal, FRANCFURT above, AD NORMAM CONVENTIONIS at sides and below

Date	Mintage	VG	F	VF	XF	Unc
1763 IOT	—	60.00	100	180	350	—

KM# 229 20 KREUZER

Silver **Obverse:** Crowned displayed eagle on pedestal, value in pedestal, FRANCFVRT below **Reverse:** Cross with flourishes

Date	Mintage	VG	F	VF	XF	Unc
1764 IOT	—	30.00	50.00	100	200	—
1764 B(F)N	—	35.00	60.00	110	220	—

KM# 230.1 20 KREUZER

Silver **Reverse:** Cross in inner circle without flourishes between arms

Date	Mintage	VG	F	VF	XF	Unc
1764 D(Γ)N	—	30.00	50.00	110	240	—

KM# 230.2 20 KREUZER

Silver **Obverse:** Without FRANCFURT below pedestal

Date	Mintage	VG	F	VF	XF	Unc
1764 G PCB N	—	20.00	40.00	80.00	165	—
1765 G PCB N	—	20.00	40.00	80.00	165	—

KM# 230.3 20 KREUZER

Silver **Reverse:** With ornamentation between arms

Date	Mintage	VG	F	VF	XF	Unc
1766 G PCB N	—	40.00	90.00	180	380	—

KM# 244.1 20 KREUZER

Silver **Obverse:** Initials below pedestal in line **Reverse:** Ornate cross

Date	Mintage	VG	F	VF	XF	Unc
1766 G PCB N	—	15.00	30.00	60.00	100	—
1767 G PCB N	—	20.00	40.00	80.00	165	—

KM# 244.2 20 KREUZER

Silver **Obverse:** Initials follow coin curvature **Reverse:** Ornate cross

Date	Mintage	VG	F	VF	XF	Unc
1766 G PCB N	—	20.00	40.00	80.00	165	—
1767 G PCB N	—	20.00	40.00	80.00	165	—
1768 G PCB N	—	20.00	40.00	80.00	165	—
1770 G PCB N	—	20.00	40.00	80.00	165	—
1771 G PCB N	—	20.00	40.00	80.00	165	—
1772 G PCB N	—	20.00	40.00	80.00	165	—

KM# 255 20 KREUZER

Silver **Obverse:** Crowned eagle **Reverse:** Value within wreath, small towers above

Date	Mintage	VG	F	VF	XF	Unc
1776 G PCB N	—	30.00	50.00	90.00	180	—

KM# 266 20 KREUZER

Silver **Obverse:** Crowned eagle arms in cartouche **Reverse:** Value equivalent with date, 20 below

Date	Mintage	VG	F	VF	XF	Unc
1781 G PCB N	—	25.00	50.00	100	200	—
1784 G PCB N	—	25.00	45.00	90.00	170	—

KM# 275 20 KREUZER

Silver **Obverse:** Displayed eagle within crowned cartouche, value below **Reverse:** Value and date

Date	Mintage	VG	F	VF	XF	Unc
1790 I PCB H	—	30.00	45.00	90.00	170	—

KM# 219 30 KREUZER

Silver **Obverse:** Displayed eagle within circle **Reverse:** Ornate cross with joining garlands at angles, circle surrounds **Note:** Convention 30 Kreuzer.

Date	Mintage	VG	F	VF	XF	Unc
1762 IOT	—	40.00	80.00	160	350	—

KM# 137.2 TURNOSGROSHEN

Silver **Reverse:** Large cross with flourishes

Date	Mintage	VG	F	VF	XF	Unc
1710 IIF	—	30.00	65.00	150	200	—
1710 IIF	—	30.00	65.00	150	200	—

KM# 170 TURNOSGROSHEN

Silver **Note:** Klippe.

Date	Mintage	VG	F	VF	XF	Unc
1710 IIF	—	—	—	—	—	—

KM# 180 1/8 THALER

Silver **Subject:** 200th Anniversary of Reformation **Obverse:** Open book atop rocks within sea, radiant emblem above **Reverse:** Inscription

Date	Mintage	VG	F	VF	XF	Unc
1717 IIF	—	40.00	80.00	150	250	—

KM# 174 1/4 THALER

Silver **Subject:** Election of Karl VI **Obverse:** Eagle flying above city view, crown at top **Reverse:** 12-line inscription with date

Date	Mintage	VG	F	VF	XF	Unc
1711 IIF	—	50.00	100	200	350	—

KM# 182 1/2 THALER

Silver **Subject:** 200th Anniversary of Reformation

Date	Mintage	VG	F	VF	XF	Unc
1717 IIF	—	300	400	550	950	—

KM# 220.2 1/2 THALER

Silver **Obverse:** Crowned eagle within cartouche **Reverse:** Cross with florals at angles

Date	Mintage	VG	F	VF	XF	Unc
1762 IOT	—	50.00	120	230	450	—
1764 BFN	—	40.00	100	220	430	—

KM# 220.1 1/2 THALER

Silver **Obverse:** Crowned eagle within circle **Reverse:** Ornate cross with joining garlands at angles **Note:** Convention 1/2 Thaler. Varieties of style of eagle exist.

Date	Mintage	VG	F	VF	XF	Unc
1762 IOT	—	60.00	125	250	500	—

KM# 231 1/2 THALER

Silver

Date	Mintage	VG	F	VF	XF	Unc
1764 G PCB N	—	40.00	80.00	150	300	—

KM# 232 1/2 THALER

Silver

Date	Mintage	VG	F	VF	XF	Unc
1764 G PCB N	—	50.00	100	180	360	—

KM# 243 1/2 THALER

Silver **Obverse:** Crowned eagle **Reverse:** Ornate cross

Date	Mintage	VG	F	VF	XF	Unc
1765 G PCB N	—	50.00	100	220	500	—

KM# 245 1/2 THALER

Silver **Obverse:** Crowned eagle **Reverse:** Ornate cross, date in legend

Date	Mintage	VG	F	VF	XF	Unc
1766 G PCB N	—	50.00	100	250	580	—

KM# 280 1/2 THALER

Silver **Obverse:** Crowned eagle **Reverse:** Value and date within wreath of palm and laurel branches

Date	Mintage	VG	F	VF	XF	Unc
1791	—	30.00	70.00	160	320	—

KM# 171 THALER

Silver **Obverse:** Crowned eagle within circle **Obv. Legend:** .MONETA NOVA ARGENTEA. REIP • FRANCOFURTENSIS. **Reverse:** Ornate cross with joining garlands at angles, circle surrounds **Rev. Legend:** NOMEN. DOMINI. TURRIS. FORTISSIMA. **Note:** Dav. #2215.

Date	Mintage	VG	F	VF	XF	Unc
1710 IIF	—	—	1,800	3,000	5,000	—
1716/0 IIF	—	—	1,800	3,000	5,000	—

KM# 175 THALER

Silver **Subject:** Coronation of Karl VI **Obverse:** Hand bestowing crown on Karl VI's head **Obv. Legend:** qVIs haC IMperII Corona - DIgnIorle **Reverse:** 10-line inscription, date below **Rev. Inscription:** VIVAT/CAROLVS SEXTVS/IMPERATOR CAESAR/AVGVSTVS/PIVS FELIX/LEOPOLDI MAGNI FILIVS/ET IPSE MAGNVS/ELECTVS ET CORONATVS/HIC FRANCOFVRTI AD MOENVM/ANNO 1711/I.I.F. **Note:** Dav. #2216.

Date	Mintage	VG	F	VF	XF	Unc
1711 IIF	—	—	6,000	10,000	13,500	—

KM# 179 THALER

Silver **Subject:** Shooting Festival **Obverse:** Crowned eagle **Obv. Legend:** MONETA NOVA REIPUBLICAE FRANCOFURTENSIS **Reverse:** Inscription **Rev. Inscription:** IM/1716 */DES THEUREN ERZHERZOGS/VON OESTERREICH. U. PRIN/ZENS VON ASTURIEN/LEOPOLDI/ GEBURTHS IAHR/DIESER FUNFFZIG UND EIN/BEYM HIESIGEN STUCK:/SCHIESSEN DAS BESTE/WAR **Note:** Dav. #2217.

Date	Mintage	VG	F	VF	XF	Unc
1716 IIF	—	—	2,200	3,200	5,000	—

KM# 183 THALER

Silver **Subject:** 200th Anniversary of Reformation **Obverse:** Open book atop rocks within sea, all seeing eye above **Obv. Legend:** * DOMINE ! CONSERVA NOBIS LUMEN EVANGELII **Reverse:** Inscription **Rev. Inscription:** * IN */MEMORIAM/ SECUNDI IUBILÆI/EVANGELICI/ANNO SECULARI/ MDCCXVII DIE 31 OCT:/CELEBRATI/SENAT, FRANCOFURT:/ *FF*/I.I.F. **Note:** Dav. #2218. Varieties exist.

Date	Mintage	VG	F	VF	XF	Unc
1717 IIF	—	200	400	700	1,250	—

KM# 221 THALER

Silver **Obverse:** Crowned eagle **Obv. Legend:** * AD NORMAM CONVENTIONIS X • E • F • MARK • **Reverse:** Ornate cross with joining garlands at angles **Rev. Legend:** * NOMEN DOMINI TURRIS FORTISSIMA **Note:** Convention Thaler. Dav. #2219. Many varieties of the imperial eagle exist.

Date	Mintage	VG	F	VF	XF	Unc
1762 IOT	—	120	220	450	900	—
1762 O=T	—	150	300	600	1,200	—
1763 IOT	—	200	400	800	1,600	—

KM# A233 THALER

Silver **Obverse:** Similar to KM#233 **Reverse:** Similar to KM#221 **Note:** Dav. #2220.

Date	Mintage	VG	F	VF	XF	Unc
1764 IOT	—	80.00	180	360	700	—
1764 BFN	—	120	220	420	750	—

KM# 233 THALER

Silver **Obverse:** Eagle in Roccoco cartouche **Obv. Legend:** * AD NORMAM CONVENTIONIS • X • E • F • MARK • **Reverse:** Cross with flourishes **Rev. Legend:** * NOMEN DOMINI TURRIS FORTISSIMA **Note:** Dav. #2221. Varieties exist.

Date	Mintage	VG	F	VF	XF	Unc
1764 IOT	—	140	250	500	1,000	—

KM# 234.1 THALER

Silver **Obverse:** Thin eagle in circle with G*P.C.B.*N. below **Obv. Legend:** * AD NORMAM CONVENTIONIS X • E • F • MARK • FRANCOFURTI **Reverse:** Cross with flourishes **Rev. Legend:** * NOMEN DOMINI TURRIS FORTISSIMA **Note:** Dav. #2222.

Date	Mintage	VG	F	VF	XF	Unc
1764 G PCB N	—	120	250	500	900	—

KM# 234.2 THALER

Silver **Obverse:** Crowned eagle **Obv. Legend:** * AD NORMAM CONVENTIONIS X • E • F • MARK • FRANCOFURTI • **Reverse:** Cross without flourishes **Rev. Legend:** * NOMEN DOMINI TURRIS FORTISSIMA **Note:** Dav. #2223

Date	Mintage	VG	F	VF	XF	Unc
1764 G PCB N	—	100	160	280	520	—
1765 G PCB N	—	100	175	350	650	—

KM# 246 THALER

Silver **Obverse:** No border, different eagle,and G.P.C.B.N. on a band under the eagle **Obv. Legend:** * AD NORMAM CONVENTIONIS X • E • F • MARK • FRANCOFURTI **Reverse:** Ornate cross, no border **Rev. Legend:** * NOMEN DOMINI TURRIS FORTISSIMA **Note:** Dav. #2225.

Date	Mintage	VG	F	VF	XF	Unc
1766 G PCB N	—	200	500	1,000	2,000	—
1767 G PCB N	—	200	400	800	1,600	—

KM# 234.3 THALER

Silver **Obverse:** Crowned eagle **Reverse:** No inner circle

Date	Mintage	VG	F	VF	XF	Unc
1766 G PCB N	—	150	250	500	1,000	—

KM# 251 THALER

Silver **Obverse:** Crowned eagle within cartouche **Obv. Legend:** MONETA REIPVBL • FRANCOFURT • AD LEGEM CONBENTIONIS, below: X • ST • EINE F • M • MDCCLXXII **Reverse:** City view, caduceus with cornucopia in foreground **Rev. Legend:** * NOMEN DOMINI TURRIS FORTISSIMA **Note:** Dav. #2226. Reverse varieties exist.

Date	Mintage	VG	F	VF	XF	Unc
1772 PCB	—	60.00	120	280	450	—

KM# 256 THALER

Silver **Subject:** Opening of the Bridge at Hausen **Obverse:** Three figures and arms at waters edge **Obv. Legend:** A DEO ET - CAESARE, below: FRANCFURT **Reverse:** Inscription within wreath with small towers above **Rev. Legend:** X. EINE FEINE MARCK •, AD/NORMAM/CONVEN/TIONIS in wreath **Note:** Dav. #2227.

Date	Mintage	VG	F	VF	XF	Unc
1776 BN	—	80.00	220	380	550	—

KM# 286 THALER

Silver **Obverse:** Crowned eagle **Obv. Legend:** STADT FRANCKFVRT, below: H•G•B•H• **Reverse:** Value and date within laurel branches **Rev. Legend:** X/EINE FEINE/MARK/date in wreath **Note:** Dav. #2228. Varieties exist.

Date	Mintage	VG	F	VF	XF	Unc
1793 HGBH	—	60.00	120	240	480	—
1796 HGBH	—	60.00	120	240	480	—

KM# 288 THALER

Silver **Obverse:** Crowned eagle within beaded circle **Obv. Legend:** DER STADT FRANCKFURT H • G • B • H • **Reverse:** Value and date within beaded circle **Rev. Legend:** * AUS DEN GEFAESEN DER KIRCHEN UND BURGER, *X*/EINE FEINE/MARK/1796. in center **Note:** Contribution Thaler. Dav. #2229. Varieties of eagle and value exist.

Date	Mintage	F	VF	XF	Unc
1796 HGBH	—	90.00	180	300	600

TOKEN COINAGE

KM# Tn14 THELER

Copper **Obverse:** Crossed swords on shield, 3 circles above **Reverse:** Value, date

Date	Mintage	F	VF	XF	Unc
1703	—	4.00	9.00	18.00	50.00

TRADE COINAGE

KM# A176 1/4 DUCAT

0.8750 g., 0.9860 Gold 0.0277 oz. AGW **Subject:** Coronation of Karl VI **Obverse:** Bust right **Reverse:** Globe in circle of clouds

Date	Mintage	VG	F	VF	XF	Unc
1711	—	50.00	100	175	300	—

KM# B176 1/2 DUCAT

1.7500 g., 0.9860 Gold 0.0555 oz. AGW **Subject:** Coronation of Karl VI **Obverse:** Bust right **Reverse:** Globe in circle of clouds

Date	Mintage	VG	F	VF	XF	Unc
1711	—	87.50	175	300	500	—

KM# 195 1/2 DUCAT

1.7500 g., 0.9860 Gold 0.0555 oz. AGW **Obverse:** Crowned displayed eagle **Reverse:** Value and date

Date	Mintage	VG	F	VF	XF	Unc
1740 BIB	—	175	400	750	1,200	—

KM# 176 3/4 DUCAT

2.6250 g., 0.9860 Gold 0.0832 oz. AGW **Subject:** Coronation of Karl VI **Obverse:** Glove in circle of clouds **Reverse:** Crown above 7-line inscription and date

Date	Mintage	VG	F	VF	XF	Unc
1711	—	100	200	350	550	—

KM# 202 3/4 DUCAT

2.6250 g., 0.9860 Gold 0.0832 oz. AGW **Subject:** Coronation of Franz I **Obverse:** Crown above inscription **Reverse:** Coronation items on pedestal, all seeing eye above

Date	Mintage	VG	F	VF	XF	Unc
1745	—	75.00	150	275	450	—

KM# 236 3/4 DUCAT

2.6250 g., 0.9860 Gold 0.0832 oz. AGW **Subject:** Coronation of Josef II **Obverse:** Crown above inscription **Reverse:** Coronation items on altar, all seeing eye above

Date	Mintage	F	VF	XF	Unc
1764	—	200	350	600	1,000

KM# 276 3/4 DUCAT

2.6250 g., 0.9860 Gold 0.0832 oz. AGW **Subject:** Coronation of Leopold II **Obverse:** Inscription **Reverse:** Coronation items

Date	Mintage	F	VF	XF	Unc
1790	—	150	275	400	650

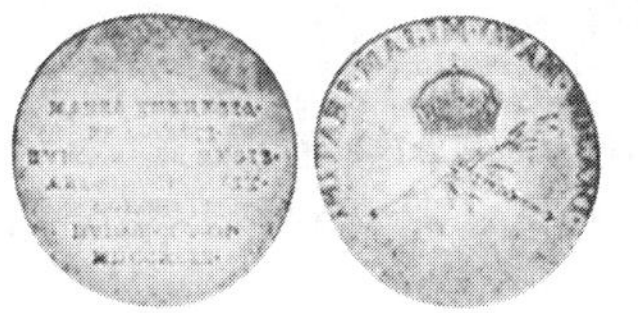

KM# 281 3/4 DUCAT

2.6250 g., 0.9860 Gold 0.0832 oz. AGW **Subject:** Coronation of Franz II **Obverse:** Inscription **Reverse:** Coronation items

Date	Mintage	F	VF	XF	Unc
1792	—	200	400	700	1,000

KM# 165 DUCAT

3.5000 g., 0.9860 Gold 0.1109 oz. AGW **Obverse:** Crowned eagle, head left, in oval baroque frame **Reverse:** 6-line inscription with date in oval baroque frame

Date	Mintage	VG	F	VF	XF	Unc
1704 IIF	—	350	550	1,000	1,750	—

KM# 166 DUCAT

3.5000 g., 0.9860 Gold 0.1109 oz. AGW **Obverse:** Crowned eagle, head left, in circle **Note:** Varieties exist.

Date	Mintage	VG	F	VF	XF	Unc
1705 IIF	—	400	600	1,200	2,000	—

KM# A172 DUCAT

3.5000 g., 0.9860 Gold 0.1109 oz. AGW **Obverse:** Crowned eagle, head left **Reverse:** Tower by sea

Date	Mintage	VG	F	VF	XF	Unc
1710 IF	—	450	800	1,500	2,500	—

KM# 172 DUCAT

3.5000 g., 0.9860 Gold 0.1109 oz. AGW **Obverse:** Crowned eagle within circle **Reverse:** Tower in sea during storm, all seeing eye above

Date	Mintage	VG	F	VF	XF	Unc
1710 IF	—	450	800	1,500	2,500	—
1711 IF	—	450	1,000	1,800	3,500	—

KM# 184 DUCAT

3.5000 g., 0.9860 Gold 0.1109 oz. AGW **Subject:** Bicentennial of the Reformation **Obverse:** Inscription **Reverse:** Open book atop rocks within sea, all seeing eye above

Date	Mintage	VG	F	VF	XF	Unc
1717 IIF	—	200	325	700	1,200	—

KM# 190.1 DUCAT

3.5000 g., 0.9860 Gold 0.1109 oz. AGW **Obverse:** Crowned eagle with head left in oval baroque frame **Reverse:** 6-line inscription with date in circle

Date	Mintage	VG	F	VF	XF	Unc
1725 IIF	—	250	400	850	1,500	—

KM# 190.2 DUCAT

3.5000 g., 0.9860 Gold 0.1109 oz. AGW **Obverse:** Crowned eagle within circle **Reverse:** Without flourish above text

Date	Mintage	VG	F	VF	XF	Unc
1742 EIK	—	200	350	750	1,350	—

KM# 196 DUCAT

3.5000 g., 0.9860 Gold 0.1109 oz. AGW **Subject:** Coronation of Karl VII **Obverse:** Laureate bust of Karl VII right **Reverse:** Bust of Maria Amalia right

Date	Mintage	VG	F	VF	XF	Unc
ND(1742) ILOE	—	125	225	500	950	—
ND(1742) OE	—	125	225	500	950	—
ND(1742) ILOE RW	—	125	225	500	950	—

KM# 197 DUCAT

3.5000 g., 0.9860 Gold 0.1109 oz. AGW **Subject:** Election fo Karl VII **Obverse:** Bust right **Reverse:** Open book with DECA/LOGVS on Ark of the Covenant

Date	Mintage	VG	F	VF	XF	Unc
1742	—	225	375	750	1,250	—

KM# 198 DUCAT

3.5000 g., 0.9860 Gold 0.1109 oz. AGW **Obverse:** Head of Carl VII right **Reverse:** Imperial crown, below ELECT. D. 24 IAN/1742 **Note:** Varieties exist.

Date	Mintage	VG	F	VF	XF	Unc
1742	—	300	650	1,350	2,000	—
1742 I.L. OE	—	300	650	1,350	2,000	—

KM# 199 DUCAT

3.5000 g., 0.9860 Gold 0.1109 oz. AGW **Subject:** Coronation of Karl VII **Obverse:** Crowned eagle within circle **Reverse:** Imperial crown above 7-line inscription with titles and date

Date	Mintage	VG	F	VF	XF	Unc
1742 EK	—	400	750	1,500	2,500	—

KM# 203 DUCAT

3.5000 g., 0.9860 Gold 0.1109 oz. AGW **Subject:** Election of Franz I as H.R. Emperor **Obverse:** Bust right **Reverse:** Royal regalia on draped table, date in exergue

Date	Mintage	VG	F	VF	XF	Unc
1745	—	125	250	550	950	—

KM# 204 DUCAT

3.5000 g., 0.9860 Gold 0.1109 oz. AGW **Subject:** Election of Franz I **Obverse:** Crowned eagle **Reverse:** 5-line inscription and date

Date	Mintage	VG	F	VF	XF	Unc
1745	—	125	225	500	900	—

KM# 206 DUCAT

3.5000 g., 0.9860 Gold 0.1109 oz. AGW **Obverse:** Crowned eagle, head left **Reverse:** 6-line inscription with date, initials

Date	Mintage	VG	F	VF	XF	Unc
1749 IIE	—	225	450	625	1,000	—

KM# 222 DUCAT

3.5000 g., 0.9860 Gold 0.1109 oz. AGW **Obverse:** Crown displayed eagle **Reverse:** Cross with ends joined by garlands

Date	Mintage	F	VF	XF	Unc
1762 IOT	—	400	800	1,500	2,500

KM# 237 DUCAT

3.5000 g., 0.9860 Gold 0.1109 oz. AGW **Subject:** Coronation of Josef II **Obverse:** Bust of Josef II **Reverse:** Peace standing over fallen knight (War)

Date	Mintage	F	VF	XF	Unc
1764	—	200	350	800	1,500

KM# 277 DUCAT

3.5000 g., 0.9860 Gold 0.1109 oz. AGW **Subject:** Coronation of Leopold II **Obverse:** Head right **Reverse:** Coronation items atop altar

Date	Mintage	F	VF	XF	Unc
1790	—	150	250	550	950

KM# 282 DUCAT

3.5000 g., 0.9860 Gold 0.1109 oz. AGW **Subject:** Coronation of Franz II **Obverse:** Head right **Reverse:** Radiant altar with coronation items on top

Date	Mintage	F	VF	XF	Unc
1792	—	200	350	800	1,750

KM# 283 DUCAT

3.5000 g., 0.9860 Gold 0.1109 oz. AGW **Obverse:** Bust of Franz II **Reverse:** 2 standing figures

Date	Mintage	F	VF	XF	Unc
ND(1792)	—	400	800	1,250	2,250

KM# 289 DUCAT

3.5000 g., 0.9860 Gold 0.1109 oz. AGW **Subject:** Contribution Ducat - French Revolutionary Army **Obverse:** Inscription within laurel wreath **Reverse:** City view

Date	Mintage	F	VF	XF	Unc
1796	—	150	275	450	750

KM# 290 DUCAT

3.5000 g., 0.9860 Gold 0.1109 oz. AGW **Obverse:** Inscription within laurel wreath **Reverse:** City view

Date	Mintage	F	VF	XF	Unc
1796	—	85.00	145	275	550

KM# 177 1-1/4 DUCAT

4.3750 g., 0.9860 Gold 0.1387 oz. AGW **Subject:** Coronation of Karl VI **Obverse:** Globe in circle of clouds **Reverse:** Crown above 7-line inscription and date

Date	Mintage	VG	F	VF	XF	Unc
1711	—	100	200	400	600	—

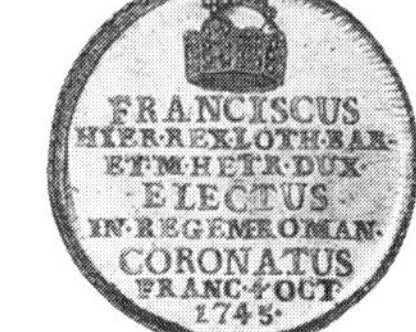

KM# 205 1-1/4 DUCAT

4.3750 g., 0.9860 Gold 0.1387 oz. AGW **Subject:** Coronation of Franz I **Obverse:** Crown above inscription **Reverse:** Coronation items on altar, all seeing eye above

Date	Mintage	VG	F	VF	XF	Unc
1745	—	150	250	450	700	—

KM# 284 1-1/4 DUCAT
4.3750 g., 0.9860 Gold 0.1387 oz. AGW **Subject:** Coronation of Franz II **Obverse:** Regal insignia **Reverse:** 8-line inscription

Date	Mintage	F	VF	XF	Unc
1792	—	225	400	700	1,400

KM# 238 1-1/2 DUCAT
5.2500 g., 0.9860 Gold 0.1664 oz. AGW **Subject:** Coronation of Josef II **Obverse:** Crown above 9-line inscription **Reverse:** Globe with coronation items on top

Date	Mintage	F	VF	XF	Unc
1764	—	200	400	600	1,250

KM# 278 1-1/2 DUCAT
5.2500 g., 0.9860 Gold 0.1664 oz. AGW **Subject:** Coronation of Leopold II **Obverse:** Coronation items **Reverse:** Inscription

Date	Mintage	F	VF	XF	Unc
1790	—	200	350	550	1,000

KM# 167 2 DUCAT
7.0000 g., 0.9860 Gold 0.2219 oz. AGW **Obverse:** Crowned displayed eagle divides date in inner circle **Reverse:** Storm above city, all-seeing eye at top

Date	Mintage	VG	F	VF	XF	Unc
1705	—	400	1,000	2,500	4,000	—
1710	—	400	1,000	2,500	4,000	—

KM# 173 2 DUCAT
7.0000 g., 0.9860 Gold 0.2219 oz. AGW **Obverse:** Crowned eagle within circle **Reverse:** Tower in sea during storm

Date	Mintage	VG	F	VF	XF	Unc
1710	—	450	1,000	2,500	4,000	—

KM# 178 2 DUCAT
7.0000 g., 0.9860 Gold 0.2219 oz. AGW **Subject:** Coronation of Karl VI **Obverse:** Inscription **Reverse:** City of Sachsenhausen

Date	Mintage	VG	F	VF	XF	Unc
1711	—	400	800	1,500	2,500	—

KM# 200 2 DUCAT
7.0000 g., 0.9860 Gold 0.2219 oz. AGW **Subject:** Coronation of Karl VII **Obverse:** Bust right **Reverse:** Standing figure with arms at right, altar at left

Date	Mintage	VG	F	VF	XF	Unc
1742	—	350	700	1,250	2,200	—

KM# 239 2 DUCAT
7.0000 g., 0.9860 Gold 0.2219 oz. AGW **Subject:** Coronation of Josef II **Obverse:** Bust of Josef II **Reverse:** Peace standing above fallen knight (War)

Date	Mintage	F	VF	XF	Unc
1764	—	650	1,500	2,500	4,000

KM# 279 2 DUCAT
7.0000 g., 0.9860 Gold 0.2219 oz. AGW **Subject:** Coronation of Leopold II **Obverse:** Head of Leopold II **Reverse:** Altar

Date	Mintage	F	VF	XF	Unc
1790	—	300	600	1,200	2,000

KM# 285 2 DUCAT
7.0000 g., 0.9860 Gold 0.2219 oz. AGW **Subject:** Coronation of Franz II **Obverse:** Head of Franz II **Reverse:** Figure at altar

Date	Mintage	F	VF	XF	Unc
1792	—	500	1,250	2,000	3,000

KM# 201 4 DUCAT
14.0000 g., 0.9860 Gold 0.4438 oz. AGW **Subject:** Coronation of Karl VII **Obverse:** Laureate bust of Karl VII right **Reverse:** Standing female figure with altar left, date in exergue

Date	Mintage	VG	F	VF	XF	Unc
1742 Rare	—	—	—	—	—	—

PATTERNS

Including off metal strikes

KM#	Date	Mintage	Identification	Mkt Val
Pn19	1710	—	Turnosgroshen. Gold. . Klippe, KM#170.	—
Pn20	1711	—	3/4 Ducat. Silver. KM#176, Karl VI.	75.00
Pn21	1711	—	1-1/4 Ducat. Silver. KM#177, Karl VI.	70.00
PnA22	1742	—	Ducat. Silver. KM#196, Karl VII.	150
Pn22	1742	—	Ducat. Silver. KM#197, Karl VII.	135
Pn23	1742	—	Ducat. Silver. KM#198.	150
Pn24	1742	—	Ducat. Silver. KM#198.	150
Pn25	1742	—	Ducat. Silver. KM#199, Karl VII.	225
Pn26	1742	—	2 Ducat. Silver. KM#200.	100
Pn27	1745	—	3/4 Ducat. Silver KM#202, Franz I.	75.00
Pn28	1745	—	3/4 Ducat. Copper. KM#202, Franz I.	60.00
Pn29	1745	—	Ducat. Silver. KM#203, Franz I.	150
Pn30	1745	—	Ducat. Bronze. KM#203.	125
Pn31	1745	—	1-1/4 Ducat. Silver. KM#205, Franz I.	70.00
Pn32	1749	—	Ducat. Copper. KM#206.	150
Pn33	1764	—	3/4 Ducat. Silver. KM#236, Josef II.	65.00
Pn34	1764	—	Ducat. Silver. KM#237, Josef II.	65.00
Pn35	1764	—	1-1/2 Ducat. Silver. KM#238, Josef II.	70.00
Pn36	1764	—	2 Ducat. Silver. KM#239, Josef II.	75.00
Pn37	1765	—	1/4 Kreuzer. Gold. KM#240.	—
Pn38	1773	—	Kreuzer. Gold. Crowned displayed eagle. KM#254.	—

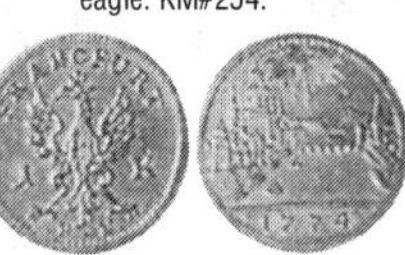

KM#	Date	Mintage	Identification	Mkt Val
Pn40	1774	—	Kreuzer. Gold. KM#253.	—
Pn39	1774	—	Heller. Silver. KM#247.	85.00
PnA40	1774	—	Kreuzer. Gold. KM#228.1.	300
Pn41	1790	—	3/4 Ducat. Silver. KM#276, Leopold II.	65.00
Pn42	1790	—	Ducat. Silver. . KM#277, Leopold II.	65.00
Pn43	1790	—	1-1/2 Ducat. Silver. KM#278, Leopold II.	70.00
Pn44	1790	—	2 Ducat. Silver. KM#279, Leopold II.	75.00
PnA45	1792	—	3/4 Ducat. Silver. KM#281, Franz II.	185
Pn45	1792	—	Ducat. Silver. KM#282, Franz II.	65.00
Pn46	1792	—	1-1/2 Ducat. Silver. KM#284, Franz II.	70.00
Pn47	1792	—	2 Ducat. Silver. KM#285, Franz II.	100

FREIBURG IM BREISGAU

CITY

Located in Baden about 35 miles north of Basel and east of the Rhine, Freiburg was a free city in the early 12th century. A century later the city lost its free status when it fell to the counts of Urach. In 1368, Freiburg became a Hapsburg possession and it remained so until 1803. In 1805 the city was united to Baden. Freiburg struck coins from the 14th century until 1739. As a member of the Rappenmünzbund from 1387 until 1584, Freiburg struck coins in accordance with the provisions of that monetary union of South German and Swiss entities.

ARMS

Raven's head, usually turned to the left.

REGULAR COINAGE

KM# 60 KREUZER
Silver **Obverse:** Raven's head left in shield, 1 below, date in legend **Reverse:** Cross in shield **Rev. Legend:** GLORIA IN..

Date	Mintage	VG	F	VF	XF	Unc
1706	—	12.00	25.00	50.00	90.00	—
1707	—	12.00	25.00	50.00	90.00	—

KM# 65 KREUZER
Silver **Obverse:** Raven's head left in oval cartouche, I below, date in legend **Reverse:** Cross in shield in round cartouche **Rev. Legend:** GLORIA IN..

Date	Mintage	VG	F	VF	XF	Unc
1710	—	12.00	25.00	50.00	90.00	—
1736	—	12.00	25.00	50.00	90.00	—

KM# 66 KREUZER
Silver **Obverse:** Raven's head right

Date	Mintage	VG	F	VF	XF	Unc
1710	—	18.00	30.00	65.00	100	—

KM# 70 KREUZER
Silver **Obverse:** Raven's head left in circle, 1 above, K below, date in legend **Reverse:** Cross in ornamented shield in circle **Rev. Legend:** GLORIA IN..

Date	Mintage	VG	F	VF	XF	Unc
1712	—	10.00	20.00	40.00	75.00	—
1713	—	10.00	20.00	40.00	75.00	—

KM# 73 KREUZER
Silver **Obverse:** Raven's head, date in legend **Reverse:** Cross in shield, 1 above, K. below

Date	Mintage	VG	F	VF	XF	Unc
1713	—	15.00	30.00	60.00	95.00	—

KM# 75 KREUZER
Silver **Obverse:** Raven's head left **Reverse:** Arms within branches **Note:** Similar to KM#70 but branches around arms on reverse.

Date	Mintage	VG	F	VF	XF	Unc
1714	—	10.00	20.00	40.00	75.00	—
1715	—	10.00	20.00	40.00	75.00	—

KM# 77 KREUZER
Silver **Obverse:** Raven's head left **Reverse:** Arms **Note:** Similar to KM#70 without circles around obverse and reverse centers.

Date	Mintage	VG	F	VF	XF	Unc
1715	—	10.00	20.00	40.00	75.00	—

KM# 92 KREUZER
Silver **Obverse:** Raven's head divides date, 1 above, K below **Reverse:** Cross in ornamented shield

Date	Mintage	VG	F	VF	XF	Unc
1722	—	15.00	30.00	60.00	95.00	—
1728	—	15.00	30.00	60.00	95.00	—
1731	—	15.00	30.00	60.00	95.00	—

KM# 95 KREUZER
Silver **Obverse:** Raven's head in oval cartouche, date above, 1K in oval below **Reverse:** Eagle **Rev. Legend:** DA.PAC.DO..

Date	Mintage	VG	F	VF	XF	Unc
1725	—	15.00	30.00	60.00	95.00	—

KM# 106 KREUZER
Silver **Obverse:** Arms divide 1 - K, date in legend **Reverse:** Eagle **Rev. Legend:** GLORIA IN..

Date	Mintage	VG	F	VF	XF	Unc
1733	—	10.00	20.00	40.00	65.00	—

KM# 67 2 KREUZER
Silver **Obverse:** Raven's head divides date in cartouche, 2 above, K below **Reverse:** Crowned eagle in circle

Date	Mintage	VG	F	VF	XF	Unc
1711	—	8.00	15.00	30.00	55.00	—

KM# 71 2 KREUZER
Silver **Reverse:** Eagle in circle without crown

Date	Mintage	VG	F	VF	XF	Unc
1712	—	12.00	25.00	50.00	85.00	—

Date	Mintage	VG	F	VF	XF	Unc
1713	—	12.00	25.00	50.00	85.00	—

KM# 78 2 KREUZER

Silver **Obverse:** Raven's head in cartouche, 2 above, K below, date in legend **Reverse:** Eagle, arabesque above head **Rev. Legend:** DA. PACEM..

Date	Mintage	VG	F	VF	XF	Unc
1715	—	10.00	20.00	40.00	75.00	—

KM# 79 2 KREUZER

Silver **Obverse:** Raven's head, 2 above, K below, date in legend **Reverse:** Eagle **Rev. Legend:** DA.PAC..

Date	Mintage	VG	F	VF	XF	Unc
1715	—	15.00	30.00	60.00	95.00	—
1716	—	15.00	30.00	60.00	95.00	—
1719	—	15.00	30.00	60.00	95.00	—

KM# 90 2 KREUZER

Silver **Obverse:** Raven's head in oval cartouche, date above, 2 K. in oval below

Date	Mintage	VG	F	VF	XF	Unc
1720	—	12.00	25.00	50.00	85.00	—
1721	—	12.00	25.00	50.00	85.00	—
1723	—	12.00	25.00	50.00	85.00	—

KM# 93 2 KREUZER

Silver **Obverse:** Raven's head divides date, 1 above, K below **Reverse:** Cross in ornamented shield

Date	Mintage	VG	F	VF	XF	Unc
1722	—	15.00	30.00	60.00	95.00	—

KM# 99 2 KREUZER

Silver **Obverse:** Raven's head divides date **Reverse:** Cross in shield **Rev. Legend:** DA PACEM..

Date	Mintage	VG	F	VF	XF	Unc
1729	—	15.00	30.00	60.00	95.00	—
1732	—	15.00	30.00	60.00	95.00	—

KM# 100 2 KREUZER

Silver **Obverse:** Raven's head divides 2 - K, date in legend **Reverse:** Cross on shield

Date	Mintage	VG	F	VF	XF	Unc
1729	—	15.00	30.00	60.00	95.00	—
1732	—	15.00	30.00	60.00	95.00	—
1735	—	15.00	30.00	60.00	95.00	—

KM# 105 2 KREUZER

Silver **Obverse:** Raven's head in cartouche with 2 above, K below

Date	Mintage	VG	F	VF	XF	Unc
1732	—	15.00	30.00	60.00	95.00	—

KM# 96 3 KREUZER (Groschen)

Silver **Obverse:** Raven's head divides date, 3 above, K below **Reverse:** Cross in shield **Rev. Legend:** DA.PACE..

Date	Mintage	VG	F	VF	XF	Unc
1726	—	15.00	30.00	60.00	95.00	—
1727	—	15.00	30.00	60.00	95.00	—

KM# 82 5 KREUZER

Silver **Obverse:** Raven's head in oval baroque frame, angel's head above, date in legend **Reverse:** Eagle, 5 above, KR below **Rev. Legend:** DOMINE CONSER..

Date	Mintage	VG	F	VF	XF	Unc
1717	—	—	—	—	—	—

KM# 107 5 KREUZER

Silver **Obverse:** Cross in oval cartouche, date above, V. K in oval below **Reverse:** Austrian arms in oval cartouche

Date	Mintage	VG	F	VF	XF	Unc
1733	—	15.00	30.00	60.00	145	—

KM# 80 10 KREUZER

Silver **Obverse:** Raven's head in oval baroque frame, angel's head above, date in legend **Reverse:** Eagle 10 above, KR below **Rev. Legend:** DOMINE CONSER..

Date	Mintage	VG	F	VF	XF	Unc
1716	—	—	—	—	—	—
1717	—	—	—	—	—	—
1718	—	—	—	—	—	—

KM# 110 10 KREUZER

Silver **Obverse:** 2 oval arms in baroque frame **Reverse:** Date in cartouche **Rev. Legend:** X/KREV/ZER

Date	Mintage	VG	F	VF	XF	Unc
1735	—	65.00	125	225	375	—

KM# 81 20 KREUZER

Silver **Obverse:** Raven's head in oval baroque frame, angel's head above, date in legend **Reverse:** Eagle, 20 above, KR below **Rev. Legend:** DOMINE CONSER..

Date	Mintage	VG	F	VF	XF	Unc
1716	—	475	850	1,600	2,250	—
ND	—	475	850	1,600	2,250	—

KM# 55 THALER

Silver **Obverse:** Raven's head left in oval baroque frame, angel's head above **Note:** Dav. #2230.

Date	Mintage	VG	F	VF	XF	Unc
ND Rare	—	—	—	—	—	—

KM# 68.1 THALER

Silver **Obverse:** City view, inscription and date below **Reverse:** Eagle with sword and 2 oval city arms on pedestal, large crown above **Note:** Dav. #2232.

Date	Mintage	VG	F	VF	XF	Unc
1711	—	850	1,600	2,500	3,750	—

KM# 68.2 THALER

Silver **Obverse:** City view, inscription and date below **Reverse:** Smaller crown above eagle **Note:** Dav. #2232A.

Date	Mintage	VG	F	VF	XF	Unc
1711	—	850	1,650	2,550	4,000	—

KM# 74 THALER

Silver **Obverse:** City view, inscription and date in cartouche below **Reverse:** Eagle with 2 swords and 2 oval city arms, crown above, branches below **Note:** Dav. #2233.

Date	Mintage	VG	F	VF	XF	Unc
1713	—	1,350	2,500	4,000	6,000	—

KM# 76 THALER

Silver **Subject:** Peace of Baden **Obv. Legend:** SVB VMBRA ALA - RVMTVARVM **Reverse:** City view, PAX in cartouche below **Rev. Legend:** CIVITAS • AC • MVNIMENTVM • / FRIBVRGEN • BRISGOICVM • **Note:** Dav. #2234.

Date	Mintage	VG	F	VF	XF	Unc
ND(1714)	—	850	1,650	2,550	4,000	—

KM# 83 THALER

Silver **Obverse:** Raven's head in oval baroque frame, eagle with wings extended above, date in legend **Reverse:** Round cross in shield arms in baroque frame, angel's head above **Note:** Dav. #--.

Date	Mintage	VG	F	VF	XF	Unc
1717	—	—	—	—	—	—

KM# 91 THALER

Silver **Obverse:** Raven's head in oval baroque frame, angel's head above **Reverse:** Eagle, head left **Note:** Dav. #--.

Date	Mintage	VG	F	VF	XF	Unc
ND(1720)	—	—	—	—	—	—

KM# 94 THALER

Silver **Obverse:** Raven's head within oval baroque frame **Obv. Legend:** MON • NO • FRIBVRG - EN • BRISGOIAE 1723 • **Reverse:** Eagle **Rev. Legend:** DA • PACEM • DOMINE - IN DIEB • NOSTRIS • **Note:** Dav. #2236.

Date	Mintage	VG	F	VF	XF	Unc
1723 Rare	—	—	—	—	—	—

KM# 97 THALER

Silver **Obverse:** Raven's head within ornate cartouche **Obv. Legend:** MON • NOVA • FRI - BVRG • BRISGOIAE **Reverse:** Eagle with sword and sceptre **Rev. Legend:** DA • PACEM • KOMINE • - • IN • DIEB • NOSTRIS **Note:** Dav. #2237.

Date	Mintage	VG	F	VF	XF	Unc
1726	—	950	1,750	3,000	5,000	—

KM# 98 THALER

Silver **Reverse:** Cross in baroque frame, angel's head above **Note:** Dav. #2238.

Date	Mintage	VG	F	VF	XF	Unc
1726	—	950	1,750	3,000	5,000	—

KM# 108 THALER

Silver **Obverse:** Raven's head divides date **Note:** Dav. #2239.

Date	Mintage	VG	F	VF	XF	Unc
1733 Rare	—	—	—	—	—	—

KM# 109 THALER

Silver **Reverse:** Eagle with head left, crown above **Note:** Dav. #2240.

Date	Mintage	VG	F	VF	XF	Unc
1733 Rare	—	—	—	—	—	—

KM# 111 THALER

Silver **Obverse:** Date in chronogram **Obv. Legend:** LaMbertI aLeXanDrIqVe / aVXILIo fLorebIt (all capitals), in exergue: FRIBVRGVM/BRISGOIAE **Reverse:** Two saints with arms **Rev. Legend:** S. LAMBERTVS - S. ALEXANDER, below: PROTECTORES CIVIT: FRIBVRG BRISG: **Note:** Dav. #2241.

Date	Mintage	VG	F	VF	XF	Unc
1735 Rare	—	—	—	—	—	—

KM# 112 THALER

Silver **Obverse:** City view **Obv. Legend:** LAMBERTI ALEXANDRIQUE/AVXILIO FLOREBIT, below: FRIBVRGVM/ BRISGOIAE **Reverse:** Saints face forward, date above **Rev. Legend:** S. LANBERTVS - S. ALEXANDER, below: PROTECTORES CIVIT: FRIBVRG BRISG: **Note:** Dav. #2245.

Date	Mintage	VG	F	VF	XF	Unc
1737	—	450	900	1,750	3,250	—
1739	—	450	900	1,750	3,250	—

KM# 113 THALER

Silver **Obverse:** Raven's head within baroque frame **Obv. Legend:** • MON NOVA • FRIB - FRG • BRISGOIAE **Reverse:** Eagle with sword and sceptre, arms on breast **Rev. Legend:** • DA • PACEM • DOMINE - IN • DIEB • NOSTRIS • **Note:** Dav. #2244.

Date	Mintage	VG	F	VF	XF	Unc
1738	—	850	1,600	2,500	4,250	—

KM# 69 2 THALER

Silver **Obverse:** City view, inscription and date below **Reverse:** Eagle with sword and 2 oval city arms on pedestal with large crown above **Note:** Dav. #2231.

Date	Mintage	VG	F	VF	XF	Unc
1711 Rare	—	—	—	—	—	—

KM# 114 2 THALER

Silver **Obverse:** Raven's head left in baroque frame, date divided below **Reverse:** Eagle with head left with large crown above, cross in shield on breast **Note:** Dav. #2243.

Date	Mintage	VG	F	VF	XF	Unc
1738	—	1,000	2,000	3,500	6,500	—

TRADE COINAGE

KM# 72 DUCAT

3.5000 g., 0.9860 Gold 0.1109 oz. AGW **Obverse:** City view, 1 and date divided below **Reverse:** St. Leopold standing

Date	Mintage	VG	F	VF	XF	Unc
1712 Rare	—	—	—	—	—	—

KM# 84 DUCAT

3.5000 g., 0.9860 Gold 0.1109 oz. AGW **Obverse:** Large crown above eagle with head right, two shields of arms **Reverse:** City view above date

Date	Mintage	VG	F	VF	XF	Unc
1717	—	800	1,600	3,250	5,500	—

KM# 115 6 DUCAT

21.0000 g., 0.9860 Gold 0.6657 oz. AGW **Obverse:** City view **Reverse:** Two standing figures with shields **Note:** Struck with 1 Thaler dies, KM#112.

Date	Mintage	VG	F	VF	XF	Unc
1739	—	—	—	13,500	20,000	—

FREISING

BISHOPRIC

A Bishopric located in central Bavaria, was founded in 724. It became the site of an Imperial Mint in the 11th century. Bracteates of the bishops appeared c. 1150. The bishops were made princes of the empire in the 17th century. It became secularized in 1802 with part of the territories going to Bavaria and the rest to Salzburg.

RULERS

Johann Franz Eckher Freiherr von Kapfing, 1695-1727
Johann Theodor von Bayern, 1727-1763
Clemens Wenzel von Sachsen, 1763-1768
Ludwig Joseph, Freiherr von Welden, 1769-1788
Josef Conrad, 1790-1803

MINT OFFICIALS' INITIALS

Initials	Date	Name
CM	1724-60	Christian Ernst Muller, medailleur in Augsburg
K, KORNLEIN	1758-1801	Johann Nikolaus Kornlein, medailleur in Regensburg
*, PHM	Ca.1685-1719	Philipp Heinrich Müller, medailleur in Augsburg

REGULAR COINAGE

KM# 15 THALER

Silver **Ruler:** Johann Franz **Subject:** Johann Franz **Obverse:** Armored bust right **Obv. Legend:** IOANNES FRANCIS, D: G: EPISCOP, FRISING **Reverse:** Helmeted and mitred four-fold arms, date in legend **Rev. Legend:** * SAC: ROM: IMP: - PRINCEPS * 1709 * **Note:** Dav. #2247.

Date	Mintage	F	VF	XF	Unc
1709	—	350	550	950	1,600

KM# 32 THALER

Silver **Ruler:** Josef Conrad **Obverse:** Draped bust right **Obv. Legend:** * IOS • CONR • D • G • EP • FRISING • & RATISB • PRAEP • BERCHTESG • S • R • I • PRINC • **Reverse:** Crowned complex multi-arms within crowned mantle **Rev. Legend:** * X • EINE FEINE MARK * **Note:** Convention Thaler. Dav. #2248.

Date	Mintage	VG	F	VF	XF	Unc
1790 K	—	150	300	500	850	—

KM# 33 THALER

Silver **Ruler:** Josef Conrad **Obverse:** Draped bust right **Obv. Legend:** * IOS • CONR • D • G • EP • FRISING • & RATISB • PRAEP • BERCHTESG • S • R • I • PRINC • **Reverse:** Crowned complex multi-arms within crowned mantle **Rev. Legend:** * X • EINE FEINE MARK * **Note:** Dav. #2249.

Date	Mintage	VG	F	VF	XF	Unc
ND(1790) KORNLEIN	—	150	300	500	850	—

TRADE COINAGE

KM# 25 DUCAT

3.5000 g., 0.9860 Gold 0.1109 oz. AGW **Ruler:** Johann Theodor **Obverse:** Bust left **Reverse:** Crowned arms

Date	Mintage	VG	F	VF	XF	Unc
1749	—	750	1,500	3,000	5,500	—

KM# 30 DUCAT

3.5000 g., 0.9860 Gold 0.1109 oz. AGW **Ruler:** Clemens Wenzel **Obverse:** Clemens Wenzel **Reverse:** Mitre above crowned complex arms

Date	Mintage	VG	F	VF	XF	Unc
1765	—	500	1,000	2,000	4,000	—

KM# 31 DUCAT

3.5000 g., 0.9860 Gold 0.1109 oz. AGW **Ruler:** Clemens Wenzel **Reverse:** Crowned arms

Date	Mintage	VG	F	VF	XF	Unc
1766	—	550	1,150	2,250	4,500	—

KM# 20 2 DUCAT

7.0000 g., 0.9860 Gold 0.2219 oz. AGW **Ruler:** Johann Franz **Obverse:** Crowned arms in inner circle **Reverse:** St. Corbinianus in inner circle

Date	Mintage	VG	F	VF	XF	Unc
1724 CM Rare	100	—	—	—	—	—

FRIEDBERG

BURGRAVESHIP

The fortified town of Friedberg, located in Hesse about 15 miles (25 kilometers) north of Frankfurt am Main, dates from Roman times. It attained free status in 1211 and was the site of an imperial mint until the mid-13th century. In 1349 Friedberg passed to the countship of Schwarzburg, losing its free status shortly thereafter. Local nobles began electing one among themselves to the office of burgrave-for-life. The burgraves obtained the mint right in 1541 and recognized only the emperor as overlord. In 1802 Friedberg passed in fief to Hesse-Darmstadt and was mediatized in 1818.

RULERS

Adolf Johann Karl von Bettendorf, 1700-1705
Johann V Löw von Steinfurt, 1706-1710
Johann Erwin von Greiffenklau-Vollraths, 1710-1727
Hermann II von Riedesel zu Lauterbach, 1727-1745
Johann Eitel II von Diede zu Fürstenstein, 1745-1748
Ernst Ludwig von Breidenbach zu Breidenstein, 1749-1755
Franz Heinrich von Dalberg, 1755-1776
Johann Maria Rudolph von Waldbott-Bassenheim, 1777-1805

MINT OFFICIALS' INITIALS

Initials	Date	Name
CPS	1729-51	Christian Phillip Spangenberg, coinage director in Clausthal
GB(F)GH	1790-1833	Johann Georg Bunsen in Frankfurt
	1798-1816	Georg Hille, warden in Frankfurt
S(N)R	1760-74	Siegmund Scholz, warden in Nüremberg
	1764-93	Georg Nikolaus Riedner in Nüremberg
VBW	1684-1688, 1702-14	Ulrich Burkhard Willerding in Mainz

REGULAR COINAGE

KM# 70 20 KREUZER

Silver **Ruler:** Franz Heinrich **Obverse:** Towers on pedestal with value, laurel branch at left, palm branch at right **Reverse:** Crowned double-headed eagle with two shields below and one on breast

Date	Mintage	F	VF	XF	Unc
1766 S(N)R	—	50.00	100	200	350

KM# 71 1/2 THALER

Silver **Ruler:** Franz Heinrich **Obverse:** Crowned double-headed eagle with two shields below and one on breast **Reverse:** St. George standing on dragon, shields at left and right

Date	Mintage	F	VF	XF	Unc
1766 S(N)R	—	100	150	250	500

KM# 65 2/3 THALER (60 Kreuzer)

Silver **Ruler:** Johann Eitel II **Obverse:** Crowned double-headed eagle with two shields below and one on breast **Reverse:** St. George standing on dragon, shields at left and right

Date	Mintage	VG	F	VF	XF	Unc
1747 CPS	—	60.00	100	150	285	—

KM# 66 THALER

Silver **Ruler:** Johann Eitel II **Obverse:** Titles of Francis I **Obv. Legend:** MONETA CASTRI - IMP. FRIDBERG. **Rev. Legend:** FRANCISCVS • - D • G • - ROM - • IMP • S • A •, inner row: NACH DEM - REICHS FVS• **Note:** Dav. #2250.

Date	Mintage	F	VF	XF	Unc
1747 CPS	—	350	550	900	1,650

KM# 72 THALER

Silver **Ruler:** Franz Heinrich **Obverse:** Crowned double-headed eagle with two shields below and one on breast **Obv. Legend:** MONETA - NOVA CASTRI IMP • FRIDBERG • IN - WETTER •, in exergue: X EINE FEINE MARK •/S• (N) R• **Reverse:** St. George on horseback slaying the dragon, shields at left and right **Rev. Legend:** IOSEPHUS II • - D • G • - ROM • - IMP • S • A • 1766 •, inner row: AD NORM • - CONVENT • **Note:** Dav. #2251.

Date	Mintage	F	VF	XF	Unc
1766 S(N)R	—	400	675	1,000	1,750

FUGGER

A wealthy banking and commercial family of Augsburg, which first came into prominence about 1370 and became the bankers of the Hapsburgs by 1475. In 1500 they were given the county of Kirchberg and the lordship of Weissenborn (in Swabia) as security for a loan. The emperor made them hereditary counts of these areas and gave them the mint right in 1534. There was a complicated succession with many lines and few coin issuers. The land was mediatized to Bavaria and Württemberg in 1806.

RULERS

Cajetan zu Zinnenberg, (Elder line), 1751-91 and
Carl zu Nordendorf, (Younger line), 1710-84

FAMILY ARMS

2 lilies on adjacent fields

COUNTY

JOINT COINAGE

KM# 1 THALER

Silver **Ruler:** Cajetan zu Zinnenberg, (elder line) and Carl zu Nordendorf, (Younger line) **Obverse:** Helmeted four-fold arms **Obv. Legend:** * CAI • & CAR • COM • DE FVGGER • IN ZIN • & NORN • SEN • & ADM • FAM • **Reverse:** Titles of Josef II **Rev. Legend:** IOSEPH • II • ROM • IMP • - SEMPER AVGVST • **Note:** Dav. #2252.

Date	Mintage	Good	VG	F	VF	XF
1781	—	—	375	650	1,000	2,000

FUGGER-PFIRT

DUCHY

JOINT COINAGE

KM# 1 THALER

Silver **Obverse:** Titles of Josef II **Note:** Dav #2252.

Date	Mintage	VG	F	VF	XF	Unc
1781	—	375	650	1,000	2,000	—

FULDA

ABBEY

Located in central Germany, the abbey was founded in 744. The abbot became prince of the empire in the late 10th century. The first coins were struck in the 11th century. It became a bishopric in 1752 and in 1803, Fulda was secularized and passed successively to Orange-Nassau, Westphalia, Hesse-Cassel and Prussia.

RULERS

Adalbert I von Schleifras, 1700-1714
Konstantin von Buttlar, 1714-1726
Adolph von Dalberg, 1726-1737
Amandus Freiherr von Buseck, 1737-1756
as Bishop, 1752
Adalbert II von Walderdorf, 1757-1759
Heinrich VIII Freiherr von Bibra, ...1759-1788
Sede Vacante, 1788
Adalbert III von Harstall, 1788-1803

MINT OFFICIALS' INITIALS

Initials	Date	Name
D, IND, ND	1727-64	Nicolaus Dittmar
HM	1765-70	Heinrich Meidinger, director
ICK, K	1706-42	Johann Christian Koch, die-cutter in Gotha
IFM	1758-69	Johann Friedrich Müller, die-cutter in Bayreuth
PPW	(d.1771)	Peter Paul Werner, die-cutter in Nüremberg
VH	1765-96	Von Hoven

ARMS

Plain cross, sometimes in shield divided vertically with 3 long-stemmed flowers of cathedral chapter.

REGULAR COINAGE

KM# 105 2 HELLER

Copper **Ruler:** Adalbert II **Obverse:** Crowned AEF script monogram **Reverse:** FFLM, value, date

Date	Mintage	VG	F	VF	XF	Unc
1759	—	5.00	10.00	15.00	30.00	—

KM# 45 PFENNIG

Billon **Ruler:** Konstantin **Obverse:** Crowned oval 2-fold arms of Fulda and Buttlar **Reverse:** Date in wreath **Rev. Legend:** I/PFEN/NING

Date	Mintage	VG	F	VF	XF	Unc
1723	—	15.00	30.00	60.00	100	—
1724	—	15.00	30.00	60.00	100	—
1726	—	15.00	30.00	60.00	100	—

KM# 47 PFENNIG

Billon **Ruler:** Konstantin **Rev. Legend:** PFEN/NIGE

Date	Mintage	VG	F	VF	XF	Unc
1724	—	7.00	15.00	30.00	65.00	—

KM# 60 PFENNIG

Billon **Ruler:** Adolph **Obverse:** Crowned round arms in cartouche **Reverse:** Date in wreath **Rev. Legend:** 1/PFEN/NING

Date	Mintage	VG	F	VF	XF	Unc
1726	—	5.00	10.00	12.00	28.00	—
1727	—	5.00	10.00	12.00	28.00	—

KM# 85 PFENNIG

Billon **Ruler:** Amandus Freiherr **Obverse:** Crowned round ornamented arms **Reverse:** Value, date

Date	Mintage	VG	F	VF	XF	Unc
1737	—	6.00	12.00	22.00	50.00	—
1738	—	6.00	12.00	22.00	50.00	—
1739	—	6.00	12.00	22.00	50.00	—
1744	—	9.00	18.00	35.00	75.00	—
1745	—	6.00	12.00	22.00	50.00	—
1746	—	6.00	12.00	22.00	50.00	—
1747	—	6.00	12.00	22.00	50.00	—
1748	—	6.00	12.00	22.00	50.00	—
1749	—	6.00	12.00	22.00	50.00	—

KM# 134 PFENNIG

Copper **Ruler:** Heinrich VIII **Obverse:** Crowned HEF monogram **Reverse:** Value and date

Date	Mintage	VG	F	VF	XF	Unc
1769	—	5.00	10.00	20.00	42.00	—

KM# 135 2 PFENNIG

Billon **Ruler:** Heinrich VIII **Obverse:** Crowned HEF monogram **Reverse:** Value and date

Date	Mintage	VG	F	VF	XF	Unc
1769	—	5.00	10.00	20.00	42.00	—

KM# 48 3 PFENNIG

Billon **Ruler:** Konstantin **Obverse:** Crowned oval 2-fold arms of Fulda and Buttlar **Reverse:** Date in wreath **Rev. Legend:** III/PFEN/NING

Date	Mintage	VG	F	VF	XF	Unc
1724	—	6.00	12.00	22.00	45.00	—

KM# 106 3 PFENNIG

Billon **Ruler:** Adalbert II **Obverse:** Crowned monogram **Reverse:** Value within orb **Note:** Simiilar to 6 Pfennig, KM#102 but with 3 in orb.

Date	Mintage	VG	F	VF	XF	Unc
1759 Rare	—	—	—	—	—	—

KM# 49 4 PFENNIG

Silver **Ruler:** Konstantin **Obverse:** Crowned round arms **Reverse:** Value, date

Date	Mintage	VG	F	VF	XF	Unc
1724	—	7.00	12.00	20.00	45.00	—
1725	—	7.00	12.00	20.00	45.00	—

KM# 61 4 PFENNIG

Silver **Ruler:** Adolph **Obverse:** Crowned round ornate arms **Reverse:** Value and date within branches **Note:** Similar to 1 Pfennig KM#60, but value IIII.

Date	Mintage	VG	F	VF	XF	Unc
1726	—	20.00	40.00	75.00	125	—
1727	—	20.00	40.00	75.00	125	—
1728	—	20.00	40.00	75.00	125	—
1729	—	20.00	40.00	75.00	125	—

KM# 124 4 PFENNIG

Billon **Ruler:** Heinrich VIII **Obverse:** Crowned arms **Reverse:** Value and date

Date	Mintage	VG	F	VF	XF	Unc
1763	—	5.00	10.00	25.00	50.00	—

KM# 50 6 PFENNIG

Silver **Ruler:** Konstantin **Obverse:** Crowned round arms **Reverse:** Value and date within branches **Note:** Similar to 4 Pfennig KM#49, but value VI.

Date	Mintage	VG	F	VF	XF	Unc
1724	—	8.00	15.00	25.00	45.00	—
1726	—	8.00	15.00	25.00	45.00	—

KM# 62 6 PFENNIG

Silver **Ruler:** Adolph **Obverse:** Crowned round arms within cartouche **Reverse:** Value and date within wreath **Note:** Similar to 1 Pfennig KM#60, but value VI.

Date	Mintage	VG	F	VF	XF	Unc
1726	—	7.00	12.00	20.00	45.00	—
1727	—	7.00	12.00	20.00	45.00	—
1728	—	7.00	12.00	20.00	45.00	—

KM# 102 6 PFENNIG

Billon **Ruler:** Adalbert II **Obverse:** Crowned monogram **Reverse:** Value within orb

Date	Mintage	VG	F	VF	XF	Unc
1758	—	7.00	16.00	28.00	45.00	—
1759	—	20.00	50.00	100	200	—

KM# 46 KREUZER

Billon **Ruler:** Konstantin **Obverse:** Crowned round arms **Reverse:** Value within cartouche

Date	Mintage	VG	F	VF	XF	Unc
1723	—	6.00	12.00	22.00	45.00	—
1724	—	6.00	12.00	22.00	45.00	—

KM# 103 KREUZER

Billon **Ruler:** Adalbert II **Obverse:** Bust right **Reverse:** Value, date in cartouche

Date	Mintage	VG	F	VF	XF	Unc
1758	—	6.00	15.00	25.00	50.00	—
1759	—	6.00	15.00	25.00	50.00	—

KM# 107 KREUZER

Billon **Ruler:** Adalbert II **Obverse:** Crowned monogram **Reverse:** Value, date in cartouche, FFLM

Date	Mintage	VG	F	VF	XF	Unc
1759	—	6.00	15.00	25.00	50.00	—

KM# 128 KREUZER

Billon **Ruler:** Heinrich VIII **Obverse:** Crowned arms **Reverse:** Value and date **Note:** Varieties exist.

Date	Mintage	VG	F	VF	XF	Unc
1765 HM	—	8.00	17.00	40.00	70.00	—
1769 VH	—	8.00	17.00	40.00	70.00	—

KM# 95 3 KREUZER (Groschen)

Silver **Ruler:** Amandus Freiherr **Obverse:** Crowned oval 4-fold arms, value 3 in frame below divides date, LAND-MUNZ **Reverse:** 1/2 length facing figure of St. Boniface

Date	Mintage	VG	F	VF	XF	Unc
1750 ND	—	9.00	18.00	30.00	55.00	—
1751 ND	—	9.00	18.00	30.00	55.00	—

KM# 96 4 KREUZER

Billon **Ruler:** Adalbert II **Obverse:** FURST.FULD., 3 shields around **Reverse:** LAND MUNZ, value, date

Date	Mintage	VG	F	VF	XF	Unc
1757 ND	—	10.00	25.00	40.00	75.00	—

KM# 97 4 KREUZER

Billon **Ruler:** Adalbert II **Obverse:** F.F., 3 shields around **Reverse:** Value within round frame

Date	Mintage	VG	F	VF	XF	Unc
1757 ND	—	12.00	25.00	40.00	65.00	—
1758 ND	—	12.00	25.00	40.00	65.00	—

KM# 125 5 KREUZER

Billon **Ruler:** Heinrich VIII **Obverse:** Crowned arms in palm branches **Reverse:** Value and date in ornamental border

Date	Mintage	VG	F	VF	XF	Unc
1763 ND	—	7.50	15.00	30.00	50.00	—
1764	—	7.50	15.00	30.00	50.00	—
1765	—	7.50	15.00	30.00	50.00	—

KM# 129 5 KREUZER

Billon **Ruler:** Heinrich VIII **Obverse:** Crowned arms within ornate square **Reverse:** Value and date within ornate square

Date	Mintage	VG	F	VF	XF	Unc
1765	—	9.00	18.00	35.00	60.00	—

KM# 130 5 KREUZER

Billon **Ruler:** Heinrich VIII **Obverse:** Crowned monogram within ornate square **Reverse:** Value, date within ornate square

Date	Mintage	VG	F	VF	XF	Unc
1765	—	15.00	25.00	50.00	80.00	—

KM# 108 6 KREUZER

Silver **Ruler:** Heinrich VIII **Obverse:** Crowned monogram **Reverse:** Value, date, mintmaster's initials in 5 lines

Date	Mintage	VG	F	VF	XF	Unc
1759 IFM Rare	—	—	—	—	—	—

KM# 71 10 KREUZER

Silver **Ruler:** Adolph **Obverse:** Crowned shield divides date **Reverse:** Value within branches **Note:** Similar to 20 Kreuzer, KM#82 but value 10 KR.

Date	Mintage	VG	F	VF	XF	Unc
1727 IND	—	—	—	—	—	—

KM# 120 10 KREUZER

Silver **Ruler:** Heinrich VIII **Obverse:** Crowned arms **Reverse:** Value and date

Date	Mintage	VG	F	VF	XF	Unc
1761	—	—	—	—	—	—

Note: Reported, not confirmed

KM# A131 10 KREUZER

Silver **Ruler:** Heinrich VIII **Note:** Similar to 20 Kreuzer, KM#A126.

Date	Mintage	VG	F	VF	XF	Unc
1763	—	20.00	40.00	125	200	—

KM# 131 10 KREUZER

Silver **Ruler:** Heinrich VIII **Obverse:** Crowned 4-fold arms on pedestal with value **Reverse:** Date within ornaments

Date	Mintage	VG	F	VF	XF	Unc
1765	—	12.00	25.00	50.00	80.00	—
1766	—	12.00	25.00	50.00	80.00	—

KM# 145 10 KREUZER

Silver **Ruler:** Heinrich VIII **Subject:** Death of the Bishop **Obverse:** Helmeted 4-fold arms with ornaments **Reverse:** Inscription

Date	Mintage	VG	F	VF	XF	Unc
1788	—	15.00	35.00	70.00	120	—

KM# 98 12 KREUZER

Silver **Ruler:** Adalbert II **Obverse:** 3 crowned shields dividing date below **Reverse:** Value in baroque frame **Rev. Legend:** FURST FULD LAND MUNZ

Date	Mintage	VG	F	VF	XF	Unc
1757 ND	—	45.00	80.00	135	200	—

KM# 109 12 KREUZER

Silver **Ruler:** Adalbert II **Obverse:** 3 crowned ornate shields **Reverse:** Value, date, mintmaster's initials in 5 lines

Date	Mintage	VG	F	VF	XF	Unc
1759 IFM	—	45.00	80.00	135	200	—

KM# 110 12 KREUZER

Silver **Ruler:** Adalbert II **Obverse:** Crown above three shields of arms **Reverse:** In cartouche

Date	Mintage	VG	F	VF	XF	Unc
1759 IFM	—	45.00	80.00	135	200	—

KM# 82 20 KREUZER

Silver **Ruler:** Adolph **Obverse:** Crowned 4-fold arms **Reverse:** Value, date and legend within branches

Date	Mintage	VG	F	VF	XF	Unc
1735 IND	—	25.00	50.00	100	175	—
1736 IND	—	25.00	50.00	100	175	—

KM# 104 20 KREUZER

Silver **Ruler:** Adalbert II **Obverse:** Bust right, inscription completely around **Reverse:** NACH DEM... around 3 crowned shields, date **Note:** Convention 20 Kreuzer.

Date	Mintage	VG	F	VF	XF	Unc
1758	—	20.00	35.00	65.00	125	—

KM# 111 20 KREUZER

Silver **Ruler:** Adalbert II **Obverse:** Inscription only part way around

Date	Mintage	VG	F	VF	XF	Unc
1759 IFM	—	—	—	—	—	—

KM# 121 20 KREUZER

Silver **Ruler:** Heinrich VIII **Obverse:** Draped bust right **Reverse:** Mitres and Cardinal's hat above 4-fold arms on pedestal with value

Date	Mintage	VG	F	VF	XF	Unc
1761	—	20.00	50.00	125	200	—
1762	—	20.00	50.00	125	200	—
1763	—	20.00	50.00	125	200	—
1764	—	20.00	50.00	125	200	—
1765	—	20.00	50.00	125	200	—
1766	—	20.00	50.00	125	200	—
1767	—	20.00	50.00	125	200	—
1768	—	20.00	50.00	125	200	—
1769	—	20.00	50.00	125	200	—
1770	—	20.00	50.00	125	200	—

KM# A126 20 KREUZER

Silver **Ruler:** Heinrich VIII

Date	Mintage	VG	F	VF	XF	Unc
1763	—	20.00	50.00	125	200	—

KM# 126 20 KREUZER

Silver **Ruler:** Heinrich VIII **Obverse:** Crowned round arms within branches **Reverse:** Vaue and date within ornate wreath

Date	Mintage	VG	F	VF	XF	Unc
1763	—	20.00	50.00	125	200	—

KM# 146 20 KREUZER

Silver **Ruler:** Heinrich VIII **Subject:** Death of the Bishop **Obverse:** Helmeted 4-fold arms with ornaments **Reverse:** Inscription

Date	Mintage	VG	F	VF	XF	Unc
1788	—	20.00	40.00	65.00	100	—

KM# 51 GROSCHEN (1/24 Thaler)

Silver **Ruler:** Konstantin **Obverse:** Crowned round 4-fold arms **Reverse:** Full figure of St. Boniface turned left divides date

Date	Mintage	VG	F	VF	XF	Unc
1724	—	10.00	20.00	40.00	70.00	—

KM# 52 GROSCHEN (1/24 Thaler)

Silver **Ruler:** Konstantin **Reverse:** Full facing figure of standing St. Boniface

Date	Mintage	VG	F	VF	XF	Unc
1724	—	15.00	30.00	60.00	95.00	—

KM# 53 GROSCHEN (1/24 Thaler)

Silver **Ruler:** Konstantin **Obverse:** Date divided below arms

Date	Mintage	VG	F	VF	XF	Unc
1724	—	10.00	20.00	40.00	70.00	—

KM# 59 GROSCHEN (1/24 Thaler)

Silver **Ruler:** Konstantin **Obverse:** Date divided by arms

Date	Mintage	VG	F	VF	XF	Unc
1725	—	10.00	20.00	40.00	70.00	—
1726	—	10.00	20.00	40.00	70.00	—

KM# 63 GROSCHEN (1/24 Thaler)

Silver **Ruler:** Adolph **Obverse:** Small oval central shield in arms **Reverse:** Standing figure of Saint

Date	Mintage	VG	F	VF	XF	Unc
1726	—	10.00	20.00	40.00	70.00	—
1728	—	10.00	20.00	40.00	70.00	—
1735	—	10.00	20.00	40.00	70.00	—
1736	—	10.00	20.00	40.00	70.00	—

KM# 90 GROSCHEN (1/24 Thaler)

Silver **Ruler:** Amandus Freiherr **Subject:** Millennium of Abbey **Obverse:** Standing figure of Saint **Reverse:** Inscription and date

Date	Mintage	VG	F	VF	XF	Unc
1744 D	—	20.00	40.00	80.00	135	—

KM# 122 GROSCHEN (1/24 Thaler)

Billon **Ruler:** Heinrich VIII **Obverse:** F above arms **Reverse:** Figure of St. Boniface

Date	Mintage	VG	F	VF	XF	Unc
1762	—	7.50	15.00	30.00	50.00	—
1763	—	7.50	15.00	30.00	50.00	—
1764	—	7.50	15.00	30.00	50.00	—

KM# 54 BOHMISCH

Silver **Ruler:** Konstantin **Obverse:** Crowned round 4-fold arms **Reverse:** Value, date

Date	Mintage	VG	F	VF	XF	Unc
1724	—	10.00	20.00	35.00	65.00	—

KM# 55 2 BOHMISCH

Silver **Ruler:** Konstantin **Obverse:** Crowned round 4-fold arms **Reverse:** Value, date

Date	Mintage	VG	F	VF	XF	Unc
1724	—	10.00	20.00	35.00	65.00	—

KM# 56 1/2 KOPFSTUCK (10 Kreuzer)

Silver **Ruler:** Konstantin **Obverse:** Crowned round arms **Reverse:** Value, date

Date	Mintage	VG	F	VF	XF	Unc
1724	—	15.00	30.00	50.00	90.00	—

KM# 64 1/2 KOPFSTUCK (10 Kreuzer)

Silver **Ruler:** Adolph **Obverse:** Crowned round 4-fold arms, small central shield **Reverse:** Value, date

Date	Mintage	VG	F	VF	XF	Unc
1726	—	18.00	35.00	60.00	110	—
1727	—	18.00	35.00	60.00	110	—

KM# 57 KOPFSTUCK (20 Kreuzer)

Silver **Ruler:** Konstantin **Obverse:** Crowned shielded 4-fold arms **Reverse:** Value, date

Date	Mintage	VG	F	VF	XF	Unc
1724	—	20.00	40.00	80.00	125	—
1725	—	20.00	40.00	80.00	125	—

KM# 65 KOPFSTUCK (20 Kreuzer)

Silver **Ruler:** Adolph **Obverse:** Crowned oval 4-fold arms, small central shield **Reverse:** Value, date within laurel wreath

Date	Mintage	VG	F	VF	XF	Unc
1726	—	12.00	25.00	45.00	85.00	—
1727	—	12.00	25.00	45.00	85.00	—
1728	—	12.00	25.00	45.00	85.00	—

KM# 58 1/32 THALER (Schilling)

Silver **Ruler:** Konstantin **Obverse:** Crowned oval 4-fold arms **Reverse:** Value, date **Rev. Legend:** 32/EINEN/THALER

Date	Mintage	VG	F	VF	XF	Unc
1724	—	—	—	—	—	—

KM# 99 1/6 THALER

Silver **Ruler:** Adalbert II **Obverse:** Bust right **Reverse:** Value, date

Date	Mintage	VG	F	VF	XF	Unc
1757	—	20.00	40.00	70.00	120	—

KM# 100 1/6 THALER

Silver **Ruler:** Adalbert II **Obverse:** 3 crowned shields **Reverse:** Value, date

Date	Mintage	VG	F	VF	XF	Unc
1757	—	25.00	45.00	90.00	140	—

KM# 101 1/6 THALER

Silver **Ruler:** Adalbert II **Obverse:** Crowned monogram **Reverse:** Value, date

Date	Mintage	VG	F	VF	XF	Unc
1757 ND	—	20.00	35.00	60.00	100	—
1758 ND	—	20.00	35.00	60.00	100	—
1759 ND	—	20.00	35.00	60.00	100	—

KM# 123 1/2 THALER

Silver **Ruler:** Heinrich VIII **Obverse:** Draped bust right **Reverse:** Crown, mitre and helmet above two shields **Note:** Convention 1/2 Thaler.

Date	Mintage	VG	F	VF	XF	Unc
1762	—	25.00	50.00	100	200	—

KM# 154 1/2 THALER

Silver **Ruler:** Adalbert III **Obverse:** Crowned 4-fold arms **Reverse:** Legend within wreath

Date	Mintage	VG	F	VF	XF	Unc
1796	—	35.00	60.00	110	220	—

KM# 153 1/2 THALER
Silver **Ruler:** Adalbert III **Obverse:** Bust right **Reverse:** Crowned 4-fold arms **Note:** Contribution 1/2 Thaler.

Date	Mintage	VG	F	VF	XF	Unc
1796	—	60.00	120	200	350	—

KM# 112 2/3 THALER (1/2 Konventionstaler)
Silver **Ruler:** Heinrich VIII **Obverse:** Bust right, inscription completely around **Reverse:** NACH DEM... around 3 crowned shields, date

Date	Mintage	VG	F	VF	XF	Unc
1759 IFM	—	30.00	60.00	100	200	—

KM# 41 THALER
Silver **Ruler:** Konstantin **Obverse:** Helmeted oval arms, crowned mantle behind, date below **Reverse:** 2 ships in harbor entrance

Date	Mintage	VG	F	VF	XF	Unc
1718 Rare	—	—	—	—	—	—

KM# 66 THALER
Silver **Ruler:** Konstantin **Obverse:** Bust of Abbot Konstantin right **Reverse:** Helmeted arms in front of crowned mantle, date below **Rev. Legend:** CONSILIO ET CONSTANTIA

Date	Mintage	VG	F	VF	XF	Unc
1726 Rare	—	—	—	—	—	—

KM# 67 THALER
Silver **Ruler:** Konstantin **Obverse:** Bust of Adolph right **Reverse:** Helmeted oval 4-fold arms, crowned mantle behind, divide date **Note:** Dav. #2253.

Date	Mintage	VG	F	VF	XF	Unc
1726 Rare	—	—	—	—	—	—

KM# 68 THALER
Silver **Ruler:** Konstantin **Reverse:** Crowned and mantled oval 4-fold arms with central shield divide date **Note:** Dav. #2254.

Date	Mintage	VG	F	VF	XF	Unc
1726 Rare	—	—	—	—	—	—

KM# 69 THALER
Silver **Ruler:** Konstantin **Reverse:** Helmeted oval arms, date divided below **Note:** Dav. #2255.

Date	Mintage	VG	F	VF	XF	Unc
1726 ICK Rare	—	—	—	—	—	—

KM# 72 THALER
Silver **Ruler:** Adolph **Reverse:** Helmeted 4-fold arms with central shield, date divided below **Note:** Dav. #2256.

Date	Mintage	VG	F	VF	XF	Unc
1728 K Rare	—	—	—	—	—	—

KM# 74.1 THALER
Silver **Ruler:** Adolph **Obverse:** Cloaked bust right **Obv. Legend:** ADOLPHVS • D • G • S • R • I • PR • & • AB • FVLD • D • A • A • P • G • & G • P • **Reverse:** Helmeted and mitred arms with small central shield **Rev. Legend:** CANDORE ET AMORE **Note:** Dav. #2257.

Date	Mintage	VG	F	VF	XF	Unc
1729	—	300	550	900	1,500	—

KM# 74.3 THALER
Silver **Ruler:** Adolph **Obverse:** Larger bust, larger letters in legend **Reverse:** Helmeted and mitred arms with small central shield **Note:** Dav. #2258.

Date	Mintage	VG	F	VF	XF	Unc
1729	—	300	550	900	1,500	—

KM# 74.2 THALER
Silver **Ruler:** Adolph **Obverse:** Cloaked bust right **Obv. Legend:** ...PRINCE*++*ABB+FVLD **Reverse:** Helmeted and mitred arms with small central shield **Note:** Dav. #2259.

Date	Mintage	VG	F	VF	XF	Unc
1737 PPW Rare	—	—	—	—	—	—

KM# 84 THALER
Silver **Ruler:** Adolph **Reverse:** Crowned and mantled arms supported by 2 lions, date divided below **Note:** Dav. #2260.

Date	Mintage	VG	F	VF	XF	Unc
1737 Rare	—	—	—	—	—	—

KM# 86 THALER
Silver **Ruler:** Amandus Freiherr **Obverse:** Capped, draped bust right **Obv. Legend:** ANANDVS • D • G • S • R • I • PRINC • ET • ABB • FVLD • **Reverse:** Helmeted ornate 4-fold arms, date below **Rev. Legend:** ...IVSTITIA •

Date	Mintage	VG	F	VF	XF	Unc
1738 ND	—	1,200	2,000	3,500	5,500	—

KM# 127 THALER
Silver **Ruler:** Heinrich VIII **Obverse:** Draped bust with cloak below right **Reverse:** Crowned and helmeted arms, value in exergue, value stated X **Note:** Dav. #2261.

Date	Mintage	VG	F	VF	XF	Unc
1764 ND Rare	—	—	—	—	—	—

KM# 133 THALER
Silver **Ruler:** Heinrich VIII **Reverse:** Date in legend **Note:** Dav. #2262A.

Date	Mintage	VG	F	VF	XF	Unc
1765 VH	—	200	400	800	1,400	—

KM# 132 THALER
Silver **Ruler:** Heinrich VIII **Obverse:** Draped bust with cloak below right **Obv. Legend:** HENRICUS D • G • EPIS • ET ABB • FULD • S • R • I • PR • **Reverse:** Crowned and helmeted arms, date below in exergue **Rev. Legend:** CONSILIO ET AEQUITATE, below: 10/EINE FEINE MARCK/H•M• **Note:** Value stated "10". Dav. #2262.

Date	Mintage	VG	F	VF	XF	Unc
1765 HM	—	200	400	800	1,400	—

KM# 147 THALER
Silver **Ruler:** Heinrich VIII **Obverse:** St. Boniface in ornamented frame **Obv. Legend:** MONETA CAPIT CATHEDR: FULD: SEDE VACANTE. 1788., X/E.F.M. in frame below **Reverse:** Arms within crowned mantle, 15 shields surround **Note:** Sede vacante issue. Dav. #2263.

Date	Mintage	VG	F	VF	XF	Unc
1788	—	150	200	300	500	—

KM# 150 THALER
Silver **Ruler:** Adalbert III **Obverse:** Ruffed collar bust right **Obv. Legend:** ADALBERTUS D. G. EPIS: ET ABB: FULD: S. R. I. PR: **Reverse:** Crowned 4-fold arms **Rev. Legend:** PRO DEO ET PATRIA, X EINE FEINE MARCK and date below **Note:** Contribution Thaler. Adalbert. Dav. #2264.

Date	Mintage	VG	F	VF	XF	Unc
1795	—	100	200	325	550	—
1796	—	75.00	150	275	450	—

KM# 151 THALER
Silver **Ruler:** Adalbert III **Obverse:** Helmeted 4-fold arms **Obv. Legend:** ADALBERTUS D. G. EPIS: ET ABB: FULD: S. R. I. PR: **Reverse:** Legend and date within palm and laurel branches, value below **Rev. Legend:** PRO DEO/ET/PATRIA./1795., X/EINE F:/MARCK. below **Note:** Dav. #2265.

Date	Mintage	VG	F	VF	XF	Unc
1795	—	90.00	180	300	500	—

KM# 152 THALER
Silver **Ruler:** Adalbert III **Obverse:** Ruffed collar bust right **Obv. Legend:** ADALBERTUS D. G. EPIS: ET ABB: FULD: S. R. I. PR: **Reverse:** Legend and date within palm and laurel branches, value below **Rev. Legend:** PRO DEO/ET PATRIA./1795., X/EINE F:/MARCK. below **Note:** Dav. #2266.

Date	Mintage	VG	F	VF	XF	Unc
1795	—	115	225	375	625	—

KM# 80 1/2 CAROLIN (5 Gulden)

4.8500 g., 0.7700 Gold 0.1201 oz. AGW **Ruler:** Adolph
Obverse: Bust of Adolph right **Reverse:** Cruciform crowned monograms around value, date below

Date	Mintage	VG	F	VF	XF	Unc
1734	—	350	850	1,600	2,750	—
1735	—	350	850	1,600	2,750	—

KM# 81 CAROLIN (10 Gulden)
9.7000 g., 0.7700 Gold 0.2401 oz. AGW **Ruler:** Adolph
Obverse: Bust right **Reverse:** Crowned monograms in cruciform, value at center

Date	Mintage	VG	F	VF	XF	Unc
1734	—	200	450	1,000	2,000	—
1735	—	200	450	1,000	2,000	—

KM# 83 CAROLIN (10 Gulden)
9.7000 g., 0.7700 Gold 0.2401 oz. AGW **Ruler:** Adolph
Obverse: Bust right **Reverse:** Crowned monograms in cruciform

Date	Mintage	VG	F	VF	XF	Unc
1735	—	200	450	1,000	2,000	—

TRADE COINAGE

KM# 40 DUCAT
3.5000 g., 0.9860 Gold 0.1109 oz. AGW **Ruler:** Konstantin
Obverse: Bust of Constantine right

Date	Mintage	VG	F	VF	XF	Unc
1715	—	450	1,200	2,250	4,250	—
1716	—	450	1,200	2,250	4,250	—
1717	—	450	1,200	2,250	4,250	—
1721	—	450	1,200	2,250	4,250	—
1726	—	450	1,200	2,250	4,250	—

KM# 70 DUCAT
3.5000 g., 0.9860 Gold 0.1109 oz. AGW **Ruler:** Adolph
Obverse: Bust right **Reverse:** Arms topped by 4 helmets **Note:** Varieties exist.

Date	Mintage	VG	F	VF	XF	Unc
1726	—	325	750	1,650	3,000	—
1728	—	325	750	1,650	3,000	—
1730	—	350	800	1,750	3,200	—

KM# 87 DUCAT
3.5000 g., 0.9860 Gold 0.1109 oz. AGW **Ruler:** Amandus Freiherr **Obverse:** Bust right **Reverse:** Helmeted 4-fold arms

Date	Mintage	VG	F	VF	XF	Unc
1738 ND	—	450	1,150	2,000	4,000	—

KM# 91 DUCAT
3.5000 g., 0.9860 Gold 0.1109 oz. AGW **Ruler:** Amandus Freiherr **Subject:** 1000th Anniversary of the Abbey **Obverse:** Bust right **Reverse:** Radiant arms above inscription

Date	Mintage	VG	F	VF	XF	Unc
1744 ND	—	350	800	1,600	3,000	—

KM# 140 DUCAT
3.5000 g., 0.9860 Gold 0.1109 oz. AGW **Ruler:** Heinrich VIII
Obverse: Draped bust with cloak below right **Reverse:** Helmeted 4-fold arms

Date	Mintage	F	VF	XF	Unc
1779	—	450	900	1,500	2,500

KM# 141 DUCAT
3.5000 g., 0.9860 Gold 0.1109 oz. AGW **Ruler:** Heinrich VIII
Obverse: Bust right **Reverse:** Inscription

Date	Mintage	F	VF	XF	Unc
1779	—	450	900	1,250	2,250

KM# 142 DUCAT
3.5000 g., 0.9860 Gold 0.1109 oz. AGW **Ruler:** Heinrich VIII
Obverse: 3 helmeted arms **Reverse:** 9-line inscription

Date	Mintage	F	VF	XF	Unc
1779	—	500	1,000	2,000	3,000

KM# 73 2 DUCAT
7.0000 g., 0.9860 Gold 0.2219 oz. AGW **Ruler:** Adolph
Obverse: Adolph

Date	Mintage	VG	F	VF	XF	Unc
1728	—	850	1,750	3,500	6,000	—
1730	—	900	1,850	3,750	6,500	—

KM# 113 2 DUCAT
7.0000 g., 0.9860 Gold 0.2219 oz. AGW **Ruler:** Adalbert II
Obverse: Bust right **Reverse:** Crowned arms with lion supporters

Date	Mintage	F	VF	XF	Unc
1759	—	850	1,750	3,500	6,000

KM# 75 8 DUCAT
28.0000 g., 0.9860 Gold 0.8876 oz. AGW **Ruler:** Adolph

Date	Mintage	VG	F	VF	XF	Unc
1729	—	—	—	17,500	26,000	—

KM# 88 8 DUCAT
28.0000 g., 0.9860 Gold 0.8876 oz. AGW **Ruler:** Amandus Freiherr **Note:** Struck with 1 Thaler dies, KM#86.

Date	Mintage	VG	F	VF	XF	Unc
1738 Rare	—	—	—	—	—	—

KM# 42 10 DUCAT (Portugalöser)
35.0000 g., 0.9860 Gold 1.1095 oz. AGW **Ruler:** Konstantin
Note: Struck with 1 Thaler dies, KM#41.

Date	Mintage	VG	F	VF	XF	Unc
1718 Rare	—	—	—	—	—	—

KM# 76 12 DUCAT
42.0000 g., 0.9860 Gold 1.3314 oz. AGW **Ruler:** Adolph **Note:** Struck with 1 Thaler dies, KM#74.

Date	Mintage	VG	F	VF	XF	Unc
1729 Rare	—	—	—	—	—	—

PATTERNS
Including off metal strikes

KM#	Date	Mintage	Identification	Mkt Val
Pn2	1726	—	Ducat. Silver. KM#40, Constantine.	—
Pn3	1726	—	Ducat. Lead. KM#70, Adolph.	—
Pn4	1726	—	Ducat. Silver. KM#70.	—
Pn8	1738	—	Ducat. Silver. KM#87, Amandus.	—
Pn9	1744	—	Ducat. Silver. KM#91, Amandus.	150
Pn10	1758	—	1/6 Thaler. Tin. KM#101.	—
Pn11	1759	—	2 Ducat. Silver. KM#113, Adalbert.	—
Pn12	1779	—	Ducat. Silver. KM#140.	—

FURSTENBERG

A noble family with holdings in Baden and Württemberg. The lord of Fürstenberg assumed the title of Count in the 13th century, which was raised to the rank of Prince in 1664. The Fürstenberg possessions were mediatized in 1806.

FURSTENBERG-PURGLITZ

RULERS
Karl Egon I, 1762-1787
Philipp Maria Josef, 1787-1790
Karl Gabriel Maria, 1790-1799
Karl Egon II, 1799-1804

PRINCIPALITY

TRADE COINAGE

KM# 5 DUCAT
3.5000 g., 0.9860 Gold 0.1109 oz. AGW **Ruler:** Karl Egon I
Obverse: Bust right **Reverse:** Crowned and mantled arms

Date	Mintage	VG	F	VF	XF	Unc
1772	—	400	850	1,750	3,000	—

FURSTENBERG-STUHLINGEN

RULERS
Prosper Ferdinand, 1681-1704
Josef Wilhelm Ernst, 1704-1762
Josef Wenzel, 1762-1783
Josef Maria Benedict, 1783-1796
Karl Joachim, 1796-1804

MINT MARKS
G - Gunzburg

MINT OFFICIALS' INITIALS

Initials	Date	Name
ARW	1742-84	Adam Rudolph Werner, die-cutter in Stüttgart
CH	1784-1808	Christian Heugelin, warden in Stüttgart
ILW, W	1798-1845	Johann Ludwig Wagner, die-cutter in Stüttgart
V	?-1740	Georg Wilhelm Vestner, die-cutter in Nüremberg

PRINCIPALITY

REGULAR COINAGE

KM# 25 1/2 KREUZER
Copper **Ruler:** Josef Wenzel **Obverse:** Crowned arms **Reverse:** Value, date

Date	Mintage	VG	F	VF	XF	Unc
1772	—	10.00	20.00	35.00	60.00	—

KM# 26 KREUZER
Copper **Ruler:** Josef Wenzel **Obverse:** Crowned arms **Reverse:** Value and date

Date	Mintage	VG	F	VF	XF	Unc
1772 G	—	10.00	20.00	35.00	60.00	—
1773 G	—	10.00	20.00	35.00	60.00	—

KM# 29 3 KREUZER (Groschen)
1.4200 g., 0.3120 Silver 0.0142 oz. ASW **Ruler:** Josef Wenzel

Date	Mintage	F	VF	XF	Unc
1772	—	—	—	—	—

KM# 27 1/48 THALER
Billon **Ruler:** Josef Wenzel **Obverse:** Crowned arms **Reverse:** Value, date

Date	Mintage	VG	F	VF	XF	Unc
1772 G	—	30.00	60.00	110	220	—

KM# 28 1/24 THALER (Groschen)
Billon **Ruler:** Josef Wenzel **Obverse:** Crowned arms **Reverse:** Value, date

Date	Mintage	VG	F	VF	XF	Unc
1772 G	—	35.00	70.00	135	245	—

KM# 5 THALER
Silver **Ruler:** Josef Wilhelm Ernst **Obverse:** Armored bust right **Obv. Legend:** IOS: WILH: ERN: S.R.I. PRINC. IN FURSTENBERG: LANDGRAV: IN BAAR & STUHLINGEN **Reverse:** View of mines and valley with figures at work **Rev. Legend:** AVSBEUT THALER VON S. IOSEPHS COBOLD / UND SILBER ZECHE. **Note:** Mining Thaler. Dav. #2267.

Date	Mintage	F	VF	XF	Unc
1729 V	1,167	475	800	1,400	2,500

KM# 15 THALER
Silver **Ruler:** Josef Wilhelm Ernst **Obverse:** Armored bust right **Obv. Legend:** IOSEPH WILH • ERNEST • S • R • I • PR • DE FURSTENBERG **Reverse:** Crowned arms within Order chain and ornate frame **Rev. Legend:** AD LEGEM CONVENTIONIS., in exergue: AUSBEUT THALER/VON S. SOPHIA KOBOLD/UND SILBER ZECHE/BEY WITICHEN/1762 **Note:** Dav. #2268.

Date	Mintage	F	VF	XF	Unc
1762	725	425	700	1,100	1,800

KM# 16 THALER
Silver **Ruler:** Josef Wenzel **Obverse:** Armored bust right **Obv. Legend:** IOSEPHUS WENCESLAUS • S • R • I • PR • DE FURSTENBERG • **Reverse:** Mining scene with St. Wenzel to right, legend and date in exergue **Rev. Legend:** AD LEGEM CONVENTIONIS, in exergue: DIE. GRUB S. WENCESLAUS/BEY WOLFFACH KAME IN/AUSBEUTH IM QUAR/TAL REMINISCERE/•1767• **Note:** Dav. #2270.

Date	Mintage	F	VF	XF	Unc
1767 ARW	500	250	500	1,000	1,700

KM# 17 THALER
Silver **Ruler:** Josef Wenzel **Obverse:** Plainer armor breast plate **Obv. Legend:** IOSEPHUS WENCESLAUS • S • R • I • PR • DE FURSTENBERG **Reverse:** Mining scene with St. Wenzel to right, legend and date in exergue **Rev. Legend:** AD LEGEM CONVENTIONIS, in exergue: DIE. GRUB S. WENCESLAUS/ BEY WOLFFACH KAME IN /AUSBEUTH IM QUAR/TAL REMINISCERE/•1767• **Note:** Dav. #2270A.

Date	Mintage	F	VF	XF	Unc
1767 ARW	—	250	500	1,000	1,700

KM# 30 THALER
Silver **Ruler:** Josef Maria Benedict **Obverse:** Armored bust left **Obv. Legend:** IOS • M • B • FURST ZU FURSTENBERG L • I • D • B • U • Z • ST • H • Z • HAUSEN I • KINZ • THAL, in exergue: X EINE FEINE MARK **Reverse:** View of the mines, inscription below **Rev. Legend:** MIT GOTT DURCH KUNST U • ARBEIT, in exergue: DIE GRUBE FRIED • CHRIST • GABS/ZUR AUSBEUT IM QUARTAL/CRUCIS •1790• **Note:** Dav. #2271.

Date	Mintage	F	VF	XF	Unc
1790	806	250	475	975	1,650

KM# 18 3 THALER
Silver, 65 mm. **Ruler:** Josef Wenzel **Obverse:** Large armored bust right **Obv. Legend:** IOSEPHUS WENCESLAUS • S • R • I • PRINCEPS • DE FURSTENBERG • **Reverse:** Mining scene with St. Wenzel to right, legend and date in exergue **Rev. Legend:** SYDERA FAVENT INDUSTRIAE., in exergue; DIE GRUB S• WENCESLAUS:•/BEY WOLFFACH KAME IN AUS/BEUT IM QUARTAL REMI/NISCERE/•1767• **Note:** Dav. #LS277. Illustration reduced.

Date	Mintage	VG	F	VF	XF	Unc
1767 ARW	—	1,500	2,250	3,000	5,000	—

KM# 19 4 THALER
Silver **Ruler:** Josef Wenzel **Obverse:** Armored bust right **Reverse:** Mining scene with St. Wenzel to right, legend and date in exergue **Note:** Dav. #LS276.

Date	Mintage	VG	F	VF	XF	Unc
1767 ARW Rare	150	—	—	—	—	—

KM# 20 8 THALER
Silver **Ruler:** Josef Wenzel **Obverse:** Armored bust right **Reverse:** Mining scene with St. Wenzel to right, legend and date in exergue

Date	Mintage	VG	F	VF	XF	Unc
1767 ARW Rare	—	—	—	—	—	—

TRADE COINAGE

KM# 10 DUCAT
3.5000 g., 0.9860 Gold 0.1109 oz. AGW **Ruler:** Josef Wilhelm Ernst **Obverse:** Armored bust right **Reverse:** Arms within Order chain and crowned mantle

Date	Mintage	VG	F	VF	XF	Unc
1750	—	700	1,250	2,850	5,000	—
1751	—	700	1,250	2,850	5,000	—
1754	—	1,500	2,200	3,600	6,000	—

PATTERNS

Including off metal strikes

KM#	Date	Mintage	Identification	Mkt Val
Pn1	1729	—	Thaler. Tin. KM#5	175

FURTHER AUSTRIA

(Vorderösterreich)

Name given to imperial lands in South Swabia in the 18th century. In 1805 it was divided by Baden and Bavaria.

RULERS
Josef II, 1780-1790
Leopold II, 1790-1792
Franz II (Austria), 1792-1805

MINT MARKS
A - Wien
F - Hall
G - Baia Mare (Nagybanya)
H - Günzburg

PROVINCE

REGULAR COINAGE

KM# 5 HELLER
Copper **Ruler:** Josef II **Mint:** Gunzburg **Note:** Varieties exist with and without period after date.

Date	Mintage	VG	F	VF	XF	Unc
1783H	—	—	7.50	15.00	30.00	75.00
1784H	—	—	5.00	10.00	20.00	50.00
1785H	—	—	5.00	10.00	20.00	50.00
1787H	—	—	7.50	15.00	30.00	75.00
1788H	—	—	5.00	10.00	20.00	50.00
1789H	—	—	5.00	10.00	20.00	50.00
1790H	—	—	5.00	10.00	20.00	50.00
1791H	—	—	5.00	10.00	20.00	75.00
1792H	—	—	5.00	10.00	20.00	75.00

KM# 21 HELLER
Copper **Ruler:** Franz II (Austria) **Mint:** Gunzburg **Note:** Varieties exist with and without period after date.

Date	Mintage	VG	F	VF	XF	Unc
1793H	—	—	6.00	12.00	22.00	80.00
1797H	—	—	6.00	12.00	22.00	80.00
1798H	—	—	—	—	—	—
1799H	—	—	8.00	20.00	30.00	125
1801H	—	—	8.00	20.00	30.00	125
1803H	—	—	8.00	20.00	30.00	125

KM# 6 1/4 KREUTZER
Copper **Ruler:** Josef II **Mint:** Gunzburg **Obverse:** Crowned arms **Reverse:** Value and date

Date	Mintage	VG	F	VF	XF	Unc
1783H	—	6.00	12.00	25.00	50.00	—
1784H	—	7.50	20.00	40.00	75.00	—
1789H	—	6.00	12.00	25.00	50.00	—
1790H	—	7.50	20.00	40.00	75.00	—

KM# 17 1/4 KREUTZER

1.9900 g., Copper **Ruler:** Franz II (Austria) **Mint:** Gunzburg **Obverse:** Crowned arms **Reverse:** Value and date

Date	Mintage	VG	F	VF	XF	Unc
1792H Rare	—	—	—	—	—	—
1793H	—	—	10.00	25.00	50.00	150
1797H	—	—	10.00	25.00	50.00	150
1798H Rare	—	—	—	—	—	—
1799H Rare	—	—	—	—	—	—
1800H Rare	—	—	—	—	—	—

KM# 8 1/2 KREUTZER

Copper **Ruler:** Josef II **Mint:** Gunzburg **Obverse:** Crowned arms, legend of Josef II **Reverse:** Value and date in cartouche **Note:** Varieties exist.

Date	Mintage	VG	F	VF	XF	Unc
1784H	—	10.00	22.00	45.00	100	—
1789H	—	8.00	20.00	40.00	90.00	—

KM# 15 1/2 KREUTZER

Copper **Mint:** Gunzburg **Obverse:** Crowned arms, legend of Leopold II

Date	Mintage	VG	F	VF	XF	Unc
1791H Rare	—	—	—	—	—	—
1792H Rare	—	—	—	—	—	—

KM# 18 1/2 KREUTZER

3.8800 g., Copper **Mint:** Gunzburg **Obverse:** Crowned arms, legend of Leopold II

Date	Mintage	VG	F	VF	XF	Unc
1792H Rare	—	—	—	—	—	—
1793H	—	—	25.00	100	135	225
1795H	—	—	25.00	100	135	225
1797H Rare	—	—	—	—	—	—
1798H Rare	—	—	—	—	—	—
1799H Rare	—	—	—	—	—	—
1800H Rare	—	—	—	—	—	—

KM# 7 KREUTZER

Copper **Ruler:** Josef II **Obverse:** Crowned arms, legend of Josef II **Reverse:** Value and date in cartouche

Date	Mintage	VG	F	VF	XF	Unc
1783	—	—	15.00	30.00	75.00	150
1784	—	—	15.00	40.00	80.00	160
1789	—	—	15.00	40.00	80.00	160

KM# 16 KREUTZER

Copper **Ruler:** Leopold II **Mint:** Gunzburg **Obverse:** Legend of Leopold II

Date	Mintage	VG	F	VF	XF	Unc
1791H Rare	—	—	—	—	—	—
1792H	—	—	20.00	45.00	90.00	175

KM# 19 KREUTZER

7.7700 g., Copper **Ruler:** Franz II (Austria) **Mint:** Gunzburg **Obverse:** Crowned divided arms within ornate shield **Reverse:** Value and date within cartouche

Date	Mintage	VG	F	VF	XF	Unc
1792H	—	—	4.00	12.00	25.00	50.00
1793H	—	—	4.00	12.00	25.00	50.00
1794H	—	—	4.00	12.00	25.00	50.00
1795H	—	—	4.00	12.00	25.00	50.00

KM# 9 3 KREUTZER

Billon **Ruler:** Josef II **Mint:** Gunzburg

Date	Mintage	VG	F	VF	XF	Unc
1786H	—	—	15.00	35.00	75.00	165
1787H	—	—	15.00	35.00	75.00	165
1791H	—	—	15.00	35.00	75.00	165
1792H	—	—	15.00	35.00	75.00	165

KM# 22 3 KREUTZER

1.4600 g., 0.3120 Silver 0.0146 oz. ASW **Ruler:** Franz II (Austria)

Date	Mintage	VG	F	VF	XF	Unc
1793A	—	—	15.00	30.00	65.00	185
1793H	—	—	15.00	30.00	65.00	185
1794H	—	—	10.00	25.00	50.00	150
1794A Rare	—	—	—	—	—	—
1795H	—	—	10.00	25.00	50.00	150
1796H	—	—	10.00	30.00	65.00	185
1797H	—	—	10.00	25.00	50.00	150
1799H Rare	—	—	—	—	—	—
1800H Rare	—	—	—	—	—	—

KM# 10 6 KREUTZER

Billon **Mint:** Gunzburg **Obverse:** 3 Shields of arms, lower on divides date **Reverse:** Value above sprays **Note:** Similar to KM#20.

Date	Mintage	VG	F	VF	XF	Unc
1786H	—	5.00	10.00	22.50	50.00	—
1787H	—	5.00	10.00	22.50	50.00	—
1788H	—	5.00	10.00	22.50	50.00	—
1792H	—	7.50	15.00	35.00	80.00	—

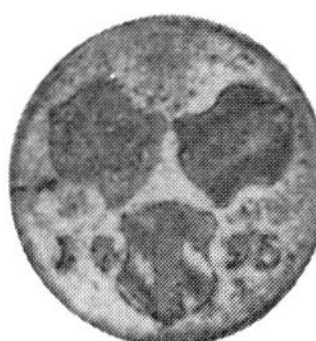

KM# 20 6 KREUTZER

2.4500 g., 0.3750 Silver 0.0295 oz. ASW **Ruler:** Franz II (Austria) **Obverse:** 3 Shields of arms, lower one divides date **Reverse:** Value above sprays

Date	Mintage	VG	F	VF	XF	Unc
1792H	—	—	4.50	12.50	30.00	75.00
1793A	—	—	4.50	12.50	30.00	75.00
1793H	—	—	4.50	12.50	30.00	75.00
1794H	—	—	4.50	12.50	30.00	75.00
1794A Rare	—	—	—	—	—	—
1795H	—	—	4.50	12.50	30.00	75.00
1796H	—	—	4.50	12.50	30.00	75.00
1797H	—	—	4.50	12.50	30.00	75.00
1798H	—	—	4.50	12.50	30.00	75.00
1799H	—	—	4.50	12.50	30.00	75.00
1800H	—	—	4.50	12.50	30.00	75.00

GOSLAR

FREE CITY

The small city of Goslar is located on the northern flank of the Harz Mountains, about 26 miles (44 kilometers) west of Halberstadt. It was founded as a free city by Emperor Heinrich I (918-936) about the year 920 and was later a royal residence, as well as the site of an imperial mint. Goslar was ideally situated close to mines in the Harz Mountains which produced an abundance of metals including copper and silver among others. The growing town became a member of the Hanseatic League in the mid-14th century and was soon producing its own coinage. The free imperial status of Goslar came to an end in 1802 when it passed to the rule of Prussia. It became a part of the Kingdom of Westphalia from 1807 until 1813, after which it was returned to Prussia for a short time. It was then assigned to Hannover in the peace which ended the Napoleonic Wars in 1815. When Hannover was annexed by Prussia in 1866, Goslar was once again in the Prussian fold.

MINT OFFICIALS' INITIALS

Initials	Date	Name
FRH	Ca.1717	Unknown
HAH	Ca.1716-18	Unknown
HCRF	1734-64	Heinrich Christoph Rudolph Friese
IAB	1705	Johann Albert Bar
IAH	Ca.1712-16	Unknown, possibly Johann Anselm Hallaicher

ARMS

Crowned eagle.

REGULAR COINAGE

KM# 116 LEICHTER PFENNIG (Light Pfenning)

Copper **Obverse:** Madonna with rays, GOSLAR below **Reverse:** Value, date in 4 lines

Date	Mintage	VG	F	VF	XF	Unc
1749	—	5.00	10.00	16.00	30.00	—
1753	—	5.00	10.00	16.00	30.00	—
1757	—	5.00	10.00	16.00	30.00	—
1758	—	5.00	10.00	16.00	30.00	—

KM# 125 LEICHTER PFENNIG (Light Pfenning)

Copper **Obverse:** Madonna in rays **Reverse:** Value, date **Note:** Similar to KM#116.

Date	Mintage	VG	F	VF	XF	Unc
1763	—	6.00	12.00	20.00	35.00	—
1764	—	6.00	12.00	20.00	35.00	—

KM# 61 PFENNIG

Billon **Note:** Uniface, GOS/date. Varieties exist.

Date	Mintage	VG	F	VF	XF	Unc
1664	—	25.00	40.00	75.00	125	—
1668	—	25.00	40.00	75.00	125	—
1707	—	25.00	40.00	75.00	125	—
1707	—	25.00	40.00	75.00	125	—
1708	—	25.00	40.00	75.00	125	—

KM# 89 PFENNIG

Billon **Obv. Legend:** GOS/LAR **Reverse:** Imperial orb divides date

Date	Mintage	VG	F	VF	XF	Unc
1716	—	10.00	20.00	35.00	55.00	—
1728	—	10.00	20.00	35.00	55.00	—

KM# 105 PFENNIG

Copper **Obverse:** Eagle, GOSLAR on band below **Reverse:** Value, date **Rev. Legend:** I/PFENNIG/SCHEIDE/MUNTZ

Date	Mintage	VG	F	VF	XF	Unc
1734 HCRF	—	7.00	15.00	30.00	55.00	—
1735 HCRF	—	7.00	15.00	30.00	55.00	—

KM# 106 PFENNIG

Copper **Rev. Legend:** PFENNING..

Date	Mintage	VG	F	VF	XF	Unc
1734 HCRF	—	5.00	12.00	20.00	35.00	—
1735 HCRF	—	5.00	12.00	20.00	35.00	—
1737 HCRF	—	5.00	12.00	20.00	35.00	—

KM# 107 PFENNIG

Copper **Obverse:** Madonna in rays, divides GOS-LAR, city arms below **Reverse:** Value, date, mintmaster's initials in 6 lines

Date	Mintage	VG	F	VF	XF	Unc
1737 HCRF	—	4.00	10.00	18.00	32.00	—
1738 HCRF	—	4.00	10.00	18.00	32.00	—
1741 HCRF	—	4.00	10.00	18.00	32.00	—
1742 HCRF	—	4.00	10.00	18.00	32.00	—
1743 HCRF	—	4.00	10.00	18.00	32.00	—
1744 HCRF	—	4.00	10.00	18.00	32.00	—
1745 HCRF	—	4.00	10.00	18.00	32.00	—
1746 HCRF	—	4.00	10.00	18.00	32.00	—
1748 HCRF	—	4.00	10.00	18.00	32.00	—
1749 HCRF	—	4.00	10.00	18.00	32.00	—
1750 HCRF	—	4.00	10.00	18.00	32.00	—
1751 HCRF	—	4.00	10.00	18.00	32.00	—
1763 HCRF	—	4.00	10.00	18.00	32.00	—

KM# 120 PFENNIG

Copper **Obverse:** Full-length Madonna in wide mantle **Obv. Legend:** MARIA MATER **Reverse:** Value, date in 5 lines

Date	Mintage	VG	F	VF	XF	Unc
1752	—	3.50	9.00	16.00	30.00	—
1753	—	3.50	9.00	16.00	30.00	—

KM# 121 PFENNIG

Copper **Obverse:** Madonna with narrow mantle **Reverse:** Value, date

Date	Mintage	VG	F	VF	XF	Unc
1752	—	3.50	9.00	16.00	30.00	—
1753	—	3.50	9.00	16.00	30.00	—
1756	—	3.50	9.00	16.00	30.00	—
1759	—	3.50	9.00	16.00	30.00	—
1760	—	3.50	9.00	16.00	30.00	—

KM# 126 PFENNIG

Copper **Obverse:** Rays on both sides of Madonna **Obv. Legend:** DOMINI MARIA MA.. **Reverse:** Value, date

Date	Mintage	VG	F	VF	XF	Unc
1763 HCRF	—	3.50	9.00	16.00	30.00	—
1764 HCRF	—	3.50	9.00	16.00	30.00	—

KM# 85 2 PFENNIG (Gute)
Silver **Obverse:** Eagle, GOSLAR in band below **Reverse:** Date **Rev. Legend:** II/GUTE/PFENNIG

Date	Mintage	VG	F	VF	XF	Unc
1712	—	—	—	—	—	—

KM# 98 2 PFENNIG (Gute)
Silver **Rev. Legend:** PFENNIGE

Date	Mintage	VG	F	VF	XF	Unc
1726	—	20.00	40.00	65.00	100	—
1749	—	20.00	40.00	65.00	100	—
1753	—	20.00	40.00	65.00	100	—
1754	—	20.00	40.00	65.00	100	—

KM# 109 2 PFENNIG (Gute)
Silver **Reverse:** Date **Rev. Legend:** 2/PFENN

Date	Mintage	VG	F	VF	XF	Unc
1739	—	20.00	40.00	65.00	100	—
1740	—	20.00	40.00	65.00	100	—

KM# 77 3 PFENNIG (Dreier)
Silver **Obv. Legend:** GOS/LAR **Reverse:** Imperial orb with 3 divides date

Date	Mintage	VG	F	VF	XF	Unc
1709	—	10.00	20.00	40.00	70.00	—
1710	—	10.00	20.00	40.00	70.00	—
1711	—	10.00	20.00	40.00	70.00	—
1716	—	10.00	20.00	40.00	70.00	—
1735	—	10.00	20.00	40.00	70.00	—
1743	—	10.00	20.00	40.00	70.00	—

KM# 87 4 PFENNIG (Gute)
Billon **Obverse:** Eagle **Reverse:** Date **Rev. Legend:** IIII/GUTE/PFEN **Note:** Mattier 4 Pfennig.

Date	Mintage	VG	F	VF	XF	Unc
1713	—	15.00	35.00	60.00	100	—
1714	—	15.00	35.00	60.00	100	—
1716	—	15.00	35.00	60.00	100	—
1718	—	15.00	35.00	60.00	100	—
1721	—	15.00	35.00	60.00	100	—
1722	—	15.00	35.00	60.00	100	—
1723	—	15.00	35.00	60.00	100	—
1725	—	15.00	35.00	60.00	100	—
1728	—	15.00	35.00	60.00	100	—
1733	—	15.00	35.00	60.00	100	—
1734	—	15.00	35.00	60.00	100	—

KM# 108 4 PFENNIG (Gute)
Billon **Obverse:** Eagle, GOSLAR in band below **Reverse:** Date **Rev. Legend:** IIII/GUTE/PFENN

Date	Mintage	VG	F	VF	XF	Unc
1734 HCRF	—	—	—	—	—	—
1738 HCRF	—	10.00	25.00	45.00	80.00	—
1741 HCRF	—	10.00	25.00	45.00	80.00	—
1742 HCRF	—	10.00	25.00	45.00	80.00	—
1744 HCRF	—	10.00	25.00	45.00	80.00	—
1745 HCRF	—	10.00	25.00	45.00	80.00	—
1746 HCRF	—	10.00	25.00	45.00	80.00	—
1748 HCRF	—	10.00	25.00	45.00	80.00	—
1752 HCRF	—	10.00	25.00	45.00	80.00	—

KM# 128 4 PFENNIG (Gute)
Billon **Obverse:** Eagle above ribbon with GOSLAR imprinted **Reverse:** Date and value in center **Rev. Legend:** NACH DEM

Date	Mintage	VG	F	VF	XF	Unc
1764 HCRF	—	25.00	35.00	60.00	100	—

KM# 78 6 PFENNIG
Silver **Obverse:** Eagle, GOSLAR in band below **Reverse:** Imperial orb with VI divides date **Note:** Varieties exist.

Date	Mintage	VG	F	VF	XF	Unc
1709	—	8.00	16.00	30.00	60.00	—
1710	—	8.00	16.00	30.00	60.00	—
1711	—	8.00	16.00	30.00	60.00	—
1712	—	8.00	16.00	30.00	60.00	—
1712 IAH	—	8.00	16.00	30.00	60.00	—
1713 IAH	—	8.00	16.00	30.00	60.00	—
1714 IAH	—	8.00	16.00	30.00	60.00	—
1715	—	8.00	16.00	30.00	60.00	—
1722	—	8.00	16.00	30.00	60.00	—
1723	—	8.00	16.00	30.00	60.00	—
1724	—	8.00	16.00	30.00	60.00	—
1725	—	8.00	16.00	30.00	60.00	—
1726	—	8.00	16.00	30.00	60.00	—
1727	—	8.00	16.00	30.00	60.00	—
1728	—	8.00	16.00	30.00	60.00	—
1734	—	8.00	16.00	30.00	60.00	—
1735	—	8.00	16.00	30.00	60.00	—
1736	—	8.00	16.00	30.00	60.00	—
1736 HCRF	—	8.00	16.00	30.00	60.00	—
1737 HCRF	—	8.00	16.00	30.00	60.00	—
1738 HCRF	—	8.00	16.00	30.00	60.00	—
1739 HCRF	—	8.00	16.00	30.00	60.00	—
1740 HCRF	—	8.00	16.00	30.00	60.00	—
1742 HCRF	—	8.00	16.00	30.00	60.00	—
1743 HCRF	—	8.00	16.00	30.00	60.00	—
1744 HCRF	—	8.00	16.00	30.00	60.00	—
1747 HCRF	—	8.00	16.00	30.00	60.00	—
1748 HCRF	—	8.00	16.00	30.00	60.00	—

KM# 127 6 PFENNIG
Billon **Obverse:** City arms, plumed helmet above, GOSLAR below **Reverse:** Imperial orb with VI, date **Rev. Legend:** NACH DEM

Date	Mintage	VG	F	VF	XF	Unc
1763 HCRF	—	28.00	38.00	65.00	120	—
1764 HCRF	—	28.00	38.00	65.00	120	—

KM# 129 6 PFENNIG
Billon **Obverse:** Eagle above ribbon with GOSLAR imprinted **Reverse:** Imperial orb with value divides date

Date	Mintage	VG	F	VF	XF	Unc
1763 HCRF	—	8.00	15.00	25.00	50.00	—
1764 HCRF	—	8.00	15.00	25.00	50.00	—

KM# 88 MARIENGROSCHEN
Silver **Reverse:** Date in legend at top

Date	Mintage	VG	F	VF	XF	Unc
1714 IAH	—	18.00	35.00	65.00	120	—
1715 IAH	—	18.00	35.00	65.00	120	—
1723	—	18.00	35.00	65.00	120	—
1738 HCRF	—	18.00	35.00	65.00	120	—

KM# 130 MARIENGROSCHEN
Billon **Obverse:** Helmeted city arms, inscription around **Reverse:** Value, date **Rev. Legend:** NACH DEM

Date	Mintage	VG	F	VF	XF	Unc
1764 HCRF	—	25.00	40.00	75.00	140	—

KM# 110 12 MARIENGROSCHEN (1/3 Thaler)
Silver **Obverse:** Helmeted eagle arms, value 1/3 below **Reverse:** Date in legend **Rev. Legend:** XII/MARIEN/GROSCH, NACH DEM

Date	Mintage	VG	F	VF	XF	Unc
1739 HCRF	—	80.00	150	225	475	—

KM# 69 24 MARIENGROSCHEN (2/3 Thaler)
Silver **Obverse:** Helmeted arms with plumes **Reverse:** Value and date within inner circle **Note:** Similar to KM#99.

Date	Mintage	VG	F	VF	XF	Unc
1709	—	60.00	100	175	285	—
1709	—	60.00	100	175	285	—
1713 IAH	—	60.00	100	175	285	—

KM# 99 24 MARIENGROSCHEN (2/3 Thaler)
Silver **Obverse:** Without 2/3 **Reverse:** Value and date within inner circle

Date	Mintage	VG	F	VF	XF	Unc
1727	—	60.00	100	175	285	—

KM# 79 1/24 THALER (Groschen)
Silver **Rev. Legend:** IMPERIALIS GOSLARIENSIS

Date	Mintage	VG	F	VF	XF	Unc
1709	—	35.00	65.00	100	155	—
1714	—	35.00	65.00	100	155	—
1716 HAH	—	35.00	65.00	100	155	—
1717 FRH	—	35.00	65.00	100	155	—
1718 HAH	—	35.00	65.00	100	155	—
1722	—	35.00	65.00	100	155	—
1724	—	35.00	65.00	100	155	—
1725	—	35.00	65.00	100	155	—
1726	—	35.00	65.00	100	155	—
1727	—	20.00	40.00	65.00	100	—
1728	—	20.00	40.00	65.00	100	—
1729	—	20.00	40.00	65.00	100	—
1737 HCRF	—	20.00	40.00	65.00	100	—

KM# 115 1/24 THALER (Groschen)
Silver **Reverse:** Date divided in legend at top

Date	Mintage	VG	F	VF	XF	Unc
1740 HCRF	—	20.00	40.00	65.00	100	—

KM# 131 1/24 THALER (Groschen)
Billon **Obverse:** Helmeted city arms, inscription around **Reverse:** Value, date **Rev. Legend:** NACH DEM..

Date	Mintage	VG	F	VF	XF	Unc
1764 HCRF	—	20.00	32.00	55.00	100	—

KM# 86 1/12 THALER (2 Groschen)
Silver **Obverse:** Helmeted arms with plumes **Reverse:** Value and date within inner circle **Note:** Similar to KM#96 but different reverse value: XII/EINEN/THALER.

Date	Mintage	VG	F	VF	XF	Unc
1712 IAH	—	12.00	35.00	65.00	110	—
1713 IAH	—	12.00	35.00	65.00	110	—
1716 IAH	—	12.00	35.00	65.00	110	—

KM# 96 1/12 THALER (2 Groschen)
Silver **Obverse:** Helmeted arms with plumes **Reverse:** Value and date within inner circle

Date	Mintage	VG	F	VF	XF	Unc
1722	—	15.00	35.00	65.00	115	—
1724	—	15.00	35.00	65.00	115	—
1738	—	15.00	35.00	65.00	115	—

KM# 95 1/12 THALER (2 Groschen)
Silver **Obverse:** Helmeted arms **Reverse:** Value and date **Rev. Legend:** IMPERIALIS GOSLARIENSIS **Note:** Similar to KM#96, different reverse legend.

Date	Mintage	VG	F	VF	XF	Unc
ND(1723)	—	20.00	35.00	65.00	115	—

KM# 132 1/12 THALER (2 Groschen)
Silver **Obverse:** Helmeted city arms, inscripton around **Reverse:** Value and date **Rev. Legend:** NACH DEM...

Date	Mintage	Good	VG	F	VF	XF
1764 HCRF	—	—	20.00	35.00	65.00	115

KM# 75 1/2 THALER (12 Groschen)
Silver **Obverse:** Radiant Madonna above arms **Reverse:** Titles of Josef I

Date	Mintage	VG	F	VF	XF	Unc
1705 IAB	—	200	325	525	875	—

KM# 90 1/2 THALER (12 Groschen)
Silver **Obverse:** Radiant Madonna above arms **Reverse:** Titles of Karl VI

Date	Mintage	VG	F	VF	XF	Unc
1717	—	125	200	350	625	—

KM# 97 2/3 THALER (Gulden)
Silver **Obverse:** Helmeted arms with plumes **Reverse:** Radiant Madonna

Date	Mintage	VG	F	VF	XF	Unc
1723	—	225	400	725	1,150	—
1725	—	225	400	725	1,150	—

KM# 76.1 THALER
Silver **Obverse:** Madonna and child divide RESP - GOSL, arms below **Obv. Legend:** SPES NOSTRA IESUS - DEI ET MARIAE FILIUS **Reverse:** Titles of Josef I **Rev. Legend:** IOSEPHUS. I. D. G. ROM. IMPERATOR. SEMP. AUGUSTUS. **Note:** Dav. #2272.

Date	Mintage	F	VF	XF	Unc
1705	—	400	700	1,200	1,850

KM# 76.2 THALER
Silver **Obverse:** Madonna and child divide RESP - GOSL, arms below **Obv. Legend:** SPES NOSTRA IESUS - DEI ET MARIAE FILIUS **Reverse:** Titles of Josef I, imperial eagle with ob on breast **Rev. Legend:** IOSEPHUS. I. D. G. ROM. IMPERATOR. SEMP. AUGUSTUS. **Note:** Dav. #2272A.

Date	Mintage	F	VF	XF	Unc
1705 IAB	—	400	700	1,200	1,850

KM# 91 THALER
Silver **Obverse:** Madonna and child divide RESP: - GOSL:, arms below **Obv. Legend:** SPES NOSTRA IESUS - DEI ET MARIAE FILIUS **Reverse:** Titles of Karl VI **Rev. Legend:** CAROL • VI • D • G • ROM • IMP • SEMP • AUG • HISP • HUNG • & BOH • REX • **Note:** Dav. #2273.

Date	Mintage	F	VF	XF	Unc
1717	—	500	900	1,500	2,250

HALL

(Schwabisch Hall)
(Hall am Kocher)

This city in Swabia, situated on the River Kocher 34 miles (56 kilometers) northeast of Stüttgart, was founded at an early date, probably because of the presence of natural salt in the area. Small silver coins struck beginning in the second half of the 12th century and called *haller* were the origin of both the denomination and its name which has come down over the centuries as *heller*. Hall was made a free imperial city in 1276 and was given the right to strike its own coins in 1396. The city soon began to mint hellers with an open hand on the obverse and a cross on the reverse. These coins became known as *handelshellers* and the hand became the symbol of the city. Hall produced some coins during each of the following centuries, but total mintages were never very high. Most coins issued during the 18th century were commemorative in nature and usually only struck in a single year. The last city coins were produced in 1798. Württemberg annexed the city in 1803 as part of Napoleon's consolidation plans for Germany.

MINT OFFICIALS' INITIALS

Initials	Date	Name
CGL, L	1746-55	Carl Gottlieb Laufer in Nüremberg
GFN, N	1709-21	Georg Friedrich Nürnberger in Nüremberg
K-R	1764-93	G. Knoll, warden and Georg Nikolaus Riedner in Nüremberg
MB	1659-1725	Martin Brunner
OE, OEXLEIN	1740-87	Johann Leonhard Oexlein, die-cutter in Nüremberg
PPW, P.P.WERNER	1711-71	Peter Paul Werner, die-cutter in Nüremberg

ARMS

Usually 2-fold, but also found in separate shields, Open-palmed hand with fingers pointed upwards or a cross.

FREE CITY

REGULAR COINAGE

KM# 7 PFENNIG
Silver **Obverse:** Imperial eagle rising above arms **Note:** Uniface

Date	Mintage	VG	F	VF	XF	Unc
1696	—	4.00	10.00	22.00	50.00	—
1712	—	4.00	10.00	22.00	50.00	—

KM# 43 PFENNIG
Billon **Obverse:** Imperial double-headed eagle rising above two shields of arms **Note:** Uniface.

Date	Mintage	F	VF	XF	Unc
1751	—	10.00	20.00	40.00	80.00
1754	—	10.00	20.00	40.00	80.00
1774	36,000	10.00	20.00	40.00	80.00
1798	—	10.00	20.00	40.00	80.00

KM# 16 1/2 KREUZER
Silver **Subject:** Coronation of Karl VI in 1711 **Obverse:** Imperial double-headed eagle rising above two shields of arms **Reverse:** 5-line inscription with date

Date	Mintage	VG	F	VF	XF	Unc
1712	—	12.00	30.00	60.00	100	—

KM# 15 1/2 KREUZER
Silver **Obverse:** Imperial double-headed eagle rising above shields, 1/2 in oval below divides date **Note:** Uniface

Date	Mintage	VG	F	VF	XF	Unc
1712	—	4.00	8.00	17.00	35.00	—

KM# 36 KREUZER
Silver **Subject:** Centenary - Peace of Westphalia **Obverse:** 2 Ornate shields in laurel wreath **Reverse:** 5-Line inscription with date in laurel wreath

Date	Mintage	VG	F	VF	XF	Unc
1748	—	12.00	30.00	60.00	100	—

KM# 37 KREUZER
Silver **Note:** Klippe.

Date	Mintage	VG	F	VF	XF	Unc
1748	—	25.00	60.00	100	165	—

KM# 38 3 KREUZER
Silver **Subject:** Centenary - Peace of Westphalia **Obverse:** 3 Ornate shields in laurel wreath **Reverse:** 6-Line inscription with date in laurel wreath

Date	Mintage	VG	F	VF	XF	Unc
1748 L	—	25.00	50.00	100	160	—

KM# 39 3 KREUZER
Silver **Note:** Klippe.

Date	Mintage	VG	F	VF	XF	Unc
1748 L	—	30.00	75.00	120	200	—

KM# 25 1/2 THALER

Silver **Subject:** Charles VII **Obverse:** Draped bust right **Reverse:** 3 Ornate shields, laurels flank top shield

Date	Mintage	VG	F	VF	XF	Unc
1742 PGN-I.L. OE	400	400	850	1,600	2,750	—

KM# 30 1/2 THALER

Silver **Subject:** Francis I **Obverse:** Bust right **Reverse:** 3 Ornate shields, laurels flank top shield

Date	Mintage	VG	F	VF	XF	Unc
1746 CGL-P.P. WERNER	700	100	225	400	750	—

KM# 31 1/2 THALER

Silver **Obverse:** Bust right **Reverse:** 3 Ornate shields, laurels flank top shield **Note:** Klippe.

Date	Mintage	VG	F	VF	XF	Unc
1746 CGL-P.P.WERNER	—	650	1,200	2,000	3,250	—

KM# 46 1/2 THALER

Silver **Note:** Klippe.

Date	Mintage	VG	F	VF	XF	Unc
1777 OEXLEIN-K-R	—	—	—	—	—	—

KM# 45.2 1/2 THALER

Silver

Date	Mintage	F	VF	XF	Unc
1777 OE-K-R	Inc. above	200	350	500	900

KM# 45.1 1/2 THALER

Silver **Obverse:** 3 ornate shields, laurels flank top shield **Reverse:** Draped, laureate bust right **Note:** Convention 1/2 Thaler.

Date	Mintage	F	VF	XF	Unc
1777 OEXLEIN-K-R	437	200	350	500	900

KM# 10 THALER

Silver **Obverse:** Joseph I right **Obv. Legend:** IOSEPHUS I • D • G • ROMANORVM IMPERATOR SEMPER AVG **Reverse:** 3 Ornate shields **Rev. Legend:** MONETA NOVA REIPUBLICAE HALAE SUEVICAE * 1705 * **Note:** Dav. #2274.

Date	Mintage	F	VF	XF	Unc
1705 GFN	400	450	750	1,250	1,850

KM# 17 THALER

Silver **Obverse:** Charles VI right **Obv. Legend:** CAROLVS SI • D • G • - ROM • IMP • SEMP • AVG • **Rev. Legend:** MONETA NOVA REPUBLICAE HALAE SUEVICAE, G.F.N. at center **Note:** Dav. #2276.

Date	Mintage	F	VF	XF	Unc
1712 GFN	—	350	600	900	1,500

KM# 26 THALER

Silver **Obverse:** 3 Ornate shields, laurels flank top shield **Obv. Legend:** MONETA NOVA REPUBLICAE HALAE SUEVICAE, P.G.N. at center **Reverse:** Charles VII right **Rev. Legend:** CAROLVS VII•D•G•ROM•IMP•SEMP•AVG• **Note:** Dav. #2278.

Date	Mintage	F	VF	XF	Unc
1742 PGN-I.L. OE	400	725	1,200	1,700	2,600

KM# 27 THALER

Silver **Reverse:** 3 shields of arms, date in legend **Note:** Dav. #2278A.

Date	Mintage	F	VF	XF	Unc
1742 GFN-I.L. OE	Inc. above	725	1,200	1,700	2,600

KM# 32 THALER

Silver **Obverse:** 3 Ornate shields, laurels flank top shield **Obv. Legend:** MONETA NOVA REPUBLICAE HALAE SUEVICAE, C.G.L. at center **Reverse:** Francis I right **Rev. Legend:** FRANCISCVS D • - G • ROM • IMP • SEMP • AVG •, P.P. WERNER on arm **Note:** Dav. #2279.

Date	Mintage	F	VF	XF	Unc
1746 CGL-P.P. WERNER	800	350	600	900	1,500

KM# 33 THALER

Silver **Obverse:** 3 Ornate shields, laurels flank top shield **Obv. Legend:** MONETA NOVA REPUBLICAE HALAE SUEVICAE, G.C.L. at center **Reverse:** Francis I right **Rev. Legend:** FRANCISCVS D • - G • ROM • IMP • SEMP • AVG • **Note:** Klippe. Dav. #2279A.

Date	Mintage	F	VF	XF	Unc
1746 GCL-P.P. WERNER	—	1,650	2,750	4,250	6,000

KM# 48 THALER

Silver **Note:** Klippe. Dav. #2280A.

Date	Mintage	F	VF	XF	Unc
1777 OEXLEIN-K-R	—	—	—	—	—

KM# 47 THALER

Silver **Obverse:** Joseph II right **Obv. Legend:** IOSEPHVS II. D.G. - ROM. IMP. SEMP. AVG., OEXLEIN. F. below **Reverse:** 3 Ornate shields, laurels flank top shield **Rev. Legend:** MONETA NOVA REPUBLICAE HALAE SUEVICAE, E.(N)K. below shields **Note:** Convention Thaler. Dav. #2280.

Date	Mintage	F	VF	XF	Unc
1777 OEXLEIN-K-R	406	200	400	850	1,350

KM# 18 2 THALER

Silver **Obverse:** 3 shields of arms, date in legend **Obv. Legend:** MONETA NOVA REPUBLICAE HALAE SUEVICAE, G.F.N. at center **Reverse:** Joseph I right **Rev. Legend:** CAROLVS VI • D • G • - ROM • IMP • SEMP • AVG • **Note:** Dav. #2275.

Date	Mintage	F	VF	XF	Unc
1712 GFN	—	1,800	3,000	5,000	—

KM# 28 2 THALER

Silver **Obverse:** Charles VII right **Reverse:** 3 Ornate shields, laurels flank top shield **Note:** Similar to 1 Thaler, KM#26. Dav. #2277.

Date	Mintage	F	VF	XF	Unc
1742 PGN-I.L. OE Rare	—	—	—	—	—

KM# 34 2 THALER

Silver **Obverse:** Bust of Franz I **Reverse:** 3 shields of arms, date in legend **Note:** Dav. #A2279.

Date	Mintage	F	VF	XF	Unc
1746 CGL-P.P. WERNER Rare	—	—	—	—	—

TRADE COINAGE

KM# 20 1/4 DUCAT

0.8750 g., 0.9860 Gold 0.0277 oz. AGW **Subject:** Peace of Baden **Obverse:** Two shields with laurels above **Reverse:** Date within wreath

Date	Mintage	VG	F	VF	XF	Unc
1714 N	—	85.00	165	325	550	—

KM# 11 DUCAT

3.5000 g., 0.9860 Gold 0.1109 oz. AGW **Obverse:** Three ornate shields **Reverse:** Joseph I right

Date	Mintage	VG	F	VF	XF	Unc
1705	300	600	1,200	2,500	4,500	—

KM# 19 DUCAT

3.5000 g., 0.9860 Gold 0.1109 oz. AGW **Subject:** Charles VI

Date	Mintage	VG	F	VF	XF	Unc
1712	—	400	900	1,650	2,850	—

KM# 21 DUCAT

3.5000 g., 0.9860 Gold 0.1109 oz. AGW **Subject:** Peace of Baden **Obverse:** 3 Ornate shields, laurels flank top shield **Reverse:** Inscription and date within wreath

Date	Mintage	VG	F	VF	XF	Unc
1714 N	—	300	700	1,200	2,150	—

KM# 29 DUCAT

3.5000 g., 0.9860 Gold 0.1109 oz. AGW **Obverse:** Bust of Charles VII right **Reverse:** 3 Ornate shields, laurels flank top shield

Date	Mintage	VG	F	VF	XF	Unc
1742	200	400	900	1,650	2,850	—

KM# 35 DUCAT

3.5000 g., 0.9860 Gold 0.1109 oz. AGW **Obverse:** 3 ornate shields, laurels flank top shield **Reverse:** Bust of Francis I right

Date	Mintage	VG	F	VF	XF	Unc
1746 PPW-CGL	550	250	550	1,000	1,850	—

KM# 49 DUCAT

3.5000 g., 0.9860 Gold 0.1109 oz. AGW **Obverse:** 3 ornate shields, laurels flank top shield **Reverse:** Bust of Joseph II right

Date	Mintage	F	VF	XF	Unc
1777 OE-K-R	402	300	700	1,200	2,150

KM# A36 5 DUCAT (1/2 Portugalöser)

17.5000 g., 0.9860 Gold 0.5547 oz. AGW **Note:** Struck with 1/2 Thaler dies, KM#30.

Date	Mintage	VG	F	VF	XF	Unc
1746 CGL-P.P. Werner Rare	—	—	—	—	—	—

KM# A20 10 DUCAT (Portugalöser)

35.0000 g., 0.9860 Gold 1.1095 oz. AGW **Note:** Struck with 1 Thaler dies, KM#17.

Date	Mintage	VG	F	VF	XF	Unc
1712 GFN Rare	—	—	—	—	—	—

KM# B36 10 DUCAT (Portugalöser)

35.0000 g., 0.9860 Gold 1.1095 oz. AGW **Note:** Struck with 1 Thaler dies, KM#32.

Date	Mintage	VG	F	VF	XF	Unc
1746 CGL-P.P. Werner Rare	—	—	—	—	—	—

KM# C36 12 DUCAT

42.0000 g., 0.9860 Gold 1.3314 oz. AGW **Note:** Struck with 1 Thaler dies, KM#17.

Date	Mintage	VG	F	VF	XF	Unc
1746 CGL-P.P. Werner Rare	—	—	—	—	—	—

PATTERNS

Including off metal strikes

KM#	Date	Mintage	Identification	Mkt Val
Pn2	1712	—	1/2 Kreuzer. Copper. KM#15.	—
Pn4	1712	—	Thaler. Gold. KM#17, Karl VI.	—
Pn3	1712	—	1/2 Kreuzer. Gold. KM#16.	1,000
Pn5	1714	—	1/4 Ducat. Silver. KM#20.	65.00
Pn6	1714	—	Ducat. Silver. KM#21.	75.00
Pn7	1742	—	Ducat. Silver. KM#29.	—
Pn9	1748	—	Kreuzer. Gold. KM#36.	—

HAMBURG

The city of Hamburg is located on the Elbe River about 75 miles from the North Sea. It was founded by Charlemagne in the 9th century. In 1241 it joined Lübeck to form the Hanseatic League. The mint right was leased to the citizens in 1292. However, the first local halfpennies had been struck almost 50 years earlier. In 1510 Hamburg was formally made a Free City, though, in fact, it had been free for about 250 years. It was occupied by the French during the Napoleonic period. In 1866 it joined the North German Confederation and became a part of the German Empire in 1871. The Hamburg coinage is almost continuous up to the time of World War I.

MINT OFFICIALS' INITIALS

Initials	Date	Name
IHL	1725-59	Johann Hinrich Löwe
IR	1692-1724	Jochim Rustmeyer
OHK	1761-1805	Otto Heinrich Knorre
	1691-1718	Jacob Schroeder, warden
	1718-29	Wichmann Schroeder, warden
	1729-72	Andreas Christoph Cramer, warden
	1772-1806	Johann Joachim Struve, warden

CITY ARMS

A triple-turreted gate, often includes nettleleaf of Holstein.

FREE CITY

REGULAR COINAGE

KM# 163 DREILING (3 Pfennig)

0.5100 g., 0.1870 Silver 0.0031 oz. ASW **Obverse:** Castle with I•H•L below within branches **Reverse:** Value and date within branches

Date	Mintage	VG	F	VF	XF	Unc
1726 IHL	269,000	3.00	6.00	12.00	25.00	—
1727 IHL	230,000	3.00	6.00	12.00	25.00	—
1728 IHL	158,000	3.00	6.00	12.00	25.00	—
1731 IHL	144,000	3.00	6.00	12.00	25.00	—
1734 IHL	227,000	3.00	6.00	12.00	25.00	—
1737 IHL	211,000	3.00	6.00	12.00	25.00	—
1742 IHL	339,000	3.00	6.00	12.00	25.00	—
1745 IHL	—	3.00	6.00	12.00	25.00	—
1746 IHL	443,000	3.00	6.00	12.00	25.00	—
1750 IHL	436,000	3.00	6.00	12.00	25.00	—
1752 IHL	298,000	3.00	6.00	12.00	25.00	—
1756 IHL	348,000	3.00	6.00	12.00	25.00	—
1758 IHL	—	3.00	6.00	12.00	25.00	—
1759 IHL	—	3.00	6.00	12.00	25.00	—
1761 OHK	—	3.00	6.00	12.00	25.00	—
1762 OHK	—	3.00	6.00	12.00	25.00	—
1763 OHK	—	3.00	6.00	12.00	25.00	—

KM# 204 DREILING (3 Pfennig)

0.5100 g., 0.1870 Silver 0.0031 oz. ASW **Reverse:** Without wreath

Date	Mintage	VG	F	VF	XF	Unc
1765 OHK	—	6.00	12.00	25.00	45.00	—
1766 OHK	—	6.00	12.00	25.00	45.00	—

KM# 220 DREILING (3 Pfennig)

0.5100 g., 0.1870 Silver 0.0031 oz. ASW **Obverse:** Castle with O.H.K. below **Reverse:** "1" between rosettes

Date	Mintage	F	VF	XF	Unc
1783 OHK	272,000	4.00	8.00	25.00	35.00
1786 OHK	394,000	4.00	8.00	25.00	35.00
1793 OHK	768,000	4.00	8.00	25.00	35.00
1794 OHK	Inc. above	4.00	8.00	25.00	35.00
1796 OHK	172,000	4.00	8.00	25.00	35.00
1797 OHK	529,000	4.00	8.00	25.00	35.00
1798 OHK	—	4.00	8.00	25.00	35.00
1800 OHK	656,000	4.00	8.00	25.00	35.00
1803 OHK	355,000	4.00	8.00	25.00	35.00

KM# 164 SECHSLING (6 Pfennig)

0.7600 g., 0.2500 Silver 0.0061 oz. ASW **Obverse:** Triple-towered city between legends **Obv. Legend:** HAMBURGER, HAMBURGER **Reverse:** Value, date in wreath

Date	Mintage	VG	F	VF	XF	Unc
1726 IHL	336,000	3.00	6.00	12.00	25.00	—
1727 IHL	146,000	3.00	6.00	12.00	25.00	—
1728 IHL	—	3.00	6.00	12.00	25.00	—
1731 IHL	105,000	3.00	6.00	12.00	25.00	—
1751 IHL	—	3.00	6.00	12.00	25.00	—
1752 IHL	205,000	3.00	6.00	12.00	25.00	—
1756 IHL	244,000	3.00	6.00	12.00	25.00	—
1757 IHL	150,000	3.00	6.00	12.00	25.00	—
1759 IHL	—	3.00	6.00	12.00	25.00	—
1761 OHK	—	3.00	6.00	12.00	25.00	—
1762 OHK	—	3.00	6.00	12.00	25.00	—
1763 OHK	—	3.00	6.00	12.00	25.00	—
1764 OHK	—	3.00	6.00	12.00	25.00	—

KM# 213 SECHSLING (6 Pfennig)
0.7600 g., 0.2500 Silver 0.0061 oz. ASW **Obverse:** Castle with O. H. K. below **Reverse:** "I" between rosettes

Date	Mintage	F	VF	XF	Unc
1778 OHK	259,000	8.00	20.00	27.00	50.00
1783 OHK	182,000	8.00	20.00	27.00	50.00
1794 OHK	256,000	8.00	20.00	27.00	50.00
1797 OHK	163,000	8.00	20.00	27.00	50.00
1800 OHK	227,000	8.00	20.00	27.00	50.00
1803 OHK	182,000	8.00	20.00	27.00	50.00

KM# 160 SCHILLING (12 Pfennig)
1.0800 g., 0.3750 Silver 0.0130 oz. ASW **Obverse:** Castle within branches **Reverse:** Value, date and I•H•L below

Date	Mintage	VG	F	VF	XF	Unc
1725 IHL	—	3.00	6.50	12.50	28.00	—
1726 IHL	1,267,000	3.00	6.50	12.50	28.00	—
1727 IHL	1,308,000	3.00	6.50	12.50	28.00	—
1738 IHL	797,000	3.00	6.50	12.50	28.00	—
1749 IHL	288,000	3.00	6.50	12.50	28.00	—
1750 IHL	120,000	3.00	6.50	12.50	28.00	—
1752 IHL	827,000	3.00	6.50	12.50	28.00	—
1753 IHL	238,000	3.00	6.50	12.50	28.00	—
1754 IHL	558,000	3.00	6.50	12.50	28.00	—
1757 IHL	308,000	3.00	6.50	12.50	28.00	—
1758 IHL	—	3.00	6.50	12.50	28.00	—
1759 IHL	—	3.00	6.50	12.50	28.00	—
1762 OHK	—	3.00	6.50	12.50	28.00	—
1763 OHK	—	3.00	6.50	12.50	28.00	—
1765 OHK	—	3.00	6.50	12.50	28.00	—
1768 OHK	—	3.00	6.50	12.50	28.00	—

KM# 214 SCHILLING (12 Pfennig)
1.0800 g., 0.3750 Silver 0.0130 oz. ASW **Obverse:** Castle with O. H. K. below **Reverse:** "I" between rosettes

Date	Mintage	F	VF	XF	Unc
1778 OHK	2,320,000	2.00	4.00	10.00	40.00
1790 OHK	570,000	2.00	4.00	10.00	40.00
1794 OHK	1,200,000	2.00	4.00	10.00	40.00
1795 OHK	664,000	2.00	4.00	10.00	40.00

KM# 161 2 SCHILLING (1/16 Thaler)
Silver **Obverse:** Crowned imperial eagle, orb on breast, titles of Karl VI **Reverse:** City arms between two laurel branches, II/SCHILL in oval below, date in legend

Date	Mintage	VG	F	VF	XF	Unc
1725 IHL	60,000	12.00	25.00	50.00	85.00	—
1726 IHL	1,044,000	12.00	25.00	50.00	85.00	—
1727 IHL	1,380,000	12.00	25.00	50.00	85.00	—

KM# 197 2 SCHILLING (1/16 Thaler)
1.9600 g., 0.4370 Silver 0.0275 oz. ASW **Obverse:** Crowned imperial eagle **Obv. Legend:** FRANCISCVS D. G... **Reverse:** Three towers in wreath **Rev. Legend:** HAMBURGER COURANT

Date	Mintage	VG	F	VF	XF	Unc
1762 OHK	—	6.00	10.00	20.00	45.00	—
1763 OHK	—	6.00	10.00	20.00	45.00	—

KM# 141 4 SCHILLING
Silver **Obverse:** Crowned imperial double-headed eagle with value on breast **Reverse:** 4/SCHIL/LING between two branches, city arms in small shield below, date in legend

Date	Mintage	VG	F	VF	XF	Unc
1702 IR	—	18.00	35.00	70.00	120	—
1703 IR	—	18.00	35.00	70.00	120	—
1705 IR	—	18.00	35.00	70.00	120	—

KM# 162.1 4 SCHILLING
Silver **Obverse:** Crowned imperial double-headed eagle with orb on breast **Reverse:** Castle within branches above value within circle

Date	Mintage	VG	F	VF	XF	Unc
1725 IHL	558,000	6.00	12.00	25.00	50.00	—
1727 IHL	1,248,000	6.00	12.00	25.00	50.00	—
1728 IHL	545,000	6.00	12.00	25.00	50.00	—

KM# 162.2 4 SCHILLING
Silver **Obverse:** Revised design **Reverse:** Revised design

Date	Mintage	VG	F	VF	XF	Unc
1738 IHL	212,000	8.00	15.00	30.00	55.00	—

KM# 186 4 SCHILLING
3.0500 g., 0.5620 Silver 0.0551 oz. ASW **Obverse:** Crowned imperial eagle **Obv. Legend:** FRANCISCVS D. G.... **Reverse:** Three towers in wreath **Rev. Legend:** HAMBURGER COURANT

Date	Mintage	VG	F	VF	XF	Unc
1749 IHL	—	15.00	30.00	60.00	95.00	—
1761 OHK	—	15.00	30.00	60.00	95.00	—
1762 OHK	—	15.00	30.00	60.00	95.00	—
1765 OHK	—	15.00	30.00	60.00	95.00	—

KM# 230 4 SCHILLING
3.0500 g., 0.5620 Silver 0.0551 oz. ASW **Obverse:** Crowned imperial double-headed eagle with orb on breast **Reverse:** Castle above O.H.K.

Date	Mintage	F	VF	XF	Unc
1797 CHK	236,000	10.00	20.00	40.00	100

KM# 198 6 SCHILLING (1/8 Thaler)
3.6500 g., 0.8880 Silver 0.1042 oz. ASW **Obverse:** Value: 6 SCHILL SPEC in cartouche, arms supported by two lions **Obv. Legend:** MONETA NOVA HAMBVRGENSIS **Reverse:** Crowned imperial eagle, divided date below **Rev. Legend:** FRANCISCVS D. G. ...

Date	Mintage	VG	F	VF	XF	Unc
1762 OHK	—	90.00	150	300	575	—

KM# 165 8 SCHILLING (1/2 Mark)
Silver **Obverse:** Crowned imperial double-headed eagle with orb on breast **Reverse:** Castle within helmeted shield, value within oval below

Date	Mintage	VG	F	VF	XF	Unc
1726 IHL	162,000	12.50	28.00	45.00	90.00	—
1727 IHL	695,000	12.50	28.00	45.00	90.00	—
1728 IHL	273,000	12.50	28.00	45.00	90.00	—

KM# 174 8 SCHILLING (1/2 Mark)
Silver **Obverse:** Mintmaster's initials **Reverse:** Value: 8. SCHIL

Date	Mintage	VG	F	VF	XF	Unc
1738 IHL	199,000	17.50	35.00	60.00	100	—

KM# 195 8 SCHILLING (1/2 Mark)
5.5000 g., 0.6250 Silver 0.1105 oz. ASW **Obverse:** Crowned imperial eagle, date in legend **Obv. Legend:** FRANICSCVS... **Reverse:** Arms **Rev. Legend:** HAMBURGER CURRENT GELD

Date	Mintage	VG	F	VF	XF	Unc
1761 OHK	—	90.00	150	300	575	—

KM# 199 8 SCHILLING (1/2 Mark)
5.5000 g., 0.6250 Silver 0.1105 oz. ASW **Obverse:** Divided date below eagle

Date	Mintage	VG	F	VF	XF	Unc
1762 OHK	—	25.00	45.00	80.00	150	—
1763 OHK	—	25.00	45.00	80.00	150	—
1764 OHK	—	20.00	40.00	70.00	145	—

KM# 231 8 SCHILLING (1/2 Mark)
5.5000 g., 0.6250 Silver 0.1105 oz. ASW **Obverse:** Crowned imperial double-headed eagle with orb on breast **Reverse:** Castle above O.H.K.

Date	Mintage	F	VF	XF	Unc
1797 OHK	206,000	20.00	40.00	80.00	160

KM# 232 8 SCHILLING (1/2 Mark)
5.5000 g., 0.6250 Silver 0.1105 oz. ASW **Obverse:** Castle above O.H.K. **Reverse:** Crowned imperial double-headed eagle with orb on breast **Note:** Varieties exist.

Date	Mintage	F	VF	XF	Unc
1797 OHK	Inc. above	20.00	40.00	80.00	160

KM# 200 12 SCHILLING (1/4 Thaler)
7.3000 g., 0.8880 Silver 0.2084 oz. ASW **Obverse:** Crowned imperial eagle, divided date below **Obv. Legend:** FRANCISCUS D. G.... **Reverse:** Value: 12 SCHILL SPEC in cartouche, arms supported by two lions **Rev. Legend:** MONETA NOVA HAMBVRGENSIS **Note:** Varieties exist.

Date	Mintage	VG	F	VF	XF	Unc
1762 OHK	—	200	400	650	1,000	—

KM# 166 16 SCHILLING (Mark)
Silver **Obverse:** Crowned imperial double-headed eagle with orb on breast **Reverse:** Helmeted arms above value within oval **Note:** Value: 16. SCHILL, similar to 8 Schilling, KM#165.

Date	Mintage	VG	F	VF	XF	Unc
1726 IHL	161,000	20.00	40.00	70.00	125	—
1727 IHL	93,000	20.00	40.00	70.00	125	—
1728 IHL	75,000	20.00	40.00	70.00	125	—

KM# 171 16 SCHILLING (Mark)

Silver **Obverse:** Mintmaster's initials **Reverse:** Value: 16. SCHIL

Date	Mintage	VG	F	VF	XF	Unc
1731	135,000	20.00	40.00	70.00	125	—

KM# 201 16 SCHILLING (Mark)

9.1600 g., 0.7500 Silver 0.2209 oz. ASW **Obverse:** Crowned imperial eagle, divided date below **Obv. Legend:** FRANCISCVS **Reverse:** Arms **Rev. Legend:** HAMBURGER CURRENT GELD

Date	Mintage	VG	F	VF	XF	Unc
1762 OHK	—	50.00	90.00	160	250	—
1763 OHK	—	50.00	90.00	160	250	—
1764 OHK	—	50.00	90.00	160	250	—

KM# 222 16 SCHILLING (Mark)

9.1600 g., 0.7500 Silver 0.2209 oz. ASW **Obverse:** Titles of Josef II **Reverse:** Helmet above castle within frame

Date	Mintage	F	VF	XF	Unc
1789 OHK	80,000	30.00	60.00	100	175

KM# 202 24 SCHILLING (1/2 Thaler)

14.6000 g., 0.8880 Silver 0.4168 oz. ASW **Obverse:** Crowned imperial eagle, divided date below **Obv. Legend:** FRANCISCVS D. G. ... **Reverse:** Value: 6 SCHILL SPEC in cartouche, arms supported by two lions **Rev. Legend:** MONETA NOVA HAMBVRGENSIS

Date	Mintage	VG	F	VF	XF	Unc
1762 OHK	—	500	1,000	1,500	3,000	—

KM# 167 32 SCHILLING (2 Mark)

Silver **Obverse:** Titles of Karl VI **Reverse:** Crowned imperial double-headed eagle with orb on breast

Date	Mintage	VG	F	VF	XF	Unc
1726 IHL	188,000	30.00	65.00	120	180	—
1727 IHL	164,000	30.00	65.00	120	180	—
1728 IHL	39,000	30.00	65.00	120	180	—

KM# 172 32 SCHILLING (2 Mark)

Silver **Obverse:** 32 SCHIL **Reverse:** Mintmaster's initials

Date	Mintage	VG	F	VF	XF	Unc
1731 IHL	113,000	35.00	85.00	160	235	—
1733 IHL	110,000	35.00	85.00	160	235	—
1734 IHL	—	35.00	85.00	160	235	—
1737 IHL	110,000	35.00	85.00	160	235	—

KM# 184 32 SCHILLING (2 Mark)

18.3200 g., 0.7500 Silver 0.4417 oz. ASW **Obverse:** Titles of Franz I **Reverse:** Helmet with plumes above arms

Date	Mintage	VG	F	VF	XF	Unc
1748 IHL	55,000	25.00	45.00	80.00	150	—
1751 IHL	6,000	25.00	45.00	80.00	150	—
1752 IHL	54,000	25.00	45.00	80.00	150	—
1754 IHL	36,000	25.00	45.00	80.00	150	—
1755 IHL	34,000	25.00	45.00	80.00	150	—
1757 IHL	29,000	25.00	45.00	80.00	150	—
1758 IHL	—	25.00	45.00	80.00	150	—
1759 IHL	—	25.00	45.00	80.00	150	—
1761 OHK	—	25.00	45.00	80.00	150	—

KM# 203 32 SCHILLING (2 Mark)

18.3200 g., 0.7500 Silver 0.4417 oz. ASW **Obverse:** Crowned imperial double-headed eagle with orb on breast **Reverse:** Helmeted arms

Date	Mintage	VG	F	VF	XF	Unc
1762 OHK	—	25.00	50.00	85.00	160	—
1763 OHK	—	25.00	50.00	85.00	160	—
1764 OHK	—	25.00	50.00	85.00	160	—

KM# 205 32 SCHILLING (2 Mark)

18.3200 g., 0.7500 Silver 0.4417 oz. ASW **Obverse:** Crowned imperial double-headed eagle with orb on breast **Obv. Legend:** JOSEPHVS. II. D. G... **Reverse:** Helmeted arms **Note:** Similar to KM#229.

Date	Mintage	F	VF	XF	Unc
1766 OHK	18,000	60.00	125	175	300
1767 OHK	—	60.00	125	175	300

KM# 221 32 SCHILLING (2 Mark)

18.3200 g., 0.7500 Silver 0.4417 oz. ASW **Obverse:** Crowned imperial double-headed eagle with orb on breast **Reverse:** Helmeted arms

Date	Mintage	F	VF	XF	Unc
1788 OHK	60,000	50.00	80.00	120	200
1789 OHK	315,000	40.00	70.00	110	185

KM# 229 32 SCHILLING (2 Mark)

18.3200 g., 0.7500 Silver 0.4417 oz. ASW **Obverse:** Titles of Franz II; Helmeted arms **Reverse:** Crowned imperial eagle **Rev. Legend:** FRANCISCUS•II•D•G•ROM•IMP•SEMP•AUGUSTUS

Date	Mintage	F	VF	XF	Unc
1794 OHK	130,000	30.00	60.00	100	175
1795 OHK	951,000	30.00	60.00	100	175
1796 OHK	1,138,000	30.00	60.00	100	175
1797 OHK	180,000	30.00	60.00	100	175

KM# 196.1 48 SCHILLING (Thaler)

29.2000 g., 0.8880 Silver 0.8336 oz. ASW **Obverse:** Medium-sized crown, orb and crowned imperial eagle **Obv. Legend:** FRANCISCVS D • G • ROM • IMP • SEMP • AVGVSTVS **Reverse:** Large lions supporting ornate shield, large 48 **Rev. Legend:** MONETA NOVA - HAMBVRGENSIS, 48 SCHILL•SPEC/O.H.K. in frame below **Note:** Dav. #2285.

Date	Mintage	VG	F	VF	XF	Unc
1761 OHK	—	65.00	125	250	400	—

KM# 196.2 48 SCHILLING (Thaler)

29.2000 g., 0.8880 Silver 0.8336 oz. ASW **Obverse:** Large lions supporting ornate shield **Obv. Legend:** MONETA NOVA - HAMBVRGENSIS, 48 SCHILL • SPEC/O.H.K. below in frame **Reverse:** Large crown, orb and crowned imperial eagle **Rev. Legend:** FRANCISCVS D • G • ROM • IMP • SEMP • AVGVSTVS **Note:** Dav. #2285A.

Date	Mintage	VG	F	VF	XF	Unc
1763 OHK	—	50.00	100	200	350	—

KM# 196.3 48 SCHILLING (Thaler)

29.2000 g., 0.8880 Silver 0.8336 oz. ASW **Obverse:** Medium-sized crown, orb and crowned imperial eagle **Obv. Legend:** FRANCISCVS D • G • ROM • IMP • SEMP • AVGVSTVS **Reverse:** Small lions supporting plain shield **Rev. Legend:** MONETA NOVA - HAMBVRGENSIS, 48 SCHILL • SPEC/O.H.K. below in frame **Note:** Dav. #2285B.

Date	Mintage	VG	F	VF	XF	Unc
1763 OHK	—	50.00	100	200	350	—

KM# 196.4 48 SCHILLING (Thaler)

29.2000 g., 0.8880 Silver 0.8336 oz. ASW **Obverse:** Small lions supporting plain shild **Obv. Legend:** MONETA NOVA - HAMBVRGENSIS, 48 SCHILL • SPEC/O.H.K. below in frame **Reverse:** Small crown, orb and crowned imperial eagle **Rev. Legend:** FRANCISCVS D • G • ROM • IMP • SEMP • AVGVSTVS **Note:** Dav. #2285C.

Date	Mintage	VG	F	VF	XF	Unc
1764 OHK	—	50.00	100	200	350	—

KM# 152 1/2 THALER

Silver **Subject:** 200th Anniversary of the Reformation **Obverse:** City scene **Obv. Legend:** SUB UMBRA ALARUM TUARUM, HAMBURG in cartouche below **Reverse:** Date in Roman numerals **Rev. Legend:** IN/MEMORIAM/IUBILÆ EVANGE/LICI SECUNDI/CELEBRATI/ANNO SECLARI/MDCCXVII

Date	Mintage	VG	F	VF	XF	Unc
ND(1717) IR	—	150	325	600	950	—

KM# 153 1/2 THALER

Silver **Obverse:** Facing bust of Martin Luther, date below **Reverse:** Altar with Bible, storm raging about

Date	Mintage	VG	F	VF	XF	Unc
1717	—	75.00	140	240	375	—

KM# 154 THALER

Silver **Subject:** 200th Anniversary of the Reformation **Obverse:** City scene **Obv. Legend:** SUB UMBRA ALARUM TUARUM, HAMBURG in cartouche below **Note:** Dav. #2281.

Date	Mintage	F	VF	XF	Unc
ND(1717) IR	—	500	900	1,500	2,500

KM# 170 THALER

Silver **Subject:** 200th Anniversary of the Augsburg Confession **Obverse:** Titles of Karl VI **Obv. Legend:** CAROLVS VI. D.G. ROM. - IMP. SEMP. AVGVST. **Reverse:** Helmeted arms on shield, branches at left and right **Rev. Legend:** MONET. NOV. CIVITAT. HAMBVRG. ANNO IVBIL. II. **Note:** Dav. #2282.

Date	Mintage	F	VF	XF	Unc
1730 IHL	5,000	110	225	375	800

KM# 173 THALER

Silver **Obverse:** Helmeted arms with branches at left and right **Obv. Legend:** MONETA • NOVA • CIVITATIS • HAMBVRGENSIS • **Reverse:** Crowned imperial double-headed eagle with orb on breast **Rev. Legend:** CAROLVS • VI • D• G • ROM • IMP • SEMP • AVGVST • **Note:** Dav. #2283.

Date	Mintage	F	VF	XF	Unc
1735 IHL	8,000	125	250	400	850

KM# 185 THALER

Silver **Subject:** Centenary - Peace of Westphalia **Obverse:** Helmeted arms with lion supporters, date in exergue below **Obv. Legend:** SAECVLO A PACE WESTPHALICA EXACTO **Reverse:** Titles of Franz I **Rev. Legend:** FRANCISCVS D • G • ROM • IMP • SEMP • AVGVST • **Note:** Dav. #2284.

Date	Mintage	F	VF	XF	Unc
1748 IHL	7,000	125	250	400	800

TRADE COINAGE

KM# 168 1/4 DUCAT

0.8750 g., 0.9860 Gold 0.0277 oz. AGW **Obverse:** Crowned imperial eagle, titles of Karl VI **Reverse:** Arms

Date	Mintage	VG	F	VF	XF	Unc
1729 IHL	—	100	175	350	500	—

KM# 121 DUCAT

3.5000 g., 0.9860 Gold 0.1109 oz. AGW **Obverse:** Arms in branches **Reverse:** Crowned imperial eagle

Date	Mintage	VG	F	VF	XF	Unc
1701	—	150	250	625	1,150	—
1704	—	150	250	625	1,150	—
1705 IR	—	150	250	625	1,150	—

KM# 142 DUCAT

3.5000 g., 0.9860 Gold 0.1109 oz. AGW **Obverse:** Castle within branches **Reverse:** Bust of Josef I right

Date	Mintage	VG	F	VF	XF	Unc
1705 IR	—	300	500	1,300	2,250	—
1706 IR	—	300	500	1,300	2,250	—
1708 IR	—	300	500	1,300	2,250	—
1710 IR	—	300	500	1,300	2,250	—

KM# 145 DUCAT

3.5000 g., 0.9860 Gold 0.1109 oz. AGW **Obverse:** Eage, titles of Josef I

Date	Mintage	VG	F	VF	XF	Unc
1706 IR	—	150	250	600	1,000	—
1707 IR	—	150	250	600	1,000	—
1708 IR	—	150	250	600	1,000	—
1710 IR	—	150	250	600	1,000	—
1711 IR	—	150	250	600	1,000	—

KM# 150 DUCAT

3.5000 g., 0.9860 Gold 0.1109 oz. AGW **Obverse:** Titles of Karl VI **Reverse:** Castle within shield, lion supporters

Date	Mintage	VG	F	VF	XF	Unc
1713 IR	—	150	250	550	900	—
1714 IR	—	150	250	550	900	—
1717 IR	—	150	250	550	900	—
1721	—	150	250	550	900	—
1726 IHL	1,700	150	250	550	900	—
1727 IHL	5,078	150	250	550	900	—
1728 IHL	3,798	150	250	550	900	—
1729 IHL	3,454	150	250	550	900	—
1730 IHL	2,429	150	250	550	900	—
1731 IHL	2,114	150	250	550	900	—
1732 IHL	5,171	150	250	550	900	—
1733 IHL	2,235	150	250	550	900	—
1734 IHL	3,184	150	250	550	900	—
1735 IHL	3,945	150	250	550	900	—
1736 IHL	4,215	150	250	550	900	—
1737 IHL	5,165	150	250	550	900	—
1738 IHL	1,947	150	250	550	900	—
1739 IHL	2,221	150	250	550	900	—
1740 IHL	4,942	150	250	550	900	—

KM# 180 DUCAT

3.5000 g., 0.9860 Gold 0.1109 oz. AGW **Obverse:** Crowned imperial eagle, titles of Karl VII **Reverse:** Arms in cartouche

Date	Mintage	VG	F	VF	XF	Unc
1742 IHL	4,506	125	250	600	1,000	—
1743 IHL	2,810	125	250	600	1,000	—
1744 IHL	5,343	125	250	600	1,000	—
1745 IHL	3,232	125	250	600	1,000	—

KM# 182 DUCAT

3.5000 g., 0.9860 Gold 0.1109 oz. AGW **Obverse:** Crowned imperial double-headed eagle with orb on breast **Reverse:** Arms within ornate frame

Date	Mintage	VG	F	VF	XF	Unc
1746 IHL	2,645	125	250	550	900	—
1747 IHL	2,529	125	250	550	900	—
1748 IHL	2,479	125	250	550	900	—
1749 IHL	3,749	125	250	550	900	—
1750 IHL	5,166	125	250	550	900	—
1751 IHL	2,114	125	250	550	900	—
1752 IHL	4,379	125	250	550	900	—
1753 IHL	4,866	125	250	550	900	—

KM# 190 DUCAT

3.5000 g., 0.9860 Gold 0.1109 oz. AGW **Obverse:** Crowned imperial double-headed eagle with orb on breast **Reverse:** Shielded arms

Date	Mintage	VG	F	VF	XF	Unc
1754 IHL	5,047	125	250	550	900	—
1755 IHL	3,750	125	250	550	900	—
1756 IHL	15,000	125	250	550	900	—
1757 IHL	—	125	250	550	900	—
1758 IHL	—	125	250	550	900	—
1759 IHL	—	125	250	550	900	—
1760 IHL	—	125	250	550	900	—
1761 OHK	—	125	250	550	900	—
1762 OHK	—	125	250	550	900	—
1763 OHK	—	125	250	550	900	—
1764 OHK	—	125	250	550	900	—
1765 OHK	—	125	250	550	900	—

KM# 206 DUCAT

3.5000 g., 0.9860 Gold 0.1109 oz. AGW **Obverse:** Castle within decorative frame **Reverse:** Titles of Josef II

Date	Mintage	F	VF	XF	Unc
1766 OHK	2,904	250	350	600	1,000
1767 OHK	3,640	250	350	600	1,000
1768 OHK	—	250	350	600	1,000
1769 OHK	—	250	350	600	1,000
1770 OHK	3,192	250	350	600	1,000
1771 OHK	—	250	350	600	1,000
1772 OHK	—	250	350	600	1,000

KM# 211 DUCAT

3.4900 g., 0.9790 Gold 0.1098 oz. AGW **Obverse:** Crowned imperial double-headed eagle with orb on breast **Reverse:** Legend within square, castle above, ornaments around

Date	Mintage	F	VF	XF	Unc
1773	—	250	350	600	950
1774	—	250	350	600	950
1775	—	250	350	600	950
1776	—	250	350	600	950
1777	—	250	350	600	950
1778	—	250	350	600	950
1779	3,192	250	350	600	950
1780	4,471	250	350	600	950
1781	4,414	250	350	600	950
1782	4,500	250	350	600	950
1783	4,500	250	350	600	950
1784	3,231	250	350	600	950
1785	3,714	250	350	600	950
1786	4,500	250	350	600	950
1787	4,689	250	350	600	950
1788	4,500	250	350	600	950

KM# 225 DUCAT

3.4900 g., 0.9790 Gold 0.1098 oz. AGW **Obverse:** Legend within square, castle above, ornaments around **Reverse:** Titles of Leopold II

Date	Mintage	F	VF	XF	Unc
1791	5,633	350	575	900	1,275
1792	5,054	350	575	900	1,275

KM# 227.1 DUCAT

3.4900 g., 0.9790 Gold 0.1098 oz. AGW **Obverse:** Legend within square, castle above, ornaments surround **Reverse:** Titles of Franz II

Date	Mintage	F	VF	XF	Unc
1793	3,303	375	625	1,100	1,650
1794	5,397	375	625	1,000	1,500
1795	5,000	375	625	1,000	1,500
1796	5,142	375	625	1,000	1,500
1797	4,824	375	625	1,000	1,500
1798	6,287	375	625	1,000	1,500
1799	7,325	375	625	1,000	1,500
1800	3,370	375	625	1,100	1,650
1801	7,236	375	625	1,000	1,500
1802	9,199	375	625	1,000	1,500
1803	6,365	375	625	1,000	1,500
1804	7,284	375	625	1,000	1,500
1805	9,466	375	625	1,000	1,500

KM# 122 2 DUCAT

7.0000 g., 0.9860 Gold 0.2219 oz. AGW **Obverse:** Crowned imperial eagle, titles of Leopold I **Reverse:** Arms in cartouche

Date	Mintage	VG	F	VF	XF	Unc
1689 HL	—	400	900	2,000	3,000	—
1692	—	400	900	2,000	3,000	—
1696	—	400	900	2,000	3,000	—
1698	—	400	900	2,000	3,000	—
1701	—	400	900	2,000	3,000	—
1705	—	400	900	2,000	3,000	—

KM# 143 2 DUCAT

7.0000 g., 0.9860 Gold 0.2219 oz. AGW **Obverse:** Bust of Josef I right **Reverse:** Arms in cartouche

Date	Mintage	VG	F	VF	XF	Unc
1705	—	500	1,000	2,500	4,000	—

KM# 144 2 DUCAT

7.0000 g., 0.9860 Gold 0.2219 oz. AGW **Obverse:** Crowned imperial eagle, titles of Josef I **Reverse:** Arms in palm branches

Date	Mintage	VG	F	VF	XF	Unc
1705 IR	—	300	650	1,250	2,250	—
ND IR	—	300	650	1,250	2,250	—

KM# 151 2 DUCAT

7.0000 g., 0.9860 Gold 0.2219 oz. AGW **Obverse:** Titles of Karl VI **Reverse:** Castle within oval ornate frame

Date	Mintage	VG	F	VF	XF	Unc
1713 IR	—	250	550	1,200	2,000	—
1717 IR	—	250	550	1,200	2,000	—
1725 IHL	1,073	250	550	1,200	2,000	—
1726 IHL	842	250	550	1,200	2,000	—
1727 IHL	1,005	250	550	1,200	2,000	—
1728 IHL	396	250	550	1,200	2,000	—
1729 IHL	566	250	550	1,200	2,000	—
1730 IHL	502	250	550	1,200	2,000	—
1732 IHL	1,078	250	550	1,200	2,000	—
1733 IHL	—	250	550	1,200	2,000	—
1734 IHL	471	250	550	1,200	2,000	—
1735 IHL	679	250	550	1,200	2,000	—
1736 IHL	260	250	550	1,200	2,000	—
1737 IHL	545	250	550	1,200	2,000	—
1738 IHL	335	250	550	1,200	2,000	—
1739	352	250	550	1,200	2,000	—
1740	435	250	550	1,200	2,000	—

KM# 181 2 DUCAT

7.0000 g., 0.9860 Gold 0.2219 oz. AGW **Obverse:** Crowned imperial eagle, titles of Karl VII **Reverse:** Arms in cartouche

Date	Mintage	VG	F	VF	XF	Unc
1742 IHL	1,080	300	650	1,250	2,250	—
1744 IHL	336	300	650	1,250	2,250	—
1745 IHL	775	300	650	1,250	2,250	—

KM# 183 2 DUCAT

7.0000 g., 0.9860 Gold 0.2219 oz. AGW **Obverse:** Arms within ornate frame **Reverse:** Titles of Franz

Date	Mintage	F	VF	XF	Unc
1746 IHL	450	600	1,250	1,750	2,650
1748 IHL	292	600	1,250	1,750	2,650
1746 IHL	543	600	1,250	1,750	2,650
1750 IHL	446	600	1,250	1,750	2,650
1751 IHL	1,207	600	1,250	1,750	2,650
1753 IHL	1,094	600	1,250	1,750	2,650

KM# 191 2 DUCAT

7.0000 g., 0.9860 Gold 0.2219 oz. AGW **Obverse:** Crowned imperial double-headed eagle with orb on breast **Reverse:** Casstle within cartouche

Date	Mintage	F	VF	XF	Unc
1754 IHL	—	600	1,250	1,750	2,650
1755 IHL	505	600	1,250	1,750	2,650
1756 IHL	767	600	1,250	1,750	2,650
1757 IHL	—	600	1,250	1,750	2,650
1758 IHL	—	600	1,250	1,750	2,650
1759 IHL	—	600	1,250	1,750	2,650
1760 IHL	—	600	1,250	1,750	2,650
1762 OHK	—	600	1,250	1,750	2,650
1763 OHK	—	600	1,250	1,750	2,650
1764 OHK	—	600	1,250	1,750	2,650
1765 OHK	—	600	1,250	1,750	2,650

KM# 207 2 DUCAT

7.0000 g., 0.9860 Gold 0.2219 oz. AGW **Obverse:** Titles of Josef II **Reverse:** Castle within ornate frame, O.H.K. in frame below

Date	Mintage	F	VF	XF	Unc
1766 OHK	613	650	1,250	1,750	2,650
1767 OHK	584	650	1,250	1,750	2,650
1768 OHK	—	650	1,250	1,750	2,650
1769 OHK	—	650	1,250	1,750	2,650
1770 OHK	536	650	1,250	1,750	2,650
1771 OHK	—	650	1,250	1,750	2,650

KM# 210 2 DUCAT

7.0000 g., 0.9860 Gold 0.2219 oz. AGW **Obverse:** Without frame for O. H. K. **Reverse:** Crowned imperial double-headed eagle with orb on breast

Date	Mintage	F	VF	XF	Unc
1772 OHK	—	1,000	1,500	1,950	2,800

KM# 212 2 DUCAT

6.9800 g., 0.9790 Gold 0.2197 oz. AGW **Obverse:** Crowned imperial double-headed eagle with orb on breast **Reverse:** Legend within square, castle above, ornaments around **Note:** Varieties exist.

Date	Mintage	F	VF	XF	Unc
1773	—	650	1,000	1,500	2,500
1774	—	650	1,000	1,500	2,500
1775	—	650	1,000	1,500	2,500
1776	—	650	1,000	1,500	2,500
1777	—	650	1,000	1,500	2,500

Date	Mintage	F	VF	XF	Unc
1778	—	750	1,150	1,750	2,850
1779	479	650	1,100	1,650	2,750
1780	875	650	1,000	1,500	2,500
1781	231	800	1,200	1,800	3,000
1782	450	750	1,100	1,650	2,750
1783	450	750	1,100	1,650	2,750
1784	455	750	1,100	1,650	2,750
1785	879	650	1,000	1,500	2,500
1786	400	750	1,100	1,650	2,750
1787	320	750	1,150	1,750	2,850
1788	400	750	1,100	1,650	2,750

KM# 223 2 DUCAT
6.9800 g., 0.9790 Gold 0.2197 oz. AGW **Obverse:** Legend within square, castle above, ornaments around **Reverse:** Crowned small imperial eagle, date above

Date	Mintage	F	VF	XF	Unc
1789	402	600	1,100	1,500	2,500
1790	500	600	1,100	1,500	2,500

KM# 226 2 DUCAT
6.9800 g., 0.9790 Gold 0.2197 oz. AGW **Obverse:** Legend within square, castle above, ornaments around **Reverse:** Crowned imperial double-headed eagle with orb on breast

Date	Mintage	F	VF	XF	Unc
1791	502	600	1,100	1,500	2,500
1792	701	600	1,100	1,500	2,500

KM# 228.1 2 DUCAT
6.9800 g., 0.9790 Gold 0.2197 oz. AGW **Obverse:** Legend within square ornamental frame **Reverse:** Crowned orb at center of double eagle with sword and sceptre **Rev. Legend:** FRANCISVS II D. G. ROM. IMP...

Date	Mintage	F	VF	XF	Unc
1793	360	650	1,450	2,500	3,250
1794	673	650	1,300	1,950	2,650
1795	600	650	1,300	1,950	2,650
1796	547	650	1,350	2,350	3,000
1797	670	650	1,300	1,950	2,650
1798	670	650	1,300	1,950	2,650
1799	765	650	1,300	1,950	2,650
1800	811	650	1,350	2,350	3,000
1801	1,273	650	1,250	1,750	2,450
1802	1,256	650	1,250	1,750	2,450
1803	837	650	1,350	2,350	3,000
1804	—	650	1,300	2,000	2,750
1805	—	650	1,250	1,750	2,450

Note: Mintage included in KM#227.1

KM# 233 4 DUCAT
13.9600 g., 0.9790 Gold 0.4394 oz. AGW **Obverse:** Three towers **Reverse:** Crowned eagle

Date	Mintage	F	VF	XF	Unc
1797	—	1,250	2,500	4,000	7,500

PATTERNS

Including off metal strikes

KM#	Date	Mintage	Identification	Mkt Val
Pn1	1730	—	2 Ducat. Silver. KM#151	180
Pn2	1733	—	Ducat. Silver. KM#150	120
Pn3	1734	—	2 Ducat. Silver. KM#151	180
Pn4	1735	—	Ducat. Silver. KM#150	120
Pn5	1735	—	2 Ducat. Silver. KM#151	180
Pn6	1740	—	Ducat. Silver. KM#150	120
Pn7	1740	—	2 Ducat. Silver. KM#151	180
Pn8	1742	—	2 Ducat. Silver. KM#181	275

KM#	Date	Mintage	Identification	Mkt Val
Pn9	1746	—	2 Ducat. Silver. KM#183	180
Pn10	1778	—	Schilling. Gold. KM#214	400
Pn11	1778	—	Schilling. 0.9990 Gold. KM#214	425
Pn12	1790	—	Schilling. Gold. KM#214	400
PnA13	1795	—	4 Schilling. Gold. 6.9600 g. KM#230.	—

KM#	Date	Mintage	Identification	Mkt Val
Pn13	1796	—	Dreiling. Gold. . KM#220	175
Pn14	1798	—	Schilling. 0.9990 Gold. . KM#214	425

HAMM

A provincial city located in Westphalia, some 20 miles northeast of Dortmund, in the county of Mark. When the ruling house of Mark (see Cleves and Julich-Berg) became extinct in 1609, its territories, including Hamm, went to Brandenburg-Prussia in 1624 after a dispute with Pfalz-Neuburg. Hamm struck a local copper coinage from 1609 to 1749.

ARMS
Fesse of checkerboard

CITY

REGULAR COINAGE

KM# 71 3 PFENNIG
Copper **Obverse:** Arms **Reverse:** Value within wreath

Date	Mintage	VG	F	VF	XF	Unc
1687	—	5.00	15.00	25.00	40.00	—
1699	—	5.00	15.00	25.00	40.00	—
1700	—	5.00	15.00	25.00	40.00	—
1701	—	5.00	15.00	25.00	40.00	—
1701	—	5.00	15.00	25.00	40.00	—
1703	—	5.00	15.00	25.00	40.00	—
1705	—	5.00	15.00	25.00	40.00	—
1711	—	5.00	15.00	25.00	40.00	—
1744	—	5.00	15.00	25.00	40.00	—

KM# 72 3 PFENNIG
Copper **Obverse:** Date above arms

Date	Mintage	VG	F	VF	XF	Unc
1687	—	5.00	15.00	25.00	40.00	—
1692	—	5.00	15.00	25.00	40.00	—
1693	—	5.00	15.00	25.00	40.00	—
1696	—	5.00	15.00	25.00	40.00	—
1727	—	5.00	15.00	25.00	40.00	—
1727	—	5.00	15.00	25.00	40.00	—
1741	—	5.00	15.00	25.00	40.00	—
1746	—	5.00	15.00	25.00	40.00	—

KM# 75 3 PFENNIG
Copper **Obverse:** Arms **Reverse:** Value within wreath **Note:** Varieties exist.

Date	Mintage	VG	F	VF	XF	Unc
1690	47,000	5.00	15.00	25.00	40.00	—
1699	—	5.00	15.00	25.00	40.00	—
1710	—	5.00	15.00	25.00	40.00	—
1710	—	5.00	15.00	25.00	40.00	—
1713	—	5.00	15.00	25.00	40.00	—
1714	—	5.00	15.00	25.00	40.00	—
1715	—	5.00	15.00	25.00	40.00	—
1717	—	5.00	15.00	25.00	40.00	—
1719	228,000	5.00	15.00	25.00	40.00	—
1720	—	5.00	15.00	25.00	40.00	—
1721	232,000	5.00	15.00	25.00	40.00	—
1725	156,000	5.00	15.00	25.00	40.00	—
1727	Inc. above	5.00	15.00	25.00	40.00	—
1729	361,000	5.00	15.00	25.00	40.00	—
1730	—	5.00	15.00	25.00	40.00	—
1732	105,000	5.00	15.00	25.00	40.00	—
1733	232,000	5.00	15.00	25.00	40.00	—
1734	245,000	5.00	15.00	25.00	40.00	—
1736	295,000	5.00	15.00	25.00	40.00	—
1737	172,000	5.00	15.00	25.00	40.00	—
1739	—	5.00	15.00	25.00	40.00	—
1742	—	5.00	15.00	25.00	40.00	—
1743	—	5.00	15.00	25.00	40.00	—
1745	—	5.00	15.00	25.00	40.00	—
1747	—	5.00	15.00	25.00	40.00	—
1749	—	5.00	15.00	25.00	40.00	—

KM# 76 3 PFENNIG
Copper **Obv. Legend:** STADT/date/HAMM

Date	Mintage	VG	F	VF	XF	Unc
1696	—	5.00	15.00	25.00	40.00	—
1713	—	5.00	15.00	25.00	40.00	—
1713	—	5.00	15.00	25.00	40.00	—
1746	—	5.00	15.00	25.00	40.00	—

HANAU

Located 14 miles east of Frankfurt am Main, Hanau is the site of a Roman frontier settlement. The line of counts can be traced back to the mid-11th century. The county was divided into the lines of Hanau-Lichtenberg and Hanau-Münzenberg in 1451.

HANAU-LICHTENBERG

The younger line of the counts of Hanau. Lands in Alsace, acquired through marriage, the counts taking up residence in Buchsweiler, some 14 miles west of Hagenau. The elder Münzenberg line became extinct in 1642 and all lands passed to Lichtenberg. Raised to the rank of prince in 1696. Became extinct in 1736 and passed to Hesse-Darmstadt in 1785.

RULERS
Philipp Reinhard, 1685-1712
Johann Reinhard III, 1712-1736
Ludwig IX of Hesse-Darmstadt, 1736-1785

MINT OFFICIALS' INITIALS

Darmstadt

Initials	Date	Name
BIB	1707-33	Balthasar Johann Benthmann
R	1696-1727	Johann C. Roth, die-cutter

Hanau

Initials	Date	Name
CHS	1757-58	Conrad Heinrich Schwertner
EGF	1758-59	Eberhard Gregorius Fleischheld

Heidelberg

Initials	Date	Name
IL, JL	1659-1711	Johann Link, die-cutter

Mannheim

Initials	Date	Name
AS	d.1799	Anton Schaeffer, die-cutter
MC		Manhemi Cusa

ARMS
Hanau only - 3 chevrons, but often 4-fold arms with central chevron shield.
Hanau-Lichtenberg - 3 chevrons on left, rampant lion on right.
Ochsenstein – 2 horizontal bars.

COUNTY

REGULAR COINAGE

KM# 110 PFENNIG
Silver **Ruler:** Johann Reinhard III **Obverse:** Hanau arms in shield **Note:** Uniface

Date	Mintage	VG	F	VF	XF	Unc
ND(1712-36)	—	12.00	25.00	45.00	85.00	—

KM# 123 KREUZER
Billon **Ruler:** Ludwig IX of Hesse-Darmstadt **Obverse:** Crowned lion shield in cartouche, HD above, HL below **Reverse:** Value, date in 4 lines between 2 branches

Date	Mintage	VG	F	VF	XF	Unc
1759	—	75.00	165	375	650	—

KM# 124 2 KREUZER (1/2 Batzen)

Billon **Ruler:** Ludwig IX of Hesse-Darmstadt **Obverse:** Crowned lion shield in cartouche, HD above, HL below **Reverse:** Value, date in 4 lines between 2 branches

Date	Mintage	VG	F	VF	XF	Unc
1759	—	75.00	165	375	650	—

KM# 125 4 KREUZER

Billon **Ruler:** Ludwig IX of Hesse-Darmstadt **Obverse:** Crowned rampant lion left within branches **Reverse:** Value within cartouche, date below

Date	Mintage	VG	F	VF	XF	Unc
1759 EGF	—	60.00	145	350	550	—

KM# 120 2 ALBUS (Batzen)

Billon **Ruler:** Ludwig IX of Hesse-Darmstadt **Obverse:** 3 oval arms in cartouche, HD above, HL below **Reverse:** Value in cartouche, date below **Rev. Legend:** LAND MUNZ

Date	Mintage	VG	F	VF	XF	Unc
1757 CHS	—	22.00	40.00	70.00	135	—

KM# 130 10 KREUZER

Silver **Ruler:** Ludwig IX of Hesse-Darmstadt **Obverse:** Bust right in wreath, legend around **Reverse:** Crowned lion shield on pedestal, value, date at left and right **Rev. Legend:** AD NORMAM.. **Note:** Convention 10 Kreuzer.

Date	Mintage	VG	F	VF	XF	Unc
1760 MC-AS	—	85.00	200	425	750	—

KM# 121 1/6 THALER

Silver **Ruler:** Ludwig IX of Hesse-Darmstadt **Obverse:** Crowned monogram **Reverse:** Value, date in 5 lines

Date	Mintage	VG	F	VF	XF	Unc
1758	—	40.00	75.00	125	235	—
1758 EGF	—	40.00	75.00	125	235	—

KM# 115 60 KREUZER (2/3 Thaler)

Silver **Ruler:** Johann Reinhard III **Obverse:** Armored bust right **Reverse:** Crowned complex arms within Order chain, date divided below

Date	Mintage	VG	F	VF	XF	Unc
1721 BIB Unique	—	—	—	—	—	—

TRADE COINAGE

KM# 118 GOLDGULDEN

3.5000 g., 0.9860 Gold 0.1109 oz. AGW **Ruler:** Ludwig IX of Hesse-Darmstadt **Obverse:** Bust right **Reverse:** Crowned arms

Date	Mintage	VG	F	VF	XF	Unc
1737	—	1,000	2,000	3,500	6,000	—
1739	—	1,000	2,000	3,500	6,000	—
1740	—	1,000	2,000	3,500	6,000	—

KM# 122 GOLDGULDEN

3.5000 g., 0.9860 Gold 0.1109 oz. AGW **Ruler:** Ludwig IX of Hesse-Darmstadt **Obverse:** Bust right, legend around **Reverse:** Crowned arms, date below

Date	Mintage	VG	F	VF	XF	Unc
1758	—	1,250	2,500	4,250	7,000	—

KM# 116 DUCAT

3.5000 g., 0.9860 Gold 0.1109 oz. AGW **Ruler:** Johann Reinhard III **Obverse:** Bust right **Reverse:** Crowned oval 7-fold arms within Order chain, date divided below

Date	Mintage	VG	F	VF	XF	Unc
1721 Rare	—	—	—	—	—	—
1731	—	1,150	2,250	4,000	6,500	—

KM# 117 DUCAT

3.5000 g., 0.9860 Gold 0.1109 oz. AGW **Ruler:** Johann Reinhard III **Obverse:** Bust right in inner circle

Date	Mintage	VG	F	VF	XF	Unc
1733	—	1,000	2,000	3,500	6,000	—
ND	—	1,000	2,000	3,500	6,000	—

PATTERNS

Including off metal strikes

KM#	Date	Mintage	Identification	Mkt Val
Pn3	ND1758	—	1/6 Thaler. Gold. KM#121.	3,250

HANAU-MUNZENBERG

Elder line of Hanau founded in division of 1451, but became extinct in 1642 and fell to the Lichtenberg line. Hanau-Münzenberg passed to Hesse-Cassel in 1736 upon extinction of Hanau-Lichtenberg.

RULERS

Wilhelm VIII of Hesse-Cassel, 1736-1760
Wilhelm IX of Hesse-Cassel, Count (under regency of mother, Mary of England) 1760-1764
Wilhelm IX, Alone, 1764-1803

MINT OFFICIALS' INITIALS

Initials	Date	Name
CLR	1771-84	Christian Ludwig Ruden
EIK, EK	1737-42	Engelhard Johann Krull
IIE	1740-70	Johann Jacob Encke

COUNTSHIP

REGULAR COINAGE

KM# 72 HELLER

Copper **Ruler:** Wilhelm VIII of Hesse-Cassel **Obverse:** Crowned monogram **Reverse:** Value, date **Rev. Legend:** HANAU/SCHEIDE/MUNZ

Date	Mintage	VG	F	VF	XF	Unc
1739	—	4.00	8.00	16.00	35.00	—
1741	—	4.00	8.00	16.00	35.00	—
1743	—	4.00	8.00	16.00	35.00	—
1745	—	4.00	8.00	16.00	35.00	—
1746	—	4.00	8.00	16.00	35.00	—

KM# 85 HELLER

Copper **Ruler:** Wilhelm VIII of Hesse-Cassel **Obverse:** Crowned WL monogram, ZH at upper left and right **Reverse:** Value, date in 5 lines

Date	Mintage	VG	F	VF	XF	Unc
1752	—	7.00	12.00	25.00	45.00	—
1753	—	7.00	12.00	25.00	45.00	—
1754	—	7.00	12.00	25.00	45.00	—
1755	—	7.00	12.00	25.00	45.00	—
1756	—	7.00	12.00	25.00	45.00	—
1757	—	7.00	12.00	25.00	45.00	—

KM# 101 HELLER

Copper **Ruler:** Wilhelm IX Alone **Obverse:** Crowned complex arms with lion shield at center **Reverse:** Value, date

Date	Mintage	VG	F	VF	XF	Unc
1768	—	3.50	7.00	14.00	30.00	—
1769	—	3.50	7.00	14.00	30.00	—
1770	—	3.50	7.00	14.00	30.00	—
1771	—	3.50	7.00	14.00	30.00	—
1772	—	3.50	7.00	14.00	30.00	—
1773	—	3.50	7.00	14.00	30.00	—

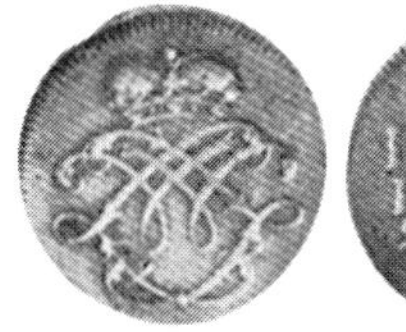

KM# 83 2 HELLER

Copper **Ruler:** Wilhelm VIII of Hesse-Cassel **Obverse:** Crowned monogram **Reverse:** Value, date

Date	Mintage	VG	F	VF	XF	Unc
1745	—	6.00	10.00	22.00	40.00	—

KM# 71 KREUZER

Billon **Ruler:** Wilhelm VIII of Hesse-Cassel **Obverse:** Lion left in crowned baroque frame, value as 1K **Reverse:** Value, date in circle **Rev. Legend:** HANAU LAND MUNTZ

Date	Mintage	VG	F	VF	XF	Unc
1738	—	60.00	100	200	300	—
1739	—	60.00	100	200	300	—

KM# 73 KREUZER

Billon **Ruler:** Wilhelm VIII of Hesse-Cassel **Obverse:** Crowned lion shield **Reverse:** Value, date, mintmaster's initials in 5 lines

Date	Mintage	VG	F	VF	XF	Unc
1739 EK	—	40.00	75.00	150	250	—

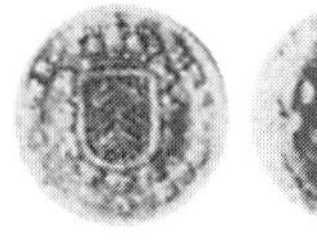

KM# 95 KREUZER

Billon **Ruler:** Wilhelm IX Alone **Obverse:** Arms **Reverse:** Value and date

Date	Mintage	VG	F	VF	XF	Unc
1765	—	6.00	10.00	20.00	40.00	—
1766 IIE	—	35.00	75.00	125	—	—

KM# 111 KREUZER

Copper **Ruler:** Wilhelm IX Alone **Obverse:** Crowned arms **Reverse:** Value and date in ornate circle

Date	Mintage	VG	F	VF	XF	Unc
1773	—	5.00	9.00	17.50	35.00	—

KM# 112 KREUZER

Billon **Ruler:** Wilhelm IX Alone **Obverse:** Crowned arms **Reverse:** Value and date in ornate circle

Date	Mintage	VG	F	VF	XF	Unc
1773	—	6.00	10.00	20.00	40.00	—

KM# 81 2 ALBUS

Billon **Ruler:** Wilhelm VIII of Hesse-Cassel **Obverse:** Crowned oval arms in cartouche **Reverse:** Value, date in laurel wreath

Date	Mintage	VG	F	VF	XF	Unc
1740 Rare	—	—	—	—	—	—
1741 Rare	—	—	—	—	—	—

KM# 80 5 KREUZER

Silver **Ruler:** Wilhelm VIII of Hesse-Cassel **Obverse:** Arms in baroque shield **Reverse:** Value, date, mintmaster's initials in laurel wreath

Date	Mintage	VG	F	VF	XF	Unc
1740 EK	—	—	—	1,500	2,500	—

KM# 96 5 KREUZER

Billon **Ruler:** Wilhelm IX Alone **Obverse:** Arms **Reverse:** Value and date

Date	Mintage	VG	F	VF	XF	Unc
1765	—	6.00	10.00	17.50	35.00	—
1766	—	6.00	10.00	17.50	35.00	—

KM# 116 5 KREUZER

Silver **Ruler:** Wilhelm IX Alone **Obverse:** Head left **Reverse:** Crowned arms

Date	Mintage	F	VF	XF	Unc
1775 CLR	—	25.00	40.00	75.00	135

KM# 90 10 KREUZER

Silver **Ruler:** Wilhelm IX of Hesse-Cassel, Count Under regency of mother, Mary of England **Obverse:** Monogram within wreath **Reverse:** Crowned column divides arms

Date	Mintage	F	VF	XF	Unc
1763 IIE	—	30.00	50.00	80.00	140

KM# 100.1 10 KREUZER

Silver **Ruler:** Wilhelm IX Alone **Obverse:** Head right **Reverse:** Crowned arms with lion shield at center

Date	Mintage	F	VF	XF	Unc
1765 IE	—	—	—	—	375

KM# 100.2 10 KREUZER

Silver **Ruler:** Wilhelm IX Alone **Reverse:** Crowned arms with lion shield at center **Note:** Similar to 20 Kreuzer, KM#97.2.

Date	Mintage	F	VF	XF	Unc
1766 IIE	—	25.00	40.00	60.00	100

KM# 82 6 ALBUS

Silver **Ruler:** Wilhelm VIII of Hesse-Cassel **Obverse:** Crowned complex arms within cartouche **Reverse:** Value, date within circle

Date	Mintage	VG	F	VF	XF	Unc
1740 IIE	—	25.00	50.00	100	225	—
1741 IIE	—	25.00	50.00	100	225	—
1743 IIE	—	25.00	50.00	100	225	—
1744 IIE	—	25.00	50.00	100	225	—

KM# 92 20 KREUZER

Silver **Ruler:** Wilhelm IX Alone **Obverse:** Crowned column divides arms **Reverse:** Value, date within cartouche

Date	Mintage	F	VF	XF	Unc
1764 IIE	—	100	155	250	425

KM# 97.1 20 KREUZER

Silver **Ruler:** Wilhelm IX Alone **Obverse:** Head right **Reverse:** Crowned arms with lion shield at center

Date	Mintage	F	VF	XF	Unc
1765 IIE	—	75.00	125	220	400

KM# 97.2 20 KREUZER

Silver **Ruler:** Wilhelm IX Alone **Obverse:** Bust right **Reverse:** Crowned arms with lion shield at center

Date	Mintage	F	VF	XF	Unc
1766 IIE	—	25.00	60.00	135	285

KM# 91 1/2 THALER

Silver **Ruler:** Wilhelm IX of Hesse-Cassel, Count Under regency of mother, Mary of England **Obverse:** Bust with décolletage right **Reverse:** Crowned bow above two shields of arms

Date	Mintage	F	VF	XF	Unc
1763 iie	—	325	525	900	1,600

KM# 98 1/2 THALER

Silver **Ruler:** Wilhelm IX Alone **Obverse:** Draped bust right **Reverse:** Crowned complex arms with supporters

Date	Mintage	F	VF	XF	Unc
1765 ie	—	110	185	300	550

KM# 103 1/2 THALER

Silver **Ruler:** Wilhelm IX Alone **Obverse:** Armored bust right **Reverse:** Crowned complex arms with supporters **Note:** Mining 1/2 Thaler - Bieber Mint.

Date	Mintage	F	VF	XF	Unc
1769	—	135	250	425	800
1770 IIE	—	135	250	425	800

KM# 115 THALER

Silver **Ruler:** Wilhelm IX Alone **Obverse:** Large head right **Obv. Legend:** WILHELMUS D: G: LANDG. & PR: HER: HASS: COM: HAN: **Reverse:** Crowned oval complex arms with supporters **Rev. Legend:** X. EINE FEINE MARCK. **Note:** Dav. #2289.

Date	Mintage	F	VF	XF	Unc
1774 CLR	—	145	225	375	850
1775 CLR	—	145	225	375	850
1775 CLK Error	—	150	225	375	850
1777 CLR	—	145	225	375	850
1778 CLR	—	145	225	375	850

KM# 93 THALER

Silver **Ruler:** Wilhelm IX Alone **Subject:** Maria, Regent **Obverse:** Bust with décolletage right **Obv. Legend:** MARIA D: G: LANDGR: HAS: N: PR: M: B: FR: & H: T: & COM: HAN: ADMINISTR * **Reverse:** Crowned complex arms within wreath **Note:** Dav. #2286.

Date	Mintage	F	VF	XF	Unc
1764 IIE	—	650	1,000	2,000	3,250

KM# 99 THALER

Silver **Ruler:** Wilhelm IX Alone **Subject:** Wilhelm IX **Obverse:** Armored, draped bust right **Obv. Legend:** WILHELM9 D.G.LANDG. & PR. HER. HASS. COM. HAN **Reverse:** Crowned complex arms with supporters **Rev. Legend:** X. EINE FEINE MARCK **Note:** Dav. #2287.

Date	Mintage	F	VF	XF	Unc
1765 IE	—	200	300	550	1,750
1765 IR	—	200	300	550	1,750

KM# 104 THALER

Silver **Ruler:** Wilhelm IX Alone **Obverse:** Armored bust right **Obv. Legend:** WILHELM9 D.G. LANDG. & PR. HER. HASS. COM. HAN. **Reverse:** Crowned complex arms with supporters **Rev. Legend:** EX VISCERIBUS FODINAE BIEBER., X. EINE F. MARCK below **Note:** Mining Thaler - Bieber Mines. Dav. #2288.

Date	Mintage	F	VF	XF	Unc
1769 IIE	—	150	225	375	850
1770 IIE	—	150	225	375	850
1771 CLR	—	150	225	375	850

KM# 110 THALER
Silver **Ruler:** Wilhelm IX Alone **Obverse:** Bust with mantle right **Obv. Legend:** WILHELM9 D.G. LANDG. & PR. HER. HASS. COM. HAN. **Reverse:** Crowned complex arms with supporters **Rev. Legend:** EX VISCERIBUS FODINAE BIEBER., X. EINE F. MARCK below **Note:** Dav. #2288A.

Date	Mintage	F	VF	XF	Unc
1771 CLR*	—	125	250	400	900

KM# 114 THALER
Silver **Ruler:** Wilhelm IX Alone **Obverse:** Small head right **Obv. Legend:** WILHELMUS D: G: LANDG • & PR: HER: HASS: COM; HAN: **Reverse:** Crowned oval arms with supporters **Rev. Legend:** X. EINE FEINE MARCK, BIEBERER SILBER in cartouche below **Note:** Dav. #2289B.

Date	Mintage	F	VF	XF	Unc
1774 CLR	—	145	225	375	850
1777 CLR	—	145	225	375	850
1778 CLR	—	145	225	375	850

KM# 113 THALER
Silver **Ruler:** Wilhelm IX Alone **Obverse:** Head right **Obv. Legend:** WILH.D.G.LANDG.. **Reverse:** Crowned complex arms with supporters **Note:** Mining Thaler - Bieber Mines. Dav. #2289A.

Date	Mintage	F	VF	XF	Unc
1774 CLR	—	145	225	375	850

KM# 117 THALER
Silver **Ruler:** Wilhelm IX Alone **Reverse:** BIBERER SILBER in square **Note:** Dav. #2289D.

Date	Mintage	F	VF	XF	Unc
1778 CLR	—	155	225	375	850

KM# 118 THALER
Silver **Ruler:** Wilhelm IX Alone **Obverse:** Larger head right **Obv. Legend:** WILHELMUS D:G: LANDG • & PR: GER: HASS; COM: HAN: **Reverse:** Crowned complex arms with supporters **Rev. Legend:** X. EINE FEINE MARCK, BIBERER SILBER in box below **Note:** Mining Thaler - Bieber Mines. Dav. #2290.

Date	Mintage	F	VF	XF	Unc
1784 CLR	—	225	400	825	1,650

TRADE COINAGE

KM# 74 1/2 DUCAT
1.7500 g., 0.9860 Gold 0.0555 oz. AGW **Ruler:** Wilhelm VIII of Hesse-Cassel **Obverse:** Bust right **Reverse:** Crowned complex arms

Date	Mintage	VG	F	VF	XF	Unc
1739	—	250	650	1,250	2,500	—

KM# 70 DUCAT
3.5000 g., 0.9860 Gold 0.1109 oz. AGW **Ruler:** Wilhelm VIII of Hesse-Cassel **Subject:** Wilhelm VIII **Obverse:** Head right **Reverse:** Crowned complex arms

Date	Mintage	VG	F	VF	XF	Unc
1737	—	450	950	2,000	3,500	—
1738	—	450	950	2,000	3,500	—
1739	—	450	950	2,000	3,500	—
1740	—	450	950	2,000	3,500	—

KM# 94 DUCAT
3.5000 g., 0.9860 Gold 0.1109 oz. AGW **Ruler:** Wilhelm IX Alone **Subject:** Marriage of Wilhelm to Wilhelmine Caroline of Denmark **Obverse:** Bust with décolletage right **Reverse:** Inscription

Date	Mintage	F	VF	XF	Unc
1764 IIE	—	600	1,200	2,500	4,500

KM# 102 DUCAT
3.5000 g., 0.9860 Gold 0.1109 oz. AGW **Ruler:** Wilhelm IX Alone **Obverse:** Bust right **Reverse:** Arms and date

Date	Mintage	F	VF	XF	Unc
1768	—	750	1,500	3,000	5,000

KM# 120 DUCAT
3.5000 g., 0.9860 Gold 0.1109 oz. AGW **Ruler:** Wilhelm IX Alone

Date	Mintage	F	VF	XF	Unc
1775 CLR	—	1,000	2,000	3,500	6,000

HEILBRONN

First mentioned around 741, Heilbronn is about 30 miles north of Stüttgart in Württemberg. It became a free imperial city in 1360 and passed to Württemberg in 1803.

FREE CITY

TRADE COINAGE

KM# 1 DUCAT
3.5000 g., 0.9860 Gold 0.1109 oz. AGW **Subject:** 200th Anniversary of the Reformation **Obverse:** 4-Line inscription, date in cartouche below **Reverse:** 7-Streamed fountain, date in chronogram

Date	Mintage	VG	F	VF	XF	Unc
1717	—	300	600	1,200	2,000	—

PATTERNS

Including off metal strikes

KM#	Date	Mintage	Identification	Mkt Val
Pn1	1717	—	Ducat. Silver. . KM#1.	150

HENNEBERG

The line of counts of Henneberg in southern Thuringia, who traced their ancestors back to the late eighth century became extinct in 1583. The territories went mostly to Saxony with smaller parts to Hesse-Cassel and Brandenburg. Several Saxon duchies issued coins at Ilmenau. In 1660 Henneberg was divided again and redistributed among the duchies of both Albertine Saxony (Electoral Saxony and Saxe-Zeitz) and Ernestine Saxony (Saxe-Gotha and Saxe-Weimar). Each struck coins for its portion.

RULER
Friedrich August III of Electoral Saxony, 1763-1806

MINT OFFICIALS' INITIALS

Initials	Date	Name
EDC	1764-78	Ernst Dietrich Croll in Dresden
IEC	1779-1804	Johann Ernst Croll in Dresden

DIVISION OF 1660

Albertine Line

REGULAR COINAGE

KM# 41 KREUZER
Billon **Ruler:** Friedrich August III of Electoral Saxony **Obverse:** Crowned monogram **Reverse:** Value, date **Note:** Listed by Craig under Saxony as Cr#96.

Date	Mintage	F	VF	XF	Unc
1765 EDC	—	5.00	10.00	25.00	80.00
1780 JEC	—	5.00	10.00	25.00	80.00

KM# 42 5 KREUZER
Billon **Ruler:** Friedrich August III of Electoral Saxony **Obverse:** Crowned monogram **Reverse:** Value, date **Note:** Listed by Craig under Saxony as Cr#99.

Date	Mintage	F	VF	XF	Unc
1765 EDC	—	8.00	16.00	35.00	100

HENNEBERG-ILMENAU

SUCCESSION TO SAXE-GOTHA AND WEIMAR

RULERS
Friedrich II of Saxe-Gotha, 1691-1732
Wilhelm Ernst of Saxe-Weimar, 1683-1728
Johann Ernst of Saxe-Weimar, 1683-1707

MINT OFFICIALS' INITIALS

Initials	Date	Name
BA	1691-1702	Bastian Altmann at Ilmenau

REGULAR COINAGE

KM# 40 1/4 THALER
Silver **Ruler:** Johann Ernst o Saxe-Weimar **Obverse:** 2 Helmets with plumes and supporters, date below **Reverse:** Crown above 2 shields

Date	Mintage	VG	F	VF	XF	Unc
1701 BA	—	—	—	—	—	—

KM# 41 1/2 THALER
Silver **Ruler:** Johann Ernst o Saxe-Weimar **Obverse:** 2 Helmets with plumes and supporters, date below **Reverse:** Crown above 2 shields

Date	Mintage	VG	F	VF	XF	Unc
1701 BA	—	450	800	1,200	1,850	—

KM# 35 THALER

Silver **Ruler:** Bernard III **Obverse:** 2 ornate helmets, figures at right and left **Reverse:** Crown above two shields of arms **Note:** Dav. #7491.

Date	Mintage	F	VF	XF	Unc
1700 BA	—	250	400	700	1,250
1701 BA	—	250	400	700	1,250
1701 BA	—	250	400	700	1,250
1702 BA	—	250	400	700	1,250

SUCCESSION TO SAXE-MEININGEN

RULER

Bernhard III, 1680-1706

REGULAR COINAGE

KM# 43 HELLER

Copper **Obverse:** Hen right

Date	Mintage	VG	F	VF	XF	Unc
1701	—	4.00	10.00	18.00	30.00	—

KM# 42 HELLER

Copper **Ruler:** Wilhelm Ernst of Saxe-Weimar **Obverse:** Crowned hen left on 3 mounds **Reverse:** Date **Rev. Legend:** H./MEINING/HELLER **Note:** Varieties exist.

Date	Mintage	VG	F	VF	XF	Unc
1701	—	4.00	10.00	18.00	30.00	—
1702	—	4.00	10.00	18.00	30.00	—
1703	—	4.00	10.00	18.00	30.00	—

KM# 46 HELLER

Copper **Ruler:** Anton Ulrich **Obverse:** Crowned hen left **Reverse:** Date **Rev. Legend:** I/MEININ/HELLER

Date	Mintage	VG	F	VF	XF	Unc
1761	—	—	—	—	—	—
Note: Reported, not confirmed						
1762	—	4.00	8.00	16.00	30.00	—

KM# 47 HELLER

Copper **Ruler:** Anton Ulrich **Obverse:** Hen right

Date	Mintage	VG	F	VF	XF	Unc
1762	—	4.00	8.00	16.00	30.00	—

KM# 48 HELLER

Copper **Ruler:** Charlotte Amalie Regent for Karl 1763-1775 **Reverse:** Date **Rev. Legend:** I/MEINING/HELLER

Date	Mintage	VG	F	VF	XF	Unc
1768	—	7.00	12.00	25.00	45.00	—

KM# 44 2 PFENNIG

Billon **Ruler:** Ernst Ludwig I **Obverse:** 2-Fold arms of Henneberg and Saxony in palm branches, S-M-L around **Reverse:** Imperial orb with 2, cross on orb divides date

Date	Mintage	VG	F	VF	XF	Unc
1707	—	60.00	100	185	300	—

SUCCESSION TO SAXE-HILDBURGHAUSEN

RULER

Ernst Friedrich I, 1715-24

REGULAR COINAGE

KM# 45 1/18 THALER

Silver **Ruler:** Ernst Friedrich I **Obverse:** 2 Oval arms in cartouches, crown above **Reverse:** Date **Rev. Legend:** 18/EIN.R./THALER

Date	Mintage	VG	F	VF	XF	Unc
1719	—	75.00	150	275	400	—

HENNEBERG-SCHLEUSINGEN

Part of the Henneberg lands belonging to Electoral Saxony, the princely countship of Schleusingen came under the control of the duke of Saxe-Zeitz after the division of 1660. A small number of coins were minted for use in the district during the early 18th century. When the line became extinct in 1718, the territory returned to the direct control of Saxony, which issued coins for all Henneberg later in the century.

RULER

Moritz Wilhelm von Sachsen-Zeitz-Naumburg, 1681-1718

MINT OFFICIALS' INITIALS

Initials	Date	Name
HEA	1686-1705	Heinrich Ernst Angerstein, Mintmaster in Coburg

DUCHY

REGULAR COINAGE

KM# 5 HELLER

Copper **Ruler:** Moritz Wilhelm **Obverse:** Crowned 'MW' monogram between two palm fronds **Reverse:** 5-line inscription with date **Rev. Inscription:** 1/SCHLEU/SINGER/HELLER/(date)

Date	Mintage	Good	VG	F	VF	XF
1705	—	—	6.00	12.00	25.00	50.00
1712	—	—	6.00	12.00	25.00	50.00
1713	—	—	6.00	12.00	25.00	50.00
1714	—	—	6.00	12.00	25.00	50.00
1715	—	—	6.00	12.00	25.00	50.00
1716	—	—	6.00	12.00	25.00	50.00
1717	—	—	6.00	12.00	25.00	50.00
1718	—	—	6.00	12.00	25.00	50.00

KM# 6 3 PFENNIG (Dreier)

Silver **Ruler:** Moritz Wilhelm **Obverse:** Crown above 3 oval arms within legend **Reverse:** Orb divides date in legend

Date	Mintage	Good	VG	F	VF	XF
1702 HEA Rare	—	—	—	—	—	—

HESSE-CASSEL

(Hessen-Kassel)

The Hesse principalities were located for the most part north of the Main River, bounded by Westphalia on the west, the Brunswick duchies on the north, the Saxon-Thuringian duchies on the east and Rhine Palatinate and the bishoprics of Mainz and Fulda on the south. The rule of the landgraves of Hesse began in the second half of the 13th century, the dignity of Prince of the Empire being acquired in 1292. In 1567 the patrimony was divided by four surviving sons, only those of Cassel and Darmstadt surviving for more than a generation in Hesse-Cassel the landgrave was raised to the rank of elector in 1803. The electorate formed part of the Kingdom of Westphalia from 1806 to 1813. In 1866 Hesse-Cassel was annexed by Prussia and became the province of Hesse-Nassau.

RULERS

Karl, 1670-1730
Friedrich I, 1730-51
(also King of Sweden)
Wilhelm VIII, 1751-60
Friedrich II, 1760-85
Wilhelm IX, 1785-1803

MINT MARKS

C – Cassel
(L.) – Lippoldsberg

MINT OFFICIALS' INITIALS

Initials	Date	Name
AD	1701-04	Andreas Dittmar
BR	1765-83	Balthasar Reinhard
CLR	1771-84	Christian Ludwig Rüder, mintmaster in Hanau
D.F., F.	1774-1831	Dietrich Flalda
FH	1786-1821	Friedrich Heenwagen
FH	1760-94	Friedrich Henglin
FU	1764-73	Friedrich Ulrich
H	1775-1820	Carl Ludwig Holzemer, die-cutter
ICB	1744-63	Johann Conrad Bandel
ICH	1719-46	Johann Carl Hedlinger, medailleur in Swedish service
	1746-71	Medailleur in Switzerland
ICS, S	1749-70	Johann Christoph Schepp, die-cutter
I.LE CLERC	1701-46	Isaac Le Clerc, medailleur and die-cutter
Kohler	1706-11	E. Pomponius K.F. Kohler, medailleur, possibly in Hannover or Berlin
LR	1724-44	Ludwig Rollin

ARMS

Hessian lion rampant left.
Diez – 2 leopards passant to left, one above the other.
Katzenelnbogen – Crowned lion springing to left.
Nidda – 2-fold divided horizontally, two 8-pointed stars in upper half, lower half shaded.
Ziegenhain – 2-fold divided horizontally, 6-pointed star in upper half, lower half shaded.

LANDGRAVIATE

REGULAR COINAGE

KM# 347 HELLER

Billon **Ruler:** Karl **Note:** Date divided as 17-02 by monogram.

Date	Mintage	VG	F	VF	XF	Unc
1702 AD	—	6.00	12.00	25.00	50.00	—
1704	—	6.00	12.00	25.00	50.00	—
1705	—	6.00	12.00	25.00	50.00	—
1723	—	7.00	15.00	30.00	60.00	—

KM# 380 HELLER

Copper **Ruler:** Karl **Obverse:** Crowned Hessian lion **Reverse:** Value, date

Date	Mintage	VG	F	VF	XF	Unc
1723	—	7.00	14.00	28.00	55.00	—
1724	—	7.00	14.00	28.00	55.00	—

KM# 393 HELLER

Copper **Ruler:** Karl **Obverse:** Crowned monogram **Reverse:** Value, date

Date	Mintage	VG	F	VF	XF	Unc
1725	—	7.00	14.00	28.00	55.00	—
1726	—	7.00	14.00	28.00	55.00	—
1727	—	7.00	14.00	28.00	55.00	—
1728	—	7.00	14.00	28.00	55.00	—
1729	—	7.00	14.00	28.00	55.00	—
1730	—	7.00	14.00	28.00	55.00	—

KM# 401 HELLER

Copper **Ruler:** Friedrich I (also King of Sweden) **Obverse:** Crowned monogram **Reverse:** Value, date

Date	Mintage	VG	F	VF	XF	Unc
1730	—	7.00	14.00	28.00	55.00	—
1731	—	7.00	14.00	28.00	55.00	—
1732	—	7.00	14.00	28.00	55.00	—
1733	—	7.00	14.00	28.00	55.00	—
1734	—	7.00	14.00	28.00	55.00	—
1735	—	7.00	14.00	28.00	55.00	—
1736	—	7.00	14.00	28.00	55.00	—
1737	—	7.00	14.00	28.00	55.00	—
1738	—	7.00	14.00	28.00	55.00	—
1739	—	7.00	14.00	28.00	55.00	—
1740	—	7.00	14.00	28.00	55.00	—
1741	—	7.00	14.00	28.00	55.00	—
1742	—	7.00	14.00	28.00	55.00	—
1743	—	7.00	14.00	28.00	55.00	—

KM# A401 HELLER

Copper **Ruler:** Karl **Obverse:** Monogram divides date **Note:** Similar to KM#400 ornamented

Date	Mintage	VG	F	VF	XF	Unc
1730	—	20.00	35.00	70.00	150	—

KM# 400 HELLER

Copper **Ruler:** Friedrich I (also King of Sweden) **Obverse:** Crowned monogram **Reverse:** Value, date

Date	Mintage	VG	F	VF	XF	Unc
1743	—	7.00	14.00	28.00	55.00	—
1744	—	7.00	14.00	28.00	55.00	—
1745	—	7.00	14.00	28.00	55.00	—
1746	—	7.00	14.00	28.00	55.00	—
1747	—	7.00	14.00	28.00	55.00	—
1748	—	7.00	14.00	28.00	55.00	—
1749	—	7.00	14.00	28.00	55.00	—
1750	—	7.00	14.00	28.00	55.00	—

KM# 445 HELLER

Copper **Ruler:** Wilhelm VIII **Obverse:** Crowned monogram **Reverse:** Value, date

Date	Mintage	VG	F	VF	XF	Unc
1751	—	4.00	9.00	20.00	45.00	—
1752	—	4.00	9.00	20.00	45.00	—
1753	—	4.00	9.00	20.00	45.00	—
1754	—	4.00	9.00	20.00	45.00	—
1755	—	4.00	9.00	20.00	45.00	—
1756	—	4.00	9.00	20.00	45.00	—
1757	—	4.00	9.00	20.00	45.00	—
1758	—	4.00	9.00	20.00	45.00	—
1759	—	4.00	9.00	20.00	45.00	—

KM# 458 HELLER

Copper **Ruler:** Wilhelm VIII **Obverse:** Crowned monogram **Reverse:** Value, date

Date	Mintage	VG	F	VF	XF	Unc
1759	—	7.00	12.00	25.00	50.00	—

KM# 465 HELLER

Copper **Ruler:** Wilhelm VIII **Obverse:** Crowned monogram **Reverse:** Value, date **Rev. Legend:** I/HELLER/SCHEIDE/MUNTZ

Date	Mintage	VG	F	VF	XF	Unc
1760	—	4.00	9.00	20.00	50.00	—

KM# 497 HELLER

Copper **Ruler:** Friedrich II **Obverse:** Crowned monogram **Reverse:** Value, date **Note:** Similar to KM#465 without SCHEIDE MUNTZ.

Date	Mintage	VG	F	VF	XF	Unc
1772	—	6.00	15.00	40.00	90.00	—

KM# 505 HELLER

Copper **Ruler:** Friedrich II **Obverse:** Crowned lion left on pedestal **Reverse:** Value above date

Date	Mintage	VG	F	VF	XF	Unc
1774	—	3.00	7.00	18.00	40.00	—
1775	—	3.00	7.00	18.00	40.00	—

KM# 540 HELLER

Copper **Ruler:** Wilhelm IX **Obverse:** Crowned lion on pedestal **Reverse:** Value, date **Note:** Similar to KM#505.

Date	Mintage	VG	F	VF	XF	Unc
1790	—	1.00	3.00	6.00	15.00	—

KM# 543 HELLER

Copper, 19 mm. **Ruler:** Wilhelm IX **Obverse:** Crowned monogram **Reverse:** Denomination, date

Date	Mintage	F	VF	XF	Unc
1791	—	4.50	12.00	28.00	70.00
1792	—	4.50	12.00	28.00	70.00
1793	—	4.50	12.00	28.00	70.00
1797	—	4.50	12.00	28.00	70.00
1798	—	4.50	12.00	28.00	70.00
1799	—	4.50	12.00	28.00	70.00
1800	—	4.50	12.00	28.00	70.00
1801	—	10.00	25.00	55.00	85.00
1802	—	10.00	25.00	55.00	85.00
1803	—	10.00	25.00	55.00	85.00

KM# 437 1-1/2 HELLER

Copper **Ruler:** Friedrich I (also King of Sweden) **Obverse:** Crowned monogram **Reverse:** Value, date **Note:** Similar to 1 Heller, KM#400, but value 1-1/2.

Date	Mintage	VG	F	VF	XF	Unc
1746	—	12.00	28.00	55.00	120	—

KM# 359 2 HELLER

Billon **Ruler:** Karl **Obverse:** Crowned Hessian arms between palm branches **Reverse:** Value, 2 in cartouche, date above

Date	Mintage	VG	F	VF	XF	Unc
1712	—	15.00	30.00	60.00	125	—
1713	—	15.00	30.00	60.00	125	—
1714	—	15.00	30.00	60.00	125	—

KM# 370 2 HELLER

Billon **Ruler:** Karl **Obverse:** Crowned arms between palm branches **Reverse:** Value, II/date

Date	Mintage	VG	F	VF	XF	Unc
1720	—	12.00	25.00	50.00	85.00	—

KM# 395 2 HELLER

Copper **Ruler:** Karl **Obverse:** Crowned CL monogram, Z-H divided below **Reverse:** Value, date **Rev. Legend:** II/HELLER/SCHEIDE/MUNTZ

Date	Mintage	VG	F	VF	XF	Unc
1727	—	7.00	15.00	30.00	55.00	—

KM# 412 2 HELLER

Copper **Ruler:** Friedrich I (also King of Sweden) **Obverse:** Crowned mirror-image script F monogram

Date	Mintage	VG	F	VF	XF	Unc
1733	—	10.00	20.00	50.00	90.00	—
1734	—	10.00	20.00	50.00	90.00	—
1735	—	10.00	20.00	50.00	90.00	—
1739	—	10.00	20.00	50.00	90.00	—
1741	—	10.00	20.00	50.00	90.00	—
1742	—	10.00	20.00	50.00	90.00	—
1746	—	10.00	20.00	50.00	90.00	—
1749	—	10.00	20.00	50.00	90.00	—
1750	—	10.00	20.00	50.00	90.00	—
1751	—	10.00	20.00	50.00	90.00	—

KM# 446 2 HELLER

Copper **Ruler:** Wilhelm VIII **Obverse:** Crowned monogram **Reverse:** Value, date **Note:** Similar to 1 Heller, KM#445.

Date	Mintage	VG	F	VF	XF	Unc
1751	—	5.00	10.00	20.00	60.00	—
1752	—	5.00	10.00	20.00	60.00	—
1753	—	5.00	10.00	20.00	60.00	—
1754	—	5.00	10.00	20.00	60.00	—
1755	—	5.00	10.00	20.00	60.00	—
1756	—	5.00	10.00	20.00	60.00	—
1758	—	5.00	10.00	20.00	60.00	—

KM# 472 2 HELLER

Copper **Ruler:** Friedrich II **Obverse:** Crowned script FL monogram **Reverse:** Value, date **Rev. Legend:** II/HELLER/ SCHEIDE/ MUNTZ

Date	Mintage	VG	F	VF	XF	Unc
1765	—	6.00	12.00	25.00	60.00	—

KM# 498 2 HELLER

Copper **Ruler:** Friedrich II **Obverse:** Crowned double FL monogram **Reverse:** Without SCHEIDE/MUNTZ

Date	Mintage	VG	F	VF	XF	Unc
1772	—	3.00	7.00	25.00	60.00	—

KM# 506 2 HELLER

Copper **Ruler:** Friedrich II **Obverse:** Lion holding shield with FL monogram **Reverse:** Value above date

Date	Mintage	VG	F	VF	XF	Unc
1774	—	2.50	6.00	15.00	30.00	—

KM# 541 2 HELLER

Copper **Ruler:** Wilhelm IX **Obverse:** Lion holding shield with WL monogram **Reverse:** Value, date

Date	Mintage	VG	F	VF	XF	Unc
1790	—	1.00	3.00	8.00	20.00	—
1791	—	1.00	3.00	8.00	20.00	—
1792	—	1.00	3.00	8.00	20.00	—
1795	—	1.00	3.00	8.00	20.00	—

KM# 396 PFENNIG

Billon **Ruler:** Karl **Obverse:** Crowned Hessian lion in heart-shaped cartouche, date divided above **Note:** Uniface

Date	Mintage	VG	F	VF	XF	Unc
1728	—	15.00	30.00	55.00	90.00	—

KM# 348 3 HELLER

Billon **Ruler:** Karl **Reverse:** Date above cartouche with 3

Date	Mintage	VG	F	VF	XF	Unc
1702 AD	—	12.00	30.00	70.00	150	—
1704	—	12.00	30.00	70.00	150	—
1705	—	12.00	30.00	70.00	150	—

KM# 363 3 HELLER

Billon **Ruler:** Karl **Obverse:** Crowned shield with Hessian lion between palm branches **Reverse:** Value 3 in cartouche, date above

Date	Mintage	VG	F	VF	XF	Unc
1713	—	12.00	30.00	60.00	130	—

KM# 371 3 HELLER

Billon **Ruler:** Karl **Obverse:** Crowned shield with arms between palm branches **Reverse:** III/date

Date	Mintage	VG	F	VF	XF	Unc
1720	—	12.00	25.00	60.00	130	—

KM# 381 3 HELLER

Billon **Ruler:** Karl **Obverse:** Crowned Hessian lion **Reverse:** Value 3 in shield, date above

Date	Mintage	VG	F	VF	XF	Unc
1723	—	15.00	30.00	65.00	145	—
1725	—	15.00	30.00	65.00	145	—

KM# 394 3 HELLER

Copper **Ruler:** Karl **Obverse:** Head right **Reverse:** Value, date

Date	Mintage	VG	F	VF	XF	Unc
1726	—	14.00	28.00	55.00	90.00	—
1728	—	14.00	28.00	55.00	90.00	—

KM# 413 3 HELLER

Copper **Ruler:** Friedrich I (also King of Sweden) **Obverse:** Crowned monogram **Reverse:** Value, date

Date	Mintage	VG	F	VF	XF	Unc
1733	—	10.00	20.00	40.00	75.00	—

KM# 414 3 HELLER

Copper **Ruler:** Friedrich I (also King of Sweden) **Obverse:** Draped bust right **Reverse:** Value, date

Date	Mintage	VG	F	VF	XF	Unc
1733	—	7.00	15.00	32.00	70.00	—
1735	—	7.00	15.00	32.00	70.00	—

KM# 422 3 HELLER

Copper **Ruler:** Friedrich I (also King of Sweden) **Obverse:** Laureate head right **Reverse:** Value, date

Date	Mintage	VG	F	VF	XF	Unc
1737	—	7.00	15.00	32.00	70.00	—
1739	—	7.00	15.00	32.00	70.00	—
1740	—	7.00	15.00	32.00	70.00	—

Date	Mintage	VG	F	VF	XF	Unc
1748	—	7.00	15.00	32.00	70.00	—

KM# 450 3 HELLER

Copper **Ruler:** Wilhelm VIII **Obverse:** Crowned monogram **Reverse:** Value, date **Note:** Similar to 1 Heller, KM#445.

Date	Mintage	VG	F	VF	XF	Unc
1752	—	—	—	—	—	—

Note: Reported, not confirmed

KM# 456 3 HELLER

Copper **Ruler:** Wilhelm VIII **Obverse:** Bust right, inscription around **Reverse:** Value, date

Date	Mintage	VG	F	VF	XF	Unc
1755	—	15.00	30.00	60.00	110	—

KM# 459 3 HELLER

Copper **Ruler:** Wilhelm VIII **Obverse:** Crowned monogram **Reverse:** Value, date

Date	Mintage	VG	F	VF	XF	Unc
1758	—	7.00	15.00	32.00	65.00	—

KM# 466 3 HELLER

Copper **Ruler:** Wilhelm VIII **Obverse:** Crowned double FL monogram **Reverse:** Value, date **Rev. Legend:** III/HELLER/SCHEIDE/MUNTZ

Date	Mintage	VG	F	VF	XF	Unc
1760	—	3.00	7.00	18.00	40.00	—
1761	—	3.00	7.00	18.00	40.00	—

KM# 499 3 HELLER

Copper **Ruler:** Friedrich II **Reverse:** Value 3 and date

Date	Mintage	VG	F	VF	XF	Unc
1772	—	5.00	10.00	15.00	50.00	—

KM# 507 3 HELLER

Copper **Ruler:** Friedrich II **Obverse:** Crowned script FL monogram **Reverse:** Value 3 and date, 2 palm branches

Date	Mintage	VG	F	VF	XF	Unc
1774	—	7.00	15.00	20.00	50.00	—

KM# 544 3 HELLER

Copper **Ruler:** Wilhelm IX **Obverse:** Crowned WL monogram **Reverse:** Value over date

Date	Mintage	VG	F	VF	XF	Unc
1791	—	3.00	8.00	15.00	40.00	—

KM# 350 4 HELLER

Silver **Ruler:** Karl **Reverse:** Value, date above **Rev. Legend:** IIII/HELLER

Date	Mintage	VG	F	VF	XF	Unc
1704	—	7.00	15.00	30.00	55.00	—
1705	—	7.00	15.00	30.00	55.00	—
1707	—	7.00	15.00	30.00	55.00	—

KM# 361 4 HELLER

Billon **Ruler:** Karl **Obverse:** Value, IIII HELLER below monogram **Reverse:** Hessian lion in crowned shield divides date

Date	Mintage	VG	F	VF	XF	Unc
1712	—	—	—	—	—	—

KM# 360 4 HELLER

Billon **Ruler:** Karl **Obverse:** Crowned double mirror-script C monogram divides date, IIII below **Reverse:** Hessian lion in crowned shield between palm branches **Note:** Varieties exist.

Date	Mintage	VG	F	VF	XF	Unc
1712	—	8.00	16.00	32.00	60.00	—
1713	—	8.00	16.00	32.00	60.00	—
1714	—	8.00	16.00	32.00	60.00	—
1716	—	8.00	16.00	32.00	60.00	—
1717	—	—	—	—	—	—

Note: Reported, not confirmed

KM# 365 4 HELLER

Billon **Ruler:** Karl **Obverse:** Hessian lion in crowned shield between palm branches **Reverse:** Value, 4 in shield, date above

Date	Mintage	VG	F	VF	XF	Unc
1719	—	10.00	20.00	40.00	65.00	—

KM# 372 4 HELLER

Billon **Ruler:** Karl **Reverse:** Date **Rev. Legend:** IIII

Date	Mintage	VG	F	VF	XF	Unc
1720	—	12.00	25.00	50.00	85.00	—
1721	—	12.00	25.00	50.00	85.00	—

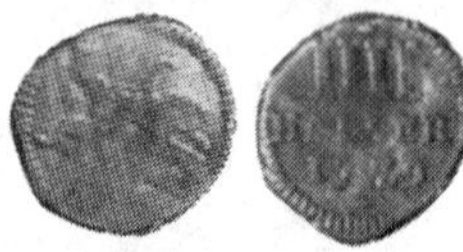

KM# 382 4 HELLER

Billon **Ruler:** Karl **Obverse:** Crowned Hessian lion left without shield **Reverse:** Value, date **Rev. Legend:** IIII/HELLER

Date	Mintage	VG	F	VF	XF	Unc
1723	—	7.00	15.00	30.00	55.00	—
1724	—	7.00	15.00	30.00	55.00	—
1725	—	7.00	15.00	30.00	55.00	—
1726	—	7.00	15.00	30.00	55.00	—
1727	—	7.00	15.00	30.00	55.00	—
1728	—	7.00	15.00	30.00	55.00	—
1729	—	7.00	15.00	30.00	55.00	—
1730	—	7.00	15.00	30.00	55.00	—

KM# 402.1 4 HELLER

Billon **Ruler:** Friedrich I (also King of Sweden) **Obverse:** Crowned shield with Hessian lion between palm branches **Reverse:** Value, date **Rev. Legend:** IIII/HELLER

Date	Mintage	VG	F	VF	XF	Unc
1730	—	6.00	12.00	25.00	45.00	—
1731	—	6.00	12.00	25.00	45.00	—
1732	528,000	6.00	12.00	25.00	45.00	—
1732	—	7.00	15.00	30.00	50.00	—
1733	1,044,999	6.00	12.00	25.00	45.00	—
1734	1,498,000	6.00	12.00	25.00	45.00	—
1735	1,461,000	6.00	12.00	25.00	45.00	—
1736	633,000	6.00	12.00	25.00	45.00	—
1737	912,000	6.00	12.00	25.00	45.00	—
1738	1,104,000	6.00	12.00	25.00	45.00	—
1739	749,000	6.00	12.00	25.00	45.00	—
1740	—	6.00	12.00	25.00	45.00	—
1741	—	6.00	12.00	25.00	45.00	—
1742	—	6.00	12.00	25.00	45.00	—
1743	—	6.00	12.00	25.00	45.00	—
1743	—	7.00	15.00	30.00	50.00	—
1744	—	6.00	12.00	25.00	45.00	—
1745	—	6.00	12.00	25.00	45.00	—
1746	—	6.00	12.00	25.00	45.00	—
1747	—	7.00	15.00	30.00	50.00	—
1748	—	7.00	15.00	30.00	50.00	—
1749	—	7.00	15.00	30.00	50.00	—
1750	—	7.00	15.00	30.00	50.00	—
1751	—	7.00	15.00	30.00	50.00	—

KM# 402.3 4 HELLER

Billon **Ruler:** Friedrich I (also King of Sweden) **Obverse:** Lion with only one tail **Reverse:** Value, date

Date	Mintage	VG	F	VF	XF	Unc
1740	—	7.00	15.00	30.00	50.00	—
1741	—	7.00	15.00	30.00	50.00	—
1742	—	7.00	15.00	30.00	50.00	—
1743	—	7.00	15.00	30.00	50.00	—
1744	—	7.00	15.00	30.00	50.00	—
1751	—	7.00	15.00	30.00	50.00	—

KM# 447 4 HELLER

Billon **Ruler:** Wilhelm VIII **Subject:** Issued under Wilhelm VIII **Obverse:** Crowned shield with lion shield **Reverse:** Date **Rev. Legend:** IIII/HELLER

Date	Mintage	VG	F	VF	XF	Unc
1751	—	7.00	14.00	28.00	50.00	—
1752	—	7.00	14.00	28.00	50.00	—
1753	—	7.00	14.00	28.00	50.00	—
1754	—	7.00	14.00	28.00	50.00	—
1755	—	7.00	14.00	28.00	50.00	—
1756	—	7.00	14.00	28.00	50.00	—
1757	—	7.00	14.00	28.00	50.00	—
1758	—	7.00	14.00	28.00	50.00	—
1759	—	7.00	14.00	28.00	50.00	—
1760	—	7.00	14.00	28.00	50.00	—

KM# 467 4 HELLER

Copper **Ruler:** Friedrich II **Obverse:** Crowned double FL monogram **Reverse:** Value IIII and date **Rev. Legend:** SCHEIDEMUNT

Date	Mintage	VG	F	VF	XF	Unc
1760	—	3.00	7.00	15.00	35.00	—
1762	—	3.00	7.00	15.00	35.00	—

KM# 473 4 HELLER

Copper **Ruler:** Friedrich II **Obverse:** Crowned script FL monogram **Reverse:** Value 4; date **Rev. Legend:** SCHEIDE MUNTZ

Date	Mintage	VG	F	VF	XF	Unc
1765	—	5.00	10.00	20.00	40.00	—

KM# 502 4 HELLER

Copper **Ruler:** Friedrich II **Obverse:** Crowned double FL monogram **Reverse:** Value 4 and date **Rev. Legend:** SCHEIDEMUNTZ

Date	Mintage	VG	F	VF	XF	Unc
1773	—	4.00	9.00	20.00	40.00	—

KM# 508 4 HELLER

Copper **Ruler:** Friedrich II **Obverse:** Crowned lion left holding shield with FL monogram **Reverse:** Value 4 above date

Date	Mintage	VG	F	VF	XF	Unc
1774	—	3.00	7.00	15.00	35.00	—
1778	—	3.00	7.00	15.00	35.00	—
1782	—	3.00	7.00	15.00	35.00	—

KM# 533 4 HELLER

Copper **Ruler:** Wilhelm IX **Obverse:** Lion holding shield with WL monogram

Date	Mintage	VG	F	VF	XF	Unc
1788	—	2.00	5.00	10.00	25.00	—
1789	—	2.00	5.00	10.00	25.00	—
1790	—	2.00	5.00	10.00	25.00	—
1794	—	2.00	5.00	10.00	25.00	—

KM# 290 4 HELLER (1/3 Albus)

Silver **Ruler:** Karl **Obverse:** Crowned shield with Hessian lion left, palm branches flank **Reverse:** Value, date **Note:** Varieties exist.

Date	Mintage	VG	F	VF	XF	Unc
1702 AD	—	6.00	12.00	25.00	40.00	—
1703 AD	—	6.00	12.00	25.00	40.00	—

KM# 298 6 HELLER (1/2 Albus)

Silver **Ruler:** Karl **Obverse:** Crowned script C, date below, palm branches at sides **Reverse:** Hessian lion, value VI below **Note:** Varieties exist in date numeral placement.

Date	Mintage	VG	F	VF	XF	Unc
1701 AD	—	7.00	15.00	30.00	50.00	—
170Z AD	—	7.00	15.00	30.00	50.00	—
1703 AD	—	7.00	15.00	30.00	50.00	—
1706	—	7.00	15.00	30.00	50.00	—
1713	—	7.00	15.00	30.00	50.00	—
1714	—	7.00	15.00	30.00	50.00	—

KM# 415 6 HELLER (1/2 Albus)

Silver **Ruler:** Friedrich I (also King of Sweden) **Obverse:** Crowned Hessian lion beneath large crown **Reverse:** Date, value **Rev. Legend:** VI/HELLER

Date	Mintage	VG	F	VF	XF	Unc
1733	134,000	7.00	15.00	30.00	50.00	—
1736	374,000	7.00	15.00	30.00	50.00	—
1737	283,000	7.00	15.00	30.00	50.00	—
1738	141,000	7.00	15.00	30.00	50.00	—
1743	—	7.00	15.00	30.00	50.00	—
1745	—	7.00	15.00	30.00	50.00	—
1746	—	7.00	15.00	30.00	50.00	—
1750	—	7.00	15.00	30.00	50.00	—

KM# 457 6 HELLER (1/2 Albus)

Billon **Ruler:** Wilhelm VIII **Obverse:** Hessian lion rampant left **Reverse:** Value, date

Date	Mintage	VG	F	VF	XF	Unc
1756	—	6.00	12.00	25.00	48.00	—
1757	—	6.00	12.00	25.00	48.00	—
1758	—	6.00	12.00	25.00	48.00	—
1759	—	6.00	12.00	25.00	48.00	—

KM# 495 6 HELLER (1/2 Albus)

Billon **Ruler:** Friedrich II **Obverse:** Crowned script F **Reverse:** Value and date

Date	Mintage	VG	F	VF	XF	Unc
1770	—	8.00	20.00	35.00	80.00	—

KM# 500 6 HELLER (1/2 Albus)

Copper **Ruler:** Friedrich II **Obverse:** Crowned double FL monogram

Date	Mintage	VG	F	VF	XF	Unc
1772	—	10.00	25.00	40.00	90.00	—

KM# 510 6 HELLER (1/2 Albus)

Copper **Ruler:** Friedrich II **Obverse:** Crowned FL monogram **Reverse:** Large value, date

Date	Mintage	VG	F	VF	XF	Unc
1775	—	10.00	25.00	45.00	100	—

KM# 416 8 HELLER (1/48 Thaler)

Silver **Ruler:** Friedrich I (also King of Sweden) **Obverse:** Hessian lion in crowned shield, palm branches at sides **Reverse:** Value, date below **Rev. Legend:** VIII/HELLER

Date	Mintage	VG	F	VF	XF	Unc
1733 LR	113,000	8.00	18.00	40.00	90.00	—

KM# 423 8 HELLER (1/48 Thaler)

Silver **Ruler:** Friedrich I (also King of Sweden) **Obverse:** Crowned script FR monogram

Date	Mintage	VG	F	VF	XF	Unc
1737	118,000	7.00	16.00	35.00	85.00	—
1737 LR	Inc. above	7.00	16.00	35.00	85.00	—
1743	—	7.00	16.00	35.00	85.00	—

KM# 492 8 HELLER (1/48 Thaler)
Billon **Ruler:** Friedrich II **Obverse:** Crowned lion **Reverse:** Value and date

Date	Mintage	VG	F	VF	XF	Unc
1769 FU	—	3.00	8.00	20.00	45.00	—

KM# 501 8 HELLER (1/48 Thaler)
Copper **Ruler:** Friedrich II **Obverse:** Crowned monogram **Reverse:** Value, date

Date	Mintage	VG	F	VF	XF	Unc
1772	—	5.00	10.00	25.00	55.00	—

KM# 509 8 HELLER (1/48 Thaler)
Copper **Ruler:** Friedrich II **Obverse:** Hessian lion left with monogram in frame at left **Reverse:** Value, date

Date	Mintage	VG	F	VF	XF	Unc
1774	—	3.00	8.00	18.00	40.00	—
1777	—	3.00	8.00	18.00	40.00	—

KM# 364 ALBUS
Silver **Ruler:** Karl **Obverse:** Crowned double, mirror-image CL monogram **Reverse:** Crowned Hessian lion divides date **Note:** Varieties exist.

Date	Mintage	VG	F	VF	XF	Unc
1716	—	10.00	22.00	45.00	75.00	—
1719	—	10.00	22.00	45.00	75.00	—
1720	—	10.00	22.00	45.00	75.00	—
1721	—	10.00	22.00	45.00	75.00	—
1722	—	10.00	22.00	45.00	75.00	—
1723	—	10.00	22.00	45.00	75.00	—

KM# 383 ALBUS
Silver **Ruler:** Karl **Obverse:** Crowned script CL monogram divides date **Reverse:** Crowned Hessian lion **Note:** Varieties exist.

Date	Mintage	VG	F	VF	XF	Unc
1723	—	8.00	20.00	40.00	65.00	—
1724	—	8.00	20.00	40.00	65.00	—
1724 LR	—	8.00	20.00	40.00	65.00	—
1725 LR	—	8.00	20.00	40.00	65.00	—
1726 LR	—	8.00	20.00	40.00	65.00	—
1727 LR	—	8.00	20.00	40.00	65.00	—
1728 LR	—	8.00	20.00	40.00	65.00	—
1729 LR	—	8.00	20.00	40.00	65.00	—

KM# 384 ALBUS
Silver **Ruler:** Karl **Obverse:** Bust right **Reverse:** Spring flowing into natural basin **Rev. Legend:** INDUSTRIAE PRAEMIUM

Date	Mintage	VG	F	VF	XF	Unc
ND	—	20.00	45.00	85.00	120	—

KM# 403 ALBUS
Silver **Ruler:** Karl **Obverse:** Crowned script FR monogram divides date **Reverse:** Crowned Hessian lion

Date	Mintage	VG	F	VF	XF	Unc
1730 LR	—	12.00	25.00	50.00	90.00	—

KM# 404 ALBUS
Silver **Ruler:** Friedrich I (also King of Sweden) **Reverse:** Lion in baroque shield

Date	Mintage	VG	F	VF	XF	Unc
1731 LR	—	15.00	35.00	70.00	145	—

KM# 435 ALBUS
Silver **Ruler:** Friedrich I (also King of Sweden) **Obverse:** Crowned script FR monogram **Reverse:** Hessian lion divides date

Date	Mintage	VG	F	VF	XF	Unc
1743 LR	—	12.00	25.00	45.00	85.00	—
1744 LR	—	12.00	25.00	45.00	85.00	—
1744	—	12.00	25.00	45.00	85.00	—
1745	—	12.00	25.00	45.00	85.00	—
1746 ICB	—	12.00	25.00	45.00	85.00	—
1747 ICB	—	12.00	25.00	45.00	85.00	—
1748 ICB	—	12.00	25.00	45.00	85.00	—
1749 ICB	—	12.00	25.00	45.00	85.00	—
1750 ICB	—	12.00	25.00	45.00	85.00	—
1751 ICB	—	12.00	25.00	45.00	85.00	—

KM# 451 ALBUS
Billon **Ruler:** Wilhelm VIII **Obverse:** Crowned monogram **Reverse:** Crowned lion divides date

Date	Mintage	VG	F	VF	XF	Unc
1752 ICB	—	8.00	15.00	30.00	70.00	—
1753 ICB	—	8.00	15.00	30.00	70.00	—
1754 ICB	—	8.00	15.00	30.00	70.00	—
1755 ICB	—	8.00	15.00	30.00	70.00	—
1757 ICB	—	8.00	15.00	30.00	70.00	—
1758 ICB	—	8.00	15.00	30.00	70.00	—

KM# 464 ALBUS
Billon **Ruler:** Friedrich II **Obverse:** Crowned script FFLL monogram **Reverse:** Crowned rampant lion left

Date	Mintage	VG	F	VF	XF	Unc
1761 ICB	—	8.00	15.00	32.00	75.00	—
1762 ICB	—	8.00	15.00	32.00	75.00	—

KM# A489 ALBUS
Billon **Ruler:** Friedrich II **Obverse:** Crowned script F with .I.Z.H. below

Date	Mintage	VG	F	VF	XF	Unc
1763 FU	—	9.00	18.00	40.00	90.00	—
1764 FU	—	9.00	18.00	40.00	90.00	—

KM# B489 ALBUS
Billon **Ruler:** Friedrich II **Obverse:** Script FL, legend around **Reverse:** Lion in oval

Date	Mintage	VG	F	VF	XF	Unc
1765 FU	—	10.00	20.00	50.00	110	—

KM# 489 ALBUS
Billon **Ruler:** Friedrich II **Obverse:** Crowned monogram **Reverse:** Value, date

Date	Mintage	VG	F	VF	XF	Unc
1768 FU	—	5.00	12.00	25.00	50.00	—
1769 FU	—	5.00	12.00	25.00	50.00	—
1770 FU	—	5.00	12.00	25.00	50.00	—
1771 FU	—	5.00	12.00	25.00	50.00	—
1777 BR	—	5.00	12.00	25.00	50.00	—

KM# 342 ALBUS (12 Heller)
Silver **Ruler:** Karl **Obverse:** Crowned double-script C monogram, L-Z-H **Reverse:** Hessian lion divides date **Note:** Varieties exist in date numeral placement.

Date	Mintage	VG	F	VF	XF	Unc
1700	—	10.00	20.00	35.00	65.00	—
1701	—	10.00	20.00	35.00	65.00	—
1703 AD	—	10.00	20.00	35.00	65.00	—

KM# 511 2 ALBUS (4 Kreuzer)
Billon **Ruler:** Friedrich II **Obverse:** Crowned monogram **Reverse:** Value, date

Date	Mintage	VG	F	VF	XF	Unc
1768 FU	—	6.00	12.00	28.00	60.00	—
1771 FU	—	6.00	12.00	28.00	60.00	—
1774 BR	—	6.00	12.00	28.00	60.00	—
1775 BR	—	6.00	12.00	28.00	60.00	—
1776 BR	—	6.00	12.00	28.00	60.00	—
1777 BR	—	6.00	12.00	28.00	60.00	—
1778 BR	—	6.00	12.00	28.00	60.00	—
1779 BR	—	6.00	12.00	28.00	60.00	—
1780 BR	—	6.00	12.00	28.00	60.00	—
1781 BR	—	6.00	12.00	28.00	60.00	—
1782 BR	—	6.00	12.00	28.00	60.00	—
1783 BR	—	6.00	12.00	28.00	60.00	—

KM# 385 4 ALBUS (1/8 Thaler)
Silver **Ruler:** Karl **Obverse:** Crowned arms **Reverse:** Value, date **Rev. Legend:** IV/ALBUS

Date	Mintage	VG	F	VF	XF	Unc
1723	—	25.00	60.00	150	350	—

KM# A468 4 ALBUS (1/8 Thaler)
Silver **Ruler:** Friedrich II **Reverse:** Denomination **Rev. Legend:** IIII HESSEN ALBUS

Date	Mintage	VG	F	VF	XF	Unc
1761 ICB	—	35.00	75.00	165	300	—
1762 ICB	—	32.00	70.00	160	290	—
1768 U	—	40.00	80.00	175	320	—

KM# 468 4 ALBUS (1/8 Thaler)
Silver **Ruler:** Friedrich II **Obverse:** Hessian lion within crowned cartouche **Reverse:** Denomination **Rev. Legend:** 4 HESSEN ALBUS

Date	Mintage	VG	F	VF	XF	Unc
1763 FU	—	30.00	60.00	130	250	—
1764 FU	—	30.00	60.00	130	250	—
1765 FU	—	30.00	60.00	130	250	—

KM# 420 8 ALBUS (1/4 Thaler)
Silver **Ruler:** Friedrich I (also King of Sweden) **Obverse:** Bust right

Date	Mintage	VG	F	VF	XF	Unc
1734 LR	—	40.00	90.00	250	525	—
1738 LR	50,000	40.00	90.00	250	525	—

KM# 424 8 ALBUS (1/4 Thaler)
Silver **Ruler:** Friedrich I (also King of Sweden) **Obverse:** Head right **Reverse:** Value and date within wreath

Date	Mintage	VG	F	VF	XF	Unc
1737 LR	13,000	25.00	60.00	125	265	—
1738 LR	Inc. above	25.00	60.00	125	265	—
1740 LR	—	25.00	60.00	125	265	—

KM# 345 1/32 THALER (Albus)
Silver **Ruler:** Karl **Obverse:** Hessian lion, large crown above **Reverse:** Value, date below, legend around **Rev. Legend:** 32/EIN.THA/LER **Note:** Varieties exist.

Date	Mintage	VG	F	VF	XF	Unc
1704	—	15.00	30.00	60.00	110	—
1705	—	15.00	30.00	60.00	110	—
1706	—	15.00	30.00	60.00	110	—
1707	—	15.00	30.00	60.00	110	—

Date	Mintage	VG	F	VF	XF	Unc
1710	—	15.00	30.00	60.00	110	—

KM# 362 1/32 THALER (Albus)

Silver **Ruler:** Karl **Obverse:** Crowned double, mirror-image CLG monogram, value 32 below **Reverse:** Crowned Hessian lion divides date

Date	Mintage	VG	F	VF	XF	Unc
1712	—	12.00	28.00	55.00	100	—

KM# 410 1/32 THALER (Albus)

Silver **Ruler:** Friedrich I (also King of Sweden) **Obverse:** Crowned script FR monogram **Reverse:** Value, date below **Rev. Legend:** 32/EINEN/F. THAL

Date	Mintage	VG	F	VF	XF	Unc
1732 LR	—	12.00	28.00	55.00	100	—
1736 LR	24,000	12.00	28.00	55.00	100	—

KM# 425 1/32 THALER (Albus)

Silver **Ruler:** Friedrich I (also King of Sweden) **Obverse:** Hessian lion in crowned oval baroque frame **Reverse:** Value, date **Note:** Varieties exist with one or two tailed lion.

Date	Mintage	VG	F	VF	XF	Unc
1737 LR	86,000	10.00	20.00	45.00	75.00	—
1738 LR	218,000	10.00	20.00	45.00	75.00	—
1739 LR	262,000	10.00	20.00	45.00	75.00	—
1740 LR	—	10.00	20.00	45.00	75.00	—
1740 LR Error	—	10.00	20.00	45.00	75.00	—
1741 LR	—	10.00	20.00	45.00	75.00	—

KM# 520 1/24 THALER (Groschen)

Billon **Ruler:** Friedrich II **Obverse:** Rampant lion left, mintmaster's initials in exergue **Reverse:** Value 24/EINEN/THAL above date

Date	Mintage	VG	F	VF	XF	Unc
1768 FU	—	4.00	8.00	18.00	40.00	—
1769 FU	—	4.00	8.00	18.00	40.00	—
1780 BR	—	5.00	10.00	20.00	45.00	—

KM# 525 1/24 THALER (Groschen)

Billon **Ruler:** Friedrich II **Obverse:** Rampant lion left **Reverse:** Value 24/EINEN/THALER above date, mintmaster's initials in exergue

Date	Mintage	VG	F	VF	XF	Unc
1782 DF	—	3.00	7.00	15.00	36.00	—
1783 DF	—	3.00	7.00	15.00	36.00	—
1784 DF	—	3.00	7.00	15.00	36.00	—
1785 DF	—	3.00	7.00	15.00	36.00	—

KM# 529 1/24 THALER (Groschen)

Billon **Ruler:** Wilhelm IX **Obverse:** Rampant lion left, garland below **Reverse:** Denomination, date below, mintmaster's initials in exergue

Date	Mintage	F	VF	XF	Unc
1786 DF	—	12.00	25.00	50.00	150
1787 DF	—	12.00	25.00	50.00	150
1788 DF	—	12.00	25.00	50.00	150
1789 DF	—	12.00	25.00	50.00	150
1792 F	—	10.00	20.00	40.00	80.00
1793 F	—	10.00	20.00	40.00	80.00
1794 F	—	10.00	20.00	40.00	80.00
1795 F	—	10.00	20.00	40.00	80.00
1796 F	—	10.00	20.00	40.00	80.00
1797 F	—	10.00	20.00	40.00	80.00
1798 F	—	10.00	20.00	40.00	80.00
1799 F	—	10.00	20.00	40.00	80.00
1800 F	—	10.00	20.00	40.00	80.00
1801 F	—	12.00	24.00	45.00	120
1802 F	—	10.00	20.00	40.00	90.00

KM# 417 1/16 THALER

Silver **Ruler:** Friedrich I (also King of Sweden) **Obverse:** Crowned script FR monogram **Reverse:** Value, date **Rev. Legend:** 16/EINEN/R. THAL

Date	Mintage	VG	F	VF	XF	Unc
1733 LR	32,000	25.00	60.00	125	225	—
1737 LR	16,000	25.00	60.00	125	225	—

KM# 421 1/12 THALER (2 Groschen)

Silver **Ruler:** Friedrich I (also King of Sweden) **Obverse:** Crowned oval arms in cartouche **Reverse:** Value, date in wreath-like cartouche **Rev. Legend:** 12/EINEN/THAL

Date	Mintage	VG	F	VF	XF	Unc
1734 LR	—	50.00	120	225	350	—
1734	—	50.00	120	225	350	—
1742	—	—	—	—	—	—

Note: Reported, not confirmed

KM# 471 1/12 THALER (2 Groschen)

Silver **Ruler:** Friedrich II **Obverse:** Arms **Reverse:** Value and date

Date	Mintage	VG	F	VF	XF	Unc
1764 FU	—	15.00	25.00	60.00	140	—
1765 FU	—	15.00	25.00	60.00	140	—

KM# 474.1 1/12 THALER (2 Groschen)

Silver **Ruler:** Friedrich II **Obverse:** Rampant lion left **Reverse:** Value, date

Date	Mintage	VG	F	VF	XF	Unc
1766 FU	—	10.00	20.00	40.00	80.00	—

KM# 474.2 1/12 THALER (2 Groschen)

Silver **Ruler:** Friedrich II **Obverse:** Lion faces right **Reverse:** Value, date **Note:** Varieties exist.

Date	Mintage	VG	F	VF	XF	Unc
1766 FU	—	6.50	12.50	28.00	60.00	—
1767 FU	—	6.50	12.50	28.00	60.00	—
1768 FU	—	6.50	12.50	28.00	60.00	—
1769 FU	—	6.50	12.50	28.00	60.00	—
1771	—	6.50	12.50	28.00	60.00	—

KM# 336 1/8 THALER

Silver **Ruler:** Karl **Obverse:** Crowned arms **Reverse:** Value **Rev. Inscription:** VIII/EINEN/THALER **Note:** Varieties exist.

Date	Mintage	VG	F	VF	XF	Unc
1693 IVF	—	20.00	40.00	80.00	135	—
1702 AD	—	20.00	40.00	85.00	145	—
1703 AD	—	20.00	40.00	85.00	145	—
1704	—	20.00	40.00	85.00	145	—

KM# 386 1/8 THALER

Silver **Ruler:** Karl **Obverse:** Head right, date below **Reverse:** Crowned Hessian lion, VIGILAT above, 1/8 in cartouche below

Date	Mintage	VG	F	VF	XF	Unc
1723	—	65.00	135	275	450	—

KM# 387 1/8 THALER

Silver **Ruler:** Karl **Obverse:** Head right **Reverse:** Crowned Hessian lion on pedestal with value 8

Date	Mintage	VG	F	VF	XF	Unc
1723	—	15.00	30.00	65.00	120	—

KM# 388 1/8 THALER

Silver **Ruler:** Karl **Obverse:** Head right **Reverse:** Value, 1/8 on pedestal

Date	Mintage	VG	F	VF	XF	Unc
1723	—	15.00	30.00	65.00	120	—
1724	—	15.00	30.00	65.00	120	—

KM# 389 1/8 THALER

Silver **Ruler:** Karl **Reverse:** Crowned 6-fold arms

Date	Mintage	VG	F	VF	XF	Unc
1723	—	50.00	125	250	375	—

KM# 390 1/8 THALER

Silver **Ruler:** Karl **Obverse:** Crowned complex oval arms within cartouche **Reverse:** Hessian lion on pedestal with value 1/8

Date	Mintage	VG	F	VF	XF	Unc
1724	—	20.00	45.00	100	200	—

KM# 391 1/8 THALER

Silver **Ruler:** Karl **Obverse:** Crowned complex oval arms within cartouche **Reverse:** Value and date within inner circle **Note:** Varieties exist.

Date	Mintage	VG	F	VF	XF	Unc
1724 LR	—	15.00	30.00	65.00	135	—
1726 LR	—	15.00	30.00	65.00	135	—
1727 LR	—	15.00	30.00	65.00	135	—

KM# 411 1/8 THALER

Silver **Ruler:** Friedrich I (also King of Sweden) **Obverse:** Crowned monogram **Reverse:** Value, date

Date	Mintage	VG	F	VF	XF	Unc
1732 LR	—	15.00	30.00	65.00	135	—

KM# 427 1/8 THALER

Silver **Ruler:** Friedrich I (also King of Sweden) **Obverse:** Crowned oval arms in cartouche **Reverse:** Value, date within inner circle

Date	Mintage	VG	F	VF	XF	Unc
1737 LR	61,000	20.00	40.00	80.00	145	—

KM# 428 1/8 THALER

Silver **Ruler:** Friedrich I (also King of Sweden) **Obverse:** Rampant lion left within crowned cartouche **Reverse:** Value, date within inner circle

Date	Mintage	VG	F	VF	XF	Unc
1737 LR	—	15.00	30.00	65.00	135	—
Note: Mintage included in KM#427						
1738 LR	120,000	15.00	30.00	65.00	135	—
1743 LR	—	15.00	30.00	65.00	135	—
1745	—	15.00	30.00	65.00	135	—

KM# 438 1/8 THALER

Silver **Ruler:** Friedrich I (also King of Sweden) **Obverse:** Crowned and mantled lion arms **Note:** Varieties in mantle exist.

Date	Mintage	VG	F	VF	XF	Unc
1748 ICB	—	22.00	50.00	100	165	—

KM# 477 1/8 THALER

Silver **Ruler:** Friedrich II **Obverse:** Crowned lion left within ornate crowned shield **Reverse:** Value, date within inner circle

Date	Mintage	VG	F	VF	XF	Unc
1766 FU	—	7.00	15.00	30.00	65.00	—
1767 FU	—	7.00	15.00	30.00	65.00	—
1768 FU	—	7.00	15.00	30.00	65.00	—
1769 FU	—	7.00	15.00	30.00	65.00	—

KM# 514 1/8 THALER

Silver **Ruler:** Friedrich II **Obverse:** Lion in crowned cartouche **Reverse:** Value above wreath

Date	Mintage	VG	F	VF	XF	Unc
1771	—	7.00	15.00	30.00	65.00	—
1775	—	7.00	15.00	30.00	65.00	—
1776	—	7.00	15.00	30.00	65.00	—

KM# 475 1/6 THALER

Silver **Ruler:** Friedrich II **Obverse:** Rampant lion left standing on pedestal holding shield **Reverse:** Value, date within inner circle

Date	Mintage	VG	F	VF	XF	Unc
1765 FU	—	25.00	50.00	100	220	—

KM# 478 1/6 THALER

Silver **Ruler:** Friedrich II **Obverse:** Rampant lion left standing on pedestal holding shield **Reverse:** Value, date within inner circle

Date	Mintage	VG	F	VF	XF	Unc
1766 FU	—	22.00	45.00	90.00	200	—

KM# 479 1/6 THALER

Silver **Ruler:** Friedrich II **Obverse:** Rampant lion left holding monogrammed shield **Reverse:** Value, date within inner circle

Date	Mintage	VG	F	VF	XF	Unc
1766 FU	—	15.00	30.00	60.00	120	—

KM# 480 1/6 THALER

Silver **Ruler:** Friedrich II **Obverse:** Rampant lion left holding monogrammed shield **Reverse:** Value, date within inner circle

Date	Mintage	VG	F	VF	XF	Unc
1766	—	15.00	30.00	60.00	120	—
1766 FU	—	10.00	20.00	50.00	100	—

KM# 486 1/6 THALER

Silver **Ruler:** Friedrich II **Obverse:** Rampant lion left holding monogrammed shield **Reverse:** Legend around garland ring

Date	Mintage	VG	F	VF	XF	Unc
1767 FU	—	10.00	22.50	45.00	85.00	—
1768 FU	—	10.00	22.50	45.00	85.00	—

KM# 490 1/6 THALER

Silver **Ruler:** Friedrich II **Obverse:** Rampant lion left holding monogrammed shield **Reverse:** Legend around ring

Date	Mintage	VG	F	VF	XF	Unc
1768 FU	—	10.00	22.50	45.00	85.00	—
1769 FU	—	10.00	22.50	45.00	85.00	—

Date	Mintage	VG	F	VF	XF	Unc
1771 FU	—	10.00	22.50	45.00	85.00	—

KM# 503 1/6 THALER

Silver **Ruler:** Friedrich II **Rev. Legend:** 6 EINEN **Note:** Similar to KM#479.

Date	Mintage	VG	F	VF	XF	Unc
1772 FU	—	10.00	22.50	45.00	85.00	—
1773 FU	—	10.00	22.50	45.00	85.00	—

KM# 542 1/6 THALER

Silver **Ruler:** Wilhelm IX **Obverse:** Crowned arms **Reverse:** Value above date

Date	Mintage	F	VF	XF	Unc
1790 F	—	12.00	35.00	90.00	200
1791 F	—	12.00	35.00	90.00	200
1792 F	—	12.00	35.00	90.00	200
1793 F	—	12.00	35.00	90.00	200
1794 F	—	12.00	35.00	90.00	200
1795 F	—	12.00	35.00	90.00	200
1796 F	—	12.00	35.00	90.00	200
1798 F	—	12.00	35.00	90.00	200
1799 F	—	12.00	35.00	90.00	200
1800 F	—	12.00	35.00	90.00	200
1801 F	—	15.00	40.00	120	240
1802 F	—	20.00	50.00	150	300

KM# 373 1/4 THALER (Ortstaler)

Silver **Ruler:** Karl **Obverse:** Crowned C monogram **Reverse:** Swan on pedestal **Rev. Legend:** CANDIDE ET-CONSTANTER

Date	Mintage	VG	F	VF	XF	Unc
ND(ca.1720)	—	—	—	—	—	—

KM# 469 1/4 THALER (Ortstaler)

Silver **Ruler:** Friedrich II **Obverse:** Rampant lion left within crowned ornate shield **Reverse:** Value, date within ornate frame

Date	Mintage	VG	F	VF	XF	Unc
1763	—	12.00	22.00	45.00	90.00	—
1764	—	12.00	22.00	45.00	90.00	—
1765	—	12.00	22.00	45.00	90.00	—
1766	—	12.00	22.00	45.00	90.00	—
1767 FU	—	12.00	22.00	45.00	90.00	—

KM# 481 1/4 THALER (Ortstaler)

Silver **Ruler:** Friedrich II **Obverse:** Rampant lion left within ornate shield **Reverse:** Value, date within ornate frame

Date	Mintage	VG	F	VF	XF	Unc
1766	—	12.00	22.00	45.00	90.00	—

KM# 491 1/4 THALER (Ortstaler)

Silver **Ruler:** Friedrich II **Obverse:** Rampant lion left within crowned shield **Reverse:** Value, date within inner circle

Date	Mintage	VG	F	VF	XF	Unc
1768 FU	—	12.00	22.00	45.00	90.00	—
1769 FU	—	12.00	22.00	45.00	90.00	—
1770 FU	—	12.00	22.00	45.00	90.00	—
1771 FU	—	12.00	22.00	45.00	90.00	—
1771 FU	—	12.00	22.00	45.00	90.00	—
1772 FU	—	12.00	22.00	45.00	90.00	—

KM# 539 1/4 THALER (Ortstaler)

7.7300 g., Silver **Ruler:** Wilhelm IX **Obverse:** Head right **Reverse:** Value, date

Date	Mintage	VG	F	VF	XF	Unc
1790 F	—	60.00	120	250	450	—

KM# 482 1/3 THALER

Silver **Ruler:** Friedrich II **Obverse:** Head right **Reverse:** Crowned shield with supporters

Date	Mintage	VG	F	VF	XF	Unc
1766 fu	—	25.00	50.00	85.00	165	—

KM# 487 1/3 THALER

Silver **Ruler:** Friedrich II **Obverse:** Head right **Reverse:** Crowned shield with supporters

Date	Mintage	VG	F	VF	XF	Unc
1767	—	25.00	45.00	75.00	150	—
1768	—	25.00	45.00	75.00	150	—
1769	—	25.00	45.00	75.00	150	—
1770	—	25.00	45.00	75.00	150	—
1771	—	25.00	45.00	75.00	150	—

KM# 355 1/2 THALER

Silver **Ruler:** Karl **Subject:** Death of Maria Amalia, Wife of Karl **Obverse:** Crowned conjoined oval arms of Hesse and Courland **Reverse:** Bust left, inscription below

Date	Mintage	VG	F	VF	XF	Unc
1711 Kohler	—	200	400	600	1,000	—

KM# 366 1/2 THALER

Silver **Ruler:** Karl **Subject:** Coronation of Ulrike Eleonore, Second Wife of Friedrich I **Obverse:** Bust of Ulrike Eleonore **Reverse:** Shining star **Rev. Legend:** SECUR FUTURI **Rev. Inscription:** Roman numeral date below

Date	Mintage	VG	F	VF	XF	Unc
1719 Rare	—	—	—	—	—	—

KM# 515 1/2 THALER

Silver **Ruler:** Friedrich II **Obverse:** Head right **Reverse:** Lion arms within inner circle of star, value above, date below **Note:** Reichs 1/2 Thaler.

Date	Mintage	VG	F	VF	XF	Unc
1776 BR	—	35.00	65.00	125	250	—

KM# 530 1/2 THALER

Silver **Ruler:** Wilhelm IX **Subject:** Bieber Mines **Obverse:** Head right **Reverse:** Crowned arms on pedestal with supporters **Note:** Convention 1/2 Thaler.

Date	Mintage	VG	F	VF	XF	Unc
1786	—	125	225	375	650	—

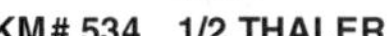

KM# 534 1/2 THALER

Silver **Ruler:** Wilhelm IX **Obverse:** Head right **Reverse:** Crowned arms with ornaments, branches below **Note:** Reichs 1/2 Thaler.

Date	Mintage	VG	F	VF	XF	Unc
1789 F	—	25.00	60.00	100	160	—

KM# 483 2/3 THALER

Silver **Ruler:** Friedrich II **Obverse:** Bust right **Reverse:** Arms **Note:** Reichs 2/3 Thaler.

Date	Mintage	VG	F	VF	XF	Unc
1766 FU	—	25.00	55.00	135	245	—

KM# 488 2/3 THALER

Silver **Ruler:** Friedrich II **Obverse:** Head right **Reverse:** Crowned arms with supporters

Date	Mintage	VG	F	VF	XF	Unc
1767 FU	—	25.00	55.00	120	225	—

KM# 527 2/3 THALER

Silver **Ruler:** Friedrich II **Obverse:** Head right **Reverse:** Crowned arms with supporters

Date	Mintage	VG	F	VF	XF	Unc
1785 DF	—	35.00	75.00	160	275	—

KM# 346 THALER

Silver **Ruler:** Karl **Obverse:** Bust right **Reverse:** Crowned oval arms with trophies

Date	Mintage	VG	F	VF	XF	Unc
ND(1701) Rare	—	—	—	—	—	—

KM# 357 THALER

Silver **Ruler:** Karl **Obverse:** Bust right **Obv. Legend:** PIETATE - INSIGNIS, I LE CLERC below **Reverse:** Inscription **Rev. Inscription:** SERMA./PRINC. ET. DNA./DNA: MARIA AMAL:/EX. SERMA. DUCAL. STIRP./CHURL. ORIUNDA. NATA./AO. M.DC.LIII. DIE. XII. IVNY./NUPTA. SERMO. ET. POTENT./PRINC. AC. DNO. DNO. CAROLO./HASS: LANDG. PR: H.C.C.D.Z./N. ET. S. DIE. XXI. MAY. AO./M.DC.LXXIII. DENATA. **Note:** Dav. #2292

Date	Mintage	VG	F	VF	XF	Unc
1711 I.LE CLERC	Inc. above	600	1,200	2,000	3,700	—

KM# 356 THALER

Silver **Ruler:** Karl **Subject:** Death of Maria Amalia, Wife of Karl **Obverse:** Bust left **Reverse:** 13-line inscription with Roman numeral date **Note:** Dav. #2292.

Date	Mintage	VG	F	VF	XF	Unc
1711	400	600	1,200	2,000	3,700	—

KM# 418 THALER

Silver **Ruler:** Friedrich I (also King of Sweden) **Obverse:** Armored, draped bust right **Obv. Legend:** FRIDERICUS D - G: REX SUECIAE **Reverse:** Crowned arms with supporters **Rev. Legend:** HASSIAE - LANDGR. **Note:** Dav. #2294.

Date	Mintage	VG	F	VF	XF	Unc
1733 LR	1,000	500	1,000	1,850	3,250	—
1733 JR (error)	—	500	1,000	1,850	3,250	—

KM# 419 THALER

Silver **Ruler:** Friedrich I (also King of Sweden) **Obverse:** Bust left **Reverse:** CASSEL below arms **Note:** Dav. #2294A.

Date	Mintage	VG	F	VF	XF	Unc
1733 LR	Inc. above	500	1,000	1,850	3,250	—

KM# 432 THALER

Silver **Ruler:** Friedrich I (also King of Sweden) **Obverse:** Crowned lion arms within cartouche **Reverse:** Value, date within inner circle **Note:** Similar to 1/8 Thaler, KM#428, struck with same dies on large flan.

Date	Mintage	VG	F	VF	XF	Unc
1738 LR Rare	—	—	—	—	—	—

KM# 448 THALER

Silver **Ruler:** Friedrich I (also King of Sweden) **Subject:** Death of Friedrich I **Obverse:** Bust right **Reverse:** 11-line inscription with date

Date	Mintage	VG	F	VF	XF	Unc
1751 ICH	—	—	—	—	—	—

KM# 453 THALER

Silver **Ruler:** Wilhelm VIII **Obverse:** Bust right, inscription around **Reverse:** Value, 1/9 I. MARCK - F. SILBER below, crowned and supported arms, date in Roman numerals in lower panel **Note:** Species Thaler. Dav. #2295.

Date	Mintage	VG	F	VF	XF	Unc
1754 SICB	—	500	1,000	2,000	3,000	—

KM# 454 THALER

Silver **Ruler:** Wilhelm VIII **Reverse:** Value 1/9 MARCK F. SILBER AUS BIEBER in 4-line inscription, date divided by mintmaster's initials below **Note:** Dav. #2296.

Date	Mintage	VG	F	VF	XF	Unc
1754 S-ICB	—	300	750	1,400	2,000	—

KM# 455 THALER

Silver **Ruler:** Wilhelm VIII **Obverse:** Cloaked bust right **Obv. Legend:** WILHELM • VIII • D • G • - HAS • LANDG • HAN • COM • **Reverse:** 5-Line inscription in panel below arms **Rev. Legend:** RECTUS ET IMMOTUS, 1/9/MARCK/F:SILBER/AUS/BIEBER below arms in frame **Note:** Dav. #2297.

Date	Mintage	VG	F	VF	XF	Unc
1754 S-ICB	—	300	750	1,400	2,000	—

KM# 460 THALER

Silver **Ruler:** Wilhelm VIII **Obverse:** Cloaked bust right **Obv. Legend:** WILHELM • VIII • D • G • - HASS • LANDG • HAN • COM • **Reverse:** 3-Line inscription in panel below arms **Rev. Legend:** RECTUS ET IMMOTUS, 1/9/MARCK./F.SILB: AUS/BIEBER below arms **Note:** Dav. #2298.

Date	Mintage	VG	F	VF	XF	Unc
1759 S-ICB	—	350	900	1,600	2,250	—

KM# 470 THALER

Silver **Ruler:** Friedrich II **Obverse:** Armored bust left **Obv. Legend:** FRIDERICUS II. D.G. HASS. LANDG. HAN. COM. **Reverse:** Crowned oval arms with supporters **Note:** Convention Thaler. Dav. #2299.

Date	Mintage	VG	F	VF	XF	Unc
1763 U	—	250	600	1,000	1,750	—

KM# 476 THALER

Silver **Ruler:** Friedrich II **Obverse:** Armored bust right **Obv. Legend:** FRIDERICUS II. D.G. HASS. LANDG. HAN. COM. **Reverse:** Crowned oval complex arms with supporters **Rev. Legend:** X. EINE MARCK - FEIN SILBER

Date	Mintage	F	VF	XF	Unc
1765 FU	—	150	300	550	950

KM# 484 THALER
Silver **Ruler:** Friedrich II **Obverse:** Draped, armored bust right **Obv. Legend:** FRIDERICUS II. D.G. HASS. LANDG. HAN. COM. **Reverse:** Crowned oval arms wtih supporters **Rev. Legend:** X. ST: EINE - FEINE MARK., 17.IUSTIRT.66 below **Note:** Dav. #2301.

Date	Mintage	F	VF	XF	Unc
1766 FU	—	85.00	175	325	725

KM# 485 THALER
Silver **Ruler:** Friedrich II **Obverse:** Head right **Obv. Legend:** FRIDERICUS II. D.G. HASS. LANDG. HAN. COM. **Reverse:** Crowned oval arms with supporters **Rev. Legend:** X. ST: EINE - MARK FEIN., 17.IUSTIRT.66 **Note:** Dav. #2302.

Date	Mintage	F	VF	XF	Unc
1766 FU	—	85.00	175	325	725

KM# 516 THALER
Silver **Ruler:** Friedrich II **Obverse:** Head right **Obv. Legend:** FRIDERICUS II. D. G. HASS. LANDG. HAN. COM. **Reverse:** Lion arms within inner circle of star, value above, date below **Rev. Legend:** EIN THALER, VIRTUTE ET FIDELITATE around lion **Note:** Reichs Thaler. Dav. #2303. Varieties exist.

Date	Mintage	F	VF	XF	Unc
1776 BR	—	70.00	125	225	450
1778 BR	—	70.00	125	225	450
1779 BR	—	70.00	125	225	450

KM# 528 THALER
Silver **Ruler:** Friedrich II **Obverse:** Head right **Obv. Legend:** WILHELMUS IX. D. G. HASS. LANDG. COM. HAN. **Reverse:** BIBERER SILBER on pedestal below arms **Rev. Legend:** X. EINE FEINE MARCK. **Note:** Mining Thaler. Dav. #2304.

Date	Mintage	F	VF	XF	Unc
1784 CLR	—	100	200	350	750
1785 IFH	—	100	200	375	750

KM# 532 THALER
Silver **Ruler:** Wilhelm IX **Obverse:** Bust right **Obv. Legend:** WILHELMUS IX D:G: HASS: LANDG: COM. HAN **Reverse:** Crowned oval arms with griffin supporters **Rev. Legend:** X EINE FEINE MARCK, BEBERER SILBER below **Note:** Dav. #2305. Many varieties exist. Prev. KM#552.

Date	Mintage	F	VF	XF	Unc
1787 FH	—	100	200	375	750
1789 FH	—	100	200	375	750
1791 FH	—	100	200	375	750
1793 FH	—	100	200	375	750
1794 FH	—	100	200	375	750
1796 FH	—	100	200	375	750
1798 FH	—	100	200	375	750
1800 FH	—	1,000	2,000	5,000	12,000
1802 FH Rare	—	—	—	—	—

KM# 535 THALER
Silver **Ruler:** Wilhelm IX **Obverse:** Head right **Obv. Legend:** WILHELMUS IX D. G. HASS. LANDG. HAN. COM. **Reverse:** Crowned arms with ornaments, branches below **Rev. Legend:** EIN THALER **Note:** Reichs Thaler. Dav. #2307.

Date	Mintage	F	VF	XF	Unc
1789 K//F	—	90.00	150	325	825
1789 K//DF	—	90.00	150	325	825

KM# 536 2 THALER (3-1/2 Gulden)
Silver **Ruler:** Wilhelm IX **Obverse:** Head right **Obv. Legend:** WILHELMUS IX D. G. HASS. LANDG. HAN. COM. **Reverse:** Arms within Order chain and mantle, value above, date below **Rev. Legend:** ZWEY THALER **Note:** Reichs 2 Thaler. Dav. #2306.

Date	Mintage	VG	F	VF	XF	Unc
1789	250	1,000	1,500	2,000	3,000	—

KM# 496 5 THALER (Friedrich d'or)
6.6500 g., 0.9000 Gold 0.1924 oz. AGW **Ruler:** Friedrich II **Obverse:** Head right **Reverse:** Lion arms within inner circle of star, date below

Date	Mintage	F	VF	XF	Unc
1771 BR	—	500	1,200	2,000	4,000
1777 BR	—	500	1,200	2,000	4,000
1778 BR	—	500	1,200	2,000	4,000

KM# 526 5 THALER (Friedrich d'or)
6.6500 g., 0.9000 Gold 0.1924 oz. AGW **Ruler:** Friedrich II **Obverse:** Head right **Reverse:** Lion arms within inner circle of star, date below

Date	Mintage	F	VF	XF	Unc
1783 DF	—	250	500	1,500	2,500
1784 DF	—	250	500	1,500	2,500
1785 DF	—	250	500	1,500	2,500

KM# 531 5 THALER (Friedrich d'or)
6.6500 g., 0.9000 Gold 0.1924 oz. AGW **Ruler:** Wilhelm IX **Obverse:** Head right **Reverse:** Lion arms within inner circle of star

Date	Mintage	F	VF	XF	Unc
1786	—	300	600	1,000	1,750
1787	—	300	600	1,000	1,750
1788	—	300	600	1,000	1,750
1790	—	300	600	1,000	1,750

KM# 545 5 THALER (Friedrich d'or)
6.6500 g., 0.9000 Gold 0.1924 oz. AGW **Ruler:** Wilhelm IX **Obverse:** Head right **Reverse:** Lion lying at front of crowned arms, flags at left, fasces and swords at right

Date	Mintage	F	VF	XF	Unc
1791 F	—	300	600	1,000	1,750
1792 F	—	300	600	1,000	1,750
1793 F	—	300	600	1,000	1,750
1794 F	—	300	600	1,000	1,750
1795 F	—	300	600	1,000	1,750
1796 F	—	300	600	1,000	1,750
1797 F	—	300	600	1,000	1,750
1798 F	—	300	600	1,000	1,750
1799 F	—	300	600	1,000	1,750
1800 F	—	300	600	1,000	1,750
1801 F	—	900	1,800	2,600	3,600

KM# 504 10 THALER (2 Friedrich d'or)
13.3000 g., 0.9000 Gold 0.3848 oz. AGW **Ruler:** Friedrich II **Obverse:** Head right **Reverse:** Lion arms within inner circle of star, date below

Date	Mintage	F	VF	XF	Unc
1773 FU	—	750	1,250	2,750	4,500

KM# 512 10 THALER (2 Friedrich d'or)
13.3000 g., 0.9000 Gold 0.3848 oz. AGW **Ruler:** Friedrich II **Obverse:** Head right **Reverse:** Lion arms within inner circle of star, date below

Date	Mintage	F	VF	XF	Unc
1775 BR	—	750	1,250	2,750	4,500
1776 BR	—	750	1,250	2,750	4,500
1777 BR	—	750	1,250	2,750	4,500

KM# 521 10 THALER (2 Friedrich d'or)
13.3000 g., 0.9000 Gold 0.3848 oz. AGW **Ruler:** Friedrich II **Obverse:** Head right **Reverse:** Lion arms within inner circle of star, date below

Date	Mintage	F	VF	XF	Unc
1780 DF	—	750	1,250	2,750	4,500
1785 DF	—	750	1,250	2,750	4,500

REGIONAL COINAGE

Ober-Hessen

Under Wilhelm II

KM# 522 1/4 KREUZER
Copper **Ruler:** Friedrich II **Obverse:** Crowned arms **Reverse:** Value above date

Date	Mintage	VG	F	VF	XF	Unc
1783	—	3.00	6.00	12.00	28.00	—

KM# 523 1/2 KREUZER
Copper **Ruler:** Friedrich II **Obverse:** Crowned arms **Reverse:** Value above date

Date	Mintage	VG	F	VF	XF	Unc
1783	—	2.50	5.00	10.00	25.00	—

KM# 524 KREUZER
Copper **Ruler:** Friedrich II **Obverse:** Crowned arms **Reverse:** Value above date

Date	Mintage	VG	F	VF	XF	Unc
1783	—	2.50	5.00	10.00	40.00	—

TRADE COINAGE

KM# 374 1/4 DUCAT
0.8750 g., 0.9860 Gold 0.0277 oz. AGW **Ruler:** Karl **Obverse:** Head right **Reverse:** Rampant lion left

Date	Mintage	VG	F	VF	XF	Unc
1720	—	75.00	150	285	450	—

KM# 375 1/4 DUCAT
0.8750 g., 0.9860 Gold 0.0277 oz. AGW **Ruler:** Karl **Obverse:** Head right **Reverse:** Swan on pedestal

Date	Mintage	VG	F	VF	XF	Unc
ND	—	75.00	150	285	450	—

KM# 405 1/4 DUCAT
0.8750 g., 0.9860 Gold 0.0277 oz. AGW **Ruler:** Friedrich I (also King of Sweden) **Obverse:** Head right **Reverse:** Crowned Hessian lion, date **Rev. Legend:** EDDER GOLD

Date	Mintage	VG	F	VF	XF	Unc
1731	—	—	—	—	—	—

KM# 406 1/4 DUCAT
0.8750 g., 0.9860 Gold 0.0277 oz. AGW **Ruler:** Friedrich I (also King of Sweden) **Obverse:** Head right **Reverse:** Crowned rampant lion

Date	Mintage	VG	F	VF	XF	Unc
ND	—	100	200	350	500	—

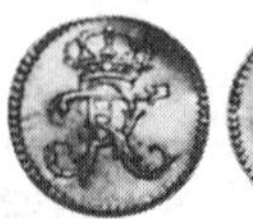

KM# 436 1/4 DUCAT
0.8750 g., 0.9860 Gold 0.0277 oz. AGW **Ruler:** Friedrich I (also King of Sweden) **Obverse:** Crowned FR monogram **Reverse:** Crowned rampant lion, value divides date below

Date	Mintage	VG	F	VF	XF	Unc
1744	—	100	200	350	500	—
1750	—	100	200	350	500	—

KM# 452 1/4 DUCAT
0.8750 g., 0.9860 Gold 0.0277 oz. AGW **Ruler:** Wilhelm VIII **Obverse:** Crowned WL monogram **Reverse:** Crowned rampant lion, value, date

Date	Mintage	VG	F	VF	XF	Unc
1752	—	75.00	125	250	400	—

KM# 376 1/2 DUCAT
1.7500 g., 0.9860 Gold 0.0555 oz. AGW **Ruler:** Friedrich I (also King of Sweden) **Obverse:** Bust right **Reverse:** Pastoral scene with spring

Date	Mintage	VG	F	VF	XF	Unc
ND	—	125	275	450	700	—

KM# 407 1/2 DUCAT
1.7500 g., 0.9860 Gold 0.0555 oz. AGW **Ruler:** Friedrich I (also King of Sweden) **Obverse:** Head right **Reverse:** Date in exergue, inscription **Rev. Inscription:** EDDER GOLD

Date	Mintage	VG	F	VF	XF	Unc
1731	—	225	450	950	1,750	—
1737	—	225	450	950	1,750	—

KM# 377 1/2 DUCAT
1.7500 g., 0.9860 Gold 0.0555 oz. AGW **Ruler:** Friedrich I (also King of Sweden) **Reverse:** Crowned rampant lion, legend in exergue **Rev. Legend:** EDDER GOLD

Date	Mintage	VG	F	VF	XF	Unc
ND	—	250	500	1,200	2,000	—

KM# 408 1/2 DUCAT
1.7500 g., 0.9860 Gold 0.0555 oz. AGW **Ruler:** Friedrich I (also King of Sweden) **Obverse:** Bust right **Reverse:** Value in exergue

Date	Mintage	VG	F	VF	XF	Unc
1731	—	225	450	950	1,750	—

KM# 439 1/2 DUCAT
1.7500 g., 0.9860 Gold 0.0555 oz. AGW **Ruler:** Friedrich I (also King of Sweden) **Obverse:** Head right **Reverse:** Crowned rampant lion left

Date	Mintage	VG	F	VF	XF	Unc
1748	—	125	275	450	800	—

KM# 378 DUCAT
3.5000 g., 0.9860 Gold 0.1109 oz. AGW **Ruler:** Karl **Obverse:** Head right **Reverse:** Crowned rampant lion holding book and sword

Date	Mintage	VG	F	VF	XF	Unc
1720	—	175	375	800	1,500	—
ND	—	175	375	800	1,500	—

KM# 379 DUCAT
3.5000 g., 0.9860 Gold 0.1109 oz. AGW **Ruler:** Karl **Obverse:** Head right **Reverse:** Without book in lion's paw

Date	Mintage	VG	F	VF	XF	Unc
1720	—	175	375	800	1,500	—

KM# 392 DUCAT
3.5000 g., 0.9860 Gold 0.1109 oz. AGW **Ruler:** Karl **Obverse:** Head right **Reverse:** Crowned round arms

Date	Mintage	VG	F	VF	XF	Unc
1724	—	150	325	675	1,350	—
1725	—	150	325	675	1,350	—
ND	—	150	325	675	1,350	—

KM# 409 DUCAT
3.5000 g., 0.9860 Gold 0.1109 oz. AGW **Ruler:** Friedrich I (also King of Sweden) **Obverse:** Bust of Friedrich right **Reverse:** Crowned arms of Sweden

Date	Mintage	VG	F	VF	XF	Unc
1731	—	150	325	675	1,350	—
1737	—	150	325	675	1,350	—
1746	—	150	325	675	1,350	—
1749	—	150	325	675	1,350	—
1750	—	150	325	675	1,350	—

KM# 429 DUCAT
3.5000 g., 0.9860 Gold 0.1109 oz. AGW **Ruler:** Friedrich I (also King of Sweden) **Obverse:** Crowned FR monogram divides date **Reverse:** Crowned Hessian arms

Date	Mintage	VG	F	VF	XF	Unc
1737 LR	—	150	325	675	1,350	—

KM# 431 DUCAT
3.5000 g., 0.9860 Gold 0.1109 oz. AGW **Ruler:** Friedrich I (also King of Sweden) **Obverse:** Laureate head right **Reverse:** Crowned complex arms divide date

Date	Mintage	VG	F	VF	XF	Unc
1737	—	200	400	850	1,600	—
1746	—	200	400	850	1,600	—

KM# 449 DUCAT
3.5000 g., 0.9860 Gold 0.1109 oz. AGW **Ruler:** Wilhelm VIII **Obverse:** Wilhelm VIII

Date	Mintage	VG	F	VF	XF	Unc
1751 ICB	—	250	550	1,000	1,800	—
1754 ICB	—	250	550	1,000	1,800	—

KM# A513 DUCAT
3.5000 g., 0.9860 Gold 0.1109 oz. AGW **Ruler:** Friedrich II **Obverse:** Armored bust right **Reverse:** River god reclining **Note:** Fr. #1284.

Date	Mintage	F	VF	XF	Unc
MDCCLXXV (1775)	—	750	1,500	3,000	5,000

KM# 314 2 DUCAT
7.0000 g., 0.9860 Gold 0.2219 oz. AGW **Ruler:** Karl **Obverse:** Head right **Reverse:** Crowned rampant lion holding book and sword

Date	Mintage	VG	F	VF	XF	Unc
ND	—	500	1,000	2,200	3,500	—

KM# 315 2 DUCAT
7.0000 g., 0.9860 Gold 0.2219 oz. AGW **Ruler:** Karl **Reverse:** Crowned arms

Date	Mintage	VG	F	VF	XF	Unc
ND	—	400	900	1,850	3,000	—

KM# 513 4 DUCAT
14.0000 g., 0.9860 Gold 0.4438 oz. AGW **Ruler:** Friedrich II **Subject:** 50th Anniversary of Reign **Obverse:** Bust right **Reverse:** Roman numeral date at bottom

Date	Mintage	F	VF	XF	Unc
ND(1777) Rare	—	—	—	—	—

PATTERNS

Including off metal strikes

KM#	Date	Mintage	Identification	Mkt Val
Pn1	ND1734	—	1/12 Thaler. Copper. KM#421.	150
Pn11	ND1723	—	Heller. Copper. KM#347.	—
Pn12	ND1723	—	1/8 Thaler. Gold. KM#388.	—
Pn13	ND1725	—	Ducat. Copper. KM#392.	—
Pn14	ND1729	—	4 Heller. Copper. KM#382.	—
Pn15	ND1729	—	4 Heller. Gold. KM#382.	—
Pn16	ND1730	—	4 Heller. Silver. KM#382.	—

KM#	Date	Mintage	Identification	Mkt Val
Pn17	ND1730	—	4 Heller. Silver. KM#402.	—
Pn18	ND1734	—	1/12 Thaler. Copper. KM#421.	150
Pn19	ND1737	—	1/16 Thaler. Gold. KM#417.	—
Pn20	ND1738	—	Heller. Silver. KM#401.	—
Pn21	ND1738	—	1/32 Thaler. Copper. KM#425.	—
Pn22	ND1741	—	Heller. Gold. KM#401.	—
Pn23	ND1741	—	4 Heller. Gold. KM#402.	950
Pn24	ND(1743)	—	Albus. Copper. KM#435.	—
Pn25	ND1746	—	4 Heller. Gold. KM#402.	950
Pn26	ND1747	—	4 Heller. Gold. KM#402.	950
Pn27	ND1754	—	4 Heller. Gold. KM#447.	—
Pn28	ND1754	—	Ducat. Copper. KM#449.	—
Pn29	ND1755	—	3 Heller. Silver. KM#456.	250
Pn30	ND1755	—	4 Heller. Gold. KM#447.	—
Pn31	ND1756	—	4 Heller. Gold. KM#447.	25,000
Pn32	ND1756	—	6 Heller. Gold. KM#457.	—
Pn33	ND1759	—	Thaler. Copper. KM#460.	—

TRIAL STRIKES

KM#	Date	Mintage	Identification	Mkt Val
TS1	ND1752	—	8 Albus. Silver. .	—

HESSE-DARMSTADT

Established by the division of the Landgraviate of Hesse in 1567, Hesse-Darmstadt was the territorially smaller of the two surviving branches of the family. The ruler was raised to the rank of Grand Duke in 1806. In 1815 the Congress of Vienna awarded Hesse-Darmstadt the cities of Mainz and Worms, which were relinquished along with the newly acquired Hesse-Homburg, to the Prussians in 1866. It became part of the German Empire in 1871.

RULERS

Ernst Ludwig, 1678-1739
Ludwig VIII, 1739-1768
Ludwig IX, 1768-1790
Ludwig X, 1790-1806
As Grand Duke Ludwig I, 1806-1830

MINT OFFICIALS' INITIALS

Initials	Date	Name
AK	1744-71	Andreas Koch
BIB	1707-33	Balthasar Johann Bethmann
CF, GCF	1741-43, 1752-66	George Conrad Fehr
CHK, K	1763-77	Conrad Heinrich Kuchler, die-cutter
GK	1733-40	Georg Christoph Kuster
GLC	1695-1708	Gabriel Le Clerc, die-cutter, medailleur in Cassel
IAR	1693-1705	Johann Adam Rephun
IAR, R	1741-65	J.A. Roth, die-cutter
ICR, R	1696-1707	J.C. Roth, medailleur
PB	1765-66	Philipp Bischof, warden
RF	1772-1809	Remigius Fehr
S	1750-60	Johann Heinrich Schepp, engraver in Cassel

GRAND DUCHY

REGULAR COINAGE

KM# 177 HELLER (Pfennig)

Billon **Ruler:** Ludwig VIII **Obverse:** Lion in German shield in laurel wreath, H.D. above **Note:** Uniface

Date	Mintage	VG	F	VF	XF	Unc
ND(1743-44) AK Rare	—	—	—	—	—	—

KM# 251 PFENNIG

Copper **Ruler:** Ludwig X **Obverse:** Crowned oval arms, H. D. flank crown **Reverse:** Denomination above date, stars

Date	Mintage	F	VF	XF	Unc
1797	—	4.00	18.00	40.00	90.00
1798	—	4.00	18.00	40.00	90.00
1799	—	4.00	18.00	40.00	90.00

KM# 163 PFENNIG (Heller)

Copper **Ruler:** Ernst Ludwig **Obverse:** Crowned EL monogram **Reverse:** Value within cartouche **Note:** Similar to IIII Pfennig KM#166 but value I.

Date	Mintage	VG	F	VF	XF	Unc
1735	—	20.00	45.00	55.00	80.00	—

KM# A177 PFENNIG (Heller)

Billon **Ruler:** Ludwig VIII **Obverse:** Lion in French shield, H.D. above **Note:** Uniface

Date	Mintage	Good	VG	F	VF	XF
ND(1743-1744) Rare	—	—	—	—	—	—

KM# B177 PFENNIG (Heller)

Billon **Ruler:** Ludwig VIII **Obverse:** Lion in dot circle, H.D. above **Note:** Uniface

Date	Mintage	Good	VG	F	VF	XF
ND(1743-1744) Rare	—	—	—	—	—	—

KM# 183 PFENNIG (Heller)

Billon **Ruler:** Ludwig VIII **Obverse:** Crowned lion shield, branches below, H.D. above **Reverse:** Value above date in oval cartouche

Date	Mintage	VG	F	VF	XF	Unc
1748 AK Rare	—	—	—	—	—	—

KM# 182 PFENNIG (Heller)

Billon **Ruler:** Ludwig VIII **Obverse:** Lion left, divided date below, H.D. PFENNIG. above **Note:** Uniface

Date	Mintage	VG	F	VF	XF	Unc
1748 AK Rare	—	—	—	—	—	—

KM# 231 PFENNIG (Heller)

Copper **Ruler:** Ludwig IX **Obverse:** Lion in rococo cartouche, H.D. flanking crown above, flags at sides, cannons below **Reverse:** Value above date

Date	Mintage	VG	F	VF	XF	Unc
1773 RF	—	2.00	5.00	10.00	25.00	—

KM# 232 PFENNIG (Heller)

Copper **Ruler:** Ludwig IX **Obverse:** Lion in thick oval shield, H.D. flanking crown above, flags at side **Reverse:** Value 1 ZOLL PFENNIG above date

Date	Mintage	VG	F	VF	XF	Unc
1774 .R.F.	—	3.00	8.00	16.00	40.00	—

KM# 234 PFENNIG (Heller)

Copper **Ruler:** Ludwig IX **Obverse:** Lion in crowned oval wreath, HESSEN DARMST at side **Reverse:** Value above date (Zoll = Toll)

Date	Mintage	VG	F	VF	XF	Unc
1777 .R.F.	—	3.00	6.00	15.00	35.00	—

KM# 240 PFENNIG (Heller)

Copper **Ruler:** Ludwig IX **Obverse:** Lion in circle wreath with crown, HESSEN DARMST at side **Reverse:** Value 1 PFENNIG above date **Note:** Varieties exist.

Date	Mintage	VG	F	VF	XF	Unc
1784 .R.F.	—	1.00	3.00	7.00	18.00	—
1785 .R.F.	—	1.00	3.00	7.00	18.00	—
1786 .R.F.	—	1.00	3.00	7.00	18.00	—
1787 .R.F.	—	1.00	3.00	7.00	18.00	—
1788 .R.F.	—	1.00	3.00	7.00	18.00	—
1789	—	1.00	3.00	7.00	18.00	—
1790	—	1.00	3.00	7.00	18.00	—

KM# 242 PFENNIG (Heller)

Copper **Ruler:** Ludwig X **Obverse:** Crowned oval arms, crown divides H. D. **Reverse:** Value above date, no stars

Date	Mintage	VG	F	VF	XF	Unc
1789	—	2.00	5.00	10.00	20.00	—
1806 RF	—	10.00	30.00	90.00	160	—

KM# A240 PFENNIG (Heller)

Copper **Ruler:** Ludwig IX **Obverse:** Lion in oval with ornaments at sides

Date	Mintage	VG	F	VF	XF	Unc
1789 RF	—	1.00	3.00	7.00	18.00	—
1790 RF	—	1.00	3.00	7.00	18.00	—
1790	—	1.00	3.00	7.00	18.00	—
1794	—	1.00	3.00	7.00	18.00	—
1796	—	1.00	3.00	7.00	18.00	—
1797	—	1.00	3.00	7.00	18.00	—

KM# 164 2 PFENNIG (2 Heller)

Copper **Ruler:** Ernst Ludwig **Obverse:** Crowned EL monogram **Reverse:** Value within cartouche

Date	Mintage	VG	F	VF	XF	Unc
1735	—	8.00	18.00	28.00	60.00	—

KM# 233 2 PFENNIG (2 Heller)

Copper **Ruler:** Ludwig IX **Obverse:** Crowned arms, H.D. above, flags and cannons at sides **Reverse:** Value above date

Date	Mintage	VG	F	VF	XF	Unc
1776 R.F.	—	4.00	8.00	15.00	30.00	—

KM# 165 3 PFENNIG

Copper **Ruler:** Ernst Ludwig **Obverse:** Crowned EL monogram **Reverse:** Value within cartouche **Note:** Similar to IIII Pfennig, KM#166, but value III.

Date	Mintage	VG	F	VF	XF	Unc
1735	—	10.00	20.00	40.00	80.00	—

KM# 166 4 PFENNIG

Copper **Ruler:** Ernst Ludwig **Obverse:** Crowned EL monogram **Reverse:** Value within cartouche

Date	Mintage	VG	F	VF	XF	Unc
1735	—	10.00	20.00	45.00	80.00	—

KM# 167 6 PFENNIG

Copper **Ruler:** Ernst Ludwig **Obverse:** Crowned EL monogram **Reverse:** Value within cartouche **Note:** Similar to IIII Pfennig, KM #166 but value VI.

Date	Mintage	VG	F	VF	XF	Unc
1735	—	7.00	15.00	30.00	55.00	—

KM# 71.4 ALBUS

Silver **Ruler:** Ernst Ludwig **Obverse:** Hessian lion in shield within laurel wreath, H.D. above **Note:** Varieties exist with Spanish or French shield.

Date	Mintage	VG	F	VF	XF	Unc
1702 IAR	—	7.00	12.00	20.00	50.00	—
1703 IAR	—	7.00	12.00	20.00	50.00	—
1703 IAR	—	—	—	—	—	—
1704	—	—	—	—	—	—
1705	—	—	—	—	—	—

KM# 82 2 ALBUS

Silver **Ruler:** Ernst Ludwig **Obverse:** Manifold Hessian arms in Spanish shield within laurel wreath, HD above **Reverse:** Value, date within branches **Note:** Varieties exist with Spanish or French shield.

Date	Mintage	VG	F	VF	XF	Unc
1703 IAR	—	10.00	18.00	28.00	55.00	—
1703 IAR	—	10.00	18.00	28.00	55.00	—
1704 IAR	—	10.00	18.00	28.00	55.00	—
1705 IAR	—	10.00	18.00	28.00	55.00	—
1707 BIB	—	10.00	18.00	28.00	55.00	—
1708 BIB	—	10.00	18.00	28.00	55.00	—
1780 BIB (error)	—	10.00	18.00	28.00	55.00	—

KM# 179 2 ALBUS

Billon **Ruler:** Ludwig VIII **Obverse:** Arms in cartouche **Reverse:** Value, date **Note:** Similar to KM#82.

Date	Mintage	VG	F	VF	XF	Unc
1745 AK	—	12.00	25.00	50.00	95.00	—
1746 AK	—	12.00	25.00	50.00	95.00	—
1747 AK	—	12.00	25.00	50.00	95.00	—
1750 AK	—	12.00	25.00	50.00	95.00	—

KM# 70.2 KREUZER

Silver **Ruler:** Ernst Ludwig **Obverse:** Lion in shield, H.D. above, laurel branches around **Reverse:** I/KREV/TZER/date, laurel branches around

Date	Mintage	VG	F	VF	XF	Unc
1702 IAR	—	4.00	10.00	20.00	35.00	—
1702 IAR	—	4.00	10.00	20.00	35.00	—
1720 BIB	—	4.00	10.00	20.00	35.00	—
17Z1 BIB	—	4.00	10.00	20.00	35.00	—
1721 BIB	—	4.00	10.00	20.00	35.00	—
1722 BIB	—	4.00	10.00	20.00	35.00	—
1723 BIB	—	4.00	10.00	20.00	35.00	—
1726 BIB	—	4.00	10.00	20.00	35.00	—
1733 GK	—	4.00	10.00	20.00	35.00	—
1741 GCF	—	5.00	10.00	20.00	45.00	—

KM# 172 KREUZER

Billon **Ruler:** Ludwig VIII **Obverse:** Lion in Spanish shield, HD above, laurel branches around **Reverse:** I/KREU/TZER/date

Date	Mintage	VG	F	VF	XF	Unc
1742	—	6.00	15.00	30.00	70.00	—
1759	—	6.00	15.00	30.00	70.00	—

KM# 170 KREUZER

Billon **Ruler:** Ludwig VIII **Obverse:** Lion shield on monogram, crown above **Reverse:** I/KREV/TZER/date/AK, laurel branches around date

Date	Mintage	VG	F	VF	XF	Unc
1746 AK	—	5.00	8.00	16.00	35.00	—
1759 AK	—	6.00	15.00	30.00	70.00	—

KM# 207 KREUZER

Billon **Ruler:** Ludwig VIII **Obverse:** Lion in baroque shield, crown above, HD at its sides, date below **Reverse:** I/KR/AK in cartouche **Rev. Legend:** AD NORM: CONVENT **Note:** Convention - Kreuzer.

Date	Mintage	VG	F	VF	XF	Unc
1763 AK	—	6.00	10.00	20.00	40.00	—

KM# 216 KREUZER

Billon **Ruler:** Ludwig VIII **Obverse:** Lion in Spanish shield, DH above, laurel branches around **Reverse:** I/KREU/TZER, date

Date	Mintage	VG	F	VF	XF	Unc
1765 GCF-PB	—	6.00	12.00	25.00	50.00	—

KM# 228 KREUZER

0.7700 g., 0.1870 Silver 0.0046 oz. ASW **Ruler:** Ludwig IX **Obverse:** Lion in cartouche, crown above. HESSEN-DARMST at sides **Reverse:** I/KREUZER/date/AK, cartouche around

Date	Mintage	VG	F	VF	XF	Unc
1771 AK	—	7.00	15.00	30.00	60.00	—
1772 RF	—	7.00	15.00	30.00	60.00	—
1773 RF	—	7.00	15.00	30.00	60.00	—
1775 RF	—	7.00	15.00	30.00	60.00	—

KM# 241 KREUZER

0.7700 g., 0.1870 Silver 0.0046 oz. ASW **Ruler:** Ludwig IX **Obverse:** Lion in circle cartouche, crown above, H.D. at its sides **Reverse:** I/KREUZ/date/R.F., branch around

Date	Mintage	F	VF	XF	Unc
1776 RF	—	18.00	40.00	80.00	—
1783 RF	—	18.00	40.00	80.00	—
1784	—	14.00	30.00	65.00	—

KM# 255 KREUZER

0.7700 g., 0.1870 Silver 0.0046 oz. ASW **Ruler:** Ludwig X **Obverse:** Lion on pedestal, H.D. within, LAND-MUNZ and branches at sides **Reverse:** I/KREUZER/date

Date	Mintage	F	VF	XF	Unc
1800	—	2.00	6.00	14.00	50.00

KM# 173 2 KREUZER

Billon **Ruler:** Ludwig VIII **Obverse:** Crowned rampant lion left within shield, branches surround **Reverse:** Value and date within branches

Date	Mintage	VG	F	VF	XF	Unc
1741 GCF	—	8.00	12.00	25.00	45.00	—
1743 GCF	—	8.00	12.00	25.00	45.00	—
1744 AK	—	8.00	12.00	25.00	45.00	—

KM# 208 2 KREUZER

Billon **Ruler:** Ludwig VIII **Obverse:** Crowned lion in rococo cartouche, HESSEN-DARMST around **Reverse:** 2/KREUZ/date, LAND-MUNZ at sides

Date	Mintage	VG	F	VF	XF	Unc
1763 AK Rare	—	—	—	—	—	—

KM# 184 4 KREUZER

Billon **Ruler:** Ludwig VIII **Obverse:** Crowned lion left **Reverse:** Value in baroque frame, date below

Date	Mintage	VG	F	VF	XF	Unc
1748 AK	—	7.00	15.00	30.00	65.00	—
1750 AK	—	—	—	—	—	—
1759 AK	—	7.00	15.00	30.00	65.00	—

KM# 209 4 KREUZER

Billon **Ruler:** Ludwig VIII **Obverse:** Lion on pedestal with HD on it, date below **Obv. Legend:** AD NORMAN CONVENTIONIS **Reverse:** IIII/KR:EUZER, 360 E.F.M below **Rev. Legend:** LAND MUNZ

Date	Mintage	VG	F	VF	XF	Unc
1763	—	25.00	40.00	80.00	170	—
1764 GCF	—	25.00	45.00	90.00	180	—

KM# 217 4 KREUZER

Billon **Ruler:** Ludwig VIII **Obverse:** Lion on pedestal with monogram, date below, branches and HESSEN-DARMST at sides **Reverse:** IIII/KREU/ZER in baroque frame, 300 E.F.M., LAND-MUNZ

Date	Mintage	VG	F	VF	XF	Unc
1765 GCF-PB	—	30.00	50.00	120	250	—

KM# 210 5 KREUZER

Silver **Ruler:** Ludwig VIII **Obverse:** Script monogram LL with crown; 240 STUK EINE FEINE MARK **Reverse:** Crowned lion shield, branches and HD at sides **Rev. Legend:** AD NORMAN **Note:** Convention 5 Kreuzer.

Date	Mintage	VG	F	VF	XF	Unc
1763 AK	—	25.00	40.00	75.00	140	—

KM# 218 5 KREUZER

Silver **Ruler:** Ludwig VIII **Obverse:** Crowned lion shield, branches and HESSEN-DARMST at sides, date below **Reverse:** Value in rhombus; 240/EINE/FEINE/MARK

Date	Mintage	VG	F	VF	XF	Unc
1765 GCF-PB	—	35.00	55.00	110	225	—

KM# 193 6 KREUZER

Billon **Ruler:** Ludwig VIII **Obverse:** Lion in German shield, crown above; HESSEN-DARMST at sides **Reverse:** VI/KREUZ, date in cartouche, LAND-MUNZ in the upper half

Date	Mintage	VG	F	VF	XF	Unc
1759 AK	—	100	160	300	550	—
1762 AK	—	100	160	300	550	—

KM# 127 10 KREUZER

Silver **Ruler:** Ernst Ludwig **Subject:** 200th Anniversary of the Reformation **Obverse:** Crowned shield divides dates **Reverse:** Inscription within inner circle

Date	Mintage	VG	F	VF	XF	Unc
1717 BIB	—	8.00	20.00	40.00	75.00	—

KM# 148 10 KREUZER

Silver **Ruler:** Ernst Ludwig **Obverse:** Hesse arms with crown; ERNEST.LVD.D.G.HASS... **Reverse:** X/KREU/TZER/date in ring; FURSTL.HESS.DARMST...

Date	Mintage	VG	F	VF	XF	Unc
1726 BIB	—	8.00	15.00	30.00	55.00	—
1727 BIB	—	8.00	15.00	30.00	55.00	—
1728 BIB	—	8.00	15.00	30.00	55.00	—
1729 BIB	—	8.00	15.00	30.00	55.00	—
1733 GK	—	8.00	15.00	30.00	55.00	—

KM# 211 10 KREUZER

Silver **Ruler:** Ludwig VIII **Obverse:** Head right **Obv. Legend:** LUDOVICUS VIII.D.G.LANDG.HASS. **Reverse:** Lion in German shield with crown above, 7 small shields around **Rev. Legend:** NACH DEM CONVENTIONS FUS **Note:** Convention 10 Kreuzer. Die varieties exist.

Date	Mintage	VG	F	VF	XF	Unc
1763 AK	—	18.00	30.00	70.00	150	—
1764 AK	—	18.00	30.00	70.00	150	—
1765 GCF	—	18.00	30.00	70.00	150	—
1765 CF	—	18.00	30.00	70.00	150	—
ND AK Rare	—	—	—	—	—	—

KM# 219 10 KREUZER

Silver **Ruler:** Ludwig VIII **Obverse:** Script monogram LL with crown; HESSEN-DARMST in upper half **Reverse:** X KREUZER, date, NACH DEM

Date	Mintage	VG	F	VF	XF	Unc
1765 GCF-PB	—	12.00	20.00	45.00	95.00	—
1766 GCF-PB	—	15.00	25.00	50.00	110	—

KM# 110 12 KREUZER (1/8 Thaler)

Silver **Ruler:** Ernst Ludwig **Obverse:** Crowned arms with lion shield at center **Reverse:** Value, date within circle

Date	Mintage	VG	F	VF	XF	Unc
1705 IAR	—	12.00	30.00	60.00	100	—

KM# 178 12 KREUZER (1/8 Thaler)

Silver **Ruler:** Ludwig VIII **Obverse:** Crowned arms with lion shield at center **Reverse:** Value and date within inner circle

Date	Mintage	VG	F	VF	XF	Unc
1745 AK	—	20.00	35.00	70.00	135	—
1746 AK	—	20.00	35.00	70.00	135	—
1747 AK	—	20.00	35.00	70.00	135	—
1748 AK	—	20.00	35.00	70.00	135	—
1751 AK	—	20.00	35.00	70.00	135	—
1759 AK	—	12.00	25.00	55.00	120	—

KM# 206 20 KREUZER

Silver **Ruler:** Ludwig VIII **Obverse:** 4 crowned double L monograms in cruciform, script HD in center **Obv. Legend:** 60 STUK-EINE-FEINE-MARK **Reverse:** Crowned lion shield, 7 small shields around **Rev. Legend:** NACH DEM CONVENTIONS FUS, A(20)K below **Note:** Convention 20 Kreuzer. Die varieties exist.

Date	Mintage	VG	F	VF	XF	Unc
1760 AK	—	20.00	75.00	180	400	—
1762 AK	—	25.00	75.00	160	360	—

KM# 212 20 KREUZER

Silver **Ruler:** Ludwig VIII **Obverse:** Head right **Obv. Legend:** LUDOVICUS VIII D G LANDGR HASS(IAE) **Reverse:** Lion in German shield with crown above, 7 small shields around; date and 20 below.

Date	Mintage	VG	F	VF	XF	Unc
1763 AK	—	35.00	70.00	150	275	—
1766 CF-PB	—	35.00	70.00	150	275	—
1766 PB Rare	—	—	—	—	—	—

KM# 222 20 KREUZER

Silver **Ruler:** Ludwig VIII **Obverse:** Crowned lion shield, 7 small shields around **Reverse:** Value, date

Date	Mintage	VG	F	VF	XF	Unc
1766 GCF-PB	—	25.00	40.00	80.00	130	—

KM# 230.1 20 KREUZER

Silver, 29.5 mm. **Ruler:** Ludwig IX **Obverse:** Head right **Obv. Legend:** LUDOVICUS IX D G LANDGRAVIUS HASS **Reverse:** Lion in cartouche with crown and flags, arms, trophies and date at sides **Rev. Legend:** NACH DEM CONVENT FUS

Date	Mintage	VG	F	VF	XF	Unc
1772	—	17.50	50.00	150	300	—

KM# 230.2 20 KREUZER

Silver, 28.5 mm. **Ruler:** Ludwig IX **Obverse:** Head right **Reverse:** Lion in cartouche with crown and flags, arms, trophies and date at sides **Note:** Similar to KM#230.1, but with reduced size.

Date	Mintage	Good	VG	F	VF	XF
1772 B RF Rare	—	—	—	—	—	—

KM# 224 20 KREUZER

Silver **Ruler:** Ludwig IX **Obverse:** Bust in breast-armour right in rhombus **Obv. Legend:** LUDOVICUS( )IX D G LAND( )GRAVIUS( )HASSIAE **Reverse:** Hessian arms in cartouche, crown above, Imperial eagle and date at sides, order below, all in rhombus **Rev. Legend:** SECHZIG(=60)( )EINE( )FEINE( )MARK

Date	Mintage	Good	VG	F	VF	XF
1772 K RF	—	—	80.00	150	275	500

KM# A224 20 KREUZER

Silver **Ruler:** Ludwig IX **Obverse:** Bust in breast-armour right **Obv. Legend:** LUDOVICUS IX D G LANDGRAV HASS **Reverse:** Lion in cartouche, crown above, flags, armatures and date at sides, (20) below, legend around the upper half **Rev. Legend:** NACH DEM CONVENT FUS

Date	Mintage	Good	VG	F	VF	XF
1772 B RF	—	—	70.00	150	250	450

KM# 194 30 KREUZER

Silver **Ruler:** Ludwig VIII **Obverse:** 4 crowned double 'L' monograms in cruciform, script HD in center **Reverse:** Crowned arms, rococo in cartouche, value 30-KR above, date below

Date	Mintage	VG	F	VF	XF	Unc
1759	—	300	400	800	1,500	—

KM# 128 1/4 THALER
Silver **Ruler:** Ernst Ludwig **Subject:** 200th Anniversary of the Reformation **Obverse:** Bust right **Obv. Legend:** ERNEST LVD... **Reverse:** Oval arms with 5 helmets divide date **Rev. Legend:** PIETATE ET IVSTITIA

Date	Mintage	VG	F	VF	XF	Unc
1717 BIB Rare	—	—	—	—	—	—

KM# 129 1/2 THALER
Silver **Ruler:** Ernst Ludwig **Subject:** 200th Anniversary of the Reformation **Obverse:** Bust right **Obv. Legend:** ERNEST LVD D G HASS LANDG PR HERSF **Reverse:** Oval arms with 5 helmets divide date **Rev. Legend:** PIETATE ET IVSTITIA

Date	Mintage	VG	F	VF	XF	Unc
1717 BIB Rare	—	—	—	—	—	—

KM# 130 1/2 THALER
Silver **Ruler:** Ernst Ludwig **Obverse:** Bust right **Obv. Legend:** ERNEST LVD DG( )HASS LANDG PR HERSF **Reverse:** 4 crowned reversed E and L monograms, crowned Hesse lion in center, date divided at top **Rev. Legend:** SIC DEO PLACUIT IN TRIBULATIONIBVS

Date	Mintage	VG	F	VF	XF	Unc
1717 BIB Rare	—	—	—	—	—	—

KM# 145 1/2 THALER
Silver **Ruler:** Ernst Ludwig **Obverse:** Bust right **Reverse:** Date undivided in legend **Rev. Legend:** MONETA ARGENTEA DARMSTADINA **Note:** Similar to KM#130, but with different reverse legend.

Date	Mintage	VG	F	VF	XF	Unc
1721 BIB Rare	—	—	—	—	—	—

KM# 146 1/2 THALER
Silver **Ruler:** Ernst Ludwig **Obverse:** Bust right and title in legend **Rev. Legend:** Like KM#130, but no legend **Note:** Existence of this type is questionable.

Date	Mintage	VG	F	VF	XF	Unc
ND BIB Rare	—	—	—	—	—	—

KM# 174 1/2 THALER
Silver **Ruler:** Ludwig VIII **Obverse:** Crowned 'double L'monogram **Reverse:** Lion holds arms, date in Roman numerals **Rev. Legend:** PRO-PATRIA **Note:** Varieties exist in size and edge.

Date	Mintage	VG	F	VF	XF	Unc
1742	—	100	160	320	500	—
1744	—	100	160	320	500	—
1748	—	100	160	320	500	—
1750	—	100	160	320	500	—

KM# 213 1/2 THALER
Silver **Ruler:** Ludwig VIII **Obverse:** Harness bust right **Obv. Legend:** LUDOVICUS VIII D G LANDGR HASS **Reverse:** Crowned arms supported by 2 lions, date above, value XX/EINE FEINE/MARCK below **Note:** Convention 1/2 Thaler.

Date	Mintage	VG	F	VF	XF	Unc
1763 CHK Rare	—	—	—	—	—	—

KM# 229 1/2 THALER
Silver **Ruler:** Ludwig IX **Obverse:** Bust in armour right **Obv. Legend:** LUDOVICUS IX D G LANDGRAVIUS HASS **Reverse:** Arms in shield, crown above, trophies at sides, date and value "XX EINE FEINE MARCK" below

Date	Mintage	VG	F	VF	XF	Unc
1771 K AK	—	100	200	350	900	—
1772 K RF	—	100	200	350	900	—

KM# 239 1/2 THALER
Silver **Ruler:** Ludwig IX **Note:** Similar to KM#229.

Date	Mintage	Good	VG	F	VF	XF
1772 K RF	—	—	100	200	350	900

KM# 245 1/2 THALER
Silver **Ruler:** Ludwig X **Obverse:** Bust right in plain clothes **Obv. Legend:** LUDOVICUS X D G LANDGRAVIUS HASS **Reverse:** Arms in oval, crown above, 2 lions at sides, value "XX EINE FEINE MARCK" above, date in segment below

Date	Mintage	VG	F	VF	XF	Unc
1793 RF	—	350	625	1,000	1,800	—

KM# 246 1/2 THALER
Silver **Ruler:** Ludwig X **Obverse:** Bust right **Reverse:** Crowned multiple arms flanked by trophies

Date	Mintage	VG	F	VF	XF	Unc
1793 RF	—	550	1,000	1,600	2,400	—

KM# 120 THALER (Species)
Silver **Ruler:** Ernst Ludwig **Obverse:** Armored bust right **Obv. Legend:** ERNEST. LVD. D. G. - HASS. LANDG. PR. HERSF. **Reverse:** Crowned complex arms with supporters **Rev. Legend:** MONETA • NOVA • ARGENTEA • DARMSTADINA **Note:** Dav. #2313.

Date	Mintage	F	VF	XF	Unc
1710 BIB	—	300	500	1,000	2,000

KM# 121 THALER (Species)
Silver **Ruler:** Ernst Ludwig **Obverse:** Similar to KM#120, but with "BIB" below shoulder **Reverse:** 5 helmets above arms in oval cartouche, order below, date in legend **Note:** Dav. #2314.

Date	Mintage	F	VF	XF	Unc
1710 BIB	—	300	500	1,000	2,000

KM# 125 THALER (Species)
Silver **Ruler:** Ernst Ludwig **Obverse:** Similar to KM#212, but with BIB below shoulder **Obv. Legend:** ERNEST: LVD: D: G: - HASS: LANDG: PR: HERSF: **Reverse:** Itter Mine, small crowned oval arms below, 2 inscriptions above, inner one has date at end **Rev. Legend:** GOTT HAT SEINEN REICHEN SEEGEN / ITTER IN DICH WOLLEN LEGEN 1714 **Note:** Mining Thaler. Dav. #2315. Exists in 2 different sizes - 41.5 and 45.5mm with 3 different dies for each.

Date	Mintage	F	VF	XF	Unc
1714 BIB	—	500	1,000	1,600	2,500

KM# 126 THALER (Species)
Silver **Ruler:** Ernst Ludwig **Obverse:** Bust right, legend, name and title **Reverse:** Crowned arms, supported by 2 lions, divide date **Rev. Legend:** MONETA... **Note:** Dav. #2316.

Date	Mintage	F	VF	XF	Unc
1715 BIB	—	300	500	1,000	2,000

KM# 131 THALER (Species)
Silver **Ruler:** Ernst Ludwig **Subject:** 200th Anniversary of the Reformation **Obverse:** Armored bust right **Obv. Legend:** ERNEST: LVD: D: G. - HASS: LANDG: PR: HERSF: **Reverse:** Kneeling figure at altar **Rev. Legend:** FESTVM. SECVLARE. SECVNDVM. ECCLESIAE. EVANG. LVTHER. 31. OCT. 1717., in exergue; HASSIA VOTORVM COMPOS/DEO: GRATA: **Note:** Dav. #2317.

Date	Mintage	F	VF	XF	Unc
1717 BIB	—	250	550	800	1,600

KM# 133 THALER (Species)
Silver **Ruler:** Ernst Ludwig **Reverse:** E's in monogram normal **Note:** Dav. #2318. Existence of this type is questionable.

Date	Mintage	F	VF	XF	Unc
1717 BIB	—	400	650	1,200	2,250

KM# 132 THALER (Species)
Silver **Ruler:** Ernst Ludwig **Obverse:** Similar to KM#212, legend, name and title above, smaller legend below **Obv. Legend:** NACH ALT REICHS SCHROTH V KORN **Reverse:** 4 crowned reversed E and L monograms, crowned Hesse lion in center, date divided at top **Rev. Legend:** SIC DEO PLACVIT IN TRIBVLATIONIBVS BIB **Note:** Dav. #2318A.

Date	Mintage	F	VF	XF	Unc
1717 BIB	—	400	650	1,200	2,250

KM# 134 THALER (Species)
Silver **Ruler:** Ernst Ludwig **Obverse:** Legend, name and title above, smaller legend below **Reverse:** Arms, 5 helmets above, divide date **Rev. Legend:** PIETATE ET IVISTITIA **Note:** Dav. #2319.

Date	Mintage	F	VF	XF	Unc
1717 BIB	—	300	500	1,000	2,000

KM# 147 THALER (Species)
Silver **Ruler:** Ernst Ludwig **Obverse:** Legend, name and title above, smaller legend below **Reverse:** 4 crowned reversed E and L monograms, crowned Hesse lion in center, date undivided in legend **Rev. Legend:** MONETA NOVA ARGENTEA...BIB **Note:** Dav. #2320.

Date	Mintage	F	VF	XF	Unc
1721 BIB	—	1,200	2,000	3,250	—

KM# 149 THALER (Species)
Silver **Ruler:** Ernst Ludwig **Obverse:** Legend, name and title above, smaller legend below **Reverse:** Similar to KM#132, but cross with lilies in the angles, date at bottom **Note:** Dav. #2321.

Date	Mintage	F	VF	XF	Unc
1728 BIB	—	400	650	1,200	2,250

KM# 150 THALER (Species)
Silver **Ruler:** Ernst Ludwig **Obverse:** Bust right

Date	Mintage	F	VF	XF	Unc
1728 BIB	—	400	650	1,200	2,250

KM# 151 THALER (Species)
Silver **Ruler:** Ernst Ludwig **Obverse:** Bust right **Reverse:** Hessian lion holds sword and Hesse arms

Date	Mintage	F	VF	XF	Unc
ND Rare	—	—	—	—	—

KM# 152 THALER (Species)
Silver **Ruler:** Ernst Ludwig **Reverse:** Crowned arms supported by 2 lions

Date	Mintage	F	VF	XF	Unc
ND Rare	—	—	—	—	—

KM# 153 THALER (Species)
Silver **Ruler:** Ernst Ludwig **Reverse:** 4 crowned reversed E and L monograms, crowned Hesse lion in center

Date	Mintage	F	VF	XF	Unc
ND BIB Rare	—	—	—	—	—

KM# 154 THALER (Species)
Silver **Ruler:** Ernst Ludwig **Obverse:** 4 crowned double L monograms in cruciform, script HD in center **Reverse:** Leaping horse, hand from clouds

Date	Mintage	F	VF	XF	Unc
ND	—	1,000	1,400	2,400	3,500

KM# 155 THALER (Species)
Silver **Ruler:** Ernst Ludwig **Obverse:** Bust right **Reverse:** Leaping horse, hand from clouds

Date	Mintage	F	VF	XF	Unc
ND	—	1,000	1,400	2,400	3,500

KM# 190 THALER (Species)
Silver **Ruler:** Ludwig VIII **Obverse:** Draped bust right **Obv. Legend:** LUDOVICUS VIII D • G • LANDGRAVIUS HASS **Reverse:** Helmeted arms divide date **Rev. Legend:** SINCERE ET CONSTANTER **Note:** Dav. #2322.

Date	Mintage	F	VF	XF	Unc
1751 AK	—	700	1,050	2,000	3,200
1758 R	—	700	1,050	2,000	3,200

KM# 201 THALER (Convention)
Silver **Ruler:** Ludwig VIII **Obverse:** Small bust right **Obv. Legend:** LUDOVICUS VIII D • G • LANDGRAVIUS HASS **Reverse:** Helmeted and supported arms, legend above **Rev. Legend:** SINCERE ET CONSTANTER, X EINE FEINE MARCK/A•1760 K• below **Note:** Convention Thaler. Dav. #2323.

Date	Mintage	F	VF	XF	Unc
1760 AK	—	500	800	1,600	2,750
1763 AK	—	500	800	1,600	2,750
1764 AK	—	500	800	1,600	2,750

KM# 202 THALER (Convention)
Silver **Ruler:** Ludwig VIII **Obverse:** Large bust right **Reverse:** Helmeted and supported arms **Note:** Dav. #2324.

Date	Mintage	F	VF	XF	Unc
1760 S-AK	—	1,200	1,800	3,200	5,000

KM# 214 THALER (Convention)
Silver **Ruler:** Ludwig VIII **Obverse:** Small bust right **Obv. Legend:** LUDOVICUS VIII... **Reverse:** Helmeted and supported arms **Rev. Legend:** AD NORMAM.. **Note:** Dav. #2326.

Date	Mintage	F	VF	XF	Unc
1764 R	—	500	800	1,600	2,750
1764	—	500	800	1,600	2,750
1764 AK	—	500	800	1,600	2,750

KM# 215 THALER (Convention)
Silver **Ruler:** Ludwig VIII **Obverse:** Small bust right **Obv. Legend:** LUDOVICUS VIII... **Reverse:** Crowned lion shield, 7 shields around, date below **Rev. Legend:** AD NORMAM... **Note:** Dav. #2327.

Date	Mintage	F	VF	XF	Unc
1764	—	500	800	1,600	2,750

KM# 220 THALER (Convention)
Silver **Ruler:** Ludwig VIII **Obverse:** Small bust right, 'K' on arm **Obv. Legend:** LUDOVICUS VIII... **Reverse:** Crowned arms in nicely decorated rokoko shield **Note:** Dav. #2328.

Date	Mintage	F	VF	XF	Unc
1765 K GCF-PB	—	500	800	1,600	2,750

KM# 221 THALER (Convention)
Silver **Ruler:** Ludwig VIII **Obverse:** Similar to KM#220, but with 'R' on arm **Reverse:** Arms with 5 helmets, supported by 2 lions, value X EINE FEINE MARCK/date/GCF PB **Rev. Legend:** AD NORMAM... **Note:** Dav. #2331.

Date	Mintage	F	VF	XF	Unc
1765 R-GCF-PB	—	500	800	1,600	2,750

KM# 225 THALER (Convention)
Silver **Ruler:** Ludwig IX **Obverse:** Armored bust right **Obv. Legend:** LUDOVICUS • IX • D: G • LANDGRAVIUS • HASS • **Reverse:** Crowned arms with flags and trophies **Rev. Legend:** X. EINE FEINE MARCK below **Note:** Dav. #2332. Varieties exist, including one without the 'K'.

Date	Mintage	F	VF	XF	Unc
1770 K AK	—	140	250	550	1,200

KM# 226 THALER (Convention)
Silver **Ruler:** Ludwig IX **Obverse:** Armored bust right **Obv. Legend:** LUDOVICUS IX... **Reverse:** Arms with 8 helmets supported by 2 lions and trophies at sides, order and legend below, date above **Rev. Legend:** X EINE FEINE MARCK **Note:** Dav. #2333; reverse varieties exist.

Date	Mintage	F	VF	XF	Unc
1770 B AK	—	350	600	1,200	2,500
1772 RF	—	150	250	600	1,300

KM# 247 THALER (Convention)
Silver **Ruler:** Ludwig X **Obverse:** Bust right **Obv. Legend:** LUDOVICUS • X • D • G • LANDGRAVIUS HASS • **Reverse:** Crowned arms with lion supporters, date below **Rev. Legend:** X • EINE FEINE MARK **Note:** Dav. #2336.

Date	Mintage	F	VF	XF	Unc
1793 RF	—	850	1,550	2,350	3,500

KM# 248 THALER (Convention)
Silver **Ruler:** Ludwig X **Obverse:** Civilian bust right **Reverse:** Crowned oval arms with lion supporters, date below **Note:** Dav. #2337.

Date	Mintage	F	VF	XF	Unc
1793 RF	—	850	1,550	2,350	3,500

KM# 249 THALER (Convention)
Silver **Ruler:** Ludwig X **Obverse:** Armored bust right **Reverse:** Crowned oval arms with lion supporters, date below **Note:** Dav. #2338.

Date	Mintage	F	VF	XF	Unc
1793 RF	—	1,350	2,450	3,750	5,500

KM# 250 THALER (Convention)
Silver **Ruler:** Ludwig X **Obverse:** Armored bust right **Obv. Legend:** LUDOVICUS • X • D • G • LANDGRAVIUS HASS **Reverse:** Crowned oval arms with flags and trophies **Rev. Legend:** X • EINE FEINE MARK **Note:** Dav. #2339.

Date	Mintage	F	VF	XF	Unc
1793 RF	—	850	1,550	2,350	3,500

KM# 160 1/4 CAROLIN
2.4250 g., 0.7700 Gold 0.0600 oz. AGW **Ruler:** Ernst Ludwig **Obverse:** Head right **Reverse:** Crowned monograms in cruciform, value at center **Note:** Similar to 1/2 Carolin KM#161, but 1/4 in center.

Date	Mintage	VG	F	VF	XF	Unc
1733 G-K	—	125	250	600	1,200	—
ND	—	125	250	600	1,200	—

KM# 161 1/2 CAROLIN (5 Thaler)
4.8500 g., 0.7700 Gold 0.1201 oz. AGW **Ruler:** Ernst Ludwig **Obverse:** Head right **Reverse:** Crowned monograms in cruciform, value at center

Date	Mintage	VG	F	VF	XF	Unc
1733 G-K	—	100	200	500	950	—
ND	—	100	200	500	950	—

KM# 162 CAROLIN (10 Thaler)
9.7000 g., 0.7700 Gold 0.2401 oz. AGW **Ruler:** Ernst Ludwig **Obverse:** Head right **Reverse:** Crowned monograms in cruciform, value at center

Date	Mintage	VG	F	VF	XF	Unc
1733 G-K	—	150	350	750	1,500	—
ND	—	150	350	750	1,500	—

TRADE COINAGE

KM# 111 1/8 DUCAT
0.4375 g., 0.9860 Gold 0.0139 oz. AGW **Ruler:** Ernst Ludwig **Obverse:** Crowned arms in oval cartouche **Reverse:** Value and date in 3 lines

Date	Mintage	VG	F	VF	XF	Unc
1705	—	65.00	120	285	550	—

KM# 101 1/4 DUCAT
0.8750 g., 0.9860 Gold 0.0277 oz. AGW **Ruler:** Ernst Ludwig **Obverse:** Crowned arms in oval cartouche **Reverse:** Value and date in 3 lines

Date	Mintage	VG	F	VF	XF	Unc
1703 IAR	—	75.00	125	300	600	—

KM# 112 1/4 DUCAT
0.8750 g., 0.9860 Gold 0.0277 oz. AGW **Ruler:** Ernst Ludwig **Obverse:** Bust right, 1/4 below **Reverse:** Crowned arms in oval cartouche, date in legend

Date	Mintage	VG	F	VF	XF	Unc
1705	—	75.00	125	300	600	—

KM# 113 1/4 DUCAT
0.8750 g., 0.9860 Gold 0.0277 oz. AGW **Ruler:** Ernst Ludwig **Obverse:** Bust right **Reverse:** Crowned oval arms supported by 2 lions, date divided above

Date	Mintage	VG	F	VF	XF	Unc
1706	—	—	—	—	—	—

KM# 102 1/2 DUCAT
1.7500 g., 0.9860 Gold 0.0555 oz. AGW **Ruler:** Ernst Ludwig **Obverse:** Bust right **Reverse:** Crowned arms in oval cartouche within palm branches, crown divides date

Date	Mintage	VG	F	VF	XF	Unc
1703	—	100	200	500	950	—

KM# 122 1/2 DUCAT
1.7500 g., 0.9860 Gold 0.0555 oz. AGW **Ruler:** Ernst Ludwig **Obverse:** Rampant lion **Reverse:** Value and date

Date	Mintage	VG	F	VF	XF	Unc
1710 BIB	—	100	200	500	950	—

KM# 100 DUCAT
3.5000 g., 0.9860 Gold 0.1109 oz. AGW **Ruler:** Ernst Ludwig **Obverse:** Bust right **Reverse:** Crowned arms with lion supporters, date in legend

Date	Mintage	VG	F	VF	XF	Unc
1702	—	175	350	800	1,550	—
1704	—	175	350	800	1,550	—
1705	—	175	350	800	1,550	—
ND	—	175	350	800	1,550	—

KM# 104 DUCAT
3.5000 g., 0.9860 Gold 0.1109 oz. AGW **Ruler:** Ernst Ludwig **Reverse:** Arms divide date

Date	Mintage	VG	F	VF	XF	Unc
1703	—	175	350	800	1,550	—
1703 IAR	—	175	350	800	1,550	—

KM# 105 DUCAT
3.5000 g., 0.9860 Gold 0.1109 oz. AGW **Ruler:** Ernst Ludwig **Reverse:** Crown above arms divides date

Date	Mintage	VG	F	VF	XF	Unc
1703	—	175	350	800	1,550	—
1706	—	175	350	800	1,550	—
1718 BIB	—	175	350	800	1,550	—

KM# 135 DUCAT
3.5000 g., 0.9860 Gold 0.1109 oz. AGW **Ruler:** Ernst Ludwig **Obverse:** Bust right **Reverse:** Arms, date in legend

Date	Mintage	VG	F	VF	XF	Unc
1717	—	200	450	1,000	2,000	—

KM# 136 DUCAT
3.5000 g., 0.9860 Gold 0.1109 oz. AGW **Ruler:** Ernst Ludwig **Subject:** Reformation Bicentennial **Obverse:** Bust right **Reverse:** Woman kneeling at altar, date below

Date	Mintage	VG	F	VF	XF	Unc
1717	—	250	600	1,500	2,500	—

KM# 137 DUCAT
3.5000 g., 0.9860 Gold 0.1109 oz. AGW **Ruler:** Ernst Ludwig **Obverse:** Bust right **Reverse:** Cruciform crowned EL monograms **Note:** Alchemy Ducat.

Date	Mintage	VG	F	VF	XF	Unc
ND	—	250	600	1,500	2,500	—

KM# 139 DUCAT
3.5000 g., 0.9860 Gold 0.1109 oz. AGW **Ruler:** Ernst Ludwig **Obverse:** Bust right **Reverse:** Arms, date below

Date	Mintage	VG	F	VF	XF	Unc
1718	—	200	450	1,000	2,000	—

KM# 204 DUCAT
3.5000 g., 0.9860 Gold 0.1109 oz. AGW **Ruler:** Ludwig VIII **Obverse:** Crowned monogram **Reverse:** 5-line inscription

Date	Mintage	VG	F	VF	XF	Unc
ND	—	175	350	800	1,600	—

KM# 171 DUCAT
3.5000 g., 0.9860 Gold 0.1109 oz. AGW **Ruler:** Ludwig VIII **Obverse:** Cruciform crowned double L monograms **Reverse:** Rampant lion holds arms

Date	Mintage	VG	F	VF	XF	Unc
1740	—	175	300	750	1,500	—
1741 GCF	—	200	400	950	1,750	—

KM# 175 DUCAT

3.5000 g., 0.9860 Gold 0.1109 oz. AGW **Ruler:** Ludwig VIII **Obverse:** Crowned monogram **Reverse:** Rampant lion left holding arms and sword

Date	Mintage	VG	F	VF	XF	Unc
1742 GCF	—	200	400	950	1,750	—
1743	—	200	400	950	1,750	—
1752 GCF	—	—	—	—	—	—
1753	—	200	400	950	1,750	—
ND	—	200	400	950	1,750	—

KM# 180 DUCAT

3.5000 g., 0.9860 Gold 0.1109 oz. AGW **Ruler:** Ludwig VIII **Obverse:** Armored bust right **Reverse:** Crowned arms within ornate oval

Date	Mintage	VG	F	VF	XF	Unc
1746 AK	—	200	400	950	1,750	—
1748 S-AK	—	200	400	950	1,750	—
1749 S-AK	—	200	400	950	1,750	—
1751	—	200	400	950	1,750	—
1753	—	200	400	950	1,750	—
1755	—	200	400	950	1,750	—
ND	—	200	400	950	1,750	—

KM# 181 DUCAT

3.5000 g., 0.9860 Gold 0.1109 oz. AGW **Ruler:** Ludwig VIII **Obverse:** Draped bust right **Reverse:** Rampant lion holding crowned arms

Date	Mintage	VG	F	VF	XF	Unc
1746	—	200	400	1,000	1,850	—

KM# 176 DUCAT

3.5000 g., 0.9860 Gold 0.1109 oz. AGW **Ruler:** Ludwig VIII **Obverse:** Double L monogram **Reverse:** Reclining lion

Date	Mintage	VG	F	VF	XF	Unc
ND	—	200	400	1,000	1,850	—

KM# 203 DUCAT

3.5000 g., 0.9860 Gold 0.1109 oz. AGW **Ruler:** Ludwig VIII **Obverse:** Cruciform crowned double L monograms **Reverse:** Crowned arms in arc of 7 shields, date at bottom

Date	Mintage	VG	F	VF	XF	Unc
1760	—	200	400	1,000	1,850	—
1761	—	200	400	1,000	1,850	—

KM# 106 2 DUCAT

7.0000 g., 0.9860 Gold 0.2219 oz. AGW **Ruler:** Ernst Ludwig **Obverse:** Bust right **Reverse:** Crowned arms with lion supporters divide date

Date	Mintage	VG	F	VF	XF	Unc
1703	—	400	1,000	2,500	4,500	—
1707	—	400	1,000	2,500	4,500	—
1709 BIB	—	400	1,000	2,500	4,500	—

KM# 109 2 DUCAT

7.0000 g., 0.9860 Gold 0.2219 oz. AGW **Ruler:** Ernst Ludwig **Obverse:** Armored bust right **Reverse:** Arms topped by 5 helmets divide date

Date	Mintage	VG	F	VF	XF	Unc
1704	—	500	1,150	2,750	5,000	—
1704 IAR	—	500	1,150	2,750	5,000	—

KM# 123 2 DUCAT

7.0000 g., 0.9860 Gold 0.2219 oz. AGW **Ruler:** Ernst Ludwig **Obverse:** Armored bust right **Reverse:** Crowned arms with supporters, date below **Note:** Similar to KM#106, but date below arms on reverse.

Date	Mintage	VG	F	VF	XF	Unc
1710 BIB	—	400	1,000	2,500	4,500	—

KM# 124 2 DUCAT

7.0000 g., 0.9860 Gold 0.2219 oz. AGW **Ruler:** Ernst Ludwig **Reverse:** Cruciform crowned EL monograms

Date	Mintage	VG	F	VF	XF	Unc
ND	—	850	1,750	3,500	6,000	—

KM# 205 2 DUCAT

7.0000 g., 0.9860 Gold 0.2219 oz. AGW **Ruler:** Ernst Ludwig **Obverse:** Cruciform crowned double L monograms **Reverse:** Crowned arms in arc of 7 shields, date at bottom

Date	Mintage	VG	F	VF	XF	Unc
1760 AK	—	850	1,750	3,500	6,000	—

KM# 138 4 DUCAT

14.0000 g., 0.9860 Gold 0.4438 oz. AGW **Ruler:** Ernst Ludwig **Obverse:** Bust right **Reverse:** Cruciform crowned EL monograms, date in legend at bottom

Date	Mintage	VG	F	VF	XF	Unc
1717 Rare	—	—	—	—	—	—

KM# A139 25 DUCAT

Gold **Ruler:** Ernst Ludwig **Obverse:** Bust right, titles of Ernst Ludwig **Reverse:** Ornate oval 6-fold arms with central shield, 5 helmets above

Date	Mintage	Good	VG	F	VF	XF
ND(1696-1707) R Rare	—	—	—	—	—	—

PATTERNS

Including off metal strikes

KM#	Date	Mintage	Identification	Mkt Val
Pn3	ND1710	—	Thaler. Copper. KM#120.	—
Pn4	ND1710	—	Thaler. Lead. KM#121.	—
PnA5	ND(1739-68)	—	Ducat. Silver. KM#A204.	—
PnB5	ND(1739-68)	—	Ducat. Silver. Weight of 1 Thaler, KM#A204.	—
PnC5	ND(1739-68)	—	Ducat. Copper. KM#A204.	—
Pn5	ND1740	—	Kreuzer. Gold. KM#170.	325
Pn6	ND1740	—	Ducat. Copper.. KM#171.	—
Pn7	ND1740	—	Ducat. Silver. KM#171.	80.00
Pn8	ND1742	—	1/2 Thaler. Copper. KM#174.	—
Pn9	ND1742	—	Ducat. Copper. KM#175.	—
Pn10	ND1742	—	Ducat. Silver. KM#175.	—
PN11	ND	—	Ducat. Silver. KM#175.	—
Pn12	ND1745	—	2 Kreuzer. Copper. KM#173.	—
Pn13	ND1746	—	Kreuzer. Gold. KM#170.	325
Pn14	ND1746	—	Ducat. Silver. KM#181.	—
Pn15	ND1748	—	Pfennig. Gold. KM#183.	—
Pn16	ND1750	—	1/2 Thaler. Copper. KM#174.	—
Pn17	ND1754	—	Ducat. Copper. KM#180.	—
Pn18	ND1755	—	Ducat. Copper. KM#180.	—
Pn19	ND	—	Ducat. Copper. KM#180.	—
Pn20	ND	—	Ducat. Silver. KM#180.	60.00
Pn21	ND1756	—	Thaler. Copper. KM#181.	—
PnA22	ND1759	—	4 Kreuzer. Copper. KM#184.	—
Pn22	ND1760	—	Ducat. Silver. KM#203.	—
Pn23	ND	—	Ducat. Copper. KM#204.	—
Pn24	ND	—	Ducat. Silver. KM#204.	80.00
Pn25	ND1763	—	1/2 Thaler. Copper. . KM#213.	—
Pn26	ND1764	—	Thaler. Copper. KM#214.	—
Pn27	ND1764	—	Thaler. Copper. KM#215.	900
Pn28	ND1765	—	Thaler. Copper. KM#220.	—
Pn29	ND1765	—	Thaler. Copper. KM#221.	800
Pn30	ND1793	—	Thaler. Bronze. KM#248.	1,000
Pn34	ND1760	—	2 Ducat. Silver. 4 crowned double L monograms in cruciform, script HD in center. Crowned lion shield, 7 small shields around, date below.	—

HESSE-HOMBURG

Located in west central Germany, Hesse-Homburg was created from part of Hesse-Darmstadt in 1622. It had six villages along with Homburg (today Bad Homburg) and is mostly known for its famous landgrave, Friedrich II. Commander of the Brandenburg cavalry, Friedrich II (with the silver leg) won the Battle of Fehrbellin in 1675. Hesse-Homburg was mediatized to Hesse-Darmstadt in 1806 and by 1816 had acquired full sovereignty and the lordship of Meisenheim. The Homburg line became extinct in 1866, and along with Hesse-Darmstadt, was annexed by Prussia.

RULERS

Friedrich II, 1681-1708
Friedrich III Jacob, 1708-1746
Friedrich IV Karl, 1746-1751
Friedrich V Ludwig, 1751-1820

LANDGRAVIATE

REGULAR COINAGE

KM# 10 1/24 THALER (Groschen)

Silver **Ruler:** Friedrich V Ludwig **Obverse:** Crowned F, H.H.S.M. below **Reverse:** 24/EINEN/THALER/date

Date	Mintage	Good	VG	F	VF	XF
1760	—	—	—	—	—	—

HILDESHEIM

BISHOPRIC

A bishopric located in Westphalia, about 18 miles southeast of Hannover, was established in 822. The first mint was installed in the Mundburg Castle c. 977. Hildesheim coins were minted there although the bishopric didn't legally receive the mint right until 1054. There was no episcopal coinage during most of the 16th century, the first being produced only during the reign of Ernst of Bavaria. In 1803 it was secularized and assigned to Prussia. From 1807-1813 it formed part of the Kingdom of Westphalia and in 1813 was given to Hannover.

RULERS

Jobst Edmund von Brabeck, 1688-1702
Josef Clemens of Bavaria, elected 1702
¬¬installed 1714-1723
Clemens August of Bavaria, 1724-1761
Sede Vacante, 1761-1763
Friedrich Wilhelm, Bishop, 1763-1789
Franz Egon, 1789-1803

MINT OFFICIALS' INITIALS

Hildesheim Mint

Initials	Date	Name
HB	1674-1711	Heinrich Bonhorst in Clausthal
HS, HIS	1692, 1694-1702	Heinrich Justus Sebastiani
IhvU	1764-84	Johann Heinrich von Uslar, director
IL, L	1764-68	Joseph Luckner, die-cutter
S, SCHMIDT	1760-76	Schmidt, die-cutter

ARMS

Hildesheim (bishopric): Parted per pale gold and red.
Peine: Wolf leaping left above two corn sheaves.

REGULAR COINAGE

KM# 93 6 PFENNIG

Silver **Ruler:** Jobst Edmund von Brabeck **Obverse:** Crowned script JE monogram **Reverse:** Imperial orb with 6 divides date

Date	Mintage	VG	F	VF	XF	Unc
1701	—	—	—	—	—	—

KM# 101 MARIENGROSCHEN

Billon **Ruler:** Sede Vacante **Obverse:** Crowned arms **Reverse:** Value and date

Date	Mintage	VG	F	VF	XF	Unc
1762	—	2.00	4.00	10.00	20.00	—
1763	—	2.00	4.00	10.00	20.00	—

KM# 104 2 MARIENGROSCHEN
Billon **Ruler:** Sede Vacante **Obverse:** Crowned arms **Reverse:** Value and date

Date	Mintage	VG	F	VF	XF	Unc
1763	—	5.00	10.00	20.00	40.00	—

KM# 105 2 MARIENGROSCHEN
Billon **Ruler:** Sede Vacante **Obverse:** Crowned arms; crozier and sword behind

Date	Mintage	VG	F	VF	XF	Unc
1763	—	4.00	7.00	15.00	30.00	—

KM# 106 4 MARIENGROSCHEN
Billon **Ruler:** Sede Vacante **Obverse:** Crowned arms; crozier and sword behind **Reverse:** Value and date

Date	Mintage	VG	F	VF	XF	Unc
1763	—	10.00	20.00	40.00	85.00	—

KM# 90 24 MARIENGROSCHEN (2/3 Thaler)
Silver **Ruler:** Jobst Edmund von Brabeck **Obverse:** Bust right **Reverse:** Date in legend **Rev. Legend:** XXIIII / MARIEN / GROSCH / VIFEINEM SILVER / HIS

Date	Mintage	VG	F	VF	XF	Unc
1701 HIS	—	175	350	700	1,100	—

KM# 107 1/48 THALER (Schilling)
Billon **Ruler:** Sede Vacante **Obverse:** Crowned arms **Reverse:** Value and date

Date	Mintage	VG	F	VF	XF	Unc
1763	—	2.00	4.00	10.00	25.00	—

KM# 102 1/24 THALER
Billon **Ruler:** Sede Vacante **Obverse:** Crowned arms **Reverse:** Value and date

Date	Mintage	VG	F	VF	XF	Unc
1762	—	4.00	7.00	15.00	50.00	—
1763	—	4.00	7.00	15.00	50.00	—

KM# 108 1/24 THALER
Billon **Ruler:** Sede Vacante **Obverse:** Crowned arms; crozier and sword behind **Reverse:** Value, date

Date	Mintage	VG	F	VF	XF	Unc
1763	—	3.00	7.00	10.00	40.00	—

KM# 103 1/12 THALER (2 Groschen)
Billon **Ruler:** Sede Vacante **Obverse:** Crowned arms **Reverse:** Value, date

Date	Mintage	VG	F	VF	XF	Unc
1762	—	7.00	20.00	35.00	75.00	—
1763	—	7.00	20.00	35.00	75.00	—

KM# 109 1/12 THALER (2 Groschen)
Billon **Ruler:** Friedrich Wilhelm, Bishop **Obverse:** Crowned arms; crozier and sword behind **Reverse:** Value, date

Date	Mintage	VG	F	VF	XF	Unc
1763	—	6.00	12.00	30.00	65.00	—
1764	—	6.00	12.00	30.00	65.00	—
1765	—	6.00	12.00	30.00	65.00	—

KM# 123 1/12 THALER (2 Groschen)
Billon **Ruler:** Friedrich Wilhelm, Bishop **Obverse:** Arms with crozier and sword within crowned mantle

Date	Mintage	VG	F	VF	XF	Unc
1763	—	6.00	12.00	30.00	65.00	—

KM# 110 1/6 THALER
Silver **Ruler:** Friedrich Wilhelm, Bishop **Obverse:** Arms with crozier and sword behind within crowned mantle **Reverse:** Value, date

Date	Mintage	VG	F	VF	XF	Unc
1763	—	25.00	40.00	75.00	150	—

KM# 111 1/6 THALER
Silver **Ruler:** Friedrich Wilhelm, Bishop **Obverse:** Arms with crozier and sword behind within crowned mantle **Reverse:** Value, date

Date	Mintage	VG	F	VF	XF	Unc
1763	—	20.00	35.00	65.00	135	—
1764	—	20.00	35.00	65.00	135	—
1764 IHvU	—	40.00	60.00	90.00	175	—

KM# 114 1/3 THALER
Silver **Ruler:** Friedrich Wilhelm, Bishop **Obverse:** Armored bust right **Reverse:** Arms with crozier and sword behind, value within frame below

Date	Mintage	VG	F	VF	XF	Unc
1764 IHvU	—	55.00	100	200	325	—

KM# 115 1/3 THALER
Silver **Ruler:** Friedrich Wilhelm, Bishop **Obverse:** Arms with crozier and sword behind, branches flank **Reverse:** Value, date

Date	Mintage	VG	F	VF	XF	Unc
1764	—	50.00	90.00	185	300	—

KM# 100 2/3 THALER (Gulden)
Silver **Ruler:** Sede Vacante **Obverse:** Armored, laureate bust right with Order chain on breast **Reverse:** Arms, value within frame below

Date	Mintage	VG	F	VF	XF	Unc
1761 S	—	175	275	425	800	—
1761 SCHMIDT	—	175	275	425	800	—

KM# 116 2/3 THALER (Gulden)
Silver **Ruler:** Friedrich Wilhelm, Bishop **Obverse:** Draped bust left **Reverse:** Arms with crozier and sword behind, value in frame below

Date	Mintage	F	VF	XF	Unc
1764	—	150	225	375	650

KM# 92 THALER
Silver **Ruler:** Jobst Edmund von Brabeck **Obverse:** Ornately-helmeted 4-fold arms **Reverse:** St. Anthony in circle **Note:** Mining Thaler. Dav. #5415.

Date	Mintage	VG	F	VF	XF	Unc
1700 HIS Rare	—	—	—	—	—	—
1701 HIS Rare	—	—	—	—	—	—

KM# 97 THALER
Silver **Ruler:** Clemens August of Bavaria **Subject:** Sede Vacante Issue **Obverse:** Bust of Karl VI right **Reverse:** Ornately-helmeted Hildesheim arms, Madonna and child above, date in legend **Note:** Dav. #2343.

Date	Mintage	F	VF	XF	Unc
1724	4,000	450	750	1,250	2,000

KM# 119 THALER
Silver **Ruler:** Friedrich Wilhelm, Bishop **Obverse:** Draped bust right **Obv. Legend:** FRID: WILH: D: G: EP: HELD: S: R: I: P: **Reverse:** Arms with crozier and sword behind within crowned mantle **Rev. Legend:** CONCORDIA STABILI •, I.H. - V.U./X STÜCK EINE FEINE/*MARCK*/1766 below **Note:** Dav. #2344.

Date	Mintage	F	VF	XF	Unc
1766 L-IHvU	—	375	750	1,250	2,500

KM# 120 THALER
Silver **Ruler:** Friedrich Wilhelm, Bishop **Obverse:** Larger bust right **Obv. Legend:** FRID: WILH: D:G: EP: HILD: S: R: I: P: **Reverse:** Large crown on mantled arms, crozier and sword behind **Rev. Legend:** CONCORDIA STABILI •, I•H• - V•U•/X STÜCK EINE FEINE/*MARCK*/1766 below **Note:** Dav. #2345.

Date	Mintage	F	VF	XF	Unc
1766 L-IHvU	—	600	1,000	1,500	2,750

KM# 122 THALER

Silver **Ruler:** Friedrich Wilhelm, Bishop **Obverse:** Draped bust right **Obv. Legend:** FRID: WILH: D: G: EP: HILD: S: R: I: P: **Reverse:** Smaller mantle on crowned arms **Rev. Legend:** CONCORDIA STABILI •, I•H• - V•U•/X STÜCK EINE FEINE/*MARCK*/1766 below **Note:** Dav. #2345.

Date	Mintage	F	VF	XF	Unc
1768 L-IHvU	—	550	900	1,400	2,500

KM# 94 2 THALER

Silver **Ruler:** Jobst Edmund von Brabeck **Note:** Similar to 1 Thaler, KM#84 but St. Anthony in circle. Dav. #2341.

Date	Mintage	VG	F	VF	XF	Unc
1701 HIS Rare	—	—	—	—	—	—

KM# 117 5 THALER

6.6500 g., 0.9000 Gold 0.1924 oz. AGW **Ruler:** Friedrich Wilhelm, Bishop **Obverse:** Bust left **Reverse:** Crowned and mantled arms, value and date below

Date	Mintage	F	VF	XF	Unc
1764 IHvU	—	600	1,200	2,500	4,500
1765 IHvU	—	600	1,200	2,500	4,500

KM# 118 5 THALER

6.6500 g., 0.9000 Gold 0.1924 oz. AGW **Ruler:** Friedrich Wilhelm, Bishop **Obverse:** Cloaked bust right **Reverse:** Arms with crozier and sword behind within crowned mantle

Date	Mintage	F	VF	XF	Unc
1765	—	600	1,200	2,500	4,500

KM# 121 10 THALER

13.3000 g., 0.9000 Gold 0.3848 oz. AGW **Ruler:** Friedrich Wilhelm, Bishop **Obverse:** Bust left **Reverse:** Crowned and mantled arms, value and date below

Date	Mintage	F	VF	XF	Unc
1766	—	2,500	4,500	6,000	9,000

KM# 112 1/2 PISTOLE

6.6500 g., 0.9000 Gold 0.1924 oz. AGW **Ruler:** Friedrich Wilhelm, Bishop **Subject:** Sede Vacante Issue **Obverse:** Crowned arms within branches **Reverse:** Value, date within ornate frame

Date	Mintage	F	VF	XF	Unc
1763	—	400	900	1,500	2,500

KM# 113 1/2 PISTOLE

6.6500 g., 0.9000 Gold 0.1924 oz. AGW **Ruler:** Friedrich Wilhelm, Bishop **Obverse:** Crowned and mantled arms

Date	Mintage	F	VF	XF	Unc
1763	—	600	1,200	2,000	3,000

TRADE COINAGE

KM# 125 DUCAT

3.5000 g., 0.9860 Gold 0.1109 oz. AGW **Ruler:** Friedrich Wilhelm, Bishop **Obverse:** Bust left **Reverse:** Arms with crozier and sword behind within crowned mantle

Date	Mintage	F	VF	XF	Unc
1778 K	—	600	1,250	2,500	4,000

FREE CITY

The town of Hildesheim grew up around the seat of the bishopric and was made a free imperial city in the mid-13th century. The first civic coinage was struck in 1428 and continued more or less continually until the second half of the 18th century. The last silver coins were struck for the city in 1764 and copper coinage was last produced in 1772. Hildesheim came under the control of Prussia in 1803 and like the bishopric, became part of the Kingdom of Westphalia 1807-13. It was awarded to the Kingdom of Hannover in 1813 and reverted to Prussia when the latter absorbed Hannover in 1866.

MINTMASTERS' INITIALS

Initials	Date	Name
HL	1696-1710	Hans Luders
II, JJ	1710-31	Jonas Jaster
ITW	1756-65	Johann Thomas Woeltgen
UAW	1732-56	Ulrich Andreas Willerding

SUPERVISORS

Date	Name
1709	Joachim Bose and Herr Schaefer
1717-18	Johann Christoph Bose

MINT WARDENS

Date	Name
1701-04	Georg Bose
1707-08	Jonas Jaster
1721-31	Ulrich Andreas Willerding
1734-56	Johann Thomas Woltgen
1756-72	Johann Heinrich Willerding

DIE-CUTTERS

Date	Name
1732	C.E. Harbords
1732	B.C. Jaster
1734-37	Johann Ludolf Brandes
1735	Johann Peter Meyer
1736	Bernhard J. Dedekind in Brunswick
1737-50, 1756-59	Christian Kretzer
1759-62	Herr Wiehen
1762	Herr Fincke in Clausthal
1763	Herr Dobicht
1764	Zum Hagen

ARMS

Old style are quartered red and gold, new style have upper half of crowned eagle above quarterly.

REGULAR COINAGE

KM# 280 PFENNIG

Copper **Obverse:** City arms **Reverse:** Value, date

Date	Mintage	VG	F	VF	XF	Unc
1762	—	5.00	10.00	20.00	35.00	—
1772	—	5.00	10.00	20.00	35.00	—

KM# 252 2 PFENNIG (Stadt)

Billon **Obverse:** City arms **Reverse:** Value, date **Note:** Varieties exist.

Date	Mintage	VG	F	VF	XF	Unc
1702	—	8.00	15.00	30.00	60.00	—
1707	—	8.00	15.00	30.00	60.00	—
1707	—	8.00	15.00	30.00	60.00	—
1709	—	8.00	15.00	30.00	60.00	—
1710	—	8.00	15.00	30.00	60.00	—
1712	—	8.00	15.00	30.00	60.00	—
1713	—	8.00	15.00	30.00	60.00	—
1716	—	8.00	15.00	30.00	60.00	—
1719	—	8.00	15.00	30.00	60.00	—
1722	—	8.00	15.00	30.00	60.00	—
1723	—	8.00	15.00	30.00	60.00	—
1724	—	8.00	15.00	30.00	60.00	—
1727	—	8.00	15.00	30.00	60.00	—
1728	—	8.00	15.00	30.00	60.00	—
1729	—	8.00	15.00	30.00	60.00	—
1730	—	8.00	15.00	30.00	60.00	—
1731	—	8.00	15.00	30.00	60.00	—
1732	—	8.00	15.00	30.00	60.00	—
1733	—	8.00	15.00	30.00	60.00	—
1734	—	8.00	15.00	30.00	60.00	—
1735	—	8.00	15.00	30.00	60.00	—
1736	—	8.00	15.00	30.00	60.00	—
1737	—	8.00	15.00	30.00	60.00	—
1738	—	8.00	15.00	30.00	60.00	—
1739	—	8.00	15.00	30.00	60.00	—
1740	—	8.00	15.00	30.00	60.00	—
1741	—	8.00	15.00	30.00	60.00	—
1742	—	8.00	15.00	30.00	60.00	—
1743	—	8.00	15.00	30.00	60.00	—
1744	—	8.00	15.00	30.00	60.00	—
1745	—	8.00	15.00	30.00	60.00	—
1746	—	8.00	15.00	30.00	60.00	—
1747	—	8.00	15.00	30.00	60.00	—
1748	—	8.00	15.00	30.00	60.00	—
1749	—	8.00	15.00	30.00	60.00	—
1750	—	8.00	15.00	30.00	60.00	—
1751	—	8.00	15.00	30.00	60.00	—
1752	—	8.00	15.00	30.00	60.00	—
1753	—	8.00	15.00	30.00	60.00	—
1755	—	8.00	15.00	30.00	60.00	—
1756	—	8.00	15.00	30.00	60.00	—
1757	—	8.00	15.00	30.00	60.00	—
1758	—	8.00	15.00	30.00	60.00	—
1759	—	8.00	15.00	30.00	60.00	—
1760	—	8.00	15.00	30.00	60.00	—

KM# 274 3 PFENNIG

Billon **Ruler:** Clemens August of Bavaria **Obverse:** City arms, HILDESH above **Reverse:** Imperial orb with 3 divides date

Date	Mintage	VG	F	VF	XF	Unc
1745	—	7.00	12.00	20.00	45.00	—
1754	—	7.00	12.00	20.00	45.00	—
1759	—	7.00	12.00	20.00	45.00	—

KM# 220 3 PFENNIG (1/96 Thaler)

Billon **Obverse:** HILDES above ornately-shaped arms **Reverse:** Imperial orb with value divides date **Note:** Varieties exist.

Date	Mintage	VG	F	VF	XF	Unc
1700	—	5.00	15.00	27.00	45.00	—
1702	—	5.00	15.00	27.00	45.00	—
1703	—	5.00	15.00	27.00	45.00	—
1704	—	5.00	15.00	27.00	45.00	—
1705	—	5.00	15.00	27.00	45.00	—
1706	—	5.00	15.00	27.00	45.00	—
1708	—	5.00	15.00	27.00	45.00	—
1709	—	5.00	15.00	27.00	45.00	—
1710	—	5.00	15.00	27.00	45.00	—
1711	—	5.00	15.00	27.00	45.00	—
1712	—	5.00	15.00	27.00	45.00	—
1713	—	5.00	15.00	27.00	45.00	—
1714	—	5.00	15.00	27.00	45.00	—
1715	—	5.00	15.00	27.00	45.00	—
1717	—	5.00	15.00	27.00	45.00	—
1718	—	5.00	15.00	27.00	45.00	—
1719	—	5.00	15.00	27.00	45.00	—
1721	—	5.00	15.00	27.00	45.00	—
1722	—	5.00	15.00	27.00	45.00	—
1723	—	5.00	15.00	27.00	45.00	—
1724	—	5.00	15.00	27.00	45.00	—
1726	—	5.00	15.00	27.00	45.00	—
1728	—	5.00	15.00	27.00	45.00	—
1729	—	5.00	15.00	27.00	45.00	—
1737	—	5.00	15.00	27.00	45.00	—

KM# 251 4 PFENNIG

Billon **Obverse:** Arms within square **Reverse:** Value with PF dividing date below **Rev. Legend:** IIII/STADT/17PF16 **Note:** Varieties exist.

Date	Mintage	VG	F	VF	XF	Unc
1702	—	8.00	16.00	35.00	65.00	—
170Z	—	8.00	16.00	35.00	65.00	—
1703	—	8.00	16.00	35.00	65.00	—
1704	—	8.00	16.00	35.00	65.00	—
1705	—	8.00	16.00	35.00	65.00	—
1706	—	8.00	16.00	35.00	65.00	—
1707	—	8.00	16.00	35.00	65.00	—
1709	—	8.00	16.00	35.00	65.00	—
1710	—	8.00	16.00	35.00	65.00	—
1711	—	8.00	16.00	35.00	65.00	—
1713	—	8.00	16.00	35.00	65.00	—
1715	—	8.00	16.00	35.00	65.00	—
1716	—	8.00	16.00	35.00	65.00	—
1717	—	8.00	16.00	35.00	65.00	—
1718	—	8.00	16.00	35.00	65.00	—
1719	—	8.00	16.00	35.00	65.00	—
1720	—	8.00	16.00	35.00	65.00	—
1721	—	8.00	16.00	35.00	65.00	—
1723	—	8.00	16.00	35.00	65.00	—
1724	—	8.00	16.00	35.00	65.00	—
1725	—	8.00	16.00	35.00	65.00	—
1726	—	8.00	16.00	35.00	65.00	—
1727	—	8.00	16.00	35.00	65.00	—
1728	—	8.00	16.00	35.00	65.00	—
1729	—	8.00	16.00	35.00	65.00	—
1730	—	8.00	16.00	35.00	65.00	—
1731	—	8.00	16.00	35.00	65.00	—
1732	—	8.00	16.00	35.00	65.00	—
1733	—	8.00	16.00	35.00	65.00	—

KM# 270 4 PFENNIG

Billon **Obverse:** City arms in mutli-arched shield **Reverse:** Value, date below **Rev. Legend:** IIII/STADT/PFENN

Date	Mintage	VG	F	VF	XF	Unc
1730	—	8.00	15.00	28.00	55.00	—
1731	—	8.00	15.00	28.00	55.00	—
1732	—	8.00	15.00	28.00	55.00	—
1733	—	8.00	15.00	28.00	55.00	—
1734	—	8.00	15.00	28.00	55.00	—
1735	—	8.00	15.00	28.00	55.00	—
1736	—	8.00	15.00	28.00	55.00	—
1737	—	8.00	15.00	28.00	55.00	—
1738	—	8.00	15.00	28.00	55.00	—
1739	—	8.00	15.00	28.00	55.00	—
1740	—	8.00	15.00	28.00	55.00	—
1741	—	8.00	15.00	28.00	55.00	—
1742	—	8.00	15.00	28.00	55.00	—
1743	—	8.00	15.00	28.00	55.00	—
1744	—	8.00	15.00	28.00	55.00	—
1745	—	8.00	15.00	28.00	55.00	—
1746	—	8.00	15.00	28.00	55.00	—
1747	—	8.00	15.00	28.00	55.00	—
1748	—	8.00	15.00	28.00	55.00	—
1749	—	8.00	15.00	28.00	55.00	—
1750	—	8.00	15.00	28.00	55.00	—
1751	—	8.00	15.00	28.00	55.00	—
1752	—	8.00	15.00	28.00	55.00	—
1753	—	8.00	15.00	28.00	55.00	—
1754	—	8.00	15.00	28.00	55.00	—
1755	—	8.00	15.00	28.00	55.00	—
1756	—	8.00	15.00	28.00	55.00	—
1757	—	8.00	15.00	28.00	55.00	—
1758	—	8.00	15.00	28.00	55.00	—
1759	—	8.00	15.00	28.00	55.00	—
1763	—	8.00	15.00	28.00	55.00	—
1764	—	8.00	15.00	28.00	55.00	—

KM# 275 6 MARIENGROSCHEN

Silver **Obverse:** Ornate helmeted arms **Obv. Legend:** DA PACEM.. **Reverse:** Value, date in 4 lines within legend

Date	Mintage	VG	F	VF	XF	Unc
1739 UAW	—	35.00	80.00	150	275	—
1763	—	35.00	80.00	150	275	—

KM# 236 12 MARIENGROSCHEN (1/3 Thaler)

Silver

Date	Mintage	VG	F	VF	XF	Unc
1700 HL	—	50.00	125	200	350	—
1702 HL	—	50.00	125	200	350	—
1702 HL	—	50.00	125	200	350	—
1716 JJ	—	50.00	125	200	350	—

KM# 273 12 MARIENGROSCHEN (1/3 Thaler)

Silver **Ruler:** Clemens August of Bavaria **Obverse:** Ornate helmeted arms **Obv. Legend:** DA PACEM.. **Reverse:** Value, date in 4 lines within legend

Date	Mintage	VG	F	VF	XF	Unc
1735 UAW	—	90.00	150	300	400	—
1737 UAW	—	90.00	150	300	400	—
1741 UAW	—	90.00	150	300	400	—

KM# 237 24 MARIENGROSCHEN (2/3 Thaler)

Silver **Obverse:** Small arms in ovoid shield, pointed at bottom, ornate helmet above, 3/4 length figure of maiden above helmet **Reverse:** Value, date below **Rev. Legend:** 24/MARIEN/GROSCH **Note:** Varietes exist.

Date	Mintage	VG	F	VF	XF	Unc
1700 HL	—	60.00	125	220	400	—
1701 HL	—	60.00	125	220	400	—
1701 HL	—	60.00	125	220	400	—
1702 HL	—	60.00	125	220	400	—
170Z HL	—	60.00	125	220	400	—
1703 HL	—	60.00	125	220	400	—
1709 HL	—	60.00	125	220	400	—
1710 JJ	—	60.00	125	220	400	—
1712 II	—	60.00	125	220	400	—
1713 JJ	—	60.00	125	220	400	—
1714 JJ	—	60.00	125	220	400	—
1718 JJ	—	60.00	125	220	400	—
1721 JJ	—	60.00	125	220	400	—

KM# 272 24 MARIENGROSCHEN (2/3 Thaler)

Silver **Obverse:** Ornate helmeted arms **Obv. Legend:** DA PACEM... **Reverse:** Value, date in 4 lines within legend

Date	Mintage	VG	F	VF	XF	Unc
1733 UAW	—	80.00	135	225	350	—
1735 UAW	—	80.00	135	225	350	—
1737 UAW	—	80.00	135	225	350	—
1741 UAW	—	80.00	135	225	350	—
1742 UAW	—	80.00	135	225	350	—
1746 UAW	—	80.00	135	225	350	—
1763 ITW	—	80.00	135	225	350	—

KM# 255 1/24 THALER

Silver **Ruler:** Jobst Edmund von Brabeck **Obverse:** Helmeted arms in rectangular shield

Date	Mintage	VG	F	VF	XF	Unc
1701 HL	—	15.00	40.00	75.00	120	—

KM# 265 1/24 THALER

Silver **Ruler:** Clemens August of Bavaria **Obverse:** Helmeted arms in shield with flat top and rounded bottom

Date	Mintage	VG	F	VF	XF	Unc
1726 JJ	—	15.00	20.00	36.00	65.00	—
1727 JJ	—	15.00	20.00	36.00	65.00	—

KM# 271 1/24 THALER

Silver **Obverse:** City arms in multi-faceted shield **Obv. Legend:** DA PA... or DA PAC...

Date	Mintage	VG	F	VF	XF	Unc
1732 UAW	—	15.00	20.00	36.00	65.00	—
1733 UAW	—	15.00	20.00	36.00	65.00	—
1734 UAW	—	15.00	20.00	36.00	65.00	—
1736 UAW	—	15.00	20.00	36.00	65.00	—
1737 UAW	—	15.00	20.00	36.00	65.00	—
1743 UAW	—	15.00	20.00	36.00	65.00	—
1745 UAW	—	15.00	20.00	36.00	65.00	—
1746 UAW	—	15.00	20.00	36.00	65.00	—
1747 UAW	—	15.00	20.00	36.00	65.00	—
1748 UAW	—	15.00	20.00	36.00	65.00	—
1749 UAW	—	15.00	20.00	36.00	65.00	—
1756 ITW	—	15.00	20.00	36.00	65.00	—
1762 ITW	—	15.00	20.00	36.00	65.00	—
1763 ITW	—	15.00	20.00	36.00	65.00	—
1764 ITW	—	15.00	20.00	36.00	65.00	—

KM# 281 1/24 THALER

Silver **Ruler:** Friedrich Wilhelm, Bishop **Obverse:** Helmeted city arms in multi-arched shield **Obv. Legend:** DA PAC...

Date	Mintage	VG	F	VF	XF	Unc
1763 ITW	—	20.00	35.00	60.00	95.00	—

KM# 246 1/24 THALER (Reichsgroschen)

Silver **Obverse:** Oval arms with pointed bottom, ornate helmet and figure of maiden above **Obv. Legend:** DA PACEM... **Reverse:** Imperial orb with 24 or Z4 divides date **Rev. Legend:** HILDESHEI STADT GELDT **Note:** Varieties exist.

Date	Mintage	VG	F	VF	XF	Unc
1700 HL	—	12.00	20.00	36.00	60.00	—
1701 HL	—	12.00	20.00	36.00	60.00	—
1701 HL	—	12.00	18.00	32.00	60.00	—
1702 HL	—	12.00	18.00	32.00	60.00	—
1703 HL	—	12.00	18.00	32.00	60.00	—
1704/3 HL	—	12.00	18.00	32.00	60.00	—
1704 HL	—	12.00	18.00	32.00	60.00	—
1705 HL	—	12.00	18.00	32.00	60.00	—
1706 HL	—	12.00	18.00	32.00	60.00	—
1707 HL	—	12.00	18.00	32.00	60.00	—
1708 HL	—	12.00	18.00	32.00	60.00	—
1709 HL	—	12.00	18.00	32.00	60.00	—
1710 HL	—	12.00	18.00	32.00	60.00	—
1710 JJ	—	12.00	18.00	32.00	60.00	—
1710 II	—	12.00	18.00	32.00	60.00	—
1711 II	—	12.00	18.00	32.00	60.00	—
1712 II	—	12.00	18.00	32.00	60.00	—
1713 II	—	12.00	18.00	32.00	60.00	—
1713 JJ	—	12.00	18.00	32.00	60.00	—
1714 JJ	—	12.00	18.00	32.00	60.00	—
1715 JJ	—	12.00	18.00	32.00	60.00	—
1716 JJ	—	12.00	18.00	32.00	60.00	—
1717 JJ	—	12.00	18.00	32.00	60.00	—
1718 JJ	—	12.00	18.00	32.00	60.00	—
1718 II	—	12.00	18.00	32.00	60.00	—
1719 II	—	12.00	18.00	32.00	60.00	—
1720 II	—	12.00	18.00	32.00	60.00	—
1721 II	—	12.00	18.00	32.00	60.00	—
1722 II	—	12.00	18.00	32.00	60.00	—
1723 II	—	12.00	18.00	32.00	60.00	—
1727 JJ	—	12.00	18.00	32.00	60.00	—
1728 JJ	—	12.00	18.00	32.00	60.00	—
1729 JJ	—	12.00	20.00	36.00	65.00	—
1731 JJ	—	12.00	20.00	36.00	65.00	—
1750 UAW	—	12.00	20.00	36.00	65.00	—
1751 UAW	—	12.00	20.00	36.00	65.00	—
1752 UAW	—	12.00	20.00	36.00	65.00	—
1753 UAW	—	12.00	20.00	36.00	65.00	—
1754 UAW	—	12.00	20.00	36.00	65.00	—
1755 UAW	—	12.00	20.00	36.00	65.00	—

KM# 260.1 THALER

Silver **Obverse:** Helmeted arms with ornaments **Obv. Legend:** MONETA NOVA - HILDESIENSIS * **Reverse:** Crowned double-headed eagle, date divided by legs **Rev. Legend:** CAROL. VI. D. G. ROM. IMP. S. A. G. H. H. ET B. REX **Note:** Dav. #2346.

Date	Mintage	VG	F	VF	XF	Unc
1712 II	—	450	900	1,500	2,500	—
1720 II	—	450	900	1,500	2,500	—
1724/0 II	—	450	900	1,500	2,500	—
1740 UA-W	—	450	900	1,500	2,500	—

KM# 260.2 THALER

Silver **Obverse:** Pointed shield with different scrollwork around the shield **Reverse:** Crowned double-headed eagle, legs divide date **Note:** Dav. #2347. Varieties exist.

Date	Mintage	VG	F	VF	XF	Unc
1736 UA-W	—	450	900	1,500	2,500	—

PATTERNS

Including off metal strikes

KM#	Date	Mintage	Identification	Mkt Val
Pn5	1703	—	4 Pfennig. Copper.	—
Pn6	1704	—	3 Pfennig. Copper.	—
Pn7	1705	—	1/24 Thaler. Copper.	—
Pn8	1710	—	1/24 Thaler. Copper.	—
Pn9	1711	—	3 Pfennig. Copper.	—
Pn10	1713	—	4 Pfennig. Copper.	—
Pn11	1724	—	4 Pfennig. Copper.	—
Pn12	1730	—	4 Pfennig. Copper.	—
Pn13	1741	—	4 Pfennig. Copper.	—
Pn14	1745	—	2 Pfennig. Gold.	—
Pn15	1748	—	1/24 Thaler. Gold.	—
Pn16	1751	—	1/24 Thaler. Gold.	—
Pn17	1756	—	1/24 Thaler. Gold.	—
Pn18	1762	—	Pfennig. Gold.	—
Pn19	1763	—	4 Pfennig. Copper.	—
Pn20	1763	—	4 Pfennig. Gold.	—
Pn21	1763	—	1/24 Thaler. Gold.	—

HOHENLOHE

A countship located in the vicinity of Uffenheim in Franconia and originally centered on the village and castle of present-day Hohlach. The ruling family derived its name from the placename and has been traced back as far as the 10th century. The counts gradually acquired various territories between Offenheim to Bad Mergentheim and beyond that became the basis for the many branches of the dynasty. The first of these was Weikersheim with its castle overlooking the confluence of the Vorbach with the Tauber River. In 1472, the surviving elder branch of counts was divided into Hohenlohe-Weikersheim and Hohenlohe Neuenstein. The former became extinct in 1545 and its lands reverted to Hohenlohe-Neuenstein, which itself was divided once again into Hohenlohe-Neuenstein-Neuenstein (Protestant) and Hohenlohe-Neuenstein-Waldenburg (Catholic) in 1551. Hohenlohe-Neuenstein-Neuenstein was further divided in 1610 (see) and Hohenlohe-Neuenstein-Waldenburg underwent the same process in 1600 with the establishment of Hohenlohe-Waldenburg-Pfedelbach, Hohenlohe-Waldenburg-Schillingsfürst and Hohenlohe-Waldenburg-Waldenburg. See the sections under each of these branches for the subsequent history of each. The lands of all branches of Hohenlohe were mediatized in 1806 and passed to Bavaria and Württemberg.

MINT MARKS

S - Schwabach

MINT OFFICIALS' INITIALS

Initials	Date	Name
CGL	1746-55	Carl Gottlieb Laufer in Nuremberg
F	1755-64	Johann Martin Forster in Nuremberg
G	1752-91	Johann Samuel Gotzinger, die-cutter in Ansbach
KNR, KRN	1777-93	Knoll, warden and Georg Nikolaus Riedner, mintmaster in Nuremberg
N	1721-43	Paul Gottlieb Nürnberger in Nuremberg
OE, OEXLEIN, I.L. OEXLEIN	1740-87	Johann Leonard Oexlein, die-cutter in Nuremberg
PPW, PW	(d.1771)	Peter Paul Werner, medailleur in Nuremberg
SNR, SRN, NSR	1764-70	Siegmund Scholz, warden and Georg Nikolaus Riedner, mintmaster in Nuremberg
W	1761-90	Jeremias Paul Werner, die-cutter in Nuremberg
WKS	1768-81	Westphal, mintmaster and Kern, warden in Schwabach

HOHENLOHE-BARTENSTEIN

Of the many branches of the house of Hohenlohe, this branch was founded in 1656 by Christian, the 4th son of Georg Friedrich II (1600-1635) of Hohenlohe-Schillingfürst. It is one of the surviving lines from when Hohenlohe was mediatized and divided between Bavaria and Württemberg in 1806.

RULER

Karl Philipp Franz, 1729-1763

PRINCIPALITY

TRADE COINAGE

KM# 1 GOLDGULDEN

3.5000 g., 0.9860 Gold 0.1109 oz. AGW **Ruler:** Karl Philipp Franz **Obverse:** Bust right **Reverse:** Crowned arms

Date	Mintage	Good	VG	F	VF	XF
1735	—	—	800	1,650	3,000	5,000

KM# 2 DUCAT

3.5000 g., 0.9860 Gold 0.1109 oz. AGW **Ruler:** Karl Philipp Franz **Obverse:** Bust left **Reverse:** Eagle above crowned and mantled arms

Date	Mintage	Good	VG	F	VF	XF
1747 PPW	—	—	550	1,150	2,000	3,500
1750 PPW	—	—	—	—	—	—

HOHENLOHE-BARTENSTEIN-PFEDELBACH

Upon the extinction of the line of Hohenlohe-Pfedelbach in 1728, its properties and titles passed to Bartenstein, thus establishing a new cadet descendancy.

RULERS

Philipp Karl Kaspar, 1728-1729
Ferdinand Ruprecht Franz, 1729-1745
Josef Anton, 1745-1764

PRINCIPALITY

TRADE COINAGE

KM# 2 DUCAT

3.5000 g., 0.9860 Gold 0.1109 oz. AGW **Ruler:** Josef Anton **Obverse:** Bust left **Reverse:** Phoenix rising from flames, Hohenlohe arms in front, crown and mantle below divide date

Date	Mintage	Good	VG	F	VF	XF
1747 PPW	—	—	350	700	1,350	2,750

KM# 1 4 DUCAT

14.0000 g., 0.9860 Gold 0.4438 oz. AGW **Ruler:** Philipp Karl Kaspar **Subject:** Division of Hohenlohe-Pfedeloh **Obverse:** Crowned 4-fold arms within circular thick wreath **Reverse:** Flame atop altar, inscription below **Note:** Joint issue with Hohenlohe-Bartenstein.

Date	Mintage	Good	VG	F	VF	XF
1729 PW Rare	—	—	—	—	—	—

PATTERNS

Including off metal strikes

KM#	Date	Mintage	Identification	Mkt Val
Pn1	1729	—	4 Ducat. Silver.	750

HOHENLOHE-INGELFINGEN

The Ingelfingen line was founded in 1701 upon the division of Hohenlohe-Langenburg. The count was raised to the rank of prince of the empire in 1764 and the last ruler abdicated in 1806.

RULERS

Christian Krato, 1701-1743
Philipp Heinrich, 1743-1781, Prince from 1764
with Heinrich August, 1765-1796
Friedrich Ludwig, 1796-1806 (died 1818)

PRINCIPALITY

REGULAR COINAGE

KM# 2 10 KREUZER

Silver **Ruler:** Philipp Heinrich as Prince **Obverse:** Arms within crowned mantle **Reverse:** Value and date within ornaments **Note:** Convention 10 Kreuzer; Similar to 20 Kreuzer, KM#3.

Date	Mintage	Good	VG	F	VF	XF
1770 SRN	—	—	45.00	80.00	160	325

KM# 3 20 KREUZER

Silver **Ruler:** Philipp Heinrich as Prince **Obverse:** Arms within crowned mantle **Obv. Legend:** FURSTLICH HOHENL: NEUENST • CONV: MUNZ **Reverse:** Value and date within crowned mantle **Rev. Legend:** 60/EINE FEINE/MARCK/1770 **Note:** Convention 20 Kreuzer.

Date	Mintage	Good	VG	F	VF	XF
1770 SRN	—	—	35.00	70.00	135	285

KM# 5 THALER

Silver **Ruler:** Friedrich Ludwig **Obverse:** Bust right, Order cross below **Obv. Legend:** FREID • LUDWIG FRUST ZU HOHENLOHE INGELFINGEN **Reverse:** Value, date **Rev. Legend:** * X */EINE/FEINE/MARK/1796 **Note:** Convention Thaler; Dav. #2356.

Date	Mintage	Good	VG	F	VF	XF
1796	—	—	200	350	650	1,200

TRADE COINAGE

KM# 7 DUCAT

3.5000 g., 0.9860 Gold 0.1109 oz. AGW **Ruler:** Friedrich Ludwig **Obverse:** Bust right **Obv. Legend:** FRIED • LUD • FÜRST ZU HOHENLOHE INGELF • **Reverse:** Value above date **Rev. Legend:** * I */DUCATEN/1796

Date	Mintage	Good	VG	F	VF	XF
1796	—	—	650	1,350	2,750	4,750

HOHENLOHE-KIRCHBERG

Another line founded upon the division of Hohenlohe-Langenburg in 1701, Kirchberg lasted for a little over a century. Like his older brothers, the count was raised to the rank of prince of the empire in 1764. The last prince had his territories mediatized in 1806, but lived until 1819.

RULERS

Christian Friedrich Karl, 1767-1806 (died 1819)

PRINCIPALITY

REGULAR COINAGE

KM# 10 1/2 THALER

Silver **Ruler:** Christian Friedrich Karl **Obverse:** Armored bust right **Reverse:** Helmeted arms within crowned mantle **Rev. Legend:** ZWANZIG EINE... **Note:** Convention 1/2 Thaler.

Date	Mintage	VG	F	VF	XF	Unc
1781 G-WKS	—	—	275	500	900	1,550

KM# 13 1/2 THALER

Silver **Ruler:** Christian Friedrich Karl **Obverse:** Armored bust right **Reverse:** Arms within crowned mantle

Date	Mintage	VG	F	VF	XF	Unc
1786 W-S	—	—	275	475	850	1,450
1786 G-S	—	—	—	—	—	—

KM# 5 THALER

Silver **Ruler:** Friedrich Eberhard **Subject:** Death of Friedrich Eberhard **Obverse:** Armored bust right **Obv. Legend:** CAROL • AUG • COM • HOHENLOH • & GLEICH • DYN • LB: & CR • **Reverse:** Phoenix above inscription **Rev. Inscription:** EX CINERIBUS ORIOR, CINERIBUS/DIVI PARENTIS/FRIDERICI EBERHARDI/DEF• D• XXIII• AUG• MDCCXXXVII•/ANNO AET• LXV•/PARENTAT•/•N• **Note:** Dav. #2357. Date of death in Roman numerals.

Date	Mintage	VG	F	VF	XF	Unc
MDCCXXXVII (1737) W-N	—	—	500	850	1,500	2,500

KM# 6 THALER

Silver **Ruler:** Karl August **Obverse:** Armored bust right **Obv. Legend:** CAROL • AUG • COM • HOHENLOH • & GLEICH • DYN • LB: & CR • **Reverse:** Helmeted arms with ornaments **Rev. Legend:** CVM DEO ET DIE **Note:** Dav. #2358.

Date	Mintage	VG	F	VF	XF	Unc
1738 W-N	—	—	350	600	950	1,750

KM# 11 THALER

Silver **Ruler:** Christian Friedrich Karl **Obverse:** Small young bust **Obv. Legend:** CHRIST • FR • CAR • D • G • S • R • I • PRINC • HOHENL • KIRCHB **Reverse:** Helmeted arms with supporters within crowned mantle **Rev. Legend:** ZEHEN - EINE - FEINE - MARK **Note:** Convention Thaler; Dav. #2359.

Date	Mintage	VG	F	VF	XF	Unc
1781 G-WKS	—	—	400	750	1,250	2,250

KM# 12 THALER

Silver **Ruler:** Christian Friedrich Karl **Obverse:** Larger older bust **Obv. Legend:** CHRIST • FR • CAR • D • G • S • R • I • PRINC • HOHENL • KIRCHB **Reverse:** Helmeted arms with supporters within crowned mantle **Rev. Legend:** ZEHEN - EINE - FEINE - MARK **Note:** Dav. #2359A.

Date	Mintage	VG	F	VF	XF	Unc
1781 W-WKS	—	—	400	750	1,250	2,250

TRADE COINAGE

KM# 7 12 DUCAT

42.0000 g., 0.9860 Gold 1.3314 oz. AGW **Ruler:** Karl August **Obverse:** Bust right **Reverse:** Eagle flanked by crowned lions atop arms **Note:** Similar to 1 Thaler, KM#6.

Date	Mintage	VG	F	VF	XF	Unc
1738 W-N Rare	—	—	—	—	—	—

HOHENLOHE-LANGENBURG

A branch of Hohenlohe-Neuenstein founded in 1610 and was the Protestant line of the family. It was divided again in 1701, Langenburg being one of the cointinuing entities. The count gained princely rank in 1764, but lost his territory as a result of the mediatization of 1806.

RULERS

Albrecht Wolfgang, 1699-1715

MINT MARKS

K - Kirchberg
L - Langenburg

PRINCIPALITY

REGULAR COINAGE

KM# 20 THALER

Silver **Ruler:** Ludwig **Obverse:** 3 females with shields **Obv. Legend:** ARMAT CONCORDIA FRATRES, below; LANGENB. INGELFING. KIRCHB, in exergue; PATRIMON. HENR. FRID/ SORTE DIVISUM/D. 10 IUNII./P.P W f. **Reverse:** Date in chronogram **Rev. Inscription:** *LVDOVICVS/ET PHILIPPVS/ CHRISTIANVS. ET. CAROLVS/HENRICVS. ATQUE. AVGVSTVS/ HIS. EX. FRATRIBVS/NATI. IN. VNIONE. FELICES/ SVNT. CAPITA. LINEAE. HOHEN/LOICAE LANGENBVRGICAE, in exergue; SIT. VNIO. HAEC/ PERENNIS/C.G.L. **Note:** Dav. #2355.

Date	Mintage	VG	F	VF	XF	Unc
1751 PPW-CGL	—	200	400	700	1,250	—

TRADE COINAGE

KM# 21 DUCAT

1.5000 g., 0.9860 Gold 0.0475 oz. AGW **Subject:** 50th Anniversary of Territorial Division **Obverse:** 3 Females with shields **Reverse:** Date in chronogram

Date	Mintage	VG	F	VF	XF	Unc
ND(1751) PPW-CGL	—	200	400	850	1,650	—

HOHENLOHE-NEUENSTEIN-OEHRINGEN

This principality was located in southern Germany. The Neuenstein-Öhringen line was founded in 1610 and the first prince of the empire from this line was proclaimed in 1764. The line became extinct in 1805 and the lands passed to Ingelfingen.

RULERS

Johann Friedrich I, 1641-1702
Friedrich Krato, 1702-1709
Karl Ludwig von Weikersheim, 1702-1756
Johann Friedrich II, 1702-1765
Ludwig Friedrich Karl, 1765-1805

COUNTSHIP

REGULAR COINAGE

KM# 30 GROSCHEN (3 Kreuzer)

Silver **Ruler:** Johann Friedrich II **Mint:** Nuremberg **Subject:** Bicentennial - Augsburg Confession **Obverse:** Inscription within inner circle **Reverse:** Inscription **Note:** Similar to 2 Groschen, KM#31.

Date	Mintage	VG	F	VF	XF	Unc
1730 N	—	45.00	75.00	150	280	—

KM# 31 2 GROSCHEN

Silver **Ruler:** Johann Friedrich II **Mint:** Nuremberg **Subject:** Bicentennial - Augsburg Confession **Obverse:** 7-line inscription, date in chronogram, mintmaster's initial below **Obv. Legend:** IOH. FRID. G. V. H. V. G. H. Z. L. V. C. ÆT. XLVIII. **Obv. Inscription:** CHRISTI/WORT/IST LVTHERS/LEHR/DIE VERGEHET/NUN NIT/MEHR. **Reverse:** 9-line inscription with date in laurel wreath **Rev. Inscription:** MEIN CHRIST/DAMIT DV NIE/VERGIST/WAS GOTT AN ZION/HAT GETHAN/SO SCHAVE DIESE/DENCKMUNTZ AN./(1730)

Date	Mintage	VG	F	VF	XF	Unc
1730 N	—	55.00	85.00	165	300	—

KM# 40 20 KREUZER

Silver **Ruler:** Johann Friedrich II **Mint:** Nuremberg **Obverse:** Bust left, double legend inscriptions **Reverse:** Order chain around 3 oval arms within crowned baroque frame, value divides date below **Note:** Convention 20 Kreuzer.

Date	Mintage	VG	F	VF	XF	Unc
1760 PPW-F	—	85.00	130	240	450	—

KM# 41 1/4 THALER

7.2000 g., Silver **Ruler:** Johann Friedrich II **Mint:** Nuremberg **Obverse:** Armored bust left **Reverse:** Order chain around 3 oval arms within crowned baroque frame, cross divides date below **Note:** Convention 1/4 Thaler.

Date	Mintage	VG	F	VF	XF	Unc
1760 PPW-F	—	100	160	350	600	—

KM# 32 1/2 THALER

Silver **Ruler:** Johann Friedrich II **Mint:** Nuremberg **Subject:** Bicentennial - Augsburg Confession **Obverse:** Phoenix rising from flames on altar, date in chronogram **Obv. Legend:** IOH: FRIDERICVS. COMES HOHEN: EX PIO VOTO POSVIT. **Reverse:** Full-length facing female figure holding Bible and Augsburg Confession, hand from clouds above holding crown above head, date in chronogram continued **Rev. Legend:** IESVS CHRISTVS EST DOMINVS. qVI CORONABIT SVOS.

Date	Mintage	VG	F	VF	XF	Unc
ND(1730) N	—	280	400	725	1,200	—

KM# 42 1/2 THALER

Silver **Ruler:** Johann Friedrich II **Mint:** Nuremberg **Obverse:** Armored bust left **Reverse:** Order chain around 3 oval arms within crowned baroque frame **Note:** Convention 1/2 Thaler.

Date	Mintage	VG	F	VF	XF	Unc
1760 PPW-F	—	125	200	400	650	—

KM# 33 THALER

Silver **Ruler:** Johann Friedrich II **Mint:** Nuremberg **Subject:** Bicentennial - Augsburg Confession **Obverse:** Crowned lion seated left holding shield of arms **Obv. Legend:** IOH. FRIDERICVS LINEAE HOHENLOH - NEVENSTEINENSIS DEDIT ET EREXIT PIIS*, above lion in 3 lines; GOTT SEY GEDANCKET. DER VNS SIEG GIBT IN CHRISTO./VND OFFENBAHRET SEINE VVAHRE/ERKANTNVS • 2 • COR • 2• **Reverse:** Date in chronogram **Rev. Legend:** FIDEI PIETATI HVIC ET FVTVRO AEVO SACRVM. *, below angel in 3 lines; IN ALLE LANDE GIENG/IHR SCHALL. VND IN ALLE/VVELT IHRE VVORT. **Note:** Dav. #2350.

Date	Mintage	F	VF	XF	Unc
1730 N	—	300	550	950	1,850

KM# 43 THALER
Silver **Ruler:** Johann Friedrich II **Mint:** Nuremberg **Obverse:** Armored bust left **Obv. Legend:** IOANN: FRID: COM: DE HOHENL: ET GLEICH: DOM: IN LANGENB: ET CRANICHF:/ SENIOR ET FEUD: ADMINISTRATOR AETAT: S: 77. **Reverse:** Order chain around 3 oval arms within crowned baroque frame **Rev. Legend:** RECTE FACIENDO NEMINEM TIMEAS, 10 EINE FEINE MARCK in band below **Note:** Convention Thaler. Dav. #2351.

Date	Mintage	F	VF	XF	Unc
1760 PPW-F	—	300	600	1,000	2,000

TRADE COINAGE

KM# 44 DUCAT
3.5000 g., 0.9860 Gold 0.1109 oz. AGW **Ruler:** Johann Friedrich II **Mint:** Nuremberg **Obverse:** Armored bust left **Reverse:** Order chain around 3 oval arms within crowned baroque frame, date below

Date	Mintage	VG	F	VF	XF	Unc
1760 PPW-F	—	400	850	1,750	3,000	—

KM# 26 7 DUCAT
24.5000 g., 0.9860 Gold 0.7766 oz. AGW **Ruler:** Johann Friedrich I **Mint:** Augsburg **Note:** Age of count is 84 in reverse legend.

Date	Mintage	VG	F	VF	XF	Unc
1701 (a) Rare	—	—	—	—	—	—

PRINCIPALITY

REGULAR COINAGE

KM# 54 KREUZER
Billon **Ruler:** Ludwig Friedrich Karl **Mint:** Nuremberg **Obverse:** Monogram above date **Reverse:** Crowned arms within branches, value below **Note:** Convention Kreuzer.

Date	Mintage	VG	F	VF	XF	Unc
1774 SNR	—	7.00	15.00	30.00	70.00	—

KM# 55 2-1/2 KREUZER
Billon **Ruler:** Ludwig Friedrich Karl **Mint:** Nuremberg **Obverse:** Monogram above date **Reverse:** Crowned arms within branches, value below **Note:** Convention 2-1/2 Kreuzer.

Date	Mintage	VG	F	VF	XF	Unc
1774 SNR	—	10.00	20.00	40.00	80.00	—

KM# 50 10 KREUZER
Silver **Ruler:** Ludwig Friedrich Karl **Mint:** Nuremberg **Obverse:** Arms within crowned mantle **Reverse:** Value and date within ornate frame **Note:** Convention 10 Kreuzer.

Date	Mintage	VG	F	VF	XF	Unc
1770 SNR	—	15.00	30.00	75.00	160	—

KM# 60 10 KREUZER
Silver **Ruler:** Ludwig Friedrich Karl **Mint:** Nuremberg **Obverse:** Complex arms within crowned mantle **Reverse:** Value and date within ornate frame

Date	Mintage	VG	F	VF	XF	Unc
1785 KRN	—	15.00	30.00	75.00	160	—

KM# 51 20 KREUZER
Silver **Ruler:** Ludwig Friedrich Karl **Mint:** Nuremberg **Obverse:** Arms within crowned mantle **Reverse:** Value and date within ornate frame

Date	Mintage	VG	F	VF	XF	Unc
1770 SNR	—	25.00	50.00	100	200	—

KM# 61 20 KREUZER
Silver **Ruler:** Ludwig Friedrich Karl **Mint:** Nuremberg **Obverse:** Complex arms within crowned mantle **Reverse:** Value and date within ornate frame

Date	Mintage	VG	F	VF	XF	Unc
1785 KRN	—	25.00	50.00	100	200	—

KM# 52 THALER
Silver **Ruler:** Ludwig Friedrich Karl **Mint:** Nuremberg **Obverse:** Armored bust right **Obv. Legend:** LVDM• FRID • CAROL • D • G • PRINC • AB HOHENL • COM • DE GLEICK • D • IN LANGENB • & • CRANICHFELD * **Reverse:** Order chain surrounds arms within crowned mantle, date divided below **Rev. Legend:** X • EINE FEINE MARCK **Note:** Dav. #2352.

Date	Mintage	F	VF	XF	Unc
1770 OEXLEIN-NSR	—	175	325	600	1,300

KM# 62 THALER
Silver **Ruler:** Ludwig Friedrich Karl **Mint:** Nuremberg **Obverse:** Armored bust right **Obv. Legend:** SVD • FRID • CAROL • D • G • PRINC • AB HOHENL • COM • DE GLEICH • IN LANGENB • ET CRANICHFELD * **Reverse:** Helmeted complex arms with supporters within crowned mantle **Rev. Legend:** ZEHEN - EINE - FEINE - MARK **Note:** Dav. #2353.

Date	Mintage	F	VF	XF	Unc
1785 OE-KRN	—	150	300	550	1,200

KM# 65 THALER
Silver **Ruler:** Ludwig Friedrich Karl **Obverse:** Armored bust left **Obv. Legend:** LUD: FRID: CAROL: D:G: PRINC: AB HOHENLOHE. COM: DE GLEICH. **Reverse:** Helmeted complex arms within crowned mantle **Rev. Legend:** DOM: IN LANGENB: ET CRANICHF: SEN: FAM: ET FEUDOR: ADMIN. AE. 74, below; X EINE F MARK 1797 **Note:** Dav. #2354.

Date	Mintage	F	VF	XF	Unc
1797	—	125	225	400	950

TRADE COINAGE

KM# 53 DUCAT
3.5000 g., 0.9860 Gold 0.1109 oz. AGW **Ruler:** Ludwig Friedrich Karl **Mint:** Nuremberg **Obverse:** Armored bust right **Reverse:** Order chain surrounds arms within crowned mantle, value divides date below

Date	Mintage	F	VF	XF	Unc
1770 OE-SNR	—	550	1,150	2,000	3,500

KM# 63 DUCAT
3.5000 g., 0.9860 Gold 0.1109 oz. AGW **Ruler:** Ludwig Friedrich Karl **Obverse:** Armored bust right **Reverse:** Crowned and mantled arms **Note:** Similar to KM#71.

Date	Mintage	F	VF	XF	Unc
1787	—	550	1,150	2,000	3,500

HOHENLOHE-NEUENSTEIN-WEIKERSHEIM

Established as a branch of Hohenlohe-Neuenstein in the division of 1610, it became extinct in one generation and passed to Hohenlohe-Neuenstein-Neuenstein from which line the younger brothers ruled Weikersheim until 1756.

RULERS
Karl Ludwig, 1702-1756

MINT MARK
N - Nuremberg

MINT OFFICIALS' INITIALS

Initials	Date	Name
N, PGN	1721-43	Paul Gottlieb Nürnberger in Nuremberg
PPW	(d.1771)	Peter Paul Werner, die-cutter in Nuremberg

PRINCIPALITY

REGULAR COINAGE

KM# 15 1/2 THALER
Silver **Ruler:** Karl Ludwig **Obverse:** Armored bust right **Obv. Legend:** CAROL • LUD • COM • DE HOHENLO & GLEICH • DOM • IN • LANGENB • & CRANICHF • Æ68 **Reverse:** Helmeted arms within Order chain **Rev. Legend:** SOLA BONA QUÆ HONESTA

Date	Mintage	VG	F	VF	XF	Unc
1742	—	200	400	800	1,650	—

KM# 16 THALER
Silver **Ruler:** Karl Ludwig **Obverse:** Armored bust right **Obv. Legend:** CAROL • LUD • COM • DE HOHENLO • & GLEICH • DOM • IN LANGENB • & CRANICHF • Æ68 **Reverse:** Helmeted arms within Order chain, date divided below **Rev. Legend:** SOLA BONA QUÆ HONESTA **Note:** Struck from 1/2 Thaler dies, KM#15. Dav. #2349.

Date	Mintage	VG	F	VF	XF	Unc
1742 PPW-PGN	—	1,800	3,000	4,500	6,500	—

KM# 17 2 THALER
Silver **Ruler:** Karl Ludwig **Note:** Struck from 1/2 Thaler dies, KM#15. Dav. #2348.

Date	Mintage	VG	F	VF	XF	Unc
1742 PPW-PGN	—	1,500	2,500	4,000	6,500	—

TRADE COINAGE

KM# 12 DUCAT
3.5000 g., 0.9860 Gold 0.1109 oz. AGW **Ruler:** Karl Ludwig **Obverse:** Armored bust right **Reverse:** Helmeted arms within Order chain, date below

Date	Mintage	VG	F	VF	XF	Unc
1737 N	—	300	650	1,350	2,750	—

KM# 20 8 DUCAT
28.0000 g., 0.9860 Gold 0.8876 oz. AGW **Ruler:** Karl Ludwig **Subject:** 50th Anniversary of Reign **Obverse:** Armored bust right **Reverse:** Inscription within ornate frame

Date	Mintage	VG	F	VF	XF	Unc
1752 PPW Rare	—	—	—	—	—	—

PATTERNS

Including off metal strikes

KM#	Date	Mintage	Identification	Mkt Val
Pn1	1737	—	1/8 Thaler. Silver. KM#12.	—
Pn2	1737	—	1/4 Thaler. Silver. KM#12.	—
Pn3	1752	—	Thaler. Silver.	1,250

HOHENLOHE-PFEDELBACH

Established as one of three lines of the Waldenburg (Catholic) branch of Hohenlohe in 1600. It became extinct in 1728, passed to Hohenlohe-Bartenstein. A new line was established as Hohenlohe-Bartenstein-Pfedelbach (which see).

RULER
Ludwig Gottfried, 1685-1728

PRINCIPALITY

REGULAR COINAGE

KM# 20 1/2 GROSCHEN (6 Pfennig)
Silver **Ruler:** Ludwig Gottfried **Subject:** 200th Anniversary of the Reformation **Obverse:** Shield of Hohenlohe arms leaning to left, large crown above **Reverse:** Legend in wreath **Rev. Legend:** EVAN/GELISCHE/IVEL. MUNZ/D. 31. OCT/1717

Date	Mintage	VG	F	VF	XF	Unc
1717	—	30.00	60.00	100	175	—

KM# 21 GROSCHEN (3 Kreuzer)
Silver **Ruler:** Ludwig Gottfried **Subject:** 200th Anniversary of the Reformation **Obverse:** Crowned four-fold arms in cartouche **Reverse:** Six-line inscription with Roman numeral date

Date	Mintage	VG	F	VF	XF	Unc
1717	—	35.00	75.00	125	200	—

KM# 22 2 GROSCHEN
Silver **Ruler:** Ludwig Gottfried **Subject:** 200th Anniversary of the Reformation **Obverse:** Crowned 4-fold arms within cartouche **Reverse:** 6-Line inscription with Roman numeral date **Note:** Similar to 1 Groschen, KM#21. Struck from 1 Groschen dies, KM#21.

Date	Mintage	VG	F	VF	XF	Unc
1717	—	—	—	—	—	—

KM# 23 1/8 THALER
Silver **Ruler:** Ludwig Gottfried **Subject:** 200th Anniversary of the Reformation **Obverse:** Four-line inscription with date in chronogram **Reverse:** Phoenix and flan in boat **Rev. Legend:** REPARATIO VERIT EVANGEL **Rev. Inscription:** SANCTIFICA/VERO NOS/SERMONE/TVO DEVS

Date	Mintage	VG	F	VF	XF	Unc
1717	—	45.00	90.00	150	250	—

KM# 24 1/4 THALER
Silver **Ruler:** Ludwig Gottfried **Subject:** 200th Anniversary of the Reformation **Obverse:** 4-Line inscription with date in chronogram **Reverse:** Phoenix and flan in boat **Note:** Similar to 1/8 Thaler, KM#23.

Date	Mintage	VG	F	VF	XF	Unc
1717	—	80.00	160	275	450	—

TRADE COINAGE

KM# 25 DUCAT
3.5000 g., 0.9860 Gold 0.1109 oz. AGW **Ruler:** Ludwig Gottfried **Subject:** Bicentennial of the Reformation **Obverse:** Crowned arms within cartouche **Reverse:** Inscription within branches

Date	Mintage	VG	F	VF	XF	Unc
1717	—	400	850	1,750	3,000	—

KM# 30 DUCAT
3.5000 g., 0.9860 Gold 0.1109 oz. AGW **Obverse:** Bust of Josef Anton right **Reverse:** Phoenix rising from flames, date in exergue

Date	Mintage	VG	F	VF	XF	Unc
1747 PPW	—	425	900	1,850	3,250	—

KM# 26 2 DUCAT
7.0000 g., 0.9860 Gold 0.2219 oz. AGW **Ruler:** Ludwig Gottfried **Note:** Struck from 1 Ducat dies, KM#25.

Date	Mintage	VG	F	VF	XF	Unc
1717	—	4,500	6,500	9,000	12,500	—

HOHENLOHE-WALDENBURG-SCHILLINGSFURST

In 1600 the Pfedelbach, Waldenburg and Schillingsfürst lines of Hohenlohe were established from Waldenburg, the Catholic branch of the family. Waldenburg became extinct in 1679 with all lands passing to Schillingsfurst. The count gained the rank of prince in 1744, but the line only lasted until mediatization in 1806.

RULERS
Philipp Ernst, 1697-1753
Karl Albrecht, 1753-1793
Karl Albrecht Christian, 1793-1796
Karl Albrecht Philipp Josef, 1796-1806

MINT MARKS
F - Friedberg

MINTMASTER'S INITIALS

Initial	Date	Name
GFN	1682-1724	Georg Friedrich Nürnberger in Nuremberg

NOTE: Mints functioned at Bartenstein and Schillingsfürst during the Kipper Period.

PRINCIPALITY

REGULAR COINAGE

KM# 45 KREUZER
Billon **Ruler:** Karl Albrecht **Obverse:** Legend and date **Reverse:** Phoenix

Date	Mintage	VG	F	VF	XF	Unc
1768 SNR	—	10.00	20.00	32.00	70.00	—

KM# 50 2-1/2 KREUZER
Billon **Ruler:** Karl Albrecht **Obverse:** Legend, date **Reverse:** Phoenix **Note:** Similar to 1 Kreuzer, KM#45.

Date	Mintage	VG	F	VF	XF	Unc
1770 SNR	—	16.00	32.00	60.00	120	—

KM# 46 5 KREUZER
Billon **Ruler:** Karl Albrecht **Obverse:** Legend, date with branches **Reverse:** Phoenix

Date	Mintage	VG	F	VF	XF	Unc
1768 SNR	—	20.00	40.00	70.00	150	—
1770	—	20.00	40.00	70.00	150	—

KM# 51 1/2 THALER
Silver **Ruler:** Karl Albrecht **Obverse:** Armored bust right **Reverse:** Phoenix

Date	Mintage	VG	F	VF	XF	Unc
1770 OEXLEIN-SNR	—	75.00	165	350	650	—

KM# 41 THALER
Silver **Ruler:** Karl Albrecht **Obverse:** Large lettering **Obv. Legend:** CAR: ALB: D:G: PR: REGN: AB HOHENL: ET WALDENB: D: IN LANGENBURG., inner row; DEO PATRIÆ - NON NOBIS, below; I. L. OEXLEIN f. **Reverse:** Phoenix rising from ashes **Rev. Legend:** EX FLAMMIS ORIOR, in exergue; 10 EINE FEINE MARCK MDCCLVII/M.F **Note:** Dav. #2360.

Date	Mintage	VG	F	VF	XF	Unc
1757 I.L. OEXLEIN-MF	—	175	350	700	1,200	—

KM# 42 THALER

Silver **Ruler:** Karl Albrecht **Obverse:** Small lettering **Obv. Legend:** CAR: ALB: D:G: PR: REG: AB HOHENLOHE WALD: DOM: IN LANG: ET SCHILLINGS • FVRST •, in inner row; DEO PATRIÆ - NON NOBIS, below; I. L. OEXLEIN. F. **Reverse:** Phoenix rising from ashes **Rev. Legend:** EX FLAMMIS ORIOR, in exergue; 10 EINE FEINE MARCK/MDCCLVII/M. F. **Note:** Dav. #2361.

Date	Mintage	VG	F	VF	XF	Unc
1757 I.L. OEXLEIN-MF	—	175	350	700	1,200	—

TRADE COINAGE

KM# 40 DUCAT

3.5000 g., 0.9860 Gold 0.1109 oz. AGW **Ruler:** Philipp Ernst **Obverse:** Bust left **Reverse:** Phoenix

Date	Mintage	VG	F	VF	XF	Unc
1750 PW	—	850	1,750	3,000	5,000	—

KM# 52 DUCAT

3.5000 g., 0.9860 Gold 0.1109 oz. AGW **Ruler:** Karl Albrecht **Obverse:** Armored bust right **Reverse:** Phoenix

Date	Mintage	VG	F	VF	XF	Unc
1776 OE	—	1,200	2,500	4,500	7,000	—

PATTERNS

Including off metal strikes

KM#	Date	Mintage	Identification	Mkt Val
Pn2	1750	—	Ducat. Silver. KM#40.	275

HOHENZOLLERN-HECHINGEN

Located in southern Germany, the Hechingen line was founded in 1576. The family received the mint right in 1471 and the counts were raised to the rank of prince of the empire in 1623. As a result of the 1848 revolutions the prince abdicated in favor of Prussia in 1849.

RULERS

Friedrich Wilhelm, 1671-1735
Friedrich Ludwig, 1735-1750
Josef Wilhelm, 1750-1798
Hermann Friedrich Otto, 1798 - 1810

MINT OFFICIALS' INITIALS

Initials	Date	Name
ARW	1742-84	Adam Rudolf Werner, die-cutter
CH, ICH	1783-1808	Johann Christian Heuglin
DFH	1760-84	Daniel Friedrich Heuglin, warden
ILW, W	1798-1845	Johann Ludwig Wagner, die-cutter

ARMS

Hohenzollern: Quartered square, upper left and lower right dark, upper right and lower left light (black and silver).

Hereditary Imperial Chamberlain: Two crossed sceptres.

REFERENCE:

B = Emil Bahrfeldt, *Das Münz- und Geldwesen der Fürstenthümer Hohenzollern,* Berlin, 1900.

PRINCIPALITY

REGULAR COINAGE

KM# 30 THALER

Silver **Ruler:** Josef Wilhelm **Obverse:** Bust right **Obv. Legend:** IOS: WILH: D:G: PR: DE - HOHENZOLLERN. BVRGG: N: **Reverse:** Crowned arms withini Order chain, cross divides date below **Rev. Legend:** AD NORMAM - CONVENTIONIS **Note:** Convention Thaler.

Date	Mintage	VG	F	VF	XF	Unc
1783 ARW-DFH-ICH	—	—	225	450	850	1,650

TRADE COINAGE

KM# 25 1/4 CAROLIN

2.4250 g., 0.7700 Gold 0.0600 oz. AGW **Ruler:** Friedrich Wilhelm **Obverse:** Bust right **Reverse:** Crowned and mantled arms, date below

Date	Mintage	VG	F	VF	XF	Unc
1734	—	350	700	1,500	3,000	—
1735	—	350	700	1,500	3,000	—

KM# 26 1/2 CAROLIN

4.8500 g., 0.7700 Gold 0.1201 oz. AGW **Ruler:** Friedrich Wilhelm **Obverse:** Bust right **Reverse:** Crowned and mantled arms, date below

Date	Mintage	VG	F	VF	XF	Unc
1734	—	400	800	1,650	3,250	—
1735	—	400	800	1,650	3,250	—

KM# 27 CAROLIN

9.7000 g., 0.7700 Gold 0.2401 oz. AGW **Ruler:** Friedrich Wilhelm **Obverse:** Bust right **Reverse:** Crowned and mantled arms, date below

Date	Mintage	VG	F	VF	XF	Unc
1734	—	600	1,200	2,500	4,500	—
1735	—	600	1,200	2,500	4,500	—

ISNY

FREE CITY

This south German city, some 17 miles NE of Lindau and the shore of the Bodensee, is first mentioned in the 11th century. It acquired its imperial city status from Emperor Karl IV in 1365 and the mint right in 1507 from Maximilian I. A regular coinage began the following year and continued, on-and-off, until the early 18th century. The city was acquired by Württemberg in 1803 and lost its position as a free city.

MINT OFFICIALS' INITIALS

Initials	Date	Name
PI	1695-1702	Hans Jakob Hau
PPW, W	(d.1771)	Peter Paul Werner, die-cutter in Nüremberg

ARMS

Crowned eagle with horseshoe in shield on breast.

REGULAR COINAGE

KM# 15 PFENNIG

Copper **Note:** Crowned city eagle arms.

Date	Mintage	VG	F	VF	XF	Unc
ND(ca.1701-2)	—	12.00	20.00	30.00	50.00	—

KM# 16 KREUZER

Silver **Obverse:** Crowned imperial eagle, value I in orb on breast **Reverse:** Crowned city eagle arms

Date	Mintage	VG	F	VF	XF	Unc
ND(ca.1701-02)	—	18.00	35.00	70.00	125	—

KM# 21 GROSCHEN

Silver **Subject:** 200th Anniversary of Augsburg Confession **Obverse:** Eye of God in clouds above figure with cart of grapes **Reverse:** Eight-line inscription, VII.KAL. IVL. in exergue, W below

Date	Mintage	VG	F	VF	XF	Unc
ND(1730) W Rare	—	—	—	—	—	—

KM# 25 GROSCHEN

Silver **Subject:** Centennial of Peace of Westphalia **Obverse:** Allegorical figure standing with garlanded altar left **Reverse:** Six-line inscription within laurel wreath

Date	Mintage	VG	F	VF	XF	Unc
1748 PPW Rare	—	—	—	—	—	—

COUNTERMARKED COINAGE

KM# 30 KREUZER

Copper **Countermark:** Broad horseshoe **Note:** Countermark on Furstenberg, KM#26.

CM Date	Host Date	Good	VG	F	VF	XF
ND	1772 G	—	—	—	—	—

KM# 20 GROSCHEN

Silver **Countermark:** Horseshoe in a circle **Note:** Countermark on Bavaria, KM#167.

CM Date	Host Date	Good	VG	F	VF	XF
ND	ND(1726)	—	—	—	—	—

TRADE COINAGE

KM# 26 3 DUCAT

10.5000 g., 0.9860 Gold 0.3328 oz. AGW **Subject:** Centennial - Peace of Westphalia **Obverse:** Allegorical figure standing with garlanded altar left **Reverse:** Six-line inscription within laurel wreath

Date	Mintage	VG	F	VF	XF	Unc
1748 PPW Rare	—	—	—	—	—	—

KM# 27 6 DUCAT

21.0000 g., 0.9860 Gold 0.6657 oz. AGW **Subject:** Centennial - Peace of Westphalia **Obverse:** Allegorical figure standing with garlanded altar left **Reverse:** Six-line inscription within laurel wreath

Date	Mintage	VG	F	VF	XF	Unc
1748 PPW Rare	—	—	—	—	—	—

PATTERNS

Including off metal strikes

KM#	Date	Mintage	Identification	Mkt Val
Pn1	1748	—	3 Ducat. Silver. KM#26	—

JEVER

A lordship lying on the North Sea coast, Jever's earliest coinage dates from the late 10th and early 11th centuries. For several centuries Jever experienced political disintegration until one powerful lord united the district in the early 15th century. The noble line fell extinct in 1575 and Jever passed by marriage to Oldenburg, then successively to Anhalt-Zerbst in 1667, Russia in 1793, Holland in 1807, Russia again in 1813, and finally to Oldenburg again in 1818.

The coinage struck for Jever under Oldenburg can be distinguished by prominence given to the Jever arms - a lion rampant to the left usually in a central shield imposed over the four-fold arms of Oldenburg and Delmenhorst.

RULERS

Karl Wilhelm von Anhalt-Zerbst, 1667-1718
Johann August von Anhalt-Zerbst, 1718-1742
Johann Ludwig von Anhalt-Zerbst, 1742-1746 and
Christian August von Anhalt-Zerbst, 1742-1747
Johanna Elisabeth von Schleswig-Holstein-Gottorp, 1747-1752
Friedrich August of Anhalt-Zerbst, 1753-1793
Friederike Auguste Sophie, 1793-1807

DUCHY

REGULAR COINAGE

KM# 96 HELLER

Copper **Ruler:** Friedrich August **Obverse:** Bust right **Reverse:** Arms divide date, JEVER above, value below

Date	Mintage	VG	F	VF	XF	Unc
1764	—	15.00	25.00	40.00	70.00	—

KM# 97 PFENNIG

Copper **Ruler:** Friedrich August **Obverse:** Bust right **Reverse:** Arms divide date, JEVER above, value below

Date	Mintage	VG	F	VF	XF	Unc
1764	—	7.50	15.00	25.00	45.00	—

KM# 111 1/4 STUBER (Örtgen)

Copper **Ruler:** Friederike Auguste Sophie **Obverse:** Arms **Reverse:** Value above date

Date	Mintage	VG	F	VF	XF	Unc
1799	—	12.00	22.00	35.00	65.00	—

KM# 105 STUBER (10 Witten)

1.5400 g., 0.1870 Silver 0.0093 oz. ASW **Ruler:** Friederike Auguste Sophie **Obverse:** Arms **Reverse:** Value above date

Date	Mintage	VG	F	VF	XF	Unc
1798	—	12.00	22.50	37.50	70.00	—

KM# 106 2 STUBER (Schaf)
1.8500 g., 0.1870 Silver 0.0111 oz. ASW **Ruler:** Friederike Auguste Sophie **Obverse:** Arms **Reverse:** Value above date

Date	Mintage	VG	F	VF	XF	Unc
1798	—	22.00	45.00	65.00	110	—

KM# 98 GROTEN (4 Pfennig)
1.5200 g., 0.1600 Silver 0.0078 oz. ASW **Ruler:** Friedrich August **Obverse:** Bust right **Reverse:** Arms divide date, value below

Date	Mintage	VG	F	VF	XF	Unc
1764	—	12.50	25.00	40.00	75.00	—

KM# 107 GROTEN (4 Pfennig)
1.1500 g., 0.1870 Silver 0.0069 oz. ASW **Ruler:** Friederike Auguste Sophie **Obverse:** Arms **Reverse:** Value above date

Date	Mintage	VG	F	VF	XF	Unc
1798	—	17.50	32.50	55.00	110	—

KM# 108 3 GROTE
2.0800 g., 0.3120 Silver 0.0209 oz. ASW **Ruler:** Friederike Auguste Sophie **Obverse:** Arms **Reverse:** Value above date

Date	Mintage	VG	F	VF	XF	Unc
1798	—	20.00	40.00	70.00	130	—

KM# 99 4 GROTE (1/18 Thaler)
2.4100 g., 0.4000 Silver 0.0310 oz. ASW **Ruler:** Friedrich August **Obverse:** Bust right **Reverse:** Arms divide date; value below

Date	Mintage	VG	F	VF	XF	Unc
1764	—	15.00	30.00	50.00	100	—

KM# 100 4 GROTE (1/18 Thaler)
2.4100 g., 0.4000 Silver 0.0310 oz. ASW **Ruler:** Friedrich August **Obverse:** Bust right **Reverse:** Arms divide 16-P, date, 5-K, "JEVER" above, value below

Date	Mintage	VG	F	VF	XF	Unc
1764	—	25.00	50.00	90.00	150	—

KM# 101 12 GROTE (1/6 Thaler)
4.0200 g., 0.7200 Silver 0.0931 oz. ASW **Ruler:** Friedrich August **Obverse:** Bust right **Reverse:** Lion arms divide date, name and value below

Date	Mintage	VG	F	VF	XF	Unc
1764	—	25.00	45.00	70.00	145	—

KM# 102 12 GROTE (1/6 Thaler)
4.0200 g., 0.7200 Silver 0.0931 oz. ASW **Ruler:** Friedrich August **Reverse:** Arms divide 48-P, date, 15-K, "JEVER" above **Note:** C5a.

Date	Mintage	VG	F	VF	XF	Unc
1764	—	35.00	65.00	120	200	—

KM# 109 1/2 THALER
11.1400 g., 0.7500 Silver 0.2686 oz. ASW **Ruler:** Friederike Auguste Sophie **Obverse:** Crowned imperial eagle with lion arms on breast **Reverse:** Value, date within branches **Note:** Reichs 1/2 Thaler.

Date	Mintage	VG	F	VF	XF	Unc
1798	—	125	250	450	650	—

KM# 95 2/3 THALER (Gulden)
12.9600 g., 0.9000 Silver 0.3750 oz. ASW **Ruler:** Friedrich August **Obverse:** Armored bust right **Reverse:** Helmeted lion arms, Roman numeral date below

Date	Mintage	VG	F	VF	XF	Unc
1763	—	400	800	1,200	1,800	—

KM# 110 THALER
22.2700 g., 0.7500 Silver 0.5370 oz. ASW **Ruler:** Friederike Auguste Sophie **Obverse:** Crowned double-headed imperial eagle with lion arms on breast **Obv. Legend:** SUB • UMBRA • ALARUM • TUARUM • **Reverse:** Value, date within branches **Rev. Legend:** * FRIED • AVG • SOPH • PRINC • ANH • DYN • IEVER • ADMIN • **Note:** Reichs Thaler; Dav.#2363.

Date	Mintage	VG	F	VF	XF	Unc
1798	—	200	350	600	900	—

JULICH-BERG

The earliest counts of Jülich, located between Aachen and the Rhine (see Jülich, City), are known from the mid-9th century. Successive counts added territories to the nucleus of their domains and obtained the mint right in 1237. Count Wilhelm V (1328-62) attained the rank of Margrave in 1336 and was raised to that of Duke as Wilhelm I in 1356. His son, Wilhelm II, married Maria of Geldern, thus enlarging the duchy greatly. His younger brother married the heiress of Berg (along the east bank of the Rhine) and Ravensberg (in Westphalia). Geldern passed to the Egmont family in 1423 for lack of legitimate heirs in the Jülich line. Jülich itself fell to the younger branch of the family in Berg-Ravensberg in the same year. From this time on, the duchy was known as Jülich-Berg. Wilhelm IV died in 1511 without a male heir and his daughter, Maria, had married Duke Johann III of Cleve the year before. In 1521, the three duchies were united as Jülich-Cleve Berg (see). Following the great controversy after the death of Duke Johann Wilhelm in 1609, Jülich and Berg were occupied jointly by Brandenburg and Pfalz-Neuburg. The latter acquired Jülich-Berg outright in 1624, while Cleve, Mark and Ravensberg went to Brandenburg-Prussia. The dual duchy remained with the Wittelsbachs of the Palatinate until 1801, in which year France occupied it. In the peace settlement at the end of the Napoleonic Wars in 1815, Jülich-Berg was given to Prussia.

RULERS

Johann Wilhelm von Pfalz-Neuburg, 1679-1716
Karl Philipp von Pfalz-Neuburg, 1716-1742
Karl Theodor, 1742-1799

MINT MARKS

D - Dusseldorf

MINT OFFICIALS' INITIALS

Initials	Date	Name
AK	1748-66	Anton Kamphausen
CLS	1767-70	Carl Ludwig Selche
FM	1735-48	Friedrich Maul
FO	1736-37	Franz Offner
GB	1765-1803	Georg Barbier, die-cutter
HLO	1700-01	Heinrich Lorenz Odenthal
IAL	1707-09	Johann Adam Longerich
ICM, M, MARME	1737-51	Johann Konrad Marme, die-cutter in Mannheim
IH	1724-26	Johann Hittorff
L, LC	1706-14	Gabriel Leclerc, die-cutter
NP	1710-21	Nikolaus Pruck
PM	1771-84	Paul Maassen
PR	1785-1804	Peter Ruedesheim
RF	1728-35	Richard Fehr
S	1748-51	Anton Schafer, die-cutter in Mannheim

ARMS

Berg and Pfalz: Lion rampant left.

DUCHY

REGULAR COINAGE

KM# 135 HELLER
Billon **Ruler:** Johann Wilhelm von Pfalz-Neuburg **Obverse:** Lion rampant right in circle **Note:** Uniface

Date	Mintage	VG	F	VF	XF	Unc
ND(ca.1710)	—	10.00	20.00	40.00	75.00	—

KM# 172 HELLER
Billon **Ruler:** Karl Philipp von Pfalz-Neuburg **Obverse:** Lion rampant right in circle. H between hind legs. **Note:** Varieties exist.

Date	Mintage	VG	F	VF	XF	Unc
ND(ca.1725)	—	10.00	20.00	40.00	75.00	—

KM# 186 8 HELLER (1/2 Stüber)
Billon **Ruler:** Karl Philipp von Pfalz-Neuburg **Obverse:** Crowned rampant lion left in square shield, palm fronds at sides, large crown above **Reverse:** Value, VIII, date in circle **Rev. Legend:** GULICH.UND.BERG.LANDMUNZ **Note:** Varieties exist.

Date	Mintage	VG	F	VF	XF	Unc
1736 FO	—	10.00	20.00	35.00	60.00	—
1737 FO	—	10.00	20.00	35.00	60.00	—

KM# 200 1/4 STUBER
Copper **Ruler:** Karl Theodor **Obverse:** Crowned lion shield **Reverse:** Value, date

Date	Mintage	VG	F	VF	XF	Unc
1750 AK	—	5.00	10.00	25.00	50.00	—
1751 AK	—	5.00	10.00	25.00	50.00	—
1752 AK	—	5.00	10.00	25.00	50.00	—
1753 AK	—	5.00	10.00	25.00	50.00	—

KM# 205 1/4 STUBER
Copper **Ruler:** Karl Theodor **Obverse:** Floriated monogram **Reverse:** Value, date **Note:** Varieties exist.

Date	Mintage	VG	F	VF	XF	Unc
1765 AK	—	3.00	5.00	10.00	25.00	—
1766 AK	—	3.00	5.00	10.00	25.00	—
1767 CLS	—	3.00	5.00	10.00	25.00	—
1768 CLS	—	3.00	5.00	10.00	25.00	—
1769 CLS	—	3.00	5.00	10.00	25.00	—
1770 CLS	—	3.00	5.00	10.00	25.00	—
1771 PM	—	3.00	5.00	10.00	25.00	—
1772 PM	—	3.00	5.00	10.00	25.00	—
1773 PM	—	3.00	5.00	10.00	25.00	—
1774 PM	—	3.00	5.00	10.00	25.00	—
1775 PM	—	3.00	5.00	10.00	25.00	—
1776 PM	—	3.00	5.00	10.00	25.00	—
1777 PM	—	3.00	5.00	10.00	25.00	—
1778 PM	—	3.00	5.00	10.00	25.00	—
1779 PM	—	3.00	5.00	10.00	25.00	—

Date	Mintage	VG	F	VF	XF	Unc
1780 PM	—	3.00	5.00	10.00	25.00	—
1781 PM	—	3.00	5.00	10.00	25.00	—
1782 PM	—	3.00	5.00	10.00	25.00	—
1783 PM	—	3.00	5.00	10.00	25.00	—
1784 PM	—	3.00	5.00	10.00	25.00	—
1784/3 PM	—	3.00	5.00	10.00	25.00	—
1785 PR	—	3.00	5.00	10.00	25.00	—
1786 PR	—	3.00	5.00	10.00	25.00	—
1787 PR	—	3.00	5.00	10.00	25.00	—
1792 PR	—	3.00	5.00	10.00	25.00	—
1794 PR	—	3.00	5.00	10.00	25.00	—

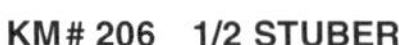

KM# 206 1/2 STUBER

Copper **Ruler:** Karl Theodor **Obverse:** Floriated monogram **Reverse:** Value, date

Date	Mintage	VG	F	VF	XF	Unc
1765 AK	—	3.50	6.00	12.00	28.00	—
1766 AK	—	3.50	6.00	12.00	28.00	—
1767 CLS	—	3.50	6.00	12.00	28.00	—
1768 CLS	—	3.50	6.00	12.00	28.00	—
1769 CLS	—	3.50	6.00	12.00	28.00	—
1770 CLS	—	3.50	6.00	12.00	28.00	—
1771 PM	—	3.50	6.00	12.00	28.00	—
1772 PM	—	3.50	6.00	12.00	28.00	—
1773 PM	—	3.50	6.00	12.00	28.00	—
1774 PM	—	3.50	6.00	12.00	28.00	—
1775 PM	—	3.50	6.00	12.00	28.00	—
1776 PM	—	3.50	6.00	12.00	28.00	—
1777 PM	—	3.50	6.00	12.00	28.00	—
1778 PM	—	3.50	6.00	12.00	28.00	—
1779 PM	—	3.50	6.00	12.00	28.00	—
1780 PM	—	3.50	6.00	12.00	28.00	—
1781 PM	—	3.50	6.00	12.00	28.00	—
1782 PM	—	3.50	6.00	12.00	28.00	—
1783 PM	—	3.50	6.00	12.00	28.00	—
1784 PR	—	3.50	6.00	12.00	28.00	—
1785 PR	—	3.50	6.00	12.00	28.00	—
1786 PR	—	3.50	6.00	12.00	28.00	—
1787 PR	—	3.50	6.00	12.00	28.00	—
1790 PR	—	3.50	6.00	12.00	28.00	—
1794 PR	—	3.50	6.00	12.00	28.00	—

KM# 187 STUBER

Billon **Ruler:** Karl Philipp von Pfalz-Neuburg **Obverse:** Crowned lion rampant left in square shield, palm fronds at sides, large crown above **Reverse:** Value, date **Rev. Legend:** I/STVBER **Note:** Varieties exist.

Date	Mintage	VG	F	VF	XF	Unc
1736 FO	—	7.00	12.00	25.00	55.00	—
1737 FO	—	7.00	12.00	25.00	55.00	—

KM# 191 STUBER

Billon **Ruler:** Karl Philipp von Pfalz-Neuburg **Obverse:** Crowned lion rampant left in circle **Obv. Legend:** GULICH.UND.BERG.LANDMUNZ **Reverse:** Value, date and initials **Rev. Legend:** I/STUBER **Note:** Varieties exist.

Date	Mintage	VG	F	VF	XF	Unc
1738 FM	—	8.00	15.00	30.00	65.00	—

KM# 207 STUBER

Billon **Ruler:** Karl Theodor **Obverse:** Crowned CT monogram **Reverse:** Value, date

Date	Mintage	VG	F	VF	XF	Unc
1765 AK	—	10.00	20.00	45.00	80.00	—

KM# 215 2 STUBER

Billon **Ruler:** Karl Theodor **Obverse:** Crowned arms **Reverse:** Value above date

Date	Mintage	VG	F	VF	XF	Unc
1792	—	7.00	15.00	30.00	60.00	—
1794	—	7.00	15.00	30.00	60.00	—

KM# 208 3 STUBER

Billon **Ruler:** Karl Theodor **Obverse:** CT monogram **Reverse:** Value, date

Date	Mintage	VG	F	VF	XF	Unc
1765 AK	—	20.00	35.00	65.00	100	—
1766 AK	—	20.00	35.00	65.00	100	—

KM# 216 3 STUBER

Billon **Ruler:** Karl Theodor **Obverse:** Crowned arms **Reverse:** Value above date

Date	Mintage	VG	F	VF	XF	Unc
1792 PR	—	6.00	12.00	28.00	55.00	—
1793 PR	—	6.00	12.00	28.00	55.00	—
1794 PR	—	6.00	12.00	28.00	55.00	—

KM# 209 12 STUBER

Silver **Ruler:** Karl Theodor **Obverse:** Bust right **Reverse:** Crowned large oval arms, value, date

Date	Mintage	VG	F	VF	XF	Unc
1765 GB	—	50.00	90.00	180	300	—

KM# 210 12 STUBER

Silver **Ruler:** Karl Theodor **Reverse:** Smaller arms

Date	Mintage	VG	F	VF	XF	Unc
1765 AK	—	45.00	85.00	160	275	—
1766 AK	—	45.00	85.00	160	275	—

KM# 192 8 ALBUS (6 Stüber)

Silver **Ruler:** Karl Philipp von Pfalz-Neuburg **Obverse:** Crowned complex round arms **Reverse:** Value, date within inner circle **Note:** Varieties exist.

Date	Mintage	VG	F	VF	XF	Unc
1738 FM	—	22.00	45.00	90.00	165	—

KM# 162 3 KREUZER (4 Fettmännchen)

Billon **Ruler:** Karl Philipp von Pfalz-Neuburg **Obverse:** Crowned lion rampant left in baroque frame divides date, large crown above **Reverse:** Value in palm wreath **Rev. Legend:** 3.KR/LAND/MUNTZ/4. FET **Note:** Varieties exist.

Date	Mintage	VG	F	VF	XF	Unc
1718 NP	—	40.00	80.00	165	250	—
1719 NP	—	40.00	80.00	165	250	—
1721 NP	—	40.00	80.00	165	250	—

KM# 163 12 KREUZER (16 Fettmännchen)

Silver **Ruler:** Karl Philipp von Pfalz-Neuburg **Obverse:** Crowned lion rampant left in ornate frame divides date, large crown above **Reverse:** Value in palm wreath **Rev. Legend:** 12.KR/LAND/MUNTZ/16. FET

Date	Mintage	VG	F	VF	XF	Unc
1718 NP	—	35.00	75.00	150	225	—

KM# 164 20 KREUZER (26 Fettmännchen)

Silver **Ruler:** Karl Philipp von Pfalz-Neuburg **Obverse:** Crowned lion arms divide date **Reverse:** Value within wreath **Note:** Varieties exist.

Date	Mintage	VG	F	VF	XF	Unc
1718 NP	—	30.00	65.00	125	180	—
1719 NP	—	30.00	65.00	125	180	—
1720 NP	—	30.00	65.00	125	180	—
1721 NP	—	30.00	65.00	125	180	—

KM# 171 20 KREUZER (26 Fettmännchen)

Silver **Ruler:** Karl Philipp von Pfalz-Neuburg **Obverse:** Crowned arms of Pfalz and Bavaria divide date **Reverse:** Value, legend in palm wreath **Rev. Legend:** 20.KR/CHVR/PFALZ/LAND/MVNZ **Note:** Varieties exist.

Date	Mintage	VG	F	VF	XF	Unc
1724 IH	—	12.00	30.00	60.00	100	—

KM# 173 20 KREUZER (26 Fettmännchen)

Silver **Ruler:** Karl Philipp von Pfalz-Neuburg **Obverse:** Crowned 3-fold arms divide date **Reverse:** In willow wreath

Date	Mintage	VG	F	VF	XF	Unc
1725 IH	—	12.00	30.00	60.00	100	—

KM# 174 20 KREUZER (26 Fettmännchen)

Silver **Ruler:** Karl Philipp von Pfalz-Neuburg **Obverse:** Crowned oval arms of Pfalz and Bavaria divide date **Reverse:** Value inscription in round baroque frame **Note:** Varieties exist.

Date	Mintage	VG	F	VF	XF	Unc
1726 IH	—	18.00	40.00	80.00	125	—
1728 RF	—	18.00	40.00	80.00	125	—

KM# 180 20 KREUZER (26 Fettmännchen)

Silver **Ruler:** Karl Philipp von Pfalz-Neuburg **Obverse:** Crowned oval ams of Pfalz and Bavaria **Reverse:** Value, date in round baroque frame **Rev. Legend:** 20.KR/CHVR/PFALZ/LANDMVNZ **Note:** Varieties exist.

Date	Mintage	VG	F	VF	XF	Unc
1731 RF	—	18.00	40.00	80.00	125	—
1732 RF	—	18.00	40.00	80.00	125	—
1733 RF	—	18.00	40.00	80.00	125	—
1734 RF	—	18.00	40.00	80.00	125	—
1735 FM	—	18.00	40.00	80.00	125	—
1736 FM	—	18.00	40.00	80.00	125	—

KM# 165 24 KREUZER (32 Fettmännchen)

Silver **Ruler:** Karl Philipp von Pfalz-Neuburg **Obverse:** Crowned rampant lion left in ornate frame divides date, large crown above

Date	Mintage	VG	F	VF	XF	Unc
1718 NP	—	60.00	125	225	350	—

KM# 154 1/24 THALER (1/16 Gulden)

Silver **Ruler:** Johann Wilhelm von Pfalz-Neuburg **Obverse:** Crowned imperial orb in shield divides mintmaster's initials **Reverse:** Value, date **Rev. Legend:** 24/EINEN/REICHS/THAL **Note:** Varieties exist.

Date	Mintage	VG	F	VF	XF	Unc
1712 NP	—	28.00	60.00	120	200	—
1713 NP	—	28.00	60.00	120	200	—

KM# 136.1 1/12 THALER (1/8 Gulden)

Silver **Ruler:** Johann Wilhelm von Pfalz-Neuburg **Obverse:** Crowned arms divide date **Reverse:** Value

Date	Mintage	VG	F	VF	XF	Unc
1710 NP	—	22.00	50.00	100	165	—
1713 NP	—	22.00	50.00	100	165	—

KM# 136.2 1/12 THALER (1/8 Gulden)
Silver **Ruler:** Johann Wilhelm von Pfalz-Neuburg **Obverse:** Baroque frame around oval arms **Reverse:** Value

Date	Mintage	VG	F	VF	XF	Unc
1714 NP	—	35.00	75.00	150	245	—

KM# 108 1/6 THALER (1/4 Gulden)
Silver **Ruler:** Johann Wilhelm von Pfalz-Neuburg **Obverse:** Bust right **Reverse:** Crowned oval 9-fold arms with central shield, value "1/6" near bottom, date in legend

Date	Mintage	VG	F	VF	XF	Unc
1707 IAL	—	60.00	100	175	275	—

KM# 109 1/6 THALER (1/4 Gulden)
Silver **Ruler:** Johann Wilhelm von Pfalz-Neuburg **Obverse:** Head right **Reverse:** Large crown above 4 small oval arms in cruciform, smaller oval arms in center, value (1/6) in lower part of bottom shield, date in legend

Date	Mintage	VG	F	VF	XF	Unc
1707 IAL	—	28.00	60.00	120	200	—

KM# 110 1/6 THALER (1/4 Gulden)
Silver **Ruler:** Johann Wilhelm von Pfalz-Neuburg **Reverse:** 9 small oval arms in circle around small central shield, crown above, value 1/6 below, date in legend

Date	Mintage	VG	F	VF	XF	Unc
1707 IAL	—	35.00	75.00	150	250	—

KM# 118 1/6 THALER (1/4 Gulden)
Silver **Ruler:** Johann Wilhelm von Pfalz-Neuburg **Reverse:** 2 ornate shields of arms separated by 1/6 in oval, large crown above, third shield below with imperial orb, date in chronogram in legend

Date	Mintage	VG	F	VF	XF	Unc
1708 IAL	—	28.00	60.00	120	200	—

KM# 125 1/6 THALER (1/4 Gulden)
Silver **Ruler:** Johann Wilhelm von Pfalz-Neuburg **Obverse:** Bust right **Reverse:** Date in legend

Date	Mintage	VG	F	VF	XF	Unc
1709	—	22.00	50.00	100	175	—
1709 IAL	—	28.00	60.00	120	200	—

KM# 137 1/6 THALER (1/4 Gulden)
Silver **Ruler:** Johann Wilhelm von Pfalz-Neuburg **Obverse:** Head right **Reverse:** Shield with imperial orb smaller and between 2 larger shields

Date	Mintage	VG	F	VF	XF	Unc
1710	—	22.00	50.00	100	175	—

KM# 138 1/6 THALER (1/4 Gulden)
Silver **Ruler:** Johann Wilhelm von Pfalz-Neuburg **Reverse:** Small shield in center blank

Date	Mintage	VG	F	VF	XF	Unc
1710	—	30.00	65.00	140	225	—

KM# 139 1/6 THALER (1/4 Gulden)
Silver **Ruler:** Johann Wilhelm von Pfalz-Neuburg **Obverse:** Head right **Reverse:** Imperial orb in oval baroque frame, date divided at top, large crown above, value (1/6) in oval below. **Note:** Varieties exist.

Date	Mintage	VG	F	VF	XF	Unc
1710	—	20.00	45.00	90.00	150	—
1710 NP	—	20.00	40.00	75.00	140	—
1711 NP	—	20.00	40.00	75.00	140	—
1712 NP	—	20.00	40.00	75.00	140	—
1714 NP	—	20.00	40.00	75.00	140	—
1715 NP	—	20.00	40.00	75.00	140	—

KM# 142 1/6 THALER (1/4 Gulden)
Silver **Ruler:** Johann Wilhelm von Pfalz-Neuburg **Obverse:** Head right **Reverse:** Double-headed eagle with two shields on breast **Note:** Vicariat issue.

Date	Mintage	VG	F	VF	XF	Unc
1711 NP	—	22.00	50.00	100	175	—

KM# 157 1/6 THALER (1/4 Gulden)
Silver **Ruler:** Johann Wilhelm von Pfalz-Neuburg **Subject:** Death of Johann Wilhelm II **Obverse:** Bust right **Reverse:** 7-line inscription with date

Date	Mintage	VG	F	VF	XF	Unc
1716	—	35.00	75.00	150	250	—

KM# 159 1/6 THALER (1/4 Gulden)
Silver **Ruler:** Karl Philipp von Pfalz-Neuburg **Obverse:** Bust and titles of Karl Philipp **Reverse:** Imperial orb in oval baroque frame, date divided at top, large crown above, value "1/6" in oval below

Date	Mintage	VG	F	VF	XF	Unc
1717 NP	—	60.00	125	225	375	—

KM# 166 1/6 THALER (1/4 Gulden)
Silver **Ruler:** Karl Philipp von Pfalz-Neuburg **Obverse:** Bust right **Reverse:** Large crown above ornate CP monogram, date divided at lower left and right, 1/6 - NP divided at bottom

Date	Mintage	VG	F	VF	XF	Unc
1718 NP	—	100	250	550	875	—

KM# 111 1/3 THALER (1/2 Gulden)
Silver **Ruler:** Johann Wilhelm von Pfalz-Neuburg

Date	Mintage	VG	F	VF	XF	Unc
1707 IAL	—	600	1,000	1,850	2,500	—

KM# 155 1/3 THALER (1/2 Gulden)
Silver **Ruler:** Johann Wilhelm von Pfalz-Neuburg **Reverse:** 2 ornate shields of arms separted by 1/3 in oval, large crown above, 3rd shield below with imperial orb, date in legend

Date	Mintage	VG	F	VF	XF	Unc
1712 L	—	100	225	400	750	—

KM# 107 2/3 THALER (Gulden)
Silver **Ruler:** Johann Wilhelm von Pfalz-Neuburg **Obverse:** Draped bust right **Reverse:** Round arms

Date	Mintage	VG	F	VF	XF	Unc
1701 HLO	—	600	900	1,250	1,800	—

KM# 112 2/3 THALER (Gulden)
Silver **Ruler:** Johann Wilhelm von Pfalz-Neuburg **Reverse:** Large crown above 4 small oval arms in cruciform, smaller oval arms in center, value 2/3 in lower part of bottom shield, date in legend

Date	Mintage	VG	F	VF	XF	Unc
1707 IAL	—	800	1,350	1,750	2,250	—

KM# 119 2/3 THALER (Gulden)
Silver **Ruler:** Johann Wilhelm von Pfalz-Neuburg **Reverse:** 2 ornate shields of arms separated by 2/3 in oval, large crown above, 3rd shield below with imperial orb, date in chronogram in legend

Date	Mintage	VG	F	VF	XF	Unc
1708 IAL	—	800	1,350	1,750	2,250	—

KM# 126 2/3 THALER (Gulden)
Silver **Ruler:** Johann Wilhelm von Pfalz-Neuburg **Obverse:** Head right **Reverse:** Date in legend

Date	Mintage	VG	F	VF	XF	Unc
1709	—	650	1,000	1,450	2,000	—

KM# 127 2/3 THALER (Gulden)
Silver **Ruler:** Johann Wilhelm von Pfalz-Neuburg **Obverse:** Bust right **Reverse:** Shield with imperial orb smaller

Date	Mintage	VG	F	VF	XF	Unc
1709	—	650	1,000	1,450	2,000	—
1710	—	—	—	—	—	—

Note: Reported, not confirmed

KM# 143 2/3 THALER (Gulden)
Silver **Ruler:** Johann Wilhelm von Pfalz-Neuburg **Obverse:** Head right **Reverse:** Double-headed eagle with two crowned shields on breast, value above tail **Note:** Vicariat issue.

Date	Mintage	VG	F	VF	XF	Unc
1711 NP	—	675	1,000	1,850	2,650	—

KM# 156 2/3 THALER (Gulden)
Silver **Ruler:** Johann Wilhelm von Pfalz-Neuburg **Obverse:** Bust right **Reverse:** 2 ornate shields of arms separated by 1/3 in oval, large crown above, 3rd shield below with imperial orb, date in legend

Date	Mintage	VG	F	VF	XF	Unc
1712 L	—	650	1,000	1,450	2,000	—

KM# 158 2/3 THALER (Gulden)
Silver **Ruler:** Johann Wilhelm von Pfalz-Neuburg **Subject:** Death of Johann Wilhelm II **Obverse:** Bust right **Reverse:** 7-line inscription with date

Date	Mintage	VG	F	VF	XF	Unc
1716	—	450	750	1,000	1,550	—

KM# 188 2/3 THALER (Gulden)
Silver **Ruler:** Karl Philipp von Pfalz-Neuburg **Obverse:** Bust right **Reverse:** Similar to obverse of KM#193 but value "2/3" in oval below arms dividing date and mintmaster's initials

Date	Mintage	VG	F	VF	XF	Unc
1737 M/FO	—	800	1,250	2,250	3,500	—

KM# 189 2/3 THALER (Gulden)
Silver **Ruler:** Karl Philipp von Pfalz-Neuburg **Obverse:** Large crowned ornate CP monogram **Reverse:** Date divided below arms, value divides FEIN - SILB and mintmaster's initials

Date	Mintage	VG	F	VF	XF	Unc
1737 FO	—	800	1,250	2,250	3,500	—

KM# 190 2/3 THALER (Gulden)
Silver **Ruler:** Karl Philipp von Pfalz-Neuburg **Reverse:** Large rampant lion of Berg left, date divided above, M between hind legs, value "2/3" in oval below divides FEIN - SILB and mintmaster's initials

Date	Mintage	VG	F	VF	XF	Unc
1737 M/FO Rare	—	—	—	—	—	—

KM# 193 2/3 THALER (Gulden)
Silver **Ruler:** Karl Philipp von Pfalz-Neuburg **Obverse:** Crown above 3 shields, Order chain below **Reverse:** Value, date within inner circle

Date	Mintage	VG	F	VF	XF	Unc
1738 FM	—	400	750	1,350	2,000	—

KM# 128 THALER
Silver **Ruler:** Johann Wilhelm von Pfalz-Neuburg **Obverse:** Bust right **Reverse:** 3 Coats of arms crowned **Note:** Dav. #2364.

Date	Mintage	VG	F	VF	XF	Unc
1709	—	1,000	1,650	2,600	3,800	—

KM# 144 THALER
Silver **Ruler:** Johann Wilhelm von Pfalz-Neuburg **Obverse:** Head right **Obv. Legend:** D • G • IOH: WILH: C • P • R • S • - R • I • ARCHID: EL: EIUSQ: **Reverse:** Double eagle with 2 crowned arms **Rev. Legend:** B • I • C & M • D • PR • M • C • V - S • M • & R • D • I • R • 1709 **Note:** Dav. #2365.

Date	Mintage	VG	F	VF	XF	Unc
1711 NP	—	800	1,350	2,250	3,750	—

KM# 145 THALER
Silver **Ruler:** Johann Wilhelm von Pfalz-Neuburg **Obverse:** LC below head **Note:** Dav. #2365A.

Date	Mintage	VG	F	VF	XF	Unc
1711 LC//NP	—	800	1,350	2,250	3,750	—

KM# 211 THALER
Silver **Ruler:** Karl Theodor **Obverse:** Draped bust **Reverse:** 3 shields **Note:** Convention Thaler. Dav. #2366.

Date	Mintage	F	VF	XF	Unc
1765 AK	—	125	250	450	950

KM# 212 THALER
Silver **Ruler:** Karl Theodor **Reverse:** 3 coats of arms crowned, supported by lion **Note:** Dav. #2367.

Date	Mintage	F	VF	XF	Unc
1767 CLS	—	100	200	375	850

KM# 213 THALER
Silver **Ruler:** Karl Theodor **Obverse:** Bust right **Obv. Legend:** CAR • THEODOR • D: G • C • P • R • S • R • I • A • T • & • EL • **Reverse:** 3 Shields of arms **Rev. Legend:** 10 EINE FEINE MARCK **Note:** Dav. #2368.

Date	Mintage	F	VF	XF	Unc
1771 PM	—	85.00	175	325	750

KM# 214 THALER
Silver **Ruler:** Karl Theodor **Obverse:** Head right **Obv. Legend:** CAR • THEODOR • D: G • C • P • R • S • R • I • A • T • & • EL • **Reverse:** Crowned shield in sprays on ornate base separate date **Rev. Legend:** 10 EINE • FEI - NE • MARCK **Note:** Dav. #2369.

Date	Mintage	F	VF	XF	Unc
1772 PM	—	85.00	175	325	750

KM# 217 THALER
Silver **Ruler:** Karl Theodor **Obverse:** Head right **Obv. Legend:** CAR • THEODOR • D: G • C • P • R • S • R • I • A • T • & • EL • **Reverse:** Designs altered slightly **Rev. Legend:** 10 EINE • FEI - NE • MARCK **Note:** Dav. #2370. Varieties exist.

Date	Mintage	F	VF	XF	Unc
1774 PM	—	100	200	350	800

KM# 167 1/2 GOLDGULDEN
1.7500 g., 0.9860 Gold 0.0555 oz. AGW **Ruler:** Karl Philipp von Pfalz-Neuburg **Obverse:** Bust right, date in legend **Reverse:** Crowned large ornate CP monogram **Rev. Legend:** EIN HALB GOLT - GVLDEN

Date	Mintage	F	VF	XF	Unc
1718 Rare	—	—	—	—	—

KM# 168 GOLDGULDEN
3.5000 g., 0.9860 Gold 0.1109 oz. AGW **Ruler:** Karl Philipp von Pfalz-Neuburg **Obverse:** Bust right **Reverse:** Crowned CP monogram

Date	Mintage	VG	F	VF	XF	Unc
1718	—	200	500	1,000	1,700	—

KM# 182 1/2 CAROLIN
4.8500 g., 0.7700 Gold 0.1201 oz. AGW **Ruler:** Karl Philipp von Pfalz-Neuburg **Obverse:** Bust right, date below **Reverse:** Small round 9-fold arms with central shield, 4 sets of crowned double initials, 1 correct and 1 backwards, 2 C's at top and bottom, 2 P's at left and right **Note:** Varieties exist.

Date	Mintage	F	VF	XF	Unc
1733	—	475	700	1,100	1,650

KM# 183 1/2 CAROLIN
4.8500 g., 0.7700 Gold 0.1201 oz. AGW **Ruler:** Karl Philipp von Pfalz-Neuburg **Reverse:** Arms larger and oval

Date	Mintage	F	VF	XF	Unc
1733	—	475	700	1,100	1,650

KM# 184 1/2 CAROLIN
4.8500 g., 0.7700 Gold 0.1201 oz. AGW **Ruler:** Karl Philipp von Pfalz-Neuburg **Reverse:** Arms in square shield

Date	Mintage	F	VF	XF	Unc
1733	—	475	700	1,100	1,650

KM# 181 CAROLIN
9.7000 g., 0.7700 Gold 0.2401 oz. AGW **Ruler:** Karl Philipp von Pfalz-Neuburg **Obverse:** Head right **Reverse:** 5 shields of arms

Date	Mintage	VG	F	VF	XF	Unc
1732	—	350	700	1,350	2,500	—

KM# 185 CAROLIN
9.7000 g., 0.7700 Gold 0.2401 oz. AGW **Ruler:** Karl Philipp von Pfalz-Neuburg **Reverse:** Small round 9-fold arms with central shield, 4 sets of crowned double initials, 1 correct and 1 backwards, 2 C's at top and bottom, 2 P's at left and right **Note:** Varieties exist.

Date	Mintage	F	VF	XF	Unc
1733	—	300	650	1,200	2,000

TRADE COINAGE

KM# 140 1/4 DUCAT
0.8750 g., 0.9860 Gold 0.0277 oz. AGW **Ruler:** Johann Wilhelm von Pfalz-Neuburg **Obverse:** Bust right **Reverse:** Imperial orb in crowned shield divides date

Date	Mintage	F	VF	XF	Unc
1710	—	150	300	600	1,000

KM# 146 1/4 DUCAT
0.8750 g., 0.9860 Gold 0.0277 oz. AGW **Ruler:** Johann Wilhelm von Pfalz-Neuburg **Reverse:** Imperial orb in oval baroque frame, date divided without indication of value, large crown above **Rev. Legend:** REDIT.VNDE.VENIT.Ao.1708

Date	Mintage	F	VF	XF	Unc
1711	—	275	450	850	1,350

KM# 113 DUCAT
3.5000 g., 0.9860 Gold 0.1109 oz. AGW **Ruler:** Johann Wilhelm von Pfalz-Neuburg **Reverse:** 9 small oval arms in circle around small central shield, crown above, date in Roman numerals **Rev. Legend:** HOC.BELLONAE - STIPENDIVM

Date	Mintage	VG	F	VF	XF	Unc
1707 IAL	—	850	1,800	3,000	4,500	—

KM# 114 DUCAT
3.5000 g., 0.9860 Gold 0.1109 oz. AGW **Ruler:** Johann Wilhelm von Pfalz-Neuburg **Reverse:** Crowned round 9-fold arms with central shield, legend in Roman numerals

Date	Mintage	VG	F	VF	XF	Unc
1707 IAL	—	850	1,800	3,000	4,500	—

KM# 115 DUCAT
3.5000 g., 0.9860 Gold 0.1109 oz. AGW **Ruler:** Johann Wilhelm von Pfalz-Neuburg **Reverse:** 9 small oval arms in circle around small central shield, crown above **Rev. Legend:** MON.NOV.AVR - PALAT

Date	Mintage	VG	F	VF	XF	Unc
1707 IAL	—	850	1,800	3,000	4,500	—

KM# 120 DUCAT
3.5000 g., 0.9860 Gold 0.1109 oz. AGW **Ruler:** Johann Wilhelm von Pfalz-Neuburg **Reverse:** Crown above imperial orb in shield, date in legend

Date	Mintage	VG	F	VF	XF	Unc
1708 IAL	—	650	1,000	2,000	3,250	—

KM# 121 DUCAT
3.5000 g., 0.9860 Gold 0.1109 oz. AGW **Ruler:** Johann Wilhelm von Pfalz-Neuburg **Reverse:** 9 small oval arms in circle around small central shield, crown above, date divided at bottom **Rev. Legend:** B.I.C.&M..

Date	Mintage	VG	F	VF	XF	Unc
1708 IAL	—	850	1,800	3,000	4,500	—

KM# 122 DUCAT
3.5000 g., 0.9860 Gold 0.1109 oz. AGW **Ruler:** Johann Wilhelm von Pfalz-Neuburg **Reverse:** 2 ornate shields of arms, large crown above, 3rd shield below with imperial orb, date in chronogram

Date	Mintage	VG	F	VF	XF	Unc
1708 IAL	—	650	1,000	2,000	3,250	—

KM# 123 DUCAT
3.5000 g., 0.9860 Gold 0.1109 oz. AGW **Ruler:** Johann Wilhelm von Pfalz-Neuburg **Reverse:** Date in chronogram in legend

Date	Mintage	VG	F	VF	XF	Unc
1708	—	800	1,350	2,400	4,000	—

KM# 129 DUCAT
3.5000 g., 0.9860 Gold 0.1109 oz. AGW **Ruler:** Johann Wilhelm von Pfalz-Neuburg **Reverse:** Date **Rev. Legend:** B.I.C.&M..

Date	Mintage	VG	F	VF	XF	Unc
1709	—	350	750	1,350	1,800	—

KM# 141 DUCAT
3.5000 g., 0.9860 Gold 0.1109 oz. AGW **Ruler:** Johann Wilhelm von Pfalz-Neuburg **Reverse:** Imperial orb in baroque frame divides date, large crown above **Rev. Legend:** REDIT.VNDE.VENIT.23.IVN.1708 **Note:** Varieties exist.

Date	Mintage	VG	F	VF	XF	Unc
1710	—	800	1,350	2,400	4,000	—

KM# 147 DUCAT
3.5000 g., 0.9860 Gold 0.1109 oz. AGW **Ruler:** Johann Wilhelm von Pfalz-Neuburg **Reverse:** 2 ornate shields of arms, smaller shield with imperial orb between large crown above

Date	Mintage	VG	F	VF	XF	Unc
1711	—	400	850	1,600	2,500	—

KM# 148 DUCAT
3.5000 g., 0.9860 Gold 0.1109 oz. AGW **Ruler:** Johann Wilhelm von Pfalz-Neuburg **Obverse:** Head right **Reverse:** Double eagle with 2 crowned arms

Date	Mintage	VG	F	VF	XF	Unc
1711 NP	—	400	850	1,600	2,500	—

Note: Struck with 1 Thaler dies, KM#144

KM# 170 DUCAT
3.5000 g., 0.9860 Gold 0.1109 oz. AGW **Ruler:** Karl Philipp von Pfalz-Neuburg **Obverse:** Bust right **Reverse:** Crowned CP monogram

Date	Mintage	VG	F	VF	XF	Unc
1720 NP	—	225	550	1,000	1,800	—

KM# 195 DUCAT
3.5000 g., 0.9860 Gold 0.1109 oz. AGW **Ruler:** Karl Theodor **Obverse:** Bust right **Reverse:** Crowned ornate arms in baroque frame, date

Date	Mintage	VG	F	VF	XF	Unc
1749 AK//ICM	—	350	750	1,750	2,500	—
1750 AK//MARME	—	350	750	1,750	2,500	—
1750 AK//S	—	350	750	1,750	2,500	—
1751 AK	—	350	750	1,750	2,500	—

KM# 201 DUCAT
3.5000 g., 0.9860 Gold 0.1109 oz. AGW **Ruler:** Karl Theodor **Obverse:** Bust right **Reverse:** Crowned Order of St. Hubert, date

Date	Mintage	VG	F	VF	XF	Unc
1750 AK	—	250	500	1,100	1,800	—

KM# 116 2 DUCAT
7.0000 g., 0.9860 Gold 0.2219 oz. AGW **Ruler:** Johann Wilhelm von Pfalz-Neuburg **Reverse:** 9 small oval arms in circle around small central shield, crown above, date in Roman numerals **Rev. Legend:** HOC.BELLONAE-STIPENDIVM

Date	Mintage	VG	F	VF	XF	Unc
1707 IAL	—	1,750	3,250	6,000	9,000	—

KM# 117 2 DUCAT
7.0000 g., 0.9860 Gold 0.2219 oz. AGW **Ruler:** Johann Wilhelm von Pfalz-Neuburg **Reverse:** Date **Rev. Legend:** MON.NOV.AVR - PALAT

Date	Mintage	VG	F	VF	XF	Unc
1707 IAL	—	1,750	3,250	6,000	9,000	—

KM# 124 2 DUCAT
7.0000 g., 0.9860 Gold 0.2219 oz. AGW **Ruler:** Johann Wilhelm von Pfalz-Neuburg **Reverse:** 2 ornate shields of arms, large crown above, 3rd shield below with imperial orb, date in chronogram

Date	Mintage	VG	F	VF	XF	Unc
1708 Rare	—	—	—	—	—	—

KM# 130 2 DUCAT
7.0000 g., 0.9860 Gold 0.2219 oz. AGW **Ruler:** Johann Wilhelm von Pfalz-Neuburg **Reverse:** Date **Rev. Legend:** B.I.C.&M

Date	Mintage	VG	F	VF	XF	Unc
1709	—	950	1,800	3,200	6,500	—

KM# 149 2 DUCAT
7.0000 g., 0.9860 Gold 0.2219 oz. AGW **Ruler:** Johann Wilhelm von Pfalz-Neuburg **Reverse:** 2 ornate shields of arms, smaller shield with imperial orb between, large crown above

Date	Mintage	VG	F	VF	XF	Unc
1711	—	950	1,800	3,200	6,500	—

KM# 150 2 DUCAT
7.0000 g., 0.9860 Gold 0.2219 oz. AGW **Ruler:** Johann Wilhelm von Pfalz-Neuburg **Obverse:** Head right **Reverse:** Double eagle with 2 crowned arms **Note:** Struck with 1 Thaler dies, KM#144.

Date	Mintage	VG	F	VF	XF	Unc
1711 NP	—	950	1,800	3,200	6,500	—

KM# 202 2 DUCAT
7.0000 g., 0.9860 Gold 0.2219 oz. AGW **Ruler:** Karl Theodor **Obverse:** Draped bust right **Reverse:** 3 Coats of arms within crowned shield

Date	Mintage	VG	F	VF	XF	Unc
1750 AK//SD	—	400	1,000	2,000	3,500	—

KM# 151 3 DUCAT
10.5000 g., 0.9860 Gold 0.3328 oz. AGW **Ruler:** Johann Wilhelm von Pfalz-Neuburg **Obverse:** Head right **Reverse:** Double eagle with 2 crowned arms, thin flan **Note:** Struck with 1 Thaler dies, KM#144.

Date	Mintage	VG	F	VF	XF	Unc
1711 NP Rare	—	—	—	—	—	—

KM# 152 3 DUCAT
10.5000 g., 0.9860 Gold 0.3328 oz. AGW **Ruler:** Johann Wilhelm von Pfalz-Neuburg **Note:** Thick flan.

Date	Mintage	VG	F	VF	XF	Unc
1711 NP Rare	—	—	—	—	—	—

KM# 153 5 DUCAT
17.5000 g., 0.9860 Gold 0.5547 oz. AGW **Ruler:** Johann Wilhelm von Pfalz-Neuburg

Date	Mintage	VG	F	VF	XF	Unc
1711 LC//NP Rare	—	—	—	—	—	—

KM# 160 5 DUCAT
17.5000 g., 0.9860 Gold 0.5547 oz. AGW **Ruler:** Karl Philipp von Pfalz-Neuburg **Obverse:** Date in legend

Date	Mintage	VG	F	VF	XF	Unc
1717	—	2,500	4,250	8,000	13,500	—

KM# A132 10 DUCAT
35.0000 g., 0.9860 Gold 1.1095 oz. AGW **Ruler:** Johann Wilhelm von Pfalz-Neuburg **Obverse:** Bust right **Reverse:** 3 coats of arms crowned **Note:** Struck with 1 Thaler dies, KM#128.

Date	Mintage	VG	F	VF	XF	Unc
1709 Rare	—	—	—	—	—	—

KM# A162 10 DUCAT
35.0000 g., 0.9860 Gold 1.1095 oz. AGW **Ruler:** Johann Wilhelm von Pfalz-Neuburg **Obverse:** LC below head **Note:** Struck with 1 Thaler dies, KM#145.

Date	Mintage	VG	F	VF	XF	Unc
1711 LC//NP Rare	—	—	—	—	—	—

KM# 161 10 DUCAT
35.0000 g., 0.9860 Gold 1.1095 oz. AGW **Ruler:** Johann Wilhelm von Pfalz-Neuburg **Obverse:** Head right **Reverse:** Double eagle with 2 crowned arms **Note:** Struck with 1 Thaler dies, KM#144.

Date	Mintage	VG	F	VF	XF	Unc
1717 NP Rare	—	—	—	—	—	—

PATTERNS

Including off metal strikes

KM#	Date	Mintage	Identification	Mkt Val
Pn3	1708	—	2 Ducat. Silver.	1,000
Pn4	1709	—	2 Ducat. Silver. 1/6 Thaler flan, KM#130.	250
Pn6	1710	—	1/4 Ducat. Silver. KM#140.	175
Pn8	1716	—	1/6 Thaler. Gold. Weight of 1 Ducat, KM#157.	2,500
Pn9	1716	—	1/6 Thaler. Gold. Weight of 4 Ducat, KM#157.	6,000
Pn10	1736	—	Stuber. Gold. KM#187.	—
Pn11	1737	—	Stuber. Gold. KM#187.	—
Pn12	1750	—	1/4 Stuber. Gold. KM#200.	100
Pn13	1783	—	1/2 Stuber. Gold. KM#206.	—
Pn14	1793	—	1/2 Stuber. Gold. KM#206.	—
Pn15	1793	—	3 Stuber. Silver. KM#216.	—
Pn16	1794	—	1/2 Stuber. Tin. KM#216.	—

KAUFBEUREN

(Kaufburen)

As a free city in Bavaria 55 miles southwest of Munich Kaufbeuren was established c. 842. It was an imperial city from 1286 to 1803 when it passed to Bavaria, and struck a local coinage from about 1540 until 1748.

ARMS

Divided vertically, half of imperial eagle on left, right side divided diagonally from upper left to lower right by band, a 6-pointed star above and below.

FREE CITY

TRADE COINAGE

KM# 10 DUCAT
3.5000 g., 0.9860 Gold 0.1109 oz. AGW **Subject:** Bicentennial of Augsburg Confession **Obverse:** Seated figure at left, standing figure at right, kneeling figures between **Reverse:** 5-line legend **Note:** FR. #1421.

Date	Mintage	Good	VG	F	VF	XF
1730	—	—	600	1,250	2,500	4,000

PATTERNS

Including off metal strikes

KM#	Date	Mintage	Identification	Mkt Val
Pn1	1730	—	Ducat. Silver. KM#10.	150

KEMPTEN

ABBEY

The site of Kempten, 81 miles southwest of Munich, predates the Roman town known as Cambodunum. A monastery was founded there as early as 752 from St. Gall (in present-day Switzerland), but the famous abbey was refounded in 773/4 by Hildegard, wife of Charlemagne. A town grew up around the abbey and was the site of an imperial mint from the early 13th century. In 1289 Kempten became a free imperial city and in 1348 the abbot became a prince of the empire. The city obtained the right to mint coins in 1510 and struck a series from 1511 until 1730. The abbots struck coins in the 12th and 13th centuries, then again from 1572 infrequently until 1748. In 1803 the abbey was secularized and, together with the city, was joined to Bavaria.

RULERS

Ruprecht von Bodnau (Bodman), 1678-1728
Anselm Reichlin von Meldegg, 1728-1747
Engelbert von Surgenstein, 1747-1760
Honorius Roth von Schreckenstein, 1760-1785
Ruprecht von Neuenstein, 1785-1793
Castolus Reichlin von Meldegg, 1793-1802

MINT OFFICIALS' INITIALS

Initials	Date	Name
CM	1714-41	Christian Ernst Müller, die-cutter
MW	?	?
(h) – 2 horseshoes		Mintmasters at Augsburg

ARMS

Facing bust of St. Hildegard, usually in shield

REGULAR COINAGE

KM# 35 THALER
Silver **Ruler:** Anselm Reichlin **Obverse:** Bust right, CM below **Obv. Legend:** ANSELM • S • R • I • PR • ABB • CAMPID • A • R • IMP cis ARCHIMAR **Reverse:** Hand out of cloud guiding horse, 2 shields dividing date below **Rev. Legend:** MODERATIONE ET INDUSTRIA **Note:** Dav. #2371.

Date	Mintage	VG	F	VF	XF	Unc
1729 CM Rare	—	—	—	—	—	—

KM# 40 THALER

Silver **Ruler:** Engelbert **Obverse:** Bust right, MW below **Obv. Legend:** ENGELBERT • D • G • S • R • I • P • AB • CAM • A • R • IMP • ARCHIMAR • **Reverse:** Female with cross and arms before altar, Roman numeral date below **Rev. Legend:** PEITATE ET - ÆQUITATE, below; .MDCCXXXXVIII. **Note:** Dav. #2372.

Date	Mintage	VG	F	VF	XF	Unc
1748 MW	—	400	750	1,250	2,250	—

TRADE COINAGE

KM# 36 DUCAT

3.5000 g., 0.9860 Gold 0.1109 oz. AGW **Ruler:** Anselm Reichlin **Obverse:** Bust right **Reverse:** Arms with horse **Note:** Fr. #1424.

Date	Mintage	VG	F	VF	XF	Unc
1729	—	1,450	2,750	5,000	8,000	—

KM# 41 DUCAT

3.5000 g., 0.9860 Gold 0.1109 oz. AGW **Ruler:** Engelbert **Obverse:** Bust right **Reverse:** Arms in inner circle **Note:** Fr. #1426.

Date	Mintage	VG	F	VF	XF	Unc
1748 MW/ /H	—	600	1,200	2,500	4,500	—

KM# 42 2 DUCAT

7.0000 g., 0.9860 Gold 0.2219 oz. AGW **Ruler:** Engelbert **Obverse:** Bust right **Reverse:** Arms in inner circle **Note:** Fr. #1425.

Date	Mintage	VG	F	VF	XF	Unc
1748	—	1,500	2,850	5,500	9,000	—

FREE CITY

REGULAR COINAGE

KM# 75 GROSCHEN

Silver **Subject:** 200th Anniversary of Reformation **Obverse:** Inscription within circle **Reverse:** Winged figure with banner

Date	Mintage	VG	F	VF	XF	Unc
1717	—	15.00	30.00	50.00	85.00	—

KM# 76 2 GROSCHEN

Silver **Subject:** 200th Anniversary of Reformation **Obverse:** Inscription **Reverse:** Winged figure with banner

Date	Mintage	VG	F	VF	XF	Unc
1717	—	25.00	50.00	90.00	150	—

TRADE COINAGE

KM# 80 DUCAT

3.5000 g., 0.9860 Gold 0.1109 oz. AGW **Subject:** Bicentennial of the Augsburg Confession **Obverse:** Standing pillar **Reverse:** Castle with sun above **Note:** Fr. #1429.

Date	Mintage	VG	F	VF	XF	Unc
1730	—	500	1,000	2,000	3,500	—

PATTERNS

Including off metal strikes

KM#	Date	Mintage	Identification	Mkt Val
Pn3	1717	—	Ducat. Gold. Fr.1428; prev. KM#Pn1.	2,000
Pn4	1730	—	Ducat. Silver. KM#80; prev. KM#Pn2.	200

KIRCHBERG

Kirchberg, the oldest town in the Hunsruck Mountains is located about 30 miles northeast of Trier. At first it belonged to the Counts of Sponheim, but at their extinction passed into joint possession of Pfalz and Baden and in the 18th century wholly to Baden.

RULER

Georg Friedrich of Sayn-Wittgenstein, 1695-1749

PRINCIPALITY

REGULAR COINAGE

KM# 5 THALER

Silver **Ruler:** Georg Friedrich of Sayn-Wittgenstein **Subject:** Death of Georg Friedrich **Obverse:** Bust right, 4-line inscription below **Reverse:** Sun above mining scene, inscription below **Note:** Dav. #2373.

Date	Mintage	Good	VG	F	VF	XF
ND(1749)	—	—	1,500	2,500	4,500	6,500

KONIGSEGG-ROTHENFELS

(Königseck)

A Swabian family that came into prominence c.1200, the house was divided in 1622 and the head of each branch was made a count in 1665. This coin issue was the only one for this particular house. Königsegg was mediatized to Bavaria shortly after 1800.

RULERS

Franz Hugo, 1736-1771
Karl Ferdinand, 1736-1759 and
Christian Moritz Eugen, 1736-1778 and
Maximilian Friedrich, 1736-1784

MINTMASTERS' INITIALS

Initials	Date	Name
GTF, G.TODA.F	1739-45	Giovanni Toda, die-cutter from Florence in Vienna

COUNTY

REGULAR COINAGE

KM# 6 THALER

Silver **Ruler:** Karl Ferdinand, Christian Moritz Eugen and Maximilian Friedrich **Obverse:** Date in Roman numerals **Obv. Legend:** S•R•I• COMITES• A• KÖNIGSEGG• ET• ROTTENFELS• KOMINI• IN / AULENDORF• & STAUFFEN• / FRATRES•, in exergue; UTI• SNAGUINE• ITA• ET•/ AMICITIA• IUNCTI • / M•D•C•C•L•IX• **Reverse:** 22 Lines of inscription with names, birthdays and titles of the four brothers **Note:** Dav. #2374.

Date	Mintage	Good	VG	F	VF	XF
ND(1759	—	—	750	1,250	2,200	3,750

TRADE COINAGE

KM# 5 DUCAT

3.5000 g., 0.9860 Gold 0.1109 oz. AGW **Ruler:** Karl Ferdinand, Christian Moritz Eugen and Maximilian Friedrich **Obverse:** Bust of Franz Hugo right **Reverse:** Helmeted arms

Date	Mintage	Good	VG	F	VF	XF
1756	—	—	1,000	2,000	4,000	6,500

KM# 7 10 DUCAT (Portugalöser)

35.0000 g., 0.9860 Gold 1.1095 oz. AGW **Ruler:** Karl Ferdinand, Christian Moritz Eugen and Maximilian Friedrich **Obverse:** Date in Roman numerals **Note:** Struck with 1 Thaler dies, KM#6.

Date	Mintage	VG	F	VF	XF	Unc
ND(1759) Rare, G.TODA F.	—	—	—	—	—	—

PATTERNS

Including off metal strikes

KM#	Date	Mintage	Identification	Mkt Val
Pn1	ND1759	—	Thaler. Lead.	—

KOSEL

A city in Silesia located on the Oder River 74 miles southeast of Breslau, local coinage was struck here in 1761 during the Austrian offensive into Silesia as part of the Seven-Years' War.

CITY

REGULAR COINAGE

KM# 5 KREUZER

Copper **Note:** Uniface; 2 opposing goat's heads, COSEL below divides I-X, date below.

Date	Mintage	Good	VG	F	VF	XF
1761 Rare	—	—	—	—	—	—

KM# 7 GROSCHEN

Note: Gute Groschen; 3 Goat's heads, COSEL/I above, date divided below, GG at bottom.

Date	Mintage	Good	VG	F	VF	XF
1761 Rare	—	—	—	—	—	—

KM# 6 GROSCHEN

Copper **Note:** Uniface; Goat's head to left divides I-GR, COSEL/ date below.

Date	Mintage	Good	VG	F	VF	XF
1761 Rare	—	—	—	—	—	—

LANDAU

First mentioned in 1106, this city in Bavaria was 30 miles southwest of Mannheim. A monastery was founded there in 1276 and it became an imperial free city in 1291. It was occupied by the French from 1680-1815. Two sieges took place, 1702 and 1713, during both of which coins were struck.

With Prince Charles Alexander of Württemberg as commander, Landau was besieged from June 25, 1713 to August 20, 1713, by the French, commanded by the Duc de Villars.

FREE CITY

SIEGE COINAGE

1702

Issued by the French General Graf von Melac

KM# 6 1 LIVRE 1 SOL

Silver **Obverse:** Round arms with ornaments above 3 fleur-de-lis, all within circle, legend below, 8 fleur-de-lis around rim **Shape:** Irregular

Date	Mintage	VG	F	VF	XF	Unc
1702	—	400	700	1,100	1,500	—

KM# 5 1 LIVRE 1 SOL

Silver **Obverse:** Round arms with ornaments above 3 fleur-de-lis, circle surrounds all, fleurs at corners **Shape:** 4-Sided **Note:** Uniface. Klippe.

Date	Mintage	VG	F	VF	XF	Unc
1702	—	350	600	800	1,200	—

KM# 8 2 LIVRES 2 SOLS
Silver **Obverse:** Round arms with ornaments above 3 fleur-de-lis, all within circle, legend below, fleurs at corners **Shape:** Irregular

Date	Mintage	VG	F	VF	XF	Unc
1702	—	550	1,000	1,700	2,300	—

KM# 7 2 LIVRES 2 SOLS
Silver **Obverse:** Round arms, date below, fleur-de-lis around rim **Shape:** Irregular **Note:** Uniface. Klippe.

Date	Mintage	VG	F	VF	XF	Unc
1702	—	600	1,000	1,500	2,200	—

KM# 10a 4 LIVRES 4 SOLS
Gold **Obverse:** Round arms, value and date below, fleur-de-lis around rim

Date	Mintage	VG	F	VF	XF	Unc
1702 Rare	—	—	—	—	—	—

KM# 9 4 LIVRES 4 SOLS
Silver **Note:** Dav. #2375. Uniface. Klippe.

Date	Mintage	VG	F	VF	XF	Unc
1702	—	650	1,100	1,850	3,000	—

KM# 10 4 LIVRES 4 SOLS
Silver **Obverse:** Round arms, value and date below, fleur-de-lis around rim **Shape:** Irregular **Note:** Dav. #2376.

Date	Mintage	VG	F	VF	XF	Unc
1702	—	900	1,400	1,900	3,000	—

SIEGE COINAGE

1709-1713

Issued by Prince Karl Alexander of Wurttemberg

KM# 11 1/2 FLORIN 2 KREUZER
Silver **Obverse:** Crowned monogram at center and corners **Shape:** Irregular **Note:** Uniface. Klippe.

Date	Mintage	VG	F	VF	XF	Unc
1713	—	300	500	850	1,350	—

KM# 12 1 FLORIN 4 KREUZER
Silver **Obverse:** Arms at center, crowned monograms at corners **Shape:** Irregular **Note:** Uniface. Klippe.

Date	Mintage	VG	F	VF	XF	Unc
1713	—	285	475	800	1,250	—

KM# 13 2 FLORIN 8 KREUZER
Silver **Obverse:** Round arms, crowned monograms at corners **Shape:** Irregular **Note:** Dav. #2377. Uniface. Klippe.

Date	Mintage	VG	F	VF	XF	Unc
1713	—	750	1,000	1,700	2,500	—

KM# 14 DOPPIA
7.0000 g., 0.9860 Gold 0.2219 oz. AGW **Obverse:** Crowned monogram at center and four corners **Note:** Uniface. Similar to 1/2 Florin 2 Kreuzer, KM#11. Crowned CA monogram at center and at corners.

Date	Mintage	VG	F	VF	XF	Unc
1713	—	2,000	3,000	5,000	7,000	—

KM# 15 DOPPIA
7.0000 g., 0.9860 Gold 0.2219 oz. AGW **Obverse:** Five large crowned CA monogram stampings **Note:** Similar to KM#14 but with five large crowned CA monogram stampings.

Date	Mintage	VG	F	VF	XF	Unc
1713	—	2,000	3,000	5,000	7,000	—

KM# 16 2 DOPPIA
Gold **Obverse:** Crowned Wurttemberg arms at center, crowned CA monograms at corners, value at bottom **Note:** Uniface. Klippe

Date	Mintage	VG	F	VF	XF	Unc
1713 Rare	—	—	—	—	—	—

KM# 17 4 DOPPIA
28.0000 g., 0.9860 Gold 0.8876 oz. AGW **Obverse:** Crowned Wurttemberg arms at center, crowned CA monograms at corners, value at bottom **Note:** Uniface

Date	Mintage	VG	F	VF	XF	Unc
1713 Rare	—	—	—	—	—	—

LAUENBURG

The line of rulers of this Saxon duchy became extinct in 1689 and passed to Brunswick-Lüneburg-Celle, then to Brunswick-Lüneburg-Calenberg-Hannover in 1705. After the Napoleonic Wars, Lauenburg went to Prussia in 1813, to Denmark in 1814, and was regained by Prussia as part of the latter's annexation of Holstein in 1864. The Brunswick duches struck special coins for Lauenburg. See Saxe-Lauenburg for coinage prior to 1689.

RULERS

Georg II Wilhelm von Brunswick-Lüneburg-Celle, 1689-1705
Georg I Ludwig von Brunswick-Lüneburg-Calenberg-Hannover, 1705-1727
Georg II August von Brunswick-Lüneburg-Calenberg-Hannover, 1727-1760
Georg III von Brunswick-Lüneburg-Calenberg-Hannover, 1760-1818

MINT OFFICIALS' INITIALS

Initials	Date	Name
CPS, S	1725-53	Christian Philipp Spangenberg in Clausthal
JJJ	1687-1705	Jobst Jakob Janisch in Celle

DUCHY

REGULAR COINAGE

KM# 18 1/2 DREILING (1-1/2 Pfennig)
Copper **Ruler:** George II August von Brunswick-Luneburg-Celle-Callenberg-Hannover **Obverse:** Horse leaping left **Reverse:** Value: 1/2 / DREILING/ date **Rev. Legend:** LAVENBVRGISCHE SCHEIDEMVNTZ

Date	Mintage	VG	F	VF	XF	Unc
1739 S	—	6.00	12.00	20.00	45.00	—
1740 S	—	6.00	12.00	20.00	45.00	—

KM# 19 1/2 DREILING (1-1/2 Pfennig)
Copper **Ruler:** George II August von Brunswick-Luneburg-Celle-Callenberg-Hannover **Obverse:** Crowned GR script monogram **Reverse:** Value, date within inner circle

Date	Mintage	VG	F	VF	XF	Unc
1739 S	—	12.00	25.00	50.00	85.00	—
1740 S	—	8.00	15.00	30.00	55.00	—

KM# 13 DREILING (3 Pfennig)
Silver **Ruler:** George II August von Brunswick-Luneburg-Celle-Callenberg-Hannover **Obverse:** Horse leaping left, mintmaster's initials below **Obv. Legend:** MONETA NOVA LAVENBURGICA **Reverse:** Value: +I+/DREI/LING/date **Rev. Legend:** +NACH DEM LVBSCHEN FVS

Date	Mintage	VG	F	VF	XF	Unc
1738 CPS	—	9.00	20.00	35.00	60.00	—

KM# 14 SECHSLING (Soesling = 6 Pfennig)

Silver **Obverse:** Horse leaping left **Reverse:** I/SOES/LING/date **Note:** Similar to 4 Schilling, KM#11. Varieties exist.

Date	Mintage	VG	F	VF	XF	Unc
1738 CPS	—	12.00	25.00	40.00	70.00	—

KM# 12 SCHILLING

Silver **Ruler:** George II August von Brunswick-Luneburg-Celle-Callenberg-Hannover **Obverse:** Horse leaping left **Reverse:** I/SCHILLING/date **Note:** Similar to 4 Schilling, KM#11. Varieties exist.

Date	Mintage	VG	F	VF	XF	Unc
1737 CPS	—	6.00	12.00	20.00	45.00	—
1738 CPS	—	12.00	25.00	40.00	70.00	—

KM# 10 2 SCHILLING

Silver **Ruler:** George II August von Brunswick-Luneburg-Celle-Callenberg-Hannover **Obverse:** Horse leaping left within inner circle **Reverse:** II/SCHILLING/date **Note:** Varieties exist.

Date	Mintage	VG	F	VF	XF	Unc
1736 CPS	—	8.00	15.00	30.00	55.00	—
1738 CPS	—	18.00	30.00	45.00	75.00	—

KM# 5 4 SCHILLING

Silver **Ruler:** Georg II Wilhelm von Brunswick-Luneburg-Celle **Obverse:** Horse leaping left within inner circle **Reverse:** Value, date

Date	Mintage	VG	F	VF	XF	Unc
1704 JJJ	—	35.00	65.00	100	150	—

KM# 11 4 SCHILLING

Silver **Ruler:** George II August von Brunswick-Luneburg-Celle-Callenberg-Hannover **Obverse:** Horse leaping left within inner circle **Reverse:** Value, date **Note:** Varieties exist.

Date	Mintage	VG	F	VF	XF	Unc
1736 CPS	—	28.00	55.00	95.00	140	—
1738 CPS	—	12.00	30.00	55.00	85.00	—

KM# 15 8 SCHILLING

Silver **Ruler:** George II August von Brunswick-Luneburg-Celle-Callenberg-Hannover **Obverse:** Horse leaping left within inner circle **Reverse:** Value, date

Date	Mintage	VG	F	VF	XF	Unc
1738 CPS	—	20.00	50.00	85.00	140	—

KM# 16 16 SCHILLING (Mark)

Silver **Ruler:** George II August von Brunswick-Luneburg-Celle-Callenberg-Hannover **Obverse:** Horse leaping left within inner circle **Reverse:** Value, date

Date	Mintage	VG	F	VF	XF	Unc
1738 CPS	—	30.00	65.00	100	175	—

KM# 17 32 SCHILLING (2 Mark)

Silver **Ruler:** George II August von Brunswick-Luneburg-Celle-Callenberg-Hannover **Obverse:** Horse leaping left within inner circle **Reverse:** Value, date

Date	Mintage	VG	F	VF	XF	Unc
1738 CPS	—	160	300	500	750	—

LEUTKIRCH

This free imperial city in Swabia, about 15 miles north of Isny, is mentioned in the mid-8th century. Its imperial city status dates from the 13th century. Leutkirch rarely exercised its right of coinage, preferring rather to join other Swabian towns in currency unions.

FREE CITY

TRADE COINAGE

KM# 5 DUCAT

3.5000 g., 0.9860 Gold 0.1109 oz. AGW **Subject:** Centennial - Peace of Westphalia **Obverse:** Eye of God above city view with legends above and below **Obv. Legend:** PROVIDENTE DEO ... R. I. L. I. B. CIV / LEUTKIRCH **Reverse:** Imperial eagle on roof of church, legend above **Rev. Legend:** DEUS IN MEDIO EIUS NON COMMOVEBITUR ... MEMOR. IUB. I. PAC / WESTPH. 1748.

Date	Mintage	Good	VG	F	VF	XF
1748	—	—	750	1,600	3,000	5,000

PATTERNS

Including off metal strikes

KM#	Date	Mintage	Identification	Mkt Val
Pn1	1748	—	Ducat. Silver. KM#5.	225

LINDAU

A city located on the northeast shore of Lake Constance, Lindau dates from the early 9th century. After acquiring the status of free imperial city in 1274, a local coinage was produced for Lindau on and off during the next 5 centuries. During the Kipper Period of the Thirty Years' War, a variety of coins from South German issuing authorities were counterstamped with the linden tree symbol of Lindau. These are not listed here. In 1732 a joint coinage with the towns of Isny, Wangen, and Leutkirch was struck. After the Napoleonic Wars, in 1805, Lindau was made a part of Bavaria.

MINT

Langenargen, mint of the Swabian imperial circle located in Montfort.

MINT OFFICIALS' INITIALS

Initials	Date	Name
	1682-1712	Hans Jakob Kickh
	1685, 1712-19	Johann Albrecht Riedlin von Ulm, die-cutter
T	1740-69	Jonas Thiebaud, die-cutter in Augsburg

IMPERIAL CITY

REGULAR COINAGE

KM# 10 1/4 KREUZER (Pfennig)

Silver **Obverse:** Nine-leaved Linden tree **Reverse:** Value 1/4 **Note:** Varieties exist.

Date	Mintage	VG	F	VF	XF	Unc
ND(1712)	288,000	22.00	50.00	90.00	140	—

KM# 11 1/2 KREUZER (2 Pfennig)

Silver **Obverse:** Two adjacent oval arms, imperial eagle on left, three-leaved Linden tree on right, value 1/2 in smaller oval above **Reverse:** Value 1/2 **Note:** Varieties exist.

Date	Mintage	VG	F	VF	XF	Unc
ND(1712)	348,000	12.00	30.00	65.00	120	—

KM# 12 1/8 THALER

Silver **Subject:** Bicentennial of the Reformation **Obverse:** Linden branches spreading above open book **Obv. Legend:** VERBVM. DOMINI. MANET. IN. AETERNVM. **Reverse:** Six-line inscription **Rev. Inscription:** IVBILAE/VM/EVANGELICO/RVM/SECVNDVM/1717

Date	Mintage	VG	F	VF	XF	Unc
1717	—	—	—	—	—	—

TRADE COINAGE

KM# 15 1/2 DUCAT

1.7500 g., 0.9860 Gold 0.0555 oz. AGW **Subject:** Centennial - Peace of Westphalia **Obverse:** Linden tree in baroque frame, laurel and palm branches at sides **Obv. Legend:** SERVATA LIBERTATE VIRESCIT **Reverse:** Seven-line inscription, crossed laurel and palm branches below **Rev. Inscription:** PACIS / WESTPHAL. / IUBILA PRIMA / LINDAV. III / ID. AUG. / MDCCXLVIII / CELEBRATA

Date	Mintage	VG	F	VF	XF	Unc
1748 T	—	—	—	—	—	—

KM# 16 2 DUCAT

7.0000 g., 0.9860 Gold 0.2219 oz. AGW **Subject:** Centennial - Peace of Westphalia **Obverse:** Linden tree in baroque frame **Obv. Legend:** MNEMOSYNON. ANN. LIBERTAT. IVBIL. MDCCXLVIII:LINDAV. III. ID. AUG. **Reverse:** Rays streaming down from clouds onto altar **Rev. Legend:** ARA + PACIS - WEST - PHALICAE

Date	Mintage	VG	F	VF	XF	Unc
1748 T	—	1,000	2,000	3,500	6,000	—

JOINT COINAGE

with Isny, Wangen, and Leutkirch

KM# 20 1/4 KREUZER (Pfennig)

Silver **Mint:** Langenargen **Obverse:** Date above crowned imperial eagle on pedestal with M(ontfort), below crossed branches, letters L, Y, W, and L around in four small ovals **Reverse:** Value 1/4

Date	Mintage	VG	F	VF	XF	Unc
1732	—	20.00	45.00	85.00	125	—

KM# 21 1/4 KREUZER (Pfennig)

Silver **Mint:** Langenargen **Obverse:** Date above crowned imperial eagle on pedestal with M(ontfort), below crossed branches, letters L, Y, W, and L around in four small ovals **Reverse:** Value 1/2

Date	Mintage	VG	F	VF	XF	Unc
1732	—	30.00	55.00	100	185	—

PATTERNS

Including off metal strikes

KM#	Date	Mintage	Identification	Mkt Val
Pn1	1748	—	1/2 Ducat. Silver. KM#15	90.00
Pn2	1748	—	2 Ducat. Silver. KM#16	150

LIPPE-DETMOLD

The Counts of Lippe ruled over a small state in northwestern Germany. In 1528/9 they became counts; in 1720 they were raised to the rank of princes, but did not use the title until 1789. Another branch of the family ruled the even smaller Schaumburg-Lippe. Lippe joined North German Confederation in 1866, and became part of the German Empire in 1871. When the insane Prince Alexander succeeded to the throne in 1895, the main branch reached an end, and a ten-year testamentary dispute between the Biesterfeld and the Schaumburg-Lippe lines followed - a Wilhelmine cause celebre. The Biesterfeld line gained the principality in 1905, but abdicated in 1918. In 1947 Lippe was absorbed by the German Land of North Rhine-Westphalia.

RULERS

Friedrich Adolf, 1697-1718
Simon Heinrich Adolf, 1718-1734
Simon August, 1734-1782
Friedrich Wilhelm Leopold
under Regency of Ludwig
Heinrich Adolf, 1782-1789
Alone, 1789-1802

MINT OFFICIALS' INITIALS

Initials	Date	Name
B, TB	1678-1716	Thomas (or Tobias) Bernard, die-cutter in Paris
HL	1710-16	Hans (Johann) Luders
LHL	1716-27	Ludolf Heinrich Luders in Detmold and Brake
	1711	Johann Heinrich Siegel, warden
	1763-71	Johann Conrad Bandel
	1763, 1771	Heinrich Daniel Sturner, warden & mintmaster
	1789-1803	Balthasar Reinhard

PRINCIPALITY

REGULAR COINAGE

KM# 175 HELLER

Copper **Ruler:** Simon August **Obverse:** Rose surrounded by rosettes **Reverse:** I in circle, date around border

Date	Mintage	VG	F	VF	XF	Unc
1760	—	2.00	4.00	7.00	20.00	—

KM# 192 HELLER

Copper **Ruler:** Simon August **Obverse:** Rose **Reverse:** Value above date

Date	Mintage	VG	F	VF	XF	Unc
1767	—	1.00	2.00	4.00	10.00	—
1768	—	1.00	2.00	4.00	10.00	—

KM# 205 HELLER

Copper **Ruler:** Friedrich Wilhelm Leopold under Regency of Ludwig Hienrich Adolf **Obverse:** Rose displayed **Reverse:** Value stated in 5 lines, date below

Date	Mintage	VG	F	VF	XF	Unc
1783	—	1.00	2.00	4.00	10.00	—

KM# 216 HELLER

Copper **Ruler:** Friedrich Wilhelm Leopold Alone **Reverse:** Value above date

Date	Mintage	VG	F	VF	XF	Unc
1791	—	1.00	2.00	4.00	10.00	—
1798	—	1.00	2.00	4.00	10.00	—

KM# 145 1/2 PFENNIG (Groschen)

Copper **Ruler:** Friedrich Adolf **Obverse:** Rose

Date	Mintage	VG	F	VF	XF	Unc
ND(1715)	Inc. above	5.00	12.00	20.00	35.00	—

KM# 146 1/2 PFENNIG (Groschen)

Copper **Ruler:** Friedrich Adolf **Obverse:** Rose in plain circle, rosettes and/or clover leaves in field **Reverse:** Value within oval, crowned ring above and below **Note:** Varieties exist.

Date	Mintage	VG	F	VF	XF	Unc
ND(1715)	Inc. above	5.00	12.00	20.00	35.00	—

KM# 144 1/2 PFENNIG (Groschen)

Copper **Ruler:** Friedrich Adolf **Obverse:** Rose in plain circle, rosettes and/or clover leaves in field **Reverse:** Value 1/2 in plain circle, 4 rosettes and clover leaves in field **Note:** Varieties exist. Goschen 1/2 Pfennig.

Date	Mintage	VG	F	VF	XF	Unc
ND(1715)	306,000	5.00	12.00	20.00	35.00	—

KM# 167 1/2 PFENNIG (Groschen)

Copper **Ruler:** Simon Heinrich Adolf **Obverse:** Rose in circle, 4 rosettes and 4 clover leaves around **Reverse:** Value 1/2 in circle, date in legend with ornament between each digit

Date	Mintage	VG	F	VF	XF	Unc
1724	—	10.00	20.00	40.00	75.00	—

KM# 176 1/2 PFENNIG (Groschen)

Copper **Ruler:** Simon August **Obverse:** SA script monogram **Reverse:** Value above date

Date	Mintage	VG	F	VF	XF	Unc
1763	—	2.00	4.00	7.00	20.00	—

KM# 152 PFENNING

Copper, 15.3 mm. **Ruler:** Friedrich Adolf **Obverse:** Rose in circle, 4 rosettes and 4 clover leaves around **Rev. Legend:** 1/PFEN/NING

Date	Mintage	VG	F	VF	XF	Unc
ND(1716-17)	151,000	5.00	12.00	20.00	35.00	—

KM# 168 PFENNING

Copper **Ruler:** Simon Heinrich Adolf **Obverse:** 8 rosettes alternating with 8 stars **Reverse:** Value 1

Date	Mintage	VG	F	VF	XF	Unc
1724	—	10.00	25.00	50.00	85.00	—

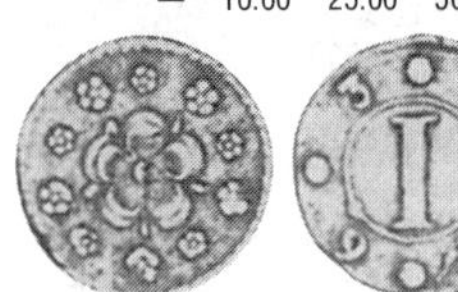

KM# 177 PFENNING

Copper **Ruler:** Simon August **Obverse:** Rose in circle of rosettes **Reverse:** I in circle; date around border

Date	Mintage	VG	F	VF	XF	Unc
1763	—	2.00	4.00	7.00	15.00	—

KM# 178 PFENNING

Copper **Ruler:** Simon August **Obverse:** SA script monogram **Reverse:** Value in center

Date	Mintage	VG	F	VF	XF	Unc
1763	—	2.00	4.00	7.00	15.00	—

KM# 193 PFENNING

Copper **Ruler:** Simon August **Obverse:** Rose **Reverse:** Value above date

Date	Mintage	VG	F	VF	XF	Unc
1767	—	1.00	3.00	6.00	10.00	—
1768	—	1.00	3.00	6.00	10.00	—

KM# 217 PFENNING

Copper **Ruler:** Friedrich Wilhelm Leopold Alone **Obverse:** Rose displayed **Reverse:** Value above date

Date	Mintage	VG	F	VF	XF	Unc
1791	—	1.00	3.00	6.00	10.00	—

KM# 153 1-1/2 PFENNING (1/192 Thaler)

Copper **Ruler:** Friedrich Adolf **Obverse:** Rose, large rosettes and small stars around **Reverse:** 1-1/2 in circle, rosettes and stars around

Date	Mintage	VG	F	VF	XF	Unc
ND(1716-17)	—	5.00	12.00	20.00	35.00	—

Note: Number of rosettes and stars varies between 5 and 10

KM# 147 2 PFENNING

Copper **Ruler:** Friedrich Adolf **Obverse:** Legend around rose **Obv. Legend:** G.LIPP.LANT.MVNTZ **Reverse:** II in center, 4 vine leaves and 4 rosettes around **Note:** Varieties exist.

Date	Mintage	VG	F	VF	XF	Unc
ND(1715-17)	—	7.00	15.00	25.00	45.00	—

KM# 179 2 PFENNING

Copper **Ruler:** Simon August **Obverse:** Script monogram **Reverse:** II within flower

Date	Mintage	VG	F	VF	XF	Unc
1763	—	2.00	4.00	7.00	15.00	—

KM# 180 2 PFENNING

Copper **Ruler:** Simon August **Obverse:** Rose **Obv. Legend:** FRIE • ADOLPH • - COM • & • NOB • D • LIPP • **Reverse:** Value **Rev. Legend:** • IVSTVM • & DECORVM •

Date	Mintage	VG	F	VF	XF	Unc
1763	—	3.00	6.00	10.00	20.00	—

KM# 191 2 PFENNING

Billon **Ruler:** Simon August **Obverse:** Rose **Reverse:** Value above date

Date	Mintage	VG	F	VF	XF	Unc
1766	—	2.00	4.00	7.00	15.00	—
1769	—	2.00	4.00	7.00	15.00	—

KM# 208 2 PFENNING

Billon **Ruler:** Friedrich Wilhelm Leopold under Regency of Ludwig Hienrich Adolf **Obverse:** Rose **Reverse:** Value above date

Date	Mintage	VG	F	VF	XF	Unc
1785	—	3.00	6.00	10.00	20.00	—

KM# 206 4 PFENNING

Billon **Ruler:** Friedrich Wilhelm Leopold under Regency of Ludwig Hienrich Adolf **Obverse:** Rose **Reverse:** Value above date

Date	Mintage	VG	F	VF	XF	Unc
1784	—	3.00	6.00	10.00	20.00	—

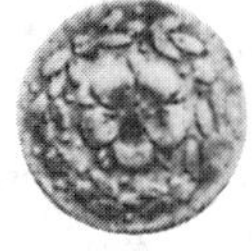

KM# 115 MATTIER (4 Pfennig)

Silver **Ruler:** Friedrich Adolf **Obverse:** Rose in wreath of laurel and rosettes **Reverse:** Date **Rev. Legend:** I/MATTIER/GR:LIPP/LM **Note:** Varieties exist.

Date	Mintage	VG	F	VF	XF	Unc
1710	162,000	10.00	25.00	45.00	85.00	—
1711	—	10.00	25.00	45.00	85.00	—
1712	144,000	10.00	25.00	45.00	85.00	—
1714	783,000	10.00	25.00	45.00	85.00	—

KM# 181 MATTIER (4 Pfennig)

Billon **Ruler:** Simon August **Obverse:** Rose **Reverse:** Value above date

Date	Mintage	VG	F	VF	XF	Unc
1763	—	2.00	4.00	8.00	20.00	—

KM# 189 MATTIER (4 Pfennig)

Billon **Ruler:** Simon August

Date	Mintage	VG	F	VF	XF	Unc
1766	—	2.00	4.00	8.00	20.00	—
1767	—	2.00	4.00	8.00	20.00	—
1768	—	2.00	4.00	8.00	20.00	—

KM# 196 MATTIER (4 Pfennig)

Billon **Ruler:** Simon August **Obverse:** SA script monogram in rose **Reverse:** Value

Date	Mintage	VG	F	VF	XF	Unc
1769	—	2.00	4.00	8.00	20.00	—

KM# 209 MATTIER (4 Pfennig)

Billon **Ruler:** Friedrich Wilhelm Leopold under Regency of Ludwig Hienrich Adolf **Obverse:** L H A C monogram in rose **Reverse:** Value above date

Date	Mintage	VG	F	VF	XF	Unc
1785	—	3.00	5.00	10.00	25.00	—

KM# 210 MATTIER (4 Pfennig)

Billon **Ruler:** Friedrich Wilhelm Leopold under Regency of Ludwig Hienrich Adolf **Note:** Similar to KM#218.

Date	Mintage	VG	F	VF	XF	Unc
1789	—	3.00	5.00	10.00	25.00	—

KM# 218 MATTIER (4 Pfennig)

Billon **Ruler:** Friedrich Wilhelm Leopold Alone **Obverse:** Rose **Reverse:** Value, date

Date	Mintage	VG	F	VF	XF	Unc
1791	—	2.00	4.00	8.00	20.00	—
1792	—	2.00	4.00	8.00	20.00	—
1793	—	2.00	4.00	8.00	20.00	—
1794	—	2.00	4.00	8.00	20.00	—
1795	—	2.00	4.00	8.00	20.00	—
1796	—	2.00	4.00	8.00	20.00	—
1797	—	2.00	4.00	8.00	20.00	—
1798	—	2.00	4.00	8.00	20.00	—
1799	—	2.00	4.00	8.00	20.00	—

KM# 121 MARIENGROSCHEN (1/36 Thaler)

Silver **Ruler:** Friedrich Adolf **Obverse:** Rose in circle, titles of Friedrich Adolf **Reverse:** I/MARI.HEROS/HL, date **Rev. Legend:** G.LIPP.LANT.MVN(T)Z **Note:** Varieties exist.

Date	Mintage	VG	F	VF	XF	Unc
1711 HL	287,000	12.00	30.00	60.00	100	—
1712 HL	295,000	12.00	30.00	60.00	100	—
1713 HL	722,000	12.00	30.00	60.00	100	—
1714 HL	1,024,000	12.00	30.00	60.00	100	—
1715 HL	789,000	12.00	30.00	60.00	100	—

KM# 148 MARIENGROSCHEN (1/36 Thaler)

Silver **Ruler:** Friedrich Adolf **Reverse:** Date at bottom, 17HL15

Date	Mintage	VG	F	VF	XF	Unc
1715 HL	Inc. above	12.00	30.00	60.00	100	—

KM# 182 MARIENGROSCHEN (1/36 Thaler)

Billon **Ruler:** Simon August **Obverse:** SA script monogram **Reverse:** Value and date

Date	Mintage	VG	F	VF	XF	Unc
1764	—	3.00	5.00	10.00	25.00	—
1765	—	3.00	5.00	10.00	25.00	—
1766	—	3.00	5.00	10.00	25.00	—
1767	—	3.00	5.00	10.00	25.00	—
1768	—	3.00	5.00	10.00	25.00	—

KM# 200 MARIENGROSCHEN (1/36 Thaler)

Billon **Ruler:** Simon August **Obverse:** SA script monogram in rose **Reverse:** Value

Date	Mintage	VG	F	VF	XF	Unc
1770	—	3.00	5.00	10.00	25.00	—

KM# 207 MARIENGROSCHEN (1/36 Thaler)

Billon **Ruler:** Friedrich Wilhelm Leopold under Regency of Ludwig Hienrich Adolf **Obverse:** L H A C monogram in rose **Reverse:** Value above date

Date	Mintage	VG	F	VF	XF	Unc
1784	—	4.00	8.00	16.00	35.00	—
1786	—	4.00	8.00	16.00	35.00	—

KM# 211 MARIENGROSCHEN (1/36 Thaler)

Billon **Ruler:** Friedrich Wilhelm Leopold under Regency of Ludwig Hienrich Adolf **Obverse:** Rose displayed

Date	Mintage	VG	F	VF	XF	Unc
1789	—	3.00	5.00	10.00	25.00	—

KM# 215 MARIENGROSCHEN (1/36 Thaler)

Billon **Ruler:** Friedrich Wilhelm Leopold Alone **Obverse:** Rose displayed **Note:** Similar to KM#211.

Date	Mintage	VG	F	VF	XF	Unc
1790	—	2.00	4.00	8.00	20.00	—
1791	—	2.00	4.00	8.00	20.00	—
1792	—	2.00	4.00	8.00	20.00	—
1793	—	2.00	4.00	8.00	20.00	—
1794	—	2.00	4.00	8.00	20.00	—
1795	—	2.00	4.00	8.00	20.00	—

KM# 190 4 MARIENGROSCHEN (1/9 Thaler)

Billon **Ruler:** Simon August **Obverse:** SA script monogram in rose **Reverse:** Value and date

Date	Mintage	VG	F	VF	XF	Unc
1766	—	20.00	35.00	70.00	125	—

KM# 219 GULDEN

Silver **Ruler:** Friedrich Wilhelm Leopold Alone **Obverse:** Helmeted arms within crowned mantle **Reverse:** Inscription within oak leaf wreath **Note:** Prize Gulden.

Date	Mintage	VG	F	VF	XF	Unc
1793	—	125	200	300	450	—

KM# 116 1/48 THALER (4-1/2 Pfennig)

Silver **Ruler:** Friedrich Adolf **Obverse:** Ornate script FA monogram, large crown above **Reverse:** Date, value in circle **Rev. Legend:** L.KIP.L.MVNTZ; 48/I/REICHS/TH

Date	Mintage	VG	F	VF	XF	Unc
1710 HL	36,000	80.00	150	275	450	—

KM# 122 1/48 THALER (4-1/2 Pfennig)

Silver **Ruler:** Friedrich Adolf **Obverse:** Date, rose in circle **Obv. Legend:** G.LIP.L.MUNTZ **Reverse:** Value **Rev. Legend:** 48/I/REICHS/TH/HL **Note:** Varieties exist.

Date	Mintage	VG	F	VF	XF	Unc
1711 HL	142,000	10.00	25.00	50.00	85.00	—
1713 HL	191,000	10.00	25.00	50.00	85.00	—
1714 HL	377,000	10.00	25.00	50.00	85.00	—

KM# 126 1/48 THALER (4-1/2 Pfennig)

Silver **Ruler:** Friedrich Adolf **Reverse:** Date as ...REICHS/17 TH 12/HL **Note:** Varieties exist.

Date	Mintage	VG	F	VF	XF	Unc
1712 HL	—	10.00	25.00	50.00	85.00	—
1713 HL	Inc. above	10.00	25.00	50.00	85.00	—
1714 HL	Inc. above	10.00	25.00	50.00	85.00	—

KM# 183 1/48 THALER (4-1/2 Pfennig)

Billon **Ruler:** Simon August **Obverse:** SA script monogram **Reverse:** Value and date

Date	Mintage	VG	F	VF	XF	Unc
1764	—	3.00	7.00	15.00	35.00	—

KM# 174 1/24 THALER (Furstengroschen)

Billon **Ruler:** Simon August **Obverse:** SA script monogram **Reverse:** Value and date

Date	Mintage	VG	F	VF	XF	Unc
1764	—	3.00	5.00	10.00	25.00	—

KM# 117 1/12 THALER (2 Groschen)

Silver **Ruler:** Friedrich Adolf **Obverse:** Crowned 4-fold oval arms with 4-fold central shield **Reverse:** Date **Rev. Legend:** 12/EINEN/REICHS/THALER **Note:** Varieties exist.

Date	Mintage	VG	F	VF	XF	Unc
1710 HL	36,000	12.00	30.00	60.00	120	—
1711 HL	15,000	12.00	30.00	60.00	120	—
1712 HL	—	12.00	30.00	60.00	120	—
1713 HL	28,000	16.00	35.00	70.00	140	—
1714 HL	45,000	16.00	35.00	70.00	140	—
1715 HL	206,000	12.00	30.00	60.00	120	—
1716 HL	Inc. above	16.00	35.00	70.00	140	—
1716 LHL	Inc. above	16.00	35.00	70.00	140	—
1717 LHL	148,000	16.00	35.00	70.00	140	—

KM# 136 1/12 THALER (2 Groschen)

Silver **Ruler:** Friedrich Adolf **Note:** Similar to KM#117, but date divided by crown.

Date	Mintage	VG	F	VF	XF	Unc
1714 HL	Inc. above	12.00	30.00	60.00	120	—

KM# 154 1/12 THALER (2 Groschen)

Silver **Ruler:** Friedrich Adolf **Obverse:** Crowned 4-fold arms in shape of shield **Reverse:** Value, date within inner circle

Date	Mintage	VG	F	VF	XF	Unc
1716 HL	Inc. above	—	—	—	—	—

KM# 165 1/12 THALER (2 Groschen)

Silver **Ruler:** Simon Heinrich Adolf **Obverse:** Crowned 4-fold arms in baroque frame **Reverse:** Mintmaster's intials NACH - DEM, date in legend **Rev. Legend:** 12/EINEN/REICHS/THALER **Note:** Varieties exist.

Date	Mintage	VG	F	VF	XF	Unc
1720 LHL	3,360	18.00	40.00	80.00	165	—

KM# 184 1/12 THALER (2 Groschen)

Billon **Ruler:** Simon August **Obverse:** Crowned 4-fold arms within cartouche **Reverse:** Value, date

Date	Mintage	VG	F	VF	XF	Unc
1764	—	7.00	15.00	50.00	110	—
1765 BS	—	7.00	15.00	50.00	110	—
1765 TAHLER (Error)	—	15.00	30.00	100	300	—
1766	—	7.00	15.00	50.00	110	—
1767	—	7.00	15.00	50.00	110	—
1768	—	15.00	30.00	90.00	200	—
1769	—	15.00	30.00	90.00	250	—

KM# A184 1/12 THALER (2 Groschen)

Silver, 22.2 mm. **Ruler:** Simon August **Obverse:** Crowned shield of arms **Reverse:** 5-line inscription **Rev. Inscription:** 12/ EINEN/ REICHS/ THALER/B S

Date	Mintage	VG	F	VF	XF	Unc
1764 BS	—	7.00	15.00	50.00	110	—

KM# 212 1/12 THALER (2 Groschen)

Billon **Ruler:** Friedrich Wilhelm Leopold Alone **Obverse:** Complex arms within crowned mantle **Reverse:** Value, date

Date	Mintage	VG	F	VF	XF	Unc
1789	—	8.00	16.50	50.00	115	—
1790 BR	—	9.00	17.50	60.00	120	—

KM# 127 1/6 THALER (1/4 Gulden)

Silver **Ruler:** Friedrich Adolf **Obverse:** Armored bust right **Reverse:** Quartered arms with crown above and value in oval below **Note:** Similar to 1/3 Thaler, KM#128 but value 1/6 in oval at bottom on reverse. Varieties exist.

Date	Mintage	VG	F	VF	XF	Unc
1712 HL	3,852	50.00	125	250	500	—
1713 HL	10,000	50.00	125	250	500	—

KM# 137 1/6 THALER (1/4 Gulden)

Silver **Ruler:** Friedrich Adolf **Reverse:** Arms in shield with straight sides divide date

Date	Mintage	VG	F	VF	XF	Unc
1714 HL	13,000	50.00	125	250	500	—

KM# 166 1/6 THALER (1/4 Gulden)

Silver **Ruler:** Simon Heinrich Adolf **Obverse:** Armored bust right **Reverse:** Value, date within inner circle **Note:** Varieties exist.

Date	Mintage	VG	F	VF	XF	Unc
1720 LHL	48,000	32.00	70.00	135	250	—

KM# 185 1/6 THALER (1/4 Gulden)

Silver **Ruler:** Simon August **Obverse:** Head right **Reverse:** Value, date within inner circle

Date	Mintage	VG	F	VF	XF	Unc
1765 BS	—	20.00	40.00	90.00	225	—
1766	—	20.00	40.00	90.00	225	—
1767	—	20.00	40.00	90.00	225	—
1768	—	20.00	40.00	90.00	225	—
1769	—	20.00	40.00	90.00	225	—
1770	—	20.00	40.00	90.00	225	—

KM# 201 1/6 THALER (1/4 Gulden)

Silver **Ruler:** Simon August **Obverse:** Head right **Reverse:** Value

Date	Mintage	VG	F	VF	XF	Unc
1770 HDS	—	20.00	40.00	90.00	225	—

KM# 133 1/4 THALER

Silver **Ruler:** Friedrich Adolf **Subject:** 46th Birthday of Friedrich Adolf **Obverse:** Armored bust right **Reverse:** Inscription **Note:** Klippe. Varieties exist.

Date	Mintage	VG	F	VF	XF	Unc
1713	—	150	325	650	1,000	—
1713 B	—	150	325	650	1,000	—

KM# 128 1/3 THALER (1/2 Gulden)

Silver **Ruler:** Friedrich Adolf **Obverse:** Armored bust right **Reverse:** Quartered arms with crown above and value in oval below **Note:** Varieties exist.

Date	Mintage	VG	F	VF	XF	Unc
1712 HL	—	80.00	200	400	650	—
1713 HL	5,703	80.00	200	400	650	—
1715 HL	—	80.00	200	400	650	—
1716 HL	—	80.00	200	400	650	—

KM# 134.1 1/3 THALER (1/2 Gulden)

Silver **Ruler:** Friedrich Adolf **Obverse:** Armored bust right **Reverse:** Small crown above shield, date in legend **Note:** Varieties exist.

Date	Mintage	VG	F	VF	XF	Unc
1713 HL	Inc. above	80.00	200	400	650	—

KM# 134.2 1/3 THALER (1/2 Gulden)

Silver **Ruler:** Friedrich Adolf **Obv. Legend:** Large crown above shield **Reverse:** Large crown above shield **Note:** Varieties exist.

Date	Mintage	VG	F	VF	XF	Unc
1717 LHL	8,388	80.00	200	400	650	—

KM# 138 1/3 THALER (1/2 Gulden)
Silver **Ruler:** Friedrich Adolf **Reverse:** Arms in shield with straight sides divide date **Note:** Varieties exist.

Date	Mintage	VG	F	VF	XF	Unc
1714 HL	2,565	80.00	200	400	650	—

KM# 158 1/3 THALER (1/2 Gulden)
Silver **Ruler:** Simon Heinrich Adolf **Obverse:** Armored bust right **Reverse:** Date divided above arms, value (1/3) below

Date	Mintage	VG	F	VF	XF	Unc
1719 LHL	—	150	325	675	1,000	—

KM# 202 1/3 THALER (1/2 Gulden)
Silver **Ruler:** Simon August **Obverse:** Crowned arms within cartouche **Reverse:** Value, date

Date	Mintage	VG	F	VF	XF	Unc
1772	—	30.00	60.00	100	185	—

KM# 149 1/2 THALER
Silver **Ruler:** Friedrich Adolf **Subject:** 47th Birthday of Friedrich Adolf **Obverse:** Bust right, titles in legend **Reverse:** Crowned oval arms, supported by 2 lions, IVSTVM ER DECORVM above, date divided below **Note:** Octagonal klippe.

Date	Mintage	VG	F	VF	XF	Unc
1715	—	575	1,200	2,400	5,000	—

KM# 169 1/2 THALER
Silver **Ruler:** Simon Heinrich Adolf **Subject:** 33rd Birthday of Simon Heinrich Adolf **Obverse:** Bust right, titles in legend **Obv. Legend:** XXXIII AET.ANNO/COMPLETO **Reverse:** 9-line inscription with date **Rev. Legend:** GOTT ERHALTE **Note:** Octagonal klippe.

Date	Mintage	VG	F	VF	XF	Unc
1727	—	500	1,100	2,200	4,500	—

KM# 118 2/3 THALER (Gulden)
Silver **Ruler:** Friedrich Adolf **Obverse:** Bust right **Reverse:** Helmeted curved-sided arms, date divided above, value 2/3 below

Date	Mintage	VG	F	VF	XF	Unc
1710 HL	2,230	150	325	650	1,000	—

KM# 123 2/3 THALER (Gulden)
Silver **Ruler:** Friedrich Adolf **Obverse:** Armored, draped bust right **Reverse:** Oval 4-fold arms with 4-fold central shield, 5 helmets above with date divided above **Note:** Varieties exist.

Date	Mintage	VG	F	VF	XF	Unc
1711 HL	4,682	100	250	500	900	—
1712 HL	1,472	100	250	500	900	—
1713 HL	3,975	100	250	500	900	—
1714 HL	9,163	100	250	500	900	—
1715 HL	5,852	100	250	500	900	—
1716 HL	Inc. above	100	250	500	900	—
1717 LHL	8,113	100	250	500	900	—

KM# 159 2/3 THALER (Gulden)
Silver **Ruler:** Simon Heinrich Adolf **Obverse:** Armored bust right **Reverse:** Date divided by value at bottom **Note:** Varieties exist.

Date	Mintage	VG	F	VF	XF	Unc
1719 LHL	120	175	400	750	1,250	—
1722 LHL	421	125	300	600	1,000	—

KM# 186 2/3 THALER (Gulden)
Silver **Ruler:** Simon August **Subject:** Second Marriage of the Prince **Obverse:** Head right **Reverse:** Crowned quartered arms with rosettes, within cartouche, value in oval below

Date	Mintage	VG	F	VF	XF	Unc
1765 BS	—	175	300	500	850	—

KM# 187 2/3 THALER (Gulden)
Silver **Ruler:** Simon August **Obverse:** Bust right **Reverse:** Crowned quartered arms with quartered shield at center, value in oval below

Date	Mintage	VG	F	VF	XF	Unc
1765 BS	—	125	250	400	700	—

KM# 197 2/3 THALER (Gulden)
Silver **Ruler:** Simon August **Obverse:** Bust right **Reverse:** Crowned arms

Date	Mintage	VG	F	VF	XF	Unc
1769	—	350	525	800	1,400	—

KM# 130 THALER
Silver **Ruler:** Friedrich Adolf **Obverse:** Bust right **Obv. Legend:** FRID • ADOLPH • COM • ET • NOB • D • LIP • **Reverse:** Crowned arms **Rev. Inscription:** IVSTVM ET DECORVM 17 • 12 **Note:** Dav. #2378.

Date	Mintage	VG	F	VF	XF	Unc
1712	300	800	1,500	2,500	4,500	—

KM# 131 THALER
Silver **Ruler:** Friedrich Adolf **Obverse:** Bust right **Obv. Legend:** FRIED • ADOLPH • - COM • & • NOB • D • LIPP • **Reverse:** Crowned arms, date and HL below **Rev. Legend:** IVSTVM • & • - DECORVM • **Note:** Dav. #2379.

Date	Mintage	VG	F	VF	XF	Unc
1712 B	Inc. above	400	700	1,200	1,850	—
1713 HL	2,057	400	700	1,200	1,850	—

KM# 129 THALER
Silver **Ruler:** Friedrich Adolf **Subject:** 45th Birthday of Friedrich Adolf **Obverse:** Bust right **Reverse:** Crown above 11-line inscription with date

Date	Mintage	VG	F	VF	XF	Unc
1712 TB	125	1,500	3,000	4,850	7,500	—

KM# 135 THALER
Silver **Ruler:** Friedrich Adolf **Subject:** 46th Birthday of Friedrich Adolt **Obverse:** Bust right **Reverse:** 12-line inscription with date

Date	Mintage	VG	F	VF	XF	Unc
1713 TB	228	750	1,500	2,850	5,500	—

KM# 139 THALER
Silver **Ruler:** Friedrich Adolf **Subject:** 47th Birthday of Friedrich Adolt **Obverse:** Bust right **Reverse:** 13-line inscription, crown above, date in chronogram of legend

Date	Mintage	VG	F	VF	XF	Unc
1714 TB	—	650	1,100	2,350	4,750	—

KM# 140 THALER
Silver **Ruler:** Friedrich Adolf **Obverse:** Bust right **Reverse:** Crowned arms, date and HL below **Rev. Legend:** SUPR.D.VIAN.ET.. **Note:** Dav. #2380.

Date	Mintage	VG	F	VF	XF	Unc
1714 HL	—	1,150	2,000	3,250	—	—

KM# 155 THALER

Silver **Ruler:** Friedrich Adolf **Obverse:** Armored bust right **Obv. Legend:** FRID • ADOLPH • - COM • ET • NOB • D • LIPP • **Reverse:** Crowned quartered arms surrounded by monograms in cruciform within small circles, Order chain surrounds all **Rev. Legend:** IVSTVM • & • - DECORVM • **Note:** Dav. #2382.

Date	Mintage	VG	F	VF	XF	Unc
1716 HL	—	450	800	1,400	2,500	—

KM# 156 THALER

Silver **Ruler:** Friedrich Adolf **Obverse:** Armored bust right **Note:** Dav. #2382A.

Date	Mintage	VG	F	VF	XF	Unc
1716 HL	190	—	—	—	—	—

KM# 160 THALER

Silver **Ruler:** Simon Heinrich Adolf **Obverse:** Bust right **Obv. Legend:** SIMON • HENRICH • - ADOLPH • COM • & • N • D • LIPP • **Reverse:** Helmeted arms, date in legend **Rev. Legend:** SVPR • D • VIAN • & AMEID BVRG • H • VLTR • 1719 **Note:** Dav. #2383.

Date	Mintage	VG	F	VF	XF	Unc
1719	80	750	1,500	3,500	6,500	—

KM# 161 THALER

Silver **Ruler:** Simon Heinrich Adolf **Obverse:** Armored, draped bust right **Obv. Legend:** SIMON • HENRICH • - ADOLPH • C • & • N • D • LIPP • **Reverse:** Date divided below arms **Rev. Legend:** SVPR • D • VIAN • & AMEID BVRG • H • VLTR • **Note:** Dav. #2384.

Date	Mintage	VG	F	VF	XF	Unc
1719 LHL	Inc. above	750	1,450	2,650	4,750	—

KM# 194 THALER

Silver **Ruler:** Simon August **Subject:** 41st Birthday of the Prince **Obverse:** Armored bust right **Obv. Legend:** SIMON AUGUST. COM & NOB • D • LIPP • S • D • V • & A • B • H • VLTR • **Reverse:** Legend within square, ornaments surround **Rev. Legend:** QUEM/QUADRAGESIES ET/SEMEL PATRIAE/NATUM ESSE/ GRATULAMUR/d: XII Jun./MDCCLXVII **Note:** Dav. #2385. Vereins Thaler.

Date	Mintage	VG	F	VF	XF	Unc
1767 BS	—	300	600	1,250	2,000	—

KM# 150 1-1/4 THALER

Silver **Ruler:** Friedrich Adolf **Obverse:** Armored bust right **Reverse:** Quartered arms within crowned quartered arms with supporters **Note:** Dav. #2381. Klippe.

Date	Mintage	F	VF	XF	Unc
1715 B	200	2,000	4,000	6,500	10,000

KM# 151 1-1/4 THALER

Silver **Ruler:** Friedrich Adolf **Obverse:** Armored bust right **Note:** Dav. #2381A.

Date	Mintage	F	VF	XF	Unc
1715 HL Rare	Inc. above	—	—	—	—

TRADE COINAGE

KM# 141 1/4 DUCAT

0.8750 g., 0.9860 Gold 0.0277 oz. AGW **Ruler:** Friedrich Adolf **Obverse:** Bust right **Reverse:** Value

Date	Mintage	VG	F	VF	XF	Unc
1714 HL	—	150	300	550	1,000	—
1715	—	150	300	550	1,000	—

KM# 119 DUCAT

3.5000 g., 0.9860 Gold 0.1109 oz. AGW **Ruler:** Friedrich Adolf **Subject:** 43rd Birthday of the Prince **Obverse:** Armored bust right **Reverse:** Legend

Date	Mintage	VG	F	VF	XF	Unc
1710	—	400	900	1,700	3,000	—
ND	—	400	900	1,700	3,000	—

KM# 120 DUCAT

3.5000 g., 0.9860 Gold 0.1109 oz. AGW **Ruler:** Friedrich Adolf **Obverse:** Bust right **Reverse:** Crowned squarish 4-fold arms with 4-fold central shield in baroque frame divide date **Note:** Varieties exist.

Date	Mintage	VG	F	VF	XF	Unc
ND(ca. 1710)	—	500	1,000	2,000	4,000	—
1711 HL	Inc. above	500	1,000	2,000	4,000	—
1712 HL	70	500	1,000	2,000	4,000	—

KM# 124 DUCAT

3.5000 g., 0.9860 Gold 0.1109 oz. AGW **Ruler:** Friedrich Adolf **Reverse:** Helmeted oval arms

Date	Mintage	VG	F	VF	XF	Unc
1711 HL	70	450	950	1,800	3,500	—
1712 HL	—	450	950	1,800	3,500	—
1714 HL	100	450	950	1,800	3,500	—
1715 HL	—	450	950	1,800	3,500	—
1716 HL	116	450	950	1,800	3,500	—

KM# 142 DUCAT

3.5000 g., 0.9860 Gold 0.1109 oz. AGW **Ruler:** Friedrich Adolf **Obverse:** Bust right **Reverse:** 7-line inscription below crown

Date	Mintage	VG	F	VF	XF	Unc
ND(1714)	—	900	1,600	3,200	6,000	—

KM# 157 DUCAT

3.5000 g., 0.9860 Gold 0.1109 oz. AGW **Ruler:** Simon Heinrich Adolf **Obverse:** Bust right

Date	Mintage	VG	F	VF	XF	Unc
1718 LHL	73	450	950	1,800	3,500	—
1719 LHL	100	450	950	1,800	3,500	—

KM# 188 DUCAT

3.5000 g., 0.9860 Gold 0.1109 oz. AGW **Ruler:** Simon August **Obverse:** Head right **Reverse:** Crowned arms in sprays

Date	Mintage	VG	F	VF	XF	Unc
1765	—	350	750	1,250	2,500	—

KM# 195 DUCAT

3.5000 g., 0.9860 Gold 0.1109 oz. AGW **Ruler:** Simon August **Reverse:** Arms and date

Date	Mintage	VG	F	VF	XF	Unc
1767	—	400	900	1,600	3,000	—

KM# 198 DUCAT

3.5000 g., 0.9860 Gold 0.1109 oz. AGW **Ruler:** Simon August **Subject:** Prince's 3rd Marriage **Obverse:** Busts facing each other **Reverse:** Hands held at center

Date	Mintage	VG	F	VF	XF	Unc
1769	—	400	900	1,500	2,250	—

KM# 143 2 DUCAT

7.0000 g., 0.9860 Gold 0.2219 oz. AGW **Ruler:** Friedrich Adolf **Obverse:** Bust right **Reverse:** Crowned arms

Date	Mintage	VG	F	VF	XF	Unc
1714 IHL	—	2,500	4,000	6,000	9,500	—

KM# 163 4 DUCAT

14.0000 g., 0.9860 Gold 0.4438 oz. AGW **Ruler:** Simon Heinrich Adolf **Obverse:** Bust right **Reverse:** Crowned arms

Date	Mintage	VG	F	VF	XF	Unc
1719 LHL Rare	—	—	—	—	—	—

KM# 125 5 DUCAT

17.5000 g., 0.9860 Gold 0.5547 oz. AGW **Ruler:** Friedrich Adolf **Obverse:** Bust right **Reverse:** Crowned arms

Date	Mintage	VG	F	VF	XF	Unc
1711 LHL Rare	—	—	—	—	—	—
1715 LHL Rare	—	—	—	—	—	—
1716 LHL Rare	—	—	—	—	—	—

KM# A143 5 DUCAT

17.5000 g., 0.9860 Gold 0.5547 oz. AGW **Ruler:** Friedrich Adolf **Subject:** 47th Birthday of Friedrich Adolf

Date	Mintage	VG	F	VF	XF	Unc
1715	—	—	—	7,500	12,500	—

Note: Struck with 1/2 Thaler dies, KM#149

KM# 132 10 DUCAT

35.0000 g., 0.9860 Gold 1.1095 oz. AGW **Ruler:** Friedrich Adolf **Obverse:** Bust right **Obv. Legend:** FRID • ADOLF • - COM • ET • NOB • D • LIPP • **Reverse:** Crowned arms in order ribbon **Rev. Legend:** IVSTVM • ET • DECORVM • 1712

Date	Mintage	VG	F	VF	XF	Unc
1712 LHL Rare	—	—	—	—	—	—

Note: Stacks International sale 3-88 AU realized $16,500

Date	Mintage	VG	F	VF	XF	Unc
1715 LHL Rare	—	—	—	—	—	—

PATTERNS

Including off metal strikes

KM#	Date	Mintage	Identification	Mkt Val
Pn8	1710	—	1/48 Thaler. Gold. KM#116.	—
Pn9	1710	—	Ducat. Silver. Weight of 1/4 Thaler, KM#119.	150
Pn10	1711	—	Ducat. Silver. KM#120.	—
Pn11	1712	—	Ducat. Silver. KM#124.	—
Pn13	1716	—	Ducat. Copper. KM#124.	—

KM#	Date	Mintage	Identification	Mkt Val
Pn14	1722	—	2/3 Thaler. Copper. . KM#159.	—

LORRAINE

(Lothringen)

Lorraine was established as a kingdom for Lothaire in the mid-9th century and was a part of the Carolingian Empire. It emerged as a duchy in the early 10th century and eventually became a buffer state between Germany and France. By 955, following several revolts which had their roots in Lorraine, Emperor Otto I (936-73) divided the territory in Lower Lorraine, which later became Brabant, and Upper Lorraine, the region which stretched along the Meuse and Mosel Rivers southwards to Burgundy. It is the latter entity, often associated with Alsace (see), which has come down to modern Europe as Lorraine.

The duchy was often a source of contention between the emperors and the kings of France, especially in the 17th century. France occupied it several times, from 1634-41, 1643-44, 1654-61, and 1673-75, and then again 1690-97. In 1736, duke Franz III married Maria Theresa, daughter of Emperor Karl VI and reigned as Emperor Franz I (1745-65). He exchanged Lorraine with France at the end of 1736 and received the Grand Duchy of Tuscany as compensation in the following year. The former King of Poland, Stanislaw Leszczinski, succeeded Franz III (I) in Lorraine, but the duchy was finally incorporated into France upon his death in 1766. Along with Alsace, Lorraine was acquired by the German Empire after the defeat of France by Prussia in the Franco-Prussian War of 1870-71. The Treaty of Versailles returned Alsace and Lorraine to France in 1919.

RULERS

Leopold, (1690) 1697-1729
Franz III, 1729-1736

MINTS

Badenweiler
Florence
Nancy
Romarti (Remiremont)
Stenay

MINT MARKS

G – Unknown mint official at Nancy, late 16th-early 17th c.
A – Paris

ARMS

Lorraine – band from upper left to lower right on which 3 small eagles
Bar – two fish standing on tails, four small crosses around

MONETARY SYSTEM

3 Deniers = 1 Liard
4 Liards = 1 Sol
25 Sols = 1 Livre
6 Livres = 1 Ecu
4 Ecus = 1 Louis D'or

DUCHY

STANDARD COINAGE

KM# 70 DENIER

Copper **Ruler:** Leopold Joseph as Leopold I **Obverse:** Crowned arms **Reverse:** Monogram within four crosses

Date	Mintage	VG	F	VF	XF	Unc
ND(1697-1729)	—	12.00	22.00	45.00	90.00	—

KM# 71 DENIER

Copper **Ruler:** Leopold Joseph as Leopold I **Reverse:** Monogram with cross above and eagles at sides and bottom

Date	Mintage	VG	F	VF	XF	Unc
ND(1697-1729)	—	12.00	22.00	45.00	90.00	—

KM# 72 DENIER

Silver **Ruler:** Leopold Joseph as Leopold I **Obverse:** Head right **Obv. Legend:** LEOP • I • D • G • D • LOT • BA • REX • IE • **Reverse:** Radiant cross of Lorraine with four crowned eagles

Date	Mintage	VG	F	VF	XF	Unc
1728	—	25.00	50.00	90.00	180	—

KM# 73 12 DENIERS

Silver **Ruler:** Leopold Joseph as Leopold I **Obverse:** Crowned cross of Lorraine in field of eagles **Reverse:** Cross of Lorraine within three monograms and eagles

Date	Mintage	VG	F	VF	XF	Unc
1726	—	20.00	40.00	85.00	175	—
1727	—	20.00	40.00	85.00	175	—
1728	—	20.00	40.00	85.00	175	—

KM# 74 15 DENIERS

Silver **Ruler:** Leopold Joseph as Leopold I **Obverse:** Crowned double L monogram, three small eagles in field **Obv. Legend:** LEOP • I • D • G • D • LOT • BA • REX • IER • **Reverse:** Cross of Lorraine with eagles in angles

Date	Mintage	VG	F	VF	XF	Unc
ND(1697-1729)	—	15.00	35.00	75.00	150	—

KM# 76 30 DENIERS

Silver **Ruler:** Leopold Joseph as Leopold I **Obverse:** Crowned double L monogram, three small eagles in field **Reverse:** Cross of Lorraine with eagles in angles **Note:** Similar to 15 Deniers, KM#74.

Date	Mintage	VG	F	VF	XF	Unc
ND(1697-1729)	—	20.00	35.00	75.00	160	—

KM# 77 30 DENIERS

Silver **Ruler:** Leopold Joseph as Leopold I **Obverse:** Monogram in block letters **Reverse:** Cross of Lorraine with eagles in angles **Note:** Similar to 15 Deniers, KM#74.

Date	Mintage	VG	F	VF	XF	Unc
ND(1697-1729)	—	12.00	25.00	50.00	120	—

KM# 75 30 DENIERS

Silver **Ruler:** Leopold Joseph as Leopold I **Obverse:** Crowned cross of Lorraine in field of eagles **Reverse:** Cross of Lorraine within three monograms and eagles

Date	Mintage	VG	F	VF	XF	Unc
1726	—	12.00	25.00	50.00	120	—
1727	—	12.00	25.00	50.00	120	—

KM# 78 30 DENIERS

Silver **Ruler:** Leopold Joseph as Leopold I **Obverse:** Crowned eagle **Reverse:** Cross with four small crosses

Date	Mintage	VG	F	VF	XF	Unc
1728	—	12.00	25.00	50.00	120	—
1729	—	12.00	25.00	50.00	120	—

KM# 125 30 DENIERS

Silver **Ruler:** Franz III **Obverse:** Crowned eagle **Reverse:** Cross with four small crosses

Date	Mintage	VG	F	VF	XF	Unc
1729	—	12.50	27.50	60.00	140	—

KM# 79 60 DENIERS

Silver **Ruler:** Leopold Joseph as Leopold I **Obverse:** Crowned cross of Lorraine in field of eagles **Reverse:** Cross of Lorraine within three monograms and eagles

Date	Mintage	VG	F	VF	XF	Unc
1726	—	25.00	50.00	125	225	—

KM# 80 LIARD

Copper **Ruler:** Leopold Joseph as Leopold I **Obverse:** Bust right **Reverse:** Crowned cross

Date	Mintage	VG	F	VF	XF	Unc
1704	—	7.00	15.00	30.00	60.00	—

KM# 81 LIARD

Copper **Ruler:** Leopold Joseph as Leopold I **Rev. Inscription:** LIARD/DE/LORRAINE

Date	Mintage	VG	F	VF	XF	Unc
1706	—	6.00	12.00	25.00	50.00	—
1707	—	6.00	12.00	25.00	50.00	—
1708	—	6.00	12.00	25.00	50.00	—
1710	—	6.00	12.00	25.00	50.00	—
1711	—	6.00	12.00	25.00	50.00	—
1713	—	6.00	12.00	25.00	50.00	—
1714	—	6.00	12.00	25.00	50.00	—
1715	—	6.00	12.00	25.00	50.00	—
1726	—	6.00	12.00	25.00	50.00	—
1727	—	6.00	12.00	25.00	50.00	—
1728	—	6.00	12.00	25.00	50.00	—
1729	—	6.00	12.00	25.00	50.00	—

KM# 82 SOL

Silver **Ruler:** Leopold Joseph as Leopold I **Mint:** Nancy **Obverse:** Crown above two oval arms **Reverse:** Crowned eagle

Date	Mintage	VG	F	VF	XF	Unc
ND(1697-1729)	—	10.00	20.00	40.00	80.00	—

KM# 83 SOL

Silver **Ruler:** Leopold Joseph as Leopold I **Obverse:** Crowned two-part arms **Reverse:** Eagle

Date	Mintage	VG	F	VF	XF	Unc
ND(1697-1729)	—	10.00	20.00	40.00	80.00	—

KM# 84 1/2 TESTON

Silver **Ruler:** Leopold Joseph as Leopold I **Obverse:** Bust right **Reverse:** Crowned arms

Date	Mintage	VG	F	VF	XF	Unc
1700	—	35.00	85.00	175	325	—
1709	—	35.00	85.00	175	325	—

KM# 85 1/2 TESTON

Silver **Ruler:** Leopold Joseph as Leopold I **Obverse:** Bust right **Reverse:** Crowned arms with two crosses above

Date	Mintage	VG	F	VF	XF	Unc
1702	—	35.00	75.00	150	300	—

KM# 86 1/2 TESTON

Silver **Ruler:** Leopold Joseph as Leopold I **Obverse:** Bust right **Obv. Legend:** LEOP • I • D • G • D • LOT • BA • REX • IER • **Reverse:** Crowned shield

Date	Mintage	VG	F	VF	XF	Unc
1705	—	35.00	75.00	150	300	—

KM# 87 1/2 TESTON

Silver **Ruler:** Leopold Joseph as Leopold I **Reverse:** Crowned cross of Lorraine

Date	Mintage	VG	F	VF	XF	Unc
1710	—	35.00	75.00	150	300	—
1711	—	35.00	75.00	150	300	—
1712	—	35.00	75.00	150	300	—

KM# 88 1/2 TESTON

Silver **Ruler:** Leopold Joseph as Leopold I **Obverse:** Head right **Obv. Legend:** LEOP•I•D•G•D•LOT•BA•REX•IER• **Reverse:** Crowned shielded Cross of Lorraine with crosses at angles

Date	Mintage	VG	F	VF	XF	Unc
1716	—	35.00	75.00	150	300	—
1717	—	35.00	75.00	150	300	—

KM# 89 1/2 TESTON

Silver **Ruler:** Leopold Joseph as Leopold I **Obverse:** Head right **Obv. Legend:** LEOP • I • D • G • D • LOT • BA • REX • IE • **Reverse:** Crowned shield

Date	Mintage	VG	F	VF	XF	Unc
1718	—	35.00	75.00	150	300	—
1719	—	35.00	75.00	150	300	—
1720	—	35.00	75.00	150	300	—
1722	—	35.00	75.00	150	300	—

KM# 90 TESTON

Silver **Ruler:** Leopold Joseph as Leopold I **Mint:** Nancy **Obverse:** Bust right **Reverse:** Crowned plain oval arms

Date	Mintage	VG	F	VF	XF	Unc
1700	—	75.00	150	325	650	—
1701	—	75.00	150	325	650	—
1702	—	75.00	150	325	650	—
1703	—	75.00	150	325	650	—
1704	—	75.00	150	325	650	—
1709	—	65.00	125	250	500	—

Date	Mintage	VG	F	VF	XF	Unc
1710	—	65.00	125	250	500	—

KM# 91 TESTON

Silver **Ruler:** Leopold Joseph as Leopold I **Reverse:** Cross of Lorraine on crowned ornate oval arms

Date	Mintage	VG	F	VF	XF	Unc
1700	—	75.00	150	325	650	—
1701	—	75.00	150	325	650	—
1702	—	75.00	150	325	650	—

KM# 92 TESTON

Silver **Ruler:** Leopold Joseph as Leopold I **Obverse:** Bust right **Obv. Legend:** LEOP • I • D • G • D • LOT • BA • REX • IE • **Reverse:** Crowned oval shield within cartouche **Rev. Legend:** IN • TE • DOMINE • SPERAVI •

Date	Mintage	VG	F	VF	XF	Unc
1700	—	75.00	150	325	650	—
1702	—	75.00	150	325	650	—
1704	—	75.00	150	325	650	—

KM# 93 TESTON

Silver **Ruler:** Leopold Joseph as Leopold I **Obverse:** Bust right **Obv. Legend:** LEOP • I • D • G • D • LOT • BA • REX • IER • **Reverse:** Crowned two-fold shield **Rev. Legend:** IN • TE • DOMINE • SPERAVI •

Date	Mintage	VG	F	VF	XF	Unc
1704	—	75.00	150	325	650	—

KM# 94 TESTON

Silver **Ruler:** Leopold Joseph as Leopold I **Obverse:** Bust right **Obv. Legend:** LEOP • I • D • G • D • LOT • BA • REX • IER • **Reverse:** Crowned shield, small crosses at left and right **Rev. Legend:** IN • TE • DOMINE • SPERAVI •

Date	Mintage	VG	F	VF	XF	Unc
1704	—	65.00	125	250	500	—
1705	—	65.00	125	250	500	—

KM# 95 TESTON

Silver **Ruler:** Leopold Joseph as Leopold I **Obverse:** Head right **Obv. Legend:** LEOP • I • D • G • D • LOT • BA • REX • IER • **Reverse:** Crowned cross of Lorraine **Rev. Legend:** IN • TE • DOMINE • SPERAVI •

Date	Mintage	VG	F	VF	XF	Unc
1709	—	50.00	100	200	400	—
1710	—	50.00	100	200	400	—
1711	—	50.00	100	200	400	—
1712	—	50.00	100	200	400	—
1713	—	50.00	100	200	400	—
1714	—	50.00	100	200	400	—
1715	—	50.00	100	200	400	—
1716	—	50.00	100	200	400	—

KM# 96 TESTON

Silver **Ruler:** Leopold Joseph as Leopold I **Obverse:** Head right **Obv. Legend:** LEOP • I • D • G • D • LOT • BA • REX • IE • **Reverse:** Crowned shield holds Cross of Lorraine with crosses at angles **Rev. Legend:** IN • TE • DOMINE • SPERAVI •

Date	Mintage	VG	F	VF	XF	Unc
1716	—	50.00	100	200	400	—
1717	—	50.00	100	200	400	—

KM# 97 TESTON

Silver **Ruler:** Leopold Joseph as Leopold I **Obverse:** Head right **Reverse:** Crowned arms in cartouche

Date	Mintage	VG	F	VF	XF	Unc
1716 Rare	—	—	—	—	—	—

KM# 98 TESTON

Silver **Ruler:** Leopold Joseph as Leopold I **Obverse:** Head right **Obv. Legend:** LEOP • I • D • G • D • LOT • BA • REX • IE • **Reverse:** Crowned shield **Rev. Legend:** IN • TE • DOMINE • SPERAVI •

Date	Mintage	VG	F	VF	XF	Unc
1718	—	35.00	75.00	150	300	—
1719	—	35.00	75.00	150	300	—
1720	—	35.00	75.00	150	300	—
1722	—	35.00	75.00	150	300	—
1723	—	35.00	75.00	150	300	—

KM# 99 TESTON

Silver **Ruler:** Leopold Joseph as Leopold I **Obverse:** Head right **Obv. Legend:** LEOP • I • D • G • D • LOT • BAR • REX • IER • **Reverse:** Crowned shield **Rev. Legend:** IN • TE • DOMINE • SPERAVI •

Date	Mintage	VG	F	VF	XF	Unc
1722	—	30.00	65.00	125	250	—
1723	—	30.00	65.00	125	250	—

KM# 126 TESTON

Silver **Ruler:** Franz III **Obverse:** Armored bust right **Obv. Legend:** FRANC • III • D • G • DVX • LOT • BAR • REX • IER • **Reverse:** Crowned shield, double crosses at left and right **Rev. Legend:** IN • TE • DOMINE • SPERAVI •

Date	Mintage	VG	F	VF	XF	Unc
1736	—	50.00	110	240	500	—

KM# 100 1/8 THALER

Silver **Ruler:** Leopold Joseph as Leopold I **Note:** Similar to 1/4 Thaler, KM#101.

Date	Mintage	VG	F	VF	XF	Unc
1718	—	25.00	50.00	85.00	175	—
1719	—	25.00	50.00	85.00	175	—
1720	—	25.00	50.00	85.00	175	—
1724	—	25.00	50.00	85.00	175	—

KM# 101 1/4 THALER

Silver **Ruler:** Leopold Joseph as Leopold I **Obverse:** Head right **Obv. Legend:** LEOP • I • D • G • D • LOT • BAR • REX • IER • **Reverse:** Crowned shield **Rev. Legend:** IN • TE • DOMINE • SPERAVI •

Date	Mintage	VG	F	VF	XF	Unc
1718	—	—	—	—	—	—
1724	—	30.00	60.00	120	250	—
1725	—	30.00	60.00	120	250	—

KM# 127 1/4 THALER

Silver **Ruler:** Franz III **Note:** Similar to 1 Teston, KM#126.

Date	Mintage	VG	F	VF	XF	Unc
1736	—	—	—	—	—	—

KM# 102 1/2 THALER

Silver **Ruler:** Leopold Joseph as Leopold I **Obverse:** Bust right **Obv. Legend:** LEOPOLDVS • I • D • G • D • LOT • BA • REX • IE **Reverse:** Crowned shield **Rev. Legend:** IN • TE • DOMINE • SPERAVI •

Date	Mintage	VG	F	VF	XF	Unc
1718	—	100	200	350	700	—
1719	—	100	200	350	700	—
1720	—	100	200	350	700	—

KM# 103 1/2 THALER

Silver **Ruler:** Leopold Joseph as Leopold I **Obverse:** Head right **Obv. Legend:** LEOP • I • D • G • D • LOT • BA • REX • IER • **Reverse:** Crowned shield **Rev. Legend:** IN • TE • DOMINE • SPERAVI •

Date	Mintage	VG	F	VF	XF	Unc
1724	—	150	250	400	800	—
1725	—	150	250	400	800	—

KM# 128 1/2 THALER

Silver **Ruler:** Franz III **Obverse:** Armored bust right **Obv. Legend:** FRANC • III • D • G • DVX • LOT • BAR • REX • IER • **Reverse:** Crowned two-fold arms, double crosses at right and left **Rev. Legend:** IN • TE • DOMINE • SPERAVI •

Date	Mintage	VG	F	VF	XF	Unc
1736	—	200	350	700	1,450	—

KM# 105 THALER

Silver **Ruler:** Leopold Joseph as Leopold I **Reverse:** Crowned shield arms **Note:** Dav. #2386.

Date	Mintage	VG	F	VF	XF	Unc
1702	—	600	1,000	1,600	3,000	—

KM# 106 THALER

Silver **Ruler:** Leopold Joseph as Leopold I **Obverse:** Draped bust right **Obv. Legend:** LEOP • I • D • G • D • LOT • BA • REX • IER • **Reverse:** Crowned arms of Lorraine and bar among branches and plumes **Rev. Legend:** IN • TE • DOMINE • SPERAVI • **Note:** Dav. #2387.

Date	Mintage	VG	F	VF	XF	Unc
1704	—	450	800	1,350	2,250	—
1705	—	450	800	1,350	2,250	—

KM# 107 THALER

Silver **Ruler:** Leopold Joseph as Leopold I **Obverse:** Head right **Obv. Legend:** LEOPOLDVS • I • D • G • D • LOT • BA • REX • IE • **Reverse:** Crowned round arms in palm sprays **Rev. Legend:** IN • TE • DOMINE • SPERAVI • **Note:** Dav. #2388.

Date	Mintage	VG	F	VF	XF	Unc
1710	—	500	850	1,450	2,350	—

KM# 108 THALER

20.0000 g., Silver **Ruler:** Leopold Joseph as Leopold I **Obverse:** Head right **Obv. Legend:** LEOP • I • D • G • D • LOT • BAR • REX • IER • **Reverse:** Crowned shield arms **Rev. Legend:** IN • TE • DOMINE • SPERAVI • **Note:** Dav. #2389.

Date	Mintage	VG	F	VF	XF	Unc
1724	—	350	600	1,000	1,750	—
1725	—	350	600	1,000	1,750	—

KM# 109 THALER

Silver **Ruler:** Leopold Joseph as Leopold I **Obverse:** Head right **Obv. Legend:** LEOP • I • D • G • D • LOT • BAR • REX • IER • **Reverse:** Crowned L's in cruciform **Rev. Legend:** IN • TE • DOMINE • SPERAVI • **Note:** Dav. #2390.

Date	Mintage	VG	F	VF	XF	Unc
1725	—	400	700	1,200	2,000	—
1726	—	400	700	1,200	2,000	—

KM# 129 THALER

16.0000 g., Silver **Ruler:** Franz III **Obverse:** Armored bust right **Obv. Legend:** FRANC • III • D • G • DVX • LOT • BAR • REX • IER • **Reverse:** Crowned two-fold shield **Rev. Legend:** IN • TE • DOMINE • SPERAVI • **Note:** Dav. #2940.

Date	Mintage	VG	F	VF	XF	Unc
1736	—	600	1,000	2,000	3,500	—

KM# 130 THALER

16.0000 g., Silver **Ruler:** Franz III **Reverse:** Crowned eight-section arms **Note:** Dav. #2941.

Date	Mintage	VG	F	VF	XF	Unc
1736 Rare	—	—	—	—	—	—

KM# 131 THALER

16.0000 g., Silver **Ruler:** Franz III **Reverse:** Crowned oval arms

Date	Mintage	VG	F	VF	XF	Unc
1736 Rare	—	—	—	—	—	—

KM# 110 2 THALER

42.0000 g., Silver **Ruler:** Leopold Joseph as Leopold I **Obverse:** Bust right **Reverse:** Crowned shield arms **Note:** Dav. #2989A.

Date	Mintage	VG	F	VF	XF	Unc
1725 Rare	—	—	—	—	—	—

KM# 111 1/2 LEOPOLD D'OR

3.3450 g., 0.9170 Gold 0.0986 oz. AGW **Ruler:** Leopold Joseph as Leopold I **Mint:** Nancy **Note:** Similar to 1 Leopold D'or, KM#118.

Date	Mintage	VG	F	VF	XF	Unc
1717 Rare	—	—	—	—	—	—
1718 Rare	—	—	—	—	—	—

KM# 112 1/2 LEOPOLD D'OR

3.3450 g., 0.9170 Gold 0.0986 oz. AGW **Ruler:** Leopold Joseph as Leopold I **Obverse:** Large laureate head right, date below **Reverse:** Crowned arms **Note:** Fr.161.

Date	Mintage	VG	F	VF	XF	Unc
1718	—	450	1,000	1,750	2,850	—
1719	—	450	1,000	1,750	2,850	—

KM# 112A 1/2 LEOPOLD D'OR

3.3450 g., 0.9170 Gold 0.0986 oz. AGW **Ruler:** Leopold Joseph as Leopold I **Obverse:** Small laureate head right **Obv. Legend:** LEOP • I • D • G • D • LOT • BAR • REX • IE • **Reverse:** Crowned shield **Rev. Legend:** TV • DOMINE • SPES • MEA

Date	Mintage	VG	F	VF	XF	Unc
1720	—	550	1,150	2,000	3,000	—

KM# 113 1/2 LEOPOLD D'OR

3.3450 g., 0.9170 Gold 0.0986 oz. AGW **Ruler:** Leopold Joseph as Leopold I **Reverse:** Crowned complex arms

Date	Mintage	VG	F	VF	XF	Unc
1724	—	450	1,000	1,750	2,850	—

KM# 115 LEOPOLD D'OR

6.6900 g., 0.9170 Gold 0.1972 oz. AGW **Ruler:** Leopold Joseph as Leopold I **Mint:** Nancy **Obverse:** Laureate head right **Obv. Legend:** LEOP • I • D • G • D • LOT • BAR • REX • IE • **Reverse:** Crowned L's in cruciform, double crosses at angles **Rev. Legend:** TV • DOMINE • SPES • MEA **Note:** Fr. #158.

Date	Mintage	VG	F	VF	XF	Unc
1700	—	1,000	2,250	3,750	5,500	—
1702	—	500	1,100	2,000	4,500	—
1703	—	500	1,100	2,000	4,500	—

KM# 116 LEOPOLD D'OR

6.6900 g., 0.9170 Gold 0.1972 oz. AGW **Ruler:** Leopold Joseph as Leopold I **Obverse:** Older laureate head right **Reverse:** Eagle in center of monogram **Note:** Similar to KM#117, but eagle in center of monogram.

Date	Mintage	VG	F	VF	XF	Unc
1710	—	1,000	2,250	3,750	5,500	—

KM# 117 LEOPOLD D'OR

6.6900 g., 0.9170 Gold 0.1972 oz. AGW **Ruler:** Leopold Joseph as Leopold I **Obverse:** Older laureate head right **Obv. Legend:** LEOP • I • D • G • D • LOT • BA • REX • IER • **Reverse:** Crowned L's in cruciform, eagles at angles **Rev. Legend:** TV • DO MINE SPES MEA

Date	Mintage	VG	F	VF	XF	Unc
1713	—	500	1,200	2,150	3,750	—

KM# 118 LEOPOLD D'OR

6.6900 g., 0.9170 Gold 0.1972 oz. AGW **Ruler:** Leopold Joseph as Leopold I **Obverse:** Laureate head right **Obv. Legend:** LEOP • I • D • G • D • LOT • BAR • REX • IE • **Reverse:** Crowned shields in cruciform, eagles at angles **Rev. Legend:** TV • DO MINE SPES MEA

Date	Mintage	VG	F	VF	XF	Unc
1717N	—	550	1,200	2,450	3,750	—

KM# 119 LEOPOLD D'OR

6.6900 g., 0.9170 Gold 0.1972 oz. AGW **Ruler:** Leopold Joseph as Leopold I **Obverse:** Head right **Obv. Legend:** LEOPOLDVS • I • D • G • D • LOT • BAR • REX • IE • **Reverse:** Crowned shield **Rev. Legend:** TV • DOMINE SPES • MEA **Note:** Fr.160.

Date	Mintage	VG	F	VF	XF	Unc
1718	—	650	1,850	3,250	4,000	—
1719	—	650	1,850	3,250	4,000	—

KM# 120 LEOPOLD D'OR

6.6900 g., 0.9170 Gold 0.1972 oz. AGW **Ruler:** Leopold Joseph as Leopold I **Obverse:** Head right **Obv. Legend:** LEOP • I • D • G • D • LOT • BA • REX • IE • **Reverse:** Crowned two-fold arms **Rev. Legend:** TV • DOMINE SPES • MEA

Date	Mintage	VG	F	VF	XF	Unc
1722	—	800	2,000	3,500	5,000	—
1724 Rare	—	—	—	—	—	—
1725 Rare	—	—	—	—	—	—

KM# 119A 1-1/2 LEOPOLD D'OR

9.7200 g., 0.9170 Gold 0.2866 oz. AGW **Ruler:** Leopold Joseph as Leopold I **Obverse:** Laureate head right **Obv. Legend:** LEOPOLDVS • I • D • G • D • LOT • BAR • REX • IE • **Reverse:** Crowned shield **Rev. Legend:** TV • DOMINE SPES • MEA

Date	Mintage	VG	F	VF	XF	Unc
1719	—	800	2,000	3,500	5,000	—

KM# 121 2 LEOPOLD D'OR
13.3800 g., 0.9170 Gold 0.3945 oz. AGW **Ruler:** Leopold Joseph as Leopold I **Mint:** Nancy **Obverse:** Laureate head right **Obv. Legend:** LEOPOLDVS • I • D • G • D • LOT • BAR • REX • IE • **Reverse:** Crowned shield **Rev. Legend:** TV • DOMINE SPES • MEA **Note:** Fr.159.

Date	Mintage	VG	F	VF	XF	Unc
1720	—	1,100	2,700	4,500	6,500	—

KM# 122 2 LEOPOLD D'OR
13.3800 g., 0.9170 Gold 0.3945 oz. AGW **Ruler:** Leopold Joseph as Leopold I **Obverse:** Laureate head right **Obv. Legend:** LEOPOL • I • D • G • D • LOT • BAR • REX • IER • **Reverse:** Crowned complex arms **Rev. Legend:** TV • DOMINE SPES • MEA **Note:** Fr.159.

Date	Mintage	VG	F	VF	XF	Unc
1724	—	1,200	3,300	5,500	8,000	—
1725	—	1,100	2,700	4,500	7,000	—
1726	—	750	1,850	3,250	5,500	—

KM# 132 DUCAT
3.3450 g., 0.9170 Gold 0.0986 oz. AGW **Ruler:** Franz III **Obverse:** Laureate bust right **Reverse:** Crowned oval arms **Note:** Fr.163.

Date	Mintage	VG	F	VF	XF	Unc
1736	—	800	1,700	2,950	4,500	—

KM# 134 2 DUCAT
6.6900 g., 0.9170 Gold 0.1972 oz. AGW **Ruler:** Franz III **Obverse:** Laureate armored bust right **Obv. Legend:** FRANC • III • D • G • DVX • LOT • BAR • REX • IER • **Reverse:** Crowned ornate arms **Rev. Legend:** TV • DOMINE • SPES • MEA **Note:** Fr.162.

Date	Mintage	VG	F	VF	XF	Unc
1736	—	1,450	3,250	5,500	8,000	—

LOWENSTEIN-WERTHEIM-ROCHEFORT

Rochefort was the Catholic branch of Lowenstein-Wertheim, established in 1635. From 1622 until about 1650, coinage for Lowenstein-Wertheim-Rochefort was struck at the mint of Cugnon in Luxembourg. The ruler was made Prince of the Empire in 1711. All lands in his possession were mediatized in 1806.

RULERS

Maximilian Charles, 1672-1718
Dominik Marquard, 1718-1735
Karl Thomas, 1735-1789
Dominik Constantin, 1789-1806

MINT

Cugnon Mint in Luxembourg

MINT OFFICIALS' INITIALS

Initials	Date	Name
(a)	1677-1718	Philipp Heinrich Muller, die-cutter in Augsburg
(b) – 2 horshoes	Ca.1712	Christian Holeisen in Augsburg
E(w)w	1765-77	Eberhard (Wertheim) Weber
IS	Ca.1703	
WE	1765-77	Weber & Eberhard

PRINCIPALITY
Catholic Branch

REGULAR COINAGE

KM# 85 PFENNING
Copper **Ruler:** Karl Thomas **Obverse:** CFZL monogram **Reverse:** Value above date

Date	Mintage	VG	F	VF	XF	Unc
1781	—	5.00	10.00	20.00	50.00	—

KM# 90 PFENNING
Copper **Ruler:** Dominik Constantin

Date	Mintage	VG	F	VF	XF	Unc
1790	—	3.00	7.00	15.00	35.00	—

KM# 91 PFENNING
Copper **Ruler:** Dominik Constantin

Date	Mintage	F	VF	XF	Unc
1790	—	5.00	10.00	30.00	150
1791	—	5.00	10.00	30.00	150
1792	—	5.00	10.00	30.00	150
1793	—	5.00	10.00	30.00	150
1794	—	5.00	10.00	30.00	150
1795	—	5.00	10.00	30.00	150
1796	—	5.00	10.00	30.00	150
1797	—	5.00	10.00	30.00	150
1798	—	5.00	10.00	30.00	150
1799	—	5.00	10.00	30.00	150
1800	—	5.00	10.00	30.00	150

KM# 92 PFENNING
Copper **Ruler:** Dominik Constantin **Obverse:** Crowned CF monogram

Date	Mintage	F	VF	XF	Unc
1790	—	5.00	10.00	35.00	175
1800	—	5.00	10.00	35.00	175

KM# 100 PFENNING
Copper **Ruler:** Dominik Constantin **Obverse:** Crowned C monogram on shield **Reverse:** Denomination, date

Date	Mintage	F	VF	XF	Unc
1800	—	6.00	12.00	40.00	185
1801	—	6.00	12.00	40.00	185
1802	—	6.00	12.00	40.00	185

KM# 45 1/4 KREUZER
Billon **Ruler:** Dominik Marquard **Mint:** Wertheim **Obverse:** Crowned imperial eagle on pedestal between palm branches, 4 small circles with L - Y - L - W around, date above **Reverse:** Value 1/4 in center

Date	Mintage	VG	F	VF	XF	Unc
1732	—	10.00	18.00	35.00	60.00	—

KM# 46 1/2 KREUZER
Billon **Ruler:** Dominik Marquard **Mint:** Wertheim **Obverse:** Crowned imperial eagle on pedestal between palm branches, 4 small circles with L - Y - L - W around, date above **Reverse:** Value 1/2 in center

Date	Mintage	VG	F	VF	XF	Unc
1732	—	10.00	18.00	35.00	60.00	—

KM# 35 KREUZER
Billon **Ruler:** Maximilian Charles **Mint:** Wertheim **Obverse:** Crowned 3-fold arms **Reverse:** I/KREU/TZER/date **Note:** Varieties exist.

Date	Mintage	VG	F	VF	XF	Unc
1697 FS	—	10.00	22.00	45.00	80.00	—
1703 FS	—	10.00	22.00	45.00	80.00	—

KM# 47 KREUZER
Billon **Ruler:** Dominik Marquard **Obverse:** Crowned imperial eagle on pedestal between palm branches, 4 small circles with L - I - L - W around, date above **Note:** Uniface.

Date	Mintage	VG	F	VF	XF	Unc
1732	—	—	—	—	—	—

KM# 57 KREUZER
Billon **Ruler:** Karl Thomas **Obverse:** Arms **Reverse:** Value and date

Date	Mintage	VG	F	VF	XF	Unc
1765	—	1.00	3.00	6.00	12.00	—

KM# 58 KREUZER
Copper **Ruler:** Karl Thomas **Obverse:** Crowned monogram **Reverse:** Value and date within baroque frame

Date	Mintage	VG	F	VF	XF	Unc
1767	—	3.00	5.00	10.00	25.00	—

KM# 59 KREUZER
Copper **Ruler:** Karl Thomas **Obverse:** Head right **Reverse:** Value and date within baroque frame

Date	Mintage	VG	F	VF	XF	Unc
1767	—	5.00	10.00	20.00	60.00	—
1768	—	5.00	10.00	20.00	60.00	—
1769	—	5.00	10.00	20.00	60.00	—

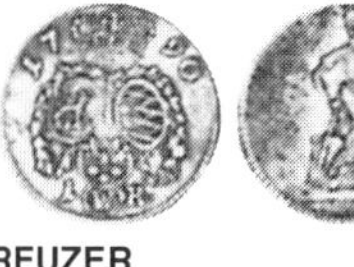

KM# 93 KREUZER
Billon **Ruler:** Dominik Constantin **Obverse:** Arms, 1 W K below **Reverse:** Ceres

Date	Mintage	F	VF	XF	Unc
ND	—	7.00	14.00	35.00	75.00
1790	—	7.00	14.00	35.00	75.00

KM# 96 KREUZER
Billon **Ruler:** Dominik Constantin **Obverse:** 1 below crowned arms **Reverse:** Ceres

Date	Mintage	F	VF	XF	Unc
ND(1798)	—	6.00	12.00	28.00	65.00

KM# 97 KREUZER
Billon **Ruler:** Dominik Constantin **Obverse:** Prince's crown above CFZL monogram

Date	Mintage	F	VF	XF	Unc
1798	—	5.00	10.00	28.00	70.00

KM# 60 2 KREUZER
Billon **Ruler:** Karl Thomas **Obverse:** Arms **Reverse:** Value and date

Date	Mintage	VG	F	VF	XF	Unc
1767	—	45.00	75.00	125	200	—

KM# 73 2-1/2 KREUZER
Billon **Ruler:** Karl Thomas **Obverse:** Bust right **Reverse:** Value and date

Date	Mintage	VG	F	VF	XF	Unc
1769	—	20.00	40.00	70.00	150	—

KM# 94 3 KREUZER (Groschen)
Billon **Ruler:** Dominik Constantin **Obverse:** Crowned arms **Reverse:** Seated lion with "C" shield

Date	Mintage	F	VF	XF	Unc
1790	—	10.00	25.00	60.00	175

KM# 36 4 KREUZER (Batzen)
Silver **Ruler:** Maximilian Charles **Mint:** Wertheim **Obverse:** Crowned imperial eagle, 4 in orb on breast, titles of Leopold I **Reverse:** Crowned oval 8-fold arms, date divided by crown in legend **Note:** Varieties exist.

Date	Mintage	VG	F	VF	XF	Unc
1702 IS	—	30.00	70.00	125	185	—

KM# 61 5 KREUZER

Billon **Ruler:** Karl Thomas **Obverse:** Head right **Reverse:** Crown above three oval arms, value in frame below

Date	Mintage	VG	F	VF	XF	Unc
1767	—	7.00	20.00	35.00	100	—
1769	—	7.00	20.00	35.00	100	—

KM# 62 10 KREUZER

Silver **Ruler:** Karl Thomas **Obverse:** Head right **Reverse:** Arms

Date	Mintage	F	VF	XF	Unc
1767	—	50.00	125	200	350

KM# 63 10 KREUZER

Silver **Ruler:** Karl Thomas **Obverse:** Arms **Reverse:** Value and date

Date	Mintage	F	VF	XF	Unc
1767	—	50.00	115	175	300

KM# 55 20 KREUZER

Silver **Ruler:** Karl Thomas **Obverse:** Draped bust right **Reverse:** Crowned complex arms within ornate frame atop pedestal with value

Date	Mintage	F	VF	XF	Unc
1762	—	25.00	60.00	100	375
1763	—	25.00	60.00	100	375
1764	—	25.00	60.00	100	375
1765	—	25.00	60.00	100	375
1766	—	25.00	60.00	100	375

KM# 64 20 KREUZER

Silver **Ruler:** Karl Thomas **Obverse:** Head right **Reverse:** Crowned complex arms above framed value

Date	Mintage	F	VF	XF	Unc
1767	—	25.00	60.00	100	375
1768	—	25.00	60.00	100	375
1769	—	25.00	60.00	100	375

KM# 65 20 KREUZER

Silver **Ruler:** Karl Thomas **Obverse:** Crown above 3 shields of arms, value framed below **Reverse:** Inscription within branches

Date	Mintage	F	VF	XF	Unc
1767	—	25.00	60.00	100	375

KM# 66 30 KREUZER

Silver **Ruler:** Karl Thomas **Obverse:** Bust right within square **Reverse:** Crown above 3 shields, value below, all within square

Date	Mintage	F	VF	XF	Unc
1767	—	25.00	60.00	125	400

KM# 71 1/2 THALER

Silver **Ruler:** Karl Thomas

Date	Mintage	F	VF	XF	Unc
1768 WE	—	275	450	750	1,300

KM# 74 1/2 THALER

Silver **Ruler:** Karl Thomas **Obverse:** Armored bust right **Reverse:** Crowned divided arms within Order chain, supporters at left and right

Date	Mintage	F	VF	XF	Unc
1769 WE	—	175	325	575	1,000

KM# 86 1/2 THALER

Silver **Ruler:** Karl Thomas **Obverse:** Head right **Reverse:** Crowned divided arms within Order chain **Note:** Convention 1/2 Thaler.

Date	Mintage	F	VF	XF	Unc
1789	—	150	275	475	850

KM# 40 THALER

Silver **Ruler:** Maximilian Charles **Obverse:** Armored bust right **Obv. Legend:** MAX • CAR • COM • in. LOWENSTEIN WERTH **Reverse:** Lion with date below **Rev. Legend:** IN CASVS PERVIGIL OMNES

Date	Mintage	VG	F	VF	XF	Unc
1711	—	450	850	1,750	3,000	—

KM# 41 THALER

Silver **Ruler:** Maximilian Charles **Obverse:** Armored, draped bust right **Obv. Legend:** D • G • MAX • - CAROL • S • R • IMP • **Reverse:** Crowned and mantled arms, date divided below **Rev. Legend:** * PRINC • IN LOWENSTEIN WERTH * **Note:** Dav.#2399.

Date	Mintage	VG	F	VF	XF	Unc
1712	—	350	600	1,100	1,750	—

KM# 50 THALER

Silver **Ruler:** Karl Thomas **Obverse:** Armored bust right with Order ribbon around neck **Obv. Legend:** CAROL D • G • S • R • IMP • PRINC • IN LOWENST • & WERTH • **Reverse:** Crowned arms with supporters **Rev. Legend:** CONSTANTIA ET PRUDENTIA **Note:** Dav.#2401.

Date	Mintage	F	VF	XF	Unc
1754	—	350	600	1,100	1,750

KM# 56 THALER

Silver **Ruler:** Karl Thomas **Obverse:** Armored bust right **Obv. Legend:** CAROL. D. G. S. R. IMP. PRINC. IN LÖWENST. & WERTH. **Reverse:** Crowned complex arms with supporters; one standing, one sitting **Rev. Legend:** X • EINE FFEINE - MARK • 1766. **Note:** Dav.#2402.

Date	Mintage	F	VF	XF	Unc
1766 N-SR	—	200	350	650	1,300

KM# 67 THALER
Silver **Ruler:** Karl Thomas **Obverse:** Larger bust right **Note:** Dav.#2404.

Date	Mintage	F	VF	XF	Unc
1767 E(W)W	—	200	275	500	1,150

KM# 69 THALER
Silver **Ruler:** Karl Thomas **Obverse:** Head right **Obv. Legend:** CAROL: D: G: S: R: I: PRIN: IN LOEWENST: & WERTH: **Reverse:** Crowned and supported arms on elaborate base **Rev. Legend:** X: EINE FEINE - MARK: **Note:** Dav.#2405.

Date	Mintage	F	VF	XF	Unc
1767 ST	—	125	200	450	900

KM# 68 THALER
Silver **Ruler:** Karl Thomas **Reverse:** Crowned and supported arms on base **Note:** Similar to KM#75 but crowned and supported arms on base. Dav.#2403.

Date	Mintage	F	VF	XF	Unc
1767 WEW	—	150	200	400	1,000

KM# 70 THALER
Silver **Ruler:** Karl Thomas **Obv. Legend:** ... ET WERTH **Note:** Dav#2405A.

Date	Mintage	F	VF	XF	Unc
1767 WEW	—	125	200	450	900

KM# 70A THALER
Silver **Ruler:** Karl Thomas **Obverse:** Head right **Reverse:** KM#70 **Note:** Mule. Dav#2405B.

Date	Mintage	F	VF	XF	Unc
1767 ST//WEW	—	125	200	450	900

KM# 72 THALER
Silver **Ruler:** Karl Thomas **Obverse:** Armored, draped bust right **Obv. Legend:** CAROL. D. G. S. R. I. PRIN. DE LOEWENST. WERTH. &. **Reverse:** Crowned and supported arms **Rev. Legend:** X. EINE FEINE MARCK. **Note:** Similar to KM#75; Dav.#2406.

Date	Mintage	F	VF	XF	Unc
1768 WWE	—	175	250	450	1,100

KM# 72A THALER
Silver **Ruler:** Karl Thomas **Obverse:** Head right **Reverse:** Crowned and supported arms **Note:** Mule. Dav#2406A.

Date	Mintage	F	VF	XF	Unc
1768 ST//WWE	—	175	250	450	1,100

KM# 79 THALER
Silver **Ruler:** Karl Thomas **Obverse:** Head right **Obv. Legend:** CAROL D: G: S: R: I: PRIN: IN LOEWENST: & WERTH: **Reverse:** Crowned and supported arms with Order chain **Rev. Legend:** X. EINE FEINE MARCK. **Note:** Dav.#2408.

Date	Mintage	F	VF	XF	Unc
1769 WWE	—	125	200	450	900

KM# 75 THALER
Silver **Ruler:** Karl Thomas **Obverse:** Armored, draped bust right **Obv. Legend:** CAROL. D. G. S. R. I. PRIN. DE LOEWENST. WERTH. &. **Reverse:** Crowned and supported arms **Rev. Legend:** X. EINE FEINE MARCK. **Note:** Dav.#2407.

Date	Mintage	F	VF	XF	Unc
1769 WWE	—	100	175	300	700

KM# 76 THALER
Silver **Ruler:** Karl Thomas **Reverse:** 1 tail on left lion **Note:** Dav#2407A.

Date	Mintage	F	VF	XF	Unc
1769 WWE	—	125	200	450	800

KM# 80 THALER
Silver **Ruler:** Karl Thomas **Obv. Legend:** ... LOEWENST: WERTH: **Note:** Dav#2408A.

Date	Mintage	F	VF	XF	Unc
1769 WWE	—	125	200	450	900

KM# 81 THALER
Silver **Ruler:** Karl Thomas **Reverse:** Left lion with 2 tails **Note:** Dav#2408B.

Date	Mintage	F	VF	XF	Unc
1769 WWE	—	125	200	450	900

KM# 77 THALER
Silver **Ruler:** Karl Thomas **Obverse:** Armored, draped bust right **Obv. Legend:** CAROL. D. G. S. R. I. PRIN. DE LOEWENST. WERTH. &. **Reverse:** Left lion looks up, not down **Rev. Legend:** X. EINE FEINE MARCK. **Note:** Dav#2407B.

Date	Mintage	F	VF	XF	Unc
1769 WWE	—	110	200	350	750

KM# 78 THALER
Silver **Ruler:** Karl Thomas **Obverse:** Without "&" **Note:** Dav.#2407C.

Date	Mintage	F	VF	XF	Unc
1769 WWE	—	110	200	350	750

KM# 51 2 THALER (Thick)
Silver **Ruler:** Karl Thomas **Obverse:** Armored bust of Karl Thomas right **Reverse:** Crowned and supported arms, date below **Note:** Dav.#2400.

Date	Mintage	F	VF	XF	Unc
1754	—	950	1,250	2,000	4,500

TRADE COINAGE

KM# 42 DUCAT
3.5000 g., 0.9860 Gold 0.1109 oz. AGW **Ruler:** Maximilian Charles **Subject:** Birth of Prince Leopold **Obverse:** Inscription

Date	Mintage	VG	F	VF	XF	Unc
1716	—	500	1,100	2,000	3,250	—

KM# 52 DUCAT
3.5000 g., 0.9860 Gold 0.1109 oz. AGW **Ruler:** Karl Thomas **Subject:** Karl Thomas **Obverse:** Bust left **Reverse:** Crowned arms with supporters

Date	Mintage	F	VF	XF	Unc
1754	—	600	1,200	2,200	3,750

KM# 95 DUCAT
3.5000 g., 0.9860 Gold 0.1109 oz. AGW **Ruler:** Dominik Constantin **Obverse:** Bust **Reverse:** Allegory

Date	Mintage	F	VF	XF	Unc
1791	—	1,650	3,000	5,000	7,500

PATTERNS

Including off metal strikes

KM#	Date	Mintage	Identification	Mkt Val
Pn1	1716	—	Ducat. Silver. KM42.	175
Pn2	1754	—	Ducat. Silver. KM52.	150

LOWENSTEIN-WERTHEIM-VIRNEBURG

The Protestant branch of the family dates from the division of 1635. There was a further division in 1721 into 3 branches, 2 of which survived more than one generation, only to be mediatized in 1806.

RULERS
Heinrich Friedrich, 1683-1721
I Johann Ludwig Vollrath, 1721-1790
Johann Karl Ludwig, 1790-1806
II Friedrich Ludwig, 1721-1796
III Karl Ludwig, 1721-1779
Friedrich Karl, 1779-1806

MINT OFFICIALS' INITIALS

Initials	Date	Name
IS	Ca.1703	
WE	1765-77	Weber & Eberhard

COUNTY
Protestant Branch

REGULAR COINAGE

KM# 20 KREUZER
Silver **Ruler:** Heinrich Friedrich **Obverse:** Titles of Heinrich Friedrich

Date	Mintage	VG	F	VF	XF	Unc
1703 IS	—	8.00	15.00	30.00	55.00	—
1704 IS	—	10.00	20.00	40.00	75.00	—

KM# 43 KREUZER
Billon **Ruler:** Johann Ludwig Vollrath Branch I **Obverse:** JLVGIL monogram **Reverse:** Arms

Date	Mintage	VG	F	VF	XF	Unc
1772	—	3.50	8.00	15.00	35.00	—

KM# 55 KREUZER
Billon **Obverse:** Crowned three-fold arms **Reverse:** Value above date

Date	Mintage	VG	F	VF	XF	Unc
1798	—	2.00	5.00	7.00	20.00	—

KM# 44 2-1/2 KREUZER
Billon **Ruler:** Johann Ludwig Vollrath Branch I **Obverse:** JLVGIL monogram

Date	Mintage	VG	F	VF	XF	Unc
1772	—	20.00	40.00	80.00	120	—

KM# 45 3 KREUZER (Groschen)
Billon **Ruler:** Johann Ludwig Vollrath Branch I **Obverse:** Bust right **Reverse:** Arms

Date	Mintage	VG	F	VF	XF	Unc
1772	—	4.00	9.00	16.00	38.00	—

KM# 21 4 KREUZER (Batzen)
Silver **Obverse:** Date divided by crown above arms, titles of Heinrich Friedrich in legend **Reverse:** Titles of Leopold I

Date	Mintage	VG	F	VF	XF	Unc
1703	—	15.00	35.00	65.00	100	—

KM# 27 10 KREUZER
Silver **Obverse:** Three shields of arms **Reverse:** Arms

Date	Mintage	F	VF	XF	Unc
1767	—	10.00	20.00	75.00	200

KM# 28 10 KREUZER

Silver **Obverse:** Head right **Reverse:** Crowned arms within branches

Date	Mintage	F	VF	XF	Unc
1767	—	10.00	20.00	75.00	200
1771 WE	—	10.00	20.00	75.00	200

KM# 29 20 KREUZER

Silver **Obverse:** Armored bust right **Reverse:** 4 Shields circle center shield, crown above, value in frame below

Date	Mintage	F	VF	XF	Unc
1767 WE	—	10.00	20.00	75.00	175

KM# 40 20 KREUZER

Silver

Date	Mintage	F	VF	XF	Unc
1770 WE	—	75.00	125	250	500

KM# 32 1/2 THALER

Silver **Obverse:** Armored bust right **Reverse:** 4 Shields circle center shield, crown above

Date	Mintage	F	VF	XF	Unc
1768 WR	—	300	500	1,000	1,700

KM# 36 1/2 THALER

Silver **Obverse:** Armored bust right **Reverse:** 5 shields circle center shield, crown above

Date	Mintage	F	VF	XF	Unc
1769	—	650	1,200	2,000	4,200
1770 WE	—	650	1,200	2,000	4,200

KM# 41 1/2 THALER

Silver **Obverse:** Armored, draped bust right **Reverse:** 4 Shields circle central shield, crown above

Date	Mintage	F	VF	XF	Unc
1770 WE	—	200	350	750	1,500

KM# 26 THALER

Silver **Obverse:** Bust of Johann LUdwig Vollrath right, ST on arm **Reverse:** Crowned and supported arms, date below **Note:** Dav. #2391.

Date	Mintage	F	VF	XF	Unc
1766 ST//WE	—	600	1,100	1,700	3,000

KM# 30 THALER

Silver **Reverse:** Date divided at bottom 17 W. 67 **Note:** Dav. #2392.

Date	Mintage	F	VF	XF	Unc
1767 ST//WE	—	500	800	1,400	2,300

KM# 33 THALER

Silver **Obverse:** Bust of Johannn Ludwig Vollrath right **Obv. Legend:** IN LOW WERTH **Reverse:** SUUM CUIQUE in crowned cartouche, lion below **Note:** Dav. #2393.

Date	Mintage	F	VF	XF	Unc
1768 WE	—	600	1,100	1,700	3,000

KM# 38 THALER

Silver **Ruler:** Friedrich Ludwig Branch II **Obverse:** Armored bust right **Obv. Legend:** FRIED • LUD • S • R • I • COM • IN • LOEWENST • WERTH • **Reverse:** 6 Shields circle center shield, crown above **Rev. Legend:** CONCORDIA RES PARVAE CRESCUNT, DISCORDIA DILABUNTUR, in inner row; X. EINE FEINE MARCK. **Note:** Dav. #2396.

Date	Mintage	F	VF	XF	Unc
1768 WE	—	300	500	950	1,750

KM# 37 THALER

Silver **Ruler:** Johann Ludwig Vollrath Branch I **Obverse:** Draped bust right **Obv. Legend:** IOH • LUD • VOLR • S • R • I • COM • IN LOEW • WERTH • **Reverse:** Lion lying beneath ornate frame **Rev. Legend:** X • EINE FEINE - MARCK • 1769 •, SUUM CUIQUE in cartouche **Note:** Dav. #2394.

Date	Mintage	F	VF	XF	Unc
1769 WE	—	300	500	950	1,600

KM# 42 THALER

Silver **Ruler:** Karl Ludwig Branch III **Obverse:** Draped bust right **Obv. Legend:** CAROL. LUD. S. R. I. COM. IN LOEWENST. WERTH. & C. **Reverse:** 4 Shields circle center shield, crown above **Rev. Legend:** * DEUS PROVIDEBIT *, below; X. EINE FEINE(W) MARCK. 1770 **Note:** Dav. #2397.

Date	Mintage	F	VF	XF	Unc
1770 WE	—	300	500	950	1,600

KM# 46 THALER

Silver **Obv. Legend:** IN LOW. WERTH **Note:** Dav. #2395.

Date	Mintage	F	VF	XF	Unc
1776 WE	—	300	500	900	1,500

TRADE COINAGE

KM# 25 1/4 DUCAT

0.8750 g., 0.9860 Gold 0.0277 oz. AGW **Obverse:** Arms **Reverse:** Crouching lion

Date	Mintage	VG	F	VF	XF	Unc
ND(1765-84)	—	200	400	750	1,250	—

KM# 31 DUCAT

3.5000 g., 0.9860 Gold 0.1109 oz. AGW **Ruler:** Karl Ludwig Branch III **Obverse:** Bust right **Reverse:** Five shields of arms, crowned

Date	Mintage	F	VF	XF	Unc
1767 WE	—	750	1,500	2,500	4,000

KM# 34 DUCAT

3.5000 g., 0.9860 Gold 0.1109 oz. AGW **Ruler:** Johann Ludwig Vollrath Branch I **Obverse:** Bust right **Reverse:** Arms

Date	Mintage	F	VF	XF	Unc
1768 WE	—	550	1,100	2,000	3,250
1769 WE	—	550	1,100	2,000	3,250
1771 WE	—	550	1,100	2,000	3,250

KM# 35 DUCAT

3.5000 g., 0.9860 Gold 0.1109 oz. AGW **Reverse:** Lion

Date	Mintage	F	VF	XF	Unc
ND	—	550	1,100	2,000	3,250

KM# 50 DUCAT

3.5000 g., 0.9860 Gold 0.1109 oz. AGW **Subject:** 50th Year of Reign **Obverse:** Bust **Reverse:** Kneeling figure

Date	Mintage	F	VF	XF	Unc
1780	—	550	1,100	2,000	3,250

KM# 56 DUCAT

3.5000 g., 0.9860 Gold 0.1109 oz. AGW **Obverse:** Armored bust right **Reverse:** Crowned arms divide date

Date	Mintage	F	VF	XF	Unc
1799	—	850	1,650	3,000	5,000

KM# 57 2 DUCAT

7.0000 g., 0.9860 Gold 0.2219 oz. AGW **Obverse:** Bust right **Reverse:** Crowned arms **Note:** Thick planchet.

Date	Mintage	F	VF	XF	Unc
1799	—	2,000	3,500	5,500	8,500

PATTERNS

Including off metal strikes

KM#	Date	Mintage	Identification	Mkt Val
Pn1	1780	—	2 Ducat. Silver. KM#50	400
Pn2	1799	—	2 Ducat. Silver. KM#56	200

LOWENSTEIN-WERTHEIM-VIRNEBURG & ROCHEFORT

COUNTY

JOINT COINAGE

KM# 5 PFENNING
Copper **Obverse:** L.W. with arms of Werthein below **Reverse:** Value and date

Date	Mintage	VG	F	VF	XF	Unc
1765	—	3.00	6.00	12.00	30.00	—

KM# 6 PFENNING
Copper **Obverse:** L.W. above three shields of arms **Reverse:** Value and date in branches

Date	Mintage	VG	F	VF	XF	Unc
1766	—	3.00	6.00	12.00	30.00	—

KM# 7 PFENNING
Copper **Obverse:** Arms on cartouche

Date	Mintage	VG	F	VF	XF	Unc
1766	—	4.00	8.00	16.00	35.00	—
1776	—	4.00	8.00	16.00	35.00	—
1780	—	4.00	8.00	16.00	35.00	—
1799	—	4.00	8.00	16.00	35.00	—

KM# 10 PFENNING
Copper **Obverse:** L.W. above 3 oval arms **Reverse:** Value in cartouche

Date	Mintage	VG	F	VF	XF	Unc
1769-81	—	4.00	8.00	16.00	35.00	—
1770	—	4.00	8.00	16.00	35.00	—
1776	—	4.00	8.00	16.00	35.00	—
1780	—	4.00	8.00	16.00	35.00	—
1781	—	4.00	8.00	16.00	35.00	—

KM# 20 PFENNING
Copper **Obverse:** Three-fold arms below L.W. **Reverse:** Value above date in ornamental border

Date	Mintage	VG	F	VF	XF	Unc
1791	—	3.00	6.00	12.00	30.00	—

KM# 21 PFENNING
Billon **Obverse:** Arms **Reverse:** Value above date

Date	Mintage	VG	F	VF	XF	Unc
1794	—	4.00	8.00	16.00	35.00	—
1795	—	4.00	8.00	16.00	35.00	—

KM# 25 PFENNING
Copper **Subject:** Eagle above three roses, value: 1 PF above **Note:** Uniface

Date	Mintage	F	VF	XF	Unc
1798	—	5.00	10.00	32.00	80.00
1799	—	5.00	10.00	32.00	80.00
1800	—	5.00	10.00	32.00	80.00
1801	—	5.00	10.00	32.00	80.00
1802	—	5.00	10.00	32.00	80.00
1803	—	5.00	10.00	32.00	80.00
1804	—	5.00	10.00	32.00	80.00

KM# 8 2 PFENNING
Copper **Obverse:** L.W. above 3 oval arms **Reverse:** Value, date

Date	Mintage	VG	F	VF	XF	Unc
1766	—	4.00	9.00	18.00	40.00	—

KM# 15 2 PFENNING
Copper **Obverse:** Arms on cartouche **Reverse:** Value in cartouche

Date	Mintage	VG	F	VF	XF	Unc
1776	—	4.00	9.00	18.00	40.00	—
1777	—	4.00	9.00	18.00	40.00	—
1778	—	4.00	9.00	18.00	40.00	—
1779	—	4.00	9.00	18.00	40.00	—
1780	—	4.00	9.00	18.00	40.00	—
1781	—	4.00	9.00	18.00	40.00	—

KM# 16 KREUZER
Billon **Obverse:** Arms **Reverse:** Value above date

Date	Mintage	VG	F	VF	XF	Unc
1776	—	5.00	10.00	20.00	45.00	—

KM# 26 KREUZER
Billon **Obverse:** Arms **Reverse:** Denomination, date **Note:** Varieties exist.

Date	Mintage	F	VF	XF	Unc
1800	—	5.00	10.00	30.00	75.00

KM# 17 2-1/2 KREUZER (3 Kreuzer Land Munze)
Billon **Obverse:** Three-fold arms **Reverse:** Three-line inscription above date **Note:** Convention 2-1/2 Kreuzer.

Date	Mintage	VG	F	VF	XF	Unc
1776	—	8.00	16.00	30.00	65.00	—

KM# 27.1 3 KREUZER
Billon **Obverse:** Arms **Reverse:** Denomination

Date	Mintage	F	VF	XF	Unc
1800	—	8.00	16.00	48.00	160

KM# 9 5 KREUZER
Billon **Obverse:** Arms **Reverse:** Value and date

Date	Mintage	VG	F	VF	XF	Unc
1767	—	12.00	25.00	40.00	75.00	—

LUBECK

BISHOPRIC

The bishopric was established at Lubeck ca. 1160. The first coins were struck ca. 1190. The bishops became Protestant during the Reformation. Territories were absorbed into Oldenburg during the reign of the last bishop. All the bishops of Lübeck from 1586 until 1802 were dukes of Schleswig-Holstein-Gottorp.

RULERS

August Friedrich, 1666-1705
Christian August, 1706-1726
Karl, 1726-1727
Adolf Friedrich, 1727-1750
Friedrich August, 1750-1785
Peter Friedrich Ludwig, 1785-1802

MINT OFFICIALS' INITIALS

Initials	Date	Name
AW	1702-24	Andreas Woltereck in Gluckstadt and Eutin
B	Ca.1776	
HR	1673-1715	Hans Ridder
III, JJJ	1727-58	Johann Justus Jaster

ARMS

Lübeck: A cross.
Schleswig: 2 lions walking left.
Holstein: Nettleleaf.

REGULAR COINAGE

KM# 75 DREILING (1/192 Thaler = 3 Pfennig)
Silver **Ruler:** Christian August **Obverse:** Crowned CA monogram **Reverse:** Value: I/DREI/LING/date/initials **Note:** Varieties exist.

Date	Mintage	VG	F	VF	XF	Unc
1723 AW	—	8.00	20.00	45.00	80.00	—
1724 AW	—	8.00	20.00	45.00	80.00	—
1724 JJJ	—	8.00	20.00	45.00	80.00	—
1724 III	—	8.00	20.00	45.00	80.00	—

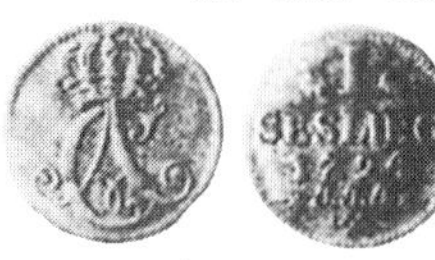

KM# 76 SECHSLING (1/96 Thaler = 6 Pfennig)
Silver **Ruler:** Christian August **Obverse:** Crowned monogram **Reverse:** Value, date **Note:** Similar to 1 Dreiling, KM#75, but SESLING on reverse.

Date	Mintage	VG	F	VF	XF	Unc
1723 AW	—	10.00	25.00	50.00	95.00	—
1724 AW	—	10.00	25.00	50.00	95.00	—
1724 JJJ	—	10.00	25.00	50.00	95.00	—
1724 III	—	10.00	25.00	50.00	95.00	—

KM# 77 6 SCHILLING
Silver **Ruler:** Christian August **Obverse:** Crowned CA monogram **Reverse:** Value: VI/SCHILLING/LUB: /date/initials **Note:** Varieties exist.

Date	Mintage	VG	F	VF	XF	Unc
1723 AW	—	15.00	32.00	60.00	100	—
1724 AW	—	15.00	32.00	60.00	100	—
1724 JJJ	—	15.00	32.00	60.00	100	—
1724 III	—	15.00	32.00	60.00	100	—
1725 JJJ	—	15.00	32.00	60.00	100	—

KM# 78 2 MARCK (Gulden)
Silver **Ruler:** Christian August **Obverse:** Bust right **Reverse:** Crowned arms with central shield of Lubeck cross divides date and initials, value: 2/MARCK below **Note:** Varieties exist.

Date	Mintage	Good	VG	F	VF	XF
1723 AW	—	800	1,600	2,800	4,000	—

KM# 79 THALER
Silver **Ruler:** Christian August **Obverse:** Bust right **Obv. Legend:** CHRISTIAN • AVG • D • G • EL • EP • LVB • H • N • DVX • S • ET • H • **Reverse:** Crowned arms, date in legend **Rev. Legend:** STORM • ET • DIT • COM • IN • OLD • ET • DELM • 1724 **Note:** Dav. #2409.

Date	Mintage	VG	F	VF	XF	Unc
1724	—	850	1,650	3,000	5,000	—

KM# 81 THALER
Silver **Ruler:** Karl **Subject:** Sede Vacante **Obverse:** Bust right **Obv. Legend:** CAROLUS. VG.D.G.ROM.I.S.A **Reverse:** Helmeted arms **Rev. Legend:** SEDE VACANTE.1727 MON.CAPIT:LUBEC: **Note:** Dav. #2410.

Date	Mintage	VG	F	VF	XF	Unc
1727	—	425	850	1,500	2,500	—

KM# 86 THALER
Silver **Ruler:** Friedrich August **Obverse:** Bust left **Obv. Legend:** FRID • AUG • D • G • HAER • N • EP • LUB • DUX S • G • ST • & D • DUX • REGN • OLD • **Reverse:** Crowned and mantled arms **Rev. Legend:** SUBDITORUM • SALUS - FELICITAS • SUMMA **Note:** Dav. #2412.

Date	Mintage	VG	F	VF	XF	Unc
1775 Rare	10	—	—	—	—	—

KM# 85 THALER
Silver **Ruler:** Friedrich August **Obverse:** Crowned monogram **Obv. Legend:** D • G • EP • LUB• HAER • NORV • DUX • S • H • ST • & D • DUX • REGN • OLD • **Reverse:** Crowned arms within Order chain **Rev. Legend:** SUBDITORUM • SALUS - FELICITAS • SUMMA • **Note:** Albertus Thaler. Dav. #2411.

Date	Mintage	VG	F	VF	XF	Unc
1775	1,000	350	650	1,150	2,000	—

KM# 87 5 THALER
6.5000 g., 0.9000 Gold 0.1881 oz. AGW **Ruler:** Friedrich August **Obverse:** Bust left **Reverse:** Oval arms within crowned mantle

Date	Mintage	VG	F	VF	XF	Unc
1776 B	—	500	1,250	2,000	3,250	—

TRADE COINAGE

KM# 80 DUCAT
3.5000 g., 0.9860 Gold 0.1109 oz. AGW **Ruler:** Christian August **Obverse:** Armored bust right in inner circle **Reverse:** Lion walking to right

Date	Mintage	VG	F	VF	XF	Unc
1724	—	750	1,500	2,750	4,500	—
1726	—	—	—	—	—	—

Note: Reported, not confirmed

FREE CITY

REGULAR COINAGE

KM# 140 DREILING (1/192 Thaler = 3 Pfennig)
0.5100 g., 0.1870 Silver 0.0031 oz. ASW **Obverse:** Crowned imperial eagle, city arms on breast, inscription around **Reverse:** Value, date in wreath

Date	Mintage	VG	F	VF	XF	Unc
1727 JJJ	—	4.00	8.00	16.00	35.00	—
1728 JJJ	—	4.00	8.00	16.00	35.00	—
1733 JJJ	—	4.00	8.00	16.00	35.00	—
1737 JJJ	—	4.00	8.00	16.00	35.00	—
1742 JJJ	—	4.00	8.00	16.00	35.00	—
1747 JJJ	—	4.00	8.00	16.00	35.00	—

KM# 166 DREILING (1/192 Thaler = 3 Pfennig)
0.5100 g., 0.1870 Silver 0.0031 oz. ASW **Obverse:** Without inscription **Reverse:** Value, date within branches

Date	Mintage	VG	F	VF	XF	Unc
1752 JJJ	—	4.00	8.00	16.00	35.00	—
1762 DPZ	—	4.00	8.00	16.00	35.00	—

KM# 165 SECHSLING (1/64 Gulden = 6 Pfennig)
Silver **Obverse:** Value: 1/SECHS/LING/initials, date in legend **Reverse:** Crowned imperial eagle, city arms on breast **Rev. Legend:** CIVITATIS - IMPERIAL

Date	Mintage	VG	F	VF	XF	Unc
1750 JJJ	—	8.00	15.00	30.00	50.00	—

KM# 141 SCHILLING
1.0800 g., 0.3750 Silver 0.0130 oz. ASW **Obverse:** City arms on breast of eagle **Reverse:** Value, date within inner circle

Date	Mintage	VG	F	VF	XF	Unc
1727 JJJ	—	4.00	8.00	15.00	30.00	—
1728 JJJ	—	4.00	8.00	15.00	30.00	—
1729 JJJ	—	4.00	8.00	15.00	30.00	—
1733 JJJ	—	4.00	8.00	15.00	30.00	—
1758 JJJ	—	4.00	8.00	15.00	30.00	—

KM# 190 SCHILLING
1.0800 g., 0.3750 Silver 0.0130 oz. ASW **Obverse:** Crowned double-headed eagle **Reverse:** Value, date

Date	Mintage	VG	F	VF	XF	Unc
1789 HDF	554,000	2.00	4.00	7.00	20.00	—

KM# 142 2 SCHILLING
1.9600 g., 0.4370 Silver 0.0275 oz. ASW **Obverse:** Crowned imperial eagle, 2 on breast, inscription around **Reverse:** Value in two branches above city arms, inscription with date around

Date	Mintage	VG	F	VF	XF	Unc
1727 JJJ	—	8.00	16.00	30.00	65.00	—

KM# 175 2 SCHILLING
1.9600 g., 0.4370 Silver 0.0275 oz. ASW **Obverse:** Crowned double-headed eagle **Reverse:** Value within branches above city arms **Note:** Similar to KM#142, but legend differs.

Date	Mintage	VG	F	VF	XF	Unc
1758 JJJ	—	8.00	16.00	30.00	65.00	—

KM# 131 4 SCHILLING (1/8 Thaler = 1/2 Orststaler)
Silver **Obverse:** Crowned imperial eagle, value: 4 in circle on breast **Obv. Legend:** CIVITAT - IMPERIALIS **Reverse:** Value 4/SCHIL/LING between palm branches divide date, city arms below **Rev. Legend:** LUBECKS. STADT. GELDT.

Date	Mintage	VG	F	VF	XF	Unc
1711 (f)	—	—	—	—	—	—

KM# 143 4 SCHILLING (1/8 Thaler = 1/2 Orststaler)
3.0500 g., 0.5620 Silver 0.0551 oz. ASW **Obverse:** Crowned double-headed eagle with value on breast **Reverse:** Value within branches above city arms

Date	Mintage	VG	F	VF	XF	Unc
1727 JJJ	—	6.00	12.00	25.00	60.00	—
1728 JJJ	—	6.00	12.00	25.00	60.00	—
1729 JJJ	—	6.00	12.00	25.00	60.00	—

KM# 156 4 SCHILLING (1/8 Thaler = 1/2 Orststaler)
3.0500 g., 0.5620 Silver 0.0551 oz. ASW **Obverse:** Crowned double-headed eagle **Reverse:** Bottom of city arms lined vertically

Date	Mintage	VG	F	VF	XF	Unc
1732 JJJ	—	10.00	20.00	40.00	85.00	—
1752 JJJ	—	10.00	20.00	40.00	85.00	—

KM# 144 8 SCHILLING (1/4 Thaler = 1 Orststaler)
5.5000 g., 0.6250 Silver 0.1105 oz. ASW **Obverse:** Value in two branches above city arms with squares in bottom, inscription with date around **Reverse:** Crowned imperial eagle, 8 on breast, inscription around

Date	Mintage	VG	F	VF	XF	Unc
1727 JJJ	—	9.00	16.00	32.00	70.00	—
1728 JJJ	—	9.00	16.00	32.00	70.00	—
1729 JJJ	—	9.00	16.00	32.00	70.00	—
1730 JJJ	—	9.00	16.00	32.00	70.00	—
1758 JJJ	—	9.00	16.00	32.00	70.00	—

KM# 152 8 SCHILLING (1/4 Thaler = 1 Orststaler)
5.5000 g., 0.6250 Silver 0.1105 oz. ASW **Obverse:** 8 on eagle's breast **Reverse:** Bottom of city arms lined vertically

Date	Mintage	VG	F	VF	XF	Unc
1731 JJJ	—	8.00	16.00	28.00	55.00	—
1732 JJJ	—	8.00	16.00	28.00	55.00	—
1733 JJJ	—	8.00	16.00	28.00	55.00	—
1734 JJJ	—	8.00	16.00	28.00	55.00	—
1738 JJJ	—	8.00	16.00	28.00	55.00	—
1741 JJJ	—	8.00	16.00	28.00	55.00	—
1747 JJJ	—	8.00	16.00	28.00	55.00	—
1749 JJJ	—	8.00	16.00	28.00	55.00	—
1752 JJJ	—	8.00	16.00	28.00	55.00	—
1758 JJJ	—	8.00	16.00	28.00	55.00	—

KM# 146 16 SCHILLING (1/2 Thaler)
9.1600 g., 0.7500 Silver 0.2209 oz. ASW **Obverse:** Crowned imperial eagle, city arms on breast, inscription around **Reverse:** Value in two branches above city arms, inscription with date around

Date	Mintage	VG	F	VF	XF	Unc
1728 JJJ	—	20.00	35.00	60.00	135	—

KM# 153 16 SCHILLING (1/2 Thaler)
9.1600 g., 0.7500 Silver 0.2209 oz. ASW **Obverse:** 16 on eagle's breast **Reverse:** Value within branches above city arms

Date	Mintage	VG	F	VF	XF	Unc
1731 JJJ	—	20.00	35.00	60.00	135	—
1732 JJJ	—	20.00	35.00	60.00	135	—
1733 JJJ	—	20.00	35.00	60.00	135	—
1737 JJJ	—	20.00	35.00	60.00	135	—
1738 JJJ	—	20.00	35.00	60.00	135	—
1752 JJJ	—	20.00	35.00	60.00	135	—
1758 JJJ	—	20.00	35.00	60.00	135	—

KM# 147 32 SCHILLING (2/3 Thaler = Gulden)
Silver **Obverse:** 32 on eagle's breast, wtihout shield on tail **Reverse:** Value in wreath above shield

Date	Mintage	VG	F	VF	XF	Unc
1728 JJJ	—	40.00	65.00	125	250	—

KM# 154 32 SCHILLING (2/3 Thaler = Gulden)
Silver **Obverse:** Shield below eagle **Reverse:** Vertical lines in arms

Date	Mintage	VG	F	VF	XF	Unc
1731 JJJ	—	20.00	40.00	80.00	165	—
1732 JJJ	—	20.00	40.00	80.00	165	—
1738 JJJ	—	20.00	40.00	80.00	165	—

KM# 162 32 SCHILLING (2/3 Thaler = Gulden)
Silver **Obverse:** Ornate arms **Reverse:** Crowned double-headed eagle, 32 on breast

Date	Mintage	VG	F	VF	XF	Unc
1747 JJJ	—	25.00	50.00	100	200	—
1748 JJJ	—	25.00	50.00	100	200	—

KM# 163 32 SCHILLING (2/3 Thaler = Gulden)
Silver **Obverse:** Crowned double-headed eagle **Reverse:** Large ornate arms in palm sprays

Date	Mintage	VG	F	VF	XF	Unc
1749 JJJ	—	30.00	55.00	110	225	—
1750 JJJ	—	30.00	55.00	110	225	—

KM# 167 32 SCHILLING (2/3 Thaler = Gulden)
Silver **Obverse:** Wheat stalks in shield **Reverse:** Small ornate arms

Date	Mintage	VG	F	VF	XF	Unc
1752 JJJ	—	25.00	50.00	100	200	—

KM# 176 32 SCHILLING (2/3 Thaler = Gulden)
Silver **Obverse:** City arms below value within branches **Reverse:** Revised shield

Date	Mintage	VG	F	VF	XF	Unc
1758 JJJ	—	30.00	55.00	110	225	—

KM# 177 32 SCHILLING (2/3 Thaler = Gulden)
Silver **Obverse:** Revised eagle and shield **Reverse:** Wide arms in branches

Date	Mintage	VG	F	VF	XF	Unc
1758 JJJ	—	40.00	65.00	125	250	—

KM# 178 32 SCHILLING (2/3 Thaler = Gulden)
Silver **Obverse:** Narrow plain arms in branches **Reverse:** Crowned double-headed eagle, 32 on breast, small shield below

Date	Mintage	VG	F	VF	XF	Unc
1758 DPZ	—	40.00	65.00	125	250	—

KM# 199 32 SCHILLING (2/3 Thaler = Gulden)
Silver **Obverse:** Crowned double-headed eagle with pointed shield on breast **Reverse:** Value, date divided by shield below

Date	Mintage	F	VF	XF	Unc
1796 HDF	—	40.00	80.00	150	300
1797 HDF	—	40.00	80.00	150	300

KM# 27 1/192 THALER
Silver **Obverse:** Value: 192 in imperial orb **Reverse:** Crowned double-headed imperial eagle within circle **Note:** Varieties exist.

Date	Mintage	VG	F	VF	XF	Unc
(170)1 (f)	—	5.00	10.00	25.00	45.00	—
(17)03 (f)	—	5.00	10.00	25.00	45.00	—
(17)05 (f)	—	5.00	10.00	25.00	45.00	—
(17)06 (f)	—	5.00	10.00	25.00	45.00	—
(17)07 (f)	—	5.00	10.00	25.00	45.00	—
(17)09 (f)	—	5.00	10.00	25.00	45.00	—
(17)10 (f)	—	5.00	10.00	25.00	45.00	—

Date	Mintage	VG	F	VF	XF	Unc
(17)12 (f)	—	5.00	10.00	25.00	45.00	—

KM# A79 1/24 THALER (2 Schilling)
Silver **Obv. Legend:** CIVITAT-IMPERIAL **Reverse:** Crowned imperial eagle **Note:** Varieties exist. Prev. KM#79.

Date	Mintage	VG	F	VF	XF	Unc
1700 (f)	—	15.00	30.00	60.00	100	—
1701 (f)	—	15.00	30.00	60.00	100	—
1702 (f)	—	15.00	30.00	60.00	100	—
1703 (f)	—	15.00	30.00	60.00	100	—
1705 (f)	—	15.00	30.00	60.00	100	—
1707 (f)	—	15.00	30.00	60.00	100	—
1709 (f)	—	15.00	30.00	60.00	100	—
1710 (f)	—	15.00	30.00	60.00	100	—
1712 (f)	—	15.00	30.00	60.00	100	—
1714 (f)	—	15.00	30.00	60.00	100	—
1715 (f)	—	15.00	30.00	60.00	100	—

KM# 130 THALER OF 32 SCHILLING
Silver **Obverse:** St. John with lamb and book, city arms below **Obv. Legend:** MONETA. NOVA. - LUBECENSIS. **Reverse:** Crowned double-headed imperial eagle, 32 on breast, small shield below **Rev. Legend:** IOSEPHUS. D: G: - ROMA: IMP: SE: AUG. **Note:** Dav. #2413.

Date	Mintage	VG	F	VF	XF	Unc
1710 IF//(f)	—	350	750	1,350	2,250	—

KM# 132 THALER OF 32 SCHILLING
Silver **Subject:** Election of Karl VI **Obverse:** St. John with lamb and book, city arms below **Obv. Legend:** MONETA • NOVA •- LUBECENSIS •/ SALVO • CAES •- SALVA • RESPVB• in inner row **Reverse:** Crowned double-headed eagle, 32 on breast, small shield below **Rev. Legend:** CAROLUS. VI. D:G:- ROMA: IMP: SEM: AUG:/ELECT. FRANCOFURT:- XII. OCT. MDCCXI in inner row **Note:** Dav. #2414.

Date	Mintage	VG	F	VF	XF	Unc
1712 IHF//(f)	—	2,000	3,500	6,000	9,000	—

KM# 145 THALER

29.2000 g., 0.8880 Silver 0.8336 oz. ASW **Obverse:** St. John with lamb and book, two shields below, JJJX at bottom, date in legend **Obv. Legend:** MONETA * NOVA * - LUBECENS * 1727 * **Reverse:** Crowned double-headed eagle, titles of Karl VI **Rev. Legend:** CAROLUS * VI * D * G* - ROM * IMP * S * AUG * **Note:** Dav. #2415.

Date	Mintage	VG	F	VF	XF	Unc
1727 IHL//JJJ	—	250	500	900	1,500	—

KM# 150 THALER

29.2000 g., 0.8880 Silver 0.8336 oz. ASW **Subject:** 200th Anniversary - Augsburg Confession **Obverse:** Crowned double-headed eagle with arms on breast and shield below **Obv. Legend:** IMPERIAL • CIVIT • LUBECENSIS 1730 • **Reverse:** Religion standing with book and cross **Rev. Legend:** CONFESS. EVANG. IN. COMIT. AUG. EXHIBITAE, figure separates; SACRA-SAECU/LARIA-SECUNDA/XXV-IUN. **Note:** Dav. #2416. Varieties exist.

Date	Mintage	F	VF	XF	Unc
1730 JJJ	—	125	275	600	1,000

KM# 155 THALER

29.2000 g., 0.8880 Silver 0.8336 oz. ASW **Obverse:** Titles of Karl VI **Obv. Legend:** CAROLUS • VI • D • G • - ROM • IMP • S • AUG • **Reverse:** St. John with lamb and book, full-length

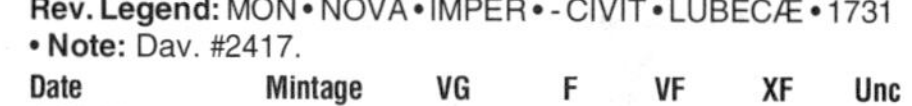

Rev. Legend: MON • NOVA • IMPER • - CIVIT • LUBECÆ • 1731 • **Note:** Dav. #2417.

Date	Mintage	VG	F	VF	XF	Unc
1731 JJJ	—	200	400	800	1,800	—

KM# 160 THALER

29.2000 g., 0.8880 Silver 0.8336 oz. ASW **Obverse:** Titles of Karl VI **Obv. Legend:** CAROLUS • VII • D • G • - ROM • IMP • S • AUG • 1742 • **Reverse:** St. John with lamb and book, full-length **Note:** Dav. #2418.

Date	Mintage	VG	F	VF	XF	Unc
1742 JJJ	—	150	350	750	1,750	—

KM# 185 THALER

29.2000 g., 0.8880 Silver 0.8336 oz. ASW **Obverse:** Titles of Josef **Obv. Legend:** IOSEPHUS. II. - ROM. IMP. S. AUG. **Reverse:** St. John with lamb and book, shield below **Rev. Legend:** MONETA. NOVA - LUBECENSIS. 1776 **Note:** Specie Thaler. Dav. #2422.

Date	Mintage	F	VF	XF	Unc
1776 HDF	—	150	250	400	750

KM# 161 THALER OF 48 SCHILLING

Silver **Obverse:** St. John with lamb and book, full-length **Obv. Legend:** MON. NOVA. IMPER. - CIVIT. LUBECÆ. **Reverse:** Crowned double-headed eagle, shield below **Rev. Legend:** FRANCISCUS. D. G. - ROM. IMP. S. AUG. 1745 **Note:** Dav. #2419.

Date	Mintage	VG	F	VF	XF	Unc
1745 JJJ	—	300	600	1,200	2,000	—

KM# 168.1 THALER OF 48 SCHILLING

27.5100 g., 0.7500 Silver 0.6633 oz. ASW **Obverse:** City arms within ornate frame **Obv. Legend:** 48 • SCHILLING • COURANT •- GELDT • ANNO • 1752 • **Reverse:** Crowned double-headed eagle with 48 on breast, shield below **Rev. Legend:** MON • NOVA • IMP •- CIVITAT • LUBECAE • **Note:** Dav. #2420.

Date	Mintage	VG	F	VF	XF	Unc
1752 JJJ	—	40.00	65.00	120	220	—

KM# 168.2 THALER OF 48 SCHILLING

27.5100 g., 0.7500 Silver 0.6633 oz. ASW **Obverse:** Crowned double-headed eagle with 48 on breast and shield below **Obv. Legend:** MON • NOVA • IMP • - CIVITAT • LUBECÆ **Reverse:** Revised arms **Rev. Legend:** 48 SCHILLING • COURANT • - GELDT • ANNO • **Note:** Dav. #2420A.

Date	Mintage	VG	F	VF	XF	Unc
1752 JJJ	—	30.00	55.00	100	185	—

KM# 168.3 THALER OF 48 SCHILLING

27.5100 g., 0.7500 Silver 0.6633 oz. ASW **Obverse:** Crowned double-headed eagle with 48 on breast and shield below **Obv. Legend:** MON • NOVA • IMP • 1752 - CIVITAT • LUBECÆ • **Reverse:** Revised arms **Rev. Legend:** 48 • SCHILLING • COURANT • - GELDT • ANNO • 1752 • **Note:** Dav. #2420B.

Date	Mintage	VG	F	VF	XF	Unc
1752 JJJ	—	30.00	55.00	100	185	—

KM# 168.4 THALER OF 48 SCHILLING
27.5100 g., 0.7500 Silver 0.6633 oz. ASW **Obverse:** City arms within baroque frame **Obv. Legend:** 48 • SCHILLING • COURANT •- GELDT • ANNO • 1752 • **Reverse:** Crowned double-headed eagle with 48 on breast and shield below **Rev. Legend:** MON • NOVA • IMP • CIVITAT • LUBECÆ • **Note:** Dav. #2420C.

Date	Mintage	VG	F	VF	XF	Unc
1752 JJJ	—	30.00	55.00	100	185	—

KM# 168.5 THALER OF 48 SCHILLING
27.5100 g., 0.7500 Silver 0.6633 oz. ASW **Obverse:** Large 48, small wheat stalks **Obv. Legend:** MON • NOVA • IMP • - CIVITAT • LUBECÆ • **Reverse:** City arms within baroque frame **Rev. Legend:** 48 • SCHILLING • COURANT • - GELDT • ANNO • 1752 • **Note:** Dav. #2420D.

Date	Mintage	VG	F	VF	XF	Unc
1752 JJJ	—	30.00	55.00	100	185	—

KM# 168.6 THALER OF 48 SCHILLING
27.5100 g., 0.7500 Silver 0.6633 oz. ASW **Obverse:** Revised arms **Obv. Legend:** 48 • SCHILLING • COURANT •- GELDT • ANNO • 1752 • **Reverse:** Crowned double-headed eagle with 48 on breast and shield below **Rev. Legend:** MON • NOVA • IMP • - CIVITAT • LUBECÆ • **Note:** Dav. #2420E.

Date	Mintage	VG	F	VF	XF	Unc
1752 JJJ	—	35.00	60.00	110	200	—

KM# 180 2 THALER
Silver **Obverse:** Crowned double-headed eagle with shield on breast **Reverse:** St. John with lamb and book, shield below **Note:** Similar to 1 Thaler, KM#185. Dav. #2421.

Date	Mintage	VG	F	VF	XF	Unc
1766 Rare	—	—	—	—	—	—

TRADE COINAGE

KM# 110 1/4 DUCAT
0.8750 g., 0.9860 Gold 0.0277 oz. AGW **Obverse:** Emperor standing **Reverse:** Crowned imperial eagle

Date	Mintage	VG	F	VF	XF	Unc
1701 (f)	—	125	250	400	750	—
1702	—	125	250	400	750	—
1707	—	125	250	400	750	—
1712	—	125	250	400	750	—
1714 (f)	—	125	250	400	750	—
1715	—	125	250	400	750	—
1716 (f)	—	125	250	400	750	—
1721	—	125	250	400	750	—
1725	—	125	250	400	750	—
1728	—	125	250	400	750	—

KM# 111 1/2 DUCAT
1.7500 g., 0.9860 Gold 0.0555 oz. AGW **Obverse:** Emperor standing **Reverse:** Crowned imperial eagle

Date	Mintage	VG	F	VF	XF	Unc
1703	—	150	300	600	1,000	—
1706	—	150	300	600	1,000	—
1710 (f)	—	150	300	600	1,000	—
1711	—	150	300	600	1,000	—
1714 (f)	—	150	300	600	1,000	—
1716 (f)	—	150	300	600	1,000	—

KM# A36 DUCAT
3.5000 g., 0.9860 Gold 0.1109 oz. AGW **Obverse:** Emperor standing **Reverse:** Crowned imperial eagle, date divided **Note:** Varieties exist. Prev. KM#36.

Date	Mintage	VG	F	VF	XF	Unc
1701	—	200	400	750	1,250	—
1707 (f)	—	200	400	750	1,250	—
1710 (f)	—	200	400	750	1,250	—
1712 (f)	—	200	400	750	1,250	—
1713 (f)	—	200	400	750	1,250	—
1714 (f)	—	200	400	750	1,250	—
1716 (f)	—	200	400	750	1,250	—
1722	—	200	400	750	1,250	—
1727 JJJ	—	200	400	750	1,250	—
1728	—	200	400	750	1,250	—
1733	—	200	400	750	1,250	—
1737	—	200	400	750	1,250	—
1743	—	200	400	750	1,250	—
1749	—	200	400	750	1,250	—
1751	—	200	400	750	1,250	—
1759 DPZ	—	200	400	750	1,250	—

KM# 125 DUCAT
3.5000 g., 0.9860 Gold 0.1109 oz. AGW **Obverse:** Solid rock in sea **Reverse:** All-seeing eye

Date	Mintage	VG	F	VF	XF	Unc
1707	—	300	600	1,250	2,500	—

KM# 133 DUCAT
3.5000 g., 0.9860 Gold 0.1109 oz. AGW **Subject:** Bicentennial of the Reformation **Obverse:** Crowned double-headed eagle with city arms on breast **Reverse:** Inscription

Date	Mintage	VG	F	VF	XF	Unc
1717	—	350	550	1,200	1,800	—

KM# 148 DUCAT
3.5000 g., 0.9860 Gold 0.1109 oz. AGW **Obverse:** Armored bust of Karl VI right **Reverse:** Crowned imperial eagle with Lubeck arms on breast, date divided at bottom

Date	Mintage	VG	F	VF	XF	Unc
1729 JJJ	—	375	650	1,400	2,200	—
1730 JJJ	—	375	650	1,400	2,200	—

KM# 151 DUCAT
3.5000 g., 0.9860 Gold 0.1109 oz. AGW **Subject:** Bicentennial of the Augsburg Confession **Obverse:** Crowned double-headed eagle with city arms on breast **Reverse:** Standing figure with book and cross

Date	Mintage	VG	F	VF	XF	Unc
1730 JJJ	—	200	350	700	1,200	—

KM# 191 DUCAT
3.5000 g., 0.9860 Gold 0.1109 oz. AGW **Obverse:** Crowned eagle, titles of Josef II **Reverse:** Four-line inscription and date in tablet

Date	Mintage	F	VF	XF	Unc
1789 HDF	—	—	—	—	—
1790 HDF	—	500	900	1,500	2,500

KM# 195 DUCAT
3.5000 g., 0.9860 Gold 0.1109 oz. AGW **Obverse:** Eagle **Rev. Legend:** MON AVR LVBECENS

Date	Mintage	F	VF	XF	Unc
1791 HDF	1,800	400	650	1,250	1,850
1792 HDF	—	400	650	1,250	1,850

KM# 196 DUCAT
3.5000 g., 0.9860 Gold 0.1109 oz. AGW **Obverse:** Titles of Franz II **Obv. Legend:** ... AVG

Date	Mintage	F	VF	XF	Unc
1792 HDF	—	400	650	1,250	1,850

KM# 197 DUCAT
3.5000 g., 0.9860 Gold 0.1109 oz. AGW **Obv. Legend:** ... AVGVST

Date	Mintage	F	VF	XF	Unc
1792 HDF	—	400	650	1,250	1,850

KM# 198 DUCAT
3.5000 g., 0.9860 Gold 0.1109 oz. AGW **Obverse:** Crowned double-headed eagle with shield on breast **Reverse:** Legend and date within square

Date	Mintage	F	VF	XF	Unc
1793 HDF	1,200	400	550	1,150	2,000
1794 HDF	1,953	400	550	1,100	1,850
1797 HDF	1,490	400	550	1,150	2,000

KM# 89 2 DUCAT
7.0000 g., 0.9860 Gold 0.2219 oz. AGW **Obverse:** Crowned double-headed eagle with city arms on breast **Reverse:** Knight with imperial orb and sceptre

Date	Mintage	VG	F	VF	XF	Unc
1701 (f)	—	450	800	1,900	3,200	—
1706	—	450	800	1,900	3,200	—
1707 (f)	—	450	800	1,900	3,200	—
1711	—	450	800	1,900	3,200	—
1713	—	450	800	1,900	3,200	—
1714	—	450	800	1,900	3,200	—
1716 (f)	—	450	800	1,900	3,200	—

KM# 134 2 DUCAT
7.0000 g., 0.9860 Gold 0.2219 oz. AGW **Subject:** Bicentennial of the Reformation

Date	Mintage	VG	F	VF	XF	Unc
1717 IF//(f)	—	600	1,200	2,500	4,000	—

KM# A160 10 DUCAT

35.0000 g., 0.9860 Gold 1.1095 oz. AGW **Obverse:** Titles of Karl VII, date in legend **Note:** Struck with 1 Thaler dies, KM#161.

Date	Mintage	VG	F	VF	XF	Unc
1745 JJJ	—	—	—	6,500	10,000	—

PATTERNS

Including off metal strikes

KM#	Date	Mintage	Identification	Mkt Val
Pn2	1724	—	Dreiling. Gold. KM#75.	—
Pn3	1724	—	Sechsling. Gold. Weight of 1/2 Ducat, KM#76.	—
Pn4	1776	—	5 Thaler. Silver. KM#87.	—
Pn12	1701	—	1/24 Thaler. Gold. Weight of 1 Ducat, KM#79.	—
Pn13	(17)09	—	Dreiling. Gold. KM#27	—
Pn14		—	Dreiling. Gold. KM#27	—
Pn15	1711	—	4 Schilling. Gold. Weight of 1 Ducat, KM#131.	—

KM#	Date	Mintage	Identification	Mkt Val
Pn16	1717	—	Ducat. Silver. KM#133.	125

KM#	Date	Mintage	Identification	Mkt Val
Pn17	1717	—	2 Ducat. Silver. KM#134.	450
Pn18	1726	—	8 Schilling. Gold. KM#144.	—
Pn19	1727	—	Dreiling. Gold. KM#140.	225
PnA20	1730	—	Ducat. Silver. KM#151.	125
Pn20	1732	—	16 Schilling. Gold. KM#153.	12,000
Pn21	1737	—	Dreiling. Gold. KM#140.	225
Pn22	1742	—	Dreiling. Gold. KM#140.	225
Pn24	1750	—	Sechsling. Gold. KM#165.	450

KM#	Date	Mintage	Identification	Mkt Val
Pn25	1752	—	48 Schilling. Gold. KM#168.	18,700
Pn26	1776	—	1/2 Thaler. Silver. 14.4000 g. Thaler dies. KM#185	—
Pn27	1776	—	1/2 Thaler. Tin. Thaler dies. KM#185.	3,000
Pn28	1776	—	Thaler. Gold. 35.0000 g. KM#185.	—
Pn29	1776	—	2 Thaler. Silver. Thaler dies. KM#180.	—
Pn30	1789	—	Schilling. Silver. Broad planchet. KM#190.	250
Pn31	1789	—	Schilling. Gold. KM#190.	425
Pn32	1789	—	Ducat. Silver. KM#191.	125
Pn33	1790	—	Ducat. Silver. KM#191.	125
Pn34	1792	—	Ducat. Silver. KM#195.	125
Pn35	1794	—	Ducat. Silver. KM#198.	125
Pn36	1797	—	Ducat. Copper. KM#198.	85.00
Pn37		—	2 Mark. Silver. Uniface.	—

LUNEBURG

This city 50 miles southeast of Hamburg, chartered in 1247, became a powerful member of The Hanseatic League and received the mint right in 1293. It was passed to Hannover in 1705 and to Prussia in 1866. Using a pun on the city name "luna" they showed a half moon on larger coins. Lüneburg had a local coinage, which was produced intermittently from 1293 until 1777.

MINT OFFICIALS' INITIALS

Initials	Date	Name
JJJ	1687-1705	Jobst Jakob Janisch in Celle

ARMS

City gate, usually w/3 towers, lion rampant or leopard left in portal. Often depicted w/St. John (patron saint) above towers.

CITY

REGULAR COINAGE

KM# 90 SCHERF (1/2 Pfennig)

Copper **Obverse:** Lion rampant left **Reverse:** Large S divides date, value 1 above, LVN below **Note:** Varieties exist.

Date	Mintage	VG	F	VF	XF	Unc
1701	—	6.00	12.00	25.00	50.00	—
1710	—	6.00	12.00	25.00	50.00	—
1714	—	6.00	12.00	25.00	50.00	—
1716	—	6.00	12.00	25.00	50.00	—
1718	—	6.00	12.00	25.00	50.00	—
1741	—	6.00	12.00	25.00	50.00	—
1743	—	6.00	12.00	25.00	50.00	—
1745	—	6.00	12.00	25.00	50.00	—
1751	—	6.00	12.00	25.00	50.00	—
1757	—	6.00	12.00	25.00	50.00	—
1777	—	6.00	12.00	25.00	50.00	—

KM# 95 2/3 THALER (Gulden)

Silver **Obverse:** Helmeted arms with plumes **Reverse:** Value

Date	Mintage	VG	F	VF	XF	Unc
1702 JJJ	—	65.00	120	225	350	—

TRADE COINAGE

KM# 96 10 DUCAT

35.0000 g., 0.9860 Gold 1.1095 oz. AGW **Subject:** 80th Birthday of Duke Georg Wilhelm of Brunswick-Luneburg-Celle **Obverse:** Bust right, double legend **Reverse:** Fourteen-line inscription with Roman numeral date

Date	Mintage	VG	F	VF	XF	Unc
1703 TKS Rare	—	—	—	—	—	—

PATTERNS

Including off metal strikes

KM#	Date	Mintage	Identification	Mkt Val
Pn2	1703	—	10 Ducat. Silver. KM#96	325

MAINZ

Mainz, located on the Rhine 25 miles west of Frankfurt, became an archbishopric in 747. It was a residence and mint of Charlemagne, and the Imperial Mint established then functioned into the 11th century. The archbishops were recognized as presidents of the electoral college and arch-chancellors of the Empire by the Golden Bull of 1356. In 1797, Mainz was ceded to France and in 1801 the French annexed all of the territories on the left bank of the Rhine. The remaining lands were secularized in 1803 and portions were divided between Hesse-Darmstadt, Nassau and Prussia.

Mainz became a Free City of the Empire in 1118 but lost the title in 1163 through an unsuccessful revolt against ecclesiastical authority. They obtained the mint right in 1420 but rarely availed itself of the privilege. It was occupied by Sweden from 1631 to 1635 during the 30 Years War. Siege coins were struck in 1793 when the French garrison was beseiged by the Prussians.

RULERS

Lothar Franz, Graf von Schoenborn, 1695-1729
Franz Ludwig von Pfalz-Neuburg, 1729-1732
Philipp Karl, Freiherr von Eltz, 1732-1743
Johann Friedrich Karl, Graf von Ostein, 1743-1763
Emeric Josef, 1763-1774
Friedrich Karl Josef, 1774-1802

MINT OFFICIALS' INITIALS

Initials	Date	Name
AE, AEF	1765	Andreas Eplie
AFS, AS, FS, S, ST	1765-89	August Friedrich Stieler
AK	1714-23	Andreas Kotzner in Mainz
B, BECKER	1702-43	Philipp Christoph Becker, die-cutter in Vienna
BIB	1707-33	Balthasar Johann Bethmann in Darmstadt
CS	Ca.1744	-
DF	1765-95	Damian Fritsch
EG	1750-75	Elias Gervais
FB	1765-68	Damian Fritsch and Peter Moritz Brahm, warden
GFN	1682-1724	Georg Friedrich Nurnberger in Nüremberg
IA	1794-96	Joseph Aatz, mint-inspector
IL	1790-96	Johann Lindenschmitt, die-cutter
S	1751-63	Johann Franz Schmitt
S	1716-44	Wiegand Schaffer, die-cutter in Mainz and Heidelberg
S	1744-99	Anton Schafer in Mannheim
VBW	1684-88, 1702-14	Ulrich Burkhard Willerding
W	1732-62	Johann Heinrich Werner, die-cutter in Erfurt

ARCHBISHOPRIC

REGULAR COINAGE

KM# 230 PFENNIG

Silver **Ruler:** Lothar Franz, Graf von Schoenborn **Note:** Uniface. Schussel-type. 2-fold arms of Mainz and Schonborn, mintmaster's initials above.

Date	Mintage	VG	F	VF	XF	Unc
ND(1702-14) VBW	—	6.00	10.00	20.00	35.00	—

KM# 242 PFENNIG

Silver **Ruler:** Lothar Franz, Graf von Schoenborn **Note:** 3 small shields, those of Mainz and Bamberg above Schonborn, value 1 above, date divided below.

Date	Mintage	VG	F	VF	XF	Unc
1713	—	6.00	10.00	20.00	35.00	—
1714	—	6.00	10.00	20.00	35.00	—

KM# 243 PFENNIG

Silver **Ruler:** Lothar Franz, Graf von Schoenborn **Note:** Schussel-type. 2-fold arms of Mainz and Schonborn, mintmaster's initials above.

Date	Mintage	VG	F	VF	XF	Unc
ND(1714-23) AK	—	6.00	10.00	20.00	35.00	—

KM# 244 PFENNIG

Silver **Ruler:** Lothar Franz, Graf von Schoenborn **Note:** 2-fold arms of Mainz and Schonborn in laurel wreath, rosette above.

Date	Mintage	VG	F	VF	XF	Unc
ND	—	6.00	10.00	20.00	35.00	—

KM# 293 PFENNIG

Copper **Ruler:** Johann Friedrich Karl, Graf von Ostein **Obverse:** Crowned arms **Reverse:** Date in floral sprays

Date	Mintage	VG	F	VF	XF	Unc
1756	—	3.00	6.00	12.00	25.00	100

KM# 294 PFENNIG

Copper **Ruler:** Johann Friedrich Karl, Graf von Ostein **Obverse:** Sword and crozier back of crowned arms within baroque frame **Reverse:** Value, date

Date	Mintage	VG	F	VF	XF	Unc
1757	—	3.00	6.00	12.00	25.00	—
1758	—	3.00	6.00	12.00	25.00	—
1759	—	3.00	6.00	12.00	25.00	—
1760	—	3.00	6.00	12.00	25.00	—

KM# 296 PFENNIG

Copper **Ruler:** Johann Friedrich Karl, Graf von Ostein **Obverse:** Crowned arms between branches **Reverse:** Value, date

Date	Mintage	VG	F	VF	XF	Unc
1759	—	3.00	6.00	12.00	25.00	—
1760	—	3.00	6.00	12.00	25.00	—

KM# 297 PFENNIG

Copper **Ruler:** Johann Friedrich Karl, Graf von Ostein **Obverse:** Crowned arms in baroque frame with greyhound at left of arms

Date	Mintage	VG	F	VF	XF	Unc
1759	—	3.00	6.00	12.00	25.00	—
1760	—	3.00	6.00	12.00	25.00	—

KM# 316 PFENNIG

Copper **Ruler:** Johann Friedrich Karl, Graf von Ostein **Obverse:** Greyhound at right of arms

Date	Mintage	VG	F	VF	XF	Unc
1760	—	3.00	6.00	12.00	25.00	—

KM# 317 PFENNIG

Copper **Ruler:** Johann Friedrich Karl, Graf von Ostein
Obverse: Crowned monogram above wheel **Reverse:** Value, date

Date	Mintage	VG	F	VF	XF	Unc
1760	—	3.00	6.00	12.00	25.00	—

KM# 334 PFENNIG

Copper **Ruler:** Johann Friedrich Karl, Graf von Ostein
Obverse: Crowned arms **Reverse:** Value and date in cartouche

Date	Mintage	VG	F	VF	XF	Unc
1761	—	3.00	6.00	12.00	25.00	—

KM# 355 PFENNIG

Copper **Ruler:** Emeric Josef **Obverse:** Sword and crozier back of crowned arms **Reverse:** Value, C.M.L.M. and date

Date	Mintage	VG	F	VF	XF	Unc
1766	—	2.00	4.00	10.00	20.00	—

KM# 364 PFENNIG

Copper **Ruler:** Emeric Josef **Obverse:** Sword and crozier back of crowned arms within baroque frame **Reverse:** Value, date

Date	Mintage	VG	F	VF	XF	Unc
1768	—	2.00	4.00	10.00	25.00	—
1769	—	2.00	4.00	10.00	25.00	—
1770	—	2.00	4.00	10.00	25.00	100

KM# 374 PFENNIG

Copper **Ruler:** Emeric Josef **Obverse:** Without legend

Date	Mintage	VG	F	VF	XF	Unc
1769	—	2.00	4.00	10.00	25.00	—
1770	—	2.00	4.00	10.00	25.00	100

KM# 381 PFENNIG

Copper **Ruler:** Emeric Josef **Obverse:** Arms within cartouche
Obv. Legend: EM.10.D.G.EL.M.E.W

Date	Mintage	VG	F	VF	XF	Unc
1771	—	2.00	4.00	10.00	25.00	100

KM# 387 PFENNIG

Copper **Ruler:** Friedrich Karl Josef **Obverse:** Sword and crozier back of crowned arms withinh ornate frame **Reverse:** Value, date

Date	Mintage	VG	F	VF	XF	Unc
1779	—	2.00	4.00	10.00	25.00	—
1781	—	2.00	4.00	10.00	25.00	100

KM# 390 PFENNIG

Copper **Ruler:** Friedrich Karl Josef **Obverse:** F C I K monogram

Date	Mintage	VG	F	VF	XF	Unc
1781	—	2.00	4.00	10.00	25.00	100

KM# 298 2 PFENNIG

Copper **Ruler:** Johann Friedrich Karl, Graf von Ostein
Obverse: Crowned 5-fold arms supported by 2 greyhounds
Reverse: Value, date

Date	Mintage	VG	F	VF	XF	Unc
1759	—	5.00	8.00	12.00	25.00	150
1760	—	5.00	8.00	12.00	25.00	150

KM# 299 2 PFENNIG

Copper **Ruler:** Johann Friedrich Karl, Graf von Ostein
Obverse: Crowned and mantled arms **Reverse:** Value, date

Date	Mintage	VG	F	VF	XF	Unc
1759	—	7.00	10.00	20.00	35.00	150

KM# 300 2 PFENNIG

Copper **Ruler:** Johann Friedrich Karl, Graf von Ostein
Obverse: Crowned and mantled monogram above wheel
Reverse: Value, date

Date	Mintage	VG	F	VF	XF	Unc
1759	—	7.00	10.00	20.00	35.00	150

KM# 301 2 PFENNIG

Copper **Ruler:** Johann Friedrich Karl, Graf von Ostein **Obverse:** Crowned arms in baroque frame **Reverse:** Value as II, date

Date	Mintage	VG	F	VF	XF	Unc
1759	—	5.00	8.00	15.00	30.00	150
1760	—	5.00	8.00	15.00	30.00	150

KM# 302 2 PFENNIG

Copper **Ruler:** Johann Friedrich Karl, Graf von Ostein
Reverse: Value as 2

Date	Mintage	VG	F	VF	XF	Unc
1759	—	5.00	8.00	15.00	30.00	150
1761	—	5.00	8.00	15.00	30.00	150

KM# 318 2 PFENNIG

Copper **Ruler:** Johann Friedrich Karl, Graf von Ostein **Obverse:** Crowned and mantled arms **Reverse:** Value, date in cartouche

Date	Mintage	VG	F	VF	XF	Unc
1760	—	7.00	10.00	20.00	35.00	150

KM# 319 2 PFENNIG

Copper **Ruler:** Johann Friedrich Karl, Graf von Ostein
Obverse: Crowned monogram above wheel **Reverse:** Value, date

Date	Mintage	VG	F	VF	XF	Unc
1760	—	3.00	6.00	10.00	25.00	125
1761	—	3.00	6.00	10.00	25.00	125

KM# 320 2 PFENNIG

Copper **Ruler:** Johann Friedrich Karl, Graf von Ostein
Obverse: Crowned 5-fold arms supported by 2 greyhounds
Reverse: Value as 2

Date	Mintage	VG	F	VF	XF	Unc
1760	—	3.00	6.00	10.00	25.00	125

KM# 321 2 PFENNIG

Copper **Ruler:** Johann Friedrich Karl, Graf von Ostein
Obverse: Bust right **Reverse:** Value, date

Date	Mintage	VG	F	VF	XF	Unc
1760	—	8.00	16.00	35.00	65.00	250

KM# 322 2 PFENNIG

Copper **Ruler:** Johann Friedrich Karl, Graf von Ostein
Obverse: Bust right **Reverse:** Value, date in cartouche

Date	Mintage	VG	F	VF	XF	Unc
1760	—	8.00	16.00	35.00	65.00	200

KM# 323 2 PFENNIG

Copper **Ruler:** Johann Friedrich Karl, Graf von Ostein
Obverse: Crowned arms in baroque frame

Date	Mintage	VG	F	VF	XF	Unc
1760	—	6.00	12.00	25.00	45.00	200

KM# 335 2 PFENNIG

Copper **Ruler:** Johann Friedrich Karl, Graf von Ostein
Reverse: Date in floral sprays

Date	Mintage	VG	F	VF	XF	Unc
1761	—	6.00	12.00	25.00	45.00	200

KM# 356 2 PFENNIG

Copper **Ruler:** Emeric Josef **Obverse:** Sword and crozier back of crowned arms **Reverse:** Value, C.M.L.M. and date

Date	Mintage	VG	F	VF	XF	Unc
1766	—	2.00	4.00	12.00	20.00	125

KM# 365 2 PFENNIG

Copper **Ruler:** Emeric Josef **Obverse:** Quartered arms with dragon supporters, elector's cap above **Reverse:** Value and date
Rev. Legend: SCHEIDE MUNZ

Date	Mintage	VG	F	VF	XF	Unc
1768	—	2.00	4.00	12.00	20.00	125

KM# 303 3 PFENNIG (Dreier)

Copper **Ruler:** Johann Friedrich Karl, Graf von Ostein
Obverse: Bust right **Reverse:** Value III, date

Date	Mintage	VG	F	VF	XF	Unc
1759	—	8.00	12.00	25.00	50.00	175

KM# 304 3 PFENNIG (Dreier)

Copper **Ruler:** Johann Friedrich Karl, Graf von Ostein
Reverse: Value as 3

Date	Mintage	VG	F	VF	XF	Unc
1759	—	8.00	12.00	25.00	50.00	175
1760	—	8.00	12.00	25.00	50.00	175

KM# 305 3 PFENNIG (Dreier)

Copper **Ruler:** Johann Friedrich Karl, Graf von Ostein
Obverse: Crowned arms in baroque frame, greyhound at right
Reverse: Value, date

Date	Mintage	VG	F	VF	XF	Unc
1759	—	2.00	5.00	20.00	40.00	150

KM# 306 3 PFENNIG (Dreier)

Copper **Ruler:** Johann Friedrich Karl, Graf von Ostein
Obverse: Crowned 5-fold arms supported by greyhounds, branches below **Reverse:** Value, date

Date	Mintage	VG	F	VF	XF	Unc
1759	—	2.00	5.00	12.00	35.00	150
1760	—	2.00	5.00	12.00	35.00	150

KM# 307 3 PFENNIG (Dreier)

Copper **Ruler:** Johann Friedrich Karl, Graf von Ostein
Obverse: Crowned 5-fold arms supported by 2 greyhounds
Reverse: Value III, date

Date	Mintage	VG	F	VF	XF	Unc
1759	—	5.00	8.00	15.00	35.00	150

KM# 308 3 PFENNIG (Dreier)

Copper **Ruler:** Johann Friedrich Karl, Graf von Ostein
Obverse: Crowned and mantled arms **Reverse:** Value, date

Date	Mintage	VG	F	VF	XF	Unc
1759	—	4.00	7.00	12.00	30.00	125
1760	—	4.00	7.00	12.00	30.00	125
1761	—	4.00	7.00	12.00	30.00	125

KM# 324 3 PFENNIG (Dreier)

Copper **Ruler:** Johann Friedrich Karl, Graf von Ostein
Obverse: Bust right **Reverse:** Value and date in cartouche

Date	Mintage	VG	F	VF	XF	Unc
1760	—	8.00	12.00	20.00	40.00	150
1761	—	8.00	12.00	20.00	40.00	150

KM# 325 3 PFENNIG (Dreier)

Copper **Ruler:** Johann Friedrich Karl, Graf von Ostein
Obverse: Sword and crozier back of crowned arms within baroque frame **Reverse:** Value and date within cartouche

Date	Mintage	VG	F	VF	XF	Unc
1760	—	7.00	10.00	17.50	40.00	150
1761	—	7.00	10.00	17.50	40.00	150

KM# 326 3 PFENNIG (Dreier)

Copper **Ruler:** Johann Friedrich Karl, Graf von Ostein
Obverse: Crowned monogram above wheel **Reverse:** Value, date

Date	Mintage	VG	F	VF	XF	Unc
1760	—	3.00	6.00	15.00	40.00	125

KM# 327 3 PFENNIG (Dreier)

Copper **Ruler:** Johann Friedrich Karl, Graf von Ostein
Obverse: Ruler's titles in legend **Reverse:** Value, date

Date	Mintage	VG	F	VF	XF	Unc
1760	—	5.00	8.00	20.00	35.00	2.00

KM# 328 3 PFENNIG (Dreier)

Copper **Ruler:** Johann Friedrich Karl, Graf von Ostein **Obverse:** Without ruler's titles **Reverse:** Value and date in cartouche

Date	Mintage	VG	F	VF	XF	Unc
1760	—	5.00	8.00	15.00	25.00	125
1761	—	5.00	8.00	15.00	25.00	125

KM# 329 3 PFENNIG (Dreier)
Copper **Ruler:** Johann Friedrich Karl, Graf von Ostein **Obverse:** Sword and crozier back of crowned arms within baroque frame **Reverse:** Value, date

Date	Mintage	VG	F	VF	XF	Unc
1760	—	7.00	10.00	17.50	30.00	100
1761	—	7.00	10.00	17.50	30.00	100

KM# 330 3 PFENNIG (Dreier)
Copper **Ruler:** Johann Friedrich Karl, Graf von Ostein **Obverse:** Sword and crozier back of crowned arms within baroque frame **Reverse:** Value and date in cartouche

Date	Mintage	VG	F	VF	XF	Unc
1760	—	7.00	10.00	17.50	30.00	100
1761	—	7.00	10.00	17.50	30.00	100

KM# 331 3 PFENNIG (Dreier)
Copper **Ruler:** Johann Friedrich Karl, Graf von Ostein **Obverse:** Crowned arms between branches

Date	Mintage	VG	F	VF	XF	Unc
1760	—	7.00	10.00	17.50	30.00	100

KM# 336 3 PFENNIG (Dreier)
Copper **Ruler:** Johann Friedrich Karl, Graf von Ostein **Obverse:** Crowned and mantled arms, sword and crozier below **Reverse:** Value and date in floral sprigs

Date	Mintage	VG	F	VF	XF	Unc
1761	—	7.00	10.00	17.50	30.00	100

KM# 337 3 PFENNIG (Dreier)
Copper **Ruler:** Johann Friedrich Karl, Graf von Ostein **Reverse:** Date in floral sprigs

Date	Mintage	VG	F	VF	XF	Unc
1761	—	7.00	10.00	17.50	30.00	100

KM# 366 3 PFENNIG (Dreier)
Copper **Ruler:** Emeric Josef **Obverse:** Quartered arms with dragon supporters, elector's cap above **Reverse:** Value and date **Rev. Legend:** SCHEIDE MUNZ

Date	Mintage	VG	F	VF	XF	Unc
1768	—	3.00	6.00	12.00	20.00	100

KM# 357 4 PFENNIG
Copper **Ruler:** Emeric Josef **Obverse:** Large wheel, sword and crozier, elector's cap above **Reverse:** Value and date **Rev. Legend:** C.M.L.M

Date	Mintage	VG	F	VF	XF	Unc
1766	—	5.00	10.00	20.00	40.00	125

KM# 402 1/4 KREUTZER
Copper **Ruler:** Friedrich Karl Josef **Obverse:** Bust right **Reverse:** Value and date within beaded circle

Date	Mintage	VG	F	VF	XF	Unc
1795 IA	—	6.00	12.50	30.00	60.00	100

KM# 403 1/2 KREUTZER
Copper **Ruler:** Friedrich Karl Josef **Obverse:** Bust right **Reverse:** Value and date within beaded circle

Date	Mintage	VG	F	VF	XF	Unc
1795 S-IA	—	5.00	10.00	25.00	50.00	80.00
1796 S-IA	—	5.00	10.00	25.00	50.00	80.00

KM# 231 KREUZER
Silver **Ruler:** Lothar Franz, Graf von Schoenborn **Obverse:** 2-fold arms of Mainz and Schonborn in laurel wreath **Reverse:** Value, date, initials in laurel wreath **Rev. Legend:** I/KREVTZ **Note:** Varieties exist.

Date	Mintage	VG	F	VF	XF	Unc
1703 VBW	—	6.00	10.00	20.00	35.00	80.00
1704 VBW	—	6.00	10.00	20.00	35.00	80.00
1716 AK	—	6.00	10.00	20.00	35.00	80.00
1717 AK	—	6.00	10.00	20.00	35.00	80.00
1718 AK	—	6.00	10.00	20.00	35.00	80.00
1720 AK	—	6.00	10.00	20.00	35.00	80.00
1721 AK	—	6.00	10.00	20.00	35.00	80.00
1722 AK	—	6.00	10.00	20.00	35.00	80.00

KM# 338 KREUZER
Silver **Ruler:** Johann Friedrich Karl, Graf von Ostein **Subject:** Death of Archbishop **Obverse:** Arms within crowned mantle, sword and crozier behind **Reverse:** Inscription

Date	Mintage	VG	F	VF	XF	Unc
1763	—	25.00	60.00	125	175	300

KM# 348 KREUZER
Billon **Ruler:** Emeric Josef **Obverse:** Arms **Reverse:** Value and date

Date	Mintage	VG	F	VF	XF	Unc
1765 FB	—	3.00	7.00	20.00	40.00	100

KM# 404 KREUZER
Billon **Ruler:** Friedrich Karl Josef **Obverse:** Bust right **Reverse:** Crowned arms

Date	Mintage	VG	F	VF	XF	Unc
1795 IA	—	4.00	9.00	22.00	45.00	80.00

KM# 250 3 KREUZER (Groschen)
Silver **Ruler:** Lothar Franz, Graf von Schoenborn **Subject:** Death of Lothar Franz **Obverse:** Crowned oval 6-fold arms with central shield of Schonborn in cartouche **Reverse:** 10-line inscription with dates, small imperial orb with 3 at bottom

Date	Mintage	VG	F	VF	XF	Unc
1729 BIB	—	20.00	60.00	125	200	400

KM# 413 3 KREUZER (Groschen)
Billon **Ruler:** Friedrich Karl Josef **Obverse:** Bust right **Reverse:** Crowned complex arms on pedestal

Date	Mintage	VG	F	VF	XF	Unc
1796 S-IA	—	5.00	10.00	25.00	50.00	80.00

KM# 339 5 KREUZER
Silver **Ruler:** Emeric Josef **Obverse:** Arms supported by dragon **Reverse:** EJC monogram on pedestal **Note:** Convention 5 Kreuzer.

Date	Mintage	VG	F	VF	XF	Unc
1763	—	15.00	30.00	65.00	125	—

KM# 349 5 KREUZER
Silver **Ruler:** Emeric Josef **Obverse:** Arms on pedestal **Reverse:** Value and date

Date	Mintage	VG	F	VF	XF	Unc
1765 FB	—	10.00	20.00	50.00	100	200

KM# 362 5 KREUZER
Silver **Ruler:** Emeric Josef **Obverse:** 2-fold arms

Date	Mintage	VG	F	VF	XF	Unc
1767	—	17.00	35.00	70.00	150	250

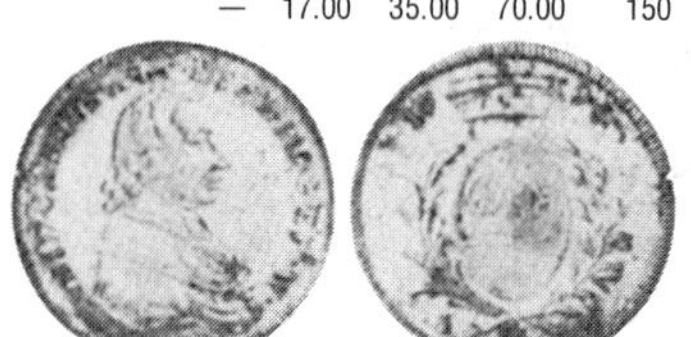

KM# 405 5 KREUZER
Silver **Ruler:** Friedrich Karl Josef **Obverse:** Bust right **Reverse:** Crowned 3-fold arms

Date	Mintage	VG	F	VF	XF	Unc
1795 FS-IA	—	7.00	15.00	35.00	70.00	125

KM# 406 5 KREUZER
Silver **Ruler:** Friedrich Karl Josef **Obverse:** Arms **Reverse:** Inscription

Date	Mintage	VG	F	VF	XF	Unc
1795 IA-S	—	7.00	15.00	35.00	70.00	125

KM# 346 10 KREUZER
Silver **Ruler:** Emeric Josef **Obverse:** Bust right **Reverse:** Quartered arms and date **Note:** Convention 10 Thaler.

Date	Mintage	VG	F	VF	XF	Unc
1764	—	10.00	20.00	50.00	100	200

KM# 350 10 KREUZER
Silver **Ruler:** Emeric Josef **Reverse:** 2-fold arms

Date	Mintage	VG	F	VF	XF	Unc
1765 S-FB	—	9.00	18.00	40.00	100	200
1766	—	9.00	18.00	40.00	100	200

KM# 383 10 KREUZER
Silver **Ruler:** Emeric Josef **Reverse:** 3-fold arms

Date	Mintage	VG	F	VF	XF	Unc
1773 DF	—	9.00	18.00	40.00	100	200
1774	—	9.00	18.00	40.00	100	200

KM# 407 10 KREUZER
Silver **Ruler:** Friedrich Karl Josef **Obverse:** Bust right **Reverse:** Crowned complex arms divide date **Note:** Varieties exist.

Date	Mintage	VG	F	VF	XF	Unc
1795 FS-IA	—	10.00	20.00	50.00	100	200

KM# 351 20 KREUZER
Silver **Ruler:** Emeric Josef **Obverse:** Bust right **Reverse:** Quartered arms and date

Date	Mintage	VG	F	VF	XF	Unc
1765 EG-FB	—	15.00	35.00	70.00	125	200
1765 SA-FB	—	15.00	35.00	70.00	125	200

KM# 358 20 KREUZER
Silver **Ruler:** Emeric Josef **Reverse:** 2-fold arms

Date	Mintage	VG	F	VF	XF	Unc
1766 A	—	15.00	32.00	65.00	125	200

KM# 367 20 KREUZER

Silver **Ruler:** Emeric Josef **Obverse:** Bust right **Reverse:** 3-fold arms

Date	Mintage	VG	F	VF	XF	Unc
1768 FB	—	15.00	30.00	60.00	125	225
1771 DF	—	15.00	30.00	60.00	125	225
1772 DF	—	15.00	30.00	60.00	125	225

KM# 395 20 KREUZER

Silver **Ruler:** Friedrich Karl Josef **Obverse:** Bust right **Reverse:** Crowned complex arms divide date, value below

Date	Mintage	VG	F	VF	XF	Unc
1794 IA	—	20.00	40.00	80.00	160	250

KM# 352 30 KREUZER (1/3 Thaler - 1/2 Gulden)

Silver **Ruler:** Emeric Josef **Obverse:** Bust right **Reverse:** Quartered arms and date

Date	Mintage	VG	F	VF	XF	Unc
1765	—	30.00	60.00	150	250	500

KM# 359 30 KREUZER (1/3 Thaler - 1/2 Gulden)

Silver **Ruler:** Emeric Josef **Reverse:** 2 shields of arms

Date	Mintage	VG	F	VF	XF	Unc
1766	—	35.00	70.00	150	275	500

KM# 232 ALBUS (2 Kreuzer - 1/2 Batzen)

Silver **Ruler:** Lothar Franz, Graf von Schoenborn **Obverse:** 6-fold arms with central shield of Schonborn in laurel wreath **Reverse:** Value, date and initials in laurel wreath **Rev. Legend:** I/ALBUS

Date	Mintage	VG	F	VF	XF	Unc
1704 VBW	—	8.00	15.00	30.00	55.00	—

KM# 233 2 ALBUS (4 Kreuzer - Batzen)

Silver **Ruler:** Lothar Franz, Graf von Schoenborn **Obverse:** 6-fold arms with central shield of Schonborn in wreath **Reverse:** Value, date within branches

Date	Mintage	VG	F	VF	XF	Unc
1704 VBW	—	7.00	12.00	25.00	45.00	—

KM# 258 GROSCHEN (3 Kreuzer)

Silver **Ruler:** Franz Ludwig von Pfalz-Neuburg **Subject:** Death of Franz Ludwig **Obverse:** Crowned oval 9-fold arms with central shield of 4-fold arms (Worms, Ellwangen and Breslau) mounted on cross **Reverse:** 9-line inscription with dates, birthdate given as 26 July 1664

Date	Mintage	VG	F	VF	XF	Unc
1732	—	35.00	65.00	120	200	300

KM# 259 GROSCHEN (3 Kreuzer)

Silver **Ruler:** Franz Ludwig von Pfalz-Neuburg **Reverse:** Birthdate given as 24 July 1664

Date	Mintage	VG	F	VF	XF	Unc
1732	—	65.00	125	250	350	—

KM# 275 GROSCHEN (3 Kreuzer)

Silver **Ruler:** Philipp Karl, Freiherr von Eltz **Subject:** Death of Philipp Karl **Obverse:** Crowned 4-fold arms of Mainz and Eltz in baroque frame **Reverse:** 7-line inscription with dates

Date	Mintage	VG	F	VF	XF	Unc
1743	—	20.00	50.00	100	150	250

KM# 384 1/12 THALER (Doppelgroschen)

Silver **Ruler:** Emeric Josef **Subject:** Death of Archbishop **Obverse:** Arms **Reverse:** 10-line inscription

Date	Mintage	VG	F	VF	XF	Unc
1774	—	17.00	35.00	75.00	150	250

KM# 251 1/8 THALER

Silver **Ruler:** Franz Ludwig von Pfalz-Neuburg **Subject:** Death of Lothar Franz **Obverse:** Crowned round 6-fold arms with central shield of Schonborn **Reverse:** 10-line inscription with date

Date	Mintage	VG	F	VF	XF	Unc
1729 BIB	—	22.00	50.00	100	200	350

KM# 260 1/8 THALER

Silver **Ruler:** Franz Ludwig von Pfalz-Neuburg **Subject:** Death of Franz Ludwig **Obverse:** Crowned oval 9-fold arms with central shield of 4-fold arms mounted on cross **Reverse:** 9-line inscription with dates, birthdate given as 26 July 1664

Date	Mintage	VG	F	VF	XF	Unc
1732	—	120	250	400	600	1,000

KM# 261 1/8 THALER

Silver **Ruler:** Franz Ludwig von Pfalz-Neuburg **Obverse:** St. Martin on horse riding left, beggar at lower rear, Mainz arms below **Reverse:** Date in laurel wreath **Rev. Inscription:** CAPITVLVM / METROPOLI / TANVM / MOGVN / TINVM SEDE / VACANTE **Note:** Sede vacante issue.

Date	Mintage	VG	F	VF	XF	Unc
1732	200	75.00	150	250	350	—

KM# 277 1/8 THALER

Silver **Ruler:** Philipp Karl, Freiherr von Eltz **Obverse:** St. Martin on horse left, beggar below at right, date at bottom **Reverse:** Ornate oval arms of Mainz **Note:** Sede vacante issue.

Date	Mintage	VG	F	VF	XF	Unc
1743	—	50.00	100	175	300	—

KM# 276 1/8 THALER

Silver **Ruler:** Philipp Karl, Freiherr von Eltz **Subject:** Death of Philipp Karl **Obverse:** Crowned 4-fold arms in baroque frame **Reverse:** 7-Line inscription with dates **Note:** Similar to 1 Groschen, KM#275.

Date	Mintage	VG	F	VF	XF	Unc
1743	—	40.00	90.00	155	300	—

KM# 341 1/8 THALER

Silver **Ruler:** Johann Friedrich Karl, Graf von Ostein **Obverse:** St. Martin on horse, beggar on ground **Reverse:** Oval arms in cartouche, date **Note:** Sede vacante issue.

Date	Mintage	VG	F	VF	XF	Unc
1763	—	40.00	75.00	150	300	—

KM# 340 1/8 THALER

Silver **Ruler:** Johann Friedrich Karl, Graf von Ostein **Subject:** Death of Archbishop **Obverse:** Sword and crozier back of crowned complex arms within mantle **Reverse:** Inscription

Date	Mintage	VG	F	VF	XF	Unc
1763	—	40.00	75.00	150	300	—

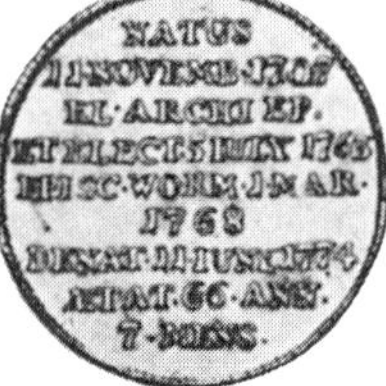

KM# 385 1/6 THALER

Silver **Ruler:** Emeric Josef **Subject:** Death of Archbishop **Obverse:** Sword and crozier back of crowned arms within mantle **Reverse:** Inscription

Date	Mintage	VG	F	VF	XF	Unc
1774	—	30.00	50.00	100	200	—

KM# 252 1/4 THALER

Silver **Ruler:** Emeric Josef **Subject:** Death of Lothar Franz **Obverse:** Crowned oval 6-fold arms with central shield of Schonborn in cartouche **Reverse:** 10-line inscription with dates, small imperial orb without indication of value

Date	Mintage	VG	F	VF	XF	Unc
1729	—	65.00	150	300	475	—

KM# 262 1/4 THALER

Silver **Ruler:** Franz Ludwig von Pfalz-Neuburg **Subject:** Death of Lothar Franz **Obverse:** Crowned oval 9-fold arms with central shield of 4-fold arms mounted on cross **Reverse:** 9-line inscription with dates, birthday as 26 July 1664

Date	Mintage	VG	F	VF	XF	Unc
1732	—	200	400	650	1,000	—

KM# 263 1/4 THALER

Silver **Ruler:** Franz Ludwig von Pfalz-Neuburg

Date	Mintage	VG	F	VF	XF	Unc
1732	—	350	700	1,000	1,500	—

KM# 264 1/4 THALER

Silver **Ruler:** Franz Ludwig von Pfalz-Neuburg **Obverse:** St. Martin on horse left, shield of arms below, beggar at lower right **Reverse:** Inscription within branches **Note:** Sede vacante issue.

Date	Mintage	VG	F	VF	XF	Unc
1732	200	80.00	140	250	500	—

KM# 279 1/4 THALER

Silver **Ruler:** Philipp Karl, Freiherr von Eltz **Obverse:** St. Martin on horse left, beggar below right, date at bottom **Reverse:** Ornate oval arms of Mainz **Note:** Sede vacante issue.

Date	Mintage	VG	F	VF	XF	Unc
1743	—	80.00	140	240	450	—

KM# 278 1/4 THALER

Silver **Ruler:** Philipp Karl, Freiherr von Eltz **Subject:** Death of Philipp Karl **Obverse:** Crowned 4-fold arms of Mainz and Eltz in baroque frame **Reverse:** 7-line inscription with dates

Date	Mintage	VG	F	VF	XF	Unc
1743	—	80.00	140	240	450	—

KM# 343 1/4 THALER

Silver **Ruler:** Johann Friedrich Karl, Graf von Ostein **Obverse:** St. Martin on horse, beggar on ground, date **Reverse:** Oval arms in cartouche **Note:** Sede vacante issue.

Date	Mintage	VG	F	VF	XF	Unc
1763	—	50.00	90.00	165	350	—

KM# 342 1/4 THALER

Silver **Ruler:** Johann Friedrich Karl, Graf von Ostein **Subject:** Death of Archbishop **Obverse:** Sword and crozier back of crowned arms within mantle **Reverse:** 10-Line inscription **Note:** Similar to 1/8 Thaler, KM#340 but 10 lines on reverse.

Date	Mintage	VG	F	VF	XF	Unc
1763	—	70.00	120	220	450	—

KM# 353 1/4 THALER

Silver **Ruler:** Emeric Josef **Obverse:** Bust right **Reverse:** Crowned arms, date **Note:** Convention 1/4 Thaler.

Date	Mintage	VG	F	VF	XF	Unc
1765 A-FB	—	30.00	70.00	140	220	—
1766 ST	—	30.00	70.00	140	220	—

KM# 386 1/3 THALER (30 Kreuzer - 1/2 Gulden)

Silver **Ruler:** Emeric Josef **Obverse:** Sword and crozier back of arms within crowned mantle **Reverse:** Inscription

Date	Mintage	VG	F	VF	XF	Unc
1774	—	45.00	90.00	180	350	—

KM# 265 1/2 THALER

Silver **Ruler:** Franz Ludwig von Pfalz-Neuburg **Obverse:** St. Martin on horse riding left, beggar to lower rear, Mainz arms below **Reverse:** Date in laurel wreath **Rev. Legend:** CAPITVLVM / METROPOLI / TANVM MOGVN / TINVM SEDE / VACANTE **Note:** Sede vacante issue.

Date	Mintage	VG	F	VF	XF	Unc
1732	200	120	200	350	650	—

KM# 280 1/2 THALER

Silver **Ruler:** Philipp Karl, Freiherr von Eltz **Obverse:** St. Martin on horse left, beggar below right, ornate oval arms of Mainz below **Reverse:** Date **Rev. Legend:** CAPITULUM / METROPOLI / TANUM MOGUN / TINUM SEDE / VACANTE **Note:** Sede vacante issue.

Date	Mintage	VG	F	VF	XF	Unc
1743	—	100	175	325	600	—

KM# 332 1/2 THALER

Silver **Ruler:** Johann Friedrich Karl, Graf von Ostein **Obverse:** Bust right **Reverse:** Crowned 5-fold arms supported by 2 greyhounds

Date	Mintage	VG	F	VF	XF	Unc
1760	—	100	175	325	600	—

KM# 344 1/2 THALER

Silver **Ruler:** Johann Friedrich Karl, Graf von Ostein **Obverse:** Arms within branches atop pedestal **Reverse:** St. Martin on horseback left, beggar on ground at right **Note:** Sede vacante issue.

Date	Mintage	VG	F	VF	XF	Unc
1763	—	100	200	350	750	—

KM# 354 1/2 THALER

Silver **Ruler:** Emeric Josef **Obverse:** Bust right **Reverse:** Arms **Note:** Convention 1/2 Thaler.

Date	Mintage	VG	F	VF	XF	Unc
1765 EG	—	65.00	125	225	500	—

KM# 360 1/2 THALER

Silver **Ruler:** Emeric Josef **Reverse:** 2-fold arms

Date	Mintage	VG	F	VF	XF	Unc
1766 ST-FB	—	100	175	250	500	—

KM# 368 1/2 THALER

Silver **Ruler:** Emeric Josef **Obverse:** Bust right **Reverse:** Sword and crozier back of crowned arms with supporters, value below

Date	Mintage	VG	F	VF	XF	Unc
1768	—	45.00	85.00	200	450	—
1769	—	45.00	85.00	200	450	—

KM# 408 1/2 THALER

Silver **Ruler:** Friedrich Karl Josef **Obverse:** Bust right **Reverse:** Crowned arms within branches

Date	Mintage	VG	F	VF	XF	Unc
1795 IA	—	100	175	250	500	—

KM# 234 THALER

Silver **Ruler:** Lothar Franz, Graf von Schoenborn **Obv. Legend:** LOTHAR FRANC D.G.A **Rev. Legend:** IN MANIBV-S DOMI-NI **Note:** Dav. #2423.

Date	Mintage	VG	F	VF	XF	Unc
1708	—	—	—	—	—	—

Note: Reported, not confirmed

KM# 266 THALER

Silver **Ruler:** Franz Ludwig von Pfalz-Neuburg **Obverse:** St. Martin on horseback left, shield below, beggar at right **Reverse:** Inscription within branches **Note:** Sede vacante issue.

Date	Mintage	F	VF	XF	Unc
1732	200	—	500	1,000	1,750

KM# 281 THALER

Silver **Ruler:** Philipp Karl, Freiherr von Eltz **Obverse:** Ornate oval arms of Mainz **Obv. Legend:** CAPITUL: METROP: MOGUNT **Note:** Sede vacante issue.

Date	Mintage	F	VF	XF	Unc
1743	—	—	1,000	2,000	3,500

KM# 282 THALER

Silver **Ruler:** Johann Friedrich Karl, Graf von Ostein **Obverse:** Bust right **Reverse:** Crowned 4-fold arms of Mainz and Ostein, date below **Rev. Legend:** DOCE ME FACERE VOLUNTATEM TUAM QUIA DEUS MEUS ES

Date	Mintage	F	VF	XF	Unc
1744 CS	—	1,250	2,250	3,500	4,750

KM# 285 THALER

Silver **Ruler:** Johann Friedrich Karl, Graf von Ostein **Obverse:** Bust right **Reverse:** Crowned and mantled 5-fold arms divides date **Note:** Convention Thaler.

Date	Mintage	VG	F	VF	XF	Unc
1747	—	300	600	1,000	2,000	—
1748	—	300	600	1,000	2,000	—

KM# 345 THALER

Silver **Ruler:** Johann Friedrich Karl, Graf von Ostein **Obverse:** St. Martin and beggar within inner circle, 12 shields of arms surround **Reverse:** Various shields surround center circle **Note:** Sede vacante issue.

Date	Mintage	VG	F	VF	XF	Unc
1763	—	325	750	1,200	2,500	—

KM# 347 THALER

Silver **Ruler:** Emeric Josef **Obverse:** Cloaked bust right **Obv. Legend:** EMERIC • IOSEPH • D • G • A • EP • MOG • S • R • I • P • G • A • CAN • P • EL • **Reverse:** Crowned quartered arms with supporters, value and date below **Rev. Legend:** AD NORMAM - CONVENTIONIS, 10/EINE FEINE MARK/date **Note:** Dav. #2424.

Date	Mintage	F	VF	XF	Unc
1764 EG	—	100	200	350	1,000
1765 EG	—	100	200	350	1,000

KM# 361 THALER

Silver **Ruler:** Emeric Josef **Obverse:** Bust right **Obv. Legend:** EMERIC • IOSEPH • D • G • A • EP • MOG • S • R • I • P • G • A • C • P • EL • **Reverse:** Sword and crozier back of crowned divided arms **Rev. Legend:** EINE FEINE - MARK 1766 **Note:** Dav. #2425.

Date	Mintage	F	VF	XF	Unc
1766 A-FB	—	100	200	350	1,000

KM# 363 THALER

Silver **Ruler:** Emeric Josef **Obverse:** Draped bust right **Obv. Legend:** EMERIC IOSEPH • D • G • A • EP • MOG • S • R • I • G • A • C • P • EL • **Reverse:** Crown above two shields within baroque frame **Rev. Legend:** EINE FEINE - MARK date **Note:** Dav. #2426.

Date	Mintage	F	VF	XF	Unc
1767 FB	—	100	200	350	1,000
1768 FB	—	100	200	350	1,000

KM# 369 THALER

Silver **Ruler:** Emeric Josef **Obverse:** Bust right **Obv. Legend:** EMERIC • IOSEPH • D • G • A • EP • MOG • S • R • I • P • G • A • C • P • EL • EP • W • **Reverse:** Crowned quartered arms with central shield and supporters **Rev. Legend:** X/EINE/FEINE/MARK below **Note:** Dav. #2427.

Date	Mintage	F	VF	XF	Unc
1768 DF	—	100	200	350	1,000
1769 DF	—	100	200	350	1,000

KM# 370 THALER

Silver **Ruler:** Emeric Josef **Note:** Dav. #2427A.

Date	Mintage	F	VF	XF	Unc
1768 FB	—	100	200	350	1,000

KM# 380 THALER

Silver **Ruler:** Emeric Josef **Obverse:** Bust right **Obv. Legend:** EMERIC • IOSEP • D • G • A • EP • MOG • S • R • I • P • G • A • C • P • EL • EP • W • **Reverse:** Crowned 3-fold oval arms within branches **Rev. Legend:** ZEHEN EINE - FEINE MARK **Note:** Dav. #2428.

Date	Mintage	F	VF	XF	Unc
1770 DF	—	100	200	350	1,000
1771 DF	—	100	200	350	1,000

KM# 396 THALER

Silver **Ruler:** Friedrich Karl Josef **Obverse:** Bust right **Obv. Legend:** FRID • CAR • IOS • D • G • A • E • MOG • S • R • I • P • G • A • C • ET • L • E • W • **Reverse:** Crowned complex arms within Order chain **Rev. Legend:** ZEHEN EINE - FEINE MARK **Note:** Dav. #2429.

Date	Mintage	F	VF	XF	Unc
1794 IFS//IA	—	125	250	400	800

KM# 397 THALER

Silver **Ruler:** Friedrich Karl Josef **Obverse:** Bust 1/4 right **Obv. Legend:** FRID • CAR • IOS • AEP • ET • EL • MOG • EP • WOR •, I • LINDENSCHMIT • below bust **Reverse:** Electors hat above arms **Rev. Legend:** ZEHEN EINE - FEINE MARK **Note:** Dav. #2430.

Date	Mintage	F	VF	XF	Unc
1794 IL-IA	—	150	300	500	1,500

KM# 400 THALER

Silver **Ruler:** Friedrich Karl Josef **Obverse:** Crown above complex arms with Order chain **Obv. Legend:** CHVR MAINZ **Reverse:** Value, date above branches **Rev. Legend:** * X */EINE FEINE/MARCK/1794 **Note:** Dav. #2432A.

Date	Mintage	F	VF	XF	Unc
1794 FS//IA	—	125	200	375	750

KM# 401 THALER

Silver **Ruler:** Friedrich Karl Josef **Obverse:** Crowned pointed arms with tassels **Obv. Legend:** CHVR MAINZ **Reverse:** Value, date above branches **Rev. Legend:** X/EINE FEINE/MARK•/ 1794•/L•A• **Note:** Dav. #2433.

Date	Mintage	F	VF	XF	Unc
1794 IL//IA	—	125	200	375	750

KM# 398 THALER

Silver **Ruler:** Friedrich Karl Josef **Obverse:** Bust 1/4 right **Obv. Legend:** FRID • CAR • IOS • AEP • ET • EL • MOG • EP • WOR •, I• LINDENSCHMIT • below **Reverse:** Inscription within branches **Rev. Legend:** X EINE FEINE MARK •, in sprays; EX VASIS/ARGENT • CLERI/MOGVNT • PRO/ARIS ET FOCIS/A • MDCCXCIV/ I • A • **Note:** Contribution Thaler. Dav. #2431.

Date	Mintage	F	VF	XF	Unc
MDCCXCIV IL-IA	—	125	250	400	1,000

KM# 399 THALER

Silver **Ruler:** Friedrich Karl Josef **Obverse:** Crowned quartered arms with central shield and Order chain **Obv. Legend:** CHVR MAINZ **Reverse:** Value, date above branches **Rev. Legend:** * X */EINE FEINE/MARCK/1794/I•A• **Note:** Convention Thaler. Dav. #2432.

Date	Mintage	F	VF	XF	Unc
1794 IA	—	125	250	400	1,000

KM# 409 THALER

Silver **Ruler:** Friedrich Karl Josef **Obverse:** Crowned pointed arms with tassels **Obv. Legend:** DEUTSCHLANDS - SCHUTZWEHR •, in exergue; DURCH CLAIRFAIT ENTSETZT/DEN 29TEN OKT•/1795 **Reverse:** Value, date within branches **Rev. Legend:** DEN ERRETTERN - DES VATERLANDS **Note:** Dav. #2434.

Date	Mintage	F	VF	XF	Unc
1795 FS-IA	—	300	600	1,000	2,000

KM# 414 THALER

Silver **Ruler:** Friedrich Karl Josef **Reverse:** Capped arms in sprays, date and I.A. below **Note:** Dav. #2434A.

Date	Mintage	F	VF	XF	Unc
1796 FS//IA	—	200	400	600	1,000

KM# 415 THALER

Silver **Ruler:** Friedrich Karl Josef **Obverse:** Bust right, F.S. below **Reverse:** Monument with I.A. below **Note:** Dav. #2434B.

Date	Mintage	F	VF	XF	Unc
1796 FS//IA	—	200	325	500	1,000

KM# 416 THALER

Silver **Ruler:** Friedrich Karl Josef **Obverse:** Bust right **Obv. Legend:** FRID • CAR • IOS • ERZB • V • KVRF • Z • MAINZ F • B • Z • W • **Reverse:** Cap above oval arms within palm and laurel branches **Rev. Legend:** ZEHEN EINE - FEINE MARK **Note:** Dav. #2435.

Date	Mintage	F	VF	XF	Unc
1796 FS//IA	—	100	200	350	700

TRADE COINAGE

KM# 240 3/4 DUCAT

2.6250 g., 0.9860 Gold 0.0832 oz. AGW **Ruler:** Lothar Franz, Graf von Schoenborn **Obverse:** Bust right in inner circle **Reverse:** Crowned arms in inner circle

Date	Mintage	VG	F	VF	XF	Unc
1712	—	300	650	1,500	2,250	—

KM# 241 DUCAT

3.5000 g., 0.9860 Gold 0.1109 oz. AGW **Ruler:** Lothar Franz, Graf von Schoenborn **Obverse:** Bust right in circle **Reverse:** Crowned oval 6-fold arms with central shield of Schonborn, date in margin at bottom

Date	Mintage	VG	F	VF	XF	Unc
1712	—	1,250	2,250	3,500	5,000	—

KM# 245 DUCAT

3.5000 g., 0.9860 Gold 0.1109 oz. AGW **Ruler:** Lothar Franz, Graf von Schoenborn **Obverse:** Bust right in inner circle **Reverse:** Crowned arms in inner circle

Date	Mintage	VG	F	VF	XF	Unc
1716 AK	—	475	1,100	2,500	3,500	—
1728	—	475	1,100	2,500	3,500	—

KM# 255 DUCAT

3.5000 g., 0.9860 Gold 0.1109 oz. AGW **Ruler:** Franz Ludwig von Pfalz-Neuburg **Obverse:** Bust right **Reverse:** Hand from heaven leads lion

Date	Mintage	VG	F	VF	XF	Unc
1730	—	250	600	1,250	2,250	—

KM# 256 DUCAT

3.5000 g., 0.9860 Gold 0.1109 oz. AGW **Ruler:** Franz Ludwig von Pfalz-Neuburg **Obverse:** Bust right **Reverse:** Crowned 4-fold arms of Worms, Ellwangen and Breslau with central shield of Mainz, date divided by crown

Date	Mintage	VG	F	VF	XF	Unc
1730	—	1,500	2,400	3,500	5,000	—
1731	—	1,500	2,400	3,500	5,000	—
1732	—	1,500	2,400	3,500	5,000	—

KM# 268 DUCAT

3.5000 g., 0.9860 Gold 0.1109 oz. AGW **Ruler:** Philipp Karl, Freiherr von Eltz **Subject:** Philipp Karl **Obverse:** Bust right **Reverse:** Arms within crowned mantle, sword and crozier behind

Date	Mintage	VG	F	VF	XF	Unc
1738	—	200	500	1,000	2,000	—

KM# 283 DUCAT

3.5000 g., 0.9860 Gold 0.1109 oz. AGW **Ruler:** Johann Friedrich Karl, Graf von Ostein **Subject:** Johann Friedrich Karl **Obverse:** Bust right **Reverse:** Arms within crowned mantle, sword and crozier behind

Date	Mintage	VG	F	VF	XF	Unc
1745	—	225	500	1,100	2,000	—
1747	—	225	500	1,100	2,000	—
1753	—	225	500	1,100	2,000	—

KM# 309 DUCAT

3.5000 g., 0.9860 Gold 0.1109 oz. AGW **Ruler:** Johann Friedrich Karl, Graf von Ostein **Reverse:** Crowned arms with dog supporters

Date	Mintage	VG	F	VF	XF	Unc
1759	—	225	650	1,200	2,000	—
1760	—	225	650	1,200	2,000	—

KM# 371 DUCAT

3.5000 g., 0.9860 Gold 0.1109 oz. AGW **Ruler:** Emeric Josef **Subject:** Emeric Josef **Obverse:** Bust right **Reverse:** Crown above 3 shields of arms within branches, sword and crozier behind

Date	Mintage	F	VF	XF	Unc
1768	—	300	750	1,000	2,000
1769	—	300	750	1,000	2,000
1771 DF	—	300	750	1,000	2,000

KM# 382 DUCAT

3.5000 g., 0.9860 Gold 0.1109 oz. AGW **Ruler:** Emeric Josef **Obverse:** Bust right **Reverse:** Value, date

Date	Mintage	F	VF	XF	Unc
1772 S-DF	—	1,000	1,750	3,500	5,000

KM# 410 DUCAT

3.5000 g., 0.9860 Gold 0.1109 oz. AGW **Ruler:** Friedrich Karl Josef **Subject:** Friedrich Karl Josef **Obverse:** Bust right **Reverse:** Cap above oval arms within palm and laurel branches

Date	Mintage	F	VF	XF	Unc
1795 FS-IA	—	250	425	600	850

KM# 411 DUCAT

3.5000 g., 0.9860 Gold 0.1109 oz. AGW **Ruler:** Friedrich Karl Josef **Obverse:** Bust right **Obv. Legend:** FRID • CAR • JOS • A EP • ET EL • MOG • EP • W **Reverse:** City view **Rev. Legend:** AVREA MOGVNTIA **Note:** Roman numeral date: MDCCLXXXXV.

Date	Mintage	F	VF	XF	Unc
(1795) FS-IA	—	300	450	650	1,000

KM# 412 DUCAT

3.5000 g., 0.9860 Gold 0.1109 oz. AGW **Ruler:** Friedrich Karl Josef **Subject:** Contribution Ducat **Reverse:** Arms

Date	Mintage	F	VF	XF	Unc
1795 Rare	—	—	—	5,000	—

KM# 269 2 DUCAT
7.0000 g., 0.9860 Gold 0.2219 oz. AGW **Ruler:** Philipp Karl, Freiherr von Eltz **Subject:** Philipp Karl **Obverse:** Bust right **Reverse:** Arms within crowned mantle, sword and crozier behind

Date	Mintage	VG	F	VF	XF	Unc
1738	—	550	1,200	2,500	5,000	—

KM# 284 2 DUCAT
7.0000 g., 0.9860 Gold 0.2219 oz. AGW **Ruler:** Johann Friedrich Karl, Graf von Ostein **Subject:** Johann Friedrich Karl **Obverse:** Bust right **Reverse:** Arms within crowned mantle, sword and crozier behind

Date	Mintage	VG	F	VF	XF	Unc
1745	—	400	800	2,000	3,500	4,500
1748	—	400	800	2,000	3,500	4,500

KM# 314 2 DUCAT
7.0000 g., 0.9860 Gold 0.2219 oz. AGW **Ruler:** Johann Friedrich Karl, Graf von Ostein **Reverse:** Crowned arms with dog supporters, date below

Date	Mintage	VG	F	VF	XF	Unc
1760 S	—	600	1,450	3,750	6,500	8,000

KM# 333 5 DUCAT (1/2 Portugaloser)
17.5000 g., 0.9860 Gold 0.5547 oz. AGW **Ruler:** Johann Friedrich Karl, Graf von Ostein **Obverse:** Bust right **Reverse:** Crowned 5-fold arms supported by 2 greyhounds

Date	Mintage	VG	F	VF	XF	Unc
1760	—	5,500	8,500	12,000	20,000	—

KM# 257 6 DUCAT
21.0000 g., 0.9860 Gold 0.6657 oz. AGW **Ruler:** Franz Ludwig von Pfalz-Neuburg **Obverse:** Bust right **Reverse:** Crowned ornate 9-fold arms with central shield of Mainz, crown divides date

Date	Mintage	VG	F	VF	XF	Unc
1730 BECKER	—	6,500	10,000	15,000	20,000	—
1732 BECKER	—	6,500	10,000	15,000	20,000	—

KM# 267 10 DUCAT (Portugaloser)
35.0000 g., 0.9860 Gold 1.1095 oz. AGW **Ruler:** Franz Ludwig von Pfalz-Neuburg **Obverse:** Bust right **Reverse:** Lion reclining right, looking back over shoulder, Eye of God with rays streaming down in clouds at top, Roman numeral date below

Date	Mintage	VG	F	VF	XF	Unc
(1732) BECKER	—	—	—	25,000	30,000	—

KM# 286 10 DUCAT (Portugaloser)
35.0000 g., 0.9860 Gold 1.1095 oz. AGW **Ruler:** Johann Friedrich Karl, Graf von Ostein **Obverse:** Bust right **Reverse:** Crowned and mantled 5-fold arms divide date

Date	Mintage	VG	F	VF	XF	Unc
1748	18	—	—	25,000	30,000	—

FRENCH OCCUPATION

SIEGE COINAGE

1793

KM# 601 SOL
Copper **Ruler:** Friedrich Karl Josef **Obverse:** Capped fasces within oak leaf wreath, date below **Reverse:** Value

Date	Mintage	VG	F	VF	XF	Unc
1793	—	15.00	25.00	45.00	95.00	—

KM# 602 2 SOLS
Copper **Ruler:** Friedrich Karl Josef **Obverse:** Capped fasces within oak leaf wreath **Reverse:** Value

Date	Mintage	VG	F	VF	XF	Unc
1793	—	20.00	30.00	55.00	85.00	—

KM# 603 5 SOLS
Copper **Ruler:** Friedrich Karl Josef **Obverse:** Capped fasces within oak leaf wreath **Reverse:** Value

Date	Mintage	VG	F	VF	XF	Unc
1793	—	30.00	45.00	75.00	110	—

PATTERNS

Including off metal strikes

KM#	Date	Mintage	Identification	Mkt Val
Pn14	(1702-14)	—	Pfennig. Gold. KM#230.	350
Pn15	1703	—	Kreuzer. Gold. KM#231.	350
Pn16	1712	—	Ducat. Lead. KM#241.	130
Pn17	1732	—	6 Ducat. Silver. KM#257.	1,500
Pn18	1732	—	10 Ducat. Silver. KM#267.	1,500
Pn19	1756	—	Pfennig. Silver. KM#293.	250
Pn20	1759	—	Pfennig. Silver. KM#297.	250
Pn21	1760	—	2 Pfennig. Silver. KM#301.	350
Pn22	1795	—	Kreuzer. Gold. 1/4 Ducat weight, KM#404.	600
Pn23	1795	—	Kreuzer. Gold. 1/2 Ducat weight, KM#404.	800

MANSFELD

A small, silver mining state, located between Anhalt and Thuringia. Bracteats were struck c. 1200. The ruling family of Mansfeld was much divided during the 15th and 16th centuries and they were prolific coin issuers during this period. The county of Mansfeld was annexed to Electoral Saxony in 1780 and then passed to Prussia in 1815.

RULERS

Vorderort Line

BORNSTEDT

Heinrich Franz, 1644-1715
Karl Franz, 1692-1717
Heinrich Paul Franz, 1717-1780
Josef Wenzel Nepomuk, 1780

MINT OFFICIALS' INITIALS

Initials	Date	Name
CW	1688-1739	Christian Wermuth, die-cutter in Gotha
IIG	1710-47	Johann Jeremias Grundler in Stolberg

ARMS

Usually 4-fold with Mansfeld and Heldrungen prominent. Other side normally has St. George slaying dragon.

MANSFELD-BORNSTEDT

Founded upon the division of Mansfeld in 1530/32. Raised to the rank of Prince of the Empire in 1709. The line became extinct in 1780 and its titles fell to Colloredo.

RULER

Henry, Prince of Fondi, 1717-1780

PRINCIPALITY

STANDARD COINAGE

KM# 140 1/4 THALER
Silver **Ruler:** Henry, Prince of Fondi **Obverse:** Bust right **Reverse:** Crowned arms, date **Note:** Species 1/4 Thaler

Date	Mintage	VG	F	VF	XF	Unc
1747 IIG	—	130	200	400	750	—

KM# 141 1/2 THALER
Silver **Ruler:** Henry, Prince of Fondi **Obverse:** Bust right **Reverse:** Crowned arms, date **Note:** Species 1/2 Thaler

Date	Mintage	VG	F	VF	XF	Unc
1747 IIG	—	185	300	600	1,100	—

KM# 150 1/2 THALER
Silver **Ruler:** Henry, Prince of Fondi **Mint:** Prague **Obverse:** Arms within crowned mantle **Reverse:** Horseman slaying dragon

Date	Mintage	VG	F	VF	XF	Unc
1774	—	135	200	275	375	—

KM# 142 THALER
Silver **Ruler:** Henry, Prince of Fondi **Obverse:** Bust right **Reverse:** Crowned arms, date **Note:** Dav. #2437. Species Thaler.

Date	Mintage	F	VF	XF	Unc
1747 IIG	—	600	1,000	1,750	3,000

KM# 151 THALER
Silver **Ruler:** Henry, Prince of Fondi **Mint:** Prague **Obverse:** Arms within crowned mantle **Obv. Legend:** HENRI: S: R: I: P: C: MANSFELD Æ • N • D • IN • HELD: SEEB: & SCHRAPPLAU • **Reverse:** Horseman slaying dragon **Rev. Legend:** BEY GOTT IST RATH - UND THAT **Note:** Dav. #2438.

Date	Mintage	F	VF	XF	Unc
1774	—	150	250	475	1,200

TRADE COINAGE

KM# 143 DUCAT
3.5000 g., 0.9860 Gold 0.1109 oz. AGW **Ruler:** Henry, Prince of Fondi **Obverse:** Armored bust of Heinrich right **Reverse:** Crowned arms, date

Date	Mintage	VG	F	VF	XF	Unc
1747 IIG	—	750	1,000	2,000	3,500	—

KM# 152 DUCAT
3.5000 g., 0.9860 Gold 0.1109 oz. AGW **Ruler:** Henry, Prince of Fondi **Mint:** Prague **Obverse:** Arms within crowned mantle **Reverse:** Horseman slaying dragon

Date	Mintage	VG	F	VF	XF	Unc
1774	—	150	350	700	1,300	—

MANSFELD-EISLEBEN

This line resulted from the division of 1530/32. Upon the extinction of Eisleben in 1710, all lands and titles reverted to the Bornstedt line.

RULER

Johann Georg III, 1663-1710

PRINCIPALITY

REGULAR COINAGE

KM# 80 GROSCHEN (1/24 Thaler)
Silver **Subject:** Death of Johann Georg III **Obverse:** Bust right **Reverse:** Nine line inscription **Note:** Varieties exist.

Date	Mintage	VG	F	VF	XF	Unc
1710 IIG	—	30.00	65.00	125	185	—

KM# 81 4 GROSCHEN (1/6 Thaler)

Silver **Subject:** Death of Johann Georg III **Obverse:** Bust right **Reverse:** Inscription **Note:** Similar to Groschen KM#80.

Date	Mintage	VG	F	VF	XF	Unc
1710 IIG Rare	—	—	—	—	—	—

KM# 82 1/4 THALER

Silver **Subject:** Death of Johann Georg III **Obverse:** Thirteen-line inscription with dates **Reverse:** Two helmets above four-fold arms **Note:** Varieties exist.

Date	Mintage	VG	F	VF	XF	Unc
1710 IIG	—	85.00	150	300	475	—

KM# 83 1/2 THALER

Silver **Subject:** Death of Johann George III **Obverse:** St. George right slaying dragon **Obv. Legend:** IOH •GEORG • III • COM • & DN • I • MANSF • NOB • D • I • H • S • & • SCH • SENIOR • **Reverse:** Fourteen-line inscription with dates **Note:** Dav. #4236. Varieties exist.

Date	Mintage	VG	F	VF	XF	Unc
1710 IIG	—	75.00	140	275	450	—

KM# 84 THALER

Silver **Subject:** Death of John Georg **Obverse:** Bust right **Obv. Legend:** IOH • GEORG: III • COM • ET • DN • I • MANSF • NOB • D • I • G • S • ET SCHR • SENIOR • **Reverse:** 19-line inscription **Note:** Dav. #2436. Varieties exist.

Date	Mintage	F	VF	XF	Unc
1710 CW/IIG	—	400	800	1,600	3,000

TRADE COINAGE

KM# 85 DUCAT

3.5000 g., 0.9860 Gold 0.1109 oz. AGW **Subject:** Death of Johann Georg III **Obverse:** Bust right **Reverse:** 9-line inscription **Note:** An off-metal strike using Groschen dies of KM#80.

Date	Mintage	VG	F	VF	XF	Unc
1710 IIG Unique	—	—	—	—	—	—

MECKLENBURG-SCHWERIN

The duchy of Mecklenburg was located along the Baltic coast between Holstein and Pomerania. Schwerin was annexed to Mecklenburg in 1357. During the Thirty Years' War, the dukes of Mecklenburg sided with the Protestant forces against the emperor. Albrecht von Wallenstein, the imperialist general, ousted the Mecklenburg dukes from their territories in 1628. They were restored to their lands in 1632. In 1658 the Mecklenburg dynasty was divided into two lines. No coinage was produced for Mecklenburg-Schwerin from 1708 until 1750. The 1815 Congress of Vienna elevated the duchy to the status of grand duchy and it became a part of the German Empire in 1871 until 1918 when the last grand duke abdicated.

RULERS

Friedrich Wilhelm, 1692-1713
Karl Leopold, 1713-1747
Christian Ludwig II, 1747-1756
Friedrich II, 1756-1785
Friedrich Franz I, 1785-1837

MINT MARKS

A - Berlin
B - Hannover

MINT OFFICIALS' INITIALS

SCHWERIN MINT

Initials	Date	Name
IFH, IHF	1703-17	Johann Friedrich Hilcken, die-cutter
OHK	1751-56	Otto Heinrich Knorre
ZDK	1695-1708	Zacharias Daniel Kelpe

GRAND DUCHY

REGULAR COINAGE

KM# 188 PFENNIG

Copper **Ruler:** Friedrich II **Obverse:** Steer head, without legend **Reverse:** Value and date

Date	Mintage	VG	F	VF	XF	Unc
1758	—	4.00	9.00	18.00	35.00	—

KM# 158 1-1/2 PFENNIG

Copper **Ruler:** Friedrich Wilhelm **Obverse:** Crowned FW monogram, crossed palm branches below **Reverse:** Value: 1 1/2/PFENN/date/initials **Note:** Varieties exist.

Date	Mintage	VG	F	VF	XF	Unc
1704 ZDK	154,000	10.00	24.00	36.00	75.00	—

KM# 171 3 PFENNIG (Dreiling)

Copper **Ruler:** Christian Ludwig II **Obverse:** Steer head with legend **Reverse:** Value and date

Date	Mintage	VG	F	VF	XF	Unc
1752	—	3.00	6.00	10.00	30.00	—
1753	—	3.00	6.00	10.00	30.00	—
1754	—	3.00	6.00	10.00	30.00	—
1755	—	3.00	6.00	10.00	30.00	—

KM# 172 3 PFENNIG (Dreiling)

Copper **Ruler:** Christian Ludwig II **Obv. Legend:** FR.MECKLENB

Date	Mintage	VG	F	VF	XF	Unc
1752	—	3.00	6.00	12.00	35.00	—

KM# 189 3 PFENNIG (Dreiling)

Copper **Ruler:** Friedrich II **Obverse:** Steer head, without legend

Date	Mintage	VG	F	VF	XF	Unc
1758	—	2.00	5.00	9.00	28.00	—

KM# 192 3 PFENNIG (Dreiling)

0.5000 g., 0.1870 Silver 0.0030 oz. ASW **Ruler:** Friedrich II **Obverse:** Crowned script F

Date	Mintage	VG	F	VF	XF	Unc
1759	—	3.00	6.00	10.00	30.00	—

KM# 202 3 PFENNIG (Dreiling)

0.5000 g., 0.1870 Silver 0.0030 oz. ASW **Ruler:** Friedrich II **Obverse:** Crowned F **Reverse:** Value above date

Date	Mintage	VG	F	VF	XF	Unc
1763	245,000	2.00	5.00	8.00	25.00	—
1764	572,000	2.00	5.00	8.00	25.00	—
1765	166,000	2.00	5.00	8.00	25.00	—
1766	142,000	2.00	5.00	8.00	25.00	—
1767	163,000	2.00	5.00	8.00	25.00	—
1775	386,000	2.00	5.00	8.00	25.00	—
1779	110,000	2.00	5.00	8.00	25.00	—
1780	131,000	2.00	5.00	8.00	25.00	—
1781	126,000	2.00	5.00	8.00	25.00	—
1782	143,000	2.00	5.00	8.00	25.00	—
1783	113,000	2.00	5.00	8.00	25.00	—
1784	189,000	2.00	5.00	8.00	25.00	—

KM# 224 3 PFENNIG (Dreiling)

0.5000 g., 0.1870 Silver 0.0030 oz. ASW **Ruler:** Friedrich Franz I **Obverse:** Crowned FF monogram **Reverse:** Legend ends ...MECK:SCHW:MUNZE, value

Date	Mintage	F	VF	XF	Unc
1787	156,000	5.00	10.00	25.00	100
1790	103,000	5.00	10.00	25.00	100
1791	126,000	5.00	10.00	25.00	100
1793	78,000	5.00	10.00	25.00	100
1797	168,000	5.00	10.00	25.00	100

KM# 190 6 PFENNIG

Copper **Ruler:** Friedrich II **Obverse:** Steer head, without legend **Reverse:** Value and date

Date	Mintage	VG	F	VF	XF	Unc
1758	—	6.00	12.00	25.00	55.00	—

KM# 193 6 PFENNIG

Copper **Ruler:** Friedrich II **Obverse:** Crowned script F

Date	Mintage	VG	F	VF	XF	Unc
1759	—	4.00	8.00	16.00	45.00	—

KM# 203 6 PFENNIG

0.7600 g., 0.2500 Silver 0.0061 oz. ASW **Ruler:** Friedrich II **Obverse:** Crowned F **Reverse:** Value and date

Date	Mintage	VG	F	VF	XF	Unc
1763	231,000	3.00	6.00	12.00	35.00	—
1764	674,000	3.00	6.00	12.00	35.00	—
1765	549,000	3.00	6.00	12.00	35.00	—
1766	542,000	3.00	6.00	12.00	35.00	—
1767	294,000	3.00	6.00	12.00	35.00	—
1769	101,000	3.00	6.00	12.00	35.00	—
1775	252,000	3.00	6.00	12.00	35.00	—
1778	230,000	3.00	6.00	12.00	35.00	—
1779	143,000	3.00	6.00	12.00	35.00	—
1780	201,000	3.00	6.00	12.00	35.00	—
1783	154,000	3.00	6.00	12.00	35.00	—
1784	134,000	3.00	6.00	12.00	35.00	—
1785	150,000	3.00	6.00	12.00	35.00	—

KM# 222 6 PFENNIG

0.7600 g., 0.2500 Silver 0.0061 oz. ASW **Ruler:** Friedrich Franz I **Obverse:** Crowned FF monogram **Reverse:** Value

Date	Mintage	F	VF	XF	Unc
1786	147,000	6.00	12.00	30.00	100
1788	201,000	6.00	12.00	30.00	100
1790	97,000	6.00	12.00	30.00	100
1792	58,000	6.00	12.00	32.00	110
1793	85,000	6.00	12.00	30.00	100
1794	96,000	6.00	12.00	30.00	100

KM# 185 SCHILLING

Billon **Ruler:** Friedrich II **Obverse:** Steer head **Reverse:** Value, date

Date	Mintage	VG	F	VF	XF	Unc
1757	—	5.00	10.00	20.00	40.00	—

KM# 204 SCHILLING

1.0800 g., 0.3750 Silver 0.0130 oz. ASW **Ruler:** Friedrich II **Obverse:** Crowned F **Reverse:** Value above date

Date	Mintage	VG	F	VF	XF	Unc
1763	890,000	3.00	6.00	10.00	25.00	—
1764	977,000	3.00	6.00	10.00	25.00	—
1765	1,308,000	3.00	6.00	10.00	25.00	—
1766	2,041,000	3.00	6.00	10.00	25.00	—
1767	2,897,000	3.00	6.00	10.00	25.00	—
1768	1,601,000	3.00	6.00	10.00	25.00	—
1769	1,521,000	3.00	6.00	10.00	25.00	—
1770	1,811,000	3.00	6.00	10.00	25.00	—
1771	2,150,000	3.00	6.00	10.00	25.00	—
1772	2,354,000	3.00	6.00	10.00	25.00	—
1773	1,562,000	3.00	6.00	10.00	25.00	—
1774	2,437,000	3.00	6.00	10.00	25.00	—
1775	2,126,000	3.00	6.00	10.00	25.00	—
1778	759,000	3.00	6.00	10.00	25.00	—
1779	642,000	3.00	6.00	10.00	25.00	—
1780	286,000	3.00	6.00	10.00	25.00	—
1781	526,000	3.00	6.00	10.00	25.00	—
1782	350,000	3.00	6.00	10.00	25.00	—
1783	283,000	3.00	6.00	10.00	25.00	—
1784	379,000	3.00	6.00	10.00	25.00	—
1785	167,000	3.00	6.00	10.00	25.00	—

KM# 220 SCHILLING

1.0800 g., 0.3750 Silver 0.0130 oz. ASW **Ruler:** Friedrich Franz I **Obverse:** Crowned FF monogram **Reverse:** Denomination, date **Rev. Legend:** 1/SCHILLING/COURANT/MECKLENB/SCHWERIN/MUNZE

Date	Mintage	F	VF	XF	Unc
1785	74,000	4.00	10.00	25.00	45.00
1786	237,000	4.00	10.00	25.00	45.00
1787	169,000	4.00	10.00	25.00	45.00
1788	167,000	4.00	10.00	25.00	45.00
1789	362,000	4.00	10.00	25.00	45.00
1790	1,207,000	4.00	10.00	25.00	45.00
1791	260,000	4.00	10.00	25.00	45.00
1792	821,000	4.00	10.00	25.00	45.00

Date	Mintage	F	VF	XF	Unc
1793	460,000	4.00	10.00	25.00	45.00
1794	1,195,000	4.00	10.00	25.00	45.00
1795	1,093,000	4.00	10.00	25.00	45.00
1796	142,000	4.00	10.00	25.00	45.00
1797	1,065,000	4.00	10.00	25.00	45.00
1798	2,020,000	4.00	10.00	25.00	45.00
1799	2,438,000	4.00	10.00	25.00	45.00
1800	1,546,000	4.00	10.00	25.00	45.00
1801	1,301,000	4.00	10.00	25.00	45.00
1802	2,431,000	4.00	10.00	25.00	45.00
1803	2,348,000	4.00	10.00	25.00	45.00
1804	2,603,000	4.00	10.00	20.00	40.00
1805	2,501,000	4.00	10.00	20.00	40.00
1806	1,766,000	4.00	10.00	20.00	40.00
1807	585,000	4.00	10.00	25.00	45.00
1808	243,000	4.00	15.00	30.00	65.00
1809	342,000	4.00	20.00	40.00	85.00
1810	250,000	4.00	15.00	30.00	65.00
1812	—	50.00	100	175	350

KM# 130 2 SCHILLING (Doppelschilling)

Silver **Ruler:** Friedrich Wilhelm **Obverse:** Crowned 7-fold arms **Reverse:** Date, mintmaster's initials **Rev. Legend:** II/SCHIL/LING **Note:** Varieties exist.

Date	Mintage	VG	F	VF	XF	Unc
1696 ZDK	—	12.00	25.00	45.00	90.00	—
1699 ZDK	10,000	12.00	25.00	45.00	90.00	—
1703 ZDK	96,000	12.00	25.00	45.00	90.00	—
1703 ZDK	96,000	12.00	25.00	45.00	90.00	—

KM# 153 2 SCHILLING (Doppelschilling)

Silver **Ruler:** Friedrich Wilhelm **Obverse:** Crowned ornate FW monogram **Reverse:** Value **Rev. Legend:** 2/SCHIL.. **Note:** Varieties exist.

Date	Mintage	VG	F	VF	XF	Unc
1703 ZDK	Inc. above	14.00	28.00	50.00	100	—
1704 ZDK	37,000	14.00	28.00	50.00	100	—

KM# 186 2 SCHILLING (Doppelschilling)

Billon **Ruler:** Friedrich II **Obverse:** Crowned steer head facing **Reverse:** Value above date

Date	Mintage	VG	F	VF	XF	Unc
1757	—	10.00	20.00	40.00	80.00	—

KM# 205 2 SCHILLING (Doppelschilling)

1.9700 g., 0.4370 Silver 0.0277 oz. ASW **Ruler:** Friedrich II **Obverse:** Crowned F monogram **Reverse:** Value above date

Date	Mintage	VG	F	VF	XF	Unc
1763	546,000	3.00	6.00	10.00	25.00	—
1764	1,072,000	3.00	6.00	10.00	25.00	—
1765	1,820,000	3.00	6.00	10.00	25.00	—
1766	695,000	3.00	6.00	10.00	25.00	—
1767	505,000	3.00	6.00	10.00	25.00	—
1768	400,000	3.00	6.00	10.00	30.00	—
1769	195,000	3.00	6.00	10.00	30.00	—
1777	60,000	4.00	8.00	15.00	35.00	—
1778	49,000	4.00	8.00	15.00	35.00	—

KM# 223 2 SCHILLING (Doppelschilling)

1.9700 g., 0.4370 Silver 0.0277 oz. ASW **Ruler:** Friedrich Franz I **Obverse:** Crowned FF monogram on baroque shield **Reverse:** Value

Date	Mintage	VG	F	VF	XF	Unc
1786	18,000	55.00	90.00	120	200	—

KM# 206 4 SCHILLING

3.0600 g., 0.5620 Silver 0.0553 oz. ASW **Ruler:** Friedrich II **Obverse:** Crowned shield with F within **Reverse:** Value above date

Date	Mintage	VG	F	VF	XF	Unc
1763	169,000	7.00	12.00	30.00	70.00	—
1764	275,000	7.00	12.00	30.00	70.00	—
1765	36,000	9.00	18.00	45.00	90.00	—
1766	115,000	7.00	12.00	30.00	70.00	—
1774	34,000	9.00	18.00	45.00	90.00	—
1782	20,000	9.00	18.00	45.00	90.00	—
1783	29,000	9.00	18.00	45.00	90.00	—

KM# 221 4 SCHILLING

3.0600 g., 0.5620 Silver 0.0553 oz. ASW **Ruler:** Friedrich Franz I **Obverse:** Crowned FF monogram on cartouche **Reverse:** Denomination

Date	Mintage	F	VF	XF	Unc
1785	12,000	25.00	45.00	100	350
1809	1,408	50.00	90.00	150	300

KM# 187 8 SCHILLING

5.5000 g., 0.6250 Silver 0.1105 oz. ASW **Ruler:** Friedrich II **Obverse:** Steer head in crowned cartouche **Reverse:** Value, date

Date	Mintage	VG	F	VF	XF	Unc
1757	—	15.00	30.00	60.00	150	—

KM# 207 8 SCHILLING

5.5000 g., 0.6250 Silver 0.1105 oz. ASW **Ruler:** Friedrich II **Obverse:** Crowned arms, date below **Reverse:** Value

Date	Mintage	VG	F	VF	XF	Unc
1763	—	12.00	25.00	50.00	125	—
1764	—	12.00	25.00	50.00	125	—

KM# 215 12 SCHILLING

8.8000 g., 0.5620 Silver 0.1590 oz. ASW **Ruler:** Friedrich II **Obverse:** Crowned arms within Order chain **Reverse:** Value above date

Date	Mintage	VG	F	VF	XF	Unc
1774	74,000	10.00	20.00	40.00	100	—
1775	99,000	10.00	20.00	40.00	100	—
1776	26,000	12.00	25.00	50.00	125	—
1777	32,000	12.00	25.00	50.00	125	—

KM# 231 12 SCHILLING

8.8000 g., 0.5620 Silver 0.1590 oz. ASW **Ruler:** Friedrich Franz I **Obverse:** Crowned arms

Date	Mintage	F	VF	XF	Unc
1791	19,000	25.00	45.00	125	375
1792	Inc. above	25.00	45.00	125	375

KM# 191 16 SCHILLING

Silver **Ruler:** Friedrich II **Obverse:** Steer head arms **Reverse:** Value, date

Date	Mintage	VG	F	VF	XF	Unc
1758	—	60.00	120	250	650	—

KM# 208 16 SCHILLING

9.1600 g., 0.7500 Silver 0.2209 oz. ASW **Ruler:** Friedrich II **Obverse:** Crowned arms, date below **Reverse:** Value

Date	Mintage	VG	F	VF	XF	Unc
1763	—	25.00	45.00	85.00	200	—
1764	—	25.00	45.00	85.00	200	—

KM# 209 32 SCHILLING

18.3400 g., 0.7500 Silver 0.4422 oz. ASW **Ruler:** Friedrich II **Obverse:** Crowned arms within Order chain, date below **Reverse:** Value above date

Date	Mintage	F	VF	XF	Unc
1763	—	45.00	90.00	225	450
1764	—	45.00	90.00	225	450

KM# 233 32 SCHILLING

18.3400 g., 0.7500 Silver 0.4422 oz. ASW **Ruler:** Friedrich Franz I **Obverse:** Crowned arms **Reverse:** Value

Date	Mintage	F	VF	XF	Unc
1797	59,000	50.00	100	250	500

KM# 176 8 GUTE GROSCHEN

Silver **Ruler:** Christian Ludwig II **Obverse:** Armored bust right **Reverse:** Value above date

Date	Mintage	VG	F	VF	XF	Unc
1753 OHK	—	15.00	25.00	50.00	125	—
1754 OHK	—	15.00	25.00	50.00	125	—

KM# 162 1/192 THALER (Dreiling)

Silver **Ruler:** Friedrich Wilhelm **Obverse:** Crowned ornate FW monogram **Reverse:** Imperial orb with 192

Date	Mintage	VG	F	VF	XF	Unc
ND(1706)	384,000	7.00	15.00	30.00	50.00	—

KM# 163 1/192 THALER (Dreiling)

Silver **Ruler:** Friedrich Wilhelm **Obverse:** 2-fold arms divided horizontally

Date	Mintage	VG	F	VF	XF	Unc
ND	3,885,000	8.00	18.00	35.00	75.00	—

KM# 164 1/192 THALER (Dreiling)

Silver **Ruler:** Friedrich Wilhelm **Obverse:** 2-fold arms divided vertically

Date	Mintage	VG	F	VF	XF	Unc
ND	Inc. above	9.00	20.00	40.00	85.00	—

KM# 137 1/96 THALER (Sechsling)

Silver **Ruler:** Friedrich Wilhelm **Mint:** Schwerin **Obverse:** Date in legend **Reverse:** Value: 96 on imperial orb **Note:** Varieties exist.

Date	Mintage	VG	F	VF	XF	Unc
1702	398,000	8.00	18.00	35.00	75.00	—
1702	398,000	8.00	18.00	35.00	75.00	—

KM# 159 1/96 THALER (Sechsling)

Silver **Ruler:** Friedrich Wilhelm **Obverse:** Crowned ornate FW monogram divides date

Date	Mintage	VG	F	VF	XF	Unc
1704	—	—	—	—	—	—
1706	288,000	9.00	20.00	40.00	85.00	—

KM# 145 1/48 THALER (Schilling)

Silver **Ruler:** Friedrich Wilhelm **Obverse:** Crowned 7-fold arms **Reverse:** Value, date in legend **Rev. Legend:** 48/EINEN/ REICHS/ TALER

Date	Mintage	VG	F	VF	XF	Unc
1701	296,000	10.00	20.00	45.00	90.00	—
1702	140,000	10.00	20.00	45.00	90.00	—

KM# 179 1/48 THALER (Schilling)

Billon **Ruler:** Christian Ludwig II **Obverse:** Crowned script CL monogram, date **Reverse:** Value

Date	Mintage	VG	F	VF	XF	Unc
1754 OHK	—	15.00	30.00	65.00	145	—

KM# 200 1/48 THALER (Schilling)

Billon **Ruler:** Friedrich II **Obverse:** Crowned script F **Reverse:** Value, date

Date	Mintage	VG	F	VF	XF	Unc
1760	—	8.00	15.00	25.00	55.00	—

KM# 180 1/24 THALER (Doppelschilling)

Billon **Ruler:** Christian Ludwig II **Obverse:** Steer head **Reverse:** Value, date

Date	Mintage	VG	F	VF	XF	Unc
1754	—	5.00	10.00	20.00	50.00	—

KM# 181 1/24 THALER (Doppelschilling)

Billon **Ruler:** Christian Ludwig II **Obverse:** Script CL monogram

Date	Mintage	VG	F	VF	XF	Unc
1754 OHK	—	5.00	10.00	20.00	50.00	—

KM# 201 1/24 THALER (Doppelschilling)

Billon **Ruler:** Friedrich II **Obverse:** Crowned script F

Date	Mintage	VG	F	VF	XF	Unc
1760	—	5.00	10.00	20.00	50.00	—
1761	—	5.00	10.00	20.00	50.00	—

KM# 170 1/12 THALER
Billon **Ruler:** Christian Ludwig II **Obverse:** Crowned steer head facing **Reverse:** Value

Date	Mintage	VG	F	VF	XF	Unc
1750 OHK	—	7.00	16.00	35.00	90.00	—
1752 OHK	—	7.00	16.00	35.00	90.00	—
1753 OHK	—	7.00	16.00	35.00	90.00	—

KM# 177 1/12 THALER
Billon **Ruler:** Christian Ludwig II **Obverse:** Bust right **Reverse:** Value and date

Date	Mintage	VG	F	VF	XF	Unc
1753 OHK	—	4.00	10.00	20.00	65.00	—
1754 OHK	—	4.00	10.00	20.00	65.00	—

KM# 173 1/6 THALER
Silver **Ruler:** Christian Ludwig II

Date	Mintage	VG	F	VF	XF	Unc
1752 OHK	—	15.00	30.00	60.00	120	—

KM# 178 1/6 THALER
Silver **Ruler:** Christian Ludwig II **Obverse:** Bust right **Reverse:** Value and date

Date	Mintage	VG	F	VF	XF	Unc
1753 OHK	—	15.00	30.00	60.00	120	—
1754 OHK	—	15.00	30.00	60.00	120	—

KM# 230 1/3 THALER (1/2 Gulden)
8.6600 g., 0.7500 Silver 0.2088 oz. ASW **Ruler:** Friedrich Franz I **Obverse:** Crowned arms within cartouche **Reverse:** Fraction above date

Date	Mintage	F	VF	XF	Unc
1790	21,000	150	300	450	750

KM# 182 2/3 THALER (Gulden)
Silver **Ruler:** Christian Ludwig II **Obverse:** Draped bust right **Reverse:** Crowned arms within Order chain and 3/4 circle of small assorted arms

Date	Mintage	VG	F	VF	XF	Unc
1754	—	75.00	145	275	450	—

KM# 225 2/3 THALER (Gulden)
17.3200 g., 0.7500 Silver 0.4176 oz. ASW **Ruler:** Friedrich Franz I **Obverse:** Arms within crowned cartouche **Reverse:** Fraction above date

Date	Mintage	F	VF	XF	Unc
1789	89,000	35.00	75.00	135	275
1790	158,000	30.00	70.00	120	260
1791	14,000	50.00	90.00	150	300
1795	132,000	30.00	70.00	120	260
1796	552,000	30.00	70.00	120	260
1797	60,000	50.00	90.00	150	300
1800	162,000	45.00	95.00	175	300
1801	169,000	30.00	55.00	75.00	175
1808	655,000	20.00	45.00	70.00	150
1810	338,000	45.00	95.00	175	275

KM# 161 THALER
Silver **Ruler:** Friedrich Wilhelm **Obverse:** Bust right **Obv. Legend:** FRIDER • WILHEL • D • B • DVX • MEGAP • PRINC • VAND **Reverse:** Crowned arms in elaborate frame separating date **Rev. Legend:** PROVIDE • ET • CONSTANTER • **Note:** Dav. #2439.

Date	Mintage	F	VF	XF	Unc
1705 ZDK	—	650	1,250	2,200	3,750
1706 ZDK	—	650	1,250	2,200	3,750

KM# 165 THALER
Silver **Ruler:** Friedrich Wilhelm **Obverse:** ZDK on arm **Reverse:** Crowned arms in frame separating date on ribbon **Note:** Dav. #2440.

Date	Mintage	F	VF	XF	Unc
1707 ZDK Rare	—	—	—	—	—

KM# 166 THALER
Silver **Ruler:** Friedrich Wilhelm **Obverse:** Armored bust right **Obv. Legend:** FRIEDE WILHEL D G - DVX MEGAPO PRINC VAND, Z D K below **Reverse:** Date below arms **Rev. Legend:** PROVIDE ET CONSTANTERE **Note:** Dav. #2441.

Date	Mintage	F	VF	XF	Unc
1707 ZDK	—	850	1,500	2,650	4,250
1708 ZDK	—	850	1,500	2,650	4,250

KM# 167 THALER
Silver **Ruler:** Friedrich Wilhelm **Reverse:** Motto below arms without ribbon **Note:** Dav. #2442.

Date	Mintage	F	VF	XF	Unc
1708 ZDK Rare	—	—	—	—	—

KM# 210 2 THALER
3.1200 g., 0.8750 Gold 0.0878 oz. AGW **Ruler:** Friedrich II **Obverse:** Armored bust right **Reverse:** Value above date

Date	Mintage	F	VF	XF	Unc
1769	1,144	300	550	950	2,250
1778	2,417	300	550	950	2,250
1782	1,625	300	550	950	2,250
1783	441	600	1,250	2,500	4,000

KM# 232 2 THALER
3.1200 g., 0.8750 Gold 0.0878 oz. AGW **Ruler:** Friedrich Franz I **Obverse:** Crowned arms within Order chain **Reverse:** Value above date

Date	Mintage	F	VF	XF	Unc
1792	1,638	325	650	1,000	1,750

KM# 234 2 THALER
3.1200 g., 0.8750 Gold 0.0878 oz. AGW **Ruler:** Friedrich Franz I **Obverse:** Crowned arms within cartouche **Reverse:** Value above date

Date	Mintage	F	VF	XF	Unc
1797	12,000	250	375	750	1,100

KM# 183 5 THALER

6.6600 g., 0.8960 Gold 0.1918 oz. AGW **Ruler:** Christian Ludwig II **Obverse:** Bust right **Obv. Legend:** CHRIST. LVDOV. D. G. DVX MECKL. **Reverse:** Crowned arms in Order chain

Date	Mintage	VG	F	VF	XF	Unc
1754	—	350	700	1,500	3,000	—

KM# 174 2 PISTOLES

13.3200 g., 0.8960 Gold 0.3837 oz. AGW **Ruler:** Christian Ludwig II **Obverse:** Armored bust right **Reverse:** Crowned oval arms within Order chain and 3/4 circle of small shields

Date	Mintage	VG	F	VF	XF	Unc
1752	—	450	1,200	2,250	4,500	—

KM# 175 2 PISTOLES

13.3200 g., 0.8960 Gold 0.3837 oz. AGW **Ruler:** Christian Ludwig II **Obverse:** Armored bust right **Reverse:** Crowned arms within Order chain and 3/4 circle of small shields

Date	Mintage	VG	F	VF	XF	Unc
1752	—	450	1,200	2,250	4,500	—

TRADE COINAGE

KM# 146 1/4 DUCAT

0.8750 g., 0.9860 Gold 0.0277 oz. AGW **Ruler:** Friedrich Wilhelm **Obverse:** Crowned and draped arms **Reverse:** Crowned steer head in laurel wreath, date below

Date	Mintage	VG	F	VF	XF	Unc
1701	384	150	325	550	950	—

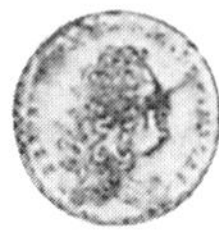

KM# 147 1/4 DUCAT

0.8750 g., 0.9860 Gold 0.0277 oz. AGW **Ruler:** Friedrich Wilhelm **Obverse:** Head right **Reverse:** Steer head within wreath

Date	Mintage	VG	F	VF	XF	Unc
ND	—	125	225	375	750	—

KM# 184 1/4 DUCAT

0.8750 g., 0.9860 Gold 0.0277 oz. AGW **Ruler:** Christian Ludwig II **Obverse:** Bust right **Reverse:** Value and date

Date	Mintage	VG	F	VF	XF	Unc
1756	—	175	350	600	1,000	—

KM# 148 1/2 DUCAT

1.7500 g., 0.9800 Gold 0.0551 oz. AGW **Ruler:** Friedrich Wilhelm **Obverse:** Crowned and draped arms **Reverse:** Crowned steer head in laurel wreath, date below

Date	Mintage	VG	F	VF	XF	Unc
1701	—	—	—	—	—	—

Note: Reported, not confirmed

KM# 150 1/2 DUCAT

1.7500 g., 0.9800 Gold 0.0551 oz. AGW **Ruler:** Friedrich Wilhelm **Obverse:** Bust right **Reverse:** Value **Rev. Legend:** 1/2/DVCA.TEN

Date	Mintage	VG	F	VF	XF	Unc
ND	—	—	—	—	—	—

Note: Reported, not confirmed

KM# 149 1/2 DUCAT

1.7500 g., 0.9800 Gold 0.0551 oz. AGW **Ruler:** Friedrich Wilhelm **Obverse:** Bust right **Reverse:** Crowned 7-fold arms, date in legend

Date	Mintage	VG	F	VF	XF	Unc
1701	—	—	—	—	—	—

Note: Reported, not confirmed

KM# 151 DUCAT

3.5000 g., 0.9860 Gold 0.1109 oz. AGW **Ruler:** Friedrich Wilhelm **Rev. Legend:** QUO DEUS ET..

Date	Mintage	VG	F	VF	XF	Unc
1701	3,645	400	850	1,750	3,500	—

KM# 152 DUCAT

3.5000 g., 0.9860 Gold 0.1109 oz. AGW **Ruler:** Friedrich Wilhelm **Obverse:** Crowned and draped arms **Reverse:** Crowned steer head in laurel wreath, date below

Date	Mintage	VG	F	VF	XF	Unc
1701	Inc. above	400	800	1,600	3,000	—

KM# 154 DUCAT

3.5000 g., 0.9860 Gold 0.1109 oz. AGW **Ruler:** Friedrich Wilhelm **Obverse:** Monogram **Rev. Legend:** PROVIDE ET-CONSTANTER..

Date	Mintage	VG	F	VF	XF	Unc
1703 ZDK	—	400	800	1,600	3,000	—

KM# 155 DUCAT

3.5000 g., 0.9860 Gold 0.1109 oz. AGW **Ruler:** Friedrich Wilhelm **Obverse:** Bust right **Rev. Legend:** PROVIDE ET-CONSTANTER..

Date	Mintage	VG	F	VF	XF	Unc
1703 ZDK	—	450	950	2,000	3,750	—
1705	—	450	950	2,000	3,750	—

KM# 156 DUCAT

3.5000 g., 0.9860 Gold 0.1109 oz. AGW **Ruler:** Friedrich Wilhelm **Obverse:** Bust right **Reverse:** Duke and Duchess in boat

Date	Mintage	VG	F	VF	XF	Unc
1703 ZDK	—	450	950	2,000	3,750	—
1704 ZDK	—	450	950	2,000	3,750	—

KM# 157 2 DUCAT

7.0000 g., 0.9860 Gold 0.2219 oz. AGW **Ruler:** Friedrich Wilhelm **Obverse:** Bust right **Reverse:** Crowned arms

Date	Mintage	VG	F	VF	XF	Unc
1703 ZDK	—	1,000	2,000	4,500	7,000	—

KM# 160 2 DUCAT

7.0000 g., 0.9860 Gold 0.2219 oz. AGW **Ruler:** Friedrich Wilhelm **Reverse:** Duke and Duchess in boat

Date	Mintage	VG	F	VF	XF	Unc
1704 ZDK	—	1,000	2,000	4,500	7,000	—

KM# A165 12 DUCAT

42.0000 g., 0.9860 Gold 1.3314 oz. AGW **Ruler:** Friedrich Wilhelm

Date	Mintage	VG	F	VF	XF	Unc
1706 Rare	—	—	—	—	—	—

Note: Struck with 1 Thaler dies, KM#161

KM# A167 16 DUCAT

57.0000 g., 0.9860 Gold 1.8069 oz. AGW **Ruler:** Friedrich Wilhelm

Date	Mintage	VG	F	VF	XF	Unc
1707 Rare	—	—	—	—	—	—

Note: Struck with 1 Thaler dies, KM#165

PATTERNS

Including off metal strikes

KM#	Date	Mintage	Identification	Mkt Val
Pn11	1704	—	Ducat. Silver. Fr1718.	200
Pn12	1705	—	Thaler. Gold. KM#161.	—
Pn15	1709	—	Ducat. Silver. 3.6300 g. KM#156.	—
Pn16	1752	—	3 Pfennig. Gold. KM#172.	—

KM#	Date	Mintage	Identification	Mkt Val
Pn17	1752	—	2 Pistoles. Silver. KM#174.	250
Pn18	1752	—	2 Pistoles. Silver. KM#175.	250
Pn19	1753	—	1/12 Thaler. Gold. KM#177.	—
Pn20	1754	—	1/6 Thaler. Gold. KM#178.	—
Pn21	1755	—	1/6 Thaler. Gold. KM#178.	—
Pn22	1766	—	2 Schillinge. Gold. KM#205.	—
Pn23	1769	—	2 Thaler. Silver. KM#210.	—

MECKLENBURG-STRELITZ

The duchy of Mecklenburg was located along the Baltic Coast between Holstein and Pomerania. The Strelitz line was founded in 1658 when the Mecklenburg line was divided into two lines. The 1815 Congress of Vienna elevated the duchy to the status of grand duchy. It became a part of the German Empire in 1871 until 1918 when the last grand duke died.

RULERS

Adolf Friedrich II, 1692-1708
Adolf Friedrich III, 1708-1752
Adolf Friedrich IV, 1752-1794
Karl II, 1794-1816

MINT OFFICIALS' INITIALS

Initials	Date	Name
CH, CHB	1703-05	Conrad Hasselbrink in Mirow
CHI	1746-49	Christoph Henning Jaster
	1746	In Neustrelitz
	1745	In Stargard
HCB	1749-60	Heinrich Christoph Baumgarten in Neustrelitz
IFF	1760-63	Johann Friedrich Funck in Schwerin
IHL	1725-59	Johann Heinrich Lowe in Hamburg
	1761-63	In Stralsund
	1763-86	In Neustrelitz
JCA	1717	Julius Christian Arensburg in Stettin

GRAND DUCHY

REGULAR COINAGE

KM# 37 PFENNIG

Copper **Obverse:** Crowned AF monogram, date below **Reverse:** Value: I/PFENNIG/MSSM/initials below

Date	Mintage	VG	F	VF	XF	Unc
1752 HCB	—	8.00	16.00	35.00	65.00	—

KM# 24 3 PFENNIG

Copper **Ruler:** Adolph Friedrich III **Obverse:** Facing steer head **Reverse:** Value: III/PFENNIG/date/initials

Date	Mintage	VG	F	VF	XF	Unc
1747 CHI	—	12.00	25.00	50.00	110	—

KM# 25 3 PFENNIG

Billon **Ruler:** Adolph Friedrich III **Obverse:** AF monogram, crown above divides date, mintmaster's initials below **Reverse:** Value: 3/GUTE/PFENNIG/MSLM

Date	Mintage	VG	F	VF	XF	Unc
1747 CHI	326,000	15.00	30.00	60.00	125	—

KM# 40 3 PFENNIG

Copper **Ruler:** Adolph Friedrich IV **Obverse:** Crowned steer head arms, date below **Reverse:** Value

Date	Mintage	VG	F	VF	XF	Unc
1753 B	175,000	4.00	9.00	20.00	45.00	—
1755 B	—	6.00	12.00	25.00	55.00	—

KM# 50 3 PFENNIG

Copper **Ruler:** Adolph Friedrich IV **Obverse:** Crowned AF script monogram, date below

Date	Mintage	VG	F	VF	XF	Unc
1760 F	—	4.00	9.00	20.00	45.00	—

KM# 58 3 PFENNIG

Copper **Ruler:** Adolph Friedrich IV **Obverse:** Crowned block AF monogram, date below **Reverse:** Value

Date	Mintage	VG	F	VF	XF	Unc
1764 IHL	16,000	5.00	10.00	22.00	50.00	—
1766 IHL	52,000	5.00	10.00	22.00	50.00	—
1785 IHL	18,000	5.00	10.00	22.00	50.00	—

KM# 76 3 PFENNIG

Copper **Ruler:** Adolph Friedrich IV **Obverse:** Crowned AF monogram, date below **Reverse:** Value above S.M. **Note:** 1793 restrikes made in 1825-1826; mintage: 99,455

Date	Mintage	VG	F	VF	XF	Unc
1793	40,000	5.00	10.00	22.00	50.00	—

KM# 75 3 PFENNIG

Copper **Ruler:** Adolph Friedrich IV **Obverse:** Crowned AF monogram, date below **Reverse:** Value **Note:** Similar to KM#58 but with finer die work. Struck in 1825-1826.

Date	Mintage	VG	F	VF	XF	Unc
1793 IHL	—	5.00	10.00	22.00	50.00	—

KM# 51 6 PFENNIG (Sechsling)

Billon **Ruler:** Adolph Friedrich IV **Obverse:** Crowned AF monogram, date below **Reverse:** Value: VI/PFENNING/MSLM/initials below

Date	Mintage	VG	F	VF	XF	Unc
1760 IFF	—	12.00	28.00	50.00	90.00	—

KM# 59 6 PFENNIG (Sechsling)

8.0000 g., 0.1870 Silver 0.0481 oz. ASW **Ruler:** Adolph Friedrich IV **Obverse:** Crowned AF monogram, date below **Reverse:** Value, initials below

Date	Mintage	VG	F	VF	XF	Unc
1764 IHL	175,000	6.00	12.00	28.00	60.00	—
1766 IHL	264,000	6.00	12.00	28.00	60.00	—

KM# 44 8 GUTE GROSCHEN (1/13 Thaler)

Silver **Ruler:** Adolph Friedrich IV **Obverse:** Head right **Reverse:** Value, date

Date	Mintage	VG	F	VF	XF	Unc
1755 HCB	13,000	30.00	60.00	140	300	—

KM# 52 8 GUTE GROSCHEN (1/13 Thaler)

Silver **Ruler:** Adolph Friedrich IV

Date	Mintage	VG	F	VF	XF	Unc
1760 IFF	32,000	15.00	25.00	42.00	80.00	—

KM# 56 8 GUTE GROSCHEN (1/13 Thaler)

Silver **Ruler:** Adolph Friedrich IV

Date	Mintage	VG	F	VF	XF	Unc
1761 IFF	10,091,000	15.00	25.00	42.00	80.00	—

KM# 26 16 GUTE GROSCHEN (2/3 Thaler - Gulden)

Silver **Ruler:** Adolph Friedrich III **Obverse:** Crowned ornate AF monogram **Reverse:** Value: XVI/GUTE GRO/SCHEN/ MDCCXLVII/initials in chain

Date	Mintage	VG	F	VF	XF	Unc
1747 CHI	—	75.00	150	300	550	—

KM# 53 16 GUTE GROSCHEN (2/3 Thaler - Gulden)

Silver **Ruler:** Adolph Friedrich IV **Obverse:** Head right **Reverse:** Value and date

Date	Mintage	VG	F	VF	XF	Unc
1760 HCB	130,000	45.00	90.00	185	375	—
1760 IFF	Inc. above	45.00	90.00	185	375	—

KM# 5 1/192 THALER (Dreiling - 3 Pfennig)

Silver **Ruler:** Adolph Friedrich II **Mint:** Mirow **Obverse:** 2-fold arms divided vertically **Reverse:** Value: 192 on imperial orb **Note:** Varieties exist.

Date	Mintage	VG	F	VF	XF	Unc
ND(1703)	811,000	15.00	30.00	60.00	100	—

KM# 6 1/96 THALER (Sechsling - 6 Pfennig)

Silver **Ruler:** Adolph Friedrich II **Mint:** Mirow **Obverse:** 2-fold arms divided vertically **Reverse:** Value: 96 on imperial orb **Note:** Varieties exist.

Date	Mintage	VG	F	VF	XF	Unc
1703	128,000	20.00	40.00	75.00	120	—

KM# 7 1/48 THALER (Schilling)

Silver **Ruler:** Adolph Friedrich II **Obverse:** Crowned 7-fold arms **Reverse:** Value: 48/EINEN/REICHS/TALER, date in legend **Note:** Struck at Mirow. Varieties exist.

Date	Mintage	VG	F	VF	XF	Unc
1703	229,000	20.00	40.00	75.00	120	—

KM# 20 1/48 THALER (Schilling)

Billon **Ruler:** Adolph Friedrich III **Obverse:** Crowned AF monogram, date below **Reverse:** Value: 48/EINEN/R THAL/MSLM/initials **Note:** Varieties exist.

Date	Mintage	VG	F	VF	XF	Unc
1745 CHI	—	8.00	16.00	30.00	55.00	—
1746 CHI	104,000	8.00	16.00	30.00	55.00	—
1747 CHI	178,000	8.00	16.00	30.00	55.00	—

KM# 27 1/48 THALER (Schilling)

Billon **Ruler:** Adolph Friedrich III **Obverse:** Crowned AF monogram, date below **Reverse:** Value: 48/EINEN/R THALER/MSLM/initials **Note:** Varieties exist.

Date	Mintage	VG	F	VF	XF	Unc
1747 CHI	93,000	6.50	12.50	25.00	50.00	—
1748 CHI	492,000	6.50	12.50	25.00	50.00	—
1748 HCB	840,000	6.50	12.50	25.00	50.00	—
1749 HCB	815,000	6.50	12.50	25.00	50.00	—
1750 HCB	—	6.50	12.50	25.00	50.00	—
1751 HCB	—	6.50	12.50	25.00	50.00	—

KM# 45 1/48 THALER (Schilling)

Billon **Ruler:** Adolph Friedrich IV **Obverse:** Crowned script AF monogram, date below **Reverse:** Value

Date	Mintage	VG	F	VF	XF	Unc
1754 HCB	3,476,000	3.00	7.00	18.00	35.00	—
1755 HCB	2,197,000	3.00	7.00	18.00	35.00	—
1756 HCB	955,000	3.00	7.00	18.00	35.00	—
1757 HCB	8,590,000	3.00	7.00	18.00	35.00	—
1760 HCB	2,277,000	3.00	7.00	18.00	35.00	—
1760 IFF	Inc. above	3.00	7.00	18.00	35.00	—

KM# 60 1/48 THALER (Schilling)

1.3300 g., 0.2500 Silver 0.0107 oz. ASW **Ruler:** Adolph Friedrich IV **Obverse:** Crowned block AF monogram, date below **Reverse:** Value with 5 pointed stars

Date	Mintage	VG	F	VF	XF	Unc
1763 IHL	—	7.00	15.00	30.00	60.00	—
1764 IHL	1,381,000	7.00	15.00	30.00	60.00	—
1766 IHL	4,565,000	7.00	15.00	30.00	60.00	—

KM# 63 1/48 THALER (Schilling)

1.3300 g., 0.2500 Silver 0.0107 oz. ASW **Ruler:** Adolph Friedrich IV **Reverse:** Value with 6 pointed stars

Date	Mintage	VG	F	VF	XF	Unc
1766 (1809)	144,000	3.00	7.00	18.00	35.00	—
1766 (1813)	204,000	3.00	7.00	18.00	35.00	—
1766 (1825)	245,000	3.00	7.00	18.00	35.00	—
1766 (1826)	Inc. above	3.00	7.00	18.00	35.00	—

Note: Original mintage unknown, restruck in several different years

KM# 8 1/24 THALER (2 Schilling)

Silver **Ruler:** Adolph Friedrich II **Reverse:** Value: 24/EINEN/ REICHS/TALER/initials, date in legend **Note:** Varieties exist.

Date	Mintage	VG	F	VF	XF	Unc
1703 CHB	107,000	40.00	85.00	135	200	—

KM# 28 1/24 THALER (2 Schilling)

Silver **Ruler:** Adolph Friedrich III **Obverse:** AF monogram, crown above divides date, initials below **Reverse:** Value: 24/EINEN/R TAL.

Date	Mintage	VG	F	VF	XF	Unc
1747 CHI	115,000	30.00	65.00	100	175	—

KM# 29 1/24 THALER (2 Schilling)

Silver **Ruler:** Adolph Friedrich III **Reverse:** Value: 24/EINEN/R TAL.

Date	Mintage	VG	F	VF	XF	Unc
1747 CHI	—	15.00	30.00	55.00	100	—
1749 CHI	59,000	15.00	30.00	55.00	100	—

KM# A64 1/24 THALER (2 Schilling)

Silver **Ruler:** Adolph Friedrich IV **Obverse:** Crowned AF monogram, date below **Reverse:** Value: 24/EINEN/THALER/M.S.L.M.

Date	Mintage	VG	F	VF	XF	Unc
1755 HCB	—	8.00	16.00	35.00	70.00	—
1756 HCB	—	8.00	16.00	35.00	70.00	—
1757 HCB	—	8.00	16.00	35.00	70.00	—
1760 HCB	—	8.00	16.00	35.00	70.00	—

KM# 64 1/24 THALER (2 Schilling)

1.6700 g., 0.4370 Silver 0.0235 oz. ASW **Obverse:** Crowned AF monogram, date below **Reverse:** Value, initials below **Note:** Restruck in 1813; mintage: 96,000.

Date	Mintage	VG	F	VF	XF	Unc
1766 IHL	737,000	7.00	14.00	28.00	60.00	—

KM# 9 1/12 THALER

Silver **Ruler:** Adolph Friedrich II **Obverse:** Crowned and mantled 7-fold arms. **Reverse:** Value: 12/EINEN/REICHS/TALER/initials, date in legend

Date	Mintage	VG	F	VF	XF	Unc
1703 CH	13,000	30.00	75.00	135	200	—

KM# 21 1/12 THALER

Silver **Ruler:** Adolph Friedrich III **Obverse:** Crowned AF monogram, date below **Reverse:** Value: 12/EINEN/REICHS/THAL.

Date	Mintage	VG	F	VF	XF	Unc
1746 CHI	35,000	20.00	45.00	90.00	165	—

KM# 31 1/12 THALER

Silver **Ruler:** Adolph Friedrich III **Reverse:** Value: 12/EINEN/THALER/initials

Date	Mintage	VG	F	VF	XF	Unc
1748 CHI	—	15.00	30.00	50.00	85.00	—
1749 CHI	164,000	15.00	30.00	50.00	85.00	—
1749 HCB	Inc. above	15.00	30.00	50.00	85.00	—

KM# 35 1/12 THALER

Silver **Ruler:** Adolph Friedrich III **Obverse:** Crown divides VGG -- HXM **Reverse:** Last 2 lines MSLM/initials **Note:** Varieties exist.

Date	Mintage	VG	F	VF	XF	Unc
1750 HCB	—	12.00	22.00	45.00	70.00	—
1751 HCB	—	12.00	22.00	45.00	70.00	—
1752 HCB	—	12.00	22.00	45.00	70.00	—

KM# 38 1/12 THALER

Silver **Reverse:** Value: 12/EINEN/THALER/LM/initials

Date	Mintage	VG	F	VF	XF	Unc
1752 HCB	—	12.00	22.00	45.00	70.00	—

KM# 41 1/12 THALER

Silver **Ruler:** Adolph Friedrich IV **Obverse:** Crowned script AF monogram, date below **Reverse:** Value

Date	Mintage	VG	F	VF	XF	Unc
1752 HCB	—	5.00	10.00	22.00	50.00	—
1753 HCB	432,000	5.00	10.00	22.00	50.00	—
1754 HCB	285,000	5.00	10.00	22.00	50.00	—
1755 HCB	355,000	5.00	10.00	22.00	50.00	—
1756 HCB	1,391,000	5.00	10.00	22.00	50.00	—
1759 HCB	2,890,000	5.00	10.00	22.00	50.00	—

KM# 57 1/12 THALER

3.3400 g., 0.4370 Silver 0.0469 oz. ASW **Ruler:** Adolph Friedrich IV **Obverse:** Crowned block AF monogram, date below **Reverse:** Value within inner circle

Date	Mintage	VG	F	VF	XF	Unc
1763 IHL	—	6.00	12.00	32.00	60.00	—
1764 IHL	688,000	6.00	12.00	32.00	60.00	—

KM# 61 1/12 THALER

3.3400 g., 0.4370 Silver 0.0469 oz. ASW **Ruler:** Adolph Friedrich IV **Obverse:** Legend, crowned arms **Obv. Legend:** Ends with "... MEG"

Date	Mintage	VG	F	VF	XF	Unc
1764 IHL	Inc. above	6.00	12.00	32.00	60.00	—

KM# 65 1/12 THALER

3.3400 g., 0.4370 Silver 0.0469 oz. ASW **Ruler:** Adolph Friedrich IV **Obv. Legend:** Ends with "... MECKL"

Date	Mintage	VG	F	VF	XF	Unc
1766 IHL	68,000	6.00	12.00	32.00	60.00	—
1768 IHL	2,293	6.00	12.00	32.00	60.00	—
1773 IHL	5,172	6.00	12.00	32.00	60.00	—

KM# 10 1/6 THALER (1/4 Gulden)

Silver **Ruler:** Adolph Friedrich II **Obverse:** Bust right, date in legend **Reverse:** Crowned and supported 7-fold arms, (1/6) in oval below

Date	Mintage	VG	F	VF	XF	Unc
1703 CH	3,042	275	450	750	1,200	—

KM# 36 1/6 THALER (1/4 Gulden)

Silver **Ruler:** Adolph Friedrich III **Obverse:** Crowned AF monogram, date below **Reverse:** Value: VI/EINEN/THALER **Note:** Varieties exist.

Date	Mintage	VG	F	VF	XF	Unc
1751 HCB	—	15.00	28.00	55.00	125	—
1752 HCB	76,000	15.00	28.00	55.00	125	—

KM# A39 1/6 THALER (1/4 Gulden)

Silver **Obverse:** Crowned AF monogram, date below **Reverse:** Value: VI/EINEN/THALER/L.M. in circle, legend around

Date	Mintage	VG	F	VF	XF	Unc
1752 HCB	—	25.00	50.00	90.00	185	—

KM# 39 1/6 THALER (1/4 Gulden)

Silver **Ruler:** Adolph Friedrich IV **Obverse:** Crowned AF monogram, date below **Reverse:** Value

Date	Mintage	VG	F	VF	XF	Unc
1752 HCB	138,000	12.00	25.00	45.00	100	—
1753 HCB	3,090,000	12.00	25.00	45.00	100	—
1754 HCB	5,116,000	12.00	25.00	45.00	100	—
1755 HCB	4,060,000	12.00	25.00	45.00	100	—
1756 HCB	4,645,000	12.00	25.00	45.00	100	—
1757 HCB	9,539,000	12.00	25.00	45.00	100	—
1758 HCB	3,670,000	12.00	25.00	45.00	100	—
1759 HCB	14,396,000	12.00	25.00	45.00	100	—
1760 HCB	931,000	10.00	20.00	40.00	90.00	—
1760 IFF	Inc. above	10.00	20.00	40.00	90.00	—
1761 IFF	4,175,000	15.00	28.00	50.00	120	—

KM# 46 1/6 THALER (1/4 Gulden)

Silver **Ruler:** Adolph Friedrich IV **Reverse:** Date added

Date	Mintage	VG	F	VF	XF	Unc
1759 IFF	—	—	—	—	—	—

KM# 54 1/6 THALER (1/4 Gulden)

Silver **Ruler:** Adolph Friedrich IV **Obverse:** Bust right **Note:** Varieties exist.

Date	Mintage	VG	F	VF	XF	Unc
1760 IFF	—	—	—	—	—	—
1761 IFF	—	—	—	—	—	—

KM# 62 1/6 THALER (1/4 Gulden)

5.8500 g., 0.5000 Silver 0.0940 oz. ASW **Ruler:** Adolph Friedrich IV **Obverse:** Head right **Obv. Legend:** Ends with "... MEGAR" **Reverse:** Crowned arms

Date	Mintage	VG	F	VF	XF	Unc
1764 IHL	186,000	15.00	28.00	50.00	120	—
1768 IHL	1,527	15.00	28.00	50.00	120	—

KM# 70 1/6 THALER (1/4 Gulden)

Silver **Ruler:** Adolph Friedrich IV **Obv. Legend:** Ends with "... MECKLEN"

Date	Mintage	VG	F	VF	XF	Unc
1773 IHL	11,000	15.00	30.00	55.00	125	—

KM# 11 1/3 THALER (1/2 Gulden)

Silver **Ruler:** Adolph Friedrich II **Obverse:** Bust right, date in legend **Reverse:** Crowned and supported 7-fold arms, value: 1/3 in oval below

Date	Mintage	VG	F	VF	XF	Unc
1703 CH	1,929	200	350	650	1,000	—

KM# 71 1/3 THALER (1/2 Gulden)

9.3500 g., 0.6250 Silver 0.1879 oz. ASW **Ruler:** Adolph Friedrich IV

Date	Mintage	VG	F	VF	XF	Unc
1773 IHL	3,727	25.00	50.00	100	185	—

DAV# 677 2/3 THALER (Gulden)

Silver **Ruler:** Adolph Friedrich II **Obverse:** Bust right, date in legend **Reverse:** Crowned and supported 7-fold arms, value 2/3 in oval below **Note:** Varieties exist.

Date	Mintage	VG	F	VF	XF	Unc
1703 CH	697	1,650	3,000	4,800	6,500	—
1704 CH	—	600	1,000	1,600	3,500	—

KM# 55 2/3 THALER (Gulden)

Silver **Ruler:** Adolph Friedrich IV

Date	Mintage	VG	F	VF	XF	Unc
1760 IFF	—	85.00	175	350	650	—

KM# 22 THALER

1.3300 g., 0.9000 Gold 0.0385 oz. AGW **Ruler:** Adolph Friedrich IV **Obverse:** Monogram within shield, crown above divides date **Reverse:** Value within inner circle

Date	Mintage	VG	F	VF	XF	Unc
1746 CHI	—	250	600	1,250	2,250	—
1747 CHI	223	250	600	1,250	2,250	—
1749 CHI	60	275	650	1,350	2,500	—

KM# 23 2 THALER

2.6600 g., 0.9000 Gold 0.0770 oz. AGW **Ruler:** Adolph Friedrich III **Obverse:** Monogram within shield, crown above divides date **Reverse:** Value within inner circle

Date	Mintage	VG	F	VF	XF	Unc
1746 CHI	—	275	650	1,250	2,250	—
1747 CHI	83	275	650	1,250	2,250	—

KM# 30 5 THALER

6.6500 g., 0.9000 Gold 0.1924 oz. AGW **Ruler:** Adolph Friedrich III **Obverse:** Head right **Reverse:** Date divided at sides of shield

Date	Mintage	VG	F	VF	XF	Unc
1747 CHI	730	500	1,150	2,250	3,750	—

KM# 32 5 THALER

6.6500 g., 0.9000 Gold 0.1924 oz. AGW **Ruler:** Adolph Friedrich III **Obverse:** Crowned script AF monogram **Reverse:** Crowned steer head arms

Date	Mintage	VG	F	VF	XF	Unc
1748 CHI	2,616	450	1,000	2,000	3,500	—

KM# A32 5 THALER

6.6500 g., 0.9000 Gold 0.1924 oz. AGW **Ruler:** Adolph Friedrich III **Obverse:** Crowned monogram **Reverse:** Date divided at top of revised shield

Date	Mintage	VG	F	VF	XF	Unc
1749 CHB	1,951	550	1,200	2,350	3,850	—

KM# 42 PISTOLE

6.6500 g., 0.9000 Gold 0.1924 oz. AGW **Ruler:** Adolph Friedrich IV **Obverse:** Head right **Reverse:** Crowned arms

Date	Mintage	VG	F	VF	XF	Unc
1754 HCB	700	1,150	2,250	4,250	7,000	—

KM# 43 PISTOLE

6.6500 g., 0.9000 Gold 0.1924 oz. AGW **Ruler:** Adolph Friedrich IV **Obverse:** Armored bust right **Reverse:** Crowned arms within ornate shield

Date	Mintage	VG	F	VF	XF	Unc
1754 HCB	—	1,250	2,500	4,500	7,500	—

TRADE COINAGE

KM# 15 DUCAT

3.5000 g., 0.9860 Gold 0.1109 oz. AGW **Ruler:** Adolph Friedrich III **Subject:** Bicentennial of the Reformation **Obverse:** Bust right **Reverse:** Figure of Faith at left, temple at right

Date	Mintage	VG	F	VF	XF	Unc
1717	—	450	1,150	2,500	4,500	—

KM# 16 DUCAT

3.5000 g., 0.9860 Gold 0.1109 oz. AGW **Ruler:** Adolph Friedrich III **Reverse:** City of Jerusalem on mountain

Date	Mintage	VG	F	VF	XF	Unc
1717	—	500	1,250	2,750	4,750	—

KM# 17 DUCAT

3.5000 g., 0.9860 Gold 0.1109 oz. AGW **Ruler:** Adolph Friedrich III **Reverse:** City located on rock in midst of ocean

Date	Mintage	VG	F	VF	XF	Unc
1717	—	500	1,250	2,750	4,750	—

PATTERNS

Including off metal strikes

KM#	Date	Mintage	Identification	Mkt Val
Pn1	1745	—	1/48 Thaler. Gold. 1.7500 g. KM20.	—
Pn2	1745	—	1/48 Thaler. Gold. 1.8800 g. KM20.	—
Pn3	1745	—	1/48 Thaler. Gold. 2.5000 g. KM20.	—
Pn4	1746	—	1/48 Thaler. Gold. 1.7500 g. KM20.	—
Pn5	1746	—	1/48 Thaler. Gold. 1.8800 g. KM20.	—
Pn6	1746	—	1/48 Thaler. Gold. 2.5000 g. KM20.	—
Pn7	1746	—	1/12 Thaler. Gold. 3.4500 g. KM21.	—
Pn8	1747	—	3 Pfennig. Gold. 3.6300 g. KM24.	—
Pn9	1747	—	3 Pfennig. Gold. 3.5500 g. KM24.	—
Pn10	1747	—	3 Pfennig. Gold. 0.9000 g. KM25.	1,000
Pn11	1747	—	3 Pfennig. Gold. 1.6400 g. KM25.	1,200
Pn12	1747	—	3 Pfennig. Gold. 1.7500 g. KM25.	1,500
Pn13	1747	—	1/48 Thaler. Gold. 1.7500 g. KM20.	—
Pn14	1747	—	1/48 Thaler. Gold. 1.8800 g. KM20.	—
Pn15	1747	—	1/48 Thaler. Gold. 2.5000 g. KM20.	—
Pn16	1747	—	1/48 Thaler. Gold. 1.7500 g. KM27.	—
Pn17	1747	—	1/48 Thaler. Gold. 2.0000 g. KM27.	—
Pn18	1747	—	1/48 Thaler. Gold. 3.4100 g. KM27.	—
Pn19	1747	—	1/24 Thaler. Gold. 3.0400 g. KM28.	—
Pn20	1747	—	1/24 Thaler. Gold. 2.3000 g. KM29.	—
Pn21	1748	—	1/48 Thaler. Gold. 1.7500 g. KM27.	—
Pn22	1748	—	1/48 Thaler. Gold. 2.0000 g. KM27.	—
Pn23	1748	—	1/48 Thaler. Gold. 3.4100 g. KM27.	—
Pn24	1748	—	1/12 Thaler. Gold. 3.4900 g. KM31.	—
Pn25	1749	—	1/48 Thaler. Gold. 1.7500 g. KM27.	—
Pn26	1749	—	1/48 Thaler. Gold. 2.0000 g. KM27.	—
Pn27	1749	—	1/48 Thaler. Gold. 3.4100 g. KM27.	—
Pn28	1749	—	1/24 Thaler. Gold. 2.3000 g. KM29.	—
Pn29	1749	—	1/12 Thaler. Gold. 3.7900 g. KM31.	—
Pn30	1749	—	1/12 Thaler. Gold. 3.4900 g. KM31.	—
Pn31	1750	—	1/48 Thaler. Gold. 1.7500 g. KM27.	—
Pn32	1750	—	1/48 Thaler. Gold. 2.0000 g. KM27.	—
Pn33	1750	—	1/48 Thaler. Gold. 3.4100 g. KM27.	—

KM#	Date	Mintage	Identification	Mkt Val
Pn34	1751	—	1/48 Thaler. Gold. 1.7500 g. KM27.	—
Pn35	1751	—	1/48 Thaler. Gold. 2.0000 g. KM27.	—
Pn36	1751	—	1/48 Thaler. Gold. 3.4100 g. KM27.	—
Pn37	1751	—	1/6 Thaler. Gold. 8.6000 g. KM36.	—
Pn38	1752	—	1/6 Thaler. Gold. 8.6000 g. KM36.	—
Pn39	1768	—	1/6 Thaler. Copper. KM62.	120
Pn40	1793	—	3 Pfennig. Silver. KM75.	70.00

MEMMINGEN

This former free imperial city is located in southern Bavaria, about 35 miles southwest of Augsburg. It is the site of an early church foundation of the mid-8th century, but the town itself is mentioned only from the first part of the 11th century. In 1286, free city status and mint rights were granted.

The town struck bracteates into the 14th century. A local town coinage was also issued in the 17th and early 18th centuries. The city was annexed to Bavaria in 1802.

MINTMASTER

Hieronymous Hueber, 1716

ARMS

Normally 2-fold, divided vertically, half of imperial eagle on left, cross on right.

FREE CITY

REGULAR COINAGE

KM# 15 HELLER

Copper **Note:** City arms.

Date	Mintage	Good	VG	F	VF	XF
ND(1700-1716)	—	—	20.00	40.00	100	250

KM# 16 KREUZER

Billon **Obverse:** City arms in oval baroque frame **Reverse:** Legend in double cross (++ above X) **Rev. Legend:** STATT MVNTZ

Date	Mintage	Good	VG	F	VF	XF
ND(1700-1716)	—	—	25.00	50.00	125	275

KM# 20 THALER

Silver **Obverse:** Bust of Karl V right **Obv. Legend:** CAROL • VI • D • G • R • - I • S • A • G • H • H • B • REX • **Reverse:** Arms **Rev. Legend:** * MUNUS REIPUBLICÆ MEMMINGENSIS **Note:** Dav. #2447

Date	Mintage	Good	VG	F	VF	XF
ND(1712)	—	—	—	—	—	9,000

TRADE COINAGE

KM# 25 DUCAT

3.5000 g., 0.9860 Gold 0.1109 oz. AGW **Subject:** Augsburg Confession **Obverse:** Eagle above city view **Reverse:** Standing figure left of column

Date	Mintage	Good	VG	F	VF	XF
1730	—	—	450	750	1,250	2,250

KM# 30 DUCAT

3.5000 g., 0.9860 Gold 0.1109 oz. AGW **Subject:** Centennial - Peace of Westphalia **Obverse:** Eagle above city view **Reverse:** Inscription

Date	Mintage	Good	VG	F	VF	XF
1748	—	—	650	1,100	1,850	3,500

PATTERNS

Including off metal strikes

KM#	Date	Mintage	Identification	Mkt Val
Pn1	1730	—	Ducat. Silver. KM#25.	135
Pn2	1748	—	Ducat. Silver. KM#30.	135

MONTFORT

Montfort struck their first coins, bracteates, in the 13th century. The first Count of Montfort ruled ca. 1200.

After many divisions and consolidations, Montfort was sold to Austria in 1780.

RULERS

Anton III, the Younger, 1693-1734
Ernst Josef, 1734-1758
Franz Xavier, 1758-1780

MINTMASTERS' INITIALS

FIG - Franz Josef Gully

ENGRAVER'S INITIALS

H, IH - Johann Haag, 1736-1752

COUNTY

STANDARD COINAGE

KM# 112 HELLER

Copper **Ruler:** Anton III, the Younger **Obverse:** Two oval arms above date **Note:** Uniface.

Date	Mintage	VG	F	VF	XF	Unc
1714	—	8.00	17.50	35.00	75.00	—
1715	—	8.00	17.50	35.00	75.00	—
1730	—	8.00	17.50	35.00	75.00	—

KM# 102 PFENNIG

Silver **Ruler:** Anton III, the Younger **Obverse:** Crowned oval arms divide date

Date	Mintage	VG	F	VF	XF	Unc
1703	—	20.00	35.00	65.00	125	—
1732	—	20.00	35.00	65.00	125	—

KM# 182 PFENNIG

Silver **Ruler:** Ernst Josef **Obverse:** Arms

Date	Mintage	VG	F	VF	XF	Unc
1756	—	10.00	20.00	45.00	85.00	—

KM# 105 1/4 KREUZER

Copper **Ruler:** Anton III, the Younger **Obverse:** Oval arms above date **Reverse:** Value

Date	Mintage	VG	F	VF	XF	Unc
1706	—	15.00	30.00	60.00	100	—

KM# 126 1/4 KREUZER

Silver **Ruler:** Anton III, the Younger **Obverse:** Oval arms divide date **Reverse:** Value

Date	Mintage	VG	F	VF	XF	Unc
1726	—	20.00	35.00	65.00	125	—

KM# 103 1/2 KREUZER (2 Pfennig)

Silver **Ruler:** Anton III, the Younger **Obverse:** Two oval arms below value, value divides date **Note:** Uniface.

Date	Mintage	VG	F	VF	XF	Unc
1703	—	25.00	45.00	85.00	150	—
1704	—	25.00	45.00	85.00	150	—
1705	—	25.00	45.00	85.00	150	—

KM# 111 1/2 KREUZER (2 Pfennig)

Silver **Ruler:** Anton III, the Younger **Obverse:** Value above two oval arms

Date	Mintage	VG	F	VF	XF	Unc
1712	—	25.00	45.00	85.00	150	—
1713	—	25.00	45.00	85.00	150	—
1714	—	25.00	45.00	85.00	150	—
1715	—	25.00	45.00	85.00	150	—
1717	—	25.00	45.00	85.00	150	—
1724	—	25.00	45.00	85.00	150	—

KM# 127 1/2 KREUZER (2 Pfennig)

Silver **Ruler:** Anton III, the Younger **Obverse:** Fancy oval arms divide date **Reverse:** Value

Date	Mintage	VG	F	VF	XF	Unc
1726	—	35.00	55.00	95.00	175	—

KM# 128 1/2 KREUZER (2 Pfennig)

Silver **Ruler:** Anton III, the Younger **Obverse:** Value at top divides date

Date	Mintage	VG	F	VF	XF	Unc
1726	—	8.50	18.50	40.00	85.00	—
1727	—	8.50	18.50	40.00	85.00	—
1729	—	8.50	18.50	40.00	85.00	—
1730	—	8.50	18.50	40.00	85.00	—
1731	—	8.50	18.50	40.00	85.00	—
1732	—	8.50	18.50	40.00	85.00	—
1733	—	8.50	18.50	40.00	85.00	—

KM# 150 1/2 KREUZER (2 Pfennig)

Billon **Ruler:** Anton III, the Younger **Obverse:** Two shields of arms **Reverse:** Value and date

Date	Mintage	VG	F	VF	XF	Unc
1733	—	8.50	17.50	35.00	75.00	—
1734	—	8.50	17.50	35.00	75.00	—
1735	—	8.50	17.50	35.00	75.00	—
1736	—	8.50	17.50	35.00	75.00	—
1737	—	8.50	17.50	35.00	75.00	—
1738	—	8.50	17.50	35.00	75.00	—
1739	—	8.50	17.50	35.00	75.00	—
1750	—	8.50	17.50	35.00	75.00	—
1753	—	8.50	17.50	35.00	75.00	—

KM# 100 KREUZER

Silver **Ruler:** Anton II. Regent **Obverse:** Arms divide date **Reverse:** Crowned imperial eagle with 1 on breast

Date	Mintage	VG	F	VF	XF	Unc
1702	—	25.00	40.00	80.00	165	—

KM# 101 KREUZER

Silver **Ruler:** Anton III, the Younger **Reverse:** K on eagle's breast

Date	Mintage	VG	F	VF	XF	Unc
1702	—	25.00	40.00	80.00	165	—

KM# 104 KREUZER

Silver **Ruler:** Anton III, the Younger **Obverse:** Oval arms **Reverse:** Eagle shield slanting in cross design

Date	Mintage	VG	F	VF	XF	Unc
1703	—	15.00	30.00	65.00	125	—
1704	—	15.00	30.00	65.00	125	—
1706	—	15.00	30.00	65.00	125	—

KM# 110 KREUZER

Silver **Obverse:** Crowned imperial eagle with 1 on breast **Reverse:** Fancy oval arms

Date	Mintage	VG	F	VF	XF	Unc
1711	—	12.50	25.00	50.00	100	—
1714	—	12.50	25.00	50.00	100	—
1715	—	7.50	17.50	35.00	70.00	—
1716	—	7.50	17.50	35.00	70.00	—
1717	—	7.50	15.00	30.00	65.00	—
1718	—	7.50	15.00	30.00	65.00	—
1721	—	7.50	15.00	30.00	65.00	—
1722	—	7.50	15.00	30.00	65.00	—
1723	—	7.50	15.00	30.00	65.00	—
1724	—	7.50	15.00	30.00	65.00	—
1726	—	7.50	15.00	30.00	65.00	—
1727	—	7.50	15.00	30.00	65.00	—
1728	—	7.50	17.50	35.00	70.00	—
1729	—	7.50	17.50	35.00	70.00	—
1730	—	7.50	17.50	35.00	70.00	—
1731	—	7.50	17.50	35.00	70.00	—

KM# 129 KREUZER

Silver **Ruler:** Anton III, the Younger **Obverse:** "K" in orb on double eagle's breast **Reverse:** Arms

Date	Mintage	VG	F	VF	XF	Unc
1726 Rare	—	—	—	—	—	—

KM# 148 KREUZER

Silver **Ruler:** Anton III, the Younger **Obverse:** Bust **Reverse:** Crowned imperial eagle shield above date 17-32

Date	Mintage	VG	F	VF	XF	Unc
1732	—	7.50	15.00	30.00	65.00	—

KM# 159 KREUZER

Billon **Ruler:** Ernst Josef **Obverse:** Bust right **Reverse:** Helmeted arms and date

Date	Mintage	VG	F	VF	XF	Unc
1736	—	12.00	25.00	40.00	75.00	—

KM# 161 KREUZER

Billon **Ruler:** Anton III, the Younger **Obverse:** Shield of arms **Reverse:** Value and date **Note:** Tax Kreuzer.

Date	Mintage	VG	F	VF	XF	Unc
1737	—	25.00	50.00	75.00	125	—

KM# 164 KREUZER

Billon **Ruler:** Ernst Josef **Obverse:** Bust right **Reverse:** Arms on cross **Note:** Tax Kreuzer.

Date	Mintage	VG	F	VF	XF	Unc
1739	—	25.00	50.00	75.00	125	—

KM# 165 KREUZER

Billon **Ruler:** Ernst Josef **Obverse:** Bust right **Reverse:** Oval arms on cross

Date	Mintage	VG	F	VF	XF	Unc
1739	—	25.00	50.00	75.00	125	—

KM# 170 KREUZER

Billon **Ruler:** Ernst Josef **Obverse:** Bust right **Reverse:** Two shields of arms in cartouche; value below

Date	Mintage	VG	F	VF	XF	Unc
1741	—	6.25	12.50	20.00	40.00	—
1742	—	6.25	12.50	20.00	40.00	—
1743	—	6.25	12.50	20.00	40.00	—
1744	—	6.25	12.50	20.00	40.00	—
1745	—	6.25	12.50	20.00	40.00	—
1746	—	6.25	12.50	20.00	40.00	—
1747	—	6.25	12.50	20.00	40.00	—
1748	—	6.25	12.50	20.00	40.00	—
1749	—	6.25	12.50	20.00	40.00	—
1750	—	25.00	50.00	150	200	—
1751	—	7.50	15.00	30.00	55.00	—
1752	—	6.25	12.50	20.00	40.00	—
1753	—	6.25	12.50	20.00	40.00	—
1754 Rare	—	—	—	—	—	—
1755	—	6.25	12.50	20.00	40.00	—
1756	—	6.25	12.50	20.00	40.00	—
1757	—	6.25	12.50	20.00	40.00	—
1758	—	6.25	12.50	20.00	40.00	—

KM# 183 KREUZER

Billon **Ruler:** Franz Xavier **Obverse:** Bust right **Reverse:** Arms

Date	Mintage	VG	F	VF	XF	Unc
1758	—	7.50	12.00	20.00	40.00	—
1759	—	7.50	12.00	20.00	40.00	—

KM# 193 KREUZER

Billon **Ruler:** Franz Xavier **Reverse:** Crowned imperial eagle with value on breast

Date	Mintage	VG	F	VF	XF	Unc
1763	—	12.50	20.00	35.00	60.00	—

KM# 130 2 KREUZER

Silver **Ruler:** Anton III, the Younger **Reverse:** Value in orb on double eagle's breast

Date	Mintage	VG	F	VF	XF	Unc
1726	—	20.00	40.00	75.00	165	—
1728	—	20.00	40.00	75.00	165	—
1732	—	20.00	40.00	75.00	165	—

KM# 131 2 KREUZER

Silver **Obverse:** Oval arms with OCV at top

Date	Mintage	VG	F	VF	XF	Unc
1726	—	20.00	40.00	75.00	165	—

KM# 146 3 KREUZER

Silver **Ruler:** Anton III, the Younger **Obverse:** St. Johann with flag and sword **Reverse:** Value in orb on crowned imperial eagle's breast

Date	Mintage	VG	F	VF	XF	Unc
1731	—	35.00	75.00	150	300	—

KM# 171 3 KREUZER

Billon **Ruler:** Ernst Josef **Obverse:** Bust right **Reverse:** Value and date

Date	Mintage	VG	F	VF	XF	Unc
1741	—	25.00	50.00	75.00	135	—
1744	—	25.00	50.00	75.00	135	—

KM# 172 3 KREUZER

Billon **Ruler:** Ernst Josef **Reverse:** Crowned imperial eagle, value below

Date	Mintage	VG	F	VF	XF	Unc
1744	—	25.00	50.00	75.00	135	—

KM# 173 3 KREUZER

Billon **Ruler:** Ernst Josef **Reverse:** Helmeted arms, value below

Date	Mintage	VG	F	VF	XF	Unc
1744	—	25.00	50.00	75.00	135	—
1745	—	25.00	50.00	75.00	135	—
1747	—	25.00	50.00	75.00	135	—
1749	—	25.00	50.00	75.00	135	—

KM# 85 4 KREUZER

4.0000 g., Silver **Ruler:** Anton III, the Younger **Obv. Legend:** "COM:" **Note:** Many varieties exist.

Date	Mintage	VG	F	VF	XF	Unc
1702	—	15.00	30.00	75.00	165	—
1714	—	15.00	30.00	65.00	145	—
1717	—	15.00	30.00	65.00	145	—
1718	—	15.00	30.00	65.00	145	—
1721	—	15.00	30.00	65.00	145	—
1722	—	15.00	30.00	65.00	145	—
1724	—	15.00	30.00	65.00	145	—
1728	—	15.00	30.00	65.00	145	—
1730	—	15.00	30.00	65.00	145	—
1731	—	15.00	30.00	65.00	145	—
1732	—	12.50	25.00	45.00	100	—

KM# 132 4 KREUZER

Silver **Ruler:** Anton III, the Younger **Obverse:** OCV above arms

Date	Mintage	VG	F	VF	XF	Unc
1726	—	20.00	40.00	80.00	175	—

KM# 155 4 KREUZER

Billon **Ruler:** Anton III, the Younger **Obverse:** Helmeted arms **Reverse:** Crowned imperial eagle, value below

Date	Mintage	VG	F	VF	XF	Unc
1735	—	35.00	75.00	125	200	—

KM# 186 6 KREUZER

Billon **Ruler:** Franz Xavier **Reverse:** Mitred, helmeted and draped arms, value and date below

Date	Mintage	VG	F	VF	XF	Unc
1759	—	20.00	45.00	90.00	200	—

KM# 190 10 KREUZER

Silver **Ruler:** Franz Xavier **Obverse:** Bust right **Reverse:** Crowned imperial eagle, value below

Date	Mintage	VG	F	VF	XF	Unc
1761	—	30.00	60.00	125	250	—
1763	—	30.00	60.00	125	250	—

KM# 124 20 KREUZER

Silver **Ruler:** Anton III, the Younger **Obverse:** Oval arms **Reverse:** Three-line inscription **Note:** Tax Kreuzer.

Date	Mintage	VG	F	VF	XF	Unc
ND(1723)	—	100	175	250	450	—

KM# 191 20 KREUZER

Silver **Ruler:** Ernst Josef **Obverse:** Armored bust right **Reverse:** Imperial orb on eagle's breast, value within pedestal below arms

Date	Mintage	VG	F	VF	XF	Unc
1761	—	35.00	75.00	150	350	—
1762	—	35.00	75.00	150	350	—
1763	—	35.00	75.00	150	350	—

KM# 149 30 KREUZER (1/2 Gulden)

Silver **Ruler:** Anton III, the Younger **Obverse:** Head right **Reverse:** Value framed below arms, mitred mantle above

Date	Mintage	VG	F	VF	XF	Unc
1732	—	125	200	375	675	—

KM# 151 30 KREUZER (1/2 Gulden)

Silver **Ruler:** Ernst Josef **Obverse:** Bust right **Reverse:** Helmeted arms

Date	Mintage	VG	F	VF	XF	Unc
1734	—	85.00	175	350	625	—
1735	—	85.00	175	350	625	—
1736	—	85.00	175	350	625	—

KM# 133 1/8 THALER (1/2 Ort)

Silver **Ruler:** Anton III, the Younger **Obverse:** Oval arms with "Halb Ort" denomination **Reverse:** 1/8 in orb on crowned imperial eagle's breast

Date	Mintage	VG	F	VF	XF	Unc
1726	—	150	250	400	700	—

KM# 184 1/6 THALER

Silver **Ruler:** Ernst Josef **Obverse:** Bust right **Reverse:** Value, date

Date	Mintage	VG	F	VF	XF	Unc
1758	—	40.00	80.00	150	275	—

KM# 121 1/4 THALER

Silver **Ruler:** Anton III, the Younger **Obverse:** Bust right **Reverse:** Arms

Date	Mintage	VG	F	VF	XF	Unc
1722	—	125	225	375	600	—
1723	—	125	225	375	600	—

KM# 87 1/2 THALER

14.6500 g., Silver, 36 mm. **Ruler:** Anton III, the Younger **Obverse:** Draped armored bust right **Reverse:** Arms

Date	Mintage	VG	F	VF	XF	Unc
1695	—	300	600	1,000	1,750	—
Note: Contemporary counterfeit of 1695 coin is struck from smaller oval shaped dies in lower grade silver						
1714	—	300	600	1,000	1,750	—
1715	—	300	600	1,000	1,750	—

KM# A88 1/2 THALER
14.6500 g., Silver, 36 mm. **Ruler:** Anton III, the Younger **Obverse:** Large bust **Reverse:** Arms

Date	Mintage	VG	F	VF	XF	Unc
1717	—	300	600	1,000	1,750	—
1730	—	300	600	1,000	1,750	—

KM# 141 1/2 THALER
Silver **Ruler:** Anton III, the Younger **Obverse:** Armored bust right **Reverse:** Helmeted, mitred and mantled arms **Note:** Varieties exist.

Date	Mintage	VG	F	VF	XF	Unc
1730	—	250	450	800	1,500	—
1736	—	250	500	800	1,200	—
1740	—	150	250	450	800	—
1746	—	150	250	450	800	—
1753	—	800	1,500	2,000	2,500	—

KM# 140 1/2 THALER
14.6500 g., Silver, 36 mm. **Ruler:** Anton III, the Younger **Obverse:** St. Johann **Reverse:** Madonna with child divides date

Date	Mintage	VG	F	VF	XF	Unc
1730	—	250	475	900	1,650	—

KM# 120 THALER
Silver **Ruler:** Anton III, the Younger **Obverse:** Larger bust right **Obv. Legend:** ANTONIUS. COMES. IN MONTFORT **Reverse:** Mitred, helmeted and mantled arms **Rev. Legend:** * PRO DEO - ET LEGE. * **Note:** Dav. #2448.

Date	Mintage	F	VF	XF	Unc
1720	—	2,500	3,500	6,500	10,000

KM# 125 THALER
Silver **Ruler:** Anton III, the Younger **Obverse:** Head right **Obv. Legend:** ANTONI. COM: *IN MONTFORT* **Note:** Dav. #2449.

Date	Mintage	F	VF	XF	Unc
1723	—	2,500	3,500	6,500	10,000
1728	—	2,500	3,500	6,500	10,000

KM# 143 THALER
Silver **Ruler:** Anton II. Regent **Obverse:** St. Johann with standard and shield **Obv. Legend:** MONETA: NOV: COMITATVS DE MONFORT *, in inner row; IN HONOREM DIV • IOAN • - COM DE MONT • CYP • PATR • **Reverse:** Virgin with child divides date **Rev. Legend:** DVRCH GOTT, VNTER MARIA SCHVTZ WURDT DIS GETRVCKHT DEM FEINDT ZU TRVTZ **Note:** Dav. #2452.

Date	Mintage	VG	F	VF	XF	Unc
1730	—	800	1,000	1,500	2,000	—

KM# 142 THALER
Silver **Ruler:** Anton III, the Younger **Obv. Legend:** ANTONIVS. COMES... **Note:** Dav. #2453.

Date	Mintage	VG	F	VF	XF	Unc
1730	—	2,000	3,000	5,000	8,000	—

KM# 147 THALER
Silver **Ruler:** Anton II. Regent **Obv. Legend:** ANTONIUS. COMES. IN MONTFORT **Note:** Dav. #2454.

Date	Mintage	VG	F	VF	XF	Unc
1731	—	2,000	3,000	5,000	8,000	—

KM# 162 THALER
Silver **Ruler:** Ernst Josef **Obverse:** Bust right, I. THIEBAUD. F. below **Obv. Legend:** ERN • COM • DE MONTF • - D • IN BREG • TETT • ET AR • **Reverse:** Helmeted and mantled arms with standard **Rev. Legend:** AVITA RELIGIONE ET IUSTITIA **Note:** Dav. #2456.

Date	Mintage	VG	F	VF	XF	Unc
1738	—	700	1,200	1,750	2,500	—

KM# 174 THALER
Silver **Ruler:** Ernst Josef **Obverse:** Cloaked, armored bust right, I: HAAG. F. below **Obv. Legend:** ERNESTVS • CO - MES • DE • MONTFORT • **Reverse:** Helmeted and mantled arms with standard **Rev. Legend:** * PRO DEO - ET - LEGE * **Note:** Dav. #2458.

Date	Mintage	VG	F	VF	XF	Unc
1749	—	500	1,200	1,500	2,000	—
1752	—	500	1,200	1,500	2,000	—

KM# 188 THALER
Silver **Ruler:** Franz Xavier **Obverse:** Armored bust right **Obv. Legend:** FRANC: XAV: COM: - DE MONTFORT **Reverse:** Date divided below mantle **Note:** Dav. #2459.

Date	Mintage	VG	F	VF	XF	Unc
1759	—	250	500	750	1,250	—

KM# 187 THALER
Silver **Ruler:** Franz Xavier **Obverse:** Armored bust right **Obv. Legend:** FR: XAV: COM: - DE MONTFORT • **Reverse:** Date divided by mantle **Note:** Dav. #2460.

Date	Mintage	VG	F	VF	XF	Unc
1759	—	250	500	750	1,250	—

KM# 192 THALER
Silver **Ruler:** Franz Xavier **Obverse:** Armored bust right **Obv. Legend:** FRANC: XAV: COM: - IN MONTFORT • **Reverse:** Mitred, helmeted and mantled arms **Note:** Dav. #2461.

Date	Mintage	VG	F	VF	XF	Unc
1761	—	250	500	750	1,250	—

KM# 144 2 THALER
Silver **Ruler:** Anton III, the Younger **Note:** Similar to 1 Thaler, KM#143. Dav. #2451.

Date	Mintage	VG	F	VF	XF	Unc
1730 Rare	—	—	—	—	—	—

KM# A162 2 THALER
Silver **Ruler:** Ernst Josef **Obverse:** Armored bust right **Reverse:** Helmeted and mantled arms with standard **Note:** Similar to 1 Thaler, KM#162. Dav. #2455.

Date	Mintage	VG	F	VF	XF	Unc
1738 Rare	—	—	—	—	—	—

KM# A182 2 THALER
Silver **Ruler:** Ernst Josef **Obverse:** Armored, cloaked bust right **Reverse:** Helmeted and mantled arms with standard **Note:** Similar to 1 Thaler, KM#174. Dav. #2457.

Date	Mintage	VG	F	VF	XF	Unc
1752 Rare	—	—	—	—	—	—

KM# 152 1/4 CAROLIN
2.4250 g., 0.7500 Gold 0.0585 oz. AGW **Ruler:** Ernst Josef

Date	Mintage	VG	F	VF	XF	Unc
1734	—	350	650	1,500	2,650	—
1735	—	350	650	1,500	2,650	—

KM# 160 1/4 CAROLIN
2.4250 g., 0.7500 Gold 0.0585 oz. AGW **Ruler:** Ernst Josef **Obverse:** Draped bust right **Reverse:** Monograms in cruciform, value at center

Date	Mintage	VG	F	VF	XF	Unc
1736	—	450	750	1,650	2,850	—

KM# 153 1/2 CAROLIN
4.8500 g., 0.7500 Gold 0.1169 oz. AGW **Ruler:** Ernst Josef **Obverse:** Bust right **Reverse:** Mitred, helmeted and mantled arms

Date	Mintage	VG	F	VF	XF	Unc
1734	—	475	975	2,000	3,250	—
1735	—	475	975	2,000	3,250	—

KM# 154 CAROLIN
9.7000 g., 0.7500 Gold 0.2339 oz. AGW **Ruler:** Ernst Josef **Obverse:** Draped bust right **Reverse:** Helmeted, mitred and mantled arms

Date	Mintage	VG	F	VF	XF	Unc
1734	—	325	800	1,750	3,000	—
1735	—	325	800	1,750	3,000	—
1736	—	325	800	1,750	3,000	—

KM# 156 CAROLIN
9.7000 g., 0.7500 Gold 0.2339 oz. AGW **Ruler:** Ernst Josef **Note:** Similar to 1/4 Carolin, KM#152.

Date	Mintage	VG	F	VF	XF	Unc
1735	—	1,000	1,800	3,500	5,000	—

KM# 157 10 GULDEN
Gold **Ruler:** Ernst Josef **Reverse:** Monograms in cruciform, value at center

Date	Mintage	VG	F	VF	XF	Unc
1735	—	1,500	2,500	4,500	9,000	—

TRADE COINAGE

KM# 122 1/4 DUCAT
0.8750 g., 0.9860 Gold 0.0277 oz. AGW **Ruler:** Anton III, the Younger **Obverse:** Head right **Reverse:** Helmeted, mitred and mantled arms

Date	Mintage	VG	F	VF	XF	Unc
1722	—	275	725	1,600	2,750	—
1728	—	275	725	1,600	2,750	—
1730	—	275	725	1,600	2,750	—

KM# 123 1/2 DUCAT
1.7500 g., 0.9860 Gold 0.0555 oz. AGW **Ruler:** Anton III, the Younger **Obverse:** Head right **Reverse:** Helmeted, mitred and mantled arms **Note:** Similar to 1/4 Ducat, KM#122.

Date	Mintage	VG	F	VF	XF	Unc
1722	—	800	1,200	3,250	5,500	—

KM# 114 DUCAT
3.5000 g., 0.9860 Gold 0.1109 oz. AGW **Ruler:** Anton III, the Younger **Obverse:** Helmeted, mitred and draped arms **Reverse:** Crowned imperial eagle, orb on breast

Date	Mintage	VG	F	VF	XF	Unc
1715 Rare	—	—	—	—	—	—
1716 Rare	—	—	—	—	—	—

KM# 115 DUCAT
3.5000 g., 0.9860 Gold 0.1109 oz. AGW **Ruler:** Anton III, the Younger **Obverse:** Head right **Reverse:** Helmeted, mitred and mantled arms

Date	Mintage	VG	F	VF	XF	Unc
1717	—	1,750	2,750	4,750	9,000	—
1718	—	1,750	2,750	4,750	9,000	—
1730	—	1,750	2,750	4,750	9,000	—
1732	—	1,750	2,750	4,750	9,000	—

KM# 158 DUCAT
3.5000 g., 0.9860 Gold 0.1109 oz. AGW **Ruler:** Ernst Josef **Obverse:** Armored bust right **Reverse:** Date divided at sides

Date	Mintage	VG	F	VF	XF	Unc
1735	—	1,000	2,000	4,000	6,500	—
1736	—	1,000	2,000	4,000	6,500	—
1745	—	1,000	2,000	4,000	6,500	—

KM# 180 DUCAT
3.5000 g., 0.9860 Gold 0.1109 oz. AGW **Ruler:** Ernst Josef **Obverse:** Armored bust right **Reverse:** Date divided by arms at bottom

Date	Mintage	VG	F	VF	XF	Unc
1750 H	—	750	1,650	3,000	5,500	—
1756	—	750	1,650	3,000	5,500	—

KM# 185 DUCAT
3.5000 g., 0.9860 Gold 0.1109 oz. AGW **Obverse:** Bust right **Reverse:** Mitred, helmeted and mantled arms; date divided at bottom

Date	Mintage	VG	F	VF	XF	Unc
1758	—	650	1,450	2,800	5,000	—

KM# 145 2 DUCAT
7.0000 g., 0.9860 Gold 0.2219 oz. AGW **Ruler:** Anton III, the Younger **Obverse:** St. Johann with flag and shield **Reverse:** Madonna and child below God

Date	Mintage	VG	F	VF	XF	Unc
1730 Rare	—	—	—	—	—	—

KM# 181 3 DUCATS
10.5200 g., Gold, 27.5 mm. **Ruler:** Ernst Josef **Obverse:** Armored bust right **Obv. Legend:** ERNEST: COM - IN MONTFORT • **Reverse:** Cardinal's hat above helmet, draperies and shield divide date **Rev. Legend:** PRO - DEO - ET - LEGE •

Date	Mintage	F	VF	XF	Unc
1752 Rare	—	—	—	—	—

PATTERNS

Including off metal strikes

KM#	Date	Mintage	Identification	Mkt Val
Pn2	1720	—	Thaler. Copper. KM#120	1,500
Pn3	1732	—	Pfennig. Copper. KM#102	—
Pn4	1736	—	1/2 Kreuzer. Copper. KM#150	—

MUHLHAUSEN ALSACE

FREE CITY

(Mulhouse)

Not to be confused with the Mühlhausen in Thüringen, this town is located in southern Alsace, 58 miles (96 km) south of Strassburg. Mühlhausen was made a free imperial city during the 14th century. The town did not exercise its right to strike coins until the early phase of the Thirty Years' War. At the conclusion of hostilities in 1648, Mühlhausen joined the Swiss Confederation, but was annexed to France in 1798.

ARM

A millwheel, sometimes just half a millwheel and half an eagle.

REGULAR COINAGE

KM# 10.1 THALER
Silver **Obverse:** Rappant Lion left holding city arms, MONETA, etc. **Reverse:** Crowned imperial eagle **Rev. Legend:** EX VNO OMNIS NOSTRA SAL

Date	Mintage	VG	F	VF	XF	Unc
1623	—	900	1,650	2,750	4,000	—
1623(ca.1800) Restrike	—	—	—	350	600	1,000

Note: Identified by the leafy ornamentation on the edge and generally streaky fields

KM# 11 THALER
Silver **Obverse:** Ornate city arms, date in margin above, MONETA, etc. **Reverse:** Crowned imperial eagle **Rev. Legend:** EX VNO OMNIS NOSTRA SAL **Note:** Klippe.

Date	Mintage	VG	F	VF	XF	Unc
1623	—	500	900	1,500	2,500	—
1623(ca.1800) Restrike	—	—	—	250	400	700

Note: Identified by the leafy ornamentation on the edge and generally streaky fields

MUHLHAUSEN THURINGEN

The city of Mühlhausen is located 20 miles (34km) north-northwest of Gotha and is one of the oldest towns in Thuringia (Thüringen). Walls and fortifications were built during the reign of Emperor Heinrich I (918-36), who gave Mühlhausen a number of special privileges. An imperial mint was located there in the 12th and 13th centuries. After obtaining the right to mint its own coinage, Mühlhausen issued a long series dated from 1496-1767. Mühlhausen came under Prussian rule in 1802, then was dominated by Westphalia from 1807. It was returned to Prussia in 1815, by the terms of the peace which ended the Napoleonic Wars.

RULERS

Josef II, 1765-1790

MINT OFFICIALS' INITIALS

Initials	Date	Name
ID	1701-10	Johann Dietmar
	1701-03	Johann Gottfried Hermann, warden
	1701-09	Jeremias Balthaser Wilhelmi, die-cutter
	1704-09	Christoph Muller, warden
	1705-41	Ehrenfried Hannibal, die-cutter in Clausthal
	1707-09	Nikolaus Pitsch, mint official
	1753-90	Johann Wilhelm Schlemm of Clausthal
	1767-68	J.P. Luttmer, die-cutter in Clausthal

NOTE: Coinage of 1737 and 1767 minted in Clausthal, Brunswick-Hannover.

ARMS

Eagle with mill-rind on breast.

FREE CITY

REGULAR COINAGE

KM# 40 2 PFENNINGE

Silver **Obverse:** Mulhausen eagle, tail divides initials **Obv. Legend:** MUHLHAUSER STADT MUNTZ **Reverse:** Value: II/LEUCHTE/PFENNGE/date

Date	Mintage	VG	F	VF	XF	Unc
1702 ID	—	25.00	50.00	85.00	140	—
1706 ID	113,000	25.00	50.00	85.00	140	—

KM# 55 2 PFENNINGE

Copper **Obv. Legend:** MVHLHAVSER/STAADT MVNTZ/1737 **Reverse:** Similar to KM#65

Date	Mintage	VG	F	VF	XF	Unc
1737	—	8.00	12.00	20.00	40.00	—

KM# 70 2 PFENNINGE

Copper **Ruler:** Josef II **Obverse:** Name, date **Reverse:** Value

Date	Mintage	VG	F	VF	XF	Unc
1767	—	5.00	8.00	15.00	30.00	—

KM# 42 3 PFENNINGE (Dreier)

Copper **Obverse:** Muhlhausen eagle, initials divided below **Obv. Legend:** MVLHAVSEN **Reverse:** Value: 3 on imperial orb, cross divides date

Date	Mintage	VG	F	VF	XF	Unc
1703 ID	—	20.00	40.00	75.00	120	—
1704 ID	—	20.00	40.00	75.00	120	—

KM# 45 3 PFENNINGE (Dreier)

Copper **Obverse:** Muhlhausen eagle in shield divides initials, ornate helmet above **Obv. Legend:** MVHL - HAVSEN

Date	Mintage	VG	F	VF	XF	Unc
1707 ID	363,000	18.00	35.00	65.00	100	—

KM# 56.1 3 PFENNINGE (Dreier)

Billon **Obverse:** Mulhausen eagle in shield divides initials, ornate helmet above **Reverse:** Value within Palm branches, circle surrounds

Date	Mintage	VG	F	VF	XF	Unc
1737	—	10.00	15.00	25.00	50.00	—

KM# 56.2 3 PFENNINGE (Dreier)

Billon **Ruler:** Josef II

Date	Mintage	VG	F	VF	XF	Unc
1767	—	7.00	12.00	20.00	40.00	—

KM# 41 4 PFENNINGE

Silver **Obverse:** Muhlhausen eagle in oval shield, ornate helmet above, date **Obv. Legend:** MUHLHAUSEN **Reverse:** Value: III/LEICHTE/PFENGE/initials, all in palm wreath

Date	Mintage	VG	F	VF	XF	Unc
1702 ID	—	30.00	60.00	100	170	—

KM# 57.1 6 PFENNINGE

Billon **Obverse:** Helmeted arms **Reverse:** Imperial orb with VI dividing date

Date	Mintage	VG	F	VF	XF	Unc
1737	—	14.00	20.00	30.00	65.00	—

KM# 57.2 6 PFENNINGE

Billon **Ruler:** Josef II **Obverse:** Muhlhausen eagle in shield, ornate helmet above **Reverse:** Value on imperial orb dividing date

Date	Mintage	VG	F	VF	XF	Unc
1767	—	10.00	18.00	28.00	55.00	—

KM# 35 1/24 THALER (Groschen)

Silver **Obverse:** Muhlhausen eagle in shield divides initials, ornate helmet above **Obv. Legend:** SUB DEO ET - CESARAE **Reverse:** Value: 24 in imperial orb divides date **Rev. Legend:** CIVIT. IMPERIALIS MOLHUSINAE

Date	Mintage	VG	F	VF	XF	Unc
1701 ID	—	40.00	80.00	160	320	—
1702 ID	—	40.00	80.00	160	320	—
1707 ID	3,437	30.00	60.00	120	250	—

Note: Altered from 2

KM# 58 1/24 THALER (Groschen)

Billon **Obverse:** Helmeted arms **Reverse:** Value, date

Date	Mintage	VG	F	VF	XF	Unc
1737	—	10.00	16.00	32.00	70.00	—

KM# 72 1/24 THALER (Groschen)

Billon **Ruler:** Josef II **Obverse:** Muhlhausen eagle in shield, ornate helmet above **Reverse:** Value, date

Date	Mintage	VG	F	VF	XF	Unc
1767	—	7.00	14.00	30.00	60.00	—

KM# 36 1/12 THALER (Doppelgroschen)

Silver **Obv. Legend:** MONETA NOVA - ARGENTEA **Reverse:** Date. value: 12/EINEN/THALER in palm wreath **Rev. Legend:** CIVIT. IMPERIALIS MOLHUSINAE **Note:** Varieties exist.

Date	Mintage	VG	F	VF	XF	Unc
1701 ID	—	22.00	50.00	80.00	135	—
1702 ID	—	22.00	50.00	80.00	135	—
1703 ID	—	22.00	50.00	80.00	135	—
1704 ID	—	22.00	50.00	80.00	135	—

KM# 43 1/12 THALER (Doppelgroschen)

Silver **Reverse:** Value: 12/EINEN/THALER/ at center, date

Date	Mintage	VG	F	VF	XF	Unc
1704 ID	—	22.00	50.00	80.00	135	—

KM# 44 1/12 THALER (Doppelgroschen)

Silver **Obverse:** Muhlhausen eagle in shield, ornate helmet above **Reverse:** Value, date within inner circle **Rev. Legend:** SUB DEO ET - CAESARE

Date	Mintage	VG	F	VF	XF	Unc
1706 ID	11,000	22.00	50.00	80.00	135	—
1707 ID	47,000	22.00	50.00	80.00	135	—

KM# 46 1/12 THALER (Doppelgroschen)

Silver **Obverse:** Muhlhausen eagle in shield, ornate helmet above **Reverse:** Value: 12/EINEN/THALER/date **Note:** Similar to 1/24 Thaler, KM#35

Date	Mintage	VG	F	VF	XF	Unc
1707 ID	Inc. above	22.00	50.00	80.00	135	—

KM# 59 1/12 THALER (Doppelgroschen)

Silver **Obverse:** Helmeted arms **Reverse:** Value, date

Date	Mintage	VG	F	VF	XF	Unc
1737	—	15.00	20.00	40.00	85.00	—

KM# 73 1/12 THALER (Doppelgroschen)

Silver **Ruler:** Josef II **Obverse:** Helmeted arms **Reverse:** Value and date

Date	Mintage	VG	F	VF	XF	Unc
1767	—	12.00	18.00	35.00	70.00	—

KM# 37 8 GUTE GROSCHEN (1/2 Gulden)

Silver **Obverse:** Muhlhausen eagle in shield divides initials, ornate helmet above, all in partial circle **Obv. Legend:** NOMETA NOVA - ARGENTEA **Reverse:** Legend, value: VII/GUTE/GROSCHEN in palm wreath **Rev. Legend:** CIVIT: value, IMPERIALIS MOLHUSINAE, date

Date	Mintage	VG	F	VF	XF	Unc
1701 ID Rare	—	—	—	—	—	—
1702 ID Rare	—	—	—	—	—	—

KM# 39 16 GUTE GROSCHEN (2/3 Thaler = Gulden)
Silver **Obverse:** Without circle **Reverse:** Value: SVI/GUTE/GROSCH/EN palm wreath in circle

Date	Mintage	VG	F	VF	XF	Unc
1701 ID Rare	—	—	—	—	—	—

KM# 38 16 GUTE GROSCHEN (2/3 Thaler = Gulden)
Silver **Obverse:** Center in partial circle **Reverse:** GROSCHEN in one line **Note:** Dav. #690.

Date	Mintage	VG	F	VF	XF	Unc
1701 ID	—	400	725	1,125	1,750	—
1703 ID	—	400	725	1,125	1,750	—

KM# 60 2/3 THALER (Gulden)
Silver **Obverse:** Helmeted arms **Reverse:** Value: Large 2/3 in field, date **Note:** Dav. #689.

Date	Mintage	VG	F	VF	XF	Unc
1737	600	275	400	650	1,000	—

KM# 74 2/3 THALER (Gulden)
Silver **Ruler:** Josef II **Obverse:** Muhlhausen eagle in shield, ornate helmet above **Reverse:** Fraction, date above

Date	Mintage	VG	F	VF	XF	Unc
1767	—	150	250	450	800	—

KM# 75 THALER
Silver **Ruler:** Josef II **Obverse:** Armored bust right **Obv. Legend:** IOSEPH II • D • G • R • I • S • A • - COR • & HER • R • G • B • & C • **Reverse:** Muhlhausen eagle in shield, ornate helmet above **Rev. Legend:** CIVIT • IMPERIALIS MULHUSINÆ, X • EINE FEINE MARCK below arms **Note:** Dav. #2462.

Date	Mintage	VG	F	VF	XF	Unc
1767	—	250	500	800	1,500	—

MUNSTER

BISHOPRIC

A Bishopric, located in Westphalia, was established c.802. The first Munster coinage was struck c. 1228. In 1802 the bishopric was secularized and divided. From 1806-1810 most of Munster belonged to Berg, from 1810-1814 to France and from 1814 onward, to Prussia.

During the 16th and 17th centuries treasury tokens, mostly counterstamped with the arms or initials of the current treasurer were issued. These were replaced in the middle of the 17th century by Cathedral coins, showing St. Paul with a sword. They last appeared at the end of the 18th century.

RULERS

Friedrich Christian von Plettenberg, 1688-1706
Franz Arnold von Wolff-Metternich, 1706-1718
Clemens August von Bavaria, 1719-1761
Sede Vacante, 1761
Maximilian Friedrich, Graf von ¬¬Konigsegg-Rothenees, 1762-1784
Maximilian Franz of Austria, 1784-1801

MINT OFFICIALS' INITIALS & PRIVY MARKS

Initials or Privy Mark	Date	Name
AGP	1714-23	Anton Gottfried Pott
GLC	1708-37	Gabriel Le Clerc, die-cutter in Berlin
HLO, HO	1696-1700, 1704, 1706	Heinrich Lorenz Odendahl
IK	1739-67	Jacob Kohlhaas
IW, JW	1709-13	Johann Willerding
W	d.1771	Peter Paul Werner, die-cutter in Nürnberg
WR	1713-18	Wilhelm Ritter
(a) – bird		
(b) – flower		
(c) - rosette		

REGULAR COINAGE

KM# 130 3 PFENNIG (1/112 Thaler)
Copper **Ruler:** Friedrich Christian von Plettenberg
Obverse: Crowned ornate double FC monogram
Reverse: Value and date **Rev. Legend:** F. MUNSTERISCHE. SCHEIDMUNTZ, III/PFEN **Note:** Varieties exist.

Date	Mintage	VG	F	VF	XF	Unc
1701	—	3.00	7.00	15.00	35.00	—
1703	—	3.00	7.00	15.00	35.00	—

KM# 132 3 PFENNIG (1/112 Thaler)
Copper **Ruler:** Friedrich Christian von Plettenberg **Reverse:** Date and value **Rev. Legend:** F.M. SCHEIDE. MUNTZ, III/PFEN

Date	Mintage	VG	F	VF	XF	Unc
1703	—	65.00	150	300	475	—

KM# 149 3 PFENNIG (1/112 Thaler)
Copper **Ruler:** Franz Arnold von Wolff-Metternich **Obverse:** Crowned double FA monogram **Reverse:** Value and date within inner circle **Note:** Varieties exist.

Date	Mintage	VG	F	VF	XF	Unc
1712	—	6.00	10.00	20.00	40.00	—
1714	—	6.00	10.00	20.00	40.00	—

KM# 170 3 PFENNIG (1/112 Thaler)
Copper **Ruler:** Clemens August von Bayern **Obverse:** Crowned monogram **Reverse:** Value and date within inner circle **Rev. Legend:** FURSTL

Date	Mintage	VG	F	VF	XF	Unc
1735	—	3.00	6.00	12.00	22.00	—
1736	—	3.00	6.00	12.00	22.00	—
1737	—	3.00	6.00	12.00	22.00	—
1738	—	3.00	6.00	12.00	22.00	—
1739	—	3.00	6.00	12.00	22.00	—
1740	—	3.00	6.00	12.00	22.00	—
1741	—	3.00	6.00	12.00	22.00	—

KM# 171 3 PFENNIG (1/112 Thaler)
Copper **Ruler:** Clemens August von Bayern
Obverse: Monogram within crowned mantle **Reverse:** Value, date within inner circle **Rev. Legend:** HOCHFURST

Date	Mintage	VG	F	VF	XF	Unc
1735	—	3.00	6.00	12.00	22.00	—
1736	—	3.00	6.00	12.00	22.00	—
1737	—	3.00	6.00	12.00	22.00	—
1738	—	3.00	6.00	12.00	22.00	—
1739	—	3.00	6.00	12.00	22.00	—
1740	—	3.00	6.00	12.00	22.00	—
1741	—	3.00	6.00	12.00	22.00	—
1742	—	3.00	6.00	12.00	22.00	—
1743	—	3.00	6.00	12.00	22.00	—
1744	—	3.00	6.00	12.00	22.00	—
1745	—	3.00	6.00	12.00	22.00	—
1746	—	3.00	6.00	12.00	22.00	—

KM# 178 3 PFENNIG (1/112 Thaler)
Copper **Ruler:** Clemens August von Bayern **Obverse:** Crowned monogram **Reverse:** Value, date within inner circle

Date	Mintage	VG	F	VF	XF	Unc
1748	—	4.00	8.00	16.00	25.00	—
1749	—	4.00	8.00	16.00	25.00	—
1750	—	4.00	8.00	16.00	25.00	—
1751	—	4.00	8.00	16.00	25.00	—
1752	—	4.00	8.00	16.00	25.00	—
1753	—	4.00	8.00	16.00	25.00	—
1754	—	4.00	8.00	16.00	25.00	—
1755	—	4.00	8.00	16.00	25.00	—

KM# 133 4 PFENNIG (1/84 Thaler)
Copper **Ruler:** Friedrich Christian von Plettenberg **Obverse:** FC monogram within palm branches **Reverse:** Value, IIII

Date	Mintage	VG	F	VF	XF	Unc
1703	—	5.00	10.00	18.00	38.00	—

KM# 152 4 PFENNIG (1/84 Thaler)
Copper **Ruler:** Franz Arnold von Wolff-Metternich **Obverse:** FA monogram within palm branches **Reverse:** Value, IIII

Date	Mintage	VG	F	VF	XF	Unc
1715	—	6.00	12.00	20.00	42.00	—
1716	—	6.00	12.00	20.00	42.00	—

KM# 172 4 PFENNIG (1/84 Thaler)
Copper **Ruler:** Clemens August von Bayern **Obverse:** Crowned monogram **Reverse:** Value, date within inner circle **Note:** Similar to 3 Pfennig, KM#170.

Date	Mintage	VG	F	VF	XF	Unc
1735 Rare	—	—	—	—	—	—

KM# 175 4 PFENNIG (1/84 Thaler)
Copper **Ruler:** Clemens August von Bayern **Obverse:** Monogram within crowned mantle **Reverse:** Value, date within inner circle

Date	Mintage	VG	F	VF	XF	Unc
1743	—	4.00	8.00	16.00	25.00	—
1744	—	4.00	8.00	16.00	25.00	—
1745	—	4.00	8.00	16.00	25.00	—

KM# 179 4 PFENNIG (1/84 Thaler)
Copper **Ruler:** Clemens August von Bayern **Obverse:** Crowned monogram within branches **Reverse:** Value, date within inner circle

Date	Mintage	VG	F	VF	XF	Unc
1748	—	4.00	8.00	16.00	25.00	—
1749	—	4.00	8.00	16.00	25.00	—
1750	—	4.00	8.00	16.00	25.00	—
1751	—	4.00	8.00	16.00	25.00	—
1752	—	4.00	8.00	16.00	25.00	—
1753	—	4.00	8.00	16.00	25.00	—
1754	—	4.00	8.00	16.00	25.00	—
1755	—	4.00	8.00	16.00	25.00	—

KM# 180 SCHILLING (1/28 Thaler)
Billon **Ruler:** Clemens August von Bayern **Obverse:** Crowned round arms in cartouche, value below **Reverse:** Bust of St. Paul, value, date

Date	Mintage	VG	F	VF	XF	Unc
1748 IK	—	4.00	8.00	16.00	25.00	—

KM# 203 SCHILLING (1/28 Thaler)
Billon **Ruler:** Sede Vacante **Obverse:** MF monogram **Reverse:** St. Paul, value and date

Date	Mintage	VG	F	VF	XF	Unc
1764	—	4.50	10.00	17.50	30.00	—

KM# 146 2 SCHILLING (1/14 Thaler)
Silver **Ruler:** Franz Arnold von Wolff-Metternich **Obverse:** Crowned 8-fold arms with central shield of Metternich divide date, titles of Franz Arnold, (14) in legend at bottom **Reverse:** Without date

Date	Mintage	VG	F	VF	XF	Unc
1711 JW	—	40.00	80.00	150	—	—

KM# 159 2 SCHILLING (1/14 Thaler)
Silver **Ruler:** Clemens August von Bayern **Obverse:** Facing bust of St. Paul with sword and book in round baroque frame **Reverse:** Value, date and initials **Rev. Legend:** XIIII EIN:RTH **Note:** Sede vacante issue.

Date	Mintage	VG	F	VF	XF	Unc
1719 AGP	—	18.00	40.00	80.00	135	—

KM# 181 2 SCHILLING (1/14 Thaler)
Billon **Ruler:** Clemens August von Bayern **Obverse:** Crowned round arms in cartouche, value below **Reverse:** St. Paul standing with sword and bible, divides date

Date	Mintage	VG	F	VF	XF	Unc
1748 IK	—	18.00	25.00	50.00	110	—

KM# 182 2 SCHILLING (1/14 Thaler)
Billon **Ruler:** Clemens August von Bayern **Reverse:** Without value showing

Date	Mintage	VG	F	VF	XF	Unc
1748 IK	—	10.00	16.00	35.00	75.00	—

KM# 188 2 SCHILLING (1/14 Thaler)
Billon **Ruler:** Clemens August von Bayern **Obverse:** ST. Paul standing with sword and bible **Reverse:** Value, date **Rev. Legend:** FURSTL

Date	Mintage	VG	F	VF	XF	Unc
1755 IK	—	20.00	35.00	60.00	120	—

KM# 189 2 SCHILLING (1/14 Thaler)
Billon **Ruler:** Clemens August von Bayern **Rev. Legend:** HOCHFURST

Date	Mintage	VG	F	VF	XF	Unc
1755 IK	—	20.00	35.00	60.00	120	—

KM# 151 MARIENGROSCHEN (1/24 Gulden - 1/36 Thaler)
Silver **Ruler:** Franz Arnold von Wolff-Metternich **Obverse:** Crowned 8-fold arms with central shield of Metternich **Reverse:** Value, date

Date	Mintage	VG	F	VF	XF	Unc
1714	—	—	—	—	—	—

KM# 147 6 MARIENGROSCHEN (1/4 Gulden - 1/6 Thaler)
Silver **Ruler:** Franz Arnold von Wolff-Metternich **Obverse:** Crowned oval 8-fold arms with central shield of Metterich **Reverse:** Value, date within inner circle **Note:** Similar to 1/12 Thaler, KM#138, but value: VI/MARIEN/GROS, date. Varieties exist.

Date	Mintage	VG	F	VF	XF	Unc
1711 JW	—	18.00	28.00	50.00	85.00	—
1715 WR	—	18.00	28.00	50.00	85.00	—
1718 WR	—	18.00	28.00	50.00	85.00	—
1718 AGP	—	18.00	28.00	50.00	85.00	—

KM# 185 6 MARIENGROSCHEN (1/4 Gulden - 1/6 Thaler)
Silver **Ruler:** Clemens August von Bayern **Obverse:** Crowned complex arms with central shield **Reverse:** Value, date within inner circle

Date	Mintage	VG	F	VF	XF	Unc
1754 IK	—	18.00	28.00	60.00	110	—

KM# 145 12 MARIENGROSCHEN (1/2 Gulden - 1/3 Thaler)
Silver **Ruler:** Franz Arnold von Wolff-Metternich **Obverse:** Crowned oval 8-fold arms with central shield of Metterich **Reverse:** Value, date within inner circle **Note:** Similar to 1/12 Thaler, KM#138, but value: XII/MARIEN/GROS/date.

Date	Mintage	VG	F	VF	XF	Unc
1710 JW	—	60.00	100	200	325	—

KM# 134 24 MARIENGROSCHEN (Gulden - 2/3 Thaler)
Silver **Ruler:** Franz Arnold von Wolff-Metternich **Obverse:** Crowned oval 8-fold arms with central shield of Metternich, titles of Franz Arnold **Reverse:** Value and date within inner circle **Note:** Varieties exist.

Date	Mintage	VG	F	VF	XF	Unc
1706	—	100	185	325	550	—
1709 JW	—	100	185	325	550	—
1710 JW	—	100	185	325	550	—
1715 WR	—	100	185	325	550	—

KM# 200 24 MARIENGROSCHEN (Gulden - 2/3 Thaler)
Silver **Ruler:** Maximilian Friedrich, Graf von Königsegg-Rothenfels **Obverse:** Arms **Reverse:** Value and date

Date	Mintage	VG	F	VF	XF	Unc
1763	—	40.00	75.00	110	200	—

KM# 137 1/48 THALER (Halbgroschen)
Silver **Ruler:** Franz Arnold von Wolff-Metternich **Obverse:** Crowned FA monogram **Reverse:** Value within inner circle **Rev. Legend:** F.M. & P.L **Note:** Varieties exist.

Date	Mintage	VG	F	VF	XF	Unc
1709 JW	—	10.00	20.00	35.00	55.00	—
1710 JW	—	10.00	20.00	35.00	55.00	—
1711 JW	—	10.00	20.00	35.00	55.00	—
1717 WR	—	10.00	20.00	35.00	55.00	—

KM# 165 1/48 THALER (Halbgroschen)
Billon **Ruler:** Clemens August von Bayern **Obverse:** Crowned CAC monogram **Reverse:** Value, date

Date	Mintage	VG	F	VF	XF	Unc
1723 AGP	—	10.00	16.00	35.00	65.00	—

KM# 176 1/48 THALER (Halbgroschen)
Billon **Ruler:** Clemens August von Bayern **Obverse:** CA monogram **Reverse:** Value, date

Date	Mintage	VG	F	VF	XF	Unc
1745 IK	—	10.00	16.00	30.00	60.00	—
1748 IK	—	10.00	16.00	30.00	60.00	—

KM# 206 1/48 THALER (Halbgroschen)
Billon **Ruler:** Maximilian Friedrich, Graf von Königsegg-Rothenfels **Obverse:** MF monogram **Reverse:** Value and date

Date	Mintage	VG	F	VF	XF	Unc
1766	—	5.00	10.00	20.00	35.00	—

KM# 160 1/24 THALER (Groschen)
Silver **Ruler:** Clemens August von Bayern **Obverse:** Facing bust of St. Paul with sword and book in oval baroque frame **Reverse:** Value, initials and date **Rev. Legend:** NACH. DEN. LEIPZIGER. FUES, 24/I/REICHS/THAL **Note:** Sede vacante issue.

Date	Mintage	VG	F	VF	XF	Unc
1719 AGP	—	10.00	20.00	40.00	65.00	—

KM# 186 1/24 THALER (Groschen)
Billon **Ruler:** Clemens August von Bayern **Obverse:** Crowned CAC monogram **Reverse:** Five-line inscription with date **Rev. Legend:** HOCHFURST.MUNST.LANDTMUNTZ **Rev. Inscription:** 24/ EINEN/ REICHS/THALER/1754

Date	Mintage	VG	F	VF	XF	Unc
1754 IK	—	8.00	12.00	25.00	40.00	—

KM# 190 1/24 THALER (Groschen)
Billon **Ruler:** Clemens August von Bayern **Obverse:** Crowned monogram **Reverse:** Value, date within inner circle

Date	Mintage	VG	F	VF	XF	Unc
1755 IK	—	8.00	12.00	25.00	40.00	—

KM# 191 1/24 THALER (Groschen)

Billon, 19.5 mm. **Ruler:** Clemens August von Bayern **Note:** Larger size.

Date	Mintage	VG	F	VF	XF	Unc
1755 IK	—	10.00	15.00	30.00	50.00	—

KM# 153 1/12 THALER (Doppelgroschen)

Silver **Ruler:** Franz Arnold von Wolff-Metternich **Obverse:** Crowned flat-top shield **Reverse:** Value, date

Date	Mintage	VG	F	VF	XF	Unc
1710 WR	—	12.00	22.00	45.00	85.00	—
1711 WR	—	12.00	22.00	45.00	85.00	—
1712 WR	—	12.00	22.00	45.00	85.00	—
1713 WR	—	12.00	22.00	45.00	85.00	—
1714 WR	—	12.00	22.00	45.00	85.00	—
1715 WR	—	12.00	22.00	45.00	85.00	—
1716 WR	—	12.00	22.00	45.00	85.00	—
1717 WR	—	12.00	22.00	45.00	85.00	—

KM# 138 1/12 THALER (Doppelgroschen)

Silver **Ruler:** Franz Arnold von Wolff-Metternich **Obverse:** Crowned oval 8-fold arms with central shield of Metternich, titles of Franz Arnold **Reverse:** Value, date, titles in legend **Rev. Legend:** 12/EINEN/REICHS/THAL(ER) **Note:** Varieties exist.

Date	Mintage	VG	F	VF	XF	Unc
1710 JW	—	40.00	125	250	400	—

KM# 166 1/12 THALER (Doppelgroschen)

Silver **Ruler:** Clemens August von Bayern **Obverse:** Crowned CAC monogram **Reverse:** Value, date, titles

Date	Mintage	VG	F	VF	XF	Unc
1723 AGP	—	12.00	25.00	50.00	90.00	—

KM# 167 1/12 THALER (Doppelgroschen)

Silver **Ruler:** Clemens August von Bayern **Obverse:** Crowned arms, titles in legend **Reverse:** Value, date within inner circle

Date	Mintage	VG	F	VF	XF	Unc
1728	—	25.00	40.00	80.00	150	—

KM# 177 1/12 THALER (Doppelgroschen)

Silver **Ruler:** Clemens August von Bayern **Obverse:** Crowned monogram **Reverse:** Value, date within inner circle

Date	Mintage	VG	F	VF	XF	Unc
1745 IK	—	10.00	20.00	40.00	85.00	—
1746 IK	—	12.00	25.00	50.00	85.00	—
1747 IK	—	12.00	25.00	50.00	85.00	—
1748 IK	—	12.00	25.00	50.00	85.00	—
1749 IK	—	12.00	25.00	50.00	85.00	—
1754 IK	—	12.00	25.00	50.00	85.00	—

KM# 187 1/12 THALER (Doppelgroschen)

Silver **Ruler:** Clemens August von Bayern **Obverse:** Crowned CAC monogram **Reverse:** Value, date within inner circle

Date	Mintage	VG	F	VF	XF	Unc
1754 IK	—	12.00	25.00	50.00	85.00	—
1755 IK	—	12.00	25.00	50.00	85.00	—

KM# 201 1/12 THALER (Doppelgroschen)

Billon **Ruler:** Maximilian Friedrich, Graf von Königsegg-Rothenfels **Obverse:** MF monogram **Reverse:** Value and date

Date	Mintage	VG	F	VF	XF	Unc
1763	—	6.00	13.50	22.50	40.00	—
1764	—	6.00	13.50	22.50	40.00	—
1765	—	6.00	13.50	22.50	40.00	—
1766	—	6.00	13.50	22.50	40.00	—
1767	—	6.00	13.50	22.50	40.00	—
1768	—	6.00	13.50	22.50	40.00	—
1769	—	6.00	13.50	22.50	40.00	—

KM# 196 1/6 THALER

Silver **Ruler:** Sede Vacante **Obverse:** St. Paul in chapter arms **Reverse:** Charlemagne with sword and orb above framed value

Date	Mintage	VG	F	VF	XF	Unc
1761	—	25.00	50.00	100	200	—

KM# 195 1/6 THALER

Silver **Obverse:** St. Paul in baroque frame **Reverse:** Charlemange with sword and orb, framed value below **Note:** Sede vacante issue.

Date	Mintage	VG	F	VF	XF	Unc
1761	—	25.00	50.00	100	200	—

KM# 202 1/6 THALER

Silver **Ruler:** Maximilian Friedrich, Graf von Königsegg-Rothenfels **Obverse:** Crowned arms **Reverse:** Value, date

Date	Mintage	VG	F	VF	XF	Unc
1763 IK	—	15.00	25.00	50.00	90.00	—
1764 IK	—	15.00	25.00	50.00	90.00	—

KM# 198 1/3 THALER

Silver **Ruler:** Sede Vacante **Obverse:** St. Paul in chapter arms **Reverse:** Charlemagne with sword and orb above framed value

Date	Mintage	VG	F	VF	XF	Unc
1761	—	35.00	75.00	150	250	—

KM# 197 1/3 THALER

Silver **Obverse:** St. Paul within baroque frame **Reverse:** Charlemagne with sword and orb, framed value below **Note:** Sede vacante issue.

Date	Mintage	VG	F	VF	XF	Unc
1761	—	35.00	75.00	150	250	—

KM# 204 1/3 THALER

Silver **Ruler:** Maximilian Friedrich, Graf von Königsegg-Rothenfels **Obverse:** Crowned arms with supporters **Reverse:** Value, date

Date	Mintage	VG	F	VF	XF	Unc
1764	—	25.00	40.00	75.00	135	—
1765	—	25.00	40.00	75.00	135	—

KM# 205 2/3 THALER (Gulden)

Silver **Ruler:** Maximilian Friedrich, Graf von Königsegg-Rothenfels **Obverse:** Draped bust right **Reverse:** Crowned arms with supporters above framed value **Note:** Reichs 2/3 Thaler.

Date	Mintage	F	VF	XF	Unc
1764	—	85.00	175	250	400

KM# 135 THALER

Silver **Ruler:** Friedrich Christian von Plettenberg **Subject:** Death of Bishop **Obverse:** Sword and crozier back of crowned arms on ornate frame **Obv. Legend:** * CONSILIO ET CONSTANTIA **Reverse:** Inscription **Rev. Legend:** FRIDERIC9/ CHRISTIANUS/L•B•A PLETTENBERG/ NATUS/ANNO 1664 • DIE 8 AUG/ELECTUS/ EPISCOPUS• AC•PRINCEPS/ MONASTERIENSIS/ANNO 1688 DIE 29 IULY/DENATUS/ ANNO 1706 DIE/5 MAY **Note:** Dav. #2464.

Date	Mintage	F	VF	XF	Unc
1706	—	135	275	575	1,000

KM# 136 THALER
Silver **Ruler:** Friedrich Christian von Plettenberg **Obverse:** Cathedral view **Obv. Legend:** DEUS • ADIUTOR • ET • PROTECTOR • NOSTER * **Reverse:** St. Paul on shield below ornamental helmet **Rev. Legend:** CAPITULUM • CATH • MONAST • SEDE • VACANT * **Note:** Sede Vacante. Dav. #2465.

Date	Mintage	F	VF	XF	Unc
1706	—	160	325	650	1,150

KM# 139 THALER
Silver **Ruler:** Franz Arnold von Wolff-Metternich **Obverse:** Crowned complex arms with central shield divides date **Obv. Legend:** FRANC • ARNOL • DG • EP • MON • & PAD • BUR • STR • S • R • I • P • C • PYR • & D • IN BOR • **Reverse:** 2 saints **Rev. Legend:** FRAN • ARN • EL • COA • PA • 15 • SEP • 1703 • SUC • PATRUO • 21 • MAY • 1704 • EL • EP • MO • 30 • SEP • 1706 *, PRO/LEGE & GREGE below busts **Note:** Dav. #2466.

Date	Mintage	F	VF	XF	Unc
1709 JW	—	250	500	900	1,500
1710 JW	—	250	500	900	1,500
1711 JW	—	250	500	900	1,500

KM# 150 THALER
Silver **Ruler:** Franz Arnold von Wolff-Metternich **Obverse:** Armored bust right **Obv. Legend:** FRANC • ARNOLD • D • G • EPISC • MONAST • ET • PADERB * **Reverse:** Crowned complex arms with sword and crozier behind **Rev. Legend:** BURGG • STROMB • S • R • I • P • COM • PYRM • DOM • IN • BORK • ET • WEHRT •, PRO LEGE ET GREGE on ribbon below **Note:** Dav. #2467.

Date	Mintage	F	VF	XF	Unc
1712 IW	—	750	1,350	2,200	3,250
1713 WR	—	750	1,350	2,200	3,250
1714 WR	—	750	1,350	2,200	3,250
1715 WR	—	750	1,350	2,200	3,250

KM# 154 THALER
Silver **Ruler:** Franz Arnold von Wolff-Metternich **Obverse:** Cloaked bust right, G.L.C. below **Obv. Legend:** FRANC: ARNOLD: D: G: EP: MONAST: ET PAD: **Reverse:** Crowned arms within legend **Rev. Legend:** BVRGG: ST: S. R. I. PR: C. PYRMON: ET DOM: IN BORKEL: 1716 **Note:** Dav. #2468.

Date	Mintage	F	VF	XF	Unc
1716 WR	—	400	800	1,500	2,500
1717 WR	—	400	800	1,500	2,500

KM# 158 THALER
Silver **Ruler:** Franz Arnold von Wolff-Metternich **Rev. Legend:** BURGG: STROMB: S: R: I.P: COM: PYRM **Note:** Dav. #2469.

Date	Mintage	F	VF	XF	Unc
1718 AGP Rare	—	—	—	—	—

KM# 161 THALER
Silver **Ruler:** Clemens August von Bayern **Obverse:** St. Paul standing with sword and book, divides date, 19 small shields around **Reverse:** Charlemagne standing with sword and imperial orb, 19 small shields around **Note:** Sede vacante issue.

Date	Mintage	F	VF	XF	Unc
1719 W Rare	—	—	—	—	—

KM# 199 THALER
Silver **Obverse:** Cathedral view **Obv. Legend:** CAPIT: CATH: ECCLESIA MONASTERIENSIS * SEDE VACANTE *, EIN SPECIES/REICHS THALER below **Reverse:** Charlemagne standing with sword and imperial orb **Rev. Legend:** * S. CAROLUS * MAGNUS * FUNDATOR * **Note:** Sede vacante issue. Species Thaler.Dav. #2470.

Date	Mintage	F	VF	XF	Unc
1761	—	150	300	600	1,200

KM# 131 2 THALER
Silver **Ruler:** Friedrich Christian von Plettenberg **Obverse:** Bust right breaks through legend at top and bottom **Reverse:** Crowned arms in frame **Note:** Dav. #2463.

Date	Mintage	VG	F	VF	XF	Unc
1702	—	1,000	2,000	3,500	6,000	—

TRADE COINAGE

KM# 148 DUCAT
3.5000 g., 0.9860 Gold 0.1109 oz. AGW **Ruler:** Franz Arnold von Wolff-Metternich **Obverse:** Bust right **Reverse:** Crowned arms, date in legend

Date	Mintage	VG	F	VF	XF	Unc
1711	—	—	—	—	—	—
1713	—	—	—	—	—	—

KM# 155 DUCAT
3.5000 g., 0.9860 Gold 0.1109 oz. AGW **Ruler:** Franz Arnold von Wolff-Metternich **Obverse:** Bust right **Reverse:** Crowned arms divide date

Date	Mintage	VG	F	VF	XF	Unc
1717 WR	—	650	1,200	2,800	4,500	—

KM# 156 2 DUCAT
7.0000 g., 0.9860 Gold 0.2219 oz. AGW **Ruler:** Franz Arnold von Wolff-Metternich **Obverse:** Bust right **Reverse:** Crowned arms divide date

Date	Mintage	VG	F	VF	XF	Unc
1717 WR Rare	—	—	—	—	—	—

KM# 157 3 DUCAT
10.5000 g., 0.9860 Gold 0.3328 oz. AGW **Ruler:** Franz Arnold von Wolff-Metternich **Obverse:** Bust right **Reverse:** Crowned oval 8-fold arms with central shield of Metternich divide date

Date	Mintage	VG	F	VF	XF	Unc
1717 WR Rare	—	—	—	—	—	—

KM# 162 15 DUCAT
52.5000 g., 0.9860 Gold 1.6642 oz. AGW **Ruler:** Clemens August von Bayern **Obverse:** St. Paul with sword and book at center, 19 small shields surround **Reverse:** Charlemagne at center, 19 small shields surround **Note:** Sede vacante issue. Similar to 1-1/2 Thaler, KM#M2.

Date	Mintage	VG	F	VF	XF	Unc
1719 AGP Rare	—	—	—	—	—	—

CITY

The history of the city is one of continuous struggle with the bishops for recognition of its autonomy. It was an important member of the Hanseatic League in the 13th and 14th centuries. Figured as the center of the Anabaptist revolt of 1534-35. Bishop took the city as his seat in 1660 and deprived it of free status, yet local coinage was struck from the mid-16th-18th century.

NOTE: Numbers on some 3 Schilling and 12 Pfennig coins ranging from 1 to 11 are die-numbers.

REGULAR COINAGE

KM# 330 HELLER
Copper **Obverse:** Small, plain city arms with point in center **Obv. Legend:** STADT. MVNSTER **Reverse:** Value, I/H in ornamented circle

Date	Mintage	Good	VG	F	VF	XF
ND(1700-1740)	—	3.00	6.00	18.00	30.00	—

KM# 340 HELLER
Copper **Obverse:** Larger shield of arms, without point in center

Date	Mintage	Good	VG	F	VF	XF
ND(ca.1750)	—	3.00	6.00	12.00	28.00	—

KM# 345 HELLER
Copper **Obverse:** Arms in cartouche **Reverse:** ++ on sides of I

Date	Mintage	Good	VG	F	VF	XF
ND(ca.1790-1810)	—	3.00	6.00	12.00	28.00	—

KM# 335 PFENNIG
Copper **Obverse:** Arms **Reverse:** Value divides date

Date	Mintage	VG	F	VF	XF	Unc
1740	—	5.00	10.00	15.00	30.00	—
1750	—	5.00	10.00	15.00	30.00	—
1758	—	5.00	10.00	15.00	30.00	—

KM# 336 1-1/2 PFENNING
Copper **Obverse:** Monogram **Reverse:** Value, date

Date	Mintage	VG	F	VF	XF	Unc
1740	—	9.00	16.00	30.00	55.00	—
1750	—	9.00	16.00	30.00	55.00	—
1758	—	9.00	16.00	30.00	55.00	—

KM# 337 2 PFENNING

Copper **Obverse:** Supported city arms **Reverse:** Value, date

Date	Mintage	VG	F	VF	XF	Unc
1740	—	3.00	6.00	12.00	28.00	—
1750	—	3.00	6.00	12.00	28.00	—
1758	—	3.00	6.00	12.00	28.00	—
1759	—	3.00	6.00	12.00	28.00	—

CATHEDRAL CHAPTER

Coinage until after 1633 consisted of bursary tokens issued by cathedral chapter members of local nobility.

RULER

EVB = Engelbert von Brabeck, leader of cathedral chapter.

MINT OFFICIALS' INITIALS

Initials	Date	Name
GS	Ca. 1714	Gottfried Storp?

REGULAR COINAGE

KM# 416 PFENNIG

Copper **Obverse:** Full-length facing figure of St. Paul divides S-P near bottom. **Obv. Legend:** M:CATHED:ECCL:MONASTA **Reverse:** Large 'I' divides date in wreath

Date	Mintage	Good	VG	F	VF	XF
1707	—	6.00	12.00	25.00	40.00	—

KM# 425 PFENNIG

Copper **Obverse:** Full-length figure of St. Paul with sword and book **Obv. Legend:** S.PAVLVS.APOS.-PATR:MONAS **Reverse:** Value and date **Rev. Legend:** M.CATHED. ECCLE.MONASTER, 1/PFEN **Note:** Uniface. Varieties exist.

Date	Mintage	Good	VG	F	VF	XF
1714 GS	—	—	—	—	—	—

KM# 435 PFENNIG

Copper **Obverse:** Half-length figure of St. Paul with sword and book, below S. PAVLVS **Obv. Legend:** MON:CATHED: ECCLES: MONASTE **Reverse:** Value, date in circle with baroque frame **Rev. Legend:** I/PFENNIG

Date	Mintage	Good	VG	F	VF	XF
1740	—	6.00	10.00	20.00	35.00	—

KM# 450 PFENNIG

Copper **Obverse:** Legend **Reverse:** Value, date

Date	Mintage	VG	F	VF	XF	Unc
1790	—	2.00	4.00	9.00	18.00	—

KM# 417 2 PFENNING

Copper **Obverse:** 3/4-length figure of St. Paul with sword and book, S.P. below **Obv. Legend:** MO.CATH.ECCL.MONAS **Reverse:** Value, II in center divides date, wreath of palm leaves **Note:** Varieties exist.

Date	Mintage	VG	F	VF	XF	Unc
1707	—	7.00	15.00	30.00	55.00	—

KM# 436 2 PFENNING

Copper **Obverse:** St. Paul **Reverse:** Value, date

Date	Mintage	Good	VG	F	VF	XF
1740	—	6.00	10.00	20.00	35.00	—

KM# 451 2 PFENNING

Copper **Obverse:** Legend **Reverse:** Value, date

Date	Mintage	VG	F	VF	XF	Unc
1790	—	2.00	4.00	9.00	18.00	—

KM# 426 3 PFENNING

Copper

Date	Mintage	Good	VG	F	VF	XF
1714 GS	—	12.00	25.00	40.00	65.00	—

KM# 430 3 PFENNING

Copper **Obverse:** St. Paul **Reverse:** Value, date

Date	Mintage	VG	F	VF	XF	Unc
1739	—	2.00	4.00	9.00	18.00	—
1740	—	2.00	4.00	9.00	18.00	—
1743	—	2.00	4.00	9.00	18.00	—
1748	—	2.00	4.00	9.00	18.00	—
1753	—	2.00	4.00	9.00	18.00	—
1759	—	2.00	4.00	9.00	18.00	—
1760	—	2.00	4.00	9.00	18.00	—

KM# 445 3 PFENNING

Copper **Obverse:** St. Paul **Reverse:** Value above date

Date	Mintage	VG	F	VF	XF	Unc
1787	—	2.50	5.00	10.00	20.00	—

KM# 427 4 PFENNIG

Copper **Obverse:** St. Paul **Reverse:** Value, date

Date	Mintage	Good	VG	F	VF	XF
1714 GS	—	7.00	12.00	25.00	40.00	—

K# 431 4 PFENNIG

Copper **Obverse:** 1/2 length figure of St. Paul facing holding sword, S. PAVLVS below **Obv. Legend:** MON: CATHED: ECCLES: MONESTE: **Reverse:** Value, date in ornate border

Date	Mintage	Good	VG	F	VF	XF
1739	—	0.75	2.00	4.00	9.00	18.00

KM# 431 4 PFENNIG

Copper **Obverse:** With S.P. below bust **Reverse:** Value, date

Date	Mintage	VG	F	VF	XF	Unc
1739	—	2.00	4.00	9.00	18.00	—
1762	—	2.00	4.00	9.00	18.00	—

K# 439 4 PFENNIG

Copper **Obverse:** 1/2 length figure of St. Paul facing holding sword, S • below **Obv. Legend:** MON: CATHED: ECCLES: MONESTE • **Reverse:** Value, date in ornate border **Note:** Prev. KM#431.

Date	Mintage	Good	VG	F	VF	XF
1762	—	0.75	2.00	4.00	9.00	18.00

KM# 446 4 PFENNIG

Copper

Date	Mintage	VG	F	VF	XF	Unc
1787	—	2.00	4.00	9.00	18.00	—
1788	—	—	—	—	—	—
Note: Reported, not confirmed						
1789	—	—	—	—	—	—
Note: Reported, not confirmed						
1790	—	2.00	4.00	9.00	18.00	—

KM# 440 6 PFENNIG

Copper **Obverse:** With S. PAULUS/6*P below bust **Reverse:** Value, date

Date	Mintage	VG	F	VF	XF	Unc
1762	—	2.00	4.00	9.00	18.00	—

KM# 441 6 PFENNIG

Copper **Obverse:** With 6*P below bust **Reverse:** Value, date

Date	Mintage	VG	F	VF	XF	Unc
1762	—	2.00	4.00	9.00	18.00	—

KM# 447 6 PFENNIG

Copper **Obverse:** St. Paul **Reverse:** Value above date

Date	Mintage	VG	F	VF	XF	Unc
1787	—	2.00	4.00	9.00	18.00	—
1788	—	2.00	4.00	9.00	18.00	—
1789	—	2.00	4.00	9.00	18.00	—
1790	—	2.00	4.00	9.00	18.00	—

PATTERNS

Including off metal strikes

KM#	Date	Mintage	Identification	Mkt Val
Pn1	1717	—	1/48 Thaler. Gold. KM#137.	—
Pn2	1754	—	1/24 Thaler. Copper. C#12.1.	—

NASSAU

The Countship of Nassau had its origins in the area of the Lahn of the central Rhineland, with territory on both sides of that river. The first count who attained the title with recognition from the emperor was Walram in 1158. His grandsons, Walram I (1255-88) and Otto I (1255-90), divided their patrimony. Walram claimed the left bank of the lahn and made Weisbaden his principal seat, whereas Otto took the right bank and ruled from Siegen. Thus, the division of 1255 established the two main lines over the ensuing centuries.

Several times, various branches of the family issued joint coinage, notably in the late 17th and again in the early 19th centuries. Eventually, through extinction of the various lines and the elevation of one ruler to the throne of the Netherlands, all Nassau was reunited under the house of Nassau-Weilburg.

ARMS

Nassau – lion rampant left on field of billets (small vertical rectangles)
Holzappel – griffin rampant left holding apple

DUCHY

Nassau-Dietz

STANDARD COINAGE

C# 1 HELLER

Copper **Ruler:** Wilhelm V **Obverse:** Crowned monogram **Reverse:** Value, date **Note:** Similar to 2 Heller, C#2.

Date	Mintage	F	VF	XF	Unc
1766	—	15.00	28.00	45.00	85.00
1791	—	12.50	22.50	35.00	65.00

C# 2 2 HELLER

Copper **Ruler:** Wilhelm V **Obverse:** Crowned monogram **Reverse:** Value, date

Date	Mintage	F	VF	XF	Unc
1766	—	15.00	25.00	40.00	80.00
1791	—	12.50	22.00	32.50	60.00

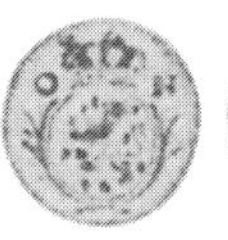

C# 3 KREUZER

Billon **Ruler:** Wilhelm V **Obverse:** Crowned lion shield between branches divides O - N **Reverse:** Value, date **Note:** Convention Kreuzer.

Date	Mintage	VG	F	VF	XF	Unc
1766 IIE	—	8.00	15.00	25.00	45.00	—

C# 4 5 KREUZER

Billon **Ruler:** Wilhelm V **Obverse:** Crowned arms within branches **Reverse:** Date within square, value around rim **Note:** Convention 5 Kreuzer.

Date	Mintage	F	VF	XF	Unc
1766 IIE	—	70.00	120	185	—

NASSAU-WEILBURG

Duchy

RULERS

Carl August, 1719-53
Friedrich Wilhelm II, 1788-1816

MINT OFFICIALS' INITIALS

Initials	Date	Name
C, EC, EDC	1749-52	Ernst Dietrich Croll
FS, S	1749-54	Friedrich Siegmund Schaefer, die-cutter
ICS	1749-50	Johann Christoph Schepp, die-cutter
VDK	1749-54	Von der Koers, die-cutter and warden

STANDARD COINAGE

C# 15 1/4 KREUZER

Copper **Ruler:** Karl August **Obverse:** Crowned CA monogram **Reverse:** Value, date

Date	Mintage	VG	F	VF	XF	Unc
1752	—	10.00	20.00	35.00	60.00	—

C# 16 1/2 KREUZER

Copper **Ruler:** Karl August **Obverse:** Crowned CA monogram **Reverse:** Value, date

Date	Mintage	VG	F	VF	XF	Unc
1752	—	10.00	17.50	30.00	50.00	—

C# 18 KREUZER

Billon **Ruler:** Karl August **Obverse:** Lion shield in baroque frame **Reverse:** Value in baroque frame, date

Date	Mintage	VG	F	VF	XF	Unc
1749 C	—	8.00	15.00	30.00	50.00	—
1749 S	—	8.00	15.00	30.00	50.00	—
1750 S	—	8.00	15.00	30.00	50.00	—
1751 S	—	10.00	20.00	35.00	60.00	—

C# 20 4 KREUZER

Billon **Ruler:** Karl August **Obverse:** 3 Oval shields within crowned frame **Reverse:** Value within cartouche, date below

Date	Mintage	VG	F	VF	XF	Unc
1749 EC	—	15.00	25.00	35.00	80.00	—
1749 EDC	—	15.00	25.00	35.00	80.00	—
1749 FS	—	15.00	25.00	35.00	80.00	—
1750 FS	—	15.00	25.00	35.00	80.00	—
1751 FS	—	15.00	25.00	35.00	80.00	—

C# 22 12 KREUZER

Billon **Ruler:** Karl August **Obverse:** 3 Oval shields within crowned frame **Reverse:** Value within cartouche, date below

Date	Mintage	VG	F	VF	XF	Unc
1749 EDC	—	50.00	100	160	225	—
1749 FS	—	50.00	100	160	225	—
1750 FS	—	50.00	100	160	225	—
1751 FS	—	50.00	100	160	225	—

C# 24 2/3 THALER

Billon **Ruler:** Friedrich Wilhelm **Obverse:** Crowned eight-fold arms in baroque frame, supported by two lions, date **Reverse:** Mining scene, with rays from eye of God, value below **Note:** Mining 2/3 Thaler.

Date	Mintage	VG	F	VF	XF	Unc
1750 ICS-EC	—	110	280	550	800	1,250

C# 24.5 2/3 THALER

Billon **Ruler:** Karl August **Obverse:** Bust right, titles around **Reverse:** Crowned eight-fold arms in baroque frame, supported by two lions and set on pedestal

Date	Mintage	VG	F	VF	XF	Unc
1752 VDK-FS	—	200	525	800	1,200	1,750

C# 25 THALER

Silver **Ruler:** Karl August **Obverse:** Draped bust right **Obv. Legend:** CAR•AUG•D:G•-PR•NASS•WEILB: **Reverse:** Crowned 8-fold arms in baroque frame with lion supporters **Rev. Legend:** EX•VISCERIBUS•FODINÆ•MEHLBAC•1752, FEIN SILBER below **Note:** Mining Thaler. Dav. #2471.

Date	Mintage	VG	F	VF	XF	Unc
1752 VDK-FS	—	225	600	1,200	2,000	2,800

TRADE COINAGE

Separate coinage of Nassau-Weilburg

C# 28 10 GULDEN

Gold **Ruler:** Karl August **Obverse:** Bust right **Reverse:** Value: X in oval, surrounded by four crowned CA monograms, MONET. AUREA, date below

Date	Mintage	VG	F	VF	XF	Unc
1751 EC Rare	—	—	—	—	—	—

C# 26 DUCAT

3.5000 g., 0.9860 Gold 0.1109 oz. AGW **Ruler:** Karl August **Obverse:** Draped bust right **Reverse:** Crowned baroque shield of arms

Date	Mintage	VG	F	VF	XF	Unc
1750 S-EC	—	700	1,650	3,500	6,000	—

C# 27 DUCAT

3.5000 g., 0.9860 Gold 0.1109 oz. AGW **Ruler:** Karl August **Obverse:** Karl August standing facing **Reverse:** Crowned baroque shield of arms

Date	Mintage	VG	F	VF	XF	Unc
1750 EC	—	600	1,250	3,000	5,500	—

PATTERNS

Including off metal strikes

KM#	Date	Mintage	Identification	Mkt Val
Pn1	1750	—	Ducat. Silver. C#27	800

NURNBERG

Nürnberg, (Nuremberg) in Franconia, was made a Free City in 1219. In that same year an Imperial mint was established there and continued throughout the rest of the century. The mint right was obtained in 1376 and again in 1422. City coins were struck from ca.1390 to 1806 when the city was made part of Bavaria. It was briefly occupied by Swedish forces until the death of Gustav II Adolfus in 1632.

MINT OFFIIALS' INITIALS

Initials	Date	Name
CGL	1746-55	Carl Gottleib Lauffer
F, I.M.F.	1755-64	Johann Martin Forster
G.N.R., R.	1764-93	Georg Nikolaus Riedner
H, GH	1679-1712	George Hautsch (1745), die-cutter
I.L.OE., OEXELEIN		Johann Leonhard Oexelein, die-cutter
P.P.W.	1760-96	Johann Peter Werner, die-cutter
K	1779-?	Georg Knoll, warden
K.R.		Georg Knoll and Riedner
LOOS, L, Lf	1742-62	Carl Friedrich Loos, die-cutter
	Ca.1745-76	Georg Friedrich Loos, die-cutter
M	1755-60	Georg Michael Mann, warden
PHM	(1719)	Philipp Heinrich Muller, die-cutter
PPW	(1771)	Peter Paul Werner, die-cutter
R	1794-?	Adam Nikalaus Riedner
S.F.	1760-64	Scholz and Forster
S.R.	1764-70	Scholz and Riedner
S.S.	1760-79	Sigmund Scholz, warden
	1677-1716	Georg Friedrich Nürnberger
(g) and/or	1716-46	Paul Gottlieb Nürnberger
PGN – cross		

CITY ARMS

Divided vertically, eagle (or half eagle) on left, six diagonal bars downward to right on right side.

Paschal Lamb

The paschal lamb, Lamb of God or Agnes Dei was used in the gold Ducat series. It appears standing on a globe holding a banner with the word "PAX" (peace).

FREE CITY

REGULAR COINAGE

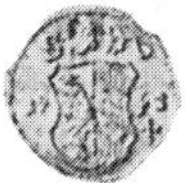

KM# 193a PFENNIG

Copper **Obverse:** City arms divide date **Note:** Uniface. Varieties exist.

Date	Mintage	VG	F	VF	XF	Unc
1701 (f)	—	5.00	10.00	18.00	35.00	—
1702 (f)	—	5.00	10.00	18.00	35.00	—

Date	Mintage	VG	F	VF	XF	Unc
1703 (f)	—	5.00	10.00	18.00	35.00	—
1704 (f)	—	5.00	10.00	18.00	35.00	—
1705 (f)	—	5.00	10.00	18.00	35.00	—
1706 (f)	—	5.00	10.00	18.00	35.00	—
1707 (f)	—	5.00	10.00	18.00	35.00	—
1708 (f)	—	5.00	10.00	18.00	35.00	—
1709 (f)	—	5.00	10.00	18.00	35.00	—
1710 (f)	—	5.00	10.00	18.00	35.00	—
1711 (f)	—	5.00	10.00	18.00	35.00	—
1712 (f)	—	5.00	10.00	18.00	35.00	—
1713 (f)	—	5.00	10.00	18.00	35.00	—
1714 (f)	—	5.00	10.00	18.00	35.00	—
1715 (f)	—	5.00	10.00	18.00	35.00	—
1716 (f)	—	5.00	10.00	18.00	35.00	—
1717 (g)	—	5.00	10.00	18.00	35.00	—
1718 (g)	—	5.00	10.00	18.00	35.00	—
1719 (g)	—	5.00	10.00	18.00	35.00	—
1720 (g)	—	5.00	10.00	18.00	35.00	—
1721 (g)	—	5.00	10.00	18.00	35.00	—
1722 (g)	—	5.00	10.00	18.00	35.00	—
1723 (g)	—	5.00	10.00	18.00	35.00	—
1724 (g)	—	5.00	10.00	18.00	35.00	—
1725 (g)	—	5.00	10.00	18.00	35.00	—
1726 (g)	—	5.00	10.00	18.00	35.00	—
1727 (g)	—	5.00	10.00	18.00	35.00	—
1728 (g)	—	5.00	10.00	18.00	35.00	—
1729 (g)	—	5.00	10.00	18.00	35.00	—
1730 (g)	—	5.00	10.00	18.00	35.00	—
1731 (g)	—	5.00	10.00	18.00	35.00	—
1732 (g)	—	5.00	10.00	18.00	35.00	—
1733 (g)	—	5.00	10.00	18.00	35.00	—
1734 (g)	—	5.00	10.00	18.00	35.00	—
1735 (g)	—	5.00	10.00	18.00	35.00	—
1736 (g)	—	5.00	10.00	18.00	35.00	—
1737 (g)	—	5.00	10.00	18.00	35.00	—
1738 (g)	—	5.00	10.00	18.00	35.00	—
1739 (g)	—	5.00	10.00	18.00	35.00	—
1740 (g)	—	5.00	10.00	18.00	35.00	—
1741 (g)	—	5.00	10.00	18.00	35.00	—
1742 (g)	—	5.00	10.00	18.00	35.00	—
1743 (g)	—	5.00	10.00	18.00	35.00	—
1744 (g)	—	5.00	10.00	18.00	35.00	—
1745 (g)	—	5.00	10.00	18.00	35.00	—
1746 (g)	—	5.00	10.00	18.00	35.00	—
1747	—	5.00	10.00	18.00	35.00	—
1748	—	5.00	10.00	18.00	35.00	—
1749	—	5.00	10.00	18.00	35.00	—
1750	—	5.00	10.00	18.00	35.00	—
1751	—	5.00	10.00	18.00	35.00	—
1752	—	5.00	10.00	18.00	35.00	—
1753	—	5.00	10.00	18.00	35.00	—

KM# 315 PFENNIG

Billon **Obverse:** Arms divide date, value above **Reverse:** Crowned imperial eagle **Note:** Uniface.

Date	Mintage	VG	F	VF	XF	Unc
1754	—	2.00	4.00	6.00	12.00	—
1755	—	2.00	4.00	6.00	12.00	—
1756	—	2.00	4.00	6.00	12.00	—
1757	—	2.00	4.00	6.00	12.00	—
1758	—	2.00	4.00	6.00	12.00	—
1759	—	2.00	4.00	6.00	12.00	—
1760	—	2.00	4.00	6.00	12.00	—
1761	—	2.00	4.00	6.00	12.00	—
1762	—	2.00	4.00	6.00	12.00	—
1763	—	2.00	4.00	6.00	12.00	—
1764	—	2.00	4.00	6.00	12.00	—
1765	—	2.00	4.00	6.00	12.00	—
1766	—	2.00	4.00	6.00	12.00	—
1767	—	2.00	4.00	6.00	12.00	—
1768	—	2.00	4.00	6.00	12.00	—
1769	—	2.00	4.00	6.00	12.00	—
1770	—	2.00	4.00	6.00	12.00	—
1771	—	2.00	4.00	6.00	12.00	—
1772	—	2.00	4.00	6.00	12.00	—
1773	—	2.00	4.00	6.00	12.00	—
1775	—	2.00	4.00	6.00	12.00	—
1776	—	2.00	4.00	6.00	12.00	—
1777	—	2.00	4.00	6.00	12.00	—
1778	—	2.00	4.00	6.00	12.00	—
1779	—	2.00	4.00	6.00	12.00	—
1780	—	2.00	4.00	6.00	12.00	—
1781	—	2.00	4.00	6.00	12.00	—
1782	—	2.00	4.00	6.00	12.00	—
1783	—	2.00	4.00	6.00	12.00	—
1784	—	2.00	4.00	6.00	12.00	—
1785	—	2.00	4.00	6.00	12.00	—
1786	—	2.00	4.00	6.00	12.00	—
1787	—	2.00	4.00	6.00	12.00	—
1790	—	2.00	4.00	6.00	12.00	—

KM# 318 PFENNIG

Billon **Obverse:** Crowned imperial eagle

Date	Mintage	VG	F	VF	XF	Unc
1756	—	2.00	4.00	7.00	15.00	—
1757	—	2.00	4.00	7.00	15.00	—
1758	—	2.00	4.00	7.00	15.00	—
1759	—	2.00	4.00	7.00	15.00	—
1767	—	2.00	4.00	7.00	15.00	—
1768	—	2.00	4.00	7.00	15.00	—
1769	—	2.00	4.00	7.00	15.00	—
1770	—	2.00	4.00	7.00	15.00	—
1771	—	2.00	4.00	7.00	15.00	—
1772	—	2.00	4.00	7.00	15.00	—
1773	—	2.00	4.00	7.00	15.00	—
1774	—	2.00	4.00	7.00	15.00	—
1775	—	2.00	4.00	7.00	15.00	—
1776	—	2.00	4.00	7.00	15.00	—
1777	—	2.00	4.00	7.00	15.00	—
1778	—	2.00	4.00	7.00	15.00	—
1779	—	2.00	4.00	7.00	15.00	—
1780	—	2.00	4.00	7.00	15.00	—

KM# 366 PFENNIG

Billon **Obverse:** Arms with value and date above **Reverse:** Crowned double-headed imperial eagle

Date	Mintage	VG	F	VF	XF	Unc
1772	—	2.00	4.00	7.00	15.00	—
1778	—	2.00	4.00	7.00	15.00	—
1779	—	2.00	4.00	7.00	15.00	—
1781	—	2.00	4.00	7.00	15.00	—
1782	—	2.00	4.00	7.00	15.00	—
1784	—	2.00	4.00	7.00	15.00	—
1789	—	2.00	4.00	7.00	15.00	—

KM# 376 PFENNIG

Billon **Obverse:** Arms draped with garlands, value and date above **Note:** Uniface

Date	Mintage	VG	F	VF	XF	Unc
1788	—	2.00	4.00	7.00	15.00	—
1789	—	2.00	4.00	7.00	15.00	—

KM# 377 PFENNIG

Billon **Obverse:** Oval arms with value and date above

Date	Mintage	VG	F	VF	XF	Unc
1789	—	2.00	4.00	7.00	15.00	—
1790	—	2.00	4.00	7.00	15.00	—
1791	—	2.00	4.00	7.00	15.00	—
1792	—	2.00	4.00	7.00	15.00	—
1793	—	2.00	4.00	7.00	15.00	—
1797	—	2.00	4.00	7.00	15.00	—

KM# 381 PFENNIG

Billon **Obverse:** Two shields of arms, value and date above

Date	Mintage	VG	F	VF	XF	Unc
1793	—	2.00	4.00	7.00	15.00	—
1794	—	2.00	4.00	7.00	15.00	—

KM# 383 PFENNIG

Billon **Obverse:** Two shields of arms, date above, value below

Date	Mintage	VG	F	VF	XF	Unc
1795	—	2.00	4.00	7.00	15.00	—

KM# 384 PFENNIG

Billon **Obverse:** Three shields of arms divide date

Date	Mintage	VG	F	VF	XF	Unc
1795	—	2.00	4.00	7.00	15.00	—
1796	—	2.00	4.00	7.00	15.00	—
1797	—	2.00	4.00	7.00	15.00	—

KM# 386 PFENNIG

Billon **Obverse:** Arms with mural crown above divides date

Date	Mintage	VG	F	VF	XF	Unc
1796	—	2.00	4.00	7.00	15.00	—

KM# 393 PFENNIG

Billon **Obverse:** Arms with value and date above

Date	Mintage	VG	F	VF	XF	Unc
1798	—	2.00	4.00	7.00	15.00	—
1799	—	2.00	4.00	7.00	15.00	—

KM# 397 PFENNIG

Billon **Obverse:** State shield between branches above denomination and date **Note:** Uniface.

Date	Mintage	F	VF	XF	Unc
1799	—	3.00	6.00	15.00	25.00
1806	—	3.00	6.00	15.00	25.00

KM# 340 4 PFENNIG

Billon **Obverse:** Eagle on pointed shield **Reverse:** City arms within square, date divided below

Date	Mintage	VG	F	VF	XF	Unc
1764	—	10.00	20.00	35.00	75.00	—
1765	—	10.00	20.00	35.00	75.00	—
1766	—	10.00	20.00	35.00	75.00	—
1774	—	10.00	20.00	35.00	75.00	—
1776	—	10.00	20.00	35.00	75.00	—
1783	—	10.00	20.00	35.00	75.00	—

KM# 215 KREUZER (4 Pfennig)

Silver **Obverse:** Double cross, date in margin, mint mark (++) at top **Reverse:** Two adjacent arms, angel's head above, N below **Note:** Varieties exist.

Date	Mintage	VG	F	VF	XF	Unc
1700 (f)	—	7.00	15.00	25.00	45.00	—
1702 (f)	—	7.00	15.00	25.00	45.00	—
1703 (f)	—	7.00	15.00	25.00	45.00	—
1705 (f)	—	7.00	15.00	25.00	45.00	—
1709 (f)	—	7.00	15.00	25.00	45.00	—
1726 (g)	—	7.00	15.00	25.00	45.00	—
1732 (g)	—	7.00	15.00	25.00	45.00	—

KM# 322.1 KREUZER (4 Pfennig)

Silver **Obverse:** Two adjacent oval arms, 1-K above, F below **Reverse:** Double cross, date in margin, mintmark at top

Date	Mintage	VG	F	VF	XF	Unc
1758 F	—	32.00	65.00	120	175	—
1759 F	—	32.00	65.00	120	175	—

KM# 322.2 KREUZER (4 Pfennig)

Silver **Obverse:** Double cross, date in margin, mintmark at top **Reverse:** Arms in ornate cartouche

Date	Mintage	VG	F	VF	XF	Unc
1758	—	32.00	65.00	120	175	—

KM# 323 KREUZER (4 Pfennig)

Silver **Obverse:** Bust of Franz I to right **Reverse:** Two adjacent arms, date in margin

Date	Mintage	VG	F	VF	XF	Unc
1758	—	20.00	50.00	100	160	—

KM# 324 KREUZER (4 Pfennig)

Silver **Obverse:** Draped bust right **Reverse:** Arms ornately shaped

Date	Mintage	VG	F	VF	XF	Unc
1758 F	—	20.00	50.00	100	160	—

KM# 325 KREUZER (4 Pfennig)

Silver **Obverse:** Double cross, date in margin **Reverse:** Two adjacent arms

Date	Mintage	VG	F	VF	XF	Unc
1759 F	—	32.00	65.00	120	175	—

KM# 336 KREUZER (4 Pfennig)

Billon **Obverse:** Mural crown above arms in branches, F in pedestal below **Reverse:** Value and date in inner circle

Date	Mintage	VG	F	VF	XF	Unc
1763 F	—	5.00	10.00	18.00	38.00	—

KM# 367 KREUZER (4 Pfennig)

Billon **Obverse:** 1 (N) KR below **Reverse:** Garland above 3 ornate shields

Date	Mintage	VG	F	VF	XF	Unc
1773	—	3.50	6.00	10.00	25.00	—

KM# 375 KREUZER (4 Pfennig)
Billon **Obverse:** Two shields **Reverse:** Value above date

Date	Mintage	VG	F	VF	XF	Unc
1786	—	3.00	6.00	10.00	25.00	—

KM# 387 KREUZER (4 Pfennig)
Billon **Obverse:** Larger city view **Reverse:** Garland above 3 ornate shields

Date	Mintage	VG	F	VF	XF	Unc
1796	—	3.50	6.00	10.00	25.00	—

KM# 388 KREUZER (4 Pfennig)
Billon **Obverse:** Divided shield **Reverse:** Garland above value, date below

Date	Mintage	VG	F	VF	XF	Unc
1796	—	3.00	6.00	10.00	25.00	—
1797	—	3.00	6.00	10.00	25.00	—
1798	—	3.00	6.00	10.00	25.00	—
1799	—	3.00	6.00	10.00	25.00	—

KM# 389 KREUZER (4 Pfennig)
Billon **Obverse:** Arms with mural crown and garlands **Reverse:** Garlands surround value, date above

Date	Mintage	VG	F	VF	XF	Unc
1796	—	3.50	6.00	10.00	25.00	—

KM# 390 KREUZER (4 Pfennig)
Billon **Obverse:** Seated female with shield **Reverse:** Value within garland, date divided above

Date	Mintage	VG	F	VF	XF	Unc
1797	—	3.00	6.00	10.00	25.00	—

KM# 391 KREUZER (4 Pfennig)
Billon **Obverse:** Oval arms in drapery

Date	Mintage	VG	F	VF	XF	Unc
1797	—	4.00	6.50	10.00	25.00	—

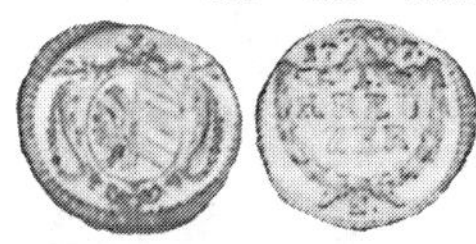

KM# 392 KREUZER (4 Pfennig)
Billon **Obverse:** Oval arms in branches **Reverse:** Value and date above sprays, N below

Date	Mintage	VG	F	VF	XF	Unc
1797	—	3.50	6.00	10.00	25.00	—

KM# 394 KREUZER (4 Pfennig)
Billon **Obverse:** Oval arms in garlands and sprays **Reverse:** Value and date in cartouche

Date	Mintage	VG	F	VF	XF	Unc
1798	—	3.50	6.00	10.00	25.00	—

KM# 395 KREUZER (4 Pfennig)
Billon **Reverse:** Garlands above value and date

Date	Mintage	VG	F	VF	XF	Unc
1798	—	3.50	6.00	10.00	25.00	—
1799	—	3.50	6.00	10.00	25.00	—

KM# 396 KREUZER (4 Pfennig)
Billon **Obverse:** Female figure holding arms at right, beside altar left

Date	Mintage	VG	F	VF	XF	Unc
1798	—	4.00	6.50	10.00	25.00	—

KM# 398 KREUZER (4 Pfennig)
Billon **Obverse:** Four-line inscription in wreath **Obv. Inscription:** •I•/ NÜRNB/ KREÜ/ ZER **Reverse:** Father Time seated, reaching out to circle with date in upper left

Date	Mintage	VG	F	VF	XF	Unc
1799	—	2.50	4.00	9.00	25.00	—

KM# 330 2-1/2 KREUZER
Billon **Obverse:** Crowned imperial eagle **Obv. Legend:** FRANCISCUS... **Reverse:** Square arms, date below **Note:** Convention 2-1/2 Kreuzer.

Date	Mintage	VG	F	VF	XF	Unc
1760 R	—	3.00	8.00	15.00	32.00	—
1763 R	—	3.00	8.00	15.00	32.00	—
1764 R	—	3.00	8.00	15.00	32.00	—

KM# 352 2-1/2 KREUZER
Billon **Obv. Legend:** JOSEPHUS...

Date	Mintage	VG	F	VF	XF	Unc
1766 R	—	4.00	9.00	16.00	35.00	—
1767 R	—	4.00	9.00	16.00	35.00	—
1776 R	—	4.00	9.00	16.00	35.00	—

KM# 369 2-1/2 KREUZER
Billon **Obverse:** Crowned double-headed eagle with shield on breast **Reverse:** City arms

Date	Mintage	VG	F	VF	XF	Unc
1774 R	—	3.00	8.00	14.00	30.00	—
1778 R	—	3.00	8.00	14.00	30.00	—
1779 R	—	3.00	8.00	14.00	30.00	—

KM# 265 4 KREUZER (Batzen)
Silver **Obverse:** Crowned imperial eagle, Nurnberg arms on breast, titles of Leopold I **Reverse:** Nurnberg arms divide date, value: K/IIII above

Date	Mintage	VG	F	VF	XF	Unc
1704 GFN	—	12.00	25.00	50.00	90.00	—

KM# 310 4 KREUZER (Batzen)
Silver **Obverse:** Value above city arms **Reverse:** Titles of Franz I **Note:** Varieties exist.

Date	Mintage	VG	F	VF	XF	Unc
1748 CGL	—	9.00	16.00	30.00	55.00	—
1749 CGL	—	9.00	16.00	30.00	55.00	—
1759 F	—	9.00	16.00	30.00	55.00	—

KM# 317 4 KREUZER (Batzen)
Silver **Obverse:** Oval arms in cartouche, value: K./IIII divides date **Reverse:** Value above city arms **Note:** Varieties exist.

Date	Mintage	VG	F	VF	XF	Unc
1755 IMF	—	10.00	20.00	40.00	65.00	—
1756 IMF	—	10.00	20.00	40.00	65.00	—
1758 IMF	—	10.00	20.00	40.00	65.00	—

KM# 337 5 KREUZER
Billon **Obverse:** Value above city arms, date divided below **Reverse:** Crowned double-headed eagle with shield on breast **Rev. Legend:** FRANCISCUS...

Date	Mintage	VG	F	VF	XF	Unc
1763 F	—	12.00	25.00	40.00	80.00	—
1764 R	—	12.00	25.00	40.00	80.00	—
1765 R	—	12.00	25.00	40.00	80.00	—

KM# 353 5 KREUZER
Billon **Obverse:** Crowned double-headed eagle with shield on breast **Obv. Legend:** JOSEPHUS... **Reverse:** Value above city arms, date divided below

Date	Mintage	VG	F	VF	XF	Unc
1766 R	—	15.00	30.00	55.00	90.00	—

KM# 201 6 KREUZER
Silver **Obverse:** Shield of city arms divides date, value K/VI in two lines above **Obv. Legend:** +MON:NOV:ARGENT:REIP: NORIMBERG **Reverse:** Crowned imperial eagle with small shield of Nürnberg arms on breast **Rev. Legend:** LEOPOLDVS: D:G: ROM:IMPER:S:A. **Note:** Varieties exist.

Date	Mintage	VG	F	VF	XF	Unc
1680 (f)	—	15.00	30.00	50.00	90.00	—
1704 GFN	—	15.00	30.00	50.00	90.00	—

KM# 298 6 KREUZER
Silver **Obverse:** Titles of Karl VI

Date	Mintage	VG	F	VF	XF	Unc
1736 PGN	—	55.00	100	200	325	—

KM# 266 8 KREUZER
Silver **Obverse:** Crowned imperial eagle, Nurnberg arms on breast, titles of Leopold I **Reverse:** Nurnberg arms divide date, value: K./IIII above

Date	Mintage	VG	F	VF	XF	Unc
1704 GFN	—	15.00	30.00	60.00	100	—

KM# 299 8 KREUZER
Silver **Obverse:** Titles of Karl VI **Reverse:** City arms divide date, value above

Date	Mintage	VG	F	VF	XF	Unc
1736 PGN	—	45.00	80.00	150	300	—

KM# 319 10 KREUZER (1/12 Thaler)
Silver **Obverse:** Bust of Franz I right in laurel wreath **Reverse:** Crowned N arms on pedestal, value: 10 on front panel, date below **Note:** Varieties exist.

Date	Mintage	VG	F	VF	XF	Unc
1756 MF	—	32.00	70.00	140	225	—
1759 MF	—	32.00	70.00	140	225	—
1760 SF	—	32.00	70.00	140	225	—

KM# 338 10 KREUZER (1/12 Thaler)
Silver **Obverse:** Crowned imperial eagle **Obv. Legend:** FRANCISCUS... **Reverse:** Crowned arms on pedestal between branches **Note:** Convention 10 Kreuzer.

Date	Mintage	VG	F	VF	XF	Unc
1763 SF	—	65.00	125	175	300	—
1764 SF	—	65.00	125	175	300	—

KM# 354 10 KREUZER (1/12 Thaler)
Silver **Obv. Legend:** JOSEPHUS...

Date	Mintage	VG	F	VF	XF	Unc
1766 SR	—	65.00	125	175	300	—

KM# 267 12 KREUZER (Dreibatzner)
Silver **Obverse:** Nurnberg arms divide date, value: K./XII above **Reverse:** Crowned imperial eagle, Nurnberg arms on breast, titles of Leopold I

Date	Mintage	VG	F	VF	XF	Unc
1704 GFN	—	22.00	50.00	85.00	145	—

KM# 295 12 KREUZER (Dreibatzner)
Silver **Obverse:** Titles of Karl VI **Reverse:** City arms divide date, value above

Date	Mintage	VG	F	VF	XF	Unc
1732 PGN	—	30.00	60.00	120	225	—
1736 PGN	—	30.00	60.00	120	225	—

KM# 320 20 KREUZER

Silver **Obverse:** Bust right within laurel branch wreath **Reverse:** Crowned city arms within baroque frame on pedestal with value, date below **Note:** Convention 20 Kreuzer.

Date	Mintage	VG	F	VF	XF	Unc
1753 L/MF	—	8.00	18.00	35.00	65.00	—
1759 L/MF	—	8.00	18.00	35.00	65.00	—
1760 OE/SF	—	10.00	20.00	35.00	65.00	—
1762 OE/SF	—	10.00	20.00	35.00	65.00	—
1763 OE/SF	—	10.00	20.00	35.00	65.00	—
1764 L/SR	—	10.00	20.00	35.00	65.00	—
1764 OE/SR	—	10.00	20.00	35.00	65.00	—
1765 OE/SR	—	10.00	20.00	35.00	65.00	—

KM# 334 20 KREUZER

Silver **Obverse:** Crowned shield on eagles breast, value within pedestal **Reverse:** Laureate head right within branches

Date	Mintage	VG	F	VF	XF	Unc
1761 SF	—	15.00	30.00	50.00	100	—

KM# 341.1 20 KREUZER

Silver **Obverse:** City arms within baroque frame **Reverse:** Crowned shield on eagle's breast **Rev. Legend:** FRANCISCVS...

Date	Mintage	VG	F	VF	XF	Unc
1764 SR	—	12.00	25.00	40.00	70.00	—
1765 SR	—	12.00	25.00	40.00	70.00	—

KM# 341.2 20 KREUZER

Silver **Obverse:** Crowned shield on eagle's breast **Reverse:** Crowned arms above pedestal with value, date below

Date	Mintage	VG	F	VF	XF	Unc
1765 SR	—	12.00	25.00	40.00	70.00	—

KM# 343 20 KREUZER

Silver **Obverse:** Bust of Josef right in wreath **Reverse:** Crowned arms on pedestal between branches, value and date below

Date	Mintage	VG	F	VF	XF	Unc
1765 SR	—	14.00	28.00	45.00	80.00	—

KM# 344 20 KREUZER

Silver **Obverse:** Crowned shield within Order chain on eagle's breast **Obv. Legend:** JOSEPHUS... **Reverse:** City arms atop pedestal with value, date below

Date	Mintage	VG	F	VF	XF	Unc
1765 SR	—	12.00	25.00	40.00	70.00	—

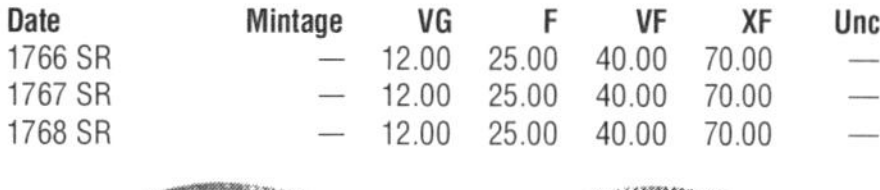

Date	Mintage	VG	F	VF	XF	Unc
1766 SR	—	12.00	25.00	40.00	70.00	—
1767 SR	—	12.00	25.00	40.00	70.00	—
1768 SR	—	12.00	25.00	40.00	70.00	—

KM# 360 20 KREUZER

Silver **Obverse:** Three shields, date divided at top, value below **Reverse:** Crowned shield within Order chain on eagle's breast

Date	Mintage	F	VF	XF	Unc
1769 SR	—	20.00	40.00	85.00	200

KM# 365 20 KREUZER

Silver **Obverse:** Crowned imperial eagle in diamond **Reverse:** Crowned arms, date and value in diamond

Date	Mintage	F	VF	XF	Unc
1770 SR	—	15.00	35.00	70.00	175
1772 SR	—	15.00	35.00	70.00	175
1774 SR	—	15.00	35.00	70.00	175
1776 SR	—	15.00	35.00	70.00	175

KM# 370 20 KREUZER

Silver **Obverse:** City arms within baroque frame **Reverse:** Crowned shield within Order chain on eagle's breast

Date	Mintage	F	VF	XF	Unc
1774 SR	—	25.00	50.00	100	250

KM# 345 30 KREUZER (1/2 Gulden)

Silver **Obverse:** Crowned arms within Order chain on eagle's breast **Reverse:** Crowned city arms within baroque frame **Note:** Convention 30 Kreuzer

Date	Mintage	F	VF	XF	Unc
1765 SR	—	50.00	75.00	125	275

KM# 332 1/2 THALER

Silver **Obverse:** River god holding arms **Reverse:** Crowned shield within Order chain on eagle's breast **Note:** Convention 1/2 Thaler.

Date	Mintage	F	VF	XF	Unc
1760 SF/OE	—	85.00	175	250	425

KM# 355 1/2 THALER

Silver **Obverse:** Crowned city arms within baroque frame **Reverse:** Crowned imperial double-headed eagle with orb on breast

Date	Mintage	F	VF	XF	Unc
1766 SR	—	65.00	125	175	350
1768 SR	—	65.00	125	175	350

KM# 382 THALER

Silver **Obverse:** City view similar to KM#350 **Reverse:** Bust of Franz II right

Date	Mintage	F	VF	XF	Unc
1794 IPW/KR	—	—	—	—	—

KM# 268 THALER

Silver **Obverse:** Standing female with two-branch palm frond and three shields **Obv. Legend:** MONETA NOVA REIPVB • NORIBERGENSIS •, in exergue; MDCCVI•/GFN• **Reverse:** Imperial eagle, titles of Josef **Rev. Legend:** IOSEPHVS • D • G • ROM • IMP • S • A • GER • H • B • R • AR • A • **Note:** Dav. #2474.

Date	Mintage	F	VF	XF	Unc
1706 GFN	—	950	1,750	3,000	5,000

KM# 275 THALER

Silver **Obverse:** Eagle with two shields of arms above city view **Obv. Legend:** SVB VMBRA - ALARVM TVARVM, in exergue; MONETA REIP•/NORIMB • 1711 **Reverse:** Armored, laureate bust of Karl VI right **Rev. Legend:** CAROLVS SI • D • G • - ROM • IMP • SEMP • AVG, GFN below **Note:** Dav. #2475.

Date	Mintage	F	VF	XF	Unc
1711 GFN	—	375	750	1,350	2,250

KM# 285 THALER

Silver **Obverse:** Eagle wearing German crown above city view, NORIMERGA below, date in chronogram **Obv. Legend:** AVGVSTO DOMINO TVTA AC SECVRA PARENTE EST, below; NORIMBERGA * **Reverse:** Laureate bust of Karl VI right **Rev. Legend:** CAROLVS VI. D. G. ROM. IMP. SEMP. AVG. **Note:** Dav. #2476.

Date	Mintage	F	VF	XF	Unc
ND(1721) PGN	—	300	550	950	1,750

KM# 305 THALER

Silver **Obverse:** City view **Obv. Legend:** TVTA HIS - AVSPICIIS, NORIMBERGA/1742 below **Reverse:** Armored bust of Karl VI right **Rev. Legend:** CAROLVS VII • - D • G • ROM • IMP • S • A • **Note:** Dav. #2482.

Date	Mintage	F	VF	XF	Unc
1742 PGN	—	325	600	1,100	1,900

KM# 321 THALER

Silver **Obverse:** Imperial eagle above two shields dividing date **Obv. Legend:** MONETA NOVA - REIPVBL • NORIM • BERGENSIS •, below; X EINE FEINE/MARK **Reverse:** Armored, laureate bust of Franz right **Rev. Legend:** FRANCISCUS • D: G - ROM • IMO • SEMP • AVG • **Note:** Dav. #2485.

Date	Mintage	F	VF	XF	Unc
1757 L-MF	—	100	200	300	700
1758 L-MF	—	100	200	300	700
1759 OEXLEIN-MF	—	100	200	300	700
1760 OEXLEIN-SF	—	100	200	300	700

KM# 296 THALER

Silver **Subject:** Artillery Shooting of 1733 **Obverse:** Six shields of arms on sprays around central shield of arms **Reverse:** Roman numeral date in exergue **Note:** Dav. #2480.

Date	Mintage	F	VF	XF	Unc
1733 PPW	—	950	1,750	3,000	5,000

KM# 307 THALER

Silver **Obverse:** City view **Obv. Legend:** TVTA HIS - AVSPICIIS, below; NORIMBERGA **Reverse:** Armored, laureate bust of Franz right **Rev. Legend:** FRANCIVCVS D •- G • ROM • IMP • SEMP • Avg • **Note:** Species Thaler. Dav. #2483.

Date	Mintage	F	VF	XF	Unc
1745 PPW	—	250	500	850	1,500

KM# 333 THALER

Silver **Obverse:** Large crowned complex arms within Order chain on eagle's breast **Obv. Legend:** 10 EINE FEINE - MARCK, below; LEGE VINDICE•/S•S•(N)I•M•F• **Reverse:** Armored, laureate bust of Franz right **Rev. Legend:** FRANC • D • G • R • I • S • - A • GE • IER • R • LO • B • M • H • D • **Note:** Dav. #2486.

Date	Mintage	F	VF	XF	Unc
1760 SS-IMF	—	125	200	400	800
1762 SS-IMF	—	125	200	400	800
1763 SS-IMF	—	125	200	400	800

KM# 300 THALER

Silver **Obverse:** Bust of Karl VI right **Obv. Legend:** CAROLVS VI. D. G. - ROM. IMP. SEMP. AVG **Reverse:** City view with NORIMBERGA below **Rev. Legend:** GLORIA IN EXCELSIS DEO ATQUE IN TERRA PAX HOMINIBVS **Note:** Dav. #2481.

Date	Mintage	F	VF	XF	Unc
1736 pgn	—	275	550	950	1,600

KM# 316 THALER

Silver **Obverse:** Armored, laureate bust of Franz right **Obv. Legend:** FRANCISCVS • D • - G • ROM • IMP • SEMP • AVG • **Reverse:** City view **Rev. Legend:** X EINE FEINE MARK, below; NORIMBERGA/1754 **Note:** Convention Thaler. Dav. #2484.

Date	Mintage	F	VF	XF	Unc
1754 PPW-CGL	—	—	—	—	—

KM# 335 THALER

Silver **Obverse:** Crowned, divided shield on eagle's breast **Obv. Legend:** FRANCISCVS • D • G • - ROM • IMP • SEMP • AVG • **Reverse:** Seated Peace with shield at left, laurel branch at right **Rev. Legend:** DA. PACEM DOMINE IN - DIEBVS NOSTRIS • 1761, in exergue; X• EINE FEINE/MARK•/S•F• **Note:** Dav. #2487.

Date	Mintage	F	VF	XF	Unc
1761 SF	—	65.00	125	250	500

KM# 339 THALER

Silver **Subject:** Peace of Hubertusburg **Obverse:** Crowned, divided shield on eagle's breast **Obv. Legend:** FRANCISCVS • D • G • - ROM • IMP • SEMP • AVG • **Reverse:** Peace standing with laurel branch, shield left of altar **Rev. Legend:** BENEDICTVS DOMINVS QVI DEDIT PACEM IN FINIBVS NOSTRIS, in exergue; X • ST • E • F • MARK/1763/ S • F • **Note:** Dav. #2488.

Date	Mintage	F	VF	XF	Unc
1763 SF-ILOE	—	65.00	125	250	500

KM# 342 THALER

Silver **Obverse:** Large crowned complex arms within Order chain on eagle's breast **Obv. Legend:** FRANC • D • G • R • I • S • - A • GE • IER • R • LO • B • M • H • D • **Reverse:** Armored, laureate bust right **Rev. Legend:** 10 • EINE FEINE - MARCK • **Note:** Dav. #2489.

Date	Mintage	F	VF	XF	Unc
1764 SS-GNR	—	125	200	400	800

KM# 347 THALER

Silver **Obverse:** Crowned, divided shield within Order chain on eagle's breast **Obv. Legend:** FRANCISCVS • D • G • - ROM • IMP • SEMP • AVG • **Reverse:** Standing Peace with laurel branch, shield left of altar **Rev. Legend:** DOMINE CONSERVA NOS IN PACE, below; X • ST • E • F • MARK •/1765/ S • S • G • N • R • **Note:** Dav. #2490.

Date	Mintage	F	VF	XF	Unc
1765 SS-GNR	—	75.00	150	275	650

KM# 346 THALER

Silver **Obverse:** Legend at bottom **Obv. Legend:** LEGE-VINDICE **Reverse:** Armored, laureate bust of Franz right **Rev. Legend:** FRANC • D • G • R • I • S • - A • GE • IER • R • LO • B • M • H • D • **Note:** Dav. #2491.

Date	Mintage	F	VF	XF	Unc
1765 SR	—	150	275	600	1,400

KM# 348 THALER

Silver **Obverse:** City arms on breast of eagle **Obv. Legend:** X. EINE FEINE - MARCK • 1765 **Reverse:** Armored, laureate bust of Josef II right **Rev. Legend:** IOSEPHVS II • D • G • - ROM • IMP • SEMP • AVG • **Note:** Dav. #2492.

Date	Mintage	F	VF	XF	Unc
1765 SR	—	150	250	450	1,000

KM# 349 THALER

Silver **Obverse:** Armored, laureate bust of Josef II right **Obv. Legend:** IOSEPHVS II • D • G • - ROM • IMP • SEMP • AVG • **Reverse:** City view **Rev. Legend:** X • EINE FEINE - MARCK • 1765 • **Note:** Dav. #2493.

Date	Mintage	F	VF	XF	Unc
1765 SR	—	150	250	450	1,000

KM# 350 THALER

Silver **Obverse:** City view **Obv. Legend:** X • EINE FEINE - MARCK • date, below; NURNBERG •/ K•R• **Reverse:** Imperial orb on eagle's breast **Rev. Legend:** IOSEPHVS II • D •G • - ROM • IMP • SEMP • AVG • **Note:** Dav. #2494.

Date	Mintage	F	VF	XF	Unc
1765 SR	—	100	175	300	700
1768 SR	—	100	175	300	700
1780 KR	—	100	175	300	700

KM# 351 THALER

Silver **Obverse:** Crowned, divided arms within Order chain on breast of eagle **Obv. Legend:** IOSEPHVS II • D • G • - ROM • IMP • SEMP • AVG • **Reverse:** City view **Rev. Legend:** X • EINE FEINE - MARCK •, below; NURNBERG •/K•R• **Note:** Dav. #2495.

Date	Mintage	F	VF	XF	Unc
1765 SR	—	100	175	300	700
1768 SR	—	100	175	300	700
1779 KR	—	100	200	325	750

KM# 357 THALER

Silver **Obverse:** Imperial orb on eagle's breast **Obv. Legend:** IOSEPHVS II • D • G • - ROM • IMP • SEMP • AVG • **Reverse:** City arms within baroque frame **Rev. Legend:** MONETA REIPVBL • - NORIMBERG • date •, below; X • E • FEINE • M • / S • R • **Note:** Dav. #2497.

Date	Mintage	F	VF	XF	Unc
1766 SR	—	135	250	450	800
1767 SR	—	135	250	450	800

KM# 359 THALER

Silver **Obverse:** Imperial double-headed eagle, orb on breast **Obv. Legend:** IOSEPHVS II • D • G • - ROM • IMP • SEMP • AVG • **Reverse:** Crowned city arms within baroque frame **Rev. Legend:** MONETA REIPVBL • NORIMBERG •, below; * X • E • FEINE • M • **Note:** Dav. #2498.

Date	Mintage	F	VF	XF	Unc
1767 SR	—	100	200	325	750
1768 SR	—	100	200	325	750
1776 SR	—	100	200	325	750

KM# 385 THALER

Silver **Obverse:** Value within Order chain, date above **Obv. Legend:** X/EINE FEINE/MARK., K. - R. below **Reverse:** Armored bust right **Rev. Legend:** FRANZ DER ZWEITE DEUTSCHER KAISER. **Note:** Dav. #2499.

Date	Mintage	F	VF	XF	Unc
1795 KR-IPW	—	500	900	1,500	2,200

KM# 211 2 THALER

Silver **Obverse:** Three cupids with three shields above city view **Obv. Legend:** MONETA NOVA - REIPBV • NORIBERG •, below; NACH DEM ALTEN/SCHROT VND KORN•/G.F.N. **Reverse:** Laureate bust of Leopold right **Rev. Legend:** LEOPOLD D • G • ROM • IMP • - S • A • GER • H • B • REX • ARCHID • AVST • **Note:** Dav. #2472.

Date	Mintage	F	VF	XF	Unc
ND GH-GFN	—	2,000	3,750	6,250	9,000

KM# 212 2 THALER

Silver **Reverse:** Bust of Josef right **Note:** Dav. #2473.

Date	Mintage	F	VF	XF	Unc
ND H-GFN	—	2,000	3,750	6,250	9,000

KM# 213 2 THALER

Silver **Obverse:** Bust of Karl VI right **Obv. Legend:** CAROLVS • VI • D • G • ROM • IMP • - S • A • GERM • H • H • & B • R • AR • A • **Reverse:** Two cherubs with three shields of arms above city view **Rev. Legend:** MONETA NOVA - REIPVB • NORIBERG •, below; NACH DEM ALTEN/SCHROT VND KORN•/ G.F.N. **Note:** Dav. #2478.

Date	Mintage	F	VF	XF	Unc
ND H-GFN	—	2,000	3,750	6,150	8,750

KM# 297 2 THALER

Silver **Obverse:** Six shields of arms on sprays around central shield of arms **Reverse:** Roman numeral date in exergue **Note:** Similar to 1 Thaler, KM#296.

Date	Mintage	VG	F	VF	XF	Unc
1733 PPW	—	2,400	4,000	6,000	8,250	—

KM# 214 3 THALER

Silver **Obverse:** Bust of Karl VI right **Reverse:** Two cherubs with three shields of arms above city view **Note:** Dav. #2477.

Date	Mintage	F	VF	XF	Unc
ND N-GFN Rare	—	—	—	—	—

KM# 207 4 THALER

Silver **Obverse:** Laureaatae bust of Leopold right **Reverse:** Three cupids with three shields above city view **Note:** Similar to 2 Thaler, KM#211.

Date	Mintage	VG	F	VF	XF	Unc
ND GH/GFN	—	—	—	—	—	—

TRADE COINAGE

KM# 368 1/2 DUCAT

1.7500 g., 0.9860 Gold 0.0555 oz. AGW **Obverse:** Three shields of arms **Reverse:** City view, date in exergue

Date	Mintage	F	VF	XF	Unc
1773	—	150	300	600	900

KM# 276 DUCAT

3.5000 g., 0.9860 Gold 0.1109 oz. AGW **Obverse:** Laureate bust of Karl VI right **Reverse:** Three shields of arms, date at bottom

Date	Mintage	VG	F	VF	XF	Unc
1711	—	950	1,850	3,250	5,500	—

KM# 277 DUCAT

3.5000 g., 0.9860 Gold 0.1109 oz. AGW **Obverse:** Altar, date in chronogram **Reverse:** Crowned bust of Karl VI right

Date	Mintage	VG	F	VF	XF	Unc
MDCCVIIIIIII (1712) GFN	—	600	1,300	2,400	3,500	—

KM# 306 DUCAT

3.5000 g., 0.9860 Gold 0.1109 oz. AGW **Obverse:** Crowned bust of Karl VI right **Reverse:** Personification of city holding shield to her left

Date	Mintage	VG	F	VF	XF	Unc
1742	—	1,000	2,250	4,000	6,000	—

KM# 308 DUCAT

3.5000 g., 0.9860 Gold 0.1109 oz. AGW **Obverse:** Standing figure with shield at right **Reverse:** Bust of Franz right

Date	Mintage	VG	F	VF	XF	Unc
1745	—	950	1,850	3,250	5,500	—

KM# 358 DUCAT

3.5000 g., 0.9860 Gold 0.1109 oz. AGW **Obverse:** Bust of Josef II right **Reverse:** Crowned ornate oval arms

Date	Mintage	F	VF	XF	Unc
1766 SR	—	500	1,000	2,000	3,250

KM# 379 DUCAT

3.5000 g., 0.9860 Gold 0.1109 oz. AGW **Obverse:** City view **Reverse:** Bust of Leopold II right

Date	Mintage	F	VF	XF	Unc
1790	—	750	1,500	3,000	5,000

KM# 380 DUCAT

3.5000 g., 0.9860 Gold 0.1109 oz. AGW **Obverse:** Bust of Franz II right **Reverse:** City view

Date	Mintage	F	VF	XF	Unc
ND(1792)	—	750	1,500	3,000	5,000

KM# A381 DUCAT

3.5000 g., 0.9860 Gold 0.1109 oz. AGW **Obverse:** Bust of Franz II right **Reverse:** Female standing with emperor

Date	Mintage	VG	F	VF	XF	Unc
ND(1792)	—	650	1,250	2,750	4,750	—

KM# 262 3 DUCAT

10.5000 g., 0.9860 Gold 0.3328 oz. AGW **Obverse:** Three shields of arms in ribbons **Reverse:** Facing paschal lamb, date in chronogram

Date	Mintage	VG	F	VF	XF	Unc
ND(1703) GFN	—	600	1,000	1,800	2,200	—

KM# 263 4 DUCAT

14.0000 g., 0.9860 Gold 0.4438 oz. AGW **Obverse:** Three shields of arms in ribbons **Reverse:** Facing paschal lamb, date in chronogram **Note:** Similar to 3 Ducat, KM#262.

Date	Mintage	VG	F	VF	XF	Unc
1703	—	600	1,200	2,000	3,000	—

KM# 264 5 DUCAT

17.5000 g., 0.9860 Gold 0.5547 oz. AGW **Obverse:** Three shields of arms in ribbons **Reverse:** Facing paschal lamb, date in chronogram **Note:** Similar to 3 Ducat, KM#262.

Date	Mintage	VG	F	VF	XF	Unc
1703	—	—	—	3,000	5,000	—

KM# 269 5 DUCAT

17.5000 g., 0.9860 Gold 0.5547 oz. AGW **Obverse:** Standing female with branch palm frond and three shields of arms, Roman numeral date below **Reverse:** Imperial eagle, titles of Josef

Date	Mintage	VG	F	VF	XF	Unc
MDCCVI (1706) GFN	—	—	—	4,500	7,000	—

KM# 301 5 DUCAT

17.5000 g., 0.9860 Gold 0.5547 oz. AGW **Obverse:** Bust of Karl VI right **Reverse:** City view with NORIMBERGA below **Rev. Legend:** FLORIA IN EXCELSIS DEO...

Date	Mintage	VG	F	VF	XF	Unc
1736 PGN	—	—	—	4,500	7,000	—

Note: Struck with 1 Thaler dies, KM#300

KM# 270 6 DUCAT

21.0000 g., 0.9860 Gold 0.6657 oz. AGW **Obverse:** Imperial eagle, titles of Josef **Reverse:** Standing female with branch palm frond and 3 shields of arms **Note:** Similar to 5 Ducat, KM#269.

Date	Mintage	VG	F	VF	XF	Unc
1706 GFN	—	—	—	5,000	8,500	—

KM# 286 6 DUCAT

21.0000 g., 0.9860 Gold 0.6657 oz. AGW **Obverse:** Bust of Karl VI right **Reverse:** Eagle wearing German crown above city view, NORINBERGA below, date in chronogram

Date	Mintage	VG	F	VF	XF	Unc
ND(1721) PGN	—	—	—	5,000	8,500	—

Note: Struck with 1 Thaler dies, KM#285

KM# 309 6 DUCAT

21.0000 g., 0.9860 Gold 0.6657 oz. AGW **Obverse:** Bust of Franz right **Reverse:** Eye of God above city view

Date	Mintage	VG	F	VF	XF	Unc
1745 PPW	—	—	—	5,000	8,500	—

Note: Struck with 1 Thaler dies, KM#307; Bowers and Merena Guia sale 3-88 AU realized $13,200

KM# 287 8 DUCAT

28.0000 g., 0.9860 Gold 0.8876 oz. AGW **Obverse:** Bust of Karl VI right **Reverse:** City view **Note:** Similar to 6 Ducat, KM#286.

Date	Mintage	VG	F	VF	XF	Unc
1721 PGN	—	—	—	5,500	9,000	—

KM# 288 10 DUCAT

35.0000 g., 0.9860 Gold 1.1095 oz. AGW **Obverse:** Standing female with palm and 3 shields **Reverse:** Imperial eagle **Note:** Similar to 6 Ducat, KM#286.

Date	Mintage	VG	F	VF	XF	Unc
1721 PGN	—	—	—	6,000	10,000	—

KM# 289 10 DUCAT

35.0000 g., 0.9860 Gold 1.1095 oz. AGW **Obverse:** Bust of Karl VI **Reverse:** Two cherubs with three shields above city view

Date	Mintage	VG	F	VF	XF	Unc
ND H/GFN	—	—	—	16,000	20,000	—

Note: Struck with 2 Thaler dies, KM#213

PATTERNS

Including off metal strikes

KM#	Date	Mintage	Identification	Mkt Val
Pn11	ND1711	—	Ducat. Silver. KM#276	150
Pn12	ND(1712)	—	Ducat. Silver. KM#277. Date in chronogram, Karl VI.	150
Pn14	ND1739	—	Pfennig. Gold.	600
Pn15	ND1740	—	Pfennig. Gold.	600
Pn17	ND1756	—	20 Kreuzer. Gold. Weight of 3 Ducat.	4,250
Pn18	ND1756	—	20 Kreuzer. Gold. Weight of 6 Ducat.	6,500
Pn19	ND1758	—	Kreuzer. Gold. Weight of 1/2 Ducat.	—
Pn20	ND1759	—	10 Kreuzer. Gold. Weight of 2 Ducat.	3,200

PIEFORTS

KM#	Date	Mintage	Identification	Mkt Val
P1	ND	—	2 Thaler. Silver. KM#211.	—

OLDENBURG

The county of Oldenburg was situated on the North Sea coast, to the east of the principality of East Friesland. It was originally part of the old duchy of Saxony and the first recorded lord ruled from the beginning of the 11th century. The first count was named in 1091 and had already acquired the county of Delmenhorst prior to that time. The first identifiable Oldenburg coinage was struck in the first half of the 13th century. Oldenburg was divided into Oldenburg and Delmenhorst in 1270, but the two lines were reunited by marriage five generations later. Through another marriage to the heiress of the duchy of Schleswig and county of Holstein, the royal house of Denmark descended through the Oldenburg line beginning in 1448, while a junior branch continued as counts of Oldenburg. The lordship of Jever was added to the county's domains in 1575. In 1667, the last count died without a direct heir and Oldenburg reverted to Denmark until 1773. In the following year, Oldenburg was given to the bishop of Lübeck, of the Holstein-Gottorp line, and raised to the status of a duchy. Oldenburg was occupied several times during the Napoleonic Wars and became a grand duchy in 1829. In 1817, Oldenburg acquired the principality of Birkenfeld from Prussia and struck coins in denominations used there. World War I spelled the end of temporal power for the grand duke in 1918, but the title has continued up to the present time. Grand Duke Anton Gunther was born in 1923.

RULERS

Friedrich IV of Denmark, 1699-1730
Christian VI of Denmark, 1730-1746
Friedrich V of Denmark, 1746-1766
Christian VII of Denmark, 1766-1773
Friedrich August
as Count, 1773
as Duke, 1774-1785
Peter Friedrich Wilhelm, 1785-1823
Peter Friedrich Ludwig, as Administrator 1785-1823, as Duke, 1823-1829

MINT OFFICIALS' INITIALS

Initials	Date	Name
B	1760-94	Johann Ephraim Bauert, die-cutter in Copenhagen
CW	1680-1702	Christopher Woltereck in Gluckstadt
IHM, JHM	1760-66	Johann Heinrich Madelung
N	1760-82	Samuel Mathias Neudorff, warden
	ca.1760	Georg Wilhelm Wahl, die-cutter in Hamburg

ARMS

Oldenburg: Two bars on field.
Delmenhorst: Cross with pointed bottom bar.
Jever: Lion rampant to left.

NOTE:

Coins struck for lordship of Jever are listed under the latter.

DUCHY

REGULAR COINAGE

KM# 133 2 PFENNIG

0.4300 g., 0.2500 Silver 0.0035 oz. ASW **Ruler:** Friedrich V of Denmark **Obverse:** Crowned FV monogram **Reverse:** Value and date

Date	Mintage	VG	F	VF	XF	Unc
1764	14,000	37.50	90.00	220	—	—

KM# 124 4 PFENNIG

0.8700 g., 0.2500 Silver 0.0070 oz. ASW **Ruler:** Friedrich V of Denmark **Obverse:** Crowned F5R monogram, A.D.M.F. below **Reverse:** Value and date, initials below date

Date	Mintage	VG	F	VF	XF	Unc
1762 IHM	629,000	25.00	50.00	100	—	—
1763 IHM	16,000	13.50	32.50	70.00	—	—

KM# 105 GROTEN (1/144 Thaler)

0.8700 g., 0.2500 Silver 0.0070 oz. ASW **Ruler:** Friedrich V of Denmark **Obverse:** Crowned F5R monogram, 15TH A.D.M.F. below **Reverse:** Value and date

Date	Mintage	VG	F	VF	XF	Unc
1761	181,000	125	275	425	—	—

KM# 106 GROTEN (1/144 Thaler)

0.8700 g., 0.2500 Silver 0.0070 oz. ASW **Ruler:** Friedrich V of Denmark **Obverse:** Crowned F5R monogram, 15TH at sides, A.D.M.F. below

Date	Mintage	VG	F	VF	XF	Unc
1761	Inc. above	32.50	85.00	160	—	—

KM# 141 GROTEN (1/144 Thaler)

0.8700 g., 0.2500 Silver 0.0070 oz. ASW **Ruler:** Peter Friedrich Wilhelm **Obverse:** Crowned arms **Reverse:** Value and date

Date	Mintage	VG	F	VF	XF	Unc
1792	72,000	6.00	12.50	25.00	45.00	—

KM# 107 1-1/2 GROTE

1.0400 g., 0.3120 Silver 0.0104 oz. ASW **Ruler:** Friedrich V of Denmark **Obverse:** Crowned F5R monogram, 15th and a.d.m.f. in script below monogram **Reverse:** Value and date

Date	Mintage	VG	F	VF	XF	Unc
1761	230,000	50.00	125	220	—	—

KM# 108 1-1/2 GROTE

1.0400 g., 0.3120 Silver 0.0104 oz. ASW **Ruler:** Friedrich V of Denmark **Obverse:** 15-TH at sides of monogram

Date	Mintage	VG	F	VF	XF	Unc
1761	Inc. above	50.00	125	220	—	—

KM# 109 1-1/2 GROTE

1.0400 g., 0.3120 Silver 0.0104 oz. ASW **Ruler:** Friedrich V of Denmark **Obverse:** Large letters below monogram

Date	Mintage	VG	F	VF	XF	Unc
1761	Inc. above	50.00	125	220	—	—

KM# 140 1-1/2 GROTE

1.0400 g., 0.3120 Silver 0.0104 oz. ASW **Ruler:** Peter Friedrich Wilhelm **Obverse:** Crowned arms **Reverse:** Value and date

Date	Mintage	VG	F	VF	XF	Unc
1792	48,000	10.00	20.00	40.00	80.00	—

KM# 110 2 GROTE (1/36 Thaler - 18 Witten)

1.3900 g., 0.3120 Silver 0.0139 oz. ASW **Ruler:** Friedrich V of Denmark **Obverse:** Crowned F5R monogram, A.D.M.F. below **Reverse:** Value and date

Date	Mintage	VG	F	VF	XF	Unc
1761	548,000	16.00	42.50	110	—	—
Note: Rosettes on reverse						
1761	Inc. above	100	160	240	—	—
Note: No rosettes on reverse						

KM# 142 2 GROTE (1/36 Thaler - 18 Witten)

1.3900 g., 0.3120 Silver 0.0139 oz. ASW **Ruler:** Peter Friedrich Wilhelm **Obverse:** Crowned 2-fold arms **Reverse:** Value, date

Date	Mintage	VG	F	VF	XF	Unc
1792	396,000	6.00	12.00	25.00	50.00	—

KM# 111 3 GROTE (1/24 Thaler)

1.7900 g., 0.3750 Silver 0.0216 oz. ASW **Ruler:** Friedrich V of Denmark **Obverse:** Crowned F5R monogram, 14-1/2 TH A.D.M.F. below **Reverse:** Value and date

Date	Mintage	VG	F	VF	XF	Unc
1761	119,000	42.50	75.00	160	—	—

KM# 112 4 GROTE (1/18 Thaler)

2.3900 g., 0.3750 Silver 0.0288 oz. ASW **Ruler:** Friedrich V of Denmark **Obverse:** Crowned F5R monogram, 14-1/2 TH A.D.M.F. below **Reverse:** Value and date

Date	Mintage	VG	F	VF	XF	Unc
1761	409,000	90.00	180	375	—	—

KM# 143 4 GROTE (1/18 Thaler)

2.3900 g., 0.3750 Silver 0.0288 oz. ASW **Ruler:** Peter Friedrich Wilhelm **Obverse:** Crowned arms

Date	Mintage	VG	F	VF	XF	Unc
1792	36,000	8.00	16.50	35.00	70.00	—

KM# 115 MARIENGROSCHEN

1.3900 g., 0.3120 Silver 0.0139 oz. ASW **Ruler:** Friedrich V of Denmark **Obverse:** Crowned monogram **Reverse:** Value, date

Date	Mintage	VG	F	VF	XF	Unc
1761	—	13.50	37.50	85.00	—	—
1762	1,967,000	27.50	75.00	150	—	—

KM# 123 MARIENGROSCHEN

1.3900 g., 0.3120 Silver 0.0139 oz. ASW **Ruler:** Friedrich V of Denmark **Reverse:** Initials below date

Date	Mintage	VG	F	VF	XF	Unc
1762 IHM	—	22.50	42.50	90.00	—	—
1763 IHM	232,000	27.50	50.00	110	—	—

KM# 125 MARIENGROSCHEN

1.3900 g., 0.3120 Silver 0.0139 oz. ASW **Ruler:** Friedrich V of Denmark **Reverse:** Value, GROSCH

Date	Mintage	VG	F	VF	XF	Unc
1762 Rare	—	—	—	—	—	—

KM# 116 2 MARIENGROSCHEN

2.3900 g., 0.3750 Silver 0.0288 oz. ASW **Ruler:** Friedrich V of Denmark **Obverse:** Crowned F5R monogram, 14-1/2 TH A.D.M.F. below **Reverse:** Value and date

Date	Mintage	VG	F	VF	XF	Unc
1761	—	22.50	55.00	140	—	—

KM# 117 2 MARIENGROSCHEN

2.3900 g., 0.3750 Silver 0.0288 oz. ASW **Ruler:** Friedrich V of Denmark **Obverse:** 2 to left of monogram **Reverse:** Without letters below date

Date	Mintage	VG	F	VF	XF	Unc
1761	—	11.00	42.50	110	—	—
1762 Rare	Inc. below	—	—	—	—	—

KM# 126 2 MARIENGROSCHEN

2.3900 g., 0.3750 Silver 0.0288 oz. ASW **Ruler:** Friedrich V of Denmark **Obverse:** Crowned F5R monogram **Reverse:** Initials below date

Date	Mintage	VG	F	VF	XF	Unc
1762 IHM	874,000	275	450	600	—	—
1763 IHM Rare	523,000	—	—	—	—	—

KM# 127 2 MARIENGROSCHEN

2.3900 g., 0.3750 Silver 0.0288 oz. ASW **Ruler:** Friedrich V of Denmark **Obverse:** Crowned monogram **Reverse:** Initials below date

Date	Mintage	VG	F	VF	XF	Unc
1762 IHM	Inc. above	22.50	42.50	100	—	—
1763 IHM	Inc. above	22.50	55.00	110	—	—

KM# 128 1/48 THALER

1.0400 g., 0.3120 Silver 0.0104 oz. ASW **Ruler:** Friedrich V of Denmark **Obverse:** Crowned F5R monogram, A.D.M.F. below date at sides **Reverse:** Value, OLM below (large letters)

Date	Mintage	VG	F	VF	XF	Unc
1762 IHM	634,000	42.50	100	175	—	—

KM# 129 1/24 THALER

1.7900 g., 0.3750 Silver 0.0216 oz. ASW **Ruler:** Friedrich V of Denmark **Obverse:** Crowned F5R monogram, 14-1/2 TH A.D.M.F. below, date at sides **Reverse:** Value, OLM below (small letters)

Date	Mintage	VG	F	VF	XF	Unc
1762 IHM	277,000	32.50	65.00	150	—	—

KM# 118 1/12 THALER

2.9200 g., 0.5000 Silver 0.0469 oz. ASW **Ruler:** Friedrich V of Denmark **Obverse:** Head of Friedrich right **Reverse:** Legend starts at upper right, with inner circle

Date	Mintage	VG	F	VF	XF	Unc
1761 N Rare	Inc. above	—	—	—	—	—
1761	137,000	75.00	175	450	—	—

KM# 131 1/12 THALER

2.9200 g., 0.5000 Silver 0.0469 oz. ASW **Ruler:** Friedrich V of Denmark **Reverse:** Value and date; legend starts at lower left, without inner circle

Date	Mintage	VG	F	VF	XF	Unc
1763 B Rare	70,000	—	—	—	—	—
1764 N	Inc. above	110	240	450	—	—

KM# 119 1/6 THALER

5.8500 g., 0.5000 Silver 0.0940 oz. ASW **Ruler:** Friedrich V of Denmark **Obverse:** Head of Friedrich right **Reverse:** Value and date in circle

Date	Mintage	VG	F	VF	XF	Unc
1761	145,000	70.00	140	275	550	—
1761 N	Inc. above	70.00	140	275	550	—
1761 B	Inc. above	70.00	140	275	550	—

KM# 132 1/6 THALER

5.8500 g., 0.5000 Silver 0.0940 oz. ASW **Ruler:** Friedrich V of Denmark **Obverse:** Head right **Reverse:** Initials at bottom

Date	Mintage	VG	F	VF	XF	Unc
1763 IHM	232,000	50.00	100	225	450	—
1763 B	Inc. above	50.00	100	225	450	—
1763 N	Inc. above	50.00	100	225	450	—
1764	Inc. above	50.00	100	225	450	—
1764 N	Inc. above	50.00	100	225	450	—
1765 N	Inc. above	50.00	100	225	450	—

KM# 120.1 1/3 THALER

8.6600 g., 0.7500 Silver 0.2088 oz. ASW **Ruler:** Friedrich V of Denmark **Obverse:** Head of Friedrich right **Reverse:** Large fraction in center, date top left; legend starts at upper right

Date	Mintage	VG	F	VF	XF	Unc
1761 B	8,358	600	1,000	2,000	—	—

KM# 120.2 1/3 THALER

8.6600 g., 0.7500 Silver 0.2088 oz. ASW **Ruler:** Friedrich V of Denmark **Obverse:** Head right **Reverse:** Date divided below denomination; legend starts at lower left

Date	Mintage	VG	F	VF	XF	Unc
1762 B/IHM	5,538	600	1,000	2,000	—	—

KM# 121 2/3 THALER (Gulden)

17.3200 g., 0.7500 Silver 0.4176 oz. ASW **Ruler:** Friedrich V of Denmark **Obverse:** Head of Friedrich right **Reverse:** Large fraction in circle, date at top left, legend starts at upper right

Date	Mintage	VG	F	VF	XF	Unc
1761 B Rare	33,000	—	—	—	750	—
1761 N Rare	Inc. above	—	—	—	750	—

KM# 122 2/3 THALER (Gulden)

17.3200 g., 0.7500 Silver 0.4176 oz. ASW **Ruler:** Friedrich V of Denmark **Reverse:** Date divided by initials IHM at bottom, legend starts at lower left

Date	Mintage	VG	F	VF	XF	Unc
1761 B Rare	Inc. above	—	—	—	—	—
1761 N Rare	Inc. above	—	—	—	—	—
1762 B	115,000	550	1,100	2,200	—	—
1762 N Rare	Inc. above	—	—	—	—	—
1763 B Rare	—	—	—	—	—	—
1763 N	—	550	1,100	2,300	—	—
1764 N Rare	34,000	—	—	—	—	—
1765 N Rare	—	—	—	—	—	—

OSNABRUCK

A bishopric was established in the town, 30 miles (50 km) northeast of Munster, in 804. The town grew into a small, fortified city around the cathedral and the bishopric expanded its territory north and east of the county of Tecklenburg. The bishops enjoyed the right of coinage from 889 and extended it to their mint in Wiedenbruck (q.v.) in 952. The cathedral chapter issued its own coins in the 17th and 18th centuries. After joining the Hanseatic League independently of the bishops, the city itself minted coins from the mid-16th century until 1805. Both the bishopric and city became part of the kingdom of Hannover in 1803.

Arms as found on coins of Osnabrück (both bishopric and city): wheel with (usually) six spokes.

BISHOPRIC

RULERS

Karl of Lorraine, 1698-1715
Sede Vacante, 1715-1716
Ernst August II of Brunswick, 1716-1728
Clemens August of Bavaria, 1728-1761
Friedrich August, 1764-1802

ARMS

Wheel w/6 spokes (usually) and also on city
Braunschweig (Brunswick): 2 leopards
Hoya: 2 bear paws
Minden: 2 crossed keys
Munster: Broad horizontal bar
Paderborn: Cross
Rietburg: Eagle
Waldeck: 8-pointed star
Wartenberg: Crowned lion rampant left

MINT OFFICIALS' INITIALS

Initials	Date	Name
HLO	1699-1705	Heinrich Lorenz Odendahl, mintmaster
GG	1698-1734	Gerhard Gödt, mintmaster in Koblenz
	1712-?	Gottfried Binnenboss
AWH	1717-20	Anton Wilhelm Hüpenden, mintmaster
	ca.1717	Johann Friedrich Howindt, die-cutter in Hannover
Iii, JJJ	1720-25	Jobst Jakob Jenisch
C	Ca.1766	Claus, die-cutter

REGULAR COINAGE

KM# 160 3 PFENNIG (1/4 Schilling)

Silver **Ruler:** Karl von Lothringen **Mint:** Melle **Obverse:** Osnabrück arms in circle, date in margin **Rev. Inscription:** 1657 / PFEN / HLO **Note:** Varieties exist.

Date	Mintage	VG	F	VF	XF	Unc
1702 HLO	—	8.00	20.00	40.00	70.00	—
1703 HLO	—	8.00	20.00	40.00	70.00	—

KM# 205 3 PFENNIG (1/4 Schilling)

Silver **Ruler:** Ernst August II of Brunswick **Mint:** Melle **Obverse:** Crowned EA monogram **Rev. Inscription:** III / PFEN / NING / date

Date	Mintage	VG	F	VF	XF	Unc
1718 AWH	54,000	5.00	10.00	20.00	35.00	—

KM# 265 3 PFENNIG

Billon **Note:** Similar to 12 Pfennig, KM#270. Prev. C#1.

Date	Mintage	VG	F	VF	XF	Unc
1766 C	230,000	7.50	15.00	30.00	55.00	—

KM# 162 4 PFENNIG (1/3 Schilling)

Silver **Ruler:** Karl von Lothringen **Mint:** Melle **Obverse:** Osnabrück arms in circle, date in margin **Note:** Varieties exist.

Date	Mintage	VG	F	VF	XF	Unc
1702	—	5.00	12.00	25.00	45.00	—
1703	—	5.00	12.00	25.00	45.00	—

KM# 207 4 PFENNIG (1/3 Schilling)

Silver **Ruler:** Ernst August II of Brunswick **Mint:** Melle **Obverse:** Crowned script EA monogram divides date **Rev. Inscription:** IIII / PFEN / NING / AWH

Date	Mintage	VG	F	VF	XF	Unc
1718 AWH	153,000	10.00	22.00	45.00	75.00	—

KM# 208 4 PFENNIG (1/3 Schilling)

Silver **Ruler:** Ernst August II of Brunswick **Mint:** Melle **Obverse:** Similar to KM#207, but date on reverse **Rev. Inscription:** IIII / PFEN / NING / (date) / AWH

Date	Mintage	VG	F	VF	XF	Unc
1718 AWH	Inc. above	10.00	22.00	45.00	75.00	—

KM# 267 4 PFENNIG

Billon **Note:** Similar to 12 Pfennig, KM#270. Prev. C#2.

Date	Mintage	VG	F	VF	XF	Unc
1766 C	172,000	10.00	20.00	35.00	65.00	—

KM# 164.2 5 PFENNIG (1/50 Thaler)

Silver **Ruler:** Karl von Lothringen **Mint:** Melle **Obverse:** Similar to KM#164.1, small maltese cross behind wheel in center

Date	Mintage	VG	F	VF	XF	Unc
1702 HLO	Inc. above	10.00	22.00	45.00	75.00	—

KM# 164.1 5 PFENNIG (1/50 Thaler)

Silver **Ruler:** Karl von Lothringen **Mint:** Melle **Obverse:** Crowned CC monogram, first C reversed, crossed with second, Osnabrück arms in center **Reverse:** 3-line inscription **Rev. Inscription:** V / PFEN / HLO **Note:** Varieties exist.

Date	Mintage	VG	F	VF	XF	Unc
1702 HLO	181,000	7.00	16.00	32.00	55.00	—
1703 HLO	Inc. above	7.00	16.00	32.00	55.00	—
1704 HLO	—	7.00	16.00	32.00	55.00	—

KM# 210 5 PFENNIG (1/50 Thaler)

Silver-Billon **Ruler:** Ernst August II of Brunswick **Mint:** Melle **Obverse:** Crowned EA monogram **Rev. Inscription:** V / PFEN / NING / AWH

Date	Mintage	VG	F	VF	XF	Unc
1718	101,000	15.00	32.00	65.00	100	—

KM# 168.2 6 PFENNIG (1/2 Schilling)
Silver **Ruler:** Karl von Lothringen **Mint:** Melle **Obverse:** Similar to 5 Pfennig, KM#164.2 **Rev. Inscription:** VI / PFEN / HLO

Date	Mintage	VG	F	VF	XF	Unc
1702 HLO	Inc. above	12.00	25.00	50.00	85.00	—

KM# 168.1 6 PFENNIG (1/2 Schilling)
Silver **Ruler:** Karl von Lothringen **Mint:** Melle **Obverse:** Similar to 5 Pfennig, KM#164.1. **Rev. Inscription:** VI / PFEN / HLO
Note: Varieties exist.

Date	Mintage	VG	F	VF	XF	Unc
1702 HLO	133,000	12.00	25.00	50.00	85.00	—
1703 HLO	Inc. above	12.00	25.00	50.00	85.00	—

KM# 232 6 PFENNIG (1/2 Schilling)
Silver **Ruler:** Ernst August II of Brunswick **Mint:** Melle **Obverse:** Crowned EA monogram, value 6 to right **Reverse:** 4-line inscription, date on last line **Rev. Inscription:** VI / PFEN / NING /

Date	Mintage	VG	F	VF	XF	Unc
1721 iii	250,000	5.00	12.00	25.00	45.00	—

KM# 269 6 PFENNIG
Billon **Note:** Similar to 12 Pfennig, KM#270. Prev. C#3.

Date	Mintage	VG	F	VF	XF	Unc
1766 C	222,000	10.00	22.50	40.00	70.00	—

KM# 234 12 PFENNIG (Schilling)
Silver **Ruler:** Ernst August II of Brunswick **Obverse:** Crowned EA monogram divides 12 - PF **Reverse:** 4-line inscription, date on last line **Rev. Inscription:** XII / PFEN / NI(N)G /

Date	Mintage	VG	F	VF	XF	Unc
1721	235,000	18.00	35.00	65.00	100	—

KM# 270 12 PFENNIG
Billon **Ruler:** Friedrich August **Note:** Prev. C#4.

Date	Mintage	VG	F	VF	XF	Unc
1766 C	321,000	12.50	25.00	45.00	80.00	—

MB# 21 1/8 SCHILLING
Silver **Ruler:** Erich II, Herzog von Braunschweig-Grubenhagen **Mint:** Wiedenbrück **Obverse:** 4-fold arms, central shield of Osnabrück **Reverse:** Similar to MB#20

Date	Mintage	Good	VG	F	VF	XF
ND(1508-32)	—	—	—	—	—	—

KM# 170 SCHILLING (1/21 Thaler)
Silver **Ruler:** Karl von Lothringen **Mint:** Melle **Obverse:** Similar to 5 Pfennig, KM#164.2 **Reverse:** 5-line inscription, date in margin **Rev. Inscription:** XXI / EINEN / REICHS / THAL / HLO

Date	Mintage	VG	F	VF	XF	Unc
1702 HLO	99,000	12.00	30.00	60.00	95.00	—

KM# 172 2 FURSTENGROSCHEN (18 Pfennig)
Silver **Ruler:** Karl von Lothringen **Obverse:** Crowned manifold arms with central shield of Lorraine arms, maltese cross behind **Reverse:** 5-line inscription, date in margin **Rev. Inscription:** XIIII / EINEN / REICHS / THAL / HLO **Note:** Varieties exist.

Date	Mintage	VG	F	VF	XF	Unc
1702 HLO	225,000	12.00	25.00	50.00	85.00	—
1703 HLO	Inc. above	12.00	25.00	50.00	85.00	—

KM# 190 2 FURSTENGROSCHEN (18 Pfennig)
Silver **Ruler:** Karl von Lothringen **Mint:** Coblenz **Note:** Similar to KM#172.

Date	Mintage	VG	F	VF	XF	Unc
1714 GG	112,000	12.00	25.00	50.00	85.00	—

KM# 236 2 FURSTENGROSCHEN (18 Pfennig)
Silver **Ruler:** Ernst August II of Brunswick **Mint:** Coblenz **Obverse:** Crowned script EA monogram divides 18 - PF **Reverse:** 3-line inscription, date **Rev. Inscription:** XIIII / EINEN / R: TH: /

Date	Mintage	VG	F	VF	XF	Unc
1721 JJJ	105,000	12.00	25.00	50.00	85.00	—

KM# 237 2 FURSTENGROSCHEN (18 Pfennig)
Silver **Ruler:** Ernst August II of Brunswick **Mint:** Coblenz **Obverse:** Crowned 4-fold arms in Order of the Garter divides 18 - PF **Reverse:** Similar to KM#236

Date	Mintage	VG	F	VF	XF	Unc
1721 JJJ	Inc. above	12.00	25.00	50.00	85.00	—

KM# 238 2 FURSTENGROSCHEN (18 Pfennig)
Silver **Ruler:** Ernst August II of Brunswick **Mint:** Coblenz **Obverse:** Crowned 4-fold arms in Order of the Garter, in exergue 14E. - R. TH. **Reverse:** 4-line inscription, date on last line **Rev. Inscription:** 18 / PFEN / NIG /

Date	Mintage	VG	F	VF	XF	Unc
1721 JJJ	Inc. above	12.00	25.00	50.00	85.00	—

KM# 188 MATIER (1/2 Mariengroschen)
Silver **Ruler:** Karl von Lothringen **Mint:** Melle **Obverse:** Osnabrück arms, date in margin **Rev. Inscription:** I / MAT: / TIER / HLO

Date	Mintage	VG	F	VF	XF	Unc
1704 HLO	—	15.00	28.00	55.00	85.00	—
1709	—	—	—	—	—	—

Note: Reported, not confirmed

KM# 179 MARIENGROSCHEN (1/36 Thaler)
Silver **Ruler:** Karl von Lothringen **Mint:** Melle **Obverse:** Crowned manifold arms with central shield of Lorraine, maltese cross behind **Reverse:** 4-line inscription, mintmaster's initials on 4th line, date in margin **Rev. Inscription:** I / MARIEN / GROS / HLO

Date	Mintage	VG	F	VF	XF	Unc
1703 HLO	353,000	10.00	22.00	40.00	65.00	—
1704 HLO	Inc. above	10.00	22.00	40.00	65.00	—

KM# 192 MARIENGROSCHEN (1/36 Thaler)
Silver **Ruler:** Karl von Lothringen **Mint:** Coblenz **Note:** Similar to KM#179. Varieties exist.

Date	Mintage	VG	F	VF	XF	Unc
1714 GG	720,000	10.00	22.00	40.00	65.00	—
1715 GG	486,000	10.00	22.00	40.00	65.00	—

KM# 214 MARIENGROSCHEN (1/36 Thaler)
Silver **Ruler:** Ernst August II of Brunswick **Mint:** Coblenz **Obverse:** Crowned 4-fold arms with Order of the Garter **Reverse:** Similar to KM#213. **Note:** Varieties exist.

Date	Mintage	VG	F	VF	XF	Unc
1718 AWH	Inc. above	6.00	14.00	28.00	50.00	—

KM# 213 MARIENGROSCHEN (1/36 Thaler)
Silver **Ruler:** Ernst August II of Brunswick **Mint:** Coblenz **Obverse:** Crowned doubled (1reversed) script EA monograms **Reverse:** 5-line inscription, date on 4th line, mintmaster's initials on 5th line **Rev. Inscription:** I / MARIEN / GROS / / AWH

Date	Mintage	VG	F	VF	XF	Unc
1718 AWH	139,000	5.00	12.00	25.00	45.00	—

KM# 240 MARIENGROSCHEN (1/36 Thaler)
Silver **Ruler:** Ernst August II of Brunswick **Mint:** Coblenz **Obverse:** Crowned EA monogram, value 1 to right **Reverse:** Similar to KM#213

Date	Mintage	VG	F	VF	XF	Unc
1721 iii	323,000	5.00	12.00	25.00	45.00	—

KM# 241 MARIENGROSCHEN (1/36 Thaler)
Silver **Ruler:** Ernst August II of Brunswick **Mint:** Coblenz **Obverse:** Crowned 4-fold arms in Order of the Garter, value 1 to right **Reverse:** Similar to KM#240

Date	Mintage	VG	F	VF	XF	Unc
1721 iii	Inc. above	6.00	14.00	28.00	50.00	—

KM# 248 MARIENGROSCHEN (1/36 Thaler)
Silver **Ruler:** Ernst August II of Brunswick **Mint:** Coblenz **Obverse:** Script EA monogram **Note:** Similar to KM#240.

Date	Mintage	VG	F	VF	XF	Unc
1724 JJJ	402,000	5.00	12.00	25.00	45.00	—

KM# 180 2 MARIENGROSCHEN (1/18 Thaler)
Silver **Ruler:** Karl von Lothringen **Mint:** Melle **Reverse:** Inscription, mintmaster's initials **Rev. Inscription:** II / MARIEN / GROS / HLO **Note:** Similar to Mariengroschen, KM#179.

Date	Mintage	VG	F	VF	XF	Unc
1703 HLO	—	10.00	22.00	45.00	70.00	—
1704 HLO	38,000	10.00	22.00	45.00	70.00	—
1708	—	—	—	—	—	—

Note: Reported, not confirmed

Date	Mintage	VG	F	VF	XF	Unc
1711	—	—	—	—	—	—

Note: Reported, not confirmed

KM# 194 2 MARIENGROSCHEN (1/18 Thaler)
Silver **Ruler:** Karl von Lothringen **Mint:** Coblenz **Reverse:** 5-line inscription, 4th line date, 5th line mintmaster's initials **Rev. Inscription:** II / MARIEN / GROS / / AWH **Note:** Similar to Mariengroschen, KM#213.

Date	Mintage	VG	F	VF	XF	Unc
1714 GG	360,000	7.00	16.00	30.00	48.00	—

KM# 200 2 MARIENGROSCHEN (1/18 Thaler)
Silver **Ruler:** Ernst August II of Brunswick **Mint:** Coblenz **Reverse:** 5-line inscription, 4th line date, 5th line mintmaster's initials **Rev. Inscription:** II / MARIEN / GROS / / AWH **Note:** Similar to Mariengroschen, KM#213. Varieties exist.

Date	Mintage	VG	F	VF	XF	Unc
1717	—	—	—	—	—	—
1718 AWH	157,000	12.00	26.00	55.00	85.00	—
1720	—	—	—	—	—	—

Note: Reported, not confirmed

KM# 201 2 MARIENGROSCHEN (1/18 Thaler)
Silver **Ruler:** Ernst August II of Brunswick **Mint:** Coblenz **Obverse:** Similar to Mariengroschen, KM#214 **Reverse:** Similar to KM#200

Date	Mintage	VG	F	VF	XF	Unc
1717	—	12.00	26.00	48.00	75.00	—
1718 AWH	Inc. above	12.00	26.00	48.00	75.00	—

KM# 218 2 MARIENGROSCHEN (1/18 Thaler)
Silver **Ruler:** Ernst August II of Brunswick **Mint:** Melle **Obverse:** Value 2 on obverse **Reverse:** Value II on reverse **Note:** Similar to Mariengroschen, KM#240. Varieties exist.

Date	Mintage	VG	F	VF	XF	Unc
1720 iii	—	7.00	16.00	32.00	60.00	—
1721 iii	297,000	7.00	16.00	32.00	60.00	—
1722 JJJ	—	7.00	16.00	32.00	60.00	—

KM# 219 2 MARIENGROSCHEN (1/18 Thaler)
Silver **Ruler:** Ernst August II of Brunswick **Mint:** Melle **Obverse:** Value 2 on obverse **Reverse:** Value II on reverse **Note:** Similar to Mariengroschen, KM#241.

Date	Mintage	VG	F	VF	XF	Unc
1720 iii	—	12.00	26.00	48.00	75.00	—
1721 iii	Inc. above	12.00	26.00	48.00	75.00	—

KM# 250 2 MARIENGROSCHEN (1/18 Thaler)
Silver **Ruler:** Ernst August II of Brunswick **Mint:** Melle **Obverse:** Script EA monogram **Note:** Similar to KM#218.

Date	Mintage	VG	F	VF	XF	Unc
1724 JJJ	274,000	7.00	16.00	32.00	60.00	—

KM# 203 3 MARIENGROSCHEN (1/12 Thaler)
Silver **Ruler:** Ernst August II of Brunswick **Obverse:** Similar to Mariengroschen, KM#214 but arms supported by lion and unicorn **Reverse:** 4-line inscription, date on last line **Rev. Inscription:** III / MARIEN / GROS / **Note:** Varieties exist.

Date	Mintage	VG	F	VF	XF	Unc
1717	—	12.00	26.00	55.00	85.00	—
1718 AWH	17,000	12.00	26.00	55.00	85.00	—

KM# 221 3 MARIENGROSCHEN (1/12 Thaler)
Silver **Ruler:** Ernst August II of Brunswick **Note:** Similar to KM#203. Varieties exist.

Date	Mintage	VG	F	VF	XF	Unc
1720 iii	—	12.00	26.00	55.00	85.00	—
1721 JJJ	116,000	12.00	26.00	55.00	85.00	—
1722 JJJ	—	12.00	26.00	55.00	85.00	—
1724 JJJ	183,000	12.00	26.00	55.00	85.00	—

KM# 225 6 MARIENGROSCHEN (1/6 Thaler)
Silver **Ruler:** Ernst August II of Brunswick **Reverse:** Value VI and date in margin **Note:** Similar to 3 Mariengroschen, KM#221. Varieties exist.

Date	Mintage	VG	F	VF	XF	Unc
1720 JJJ	—	—	—	—	—	—

Note: Reported, not confirmed

Date	Mintage	VG	F	VF	XF	Unc
1721 JJJ	167,000	15.00	32.00	65.00	100	—
1721 iii	Inc. above	15.00	32.00	65.00	100	—
1722 JJJ	—	15.00	32.00	65.00	100	—

KM# 244 12 MARIENGROSCHEN (1/3 Thaler)
Silver **Ruler:** Ernst August II of Brunswick **Mint:** Melle **Reverse:** Legend, date **Rev. Legend:** XII / MARIEN / GROSCH / **Note:** Similar to 3 Mariengroschen, KM#221.

Date	Mintage	VG	F	VF	XF	Unc
1721 JJJ	—	—	—	—	—	—

Note: Reported, not confirmed

Date	Mintage	VG	F	VF	XF	Unc
1722 JJJ	61,000	30.00	65.00	120	200	—
1724 JJJ	24,000	30.00	65.00	120	200	—

KM# 174.1 24 MARIENGROSCHEN (2/3 Thaler)
Silver **Ruler:** Karl von Lothringen **Mint:** Melle **Reverse:** Legend ends with mintmaster's initials **Rev. Legend:** XXIIII / MARIEN / GROSCH / HLO **Note:** Dav. #724. Similar to Mariengroschen, KM#179. Varieties exist.

Date	Mintage	VG	F	VF	XF	Unc
1702 HLO	46,000	65.00	130	250	400	—
1703 HLO	Inc. above	65.00	130	250	400	—

KM# 174.2 24 MARIENGROSCHEN (2/3 Thaler)
Silver **Ruler:** Karl von Lothringen **Mint:** Melle **Obverse:** Crowned oval 4-fold arms, maltese cross behind, eagle supporters to left and right **Reverse:** Legend, date **Rev. Legend:** XXIIII / MARIEN / GROSCH: /

Date	Mintage	VG	F	VF	XF	Unc
1703 HLO	Inc. above	65.00	130	250	400	—

KM# 246 24 MARIENGROSCHEN (2/3 Thaler)
Silver **Ruler:** Ernst August II of Brunswick **Mint:** Melle **Note:** Dav. #725. Similar to 3 Mariengroschen, KM#221, but value on reverse is XXIIII. Varieties exist.

Date	Mintage	VG	F	VF	XF	Unc
1721 JJJ	95,000	60.00	100	180	275	—
1724 JJJ	60,000	60.00	100	180	275	—

KM# 177 1/12 THALER (3 Mariengroschen)
Silver **Ruler:** Karl von Lothringen **Obverse:** Similar to Mariengroschen, KM#179 **Reverse:** Legend around inscription, date **Rev. Legend:** 12 / EINEN / REICHS / THAL / HLO **Rev. Inscription:** NACH DEM LEIPZIGER FUES **Note:** Varieties exist.

Date	Mintage	VG	F	VF	XF	Unc
1702 HLO	99,000	18.00	32.00	65.00	110	—
1703 HLO	Inc. above	18.00	32.00	65.00	110	—
1704 HLO	Inc. above	18.00	32.00	65.00	110	—

KM# 196 1/12 THALER (3 Mariengroschen)
Silver **Ruler:** Karl von Lothringen **Mint:** Coblenz **Note:** Similar to KM#177.

Date	Mintage	VG	F	VF	XF	Unc
1714 GG	36,000	16.00	30.00	60.00	100	—

KM# 158 THALER
Silver **Obverse:** Bust of Karl right **Reverse:** Crowned arms, HL-O below, date in legend **Note:** Dav. #2503.

Date	Mintage	VG	F	VF	XF	Unc
1701 HLO	—	1,200	2,000	3,500	6,000	—

KM# 198 THALER
Silver **Ruler:** Sede Vacante **Obverse:** Saint holding keys standing behind shield **Reverse:** Charlemagne, cathedral behind **Note:** Dav. #2504.

Date	Mintage	VG	F	VF	XF	Unc
1715	—	125	225	400	—	850

KM# 255 THALER
Silver **Ruler:** Ernst August II of Brunswick **Obverse:** Crowned and supported arms **Reverse:** Horse running left, JJJ below date in legend **Note:** Dav. #2505.

Date	Mintage	F	VF	XF	Unc
1724 JJJ	7,600	1,250	2,250	3,500	—
1725 JJJ	—	1,250	2,250	3,500	—

CATHEDRAL CHAPTER

MINT
Eversburg

REGULAR COINAGE

KM# 261 3 PFENNIG
Copper **Mint:** Eversburg **Obverse:** St. Peter standing behind Osnabrück arms which divide S - P, holding 2 keys and book **Reverse:** 3-line inscription in ornamented circle, date is last line **Rev. Inscription:** III / PFENNIG / /

Date	Mintage	VG	F	VF	XF	Unc
1740	—	18.00	40.00	80.00	135	—

KM# 263 4 PFENNIG
Copper **Mint:** Eversburg **Reverse:** Inscription with different value **Rev. Inscription:** IIII **Note:** Similar to 3 Pfennig, KM#261

Date	Mintage	VG	F	VF	XF	Unc
1740	—	22.00	50.00	100	165	—

CITY

The city of Osnabrück is located northeast of Münster. Although the city owed its original growth to the bishopric, it achieved considerable independence from the bishops and joined the Hanseatic League. It had its own local coinage from the early 16th century until 1805. It was absorbed by Hannover in 1803.

MINT OFFICIALS' INITIALS

Initials	Date	Name
IHP	1704-21	Johann Henrich Polking, mintmaster
	1736-46	Jobst, Christian and Berendt Henrich Brockmann
CB	1748-?	Christian Brockmann, mintmaster
IW	Ca.1726-60	?
GGWF	1790	G.G. Wessel (F=fecit=made this), die-cutter

REGULAR COINAGE

KM# 273 HELLER
Copper **Obverse:** Arms **Reverse:** Value above date **Note:** Prev. C#1.

Date	Mintage	VG	F	VF	XF	Unc
1790	—	4.00	6.00	12.00	35.00	—

KM# 273a HELLER
Copper **Obverse:** Wheel **Reverse:** Denomination and date **Note:** Prev. C#1a.

Date	Mintage	F	VF	XF	Unc
1791	15,000	4.00	8.00	20.00	75.00
1794	1,570	4.00	8.00	20.00	75.00
1795	—	4.00	8.00	20.00	75.00
1805	—	4.00	8.00	20.00	75.00

KM# 259 PFENNIG
Copper **Obverse:** OSNABRVCK on obverse **Note:** Similar to KM#139.1.

Date	Mintage	VG	F	VF	XF	Unc
1731	23,000	8.00	16.00	35.00	60.00	—

KM# 275 PFENNIG
Copper **Obverse:** Arms **Reverse:** Value above date **Note:** Craig #2.

Date	Mintage	VG	F	VF	XF	Unc
1790	—	4.00	6.00	12.00	35.00	—

KM# 280 PFENNIG
Copper **Obverse:** Wheel **Reverse:** Denomination and date **Note:** Craig #3.

Date	Mintage	F	VF	XF	Unc
1791	17,000	4.00	8.00	20.00	75.00
1794	2,449	4.00	8.00	20.00	75.00
1795	—	4.00	8.00	20.00	75.00
1805	—	4.00	8.00	20.00	75.00

KM# 216 1-1/2 PFENNIG
Copper **Obverse:** City arms in circle, date in legend **Reverse:** Horizontal 'I' over vertical 'I,' all in cartouche

Date	Mintage	VG	F	VF	XF	Unc
1719	—	—	—	—	—	—
1731	4,891	7.00	15.00	25.00	55.00	—

KM# 284 1-1/2 PFENNIG
Copper **Note:** Craig #5.

Date	Mintage	F	VF	XF	Unc
1791	25,000	4.00	8.00	20.00	75.00
1794	—	4.00	8.00	20.00	75.00
1795	—	4.00	8.00	20.00	75.00
1805	—	4.00	8.00	20.00	75.00

KM# 286 2 PFENNIG
Copper **Obverse:** Wheel **Reverse:** Denomination and date **Note:** Craig #7

Date	Mintage	F	VF	XF	Unc
1791	19,000	5.00	9.00	25.00	100
1794	3,549	5.00	9.00	25.00	100
1795	—	5.00	9.00	25.00	100
1805	—	5.00	9.00	25.00	100

KM# 182 3 PFENNIG
Copper **Obverse:** Date, legend, arms in cartouche **Obv. Legend:** STADT OSNABRVCK **Reverse:** Value between branches **Note:** Varieties exist. Craig #9.

Date	Mintage	VG	F	VF	XF	Unc
1704 IHP	26,000	6.00	10.00	30.00	110	—
1720 IHP	—	6.00	10.00	30.00	110	—
1721 IHP	—	6.00	10.00	30.00	110	—
1725	—	6.00	10.00	30.00	110	—
1726 IW	160,000	6.00	10.00	30.00	110	—
1731	—	6.00	10.00	30.00	110	—
1752 IW	109,000	6.00	10.00	30.00	110	—
1759	—	6.00	10.00	25.00	110	—
1759 IW	—	6.00	10.00	25.00	110	—
1759 IHS	—	6.00	10.00	25.00	110	—
1760	57,000	6.00	10.00	30.00	110	—

KM# 278 3 PFENNIG
Copper **Obverse:** Wheel between two wildmen **Reverse:** Value above date **Note:** Craig #10.

Date	Mintage	VG	F	VF	XF	Unc
1790 GGWF	—	25.00	45.00	80.00	150	—

KM# 184 4 PFENNIG
Copper **Obverse:** Date, legend, arms in cartouche **Obv. Legend:** STADT OSNABRUCK **Reverse:** Value between branches **Note:** Varieties exist. Craig #13.

Date	Mintage	VG	F	VF	XF	Unc
1704 IHP	19,000	7.00	12.00	30.00	125	—
1719	—	7.00	12.00	30.00	125	—
1720	—	7.00	12.00	30.00	125	—
1722 IW	—	7.00	12.00	30.00	125	—
1726 IW	117,000	7.00	12.00	30.00	125	—
1750	—	7.00	12.00	30.00	125	—
1752	75,000	7.00	12.00	30.00	125	—
1759	—	7.00	12.00	30.00	125	—
1760	36,000	7.00	12.00	30.00	125	—
1790	—	7.00	12.00	30.00	125	—

C# 13 4 PFENNIG
Copper **Obverse:** Date, arms in cartouche **Obv. Legend:** STADT OSNABRUCK **Reverse:** Value between branches

Date	Mintage	VG	F	VF	XF	Unc
1704	—	7.00	12.00	30.00	125	—
1719	—	7.00	12.00	30.00	125	—
1720	—	7.00	12.00	30.00	125	—
1722	—	7.00	12.00	30.00	125	—
1726	—	7.00	12.00	30.00	125	—
1750	—	7.00	12.00	30.00	125	—
1752	—	7.00	12.00	30.00	125	—
1759	—	7.00	12.00	30.00	125	—
1760	—	7.00	12.00	30.00	125	—
1790	—	7.00	12.00	30.00	125	—

KM# 166 5 PFENNIG (Stüber)
Copper **Note:** As MB#91 dated (16)25, but countermarked with Osnabrück wheel and date 1702.

Date	Mintage	VG	F	VF	XF	Unc
1702	—	20.00	45.00	80.00	125	—

KM# 186 5 PFENNIG
Copper **Note:** Craig #14.

Date	Mintage	VG	F	VF	XF	Unc
1704 IHP	—	—	7.00	12.00	30.00	125
1721 IHP	—	—	7.00	12.00	30.00	125
1726 CB	—	—	7.00	12.00	30.00	125
1726 IW	—	—	7.00	12.00	30.00	125

KM# 185 5 PFENNIG
Copper **Obverse:** Osnabrück arms in ornamented circle, around inscription, mintmaster's initials, date. **Obv. Inscription:** STADT OSNABRVCK A-O **Note:** Varieties exist.

Date	Mintage	VG	F	VF	XF	Unc
1704 IHP	3,092	5.00	9.00	20.00	35.00	—
1719 IHP	—	5.00	9.00	20.00	35.00	—
1721 IHP	—	5.00	9.00	20.00	35.00	—
1726 CB	96,000	5.00	9.00	20.00	35.00	—
1726 IW	—	5.00	9.00	20.00	35.00	—
1728	—	5.00	9.00	20.00	35.00	—

OTTINGEN

The counts of Öttingen, with lands in Swabia north of Nordlingen, trace their descent in a long line back to the early 10th century. The counts obtained the right to coin money in 1393. During the Reformation, Öttingen was divided into the Protestant Öttingen-Öttingen and the Catholic Öttingen-Wallerstein lines of counts. Öttingen-Öttingen gained the rank of prince in 1674, but became extinct in 1731 and was divided between Öttingen-Wallerstein-Spielberg and Öttingen-Wallerstein-Wallerstein. In 1602 Öttingen-Wallerstein was split into 3 lines: Öttingen-Wallerstein-Spielberg (prince in 1734, mediatized in the early 19th century), Öttingen-Wallerstein-Wallerstein (prince in 1774, mediatized in the early 19th century) and Öttingen-Wallerstein-Katzenstein, which became extinct in 1798. Only 3 lines actually struck coins during the 16th to 19th centuries.

OTTINGEN-OTTINGEN

This line of Öttingen counts was founded as the Protestant branch in 1557 during the Reformation. The count was granted the rank of prince in 1674. When it became extinct in 1731, its holdings were divided between Öttingen-Wallerstein-Spielberg and Öttingen-Wallerstein-Wallerstein.

RULERS
Albrecht Ernst II, 1683-1731

MINT OFFICIALS' INITIALS

Initials	Date	Name
GS, S	?	
PGN	1721-43	Paul Gottlieb Numberger in Nüremberg

PRINCIPALITY

TRADE COINAGE

KM# 80 DUCAT
3.5000 g., 0.9860 Gold 0.1109 oz. AGW **Subject:** Death of Albrecht Ernst II **Obverse:** Bust of Albrecht Ernst II right **Reverse:** Six-line inscription

Date	Mintage	VG	F	VF	XF	Unc
ND(1731)	—	1,150	2,250	3,750	6,000	—

KM# 75 5 DUCAT
17.5000 g., 0.9860 Gold 0.5547 oz. AGW **Ruler:** Albrecht Ernst II **Subject:** Marriage of Elisabeth Friderike Sophie and Karl Ludwig von Hohenlohe-Weikersheim **Obverse:** Bust right **Reverse:** Dove above falls, crowned arms with trophies

Date	Mintage	VG	F	VF	XF	Unc
ND(1713) Rare	—	—	—	—	—	—

KM# 76 10 DUCAT
35.0000 g., 0.9860 Gold 1.1095 oz. AGW **Ruler:** Albrecht Ernst II **Subject:** Marriage of Elisabeth Friderike Sophie and Karl Ludwig von Hohenlohe-Weikersheim **Obverse:** Bust right **Reverse:** Dove above falls, crowned arms with trophies

Date	Mintage	VG	F	VF	XF	Unc
ND(1713) Rare	—	—	—	—	—	—

PATTERNS

Including off metal strikes

KM#	Date	Mintage	Identification	Mkt Val
Pn2	ND(1713)	—	5 Ducat. Silver. KM#75	—
Pn3	ND(1713)	—	10 Ducat. Silver. KM#76	—

OTTINGEN-WALLERSTEIN-SPIELBERG

Öttingen-Wallenstein was divided into three branches in 1602 with Öttingen-Wallenstein-Spielberg being the senior line. The count achieved the rank of prince in 1734 and the lands were mediatized at the beginning of the 19th century.

RULERS
Franz Albrecht, 1685-1737
Johann Aloys I, 1737-1780
Johann Aloys II, 1780-1797
Johann Aloys III, 1797-1843

MINT OFFICIALS' INITIALS

Initials	Date	Name
B	1743-63	Johann Christoph Busch in Regensburg
GOZ	d.1786	Georg Christoph Gotz, die-cutter in Nüremberg
M	1759-61	Christian Ernst Muller, warden in Öttingen

PRINCIPALITY

REGULAR COINAGE

KM# 6 KREUZER
Billon **Ruler:** Johann Aloys I **Reverse:** Value in small cartouche I • KR

Date	Mintage	VG	F	VF	XF	Unc
1759	—	25.00	65.00	145	275	—

KM# 7 KREUZER
Billon **Ruler:** Johann Aloys I **Obverse:** Crowned and mantled arms, without legend **Reverse:** Value: I/KREUZER/LANMUNZ/date

Date	Mintage	VG	F	VF	XF	Unc
1759	—	45.00	75.00	155	285	—

KM# 5 KREUZER
Billon **Ruler:** Johann Aloys I **Obverse:** Armored bust right **Reverse:** Crown divides date above arms with supporters **Note:** Varieties exist.

Date	Mintage	VG	F	VF	XF	Unc
1759	—	25.00	65.00	145	275	—
1759 GOZ	—	25.00	65.00	145	275	—

KM# 8 6 KREUZER
Billon **Ruler:** Johann Aloys I **Obverse:** Armored bust right **Reverse:** Crowned arms with supporters, date divided below **Note:** Varieties exist.

Date	Mintage	VG	F	VF	XF	Unc
1759	—	35.00	90.00	185	375	—
1759 B	—	35.00	90.00	185	375	—
1759 GOZ	—	35.00	90.00	185	375	—

KM# 9 12 KREUZER
Silver **Ruler:** Johann Aloys I **Obverse:** Crowned arms with supporters **Reverse:** Value within cartouche, star divides date below **Note:** Varieties exist.

Date	Mintage	VG	F	VF	XF	Unc
1759	—	40.00	100	200	400	—

KM# 10 1/2 THALER
Silver **Ruler:** Johann Aloys I **Obverse:** ARmored bust right **Reverse:** Crowned arms with supporters, value in frame below

Date	Mintage	VG	F	VF	XF	Unc
1759	—	200	350	700	1,250	—

KM# 11 1/2 THALER
Silver **Ruler:** Johann Aloys I **Obverse:** Crowned arms with supporters, value in frame below **Reverse:** St. Sebastian

Date	Mintage	VG	F	VF	XF	Unc
1759	—	285	500	950	1,650	—

KM# 13 2/3 THALER
Silver **Ruler:** Johann Aloys I **Obverse:** Armored bust right **Reverse:** Crowned arms with supporters, value in frame below

Date	Mintage	VG	F	VF	XF	Unc
1759 B-M	—	150	275	500	900	—

KM# 14 2/3 THALER
Silver **Ruler:** Johann Aloys I **Obverse:** Armored bust right **Reverse:** Crowned arms with supporters, value in frame below

Date	Mintage	VG	F	VF	XF	Unc
1759	—	175	300	600	1,000	—

KM# 15 2/3 THALER
Silver **Ruler:** Johann Aloys I **Obverse:** Armored bust right **Reverse:** Crowned arms with supporters on pedestal, framed value below

Date	Mintage	VG	F	VF	XF	Unc
1759	—	250	400	750	1,350	—

KM# 16 THALER

Silver **Ruler:** Johann Aloys I **Obverse:** Armored bust right **Obv. Legend:** IOAN • ALOYS • I • PRINC • DE ET IN OTTINGEN **Reverse:** Crowned, mantled and supported arms **Rev. Legend:** EINE FEINE/MARCK • **Note:** Dav. #2500.

Date	Mintage	F	VF	XF	Unc
1759 M	—	500	900	1,500	2,500

KM# 17 THALER

Silver **Ruler:** Johann Aloys I **Reverse:** Value: X/EINE FEINE/MARK **Note:** Dav. #2500A.

Date	Mintage	F	VF	XF	Unc
1759	—	450	800	1,400	2,350

KM# 18 THALER

Silver **Ruler:** Johann Aloys I **Obverse:** Armored bust right **Obv. Legend:** IOAN • ALOYS • I • PRINC • DE ET IN OTTINGEN **Reverse:** Crowned arms with supporters, value in frame below **Rev. Legend:** • X •/EINE FEINE/MARCK • **Note:** Dav. #2501.

Date	Mintage	F	VF	XF	Unc
1759	—	500	900	1,500	2,500

KM# 19 THALER

Silver **Ruler:** Johann Aloys I **Obverse:** Crowned arms with supporters, value in frame below **Obv. Legend:** • X •/EINE FEINE/MARCK • **Reverse:** St. Sebastian at stake with clouds in front **Rev. Legend:** S: SEBAST: PATRONUS RHÆTIÆ **Note:** Dav. #2502.

Date	Mintage	F	VF	XF	Unc
1759	—	650	1,100	1,750	3,000

KM# 20 THALER

Silver **Ruler:** Johann Aloys I **Reverse:** Value: X/EINE FEINE/MARK **Note:** Dav. #2502A.

Date	Mintage	F	VF	XF	Unc
1759	—	600	1,000	1,600	2,750

PADERBORN

One of the principal cities of Westphalia and the seat of a bishopric from its founding by Charlemagne in 795, Paderborn is situated 23 miles (38 kilometers) south-southeast of Bielefeld and about 50 miles (80 kilometers) southeast of Münster. The bishop received the right to strike coins in 1028 and was raised to the rank of Prince of the Empire in about 1100. By the late 12th to early 13th century, the bishops were employing nine different mints in their territories. In 1802, the bishopric was secularized and its domains, as well as the city of Paderborn, were annexed to Prussia. The former bishopric was part of the Kingdom of Westphalia from 1807 to 1813, after which it was returned to Prussia. In addition to the episcopal coinage, the cathedral chapter issued a series of coins in the early 17th century and during the several interregnal years.

The town, and later city, of Paderborn grew up around the cathedral and became a member of the Hanseatic League, but failed to obtain the mint right. Eventually, the townspeople converted to Protestantism and found themselves in opposition to the Catholic bishop. The bishop prevailed and had a series of coins struck for the city in 1605. Paderborn also issued a local coinage during the early period of the Thirty Years' War.

RULERS

Hermann Werner, Wolff-Metternich zu Gracht,1683-1704
Franz Arnold, Wolff-Metternich zu Gracht, 1704-1718
Clemens August, Herzog von Bayern, 1719-1761
Sede Vacante, 1761-1763
Wilhelm Anton von der Asseburg, 1763-1782
Friedrich Wilhelm von Westfalen, 1782-1789
Franz Egon von Fürstenberg, 1789-1802

MINT OFFICIALS' INITIALS

Initials	Date	Name
AS, IAS	1764-91	Johann Anton Schroder
IW or JW	1709-13	Johann Willerding, mintmaster in Münster
AGP or AP	1712-24 (d.1742)	Anton Gerhard Pott, mintmaster
AGP or AP	1714-23	Johann Pott, mintmaster
WR	1714-18	Wilhelm Ritter, mintmaster
ABR	1783-1811	Abraham Abramson, die-cutter in Berlin
LOOS	1787-1818	Daniel Friedrich Loos, die-cutter in Berlin
PPW	Ca.1720-71	Peter Paul Werner, die-cutter in Nürnberg

ARMS

Bishopric – Maltese cross.
City – 2-fold, divided horizontally, top half with cross, bottom half has 4 vertical bars on light background.

BISHOPRIC

REGULAR COINAGE

C# 4.1 PFENNIG

Copper **Ruler:** Wilhelm Anton **Obverse:** Crowned arms **Reverse:** Value: PFENNING

Date	Mintage	VG	F	VF	XF	Unc
1766 AS	—	4.00	8.00	16.00	35.00	—
1767 AS	—	4.00	8.00	16.00	35.00	—

C# 4.2 PFENNIG

Copper **Ruler:** Wilhelm Anton **Obverse:** Crowned arms **Reverse:** Value: PFENN.

Date	Mintage	VG	F	VF	XF	Unc
1766 AS	—	4.00	8.00	16.00	35.00	—

C# 40 PFENNIG

Copper **Ruler:** Friedrich Wilhelm **Obverse:** Arms **Reverse:** Value

Date	Mintage	VG	F	VF	XF	Unc
1786	—	5.00	9.00	15.00	27.50	—

C# 1 3 PFENNING

Copper **Ruler:** Sede Vacante **Obverse:** St. Liborius **Reverse:** Value, date

Date	Mintage	VG	F	VF	XF	Unc
1761	—	8.00	15.00	25.00	40.00	—

C# A2 4 PFENNING

Copper **Ruler:** Clemens August **Obverse:** Crowned oval arms divide 4-P **Reverse:** Value, date

Date	Mintage	VG	F	VF	XF	Unc
1743	—	6.00	12.00	20.00	35.00	—

C# 2 4 PFENNING

Copper **Ruler:** Sede Vacante **Obverse:** St. Liborius **Reverse:** Value, date

Date	Mintage	VG	F	VF	XF	Unc
1761	—	8.00	15.00	25.00	40.00	—

C# 6 4 PFENNING

Billon **Ruler:** Wilhelm Anton **Obverse:** Crowned WA monogram **Reverse:** Value, date

Date	Mintage	VG	F	VF	XF	Unc
1763	—	10.00	16.00	30.00	65.00	—

KM# A1 6 PFENNING

2.2100 g., Copper, 24.6 mm. **Obverse:** Coat of arms **Reverse:** Value "VI"

Date	Mintage	F	VF	XF	Unc
1706	—	—	—	—	150

KM# A2 6 PFENNING

3.3500 g., Copper, 24.5 mm. **Ruler:** Franz Arnold **Obverse:** Crowned arms **Reverse:** Value and date

Date	Mintage	F	VF	XF	Unc
1718	—	15.00	25.00	40.00	—

C# 3 6 PFENNING

Copper **Ruler:** Sede Vacante **Obverse:** St. Liborius **Reverse:** Value, date

Date	Mintage	VG	F	VF	XF	Unc
1761	—	8.00	15.00	25.00	40.00	—

C# 12 6 PFENNING

Billon **Ruler:** Wilhelm Anton **Obverse:** Crowned monogram

Date	Mintage	VG	F	VF	XF	Unc
1764 IAS	—	18.00	32.00	65.00	110	—
1765 IAS	—	18.00	32.00	65.00	110	—

C# 10 MATTIER

Billon **Ruler:** Wilhelm Anton **Obverse:** Crowned monogram **Reverse:** Value, date

Date	Mintage	VG	F	VF	XF	Unc
1767 IAS	—	20.00	35.00	65.00	120	—

C# 8 1/2 MARIENGROSCHEN

Billon **Ruler:** Wilhelm Anton **Obverse:** Crowned monogram **Reverse:** Value, date

Date	Mintage	VG	F	VF	XF	Unc
1763	—	15.00	30.00	60.00	110	—

C# 15 MARIENGROSCHEN

Billon **Ruler:** Wilhelm Anton **Obverse:** Crowned monogram **Reverse:** Value, date

Date	Mintage	VG	F	VF	XF	Unc
1763	—	12.00	25.00	50.00	85.00	—

C# 17 MARIENGROSCHEN

Billon **Ruler:** Wilhelm Anton **Reverse:** Value: 504 EINE ...

Date	Mintage	VG	F	VF	XF	Unc
1770 IAS	—	18.00	30.00	60.00	100	—
1771 IAS	—	18.00	30.00	60.00	100	—
1774 IAS	—	10.00	20.00	40.00	65.00	—

C# 18 2 MARIENGROSCHEN

Billon **Ruler:** Wilhelm Anton **Obverse:** Crowned monogram in cartouche **Reverse:** Value, date

Date	Mintage	VG	F	VF	XF	Unc
1763 IAS	—	15.00	28.00	55.00	95.00	—
1765 IAS	—	15.00	28.00	55.00	95.00	—

C# 19 2 MARIENGROSCHEN

Billon **Ruler:** Wilhelm Anton **Obverse:** Crowned monogram

Date	Mintage	VG	F	VF	XF	Unc
1764 IAS	—	12.00	25.00	50.00	85.00	—
1765 IAS	—	12.00	25.00	50.00	85.00	—
1766 IAS	—	12.00	25.00	50.00	85.00	—

C# 44 16 GUTE GROSCHEN

Silver **Ruler:** Friedrich Wilhelm **Obverse:** Crowned arms within Order chain **Reverse:** Value, date

Date	Mintage	VG	F	VF	XF	Unc
1785	—	37.50	65.00	100	160	—

C# 32 24 MARIENGROSCHEN

Silver **Ruler:** Wilhelm Anton **Obverse:** Arms within crowned mantle **Reverse:** Value, date

Date	Mintage	VG	F	VF	XF	Unc
1765 IAS	—	70.00	110	200	500	—

C# 28 20 KREUZER

Silver **Ruler:** Wilhelm Anton **Obverse:** Arms within crowned mantle **Reverse:** Value, date **Note:** Convention 20 Kreuzer.

Date	Mintage	VG	F	VF	XF	Unc
1764 IAS	—	30.00	50.00	90.00	150	—
1765 IAS	—	30.00	50.00	90.00	150	—
1766 IAS	—	25.00	45.00	85.00	140	—
1767 IAS	—	25.00	45.00	85.00	140	—

C# 21 1/12 THALER

Billon **Ruler:** Wilhelm Anton **Obverse:** Crowned and mantled arms **Reverse:** Value, date

Date	Mintage	VG	F	VF	XF	Unc
1764 IAS	—	15.00	25.00	45.00	90.00	—
1765 IAS	—	15.00	25.00	45.00	90.00	—
1766 IAS	—	15.00	25.00	45.00	90.00	—
1767 IAS	—	15.00	25.00	45.00	90.00	—
1776 IAS	—	15.00	25.00	45.00	90.00	—

C# 23 1/12 THALER

Billon **Ruler:** Wilhelm Anton **Obverse:** Crowned monogram in cartouche **Reverse:** Value, date

Date	Mintage	VG	F	VF	XF	Unc
1764	—	17.50	30.00	60.00	110	—
1765	—	17.50	30.00	60.00	110	—
1766	—	17.50	30.00	60.00	110	—

C# 22 1/12 THALER

Billon **Ruler:** Wilhelm Anton **Obverse:** Crowned arms in cartouche **Reverse:** Value, date

Date	Mintage	VG	F	VF	XF	Unc
1765 IAS	—	17.50	35.00	60.00	115	—

C# 24 1/12 THALER

Billon **Ruler:** Wilhelm Anton **Obverse:** Bust right **Reverse:** Value, date

Date	Mintage	VG	F	VF	XF	Unc
1767 IAS Rare	—	—	—	—	—	—

C# 42 1/12 THALER

Billon **Ruler:** Friedrich Wilhelm **Obverse:** Arms **Reverse:** Value

Date	Mintage	VG	F	VF	XF	Unc
1783	—	10.00	20.00	40.00	80.00	—

C# 26 1/6 THALER

Silver **Ruler:** Wilhelm Anton **Obverse:** Crowned and mantled arms **Reverse:** Value, date

Date	Mintage	VG	F	VF	XF	Unc
1764 IAS	—	20.00	35.00	60.00	115	—
1766 IAS	—	20.00	35.00	60.00	115	—
1769 IAS	—	20.00	35.00	60.00	115	—
1772 IAS	—	20.00	35.00	60.00	115	—

C# 46 1/2 THALER

Silver **Ruler:** Friedrich Wilhelm **Obverse:** Crowned arms within Order chain divide date **Reverse:** St. Liborius **Note:** Convention 1/2 Thaler.

Date	Mintage	VG	F	VF	XF	Unc
1786	—	45.00	90.00	165	300	—

C# 30 2/3 THALER

Silver **Ruler:** Wilhelm Anton **Obverse:** Draped bust right **Reverse:** Arms within crowned mantle, framed value below

Date	Mintage	VG	F	VF	XF	Unc
1764 AS	—	85.00	135	275	550	—
1765 AS	—	85.00	135	275	550	—
1770 AS	—	85.00	135	275	550	—

DAV# 2509 THALER

Silver **Ruler:** Franz Arnold **Obverse:** Crowned arms divide date **Obv. Legend:** FRANC • ARNOL • DG • EP • PAD • & MON • BVR • STR • S • R • I • P • C • PY • & D • IN BOR • **Reverse:** 2 saints **Rev. Legend:** FRAN: ARM: EL. COA. PA. 15 SEP. 1703. SVC • PATRVO • 21 MAY • 1704 • EL • EP • MO • 30 SEP: 1706, PRO/LEGE & GREGE below saints

Date	Mintage	F	VF	XF	Unc
1709 JW	—	300	600	1,150	2,000
1710 JW	—	300	600	1,150	2,000
1711 JW	—	300	600	1,150	2,000

DAV# 2510 THALER

Silver **Ruler:** Franz Arnold **Obverse:** Armored bust right **Obv. Legend:** FRANC • ARNOLD • D • G • EPISC • PADERB • ET MONASTER • **Reverse:** Crowned arms divide initials, date in legend **Rev. Legend:** BURGG • STROMB • S • R • I • P • COM • PYRM • DOM • IN • BOR(C)K. ET WEHRT: date

Date	Mintage	F	VF	XF	Unc
1712 IW	—	450	850	1,500	2,500
1713 AP	—	450	850	1,500	2,500
1714 AP	—	450	850	1,500	2,500
1715 AP	—	450	850	1,500	2,500

DAV# 2511 THALER

Silver **Ruler:** Franz Arnold **Obverse:** Bust right with plainer cloak **Obv. Legend:** FRANC: ARNOLD: D • G: EP: PADERB: ET MON: **Reverse:** Crowned ornate arms divide initials **Rev. Legend:** BURGG: STROMB: S: R: I: P: COM: PYRM: ET: DOM: IN: BORK: date *

Date	Mintage	F	VF	XF	Unc
1716 AGP	—	450	850	1,500	2,500
1717 AGP	—	450	850	1,500	2,500
1718 AGP	—	450	850	1,500	2,500

DAV# 2512 THALER

Silver **Ruler:** Clemens August **Subject:** Sede Vacante **Obverse:** St. Liboris with mottos above church **Obv. Legend:** CAPITVLVM CATHEDRALE PADERBORNENSE SEDE VACANTE 1719 **Reverse:** Inscription in border above bishop's mitre on cushion **Rev. Legend:** * REDDE MIHI LAETITIAM SALVTARIS TVI ET SPIRITV PRINCIPALI CONFIRMA ME., in border; IN/CHARITATE/NON FICTA/2. AD. COR. 6 v.6, on band; CVM CECIDERIT NON COLLIDETVR. Ps. 36 v. 24

Date	Mintage	F	VF	XF	Unc
1719 AGP	—	250	450	800	1,400

DAV# 2513 THALER

Silver **Ruler:** Clemens August **Obverse:** Draped bust right **Obv. Legend:** CLEM • AVG: D • G • EP • - PAD & MON • C • COL • V • B • ET S • P • D • **Reverse:** Crowned and mantled arms divide date **Rev. Legend:** COM • PAL • RH • L • LEVCHT • B • STR • - S • R • I • P • COM • PYRM • D • IN • BORCK • & W •

Date	Mintage	F	VF	XF	Unc
1723 AGP	—	450	850	1,500	2,500

C# 35 THALER

Silver **Ruler:** Wilhelm Anton **Obverse:** Draped bust right **Obv. Legend:** WILH • ANT • D • G • EPS • PADERB • S • R • I • PR • COM • PYRM • **Reverse:** Arms within crowned mantle **Rev. Legend:** X • STUCK EINE - FEINE MARCK, on a band below; IUSTE ET CONSTANTER **Note:** Convention Thaler; Dav.#2514.

Date	Mintage	F	VF	XF	Unc
1764	—	250	600	1,000	1,850
1765 AS	—	250	600	1,000	1,850

C# 36 THALER

Silver **Ruler:** Wilhelm Anton **Reverse:** Crowned and mantled arms divide date, value **Note:** Dav.#2515.

Date	Mintage	F	VF	XF	Unc
1766 AS	—	650	1,250	2,250	3,500

C# 36.5 THALER

Silver **Ruler:** Wilhelm Anton **Obverse:** Seated St. Liborius **Reverse:** Crowned and mantled arms, date, value **Note:** Dav.#A2515.

Date	Mintage	F	VF	XF	Unc
1766 AS Rare	—	—	—	—	—

C# 37 THALER

Silver **Ruler:** Wilhelm Anton **Obverse:** Arms within crowned mantle, date divided below **Obv. Legend:** WILHELMUS ANTONIUS D • G • EPIS C• PAD • S • R • I • P • COM • PYRM •, X/EINE FEINE MARCK below **Reverse:** St. Liborius **Rev. Legend:** * S•LIBORIUS - PATR•PADERB•*, HIC EST QUI MULTUM ORAT PRO POPULO • MACK • L• 2•15•12 **Note:** Dav.#2516.

Date	Mintage	F	VF	XF	Unc
1767 AS	—	200	450	800	1,500

C# 39 5 THALER

6.6500 g., 0.9000 Gold 0.1924 oz. AGW **Ruler:** Wilhelm Anton **Obverse:** Bust right **Reverse:** Crowned and mantled arms, value, date

Date	Mintage	F	VF	XF	Unc
1765 AS	—	650	1,250	2,250	3,500

Date	Mintage	F	VF	XF	Unc
1767 AS	—	650	1,250	2,250	3,500

TRADE COINAGE

FR# 1962 DUCAT

3.5000 g., 0.9860 Gold 0.1109 oz. AGW **Ruler:** Franz Arnold **Obverse:** Armored bust right **Reverse:** Crowned arms

Date	Mintage	VG	F	VF	XF	Unc
1713 AP	—	400	900	2,000	3,500	—

FR# 1963 DUCAT

3.5000 g., 0.9860 Gold 0.1109 oz. AGW **Ruler:** Clemens August **Obverse:** Bust right

Date	Mintage	VG	F	VF	XF	Unc
1720 AP	—	500	1,000	2,250	4,000	—

C# 38 DUCAT

3.5000 g., 0.9860 Gold 0.1109 oz. AGW **Ruler:** Wilhelm Anton **Obverse:** Bust right **Reverse:** Arms within crowned mantle **Note:** Fr. #1965.

Date	Mintage	F	VF	XF	Unc
1770	—	—	—	—	—
1776	—	450	850	1,650	3,250
1777	—	450	850	1,650	3,250

C# 48 DUCAT

3.5000 g., 0.9860 Gold 0.1109 oz. AGW **Ruler:** Friedrich Wilhelm **Obverse:** Titles of Friedrich Wilhelm **Reverse:** Value, date

Date	Mintage	F	VF	XF	Unc
1784	—	550	1,000	2,150	3,750

PATTERNS

Including off metal strikes

KM#	Date	Mintage	Identification	Mkt Val
Pn1	1763	—	Thaler. Copper. C34.	—
Pn2	1767	—	Pfennig. Silver. C4.1	—
Pn3	1767	—	5 Thaler. Copper. C39.	—

PASSAU

The Bishopric, in Bavaria, near the Austrian border, was established in 738. The bishops obtained the mint right prior to 999 but they originally struck coins jointly at the imperial mint in Passau. Ecclesiastical coinage began in the 12th century. In 1803, Passau was secularized and divided between Bavaria and Salzburg. In 1805 Bavaria absorbed the Salzburg portion.

RULERS

Johann Philipp, Graf von Lamberg, 1689-1712
Raimund Ferdinand, Graf von Rabatta, 1713-1722
Josef Dominik, Graf von Lamberg, 1723-1761
Josef Maria, Graf von Thun, administrator, 1761-1763
Leopold Ernst Joseph, Graf von Firmian, 1763-1783, Cardinal in 1772
Josef Franz Anton, Fürst von Auersberg, 1783-1795
Thomas, Graf von Thun, 1795-1796
Leopold, Graf von Thun, 1796-1803

ARMS

Springing or rampant wolf, usually 1 and w/arms of bishop's own family.

MINT OFFICIALS' INITIALS

Initials	Date	Name
PHM or star (b)	1677-1718	Philipp Heinrich Müller, die-cutter in Augsburg
SEIZ	ca.1688-1706	V. Seiz, die-cutter in Passau and Salzburg
(c) – 1 or 2 wings or IMF	1700-38	Johann Michael Federer, mintmaster in Regensburg
	1700-05	Johann Georg Fischer, warden in Augsburg
D	? – ca.1730	Daniel Sigmund Dockler, die-cutter in Nürnberg
D	1730-40 (Vienna), 1745- (Nürnberg)	Matthias Donner, medailleur
HS or H. ST	ca.1767-82	Johann Heinrich Straub, die-cutter in Munich
I S V AHAM F	1768-1812	Ignaz Joseph Schäufel v. Aham, die-cutter in Munich

BISHOPRIC

REGULAR COINAGE

KM# 4 2 KREUZER

Silver **Obverse:** Cardinal's hat above script JP monogram **Reverse:** Crowned 4-fold arms with central shield divide date, value 2 below

Date	Mintage	VG	F	VF	XF	Unc
1711	—	60.00	100	200	325	—

C# 6 1/8 THALER

Silver **Ruler:** Leopold Ernst Joseph **Subject:** Homage Commemorative **Obverse:** Crowned and mantled arms at top, animals in frame below **Reverse:** Inscription

Date	Mintage	VG	F	VF	XF	Unc
1764	—	35.00	70.00	150	250	—

C# 6.5 1/4 THALER

Silver **Ruler:** Leopold Ernst Joseph **Subject:** Homage Commemorative **Obverse:** Crowned and mantled arms at top, animals in frame below **Reverse:** Inscription

Date	Mintage	VG	F	VF	XF	Unc
1764	—	40.00	80.00	165	275	—

DAV# 2517 THALER

Silver **Ruler:** Johann Philipp **Obverse:** Bust right **Obv. Legend:** IOAN: PHILIP: CARDINAL: DE LAMBERG * **Reverse:** Cardinal's hat above arms **Rev. Legend:** D • G • EP • PATAV • - S • R • I • PRINCEPS

Date	Mintage	VG	F	VF	XF	Unc
1701 (b)/(a)	—	200	400	700	1,400	—

DAV# 2518 THALER
Silver **Ruler:** Johann Philipp **Obverse:** Capped bust right **Obv. Legend:** IOAN: PHILP: CARDINAL: DE LAMBERG •, SEIZ below bust **Reverse:** Cardinal's hat and head above arms **Rev. Legend:** D • G • EP • PATAV • - S • R • I • PRINCEPS •

Date	Mintage	VG	F	VF	XF	Unc
1703	—	200	400	700	1,400	—

DAV# 2519 THALER
Silver **Ruler:** Johann Philipp **Obverse:** Bust right, SIEZ. F below **Reverse:** Taller capped arms, date above

Date	Mintage	VG	F	VF	XF	Unc
1706	—	900	1,500	2,500	—	—

DAV# 2520 THALER
Silver **Ruler:** Johann Philipp **Obverse:** Bust right **Obv. Legend:** IOAN: PHILIP: CARDINAL: DE LAMBERG, SEIZE below bust **Reverse:** Cardinal's hat above arms **Rev. Legend:** D • G • EP • PATAV • - S • R • I • PRINCEPS •

Date	Mintage	VG	F	VF	XF	Unc
1712	—	225	450	800	1,450	—

DAV# 2521 THALER
Silver **Ruler:** Raimund Ferdinand **Obverse:** Bust right **Obv. Legend:** RAYMVND: FERD: D: G: EPISC: PASSAV: **Reverse:** Crowned arms in frame divide date **Rev. Legend:** SAC: ROM: IMP: PRINC: EX COMITIBVS: DE RABATTA *

Date	Mintage	VG	F	VF	XF	Unc
1714	—	300	650	1,200	2,000	—

Date	Mintage	VG	F	VF	XF	Unc
1716	—	300	650	1,200	2,000	—
1717	—	300	650	1,200	2,000	—

C# 1 THALER
Silver **Ruler:** Josef Dominik **Obverse:** Bust right **Obv. Legend:** IOSEPH • DOMINIC • D • G • EPISC • PATAV • **Reverse:** Crowned imperial eagle with crowned arms on breast, date **Rev. Legend:** SAC • ROM • IMP • PRINCEPS • - COM • DE LAMBERG 1723 **Note:** Dav. #2522.

Date	Mintage	F	VF	XF	Unc
1723	—	250	500	900	1,500
1723 ICB	—	250	500	900	1,500

C# 2 THALER
Silver **Ruler:** Josef Dominik **Obverse:** Bust right, title of cardinal **Obv. Legend:** IOS • DOMINIC • CARDINAL • DE LAMBERG **Reverse:** Cardinal's hat above arms on eagle's breast **Rev. Legend:** D • G • EPISC • PATAV • - S • R • I • PRINC • 1753 **Note:** Dav. #2523.

Date	Mintage	F	VF	XF	Unc
1753	—	300	650	1,200	2,000

C# 7 THALER
Silver **Ruler:** Leopold Ernst Joseph **Obverse:** Bust right **Reverse:** Crowned and mantled arms **Note:** Dav. #2524.

Date	Mintage	F	VF	XF	Unc
1767	—	225	525	1,000	1,850

C# 8 THALER
Silver **Ruler:** Leopold Ernst Joseph **Obverse:** Bust right **Reverse:** Cardinal's hat above arms within mantle **Note:** Dav. #2525.

Date	Mintage	F	VF	XF	Unc
1779 H. ST	—	200	400	800	1,500

C# 10 THALER
Silver **Ruler:** Josef Franz Anton **Obverse:** Bust right **Obv. Legend:** IOSEPH • EX PRIN • DE AVERSBERG S • R • ECCL • CARDIN • *, I: S: V: AHAM: F: below **Reverse:** Oval arms within crowned mantle **Rev. Legend:** EXEMTAE ECCLE • PASSAV • EPISC • ET S • R • I • PRINC • 1792 • **Note:** Dav. #2526.

Date	Mintage	F	VF	XF	Unc
1792 I.S.V. AHAM. F.	—	200	400	750	1,450

TRADE COINAGE

FR# 2070 1/2 DUCAT
1.7500 g., 0.9860 Gold 0.0555 oz. AGW **Ruler:** Johann Philipp **Obverse:** Monogram below cardinal's hat **Reverse:** Capped arms divide date

Date	Mintage	VG	F	VF	XF	Unc
1709 (c)	—	250	500	900	1,600	—

FR# 2072 1/2 DUCAT
1.7500 g., 0.9860 Gold 0.0555 oz. AGW **Ruler:** Raimund Ferdinand **Obverse:** Crowned RF monogram **Reverse:** Wolf holding oval shield, date above

Date	Mintage	VG	F	VF	XF	Unc
1716 D	—	300	600	1,250	2,250	—

FR# 2069.1 DUCAT
3.5000 g., 0.9860 Gold 0.1109 oz. AGW **Ruler:** Johann Philipp **Reverse:** Arms below cardinal's hat, date above

Date	Mintage	VG	F	VF	XF	Unc
1705 (b)/(c)	—	400	800	1,600	2,750	—
1706 (b)/(c)	—	400	800	1,600	2,750	—

FR# 2069.2 DUCAT
3.5000 g., 0.9860 Gold 0.1109 oz. AGW **Ruler:** Johann Philipp **Obverse:** Large bust of Johann Philip

Date	Mintage	VG	F	VF	XF	Unc
1709 (b)	—	400	800	1,600	2,750	—

FR# 2071 DUCAT
3.5000 g., 0.9860 Gold 0.1109 oz. AGW **Ruler:** Raimund Ferdinand **Obverse:** Bust right **Reverse:** Crowned round arms, date at top

Date	Mintage	VG	F	VF	XF	Unc
1716	—	500	1,000	2,000	3,250	—

C# 3 DUCAT
3.5000 g., 0.9860 Gold 0.1109 oz. AGW **Ruler:** Josef Dominik **Obverse:** Bust right **Reverse:** Cardinal's hat above arms

Date	Mintage	VG	F	VF	XF	Unc
1747 D	—	400	800	1,600	2,750	—

C# 9 DUCAT

3.5000 g., 0.9860 Gold 0.1109 oz. AGW **Ruler:** Leopold Ernst Joseph **Obverse:** Bust right **Reverse:** Capped and mantled arms, date below

Date	Mintage	F	VF	XF	Unc
1779 HS	—	500	1,000	2,000	3,000

FR# 2068.1 2 DUCAT

7.0000 g., 0.9860 Gold 0.2219 oz. AGW **Ruler:** Johann Philipp **Reverse:** Arms below cardinal's hat, date above

Date	Mintage	VG	F	VF	XF	Unc
1701 (b)/(a)	—	1,000	2,000	4,000	6,500	—

C# 4 5 DUCAT

17.5000 g., 0.9860 Gold 0.5547 oz. AGW **Ruler:** Josef Dominik **Obverse:** Bust right, title of cardinal **Reverse:** Crowned imperial eagle with cardinal's hat above arms

Date	Mintage	VG	F	VF	XF	Unc
1753	—	—	—	12,500	20,000	—

Note: Struck with 1 Thaler dies, C#2

C# 5 6 DUCAT

21.0000 g., 0.9860 Gold 0.6657 oz. AGW **Ruler:** Josef Dominik **Obverse:** Bust right, titles of cardinal **Reverse:** Crowned imperial eagle, cardinal's hat above arms **Note:** Struck with 1 Thaler dies, C#2.

Date	Mintage	F	VF	XF	Unc
1753	—	—	—	15,000	22,500

KM# 110 10 DUCAT

35.0000 g., 0.9860 Gold 1.1095 oz. AGW **Note:** Struck with 1 Thaler dies, Dav. #5718.

Date	Mintage	VG	F	VF	XF	Unc
1703 SEIZ/MF Rare	—	—	—	—	—	—

PATTERNS

Including off metal strikes

KM#	Date	Mintage	Identification	Mkt Val
Pn1	1723	—	Thaler. Copper. C#1.	—
Pn2	1747	—	Ducat. Tin. C#3.	100
Pn3	1747	—	Ducat. Lead. C#3.	—
Pn4	1747	—	Ducat. Silver. C#3.	125
Pn6	1764	—	1/8 Thaler. Gold. C#6.	—
Pn7	1779	—	Thaler. Tin. C#8.	—
Pn8	1779	—	Ducat. Tin. C#9.	—
Pn9	1779	—	Ducat. Copper. C#9.	—
Pn10	1792	—	Thaler. Lead. C#10.	—

PFALZ

(Rhenish Palatinate, Rheinpfalz)

The Counts Palatine originally administered and exercised judicial functions over the imperial household of the Holy Roman Emperor, based at the center of Charlemagne's empire, Aachen. They gradually acquired territories in the middle Rhine. From1214 onwards the position was hereditary in the Wittelsbach family, who also controlled Bavaria. For a time the electoral dignity alternated between the Bavarian and Palatinate branches of the Wittelsbach family, until the Golden Bull in1356 settled it upon the Palatinate branch.

When the Protestant nobles in Prague elected Friedrich V, who was also a Protestant, as King of Bohemia in 1618, it precipitated a conflict which became known as the Thirty Years' War. Bohemia had been ruled by the Catholic Habsburg Emperors from Vienna since 1527 and Ferdinand II, was incensed at being rebuffed for the crown. Friedrich V lost his battles with Ferdinand II's armies and had to flee to the Hague and to the protection of his father-in-law, King James I of England. He would forever after be known as "The Winter King" in ridicule of his short reign. As punishment, the electoral dignity was taken from the Pfalz branch of the Wittelsbachs and given to the rival branch, the Catholic Duke of Bavaria. As one of the general conditions set forth in the Peace of Westphalia in 1648-50, an eighth electorship was created for Pfalz and thus the dignity was restored to the family.

The conversion of the electors to Roman Catholicism led to the expulsion of Huguenots and other Protestants from their territories, many of whom made their way to America, founding New Paltz, New York. In the course of the later seventeenth and eighteenth centuries, the various branches of the Palatinate were left without any legitimate heirs, so that Karl The odor was able to combine the thrones of Jülich-Berg, the Palatinate, and Bavaria after the War of the Bavarian Succession.

Karl Theodor was a great Maecenas, whose orchestra at Mannheim was one of the greatest in Europe. He was a patron of Mozart, who wrote *Idomeneo* for the opera house in Munich, and of the chemist Benjamin Thompson, later Count Rumford, who fled Massachusetts when the American Revolution broke out and sought refuge in Bavaria.

The Palatinate was administered as part of Bavaria from1777, and did not mint any separate coins after 1802. The territories which composed the Palatinate were scattered over central Germany, and now form part of the West German states of Bavaria, Baden, Hesse, and Rheinland-Pfalz. The chief industry is bulk chemicals, from the great BASF factory at Ludwigshafen.

In 1753 Bavaria and Austria concluded a monetary convention, reducing the fineness of the thaler to the point that 20 gulden could be coined from a Mark of fine silver. The most important result was that henceforth the gulden, rather than being worth 2/3 of a thaler, was henceforth worth half a thaler. This Convention standard was soon afterwards adopted by most of the states of southwest Germany, including the Palatinate.

The Electors Palatine and the Saxon Elector acted as Vicars of the Empire after the death of a Holy Roman Emperor and before a new one was elected; the Elector Palatine in the areas of Franconian and Suevic law, the Saxon Elector in the areas where Saxon law applied. Both principalities issued coins commemorating the vicariates. Thus the Elector, Palatine Karl Theodor Actedas, Vicar of the Empire in 1790, after the death of Josef II, and again in 1792, after the early death of Leopold II, and issued coins in those two years. These coins are analogous to the "Sede Vacante" coins of ecclesiastical principalities.

ELECTORAL PFALZ

(Rhenish Pfalz, Rheinpfalz, Churpfalz, Kurpfalz)
Line of Succession in the Electoral Dignity

Once the electorship was vested in the Palatine line of the Wittelsbachs, it passed by right of succession through the senior male line until the death of Friedrich II in 1556. His nephew Otto Heinrich then received the dignity, but this failed at his death three years later. The branch of the family with the highest seniority at this time was that of Pfalz-Simmern and it was to it that the electoral office passed. The electorship was lost, as stated above, in 1623 as a result of Friedrich V's actions and not restored until the end of the Thirty Years' War in 1648 as part of the peace settlement. The royal coinage of Friedrich V for Bohemia is listed under that entity. From 1622 until 1648, the Upper Palatinate and part of the Rhenish Palatinate were administered by Bavaria, which struck coins for use in those territories. See Bavaria for listings of those issues. The Simmern line died out in 1685 and the office of elector fell to Pfalz-Neuburg, the rulers of which were also dukes of Jülich-Berg. The coinage issued of these Pfalz-Neuburg rulers are often confused one with the other and it is sometimes difficult to separate issues for Electoral Pfalz from those of Jülich-Berg, particularly because some issues for one principality were produced or at least the dies were made in the mint of the other territory. The fate of extinction befell the Pfalz-Neuburg line in 1742 and all its lands and titles passed to Pfalz-Sulzbach for one generation. The Elector also became duke and elector in Bavaria when the Wittelsbach line in that principality became extinct and the two branches of the family were finally united after a breach of centuries. Once again the electoral dignity passed to another branch of the Palatine family, this time to Pfalz-Birkenfeld in 1799. With the abolition of the Holy Roman Empire by Napoleon in 1806, the electoral college was no longer needed and passed quietly away.

RULERS

Johann Wilhelm von Neuburg, 1690-1716
Karl Philipp von Neuburg, 1716-1742
Karl Theodor von Sulzbach, 1742-1799
Maximilian I Joseph von Birkenfeld, 1799-1805

MINT OFFICIALS' INITIALS

DÜSSELDORF MINT

Initials	Date	Name
IH	1724-26	Johann Hitorff, mintmaster
RF	1728-35	Richard Fehr, mintmaster
FM	1735-48	Friedrich Maul, mintmaster
CLS	1767-70	Karl Ludwig Selche, mintmaster
PM	1771-83	Paul Maassen, mintmaster

HEIDELBERG MINT

Initials	Date	Name
	1620	Johan Ludwig Eichesstein, mintmaster
GP	1650-63	Georg Pfründt, die-cutter in Nürnberg
(a)	1656-59	Johan Kasimir Herman, mintmaster
	1659-76	Johann Kaspar Herman, mintmaster
	1657-?	Michael Koch, warden
ISS	1658-59	Unknown die-cutter
	1659-76	Sebastian Müller, warden
IL, L	1659-1711	Johann Linck, die-cutter and mintmaster
GB	1684-92	Johann Gerhard Bender, mintmaster
IMW, MW	1694-1709	Johann Michael Wunsch, mintmaster
	1705-16	Johann Selter, die-cutter
IGW, GW	1711-28	Johann Georg Wunsch, mintmaster
AC	1716-35	Anton Cajet, die-cutter and warden
WS	1716-35	Wigand Schäffer, die-cutter
W	1728-35	Johann Melcior Wunsch, mintmaster
RF	1731-35	Richard Fehr, mintmaster
	1733-35	Johann Konrad Kaltschmidt, mintmaster

MANNHEIM MINT

Initials	Date	Name
	1607-10	Johann Ludwig Eichelstein, mintmaster
WS	1735-45	Wigand Schäffer, die-cutter
	1745-58	As warden and mintmaster
	1735-36	Johann Konrad Kaltschmidt, warden
	1736-38	Adam Palm, warden
FO, O	1743-50	Franz Offner, mintmaster
N	1746-47	C. Niesner, mintmaster
	1746-?	Georg Christof Deyl, warden
AS, S	1748-64	Anton Schäffer, die-cutter
	1764-99	As mintmaster
AK	1749-71	Andreas Koch, mintmaster
	1764-66	Joseph Schäffer, die-cutter
	1770-71	Georg Christoph Wächter, die-cutter
	?-1776	Friedrich Schäffer, die-cutter
	1778-89	Johann Georg Dieze (Dietz), warden
	1789-1812	Heinrich Boltschauser, die-cutter
FE	1799-1805	Friedrich Christof Eberle, warden

ARMS

Pfalz – rampant lion to left or right
Bavaria or old Wittelsbach – field of lozenges (diamond shapes)
Electorate – blank shield, sometimes shaded with closely spaced horizontal lines or ..arabesques
..- also, an imperial orb

MONETARY SYSTEMS

8 Pfenning = 2 Kreuzer = 1 Albus
16 Pfenning = 4 Kreuzer = 2 Albus = 1 Batzen

PFALZ-BIRKENFELD-ZWEIBRUCKEN

RULERS

Christian IV, 1735-1775
Karl II, 1775-1795
Maximilian I Joseph, 1795-1799

MINT OFFICIALS' INITIALS

Initials	Date	Name
EHF	Ca.1760	Eberhard Gregorius Fleischhold, die-cutter
IM, M	1758-69	Joseph Mellinger
IW, W	1765-90	Johann Weichinger
S	1744-99	Anton Schäffer, die-cutter

COUNTY

REGULAR COINAGE

KM# 60 HELLER

Copper **Ruler:** Karl II **Obverse:** Crowned lion arms **Reverse:** Value, date

Date	Mintage	VG	F	VF	XF	Unc
1788	—	18.00	30.00	55.00	110	—

KM# 23 1/4 KREUZER

Copper **Ruler:** Christian IV **Obverse:** Crowned CP monogram, P-Z **Reverse:** Value, date

Date	Mintage	VG	F	VF	XF	Unc
1759 M	—	10.00	20.00	40.00	70.00	—
1764 M	—	10.00	20.00	40.00	70.00	—
1767 M	—	10.00	20.00	40.00	70.00	—
1774	—	10.00	20.00	40.00	70.00	—

KM# 24 1/2 KREUZER

Copper **Ruler:** Christian IV **Obverse:** Crowned CP monogram, P-Z **Reverse:** Value, date

Date	Mintage	VG	F	VF	XF	Unc
1759	—	10.00	20.00	45.00	90.00	—

KM# 61 1/2 KREUZER

Copper **Ruler:** Karl II **Obverse:** Crowned C P monogram **Reverse:** Value above date

Date	Mintage	VG	F	VF	XF	Unc
1788	—	12.00	25.00	50.00	100	—

KM# 5 KREUZER

Billon **Ruler:** Christian IV **Obverse:** Crowned monogram **Reverse:** Value, date in cartouche

Date	Mintage	VG	F	VF	XF	Unc
1747 Rare	108	—	—	—	—	—

KM# 44 KREUZER

Silver **Ruler:** Christian IV **Obverse:** Crowned oval arms between 2 branches divide P-Z near top **Reverse:** 1/KR/M in cartouche, date in legend **Rev. Legend:** NACH DEM CONV. FVS **Note:** Convention Kreuzer. Similar to KM#55.

Date	Mintage	VG	F	VF	XF	Unc
1765 M	—	7.00	14.00	32.00	65.00	—

KM# 55 KREUZER

Copper **Ruler:** Christian IV **Obverse:** Crowned lion arms **Reverse:** Value, legend and date

Date	Mintage	VG	F	VF	XF	Unc
1774 W	—	8.00	16.00	35.00	70.00	—

KM# 56 KREUZER

Copper **Ruler:** Christian IV **Obverse:** Crowned oval lion shield in wreath

Date	Mintage	VG	F	VF	XF	Unc
1774	—	30.00	60.00	125	225	—

KM# 62 KREUZER

Copper **Ruler:** Karl II **Obverse:** Crowned lion arms, PZ divided above **Reverse:** Value, date within wreath

Date	Mintage	VG	F	VF	XF	Unc
1788	—	10.00	20.00	40.00	80.00	—

KM# 6 2 KREUZER

Billon **Ruler:** Christian IV **Obverse:** Crowned C4 monogram **Reverse:** Value, date in cartouche

Date	Mintage	VG	F	VF	XF	Unc
1747	300	60.00	100	200	450	—

KM# 25 2 KREUZER

Billon **Ruler:** Christian IV **Obverse:** Crowned monogram **Reverse:** Value, date

Date	Mintage	VG	F	VF	XF	Unc
1759	—	8.00	16.00	35.00	70.00	—
1763	—	8.00	16.00	35.00	70.00	—

KM# 7 4 KREUZER

Billon **Ruler:** Christian IV **Obverse:** Crowned monogram **Reverse:** Value, date in cartouche

Date	Mintage	VG	F	VF	XF	Unc
1747 Rare	190	—	—	—	—	—

KM# 8 4 KREUZER

Billon **Ruler:** Christian IV **Obverse:** Angular lion shield on crowned C4 monogram **Reverse:** Value, date

Date	Mintage	VG	F	VF	XF	Unc
1747 Rare	Inc. above	—	—	—	—	—

KM# 26 4 KREUZER

Billon **Ruler:** Christian IV **Obverse:** Crowned CP monogram, P-Z

Date	Mintage	VG	F	VF	XF	Unc
1759	—	18.00	30.00	55.00	120	—

KM# 39 5 KREUZER

Silver **Ruler:** Christian IV **Obverse:** Crowned lion arms within branches **Reverse:** Value, date within frame **Note:** Convention 5 Kreuzer.

Date	Mintage	VG	F	VF	XF	Unc
1763 M	—	90.00	140	250	475	—
1764 M	—	90.00	140	250	475	—
1765 M	—	90.00	140	250	475	—

KM# 48 5 KREUZER

Silver **Ruler:** Christian IV **Obverse:** Crowned lion arms on pedestal **Reverse:** Value around outer edges of ornamental square

Date	Mintage	VG	F	VF	XF	Unc
1766 M	—	28.00	50.00	100	225	—
1767 M	—	28.00	50.00	100	225	—

KM# 35 10 KREUZER

Silver **Ruler:** Christian IV **Obverse:** Head right between branches **Reverse:** Crowned lion shield on pedestal, value, date **Rev. Legend:** NACH DEM.. **Note:** Convention 10 Kreuzer.

Date	Mintage	VG	F	VF	XF	Unc
1760	—	18.00	30.00	60.00	100	—

KM# 40 10 KREUZER

Silver **Ruler:** Christian IV **Obverse:** Head right **Reverse:** Crowned lion arms on pedestal sith value

Date	Mintage	VG	F	VF	XF	Unc
1763 IM	—	18.00	30.00	60.00	100	—
1764 M	—	18.00	30.00	60.00	100	—
1765 M	—	18.00	30.00	60.00	100	—

KM# 42 10 KREUZER

Silver **Ruler:** Christian IV **Reverse:** Crowned lion shield between branches, value, date

Date	Mintage	VG	F	VF	XF	Unc
1763	—	18.00	30.00	60.00	100	—

KM# 49 10 KREUZER

Silver **Ruler:** Christian IV **Obverse:** Head right **Reverse:** Crowned lion arms

Date	Mintage	VG	F	VF	XF	Unc
1767 IW-M	—	25.00	40.00	80.00	125	—

KM# 9 12 KREUZER

Silver **Ruler:** Christian IV **Obverse:** Crowned double C monogram between branches **Reverse:** Value, date in cartouche **Rev. Legend:** LAND MUNZ

Date	Mintage	VG	F	VF	XF	Unc
1747 Rare	118	—	—	—	—	—

KM# 10 12 KREUZER

Silver **Ruler:** Christian IV **Obverse:** Crowned monogram **Reverse:** Value, date within cartouche

Date	Mintage	VG	F	VF	XF	Unc
1747	Inc. above	375	525	1,000	1,650	—

KM# 11 12 KREUZER

Silver **Ruler:** Christian IV **Obverse:** Crowned C4 monogram

Date	Mintage	VG	F	VF	XF	Unc
1747 Rare	Inc. above	—	—	—	—	—

KM# 27 12 KREUZER

Silver **Ruler:** Christian IV **Obverse:** Crowned 4-fold arms **Reverse:** Value within frame

Date	Mintage	VG	F	VF	XF	Unc
1759 M	—	30.00	50.00	80.00	150	—

KM# 36 20 KREUZER

Silver **Ruler:** Christian IV **Obverse:** Head right between branches **Reverse:** Crowned lion shield on pedestal, value, date **Rev. Legend:** NACH DEM.. **Note:** Convention 20 Kreuzer.

Date	Mintage	VG	F	VF	XF	Unc
1760	—	20.00	35.00	75.00	125	—

KM# 38 20 KREUZER

Silver **Ruler:** Christian IV **Obverse:** Head right within palm and laurel branches **Reverse:** Crowned lion arms atop pedestal with value

Date	Mintage	VG	F	VF	XF	Unc
1762 M	—	20.00	35.00	75.00	125	—
1763 M	—	20.00	35.00	75.00	125	—

KM# 41 20 KREUZER

Silver **Ruler:** Christian IV **Obverse:** Head right

Date	Mintage	VG	F	VF	XF	Unc
1763	—	45.00	75.00	150	275	—

KM# 45 20 KREUZER

Silver **Ruler:** Christian IV **Obverse:** Head right between branches **Reverse:** 2 wavery arms in crowned cartouche, value, date

Date	Mintage	VG	F	VF	XF	Unc
1765 M Rare	—	—	—	—	—	—

KM# 46 20 KREUZER

Silver **Ruler:** Christian IV **Obverse:** Head right within branches **Reverse:** Crown above two shields of arms, value divides date below

Date	Mintage	VG	F	VF	XF	Unc
1765 M	—	20.00	30.00	70.00	120	—
1766 M	—	20.00	30.00	70.00	120	—
1768 M	—	20.00	30.00	70.00	120	—

KM# 50 20 KREUZER

Silver **Ruler:** Christian IV **Reverse:** Lion left between 2 crowned laurel garlands, value, date

Date	Mintage	VG	F	VF	XF	Unc
1769 Rare	—	—	—	—	—	—

KM# 12 24 KREUZER

Silver **Ruler:** Christian IV **Obverse:** Head right **Reverse:** Value, date within cartouche

Date	Mintage	VG	F	VF	XF	Unc
1747	18	400	650	1,200	2,000	—

KM# 13 36 KREUZER

Silver **Ruler:** Christian IV **Obverse:** Head right **Reverse:** Value, date within cartouche

Date	Mintage	VG	F	VF	XF	Unc
1747	1,683	375	525	1,000	1,650	—

KM# 22 1/6 THALER

Silver **Ruler:** Christian IV **Obverse:** Crowned monogram **Reverse:** Value, date

Date	Mintage	VG	F	VF	XF	Unc
1757	—	30.00	45.00	75.00	120	—
1758	—	30.00	45.00	75.00	120	—
1759	—	30.00	45.00	75.00	120	—

KM# 14 THALER

Silver **Ruler:** Christian IV **Obverse:** Bust right **Reverse:** Crowned 8-fold arms in baroque frame, date **Note:** Dav. #2545.

Date	Mintage	VG	F	VF	XF	Unc
1747	17	1,650	2,200	4,000	8,500	—

KM# 21 THALER

Silver **Ruler:** Christian IV **Obverse:** Bust right **Obv. Legend:** CHRISTIAN • IV • - D: G • C • P • R • BAV • D • **Reverse:** Crowned complex arms within baroque frame with Order chain **Rev. Legend:** EX • FODINIS • BIPONTINO • SEELBERGENSIBUS • 1754, E.H. - F. and FEIN: SILB below arms **Note:** Mining Thaler. Dav. #2546.

Date	Mintage	VG	F	VF	XF	Unc
1754 EGF	280	1,200	1,800	3,200	5,500	—

KM# 30 THALER

Silver **Ruler:** Christian IV **Obverse:** Bust right **Reverse:** Crowned 8-fold arms in ornate baroque frame, value, date **Note:** Convention Thaler. Dav. #2549.

Date	Mintage	VG	F	VF	XF	Unc
1759 IM	—	325	450	800	1,400	—

KM# 28 THALER

Silver **Ruler:** Christian IV **Obverse:** Head right **Note:** Dav. #2547.

Date	Mintage	VG	F	VF	XF	Unc
1759 IM	—	325	450	800	1,400	—

KM# 29 THALER

Silver **Ruler:** Christian IV **Obverse:** Draped bust **Note:** Dav. #2548.

Date	Mintage	VG	F	VF	XF	Unc
1759 S-IM	—	325	450	800	1,400	—

KM# 31 THALER

Silver **Ruler:** Christian IV **Obverse:** Head right **Obv. Legend:** CHRISTIAN • IV • - D: G • C • P • R • BAV • DUX • **Reverse:** Crowned oval arms within Order chain and branches **Rev. Legend:** AUF EINE - MARC FEIN **Note:** Dav. #2550.

Date	Mintage	VG	F	VF	XF	Unc
1759 IM	—	90.00	150	280	450	—
1760 IM	—	90.00	150	280	450	—
1762 IM	—	90.00	150	280	450	—
1763	—	90.00	150	280	450	—

KM# 37 THALER

Silver **Ruler:** Christian IV **Obverse:** Head left **Reverse:** Crowned oval arms in wreath, value, date **Note:** Dav. #2551.

Date	Mintage	VG	F	VF	XF	Unc
1760 IM	—	400	650	1,200	1,800	—

KM# 47 THALER

Silver **Ruler:** Christian IV **Obverse:** Head right **Obv. Legend:** CHRISTIAN IV. - D. G. C. P. R. BAV. DUX. **Reverse:** Crowned oval arms within branches, crown divides date **Rev. Legend:** 10 AUF EINE MARCK FEIN **Note:** Dav. #2552. Varieties exist.

Date	Mintage	VG	F	VF	XF	Unc
1765 IM	—	110	200	375	600	—
1775 IM	—	110	200	375	600	—

TRADE COINAGE

KM# 15 DUCAT

3.5000 g., 0.9860 Gold 0.1109 oz. AGW **Ruler:** Christian IV **Obverse:** Bust right **Reverse:** Crowned 8-fold arms in ornate baroque frame, date **Rev. Legend:** DUCAT BIPONT

Date	Mintage	VG	F	VF	XF	Unc
1747	—	800	1,650	3,250	5,500	—

KM# 20 DUCAT

3.5000 g., 0.9860 Gold 0.1109 oz. AGW **Ruler:** Christian IV **Reverse:** Round arms, supported by 2 lions

Date	Mintage	VG	F	VF	XF	Unc
1751 S	—	800	1,650	3,250	5,500	—

KM# 63 DUCAT

3.5000 g., 0.9860 Gold 0.1109 oz. AGW **Ruler:** Karl II **Obverse:** Bust right **Reverse:** Crowned arms supported by lions

Date	Mintage	F	VF	XF	Unc
1788 W	—	500	1,000	2,000	3,500

KM# 70 DUCAT

3.5000 g., 0.9860 Gold 0.1109 oz. AGW **Ruler:** Karl II **Obverse:** Head right **Reverse:** Lion at right standing on 4 legs

Date	Mintage	F	VF	XF	Unc
1790 W	—	500	1,000	2,000	3,500

KM# 64 2 DUCAT

7.0000 g., 0.9860 Gold 0.2219 oz. AGW **Ruler:** Karl II **Obverse:** Head right **Obv. Legend:** CAROLVS II • D • G • C: PAL • RH •D • BAV • IC • & • M • **Reverse:** Crowned and mantled arms

Date	Mintage	F	VF	XF	Unc
1788	—	1,250	2,250	4,000	6,500

PATTERNS

Including off metal strikes

KM#	Date	Mintage	Identification	Mkt Val
Pn1	1757	—	1/6 Thaler. Copper. KM#22.	—
Pn2	1759	—	1/4 Kreuzer. Silver. KM#23.	150
Pn3	1759	—	1/2 Kreuzer. Silver. KM#24.	350
Pn4	1759	—	12 Kreuzer. Copper. KM#27.	—
Pn5	1765	—	Kreuzer. Gold. KM#44.	—
Pn6	1767	—	5 Kreuzer. Copper. KM#48.	—
Pn7	1774	—	Kreuzer. Silver. KM#55.	—

PFALZ-NEUBURG

Pfalz-Neuburg takes its name designation from the town Neuburg on the Danube, 11 miles (18 kilometers) west of Ingolstadt, in the Upper Palatinate (Oberpfalz). It was acquired by Electoral Pfalz from Bavaria-Landshut when the ducal line of that principality became extinct in 1504. Two nephews of the elector ruled in Pfalz-Neuburg jointly, then the survivor continued until he succeeded to the electorate in 1556. In the following year, Wolfgang, the count Palatine (Pfalzgraf) of Pfalz-Zweibrücken purchased Neuburg and Sulzbach. The new line of Pfalz-Neuburg was founded by the eldest son of Wolfgang in the division of 1569. Pfalz-Neuburg acquired Pfalz-Sulzbach in 1604, then divided into Pfalz-Neuburg and Pfalz-Sulzbach in 1614. In 1685, the male line of descent in the Electoral Line from Pfalz-Simmern failed and the electoral dignity passed to Pfalz-Neuburg. See Electoral Pfalz for coinage after 1685.

RULERS

Johann Wilhelm, 1690-1716
Karl Philipp, 1716-1742

COUNTY

REGULAR COINAGE

KM# 99 1/4 KREUZER

Silver **Ruler:** Karl Philipp **Note:** Uniface

Date	Mintage	VG	F	VF	XF	Unc
1741	—	12.00	25.00	50.00	100	—

KM# 65.1 1/2 KREUZER

0.4100 g., Billon **Ruler:** Karl Philipp **Obverse:** Three shields with Palatine arms, CP and denomination above **Note:** Uniface

Date	Mintage	VG	F	VF	XF	Unc
1718	—	10.00	20.00	40.00	85.00	—
1721	—	10.00	20.00	40.00	85.00	—
1723	—	10.00	20.00	40.00	85.00	—
1728	—	10.00	20.00	40.00	85.00	—
1734	—	10.00	20.00	40.00	85.00	—

KM# 65.2 1/2 KREUZER

Billon **Ruler:** Karl Philipp **Obverse:** Three shields in circle, denomination in inner circle

Date	Mintage	VG	F	VF	XF	Unc
1728	—	10.00	20.00	40.00	85.00	—

KM# 72 KREUZER

Billon **Ruler:** Karl Philipp **Mint:** Heidelberg **Obverse:** Script CP monogram **Reverse:** Crowned rampant lion right in circle

Date	Mintage	VG	F	VF	XF	Unc
1723 GW	—	6.00	12.00	25.00	55.00	—
1724 GW	—	6.00	12.00	25.00	55.00	—
1725 GW	—	6.00	12.00	25.00	55.00	—
1728 GW	—	6.00	12.00	25.00	55.00	—
1736	—	6.00	12.00	25.00	55.00	—

KM# 82 KREUZER

Billon **Ruler:** Karl Philipp **Obverse:** Value: EINEN KRUZ, crowned CP monogram **Reverse:** Lion rampant right dividing CP, date in exergue

Date	Mintage	VG	F	VF	XF	Unc
1737	—	6.00	12.00	25.00	55.00	—

KM# 83 KREUZER

Billon **Ruler:** Karl Philipp **Obverse:** Rampant lion to right in circle **Obv. Legend:** CHVR PFALZ. LAND. MVNZ **Reverse:** Script 'CP' in circle, date at end of legend **Rev. Legend:** EINEN. KREVZER

Date	Mintage	VG	F	VF	XF	Unc
1737	—	6.00	12.00	25.00	55.00	—
1738	—	6.00	12.00	25.00	55.00	—
1739	—	6.00	12.00	25.00	55.00	—
1740 W	—	6.00	12.00	25.00	55.00	—

KM# 100 KREUZER

Billon **Ruler:** Karl Philipp **Obverse:** Lion rampant right **Obv. Legend:** CHUR PFALTZ LAND MVNTZ **Rev. Legend:** LAND MUNZEINEN KREUTZER

Date	Mintage	VG	F	VF	XF	Unc
1741	—	12.00	25.00	55.00	110	—

KM# 101 KREUZER

Billon **Ruler:** Karl Philipp **Obverse:** Lion rampant right **Obv. Legend:** LAND MUNZ **Reverse:** Value: EINEN. KREUZER, CP monogram

Date	Mintage	VG	F	VF	XF	Unc
1742 O	—	5.00	10.00	22.00	45.00	—

KM# 84 2 KREUZER (1 Albus)

Silver **Ruler:** Karl Philipp **Obverse:** Lion rampant **Reverse:** Denomination, date

Date	Mintage	VG	F	VF	XF	Unc
1737	—	10.00	20.00	40.00	70.00	—
1738	—	10.00	20.00	40.00	70.00	—
1740	—	10.00	20.00	40.00	70.00	—
1741	—	10.00	20.00	40.00	70.00	—

KM# 85 2 KREUZER (1 Albus)

Silver **Ruler:** Karl Philipp **Obverse:** Lion rampant right in circle of berries **Obv. Legend:** CHVRPFALZ **Reverse:** Value: LANDMVNZ 2 KREUZER, date, in circle of berries

Date	Mintage	VG	F	VF	XF	Unc
1737 0	—	5.00	12.00	25.00	45.00	—
1742 0	—	5.00	12.00	25.00	45.00	—

KM# 86 4 KREUZER (2 Albus = 1/2 Batzen)

Billon **Ruler:** Karl Philipp **Obverse:** Palatine lion **Reverse:** CP monogram

Date	Mintage	VG	F	VF	XF	Unc
1737	—	25.00	50.00	100	200	—

KM# 73 5 KREUZER

Billon **Ruler:** Karl Philipp **Obverse:** Three-fold Palatine arms in oval electoral cap above **Reverse:** Value: V KREVZER in wreath **Rev. Legend:** CHVR. PFALZ. LAND.

Date	Mintage	VG	F	VF	XF	Unc
1727	—	30.00	70.00	150	275	—
1736	—	30.00	70.00	150	275	—

KM# 70 10 KREUZER

Silver **Ruler:** Karl Philipp **Obverse:** Three-fold shield - lion, stylized orb, and lozenge - divide date inside oval, crown above **Reverse:** Value: 10.KR. CHVRPFALZ LANDMVNZ within wreath

Date	Mintage	VG	F	VF	XF	Unc
1721 IGW	—	25.00	50.00	115	225	—
1722 IGW	—	25.00	50.00	115	225	—
1727 IGW	—	25.00	50.00	115	225	—

KM# 74 10 KREUZER

Silver **Ruler:** Karl Philipp **Obverse:** Without inner oval **Reverse:** Value: X KR. CHVRPFALZ...

Date	Mintage	VG	F	VF	XF	Unc
1727	—	30.00	65.00	135	275	—
1735	—	30.00	65.00	135	275	—
1736	—	30.00	65.00	135	275	—

KM# 71 20 KREUZER

Silver **Ruler:** Karl Philipp **Mint:** Heidelberg **Obverse:** Three-fold squarish shield - lion, stylized orb, lozenge **Obv. Legend:** D. G. C. P. CP... **Reverse:** Value: 20. KR. CHURPFALZ LANDMVNZ., in palm wreath

Date	Mintage	VG	F	VF	XF	Unc
17Z1	—	12.00	30.00	60.00	120	—
1722 IGW	—	12.00	30.00	60.00	120	—
1723 IGW	—	12.00	30.00	60.00	120	—
1724 IGW	—	12.00	30.00	60.00	120	—
1725 IGW	—	12.00	30.00	60.00	120	—
1726 IGW	—	12.00	30.00	60.00	120	—
1727 IGW	—	12.00	30.00	60.00	120	—

KM# 80 20 KREUZER

Silver **Ruler:** Karl Philipp **Obverse:** Three-fold baroque, oval shield - lion, stylized orb, and lozenge **Obv. Legend:** CAR. PJIL. D. G. C. P... **Reverse:** Value: 20 KRZ. CHVRPFALZ..., in cartouche

Date	Mintage	VG	F	VF	XF	Unc
1731	—	15.00	35.00	75.00	150	—
1732	—	15.00	35.00	75.00	150	—
1733	—	15.00	35.00	75.00	150	—

KM# 81 20 KREUZER

Silver **Ruler:** Karl Philipp **Obverse:** Shield squared off

Date	Mintage	VG	F	VF	XF	Unc
1736	—	15.00	35.00	75.00	150	—

KM# 87 60 KREUZER (1 Gulden)

Silver **Ruler:** Karl Philipp **Obverse:** Bust right **Reverse:** Legend, arms **Rev. Legend:** CHVR PFALZ

Date	Mintage	VG	F	VF	XF	Unc
1737 Rare	—	—	—	—	—	—

KM# 88 60 KREUZER (1 Gulden)

Silver **Ruler:** Karl Philipp **Rev. Legend:** FEIN SILBER

Date	Mintage	VG	F	VF	XF	Unc
1737 Rare	—	—	—	—	—	—
1740 Rare	—	—	—	—	—	—

KM# 45 ALBUS

Silver **Ruler:** Johann Wilhelm **Obverse:** Lion rampant left **Obv. Legend:** I. W. C. P... **Reverse:** Value: I/ALBUS **Rev. Legend:** C. M. D. C. V. S.

Date	Mintage	VG	F	VF	XF	Unc
1712	—	12.00	25.00	55.00	115	—

KM# 51 2 ALBUS

1.7500 g., Billon **Ruler:** Johann Wilhelm **Obverse:** Crowned lion rampant left in laurel wreath divides C-P **Reverse:** Value: II ALBUS in laurel wreath **Note:** Varieties exist, some are counterfeits of the time.

Date	Mintage	VG	F	VF	XF	Unc
1700 IMW	—	20.00	30.00	65.00	135	—
1701 IMW	—	7.00	15.00	35.00	80.00	—
1702 IMW	—	7.00	15.00	35.00	80.00	—
1703 IMW	—	9.00	18.00	40.00	90.00	—
1704 IMW	—	7.00	15.00	35.00	80.00	—
1706 IMW	—	7.00	15.00	35.00	80.00	—
1707 IMW	—	7.00	15.00	35.00	80.00	—
1708 IMW	—	9.00	18.00	40.00	90.00	—

KM# 52 6 ALBUS

Billon **Ruler:** Johann Wilhelm **Obverse:** Crowned complex arms **Reverse:** Value, date within inner circle

Date	Mintage	VG	F	VF	XF	Unc
1700	—	35.00	70.00	145	250	—
1701	—	30.00	60.00	125	225	—
1702	—	30.00	60.00	125	225	—

KM# 60 1/12 THALER

Silver **Ruler:** Johann Wilhelm **Obverse:** Crown above shield with orb dividing date **Reverse:** Value: 12 EINEN REICHSTAHL. N. P. NACH...

Date	Mintage	VG	F	VF	XF	Unc
1710	—	—	—	—	—	—

Note: Variety may exist with correct legend: REICHSTHAL

KM# 61 1/6 THALER

Silver **Ruler:** Johann Wilhelm **Obverse:** Bust right **Obv. Legend:** D. G. I. W. C. P. R... **Reverse:** Orb in cartouche, electoral cap above **Rev. Legend:** B. I. C. et. M. D. P. M. C. V. S...

Date	Mintage	VG	F	VF	XF	Unc
1710	—	85.00	165	300	500	—
1715	—	85.00	165	300	500	—

KM# 63 1/6 THALER

Silver **Subject:** Death of Johann Wilhelm **Reverse:** Inscription for Johann Wilhelm

Date	Mintage	VG	F	VF	XF	Unc
1716	—	—	—	—	—	—

KM# 64 1/6 THALER

Silver **Ruler:** Karl Philipp **Obverse:** Armored bust right **Obv. Legend:** D. G. CAR. PHIL... **Reverse:** Crown above orb in baroque cartouche, denomination below **Rev. Legend:** B. I. C. ET...

Date	Mintage	VG	F	VF	XF	Unc
1717	—	75.00	150	275	450	—

KM# 95 1/4 THALER

Silver **Ruler:** Karl Philipp **Obverse:** Jugate busts of Karl Philipp and Karl Albrecht **Reverse:** Double-headed eagle **Note:** Vicariate.

Date	Mintage	VG	F	VF	XF	Unc
1740	—	225	450	850	1,400	—

KM# 96 1/2 THALER

Silver **Ruler:** Karl Philipp **Obverse:** Jugate busts of Karl Philipp and Karl Albrecht **Reverse:** Double-headed eagle **Note:** Vicariate.

Date	Mintage	VG	F	VF	XF	Unc
1740	—	250	500	950	1,600	—

KM# 55 THALER

Silver **Ruler:** Johann Wilhelm **Obverse:** Bust right **Obv. Legend:** I. W. D. G. C. P. R. S. - R. I. ARCHID. &. EL. **Reverse:** Three shields crowned, date divided at top **Rev. Legend:** B. I. C. & M. D. PR. M. - C. V. S. M.& R. D. I. R. **Note:** Dav. #2527.

Date	Mintage	VG	F	VF	XF	Unc
1708	—	700	1,250	2,250	3,750	—

KM# 62 THALER

Silver **Ruler:** Johann Wilhelm **Obverse:** Head right **Obv. Legend:** D. G. I. W. C. P. R. S. R. I. ARCHID. ET EL. EIUSQ. **Reverse:** Imperial eagle with two crowned shields on breast **Rev. Legend:** IN. PR. S. ET FR. I. PROV. ET VICARIVS. 1711 **Note:** Dav. #2528.

Date	Mintage	VG	F	VF	XF	Unc
1711	—	550	1,000	1,650	2,750	—

KM# 97 THALER

Silver **Ruler:** Karl Philipp **Obverse:** Jugate busts of Albert and Karl Philipp right **Obv. Legend:** D: G. C: ALB. &. C: PHIL. ELECT. PROV. & VICARII **Reverse:** Imperial eagle with two shields on breast **Rev. Legend:** IN. PART. RHENI. SUEV. ET IUR. FRANCON. 1740 **Note:** Dav. #2530.

Date	Mintage	F	VF	XF	Unc
1740	—	350	650	1,100	1,850

KM# 98 1-1/2 THALER

Silver **Ruler:** Karl Philipp **Obverse:** Bust of Karl Philipp right **Obv. Legend:** D: G • C • PHIL: D: B • C • P • R • S • R • I • A • T • & EL • PROVISOR & VICARIUS **Reverse:** Imperial eagle with three crowned shields on breast **Rev. Legend:** IN • PART • RHENI • SUEV • ET IUR • FRANCON • 1740 **Note:** Dav. #2529.

Date	Mintage	VG	F	VF	XF	Unc
1740	—	550	1,000	1,750	3,000	—

PFALZ-SULZBACH

Originally one of the four lines established in 1569, the first ruler died childless in 1604 and Sulzbach went to the eldest brother in Pfalz-Neuburg. The latter's younger son began a new line in 1614 upon the division of Pfalz-Neuburg. Early in the 18th century, the electoral dignity had passed to Pfalz-Neuburg, but that line also became extinct and all titles, including the electorate, reverted to Pfalz-Sulzbach in 1742 (see Electoral Pfalz for listings after this date).

RULERS

Christian August, 1632-1708
Theodor Eustach, 1708-32
Johann Christian, 1732-33
Karl IV Philipp Theodor, 1733-42 (died 1777)

MINT MARKS

D - Dusseldorf Mint
M - Mannheim Mint

MINT OFFICIALS' INITIALS

Initials	Date	Name
AK	1749-71	Andreas Kock
AS, S	1744-99	Anton Schäffer, die-cutter and mintmaster
CLS	1767-70	Karl Ludwig Selche
FO, O	1732-50	Franz Offner, in Heidelberg
	1743-50	In Mannheim
N	1746-47	C.Niesner
PM	1771-83	Paul Maasen
WS	1716-58	Wigand Schäffer, die-cutter

REFERENCE

N = Alfred Noss, Die pfälzischen Münzen des Hauses Wittelsbach, v. 4, Pfalz-Veldenz, Pfalz-Neuburg, Pfalz-Sulzbach, Munich, 1938.

ELECTORATE

Chur Pfalz

REGULAR COINAGE

KM# 75 1/2 KREUZER

Billon **Ruler:** Karl Theodor **Obverse:** Divided arms
Note: Convention 1/2 Kreuzer.

Date	Mintage	VG	F	VF	XF	Unc
1747 FO	—	15.00	30.00	60.00	120	—
1748 FO	—	15.00	30.00	60.00	120	—
1750 FO	—	15.00	30.00	60.00	120	—

KM# 96 1/2 KREUZER

Billon **Ruler:** Karl Theodor **Obverse:** Lion left in cartouche, date **Reverse:** Value

Date	Mintage	VG	F	VF	XF	Unc
1758 AS	—	18.00	35.00	70.00	145	—
1759 AS	—	18.00	35.00	70.00	145	—
1764 AS	—	18.00	35.00	70.00	145	—

KM# 59 KREUZER

Billon **Ruler:** Karl Theodor **Obverse:** Lion left in crowned cartouche **Reverse:** Value in cartouche, date

Date	Mintage	VG	F	VF	XF	Unc
1745	—	25.00	40.00	80.00	150	—
1746	—	25.00	40.00	80.00	150	—
1747	—	25.00	40.00	80.00	150	—
1748	—	25.00	40.00	80.00	150	—

KM# 62 KREUZER

Billon **Ruler:** Karl Theodor **Obverse:** Crowned oval three-fold arms **Reverse:** Value, date

Date	Mintage	VG	F	VF	XF	Unc
1746 FO	—	75.00	140	265	400	—

KM# 80 KREUZER

Billon **Ruler:** Karl Theodor **Rev. Legend:** LAND MVNZ

Date	Mintage	VG	F	VF	XF	Unc
1749 FO	—	25.00	40.00	80.00	150	—
1750 AK	—	25.00	40.00	80.00	150	—

KM# 97 KREUZER

Billon **Ruler:** Karl Theodor **Obverse:** Crowned lion arms **Obv. Legend:** CHUR. PFALZ. **Reverse:** Value, date within frame

Date	Mintage	VG	F	VF	XF	Unc
1758 AS	—	5.00	9.00	18.00	30.00	—
1762 AS	—	5.00	9.00	18.00	30.00	—
1763 AS	—	5.00	9.00	18.00	30.00	—
1764 AS	—	5.00	9.00	18.00	30.00	—
1765 AS	—	5.00	9.00	18.00	30.00	—
1768 AS	—	5.00	9.00	18.00	30.00	—
1773 AS	—	5.00	9.00	18.00	30.00	—
1774 AS	—	5.00	9.00	18.00	30.00	—
1775 AS	—	5.00	9.00	18.00	30.00	—

KM# 98 KREUZER

Billon **Ruler:** Karl Philip **Obv. Legend:** C. P. **Reverse:** Value, date

Date	Mintage	VG	F	VF	XF	Unc
1758	—	30.00	50.00	100	185	—

KM# 52 2 KREUZER

Billon **Obverse:** Lion rampant right in baroque oval of berries **Reverse:** LANDMVNZ 2 KREUZER, date

Date	Mintage	VG	F	VF	XF	Unc
1742 FO	—	6.00	12.00	25.00	40.00	—

KM# 54 2 KREUZER

Billon **Ruler:** Karl Theodor **Obverse:** Lion right **Reverse:** Value within inner circle

Date	Mintage	VG	F	VF	XF	Unc
1743 O	—	10.00	20.00	40.00	65.00	—
1744 O	—	10.00	20.00	40.00	65.00	—
1745 O	—	10.00	20.00	40.00	65.00	—

KM# 77 2 KREUZER

Billon **Ruler:** Karl Theodor **Obverse:** Crowned lion arms **Reverse:** Value within frame, date below

Date	Mintage	VG	F	VF	XF	Unc
1745 FO	—	7.00	15.00	30.00	55.00	—
1749 FO	—	7.00	15.00	30.00	55.00	—
1750 AK	—	7.00	15.00	30.00	55.00	—
1759 AK	—	7.00	15.00	30.00	55.00	—

KM# 60 2 KREUZER

Billon **Ruler:** Karl Theodor **Obverse:** Lion right **Reverse:** Value within shield **Note:** Similar to KM#52.

Date	Mintage	VG	F	VF	XF	Unc
1745 O	—	6.00	12.00	25.00	40.00	—
1746 O	—	6.00	12.00	25.00	40.00	—

KM# 76 2 KREUZER

Billon **Ruler:** Karl Theodor **Obverse:** Lion rampant in baroque cartouche **Obv. Legend:** CHVR. PFALZ **Reverse:** Denomination in baroque cartouche **Rev. Legend:** LANDMVNZ 2 KR

Date	Mintage	VG	F	VF	XF	Unc
1747 O	—	6.00	12.00	25.00	40.00	—
1748 FO	—	6.00	12.00	25.00	40.00	—

KM# 55 3 KREUZER

Billon **Ruler:** Karl Theodor **Obverse:** Lion right in crowned cartouche **Reverse:** Value, date

Date	Mintage	VG	F	VF	XF	Unc
1743 FO	—	100	180	325	550	—
1745	—	—	—	—	—	—

Note: Reported, not confirmed

KM# 63 4 KREUZER

Billon **Ruler:** Karl Theodor **Obverse:** Crown above three shields **Reverse:** Value within ornate frame

Date	Mintage	VG	F	VF	XF	Unc
1746 FO	—	10.00	20.00	45.00	75.00	—
1746	—	10.00	20.00	45.00	75.00	—
1747 FO	—	10.00	20.00	45.00	75.00	—
1748 FO	—	10.00	20.00	45.00	75.00	—
1749 FO	—	10.00	20.00	45.00	75.00	—
1750 FO	—	—	—	—	—	—
Note: Reported, not confirmed						
1750 AK	—	10.00	20.00	45.00	75.00	—
1705	—	—	—	—	—	—
Note: Error for 1750						

KM# 64 12 KREUZER (1 Batzen)

Silver **Ruler:** Karl Theodor **Obverse:** Head right **Reverse:** Lion, lozenge and stylized orb in three oval shields, value in cartouche, date

Date	Mintage	VG	F	VF	XF	Unc
1746 FO	—	65.00	125	240	400	—
1746 AK	—	65.00	125	240	400	—
1746 N	—	65.00	125	240	400	—

KM# 65 12 KREUZER (1 Batzen)

Silver **Ruler:** Karl Theodor **Obverse:** Armored bust right

Date	Mintage	VG	F	VF	XF	Unc
1746	—	80.00	130	240	380	—

KM# 66 12 KREUZER (1 Batzen)

Silver **Ruler:** Karl Theodor **Obverse:** Arms of Pfalz at top **Reverse:** Value: XII/KREU/TZER in cartouche

Date	Mintage	VG	F	VF	XF	Unc
1746	—	35.00	60.00	120	200	—
1746 CN	—	35.00	60.00	120	200	—
1746 O	—	35.00	60.00	120	200	—
1746 FO	—	35.00	60.00	120	200	—
1747 FO	—	35.00	60.00	120	200	—
1748 FO	—	35.00	60.00	120	200	—
1749 FO	—	35.00	60.00	120	200	—
1750 FO	—	35.00	60.00	120	200	—

KM# 67 12 KREUZER (1 Batzen)

Silver **Ruler:** Karl Theodor **Obverse:** Arms of Bavaria at top **Reverse:** Value within cartouche **Note:** Varieties exist, including copper counterfeits.

Date	Mintage	VG	F	VF	XF	Unc
1746 FO	—	45.00	90.00	185	325	—
1747 FO	—	45.00	90.00	185	325	—
1748 FO	—	45.00	90.00	185	325	—
1749 FO	—	45.00	90.00	185	325	—
1750 FO	—	45.00	90.00	185	325	—

KM# 68 24 KREUZER (6 Batzen)

Silver **Ruler:** Karl Theodor **Obverse:** Bust right **Reverse:** Three joined oval arms in crowned cartouche, value, date

Date	Mintage	VG	F	VF	XF	Unc
1746 S	—	70.00	130	250	450	—

KM# 69 24 KREUZER (6 Batzen)

Silver **Ruler:** Karl Theodor **Obverse:** Three oval arms in crowned cartouche **Reverse:** Value, date

Date	Mintage	VG	F	VF	XF	Unc
1746	—	70.00	130	250	450	—

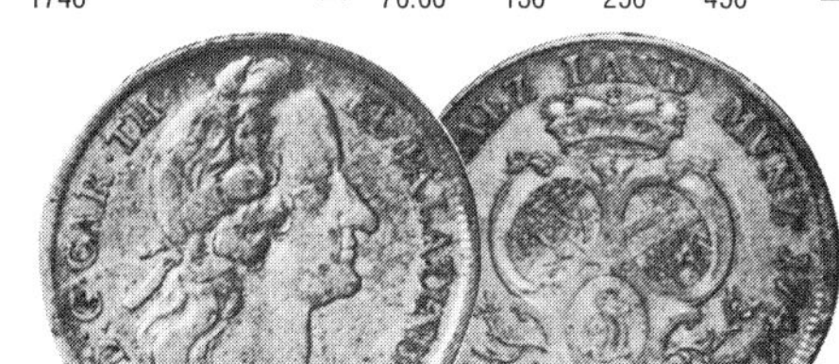

KM# 70 36 KREUZER (9 Batzen)

Silver **Ruler:** Karl Theodor **Obverse:** Bust right **Reverse:** Three joined oval arms in crowned cartouche, value, date

Date	Mintage	VG	F	VF	XF	Unc
1746	—	200	300	550	1,000	—

KM# 71 36 KREUZER (9 Batzen)

Silver **Obverse:** Three oval arms in crowned cartouche **Reverse:** Value, date

Date	Mintage	VG	F	VF	XF	Unc
1746 S	—	200	300	550	1,000	—

KM# 72 1/2 THALER

Silver **Ruler:** Karl Theodor **Subject:** Homage of Heidelberg **Obverse:** Date in chronogram **Reverse:** City view

Date	Mintage	VG	F	VF	XF	Unc
1746 S	—	250	500	900	1,500	—

KM# 78 2/3 THALER

Silver **Ruler:** Karl Theodor **Subject:** Karl Theodor **Obverse:** Armored bust right **Reverse:** Crowned complex arms within Order chain, value below **Note:** Mining 2/3 Thaler.

Date	Mintage	VG	F	VF	XF	Unc
1748 S-FO	—	225	325	625	1,150	—

KM# 85 2/3 THALER

Silver **Ruler:** Karl Theodor **Obverse:** Armored bust right **Reverse:** Rococo loops on sides of arms

Date	Mintage	VG	F	VF	XF	Unc
1750 SAK	—	250	450	800	1,400	—

KM# 91 2/3 THALER

Silver **Ruler:** Karl Theodor **Obverse:** Armored bust right **Reverse:** Arms with lion supporters

Date	Mintage	VG	F	VF	XF	Unc
1751 S	—	135	250	480	850	—
1753 AS	—	135	250	480	850	—
1754 AS	—	135	250	480	850	—
1755 AS	—	135	250	480	850	—

KM# 94 2/3 THALER

Silver **Ruler:** Karl Theodor **Obverse:** Head right **Reverse:** Three oval arms in crowned cartouche, value, date

Date	Mintage	VG	F	VF	XF	Unc
1756 AS	—	100	225	425	750	—

KM# 99 2/3 THALER

Silver **Ruler:** Karl Theodor **Obverse:** Head right **Reverse:** Crown above three shields

Date	Mintage	VG	F	VF	XF	Unc
1758 AS	—	225	325	625	1,150	—

KM# 56 THALER

Silver **Ruler:** Karl Theodor **Obverse:** Bust right **Reverse:** Angular three-fold arms in crowned baroque frame, date **Note:** Cross-reference number Dav. #2531.

Date	Mintage	F	VF	XF	Unc
1744 WS	—	3,500	5,000	7,500	12,500

KM# 61 THALER

Silver **Ruler:** Karl Theodor **Obverse:** Armored bust right **Obv. Legend:** D: G • C • TH • C • P • R • S • R • I • A • T • & • EL • PROV •& VICARIUS **Reverse:** Imperial eagle with crowned arms on breast, date **Rev. Legend:** IN • PART • RHENI • SUEV • ET • IUR FRANCON • 1745 **Note:** Vicariat Thaler. Dav. #2532.

Date	Mintage	F	VF	XF	Unc
1745 S	12	1,500	3,000	5,000	8,500

KM# 92 THALER

Silver **Ruler:** Karl Theodor **Obverse:** Armored bust right **Obv. Legend:** D: G • CAR • TH • - C • P • R • S • R • I • A • T • & • EL • **Reverse:** Small crown **Rev. Legend:** EX VISCERIBUS FODINÆ WILDBERG date, A - K/ FEIN: SILB. below **Note:** Mining Thaler. Dav. #2533.

Date	Mintage	F	VF	XF	Unc
1751 AS-AK	—	350	750	1,300	2,150

KM# 93 THALER

Silver **Ruler:** Karl Theodor **Obverse:** Armored bust right **Obv. Legend:** D: G • CAR • TH • - C • P • R • S • R • I • A • T • & • EL • **Reverse:** Large crown **Rev. Legend:** EX VISCERIBUS FODINÆ WILDBERG date, A - S/ FEIN • SILB below **Note:** Dav. #2533A.

Date	Mintage	F	VF	XF	Unc
1753 AS	—	350	750	1,300	2,150

KM# 95 THALER

Silver **Ruler:** Karl Theodor **Obverse:** Bust right **Obv. Legend:** D • G • CAR • THEODOR • C • P• R • S • R • I • A • T • & ELEC • **Reverse:** Three oval arms in crowned cartouche, value, date **Rev. Legend:** EX VISCERIBUS FODINÆ WILDBERGENSIS date, .A. - .S./ FEIN - SILB: below **Note:** Dav. #2534.

Date	Mintage	F	VF	XF	Unc
1756 AS	—	250	600	1,100	2,000

KM# 100 THALER

Silver **Ruler:** Karl Theodor **Obverse:** Head right **Obv. Legend:** D: G • CAR • THEOD: - C • P • R • S • R • I • A • T • & EL • **Reverse:** Crown above three shields within frame **Rev. Legend:** EX VISCERIBUS FODINÆ WILDBERG • 1758, FEIN - SILBER below **Note:** Dav. #2535.

Date	Mintage	F	VF	XF	Unc
1758 AS	—	100	300	750	1,250

KM# 79 5 THALER

6.6500 g., 0.9000 Gold 0.1924 oz. AGW **Ruler:** Karl Theodor **Obverse:** Head right **Reverse:** Crowned monograms in cruciform

Date	Mintage	VG	F	VF	XF	Unc
1748 FO	—	500	1,000	2,500	4,000	—
1749 FO	—	800	1,750	3,500	5,000	—
1750 AK	—	500	1,000	2,500	4,000	—

KM# 44 CAROLIN

9.7000 g., 0.7700 Gold 0.2401 oz. AGW **Ruler:** Karl Philip **Obverse:** Bust right **Reverse:** 3 Shields on crowned shield with supporters

Date	Mintage	VG	F	VF	XF	Unc
1733	—	650	1,350	2,850	4,750	—

REFORM COINAGE

KM# 127 ZOLLPFENNIG

Copper **Ruler:** Karl Theodor **Obverse:** Crowned lion arms **Reverse:** Value, date within frame

Date	Mintage	VG	F	VF	XF	Unc
1766	—	12.00	25.00	50.00	100	—
1778 Rare	—	—	—	—	—	—

KM# 142 1/4 KREUZER

Copper **Ruler:** Karl Theodor **Obverse:** Crowned lion arms **Reverse:** Value, date within beaded circle

Date	Mintage	VG	F	VF	XF	Unc
1773	—	2.00	4.00	10.00	22.00	—
1774	—	—	—	—	—	—
1775	—	2.00	4.00	10.00	22.00	—
1777	—	2.00	4.00	10.00	22.00	—
1786	—	2.00	4.00	10.00	22.00	—
1793	—	2.00	4.00	10.00	22.00	—
1794	—	2.00	4.00	10.00	22.00	—
1795	—	2.00	4.00	10.00	22.00	—

KM# 143 1/2 KREUZER

Copper **Ruler:** Karl Theodor **Obverse:** Crowned arms **Reverse:** Value above date in wreath

Date	Mintage	VG	F	VF	XF	Unc
1773	—	3.00	5.00	12.00	28.00	—
1774	—	3.00	5.00	12.00	28.00	—
1775	—	3.00	5.00	12.00	28.00	—
1776	—	3.00	5.00	12.00	28.00	—
1777	—	3.00	5.00	12.00	28.00	—
1786	—	3.00	5.00	12.00	28.00	—

KM# 144 KREUZER

Copper **Ruler:** Karl Theodor **Obverse:** Three-fold arms **Reverse:** Value and date

Date	Mintage	VG	F	VF	XF	Unc
1773	—	6.50	12.50	26.50	55.00	—

KM# 145 KREUZER

Copper **Ruler:** Karl Theodor **Obverse:** Crowned lion arms **Reverse:** 1/CONVENT/KREUZ in wreath

Date	Mintage	VG	F	VF	XF	Unc
1773	—	5.00	11.50	25.00	50.00	—
1774	—	5.00	11.50	25.00	50.00	—
1775	—	5.00	11.50	25.00	50.00	—
1776	—	5.00	11.50	25.00	50.00	—
1783	—	5.00	11.50	25.00	50.00	—
1784	—	5.00	11.50	25.00	50.00	—
1786	—	5.00	11.50	25.00	50.00	—
1793	—	5.00	11.50	25.00	50.00	—

KM# 179 KREUZER

Copper **Ruler:** Karl Theodor **Obverse:** Crowned lion arms **Reverse:** Without CONVENT in wreath

Date	Mintage	VG	F	VF	XF	Unc
1794	—	7.50	13.50	28.50	60.00	—
1795	—	—	—	—	—	—

KM# 119 5 KREUZER

Billon **Ruler:** Karl Theodor **Obverse:** Bust right **Reverse:** Crowned three-fold arms, value, date

Date	Mintage	VG	F	VF	XF	Unc
1765 AS	—	28.00	45.00	85.00	135	—
1766 AS	—	28.00	45.00	85.00	135	—

KM# 148 5 KREUZER

Billon **Ruler:** Karl Theodor **Reverse:** Crowned arms hung in garland, value, date

Date	Mintage	VG	F	VF	XF	Unc
1774 AS	—	25.00	40.00	80.00	125	—
1775 AS	—	25.00	40.00	80.00	125	—
1776 AS	—	25.00	40.00	80.00	125	—
1777 AS	—	25.00	40.00	80.00	125	—

KM# 160 5 KREUZER

Billon **Ruler:** Karl Theodor **Obverse:** Head right **Reverse:** Three-fold arms and value

Date	Mintage	VG	F	VF	XF	Unc
1780 AS	—	10.00	20.00	40.00	90.00	—
1782 AS	—	10.00	20.00	40.00	90.00	—
1784 AS	—	10.00	20.00	40.00	90.00	—
1785 AS	—	10.00	20.00	40.00	90.00	—
1788 AS	—	10.00	20.00	40.00	90.00	—
1789 AS	—	10.00	20.00	40.00	90.00	—
1794 AS	—	10.00	20.00	40.00	90.00	—
1795 AS	—	10.00	20.00	40.00	90.00	—
1796 AS	—	10.00	20.00	40.00	90.00	—
1797 AS	—	10.00	20.00	40.00	90.00	—
1798 AS	—	10.00	20.00	40.00	90.00	—

KM# 105 10 KREUZER

Silver **Ruler:** Karl Theodor **Obverse:** Head right **Obv. Legend:** D. G. CAR... **Reverse:** Three-fold arms in circle, crown above, palm fronds above

Date	Mintage	VG	F	VF	XF	Unc
1761 AS	—	15.00	30.00	60.00	100	—
1762 AS	—	15.00	30.00	60.00	100	—
1763 AS	—	15.00	30.00	60.00	100	—

KM# 110 10 KREUZER

Silver **Ruler:** Karl Theodor **Obverse:** Head right **Obv. Legend:** CAR. THEODOR. D. G. **Reverse:** Crowned 3-fold arms, value below

Date	Mintage	VG	F	VF	XF	Unc
1763 AS	—	15.00	30.00	60.00	100	—
1763	—	15.00	30.00	60.00	100	—
1764 AS	—	15.00	30.00	60.00	100	—
1764	—	15.00	30.00	60.00	100	—
1765 AS	—	15.00	30.00	60.00	100	—
1766 AS	—	15.00	30.00	60.00	100	—

KM# 129 10 KREUZER

Silver **Ruler:** Karl Theodor **Obverse:** Head right **Reverse:** Crowned oval arms **Note:** Convention 10 Kreuzer.

Date	Mintage	VG	F	VF	XF	Unc
1767 AS	—	15.00	30.00	60.00	100	—
1768 AS	—	15.00	30.00	60.00	100	—
1769 AS	—	15.00	30.00	60.00	100	—
1770 AS	—	15.00	30.00	60.00	100	—
1771 AS	—	15.00	30.00	60.00	100	—
1772 AS	—	15.00	30.00	60.00	100	—
1773 AS	—	15.00	30.00	60.00	100	—
1774 AS	—	15.00	30.00	60.00	100	—

KM# 149 10 KREUZER

Billon **Ruler:** Karl Theodor **Obverse:** Head right **Reverse:** Shield curves inward

Date	Mintage	VG	F	VF	XF	Unc
1774 AS	—	25.00	40.00	80.00	130	—
1775 AS	—	25.00	40.00	80.00	130	—
1776 AS	—	25.00	40.00	80.00	130	—
1777 AS	—	25.00	40.00	80.00	130	—

KM# 150 10 KREUZER

Silver **Ruler:** Karl Theodor **Obv. Legend:** ... D. G. C. P. R. U. B. D. S. R...

Date	Mintage	VG	F	VF	XF	Unc
1777 AS	—	12.50	30.00	60.00	100	—
1778 AS	—	12.50	30.00	60.00	100	—
1779 AS	—	12.50	30.00	60.00	100	—
1780 AS	—	12.50	30.00	60.00	100	—
1780 AS	—	12.50	30.00	60.00	100	—
1780 AS	—	12.50	30.00	60.00	100	—

KM# 161 10 KREUZER

Silver **Ruler:** Karl Theodor **Obv. Legend:** ... D. G. C. P. R. V. B. D. S. R...

Date	Mintage	VG	F	VF	XF	Unc
1781 AS	—	—	—	—	—	—
1782 AS	—	—	—	—	—	—
1785 AS	—	12.50	30.00	60.00	100	—
1785 AS	—	12.50	30.00	60.00	100	—
1787 AS	—	12.50	30.00	60.00	100	—
1788 AS	—	12.50	30.00	60.00	100	—
1789 AS	—	12.50	30.00	60.00	100	—
1790 AS	—	12.50	30.00	60.00	100	—
1791 AS	—	12.50	30.00	60.00	100	—
1792 AS	—	—	—	—	—	—
Note: Reported, not confirmed						
1794 AS	—	12.50	30.00	60.00	100	—

KM# 170 10 KREUZER

Silver **Ruler:** Karl Theodor **Obverse:** Head right **Reverse:** Eagle with crowned arms on breast **Note:** Vicariat Issue.

Date	Mintage	VG	F	VF	XF	Unc
1790 AS	—	20.00	45.00	90.00	165	—
1792 AS	—	20.00	45.00	90.00	165	—

KM# 106 20 KREUZER

Silver **Ruler:** Karl Theodor **Obverse:** Bust right **Reverse:** Crowned three-fold arms, value, date **Note:** Convention 20 Kreuzer.

Date	Mintage	VG	F	VF	XF	Unc
1761 AS	—	15.00	30.00	55.00	100	—
1763 AS	—	15.00	30.00	55.00	100	—
1764 AS	—	15.00	30.00	55.00	100	—
1771 AS	—	15.00	30.00	55.00	100	—
1772 AS	—	15.00	30.00	55.00	100	—

KM# 152 20 KREUZER

Silver **Ruler:** Karl Theodor **Obverse:** Head right **Reverse:** Eagle with three fold-arms on breast

Date	Mintage	VG	F	VF	XF	Unc
1779	—	20.00	40.00	85.00	145	—
1780	—	20.00	40.00	85.00	145	—
1781	—	20.00	40.00	85.00	145	—
1782	—	20.00	40.00	85.00	145	—
1784	—	20.00	40.00	85.00	145	—
1786	—	20.00	40.00	85.00	145	—
1787	—	20.00	40.00	85.00	145	—
1789	—	20.00	40.00	85.00	145	—
1790	—	20.00	40.00	85.00	145	—
1791	—	20.00	40.00	85.00	145	—
1792	—	20.00	40.00	85.00	145	—
1793	—	20.00	40.00	85.00	145	—

KM# 171 20 KREUZER

Silver **Ruler:** Karl Theodor **Rev. Legend:** Ends: ... FRANC. **Note:** Vicariat Issue.

Date	Mintage	VG	F	VF	XF	Unc
1790	—	30.00	50.00	100	175	—

KM# 175 20 KREUZER

Silver **Ruler:** Karl Theodor **Reverse:** Eagle with three-fold arms on breast, legend, date **Rev. Legend:** Ends: ... FRANCON **Note:** Vicariat Issue.

Date	Mintage	VG	F	VF	XF	Unc
1792	—	30.00	50.00	75.00	150	—

KM# 120 1/4 THALER

Silver **Ruler:** Karl Theodor **Obverse:** Armored bust right **Reverse:** Three ornate arms below crown between branches, date, value as 40 EINE...

Date	Mintage	VG	F	VF	XF	Unc
1765 AS	—	65.00	100	200	325	—

KM# 108 1/2 THALER

Silver **Ruler:** Karl Theodor **Obverse:** Head right **Reverse:** Crown above three shields

Date	Mintage	VG	F	VF	XF	Unc
1762 AS	—	75.00	140	280	525	—
1763 AS	—	75.00	140	280	525	—

KM# 114 1/2 THALER

Silver **Ruler:** Karl Theodor **Reverse:** Three oval arms below crown between branches, date

Date	Mintage	VG	F	VF	XF	Unc
1764 AS	—	85.00	160	325	600	—

KM# 121 1/2 THALER

Silver **Ruler:** Karl Theodor **Obverse:** Head right **Reverse:** Date in legend

Date	Mintage	VG	F	VF	XF	Unc
1765 AS	—	85.00	160	325	600	—

KM# 122 1/2 THALER

Silver **Ruler:** Karl Theodor **Obverse:** Head right **Reverse:** Date divided below arms

Date	Mintage	VG	F	VF	XF	Unc
1765 AS	—	60.00	100	200	350	—

KM# 123 1/2 THALER

Silver **Ruler:** Karl Theodor **Obverse:** Bust right **Reverse:** Three crowned arms between branches, date divided above

Date	Mintage	VG	F	VF	XF	Unc
1765 AS	—	45.00	80.00	160	300	—

KM# 124 1/2 THALER

Silver **Ruler:** Karl Theodor **Reverse:** Crowned three-fold arms in cartouche between two branches, value, divided date above

Date	Mintage	VG	F	VF	XF	Unc
1765 AS	—	85.00	160	325	600	—

KM# 140 1/2 THALER

Silver **Ruler:** Karl Theodor **Obverse:** Head right **Reverse:** Crowned arms, date divided above

Date	Mintage	VG	F	VF	XF	Unc
1771 AS	—	60.00	120	225	450	—
1772 AS	—	60.00	120	225	450	—

KM# 146 1/2 THALER

Silver **Ruler:** Karl Theodor **Obverse:** Head right **Reverse:** Crowned arms, date divided above

Date	Mintage	VG	F	VF	XF	Unc
1773 AS	—	50.00	100	200	350	—
1774 AS	—	50.00	100	200	350	—
1776 AS	—	50.00	100	200	350	—

KM# 153 1/2 THALER

Silver **Ruler:** Karl Theodor **Obverse:** Head right **Reverse:** Garland draped arms

Date	Mintage	VG	F	VF	XF	Unc
1779 AS	—	60.00	120	225	450	—
1780 AS	—	60.00	120	225	450	—
1781 AS	—	60.00	120	225	450	—

KM# 162 1/2 THALER

Silver **Ruler:** Karl Theodor **Obverse:** Head right **Reverse:** Crowned arms , date divided below

Date	Mintage	VG	F	VF	XF	Unc
1782 AS	—	50.00	100	200	375	—

KM# 163 1/2 THALER

Silver **Ruler:** Karl Theodor **Obverse:** Head right **Reverse:** Crowned arms within branches, date divided below **Note:** Varieties exist.

Date	Mintage	VG	F	VF	XF	Unc
1783 AS	—	40.00	90.00	175	325	—
1784 AS	—	40.00	90.00	175	325	—
1786 AS	—	40.00	90.00	175	325	—
1788 AS	—	40.00	90.00	175	325	—
1791 AS	—	40.00	90.00	175	325	—
1792 AS	—	40.00	90.00	175	325	—
1793 AS	—	40.00	90.00	175	325	—

KM# 172 1/2 THALER
Silver **Ruler:** Karl Theodor **Obverse:** Head right **Reverse:** Crowned arms within Order chain, cross divides date below **Note:** Vicariat Issue.

Date	Mintage	VG	F	VF	XF	Unc
1790 AS	—	65.00	135	250	475	—

KM# 176 1/2 THALER
Silver **Ruler:** Karl Theodor **Obverse:** Head right **Reverse:** Crowned arms on eagle's breast, date divided below **Note:** Vicariat Issue.

Date	Mintage	VG	F	VF	XF	Unc
1792 AS	—	60.00	125	240	450	—

KM# 107 THALER
Silver **Ruler:** Karl Theodor **Obverse:** Head right **Obv. Legend:** D • G • CAR • THEODOR • C • P • R • S • R • I • A • T • & • EL • **Reverse:** Three shields within Order chain, crown above, date divided below **Rev. Legend:** AD NORMAM - CONVENTION **Note:** Convention Thaler. Dav. #2536.

Date	Mintage	F	VF	XF	Unc
1761 AS	—	200	500	1,000	2,000

KM# 111 THALER
Silver **Ruler:** Karl Theodor **Obverse:** Head right **Obv. Legend:** CAR • THEODOR • D: G • C • P • R • S • R • I • A • T • & • EL • **Reverse:** Three oval arms below crown between branches, date **Rev. Legend:** AD NORMAM CONVENTIONIS **Note:** Dav. #2537.

Date	Mintage	F	VF	XF	Unc
1763 AS	—	85.00	200	375	850
1764 AS	—	85.00	200	375	850

KM# 112 THALER
Silver **Ruler:** Karl Theodor **Obverse:** Head right **Obv. Legend:** CAR • THEODOR • D: G • C • P • R • S • R • I • A • T • & • EL • **Reverse:** Three square shields, Order chain below with cross dividing date, crown above **Rev. Legend:** * AD NORMAN - CONVENTION * **Note:** Dav. #A2537.

Date	Mintage	F	VF	XF	Unc
1763 AS	—	900	1,800	2,800	5,000

KM# 115 THALER
Silver **Ruler:** Karl Theodor **Obverse:** Head right **Obv. Legend:** CAR • THEODOR • D: G • C • P • R • S • R • I • A • T • & • EL • **Reverse:** Three shields crowned separating date and initials **Rev. Legend:** AD NORMAM CONVENTIONIS **Note:** Varieties exist. Dav. #2538.

Date	Mintage	F	VF	XF	Unc
1764 AS	—	85.00	165	300	800

KM# 116 THALER
Silver **Ruler:** Karl Theodor **Obverse:** Draped bust **Obv. Legend:** CAR • THEODOR • D: G • C • P • R • S • R • I • A • T • & • EL • **Reverse:** Three shields, crown above, lower shield divides date **Rev. Legend:** AD NORMAM CONVENTIONIS **Note:** Dav. #2539.

Date	Mintage	F	VF	XF	Unc
1764 AS	—	75.00	150	275	500

KM# 117 THALER
Silver **Ruler:** Karl Theodor **Obverse:** Head right **Obv. Legend:** CAR • THEODOR • D: G • C • P • R • S • R • I • A • T • & • EL • **Reverse:** AS below date **Rev. Legend:** AD NORMAM CONVENTIONIS **Note:** Dav. #2539A.

Date	Mintage	F	VF	XF	Unc
1764 AS	—	50.00	100	200	350
1764	—	50.00	100	200	350

KM# 125 THALER
Silver **Ruler:** Karl Theodor **Obverse:** Draped bust right **Obv. Legend:** CAR • THEODOR • D: G • C • P • R • S • R • I • A • T • & • EL • **Reverse:** Crown above three shields, value below, date divided above **Rev. Legend:** 10. EINE FEINE MARCK **Note:** Dav. #2540.

Date	Mintage	F	VF	XF	Unc
1765 AS	—	65.00	120	250	450
1765 AK	—	125	225	400	650
1771	—	65.00	120	250	450

KM# 126 THALER
Silver **Ruler:** Karl Theodor **Obverse:** Head right **Obv. Legend:** CAR • THEODOR • D: G • C • P • R • S • R • I • A • T • & • EL • **Reverse:** Date in legend **Rev. Legend:** AD NORMAM CONVENTIONIS 1765, * 10 EINE FEINE MARCK * below **Note:** Dav. #2541.

Date	Mintage	F	VF	XF	Unc
1765 AS	—	75.00	150	280	500

KM# 128 THALER
Silver **Ruler:** Karl Theodor **Obverse:** Draped bust right **Obv. Legend:** CAR • THEODOR • D: G • C • P • R • S • R • I • A • T • & • EL • **Reverse:** Crowned arms within branches, date divided above **Rev. Legend:** • X •/ EINE FEINE MARK below **Note:** Dav. #2542.

Date	Mintage	F	VF	XF	Unc
1766 AS	—	135	250	450	750

KM# 132 THALER
Silver **Ruler:** Karl Theodor **Obverse:** Draped bust right **Reverse:** Crowned arms within branches, date divided above, value below **Note:** Dav. #2543.

Date	Mintage	F	VF	XF	Unc
1768 AS	—	75.00	150	275	500

KM# 133 THALER
Silver **Ruler:** Karl Theodor **Obverse:** Head right **Obv. Legend:** CAR • THEODOR • D: G • C • P • R • S • R • I • A • T • & • EL • **Reverse:** Crowned arms within branches, date divided above, value below **Rev. Legend:** 10 EINE - FEIN MARC **Note:** Large bust.

Date	Mintage	F	VF	XF	Unc
1769 AS	—	75.00	150	275	500
1770 AS	—	75.00	150	275	500

KM# 141 THALER
Silver **Ruler:** Karl Theodor **Obverse:** Draped bust right **Obv. Legend:** CAR • THEODOR • D: G • C • P • R • S • R • I • A • T • & • EL • **Reverse:** Crowned arms within branches, date divided above, value below **Rev. Legend:** 10 EINE - FEIN MARC **Note:** Small bust.

Date	Mintage	F	VF	XF	Unc
1771 AS	—	75.00	150	275	500
1772 AS	—	75.00	150	275	500
1773 AS	—	75.00	150	275	500

KM# 147 THALER
Silver **Ruler:** Karl Theodor **Obverse:** Head right **Obv. Legend:** CAR • THEODOR • D: G • C • P • R • S • R • I • A • T • & • EL • **Reverse:** Crowned arms with tassels, date below **Rev. Legend:** AD NORMAM - CONVENTION: **Note:** Varieties exist. Dav. #2544.

Date	Mintage	F	VF	XF	Unc
1773 AS	—	80.00	160	300	600
1774 AS	—	80.00	160	300	600
1775 AS	—	80.00	160	300	600
1776 AS	—	80.00	160	300	600
1777 AS	—	80.00	160	300	600

KM# 151 THALER
Silver **Ruler:** Karl Theodor **Obverse:** Long hair, crude truncation **Obv. Legend:** CA R• THEODOR • D • G • C • P • R • UTR • BAV • DUX • **Reverse:** Crowned arms, date divided below **Note:** Dav. #1957.

Date	Mintage	F	VF	XF	Unc
1778 AS	—	70.00	145	275	500
1779 AS	—	70.00	145	275	500
1780 AS	—	70.00	145	275	500
1781 AS	—	70.00	145	275	500
1782 AS	—	70.00	145	275	500

KM# 165 THALER
Silver **Ruler:** Karl Theodor **Obverse:** Draped bust right **Obv. Legend:** CAR • THEODOR • D: G • C • P • R • V • B • D • S • R • I • A• D • & EL • **Reverse:** Crowned arms within branches **Rev. Legend:** AD NORMAM - CONVENTION **Note:** Dav. #1960.

Date	Mintage	F	VF	XF	Unc
1781 AS	—	100	185	375	650

KM# 166 THALER
Silver **Ruler:** Karl Theodor **Obverse:** Clean truncation **Obv. Legend:** CAR • THEODOR • G • C • P • R • V • B • D • S • R • I • A • D • & EL • **Reverse:** Crowned arms within branches **Rev. Legend:** AD NORMAM - CONVENTION **Note:** Dav. #1959.

Date	Mintage	F	VF	XF	Unc
1783 AS	—	70.00	145	275	500
1784 AS	—	70.00	145	275	500
1785 AS	—	70.00	145	275	500
1786 AS	—	70.00	145	275	500
1787 AS	—	70.00	145	275	500
1788 AS	—	70.00	145	275	500
1789 AS	—	70.00	145	275	500
1790 AS	—	70.00	145	275	500
1791 AS	—	100	185	375	650
1792 AS	—	70.00	135	225	400
1793 AS	—	65.00	125	200	375
1794 AS	—	65.00	125	200	375
1795 AS	—	65.00	125	200	375

KM# 173 THALER
Silver **Ruler:** Karl Theodor **Obverse:** Without hair ribbon **Obv. Legend:** CAR • THEODOR • D • G • P • R • V • B • D • S • R • I • A • D • & • EL • **Reverse:** Crowned arms within branches **Rev. Legend:** AD NORMAM - CONVENTION **Note:** Dav. #1961.

Date	Mintage	F	VF	XF	Unc
1790 AS	—	70.00	145	275	500
1791 AS	—	100	185	375	650
1792 AS	—	70.00	135	225	400
1793 AS	—	65.00	125	200	375
1794 AS	—	65.00	125	200	375
1795 AS	—	65.00	125	200	375

KM# 174 THALER
Silver **Ruler:** Karl Theodor **Obverse:** Head right **Obv. Legend:** CAR • THEODOR • D: G • C • P • R • V • B • D • S • R • I • A • D •& EL • PROV • & VICAR • **Reverse:** Crowned complex arms within order chain and eagle's breast, date below **Rev. Legend:** * IN • PART • RHENI • SVEV • ET • IVR • FRANCON * **Note:** Vicariat issue. Dav. #1972.

Date	Mintage	F	VF	XF	Unc
1790 AS	—	225	435	700	1,200

KM# 177 THALER

Silver **Ruler:** Karl Theodor **Obverse:** Head right **Obv. Legend:** CAR • THEOD • D: G • C • P • R • V • B • D • S • R • I • A • D • & EL • PROV • & VICAR **Reverse:** Crowned arms within Order chain on eagle's breast, date below **Rev. Legend:** IN • PART • RHENI • SVEV • ET • IVR • FRANCON • **Note:** Vicariat issue. Dav. #1974.

Date	Mintage	F	VF	XF	Unc
1792 AS	—	165	325	525	850

TRADE COINAGE

KM# 46 1/4 CAROLIN

2.4250 g., 0.7700 Gold 0.0600 oz. AGW **Ruler:** Karl Philip **Obverse:** Head right **Reverse:** Monograms in cruciform

Date	Mintage	VG	F	VF	XF	Unc
1735	—	125	250	450	850	—
1736	—	125	250	450	850	—
1736/1	—	—	—	—	—	—

KM# 40 1/2 CAROLIN

4.8500 g., 0.7700 Gold 0.1201 oz. AGW **Ruler:** Karl Philip **Obverse:** Head right, date below **Reverse:** Cruciform arms with 5th shield at center, CP monograms in angles

Date	Mintage	VG	F	VF	XF	Unc
1732	—	400	850	1,800	3,000	—

KM# 41 1/2 CAROLIN

4.8500 g., 0.7700 Gold 0.1201 oz. AGW **Ruler:** Karl Philip **Obverse:** Bust right **Reverse:** Crown with lion supporters above three shields of arms, date below

Date	Mintage	VG	F	VF	XF	Unc
1732	—	550	1,150	2,500	4,000	—

KM# 43 1/2 CAROLIN

4.8500 g., 0.7700 Gold 0.1201 oz. AGW **Ruler:** Karl Philip **Obverse:** Head right **Reverse:** Crowned monogram in cruciform, shield at center

Date	Mintage	VG	F	VF	XF	Unc
1733	—	200	400	800	1,750	—
1736	—	200	400	800	1,750	—

KM# 42 CAROLIN

9.7000 g., 0.7700 Gold 0.2401 oz. AGW **Ruler:** Karl Philip **Obverse:** Head to right, date below **Reverse:** Cruciform arms with fifth shield at center, CP monograms in angles

Date	Mintage	VG	F	VF	XF	Unc
1732	—	550	1,150	2,500	4,200	—

KM# 45 CAROLIN

9.7000 g., 0.7700 Gold 0.2401 oz. AGW **Ruler:** Karl Philip **Obverse:** Head right **Reverse:** Crowned monogram in cruciform, shield in center

Date	Mintage	VG	F	VF	XF	Unc
1733	—	150	300	700	1,500	—
1735	—	150	300	700	1,500	—

KM# 16 1/4 DUCAT

0.8750 g., 0.9860 Gold 0.0277 oz. AGW **Ruler:** Johann Wilhelm **Obverse:** Bust right **Reverse:** Value and date

Date	Mintage	VG	F	VF	XF	Unc
1708	—	150	325	650	1,250	—

KM# 25 1/4 DUCAT

0.8750 g., 0.9860 Gold 0.0277 oz. AGW **Ruler:** Johann Wilhelm **Obverse:** Bust right **Reverse:** Crowned shield divides date

Date	Mintage	VG	F	VF	XF	Unc
1710	—	100	200	450	1,000	—

KM# 27 1/4 DUCAT

0.8750 g., 0.9860 Gold 0.0277 oz. AGW **Ruler:** Johann Wilhelm **Reverse:** Imperial eagle with crown above two oval shields of arms on breast, date in legend

Date	Mintage	VG	F	VF	XF	Unc
1711	—	150	325	650	1,250	—

KM# 26 1/4 DUCAT

0.8750 g., 0.9860 Gold 0.0277 oz. AGW **Ruler:** Johann Wilhelm **Obverse:** Head right **Reverse:** Crowned shield, crown divides date **Note:** Vicariat Issue

Date	Mintage	VG	F	VF	XF	Unc
1711	—	125	300	600	1,100	—

KM# 11 1/2 DUCAT

1.7500 g., 0.9860 Gold 0.0555 oz. AGW **Ruler:** Johann Wilhelm **Obverse:** Armored bust right **Reverse:** Crowned complex arms

Date	Mintage	VG	F	VF	XF	Unc
1705	—	275	600	1,350	2,750	—
1708	—	275	600	1,350	2,750	—

KM# 10 DUCAT

3.5000 g., 0.9860 Gold 0.1109 oz. AGW **Ruler:** Johann Wilhelm **Obverse:** Bust right

Date	Mintage	VG	F	VF	XF	Unc
1703	—	475	950	2,100	3,500	—

KM# 12 DUCAT

3.5000 g., 0.9860 Gold 0.1109 oz. AGW **Ruler:** Johann Wilhelm **Obverse:** Crowned circle of nine shields wtih tenth at center

Date	Mintage	VG	F	VF	XF	Unc
1707	—	450	900	2,000	3,250	—

KM# 13 DUCAT

3.5000 g., 0.9860 Gold 0.1109 oz. AGW **Ruler:** Johann Wilhelm **Reverse:** Date in chronogram

Date	Mintage	VG	F	VF	XF	Unc
1707	—	475	950	2,100	3,500	—

KM# 17 DUCAT

3.5000 g., 0.9860 Gold 0.1109 oz. AGW **Ruler:** Johann Wilhelm **Reverse:** Crowned shield emblazoned with orb, date in legend

Date	Mintage	VG	F	VF	XF	Unc
1708	—	500	1,000	2,250	3,750	—

KM# 18 DUCAT

3.5000 g., 0.9860 Gold 0.1109 oz. AGW **Ruler:** Johann Wilhelm **Reverse:** Three shields of arms

Date	Mintage	VG	F	VF	XF	Unc
1708	—	550	1,100	2,500	4,000	—

KM# 28 DUCAT

3.5000 g., 0.9860 Gold 0.1109 oz. AGW **Ruler:** Johann Wilhelm **Obverse:** Head right **Reverse:** Crown above two shields on breast **Note:** Vicariat Issue.

Date	Mintage	VG	F	VF	XF	Unc
1711 NP	—	300	700	1,650	2,750	—

KM# 35 DUCAT

3.5000 g., 0.9860 Gold 0.1109 oz. AGW **Ruler:** Karl Philip **Obverse:** Bust right **Reverse:** Crown with lion supporters above three shields of arms, date divided below

Date	Mintage	VG	F	VF	XF	Unc
1721	—	900	1,850	3,250	5,500	—

KM# 36 DUCAT

3.5000 g., 0.9860 Gold 0.1109 oz. AGW **Ruler:** Karl Philip **Obverse:** Horseman right **Reverse:** Crowned shields in cruciform, monograms at angles, shield at center

Date	Mintage	VG	F	VF	XF	Unc
1721 IGW	—	200	500	1,100	1,750	—
1726	—	200	500	1,100	1,750	—

KM# 37 DUCAT

3.5000 g., 0.9860 Gold 0.1109 oz. AGW **Ruler:** Karl Philip **Mint:** Mannheim **Obverse:** Young laureate bust right **Reverse:** Standing figure facing, laurel branch at right

Date	Mintage	VG	F	VF	XF	Unc
1725	—	250	550	1,250	2,000	—

KM# 47 DUCAT

3.5000 g., 0.9860 Gold 0.1109 oz. AGW **Ruler:** Karl Philip **Obverse:** Bust right **Reverse:** Crown above three shields of arms, date in exergue

Date	Mintage	VG	F	VF	XF	Unc
1737	—	500	1,000	2,400	4,000	—

KM# 50 DUCAT

3.5000 g., 0.9860 Gold 0.1109 oz. AGW **Ruler:** Karl Philip **Obverse:** Armored bust right **Reverse:** Crowned imperial eagle over three shields of arms on breast, divided date in exergue

Date	Mintage	VG	F	VF	XF	Unc
1740	—	550	1,150	2,750	4,500	—

KM# 51 DUCAT

3.5000 g., 0.9860 Gold 0.1109 oz. AGW **Ruler:** Karl Philip **Obverse:** Armored bust right **Reverse:** City of Mannheim and Environs **Note:** Rhine Gold.

Date	Mintage	VG	F	VF	XF	Unc
ND(1742)	—	650	1,500	3,700	6,000	—

KM# 53 DUCAT

3.5000 g., 0.9860 Gold 0.1109 oz. AGW **Ruler:** Karl Theodor **Mint:** Mannheim **Subject:** Marriage of Karl Theodor and Elizabeth Augusta **Obverse:** Conjoined busts right **Reverse:** Crown above two shields of arms

Date	Mintage	VG	F	VF	XF	Unc
1742	—	300	600	1,300	2,000	—

KM# 57 DUCAT

3.5000 g., 0.9860 Gold 0.1109 oz. AGW **Ruler:** Karl Theodor **Subject:** Homage of Mannheim **Obverse:** Lion holds city arms **Reverse:** Inscription

Date	Mintage	VG	F	VF	XF	Unc
1744	—	400	850	1,600	2,500	—

KM# 73 DUCAT

3.5000 g., 0.9860 Gold 0.1109 oz. AGW **Ruler:** Karl Theodor **Subject:** Homage of Heidelberg **Obverse:** Lion arms on pedestal **Reverse:** Inscription

Date	Mintage	VG	F	VF	XF	Unc
1746 S	—	275	550	1,250	2,000	—

KM# 86 DUCAT

3.5000 g., 0.9860 Gold 0.1109 oz. AGW **Ruler:** Karl Theodor **Obverse:** Bust right **Reverse:** Order of St. Hubert

Date	Mintage	VG	F	VF	XF	Unc
1750 M-S-AK	—	250	525	1,000	1,750	—

KM# 87 DUCAT

3.5000 g., 0.9860 Gold 0.1109 oz. AGW **Ruler:** Karl Theodor **Obverse:** Bust right **Reverse:** Crowned arms with two lion heads, date

Date	Mintage	VG	F	VF	XF	Unc
1750	—	400	1,000	2,000	3,250	—

KM# 88 DUCAT

3.5000 g., 0.9860 Gold 0.1109 oz. AGW **Ruler:** Karl Theodor **Subject:** Homage of Weinheim **Obverse:** Lion with city arms in cartouche **Reverse:** Inscription in cartouche

Date	Mintage	VG	F	VF	XF	Unc
1750 Rare	—	—	—	—	—	—

KM# 89 DUCAT

3.5000 g., 0.9860 Gold 0.1109 oz. AGW **Ruler:** Karl Theodor **Subject:** Homage of Weisloch **Obverse:** City arms in cartouche **Reverse:** Inscription between branches

Date	Mintage	VG	F	VF	XF	Unc
1750 Rare	—	—	—	—	—	—

KM# 90 DUCAT

3.5000 g., 0.9860 Gold 0.1109 oz. AGW **Ruler:** Karl Theodor **Subject:** Homage of Neckargemund **Obverse:** Lion with city arms in cartouche **Reverse:** Inscription in wreath

Date	Mintage	VG	F	VF	XF	Unc
1750 Rare	—	—	—	—	—	—

KM# 109 DUCAT

3.5000 g., 0.9860 Gold 0.1109 oz. AGW **Ruler:** Karl Theodor

Date	Mintage	VG	F	VF	XF	Unc
1762 AS	—	950	1,500	2,250	3,500	—

KM# 113 DUCAT

3.5000 g., 0.9860 Gold 0.1109 oz. AGW **Ruler:** Karl Theodor **Obverse:** Bust right **Reverse:** City view of Mannheim

Date	Mintage	VG	F	VF	XF	Unc
1763 AS	—	225	500	1,000	1,750	—
1764 AS	—	225	500	1,000	1,750	—
1764 S	—	225	500	1,000	1,750	—
1767 S	—	225	500	1,000	1,750	—
1778	—	300	800	1,650	2,750	—

KM# 118 DUCAT

3.5000 g., 0.9860 Gold 0.1109 oz. AGW **Ruler:** Karl Theodor **Reverse:** Crowned arms

Date	Mintage	VG	F	VF	XF	Unc
1764 S	—	300	800	1,650	2,750	—

KM# 131 DUCAT

3.5000 g., 0.9860 Gold 0.1109 oz. AGW **Ruler:** Karl Theodor **Obverse:** Head right **Reverse:** Sun on right side

Date	Mintage	VG	F	VF	XF	Unc
1767 S	—	350	900	1,750	3,000	—
1768	—	—	—	—	—	—

KM# 130 DUCAT

3.5000 g., 0.9860 Gold 0.1109 oz. AGW **Ruler:** Karl Theodor **Obverse:** Bust right **Reverse:** Goddess Fortuna **Note:** Lottery prize.

Date	Mintage	VG	F	VF	XF	Unc
ND(1767)	—	300	800	1,650	2,750	—

KM# 134 DUCAT

3.5000 g., 0.9860 Gold 0.1109 oz. AGW **Ruler:** Karl Theodor **Obverse:** Bust right **Reverse:** Crown over three shields of arms

Date	Mintage	VG	F	VF	XF	Unc
1769 S	—	400	1,000	2,000	3,500	—

KM# 164 DUCAT

3.5000 g., 0.9860 Gold 0.1109 oz. AGW **Ruler:** Karl Theodor **Subject:** 50th Year of Reign in Pfalz-Sulzbach **Obverse:** Altar with inscription, date **Reverse:** Inscription, date in chronogram

Date	Mintage	VG	F	VF	XF	Unc
1783 Rare	—	—	—	—	—	—

KM# 178 DUCAT

3.5000 g., 0.9860 Gold 0.1109 oz. AGW **Ruler:** Karl Theodor **Subject:** 50th Year of Reign Commemorative **Obverse:** Lion left with shield **Reverse:** Five-line inscription in sprays

Date	Mintage	VG	F	VF	XF	Unc
1792	—	175	325	700	1,200	—

KM# 14 2 DUCAT

7.0000 g., 0.9860 Gold 0.2219 oz. AGW **Ruler:** Johann Wilhelm **Obverse:** Bust right **Reverse:** Crowned circle of nine shields with tenth at center

Date	Mintage	VG	F	VF	XF	Unc
1707	—	650	1,350	3,250	6,000	—

KM# 19 2 DUCAT

7.0000 g., 0.9860 Gold 0.2219 oz. AGW **Ruler:** Johann Wilhelm **Reverse:** Date in chronogram

Date	Mintage	VG	F	VF	XF	Unc
1707	—	750	1,450	3,500	6,500	—

KM# 29 2 DUCAT

7.0000 g., 0.9860 Gold 0.2219 oz. AGW **Ruler:** Johann Wilhelm **Obverse:** Head right **Reverse:** Crowned imperial eagle above two shields of arms on breast

Date	Mintage	VG	F	VF	XF	Unc
1711	—	800	1,600	3,700	6,750	—

KM# 58 2 DUCAT

7.0000 g., 0.9860 Gold 0.2219 oz. AGW **Ruler:** Karl Theodor **Subject:** Homage of Mannheim **Obverse:** Bust right **Reverse:** Crowned oval arms between branches

Date	Mintage	VG	F	VF	XF	Unc
1744 A SCHAEFFER Rare	—	—	—	—	—	—

KM# 74 2 DUCAT

7.0000 g., 0.9860 Gold 0.2219 oz. AGW **Ruler:** Karl Theodor **Subject:** Homage of Heidelberg **Obverse:** Bust right **Reverse:** Lion shield on pedestal between branches, date in chronogram

Date	Mintage	VG	F	VF	XF	Unc
1746 Rare	—	—	—	—	—	—

KM# 30 3 DUCAT

10.5000 g., 0.9860 Gold 0.3328 oz. AGW **Ruler:** Johann Wilhelm **Obverse:** Head right **Reverse:** Crowned imperial eagle above two shields of arms on breast **Note:** Vicariat Issue.

Date	Mintage	VG	F	VF	XF	Unc
1711	—	1,650	3,250	5,500	8,500	—

PATTERNS

Including off metal strikes

KM#	Date	Mintage	Identification	Mkt Val
Pn3	1737	—	2/3 Thaler. Gold. Mannheim	—
Pn4	1742	—	Ducat. Silver. Marriage.	150
Pn5	1742	—	2 Ducat. Silver. Carl Philipp	250
Pn6	1742	—	2 Ducat. Silver. Mannheim	250
Pn7	1744	—	Ducat. Silver. KM#57; Mannheim.	90.00
Pn8	1744	—	2 Ducat. Silver. KM#58; Mannheim; A SCHAEFFER.	—
Pn9	1745	—	2 Kreuzer. Copper. KM#52	—
Pn10	1746	—	2 Kreuzer. Copper. KM#52	—
Pn11	1746	—	Ducat. Silver. KM#57. Heidelberg.	150
Pn12	1746	—	2 Ducat. Silver. KM#74. Heidelberg.	150
Pn13	1750	—	2 Kreuzer. Copper. KM#77	—
Pn14	1750	—	4 Kreuzer. Copper. KM#63	—
Pn15	1750	—	Ducat. Silver. KM#88. Weinheim.	180
Pn16	1750	—	Ducat. Silver. KM#89. Wieslach.	180
Pn17	1750	—	Ducat. Silver. KM#90. Neckargemund.	180
Pn18	1761	—	Thaler. Lead. KM#107.	100
Pn19	1764	—	Thaler. Tin. KM#116.	150
Pn20	1764	—	Thaler. Tin. KM#117.	150
Pn21	1765	—	1/2 Thaler. Tin. KM#122.	150
Pn22	1765	—	Thaler. Tin. KM#125.	150
Pn23	1769	—	Thaler. Tin. KM#133.	150
Pn24	1771	—	Thaler. Tin. KM#141.	150
Pn25	1774	—	Thaler. Tin. KM#141.	180
Pn26	1775	—	1/2 Kreuzer. Silver. KM#143.	—
Pn27	1783	—	Kreuzer. Gold. KM#145.	—
Pn28	1783	—	Ducat. Silver. KM#164.	100

KM#	Date	Mintage	Identification	Mkt Val
Pn29	1792	—	Ducat. Silver. KM#178	75.00

POMERANIA

A duchy on the Baltic Sea, near modern day Poland, was founded in the late 11th century. After many divisions, Pomerania was annexed to Sweden in 1637. Brandenburg-Prussia had an interest in the area and slowly acquired bits until in 1815 all of Pomerania belonged to Prussia. The arms of Pomerania appear on coins of Brandenburg-Prussia from the 17th century onward.

RULERS

Karl XII of Sweden, 1697-1718
Adolf Fredrik of Sweden, 1751-1771
Gustav III, King of Sweden, 1771-1792
Gustav IV Adolf of Sweden, 1792-1809

MINT

Stettin

MINT OFFICIALS' INITIALS

Initials	Date	Name
IM	1705-10	Johann Memmies

SWEDISH OCCUPATION

REGULAR COINAGE

KM# 422 3 PFENNINGE

Copper **Ruler:** Gustav III, King of Sweden **Obverse:** Crowned griffin left holding sword **Obv. Legend:** K. S. P. L. M. **Reverse:** Value above date

Date	Mintage	VG	F	VF	XF	Unc
1776	384,000	5.00	10.00	22.00	50.00	—
1792	384,000	4.00	8.00	18.00	40.00	—
1806	384,000	4.00	8.00	18.00	40.00	—
1808	258,000	4.00	8.00	18.00	40.00	—

KM# 363 WITTEN (1/192 Thaler)

Silver **Ruler:** Karl XII of Sweden **Obverse:** Crowned monogram **Reverse:** Value, date

Date	Mintage	VG	F	VF	XF	Unc
1707 IM	—	20.00	40.00	80.00	160	—

KM# 399 2 GUTE GROSCHEN

Silver **Ruler:** Adolf Fredrik of Sweden **Obverse:** Crowned script AFR monogram, date below **Reverse:** Crowned griffin holding sword, value in exergue

Date	Mintage	VG	F	VF	XF	Unc
1759	—	3.00	6.00	10.00	25.00	—

KM# 397 4 GUTE GROSCHEN

Silver **Ruler:** Adolf Fredrik of Sweden **Obverse:** Crowned monogram above date **Reverse:** Crowned griffin with sword left

Date	Mintage	VG	F	VF	XF	Unc
1758 OHK	—	20.00	50.00	90.00	160	—
1759 OHK	—	20.00	50.00	90.00	160	—

KM# 398 8 GUTE GROSCHEN

Silver **Ruler:** Adolf Fredrik of Sweden **Obverse:** Crowned AFR monogram, date below **Reverse:** Crowned griffin holding sword, value in exergue

Date	Mintage	VG	F	VF	XF	Unc
1758 OHK	—	30.00	65.00	125	200	—
1759 OHK	—	30.00	65.00	125	200	—
1760 OHK	—	30.00	65.00	125	200	—

KM# 410 8 GUTE GROSCHEN
Silver **Ruler:** Adolf Fredrik of Sweden **Obverse:** Head right **Reverse:** Value, date

Date	Mintage	VG	F	VF	XF	Unc
1760 OHK	—	25.00	60.00	100	165	—
1761 LFK	—	25.00	60.00	100	165	—
1761 ICS	—	25.00	60.00	100	165	—
1761 IHL	—	25.00	60.00	100	165	—

KM# 364 1/96 THALER (Sechsling)
Silver **Ruler:** Karl XII of Sweden **Obverse:** Crowned CC XII monogram, initials below

Date	Mintage	VG	F	VF	XF	Unc
1707 IM	—	40.00	80.00	160	325	—

KM# 318 1/48 THALER (Schilling)
Silver **Ruler:** Karl XII of Sweden **Obverse:** Stralsund city arms in inner circle **Reverse:** Value in inner circle, date in legend

Date	Mintage	VG	F	VF	XF	Unc
1715	—	20.00	40.00	80.00	160	—

KM# 411 1/48 THALER (Schilling)
Billon **Ruler:** Adolf Fredrik of Sweden **Obverse:** Crowned script AFR monogram, date below **Reverse:** Value

Date	Mintage	VG	F	VF	XF	Unc
1760 OHK	—	5.00	10.00	20.00	40.00	—
1761 LFK	—	5.00	10.00	20.00	40.00	—
1761 IDL	—	5.00	10.00	20.00	40.00	—
1761 IHL	—	5.00	10.00	20.00	40.00	—
1761 LDS	—	5.00	10.00	20.00	40.00	—

KM# 416 1/48 THALER (Schilling)
Billon **Ruler:** Adolf Fredrik of Sweden **Obverse:** Crowned AF monogram, date below **Reverse:** Value in inner circle

Date	Mintage	VG	F	VF	XF	Unc
1763 IDL	—	4.00	8.00	15.00	32.00	—
1763 LDS	—	4.00	8.00	15.00	32.00	—

KM# 400 1/24 THALER (1 Groschen = 2 Schilling)
Billon **Ruler:** Adolf Fredrik of Sweden **Obverse:** Crowned monogram above date **Reverse:** Value

Date	Mintage	VG	F	VF	XF	Unc
1759 OHK	—	4.00	8.00	15.00	32.00	—
1760 OHK	—	4.00	8.00	15.00	32.00	—
1761 LFK	—	4.00	8.00	15.00	32.00	—
1761 ICS	—	4.00	8.00	15.00	32.00	—
1761 IHL	—	4.00	8.00	15.00	32.00	—
1761 IDL	—	4.00	8.00	15.00	32.00	—

KM# 417.1 1/24 THALER (1 Groschen = 2 Schilling)
Billon **Ruler:** Adolf Fredrik of Sweden **Obverse:** Crowned AF monogram, date below, K. S. P. L. M.

Date	Mintage	VG	F	VF	XF	Unc
1763 IDL	—	4.50	9.00	18.00	35.00	—

KM# 417.2 1/24 THALER (1 Groschen = 2 Schilling)
Billon **Ruler:** Adolf Fredrik of Sweden **Obverse:** Without K. S. P. L. M.

Date	Mintage	VG	F	VF	XF	Unc
1763 IDL	—	4.50	9.00	18.00	35.00	—

KM# 415 1/12 THALER (2 Groschen)
Silver **Ruler:** Adolf Fredrik of Sweden **Obverse:** Head right **Reverse:** Value and date

Date	Mintage	VG	F	VF	XF	Unc
1761 IDL	—	10.00	20.00	40.00	85.00	—

KM# 419 1/12 THALER (2 Groschen)
Silver **Ruler:** Adolf Fredrik of Sweden **Obverse:** Crowned monogram **Reverse:** Value

Date	Mintage	VG	F	VF	XF	Unc
1763 IDL	—	8.00	16.00	32.00	75.00	—
1763 IHL	—	8.00	16.00	32.00	75.00	—
1763 LDS	—	8.00	16.00	32.00	75.00	—
1767 IHL	—	8.00	16.00	32.00	75.00	—
1767 LDS	—	8.00	16.00	32.00	75.00	—
1768 LDS	—	8.00	16.00	32.00	75.00	—

KM# 412 1/6 THALER (4 Groschen)
Silver **Ruler:** Adolf Fredrik of Sweden **Obverse:** Head right **Reverse:** Value and date

Date	Mintage	VG	F	VF	XF	Unc
1760 OHK	—	12.00	25.00	55.00	120	—
1761 LFK	—	12.00	25.00	55.00	120	—
1761 ICS	—	12.00	25.00	55.00	120	—
1761 IHL	—	12.00	25.00	55.00	120	—
1761 DL	—	12.00	25.00	55.00	120	—
1761 F	—	12.00	25.00	55.00	120	—

KM# 413 1/3 THALER (1/2 Gulden - 8 Groschen)
Silver **Ruler:** Adolf Fredrik of Sweden **Obverse:** Head right **Reverse:** Value in four lines, date and initials below

Date	Mintage	VG	F	VF	XF	Unc
1760 OHK Rare	—	—	—	—	—	—

KM# 414 1/3 THALER (1/2 Gulden - 8 Groschen)
Silver **Ruler:** Adolf Fredrik of Sweden **Reverse:** Value and date in branches

Date	Mintage	VG	F	VF	XF	Unc
1760	—	90.00	175	350	550	—

KM# 420 1/3 THALER (1/2 Gulden - 8 Groschen)
Silver **Ruler:** Adolf Fredrik of Sweden **Obverse:** Head right **Reverse:** Crowned and supported arms, date and value in exergue

Date	Mintage	VG	F	VF	XF	Unc
1763 IHL	—	60.00	120	250	450	—

KM# 356 2/3 THALER (1 Gulden)
Silver **Ruler:** Karl XII of Sweden **Obverse:** Armored bust with wig right, IM on truncation **Reverse:** Crowned, supported arms, value and date below

Date	Mintage	VG	F	VF	XF	Unc
1705 IM Rare	—	—	—	—	—	—
1706 IM	—	100	200	400	800	—

KM# 357 2/3 THALER (1 Gulden)
Silver **Ruler:** Karl XII of Sweden **Obverse:** Script initials on truncation

Date	Mintage	VG	F	VF	XF	Unc
1706 IM	—	75.00	150	300	600	—
1707 IM	—	100	200	400	800	—

KM# 358 2/3 THALER (1 Gulden)
Silver **Ruler:** Karl XII of Sweden **Obverse:** Rounded truncation, initials below bust **Obv. Legend:** CAROL VS•XII•-D•G•REX•SVEC• **Reverse:** Crowned supported arms **Rev. Legend:** CITERIORIS + - MON•NOV•POMERB*

Date	Mintage	VG	F	VF	XF	Unc
1706 IM	—	100	200	400	800	—

KM# 359 2/3 THALER (1 Gulden)
Silver **Ruler:** Karl XII of Sweden **Obverse:** Bust right **Obv. Legend:** CAROL VS•XII•-D•G•REX•SVEC• **Reverse:** Crowned supported arms **Rev. Legend:** CITERIORIS + - MON•NOV• POMERB*

Date	Mintage	VG	F	VF	XF	Unc
1706 IM	—	85.00	175	350	700	—
1707 IM	—	85.00	175	350	700	—

KM# 360 2/3 THALER (1 Gulden)
Silver **Ruler:** Karl XII of Sweden **Obverse:** Bust right, different hair style and drapery **Obv. Legend:** CAROL VS•XII•-D•G•REX•SVEC• **Reverse:** Crowned supported arms **Rev. Legend:** CITERIORIS + - MON•NOV•POMERB*

Date	Mintage	VG	F	VF	XF	Unc
1706 IM	—	85.00	175	350	700	—
1707 IM	—	85.00	175	350	700	—

KM# 365 2/3 THALER (1 Gulden)
Silver **Ruler:** Karl XII of Sweden **Obverse:** Bust right with left shoulder draped **Reverse:** Crowned, supported arms with value and date below

Date	Mintage	VG	F	VF	XF	Unc
1708	—	75.00	150	300	600	—
1709	—	75.00	150	300	600	—

KM# 366 2/3 THALER (1 Gulden)
Silver **Ruler:** Karl XII of Sweden **Obverse:** Multi-folded mantle **Reverse:** Helmeted complex arms with supporters

Date	Mintage	VG	F	VF	XF	Unc
1708	—	80.00	140	280	560	—

KM# 367 2/3 THALER (1 Gulden)

Silver **Ruler:** Karl XII of Sweden **Obverse:** Mantle around neck

Date	Mintage	VG	F	VF	XF	Unc
1708	—	90.00	160	320	640	—

KM# 421 2/3 THALER (1 Gulden)

Silver **Ruler:** Adolf Fredrik of Sweden **Obverse:** Head right **Reverse:** Crowned, helmeted complex arms with supporters, value divides date below **Note:** Varieties in reverse legend DEM and DEN exist.

Date	Mintage	VG	F	VF	XF	Unc
1763 IHL	—	60.00	125	200	350	—

KM# 401 5 THALER

6.6500 g., 0.9000 Gold 0.1924 oz. AGW **Ruler:** Adolf Fredrik of Sweden **Subject:** Adolf Fredrik **Obverse:** Head right **Reverse:** Crowned griffin with sword left, value below

Date	Mintage	VG	F	VF	XF	Unc
1759 OHK	—	400	1,000	2,000	4,500	—

KM# 404 10 THALER

13.3000 g., 0.9000 Gold 0.3848 oz. AGW **Ruler:** Adolf Fredrik of Sweden **Subject:** Adolf Fredrik **Obverse:** Head right **Reverse:** Crowned griffin with sword left, value below

Date	Mintage	VG	F	VF	XF	Unc
1759 OHK	—	600	1,500	3,500	6,500	—

TRADE COINAGE

KM# 361.1 DUCAT

3.5000 g., 0.9860 Gold 0.1109 oz. AGW **Ruler:** Karl XII of Sweden **Obverse:** Armored, draped bust right **Reverse:** Helmeted, crowned complex arms with supporters

Date	Mintage	VG	F	VF	XF	Unc
1706 IM	—	750	1,650	3,000	5,000	—

KM# 361.2 DUCAT

3.5000 g., 0.9860 Gold 0.1109 oz. AGW **Ruler:** Karl XII of Sweden **Obverse:** Large bust right **Reverse:** Helmeted, crowned complex arms with supporters

Date	Mintage	VG	F	VF	XF	Unc
1706 IM	—	400	950	2,250	4,250	—

KM# 370 DUCAT

3.5000 g., 0.9860 Gold 0.1109 oz. AGW **Ruler:** Karl XII of Sweden **Obverse:** Smaller bust right **Reverse:** Helmeted, crowned complex arms with supporters **Note:** Varieties exist.

Date	Mintage	VG	F	VF	XF	Unc
1709 IM	—	400	950	2,250	4,250	—

PATTERNS

Including off metal strikes

KM#	Date	Mintage	Identification	Mkt Val
Pn1	1761	—	1/12 Thaler. Gold. 3.5000 g. KM#415	—
Pn2	1763	—	1/12 Thaler. Gold. 3.5000 g. KM#419	—

PRUSSIA

(Preussen)

The Elector and Margrave of Brandenburg-Prussia, Friedrich III (1688-1713) offered his support to the Austrian Habsburgs during the War of the Spanish Succession. In exchange, Friedrich was permitted to assume the title "King in Prussia" in 1701 and ruled from that year as Friedrich I. Prussia built itself up as one of the major military powers of Europe during the 18th century, despite its size and mostly rural population. Brandenburg-Prussia had been adroitly acquiring territories and significant increases in the number of inhabitants all during the 17th century, especially in the technologically advanced Rhineland. Her far-flung territories gave Prussia a wide operating base and a large and steady income flowed into the state treasury.

Friedrich II the Great (1740-1786) built upon his predecessors' advances and began his reign by wresting much of Silesia away from Austria. Friedrich II was handed a setback during the Seven Years' War (1756-1763) when Russia, under Tsarina Elisabeth I Petrovna, occupied the eastern Prussian territories from 1758 until 1762. A short-lived, but extensive series of coins were struck in Elisabeth's name during those years. As a result of the second partitioning of Poland in 1793, Prussia received the region between East and West Prussia designated the province of South Prussia. A number of small denomination copper coins were struck for this territory for several years late in the 18th century.

Prussia suffered greatly at the hands of Napoleon in the early 19th century, but was among the victorious allies who shared in the spoils of his defeats in 1814 and 1815. Prussia industrialized during the 19th century and added considerably to its territory after wars with Denmark and Austria in 1864 and 1866. The victory over France in the war of 1870-71 resulted in the annexation of Alsace and Lorraine, but even more importantly, it precipitated the creation of the German Empire, with Prussia leading the way. King Wilhelm I became Kaiser (Emperor) Wilhelm I of a united Germany. Defeat in World War I ended the empire and monarchy in Germany. Today, Prussia is not even part of the modern, unified country of Germany.

NOTE:

For coins of Neuchatel previously listed here, see Switzerland.

RULERS

Friedrich I, 1701-1713
Friedrich Wilhelm I, 1713-1740
Friedrich II, 1740-1786
Friedrich Wilhelm II, 1786-1797
Friedrich Wilhelm III, 1797-1840

MINT MARKS

A - Berlin = Prussia, East Friesland, East Prussia, Posen
B - Bayreuth = Brandenburg-Ansbach-Bayreuth
B - Breslau = Silesia, Posen, South Prussia
C - Cleve
D - Aurich = East Friesland, Prussia
E - Königsberg = East Prussia
F - Magdeburg
G - Stettin
G - Schwerin, Plön-Rethwisch Mint, 1763 only
S - Schwabach = Brandenburg-Ansbach-Bayreuth
Star - Dresden

MINT OFFICIALS' INITIALS

Aurich Mint

Initials	Date	Name
BID	1747-49	Bernhard Julius Dedekind
ICG	1735-47	Johann Christian Gittermann

Berlin Mint

Initials	Date	Name
ALS	1741-65	August Ludwig Siemens, warden in Berlin
B, LB, LHB	1742-54	Ludwig Heinrich Barbiez, die-cutter
CFL, L	1702-42	Christian Friedrich Luders, die-cutter
CHI	1749-64	Christoph Henning Jaster
CS	1701-13	Christoph Stricker
	1713-15	Christoph Stricker, warden
E	1754-68	Tobias Ernst, die-cutter
EGN	1725-49	Ernst Georg Neubauer
GLC	1702	Gabriel Leclerc, die-cutter
HFH	1718-19	Heinrich Friedrich Halter
IFS	1713-18	Jobst Friedrich Sauerbrei
IGN	1718-25	Johann Georg Neubauer
LCS	1682-1701	Lorenz Christoph Schneider, mint commissioner
M	1704-43	Friedrich Marl, die-cutter
R	1704-18	Stephan Reinhard, die-cutter

Breslau Mint

Initials	Date	Name
AE, AHE	1743-51	Adam Heinrich von Ehrenberg

Cleve Mint

Initials	Date	Name
AGP	1742	Anton Gottfried Pott
GK	1741-55	Georg Christoph Kuster
ICM	1741-57	Johann Christian Marme, die-cutter

Dresden Mint

Initials	Date	Name
B, IDB	1756-59	Johann David Biller

Königsberg Mint

Initials	Date	Name
A	1756-58	Jakob Abraham, die-cutter
CG	1699-1728	Caspar Geelhaar
CS	1735-49	Christian Schirmer
GM, GWM, M	1711-25	Gottfried Wilhelm Metelles, die-cutter
S	1751-56	Schwanefelder, die-cutter
ST	1752-68	Johann Julius Steinbrück, die-cutter
W	1725-52	Otto Herman Wissel, die-cutter

Leipzig Mint

Initials	Date	Name
EC, LDS	1753-63	Ernst Dietrich Croll

London Mint

Initials	Date	Name
R	Ca.1710-14	Karl Christian Reisen, die-cutter

Magdeburg Mint

Initials	Date	Name
HFH	1698-1718	Heinrich Friedrich Halter

Minden Mint

Initials	Date	Name
BH	1682-1713	Bastian Hille
GM, GWM, M	1689-1711	Gottfried Wilhelm Metelles, die-cutter

ARMS

Hohenzollern – shield divided into quarters, upper left and lower right usually shaded.

Prussia – eagle, usually crowned, with wings spread

REFERENCES

D = Kurt Dost, ***Münzen in Preussenland...1525-1821***, Essen, 1990.
M = Klaus Martin, **Die Preussischen Münzprägungen von 1701-1786,** Berlin, 1976.
N = Erich Neumann, **Brandenburg-preussische Münzprägungen unter der Herrschaft der Hohenzollern 1415-1918,** 2 vols., Cologne, 1997.
O = Manfred Olding, **Die Münzen Friedrichs des Grossen – Katalog der preussischen Münzen von 1740-1786,** Osnabrück, 1987.

KINGDOM

REGULAR COINAGE

A series of counterfeit Prussian 5, 10 and 20 Mark gold pieces all dated 1887A were being marketed in the early 1970's. They were created by a dentist in Bonn, West Germany and the previously unknown date listed above aroused the curiousity of the numismatic community and eventually exposed the scam.

KM# 30 PFENNIG

Billon **Ruler:** Friedrich I **Mint:** Magdeburg

Date	Mintage	VG	F	VF	XF	Unc
1703 HFH	Inc. above	8.00	15.00	30.00	60.00	—

KM# 29 PFENNIG

Billon **Ruler:** Friedrich I **Mint:** Berlin **Obverse:** Crowned FR monogram divides value: I-PF and date, initials below **Note:** Uniface

Date	Mintage	VG	F	VF	XF	Unc
1703 CS	423,000	8.00	15.00	30.00	60.00	—

KM# 52 PFENNIG

Billon **Ruler:** Friedrich I **Mint:** Minden **Obverse:** Crowned FR monogram divides value: I - P **Reverse:** Value, I/PFEN/date/initials.

Date	Mintage	VG	F	VF	XF	Unc
1705 BH	634,000	10.00	25.00	50.00	85.00	—

KM# 217 PFENNIG

Billon **Ruler:** Friedrich Wilhelm I **Mint:** Berlin **Obverse:** Crowned FWR monogram, initials below **Reverse:** Value: 1/GUTER/PFEN/date

Date	Mintage	VG	F	VF	XF	Unc
1735 EGN	2,878,000	12.00	30.00	60.00	95.00	—
1736 EGN	Inc. above	12.00	30.00	60.00	95.00	—

KM# 227 PFENNIG

Billon **Ruler:** Friedrich II **Mint:** Berlin **Obverse:** Crowned script FR monogram, date **Reverse:** Value: GUTER PFEN **Note:** (Guter).

Date	Mintage	VG	F	VF	XF	Unc
1741 EGN	473,000	8.00	12.00	25.00	50.00	—
1742 EGN	Inc. above	8.00	12.00	25.00	50.00	—
1743 EGN	679,000	8.00	12.00	25.00	50.00	—

KM# 262 PFENNIG

Copper **Ruler:** Friedrich II **Obverse:** Crowned script FR monogram **Reverse:** Value, date **Rev. Legend:** *1*/PFEN.SCHEID/ MUNTZ/date/initial

Date	Mintage	VG	F	VF	XF	Unc
1751A	8,640,000	4.00	8.00	20.00	35.00	—
1752A	Inc. above	4.00	8.00	20.00	35.00	—
1753A	Inc. above	4.00	8.00	20.00	35.00	—
1754F	Inc. above	12.50	25.00	50.00	100	—
1755A	Inc. above	4.00	8.00	20.00	35.00	—

KM# 319 PFENNIG

Billon **Ruler:** Friedrich II **Mint:** Berlin **Obverse:** Crowned FR monogram with date below **Reverse:** Value

Date	Mintage	VG	F	VF	XF	Unc
1768A	1,220,000	1.50	3.00	6.00	12.00	—
1769A	789,000	1.50	3.00	6.00	12.00	—
1770A	451,000	1.50	3.00	6.00	12.00	—

KM# 326 PFENNIG

Billon **Ruler:** Friedrich II **Mint:** Berlin **Obverse:** Crowned FR monogram **Reverse:** Value above date **Rev. Legend:** *1*/GUTER/PFEN/date

Date	Mintage	VG	F	VF	XF	Unc
1771A	608,000	1.50	3.00	5.00	10.00	—
1772A	431,000	1.50	3.00	5.00	10.00	—
1773A	725,000	1.50	3.00	5.00	10.00	—
1774A	804,000	1.50	3.00	5.00	10.00	—
1775A	438,000	1.50	3.00	5.00	10.00	—
1776A	963,000	1.50	3.00	5.00	10.00	—
1777A	696,000	1.50	3.00	5.00	10.00	—
1778A	659,000	1.50	3.00	5.00	10.00	—
1779A	645,000	1.50	3.00	5.00	10.00	—
1780A	685,000	1.50	3.00	5.00	10.00	—
1781A	390,000	1.50	3.00	5.00	10.00	—
1782A	944,000	1.50	3.00	5.00	10.00	—
1783A	757,000	1.50	3.00	5.00	10.00	—
1784A	750,000	1.50	3.00	5.00	10.00	—
1785A	821,000	1.50	3.00	5.00	10.00	—
1786A	164,000	1.50	3.00	5.00	10.00	—

KM# 350 PFENNIG

Billon **Ruler:** Friedrich Wilhelm II **Mint:** Berlin **Obverse:** Crowned monogram **Reverse:** Value, date **Rev. Legend:** *1*/PFENNIG/ date/initial

Date	Mintage	VG	F	VF	XF	Unc
1787A	—	1.50	3.00	5.00	10.00	—
1788A	—	1.50	3.00	5.00	10.00	—
1789A	—	1.50	3.00	5.00	10.00	—
1790A	—	1.50	3.00	5.00	10.00	—
1791A	—	1.50	3.00	5.00	10.00	—
1792A	—	1.50	3.00	5.00	10.00	—
1793A	—	1.50	3.00	5.00	10.00	—
1794A	—	1.50	3.00	5.00	10.00	—
1795A	—	1.50	3.00	5.00	10.00	—
1796A	—	1.50	3.00	5.00	10.00	—
1797A	—	1.50	3.00	5.00	10.00	—

KM# 353 PFENNIG

Copper **Ruler:** Friedrich Wilhelm II **Mint:** Berlin **Obverse:** Crowned FW monogram **Reverse:** Value, date **Rev. Legend:** *1*/PFENN•/SCHEIDE/MUNZE/date/*initial*

Date	Mintage	VG	F	VF	XF	Unc
1788A	—	1.50	3.00	5.00	10.00	—
1789A	—	1.50	3.00	5.00	10.00	—
1790A	—	1.50	3.00	5.00	10.00	—
1791A	—	1.50	3.00	5.00	10.00	—
1792A	—	1.50	3.00	5.00	10.00	—
1793A	—	1.50	3.00	5.00	10.00	—
1794A	—	1.50	3.00	5.00	10.00	—
1795A	—	1.50	3.00	5.00	10.00	—
1796A	—	1.50	3.00	5.00	10.00	—
1797A	—	1.50	3.00	5.00	10.00	—

KM# 372 PFENNIG

Copper **Ruler:** Friedrich Wilhelm III **Mint:** Berlin **Obverse:** Crowned monogram **Reverse:** Denomination and date **Rev. Legend:** *1*/PFENN/SCHEIDE/MUNZE/date/initial

Date	Mintage	F	VF	XF	Unc
1799A	—	4.00	8.00	60.00	100
1801A	—	4.00	8.00	60.00	100
1804A	—	3.00	6.00	50.00	90.00
1806A	—	8.00	15.00	120	225

KM# 373 PFENNIG

Billon **Ruler:** Friedrich Wilhelm III **Mint:** Berlin **Obverse:** Crowned FRW monogram **Reverse:** Value, date

Date	Mintage	F	VF	XF	Unc
1799A	—	4.00	8.00	45.00	80.00
1801A	—	6.00	15.00	55.00	110
1802A	—	4.00	8.00	45.00	95.00
1803A	—	4.00	8.00	45.00	95.00
1804A	—	4.00	8.00	45.00	95.00
1806A Rare	—	—	—	—	—

KM# 31 2 PFENNIG

Billon **Ruler:** Friedrich I **Mint:** Berlin **Obverse:** Crowned FR monogram, initials below **Reverse:** Value in date **Rev. Legend:** II/PF.BR./LANDT/MVNZ

Date	Mintage	VG	F	VF	XF	Unc
1703 CS	1,590,000	12.00	30.00	60.00	100	—

KM# 32 2 PFENNIG

Billon **Ruler:** Friedrich I **Mint:** Magdeburg **Obverse:** Crowned FR monogram divides dates, initials below **Reverse:** Value **Rev. Legend:** II/PF.BR/LANDT/MUNZ

Date	Mintage	VG	F	VF	XF	Unc
1703 HFH	Inc. above	12.00	30.00	60.00	100	—

KM# 53 2 PFENNIG

Billon **Ruler:** Friedrich I **Mint:** Minden **Obverse:** Crowned FR monogram **Reverse:** Value with date/initials **Rev. Legend:** II/G.PFEN

Date	Mintage	VG	F	VF	XF	Unc
1705 BH	328,000	18.00	40.00	80.00	125	—
1706 BH	Inc. above	18.00	40.00	80.00	125	—

KM# 33 3 PFENNIG

Billon **Ruler:** Friedrich I **Mint:** Berlin **Obverse:** Crowned eagle with crowned FR on breast, initials below **Reverse:** Value in date **Rev. Legend:** 3/PR.BR./LANDT (or LANDES)/MUNTZ **Note:** Varieties exist

Date	Mintage	VG	F	VF	XF	Unc
1703 CS	2,924,000	6.00	10.00	20.00	40.00	—
1705 CS	816,000	6.00	10.00	20.00	40.00	—

KM# 34 3 PFENNIG

Billon **Ruler:** Friedrich I **Mint:** Magdeburg **Note:** Varieties exist

Date	Mintage	VG	F	VF	XF	Unc
1703 HFH	Inc. above	6.00	10.00	20.00	40.00	—
1706 HFH	272,000	6.00	10.00	20.00	40.00	—

KM# 218 3 PFENNIG

Billon **Ruler:** Friedrich Wilhelm I **Mint:** Berlin **Obverse:** Crowned FWR monogram, initials below **Reverse:** Value in date **Rev. Legend:** 3/GUTE/PFEN **Note:** Gute 3 Pfenning

Date	Mintage	VG	F	VF	XF	Unc
1735 EGN	1,920,000	12.00	30.00	60.00	100	—

KM# 236 3 PFENNIG

Billon **Ruler:** Friedrich II **Obverse:** Crowned script FR monogram, date **Reverse:** Value **Rev. Legend:** 3 GUTE PFEN

Date	Mintage	VG	F	VF	XF	Unc
1742 EGN	960,000	7.50	15.00	35.00	70.00	—

KM# 267 3 PFENNIG

Copper, 26.8 mm. **Ruler:** Friedrich II **Obverse:** Crowned monogram **Reverse:** Value, date **Rev. Legend:** *3*/PFEN:/ SCHEIDE/MUNZ./date/initial

Date	Mintage	VG	F	VF	XF	Unc
1752A	5,760,000	7.50	15.00	25.00	45.00	—
1753A	Inc. above	7.50	15.00	25.00	45.00	—
1754F	Inc. above	15.00	25.00	50.00	85.00	—
1755A	Inc. above	7.50	15.00	25.00	45.00	—
1760A	Inc. above	7.50	15.00	25.00	45.00	—

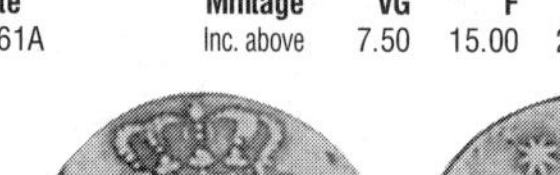

Date	Mintage	VG	F	VF	XF	Unc
1761A	Inc. above	7.50	15.00	25.00	45.00	—

KM# 290 3 PFENNIG

Copper **Ruler:** Friedrich II **Mint:** Berlin **Obverse:** Crowned monogram **Reverse:** Value, date **Rev. Legend:** *3*/PFEN./ SCHEIDE/ MUNZ/date/*initial*

Date	Mintage	VG	F	VF	XF	Unc
1762A	Inc. above	7.50	15.00	25.00	45.00	—

KM# 293 3 PFENNIG

Billon **Ruler:** Friedrich II **Obverse:** Crowned FR monogram divides date **Reverse:** Value above mint mark

Date	Mintage	VG	F	VF	XF	Unc
1764A	443,000	2.50	5.00	10.00	20.00	—
1764F	—	2.50	5.00	10.00	35.00	—
1765A	481,000	2.50	5.00	10.00	20.00	—
1765F	—	2.50	5.00	10.00	35.00	—
1767A	370,000	2.50	5.00	10.00	20.00	—
1769A	367,000	2.50	5.00	10.00	20.00	—
1770A	577,000	2.50	5.00	10.00	20.00	—

KM# 325 3 PFENNIG

Copper **Ruler:** Friedrich II **Reverse:** Value

Date	Mintage	VG	F	VF	XF	Unc
1770	—	2.50	5.00	10.00	15.00	—

KM# 328 3 PFENNIG

Billon **Ruler:** Friedrich II **Mint:** Berlin **Obverse:** Crowned FR monogram above mint mark **Reverse:** Value above date

Date	Mintage	VG	F	VF	XF	Unc
1772A	—	1.50	3.00	6.00	15.00	—
1774A	—	1.50	3.00	6.00	15.00	—
1775A	—	1.50	3.00	6.00	15.00	—
1776A	—	1.50	3.00	6.00	15.00	—
1777A	—	1.50	3.00	6.00	15.00	—
1778A	—	1.50	3.00	6.00	15.00	—
1779A	—	1.50	3.00	6.00	15.00	—
1780A	—	1.50	3.00	6.00	15.00	—
1781A	—	1.50	3.00	6.00	15.00	—
1782A	—	1.50	3.00	6.00	15.00	—
1783A	—	1.50	3.00	6.00	15.00	—
1784A	—	1.50	3.00	6.00	15.00	—
1786A	—	1.50	3.00	6.00	15.00	—

KM# 351 3 PFENNIG

0.7000 g., 0.2500 Silver 0.0056 oz. ASW **Ruler:** Friedrich Wilhelm II **Mint:** Berlin **Obverse:** Crowned monogram **Reverse:** Value, date

Date	Mintage	VG	F	VF	XF	Unc
1787A	—	1.50	3.00	6.00	15.00	—
1788A	—	1.50	3.00	6.00	15.00	—
1789A	—	1.50	3.00	6.00	15.00	—
1790A	—	1.50	3.00	6.00	15.00	—
1791A	—	1.50	3.00	6.00	15.00	—
1792A	—	1.50	3.00	6.00	15.00	—
1793A	—	1.50	3.00	6.00	15.00	—
1794A	—	1.50	3.00	6.00	15.00	—
1795A	—	1.50	3.00	6.00	15.00	—
1797A	—	1.50	3.00	6.00	15.00	—

KM# 374 3 PFENNIG

0.7000 g., 0.2500 Silver 0.0056 oz. ASW **Ruler:** Friedrich Wilhelm III **Mint:** Berlin **Obverse:** Crowned monogram **Reverse:** Denomination and date

Date	Mintage	F	VF	XF	Unc
1799A	—	8.00	15.00	40.00	125
1801A	—	8.00	15.00	40.00	125
1802A	—	8.00	15.00	30.00	100
1803A	—	8.00	15.00	45.00	150
1804A	—	6.00	12.00	30.00	100

KM# 35 4 PFENNIG

Billon **Ruler:** Friedrich I **Mint:** Berlin **Obverse:** Crowned FR monogram, initials below **Reverse:** Value in date **Rev. Legend:** IIII/PFEN.BRA/DENB.LAND/MVNTZ

Date	Mintage	VG	F	VF	XF	Unc
1703 CS	2,419,000	7.00	15.00	30.00	50.00	—

KM# 37 4 PFENNIG

Billon **Ruler:** Friedrich I **Obverse:** Date divided by monogram

Date	Mintage	VG	F	VF	XF	Unc
1703 HFH	Inc. above	7.00	15.00	30.00	50.00	—

KM# 36 4 PFENNIG

Billon **Ruler:** Friedrich I **Mint:** Magdeburg **Note:** Varieties exist

Date	Mintage	VG	F	VF	XF	Unc
1703 HFH	Inc. above	7.00	15.00	30.00	50.00	—
1705 HFH	605,000	7.00	15.00	30.00	50.00	—
1706 HFH	202,000	7.00	15.00	30.00	50.00	—

KM# 54 4 PFENNIG

Billon **Ruler:** Friedrich I **Mint:** Minden **Obverse:** Crowned FR monogram **Reverse:** Value with date/initials **Rev. Legend:** IIII/PF.BR

Date	Mintage	VG	F	VF	XF	Unc
1705 BH	294,000	12.00	30.00	60.00	100	—
1706 BH	Inc. above	12.00	30.00	60.00	100	—

KM# 323 4 PFENNIG

Billon **Ruler:** Friedrich II **Mint:** Berlin **Obverse:** Crowned FR monogram divides date **Reverse:** Value 4 **Note:** Gute 4 Pfennig.

Date	Mintage	VG	F	VF	XF	Unc
1764A	1,092,000	7.50	15.00	30.00	65.00	—
1766A	269,000	10.00	20.00	40.00	80.00	—

KM# 324 4 PFENNIG

Billon **Ruler:** Friedrich II **Mint:** Berlin **Obverse:** Crowned FR monogram in cartouche **Reverse:** Value IIII in date

Date	Mintage	VG	F	VF	XF	Unc
1774A	—	20.00	40.00	65.00	120	—

KM# A268 4 PFENNIG (Gute)

Billon, 16mm mm. **Ruler:** Friedrich II **Mint:** Magdeburg **Obverse:** Crowned script FR monogram **Reverse:** 5-line inscription of value, date, mintmark **Rev. Inscription:** IIII/GUTE/PFEN./(date)/(mintmark) **Note:** O#277

Date	Mintage	VG	F	VF	XF	Unc
1752F	—	—	—	—	—	—
1753F	—	—	—	—	—	—

KM# 294 4 PFENNIG (Gute)

Billon, 16mm mm. **Ruler:** Friedrich II **Mint:** Magdeburg **Obverse:** Crowned script FR monogram in cartouche **Reverse:** 5-line inscription with value, date, mintmark **Rev. Inscription:** IIII/GUTE/PFEN./(date)/(mintmark) **Note:** O#278

Date	Mintage	VG	F	VF	XF	Unc
1764F	180,019	—	—	—	—	—

KM# 38 6 PFENNIG

Billon **Ruler:** Friedrich I **Mint:** Berlin **Obverse:** Crowned eagle with crowned FR on breast, initials below **Reverse:** Value in date **Rev. Legend:** 6/PF.BRAN/DENB.LAND/MUNTZ **Note:** Varieties exist

Date	Mintage	VG	F	VF	XF	Unc
1703 CS	656,000	8.00	20.00	40.00	70.00	—
1704 CS	—	8.00	20.00	40.00	70.00	—
1705 CS	—	8.00	20.00	40.00	70.00	—
1706 CS	262,000	8.00	20.00	40.00	70.00	—
1707 CS	2,099,000	8.00	20.00	40.00	70.00	—
1708 CS	Inc. above	8.00	20.00	40.00	70.00	—
1709 CS	Inc. above	8.00	20.00	40.00	70.00	—
1710 CS	Inc. above	8.00	20.00	40.00	70.00	—

KM# 39 6 PFENNIG

Billon **Ruler:** Friedrich I **Mint:** Magdeburg **Obverse:** Initials divided by eagle **Reverse:** Value, date **Note:** Varieties exist

Date	Mintage	VG	F	VF	XF	Unc
1703 HFH	Inc. above	8.00	20.00	40.00	70.00	—
1705 HFH	Inc. above	8.00	20.00	40.00	70.00	—
1707 HFH	Inc. above	8.00	20.00	40.00	70.00	—
1708 HFH	Inc. above	8.00	20.00	40.00	70.00	—
1709 HFH	Inc. above	8.00	20.00	40.00	70.00	—
1710 HFH	Inc. above	8.00	20.00	40.00	70.00	—
1711 HFH	Inc. above	8.00	20.00	40.00	70.00	—

KM# 55 6 PFENNIG

Billon **Ruler:** Friedrich I **Mint:** Minden **Obverse:** Crowned FR monogram in palm branches **Reverse:** Value in date with initials **Rev. Legend:** VI/GUTE/PFENING **Note:** Mintage included in KM#58

Date	Mintage	VG	F	VF	XF	Unc
1705 BH	—	10.00	25.00	50.00	85.00	—
1706 BH	—	10.00	25.00	50.00	85.00	—

KM# 6 SCHILLING

Billon **Ruler:** Friedrich I **Obverse:** Initials below monogram **Note:** Varieties exist.

Date	Mintage	VG	F	VF	XF	Unc
1701 CG	—	5.00	8.00	20.00	45.00	—
1702 CG	—	5.00	8.00	20.00	45.00	—
1703 CG	—	5.00	8.00	20.00	45.00	—
1705 CG	—	5.00	8.00	20.00	45.00	—
1706 CG	—	5.00	8.00	20.00	45.00	—
1707 CG	—	5.00	8.00	20.00	45.00	—
1708 CG	—	5.00	8.00	20.00	45.00	—
1709 CG	—	5.00	8.00	20.00	45.00	—
1710 CG	—	5.00	8.00	20.00	45.00	—

KM# 5 SCHILLING

Billon **Ruler:** Friedrich I **Mint:** Konigsberg **Obverse:** Crowned FR monogram **Reverse:** Date, initials **Rev. Legend:** SOLID/REGNI/PRUSS

Date	Mintage	VG	F	VF	XF	Unc
1701 CG	—	8.00	15.00	25.00	50.00	—

KM# 120 SCHILLING

Billon **Ruler:** Friedrich Wilhelm I **Obverse:** Crwned FWR monogram, initials below **Reverse:** Date **Rev. Legend:** SOLID/REGNI/PRUS **Note:** Varieties exist.

Date	Mintage	VG	F	VF	XF	Unc
1714 CG	1,344,000	8.00	15.00	25.00	45.00	—
1715 CG	Inc. above	8.00	15.00	25.00	45.00	—
1717 CG	2,689,000	8.00	15.00	25.00	45.00	—
1718 CG	Inc. above	8.00	15.00	25.00	45.00	—
1719 CG	Inc. above	8.00	15.00	25.00	45.00	—
1720 CG	—	8.00	15.00	25.00	45.00	—
1721 CG	5,378,000	8.00	15.00	25.00	45.00	—
1722 CG	Inc. above	8.00	15.00	25.00	45.00	—
1723 CG	Inc. above	8.00	15.00	25.00	45.00	—
1724 CG	1,794,000	8.00	15.00	25.00	45.00	—
1725 CG	420,000	8.00	15.00	25.00	45.00	—
1726	1,370,000	8.00	15.00	25.00	45.00	—

KM# 164 SCHILLING

Billon **Ruler:** Friedrich Wilhelm I **Obverse:** Initials divided by scepter **Note:** Varieties exist.

Date	Mintage	VG	F	VF	XF	Unc
1718 CG	Inc. above	8.00	15.00	25.00	45.00	—
1720 CG	Inc. above	8.00	15.00	25.00	45.00	—
1721 CG	Inc. above	8.00	15.00	25.00	45.00	—

KM# 212 SCHILLING

Billon **Ruler:** Friedrich Wilhelm I **Obverse:** Initials below monogram **Note:** Varieties exist.

Date	Mintage	VG	F	VF	XF	Unc
1733 CS	10,788,000	8.00	15.00	25.00	45.00	—
1734 CS	Inc. above	8.00	15.00	25.00	45.00	—
1735 CS	Inc. above	8.00	15.00	25.00	45.00	—
1736 CS	8,369,999	8.00	15.00	25.00	45.00	—
1737 CS	Inc. above	8.00	15.00	25.00	45.00	—
1738 CS	Inc. above	8.00	15.00	25.00	45.00	—
1739 CS	Inc. above	8.00	15.00	25.00	45.00	—
1740 CS	Inc. above	8.00	15.00	25.00	45.00	—

KM# 223 SCHILLING

Silver, 15mm mm. **Ruler:** Friedrich II **Mint:** Konigsberg **Obverse:** Crowned cursive FR monogram **Reverse:** 4-line inscription with date **Rev. Inscription:** SOLID/REGNI/PRUSS/(date) **Note:** D#1814-45

Date	Mintage	VG	F	VF	XF	Unc
1741 CS	—	8.00	20.00	40.00	65.00	—
1742 CS	—	8.00	20.00	40.00	65.00	—
1743 CS	—	8.00	20.00	40.00	65.00	—
1752E	—	12.00	25.00	50.00	85.00	—
1753E	—	12.00	25.00	50.00	85.00	—
1754E	—	12.00	25.00	50.00	85.00	—
1755E	—	12.00	25.00	50.00	85.00	—
1756E	—	12.00	25.00	50.00	85.00	—

KM# 286 SCHILLING

0.7500 g., Silver, 14mm mm. **Ruler:** Elisabeth I of Russia **Obverse:** Crowned script EP monogram in laurel wreath **Reverse:** 4-line inscription with date **Rev. Inscription:** SOLID/REGNI/PRUSS/(date) **Note:** D#2141-44

Date	Mintage	VG	F	VF	XF	Unc
1759	734,014	20.00	40.00	100	185	—
1760	—	20.00	40.00	100	185	—
1761	390,045	20.00	40.00	100	185	—

KM# A295.1 SCHILLING

Silver **Ruler:** Friedrich II **Mint:** Konigsberg **Obverse:** Crowned FR monogram **Reverse:** 4-line inscription with date **Rev. Inscription:** SOLID/REGNI/PRUSS/(date) **Note:** D#2260-1, 2266-7, 2270-77

Date	Mintage	VG	F	VF	XF	Unc
1764E	1,595,250	7.00	15.00	28.00	45.00	—
1771E	1,445,220	7.00	15.00	28.00	45.00	—
1775E	1,972,710	7.00	15.00	28.00	45.00	—
1777E	347,265	7.00	15.00	28.00	45.00	—
1779E	757,980	7.00	15.00	28.00	45.00	—
1780E	259,460	7.00	15.00	28.00	45.00	—
1781E	639,967	7.00	15.00	28.00	45.00	—
1782E	419,266	7.00	15.00	28.00	45.00	—
1783E	467,820	7.00	15.00	28.00	45.00	—
1785E	1,121,040	7.00	15.00	28.00	45.00	—
1786E	830,250	7.00	15.00	28.00	45.00	—

KM# A316 SCHILLING

Silver **Ruler:** Friedrich II **Mint:** Konigsberg **Obverse:** Crowned FR monogram divides date **Reverse:** 4-line inscription with mintmark **Rev. Inscription:** SOLID/REGNI/PRUSS/(mintmark) **Note:** D#2262-5

Date	Mintage	VG	F	VF	XF	Unc
1766E	947,734	8.00	15.00	40.00	70.00	—
1767E	959,400	8.00	15.00	40.00	70.00	—
1768E	825,018	8.00	15.00	40.00	70.00	—
1769E	735,715	8.00	15.00	40.00	70.00	—

KM# A295.2 SCHILLING

Silver **Ruler:** Friedrich II **Mint:** Berlin **Obverse:** Crowned FR monogram **Reverse:** 4-line inscription with date **Rev. Inscription:** SOLID/REGNI/PRUSS/(date) **Note:** D#2268-9

Date	Mintage	VG	F	VF	XF	Unc
1776A	—	12.00	25.00	60.00	110	—

KM# 354 SCHILLING

0.7200 g., Billon, 14 mm. **Ruler:** Friedrich Wilhelm II **Mint:** Konigsberg **Obverse:** Crowned script FWR monogram **Reverse:** 4-line inscription with date and mintmark **Rev. Inscription:** 1/SCHILLING/(date)/(mintmark) **Note:** D#2406

Date	Mintage	VG	F	VF	XF	Unc
1788E	—	8.00	15.00	35.00	65.00	—

KM# 357 SCHILLING

2.6000 g., Copper, 20 mm. **Ruler:** Friedrich Wilhelm II **Mint:** Konigsberg **Obverse:** Crowned script FW monogram **Reverse:** 6-line inscription with date and mintmark **Rev. Inscription:** I/SCHILLING/PR:SCHEIDE/MÜNZE/(date)/(mintmark) **Note:** D#2407-22

Date	Mintage	VG	F	VF	XF	Unc
1790E	—	5.00	8.00	20.00	45.00	—
1791E	—	5.00	8.00	20.00	45.00	—
1792E	—	5.00	8.00	20.00	45.00	—
1793E	—	5.00	8.00	20.00	45.00	—
1794E	—	5.00	8.00	20.00	45.00	—
1795E	—	5.00	8.00	20.00	45.00	—
1796E	—	5.00	8.00	20.00	45.00	—
1797E	—	5.00	8.00	20.00	45.00	—

KM# 362.2 SCHILLING

1.3000 g., Copper, 15 mm. **Ruler:** Friedrich Wilhelm II **Mint:** Konigsberg **Obverse:** FW monogram in crowned oval shield **Reverse:** 4-line inscription with date **Rev. Inscription:** I/SOLID/ BOR:MER:/(date) **Note:** Coinage for South Prussia (Südpreussen). N#29

Date	Mintage	VG	F	VF	XF	Unc
1796E	—	7.00	15.00	30.00	45.00	—
1797E	—	7.00	15.00	30.00	45.00	—

KM# 362.1 SCHILLING

1.3000 g., Copper, 15 mm. **Ruler:** Friedrich Wilhelm II **Mint:** Breslau **Obverse:** FW monogram in crowned oval shield **Reverse:** 4-line inscription with date **Rev. Legend:** 1/SOLID/BOR:MER:/(date) **Note:** Coinage for South Prussia (Südpreussen). N#29

Date	Mintage	VG	F	VF	XF	Unc
1796B	—	5.00	10.00	20.00	35.00	—
1797B	—	5.00	10.00	20.00	35.00	—

KM# B362 1/2 GROSCHEN

1.9500 g., Copper, 18 mm. **Ruler:** Friedrich Wilhelm II **Obverse:** FWR monogram in crowned oval shield between 2 branches **Reverse:** 5-line inscription with date **Rev. Inscription:** 1/2/GROSSUS(S)/REGNI/BORUSS/(date) **Note:** Coinage for South Prussia (Südpreussen). N#27.

Date	Mintage	VG	F	VF	XF	Unc
1796	—	7.00	15.00	30.00	45.00	—

KM# C362.1 1/2 GROSCHEN

1.9500 g., Copper, 18 mm. **Ruler:** Friedrich Wilhelm II **Mint:** Breslau **Obverse:** FWR monogram in crowned oval shield between 2 branches **Reverse:** 5-line inscription with date **Rev. Inscription:** 1/2/GROSSUS/BORUS(S)./MERID/(date) **Note:** Coinage for South Prussia (Südpreussen). N#28.

Date	Mintage	VG	F	VF	XF	Unc
1796B	—	10.00	20.00	40.00	75.00	—
1797B	—	10.00	20.00	40.00	75.00	—

KM# C362.2 1/2 GROSCHEN

1.9500 g., Copper, 18 mm. **Ruler:** Friedrich Wilhelm II **Mint:** Konigsberg **Obverse:** FWR monogram in crowned oval shield between 2 branches **Reverse:** 5-line inscription with date **Rev. Inscription:** 1/2/GROSSUS/BORUS(S)./MERID./(date) **Note:** Coinage for South Prussia (Südpreussen). N#28.

Date	Mintage	VG	F	VF	XF	Unc
1796E	—	12.00	32.00	60.00	95.00	—
1797E	—	12.00	32.00	60.00	95.00	—

KM# B268 GRöSCHER

0.7700 g., Silver, 15 mm. **Ruler:** Friedrich II **Mint:** Konigsberg **Obverse:** Crowned Prussian eagle **Reverse:** 5-line inscription with date **Rev. Legend:** FRIDERIC. - BOR: REX **Rev. Inscription:** I/GROSSUS/REGNI/PRUSS./(date) **Note:** D#1846-7.

Date	Mintage	VG	F	VF	XF	Unc
1752E	—	18.00	40.00	80.00	135	—

KM# 287 GRöSCHER

0.8800 g., Silver, 16 mm. **Ruler:** Elisabeth I of Russia **Obverse:** Crown above Russian crowned imperial eagle **Obv. Legend:** MONETA. ARGENTEA **Reverse:** 5-line inscription with date **Rev. Inscription:** I/GROSSUS/REGNI/PRUSS/(date) **Note:** Varieties exist. D#2145-51.

Date	Mintage	VG	F	VF	XF	Unc
1759	112,650	60.00	100	200	325	—
1760	—	60.00	100	200	325	—
1761	111,804	60.00	100	200	325	—

KM# B295 GRöSCHER
0.8310 g., Silver, 16 mm. **Ruler:** Friedrich II **Mint:** Konigsberg **Obverse:** Crowned Prussian eagle **Obv. Legend:** FRIDERIC. - BOR: REX. **Reverse:** 5-line inscription with date
Rev. Inscription: I/GROSSUS/REGNI/PRUSS./(date)
Note: Varieties exist. D2278-85.

Date	Mintage	VG	F	VF	XF	Unc
1764E	1,291,305	7.00	15.00	40.00	70.00	—
1769E	876,008	7.00	15.00	40.00	70.00	—
1770E	Inc. above	7.00	15.00	40.00	70.00	—

KM# A327.2 GRöSCHER
0.8660 g., Silver, 16 mm. **Ruler:** Friedrich II **Mint:** Konigsberg **Obverse:** Crowned eagle flying left, looking right **Obv. Legend:** FRIDERIC: BORUSS: REX. **Reverse:** 5-line inscription with date **Rev. Inscription:** I/GROSSUS/REGNI/PRUSS./(date)
Note: Varieties exist. D#2286-7, 2289-96.

Date	Mintage	VG	F	VF	XF	Unc
1771E	1,619,535	5.00	12.00	30.00	55.00	—
1772E	151,489	5.00	12.00	30.00	55.00	—
1778E	316,530	5.00	12.00	30.00	55.00	—
1779E	207,810	5.00	12.00	30.00	55.00	—
1780E	Inc. above	5.00	12.00	30.00	55.00	—
1781E	78,322	5.00	12.00	30.00	55.00	—
1782E	169,365	5.00	12.00	30.00	55.00	—
1783E	525,825	5.00	12.00	30.00	55.00	—
1785E	387,450	5.00	12.00	30.00	55.00	—
1786E	Inc. above	5.00	12.00	30.00	55.00	—

KM# A327.1 GRöSCHER
0.8660 g., Silver, 16 mm. **Ruler:** Friedrich II **Mint:** Berlin **Obverse:** Crowned eagle flying left, looking right **Obv. Legend:** FRIDERIC: BORUSS: REX. **Reverse:** 5-line inscription with date **Rev. Inscription:** I/GROSSUS/REGNI/PRUSS./(date) **Note:** D#2281.

Date	Mintage	VG	F	VF	XF	Unc
1776A	—	15.00	35.00	80.00	145	—

KM# 348 GRöSCHER
0.8500 g., Silver, 17 mm. **Ruler:** Friedrich Wilhelm II **Mint:** Konigsberg **Obverse:** Armored bust to right **Obv. Legend:** FRIED. WILH. KOEN. V. PREUSS. **Reverse:** Crowned shield of Prussian eagle arms divides 1 - GR/(date) **Note:** Varieties exist. D#2423-43.

Date	Mintage	VG	F	VF	XF	Unc
1787E	—	16.00	30.00	60.00	115	—
1788E	—	16.00	30.00	60.00	115	—
1789E	121,770	16.00	30.00	60.00	115	—
Note: Ref. N#21.						
1790E	373,591	16.00	30.00	60.00	115	—
1791E	569,160	16.00	30.00	60.00	115	—
1792E	179,838	16.00	30.00	60.00	115	—
1793E	374,955	16.00	30.00	60.00	115	—
1794E	199,260	16.00	30.00	60.00	115	—
1795E	84,351	16.00	30.00	60.00	115	—
1796E	332,100	16.00	30.00	60.00	115	—
1797E	567,288	16.00	30.00	60.00	115	—
1798E	41,496	20.00	40.00	75.00	130	—
Note: Posthumous issue.						

KM# D362.1 GRöSCHER
3.9000 g., Copper, 21 mm. **Ruler:** Friedrich Wilhelm II **Mint:** Breslau **Obverse:** Bust to right **Obv. Legend:** FRIDERICUS WILHELM BORUSS REX. **Reverse:** Crowned Prussian eagle in crowned oval shield between 2 branches, date at end of legend **Rev. Legend:** GROSSUS. BORUSS. MERIDIONAL(IS) (date) **Note:** Coinage for South Prussia (Südpreussen). N#26.

Date	Mintage	VG	F	VF	XF	Unc
1796B	—	8.00	15.00	30.00	50.00	—
1797B	—	8.00	15.00	30.00	50.00	—

KM# D362.2 GRöSCHER
3.9000 g., Copper, 21 mm. **Ruler:** Friedrich Wilhelm II **Mint:** Konigsberg **Obverse:** Bust to right **Obv. Legend:** FRIDERICUS WILHELM BORUSS REX. **Reverse:** Crowned Prussian eagle in crowned oval shield between 2 branches **Rev. Legend:** GROSSUS. BORUSS. MERIDIONAL(IS) (date) **Note:** Coinage for South Prussia (Südpreussen). N#26.

Date	Mintage	VG	F	VF	XF	Unc
1796E	—	30.00	65.00	120	185	—
1797E	—	30.00	65.00	120	185	—
1798E	—	30.00	65.00	120	185	—
Note: Posthumous issue.						

KM# 56 MARIENGROSCHEN
Billon **Ruler:** Friedrich I **Mint:** Minden **Obverse:** Crowned FR monogram **Reverse:** Value in date with initials
Rev. Legend: I/MARIEN/GROSCH

Date	Mintage	VG	F	VF	XF	Unc
1705 BH	209,000	30.00	60.00	125	200	—

KM# 65 MARIENGROSCHEN
Billon **Ruler:** Friedrich I **Obverse:** Monogram divides 1 - M

Date	Mintage	VG	F	VF	XF	Unc
1706 BH	Inc. above	30.00	60.00	125	200	—

KM# E268 MARIENGROSCHEN
Silver, 17 mm. **Ruler:** Friedrich II **Mint:** Magdeburg **Obverse:** Crowned Prussian eagle in baroque frame, large crown above **Reverse:** 5-line inscription with date and mintmark
Rev. Legend: 1/MARIEN/GROS/(date)/(mintmark) **Note:** O#275

Date	Mintage	VG	F	VF	XF	Unc
1752F	—	—	—	—	—	—

KM# C295 MARIENGROSCHEN
Silver, 19 mm. **Ruler:** Friedrich II **Mint:** Magdeburg **Obverse:** Crowned Prussian eagle in baroque frame, large crown above **Reverse:** 5-line inscription with date and mintmark **Rev. Legend:** I/MARIEN/GROSCHEN/(date)/(mintmark). **Note:** O#276

Date	Mintage	VG	F	VF	XF	Unc
1764F	426,223	—	—	—	—	—

KM# 66 2 MARIENGROSCHEN
Billon **Ruler:** Friedrich I **Mint:** Minden **Obverse:** Crowned FR monogram divides 2 - M **Reverse:** Value in date with initials
Rev. Legend: II/MARIEN/GROSCH

Date	Mintage	VG	F	VF	XF	Unc
1706 BH	140,000	45.00	80.00	150	250	—

KM# F268 2 MARIENGROSCHEN
Silver, 20 mm. **Ruler:** Friedrich II **Mint:** Magdeburg **Obverse:** Crowned Prussian eagle in baroque frame, large crown above **Reverse:** 5-line inscription with date and mintmark
Rev. Legend: II/MRIEN/GROS/(date)/(mintmark). **Note:** O#273.

Date	Mintage	VG	F	VF	XF	Unc
1752F	—	—	—	—	—	—

KM# D295 2 MARIENGROSCHEN
Silver, 22 mm. **Ruler:** Friedrich II **Mint:** Magdeburg **Obverse:** Crowned Prussian eagle in baroque frame, large crown above **Reverse:** 5-line inscription with date and mintmark **Rev. Legend:** II/MARIEN/GROSCHEN/(date)/(mintmark) **Note:** O#274.

Date	Mintage	VG	F	VF	XF	Unc
1764F	230,638	—	—	—	—	—

KM# 57 4 MARIENGROSCHEN
Billon **Ruler:** Friedrich I **Mint:** Minden **Obverse:** Crowned FR monogram **Reverse:** Value in date with initials
Rev. Legend: IIII/MARIEN/GROSCH **Note:** Varieties exist

Date	Mintage	VG	F	VF	XF	Unc
1705 BH	—	75.00	160	275	375	—
1706 BH	—	75.00	160	275	375	—

KM# G268 4 MARIENGROSCHEN
Silver, 23-24 mm. **Ruler:** Friedrich II **Mint:** Magdeburg **Obverse:** Crowned Prussian eagle in baroque frame, large crown above **Reverse:** 5-line inscription with date and mintmark **Rev. Legend:** IIII/MARIEN/GROS/(date)/(mintmark). **Note:** O#272.

Date	Mintage	VG	F	VF	XF	Unc
1752F	—	—	—	—	—	—

KM# 362 4 GROSCHEN
5.3450 g., 0.5210 Silver 0.0895 oz. ASW **Ruler:** Friedrich Wilhelm II **Obverse:** Head right **Obv. Legend:** FRIDERICUS WILHELM • BORUSS • REX **Reverse:** Crowned arms divide date, value below

Date	Mintage	VG	F	VF	XF	Unc
1796A	—	5.00	10.00	25.00	50.00	—
1796B	—	5.00	10.00	25.00	50.00	—
1796E	—	5.00	10.00	25.00	50.00	—
1797A	—	5.00	10.00	25.00	50.00	—
1797E	—	5.00	10.00	25.00	50.00	—
1798E	—	5.00	10.00	25.00	50.00	—

KM# 370 4 GROSCHEN
5.3450 g., 0.5210 Silver 0.0895 oz. ASW **Ruler:** Friedrich Wilhelm III **Obverse:** Uniformed bust left **Obv. Legend:** FRIDERICUS WILHELM III BO RUSS. REX **Reverse:** Crowned arms divide date

Date	Mintage	F	VF	XF	Unc
1797A	—	5.00	15.00	35.00	55.00
1798A	—	8.00	20.00	50.00	75.00
1799A	—	5.00	15.00	40.00	65.00
1800A	—	8.00	20.00	50.00	75.00
1801A	—	5.00	15.00	40.00	65.00
1802A	—	5.00	15.00	40.00	65.00
1802B	—	10.00	25.00	65.00	100
1803A	—	5.00	15.00	35.00	55.00
1803B	—	8.00	20.00	60.00	90.00
1804A	—	5.00	15.00	35.00	55.00
1804B	—	8.00	20.00	60.00	90.00
1805A	—	5.00	15.00	35.00	55.00
1805B	—	10.00	25.00	90.00	185
1806A	—	8.00	20.00	45.00	75.00
1807A	—	7.00	15.00	45.00	70.00
1808A	—	10.00	25.00	70.00	100
1808G	—	10.00	25.00	170	320
1809A	—	10.00	25.00	70.00	100
1809G	—	25.00	60.00	240	400

KM# 274.2 8 GROSCHEN (Gute)
Silver **Ruler:** Friedrich II **Obverse:** Head right **Obv. Legend:** FREDERICHS BORUSSORUM REX **Reverse:** Drum, crossed flags, cannon (war spoils)

Date	Mintage	VG	F	VF	XF	Unc
1753F	—	80.00	140	250	425	—

Date	Mintage	VG	F	VF	XF	Unc
1753G	—	100	160	360	725	—
1754D	—	80.00	140	250	425	—
1754E	16,000	375	550	1,000	1,750	—
1754F	—	80.00	140	250	425	—
1754G	—	100	160	360	725	—
1755F	—	80.00	140	250	425	—
1756F	—	80.00	140	250	425	—
1757F	—	80.00	140	250	425	—
1759F	—	80.00	140	250	425	—
1763F	1,896,000	80.00	140	250	425	—

KM# 274.1 8 GROSCHEN (Gute)
Silver **Ruler:** Friedrich II **Obverse:** Head right **Obv. Legend:** FRIDERICVS BORVSSORVM REX **Reverse:** Value, date above flags **Rev. Legend:** *6*/GUTE/GROSCHEN/*date*
Note: Varieties exist.

Date	Mintage	VG	F	VF	XF	Unc
1753A	—	50.00	90.00	160	275	—
1754A	—	50.00	90.00	160	275	—
1755A	19,000	50.00	90.00	160	275	—
1755C	—	—	—	—	—	—
1756A	752,000	50.00	90.00	160	275	—
1757A	487,000	50.00	90.00	160	275	—
1759A	—	50.00	90.00	160	275	—
1759B	—	65.00	110	200	375	—
1763A	6,507,000	50.00	90.00	160	275	—
1763B	928,000	65.00	110	200	375	—

KM# 40 2 GROSCHER
Billon **Ruler:** Friedrich I **Mint:** Konigsberg **Obverse:** Eagle, crown above divides legend FRID - REX with initials below **Reverse:** Value in date **Rev. Legend:** II/GROSS/DUPLEX/REGNI/PRUSS

Date	Mintage	VG	F	VF	XF	Unc
1703 CG	—	12.00	25.00	45.00	85.00	—

KM# C268.1 2 GROSCHER
Silver, 19-20 mm. **Ruler:** Friedrich II **Mint:** Konigsberg **Obverse:** Crowned Prussian eagle **Obv. Legend:** FRIDERIC(US). - BOR(US). REX. **Reverse:** 5-line inscription with date **Rev. Inscription:** II/GROSSUS/REGNI/PRUSS./(date)
Note: D#1848-52, 1854-62.

Date	Mintage	VG	F	VF	XF	Unc
1752E	—	7.00	15.00	30.00	55.00	—
1753E	—	7.00	15.00	30.00	55.00	—

KM# C268.2 2 GROSCHER
Silver, 19-20 mm. **Ruler:** Friedrich II **Mint:** Konigsberg **Obverse:** Crowned Prussian eagle **Obv. Legend:** FRIDERIC(US). - BOR(US). REX. **Reverse:** 6-line inscription with date **Rev. Inscription:** II/GROSSUS/DUPLEX/REGNI/PRUSS./(date) **Note:** D#1853.

Date	Mintage	VG	F	VF	XF	Unc
1752E	—	12.00	30.00	55.00	115	—

KM# A279 2 GROSCHER
1.5400 g., Silver, 19-20 mm. **Ruler:** Friedrich II **Mint:** Konigsberg **Obverse:** Crowned Prussian eagle **Obv. Legend:** FRIDERIC(US). - BOR(US). REX. **Reverse:** 5-line inscription with date **Rev. Inscription:** II/GROSSUS/REGNI/PRUSS./(date) **Note:** D#1863-76.

Date	Mintage	VG	F	VF	XF	Unc
1755E	—	7.00	15.00	30.00	55.00	—
1756E	—	7.00	15.00	30.00	55.00	—
1757E	—	7.00	15.00	30.00	55.00	—

KM# 288 2 GROSCHER
1.4600 g., Silver, 18 mm. **Ruler:** Elisabeth I of Russia **Obverse:** Crown above Russian crowned imperial eagle **Obv. Legend:** MONETA. ARGENTEA. **Reverse:** 5-line inscription with date **Rev. Inscription:** II/GROSSUS/REGNI/PRUSS/(date)
Note: Varieties exist. D#2152-61.

Date	Mintage	VG	F	VF	XF	Unc
1759	126,657	75.00	130	240	400	—
1760	—	75.00	130	240	400	—
1761	93,634	75.00	130	240	400	—

KM# A296 2 GROSCHER
1.5400 g., Silver, 19 mm. **Ruler:** Friedrich II **Mint:** Konigsberg **Obverse:** Crowned Prussian eagle **Obv. Legend:** FRIDERIC. - BOR. REX. **Reverse:** 5-line inscription with date **Rev. Inscription:** II/GROSSUS/REGNI/PRUSS./(date) **Note:** D32297-99.

Date	Mintage	VG	F	VF	XF	Unc
1764E	960,060	7.00	15.00	40.00	70.00	—
1768E	216,045	7.00	15.00	40.00	70.00	—

KM# A329 2 GROSCHER
1.5400 g., Silver, 19 mm. **Ruler:** Friedrich II **Mint:** Konigsberg **Obverse:** Crowned flying eagle left, looking right **Obv. Legend:** FRIDERIC: BORUSS: REX. **Reverse:** 5-line inscription with date **Rev. Inscription:** II/GROSSUS/REGNI/PRUSS./(date)
Note: D#2300.

Date	Mintage	VG	F	VF	XF	Unc
1773E	4,815,975	5.00	12.00	35.00	65.00	—

KM# 41 3 GROSCHER (Düttchen)

Billon **Ruler:** Friedrich I **Mint:** Konigsberg **Obverse:** Laureate head right **Reverse:** Crowned monogram in cruciform, value at center, "R" at angles **Note:** Similar to 6 Groscher, KM#21, but with value 3 in center. Varieties exist.

Date	Mintage	VG	F	VF	XF	Unc
1703 CG	Est. 2,700,000	9.00	20.00	45.00	80.00	—
1704 CG	Inc. above	9.00	20.00	45.00	80.00	—
1705 CG	Inc. above	9.00	20.00	45.00	80.00	—
1706 CG	Inc. above	9.00	20.00	45.00	80.00	—
1709 CG	Inc. above	9.00	20.00	45.00	80.00	—
1710 CG	Inc. above	9.00	20.00	45.00	80.00	—
1711 CG	Inc. above	9.00	20.00	45.00	80.00	—
1713 CG	Inc. above	9.00	20.00	45.00	80.00	—

KM# 121 3 GROSCHER (Düttchen)

Billon **Ruler:** Friedrich Wilhelm I **Obverse:** Laureate bust right, initials below **Reverse:** 3 shields of arms below crowns, date divided below, value: 3 in oval at bottom **Note:** Varieties exist.

Date	Mintage	VG	F	VF	XF	Unc
1714 CG	555,000	22.00	50.00	80.00	150	—
1715 CG	Inc. above	22.00	50.00	80.00	150	—
1716 CG	Inc. above	22.00	50.00	80.00	150	—

KM# 165 3 GROSCHER (Düttchen)

Billon **Ruler:** Friedrich Wilhelm I **Note:** Similar to 5 Groscher but value: II at bottom of reverse. Varieties exist.

Date	Mintage	VG	F	VF	XF	Unc
1718 CG	650,000	22.00	50.00	80.00	150	—
1719 CG	Inc. above	22.00	50.00	80.00	150	—
1720 CG	Inc. above	22.00	50.00	80.00	150	—
1722 CG/M	145,000	22.00	50.00	80.00	150	—
1723 CG/M	Inc. above	22.00	50.00	80.00	150	—

KM# A263 3 GROSCHER (Düttchen)

1.5110 g., Silver, 21-22 mm. **Ruler:** Friedrich II **Mint:** Konigsberg **Obverse:** Armored bust to right **Obv. Legend:** FRIDERICVS BORVSSOR: REX. **Reverse:** Two adjacent shields with eagle in each, '3' between near top, crown above, date divided below **Rev. Legend:** MON: ARG: - REG: PRUS. **Note:** Varieties exist. Weight varies 1.511-1.596g. D#1877-94, 1897-1911, 1914-15, 1917-28.

Date	Mintage	VG	F	VF	XF	Unc
1751 W//E	—	8.00	20.00	40.00	65.00	—
1752 W//E	—	8.00	20.00	40.00	65.00	—
1752 S//E	—	8.00	20.00	40.00	65.00	—
1752 E	—	8.00	20.00	40.00	65.00	—
1753 ST//E	—	8.00	20.00	40.00	65.00	—
1753 E	—	8.00	20.00	40.00	65.00	—
1754 E	—	8.00	20.00	40.00	65.00	—

KM# 274 3 GROSCHER (Düttchen)

1.5110 g., Silver, 21-22 mm. **Ruler:** Friedrich II **Mint:** Konigsberg **Obverse:** Armored bust to right **Obv. Legend:** FRIDERICVS BORVSSOR: REX. **Reverse:** Two adjacent shields with eagle in each, '3' between near top, crown above **Rev. Legend:** MON: ARG: - REG: PRUS(S): (date) **Note:** Varieties exist. D#1895-6, 1912-13, 1916.

Date	Mintage	VG	F	VF	XF	Unc
1753 ST//E	—	8.00	20.00	40.00	65.00	—
1753 E	—	8.00	20.00	40.00	65.00	—

KM# 289.1 3 GROSCHER (Düttchen)

1.5600 g., Silver, 21 mm. **Ruler:** Elisabeth I of Russia **Obverse:** Crowned bust to right **Obv. Legend:** ELISAB: I: D:G: IMP: TOT: RUSS. **Reverse:** Crowned Prussian eagle, '3' in shield on breast, tail divides date below **Rev. Legend:** MONETA: REGNI: PRUSS. **Note:** Varieties exist. D#2162-7, 2169-71.

Date	Mintage	VG	F	VF	XF	Unc
1759	36,972	30.00	70.00	125	200	—
1760	—	18.00	40.00	100	165	—
1761	1,050,000	18.00	40.00	100	165	—

KM# 289.2 3 GROSCHER (Düttchen)

1.5600 g., Silver, 21 mm. **Ruler:** Elisabeth I of Russia **Obverse:** Crowned bust to right **Obv. Legend:** ELISAB: 1: IMP. TOT: RUSS. **Reverse:** Crowned Prussian eagle, '3' in shield on breast, tail divides date below **Rev. Legend:** MONETA: ARGENTEA: REG: PRVS. **Note:** D#2168.

Date	Mintage	VG	F	VF	XF	Unc
1759	Inc. above	18.00	40.00	100	165	—

KM# A290 3 GROSCHER (Düttchen)

Silver, 18 mm. **Ruler:** Elisabeth I of Russia **Obverse:** Smaller crowned bust to right **Obv. Legend:** ELISAB: I: D:G: IMP: TOT: RUSS. **Reverse:** Smaller crowned Prussian eagle, '3' in shield on breast, tail divides date below **Rev. Legend:** MONETA: ARGENTEA: REG: PRVS. **Note:** Varieties exist. D#2172-80.

Date	Mintage	VG	F	VF	XF	Unc
1761	Inc. above	18.00	40.00	100	165	—
1762	—	18.00	40.00	100	165	—

KM# 313.2 3 GROSCHER (Düttchen)

1.6410 g., Silver, 20 mm. **Ruler:** Friedrich II **Mint:** Konigsberg **Obverse:** Crowned head to right **Obv. Legend:** FRIDERICUS BORUSSORUM REX. **Reverse:** Crowned Prussian eagle, script FR monogram on breast, tail divides '3 - gr.' **Rev. Legend:** MONETA - (date) - ARGENTEA. **Note:** Varieties exist. D#2302-07.

Date	Mintage	VG	F	VF	XF	Unc
1765E	Inc. above	9.00	20.00	40.00	65.00	—
1766E	429,515	9.00	20.00	40.00	65.00	—
1767E	Inc. above	9.00	20.00	40.00	65.00	—

KM# 313.1 3 GROSCHER (Düttchen)

1.6410 g., Silver, 20 mm. **Ruler:** Friedrich II **Mint:** Konigsberg **Obverse:** Head to right **Obv. Legend:** FRIDERICUS BORUSS: REX. **Reverse:** Crowned Prussian eagle, script FR monogram on breast, '3' below **Rev. Legend:** MONETA - (date) - ARGENT. **Note:** D#2301.

Date	Mintage	VG	F	VF	XF	Unc
1765	2,071,405	9.00	20.00	40.00	65.00	—

KM# A328.2 3 GROSCHER (Düttchen)

1.6700 g., Silver, 20 mm. **Ruler:** Friedrich II **Mint:** Konigsberg **Obverse:** Laureate head to right **Obv. Legend:** FRIDERICUS BORUSSORUM REX. **Reverse:** Crowned eagle flying left, looking right, '3 - gr:'/date and mintmark below, legend in arc above eagle **Rev. Legend:** MONETA ARGENT **Note:** Varieties exist. D#2308-18, 2320-26.

Date	Mintage	VG	F	VF	XF	Unc
1771E	4,033,865	2.50	5.00	10.00	25.00	—
1772E	2,291,895	2.50	5.00	10.00	25.00	—
1773E	3,569,790	2.50	5.00	10.00	25.00	—
1774E	4,783,560	2.50	5.00	10.00	25.00	—
1775E	2,784,425	2.50	5.00	10.00	25.00	—
1776E	1,784,890	2.50	5.00	10.00	25.00	—
1777E	1,070,960	2.50	5.00	10.00	25.00	—
1778E	754,575	2.50	5.00	10.00	25.00	—
1779E	893,025	2.50	5.00	10.00	25.00	—
1780E	1,277,150	2.50	5.00	10.00	25.00	—
1781E	2,066,400	2.50	5.00	10.00	25.00	—
1782E	2,432,325	2.50	5.00	10.00	25.00	—
1783E	2,539,950	2.50	5.00	10.00	25.00	—
1784E	13,201,990	2.50	5.00	10.00	25.00	—
1785E	8,351,700	2.50	5.00	10.00	25.00	—
1786E	932,750	2.50	5.00	10.00	25.00	—

KM# A328.1 3 GROSCHER (Düttchen)

1.6700 g., Silver, 20 mm. **Ruler:** Friedrich II **Mint:** Berlin **Obverse:** Laureate head to right **Obv. Legend:** FRIDERICUS BORUSSORUM REX. **Reverse:** Crowned eagle flying left, looking right, '3 - gr:' date and mintmark below, legend in arc above eagle **Rev. Legend:** MONETA ARGENT **Note:** Varieties exist. D#2327-31.

Date	Mintage	VG	F	VF	XF	Unc
1774A	1,905,010	5.00	12.00	30.00	50.00	—
1775A	741,595	5.00	12.00	30.00	50.00	—
1776A	Inc. above	5.00	12.00	30.00	50.00	—

KM# 337 3 GROSCHER (Düttchen)

1.6700 g., Silver, 20 mm. **Ruler:** Friedrich II **Mint:** Berlin **Obverse:** Laureate head to right **Obv. Legend:** FRIDERICUS BORUSSORUM REX. **Reverse:** Crowned eagle flying left, looking right, '3/A' divides date below, legend in arc above **Rev. Legend:** MONETA ARGENT **Note:** Varieties exist. M#187b.

Date	Mintage	VG	F	VF	XF	Unc
1779A	25,964,596	2.50	5.00	10.00	25.00	—
1780A	27,207,560	2.50	5.00	10.00	25.00	—
1781A	44,023,765	2.50	5.00	10.00	25.00	—
1782A	38,758,010	2.50	5.00	10.00	25.00	—
1783A	43,743,700	2.50	5.00	10.00	25.00	—
1784A	23,005,400	2.50	5.00	10.00	25.00	—
1785A	5,906,220	2.50	5.00	10.00	25.00	—

KM# 338 3 GROSCHER (Düttchen)

1.6700 g., Silver, 20 mm. **Ruler:** Friedrich II **Mint:** Konigsberg **Obverse:** Laureate head to right **Obv. Legend:** FRIDERICUS BORUSSORUM REX. **Reverse:** Crowned eagle flying left, looking right, '3/E' divides date below, legend in arc above eagle **Rev. Legend:** MONETA ARGENT **Note:** D#2319.

Date	Mintage	VG	F	VF	XF	Unc
1781E	Inc. above	5.00	10.00	20.00	35.00	—

KM# E362.1 3 GROSCHER (Düttchen)

11.7000 g., Copper, 25 mm. **Ruler:** Friedrich Wilhelm II **Obverse:** Bust to right **Obv. Legend:** FRIDERICUS WILHELM BORUSS REX. **Reverse:** Crowned Prussian eagle in crowned oval shield between 2 branches, date at end of legend **Rev. Legend:** GROSSUS BORUSSIAE TRIPLEX (date) **Note:** Coinage for South Prussia (Südpreussen). N#24.

Date	Mintage	VG	F	VF	XF	Unc
1796A	—	8.00	20.00	35.00	55.00	—
1796B	—	10.00	22.00	45.00	70.00	—

KM# E362.2 3 GROSCHER (Düttchen)

11.7000 g., Copper, 25 mm. **Ruler:** Friedrich Wilhelm II **Obverse:** Bust to right **Obv. Legend:** FRIDERICUS WILHELM BORUSS REX. **Reverse:** Crowned Prussian eagle in crowned oval shield between 2 branches, date at end of legend **Rev. Legend:** GROSSUS BORUS(S). MERID. TRIPLEX (date) **Note:** N#25.

Date	Mintage	VG	F	VF	XF	Unc
1796B	—	25.00	50.00	100	185	—
1796E	—	45.00	100	200	325	—
1797A	—	10.00	20.00	40.00	75.00	—
1797B	—	25.00	50.00	100	185	—
1798E	—	45.00	100	200	325	—

KM# 376.1 3 GROSCHER (Düttchen)

1.7000 g., Silver, 18 mm. **Ruler:** Friedrich Wilhelm III **Mint:** Berlin **Obverse:** Bust to left **Obv. Legend:** FRID. WILHELM. III BORUSS. REX. **Reverse:** Crowned eagle flying right, looking left, 3/date/mintmark below, legend curved at top **Rev. Legend:** MON. ARGENT. **Note:** D#2477.

Date	Mintage	VG	F	VF	XF	Unc
1800A	—	3.00	6.00	12.00	25.00	—

KM# 376.2 3 GROSCHER (Düttchen)

1.7000 g., Silver, 18 mm. **Ruler:** Friedrich Wilhelm III **Mint:** Berlin **Obverse:** Bust to left **Obv. Legend:** FRID. WILHELM. III BORUSS. REX. **Reverse:** Crowned eagle flying right, looking left, III/date/mintmark below, legend curved at top **Rev. Legend:** MON. ARGENT. **Note:** Varieties exist. D#2478-85.

Date	Mintage	VG	F	VF	XF	Unc
1800A	—	3.00	6.00	12.00	25.00	—
1801A	—	3.00	6.00	12.00	25.00	—
1802A	—	3.00	6.00	12.00	25.00	—
1803A	—	3.00	6.00	12.00	25.00	—
1804A	—	3.00	6.00	12.00	25.00	—
1805A	—	3.00	6.00	12.00	25.00	—
1806A	—	3.00	6.00	12.00	25.00	—
1807A	—	3.00	6.00	12.00	25.00	—

KM# 21 6 GROSCHER (Szostake)

Billon **Ruler:** Friedrich I **Mint:** Konigsberg **Obverse:** Laureate head right **Obv. Legend:** FRIDERICUS REX **Reverse:** Crowned monograms in cruciform, value at center, "R" at angles **Note:** Varieties exist

Date	Mintage	VG	F	VF	XF	Unc
1702 CG	Est. 1,950,000	10.00	20.00	55.00	90.00	—
1704 CG	Inc. above	10.00	20.00	55.00	90.00	—
1709 CG	Inc. above	10.00	20.00	55.00	90.00	—

KM# 122 6 GROSCHER (Szostake)

Billon **Ruler:** Friedrich Wilhelm I **Obverse:** Laureate bust right **Reverse:** Crown above two shields, date and value below **Note:** Similar to KM#166 but laureate bust. Varieties exist.

Date	Mintage	VG	F	VF	XF	Unc
1714 CG/M	593,000	25.00	60.00	100	160	—
1715 CG/M	Inc. above	25.00	60.00	100	160	—
1716 CG/M	Inc. above	25.00	60.00	100	160	—
1717 CG/M	Inc. above	25.00	60.00	100	160	—
1718 CG/M	Inc. above	25.00	60.00	100	160	—

KM# 166 6 GROSCHER (Szostake)

Billon **Ruler:** Friedrich Wilhelm I **Obverse:** Armored bust right **Reverse:** Crown above two shields, date and value below **Note:** Varieties exist.

Date	Mintage	VG	F	VF	XF	Unc
1718 CG	—	25.00	60.00	100	160	—
1719 CG	—	25.00	60.00	100	160	—
1720 CG	—	25.00	60.00	100	160	—
1721 CG	286,000	25.00	60.00	100	160	—
1722 CG	Inc. above	25.00	60.00	100	160	—
1723 CG	Inc. above	25.00	60.00	100	160	—

KM# A277 6 GROSCHER (Szostake)

3.1180 g., Silver, 23 mm. **Ruler:** Friedrich II **Obverse:** Armored bust to right **Obv. Legend:** FRIDERICVS BORVSSORVM REX. **Reverse:** Two adjacent shields of arms, eagle in each, 'VI' in between near top, large crown above, date divided below, mintmark in cartouche at bottom **Rev. Legend:** MON(ETA): ARG(ENT). - REG: PRUS(S). **Note:** Varieties exist. D#1942-51, 1956-81, 1993-2008.

Date	Mintage	VG	F	VF	XF	Unc
1753 S//E	—	7.00	12.00	30.00	50.00	—
1753 ST//E	—	7.00	12.00	30.00	50.00	—
1753 E	—	7.00	12.00	30.00	50.00	—
1754 ST//E	—	7.00	12.00	30.00	50.00	—
1754 E	—	7.00	12.00	30.00	50.00	—
1755 E	—	7.00	12.00	30.00	50.00	—
1756 S//E	—	7.00	12.00	30.00	50.00	—
1756 A//E	—	7.00	12.00	30.00	50.00	—
1756 E	—	7.00	12.00	30.00	50.00	—
1757 E	—	7.00	12.00	30.00	50.00	—

KM# D278 6 GROSCHER (Szostake)

2.5980 g., Silver, 23 mm. **Ruler:** Friedrich II **Mint:** Konigsberg **Obverse:** Armored bust to right **Obv. Legend:** FRIDERICVS BORVSSORVM REX. **Reverse:** Two adjacent shields of arms, eagle in each, 'VI' in between near top, large crown above, date divided below, mintmark in cartouche at bottom **Rev. Legend:** MON(ETA): ARG(ENT). - REG: PRUS(S). **Note:** D#1929-41.

Date	Mintage	VG	F	VF	XF	Unc
1752 S//E	—	7.00	12.00	30.00	50.00	—
1752 ST//E	—	7.00	12.00	30.00	50.00	—

KM# B277 6 GROSCHER (Szostake)

3.1180 g., Silver, 23 mm. **Ruler:** Friedrich II **Mint:** Stettin **Obverse:** Armored bust to right **Obv. Legend:** FRIDERICVS BORVSSORVM REX. **Reverse:** Two adjacent shields of arms, eagle in each, 'VI' in between near top, large crown above, date divided below, mintmark in cartouche at bottom **Rev. Legend:** MON. NOVA - ARG. PRUS. **Note:** M#188.

Date	Mintage	VG	F	VF	XF	Unc
1753G	—	150	225	400	650	—

KM# B279 6 GROSCHER (Szostake)
3.1180 g., Silver, 24-25 mm. **Ruler:** Friedrich II **Mint:** Konigsberg **Obverse:** Crowned bust to right holding sword over right shoulder **Obv. Legend:** FRIDERICUS BORUSSOR: REX. **Reverse:** Two adjacent shields of arms, eagle in each, 'VI' in between near top, large crown above, date divided below, mintmark in cartouche at bottom **Rev. Legend:** MON: ARG. - REG: PRUS(S). **Note:** D#1982-92.

Date	Mintage	VG	F	VF	XF	Unc
1755E	—	18.00	40.00	80.00	135	—

KM# C279 6 GROSCHER (Szostake)
3.1180 g., Silver, 24-25 mm. **Ruler:** Friedrich II **Mint:** Konigsberg **Obverse:** Crowned and armored bust to right **Obv. Legend:** FRIDERICUS BORUSSORUM REX. **Reverse:** Round 4-fold arms with central shield of Prussian eagle, palm branches at left and right, large crown above divides date, value 'VI' below. **Rev. Legend:** MONETA - ARGENTEA. **Note:** Varieties exist. D#2009-13.

Date	Mintage	VG	F	VF	XF	Unc
1755E	—	80.00	130	240	425	—
1756E	—	80.00	130	240	425	—

KM# A283 6 GROSCHER (Szostake)
Silver, 24 mm. **Ruler:** Friedrich II **Mint:** Cleve **Obverse:** Crowned bust to right **Obv. Legend:** FRIDERICUS BORUSSORUM REX. **Reverse:** Two adjacent shields of arms, eagle in each, 'VI' in between near top, large crown above divides date, mintmark at bottom **Rev. Legend:** MONETA - ARGENTEA. **Note:** O#359a. Although the 'C' mintmark normally designated Cleves, these coins were struck in Berlin, Aurich, Magdeburg and Königsberg, as well as Cleves.

Date	Mintage	VG	F	VF	XF	Unc
1756C	—	—	—	—	—	—
1757C	—	—	—	—	—	—

KM# A284 6 GROSCHER (Szostake)
Silver, 24 mm. **Ruler:** Friedrich II **Mint:** Cleve **Obverse:** Crowned bust to right **Obv. Legend:** FRIDERICVS BORVSSORVM REX. **Reverse:** Two adjacent shields of arms, eagle in each, 'VI' in between near top, large crown above divides date, mintmark at bottom **Rev. Legend:** MONETA - ARGENTEA. **Note:** O#359b. Although the 'C' mintmark normally designated Cleves, this coin was struck in Berlin, Aurich, Magdeburg and Königsberg, as well as Cleves.

Date	Mintage	VG	F	VF	XF	Unc
1757C	—	—	—	—	—	—

KM# B290 6 GROSCHER (Szostake)
Silver, 22-23 mm. **Ruler:** Elisabeth I of Russia **Obverse:** Crowned bust to right **Obv. Legend:** ELISAB: I: D:G: IMP: TOT: RUSS. **Reverse:** Crowned Prussian eagle, 'VI' in shield on breast, tail divides date below. **Rev. Legend:** MONETA: REGNI: PRUSS. **Note:** Varieties exist. D#2181-2219

Date	Mintage	VG	F	VF	XF	Unc
1759	3,795,000	18.00	30.00	75.00	120	—
1760	488,782	18.00	30.00	75.00	120	—
1761	3,457,439	18.00	30.00	75.00	120	—
1762	120,000	35.00	65.00	125	220	—

KM# 291 6 GROSCHER (Szostake)
Silver, 23-24 mm. **Ruler:** Friedrich II **Mint:** Konigsberg **Obverse:** Armored bust to right **Obv. Legend:** FRIDERICUS BORUSSORUM REX. **Reverse:** Two adjacent shields of arms, eagle in each, 'VI' in between near top, large crown above, date divided below, mintmark in cartouche at bottom **Rev. Legend:** MON(ETA): ARG(ENT). - REG: PRUS(S). **Note:** D#2256-7.

Date	Mintage	VG	F	VF	XF	Unc
1763E	21,421,145	12.00	20.00	50.00	85.00	—

KM# A300 6 GROSCHER (Szostake)
Silver, 28 mm. **Ruler:** Friedrich II **Mint:** Konigsberg **Obverse:** Armored bust to right **Obv. Legend:** FRIDERICUS BORUSSORUM REX. **Reverse:** Crowned Prussian eagle, '18' in crowned round shield on breast, date divided at top **Rev. Legend:** MONETA AR - GENTEA.

Date	Mintage	VG	F	VF	XF	Unc
1763E	—	—	—	—	—	—

KM# A297 6 GROSCHER (Szostake)
3.1180 g., Silver, 22-23 mm. **Ruler:** Friedrich II **Mint:** Konigsberg **Obverse:** Crowned head to right **Obv. Legend:** FRIDERICUS BORUSSORUM REX. **Reverse:** Crowned Prussian eagle, crowned script FR monogram on breast, date divided above crown, tail divides 'V - I.' **Rev. Legend:** MONETA - (date) - ARGENTEA. **Note:** Varieties exist. D#2332-50.

Date	Mintage	VG	F	VF	XF	Unc
1764E	183,740	8.00	20.00	40.00	65.00	—
1770E	—	8.00	20.00	40.00	65.00	—
1771E	—	8.00	20.00	40.00	65.00	—
1772E	—	8.00	20.00	40.00	65.00	—
1773E	—	8.00	20.00	40.00	65.00	—
1774E	—	8.00	20.00	40.00	65.00	—
1775E	—	8.00	20.00	40.00	65.00	—
1776E	—	8.00	20.00	40.00	65.00	—
1777E	717,540	8.00	20.00	40.00	65.00	—
1778E	645,835	8.00	20.00	40.00	65.00	—
1779E	561,275	8.00	20.00	40.00	65.00	—
1780E	341,250	8.00	20.00	40.00	65.00	—
1781E	799,968	8.00	20.00	40.00	65.00	—
1782E	400,010	8.00	20.00	40.00	65.00	—
1783E	232,395	8.00	20.00	40.00	65.00	—
1784E	Inc. above	8.00	20.00	40.00	65.00	—

KM# 22 18 GROSCHER (Tympf)
Billon **Ruler:** Friedrich I **Mint:** Konigsberg **Obverse:** Bust right, initials below **Reverse:** Legend is divided, crowned eagle with FR on breast, 1-8 divided near bottom, date below
Rev. Legend: SUUM - QUIQUE

Date	Mintage	VG	F	VF	XF	Unc
1702 CG	150,000	35.00	80.00	160	275	—

KM# 123 18 GROSCHER (Tympf)
Billon **Ruler:** Friedrich Wilhelm I **Reverse:** Crowned 6-fold arms with central shield of Prussia divides 1-8, date in legend
Note: Varieties exist.

Date	Mintage	VG	F	VF	XF	Unc
1714 CG	67,000	100	225	400	625	—
1716 CG	Inc. above	100	225	400	625	—
1716 CG/M	Inc. above	100	225	400	625	—
1717 CG	38,000	100	225	400	625	—
1717 CG/M	Inc. above	100	225	400	625	—

KM# 167 18 GROSCHER (Tympf)
Billon **Ruler:** Friedrich Wilhelm I **Obverse:** Armored bust right **Reverse:** Crown above two shields, date and value below **Note:** Similar to 6 Groscher, KM#166.

Date	Mintage	VG	F	VF	XF	Unc
1718 CG	30,000	100	225	400	625	—

KM# A266 18 GROSCHER (Tympf)
5.9200 g., Silver, 26-28 mm. **Ruler:** Friedrich II **Mint:** Konigsberg **Obverse:** Armored bust to right **Obv. Legend:** FRIDERICUS BORUSSORUM REX. **Reverse:** Crowned Prussian eagle with script FR monogram on breast, tail divides 1 - 8. **Rev. Legend:** MONETA. ARGENT - REG: PRUSS. (date). **Note:** Varieties exist. D#2014-92.

Date	Mintage	VG	F	VF	XF	Unc
1751 W//E	—	10.00	25.00	50.00	90.00	—
1751 E	—	10.00	25.00	50.00	90.00	—
1752 W//E	—	10.00	25.00	50.00	90.00	—
1752 S//E	—	10.00	25.00	50.00	90.00	—
1752 ST//E	—	10.00	25.00	50.00	90.00	—
1752 E	—	10.00	25.00	50.00	90.00	—
1753 ST//E	—	10.00	25.00	50.00	90.00	—
1753 E	—	10.00	25.00	50.00	90.00	—
1754 ST//E	—	10.00	25.00	50.00	90.00	—
1754 E	—	10.00	25.00	50.00	90.00	—

KM# C277 18 GROSCHER (Tympf)
5.9200 g., Silver, 26-28 mm. **Ruler:** Friedrich II **Mint:** Stettin **Obverse:** Armored bust to right **Obv. Legend:** FRIDERICUS BORUSSORUM REX. **Reverse:** Crowned Prussian eagle with script FR monogrm on breast, tail divides 1 - 8 **Rev. Legend:** MONETA. NOVA - ARG. PRUSS. (date). **Note:** M#189.

Date	Mintage	VG	F	VF	XF	Unc
1753G	—	140	225	400	625	—

KM# D279.1 18 GROSCHER (Tympf)
5.9200 g., Silver, 28 mm. **Ruler:** Friedrich II **Mint:** Konigsberg **Obverse:** Crowned bust to right in circle, holding sword over right shoulder **Obv. Legend:** FRIDERICVS - BORVSSORVM REX. **Reverse:** Crowned Prussian eagle with script FR monogram on breast, tail divides 1 - 8. **Rev. Legend:** MONETA. ARGENT - REG: PRUSS. (date). **Note:** D#2093-2106.

Date	Mintage	VG	F	VF	XF	Unc
1754E	—	35.00	60.00	120	200	—
1755E	—	35.00	60.00	120	200	—

KM# D279.2 18 GROSCHER (Tympf)
5.9200 g., Silver, 28 mm. **Ruler:** Friedrich II **Mint:** Konigsberg **Obverse:** Crowned bust to right in circle, holding sword over right shoulder **Obv. Legend:** FRIDERICVS - BORVSSORVM REX (date). **Reverse:** Crowned Prussian eagle, '18' in crowned oval shield on breast **Rev. Legend:** MONETA. ARGENT - REG: PRUSS. **Note:** D#2107-9

Date	Mintage	VG	F	VF	XF	Unc
1755E	—	35.00	60.00	120	200	—

KM# D279.3 18 GROSCHER (Tympf)
5.8640 g., Silver, 27-28 mm. **Ruler:** Friedrich II **Mint:** Konigsberg **Obverse:** Crowned bust to right holding sword over right shoulder **Obv. Legend:** FRIDERICVS - BORVSSORVM REX. **Reverse:** Crowned Prussian eagle, '18' in crowned oval shield on breast **Rev. Legend:** MONETA AR - GENTEA (date). **Note:** D#2110-20.

Date	Mintage	VG	F	VF	XF	Unc
1755E	—	35.00	60.00	120	200	—
1756 A//E	—	35.00	60.00	120	200	—
1756E	—	35.00	60.00	120	200	—
1757E	—	35.00	60.00	120	200	—
1758E	—	35.00	60.00	120	200	—

KM# B284 18 GROSCHER (Tympf)
5.8640 g., Silver, 27-28 mm. **Ruler:** Friedrich II **Mint:** Berlin **Obverse:** Armored bust to right **Obv. Legend:** FRIDERICUS BORUSSORUM REX. **Reverse:** Crowned Prussian eagle with script FR monogram on breast, tail divides 1 - 8.
Rev. Legend: MONETA AR - GENTEA (date). **Note:** D#2121-22.

Date	Mintage	VG	F	VF	XF	Unc
1757A	—	35.00	60.00	120	200	—
1758A	—	35.00	60.00	120	200	—

KM# C284.1 18 GROSCHER (Tympf)
5.8640 g., Silver, 27-28 mm. **Ruler:** Friedrich II **Mint:** Berlin **Obverse:** Crowned and armored bust to right with sword over right shoulder. **Obv. Legend:** FRIDERICUS BORUSSORUM REX. **Reverse:** Crowned Prussian eagle with script FR monogram on breast, tail divides 1 - 8, date divided at top by eagle's head **Rev. Legend:** MONETA - ARGENTEA. **Note:** D#2123-32.

Date	Mintage	VG	F	VF	XF	Unc
1758A	—	35.00	60.00	120	200	—
1759A	—	35.00	60.00	120	200	—

KM# C284.2 18 GROSCHER (Tympf)
5.8640 g., Silver, 28 mm. **Ruler:** Friedrich II **Mint:** Magdeburg **Obverse:** Crowned and armored bust to right with sword over right shoulder **Obv. Legend:** FRIDERICVS BORVSSORVM REX. **Reverse:** Crowned Prussian eagle with script FR monogram on breast, tail divides 1 - 8, date divided at top by eagle's head. **Rev. Legend:** MONETA - ARGENTEA. **Note:** D#2133.

Date	Mintage	VG	F	VF	XF	Unc
1758F	—	35.00	60.00	120	200	—

KM# C290 18 GROSCHER (Tympf)
Silver, 27 mm. **Ruler:** Elisabeth I of Russia **Obverse:** Crowned bust to right **Obv. Legend:** ELISAB: I: D:G: IMP: TOT: RUSS. **Reverse:** Crowned Prussian eagle, '18' in shield on breast, tail divides date below **Rev. Legend:** MONETA: REGNI: PRUSS(IAE). **Note:** Varieties exist. D#2220-37.

Date	Mintage	VG	F	VF	XF	Unc
1759	268,745	85.00	150	350	600	—
1760	52,638	100	175	400	700	—
1761	—	85.00	150	350	600	—

KM# B300 18 GROSCHER (Tympf)
5.9390 g., Silver, 26.5 mm. **Ruler:** Friedrich II **Mint:** Konigsberg **Obverse:** Crowned head to right **Obv. Legend:** FRIDERICUS BORUSSORUM REX. **Reverse:** Crowned Prussian eagle, crowned FR monogram on breast, date above crown, tail divides 1 - 8. **Rev. Legend:** MONETA - (date) - ARGENTEA. **Note:** D#2351-56.

Date	Mintage	VG	F	VF	XF	Unc
1764E	989,685	12.00	30.00	60.00	100	—
1765E	1,465,515	12.00	30.00	60.00	100	—

KM# 237 1/48 THALER (1/2 Groschen)
Billon **Ruler:** Friedrich II **Obverse:** Crowned script FR monogram, date below **Reverse:** Value

Date	Mintage	VG	F	VF	XF	Unc
1743 EGN	2,560,000	15.00	25.00	40.00	65.00	—
1744 EGN	8,372,000	15.00	25.00	40.00	65.00	—
1745 EGN	1,793,000	15.00	25.00	40.00	65.00	—
1746 EGN	2,917,000	15.00	25.00	40.00	65.00	—
1747 EGN	9,600,000	15.00	25.00	40.00	65.00	—
1748 EGN	10,145,000	15.00	25.00	40.00	65.00	—
1749 EGN	6,233,000	15.00	25.00	40.00	65.00	—
1749 ALS	Inc. above	15.00	25.00	40.00	65.00	—
1749 CHI	Inc. above	15.00	25.00	40.00	65.00	—

KM# 58 1/48 THALER (1/2 Groschen)
Billon **Ruler:** Friedrich I **Mint:** Minden **Obverse:** Crowned FR monogram **Reverse:** Value in date with initials
Rev. Legend: 48/EINEN/REICHS.TH **Note:** Varieties exist

Date	Mintage	VG	F	VF	XF	Unc
1705 BH	188,000	20.00	45.00	75.00	125	—

KM# 210 1/48 THALER (1/2 Groschen)
Billon **Ruler:** Friedrich Wilhelm I **Mint:** Berlin **Obverse:** Crowned FWR monogram, initials below **Reverse:** Value in date
Rev. Legend: 48/EINEN/THALER

Date	Mintage	VG	F	VF	XF	Unc
1731 EGN	24,000,000	12.00	25.00	50.00	85.00	—
1732 EGN	Inc. above	12.00	25.00	50.00	85.00	—
1733 EGN	Inc. above	12.00	25.00	50.00	85.00	—
1734 EGN	Inc. above	12.00	25.00	50.00	85.00	—

KM# 225 1/48 THALER (1/2 Groschen)
Billon **Ruler:** Friedrich II **Mint:** Magdeburg **Obverse:** Crowned script FR monogram **Reverse:** Value, date

Date	Mintage	VG	F	VF	XF	Unc
1740 GK Rare	—	—	—	—	—	—
1753F	—	10.00	20.00	40.00	65.00	—
1754F	—	10.00	20.00	40.00	65.00	—
1755F	—	10.00	20.00	40.00	65.00	—
1756F	—	10.00	20.00	40.00	65.00	—
1757F	—	10.00	20.00	40.00	65.00	—

KM# 228 1/48 THALER (1/2 Groschen)

Billon **Ruler:** Friedrich II **Obverse:** Crowned script FR monogram, date **Reverse:** Value

Date	Mintage	VG	F	VF	XF	Unc
1741 GK	4,070,000	15.00	25.00	45.00	70.00	—
1742 GK	Inc. above	15.00	25.00	45.00	70.00	—
1742 AGP	426,000	15.00	25.00	45.00	70.00	—
1743 GK	Inc. above	15.00	25.00	45.00	70.00	—
1744 GK	Inc. above	15.00	25.00	45.00	70.00	—
1746 GK	Inc. above	15.00	25.00	45.00	70.00	—
1747 GK	Inc. above	15.00	25.00	45.00	70.00	—
1749 GK	Inc. above	15.00	25.00	45.00	70.00	—
1750 GK	Inc. above	15.00	25.00	45.00	70.00	—

KM# 229 1/48 THALER (1/2 Groschen)

Billon **Ruler:** Friedrich II **Reverse:** Crowned value in wreath

Date	Mintage	VG	F	VF	XF	Unc
1741 EGN	6,004,000	9.00	16.00	35.00	65.00	—

KM# 250 1/48 THALER (1/2 Groschen)

Billon **Ruler:** Friedrich II **Obverse:** With mint mark instead of initials **Reverse:** Value **Rev. Legend:** 48/EINEN/REICHS/THALER/ *initial*

Date	Mintage	VG	F	VF	XF	Unc
1750A	—	10.00	20.00	40.00	65.00	—
1750B	240,000	20.00	40.00	80.00	115	—
1751A	—	10.00	20.00	40.00	65.00	—
1752A	—	10.00	20.00	40.00	65.00	—
1752B	—	20.00	40.00	80.00	115	—
1753G	—	20.00	40.00	80.00	115	—

KM# 275 1/48 THALER (1/2 Groschen)

Billon **Ruler:** Friedrich II **Obverse:** Monogram divides date

Date	Mintage	VG	F	VF	XF	Unc
1753A	—	18.00	25.00	50.00	85.00	—
1756A	6,322,000	18.00	25.00	50.00	85.00	—
1760	—	18.00	25.00	50.00	85.00	—
1763G	—	20.00	35.00	60.00	100	—

KM# 295 1/48 THALER (1/2 Groschen)

0.9700 g., 0.2500 Silver 0.0078 oz. ASW **Ruler:** Friedrich II **Obverse:** Crowned monogram divides date **Reverse:** Value above spray **Rev. Legend:** *48*/EINEN/THALER/initial

Date	Mintage	VG	F	VF	XF	Unc
1764A	25,611,000	3.50	6.00	10.00	20.00	—
1764F	1,285,000	10.00	18.00	30.00	60.00	—
1765A	59,744,000	3.50	6.00	10.00	20.00	—
1765F	327,000	11.00	20.00	32.50	65.00	—
1766A	68,709,000	3.50	6.00	10.00	20.00	—
1766F	77,000	13.50	25.00	40.00	80.00	—
1767A	61,962,000	3.50	6.00	10.00	20.00	—
1768A	119,589,000	3.50	6.00	10.00	20.00	—
1769A	52,947,000	3.50	6.00	10.00	20.00	—
1770A	6,507,000	4.75	8.00	13.50	27.50	—

KM# 327 1/48 THALER (1/2 Groschen)

0.9700 g., 0.2500 Silver 0.0078 oz. ASW **Ruler:** Friedrich II **Mint:** Berlin **Obverse:** Crowned FR monogram; A below **Reverse:** Value and date **Rev. Legend:** *18*/EINEN/THALER/ date

Date	Mintage	VG	F	VF	XF	Unc
1771A	68,079,000	3.50	6.00	10.00	20.00	—
1772A	47,769,000	3.50	6.00	10.00	20.00	—
1773A	48,446,000	3.50	6.00	10.00	20.00	—
1774A	12,317,000	3.50	6.00	10.00	20.00	—
1775A	25,160,000	3.50	6.00	10.00	20.00	—
1776A	53,697,000	3.50	6.00	10.00	20.00	—
1777A	57,412,000	3.50	6.00	10.00	20.00	—
1778A	65,433,000	3.50	6.00	10.00	20.00	—
1779A	17,405,000	3.50	6.00	10.00	20.00	—
1780A	52,000	10.00	18.50	32.50	65.00	—
1781A Rare	Inc. above	—	—	—	—	—

KM# 263 1/24 THALER

Billon **Ruler:** Friedrich II **Obverse:** Crowned monogram **Reverse:** Value, date **Rev. Legend:** *24*/EINEN/REICHS/ THALER/date/initial

Date	Mintage	VG	F	VF	XF	Unc
1751C	—	20.00	35.00	75.00	110	—
1752A	27,131,000	15.00	30.00	60.00	95.00	—
1752F	—	8.00	15.00	30.00	65.00	—
1753C	—	20.00	35.00	75.00	110	—
1753F	—	8.00	15.00	30.00	65.00	—
1753G	—	10.00	20.00	35.00	75.00	—
1754C	—	20.00	35.00	75.00	110	—
1754F	—	8.00	15.00	30.00	65.00	—
1754G	—	10.00	20.00	35.00	75.00	—
1755C	—	20.00	35.00	75.00	110	—
1755F	—	8.00	15.00	30.00	65.00	—
1756F	—	8.00	15.00	30.00	65.00	—
1757F	—	8.00	15.00	30.00	65.00	—
1763B	21,119,000	15.00	25.00	60.00	100	—
1763C	2,551,000	20.00	35.00	75.00	110	—
1763F	33,660,000	8.00	15.00	30.00	65.00	—

KM# 264 1/24 THALER

Billon **Ruler:** Friedrich II **Obverse:** Crowned monogram above date **Reverse:** Value **Rev. Legend:** *24*/EINEN/REICHS/ THALER/initial

Date	Mintage	VG	F	VF	XF	Unc
1751B	533,000	10.00	20.00	45.00	85.00	—
1752A	—	8.00	12.00	25.00	50.00	—
Note: Mintage included in KM#263						
1753A	20,566,000	8.00	12.00	25.00	50.00	—
1754A	—	8.00	12.00	25.00	50.00	—

KM# 265 1/24 THALER

Billon **Ruler:** Friedrich II **Reverse:** Date added

Date	Mintage	VG	F	VF	XF	Unc
1751B	1,573,000	18.00	30.00	60.00	100	—

KM# 276 1/24 THALER

Billon **Ruler:** Friedrich II **Obverse:** Crowned monogram divides date **Reverse:** Value **Rev. Legend:** *24*/EINEN/REICHS/ THALER/*initial*

Date	Mintage	VG	F	VF	XF	Unc
1753A	—	9.00	15.00	30.00	65.00	—
1754A	—	9.00	15.00	30.00	65.00	—
1755A	1,860,000	9.00	15.00	30.00	65.00	—
1756A	14,637,000	9.00	15.00	30.00	65.00	—
1756F	—	10.00	20.00	40.00	75.00	—
1757A	16,696,000	9.00	15.00	30.00	65.00	—
1763A	88,778,000	9.00	15.00	30.00	65.00	—
1763G	—	15.00	25.00	45.00	85.00	—

KM# 296 1/24 THALER

1.9900 g., 0.3680 Silver 0.0235 oz. ASW, 19 mm. **Ruler:** Friedrich II

Date	Mintage	VG	F	VF	XF	Unc
1764A	6,311,000	7.50	12.50	25.00	50.00	—
1764F	2,795,000	1.00	2.00	4.00	10.00	—
1765F	408,000	1.00	2.00	4.00	10.00	—
1766F	55,000	1.00	2.00	4.00	10.00	—
1769A	127,000	12.50	20.00	40.00	80.00	—
1781A	3,730,000	3.50	6.00	12.00	25.00	—
1781B	—	15.00	30.00	65.00	100	—
1782A	6,041,000	3.00	5.00	10.00	20.00	—
1782E	—	20.00	37.50	80.00	130	—
1783A	4,567,000	3.25	5.50	11.00	22.00	—
1784A	1,686,000	4.00	7.00	13.50	27.50	—
1785A	16,960,000	3.00	5.00	10.00	20.00	—
1786A	16,171,000	3.00	5.00	10.00	20.00	—

KM# 7 1/12 THALER (Doppelgroschen)

Silver **Ruler:** Friedrich I **Mint:** Berlin **Obverse:** Crowned eagle in center, 4 crowned double-F monograms alternating with 4 R's **Reverse:** Crowned oval scepter arms between palm branches divide date and mintmaster's initials, value in exergue **Rev. Legend:** SUUM - CUIQUE **Rev. Inscription:** 12.EINEN/R.T.

Date	Mintage	VG	F	VF	XF	Unc
1701 CS	478,000	12.00	25.00	50.00	85.00	—
1702 CS	788,000	12.00	25.00	50.00	85.00	—
1703 CS	Inc. above	12.00	25.00	50.00	85.00	—
1704 CS	147,000	12.00	25.00	50.00	85.00	—
1705 CS	139,000	12.00	25.00	50.00	85.00	—
1706 CS	193,000	12.00	25.00	50.00	85.00	—
1707 CS	182,000	12.00	25.00	50.00	85.00	—
1708 CS	133,000	12.00	25.00	50.00	85.00	—
1709 CS	78,000	12.00	25.00	50.00	85.00	—
1710 CS	101,000	12.00	25.00	50.00	85.00	—
1711 CS	251,000	12.00	25.00	50.00	85.00	—
1712 CS	349,000	12.00	25.00	50.00	85.00	—
1713 CS	193,000	12.00	25.00	50.00	85.00	—

KM# 8 1/12 THALER (Doppelgroschen)

Silver **Ruler:** Friedrich I **Mint:** Magdeburg **Obverse:** Crowned monograms in cruciform, "R" at angles, eagle in center **Reverse:** Crowned arms divide date, value below **Note:** Varieties exist

Date	Mintage	VG	F	VF	XF	Unc
1701 HFH	—	12.00	25.00	50.00	85.00	—
1702 HFH	—	12.00	25.00	50.00	85.00	—
1703 HFH	—	12.00	25.00	50.00	85.00	—
1704 HFH	—	12.00	25.00	50.00	85.00	—
1705 HFH	—	12.00	25.00	50.00	85.00	—
1706 HFH	—	12.00	25.00	50.00	85.00	—
1707 HFH	—	12.00	25.00	50.00	85.00	—
1708 HFH	—	12.00	25.00	50.00	85.00	—
1709 HFH	—	12.00	25.00	50.00	85.00	—
1711 HFH	—	12.00	25.00	50.00	85.00	—
1712 HFH	—	12.00	25.00	50.00	85.00	—
1713 HFH	—	12.00	25.00	50.00	85.00	—

KM# 42 1/12 THALER (Doppelgroschen)

Silver **Ruler:** Friedrich I **Mint:** Berlin **Obverse:** Alternating sets of III's replace R's **Reverse:** Crowned arms divide date, value below **Note:** Varieties exist

Date	Mintage	VG	F	VF	XF	Unc
1703 CS	Inc. above	12.00	25.00	50.00	85.00	—
1704 CS	Inc. above	12.00	25.00	50.00	85.00	—
1705 CS	Inc. above	12.00	25.00	50.00	85.00	—

KM# 59 1/12 THALER (Doppelgroschen)

Silver **Ruler:** Friedrich I **Mint:** Minden **Reverse:** Crowned 5-fold arms divide date and initials **Note:** Varieties exist

Date	Mintage	VG	F	VF	XF	Unc
1705 BH	—	22.00	50.00	100	165	—
1706 BH	—	22.00	50.00	100	165	—

KM# 98 1/12 THALER (Doppelgroschen)

Silver **Ruler:** Friedrich Wilhelm I **Mint:** Magdeburg **Obverse:** Laureate bust right **Reverse:** Crowned FW monogram, initials lower left, date lower right, value below **Rev. Legend:** 12.EINEN./R.T **Note:** Varieties exist

Date	Mintage	VG	F	VF	XF	Unc
1713 HFH	—	175	300	600	1,000	—

Date	Mintage	VG	F	VF	XF	Unc
1714 HFH	—	175	300	600	1,000	—

KM# 97 1/12 THALER (Doppelgroschen)

Silver **Ruler:** Friedrich I **Reverse:** Ornately-shaped shield **Note:** Varieties exist.

Date	Mintage	VG	F	VF	XF	Unc
1713 IFS	Inc. above	25.00	60.00	120	200	—
1714 IFS	165,000	25.00	60.00	120	200	—
1715 IFS	193,000	25.00	60.00	120	200	—
1716 IFS	137,000	25.00	60.00	120	200	—

KM# 99 1/12 THALER (Doppelgroschen)

Silver **Ruler:** Friedrich Wilhelm I **Obverse:** Crowned FW monogram, value below **Obv. Legend:** 12.EINEN./R.T **Reverse:** Crowned narrow oval scepter arms in palm leaves divide date and initials below **Note:** Varieties exist.

Date	Mintage	VG	F	VF	XF	Unc
1713 HFH	—	35.00	80.00	160	325	—
1714 HFH	—	35.00	80.00	160	325	—

KM# 93 1/12 THALER (Doppelgroschen)

Silver **Ruler:** Friedrich I **Mint:** Berlin **Obverse:** Laureate bust right **Reverse:** Crowned FW monogram, initials left date right, value 12.EINEN R.T at bottom

Date	Mintage	VG	F	VF	XF	Unc
1713 CS	Inc. above	175	300	600	1,000	—

KM# 94 1/12 THALER (Doppelgroschen)

Silver **Ruler:** Friedrich I **Obverse:** Crowned FW monogram, value at bottom **Obv. Legend:** 12EIN.RT **Reverse:** Crowned oval scepter arms in palm leaves, initials and date at bottom

Date	Mintage	VG	F	VF	XF	Unc
1713 IFS	Inc. above	25.00	60.00	120	200	—

KM# 95 1/12 THALER (Doppelgroschen)

Silver **Ruler:** Friedrich I **Obverse:** Crowned FW monogram, initials and date below **Reverse:** Crowned shield of scepter arms in palm fronds, value below **Rev. Legend:** 12.EIN.RT

Date	Mintage	VG	F	VF	XF	Unc
1713 IFS	Inc. above	35.00	80.00	160	325	—
1717 IFS	231,000	35.00	80.00	160	325	—

KM# 96 1/12 THALER (Doppelgroschen)

Silver **Ruler:** Friedrich I **Obverse:** Date below initials

Date	Mintage	VG	F	VF	XF	Unc
1713 IFS	Inc. above	35.00	80.00	160	325	—

KM# 124 1/12 THALER (Doppelgroschen)

Silver **Ruler:** Friedrich Wilhelm I **Obverse:** Value below monogram **Obv. Legend:** 12.EIN.R.T **Reverse:** Crowned ornately-shaped shield of scepter arms in palm fronds, initials and date below **Note:** Varieties exist.

Date	Mintage	VG	F	VF	XF	Unc
1714 HFH	—	25.00	60.00	120	200	—
1715 HFH	—	25.00	60.00	120	200	—
1716 HFH	—	25.00	60.00	120	200	—
1717 HFH	—	25.00	60.00	120	200	—
1718 HFH	—	25.00	60.00	120	200	—

KM# 159 1/12 THALER (Doppelgroschen)

Silver **Ruler:** Friedrich Wilhelm I **Mint:** Berlin **Obverse:** Crowned FW monogram, initials, date in curved band below **Reverse:** Crowned oval scepter arms in palm leaves, value in curved band below **Rev. Legend:** 12.EIN.R.T

Date	Mintage	VG	F	VF	XF	Unc
1717 IFS	Inc. above	40.00	85.00	165	340	—
1718 IFS	180,000	40.00	85.00	165	340	—

KM# 168 1/12 THALER (Doppelgroschen)

Silver **Ruler:** Friedrich Wilhelm I **Obverse:** Value in band **Obv. Legend:** 12.EIN.R.T **Reverse:** Initials, date

Date	Mintage	VG	F	VF	XF	Unc
1718 IFS	Inc. above	30.00	65.00	125	215	—

KM# 169 1/12 THALER (Doppelgroschen)

Silver **Ruler:** Friedrich Wilhelm I **Mint:** Magdeburg **Reverse:** Round arms

Date	Mintage	VG	F	VF	XF	Unc
1718 HFH	—	30.00	65.00	125	215	—

KM# 176 1/12 THALER (Doppelgroschen)

Silver **Ruler:** Friedrich Wilhelm I **Mint:** Berlin **Note:** Varieties exist

Date	Mintage	VG	F	VF	XF	Unc
1719 IGN	459,000	30.00	65.00	125	215	—
1720 IGN	555,000	30.00	65.00	125	215	—
1721 IGN	100,000	30.00	65.00	125	215	—
1722 IGN	152,000	30.00	65.00	125	215	—
1723 IGN	204,000	30.00	65.00	125	215	—
1724 IGN	81,000	30.00	65.00	125	215	—
1725 IGN	1,062,000	30.00	65.00	125	215	—

KM# 201 1/12 THALER (Doppelgroschen)

Silver **Ruler:** Friedrich Wilhelm I **Mint:** Konigsberg **Reverse:** Oval arms **Note:** Varieties exist

Date	Mintage	VG	F	VF	XF	Unc
1724 CG	153,000	30.00	65.00	125	215	—
1725 CG	147,000	30.00	65.00	125	215	—
1726 CG	56,000	30.00	65.00	125	215	—
1727 CG	110,000	30.00	65.00	125	215	—
1728 CG	120,000	30.00	65.00	125	215	—

KM# 203 1/12 THALER (Doppelgroschen)

Silver **Ruler:** Friedrich Wilhelm I **Mint:** Berlin **Reverse:** Large round arms **Note:** Varieties exist

Date	Mintage	VG	F	VF	XF	Unc
1725 EGN	Inc. above	30.00	65.00	125	215	—
1726 EGN	815,000	30.00	65.00	125	215	—
1727 EGN	675,000	30.00	65.00	125	215	—
1728 EGN	631,000	30.00	65.00	125	215	—
1729 EGN	886,000	30.00	65.00	125	215	—

KM# 216 1/12 THALER (Doppelgroschen)

Silver **Ruler:** Friedrich Wilhelm I **Obverse:** Crowned monogram **Reverse:** Small round arms **Note:** Varieties exist.

Date	Mintage	VG	F	VF	XF	Unc
1734 EGN	118,000	30.00	65.00	125	215	—
1735 EGN	840,000	30.00	65.00	125	215	—
1736 EGN	623,000	30.00	65.00	125	215	—
1737 EGN	802,000	30.00	65.00	125	215	—
1738 EGN	876,000	30.00	65.00	125	215	—
1739 EGN	473,000	30.00	65.00	125	215	—
1740 EGN	600,000	30.00	65.00	125	215	—

KM# 226 1/12 THALER (Doppelgroschen)

Billon **Ruler:** Friedrich II **Obverse:** Crowned script FR monogram, date below **Reverse:** Value **Note:** Varieties exist.

Date	Mintage	VG	F	VF	XF	Unc
1740 EGN	505,000	20.00	35.00	65.00	100	—
1741 EGN	4,391,000	20.00	35.00	65.00	100	—
1741 GK	114,000	45.00	85.00	160	275	—
1742 EGN	Inc. above	20.00	35.00	65.00	100	—
1742 GK	Inc. above	45.00	85.00	160	275	—
1743 EGN	507,000	20.00	35.00	65.00	100	—
1745 EGN	5,735,000	20.00	35.00	65.00	100	—
1746 EGN	5,057,000	20.00	35.00	65.00	100	—

KM# 251 1/12 THALER (Doppelgroschen)

Billon **Ruler:** Friedrich II **Obverse:** Armored, laureate bust right **Obv. Legend:** FRIDERICVS BORVSSORVM REX **Reverse:** Value, date divided by initial **Rev. Legend:** *12*/EINENREICHS/THALER/date-initial

Date	Mintage	VG	F	VF	XF	Unc
1750A	—	18.00	30.00	75.00	135	—
1750B	4,567,000	18.00	30.00	75.00	135	—
1751A	—	18.00	30.00	75.00	135	—
1751B	7,696,000	18.00	30.00	75.00	135	—
1751C	—	20.00	40.00	80.00	150	—
1752A	—	18.00	30.00	75.00	135	—
1752B	Inc. above	18.00	30.00	75.00	135	—
1752C	—	20.00	40.00	80.00	150	—
1752F	—	75.00	120	250	400	—
1753C	—	20.00	40.00	80.00	150	—
1753F	—	75.00	120	250	400	—
1754C	—	20.00	40.00	80.00	150	—
1755C	—	20.00	40.00	80.00	150	—

KM# 268 1/12 THALER (Doppelgroschen)

Billon **Ruler:** Friedrich II **Obverse:** Head right **Obv. Legend:** FRIDERICVS BORVSSORVM REX **Reverse:** Value, date **Rev. Legend:** *12*/EINEN/REICHS/THALER/date/•initial•

Date	Mintage	VG	F	VF	XF	Unc
1752A	—	10.00	20.00	40.00	65.00	—
1753A	—	10.00	20.00	40.00	65.00	—
1753B	—	10.00	20.00	40.00	65.00	—

Note: Mintage included in KM#251

Date	Mintage	VG	F	VF	XF	Unc
1753G	—	40.00	65.00	120	225	—
1754A	—	10.00	20.00	40.00	65.00	—
1754B	1,301,000	10.00	20.00	40.00	65.00	—
1754E	619,000	10.00	20.00	40.00	65.00	—
1754G	—	40.00	65.00	120	225	—
1755B	—	10.00	20.00	40.00	65.00	—
1763B	3,715,000	10.00	20.00	40.00	65.00	—

KM# 297 1/12 THALER (Doppelgroschen)

3.3400 g., 0.4370 Silver 0.0469 oz. ASW **Ruler:** Friedrich II **Mint:** Berlin **Obverse:** Head right **Reverse:** Value above date, "A" below

Date	Mintage	VG	F	VF	XF	Unc
1764A	—	5.00	10.00	20.00	40.00	—

KM# 298 1/12 THALER (Doppelgroschen)

3.3400 g., 0.4370 Silver 0.0469 oz. ASW **Ruler:** Friedrich II **Obverse:** Larger head **Reverse:** Value, date **Rev. Legend:** 12/EINEN/REICHS/THALER/date/*initial*

Date	Mintage	VG	F	VF	XF	Unc
1764A	—	2.00	4.00	8.00	20.00	—
1764C	—	5.00	15.00	30.00	50.00	—
1764B	—	2.00	4.00	8.00	20.00	—
1764C	—	5.00	15.00	30.00	50.00	—
1765A	—	2.00	4.00	8.00	20.00	—
1765B	—	2.00	4.00	8.00	20.00	—
1766A	—	2.00	4.00	8.00	20.00	—
1766B	—	2.00	4.00	8.00	20.00	—
1766C	—	5.00	15.00	30.00	50.00	—
1767A	—	2.00	4.00	8.00	20.00	—
1767B	—	2.00	4.00	8.00	20.00	—
1768B	—	2.00	4.00	8.00	20.00	—
1769B	—	2.00	4.00	8.00	20.00	—
1770A	—	2.00	4.00	8.00	20.00	—
1771A	—	2.00	4.00	8.00	20.00	—

KM# 311 1/12 THALER (Doppelgroschen)

3.3400 g., 0.4370 Silver 0.0469 oz. ASW **Ruler:** Friedrich II **Obverse:** Berlin-type head **Reverse:** Value, date **Rev. Legend:** 12/EINEN/REICHS/THALER/date/initial

Date	Mintage	VG	F	VF	XF	Unc
1764E	—	2.00	3.00	6.00	20.00	—
1764F	—	4.00	8.00	20.00	50.00	—
1765E	—	2.00	3.00	6.00	20.00	—
1765F	—	4.00	8.00	20.00	50.00	—
1766E	—	2.00	3.00	6.00	20.00	—
1766F	—	4.00	8.00	20.00	50.00	—
1767E	—	2.00	3.00	6.00	20.00	—
1767F	—	4.00	8.00	20.00	50.00	—
1768E	—	2.00	3.00	6.00	20.00	—
1768F	—	4.00	8.00	20.00	50.00	—
1769E	—	2.00	3.00	6.00	20.00	—
1770E	—	2.00	3.00	6.00	20.00	—
1771E	—	2.00	3.00	6.00	20.00	—
1772E	—	2.00	3.00	6.00	20.00	—

KM# 341 1/12 THALER (Doppelgroschen)

3.3400 g., 0.4370 Silver 0.0469 oz. ASW **Ruler:** Friedrich II **Mint:** Berlin **Obverse:** Old head

Date	Mintage	VG	F	VF	XF	Unc
1786A Rare	—	—	—	—	—	—

KM# D284 6 MARIENGROSCHEN

4.8000 g., Silver, 25 mm. **Ruler:** Friedrich II **Obverse:** Head to right **Obv. Legend:** FRIDERICUS BORUSSORUM REX. **Reverse:** 4-line inscription with date in palm wreath **Rev. Legend:** VI/MARIEN/GROSCHEN/(date) **Note:** N#328.

Date	Mintage	VG	F	VF	XF	Unc
1758 (star)	—	—	—	—	—	—

KM# 252 1/6 THALER

5.3450 g., 0.5210 Silver 0.0895 oz. ASW **Ruler:** Friedrich II **Obverse:** Armored bust right **Obv. Legend:** FRIDERICVS BORVSSORVM REX **Reverse:** Value, date **Rev. Legend:** * VI */EINEN/REICHS/THALER/date/*initial*

Date	Mintage	VG	F	VF	XF	Unc
1750A	—	18.00	30.00	80.00	130	—
1750B	6,341,000	18.00	30.00	80.00	130	—
1751A	—	18.00	30.00	80.00	130	—
1751B	—	18.00	30.00	80.00	130	—
1751C	—	20.00	40.00	120	175	—
1752A	—	18.00	30.00	80.00	130	—
1752B	11,163,000	18.00	30.00	80.00	130	—
1752C	—	20.00	40.00	120	175	—
1752F	—	30.00	50.00	125	185	—
1753C	—	20.00	40.00	120	175	—
1753F	—	30.00	50.00	125	185	—
1754C	—	20.00	40.00	120	175	—
1755C	—	20.00	40.00	120	175	—

KM# 269 1/6 THALER

5.3450 g., 0.5210 Silver 0.0895 oz. ASW **Ruler:** Friedrich II **Obverse:** Head right **Obv. Legend:** FRIDERICUS BORUSSORUM REX **Reverse:** Value, date **Rev. Legend:** 6/EINEN/REICHS/THALER/date/*initial*

Date	Mintage	VG	F	VF	XF	Unc
1752A	—	18.00	30.00	60.00	110	—
1753B	Inc. above	18.00	30.00	60.00	110	—
1753G	—	85.00	130	250	400	—
1754B	911,000	18.00	30.00	60.00	110	—
1754E	538,000	120	180	325	600	—
1754F	—	18.00	30.00	60.00	110	—
1754G	—	85.00	130	250	400	—
1755C	—	85.00	130	250	400	—
1756A	282,000	18.00	30.00	60.00	110	—
1756C	—	85.00	130	250	400	—
1756F	—	18.00	30.00	60.00	110	—
1757C	—	85.00	130	250	400	—
1759F	—	18.00	30.00	60.00	110	—
1763A	9,854,000	18.00	30.00	60.00	110	—
1763B	13,546,000	18.00	30.00	60.00	110	—
1763F	4,476,000	18.00	30.00	60.00	110	—
1764A	—	18.00	30.00	60.00	110	—

KM# D290 1/6 THALER

4.3300 g., Silver, 25 mm. **Ruler:** Elisabeth I of Russia **Obverse:** Crowned bust to right **Obv. Legend:** ELISAB: I: D:G: IMP: TOT: RUSS. **Reverse:** Crowned Prussian eagle, date divided by claws to far left and right, 2-line inscription in exergue **Rev. Inscription:** 6. EIN. R. TH/COUR. **Note:** Varieties exist. D#2238-43.

Date	Mintage	VG	F	VF	XF	Unc
1761	1,342,988	30.00	55.00	130	215	—

KM# 299 1/6 THALER

5.3450 g., 0.5210 Silver 0.0895 oz. ASW **Ruler:** Friedrich II **Obverse:** Head right **Obv. Legend:** FRIDERICUS BORUSSORUM REX **Reverse:** Value, date **Rev. Legend:** 6/EINEN/REICHS/THALER/date/initial

Date	Mintage	VG	F	VF	XF	Unc
1764A	—	4.00	8.00	15.00	40.00	—
1764B	—	5.00	10.00	20.00	45.00	—
1764C	—	6.00	12.00	25.00	65.00	—
1764E	—	4.00	8.00	15.00	35.00	—
1765A	—	4.00	8.00	15.00	40.00	—
1765B	—	5.00	10.00	20.00	45.00	—
1765C	—	6.00	12.00	25.00	65.00	—
1766A	—	4.00	8.00	15.00	40.00	—
1766B	—	5.00	10.00	20.00	45.00	—
1767B	—	5.00	10.00	20.00	45.00	—
1768A	—	4.00	8.00	15.00	40.00	—
1768B	—	5.00	10.00	20.00	45.00	—
1770B	—	5.00	10.00	20.00	45.00	—
1780A Rare	—	—	—	—	—	—
1786A Rare	—	—	—	—	—	—

KM# 300 1/6 THALER

5.3450 g., 0.5210 Silver 0.0895 oz. ASW **Ruler:** Friedrich II **Obverse:** Berlin-type head **Obv. Legend:** FRIDERICUS BORUSSORUM REX **Reverse:** Value, date **Rev. Legend:** 6/EINEN/REICHS/THALER/date/initial

Date	Mintage	VG	F	VF	XF	Unc
1764E	—	4.00	8.00	15.00	35.00	—
1764F	—	6.00	12.00	25.00	50.00	—
1767E	—	4.00	8.00	15.00	35.00	—
1768E	—	4.00	8.00	15.00	35.00	—
1769E	—	4.00	8.00	15.00	35.00	—
1770E	—	4.00	8.00	15.00	35.00	—
1771E	—	4.00	8.00	15.00	35.00	—
1772E	—	4.00	8.00	15.00	35.00	—
1773E	—	4.00	8.00	15.00	35.00	—
1775E	—	4.00	8.00	15.00	35.00	—
1776E	—	4.00	8.00	15.00	35.00	—
1777E	582,000	4.00	8.00	15.00	35.00	—
1778E	174,000	4.00	8.00	15.00	35.00	—

KM# 312 1/6 THALER

5.3450 g., 0.5210 Silver 0.0895 oz. ASW **Ruler:** Friedrich II **Obverse:** Smaller head **Obv. Legend:** FRIDERICUS BORUSSORUM REX **Reverse:** Value, date **Rev. Legend:** 6/EINEN/REICHS/THALER/date/*initial*

Date	Mintage	VG	F	VF	XF	Unc
1765	—	5.00	10.00	20.00	45.00	—
1766	—	5.00	10.00	20.00	45.00	—

KM# 10 1/4 THALER

Silver **Ruler:** Friedrich I **Mint:** Berlin **Obverse:** Head right **Reverse:** Crowned F monograms divide date and initials

Date	Mintage	VG	F	VF	XF	Unc
1701 LCS	—	45.00	80.00	125	200	—

KM# 9 1/4 THALER

Silver **Ruler:** Friedrich I **Mint:** Konigsberg **Subject:** Coronation Issue **Obverse:** Bust above legend **Reverse:** Crown **Note:** Thick flan

Date	Mintage	VG	F	VF	XF	Unc
1701	—	60.00	100	150	250	—

KM# 253 1/4 THALER

Silver **Ruler:** Friedrich II **Obverse:** Armored, laureate bust right **Obv. Legend:** FRIDERICVS BORVSSORVM REX **Reverse:** Crowned eagle above flags and cannons, 'A' divides date below **Rev. Legend:** 4 EINEN R: THALER

Date	Mintage	VG	F	VF	XF	Unc
1750A	—	25.00	40.00	80.00	150	—
1751A	—	25.00	40.00	80.00	150	—
1751B	—	25.00	40.00	80.00	150	—
1752B	—	25.00	40.00	80.00	150	—

KM# 302 1/4 THALER

Silver **Ruler:** Friedrich II **Obverse:** Berlin head **Obv. Legend:** FRIDERICUS BORUSSORUM REX **Reverse:** Crowned eagle above flags and cannons, 'F' divides date below **Rev. Legend:** 4 EINEN R: THALER

Date	Mintage	VG	F	VF	XF	Unc
1764F	—	7.50	15.00	35.00	100	—

KM# 301 1/4 THALER

Silver **Ruler:** Friedrich II **Obverse:** Head right **Obv. Legend:** FRIDERICUS BORUSSORUM REX **Reverse:** Crowned eagle above flags and cannons, 'A' divides date below **Note:** Reichs 1/4 Thaler.

Date	Mintage	VG	F	VF	XF	Unc
1764A	—	7.50	15.00	30.00	100	—
1764E	—	10.00	25.00	50.00	150	—
1764F	—	7.50	15.00	35.00	100	—
1765A	—	7.50	15.00	30.00	100	—
1766A	—	7.50	15.00	30.00	100	—
1768B	—	7.50	15.00	30.00	90.00	—

KM# 342 1/4 THALER

Silver **Ruler:** Friedrich II **Obverse:** Head right **Obv. Legend:** FRIDERICUS BORUSSORUM REX **Reverse:** Crowned eagle above flags and cannons, 'A' divides date below **Rev. Legend:** 4 EINEN R: THALER

Date	Mintage	VG	F	VF	XF	Unc
1786A	—	150	275	400	600	—

KM# 343 1/4 THALER

Silver **Ruler:** Friedrich II **Mint:** Berlin **Subject:** Cornerstone Laying At Bellevue Castle **Obverse:** Old head right **Reverse:** Castle

Date	Mintage	VG	F	VF	XF	Unc
1786A	—	125	175	250	350	—

KM# E284 12 MARIENGROSCHEN

8.0640 g., Silver, 30 mm. **Ruler:** Friedrich II **Obverse:** Head to right **Obv. Legend:** FRIDERICUS BORUSSORUM REX. **Reverse:** 4-line inscription with date in palm wreath **Rev. Legend:** XII/MARIEN/GROSCHEN/(date). **Note:** N#327.

Date	Mintage	VG	F	VF	XF	Unc
1758 (star)	—	—	—	—	—	—

KM# 11 1/3 THALER (1/2 Gulden)

Silver **Ruler:** Friedrich I **Mint:** Berlin **Obverse:** Laureate bust right **Reverse:** Crowned manifold arms divide initials, value 1/3 below divides date **Rev. Legend:** SUUM - CUIQUE **Note:** Varieties exist.

Date	Mintage	VG	F	VF	XF	Unc
1701 CS	14,000	125	275	550	875	—
1702 CS	18,000	125	275	550	875	—
1703 CS	4,000	125	275	550	875	—
1705 CS	8,000	125	275	550	875	—
1706 CS	7,000	125	275	550	875	—
1707 CS	4,000	125	275	550	875	—
1711 CS	2,000	125	275	550	875	—

KM# 23 1/3 THALER (1/2 Gulden)

Silver **Ruler:** Friedrich I **Mint:** Magdeburg **Obverse:** Head right **Obv. Legend:** FRIDERICUS REX PRUSSIÆ **Reverse:** Crowned arms **Rev. Legend:** SUUM - CUIQUE • **Note:** Varieties exist

Date	Mintage	VG	F	VF	XF	Unc
1702 HFH	—	125	275	550	875	—
1712 HFH	—	125	275	550	875	—

KM# 60 1/3 THALER (1/2 Gulden)
Silver **Ruler:** Friedrich I **Mint:** Minden **Reverse:** Date, initials divided by arms

Date	Mintage	VG	F	VF	XF	Unc
1705 BH	—	200	350	600	950	—

KM# 102 1/3 THALER (1/2 Gulden)
Silver **Ruler:** Friedrich I **Mint:** Magdeburg **Reverse:** Crowned ornate 11-fold arms divide date, value: 1/3 in oval below divides initials

Date	Mintage	VG	F	VF	XF	Unc
1713 HFH	—	425	875	1,600	3,000	—

KM# 101 1/3 THALER (1/2 Gulden)
Silver **Ruler:** Friedrich I **Mint:** Berlin **Obverse:** Laureate bust right **Reverse:** Crowned 11-fold arms divide date and initials, value: 1/3 below **Note:** Varieties exist

Date	Mintage	VG	F	VF	XF	Unc
1713 IFS	1,533	425	875	1,600	3,000	—

KM# 125 1/3 THALER (1/2 Gulden)
Silver **Ruler:** Friedrich Wilhelm I **Mint:** Berlin **Reverse:** Crowned 12-fold arms divide date, value: 1/3 at bottom in oval divides initials

Date	Mintage	VG	F	VF	XF	Unc
1714 IFS	2,158	425	875	1,600	3,000	—
1715 IFS	1,270	425	875	1,600	3,000	—

KM# 152 1/3 THALER (1/2 Gulden)
Silver **Ruler:** Friedrich Wilhelm I **Obverse:** Wigged bust **Reverse:** Ornately-shaped arms

Date	Mintage	VG	F	VF	XF	Unc
1716 IFS	922	425	875	1,600	3,000	—

KM# 177 1/3 THALER (1/2 Gulden)
Silver **Ruler:** Friedrich Wilhelm I **Obverse:** Bust right **Reverse:** Oval 13-fold arms, large crown above divides date, value: 1/3 below initials divided to left, right **Note:** Varieties exist.

Date	Mintage	VG	F	VF	XF	Unc
1719 L/IGN	4,911	425	875	1,600	3,000	—
1720 L/IGL	—	425	875	1,600	3,000	—
1720 IGN	—	425	875	1,600	3,000	—
1721 IGN	—	425	875	1,600	3,000	—
1722 IGN	—	425	875	1,600	3,000	—
1723 IGN	—	425	875	1,600	3,000	—
1727 EGN	24,000	425	875	1,600	3,000	—

KM# 230 1/3 THALER (1/2 Gulden)
8.3500 g., 0.6660 Silver 0.1788 oz. ASW **Ruler:** Friedrich II **Obverse:** Bust right **Reverse:** Crowned oval eagle arms in baroque frame, value, date

Date	Mintage	VG	F	VF	XF	Unc
1741 EGN	7,704	300	525	1,000	1,750	—

KM# 284 1/3 THALER (1/2 Gulden)
8.3500 g., 0.6660 Silver 0.1788 oz. ASW **Ruler:** Friedrich II **Obverse:** Head right **Reverse:** Value, date in 2 palm branches

Date	Mintage	VG	F	VF	XF	Unc
1758 (star)	—	20.00	40.00	80.00	150	—

KM# 285 1/3 THALER (1/2 Gulden)
8.3500 g., 0.6660 Silver 0.1788 oz. ASW **Ruler:** Friedrich II **Obverse:** Head right **Obv. Legend:** FRIDERICUS BORUSSORUM REX **Reverse:** Value, date **Note:** Varieties exist.

Date	Mintage	VG	F	VF	XF	Unc
1758 (Dresden)	—	30.00	65.00	120	180	—
1759 (Dresden)	—	30.00	65.00	120	180	—
1759A	—	20.00	40.00	80.00	150	—

KM# 303 1/3 THALER (1/2 Gulden)
8.3520 g., 0.6660 Silver 0.1788 oz. ASW **Ruler:** Friedrich II **Obverse:** Head right **Obv. Legend:** FRIDERICUS BORUSSORUM REX **Reverse:** Value, date within laurel and palm branches **Rev. Legend:** 3/EINEN/REICHS/THALER/date/•initial• **Note:** Reichs 1/3 Thaler.

Date	Mintage	VG	F	VF	XF	Unc
1764A	—	5.00	10.00	20.00	60.00	—
1764F Rare	—	—	—	—	—	—
1765B	—	5.00	12.00	25.00	70.00	—
1765F Rare	—	—	—	—	—	—
1767B	—	5.00	12.00	25.00	70.00	—
1768B	—	5.00	12.00	25.00	70.00	—
1768E	—	7.00	15.00	30.00	75.00	—
1769B	—	5.00	12.00	25.00	70.00	—
1769E	—	7.00	15.00	30.00	75.00	—
1770A	—	5.00	10.00	20.00	60.00	—
1770B	—	5.00	12.00	25.00	70.00	—
1771A	—	5.00	10.00	20.00	60.00	—
1771B	—	5.00	12.00	25.00	70.00	—
1772A	—	5.00	10.00	20.00	60.00	—
1772B	—	5.00	12.00	25.00	70.00	—
1773A	—	5.00	10.00	20.00	60.00	—
1773B	—	5.00	12.00	25.00	70.00	—
1773E	—	7.00	15.00	30.00	75.00	—
1774A	—	5.00	10.00	20.00	60.00	—

KM# 329 1/3 THALER (1/2 Gulden)
8.3520 g., 0.6660 Silver 0.1788 oz. ASW **Ruler:** Friedrich II **Obverse:** Old head **Obv. Legend:** FRIDERICUS BORUSSORUM REX **Reverse:** Value, date within palm and laurel branches **Rev. Legend:** EINEN/REICHS/THALER/date/•initial•

Date	Mintage	VG	F	VF	XF	Unc
1774A	—	5.00	15.00	30.00	85.00	—
1774B	—	5.00	12.00	25.00	70.00	—
1774E	—	7.00	15.00	30.00	80.00	—
1775A	—	5.00	15.00	30.00	85.00	—
1775B	—	5.00	12.00	25.00	70.00	—
1775E	—	7.00	15.00	30.00	80.00	—
1776B	—	5.00	12.00	25.00	70.00	—
1776E	—	7.00	15.00	30.00	80.00	—
1777B	868,000	5.00	12.00	25.00	70.00	—
1778B	870,000	5.00	12.00	25.00	70.00	—
1779B	446,000	5.00	12.00	25.00	70.00	—
1779E	343,000	7.00	15.00	30.00	80.00	—
1780B	—	5.00	12.00	25.00	70.00	—
1780E	672,000	7.00	15.00	30.00	80.00	—
1781E	—	7.00	15.00	30.00	80.00	—
1783B	601,000	5.00	12.00	25.00	70.00	—
1784B	52,000	5.00	12.00	25.00	70.00	—
1786A	—	5.00	15.00	30.00	85.00	—
1786B	—	5.00	12.00	25.00	70.00	—
1786E	—	7.00	15.00	30.00	80.00	—

KM# 344 1/3 THALER (1/2 Gulden)
8.3520 g., 0.6660 Silver 0.1788 oz. ASW **Ruler:** Friedrich Wilhelm II **Obverse:** Armored bust right **Obv. Legend:** FRID. WIHELM KOENIG VON PREUSSEN **Reverse:** Crowned arms divide date, "A" below arms

Date	Mintage	VG	F	VF	XF	Unc
1786A	—	10.00	15.00	30.00	65.00	—
1787A	—	10.00	15.00	30.00	65.00	—
1787B	—	10.00	15.00	30.00	65.00	—
1787E	—	15.00	25.00	40.00	100	—
1788A	—	10.00	15.00	30.00	65.00	—
1788B	—	10.00	15.00	30.00	65.00	—
1788E	—	15.00	25.00	40.00	100	—
1789A	—	10.00	15.00	30.00	65.00	—
1789B	—	10.00	15.00	30.00	65.00	—
1789E	—	15.00	25.00	40.00	100	—
1790A	—	10.00	15.00	30.00	65.00	—
1790B	—	10.00	15.00	30.00	65.00	—
1790E	—	15.00	25.00	40.00	100	—
1791A	—	10.00	15.00	30.00	65.00	—
1791E	—	15.00	25.00	40.00	100	—
1792A	—	10.00	15.00	30.00	65.00	—
1792E	—	15.00	25.00	40.00	100	—
1793A	—	10.00	15.00	30.00	65.00	—
1793B	—	10.00	15.00	30.00	65.00	—
1793E	—	15.00	25.00	40.00	100	—
1794E	—	15.00	25.00	40.00	100	—
1795E	—	15.00	25.00	40.00	100	—
1796A	—	10.00	15.00	30.00	65.00	—
1796B	—	10.00	15.00	30.00	65.00	—
1796E	—	15.00	25.00	40.00	100	—
1797B	—	10.00	15.00	30.00	65.00	—
1797E	—	15.00	25.00	40.00	100	—
1798E	—	15.00	25.00	40.00	100	—

KM# E290 1/3 THALER
7.7900 g., Silver, 27 mm. **Ruler:** Elisabeth I of Russia **Obverse:** Crowned bust to right **Obv. Legend:** ELISAB: I: D:G: IMP: TOT: RUSS. **Reverse:** Crowned Prussian eagle, date divided by claws to far left and right, 2-line inscription in exergue **Rev. Inscription:** 3. EIN. R. TH/COUR. **Note:** D#2244-55.

Date	Mintage	VG	F	VF	XF	Unc
1761	470,059	60.00	100	250	525	—

KM# 339 1/3 THALER
Silver **Ruler:** Friedrich II **Mint:** Konigsberg **Obverse:** Laureate head to right **Obv. Legend:** FRIDERICUS BORUSSORUM REX. **Reverse:** 4-line inscription in palm and laurel wreath, date divided by mintmark below **Rev. Inscription:** 3/EINEN/REICHS/ THALER. **Note:** D#2389.

Date	Mintage	VG	F	VF	XF	Unc
1778E	—	—	—	—	—	—

KM# 126 1/2 THALER
Silver **Ruler:** Friedrich I **Mint:** Berlin **Subject:** Homage of Berlin **Obverse:** Bust right **Reverse:** 7-line inscription with Roman numeral date

Date	Mintage	VG	F	VF	XF	Unc
1714 IFS	—	350	650	1,200	2,000	—

KM# 127 1/2 THALER
Silver **Ruler:** Friedrich Wilhelm I **Mint:** Konigsberg **Subject:** Homage of Konigsberg **Obverse:** Armored bust right **Reverse:** Inscription

Date	Mintage	VG	F	VF	XF	Unc
1714 CG	—	250	525	1,000	1,850	—

KM# 195 1/2 THALER
Silver **Ruler:** Friedrich Wilhelm I **Mint:** Berlin **Subject:** Homage of Stettin **Reverse:** Inscription in straight lines

Date	Mintage	VG	F	VF	XF	Unc
1721 L	—	450	875	1,600	2,500	—

KM# 196 1/2 THALER
Silver **Ruler:** Friedrich Wilhelm I **Obverse:** Armored bust right **Obv. Legend:** FRID • WILH • D • G • REX • BORVSS • EL • BRAND • **Reverse:** Inscription in curved lines

Date	Mintage	VG	F	VF	XF	Unc
1721 L	—	450	875	1,600	2,500	—

KM# 254 1/2 THALER
11.1300 g., 0.7500 Silver 0.2684 oz. ASW **Ruler:** Friedrich II **Obverse:** Armored bust right **Obv. Legend:** FRIDERICVS BORVSSORVM REX **Reverse:** Crowned eagle above flags and cannons, 'B' divides date below **Note:** Varieties exist.

Date	Mintage	VG	F	VF	XF	Unc
1750A	—	35.00	55.00	100	180	—
1750 L-A	—	35.00	55.00	100	180	—
1750 LB-A	—	35.00	55.00	100	180	—
1751 B	—	40.00	60.00	120	225	—
1751 C	—	75.00	120	260	575	—
1752 B	—	40.00	60.00	120	225	—

KM# 304 1/2 THALER
11.1300 g., 0.7500 Silver 0.2684 oz. ASW **Ruler:** Friedrich II **Obverse:** Laureate head right **Obv. Legend:** FRIDERICUS BORUSSORUM REX **Reverse:** Crowned eagle above flags and cannons, 'A' divides date below **Note:** Reichs 1/2 Thaler.

Date	Mintage	VG	F	VF	XF	Unc
1764A	—	10.00	20.00	45.00	150	—
1764A *	—	10.00	20.00	45.00	150	—
1764E	—	45.00	110	250	450	—
1764F	—	30.00	50.00	135	300	—
1765A	—	10.00	20.00	45.00	150	—
1765A *	—	10.00	20.00	45.00	150	—
1765F	—	30.00	50.00	135	300	—
1766A	—	10.00	20.00	45.00	150	—
1767A	—	10.00	20.00	45.00	150	—
1767B	—	15.00	25.00	50.00	160	—

KM# 305 1/2 THALER
11.1300 g., 0.7500 Silver 0.2684 oz. ASW **Ruler:** Friedrich II **Mint:** Magdeburg **Obverse:** Head right **Obv. Legend:** FRIDERICUS BORUSSORUM REX. **Reverse:** Crowned eagle above flags and cannons, 'F' divides date below

Date	Mintage	VG	F	VF	XF	Unc
1764F	—	—	—	—	—	—

KM# 345 1/2 THALER
11.1300 g., 0.7500 Silver 0.2684 oz. ASW **Ruler:** Friedrich II **Mint:** Berlin **Subject:** King's Death **Obverse:** Laureate head right **Obv. Legend:** FRIDERICUS BORUSSORUM REX **Reverse:** Crowned eagle above flags and cannons, 'A' divides date below

Date	Mintage	VG	F	VF	XF	Unc
1786A	—	265	475	700	1,100	—

KM# 346 1/2 THALER
11.1300 g., 0.7500 Silver 0.2684 oz. ASW **Ruler:** Friedrich II **Subject:** Cornerstone Laying At Bellevue Castle **Obverse:** Old head **Reverse:** Castle

Date	Mintage	VG	F	VF	XF	Unc
1786	—	150	210	300	425	—

KM# 12 2/3 THALER (Gulden)
Silver **Ruler:** Friedrich I **Mint:** Berlin **Obverse:** Titles unbroken in legend **Obv. Legend:** FRID • D • G • REX BORVSSIAE • EL • BR • **Reverse:** Value: 2/3 **Rev. Legend:** SUUM - CUIQUE • **Note:** Varieties exist.

Date	Mintage	VG	F	VF	XF	Unc
1701 CS	163,000	125	300	600	1,000	—
1702 CS	246,000	125	300	600	1,000	—
1703 CS	Inc. above	125	300	600	1,000	—
1704 CS	69,000	125	300	600	1,000	—
1705 CS	152,000	125	300	600	1,000	—
1706 CS	148,000	125	300	600	1,000	—
1707 CS	105,000	125	300	600	1,000	—
1709 CS	75,000	125	300	600	1,000	—

KM# 13 2/3 THALER (Gulden)
Silver **Ruler:** Friedrich I **Mint:** Magdeburg **Obverse:** Head right **Obv. Legend:** FRIDERICUS REX PRUSSIÆ **Reverse:** Crowned complex arms, value below **Rev. Legend:** SUUM - CUIQUE **Note:** Varieties exist.

Date	Mintage	VG	F	VF	XF	Unc
1701 HFH	—	200	425	800	1,250	—
1702 HFH	—	200	425	800	1,250	—
1703 HFH	—	200	425	800	1,250	—

KM# 43 2/3 THALER (Gulden)
Silver **Ruler:** Friedrich I **Obverse:** Head right **Obv. Legend:** FRIDERICUS - REX PRUSSIÆ **Reverse:** Very large shield of arms **Note:** Varieties exist.

Date	Mintage	VG	F	VF	XF	Unc
1703 HFH	—	200	425	800	1,250	—
1704 HFH	—	200	425	800	1,250	—
1705 HFH	—	200	425	800	1,250	—
1706 HFH	—	200	425	800	1,250	—

KM# 61 2/3 THALER (Gulden)
Silver **Ruler:** Friedrich I **Mint:** Berlin **Obverse:** Titles divided by top of laurel wreath on King's head **Obv. Legend:** FRI • D • G • REX - BORUSS • EL • BR • **Reverse:** Crowned complex arms, date divided below **Note:** Varieties exist

Date	Mintage	VG	F	VF	XF	Unc
1705 CS	Inc. above	125	300	600	1,000	—
1706 CS	Inc. above	125	300	600	1,000	—
1707 CS	Inc. above	125	300	600	1,000	—
1708 CS	78,000	125	300	600	1,000	—
1709 CS	Inc. above	125	300	600	1,000	—
1710 CS	34,000	125	300	600	1,000	—

KM# 62 2/3 THALER (Gulden)
Silver **Ruler:** Friedrich I **Mint:** Minden **Reverse:** Date and initials divided by arms **Note:** Varieties exist

Date	Mintage	VG	F	VF	XF	Unc
1705 BH Rare	—	—	—	—	—	—
1706 BH Rare	—	—	—	—	—	—

KM# 67 2/3 THALER (Gulden)
Silver **Ruler:** Friedrich I **Mint:** Magdeburg **Obverse:** Draped, laureate bust right **Obv. Legend:** FRIDERICUS - REX PRUSSIÆ **Reverse:** Crowned complex arms, value below divides date **Note:** Smaller bust and shield, varieties exist

Date	Mintage	VG	F	VF	XF	Unc
1706 HFH	—	200	425	800	1,250	—
1707 HFH	—	200	425	800	1,250	—
1708 HFH	—	200	425	800	1,250	—
1709 HFH	—	200	425	800	1,250	—
1710 HFH	—	200	425	800	1,250	—
1711 HFH	—	200	425	800	1,250	—
1712 HFH	—	200	425	800	1,250	—
1713 HFH	—	200	425	800	1,250	—

KM# 77 2/3 THALER (Gulden)
Silver **Ruler:** Friedrich I **Obverse:** Thinner bust **Note:** Varieties exist.

Date	Mintage	VG	F	VF	XF	Unc
1707 CS	Inc. above	125	300	600	1,000	—
1708 CS	Inc. above	125	300	600	1,000	—
1709 CS	Inc. above	125	300	600	1,000	—
1710 CS	Inc. above	125	300	600	1,000	—

KM# 74 2/3 THALER (Gulden)
Silver **Ruler:** Friedrich I **Mint:** Berlin **Obverse:** Laureate head right **Reverse:** Crowned arms divide date, value divides initials **Note:** Similar to KM#12, but arms divide date, value divides initials

Date	Mintage	VG	F	VF	XF	Unc
1707 CS	—	125	300	600	1,000	—

Note: Mintage included in KM#12

KM# 75 2/3 THALER (Gulden)
Silver **Ruler:** Friedrich I **Obverse:** Laurel divides titles **Reverse:** Crowned arms divide date, value divides initials **Note:** Similar to KM#61, but arms divide date, value divides initials.

Date	Mintage	VG	F	VF	XF	Unc
1707 CS	—	125	300	600	1,000	—

Note: Mintage included in KM#61

KM# 76 2/3 THALER (Gulden)
Silver **Ruler:** Friedrich I **Obverse:** Full, large bust right **Reverse:** Crwoned arms, value below divides date **Note:** Similar to KM#61, with full, large bust. Varieties exist.

Date	Mintage	VG	F	VF	XF	Unc
1707 CS	Inc. above	125	300	600	1,000	—
1708 CS	Inc. above	125	300	600	1,000	—
1710 CS	Inc. above	125	300	600	1,000	—
1711 CS	31,000	125	300	600	1,000	—
1712 CS	55,000	125	300	600	1,000	—

KM# 81 2/3 THALER (Gulden)
Silver **Ruler:** Friedrich I **Obverse:** Head right **Reverse:** Crowned complex arms, value below divides date **Note:** Similar to KM#12, but unadorned bust. Varieties exist.

Date	Mintage	VG	F	VF	XF	Unc
1708 CS	Inc. above	125	300	600	1,000	—
1709 CS	Inc. above	125	300	600	1,000	—

KM# 107 2/3 THALER (Gulden)
Silver **Ruler:** Friedrich Wilhelm I **Mint:** Magdeburg **Note:** Varieties exist

Date	Mintage	VG	F	VF	XF	Unc
1713 HFH	—	200	450	800	1,250	—
1714 HFH	—	200	450	800	1,250	—
1715 HFH	—	200	450	800	1,250	—

KM# 104 2/3 THALER (Gulden)
Silver **Ruler:** Friedrich I **Obverse:** Laureate bust right **Reverse:** Crowned 11-fold arms divide date and initials, value: 2/3 below divides FEIN - SILB

Date	Mintage	VG	F	VF	XF	Unc
1713 CS	68,000	300	650	1,200	1,850	—

KM# 105 2/3 THALER (Gulden)
Silver **Ruler:** Friedrich I **Reverse:** Value 2/3

Date	Mintage	VG	F	VF	XF	Unc
1713 IFS	Inc. above	125	300	600	1,000	—

KM# 106 2/3 THALER (Gulden)
Silver **Ruler:** Friedrich I **Reverse:** Ornately-shaped arms divide date, value: 2/3 in oval divides initials

Date	Mintage	VG	F	VF	XF	Unc
1713 IFS	Inc. above	125	300	600	1,000	—

KM# 128 2/3 THALER (Gulden)
Silver **Ruler:** Friedrich Wilhelm I **Mint:** Berlin **Obverse:** Wigged bust right **Reverse:** Ornate 6-fold arms divide date, large crown above, value: 2/3 below divides initials

Date	Mintage	VG	F	VF	XF	Unc
1714 R/IFS	32,000	125	300	600	1,000	—

KM# 130 2/3 THALER (Gulden)
Silver **Ruler:** Friedrich Wilhelm I **Reverse:** 12-fold arms

Date	Mintage	VG	F	VF	XF	Unc
1714 IFS	Inc. above	200	450	800	1,250	—

KM# 129 2/3 THALER (Gulden)
Silver **Ruler:** Friedrich Wilhelm I **Obverse:** Laureate bust **Note:** Varieties exist.

Date	Mintage	VG	F	VF	XF	Unc
1714 IFS	Inc. above	200	450	800	1,250	—
1715 IFS	16,000	200	450	800	1,250	—

KM# 147 2/3 THALER (Gulden)
Silver **Ruler:** Friedrich Wilhelm I **Obverse:** Wigged bust **Note:** Varieties exist.

Date	Mintage	VG	F	VF	XF	Unc
1715 HFH	—	200	450	800	1,250	—
1716 HFH	—	200	450	800	1,250	—

KM# 145 2/3 THALER (Gulden)
Silver **Ruler:** Friedrich Wilhelm I **Reverse:** 11-fold arms

Date	Mintage	VG	F	VF	XF	Unc
1715 IFS	Inc. above	200	450	800	1,250	—

KM# 146 2/3 THALER (Gulden)
Silver **Ruler:** Friedrich Wilhelm I **Mint:** Magdeburg **Obverse:** Small, short-haired bust **Reverse:** Crowned 11-fold arms divide date and initials, value: 1/3 below

Date	Mintage	VG	F	VF	XF	Unc
1715 HFH	—	200	450	800	1,250	—

KM# 153 2/3 THALER (Gulden)
Silver **Ruler:** Friedrich Wilhelm I **Mint:** Berlin **Obverse:** Laureate bust **Reverse:** 12-fold arms **Note:** Varieties exist

Date	Mintage	VG	F	VF	XF	Unc
1716 IFS	13,000	200	450	800	1,250	—
1717 IFS	27,000	200	450	800	1,250	—

KM# 154 2/3 THALER (Gulden)
Silver **Ruler:** Friedrich Wilhelm I **Obverse:** Wigged bust **Reverse:** 12-fold arms **Note:** Varieties exist.

Date	Mintage	VG	F	VF	XF	Unc
1716 HFH	—	200	450	800	1,250	—
1717 HFH	—	200	450	800	1,250	—
1718 HFH	—	200	450	800	1,250	—

KM# 160 2/3 THALER (Gulden)
Silver **Ruler:** Friedrich Wilhelm I **Mint:** Berlin **Obverse:** Wigged bust right **Reverse:** Large oval 13-fold arms, crown above divides date, value: 2/3 below divides initials **Note:** Varieties exist

Date	Mintage	VG	F	VF	XF	Unc
1717 IFS	Inc. above	200	450	800	1,250	—
1718 IFS	49,000	200	450	800	1,250	—

KM# 170 2/3 THALER (Gulden)
Silver **Ruler:** Friedrich Wilhelm I **Mint:** Magdeburg **Obverse:** Armored bust right **Reverse:** Crowned oval 13-fold arms divide date **Note:** Varieties exist

Date	Mintage	VG	F	VF	XF	Unc
1718 HFH	—	200	450	800	1,250	—
1719 HFH	—	200	450	800	1,250	—

KM# 178 2/3 THALER (Gulden)
Silver **Ruler:** Friedrich Wilhelm I **Mint:** Berlin **Obverse:** Smaller bust **Obv. Legend:** FRID • WILH • D • G • REX • BORVSS • EL • BRAND • **Reverse:** Crowned complex arms, value below **Note:** Varieties exist

Date	Mintage	VG	F	VF	XF	Unc
1719 IGN	65,000	250	525	950	1,350	—
1719 L/IGN	Inc. above	250	525	950	1,350	—
1720 IGN	59,000	250	525	950	1,350	—
1720 L/IGN	Inc. above	250	525	950	1,350	—
1721 L/IGN	2,274	250	525	950	1,350	—
1722 L/IGN	22,000	250	525	950	1,350	—
1723 L/IGN	36,000	250	525	950	1,350	—
1724 L/IGN	26,000	250	525	950	1,350	—

KM# 179 2/3 THALER (Gulden)
Silver **Ruler:** Friedrich Wilhelm I **Mint:** Magdeburg **Obverse:** Armored bust right **Reverse:** Crowned oval 13-fold arms divide date **Note:** Similar to KM#170 but smaller bust with shorter hair

Date	Mintage	VG	F	VF	XF	Unc
1719 HFH	—	200	450	800	1,250	—

KM# 231 2/3 THALER (Gulden)
Silver **Ruler:** Friedrich II **Obverse:** Draped bust right **Obv. Legend:** FRIDERICVS BORVSSORVM REX **Reverse:** Crwoned eagle arms within baroque frame

Date	Mintage	VG	F	VF	XF	Unc
1741 EGN	3,096	750	1,050	2,000	3,500	—

KM# 363 2/3 THALER (Gulden)
17.3230 g., 0.7500 Silver 0.4177 oz. ASW **Ruler:** Friedrich Wilhelm II **Obverse:** Crowned oval arms within wreath **Reverse:** Denomination and date **Note:** Gulden 2/3 Thaler.

Date	Mintage	VG	F	VF	XF	Unc
1796	—	25.00	50.00	90.00	225	—
1797	—	25.00	50.00	90.00	225	—
1801	—	25.00	50.00	90.00	225	—

KM# 364 2/3 THALER (Gulden)
17.3230 g., 0.7500 Silver 0.4177 oz. ASW **Ruler:** Friedrich Wilhelm II **Obverse:** Crowned arms in palm branches

Date	Mintage	VG	F	VF	XF	Unc
1797	—	30.00	65.00	100	250	—

KM# 365 2/3 THALER (Gulden)
17.3230 g., 0.7500 Silver 0.4177 oz. ASW **Ruler:** Friedrich Wilhelm II **Obv. Legend:** FR. WILH. II..

Date	Mintage	VG	F	VF	XF	Unc
1797	—	30.00	65.00	100	250	—

KM# 14 THALER
Silver **Ruler:** Friedrich I **Mint:** Berlin **Subject:** Coronation of Friedrich I **Obverse:** Bust right, CG and 1701 below **Obv. Legend:** FRIDERICUS REX **Reverse:** 4 crowned double F's and R's around arms **Rev. Legend:** SUUM - CIUQUE **Note:** Dav. #2553. Varieties exist.

Date	Mintage	VG	F	VF	XF	Unc
1701 CG	—	650	1,350	2,750	5,000	—

KM# 16 THALER
Silver **Ruler:** Friedrich I **Reverse:** Eagle above 4 tents **Note:** Dav. #2554A.

Date	Mintage	VG	F	VF	XF	Unc
1701 CS	—	400	850	1,650	3,000	—

KM# 15 THALER
Silver **Ruler:** Friedrich I **Obverse:** Laureate armored bust right **Obv. Legend:** FRIDERICUS • D • G • REX BORVSS • EL • BR • **Reverse:** Crowned eagle flying above 3 mining winch supports (above shafts), SVVMCVIQVE curved over eagle **Rev. Legend:** * PRIMITIAE • METALLIFODINARVM • IN • DVCATV • MAGD • 1701 • **Note:** Rothenburger Mining Thaler. Dav. #2554.

Date	Mintage	VG	F	VF	XF	Unc
1701 CS	—	400	850	1,650	3,000	—

KM# 24 THALER
Silver **Ruler:** Friedrich I **Obverse:** Different bust right **Obv. Legend:** FRIDERICUS • D • G • REX • BORVSS • EL BR • **Reverse:** Crowned eagle holding scepter and globe divides date 1-7-0-2 and C-S **Note:** Dav. #2555.

Date	Mintage	VG	F	VF	XF	Unc
1702 CS	—	500	1,100	2,250	4,000	—

KM# 25 THALER
Silver **Ruler:** Friedrich I **Reverse:** Globe without pearls **Note:** Dav. #2555A.

Date	Mintage	VG	F	VF	XF	Unc
1702 CS	—	500	1,100	2,250	4,000	—

KM# 26 THALER
Silver **Ruler:** Friedrich I **Obverse:** Large bust **Reverse:** Larger eagle, date and initials **Note:** Dav. #2556.

Date	Mintage	VG	F	VF	XF	Unc
1702 CS Rare	—	—	—	—	—	—

KM# 27 THALER
Silver **Ruler:** Friedrich I **Obverse:** Head right **Reverse:** Large crown, smaller eagle **Note:** Dav. #2557.

Date	Mintage	VG	F	VF	XF	Unc
1702 CS	—	850	1,750	3,250	5,500	—

KM# 44 THALER
Silver **Ruler:** Friedrich I **Obverse:** Bust right **Reverse:** Smaller crown **Note:** Dav. #2558.

Date	Mintage	VG	F	VF	XF	Unc
1703 CS	—	850	1,750	3,250	5,500	—

KM# 45 THALER
Silver **Ruler:** Friedrich I **Obverse:** Large bust right **Reverse:** Large crowned eagle **Note:** Dav. #2559.

Date	Mintage	VG	F	VF	XF	Unc
1703 CS	—	850	1,750	3,250	5,500	—

KM# 46 THALER

Silver **Ruler:** Friedrich I **Obverse:** Large, laureate head right **Obv. Legend:** FRID: D • G • REX - BORUSS: EL: BR: **Reverse:** Imperial eagle with monogrammed shield on breast **Note:** Dav. #2560, variety with triangles for periods

Date	Mintage	VG	F	VF	XF	Unc
1703 CS	—	850	1,750	3,250	5,500	—

KM# 47 THALER

Silver **Ruler:** Friedrich I **Obverse:** Draped, laureate bust right **Obv. Legend:** FRIDERICUS • D • G • REX • BORVSS • EL • BR • **Reverse:** Initials divided below **Note:** Dav. #2561. Varieties exist.

Date	Mintage	VG	F	VF	XF	Unc
1703 HF-H	—	1,000	2,000	3,500	6,000	—

KM# 50 THALER

Silver **Ruler:** Friedrich I **Obverse:** Armored, laureate bust right **Reverse:** Crowned FR divides date **Note:** Dav. #2562.

Date	Mintage	VG	F	VF	XF	Unc
1704 CFL	—	650	1,350	2,500	4,250	—

KM# 51 THALER

Silver **Ruler:** Friedrich I **Obverse:** Armored, laureate bust right **Obv. Legend:** FRID • D • G • REX • - BORUSS • EL • BR •, C.F.L. below **Reverse:** Crowned FR in Order chain with divided date and C - S below **Rev. Legend:** SVVM - CVQVE **Note:** Dav. #2563. Varieties exist.

Date	Mintage	VG	F	VF	XF	Unc
1704 CS	—	450	900	1,750	3,250	—
1705	—	450	900	1,750	3,250	—

KM# 63 THALER

Silver **Ruler:** Friedrich I **Obverse:** New bust **Reverse:** Imperial eagle with monogrammmed shield on breast **Note:** Dav. #2564.

Date	Mintage	VG	F	VF	XF	Unc
1705	—	1,200	2,250	4,000	7,000	—

KM# 68 THALER

Silver **Ruler:** Friedrich I **Obverse:** Thick laureate crown, multi-layer armor **Reverse:** Crowned FR in small Order chain **Note:** Dav. #2565.

Date	Mintage	VG	F	VF	XF	Unc
1706	—	650	1,350	2,500	4,250	—

KM# 78 THALER

Silver **Ruler:** Friedrich I **Obverse:** Thick laurels, multi-layer armor **Obv. Legend:** FRID • D • G • REX • - BORUSS • EL • BR • **Reverse:** Large chain, date left and CS right below **Rev. Legend:** SVVM - CVIQVE **Note:** Dav. #2566. Varieties exist.

Date	Mintage	VG	F	VF	XF	Unc
1707	—	400	850	1,650	3,000	—
1708	—	400	850	1,650	3,000	—
1710	—	400	850	1,650	3,000	—
1711	—	400	850	1,650	3,000	—
1712	—	400	850	1,650	3,000	—

KM# 108 THALER

Silver **Ruler:** Friedrich Wilhelm I **Mint:** Magdeburg **Obverse:** Draped, laureate bust right **Obv. Legend:** FRID: WILH: - D • G • REX • BORUSSIAE • **Reverse:** Sun with rays above eagle **Rev. Legend:** NEC - SOLI CEDIT, • HFH • 1713 • below **Note:** Dav. #2568

Date	Mintage	VG	F	VF	XF	Unc
1713 HFH	—	1,000	2,000	3,500	6,000	—
1716 HFH	—	1,000	2,000	3,500	6,000	—

KM# 109 THALER

Silver **Ruler:** Friedrich Wilhelm I **Mint:** Berlin **Obverse:** Bust with mantle covering more of armband **Note:** Dav. #2568A

Date	Mintage	VG	F	VF	XF	Unc
1713	—	1,000	2,000	3,500	6,000	—

KM# 155 THALER

Silver **Ruler:** Friedrich Wilhelm I **Obverse:** Draped, laureate bust right **Reverse:** Sun without rays **Note:** Dav. #2568B.

Date	Mintage	VG	F	VF	XF	Unc
1716	—	1,000	2,000	3,500	6,000	—

KM# 161 THALER

Silver **Ruler:** Friedrich Wilhelm I **Obverse:** Bust right **Reverse:** Crowned shield divides date **Note:** Dav. #2569.

Date	Mintage	VG	F	VF	XF	Unc
1717 IFS	—	650	1,350	2,750	5,000	—

KM# 171 THALER

Silver **Ruler:** Friedrich Wilhelm I **Reverse:** Crowned circular arms in sprays, date divided above **Note:** Dav. #2570.

Date	Mintage	VG	F	VF	XF	Unc
1718 IFS	—	850	1,750	3,250	5,500	—

KM# 172 THALER

Silver **Ruler:** Friedrich Wilhelm I **Obverse:** Armored bust right **Obv. Legend:** FRID • SILH • D • - G • REX • BOR • EL • BR: **Reverse:** Shorter palm branches **Rev. Legend:** I•F•S• below **Note:** Dav. #2570A.

Date	Mintage	VG	F	VF	XF	Unc
1718 IFS	—	850	1,750	3,250	5,500	—

KM# 173 THALER

Silver **Ruler:** Friedrich Wilhelm I **Obverse:** Armored bust right **Obv. Legend:** FRID • WILH • D • G • REX • BOR • EL • BR • DVX • GELDRIAE • **Reverse:** Crowned shield separating date at top, initials at sides **Note:** Dav. #2571.

Date	Mintage	VG	F	VF	XF	Unc
1718 HF-H	—	750	1,500	2,750	4,500	—

KM# 180 THALER

Silver **Ruler:** Friedrich Wilhelm I **Reverse:** Crowned shield-shaped arms divide date above initials below **Note:** Dav. #2573.

Date	Mintage	VG	F	VF	XF	Unc
1719 IG-N Rare	—	—	—	—	—	—

KM# 181 THALER

Silver **Ruler:** Friedrich Wilhelm I **Reverse:** Initials below crowned shield **Note:** Dav. #2575.

Date	Mintage	VG	F	VF	XF	Unc
1719 L/IGN	—	850	1,750	3,250	5,500	—

KM# 183 THALER
Silver **Ruler:** Friedrich Wilhelm I **Obverse:** Armored bust right **Obv. Legend:** FRID • WILH • D • G • REX • BORVSSIAE • EL • BRAND • **Reverse:** Crowned complex arms within branches **Note:** Dav. #2577A.

Date	Mintage	VG	F	VF	XF	Unc
1719 L/IGN	—	850	1,750	3,250	5,500	—

KM# 184 THALER
Silver **Ruler:** Friedrich Wilhelm I **Mint:** Magdeburg **Obverse:** Head breaks legend **Obv. Legend:** D.G.-REX.. **Note:** Dav. #2579

Date	Mintage	VG	F	VF	XF	Unc
1719 HFH Rare	—	—	—	—	—	—

KM# 182 THALER
Silver **Ruler:** Friedrich Wilhelm I **Note:** Similar to KM#183 but obverse legends ends: ...BRANDENB. Dav. #2577.

Date	Mintage	VG	F	VF	XF	Unc
1719 L/IGN	—	850	1,750	3,250	5,500	—
1727 EGN	—	850	1,750	3,250	5,500	—

KM# 232 THALER
Silver **Ruler:** Friedrich Wilhelm I **Obverse:** Armored bust with Order chain right **Obv. Legend:** FRIDERICVS BORVSSORVM REX **Reverse:** Crowned eagle arms within cartouche, date divided above **Note:** Dav. #2581.

Date	Mintage	VG	F	VF	XF	Unc
1741 EGN	1,486	800	1,700	3,200	5,500	—

KM# 256 THALER
Silver **Ruler:** Friedrich II **Obverse:** Draped bust right **Obv. Legend:** FRIDERICVS BORVSSORVM REX

Reverse: Crowned eagle above flags, drums and cannons **Rev. Legend:** EIN REICHS THALER **Note:** Dav. #2583.

Date	Mintage	VG	F	VF	XF	Unc
1750B	175,000	60.00	120	250	450	—
1751B	107,000	60.00	120	250	450	—
1752B	Inc. above	60.00	120	250	450	—

KM# 255 THALER
Silver **Ruler:** Friedrich II **Obverse:** Armored bust right **Obv. Legend:** FRIDERICVS BORVSSORVM REX **Reverse:** Crowned eagle above flags, 'A' divides date below **Rev. Legend:** EIN REICHS THALER **Note:** Reichs Thaler. Dav. #2582.

Date	Mintage	VG	F	VF	XF	Unc
1750A	—	40.00	80.00	160	325	—
1750 L-A	—	40.00	80.00	160	325	—
1750 LB-A	—	40.00	80.00	160	325	—
1751A	220,000	40.00	80.00	160	325	—
1752A	—	40.00	80.00	160	325	—

KM# 266 THALER
Silver **Ruler:** Friedrich II **Mint:** Cleve **Obverse:** Armored, draped bust right **Obv. Legend:** FRIDERICVS BORVSSORVM REX **Reverse:** Crowned eagle above flags and cannons **Rev. Legend:** EIN REICHS THALER **Note:** Dav. #2584.

Date	Mintage	VG	F	VF	XF	Unc
1751C	—	70.00	140	325	600	—
1752C	—	70.00	140	325	600	—
1753C	—	70.00	140	325	600	—

KM# 270 THALER
Silver **Ruler:** Friedrich II **Mint:** Berlin **Obverse:** Head right **Note:** Dav. #2585.

Date	Mintage	VG	F	VF	XF	Unc
1752A Rare	—	—	—	—	—	—

Note: Some consider this a pattern

KM# 279 THALER
Silver **Ruler:** Friedrich II **Mint:** Berlin **Obverse:** Crowned bust right **Reverse:** Eagle in crowned ornate baroque frame, date **Note:** Species Thaler. Dav. #2592.

Date	Mintage	VG	F	VF	XF	Unc
1755A	16	—	—	6,000	9,000	—

Note: Some consider this a pattern

KM# 306.1 THALER
22.2720 g., 0.7500 Silver 0.5370 oz. ASW **Ruler:** Friedrich II **Mint:** Berlin **Rev. Legend:** EIN REICHS THALER **Note:** Reichs Thaler. Dav. #2586.

Date	Mintage	VG	F	VF	XF	Unc
1764A	—	30.00	65.00	125	250	—
1764 *A*	—	35.00	70.00	135	275	—
1765A	—	30.00	65.00	125	250	—
1765 *A*	—	35.00	70.00	135	275	—
1766A	—	30.00	65.00	125	250	—
1767A	—	30.00	65.00	125	250	—
1768A	255,000	30.00	65.00	125	250	—
1769A	412,000	30.00	65.00	125	250	—
1770A	621,000	30.00	65.00	125	250	—
1771A	1,085,000	30.00	65.00	125	250	—
1772A	441,000	30.00	65.00	125	250	—
1773A	109,000	30.00	65.00	125	250	—
1774A	240,000	30.00	65.00	125	250	—

KM# 306.2 THALER
22.2720 g., 0.7500 Silver 0.5370 oz. ASW **Ruler:** Friedrich II **Note:** Dav. #2586A.

Date	Mintage	VG	F	VF	XF	Unc
1764 .B.	—	40.00	85.00	175	350	—
1765 .B.	—	40.00	85.00	175	350	—
1766 .B.	—	40.00	85.00	175	350	—
1767 .B.	—	40.00	85.00	175	350	—
1768 .B.	—	40.00	85.00	175	350	—
1770 .B.	—	40.00	85.00	175	350	—
1770B	—	40.00	85.00	175	350	—
1771 .B.	—	40.00	85.00	175	350	—
1771B	—	40.00	85.00	175	350	—
1772 .B.	—	40.00	85.00	175	350	—

KM# 306.4 THALER
22.2720 g., 0.7500 Silver 0.5370 oz. ASW **Ruler:** Friedrich II **Mint:** Konigsberg **Note:** Dav. #2586C.

Date	Mintage	VG	F	VF	XF	Unc
1764E	—	65.00	150	375	1,000	—
1772E	—	65.00	150	375	1,000	—

KM# 306.5 THALER
22.2720 g., 0.7500 Silver 0.5370 oz. ASW **Ruler:** Friedrich II **Mint:** Magdeburg **Note:** Dav. #2586D.

Date	Mintage	VG	F	VF	XF	Unc
1764F	—	60.00	150	300	700	—
1765F	—	60.00	150	300	700	—
1766F	—	60.00	150	300	700	—
1767F	—	60.00	150	300	700	—

KM# 308 THALER
22.2720 g., 0.7500 Silver 0.5370 oz. ASW **Ruler:** Friedrich II **Mint:** Cleve **Obverse:** Laureate head right **Obv. Legend:** FRIDERICUS BORUSSORUM: REX. **Reverse:** Crowned eagle above flags and cannons **Rev. Legend:** EIN REICHS THALER **Note:** Dav. #2587.

Date	Mintage	VG	F	VF	XF	Unc
1764C	—	100	225	450	900	—
1765 *C*	—	75.00	175	350	750	—

KM# 307 THALER
22.2720 g., 0.7500 Silver 0.5370 oz. ASW **Ruler:** Friedrich II **Mint:** Magdeburg **Obverse:** Laureate head right **Obv. Legend:** FRIDERICUS BORUSSORUM: REX. **Reverse:** Crowned eagle above flags and drums, 'F' divides date below **Rev. Legend:** EIN REICHS THALER **Note:** Dav. #2588.

Date	Mintage	VG	F	VF	XF	Unc
1764F	—	60.00	150	300	700	—

KM# 314 THALER

22.2720 g., 0.7500 Silver 0.5370 oz. ASW **Ruler:** Friedrich II **Mint:** Berlin **Obverse:** Draped bust right **Obv. Legend:** FRIDERICUS BORUSSORUM REX **Reverse:** Crowned eagle above flags and cannons, 'A' divides date below **Rev. Legend:** EIN BANCO THALER **Note:** Banco Thaler. Dav. #2593.

Date	Mintage	F	VF	XF	Unc
1765A	—	1,000	1,600	2,800	4,800

KM# 316 THALER

22.2720 g., 0.7500 Silver 0.5370 oz. ASW **Ruler:** Friedrich II **Obverse:** Multi-layers on mantle **Obv. Legend:** FRIDERICVS BORVSSORVM REX **Reverse:** Crowned complex arms **Rev. Legend:** NACH DEM FVS DER ALBERTVS THALER **Note:** Albertus Thaler. Dav. #2594.

Date	Mintage	F	VF	XF	Unc
1766(F)	—	1,000	1,750	2,500	4,500
1767(A)	—	1,000	1,750	2,500	4,500

KM# 317 THALER

22.2720 g., 0.7500 Silver 0.5370 oz. ASW **Ruler:** Friedrich II **Obverse:** Laureate bust right **Obv. Legend:** FRIDERICVS BORVSSORVM REX **Reverse:** Crowned eagle with crowned arms on breast **Rev. Legend:** MAR: BRAN: SAC: ROM; IMP: ARCAM - ET ELEC • SVP • DVX • SILES: **Note:** Levant Trade Thaler. Dav. #2595.

Date	Mintage	F	VF	XF	Unc
1766(A)	—	1,000	1,750	2,500	4,500
1767(A)	—	1,000	1,750	2,500	4,500

KM# 318 THALER

22.2720 g., 0.7500 Silver 0.5370 oz. ASW **Ruler:** Friedrich II **Obverse:** Laureate bust right **Note:** Levant Trade Thaler. Dav. #2596.

Date	Mintage	F	VF	XF	Unc
1767(A)	—	5,000	8,500	12,000	17,500

KM# 332.1 THALER

22.2720 g., 0.7500 Silver 0.5370 oz. ASW **Ruler:** Friedrich II **Mint:** Berlin **Obverse:** Laureate head right **Obv. Legend:** FRIDERICUS BORUSSORUM REX **Reverse:** Crowned eagle above flags and cannons, 'A' divides date below **Rev. Legend:** EIN REICHS THALER **Note:** Reichsthaler. Dav. #2590.

Date	Mintage	VG	F	VF	XF	Unc
1775A	505,000	30.00	60.00	125	225	—
1776A	392,000	30.00	60.00	125	225	—
1777A	420,000	30.00	60.00	125	225	—
1778A	551,000	30.00	60.00	125	225	—
1779A	399,000	30.00	60.00	125	225	—
1780A	211,000	30.00	60.00	125	225	—
1781A	229,000	30.00	60.00	125	225	—
1782A	247,000	30.00	60.00	125	225	—
1783A	545,000	30.00	60.00	125	225	—
1784A	3,347,000	30.00	60.00	125	225	—
1785A	1,622,000	30.00	60.00	125	225	—
1786A	193,000	30.00	60.00	125	225	—

KM# 332.2 THALER

22.2720 g., 0.7500 Silver 0.5370 oz. ASW **Ruler:** Friedrich II **Note:** Dav. #2590B.

Date	Mintage	VG	F	VF	XF	Unc
1780B	189,000	30.00	65.00	135	250	—
1781B	188,000	30.00	65.00	135	250	—
1782B	72,000	30.00	65.00	135	250	—
1783B	19,000	30.00	65.00	135	250	—
1784B	348,000	30.00	65.00	135	250	—
1785B	625,000	30.00	65.00	135	250	—
1786B	234,000	30.00	65.00	135	250	—

KM# 332.3 THALER

22.2720 g., 0.7500 Silver 0.5370 oz. ASW **Ruler:** Friedrich II **Mint:** Konigsberg **Note:** Dav. #2590C.

Date	Mintage	VG	F	VF	XF	Unc
1781E	296,000	30.00	65.00	150	300	—
1782E	84,000	30.00	65.00	150	300	—
1783E	171,000	30.00	65.00	150	300	—
1784E	287,000	30.00	65.00	150	300	—
1785E	150,000	30.00	65.00	150	300	—
1786E	100,000	30.00	65.00	150	300	—

KM# 348.1 THALER

22.2720 g., 0.7500 Silver 0.5370 oz. ASW **Ruler:** Friedrich Wilhelm II **Mint:** Berlin **Obverse:** Armored, draped bust right **Obv. Legend:** FRIED: WILHELM KOENIG VON PREUSSEN **Reverse:** Imperial eagle with orb and sceptre on ledge above branches **Rev. Legend:** EIN REICHS THALER **Note:** Dav. #2597.

Date	Mintage	VG	F	VF	XF	Unc
1786A	—	30.00	50.00	100	200	—
1787A	—	30.00	50.00	100	200	—
1788A	—	30.00	50.00	100	200	—
1789A	—	30.00	50.00	100	200	—
1790A	—	30.00	50.00	100	200	—

KM# 347 THALER

22.2720 g., 0.7500 Silver 0.5370 oz. ASW **Ruler:** Friedrich II **Obverse:** Laureate head right **Obv. Legend:** FRIDERICUS BORUSSORUM REX **Reverse:** Periods at sides of "A" mint mark **Rev. Legend:** EIN REICHS THALER **Note:** Dav. #2590A.

Date	Mintage	VG	F	VF	XF	Unc
1786 .A.	—	35.00	65.00	150	300	—

KM# 348.2 THALER

22.2720 g., 0.7500 Silver 0.5370 oz. ASW **Ruler:** Friedrich Wilhelm II **Note:** Dav. #2597A.

Date	Mintage	VG	F	VF	XF	Unc
1788B	—	40.00	75.00	125	250	—
1789B	—	40.00	75.00	125	250	—
1790B	—	40.00	75.00	125	250	—
1791B	—	40.00	75.00	125	250	—

KM# 360.1 THALER

22.2720 g., 0.7500 Silver 0.5370 oz. ASW **Ruler:** Friedrich Wilhelm II **Mint:** Berlin **Obverse:** Bust right **Obv. Legend:** FRIED: WILHELM KOENIG VON PREUSSEN **Reverse:** Crowned eagle arms with supporters, value and date below **Rev. Legend:** EIN THALER **Note:** Dav. #2599.

Date	Mintage	VG	F	VF	XF	Unc
1790A	—	25.00	50.00	125	250	—
1791A	—	25.00	50.00	125	250	—
1792A	—	25.00	50.00	125	250	—
1793A	—	25.00	50.00	125	250	—
1794A Open 4	—	25.00	50.00	125	250	—
1794A Closed 4	—	25.00	50.00	125	250	—
1795A	—	25.00	50.00	125	250	—
1796A	—	25.00	50.00	125	250	—
1797A	—	25.00	50.00	125	250	—

KM# 360.2 THALER

22.2720 g., 0.7500 Silver 0.5370 oz. ASW **Ruler:** Friedrich Wilhelm II **Note:** Dav. #2599A.

Date	Mintage	VG	F	VF	XF	Unc
1791B	—	30.00	60.00	135	300	—
1792B	—	30.00	60.00	135	300	—
1793B	—	30.00	60.00	135	300	—
1794B	—	30.00	60.00	135	300	—
1795B	—	30.00	60.00	135	300	—
1796B	—	30.00	60.00	135	300	—
1797B	—	30.00	60.00	135	300	—

KM# 360.3 THALER

22.2720 g., 0.7500 Silver 0.5370 oz. ASW **Ruler:** Friedrich Wilhelm II **Mint:** Konigsberg **Note:** Dav. #2599B.

Date	Mintage	VG	F	VF	XF	Unc
1791E	—	45.00	90.00	200	500	—
1792E	—	45.00	90.00	200	500	—
1793E	—	45.00	90.00	200	500	—
1794E	—	45.00	90.00	200	500	—
1795E	—	45.00	90.00	200	500	—
1797E	—	45.00	90.00	200	500	—

KM# 361 THALER

22.2720 g., 0.7500 Silver 0.5370 oz. ASW **Ruler:** Friedrich Wilhelm II **Mint:** Berlin **Obverse:** Bust right **Obv. Legend:** FRIEDR. WILHELM II KOENIG VON PREUSSEN **Reverse:** Crowned oval arms within branches **Rev. Legend:** ZEHN EINE FEINE MARK **Note:** Convention Thaler. Dav. #2600.

Date	Mintage	VG	F	VF	XF	Unc
1795	—	25.00	50.00	125	250	—

KM# 368 THALER

22.2720 g., 0.7500 Silver 0.5370 oz. ASW **Ruler:** Friedrich Wilhelm III **Obverse:** Uniformed bust left **Obv. Legend:** FRIEDR. WILHELM III KOENIG VON PREUSSEN **Reverse:** Crowned arms with wild men supporters **Rev. Legend:** EIN THALER and date **Note:** Reichs Thaler. Dav. #2603.

Date	Mintage	F	VF	XF	Unc
1797A	—	40.00	75.00	125	400
1798A	—	45.00	85.00	150	500
1799A	—	40.00	75.00	125	400
1799B	—	50.00	120	300	800
1800A	—	40.00	75.00	125	400
1800B	—	60.00	200	550	1,200
1801A	—	35.00	65.00	110	340
1801B	—	55.00	135	400	1,100
1802A	—	35.00	65.00	110	325
1802B	—	35.00	95.00	250	800
1803A	—	35.00	65.00	110	325
1803A	—	—	—	—	—
Note: PRUSSEN, error					
1803B	—	40.00	100	375	650
1804A	—	100	650	2,500	4,250
1805A	—	45.00	110	350	800
1806A	—	45.00	125	400	1,000
1807A	—	45.00	110	325	900
1808A	—	45.00	110	350	950
1808G	33,000	90.00	300	1,500	2,500
1809A	—	40.00	75.00	300	500
1809G	—	200	350	7,500	13,000

KM# 366 THALER

28.0600 g., 0.8680 Silver 0.7830 oz. ASW **Ruler:** Friedrich Wilhelm II **Obverse:** Crowned eagle arms divide date **Obv. Legend:** FRIDER. WILHELM. BORUSS. REX **Reverse:** Crowned 4-fold arms right of wild man **Rev. Legend:** AD NORMAM TALERORUM ALBERTI **Note:** Albertus Thaler. Dav. #2601.

Date	Mintage	F	VF	XF	Unc
1797	—	1,400	2,000	3,500	6,500

KM# 367 THALER

28.0600 g., 0.8680 Silver 0.7830 oz. ASW **Ruler:** Friedrich Wilhelm III **Obverse:** Bust right **Reverse:** Crowned and supported arms with flat top **Note:** Dav. #2602.

Date	Mintage	F	VF	XF	Unc
1797 Rare	—	—	—	—	—
1798 Rare	—	—	—	—	—

KM# 197 1-1/2 THALER

Silver **Ruler:** Friedrich Wilhelm I **Obverse:** Bust right **Reverse:** Crowned oval shield in sprays, divided date above, initials below **Note:** Dav. #2580.

Date	Mintage	VG	F	VF	XF	Unc
1721 L/IGN Rare	—	—	—	—	—	—

KM# 186 2 THALER (3-1/2 Gulden)

Silver **Ruler:** Friedrich Wilhelm I **Reverse:** Initials below shield **Note:** Dav. #2574.

Date	Mintage	VG	F	VF	XF	Unc
1719 L/IGN Rare	—	—	—	—	—	—

KM# 156 2 THALER (3-1/2 Gulden)

Silver **Ruler:** Friedrich Wilhelm I **Obverse:** Draped, laureate bust right **Reverse:** Sun with rays above eagle **Note:** Similar to 1 Thaler, KM#108. Dav. #2567.

Date	Mintage	VG	F	VF	XF	Unc
1716 HFH Rare	—	—	—	—	—	—

KM# 157 2 THALER (3-1/2 Gulden)

Silver **Ruler:** Friedrich Wilhelm I **Obverse:** Draped, laureate bust right **Reverse:** Sun without rays **Note:** Similar to 1 Thaler, KM#155. Dav. #2567A.

Date	Mintage	VG	F	VF	XF	Unc
1716 HFH Rare	—	—	—	—	—	—

KM# 187 2 THALER (3-1/2 Gulden)

Silver **Ruler:** Friedrich Wilhelm I **Obverse:** Armored bust right **Reverse:** Crowned arms within branches **Note:** Similar to 1 Thaler, KM#182. Dav. #2576.

Date	Mintage	VG	F	VF	XF	Unc
1719 L/IGN Rare	—	—	—	—	—	—

KM# 188 2 THALER (3-1/2 Gulden)

Silver **Ruler:** Friedrich Wilhelm I **Obverse:** Legend ends, ...BRAND **Reverse:** Crowned arms within branches **Note:** Similar to 1 Thaler, KM#183. Dav. #2576A.

Date	Mintage	VG	F	VF	XF	Unc
1719 IGN Rare	—	—	—	—	—	—

KM# 189 2 THALER (3-1/2 Gulden)

Silver **Ruler:** Friedrich Wilhelm I **Obverse:** Bust right breaks legend **Obv. Legend:** ... DG-REX **Note:** Dav. #2578.

Date	Mintage	VG	F	VF	XF	Unc
1719 IGN Rare	—	—	—	—	—	—

KM# 185 2 THALER (3-1/2 Gulden)

Silver **Ruler:** Friedrich Wilhelm I **Reverse:** Crowned shield-shaped arms, date divided above, initials below **Note:** Dav. #2572.

Date	Mintage	VG	F	VF	XF	Unc
1719 L/IGN Rare	—	—	—	—	—	—

TRADE COINAGE

KM# 69 1/4 DUCAT

0.8750 g., 0.9860 Gold 0.0277 oz. AGW **Ruler:** Friedrich I **Mint:** Magdeburg **Subject:** Wedding of Friedrich Wilhelm and Sophia Dorothea **Obverse:** Conjoined busts of Friedrich Wilhelm and Sophia Dorothea **Reverse:** 6-line inscription and date **Note:** Varieties exist.

Date	Mintage	VG	F	VF	XF	Unc
1706 HFH	—	100	200	450	800	—
1712 HFH	—	100	200	450	800	—

KM# 110 1/4 DUCAT

0.8750 g., 0.9860 Gold 0.0277 oz. AGW **Ruler:** Friedrich I **Obverse:** Armored bust right **Reverse:** Spread eagle flying toward sun

Date	Mintage	VG	F	VF	XF	Unc
1713 HFH	—	75.00	125	225	400	—

KM# 111 1/4 DUCAT

0.8750 g., 0.9860 Gold 0.0277 oz. AGW **Ruler:** Friedrich I **Obverse:** Small laureate bust right **Reverse:** Spread eagle, sun at left

Date	Mintage	VG	F	VF	XF	Unc
1713 HFH	—	75.00	125	225	400	—

KM# 112 1/4 DUCAT

0.8750 g., 0.9860 Gold 0.0277 oz. AGW **Ruler:** Friedrich I **Obverse:** Larger laureate bust right

Date	Mintage	VG	F	VF	XF	Unc
1713 HFH	—	75.00	125	225	400	—

KM# 132 1/4 DUCAT

0.8750 g., 0.9860 Gold 0.0277 oz. AGW **Ruler:** Friedrich Wilhelm I **Obverse:** Laureate bust right **Reverse:** Crowned star of the Order of the Black Eagle

Date	Mintage	VG	F	VF	XF	Unc
1714 HFH	—	75.00	125	225	400	—
1716 HFH	—	75.00	125	225	400	—

KM# 131 1/4 DUCAT

0.8750 g., 0.9860 Gold 0.0277 oz. AGW **Ruler:** Friedrich Wilhelm I **Obverse:** Draped bust right **Reverse:** Crowned star of the Black Eagle, date at lower right **Note:** Varieties exist.

Date	Mintage	VG	F	VF	XF	Unc
1714 HFH	—	75.00	125	225	400	—
1716 HFH	—	75.00	125	225	400	—

KM# 148 1/4 DUCAT

0.8750 g., 0.9860 Gold 0.0277 oz. AGW **Ruler:** Friedrich Wilhelm I **Obverse:** Head right **Reverse:** Crowned elaborate arms of 40 fiefs, date below

Date	Mintage	VG	F	VF	XF	Unc
1715 HFH	—	75.00	125	225	400	—

KM# 149 1/4 DUCAT

0.8750 g., 0.9860 Gold 0.0277 oz. AGW **Ruler:** Friedrich Wilhelm I **Obverse:** Armored bust right **Reverse:** Crowned complex arms

Date	Mintage	VG	F	VF	XF	Unc
1715 HFH	—	75.00	125	225	400	—

KM# 70 1/2 DUCAT

1.7500 g., 0.9860 Gold 0.0555 oz. AGW **Ruler:** Friedrich I **Mint:** Magdeburg **Subject:** Wedding of Friedrich Wilhelm and Sophia Dorothea **Obverse:** Conjoined busts of Friedrich Wilhelm and Sophia Dorothea **Reverse:** 6-line inscription and date **Note:** Varieties exist.

Date	Mintage	VG	F	VF	XF	Unc
1706 HFH	—	150	300	650	1,200	—
1712 HFH	—	150	300	650	1,200	—

KM# 88 1/2 DUCAT

1.7500 g., 0.9860 Gold 0.0555 oz. AGW **Ruler:** Friedrich I **Obverse:** Laureate head **Reverse:** Crowned displayed eagle, date below

Date	Mintage	VG	F	VF	XF	Unc
1712 HFH	—	150	300	750	1,400	—

KM# 113 1/2 DUCAT

1.7500 g., 0.9860 Gold 0.0555 oz. AGW **Ruler:** Friedrich I **Obverse:** Head right **Reverse:** Spread eagle flying to sun

Date	Mintage	VG	F	VF	XF	Unc
1713 HFH	—	100	200	450	600	—

KM# 133 1/2 DUCAT

1.7500 g., 0.9860 Gold 0.0555 oz. AGW **Ruler:** Friedrich Wilhelm I **Obverse:** Head right **Reverse:** Crowned star of the Order of the Black Eagle, date at lower right

Date	Mintage	VG	F	VF	XF	Unc
1714 HFH	—	100	200	450	600	—

KM# 134 1/2 DUCAT

1.7500 g., 0.9860 Gold 0.0555 oz. AGW **Ruler:** Friedrich Wilhelm I **Reverse:** Crowned elaborate arms of 40 fiefs, date below

Date	Mintage	VG	F	VF	XF	Unc
1714 HFH	—	100	200	450	600	—

KM# 205 1/2 DUCAT

1.7500 g., 0.9860 Gold 0.0555 oz. AGW **Ruler:** Friedrich Wilhelm I **Mint:** Berlin **Obverse:** Armored bust right **Obv. Legend:** FRIDER • WILH • D • G • REX • BORVSS • **Reverse:** Crowned oval arms, crown divides date

Date	Mintage	VG	F	VF	XF	Unc
1726 EGN	—	100	200	475	700	—

KM# 17 DUCAT
3.5000 g., 0.9860 Gold 0.1109 oz. AGW **Ruler:** Friedrich I **Mint:** Konigsberg **Subject:** Coronation at Konigsberg, January 18, 1701 **Obverse:** Laureate head right **Obv. Legend:** FRIDERICUS REX... **Reverse:** Crown, date below in exergue

Date	Mintage	VG	F	VF	XF	Unc
1701	—	125	250	500	900	—

KM# 18 DUCAT
3.5000 g., 0.9860 Gold 0.1109 oz. AGW **Ruler:** Friedrich I **Mint:** Berlin **Obverse:** Laureate bust right **Reverse:** Cruciform crowned double F monograms, Rs in angles, arms at center

Date	Mintage	VG	F	VF	XF	Unc
1701 LCS	—	400	900	2,100	3,000	—

KM# 19 DUCAT
3.5000 g., 0.9860 Gold 0.1109 oz. AGW **Ruler:** Friedrich I **Obverse:** Laureate head right **Reverse:** Crowned displayed eagle with FR on breast, date divided at top **Note:** Varieties exist.

Date	Mintage	VG	F	VF	XF	Unc
1701 CS	—	400	900	2,100	3,000	—

KM# 28 DUCAT
3.5000 g., 0.9860 Gold 0.1109 oz. AGW **Ruler:** Friedrich I **Mint:** Konigsberg **Obverse:** Laureate head right **Obv. Legend:** FRIDERICUS REX **Reverse:** Crowned eagle arms within branches

Date	Mintage	VG	F	VF	XF	Unc
1702 CG	—	200	500	1,000	1,800	—
1703 CG	—	200	500	1,000	1,800	—
1704 CG	—	200	500	1,000	1,800	—
1705 CG	—	200	500	1,000	1,800	—
1706 CG	—	200	500	1,000	1,800	—

KM# 48 DUCAT
3.5000 g., 0.9860 Gold 0.1109 oz. AGW **Ruler:** Friedrich I **Mint:** Berlin **Obverse:** Thick laurels **Reverse:** Crowned displayed eagle with FR on breast divides date

Date	Mintage	VG	F	VF	XF	Unc
1703 CFL/CS	—	250	600	1,100	1,900	—
1704 CFL/CS	—	250	600	1,100	1,900	—

KM# 64 DUCAT
3.5000 g., 0.9860 Gold 0.1109 oz. AGW **Ruler:** Friedrich I **Obverse:** Laureate head right **Obv. Legend:** FRID • D • G • REX • BORVSS • EL • BR • **Reverse:** Crowned FR monogram in collar of the Order of the Black Eagle, date divided at bottom

Date	Mintage	VG	F	VF	XF	Unc
1705 L/CS	—	200	500	1,000	1,800	—
1706 L/CS	—	200	500	1,000	1,800	—
1707 L/CS	—	200	500	1,000	1,800	—
1708 L/CS	—	200	500	1,000	1,800	—

KM# 71 DUCAT
3.5000 g., 0.9860 Gold 0.1109 oz. AGW **Ruler:** Friedrich I **Mint:** Magdeburg **Subject:** Wedding of Friedrich Wilhelm and Sophia Dorothea **Obverse:** Conjoioned busts left **Obv. Legend:** FRID • WILH • ET • SOPHIA • DOROTHEA **Reverse:** Inscription, date **Note:** Varieties exist.

Date	Mintage	VG	F	VF	XF	Unc
1706 HFH	—	225	450	900	1,700	—

KM# 72 DUCAT
3.5000 g., 0.9860 Gold 0.1109 oz. AGW **Ruler:** Friedrich I **Mint:** Minden **Obverse:** Laureate bust right **Reverse:** Crowned FR monogram in collar of the Order of the Black Eagle, date divided at bottom

Date	Mintage	VG	F	VF	XF	Unc
1706 BH	—	550	1,100	3,000	5,000	—

KM# 79 DUCAT
3.5000 g., 0.9860 Gold 0.1109 oz. AGW **Ruler:** Friedrich I **Mint:** Berlin **Obverse:** Laureate head right **Obv. Legend:** FRIDERICUS REX **Reverse:** Oval frame ornamentation modified

Date	Mintage	VG	F	VF	XF	Unc
1707 CG	—	200	500	1,000	1,800	—
1708 CG	—	200	500	1,000	1,800	—
1709 CG	—	200	500	1,000	1,800	—
1710 CG	—	200	500	1,000	1,800	—
1711 CG	—	200	500	1,000	1,800	—

KM# 80 DUCAT
3.5000 g., 0.9860 Gold 0.1109 oz. AGW **Ruler:** Friedrich I **Mint:** Magdeburg

Date	Mintage	VG	F	VF	XF	Unc
1707 HFH	—	550	1,100	3,000	5,000	—
1708 HFH	—	550	1,100	3,000	5,000	—
1709 HFH	—	550	1,100	3,000	5,000	—

KM# 82 DUCAT
3.5000 g., 0.9860 Gold 0.1109 oz. AGW **Ruler:** Friedrich I **Mint:** Berlin **Obverse:** Bust right **Obv. Legend:** FRIDERICVS • D • G • REX BORVSSIAE • ELECT • BR • **Reverse:** Date at lower left of Order cross

Date	Mintage	VG	F	VF	XF	Unc
1709 L/CS	—	200	500	1,000	1,800	—
1710 L/CS	—	300	700	1,500	2,500	—
1711 L/CS	—	200	500	1,000	1,800	—

KM# 85 DUCAT
3.5000 g., 0.9860 Gold 0.1109 oz. AGW **Ruler:** Friedrich I **Obverse:** Head right **Reverse:** Crowned displayed eagle, date at lower right

Date	Mintage	VG	F	VF	XF	Unc
1710 R/CS	—	500	900	2,500	4,500	—

KM# 86 DUCAT
3.5000 g., 0.9860 Gold 0.1109 oz. AGW **Ruler:** Friedrich I **Subject:** Friendship with Saxony **Obverse:** Bust right, date below **Reverse:** Bust of August II of Saxony right

Date	Mintage	VG	F	VF	XF	Unc
1710 Rare	—	—	—	—	—	—

KM# 89 DUCAT
3.5000 g., 0.9860 Gold 0.1109 oz. AGW **Ruler:** Friedrich I **Mint:** Konigsberg **Obverse:** Thick laurels **Obv. Legend:** FRIDERICUS REX • **Reverse:** Larger eagle in oval frame

Date	Mintage	VG	F	VF	XF	Unc
1712 CG	—	200	500	1,000	1,800	—
1713 CG	—	200	500	1,000	1,500	—

KM# 91 DUCAT
3.5000 g., 0.9860 Gold 0.1109 oz. AGW **Ruler:** Friedrich I **Mint:** Konigsberg **Obverse:** Laureate bust right **Reverse:** Crowned oval arms in palm branches, date in legend

Date	Mintage	VG	F	VF	XF	Unc
1712 GWM/CG	—	500	900	2,500	4,500	—
1713 GWM/CG	—	500	900	2,500	4,500	—

KM# 90 DUCAT
3.5000 g., 0.9860 Gold 0.1109 oz. AGW **Ruler:** Friedrich I **Mint:** Berlin **Obverse:** Armored laureate bust right **Obv. Legend:** FRID • D • G • REX • - BORVSS • EL • BR • **Reverse:** Crowned monogram within Order chain

Date	Mintage	VG	F	VF	XF	Unc
1712 L/CS	—	200	500	1,000	1,800	—

KM# 114 DUCAT
3.5000 g., 0.9860 Gold 0.1109 oz. AGW **Ruler:** Friedrich I **Mint:** Berlin **Subject:** Death of Friedrich I **Obverse:** Laureate bust right **Obv. Legend:** FRID • D • G • REX • - BORVSS • EL • BR • **Reverse:** Crown on alter with Prussian arms on front **Note:** Varieties exist.

Date	Mintage	VG	F	VF	XF	Unc
1713 L/CS	—	150	325	700	1,200	—
1713 L	—	150	325	700	1,200	—

KM# 115 DUCAT
3.5000 g., 0.9860 Gold 0.1109 oz. AGW **Ruler:** Friedrich I **Obverse:** Armored bust of Friedrich Wilhelm right **Reverse:** Spread eagle flying to sun, date below **Note:** Varieties exist.

Date	Mintage	VG	F	VF	XF	Unc
1713 L/IFS	—	400	900	2,100	3,000	—

KM# 116 DUCAT
3.5000 g., 0.9860 Gold 0.1109 oz. AGW **Ruler:** Friedrich I **Mint:** Magdeburg **Obverse:** Laureate bust right **Obv. Legend:** FRID: WILH: D • G • REX • BORUSSIÆ **Reverse:** Imperial eagle in flight

Date	Mintage	VG	F	VF	XF	Unc
1713 HFH	—	200	450	900	1,600	—

KM# 117 DUCAT
3.5000 g., 0.9860 Gold 0.1109 oz. AGW **Ruler:** Friedrich I **Mint:** Konigsberg **Obverse:** Laureate head right **Obv. Legend:** FRID • WILH • REX • **Reverse:** Eagle flying toward sun at left, date below **Rev. Legend:** NEC SOLI CEDIT

Date	Mintage	VG	F	VF	XF	Unc
1713 CG	—	175	400	800	1,400	—
1713 M	—	175	400	800	1,400	—
1713 L	—	175	400	800	1,400	—

KM# 135 DUCAT
3.5000 g., 0.9860 Gold 0.1109 oz. AGW **Ruler:** Friedrich Wilhelm I **Mint:** Berlin **Obverse:** Armored bust right **Reverse:** Crowned FW monogram in shield in collar of the Order of the Black Eagle **Note:** Varieties exist.

Date	Mintage	VG	F	VF	XF	Unc
1714 L/IFS	—	300	600	1,300	2,500	—

KM# 143 DUCAT

3.5000 g., 0.9860 Gold 0.1109 oz. AGW **Ruler:** Friedrich Wilhelm I **Mint:** Magdeburg **Obverse:** Armored bust right **Obv. Legend:** FRID • WILH • D • G • - REX • BORUSSIÆ **Reverse:** Crowned star of the Order of the Black Eagle, date below **Note:** Varieties exist.

Date	Mintage	VG	F	VF	XF	Unc
1714 HFH	—	150	300	600	1,500	—
1717 HFH	—	150	300	600	1,500	—

KM# 141 DUCAT

3.5000 g., 0.9860 Gold 0.1109 oz. AGW **Ruler:** Friedrich Wilhelm I **Mint:** Konigsberg **Reverse:** Crowned star of the Order of the Black Eagle divides date

Date	Mintage	VG	F	VF	XF	Unc
1714 M/CG	—	400	900	2,000	3,500	—
1715	—	400	900	2,000	3,500	—

KM# 142 DUCAT

3.5000 g., 0.9860 Gold 0.1109 oz. AGW **Ruler:** Friedrich Wilhelm I **Obverse:** Draped, armored bust right **Obv. Legend:** FRID • WILH • D • G • - REX • BORUSSIÆ **Reverse:** Crowned arms divide date

Date	Mintage	VG	F	VF	XF	Unc
1714 L/CG	—	125	250	550	1,100	—
1714 M/CG	—	125	250	550	1,100	—
1715 M/CG	—	125	250	550	1,100	—
1716 M/CG	—	125	250	550	1,100	—
1717 M/CG	—	125	250	550	1,100	—

KM# 136 DUCAT

3.5000 g., 0.9860 Gold 0.1109 oz. AGW **Ruler:** Friedrich Wilhelm I **Reverse:** Crowned shield of arms divides date

Date	Mintage	VG	F	VF	XF	Unc
1714 L/IFS	—	400	900	2,000	3,500	—

KM# 137 DUCAT

3.5000 g., 0.9860 Gold 0.1109 oz. AGW **Ruler:** Friedrich Wilhelm I **Mint:** Magdeburg **Obverse:** Draped bust right **Obv. Legend:** FRID • WILH • D • G • - REX • BORVSSIÆ **Reverse:** Crowned arms of 40 fiefs, date below

Date	Mintage	VG	F	VF	XF	Unc
1714 HFH	—	175	350	700	1,300	—

KM# 138 DUCAT

3.5000 g., 0.9860 Gold 0.1109 oz. AGW **Ruler:** Friedrich Wilhelm I **Reverse:** Crowned displayed eagle with scepter and orb, date below

Date	Mintage	VG	F	VF	XF	Unc
1714 HFH	—	350	800	2,000	3,000	—

KM# 139 DUCAT

3.5000 g., 0.9860 Gold 0.1109 oz. AGW **Ruler:** Friedrich Wilhelm I **Reverse:** Crowned arms, date below

Date	Mintage	VG	F	VF	XF	Unc
1714 HFH	—	250	550	1,200	2,000	—

KM# 140 DUCAT

3.5000 g., 0.9860 Gold 0.1109 oz. AGW **Ruler:** Friedrich Wilhelm I **Reverse:** Crowned arms of 12 fiefs, date below

Date	Mintage	VG	F	VF	XF	Unc
1714 HFH	—	175	400	800	1,400	—

KM# 151 DUCAT

3.5000 g., 0.9860 Gold 0.1109 oz. AGW **Ruler:** Friedrich Wilhelm I **Obverse:** Armored bust right **Reverse:** Crowned star of the Order of the Black Eagle

Date	Mintage	VG	F	VF	XF	Unc
1715 L/IFS	—	150	300	600	1,000	—
1716 L/IFS	—	150	300	600	1,000	—
1717 L/IFS	—	150	300	600	1,000	—

KM# 150 DUCAT

3.5000 g., 0.9860 Gold 0.1109 oz. AGW **Ruler:** Friedrich Wilhelm I **Mint:** Berlin **Reverse:** Crowned arms divide date **Note:** Varieties exist.

Date	Mintage	VG	F	VF	XF	Unc
1715 L/IFS	—	200	500	1,100	2,000	—
1716 L/IFS	—	200	500	1,100	2,000	—

KM# 158 DUCAT

3.5000 g., 0.9860 Gold 0.1109 oz. AGW **Ruler:** Friedrich Wilhelm I **Mint:** Magdeburg **Obverse:** Head right **Obv. Legend:** FRID • WILH • D • G • - REX BORVSSIÆ **Reverse:** Crowned star of the Order of the Black Eagle, date below

Date	Mintage	VG	F	VF	XF	Unc
1716 HFH	—	125	250	550	1,100	—

KM# 163 DUCAT

3.5000 g., 0.9860 Gold 0.1109 oz. AGW **Ruler:** Friedrich Wilhelm I **Mint:** Magdeburg **Reverse:** Crowned star of the Order of the Black Eagle, date below

Date	Mintage	VG	F	VF	XF	Unc
1717 HFH	—	200	400	900	1,600	—
1718 M/HFH	—	200	400	900	1,600	—

KM# 162 DUCAT

3.5000 g., 0.9860 Gold 0.1109 oz. AGW **Ruler:** Friedrich Wilhelm I **Mint:** Berlin **Obverse:** Armored bust with pigtail **Reverse:** Crowned oval ams, crown divides date **Note:** Varieties exist.

Date	Mintage	VG	F	VF	XF	Unc
1717 L/IFS	—	150	300	650	1,300	—
1718 L/IFS	—	150	300	650	1,300	—

KM# 174 DUCAT

3.5000 g., 0.9860 Gold 0.1109 oz. AGW **Ruler:** Friedrich Wilhelm I **Reverse:** Crowned oval arms, crown divides date

Date	Mintage	VG	F	VF	XF	Unc
1718 HFH	—	175	400	800	1,400	—
1718 L/HFH	—	175	400	800	1,400	—

KM# 175 DUCAT

3.5000 g., 0.9860 Gold 0.1109 oz. AGW **Ruler:** Friedrich Wilhelm I **Mint:** Konigsberg **Obverse:** Armored bust right **Obv. Legend:** FRID • WILH • - D • G • REX • BORVSS • **Reverse:** Crowned shield at center of crowned arms , date divided above

Date	Mintage	VG	F	VF	XF	Unc
1718 CG	—	100	200	450	800	—
1719 CG	—	100	200	450	800	—
1720 M/CG	—	100	200	450	800	—
1721 M/CG	—	100	200	450	800	—
1722 M/CG	—	100	200	450	800	—
1723 M/CG	—	100	200	450	800	—
1724 M/CG	—	100	200	450	800	—
1725 M/CG	—	100	200	450	800	—
1726 M/CG	—	100	200	450	800	—
1727 M/CG	—	100	200	450	800	—
1728 M/CG	—	100	200	450	800	—

KM# 190 DUCAT

3.5000 g., 0.9860 Gold 0.1109 oz. AGW **Ruler:** Friedrich Wilhelm I **Mint:** Berlin **Obverse:** Armored bust right **Reverse:** Crowned shield at center of crowned arms, date divided above

Date	Mintage	VG	F	VF	XF	Unc
1719 L/IGN	—	150	300	700	1,400	—
1720 L/IGN	—	150	300	700	1,400	—
1721 L/IGN	—	150	300	700	1,400	—
1722 L/IGN	—	150	300	700	1,400	—
1723 L/IGN	—	150	300	700	1,400	—
1724 L/IGN	—	150	300	700	1,400	—
1725 L/IGN	—	150	300	700	1,400	—

KM# 204 DUCAT

3.5000 g., 0.9860 Gold 0.1109 oz. AGW **Ruler:** Friedrich Wilhelm I **Obverse:** Armored bust right **Obv. Legend:** FRID.WILH - D.G.REX... **Reverse:** Crowned shield at center of crowned arms, date divided above **Note:** Varieties exist.

Date	Mintage	VG	F	VF	XF	Unc
1725 EGN	—	125	225	550	1,100	—
1726 EGN	—	125	225	550	1,100	—
1727 EGN	—	125	225	550	1,100	—
1728 EGN	—	125	225	550	1,100	—
1729 EGN	—	125	225	550	1,100	—
1730 EGN	—	125	225	550	1,100	—
1731 EGN	—	125	225	550	1,100	—
1732 EGN	—	125	225	550	1,100	—

KM# 213 DUCAT

3.5000 g., 0.9860 Gold 0.1109 oz. AGW **Ruler:** Friedrich Wilhelm I **Reverse:** Flying crowned eagle, date below **Note:** Varieties exist.

Date	Mintage	VG	F	VF	XF	Unc
1733 EGN	—	125	225	550	1,100	—
1734 EGN	—	125	225	550	1,100	—

KM# 214 DUCAT

3.5000 g., 0.9860 Gold 0.1109 oz. AGW **Ruler:** Friedrich Wilhelm I **Obverse:** Armored bust right **Obv. Legend:** FRID • WILH • - D • G • REX • BOR: & • **Reverse:** Crowned star of the Order of the Black Eagle **Note:** Varieties exist.

Date	Mintage	VG	F	VF	XF	Unc
1733 EGN	—	150	300	600	1,200	—
1734 EGN	—	150	300	600	1,200	—
1735 EGN	—	150	300	600	1,200	—
1736 EGN	—	150	300	600	1,200	—
1737 EGN	—	150	300	600	1,200	—
1738 EGN	—	150	300	600	1,200	—
1739 EGN	—	150	300	600	1,200	—
1740 EGN	—	150	300	600	1,200	—

KM# 235 DUCAT

3.5000 g., 0.9860 Gold 0.1109 oz. AGW **Ruler:** Friedrich II **Obverse:** Armored bust right **Obv. Legend:** FRIDERICVS BORVSSORVM REX **Reverse:** Crown divides date above eagle arms on irregular shield

Date	Mintage	VG	F	VF	XF	Unc
1741 EGN	—	150	325	700	1,300	—
1742 EGN	—	150	325	700	1,300	—
1743 EGN	—	150	325	700	1,300	—
1744 EGN	—	150	325	700	1,300	—
1745 EGN	—	150	325	700	1,300	—

KM# 238 DUCAT

3.5000 g., 0.9860 Gold 0.1109 oz. AGW **Ruler:** Friedrich II **Reverse:** Crowned FR monogram in collar of the Order of the Black Eagle, date below

Date	Mintage	VG	F	VF	XF	Unc
1745 EGN	—	350	800	1,500	2,500	—

KM# 239 DUCAT

3.5000 g., 0.9860 Gold 0.1109 oz. AGW **Ruler:** Friedrich II **Obverse:** Armored bust right **Obv. Legend:** FRIDERICVS BORVSSORVM REX **Reverse:** Crowned displayed eagle above trophies

Date	Mintage	VG	F	VF	XF	Unc
1745 EGN	—	200	400	800	1,500	—
1746 EGN	—	200	400	800	1,500	—
1747 EGN	—	200	400	800	1,500	—
1748 EGN	—	200	400	800	1,500	—
1749 EGN	—	200	400	800	1,500	—

KM# 243 DUCAT

3.5000 g., 0.9860 Gold 0.1109 oz. AGW **Ruler:** Friedrich II **Obverse:** Armored bust right **Obv. Legend:** FRIDERICVS

BORVSSORVM REX **Reverse:** Eagle divides date above trophies **Note:** Varieties exist.

Date	Mintage	VG	F	VF	XF	Unc
1749 CHI	—	225	450	900	1,600	—

KM# 244 DUCAT

3.5000 g., 0.9860 Gold 0.1109 oz. AGW **Ruler:** Friedrich II **Reverse:** Crowned eagle on glove in palm branches, date at top

Date	Mintage	VG	F	VF	XF	Unc
1749 EGN	—	400	900	2,000	3,500	—

KM# 278 DUCAT

3.5000 g., 0.9860 Gold 0.1109 oz. AGW **Ruler:** Friedrich II **Obverse:** Head right **Obv. Legend:** FRIDERICUS BORUSSORUM REX **Reverse:** Eagle above trophies

Date	Mintage	VG	F	VF	XF	Unc
1753 A	—	150	300	700	1,200	—
1754 A	—	150	300	700	1,200	—
1757 B	—	—	—	—	—	—

KM# 292 DUCAT

3.5000 g., 0.9860 Gold 0.1109 oz. AGW **Ruler:** Friedrich II **Obverse:** Standing figure **Reverse:** Building

Date	Mintage	F	VF	XF	Unc
1763	—	—	500	750	1,000

KM# 352 DUCAT

3.5000 g., 0.9860 Gold 0.1109 oz. AGW **Ruler:** Friedrich Wilhelm II **Mint:** Berlin **Obverse:** Crowned eagle arms **Reverse:** Value and date within square, crowns at points joined by laurels

Date	Mintage	F	VF	XF	Unc
1787A	—	300	600	900	1,200
1790A	—	300	600	900	1,200

KM# 20 2 DUCAT

7.0000 g., 0.9860 Gold 0.2219 oz. AGW **Ruler:** Friedrich I **Mint:** Berlin **Obverse:** Laureate bust right **Reverse:** Cruciform crowned double F monograms, Rs in angles, arms at center **Note:** Thick planchet.

Date	Mintage	VG	F	VF	XF	Unc
1701 LCS	—	900	2,000	5,000	8,000	—

KM# 49 2 DUCAT

7.0000 g., 0.9860 Gold 0.2219 oz. AGW **Ruler:** Friedrich I **Mint:** Konigsberg **Obverse:** Laureate draped bust right **Reverse:** Crowned oval arms in palm branches, date in legend

Date	Mintage	VG	F	VF	XF	Unc
1703 CG	—	600	1,500	3,500	6,000	—
1704 CG	—	600	1,500	3,500	6,000	—

KM# 73 2 DUCAT

7.0000 g., 0.9860 Gold 0.2219 oz. AGW **Ruler:** Friedrich I **Mint:** Magdeburg **Subject:** Wedding of Friedrich Wilhelm and Sophia Dorothea **Obverse:** Conjoined busts of Friedrich Wilhelm and Sophia Dorothea left **Reverse:** 6-line inscription and date

Date	Mintage	VG	F	VF	XF	Unc
1706 HFH	—	500	1,200	3,000	5,000	—

KM# 87 2 DUCAT

7.0000 g., 0.9860 Gold 0.2219 oz. AGW **Ruler:** Friedrich I **Mint:** Berlin **Obverse:** Head right **Reverse:** Crowned displayed eagle, date at lower right

Date	Mintage	VG	F	VF	XF	Unc
1710 R/CS	—	700	1,750	4,000	7,000	—

KM# 92 2 DUCAT

7.0000 g., 0.9860 Gold 0.2219 oz. AGW **Ruler:** Friedrich I **Mint:** Magdeburg **Obverse:** Laureate head right **Reverse:** Crowned displayed eagle holding laurel wreath and lightning, date below **Note:** Varieties exist.

Date	Mintage	VG	F	VF	XF	Unc
1712 HFH	—	450	1,000	2,800	4,000	—

KM# 118 2 DUCAT

7.0000 g., 0.9860 Gold 0.2219 oz. AGW **Ruler:** Friedrich I **Mint:** Konigsberg **Obverse:** Laureate draped bust right **Reverse:** Crowned oval arms in palm branches, date in legend

Date	Mintage	VG	F	VF	XF	Unc
1713 CG	—	700	1,750	4,000	7,000	—

KM# 119 2 DUCAT

7.0000 g., 0.9860 Gold 0.2219 oz. AGW **Ruler:** Friedrich I **Mint:** Magdeburg **Obverse:** Laureate head right **Obv. Legend:** FRID • WILH • REX • **Reverse:** Eagle flying to sun at left, date below

Date	Mintage	VG	F	VF	XF	Unc
1713 HFH	—	500	1,200	3,000	5,000	—

KM# 202 2 DUCAT

7.0000 g., 0.9860 Gold 0.2219 oz. AGW **Ruler:** Friedrich Wilhelm I **Mint:** Berlin **Obverse:** Armored bust right with pigtail **Reverse:** Crowned oval arms, crown divides date

Date	Mintage	VG	F	VF	XF	Unc
1724 IGN	—	500	1,200	3,000	5,000	—

KM# 211 2 DUCAT

7.0000 g., 0.9860 Gold 0.2219 oz. AGW **Ruler:** Friedrich Wilhelm I

Date	Mintage	VG	F	VF	XF	Unc
1732 EGN	—	500	1,200	3,000	5,000	—

KM# 215 2 DUCAT

7.0000 g., 0.9860 Gold 0.2219 oz. AGW **Ruler:** Friedrich Wilhelm I **Reverse:** Flying crowned eagle, date below

Date	Mintage	VG	F	VF	XF	Unc
1733 EGN	—	500	1,200	3,000	5,000	—

KM# 245 2 DUCAT

7.0000 g., 0.9860 Gold 0.2219 oz. AGW **Ruler:** Friedrich Wilhelm I **Obverse:** Head right **Reverse:** Crowned eagle on globe in palm branches, date at top

Date	Mintage	VG	F	VF	XF	Unc
1749 EGN	—	600	1,500	3,500	6,000	—

KM# 198 5 DUCAT

17.5000 g., 0.9860 Gold 0.5547 oz. AGW **Ruler:** Friedrich Wilhelm I **Mint:** Berlin **Subject:** Homage of Stettin **Obverse:** Bust right **Reverse:** Inscription in straight lines **Note:** Struck with 1/2 Thaler dies, KM#195.

Date	Mintage	VG	F	VF	XF	Unc
1721 L	—	3,200	4,800	6,000	8,500	—

KM# 199 5 DUCAT

17.5000 g., 0.9860 Gold 0.5547 oz. AGW **Ruler:** Friedrich Wilhelm I **Reverse:** Inscription in curved lines **Note:** Struck with 1/2 Thaler dies, KM#196.

Date	Mintage	VG	F	VF	XF	Unc
1721 L	—	3,200	4,800	6,000	8,500	—

KM# 200 8 DUCAT

28.0000 g., 0.9860 Gold 0.8876 oz. AGW **Ruler:** Friedrich Wilhelm I **Mint:** Berlin **Subject:** Homage of Stettin **Reverse:** Inscription **Note:** Similar to 5 Ducat, KM#199. Struck with 1/2 Thaler dies, KM#196.

Date	Mintage	VG	F	VF	XF	Unc
1721 L	—	9,000	12,500	16,000	20,000	—

KM# 240 1/2 FREDERICK D'OR

3.3410 g., 0.9030 Gold 0.0970 oz. AGW **Ruler:** Friedrich II **Obverse:** Armored bust right **Obv. Legend:** FRIDERICVS BORVSSORVM REX **Reverse:** Crown above eagle on trophies, date at lower right

Date	Mintage	VG	F	VF	XF	Unc
1749 CHI	—	150	300	600	1,100	—

KM# 257 1/2 FREDERICK D'OR

3.3410 g., 0.9030 Gold 0.0970 oz. AGW **Ruler:** Friedrich II **Obverse:** Armored bust right **Obv. Legend:** FRIDERICVS BORVSSORVM REX **Reverse:** Date divided at bottoom

Date	Mintage	VG	F	VF	XF	Unc
1750 A	—	100	200	600	1,200	—
1751 A	—	100	150	400	800	—
1752 A	—	100	200	600	1,200	—

KM# 258 1/2 FREDERICK D'OR

3.3410 g., 0.9030 Gold 0.0970 oz. AGW **Ruler:** Friedrich II **Obverse:** Head right **Obv. Legend:** FRIDERICUS BORUSSORUM REX • **Reverse:** Crowned back to back F's

Date	Mintage	VG	F	VF	XF	Unc
1750 A	—	150	300	800	1,300	—

KM# 271 1/2 FREDERICK D'OR

3.3410 g., 0.9030 Gold 0.0970 oz. AGW **Ruler:** Friedrich II **Obverse:** Head right **Obv. Legend:** FRIDERICVS BORVSSORVM REX **Reverse:** Crowned eagle above trophies

Date	Mintage	VG	F	VF	XF	Unc
1752 A	—	100	200	600	1,200	—
1753 A	—	100	200	600	1,200	—

KM# 280 1/2 FREDERICK D'OR

3.3410 g., 0.9030 Gold 0.0970 oz. AGW **Ruler:** Friedrich II **Reverse:** A in exergue

Date	Mintage	VG	F	VF	XF	Unc
1755 A	—	100	200	600	1,000	—
1756 A	—	100	200	600	1,000	—

KM# 281 1/2 FREDERICK D'OR

3.3410 g., 0.9030 Gold 0.0970 oz. AGW **Ruler:** Friedrich II **Note:** Struck in lower grade gold during 7 Years War (1758-1763).

Date	Mintage	VG	F	VF	XF	Unc
1755 A	—	300	1,000	2,000	3,000	—

KM# 315 1/2 FREDERICK D'OR

3.3410 g., 0.9030 Gold 0.0970 oz. AGW **Ruler:** Friedrich II **Mint:** Berlin **Obverse:** Head right **Obv. Legend:** FRIDERICUS BORUSSORUM REX **Reverse:** Date above eagle with trophies

Date	Mintage	VG	F	VF	XF	Unc
1765A	—	100	200	450	900	—
1769A	—	100	200	450	900	—
1770A	—	100	200	450	900	—
1772A	—	100	200	450	900	—
1773A	—	100	200	450	900	—
1774A	—	100	200	450	900	—

KM# 340 1/2 FREDERICK D'OR

3.3410 g., 0.9030 Gold 0.0970 oz. AGW **Ruler:** Friedrich II **Mint:** Berlin **Obverse:** Laureate head right **Obv. Legend:** FRIDERICUS BORUSSORUM REX **Reverse:** Eagle with trophies

Date	Mintage	VG	F	VF	XF	Unc
1784A	—	100	200	500	1,000	—
1786A	—	100	200	500	1,000	—

KM# 233 FREDERICK D'OR

6.6820 g., 0.9030 Gold 0.1940 oz. AGW **Ruler:** Friedrich II **Obverse:** Armored bust right **Obv. Legend:** FRIDERICVS BORVSSORVM REX **Reverse:** Crown above shield

Date	Mintage	VG	F	VF	XF	Unc
1741 EGN	—	225	450	900	1,650	—
1742 EGN	—	225	450	900	1,650	—
1743 EGN	—	225	450	900	1,650	—
1744 EGN	—	225	450	900	1,650	—
1745 EGN	—	225	450	900	1,650	—

KM# 234 FREDERICK D'OR

6.6820 g., 0.9030 Gold 0.1940 oz. AGW **Ruler:** Friedrich II **Reverse:** Crown above eagle amongst trophies, date at lower right

Date	Mintage	VG	F	VF	XF	Unc
1741 EGN	—	200	400	800	1,450	—
1742 EGN	—	200	400	800	1,450	—
1743 EGN	—	200	400	800	1,450	—
1745 EGN	—	200	400	800	1,450	—
1746 EGN	—	200	400	800	1,450	—

KM# 241 FREDERICK D'OR
6.6820 g., 0.9030 Gold 0.1940 oz. AGW **Ruler:** Friedrich II **Obverse:** Armored bust left **Obv. Legend:** FRIDERICVS BORVSSORVM REX **Reverse:** Crown above eagle with trophies

Date	Mintage	VG	F	VF	XF	Unc
1749 ALS	—	200	500	1,000	2,250	—

KM# 259 FREDERICK D'OR
6.6820 g., 0.9030 Gold 0.1940 oz. AGW **Ruler:** Friedrich II **Obverse:** Mature head right **Reverse:** Crowned ornamental shield with crowned eagle and FR monogram, date divided at top

Date	Mintage	VG	F	VF	XF	Unc
1750A	—	200	500	1,000	2,250	—

KM# 260 FREDERICK D'OR
6.6820 g., 0.9030 Gold 0.1940 oz. AGW **Ruler:** Friedrich II **Mint:** Berlin **Obverse:** Armored bust right **Obv. Legend:** FRIDERICVS BORVSSORVM REX **Reverse:** Crown above eagle with trophies

Date	Mintage	VG	F	VF	XF	Unc
1750A	—	150	300	500	1,150	—
1751A	—	150	300	500	1,150	—
1752A	—	150	300	500	1,150	—
1759A	—	150	300	500	1,150	—

KM# 272 FREDERICK D'OR
6.6820 g., 0.9030 Gold 0.1940 oz. AGW **Ruler:** Friedrich II **Mint:** Berlin **Obverse:** Head right **Obv. Legend:** FRIDERICUS BORUSSORUM REX **Reverse:** Eagle with trophies **Note:** Varieties exist.

Date	Mintage	VG	F	VF	XF	Unc
1752A	—	150	300	600	1,200	—
1753A	—	400	800	1,700	2,500	—
1754A	—	150	300	600	1,200	—
1755A	—	150	300	600	1,200	—
1756A	—	150	300	600	1,200	—
1757A	—	150	300	600	1,200	—
1758A	—	150	300	600	1,200	—
1763A	—	150	300	600	1,200	—

KM# 282 FREDERICK D'OR
6.6820 g., 0.9030 Gold 0.1940 oz. AGW **Ruler:** Friedrich II **Mint:** Berlin **Reverse:** Crown above eagle with trophies, date divided below **Note:** Struck in lower grade gold during 7 Years War (1758-1763).

Date	Mintage	VG	F	VF	XF	Unc
1755A	—	200	400	800	1,350	—
1756A	—	200	400	800	1,350	—
1757A	—	200	400	800	1,350	—

KM# 309 FREDERICK D'OR
6.6820 g., 0.9030 Gold 0.1940 oz. AGW **Ruler:** Friedrich II **Mint:** Berlin **Obverse:** Head right **Obv. Legend:** FRIDERICUS BORUSSORUM REX **Reverse:** Eagle with trophies, date above

Date	Mintage	VG	F	VF	XF	Unc
1764A	—	200	350	600	1,200	—
1766A	—	200	350	600	1,200	—
1767A	—	200	350	600	1,200	—
1768A	—	200	350	600	1,200	—
1769A	—	200	350	600	1,200	—
1770A	—	200	350	600	1,200	—
1771A	—	200	350	600	1,200	—
1772A	—	200	350	600	1,200	—
1773A	—	200	350	600	1,200	—
1774A	—	200	350	600	1,200	—
1775A	—	200	350	600	1,200	—

KM# 333 FREDERICK D'OR
6.6820 g., 0.9030 Gold 0.1940 oz. AGW **Ruler:** Friedrich II **Mint:** Berlin **Obverse:** Laureate head right **Obv. Legend:** FRIDERICUS BORUSSORUM REX **Reverse:** Eagle with trophies, date above

Date	Mintage	VG	F	VF	XF	Unc
1775A	—	200	350	500	900	—
1776A	—	200	350	500	900	—
1777A	—	200	350	500	900	—
1778A	—	200	350	500	900	—
1779A	—	200	350	500	900	—
1780A	—	200	350	500	900	—
1781A	—	200	350	500	900	—
1782A	—	200	350	500	900	—
1783A	—	200	350	500	900	—
1784A	—	200	350	500	900	—
1786A	—	200	350	500	900	—

KM# 349 FREDERICK D'OR
6.6820 g., 0.9030 Gold 0.1940 oz. AGW **Ruler:** Friedrich Wilhelm II **Obverse:** Draped bust right **Obv. Legend:** FRIED: WILHELM KOENIG VON PREUSSEN **Reverse:** Eagle with trophies, date below

Date	Mintage	VG	F	VF	XF	Unc
1786A	—	200	350	500	900	—
1787B	—	200	350	500	900	—
1788A	—	200	350	500	900	—
1788B	—	200	350	500	900	—
1789A	—	200	350	500	900	—
1789B	—	200	350	500	900	—
1790A	—	200	350	500	900	—
1790B	—	200	350	500	900	—
1791A	—	200	350	500	900	—
1791B	—	200	350	500	900	—
1792A	—	200	350	500	900	—
1792B	—	200	350	500	900	—
1793A	—	200	350	500	900	—
1793B	—	200	350	500	900	—
1794A	—	200	350	500	900	—
1794B	—	200	350	500	900	—
1795A	—	200	350	500	900	—
1795B	—	200	350	500	900	—
1796A	—	200	350	500	900	—
1796B	—	200	350	500	900	—
1797A	—	200	350	500	900	—
1797B	—	200	350	500	900	—

KM# 369 FREDERICK D'OR
6.6820 g., 0.9030 Gold 0.1940 oz. AGW **Ruler:** Friedrich Wilhelm III **Mint:** Berlin **Obverse:** Armored bust left **Obv. Legend:** FRIED. WILHELM III KOENIG VON PREUSSEN **Reverse:** Eagle with trophies, 'A' divides date below

Date	Mintage	VG	F	VF	XF	Unc
1797A	—	200	400	800	1,350	—
1798A	—	200	400	800	1,350	—

KM# 371 FREDERICK D'OR
6.6820 g., 0.9030 Gold 0.1940 oz. AGW **Ruler:** Friedrich Wilhelm III **Obverse:** Armored bust left **Obv. Legend:** FRIEDR. WILHELM III KOENIG VON PREUSSEN **Reverse:** Eagle with trophies, date below

Date	Mintage	F	VF	XF	Unc
1798A	—	275	475	675	1,250
1799A	—	275	475	675	1,250
1800A	—	275	475	675	1,250
1800B	—	450	600	950	1,600

KM# 242 2 FREDERICK D'OR
13.3630 g., 0.9030 Gold 0.3879 oz. AGW **Ruler:** Friedrich II **Obverse:** Armored bust right **Obv. Legend:** FRIDERICUS • D • G • REX • BORUSSORUM **Reverse:** Crown above eagle with trophies, date at lower right

Date	Mintage	VG	F	VF	XF	Unc
1749 ALS	—	600	1,500	3,000	5,000	

KM# 261 2 FREDERICK D'OR
13.3630 g., 0.9030 Gold 0.3879 oz. AGW **Ruler:** Friedrich II **Mint:** Berlin **Obverse:** Armored bust right **Obv. Legend:** FRIDERICVS BORVSSORVM REX **Reverse:** Crown above eagle with trophies, date divided below

Date	Mintage	VG	F	VF	XF	Unc
1750A	—	600	1,500	3,000	5,000	—
1751A	—	600	1,500	3,000	5,000	—

KM# 273 2 FREDERICK D'OR
13.3630 g., 0.9030 Gold 0.3879 oz. AGW **Ruler:** Friedrich II **Mint:** Berlin **Obverse:** Differing sashes **Obv. Legend:** FRIDERICVS BORVSSORVM REX **Reverse:** Crown above eagle with trophies, date divided below

Date	Mintage	VG	F	VF	XF	Unc
1752A	—	600	1,500	3,000	5,000	—

KM# 277 2 FREDERICK D'OR
13.3630 g., 0.9030 Gold 0.3879 oz. AGW **Ruler:** Friedrich II **Mint:** Berlin **Obverse:** Mature head right **Reverse:** Crowned eagle on trophies, date at top, A in exergue

Date	Mintage	VG	F	VF	XF	Unc
1753A	—	1,000	2,000	4,500	8,500	—
1755A	—	1,000	2,000	4,500	8,500	—

KM# 283 2 FREDERICK D'OR
13.3630 g., 0.9030 Gold 0.3879 oz. AGW **Ruler:** Friedrich II **Mint:** Berlin **Note:** Struck in lower grade gold during 7 Years War (1758-1763).

Date	Mintage	VG	F	VF	XF	Unc
1756A	—	500	1,000	3,000	6,000	—
1757A	—	500	1,000	3,000	6,000	—

KM# 310 2 FREDERICK D'OR
13.3630 g., 0.9030 Gold 0.3879 oz. AGW **Ruler:** Friedrich II **Mint:** Berlin **Obverse:** Head right **Obv. Legend:** FRIDERICUS BORUSSORUM REX **Reverse:** Eagle with trophies, date above

Date	Mintage	F	VF	XF	Unc
1764A	—	700	1,400	2,350	4,000
1765A	—	700	1,400	2,350	4,000
1766A	—	700	1,400	2,350	4,000
1767A	—	700	1,400	2,350	4,000

Date	Mintage	F	VF	XF	Unc
1768A	—	700	1,400	2,350	4,000
1769A	—	700	1,400	2,350	4,000
1770A	—	700	1,400	2,350	4,000
1771A	—	700	1,400	2,350	4,000
1775A	—	700	1,400	2,350	4,000

KM# 334 2 FREDERICK D'OR

13.3630 g., 0.9030 Gold 0.3879 oz. AGW **Ruler:** Friedrich II **Mint:** Berlin **Obverse:** Old head right

Date	Mintage	F	VF	XF	Unc
1776A	—	1,250	1,750	2,500	4,250

KM# 221 1/2 WILHELM D'OR

3.3410 g., 0.9030 Gold 0.0970 oz. AGW **Ruler:** Friedrich Wilhelm I **Mint:** Berlin **Obverse:** Armored bust right **Obv. Legend:** FRID • WILH • D • G • REX • BOR • EL • BR • **Reverse:** Crowned monograms in cruciform, eagle arms at center

Date	Mintage	VG	F	VF	XF	Unc
1738 EGN	5,833	200	400	600	2,000	—
1739 EGN	Inc. above	200	400	600	2,000	—
1740 EGN	Inc. above	200	400	600	2,000	—

KM# 219 WILHELM D'OR

6.6820 g., 0.9030 Gold 0.1940 oz. AGW **Ruler:** Friedrich Wilhelm I **Mint:** Berlin **Obverse:** Armored bust right **Obv. Legend:** FRID • WILH • D • G • * REX • BOR • EL • BRAN • **Reverse:** Cruciform crowned F (block) W (script) monograms

Date	Mintage	VG	F	VF	XF	Unc
1737 EGN on obverse	5,021	250	500	1,000	2,250	—
1737 EGN on reverse	Inc. above	250	500	1,000	2,250	—
1738 EGN	Inc. above	250	500	1,000	2,250	—

KM# 220 WILHELM D'OR

6.6820 g., 0.9030 Gold 0.1940 oz. AGW **Ruler:** Friedrich Wilhelm I **Obverse:** Armored bust right **Obv. Legend:** FRID • WILH • D • G • REX • BOR • EL • BRAN • **Reverse:** Cruciform crowned block FW monograms, eagle arms at center

Date	Mintage	VG	F	VF	XF	Unc
1738 EGN	Inc. above	250	500	1,000	2,250	—
1739 EGN	Inc. above	250	500	1,000	2,250	—
1740 EGN	Inc. above	250	500	1,000	2,250	—

PATTERNS

Including off metal strikes

KM#	Date	Mintage	Identification	Mkt Val
Pn1	1701	—	Ducat. Silver. KM#17.	175
Pn2	1701	—	Ducat. Silver. KM#17.	175
Pn3	1701	—	Ducat. Silver. KM#18.	285
Pn4	1710	—	Ducat. Silver.	—
Pn5	1713	—	Ducat. Silver. KM#114.	250
Pn6	1713	—	Ducat. Silver. KM#141.	250
Pn7	1740	—	Ducat. Silver. M4.	230
Pn8	1749	—	2 Frederick D'Or. Copper. KM#242.	—

KM#	Date	Mintage	Identification	Mkt Val
Pn9	1754A	6	1/24 Thaler.	—

KM#	Date	Mintage	Identification	Mkt Val
Pn10	1755	16	Thaler.	—
PnA11	1756E	—	2 Groscher. Gold. KM#A279.	—
PnB11	1763E	—	6 Groscher. Gold. KM#291.	—
PnC11	1763E	—	18 Groscher. Gold. KM#A300.	—
Pn11	1788	—	Thaler. Silver. KM#348.	—
PnC12	1796B	—	GröScher. Silver. 21 mm. KM#362.1.	—
PnD12	1796B	—	3 Groscher. Silver. KM#E362.2.	—
PnB12	1796B	—	1/2 Groschen. Silver. 18 mm. KM#C362.1.	—
	1797B	—	1/2 Groschen. Silver. 18 mm. KM#C362.1.	—
PnD12	1797B	—	3 Groscher. Silver. KM#E362.2.	—
PnC12	1797B	—	GröScher. Silver. 21 mm. KM#362.1.	—
Pn12	1799	—	Frederick D'Or. Copper. KM#371.	85.00

PYRMONT

A county southwest of Hannover, established c.1160, Pyrmont's first coins were struck in the 13th century. In 1625, it was incorporated with Waldeck. Occasional issues of special coins for Pyrmont were struck in the 18th and 19th centuries.

RULER

Karl August Friedrich, 1728-1763

COUNTY

REGULAR COINAGE

C# 1 PFENNIG

Copper **Ruler:** Karl August Friedrich **Obverse:** Crowned cross **Reverse:** Value, date

Date	Mintage	Good	VG	F	VF	XF
1761	56,000	—	6.00	12.00	25.00	50.00

C# 2 2 PFENNIGE

Copper **Ruler:** Karl August Friedrich **Obverse:** Crowned cross **Reverse:** Value, date **Note:** Similar to 1 Pfennige, C#1.

Date	Mintage	Good	VG	F	VF	XF
1761	40,000	—	7.50	15.00	30.00	60.00

C# 3 4 PFENNIGE

Copper **Ruler:** Karl August Friedrich **Obverse:** Crowned cross **Reverse:** Value, date **Note:** Similar to 1 Pfennige, C#1.

Date	Mintage	Good	VG	F	VF	XF
1761	52,000	—	10.00	20.00	40.00	80.00

QUEDLINBURG

The small provincial town of Quedlinburg, 8 miles (13 kilometers) south-southeast of Halberstadt and slightly north of the Harz Mountains, was founded in 922. The town itself had its own coinage during the middle of the 17th century, but most of the local coinage was produced in and for the abbey. Near the village in 966, Emperor Otto I the Great (962-73) founded an abbey primarily for princesses of his imperial Saxon family. Otto I's grandson, Otto III (983-1002), established an imperial mint in the town and gave the abbesses the right to strike their own coinage at about the same time. Many of the abbesses were members of the House of Saxony or from noble families closely associated with it. When the Electorate and Duchy of Saxony itself became officially Protestant during the Reformation, Quedlinburg followed the same path in 1539. The coinage of the abbesses came to an end in 1697 when Elector Friedrich August I of Saxony (1694-1733) sold his rights over Quedlinburg to Brandenburg-Prussia in order to become King of Poland. A brief and scarce issue of a few types occurred in 1759, but otherwise the abbesses had only tier 40-square mile (65-square kilometer) territory to administer. Even this was secularized and annexed by Prussia in 1803.

RULERS

Anna Dorothea von Sachsen-Weimar, 1684-1704
Maria Elisabeth von Holstein-Gottorp, 1710-55
Anna Amalia von Preussen, 1755-87
Sophia Albertina von Schweden, 1787-1808, died 1829

MINT OFFICIALS' INITIALS

Initials	Date	Name
HCH	1689-1729	Heinrich Christoph Hille, mintmaster in Braunschweig

ARMS

Two crossed fish, but also sometimes an eagle or a three-towered city gate, or a combination of these.

Electoral and Ducal Saxony arms often appear on coins of abbesses from that family.

REFERENCE

D = Adalbert Düning, ***Übersich über die Münzgeschichte des kaiserlichen freien weltlichen Stifts Quedlinburg***, Quedlinburg, 1886.

ABBEY

REGULAR COINAGE

KM# 81 1/24 THALER (Groschen)

Silver **Ruler:** Anna Amalia von Preussen **Obverse:** Quedlinburg arms divide date in circle, titles of Anna Amalia **Reverse:** Crown above 24/EINEN/THALER in wreath **Note:** Reference D-40.

Date	Mintage	VG	F	VF	XF	Unc
1759 Rare	—	—	—	—	—	—

KM# 82 1/12 THALER (Doppelgroschen)

Silver **Ruler:** Anna Amalia von Preussen **Obverse:** Quedlinburg arms divide date in circle. **Reverse:** Crown above 3-line inscription in wreath. **Rev. Inscription:** 12/EINEN/THALER

Date	Mintage	VG	F	VF	XF	Unc
1759 Rare	—	—	—	—	—	—

KM# 75 1/8 THALER

Silver **Ruler:** Anna Dorothea von Saxe-Weimar **Subject:** Death of Anna Dorothea **Obverse:** Bust right, double legends with titles and dates. **Reverse:** Rays from setting sun at lower right over hilly landscape, inscription in curved band above **Rev. Legend:** ABITV DECORATVR AMOENO **Note:** Struck from Ducat dies, Fr. #2447. Prev. KM#Pn1.

KM# 83 1/6 THALER (1/4 Gulden)

Silver **Ruler:** Anna Amalia von Preussen **Obverse:** Crowned Prussian eagle, Quedlinburg arms on breast, divides date **Reverse:** Crown above 3-line inscription in wreath **Rev. Inscription:** VI/EINEN/THALER **Note:** Reference D-39.

Date	Mintage	VG	F	VF	XF	Unc
1759 Rare	—	—	—	—	—	—

KM# 35 1/4 THALER

Silver, 30 mm. **Ruler:** Dorothea Sophia von Saxe-Altenburg **Obverse:** Manifold arms with central shield of Quedlinburg **Obv. Legend:** MO: NO: D:G: DOR: SOPH: DV: SA: A **Reverse:** Crowned imperial eagle, orb on breast, date divided above **Rev. Legend:** FERDI: II. D:G: ROM: IMP: SEM: AVG

Date	Mintage	VG	F	VF	XF	Unc
16Z4	—	125	275	400	750	—

KM# 76 1/4 THALER (1/3 Gulden)

Silver, 28 mm. **Ruler:** Anna Dorothea von Saxe-Weimar **Subject:** Death of Anna Dorothea **Obverse:** Bust right, double legend with dates **Reverse:** Three-masted sailing ship to right, legend in curved band above, mintmaster's initials and symbol in exergue **Rev. Legend:** ADVERSIS DECOR ADDITVS

Date	Mintage	VG	F	VF	XF	Unc
1704 HCH	—	125	240	325	475	—

KM# 77 THALER
Silver **Ruler:** Anna Dorothea von Saxe-Weimar **Subject:** Death of Anna Dorothea **Obverse:** Bust right, double legends with dates **Reverse:** Scorpion and other Zodiacal signs with rays streaming down through clouds, eagle in sky above town scene, legend in curved band at top, mintmaster's initials and symbol in exergue **Rev. Legend:** ARDVA DIFFICILI ADSCENSV **Note:** Dav.2604.

Date	Mintage	F	VF	XF	Unc
1704 HCH	—	300	600	1,250	2,500

TRADE COINAGE

KM# 78 DUCAT
3.5000 g., 0.9860 Gold 0.1109 oz. AGW **Ruler:** Anna Dorothea von Saxe-Weimar **Subject:** Death of Anna Dorothea **Obverse:** Bust to right, double legends with dates **Reverse:** Rays from setting sun at lower right over hilly landscape, inscription in curved band above **Rev. Legend:** ABITV DECORATVR AMOENO **Note:** Fr. #2447. Struck from 1/8 Thaler dies, KM #75.

Date	Mintage	VG	F	VF	XF	Unc
1704 HCH	—	350	700	1,200	2,200	—

KM# 79 2 DUCAT
7.0000 g., 0.9860 Gold 0.2219 oz. AGW **Ruler:** Anna Dorothea von Saxe-Weimar **Subject:** Death of Anna Dorothea **Obverse:** Bust to right, double legends with dates **Reverse:** Three-masted sailing ship to right, legend in curved band above, mintmaster's initials and symbol in exergue **Rev. Legend:** ADVERSIS DECOR ADDITVS **Note:** Fr. #2446. Struck from 1/4 Thaler dies, KM #76.

Date	Mintage	VG	F	VF	XF	Unc
1704 HCH	—	1,000	2,000	3,500	6,000	—

REGENSBURG

(Ratisbon)

Regensburg is located in Bavaria. Coinage was first struck jointly with the dukes of Bavaria beginning in the 10th century then later on its own. It was secularized in 1810 and ceded to Bavaria.

MINT OFFICIALS' INITIALS

Initials	Date	Name
B, BF, G.C.B.	1773-1803	Georg Christoph Busch
B, I.C.B.	1741-66	Johann Christoph Busch
F, I.M.F., 2 wings, 1 wing	1700-40	Johann Michael Federer
GM	1762-94	Gotthardt Martinengo, in Coblenz
GZ, Z	1791-1802	Johann Leonhard Zollner
K, Kornlein	1773-1802	Johann Nikolaus Kornlein
O, CDO, CD OEXL, CD OEXLEIN	1714-79	Christoph Daniel Oxlein
OE, I.L OEXLEIN	1737-66 (intermittently)	Johann Leonhard Oxlein
R.	1766-67	Georg Nikolaus Riedner
RRB	1740	David Michael Busch
(Cinquefoil)	1706-12	Johann Pichler

WARDENS

Date	Name
1700-18	Johann Georg Kramer
1700-18	Johann Georg Kramer
1725-38	Christoph Matthias Baueisen
1742-61	David Michael Marenz
1775-91	Jakob Schneider

DIE-CUTTERS and ENGRAVERS

Date	Name
1691-1706	Johann Adam Seitz
1694-95, 1706	Philipp Heinrich Muller
1756	Georg Friedrich Loos
1759	Christoph Wilhelm Lehner

BISHOPRIC

RULERS
Anton Ignaz, Bishop, 1769-1787
Sede Vacante, 1787
Max Prokop, 1787-1789
Joseph Conrad, 1790-1803

REGULAR COINAGE

KM# 381 1/3 THALER (1/2 Gulden)
Silver **Obverse:** St. Peter in small boat within baroque frame **Reverse:** View of Regensburg cathedral, Roman numeral date below **Note:** Sede vacante.

Date	Mintage	VG	F	VF	XF	Unc
1763 Rare	—	—	—	—	—	—

KM# 449 THALER
Silver **Ruler:** Anton Ignaz Josef, Graf von Fugger-Glött **Obverse:** Bust right **Obv. Legend:** ANTON • IGNAT • D • G • EPISC • RATISBON •, KÖRNLEIN and date below **Reverse:** Arms within crowned mantle **Rev. Legend:** PRAEP • & D • ELVAC • - S • R • I • PR • C • FUGGER •, G• C• - B• and * X • EINE FEINE MARK • * below **Note:** Convention Thaler. Dav. #2605.

Date	Mintage	F	VF	XF	Unc
1786 KORNLEIN/GCB	—	400	650	1,150	2,000

KM# 450 THALER
Silver **Ruler:** Anton Ignaz Josef, Graf von Fugger-Glött **Obverse:** Inscription, Roman date below **Reverse:** St. Peter in small boat, 15 small shields surround **Rev. Inscription:** REGNANS/ CAPITVLVM/ ECCLESIAE/ CATHEDRALIS/ RATISBONENSIS/ SEDE VACANTE • / MDCCLXXXVII • / 10 • EINE F • MARK • below **Note:** Sede Vacante Issue. Dav. #2606.

Date	Mintage	F	VF	XF	Unc
MDCCLXXXVII (1787) BK	—	175	325	550	900

KM# 382 1-1/2 THALER
Silver **Obverse:** View of Regensburg cathedral, Roman numeral, date below **Reverse:** St. Peter in small boat, 15 small shields of arms around

Date	Mintage	VG	F	VF	XF	Unc
1763	—	150	225	400	650	—

TRADE COINAGE

KM# 415 DUCAT
3.5000 g., 0.9860 Gold 0.1109 oz. AGW **Ruler:** Anton Ignaz Josef, Graf von Fugger-Glött **Obverse:** Bust right **Reverse:** Crowned and mantled arms

Date	Mintage	VG	F	VF	XF	Unc
1770 GM	—	900	1,750	3,250	5,500	—

FREE CITY

RULER
Holy Roman until 1802

ARMS
2 crossed keys

REGULAR COINAGE

KM# 192 HELLER
Copper **Note:** Diamond-shaped with rounded corners, Regensburg arms divide date, R above, H below.

Date	Mintage	VG	F	VF	XF	Unc
1701	427,000	5.00	12.00	20.00	40.00	—
1702	459,000	5.00	12.00	20.00	40.00	—
1703	260,000	5.00	12.00	20.00	40.00	—
1704	—	5.00	12.00	20.00	40.00	—
1705	250,000	5.00	12.00	20.00	40.00	—
1706	194,000	5.00	12.00	20.00	40.00	—
1707	133,000	5.00	12.00	20.00	40.00	—

KM# 237 HELLER
Copper **Obverse:** Crossed keys divide date **Note:** Uniface. Varieties exist.

Date	Mintage	VG	F	VF	XF	Unc
1709	244,000	2.50	4.50	9.00	18.00	—
1712	177,000	2.50	4.50	9.00	18.00	—
1714	—	2.50	4.50	9.00	18.00	—
1716	—	2.50	4.50	9.00	18.00	—
1717	—	2.50	4.50	9.00	18.00	—
1718	—	2.50	4.50	9.00	18.00	—
1719	118,000	2.50	4.50	9.00	18.00	—
1721	130,000	2.50	4.50	9.00	18.00	—
1722	212,000	2.50	4.50	9.00	18.00	—
1724	94,000	2.50	4.50	9.00	18.00	—
1725	271,000	2.50	4.50	9.00	18.00	—
1727	142,000	2.50	4.50	9.00	18.00	—
1728	165,000	2.50	4.50	9.00	18.00	—
1729	201,000	2.50	4.50	9.00	18.00	—
1730	330,000	2.50	4.50	9.00	18.00	—
1732	118,000	2.50	4.50	9.00	18.00	—
1733	189,000	2.50	4.50	9.00	18.00	—
1734	236,000	2.50	4.50	9.00	18.00	—
1735	283,000	2.50	4.50	9.00	18.00	—
1736	—	2.50	4.50	9.00	18.00	—
1737	1,004,000	2.50	4.50	9.00	18.00	—

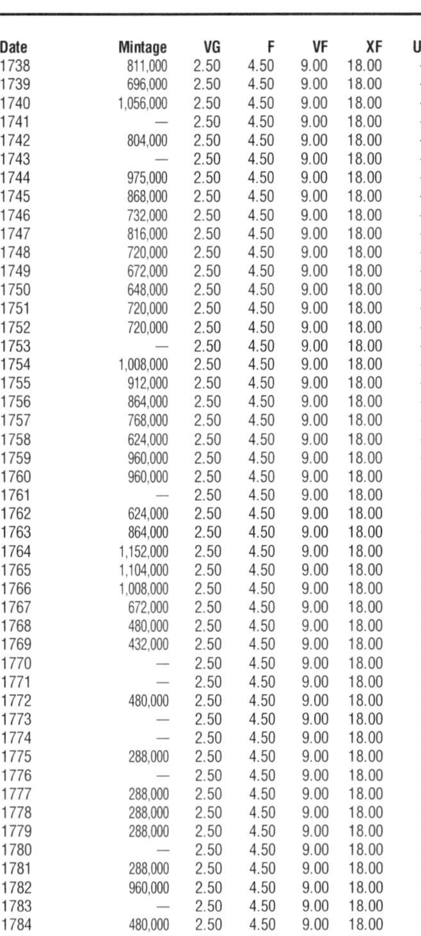
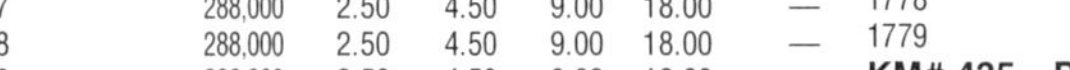

Date	Mintage	VG	F	VF	XF	Unc
1738	811,000	2.50	4.50	9.00	18.00	—
1739	696,000	2.50	4.50	9.00	18.00	—
1740	1,056,000	2.50	4.50	9.00	18.00	—
1741	—	2.50	4.50	9.00	18.00	—
1742	804,000	2.50	4.50	9.00	18.00	—
1743	—	2.50	4.50	9.00	18.00	—
1744	975,000	2.50	4.50	9.00	18.00	—
1745	868,000	2.50	4.50	9.00	18.00	—
1746	732,000	2.50	4.50	9.00	18.00	—
1747	816,000	2.50	4.50	9.00	18.00	—
1748	720,000	2.50	4.50	9.00	18.00	—
1749	672,000	2.50	4.50	9.00	18.00	—
1750	648,000	2.50	4.50	9.00	18.00	—
1751	720,000	2.50	4.50	9.00	18.00	—
1752	720,000	2.50	4.50	9.00	18.00	—
1753	—	2.50	4.50	9.00	18.00	—
1754	1,008,000	2.50	4.50	9.00	18.00	—
1755	912,000	2.50	4.50	9.00	18.00	—
1756	864,000	2.50	4.50	9.00	18.00	—
1757	768,000	2.50	4.50	9.00	18.00	—
1758	624,000	2.50	4.50	9.00	18.00	—
1759	960,000	2.50	4.50	9.00	18.00	—
1760	960,000	2.50	4.50	9.00	18.00	—
1761	—	2.50	4.50	9.00	18.00	—
1762	624,000	2.50	4.50	9.00	18.00	—
1763	864,000	2.50	4.50	9.00	18.00	—
1764	1,152,000	2.50	4.50	9.00	18.00	—
1765	1,104,000	2.50	4.50	9.00	18.00	—
1766	1,008,000	2.50	4.50	9.00	18.00	—
1767	672,000	2.50	4.50	9.00	18.00	—
1768	480,000	2.50	4.50	9.00	18.00	—
1769	432,000	2.50	4.50	9.00	18.00	—
1770	—	2.50	4.50	9.00	18.00	—
1771	—	2.50	4.50	9.00	18.00	—
1772	480,000	2.50	4.50	9.00	18.00	—
1773	—	2.50	4.50	9.00	18.00	—
1774	—	2.50	4.50	9.00	18.00	—
1775	288,000	2.50	4.50	9.00	18.00	—
1776	—	2.50	4.50	9.00	18.00	—
1777	288,000	2.50	4.50	9.00	18.00	—
1778	288,000	2.50	4.50	9.00	18.00	—
1779	288,000	2.50	4.50	9.00	18.00	—
1780	—	2.50	4.50	9.00	18.00	—
1781	288,000	2.50	4.50	9.00	18.00	—
1782	960,000	2.50	4.50	9.00	18.00	—
1783	—	2.50	4.50	9.00	18.00	—
1784	480,000	2.50	4.50	9.00	18.00	—
1786	—	2.50	4.50	9.00	18.00	—
1787	288,000	2.50	4.50	9.00	18.00	—
1788	864,000	2.50	4.50	9.00	18.00	—
1791	288,000	2.50	4.50	9.00	18.00	—
1792	288,000	2.50	4.50	9.00	18.00	—
1793	—	2.50	4.50	9.00	18.00	—
ND	—	2.50	4.50	9.00	18.00	—

KM# 470 HELLER

Copper **Obverse:** Crossed keys **Note:** Uniface

Date	Mintage	VG	F	VF	XF	Unc
1794	336,000	2.50	4.50	9.00	18.00	—
1795	288,000	2.50	4.50	9.00	18.00	—
1796	288,000	2.50	4.50	9.00	18.00	—
1797	384,000	2.50	4.50	9.00	18.00	—
1799	—	2.50	4.50	9.00	18.00	—
1801	—	2.50	4.50	9.00	18.00	—
1802	192,000	2.50	4.50	9.00	18.00	—
1803	104,000	2.50	4.50	9.00	18.00	—

KM# 236 PFENNIG

Silver **Note:** Regensburg arms in ornamented oval frame, date divided at top.

Date	Mintage	VG	F	VF	XF	Unc
1707	—	7.00	12.00	25.00	45.00	—

KM# 253 PFENNIG

Silver **Note:** Regensburg arms in cartouche, date above. Varieties exist.

Date	Mintage	VG	F	VF	XF	Unc
1712	—	6.00	10.00	20.00	40.00	—
1716	24,000	6.00	10.00	20.00	40.00	—
1722	—	6.00	10.00	20.00	40.00	—
1723	46,000	6.00	10.00	20.00	40.00	—
1725	38,000	6.00	10.00	20.00	40.00	—
1727	102,000	6.00	10.00	20.00	40.00	—
1732	71,000	6.00	10.00	20.00	40.00	—
1736	—	6.00	10.00	20.00	40.00	—
1738	128,000	6.00	10.00	20.00	40.00	—
1740	—	6.00	10.00	20.00	40.00	—
1741	—	6.00	10.00	20.00	40.00	—

KM# 299 PFENNIG

Silver **Obverse:** Date divided at top **Note:** Varieties exist. Uniface.

Date	Mintage	VG	F	VF	XF	Unc
1742	62,000	4.00	8.00	16.00	35.00	—
1745	87,000	4.00	8.00	16.00	35.00	—
1746	13,000	4.00	8.00	16.00	35.00	—
1747	6,000	4.00	8.00	16.00	35.00	—
ND B	—	4.00	8.00	16.00	35.00	—

KM# 349 PFENNIG

Silver **Obverse:** Date divided above city arms **Reverse:** Value within branches

Date	Mintage	VG	F	VF	XF	Unc
1747	32,000	4.00	7.50	12.50	25.00	—
1748	—	4.00	7.50	12.50	25.00	—
1749	17,000	4.00	7.50	12.50	25.00	—
1750	48,000	4.00	7.50	12.50	25.00	—
1752	18,000	4.00	7.50	12.50	25.00	—
1753	—	4.00	7.50	12.50	25.00	—
1754	27,000	4.00	7.50	12.50	25.00	—
1755	35,000	4.00	7.50	12.50	25.00	—
1756	11,000	4.00	7.50	12.50	25.00	—
1758	123,000	4.00	7.50	12.50	25.00	—
1759	542,000	4.00	7.50	12.50	25.00	—
1761	288,000	4.00	7.50	12.50	25.00	—
1763	41,000	4.00	7.50	12.50	25.00	—
1764	72,000	4.00	7.50	12.50	25.00	—
1765	36,000	4.00	7.50	12.50	25.00	—
1766	24,000	4.00	7.50	12.50	25.00	—

KM# 408 PFENNIG

Silver **Obverse:** Date divided above city arms **Reverse:** Value within branches

Date	Mintage	VG	F	VF	XF	Unc
1767 R	106,000	4.00	7.50	12.50	25.00	—
1774	—	4.00	7.50	12.50	25.00	—
1776	—	4.00	7.50	12.50	25.00	—
1778	39,000	4.00	7.50	12.50	25.00	—
1779	—	4.00	7.50	12.50	25.00	—

KM# 435 PFENNIG

Silver

Date	Mintage	VG	F	VF	XF	Unc
1780	—	4.00	7.50	12.50	25.00	—
1781	—	4.00	7.50	12.50	25.00	—
1783	70,000	4.00	7.50	12.50	25.00	—

KM# 447 PFENNIG

Silver

Date	Mintage	VG	F	VF	XF	Unc
1785 R	120,000	4.00	7.50	12.50	25.00	—
1790 R	48,000	4.00	7.50	12.50	25.00	—

KM# 462 PFENNIG

Silver **Obverse:** Crowned city arms **Reverse:** Value within branches

Date	Mintage	VG	F	VF	XF	Unc
1791	53,000	4.00	7.50	12.50	25.00	—
1792	24,000	4.00	7.50	12.50	25.00	—
1793	82,000	4.00	7.50	12.50	25.00	—
1797	53,000	4.00	7.50	12.50	25.00	—

KM# 205 1/2 KREUZER (2 Pfennig)

Silver **Obverse:** Regensburg arms in cartouche, value: 1/2 in ornament above divides date **Note:** Uniface

Date	Mintage	VG	F	VF	XF	Unc
Note: 1/2 Kreuzer dated 1696 reported struck in 1696, 1701 and 1734; Mintage reported only in latter year at 6,048 pieces						
1706	—	6.00	12.00	25.00	45.00	—
1738 Reported, not confirmed	—	—	—	—	—	—

KM# 176 KREUZER

Billon **Obverse:** Heart-shaped cartouche encloses arms, date above **Reverse:** Crowned imperial eagle, value: I in shield on breast **Note:** Varieties exist.

Date	Mintage	VG	F	VF	XF	Unc
1716 MF	—	7.00	15.00	30.00	60.00	—

KM# 228 KREUZER

Billon **Obverse:** Crowned imperial eagle, value: I in orb on breast **Reverse:** Regensburg arms in ornate baroque frame, date above **Note:** Varieties exist.

Date	Mintage	VG	F	VF	XF	Unc
1706	24,000	7.00	15.00	30.00	60.00	—
Note: Some of 1706 struck in 1711						
1716 IMF	20,000	7.00	15.00	30.00	60.00	—
Note: Some of 1716 struck in 1724, 1726, 1729						
1732 IMF	21,000	7.00	15.00	30.00	60.00	—
Note: Some of 1732 struck in 1734 and 1737, date altered from 1716 die						

KM# 291 KREUZER

Billon **Obverse:** Crowned imperial eagle, value: I in heart-shaped shield on breast **Reverse:** Regensburg arms, date between tops of keys, all in oval baroque frame, angel's head above

Date	Mintage	VG	F	VF	XF	Unc
1738 IMF	25,000	12.00	25.00	50.00	85.00	—

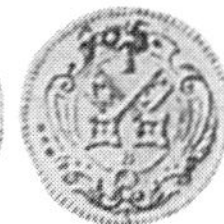

KM# 292 KREUZER

Billon **Obverse:** Value: I in orb on breast, crowned imperial eagle **Reverse:** Regensburg arms in round baroque frame **Note:** Varieties exist.

Date	Mintage	VG	F	VF	XF	Unc
ND B	32,000	—	—	—	—	—
Note: Kreuzers struck in 1744, 1745 and 1752, but whether or not date present on coins not indicated; Total mintage for this type could have included some dated 1738						

KM# 364 KREUZER

Billon **Obverse:** Crowned imperial double-headed eagle, value in orb on breast **Reverse:** City arms

Date	Mintage	VG	F	VF	XF	Unc
1754	199,000	3.00	6.00	12.00	28.00	—
1758 B	14,000	3.00	6.00	12.00	28.00	—
1764	4,500	3.00	6.00	12.00	28.00	—
1774	—	3.00	6.00	12.00	28.00	—

KM# 409 KREUZER

Billon **Obverse:** Crowned imperial double-headed eagle, value in orb on breast **Reverse:** City arms

Date	Mintage	VG	F	VF	XF	Unc
1767	13,000	3.00	6.00	12.00	28.00	—
1774	—	3.00	6.00	12.00	28.00	—

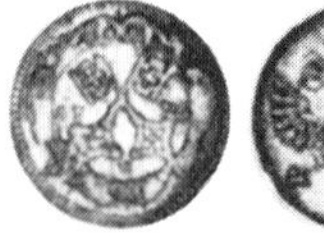

KM# 430 KREUZER

Billon **Obverse:** City arms **Reverse:** Crowned imperial double-headed eagle, value in orb on breast

Date	Mintage	VG	F	VF	XF	Unc
1776	—	3.00	6.00	12.00	28.00	—
1781	6,000	3.00	6.00	12.00	28.00	—

KM# 448 KREUZER

Billon **Obverse:** City arms **Reverse:** Crowned imperial double-headed eagle, value in orb on breast

Date	Mintage	VG	F	VF	XF	Unc
1785	49,000	3.00	6.00	12.00	28.00	—

KM# 451 KREUZER

Billon **Obverse:** Crowned imperial double-headed eagle, value in orb on breast **Reverse:** City arms

Date	Mintage	VG	F	VF	XF	Unc
1787	—	3.00	6.00	12.00	28.00	—
Note: Struck intermittantly with same date through 1803						

KM# 365 2 KREUZER

Silver

Date	Mintage	VG	F	VF	XF	Unc
1754	56,000	5.00	7.50	12.50	25.00	—

KM# 312 2 KREUZER

Silver **Obverse:** Titles of Karl VI

Date	Mintage	VG	F	VF	XF	Unc
ND(1744) B	3,984	35.00	60.00	120	200	—

KM# 229 2 KREUZER
Silver **Obverse:** Regensburg arms in oval baroque frame, date at top **Reverse:** Value: 2 on orb on breast, crowned imperial eagle, titles of Josef I

Date	Mintage	VG	F	VF	XF	Unc
1706	—	18.00	40.00	80.00	135	—

KM# 255 2 KREUZER
Silver **Obverse:** Value: 1/2 on imperial orb, titles of Karl VI
Note: Varieties exist.

Date	Mintage	VG	F	VF	XF	Unc
1714	—	12.00	20.00	40.00	75.00	—
1716/4	10,000	12.00	20.00	40.00	75.00	—
Note: Coins dated 1716/4 struck intermittantly until 1734						
1738	9,000	12.00	20.00	40.00	75.00	—

KM# 350 2 KREUZER
Silver **Obverse:** Titles of Franz I

Date	Mintage	VG	F	VF	XF	Unc
ND(1748) B	6,600	10.00	20.00	40.00	70.00	—

KM# 366 2 KREUZER
Silver **Obverse:** City arms **Reverse:** B below keys

Date	Mintage	VG	F	VF	XF	Unc
1754 B	56,000	5.00	7.50	12.50	25.00	—

KM# 410 2 KREUZER
Billon **Obverse:** Arms in cartouche, date below
Reverse: Imperial eagle, value on breast

Date	Mintage	VG	F	VF	XF	Unc
1767 R	1,950	5.00	7.50	12.50	25.00	—

KM# 426 2 KREUZER
Billon **Obverse:** Crowned imperial eagle with value on breast
Reverse: Crossed keys in cartouche over date

Date	Mintage	VG	F	VF	XF	Unc
1775 B	6,000	4.00	6.50	10.00	20.00	—

KM# 452 2 KREUZER
Billon **Obverse:** City arms, date below **Reverse:** Crowned imperial double-headed eagle, value in orb on breast

Date	Mintage	VG	F	VF	XF	Unc
1787	4,500	4.00	6.50	10.00	20.00	—

KM# 313 4 KREUZER (1 Batzen)
Silver **Obverse:** Regensburg arms in oval baroque frame
Reverse: Value: 4 on imperial orb on breast, crowned imperial eagle, titles of Karl VII

Date	Mintage	VG	F	VF	XF	Unc
ND(1744) B	1,784	30.00	50.00	100	180	—

KM# 362 4 KREUZER (1 Batzen)
Silver **Obverse:** Titles of Franz I

Date	Mintage	VG	F	VF	XF	Unc
ND(1751) B	1,185	35.00	60.00	120	200	—

KM# 367 10 KREUZER (1/6 Guldenthaler)
Silver **Obverse:** Date divided by arms atop pedestal with value
Reverse: Crowned imperial double-headed eagle within branches **Rev. Legend:** FRANCISCVS I • D • G • - ROM • IMP • SEMP • AVG •

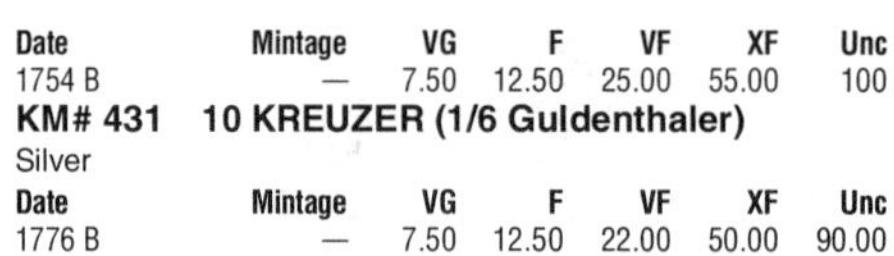

Date	Mintage	VG	F	VF	XF	Unc
1754 B	—	7.50	12.50	25.00	55.00	100

KM# 431 10 KREUZER (1/6 Guldenthaler)
Silver

Date	Mintage	VG	F	VF	XF	Unc
1776 B	—	7.50	12.50	22.00	50.00	90.00

KM# 439 10 KREUZER (1/6 Guldenthaler)
Silver **Obverse:** City arms within branches atop pedestal with value **Reverse:** Crowned imperial double-headed eagle

Date	Mintage	VG	F	VF	XF	Unc
1781 B	3,600	7.50	12.50	22.00	50.00	90.00

KM# 440 10 KREUZER (1/6 Guldenthaler)
Silver **Obverse:** Eagle holds sword in orb

Date	Mintage	VG	F	VF	XF	Unc
1781 B	3,600	7.50	12.50	22.00	50.00	90.00

KM# 441 10 KREUZER (1/6 Guldenthaler)
Silver **Obverse:** Crowned imperial double-headed eagle
Reverse: Date moved to above pedestal

Date	Mintage	VG	F	VF	XF	Unc
1781 B	3,600	7.50	12.50	22.00	50.00	90.00

KM# 442 10 KREUZER (1/6 Guldenthaler)
Silver **Obverse:** Without sword or orb held by eagle

Date	Mintage	VG	F	VF	XF	Unc
1781 B	3,600	7.50	12.50	22.00	50.00	90.00

KM# 314 15 KREUZER (1/8 Thaler)
Silver **Obverse:** Bust of Karl VII right, titles **Reverse:** Regensburg arms in oval baroque frame, value: XV at bottom

Date	Mintage	VG	F	VF	XF	Unc
ND(1744) ICB/OEXL	208	90.00	200	400	675	—

KM# 315 15 KREUZER (1/8 Thaler)
Silver **Obverse:** City arms, Roman numeral value below
Reverse: Bust of Franz I and titles **Rev. Legend:** FRAANCISC: - D • G • R • I • S • A •

Date	Mintage	VG	F	VF	XF	Unc
ND ICB/I.L.OE	—	90.00	200	400	675	—

KM# 316 15 KREUZER (1/8 Thaler)
Silver **Reverse:** City view, small Regensburg arms in cartouche below

Date	Mintage	VG	F	VF	XF	Unc
ND ICB/I.L/OE	—	90.00	200	400	675	—

KM# 368 20 KREUZER
Silver **Obverse:** Crowned imperial double-headed eagle
Obv. Legend: FRANCISCVS • I • D • G • - ROM • IMP • SEMP • AVG • **Reverse:** Arms atop pedestal with value, date divided

Date	Mintage	F	VF	XF	Unc
1754 B	—	15.00	25.00	45.00	100

KM# 417 20 KREUZER
Silver

Date	Mintage	F	VF	XF	Unc
1774 B	—	10.00	20.00	40.00	85.00

KM# 418 20 KREUZER
Silver **Obverse:** Without branches around eagle

Date	Mintage	F	VF	XF	Unc
1774 GCB	—	10.00	20.00	40.00	85.00

KM# 419 20 KREUZER
Silver **Obverse:** Date at bottom

Date	Mintage	F	VF	XF	Unc
1774 B	—	10.00	20.00	40.00	85.00

KM# 420 20 KREUZER
Silver **Obverse:** Crowned imperial double-headed eagle
Obv. Legend: IOSEPHVS II. D. G. ROM. IMP. SEMP. AVG.
Note: Convention 20 Kreuzer. Varieties exist.

Date	Mintage	F	VF	XF	Unc
1774 B	—	10.00	20.00	40.00	85.00
1775 B	4,273	12.00	25.00	45.00	100

KM# 369 1/4 THALER
Silver **Obverse:** City view **Reverse:** Armored bust right
Rev. Legend: FRANCISC: - D: G: R: I: S: A:

Date	Mintage	F	VF	XF	Unc
1754 ICB/ILOE	632	100	175	250	450

KM# 230 1/4 THALER
Silver **Obverse:** Round Regensburg arms in baroque frame, date divided at top **Reverse:** Value: 1/4 on orb on breast, crowned imperial eagle, titles of Josef I

Date	Mintage	VG	F	VF	XF	Unc
1706 (e)	—	125	300	600	1,000	—

KM# 231 1/4 THALER
Silver **Reverse:** Oval arms, date undivided at top

Date	Mintage	VG	F	VF	XF	Unc
1706 (e)	—	175	400	800	1,250	—

KM# 275 1/4 THALER
Silver **Obverse:** Bust right, titles of Karl VI **Reverse:** Value: 1/4 above crossed keys which divide date **Note:** Varieties exist.

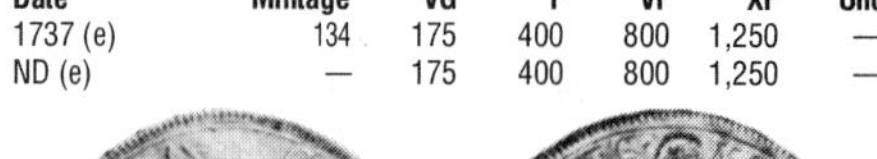

Date	Mintage	VG	F	VF	XF	Unc
1737 (e)	134	175	400	800	1,250	—
ND (e)	—	175	400	800	1,250	—

KM# 276 1/4 THALER
Silver **Obverse:** Oval Regensburg arms in baroque frame
Reverse: Bust right, titles of Karl VII **Rev. Legend:** CAROL • VII • D • G • -- R • I • S • A •

Date	Mintage	VG	F	VF	XF	Unc
ND ICB/OE	—	275	600	1,200	2,000	—

KM# 277 1/4 THALER

Silver **Obverse:** Bust right, titles of Franz I

Date	Mintage	VG	F	VF	XF	Unc
ND ICB/ILOE	—	90.00	200	400	675	—

KM# 278 1/4 THALER

Silver **Obverse:** City view **Reverse:** Armored, draped laureate bust right **Rev. Legend:** FRANCISC. - D. G. R. I. S. A. **Note:** 3 Ducat struck from same dies.

Date	Mintage	VG	F	VF	XF	Unc
ND B/ILOE	—	90.00	200	400	675	—

KM# 453 1/4 THALER

Silver **Subject:** Archery Contest **Reverse:** Inscription **Note:** Convention 1/4 Thaler.

Date	Mintage	VG	F	VF	XF	Unc
1788	—	30.00	60.00	90.00	150	—

KM# 232 1/2 THALER

Silver **Obverse:** Regensburg arms in baroque frame divide date, angel's head and wings above **Reverse:** Titles of Josef I **Rev. Legend:** IOSEPHVS • D • G • - ROM • IMP • SEMP • AVG •

Date	Mintage	VG	F	VF	XF	Unc
1706 (e)	430	150	350	700	1,500	—

KM# 233 1/2 THALER

Silver **Obverse:** Oval Regensburg arms in baroque frame **Reverse:** Crowned imperial eagle holding sword and scepter in claws, titles of Karl VI **Rev. Legend:** CAROLVS • VI • D • G • - ROM • IMP • SEMP • AVG •

Date	Mintage	VG	F	VF	XF	Unc
ND (e)	—	225	475	875	1,700	—

KM# 263 1/2 THALER

Silver **Obverse:** Regensburg arms in ribbon-like baroque frame, date in small frame below **Reverse:** Bust right, titles of Karl VI **Rev. Legend:** CAROL • VII - D • G • ROM • IMP • S • A •

Date	Mintage	VG	F	VF	XF	Unc
1716 (e)	100	300	650	1,200	1,750	—
1737 (e)	60	300	650	1,200	1,750	—

KM# 264 1/2 THALER

Silver **Obverse:** Bust right and titles of Karl VII **Obv. Legend:** CAROL • VII - D • G • ROM • IMP • S • A • **Reverse:** Oval Regensburg arms in baroque frame

Date	Mintage	VG	F	VF	XF	Unc
ND ICB/C.D. OEXL	—	250	500	1,000	1,650	—

KM# 265 1/2 THALER

Silver **Obverse:** City view, small Regensburg arms below **Reverse:** Armored laureate bust right **Rev. Legend:** CAROL • VII - D • G • ROM • IMP •S • A •

Date	Mintage	VG	F	VF	XF	Unc
ND B/I.L.OE/C.D. OEXL	—	275	525	1,050	1,700	—

KM# 266 1/2 THALER

Silver **Obverse:** Bust right, titles of Franz I

Date	Mintage	VG	F	VF	XF	Unc
ND B/ILOE	—	90.00	200	400	675	—

KM# 267 1/2 THALER

Silver **Obverse:** City view **Reverse:** Armored laureate bust right **Note:** Varieties exist.

Date	Mintage	VG	F	VF	XF	Unc
ND B/ILOE	—	70.00	120	240	400	—
ND B/ILOE/CDOEXL	—	70.00	120	240	400	—

KM# 370 1/2 THALER

Silver **Obverse:** City view **Reverse:** Laureate armored bust right **Rev. Legend:** FRANCISCUS D • G • - ROM • IMP • SEMP • AVG •

Date	Mintage	F	VF	XF	Unc
1754 ICB	1,360	125	200	300	450

KM# 383 1/2 THALER

Silver **Subject:** Peace of Hubertusburg **Obverse:** 8-line inscription **Reverse:** Globe on pedestal **Note:** Convertion 1/2 Thaler.

Date	Mintage	F	VF	XF	Unc
1763	—	150	225	325	475

KM# 421 1/2 THALER

Silver **Obverse:** City arms **Obv. Legend:** NON DORMIT CUSTOS **Reverse:** Laureate armored bust right **Rev. Legend:** IOSEPHVS II • - D • G • ROM • IMP • S • A •

Date	Mintage	F	VF	XF	Unc
1774 GCB	—	25.00	50.00	100	200

KM# 422 1/2 THALER

Silver **Obverse:** City arms, "Eye of God" above **Reverse:** Armored laureate bust right **Rev. Legend:** IOSEPHVS II - D. G. ROM. IMP. S. A.

Date	Mintage	F	VF	XF	Unc
1774 GCB	—	25.00	50.00	100	200

KM# 427 1/2 THALER

Silver **Obverse:** City view **Reverse:** Draped, laureate bust right **Rev. Legend:** IOSEPHVS II • - D • G • ROM • IMP • S • A •

Date	Mintage	F	VF	XF	Unc
1775 GCB	—	35.00	70.00	125	250

KM# 443 1/2 THALER

Silver **Obverse:** City view **Reverse:** Laureate bust right
Rev. Legend: IOSEPHVS II. D. G. ROM. IMP. SEMP. AVGVST.

Date	Mintage	F	VF	XF	Unc
1781 GCB	—	35.00	70.00	125	250

KM# 444 1/2 THALER

Silver **Obverse:** City view **Reverse:** Armored laureate bust right
Rev. Legend: IOSEPHVS II • - D • G • ROM • IMP • S • A •

Date	Mintage	F	VF	XF	Unc
1782 GCB	—	35.00	70.00	125	250

KM# 445 1/2 THALER

Silver **Obverse:** City arms, "Eye of God" above
Reverse: Laureate armored bust right **Rev. Legend:** IOSEPHVS II • - D • G • ROM • IMP • S • A • **Note:** Mule.

Date	Mintage	F	VF	XF	Unc
1782 GCB	—	60.00	100	175	300

KM# 446 1/2 THALER

Silver **Obverse:** City arms, value and date below **Reverse:** Crowned imperial double-headed eagle with orb on breast
Rev. Legend: IOSEPHVS II • D • G • - ROM • IMP • SEMP • AVG •

Date	Mintage	F	VF	XF	Unc
1784 KB	1,280	125	225	300	500

KM# 454 1/2 THALER

Silver **Subject:** Archery Contest **Obverse:** 8-line legend
Reverse: Target and crossbows

Date	Mintage	F	VF	XF	Unc
1788	—	50.00	100	150	300

KM# 463 1/2 THALER

Silver **Obverse:** City view **Reverse:** Laureate head right
Rev. Legend: LEOPOLDVS II • D • G • RUM • IMP • S • A •

Date	Mintage	F	VF	XF	Unc
1791 GCB/K	1,446	40.00	80.00	125	275

KM# 256 THALER

Silver **Obverse:** City arms in frame, date below
Obv. Legend: MONETA REIPVBLICAE - RATISBONENSIS
Reverse: Bust right **Rev. Legend:** CAROL: VI D • G • - R • I • S • A • G • H • H • & B • R • **Note:** Dav. #2609.

Date	Mintage	F	VF	XF	Unc
1714 (e) CD OXLEIN	—	275	550	1,100	1,850
1716 (e)	209	275	550	1,100	1,850
1737 (e)	82	275	550	1,100	1,850

KM# 234 THALER

Silver **Obverse:** Cupid above city arms in shield dividing date
Obv. Legend: * MONETA • REIPVBLICAE • RATISBONENSIS * **Reverse:** Titles of Josef **Rev. Legend:** IOSEPHVS • D • G • - ROM • IMP • SEMP • AVG • **Note:** Dav. #2608.

Date	Mintage	F	VF	XF	Unc
1706 (e)	—	275	550	1,100	1,850

KM# 257 THALER

Silver **Obverse:** City arms in elaborate frame
Obv. Legend: * MONETA * REIPVBLICAE * RATISBONENSIS * **Reverse:** Different bust **Rev. Legend:** CAROLVS VI • D • G • ROM • SEMP • AVG • **Note:** Dav. #2612.

Date	Mintage	F	VF	XF	Unc
ND (e)	—	650	1,200	2,250	3,750
ND (e) CDO	—	650	1,200	2,250	3,750
ND (e) O	—	650	1,200	2,250	3,750

KM# 261 THALER

Silver **Obverse:** Armored laureate bust right **Obv. Legend:** CAROL. VII. - D. G. ROM. IMP. SEMP. AVG., C. D. OEXL. below
Reverse: City arms in frame **Rev. Legend:** MONETA REIPUBL. - RATISBONENSIS **Note:** Dav. #2615.

Date	Mintage	F	VF	XF	Unc
ND ICB/C.D. OE	—	950	1,650	2,750	4,250

KM# 260 THALER

Silver **Obverse:** Armored laureate bust right
Obv. Legend: CAROL • VII • - D • G • ROM • IMP • SEMP • AVG
Reverse: Crowned eagle to left above city view, arms below
Rev. Legend: TALI SUB - CUSTODIA **Note:** Dav. #A2615.

Date	Mintage	F	VF	XF	Unc
ND ICB/C.D. OEXL Rare	280	—	—	—	—

KM# 279 THALER

Silver **Subject:** City Hall **Obverse:** Bust of Karl VI right **Reverse:** City hall, date in chronogram above, CVRIA RATISB below

Date	Mintage	VG	F	VF	XF	Unc
1737 O-F/CDO	462	650	1,200	1,850	2,750	—

KM# 280 THALER

Silver **Obverse:** Bust of Franz I right

Date	Mintage	VG	F	VF	XF	Unc
1737 O-F/I.L. OEXLEIN. F.	—	1,350	1,850	2,400	3,100	—

Note: Mule of previous coin with die of Franz I, not struck before 1745

KM# 258 THALER

Silver **Obverse:** City arms in elaborate frame **Obv. Legend:** MON • REIP •- RATISBON **Reverse:** Different bust **Rev. Legend:** CAROLVS VI • D • - G • ROM • IMP • SEMP • AVG, C D O below **Note:** Dav. #2613.

Date	Mintage	VG	F	VF	XF	Unc
ND (e)	—	250	500	1,000	2,000	—

KM# 259 THALER

Silver **Obverse:** Larger bust right, C. D. OEXL below **Obv. Legend:** CAROL • VII • - D • G • ROM • IMP • SEMP • AVG **Reverse:** City arms **Rev. Legend:** MON. REIP. - RATISBON **Note:** Dav. #2614.

Date	Mintage	VG	F	VF	XF	Unc
ND (e)	399	250	500	1,000	2,000	—

KM# 262 THALER

Silver **Note:** Similar to 2 Thaler, KM#216.

Date	Mintage	VG	F	VF	XF	Unc
ND (e)	—	750	1,125	1,500	1,950	—

KM# 317 THALER

Silver **Obverse:** Laureate bust of Franz I right **Reverse:** Interior view of city council chamber, small oval Regensburg arms below divides RATIS - PONAE/D. 29 - NOV. /17.45 **Note:** Ratssalthaler Thaler. Varieties exist.

Date	Mintage	VG	F	VF	XF	Unc
1745 C. D. OEXL	133	1,050	2,000	3,250	5,000	—
1745 C. D. OEXL/I.L. OEXLEIN. F.	—	1,050	2,000	3,250	5,000	—
174x C. D. OEXL/CDO	Inc. above	1,050	2,000	3,250	5,000	—

KM# 318 THALER

Silver **Obverse:** City view **Obv. Legend:** TALI SUB - CUSTODIA **Reverse:** Bust of Franz I right, I.L. OEXLEIN. F below **Rev. Legend:** FRANCISCUS D • G • - ROM • IMP • SEMP • AVG • **Note:** Dav. #2617.

Date	Mintage	VG	F	VF	XF	Unc
ND CDOE/C. D/ OEXL	—	150	300	600	1,200	—

KM# 319 THALER

Silver **Obverse:** Small eagle above different city view **Obv. Legend:** MONETA REIP • RATISPON •, in exergue; X•ST•EINE F•C•M•/date/ I•C•B• **Reverse:** Bust right, C.D. OEXL. below **Rev. Legend:** FRANCISCUS I • D • G • ROM IMP • SEMP • AUG • **Note:** Dav. #A2618.

Date	Mintage	F	VF	XF	Unc
ND CDOE/C.D. OEXL	—	150	300	600	1,200

KM# 371 THALER

Silver **Obverse:** City view **Obv. Legend:** MONETA REIP • RATISPON, X•ST•EINE F•C•M•/date/I•C•B• **Reverse:** Laureate bust with different wig right, I.L. OEXLEIN F below **Rev. Legend:** FRANCISCUS D: G: ROM: IMP: SEMP: AVG. **Note:** Dav. #2618B.

Date	Mintage	F	VF	XF	Unc
1754 ICB	—	75.00	150	325	650

KM# 372 THALER

Silver **Obverse:** Armored laureate bust right **Obv. Legend:** FRANCISCUS D: G: ROM: IMP: SEMP: AVG • **Reverse:** City view **Rev. Legend:** MONETA REIP • RATISPON, X•ST•EINE F•C•M•/date/I•C•B• **Note:** Dav. #2618.

Date	Mintage	F	VF	XF	Unc
1756 ICB	—	75.00	150	325	650

KM# 373 THALER

Silver **Reverse:** Similar to KM#374 **Note:** Dav. #2618A.

Date	Mintage	F	VF	XF	Unc
1756 ICB	—	75.00	150	325	650

KM# 374 THALER

Silver **Obverse:** City arms **Obv. Legend:** MONETA REIP • RATISPON, I•C• - B•, in exergue; X•ST•EINE•F•C•M•/1759/ C•D•OEXL• **Reverse:** Armored laureate bust right **Rev. Legend:** FRANCISCUS D: G: ROM: IMP: SEMP: AVG• **Note:** Dav. #2619.

Date	Mintage	F	VF	XF	Unc
1759 ICB	—	100	175	350	750

KM# 380 THALER

Silver **Obverse:** City view **Obv. Legend:** MONETA REIP • RATISPON •, X•ST•EINE F•G•M•/date/I•C•B• **Reverse:** Armored bust right **Rev. Legend:** FRANCISCUS D: G: ROM: IMP: SEMP: AVG • **Note:** Dav. #2618C.

Date	Mintage	F	VF	XF	Unc
1762 ICB	—	75.00	150	325	650

KM# 384 THALER

Silver **Subject:** Peace of Hubertusburg **Obverse:** Inscription **Obv. Inscription:** VOTIS/PRO PACE/ET/SALVTE IMPERII/ SOLVTIS/SAGITTARII/RATISBON./F. C. **Reverse:** Angel right of column **Rev. Legend:** FELICITAS - TEMPORVM, MDCCLXIII below and I.N.K. - I.C.B. at sides **Note:** Convention Thaler. Dav. #2620.

Date	Mintage	F	VF	XF	Unc
1763	—	350	700	1,200	2,000

KM# 407 THALER

Silver **Obverse:** Different portrait

Date	Mintage	F	VF	XF	Unc
1766 BF	—	300	600	950	1,800

KM# 405 THALER

Silver **Obverse:** Eagle over city arms **Obv. Legend:** MON. REIP. - RATISPON. **Reverse:** Armored laureate bust right **Rev. Legend:** IOSEPHVS II. D. G. - ROM. IMP. SEMP. AVG., OEXLEIN. below **Note:** Dav. #2621.

Date	Mintage	F	VF	XF	Unc
1766	—	275	550	900	1,700

KM# 406 THALER

Silver **Obverse:** City view **Obv. Legend:** MONETA REIP•RATISPON, in exergue; X•ST•EINE F•C•M•/1766 **Reverse:** Armored laureate bust right **Rev. Legend:** IOSEPHVS II. DD.G. - ROM. IMP. SEMP. AVG, OEXLEIN below **Note:** Dav. #2622.

Date	Mintage	F	VF	XF	Unc
1766	—	100	225	500	1,100

KM# 416 THALER

Silver **Obverse:** Keys on finely lined background **Obv. Legend:** DOMINE CONSERVA NOS IN PACE, in exergus; MON. REIP. RATISP./X. EINE F. MARK/1773 **Reverse:** Armored laureate bust right **Rev. Legend:** IOSEPHVS II D. G. - ROM. IMP. SEMP. AVG, KÖRNLEIN below **Note:** Dav. #2623.

Date	Mintage	F	VF	XF	Unc
1773 GCB	—	125	275	550	1,150

KM# 423 THALER

Silver **Obv. Legend:** DOMINE CONSERVA NOS IN PACE, in exergue: MON. REIP. RATISP./X. EINE F. MARK/1774 **Reverse:** Keys on plain background **Rev. Legend:** IOSEPHVS II D. G. - ROM. IMP. SEMP. AVG, KÖRNLEIN below **Note:** Dav. #2624.

Date	Mintage	F	VF	XF	Unc
1774 GCB	—	100	225	400	1,000

KM# 424 THALER

Silver **Obverse:** Portrait similar to KM#405 **Note:** Dav. #2624A.

Date	Mintage	F	VF	XF	Unc
1774 GCB	—	100	225	400	1,000

KM# 425 THALER

Silver **Obverse:** City arms **Obv. Legend:** DOMINE CONSERVA NOS IN PACE, in exergue; MON•REIP• RATISP•/X•EINE F•MARK/date **Reverse:** KORNLEIN on should truncation **Rev. Legend:** IOSBHVS II • D • G • ROM • IMP • SEMP • AVG

Date	Mintage	F	VF	XF	Unc
1774 GCB	—	100	225	400	1,000

KM# 429 THALER

Silver **Obverse:** Arms in wreath **Obv. Legend:** DOMINE CONSERVA NOS IN PACE, below; MON • REIP • RATISP •/X • EINE F • MARK/ **Reverse:** Armored laureate bust right **Rev. Legend:** IOSEPHVS II D • G • ROM • IMP • SEMP • AVG •, KÖRNLEIN below **Note:** Dav. #2625.

Date	Mintage	F	VF	XF	Unc
1775 GCB	—	100	225	400	1,000

KM# 428 THALER

Silver **Obverse:** Armored laureate bust right **Obv. Legend:** IOSEPHVS II D • G • ROM • IMP • SEMP • AVG •**Reverse:** City view **Rev. Legend:** MONETA REIP•RATISPON, X• ST• EINE F•C•M•/1780 **Note:** Dav. #2626.

Date	Mintage	F	VF	XF	Unc
1775	—	100	225	400	1,000

KM# 436 THALER

Silver **Obverse:** City view **Obv. Legend:** MONETA REIP • RATISPON, X • ST • EINE F•C•M/1766 **Reverse:** Armored bust right **Rev. Legend:** IOSEPHVS II D • G • ROM • IMP • SEMP • AVG • **Note:** Dav. #2627.

Date	Mintage	F	VF	XF	Unc
1780 BF	—	100	225	400	1,000

KM# 437 THALER

Silver **Obverse:** Crowned imperial eagle **Reverse:** City view with city arms of crossed keys in exerge **Note:** Dav. #2628.

Date	Mintage	F	VF	XF	Unc
ND(1780-90) Rare	—	—	—	—	—

KM# 455 THALER

Silver **Subject:** Archery Contest **Obverse:** Inscription **Obv. Inscription:** SOLEMNIVM/A. MDLXXXVI./PER ACTORVM/MEMORIAM/PATRVM/PATRIAE/INDVLGENTIA/CELEBRANT/SAGITTARII/RATISB•/A• MDCCLXXXVIII• **Reverse:** Flags left and right of column, urn on top **Rev. Legend:** REDEVNT ANTIQVI GAVDIA MORIS **Note:** Dav. #2629.

Date	Mintage	F	VF	XF	Unc
1788	—	—	—	1,250	2,000

KM# 465 THALER

Silver **Obverse:** Laureate head right **Obv. Legend:** LEOPOLDVS II. D. G. ROM. IMP. SEMP. AVG. **Reverse:** City view **Rev. Legend:** MONETA REIP. RATISPON., in exergue; X•ST•EINE F•C•M•/1791 **Note:** Dav. #2630.

Date	Mintage	F	VF	XF	Unc
1791	—	125	275	550	1,150

KM# 464 THALER

Silver **Obverse:** Arms in wreath **Obv. Legend:** MONETA REIP. RATISBONEENSIS., X. EINE FEINE MARK/1791/G.C.B. **Reverse:** Laureate head right **Rev. Legend:** LEOPOLDVS II. D. G. ROM. IMP. SEMP. AVG, KÖRNLEIN below **Note:** Dav. #2631.

Date	Mintage	F	VF	XF	Unc
1791 GCB	—	100	225	400	1,000

KM# 466 THALER

Silver **Obverse:** Sunrise over city view **Reverse:** Laureate head right **Note:** Dav. #2632.

Date	Mintage	F	VF	XF	Unc
1792	—	350	700	1,250	2,150

KM# 469 THALER

Silver **Obverse:** Laureate head right **Obv. Legend:** FRANCISCVS II • D • G • ROM • IMP • SEMP • AVG •, KÖRNLEIN below **Reverse:** City view **Rev. Legend:** MONETA REIP. RATISPON, X. ST. EINE F.C.M./1793/G.C.B. **Note:** Dav. #2633.

Date	Mintage	F	VF	XF	Unc
1793 GCB	—	125	275	550	1,150

KM# 216 2 THALER

Silver **Obverse:** City arms in elaborate frame **Obv. Legend:** * MONETA * REIPVBLICAE * RATISBONENSIS * **Reverse:** Crowned imperial eagle with arms on breast, titles of Josef **Rev. Legend:** * IOSEPHVS • D • G • - ROM • IMP • SEMP • AVG • **Note:** Dav. #2607.

Date	Mintage	F	VF	XF	Unc
ND	—	900	1,500	2,500	4,000

KM# 215 2 THALER

Silver

Date	Mintage	VG	F	VF	XF	Unc
ND IMF/HF	—	1,500	2,200	4,000	6,800	—

KM# 217 2 THALER

Silver **Obverse:** Titles of Karl VI

Date	Mintage	VG	F	VF	XF	Unc
ND Rare	—	—	—	—	—	—

KM# 281 2 THALER

Silver **Subject:** City Hall **Obverse:** Bust of Karl VI right **Reverse:** City hall, date in chronogram above, CVRIA RATISB below

Date	Mintage	VG	F	VF	XF	Unc
1737 O-F/CDO	—	4,000	6,250	8,000	12,500	—

KM# 285 2 THALER

Silver **Obverse:** City view, arms above, RATISBONA in frame below **Reverse:** Bust right, I.L. OEXLEIN below **Note:** Dav. #2616.

Date	Mintage	VG	F	VF	XF	Unc
ND	—	1,350	2,750	4,750	7,500	—

KM# 218 2 THALER

Silver **Obverse:** Back of armored laureate bust right **Obv. Legend:** FRANCISCVS II • D • G • ROM • MP • SEMP • AVG • **Reverse:** City arms **Rev. Legend:** MON • REIP • RATISP:, below; X • EINE F • MARK •/1792 **Note:** Similar to 1 Thaler, KM#257. Dav. #2611.

Date	Mintage	VG	F	VF	XF	Unc
ND (e)	—	1,500	2,500	4,000	6,500	—

KM# 219 2 THALER

Silver **Obverse:** Armored bust right **Reverse:** City view **Note:** Similar to 1 Thaler, KM#258.

Date	Mintage	VG	F	VF	XF	Unc
ND (e)	—	1,250	2,000	3,750	5,400	—

KM# 282 2 THALER

Silver **Obverse:** Armored draped bust right **Reverse:** City view **Note:** Similar to 1 Thaler, KM#259.

Date	Mintage	VG	F	VF	XF	Unc
ND C.D. OEXL	—	4,750	6,800	8,500	14,000	—

KM# 284 2 THALER

Silver **Obverse:** Armored laureate bust right **Reverse:** City view **Note:** Similar to 1 Thaler, KM#260.

Date	Mintage	VG	F	VF	XF	Unc
ND ICB-I.L. OE. /C. D. OEXL	—	4,750	6,800	8,500	14,000	—

KM# 283 2 THALER

Silver **Obverse:** Armored laureate bust right **Reverse:** City arms **Note:** Similar to 1 Thaler, KM#261.

Date	Mintage	VG	F	VF	XF	Unc
ND ICB/C.D. OE.	—	4,750	6,800	8,500	14,000	—

KM# 286 2 THALER

Silver **Obverse:** Armored bust right **Reverse:** City arms **Note:** Similar to 1 Thaler, KM#319.

Date	Mintage	VG	F	VF	XF	Unc
ND C.D. OE/C.D. OEXL	—	3,850	5,500	7,200	11,500	—

KM# 220 3 THALER

Silver **Obverse:** Draped laureate bust right **Reverse:** City arms **Note:** Similar to 1 Thaler, KM#257. Dav. #2610.

Date	Mintage	VG	F	VF	XF	Unc
ND Rare	—	—	—	—	—	—

KM# 287 4 THALER

Silver **Subject:** City Hall **Obverse:** Bust of Karl VI right **Reverse:** City hall, date in chronogram above, CVRIA RATISB below

Date	Mintage	VG	F	VF	XF	Unc
1737 O-F/CDO	—	6,500	7,850	9,500	12,000	—

KM# 288 4 THALER

Silver **Obverse:** City view, arms above, RATISBONA in frame below **Reverse:** Bust right, I.L. OEXLEIN below **Note:** Dav. #2616A.

Date	Mintage	VG	F	VF	XF	Unc
ND Rare	—	—	—	—	—	—

TRADE COINAGE

KM# A325 1/32 DUCAT

0.1090 g., 0.9860 Gold 0.0035 oz. AGW **Obverse:** City arms, 'B' below, in dotted circle **Reverse:** Crowned imperial eagle in dotted circle **Note:** FR#2547 variety; B# 528.

Date	Mintage	VG	F	VF	XF	Unc
ND(ca.1741+)	—	30.00	45.00	65.00	120	200

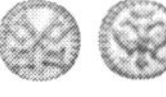

KM# 355 1/32 DUCAT

0.1094 g., 0.9860 Gold 0.0035 oz. AGW **Obverse:** Crossed key arms in inner circle **Reverse:** Crowned imperial eagle with shield on breast in inner circle **Note:** FR#2547.

Date	Mintage	VG	F	VF	XF	Unc
ND(ca.1750)	—	25.00	40.00	60.00	100	175

KM# 356 1/32 DUCAT

0.1094 g., 0.9860 Gold 0.0035 oz. AGW **Reverse:** R above keys

Date	Mintage	VG	F	VF	XF	Unc
ND(ca.1750)	—	25.00	40.00	60.00	100	175

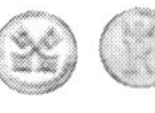

KM# 357 1/32 DUCAT

0.1094 g., 0.9860 Gold 0.0035 oz. AGW **Obverse:** Crossed keys **Reverse:** Crowned R **Note:** FR#2545a.

Date	Mintage	VG	F	VF	XF	Unc
ND(ca.1750)	—	30.00	45.00	65.00	120	200

KM# A395 1/32 DUCAT

0.1090 g., 0.9860 Gold 0.0035 oz. AGW **Obverse:** City arms in circle **Reverse:** Crowned imperial eagle **Note:** FR#2547 variety; B# 527.

Date	Mintage	VG	F	VF	XF	Unc
ND(ca.1773-)	—	30.00	45.00	65.00	120	200

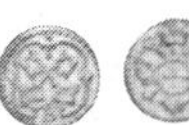

KM# 358 1/16 DUCAT

0.2188 g., 0.9860 Gold 0.0069 oz. AGW **Obverse:** Crossed keys in shallow quatrefoil, B below **Reverse:** Crowned imperial eagle with orb on breast **Note:** FR#2546.

Date	Mintage	VG	F	VF	XF	Unc
ND(ca.1750)	—	45.00	75.00	150	250	400

KM# 359 1/16 DUCAT

0.2188 g., 0.9860 Gold 0.0069 oz. AGW **Obverse:** Crowned imperial eagle in circle **Reverse:** Crossed keys in circle, B below **Note:** Klippe.

Date	Mintage	VG	F	VF	XF	Unc
ND(ca.1750)	—	50.00	100	175	300	500

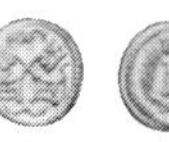

KM# 360 1/16 DUCAT

0.2188 g., 0.9860 Gold 0.0069 oz. AGW **Obverse:** Crossed keys **Reverse:** Crowned R in palm branches **Note:** FR#2545.

Date	Mintage	VG	F	VF	XF	Unc
ND(ca.1750)	—	40.00	60.00	90.00	200	350

KM# 320 1/10 DUCAT

0.3500 g., 0.9860 Gold 0.0111 oz. AGW **Obverse:** Crowned imperial eagle with orb on breast **Reverse:** Crossed keys in cartouche, R above, 1/10 below

Date	Mintage	VG	F	VF	XF	Unc
ND	—	85.00	125	325	500	800

KM# 321 1/8 DUCAT

0.4375 g., 0.9860 Gold 0.0139 oz. AGW **Obverse:** Crossed keys with B below in cartouche **Reverse:** Crowned imperial eagle with orb on breast

Date	Mintage	VG	F	VF	XF	Unc
ND	—	50.00	100	185	325	550

KM# 322 1/8 DUCAT

0.4375 g., 0.9860 Gold 0.0139 oz. AGW **Note:** Klippe.

Date	Mintage	VG	F	VF	XF	Unc
ND(1745-65)	—	100	150	350	500	—

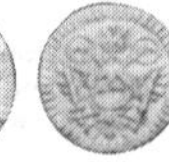

KM# 323 1/8 DUCAT

0.4375 g., 0.9860 Gold 0.0139 oz. AGW **Obverse:** Crossed keys with R above, 1/8 below in cartouche **Reverse:** Crowned imperial eagle with orb on breast

Date	Mintage	VG	F	VF	XF	Unc
ND(1745-65)	—	75.00	150	275	450	—

KM# 208 1/6 DUCAT

0.5833 g., 0.9860 Gold 0.0185 oz. AGW **Obverse:** Crowned imperial double-headed eagle with orb on breast **Reverse:** City arms

Date	Mintage	VG	F	VF	XF	Unc
ND	—	250	500	950	1,650	2,250

KM# 270 1/4 DUCAT

0.8750 g., 0.9860 Gold 0.0277 oz. AGW **Obverse:** Crossed keys in cartouche with sprigs within **Reverse:** Crowned imperial eagle, value: 1/4 on orb on breast

Date	Mintage	VG	F	VF	XF	Unc
ND(ca.1720) (e)	—	200	400	750	1,250	—

KM# 324 1/4 DUCAT

0.8750 g., 0.9860 Gold 0.0277 oz. AGW **Obverse:** B below keys **Reverse:** Without value 1/4 in orb **Note:** FR#2506.

Date	Mintage	VG	F	VF	XF	Unc
ND(1745-65)	—	100	200	325	550	850

KM# 325 1/4 DUCAT

0.8750 g., 0.9860 Gold 0.0277 oz. AGW **Note:** Klippe

Date	Mintage	VG	F	VF	XF	Unc
ND(1745-65)	—	65.00	125	200	400	650

KM# 326 1/4 DUCAT

0.8750 g., 0.9860 Gold 0.0277 oz. AGW **Obverse:** Crossed keys with R above and B below in cartouche **Reverse:** Crowned imperial eagle with crowned arms on breast **Note:** Diamond klippe; FR#2542.

Date	Mintage	VG	F	VF	XF	Unc
ND(1745-65)	—	90.00	175	300	550	900

KM# 327 1/4 DUCAT

0.8750 g., 0.9860 Gold 0.0277 oz. AGW **Obverse:** Crowned imperial eagle with orb on breast **Note:** Diamond klippe.

Date	Mintage	VG	F	VF	XF	Unc
ND(1745-65)	—	100	200	350	600	950

KM# 361 1/4 DUCAT

0.8750 g., 0.9860 Gold 0.0277 oz. AGW **Subject:** Franz I **Obverse:** Armored bust right **Reverse:** City of Regensburg, RATISBONA in exergue **Note:** FR#2539.

Date	Mintage	VG	F	VF	XF	Unc
ND(CA.1750)	—	100	200	325	550	850

KM# 385 1/4 DUCAT

0.8750 g., 0.9860 Gold 0.0277 oz. AGW **Obverse:** Crowned imperial double-headed eagle **Reverse:** City view of Regensburg **Note:** FR#2567.

Date	Mintage	F	VF	XF	Unc
ND(1765-90)	—	250	475	950	1,600

KM# B395 1/4 DUCAT

0.8750 g., 0.9860 Gold 0.0277 oz. AGW **Obverse:** City arms with 'R' above in ornate quarterfoil **Reverse:** Crowned imperial eagle, blank orb on breast

Date	Mintage	VG	F	VF	XF	Unc
ND(ca.1773-)	—	200	400	850	1,500	2,500

KM# 271 1/2 DUCAT

1.7500 g., 0.9860 Gold 0.0555 oz. AGW **Obverse:** Crowned imperial eagle, value: 1/2 in orb on breast **Reverse:** Crossed keys in cartouche

Date	Mintage	VG	F	VF	XF	Unc
ND	—	200	450	1,100	2,000	—

KM# 272 1/2 DUCAT

1.7500 g., 0.9860 Gold 0.0555 oz. AGW **Obverse:** Armored bust of Karl VI right **Reverse:** Crossed keys, value: 1/2 above in cartouche **Note:** Varieties exist.

Date	Mintage	VG	F	VF	XF	Unc
ND	—	150	300	700	1,250	—

KM# 300 1/2 DUCAT

1.7500 g., 0.9860 Gold 0.0555 oz. AGW **Obverse:** Armored bust of Karl VII right **Reverse:** Arms

Date	Mintage	VG	F	VF	XF	Unc
ND(1742-45)	—	175	350	775	1,475	—

KM# 301 1/2 DUCAT

1.7500 g., 0.9860 Gold 0.0555 oz. AGW **Reverse:** City of Regensburg, crossed keys in exergue

Date	Mintage	VG	F	VF	XF	Unc
ND	—	175	350	775	1,475	—

KM# 302 1/2 DUCAT

1.7500 g., 0.9860 Gold 0.0555 oz. AGW **Obverse:** RATISBONA in exergue **Reverse:** Armored bust of Franz I right

Date	Mintage	VG	F	VF	XF	Unc
ND	—	150	300	700	1,500	2,500

KM# 328 1/2 DUCAT

1.7500 g., 0.9860 Gold 0.0555 oz. AGW **Obverse:** Divided shield in Order chain on breast **Reverse:** City arms **Shape:** 4-Sided **Note:** Diamond klippe; Varieties exist; FR#2540.

Date	Mintage	VG	F	VF	XF	Unc
ND(1745-65) RB	—	125	200	425	750	1,250

KM# 386 1/2 DUCAT

1.7500 g., 0.9860 Gold 0.0555 oz. AGW **Obverse:** Divided shield within Order chain on breast **Obv. Legend:** IOSEPHVS II • D • G • - ROM • IMP • S • AVG • **Reverse:** City view **Note:** FR#2566.

Date	Mintage	F	VF	XF	Unc
ND(1765-90)	—	300	625	1,150	1,850

KM# 235 DUCAT

3.5000 g., 0.9860 Gold 0.1109 oz. AGW **Obverse:** Arms **Obv. Legend:** IOSEPH • D • G • ROM • - IMP • SEMP • AVG • **Reverse:** Crowned imperial eagle, titles of Josef **Note:** FR#2491.

Date	Mintage	VG	F	VF	XF	Unc
1706	826	1,000	2,000	3,750	6,250	—
ND	439	1,000	2,000	3,750	6,250	—

KM# 254 DUCAT

3.5000 g., 0.9860 Gold 0.1109 oz. AGW **Obverse:** Bust of Karl VI right **Obv. Legend:** CAROLVS VI • D • G • - R • I • S • A.... **Reverse:** Arms **Note:** FR#2500.

Date	Mintage	VG	F	VF	XF	Unc
1712	683	500	1,000	2,000	3,250	—
ND	—	500	1,000	2,000	3,250	—

KM# 268 DUCAT

3.5000 g., 0.9860 Gold 0.1109 oz. AGW **Subject:** Bicentennial of the Reformation **Obverse:** Lamb of God on column, REGENSBURG in exergue **Reverse:** Inscription

Date	Mintage	VG	F	VF	XF	Unc
1717	—	300	600	1,200	2,000	—

KM# 289 DUCAT

3.5000 g., 0.9860 Gold 0.1109 oz. AGW **Obverse:** Bust of Karl V right **Obv. Legend:** CAROL • VI • - D • G • ROM • IMP • S • A • **Reverse:** City view

Date	Mintage	VG	F	VF	XF	Unc
1737	16	600	1,200	2,000	3,500	—
ND	—	600	1,200	2,000	3,500	—

KM# 305 DUCAT

3.5000 g., 0.9860 Gold 0.1109 oz. AGW **Obverse:** Bust of Franz I right **Obv. Legend:** FRANCISC • I • D • G • ROM • IMP • SEMP • AVG • **Reverse:** City view **Note:** Varieties exist; FR#2538.

Date	Mintage	VG	F	VF	XF	Unc
ND	—	225	450	900	1,650	2,750

KM# 306 DUCAT

3.5000 g., 0.9860 Gold 0.1109 oz. AGW **Obverse:** City view **Reverse:** Armored laureate bust right **Rev. Legend:** FRANCISC • - D • G • R • I • S • A • **Note:** FR#2538.

Date	Mintage	VG	F	VF	XF	Unc
ND	—	275	550	1,000	1,850	—

KM# 303 DUCAT

3.5000 g., 0.9860 Gold 0.1109 oz. AGW **Obverse:** City view **Reverse:** Bust of Karl VII right **Rev. Legend:** CAROL • VII • - D • G • ROM • IMP • S • A •

Date	Mintage	VG	F	VF	XF	Unc
ND(1742-45) B	714	600	1,200	2,250	3,750	—

KM# 304 DUCAT

3.5000 g., 0.9860 Gold 0.1109 oz. AGW **Obverse:** Armored bust of Karl VII right

Date	Mintage	VG	F	VF	XF	Unc
ND(1742-45)	Inc. above	600	1,200	2,250	3,750	—

KM# 307 DUCAT

3.5000 g., 0.9860 Gold 0.1109 oz. AGW **Subject:** 200th Anniversary of the Reformation in Regensburg **Obverse:** Arms above four-line legend **Obv. Inscription:** RATISBONA/ EVANGELICA/ ALTERA VICE/ IVBILANS/ XV.OCT. **Reverse:** Sun above plant, date in chronogram

Date	Mintage	VG	F	VF	XF	Unc
ND(1742)	—	150	300	600	1,000	—

KM# 387 DUCAT

3.5000 g., 0.9860 Gold 0.1109 oz. AGW **Obverse:** Imperial eagle, titles of Josef II **Reverse:** City view **Note:** FR#2565.

Date	Mintage	F	VF	XF	Unc
ND(1765-90)	—	1,000	2,000	3,500	6,000

KM# 388 DUCAT

3.5000 g., 0.9860 Gold 0.1109 oz. AGW **Obverse:** Bust of Josef II **Obv. Legend:** IOSEPH • II • - D • G • R • I • S • A • **Reverse:** City view **Note:** FR#2564.

Date	Mintage	F	VF	XF	Unc
ND(1765-90)	—	400	800	1,350	2,250

KM# 389 DUCAT

3.5000 g., 0.9860 Gold 0.1109 oz. AGW **Obverse:** Crowned imperial eagle **Reverse:** Crowned imperial eagle

Date	Mintage	F	VF	XF	Unc
ND(1765-90)	—	350	700	1,200	2,000

KM# 460 DUCAT

3.5000 g., 0.9860 Gold 0.1109 oz. AGW **Obverse:** Head of Leopold II right **Reverse:** Crowned imperial eagle

Date	Mintage	VG	F	VF	XF	Unc
ND(1790-92)	—	—	—	—	—	—

KM# 467 DUCAT

3.5000 g., 0.9860 Gold 0.1109 oz. AGW **Obverse:** City view **Reverse:** Crowned imperial eagle, titles of Franz II **Rev. Legend:** FRANCISCVS II D. G. ROM. IMP. SEMP. AVG. **Note:** FR#2571.

Date	Mintage	VG	F	VF	XF	Unc
ND(1792-1803) GCB	—	250	500	900	1,500	2,500

KM# 150 2 DUCAT

7.0000 g., 0.9860 Gold 0.2219 oz. AGW **Obverse:** Crossed keys in ornate border **Reverse:** Crowned imperial eagle, titles of Leopold I

Date	Mintage	VG	F	VF	XF	Unc
ND(1657-1705) HF	—	1,350	2,750	5,000	8,500	12,000

Note: UBS Regensburg Auction 60, 9-04, XF-nearly FDC realized $10,970

KM# A235 2 DUCAT

7.0000 g., 0.9860 Gold 0.2219 oz. AGW **Obverse:** Oval city arms in baroque frame **Obv. Legend:** MONETA. REIPVBLICÆ. RATISBONENSIS **Reverse:** Armored bust to right **Rev. Legend:** IOSEPHVS. D.G. — ROM. IMP. SEMP. AVG.

Date	Mintage	VG	F	VF	XF	Unc
ND(ca.1705-)	—	—	3,000	5,000	7,500	—

KM# 240 2 DUCAT

7.0000 g., 0.9860 Gold 0.2219 oz. AGW **Obverse:** Laureate bust of Karl VI right

Date	Mintage	VG	F	VF	XF	Unc
ND(1722-40)	—	900	1,750	3,500	6,000	—

KM# A289 2 DUCAT

7.0000 g., 0.9860 Gold 0.2219 oz. AGW **Obverse:** Oval city arms in baroque frame **Obv. Legend:** MONETA. REIPVBLICÆ. RATISBONENSIS **Reverse:** Armored bust to right **Rev. Legend:** CAROL. VI — D.G. ROM. IMP. S.A.

Date	Mintage	VG	F	VF	XF	Unc
1737 Rare	—	—	—	—	—	—

Note: UBS Regensburg Auction 60, 9-04, nearly FDC realized $18,285

KM# 308 2 DUCAT

7.0000 g., 0.9860 Gold 0.2219 oz. AGW **Obverse:** Laureate head of Karl VII right **Reverse:** City view, arms in exergue **Note:** Struck with 1 Ducat dies, KM#303.

Date	Mintage	VG	F	VF	XF	Unc
ND(1742-45)	—	—	—	5,500	9,000	—

KM# 309 2 DUCAT

7.0000 g., 0.9860 Gold 0.2219 oz. AGW **Obverse:** Armored bust of Karl VII right **Reverse:** Arms in cartouche

Date	Mintage	VG	F	VF	XF	Unc
ND(1742-45) ICB	—	900	1,750	3,500	6,000	—

KM# 329 2 DUCAT
7.0000 g., 0.9860 Gold 0.2219 oz. AGW **Obverse:** City view, RATISBONA in exergue **Reverse:** Bust of Franz I right **Rev. Legend:** FRANCISCUS • I • D • G • ROM • IMP • SEMP • AVG •

Date	Mintage	VG	F	VF	XF	Unc
ND(1745-65)	—	425	850	1,750	3,250	5,500

KM# 330 2 DUCAT
7.0000 g., 0.9860 Gold 0.2219 oz. AGW **Obverse:** Bust of Franz I right **Obv. Legend:** FRANCISC • I • D • G • ROM • IMP • SEMP • AVG • **Reverse:** City view **Note:** Struck with 1 Ducat dies, KM#305.

Date	Mintage	VG	F	VF	XF	Unc
ND(1745-65)	—	—	—	2,250	3,750	—

KM# 390 2 DUCAT
7.0000 g., 0.9860 Gold 0.2219 oz. AGW **Obverse:** Titles of Josef II **Reverse:** City view **Note:** Struck with 1 Ducat dies, KM#389.

Date	Mintage	VG	F	VF	XF	Unc
ND	—	500	1,000	2,000	3,500	—

KM# 391 2 DUCAT
7.0000 g., 0.9860 Gold 0.2219 oz. AGW **Obverse:** Crowned imperial eagle, titles of Josef **Obv. Legend:** IOSEPHVS II • D • G • ROM • IMP • SEMP • AVG • **Reverse:** City view

Date	Mintage	F	VF	XF	Unc
ND(1765-90)	—	850	1,650	3,000	5,000

KM# 155 3 DUCAT
10.5000 g., 0.9860 Gold 0.3328 oz. AGW **Obverse:** Crowned imperial eagle with heart-shaped arms on breast, titles of Leopold I **Reverse:** Arms in cartouche

Date	Mintage	VG	F	VF	XF	Unc
ND(1658-1705) Rare	—	—	—	—	—	—

KM# 221 3 DUCAT
10.5000 g., 0.9860 Gold 0.3328 oz. AGW **Obverse:** Crowned imperial eagle with crowned heart-shaped arms on breast, titles of Josef I **Reverse:** Arms in cartouche

Date	Mintage	VG	F	VF	XF	Unc
ND(1705-11)	—	2,250	3,750	6,500	10,000	—

KM# 222 3 DUCAT
10.5000 g., 0.9860 Gold 0.3328 oz. AGW **Note:** Struck with 1 Ducat dies.

Date	Mintage	VG	F	VF	XF	Unc
ND(1705-11) Rare	—	—	—	—	—	—

KM# 241 3 DUCAT
10.5000 g., 0.9860 Gold 0.3328 oz. AGW **Obverse:** Bust of Karl VI right **Obv. Legend:** CAROL VI • - D • G • R • I • S • A • G • H • H • B • R • **Reverse:** Ornate arms **Note:** FR#2498.

Date	Mintage	VG	F	VF	XF	Unc
ND(1711-40)	—	2,000	3,250	5,500	9,000	—

KM# 242 3 DUCAT
10.5000 g., 0.9860 Gold 0.3328 oz. AGW **Obverse:** Bust of Karl VI **Reverse:** Arms

Date	Mintage	VG	F	VF	XF	Unc
ND(1711-40) Rare	—	—	—	—	—	—

KM# 331 3 DUCAT
10.5000 g., 0.9860 Gold 0.3328 oz. AGW **Obverse:** Bust of Franz I **Reverse:** City view

Date	Mintage	VG	F	VF	XF	Unc
ND(1745-65) Rare	—	—	—	—	—	—

KM# 332 3 DUCAT
10.5000 g., 0.9860 Gold 0.3328 oz. AGW **Note:** Struck with 1 Ducat dies.

Date	Mintage	VG	F	VF	XF	Unc
ND(1745-65)	—	1,000	2,000	4,000	7,000	—

KM# 333 3 DUCAT
10.5000 g., 0.9860 Gold 0.3328 oz. AGW **Reverse:** Different city view

Date	Mintage	VG	F	VF	XF	Unc
ND(1745-65)	—	800	1,750	3,500	6,000	—

KM# 334 3 DUCAT
10.5000 g., 0.9860 Gold 0.3328 oz. AGW **Obverse:** Bust of Franz I right **Obv. Legend:** FRANCISCUS I • D • G • ROM • IMP • SEMP • AVG • **Reverse:** City view

Date	Mintage	VG	F	VF	XF	Unc
ND(1745-65)	—	800	1,750	3,500	6,000	10,000

Note: UBS Regensburg Auction 60, 9-04, FDC-nearly FDC realized $10,510

KM# A392 3 DUCAT
10.5000 g., 0.9860 Gold 0.3328 oz. AGW **Obverse:** Arms in Order chain on breast **Obv. Legend:** IOSEPHVS II • D • G • - ROM • IMP • SEMP • AVG • **Reverse:** City view **Note:** Similar to 2 Ducat, KM#391.

Date	Mintage	F	VF	XF	Unc
ND(1765-90)	—	1,350	2,750	5,000	8,000

KM# 438 3 DUCAT
10.5000 g., 0.9860 Gold 0.3328 oz. AGW **Obverse:** Bust of Josef II right **Reverse:** Crowned imperial eagle

Date	Mintage	F	VF	XF	Unc
ND(1780-90)	—	1,000	2,000	3,500	6,000

KM# 223 4 DUCAT
14.0000 g., 0.9890 Gold 0.4451 oz. AGW **Obverse:** Crowned imperial eagle, titles of Karl VI **Reverse:** City view

Date	Mintage	VG	F	VF	XF	Unc
ND(1705-11) Rare	—	—	—	—	—	—

KM# 243 4 DUCAT
14.0000 g., 0.9890 Gold 0.4451 oz. AGW **Obverse:** Crowned imperial eagle, titles of Karl VI **Reverse:** Arms **Note:** FR#2495.

Date	Mintage	VG	F	VF	XF	Unc
ND(1711-40) Rare	—	—	—	—	—	—

Note: UBS Regensburg Auction 60, 9-04, nearly FDC-FDC realized $14,625

KM# 244 4 DUCAT
14.0000 g., 0.9890 Gold 0.4451 oz. AGW **Obverse:** Bust of Karl VI **Reverse:** Arms

Date	Mintage	VG	F	VF	XF	Unc
ND(1711-40) Rare	—	—	—	—	—	—

KM# 295 4 DUCAT
14.0000 g., 0.9890 Gold 0.4451 oz. AGW **Obverse:** Bust of Karl VII **Reverse:** City view

Date	Mintage	VG	F	VF	XF	Unc
ND(1740-45) Rare	—	—	—	—	—	—

KM# 335 4 DUCAT
14.0000 g., 0.9890 Gold 0.4451 oz. AGW **Obverse:** Laureate and armored bust of Franz I right **Reverse:** City view

Date	Mintage	VG	F	VF	XF	Unc
ND(1745-65)	—	1,250	2,500	4,500	7,500	—

KM# 336 4 DUCAT
14.0000 g., 0.9890 Gold 0.4451 oz. AGW **Reverse:** Different city view

Date	Mintage	VG	F	VF	XF	Unc
ND(1745-65)	—	1,250	2,500	4,500	7,500	—

KM# 224 5 DUCAT
17.5000 g., 0.9860 Gold 0.5547 oz. AGW **Obverse:** City arms **Reverse:** Imperial eagle, titles of Josef I **Rev. Legend:** IOSEPHVS • D • G • - ROM • IMP • SEMP • AVG •

Date	Mintage	VG	F	VF	XF	Unc
ND(1705-11) Rare	—	—	—	—	—	—

KM# 245 5 DUCAT
17.5000 g., 0.9860 Gold 0.5547 oz. AGW **Obverse:** Crowned imperial eagle, titles of Karl VI **Reverse:** City view

Date	Mintage	VG	F	VF	XF	Unc
ND(1711-40)	—	1,750	3,250	5,750	9,500	—

KM# 296 5 DUCAT
17.5000 g., 0.9860 Gold 0.5547 oz. AGW **Obverse:** Bust of Karl VII **Reverse:** City view

Date	Mintage	VG	F	VF	XF	Unc
ND(1740-45)	—	—	—	7,500	11,500	—

KM# 297 5 DUCAT
17.5000 g., 0.9860 Gold 0.5547 oz. AGW **Obverse:** Ornate arms **Reverse:** Bust of Karl VII right **Rev. Legend:** CAROL. VII - D. G. ROM. IMP. S. A.

Date	Mintage	VG	F	VF	XF	Unc
ND(1740-45) ICB	—	—	—	7,500	11,500	—

Note: Bowers and Merena Giua sale, March, 1988, choice AU, $10,450

KM# 337 5 DUCAT
17.5000 g., 0.9860 Gold 0.5547 oz. AGW **Obverse:** Bust of Franz I **Reverse:** Different city view

Date	Mintage	VG	F	VF	XF	Unc
ND(1745-65) I.L. OE/ICB	—	1,750	3,250	5,750	9,500	—

KM# 338 5 DUCAT

17.5000 g., 0.9860 Gold 0.5547 oz. AGW **Reverse:** Different city view

Date	Mintage	VG	F	VF	XF	Unc
ND(1745-65)	—	1,750	3,250	5,750	9,500	—

KM# 392 5 DUCAT

17.5000 g., 0.9860 Gold 0.5547 oz. AGW **Obverse:** Crowned imperial eagle, titles of Josef II **Reverse:** Crowned eagle in clouds above city

Date	Mintage	VG	F	VF	XF	Unc
ND(1765-90) ICB	—	1,500	3,000	5,500	9,000	—

KM# 393 5 DUCAT

17.5000 g., 0.9860 Gold 0.5547 oz. AGW **Reverse:** Name of God above city

Date	Mintage	VG	F	VF	XF	Unc
ND(1765-90)	—	1,200	2,500	5,000	8,500	—

KM# 225 6 DUCAT

21.0000 g., 0.9860 Gold 0.6657 oz. AGW

Date	Mintage	VG	F	VF	XF	Unc
ND(1705-11) Rare	—	—	—	—	—	—

KM# 246 6 DUCAT

21.0000 g., 0.9860 Gold 0.6657 oz. AGW **Obverse:** Bust of Karl VI **Reverse:** City view

Date	Mintage	VG	F	VF	XF	Unc
ND(1711-40) Rare	—	—	—	—	—	—

KM# 298 6 DUCAT

21.0000 g., 0.9860 Gold 0.6657 oz. AGW **Obverse:** Bust of Karl VII **Reverse:** City view

Date	Mintage	VG	F	VF	XF	Unc
ND(1740-45) C. D. OEXL. Rare	—	—	—	—	—	—

Note: UBS Regensburg Auction 60, 9-04, nearly FDC realized $29,250

KM# 339 6 DUCAT

21.0000 g., 0.9860 Gold 0.6657 oz. AGW **Obverse:** Laureate and armored bust of Franz I right **Reverse:** City view, RATISBONA in exergue

Date	Mintage	VG	F	VF	XF	Unc
ND(1745-65) I. L. OE/I. L. OEXLEIN	—	—	—	8,000	12,500	—

KM# 340 6 DUCAT

21.0000 g., 0.9860 Gold 0.6657 oz. AGW **Obverse:** Bust of Franz I right **Reverse:** City view

Date	Mintage	VG	F	VF	XF	Unc
ND(1745-65) I. L. OE/ICB	—	—	—	8,000	12,500	—

KM# 341 6 DUCAT

21.0000 g., 0.9860 Gold 0.6657 oz. AGW **Reverse:** Different city view

Date	Mintage	VG	F	VF	XF	Unc
ND(1745-65) Rare	3	—	—	—	—	—

Note: UBS Regensburg Auction 60, 9-04, FDC-nearly FDC realized $31,080

KM# 394 6 DUCAT

21.0000 g., 0.9860 Gold 0.6657 oz. AGW **Obverse:** Crowned imperial eagle with crowned arms on breast **Obv. Legend:** IOSEPHVS II • D • G • - NOM • IMP • SEMP • AVG • **Reverse:** City view with crowned flying eagle above, city arms below in exergue **Note:** FR#2559.

Date	Mintage	VG	F	VF	XF	Unc
ND(1765-90) I.L.OE/ICB	—	—	—	7,500	13,500	22,500

Note: UBS Regensburg Auction 60, 9-04, finest FDC realized $22,850

Date	Mintage	VG	F	VF	XF	Unc
ND IMF/HF	—	—	—	7,500	13,500	—

KM# 226 8 DUCAT

28.0000 g., 0.9860 Gold 0.8876 oz. AGW **Obverse:** Crowned imperial eagle, titles of Josef I **Reverse:** Arms

Date	Mintage	VG	F	VF	XF	Unc
ND(1705-11) Rare	8	—	—	—	—	—

KM# 247 8 DUCAT

28.0000 g., 0.9860 Gold 0.8876 oz. AGW **Obverse:** Bust of Karl VI **Reverse:** City view

Date	Mintage	VG	F	VF	XF	Unc
ND(1711-40) CDO Rare	—	—	—	—	—	—

KM# 342 8 DUCAT

28.0000 g., 0.9860 Gold 0.8876 oz. AGW **Obverse:** City of Regensburg with two angels holding two shields above, RATISBONA in cartouche in exergue **Reverse:** Laureate and armored bust of Franz I right **Rev. Legend:** FRANCISCUS I • D • G • ROM • IMP • SEMP • AVG •

Date	Mintage	VG	F	VF	XF	Unc
ND(1745-65) I. L. OE/OEXLEIN Rare	—	—	—	—	—	—

KM# 343 8 DUCAT

28.0000 g., 0.9860 Gold 0.8876 oz. AGW **Reverse:** Different city view

Date	Mintage	VG	F	VF	XF	Unc
ND(1745-65) ILOE/IL OEXLEIN Rare	—	—	—	—	—	—

KM# 395 8 DUCAT

28.0000 g., 0.9860 Gold 0.8876 oz. AGW **Reverse:** City view with crowned flying eagle above, crossed keys below in exergue **Note:** FR#2558.

Date	Mintage	VG	F	VF	XF	Unc
ND(1765-90) ICB Rare	—	—	—	—	—	—

Note: UBS Regensburg Auction 60, 9-04, FDC realized $41,135

KM# 396 8 DUCAT

28.0000 g., 0.9860 Gold 0.8876 oz. AGW **Reverse:** Eye of God above city, arms in exergue

Date	Mintage	VG	F	VF	XF	Unc
ND(1765-90) B Rare	—	—	—	—	—	—

KM# 227 10 DUCAT

35.0000 g., 0.9860 Gold 1.1095 oz. AGW **Obverse:** Crowned imperial eagle, titles of Josef I

Date	Mintage	VG	F	VF	XF	Unc
ND(1705-11) Rare	27	—	—	—	—	—

KM# 248 10 DUCAT

35.0000 g., 0.9860 Gold 1.1095 oz. AGW **Obverse:** Bust of Karl VI **Reverse:** Arms

Date	Mintage	VG	F	VF	XF	Unc
ND(1711-40) Rare	—	—	—	—	—	—

KM# 249 10 DUCAT

35.0000 g., 0.9860 Gold 1.1095 oz. AGW **Reverse:** City view

Date	Mintage	VG	F	VF	XF	Unc
ND(1711-40) CDO Rare	—	—	—	—	—	—

KM# 290 10 DUCAT

35.0000 g., 0.9860 Gold 1.1095 oz. AGW **Reverse:** City hall

Date	Mintage	VG	F	VF	XF	Unc
1737 OF/CDO Rare	—	—	—	—	—	—

KM# 468 10 DUCAT

35.0000 g., 0.9860 Gold 1.1095 oz. AGW **Obverse:** Arms in sprays **Obv. Legend:** FRANCISCVS II • D • G • ROM • IMP • SEMP • AVG • **Reverse:** Bust of Franz II right **Rev. Legend:** MONETA REIP. RATISBONENSIS. **Note:** FR#2570.

Date	Mintage	VG	F	VF	XF	Unc
ND(1742-1806) GCB Rare	—	—	—	—	—	—

Note: UBS Regensburg Auction 60, 9-04, FDC-XF realized $43,875. Stack's International Sale, 3-88, XF realized $14,300

KM# 310 10 DUCAT
35.0000 g., 0.9860 Gold 1.1095 oz. AGW **Obverse:** Bust of Karl VII right **Obv. Legend:** CAROL. VII. - D. G. ROM. IMP. SEMP. AVG **Reverse:** Eagle above city view **Rev. Legend:** TALI SUB - COSTODIA

Date	Mintage	VG	F	VF	XF	Unc
ND(1742-45) CD OEXL Rare	—	—	—	—	—	—

Note: UBS Regensburg Auction 60, 9-04, XF-FDC realized $53,015

KM# 311 10 DUCAT
35.0000 g., 0.9860 Gold 1.1095 oz. AGW **Obverse:** Armored laureate bust of Karl VII right **Obv. Legend:** CAROL. VII. - D. G. ROM. IMP. SEMP. AVG **Reverse:** Different city view without eagle **Rev. Legend:** MON • REIP • - RATISBON •

Date	Mintage	VG	F	VF	XF	Unc
ND(1742-45) CD OEXL Rare	—	—	—	—	—	—

Note: UBS Regensburg Auction 60, 9-04, XF-FDC realized $60,325; Bowers and Merena Giua sale 3-88, Choice Unc., $19,800

KM# 344 10 DUCAT
35.0000 g., 0.9860 Gold 1.1095 oz. AGW **Obverse:** Laureate and armored bust of Franz I right **Reverse:** City view with two cherubs holding two shields above, RATISBONA in cartouche in exergue

Date	Mintage	VG	F	VF	XF	Unc
ND(1745-65) IL OE/IL OEXLEIN. F. Rare	—	—	—	—	—	—

KM# 398 10 DUCAT
35.0000 g., 0.9860 Gold 1.1095 oz. AGW **Obverse:** Crowned imperial eagle **Reverse:** City view

Date	Mintage	VG	F	VF	XF	Unc
ND(1765-90) K/GCB Rare	—	—	—	—	—	—

KM# 399 10 DUCAT
35.0000 g., 0.9860 Gold 1.1095 oz. AGW **Reverse:** Eagle in clouds above city

Date	Mintage	VG	F	VF	XF	Unc
ND(1765-90) K/B Rare	—	—	—	—	—	—

KM# 397 10 DUCAT
35.0000 g., 0.9860 Gold 1.1095 oz. AGW **Obverse:** Bust of Josef II **Reverse:** Eagle above arms

Date	Mintage	VG	F	VF	XF	Unc
1766 OEXLEIN Rare	—	—	—	—	—	—

KM# 346 10 DUCAT
35.0000 g., 0.9860 Gold 1.1095 oz. AGW **Obverse:** Laureate and armored bust of Franz I right **Obv. Legend:** FRANCISCUS D • G • - ROM • IMP • SEMP • AVG • **Reverse:** City view with crowned eagle flying above city, crossed keys in exergue **Rev. Legend:** TALI SUB - CUSTODIA

Date	Mintage	VG	F	VF	XF	Unc
ND(1783) Rare	—	—	—	—	—	—

Note: Stack's International Sale 3-88 XF realized $11,000

KM# 461 10 DUCAT
35.0000 g., 0.9860 Gold 1.1095 oz. AGW **Obverse:** Bust of Leopold II **Reverse:** Arms

Date	Mintage	VG	F	VF	XF	Unc
ND(1790-92) Rare	—	—	—	—	—	—

KM# 250 12 DUCAT
42.0000 g., 0.9860 Gold 1.3314 oz. AGW **Obverse:** Arms **Reverse:** Crowned imperial eagle, titles of Karl VI **Note:** FR#2492.

Date	Mintage	VG	F	VF	XF	Unc
ND(1711-40) Rare	—	—	—	—	—	—

Note: UBS Regensburg Auction 60, 9-04, nearly FDC-XF realized $54,850

KM# 347 12 DUCAT
42.0000 g., 0.9860 Gold 1.3314 oz. AGW **Obverse:** Bust of Franz I **Reverse:** City view

Date	Mintage	VG	F	VF	XF	Unc
ND(1745-65) IL OE/IL OEXLEIN Rare	—	—	—	—	—	—

Note: UBS Regensburg Auction 60, 9-04, XF realized $59,415

KM# 401 12 DUCAT
42.0000 g., 0.9860 Gold 1.3314 oz. AGW **Obverse:** Crowned imperial eagle, titles of Josef II **Reverse:** City view

Date	Mintage	VG	F	VF	XF	Unc
ND(1765-90) K/GCB Rare	—	—	—	—	—	—

KM# 402 12 DUCAT
42.0000 g., 0.9860 Gold 1.3314 oz. AGW **Reverse:** City view with two angels

Date	Mintage	VG	F	VF	XF	Unc
ND(1765-90) ILOE-B Rare	—	—	—	—	—	—

KM# 400 12 DUCAT
42.0000 g., 0.9860 Gold 1.3314 oz. AGW **Obverse:** Bust Josef II **Reverse:** Eagle above arms

Date	Mintage	VG	F	VF	XF	Unc
1766 OEXLEIN Rare	—	—	—	—	—	—

KM# 251 16 DUCAT
56.0000 g., 0.9860 Gold 1.7752 oz. AGW **Obverse:** Bust of Karl VI **Reverse:** Arms

Date	Mintage	VG	F	VF	XF	Unc
ND(1711-40) Rare	—	—	—	—	—	—

KM# 252 20 DUCAT
70.0000 g., 0.9860 Gold 2.2190 oz. AGW **Obverse:** Bust of Karl VI **Reverse:** Arms

Date	Mintage	VG	F	VF	XF	Unc
ND(1711-40) Rare	—	—	—	—	—	—

KM# 348 20 DUCAT
70.0000 g., 0.9860 Gold 2.2190 oz. AGW **Obverse:** Bust of Franz I **Reverse:** City view

Date	Mintage	VG	F	VF	XF	Unc
ND(1745-65) Rare	—	—	—	—	—	—

KM# 403 20 DUCAT
70.0000 g., 0.9860 Gold 2.2190 oz. AGW **Obverse:** Crowned imperial eagle with crowned arms on breast **Reverse:** City view, RATISBONA in exergue

Date	Mintage	VG	F	VF	XF	Unc
ND(1765-90) K/GCB Unique	—	—	—	—	—	—

Note: UBS Regensburg Auction 60, 9-04, Unique realized $131,625

KM# 404 20 DUCAT
70.0000 g., 0.9860 Gold 2.2190 oz. AGW **Reverse:** Different city view, RATISBONA in cartouche in exergue

Date	Mintage	VG	F	VF	XF	Unc
ND(1765-90) KIB Rare	—	—	—	—	—	—

KM# A403 22 DUCAT
77.0000 g., 0.9860 Gold 2.4408 oz. AGW **Obverse:** City view, inscription in exergue **Obv. Inscription:** RATISBONA **Reverse:** Crowned imperial eagle with crowned arms on breast **Note:** Illustration reduced.

Date	Mintage	VG	F	VF	XF	Unc
ND(ca.1784) Unique	—	—	—	—	—	—

Note: UBS Regensburg Auction 60, 9-04, realized $131,630

PATTERNS

Including off metal strikes

KM#	Date	Mintage	Identification	Mkt Val
Pn15	ND1706	—	2 Kreuzer. Gold. KM#229	1,650
Pn16	ND1709	—	Heller. Gold. 1/4 Ducat weight, KM#237	—
Pn17	ND1712	—	Heller. Gold. 1/4 Ducat weight, KM#237	—
Pn18	ND1712	—	Pfennig. Gold. 1/8 Ducat weight, KM#253.	500
Pn19	ND1716	—	Pfennig. Gold. 1/8 Ducat weight, KM#253.	500
Pn20	ND1716/4	—	2 Kreuzer. Gold. 1/2 Ducat weight, KM#255.	1,500
Pn21	ND1717	—	Ducat. Silver. KM#216.	200
Pn22	ND1723	—	Pfennig. Gold. 1/8 Ducat weight, KM#253.	500
Pn23	ND1725	—	Pfennig. Gold. 1/4 Ducat weight, KM#253.	1,650
Pn24	ND1726	—	Pfennig. Gold. 1/8 Ducat weight, KM#253.	500
Pn25	ND(1738)	—	1/2 Kreuzer. Gold. 1/4 Ducat weight, KM#206.	650

KM#	Date	Mintage	Identification	Mkt Val
Pn26	ND(1738)	—	Kreuzer. Gold. 1/2 Ducat weight, KM#292.	1,375
Pn27	ND1741	—	Heller. Gold. KM#237.	—
Pn28	ND1741	—	Pfennig. Gold. 1/6 Ducat weight, KM#253.	1,250
Pn29	ND(1742)	—	Ducat. Silver. KM#303.	200
Pn30	ND	—	2 Ducat. Silver. KM#329.	200
Pn31	ND	—	2 Ducat. Silver. KM#390.	200
Pn32	ND1745	—	Thaler. Lead. KM#317.	260
PnA33	ND	—	15 Kreuzer. Gold. 2 Ducat weight, KM#316.	—
Pn33	ND(1747)	—	Pfennig. Gold. 1/4 Ducat weight, KM#299.	—
Pn34	ND1782	—	Heller. Silver. KM#237.	—
Pn35	ND1782	—	Heller. Gold. 1/4 Ducat weight, KM#237.	—
Pn36	ND	—	Heller. Gold. 1/4 Ducat weight, KM#237.	—
Pn37	ND1770	—	Ducat. Silver.	—
Pn38	ND1770	—	Ducat. Silver.	—

REUSS

The Reuss family, whose lands were located in Thuringia, was founded c. 1035. By the end of the 12th century, the custom of naming all males in the ruling house Heinrich had been established. The Elder Line modified this strange practice in the late 17th century to numbering all males from 1 to 100, then beginning over again. The Younger Line, meanwhile, decided to start the numbering of Heinrichs with the first male born in each century. Greiz was founded in1303. Upper and Lower Greiz lines were founded in 1535 and the territories were divided until 1768. In 1778 the ruler was made a prince of the Holy Roman Empire. The principality endured until 1918.

MINT MARKS

A - Berlin
B – Hannover
G – Gera Mint

MINT OFFICIALS' INITIALS

Initials	Date	Name
E, ICE	1755-65	Johann Christian Eberhard in Saalfeld
FA	1785-90	Facius, die-cutter
	1790-1835	In Eisenach
GHE	1732-40	Georg Hieronymus Eberhard, warden
	1740-54	Mintmaster in Saalfeld
ICK	1764-65	Johann Christian Knaust, warden
	1765-94	Mintmaster in Saalfeld
ILH	1698-1716	Johann Lorenz Holland in Dresden
I.L.OEXLEIN, OE	1740-87	Johann Leonhard Oexlein, die-cutter in Nurnberg
S, ST	1785-90	Johann Leonhard Stockmar, die-cutter
	1790-1835	In Eisenach

REUSS-EBERSDORF

The Reuss family, whose lands were located in Thüringia, was founded c. 1035. The Ebersdorf line was founded in 1671 from the Lobenstein branch. The county became a principality in 1806. They inherited Lobenstein in 1824and were forced to abdicate in 1849 and Lobenstein-Ebersdorf went to Schleiz.

RULERS

Heinrich XXIV, 1747-1779
Heinrich LI, 1779-1822

COUNTY

REGULAR COINAGE

KM# 17 PFENNIG

Billon **Ruler:** Heinrich XXIV **Obverse:** Crowned arms
Reverse: Value and date in cartouche

Date	Mintage	VG	F	VF	XF	Unc
1765	16,000	7.00	15.00	35.00	70.00	—

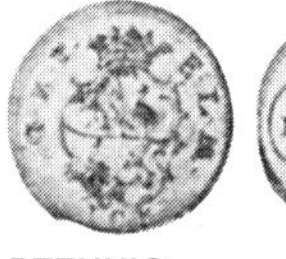

KM# 18 3 PFENNIG

Billon **Ruler:** Heinrich XXIV **Obverse:** Crowned arms
Reverse: Value and date in cartouche

Date	Mintage	VG	F	VF	XF	Unc
1765 ICK	9,696	7.00	15.00	35.00	70.00	—

KM# 19 1/48 THALER

0.9700 g., 0.2500 Silver 0.0078 oz. ASW **Ruler:** Heinrich XXIV
Obverse: Crowned arms **Reverse:** Value and date in cartouche

Date	Mintage	VG	F	VF	XF	Unc
1765 ICK	8,054	15.00	30.00	65.00	125	—

KM# 5 1/24 THALER (Groschen)

Silver **Obverse:** Four-fold arms in baroque frame, helmet above
Reverse: 24/EINEN/THAL. / date in palm branches

Date	Mintage	VG	F	VF	XF	Unc
1739 GHE	—	12.00	25.00	50.00	90.00	—

KM# 10 1/24 THALER (Groschen)

1.9800 g., 0.3680 Silver 0.0234 oz. ASW **Ruler:** Heinrich XXIV
Obverse: Crowned arms **Reverse:** Value in center, date in legend

Date	Mintage	VG	F	VF	XF	Unc
1763 ICK	44,000	8.00	16.00	38.00	75.00	—

KM# 11 1/12 THALER

3.3400 g., 0.4370 Silver 0.0469 oz. ASW **Ruler:** Heinrich XXIV
Obverse: Crowned arms **Obv. Legend:** HEINRICH XXIV
Reverse: Value and date in center

Date	Mintage	VG	F	VF	XF	Unc
1763 ICE	31,000	8.00	16.00	38.00	75.00	—
1764 ICE	Inc. above	8.00	16.00	38.00	75.00	—

KM# 14 1/12 THALER

3.3400 g., 0.4370 Silver 0.0469 oz. ASW **Ruler:** Heinrich XXIV
Obverse: Crowned arms **Obv. Legend:** HEINRICH D XXIV
Reverse: Value, date

Date	Mintage	VG	F	VF	XF	Unc
1764 ICE	Inc. above	8.00	16.00	38.00	75.00	—

KM# 15 1/12 THALER

3.3400 g., 0.4370 Silver 0.0469 oz. ASW **Ruler:** Heinrich XXIV
Obverse: I.C.E. below arms **Reverse:** Value, date

Date	Mintage	VG	F	VF	XF	Unc
1764 ICE	Inc. above	8.00	16.00	38.00	75.00	—

KM# 12 1/6 THALER

5.3600 g., 0.5410 Silver 0.0932 oz. ASW **Ruler:** Heinrich XXIV
Obverse: Crowned arms **Reverse:** Value and date in center

Date	Mintage	VG	F	VF	XF	Unc
1763 ICE	9,156	12.00	28.00	65.00	125	—
1764 ICE	Inc. above	12.00	28.00	65.00	125	—

KM# 13 1/3 THALER

7.0100 g., 0.8330 Silver 0.1877 oz. ASW **Ruler:** Heinrich XXIV
Obverse: Crowned arms **Reverse:** Value and date in center, I.C.E. below date

Date	Mintage	VG	F	VF	XF	Unc
1763 ICE	4,540	30.00	50.00	100	200	—

KM# 16 1/3 THALER

7.0100 g., 0.8330 Silver 0.1877 oz. ASW **Ruler:** Heinrich XXIV
Obverse: I.C.E. below arms **Reverse:** Value and date

Date	Mintage	VG	F	VF	XF	Unc
1764 ICE	Inc. above	25.00	45.00	85.00	165	—

KM# 20 2/3 THALER

14.0300 g., 0.8330 Silver 0.3757 oz. ASW **Ruler:** Heinrich XXIV
Obverse: Armored bust right **Reverse:** Crowned arms

Date	Mintage	VG	F	VF	XF	Unc
1765 ICK	2,366	40.00	60.00	120	250	—

KM# 21 THALER

28.0600 g., 0.8330 Silver 0.7515 oz. ASW **Ruler:** Heinrich XXIV
Obverse: Armored bust right **Obv. Legend:** HEINRICH D • XXIV • I • REUSS • GR • U • H • V • PL • H • Z • G • C • G • SVL •
Reverse: Helmeted arms **Rev. Legend:** GR • REUSS • PL • EBERSD • CONV • MUNZ • date/ * X EINE FEINE MARCK* below
Note: Convention Thaler.

Date	Mintage	F	VF	XF	Unc
1765 ICE	4,804	90.00	185	400	850
1766 ICK	Inc. above	90.00	185	400	850

REUSS-GERA

This lordship was founded in 1206 and became extinct in 1550, passing to Greiz. The Younger Line established a new branch in Gera in the same year. In 1635, Gera was divided into the lines of Gera, Lobenstein, Saalburg and Schleiz. Gera fell extinct again in 1802 and the title passed to Schleiz.

RULERS

Heinrich XVIII, 1686-1735
Heinrich XXV, 1735-1748
Heinrich XXX, 1748-1802

PRINCIPALITY

REGULAR COINAGE

KM# 65 PFENNIG

Copper **Ruler:** Heinrich XXX **Obverse:** Dog head right
Reverse: Value, date

Date	Mintage	VG	F	VF	XF	Unc
1761	—	5.00	10.00	20.00	45.00	—

KM# 66 2 PFENNIG

Copper **Ruler:** Heinrich XXV **Obverse:** Dog head right
Reverse: Value, date

Date	Mintage	VG	F	VF	XF	Unc
1761	—	6.00	12.00	25.00	50.00	—

KM# 67 1/24 THALER (12 Pfennig)
1.9800 g., 0.3680 Silver 0.0234 oz. ASW **Ruler:** Heinrich XXX
Obverse: Helmeted arms **Reverse:** Value in center, date in legend

Date	Mintage	VG	F	VF	XF	Unc
1763 ICE	—	12.00	25.00	50.00	100	—
1764 ICE	—	12.00	25.00	50.00	100	—

KM# 68 1/12 THALER
3.3400 g., 0.4370 Silver 0.0469 oz. ASW **Ruler:** Heinrich XXX
Obverse: Helmeted arms in baroque frame **Reverse:** Value with date in legend

Date	Mintage	VG	F	VF	XF	Unc
1763 ICE	—	6.00	16.00	35.00	75.00	—
1764 ICE	—	6.00	16.00	35.00	75.00	—

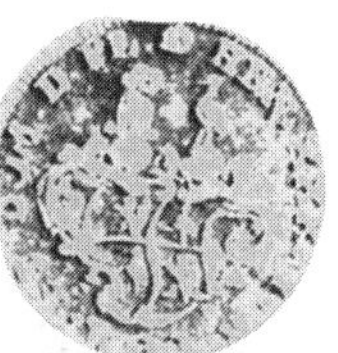

KM# 69 1/12 THALER
3.3400 g., 0.4370 Silver 0.0469 oz. ASW **Ruler:** Heinrich XXX
Obverse: Helmeted arms in baroque frame **Reverse:** Value, date

Date	Mintage	VG	F	VF	XF	Unc
1763 ICE	—	6.00	16.00	35.00	75.00	—

KM# 70 1/6 THALER
5.3600 g., 0.5410 Silver 0.0932 oz. ASW **Ruler:** Heinrich XXX
Obverse: Helmeted arms in baroque frame **Reverse:** Value with date in legend

Date	Mintage	VG	F	VF	XF	Unc
1763 ICE	—	15.00	40.00	75.00	175	—

KM# 71 1/2 THALER (30 Groschen)
14.0300 g., 0.8330 Silver 0.3757 oz. ASW **Ruler:** Heinrich XXX
Subject: Peace of Hubertusburg **Obverse:** Helmeted arms
Reverse: Figure of Freedom handing scepter to Virtue

Date	Mintage	VG	F	VF	XF	Unc
1763	—	85.00	165	325	550	—

KM# 72 THALER (Groschen)
28.0600 g., 0.8380 Silver 0.7560 oz. ASW **Ruler:** Heinrich XXX
Subject: Peace of Hubertusburg **Obverse:** Helmeted arms in baroque frame **Obv. Legend:** HENT • XXX • I • L • RVTH • COM • ET • DOM • DE • PL • D • G • C • G • S • ET • L •
Reverse: Figure of Freedom handing sceptre to Virtue
Rev. Legend: NEGLECTAE VIRTVTI DECVS RESTIT, below; MDCCLXIII/X EINE F.M. **Note:** Dav. #2639.

Date	Mintage	F	VF	XF	Unc
1763	—	300	650	1,300	2,200

REUSS-LOBENSTEIN

The Reuss family, whose lands were located in Thüringia, was founded ca. 1035. The Lobenstein line was founded in 1635. The county became a principality in 1790. In 1824 Lobenstein was given to Ebersdorf.

RULERS
Heinrich III, 1671-1710
Heinrich XV, 1710-1739
Heinrich II, 1739-1782
Heinrich XXXV, 1782-1805

COUNTY

REGULAR COINAGE

KM# 6 PFENNIG
Copper **Ruler:** Heinrich II **Obverse:** Legend, date
Obv. Legend: REUS:/ SCHEIDE/ MUNZE **Reverse:** Value
Note: Similar to 2 Pfennig, KM#7.

Date	Mintage	VG	F	VF	XF	Unc
1760	—	5.00	10.00	22.00	45.00	—
1761	—	5.00	10.00	22.00	45.00	—

KM# 7 2 PFENNIG
Copper **Ruler:** Heinrich II **Obverse:** Legend, date
Obv. Legend: REUS:/ SCHEIDE/ MUNZE **Reverse:** Value

Date	Mintage	VG	F	VF	XF	Unc
1760	—	7.00	15.00	28.00	50.00	—
1761	—	7.00	14.00	28.00	50.00	—

KM# 8 6 PFENNIG
Billon **Ruler:** Heinrich II **Obverse:** Shielded monogram
Reverse: Value within imperial orb, date above

Date	Mintage	VG	F	VF	XF	Unc
1761 ICE	—	35.00	70.00	140	250	—

KM# 5 2 GROSCHEN
Silver **Ruler:** Heinrich II **Subject:** Marriage of Count's daughter to Prince von Stolberg-Wernigerode **Obverse:** Crowned arms within baroque frame **Reverse:** Bridal pair below script RS monogram

Date	Mintage	VG	F	VF	XF	Unc
1759 ICE	—	30.00	60.00	125	225	—

KM# 10 1/48 THALER
0.9700 g., 0.2500 Silver 0.0078 oz. ASW **Ruler:** Heinrich II
Obverse: Lion on pedestal **Reverse:** Value, date in cartouche

Date	Mintage	VG	F	VF	XF	Unc
1771 ICK	9,374	15.00	30.00	70.00	120	—

REUSS-OBERGREIZ

The other branch of the division of 1635, Obergreiz went through a number of consolidations and further divisions. Upon the extinction of the Ruess-Untergreiz line in 1768, the latter passed to Reuss-Obergreiz and this line continued on into the 20th century, obtaining the rank of count back in 1673 and that of prince in 1778.

RULERS
Heinrich I, 1697-1714
Heinrich II, 1714-1722
Heinrich IX, 1722-1723
Heinrich XI, 1723-1800
Heinrich XIII, 1800-1817

PRINCIPALITY

REGULAR COINAGE

KM# 55 HELLER
Copper **Ruler:** Heinrich XI **Obverse:** Crowned lion rampant left
Reverse: Value and date

Date	Mintage	VG	F	VF	XF	Unc
1760	—	3.50	9.00	18.00	38.00	—
1761	—	3.50	9.00	18.00	38.00	—
1769	173,000	3.50	9.00	18.00	38.00	—
1770	115,000	3.50	9.00	18.00	38.00	—

KM# 70 1/2 PFENNIG
Copper **Ruler:** Heinrich XI **Obverse:** Crowned Reuss lion left
Reverse: Value above date, G. R. P. in value

Date	Mintage	VG	F	VF	XF	Unc
1775	—	6.00	12.00	28.00	50.00	—

KM# 76 1/2 PFENNIG
Copper **Ruler:** Heinrich XI **Obverse:** Rampant lion left
Reverse: Value above date, F. R. P. in value

Date	Mintage	VG	F	VF	XF	Unc
1787	89,000	6.00	12.00	28.00	50.00	—
1789	167,000	6.00	12.00	28.00	50.00	—

KM# 56 PFENNIG
Copper **Ruler:** Heinrich XI **Obverse:** Crowned Reuss lion left
Reverse: Value above date, G. R. P. in value

Date	Mintage	VG	F	VF	XF	Unc
1760	—	4.50	10.00	20.00	40.00	—
1761	—	4.50	10.00	20.00	40.00	—
1775	57,000	4.50	10.00	20.00	40.00	—

KM# 77 PFENNIG
Copper **Ruler:** Heinrich XI **Obverse:** Rampant lion left
Reverse: F. R. P. in value

Date	Mintage	VG	F	VF	XF	Unc
1787	176,000	3.00	8.00	16.00	35.00	—
1789	219,000	3.00	8.00	16.00	35.00	—

KM# 57 2 PFENNIG
Copper **Ruler:** Heinrich XI **Obverse:** Rampant lion left
Reverse: Value, date

Date	Mintage	VG	F	VF	XF	Unc
1760	—	5.00	10.00	22.00	48.00	—
1761	—	5.00	10.00	22.00	48.00	—

KM# 58 3 PFENNIG
Billon **Ruler:** Heinrich XI **Obverse:** HXIER monogram in cartouche **Reverse:** Value in orb on shield divides date

Date	Mintage	VG	F	VF	XF	Unc
1763 ICE	—	8.00	16.00	38.00	80.00	—

KM# 65 3 PFENNIG
Billon **Ruler:** Heinrich XI **Obverse:** Crowned arms **Reverse:** Value on orb within shield dividing date **Note:** Varieties exist.

Date	Mintage	VG	F	VF	XF	Unc
1764	—	8.00	16.00	38.00	80.00	—
1769	68,000	8.00	16.00	38.00	80.00	—

KM# 78 3 PFENNIG
Billon **Ruler:** Heinrich XI **Obverse:** Crowned Reuss lion left on pedestal, inscription in curve above **Obv. Inscription:** F.R.PL. G.L.M **Reverse:** Imperial orb with '3' in cartouche divides date

Date	Mintage	VG	F	VF	XF	Unc
1787	36,000	6.00	12.00	30.00	60.00	—

KM# 59 1/48 THALER
0.9700 g., 0.2500 Silver 0.0078 oz. ASW **Ruler:** Heinrich XI
Obverse: HXIER monogram in cartouche **Reverse:** Value, date

Date	Mintage	VG	F	VF	XF	Unc
1763 ICE	—	10.00	20.00	40.00	85.00	—

KM# 66 1/48 THALER
0.9700 g., 0.2500 Silver 0.0078 oz. ASW **Ruler:** Heinrich XI **Obverse:** Crowned arms within baroque frame **Reverse:** Value, date

Date	Mintage	VG	F	VF	XF	Unc
1769	36,000	8.00	16.00	38.00	80.00	—

KM# 79 1/48 THALER
0.9700 g., 0.2500 Silver 0.0078 oz. ASW **Ruler:** Heinrich XI **Obverse:** Rampant lion left **Reverse:** Value, date within cartouche

Date	Mintage	VG	F	VF	XF	Unc
1787	35,000	6.00	12.00	30.00	65.00	—
1789	86,000	6.00	12.00	30.00	65.00	—

KM# 45 1/24 THALER (Groschen)
Billon **Ruler:** Heinrich XI **Obverse:** Helmeted ornate arms **Reverse:** Value within wreath

Date	Mintage	VG	F	VF	XF	Unc
1738 GHE	—	15.00	25.00	50.00	100	—
1739 GHE	—	15.00	25.00	50.00	100	—

KM# 52 1/24 THALER (Groschen)
Billon **Ruler:** Heinrich XI **Obverse:** Crowned arms in cartouche **Reverse:** Value, date **Rev. Legend:** NACH DEM..

Date	Mintage	VG	F	VF	XF	Unc
1759 ICE	—	15.00	25.00	50.00	100	—

KM# 60 1/24 THALER (Groschen)
1.9800 g., 0.3680 Silver 0.0234 oz. ASW **Ruler:** Heinrich XI **Obverse:** Crowned arms; cornucopia on left **Reverse:** Value in center; date in outer legend

Date	Mintage	VG	F	VF	XF	Unc
1763 ICE	—	7.00	15.00	30.00	70.00	—

KM# 61 1/24 THALER (Groschen)
1.9800 g., 0.3680 Silver 0.0234 oz. ASW **Ruler:** Heinrich XI **Obverse:** Crowned arms; cornucopia on right **Reverse:** Value

Date	Mintage	VG	F	VF	XF	Unc
1763 ICE	—	7.00	15.00	30.00	70.00	—

KM# 62 1/12 THALER
3.3400 g., 0.4370 Silver 0.0469 oz. ASW **Ruler:** Heinrich XI **Obverse:** Helmeted arms **Reverse:** Value, date

Date	Mintage	VG	F	VF	XF	Unc
1763 ICE	—	10.00	20.00	40.00	85.00	—

KM# 63 1/12 THALER
3.3400 g., 0.4370 Silver 0.0469 oz. ASW **Ruler:** Heinrich XI **Obverse:** Crowned arms **Reverse:** Value in field; date in outer legend

Date	Mintage	VG	F	VF	XF	Unc
1763 ICE	—	10.00	20.00	40.00	85.00	—

KM# 80 1/12 THALER
3.3400 g., 0.4370 Silver 0.0469 oz. ASW **Ruler:** Heinrich XI **Obverse:** Arms within crowned mantle **Reverse:** Value, date

Date	Mintage	VG	F	VF	XF	Unc
1789 ICK	12,000	12.00	25.00	50.00	100	—

KM# 51 1/6 THALER (1/4 Gulden)
Silver **Ruler:** Heinrich XI **Obverse:** Helmeted arms **Reverse:** Value, date in wreath

Date	Mintage	VG	F	VF	XF	Unc
1757 ICE	1,014	45.00	70.00	130	250	—

KM# 64 1/6 THALER (1/4 Gulden)
5.3600 g., 0.5410 Silver 0.0932 oz. ASW **Ruler:** Heinrich XI **Obverse:** Helmeted arms **Reverse:** Value

Date	Mintage	VG	F	VF	XF	Unc
1763 ICE	—	30.00	60.00	100	175	—

KM# 75 1/2 THALER (Convention)
14.0300 g., 0.8330 Silver 0.3757 oz. ASW **Ruler:** Heinrich XI **Obverse:** Head right **Reverse:** Arms within crowned mantle

Date	Mintage	F	VF	XF	Unc
1786 ICK	1,694	100	175	300	650

KM# 50 2/3 THALER (1 Gulden)
Silver **Ruler:** Heinrich XI **Obverse:** Bust right, value below **Reverse:** Rampant lion left at top **Note:** Mining 2/3 Thaler.

Date	Mintage	VG	F	VF	XF	Unc
1754 GHE	440	100	250	475	800	—

KM# 67 THALER
28.0600 g., 0.8330 Silver 0.7515 oz. ASW **Ruler:** Heinrich XI **Obverse:** Head right **Obv. Legend:** HENRICVS • XI • S • L • RVTH • COM • ET DOM • DE PL • DOM • GR • C • G • S • ET L • **Reverse:** Helmeted arms, date divided below **Rev. Legend:** X. EINE FEINE MARCK **Note:** Convention Thaler. Dav. #2634.

Date	Mintage	F	VF	XF	Unc
1769 ST-ICK	2,075	150	325	575	1,200

KM# 71 THALER
28.0600 g., 0.8330 Silver 0.7515 oz. ASW **Ruler:** Heinrich XI **Obverse:** Head right **Obv. Legend:** HENRICVS • XI • S • L • RVTH • COM • ET DOM • DE PL • DOM • GR • C • G • S • ET L • **Reverse:** Helmeted arms **Rev. Legend:** BERG SEGEN DER NEUEN HOFNUNG., I.C. - K. and X EINE FEINE MARK• below **Note:** Mining Thaler from Neue Hoffnung Mine. Dav. #2635.

Date	Mintage	F	VF	XF	Unc
1775 ST-ICK	132	225	450	800	1,600

KM# 72 THALER
28.0600 g., 0.8330 Silver 0.7515 oz. ASW **Ruler:** Heinrich XI **Obverse:** Head right **Obv. Legend:** D.G. HENR. XI. S. L. RVTH. S.R.I. PRINC. COM. ET DOM. PLAV: **Reverse:** Arms within crowned mantle **Rev. Legend:** X. EINE FEINE MARCK, 17-78 **Note:** Dav. #2636.

Date	Mintage	F	VF	XF	Unc
1778 ST-ICK	1,418	150	350	550	1,350

KM# 85 THALER
28.0600 g., 0.8330 Silver 0.7515 oz. ASW **Ruler:** Heinrich XI **Obverse:** Head right **Obv. Legend:** D.G. HENR. XI. S. L. RVTH. S.R.I. PRINC. COM. ET DOM. PLAV:, FA below **Reverse:** Arms within crowned mantle **Rev. Legend:** X. EINE FEINE MARCK **Note:** Dav. #2637.

Date	Mintage	VG	F	VF	XF	Unc
1790 FA-ICK	150	250	500	750	1,400	—

PATTERNS

Including off metal strikes

KM#	Date	Mintage	Identification	Mkt Val
Pn1	1769	—	Heller. Silver. KM#55.	180
Pn2	1769	—	1/48 Thaler. Gold. KM#66.	—
Pn3	1775	—	Pfennig. Silver. KM#56.	—

REUSS-SCHLEIZ

Originally part of the holdings of Reuss-Gera, Schleiz was ruled separately on and off during the first half of the 16th century. When the Gera line died out in 1550, Schleiz passed to Obergreiz. Schleiz was reintegrated into a new line of Gera and a separate countship at Schleiz was founded in 1635, only to last one generation. At its extinction in 1666, Schleiz passed to Reuss-Saalburg which thereafter took the name of Reuss-Schleiz.

RULERS

Heinrich XI, 1692-1726
Heinrich I, 1726-1744
Heinrich XII, 1744-1784
Heinrich XLII, 1784-1818

PRINCIPALITY

REGULAR COINAGE

KM# 35 1/24 THALER (Groschen)
1.9800 g., 0.3680 Silver 0.0234 oz. ASW **Ruler:** Heinrich XII **Obverse:** Helmeted arms **Reverse:** Value, date within inner circle

Date	Mintage	VG	F	VF	XF	Unc
1763 ICE	139,000	7.00	15.00	30.00	70.00	—
1764 ICE	Inc. above	7.00	15.00	30.00	70.00	—

KM# 36 1/24 THALER (Groschen)
1.9800 g., 0.3680 Silver 0.0234 oz. ASW **Ruler:** Heinrich XII **Obverse:** Helmeted arms **Reverse:** Rosette below date

Date	Mintage	VG	F	VF	XF	Unc
1763 ICE	Inc. above	7.00	15.00	30.00	70.00	—

KM# 3 1/12 THALER
3.3400 g., 0.4370 Silver 0.0469 oz. ASW **Ruler:** Heinrich XII **Obverse:** Helmeted arms **Reverse:** Value, date

Date	Mintage	VG	F	VF	XF	Unc
1763 ICE	—	8.00	18.00	35.00	80.00	—

KM# 38 1/6 THALER
5.3600 g., 0.5410 Silver 0.0932 oz. ASW **Ruler:** Heinrich XII **Obverse:** Helmeted arms **Reverse:** Value, date **Note:** Reichs 1/6 Thaler.

Date	Mintage	VG	F	VF	XF	Unc
1763 ICE	6,520	25.00	45.00	75.00	160	—

KM# 39 1/3 THALER (1/2 Gulden)
7.0100 g., 0.8330 Silver 0.1877 oz. ASW **Ruler:** Heinrich XII **Obverse:** Helmeted arms **Reverse:** Value, date **Note:** Reichs 1/3 Thaler.

Date	Mintage	VG	F	VF	XF	Unc
1763 ICE	560	150	225	300	500	—

KM# 40 2/3 THALER (Gulden)
14.0300 g., 0.8330 Silver 0.3757 oz. ASW **Ruler:** Heinrich XII **Subject:** Peace of Hubertusberg **Obverse:** Armored bust left **Reverse:** Helmeted arms **Note:** Reichs 2/3 Thaler.

Date	Mintage	VG	F	VF	XF	Unc
1763 ST-ICE	—	45.00	90.00	185	375	—

KM# 43 2/3 THALER (Gulden)
14.0300 g., 0.8330 Silver 0.3757 oz. ASW **Ruler:** Heinrich XII **Reverse:** Different helmeted arms, value below

Date	Mintage	VG	F	VF	XF	Unc
1764 ICE	—	45.00	90.00	185	375	—

KM# 41 THALER
28.0600 g., 0.8330 Silver 0.7515 oz. ASW **Ruler:** Heinrich XII **Subject:** Peace of Hubertusberg **Obverse:** Armored bust left **Obv. Legend:** HEINRICH D. XII. I. REUSS. G. U. H. V. PLAUEN. **Reverse:** Helmeted arms **Rev. Legend:** QUF KRIEGES LAST FOLGT RUH UND RAST, below; X. EINE MARCK FEIN. **Note:** Convention Thaler. Dav. #2640.

Date	Mintage	F	VF	XF	Unc
1763 ICE	—	200	350	650	1,350

KM# 44 THALER
28.0600 g., 0.8330 Silver 0.7515 oz. ASW **Ruler:** Heinrich XII **Obverse:** Armored bust left **Obv. Legend:** HEINRICH D. XII. I. REUSS. G. U. H. V. PLAUEN. **Reverse:** Helmeted arms **Rev. Legend:** IN IESV VIVO ET MORIAR., X. EINE MARCK FEIN. below **Note:** Dav. #2641.

Date	Mintage	F	VF	XF	Unc
1764 ICE	—	200	375	700	1,450

TRADE COINAGE

KM# 42 DUCAT
3.5000 g., 0.9860 Gold 0.1109 oz. AGW **Ruler:** Heinrich XII **Subject:** Peace of Hubertusberg **Obverse:** Crowned monogram **Reverse:** Arms

Date	Mintage	F	VF	XF	Unc
1763 ICE	485	300	750	1,350	2,250

KM# 45 DUCAT
3.5000 g., 0.9860 Gold 0.1109 oz. AGW **Ruler:** Heinrich XII **Obverse:** Armored bust left **Reverse:** Arms

Date	Mintage	F	VF	XF	Unc
1764	224	550	1,150	2,150	3,500

REUSS-UNTERGREIZ

Founded in 1535, inherited Burgk in 1550. After several acquisitions and subsequent divisions, the line died out in 1768 and all holdings passed to Reuss-Obergreiz.

RULERS

Heinrich XIII, 1675-1733
Heinrich III, 1733-1768

PRINCIPALITY

REGULAR COINAGE

KM# 24 PFENNIG
Copper **Ruler:** Heinrich III **Obverse:** h3 monogram in crowned cartouche

Date	Mintage	VG	F	VF	XF	Unc
1752	—	8.00	15.00	30.00	55.00	—

KM# 25 3 PFENNIG (1/84 Thaler)
Silver **Ruler:** Heinrich III **Obverse:** Crowned baroque frame with gothic h3 **Obv. Legend:** G. R. P. UNTER-GREIZER L.M. **Reverse:** Value: 3 on imperial orb divides date in ornamented shield

Date	Mintage	VG	F	VF	XF	Unc
1751	—	15.00	25.00	50.00	100	—

KM# 28 3 PFENNIG (1/84 Thaler)
Billon **Ruler:** Heinrich III **Obverse:** h3 monogram in crowned cartouche **Reverse:** Value, date **Note:** Gute 3 Pfennig

Date	Mintage	VG	F	VF	XF	Unc
1752 GHE	—	15.00	25.00	50.00	100	—

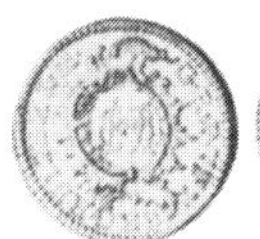

KM# 31 3 PFENNIG (1/84 Thaler)
Billon **Ruler:** Heinrich III **Obverse:** Monogram within cartouche **Reverse:** Value on imperial orb within shield dividing date

Date	Mintage	VG	F	VF	XF	Unc
1753	—	10.00	20.00	40.00	80.00	—
1755	—	10.00	20.00	40.00	80.00	—
1763	—	10.00	20.00	40.00	80.00	—

KM# 29 6 PFENNIG
Billon **Ruler:** Heinrich III **Obverse:** Monogram within cartouche **Reverse:** Value on orb, date above

Date	Mintage	VG	F	VF	XF	Unc
1752 GHE	—	8.00	15.00	30.00	70.00	—
1753 GHE	—	8.00	15.00	30.00	70.00	—
1754 GHE	—	8.00	15.00	30.00	70.00	—
1755 ICE	—	8.00	15.00	30.00	70.00	—
1756 ICE	—	8.00	15.00	30.00	70.00	—
1757 ICE	—	8.00	15.00	30.00	70.00	—
1758 ICE	—	8.00	15.00	30.00	70.00	—

KM# 40 1/48 THALER (6 Pfennig)
39700.0000 g., 0.2500 Silver 319.08 oz. ASW **Ruler:** Heinrich III **Obverse:** HER III monogram in cartouche **Reverse:** Value, date

Date	Mintage	VG	F	VF	XF	Unc
1763 E	—	10.00	20.00	40.00	75.00	—

KM# 41 1/48 THALER (6 Pfennig)
39700.0000 g., 0.2500 Silver 319.08 oz. ASW **Ruler:** Heinrich III **Obverse:** Crowned rampant lion left **Reverse:** Value and date

Date	Mintage	VG	F	VF	XF	Unc
1763 E	—	7.00	15.00	25.00	65.00	—

KM# 20 1/24 THALER (1 Groschen)
Billon **Ruler:** Heinrich III **Obverse:** Helmeted arms **Reverse:** Value, date within branches

Date	Mintage	VG	F	VF	XF	Unc
1738 GHE	—	12.00	25.00	50.00	90.00	—
1739 GHE	—	12.00	25.00	50.00	90.00	—

KM# 32 1/24 THALER (1 Groschen)
Billon **Ruler:** Heinrich III **Obverse:** Crowned arms **Reverse:** Value, date

Date	Mintage	VG	F	VF	XF	Unc
1753 GHE	—	10.00	20.00	40.00	80.00	—

KM# 42 1/24 THALER (1 Groschen)
1.9800 g., 0.3680 Silver 0.0234 oz. ASW **Ruler:** Heinrich III **Obverse:** Crowned arms **Reverse:** Value, date in legend **Note:** Varieties exist.

Date	Mintage	VG	F	VF	XF	Unc
1763 ICE	—	8.00	16.00	32.00	75.00	—
1764 ICE	—	8.00	16.00	32.00	75.00	—

KM# 33 1/12 THALER
Silver **Ruler:** Heinrich III **Obverse:** Crowned arms **Reverse:** Value

Date	Mintage	VG	F	VF	XF	Unc
1753 GHE	—	12.00	25.00	50.00	100	—

KM# 44 1/12 THALER
3.3400 g., 0.4370 Silver 0.0469 oz. ASW **Ruler:** Heinrich III **Reverse:** Value and date in center

Date	Mintage	VG	F	VF	XF	Unc
1763 ICE	—	12.00	25.00	50.00	100	—

KM# 43 1/12 THALER
3.3400 g., 0.4370 Silver 0.0469 oz. ASW **Ruler:** Heinrich III **Obverse:** Crowned arms **Reverse:** Value in center; date in outer legend **Note:** Varieties exist.

Date	Mintage	VG	F	VF	XF	Unc
1763 ICE	—	12.00	25.00	50.00	100	—

KM# 26 1/8 THALER (4 Groschen)
Silver **Ruler:** Heinrich III **Obverse:** Helmeted arms **Reverse:** Miners and mines **Note:** Mining-Species 1/8 Thaler.

Date	Mintage	VG	F	VF	XF	Unc
1751 GHE	—	30.00	60.00	135	285	—

KM# 30 1/8 THALER (4 Groschen)
Silver **Ruler:** Heinrich III **Obverse:** Crowned arms **Reverse:** View of the mine

Date	Mintage	VG	F	VF	XF	Unc
1752 GHE	—	30.00	60.00	135	285	—
1753 GHE	—	30.00	60.00	135	285	—

KM# 34 1/8 THALER (4 Groschen)
Silver **Ruler:** Heinrich III **Obverse:** Date in one line at bottom

Date	Mintage	VG	F	VF	XF	Unc
1753 GHE	—	25.00	50.00	110	225	—

KM# 45 1/6 THALER
5.3600 g., 0.5410 Silver 0.0932 oz. ASW **Ruler:** Heinrich III

Date	Mintage	VG	F	VF	XF	Unc
1763 ICE	—	30.00	60.00	100	175	—

KM# 27 1/4 THALER
Silver **Ruler:** Heinrich III **Obverse:** Crowned arms in baroque frame, date **Reverse:** Mining scene, value **Rev. Legend:** GOTT SEEGNE...

Date	Mintage	VG	F	VF	XF	Unc
1751 GHE	—	35.00	75.00	185	375	—

KM# 35 2/3 THALER (Gulden)
Silver **Ruler:** Heinrich III **Note:** Reichs 2/3 Thaler.

Date	Mintage	VG	F	VF	XF	Unc
1759	—	100	200	400	750	—

KM# 46 THALER
28.0600 g., 0.8330 Silver 0.7515 oz. ASW **Ruler:** Heinrich III **Obverse:** Armored bust right **Obv. Legend:** HENRICVS. III. S. L. RVTHENOR. TOTIVS STEMMAT. SENIOR, I.L.OEXLEIN below bust **Reverse:** Helmeted arms **Rev. Legend:** COM • ET • DOMIN • DE PL • D • DE GREITZ C • G • S • ET LOBENSTL •,X•EINE FEINE MARCK below **Note:** Dav. #2638.

Date	Mintage	F	VF	XF	Unc
1763 I. L. OEXLEIN	—	150	325	600	1,200
1764 I. L. OEXLEIN	—	150	325	600	1,200

TRADE COINAGE

KM# 47 DUCAT
3.5000 g., 0.9860 Gold 0.1109 oz. AGW **Ruler:** Heinrich III **Obverse:** Bust right **Reverse:** Arms

Date	Mintage	VG	F	VF	XF	Unc
1764 DE	—	500	1,000	1,750	3,000	—

PATTERNS

Including off metal strikes

KM#	Date	Mintage	Identification	Mkt Val
Pn1	1752	—	3 Pfennig. Gold. 1.7300 g. KM#28	—

RIETBERG

The counts of Rietberg held lands along the River Ems in Westphalia. Rietberg castle and town are located on the river about 15 miles (25 km) west-northwest of Paderborn. The line of Rietberg counts was established by Heinrich II (1185-1207), the younger brother of Count Gottfried II of Arnsberg (1185-1235). The line in Rietberg had the misfortune to become extinct in the male line more than once. When Konrad IV died in 1439, he was succeeded by his grandson through his daughter. In the mid-16th century, Johann II left only two daughters. Irmgard married first Erich von Hoya, second Simon von Lippe, who ruled Rietberg briefly after his wife died in 1583. Meanwhile, Walburg had married Enno III von Ostfriesland and their daughter Sabina Katharina eventually married her uncle, Johann III von Ostfriesland. Johann III ruled Rietberg and their son was the first of a new line of counts there. When that line became extinct as well in 1690, Rietberg passed in marriage to the counts of Kaunitz. The countship was raised to a principality in 1764 and was mediatized in 1807, passing to Westphalia thereafter.

RULERS

Maria Ernestine Franziska, 1690-1758
Maximilian Ulrich von Kaunitz, 1699-1746
Wenzel Anton, 1746-1794, Prince 1764
Ernst Christof II, 1794-1797
Dominikus Anon, 1797-1807 (d. 1812)

REFERENCE

B = W. Buse, "Münzgeschichte der Grafschaft Rietberg,, *Zeitschrift für Numismatik* 29 (1912), pp. 254-362, pls. 6-9.

COUNTY

REGULAR COINAGE

KM# 105 MATTIER
Silver **Ruler:** Maximilian Ulrich von Kaunitz **Obverse:** Crowned eagle **Reverse:** Denomination and date

Date	Mintage	VG	F	VF	XF	Unc
1706	—	120	250	450	—	—

KM# 96 PFENNIG
Copper **Ruler:** Maximilian Ulrich von Kaunitz **Obverse:** Denomination **Reverse:** Crowned eagle divides date

Date	Mintage	VG	F	VF	XF	Unc
1703	—	12.00	25.00	45.00	90.00	—

KM# 130 PFENNIG

Copper **Ruler:** Wenzel Anton **Obverse:** Crowned script WA monogram dividing date **Reverse:** Value

Date	Mintage	VG	F	VF	XF	Unc
1766	—	20.00	30.00	65.00	125	—

KM# 97.1 2 PFENNIG

Copper **Ruler:** Maximilian Ulrich von Kaunitz **Obverse:** Denomination **Obv. Legend:** ... LAND... **Reverse:** Crowned eagle

Date	Mintage	VG	F	VF	XF	Unc
1703	—	15.00	30.00	50.00	100	—

KM# 97.2 2 PFENNIG

Copper **Ruler:** Maximilian Ulrich von Kaunitz **Obverse:** Legend variation **Obv. Legend:** ... LANDT...

Date	Mintage	VG	F	VF	XF	Unc
1703	—	15.00	30.00	50.00	100	—

KM# 131 2 PFENNIG

Copper **Ruler:** Wenzel Anton **Obverse:** Crowned script WA monogram dividing date **Reverse:** Value

Date	Mintage	VG	F	VF	XF	Unc
1766	—	30.00	40.00	70.00	135	—

KM# 98 3 PFENNIG

Copper **Ruler:** Maximilian Ulrich von Kaunitz **Obverse:** Crowned eagle divides date **Reverse:** Denomination

Date	Mintage	VG	F	VF	XF	Unc
1703	—	15.00	30.00	50.00	100	—

KM# 106 3 PFENNIG

Silver **Ruler:** Maximilian Ulrich von Kaunitz **Obverse:** Crowned eagle **Reverse:** Denomination

Date	Mintage	VG	F	VF	XF	Unc
1706 HLO	—	45.00	90.00	185	—	—

KM# 99 4 PFENNIG

Copper **Ruler:** Maximilian Ulrich von Kaunitz **Obverse:** Denomination **Reverse:** Crowned eagle divides date

Date	Mintage	VG	F	VF	XF	Unc
1703	—	20.00	35.00	60.00	120	—

KM# 107 4 PFENNIG

Silver **Ruler:** Maximilian Ulrich von Kaunitz **Obverse:** Crowned eagle divides date **Reverse:** Denomination

Date	Mintage	VG	F	VF	XF	Unc
1706 HLO	—	50.00	100	200	—	—

KM# 100 5 PFENNIG

Silver **Ruler:** Maximilian Ulrich von Kaunitz **Obverse:** Crowned eagle divides date **Reverse:** Denomination

Date	Mintage	VG	F	VF	XF	Unc
1703	—	75.00	150	300	—	—

KM# 101 6 PFENNIG

Silver **Ruler:** Maximilian Ulrich von Kaunitz **Obverse:** Crowned eagle **Reverse:** Denomination

Date	Mintage	VG	F	VF	XF	Unc
1703 HLO	—	60.00	120	250	—	—

KM# 102 MARIENGROSCHEN

Silver **Ruler:** Maximilian Ulrich von Kaunitz **Obverse:** Crowned eagle **Reverse:** Denomination

Date	Mintage	VG	F	VF	XF	Unc
1703 HLO	—	—	—	—	—	—

KM# 103 24 MARIENGROSCHEN
(Gulden = 2/3 Thaler)

17.2000 g., Silver **Ruler:** Maximilian Ulrich von Kaunitz **Obverse:** Crowned arms **Reverse:** Denomination

Date	Mintage	VG	F	VF	XF	Unc
1703 HLO Rare	—	—	—	—	—	—

KM# 104 THALER

29.2000 g., Silver **Ruler:** Maximilian Ulrich von Kaunitz **Obverse:** Accolated busts of Maximilian and Maria right **Obv. Legend:** MAXIMIL • - VLR • & MAR • ERN • FRAN • S • R • I • **Reverse:** Crowned shield **Rev. Legend:** • COM • A • CAUN • RITB • & F • O • D • IN • E • S • W • & MELRICH • 1703 **Note:** Dav. #2643.

Date	Mintage	VG	F	VF	XF	Unc
1703 HLO	—	700	1,400	2,500	4,500	—

ROSTOCK

The town of Rostock is first mentioned in 1030 and was the seat of a lordship of the same name in the 13th century. It is located just a few miles inland from where the Warnow River enters the Baltic Sea and was an important trading center from earliest times. Although Rostock was usually under some control by the Mecklenburg dukes, it functioned somewhat as a free city, gaining a municipal charter as early as 1218. The city obtained control of its own coinage in 1323 and received the mint right unconditionally in 1361. From 1381, Rostock was a member of the Wendischen Münzverein (Wendish Monetary Union) and joined the Hanseatic League not long afterwards. The city coinage was struck from the 14th century until 1864.

MINT OFFICIALS' INITIALS

Initials	Date	Name
B, IHB	1750-1758	Johann Heinrich Berg
DB	ca. 1762	David Behrent, mint director
FB, FHB	1782-1795	Franz Heinrich Brandt
FL	1796-1802	Friedrich Lautersack
FS	1779-1784	Joachim Friedrich Schulze, city councilman
IG	1786-1797	Joachim Hinrich Garlieb, city councilman
IM	1679-1711	Johann Memmies
	1711	Mathias Babst
	1727-1742	Simon Siemssen

ARMS

Griffin, usually rampant to left. Also, shield divided by horizontal band above griffin walking left, below arabesques or sometimes an arrow.

FREE CITY

REGULAR COINAGE

KM# 95 PFENNIG

Copper **Obverse:** Griffin **Obv. Legend:** ROSTOCKER **Reverse:** Denomination, date, 3 rosettes **Note:** Prev. C#A1.

Date	Mintage	VG	F	VF	XF	Unc
1705	—	6.00	12.00	28.00	60.00	—
1710	—	6.00	12.00	28.00	60.00	—

KM# 114 PFENNIG

Copper **Obverse:** Griffin, "ROSTOCKER" **Reverse:** "1/date/R" and rosettes **Edge:** Plain

Date	Mintage	F	VF	XF	Unc
1725	—	6.00	10.00	22.00	—
1735	—	6.00	10.00	22.00	—

KM# 117 PFENNIG

Copper **Obverse:** Griffin, "ROSTOCKER" **Reverse:** "1/1747/R" in ornamented frame **Edge:** Plain

Date	Mintage	F	VF	XF	Unc
1747	—	5.00	8.00	15.00	—

KM# 120 PFENNIG

Copper **Obverse:** Griffin left in circle. **Obv. Legend:** ROSTOCKER **Reverse:** Four-line inscription with date **Rev. Legend:** I/PFENN./(date)/R

Date	Mintage	F	VF	XF	Unc
1753	—	6.00	10.00	22.00	—
1757	—	6.00	10.00	22.00	—

KM# 126 PFENNIG

Copper **Obverse:** ROSTOCHIENSIS in outer circle

Date	Mintage	VG	F	VF	XF	Unc
1782 FHB	—	5.00	10.00	20.00	40.00	—
1793 FHB	—	5.00	10.00	20.00	40.00	—

KM# 125 PFENNIG

Copper **Obverse:** ROSTOCKER in outer circle **Note:** Varieties exist; Prev. C#1.1.

Date	Mintage	VG	F	VF	XF	Unc
1782 FHB	—	5.00	10.00	20.00	45.00	—

KM# 128 PFENNIG

Copper **Obverse:** ROSTOCKER MUNTZ in outer circle **Note:** Varieties exist.

Date	Mintage	VG	F	VF	XF	Unc
1793 FHB	—	3.00	5.00	10.00	25.00	—
1794 FHB	—	3.00	5.00	10.00	25.00	—
1796 FL	—	3.00	5.00	10.00	25.00	—
1797 FL	—	3.00	5.00	10.00	25.00	—

KM# 132 PFENNIG

Copper **Obverse:** Griffin within ring **Reverse:** Denomination

Date	Mintage	F	VF	XF	Unc
1796 FL	—	5.00	10.00	25.00	100
1797 FL	—	5.00	10.00	25.00	100
1798 FL	—	5.00	10.00	25.00	100
1800 FL	—	5.00	10.00	25.00	100
1801 FL	—	5.00	10.00	25.00	100
1802 FL	—	5.00	10.00	25.00	100

KM# 129 PFENNIG

Copper **Obverse:** Griffin in ring **Reverse:** Value and date in garlanded rectangle, FL below

Date	Mintage	F	VF	XF	Unc
1798 FL	—	5.00	10.00	25.00	70.00

KM# 133 PFENNIG

Copper **Obverse:** Griffin shield **Reverse:** Denomination and date in garlanded rectangle above "FL" **Note:** Varieties exist.

Date	Mintage	VG	F	VF	XF	Unc
1798 FL	—	6.00	12.00	25.00	50.00	—

C# 2b PFENNIG

Copper **Obverse:** Griffin shield within ring **Reverse:** Value and date, rectangle, FL below

Date	Mintage	VG	F	VF	XF	Unc
1798 FL	—	—	5.00	10.00	25.00	70.00

KM# 115 3 PFENNIG

Copper **Obverse:** Griffin,"CIVIT ROSTOCH" **Reverse:** "III/date/R" in two rope circles **Edge:** Plain

Date	Mintage	F	VF	XF	Unc
1729	—	8.00	12.00	22.00	—
1735	—	8.00	12.00	22.00	—
1741	—	8.00	12.00	22.00	—

KM# 116 3 PFENNIG

Copper **Obverse:** Legend, city arms **Obv. Legend:** CIVIT.ROSTOCH. **Note:** Prev. C#7.

Date	Mintage	VG	F	VF	XF	Unc
1744 R	—	6.00	12.00	25.00	55.00	—
1747 R	—	6.00	12.00	25.00	55.00	—
1749 R	—	6.00	12.00	25.00	55.00	—
1750 R	—	6.00	12.00	25.00	55.00	—
1750 IHB	—	6.00	12.00	25.00	55.00	—
1751 IHB	—	6.00	12.00	25.00	55.00	—
1759 RIB	—	6.00	12.00	25.00	55.00	—

KM# 118 3 PFENNIG

Copper **Obv. Legend:** CIVITATIS ROSTOCH **Note:** Prev. C#7a.

Date	Mintage	VG	F	VF	XF	Unc
1750 RB	—	6.00	12.00	25.00	55.00	—
1750 RIHB	—	6.00	12.00	25.00	55.00	—

KM# 121 3 PFENNIG

Copper **Note:** Prev. C#8.

Date	Mintage	VG	F	VF	XF	Unc
1760 R	—	6.00	12.00	25.00	55.00	—
1761 IHB	—	6.00	12.00	25.00	55.00	—

KM# 122 3 PFENNIG

Copper **Obverse:** Griffin rampant **Note:** Prev. C#9.

Date	Mintage	VG	F	VF	XF	Unc
1761 IHB	—	6.00	12.00	25.00	55.00	—

KM# 123 6 PFENNIG

Copper **Note:** Prev. C#14.

Date	Mintage	VG	F	VF	XF	Unc
1761	—	7.50	15.00	30.00	80.00	—
1762	—	7.50	15.00	30.00	80.00	—

TRADE COINAGE

KM# 90 DUCAT

3.5000 g., 0.9860 Gold 0.1109 oz. AGW **Obverse:** Arms in inner circle, date in legend **Reverse:** Crowned imperial eagle in inner circle, titles of Leopold I **Note:** Fr. #2591. Varieties exist.

Date	Mintage	VG	F	VF	XF	Unc
1704 IM	—	300	600	1,200	2,000	—

KM# 124 DUCAT

3.5000 g., 0.9860 Gold 0.1109 oz. AGW **Obverse:** Crowned imperial eagle, titles of Franz I **Reverse:** Arms **Note:** Prev. C#16.

Date	Mintage	VG	F	VF	XF	Unc
1762 DB/IHB Rare	25	—	—	—	—	—

KM# 127 DUCAT

3.5000 g., 0.9860 Gold 0.1109 oz. AGW **Obverse:** Titles of Josef **Note:** Prev. C#17

Date	Mintage	VG	F	VF	XF	Unc
1783 FS/FB	200	—	500	800	1,250	2,500

KM# 130 DUCAT

3.5000 g., 0.9860 Gold 0.1109 oz. AGW **Reverse:** Titles of Franz II **Note:** Prev. C#18.

Date	Mintage	VG	F	VF	XF	Unc
1796 IG	200	—	500	800	1,250	2,500

PATTERNS

Including off metal strikes

KM#	Date	Mintage	Identification	Mkt Val

Pn2	1782	—	Pfennig. Silver. C1.2.	135

Pn3	1793	—	Pfennig. Silver. C1.3.	135
Pn4	1796	—	Ducat. Silver. C18.	—

ROTHENBURG

A city located in Bavaria on the Tauber River southeast of Wurzburg. Population: 11,882. Exports include soap and textiles.

Nobles of Rothenburg, whose castle lay in the Harz Mountains, were the cadet line of the counts of Beichlingen. Founded by Friedrich IV (1252-1313) the city became an imperial city in 1274 and reached the height of its prosperity at the end of the 14th century.

CITY

TRADE COINAGE

KM# 5 DUCAT

3.5000 g., 0.9860 Gold 0.1109 oz. AGW **Subject:** 200th Anniversary of Reformation **Obverse:** Castle reflected within inner circle **Obv. Legend:** GLORIA... **Reverse:** Inscription

Date	Mintage	VG	F	VF	XF	Unc
1717	—	—	—	—	1,200	2,000

KM# 6 DUCAT

3.5000 g., 0.9860 Gold 0.1109 oz. AGW **Obverse:** Castle reflected within inner circle **Reverse:** Bust of Luther right within inner circle **Note:** Similar to 2 Ducat, KM#7.

Date	Mintage	VG	F	VF	XF	Unc
1717 Rare	—	—	—	—	—	—

KM# 8 DUCAT

3.5000 g., 0.9860 Gold 0.1109 oz. AGW **Obverse:** Castle reflected with sun above **Reverse:** Inscription

Date	Mintage	VG	F	VF	XF	Unc
1744 Rare	—	—	—	—	—	—

KM# 9 DUCAT
3.5000 g., 0.9860 Gold 0.1109 oz. AGW **Subject:** School Jubilee **Obverse:** Castle reflected within inner circle **Obv. Legend:** PIETATE... **Reverse:** Inscription

Date	Mintage	VG	F	VF	XF	Unc
1792 Rare	—	—	—	—	—	—

KM# 7 2 DUCAT
7.0000 g., 0.9860 Gold 0.2219 oz. AGW **Subject:** 200th Anniversary of Reformation **Obverse:** Castle reflected within inner circle **Reverse:** Bust of Luther right within inner circle

Date	Mintage	VG	F	VF	XF	Unc
1717	—	—	—	1,200	2,000	3,500

PATTERNS

Including off metal strikes

KM#	Date	Mintage	Identification	Mkt Val
Pn3	1717	—	Ducat. Silver. KM#6.	180
Pn4	1717	—	2 Ducat. Silver. KM#7.	200
Pn5	1744	—	Ducat. Silver. KM#8.	100
Pn6	1792	—	Ducat. Silver. KM#9.	180

SAINT ALBAN

A priory, near Mainz, received the mint right in 1518, however, only coins of the 18th century are known.

PRIORY

TRADE COINAGE

C# 1 DUCAT
3.5000 g., 0.9860 Gold 0.1109 oz. AGW **Obverse:** St. Albanus standing **Reverse:** Arms

Date	Mintage	VG	F	VF	XF	Unc
1712	—	—	400	900	1,750	3,000
1716	—	—	350	800	1,500	2,750
1720	—	—	350	800	1,500	2,750
1724	—	—	400	900	1,750	3,000
1725	—	—	350	800	1,500	2,750
1744	—	—	400	900	1,750	3,000
1778	—	—	350	800	1,500	2,750
1779	—	—	350	750	1,250	2,250
1780	—	—	350	750	1,250	2,250

SALM

The earliest rulers of this county, with widely scattered territories in the border region of present-day Germany, France and Belgium, descended from the counts of Luxembourg in the second half of the 11th century. The patrimony was divided between two succeeding sons about 1130-35. Lower Salm was located in the Ardenne region of France and became extinct in 1416 with the death of Heinrich VI. It passed by marriage to the lord of Reifferscheidt who in turn established the line of Salm-Reifferscheidt in 1455. The other division of old Salm was Upper Salm and was located in the Vosges to the southwest of Strassburg. This line underwent several divisions, one of which died out and passed to Lorrainein 1503. Another branch subdivided and half passed to as on who left the area and established himself as progenitor of the Salm-Neuburg line in Austria. The remaining half of Salm went to the older son and was inherited through marriage upon his death in 1475 by a ruler styled Wild and Rhinegrave. This latter individual was well-established in lands which stretched along the Rhine between Trier and Mainz. Thus, the early modern lines of Salm and its subdivisions in Germany came into being. The old castle of Salm, seat of the earliest counts is located southwest of Strassburg, but the dynastic name was transferred to the Rhineland counts, who became from that point on, the Wild- and Rhinegraves of Salm. Two main lines were founded in 1499.

ARMS
Salm - 2 fish (salmon) standing on tails
Rhinegraves - lion with double tail
Wildgraves - crowned lion
Kyrburg - 3 lions, 2 above 1

SALM-KYRBURG

Founded in 1499, this branch took its name from Kyrburg Castle, the ruins of which are located three miles (5 km) west-southwest of Dhaun. A further subdivision was made in 1607, resulting in the lines of Salm-Kyrburg, Salm-Morchingen and Salm-Tronecken, the latter lasting only one generation. The main line became extinct in 1681 and fell to S-Mörchingen, which in turn ended in the male line in 1688. All Salm-Kyrburg lands and titles then reverted to Salm-Salm. After several subdivisions of that senior branch, a new line of Salm-Kyrburg was established from Salm-Neuweiler-Lenze in 1738. The count was raised to the rank of Prince of the Empire in 1742. All territories of the family were mediatized in 1806, but the Salm-Kyrburg line has survived down to modern times.

RULERS
Philipp Joseph, 1738-1779 as prince, 1742
Marie Therese von Hornes, 1779-1783
Friedrich III, (1779) 1783-1794
Friedrich IV, 1794-(1806)-1859

MINT OFFICIALS' INITIALS

Initials	Date	Name
BFN	1764-90	Philipp Christian Bunsen, mintmaster and Georg Neumeister, warden in Frankfurt
RF	1772-1809	Remegius Fehr

PRINCIPALITY

REGULAR COINAGE

C# 2 10 KREUZER
Silver **Ruler:** Marie Therese von Hornes **Obverse:** Head right **Reverse:** Crowned and mantled arms **Note:** Convention 10 Kreuzer.

Date	Mintage	VG	F	VF	XF	Unc
1780 BFN	—	60.00	120	250	450	—

C# 3 20 KREUZER
Silver **Ruler:** Marie Therese von Hornes **Obverse:** Head right **Reverse:** Crowned and mantled arms **Note:** Convention 20 Kreuzer.

Date	Mintage	VG	F	VF	XF	Unc
1780 BFN	—	100	180	320	575	—

C# 4 1/2 THALER
Silver **Ruler:** Marie Therese von Hornes **Obverse:** Bust right **Reverse:** Crowned oval arms between two branches, date **Note:** Convention 1/2 Thaler.

Date	Mintage	VG	F	VF	XF	Unc
1782 RF	—	275	550	1,150	2,500	—

C# 5 THALER
Silver **Ruler:** Marie Therese von Hornes **Obverse:** Head of Friedrich III right **Obv. Legend:** FRID • D • G • PR • A • SATM • KYRB • COM • RH • & • SYL • **Reverse:** Crowned and mantled arms **Rev. Legend:** AD NORMAM CONVENTIONIS • 1780 **Note:** Convention Thaler. Dav. #2644.

Date	Mintage	VG	F	VF	XF	Unc
1780 BFN	—	250	500	1,000	2,000	—

C# 6 THALER
Silver **Ruler:** Marie Therese von Hornes **Obverse:** Head right **Obv. Legend:** FRID • III • D • G • PR • A • SALM • KYRB COM • RH • & • SYLV • **Reverse:** Crowned arms in sprays, F.F. and date below **Rev. Legend:** AD NORMAM - CONVENTIONIS **Note:** Dav. #2645.

Date	Mintage	VG	F	VF	XF	Unc
1782 RF	—	225	450	900	1,800	—

TRADE COINAGE

C# 10 CAROLIN
9.7000 g., 0.7700 Gold 0.2401 oz. AGW **Ruler:** Marie Therese von Hornes **Obverse:** Head of Friedrich III right **Reverse:** Arms

Date	Mintage	F	VF	XF	Unc
1782 (g)	—	3,500	6,000	9,500	—

C# 8 DUCAT
3.5000 g., 0.9860 Gold 0.1109 oz. AGW **Ruler:** Marie Therese von Hornes **Obverse:** Head of Friedrich III right **Reverse:** Crowned and mantled arms

Date	Mintage	F	VF	XF	Unc
1780 (f)	—	1,500	3,000	5,500	8,500
1782 (g)	—	1,500	3,000	5,500	8,500

SAXE-COBURG-SAALFELD

When Saxe-Saalfeld obtained Coburg in 1735, the duchy was henceforth called Saxe-Coburg-Saalfeld. In 1826, Saalfeld was transferred to Saxe-Meiningen and the duke was given Gotha. The new creation was then known as Saxe-Coburg-Gotha.

RULERS
Christian Ernst, 1735-1745
Franz Josias, 1735-1764
....Joint Coinage until 1745
Ernst Friedrich, 1764-1800

MINT OFFICIALS' INITIALS

Initials	Date	Name
G		Bergrichter Graupner
GHE	1740-54	Georg Hieronymus Eberhard
ICE, IC-E, I-CE	1755-65	Johann Christian Eberhard
ICK, IC-K, I-CK	1765-94	Johann Christian Knaust

DUCHY

REGULAR COINAGE

KM# 10 HELLER
Copper **Ruler:** Christian Ernst **Obverse:** Crowned oval arms between palm fronds **Reverse:** 1/SAAL/FELDER/HELLER/date **Note:** Varieties exist.

Date	Mintage	VG	F	VF	XF	Unc
1733	—	5.00	10.00	20.00	35.00	—
1735	—	5.00	10.00	20.00	35.00	—
1736	—	5.00	10.00	20.00	35.00	—
1737	—	5.00	10.00	20.00	35.00	—
1738	—	5.00	10.00	20.00	35.00	—
1739	—	5.00	10.00	20.00	35.00	—
1740	—	5.00	10.00	20.00	35.00	—
1741	—	5.00	10.00	20.00	35.00	—
1742	—	5.00	10.00	20.00	35.00	—
1743	—	5.00	10.00	20.00	35.00	—
1744	—	5.00	10.00	20.00	35.00	—
1745	—	5.00	10.00	20.00	35.00	—

KM# 32 HELLER

Copper **Ruler:** Franz Josias **Obverse:** Crowned arms within branches **Reverse:** Value above date, small floral crosses flank 1

Date	Mintage	VG	F	VF	XF	Unc
1746	—	3.00	6.00	12.00	20.00	—
1747	—	3.00	6.00	12.00	20.00	—
1748	—	3.00	6.00	12.00	20.00	—
1749	—	3.00	6.00	12.00	20.00	—
1750	—	3.00	6.00	12.00	20.00	—

KM# 39 HELLER

Copper **Ruler:** Franz Josias **Obverse:** Plumes surround crowned oval arms

Date	Mintage	VG	F	VF	XF	Unc
1748	—	3.00	6.00	12.00	20.00	—
1752	—	3.00	6.00	12.00	20.00	—
1760	—	3.00	6.00	12.00	20.00	—

KM# 46 HELLER

Copper **Ruler:** Franz Josias **Obverse:** Different crowned arms **Reverse:** Value above date, rosettes flank 1

Date	Mintage	VG	F	VF	XF	Unc
1750	—	3.00	6.00	12.00	20.00	—
1751	—	3.00	6.00	12.00	20.00	—

KM# 47 HELLER

Copper **Ruler:** Franz Josias **Obverse:** Crowned arms within branches **Reverse:** Large floral crosses flank 1

Date	Mintage	VG	F	VF	XF	Unc
1751	—	3.00	6.00	12.00	20.00	—
1752	—	3.00	6.00	12.00	20.00	—

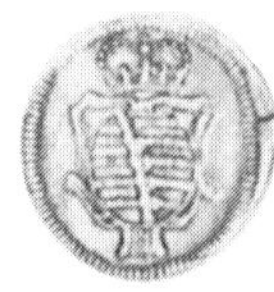

KM# 52 HELLER

Copper **Ruler:** Franz Josias **Obverse:** Crowned arms in ornamental cartouche **Reverse:** Value above date

Date	Mintage	VG	F	VF	XF	Unc
1752	—	3.00	5.00	10.00	18.00	—
1753	—	3.00	5.00	10.00	18.00	—
1754	—	3.00	5.00	10.00	18.00	—

KM# 54.1 HELLER

Copper **Ruler:** Franz Josias **Obverse:** Crowned arms in different cartouche **Reverse:** Value, date

Date	Mintage	VG	F	VF	XF	Unc
1755	—	3.00	5.00	10.00	18.00	—
1756	—	3.00	5.00	10.00	18.00	—
1757	—	3.00	5.00	10.00	18.00	—
1758	—	3.00	5.00	10.00	18.00	—
1759	—	3.00	5.00	10.00	18.00	—

KM# 54.2 HELLER

Copper **Ruler:** Franz Josias **Obverse:** Crowned arms in different cartouche **Reverse:** Without ornamentation flanking 1

Date	Mintage	VG	F	VF	XF	Unc
1760	—	3.00	5.00	10.00	18.00	—
1761	—	3.00	5.00	10.00	18.00	—
1762	—	3.00	5.00	10.00	18.00	—
1763	—	3.00	5.00	10.00	18.00	—

KM# 96 1/2 PFENNIG

Copper **Obverse:** Crowned arms **Reverse:** Value, date

Date	Mintage	VG	F	VF	XF	Unc
1772	—	6.00	12.00	25.00	65.00	—

KM# 111 1/2 PFENNIG

Copper **Obverse:** Crowned arms **Reverse:** Value, date

Date	Mintage	VG	F	VF	XF	Unc
1798	—	3.00	7.00	15.00	35.00	—
1800	—	3.00	7.00	15.00	35.00	—

KM# 62 PFENNIG

Copper **Ruler:** Franz Josias **Obverse:** Crowned monogram **Reverse:** Value, date

Date	Mintage	VG	F	VF	XF	Unc
1761	—	4.00	8.00	17.00	40.00	—
1762	—	4.00	8.00	17.00	40.00	—

KM# 80 PFENNIG

Billon **Obverse:** Crowned arms **Reverse:** Value and date in cartouche

Date	Mintage	VG	F	VF	XF	Unc
1765	—	5.00	10.00	20.00	50.00	—

KM# 95 PFENNIG

Copper **Obverse:** Crowned arms **Reverse:** Value, date

Date	Mintage	VG	F	VF	XF	Unc
1770	—	2.00	5.00	10.00	25.00	—
1772	—	2.00	5.00	10.00	25.00	—
1798	—	2.00	5.00	10.00	25.00	—

KM# 97 1-1/2 PFENNIG

Copper **Obverse:** Crowned arms **Reverse:** Value, date

Date	Mintage	VG	F	VF	XF	Unc
1772	—	3.00	7.00	15.00	35.00	—

KM# 112 1-1/2 PFENNIG

Copper **Obverse:** Crowned arms **Reverse:** Value, date

Date	Mintage	VG	F	VF	XF	Unc
1799	—	2.00	6.00	12.00	30.00	—

KM# 12 3 PFENNIG

Billon **Ruler:** Christian Ernst **Obverse:** Crowned four-fold arms between palm fronds, mintmaster's initials below, F. S. S. - L. M. divided at top **Reverse:** Imperial orb with 3 in cartouche divides date **Note:** Dreier 3 Pfennig.

Date	Mintage	VG	F	VF	XF	Unc
1736 GHE	—	10.00	20.00	40.00	65.00	—
1737 GHE	—	10.00	20.00	40.00	65.00	—
1738 GHE	—	10.00	20.00	40.00	65.00	—

KM# 25 3 PFENNIG

Billon **Ruler:** Christian Ernst **Note:** Similar to KM#12 but obverse: F. S. - S. M.

Date	Mintage	VG	F	VF	XF	Unc
1740 GHE	—	10.00	20.00	40.00	65.00	—

KM# 28 3 PFENNIG

Billon **Ruler:** Christian Ernst **Obverse:** Crowned oval with monogram FJ between palm fronds, F. S. - S. M. divided at top, mintmaster's initials at bottom **Reverse:** Value, date

Date	Mintage	VG	F	VF	XF	Unc
1742 GHE	—	7.00	15.00	30.00	55.00	—
1743 GHE	—	7.00	15.00	30.00	55.00	—
1745 GHE	—	7.00	15.00	30.00	55.00	—

KM# 37 3 PFENNIG

Billon **Ruler:** Franz Josias **Obverse:** Crowned arms in branches **Reverse:** Value in orb in cartouche divides date

Date	Mintage	VG	F	VF	XF	Unc
1747 GHE	—	6.00	12.00	28.00	50.00	—

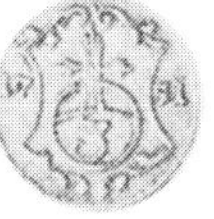

KM# 47.1 3 PFENNIG

Billon **Ruler:** Franz Josias **Obverse:** Crowned FJ monogram in cartouche; F.S.S.M. at top **Reverse:** Value on imperial orb within shield dividing date

Date	Mintage	VG	F	VF	XF	Unc
1751 GHE	—	6.00	12.00	28.00	50.00	—

KM# 47.2 3 PFENNIG

Billon **Ruler:** Franz Josias **Obverse:** Crowned FJ monogram in ornamental cartouche, F. S. S. L. M. at top **Reverse:** Value on imperial orb within shield dividing date

Date	Mintage	VG	F	VF	XF	Unc
1753 ICE	—	6.00	12.00	28.00	50.00	—
1755 ICE	—	6.00	12.00	28.00	50.00	—

KM# 65.1 3 PFENNIG

Billon **Ruler:** Franz Josias **Obverse:** Without legend above arms

Date	Mintage	VG	F	VF	XF	Unc
1764 ICE	—	6.00	12.00	28.00	50.00	—

KM# 65.2 3 PFENNIG

Billon **Obverse:** Crowned arms

Date	Mintage	VG	F	VF	XF	Unc
1764 ICE	—	7.00	15.00	30.00	55.00	—
1765 ICK	—	7.00	15.00	30.00	55.00	—

KM# 11 6 PFENNIG

Billon **Obverse:** Crowned arms **Reverse:** Imperial orb with VI divides date, mintmaster's initials below

Date	Mintage	VG	F	VF	XF	Unc
1735 GHE	—	45.00	95.00	150	200	—

KM# 33 6 PFENNIG

Billon **Ruler:** Christian Ernst **Obverse:** Crowned ornate four-fold arms between palm fronds, F. S. - S. M. divided at top, mintmaster's initials at bottom **Reverse:** Imperial orb with value divides date

Date	Mintage	VG	F	VF	XF	Unc
1738 GHE	—	45.00	95.00	150	200	—
1744 GHE	—	45.00	95.00	150	200	—

KM# 38 6 PFENNIG

Billon **Ruler:** Franz Josias **Obverse:** Crowned arms in branches, F.S.S.M. at top **Reverse:** Value in orb divides date

Date	Mintage	VG	F	VF	XF	Unc
1746 GHE	—	12.00	25.00	50.00	100	—

KM# 48.1 6 PFENNIG

Billon **Ruler:** Franz Josias **Obverse:** Crowned FJ monogram in cartouche **Reverse:** 6 in orb divides date

Date	Mintage	VG	F	VF	XF	Unc
1751 GHE	—	8.00	20.00	40.00	80.00	—
1752 GHE	—	8.00	20.00	40.00	80.00	—

KM# 48.2 6 PFENNIG

Billon **Ruler:** Franz Josias **Obverse:** Without dots after initials

Date	Mintage	VG	F	VF	XF	Unc
1754 GHE	—	9.00	22.00	45.00	90.00	—
1755 ICE	—	8.00	22.00	40.00	80.00	—
1756 ICE	—	8.00	22.00	40.00	80.00	—

KM# 61 6 PFENNIG

Billon **Ruler:** Franz Josias **Obverse:** Crowned FJ monogram in cartouche **Reverse:** Value in orb divides date

Date	Mintage	VG	F	VF	XF	Unc
1760 ICE	—	8.00	22.00	40.00	80.00	—
1761 ICE	—	8.00	22.00	40.00	80.00	—
1763 ICE	—	8.00	22.00	40.00	80.00	—

C# 81 KREUZER

Billon **Obverse:** Crowned arms **Reverse:** Value and date in ornamental border

Date	Mintage	VG	F	VF	XF	Unc
1765 ICK	—	6.00	15.00	30.00	65.00	—
1767 ICK	—	6.00	15.00	30.00	65.00	—

C# 105 KREUZER

Billon **Obverse:** Crowned arms in branches **Reverse:** Value above date

Date	Mintage	VG	F	VF	XF	Unc
1787	—	6.00	15.00	30.00	65.00	—
1794	—	6.00	15.00	30.00	65.00	—

KM# 82 2-1/2 KREUZER

Billon **Obverse:** Crowned arms **Reverse:** Value and date in cartouche

Date	Mintage	VG	F	VF	XF	Unc
1765 ICK	—	12.00	25.00	55.00	125	—

KM# 83 5 KREUZER

Silver **Obverse:** Crowned arms **Reverse:** Weight and date in cartouche, value below

Date	Mintage	VG	F	VF	XF	Unc
1765 ICK	—	25.00	60.00	125	250	—

KM# 84 20 KREUZER

Silver **Obverse:** Bust of Ernst Friedrich right in wreath **Reverse:** Crowned arms on pedestal divide date, value in pedestal

Date	Mintage	VG	F	VF	XF	Unc
1765 ICK	—	20.00	45.00	100	200	—

KM# A10 1/48 THALER

0.9700 g., 0.2500 Silver 0.0078 oz. ASW **Obverse:** Crowned arms **Reverse:** Value and date

Date	Mintage	VG	F	VF	XF	Unc
1764 ICE	—	12.00	25.00	45.00	100	—

KM# 85 1/48 THALER

0.9700 g., 0.2500 Silver 0.0078 oz. ASW **Obverse:** Crowned arms **Reverse:** Value and date in cartouche

Date	Mintage	VG	F	VF	XF	Unc
1765 ICK	—	6.00	12.00	25.00	75.00	—
1766 ICK	—	6.00	12.00	25.00	75.00	—
1767 ICK	—	6.00	12.00	25.00	75.00	—
1768 ICK	—	6.00	12.00	25.00	75.00	—
1770 ICK	—	6.00	12.00	25.00	75.00	—
1771 ICK	—	6.00	12.00	25.00	75.00	—
1779 ICK	—	6.00	12.00	25.00	75.00	—
1782 ICK	—	6.00	12.00	25.00	75.00	—
1787 ICK	—	6.00	12.00	25.00	75.00	—
1788 ICK	—	6.00	12.00	25.00	75.00	—
1791 ICK	—	6.00	12.00	25.00	75.00	—

KM# 13 GROSCHEN (1/24 Thaler)

Silver **Ruler:** Christian Ernst **Obverse:** Crowned CD and FJ monograms, date below **Reverse:** Crowned four-fold arms between palm fronds, mintmaster's initials below

Date	Mintage	VG	F	VF	XF	Unc
1737 GHE	—	18.00	40.00	80.00	125	—

KM# 27 2 GROSCHEN (1/12 Thaler)

Silver **Ruler:** Christian Ernst **Obverse:** Crowned CE and FJ monograms divide mintmaster's initials, 2 GR. below **Reverse:** Crowned oval four-fold arms in baroque frame, date divided at top

Date	Mintage	VG	F	VF	XF	Unc
1741 GHE	—	22.00	50.00	100	165	—

KM# 16 1/24 THALER (Groschen)

Silver **Ruler:** Christian Ernst **Obverse:** Crowned CE and FJ monograms, mintmaster's initials below, FVRST. SACHS. etc. around **Reverse:** 24/EINEN/THAL/date between branches, NACH DEN... around **Note:** Varieties exist.

Date	Mintage	VG	F	VF	XF	Unc
1738 GHE	—	18.00	40.00	80.00	125	—
1740 GHE	—	18.00	40.00	80.00	125	—
1743 GHE	—	18.00	40.00	80.00	125	—
1744 GHE	—	18.00	40.00	80.00	125	—
1745 GHE	—	18.00	40.00	80.00	125	—

KM# 34 1/24 THALER (Groschen)

Billon **Ruler:** Franz Josias **Obverse:** Monogram within baroque frame **Reverse:** Value, date

Date	Mintage	VG	F	VF	XF	Unc
1746 GHE	—	12.00	30.00	60.00	100	—
1748 GHE	—	12.00	30.00	60.00	100	—

KM# A38 1/24 THALER (Groschen)

Billon **Ruler:** Franz Josias **Obverse:** Monogram in larger oval **Rev. Legend:** NACH DEM LEIPZIGER FUS.

Date	Mintage	VG	F	VF	XF	Unc
1747 GHE	—	—	15.00	35.00	70.00	120
1748 GHE	—	—	15.00	35.00	70.00	120

KM# 49 1/24 THALER (Groschen)

Billon **Ruler:** Franz Josias

Date	Mintage	VG	F	VF	XF	Unc
1751 GHE	—	25.00	55.00	100	185	—

KM# 50 1/24 THALER (Groschen)

Billon **Ruler:** Franz Josias **Obverse:** Crowned monogram within frame **Reverse:** Value, date **Note:** Varieties of shields and legends exist.

Date	Mintage	VG	F	VF	XF	Unc
1751 GHE	—	8.00	20.00	45.00	85.00	—
1753 GHE	—	8.00	20.00	45.00	85.00	—
1754 GHE	—	8.00	20.00	45.00	85.00	—
1755 GHE	—	8.00	20.00	45.00	85.00	—
1758 GHE	—	8.00	20.00	45.00	85.00	—

KM# 63.1 1/24 THALER (Groschen)

1.9800 g., 0.3680 Silver 0.0234 oz. ASW **Ruler:** Franz Josias **Obverse:** Crowned arms **Reverse:** Value, within inner circle **Note:** Varieties of shields and legends exist.

Date	Mintage	VG	F	VF	XF	Unc
1763 GHE	—	6.00	15.00	35.00	70.00	—
1763 ICE	—	6.00	15.00	35.00	70.00	—

KM# 63.2 1/24 THALER (Groschen)

1.9800 g., 0.3680 Silver 0.0234 oz. ASW **Ruler:** Franz Josias **Obverse:** Crowned arms **Reverse:** Small rosette below value

Date	Mintage	VG	F	VF	XF	Unc
1763 GHE	—	6.00	15.00	35.00	70.00	—
1763 ICE	—	6.00	15.00	35.00	70.00	—

KM# 67 1/24 THALER (Groschen)

1.9800 g., 0.3680 Silver 0.0234 oz. ASW **Obverse:** Crowned arms **Reverse:** I.C.E. below value

Date	Mintage	VG	F	VF	XF	Unc
1764 ICE	—	9.00	22.00	50.00	90.00	—

KM# 68.1 1/24 THALER (Groschen)

1.9800 g., 0.3680 Silver 0.0234 oz. ASW **Obverse:** Crowned arms **Reverse:** Value

Date	Mintage	VG	F	VF	XF	Unc
1764 ICK	—	8.00	18.00	40.00	80.00	—
Note: Dot after date						
1764 ICK	—	8.00	18.00	40.00	80.00	—
Note: Rosette after date						
1765 ICK	—	8.00	18.00	40.00	80.00	—

KM# 68.2 1/24 THALER (Groschen)

1.9800 g., 0.3680 Silver 0.0234 oz. ASW **Obverse:** Crowned arms **Reverse:** Date below value

Date	Mintage	VG	F	VF	XF	Unc
1765 ICK	—	5.00	10.00	20.00	50.00	—
1772 ICK	—	5.00	10.00	20.00	50.00	—
1774 ICK	—	5.00	10.00	20.00	50.00	—

KM# 98 1/24 THALER (Groschen)

1.9800 g., 0.3680 Silver 0.0234 oz. ASW **Reverse:** Date **Rev. Legend:** 24 EINEN REICHS THALER

Date	Mintage	VG	F	VF	XF	Unc
1774 ICK	—	5.00	10.00	20.00	50.00	—

KM# 14 1/12 THALER (Doppelgroschen)

Silver **Ruler:** Christian Ernst **Obverse:** Crowned oval four-fold arms with central shield within branches, mintmaster's initials below, V. G. G. CHR. ERN etc. around **Reverse:** 12/EINEN/THALER/date within branches, NACHDEN... around

Date	Mintage	VG	F	VF	XF	Unc
1737 GHE	—	35.00	80.00	160	250	—
1739 GHE	—	35.00	80.00	160	250	—

KM# A11 1/12 THALER (Doppelgroschen)

Silver **Ruler:** Christian Ernst **Note:** Similar to 1/24 Thaler, KM#9, but reverse: 12/EINEN...

Date	Mintage	VG	F	VF	XF	Unc
1742 GHE	—	20.00	45.00	90.00	175	—

KM# 35.1 1/12 THALER (Doppelgroschen)

Billon **Ruler:** Franz Josias **Obverse:** Crowned FJ monogram in oval in inner circle **Reverse:** Value above date in inner circle

Date	Mintage	VG	F	VF	XF	Unc
1746 GHE	—	25.00	55.00	120	220	—
1747 GHE	—	25.00	55.00	120	220	—

KM# 35.2 1/12 THALER (Doppelgroschen)

Billon **Ruler:** Franz Josias **Obverse:** Crowned monogram within cartouche **Reverse:** Value, date within inner circle **Rev. Legend:** NACH CHURFURSTL...

Date	Mintage	VG	F	VF	XF	Unc
1751 GHE	—	20.00	45.00	85.00	165	—

KM# 35.3 1/12 THALER (Doppelgroschen)

Billon **Ruler:** Franz Josias **Obverse:** Crowned monogram within cartouche **Reverse:** Value, date within inner circle **Rev. Legend:** NACH CHVRFVRSTL...

Date	Mintage	VG	F	VF	XF	Unc
1753 GHE	—	20.00	45.00	85.00	165	—
1755 GHE	—	20.00	45.00	85.00	165	—
1758 GHE	—	20.00	45.00	85.00	165	—

KM# 64 1/12 THALER (Doppelgroschen)

3.3400 g., 0.4370 Silver 0.0469 oz. ASW **Ruler:** Franz Josias **Obverse:** Crowned oval arms **Reverse:** Value within inner circle

Date	Mintage	VG	F	VF	XF	Unc
1763	—	6.00	15.00	35.00	75.00	—

KM# 69.1 1/12 THALER (Doppelgroschen)

3.3400 g., 0.4370 Silver 0.0469 oz. ASW **Obverse:** Crowned arms **Reverse:** Value within inner circle

Date	Mintage	VG	F	VF	XF	Unc
1764 ICE	—	8.00	18.00	40.00	85.00	—

KM# 69.2 1/12 THALER (Doppelgroschen)

3.3400 g., 0.4370 Silver 0.0469 oz. ASW **Obverse:** Crowned arms **Reverse:** Without inner circle

Date	Mintage	VG	F	VF	XF	Unc
1764 ICE	—	8.00	18.00	40.00	85.00	—

KM# 86 1/12 THALER (Doppelgroschen)

3.3400 g., 0.4370 Silver 0.0469 oz. ASW **Obverse:** Crowned arms **Reverse:** Value in inner circle **Rev. Legend:** 12 EINEN THALER

Date	Mintage	VG	F	VF	XF	Unc
1765	—	6.00	15.00	35.00	75.00	—

KM# 88.1 1/12 THALER (Doppelgroschen)

3.3400 g., 0.4370 Silver 0.0469 oz. ASW **Obverse:** Crowned arms **Reverse:** Value, date

Date	Mintage	VG	F	VF	XF	Unc
1766 ICK	—	6.00	15.00	32.00	70.00	—
1771 ICK	—	6.00	15.00	32.00	70.00	—
1774 ICK	—	6.00	15.00	32.00	70.00	—
1775 ICK	—	6.00	15.00	32.00	70.00	—
1776 ICK	—	6.00	15.00	32.00	70.00	—
1778 ICK	—	6.00	15.00	32.00	70.00	—
1779 ICK	—	6.00	15.00	32.00	70.00	—
1780 ICK	—	6.00	15.00	32.00	70.00	—
1782 ICK	—	6.00	15.00	32.00	70.00	—
1785 ICK	—	6.00	15.00	32.00	70.00	—

KM# 88.2 1/12 THALER (Doppelgroschen)
3.3400 g., 0.4370 Silver 0.0469 oz. ASW **Obverse:** Crowned arms **Reverse:** ICK below year

Date	Mintage	VG	F	VF	XF	Unc
1780 ICK	—	8.00	18.00	38.00	80.00	—

KM# 70 1/6 THALER
5.3900 g., 0.5410 Silver 0.0937 oz. ASW **Ruler:** Franz Josias **Obverse:** Bust right **Reverse:** Crowned arms above value

Date	Mintage	VG	F	VF	XF	Unc
1764 ICE	—	20.00	40.00	80.00	135	—

KM# 71 1/4 THALER
Silver **Ruler:** Franz Josias **Subject:** Death of the Duke **Obverse:** Bust right, inscription below **Reverse:** Pointed stone with inscription within branches

Date	Mintage	VG	F	VF	XF	Unc
1764	—	60.00	120	250	400	—

KM# 87.1 1/2 THALER
14.0300 g., 0.8330 Silver 0.3757 oz. ASW **Obverse:** Bust of Ernst Friedrich right **Reverse:** Crowned arms

Date	Mintage	VG	F	VF	XF	Unc
1765 ICK	—	125	250	450	750	—

KM# 87.2 1/2 THALER
14.0300 g., 0.8330 Silver 0.3757 oz. ASW **Obverse:** Bust of Ernst Friedrich right with order cross below **Reverse:** Crowned arms

Date	Mintage	VG	F	VF	XF	Unc
1765 ICK	—	125	250	450	775	—

KM# 72 THALER
28.0600 g., 0.8330 Silver 0.7515 oz. ASW **Ruler:** Franz Josias **Obverse:** ST below bust **Obv. Legend:** FRANCISCVS IOSIAS D.G.D. S. COBVRG SAALFELD. **Reverse:** Mintmaster's initials below arms **Rev. Legend:** X. EINE FEINE MARCK, I.C.E. below **Note:** Dav. #2750.

Date	Mintage	VG	F	VF	XF	Unc
1764 E ICE	—	75.00	150	285	450	—

KM# 73 THALER
28.0600 g., 0.8330 Silver 0.7515 oz. ASW **Ruler:** Franz Josias **Obverse:** Without ST below bust **Reverse:** Mintmaster's initials split by arms **Note:** Dav. #2750A.

Date	Mintage	VG	F	VF	XF	Unc
1764 IC-E	—	100	200	400	650	—

KM# 74 THALER
28.0600 g., 0.8330 Silver 0.7515 oz. ASW **Obverse:** Small bust with order cross incircled **Obv. Legend:** ERNESTVS FRIDERICUS... **Reverse:** Small rounded arms, ICE below **Note:** Dav. #2751.

Date	Mintage	VG	F	VF	XF	Unc
1764 ICE	—	70.00	135	275	400	—

KM# 75 THALER
28.0600 g., 0.8330 Silver 0.7515 oz. ASW **Obverse:** Medium revised bust without order cross **Obv. Legend:** ERNESTVS FRIDERICVS D • G • D • S • COBVRG SAALFELD **Reverse:** Cornered arms divide I-CE **Rev. Legend:** X. EINE FEINE MARCK. 1764, I.-C.E. below **Note:** Dav. #2751A.

Date	Mintage	VG	F	VF	XF	Unc
1764 I-CE	—	65.00	125	250	350	—

KM# 76.1 THALER
28.0600 g., 0.8330 Silver 0.7515 oz. ASW **Obverse:** Large revised bust with order cross **Reverse:** Large ornate arms divide IC-E **Note:** Dav. #2751B.

Date	Mintage	VG	F	VF	XF	Unc
1764 IC-E	—	75.00	150	285	450	—

KM# 76.2 THALER
28.0600 g., 0.8330 Silver 0.7515 oz. ASW **Obverse:** Large fancy bust with order cross encircled **Note:** Dav. #2751C.

Date	Mintage	VG	F	VF	XF	Unc
1764 IC-E	—	75.00	150	285	450	—

KM# 77 THALER
28.0600 g., 0.8330 Silver 0.7515 oz. ASW **Obverse:** Large heavy bust with order cross **Obv. Legend:** ERNESTVS FRIDERICVS D • G • D • S • COBVRG SAALFELD • **Reverse:** Small arms divide I-CE **Rev. Legend:** X EINE FEINE MARCK. date, I.C. - K. below **Note:** Dav. #2752.

Date	Mintage	VG	F	VF	XF	Unc
1764 I-CE	—	65.00	125	250	350	—
1765	—	65.00	125	250	350	—
1765 I-CK Rare	—	—	—	—	—	—

KM# 78 THALER
28.0600 g., 0.8330 Silver 0.7515 oz. ASW **Obverse:** Narrow refined bust without order cross **Obv. Legend:** ERNESTVS FRIDERICVS • D • G • D • S • COBVRG SAALFELD • **Reverse:** Crowned arms **Rev. Legend:** X EINE FEINE MARCK. date, I.C. - K. **Note:** Dav. #2752A.

Date	Mintage	VG	F	VF	XF	Unc
1764 I-CE Rare	—	—	—	—	—	—
1765 I-CK	—	65.00	125	250	350	—

Note: Bust varieties exist for the 1765 IC-K

KM# 79 THALER
28.0600 g., 0.8330 Silver 0.7515 oz. ASW **Obverse:** Large refined bust without order cross **Reverse:** Smaller curved arms divide IC-K **Note:** Dav. #2752B.

Date	Mintage	VG	F	VF	XF	Unc
1765 IC-K Rare	—	—	—	—	—	—

Note: Bust varieties exist for the 1765 IC-K

TRADE COINAGE

KM# 17 1/4 DUCAT
0.8750 g., 0.9860 Gold 0.0277 oz. AGW **Ruler:** Christian Ernst **Obverse:** Crowned CE-JF monogram divides date **Reverse:** Crowned oval arms in palm fronds

Date	Mintage	VG	F	VF	XF	Unc
1738 GHE	—	100	200	450	750	—

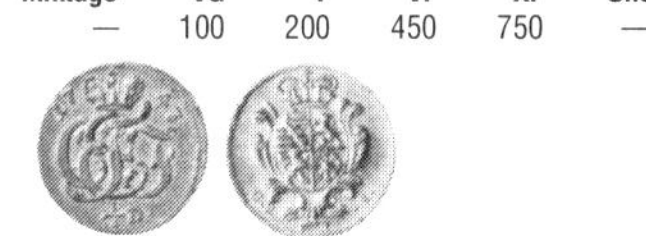

KM# 29 1/4 DUCAT
0.8750 g., 0.9860 Gold 0.0277 oz. AGW **Ruler:** Christian Ernst **Obverse:** Crowned divides date **Reverse:** Crowned oval arms in cartouche

Date	Mintage	VG	F	VF	XF	Unc
1743 GHE	—	100	200	450	750	—

KM# 51 1/4 DUCAT
0.8750 g., 0.9860 Gold 0.0277 oz. AGW **Ruler:** Franz Josias **Obverse:** Crowned FJ monogram in cartouche **Reverse:** Crowned arms

Date	Mintage	VG	F	VF	XF	Unc
1752 GHE	—	100	175	350	600	—

KM# 26 DUCAT
3.5000 g., 0.9860 Gold 0.1109 oz. AGW **Ruler:** Christian Ernst **Obverse:** CE and JF in ornamented ovals, crown on top divides date **Reverse:** Lions support crowned and ornamented four-fold arms in oval

Date	Mintage	VG	F	VF	XF	Unc
1740	—	350	700	1,400	2,500	—

KM# 30 DUCAT
3.5000 g., 0.9860 Gold 0.1109 oz. AGW **Ruler:** Christian Ernst **Subject:** Death of the Duke **Obverse:** Duke kneeling before Christ on cross **Reverse:** Crown, eagle in clouds, globe below

Date	Mintage	VG	F	VF	XF	Unc
ND(1745)	—	175	350	700	1,200	—

KM# 36 DUCAT
3.5000 g., 0.9860 Gold 0.1109 oz. AGW **Ruler:** Franz Josias **Obverse:** Crowned arms left of rampant lion **Reverse:** Crowned arms within Order cross

Date	Mintage	VG	F	VF	XF	Unc
1746 GHE	—	300	650	1,200	2,000	—

Date	Mintage	VG	F	VF	XF	Unc
1749 GHE	—	300	650	1,200	2,000	—
1749 ICE	—	300	650	1,200	2,000	—
1755 ICE	—	300	650	1,200	2,000	—

KM# 53 DUCAT

3.5000 g., 0.9860 Gold 0.1109 oz. AGW **Ruler:** Franz Josias **Subject:** Marriage of Friederike Caroline and Christian Friedrich of Brandenburg-Ansbach **Obverse:** Two cherubs above two shields of arms **Reverse:** Three-line legend, date in roman numerals

Date	Mintage	VG	F	VF	XF	Unc
ND(1754)	—	300	650	1,250	2,200	—

KM# 89 DUCAT

7.0000 g., 0.9860 Gold 0.2219 oz. AGW **Obverse:** Bust of Ernst Friedrich right **Reverse:** View of Reichmannsdorf **Note:** Mining Ducat.

Date	Mintage	VG	F	VF	XF	Unc
1766 K	—	1,000	2,000	4,000	6,500	—

KM# A29 2 DUCAT

3.5000 g., 0.9860 Gold 0.1109 oz. AGW **Subject:** Death of Christine Friederike **Obverse:** Crowned tomb with two arms at base, two line legend **Reverse:** Commemorative legend in outer circle, dates within circle

Date	Mintage	VG	F	VF	XF	Unc
1743 Rare	—	—	—	—	—	—

KM# 31 2 DUCAT

7.0000 g., 0.9860 Gold 0.2219 oz. AGW **Subject:** Death of the Duke **Obverse:** Duke kneeling before Christ on cross **Reverse:** Crown, eagle in clouds, globe below **Note:** Similar to 1 Ducat, KM#30.

Date	Mintage	VG	F	VF	XF	Unc
ND(1745)	—	800	1,500	2,500	4,000	—

KM# A36 2 DUCAT

7.0000 g., 0.9860 Gold 0.2219 oz. AGW **Ruler:** Franz Josias **Subject:** Marriage of Friederike Caroline and Christian Friedrich of Brandenburg-Angbach **Note:** Struck with 1 Ducat dies, KM#53.

Date	Mintage	VG	F	VF	XF	Unc
1754	—	—	—	—	1,200	2,000	—

PATTERNS

Including off metal strikes

KM#	Date	Mintage	Identification	Mkt Val
Pn1	1743	—	2 Ducat. Silver. KM29.	—
Pn2	(1745)	—	Ducat. Silver. KM#30.	125
Pn3	(1745)	—	2 Ducat. Silver. KM#31.	175
Pn4	1754	—	Ducat. Silver. KM#53.	150
Pn6	1765	—	Pfennig. Gold. KM#80.	—
Pn7	1765	—	Thaler. Silver. OEXLEIN below bust.	—

SAXE-EISENACH

(Sachsen-Eisenach)

One of the Ernestine Saxon duchies in Thuringia (Thüringen), Saxe-Eisenach was first ruled separately by one of eight brothers beginning in 1640. It reverted back to Saxe-Middle-Weimar in 1644, but a new line was established by the second son of Duke Wilhelm IV as Saxe-(New)-Weimar in 1622. This second line became extinct very shortly thereafter and Eisenach passed to Wilhelm IV's third son in 1671. Sayn-Altenkirchen (q.v.) was added to the duke's possessions through marriage in 1686. Again, the line passed out of existence and Eisenach was returned to Saxe-Weimar in 1741. See Saxe-Weimar-Eisenach for subsequent coinages.

RULERS

Johann Wilhelm, 1698-1729
Wilhelm Heinrich, 1729-1741

MINT OFFICIALS' INITIALS

Initial	Date	Name
CM	1711-15	Christoph Müller
CW	1688-1739	Christian Wermuth, die-cutter in Gotha
HD	1693-?	Hubertus Dönnigke
IAB	1717-50 (1728?)	Johann Albert Bähr (Bär), warden
	1692-?	Johann Matthias Obermüller
IHS	1715-17	Johann Heinrich Siegel, warden
	1715-?	Johann Heinrich Göckel, mint contractor
SC	1700-01	Simon Conradi

DUCHY

REGULAR COINAGE

KM# 33 2 PFENNIG (Leuchte)

Silver **Ruler:** Johann Wilhelm **Obverse:** 3 small oval shields of arms, crown above **Reverse:** 2/LEUCHTE/PFENN/F.E.L.M., date

Date	Mintage	VG	F	VF	XF	Unc
1700	—	9.00	20.00	40.00	70.00	—
1713	—	9.00	20.00	40.00	70.00	—

KM# 71 GROSCHEN

Silver **Ruler:** Johann Wilhelm **Subject:** Death of Johann Wilhelm **Obverse:** Bust to right **Reverse:** 8-line inscription with dates **Note:** Struck at Eisenach.

Date	Mintage	VG	F	VF	XF	Unc
1729	—	25.00	45.00	90.00	175	—

KM# 44 THALER

Silver **Ruler:** Johann Wilhelm **Subject:** Third Marriage of Duke Johann Wilhelm to Magdalene Sibylla **Obverse:** Three shields crowned separating date **Reverse:** Eagle on perch, rifle range and woods **Note:** Klippe. Dav# 2705.

Date	Mintage	VG	F	VF	XF	Unc
1708	—	350	650	1,200	2,000	—

TRADE COINAGE

FR# 2917 DUCAT

3.5000 g., 0.9860 Gold 0.1109 oz. AGW **Ruler:** Johann Wilhelm **Obverse:** Crowned cruciform JW monograms with arms at center **Reverse:** Crane on pedestal, date in exergue

Date	Mintage	VG	F	VF	XF	Unc
1716	—	500	1,000	2,000	3,500	—

KM# 59 DUCAT

3.5000 g., 0.9860 Gold 0.1109 oz. AGW **Ruler:** Johann Wilhelm **Obverse:** 4 crowned cruciform JW monograms with small oval arms of ducal Saxony in center **Reverse:** Crane on pedestal, date in exergue **Note:** Fr# 2917.

Date	Mintage	VG	F	VF	XF	Unc
1716	—	500	1,000	2,000	3,500	—

SAXE-EISENBERG

Short-lived branch of the Ernestine Saxon house which was created for Christian, fifth son of Ernst the Pious of Saxe-Gotha. The line became extinct with the death of Christian in 1707 and passed to Saxe-Hildburghausen.

RULER

Christian, 1680-1707

MINT OFFICIALS' INITIALS

Initials	Date	Name
IA	1692-1706	Julius Angerstein, die-cutter and mintmaster

DUCHY

REGULAR COINAGE

KM# 41 1/96 THALER (Dreier, 4 Pfennig)

Silver **Ruler:** Christian **Obverse:** Helmeted oval arms of ducal Saxony **Obv. Legend:** D:G. CHRISTIANUS. SAX. I. C. M. A. & W. DUX. **Reverse:** Imperial orb with 96 divides date and mintmaster's initials **Rev. Legend:** NACH REICHS SCHROTT UND KORN

Date	Mintage	VG	F	VF	XF	Unc
1701 IA	—	35.00	60.00	140	225	—

KM# 45 1/96 THALER (Dreier, 4 Pfennig)

Silver **Ruler:** Christian **Obverse:** Helmeted oval arms of ducal Saxony **Reverse:** Imperial orb with 96, date divided at top **Rev. Legend:** VON FEINE SILBER

Date	Mintage	VG	F	VF	XF	Unc
1703 IA	—	45.00	80.00	150	250	—

KM# 46 1/48 THALER (Sechser, 8 Pfennig)

Silver **Ruler:** Christian **Obverse:** Helmeted oval arms of ducal Saxony **Reverse:** Imperial orb with 48, date divided above **Rev. Legend:** VON FEINEN SILBER

Date	Mintage	VG	F	VF	XF	Unc
1703 IA	—	45.00	80.00	150	250	—

KM# 39 1/24 THALER (Groschen, 16 Pfennig)

Silver **Ruler:** Christian **Obverse:** Helmeted oval arms of ducal Saxony **Obv. Legend:** D:G. CHRISTIANUS SAX. I. C. M. A. &. W. DUX **Reverse:** Imperial orb with 24 divides date and mintmaster's initials **Rev. Legend:** NACH REICHS SCHROTT UND KORN

Date	Mintage	VG	F	VF	XF	Unc
1698 IA	—	30.00	60.00	125	185	—
1701 IA	—	30.00	60.00	125	185	—

KM# 43 1/8 THALER

Silver **Ruler:** Christian **Obverse:** Armored bust to right **Obv. Legend:** D:G. CHRISTIAN: SAX. I. C. M. A. &. W. DUX: **Reverse:** Mantled oval manifold arms of Saxony, crown above divides date, value 1/8 in oval below

Date	Mintage	VG	F	VF	XF	Unc
1701 IA	—	150	300	750	1,250	—
1703 IA	—	125	250	600	1,000	—

KM# 48 2 THALER

Silver **Ruler:** Christian **Obverse:** Bust to right **Reverse:** 10-line inscription with date **Rev. Legend:** SCHMECKET UND SEHET WIE FREUNDLICH DER HERR IST

Date	Mintage	VG	F	VF	XF	Unc
1705 IA Rare	—	—	—	—	—	—

SAXE-GOTHA-ALTENBURG

(Sachsen-Gotha-Altenburg)

When the seven sons of Ernst the Pious of Saxe-New-Gotha divided the lands of their father in 1680, the eldest established the line of Saxe-Gotha-Altenburg. The line became extinct in 1825 and the following year witnessed the division of the territory which resulted in a general reorganization of the Thuringian duchies. Altenburg itself was inherited by the duke of Saxe-Hildburghausen, who transferred Hildburghausen to Saxe-Meiningen and became the founder of a new line of Saxe-Altenburg. Saxe-Meiningen also received Saalfeld from Saxe-Coburg, which in turn had acquired Gotha as part of the proceedings. The line of Saxe-Coburg-Gotha was established as a result. See under each of the foregoing regarding developments after the realignment of 1826. For a short period of time, from 1688 to 1692, the duke leased the abbey of Walkenried from Brunswick-Wolfenbüttel and struck a series of coins for that district.

RULERS

Friedrich II, 1691-1732
Jointly with brother Johann Wilhelm, 1691-1707
Friedrich III, 1732-1772
Ernst II Ludwig, 1772-1804

MINT OFFICIALS' INITIALS

Initials	Date	Name
CW or W	1688-1739	Christian Wermuth, die-cutter in Gotha
IT	1690-1723	Johann Thun, mintmaster in Gotha
K, ICK or KOCH	1706-42	Johann Christian Koch, die-cutter
	1706-32?	Christian Andreas Roth, mint technician
AH	1718-50	Andreas Helbig, mint director
	1733-?	Tobias Gräfenstein, die-cutter
LCK	1750-66	Ludwig Christian Koch, die-cutter in Gotha
	1766-93	mintmaster

DUCHY

REGULAR COINAGE

C# 1 HELLER

Copper **Ruler:** Friedrich III **Obverse:** Crowned script F monogram **Reverse:** Value, date

Date	Mintage	VG	F	VF	XF	Unc
1738	—	3.00	6.00	12.00	20.00	—
1739	—	3.00	6.00	12.00	20.00	—
1740	—	3.00	6.00	12.00	20.00	—
1741	—	3.00	6.00	12.00	20.00	—
1742	—	3.00	6.00	12.00	20.00	—
1743	176,000	3.00	6.00	12.00	20.00	—
1744	426,000	3.00	6.00	12.00	20.00	—
1745	—	3.00	6.00	12.00	20.00	—

C# 2 HELLER

Copper **Ruler:** Friedrich III **Obverse:** Helmeted arms **Reverse:** Name, value and date

Date	Mintage	VG	F	VF	XF	Unc
1744	Inc. above	4.00	8.00	15.00	25.00	—
1745	—	4.00	8.00	15.00	25.00	—
1746	—	4.00	8.00	15.00	25.00	—
1747	—	4.00	8.00	15.00	25.00	—
1749	187,000	4.00	8.00	15.00	25.00	—
1750	—	4.00	8.00	15.00	25.00	—

C# 4 HELLER

Copper **Ruler:** Friedrich III **Obverse:** SGVA monogram **Reverse:** Value, date

Date	Mintage	VG	F	VF	XF	Unc
1770 LCK	—	4.00	8.00	16.00	30.00	—

C# 5 PFENNIG

Copper **Ruler:** Friedrich III **Obverse:** Helmeted arms **Reverse:** Value, date

Date	Mintage	VG	F	VF	XF	Unc
1747	49,000	4.00	8.00	16.00	30.00	—

C# 6.1 PFENNIG

Copper **Ruler:** Friedrich III **Obverse:** Crowned monogram **Reverse:** Value, date within cartouche **Note:** Varieties exist.

Date	Mintage	VG	F	VF	XF	Unc
1753 LCK	59,000	6.00	12.00	25.00	45.00	—
1757 LCK	—	6.00	12.00	25.00	45.00	—
1757 K	—	6.00	12.00	25.00	45.00	—
1760 LCK	378,000	6.00	12.00	25.00	45.00	—
1760 K	Inc. above	—	—	—	—	—

C# 6.3 PFENNIG

Copper **Ruler:** Friedrich III **Obverse:** Crowned monogram **Reverse:** Without cartouche

Date	Mintage	VG	F	VF	XF	Unc
1770 K	—	4.00	8.00	16.00	30.00	—

C# 7 1-1/2 PFENNIG

Copper **Ruler:** Friedrich III **Obverse:** Crowned script F monogram **Reverse:** Value, date

Date	Mintage	VG	F	VF	XF	Unc
1733	52,000	5.00	10.00	20.00	35.00	—
1735	29,000	5.00	10.00	20.00	35.00	—
1737	161,000	5.00	10.00	20.00	35.00	—

C# 8 1-1/2 PFENNIG

Copper **Ruler:** Friedrich III **Obverse:** Helmeted arms **Reverse:** Value, date

Date	Mintage	VG	F	VF	XF	Unc
1744	70,000	4.00	8.00	16.00	30.00	—
1745	—	4.00	8.00	16.00	30.00	—
1746	—	4.00	8.00	16.00	30.00	—
1749	—	4.00	8.00	16.00	30.00	—
1750	—	4.00	8.00	16.00	30.00	—

C# 9 1-1/2 PFENNIG

Copper **Ruler:** Friedrich III **Obverse:** Crowned arms in cartouche **Reverse:** Value, date in cartouche

Date	Mintage	VG	F	VF	XF	Unc
1752 LCK	159,000	5.00	10.00	20.00	38.00	—
1753 LCK	345,000	5.00	10.00	20.00	38.00	—
1755 LCK	761,000	5.00	10.00	20.00	38.00	—
1756 LCK	Inc. above	5.00	10.00	20.00	38.00	—
1757 LCK	Inc. above	5.00	10.00	20.00	38.00	—
1758 LCK	Inc. above	5.00	10.00	20.00	38.00	—
1759 LCK	Inc. above	5.00	10.00	20.00	38.00	—
1760 LCK	Inc. above	5.00	10.00	20.00	38.00	—
1761 LCK	Inc. above	5.00	10.00	20.00	38.00	—

C# 11 2 PFENNIG

Billon **Ruler:** Friedrich III **Obverse:** Crowned arms in cartouche **Reverse:** Value in cartouche divides date

Date	Mintage	VG	F	VF	XF	Unc
1752	28,000	8.00	15.00	30.00	55.00	—

C# 12 3 PFENNIG

Billon **Ruler:** Friedrich III **Obverse:** Crowned arms in cartouche **Reverse:** Value in cartouche divides date **Note:** Varieties exist.

Date	Mintage	VG	F	VF	XF	Unc
1752	67,000	8.00	15.00	30.00	55.00	—
1753 LCK	128,000	8.00	15.00	30.00	55.00	—

C# 10 3 PFENNIG

Copper **Ruler:** Friedrich III **Obverse:** Crowned arms **Reverse:** Value, date in cartouche **Note:** Varieties exist.

Date	Mintage	VG	F	VF	XF	Unc
1761 LCK	—	3.00	7.00	16.00	30.00	—

C# 13 6 PFENNIG

Billon **Ruler:** Friedrich III **Obverse:** Crowned script F monogram **Reverse:** Imperial orb with value VI, date below

Date	Mintage	VG	F	VF	XF	Unc
1734 AH	200,000	12.00	20.00	40.00	70.00	—
1735 AH	49,000	12.00	20.00	40.00	70.00	—
1736 AH	49,000	12.00	20.00	40.00	70.00	—
1737 AH	202,000	12.00	20.00	40.00	70.00	—
1745 AH	195,000	12.00	20.00	40.00	70.00	—
1747 AH	223,000	12.00	20.00	40.00	70.00	—
1749 AH	253,000	12.00	20.00	40.00	70.00	—
1750 AH	83,000	12.00	20.00	40.00	70.00	—

C# 14 6 PFENNIG

Billon **Ruler:** Friedrich III **Obverse:** Crowned ornate shield of ducal arms of Saxony **Obv. Legend:** FRIEDER. — HERZ. Z. S. **Reverse:** 3-line inscription with value and date in cartouche, mintmaster's initials below **Rev. Legend:** H.S.G.V.A.L.M. **Rev. Inscription:** 6/PFENN:/(date)

Date	Mintage	VG	F	VF	XF	Unc
1752 LCK	90,000	10.00	18.00	35.00	60.00	—
1753 LCK	26,000	10.00	18.00	35.00	60.00	—
1754 LCK	389,000	10.00	18.00	35.00	60.00	—
1755 LCK	254,000	9.00	16.00	30.00	55.00	—
1756 LCK	—	9.00	16.00	30.00	55.00	—
1757 LCK	—	9.00	16.00	30.00	55.00	—
1758 LCK	—	9.00	16.00	30.00	55.00	—
1759 LCK	—	9.00	16.00	30.00	55.00	—
1760 LCK	—	9.00	16.00	30.00	55.00	—

C# 15 1/48 THALER

Billon **Ruler:** Friedrich III **Obverse:** Crowned oval arms between branches, date **Reverse:** Value

Date	Mintage	VG	F	VF	XF	Unc
1767	409,000	7.50	15.00	25.00	50.00	—
1768	486,000	7.50	15.00	25.00	50.00	—
1769	—	7.50	15.00	25.00	50.00	—
1770	—	7.50	15.00	25.00	50.00	—
1771	—	7.50	15.00	25.00	50.00	—
1772	—	7.50	15.00	25.00	50.00	—

C# 16 1/24 THALER

Billon **Ruler:** Friedrich III **Obverse:** Crowned arms of ducal Saxony in baroque frame **Obv. Legend:** FRIEDRICH — HERZ.Z.SACHS. **Reverse:** Value, date in cartouche, legend curved above **Rev. Legend:** H.S.G.V.A.L.M. **Rev. Inscription:** 24/EINEN THA/LER/(date) **Note:** Varieties exist.

Date	Mintage	VG	F	VF	XF	Unc
1752 LCK	—	10.00	20.00	35.00	65.00	—
1753 LCK	6,989	10.00	20.00	35.00	65.00	—
1754 LCK	296,000	10.00	20.00	35.00	65.00	—
1755 LCK	3,600	10.00	20.00	35.00	65.00	—
1756 LCK	—	10.00	20.00	35.00	65.00	—

C# 17 1/24 THALER

Billon **Ruler:** Friedrich III **Subject:** 200th Anniversary - Religious Peace of Augsburg **Obverse:** Complex arms **Reverse:** Inscription within vines

Date	Mintage	VG	F	VF	XF	Unc
1755	59,000	12.00	20.00	40.00	70.00	—

C# 18.1 1/24 THALER

Billon **Ruler:** Friedrich III **Obverse:** Crowned arms in cartouche **Reverse:** Value in cartouche, date, 400 EINE...

Date	Mintage	VG	F	VF	XF	Unc
1762 LCK	305,000	30.00	45.00	80.00	140	—

C# 18.2 1/24 THALER

Billon **Ruler:** Friedrich III **Obverse:** Arms encircled by Order chain **Reverse:** Value in cartouche, date

Date	Mintage	VG	F	VF	XF	Unc
1762 LCK	Inc. above	10.00	20.00	40.00	70.00	—

C# 19 1/24 THALER

Billon **Ruler:** Friedrich III **Obverse:** Crowned arms in cartouche **Reverse:** Value, date, CCCXX EINE...

Date	Mintage	VG	F	VF	XF	Unc
1763 LCK	128,000	5.00	10.00	20.00	40.00	—
1764 LCK	489,000	5.00	10.00	20.00	40.00	—
1765 LCK	365,000	5.00	10.00	20.00	40.00	—
1766 LCK	84,000	5.00	10.00	20.00	40.00	—
1767 LCK	113,000	5.00	10.00	20.00	40.00	—
1768 LCK	22,000	5.00	10.00	20.00	40.00	—
1771 LCK	—	5.00	10.00	20.00	40.00	—

C# 20.1 1/24 THALER

Silver **Ruler:** Friedrich III **Subject:** Death of Friedrich III **Obverse:** Head right **Obv. Legend:** FRIDER. III. GOTHAN. SAXONVM. DVX. **Reverse:** Eleven-line inscription, date in Roman numerals

Date	Mintage	VG	F	VF	XF	Unc
1772 Crane	—	9.00	17.50	35.00	60.00	—

C# 20.2 1/24 THALER

Silver **Obverse:** Head right **Reverse:** Twelve-line inscription, date in Roman numerals

Date	Mintage	VG	F	VF	XF	Unc
1772 Crane	—	9.00	17.50	35.00	60.00	—

C# 36 1/24 THALER

Billon **Ruler:** Ernst Ludwig **Obverse:** Crowned arms **Reverse:** Value, date

Date	Mintage	VG	F	VF	XF	Unc
1773 LCK	—	3.00	8.00	20.00	40.00	—

C# 21 1/12 THALER

Silver **Ruler:** Friedrich III **Obverse:** Crowned arms in cartouche **Reverse:** Value: CLX EINE..., date

Date	Mintage	VG	F	VF	XF	Unc
1763 LCK	309,000	15.00	25.00	50.00	90.00	—
1764 LCK	148,000	15.00	25.00	50.00	90.00	—

C# 22.1 1/12 THALER

Silver **Ruler:** Friedrich III **Obverse:** Head right **Reverse:** Eleven-line inscription, date in Roman numerals **Note:** Double-thick flan.

Date	Mintage	VG	F	VF	XF	Unc
1772 Crane	—	15.00	25.00	50.00	100	—

C# 22.2 1/12 THALER

Silver **Obverse:** Head right **Reverse:** Twelve-line inscription **Note:** Double-thick flan.

Date	Mintage	VG	F	VF	XF	Unc
1772 Crane	—	15.00	25.00	50.00	100	—

KM# A22 1/8 THALER

Silver **Ruler:** Friedrich II **Subject:** Bicentennial of the Reformation **Obverse:** Armored bust right **Reverse:** Radiant sun, inscription below

Date	Mintage	VG	F	VF	XF	Unc
1717 CWIT	—	70.00	110	210	400	—

C# 23 1/6 THALER

Silver **Ruler:** Ernst Ludwig **Subject:** 200th Anniversary - Religious Peace of Augsburg **Obverse:** Draped bust right **Reverse:** Inscription within branches

Date	Mintage	VG	F	VF	XF	Unc
1755	14,000	20.00	45.00	80.00	145	—

C# 24.1 1/6 THALER

Silver **Ruler:** Friedrich III **Obverse:** Bust to right **Reverse:** Crowned ornate 20-fold arms in baroque frame divides L — M and date, value 1/6 in bottom of frame

Date	Mintage	VG	F	VF	XF	Unc
1757 LCK	34,000	80.00	130	250	525	—

C# 24.2 1/6 THALER

Silver **Ruler:** Friedrich III **Reverse:** Ordinary Saxon arms only

Date	Mintage	VG	F	VF	XF	Unc
1757 LCK	Inc. above	45.00	80.00	180	325	—
1758 LCK	Inc. above	45.00	80.00	180	325	—

C# 25 1/6 THALER

Silver **Ruler:** Friedrich III **Note:** 1/8 Conventions Thaler.

Date	Mintage	VG	F	VF	XF	Unc
1761 LCK	—	20.00	35.00	65.00	125	—
1762 LCK	—	20.00	35.00	65.00	125	—

C# 25a 1/6 THALER

Silver **Ruler:** Friedrich III **Obverse:** Head right **Obv. Legend:** FRIDER. III. D. G. GOTHAN. SAXONVM DVX. **Reverse:** Crowned ornate 20-fold arms in baroque frame, value 1/6 in scalloped ornament below arms **Rev. Legend:** 80. EINE FEINE — MARK. (date)

Date	Mintage	VG	F	VF	XF	Unc
1764 LCK	47,000	25.00	40.00	75.00	135	—
1765 LCK	16,000	25.00	40.00	75.00	135	—

C# 26 1/3 THALER

Silver **Ruler:** Friedrich II and Johann Wilhelm **Subject:** 200th Anniversary - Religious Peace of Augsburg **Obverse:** Draped bust right **Obv. Legend:** FRIDER. III. GOTHAN. SAXONVM. DVX. **Reverse:** Crowned arms

Date	Mintage	VG	F	VF	XF	Unc
1755	2,220	60.00	100	180	275	—
1755 LCK	2,220	60.00	100	180	275	—

C# 27 1/3 THALER

Silver **Ruler:** Friedrich III **Obverse:** Head right **Reverse:** Crowned arms **Note:** 1/4 Conventions Thaler.

Date	Mintage	VG	F	VF	XF	Unc
1765 Crane	2,704	50.00	80.00	160	250	—
1766 Crane	Inc. above	50.00	80.00	160	250	—

C# 37 1/3 THALER

Silver **Ruler:** Ernst Ludwig **Obverse:** Draped bust right **Reverse:** Crowned arms within branches

Date	Mintage	VG	F	VF	XF	Unc
1774	—	35.00	65.00	125	250	—

C# 38a 1/2 THALER

Silver **Ruler:** Ernst Ludwig **Obverse:** Crane below bust **Obv. Legend:** ERNESTVS. D. G. GOTHAN. SAXONVM. DVX. **Reverse:** Crowned arms within branches

Date	Mintage	VG	F	VF	XF	Unc
1774	—	55.00	115	200	350	—
1776	—	55.00	115	200	350	—

C# 38 1/2 THALER

Silver **Ruler:** Ernst Ludwig **Obverse:** L.C.K. below bust **Obv. Legend:** ERNESTVS. D. G. GOTHAN. SAXONVM. DVX. **Reverse:** Crowned arms within branches **Note:** Convention 1/2 Thaler

Date	Mintage	VG	F	VF	XF	Unc
1774 LCK	—	55.00	115	200	350	—
1776 LCK	—	55.00	115	200	350	—

C# 28 2/3 THALER

Silver **Ruler:** Friedrich III **Obverse:** Head right **Obv. Legend:** FRIDER. III. GOTHAN. SAXONVM. DVX. **Reverse:** Crowned arms with supporters **Note:** Reichs 2/3 Thaler

Date	Mintage	VG	F	VF	XF	Unc
1764 Crane	14,000	45.00	65.00	120	200	—

C# 39 2/3 THALER

Silver **Ruler:** Ernst Ludwig **Obverse:** Armored bust right **Obv. Legend:** ERNESTVS D • G • GOTHAN • SAXONVM DVX, L•C•R• below **Reverse:** Crowned arms with supporters **Rev. Legend:** XV. EINE - FEINE MARK **Note:** Called "Light Thaler". Dav. #2724.

Date	Mintage	F	VF	XF	Unc
1774 LCK	—	250	500	875	1,650

DAV# 2707 THALER

Silver **Ruler:** Friedrich II and Johann Wilhelm **Obverse:** Bust of Friedrich II right **Obv. Legend:** FRIDERICVS • D • G • D • S • I • C • M • A • ET W •, C.W. on arm **Reverse:** Helmeted arms divide date at bottom **Rev. Legend:** LANDG • TH • M • M • PR • D • C • HEN • C • M • E • R • D • R • E • TON •, I-T and 1704 below

Date	Mintage	F	VF	XF	Unc
1704 CW//IT	—	300	600	1,250	2,500

DAV# 2708 THALER

Silver **Ruler:** Friedrich II and Johann Wilhelm **Subject:** Death of Christina, second wife of Friedrich I **Obverse:** Crowned heart-shaped arms in frame **Reverse:** 21-line inscription with date in Roman numerals

Date	Mintage	F	VF	XF	Unc
MDCCV (1705) Rare	—	—	—	—	—

DAV# 2709 THALER

Silver **Ruler:** Friedrich II and Johann Wilhelm **Subject:** Death of Johann Wilhelm, Brother of Friedrich II **Obverse:** Bust of Johann Wilhelm right **Reverse:** Eleven-line inscription in double legend with date in Roman numerals

Date	Mintage	F	VF	XF	Unc
MDCCVII (1707) CW//IT	100	300	600	1,250	2,500

DAV# 2710 THALER

Silver **Ruler:** Friedrich II **Obverse:** Draped bust right **Obv. Legend:** FRIDERIC9 - D • G • D • S • I • C • M • A • ET W

•, C.W. on arm **Reverse:** Helmeted arms divide I-T at sides, date at bottom **Rev. Legend:** LANDG • TH • M • M • PR • D • C • HEN • C • M • E • R • D • R • E • TON •

Date	Mintage	F	VF	XF	Unc
1712 CW//IT	415	300	600	1,250	2,500

DAV# 2711 THALER

Silver **Ruler:** Friedrich II **Subject:** Bicentennial of the Reformation **Obverse:** Draped bust right **Obv. Legend:** FRIDERICVS II. DVX SAXO-GOTHANVS • **Reverse:** Sun above palm tree **Rev. Legend:** VIXI ANNOS BIS CENTVM: - NVNC TERTIA VIVITVR AETAS, in exergue; IVBIL• II• EVANGEL./MDCCXVII•

Date	Mintage	F	VF	XF	Unc
MDCCXVII (1717) K	110	275	550	1,000	1,800

DAV# 2712 THALER

Silver **Ruler:** Friedrich II **Subject:** Bicentennial of the Reformation **Obverse:** Armored bust right **Obv. Legend:** FRIDERICVS II • D • G • DVX SAXO-GOTHANVS • **Reverse:** Sun above vineyard, Roman numeral date in exergue **Rev. Legend:** NON DORMIT CVSTOS., in exergue; IVBIL• IL EVANGEL•/MDCCXVII•

Date	Mintage	F	VF	XF	Unc
MDCCXVII (1717) CW//IT	692	250	500	900	1,700

DAV# 2712A THALER

Silver **Ruler:** Friedrich II **Obverse:** Armored, draped bust right **Obv. Legend:** FRIDERICVS II. D.G. DVX SAXO-GOTHANVS **Reverse:** Sun above vineyard **Rev. Legend:** CVSTOS NON DORMIT.

Date	Mintage	F	VF	XF	Unc
MDCCXVII (1717) CW//IT	Inc. above	250	500	900	1,700

DAV# 2713 THALER

Silver **Ruler:** Friedrich II **Subject:** Laying Foundation Stone of Church at Rehestädt **Obverse:** Armored draped bust right **Reverse:** Fourteen-line inscription with Roman numeral date

Date	Mintage	F	VF	XF	Unc
MDCCXIX (1719) CW//IT Rare	20	—	—	—	—

DAV# 2714 THALER

Silver **Subject:** Laying Foundation Stone of Church at Waltershausen **Obverse:** Armored draped bust right **Reverse:** 16-line inscription with Roman numeral date

Date	Mintage	F	VF	XF	Unc
MDCCXIX (1719) CW//IT Rare	—	—	—	—	—

DAV# 2715 THALER

Silver **Ruler:** Friedrich II **Subject:** Laying Foundation Stone of Church at Waltershausen **Obverse:** Armored bust right **Obv. Legend:** FRIDERICVS II. DVX SAXO-GOTHANVS **Reverse:** 18-line inscription with Roman numeral date **Rev. Inscription:** RELIGIONIS. EVANGELICAE.....POSVIT. VIII. NOV. A.O.R. MDCCXIX

Date	Mintage	F	VF	XF	Unc
MDCCXIX (1719) K Rare	24	—	—	—	—

DAV# 2716 THALER

Silver **Ruler:** Friedrich II **Subject:** Family Group **Obverse:** Head right **Obv. Legend:** FRIDERICVS II. D.G. DVX. SAXO-GOTHANVS, * CARI GENITORIS IMAGO * at bottom **Reverse:** Seven medallion portraits, date below **Rev. Legend:** SEPTENARIVS FRATRVM ET DVCVM SAXONIAE

Date	Mintage	F	VF	XF	Unc
1723 K	101	300	600	1,250	2,200

DAV# 2717 THALER

Silver **Ruler:** Friedrich II **Subject:** Dedication of Church at Waltershausen **Obverse:** Draped bust right **Reverse:** Grapevine, Roman numeral date in exergue

Date	Mintage	VG	F	VF	XF	Unc
MDCCXXIII (1723) K	60	400	800	1,600	3,250	—

C# 29 THALER

Silver **Ruler:** Friedrich III **Subject:** Bestowal - Order of the Garter on Friedrich III **Obverse:** Bust right **Reverse:** Crowned and mantled arms with Order band, date in Roman numerals **Note:** Dav. #2718.

Date	Mintage	F	VF	XF	Unc
ND(1741) KOCH	—	900	1,650	2,750	—

C# 30 THALER

Silver **Ruler:** Friedrich III **Subject:** 200th Anniversary - Religious Peace of Augsburg **Obverse:** Order chain on bust right **Obv. Legend:** FRIDER • III • GOTHAN • SAXON • DVX • **Reverse:** Crowned arms within mantle **Rev. Legend:** PIETATE ET - IVSTITIA, in exergue; ANNO IVBIL II • PAC •/ RELIG •/MDCCLV •/LCK • **Note:** Dav. #2721.

Date	Mintage	F	VF	XF	Unc
1755 LCK	537	300	600	1,200	2,150

KM# A30 THALER

Silver **Ruler:** Friedrich III **Obverse:** Smaller bust **Note:** Dav. #2721A.

Date	Mintage	F	VF	XF	Unc
1755 LCK	—	300	600	1,200	2,150

C# 31 THALER

Silver **Ruler:** Friedrich III **Obverse:** Crane below bust **Obv. Legend:** FRIDER. III. D. G. GOTHAN. SAXONVM DVX • **Reverse:** Crowned arms with supporters, date below **Rev. Legend:** X • EINE - FEINE MARK • **Note:** Convention Thaler. Dav. #2722.

Date	Mintage	F	VF	XF	Unc
1764	29,000	100	175	350	750

C# 32 THALER

Silver **Ruler:** Friedrich III **Obverse:** Head right **Obv. Legend:** FRIDER • III • D • G • GOTHAN • SAXONVM DVX

• **Reverse:** Crowned oval arms in band with motto **Rev. Legend:** X • EINE FEINE MARK below **Note:** Dav. #2723.

Date	Mintage	F	VF	XF	Unc
1765	28,000	100	175	350	750
1768	—	100	175	350	750

C# 40 THALER

Silver **Ruler:** Ernst Ludwig **Obverse:** Crane below bust **Obv. Legend:** ERNESTVS D • G • GOTHAN • SAXONVM DVX • **Reverse:** Crowned arms within branches **Rev. Legend:** X • EINE FEINE MARK • **Note:** Dav. #2725.

Date	Mintage	F	VF	XF	Unc
1775	—	125	250	450	1,100
1776	—	125	250	450	1,100

DAV# 2711A 1-1/4 THALER

Silver **Ruler:** Friedrich II **Subject:** 200th Anniversary of the Reformation **Obverse:** Draped bust right **Reverse:** Sun above palm tree **Note:** Similar to 1 Thaler, Dav. #2711.

Date	Mintage	VG	F	VF	XF	Unc
MDCCXVII (1717) K Rare	—	—	—	—	—	—

DAV# 2711B 1-1/2 THALER

Silver **Subject:** 200th Anniversary of the Reformation **Note:** Similar to 1 Thaler, Dav. #2711.

Date	Mintage	VG	F	VF	XF	Unc
MDCCXVII (1717) K Rare	—	—	—	—	—	—

DAV# 2716A 1-1/2 THALER

Silver **Note:** Similar to 1 Thaler, Dav. #2716.

Date	Mintage	VG	F	VF	XF	Unc
1723 K Rare	—	—	—	—	—	—

TRADE COINAGE

FR# 2971 1/2 DUCAT

1.7500 g., 0.9860 Gold 0.0555 oz. AGW **Ruler:** Friedrich II and Johann Wilhelm **Obverse:** Bust of Friedrich II right **Reverse:** Crowned arms

Date	Mintage	VG	F	VF	XF	Unc
1702 IT	69	150	300	550	950	—

FR# 2970 DUCAT

3.5000 g., 0.9860 Gold 0.1109 oz. AGW **Ruler:** Friedrich II and Johann Wilhelm **Obverse:** Bust with high coiffure facing right **Reverse:** Crowned oval manifold arms in baroque frame **Rev. Legend:** LANDGR. TH. etc.

Date	Mintage	VG	F	VF	XF	Unc
1707	—	300	650	1,400	2,750	—

FR# 2973 DUCAT

3.5000 g., 0.9860 Gold 0.1109 oz. AGW **Ruler:** Friedrich II **Subject:** Bicentennial of the Reformation **Obverse:** Bust right **Reverse:** Tree on mound, date in exergue

Date	Mintage	VG	F	VF	XF	Unc
1717 K//IT	—	250	500	1,000	1,800	—

C# 33 DUCAT

3.5000 g., 0.9860 Gold 0.1109 oz. AGW **Ruler:** Friedrich III **Subject:** Granting the Polish Order of the White Eagle upon Friedrich III **Obverse:** Bust right **Reverse:** Complex arms within crowned mantle **Note:** Fr# 2975.

Date	Mintage	VG	F	VF	XF	Unc
1732 AH	300	300	650	1,400	2,750	—

C# 34 DUCAT

3.5000 g., 0.9860 Gold 0.1109 oz. AGW **Ruler:** Friedrich III **Subject:** 200 Years of Religious Peace **Obverse:** Bust right **Reverse:** Crowned arms in baroque frame

Date	Mintage	VG	F	VF	XF	Unc
1755 LCK	—	250	550	1,200	2,000	—

FR# 2969 2 DUCAT

7.0000 g., 0.9860 Gold 0.2219 oz. AGW **Ruler:** Friedrich II and Johann Wilhelm **Subject:** 32nd Birthday of Friedrich II **Obverse:** Bust of Friedrich II right **Reverse:** Crowned oval arms

Date	Mintage	VG	F	VF	XF	Unc
1707 IT	—	950	1,850	3,250	5,500	—

FR# 2972 2 DUCAT

7.0000 g., 0.9860 Gold 0.2219 oz. AGW **Ruler:** Friedrich II **Subject:** Bicentennial of the Reformation **Reverse:** Five-line inscription

Date	Mintage	VG	F	VF	XF	Unc
1717	—	600	1,000	2,000	3,500	—

FR# 2974 2 DUCAT

7.0000 g., 0.9860 Gold 0.2219 oz. AGW **Ruler:** Friedrich II **Subject:** Bicentennial of the Augsberg Confession **Obverse:** Bust right, Roman numeral date below **Reverse:** Legend

Date	Mintage	VG	F	VF	XF	Unc
ND(1730) AH	20	500	900	1,800	3,250	—

C# 35 2 DUCAT

7.0000 g., 0.9860 Gold 0.2219 oz. AGW **Ruler:** Friedrich III **Subject:** 200 Years of Religious Peace **Obverse:** Bust right **Reverse:** Four-line inscription, Roman numeral date

Date	Mintage	VG	F	VF	XF	Unc
ND(1755)	—	650	1,250	2,500	4,000	—

SAXE-HILDBURGHAUSEN

Saxe-Hildburghausen was founded from the division of Saxe-Gotha, by the sixth son of Ernst the Pious. In 1826, the last duke assigned Hildburghausen to Saxe-Meiningen in exchange for Altenburg.

RULERS

Ernst, 1680-1715
Ernst Friedrich I, 1715-1724
Ernst Friedrich II, 1724-1745
Ernst Friedrich III Carl, 1745-1780
Joseph Prince Regent, 1780-1787
Friedrich I, 1780-1826

MINT OFFICIALS' INITIALS

Initials	Date	Name
F	1718	Johann Georg Feuchter
FEW	1716-18	Friedrich Ernst Wermuth
	1686-1705	Heinrich Ernst Angerstein at Coburg
IVF	1770-84	Johann Weber (Fecit), die-cutter in Florence
K, KL	1760-63	Johann Anton David Klinghammer, die-cutter
WF	1718-19	Friedrich Ernst Wermuth and Johann Georg Feuchter

DUCHY

REGULAR COINAGE

KM# 5 HELLER

Copper **Ruler:** Ernst **Obverse:** Crowned E between palm branches **Reverse:** Value: HILD/BURG: H:/HELLER/date **Note:** Varieties exist.

Date	Mintage	VG	F	VF	XF	Unc
1703	—	3.00	6.00	12.00	25.00	—
1704	—	3.00	6.00	12.00	25.00	—
1707	—	3.00	6.00	12.00	25.00	—
1708	—	3.00	6.00	12.00	25.00	—
1711	—	3.00	6.00	12.00	25.00	—
1712	—	3.00	6.00	12.00	25.00	—
1713	—	3.00	6.00	12.00	25.00	—

KM# 10 HELLER

Copper **Ruler:** Ernst **Reverse:** Value: *1*/HILD: B./HELLER/date

Date	Mintage	VG	F	VF	XF	Unc
1714	—	4.00	8.00	15.00	32.00	—

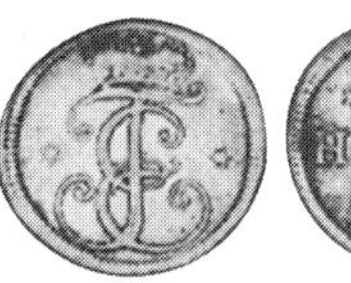

KM# 14 HELLER

Copper **Ruler:** Ernst Friedrich I **Obverse:** Crowned script EF monogram **Reverse:** Value HH (joined together)/HELLER/date

Date	Mintage	VG	F	VF	XF	Unc
1716	—	5.00	10.00	20.00	42.00	—
1717	—	5.00	10.00	20.00	42.00	—

KM# 25 HELLER

Copper **Ruler:** Ernst Friedrich II **Obverse:** Crowned monogram **Reverse:** Value, date

Date	Mintage	VG	F	VF	XF	Unc
1736	—	10.00	20.00	40.00	65.00	—

KM# 46 HELLER

Copper **Ruler:** Ernst Friedrich III Carl **Obverse:** Crowned script EFC monogram **Reverse:** Value, date

Date	Mintage	VG	F	VF	XF	Unc
1759	—	4.00	8.00	16.00	35.00	—
1761	—	4.00	8.00	16.00	35.00	—
1763	—	4.00	8.00	16.00	35.00	—
1766	—	—	—	—	—	—

KM# 80 HELLER

Copper **Ruler:** Ernst Friedrich III Carl **Obverse:** Crowned arms in baroque frame

Date	Mintage	VG	F	VF	XF	Unc
1761	—	5.00	10.00	20.00	40.00	—

KM# 83 HELLER

Copper **Ruler:** Ernst Friedrich III Carl **Obverse:** Crowned arms between 2 branches **Reverse:** Value, date **Note:** Formerly listed as Saxe-Gotha-Altenburg C#3.

Date	Mintage	VG	F	VF	XF	Unc
1763	—	5.00	10.00	20.00	40.00	—
1770	—	5.00	10.00	20.00	40.00	—

KM# 104 HELLER

Copper **Ruler:** Ernst Friedrich III Carl **Obverse:** Crowned arms **Reverse:** Value **Note:** C3a.

Date	Mintage	VG	F	VF	XF	Unc
1772	—	5.00	10.00	20.00	40.00	—

Date	Mintage	VG	F	VF	XF	Unc
1774	—	5.00	10.00	20.00	40.00	—
1778	—	5.00	10.00	20.00	40.00	—

KM# 103 HELLER

Copper **Ruler:** Ernst Friedrich III Carl **Obverse:** Crowned oval arms between 2 branches **Note:** Uniface. Klippe.

Date	Mintage	VG	F	VF	XF	Unc
1772	—	5.00	10.00	20.00	40.00	—
1774	—	5.00	10.00	20.00	40.00	—

KM# 110 HELLER

Copper **Ruler:** Joseph Prince Regent **Obverse:** Crowned arms in sprays, date below **Reverse:** Value **Note:** Klippe.

Date	Mintage	VG	F	VF	XF	Unc
1781	—	4.00	8.00	12.50	20.00	—
1784	—	4.00	8.00	12.50	20.00	—

KM# 118 HELLER

Copper **Ruler:** Friedrich I **Obverse:** Crowned arms **Reverse:** Value, date

Date	Mintage	VG	F	VF	XF	Unc
1787	—	4.00	8.00	12.50	20.00	—
1788	—	4.00	8.00	12.50	20.00	—

KM# 127 2 HELLER

Copper **Ruler:** Friedrich I **Obverse:** Crowned script F monogram **Reverse:** Value: II/HH/S.M. divides date

Date	Mintage	VG	F	VF	XF	Unc
1791	—	7.00	12.00	25.00	55.00	—

KM# 47 PFENNIG

Copper **Ruler:** Ernst Friedrich III Carl **Obverse:** Crowned arms surrounded by trophies **Reverse:** Value, date

Date	Mintage	VG	F	VF	XF	Unc
1759	—	5.00	10.00	20.00	40.00	—

KM# 15 3 PFENNIG

Silver **Ruler:** Ernst Friedrich I **Obverse:** Bust right **Reverse:** Value: 3 on imperial orb divides date

Date	Mintage	VG	F	VF	XF	Unc
1716	—	6.00	15.00	30.00	60.00	—
1717	—	6.00	15.00	30.00	60.00	—

KM# 84 3 PFENNIG

Copper **Ruler:** Ernst Friedrich III Carl **Obverse:** Crowned arms in cartouche **Reverse:** Value, date

Date	Mintage	VG	F	VF	XF	Unc
1763	—	55.00	90.00	160	275	—

KM# 16 6 PFENNIG (Sechser - 1/2 Groschen)

Silver **Ruler:** Ernst Friedrich I **Obverse:** Bust right **Reverse:** Value: VI on imperial orb divides date

Date	Mintage	VG	F	VF	XF	Unc
1716	—	15.00	30.00	50.00	90.00	—

KM# 30 KREUZER

Billon **Ruler:** Ernst Friedrich III Carl **Obverse:** Bust right **Reverse:** Crowned arms

Date	Mintage	VG	F	VF	XF	Unc
1753	—	10.00	20.00	40.00	70.00	—
1758	—	10.00	20.00	40.00	70.00	—

KM# 70 KREUZER

Billon **Ruler:** Ernst Friedrich III Carl **Reverse:** Value: '1' in baroque frame, date **Note:** C#9a.

Date	Mintage	VG	F	VF	XF	Unc
1760	—	15.00	25.00	45.00	80.00	—

KM# 89 KREUZER

Billon **Ruler:** Ernst Friedrich III Carl **Obverse:** Crowned EFC monogram **Reverse:** Value, date **Note:** Convention Kreuzer.

Date	Mintage	VG	F	VF	XF	Unc
1765	—	15.00	25.00	45.00	80.00	—

KM# 106 KREUZER

Billon **Ruler:** Ernst Friedrich III Carl **Obverse:** Arms **Reverse:** Value above date **Note:** C#12a.

Date	Mintage	VG	F	VF	XF	Unc
1774	—	5.00	10.00	25.00	50.00	—
1775	—	5.00	10.00	25.00	50.00	—
1776	—	5.00	10.00	25.00	50.00	—
1777	—	5.00	10.00	25.00	50.00	—
1778	—	5.00	10.00	25.00	50.00	—

KM# 105 KREUZER

Billon **Ruler:** Ernst Friedrich III Carl **Obverse:** Crowned arms between 2 branches on pedestal, value, date **Reverse:** Value

Date	Mintage	VG	F	VF	XF	Unc
1774	—	20.00	32.00	65.00	120	—
1775	—	20.00	32.00	65.00	120	—
1778	—	20.00	32.00	65.00	120	—

KM# 111 KREUZER

Billon **Ruler:** Joseph Prince Regent **Obverse:** Crowned I F monogram separates H H

Date	Mintage	VG	F	VF	XF	Unc
1781	—	5.00	10.00	25.00	50.00	—

KM# 117 KREUZER

Billon **Ruler:** Joseph Prince Regent **Obverse:** Saxon arms separate H H

Date	Mintage	VG	F	VF	XF	Unc
1784	—	4.00	8.00	16.00	35.00	—
1794	—	4.00	8.00	16.00	35.00	—

KM# 81 2 KREUZER

Billon **Ruler:** Ernst Friedrich III Carl **Obverse:** Arms in cartouche on crowned mantle **Reverse:** Value, date in cartouche

Date	Mintage	VG	F	VF	XF	Unc
1761	—	15.00	25.00	45.00	80.00	—

KM# 112 2-1/2 KREUZER

Billon **Ruler:** Joseph Prince Regent **Obverse:** Crowned I F monogram, date **Reverse:** Value

Date	Mintage	VG	F	VF	XF	Unc
1781	—	15.00	25.00	45.00	80.00	—

KM# 82 4 KREUZER

Billon **Ruler:** Ernst Friedrich III Carl **Obverse:** Arms in cartouche on crowned mantle **Reverse:** Value, date in cartouche

Date	Mintage	VG	F	VF	XF	Unc
1761	—	18.00	30.00	60.00	110	—

KM# 85 4 KREUZER

Billon **Ruler:** Ernst Friedrich III Carl **Obverse:** Head right **Reverse:** Crowned arms, value, date **Note:** Convention Kreuzer.

Date	Mintage	VG	F	VF	XF	Unc
1763	—	18.00	30.00	60.00	110	—

KM# 90 5 KREUZER

Billon **Ruler:** Ernst Friedrich III Carl **Obverse:** Crowned EFC monogram in rhombus **Reverse:** Value, date in rhombus **Note:** Convention 5 Kreuzer.

Date	Mintage	VG	F	VF	XF	Unc
1765	—	30.00	55.00	125	275	—

KM# 100 5 KREUZER

Billon **Ruler:** Ernst Friedrich III Carl **Obverse:** Crowned arms in cartouche between 2 branches on pedestal **Reverse:** IUS/TIRT, date in rhombus, value

Date	Mintage	VG	F	VF	XF	Unc
1770	—	20.00	40.00	80.00	175	—

KM# 48 6 KREUZER

Billon **Ruler:** Ernst Friedrich III Carl **Obverse:** Bust right **Reverse:** Crowned arms in baroque frame, value, date

Date	Mintage	VG	F	VF	XF	Unc
1759	—	18.00	32.00	65.00	135	—

KM# 49 10 KREUZER

Silver **Ruler:** Ernst Friedrich III Carl

Date	Mintage	VG	F	VF	XF	Unc
1759	—	30.00	45.00	90.00	185	—

KM# 71 10 KREUZER

Silver **Ruler:** Ernst Friedrich III Carl **Obverse:** Bust right between branches **Reverse:** Crowned arms in cartouche on pedestal between branches, value, date

Date	Mintage	VG	F	VF	XF	Unc
1760	—	30.00	45.00	90.00	185	—

KM# 94 10 KREUZER

Silver **Ruler:** Ernst Friedrich III Carl **Obverse:** Head right between branches **Reverse:** Value: 120 EINE ...

Date	Mintage	VG	F	VF	XF	Unc
1769 WR	—	50.00	100	200	350	—

KM# 31 15 KREUZER

Silver **Ruler:** Ernst Friedrich III Carl **Obverse:** Bust right **Reverse:** Crowned arms in cartouche, value divides date

Date	Mintage	VG	F	VF	XF	Unc
1758	—	80.00	150	275	500	—

KM# 72 20 KREUZER

Silver **Ruler:** Ernst Friedrich III Carl **Obverse:** Bust left **Reverse:** Crowned arms in cartouche on pedestal between branches, value, date **Note:** Convention 20 Kreuzer.

Date	Mintage	VG	F	VF	XF	Unc
1760	—	35.00	65.00	125	245	—

KM# 91 20 KREUZER

Silver **Ruler:** Ernst Friedrich III Carl **Obverse:** Bust between branches **Reverse:** Crowned arms, value, date

Date	Mintage	VG	F	VF	XF	Unc
1766	—	35.00	65.00	125	245	—

KM# 95 20 KREUZER

Silver **Ruler:** Ernst Friedrich III Carl **Obverse:** Head right between branches **Reverse:** Crowned arms in cartouche on pedestal between branches, value: LX ST. EINE ..., date

Date	Mintage	VG	F	VF	XF	Unc
1769 WK	—	50.00	100	200	400	—

KM# 113 20 KREUZER

Billon **Ruler:** Joseph Prince Regent **Obverse:** Bust right **Reverse:** Arms above date

Date	Mintage	VG	F	VF	XF	Unc
1781	—	30.00	70.00	150	300	—

KM# 128 20 KREUZER

Billon **Ruler:** Friedrich I **Obverse:** Head right

Date	Mintage	VG	F	VF	XF	Unc
1796	—	35.00	75.00	165	350	—

KM# 73 GROSCHEN

Billon **Ruler:** Ernst Friedrich III Carl **Obverse:** Crowned script EFC monogram **Reverse:** Value, date **Note:** C#29a.

Date	Mintage	VG	F	VF	XF	Unc
1760	—	45.00	85.00	150	325	—

KM# 74 GROSCHEN

Billon **Ruler:** Ernst Friedrich III Carl **Subject:** Birth of Princess Ernestine Friderike Sophie

Date	Mintage	VG	F	VF	XF	Unc
1760	—	45.00	85.00	165	350	—

KM# 86 GROSCHEN

Billon **Ruler:** Ernst Friedrich III Carl **Subject:** Birth of Prince Friedrich **Obverse:** Head right **Reverse:** 5-line inscription, date

Date	Mintage	VG	F	VF	XF	Unc
1763	—	20.00	40.00	80.00	165	—

KM# 11 2 GROSCHEN

Silver **Ruler:** Ernst **Subject:** Death of Duke Ernst **Obverse:** Bust right, legend in Roman letters **Reverse:** 8-line inscription with Roman letters and dates

Date	Mintage	VG	F	VF	XF	Unc
1715	—	30.00	50.00	90.00	150	—

KM# 12 2 GROSCHEN

Silver **Ruler:** Ernst **Subject:** Death of Duke Ernst **Obverse:** Legend in gothic letters **Reverse:** Inscription in gothic letters

Date	Mintage	VG	F	VF	XF	Unc
1715	—	25.00	45.00	80.00	135	—

KM# 17 2 GROSCHEN

Silver **Ruler:** Ernst Friedrich I **Obverse:** Bust right **Reverse:** Crowned oval 4-fold arms with central shield of Saxony arms in chain of Order, value (2GR) below, date divided near bottom

Date	Mintage	VG	F	VF	XF	Unc
1717 WF	—	20.00	40.00	75.00	125	—
1718 WF	—	20.00	40.00	75.00	125	—

KM# 23 2 GROSCHEN

Silver **Ruler:** Ernst Friedrich I **Subject:** Homage and Fealty **Obv. Legend:** Z. GED. D. ERB. U.L. -AND. HUL. I. SEPT.

Date	Mintage	VG	F	VF	XF	Unc
1718 WF	—	20.00	40.00	75.00	125	—
1718 F	—	20.00	40.00	75.00	125	—

KM# 87 2 GROSCHEN

Silver **Ruler:** Ernst Friedrich III Carl **Subject:** Birth of Prince Friedrich **Obverse:** Head right **Reverse:** 5-line inscription, date

Date	Mintage	VG	F	VF	XF	Unc
1763 Rare	—	—	—	—	—	—

KM# 92 1/48 THALER

Billon **Ruler:** Ernst Friedrich III Carl **Obverse:** Crowned oval arms between 2 branches on pedestal, value, date, CONV MUNZ **Reverse:** Value in cartouche **Note:** Convention 1/48 Thaler.

Date	Mintage	VG	F	VF	XF	Unc
1768	—	20.00	35.00	65.00	110	—

KM# 101 1/48 THALER

Billon **Ruler:** Ernst Friedrich III Carl **Obverse:** Crowned arms **Reverse:** Value

Date	Mintage	VG	F	VF	XF	Unc
1770	—	15.00	28.00	55.00	90.00	—

KM# 120 1/48 THALER

Billon **Ruler:** Friedrich I

Date	Mintage	VG	F	VF	XF	Unc
1788	—	5.00	10.00	20.00	50.00	—

KM# 121 1/48 THALER

Billon **Ruler:** Friedrich I **Obverse:** Saxon arms **Reverse:** Value above date **Note:** Reichs 1/48 Thaler.

Date	Mintage	VG	F	VF	XF	Unc
1788	—	5.00	10.00	20.00	50.00	—

Date	Mintage	VG	F	VF	XF	Unc
1790	—	5.00	10.00	20.00	50.00	—

KM# 13 1/24 THALER (Groschen)

Silver **Ruler:** Ernst Friedrich I **Obverse:** Bust right **Reverse:** 24/EINEN/THALER/DATE/mintmaster's initials

Date	Mintage	VG	F	VF	XF	Unc
1716 FEW	—	18.00	30.00	55.00	100	—

KM# 50 1/24 THALER (Groschen)

Billon **Ruler:** Ernst Friedrich III Carl **Obverse:** Crowned monogram **Reverse:** Value, date

Date	Mintage	VG	F	VF	XF	Unc
1759	—	15.00	25.00	50.00	90.00	—
1760	—	15.00	25.00	50.00	90.00	—

KM# 75 1/24 THALER (Groschen)

Billon **Ruler:** Ernst Friedrich III Carl **Obverse:** Crowned arms **Reverse:** Imperial orb with value "24", date

Date	Mintage	VG	F	VF	XF	Unc
1760	—	20.00	35.00	70.00	120	—

KM# 76 1/24 THALER (Groschen)

Billon **Ruler:** Ernst Friedrich III Carl **Obverse:** Crowned F monogram **Reverse:** Value, date

Date	Mintage	VG	F	VF	XF	Unc
1760	—	20.00	32.00	65.00	110	—
1764	—	20.00	32.00	65.00	110	—

KM# 122 1/24 THALER (Groschen)

Billon **Ruler:** Friedrich I **Obverse:** Crowned oval arms between branches **Reverse:** 24/EINEN/THALER/S.M./date

Date	Mintage	VG	F	VF	XF	Unc
1788	—	10.00	22.00	40.00	75.00	—

KM# 126 1/24 THALER (Groschen)

Billon **Ruler:** Friedrich I **Obverse:** Crowned F divides date **Reverse:** 24/EINEN/THALER/S.M./date

Date	Mintage	VG	F	VF	XF	Unc
1790	—	10.00	22.00	40.00	75.00	—

KM# 18 1/12 THALER (2 Groschen)

Silver **Ruler:** Ernst Friedrich I **Obverse:** Bust right **Reverse:** 12/EINEN/THALER/date/initials

Date	Mintage	VG	F	VF	XF	Unc
1717 F	—	25.00	50.00	90.00	160	—
1717 WF	—	25.00	50.00	90.00	160	—

KM# 19 1/12 THALER (2 Groschen)

Silver **Ruler:** Ernst Friedrich I **Subject:** Bicentennial of Reformation **Reverse:** Legend, value: XII/EINEN/THALER/ Roman numeral date/initials **Rev. Legend:** SAECVLVM LVTHERANVM SECVNDVM

Date	Mintage	VG	F	VF	XF	Unc
1717 FEW	—	30.00	60.00	120	200	—

KM# 20 1/12 THALER (2 Groschen)

Silver **Ruler:** Ernst Friedrich I **Reverse:** Value: 12

Date	Mintage	VG	F	VF	XF	Unc
1717	—	30.00	60.00	120	200	—

KM# 21 1/12 THALER (2 Groschen)

Silver **Ruler:** Ernst Friedrich I **Reverse:** Date in Arabic numerals

Date	Mintage	VG	F	VF	XF	Unc
1717	—	30.00	60.00	120	200	—

KM# 32 1/12 THALER (2 Groschen)

Silver **Ruler:** Ernst Friedrich III Carl **Obverse:** Bust right **Reverse:** Value, date **Note:** Varieties exist.

Date	Mintage	VG	F	VF	XF	Unc
1758	—	25.00	50.00	100	175	—
1760	—	25.00	50.00	100	175	—

KM# 60 1/12 THALER (2 Groschen)

Silver **Ruler:** Ernst Friedrich III Carl **Obverse:** Bust left **Reverse:** Crowned arms in baroque frame surrounded by trophies, value, date

Date	Mintage	VG	F	VF	XF	Unc
1759	—	30.00	60.00	120	200	—

KM# 61 1/12 THALER (2 Groschen)

Silver **Ruler:** Ernst Friedrich III Carl **Obverse:** Bust right

Date	Mintage	VG	F	VF	XF	Unc
1759	—	30.00	60.00	120	200	—

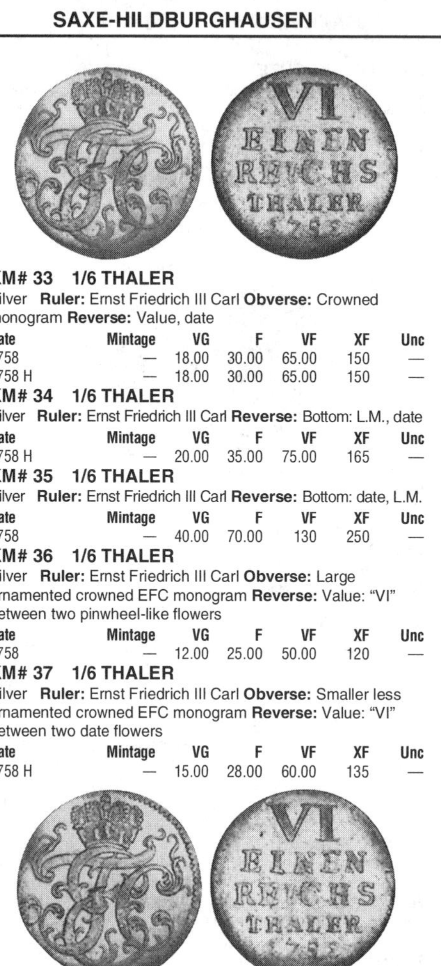

KM# 33 1/6 THALER

Silver **Ruler:** Ernst Friedrich III Carl **Obverse:** Crowned monogram **Reverse:** Value, date

Date	Mintage	VG	F	VF	XF	Unc
1758	—	18.00	30.00	65.00	150	—
1758 H	—	18.00	30.00	65.00	150	—

KM# 34 1/6 THALER

Silver **Ruler:** Ernst Friedrich III Carl **Reverse:** Bottom: L.M., date

Date	Mintage	VG	F	VF	XF	Unc
1758 H	—	20.00	35.00	75.00	165	—

KM# 35 1/6 THALER

Silver **Ruler:** Ernst Friedrich III Carl **Reverse:** Bottom: date, L.M.

Date	Mintage	VG	F	VF	XF	Unc
1758	—	40.00	70.00	130	250	—

KM# 36 1/6 THALER

Silver **Ruler:** Ernst Friedrich III Carl **Obverse:** Large ornamented crowned EFC monogram **Reverse:** Value: "VI" between two pinwheel-like flowers

Date	Mintage	VG	F	VF	XF	Unc
1758	—	12.00	25.00	50.00	120	—

KM# 37 1/6 THALER

Silver **Ruler:** Ernst Friedrich III Carl **Obverse:** Smaller less ornamented crowned EFC monogram **Reverse:** Value: "VI" between two date flowers

Date	Mintage	VG	F	VF	XF	Unc
1758 H	—	15.00	28.00	60.00	135	—

KM# 38 1/6 THALER

Silver **Ruler:** Ernst Friedrich III Carl **Obverse:** Crowned monogram **Reverse:** Value: "VI" between two diamond-shaped flowers

Date	Mintage	VG	F	VF	XF	Unc
1758 H	—	30.00	60.00	120	200	—

KM# 39 1/6 THALER

Silver **Ruler:** Ernst Friedrich III Carl **Reverse:** Inscription ends H:L:M:

Date	Mintage	VG	F	VF	XF	Unc
1758 (?)	—	20.00	35.00	75.00	165	—

KM# 40 1/6 THALER

Silver **Ruler:** Ernst Friedrich III Carl **Reverse:** Inscription ends with L.M. below date

Date	Mintage	VG	F	VF	XF	Unc
1758 (?)	—	40.00	70.00	130	250	—

KM# 41 1/6 THALER

Silver **Ruler:** Ernst Friedrich III Carl **Obverse:** Bust right **Reverse:** Value, date

Date	Mintage	VG	F	VF	XF	Unc
1758 H	—	35.00	65.00	120	225	—

KM# 42 1/6 THALER

Silver **Ruler:** Ernst Friedrich III Carl **Reverse:** Bottom: L.M., date

Date	Mintage	VG	F	VF	XF	Unc
1758 H	—	20.00	35.00	75.00	165	—

KM# 43 1/6 THALER

Silver **Ruler:** Ernst Friedrich III Carl **Obverse:** Bust right **Reverse:** Crowned ornate arms in baroque frame divide L-M and date, value below

Date	Mintage	VG	F	VF	XF	Unc
1758	—	80.00	150	250	475	—

KM# 77 1/3 THALER

Silver **Ruler:** Ernst Friedrich III Carl **Obverse:** Bust right **Reverse:** Crowned arms in cartouche with trophies, value, date

Date	Mintage	VG	F	VF	XF	Unc
1760	—	90.00	225	400	750	—

KM# 44 2/3 THALER

Silver **Ruler:** Ernst Friedrich III Carl **Obverse:** Armored bust right **Obv. Legend:** ERN•FRID•CAR•D•G•DVX•SAXON• **Reverse:** Crowned arms with wildmen supporters, value framed below

Date	Mintage	VG	F	VF	XF	Unc
1758	—	80.00	180	325	675	—

KM# 45 2/3 THALER

Silver **Ruler:** Ernst Friedrich III Carl **Reverse:** Oval arms between wildmen **Note:** C46a.

Date	Mintage	VG	F	VF	XF	Unc
1758	—	90.00	225	400	750	—

KM# 62 2/3 THALER

Silver **Ruler:** Ernst Friedrich III Carl **Reverse:** Knight with crowned arms and trophies, value, date

Date	Mintage	VG	F	VF	XF	Unc
1759	—	90.00	225	400	750	—

C# 47.5 2/3 THALER

Silver **Ruler:** Ernst Friedrich III Carl **Reverse:** Crowned arms in cartouche with trophies, value, date

Date	Mintage	VG	F	VF	XF	Unc
1759	—	125	325	600	1,000	—

KM# 78 2/3 THALER

Silver **Ruler:** Ernst Friedrich III Carl **Obverse:** Head right **Obv. Legend:** ERN • FRID • CAR • D • G • DVX • SAXON • **Reverse:** Knight seated left with shield and trophies, value below **Note:** 1/2 Convention Thaler.

Date	Mintage	VG	F	VF	XF	Unc
1760	—	80.00	180	325	675	—

KM# 6 THALER

Silver **Ruler:** Ernst **Obverse:** Bust right **Reverse:** Helmeted arms above date **Note:** Dav.#2727.

Date	Mintage	VG	F	VF	XF	Unc
1708 (a)	—	700	1,400	2,500	4,000	—

KM# 7 THALER

Silver **Ruler:** Ernst **Obverse:** Accolated busts right **Note:** Dav.#2727.

Date	Mintage	VG	F	VF	XF	Unc
1708 (a)	—	550	1,100	2,000	3,250	—

KM# 79 THALER

Silver **Ruler:** Ernst Friedrich III Carl **Obverse:** Bust right **Obv. Legend:** ERN • FRID • CAR • D • G • DVX SAXON • **Reverse:** Knight seated left with shield and trophies, date below **Rev. Legend:** ZEHEN EINE FEINE MARCK **Note:** Convention Thaler. Varieties exist; Dav.#2729.

Date	Mintage	VG	F	VF	XF	Unc
1760	—	100	250	500	850	—

KM# 88 THALER
Silver **Ruler:** Ernst Friedrich III Carl **Subject:** Peace of Hubertusburg **Obverse:** Head right **Obv. Legend:** ERN • FRID • CAR • D • G • DVX SAXON **Reverse:** Crowned arms with trophies **Rev. Legend:** ZEHEN EINE FEINE MARCK **Note:** Dav.#2730.

Date	Mintage	VG	F	VF	XF	Unc
1763 WK	—	125	325	600	1,000	—

KM# 96 THALER
Silver **Ruler:** Ernst Friedrich III Carl **Obverse:** Bust right **Reverse:** Lion at left holds crowned arms, value, date **Note:** Dav.#2731.

Date	Mintage	VG	F	VF	XF	Unc
1769	—	100	300	550	900	—

KM# 114 THALER
Silver **Ruler:** Joseph Prince Regent **Obverse:** Bust right **Obv. Legend:** V:G:G: IOSEPH: FRIED: II: H:Z:S:&.&. OBERVORMUND: U: LANDES REG: **Reverse:** Knight standing with sword and shield **Rev. Legend:** ZEHEN EINE FEINE MARK **Note:** Dav.#2732.

Date	Mintage	VG	F	VF	XF	Unc
1781	—	90.00	175	350	525	—

KM# 115 THALER
Silver **Ruler:** Joseph Prince Regent **Obverse:** Head right **Obv. Legend:** V • G • G • IOS • FRIED • H • ZV • SACHSEN • & • & • OBERVORMVND V • LANDES REGENT **Reverse:** Knight standing with sword and shield, helmet at foot **Rev. Legend:** X • EINE • FEINE • /MARK • **Note:** Dav.#2733.

Date	Mintage	VG	F	VF	XF	Unc
ND IYF	—	90.00	175	350	525	—

KM# 116 2 THALER
Silver **Ruler:** Joseph Prince Regent **Obverse:** Head right **Reverse:** Knight standing with sword and shield **Note:** Similar to KM#115. Struck on thick flan.

Date	Mintage	VG	F	VF	XF	Unc
ND IVF	—	—	—	—	—	—

TRADE COINAGE

KM# 22 1/2 DUCAT
1.7500 g., 0.9860 Gold 0.0555 oz. AGW **Ruler:** Ernst Friedrich I **Subject:** Bicentennial of the Reformation **Obverse:** Bust right **Reverse:** 4-line inscription, date

Date	Mintage	VG	F	VF	XF	Unc
1717	—	350	650	1,250	2,000	—

KM# 102 DUCAT
3.5000 g., 0.9860 Gold 0.1109 oz. AGW **Ruler:** Ernst Friedrich III Carl **Obverse:** Bust right **Reverse:** Crowned arms

Date	Mintage	VG	F	VF	XF	Unc
1771 H	—	500	1,000	2,150	3,750	—

PATTERNS

Including off metal strikes

KM#	Date	Mintage	Identification	Mkt Val
Pn1	1760	—	Groschen. Gold. KM74.	—
Pn2	1763	—	Groschen. Gold. KM86.	—

SAXE-MEININGEN

(Sachsen-Meiningen)

The duchy of Saxe-Meiningen was located in Thuringia, sandwiched between Saxe-Weimar-Eisenach on the west and north and the enclave of Schmalkalden belonging to Hesse-Cassel on the east. It was founded upon the division of the Ernestine line in Saxe-Gotha in 1680.In 1735, due to an exchange of some territory, the duchy became known as Saxe-Coburg-Meiningen. In 1826, Saxe-Coburg-Gotha assigned Saalfeld toSaxe-Meiningen. The duchy came under the strong influence of Prussia from 1866, when Bernhard II was forced to abdicate because of his support of Austria. The monarchy ended with the defeat of Germany in 1918.

RULERS
Bernhard, 1680-1706
Ernst Ludwig I, 1706-1724
Ernst Ludwig II, 1724-1729
Karl Friedrich, 1729-1743
Friedrich Wilhelm, 1743-1746
Anton Ulrich, 1746-1763
August Friedrich Karl, under Regency of Charlotte Amalie, 1763-1775
Alone as Karl, 1775-1782
Georg I, 1782-1803

MINT OFFICIALS' INITIALS

Initials	Date	Name
CW, W	1688-1739	Christian Wermuth, die-cutter in Gotha
HEA	1686-1705	Heinrich Ernst Angerstein in Coburg, and
	1687-1714	Ernst Friedrich Angerstein in Coburg
HMO	1714-17	Heinrich Ernst Obermuller in Meiningen
ICK	1765-94	Johann christian Knaust
IT	1690-1723	Johann Thun in Gotha
PFC	1685-1714	Paul Friedrich Crum in Coburg
SNR	1760-74	Siegmund Scholz, warden and
	1764-93	Georg Nikolaus Riedner, mintmaster
VOIGT		J.C. Voigt, die-cutter and medailleur

NOTE: Between 1691 and 1703, Saxe-Meiningen struck coins in various denominations for its part of Henneberg-Ilmenau.

DUCHY

REGULAR COINAGE

KM# 40 HELLER
Copper **Ruler:** Ernst Ludwig I **Obverse:** Intertwined EL monogram **Reverse:** Value, date **Rev. Legend:** I/HELLER

Date	Mintage	VG	F	VF	XF	Unc
1714	—	5.00	10.00	18.00	35.00	—

KM# 41 HELLER
Copper **Ruler:** Ernst Ludwig I **Obverse:** Ducal crown above monogram **Note:** Varieties exist.

Date	Mintage	VG	F	VF	XF	Unc
1714	—	5.00	10.00	18.00	35.00	—

KM# 55 HELLER
Copper **Ruler:** Karl Friedrich **Obverse:** Crowned round arms in cartouche **Reverse:** Value, date **Rev. Legend:** I/MEINING/HELLER **Note:** Varieties exist.

Date	Mintage	VG	F	VF	XF	Unc
1738	—	3.00	8.00	15.00	28.00	—
1740	—	3.00	8.00	15.00	28.00	—
1741	—	3.00	8.00	15.00	28.00	—
1742	—	3.00	8.00	15.00	28.00	—

KM# 60 HELLER
Copper **Ruler:** Karl Friedrich **Reverse:** Intertwined H: M (Herzogtum Meiningen), ducal crown above

Date	Mintage	VG	F	VF	XF	Unc
ND(1743)	—	—	—	—	—	—

KM# 61 HELLER
Copper **Ruler:** Friedrich Wilhelm **Obverse:** Crowned arms within cartouche **Reverse:** Value, date **Note:** Similar to KM#55.

Date	Mintage	VG	F	VF	XF	Unc
1743	—	2.50	6.00	12.00	25.00	—
1744	—	2.50	6.00	12.00	25.00	—
1745	—	2.50	6.00	12.00	25.00	—

KM# 65 HELLER
Copper **Ruler:** Anton Ulrich **Obverse:** Crowned oval arms in baroque frame **Reverse:** Value, date **Note:** Varieties exist.

Date	Mintage	VG	F	VF	XF	Unc
1755	—	3.00	6.00	12.00	25.00	—
1756	—	3.00	6.00	12.00	25.00	—
1761	—	3.00	6.00	12.00	25.00	—

KM# 70 HELLER
Copper **Ruler:** Anton Ulrich **Obverse:** Crowned monogram **Reverse:** Value, date **Note:** Similar to 3 Heller, KM#72.

Date	Mintage	VG	F	VF	XF	Unc
1761	—	3.00	6.00	12.00	25.00	—

KM# 75 HELLER
Copper **Ruler:** August Friedrich Karl under regency of Charlotte Amalie **Obverse:** Crowned oval arms in baroque frame **Reverse:** Value, date

Date	Mintage	VG	F	VF	XF	Unc
1769	—	5.00	10.00	20.00	35.00	—

KM# 71 2 HELLER
Copper **Ruler:** Anton Ulrich **Obverse:** Crowned monogram **Reverse:** Value, date **Note:** Similar to 3 Heller, KM#72.

Date	Mintage	VG	F	VF	XF	Unc
1761	—	5.00	10.00	20.00	35.00	—

KM# 72 3 HELLER
Copper **Ruler:** Anton Ulrich **Obverse:** Crowned monogram **Reverse:** Value, date

Date	Mintage	VG	F	VF	XF	Unc
1761	—	4.00	8.00	16.00	30.00	—

KM# 74 KREUZER
Billon **Ruler:** August Friedrich Karl under regency of Charlotte Amalie **Obverse:** Crowned shield of ducal Saxon arms in baroque frame **Obv. Legend:** CHARL.AMA.D.G.D.S.TVTRIX.REGENS

Reverse: Six-line inscription with date and mint officials' initials in cartouche **Rev. Inscription:** 1/S.MEINING./CONVENT./ KREVZER/ 1765/S.(N)R. **Note:** Convention Kreuzer.

Date	Mintage	VG	F	VF	XF	Unc
1765 SNR	—	15.00	28.00	55.00	100	—

KM# 80 KREUZER

Billon **Ruler:** August Friedrich Karl under regency of Charlotte Amalie

Date	Mintage	VG	F	VF	XF	Unc
1771 ICK	—	15.00	25.00	50.00	90.00	—

KM# 87 KREUZER

Billon **Ruler:** August Friedrich Karl alone as Karl
Obverse: Shield of ducal Saxon arms in baroque frame, crown above divides S.C.-M. **Reverse:** Six-line inscription with date and mintmaster's initials in cartouche **Rev. Inscription:** 1/S.COB.MEIN/CONVENT./KREVZER/1781/I.C.H.

Date	Mintage	VG	F	VF	XF	Unc
1781 ICK	—	4.00	10.00	20.00	40.00	—

KM# 88 KREUZER

Billon **Ruler:** Georg I **Obverse:** Crowned arms in sprays
Reverse: Value above date

Date	Mintage	VG	F	VF	XF	Unc
1786	—	4.00	10.00	20.00	40.00	—
1790	—	4.00	10.00	20.00	40.00	—
1794	—	4.00	10.00	20.00	40.00	—

KM# 90 KREUZER

Billon **Ruler:** Georg I

Date	Mintage	VG	F	VF	XF	Unc
1794 ICK	—	5.00	12.00	25.00	50.00	—

KM# 73 5 KREUZER (Convention)

Billon **Ruler:** August Friedrich Karl under regency of Charlotte Amalie **Obverse:** Crowned arms in cartouche **Reverse:** Value, date in cartouche

Date	Mintage	VG	F	VF	XF	Unc
1765 SNR	—	15.00	30.00	60.00	120	—

KM# 35 2 GROSCHEN (Gute)

Silver **Ruler:** Bernhard **Subject:** Death of Bernhard I
Obverse: All German inscriptions except dates in Gothic letters
Reverse: Value at bottom is 2ggr **Note:** 2 Gute Groschen.

Date	Mintage	VG	F	VF	XF	Unc
1706	—	28.00	50.00	100	175	—

KM# 36 1/12 THALER (Doppelgroschen)

Silver **Ruler:** Bernhard **Subject:** Death of Bernhard I **Obverse:** Wigged bust right, legend titles in Latin with Roman letters
Reverse: 5-line inscription with dates, value: 1/12 below

Date	Mintage	VG	F	VF	XF	Unc
1706	—	22.00	45.00	90.00	140	—

KM# 37 1/12 THALER (Doppelgroschen)

Silver **Ruler:** Bernhard **Subject:** Death of Bernhard I
Reverse: 6-line inscription

Date	Mintage	VG	F	VF	XF	Unc
1706	—	22.00	45.00	90.00	140	—

KM# 42 1/12 THALER (Doppelgroschen)

Silver **Ruler:** Ernst Ludwig I **Subject:** Marriage of Ernst Ludwig I and Dorothea Maria of Sase-Gotha-Altenburg **Obverse:** 2 adjacent busts facing right **Reverse:** Value, date and initials
Rev. Legend: 12/EINEN/THALER **Note:** Varieties exist.

Date	Mintage	VG	F	VF	XF	Unc
1714 HMO	—	35.00	75.00	150	225	—
1714 HEA	—	35.00	75.00	150	225	—
1714 PFC	—	35.00	75.00	150	225	—

KM# 43 1/12 THALER (Doppelgroschen)

Silver **Ruler:** Ernst Ludwig I **Obverse:** Busts left **Note:** Varieties exist.

Date	Mintage	VG	F	VF	XF	Unc
1714 HMO	—	65.00	120	225	350	—
1714 CW/HMO	—	65.00	120	225	350	—

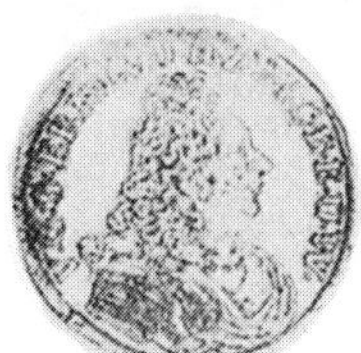

KM# 45 1/12 THALER (Doppelgroschen)

Silver **Ruler:** Ernst Ludwig I **Subject:** Reformation Bicentennial
Obverse: Bust right **Reverse:** Value, initials, legend contains date in chronogram **Rev. Legend:** 12/EINEN/THALER

Date	Mintage	VG	F	VF	XF	Unc
1717 HMO	—	60.00	100	200	325	—

KM# 46 1/4 THALER

Silver **Ruler:** Ernst Ludwig I **Subject:** Reformation Bicentennial
Obverse: Draped bust right within inner circle **Reverse:** Crowned arms within inner circle

Date	Mintage	VG	F	VF	XF	Unc
1717	—	150	250	400	650	—

TRADE COINAGE

KM# 44 DUCAT

3.5000 g., 0.9860 Gold 0.1109 oz. AGW **Ruler:** Ernst Ludwig I
Subject: Wedding of the Duke **Obverse:** Conjoined busts of Duke and Duchess, date in chronogram **Reverse:** Crown above 2 shields of arms

Date	Mintage	VG	F	VF	XF	Unc
1714	—	350	650	1,200	2,000	—

KM# 47 DUCAT

3.5000 g., 0.9860 Gold 0.1109 oz. AGW **Ruler:** Ernst Ludwig I
Subject: Bicentennial of the Reformation **Obverse:** Bust right
Reverse: Crowned arms

Date	Mintage	VG	F	VF	XF	Unc
1717	—	350	650	1,200	2,000	—

KM# 48 DUCAT

3.5000 g., 0.9860 Gold 0.1109 oz. AGW **Ruler:** Ernst Ludwig I
Subject: Bicentennial of the Reformation **Reverse:** Variation of legend, date below arms

Date	Mintage	VG	F	VF	XF	Unc
1717	—	500	850	1,450	2,250	—

KM# 85 DUCAT

3.5000 g., 0.9860 Gold 0.1109 oz. AGW **Ruler:** August Friedrich Karl alone as Karl **Subject:** Marriage of Karl and Louise
Obverse: Crowned monogram, inscription below
Reverse: Inscription

Date	Mintage	VG	F	VF	XF	Unc
1780	—	250	500	900	1,500	—

KM# 50 2 DUCAT

7.0000 g., 0.9860 Gold 0.2219 oz. AGW **Ruler:** Ernst Ludwig I
Subject: Bicentennial of the Reformation **Obverse:** Bust right within inner circle **Reverse:** Crowned arms within inner circle

Date	Mintage	VG	F	VF	XF	Unc
1717 Rare	—	—	—	—	—	—

KM# 49 2 DUCAT

7.0000 g., 0.9860 Gold 0.2219 oz. AGW **Ruler:** Ernst Ludwig I
Note: Similar to 1 Ducat, KM#48.

Date	Mintage	VG	F	VF	XF	Unc
1717 W Rare	—	—	—	—	—	—

KM# 86 2 DUCAT

7.0000 g., 0.9860 Gold 0.2219 oz. AGW **Ruler:** August Friedrich Karl alone as Karl **Subject:** Marriage of Karl and Louise
Obverse: Cupids above two shields **Reverse:** Inscription

Date	Mintage	VG	F	VF	XF	Unc
1780	—	500	1,000	2,000	3,000	—

PATTERNS

Including off metal strikes

KM#	Date	Mintage	Identification	Mkt Val
Pn2	1717	—	Ducat. Silver. KM#48.	475
Pn3	1717	—	2 Ducat. Silver. KM#49.	275
Pn4	1717	—	2 Ducat. Tin. KM#49.	225
Pn5	1744	—	Heller. Silver. KM#61.	—
Pn6	1780	—	Ducat. Copper. KM#85.	—
	Note: Rare			
Pn7	1780	—	Ducat. Silver. KM#85.	150
Pn8	1780	—	2 Ducat. Silver. KM#86.	125

SAXE-SAALFELD

As a branch of the Ernestine Saxon house, Saxe-Saalfeld was purchased from Meissen-Thuringia in 1389. It was created as a duchy for Johann Ernst VIII, 7th son of Ernst the Pious of Saxe-Gotha. Coburg was added to the holdings in 1735 and thereafter the dukes took the name of Saxe-Coburg-Saalfeld. Later coinage is listed there.

RULERS

Johann Ernst VIII, 1680-1729
Christian Ernst and Franz Josias, 1729-1745
Christian Ernst, 1729-1745

MINT OFFICIALS' INITIALS

Initials	Date	Name
ICS	Ca. 1712	Johann Christian von Selle
E, IME	1723-31	Johann Michael Edler
GHE	1732-54	Georg Hieronymus Eberhard

DUCHY

REGULAR COINAGE

DAV# 2735 THALER

Silver **Ruler:** Johann Ernst VIII **Obverse:** Bust right, helmet in front **Reverse:** Helmeted shield-shaped arms

Date	Mintage	VG	F	VF	XF	Unc
1712 ICS 3 known	—	—	—	3,500	—	—

DAV# 2736 THALER

Silver **Ruler:** Johann Ernst VIII **Obverse:** Bust right, helmet in front **Reverse:** Sun above city view, Roman numeral date in exergue **Note:** Mining Thaler.

Date	Mintage	VG	F	VF	XF	Unc
ND(1712)	—	450	900	1,650	2,750	—
ND(1714)	—	450	900	1,650	2,750	—

DAV# A2737 THALER

Silver **Ruler:** Johann Ernst VIII **Obverse:** Altered bust

Date	Mintage	VG	F	VF	XF	Unc
1715	—	450	900	1,650	2,750	—
1716	—	450	900	1,650	2,750	—
1717	—	—	—	—	—	—

DAV# 2740 THALER

Silver **Ruler:** Johann Ernst VIII **Obverse:** Bust in armor right
Reverse: Helmeted arms divide date below, I. -ME above
Note: Varieties exist.

Date	Mintage	F	VF	XF	Unc
1717	—	350	600	1,000	1,750
1720	—	350	600	1,000	1,750
1722	—	350	600	1,000	1,750
1723	—	350	600	1,000	1,750
1724	—	350	600	1,000	1,750

DAV# 2738 THALER

Silver **Ruler:** Johann Ernst VIII **Subject:** Bicentennial of the Reformation **Obverse:** Bust with long hair right **Obv. Legend:** IVBILAEVM - SAALFEL - DIA AGIT IN - LAETITIA **Reverse:** Martin Luther facing, head divides date **Rev. Legend:** DOGMATA LVTHERI STABVNT IN SECVLA

Date	Mintage	F	VF	XF	Unc
1717	—	375	750	1,350	2,250

DAV# 2738A THALER

Silver **Ruler:** Johann Ernst VIII **Subject:** Bicentennial of the Reformation **Obverse:** Without mantle and different width bust **Obv. Legend:** IVBILAEVM - SAALFEL - DIA AGIT IN - LAETITIA **Reverse:** Martin Luther facing, head divides date **Rev. Legend:** DOGMATA LVTHERI STABVNT IN SECVLA

Date	Mintage	F	VF	XF	Unc
1717	—	375	750	1,350	2,250

DAV# 2739 THALER

Silver **Ruler:** Johann Ernst VIII **Subject:** Bicentennial of the Reformation **Obverse:** Bust with short hair right **Obv. Legend:** IVBILAEVM - SAALFEL - DIA AGIT IN - LAETITIA **Reverse:** Bust of Luther is larger and coarser **Rev. Legend:** DOGMATA LVTHERI STABVNT IN SECVLA

Date	Mintage	F	VF	XF	Unc
1717	—	375	750	1,350	2,250

DAV# 2739A THALER

Silver **Ruler:** Johann Ernst VIII **Subject:** Bicentennial of the Reformation **Obverse:** Narrower bust of the Duke and the casque nearer the body **Obv. Legend:** IVBILAEVM - SAALFEL - IEA AGIT IN - LAETITIA **Reverse:** Martin Luther divides 1517 date, 1717 date in chronogram **Rev. Legend:** DOGMATA LVTHERI STABVNT IN SECVLA

Date	Mintage	F	VF	XF	Unc
1717	—	375	750	1,350	2,250

DAV# 2742 THALER

Silver **Ruler:** Johann Ernst VIII **Obverse:** Armored bust right **Obv. Legend:** D: G: IOHAN - NES ERNES - TVS VIII • DVX - SAXONIAE **Reverse:** Sun above city view **Rev. Legend:** SOLE. ET. SALE., MDCCXX below **Note:** Varieties exist.

Date	Mintage	F	VF	XF	Unc
1720	—	375	750	1,350	2,250

DAV# 2743 THALER

Silver **Ruler:** Johann Ernst VIII **Obverse:** Bust with short hair right

Date	Mintage	F	VF	XF	Unc
1720	—	500	900	1,500	2,500

DAV# 2744 THALER

Silver **Ruler:** Johann Ernst VIII **Obverse:** Thin bust right **Reverse:** Different city view, sun above crossed hammers and initials divide date **Note:** Varieties exist.

Date	Mintage	F	VF	XF	Unc
1722 IME Rare	—	—	—	—	—

DAV# 2745 THALER

Silver **Ruler:** Johann Ernst VIII **Obverse:** Larger bust **Reverse:** Different city view

Date	Mintage	F	VF	XF	Unc
1723 IME	—	1,200	2,000	3,250	—

DAV# 2746 THALER

Silver **Ruler:** Johann Ernst VIII **Obverse:** Plainer armor on bust right **Obv. Legend:** D: G: IOHAN - NES • ERNES - TVS: VIII • DVX - SAXONIÆ **Reverse:** 4 crowned monograms, VIII between, date divided by crowns

Date	Mintage	F	VF	XF	Unc
1724 IME 4 known	—	—	—	4,000	—

DAV# 2747 THALER

Silver **Ruler:** Johann Ernst VIII **Obverse:** Changed bust **Reverse:** Helmeted arms separate date below

Date	Mintage	F	VF	XF	Unc
1724 IME	—	750	1,250	2,000	3,250
1725 IME	—	750	1,250	2,000	3,250
1726 IME	—	750	1,250	2,000	3,250
1727 IME	—	750	1,250	2,000	3,250
1728 IME	—	750	1,250	2,000	3,250

DAV# 2748 THALER

Silver **Ruler:** Johann Ernst VIII **Obverse:** Sun above city view, crossed hammers in frame separate date below

Date	Mintage	F	VF	XF	Unc
1725 IME	—	750	1,250	2,000	3,250
1726 IME	—	750	1,250	2,000	3,250
1727 IME	—	750	1,250	2,000	3,250

DAV# 2749 THALER

Silver **Ruler:** Johann Ernst VIII **Subject:** Death of Johann Ernst VIII **Obverse:** 3-line inscription in exergue **Obv. Legend:** D • G • IOHANN • ERNEST - VIII D • SAX • I • C • M • A • & W •, in exergue; NAT. 22 AVG 1658. D. 17 DEC./1729 AET. 71 AN. MENS./15 DIES **Reverse:** Sarcophagus with 6-line inscription **Rev. Legend:** COELO REDVX INTAMINATIX FVLGET HONORIBVS., inscription: PARENTI OPTIMO/PRINCIPI PIO IUSTO CLEM/FILIALIS PIETAS/CONCORD. FRATRUM/MONUMENTUM/P.P.

Date	Mintage	F	VF	XF	Unc
1729	—	225	450	800	1,550

DAV# 2737 2 THALER

Silver **Ruler:** Johann Ernst VIII **Note:** Similar to Thaler, Dav. #A2737.

Date	Mintage	VG	F	VF	XF	Unc
1714	—	—	—	—	—	—

DAV# 2741 2 THALER

Silver **Ruler:** Johann Ernst VIII **Obverse:** Armored bust right **Reverse:** Sun above city view **Note:** Similar to Thaler, Dav. #2742.

Date	Mintage	VG	F	VF	XF	Unc
1720 Rare	—	—	—	—	—	—

TRADE COINAGE

FR# 3002 1/4 DUCAT

0.8750 g., 0.9860 Gold 0.0277 oz. AGW **Ruler:** Johann Ernst VIII **Obverse:** Armored bust of Johann Ernst VIII right **Reverse:** Crowned arms in branches with date divided below

Date	Mintage	VG	F	VF	XF	Unc
1725	—	125	250	475	800	—
1726	—	125	250	475	800	—
1727	—	—	—	—	—	—
1728	—	125	250	475	800	—

FR# 3001 1/2 DUCAT

1.7500 g., 0.9860 Gold 0.0555 oz. AGW **Ruler:** Johann Ernst VIII **Obverse:** Armored bust right **Reverse:** Crowned arms within branches

Date	Mintage	VG	F	VF	XF	Unc
1725	—	175	350	750	1,250	—
1726	—	175	350	750	1,250	—
1727	—	175	350	750	1,250	—
1728	—	175	350	750	1,250	—

FR# 3000 DUCAT

3.5000 g., 0.9860 Gold 0.1109 oz. AGW **Ruler:** Johann Ernst VIII **Obverse:** Young armored bust right in inner circle **Reverse:** Elaborate arms topped by 6 helmets, date divided below

Date	Mintage	VG	F	VF	XF	Unc
1698	—	350	700	1,450	2,500	—
1714	—	300	650	1,350	2,250	—
1715	—	300	650	1,350	2,250	—
1716	—	300	650	1,350	2,250	—

FR# 3004 DUCAT

3.5000 g., 0.9860 Gold 0.1109 oz. AGW **Ruler:** Johann Ernst VIII **Subject:** 200th Anniversary of the Reformation **Obverse:** Armored bust right **Reverse:** Bust of Martin Luther divides date 1517, date in chronogram

Date	Mintage	VG	F	VF	XF	Unc
ND(1717)	—	220	450	900	1,650	—

FR# 3005 DUCAT

3.5000 g., 0.9860 Gold 0.1109 oz. AGW **Ruler:** Johann Ernst VIII **Obverse:** Bust right **Reverse:** City view of Reichmansdorf

Date	Mintage	VG	F	VF	XF	Unc
1717	—	400	800	1,600	2,750	—
1719	—	400	800	1,600	2,750	—
1721	—	400	800	1,600	2,750	—
1722 E	—	400	800	1,600	2,750	—
1723	—	400	800	1,600	2,750	—
1726 IME	—	400	800	1,600	2,750	—
1727 IME	—	400	800	1,600	2,750	—
1727	—	400	800	1,600	2,750	—
1728 IME	—	400	800	1,600	2,750	—
1728 GHE	—	400	800	1,600	2,750	—

FR# A3004 DUCAT

3.5000 g., 0.9860 Gold 0.1109 oz. AGW **Ruler:** Johann Ernst VIII **Subject:** 200th Anniversary of the Reformation **Obverse:** Armored bust right **Reverse:** Bust of Martin Luther also divides IM-E

Date	Mintage	VG	F	VF	XF	Unc
ND(1717) IME	—	220	450	900	1,650	—

FR# B3004 DUCAT

3.5000 g., 0.9860 Gold 0.1109 oz. AGW **Ruler:** Johann Ernst VIII **Subject:** 200th Anniversary of the Reformation **Obverse:** Bust wearing wig right **Reverse:** Martin Luther facing divides date

Date	Mintage	VG	F	VF	XF	Unc
ND(1717)	—	175	350	750	1,350	—

FR# C3004 DUCAT

3.5000 g., 0.9860 Gold 0.1109 oz. AGW **Ruler:** Johann Ernst VIII **Subject:** 200th Anniversary of the Reformation **Obverse:** Bust wearing wig with left hand raised on helmet

Date	Mintage	VG	F	VF	XF	Unc
ND(1717)	—	175	350	750	1,350	—

FR# A3000 DUCAT

3.5000 g., 0.9860 Gold 0.1109 oz. AGW **Ruler:** Johann Ernst VIII **Reverse:** Elaborate arms topped by 6 helmets, date divided below

Date	Mintage	VG	F	VF	XF	Unc
1720	—	300	650	1,350	2,250	—
1721	—	300	650	1,350	2,250	—
1722	—	300	650	1,350	2,250	—
1723	—	300	650	1,350	2,250	—
1724	—	300	650	1,350	2,250	—
1725	—	300	650	1,350	2,250	—
1727	—	300	650	1,350	2,250	—
1728	—	300	650	1,350	2,250	—

FR# 3003 2 DUCAT

7.0000 g., 0.9860 Gold 0.2219 oz. AGW **Ruler:** Johann Ernst VIII **Subject:** 200th Anniversary of the Reformation **Obverse:** Armored bust right in inner circle **Reverse:** Facing bust of Martin Luther divides date 15 17, 1717 date in chronogram **Note:** Struck with Ducat dies, FR#3004.

Date	Mintage	VG	F	VF	XF	Unc
ND(1717)	—	700	1,400	2,750	4,750	—

SAXE-WEIMAR

(Sachsen-Neu-Weimar)

Founded from Saxe-Middle-Weimar in 1640, the division ended the joint rule of the duchy begun by all eight sons of Johann III. In 1662, the four sons of Wilhelm IV divided their inheritance into the lines of Saxe-(New)-Weimar, Saxe-Eisenach, Saxe-Marksuhl and Saxe-Jena. When the line in Eisenach became extinct in 1741, that territory and titles reverted to Weimar, which became known from that time on as Saxe-Weimar-Eisenach

RULERS

Wilhelm Ernst, 1683-1728
Johann Ernst III (VI), 1683-1707
Ernst August I, 1728-1741 (d.1748)

DUCHY

STANDARD COINAGE

DAV# 2754 THALER

Silver **Ruler:** Wilhelm Ernst **Obverse:** Different bust right **Obv. Legend:** WILH: ERNESTVS I. D:G. DVX SAX. I. C. M. A. ET W. **Reverse:** Different view of Weimar Castle, long rays from sun, Roman numeral date

Date	Mintage	VG	F	VF	XF	Unc
ND(1717)	—	300	550	900	1,550	—

DAV# 2755 THALER

Silver **Ruler:** Wilhelm Ernst **Subject:** Bicentennial of the Reformation **Obverse:** Candle on book on table with arms, hand above lighting it and winds trying to blow it out **Obv. Legend:** SIE DAEMPFFEN NICHT DES WORTES LICHT., in inner row; A DEO ACCENSVM QVIS SVPERABIT: **Reverse:** Seven-line inscription, Roman numeral date **Rev. Legend:** IN MEMORI/AM IUBILAEI/SECUNDI EVAN/GELICI VINA/RIAE CELE/BRATI XXXI/OCT.MDCCXVII

Date	Mintage	VG	F	VF	XF	Unc
ND(1717)	—	300	550	900	1,550	—

DAV# 2753 THALER

Silver **Ruler:** Wilhelm Ernst **Subject:** Duke Wilhelm Ernst's Birthday and His Pious Foundations **Note:** Similar to 1/4 Thaler with Roman numeral date; four-line inscription below.

Date	Mintage	VG	F	VF	XF	Unc
ND(1717)	—	300	550	900	1,550	—

FR# 3030 DUCAT

3.5000 g., 0.9860 Gold 0.1109 oz. AGW **Ruler:** Wilhelm Ernst **Subject:** Duke Wilhelm Ernst's Birthday and His Pious Foundations **Obverse:** Bust right in inner circle **Reverse:** Weimar Castle

Date	Mintage	VG	F	VF	XF	Unc
1717	—	400	900	1,650	2,750	—

FR# 3032 DUCAT

3.5000 g., 0.9860 Gold 0.1109 oz. AGW **Ruler:** Wilhelm Ernst **Subject:** Bicentennial of the Reformation **Obverse:** Open book and candle on table **Reverse:** Six-line inscription, Roman numeral date below

Date	Mintage	VG	F	VF	XF	Unc
ND(1717)	—	275	650	1,250	2,200	—

SAXE-WEIMAR, MIDDLE

DUCHY

TRADE COINAGE

FR# 3035 DUCAT

3.5000 g., 0.9860 Gold 0.1109 oz. AGW **Obverse:** Bust of Ernst August with military trophies in background **Reverse:** Pastorial view with sheep and rosebush

Date	Mintage	VG	F	VF	XF	Unc
ND (before 1741)	—	350	750	1,500	2,500	—

FR# 3031 2 DUCAT

7.0000 g., 0.9860 Gold 0.2219 oz. AGW **Subject:** Bicentennial of the Reformation

Date	Mintage	VG	F	VF	XF	Unc
1717	—	700	1,350	2,500	4,500	—

SAXE-WEIMAR-EISENACH

(Sachsen-Weimar-Eisenach)

When the death of the duke of Saxe-Eisenach in 1741 heralded the extinction of that line, its possessions reverted to Saxe-Weimar, which henceforth was known as Saxe-Weimar-Eisenach. Because of the strong role played by the duke during the Napoleonic Wars, Saxe-Weimar-Eisenach was raised to the rank of a grand duchy in 1814 and granted the territory of Neustadt, taken from Saxony. The last grand duke abdicated at the end of World War I.

RULERS

Ernst August I, 1741-1748
Ernst August II Konstantine, 1748-1758
under regency of Franz Josias of Saxe-Coburg-Saalfeld, regent in Weimar, 1748-1755 and Friedrich III of Saxe-Gotha-Altenburg, regent in Eisenach, 1748-1755
Karl August, 1758-1828 under regency of his mother, Anna Amalia of Brunswick, 1758-1775

MINT OFFICIALS' INITIALS

Initials	Date	Name
GHE	1740-54	Georg Hieronymus Eberhard, mintmaster in Saalfeld
IH	1750-54	Johann Heimreich, mintmaster in Eisenach
FS or S	1755-76	Friedrich Siegmund Schäfer, mintmaster in Eisenach
KL, K	1763-65	Johann Anton David Klinghammer, die-cutter
	1789-?	Johann Wolf Heinrich Stockmar, die-cutter in Ilmenau
(a)=lion or ILST, LS, LST, ST	1785-90	Johann Leonhard Stockmar, die-cutter
	1790-1835	Mintmaster in Saalfeld

DUCHY

REGULAR COINAGE

C# A1 HELLER

Copper **Ruler:** Ernst August II Konstantine **Obverse:** Crowned script FDS monogram. **Reverse:** Value, date. **Note:** Varieties exist. Prev. C#1 in Saxe-Eisenach.

Date	Mintage	Good	VG	F	VF	XF
1750	—	2.00	4.50	9.00	18.00	38.00
1751	—	2.00	4.50	9.00	18.00	38.00
1752	—	2.00	4.50	9.00	18.00	38.00
1753	—	2.00	4.50	9.00	18.00	38.00
1754	—	2.00	4.50	9.00	18.00	38.00
1755	—	2.00	4.50	9.00	18.00	38.00

C# 1.2 HELLER

Copper **Ruler:** Ernst August II Konstantine **Obverse:** Crowned ornate FDS monogram **Reverse:** Five-line inscription with date **Rev. Inscription:** I/HELLER/F.S.E.OBERV./L.MUNTZ/(date) **Note:** Coinage for Eisenach.

Date	Mintage	VG	F	VF	XF	Unc
1750	—	7.50	15.00	25.00	45.00	—
1751	—	7.50	15.00	25.00	45.00	—
1752	—	7.50	15.00	25.00	45.00	—
1753	—	7.50	15.00	25.00	45.00	—
1754	—	7.50	15.00	25.00	45.00	—
1755	—	7.50	15.00	25.00	45.00	—

C# 1.1 HELLER

Copper **Ruler:** Ernst August II Konstantine **Obverse:** Crowned script FJDS monogram **Reverse:** Five-line inscription with date **Rev. Inscription:** I/HELLER/J.V./WEIMAR/(date) **Note:** Coinage for Weimar.

Date	Mintage	VG	F	VF	XF	Unc
1750	—	7.50	15.00	25.00	45.00	—
1751	—	7.50	15.00	25.00	45.00	—
1752	—	7.50	15.00	25.00	45.00	—
1753	—	7.50	15.00	25.00	45.00	—
1754	—	7.50	15.00	25.00	45.00	—

C# 9 HELLER

Copper **Obverse:** Crowned monogram **Reverse:** Value, date **Note:** Coinage for Weimar.

Date	Mintage	VG	F	VF	XF	Unc
1756	—	3.50	8.00	15.00	30.00	—
1757	—	3.50	8.00	15.00	30.00	—
1758	—	3.50	8.00	15.00	30.00	—

C# 31 HELLER

Copper **Obverse:** Crowned Saxon arms **Reverse:** Value and date

Date	Mintage	VG	F	VF	XF	Unc
1760	—	4.00	9.00	16.00	35.00	—

C# 55 HELLER

Copper **Obverse:** Similar to C#55b but L. ST. below arms **Reverse:** Value, date

Date	Mintage	F	VF	XF	Unc
1790 LST	—	2.50	7.00	20.00	65.00

C# 55a HELLER

Copper **Obverse:** Similar to C#55b but but lion below arms **Reverse:** Value, date

Date	Mintage	F	VF	XF	Unc
1791 (a)	—	2.50	7.00	20.00	65.00

C# 55b HELLER

Copper **Obverse:** Arms **Reverse:** Value and date

Date	Mintage	F	VF	XF	Unc
1794	—	2.50	7.00	20.00	65.00

C# A3 PFENNIG

Copper **Ruler:** Ernst August II Konstantine **Rev. Legend:** GUTER.... **Note:** Guter Pfennig. Previously listed as C#3 in Saxe-Eisenach.

Date	Mintage	Good	VG	F	VF	XF
1750	—	2.00	5.00	10.00	20.00	40.00
1751	—	2.00	5.00	10.00	20.00	40.00
1752	—	2.00	5.00	10.00	20.00	40.00
1753	—	2.00	5.00	10.00	20.00	40.00
1754	—	2.00	5.00	10.00	20.00	40.00
1755	—	2.00	5.00	10.00	20.00	40.00

C# A2 PFENNIG

Copper **Ruler:** Ernst August II Konstantine **Obverse:** Crowned script FDS monogram **Reverse:** Value, date **Note:** Prev. C#2 in Saxe-Eisenach.

Date	Mintage	Good	VG	F	VF	XF
1750	—	2.00	5.00	10.00	20.00	40.00
1751	—	2.00	5.00	10.00	20.00	40.00
1752	—	2.00	5.00	10.00	20.00	40.00
1753	—	2.00	5.00	10.00	20.00	40.00
1754	—	2.00	5.00	10.00	20.00	40.00
1755	—	2.00	5.00	10.00	20.00	40.00

C# 2 PFENNIG

Copper **Obverse:** Crowned script FIDS monogram **Reverse:** Value, date

Date	Mintage	VG	F	VF	XF	Unc
1750	—	5.00	10.00	20.00	40.00	—
1751	—	5.00	10.00	20.00	40.00	—
1752	—	5.00	10.00	20.00	40.00	—
1753	—	5.00	10.00	20.00	40.00	—
1754	—	5.00	10.00	20.00	40.00	—
1755	—	5.00	10.00	20.00	40.00	—

Note: Legend varieties exist

C# 10 PFENNIG

Copper **Obverse:** Crowned monogram **Reverse:** Value, date

Date	Mintage	VG	F	VF	XF	Unc
1756	—	3.50	8.00	15.00	30.00	—
1757	—	3.50	8.00	15.00	30.00	—

C# 11 PFENNIG

Copper **Rev. Legend:** GUTER PFENNING ... **Note:** Guter Pfenning.

Date	Mintage	VG	F	VF	XF	Unc
1756	—	3.50	8.00	15.00	30.00	—
1757	—	3.50	8.00	15.00	30.00	—

C# 11a PFENNIG

Copper **Obverse:** Saxe-Eisenach C#2 **Reverse:** C#11 **Note:** Mule.

Date	Mintage	VG	F	VF	XF	Unc
1757	—	17.50	35.00	60.00	100	—

C# 32 PFENNIG

Copper **Obverse:** Crowned Saxon arms **Reverse:** Value and date

Date	Mintage	VG	F	VF	XF	Unc
1761	—	4.00	9.00	16.00	35.00	—
1762	—	4.00	9.00	16.00	35.00	—

C# 56 PFENNIG

Copper **Obverse:** Arms **Reverse:** Value, date

Date	Mintage	F	VF	XF	Unc
1790 L ST	—	3.00	8.00	20.00	60.00

C# 56a PFENNIG

Copper **Obverse:** Similar to C#56 but lion below arms **Reverse:** Value, date

Date	Mintage	F	VF	XF	Unc
1792	—	3.00	8.00	20.00	60.00

C# 56b PFENNIG

Copper **Obverse:** Similar to C#56 but without symbol below arms **Reverse:** Value, date

Date	Mintage	F	VF	XF	Unc
1796	—	3.00	8.00	20.00	60.00

C# 56c PFENNIG

Copper **Obverse:** Arms **Reverse:** Value and date; line below date

Date	Mintage	F	VF	XF	Unc
1799	—	3.00	8.00	20.00	60.00
1801	—	3.00	8.00	20.00	60.00
1801	—	3.00	8.00	20.00	60.00
1803	—	3.00	8.00	20.00	60.00
1807	30,000	3.00	8.00	20.00	60.00

C# 3 1-1/2 PFENNIG

Copper **Note:** Similar to 2 Pfenning, C#4.

Date	Mintage	VG	F	VF	XF	Unc
1750	—	8.00	15.00	25.00	45.00	—

C# A4 1-1/2 PFENNIG

Copper **Ruler:** Ernst August II Konstantine **Obverse:** Crowned script FDS monogram. **Reverse:** Value, date. **Rev. Legend:** GUTER... **Note:** Prev. C#4 in Saxe-Eisenach.

Date	Mintage	Good	VG	F	VF	XF
1751	—	2.50	6.00	12.00	25.00	45.00
1752	—	2.50	6.00	12.00	25.00	45.00
1753	—	2.50	6.00	12.00	25.00	45.00

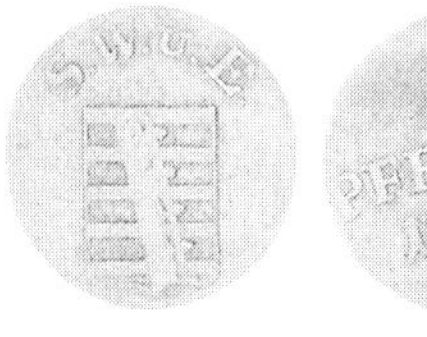

C# 57 1-1/2 PFENNIG

Copper **Obverse:** Arms **Reverse:** Value and date

Date	Mintage	F	VF	XF	Unc
1799	—	10.00	20.00	35.00	125
1807	34,000	10.00	20.00	35.00	125

C# A5 2 PFENNIG

Copper **Ruler:** Ernst August II Konstantine **Obverse:** Crowned script FDS monogram. **Note:** Prev. C#5 in Saxe-Eisenach.

Date	Mintage	Good	VG	F	VF	XF
1750	—	2.50	6.00	12.00	25.00	45.00
1751	—	2.50	6.00	12.00	25.00	45.00
1755	—	2.50	6.00	12.00	25.00	45.00

C# 4 2 PFENNIG

Copper **Obverse:** Arms **Reverse:** Value, date

Date	Mintage	VG	F	VF	XF	Unc
1750	—	8.00	15.00	25.00	45.00	—
1752	—	8.00	15.00	25.00	45.00	—

C# 13 2 PFENNIG

Copper **Rev. Legend:** GUTE . . . **Note:** Gute 2 Pfenning.

Date	Mintage	VG	F	VF	XF	Unc
1756	—	4.00	9.00	16.00	40.00	—
1757	—	4.00	9.00	16.00	40.00	—

C# 12 2 PFENNIG

Copper **Note:** Similar to Pfenning, C#10.

Date	Mintage	VG	F	VF	XF	Unc
1756	—	4.00	8.00	15.00	35.00	—
1757	—	4.00	8.00	15.00	35.00	—

C# 33 2 PFENNIG

Copper **Obverse:** Crowned arms **Reverse:** Value, date

Date	Mintage	VG	F	VF	XF	Unc
1760 FS	—	3.00	6.00	12.00	30.00	—

C# 58 2 PFENNIG

Copper **Obverse:** Arms **Reverse:** Value, date

Date	Mintage	F	VF	XF	Unc
1790	—	7.00	15.00	30.00	125
1792	—	7.00	15.00	30.00	125

C# 58a 2 PFENNIG

Copper **Obverse:** Shield with straight sides, S.W.U.E. above **Reverse:** Value, date

Date	Mintage	F	VF	XF	Unc
1792	—	7.00	15.00	30.00	125
1796	—	7.00	15.00	30.00	125

C# 58b 2 PFENNIG

Copper **Obverse:** Small U in S.W.U.E., leaf edge **Reverse:** Value, date

Date	Mintage	F	VF	XF	Unc
1799	—	7.00	15.00	30.00	125

C# A6 3 PFENNIG

Billon **Ruler:** Ernst August II Konstantine **Obverse:** Crowned script FDS monogram. **Reverse:** Imperial orb with value 3 dividing date. **Note:** Prev. C#6 in Saxe-Eisenach.

Date	Mintage	Good	VG	F	VF	XF
1751	—	6.00	15.00	25.00	50.00	100

C# A7 3 PFENNIG

Billon **Ruler:** Ernst August II Konstantine **Obverse:** Script F in crowned cartouche **Note:** Prev. C#7 in Saxe-Eisenach.

Date	Mintage	Good	VG	F	VF	XF
1751 IH	—	4.00	10.00	20.00	40.00	75.00
1752 IH	—	4.00	10.00	20.00	40.00	75.00
1753 IH	—	4.00	10.00	20.00	40.00	75.00
1754 IH	—	4.00	10.00	20.00	40.00	75.00
1755 FS	—	4.00	10.00	20.00	40.00	75.00

C# 5 3 PFENNIG

Billon **Obverse:** FI monogram in crowned cartouche **Reverse:** Value: 3 on imperial orb in cartouche dividing date

Date	Mintage	VG	F	VF	XF	Unc
1751 GHE	—	10.00	18.00	35.00	65.00	—
1753 GHE	—	10.00	18.00	35.00	65.00	—

C# 14 3 PFENNIG

Billon **Obverse:** Crowned script EAC monogram **Reverse:** Value: 3 on imperial orb, date

Date	Mintage	VG	F	VF	XF	Unc
1756 FS	—	8.00	15.00	28.00	55.00	—
1757 FS FS	—	8.00	15.00	28.00	55.00	—
1758 FS	—	8.00	15.00	28.00	55.00	—

Note: Varieties exist

C# 34 3 PFENNIG

Copper **Obverse:** Crowned Saxon arms **Reverse:** Value, date

Date	Mintage	VG	F	VF	XF	Unc
1760 FS	—	3.00	7.00	15.00	30.00	—
1761 FS	—	3.00	7.00	15.00	30.00	—
1762 FS	—	3.00	7.00	15.00	30.00	—

C# 35 3 PFENNIG

Billon **Obverse:** Crowned arms **Reverse:** Value on orb

Date	Mintage	VG	F	VF	XF	Unc
1760 FS	—	4.00	9.00	18.00	35.00	—

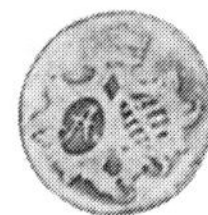

C# 36 3 PFENNIG

Billon **Obverse:** 2 shields of arms **Reverse:** Value on orb divides date

Date	Mintage	VG	F	VF	XF	Unc
1763 FS	—	4.00	9.00	18.00	35.00	—
1764 FS	—	4.00	9.00	18.00	35.00	—

C# 59 3 PFENNIG

Copper **Obverse:** Saxon arms; L.S.T. below; S.W.U.E. above **Reverse:** Value above date; rosette below; without final E in value

Date	Mintage	F	VF	XF	Unc
1791	—	3.00	7.00	20.00	65.00

C# 59a 3 PFENNIG

Copper **Obverse:** Lion below arms **Reverse:** Value, date

Date	Mintage	F	VF	XF	Unc
1792	—	3.00	7.00	20.00	65.00

C# 59b 3 PFENNIG

Copper **Obverse:** Without symbol below arms **Reverse:** Value, date

Date	Mintage	F	VF	XF	Unc
1794	—	3.00	7.00	20.00	65.00

C# 59c 3 PFENNIG

Copper **Obverse:** Arms **Reverse:** Value and date **Edge:** Leaf

Date	Mintage	F	VF	XF	Unc
1799	—	3.00	7.00	20.00	65.00
1807	49,000	5.00	10.00	30.00	100
1807	49,000	5.00	10.00	30.00	100

C# A8 6 PFENNIG

Billon **Ruler:** Ernst August II Konstantine **Obverse:** Crowned arms in cartouche **Reverse:** Imperial orb with value VI dividing date **Note:** Prev. C#8 in Saxe-Eisenach.

Date	Mintage	Good	VG	F	VF	XF
1751 IH	—	3.50	8.00	15.00	30.00	65.00
1752 IH	—	3.50	8.00	15.00	30.00	65.00
1753 IH	—	3.50	8.00	15.00	30.00	65.00
1754 IH	—	3.50	8.00	15.00	30.00	65.00
1755 FS	—	3.50	8.00	15.00	30.00	65.00

C# 6 6 PFENNIG

Billon **Obverse:** FI monogram in crowned baroque frame **Reverse:** Value: VI on imperial orb; date

Date	Mintage	VG	F	VF	XF	Unc
1751 GHE	—	18.00	30.00	55.00	100	—
1752 GHE	—	10.00	17.50	35.00	65.00	—
1754 GHE	—	10.00	17.50	35.00	65.00	—

C# 15 6 PFENNIG

Billon **Obverse:** Crowned monogram **Reverse:** Value within imperial orb

Date	Mintage	VG	F	VF	XF	Unc
1756 FS	—	12.50	25.00	40.00	70.00	—
1757 FS	—	12.50	25.00	40.00	70.00	—
1758 FS	—	12.50	25.00	40.00	70.00	—

C# 37 6 PFENNIG

Billon **Obverse:** ADS monogram **Reverse:** Value on orb divides date

Date	Mintage	VG	F	VF	XF	Unc
1759 FS	—	6.00	12.00	30.00	60.00	—
1760 FS	—	6.00	12.00	30.00	60.00	—

C# 38 6 PFENNIG

Billon **Ruler:** Karl August **Obverse:** Crowned and mantled manifold Saxon arms **Reverse:** Imperial orb with value 'VI' divides date and mintmaster's initials

Date	Mintage	VG	F	VF	XF	Unc
1760 FS	—	4.00	9.00	22.00	50.00	—

C# 39 6 PFENNIG

Billon **Obverse:** 2 shields of arms

Date	Mintage	VG	F	VF	XF	Unc
1763 FS	—	3.00	8.00	20.00	45.00	—
1764 FS	—	3.00	8.00	20.00	45.00	—

C# 18 4 GROSCHEN (1/6 Reichsthaler)

Silver **Obverse:** EAC monogram in crowned cartouche, value **Reverse:** Crowned arms in cartouche, date

Date	Mintage	VG	F	VF	XF	Unc
1756 FS	—	40.00	80.00	165	278	—

C# 67 1/48 THALER

1.0600 g., 0.2290 Silver 0.0078 oz. ASW **Obverse:** Arms **Reverse:** Value and date

Date	Mintage	F	VF	XF	Unc
1794	—	3.00	6.00	15.00	50.00
1796	—	3.00	6.00	15.00	50.00
1799	—	3.00	6.00	15.00	50.00
1801	—	3.00	6.00	15.00	50.00
1801	—	3.00	6.00	15.00	50.00
1804	—	3.00	6.00	15.00	50.00
1808	286,000	3.00	6.00	15.00	50.00
1810	327,000	3.00	6.00	15.00	50.00
1813	—	3.00	6.00	15.00	50.00
1814	—	3.00	6.00	15.00	50.00

C# 7 1/24 THALER

2.1200 g., 0.2290 Silver 0.0156 oz. ASW **Obverse:** FI monogram in crowned baroque frame **Reverse:** Value, date **Note:** Varieties exist.

Date	Mintage	VG	F	VF	XF	Unc
1751 GHE	—	10.00	20.00	40.00	75.00	—
1753 GHE	—	10.00	20.00	40.00	75.00	—

C# A9 1/24 THALER

Billon **Ruler:** Ernst August II Konstantine **Obverse:** Crowned arms in cartouche **Reverse:** Value, date **Note:** Prev. C#9 in Saxe-Eisenach.

Date	Mintage	Good	VG	F	VF	XF
1752	—	6.00	15.00	25.00	50.00	100

C# A9a.1 1/24 THALER

Billon **Ruler:** Ernst August II Konstantine **Reverse:** Imperial orb with 24 dividing date **Note:** Prev. C#9a.1 in Saxe-Eisenach. Varieties exist.

Date	Mintage	Good	VG	F	VF	XF
1753 IH	—	4.00	10.00	20.00	45.00	90.00
1754 IH	—	4.00	10.00	20.00	45.00	90.00

C# A9a.2 1/24 THALER

Billon **Ruler:** Ernst August II Konstantine **Obverse:** Crowned arms in shape of shield with rounded bottom **Note:** Prev. C#9a.2 in Saxe-Eisenach.

Date	Mintage	Good	VG	F	VF	XF
1755	—	9.00	20.00	35.00	70.00	125

C# A9b 1/24 THALER

Billon **Ruler:** Ernst August II Konstantine **Obverse:** C#A9a.1 **Reverse:** Saxe-Weimar-Eisenach C#16 **Note:** Prev. C#9b in Saxe-Eisenach.

Date	Mintage	Good	VG	F	VF	XF
1756 FS	—	9.00	20.00	40.00	75.00	135

C# 16 1/24 THALER

2.1200 g., 0.2290 Silver 0.0156 oz. ASW **Ruler:** Ernst August II Konstantine **Obverse:** Crowned arms **Reverse:** Value on imperial orb **Note:** Varieties exist.

Date	Mintage	VG	F	VF	XF	Unc
1756 FS	—	12.00	25.00	50.00	90.00	—
1757 FS	—	12.00	25.00	50.00	90.00	—

C# 40 1/24 THALER

2.1200 g., 0.2290 Silver 0.0156 oz. ASW **Obverse:** Script A and Saxon arms **Reverse:** Value and date

Date	Mintage	VG	F	VF	XF	Unc
1763 FS	—	3.00	7.00	15.00	45.00	—
1764 FS	—	3.00	7.00	15.00	45.00	—

C# 70 1/24 THALER

2.1200 g., 0.2290 Silver 0.0156 oz. ASW **Obverse:** Arms **Reverse:** Value and date

Date	Mintage	F	VF	XF	Unc
1794	—	4.00	9.00	28.00	100
1796	—	4.00	9.00	28.00	100
1799	—	4.00	9.00	28.00	100
1801	—	4.00	9.00	28.00	100
1801	—	4.00	9.00	28.00	100
1804	—	4.00	9.00	28.00	100
1808	199,000	4.00	9.00	28.00	100

Date	Mintage	F	VF	XF	Unc
1810	452,000	4.00	9.00	28.00	100
1813	—	4.00	9.00	28.00	100
1814	—	4.00	9.00	28.00	90.00

Note: Small letters

C# 8 1/12 THALER

Silver **Obverse:** FI monogram in crowned baroque frame **Reverse:** Value, date

Date	Mintage	VG	F	VF	XF	Unc
1753 GHE	—	15.00	25.00	55.00	100	—

C# 17 1/12 THALER

Silver **Ruler:** Ernst August II Konstantine **Obverse:** EAC monogram in crowned cartouche **Reverse:** Value in cartouche, date **Note:** Varieties exist.

Date	Mintage	VG	F	VF	XF	Unc
1756	—	25.00	45.00	90.00	165	—

C# 41 1/12 THALER

3.3400 g., 0.4370 Silver 0.0469 oz. ASW **Obverse:** Script A and Saxon arms **Reverse:** Value and date

Date	Mintage	VG	F	VF	XF	Unc
1763 FS	—	4.00	8.00	20.00	50.00	—
1764 FS	—	4.00	8.00	20.00	50.00	—

C# 42 1/6 THALER

5.3900 g., 0.5410 Silver 0.0937 oz. ASW **Obverse:** Crowned monogram **Reverse:** Crowned arms, value below

Date	Mintage	F	VF	XF	Unc
1763 FS	—	15.00	30.00	75.00	200

C# 42a 1/6 THALER

5.3900 g., 0.5410 Silver 0.0937 oz. ASW **Obverse:** Crowned monogram **Reverse:** Crowned arms, value below

Date	Mintage	F	VF	XF	Unc
1763 FS	—	15.00	30.00	75.00	200
1764 FS	—	15.00	30.00	75.00	200

C# A10 1/4 THALER

Silver **Ruler:** Ernst August II Konstantine **Subject:** 200th Anniversary of Religious Peace of Augsburg **Obverse:** Bust right **Reverse:** Genius with arms and altar, date **Note:** Prev. C#10 in Saxe-Eisenach.

Date	Mintage	Good	VG	F	VF	XF
1755	—	20.00	50.00	120	235	525

C# 19 1/3 THALER

Silver **Obverse:** EAC monogram in crowned cartouche on pedestal, value **Reverse:** Crowned arms in cartouche, date

Date	Mintage	VG	F	VF	XF	Unc
1756 FS	—	100	250	400	700	—

C# 43 1/3 THALER

7.0100 g., 0.8330 Silver 0.1877 oz. ASW **Ruler:** Karl August **Obverse:** Bust of Anna Amalia left **Reverse:** Crowned arms, value below

Date	Mintage	F	VF	XF	Unc
1763 FS	—	40.00	80.00	175	375
1764 FS	—	40.00	80.00	175	375
1765 FS	—	40.00	80.00	175	375

C# 20 1/2 THALER

Silver **Ruler:** Ernst August II Konstantine **Subject:** Ruler's Coming of Age **Obverse:** Crowned monogram **Reverse:** Crowned arms in baroque frame **Note:** Species 1/2 Thaler.

Date	Mintage	VG	F	VF	XF	Unc
1756	—	175	275	485	850	—

C# A11 2/3 THALER

Silver **Ruler:** Ernst August II Konstantine **Obverse:** Bust right **Reverse:** Crowned arms in baroque frame, value, date **Note:** Prev. C#11 in Saxe-Eisenach.

Date	Mintage	Good	VG	F	VF	XF
1755 FS	—	40.00	100	250	480	1,000

C# 21 2/3 THALER

Silver **Obverse:** Crowned double monogram **Reverse:** Crowned arms in cartouche, value

Date	Mintage	VG	F	VF	XF	Unc
ND FS Rare	—	—	—	—	—	—

C# 23 2/3 THALER

Silver **Obverse:** Bust right **Reverse:** Crowned ornate arms in cartouche

Date	Mintage	VG	F	VF	XF	Unc
1757	—	225	450	800	1,400	—

C# 45 2/3 THALER

Silver **Obverse:** AADS script monogram **Reverse:** Crowned arms

Date	Mintage	F	VF	XF	Unc
1760 FFS	—	1,000	1,750	3,000	4,750

C# 46 2/3 THALER

14.0300 g., 0.8330 Silver 0.3757 oz. ASW **Obverse:** Draped bust of Anna Amalia left **Obv. Legend:** AMALIA TVTRIX REG • SAX • VINAR • & ISENAC • **Reverse:** Saxon arms

Date	Mintage	F	VF	XF	Unc
1763 FS	—	60.00	125	250	500

C# 46a 2/3 THALER

14.0300 g., 0.8330 Silver 0.3757 oz. ASW **Obverse:** Draped bust of Anna Amalia left **Obv. Legend:** AMALIA TVTRIX REG • SAX • VINAR • & ISENAC • **Reverse:** Crowned complex arms, value below

Date	Mintage	F	VF	XF	Unc
1763 FS	—	50.00	100	225	475
1764 FS	—	50.00	100	225	475
1765 FS	—	50.00	100	225	475

C# 46b 2/3 THALER

14.0300 g., 0.8330 Silver 0.3757 oz. ASW **Obverse:** Draped bust of Anna Amalia left **Obv. Legend:** AMALIA TVTRIX REG • SAX • VINAR & ISENAC • **Reverse:** Crowned complex arms, value below

Date	Mintage	F	VF	XF	Unc
1764 FS	—	50.00	100	225	475

C# A25 THALER

28.9500 g., 0.8330 Silver 0.7753 oz. ASW **Obverse:** Armored bust right **Reverse:** Saxon arms within order chain **Note:** Similar to C#25 but without edge inscription. Species Thaler. Dav. 2756.

Date	Mintage	F	VF	XF	Unc
ND	—	—	—	—	—

C# A12 THALER

Silver **Ruler:** Ernst August II Konstantine **Subject:** 200th Anniversary of Religious Peace of Augsburg **Note:** Prev. C#12 in Saxe-Eisenach. Dav.#2720.

Date	Mintage	Good	VG	F	VF	XF
1755 FS	—	100	200	450	800	1,500

C# 25 THALER

28.9500 g., 0.8330 Silver 0.7753 oz. ASW **Ruler:** Ernst August II Konstantine **Subject:** Ruler's Coming of Age **Obverse:** Armored bust right **Obv. Legend:** ERN • AVG • CONSTANTIN • D: G • DVX • SAX • I • C • M • A • & W • **Reverse:** Crowned Saxon arms within Order chain **Rev. Legend:** IVSTITIA ET - CLEMENTIA **Note:** Dav. #2757.

Date	Mintage	VG	F	VF	XF	Unc
1756 S-FS	—	200	450	800	1,500	—

Note: For specimens struck on very thick flans and c/m "4-3/4" see 5 thaler, C#25a

C# 49 THALER

28.9500 g., 0.8330 Silver 0.7753 oz. ASW **Obverse:** Crowned AADS script monogram **Reverse:** Crowned Saxon arms above value **Note:** Reichs Thaler. Dav. #2758.

Date	Mintage	F	VF	XF	Unc
1760 FS	—	1,500	2,500	4,500	7,500

C# 50 THALER

28.9500 g., 0.8330 Silver 0.7753 oz. ASW **Ruler:** Karl August **Obverse:** Small bust of Anna Amalia left **Obv. Legend:** AMALIA TVTRIX REG • SAX • VINAR • & ISENAC • **Reverse:** Crowned complex arms **Rev. Legend:** F • S • W • U • E • O • - V • M *date*, 10. EINE FEINE MARCK below **Note:** Convention Thaler. Dav. #2759.

Date	Mintage	F	VF	XF	Unc
1763 K-FS	—	150	300	600	1,250
1764 K-FS	—	150	300	600	1,250
1765 K-FS	—	150	300	600	1,250

C# 50a THALER

28.9500 g., 0.8330 Silver 0.7753 oz. ASW **Obverse:** Large bust of Anna Amalia left **Obv. Legend:** AMALIA TVTRIX REG • SAX • VINAR • & ISENAC • **Reverse:** Crowned complex arms **Rev. Legend:** F • S • W • U • E • O • V • M • *date*, 10 • EINE FEINE MARCK below **Note:** Dav. #2759A.

Date	Mintage	F	VF	XF	Unc
1763 K-FS	—	175	325	600	1,250

Note: Various sizes of busts exist

C# A13 2 THALER

Silver **Ruler:** Ernst August II Konstantine **Note:** Prev. C#13 in Saxe-Eisenach. Dav.#2719. Similar to a Thaler, C#A12, but double-thick flan.

Date	Mintage	Good	VG	F	VF	XF
1755 FS	—	225	450	1,000	2,200	4,000

C# 30 5 THALER

6.6500 g., 0.9000 Gold 0.1924 oz. AGW **Obverse:** Bust right **Reverse:** Crowned arms in cartouche, value

Date	Mintage	VG	F	VF	XF	Unc
ND Rare	—	—	—	—	—	—

C# 25a 5 THALER

138.6000 g., Silver **Obverse:** Armored bust right **Reverse:** Crowned Saxon arms within Order chain **Note:** Countermark value: 4 3/4. DAV. #2757A.

Date	Mintage	F	VF	XF	Unc
1756 S-FS Rare	—	—	—	—	—

Note: Struck with 1 Thaler dies, C#25

C# 53 5 THALER

6.6500 g., 0.9000 Gold 0.1924 oz. AGW **Obverse:** Bust of Anna Amalia left **Reverse:** Crowned arms

Date	Mintage	F	VF	XF	Unc
1764 FS	—	2,000	4,000	7,000	10,000

TRADE COINAGE

FR# 3033 DUCAT

3.5000 g., 0.9860 Gold 0.1109 oz. AGW **Obverse:** Hercules strangling Nemean lion **Reverse:** Mountain

Date	Mintage	VG	F	VF	XF	Unc
ND	—	350	750	1,500	2,500	—

FR# 3034 DUCAT

3.5000 g., 0.9860 Gold 0.1109 oz. AGW **Obverse:** Crowned shield with EA monogram **Reverse:** 5-line inscription

Date	Mintage	VG	F	VF	XF	Unc
1745	—	350	750	1,500	2,500	—

C# A14 DUCAT

3.5000 g., 0.9860 Gold 0.1109 oz. AGW **Ruler:** Ernst August II Konstantine **Obverse:** Bust right **Reverse:** Felicitas standing, date **Note:** Prev. C#14 in Saxe-Eisenach.

Date	Mintage	Good	VG	F	VF	XF
1752	—	175	375	800	1,500	2,800

C# A15 DUCAT

3.5000 g., 0.9860 Gold 0.1109 oz. AGW **Ruler:** Ernst August II Konstantine **Note:** Prev. C#15 in Saxe-Eisenach.

Date	Mintage	Good	VG	F	VF	XF
1754	—	175	350	700	1,300	2,200

C# A27 DUCAT

3.5000 g., 0.9860 Gold 0.1109 oz. AGW **Obverse:** Bust of Friedrich III right **Reverse:** Crowned ornate arms

Date	Mintage	VG	F	VF	XF	Unc
1754	—	425	900	1,750	3,000	—

C# 27 DUCAT

3.5000 g., 0.9860 Gold 0.1109 oz. AGW **Ruler:** Ernst August II Konstantine **Subject:** Homage of Eisenach **Obverse:** Bust right **Reverse:** City view, LAETISSIMUS etc., date

Date	Mintage	VG	F	VF	XF	Unc
1756	—	300	700	1,500	2,500	—

C# 28 DUCAT

3.5000 g., 0.9860 Gold 0.1109 oz. AGW **Ruler:** Ernst August II Konstantine **Subject:** On Ruler's Coming of Age **Obverse:** Script EAC monogram in oval **Reverse:** Goddess, HILARITAS

Date	Mintage	VG	F	VF	XF	Unc
1756 FS	—	250	600	1,200	2,000	—

C# 29 DUCAT

3.5000 g., 0.9860 Gold 0.1109 oz. AGW **Obverse:** Bust right **Reverse:** Goddess

Date	Mintage	VG	F	VF	XF	Unc
1756 FS	—	275	650	1,350	2,250	—

C# 52 DUCAT

3.5000 g., 0.9860 Gold 0.1109 oz. AGW **Obverse:** Bust of Anna Amalia left **Reverse:** Crowned arms

Date	Mintage	F	VF	XF	Unc
1764 FS	—	1,750	3,500	6,000	9,000

TRIAL STRIKES

KM# TS1 6 PFENNIG

Billon

Date	Mintage	F	VF	XF	Unc
1751	—	—	—	—	—

PATTERNS

Including off metal strikes

KM#	Date	Mintage	Identification	Mkt Val
PnA1	1756	—	Ducat. Copper. C28.	—

SAXE-WEISSENFELS

Branch of the Albertine Saxon house, which was created in 1656 for August, 2nd son of the Elector of Saxony, John George I. The line became extinct with the death of Johann Adolf II in 1746 and the properties reverted to electoral Saxony.

RULERS

Johann Georg, 1697-1712
Christian II, 1712-1736
Johann Adolf II, 1736-46

MINT OFFICIALS' INITIALS

Initials	Date	Name
CW	1688-1739	Christian Wermuth, die-cutter in Gotha
IA	1706-10	Julius Angerstein, mintmaster

DUCHY

STANDARD COINAGE

DAV# 2760 THALER

Silver **Ruler:** Johann Georg **Obverse:** Bust right **Reverse:** Helmeted arms

Date	Mintage	F	VF	XF	Unc
1709 Rare	—	—	—	—	—

TRADE COINAGE

FR# 3048 DUCAT

3.5000 g., 0.8960 Gold 0.1008 oz. AGW **Ruler:** Christian II **Subject:** Bicentennial of the Reformation **Obverse:** Bust right **Reverse:** Martin Luther kneeling

Date	Mintage	VG	F	VF	XF	Unc
1717	—	400	800	1,650	2,800	—

FR# 3047 DUCAT

3.5000 g., 0.8960 Gold 0.1008 oz. AGW **Ruler:** Christian II **Obverse:** Bust right **Reverse:** Stag

Date	Mintage	VG	F	VF	XF	Unc
1726	—	500	1,000	2,000	3,500	—

SAXONY

Saxony, located in southeast Germany was founded in 850. The first coinage was struck c. 990. It was divided into two lines in 1464. The electoral right was obtained by the elder line in 1547. During the time of the Reformation, Saxony was one of the more powerful states in central Europe. It became a kingdom in 1806. At the Congress of Vienna in 1815, they were forced to cede half its territories to Prussia.

RULERS

Friedrich August I, 1694-1733
Friedrich August II, 1733-1763
Friedrich Christian, Elector, 1763
Xaver, Prince Regent, 1763-1768
Friedrich August III, 1763-1806
as Friedrich August I, 1806-1827

MINT MARKS

L - Leipzig

MINT OFFICIALS' INITIALS

Dresden Mint

Initials	Date	Name
C, IC, IEC	1779-1804	Johann Ernst Croll
EC, EDC	1764-78	Ernst Dietrich Croll
FwoF	1734-64	Friedrich Wilhelm o Feral
IDB	1756-59	Johann David Billert
IGS	1716-34	Johann George Schomberg
ILH	1698-1716	Johann Lorenz Holland

Leipzig Mint

Initials	Date	Name
EDC, EC	1753-63	Ernst Dietrich Croll
EPH, fish	1693-1714	Ernst Peter Hecht
IfoF	1763-65	Johann Friedrich o Feral
IGG	1752	Johann Georg Godecke

Arms of Electoral Saxony

2-fold arms divided vertically, 2 crossed swords on left, opened crown curving diagonally from upper left to lower right on right side.

DUCHY AND ELECTORATE

REGULAR COINAGE

KM# 1002.1 HELLER

Copper **Ruler:** Friedrich August III **Obverse:** Crowned arms **Reverse:** Denomination above date

Date	Mintage	F	VF	XF	Unc
1778 C	—	2.50	6.00	15.00	45.00
1779 C	—	2.50	6.00	15.00	45.00
1780 C	—	2.50	6.00	15.00	45.00
1781 C	—	2.50	6.00	15.00	45.00
1782 C	—	2.50	6.00	15.00	45.00
1783 C	—	2.50	6.00	15.00	45.00
1787 C	—	2.50	6.00	15.00	45.00
1789/7 C	—	2.50	6.00	15.00	45.00
1789 C	—	2.50	6.00	15.00	45.00
1792 C	—	2.50	6.00	15.00	45.00
1796 C	—	2.50	6.00	15.00	45.00
1799 C	—	2.50	6.00	15.00	45.00

KM# 1002.2 HELLER

Copper **Obverse:** Mint mark below arms **Reverse:** Mint mark below date

Date	Mintage	F	VF	XF	Unc
1779 C	—	2.50	6.00	15.00	45.00
1780 C	—	2.50	6.00	15.00	45.00
1781 C	—	2.50	6.00	15.00	45.00
1782 C	—	2.50	6.00	15.00	45.00
1783 C	—	2.50	6.00	15.00	45.00
1789 C	—	2.50	6.00	15.00	45.00
1792 C	—	2.50	6.00	15.00	45.00
1796 C	—	2.50	6.00	15.00	45.00

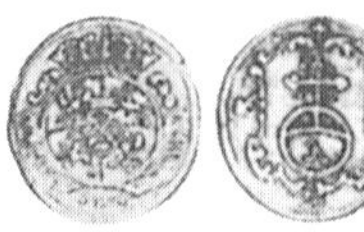

KM# 702 PFENNIG

Billon **Ruler:** Friedrich August I **Obverse:** Crowned 4-fold arms with central shield within palm branches **Reverse:** Imperial orb in cartouche divides date

Date	Mintage	VG	F	VF	XF	Unc
1701 ILH	—	5.00	10.00	18.00	35.00	—
Note: Varieties exist						
1702 ILH	—	5.00	10.00	18.00	35.00	—
1703 ILH	—	5.00	10.00	18.00	35.00	—
1704 ILH	—	5.00	10.00	18.00	35.00	—
1705 ILH	—	5.00	10.00	18.00	35.00	—
1706 ILH	—	5.00	10.00	18.00	35.00	—
1707 ILH	—	5.00	10.00	18.00	35.00	—
1708 ILH	—	5.00	10.00	18.00	35.00	—
1709 ILH	—	5.00	10.00	18.00	35.00	—
1710 ILH	—	5.00	10.00	18.00	35.00	—
1711 ILH	—	5.00	10.00	18.00	35.00	—
1711 EPH	—	5.00	10.00	18.00	35.00	—
1712 ILH	—	5.00	10.00	18.00	35.00	—
1712 EPH	—	5.00	10.00	18.00	35.00	—
1713 ILH	—	5.00	10.00	18.00	35.00	—
1713 EPH	—	5.00	10.00	18.00	35.00	—
1714 ILH	—	5.00	10.00	18.00	35.00	—
1715 ILH	—	5.00	10.00	18.00	35.00	—
1716 IGS	—	5.00	10.00	18.00	35.00	—
1717 IGS	—	5.00	10.00	18.00	35.00	—
1718 IGS	—	5.00	10.00	18.00	35.00	—
1719 IGS	—	5.00	10.00	18.00	35.00	—
1720 IGS	—	5.00	10.00	18.00	35.00	—
1721 IGS	—	5.00	10.00	18.00	35.00	—
1722 IGS	—	5.00	10.00	18.00	35.00	—
1723 IGS	—	5.00	10.00	18.00	35.00	—
1724 IGS	—	5.00	10.00	18.00	35.00	—
1725 IGS	—	5.00	10.00	18.00	35.00	—
1726 IGS	—	5.00	10.00	18.00	35.00	—
1727 IGS	—	5.00	10.00	18.00	35.00	—
1728 IGS	—	5.00	10.00	18.00	35.00	—
1729 IGS	—	5.00	10.00	18.00	35.00	—
1729 IGS	—	5.00	10.00	18.00	35.00	—
1730 IGS	—	5.00	10.00	18.00	35.00	—
1731 IGS	—	5.00	10.00	18.00	35.00	—
1731 IGS	—	5.00	10.00	18.00	35.00	—
1732 IGS	—	5.00	10.00	18.00	35.00	—
1733 IGS	—	5.00	10.00	18.00	35.00	—
Note: Varieties exist						
1733 IGS	—	5.00	10.00	18.00	35.00	—
Note: Varieties exist						

KM# 757 PFENNIG

Billon **Ruler:** Friedrich August I **Obverse:** Crowned AR monogram divides date **Reverse:** Imperial orb with symbol **Rev. Legend:** MONETA SAXONICA

Date	Mintage	VG	F	VF	XF	Unc
1708 ILH	—	6.00	12.00	25.00	45.00	—
1709 ILH	—	6.00	12.00	25.00	45.00	—

KM# 850 PFENNIG

Copper **Ruler:** Friedrich August I **Obverse:** Crowned ornate FA monogram **Reverse:** Value: 1/PFENNIG/C.S. LAND/ MUNTZ/ date

Date	Mintage	VG	F	VF	XF	Unc
1721	—	—	—	—	—	—

KM# 894 PFENNIG

Billon **Ruler:** Friedrich August II **Obverse:** Crowned arms **Reverse:** Value in orb in cartouche divides date

Date	Mintage	F	VF	XF	Unc
1733 IGS	—	3.00	6.00	12.00	60.00
1734 IGS	—	3.00	6.00	12.00	60.00
1735 FWoF	—	3.00	6.00	12.00	60.00
1736 FWoF	—	3.00	6.00	12.00	60.00
1737 FWoF	—	3.00	6.00	12.00	60.00
1738 FWoF	—	3.00	6.00	12.00	60.00
1739 FWoF	—	3.00	6.00	12.00	60.00
1739 FWoF	—	3.00	6.00	12.00	60.00
1740 FWoF	—	3.00	6.00	12.00	60.00
1741 FWoF	—	3.00	6.00	12.00	60.00
1741 FWoF	—	3.00	6.00	12.00	60.00
1742 FWoF	—	3.00	6.00	12.00	60.00
1743 FWoF	—	3.00	6.00	12.00	60.00
1744 FWoF	—	3.00	6.00	12.00	60.00
1745 FWoF	—	3.00	6.00	12.00	60.00
1746 FWoF	—	3.00	6.00	12.00	60.00
1747 FWoF	—	3.00	6.00	12.00	60.00
1748 FWoF	—	3.00	6.00	12.00	60.00
1749 FWoF	—	3.00	6.00	12.00	60.00
1750/40 FWoF	—	3.00	6.00	12.00	60.00
1750 FWoF	—	3.00	6.00	12.00	60.00
1751 FWoF	—	3.00	6.00	12.00	60.00
1752 FWoF	—	3.00	6.00	12.00	60.00
1753 FWoF	—	3.00	6.00	12.00	60.00
1754 FWoF	—	3.00	6.00	12.00	60.00
1755 FWoF	—	3.00	6.00	12.00	60.00
1756 FWoF	—	3.00	6.00	12.00	60.00

KM# 964 PFENNIG

Billon **Ruler:** Xaver **Note:** Similar to 1 Heller, KM#1002.

Date	Mintage	F	VF	XF	Unc
1764 C	—	5.00	10.00	35.00	100

KM# 980 PFENNIG

Billon **Ruler:** Xaver **Obverse:** Crowned arms **Reverse:** Value, date

Date	Mintage	F	VF	XF	Unc
1765 C	—	3.00	6.00	12.50	65.00

KM# 1000 PFENNIG

Copper **Ruler:** Friedrich August III **Obverse:** Crowned arms **Reverse:** Value above date

Date	Mintage	F	VF	XF	Unc
1772 C	—	2.50	5.00	10.00	50.00
1773 C	—	2.50	5.00	10.00	50.00
1774 C	—	2.50	5.00	10.00	50.00
1775 C	—	2.50	5.00	10.00	50.00
1776 C	—	2.50	5.00	10.00	50.00
1777 C	—	2.50	5.00	10.00	50.00
1778 C	—	2.50	5.00	10.00	50.00
1779 C	—	2.50	5.00	10.00	50.00
1780 C	—	2.50	5.00	10.00	50.00
1781 C	—	2.50	5.00	10.00	50.00
1782/72 C	—	2.50	5.00	10.00	50.00
1782 C	—	2.50	5.00	10.00	50.00
1783 C	—	2.50	5.00	10.00	50.00
1784 C	—	2.50	5.00	10.00	50.00
1785 C	—	2.50	5.00	10.00	50.00
1788 C	—	2.50	5.00	10.00	50.00
1789 C	—	2.50	5.00	10.00	50.00
1790/89 C	—	30.00	60.00	90.00	150
1790 C	—	30.00	60.00	90.00	150
1796 C	—	2.50	5.00	10.00	50.00
1797 C	—	2.50	5.00	10.00	50.00
1798/89 C	—	2.50	5.00	10.00	50.00
1799 C	—	2.50	5.00	10.00	50.00
1799 C	—	2.50	5.00	10.00	50.00
1800 C	—	2.50	5.00	10.00	50.00

KM# 711 3 PFENNIGE

Silver, 18 mm. **Ruler:** Friedrich August I **Obverse:** Crowned round 4-fold arms with central shield of 2-fold arms between 2 palm branches, initials below **Reverse:** Value: 3 on imperial orb in baroque frame, date at top

Date	Mintage	VG	F	VF	XF	Unc
1701 ILH	—	8.00	20.00	35.00	70.00	—
1702 ILH ILH	—	8.00	20.00	35.00	70.00	—
1702 ILH	—	8.00	20.00	35.00	70.00	—
1703 ILH	—	8.00	20.00	35.00	70.00	—
1704 ILH	—	8.00	20.00	35.00	70.00	—
1705 ILH	—	8.00	20.00	35.00	70.00	—
Note: Varieties exist						

KM# 745 3 PFENNIGE

Silver **Ruler:** Friedrich August I **Obverse:** Ornately-shaped arms **Reverse:** Date divided by frame

Date	Mintage	VG	F	VF	XF	Unc
1706 ILH	—	6.00	12.00	25.00	45.00	—
1707 ILH	—	6.00	12.00	25.00	45.00	—
1708 ILH	—	6.00	12.00	25.00	45.00	—
1709 ILH	—	6.00	12.00	25.00	45.00	—
1710 ILH	—	6.00	12.00	25.00	45.00	—
1710 EPH	—	6.00	12.00	25.00	45.00	—
1710 ILH	—	6.00	12.00	25.00	45.00	—
1711 EPH	—	6.00	12.00	25.00	45.00	—
1712 EPH	—	6.00	12.00	25.00	45.00	—
Note: Varieties exist.						
1711 ILH	—	6.00	12.00	25.00	45.00	—

KM# 758 3 PFENNIGE

Silver **Ruler:** Friedrich August I **Obverse:** Crowned AR monogram divides date **Rev. Legend:** MONETA SAXONICA, value: 3 in imperial orb within circle

Date	Mintage	VG	F	VF	XF	Unc
1708 ILH	—	8.00	15.00	32.00	55.00	—
1709 EPH	—	8.00	15.00	32.00	55.00	—
1709 ILH	—	8.00	15.00	32.00	55.00	—
1710 EPH	—	8.00	15.00	32.00	55.00	—
1710 ILH	—	8.00	15.00	32.00	55.00	—

KM# 819 3 PFENNIGE

Silver **Ruler:** Friedrich August I **Obverse:** Crowned round 4-fold arms with central shield of 2-fold arms between 2 palm branches, initials **Reverse:** Value: 3 on imperial orb in cartouche divides date

Date	Mintage	VG	F	VF	XF	Unc
1711 ILH	—	7.00	13.00	30.00	52.00	—
1712 ILH	—	7.00	13.00	30.00	52.00	—
1713 ILH	—	7.00	13.00	30.00	52.00	—
1714 ILH	—	7.00	13.00	30.00	52.00	—
1715 ILH	—	7.00	13.00	30.00	52.00	—
1716 ILH	—	7.00	13.00	30.00	52.00	—
1716 IGS	—	7.00	13.00	30.00	52.00	—
1717 IGS	—	7.00	13.00	30.00	52.00	—
1718 IGS	—	7.00	13.00	30.00	52.00	—
1719 IGS	—	7.00	13.00	30.00	52.00	—
1720 IGS	—	7.00	13.00	30.00	52.00	—
1721 IGS	—	7.00	13.00	30.00	52.00	—
1722 IGS	—	7.00	13.00	30.00	52.00	—
1723 IGS	—	7.00	13.00	30.00	52.00	—
1724 IGS	—	7.00	13.00	30.00	52.00	—
1725 IGS	—	7.00	13.00	30.00	52.00	—
1726 IGS	—	7.00	13.00	30.00	52.00	—
1727 IGS	—	7.00	13.00	30.00	52.00	—
1728 IGS	—	7.00	13.00	30.00	52.00	—
1729 IGS	—	7.00	13.00	30.00	52.00	—
1730 IGS	—	7.00	13.00	30.00	52.00	—
1731 IGS	—	7.00	13.00	30.00	52.00	—
1732 IGS	—	7.00	13.00	30.00	52.00	—
1733 IGS	—	7.00	13.00	30.00	52.00	—
Note: Varieties exist						

KM# 874 3 PFENNIGE

Billon **Ruler:** Friedrich August II **Obverse:** Crowned arms **Reverse:** Value on orb in cartouche divides date

Date	Mintage	F	VF	XF	Unc
1734 IGS	—	3.00	7.00	20.00	60.00
1735 FWoF	—	3.00	7.00	20.00	60.00
1736 FWoF	—	3.00	7.00	20.00	60.00
1737 FWoF	—	3.00	7.00	20.00	60.00
1738 FWoF	—	3.00	7.00	20.00	60.00
1739 FWoF	—	3.00	7.00	20.00	60.00
1740 FWoF	—	3.00	7.00	20.00	60.00
1741 FWoF	—	3.00	7.00	20.00	60.00

Date	Mintage	F	VF	XF	Unc
1742 FWoF	—	3.00	7.00	20.00	60.00
1743 FWoF	—	3.00	7.00	20.00	60.00
1744 FWoF	—	3.00	7.00	20.00	60.00
1745 FWoF	—	3.00	7.00	20.00	60.00
1746 FWoF	—	3.00	7.00	20.00	60.00
1747 FWoF	—	3.00	7.00	20.00	60.00
1748 FWoF	—	3.00	7.00	20.00	60.00
1749 FWoF	—	3.00	7.00	20.00	60.00
1750 FWoF	—	3.00	7.00	20.00	60.00
1751 FWoF	—	3.00	7.00	20.00	60.00
1752 FWoF	—	3.00	7.00	20.00	60.00
1753 FWoF	—	3.00	7.00	20.00	60.00
1754 FWoF	—	3.00	7.00	20.00	60.00
1755 FWoF	—	3.00	7.00	20.00	60.00

KM# 945 3 PFENNIGE

Billon **Ruler:** Friedrich August II **Obverse:** 3-line legend **Reverse:** Value and date in cartouche

Date	Mintage	F	VF	XF	Unc
1760 L	—	5.00	10.00	28.00	75.00
1761	—	5.00	10.00	28.00	75.00
1761 EDC	—	5.00	10.00	28.00	75.00
1761 L	—	5.00	10.00	25.00	65.00
1762	—	5.00	10.00	25.00	65.00
1762 EDC	—	5.00	10.00	25.00	65.00
1762 L	—	5.00	10.00	25.00	65.00

KM# 947 3 PFENNIGE

Billon **Ruler:** Friedrich August II **Obverse:** Crowned arms **Reverse:** Value in cartouche

Date	Mintage	F	VF	XF	Unc
1762 FWoF	—	6.00	12.00	28.00	75.00
1763 FWoF	—	6.00	12.00	28.00	75.00

KM# 965 3 PFENNIGE

Billon **Obverse:** Capped arms in sprays **Reverse:** Value above date

Date	Mintage	F	VF	XF	Unc
1764 C	—	4.50	9.00	22.00	60.00
1764 IFoF	—	4.50	9.00	22.00	60.00
1765 C	—	4.50	9.00	22.00	60.00
1779 C	—	4.50	9.00	22.00	60.00
1781 C	—	4.50	9.00	22.00	60.00
1782 C	—	4.50	9.00	22.00	60.00
1784 C	—	4.50	9.00	22.00	60.00
1785 C	—	4.50	9.00	22.00	60.00
1793 C	162,000	4.50	9.00	22.00	60.00

KM# 1037 3 PFENNIGE

Copper **Ruler:** Friedrich August III **Obverse:** Crowned oval arms within branches **Reverse:** Denomination above date

Date	Mintage	F	VF	XF	Unc
1797 C	—	3.00	6.00	18.00	55.00
1799 C	—	3.00	6.00	18.00	55.00
1800 C	—	3.00	6.00	18.00	55.00

KM# 728 6 PFENNIGE (Sechser)

Silver **Ruler:** Friedrich August I **Obverse:** 2-fold arms surrounded by 2 crossed palm branches, initials below **Reverse:** Value: 6. PF/CHUR. SACHS/LANDMUNZ/date

Date	Mintage	VG	F	VF	XF	Unc
1701 EPH	—	20.00	40.00	65.00	110	—
1702 EPH	—	20.00	40.00	65.00	110	—

KM# 995 6 PFENNIGE (Sechser)

Billon **Ruler:** Friedrich August II **Obverse:** 3-line legend **Reverse:** Value and date in cartouche

Date	Mintage	F	VF	XF	Unc
1760 L	—	6.00	12.00	30.00	80.00
1761	—	6.00	12.00	30.00	80.00

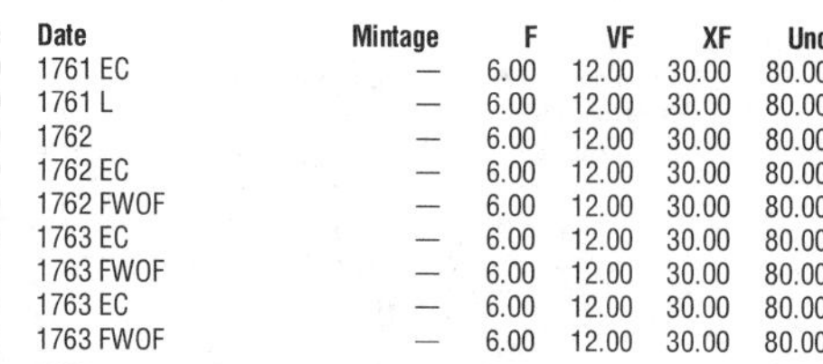

Date	Mintage	F	VF	XF	Unc
1761 EC	—	6.00	12.00	30.00	80.00
1761 L	—	6.00	12.00	30.00	80.00
1762	—	6.00	12.00	30.00	80.00
1762 EC	—	6.00	12.00	30.00	80.00
1762 FWOF	—	6.00	12.00	30.00	80.00
1763 EC	—	6.00	12.00	30.00	80.00
1763 FWOF	—	6.00	12.00	30.00	80.00
1763 EC	—	6.00	12.00	30.00	80.00
1763 FWOF	—	6.00	12.00	30.00	80.00

KM# 759 GROSCHEN (1/24 Thaler)

Silver **Ruler:** Johann Georg IV **Obverse:** Crowned script AR monogram, value 1 below **Reverse:** Butterfly in plain field

Date	Mintage	VG	F	VF	XF	Unc
ND (1709)	—	75.00	150	275	600	—

KM# 822 GROSCHEN (1/24 Thaler)

Silver **Ruler:** Friedrich August I **Subject:** Death of Friedrich August I's Mother, Anna Sophia of Denmark

Date	Mintage	VG	F	VF	XF	Unc
1717 IGS	—	25.00	50.00	85.00	140	—

KM# 900 GROSCHEN (1/24 Thaler)

Billon **Ruler:** Friedrich August II **Obverse:** Armored bust right **Reverse:** Imperial eagle divides value **Note:** Vicariat issue.

Date	Mintage	VG	F	VF	XF	Unc
1740	—	12.00	22.00	40.00	75.00	—

KM# 905 GROSCHEN (1/24 Thaler)

Billon **Ruler:** Friedrich August II **Obverse:** Friedrich August on rearing horse right **Reverse:** Empty throne on dais with symbols of office **Note:** Vicariat issue.

Date	Mintage	VG	F	VF	XF	Unc
1741	—	10.00	17.50	30.00	50.00	—
1742	—	10.00	17.50	30.00	50.00	—

KM# 948 GROSCHEN (1/24 Thaler)

Billon **Ruler:** Friedrich August II **Obverse:** Legend **Reverse:** Value, date within cartouche

Date	Mintage	VG	F	VF	XF	Unc
1762	—	7.50	12.50	25.00	50.00	—

KM# A770 2 GROSCHEN (1/12 Thaler)

Silver **Obverse:** Crowned script AR monogram, value 2 below **Reverse:** Butterfly in plain field

Date	Mintage	VG	F	VF	XF	Unc
ND	—	—	—	350	600	—

KM# 823 2 GROSCHEN (1/12 Thaler)

Silver **Ruler:** Friedrich August I **Subject:** Death of Friedrich August I's Mother, Anna Sophia of Denmark **Obverse:** Inscription **Reverse:** Ship at sea, rock in water at left **Note:** Similar to 1 Groschen, KM#822.

Date	Mintage	VG	F	VF	XF	Unc
1717 IGS	—	32.00	65.00	100	160	—

KM# 835 2 GROSCHEN (1/12 Thaler)

Silver **Ruler:** Friedrich August I **Subject:** Marriage of Prince Friedrich August (II) and Maria Josepha of Austria **Obverse:** 2 joined flaming hearts tied with ribbon held by hands at left and right, above INDISSOLVBILITER **Reverse:** 9-line inscription with Roman numeral date, mintmaster's initials and value 2 in oval

Date	Mintage	VG	F	VF	XF	Unc
1719 IGS	—	30.00	60.00	95.00	145	—
1719 IGS	—	30.00	60.00	95.00	145	—

KM# 855 2 GROSCHEN (1/12 Thaler)

Silver **Ruler:** Friedrich August I **Subject:** Death of Friedrich August I's Wife, Christiane Eberhardine **Obverse:** 11-line inscription with dates above 2 in oval dividing mintmaster's initials **Reverse:** Cyprus tree between 2 pyramids divides TOT - CORDA **Rev. Legend:** GVOT FOLIA, LVGENT below

Date	Mintage	VG	F	VF	XF	Unc
1727 IGS	—	20.00	45.00	85.00	135	—

KM# 891 2 GROSCHEN (1/12 Thaler)

Silver **Ruler:** Friedrich August II **Subject:** Marriage of Princess to King of Naple **Obverse:** 9-line inscription and date **Reverse:** Altar, holding 2 hearts, beneath crown held by hand from heaven

Date	Mintage	VG	F	VF	XF	Unc
MDCCXXXVIII (1738)	—	8.00	20.00	35.00	80.00	—

KM# 906 2 GROSCHEN (1/12 Thaler)

Silver **Ruler:** Friedrich August II **Obverse:** Friedrich August on rearing horse right **Obv. Legend:** DG FRID AUG REX POL DUX SAX ARCHIM E ELECTOR **Reverse:** Empty throne on dais with symbols of office **Note:** Vicariat issue.

Date	Mintage	VG	F	VF	XF	Unc
1741	—	10.00	20.00	45.00	90.00	—
1742	—	10.00	20.00	45.00	90.00	—

KM# 917 2 GROSCHEN (1/12 Thaler)

Silver **Ruler:** Friedrich August II **Subject:** Marriage of Princess to Dauphin of France **Obverse:** 7-line inscription and date **Reverse:** 2 hearts on altar, 2 shields of arms against altar

Date	Mintage	VG	F	VF	XF	Unc
1747	—	10.00	20.00	45.00	90.00	—

KM# 918 2 GROSCHEN (1/12 Thaler)

Silver **Ruler:** Friedrich August II **Subject:** Marriage of Prince Friedrich Christian **Obverse:** Inscription **Reverse:** Angel flying in clouds

Date	Mintage	VG	F	VF	XF	Unc
1747	—	10.00	20.00	45.00	90.00	—

KM# 1020 2 GROSCHEN (1/12 Thaler)

Silver **Ruler:** Friedrich August III **Obverse:** Head right **Reverse:** Crowned shield on eagle's breast **Note:** Vacariat issue.

Date	Mintage	VG	F	VF	XF	Unc
1790	—	6.00	12.00	28.00	55.00	—

KM# 1031 2 GROSCHEN (1/12 Thaler)

Silver **Ruler:** Friedrich August III **Obverse:** Armored bust right **Obv. Legend:** FRID • AVG • DVX • SAX • EL • ELECTOR • **Reverse:** Crowned shield on eagle's breast

Date	Mintage	VG	F	VF	XF	Unc
1792/1	—	6.00	12.00	28.00	55.00	—
1792	—	6.00	12.00	28.00	55.00	—

KM# 760 4 GROSCHEN

Silver **Ruler:** Friedrich August I **Obverse:** Crowned script AR monogram, value 4 **Reverse:** Butterfly in plain field

Date	Mintage	VG	F	VF	XF	Unc
ND (1709)	—	200	375	725	1,150	—

KM# 761 8 GROSCHEN (1/3 Thaler)

Silver **Ruler:** Friedrich August I **Obverse:** Crowned script AR monogram, value: 8 below **Reverse:** Butterfly in plain field

Date	Mintage	VG	F	VF	XF	Unc
ND (1709)	—	425	625	1,150	2,150	—

KM# 762 16 GROSCHEN

Silver **Ruler:** Friedrich August I **Obverse:** Crowned script AR monogram, value: 16 below **Reverse:** Butterfly in plain field

Date	Mintage	VG	F	VF	XF	Unc
ND (1709)	—	475	675	1,250	2,250	5,000

KM# 763 32 GROSCHEN (Thaler)

Silver **Ruler:** Johann Georg IV **Obverse:** Crowned script AR monogram, value: 32 below **Reverse:** Butterfly in plain field

Date	Mintage	VG	F	VF	XF	Unc
ND (1709)	—	750	1,150	2,200	3,650	7,500

KM# 703 1/48 THALER (1/2 Groschen)

Silver **Ruler:** Friedrich August I **Obverse:** Small branch at sides of arms **Reverse:** Crossed palm fronds

Date	Mintage	VG	F	VF	XF	Unc
1701 ILH	—	6.00	12.00	25.00	45.00	—
1702 ILH	—	6.00	12.00	25.00	45.00	—
1710 ILH	—	6.00	12.00	25.00	45.00	—
1711 ILH	—	6.00	12.00	25.00	45.00	—
1712 ILH	—	6.00	12.00	25.00	45.00	—
1713 ILH	—	6.00	12.00	25.00	45.00	—
1714 ILH	—	6.00	12.00	25.00	45.00	—
1715 ILH	—	6.00	12.00	25.00	45.00	—
1716 IGS	—	6.00	12.00	25.00	45.00	—
1717 IGS	—	6.00	12.00	25.00	45.00	—
1718 IGS	—	6.00	12.00	25.00	45.00	—
1719 IGS	—	6.00	12.00	25.00	45.00	—
1720 IGS	—	6.00	12.00	25.00	45.00	—
1721 IGS	—	6.00	12.00	25.00	45.00	—
1722 IGS	—	6.00	12.00	25.00	45.00	—
1723 IGS	—	6.00	12.00	25.00	45.00	—
1724 IGS	—	6.00	12.00	25.00	45.00	—
1725 IGS	—	6.00	12.00	25.00	45.00	—
1726 IGS	—	6.00	12.00	25.00	45.00	—
1727 IGS	—	6.00	12.00	25.00	45.00	—
1728 IGS	—	6.00	12.00	25.00	45.00	—
1729 IGS	—	6.00	12.00	25.00	45.00	—
1730 IGS	—	6.00	12.00	25.00	45.00	—
1731 IGS	—	6.00	12.00	25.00	45.00	—
1732 IGS	—	6.00	12.00	25.00	45.00	—
1733 IGS	—	6.00	12.00	25.00	45.00	—

Note: Varieties exist

KM# 712 1/48 THALER (1/2 Groschen)

Silver **Ruler:** Johann Georg IV **Obverse:** Crowned round 4-fold arms with crowned central shield of 2-fold arms, between 2 crossed palm branches, initials below **Reverse:** Value and date in palm wreath

Date	Mintage	VG	F	VF	XF	Unc
1701 ILH	—	6.00	12.00	25.00	45.00	—

KM# 773 1/48 THALER (1/2 Groschen)

Silver **Ruler:** Friedrich August I **Obverse:** Crowned AR monogram divides date, initials below **Rev. Legend:** MONETA SAXONICA, value: 48/EINEN/THAL

Date	Mintage	VG	F	VF	XF	Unc
1709 EPH	—	12.00	25.00	45.00	70.00	—

KM# 774 1/48 THALER (1/2 Groschen)

Silver **Ruler:** Friedrich August I **Obverse:** Crowned ornately-shaped arms, concave on left and right with central shield of 2-fold arms between 2 crossed branches, initials below **Reverse:** Value and date in palm wreath

Date	Mintage	VG	F	VF	XF	Unc
1709 EPH	—	10.00	20.00	35.00	60.00	—
1710 EPH	—	10.00	20.00	35.00	60.00	—
1711 EPH	—	10.00	20.00	35.00	60.00	—

Note: Varieties exist

KM# 875 1/48 THALER (1/2 Groschen)

Billon **Ruler:** Friedrich August II **Obverse:** Crowned arms **Reverse:** Value: THAL

Date	Mintage	VG	F	VF	XF	Unc
1734 IGS	—	10.00	20.00	35.00	60.00	—

KM# 883 1/48 THALER (1/2 Groschen)

Billon **Ruler:** Friedrich August II **Obverse:** Crowned arms **Reverse:** Value and date

Date	Mintage	VG	F	VF	XF	Unc
1735 FWoF	—	4.00	9.00	18.00	35.00	—
1736 FWoF	—	4.00	9.00	18.00	35.00	—
1737 FWoF	—	4.00	9.00	18.00	35.00	—
1738 FWoF	—	4.00	9.00	18.00	35.00	—
1739 FWoF	—	4.00	9.00	18.00	35.00	—
1740 FWoF	—	4.00	9.00	18.00	35.00	—
1741 FWoF	—	4.00	9.00	18.00	35.00	—
1742 FWoF	—	4.00	9.00	18.00	35.00	—
1743 FWoF	—	4.00	9.00	18.00	35.00	—
1744 FWoF	—	4.00	9.00	18.00	35.00	—
1745 FWoF	—	4.00	9.00	18.00	35.00	—
1746 FWoF	—	4.00	9.00	18.00	35.00	—
1746 FWoF	—	4.00	9.00	18.00	35.00	—
1747 FWoF	—	4.00	9.00	18.00	35.00	—
1748 FWoF	—	4.00	9.00	18.00	35.00	—
1749 FWoF	—	4.00	9.00	18.00	35.00	—
1750 FWoF	—	4.00	9.00	18.00	35.00	—
1751 FWoF	—	4.00	9.00	18.00	35.00	—
1753 FWoF	—	4.00	9.00	18.00	35.00	—
1754 FWoF	—	4.00	9.00	18.00	35.00	—
1754 FWoF	—	4.00	9.00	18.00	35.00	—
1755 FWoF	—	4.00	9.00	18.00	35.00	—
1756 FWoF	—	4.00	9.00	18.00	35.00	—

KM# 931 1/48 THALER (1/2 Groschen)

Billon **Obverse:** Script AR monogram

Date	Mintage	VG	F	VF	XF	Unc
1753 L	—	4.00	9.00	18.00	35.00	—
1754 EDC	—	4.00	9.00	18.00	35.00	—
1755 EDC	—	4.00	9.00	18.00	35.00	—

KM# 932 1/48 THALER (1/2 Groschen)

Billon **Ruler:** Friedrich August II

Date	Mintage	VG	F	VF	XF	Unc
1757 B	—	6.00	12.00	25.00	50.00	—

KM# 951 1/48 THALER (1/2 Groschen)

Billon **Obverse:** Crowned arms **Reverse:** Value; date in outer legend

Date	Mintage	VG	F	VF	XF	Unc
1763 EDC	—	5.00	10.00	20.00	45.00	—

KM# 966 1/48 THALER (1/2 Groschen)

0.9700 g., 0.2500 Silver 0.0078 oz. ASW **Ruler:** Friedrich August III **Obverse:** Crowned shield within crossed laurel branches **Reverse:** Value above date

Date	Mintage	F	VF	XF	Unc
1764 IFoF	—	—	—	—	—
1764 C	—	6.00	12.00	25.00	80.00
1765 C	—	6.00	12.00	25.00	80.00
1771 C	—	6.00	12.00	25.00	80.00
1779 C	756,000	6.00	12.00	25.00	80.00
1781 C	547,000	6.00	12.00	25.00	80.00
1781 C	547,000	6.00	12.00	25.00	80.00
1785 C	133,000	6.00	12.00	25.00	80.00
1793 C	174,000	6.00	12.00	25.00	80.00
1799 C	—	6.00	12.00	25.00	80.00
1802/799	—	6.00	12.00	25.00	80.00

KM# 682 1/24 THALER (Groschen)

Silver **Ruler:** Johann Georg IV **Obverse:** Crowned round 4-fold arms with crowned central shield of 2-fold arms **Reverse:** Value: 24/EINEN/THAI/date in palm wreath

Date	Mintage	VG	F	VF	XF	Unc
1701 ILH	—	8.00	15.00	30.00	60.00	—
1701 ILH	—	8.00	15.00	30.00	60.00	—
1702 ILH	—	8.00	15.00	30.00	60.00	—
1703 ILH	—	8.00	15.00	30.00	60.00	—
1704 ILH	—	8.00	15.00	30.00	60.00	—
1705 ILH	—	8.00	15.00	30.00	60.00	—
1709 ILH	—	8.00	15.00	30.00	60.00	—

Note: Varieties exist

KM# 743 1/24 THALER (Groschen)

Silver **Ruler:** Friedrich August I **Obverse:** Ornately-shaped arms, concave sides in 2 crossed palm branches **Reverse:** Value: 24/EINEN. . . in palm wreath

Date	Mintage	VG	F	VF	XF	Unc
1705 ILH	—	9.00	20.00	35.00	60.00	—
1706 ILH	—	9.00	20.00	35.00	60.00	—
1707 ILH	—	9.00	20.00	35.00	60.00	—
1710 ILH	—	9.00	20.00	35.00	60.00	—
1711 ILH	—	9.00	20.00	35.00	60.00	—

Note: Varieties exist.

KM# 764 1/24 THALER (Groschen)

Silver **Ruler:** Friedrich August I **Obverse:** Crowned AR monogram divides date, initials below **Rev. Legend:** MONETA SAXONICA, value: 24/EINEN/THAL

Date	Mintage	VG	F	VF	XF	Unc
1708 ILH	—	12.00	25.00	50.00	85.00	—
1709 ILH	—	12.00	25.00	50.00	85.00	—
1710 ILH	—	12.00	25.00	50.00	85.00	—

Note: Varieties exist

Date	Mintage	VG	F	VF	XF	Unc
1710 ILH	—	12.00	25.00	50.00	85.00	—

KM# 798 1/24 THALER (Groschen)

Silver **Ruler:** Friedrich August I **Obverse:** Crowned arms **Obv. Legend:** D: G: FRID: AUGUST: REX POL: **Reverse:** Value, date within branches **Rev. Legend:** DUX SAX: S•R•I•ARCH: ET ELECT•

Date	Mintage	VG	F	VF	XF	Unc
1711 ILH	—	8.00	15.00	30.00	55.00	—
1712 ILH	—	8.00	15.00	30.00	55.00	—
1713 ILH	—	8.00	15.00	30.00	55.00	—
1714 ILH	—	8.00	15.00	30.00	55.00	—
1715 ILH	—	8.00	15.00	30.00	55.00	—
1716 IGS	—	8.00	15.00	30.00	55.00	—
1717 IGS	—	8.00	15.00	30.00	55.00	—
1718 IGS	—	8.00	15.00	30.00	55.00	—
1719 IGS	—	8.00	15.00	30.00	55.00	—
1720 IGS	—	8.00	15.00	30.00	55.00	—
1721 IGS	—	8.00	15.00	30.00	55.00	—
1722 IGS	—	8.00	15.00	30.00	55.00	—
1723 IGS	—	8.00	15.00	30.00	55.00	—
1724 IGS	—	8.00	15.00	30.00	55.00	—
1725 IGS	—	8.00	15.00	30.00	55.00	—
1726 IGS	—	8.00	15.00	30.00	55.00	—
1727 IGS	—	8.00	15.00	30.00	55.00	—
1728 IGS	—	8.00	15.00	30.00	55.00	—
1729 IGS	—	8.00	15.00	30.00	55.00	—
1730 IGS	—	8.00	15.00	30.00	55.00	—
1731 IGS	—	8.00	15.00	30.00	55.00	—
1732 IGS	—	8.00	15.00	30.00	55.00	—
1733 IGS	—	8.00	15.00	30.00	55.00	—

Note: Varieties exist

KM# 876 1/24 THALER (Groschen)

Billon **Ruler:** Friedrich August II **Obverse:** Crowned arms **Reverse:** Value THAL and date in circle

Date	Mintage	VG	F	VF	XF	Unc
1734 IGS	—	10.00	20.00	40.00	75.00	—

KM# 884 1/24 THALER (Groschen)

Billon **Ruler:** Friedrich August II **Obverse:** Crowned arms **Obv. Legend:** D: G: FRID: AUGUST: REX POL • **Reverse:** Value, date **Rev. Legend:** DUX SAX: S: R: I: ARCH: ET ELECT:

Date	Mintage	VG	F	VF	XF	Unc
1734 IGS	—	6.00	12.00	25.00	50.00	—
1735 FWoF	—	6.00	12.00	25.00	50.00	—
1736 FWoF	—	6.00	12.00	25.00	50.00	—
1737 FWoF	—	6.00	12.00	25.00	50.00	—
1738 FWoF	—	6.00	12.00	25.00	50.00	—
1739 FWoF	—	6.00	12.00	25.00	50.00	—
1740 FWoF	—	6.00	12.00	25.00	50.00	—
1741 FWoF	—	6.00	12.00	25.00	50.00	—
1742 FWoF	—	6.00	12.00	25.00	50.00	—
1743 FWoF	—	6.00	12.00	25.00	50.00	—
1744 FWoF	—	6.00	12.00	25.00	50.00	—
1745 FWoF	—	6.00	12.00	25.00	50.00	—
1746 FWoF	—	6.00	12.00	25.00	50.00	—
1747 FWoF	—	6.00	12.00	25.00	50.00	—
1748 FWoF	—	6.00	12.00	25.00	50.00	—
1749 FWoF	—	6.00	12.00	25.00	50.00	—
1750 FwoF	—	6.00	12.00	25.00	50.00	—
1751 FWoF	—	6.00	12.00	25.00	50.00	—
1751/1 FWoF	—	6.00	12.00	25.00	50.00	—
1752 FWoF	—	6.00	12.00	25.00	50.00	—
1753 FWoF	—	6.00	12.00	25.00	50.00	—
1754 FWoF	—	6.00	12.00	25.00	50.00	—
1755 FWoF	—	6.00	12.00	25.00	50.00	—
1756 FWoF	—	6.00	12.00	25.00	50.00	—
1757 FWoF	—	6.00	12.00	25.00	50.00	—
1758 FWoF	—	6.00	12.00	25.00	50.00	—
1759 FWoF	—	6.00	12.00	25.00	50.00	—
1760 FWoF	—	6.00	12.00	25.00	50.00	—
1760 FWoF	—	6.00	12.00	25.00	50.00	—

KM# 910 1/24 THALER (Groschen)

Billon **Ruler:** Friedrich August II **Obv. Legend:** Ending: . . . & VIC **Note:** Vicariat issue.

Date	Mintage	VG	F	VF	XF	Unc
1745 FWoF	—	12.00	25.00	50.00	100	—

KM# A928 1/24 THALER (Groschen)

Billon **Ruler:** Friedrich August II **Obverse:** Crowned arms **Reverse:** Value: THAL and date in circle **Note:** Prev. KM#928.

Date	Mintage	VG	F	VF	XF	Unc
1753 EDC//L	—	6.00	12.00	25.00	50.00	—
1754 EDC//L	—	6.00	12.00	25.00	50.00	—
1755 EDC//L	—	6.00	12.00	25.00	50.00	—
1756 EDC//L	—	6.00	12.00	25.00	50.00	—
1757 EDC//L	—	6.00	12.00	25.00	50.00	—

KM# 927 1/24 THALER (Groschen)

Billon **Ruler:** Friedrich August II **Obverse:** Script AR monogram **Reverse:** Value and date

Date	Mintage	VG	F	VF	XF	Unc
1753L	—	10.00	20.00	40.00	75.00	—

KM# 929 1/24 THALER (Groschen)

Billon **Ruler:** Friedrich August II **Obverse:** Crowned arms **Reverse:** Value, date

Date	Mintage	VG	F	VF	XF	Unc
1753L EDC	—	6.00	12.00	25.00	50.00	—
1754L EDC	—	6.00	12.00	25.00	50.00	—
1760L EDC	—	6.00	12.00	25.00	50.00	—
1761L EDC	—	6.00	12.00	25.00	50.00	—
1767L EDC	—	6.00	12.00	25.00	50.00	—

KM# 930 1/24 THALER (Groschen)

Billon **Ruler:** Friedrich August II **Subject:** Prussian Occupation **Note:** Similar to KM#884.

Date	Mintage	VG	F	VF	XF	Unc
1756 IDB	—	6.00	12.00	25.00	50.00	—
1757 IDB	—	6.00	12.00	25.00	50.00	—

KM# 946 1/24 THALER (Groschen)

Billon **Ruler:** Friedrich August I **Obverse:** Crowned arms **Obv. Legend:** D • G • FRID • AVG • REX • POL • EL • SAX • **Reverse:** Value with rosette below **Rev. Legend:** CCCXX EINE FEINE MARCK date

Date	Mintage	VG	F	VF	XF	Unc
1760 EDC	—	6.00	12.00	25.00	50.00	—
1761 EDC	—	6.00	12.00	25.00	50.00	—
1762 EDC	—	6.00	12.00	25.00	50.00	—
1763 EDC	—	6.00	12.00	25.00	50.00	—
1763 FWoF	—	6.00	12.00	25.00	50.00	—

KM# 952 1/24 THALER (Groschen)

Billon **Obverse:** Crowned arms **Reverse:** Value, date in outer legend

Date	Mintage	VG	F	VF	XF	Unc
1763 FWoF	—	6.00	12.00	25.00	50.00	—
1763 EDC	—	6.00	12.00	25.00	50.00	—
1763 JFoF	—	6.00	12.00	25.00	50.00	—

KM# 967 1/24 THALER (Groschen)

1.9800 g., 0.3680 Silver 0.0234 oz. ASW **Ruler:** Xaver **Obverse:** Crowned arms **Obv. Legend:** XAVERIVS D G REG . . . **Reverse:** Value, date **Rev. Legend:** ELECTORATVS SAXONIÆ ADMINISTRATOR

Date	Mintage	F	VF	XF	Unc
1764 EDC	—	9.00	18.00	35.00	85.00
1765 EDC	—	9.00	18.00	35.00	85.00
1766 EDC	—	9.00	18.00	35.00	85.00
1767 EDC	—	9.00	18.00	35.00	85.00
1768 EDC	—	9.00	18.00	35.00	85.00

KM# 968 1/24 THALER (Groschen)

1.9800 g., 0.3680 Silver 0.0234 oz. ASW **Ruler:** Friedrich August III **Obverse:** Crowned oval arms within branches **Obv. Legend:** FRID. AVG. . . **Reverse:** Value above date

Date	Mintage	F	VF	XF	Unc
1764 IFoF	—	5.00	12.00	25.00	60.00
1764 EDC	—	5.00	12.00	25.00	60.00
1798 EDC	—	5.00	12.00	25.00	60.00
1800 EDC	—	5.00	12.00	25.00	60.00

KM# 683 1/12 THALER (Doppelgroschen)

Billon **Ruler:** Friedrich August I **Obverse:** Crowned arms within branches **Obv. Legend:** D • G • FRID • AUGUST • REX • POL • DUX • SAX • **Reverse:** Value, date within branches

Date	Mintage	VG	F	VF	XF	Unc
1701 ILH	—	10.00	20.00	32.00	65.00	—
1702 ILH	—	10.00	20.00	32.00	65.00	—
1702 EPH	—	10.00	20.00	32.00	65.00	—
1703 ILH	—	10.00	20.00	32.00	65.00	—
1703 EPH	—	10.00	20.00	32.00	65.00	—
1704 ILH	—	10.00	20.00	32.00	65.00	—
1704 EPH	—	10.00	20.00	32.00	65.00	—
1705 ILH	—	10.00	20.00	32.00	65.00	—
1705 EPH	—	10.00	20.00	32.00	65.00	—
1706 ILH	—	10.00	20.00	32.00	65.00	—
1707 ILH	—	10.00	20.00	32.00	65.00	—
1707 EPH	—	10.00	20.00	32.00	65.00	—
1709 ILH	—	10.00	20.00	32.00	65.00	—
1709 ILH	—	10.00	20.00	32.00	65.00	—
1709 EPH	—	10.00	20.00	32.00	65.00	—

Note: Varieties exist

KM# 746 1/12 THALER (Doppelgroschen)

Billon **Ruler:** Friedrich August I **Obverse:** Crowned arms within branches **Obv. Legend:** D • G • FRID: AUGUST: REX POL: **Reverse:** Value within branches **Rev. Legend:** DUX: SAX S: R: I: ARCH: ET ELECT:

Date	Mintage	VG	F	VF	XF	Unc
1706 ILH	—	12.00	25.00	50.00	85.00	—
1707 ILH	—	12.00	25.00	50.00	85.00	—
1709 EPH	—	12.00	25.00	50.00	85.00	—
1710 EPH	—	12.00	25.00	50.00	85.00	—
1711 EPH	—	12.00	25.00	50.00	85.00	—
1712 EPH	—	12.00	25.00	50.00	85.00	—
1713 EPH	—	12.00	25.00	50.00	85.00	—
1714 EPH	—	12.00	25.00	50.00	85.00	—
1715 EPH	—	12.00	25.00	50.00	85.00	—
1715 EPH	—	12.00	25.00	50.00	85.00	—
1716 IGS	—	12.00	25.00	50.00	85.00	—
1717 IGS	—	12.00	25.00	50.00	85.00	—

Note: Varieties exist

KM# 765 1/12 THALER (Doppelgroschen)

Billon **Ruler:** Friedrich August I **Obverse:** Crowned monogram divides date **Obv. Legend:** MONETA • SAXONICA **Reverse:** Value within inner circle

Date	Mintage	VG	F	VF	XF	Unc
1708 EPH	—	15.00	30.00	60.00	100	—
1708 ILH	—	15.00	30.00	60.00	100	—
1709 EPH	—	15.00	30.00	60.00	100	—
1710 EPH	—	15.00	30.00	60.00	100	—

Note: Varieties exist

KM# 799 1/12 THALER (Doppelgroschen)

Billon **Ruler:** Friedrich August I **Note:** Similar to 1/24 Thaler, KM#798, but reverse value: 12/EINEN.

Date	Mintage	VG	F	VF	XF	Unc
1711 ILH	—	10.00	22.00	40.00	75.00	—
1712 ILH	—	10.00	22.00	40.00	75.00	—
1713 ILH	—	10.00	22.00	40.00	75.00	—
1714 ILH	—	10.00	22.00	40.00	75.00	—
1715 ILH	—	10.00	22.00	40.00	75.00	—
1716 ILH	—	10.00	22.00	40.00	75.00	—
1716 IGS	—	10.00	22.00	40.00	75.00	—
1717 IGS	—	10.00	22.00	40.00	75.00	—
1718 IGS	—	10.00	22.00	40.00	75.00	—
1719 IGS	—	10.00	22.00	40.00	75.00	—
1720 IGS	—	10.00	22.00	40.00	75.00	—
1721 IGS	—	10.00	22.00	40.00	75.00	—
1722 IGS	—	10.00	22.00	40.00	75.00	—
1723 IGS	—	10.00	22.00	40.00	75.00	—
1724 IGS	—	10.00	22.00	40.00	75.00	—
1725 IGS	—	10.00	22.00	40.00	75.00	—
1726 IGS	—	10.00	22.00	40.00	75.00	—
1727 IGS	—	10.00	22.00	40.00	75.00	—
1728 IGS	—	10.00	22.00	40.00	75.00	—
1729 IGS	—	10.00	22.00	40.00	75.00	—
1730 IGS	—	10.00	22.00	40.00	75.00	—
1731 IGS	—	10.00	22.00	40.00	75.00	—
1732 IGS	—	10.00	22.00	40.00	75.00	—
1733 IGS	—	10.00	22.00	40.00	75.00	—

Note: Varieties exist

KM# 877 1/12 THALER (Doppelgroschen)

Silver **Ruler:** Friedrich August II **Obverse:** Crowned arms **Reverse:** Value and date in circle

Date	Mintage	VG	F	VF	XF	Unc
1734 IGS	—	7.00	16.00	30.00	60.00	—
1735 IGS	—	7.00	16.00	30.00	60.00	—
1735 FWoF	—	7.00	16.00	30.00	60.00	—
1736 FWoF	—	7.00	16.00	30.00	60.00	—
1737 FWoF	—	7.00	16.00	30.00	60.00	—
1738 FWoF	—	7.00	16.00	30.00	60.00	—
1739 FWoF	—	7.00	16.00	30.00	60.00	—
1740 FWoF	—	7.00	16.00	30.00	60.00	—
1741 FWoF	—	7.00	16.00	30.00	60.00	—
1742 FWoF	—	7.00	16.00	30.00	60.00	—
1743 FWoF	—	7.00	16.00	30.00	60.00	—
1744 FWoF	—	7.00	16.00	30.00	60.00	—
1745 FWoF	—	7.00	16.00	30.00	60.00	—
1746 FWoF	—	7.00	16.00	30.00	60.00	—
1747 FWoF	—	7.00	16.00	30.00	60.00	—
1748 FWoF	—	7.00	16.00	30.00	60.00	—
1749 FWoF	—	7.00	16.00	30.00	60.00	—
1750 FWoF	—	7.00	16.00	30.00	60.00	—
1751 FWoF	—	7.00	16.00	30.00	60.00	—
1752 FWoF	—	7.00	16.00	30.00	60.00	—
1753 FWoF	—	7.00	16.00	30.00	60.00	—
1754 FWoF	—	7.00	16.00	30.00	60.00	—
1755 FWoF	—	7.00	16.00	30.00	60.00	—
1757 FWoF	—	7.00	16.00	30.00	60.00	—
1762 FWoF	—	7.00	16.00	30.00	60.00	—
1763 FWoF	—	7.00	16.00	30.00	60.00	—

KM# 911 1/12 THALER (Doppelgroschen)

Silver **Ruler:** Friedrich August II **Obverse:** Crowned arms **Obv. Legend:** ends . . . & VICARIUS **Note:** Vicariat Issue.

Date	Mintage	VG	F	VF	XF	Unc
1745 FWoF	—	12.00	25.00	55.00	125	—

KM# 923 1/12 THALER (Doppelgroschen)

Silver **Ruler:** Friedrich August II **Subject:** Marriage of Princess Maria Josepha **Note:** Similar to 2/3 Thaler, KM#M6.

Date	Mintage	VG	F	VF	XF	Unc
1747	—	15.00	30.00	55.00	110	—

KM# 924 1/12 THALER (Doppelgroschen)

Silver **Ruler:** Friedrich August II **Subject:** Marriage of Prince Friedrich Christian **Note:** Similar to 2/3 Thaler, KM#M9.

Date	Mintage	VG	F	VF	XF	Unc
1747	—	10.00	20.00	45.00	90.00	—

KM# 949 1/12 THALER (Doppelgroschen)

Silver **Obverse:** Bust of Friedrich August right **Reverse:** Value and date

Date	Mintage	VG	F	VF	XF	Unc
1762	—	10.00	20.00	40.00	80.00	—

KM# 953 1/12 THALER (Doppelgroschen)

Silver **Obverse:** 2 crowned shields of arms **Reverse:** Value

Date	Mintage	VG	F	VF	XF	Unc
1763 EDC	—	5.00	10.00	20.00	40.00	—
1763 FWoF	—	5.00	10.00	20.00	40.00	—

KM# 954 1/12 THALER (Doppelgroschen)

Billon **Obverse:** Crowned arms **Reverse:** Value

Date	Mintage	VG	F	VF	XF	Unc
1763 FWoF	—	5.00	10.00	20.00	40.00	—
1763 EDC	—	5.00	10.00	20.00	40.00	—
1763 JFoF	—	5.00	10.00	20.00	40.00	—

KM# 956 1/12 THALER (Doppelgroschen)

3.3400 g., 0.4370 Silver 0.0469 oz. ASW **Ruler:** Friedrich August III **Obverse:** Crowned large oval arms **Obv. Legend:** FRID: AVGVST: D: G: DUX SAX: ELECTOR **Reverse:** Value above date **Rev. Legend:** CLX • EINE FEINE MARCK •

Date	Mintage	F	VF	XF	Unc
1763 EDC	—	5.00	10.00	20.00	70.00
1764 FWoF	—	12.50	25.00	50.00	100
1764 FWoF	—	12.50	25.00	50.00	100
1764 EDC	—	5.00	10.00	20.00	70.00
1765 EDC	—	5.00	10.00	20.00	70.00
1765 EDC	—	5.00	10.00	20.00	70.00
1797 EDC	—	5.00	10.00	20.00	70.00
1798 EDC	—	5.00	10.00	20.00	70.00

Date	Mintage	F	VF	XF	Unc
1799 EDC	—	5.00	10.00	20.00	70.00
1800 EDC	—	5.00	10.00	20.00	70.00
1800 EDC	—	5.00	10.00	20.00	70.00

KM# 955 1/12 THALER (Doppelgroschen)

3.3400 g., 0.4370 Silver 0.0469 oz. ASW **Ruler:** Xaver **Obv. Legend:** XAVERIVS. . ., different crowned arms

Date	Mintage	VG	F	VF	XF	Unc
1764 EDC	—	6.00	12.00	25.00	50.00	—
1765 EDC	—	6.00	12.00	25.00	50.00	—
1766 EDC	—	6.00	12.00	25.00	50.00	—
1767 EDC	—	6.00	12.00	25.00	50.00	—
1768 EDC	—	6.00	12.00	25.00	50.00	—

KM# 721 1/8 THALER

Silver **Ruler:** Johann Georg IV **Obverse:** Large bust right **Reverse:** Crowned flat top 2-fold arms between palm branches divides initials, date in legend **Note:** Varieties exist.

Date	Mintage	VG	F	VF	XF	Unc
1702 ILH	—	15.00	30.00	60.00	100	—
1703 ILH	—	15.00	30.00	60.00	100	—
1703 ILH	—	15.00	30.00	60.00	100	—
1728 IGS	—	15.00	30.00	60.00	100	—

KM# 740 1/8 THALER

Silver **Ruler:** Friedrich August I **Reverse:** Round arms, date at top

Date	Mintage	VG	F	VF	XF	Unc
1704 LIH	—	20.00	35.00	70.00	125	—
1705 LIH	—	20.00	35.00	70.00	125	—
1705 ILH	—	20.00	35.00	70.00	125	—

KM# 754 1/8 THALER

Silver **Ruler:** Friedrich August I **Obverse:** Small bust right, titles of Friedrich August 1 **Reverse:** Crowned round 4-fold arms with central shield of 2-fold arms in crossed palm fronds, date in legend

Date	Mintage	VG	F	VF	XF	Unc
1707 ILH	—	15.00	30.00	60.00	100	—
1710 ILH	—	15.00	30.00	60.00	100	—
1711 ILH	—	15.00	30.00	60.00	100	—
1713 ILH	—	15.00	30.00	60.00	100	—
1714 ILH	—	15.00	30.00	60.00	100	—
1714 ILH	—	15.00	30.00	60.00	100	—
1715 ILH	—	15.00	30.00	60.00	100	—
1716 ILH	—	15.00	30.00	60.00	100	—
1717 IGS	—	15.00	30.00	60.00	100	—
1718 IGS	—	15.00	30.00	60.00	100	—
1719 IGS	—	15.00	30.00	60.00	100	—
1720 IGS	—	15.00	30.00	60.00	100	—
1726 IGS	—	15.00	30.00	60.00	100	—
1727 IGS	—	15.00	30.00	60.00	100	—
1730 IGS	—	15.00	30.00	60.00	100	—
1733 IGS	—	15.00	30.00	60.00	100	—

Note: Varieties exist

KM# 800 1/8 THALER

Silver **Ruler:** Friedrich August I **Obverse:** Equestrian figure of Duke right, ornate arms in baroque frame below **Reverse:** 2 tables holding crown, scepter and mantle, 2-line inscription above, 4-line inscription with Roman numeral date below, initials and symbol at bottom **Rev. Inscription:** FRID: AUG:/REX ELECTOR/VICARIUS/POST MORT: IOSEPHI/IMPERAT:/MDCCXI **Note:** Vicariat issue.

Date	Mintage	VG	F	VF	XF	Unc
1711 ILH	—	20.00	35.00	70.00	125	—

KM# A878 1/8 THALER

Silver **Ruler:** Friedrich August II **Obverse:** Armored bust right **Reverse:** Crowned 4-fold arms with crowned central shield of electoral Saxony, date at end of legend

Date	Mintage	VG	F	VF	XF	Unc
1734 IGS	—	60.00	100	250	425	—
1735 FWoF	—	60.00	100	250	425	—
1736 FWoF	—	60.00	100	250	425	—
1737 FWoF	—	60.00	100	250	425	—
1739 FWoF	—	60.00	100	250	425	—
1740 FWoW	—	60.00	100	250	425	—
1742 FWoF	—	60.00	100	250	425	—
1743 FWoF	—	60.00	100	250	425	—
1746 FWoF	—	60.00	100	250	425	—
1748 FWoF	—	60.00	100	250	425	—
1750 FWoF	—	60.00	100	250	425	—

Note: Varieties exist.

KM# 722 1/6 THALER (1/4 Gulden)

Silver **Ruler:** Friedrich August I **Reverse:** 2 adjacent shields between palm branches, with 4-fold arms, with central shield of electoral Saxony, large crown above, value: 1/6 in oval below, date in legend

Date	Mintage	VG	F	VF	XF	Unc
1701 ILH	—	28.00	55.00	110	180	—
1702 ILH	—	28.00	55.00	110	180	—
1703 ILH	—	28.00	55.00	110	180	—
1704 ILH	—	28.00	55.00	110	180	—

Note: Varieties exist.

KM# 747 1/6 THALER (1/4 Gulden)

Silver **Ruler:** Friedrich August I **Obverse:** Armored bust right **Obv. Legend:** D: G: AUGUST: REX POLON: **Reverse:** Shields shaped more square, date divided by value **Rev. Legend:** DUX SAX: I • C • M • A • & W • S • R • I • ARCH: & EL:

Date	Mintage	VG	F	VF	XF	Unc
1706 ILH	—	30.00	65.00	120	200	—
1707 ILH	—	30.00	65.00	120	200	—

KM# 766 1/6 THALER (1/4 Gulden)

Silver **Ruler:** Friedrich August I **Obverse:** Bust right **Reverse:** Crowned AR monogram divides date, value 1/6 in oval below

Date	Mintage	VG	F	VF	XF	Unc
1708 ILH	—	40.00	70.00	140	250	—
1709 ILH	—	40.00	70.00	140	215	—

KM# 790 1/6 THALER (1/4 Gulden)

Silver **Ruler:** Friedrich August I **Obverse:** Armored bust right **Reverse:** Crowned arms **Note:** Similar to KM#747, but arms are oval.

Date	Mintage	VG	F	VF	XF	Unc
1710 ILH	—	25.00	45.00	95.00	160	—
1711 ILH	—	25.00	45.00	95.00	160	—
1712 ILH	—	25.00	45.00	95.00	160	—
1713 ILH	—	25.00	45.00	95.00	160	—
1714 ILH	—	25.00	45.00	95.00	160	—
1715 ILH	—	25.00	45.00	95.00	160	—
1716 ILH	—	25.00	45.00	95.00	160	—
1716 IGS	—	25.00	45.00	95.00	160	—
1717 IGS	—	25.00	45.00	95.00	160	—
1718 IGS	—	25.00	45.00	95.00	160	—
1719 IGS	—	25.00	45.00	95.00	160	—
1720 IGS	—	25.00	45.00	95.00	160	—
1721 IGS	—	25.00	45.00	95.00	160	—
1722 IGS	—	25.00	45.00	95.00	160	—
1723 IGS	—	25.00	45.00	95.00	160	—
1724 IGS	—	25.00	45.00	95.00	160	—
1725 IGS	—	25.00	45.00	95.00	160	—
1726 IGS	—	25.00	45.00	95.00	160	—
1727 IGS	—	25.00	45.00	95.00	160	—
1728 IGS	—	25.00	45.00	95.00	160	—
1729 IGS	—	25.00	45.00	95.00	160	—
1730 IGS	—	25.00	45.00	95.00	160	—
1730 IGS	—	25.00	45.00	95.00	160	—
1731 IGS	—	25.00	45.00	95.00	160	—
1732 IGS	—	25.00	45.00	95.00	160	—
1733 IGS	—	25.00	45.00	95.00	160	—

Note: Varieties exist

KM# 824 1/6 THALER (1/4 Gulden)

Silver **Ruler:** Friedrich August I **Subject:** Death of Friedrich August I's Mother, Anna Sophia of Denmark **Note:** Similar to 1/3 Thaler, KM#825, but value: 1/6 on obverse.

Date	Mintage	VG	F	VF	XF	Unc
1717 IGS	—	50.00	85.00	165	250	—

KM# 836 1/6 THALER (1/4 Gulden)

Silver **Ruler:** Friedrich August I **Subject:** Marriage of Prince Friedrich August (II) and Maria Josepha of Austria **Obverse:** 2 joined flaming hearts tied with ribbon held by hands at left and right, INDISSOLVBILITER above **Reverse:** 9-line inscription with Roman numeral date, initials below

Date	Mintage	VG	F	VF	XF	Unc
MDCCXIX (1719) IGS	—	45.00	75.00	145	225	—

KM# 856 1/6 THALER (1/4 Gulden)

Silver **Ruler:** Friedrich August I **Subject:** Death of Friedrich August I's Wife, Christiane Eberhardine **Note:** Similar to 2 Groschen, KM#855, but value: 1/6 on reverse.

Date	Mintage	VG	F	VF	XF	Unc
1727 IGS	—	45.00	75.00	145	225	—

KM# 890 1/6 THALER (1/4 Gulden)

4.8000 g., Silver **Ruler:** Friedrich August II **Obverse:** Armored bust right **Obv. Legend:** D: G: FRID: AUGUST: REX POLONIARUM • **Reverse:** Crown above two shields **Rev. Legend:** DUX SAX I • C • M • A • & W • S • R • I • ARCH • & EL • **Note:** Reichs 1/6 Thaler.

Date	Mintage	VG	F	VF	XF	Unc
1734 IGS	—	10.00	20.00	40.00	90.00	—
1735 FWoF	—	10.00	20.00	40.00	90.00	—
1736 FWoF	—	10.00	20.00	40.00	90.00	—
1737 FWoF	—	10.00	20.00	40.00	90.00	—
1738 FWoF	—	10.00	20.00	40.00	90.00	—
1739 FWoF	—	10.00	20.00	40.00	90.00	—
1740 FWoF	—	10.00	20.00	40.00	90.00	—
1741 FWoF	—	10.00	20.00	40.00	90.00	—
1742 FWoF	—	10.00	20.00	40.00	90.00	—
1743 FWoF	—	10.00	20.00	40.00	90.00	—
1744 FWoF	—	10.00	20.00	40.00	90.00	—
1745 FWoF	—	10.00	20.00	40.00	90.00	—
1746 FWoF	—	10.00	20.00	40.00	90.00	—
1747 FWoF	—	10.00	20.00	40.00	90.00	—
1748 FWoF	—	10.00	20.00	40.00	90.00	—
1749 FWoF	—	10.00	20.00	40.00	90.00	—
1750 FWoF	—	10.00	20.00	40.00	90.00	—
1751 FWoF	—	10.00	20.00	40.00	90.00	—
1752 FWoF	—	10.00	20.00	40.00	90.00	—
1752 FWoF	—	10.00	20.00	40.00	90.00	—
1753 FWoF	—	10.00	20.00	40.00	90.00	—
1754 FWoF	—	10.00	20.00	40.00	90.00	—
1755 FWoF	—	10.00	20.00	40.00	90.00	—

KM# 912 1/6 THALER (1/4 Gulden)

4.8000 g., Silver **Ruler:** Friedrich August II **Reverse:** 2 crowned shields of arms; . . . & VICAR **Note:** Vicariat issue.

Date	Mintage	VG	F	VF	XF	Unc
1745 FWoF	—	50.00	90.00	175	265	—

KM# A950 1/6 THALER (1/4 Gulden)

Silver **Ruler:** Friedrich August II **Mint:** Leipzig **Obverse:** Crowned bust to right **Obv. Legend:** D: G: FRID: AUGUSTUS REX POL: EL: SAX: **Reverse:** 4-line inscription with date between two laurel branches **Rev. Inscription:** VI/EINEN/ THALER/(date)

Date	Mintage	VG	F	VF	XF	Unc
1762	—	—	—	—	—	—

KM# 950 1/6 THALER (1/4 Gulden)

4.8000 g., Silver **Ruler:** Friedrich August II **Obverse:** Armored bust right **Obv. Legend:** D: G: FRID: AVGVST: REX POL: EL: SAX: **Reverse:** Crown above two shields

Date	Mintage	VG	F	VF	XF	Unc
1762	—	8.00	16.00	32.00	75.00	—
1762 FWoF	—	8.00	16.00	32.00	75.00	—
1763 EDC	—	8.00	16.00	32.00	75.00	—
1763 FWoF	—	10.00	20.00	40.00	90.00	—

KM# 957 1/6 THALER (1/4 Gulden)

4.8000 g., Silver

Date	Mintage	F	VF	XF	Unc
1763 EDC	—	20.00	40.00	90.00	250

KM# 969 1/6 THALER (1/4 Gulden)

4.8000 g., Silver **Ruler:** Xaver **Obverse:** Bust right **Reverse:** Crowned arms, value below

Date	Mintage	F	VF	XF	Unc
1764 EDC Proof	—	—	—	—	—
1764 EDC	—	12.00	25.00	50.00	150
1765 EDC	—	12.00	25.00	50.00	150
1766 EDC	—	12.00	25.00	50.00	150
1767 EDC	—	12.00	25.00	50.00	150

KM# 970 1/6 THALER (1/4 Gulden)

5.3900 g., 0.5410 Silver 0.0937 oz. ASW **Obverse:** Young head right **Reverse:** Elector's cap above arms in branches, date in exerque

Date	Mintage	F	VF	XF	Unc
1764 FWoF	—	10.00	20.00	40.00	135
1764 EDC	—	10.00	20.00	40.00	135
1766 EDC	—	10.00	20.00	40.00	135
1767 EDC	—	10.00	20.00	40.00	135
1768 EDC	—	10.00	20.00	40.00	135

KM# 705 1/4 THALER

Silver **Ruler:** Friedrich August I **Obverse:** Large bust right **Reverse:** Round arms between palm branches dividing initials

Date	Mintage	VG	F	VF	XF	Unc
1702 ILH	—	35.00	80.00	160	325	—
1703 ILH	—	35.00	80.00	160	325	—
1704 ILH	—	35.00	80.00	160	325	—
1705 ILH	—	35.00	80.00	160	325	—
1706 ILH	—	35.00	80.00	160	325	—
1707 ILH	—	35.00	80.00	160	325	—

Note: Varieties exist

KM# 677 1/4 THALER

Silver **Ruler:** Johann Georg IV **Obverse:** Crowned bust right **Reverse:** 3 small oval shields of arms, crown above divides date, value 18 **Note:** Prev. Poland KM#134.

Date	Mintage	VG	F	VF	XF	Unc
1704 EPH	—	—	—	—	—	—

KM# 791 1/4 THALER

Silver **Ruler:** Friedrich August I **Obverse:** Small bust right, titles of Freidrich August I **Reverse:** Crowned, round 4-fold arms with central shield of 2-fold arms in crossed palm fronds, date in legend

Date	Mintage	VG	F	VF	XF	Unc
1710 ILH	—	40.00	85.00	175	350	—
1711 ILH	—	40.00	85.00	175	350	—
1713 ILH	—	40.00	85.00	175	350	—
1714 ILH	—	40.00	85.00	175	350	—
1715 ILH	—	40.00	85.00	175	350	—
1716 ILH	—	40.00	85.00	175	350	—
1717 IGS	—	40.00	85.00	175	350	—
1718 IGS	—	40.00	85.00	175	350	—
1719 IGS	—	40.00	85.00	175	350	—
1720 IGS	—	40.00	85.00	175	350	—
1723 IGS	—	40.00	85.00	175	350	—
1727 IGS	—	40.00	85.00	175	350	—
1728 IGS	—	40.00	85.00	175	350	—
1730 IGS	—	40.00	85.00	175	350	—
1733 IGS	—	40.00	85.00	175	350	—

Note: Varieties exist

KM# 801 1/4 THALER

Silver **Ruler:** Friedrich August I **Subject:** Vicariat issue **Obverse:** King on horseback right, shield below **Reverse:** Two tables, each with crown, sceptre, orb and mantle, legends above and below **Rev. Legend:** FRID: AUG•/ REX ELECTOR/ VICARIUS/ POST MORT: IOSE:/IMPERAT:/ MDCCXI • **Note:** Similar to 1/8 Thaler, KM#800.

Date	Mintage	VG	F	VF	XF	Unc
1711 OLH	—	25.00	40.00	80.00	145	—

KM# A891 1/4 THALER

Silver **Ruler:** Friedrich August II **Obverse:** Bust to right **Reverse:** Two adjacent ornate shields of arms, value 1/4 below, date at end of legend

Date	Mintage	VG	F	VF	XF	Unc
1737 FWoF	—	75.00	120	300	525	—
1738 FWoF	—	75.00	120	300	525	—

KM# 723 1/3 THALER (1/2 Gulden)

Silver **Ruler:** Friedrich August I **Obverse:** Armored bust right **Reverse:** Crown above two shields **Note:** Similar to 1/6 Thaler, KM#722, but value: 1/3 on reverse.

Date	Mintage	VG	F	VF	XF	Unc
1701 ILH	—	28.00	55.00	110	185	—
1702 EPH	—	28.00	55.00	110	185	—
1703 ILH	—	28.00	55.00	110	185	—
1704 ILH	—	28.00	55.00	110	185	—
1705 ILH	—	28.00	55.00	110	185	—

Note: Varieties exist

KM# 748 1/3 THALER (1/2 Gulden)

Silver **Ruler:** Friedrich August I **Note:** Similar to 1/6 Thaler, KM#747, but date in reverse legend and value: 1/3.

Date	Mintage	VG	F	VF	XF	Unc
1706 ILH	—	35.00	65.00	120	225	—
1707 ILH	—	35.00	65.00	120	225	—

KM# 767 1/3 THALER (1/2 Gulden)

Silver **Ruler:** Friedrich August I **Obverse:** Bust right **Reverse:** Crowned AR monogram divides date, value: 1/3 in oval below

Date	Mintage	VG	F	VF	XF	Unc
1708 ILH	—	60.00	100	200	350	—
1709 ILH	—	60.00	100	200	350	—
1710 ILH	—	60.00	100	200	350	—
1710 EPH	—	60.00	100	200	350	—

KM# 792.1 1/3 THALER (1/2 Gulden)

Silver **Ruler:** Friedrich August I **Obverse:** Armored bust to right **Obv. Legend:** D • G • FRID: AUGUST: REX POLONIARUM • **Reverse:** Crown above two adjacent shields, value in center below

Date	Mintage	VG	F	VF	XF	Unc
1710 ILH	—	45.00	80.00	160	275	—
1711 ILH	—	45.00	80.00	160	275	—
1712 ILH	—	45.00	80.00	160	275	—
1714 ILH	—	45.00	80.00	160	275	—
1715 EPH	—	45.00	80.00	160	275	—

Note: Varieties exist.

KM# 792.2 1/3 THALER (1/2 Gulden)

Silver **Ruler:** Friedrich August I **Obverse:** Armored bust right **Obv. Legend:** D • G • FRID: AUGUST: REX POLONIARUM • **Reverse:** Crown above two shields, value in center below **Note:** Similar to 1/6 Thaler, KM#790, but value: 1/3 on reverse.

Date	Mintage	VG	F	VF	XF	Unc
1717 IGS	—	45.00	80.00	160	275	—
1718 IGS	—	45.00	80.00	160	275	—
1719 IGS	—	45.00	80.00	160	275	—
1720 IGS	—	45.00	80.00	160	275	—
1721 IGS	—	45.00	80.00	160	275	—
1722 IGS	—	45.00	80.00	160	275	—
1723 IGS	—	45.00	80.00	160	275	—
1724 IGS	—	45.00	80.00	160	275	—
1725 IGS	—	45.00	80.00	160	275	—
1726 IGS	—	45.00	80.00	160	275	—
1727 IGS	—	45.00	80.00	160	275	—
1728 IGS	—	45.00	80.00	160	275	—
1729 IGS	—	45.00	80.00	160	275	—
1730 IGS	—	45.00	80.00	160	275	—
1731 IGS	—	45.00	80.00	160	275	—
1732 IGS	—	45.00	80.00	160	275	—
1733 IGS	—	45.00	80.00	160	275	—

Note: Varieties exist

KM# 825 1/3 THALER (1/2 Gulden)

Silver **Ruler:** Friedrich August I **Subject:** Death of Friedrich August's Mother, Anna Sophia of Denmark **Obverse:** Inscription **Reverse:** Ship in harbor, inscription and value below

Date	Mintage	VG	F	VF	XF	Unc
1717 IGS	—	60.00	100	200	350	—

KM# 837 1/3 THALER (1/2 Gulden)

Silver **Ruler:** Friedrich August I **Subject:** Marriage of Prince Friedrich August (II) and Maria Josepha of Austria **Obverse:** Inscription **Reverse:** Two hands binding flaming heart **Note:** Similar to 1 Thaler, KM#840, but value: 1/3 on reverse.

Date	Mintage	VG	F	VF	XF	Unc
MDCCXIX(1719) IGS	—	50.00	90.00	180	285	—

KM# 857 1/3 THALER (1/2 Gulden)

Silver **Ruler:** Friedrich August I **Subject:** Death of Friedrich Augusts I's Wife, Christiane Eberhardine **Obverse:** Inscription **Reverse:** Cyprus tree at center

Date	Mintage	VG	F	VF	XF	Unc
1727 IGS	—	22.00	45.00	90.00	165	—

KM# 878 1/3 THALER (1/2 Gulden)

9.6000 g., Silver **Ruler:** Friedrich August II **Obverse:** Armored bust right **Reverse:** Value between 2 crowned shields of arms **Note:** Reichs 1/3 Thaler.

Date	Mintage	VG	F	VF	XF	Unc
1734 IGS	—	15.00	30.00	60.00	140	—
1736/35 FWoF	—	15.00	30.00	60.00	140	—
1736 FWoF	—	15.00	30.00	60.00	140	—
1737 FWoF	—	15.00	30.00	60.00	140	—
1738 FWoF	—	15.00	30.00	60.00	140	—
1739 FWoF	—	15.00	30.00	60.00	140	—
1740 FWoF	—	15.00	30.00	60.00	140	—
1741 FWoF	—	15.00	30.00	60.00	140	—
1742 FWoF	—	15.00	30.00	60.00	140	—
1743 FWoF	—	15.00	30.00	60.00	140	—
1745 FWoF	—	15.00	30.00	60.00	140	—
1746 FWoF	—	15.00	30.00	60.00	140	—
1747 FWoF	—	15.00	30.00	60.00	140	—
1748 FWoF	—	15.00	30.00	60.00	140	—
1749 FWoF	—	15.00	30.00	60.00	140	—
1751 FWoF	—	15.00	30.00	60.00	140	—
1752/1 FWoF	—	15.00	30.00	60.00	140	—
1752 FWoF	—	15.00	30.00	60.00	140	—
1753 FWoF	—	15.00	30.00	60.00	140	—
1754 FWoF	—	15.00	30.00	60.00	140	—
1755 FWoF	—	15.00	30.00	60.00	140	—
1756 FWoF	—	15.00	30.00	60.00	140	—

KM# 913 1/3 THALER (1/2 Gulden)

9.6000 g., Silver **Ruler:** Friedrich August II **Reverse:** 2 crowned shields of arms; ...& VICAR **Note:** Vicariat issue.

Date	Mintage	VG	F	VF	XF	Unc
1745 FWoF	—	35.00	75.00	150	300	—

KM# 958 1/3 THALER (1/2 Gulden)

9.6000 g., Silver **Ruler:** Friedrich August II **Obverse:** Armored, draped bust right **Obv. Legend:** D: G: FRID: AVGVST: REX: POL: EL: SAX: **Reverse:** Crown above two shields, value at center below

Date	Mintage	VG	F	VF	XF	Unc
1763 FWoF	—	18.00	35.00	70.00	150	—

KM# 971 1/3 THALER (1/2 Gulden)

7.0160 g., 0.8330 Silver 0.1879 oz. ASW **Ruler:** Xaver **Obverse:** Armored bust right **Reverse:** Crowned shield, value below

Date	Mintage	F	VF	XF	Unc
1764 EDC	—	35.00	70.00	145	280
1765 EDC	—	35.00	70.00	145	280
1765 EDC	—	35.00	70.00	145	280
1766 EDC	—	35.00	70.00	145	280
1767 EDC	—	35.00	70.00	145	280

KM# 972 1/3 THALER (1/2 Gulden)

7.0160 g., 0.8330 Silver 0.1879 oz. ASW **Ruler:** Friedrich August III **Obverse:** Head right **Obv. Legend:** FRID: AVGVST: D: G: SAXONIA: ELECTOR **Reverse:** Crowned arms within branches

Date	Mintage	F	VF	XF	Unc
1764 EDC	—	45.00	90.00	175	350

KM# 1010 1/3 THALER (1/2 Gulden)
7.0160 g., 0.8330 Silver 0.1879 oz. ASW **Ruler:** Friedrich August III **Obverse:** Head right **Reverse:** Crowned arms within branches, value below

Date	Mintage	VG	F	VF	XF	Unc
1780 IEC	—	15.00	30.00	50.00	90.00	—
1781 IEC	—	15.00	30.00	50.00	90.00	—
1782 IEC	—	15.00	30.00	50.00	90.00	—
1783 IEC	—	15.00	30.00	50.00	90.00	—
1784 IEC	—	15.00	30.00	50.00	90.00	—
1785 IEC	—	15.00	30.00	50.00	90.00	—
1786 IEC	—	15.00	30.00	50.00	90.00	—
1787 IEC	—	15.00	30.00	50.00	90.00	—
1788 IEC	—	15.00	30.00	50.00	90.00	—
1789 IEC	—	15.00	30.00	50.00	90.00	—
1790 IEC	—	15.00	30.00	50.00	90.00	—

KM# 1021 1/3 THALER (1/2 Gulden)
7.0160 g., 0.8330 Silver 0.1879 oz. ASW **Ruler:** Friedrich August III **Obverse:** Head right **Reverse:** Crowned arms on eagle's breast, value divides date below

Date	Mintage	VG	F	VF	XF	Unc
1790 IEC	—	20.00	40.00	85.00	160	—

KM# 1024 1/3 THALER (1/2 Gulden)
7.0160 g., 0.8330 Silver 0.1879 oz. ASW **Ruler:** Friedrich August III **Obverse:** Head right **Obv. Legend:** FRID • AVGVST • D • G • DVX • SAX • ELECTOR • **Reverse:** Crowned oval arms within crossed branches

Date	Mintage	F	VF	XF	Unc
1791 IEC	—	20.00	40.00	75.00	150
1792 IEC	—	20.00	40.00	75.00	150
1793 IEC	—	20.00	40.00	75.00	150
1794 IEC	—	20.00	40.00	75.00	150
1795 IEC	—	20.00	40.00	75.00	150
1796 IEC	—	20.00	40.00	75.00	150
1797 IEC	—	20.00	40.00	75.00	150
1800 IEC	—	20.00	40.00	75.00	150

KM# 1032 1/3 THALER (1/2 Gulden)
7.0160 g., 0.8330 Silver 0.1879 oz. ASW **Ruler:** Friedrich August III **Obverse:** Armored, draped bust right **Obv. Legend:** FRID • AVGVST • D • G • DVX • SAX • ELECTOR • **Reverse:** Crowned arms on eagle's breast, value below **Note:** Vicariat issue.

Date	Mintage	VG	F	VF	XF	Unc
1792 IEC	—	20.00	40.00	85.00	160	—

KM# 724 1/2 THALER
Silver **Ruler:** Friedrich August I **Obverse:** Laureate bust right **Obv. Legend:** DG.FRID.AUG.REX.POL — DUX SAX. I.C.M.A & W. **Reverse:** Crowned, round 4-fold arms with crowned central shield of 2-fold arms, between 2 palm branches crossed at bottom, date at top **Rev. Legend:** SAC. ROMANI. IMP. ARCHIMARS. ET. ELECT. **Note:** Varieties exist.

Date	Mintage	VG	F	VF	XF	Unc
1701 ILH	—	70.00	150	275	450	—
1702 ILH	—	70.00	150	275	450	—
1703 ILH	—	70.00	150	275	450	—
1704 ILH	—	70.00	150	275	450	—
1705 ILH	—	70.00	150	275	450	—

KM# 749 1/2 THALER
Silver **Ruler:** Friedrich August I **Obverse:** Laureate armored bust right **Obv. Legend:** D. G. FRID. AUG. REX POL: — DUX SAX: I. C. M. A. & W. **Reverse:** Crowned squarish 4-fold arms with concave sides, crowned 2-fold central shield, palm branch to left and right, date at end of legend **Rev. Legend:** SAC: ROM: IMP: ARCHIM: ET ELECT:

Date	Mintage	VG	F	VF	XF	Unc
1706 ILH	—	150	300	750	1,250	—
1707 ILH	—	150	300	750	1,250	—

KM# 834 1/2 THALER
Silver **Ruler:** Friedrich August I **Obverse:** Small laureate bust right **Obv. Legend:** D. G. FRID: AUGUST. REX POL: DUX SAX. I. C. M. A. & W. **Reverse:** Crowned round 4-fold arms with crowned central shield of 2-fold arms between crossed palm branches, date at end of legend **Rev. Legend:** SAC: ROM: IMP: ARCHIM: ET ELECT.

Date	Mintage	VG	F	VF	XF	Unc
1711 ILH	—	100	200	500	950	—
1713 ILH	—	100	200	500	950	—
1714 ILH	—	100	200	500	950	—
1715 ILH	—	100	200	500	950	—
1718 IGS	—	100	200	500	950	—
1722 IGS	—	100	200	500	950	—
1723 IGS	—	100	200	500	950	—
1724 IGS	—	100	200	500	950	—
1727 IGS	—	100	200	500	950	—
1728 IGS	—	100	200	500	950	—
1729 IGS	—	100	200	500	950	—
1733 IGS	—	100	200	500	950	—

Note: Varieties exist

KM# 802 1/2 THALER
Silver **Ruler:** Friedrich August I **Subject:** Vicariat issue **Obverse:** King on horseback right, shield below **Reverse:** Two tables, each with crown, sceptre, orb and mantle, inscriptions above and below **Rev. Inscription:** FRID: AUG:/REX ELECTOR/VICARIUS/ POST MORT: IOSEPHI/IMPERAT:/MDCCXI **Note:** Vicariat Issue. Similar to 1/8 Thaler, KM#800.

Date	Mintage	VG	F	VF	XF	Unc
1711 ILH	—	35.00	80.00	160	325	—

KM# A879 1/2 THALER
Silver **Ruler:** Friedrich August II **Obverse:** Bust to right **Reverse:** Crowned 4-fold arms with crowned central shield of electoral Saxony, date at end of legend

Date	Mintage	VG	F	VF	XF	Unc
1734 IGS	—	90.00	175	375	750	—
1736 FWoF	—	90.00	175	375	750	—
1737 FWoF	—	90.00	175	375	750	—
1738 FWoF	—	90.00	175	375	750	—
1741 FWoF	—	90.00	175	375	750	—
1742 FWoF	—	90.00	175	375	750	—
1744 FWoF	—	90.00	175	375	750	—
1745 FWoF	—	90.00	175	375	750	—
1748 FWoF	—	90.00	175	375	750	—
1751 FWoF	—	90.00	175	375	750	—
1752 FWoF	—	90.00	175	375	750	—

KM# A907 1/2 THALER
Silver **Ruler:** Friedrich August II **Subject:** Vicariat issue **Obverse:** Friedrich August II on horse rearing to right **Obv. Legend:** D.G. FRID. AUG. REX POL. DUX SAX. ARCHIMARESCHALL & ELECT. **Reverse:** Empty throne on dias with symbols of office, date at end of legend **Rev. Legend:** IN PROVINCIIS IUR. SAXON. PROVISOR ET VICARIUS.

Date	Mintage	VG	F	VF	XF	Unc
1741	—	40.00	80.00	200	375	500
1742	—	40.00	80.00	200	375	500

KM# 685 2/3 THALER (Gulden)
Silver **Ruler:** Friedrich August I **Obverse:** Armored, laureate bust right **Obv. Legend:** DG • FRID • AUGUST • REX POLONIARUM **Reverse:** Crown above two shields, value below **Rev. Legend:** DUX • SAX • I • C • M • A • & • W • S • R • I • ... **Note:** Similar to 1 Thaler, KM#707, but value: 2/3 on reverse.

Date	Mintage	VG	F	VF	XF	Unc
1701 ILH	—	28.00	50.00	100	185	—
1701 EPH	—	28.00	50.00	100	185	—
1701 ILH	—	28.00	50.00	100	185	—
1702 ILH	—	28.00	50.00	100	185	—
1702 ILH	—	28.00	50.00	100	185	—
1703 EPH	—	28.00	50.00	100	185	—
1703 ILH	—	28.00	50.00	100	185	—
1704 EPH	—	28.00	50.00	100	185	—
1704 ILH	—	28.00	50.00	100	185	—
1705 EPH	—	28.00	50.00	100	185	—

Note: Varieties exist

KM# B879 2/3 THALER (Gulden)
Silver **Ruler:** Friedrich August II **Obverse:** Bust right **Reverse:** Crowned 4-fold arms within which small 4-fold arms with central shield of electoral Saxony, all divide date, value (2/3) below

Date	Mintage	VG	F	VF	XF	Unc
1734 IGS	—	100	175	325	800	—

KM# 744 2/3 THALER (Gulden)
Silver **Ruler:** Friedrich August I **Obverse:** Draped, laureate bust right **Obv. Legend:** D • G • FRID: AUGUST: REX POLONIARUM **Reverse:** Crown above two shields, value below

Date	Mintage	VG	F	VF	XF	Unc
1705 ILH ILH	—	50.00	90.00	160	275	—
1706 ILH	—	50.00	90.00	160	275	—
1707 ILH	—	50.00	90.00	160	275	—

Note: Varieties exist

KM# 768 2/3 THALER (Gulden)
Silver **Ruler:** Friedrich August I **Obverse:** Armored bust right **Obv. Legend:** AUGUST • D • G • REX • ... **Reverse:** Crowned monogram divides date **Rev. Legend:** NONETA SAXONICA

Date	Mintage	VG	F	VF	XF	Unc
1708 ILH	—	60.00	130	240	400	—
1708 EPH	—	60.00	130	240	400	—
1709 ILH	—	60.00	130	240	400	—
1709 EPH	—	60.00	130	240	400	—
1710 ILH	—	60.00	130	240	400	—

Note: Varieties exist

KM# 775 2/3 THALER (Gulden)

Silver **Ruler:** Friedrich August I **Obverse:** Bust right **Obv. Legend:** D • G • FRID: AUGUST: REX ... **Reverse:** Crown above 2 oval shields within branches **Rev. Legend:** DUX • SAX: I • C • M • A • & W • S • R • I • ARCH: & EL:

Date	Mintage	VG	F	VF	XF	Unc
1709 ILH	—	30.00	55.00	110	200	—
1710 ILH	—	30.00	55.00	110	200	—
1711 ILH	—	30.00	55.00	110	200	—
1712 ILH	—	30.00	55.00	110	200	—
1713 ILH	—	30.00	55.00	110	200	—
1714 ILH	—	30.00	55.00	110	200	—
1715 ILH	—	30.00	55.00	110	200	—
1716 ILH	—	30.00	55.00	110	200	—
1716 IGS	—	30.00	55.00	110	200	—
1717 IGS	—	30.00	55.00	110	200	—
1718 IGS	—	30.00	55.00	110	200	—
1719 IGS	—	30.00	55.00	110	200	—
1720 IGS	—	30.00	55.00	110	200	—
1721 IGS	—	30.00	55.00	110	200	—
1722 IGS	—	30.00	55.00	110	200	—
1723 IGS	—	30.00	55.00	110	200	—
1724 IGS	—	30.00	55.00	110	200	—
1725 IGS	—	30.00	55.00	110	200	—
1726 IGS	—	30.00	55.00	110	200	—
1727 IGS	—	30.00	55.00	110	200	—
1728 IGS	—	30.00	55.00	110	200	—
1729 IGS	—	30.00	55.00	110	200	—
1730 IGS	—	30.00	55.00	110	200	—
1731 IGS	—	30.00	55.00	110	200	—
1732 IGS	—	30.00	55.00	110	200	—
1733 IGS	—	30.00	55.00	110	200	—

Note: Varieties exist

KM# 826 2/3 THALER (Gulden)

Silver **Ruler:** Friedrich August I **Subject:** Death of Friedrich August I's Mother, Anna Sophia of Denmark **Obverse:** Inscription **Reverse:** Ship in harbor

Date	Mintage	VG	F	VF	XF	Unc
1717 IGS	—	125	200	350	525	—

KM# 838 2/3 THALER (Gulden)

Silver **Ruler:** Friedrich August I **Subject:** Marriage of Prince Friedrich August (II) and Maria Josepha of Austria **Obverse:** Inscription **Reverse:** 2 Hands binding flaming heart **Note:** Similar to 1 Thaler, KM#840, but value: 2/3 on reverse.

Date	Mintage	VG	F	VF	XF	Unc
MDCCXIX (1719) IGS	—	45.00	80.00	160	275	—

KM# 858 2/3 THALER (Gulden)

Silver **Ruler:** Friedrich August I **Subject:** Death of Friedrich August I's Wife, Christiane Eberhardine **Obverse:** Inscription **Reverse:** Cyprus tree at center

Date	Mintage	VG	F	VF	XF	Unc
1727 IGS	—	35.00	65.00	130	240	—

KM# 871 2/3 THALER (Gulden)

19.2000 g., Silver **Ruler:** Friedrich August I **Obverse:** Bust right, . . . PR.R.P **Obv. Legend:** D • G • FRID: AUGUST: REX • POLONIARUM • **Reverse:** Crown above 2 shields, value in lower center **Note:** Reichs 2/3 Thaler.

Date	Mintage	VG	F	VF	XF	Unc
1733 IGS	—	30.00	55.00	120	220	—

KM# 879 2/3 THALER (Gulden)

19.2000 g., Silver **Ruler:** Friedrich August II **Obverse:** Armored bust right **Obv. Legend:** D: G: FRID: AUGUST: REX POLONIARUM • **Reverse:** Crown above 2 shields, value at lower center

Date	Mintage	VG	F	VF	XF	Unc
1734 IGS	—	30.00	55.00	110	200	—
1735 FWoF	—	30.00	55.00	110	200	—
1736 FWoF	—	30.00	55.00	110	200	—
1737 FWoF	—	30.00	55.00	110	200	—
1738 FWoF	—	30.00	55.00	110	200	—
1739 FWoF	—	30.00	55.00	110	200	—
1740 FWoF	—	30.00	55.00	110	200	—
1741 FWoF	—	30.00	55.00	110	200	—
1742 FWoF	—	30.00	55.00	110	200	—
1743 FWoF	—	30.00	55.00	110	200	—
1744 FWoF	—	30.00	55.00	110	200	—
1745 FWoF	—	30.00	55.00	110	200	—
1746 FWoF	—	30.00	55.00	110	200	—
1747 FWoF	—	30.00	55.00	110	200	—
1748 FWoF	—	30.00	55.00	110	200	—
1749 FWoF	—	30.00	55.00	110	200	—
1750 FWoF	—	30.00	55.00	110	200	—
1751 FWoF	—	30.00	55.00	110	200	—
1752/1 FWoF	—	30.00	55.00	110	200	—
1753 FWoF	—	30.00	55.00	110	200	—
1754 FWoF	—	30.00	55.00	110	200	—
1755 FWoF	—	30.00	55.00	110	200	—
1760 FWoF	—	30.00	55.00	110	200	—
1761 FWoF	—	30.00	55.00	110	200	—
1762 FWoF	—	30.00	55.00	110	200	—

KM# 897 2/3 THALER (Gulden)

19.2000 g., Silver **Ruler:** Friedrich August II **Subject:** Marriage of Princess Maria Amalia and Carlos III of Spain **Obverse:** Inscription **Reverse:** 2 Hearts on altar, crown above

Date	Mintage	VG	F	VF	XF	Unc
MDCCXXXVIII(1738)	—	35.00	75.00	165	320	—

KM# 922 2/3 THALER (Gulden)

19.2000 g., Silver **Ruler:** Friedrich August II **Subject:** Marriage of Prince Friedrich Christian **Obverse:** Inscription **Reverse:** Winged figure with sceptre

Date	Mintage	VG	F	VF	XF	Unc
1747	—	40.00	80.00	175	345	—

KM# 921 2/3 THALER (Gulden)

Silver **Ruler:** Friedrich August II **Subject:** Marriage of Princess Maria Josepha to the Dauphin Louis of France **Obverse:** 8-line inscription with Roman numeral date **Obv. Inscription:** LUDOVICI/DELPHINI/ET/MARIÆ IOSEPHÆ/ REG:POL: PRINC:/CONNUBIUM/DRESDÆ/MDCCXLVII. **Reverse:** Shields of arms of the Dauphiné and Saxony-Poland leaning against flaming altar, legend curved above **Rev. Legend:** AMOR MUTUUS.

Date	Mintage	VG	F	VF	XF	Unc
MDCCXLVII (1747)	—	32.00	65.00	160	300	—

KM# A922 2/3 THALER (Gulden)

Silver **Ruler:** Friedrich August II **Subject:** Marriage of Princess Maria Anna **Obverse:** Two busts to right **Reverse:** Personification of Bavaria before pyramid

Date	Mintage	VG	F	VF	XF	Unc
MDCCXLVII (1747)	—	45.00	90.00	200	375	—

KM# 925 2/3 THALER (Gulden)

19.2000 g., Silver **Ruler:** Friedrich August II **Subject:** Prussian Occupation **Obverse:** Armored bust right **Obv. Legend:** D: G: FRID: AUGUST: REX: POLONIARUM • **Reverse:** Value below 2 crowned oval shields of arms

Date	Mintage	VG	F	VF	XF	Unc
1753	—	30.00	60.00	145	285	—
1754 EDC	—	30.00	60.00	145	285	—
1757 IDB	—	30.00	60.00	145	285	—
1763 EDC	—	30.00	60.00	135	265	—

KM# 959 2/3 THALER (Gulden)

19.2000 g., Silver **Ruler:** Friedrich August II **Obverse:** Armored bust of Friedrich August right **Obv. Legend:** D: G: FRID: AVGVST: REX POL: EL: SAX: **Reverse:** Value between 2 crowned round shields of arms

Date	Mintage	VG	F	VF	XF	Unc
1763 FWoF	—	40.00	70.00	125	250	—

KM# 960 2/3 THALER (Gulden)

19.2000 g., Silver **Ruler:** Friedrich August II **Obverse:** Armored bust right **Obv. Legend:** D: G: FRID: CHRISTIAN: PR: R: POL: & L: DVX: SAX: **Reverse:** Crown above two shields, value below **Rev. Legend:** IVL: CL: MONT: A: W: S: R: I: ARCHIM .....

Date	Mintage	F	VF	XF	Unc
1763 FWoF	—	45.00	90.00	180	345
1763 EDC	—	45.00	90.00	180	345
1763 JFoF	—	45.00	90.00	180	345

KM# 973 2/3 THALER (Gulden)

14.0310 g., 0.8330 Silver 0.3758 oz. ASW **Ruler:** Xaver **Obverse:** Armored bust right **Obv. Legend:** XAVERIVS D: G: REG PR POL & LITH DVX SAX **Reverse:** Crowned arms, value below

Date	Mintage	F	VF	XF	Unc
1764 EDC	—	50.00	100	220	450
1765 EDC	—	50.00	100	220	450
1766 EDC	—	50.00	100	220	450
1767 EDC	—	50.00	100	220	450
1768 EDC	—	50.00	100	220	450

KM# 974 2/3 THALER (Gulden)

14.0310 g., 0.8330 Silver 0.3758 oz. ASW **Ruler:** Friedrich August III **Obverse:** Head right **Obv. Legend:** FRID: AVGVST: D: G: SAXONIÆ ELECTOR **Reverse:** Date below divided arms

Date	Mintage	F	VF	XF	Unc
1764 EDC	—	50.00	100	220	450
1764 IFoF	—	50.00	100	220	450

KM# 981 2/3 THALER (Gulden)

14.0310 g., 0.8330 Silver 0.3758 oz. ASW **Ruler:** Friedrich August III **Obverse:** Bust right **Obv. Legend:** FRID: AVGVST: D: G: DVX SAX: ELECTOR **Reverse:** Crown above two shields, value divides date below

Date	Mintage	F	VF	XF	Unc
1765 EDC	—	30.00	55.00	100	235
1766 EDC	—	30.00	55.00	100	235
1767 EDC	—	30.00	55.00	100	235
1768 EDC	—	30.00	55.00	100	235

KM# 991 2/3 THALER (Gulden)

14.0310 g., 0.8330 Silver 0.3758 oz. ASW **Ruler:** Friedrich August III **Obverse:** Head right **Obv. Legend:** FRID: AVGVST: D: G: DVX SAX ELECTOR **Reverse:** Crown above two shields, value divides date below

Date	Mintage	VG	F	VF	XF	Unc
1769 EDC	—	15.00	30.00	55.00	120	—
1770 EDC	—	15.00	30.00	55.00	120	—
1771 EDC	—	15.00	30.00	55.00	120	—
1772 EDC	—	15.00	30.00	55.00	120	—
1773 EDC	—	15.00	30.00	55.00	120	—
1774 EDC	—	15.00	30.00	55.00	120	—
1775 EDC	—	15.00	30.00	55.00	120	—
1776 EDC	—	15.00	30.00	55.00	120	—
1777 EDC	—	15.00	30.00	55.00	120	—
1779 EDC	—	15.00	30.00	55.00	120	—
1780 EDC	—	15.00	30.00	55.00	120	—
1781 EDC	—	15.00	30.00	55.00	120	—
1782 EDC	—	15.00	30.00	55.00	120	—
1783 EDC	—	15.00	30.00	55.00	120	—
1784 EDC	—	15.00	30.00	55.00	120	—
1785 IEC	—	15.00	30.00	55.00	120	—
1785 EDC	—	15.00	30.00	55.00	120	—
1786 EDC	—	15.00	30.00	55.00	120	—
1787 EDC	—	15.00	30.00	55.00	120	—
1788 EDC	—	15.00	30.00	55.00	120	—

KM# 1022 2/3 THALER (Gulden)

14.0310 g., 0.8330 Silver 0.3758 oz. ASW **Ruler:** Friedrich August III **Obverse:** Head right **Obv. Legend:** FRID • AVG • D • G • DVX • SAX • ELECTOR & VICARIVS EMPERII **Reverse:** Electors cap above arms on eagle's breast, value divides date below **Note:** Vicariat issue.

Date	Mintage	VG	F	VF	XF	Unc
1790 IEC	—	35.00	70.00	110	180	—

KM# 1025 2/3 THALER (Gulden)

14.0310 g., 0.8330 Silver 0.3758 oz. ASW **Ruler:** Friedrich August III **Obverse:** Armored bust right **Obv. Legend:** FRID • AVGVST • D • G • DVX • SAX ELECTOR **Reverse:** Large crowned oval arms within branches

Date	Mintage	F	VF	XF	Unc
1791 IEC	—	35.00	75.00	150	275
1792 IEC	—	35.00	75.00	150	275
1793 EIC	—	35.00	75.00	150	275
1794 IEC	—	35.00	75.00	150	275
1795 IEC	—	35.00	75.00	150	275
1796 IEC	—	35.00	75.00	159	275
1797 IEC	—	35.00	75.00	150	275
1798 IEC	—	35.00	75.00	150	275
1799 IEC	—	35.00	75.00	150	275
1800 IEC	—	35.00	75.00	150	275

KM# 1033 2/3 THALER (Gulden)

14.0310 g., 0.8330 Silver 0.3758 oz. ASW **Ruler:** Friedrich August III **Reverse:** Imperial eagle behind crowned shield **Note:** Vicariat Issue.

Date	Mintage	VG	F	VF	XF	Unc
1792 IEC	—	40.00	75.00	120	200	—

KM# 707 THALER

Silver **Ruler:** Friedrich August I **Reverse:** 2 shields crowned between palm branches **Note:** Dav. #7656.

Date	Mintage	F	VF	XF	Unc
1701 ILH	—	100	200	350	750
1701 EPH	—	100	200	350	750
1702 ILH	—	100	200	350	750
1702 EPH	—	100	200	350	750
1703 ILH	—	100	200	350	750
1704 ILH	—	100	200	350	750
1705 ILH	—	100	200	350	750

KM# 713 THALER

Silver **Ruler:** Friedrich August I **Obverse:** Crowned A in sprays, date divided above **Reverse:** Hand with wreath from cloud above Hercules on a cloud **Rev. Legend:** VIRTUTE PARATA **Shape:** 4-Sided **Note:** Klippe. Dav. #7657 and Dav. #2648.

Date	Mintage	F	VF	XF	Unc
1705	—	175	325	550	1,000

KM# 832 THALER

Silver **Ruler:** Friedrich August I **Obverse:** Small crowned bust right **Note:** Dav.#1614. Varieties exist. Prev. Poland KM#138.

Date	Mintage	VG	F	VF	XF	Unc
1702 EPH	—	275	550	1,000	1,800	—

KM# 750 THALER

Silver **Ruler:** Friedrich August I **Obverse:** Crowned arms with 6 small shields around, date below **Obv. Legend:** D • G • FRID: AUG: REX POL: - DUX SAX: I • C • M • A • & W • **Rev. Legend:** SAC: ROM: IMP: ARCHIM: ET ELECTOR • **Note:** Dav.#2649.

Date	Mintage	F	VF	XF	Unc
1706 ILH	—	175	325	550	1,000
1707 ILH	—	175	325	550	1,000

KM# 769 THALER

Silver **Ruler:** Friedrich August I **Obverse:** Armored bust right **Obv. Legend:** AUGUSTUS D • G • REX - ELECTOR • **Reverse:** Crowned AR dividing date **Rev. Legend:** * MONETA SAXONICA * **Note:** Dav.#2650.

Date	Mintage	F	VF	XF	Unc
1708 ILH	—	225	400	650	1,150
1709 ILH	—	225	400	650	1,150

KM# 770 THALER

Silver **Ruler:** Friedrich August I **Obverse:** Crowned AR monogram **Reverse:** Shooting range in center with band around **Rev. Legend:** ZU ERGETZUNG DER VERSAMLETEN STAENDE. 13. FEBR: 1708: * **Shape:** 4-Sided **Note:** Klippe. Dav.#2651.

Date	Mintage	F	VF	XF	Unc
1708	—	250	450	700	1,250

KM# 776 THALER

Silver **Ruler:** Friedrich August I **Obverse:** Armored, draped bust right **Obv. Legend:** D • G • FRID: AUGUST: REX POL: DUX SAX: I • C • M • A • & W • **Reverse:** Crowned shields of Poland and Saxony, date and initials between at bottom **Rev. Legend:** SAC: ROM: IMP: ARCHIM: ET ELECTOR • **Shape:** 4-Sided **Note:** Dav.#2653.

Date	Mintage	F	VF	XF	Unc
1709 ILH	—	125	250	450	900
1710 ILH	—	125	250	450	900
1711 ILH	—	125	250	450	900
1712 ILH	—	125	250	450	900
1713 ILH	—	125	250	450	900
1714 ILH	—	125	250	450	900
1715 ILH	—	125	250	450	900
1716 ILH	—	125	250	450	900
1716 IGS	—	125	250	450	900
1717 ILH	—	125	250	450	900
1717 IGS	—	125	250	450	900
1718 IGS	—	125	250	450	900
1719 IGS	—	125	250	450	900
1720 IGS	—	125	250	450	900
1721 IGS	—	125	250	450	900
1722 IGS	—	125	250	450	900
1723 IGS	—	125	250	450	900
1724 IGS	—	125	250	450	900
1725 IGS	—	125	250	450	900
1726 IGS	—	125	250	450	900
1727 IGS	—	125	250	450	900
1728 IGS	—	125	250	450	900
1729 IGS	—	125	250	450	900
1730 IGS	—	125	250	450	900
1731 IGS	—	125	250	450	900
1732 IGS	—	125	250	450	900
1733 IGS	—	125	250	450	900

KM# 803 THALER

Silver **Ruler:** Friedrich August I **Obverse:** King on horseback right, shield below **Reverse:** 2 sets of crowns and scepters on tables, 5-line inscription in wreath on mantle **Rev. Legend:** FRID: AUG:/REX ELECTOR, below in wreath; ET/VICARIUS/POST MORT/IOSEPH I/IMPERAT: **Note:** Dav.#2655.

Date	Mintage	F	VF	XF	Unc
MDCCXI (1711) ILH	—	120	225	400	800

KM# 820 THALER

Silver **Ruler:** Friedrich August I **Obverse:** Crowned AR monogram, buds in corners **Reverse:** Shooting range, band around, blossoms in corners **Rev. Legend:** * QUI VISE LE MIEUX CE 8me DE FEBR: 1714 **Shape:** 4-Sided **Note:** Klippe. Dav.#2656.

Date	Mintage	F	VF	XF	Unc
1714	—	250	450	700	1,250

KM# 827 THALER

Silver **Ruler:** Friedrich August I **Obverse:** 4 crowned A's around target **Obv. Legend:** VNA.-META - OMNI: - BCVS **Reverse:** 6-line inscription **Rev. Legend:** FRID: AVGVSTO - REGE POLON: - ELECT: SAXON: - AGONOTHETA:, in center; *DOMVS/ CERTAMINI/METAM FERIENDI/APTATAE DEDICATIO./ANNO MDCCXVII./X. CAL: SEPT: * **Shape:** 4-Sided **Note:** Klippe. Dav.#2657.

Date	Mintage	F	VF	XF	Unc
1717	—	300	550	900	1,500

KM# 828 THALER

Silver **Ruler:** Friedrich August I **Subject:** Death of Anna Sophia, Mother of Friedrich August I **Obverse:** Crown above 14-line inscription **Obv. Legend:** DEO DUCE, below; PORTUM INVENIT•/I.G.S. T. **Reverse:** Ship in harbor **Note:** Dav.#2658.

Date	Mintage	F	VF	XF	Unc
1717 IGS	—	350	600	950	1,600

KM# 839 THALER

Silver **Ruler:** Friedrich August I **Obverse:** Crowned AR monogram in sprays **Reverse:** Band over arrows **Rev. Legend:** SCHNEPPER: GESELI SCHAFT * **Shape:** 6-Sided **Note:** Dav.#2659.

Date	Mintage	F	VF	XF	Unc
1719	—	400	750	1,250	2,000

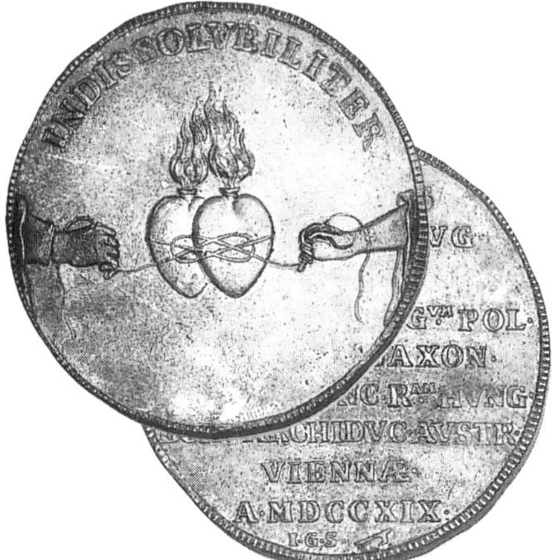

KM# 840 THALER

Silver **Ruler:** Friedrich August I **Subject:** Marriage of the Electoral Prince and Archduchess M. Josepha of Austria **Obverse:** 9-line inscription **Obv. Inscription:** SIGNATIS/PACT• CONIUG• /INTER/SER• PRINC• REGVM• POL/ET ELECT• SAXON•/ET SER• PRINC• RAM• HVNG•/BOHH• & ARCHIDVC• AVSTR•/VIENNAE•/ A• MDCCXIX•/I•G•S• **Reverse:** 2 hands binding flaming hearts **Rev. Legend:** INDISSOLVBILITER **Note:** Dav.#2660.

Date	Mintage	F	VF	XF	Unc
1719 IGS	—	150	300	500	1,000

KM# 859 THALER

Silver **Ruler:** Friedrich August I **Subject:** Death of Christiane Eberhardine, Wife of Friedrich August **Obverse:** 11-line inscription **Obv. Inscription:** IN/MEMORIAM/CHRISTIANAE/ EBERHARDINAE/REGINAE POLON: ET/ELECTRICIS SAXON:/OPTIMAE PIENTISSIMAE/NAT: BYRVTHI/A. 1671. D. 19. DEC:/DENAT: PREZSCH/A. 1727. D.S. SEPT:/I.G.S. **Reverse:** Cyprus tree dividing TOT - CORDA **Rev. Legend:** QVOT - FOLIA, LVGENT below **Note:** Dav.#2661.

Date	Mintage	F	VF	XF	Unc
1727 IGS	—	225	400	650	1,200

KM# 862 THALER

Silver **Subject:** Presence of King Friedrich Wilhelm of Prussia **Obverse:** Crowned AR, ornaments in corners **Reverse:** 8-line inscription: IN/HONOREM/GRATAMQ:ME/. . . **Shape:** 4-Sided **Note:** Dav.#2662.

Date	Mintage	F	VF	XF	Unc
1728	—	350	600	1,000	1,650

KM# 880 THALER

28.8000 g., Silver **Ruler:** Friedrich August II **Obverse:** Armored bust right **Obv. Legend:** D: G: FRID: AUGUST: REX POL: DUX SAX: I: C: M: A: & W: * **Reverse:** Crown above two shields **Rev. Legend:** SAC: ROM: IMP: ARCHIM: ET ELECTOR • **Note:** Specie Thaler. Dav.#2665.

Date	Mintage	F	VF	XF	Unc
1734 IGS	—	100	200	350	700
1735 FWoF	—	100	200	350	700
1736 FWoF	—	100	200	350	700
1737 FWoF	—	100	200	350	700
1738 FWoF	—	100	200	350	700
1739 FWoF	—	100	200	350	700
1740 FWoF	—	100	200	350	700
1741 FWoF	—	100	200	350	700
1742 FWoF	—	100	200	350	700
1743 FWoF	—	100	200	350	700
1744 FWoF	—	100	200	350	700
1745 FWoF	—	100	200	350	700
1746 FWoF	—	100	200	350	700
1747 FWoF	—	100	200	350	700
1748 FWoF	—	100	200	350	700
1749 FWoF	—	100	200	350	700
1750 FWoF	—	100	200	350	700
1751 FWoF	—	100	200	350	700
1752 FWoF	—	100	200	350	700
1753 FWoF	—	100	200	350	700
1754 FWoF	—	100	200	350	700
1755 FWoF	—	100	200	350	700
1756 FWoF	—	100	200	350	700

KM# 902 THALER

28.8000 g., Silver **Ruler:** Friedrich August II **Obverse:** Armored bust right **Obv. Legend:** D • G • FRID: AUG: REX POL: DUX SAX: ARCHIMARESCHALL: ET ELECTOR • * **Reverse:** Crowned shield on eagle's breast **Rev. Legend:** IN PROVINCIIS IVR: SAXON: PROVISOR ET VICARIUS date * **Note:** Vicariat Issue. Dav.#2668.

Date	Mintage	F	VF	XF	Unc
1740	—	175	300	500	1,000
1745	—	175	300	500	1,000

KM# 901 THALER

28.8000 g., Silver **Ruler:** Friedrich August II **Subject:** Shooting Festival **Obverse:** Crowned script ARR monogram divides date **Reverse:** Crowned A at corners, target in center **Rev. Legend:** VNA • - META - OMNI: - BVS **Shape:** 4-Sided **Note:** Klippe. Dav.#2666.

Date	Mintage	F	VF	XF	Unc
1740	—	300	450	750	1,500

KM# 907 THALER

28.8000 g., Silver **Ruler:** Friedrich August II **Obverse:** Figure on rearing horse right **Obv. Legend:** D • G • FRID • AUG • REX POL • DUX SAX • ARCHIMARESCHALL • & ELECT •* **Reverse:** Arms on tapestry back of throne **Rev. Legend:** IN PROVINCIIS IUR • SAXON • PROVISOR ET VICARIUS • 1741 • * **Note:** Vicariat Issue. Dav.#2669.

Date	Mintage	F	VF	XF	Unc
1741	—	150	250	425	850

KM# 914 THALER

28.8000 g., Silver **Ruler:** Friedrich August II **Obverse:** Armored bust right **Reverse:** 2 crowned shields of arms: . . . VICARIUS **Note:** Vicariat Issue. Dav.#2670.

Date	Mintage	F	VF	XF	Unc
1745 FWoF	—	200	325	500	1,000

KM# 929.1 THALER

28.8000 g., Silver **Subject:** Augustus III **Obverse:** Crowned bust right **Obv. Legend:** D • G • AVGVSTVS III • REX POLONIARUM • **Reverse:** Crowned arms within branches **Rev. Legend:** SAC • ROM • IMP • ARCHIM • ET ELECT • date **Note:** Dav.#1617.

Date	Mintage	F	VF	XF	Unc
1753	—	150	300	500	850
1753 EDC	—	70.00	150	300	500
1754 EDC	—	60.00	125	275	475

KM# 929.2 THALER

28.8000 g., Silver

Date	Mintage	F	VF	XF	Unc
1754 EDC L	—	60.00	125	275	475

KM# 929.3 THALER

28.8000 g., Silver **Obverse:** Crowned bust right **Obv. Legend:** D • G • AVGVSTVS III REX POLONIARVM **Reverse:** Crowned arms within branches **Rev. Legend:** SAC • ROM • IMP • ARCHIM • ET ELECT • date

Date	Mintage	F	VF	XF	Unc
1754 EDC	—	60.00	125	275	475

KM# 929.4 THALER

28.8000 g., Silver **Ruler:** Friedrich August II **Obverse:** Large legends **Obv. Legend:** DG AVGVSTVS III REX POLONIARUM **Reverse:** Large legends **Rev. Legend:** SAC • ROM • IMP • ARCHIM • ET ELECT •

Date	Mintage	F	VF	XF	Unc
1755 EDC	—	60.00	125	275	475

KM# 929.5 THALER

28.8000 g., Silver **Obverse:** Crowned bust right **Obv. Legend:** D: G: AVGVSTVS III • REX • POLONIARUM **Reverse:** Crowned arms in branches

Date	Mintage	F	VF	XF	Unc
1755 EDC	—	70.00	150	300	505

KM# 926 THALER

28.8000 g., Silver **Obverse:** Large bust right **Reverse:** Crowned shields of Poland and Sazony in decorated frame, FWOF below **Note:** Dav.#2671.

Date	Mintage	F	VF	XF	Unc
1755	—	200	400	800	1,500
1756	—	200	400	800	1,500

KM# 929.6 THALER

28.8000 g., Silver **Obverse:** Crowned bust right **Obv. Legend:** D • G • AVGVSTVS III • REX POLONIARUM • **Reverse:** Crowned arms in branches

Date	Mintage	F	VF	XF	Unc
1756 EDC	—	60.00	125	285	500
1756 EDC L	—	60.00	125	285	500
1756 EDC L LF	—	60.00	125	285	500

Note: Thalers KM#929.1-929.6 were previously listed as KM#159.1-159.6 in Poland

KM# 933 THALER

28.8000 g., Silver **Ruler:** Friedrich August II **Subject:** Prussian Occupation **Obverse:** Bust right **Reverse:** 2 crowned oval shields of arms **Note:** Dav.#2673.

Date	Mintage	F	VF	XF	Unc
1757 IDB	—	300	500	900	1,650

KM# 935 THALER

28.8000 g., Silver **Ruler:** Friedrich August II **Subject:** Prussian Occupation **Obverse:** Without curl below bust **Reverse:** Orb below shields **Note:** Dav.#2675.

Date	Mintage	F	VF	XF	Unc
1757 IDB	—	400	700	1,100	2,000

KM# 934 THALER

28.8000 g., Silver **Ruler:** Friedrich August I **Subject:** Prussian Occupation **Obverse:** Armored, draped bust right **Obv. Legend:** D: G: FRID: AUGUST: REX POL: D: S: I: C: M: A: & W: **Reverse:** FR monogram below shields **Rev. Legend:** SAC: ROM: IMP: ARCHIM: ET ELECTOR:, I.D.B. below shields **Note:** Mining Thaler. Dav.#2674.

Date	Mintage	F	VF	XF	Unc
1757 IDB	—	300	500	900	1,650

KM# 937 THALER

28.8000 g., Silver **Ruler:** Friedrich August II **Obverse:** Armored, draped bust right **Obv. Legend:** D: G: FRID: AUGUST: REX POL: D: S: I: C: M: A:& W: **Reverse:** Crowned complex arms **Rev. Legend:** SAC: ROM: IMP: ARCHIM: ELECTOR ET VICARIUS: date **Note:** Dav.#2672.

Date	Mintage	F	VF	XF	Unc
1759 FWôF	—	200	400	800	1,500
1760 FWôF	—	200	400	800	1,500
1761 FWôF	—	200	400	800	1,500
1762 FWôF	—	200	400	800	1,500

KM# 962 THALER

28.8000 g., Silver **Ruler:** Friedrich Christian **Obverse:** Bust right **Obv. Legend:** D: G: FRID: CHRIST: PR: R: POL: & L: DUX: SAX: **Reverse:** Crowned ornate arms, value below **Rev. Legend:** IUL: CL: MONT: A: & W: S: R: I: ARCHIM: & ELECTOR, X. EINE FEINE MARCK below **Note:** Convention Thaler. Dav.#2677.

Date	Mintage	F	VF	XF	Unc
1763 FWôF	—	60.00	125	250	600
1763 EDC	—	60.00	125	250	600
1763 JFôF	—	60.00	125	250	600

KM# 961 THALER

28.8000 g., Silver **Obverse:** Armored bust right **Obv. Legend:** XAVERIVS D: G: REG: PR: POL: & LITH: DVX SAX: **Reverse:** Crown above two shields **Rev. Legend:** ELECTORATVS SAXONIAE ADMINISTRATOR,E.D.C. below, X. EINE - MARCK F: below **Note:** Reichs Thaler. Dav.#2676.

Date	Mintage	F	VF	XF	Unc
1763 FWôF	—	100	175	250	650

KM# 977.2 THALER

28.0630 g., 0.8330 Silver 0.7515 oz. ASW **Obv. Legend:** ...DUX SAX ELECTOR **Reverse:** Date below shield **Rev. Legend:** D: SEEGEN D: BERGBAUES **Note:** Dav. #2681.

Date	Mintage	VG	F	VF	XF	Unc
1763 EDC	—	75.00	150	300	700	—
1764 EDC	—	75.00	150	300	700	—

KM# 977.1 THALER

28.0630 g., 0.8330 Silver 0.7515 oz. ASW **Ruler:** Friedrich August III **Obverse:** Bust right **Obv. Legend:** FRID: AUGUST: D:G: SAXONIAE ELECTOR **Reverse:** Crowned shield in sprays **Rev. Legend:** X. EINE - FEINE MARCK, E.D.C. below **Note:** Dav. #2680.

Date	Mintage	VG	F	VF	XF	Unc
1764 JFôF	—	50.00	100	175	500	—

KM# 976 THALER

28.0630 g., 0.8330 Silver 0.7515 oz. ASW **Ruler:** Xaver **Obverse:** Bust right **Obv. Legend:** XAVERIVS D:G: REG: PR: POL: & LITH: DVX SAX: **Reverse:** Crowned complex arms **Rev. Legend:** ELECTORATVS SAXONIAE ADMINISTRATOR, E.D.C. below, X. EINE - MARCK F: at sides **Note:** Dav. #2678.

Date	Mintage	F	VF	XF	Unc
1764 EDC	—	50.00	100	175	500
1765 EDC	—	50.00	100	175	500
1766 EDC	—	50.00	100	175	500
1767 EDC	—	50.00	100	175	500
1768 EDC	—	50.00	100	175	500

KM# 982 THALER

28.0630 g., 0.8330 Silver 0.7515 oz. ASW **Ruler:** Xaver **Subject:** Freiberg Mining Academy **Obverse:** Bust right **Obv. Legend:** XAVER: D: G: R: PR: POL: & L: DVX SAX: EL: ADM: **Reverse:** Mining scene **Rev. Legend:** X. EINE - ZUR ERMUNTERUNG DES FLEISSES - F. MARK, in exergue; BERG ACADEMIE ZV FREYBERG/WARD GESTIFFTET/D: 13. NOVEMBER/1765 **Note:** Dav. #2679.

Date	Mintage	F	VF	XF	Unc
1765	—	350	700	1,250	2,500

KM# 983 THALER

28.0630 g., 0.8330 Silver 0.7515 oz. ASW **Ruler:** Friedrich August III **Obverse:** Draped and armored bust right **Obv. Legend:** FRID: AUGUST: D:G: DUX SAX: ELECTOR **Reverse:** Arms within branches, date below **Rev. Legend:** X. EINE - FEINE MARCK, E.D.C. and date below **Note:** Dav. #2682.

Date	Mintage	F	VF	XF	Unc
1765 EDC	—	50.00	100	175	500
1766 EDC	—	50.00	100	175	500
1767 EDC	—	50.00	100	175	500
1768 EDC	—	50.00	100	175	500

KM# 984 THALER

28.0630 g., 0.8330 Silver 0.7515 oz. ASW **Ruler:** Friedrich August III **Obverse:** Draped bust right **Obv. Legend:** FRID: AUGUST: D:G: DUX SAX: ELECTOR **Reverse:** Electors cap above arms within branches, date below **Rev. Legend:** ZUR BELOHNUNG - DES FLEISES, E.D.C., X. EINE FEINE MARCK and date below **Note:** Dav. #2685.

Date	Mintage	F	VF	XF	Unc
1765 EDC	—	300	600	1,000	2,000

KM# 985 THALER

28.0630 g., 0.8330 Silver 0.7515 oz. ASW **Ruler:** Friedrich August III **Obverse:** Bust right **Reverse:** Similar to C#B6 **Note:** Dav. #2686.

Date	Mintage	F	VF	XF	Unc
1765	—	300	650	1,200	2,000

KM# 987.1 THALER

28.0630 g., 0.8330 Silver 0.7515 oz. ASW **Ruler:** Xaver **Obverse:** Bust of Frederic August right **Obv. Legend:** FRID: AUGUST: D:G: DUX SAX: ELECTOR **Reverse:** Bust of Xaver right **Rev. Legend:** XAVER: D:G:R: PR: POL: & L: DVX SAX: EL: ADM:, ZUR BELOHNUNG/DES FLEISSES, 1766 below **Note:** Dav. #2688.

Date	Mintage	F	VF	XF	Unc
1766	—	300	700	1,200	2,000

KM# 987.2 THALER

28.0630 g., 0.8330 Silver 0.7515 oz. ASW **Note:** Similar to KM#987, but legend ends: . . . SAX: ADM. Dav. #2689.

Date	Mintage	F	VF	XF	Unc
1766	—	300	700	1,200	2,000

KM# 990 THALER

28.0630 g., 0.8330 Silver 0.7515 oz. ASW **Ruler:** Friedrich August III **Obverse:** Bust right **Obv. Legend:** FRID: AUGUST: D: G: DUX SAX: ... **Reverse:** Arms within branches, date below **Rev. Legend:** DER SEEGEN - DES BERGBAUES, E.D.C., X.EINE FEINE MARCK and date below **Note:** Mining Thaler. Dav. #2683.

Date	Mintage	F	VF	XF	Unc
1768 EDC	—	65.00	125	225	600

KM# 993.1 THALER

28.0630 g., 0.8330 Silver 0.7515 oz. ASW **Ruler:** Friedrich August III **Rev. Legend:** DER SEEGEN. . . **Note:** Mining Thaler. Dav. #2691.

Date	Mintage	F	VF	XF	Unc
1769 EDC	—	35.00	65.00	100	300
1770 EDC	—	35.00	65.00	100	300
1771 EDC	—	35.00	65.00	100	300
1772 EDC	—	35.00	65.00	100	300
1773 EDC	—	35.00	65.00	100	300
1774 EDC	—	35.00	65.00	100	300
1775 EDC	—	35.00	65.00	100	300
1776 EDC	—	35.00	65.00	100	300
1777 EDC	—	35.00	65.00	100	300
1778 EDC	—	35.00	65.00	100	300
1779 IEC	—	35.00	65.00	100	300

KM# 992.1 THALER

28.0630 g., 0.8330 Silver 0.7515 oz. ASW **Ruler:** Friedrich August III **Obverse:** Head right **Obv. Legend:** FRID: AUGUST: D:G: DUX SAX: ELECTOR **Reverse:** Electors cap above arms within branches, date below **Rev. Legend:** X. EINE - MARCK F:, E.D.C. and date below **Note:** Convention Thaler. Dav. #2690.

Date	Mintage	F	VF	XF	Unc
1769 EDC	—	35.00	65.00	100	300
1770 EDC	—	35.00	65.00	100	300
1771 EDC	—	35.00	65.00	100	300
1772 EDC	—	35.00	65.00	100	300
1773 EDC	—	35.00	65.00	100	300
1774 EDC	—	35.00	65.00	100	300
1775 EDC	—	35.00	65.00	100	300
1776 EDC	—	35.00	65.00	100	300
1777 EDC	—	35.00	65.00	100	300
1778 EDC	—	35.00	65.00	100	300
1779 EDC	—	35.00	65.00	100	300

KM# 1011 THALER

28.0630 g., 0.8330 Silver 0.7515 oz. ASW **Ruler:** Friedrich August III **Obverse:** Head right **Obv. Legend:** FRID: AUGUST: D:G: DUX SAX: ELECTOR **Reverse:** Wreath above caduceus at left and grain sheaf back of beehive at right **Rev. Legend:** ZUR BELOHNUNG - DES FLEISSES, in exergue; 1780/X/EINE MARK FEIN **Note:** Dav. #2693.

Date	Mintage	F	VF	XF	Unc
1780	—	300	600	1,200	2,000

KM# 992.2 THALER

28.0630 g., 0.8330 Silver 0.7515 oz. ASW **Ruler:** Friedrich August III **Obverse:** Head right **Reverse:** Smaller arms **Note:** Dav. #2695.

Date	Mintage	F	VF	XF	Unc
1780 IEC	—	35.00	65.00	100	300
1781 IEC	—	35.00	65.00	100	300
1782 IEC	—	35.00	65.00	100	300
1783 IEC	—	35.00	65.00	100	300
1784 IEC	—	35.00	65.00	100	300
1785 IEC	—	35.00	65.00	100	300
1786 IEC	—	35.00	65.00	100	300
1787 IEC	—	35.00	65.00	100	300
1788 IEC	—	35.00	65.00	100	300
1789 IEC	—	35.00	65.00	100	300
1790 IEC	—	35.00	65.00	100	300

Note: Varieties exist

KM# 993.2 THALER

28.0630 g., 0.8330 Silver 0.7515 oz. ASW **Ruler:** Friedrich August III **Obverse:** Head right **Obv. Legend:** FRID: AUGUST: D:G: DUX SAX: ELECTOR **Reverse:** Smaller arms **Rev. Legend:** DER SEEGEN - DES BERGBAUES, below; I.E.C./X. EINE MARCK. F./date **Note:** Dav. #2696.

Date	Mintage	F	VF	XF	Unc
1780 IEC	—	35.00	65.00	100	300
1781 IEC	—	35.00	65.00	100	300
1782 IEC	—	35.00	65.00	100	300
1783 IEC	—	35.00	65.00	100	300
1784 IEC	—	35.00	65.00	100	300
1785 IEC	—	35.00	65.00	100	300
1786 IEC	—	35.00	65.00	100	300
1787 IEC	—	35.00	65.00	100	300
1788 IEC	—	35.00	65.00	100	300
1789 IEC	—	35.00	65.00	100	300
1790 IEC	—	35.00	65.00	100	300

KM# 1023 THALER

28.0630 g., 0.8330 Silver 0.7515 oz. ASW **Ruler:** Friedrich August III **Obverse:** Head right **Obv. Legend:** FRID • AVG • D • G • DVX SAX • ELECTOR & VICARIVS IMPERII **Reverse:** Arms on eagle's breast, date below **Rev. Legend:** X. EINE - MARCK F., below; I.E. - C./1790 **Note:** Vicariat Issue. Dav.#2697.

Date	Mintage	F	VF	XF	Unc
1790 IEC	—	50.00	100	175	450

KM# 1026 THALER

28.0630 g., 0.8330 Silver 0.7515 oz. ASW **Ruler:** Friedrich August III **Obverse:** Armored bust right **Obv. Legend:** FRID: AVGVST: D:G: DVX SAX: ELECTOR **Reverse:** Elector's cap above arms within branches, date below **Rev. Legend:** DER SEEGEN - DES BERGBAUES, below; I.E.C./X•EINE MARK F•/date **Note:** Mining Thaler. Dav.#2699.

Date	Mintage	F	VF	XF	Unc
1791 IEC	—	100	200	400	800
1792 IEC	—	100	200	400	800

KM# 1027 THALER

28.0630 g., 0.8330 Silver 0.7515 oz. ASW **Ruler:** Friedrich August III **Obverse:** Armored, draped bust right **Obv. Legend:** FRID • AVGVST • D • G • DVX SAX • ELECTOR **Reverse:** Elector's cap above arms within branches **Rev. Legend:** X • EINE • FEINE • MARK •, date **Note:** Convention Thaler. Dav.#2698.

Date	Mintage	F	VF	XF	Unc
1791 IEC	—	35.00	65.00	100	300
1792 IEC	—	35.00	65.00	100	300

KM# 1034 THALER

28.0630 g., 0.8330 Silver 0.7515 oz. ASW **Ruler:** Friedrich August III **Obverse:** Date below bust **Obv. Legend:** FRID • AVGVST • D • G • DVX SAX • ELECTOR **Reverse:** Arms on eagle's breast **Rev. Legend:** SACROM - IMP. PROVISOR - ITERVM, below; I.E.C./X • EINE MARK F • **Note:** Vicariat Issue. Dav.#2700.

Date	Mintage	F	VF	XF	Unc
1792 IEC	—	50.00	100	175	450

KM# 1027.2 THALER

28.0630 g., 0.8330 Silver 0.7515 oz. ASW **Ruler:** Friedrich August III **Obverse:** Armored bust right **Obv. Legend:** FRID. AVGVST. D. G. DVX SAX. ELECTOR **Reverse:** Crowned oval arms within branches **Rev. Legend:** X. EINE FEINE MARK. **Note:** Dav.#2701.

Date	Mintage	F	VF	XF	Unc
1793 IEC	—	35.00	65.00	100	300
1794 IEC	—	35.00	65.00	100	300
1795 IEC	—	35.00	65.00	100	300
1796 IEC	—	35.00	65.00	100	300
1797 IEC	—	35.00	65.00	100	300
1798 IEC	—	35.00	65.00	100	300
1799 IEC	—	35.00	65.00	100	300
1800 IEC	—	35.00	70.00	150	500

KM# 1026.2 THALER

28.0630 g., 0.8330 Silver 0.7515 oz. ASW **Ruler:** Friedrich August III **Obverse:** Armored bust right **Reverse:** Elector's cap above arms **Note:** Dav.#2702.

Date	Mintage	F	VF	XF	Unc
1793 IEC	—	100	200	400	800

KM# 1036 THALER

28.0630 g., 0.8330 Silver 0.7515 oz. ASW **Ruler:** Friedrich August III **Obverse:** Head right **Reverse:** Crowned oval arms **Rev. Legend:** Ends:. . . DES BERGBAVES **Note:** Dav.#2703.

Date	Mintage	F	VF	XF	Unc
1794 IEC	—	75.00	150	300	600
1795 IEC	—	75.00	150	300	600
1796 IEC	—	75.00	150	300	600
1797 IEC	—	75.00	150	300	600
1798 IEC	—	75.00	150	300	600
1799 IEC	—	75.00	150	300	600
1800 IEC	—	75.00	150	300	600

KM# 732 2 THALER

Silver **Ruler:** Friedrich August I **Note:** Thick flan; similar to 1 Thaler, KM#707.

Date	Mintage	VG	F	VF	XF	Unc
1702 ILH	—	—	—	—	—	—
1703 ILH	—	—	—	—	—	—

KM# 751 2 THALER

Silver **Ruler:** Friedrich August I **Note:** Similar to 1 Thaler, KM#750. Dav.#A2649.

Date	Mintage	VG	F	VF	XF	Unc
1706 ILH Rare	—	—	—	—	—	—

KM# 777 2 THALER

Silver **Ruler:** Friedrich August I **Note:** Similar to 1 Thaler, KM#776. Dav.#2652.

Date	Mintage	VG	F	VF	XF	Unc
1709 ILH Rare	—	—	—	—	—	—
1714 ILH Rare	—	—	—	—	—	—
1716 ILH Rare	—	—	—	—	—	—
1717 IGS Rare	—	—	—	—	—	—
1725 IGS Rare	—	—	—	—	—	—
1726 IGS Rare	—	—	—	—	—	—
1727 IGS Rare	—	—	—	—	—	—
1728 IGS Rare	—	—	—	—	—	—
1729 IGS Rare	—	—	—	—	—	—
1729 IGS Rare	—	—	—	—	—	—
1730 IGS Rare	—	—	—	—	—	—
1731 IGS Rare	—	—	—	—	—	—
1732 IGS Rare	—	—	—	—	—	—

KM# 804 2 THALER

Silver **Ruler:** Friedrich August I **Note:** Vicariat Issue. Similar to 1 Thaler, KM#803. Dav.#2654.

Date	Mintage	VG	F	VF	XF	Unc
1711 ILH	—	750	1,200	2,000	3,000	—

KM# 841 2 THALER

Silver **Ruler:** Friedrich August I **Note:** Thick flan; similar to 1 Thaler, KM#839.

Date	Mintage	VG	F	VF	XF	Unc
1719	—	—	—	—	—	—

KM# 872 2 THALER (3-1/2 Gulden)

Silver **Ruler:** Friedrich August II **Subject:** Death of Friedrich August I **Obverse:** Armored bust right **Obv. Legend:** D • G • FRID • AUGUST • PR • R • P • & L • DUX • SAX • ELECT • **Reverse:** Monument to Friedrich August I **Rev. Legend:** MEMORIÆ • ÆTERNÆ • - OPTIMI PARENTIS •, in exergue; NAT • XII • MAY MDCLXX•/OB • I • FEBR • MDCCXXXIII •/2 TH • COUR • **Note:** Dav.#2663.

Date	Mintage	VG	F	VF	XF	Unc
1733	—	300	600	1,100	1,800	—

KM# 889 2 THALER (3-1/2 Gulden)

Silver **Ruler:** Friedrich August II **Note:** Similar to 1 Thaler, KM#880. Dav.#2664.

Date	Mintage	VG	F	VF	XF	Unc
1736 FWoF	—	300	600	1,200	2,000	—
1737 FWoF	—	350	700	1,400	2,500	—
1744 FWoF	—	450	800	1,600	3,000	—

KM# 903 2 THALER (3-1/2 Gulden)

Silver **Ruler:** Friedrich August II **Reverse:** Double-headed eagle with crowned round arms on breast **Note:** Vicariat Issue. Dav.#2667.

Date	Mintage	VG	F	VF	XF	Unc
1740	—	400	800	1,400	2,200	—

Note: KM#889 and 903 struck with 1 Thaler dies, double thickness

KM# 986 2 THALER (3-1/2 Gulden)

Silver **Note:** Similar to 1 Thaler, KM#984. Dav.#2684.

Date	Mintage	VG	F	VF	XF	Unc
1765 EDC	—	400	800	1,400	2,200	—

KM# 988 2 THALER (3-1/2 Gulden)

Silver **Note:** Similar to 1 Thaler, KM#987. Dav.#2687.

Date	Mintage	VG	F	VF	XF	Unc
1766 Rare	—	—	—	—	—	—

KM# 1012 2 THALER (3-1/2 Gulden)

Silver **Ruler:** Friedrich August III **Obverse:** Head right **Obv. Legend:** FRID: AUGUSTUS D:G: DUX SAX: ELECTOR **Reverse:** Wreath above caduceus at left and wheat sheaf back of beehive at right **Rev. Legend:** ZUR BELOHNUNG - DES FLEISSES, 1780/V/EINE MARK FEIN below **Note:** Dav.#2692.

Date	Mintage	F	VF	XF	Unc
1780	—	750	1,200	2,000	3,000

KM# 1013 2 THALER (3-1/2 Gulden)

Silver **Ruler:** Friedrich August III **Obverse:** Armored bust right; F. H. KRUGER F. below **Obv. Legend:** FRID: AVGVST: D:G: DVX SAX: ELECTOR **Rev. Legend:** ZUR BELOHNUNG - DES FLEISSES, 1780/V/EINE MARK FEIN below **Note:** Dav.#2694.

Date	Mintage	F	VF	XF	Unc
1780	—	600	1,200	2,000	3,000

KM# A916 2-1/2 THALER

3.3250 g., 0.9000 Gold 0.0962 oz. AGW **Ruler:** Friedrich August II **Obverse:** Crowned, draped bust right **Obv. Legend:** D: G: AVGVSTVS III • REX POLONIARUM • **Reverse:** Crowned arms within branches **Rev. Legend:** SAC • ROM • IMP • ARCHIM • ET ELECT • **Note:** 1/2 August D'or - 2 1/2 Thaler. Previous Poland KM#161.

Date	Mintage	VG	F	VF	XF	Unc
1753 G	—	250	500	1,000	1,800	—

KM# 741 3 THALER

Silver **Ruler:** Friedrich August I **Obverse:** Armored, draped bust right **Obv. Legend:** DUX SAX • I • C • M • A • & W • - D • G • FRID • AUG • REX • POL • **Reverse:** Crown above two shields within branches **Rev. Legend:** SAC • ROM • IMP • ARCHIM • ET ELECT • date **Note:** Thick flan. Similar to 1 Thaler, KM#707. Dav.#2646.

Date	Mintage	VG	F	VF	XF	Unc
1704 Rare	—	—	—	—	—	—

KM# 860 4 THALER

Silver **Ruler:** Friedrich August I **Reverse:** Crowned shields of Poland and Saxony, date and initials between at bottom **Note:** Similar to 1 Thaler, KM#776.

Date	Mintage	VG	F	VF	XF	Unc
1727 IGS	—	—	—	—	—	—

KM# A943 5 THALER (August D'or)
6.6500 g., 0.9000 Gold 0.1924 oz. AGW **Ruler:** Friedrich August II **Obverse:** Crowned, draped bust right **Obv. Legend:** D• G • AVGVSTVS III • REX POLONIARUM • **Reverse:** Crowned arms within branches **Rev. Legend:** SAC • ROM • IMP • ARCHIM • ET ELECT • **Note:** Prev. Poland KM#162.

Date	Mintage	VG	F	VF	XF	Unc
1753 C	—	—	300	600	1,400	—
1754 EC	—	—	200	400	800	—

KM# 944 5 THALER (August D'or)
Gold **Ruler:** Friedrich August II **Note:** Debased Gold, Ephraimite Issue. Struck 1758-61 during the occupation of Poland. Prev. Poland KM#169.

Date	Mintage	VG	F	VF	XF	Unc
1755 EC	—	175	250	475	950	—
1756 EC	—	175	250	475	950	—
1758 EC	—	175	250	475	950	—

KM# 943 5 THALER (August D'or)
6.6500 g., 0.9000 Gold 0.1924 oz. AGW **Ruler:** Friedrich August II **Obverse:** Crowned, draped bust right **Obv. Legend:** D: G: AVGVSTVS III • REX POLONIARUM • **Reverse:** Crowned arms within branches **Rev. Legend:** SAC • ROM • IMP • ARCHIM • ET ELECT • **Note:** Prev. Poland KM#168.

Date	Mintage	VG	F	VF	XF	Unc
1755 EC	—	200	300	575	1,150	—
1756 EC	—	200	300	575	1,150	—

KM# 1001 5 THALER (August D'or)
6.6820 g., 0.9020 Gold 0.1938 oz. AGW **Ruler:** Friedrich August III **Obverse:** Head right **Obv. Legend:** FRID: AUGUST: D: G: DUX SAX: ELECTOR **Reverse:** Elector's cap above two shields, value and date below

Date	Mintage	VG	F	VF	XF	Unc
1777 EDC	—	250	600	1,200	1,800	—
1779 IEC	—	250	600	1,200	1,800	—
1781 IEC	—	250	600	1,200	1,800	—
1782 IEC	—	250	600	1,200	1,800	—
1785 IEC	—	250	600	1,200	1,800	—

KM# 1028 5 THALER (August D'or)
6.6820 g., 0.9020 Gold 0.1938 oz. AGW **Ruler:** Friedrich August III **Obverse:** Uniformed bust right **Obv. Legend:** FRID. AVG. D. G. DVX SAX. ELECTOR **Reverse:** Crowned oval arms within branches

Date	Mintage	F	VF	XF	Unc
1791 IEC	—	325	725	1,600	3,250
1792 IEC	—	325	725	1,600	3,250
1794 IEC	—	325	725	1,600	3,250
1795 IEC	—	325	725	1,600	3,250
1797 IEC	—	325	725	1,600	3,250
1798 IEC	—	325	725	1,600	3,250
1799 IEC	—	325	725	1,600	3,250
1800 IEC	—	400	900	1,500	3,000

KM# B916 10 THALER (2 August D'or)
13.3000 g., 0.9000 Gold 0.3848 oz. AGW **Ruler:** Friedrich August II **Obverse:** Crowned, armored bust right **Obv. Legend:** D • G • AVGVSTVS III • REX POLONIARUM • **Reverse:** Crowned arms within branches, value below **Rev. Legend:** SAC • ROM • IMP • ARCHIM • ET ELECT • **Note:** Prev. Poland KM#163.

Date	Mintage	VG	F	VF	XF	Unc
1753 G	—	300	600	1,200	2,000	3,750

KM# A944 10 THALER (2 August D'or)
13.3000 g., 0.9000 Gold 0.3848 oz. AGW **Ruler:** Friedrich August II **Obverse:** Crowned bust right **Obv. Legend:** D: G: AVGVSTVS III: REX POLONIARUM • **Reverse:** Crowned arms within branches, value below **Rev. Legend:** SAC • ROM • IMP • ARCHIM • ET ELECT • **Note:** Prev. Poland KM#164.

Date	Mintage	VG	F	VF	XF	Unc
1754 EC	—	400	800	1,400	2,500	—

KM# A975 10 THALER (2 August D'or)
Gold **Ruler:** Friedrich August II **Note:** Debased Gold. Ephraimite Issue. Struck in 1758 during the occupation of Poland. Prev. Poland KM#170.

Date	Mintage	VG	F	VF	XF	Unc
1755	—	280	550	950	1,800	—

KM# 975 10 THALER (2 August D'or)
Gold **Ruler:** Friedrich August II **Obverse:** Crowned, draped bust right **Obv. Legend:** D: G: AVGVSTVS III • REX POLONIARUM • **Reverse:** Crowned arms within branches, value below **Rev. Legend:** SAC • ROM • IMP • ARCHIM • ET ELECT • **Note:** Prev. Poland KM#171.

Date	Mintage	VG	F	VF	XF	Unc
1756 EC	—	300	600	1,200	2,000	—

KM# 1003 10 THALER (2 August D'or)
13.3640 g., 0.9020 Gold 0.3875 oz. AGW **Ruler:** Friedrich August III **Obverse:** Armored bust right **Obv. Legend:** FRID: AUGUST: D: G: DUX SAX: ELECTOR **Reverse:** Elector's cap above two shields, value and date below

Date	Mintage	VG	F	VF	XF	Unc
1778 EDC	—	250	500	1,000	2,000	—
1779 IDC	—	250	500	1,000	2,000	—

KM# 1004 10 THALER (2 August D'or)
13.3640 g., 0.9020 Gold 0.3875 oz. AGW **Ruler:** Friedrich August III **Obverse:** Head right **Obv. Legend:** FRID: AUGUST: D: G: DUX SAX: ELECTOR **Reverse:** Elector's cap above two shields, value and date below

Date	Mintage	VG	F	VF	XF	Unc
1779 IEC	—	250	500	1,000	2,000	—
1780 IEC	—	250	500	1,000	2,000	—
1782 IEC	—	250	500	1,000	2,000	—
1783 IEC	—	250	500	1,000	2,000	—
1784 IEC	—	250	500	1,000	2,000	—
1785 IEC	—	250	500	1,000	2,000	—
1786 IEC	—	250	500	1,000	2,000	—
1787 IEC	—	250	500	1,000	2,000	—
1790 IEC	—	250	500	1,000	2,000	—

KM# 1029 10 THALER (2 August D'or)
13.3640 g., 0.9020 Gold 0.3875 oz. AGW **Ruler:** Friedrich August III **Obverse:** Uniformed bust right **Obv. Legend:** FRID • AVGVST • D • G • DVX SAX • ELECTOR **Reverse:** Crowned oval arms within branches

Date	Mintage	F	VF	XF	Unc
1791 IEC	—	500	1,000	2,000	3,000
1794 IEC	—	500	1,000	2,000	3,000
1795 IEC	—	500	1,000	2,000	3,000
1796 IEC	—	500	1,000	2,000	3,000
1797 IEC	—	500	1,000	2,000	3,000
1798 IEC	—	500	1,000	2,000	3,000
1799 IEC	—	500	1,000	2,000	3,000
1800 IEC	—	500	1,000	2,000	3,000

TRADE COINAGE

KM# 725 1/4 DUCAT
0.8750 g., 0.9860 Gold 0.0277 oz. AGW **Ruler:** Friedrich August I **Mint:** Dresden **Obverse:** Bust right **Reverse:** Crowned arms

Date	Mintage	VG	F	VF	XF	Unc
1700 ILH	—	85.00	165	300	550	—
1710 ILH	—	85.00	165	300	550	—
1717 IGS	—	75.00	150	285	500	—
1722 IGS	—	75.00	150	285	500	—
1727 IGS	—	75.00	150	285	500	—
1729 IGS	—	75.00	150	285	500	—
1733 IGS	—	75.00	150	285	500	—

KM# 793 1/4 DUCAT
0.8750 g., 0.9860 Gold 0.0277 oz. AGW **Ruler:** Friedrich August I **Obverse:** Crowned FA monogram **Reverse:** Crowned arms

Date	Mintage	VG	F	VF	XF	Unc
1710	—	90.00	180	375	750	—

KM# 794 1/4 DUCAT
0.8750 g., 0.9860 Gold 0.0277 oz. AGW **Ruler:** Friedrich August I **Note:** Struck with 1/2 Ducat dies.

Date	Mintage	VG	F	VF	XF	Unc
1710	—	175	350	700	1,200	—

KM# 881 1/4 DUCAT
0.8750 g., 0.9860 Gold 0.0277 oz. AGW **Ruler:** Friedrich August II **Obverse:** Bust right **Reverse:** Crowned arms

Date	Mintage	VG	F	VF	XF	Unc
1734 IGS	—	90.00	180	375	750	—

KM# 885 1/4 DUCAT
0.8750 g., 0.9860 Gold 0.0277 oz. AGW **Ruler:** Friedrich August II **Obverse:** Bust right **Reverse:** Crowned arms

Date	Mintage	VG	F	VF	XF	Unc
1735 FWoF	—	75.00	150	300	525	—
1736 FWoF	—	75.00	150	300	525	—
1737 FWoF	—	75.00	150	300	525	—
1739 FWoF	—	75.00	150	300	525	—
1740 FWoF	—	75.00	150	300	525	—
1743 FWoF	—	75.00	150	300	525	—

KM# 714 1/2 DUCAT
1.7500 g., 0.9860 Gold 0.0555 oz. AGW **Ruler:** Friedrich August I **Mint:** Dresden **Obverse:** Bust right **Reverse:** Date in legend

Date	Mintage	VG	F	VF	XF	Unc
1701 ILH	—	85.00	190	450	800	—
1702 ILH	—	85.00	190	450	800	—

Date	Mintage	VG	F	VF	XF	Unc
1703 ILH	—	85.00	190	450	800	—
1704 ILH	—	85.00	190	450	800	—
1707 ILH	—	75.00	185	425	750	—
1710 ILH	—	75.00	185	425	750	—
1717 IGS	—	75.00	185	425	750	—
1726 IGS	—	75.00	185	425	750	—
1729 IGS	—	75.00	185	425	750	—
1733 IGS	—	75.00	185	425	750	—

KM# 733 1/2 DUCAT

1.7500 g., 0.9860 Gold 0.0555 oz. AGW **Ruler:** Friedrich August I **Mint:** Leipzig **Obverse:** Bust right **Reverse:** Crown above 2 shields of arms

Date	Mintage	VG	F	VF	XF	Unc
1702 EPH	—	125	250	550	1,100	—

KM# A795 1/2 DUCAT

1.7500 g., 0.9860 Gold 0.0555 oz. AGW **Ruler:** Friedrich August I **Obverse:** Bust right **Reverse:** Crown above three shields **Note:** Prev. Poland KM#142.

Date	Mintage	VG	F	VF	XF	Unc
1703 EPH Rare	—	—	—	—	—	—

KM# 795 1/2 DUCAT

1.7500 g., 0.9860 Gold 0.0555 oz. AGW **Mint:** Dresden **Obverse:** Crowned FA monogram **Reverse:** Crowned arms

Date	Mintage	VG	F	VF	XF	Unc
1710 ILH	—	250	450	900	1,650	—

KM# 886 1/2 DUCAT

1.7500 g., 0.9860 Gold 0.0555 oz. AGW **Ruler:** Friedrich August II **Obverse:** Bust right **Reverse:** Crown above arms

Date	Mintage	VG	F	VF	XF	Unc
1735 FWoF	—	75.00	150	300	600	—
1736 FWoF	—	75.00	150	300	600	—
1737 FWoF	—	75.00	150	300	600	—
1740 FWoF	—	75.00	150	300	600	—
1743 FWoF	—	75.00	150	300	600	—
1756 FWoF	—	75.00	150	300	600	—

KM# 942 1/2 DUCAT

1.7500 g., 0.9860 Gold 0.0555 oz. AGW **Obverse:** Crowned bust of August III **Reverse:** Crowned arms in palm branches **Note:** Prev. Poland KM#146.

Date	Mintage	VG	F	VF	XF	Unc
ND IGS	—	—	—	—	—	—
1750 FWoF	—	200	400	750	1,500	—

KM# 709 DUCAT

3.5000 g., 0.9860 Gold 0.1109 oz. AGW **Ruler:** Friedrich August I **Obverse:** Draped bust right **Obv. Legend:** D • G • FRID: AUG: REX POL DUX SAX: .. **Reverse:** Crowned arms within branches

Date	Mintage	VG	F	VF	XF	Unc
1702 ILH	—	200	450	1,000	1,700	—
1703 ILH	—	200	450	1,000	1,700	—
1704 ILH	—	200	450	1,000	1,700	—
1706 ILH	—	200	450	1,000	1,700	—
1707 ILH	—	200	450	1,000	1,700	—
1710 ILH	—	200	450	900	1,650	—
1714 ILH	—	200	450	900	1,650	—
1716 IGS	—	200	450	900	1,650	—
1720 IGS	—	200	450	900	1,650	—
1721 IGS	—	200	450	900	1,650	—
1722 IGS	—	200	450	900	1,650	—
1723 IGS	—	200	450	900	1,650	—
1724 IGS	—	200	450	900	1,650	—
1725 IGS	—	200	450	900	1,650	—
1726 IGS	—	200	450	900	1,650	—
1727 IGS	—	200	450	900	1,650	—
1729 IGS	—	200	450	900	1,650	—
1731 IGS	—	200	450	900	1,650	—
1732 IGS	—	200	450	900	1,650	—
1733 IGS	—	200	450	900	1,650	—

KM# 729 DUCAT

3.5000 g., 0.9860 Gold 0.1109 oz. AGW **Ruler:** Friedrich August I **Subject:** Gold From Freiberg Mines **Obverse:** 4-line inscription below all-seeing eye **Reverse:** 6-line inscription and date

Date	Mintage	VG	F	VF	XF	Unc
1701	—	200	450	1,000	1,800	—

KM# 735 DUCAT

3.5000 g., 0.9860 Gold 0.1109 oz. AGW **Ruler:** Friedrich August I **Obverse:** Bust right **Reverse:** Crown above 2 shields of arms

Date	Mintage	VG	F	VF	XF	Unc
1702 EPH	—	225	450	850	1,600	—
1709 EPH	—	225	450	850	1,600	—

KM# 736 DUCAT

3.5000 g., 0.9860 Gold 0.1109 oz. AGW **Ruler:** Friedrich August I **Obverse:** Figure on horseback right **Obv. Legend:** D • G • FRID • AUG • REX • POL • DUX • SAX • I • C • M • A • & W • **Reverse:** Crowned arms within flags

Date	Mintage	VG	F	VF	XF	Unc
1702 EPH	—	225	450	850	1,600	—
1712 EPH	—	225	450	850	1,600	—

KM# 734 DUCAT

3.5000 g., 0.9860 Gold 0.1109 oz. AGW **Ruler:** Friedrich August I **Mint:** Leipzig **Obverse:** Crowned bust on pedestal **Reverse:** Crown above 3 shields of arms **Note:** Prev. Poland KM#141.

Date	Mintage	VG	F	VF	XF	Unc
1702 EPH	—	450	1,000	2,000	3,750	—
1703 EPH	—	450	1,000	2,000	3,750	—

KM# 771 DUCAT

3.5000 g., 0.9860 Gold 0.1109 oz. AGW **Ruler:** Friedrich August I **Mint:** Dresden **Obverse:** Laureate bust right within inner circle **Reverse:** Crowned AR monogram divides date within inner circle

Date	Mintage	VG	F	VF	XF	Unc
1708 ILH	—	250	475	1,000	2,000	—
1709 ILH	—	250	475	1,000	2,000	—

KM# 778 DUCAT

3.5000 g., 0.9860 Gold 0.1109 oz. AGW **Ruler:** Friedrich August I **Mint:** Leipzig **Subject:** Jubilee of Leipzig University **Obverse:** Friedrich the War-like **Reverse:** View of the University

Date	Mintage	VG	F	VF	XF	Unc
1709	—	300	550	1,200	2,200	—

KM# 779 DUCAT

3.5000 g., 0.9860 Gold 0.1109 oz. AGW **Ruler:** Friedrich August I **Subject:** Gold From Freiberg Mines **Obverse:** All-seeing eye above rocks **Reverse:** 6-line inscription and date

Date	Mintage	VG	F	VF	XF	Unc
1709	—	400	900	1,750	3,000	—
1714	—	400	900	1,750	3,000	—

KM# 796 DUCAT

3.5000 g., 0.9860 Gold 0.1109 oz. AGW **Ruler:** Friedrich August I **Mint:** Dresden **Obverse:** Crowned FA monogram **Reverse:** Crowned arms, date above

Date	Mintage	VG	F	VF	XF	Unc
1710	—	250	475	1,000	2,000	—

KM# 806.1 DUCAT

3.5000 g., 0.9860 Gold 0.1109 oz. AGW **Ruler:** Friedrich August I **Obverse:** King on horseback right **Obv. Legend:** FRID. - AVGUST **Reverse:** Date curved **Rev. Legend:** D • G • REX POL • ET • EL • SAX VICARIVS • IMP **Note:** Fr. #2823.

Date	Mintage	VG	F	VF	XF	Unc
1711	—	150	300	600	1,000	—

KM# 806.2 DUCAT

3.5000 g., 0.9860 Gold 0.1109 oz. AGW **Ruler:** Friedrich August I **Obverse:** Equestrian figure right **Obv. Legend:** FRID AVGVST **Reverse:** Date straight **Rev. Legend:** DG. REX. POLON. ET. ELECT. SAXONIAE. VICARIVS. IMP.

Date	Mintage	VG	F	VF	XF	Unc
1711	—	150	300	600	1,000	—

KM# 805 DUCAT

3.5000 g., 0.9860 Gold 0.1109 oz. AGW **Ruler:** Friedrich August I **Obverse:** King on horseback right **Reverse:** Imperial regalia on tables at left and right, inscriptions above and below **Note:** Vicariat Issue.

Date	Mintage	VG	F	VF	XF	Unc
MDCCXI (1711)	—	120	250	500	850	—

KM# 821 DUCAT

3.5000 g., 0.9860 Gold 0.1109 oz. AGW **Ruler:** Friedrich August I **Subject:** Treaty of Lublin **Obverse:** Head right **Reverse:** Crown on plush pillow, date in exerque

Date	Mintage	VG	F	VF	XF	Unc
1715	—	600	1,200	2,250	3,750	—

KM# 829 DUCAT

3.5000 g., 0.9860 Gold 0.1109 oz. AGW **Subject:** Death of Ann Sophia, Mother of Friedrich August I **Obverse:** Inscription **Reverse:** Ship in water

Date	Mintage	VG	F	VF	XF	Unc
1717 IGS	—	650	1,250	2,500	4,000	—

KM# 830 DUCAT

3.5000 g., 0.9860 Gold 0.1109 oz. AGW **Ruler:** Friedrich August I **Subject:** Bicentennial of the Reformation **Obverse:** Bust of Martin Luther right **Reverse:** Flaming altar divides date, double marginal inscription

Date	Mintage	VG	F	VF	XF	Unc
1717 Rare	—	—	—	—	—	—

KM# 831 DUCAT

3.5000 g., 0.9860 Gold 0.1109 oz. AGW **Ruler:** Friedrich August I **Reverse:** Date undivided on altar

Date	Mintage	VG	F	VF	XF	Unc
1717 Rare	—	—	—	—	—	—

KM# 842 DUCAT

3.5000 g., 0.9860 Gold 0.1109 oz. AGW **Ruler:** Friedrich August I **Subject:** Wedding of the Prince to Maria Josepha of Austria **Obverse:** Inscription **Reverse:** 2 Hands binding flaming hearts

Date	Mintage	VG	F	VF	XF	Unc
1719 IGS	—	150	350	800	1,500	—

KM# 851 DUCAT

3.5000 g., 0.9860 Gold 0.1109 oz. AGW **Ruler:** Friedrich August I **Obverse:** Head right **Reverse:** Crowned arms

Date	Mintage	VG	F	VF	XF	Unc
1721 IGS	—	200	450	1,000	1,800	—

KM# 861 DUCAT

3.5000 g., 0.9860 Gold 0.1109 oz. AGW **Ruler:** Friedrich August I **Subject:** Death of Friedrich August I's Wife, Christiane

Eberhardine **Obverse:** Inscription **Reverse:** Cyprus tree at center **Note:** Similar to 2 Groschen, KM#855.

Date	Mintage	VG	F	VF	XF	Unc
1727 IGS Rare	—	—	—	—	—	—

KM# 863 DUCAT

3.5000 g., 0.9860 Gold 0.1109 oz. AGW **Ruler:** Friedrich August I **Note:** Struck from 1/2 Ducat dies.

Date	Mintage	VG	F	VF	XF	Unc
1729	—	350	750	1,500	2,500	—
1733	—	350	750	1,500	2,500	—

KM# 870 DUCAT

3.5000 g., 0.9860 Gold 0.1109 oz. AGW **Ruler:** Friedrich August II **Obverse:** Laureate bust right **Obv. Legend:** D: G: FRID: AUG: REX POL DUX SAX: ... **Reverse:** Crowned arms

Date	Mintage	VG	F	VF	XF	Unc
1732 IGS	—	200	500	1,200	2,000	—
1734 IGS	—	200	500	1,200	2,000	—

KM# 887 DUCAT

3.5000 g., 0.9860 Gold 0.1109 oz. AGW **Ruler:** Friedrich August II **Obverse:** Draped bust right **Obv. Legend:** D: G: FRID: AUGUST: REX POL DUX SAX: .... **Reverse:** Crowned arms

Date	Mintage	VG	F	VF	XF	Unc
1735 FWoF	—	150	300	700	1,250	—
1736 FWoF	—	150	300	700	1,250	—
1737 FWoF	—	150	300	700	1,250	—
1738 FWoF	—	150	300	700	1,250	—
1739 FWoF	—	150	300	700	1,250	—
1740 FWoF	—	150	300	700	1,250	—
1741 FWoF	—	150	300	700	1,250	—
1742 FWoF	—	150	300	700	1,250	—
1743 FWoF	—	150	300	700	1,250	—
1744 FWoF	—	150	300	700	1,250	—
1745 FWoF	—	150	300	700	1,250	—
1748 FWoF	—	150	300	700	1,250	—
1749 FWoF	—	150	300	700	1,250	—
1750 FWoF	—	150	300	700	1,250	—
1751 FWoF	—	150	300	700	1,250	—
1752 FWoF	—	150	300	700	1,250	—
1753 FWoF	—	150	300	700	1,250	—
1754 FWoF	—	150	300	700	1,250	—
1755 FWoF	—	150	300	700	1,250	—
1756 FWoF	—	150	300	700	1,250	—
1757 FWoF	—	200	400	850	1,450	—
1760 FWoF	—	200	400	850	1,450	—
1761 FWoF	—	200	400	850	1,450	—
1762 FWoF	—	200	400	850	1,450	—
1763 FWoF	—	200	400	850	1,450	—

KM# 896 DUCAT

3.5000 g., 0.9860 Gold 0.1109 oz. AGW **Ruler:** Friedrich August II **Subject:** Marriage of Princess Maria Amalia **Obverse:** Inscription **Reverse:** Hand with crown above hearts on altar

Date	Mintage	VG	F	VF	XF	Unc
1738	—	175	350	700	1,250	—

KM# 896a DUCAT

Silver **Ruler:** Friedrich August II **Subject:** Marrige of Princess Maria Amalia **Obverse:** Inscription **Reverse:** Hand with crown above hearts on altar

Date	Mintage	VG	F	VF	XF	Unc
1738	—	20.00	35.00	65.00	125	—

KM# 904 DUCAT

3.5000 g., 0.9860 Gold 0.1109 oz. AGW **Ruler:** Friedrich August II **Obverse:** Bust right **Reverse:** Double headed eagle with round arms on breast **Note:** Vicariat Issue.

Date	Mintage	VG	F	VF	XF	Unc
1740	—	400	800	1,500	2,500	—

KM# 908 DUCAT

3.5000 g., 0.9860 Gold 0.1109 oz. AGW **Ruler:** Friedrich August II **Obverse:** King on horseback right **Obv. Legend:** D G FRID AUG REX POL DUX SAX ARCHUM ELECTOR **Reverse:** Arms on tapestry back of throne **Note:** Vicariat Issue.

Date	Mintage	VG	F	VF	XF	Unc
1741	—	150	300	600	1,200	—
1742	—	150	300	600	1,200	—

KM# 916 DUCAT

3.5000 g., 0.9860 Gold 0.1109 oz. AGW **Ruler:** Friedrich August II **Note:** Vicariat issue. Prev. Poland KM#149.

Date	Mintage	VG	F	VF	XF	Unc
1745 FwoF	—	200	450	950	1,600	—
1752 JGG	—	250	500	1,000	1,750	—
1753 EDC	—	250	500	1,000	1,750	—
1754 EDC	—	250	500	1,000	1,750	—
1756 EDC	—	250	500	1,000	1,750	—

KM# 915 DUCAT

3.5000 g., 0.9860 Gold 0.1109 oz. AGW **Ruler:** Friedrich August II **Obverse:** King on rearing horse right **Reverse:** Eagle with sceptre in flight

Date	Mintage	VG	F	VF	XF	Unc
1745	—	300	600	1,200	2,000	—

KM# 939 DUCAT

3.5000 g., 0.9860 Gold 0.1109 oz. AGW **Ruler:** Friedrich August II **Subject:** Marriage of Prince Friedrich Christian **Obverse:** Inscription **Reverse:** Winged figure in flight

Date	Mintage	VG	F	VF	XF	Unc
MDCCXLVII (1747)	—	300	600	1,200	2,000	—

KM# 939a DUCAT

Silver **Ruler:** Friedrich August II **Subject:** Marriage of Prince Friedrich Christian **Obverse:** Inscription **Reverse:** Winged figure in flight

Date	Mintage	VG	F	VF	XF	Unc
1747	—	20.00	40.00	85.00	175	—

KM# 938 DUCAT

3.5000 g., 0.9860 Gold 0.1109 oz. AGW **Subject:** Marriage of Princess Maria Josepha **Note:** Similar to 2/3 Thaler, KM#921.

Date	Mintage	VG	F	VF	XF	Unc
1747 Rare	—	—	—	—	—	—

KM# 936 DUCAT

3.5000 g., 0.9860 Gold 0.1109 oz. AGW **Ruler:** Friedrich August I **Subject:** Prussian Occupation **Obverse:** Draped bust right **Obv. Legend:** D: G: FRID: AUGUST: REX ... **Reverse:** Crowned arms **Rev. Legend:** SAC: ROM: IMP: ARCHIM: ET: ELECT •

Date	Mintage	VG	F	VF	XF	Unc
1757 IDB	—	225	450	900	1,650	—
1757 IDB w/o FR	—	225	450	900	1,650	—

KM# 963 DUCAT

3.5000 g., 0.9860 Gold 0.1109 oz. AGW **Ruler:** Friedrich Christian **Obverse:** Head right **Reverse:** Crowned arms

Date	Mintage	F	VF	XF	Unc
1763 FWoF	—	350	650	1,200	2,250

KM# 978 DUCAT

3.5000 g., 0.9860 Gold 0.1109 oz. AGW **Ruler:** Friedrich August III **Obverse:** Head right **Obv. Legend:** FRID: AUGUST: D: G: DUX SAX: ELECTOR **Reverse:** Elector's cap above arms within branches

Date	Mintage	F	VF	XF	Unc
1764 IFOF	—	—	—	—	—

KM# 979 DUCAT

3.5000 g., 0.9860 Gold 0.1109 oz. AGW **Ruler:** Friedrich August III **Obverse:** Head right **Obv. Legend:** FRID: AVGVST: D: G: DVX SAX: ELECTOR **Reverse:** Elector's cap above arms within branches, date divided below

Date	Mintage	F	VF	XF	Unc
1764 EDC	—	200	300	650	2,000
1764 FWoF	—	200	300	650	2,000
1765 EDC	—	200	300	650	2,000
1766 EDC	—	200	300	650	2,000
1767 EDC	—	200	300	650	2,000
1768 EDC	—	200	300	650	2,000

KM# 989 DUCAT

3.5000 g., 0.9860 Gold 0.1109 oz. AGW **Ruler:** Xaver **Obverse:** Armored bust right **Obv. Legend:** XAVERIVS D: G: REG: PR: POL: & L: DVX ... **Reverse:** Elector's cap above arms within branches **Rev. Legend:** ELECTORATVS SAXON: ADMINISTRATOR •

Date	Mintage	F	VF	XF	Unc
1766 EDC	—	300	500	900	2,250
1767 EDC	—	300	500	900	2,250
1768 EDC	—	300	500	900	2,250

KM# 994 DUCAT

3.5000 g., 0.9860 Gold 0.1109 oz. AGW **Ruler:** Friedrich August III **Obverse:** Head right **Obv. Legend:** FRID: AUGUST: D: G: DUX SAX: ELECTOR **Reverse:** Elector's cap above arms within branches, date divided below

Date	Mintage	F	VF	XF	Unc
1769 EDC	—	200	300	650	2,000
1770 EDC	—	200	300	650	2,000
1771 EDC	—	200	300	650	2,000
1772 EDC	—	200	300	650	2,000
1773 EDC	—	200	300	650	2,000
1774 EDC	—	200	300	650	2,000
1775 EDC	—	200	300	650	2,000
1776 EDC	—	200	300	650	2,000
1777 EDC	—	200	300	650	2,000
1778 EDC	—	200	300	650	2,000

KM# 1005 DUCAT

3.5000 g., 0.9860 Gold 0.1109 oz. AGW **Ruler:** Friedrich August III **Obverse:** Head right **Obv. Legend:** FRID: AUGUST: D: G: DUX SAX: ELECTOR **Reverse:** Elector's cap above arms within branches, date divided below

Date	Mintage	F	VF	XF	Unc
1779 IEC	—	150	300	600	1,650
1780 IEC	—	150	300	600	1,650
1781 IEC	—	150	300	600	1,650
1782 IEC	—	150	300	600	1,650
1783 IEC	—	150	300	600	1,650
1784 IEC	—	150	300	600	1,650
1785 IEC	—	150	300	600	1,650
1786 IEC	—	150	300	600	1,650
1787 IEC	—	150	300	600	1,650
1788 IEC	—	150	300	600	1,650

Date	Mintage	F	VF	XF	Unc
1789 IEC	—	150	300	600	1,650
1790 IEC	—	150	300	600	1,650

KM# 1030 DUCAT
3.5000 g., 0.9860 Gold 0.1109 oz. AGW **Ruler:** Friedrich August III **Obverse:** Uniformed bust right **Obv. Legend:** FRID. AVG. D. G. DVX SAX. ELECTOR **Reverse:** Crowned oval arms within branches

Date	Mintage	F	VF	XF	Unc
1791 IEC	—	200	400	850	2,000
1792 IEC	—	200	400	850	2,000
1793 IEC	—	200	400	850	2,000
1794 IEC	—	200	400	850	2,000
1795 IEC	—	200	400	850	2,000
1796 IEC	—	200	400	850	2,000
1797 IEC	—	200	400	850	2,000
1798 IEC	—	200	400	850	2,000
1799 IEC	—	200	400	850	2,000
1800 IEC	—	300	600	1,250	3,000

KM# 1035 DUCAT
3.5000 g., 0.9860 Gold 0.1109 oz. AGW **Ruler:** Friedrich August III **Obverse:** Draped bust right **Obv. Legend:** FRID • AVG • D • G • DVX • SAX • ELECTOR **Reverse:** Arms on eagle's breast **Rev. Legend:** SAC • ROM • - IMP • PROVISOR - ITERVM **Note:** Vicariat Issue.

Date	Mintage	F	VF	XF	Unc
1792 IEC	—	200	400	850	2,000

KM# 710.1 2 DUCAT
7.0000 g., 0.9860 Gold 0.2219 oz. AGW **Ruler:** Friedrich August I **Obverse:** Armored, laureate bust right **Obv. Legend:** D G FRID AUG REX POL - DUX ... **Reverse:** Date above crown **Note:** Some dates struck from 1/2 Thaler dies, KM# 724.

Date	Mintage	VG	F	VF	XF	Unc
1701 ILH	—	300	700	1,500	2,750	—
1702 ILH	—	300	700	1,500	2,750	—
1704 ILH	—	300	700	1,500	2,750	—
1711 ILH	—	300	700	1,500	2,750	—
1714 ILH	—	300	700	1,500	2,750	—

KM# 739 2 DUCAT
7.0000 g., 0.9860 Gold 0.2219 oz. AGW **Ruler:** Friedrich August I **Obverse:** Bust right **Reverse:** Crowned round 4-fold arms with central shield of 2-fold arms, flanked by 2 palm branches crossed at bottom, date at top **Note:** Struck from 1/8 Thaler dies, KM# 721.

Date	Mintage	VG	F	VF	XF	Unc
1702 ILH	—	—	—	—	—	—
1703 ILH	—	—	—	—	—	—
1704 ILH	—	—	—	—	—	—
1705 ILH	—	—	—	—	—	—

KM# 737 2 DUCAT
7.0000 g., 0.9860 Gold 0.2219 oz. AGW **Ruler:** Friedrich August I **Subject:** Friedrich August I Awarded the Danish Order of the Elephant **Obverse:** Head right **Obv. Legend:** AUGUSTUS II • D • G • REX POL: ... **Reverse:** Crowned arms with 3 points at left and right, Order chain surrounds

Date	Mintage	VG	F	VF	XF	Unc
1702	—	250	500	1,200	2,000	—

KM# 738 2 DUCAT
7.0000 g., 0.9860 Gold 0.2219 oz. AGW **Ruler:** Friedrich August I **Obverse:** Equestrian figure right **Reverse:** Shield of arms on military trophies

Date	Mintage	VG	F	VF	XF	Unc
1702 EPH	—	400	800	1,800	2,800	—
1712 EPH	—	400	800	1,800	2,800	—

KM# 772 2 DUCAT
7.0000 g., 0.9860 Gold 0.2219 oz. AGW **Ruler:** Friedrich August I **Mint:** Dresden **Obverse:** Arms on breastplate **Reverse:** Crowned monogram divides date

Date	Mintage	VG	F	VF	XF	Unc
1708 ILH	—	700	1,350	2,750	4,500	—
1709 ILH	—	700	1,350	2,750	4,500	—

KM# 780 2 DUCAT
7.0000 g., 0.9860 Gold 0.2219 oz. AGW **Ruler:** Friedrich August I **Mint:** Leipzig **Subject:** Jubilee of Leipzig University **Obverse:** Bust of Friedrich the Warlike with sword and elector's cap **Reverse:** City of Leipzig

Date	Mintage	VG	F	VF	XF	Unc
1709	—	400	800	1,800	3,000	—

KM# 781 2 DUCAT
7.0000 g., 0.9860 Gold 0.2219 oz. AGW **Ruler:** Friedrich August I **Obverse:** Bust right **Reverse:** Crown above 2 shields of arms **Note:** Thick flan. Struck from Ducat dies.

Date	Mintage	VG	F	VF	XF	Unc
1709 EPH	—	400	800	1,800	3,000	—

KM# 797 2 DUCAT
7.0000 g., 0.9860 Gold 0.2219 oz. AGW **Ruler:** Friedrich August I **Mint:** Dresden **Obverse:** Crowned FA monogram **Reverse:** Crowned arms, date above

Date	Mintage	VG	F	VF	XF	Unc
1710	—	400	800	1,800	3,000	—

KM# 807 2 DUCAT
7.0000 g., 0.9860 Gold 0.2219 oz. AGW **Ruler:** Friedrich August I **Obverse:** Equestrian figure above arms **Reverse:** Altar with electoral regalia

Date	Mintage	VG	F	VF	XF	Unc
1711 ILH	—	250	550	1,200	2,000	—

KM# 809 2 DUCAT
7.0000 g., 0.9860 Gold 0.2219 oz. AGW **Ruler:** Friedrich August I **Obverse:** Equestrian figure of Duke right, ornate arms in baroque frame below **Reverse:** 2 tables holding crown, scepter and mantle, inscriptions above and below **Note:** Vicariat issue. Struck with 1/8 Thaler dies, KM#800.

Date	Mintage	VG	F	VF	XF	Unc
MDCCXI (1711) ILH	—	600	950	1,850	3,200	—

KM# 882 2 DUCAT
7.0000 g., 0.9860 Gold 0.2219 oz. AGW **Ruler:** Friedrich August I **Subject:** Bicentennial of the Reformation **Obverse:** Bust of Martin Luther right **Reverse:** Flaming altar with date above, double legend

Date	Mintage	VG	F	VF	XF	Unc
1717 Rare	—	—	—	—	—	—

KM# 710.2 2 DUCAT
7.0000 g., 0.9860 Gold 0.2219 oz. AGW **Ruler:** Friedrich August I **Obverse:** Armored, laureate bust right **Reverse:** Date at upper left

Date	Mintage	VG	F	VF	XF	Unc
1717 ILH	—	300	700	1,500	2,750	—
1721 IGS	—	300	700	1,500	2,750	—
1723 IGS	—	300	700	1,500	2,750	—
1727 IGS	—	300	700	1,500	2,750	—
1733 IGS	—	300	700	1,500	2,750	—

KM# 843 2 DUCAT
7.0000 g., 0.9860 Gold 0.2219 oz. AGW **Ruler:** Friedrich August I **Subject:** Wedding of the Prince to Maria Josepha of Austria **Obverse:** 2 flaming hearts tied by hands from each side **Reverse:** 8-line inscription and date

Date	Mintage	VG	F	VF	XF	Unc
1719 IGS	—	325	750	1,600	2,750	—

KM# 888 2 DUCAT
7.0000 g., 0.9860 Gold 0.2219 oz. AGW **Ruler:** Friedrich August II **Obverse:** Bust right **Reverse:** Crowned arms **Note:** Struck from 1/8 Thaler dies, KM# A878.

Date	Mintage	VG	F	VF	XF	Unc
1734 IGS	—	300	600	1,450	2,500	—
1735 FWoF	—	300	600	1,450	2,500	—
1739 FWoF	—	300	600	1,450	2,500	—
1742 FWoF	—	300	600	1,450	2,500	—
1743 FWoF	—	300	600	1,450	2,500	—

KM# 940 2 DUCAT
7.0000 g., 0.9860 Gold 0.2219 oz. AGW **Ruler:** Friedrich August II **Subject:** Marriage of Princess Maria Josepha **Note:** Similar to 2/3 Thaler, KM#921.

Date	Mintage	VG	F	VF	XF	Unc
1747 Rare	—	—	—	—	—	—

KM# C916 2 DUCAT
7.0000 g., 0.9860 Gold 0.2219 oz. AGW **Obverse:** Bust of Johann Casimir right **Reverse:** Crowned eagle displayed with arms on breast in inner circle, date in legend **Note:** Prev. Poland KM#160.

Date	Mintage	VG	F	VF	XF	Unc
1753 EDC	—	350	650	1,250	2,500	—
1754 EDC	—	500	800	1,650	3,500	—

KM# 810 3 DUCAT
10.5000 g., 0.9860 Gold 0.3328 oz. AGW **Ruler:** Friedrich August I **Obverse:** Horseman right on rearing horse, arms below **Reverse:** Imperial regalia on tables at left and right, inscription above and below **Note:** Vicariat Issue. Similar to 2 Ducat, KM#809. Struck with 1/4 Thaler dies, KM#801.

Date	Mintage	VG	F	VF	XF	Unc
1711 ILH	—	700	1,500	3,000	5,500	—

KM# 811 3 DUCAT
10.5000 g., 0.9860 Gold 0.3328 oz. AGW **Ruler:** Friedrich August I **Obverse:** Friedrich August I standing by table with regalia on it **Reverse:** 2 crowned arms, branches behind divided date, 3-line inscription above

Date	Mintage	VG	F	VF	XF	Unc
1711 Rare	—	—	—	—	—	—

KM# 833 3 DUCAT
10.5000 g., 0.9860 Gold 0.3328 oz. AGW **Ruler:** Friedrich August I **Obverse:** Small bust right, titles of Friedrich August I **Reverse:** Crowned round 4-fold arms with central shield of 2-fold arms in crossed palm branches, date in legend **Note:** Struck from 1/4 Thaler dies, KM#791.

Date	Mintage	VG	F	VF	XF	Unc
1717 IGS	—	1,000	2,000	4,000	6,500	—
1719 IGS	—	1,000	2,000	4,000	6,500	—
1721 IGS	—	1,000	2,000	4,000	6,500	—

KM# 844 3 DUCAT
10.5000 g., 0.9860 Gold 0.3328 oz. AGW **Ruler:** Friedrich August I **Mint:** Dresden **Subject:** Wedding of the Prince to Maria Josepha of Austria **Obverse:** 2 flaming hearts tied by hands from each side **Reverse:** 8-line inscription and date

Date	Mintage	VG	F	VF	XF	Unc
1719	—	1,000	2,000	4,000	6,500	—

KM# 892 3 DUCAT
10.5000 g., 0.9860 Gold 0.3328 oz. AGW **Ruler:** Friedrich August II **Note:** Struck from 1/2 Thaler dies, KM# A879.

Date	Mintage	VG	F	VF	XF	Unc
1738 FWoF Rare	—	—	—	—	—	—

KM# A921 3 DUCAT
10.5000 g., 0.9860 Gold 0.3329 oz. AGW 0.3328 oz. AGW **Ruler:** Friedrich August II **Subject:** Marriage of Princess Maria Josepha to the Dauphin Louis of Franc **Note:** Struck from 2/3 Thaler dies, KM# 921.

Date	Mintage	VG	F	VF	XF	Unc
MDCCXLVII(1747)	—	—	—	—	—	—

KM# 920 3 DUCAT
10.5000 g., 0.9860 Gold 0.3328 oz. AGW **Ruler:** Friedrich August II **Subject:** Marriage of Prince Friedrich Christian with Maria Antonia of Bavaria **Note:** Struck from 2/3 Thaler dies, KM# 922.

Date	Mintage	VG	F	VF	XF	Unc
MDCCXLVII(1747)	—	—	—	—	—	—

KM# 730 4 DUCAT
14.0000 g., 0.9860 Gold 0.4438 oz. AGW **Ruler:** Friedrich August I **Obverse:** Bust right **Reverse:** Crowned round 4-fold arms with central shield of 2-fold arms in 2 palm branches crossed at bottom, date at top **Note:** Struck with 1/2 Thaler dies, KM#724.

Date	Mintage	VG	F	VF	XF	Unc
1701 ILH	—	—	—	—	—	—
1704 ILH	—	—	—	—	—	—

KM# 755 4 DUCAT
14.0000 g., 0.9860 Gold 0.4438 oz. AGW **Ruler:** Friedrich August I **Reverse:** Squarish arms with concave sides **Note:** Struck with 1/2 Thaler dies, KM#749.

Date	Mintage	VG	F	VF	XF	Unc
1707 ILH	—	—	—	—	—	—

KM# 812 4 DUCAT
14.0000 g., 0.9860 Gold 0.4438 oz. AGW **Ruler:** Friedrich August I **Mint:** Dresden **Obverse:** Equestrian figure right above arms **Reverse:** 2 tables with royal and electoral regalia, inscription top and bottom **Note:** Vicariat Issue.

Date	Mintage	VG	F	VF	XF	Unc
1711 ILH Rare	—	—	—	—	—	—

KM# 813 4 DUCAT
14.0000 g., 0.9860 Gold 0.4438 oz. AGW **Ruler:** Friedrich August I **Obverse:** Horseman right **Reverse:** Imperial regalia, date below **Note:** Vicariat Issue. Similar to Ducat, KM#806. Struck with 1/2 Thaler dies, KM#802.

Date	Mintage	VG	F	VF	XF	Unc
1711 ILH	—	3,250	4,500	6,000	8,500	—

KM# 814 4 DUCAT
14.0000 g., 0.9860 Gold 0.4438 oz. AGW **Ruler:** Friedrich August I **Obverse:** Friedrich August I standing by table with regalia on it **Reverse:** 2 crowned arms, branches behind divided date, 3-line inscription above

Date	Mintage	VG	F	VF	XF	Unc
1711 Rare	—	—	—	—	—	—

KM# 852 4 DUCAT
14.0000 g., 0.9860 Gold 0.4438 oz. AGW **Ruler:** Friedrich August I **Obverse:** Armored bust right **Reverse:** Crowned arms within branches **Note:** Similar to 5 Ducat, KM#873. Struck with 1/2 Thaler dies, KM#834.

Date	Mintage	VG	F	VF	XF	Unc
1723 IGS Rare	—	—	—	—	—	—

KM# 893 4 DUCAT
14.0000 g., 0.9860 Gold 0.4438 oz. AGW **Ruler:** Friedrich August II

Date	Mintage	VG	F	VF	XF	Unc
1738 FWoF Rare	—	—	—	—	—	—

KM# 756 5 DUCAT (1/2 Portugalöser)
17.5000 g., 0.9860 Gold 0.5547 oz. AGW **Ruler:** Johann Georg IV **Obverse:** Bust right **Reverse:** Crowned squarish 4-fold arms with concave sides and central 2-fold shield in 2 palm branches crossed at bottom, date at top **Note:** Struck with 1/2 Thaler dies, KM#749.

Date	Mintage	VG	F	VF	XF	Unc
1707 ILH	—	—	—	—	—	—

KM# 815 5 DUCAT (1/2 Portugalöser)
17.5000 g., 0.9860 Gold 0.5547 oz. AGW **Ruler:** Friedrich August I **Subject:** Vicariat issue **Obverse:** Horseman right, shield below **Reverse:** Imperial regalia on tables at left and right, inscription above and below **Note:** Struck from 1/2 Thaler dies, KM# 802.

Date	Mintage	VG	F	VF	XF	Unc
1711 ILH	—	—	—	—	—	—

Note: Struck with 1/2 Thaler dies, KM#802

KM# 853 5 DUCAT (1/2 Portugalöser)
17.5000 g., 0.9860 Gold 0.5547 oz. AGW **Ruler:** Friedrich August I **Obverse:** Armored bust right **Reverse:** Crowned arms within branches **Note:** Similar to KM#873, but value "V" punched. Struck with 1/2 Thaler dies, KM#834.

Date	Mintage	VG	F	VF	XF	Unc
1723 IGS	—	—	—	—	—	—

KM# 873 5 DUCAT (1/2 Portugalöser)
17.5000 g., 0.9860 Gold 0.5547 oz. AGW **Ruler:** Friedrich August I **Obverse:** Armored bust right **Reverse:** Crowned arms within branches **Note:** Struck from 1/2 Thaler dies, KM# 834.

Date	Mintage	VG	F	VF	XF	Unc
1724 IGS Rare	—	—	—	—	—	—
1733 IGS Rare	—	—	—	—	—	—

KM# 895 5 DUCAT (1/2 Portugalöser)
17.5000 g., 0.9860 Gold 0.5547 oz. AGW **Ruler:** Friedrich August II **Subject:** Marriage of Princess Maria Amalia and Carlos III of Spain **Note:** Struck from 2/3 Thaler dies, KM# 897.

Date	Mintage	VG	F	VF	XF	Unc
MDCCXXXVIII (1738)	—	—	—	—	—	—

KM# 909 5 DUCAT (1/2 Portugalöser)
17.5000 g., 0.9860 Gold 0.5547 oz. AGW **Ruler:** Friedrich August II **Mint:** Dresden **Subject:** Vicariate issue **Obverse:** Equestrian figure right **Reverse:** Throne and arms **Note:** Struck from 1/2 Thaler dies, KM# A907.

Date	Mintage	VG	F	VF	XF	Unc
1741 Rare	—	—	—	—	—	—
1742 Rare	—	—	—	—	—	—

KM# 731 6 DUCAT
21.0000 g., 0.9860 Gold 0.6657 oz. AGW **Ruler:** Friedrich August I **Obverse:** Bust right **Reverse:** Crowned arms within branches **Note:** Similar to 4 Ducat, KM#730. Struck with 1 Thaler dies, KM#707.

Date	Mintage	VG	F	VF	XF	Unc
1701 ILH Rare	—	—	—	—	—	—

KM# 752 6 DUCAT
21.0000 g., 0.9860 Gold 0.6657 oz. AGW **Ruler:** Friedrich August I **Note:** Struck with 1 Thaler dies, KM#750.

Date	Mintage	VG	F	VF	XF	Unc
1706 ILH Rare	—	—	—	—	—	—

KM# 782 6 DUCAT
21.0000 g., 0.9860 Gold 0.6657 oz. AGW **Ruler:** Johann Georg IV **Note:** Struck with 1 Thaler dies, KM#769.

Date	Mintage	VG	F	VF	XF	Unc
1709 ILH	—	—	—	—	—	—

KM# 783 6 DUCAT
21.0000 g., 0.9860 Gold 0.6657 oz. AGW **Note:** Struck with 1 Thaler dies, KM#776.

Date	Mintage	VG	F	VF	XF	Unc
1709 ILH Rare	—	—	—	—	—	—
1719 IGS Rare	—	—	—	—	—	—

KM# 816 6 DUCAT
21.0000 g., 0.9860 Gold 0.6657 oz. AGW **Ruler:** Johann Georg IV **Note:** Vicariat issue. Struck with 1 Thaler dies, KM#803.

Date	Mintage	VG	F	VF	XF	Unc
1711 ILH	—	7,000	9,500	12,000	15,000	—

KM# A910 6 DUCAT
21.0000 g., 0.9860 Gold .6658 oz. AGW 0.6657 oz. AGW **Ruler:** Friedrich August II **Subject:** Vicariate issue **Obverse:** Friedrich August II on horse rearing to right **Reverse:** Empty throne on dias with symbols of office, date at end of legend **Note:** Struck from 1/2 Thaler dies, KM# A907.

Date	Mintage	VG	F	VF	XF	Unc
1742 Rare	—	—	—	—	—	—

KM# 817 8 DUCAT
28.0000 g., 0.9860 Gold 0.8876 oz. AGW **Ruler:** Friedrich August I **Obverse:** Equestrian rearing right, shield below **Reverse:** Imperial regalia on tables at left and right, inscription above and below **Note:** Vicariat issue. Similar to 2 Ducat, KM#809. Struck with 1 Thaler dies, KM#803.

Date	Mintage	VG	F	VF	XF	Unc
1711 ILH Rare	—	—	—	—	—	—

KM# 854 8 DUCAT
28.0000 g., 0.9860 Gold 0.8876 oz. AGW **Ruler:** Friedrich August II **Note:** Struck with 1 Thaler dies, KM#776.

Date	Mintage	VG	F	VF	XF	Unc
1725 IGS Rare	—	—	—	—	—	—
1731 IGS Rare	—	—	—	—	—	—

KM# 742 10 DUCAT (Portugalöser)
35.0000 g., 0.9860 Gold 1.1095 oz. AGW **Ruler:** Friedrich August I **Obverse:** Bust right **Reverse:** Helmeted arms **Note:** Struck with 1 Thaler dies, KM#707.

Date	Mintage	VG	F	VF	XF	Unc
1704 ILH Rare	—	—	—	—	—	—
1705 ILH Rare	—	—	—	—	—	—

KM# 753 10 DUCAT (Portugalöser)
35.0000 g., 0.9860 Gold 1.1095 oz. AGW **Ruler:** Friedrich August I **Obverse:** Bust right **Reverse:** Crowned arms with 6 small shields of arms around **Note:** Struck with 1 Thaler dies, KM#750.

Date	Mintage	VG	F	VF	XF	Unc
1706 ILH Rare	—	—	—	—	—	—

KM# 818 10 DUCAT (Portugalöser)
35.0000 g., 0.9860 Gold 1.1095 oz. AGW **Ruler:** Friedrich August I **Obverse:** Equestrian rearing right, shield below **Reverse:** Imperial regalia on tables at left and right, inscription above and below **Note:** Vicariat issue. Similar to 2 Ducat, KM#809. Struck with 1 Thaler dies, KM#803.

Date	Mintage	VG	F	VF	XF	Unc
1711 ILH Rare	—	—	—	—	—	—

KM# B907 10 DUCAT (Portugalöser)
35.0000 g., 0.9860 Gold 1.1095 oz. AGW **Ruler:** Friedrich August II **Subject:** Vicariat issue **Note:** Struck from Thaler dies, KM# 907.

Date	Mintage	VG	F	VF	XF	Unc
1741	—	—	—	—	—	—

KM# A902 12 DUCAT
42.0000 g., 0.9860 Gold 1.3314 oz. AGW **Ruler:** Friedrich August II **Subject:** Vicariat issue **Note:** Struck from Thaler dies, KM# 902.

Date	Mintage	VG	F	VF	XF	Unc
1740	—	—	—	—	—	—

KM# A908 20 DUCAT (Doppel Portugalöser)
70.0000 g., 0.9860 Gold 2.2190 oz. AGW **Ruler:** Friedrich August I **Note:** Vicariat Issue.

Date	Mintage	VG	F	VF	XF	Unc
1741 Rare	—	—	—	—	—	—

Note: Struck w/1 Thaler dies, KM#907. Bowers and Merena Guia sale 3-88 Unc realized $14,300

PATTERNS

Including off metal strikes

KM#	Date	Mintage	Identification	Mkt Val
Pn3	1701	—	Ducat. Silver. KM729.	—
Pn4	1702	—	2 Ducat. Silver. KM710.	—
Pn5	1703	—	2 Ducat. Silver. KM710.	—
Pn6	1704	—	2 Ducat. Silver. KM710.	—
Pn7	1708	—	1/3 Thaler. Copper. KM768.	—
Pn8	1708	—	1/3 Thaler. Gold. KM768.	—
Pn9	1708	—	Thaler. Lead. KM769.	—
Pn10	1709	—	Ducat. Silver. KM729.	—
Pn11	1709	—	Ducat. Silver. KM771.	—
Pn12	1709	—	Ducat. Silver. Leipzig Univ., KM778.	—
Pn13	1710	—	1/4 Ducat. Silver. KM725.	—
Pn14	1710	—	1/4 Ducat. Silver. KM793.	—
Pn15	1710	—	1/2 Ducat. Copper. KM795.	—
Pn16	1710	—	1/2 Ducat. Silver. KM795.	—
Pn17	1710	—	Ducat. Copper. KM793.	—
Pn18	1710	—	Ducat. Silver. KM796.	—
Pn20	1711	—	1/4 Thaler. Copper. KM801.	—
Pn19	1711	—	Pfennig. Gold. KM702.	325
Pn21	1711	—	Ducat. Silver. KM806.	125
Pn22	1711	—	2 Ducat. Silver. KM807.	135
Pn23	1711	—	3 Ducat. Silver. KM811.	350
Pn24	1711	—	4 Ducat. Silver. KM814.	375
Pn25	1712	—	Pfennig. Gold. KM702.	325
Pn26	1714	—	Ducat. Silver. Mining, KM779.	125
Pn27	1715	—	Ducat. Silver. Lublin, KM821.	—
Pn28	1717	—	Ducat. Silver. KM830.	—
Pn29	1717	—	Ducat. Silver. KM831.	95.00
Pn30	1717	—	2 Ducat. Silver. KM832.	125
Pn31	1721	—	Pfennig. Silver. KM850.	—
Pn32	1721	—	Pfennig. Gold. KM850.	—

KM#	Date	Mintage	Identification	Mkt Val
Pn33	1735	—	2 Ducat. Silver. KM888.	125
Pn34	1738	—	3 Ducat. Silver. KM892.	175
Pn35	1738	—	4 Ducat. Silver. KM893.	200
Pn36	1739	—	2 Ducat. Silver. KM888.	125
PnA36	1739	—	2 Ducat. Copper. KM888.	—
Pn38	1742	—	2 Ducat. Silver. KM888.	125
Pn39	1743	—	2 Ducat. Silver. KM888.	125
Pn40	1744	—	Pfennig. Gold. KM894.	600

KM#	Date	Mintage	Identification	Mkt Val
PnA41	1753	—	Thaler. Silver.	—

KM#	Date	Mintage	Identification	Mkt Val
Pn41	1763	—	Ducat. Silver. Hubertusburg Peace.	—

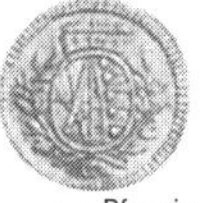

KM#	Date	Mintage	Identification	Mkt Val
Pn42	1764	—	Pfennig. Gold. KM964.	350
Pn43	1765	—	Pfennig. Gold. KM980.	350

KM#	Date	Mintage	Identification	Mkt Val
Pn44	1765	—	3 Pfennige. Billon. KM965.	65.00
Pn45	1772	—	Pfennig. Silver. KM1000.	85.00
Pn46	1779	—	Heller. Silver. KM1002.	45.00
Pn47	1779	—	Heller. Gold. KM1002.	1,200
Pn48	1779	—	Pfennig. Silver. KM1000.	85.00
Pn49	1779	—	Pfennig. Gold. KM1000.	—
Pn50	1780	—	Heller. Silver. KM1002.	45.00
Pn51	1781	—	Pfennig. Silver. KM1000.	85.00
Pn52	1781	—	3 Pfennige. Gold. KM965.	—
Pn53	1782	—	Pfennig. Silver. KM1000.	85.00
Pn54	1783	—	Heller. Silver. KM1002.	45.00
Pn55	1783	—	Pfennig. Silver. KM1000.	85.00
Pn56	1785	—	Pfennig. Silver. KM1000.	85.00
Pn57	1798	—	Pfennig. Silver. KM1000.	85.00
Pn58	1799	—	3 Pfennige. Silver. KM1037.	—
Pn59	1800	—	Pfennig. Silver. KM1000.	85.00

PIEFORTS

KM#	Date	Mintage	Identification	Mkt Val
PA1	1709	—	Ducat. Gold. 6.8900 g. KM#771.	—
P1	1799	—	Heller. Copper. KM1002.	—

SAYN-ALTENKIRCHEN

The counts of Sayn of the Rhineland are first mentioned in the 12th century. They issued a sporadic coinage from the 13th century and acquired possessions in various parts of western Germany. Divided in 1605 into the branches of Sayn-Sayn, Sayn-Wittgenstein and Sayn-Berleburg. Sayn-Altenkirchen was an offshoot of Sayn-Sayn. With the extinction of the line of Eisenach dukes in 1741, it was acquired by Brandenburg-Ansbach until 1791, went to Prussia until 1803, and finally to Nassau in 1803.

RULERS

Johanetta, 1648-1686 (1701)
Johann Wilhelm of Saxe-Eisenach, 1686-1729
Wilhelm Heinrich, 1729-1741
Karl Wilhelm Friedrich of Brandenburg-Ansbach, 1741-1757
Christian Friedrich Karl Alexander of Brandenburg-Ansbach, 1757-1791

MINT OFFICIALS' INITIALS

Initials	Date	Name
D	1750-56	Wilhelm Dobicht, die-cutter
VESTNER	(d.1754)	Andreas Vestner, die-cutter
W	(d.1771)	Peter Paul Werner, die-cutter

DUCHY

STANDARD COINAGE

KM# 15 PFENNIG

Copper **Ruler:** Karl Wilhelm Friedrich of Brandenburg - Ansbach **Mint:** Altenkirchen **Obverse:** Crowned arms of Brandenburg and Sayn in cartouche **Reverse:** Value and date

Date	Mintage	VG	F	VF	XF	Unc
1752	—	20.00	35.00	70.00	125	—
1753	—	20.00	35.00	70.00	125	—

KM# 16 1/4 STUBER

Copper **Ruler:** Karl Wilhelm Friedrich of Brandenburg - Ansbach **Mint:** Altenkirchen **Obverse:** Crowned arms of Brandenburg and Sayn in cartouche, three ermine spots on crown **Reverse:** Value and date

Date	Mintage	VG	F	VF	XF	Unc
1752	—	8.00	14.00	28.00	55.00	—
1753	—	8.00	14.00	28.00	55.00	—
1754	—	8.00	14.00	28.00	55.00	—
1755	—	8.00	14.00	28.00	55.00	—
1756	—	8.00	14.00	28.00	55.00	—

KM# 38 1/4 STUBER

Copper **Ruler:** Christian Friedrich Karl Alexander of Brandenburg - Ansbach **Obverse:** Five ermine spots on crown

Date	Mintage	VG	F	VF	XF	Unc
1757	—	6.00	12.00	25.00	50.00	—
1758	—	6.00	12.00	25.00	50.00	—

KM# 18 STUBER

Billon **Ruler:** Karl Wilhelm Friedrich of Brandenburg - Ansbach **Mint:** Altenkirchen **Obverse:** Crowned CWF monogram **Reverse:** Value and date

Date	Mintage	VG	F	VF	XF	Unc
1755	39,000	30.00	50.00	90.00	165	—

KM# 20 3 STUBER

Billon **Ruler:** Karl Wilhelm Friedrich of Brandenburg - Ansbach **Mint:** Altenkirchen **Obverse:** Crowned arms of Brandenburg and Sayn in cartouche **Reverse:** Value and date in ornamental circle

Date	Mintage	VG	F	VF	XF	Unc
1752	75,000	10.00	20.00	45.00	100	—

KM# 17 KREUZER

Billon **Ruler:** Karl Wilhelm Friedrich of Brandenburg - Ansbach **Mint:** Altenkirchen **Obverse:** Armored bust right **Reverse:** Crowned arms of Brandenburg and Sayn, value in exergue

Date	Mintage	VG	F	VF	XF	Unc
1751	13,000	45.00	90.00	185	400	—
1755	13,000	45.00	90.00	185	400	—

KM# 40 KREUZER

Billon **Ruler:** Christian Friedrich Karl Alexander of Brandenburg - Ansbach **Obverse:** Armored bust right **Note:** Prev. C#22.

Date	Mintage	VG	F	VF	XF	Unc
1757	23,000	12.00	25.00	45.00	90.00	—
1758	233,000	12.00	25.00	45.00	90.00	—

KM# 19 4 KREUZER

Billon **Ruler:** Karl Wilhelm Friedrich of Brandenburg - Ansbach **Mint:** Altenkirchen **Obverse:** Crowned compound arms in Order collar **Reverse:** Value in ornamental cartouche, date below

Date	Mintage	VG	F	VF	XF	Unc
1755	—	35.00	65.00	130	275	—

KM# 22.1 6 KREUZER

Billon **Ruler:** Karl Wilhelm Friedrich of Brandenburg - Ansbach **Mint:** Altenkirchen **Obverse:** Armored bust right **Reverse:** Crowned arms of Brandenburg and Sayn, value in exergue

Date	Mintage	VG	F	VF	XF	Unc
1751	35,000	30.00	60.00	115	225	—
1752	144,000	30.00	60.00	115	225	—
1753	493,000	30.00	60.00	115	225	—
1754	143,000	30.00	60.00	115	225	—
1755	370,000	30.00	60.00	115	225	—
1756	40,000	30.00	60.00	115	225	—

KM# 22.2 6 KREUZER

Billon **Ruler:** Karl Wilhelm Friedrich of Brandenburg - Ansbach **Obverse:** Small bust right **Reverse:** Crowned arms of Brandenburg and Sayn

Date	Mintage	VG	F	VF	XF	Unc
1751	—	35.00	65.00	120	225	—
1752	—	35.00	65.00	120	225	—

KM# 42 6 KREUZER

Billon **Ruler:** Christian Friedrich Karl Alexander of Brandenburg - Ansbach **Obverse:** Armored bust right

Date	Mintage	VG	F	VF	XF	Unc
1758	98,000	12.00	25.00	50.00	100	—

KM# 28 12 KREUZER

Silver **Ruler:** Karl Wilhelm Friedrich of Brandenburg - Ansbach **Mint:** Altenkirchen **Obverse:** Crowned arms of Brandenburg and Sayn in cartouche **Reverse:** Value and date in ornamental circle

Date	Mintage	VG	F	VF	XF	Unc
1753	645,000	35.00	65.00	120	225	—
1755	587,000	35.00	65.00	120	225	—

KM# 44 12 KREUZER

Silver **Ruler:** Christian Friedrich Karl Alexander of Brandenburg - Ansbach **Obverse:** Titles of Christian Friedrich Karl Alexander **Reverse:** Value and date within ornamental cartouche

Date	Mintage	VG	F	VF	XF	Unc
1757	278,000	100	200	325	575	—
1758	Inc. above	100	200	325	575	—

KM# 24 1/12 THALER

Silver **Subject:** Homage for Sayn **Obverse:** Bust right **Reverse:** Inscription, date in Roman numerals

Date	Mintage	VG	F	VF	XF	Unc
1741 W Rare	—	—	—	—	—	—

KM# 25 1/12 THALER

Billon **Ruler:** Karl Wilhelm Friedrich of Brandenburg - Ansbach **Mint:** Altenkirchen **Obverse:** Crowned compound arms in Order collar **Reverse:** Value and date

Date	Mintage	VG	F	VF	XF	Unc
1755	78,000	90.00	180	300	550	—

KM# 26 1/12 THALER

Billon **Ruler:** Karl Wilhelm Friedrich of Brandenburg - Ansbach **Mint:** Altenkirchen **Obverse:** Armored bust right

Date	Mintage	VG	F	VF	XF	Unc
1755	Inc. above	30.00	50.00	90.00	170	—

KM# 30 1/6 THALER

Billon **Ruler:** Karl Wilhelm Friedrich of Brandenburg - Ansbach **Mint:** Altenkirchen **Obverse:** Crowned compound arms in Order collar **Reverse:** Value and date

Date	Mintage	VG	F	VF	XF	Unc
1755	5,603	40.00	90.00	175	285	—

KM# 31 1/6 THALER

Billon **Ruler:** Karl Wilhelm Friedrich of Brandenburg - Ansbach **Obverse:** Karl Wilhelm Friedrich

Date	Mintage	VG	F	VF	XF	Unc
1755	Inc. above	50.00	100	200	320	—
1756	193,000	50.00	100	200	320	—

KM# 46 1/6 THALER

Billon **Ruler:** Christian Friedrich Karl Alexander of Brandenburg - Ansbach **Obverse:** Crowned CFA monogram **Reverse:** Value, date

Date	Mintage	VG	F	VF	XF	Unc
1757	3,197,000	25.00	45.00	90.00	165	—
1758	5,735,000	25.00	45.00	90.00	165	—

KM# 33 1/2 THALER (Mining)

Silver **Ruler:** Karl Wilhelm Friedrich of Brandenburg - Ansbach **Obverse:** Bust right **Reverse:** Figure with cornucipia standing in field, inscription, date in Roman numerals

Date	Mintage	VG	F	VF	XF	Unc
1750 D Rare	—	—	—	—	—	—

KM# 35 THALER (Convention)

Silver **Ruler:** Karl Wilhelm Friedrich of Brandenburg - Ansbach **Mint:** Altenkirchen **Obverse:** Armored bust of Karl Wilhelm Friedrich right **Reverse:** Crowned arms with eagle supporters, date in exergue

Date	Mintage	VG	F	VF	XF	Unc
1755	311	650	1,150	2,150	3,500	—

TRADE COINAGE

KM# 36.1 2 DUCAT

7.0000 g., 0.9860 Gold 0.2219 oz. AGW **Ruler:** Karl Wilhelm Friedrich of Brandenburg - Ansbach **Subject:** Succession of Brandenburg-Ansbach to Sayn-Altenkirchen **Obverse:** Bust right **Reverse:** Justice with scales and cornucopia, date in Roman numerals

Date	Mintage	VG	F	VF	XF	Unc
ND(1741) VESTNER	—	600	1,200	2,250	3,750	—

KM# 36.2 12 DUCAT

42.0000 g., 0.9860 Gold 1.3314 oz. AGW **Ruler:** Karl Wilhelm Friedrich of Brandenburg - Ansbach **Subject:** Succession of Brandenburg-Ansbach to Sayn-Altenkirchen **Reverse:** Justice with scales and cornucopia, date in Roman numerals

Date	Mintage	VG	F	VF	XF	Unc
ND(1741) VESTNER; Rare	—	—	—	—	—	—

PATTERNS

Including off metal strikes

KM#	Date	Mintage	Identification	Mkt Val
Pn1	ND(1741 VESTNER)	—	2 Ducat. Silver. C#19.	350
Pn2	ND(1741 VESTNER)	—	12 Ducat. Silver. C#19.5.	—
Pn3	ND1748	—	1/40 Thaler. Silver. Arms, value and date.	—
Pn4	ND1748	—	1/24 Thaler. Silver. Arms, value and date.	—
Pn5	ND1748	—	1/20 Thaler. Silver. Arms, value and date.	—
Pn6	ND1748	—	1/12 Thaler. Silver.Arms, value and date.	—
Pn7	ND1758	—	1/6 Thaler. Copper. C#32.	—
Pn8	ND1764	—	5 Thaler.	—
Pn9	ND1764	—	10 Thaler.	—
Pn10	ND1764	—	20 Thaler.	—

SCHAUMBURG-HESSEN

Located in northwest Germany, Schaumburg-Hessen was founded in 1640 when Schaumburg-Gehmen was divided between Hesse-Cassel and Lippe-Alverdissen. The two became known as Schaumburg-Hessen and Schaumburg--Lippe. Cassel struck coins for it half as late as 1832.

RULERS

Friedrich II (of Hesse-Cassel), 1760-1785
Wilhelm (of Hesse-Cassel), 1785-1821

MONETARY SYSTEM

12 Gute Pfennig = 1 Groschen

COUNTY

STANDARD COINAGE

C# 1 PFENNIG

Copper **Ruler:** Friedrich II **Obverse:** Crowned FL monogram **Reverse:** Value and date

Date	Mintage	VG	F	VF	XF	Unc
1769	—	6.00	12.00	25.00	45.00	—

C# 2 PFENNIG

Copper **Ruler:** Friedrich II **Obverse:** Crowned nettle, flat sides **Reverse:** Value: GUTER PFENN

Date	Mintage	VG	F	VF	XF	Unc
1772	—	3.00	6.00	12.00	25.00	—
1775	—	3.00	6.00	12.00	25.00	—
1776	—	3.00	6.00	12.00	25.00	—
1780	—	3.00	6.00	12.00	25.00	—
1785	—	3.00	6.00	12.00	25.00	—

C# 2a PFENNIG

Copper **Ruler:** Friedrich II **Obverse:** Crowned nettle **Reverse:** PFENNIG

Date	Mintage	VG	F	VF	XF	Unc
1783	—	5.00	10.00	22.00	45.00	—

C# 3 PFENNIG

Copper **Ruler:** Friedrich II **Obverse:** Crowned shield separating WL **Reverse:** Denomination

Date	Mintage	F	VF	XF	Unc
1787	—	5.00	10.00	25.00	75.00
1788	—	5.00	10.00	25.00	75.00
1789	—	5.00	10.00	25.00	75.00
1790	—	5.00	10.00	25.00	75.00
1791	—	5.00	10.00	25.00	75.00
1792	—	5.00	10.00	25.00	75.00
1793	—	5.00	10.00	25.00	75.00
1794	—	5.00	10.00	25.00	75.00
1795	—	5.00	10.00	25.00	75.00
1796	—	5.00	10.00	25.00	75.00
1797	—	5.00	10.00	25.00	75.00
1798	—	5.00	10.00	25.00	75.00
1799	—	5.00	10.00	25.00	75.00
1800	—	5.00	10.00	25.00	75.00

SCHAUMBURG-LIPPE

Located in northwest Germany, Schaumburg-Lippe was founded in 1640 when Schaumburg-Gehmen was divided between Hesse-Cassel and Lippe-Alverdissen. The two became known as Schaumburg-Hessen and Schaumburg-Lippe. They were elevated into a county independent of Lippe. Schaumburg-Lippe minted currency into the 20th century. The last prince died in 1911.

RULERS

Albert Wolfgang, 1728-1748
Wilhelm I Friedrich Ernst, 1748-1777
Philipp II Ernst, 1777-1787
Georg Wilhelm, 1787-1860

DUCHY

REGULAR COINAGE

C# 1 PFENNIG

Copper **Ruler:** Wilhelm I Friedrich Ernst

Date	Mintage	VG	F	VF	XF	Unc
1750	—	5.00	10.00	25.00	50.00	—

C# 3 4 PFENNIG

Billon **Ruler:** Wilhelm I Friedrich Ernst **Obverse:** Nettle **Reverse:** Value and date

Date	Mintage	VG	F	VF	XF	Unc
1750	—	12.00	25.00	50.00	120	—

C# 5 MARIENGROSCHEN

Billon **Ruler:** Wilhelm I Friedrich Ernst **Obverse:** Nettle **Reverse:** Value and date

Date	Mintage	VG	F	VF	XF	Unc
1750	—	10.00	20.00	45.00	115	—

C# 7 1/24 THALER

Billon **Ruler:** Wilhelm I Friedrich Ernst **Obverse:** Nettle **Reverse:** Value and date

Date	Mintage	VG	F	VF	XF	Unc
1750	—	15.00	30.00	60.00	150	—

C# 9 1/3 THALER

Silver **Ruler:** Wilhelm I Friedrich Ernst **Obverse:** Head left **Obv. Legend:** WILHELMUS • I • DEI • GRAT: C: REG: IN SCHAUMB: **Reverse:** Helmeted arms within Order collar

Date	Mintage	VG	F	VF	XF	Unc
1761	—	30.00	60.00	120	275	—

C# 11 2/3 THALER

Silver **Ruler:** Wilhelm I Friedrich Ernst **Subject:** Accession of the Count **Obverse:** Draped bust left **Reverse:** Helmeted arms

Date	Mintage	VG	F	VF	XF	Unc
1748	—	150	300	600	1,100	—

C# 13 2/3 THALER

Silver **Ruler:** Wilhelm I Friedrich Ernst **Obverse:** Head left **Obv. Legend:** WILHELMUS • I • DEI • GRAT: C: REG: IN SCHAUMB: **Reverse:** Helmeted arms within Order collar

Date	Mintage	VG	F	VF	XF	Unc
1761	—	75.00	150	300	550	—

DAV# 2761 THALER

Silver **Ruler:** Albert Wolfgang **Subject:** Marriage of Albert Wolfang to Charlotte Friederike **Obverse:** Bust right **Obv. Legend:** ALB. WOLFG. D.G. COM. SCHAVMB. LIPP. & STERNB. & C. SECUNDA. VOTA. INIIT. AO. MDCCXXX.* **Reverse:** 2 hands hold AW and CF monogram in wreath **Rev. Legend:** * SIC VOTA * SIC * PROSPERA * SECUNDA *, below; * DEO * COPULANTE *

Date	Mintage	F	VF	XF	Unc
1730	—	1,750	3,000	4,500	6,500

DAV# 2762 THALER

Silver **Ruler:** Albert Wolfgang **Obverse:** Bust left **Obv. Legend:** ALB • WOLFG • D • G • S • R • I • COM • IN • SCH • C • & • N • D • LIPP • & • ST • 1748 * **Reverse:** Helmeted arms **Rev. Legend:** GRATUS ERGA DEUM - VERUS ET SINCERUS

Date	Mintage	F	VF	XF	Unc
1748	—	900	1,650	2,750	4,500

C# 15 THALER

Silver **Ruler:** Albert Wolfgang **Subject:** Accession of the Count **Obverse:** Armored bust left **Obv. Legend:** WILHELM • FR • E • D • G • S • R • I • COM • IN • SCH • C • & • N • D • LIPP & • ST • D • 24 • SEPT • 1748 **Reverse:** Helmeted arms **Rev. Legend:** URENDO - CRRESCIT below **Note:** Dav.#2763.

Date	Mintage	F	VF	XF	Unc
1748	—	650	1,150	2,000	3,500

C# 17 THALER

19.6200 g., Silver **Ruler:** Wilhelm I Friedrich Ernst **Obverse:** Large head, hair style in waves **Obv. Legend:** WILHELMUS • I • DEI • GRAT: C: REG: IN SCHAUMB: * **Reverse:** Crowned arms within Order collar **Rev. Legend:** NOBILISSIM: DOM: AC: COM: IN LIPP: & ST: 1765, in exergue; EIN. R: THAL:/FEIN. SILB: **Note:** Dav.#2764

Date	Mintage	F	VF	XF	Unc
1765	—	70.00	150	275	550

C# 17a THALER

Silver **Ruler:** Wilhelm I Friedrich Ernst **Obverse:** Large head, hair style in curls **Obv. Legend:** WILHELMUS • I • DEI • GRAT • C: REG: IN SCHAUMB: **Reverse:** Crowned arms within Order collar **Rev. Legend:** NOBILISSIM: DOM: AC: COM: IN LIPP: & ST:, in exergue; EIN.R.THAL./FEIN.SILB: **Note:** Dav.#2764A

Date	Mintage	F	VF	XF	Unc
1765	—	70.00	150	275	550

C# 17b THALER

Silver **Ruler:** Wilhelm I Friedrich Ernst **Obverse:** Small head left **Obv. Legend:** WILHELMUS • I • DEI • GRAT: C: REG: IN SCHAUMB: * **Reverse:** Crowned arms within Order collar **Rev. Legend:** NOBILISSIM: DOM: AC: COM: IN LIPP: & ST:, in exergue; EIN.R.THAL./FEIN.SILB: **Note:** Dav.#2764B

Date	Mintage	F	VF	XF	Unc
1765	—	80.00	165	300	600

C# 20 10 THALER

13.2840 g., 0.9000 Gold 0.3844 oz. AGW **Ruler:** Wilhelm I Friedrich Ernst **Obverse:** Head left **Obv. Legend:** WILH: I • DEI • GR: C: REGN: IN SCH: N: D: .... **Reverse:** Crowned arms within Order collar **Rev. Inscription:** COPIAR: AUG: REG: LUSIT: DUX SUPREM •

Date	Mintage	VG	F	VF	XF	Unc
1763	—	900	1,750	3,500	6,000	—

PRINCIPALITY

TRADE COINAGE

C# 19 DUCAT

3.5000 g., 0.9860 Gold 0.1109 oz. AGW **Ruler:** Wilhelm I Friedrich Ernst **Obverse:** Head left **Reverse:** Helmeted arms in order collar

Date	Mintage	VG	F	VF	XF	Unc
1762	—	475	950	1,750	3,000	—

C# 25 DUCAT

3.5000 g., 0.9860 Gold 0.1109 oz. AGW **Ruler:** Wilhelm I Friedrich Ernst **Obverse:** Crowned arms in sprays **Reverse:** Tablet

Date	Mintage	VG	F	VF	XF	Unc
1777	—	650	1,450	2,750	4,500	—

C# 26 DUCAT

3.5000 g., 0.9860 Gold 0.1109 oz. AGW **Ruler:** Philipp II Ernst **Obverse:** Bust of Philipp Ernst **Reverse:** Tablet

Date	Mintage	VG	F	VF	XF	Unc
1783	—	1,000	2,000	3,500	6,000	—

SCHLESWIG-HOLSTEIN

Christian I, son of Count Dietrich of Oldenburg (1423-40), was elected King of Denmark in 1448. By virtue of his marriage to Hedwig, the last surviving heir of the countship of Holstein-Rendsburg (see Holstein), Christian I became Duke of Schleswig and Count of Holstein in 1459. His status over Holstein was raised to that of duke in 1474 and from that year onwards, the dual duchies of Schleswig-Holstein were ruled by the Danish royal house. In 1533, a separate line for one of Friedrich I's sons was established in Gottorp. Similarly, a son of Christian III was given Sonderburg as his domain in 1559. The Danish kings continued to have coins struck for their remaining portions of Schleswig-Holstein during the next several centuries. Upon the dissolution of the Holy Roman Empire by Napoleon in 1806, Holstein was made a part of Denmark. However, Holstein, without Schleswig, joined the German Confederation following the final defeat of Napoleon in 1815. After Denmark tried to annex Schleswig and Holstein in 1846, she fought a war with Prussia for three years over control of the duchies, but it was inconclusive. In 1863, Denmark declared that Schleswig was part of that country although it had a German majority in the population. A second war was fought between Denmark against Prussia and Austria and Schleswig-Holstein was occupied by the victorious Prussians. The administration of Holstein was given to Austria, while that of Schleswig was obtained by Prussia in 1865. However, Austria was forced to give up Holstein after losing a war with Prussia in 1866. Schleswig-Holstein were controlled by Prussia and became part of the German Empire in 1871. Following World War I, a plebiscite was held in Schleswig and the northern part, with its majority Danish population, was ceded to Denmark in 1920.

RULERS

Christian VII (of Denmark), 1784-1808

ALTONA MINTMASTERS INITIALS

MF, M.F, M.F. - Michael Flor

MONETARY SYSTEM

4 Dreiling = 2 Sechsling = 1 Schilling
60 Schilling = 1 Speciesdaler
N = Nypraeg = Restrike

DUCHY

JOINT COINAGE

C# 1 DREILING

Copper **Ruler:** Christian VII **Obverse:** Crowned monogram **Reverse:** Value, date

Date	Mintage	F	VF	XF	Unc
1787	2,400,000	6.00	12.00	25.00	60.00

C# 2 SECHSLING

Copper **Ruler:** Christian VII **Obverse:** Crowned monogram **Reverse:** Value, date

Date	Mintage	F	VF	XF	Unc
1787	6,000,000	8.00	16.00	35.00	80.00

C# 3 2 SECHSLING

1.4990 g., 0.2500 Silver 0.0120 oz. ASW **Ruler:** Christian VII **Obverse:** Crowned interlaced CR monogram, VII within **Reverse:** Value, date

Date	Mintage	F	VF	XF	Unc
1787 MF	761,000	9.00	18.00	40.00	100
1788 MF	—	9.00	18.00	40.00	100
1796 MF	538,000	9.00	18.00	40.00	100
1799 MF	960,000	9.00	18.00	40.00	100
1800 MF	480,000	10.00	20.00	45.00	110

C# 4 2-1/2 SCHILLING (1/24 Daler Specie)

2.8090 g., 0.3750 Silver 0.0339 oz. ASW **Ruler:** Christian VII **Obverse:** Crowned CR monogram **Reverse:** Denomination above date

Date	Mintage	F	VF	XF	Unc
1787 MF	4,800,000	8.00	16.00	35.00	90.00
1796 MF	2,880,000	8.00	16.00	35.00	90.00
1799 MF	1,440,000	8.00	16.00	35.00	90.00
1800 MF	96,000	9.00	18.00	40.00	100

C# 5 5 SCHILLING (1/12 Daler Specie)
4.2140 g., 0.5000 Silver 0.0677 oz. ASW **Ruler:** Christian VII **Obverse:** Crowned CR monogram, VII within **Reverse:** Denomination

Date	Mintage	F	VF	XF	Unc
1787 MF	1,800,000	12.00	25.00	55.00	125
1788 MF	—	12.00	25.00	55.00	125
1797 MF	527,000	12.00	25.00	55.00	125
1800 MF	48,000	14.00	28.00	60.00	135

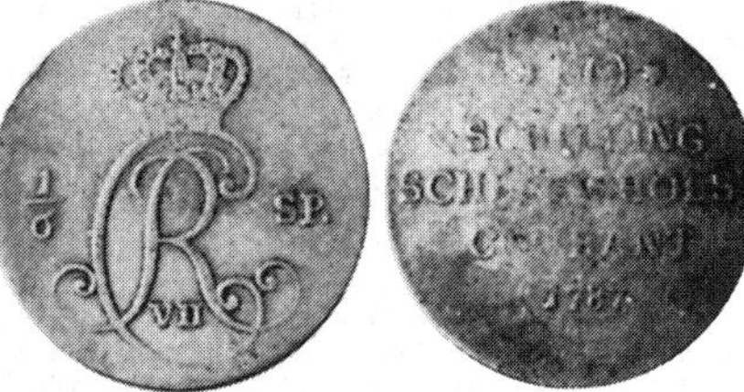

C# 6 10 SCHILLING (1/6 Daler Specie)
6.1290 g., 0.6870 Silver 0.1354 oz. ASW **Ruler:** Christian VII **Obverse:** Crowned monogram divides fraction value **Reverse:** Value, date

Date	Mintage	F	VF	XF	Unc
1787 MF	540,000	12.00	25.00	60.00	135
1788 MF	300,000	12.00	25.00	60.00	135
1789 MF	183,000	14.00	28.00	65.00	145
1796 MF	129,000	15.00	30.00	70.00	160

C# 7 20 SCHILLING (1/3 Daler Specie)
9.6310 g., 0.8750 Silver 0.2709 oz. ASW **Ruler:** Christian VII **Obverse:** Head right **Reverse:** Crowned three fold arms divide denomination

Date	Mintage	F	VF	XF	Unc
1787 MF	300,000	20.00	40.00	80.00	225
1788 MF	414,000	20.00	40.00	80.00	225
1789 MF	—	22.00	45.00	90.00	240
1797 MF	66,000	22.00	45.00	90.00	240
1799 MF Rare	—	—	—	—	—

C# 7a 20 SCHILLING (1/3 Daler Specie)
9.6310 g., 0.8750 Silver 0.2709 oz. ASW **Ruler:** Christian VII **Obverse:** "A" below head **Reverse:** Value, date

Date	Mintage	F	VF	XF	Unc
1787 MF	Inc. above	25.00	50.00	100	250

C# 8 40 SCHILLING (2/3 Daler Specie)
19.2630 g., 0.8750 Silver 0.5419 oz. ASW **Ruler:** Christian VII **Obverse:** "A" below head right **Obv. Legend:** CHRISTIANUS • VII • D • G • DAN • NORV • V • G • REX • **Reverse:** Crowned three fold arms divide denomination **Rev. Legend:** SCHILLING • SCHLESW • HOLST • COURANT •

Date	Mintage	F	VF	XF	Unc
1787 MF	333,000	65.00	125	200	450
1797 MF	70,000	65.00	125	200	450
1799 MF Rare	—	—	—	—	—

C# 9a 60 SCHILLING (Daler Specie)
28.8930 g., 0.8750 Silver 0.8128 oz. ASW **Ruler:** Christian VII **Obverse:** "DI" below head right **Reverse:** Crowned arms divide value

Date	Mintage	F	VF	XF	Unc
1787 MF Rare	—	—	—	—	—
1788 MF	—	75.00	150	350	575

C# 9b 60 SCHILLING (Daler Specie)
28.8930 g., 0.8750 Silver 0.8128 oz. ASW **Ruler:** Christian VII **Obverse:** "H" below large head right **Obv. Legend:** CHRISTIANUS • VII • D • G • DAN • NORV • V • G • REX • **Reverse:** Crowned arms divide value **Rev. Legend:** SCHILLING • SCHLESW • HOLST • COURANT •

Date	Mintage	F	VF	XF	Unc
1787 MF Rare	—	—	—	—	—
1788 MF	Inc. above	130	275	650	900

C# 9 60 SCHILLING (Daler Specie)
28.8930 g., 0.8750 Silver 0.8128 oz. ASW **Ruler:** Christian VII **Obverse:** "B" below large head right **Obv. Legend:** CHRISTIANUS • VII • D • G • DAN • NORV • V • G • REX • **Reverse:** Crowned arms divide value **Rev. Legend:** SCHILLING • SCHLESW • HOLST • COURANT • **Note:** Dav. #1311

Date	Mintage	F	VF	XF	Unc
1787 MF	412,000	65.00	125	300	500
1788 MF	644,000	65.00	125	300	500
1789 MF	—	65.00	125	300	500
1790 MF	402,000	85.00	165	550	900
1791 MF	1,000	150	275	—	—
1794 MF	1,106,000	65.00	125	300	500
1795 MF	1,774,000	50.00	100	250	450
1796 MF	1,086,000	65.00	125	400	650
1799 MF Rare	Inc. above	—	—	—	—
1800 MF	Inc. above	125	225	750	—

C# 9c 60 SCHILLING (Daler Specie)
28.8930 g., 0.8750 Silver 0.8128 oz. ASW **Ruler:** Christian VII **Obverse:** "M" below head right **Reverse:** Crowned arms divide value

Date	Mintage	F	VF	XF	Unc
1788 MF	Inc. above	150	250	450	800
1789 MF	Inc. above	250	400	—	—
1790 MF Rare	Inc. above	65.00	125	300	550
1799 MF	Inc. above	—	—	—	—

C# 9d 60 SCHILLING (Daler Specie)
28.8930 g., 0.8750 Silver 0.8128 oz. ASW **Ruler:** Christian VII **Obverse:** "PG" below head right **Obv. Legend:** CHRISTIANUS • VII • D • G • DAN • NORV • V • G • REX • **Reverse:** Crowned arms **Rev. Legend:** SCHILLING • SCHLESW • HOLST • COURANT •

Date	Mintage	F	VF	XF	Unc
1799 MF	64,000	125	200	400	750
1800 MF	146,000	75.00	150	350	600

PATTERNS

Inlcuding off metal strikes

KM#	Date	Mintage	Identification	Mkt Val
Pn4	1788	—	10 Schilling. Gold.	—
Pn6	1799	—	20 Schilling. Copper. C#7.	200

KM#	Date	Mintage	Identification	Mkt Val
Pn7	1799	—	40 Schilling. Copper. C#8.	250
Pn8	1799	—	60 Schilling. Copper. C#9.	350
Pn9	1800	—	60 Schilling. Copper. C#9.	350

SCHLESWIG-HOLSTEIN-GOTTORP

The line of Gottorp was established in 1533 as a territorial domain for the youngest son of Friedrich I, King of Denmark and Duke of Schleswig-Holstein. Many members of this line and a cadet line founded in 1702 became bishops of Lübeck (see). Duke Karl Peter Ulrich, whose father, Karl Friedrich, had married Anna of Russia, became Czar Peter III in 1762, but was killed shortly after his accession to the throne. His son, Paul, traded Gottorp to Denmark for Oldenburg in 1773 (see Oldenburg) and ruled Russia as Czar Paul I (1798-1901).

RULERS
Friedrich IV, 1694-1702
Karl Friedrich, 1702-1739
Karl Peter Ulrich, 1739-1762
Paul, 1762-1773

DUCHY

REGULAR COINAGE

KM# 102 THALER
Silver **Ruler:** Karl Friedrich **Obverse:** Armored bust right **Reverse:** Crowned arms separating B-H **Note:** Dav. #1352.

Date	Mintage	VG	F	VF	XF	Unc
1711 BH Rare	—	—	—	—	—	—

KM# 110.2 THALER
Silver **Ruler:** Karl Peter Ulrich **Mint:** Mannheim **Obverse:** Armored bust right lower to bottom rim **Obv. Legend:** PETRUS. D:G... RUSSIA **Reverse:** Imperial eagle with 2 shields on breast **Note:** Albertus Thaler, Dav. #1353A.

Date	Mintage	VG	F	VF	XF	Unc
1753 S//P	—	—	250	550	1,000	1,800

KM# 110.1 THALER
Silver **Ruler:** Karl Peter Ulrich **Mint:** Mannheim **Obverse:** Armored bust right **Obv. Legend:** PETRUS • D: G: • MAGNUS DUX TOTIUS RUSSIÆ **Reverse:** Imperial eagle with 2 shields on breast **Note:** Albertus Thaler. Dav. #1353.

Date	Mintage	VG	F	VF	XF	Unc
1753 S//P	—	—	250	550	1,000	1,800

TRADE COINAGE

KM# 98 1/4 DUCAT

0.8750 g., 0.9860 Gold 0.0277 oz. AGW **Ruler:** Karl Friedrich **Obverse:** Crowned monogram **Reverse:** Crowned shield with lions **Note:** Fr.#3094.

Date	Mintage	VG	F	VF	XF	Unc
1708 BH	—	125	225	500	800	—

KM# 103 1/4 DUCAT

0.8750 g., 0.9860 Gold 0.0277 oz. AGW **Ruler:** Karl Friedrich **Obverse:** Bust right **Reverse:** Crowned shield with lions **Note:** Fr.#3087.

Date	Mintage	VG	F	VF	XF	Unc
1711 BH	—	150	250	600	1,000	—

KM# 104 1/4 DUCAT

0.8750 g., 0.9860 Gold 0.0277 oz. AGW **Ruler:** Karl Friedrich **Note:** Modified design. Fr.#3087.

Date	Mintage	VG	F	VF	XF	Unc
1711 BH	—	150	250	600	1,000	—

KM# 96 DUCAT

3.5000 g., 0.9860 Gold 0.1109 oz. AGW **Ruler:** Karl Friedrich **Obverse:** Young head right **Reverse:** Crowned arms with lion supporters **Note:** Fr.#3088.

Date	Mintage	VG	F	VF	XF	Unc
1705 BH	—	700	1,450	2,750	4,500	—

KM# 97 DUCAT

3.5000 g., 0.9860 Gold 0.1109 oz. AGW **Ruler:** Karl Friedrich **Obverse:** Youth head right **Obv. Legend:** CAROL • FRIDER • D • G • DVX • SVPR • SIFS **Reverse:** Crowned shield with lions, date in legend **Note:** Fr.#3089.

Date	Mintage	VG	F	VF	XF	Unc
1705 BH	—	700	1,450	2,750	4,500	—
1706	—	700	1,450	2,750	4,500	—

KM# 101 DUCAT

3.5000 g., 0.9860 Gold 0.1109 oz. AGW **Ruler:** Karl Friedrich **Obverse:** Bust right **Reverse:** Crowned shield with lions, date in legend **Note:** Fr.#3092.

Date	Mintage	VG	F	VF	XF	Unc
1710 BH	—	650	1,350	2,500	4,000	—
1711 BH	—	650	1,350	2,500	4,000	—
1712 BH 3 known	—	—	—	—	—	—

KM# 100 DUCAT

3.5000 g., 0.9860 Gold 0.1109 oz. AGW **Ruler:** Karl Friedrich **Obverse:** Crowned CF monogram **Reverse:** Crowned arms **Note:** Fr.#3093.

Date	Mintage	VG	F	VF	XF	Unc
1710 BH	—	500	1,000	2,000	3,500	—

KM# 105 DUCAT

3.5000 g., 0.9860 Gold 0.1109 oz. AGW **Ruler:** Karl Friedrich **Reverse:** Crowned arms **Note:** Fr.#3091.

Date	Mintage	VG	F	VF	XF	Unc
1711	—	650	1,350	2,500	4,000	—
1712	—	650	1,350	2,500	4,000	—

KM# 106 10 DUCAT

34.6000 g., 0.9860 Gold 1.0968 oz. AGW **Ruler:** Karl Friedrich **Obverse:** Bust right **Reverse:** Arms **Note:** Struck with 1 Thaler dies, KM#102. Fr.#3090.

Date	Mintage	VG	F	VF	XF	Unc
1711 BH Rare	—	—	—	—	—	—

PATTERNS

Including off metal strikes

KM#	Date	Mintage	Identification	Mkt Val
Pn1	1705	—	Ducat. Silver. KM#97.	250
Pn2	1706	—	Ducat. Silver. KM#97.	250
Pn3	1707	—	3 Pfennig. Gold. 0.8600 g.	—
Pn4	1710	—	Ducat. Silver. KM#101.	250
Pn5	1711	—	Ducat. Silver. KM#101.	250

KM#	Date	Mintage	Identification	Mkt Val
Pn6	1711	—	1/4 Ducat. Silver. KM#103.	200

SCHLESWIG-HOLSTEIN-PLOEN

One of the branches of Schleswig-Holstein founded upon the division of Schleswig-Holstein-Sonderburg in 1622. It fell extinct in 1706 and all lands and titles reverted to Schleswig-Holstein-Norburg.

RULERS

Johann Adolf, 1671-1704
Leopold August, 1704-1706
Joachim Friedrich, 1706-1722
Danish Rule, 1722-1729
Friedrich Karl, 1729-1761
To Denmark, 1761

MINT OFFICIALS' INITIALS

Initials	Date	Name
G	Ca. 1760	Geringius, medailleur Rethwisch
GAS	1761	Georg Anton Schröder, mintmaster Rethwisch

COUNTY

REGULAR COINAGE

KM# 28 THALER

Silver **Ruler:** Friedrich Karl **Obverse:** Small bust right **Obv. Legend:** FRIDERICVS CAROLVS • D.G • H • N • D • S • H • S • ET D • C • IN • O • ETD **Reverse:** Small crown over ornate arms in sprays divides date **Note:** Dav.#1354.

Date	Mintage	VG	F	VF	XF	Unc
1761 G//GAS	—	450	900	1,500	2,500	—

KM# 30 THALER

Silver **Ruler:** Friedrich Karl **Obverse:** Large bust right, bow divides legend **Obv. Legend:** FRIDERICVS CAROLVS • D.G • H • N • G • - S • H • S • ETD • C • IN • O • ETD **Reverse:** Large crown over ornate arms in sprays divides date **Note:** Dav.#1354a.

Date	Mintage	VG	F	VF	XF	Unc
1761 G	—	450	900	1,500	2,500	—

KM# 29 THALER

Silver **Ruler:** Friedrich Karl **Obverse:** Small bust right **Obv. Legend:** FRIDERICVS CAROLVS • D.G • H • N • D • S • H • S • ET D • C • IN • O • ETD **Reverse:** Large crown over ornate arms in sprays divides date **Note:** Dav.#1355.

Date	Mintage	VG	F	VF	XF	Unc
ND(1761) G//GAS	—	450	900	1,500	2,500	—

TRADE COINAGE

KM# 26 DUCAT

3.5000 g., 0.9860 Gold 0.1109 oz. AGW **Ruler:** Friedrich Karl **Obverse:** Armored and draped bust right **Reverse:** Crowned arms, Roman numeral date below

Date	Mintage	VG	F	VF	XF	Unc
MDCCLX (1760) G	—	750	1,450	2,500	4,000	—

KM# 27 DUCAT

3.5000 g., 0.9860 Gold 0.1109 oz. AGW **Ruler:** Friedrich Karl **Obverse:** Bust right, titles of Friedrich Karl **Reverse:** Crowned 5-fold arms with central shield, laurel and palm branches to either side, value and date below **Rev. Legend:** FIDES.ET.CONSTANTIA **Note:** Specie Ducat. C13a.

Date	Mintage	VG	F	VF	XF	Unc
1760 G	—	750	1,450	2,500	4,000	—

SCHMALKALDEN

This lordship, centered on the town of the same name, became the property of Hesse-Cassel in 1583. The landgraves issued a series of copper coins for Schmalkalden during the first half of the 18th century.

RULER

Wilhelm VIII of Hesse-Cassel, 1751-1760

LORDSHIP

STANDARD COINAGE

C# 1 HELLER

Copper **Ruler:** Wilhelm VIII **Obverse:** Crowned monogram **Reverse:** Value, date

Date	Mintage	VG	F	VF	XF	Unc
1754	—	4.00	9.00	18.00	38.00	—

SCHONAU

The lordship of Schönau was centered on the Lower Rhine north of Aachen. It was ruled from the mid-15th century for several hundred years by the lords of Milendonck, themselves having originated in the mid-12th century. When the male line died out, the titles continued through marriage in the late 13th century into the line of Reifferscheidt-Malberg. After the male line again fell extinct in 1674, a surviving sister transferred ownership to the Lord of Blanche. The son of the latter struck a short-lived illegal minor coinage which was banned by the city council of Aachen in 1756. Schönau was mediatized to Jülich-Berg in 1758 and eventually sold to the Lords of Broich near the end of the 18th century.

RULER

Johann Gottfried, von Blanche, 1721-1758

BARONY

STANDARD COINAGE

KM# 1 4 HELLER

Copper **Ruler:** Johann Gottfried, Freiherr von Blanche **Obverse:** Crowned imperial eagle, rampant lion left in oval shield on breast, date divided at top **Reverse:** Rampant lion left above

3-line inscription **Rev. Inscription:** R: HERRS:/SCHÖNAW/IIII. **Note:** Previous C# 1.

Date	Mintage	VG	F	VF	XF	Unc
1755	—	15.00	30.00	55.00	100	—

SCHWARZBURG

Schwarzburg with territories in central Thuringia and Prussian Saxony was founded by a Thüringian count about 1100. After numerous divisions into separate lines, the various properties were united briefly in the late sixteenth century only to be divided again in 1583 into the two main lines of Sondershausen and Rudolstadt, each composed of several non-contiguous lands. The counts achieved absolute independence from Saxony about 1700 and were raised to the rank of princes in 1697 and 1710.

SCHWARZBURG-ARNSTADT

The seat of this branch of Schwarzburg is located about 10 miles (16 kilometers) south of Erfurt. The town, castle and surrounding territory were acquired by the counts of Schwarzburg in the early 14th century and a line was soon established separate from Schwarzburg-Blankenburg. The latter fell extinct in the mid-14th century and passed to Arnstadt. Generations later, the lines of Schwarzburg-Sondershausen and Schwarzburg-Rudolstadt were founded and Arnstadt was absorbed by the former, only to reemerge as a separate line in 1642. The last count of Schwarzburg-Arnstadt was raised to the rank of prince in 1709, but died without heirs in 1716.

RULERS

Anton Günther II, 1669-1716, Prince 1709

Arms: See under Schwarzburg

CROSS REFERENCES:

F = Ernst Fischer, *Die Münzen des Hauses Schwarzburg,* **Heidelberg, 1904.**

R = Ernst Helmuth von Bethe, *Schwarzburger Münzen und Medaillen: Sammlung des Schlossmuseums in Rudolstadt,* **Halle (Saale), 1903.**

PRINCIPALITY

REGULAR COINAGE

KM# 36 THALER

Silver, 41 mm. **Ruler:** Anton Günther II **Obverse:** Armored bust to right **Obv. Legend:** ANTHON: GVNTHER9. — D:G: PR: SCHWARTZB:. **Reverse:** Shield with crowned imperial eagle, lion arms of Schwarzburg on breast, date above, in circle, ten small oval shields of arms around **Rev. Legend:** DYN. IN. ARNS. SONDERSH. LEVT. LOH. ET. CL. **Note:** Dav#2766.

Date	Mintage	VG	F	VF	XF	Unc
1711	—	400	600	1,500	2,500	—

KM# 35 THALER

Silver, 43 mm. **Ruler:** Anton Günther II **Obverse:** Armored bust to right **Obv. Legend:** ANTHON. GVNTHERVS. D.G. PR. SCHWARTZB. **Reverse:** Ornately manifold arms supported by wildman and woman holding pennants, 6 ornate helmets above, date in cartouche at bottom **Rev. Legend:** E. IV. COM. IMP. COM. IN. HONS. D. IN. ARNS. SON. L. L. ET. C. **Note:** Dav#2765.

Date	Mintage	VG	F	VF	XF	Unc
1710	—	—	—	—	—	—

SCHWARZBURG-RUDOLSTADT

Established upon the division of Schwarzburg-Sondershausen in 1552, the younger main branch of Schwarzburg, centered on the castle and town of Rudolstadt, 17 miles (29 kilometers) south of Weimar, flourished until the end of World War I. The count was raised to the rank of prince in 1711. The three sons of Albrecht VII, the first Count of Schwarzburg-Rudolstadt, ruled and issued coinage jointly, followed by a long succession of sole rulers descended from the middle son, Ludwig Günther I.

RULERS

Albrecht Anton, 1646-1710
Ludwig Friedrich I, 1710-1718, Prince 1711
Friedrich Anton, 1718-1744
Johann Friedrich, 1744-1767
Ludwig Günther II, 1767-1790
Friedrich Karl, 1790-1793
Ludwig Friedrich II, 1793-1807

MINTMARKS AND MINT OFFICIALS' INITIALS

Initials	Date	Name
GHE, E	1732-1740, 1740-1754	Georg Hieronymus Eberhard, warden, mintmaster in Saalfeld
ICE	1755-65	Johann Christian Eberhard, mintmaster in Saalfeld
ICK	1764-1765, 1765-1794	Johann Christian Knaust, warden, mintmaster in Saalfeld

Arms: See under Schwarzburg

CROSS REFERENCES:

F = Ernst Fischer, *Die Münzen des Hauses Schwarzburg,* **Heidelberg, 1904.**

R = Ernst Helmuth von Bethe, *Schwarzburger Münzen und Medaillen: Sammlung des Schlossmuseums in Rudolstadt,* **Halle (Saale), 1903.**

COUNTSHIP

REGULAR COINAGE

KM# 100 3 PFENNIG (DREIER)

Silver, 15.5 mm. **Ruler:** Johann Friedrich **Obverse:** Script JF monogram between 2 palm branches under prince's hat, legend curved above **Obv. Legend:** F.S.R. — L.M. **Reverse:** Imperial orb with '3' divides date

Date	Mintage	VG	F	VF	XF	Unc
1751 E F#552	—	5.00	12.50	25.00	60.00	—
1752 E F#554a	—	5.00	12.50	25.00	60.00	—

PRINCIPALITY

REGULAR COINAGE

KM# 124 HELLER

Copper **Ruler:** Ludwig Günther II **Obverse:** Crowned monogram **Reverse:** Value, date **Note:** Previous C#30.

Date	Mintage	VG	F	VF	XF	Unc
1769	—	5.00	10.00	20.00	45.00	—

KM# 130 1/2 PFENNIG

Copper **Ruler:** Ludwig Günther II **Obverse:** Crowned monogram **Reverse:** Value, date **Note:** Previous C#31.

Date	Mintage	VG	F	VF	XF	Unc
1783	—	3.00	6.00	12.00	28.00	—

KM# 136 1/2 PFENNIG

Copper **Ruler:** Friedrich Karl **Obverse:** Crowned F C monogram **Note:** Previous C#41.

Date	Mintage	VG	F	VF	XF	Unc
1792	—	3.00	6.00	12.00	28.00	—

KM# 98 PFENNIG

Copper **Ruler:** Johann Friedrich **Obverse:** Crowned JF monogram **Reverse:** Value, date **Rev. Legend:** F. SCHWARZB/ RUD. L. M **Note:** Previous C#1.

Date	Mintage	VG	F	VF	XF	Unc
1751	—	2.00	5.00	10.00	25.00	—
1752	—	2.00	5.00	10.00	25.00	—

KM# 99 PFENNIG

Copper **Ruler:** Johann Friedrich **Obverse:** Crowned monogram **Reverse:** Value, date **Rev. Legend:** F. S. RUDOL/STADTI L. M **Note:** Previous C#1a.

Date	Mintage	VG	F	VF	XF	Unc
1751	—	2.00	5.00	10.00	25.00	—
1752	—	2.00	5.00	10.00	25.00	—

KM# 103 PFENNIG

Copper **Ruler:** Johann Friedrich **Obverse:** Crowned monogram **Reverse:** Value, date **Rev. Legend:** F. SCHWARZB./ RUDOLSTADT/LAND MUNZ **Note:** Previous C#1b.

Date	Mintage	VG	F	VF	XF	Unc
1752	—	2.00	5.00	10.00	25.00	—
1753	—	2.00	5.00	10.00	25.00	—

KM# 104 PFENNIG

Copper **Ruler:** Johann Friedrich **Obverse:** Crowned monogram within branches **Reverse:** Value, date **Note:** Previous C#1c.

Date	Mintage	VG	F	VF	XF	Unc
1752	—	2.00	5.00	10.00	22.00	—
1753	—	2.00	5.00	10.00	22.00	—
1756	—	2.00	5.00	10.00	22.00	—
1760	—	2.00	5.00	10.00	22.00	—
1761	—	2.00	5.00	10.00	22.00	—
1762	—	2.00	5.00	10.00	22.00	—

KM# 126 PFENNIG

Copper **Ruler:** Ludwig Günther II **Obverse:** Crowned monogram within branches **Reverse:** Value, date **Note:** Previous C#32.

Date	Mintage	VG	F	VF	XF	Unc
1772	—	3.00	7.00	14.00	30.00	—

KM# 138 PFENNIG

Copper **Ruler:** Friedrich Karl **Obverse:** Crowned F C monogram **Reverse:** Value above date **Note:** Previous C#42.

Date	Mintage	VG	F	VF	XF	Unc
1792	—	2.00	5.00	10.00	25.00	—

KM# 111 2 PFENNIG

Copper **Ruler:** Johann Friedrich **Obverse:** Crowned JF monogram in branches **Reverse:** Value and date **Note:** Prev. C#2.

Date	Mintage	VG	F	VF	XF	Unc
1760	—	3.00	7.00	14.00	30.00	—
1761	—	3.00	7.00	14.00	30.00	—

KM# 101 3 PFENNIG (DREIER)

Silver, 15.5 mm. **Ruler:** Johann Friedrich **Obverse:** Script JF monogram between 2 palm branches under prince's hat, legend curved above **Obv. Legend:** F.S. — L.M. **Reverse:** Imperial orb with '3' divides date

Date	Mintage	VG	F	VF	XF	Unc
1751 GHE F#553	—	5.00	12.50	25.00	60.00	—
1752 GHE F#554b	—	5.00	12.50	25.00	60.00	—

KM# 113 3 PFENNIG

Copper **Ruler:** Johann Friedrich **Obverse:** Crowned JF monogram **Reverse:** Value and date **Note:** Previous C#3.

Date	Mintage	VG	F	VF	XF	Unc
1761	—	4.00	9.00	18.00	38.00	—
1762	—	4.00	9.00	18.00	38.00	—

KM# 117 3 PFENNIG

0.6600 g., 0.2500 Silver 0.0053 oz. ASW **Ruler:** Johann Friedrich **Obverse:** JF monogram in crowned shield **Reverse:** Value in orb which separates date **Note:** Previous C#7.

Date	Mintage	VG	F	VF	XF	Unc
1764 ICE	—	5.00	10.00	22.00	55.00	—

KM# 102 6 PFENNIG (Sechser)

Silver, 18 mm. **Ruler:** Johann Friedrich **Obverse:** Script JF monogram between 2 palm branches under prince's hat, legend curved above **Obv. Legend:** F.S.R. — L.M. **Reverse:** Imperial orb with VI divides date and mintmaster's initials

Date	Mintage	VG	F	VF	XF	Unc
1751 GHE F#538	—	8.00	18.00	35.00	75.00	—
1752 ghe F#539	—	8.00	18.00	35.00	75.00	—

KM# 106 6 PFENNIG (Sechser)

Silver, 18 mm. **Ruler:** Johann Friedrich **Obverse:** Ornamented oval shield with script JF monogram beneath prince's hat, legend curved above **Obv. Legend:** F.S.R — L.M. **Reverse:** Imperial orb with VI divides mintmaster's initials, date divided above

Date	Mintage	VG	F	VF	XF	Unc
1753 GHE F#540	—	7.00	16.00	30.00	65.00	—
1754 GHE R#1253	—	7.00	16.00	30.00	65.00	—

KM# 108 6 PFENNIG (Sechser)

Silver, 18 mm. **Ruler:** Johann Friedrich **Obverse:** Script JF monogram in baroque frame under prince's hat, legend curved above **Obv. Legend:** F.S.R. — L.M. **Reverse:** Imperial orb with VI, mintmaster's initials below, date divided above

Date	Mintage	VG	F	VF	XF	Unc
1755 GHE F#541	—	7.00	16.00	30.00	65.00	—

KM# 109 6 PFENNIG (Sechser)

Silver, 18 mm. **Ruler:** Johann Friedrich **Obverse:** Script JF monogram in ornamented shield under prince's hat, legend curved above **Obv. Legend:** F.S.R. — L.M. **Reverse:** Imperial orb with VI divides mintmaster's initials, date above **Note:** Varieties exist.

Date	Mintage	VG	F	VF	XF	Unc
1756 ICE F#542	—	7.00	16.00	30.00	65.00	—
1757 ICE F#543	—	7.00	16.00	30.00	65.00	—
1758 ICE F#544	—	7.00	16.00	30.00	65.00	—

KM# 112 6 PFENNIG (Sechser)

Silver, 18 mm. **Ruler:** Johann Friedrich **Obverse:** Script JF monogram in ornamented shield under prince's hat, legend curved above **Obv. Legend:** F.S.R. L.M. **Reverse:** Imperial orb with VI divides date, inscription above, date divided below **Note:** Varieties exist.

Date	Mintage	VG	F	VF	XF	Unc
1760 ICE F#545	—	7.00	16.00	30.00	65.00	—
1761 ICE F#546	—	7.00	16.00	30.00	65.00	—
1762 ICE F#547	—	7.00	16.00	30.00	65.00	—
1763 ICE F#548	—	7.00	16.00	30.00	65.00	—
1766 ICK F#549	—	7.00	16.00	30.00	65.00	—

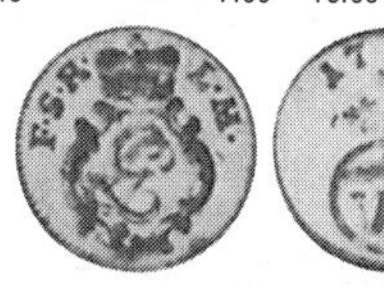

KM# 127 6 PFENNIG (Sechser)

1.3300 g., 0.2500 Silver 0.0107 oz. ASW **Ruler:** Ludwig Günther II **Obverse:** Monogram in crowned shield **Reverse:** Value in orb, date divided above **Note:** Previous C#34.

Date	Mintage	VG	F	VF	XF	Unc
1779	—	5.00	10.00	15.00	35.00	—
1780	—	5.00	10.00	15.00	35.00	—
1781	—	5.00	10.00	15.00	35.00	—
1782	—	5.00	10.00	15.00	35.00	—
1784	—	5.00	10.00	15.00	35.00	—
1785	—	5.00	10.00	15.00	35.00	—
1786	—	5.00	10.00	15.00	35.00	—

KM# 140 6 PFENNIG (Sechser)
1.3300 g., 0.2500 Silver 0.0107 oz. ASW **Ruler:** Friedrich Karl **Obverse:** Crowned cartouche with F C monogram **Reverse:** Value in orb, date divided above **Note:** Previous C#44.

Date	Mintage	VG	F	VF	XF	Unc
1792	—	5.00	10.00	15.00	35.00	—

KM# 141 6 PFENNIG (Sechser)
1.3300 g., 0.2500 Silver 0.0107 oz. ASW **Ruler:** Ludwig Friedrich II **Obverse:** Two-line inscription **Obv. Inscription:** SCHWARZ./RUD.L.M. **Reverse:** Value with script 'Pf' above date **Note:** Previous C#53.

Date	Mintage	F	VF	XF	Unc
1800	—	7.00	15.00	30.00	90.00

KM# 118 1/48 THALER
0.9700 g., 0.2500 Silver 0.0078 oz. ASW **Ruler:** Johann Friedrich **Obverse:** JF monogram in crowned shield, mintmaster's initials below **Reverse:** Value and date **Note:** Prev. C#15.

Date	Mintage	VG	F	VF	XF	Unc
1764 ICE	—	5.00	8.00	16.00	38.00	—
1766 ICK	—	6.00	9.00	18.00	40.00	—

KM# 97 1/24 THALER (Groschen)
Silver, 22 mm. **Ruler:** Friedrich Anton **Mint:** Saalfeld **Obverse:** Crowned oval manifold arms, palm branches at sides **Obv. Legend:** V.G.G. FRID. ANTH. F.Z. SCHWARZB. RVD. **Reverse:** Four-line inscription with date within palm branches **Rev. Legend:** NACH DEN LEIPZIGER FVS. **Rev. Inscription:** 24/EINEN/THAL:/(date).

Date	Mintage	VG	F	VF	XF	Unc
1737 GHE F#522	—	10.00	18.00	40.00	85.00	—

KM# 105 1/24 THALER (Groschen)
Silver, 21.5-22 mm. **Ruler:** Johann Friedrich **Obverse:** Script JF monogram in baroque frame with prince's hat above **Obv. Legend:** FVRSTL. SCHWARZB. RVDOLSTADT(L). LANDM(VNZ). **Reverse:** Imperial eagle with shield of arms on breast, prince's hat above, 4-line inscription in exergue **Rev. Inscription:** G.H. 24 E./EINEN REICHS/THALER/(date).

Date	Mintage	VG	F	VF	XF	Unc
1752 GHE F#532	—	12.00	20.00	45.00	95.00	—
1753 GHE F#533	—	12.00	20.00	45.00	95.00	—

KM# 110 1/24 THALER (Groschen)
Silver, 22 mm. **Ruler:** Johann Friedrich **Obverse:** Script JF monogram in baroque frame with prince's hat above **Obv. Legend:** FVRSTL. SCHWARZB. RVDOLSTADT. LANDM. **Reverse:** Imperial eagle with shield of arms on breast, prince's hat above, 4-line inscription in exergue **Rev. Inscription:** I.C. 24 E./EINEN REICHS/THALER/(date).

Date	Mintage	VG	F	VF	XF	Unc
1757 ICE F#534	—	12.00	20.00	45.00	95.00	—

KM# 114 1/24 THALER (Groschen)
1.9900 g., 0.3680 Silver 0.0235 oz. ASW **Ruler:** Johann Friedrich **Obverse:** Crowned imperial eagle, shield of arms on breast **Obv. Legend:** FVRSTL. SCHW. RVDOL. CONV. MVNTZ. **Reverse:** 7-line inscription with date **Rev. Inscription:** 24/EINEN/THALER/ CCCXX/EINE FEINE/MARCK/(date). **Note:** Prev. C#19.

Date	Mintage	VG	F	VF	XF	Unc
1763 ICE	—	6.00	9.00	18.00	40.00	—

KM# 115 1/24 THALER (Groschen)
1.9900 g., 0.3680 Silver 0.0235 oz. ASW **Ruler:** Johann Friedrich **Obverse:** Crowned imperial eagle, shield of arms on breast **Obv. Legend:** FVRST. SCHW. RVDOL. CONV. MVNTZ. **Reverse:** 3-line inscription with rosette below, date at end of legend **Rev. Legend:** CCCXX EINE FEINE MARCK (date). **Rev. Inscription:** 24/EINEN/THALER. **Note:** Previous C#19a.

Date	Mintage	VG	F	VF	XF	Unc
1763 ICE	—	6.00	9.00	18.00	40.00	—
1764 ICE	—	6.00	9.00	18.00	40.00	—

KM# 107 1/12 THALER (Doppelgroschen)
3.3400 g., 0.4370 Silver .0469 oz ASW 0.0469 oz. ASW **Ruler:** Johann Friedrich **Obverse:** Script JF monogram in baroque frame with prince's hat above **Obv. Legend:** FVRSTL. SCHWARZB. RVDOLSTADT (L). LANDM(VNZ). **Reverse:** Imperial eagle with shield of arms on breast, prince's hat above, 4-line inscription in exergue **Rev. Inscription:** G.H. 12 E./EINEN REICHS/THALER/(date). **Note:** Previous C#21.

Date	Mintage	VG	F	VF	XF	Unc
1753 GHE Schön 11	—	32.50	65.00	110	200	—

KM# 116 1/12 THALER (Doppelgroschen)
3.3400 g., 0.4370 Silver 0.0469 oz. ASW **Ruler:** Johann Friedrich **Obverse:** Crowned arms **Reverse:** Value **Note:** Previous C#22a.

Date	Mintage	VG	F	VF	XF	Unc
1763 ICE	—	12.50	25.00	40.00	75.00	—
1764 ICE	—	12.50	25.00	40.00	75.00	—

KM# 122 1/12 THALER (Doppelgroschen)
3.3400 g., 0.4370 Silver 0.0469 oz. ASW **Ruler:** Johann Friedrich **Obverse:** Larger crowned arms **Reverse:** Value **Note:** Previous C#22b.

Date	Mintage	VG	F	VF	XF	Unc
1766 ICK	—	12.50	25.00	40.00	75.00	—

KM# 119 1/6 THALER
5.4000 g., 0.5410 Silver 0.0939 oz. ASW **Ruler:** Johann Friedrich **Obverse:** Armored bust right **Reverse:** Value and date below eagle **Note:** Previous C#24.

Date	Mintage	VG	F	VF	XF	Unc
1764 ICE	—	20.00	40.00	80.00	165	—

KM# 120 1/2 THALER
14.0300 g., 0.8330 Silver 0.3757 oz. ASW **Ruler:** Johann Friedrich **Obverse:** Bust right **Reverse:** Crowned arms with wild man and woman supporters **Note:** Previous C#26.

Date	Mintage	F	VF	XF	Unc
1764 ICE	—	60.00	125	200	350

KM# 133 1/2 THALER
Silver **Ruler:** Friedrich Karl **Obverse:** Bust right **Reverse:** Crowned arms with supporters **Note:** Convention 1/2 Thaler. Previous C#46.

Date	Mintage	VG	F	VF	XF	Unc
1791 ICK	—	30.00	60.00	120	200	—

KM# 121 THALER
28.0600 g., 0.8330 Silver 0.7515 oz. ASW **Ruler:** Johann Friedrich **Obverse:** Armored bust right **Obv. Legend:** IOANNES FRIDERICVS • D • G • P • S • RUD • D • S • SENIOR **Reverse:** Crowned arms with wild man and woman supporters **Rev. Legend:** X. EINE FEINE MARCK, I.C. - E. above date **Note:** Convention Thaler. Dav #2768. Previous C#28.

Date	Mintage	F	VF	XF	Unc
1764 ICE	—	100	200	400	850
1765 ICE	—	100	200	400	850

KM# 123 THALER
28.0600 g., 0.8330 Silver 0.7515 oz. ASW **Ruler:** Ludwig Günther II **Obverse:** Cloaked bust right **Obv. Legend:** D • G • LVDOVICVS GVNTHERVS P • SCHWARZB • RVD: **Reverse:** Crowned arms in baroque frame, Order cross divides date below **Rev. Legend:** X. EINE FEINE MARCK, 17 I.C. - D. 68 below **Note:** Dav #2769. Previous C#37.

Date	Mintage	F	VF	XF	Unc
1768 ICK	—	100	200	425	900

KM# 128 THALER
28.0600 g., 0.8330 Silver 0.7515 oz. ASW **Ruler:** Ludwig Günther II **Subject:** Marriage of the Crown Prince **Obverse:** Draped bust right **Obv. Legend:** D • G • LVDOVICCVS GVNTHERVS PR • SCHWARZBVRG RVD **Reverse:** Inscription **Rev. Legend:** * IN MEMORIAM/CONNVB. FELICISS. INTER/PRINC. HER. FRIDER. CAROL./ET DVC. SAX./AVGVST. LOVIS. FRIDERIC/RODÆ D. 28 NOV. 1780/CELEBRATI/X. EINE FEINE MARK./I.C.K. * **Note:** Dav #2770. Previous C#38.

Date	Mintage	F	VF	XF	Unc
1780 ICK	—	100	175	350	725

KM# 132 THALER
28.0600 g., 0.8330 Silver 0.7515 oz. ASW **Ruler:** Ludwig Günther II **Obverse:** Draped bust right **Obv. Legend:** D • G • LVDOVIC • GVNTHERVS • PR • SCHWARZB • RVD • DOM • SCHW • SENIOR • **Reverse:** Crowned arms with wild man and woman supporters **Rev. Legend:** X. EINE FEINE MARCK, I. 17 - 86. C./ K. below **Note:** Dav #2771. Previous C#39.

Date	Mintage	F	VF	XF	Unc
1786 ICK	—	80.00	150	300	650

KM# 134 THALER
28.0600 g., 0.8330 Silver 0.7515 oz. ASW **Ruler:** Friedrich Karl **Obverse:** Bust right **Obv. Legend:** D • G • FRID • CAROLUS PR • SCHWARZB • RUD • DOM • SCHWARZB • SENIOR * **Reverse:** Crowned arms with wild man and woman supporters **Rev. Legend:** X. EINE - MARCK F., 17 - 91/I.C.K. below **Note:** Dav #2772. Previous C#48.

Date	Mintage	F	VF	XF	Unc
1791 ICK	—	70.00	140	275	550

PATTERNS

Including off metal strikes

KM#	Date	Mintage	Identification	Mkt Val
Pn6	1737	—	1/24 Thaler. Copper. 22 mm. KM#97.	75.00

SCHWARZBURG-SONDERSHAUSEN

As the elder main line of Schwarzburg established in 1552, the counts of Schwarzburg-Sondershausen controlled their scattered territories from the castle of Sondershausen in northern Thuringia (Thüringen), 10 miles (16 kilometers) southeast of Nordhausen. Count Christian Wilhelm I was raised to the rank of prince in 1697 and the line descended from him until it finally became extinct in 1909. All titles and territories then passed to Schwarzburg-Rudolstadt.

RULERS

Christian Wilhelm I, 1666-1721, Prince 1697
Günther XLIII (I), 1721-1740
Heinrich XLI zu Keula, 1740-1758
August zu Ebeleben, 1721-1750
Christian Günther III, 1758-1794
Günther Friedrich Karl I, 1794-1835 (died 1837)

MINT OFFICIALS' INITIALS

Initial	Date	Name
HS, HCAS, S	1763-1764	Heinrich Christian Andreas Siegel, mintmaster in Sondershausen

Arms: See under Schwarzburg

CROSS REFERENCES:

F = Ernst Fischer, *Die Münzen des Hauses Schwarzburg,* **Heidelberg, 1904.**

R = Ernst Helmuth von Bethe, *Schwarzburger Münzen und Medaillen: Sammlung des Schlossmuseums in Rudolstadt,* **Halle (Saale), 1903.**

PRINCIPALITY
REGULAR COINAGE

KM# 133 3 PFENNIG

0.6600 g., 0.2500 Silver 0.0053 oz. ASW **Ruler:** Christian Günther III **Obverse:** CG monogram **Reverse:** Value and date **Note:** Previous C#2.

Date	Mintage	VG	F	VF	XF	Unc
1764 S	—	4.00	9.00	18.00	38.00	—

KM# 134 1/48 THALER

0.9700 g., 0.2500 Silver 0.0078 oz. ASW **Ruler:** Christian Günther III **Obverse:** CG monogram **Reverse:** Value and date **Note:** Previous C#4.

Date	Mintage	VG	F	VF	XF	Unc
1764 S	—	4.00	8.00	15.00	35.00	—

KM# 128 1/24 THALER (Groschen)

1.9900 g., 0.3680 Silver 0.0235 oz. ASW **Ruler:** Christian Günther III **Obverse:** Arms in crowned cartouche **Reverse:** Value and date **Note:** Previous C#6.

Date	Mintage	Good	VG	F	VF	XF
1763 HCAS	—	7.00	15.00	30.00	65.00	—

KM# 129 1/12 THALER (Doppelgroschen)

3.3400 g., 0.4370 Silver 0.0469 oz. ASW **Ruler:** Christian Günther III **Obverse:** Arms in crowned cartouche **Reverse:** Value in circle **Note:** Previous C#8.

Date	Mintage	Good	VG	F	VF	XF
1763 HCAS	—	10.00	20.00	40.00	90.00	—

KM# 130 1/12 THALER (Doppelgroschen)

3.3400 g., 0.4370 Silver 0.0469 oz. ASW **Ruler:** Christian Günther III **Obverse:** Crowned arms **Note:** Previous C#9.

Date	Mintage	VG	F	VF	XF	Unc
1763 HCAS	—	7.00	15.00	30.00	60.00	—
1764 HCAS	—	7.00	15.00	30.00	60.00	—

KM# 131 1/6 THALER (1/4 Gulden)

5.0000 g., Silver, 25 mm. **Ruler:** Christian Günther III **Obverse:** Armored bust to right **Obv. Legend:** CHRIST. GUNTH. PR. SCHW. SOND:. **Reverse:** Crowned ornate manifold arms in baroque frame, value '1/6' divides mintmaster's initials below **Rev. Legend:** XLLL. EINE. FEINE. MARCK. (date).

Date	Mintage	VG	F	VF	XF	Unc
1763 HS R#975	—	20.00	40.00	85.00	140	—

KM# 135 1/6 THALER (1/4 Gulden)

5.4000 g., 0.5410 Silver 0.0939 oz. ASW **Ruler:** Christian Günther III **Obverse:** Bust right **Reverse:** Crowned baroque arms **Note:** Previous C#10.

Date	Mintage	VG	F	VF	XF	Unc
1764 HCAS	—	15.00	30.00	60.00	100	—

KM# 132 1/3 THALER

7.0100 g., 0.8330 Silver 0.1877 oz. ASW **Ruler:** Christian Günther III **Obverse:** Bust right **Reverse:** Crowned baroque arms **Note:** Previous C#12.

Date	Mintage	VG	F	VF	XF	Unc
1763 HS	—	30.00	60.00	120	250	—
1764 HS	—	30.00	60.00	120	250	—

KM# 136 2/3 THALER (Gulden)

14.0300 g., 0.8330 Silver 0.3757 oz. ASW **Ruler:** Christian Günther III **Obverse:** Armored bust right **Obv. Legend:** DG CHRIST GVNTHER SCHWSONDERSH **Reverse:** Crowned baroque arms **Note:** Previous C#14.

Date	Mintage	VG	F	VF	XF	Unc
1764 HCAS	—	45.00	90.00	165	350	—

KM# 137 THALER

28.0600 g., 0.8330 Silver 0.7515 oz. ASW **Ruler:** Christian Günther III **Obverse:** Armored, draped bust right **Obv. Legend:** D • G • CHRIST • GVNTH • PR • SCHWARZB • SONDERSH • **Reverse:** Crowned baroque arms **Rev. Legend:** X • EINE • FEINE • MARCK • NACH • DEM • CONVENTION • FVS • 1764, HCAS below **Note:** Convention Thaler. Dav #2767. Prev. C#16.

Date	Mintage	F	VF	XF	Unc
1764 HCAS	—	250	500	850	1,400

TRADE COINAGE

KM# 126 DUCAT

3.5000 g., 0.9860 Gold 0.1109 oz. AGW **Ruler:** Günther XLIII **Obverse:** Crowned imperial eagle, shield of arms on breast, all in cartouche **Reverse:** 7-line inscription with date **Rev. Inscription:** DEO/PROPITIO/PRIMITIAE AURI/ SCHWARTZENBURGICI/ GOLDSTHALI/PRODUCTI/(date). **Note:** Struck with gold from the Goldisthal Mines. Previous Fr#3104.

Date	Mintage	VG	F	VF	XF	Unc
1737	—	1,650	2,750	4,500	7,500	—

SCHWARZENBERG

The princes of Schwarzenberg based their land holdings in Franconia after Erkinger I of Stefansberg bought the lordship of Schwarzenberg sometime between 1405 and 1411. He became a member of the Imperial Diet in 1429 and upon his death in 1437, his two sons founded the lines of Schwarzenberg-Stefansberg and Schwarzenberg-Hohenlandsberg. The younger line, which was raised to the rank of count in 1566, became extinct in 1646. Its lands and titles reverted to Stefansberg, which attained the countship in 1599. In 1670, the count of Schwarzenberg was made a prince and, a generation later, the territories of Sulz and Kettgau were added to the family holdings through marriage, followed by Krumau in 1719. Having acquired Gimborn earlier, the prince sold that county to Wallmoden in 1783. Klettgau was sold to Baden in 1813, but not before the principality in Franconia was mediatized to Bavaria when the Holy Roman Empire came to an end in 1806. Members of the family retained their titles and held extensive lands in Bavaria, Austria and Bohemia/Czechoslovakia well into the 20th century. Several princes von Schwarzenberg distinguished themselves in both civil and military service to Austria.

RULERS

Schwarzenberg-Stefansberg

Ferdinand Wilhelm Eusebius, 1683-1703
Adam Franz Karl, 1703-1732, Duke of Krumau from 1723
Joseph Adam, 1732-1782
Johann, 1782-1789
Joseph Johann Nepomuk, 1789-(1806)-1833

MINT OFFICIALS' INITIALS

Cologne Mint

Initials	Date	Name
IAL	1700-05	Johann Adam Longerich, mintmaster
(c) =	1705-13	Franz Herrmann Hermans, mintmaster

Nuremberg Mint

Initials	Date	Name
(n)		Nuremberg mint (either struck or dies from there)
GFN	1677-1716	Georg Friedrich Nürnberg, mintmaster
	1764-93	Georg Nikolaus Riedner, mintmaster
	1760-79	Siegmund Scholz, warden
SNR	1764-79	Scholz and Riedner
OEXLEIN	1755-81	Johann Leonhard Oexlein, die-cutter

Vienna Mint

Initials	Date	Name
(b) or MM	1703-08	Matthias Mittermayer von Waffenberg, mintmaster
(d) or B	1702-43	Philipp Christoph Becker, die-cutter
	ca. 1721-?	Joseph Ignaz Keibel, mintmaster
MD	1735-67	Matthäus Donner, die-cutter
	ca. 1741	Joseph Kaschnitz von Wainberg, mintmaster
(e) or AW	1754-73 (d.1790)	Anton Wiedemann, die-cutter
	1765-83	Johann August von Kronberg, mintmaster
V.F.(=Vinazer Fecit=Vinazer made this)	ca. 1783	Joseph Vinazer, die-cutter

PRINCIPALITY
REGULAR COINAGE

KM# 60 KREUZER

Silver **Ruler:** Joseph Adam **Mint:** Nuremberg **Obverse:** Crowned arms **Reverse:** Value, NACH DEM ..., date **Note:** Previous C# 1.

Date	Mintage	VG	F	VF	XF	Unc
1765 SNR	—	15.00	30.00	50.00	80.00	145

KM# 23 GROSCHEN

2.6000 g., Silver **Ruler:** Adam Franz Karl Duke of Krumau, 1723 **Mint:** Vienna **Obverse:** Bust to right **Obv. Legend:** ADAMUS. FRANCISC. — D.G. S. R. I. PRINCEPS. **Reverse:** Four-fold arms with central shield in oval baroque frame, order chain around, princely hat above divides date **Rev. Legend:** IN. SCHWARZENBERG. LANDGR. IN. CLEGG. D. C. **Note:** Struck from Ducat dies, KM# 29.

Date	Mintage	VG	F	VF	XF	Unc
1721 B	—	—	—	—	—	—

KM# 36 GROSCHEN

2.6000 g., Silver **Ruler:** Adam Franz Karl Duke of Krumau, 1723 **Mint:** Nuremberg **Subject:** Birth of Joseph Adam Johann **Obverse:** Crowned 4-fold arms with central shield, all in palm branches **Reverse:** 9-line inscription with date in chronogram

Date	Mintage	VG	F	VF	XF	Unc
1722	—	—	—	—	—	—

KM# 25 2 GROSCHEN

Silver Weight varies 4.83-5.18 grams **Ruler:** Adam Franz Karl Duke of Krumau, 1723 **Mint:** Vienna **Subject:** Marriage of Princess Maria Anna to Ludwig Georg Wilhelm von Baden **Obverse:** Two adjacent ornate arms of Baden and Schwarzenberg. **Obv. Legend:** UTRIUSQUE GENTIS INCREMENTO. **Reverse:** 9-line inscription with Roman numeral date **Note:** Varieties exist.

Date	Mintage	VG	F	VF	XF	Unc
1721 MDCCXXI	—	35.00	65.00	115	185	—

KM# 64 20 KREUZER

Silver **Ruler:** Johann **Mint:** Vienna **Obverse:** Bust right, value below **Obv. Legend:** IOH • D • G • S • R • I • PRINCEPS • IN ... **Reverse:** Crowned arms within Order chain **Note:** Convention 20 Kreuzer. Prev. C#6.

Date	Mintage	VG	F	VF	XF	Unc
1783 VF	—	25.00	45.00	75.00	135	220

KM# 44 1/4 THALER

Silver **Ruler:** Joseph Adam **Mint:** Vienna **Subject:** Marriage of Joseph Adam to Maria Theresia of Leichtenstein **Obverse:** Flaming altar with two shields of arms, angel at right with wreath **Obv. Inscription:** TAEDIS FELICIBVS. **Reverse:** Crown above inscription **Note:** Struck from 2 Ducat dies, KM# 48.

Date	Mintage	VG	F	VF	XF	Unc
1741 MD	—	50.00	85.00	150	225	—

KM# 28 THALER

Silver **Ruler:** Adam Franz Karl Duke of Krumau, 1723 **Mint:** Vienna **Obverse:** Bust right **Obv. Legend:** ADAMUS • FRANCISC: - D: G: S: R: I: PRINCEPS • **Reverse:** Four-fold arms with central shield in oval baroque frame, chain of order around, princely hat divides date **Rev. Legend:** IN • SCHWARZENBERG • LANDGR: IN • CLEGGOV **Note:** Dav #2773.

Date	Mintage	VG	F	VF	XF	Unc
1721 B	—	200	350	600	1,000	—
1725 B	—	200	350	600	1,000	—

KM# 40 THALER

Silver **Ruler:** Adam Franz Karl Duke of Krumau, 1723 **Mint:** Nuremberg **Obverse:** Armored and draped bust to right, crossed hammers below **Obv. Legend:** ADAMUS. FRANCISC. — D:G. S.R.I. PRINCEPS. **Reverse:** Four-fold arms with central shield in oval baroque frame, chain of order around, princely hat divides date **Rev. Legend:** IN. SCHWARZENBERG. LANDGR. IN. CLEGGOV. D.C. **Note:** Mining Thaler. Dav# 2774.

Date	Mintage	VG	F	VF	XF	Unc
1729 B	—	200	450	750	1,250	—

KM# 46 THALER

Silver **Ruler:** Joseph Adam **Mint:** Vienna **Obverse:** Bust right **Obv. Legend:** IOSEPH • D • G • S • R • I • PRIN • IN • SCHWARZENBERG **Reverse:** Mantled arms within Order collar **Rev. Legend:** LANDGR • IN • CLEGGOV • COM • IN • SULZ • DUX • CRUM **Note:** Species Thaler; Dav# 2775. Prev. C# 2.

Date	Mintage	VG	F	VF	XF	Unc
1741 B	—	80.00	180	320	700	1,250

KM# 54 THALER

Silver **Ruler:** Joseph Adam **Mint:** Kremnitz **Subject:** Laying of Cornerstone for the Church of St. Mary in Postelberg **Obverse:** Bust to right **Reverse:** Crown with laurel and palm branches above 8-line inscription with Roman numeral date

Date	Mintage	VG	F	VF	XF	Unc
1746 B	—	—	—	—	—	—

KM# 56 THALER

Silver **Ruler:** Joseph Adam **Mint:** Nuremberg **Obverse:** Armored bust right **Obv. Legend:** IOSEPH • D • G • S • R • I • PRIN • IN SCHWARZENBERG, OXLEIN on arm **Reverse:** Mantled arms within Order collar **Rev. Legend:** LANDGR • IN CLEGOV • COM • IN • SULZ • DUX CRUM, X • EINE FEINE MARK •/17 - 66/S.N.R. below **Note:** Convention Thaler; Dav# 2776. Prev. C# 3.

Date	Mintage	VG	F	VF	XF	Unc
1766 OEXLEIN-SNR	—	180	400	700	1,200	—

KM# 66 THALER

Silver **Ruler:** Johann **Mint:** Vienna **Obverse:** Bust right **Obv. Legend:** IOH • D • G • S • R • I • PRINCEPS IN SCHWARZENBERG • **Reverse:** Arms within Order collar **Rev. Legend:** LANDG • IN CLEG • COM • IN SVLZ • DVX • CRVM • 1783 **Note:** Dav# 2777. Prev. C# 7.

Date	Mintage	VG	F	VF	XF	Unc
1783 VF	—	100	175	300	500	900

TRADE COINAGE

KM# 20 DUCAT

3.5000 g., 0.9860 Gold 0.1109 oz. AGW **Ruler:** Adam Franz Karl Duke of Krumau, 1723 **Mint:** Cologne **Obverse:** Bust right **Reverse:** Capped arms in Order collar, cap divides date **Note:** Fr# 95.

Date	Mintage	VG	F	VF	XF	Unc
1710 (c) Rare	—	—	—	—	—	—

KM# 29 DUCAT

3.5000 g., 0.9860 Gold 0.1109 oz. AGW **Ruler:** Adam Franz Karl Duke of Krumau, 1723 **Mint:** Vienna **Obverse:** Bust to right **Obv. Legend:** ADAMUS • FRANCISC • - D • G • S • R • I • PRINCEPS - **Reverse:** Four-fold arms with central shield in oval baroque frame, order chain around, princely hat above divides date **Rev. Legend:** LANDGR. IN CLEGG. D. C. **Note:** Prev. Fr#96.

Date	Mintage	VG	F	VF	XF	Unc
1721 B	—	400	800	1,600	2,750	—
1725 B	—	400	800	1,600	2,750	—
1728 B	—	400	800	1,500	2,500	—
1729 B	—	400	800	1,600	2,750	—
1731 B	—	400	800	1,600	2,750	—
1732 B	—	400	800	1,600	2,750	—

KM# 38 DUCAT

3.5000 g., 0.9860 Gold .1109 oz. AGW 0.1109 oz. AGW **Ruler:** Adam Franz Karl Duke of Krumau, 1723 **Mint:** Nuremberg **Subject:** Birth of Joseph Adam Johann **Obverse:** Crowned 4-fold arms with central shield, all in palm branches **Reverse:** 9-line inscription with date in chronogram **Note:** Struck from Groschen dies, KM# 36.

Date	Mintage	VG	F	VF	XF	Unc
1722 (n)	—	—	—	—	—	—

KM# 62 DUCAT

3.5000 g., 0.9860 Gold 0.1109 oz. AGW **Ruler:** Joseph Adam **Mint:** Vienna **Obverse:** Bust right **Obv. Legend:** IOS • D • G • S • R • I • PRINC • - IN SCHWARZENBERG **Reverse:** Capped arms in Order collar **Note:** Prev. C# 4.

Date	Mintage	VG	F	VF	XF	Unc
1768 (e)	500	500	1,200	2,500	3,750	—

KM# 68 DUCAT

3.5000 g., 0.9860 Gold 0.1109 oz. AGW **Ruler:** Johann **Mint:** Vienna **Obverse:** Bust right **Obv. Legend:** IOH • D • G • S • R • I • PRINC • IN SCHWARZENBERG • **Reverse:** Capped arms in Order collar **Rev. Legend:** LANDG • IN CLEG • COM • IN SVLZ • DVX • CRVM • **Note:** Prev. C# 8.

Date	Mintage	F	VF	XF	Unc
1783 VF	200	600	1,200	2,250	3,500

KM# 31 2 DUCAT

7.0000 g., 0.9860 Gold .2219 oz. AGW **Ruler:** Adam Franz Karl Duke of Krumau, 1723 **Mint:** Vienna **Subject:** Marriage of Princess Maria Anna to Ludwig Georg Wilhelm von Baden **Obverse:** Two adjacent ornate arms of Baden and Schwarzenberg **Obv. Legend:** UTRIUSQUE GENTIS INCREMENTO **Reverse:** 9-line inscription with Roman numeral date

Date	Mintage	VG	F	VF	XF	Unc
1721 (d)	—	—	—	—	—	—

KM# 48 2 DUCAT

7.0000 g., 0.9860 Gold 0.2219 oz. AGW **Ruler:** Joseph Adam **Mint:** Vienna **Subject:** Marriage of Josef Adam and Maria Theresia of Liechtenstein **Obverse:** Flaming altar with 2 arms, angel on right with wreath **Obv. Inscription:** TAEDIS FELICIBVS **Reverse:** Inscription with crown above **Note:** Previous C# 4.5.

Date	Mintage	VG	F	VF	XF	Unc
1741 MD Rare	—	—	—	—	—	—

KM# 50 3 DUCAT

10.5000 g., 0.9860 Gold 0.3328 oz. AGW **Ruler:** Joseph Adam **Subject:** Marriage of Josef Adam and Maria Theresia of Liechtenstein **Obverse:** Flaming altar with two shields of arms, angel at right with wreath **Obv. Legend:** TAEDIS FELICIBVS. **Reverse:** Crown above inscription **Note:** Struck from 2 Ducat dies, KM#48.

Date	Mintage	VG	F	VF	XF	Unc
1741 MD Rare	—	—	—	—	—	—

KM# 8 5 DUCAT

17.5000 g., 0.9860 Gold 0.5547 oz. AGW **Ruler:** Ferdinand Wilhelm Eusebius **Mint:** Cologne **Obverse:** Bust right **Obv. Legend:** FERD: D: G: PR: - SCHWARTZENB • **Reverse:** Oval 4-fold arms within chain of order, princely hat above **Note:** Fr# 93.

Date	Mintage	VG	F	VF	XF	Unc
ND IAL	—	2,500	4,500	7,000	10,000	—

KM# 33 10 DUCAT

35.0000 g., 0.9860 Gold 1.1095 oz. AGW 1.1095 oz. AGW **Ruler:** Adam Franz Karl Duke of Krumau, 1723 **Mint:** Vienna **Obverse:** Draped and armored bust to right **Obv. Legend:** ADAMUS. FRANCISC. — D:G. S. R. I. PRINCEPS. **Reverse:** Four-fold arms with central shield in oval baroque frame, chain of order around, princely hat divides date above **Rev. Legend:** IN. SCHWARZENBERG. LANDGR. IN. CLEGGOV. **Note:** Struck from Thaler dies, KM# 28 (Dav. 2773).

Date	Mintage	VG	F	VF	XF	Unc
1721 B	—	—	7,500	12,500	16,000	—

KM# 42 10 DUCAT

35.0000 g., 0.9860 Gold 1.1095 oz. AGW **Ruler:** Adam Franz Karl Duke of Krumau, 1723 **Obverse:** Armored and draped bust to right, crossed hammers below **Obv. Legend:** ADAMUS. FRANCISC. — D:G. S. R. I. PRINCEPS. **Reverse:** Four-fold arms with central shield in oval baroque frame, chain of order around, princely hat divides date **Rev. Inscription:** IN. SCHWARZENBERG. LANDGR. IN CLEGGOV. D.C. **Note:** Struck from Thaler dies, KM# 40 (Dav #2774), with altered date. Prev. KM#65.

Date	Mintage	VG	F	VF	XF	Unc
1732 B Rare	—	—	—	—	—	—

KM# 52 10 DUCAT

35.0000 g., 0.9860 Gold 1.1095 oz. AGW 1.1095 oz. AGW **Ruler:** Joseph Adam **Mint:** Vienna **Obverse:** Armored and draped bust to right **Obv. Legend:** IOSEPH. D.G. S. R. I. PRIN. IN. SCHWARZENBERG. **Reverse:** Mantled oval 4-fold arms with central shield, order chain around, princely hat above divides date **Rev. Legend:** LANDGR. IN. GLEGGOV. COM. IN. SULZ. DUX. CRUM. **Note:** Struck from Thaler dies, KM #46.

Date	Mintage	VG	F	VF	XF	Unc
1741 B	—	—	8,500	14,000	18,500	—

KM# 58 10 DUCAT

35.0000 g., 0.9860 Gold 1.1095 oz. AGW 1.1095 oz. AGW **Ruler:** Joseph Adam **Mint:** Nuremberg **Obverse:** Armored and draped bust to right **Obv. Legend:** IOSEPH. D.G. S. R. I. PRIN. IN SCHWARZENBERG. **Reverse:** Mantled oval 4-fold arms with central shield, order chain around, princely hat above, value, date and mint officials' initials in exergue **Rev. Legend:** LANDGR. IN. CLEGGOV. COM. IN. SULZ. DUX. CRUM. **Rev. Inscription:** X. EINE FEINE MARK/17 — S(N)R — 66. **Note:** Struck from Thaler dies, KM#56.

Date	Mintage	VG	F	VF	XF	Unc
1766 OEXLEIN//SNR Rare	—	—	—	—	—	—

KM# 70 10 DUCAT

35.0000 g., 0.9860 Gold 1.1095 oz. AGW 1.1095 oz. AGW **Ruler:** Johann **Mint:** Vienna **Obverse:** Bust to right **Obv. Legend:** IOH. D.G. S. R. I. PRINCEPS IN SCHWARZENBERG. **Reverse:** Round 4-fold arms with central shield, chain of order around, date at end of legend **Rev. Legend:** LANDG. IN CLEG. COM. IN SVLZ. DVX. CRVM. **Note:** Struck from Thaler dies, KM# 66.

Date	Mintage	VG	F	VF	XF	Unc
1783 VF	—	—	12,000	17,000	21,500	—

PATTERNS

Including off metal strikes

KM#	Date	Mintage	Identification	Mkt Val
Pn2	1721	—	2 Ducat. Copper. KM# 31.	—
Pn3	1741	—	2 Ducat. Silver. C#4.5.	350
Pn4	1746	—	Thaler. Copper. KM# 54.	—

SCHWEINFURT

Schweinfurt was a Free City located in Lower Franconia some 27 miles northeast of Würzburg. It was first mentioned in 790, became a Free City in the 13th century. Immediately after becoming free, Schweinfurt was the site of a short-lived royal bracteat mint.

The only Schweinfurt local coinage appeared in 1622, though a 1717 series of Reformation commemoratives may have passed as coins.

In 1803 the town was annexed to Bavaria.

FREE CITY

REGULAR COINAGE

KM# 3 2 GROSCHEN

Silver **Subject:** Reformation 200th Anniversary **Obverse:** Altar with City arms **Reverse:** Ten-line inscription

Date	Mintage	Good	VG	F	VF	XF
1717	—	—	—	100	150	200

TRADE COINAGE

KM# 4 DUCAT

Gold **Note:** Similar to KM#3.

Date	Mintage	Good	VG	F	VF	XF
1717	—	—	—	800	1,200	1,600

KM# 4a DUCAT

Silver **Note:** Similar to KM#4.

Date	Mintage	Good	VG	F	VF	XF
1717	—	—	—	50.00	80.00	120

SILESIA

The territory of Silesia was historically located between Bohemia and Poland, but was Germanic in character from an early period. The first ruling dynasty, that of the Piasts, was descended from the Polish royal line and soon had divided Silesia into a number of smaller entities. Silesia proper became a part of the Holy Roman Empire in the 14th century and came under the influence of Bohemia, which began striking coins for that territory. After the mid-14th century, Breslau (see) became the capital and the principal mint of the duchy. In 1526, Silesia, along with Bohemia, came into the possession of the Habsburg imperial family. The Austrian-style coinage of Silesia was struck from that time until 1740, with few gaps, most notably during the Thirty Years' War, when the estates struck a series of emergency coinage. All during the period of Habsburg domination, the various semi-independent small duchies, in all their branches, continued to strike their own coins. The bishops of Breslau and a number of towns and cities also issued coinages in their own names (see under Breslau and the town names).

In the 1740's, Prussia conquered the greater portion of Silesia and established a mint in Breslau which struck coins within the Prussian system from 1743 until 1797 (see under Prussia). Silesia remained a province of Prussia throughout the 18th and 19th centuries, only to be divided and partly awarded to Poland after World War I. Following the Second World War, the rest of Silesia was united with Poland and remains as part of that country up to the present day.

RULERS

Leopold I, 1657-1705
Josef I, 1705-1711
Karl VI, 1711-1740
Friedrich II, King of Prussia, 1740-1786
Friedrich Wilhelm II, 1786-1797
Friedrich Wilhelm III, 1797-1840

MINT MARKS

BRESLAU MINT

(Wroclaw, Vratislav)
(in Silesia)

Coat of arms sometimes at top center of crowned shield. Other times just Austrian arms on imperial eagle's breast. Legend usually ends: DVX S, SI or SIL.

MINT OFFICIALS' INITIALS

Initials	Years	Names
FN	1704-23	Franz Nowak

BRIEG MINT

(Breh, Brzeg)
(in Silesia)

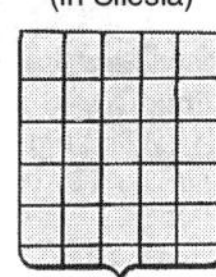

Coat of arms in legend.

MINT MARKS

MB

MINT OFFICIALS' INITIALS

Initials	Years	Names
CB	1677-1713	Christoph Brettschneider

OPPELN MINT

(in Silesia)

Large coat of arms, like Vienna, on imperial eagle's breast or coat of arms, like Breslau, on minor types without eagle. Legend usually ends CO.T or CO.TY.

MINT MARKS

(f) - - double fleur de lis

MINT OFFICIALS' INITIALS

Initials	Years	Names
FN	1699-1705	Franz Nowak

Coat of arms on imperial eagle's breast. Legend usually ends BO, BOH, BOHEMIAE REX.

NOTE: For similar gold coins dated 1787-1805 refer to Prussian listings.

REFERENCES

Ferdinand Friedensburg and Hans Seger, ***Schlesiens Münzen und Medaillen der Neueren Zeit***, Breslau, 1901 (reprint Frankfurt/Main)

Norbert Jaschke and Fritz P. Maercker, ***Schlesische Münzen und Medaillen***, Ihringen, 1985.

Viktor Miller zu Aichholz, A. Loehr, E. Holzmaair, ***Österreichische Münzprägungen 1519-1938,*** 2 vols., 2nd edn., Chicago, 1981

Hugo Frhr. Von Saurma-Jeltsch, ***Die Saurmasche Münzsammlung deutscher, schweizerischer und polnischer Gepräge von etwa dem Beginn der Groschenzeit bis zur Kipperperiode,*** Berlin, 1892

Hugo Frhr. Von Saurma-Jeltsch, ***Schlesische Münzen und Medaillen***, Breslau, 1883.

Wolfgang Schulten, ***Deutsche Münzen aus der Zeit Karls V.***, Frankfurt am Main, 1974

DUCHY

REGULAR COINAGE

KM# 927 DENAR

Billon **Ruler:** Friedrich II, King of Prussia **Obverse:** Crowned FR monogram **Reverse:** Value, date **Note:** Prev. C#1.

Date	Mintage	VG	F	VF	XF	Unc
1746 AE-W	—	12.00	25.00	50.00	90.00	—
1747 AE-W	—	12.00	25.00	50.00	90.00	—

KM# 438 3 PFENNIG

Billon **Ruler:** Leopold I **Mint:** Oppeln **Obverse:** Orb with value within divides date, ornamentation at sides **Note:** Prev. Austria KM#1279, (1184). Varieties exist.

Date	Mintage	VG	F	VF	XF	Unc
1703	—	7.00	15.00	30.00	60.00	—
1704	—	7.00	15.00	30.00	60.00	—

KM# 594 3 PFENNIG

Silver **Ruler:** Leopold I **Mint:** Brieg **Obverse:** Imperial eagle with arms on breast **Reverse:** Value within orb dividing date **Note:** Prev. Austria KM#170 (KM#1365). Varieties exist.

Date	Mintage	VG	F	VF	XF	Unc
1702MB	—	8.00	16.00	35.00	75.00	—

KM# 678 3 PFENNIG

Billon **Ruler:** Josef I **Mint:** Breslau **Obverse:** Orb with value within divides date **Reverse:** Imperial eagle with arms on breast **Note:** Prev. Austria KM#120 (KM#1420).

Date	Mintage	VG	F	VF	XF	Unc
1705	—	6.00	12.50	25.00	55.00	—
1707	—	6.00	12.50	25.00	55.00	—

KM# 681 3 PFENNIG

Billon **Ruler:** Josef I **Mint:** Breslau **Note:** Prev. KM#121 (KM#1421).

Date	Mintage	VG	F	VF	XF	Unc
1705	—	6.00	12.50	25.00	55.00	—

KM# 817 3 PFENNIG

Silver **Ruler:** Karl VI **Mint:** Brieg **Obverse:** Orb with value within divides arched date **Reverse:** Imperial eagle with arms on breast **Note:** Prev. Austria KM#195 (KM#1591).

Date	Mintage	VG	F	VF	XF	Unc
1718 Rare	—	—	—	—	—	—
1719MB	—	20.00	40.00	85.00	175	—

KM# 750 3 PFENNIG (DREIER)

17.5000 g., 0.9860 Gold 0.5547 oz. AGW **Ruler:** Josef I **Mint:** Brieg **Obverse:** Orb with value within divides date **Reverse:** Imperial eagle with arms on breast **Note:** Prev. Austria KM#185 (KM#1484). Off-metal strike.

Date	Mintage	VG	F	VF	XF	Unc
1707 Rare	—	—	—	—	—	—

KM# 1053a 1/2 KREUZER

Silver **Ruler:** Friedrich Wilhelm II **Obverse:** Crowned monogram **Reverse:** Value, date **Note:** Prev. C#47a.

Date	Mintage	VG	F	VF	XF	Unc
1787B Rare	—	—	—	—	—	—
1789B Rare	—	—	—	—	—	—

KM# 1053 1/2 KREUZER

Copper **Ruler:** Friedrich Wilhelm II **Obverse:** Crowned monogram **Reverse:** Value, date **Note:** Prev. C#47.

Date	Mintage	VG	F	VF	XF	Unc
1788B	—	4.00	8.00	16.00	35.00	—
1789B	—	4.00	8.00	16.00	35.00	—
1794B	—	4.00	8.00	16.00	35.00	—
1795B	—	4.00	8.00	16.00	35.00	—
1796B	—	4.00	8.00	16.00	35.00	—
1797B	—	4.00	8.00	16.00	35.00	—

KM# 606 KREUZER

Silver **Ruler:** Leopold I **Mint:** Brieg **Obverse:** Laureate bust right in inner circle **Reverse:** Crowned imperial eagle with value on breast, crown divides date **Note:** Prev. Austria KM#171 (1373). Varieties exist.

Date	Mintage	VG	F	VF	XF	Unc
1701 CB	—	8.00	16.00	35.00	75.00	—
1702 CB	—	8.00	16.00	35.00	75.00	—
1704 CB	—	8.00	16.00	35.00	75.00	—

KM# 612 KREUZER

Silver **Ruler:** Leopold I **Mint:** Oppeln **Obverse:** Bust right in inner circle **Obv. Legend:** LEOPOLDVS • D • G • R • I • S • ... **Reverse:** Crowned imperial eagle with value on breast in inner circle, crown divides date **Note:** Prev. Austria KM#1280 (1382). Varieties exist.

Date	Mintage	VG	F	VF	XF	Unc
1701 FN	—	8.00	16.00	35.00	70.00	—
1702 FN	—	8.00	16.00	35.00	70.00	—

KM# 774 KREUZER

Silver **Ruler:** Karl VI **Mint:** Breslau **Obverse:** Laureate bust right **Reverse:** Crowned imperial eagle, value below, crown divides date **Note:** Prev. Austria KM#140 (KM#1535). Varieties exist.

Date	Mintage	VG	F	VF	XF	Unc
1713	—	10.00	20.00	40.00	80.00	—
1726	—	10.00	20.00	40.00	80.00	—
1731	—	10.00	20.00	40.00	80.00	—

KM# 912 KREUZER

Billon **Ruler:** Friedrich II, King of Prussia **Obverse:** Bust right **Reverse:** Crowned eagle in cartouche, value, date **Note:** Prev. C#7.

Date	Mintage	VG	F	VF	XF	Unc
1745 AE	—	10.00	20.00	40.00	75.00	—
1747 AE	—	10.00	20.00	40.00	75.00	—

KM# 957 KREUZER

Billon **Ruler:** Friedrich II, King of Prussia **Obverse:** Crowned script FR monogram between 2 branches **Reverse:** Value, date **Note:** Prev. C#8.

Date	Mintage	VG	F	VF	XF	Unc
1752B	—	20.00	35.00	65.00	100	—

KM# 960.1 KREUZER

Billon **Ruler:** Friedrich II, King of Prussia **Obverse:** Bust right **Reverse:** Crowned eagle, value, date **Note:** Prev. C#9.1.

Date	Mintage	VG	F	VF	XF	Unc
1752B	—	5.00	10.00	20.00	40.00	—
1753B	—	5.00	10.00	20.00	40.00	—
1754B	2,723,000	5.00	10.00	20.00	40.00	—
1756B	—	5.00	10.00	20.00	40.00	—
1757B	—	5.00	10.00	20.00	40.00	—
1763B	432,000	5.00	10.00	20.00	40.00	—

KM# 960.2 KREUZER

Billon **Ruler:** Friedrich II, King of Prussia **Obverse:** Bust right **Reverse:** Eagle without crown **Note:** Prev. C#9.2.

Date	Mintage	VG	F	VF	XF	Unc
1757 B	—	10.00	20.00	45.00	80.00	—

KM# 1011 KREUZER

Billon **Ruler:** Friedrich II, King of Prussia **Obverse:** Head right **Obv. Legend:** FRIDERIC: BORUSS: REX **Reverse:** Crowned eagle, value above, B divides date **Note:** Prev. C#10.

Date	Mintage	VG	F	VF	XF	Unc
1766B	1,113,000	7.00	15.00	30.00	65.00	—
1767B	765,000	7.00	15.00	30.00	65.00	—

KM# 1020 KREUZER

Billon **Ruler:** Friedrich II, King of Prussia **Obverse:** Laureate head right **Obv. Legend:** FRIDERIC: BORUSS: REX **Reverse:** Crowned flying eagle above value, B divides date **Note:** Prev. C#11.

Date	Mintage	VG	F	VF	XF	Unc
1771B	—	4.00	8.00	18.00	40.00	—
1772B	—	4.00	8.00	18.00	40.00	—
1773B	—	4.00	8.00	18.00	40.00	—
1774B	—	4.00	8.00	18.00	40.00	—
1775B	—	4.00	8.00	18.00	40.00	—

Date	Mintage	VG	F	VF	XF	Unc
1776B	—	4.00	8.00	18.00	40.00	—
1777B	—	4.00	8.00	18.00	40.00	—
1778B	—	4.00	8.00	18.00	40.00	—
1779B	—	4.00	8.00	18.00	40.00	—
1780B	—	4.00	8.00	18.00	40.00	—
1781B	—	4.00	8.00	18.00	40.00	—
1782B	—	4.00	8.00	18.00	40.00	—
1783B	—	4.00	8.00	18.00	40.00	—
1784B	—	4.00	8.00	18.00	40.00	—
1785B	—	4.00	8.00	18.00	40.00	—
1786B	—	4.00	8.00	18.00	40.00	—

KM# 1047 KREUZER

Billon **Ruler:** Friedrich Wilhelm II **Obverse:** Bust right **Reverse:** Crowned arms separate value and date **Note:** Prev. C#51.

Date	Mintage	VG	F	VF	XF	Unc
1787B	—	4.00	8.00	18.00	40.00	—
1788B	—	4.00	8.00	18.00	40.00	—
1789B	—	4.00	8.00	18.00	40.00	—
1790B	—	4.00	8.00	18.00	40.00	—
1792B	—	4.00	8.00	18.00	40.00	—
1793B	—	4.00	8.00	18.00	40.00	—
1794B	—	4.00	8.00	18.00	40.00	—
1795B	—	4.00	8.00	18.00	40.00	—
1796B	—	4.00	8.00	18.00	40.00	—
1797B	—	4.00	8.00	18.00	40.00	—

KM# 471 3 KREUZER

Silver **Ruler:** Leopold I **Mint:** Breslau **Obverse:** Bust right **Obv. Legend:** LEOPOLDUS • D • G •R • I •... **Reverse:** Crowned double, eagle, crown divides date **Note:** Varieties exist. Prev. Austria KM#79 (KM#1230).

Date	Mintage	VG	F	VF	XF	Unc
1705	—	7.00	15.00	30.00	60.00	—

KM# 504 3 KREUZER

Silver **Ruler:** Leopold I **Mint:** Oppeln **Obverse:** Laureate bust right in inner circle, value below **Reverse:** Crowned imperial eagle in inner circle, crown divides date **Note:** Prev. Austria KM#1281 (KM#1273). Varieties exist.

Date	Mintage	VG	F	VF	XF	Unc
1701 FN	—	7.00	15.00	30.00	60.00	—
1702 FN	—	7.00	15.00	30.00	60.00	—
1703 FN	—	7.00	15.00	30.00	60.00	—
1704 FN	—	7.00	15.00	30.00	60.00	—

KM# 516 3 KREUZER

Silver **Ruler:** Leopold I **Mint:** Brieg **Obverse:** Laureate bust right in inner circle, value below **Reverse:** Crowned imperial eagle in inner circle, crown divides date **Note:** Prev. Austria KM#173 (KM#1287). Varieties exist.

Date	Mintage	VG	F	VF	XF	Unc
1701 CB	—	7.00	15.00	30.00	65.00	—
1702 CB	—	7.00	15.00	30.00	65.00	—
1705 CB	—	7.00	15.00	30.00	65.00	—

KM# 684 3 KREUZER

Silver **Ruler:** Leopold I **Mint:** Breslau **Note:** Klippe. Prev. Austria KM#80 (KM#1426).

Date	Mintage	VG	F	VF	XF	Unc
1705 FN Rare	—	—	—	—	—	—

KM# 687 3 KREUZER

Silver **Ruler:** Josef I **Mint:** Breslau **Obverse:** Bust right **Obv. Legend:** IOSEPHUS • D • G • R • I • S •... **Reverse:** Crowned imperial eagle in inner circle, crown divides date **Note:** Varieties exist. Prev. Austria KM#122 (KM#1427).

Date	Mintage	VG	F	VF	XF	Unc
1705 FN	—	5.00	10.00	20.00	40.00	—
1706 FN	—	5.00	10.00	20.00	40.00	—
1707 FN	—	5.00	10.00	20.00	40.00	—
1708 FN	—	5.00	10.00	20.00	40.00	—
1709 FN	—	5.00	10.00	20.00	40.00	—
1710 FN	—	5.00	10.00	20.00	40.00	—
1711 FN	—	5.00	10.00	20.00	40.00	—

KM# 690 3 KREUZER

Silver **Ruler:** Josef I **Mint:** Brieg **Obverse:** Bust right, value below **Obv. Legend:** IOSEPHVS • D • G • R • I • S •... **Reverse:** Crowned imperial double eagle with arms on breast **Note:** Varieties exist. Prev. Austria KM#186, (KM#1429).

Date	Mintage	VG	F	VF	XF	Unc
1705 CB	—	7.00	15.00	30.00	65.00	—
1706 CB	—	7.00	15.00	30.00	65.00	—
1707 CB	—	7.00	15.00	30.00	65.00	—
1708 CB	—	7.00	15.00	30.00	65.00	—
1709 CB	—	7.00	15.00	30.00	65.00	—
1710 CB	—	7.00	15.00	30.00	65.00	—
1711 CB	—	7.00	15.00	30.00	65.00	—

KM# 759 3 KREUZER

Silver **Ruler:** Karl VI **Mint:** Brieg **Obverse:** Laureate bust right in inner circle **Reverse:** Crowned imperial eagle in inner circle, crown divides date **Note:** Prev. Austria KM#196 (KM#1512).

Date	Mintage	VG	F	VF	XF	Unc
1711 CB	—	15.00	30.00	60.00	120	—
1712 CB	—	15.00	30.00	60.00	120	—
1713 CB	—	15.00	30.00	60.00	120	—

KM# 765 3 KREUZER

Silver **Ruler:** Karl VI **Mint:** Breslau **Obverse:** Without inner circle **Note:** Prev. Austria KM#1518.

Date	Mintage	VG	F	VF	XF	Unc
1712 FN	—	6.00	12.00	25.00	55.00	—

KM# 762 3 KREUZER

Silver **Ruler:** Karl VI **Mint:** Breslau **Obverse:** Laureate bust right in inner circle, value below **Obv. Legend:** CAROLUS • VI • ... **Reverse:** Crowned imperial eagle, shield on breast within inner circle, crown divides date **Rev. Legend:** ARCHID • AUS • DUX • BUR • SIL • **Note:** Prev. Austria KM#141 (1517).

Date	Mintage	VG	F	VF	XF	Unc
1712 FN	—	6.00	12.00	25.00	55.00	—
1713	—	6.00	12.00	25.00	55.00	—
1714	—	6.00	12.00	25.00	55.00	—
1715	—	6.00	12.00	25.00	55.00	—

KM# 777 3 KREUZER

Silver **Ruler:** Karl VI **Mint:** Breslau **Reverse:** Date in legend **Note:** Prev. Austria KM#142 (KM#1539).

Date	Mintage	VG	F	VF	XF	Unc
1713	—	6.00	12.00	25.00	55.00	—

KM# 804 3 KREUZER

Silver **Ruler:** Karl VI **Mint:** Breslau **Obverse:** Without inner circle **Reverse:** Without inner circle, value below eagle, date in legend **Note:** Varieties exist. Prev. Austria KM#144 (KM#1586).

Date	Mintage	VG	F	VF	XF	Unc
1716	—	6.00	12.00	25.00	55.00	—
1719	—	6.00	12.00	25.00	55.00	—
1720	—	—	—	—	—	—
Note: Reported, not confirmed						
1722	—	—	—	—	—	—
Note: Reported, not confirmed						
1723	—	6.00	12.00	25.00	55.00	—
1724	—	6.00	12.00	25.00	55.00	—
1725	—	6.00	12.00	25.00	55.00	—
1726	—	6.00	12.00	25.00	55.00	—
1727	—	6.00	12.00	25.00	55.00	—
1728	—	6.00	12.00	25.00	55.00	—
1729	—	6.00	12.00	25.00	55.00	—

KM# 869 3 KREUZER

Silver **Ruler:** Karl VI **Mint:** Breslau **Obverse:** Value below bust **Reverse:** Crowned imperial double eagle with arms on breast **Note:** Prev. Austria KM#A145 (KM#1626).

Date	Mintage	VG	F	VF	XF	Unc
1729	—	6.00	12.00	25.00	55.00	—
1730	—	6.00	12.00	25.00	55.00	—
1731	—	6.00	12.00	25.00	55.00	—
1732	—	6.00	12.00	25.00	55.00	—
1738	—	—	—	—	—	—
Note: Reported, not confirmed						
1739	—	6.00	12.00	25.00	55.00	—

KM# 891 3 KREUZER

Billon **Ruler:** Friedrich II, King of Prussia **Obverse:** Bust right, value **Reverse:** Crowned eagle in crowned cartouche, date **Note:** Prev. C#17.

Date	Mintage	VG	F	VF	XF	Unc
1743 AE-W	—	25.00	45.00	85.00	165	—

KM# 963 3 KREUZER

Billon **Ruler:** Friedrich II, King of Prussia **Obverse:** Bust right **Reverse:** Imperial eagle above value **Note:** Prev. C#19.

Date	Mintage	VG	F	VF	XF	Unc
1752B	27,390,000	10.00	20.00	40.00	70.00	—

KM# 966 3 KREUZER

Billon **Ruler:** Friedrich II, King of Prussia **Reverse:** Crowned 2 arms, value, date **Note:** Prev. C#21.

Date	Mintage	VG	F	VF	XF	Unc
1752B	Inc. above	8.00	16.00	32.00	60.00	—
1753B	Inc. above	8.00	16.00	32.00	60.00	—
1754B	6,871,000	8.00	16.00	32.00	60.00	—
1755B	—	8.00	16.00	32.00	60.00	—
1756B	—	8.00	16.00	32.00	60.00	—
1763B	12,472,000	8.00	16.00	32.00	60.00	—

KM# 1002 3 KREUZER

Billon **Ruler:** Friedrich II, King of Prussia **Obverse:** Crowned head right **Reverse:** Crowned eagle divides date at top, value and B below **Note:** Prev. C#23.

Date	Mintage	VG	F	VF	XF	Unc
1764B	3,843,000	12.00	25.00	50.00	100	—

KM# 1002a 3 KREUZER

Billon **Ruler:** Friedrich II, King of Prussia **Obverse:** Laureate head right **Obv. Legend:** FRIDERICUS BORUSS: REX **Reverse:** Imperial eagle divides date above **Note:** Prev. C#23a.

Date	Mintage	VG	F	VF	XF	Unc
1765B	Inc. above	15.00	30.00	60.00	120	—

KM# 1023 3 KREUZER

Billon **Ruler:** Friedrich II, King of Prussia **Obverse:** Laureate head right **Obv. Legend:** FRIDERICUS BORUSSORUM REX **Reverse:** A or B divides date **Rev. Legend:** MONETA ARGENT **Note:** Prev. C#24.

Date	Mintage	VG	F	VF	XF	Unc
1771B	12,300,000	4.00	7.50	14.50	22.50	—
1772B	5,559,000	4.00	7.50	14.50	22.50	—
1773B	3,353,000	4.00	7.50	14.50	22.50	—
1774B	1,088,000	4.00	7.50	14.50	22.50	—
1775B	616,000	4.00	7.50	14.50	22.50	—
1777B	511,000	4.00	7.50	14.50	22.50	—
1778B	627,000	4.00	7.50	14.50	22.50	—
1779A	—	4.00	7.50	14.50	22.50	—
1779B	379,000	4.00	7.50	14.50	22.50	—
1780A	—	4.00	7.50	14.50	22.50	—
1780B	548,000	4.00	7.50	14.50	22.50	—
1781A	—	4.00	7.50	14.50	22.50	—
1781B	662,000	4.00	7.50	14.50	22.50	—
1782A	—	4.00	7.50	14.50	22.50	—
1782B	537,000	4.00	7.50	14.50	22.50	—
1783A	—	4.00	7.50	14.50	22.50	—
1783B	3,016,000	4.00	7.50	14.50	22.50	—
1784A	—	4.00	7.50	14.50	22.50	—
1784B	1,351,000	4.00	7.50	14.50	22.50	—
1785A	—	4.00	7.50	14.50	22.50	—
1785B	1,233,000	4.00	7.50	14.50	22.50	—
1786B	549,000	4.00	7.50	14.50	22.50	—

KM# 1023a 3 KREUZER

Billon **Ruler:** Friedrich II, King of Prussia **Obverse:** Laureate head right **Reverse:** "D. 20 AUGUST" above crowned eagle **Note:** Prev. C#24a.

Date	Mintage	VG	F	VF	XF	Unc
1781B Rare	—	—	—	—	—	—

KM# 747 6 KREUZER

Silver **Ruler:** Josef I **Mint:** Brieg **Obverse:** Bust right, value below **Obv. Legend:** IOSEPHUS • D G: R: I: S: A: H: BO: REX **Reverse:** Crowned imperial double eagle with crowned arms on breast, circle surrounds **Rev. Legend:** ARCHID • AUS • DUX • BUR • SIL • ET • **Note:** Prev. Austria KM#187 (KM#1490).

Date	Mintage	VG	F	VF	XF	Unc
1707 CB	—	17.50	35.00	75.00	150	—
1708 CB	—	17.50	35.00	75.00	150	—
1709 CB	—	17.50	35.00	75.00	150	—

KM# 768 6 KREUZER

Silver **Ruler:** Karl VI **Mint:** Breslau **Obverse:** Laureate bust right in inner circle, value below **Reverse:** Crowned imperial eagle in inner circle, crown divides date **Note:** Varieties exist. Prev. Austria KM#146 (KM#1521).

Date	Mintage	VG	F	VF	XF	Unc
1712 FN	—	20.00	40.00	80.00	175	—

KM# 780 6 KREUZER

Silver **Ruler:** Karl VI **Mint:** Breslau **Obverse:** Bust right **Obv. Legend:** CAROL • VI • D • G • R • I • S • ... **Reverse:** Crowned imperial double eagle with arms on breast, date in legend **Note:** Varieties exist. Prev. Austria KM#147 (KM#1542).

Date	Mintage	VG	F	VF	XF	Unc
1713	—	10.00	20.00	45.00	90.00	—
1714	—	10.00	20.00	45.00	90.00	—
1715	—	10.00	20.00	45.00	90.00	—
1738	—	—	—	—	—	—
Note: Reported, not confirmed						
1739	—	—	—	—	—	—
Note: Reported, not confirmed						

KM# 798 6 KREUZER

Silver **Ruler:** Karl VI **Mint:** Breslau **Obverse:** Without inner circle **Reverse:** Without inner circle **Note:** Varieties exist. Prev. Austria KM#148 (KM#1575).

Date	Mintage	VG	F	VF	XF	Unc
1715	—	10.00	20.00	45.00	90.00	—

KM# 894.1 6 KREUZER

Billon **Ruler:** Friedrich II, King of Prussia **Obverse:** Bust right **Obv. Legend:** FRIDERICVS • D • G • REX • BORVSSORVM • **Reverse:** Crowned eagle in crowned cartouche, value, date **Note:** Prev. C#26.1.

Date	Mintage	VG	F	VF	XF	Unc
1743 AE-W	—	60.00	100	180	275	—
1743	—	60.00	100	180	275	—
1743 W	—	60.00	100	180	275	—
1744 AE-W	—	60.00	100	180	275	—
1744	—	60.00	100	180	275	—

KM# 894.2 6 KREUZER

Billon **Ruler:** Friedrich II, King of Prussia **Obverse:** Value: VI below bust right **Obv. Legend:** FRIDERICUS • D • G • REX • BORUSSORUM **Reverse:** Crowned eagle arms in cartouche **Note:** Prev. C#26.2.

Date	Mintage	VG	F	VF	XF	Unc
1745 AE-W	—	45.00	80.00	150	250	—
1746 AE-W	—	45.00	80.00	150	250	—
1747 AE-W	—	45.00	80.00	150	250	—

KM# 978 6 KREUZER

Billon **Ruler:** Friedrich II, King of Prussia **Obverse:** Crowned bust right **Reverse:** Crowned round arms **Note:** Prev. C#27.

Date	Mintage	VG	F	VF	XF	Unc
1755B	—	15.00	30.00	60.00	110	—
1756B	—	15.00	30.00	60.00	110	—

KM# 981 6 KREUZER

Billon **Ruler:** Friedrich II, King of Prussia **Obverse:** Armored bust right **Obv. Legend:** FRIDERICVS BORVSSOR: REX **Reverse:** Crown above value dividing shields **Note:** Prev. C#28.

Date	Mintage	VG	F	VF	XF	Unc
1755B	—	8.00	16.00	30.00	65.00	—
1756B	—	8.00	16.00	30.00	65.00	—
1757B	—	8.00	16.00	30.00	65.00	—

KM# 885 15 KREUZER

Silver **Ruler:** Karl VI **Mint:** Breslau **Obverse:** Draped bust right **Obv. Legend:** CAR • VI • D • G • R • I • S • A • GE • HI • HU • BO • REX • **Reverse:** Crowned imperial double eagle with arms on breast **Rev. Legend:** ARCHID • AVST • DVX • BVRG •... **Note:** Varieties exist. Prev. Austria KM#149 (KM#1652).

Date	Mintage	VG	F	VF	XF	Unc
1733	—	15.00	30.00	60.00	125	—
1734	—	15.00	30.00	60.00	125	—
1735	—	15.00	30.00	60.00	125	—
1736	—	15.00	30.00	60.00	125	—
1737	—	15.00	30.00	60.00	125	—
1738	—	15.00	30.00	60.00	125	—

KM# 897 15 KREUZER

Silver **Ruler:** Friedrich II, King of Prussia **Obverse:** Armored bust right **Obv. Legend:** FRIDERICUS • D • G • REX • BORUSS • **Reverse:** Crowned eagle arms within cartouche and branches **Note:** Varieties exist. Prev. C#30.

Date	Mintage	VG	F	VF	XF	Unc
1743 W	—	175	225	400	750	—
1744 D-AE-W	—	175	225	400	750	—
1745 AE-W	—	175	225	400	750	—
1746 AE-W	—	175	225	400	750	—

KM# 969.1 18 KREUZER

Silver **Ruler:** Friedrich II, King of Prussia **Obverse:** Bust right **Obv. Legend:** FRIDERICVS BORVSSORVM REX **Reverse:** Imperial eagle, tail divides value **Rev. Legend:** MONETA AR = - GENETA • 1753 **Note:** Prev. C#32.1.

Date	Mintage	VG	F	VF	XF	Unc
1752B	—	25.00	45.00	85.00	160	—
1753B	—	25.00	45.00	85.00	160	—
1754B	2,901,000	25.00	45.00	85.00	160	—

KM# 969.2 18 KREUZER

Silver **Ruler:** Friedrich II, King of Prussia **Obverse:** Crowned bust holds sword **Reverse:** Imperial eagle, tail divides value **Note:** Prev. C#32.2.

Date	Mintage	VG	F	VF	XF	Unc
1755B	—	25.00	45.00	85.00	160	—
1756B	—	25.00	45.00	85.00	160	—
1757B	—	25.00	45.00	85.00	160	—
1758B	—	25.00	45.00	85.00	160	—

KM# 990 18 KREUZER

Silver **Ruler:** Friedrich II, King of Prussia **Obverse:** Crowned bust right **Reverse:** Round arms **Note:** Similar to 6 Kreuzer, KM#978. Prev. C#33.

Date	Mintage	VG	F	VF	XF	Unc
1755B	—	60.00	100	180	275	—
1756B	—	60.00	100	180	275	—

KM# 969.3 18 KREUZER

Silver **Ruler:** Friedrich II, King of Prussia **Obverse:** Larger head **Reverse:** Different eagle **Note:** Prev. C#32.3.

Date	Mintage	VG	F	VF	XF	Unc
1755G	—	25.00	45.00	85.00	150	—

KM# 969.4 18 KREUZER

Silver **Ruler:** Friedrich II, King of Prussia **Obverse:** Bust right **Reverse:** Stars flank mint mark **Note:** Prev. C#32.4.

Date	Mintage	VG	F	VF	XF	Unc
1758A	—	25.00	45.00	85.00	150	—

KM# 972 GROSCHEL

Billon **Ruler:** Friedrich II, King of Prussia **Obverse:** Crowned monogram, date below **Reverse:** Imperial eagle with value **Note:** Prev. C#3.

Date	Mintage	VG	F	VF	XF	Unc
1752B	12,102,000	10.00	20.00	40.00	65.00	—
1753B	Inc. above	10.00	20.00	40.00	65.00	—
1754B	3,244,000	10.00	20.00	40.00	65.00	—
1755B	—	10.00	20.00	40.00	65.00	—
1756B	—	10.00	20.00	40.00	65.00	—
1757B	—	10.00	20.00	40.00	65.00	—

KM# 1014 GROSCHEL

Billon **Ruler:** Friedrich II, King of Prussia **Obverse:** Crowned block FR monogram divides date **Reverse:** Value, "B" in branches below **Note:** Prev. C#5.

Date	Mintage	VG	F	VF	XF	Unc
1769B	358,000	7.00	15.00	30.00	55.00	—

KM# 1014a GROSCHEL

Billon **Ruler:** Friedrich II, King of Prussia **Obverse:** Crowned script FR monogram divides date **Reverse:** Value, "B" in branches below **Note:** Prev. C#5a.

Date	Mintage	VG	F	VF	XF	Unc
1769B	Inc. above	6.00	12.00	25.00	45.00	—
1770B	—	6.00	12.00	25.00	45.00	—

KM# 1014b GROSCHEL

Billon **Ruler:** Friedrich II, King of Prussia **Obverse:** Crowned script FR monogram **Reverse:** Value above date **Note:** Prev. C#5b.

Date	Mintage	VG	F	VF	XF	Unc
1771B	—	5.00	10.00	20.00	40.00	—
1772B	—	5.00	10.00	20.00	40.00	—
1773B	—	5.00	10.00	20.00	40.00	—
1774B	—	5.00	10.00	20.00	40.00	—
1775B	—	5.00	10.00	20.00	40.00	—
1776B	—	5.00	10.00	20.00	40.00	—
1777B	—	5.00	10.00	20.00	40.00	—
1778B	—	5.00	10.00	20.00	40.00	—
1779B	—	5.00	10.00	20.00	40.00	—
1780B	—	5.00	10.00	20.00	40.00	—
1781B	—	5.00	10.00	20.00	40.00	—
1782B	—	5.00	10.00	20.00	40.00	—
1783B	—	5.00	10.00	20.00	40.00	—
1784B	—	5.00	10.00	20.00	40.00	—
1785B	—	5.00	10.00	20.00	40.00	—
1786B	—	5.00	10.00	20.00	40.00	—

KM# 1050 GROSCHEL

Billon **Ruler:** Friedrich Wilhelm II **Obverse:** Crowned FW monogram **Reverse:** Value and date **Note:** Prev. C#49.

Date	Mintage	VG	F	VF	XF	Unc
1787B	—	10.00	20.00	40.00	75.00	—
1788B	—	10.00	20.00	40.00	75.00	—
1789B	—	10.00	20.00	40.00	75.00	—
1790B	—	10.00	20.00	40.00	75.00	—
1791B	—	10.00	20.00	40.00	75.00	—
1792B	—	10.00	20.00	40.00	75.00	—
1793B	—	10.00	20.00	40.00	75.00	—
1794B	—	10.00	20.00	40.00	75.00	—
1795B	—	10.00	20.00	40.00	75.00	—
1796B	—	10.00	20.00	40.00	75.00	—
1797B	—	10.00	20.00	40.00	75.00	—

KM# 1050a GROSCHEL

Billon **Ruler:** Friedrich Wilhelm II **Obverse:** Crowned monogram **Reverse:** Value: GROSCHEL **Note:** Prev. C#49a.

Date	Mintage	VG	F	VF	XF	Unc
1797B	—	—	—	—	—	—

KM# 1059 GROSCHEL

Billon **Ruler:** Friedrich Wilhelm III **Obverse:** Crowned FWR monogram **Reverse:** Value **Note:** Prev. C#56.

Date	Mintage	F	VF	XF	Unc
1797B	—	20.00	40.00	75.00	150

KM# 921.1 2 GROSCHEL

Billon **Ruler:** Friedrich II, King of Prussia **Obverse:** Head right **Reverse:** Imperial eagle above value and date **Note:** Prev. C#14.1.

Date	Mintage	VG	F	VF	XF	Unc
1745 AE	—	8.00	16.00	32.00	65.00	—
1746 AE	—	8.00	16.00	32.00	65.00	—
1747 AE	—	8.00	16.00	32.00	65.00	—
1748 AE	3,000,000	8.00	16.00	32.00	65.00	—
1749 AE	6,000,000	8.00	16.00	32.00	65.00	—
1750 AE	6,000,000	8.00	16.00	32.00	65.00	—

KM# 918 2 GROSCHEL

Billon **Ruler:** Friedrich II, King of Prussia **Obverse:** Head right **Reverse:** Imperial eagle above value, date **Note:** Similar to KM#921.1 but value: GRESCHEL. Prev. C#13.

Date	Mintage	VG	F	VF	XF	Unc
1745 AE	—	10.00	20.00	40.00	75.00	—

KM# 921.2 2 GROSCHEL

Billon **Ruler:** Friedrich II, King of Prussia **Obverse:** Head right **Reverse:** Imperial eagle above value and date **Note:** Similar to KM921.1. Prev. C#14.2. Varieties exist.

Date	Mintage	VG	F	VF	XF	Unc
1751B	—	8.00	16.00	32.00	65.00	—
1752B	—	8.00	16.00	32.00	65.00	—
1753B	—	8.00	16.00	32.00	65.00	—
1754B	1,478,000	8.00	16.00	32.00	65.00	—

KM# 1029 2 GROSCHEL

Billon **Ruler:** Friedrich II, King of Prussia **Obverse:** Laureate head right **Reverse:** B below date **Note:** Prev. C#15.

Date	Mintage	VG	F	VF	XF	Unc
1771B	—	6.00	12.00	25.00	50.00	—
1772B	—	6.00	12.00	25.00	50.00	—
1773B	—	6.00	12.00	25.00	50.00	—
1774B	—	6.00	12.00	25.00	50.00	—
1775B	—	6.00	12.00	25.00	50.00	—
1776B	—	6.00	12.00	25.00	50.00	—
1777B	—	6.00	12.00	25.00	50.00	—
1778B	—	6.00	12.00	25.00	50.00	—
1779B	—	6.00	12.00	25.00	50.00	—
1780B	—	6.00	12.00	25.00	50.00	—
1781B	—	6.00	12.00	25.00	50.00	—
1782B	—	6.00	12.00	25.00	50.00	—
1783B	—	6.00	12.00	25.00	50.00	—
1784B	—	6.00	12.00	25.00	50.00	—
1785B	—	6.00	12.00	25.00	50.00	—
1786B	—	6.00	12.00	25.00	50.00	—

KM# 903 POLTURA

Billon **Ruler:** Friedrich II, King of Prussia **Obverse:** Bust right **Reverse:** Imperial eagle, value, date **Note:** Prev. C#12.

Date	Mintage	VG	F	VF	XF	Unc
1744 AE	—	45.00	80.00	155	260	—

KM# 477 1/2 THALER

Silver **Ruler:** Leopold I **Mint:** Breslau **Obverse:** Laureate bust **Reverse:** Crowned imperial eagle in inner circle, crown divides date **Note:** Varieties exist. Prev. Austria KM#89 (KM#1236).

Date	Mintage	VG	F	VF	XF	Unc
1705 FN	—	100	200	325	475	—

KM# 615 1/2 THALER

Silver **Ruler:** Leopold I **Mint:** Brieg **Obverse:** Laureate bust right in inner circle **Reverse:** Crowned imperial eagle in inner circle, crown divides date **Note:** Prev. Austria KM#176 (KM#1384).

Date	Mintage	VG	F	VF	XF	Unc
1705 CB	—	150	300	500	750	—

KM# 699 1/2 THALER

Silver **Ruler:** Josef I **Mint:** Brieg **Obverse:** Laureate armored bust right **Obv. Legend:** IOSEPHVS • DG • RO • IMP • S • A • G • E • H • B • REX • **Reverse:** Crowned imperial double eagle with arms on breast **Rev. Legend:** ARCHIDVX • AVST... **Note:** Prev. Austria KM#188 (KM#1432).

Date	Mintage	VG	F	VF	XF	Unc
1705 CB	—	150	300	500	700	—
1706 CB	—	150	300	500	700	—

KM# 696 1/2 THALER

Silver **Ruler:** Josef I **Mint:** Breslau **Note:** Similar to 1 Thaler, KM#1434.1. Prev. Austria KM#123 (KM#1431).

Date	Mintage	VG	F	VF	XF	Unc
1705 FN	—	100	200	300	500	—
1706 FN	—	100	200	300	500	—
1711 FN	—	100	200	300	500	—

KM# 783 1/2 THALER

Silver **Ruler:** Karl VI **Mint:** Breslau **Obverse:** Laureate bust right in inner circle **Reverse:** Crowned imperial eagle, date in legend **Note:** Prev. Austria KM#150 (KM#1545).

Date	Mintage	VG	F	VF	XF	Unc
1713	—	75.00	150	250	425	—
1714	—	—	—	—	—	—
Note: Reported, not confirmed						
1715	—	75.00	150	250	425	—
1717	—	75.00	150	250	425	—
1723	—	75.00	150	250	425	—
1726	—	75.00	150	250	425	—
1727	—	75.00	150	250	425	—
1728	—	75.00	150	250	425	—

KM# 870 1/2 THALER

Silver **Ruler:** Karl VI **Mint:** Breslau **Obverse:** Large laureate bust **Note:** Varieties exist. Prev. Austria KM#151 (KM#1628).

Date	Mintage	VG	F	VF	XF	Unc
1729	—	75.00	150	250	425	—
1730	—	75.00	150	250	425	—
1731	—	75.00	150	250	425	—
1736	—	75.00	150	250	425	—
1739	—	75.00	150	250	425	—

KM# 621.2 THALER

Silver **Ruler:** Leopold I **Mint:** Brieg **Obverse:** Laureate bust right in inner circle **Obv. Legend:** LEOPOLDUS. DG: ROM: IMPERATOR ... **Note:** Dav.#3305. Prev. KM#177.2 (1386.2).

Date	Mintage	VG	F	VF	XF	Unc
1705 CB	—	200	375	600	900	—

KM# 651.1 THALER

Silver **Ruler:** Leopold I **Mint:** Oppeln **Obverse:** Laureate armored bust right **Obv. Legend:** LEOPOLDUS • D • G • ROM: IMP: SEM: AVG: GER: HU: BO: REX • **Reverse:** Crowned imperial eagle with arms on breast **Rev. Legend:** ARCHIDUX • AVSTRIAE DUX • BVRG •... **Note:** Dav. #3303. Prev. Austria KM#1284.1 (KM#1398.1).

Date	Mintage	VG	F	VF	XF	Unc
1701 FN	—	200	375	550	850	—
1701 H/FN	—	200	375	550	850	—
1702 H/FN	—	200	375	550	850	—

KM# 651.2 THALER

Silver **Ruler:** Leopold I **Mint:** Oppeln **Obverse:** Laureate armored bust right **Reverse:** Imperial eagle without halos on head **Note:** Dav. #1010. Varieties exist. Prev. Austria KM#1284.2 (KM#1398.2).

Date	Mintage	VG	F	VF	XF	Unc
1703 FN	—	200	375	550	850	—

KM# 483.15 THALER

Silver **Ruler:** Leopold I **Mint:** Breslau **Obverse:** Bust right in inner circle **Obv. Legend:** LEOPOLDVS... SEM: AVG: GER: HU: BO: REX... **Reverse:** FN in different cartouche **Rev. Legend:** ...BVRG. ET. SILESIAE **Note:** Dav. #1010. Prev. Austria KM#94.15 (KM#1224.15).

Date	Mintage	VG	F	VF	XF	Unc
1704 FN	—	100	200	350	600	—

KM# 705 THALER

Silver **Ruler:** Josef I **Mint:** Brieg **Obverse:** Laureate bust right **Reverse:** Crowned imperial eagle **Note:** Similar to 1/2 Thaler, KM#1432. Dav. #1032. Prev. Austria KM#189 (KM#1436).

Date	Mintage	VG	F	VF	XF	Unc
1705 CB	—	175	350	575	850	—
1706 CB	—	—	—	—	—	—

Note: Reported, not confirmed

KM# 483.16 THALER

Silver **Ruler:** Leopold I **Mint:** Breslau **Obverse:** Armored bust right **Obv. Legend:** LEOPOLDVS • DG • ROM: IMP: SEM: AVG: GER: HV: BO: REX • **Reverse:** Halos on eagle's head **Rev. Legend:** ARCHIDUX • AUSTRIAE • DUX • BVRG • ET • SILESIAE • **Note:** Varieties exist. Dav. #1010. Prev. Austria KM#94.16 (KM#1224.16).

Date	Mintage	VG	F	VF	XF	Unc
1705 FN	—	70.00	125	250	400	—

KM# 717.1 THALER

Silver **Ruler:** Josef I **Mint:** Breslau **Obverse:** Bust right **Obv. Legend:** IOSEPHUS. DG. ROMA: IMPERATOR: SEM. AV. GE. HV. BO. REX. **Rev. Legend:** AUSTRIAE - DUX. BURG. ET. SILESIAE. **Note:** Dav. #1028. Prev. Austria KM#124.1 (KM#1434.1).

Date	Mintage	VG	F	VF	XF	Unc
1706 FN	—	150	300	500	800	—

KM# 717.2 THALER

Silver **Ruler:** Josef I **Mint:** Breslau **Obverse:** Armored bust right **Obv. Legend:** IOSEPHUS • DG • ROM • IMP • SEM • AUG • GER • HV • BO • REX • **Reverse:** Eagle with two-part arms on breast **Rev. Legend:** ARCHIDUX • AUSTRIÆ DUX • BVRG • ET SILESIÆ • **Note:** Varieties of bust exist. Dav. #1029. Prev. Austria KM#124.2 (KM#1434.2).

Date	Mintage	VG	F	VF	XF	Unc
1707 FN	—	120	225	400	700	—
1708 FN	—	120	225	400	700	—

KM# 717.3 THALER

Silver **Ruler:** Josef I **Mint:** Breslau **Obverse:** Armored bust right **Obv. Legend:** ... AU - GE. H. B. REX. **Reverse:** Legend ends; BURGU: & SILESIAE **Note:** Dav. #1030. Prev. Austria KM#124.3 (KM#1434.3).

Date	Mintage	VG	F	VF	XF	Unc
1709 GH/FN	—	120	225	400	700	—

KM# 717.4 THALER

Silver **Ruler:** Josef I **Mint:** Breslau **Obverse:** Armored bust right **Obv. Legend:** IOSEPHVS • D • G • ROM • IMP • SEM • A • G • H • B • REX • **Reverse:** Crowned imperial double eagle with crowned arms on breast **Rev. Legend:** ARCHIDVX • AVSTRIAE • DVX • BCRGV: ET SILESIA **Note:** Varieties exist. Dav. #1031. Prev. Austria KM#124.4 (KM#1434.4).

Date	Mintage	VG	F	VF	XF	Unc
1710 FN	—	200	400	750	1,250	—
1711 FN	—	200	400	750	1,250	—

KM# 786.1 THALER

Silver **Ruler:** Karl VI **Mint:** Breslau **Obverse:** Legend begins at one o'clock **Obv. Legend:** CAROL • VI: D: G: RO: IMP: S: A: GE: HIS: HU: BO • REX • **Reverse:** Crowned imperial eagle in circle **Rev. Legend:** ARCHIDVX • AVSTRIÆ • DVX • BVR •&• SIL • **Note:** Dav. #1089. Prev. Austria KM#152.1 (KM#1549.1).

Date	Mintage	VG	F	VF	XF	Unc
1713	—	60.00	125	250	450	—
1714/3	—	60.00	125	250	450	—

KM# 789 THALER

Silver **Ruler:** Karl VI **Mint:** Brieg **Obverse:** Laureate bust right in inner circle **Reverse:** Crowned imperial eagle in inner circle, crown divides date, crossed pickaxes below **Note:** Dav. #1099. Prev. Austria KM#197 (KM#1550).

Date	Mintage	VG	F	VF	XF	Unc
1713 CB Rare	—	—	—	—	—	—

KM# 786.2 THALER

Silver **Ruler:** Karl VI **Mint:** Breslau **Reverse:** Larger inner circle **Note:** Dav. #1090. Varieties exist. Prev. Austria KM#152.2 (KM#1549.2).

Date	Mintage	VG	F	VF	XF	Unc
1714	—	60.00	125	250	450	—

KM# 801.1 THALER

Silver **Ruler:** Karl VI **Mint:** Breslau **Obverse:** Laureate armored bust right **Reverse:** Without inner circle **Note:** Dav. #1091. Prev. Austria KM#153.1 (KM#1578.1).

Date	Mintage	VG	F	VF	XF	Unc
1715	—	60.00	125	250	450	—

KM# 801.2 THALER

Silver **Ruler:** Karl VI **Mint:** Breslau **Obverse:** Legend begins at nine o'clock **Obv. Legend:** CAROL • VI • D: G • R • I • S • A • G • HI • H • B • REX • **Reverse:** Crowned imperial double eagle with arms on breast **Rev. Legend:** ARCHIDVX • AVSTRIÆ • DVX • BVR •&• SILE • **Note:** Dav. #1092. Varieties exist. Prev. Austria KM#153.2 (KM#1578.2).

Date	Mintage	VG	F	VF	XF	Unc
1716	—	60.00	125	250	450	—
1717	—	60.00	125	250	450	—

KM# 801.3 THALER

Silver **Ruler:** Karl VI **Mint:** Breslau **Obverse:** Laureate armored bust right **Reverse:** Eagle with small tail and arms **Note:** Dav. #1093. Varieties exist. Prev. Austria KM#153.3 (KM#1578.3).

Date	Mintage	VG	F	VF	XF	Unc
1717	—	60.00	125	250	450	—
1718	—	60.00	125	250	450	—

KM# 819.1 THALER

Silver **Ruler:** Karl VI **Mint:** Breslau **Obverse:** New draped bust, legend divided after "D: G. R. I." **Reverse:** Large tail and arms on eagle **Note:** Dav. #1092. Prev. Austria KM#154.1 (KM#1592.1).

Date	Mintage	VG	F	VF	XF	Unc
1718	—	60.00	125	250	450	—

KM# 819.2 THALER

Silver **Ruler:** Karl VI **Mint:** Breslau **Obverse:** Legend divided between "D: G: and R.I..." **Reverse:** Crowned imperial double eagle with crowned arms on breast **Note:** Dav. #1096. Varieties exist. Prev. Austria KM#154.2 (KM#1592.2).

Date	Mintage	VG	F	VF	XF	Unc
1719	—	60.00	125	250	450	—
1720	—	60.00	125	250	450	—
1721	—	60.00	125	250	450	—
1722	—	60.00	125	250	450	—

KM# 819.3 THALER

Silver **Ruler:** Karl VI **Mint:** Breslau **Obverse:** Armored bust right **Obv. Legend:** CAROL • VI • D • G • R • I • S • A • GE • HI • HU • BO • REX • **Reverse:** Crowned imperial double eagle with crowned arms on breast **Rev. Legend:** ARCHID • AUST • DUX • BUR & SILESIÆ • **Note:** Dav. #1098. Varieties exist. Prev. Austria KM#154.3 (KM#1592.3).

Date	Mintage	VG	F	VF	XF	Unc
1723	—	60.00	125	250	450	—
1724	—	60.00	125	250	450	—
1725	—	60.00	125	250	450	—
1727	—	60.00	125	250	450	—
1728	—	60.00	125	250	450	—
1729	—	60.00	125	250	450	—
1730	—	60.00	125	250	450	—
1731	—	60.00	125	250	450	—
1732	—	60.00	125	250	450	—
1736	—	60.00	125	250	450	—
1738	—	60.00	125	250	450	—
1739	—	60.00	125	250	450	—
1740	—	60.00	125	250	450	—

KM# 834.1 2 THALER

Silver **Ruler:** Karl VI **Mint:** Breslau **Note:** Similar to 1 Thaler, KM#1578.2 Dav. #1095. Prev. Austria KM#155.1 (KM#1608.1).

Date	Mintage	VG	F	VF	XF	Unc
1722 Rare	—	—	—	—	—	—

KM# 834.2 2 THALER

Silver **Ruler:** Karl VI **Mint:** Breslau **Note:** Similar to 1 Thaler, KM#1578.2. Dav. #1097. Varieties exist. Prev. Austria KM#155.2 (KM#1608.2).

Date	Mintage	VG	F	VF	XF	Unc
1723 Rare	—	—	—	—	—	—
1725 Rare	—	—	—	—	—	—
1732 Rare	—	—	—	—	—	—

KM# 837 3 THALER

Silver **Ruler:** Karl VI **Mint:** Breslau **Obverse:** Bust right **Reverse:** Heraldic imperial eagle **Note:** Prev. Austria KM#156 (KM#1609).

Date	Mintage	VG	F	VF	XF	Unc
1722 Rare	—	—	—	—	—	—

KM# 846 3 THALER

Silver **Ruler:** Karl VI **Mint:** Breslau **Reverse:** More ornate shield on eagle **Note:** Prev. Austria KM#157 (KM#1611).

Date	Mintage	VG	F	VF	XF	Unc
1723 Rare	—	—	—	—	—	—
1725 Rare	—	—	—	—	—	—
1732 Rare	—	—	—	—	—	—

TRADE COINAGE

KM# 720 1/8 DUCAT

0.4375 g., 0.9860 Gold 0.0139 oz. AGW **Ruler:** Josef I **Mint:** Breslau **Obverse:** Large crown divides date above two shields ornamentation; value below **Note:** Prev. Austria KM#126 (KM#1465).

Date	Mintage	VG	F	VF	XF	Unc
1706	—	80.00	160	325	700	—
1707	—	80.00	160	325	700	—
1708	—	80.00	160	325	700	—
1710	—	80.00	160	325	700	—

KM# 723 1/8 DUCAT

0.4375 g., 0.9860 Gold 0.0139 oz. AGW **Ruler:** Josef I **Mint:** Breslau **Obverse:** Bust right **Reverse:** Crowned imperial eagle **Note:** Prev. Austria KM#127 (KM#1466).

Date	Mintage	VG	F	VF	XF	Unc
1706	—	70.00	140	250	600	—
1708	—	70.00	140	250	600	—
1709	—	70.00	140	250	600	—
1711	—	70.00	140	250	600	—

KM# 726 1/6 DUCAT

0.5834 g., 0.9860 Gold 0.0185 oz. AGW **Ruler:** Josef I **Mint:** Breslau **Obverse:** Laureate bust right, value at shoulder **Reverse:** Crowned imperial eagle in inner circle **Note:** Prev. Austria KM#128 (KM#1467).

Date	Mintage	VG	F	VF	XF	Unc
1706	—	75.00	150	275	500	—
1707	—	75.00	150	275	500	—
1709	—	75.00	150	275	500	—
1710	—	75.00	150	275	500	—
1711	—	75.00	150	275	500	—

KM# 879 1/6 DUCAT

0.5834 g., 0.9860 Gold 0.0185 oz. AGW, 0.0184 mm. **Ruler:** Karl VI **Mint:** Breslau **Obverse:** Laureate bust right, value at shoulder **Reverse:** Crowned imperial eagle in inner circle **Note:** Prev. Austria KM#158 (KM#1644).

Date	Mintage	VG	F	VF	XF	Unc
1731	—	70.00	140	275	500	—

KM# 597 1/4 DUCAT

0.8750 g., 0.9860 Gold 0.0277 oz. AGW **Ruler:** Leopold I **Mint:** Breslau **Obverse:** Laureate bust right in inner circle, value at shoulder **Reverse:** Crowned imperial eagle without inner circle **Note:** Prev. Austria KM#104 (KM#1369).

Date	Mintage	VG	F	VF	XF	Unc
1705	—	80.00	200	350	750	—

KM# 729 1/4 DUCAT

0.8750 g., 0.9860 Gold 0.0277 oz. AGW **Ruler:** Josef I **Mint:** Breslau **Obverse:** Laureate head right, value at shoulder **Reverse:** Crowned imperial eagle **Note:** Prev. Austria KM#129 (KM#1468).

Date	Mintage	VG	F	VF	XF	Unc
1706	—	80.00	160	300	750	—
1707	—	80.00	160	300	750	—
1708	—	80.00	160	300	750	—
1709	—	80.00	160	300	750	—
1710	—	80.00	160	300	750	—

KM# 825 1/4 DUCAT

0.8750 g., 0.9860 Gold 0.0277 oz. AGW **Ruler:** Karl VI **Mint:** Breslau **Obverse:** Laureate bust right **Reverse:** Crowned imperial eagle **Note:** Prev. Austria KM#159 (KM#1596).

Date	Mintage	VG	F	VF	XF	Unc
1719	—	70.00	140	275	650	—
1725	—	70.00	140	275	650	—
1731	—	70.00	140	275	650	—
1738	—	70.00	140	275	650	—

KM# 732 1/3 DUCAT

1.1667 g., 0.9860 Gold 0.0370 oz. AGW **Ruler:** Josef I **Mint:** Breslau **Obverse:** Laureate bust right in inner circle, value at shoulder **Reverse:** Crowned imperial eagle in inner circle **Note:** Prev. Austria KM#130 (KM#1469).

Date	Mintage	VG	F	VF	XF	Unc
1706	—	100	175	325	800	—

KM# 708 1/2 DUCAT

0.2916 g., 0.9860 Gold 0.0092 oz. AGW **Ruler:** Josef I **Mint:** Breslau **Obverse:** Laureate bust right, value at shoulder **Reverse:** Crowned imperial eagle **Note:** Prev. Austria KM#125 (KM#1448).

Date	Mintage	VG	F	VF	XF	Unc
1705	—	65.00	140	250	525	—
1706	—	65.00	140	250	525	—
1707	—	65.00	140	250	525	—
1709	—	65.00	140	250	525	—
1710	—	65.00	140	250	525	—
1711	—	65.00	140	250	525	—

KM# 735 1/2 DUCAT

1.7500 g., 0.9860 Gold 0.0555 oz. AGW **Ruler:** Josef I **Mint:** Breslau **Obverse:** Laureate bust right **Reverse:** Crowned imperial eagle **Note:** Prev. Austria KM#131 (KM#1470).

Date	Mintage	VG	F	VF	XF	Unc
1706 FN	—	125	225	400	800	—
1707 FN	—	125	225	400	800	—
1709 FN	—	125	225	400	800	—
1710 FN	—	125	225	400	800	—
1711 FN	—	125	225	400	800	—

KM# 588 DUCAT

3.5000 g., 0.9860 Gold 0.1109 oz. AGW **Ruler:** Leopold I **Mint:** Breslau **Obverse:** Fuller laureate bust right in inner circle **Reverse:** Crowned imperial eagle, crown divides date **Note:** Prev. Austria KM#111 (KM#1358).

Date	Mintage	VG	F	VF	XF	Unc
1705 FN	—	125	325	675	1,250	—

KM# 636 DUCAT

3.5000 g., 0.9860 Gold 0.1109 oz. AGW **Ruler:** Leopold I **Mint:** Brieg **Obverse:** Smaller bust right in inner circle **Reverse:** Crowned imperial eagle in inner circle, date in legend **Note:** Prev. Austria KM#179 (KM#1393).

Date	Mintage	VG	F	VF	XF	Unc
1702 CB	—	125	325	675	1,400	—
1703 CB	—	125	325	675	1,400	—
1704 CB	—	125	325	675	1,400	—

KM# 714 DUCAT

3.5000 g., 0.9860 Gold 0.1109 oz. AGW **Ruler:** Josef I **Mint:** Brieg **Note:** Prev. Austria KM#190 (KM#1451).

Date	Mintage	VG	F	VF	XF	Unc
1705 CB	—	250	600	1,200	2,500	—

KM# 711 DUCAT

3.5000 g., 0.9860 Gold 0.1109 oz. AGW **Ruler:** Josef I **Mint:** Breslau **Obverse:** Laureate bust right in inner circle **Reverse:** Crowned imperial eagle in inner circle, crown divides date **Note:** Prev. Austria KM#132 (KM#1449).

Date	Mintage	VG	F	VF	XF	Unc
1705	—	160	375	800	1,750	—
1706 FN	—	160	375	800	1,750	—
1707 FN	—	160	375	800	1,750	—
1708 FN	—	160	375	800	1,750	—
1709 FN	—	160	375	800	1,750	—
1710 FN	—	160	375	800	1,750	—
1711 FN	—	160	375	800	1,750	—

KM# 771 DUCAT

3.5000 g., 0.9860 Gold 0.1109 oz. AGW **Ruler:** Karl VI **Mint:** Breslau **Obverse:** Young laureate armored bust right in inner circle **Reverse:** Crowned imperial eagle in inner circle, crown divides date **Note:** Prev. Austria KM#160 (KM#1525).

Date	Mintage	VG	F	VF	XF	Unc
1712 FN	—	120	225	475	900	—
1713	—	120	225	475	900	—

KM# 813 DUCAT

3.5000 g., 0.9860 Gold 0.1109 oz. AGW **Ruler:** Karl VI **Mint:** Breslau **Obverse:** Young laureate armored bust right **Obv. Legend:** CAROLVS • VI • D : G • R • I • S • A • G • HI • H • B R • **Reverse:** Crowned imperial eagle, crown divides date **Rev. Legend:** : ARCHIDVX • AVSTR • DVX • BVR • &• SIL : 1717 **Note:** Prev. Austria KM#161 (KM#1589).

Date	Mintage	VG	F	VF	XF	Unc
1717	—	120	225	475	900	—
1718	—	120	225	475	900	—
1719	—	120	225	475	900	—
1720	—	120	225	475	900	—
1721	—	160	325	800	1,500	—
1722	—	120	225	475	900	—
1723	—	120	225	475	900	—
1724	—	120	225	475	900	—

KM# 858 DUCAT

3.5000 g., 0.9860 Gold 0.1109 oz. AGW **Ruler:** Karl VI **Mint:** Breslau **Obverse:** Older laureate bust right **Obv. Legend:** CAR • IV • D • G • R • I • S • A • GE • HI • H • B • REX • **Reverse:** Crowned imperial double eagle **Rev. Legend:** ARCHID • AUST • DUX • BU • COM • TYROL • **Note:** Prev. Austria KM#162 (KM#1619).

Date	Mintage	VG	F	VF	XF	Unc
1726	—	120	225	475	900	—
1727	—	120	225	475	900	—
1728	—	120	225	475	900	—
1729	—	120	225	475	900	—
1730	—	120	225	475	900	—
1731	—	120	225	475	900	—
1732	—	120	225	475	900	—
1733	—	120	225	475	900	—
1734	—	120	225	475	900	—
1735	—	120	225	475	900	—
1736	—	120	225	475	900	—
1737	—	120	225	475	900	—
1738	—	120	225	475	900	—
1739	—	120	225	475	900	—
1740	—	120	225	475	900	—

KM# 900 DUCAT

3.5000 g., 0.9860 Gold 0.1109 oz. AGW **Ruler:** Friedrich II, King of Prussia **Obverse:** Armored bust right **Obv. Legend:** FRIDERICVS • D • G • REX • BORVSSORVM **Reverse:** Crowned oval arms in cartouche and branches, crown divides date **Note:** Prev. C#36.

Date	Mintage	VG	F	VF	XF	Unc
1743W	3,220	500	900	1,650	2,500	—

KM# 900a DUCAT

3.5000 g., 0.9860 Gold 0.1109 oz. AGW **Ruler:** Friedrich II, King of Prussia **Obverse:** Armored bust right **Reverse:** AE at bottom **Note:** Prev. C#36a.

Date	Mintage	VG	F	VF	XF	Unc
1744W AE	664	550	950	1,750	2,750	—

KM# 900b DUCAT

3.5000 g., 0.9860 Gold 0.1109 oz. AGW **Ruler:** Friedrich II, King of Prussia **Obverse:** Armored bust right **Reverse:** Smaller crowned arms, date in legend, W and AE below arms **Note:** Prev. C#36b.

Date	Mintage	VG	F	VF	XF	Unc
1745W AE	—	500	900	1,650	2,500	—
1746W AE	—	500	900	1,650	2,500	—
1747W AE	—	500	900	1,650	2,500	—
1748W AE	—	500	900	1,650	2,500	—

KM# 975 DUCAT

3.5000 g., 0.9860 Gold 0.1109 oz. AGW **Ruler:** Friedrich II, King of Prussia **Obverse:** Head right **Obv. Legend:** FRIDERICUS BORUSSORUM REX **Reverse:** Eagle above military trophies, date divided above, value below **Note:** Prev. C#37.

Date	Mintage	VG	F	VF	XF	Unc
1754B	—	250	700	1,500	2,250	—
1757B	—	250	700	1,500	2,250	—

KM# 444 2 DUCAT

7.0000 g., 0.9860 Gold 0.2219 oz. AGW **Ruler:** Leopold I **Mint:** Breslau **Obverse:** Crowned bust right in inner circle **Reverse:** Crowned imperial eagle in inner circle, date in legend **Note:** Prev. Austria KM#112 (KM#1189).

Date	Mintage	VG	F	VF	XF	Unc
1705 FN	—	400	850	2,450	6,000	—
1705	—	400	850	2,450	6,000	—

KM# 738 2 DUCAT

7.0000 g., 0.9860 Gold 0.2219 oz. AGW **Ruler:** Josef I **Mint:** Breslau **Obverse:** Large laureate head right in inner circle **Reverse:** Crowned imperial eagle in inner circle, crown divides date **Note:** Prev. Austria KM#133 (KM#1472).

Date	Mintage	VG	F	VF	XF	Unc
1706 FN	—	500	1,000	3,000	7,500	—
1707 FN	—	500	1,000	3,000	7,500	—
1709 FN	—	500	1,000	3,000	7,500	—
1711 FN	—	500	1,000	3,000	7,500	—

KM# 828 2 DUCAT

7.0000 g., 0.9860 Gold 0.2219 oz. AGW **Ruler:** Karl VI **Mint:** Breslau **Obverse:** Laureate bust right **Reverse:** Crowned imperial eagle, date in legend **Note:** Prev. Austria KM#163 (KM#1597).

Date	Mintage	VG	F	VF	XF	Unc
1719	—	550	1,150	3,000	8,000	—

KM# 849 2 DUCAT

7.0000 g., 0.9860 Gold 0.2219 oz. AGW **Ruler:** Karl VI **Mint:** Breslau **Note:** Struck with 1 Ducat dies. Prev. Austria KM#164 (KM#1613).

Date	Mintage	VG	F	VF	XF	Unc
1723	—	550	1,150	3,000	8,000	—

KM# 669 3 DUCAT

10.5000 g., 0.9860 Gold 0.3328 oz. AGW **Ruler:** Leopold I **Mint:** Oppeln **Obverse:** Laureate bust right in inner circle **Reverse:** Crowned imperial eagle in inner circle **Note:** Prev. Austria KM#1290 (KM#1411).

Date	Mintage	VG	F	VF	XF	Unc
1701 FN	—	600	1,200	4,000	8,500	—

KM# 741 3 DUCAT

10.5000 g., 0.9860 Gold 0.3328 oz. AGW **Ruler:** Josef I **Mint:** Breslau **Obverse:** Laureate bust right in inner circle **Reverse:** Crowned imperial eagle in inner circle **Note:** Struck with 1/2 Thaler dies, KM#1431. Prev. Austria KM#134 (KM#1473).

Date	Mintage	VG	F	VF	XF	Unc
1706 FN	—	700	1,450	4,250	9,000	—
1707 FN	—	700	1,450	4,250	9,000	—
1711 FN	—	700	1,450	4,250	9,000	—

KM# 792.1 3 DUCAT

10.5000 g., 0.9860 Gold 0.3328 oz. AGW **Ruler:** Karl VI **Mint:** Breslau **Obverse:** Laureate bust right **Reverse:** Crowned imperial eagle in inner circle **Note:** Prev. Austria KM#165.1 (KM#1560.1).

Date	Mintage	VG	F	VF	XF	Unc
1713	—	600	1,200	4,000	7,250	—
1714	—	600	1,200	4,000	7,250	—

KM# 792.2 3 DUCAT

Gold **Ruler:** Karl VI **Mint:** Breslau **Obverse:** Draped bust right **Obv. Legend:** CAROL • VI • D.G • R • I • S • G • HI • H • B • REX • **Reverse:** Crowned imperial double eagle **Rev. Legend:** ARCHID • AVST • DVX: ... **Note:** Prev. Austria KM#165.2 (KM#1560.2).

Date	Mintage	VG	F	VF	XF	Unc
1723	—	—	—	—	—	—

KM# 855 3 DUCAT

10.5000 g., 0.9860 Gold 0.3328 oz. AGW **Ruler:** Karl VI **Mint:** Breslau **Obverse:** Laureate bust right **Reverse:** Crowned imperial eagle not enclosed in circle **Note:** Struck with 1/2 Thaler dies, KM#1545. Prev. Austria KM#A162 (KM#1614).

Date	Mintage	VG	F	VF	XF	Unc
1723	—	650	1,400	4,200	7,750	—
1723	—	650	1,400	4,200	7,750	—
1726	—	650	1,400	4,200	7,750	—

KM# 873 3 DUCAT

10.5000 g., 0.9860 Gold 0.3328 oz. AGW **Ruler:** Karl VI **Mint:** Breslau **Obverse:** Large laureate bust right **Note:** Struck with 1/2 Thaler dies, KM#1628. Prev. Austria KM#A170 (KM#1640).

Date	Mintage	VG	F	VF	XF	Unc
1730	—	650	1,400	4,200	7,750	—

KM# 861 4 DUCAT

14.0000 g., 0.9860 Gold 0.4438 oz. AGW **Ruler:** Karl VI **Mint:** Breslau **Obverse:** Laureate bust right **Reverse:** Crowned imperial eagle **Note:** Struck with 1/2 Thaler dies, KM#1545. Prev. Austria KM#A168 (KM#1620).

Date	Mintage	VG	F	VF	XF	Unc
1726	—	800	1,650	4,500	8,500	—
1727	—	800	1,650	4,500	8,500	—

KM# 876 4 DUCAT

14.0000 g., 0.9860 Gold 0.4438 oz. AGW **Ruler:** Karl VI **Mint:** Breslau **Obverse:** Large laureate bust right **Note:** Struck with 1/2 Thaler dies, KM#1628. Prev. Austria KM#B170 (KM#1641).

Date	Mintage	VG	F	VF	XF	Unc
1730	—	800	1,650	4,500	8,500	—

KM# 744 5 DUCAT

17.5000 g., 0.9860 Gold 0.5547 oz. AGW **Ruler:** Josef I **Mint:** Breslau **Obverse:** Bust right **Reverse:** Crowned imperial arms **Note:** Struck with 1/2 Thaler dies, KM#1431. Prev. Austria KM#136 (KM#1474).

Date	Mintage	VG	F	VF	XF	Unc
1706 FN	—	1,250	2,750	6,000	11,500	—

KM# 816 5 DUCAT

17.5000 g., 0.9860 Gold 0.5547 oz. AGW **Ruler:** Karl VI **Mint:** Breslau **Obverse:** Laurtea bust right **Reverse:** Crowned imperial arms **Note:** Struck with 1/2 Thaler dies, KM#1545. Prev. Austria KM#B159 (KM#1590).

Date	Mintage	VG	F	VF	XF	Unc
1717	—	1,000	2,000	5,500	9,000	—
1723	—	1,000	2,000	5,500	9,000	—
1728	—	1,000	2,000	5,500	9,000	—

KM# 831 5 DUCAT

17.5000 g., 0.9860 Gold 0.5547 oz. AGW **Ruler:** Karl VI **Mint:** Breslau **Obverse:** Laureate bust right **Obv. Legend:** CAROL: VI: D: G •• R • I • S • A • G • HI • H • B • REX • **Reverse:** Crowned imperial eagle in inner circle **Rev. Legend:** ARCHID • AVST • DVX: :BVR •&• SILESIÆ: **Note:** Struck with 1 Thaler dies, KM#1592.2. Prev. Austria KM#166 (KM#1607).

Date	Mintage	VG	F	VF	XF	Unc
1721	—	1,000	2,000	5,500	9,000	—
1722	—	1,000	2,000	5,500	9,000	—

KM# 882 5 DUCAT

17.5000 g., 0.9860 Gold 0.5547 oz. AGW **Ruler:** Karl VI **Mint:** Breslau **Obverse:** Large laureate bust right **Reverse:** Crowned imperial arms **Note:** Struck with 1 Thaler dies, KM#1592.3. Prev. Austria KM#C170 (KM#1651).

Date	Mintage	VG	F	VF	XF	Unc
1732	—	1,000	2,000	5,500	9,000	—

KM# 867 6 DUCAT

21.0000 g., 0.9860 Gold 0.6657 oz. AGW **Ruler:** Karl VI **Mint:** Breslau **Obverse:** Laureate bust right **Reverse:** Crowned imperial eagle **Note:** Struck with 1/2 Thaler dies, KM#1545. Prev. Austria KM#167 (KM#1625).

Date	Mintage	VG	F	VF	XF	Unc
1728 Rare	—	—	—	—	—	—

KM# 864 10 DUCAT

35.0000 g., 0.9860 Gold 1.1095 oz. AGW **Ruler:** Karl VI **Mint:** Breslau **Obverse:** Armored bust right **Reverse:** Crowned imperial eagle **Note:** Struck with 1 Thaler dies, KM#1592.3. Prev. Austria KM#168 (KM#1621).

Date	Mintage	VG	F	VF	XF	Unc
1726 Rare	—	—	—	—	—	—
1730 Rare	—	—	—	—	—	—

KM# 888 20 DUCAT

70.0000 g., 0.9860 Gold 2.2190 oz. AGW **Ruler:** Karl VI **Mint:** Breslau **Obverse:** Armored draped bust right **Obv. Legend:** CAROL: VI: D: G: R: I: S: A: GE: HI: HU: BO: REX • **Reverse:** Crowned imperial double eagle, crowned shield on breast **Rev. Legend:** ARCHID: AUST: DUX •• BU: COM:... **Note:** Prev. Austria KM#169 (KM#1662).

Date	Mintage	VG	F	VF	XF	Unc
1739 Rare	—	—	—	—	—	—

KM# 939 1/2 FRIEDRICH D'OR

3.3250 g., 0.9000 Gold 0.0962 oz. AGW **Ruler:** Friedrich II, King of Prussia **Obverse:** Bust right **Reverse:** Crowned eagle on military trophies, date divided below **Note:** Prev. C#38.

Date	Mintage	VG	F	VF	XF	Unc
1750B	—	200	400	750	1,200	—
1751B	—	200	400	750	1,200	—
1752B	—	200	400	750	1,200	—
1753B	—	200	400	750	1,200	—

KM# 996 1/2 FRIEDRICH D'OR

3.3250 g., 0.9000 Gold 0.0962 oz. AGW **Ruler:** Friedrich II, King of Prussia **Obverse:** Head right **Reverse:** Crowned eagle on military trophies, date divided below **Note:** Prev. C#39.

Date	Mintage	F	VF	XF	Unc
1757B	—	250	350	600	1,000
1765B	—	250	350	600	1,000
1766B	—	250	350	600	1,000
1767B	—	250	350	600	1,000
1768B	—	250	350	600	1,000
1769B	—	250	350	600	1,000
1770B	—	250	350	600	1,000
1771B	—	250	350	600	1,000
1772B	—	250	350	600	1,000
1773B	—	250	350	600	1,000
1774B	—	250	350	600	1,000
1775B	—	250	350	600	1,000

KM# 996a 1/2 FRIEDRICH D'OR

3.3250 g., 0.9000 Gold 0.0962 oz. AGW **Ruler:** Friedrich II, King of Prussia **Obverse:** Old head right **Reverse:** Crowned eagle on trophies **Note:** Prev. C#39a.

Date	Mintage	F	VF	XF	Unc
1776B	—	500	1,100	2,000	3,200
1777B	—	500	1,100	2,000	3,200

KM# 909 FRIEDRICH D'OR

6.6500 g., 0.9000 Gold 0.1924 oz. AGW **Ruler:** Friedrich II, King of Prussia **Obverse:** Armored bust right **Obv. Legend:** FRIEDERICUS D: G: REX BOR: S: SIL: D: **Reverse:** Crowned monograms with eagles at angles, date divided below **Note:** Prev. C#40. Varieties exist.

Date	Mintage	VG	F	VF	XF	Unc
1744 AE	—	250	600	1,250	2,000	—
1745 AE	—	250	600	1,250	2,000	—
1746 AE	—	250	600	1,250	2,000	—
1747 AE	—	250	600	1,250	2,000	—
1748 AE	—	250	600	1,250	2,000	—

KM# 930 FRIEDRICH D'OR

6.6500 g., 0.9000 Gold 0.1924 oz. AGW **Ruler:** Friedrich II, King of Prussia **Obverse:** Armored bust right **Obv. Legend:** FRIDERICUS • D • G • REX • BORUSSORUM **Reverse:** Crown divides date above eagle with trophies **Note:** Prev. C#41.

Date	Mintage	VG	F	VF	XF	Unc
1746 AE	—	250	600	1,250	2,000	—
1747 AE	—	250	600	1,250	2,000	—
1748 AE	—	250	600	1,250	2,000	—

KM# 930b FRIEDRICH D'OR

6.6500 g., 0.9000 Gold 0.1924 oz. AGW **Ruler:** Friedrich II, King of Prussia **Obverse:** Armored bust right **Reverse:** Date divided at bottom **Note:** Prev. C#41b.

Date	Mintage	VG	F	VF	XF	Unc
1749 AE	—	250	600	1,250	2,000	—

KM# 930c FRIEDRICH D'OR

6.6500 g., 0.9000 Gold 0.1924 oz. AGW **Ruler:** Friedrich II, King of Prussia **Obverse:** Armored bust right **Reverse:** Without W in cartouche **Note:** Prev. C#41c.

Date	Mintage	VG	F	VF	XF	Unc
1750 AE	—	175	275	400	1,000	—

KM# 948 FRIEDRICH D'OR

6.6500 g., 0.9000 Gold 0.1924 oz. AGW **Ruler:** Friedrich II, King of Prussia **Obverse:** Armored bust right **Obv. Legend:** FRIDERICVS BORVSSORVM REX **Reverse:** Eagle with trophies, date divided below **Note:** Prev. C#42.

Date	Mintage	VG	F	VF	XF	Unc
1750B	—	175	400	700	2,000	—
1751B	—	175	400	700	2,000	—
1752B	—	175	400	700	2,000	—
1753B	—	175	400	700	2,000	—
1754B	—	175	400	700	2,000	—
1755B	—	175	400	700	2,000	—
1756B	—	175	400	700	2,000	—
1757B	—	175	400	700	2,000	—
1764B	—	175	400	700	2,000	—

KM# 930a FRIEDRICH D'OR

6.6500 g., 0.9000 Gold 0.1924 oz. AGW **Ruler:** Friedrich II, King of Prussia **Obverse:** Armored bust right **Obv. Legend:** FRIDERICVS D G BORVSSORVM REX **Reverse:** B in cartouche **Note:** Prev. C#41a.

Date	Mintage	VG	F	VF	XF	Unc
1750B	—	200	500	1,000	1,650	—

KM# 1005 FRIEDRICH D'OR

6.6500 g., 0.9000 Gold 0.1924 oz. AGW **Ruler:** Friedrich II, King of Prussia **Obverse:** Head right **Reverse:** Crowned eagle on military trophies, date above **Note:** Prev. C#43.

Date	Mintage	F	VF	XF	Unc
1764B	—	400	800	1,400	2,150
1765B	—	400	800	1,400	2,150
1766B	—	400	800	1,400	2,150
1767B	—	400	800	1,400	2,150
1768B	—	400	800	1,400	2,150
1769B	—	400	800	1,400	2,150
1770B	—	400	800	1,400	2,150
1771B	—	400	800	1,400	2,150
1772B	—	400	800	1,400	2,150
1773B	—	400	800	1,400	2,150
1774B	—	400	800	1,400	2,150
1775B	—	400	800	1,400	2,150

KM# 1005a FRIEDRICH D'OR

6.6500 g., 0.9000 Gold 0.1924 oz. AGW **Ruler:** Friedrich II, King of Prussia **Obverse:** Older head right **Obv. Legend:** FRIDERICUS BORUSSORUM REX **Reverse:** Date above eagle with military trophies **Note:** Prev. C#43a.

Date	Mintage	F	VF	XF	Unc
1776B	—	300	600	1,000	1,650
1777B	—	300	600	1,000	1,650
1780B	—	300	600	1,000	1,650
1781B	—	300	600	1,000	1,650
1782B	—	300	600	1,000	1,650
1783B	—	300	600	1,000	1,650
1784B	—	300	600	1,000	1,650
1785B	—	300	600	1,000	1,650
1786B	—	300	600	1,000	1,650

KM# 1005b FRIEDRICH D'OR

6.6500 g., 0.9000 Gold 0.1924 oz. AGW **Ruler:** Friedrich II, King of Prussia **Obverse:** Laureate head right **Obv. Legend:** FRIDEICUS BORUSSORUM REX **Reverse:** "D. 20 AUGUST" above crowned eagle **Note:** Prev. C#43b.

Date	Mintage	F	VF	XF	Unc
1781B Rare	—	—	—	—	—

KM# 933 2 FRIEDRICH D'OR

13.3000 g., 0.9000 Gold 0.3848 oz. AGW **Ruler:** Friedrich II, King of Prussia **Obverse:** Armored bust right **Obv. Legend:** FRIDERICUS•D•G•REX•BORUSSORUM **Reverse:** Crowned eagle on military trophies, date divided below **Note:** Prev. C#44.

Date	Mintage	VG	F	VF	XF	Unc
1747 AHE	—	600	1,500	3,000	5,000	—
1748 AHE	—	600	1,500	3,000	5,000	—
1749 AHE	—	600	1,500	3,000	5,000	—

KM# 954 2 FRIEDRICH D'OR

13.3000 g., 0.9000 Gold 0.3848 oz. AGW **Ruler:** Friedrich II, King of Prussia **Obverse:** Armored bust right **Obv. Legend:** FRIDERICVS BORVSSORVM REX **Reverse:** Crowned eagle on military trophies, date divided below **Note:** Prev. C#45.

Date	Mintage	VG	F	VF	XF	Unc
1751B	—	400	1,000	2,000	3,500	—
1752B	—	400	1,000	2,000	3,500	—

PATTERNS

Including off metal strikes

KM#	Date	Mintage	Identification	Mkt Val
Pn1	1755B	—	Groschel. Gold. C3.	450
Pn2	1756B	—	Kreuzer. Gold. Crowned eagle. C9.1.	700
Pn3	1756B	—	3 Kreuzer. Gold. C21.	—
Pn4	1756B	—	6 Kreuzer. Gold. C28.	—
Pn5	1756B	—	Groschel. Gold. C3.	450
Pn6	1757B	—	Kreuzer. Gold. Crowned eagle. C9.1.	700
Pn7	1757B	—	Groschel. Gold. C3.	450

SOEST

Soest is a town in Westphalia, 27 miles (46 km) east of Dortmund. It was important in trade and as an imperial mint from at least the 11th-12th centuries. After Westphalia, for the most part, came under the control of the archbishops of Cologne and Soest grew in its role as a member of the Hanseatic League, the two came into increasing conflict. By the mid-15th century, Soest sought protection from the duke of Cleves. The town produced its own coinage in the late 15th century and then from the second half of the 16th until the mid-18th centuries. Prussia annexed Soest in 1813.

ARMS

A key, usually with ornate tabs, standing vertically.

MINT OFFICIALS

Date	Name
1680, 1703	Goswin Schönberg, die-cutter
Ca. 1700	Georg Harnold, mintmaster
1717-20	Heinrich Wilhelm Becker, mintmaster
1719-26, 1729-30	Helmig Simonis, mintmaster
1721-26, 1729-30	? Kilberg, mintmaster
1721-26	Johann Schotte, die-cutter
1726-50	Johann Dietrich Schooff, die-cutter
1747-49	Johann Heinrich Simons, mintmaster
1729-49	Jörg Harnold Kleinschmied, mintmaster
1728-40	Gerhard Peter Brölemann, die-cutter

CITY

REGULAR COINAGE

KM# 15 3 PFENNIG

Copper **Obverse:** Vertical key **Reverse:** Value 'III' in wreath

Date	Mintage	Good	VG	F	VF	XF
ND (1703)	7,700	—	—	—	—	—

KM# 16 3 PFENNIG

Copper **Obverse:** City key right

Date	Mintage	VG	F	VF	XF	Unc
1709	10,000	12.00	25.00	65.00	125	—

KM# 17 3 PFENNIG

Copper **Reverse:** III in wreath

Date	Mintage	VG	F	VF	XF	Unc
1709	Inc. above	12.00	25.00	65.00	125	—

KM# 20 3 PFENNIG

Copper **Obverse:** City key left, legend, date **Obv. Legend:** STADT SOEST **Reverse:** Value: III/PFEN between laurel branches

Date	Mintage	VG	F	VF	XF	Unc
1710	84,000	6.00	12.00	30.00	75.00	—

KM# 21 3 PFENNIG

Copper **Obverse:** Legend, city key right in wreath **Obv. Legend:** STADT SOEST

Date	Mintage	VG	F	VF	XF	Unc
1710	Inc. above	12.00	25.00	65.00	125	—

KM# 22 3 PFENNIG

Copper **Obverse:** Legend, key left **Obv. Legend:** STADT SOEST **Reverse:** Value: III/PFEN between palm branches

Date	Mintage	VG	F	VF	XF	Unc
171Z	76,000	5.00	10.00	20.00	50.00	—
1713	72,000	5.00	10.00	20.00	50.00	—
1714	72,000	5.00	10.00	20.00	50.00	—
1715	73,000	5.00	10.00	20.00	50.00	—
1716	79,000	5.00	10.00	20.00	50.00	—
1717	96,000	5.00	10.00	20.00	50.00	—
1718	172,000	5.00	10.00	20.00	50.00	—
1720	210,000	5.00	10.00	20.00	50.00	—
1721	109,000	5.00	10.00	20.00	50.00	—

KM# 23 3 PFENNIG

Copper **Obverse:** Key left between branches

Date	Mintage	VG	F	VF	XF	Unc
1722	129,000	5.00	10.00	20.00	50.00	—
1723	210,000	5.00	10.00	20.00	50.00	—
1725	156,000	5.00	10.00	20.00	50.00	—

KM# 24 3 PFENNIG

Copper **Obverse:** Key in oval cartouche, date above **Reverse:** Value; III/PFEN within palm branches

Date	Mintage	VG	F	VF	XF	Unc
1725	—	3.00	6.00	12.50	30.00	—
1726	225,000	3.00	6.00	12.50	30.00	—
1727	155,000	3.00	6.00	12.50	30.00	—
1728	360,000	3.00	6.00	12.50	30.00	—
1730	233,000	3.00	6.00	12.50	30.00	—
1733	235,000	3.00	6.00	12.50	30.00	—
1734	377,000	3.00	6.00	12.50	30.00	—
1735	418,000	3.00	6.00	12.50	30.00	—
1736	538,000	3.00	6.00	12.50	30.00	—
1737	487,000	3.00	6.00	12.50	30.00	—
1738	444,000	3.00	6.00	12.50	30.00	—
1739	446,000	3.00	6.00	12.50	30.00	—

KM# 25 3 PFENNIG

Copper **Obverse:** Key in crowned oval cartouche, date above **Reverse:** Value; III/PFEN in palm branches

Date	Mintage	VG	F	VF	XF	Unc
1727	Inc. above	5.00	10.00	20.00	50.00	—
1728	Inc. above	5.00	10.00	20.00	50.00	—
1736	Inc. above	5.00	10.00	20.00	50.00	—

KM# 27 3 PFENNIG

Copper **Obverse:** Key in crowned oval cartouche, date below

Date	Mintage	VG	F	VF	XF	Unc
1728	Inc. above	6.00	12.00	25.00	65.00	—
1730	Inc. above	6.00	12.00	25.00	65.00	—
1731	180,000	6.00	12.00	25.00	65.00	—
1732	209,000	6.00	12.00	25.00	65.00	—

KM# 26 3 PFENNIG

Copper **Obverse:** Crowned key in shield

Date	Mintage	VG	F	VF	XF	Unc
1728	—	6.00	12.00	30.00	75.00	—

KM# 30 3 PFENNIG

Copper **Obverse:** Key in oval cartouche, different frame; date above **Reverse:** Value; III/PFEN in palm branches

Date	Mintage	VG	F	VF	XF	Unc
1731	Inc. above	3.00	6.00	12.50	30.00	—
1732	Inc. above	3.00	6.00	12.50	30.00	—
1733	Inc. above	3.00	6.00	12.50	30.00	—

KM# 31 3 PFENNIG

Copper **Obverse:** Key in oval cartouche, date above **Reverse:** Value: III/PHEN in branches

Date	Mintage	VG	F	VF	XF	Unc
1737	Inc. above	5.00	10.00	20.00	55.00	—
1738	Inc. above	5.00	10.00	20.00	55.00	—
1739	Inc. above	5.00	10.00	20.00	55.00	—
1740	395,000	5.00	10.00	20.00	55.00	—
1741	393,000	5.00	10.00	20.00	55.00	—
1742	448,000	5.00	10.00	20.00	55.00	—
1743	466,000	5.00	10.00	20.00	55.00	—
1744	411,000	5.00	10.00	20.00	55.00	—
1745	426,000	5.00	10.00	20.00	55.00	—
1746	375,000	5.00	10.00	20.00	55.00	—
1747	288,000	5.00	10.00	20.00	55.00	—
1748	297,000	5.00	10.00	20.00	55.00	—
1749	406,000	5.00	10.00	20.00	55.00	—

KM# 32 3 PFENNIG

Copper **Obverse:** City arms in oval shield with date above **Reverse:** Two-line inscription between palm branches **Rev. Inscription:** III/PFEN **Note:** Mule of later obverse with reverse of 1710-18.

Date	Mintage	Good	VG	F	VF	XF
1739	—	—	—	—	—	—

PATTERNS

Including off metal strikes

KM#	Date	Mintage	Identification	Mkt Val
Pn1	1727	—	3 Pfennig. Silver. KM#25	125
Pn2	1738	—	3 Pfennig. Silver. KM#24	125
Pn3	1740	—	3 Pfennig. Silver. KM#31	125
Pn4	1745	—	3 Pfennig. Silver. KM#31	125

SOLMS

The earliest count of Solms whose name has come down to us was Marquard I (1129-1141). Although the original center of power may have been any one of three places, the most likely location is Burg-Solms, also known by the old name of Hohensolms. Burgsolms is located on the Lahr River about 5 miles (8 km) west of Wetzlar and 7 miles (11 km) northeast of Weilburg in the Sauerland, north of Frankfurt am Main. This region became the center of mining and smelting in medieval Germany an indication of Solms' large silver coin-issuing capability, all out of proportion to its size. Over time, the counts acquired scattered holdings near Frankfurt, in Saxony and in Bohemia. The county underwent numerous divisions from the late Middle Ages well into the 19th century. The first division occurred in 1409, when the lines of Solms-Braunfels and Solms-Lich were founded. All branches of Solms received the mint right from Emperor Karl V in 1552, but not all lines issued coins.

ARMS

Solms - crowned rampant lion left
Greiffenstein - 4 oak leaves in cruciform
Minzenberg - horizontal bar
Sonnenwalde - lion
Wildenfels - rose

SOLMS-BRAUNFELS

Established in the first division of Solms in 1409, Solms-Braunfels was further divided in 1592 into Solms-Braunfels, Solms-Greiffenstein and Solms-Hungen. Braunfels is located just 1.5 miles (3 km) south of Burgsolms (Hohensolms). Greiffenstein is a small village 7 miles (12 km) northwest of Burgsolms, whereas Hungen is further away, being 12.5 miles (21 km) southeast of Giessen or 22 miles (36 km) east-southeast of Burgsolms. The direct line of Solms-Braunfels became extinct in 1693 and passed to Greiffenstein, which was known as Braunfels from that date onwards. The count was raised to the dignity of prince in 1742. The lands were mediatized about 1806, but the counts of Solms-Braunfels descended into the present age.

RULERS

Wilhelm Moritz von Solms-Greiffenstein, 1693-1724

MINTMASTER INITIALS

Initial	Date	Name
BIB	1707-33	Balthasar Johann Bethmann in Darmstadt

COUNTSHIP

REGULAR COINAGE

KM# 21 1/2 THALER

Silver **Subject:** Death of Wilhelm Moritz' Wife, Magdalene Sophie von Hessen-Homburg **Obverse:** Crown on cross standing in open field **Obv. Legend:** UBERWUNDEN UND GEKROENT **Reverse:** Ten-line inscription with dates **Rev. Legend:** ZUM GEDAECHTNUSZWEY UND VIERZIG IAEHRIGER EHE

Date	Mintage	VG	F	VF	XF	Unc
1720 BIB Rare	—	—	—	—	—	—

KM# 20 THALER

Silver **Subject:** Death of Wilhelm Heinrich (1700), Son and Heir of Wilhelm Moritz **Obverse:** Bust right **Obv. Legend:** Titles of Wilhelm Heinrich around **Reverse:** Hand from clouds left holding cornucopia, sun above shining down, above MUNERIS OMNETUI

Date	Mintage	VG	F	VF	XF	Unc
ND(1709)	—	700	1,200	2,250	—	—

TRADE COINAGE

KM# 23 8 DUCAT

27.7000 g., Gold **Subject:** Death of Wilhelm Moritz' Wife, Magdalene Sophie von Hessen-Homburg **Obverse:** Crown on cross standing in open field **Obv. Legend:** UBERWUNDEN UND GEKROENT **Reverse:** Ten-line inscription with dates **Rev. Legend:** ZUM GEDAECHTNUS ZWEY UND VIERZIG IAEHRIGER EHE **Note:** Fr.3291a. Struck with 1/2 Thaler dies similar to 1 Thaler, KM#5.

Date	Mintage	VG	F	VF	XF	Unc
1720 BIB Rare	—	—	—	—	—	—

SOLMS-LAUBACH

Founded by a younger son of Philipp I of Solms-Lichand Hohensolms prior to 1522 and seated at the town of Laubach some 14 miles (23 km) east-southeast of Giessen, this branch lasted until at least the 20th century. The first division in 1561 resulted in the two lines of Solms-Laubach and Solms-Sonnenwalde. The next division occurred when Solms-Laubach, Solms-Baruth, Solms-Sonnenwalde and Solms-Rodelheim were established in 1600. The first Solms-Laubach died out in 1676 and titles passed to Solms-Wildenfels, from which a second line was constituted in 1696. As was the case with all other branches of Solms, Laubach was mediatized around 1806.

RULERS

Friedrich Ernst, 1696-1723
Friedrich Magnus II, 1723-1738
Christian August, 1738-1784
Friedrich Ludwig, 1784-(1806)-1822

MINT OFFICIALS' INITIALS

Initials	Date	Name
IIE/IE	1740-70	Johann Jakob Encke, mintmaster in Hanau
CGL	1746-55	Carl Gottlieb Lauffer, mintmaster in Nuremberg
AV – N	?-1754	Andreas Vestner, medailleur and die-cutter in Nuremberg
IMF	1755-64	Johann Martin Förster, mintmaster in Nuremberg
PPW	1755-64	Peter Paul Werner, die-cutter in Nuremberg
CRD	1761-65	Charlotte Rebecca Damiset, die-cutter in hanau
WWE	1767	Christian Franz Weber, warden in Wertheim
	1767	Johann Christoph Eberhard, mintmaster in Wertheim
St/CCST	Ca. 1770	C. C. Stockmar, die-cutter

COUNTY

REGULAR COINAGE

KM# 27 10 KREUZER

Silver **Note:** Prev. C#5.

Date	Mintage	VG	F	VF	XF	Unc
1762 IIE//CRD	3,470	30.00	60.00	120	250	—

KM# 31 30 KREUZER

Silver **Subject:** Death of a Grandson, Karl Christian Friedrich **Note:** Prev. C#9.

Date	Mintage	VG	F	VF	XF	Unc
1768 WWE	—	65.00	125	250	500	—

KM# 33 30 KREUZER

Silver **Subject:** Birth of a Grandson, Friedrich Ludwig Christian **Note:** Prev. #C11.

Date	Mintage	VG	F	VF	XF	Unc
1769 WWE	—	45.00	90.00	180	350	—

KM# 34 30 KREUZER

Silver **Subject:** Birth of Grandchildren, Wilahelm Ludwig Christian and Friedrich Wilhelm **Note:** Prev. #C13.

Date	Mintage	VG	F	VF	XF	Unc
1770 WWE	—	45.00	90.00	180	350	—

KM# 19 THALER

Silver **Obverse:** Bust of Christian August right **Reverse:** City view of Laubach **Note:** Dav. #2778. Prev. #C15.

Date	Mintage	F	VF	XF	Unc
ND AV-N	—	300	700	1,500	2,750

KM# 20 THALER

Silver **Subject:** First Marriage of the Count **Reverse:** Bust of E. Amalia Friedrich Graf left **Note:** Dav. #2779. Prev. #C16.

Date	Mintage	F	VF	XF	Unc
1738 AV-N	—	350	750	1,250	2,250

KM# 22 THALER

Silver **Subject:** Death of Elizabeth Amelia **Note:** Dav. #2780. Prev. #C17.

Date	Mintage	F	VF	XF	Unc
1748	202	350	750	1,250	2,250

KM# 25 THALER

Silver **Subject:** Death of Count's Third Wife, Dorothea Wilhelmina **Obverse:** Christian August and Dorothea Wilhelmina **Note:** Dav. #2781. Prev. #C18.

Date	Mintage	F	VF	XF	Unc
1754 IMF/P.P. Werner f.	—	300	650	1,150	2,000

KM# 28 THALER

Silver **Subject:** 12th Anniversary of the Wetterau Directorate **Obverse:** Crowned supported shield **Note:** Dav. #2782. Prev. #C19.

Date	Mintage	F	VF	XF	Unc
1767 WWE	—	250	500	1,000	1,750

KM# 29 THALER

Silver **Subject:** Marriage of Count's Son and Heir to Princess of Isenburg **Note:** Dav. #2783. Prev. #C20.

Date	Mintage	F	VF	XF	Unc
1767 WWE	—	250	500	1,000	1,750

KM# 32 THALER

Silver **Reverse:** View of salt mine **Note:** Dav. #2784. Prev. #C21.

Date	Mintage	F	VF	XF	Unc
1768 WWE	—	350	750	1,250	2,250

KM# 35 THALER

Silver **Ruler:** Karl Otto **Obverse:** Bust of Otto I right, founder of the Solms-Laubach Line **Reverse:** Pyramid **Note:** Dav. #2785. Prev. #C22.

Date	Mintage	F	VF	XF	Unc
1770 CCST/WWE	—	300	600	1,100	1,850

KM# 36 THALER

Silver **Obverse:** Bust of Christian August Graf right **Reverse:** SORGEN/LOOS above hunting lodge **Note:** Dav. #2786. Prev. #C23.

Date	Mintage	F	VF	XF	Unc
1770 ST/WWE	—	400	800	1,500	2,500

KM# 37 THALER

Silver **Reverse:** View of Laubach, cherub with banner LAUBACH flying above, date in exergue **Note:** Dav. #2787. Prev. #C24.

Date	Mintage	F	VF	XF	Unc
1770 ST/WWE	—	2,500	3,500	5,500	8,500

TRADE COINAGE

KM# 26 DUCAT

3.5000 g., 0.9860 Gold 0.1109 oz. AGW **Obverse:** Bust of Christian August right **Reverse:** Crowned arms **Note:** Prev. #C26.

Date	Mintage	VG	F	VF	XF	Unc
1761 IE	306	500	1,000	3,000	5,000	—

C# 27 10 DUCAT

35.0000 g., 0.9860 Gold 1.1095 oz. AGW **Subject:** Death of Elizabeth Amalia **Note:** Struck with 1 Thaler dies, Dav. #2780.

Date	Mintage	VG	F	VF	XF	Unc
1748 Rare	2	—	—	—	—	—

KM# 23 10 DUCAT

Gold **Note:** Struck with 1 Thaler dies, KM#22.

Date	Mintage	VG	F	VF	XF	Unc
1748	2	—	—	—	—	—

SPEYER

(Spires)

City and bishopric spanning the Rhine 15 miles south of Mannheim. The bishopric was founded in the 4th century, destroyed by Barbarians and re-established in 610. The city received the mint right in 1111 and became the site of the imperial mint. It became a free city of the empire in 1294 and was part of France from 1801 to 1814. In 1814 Speyer passed to Bavaria.

BISHOPRIC

RULERS

Johann Hugh von Orsbeck, 1677-1711
Heinrich Hartard von Rollingen, 1711-19
Damian Hugh Philipp von Schönborn-Puckheim, 1719-43
Franz Christof von Hutten zu Stolzenberg, 1743-70
Damian August Philipp Karl von Limburg-Vehlen-Styrum, 1770-97
Philipp Franz Wilderich Napomuk von Walderforf, 1797-1802

MINT OFFICIALS' INITIALS

Initials	Date	Name
AS	1744-99	Anton Schaffer, die-cutter and mintmaster in Mannheim

REGULAR COINAGE

C# 1 2 PFENNIG

Copper **Ruler:** Franz Christoph **Obverse:** Arms below cardinal's hat, B-S **Reverse:** Value, date

Date	Mintage	VG	F	VF	XF	Unc
1765	—	9.00	16.00	35.00	60.00	—

C# 2 KREUZER

Copper **Ruler:** Franz Christoph **Obverse:** Arms below cardinal's hat **Reverse:** Value, date

Date	Mintage	VG	F	VF	XF	Unc
1765	—	9.00	16.00	35.00	60.00	—

C# 7 5 KREUZER

Billon **Ruler:** Damian August Philipp Karl **Obverse:** 3 oval arms, crown above **Reverse:** Value, date in rhombus **Note:** Convention 5 Kreuzer.

Date	Mintage	VG	F	VF	XF	Unc
1772	—	80.00	115	200	320	—

C# 8 10 KREUZER

Silver **Ruler:** Franz Christoph **Obverse:** 3 arms, crown above **Reverse:** Value: CXX EINE ..., date in cartouche **Note:** Convention 10 Kreuzer.

Date	Mintage	VG	F	VF	XF	Unc
1770	—	40.00	65.00	145	265	—

C# 3 1/8 THALER

Silver **Ruler:** Franz Christoph **Subject:** Death of Franz Christoph **Obverse:** Cardinal's hat above crown and three shields in mantle **Reverse:** Inscription

Date	Mintage	VG	F	VF	XF	Unc
1770 AS	—	50.00	120	225	400	—

C# 4 1/4 THALER

Silver **Ruler:** Franz Christoph **Subject:** Death of Franz Christoph **Obverse:** Cardinal's hat above crown and three shields in mantle **Reverse:** Inscription

Date	Mintage	VG	F	VF	XF	Unc
1770 AS	—	60.00	135	245	450	—

C# 10 1/2 THALER

Silver **Ruler:** Damian August Philipp Karl **Subject:** Accession of August Philipp **Obverse:** Three shields with supporters within crowned mantle **Reverse:** Standing central figure with shield, staff and three cherubs **Note:** Convention 1/2 Thaler.

Date	Mintage	VG	F	VF	XF	Unc
1770 AS	5,000	30.00	60.00	120	225	—

C# 12 THALER

Silver **Ruler:** Damian August Philipp Karl **Subject:** Accession of August Philipp **Obverse:** Supporters with 3 shields within crowned mantle **Obv. Legend:** AVGVSTVS D:G: EP • SPIR • S • R • I • P • ET • PRAEP • WEISS • ELECT • 29 • MAI • CONSECR • 16 • SEPT: 1770, 10 EINE FEIN MARC below **Reverse:** Armed female with shield, staff and three cherubs **Rev. Inscription:** DEO O.M AVSPICE SVAVITER ET FORTITER SED IVSTE NEC SIBI SED SVIS **Note:** Convention Thaler. Dav.2788.

Date	Mintage	F	VF	XF	Unc
1770 AS	5,000	120	200	400	750

TRADE COINAGE

FR# 3308 DUCAT

3.5000 g., 0.9860 Gold 0.1109 oz. AGW **Ruler:** Damian Hugh Philipp **Obverse:** 2 shields of arms below crown and bishop's hat, date at bottom **Reverse:** City of Bruchsal

Date	Mintage	VG	F	VF	XF	Unc
1726	—	400	850	1,750	3,000	—

C# 5 DUCAT

3.5000 g., 0.9860 Gold 0.1109 oz. AGW **Ruler:** Franz Christoph **Obverse:** Bust right **Reverse:** One seated and one kneeling figure

Date	Mintage	VG	F	VF	XF	Unc
1745	485	350	650	1,350	2,250	—

C# 14 DUCAT

3.5000 g., 0.9860 Gold 0.1109 oz. AGW **Ruler:** Damian August Philipp Karl **Subject:** Accession of August Philipp **Obverse:** Supporters with three shields within crowned mantle **Reverse:** Standing central figure with shield, staff and three cherubs

Date	Mintage	VG	F	VF	XF	Unc
1770 AS	—	300	600	1,200	2,000	—

FR# 3306 2 DUCAT

7.0000 g., 0.9860 Gold 0.2219 oz. AGW **Ruler:** Heinrich Hartard **Obverse:** Bust right **Reverse:** Crowned arms

Date	Mintage	VG	F	VF	XF	Unc
1711	—	5,000	11,000	20,000	35,000	—

KM# 100 2 DUCAT

7.0000 g., 0.9860 Gold 0.2219 oz. AGW **Ruler:** Heinrich Hartard **Subject:** Appointment of Damian Hugo as Cardinal **Obverse:** Woman carrying magnet and olive branch, around VIS ARCANA TRAHIT

Date	Mintage	VG	F	VF	XF	Unc
ND(1716)	—	—	—	—	—	—

FR# 3307 2 DUCAT

7.0000 g., 0.9860 Gold 0.2219 oz. AGW **Ruler:** Damian Hugh Philipp **Obverse:** 2 shields of arms below crown and bishop's hat, date at bottom **Reverse:** City of Bruchsal

Date	Mintage	VG	F	VF	XF	Unc
1726	—	1,500	2,500	4,500	7,500	—

CITY

Although the city of Speyer received the mint right in 1111, very few coins were struck on its behalf over the centuries. Special coins were minted for the first and second hundred years of the Protestant Reformation. There are also a few notable countermarked coins dating from the early phase of the Thirty Years' War.

MINT OFFICIAL

LK and L.HEN.K. = Unknown, ca. 1717

REGULAR COINAGE

KM# 15 2 GROSCHEN (Doppelgroschen)

Silver **Subject:** Bicentennial of the Reformation **Obverse:** View of cathedral in laurel wreath, date below. **Reverse:** 6-line inscription with date, all in laurel wreath.

Date	Mintage	VG	F	VF	XF	Unc
1717LK	—	65.00	125	225	350	—

KM# 16 2 GROSCHEN (Doppelgroschen)

Silver **Obverse:** 6-line inscription with date. **Reverse:** 7-line inscription. **Note:** Klippe. Weight varies, 3.4-4.0 grams. Varieties exist.

Date	Mintage	VG	F	VF	XF	Unc
1717	—	45.00	90.00	175	300	—
1717LK	—	45.00	90.00	175	300	—

KM# 17 1/2 GULDEN (Halbgulden)

10.0000 g., Silver **Subject:** Bicentennial of the Reformation **Obverse:** View of cathedral, date below, double marginal inscription around **Reverse:** Bible on table, double inscription around, 3-line inscription below

Date	Mintage	VG	F	VF	XF	Unc
1717 L.HEN.K	—	175	275	475	800	—

KM# 18 1/2 GULDEN (Halbgulden)

10.9000 g., Silver **Obverse:** View of cathedral, date below, inscription around, all in wreath **Reverse:** Angel above clouds, 2-line inscription with mintmaster's initials below, inscription around, all in wreath **Note:** Klippe.

Date	Mintage	VG	F	VF	XF	Unc
1717LK	—	200	350	550	850	—

KM# 19 1/6 THALER

Silver **Subject:** Bicentennial of the Reformation **Obverse:** Open Bible on table divides date, cloud with Jehovah in Hebrew above, inscription around **Reverse:** 8-line inscription with date, inscription in margin around **Note:** Klippe. Weight varies: 5.20-6.00 grams. Varieties exist.

Date	Mintage	VG	F	VF	XF	Unc
1717LK	—	125	250	425	650	—

STOLBERG

The castle of Stolberg, located on the southern slopes of the Harz Mountains, 9 miles (15 km) northeast of Nordhausen, is the ancestral home of the counts of that name. The dynasty has a recognized line of succession from count Heinrich I (1210-1239), but the family claimed descent from Otto Colonna, an Italian noble of the 6th century. The column in the family arms signifies this supposed connection, whether historically accurate or not. Count Heinrich was the younger brother of the count of Hohnstein whose castle lay just 6 miles away. Whatever the origin of the earlier counts of Stolberg, they came to an end and the line founded by Heinrich I began in about 1222. The long series of coins, based on the rich Harz silver mine holdings of the family, began at this time. Various territories, some scattered a distance from the family home, were added to the Stolberg lands and two brothers established separate lines in 1538, Stolberg-Stolberg and Stolberg-Wernigerode. Another brother succeeded to the Dietz portion of Königstein in 1574.

MINT OFFICIALS' INITIALS

The output of the Harz silver mines belonging to the counts of Stolberg was often beyond the capacity of their several mints to turn into coins. Production of many coins frequently farmed out to mints in other territories, such as neighboring Mansfeld, or to city mints in Frankfurt am Main, Augsburg, etc. Sometimes mintmasters and die engravers were invited to work in Stolberg mints on a temporary basis. Over the centuries a bewildering number of people worked in and for Stolberg mints and many left their symbols and initials on the coins.

Stolberg Mint

Initials	Date	Name
W/CW	1700-1730	Christian Wermuth, medailleur/die-cutter in Gotha
IIG	1705-50	Johann Jeremias Gründler, mintmaster and warden
	1710	I. Thiebaud, die-cutter
IBH	1739-63	Johann Benjamin Hecht, mintmaster in Zellerfeld
C, IEVC	1750-65	Julian Eberhard Volkmar Claus, mintmaster
	1763	Jakob Abram, die-cutter in Berlin
T	1763-?	Claud François Thiébaud, die-cutter
	1764	Johann Christian Heckel, warden
	1764	Johann Veith Morgenroth, die-cutter
EFR	1766-92	Ernst Friedrich Rupstein, mintmaster
Z, EHAZ	1792-1807	Ernst Hermann Agathus Ziegler, mintmaster

ARMS

Stolberg - stag, usually to left, sometimes to right, antlers extend backwards
Wernigerode - one or two fish (trout) standing on tails
Königstein - lion left
Rochefort - eagle
Eppstein - three chevrons
Minzenberg - horizontal bar
Mark - checkerboard in horizontal bar
Agimont - five horizontal bars
Lohra - lion rampant left
Wertheim - top half of eagle above three roses
Breuberg - two horizontal bars
Hohnstein - checkerboard
Klettenberg - stag left, but antlers extend upwards

STOLBERG-GEDERN

As a cadet line of the senior house of Stolberg, Gedern was created by the division of Stolberg-Wernigerode in 1710. The count was raised to the rank of prince in 1742, but the line fell extinct in 1804 after only two generations. The lands and titles then reverted to Stolberg-Wernigerode. The castle of Gedern is located in the Wetterau some 20 miles (34 km) northeast of Friedberg.

RULERS

Friedrich Karl, 1710-1767, Prince from 1742
Karl Heinrich, 1767-1804

COUNTSHIP

TRADE COINAGE

KM# 1 DUCAT

3.5000 g., 0.9860 Gold 0.1109 oz. AGW **Ruler:** Friedrich Karl **Obverse:** Head right **Reverse:** Stag left in front of column with "S" in base

Date	Mintage	Good	VG	F	VF	XF
1719	—	—	250	500	1,200	2,000

STOLBERG-ROSSLA

The small village of Rossla is situated on the main east-west road between Nordhausen and Sangerhausen, 9 miles (15 km) southeast of Stolberg castle. It became the seat of a cadet line of the junior branch of the dynasty upon the division of Stolberg in 1704. Although Stolberg-Rossla issued a few coins in the name of the individual counts, most of its extensive coinage during the 18th century was coined jointly with the rulers of Stolberg-Stolberg, under which the issues are listed. Although the Stolberg counts surrendered their sovereignty regarding military and foreign matters to Prussia during the latter half of the 18th century, the Stolberg-Rossla line continued well into the 20th century.

RULERS

Justus Christian I, 1704-1739
Friedrich Botho, 1739-1768
Heinrich Christian Friedrich, 1768-1776, abdicated (d.1810)
Johann Wilhelm Christof, 1776-1826

Joint Coinage

of Stolberg –Rossla with Stolberg-Stolberg
C – Christof Ludwig II and Friedrich Botho, 1739-1761
D – Friedrich Botho and Karl Ludwig, 1761-1768
E – Karl Ludwig and Heinrich Christian Friedrich, 1768-1801

COUNTSHIP

REGULAR COINAGE

KM# 18 PFENNIG

Copper **Ruler:** Joint Coinage C **Obverse:** Stag left in front of column **Reverse:** Value, date **Note:** Previous C# 5.

Date	Mintage	VG	F	VF	XF	Unc
1751	—	10.00	20.00	40.00	75.00	—

KM# 20 PFENNIG

Copper **Ruler:** Joint Coinage D **Obverse:** Stag in front of column **Reverse:** Value, date in cartouche **Note:** Previous C# 5.5.

Date	Mintage	VG	F	VF	XF	Unc
1761	—	8.00	16.00	35.00	65.00	—

KM# 24 PFENNIG

Copper **Ruler:** Joint Coinage E **Obverse:** Stag left before column **Reverse:** Value above date **Note:** Previous C# 47.

Date	Mintage	VG	F	VF	XF	Unc
1799	—	6.00	15.00	35.00	60.00	—
1801 Z	—	6.00	15.00	35.00	60.00	—

TRADE COINAGE

KM# 5 1/8 DUCAT

0.4375 g., 0.9860 Gold 0.0139 oz. AGW **Ruler:** Justus Christian I **Obverse:** Crowned JC monogram **Reverse:** Stag in front of column **Note:** Fr# 3332.

Date	Mintage	VG	F	VF	XF	Unc
ND(1704)	—	80.00	150	300	500	—

KM# 12 1/8 DUCAT

0.4375 g., 0.9860 Gold 0.0139 oz. AGW **Ruler:** Friedrich Botho **Obverse:** Crowned FB monogram **Reverse:** Stag in front of column **Note:** Previous C# 25.

Date	Mintage	VG	F	VF	XF	Unc
ND(1739)	—	60.00	135	275	450	—

KM# 7 1/4 DUCAT

0.8750 g., 0.9860 Gold 0.0277 oz. AGW **Ruler:** Justus Christian I **Obverse:** Crowned JC monogram **Reverse:** Stag in front of column **Note:** Fr# 3331.

Date	Mintage	VG	F	VF	XF	Unc
ND(1704)	—	75.00	125	250	400	—

KM# 9 1/4 DUCAT

0.8750 g., 0.9860 Gold 0.0277 oz. AGW **Ruler:** Justus Christian I **Obverse:** Stag in front of column, titles of Justuc Christian **Reverse:** Crowned shield of arms **Note:** Fr# 3333.

Date	Mintage	VG	F	VF	XF	Unc
ND(1704)	—	80.00	150	300	500	—

KM# 14 1/4 DUCAT

0.8750 g., 0.9860 Gold 0.0277 oz. AGW **Ruler:** Friedrich Botho **Obverse:** Crowned FB monogram **Reverse:** Stag in front of column **Note:** Previous C# 26.

Date	Mintage	VG	F	VF	XF	Unc
ND(1739)	—	90.00	175	350	600	—

STOLBERG-STOLBERG

The old line of counts was divided into the senior (Wernigerode) and junior (Stolberg) branches in 1638. The junior branch was divided again in 1704 into Stolberg-Stolberg and Stolberg-Rossla. The two lines issued a large series of coins, mostly as joint issues, throughout the 18th century. There were still counts of Stolberg-Stolberg into the early 20th century.

RULERS

Christof Ludwig I, 1684-1704
Christof Friedrich, 1704-1738
Christof Ludwig II, 1738-1761
Karl Ludwig, 1761-1815
Josef Christian Ernst Ludwig, 1815-1839
Alfred, 1839-1903

Joint Coinage

of Stolberg-Stolberg and Stolberg-Rossla
A - Christof Friedrich and Jost Christian, 1704-1738
B - Jost Christian and Christof Ludwig II, 1738-1739
C - Christof Ludwig II and Friedrich Botho, 1739-1761
D - Friedrich Botho and Karl Ludwig, 1761-1768
E - Karl Ludwig and Heinrich Christian Friedrich, 1768-1801

COUNTSHIP

REGULAR COINAGE

KM# 144 PFENNIG

Copper **Ruler:** Christof Friedrich and Jost Christian Joint Coinage A **Obverse:** Stag left in front of column **Reverse:** 5-line inscription with date **Rev. Inscription:** 1/PFENNING/SCHEIDE/MUNTZ/(date) **Note:** Varieties exist.

Date	Mintage	VG	F	VF	XF	Unc
1715	—	6.00	12.00	25.00	45.00	—
1718	—	6.00	12.00	25.00	45.00	—
1721	—	6.00	12.00	25.00	45.00	—
1722	—	6.00	12.00	25.00	45.00	—

KM# 145 1-1/2 PFENNIG

Copper **Ruler:** Christof Friedrich and Jost Christian Joint Coinage A **Obverse:** Stag left in front of column **Reverse:** 5-line inscription with date **Rev. Inscription:** I 1/2/PFENNING/ SCHEIDE/ MUNTZ/(date). **Note:** Varieties exist.

Date	Mintage	VG	F	VF	XF	Unc
1715	—	8.00	16.00	35.00	60.00	—
1718	—	8.00	16.00	35.00	60.00	—
1722	—	8.00	16.00	35.00	60.00	—

KM# 126 1/48 THALER (1/2 Groschen)

Silver **Ruler:** Christof Friedrich and Jost Christian Joint Coinage A **Obverse:** Stag left in front of column **Obv. Legend:** GOTT SEEGNE U. ERHALTE UNSERE BERGW. **Reverse:** 4-line inscription, mintmaster's initials divide date below, all in palm wreath **Rev. Inscription:** 48/EINEN/THALER/FEIN SILB.

Date	Mintage	VG	F	VF	XF	Unc
1707 IIG	—	15.00	32.00	65.00	110	—

KM# 142 1/48 THALER (1/2 Groschen)

Silver **Ruler:** Christof Friedrich and Jost Christian Joint Coinage A **Obverse:** Stag left in front of column, end of inscription 'WERCK' in exergue **Obv. Legend:** GOTT SEEGNE U. ERHALTE UNSERE BERG. **Reverse:** 4-line inscription, mintmaster's initials divide date below **Rev. Inscription:** 48/EINEN/THALER/FEIN SILB. **Note:** Varieties exist.

Date	Mintage	VG	F	VF	XF	Unc
1711 IIG	—	8.00	16.00	35.00	60.00	—
1715 IIG	—	8.00	16.00	35.00	60.00	—
1717 IIG	—	8.00	16.00	35.00	60.00	—
1719 IIG	—	8.00	16.00	35.00	60.00	—
1722 IIG	—	8.00	16.00	35.00	60.00	—
1723 IIG	—	8.00	16.00	35.00	60.00	—
1733 IIG	—	8.00	16.00	35.00	60.00	—
1738 IIG	—	8.00	16.00	35.00	60.00	—

KM# 199 1/48 THALER (1/2 Groschen)

Silver **Ruler:** Jost Christian and Christof Ludwig II Joint Coinage B **Obverse:** Stag right in front of column, end of legend 'WERCK' in exergue **Obv. Legend:** GOTT SEEGNE U. ERHALTE UNSERE BERG. **Reverse:** 4-line inscription, mintmaster's initials divide date below **Rev. Legend:** 48/EINEN/THALER/FEIN SILB.

Date	Mintage	VG	F	VF	XF	Unc
1739 IIG	—	7.00	15.00	30.00	55.00	—

KM# 230 1/48 THALER (1/2 Groschen)

Silver **Ruler:** Christof Ludwig II and Friedrich Botho Joint Coinage C **Obverse:** Stag left before column, within legend **Reverse:** Value, date **Note:** Previous C# 6.

Date	Mintage	VG	F	VF	XF	Unc
1745 IIG	—	12.00	25.00	45.00	85.00	—
1748 IIG	—	12.00	25.00	45.00	85.00	—
1750 IEVC	—	12.00	25.00	45.00	85.00	—
1756 IEVC	—	12.00	25.00	45.00	85.00	—
ND IEVC	—	12.00	25.00	45.00	85.00	—

KM# 238 1/48 THALER (1/2 Groschen)

Silver **Ruler:** Christof Ludwig II **Obverse:** Crowned script CL monogram, date below **Reverse:** 3-line inscription beween two crossed palm branches **Rev. Inscription:** 48/EINEN/THALER

Date	Mintage	VG	F	VF	XF	Unc
1759	—	10.00	20.00	40.00	70.00	—

KM# 300.1 1/48 THALER (1/2 Groschen)

Silver **Ruler:** Friedrich Botho and Karl Ludwig Joint Coinage D **Obverse:** Stag left before column **Reverse:** Value and date **Note:** Previous C# 6a.

Date	Mintage	VG	F	VF	XF	Unc
1767 EFR	—	12.00	25.00	45.00	85.00	—
1768 EFR	—	12.00	25.00	45.00	85.00	—

KM# 300.2 1/48 THALER (1/2 Groschen)

Silver **Ruler:** Karl Ludwig and Heinrich Christian Friedrich Joint Coinage E **Obverse:** Stag left before column **Reverse:** Value, date **Note:** Previous C# 6b.

Date	Mintage	VG	F	VF	XF	Unc
1777 EFR	—	12.00	25.00	45.00	85.00	—
1791 EFR	—	12.00	25.00	45.00	85.00	—

KM# 320 1/48 THALER (1/2 Groschen)

Silver **Ruler:** Karl Ludwig and Heinrich Christian Friedrich Joint Coinage E **Obverse:** Stag right in front of column, end of legend 'WERCK' in exergue **Obv. Legend:** GOTT SEEGNE U. ERHALTE UNSERE BERG **Reverse:** 4-line inscription, date and mintmaster's initial below **Rev. Inscription:** 48/EINEN/THALER/ FEIN SILB

Date	Mintage	VG	F	VF	XF	Unc
1796 Z	—	10.00	20.00	40.00	70.00	—

KM# 128 1/24 THALER (Groschen)

Silver **Ruler:** Christof Friedrich and Jost Christian Joint Coinage A **Obverse:** Stag right in front of column **Obv. Legend:** GOTT SEEGNE U. ERHALTE UNSERE BERGW. **Reverse:** 4-line inscription, mintmaster's initials divide date below, all in palm wreath **Rev. Inscription:** 24/EINEN/THALER/FEIN SILB.

Date	Mintage	VG	F	VF	XF	Unc
1707 IIG	—	20.00	40.00	80.00	135	—

KM# 138 1/24 THALER (Groschen)

Silver **Ruler:** Christof Friedrich and Jost Christian Joint Coinage A **Obverse:** 4-line inscription, mintmaster's initials divide date below **Obv. Legend:** CHR. FRID. U. IOST. CHR. GEB. G. ZU ST. K. R. W. U. H. **Obv. Inscription:** 24/EINEN/THALER/FEIN SILB. **Reverse:** Stag left in front of column **Rev. Legend:** GOTT SEEGNE U. ERHALTE UNSERE BERGW. **Note:** Varieties exist.

Date	Mintage	VG	F	VF	XF	Unc
1709 IIG	—	10.00	20.00	40.00	70.00	—
1711 IIG	—	10.00	20.00	40.00	70.00	—
1715 IIG	—	10.00	20.00	40.00	70.00	—
1717 IIG	—	10.00	20.00	40.00	70.00	—
1719 IIG	—	10.00	20.00	40.00	70.00	—
1722 IIG	—	10.00	20.00	40.00	70.00	—
1724 IIG	—	10.00	20.00	40.00	70.00	—
1725 IIG	—	10.00	20.00	40.00	70.00	—
1726 IIG	—	10.00	20.00	40.00	70.00	—
1733 IIG	—	10.00	20.00	40.00	70.00	—
1736 IIG	—	10.00	20.00	40.00	70.00	—
1738 IIG	—	10.00	20.00	40.00	70.00	—

KM# 158 1/24 THALER (Groschen)

Silver **Ruler:** Christof Friedrich and Jost Christian Joint Coinage A **Subject:** Bicentennial of the Reformation **Obverse:** Stag left in front of column **Obv. Legend:** GOTT SEEGNE U. ERHALTE UNSERE BERGW. **Reverse:** 7-line inscription with date in chronogram, value 1/24 in oval below divides mintmaster's initials **Rev. Inscription:** KOMT/HER HÖRT/NVN ZV ALLE/DIE IHR GOTT/FVRCHTET/PS. 66 V. 16/D. 31 OCTO.

Date	Mintage	VG	F	VF	XF	Unc
1717 IIG	—	12.00	25.00	60.00	100	—

KM# 224 1/24 THALER (Groschen)

Silver **Ruler:** Christof Ludwig II and Friedrich Botho Joint Coinage C **Obverse:** Stag left in front of column **Reverse:** Value, date **Note:** Previous C# 7.

Date	Mintage	VG	F	VF	XF	Unc
1741 IIG	—	18.00	30.00	60.00	100	—
1744 IIG	—	18.00	30.00	60.00	100	—
1748 IIG	—	18.00	30.00	60.00	100	—
1750 IEVC	—	18.00	30.00	60.00	100	—
1752 IEVC	—	18.00	30.00	60.00	100	—
1758 IEVC	—	18.00	30.00	60.00	100	—

KM# 256 1/24 THALER (Groschen)

Silver **Ruler:** Friedrich Botho and Karl Ludwig Joint Coinage D **Obverse:** Titles of F. Botho and K. Ludwig **Reverse:** Value within circle, date in legend **Note:** Previous C# 28 and 28a.

Date	Mintage	VG	F	VF	XF	Unc
1763 C	—	18.00	30.00	60.00	100	—
1763	—	18.00	30.00	60.00	100	—
1764 C	—	18.00	30.00	60.00	100	—

KM# 245 1/24 THALER (Groschen)

Silver **Ruler:** Friedrich Botho and Karl Ludwig Joint Coinage D **Obverse:** Crowned 11-fold arms divide date, mintmaster's initials and F - S (Fein Silber), value 1/24 in oval below **Obv. Legend:** FR. BOTHO. V. CARL. LVDEW: GR. Z. ST: K. R. W. V. H. **Reverse:** Stag left in front of column **Rev. Legend:** GOTT SEEGNE V. ERHALTE VNSERE BERGW.

Date	Mintage	VG	F	VF	XF	Unc
1762 IEVC	—	30.00	60.00	150	250	—

KM# 288 1/24 THALER (Groschen)

Silver **Ruler:** Friedrich Botho and Karl Ludwig Joint Coinage D **Obverse:** Value and date in center **Reverse:** Stag left before column with S in base, without inner circle **Note:** Previous C# 29.

Date	Mintage	VG	F	VF	XF	Unc
1766 EFR	—	20.00	40.00	75.00	140	—

KM# 314 1/24 THALER (Groschen)

Silver **Ruler:** Karl Ludwig and Heinrich Christian Friedrich Joint Coinage E **Obverse:** Stag left before column **Reverse:** Value above date **Note:** Previous C# 48.

Date	Mintage	VG	F	VF	XF	Unc
1771 EFR	—	18.00	30.00	60.00	100	—

KM# 322 1/24 THALER (Groschen)

Silver **Ruler:** Karl Ludwig and Heinrich Christian Friedrich Joint Coinage E **Obverse:** 4-line inscription, date and mintmaster's initials below **Obv. Legend:** CARL. LVD. V. H. CHRISTI. FR. GR. STOLB. K. R. W. V. H. **Obv. Inscription:** 24/EINEN/ THALER/ FEIN SILB. **Reverse:** Stag right in front of column **Rev. Legend:** GOTT SEEGNE V. ERHALTE VNSERE BERGW.

Date	Mintage	VG	F	VF	XF	Unc
1796 Z	—	7.00	16.00	35.00	65.00	—

KM# 130 1/12 THALER (Doppelgroschen)

Silver **Ruler:** Christof Friedrich and Jost Christian Joint Coinage A **Obverse:** Stag right in front of column **Obv. Legend:** GOTT SEEGNE U. ERHALTE UNSERE BERGW. **Reverse:** 4-line inscription, mintmaster's initials divide date below, all in palm wreath **Rev. Inscription:** 12/ EINEN/ THALER./ FEIN SILB.

Date	Mintage	VG	F	VF	XF	Unc
1707 IIG	—	20.00	45.00	85.00	135	—

KM# 140 1/12 THALER (Doppelgroschen)

Silver **Ruler:** Christof Friedrich and Jost Christian Joint Coinage A **Obverse:** 4-line inscription, mintmaster's initials divide date below **Obv. Legend:** CHR. FRID. U. IOST. CHR. GEB. GR. Z. S. K. R. W. U. H. **Obv. Inscription:** 12/EINEN/THALER./FEIN SILB. **Reverse:** Stag right in front of column **Rev. Legend:** GOTT SEEGNE U. ERHALTE UNSERE BERGWERCK. **Note:** Varieties exist.

Date	Mintage	VG	F	VF	XF	Unc
1709 IIG	—	10.00	20.00	40.00	65.00	—
1711 IIG	—	10.00	20.00	40.00	65.00	—
1714 IIG	—	10.00	20.00	40.00	65.00	—
1717 IIG	—	10.00	20.00	40.00	65.00	—
1719 IIG	—	10.00	20.00	40.00	65.00	—
1722 IIG	—	10.00	20.00	40.00	65.00	—
1725 IIG	—	10.00	20.00	40.00	65.00	—
1733 IIG	—	10.00	20.00	40.00	65.00	—
1736 IIG	—	10.00	20.00	40.00	65.00	—

KM# 159 1/12 THALER (Doppelgroschen)

Silver **Ruler:** Christof Friedrich and Jost Christian Joint Coinage A **Subject:** Bicentennial of the Reformation **Obverse:** Stag right in front of column **Obv. Legend:** GOTT SEEGNE U. ERHALTE UNSERE BERGWERCK. **Reverse:** 7-line inscription with year in chronogram, value 1/12 in oval divides mintmaster's initials at bottom **Rev. Inscription:** HERZV/PREISET GOTT/DIE DA DES/HERRS WERCK/ACHTEN/IUD. 13. U. 24/D. 31 OCTO.

Date	Mintage	VG	F	VF	XF	Unc
1717 IIG	—	18.00	30.00	75.00	120	—

KM# 189 1/12 THALER (Doppelgroschen)

Silver **Ruler:** Christof Friedrich and Jost Christian Joint Coinage A **Obverse:** Stag right in front of column **Obv. Legend:** CHR. FR. U. IOST. CHR. GEB. G. Z. ST. K. R. W. U. H. **Reverse:** 3-line inscription, mintmaster's initials divide date below **Rev. Legend:** NACH DEM LEIPZIGER FUS. **Rev. Inscription:** 12/EINEN/THALER

Date	Mintage	VG	F	VF	XF	Unc
1737 IIG	—	12.00	25.00	50.00	90.00	—

KM# 191 1/12 THALER (Doppelgroschen)

Silver **Ruler:** Jost Christian and Christof Ludwig II Joint Coinage B **Obverse:** 4-line inscription, mintmaster's initials divide date below **Obv. Legend:** IOST. CHR. U. CHR. LUD. GR. Z. STOLB. K. R. W. U. H. **Reverse:** Stag right in front of column **Rev. Legend:** GOTT SEEGNE U. ERHALTE UNSERE BERGWERCK. **Note:** Varieties exist.

Date	Mintage	VG	F	VF	XF	Unc
1738 IIG	—	20.00	45.00	80.00	125	—
1739 IIG	—	20.00	45.00	80.00	125	—

KM# 232 1/12 THALER (Doppelgroschen)

Silver **Ruler:** Christof Ludwig II and Friedrich Botho Joint Coinage C **Obverse:** Value and date **Reverse:** Stag left in front of column **Note:** Previous C# 8.

Date	Mintage	VG	F	VF	XF	Unc
1746 IIG	—	30.00	50.00	100	185	—
1748 IIG	—	30.00	50.00	100	185	—
1749 IIG	—	30.00	50.00	100	185	—
1750 IEVC	—	30.00	50.00	100	185	—

KM# 247 1/12 THALER (Doppelgroschen)

Ruler: Friedrich Botho and Karl Ludwig Joint Coinage D **Obverse:** Crowned 11-fold arms divide date and mintmaster's initials, value 1/12 in oval below **Obv. Legend:** FR. BOTHO. V. CARL. LVD. G. Z. ST. K. R. W. V. H. **Reverse:** Stag right in front of column **Rev. Legend:** GOTT SEEGNE V. ERHALTE VNSERE BERGW.

Date	Mintage	VG	F	VF	XF	Unc
1762 IEVC	—	15.00	30.00	60.00	100	—

KM# 259 1/12 THALER (Doppelgroschen)

Silver **Ruler:** Friedrich Botho and Karl Ludwig Joint Coinage D **Obverse:** Value in center, C below **Reverse:** Stag left before column with S in base in inner circle **Note:** Previous C# 30.

Date	Mintage	VG	F	VF	XF	Unc
1763 C	—	8.00	25.00	50.00	150	—
1764 C	—	8.00	25.00	50.00	150	—

KM# 260 1/12 THALER (Doppelgroschen)

Silver **Ruler:** Friedrich Botho and Karl Ludwig Joint Coinage D **Obverse:** Value in cartouche **Reverse:** Stag left in front of column **Note:** Previous C# 30a.

Date	Mintage	VG	F	VF	XF	Unc
1763 C	—	8.00	25.00	50.00	150	—

KM# 302 1/12 THALER (Doppelgroschen)

Silver **Ruler:** Karl Ludwig and Heinrich Christian Friedrich Joint Coinage E **Obverse:** Value above date **Reverse:** Stag left before column **Note:** Previous C# 49.

Date	Mintage	VG	F	VF	XF	Unc
1768 EFR	—	15.00	35.00	70.00	175	—
1770 EFR	—	15.00	35.00	70.00	175	—

KM# 324 1/12 THALER (Doppelgroschen)

Silver **Ruler:** Karl Ludwig and Heinrich Christian Friedrich Joint Coinage E **Obverse:** 4-line inscription, date and mintmaster's initial below **Obv. Legend:** CARL. LUDW. U. H. CHRIST. FRIED. GR. Z. STOLB. K. R. W. U. H. **Obv. Inscription:** 12/EINEN/ THALER/FEIN SILB.

Date	Mintage	VG	F	VF	XF	Unc
1796 Z	—	15.00	30.00	60.00	100	—

KM# 132 6 MARIENGROSCHEN (1/6 Thaler)

Silver **Ruler:** Christof Friedrich and Jost Christian Joint Coinage A **Obverse:** 4-line inscription, mintmaster's initials divide date below **Obv. Legend:** CHRIST. FRID. U. IOST. CHRISTI. GEB. G. ZU. ST. K. R. W. U. H. **Obv. Inscription:** VI/MARIEN/ GROSCH:/V. FEIN. SILB. **Reverse:** Stag left in front of column **Rev. Legend:** GOTT SEEGNE UND ERHALTE UNSERE BERGWERCKE. **Note:** Varieties exist.

Date	Mintage	VG	F	VF	XF	Unc
1707 IIG	—	20.00	45.00	85.00	140	—
1708 IIG	—	20.00	45.00	85.00	140	—
1709 IIG	—	20.00	45.00	85.00	140	—
1712 IIG	—	20.00	45.00	85.00	140	—
1714 IIG	—	20.00	45.00	85.00	140	—
1715 IIG	—	20.00	45.00	85.00	140	—

Date	Mintage	VG	F	VF	XF	Unc
1716 IIG	—	20.00	45.00	85.00	140	—
1717 IIG	—	20.00	45.00	85.00	140	—
1718 IIG	—	20.00	45.00	85.00	140	—
1720 IIG	—	20.00	45.00	85.00	140	—
1721 IIG	—	20.00	45.00	85.00	140	—
1722 IIG	—	20.00	45.00	85.00	140	—
1723 IIG	—	20.00	45.00	85.00	140	—
1724 IIG	—	20.00	45.00	85.00	140	—
1725 IIG	—	20.00	45.00	85.00	140	—
1726 IIG	—	20.00	45.00	85.00	140	—
1727 IIG	—	20.00	45.00	85.00	140	—
1728 IIG	—	20.00	45.00	85.00	140	—

KM# 115 1/6 THALER

Silver **Ruler:** Christof Friedrich and Jost Christian Joint Coinage A **Obverse:** Stag left in front of column **Obv. Legend:** CHRIST: FRIED: &. IOST: CHRISTI: FRA: &. CO: ST. K: R: WE: & H:. **Reverse:** 11-fold arms divide mintmaster's initials at bottom, 3 ornate helmets above with date divided between crests **Rev. Legend:** DOM: IN. EPST: MUN: BR: AI: LOHR: &. CLET. **Note:** Struck from same dies as Ducat, KM# 124.

Date	Mintage	VG	F	VF	XF	Unc
1706 IIG	—	25.00	45.00	85.00	135	—

KM# 147 1/6 THALER

Silver **Ruler:** Christof Friedrich and Jost Christian Joint Coinage A **Obverse:** Crowned 11-fold arms divide date and mintmaster's initials, value 1/6 in oval at bottom divides FEIN — SILB. **Obv. Legend:** CHRISTO: FRID. U IOST. CHRISTI: GEBR. G. Z. ST. K. R. W. U. H. **Reverse:** Stag left in front of column **Rev. Legend:** GOTT SEEGNE UND ERHALTE UNSERE BERGWERCKE. **Note:** Varieties exist.

Date	Mintage	VG	F	VF	XF	Unc
1715 IIG	—	22.00	40.00	75.00	125	—
1717 IIG	—	22.00	40.00	75.00	125	—
1718 IIG	—	22.00	40.00	75.00	125	—
1719 IIG	—	22.00	40.00	75.00	125	—
1721 IIG	—	22.00	40.00	75.00	125	—
1722 IIG	—	22.00	40.00	75.00	125	—
1731 IIG	—	22.00	40.00	75.00	125	—
1733 IIG	—	22.00	40.00	75.00	125	—
1736 IIG	—	22.00	40.00	75.00	125	—
1737 IIG	—	22.00	40.00	75.00	125	—
1738 IIG	—	22.00	40.00	75.00	125	—

KM# 161 1/6 THALER

Silver **Ruler:** Christof Friedrich and Jost Christian Joint Coinage A **Subject:** Bicentennial of the Reformation **Obverse:** Stag left in front of column **Obv. Legend:** GOTT SEEGNE U. ERHALTE UNSERE BERGWERCKE **Reverse:** 7-line inscription with year in chronogram, value 1/6 in oval at bottom divides mintmaster's initials **Rev. Inscription:** GELOBET/ SEY NVN DER/ GOTT ISRAEL/ DER ALLEIN/ WVNDER THVT/ PS. LXXII.18/ DEN. 31 OCTOB.

Date	Mintage	VG	F	VF	XF	Unc
1717 IIG	—	30.00	55.00	90.00	140	—

KM# 193 1/6 THALER

Silver **Ruler:** Jost Christian and Christof Ludwig II Joint Coinage B **Obverse:** Crowned 11-fold arms divide date and mintmaster's initials, value 1/6 in oval below divides FEIN — SILB: **Obv. Legend:** CHRISTO. FRID. U. IOST. CHRISTI. GEBR. G. Z. ST. K. R. W. U. H. **Reverse:** Stag left in front of column **Rev. Legend:** GOTT SEEGNE U. ERHALTE UNSERE BERGWERCKE

Date	Mintage	VG	F	VF	XF	Unc
1738 IIG	—	25.00	50.00	100	175	—

KM# 218 1/6 THALER

Silver **Ruler:** Christof Ludwig II and Friedrich Botho Joint Coinage C **Obverse:** Crowned 11-fold arms divide date and mintmaster's initials, value 1/6 in oval below divides FEIN — SILB: **Reverse:** Stag left in front of column **Note:** Previous C# 9.

Date	Mintage	VG	F	VF	XF	Unc
1740 IIG	—	40.00	65.00	120	225	—
1742 IIG	—	40.00	65.00	120	225	—
1743 IIG	—	40.00	65.00	120	225	—
1744 IIG	—	40.00	65.00	120	225	—
1745 IIG	—	40.00	65.00	120	225	—
1746 IIG	—	40.00	65.00	120	225	—
1748 IIG	—	40.00	65.00	120	225	—
1749 IIG	—	40.00	65.00	120	225	—
1750 IEVC	—	40.00	65.00	120	225	—
1756 IEVC	—	40.00	65.00	120	225	—

KM# 236 1/6 THALER

Silver **Ruler:** Christof Ludwig II and Friedrich Botho Joint Coinage C **Subject:** Bicentennial of the Religious Peace of Augsburg **Obverse:** Stag left in front of column **Obv. Legend:** GOTT SEEGNE V. ERHALTE VNSERE BERGWERCKE. **Reverse:** Six-line inscription with year in chronogram, value 1/6 in oval divides last two lines **Rev. Inscription:** LAETANDO/ NUMEN LATAS/CELEBRATE PER/ORAS. PS. C. V. I./D. 25.— SEPT./I.E. — V.C. **Note:** Previous C# 10.

Date	Mintage	VG	F	VF	XF	Unc
1755 IEVC	—	275	500	1,200	2,000	—

KM# 249 1/6 THALER

Silver **Ruler:** Friedrich Botho and Karl Ludwig Joint Coinage D **Obverse:** Crowned 11-fold arms in baroque frame divide date and mintmaster's initials, value 1/6 in oval divides FEIN — SILB: below **Obv. Legend:** FR: BOTHO. V. CARL. LVDEW. GR. ZV. ST. K. R. W. V. H. **Reverse:** Stag left in front of column **Rev. Legend:** GOTT SEEGNE V. ERHALTE VNSERE BERGWERCKE

Date	Mintage	VG	F	VF	XF	Unc
1762 IEVC	—	15.00	32.00	65.00	100	—

KM# 263 1/6 THALER

Silver **Ruler:** Friedrich Botho and Karl Ludwig Joint Coinage D **Obverse:** Manifold arms, three ornate helmets above, mintmaster's initial in cartouche below **Obv. Legend:** FRID. BOTHO. U. CARL LUDW. GR. Z. ST. K. R. W. U. H. **Reverse:** Stag left in front of colume, value 1/6 in cartouche below, date at end of legend **Rev. Legend:** LXXX. EINE FEINE MARCK.

Date	Mintage	VG	F	VF	XF	Unc
1763 C	—	10.00	25.00	50.00	150	—
1764 C	—	10.00	25.00	50.00	150	—

KM# 262 1/6 THALER

Silver **Ruler:** Friedrich Botho and Karl Ludwig Joint Coinage D **Obverse:** Arms, value below **Reverse:** Stag left before column **Note:** Previous C# 32.

Date	Mintage	VG	F	VF	XF	Unc
1763 C	—	7.00	22.00	40.00	100	—

KM# 290 1/6 THALER

Silver **Ruler:** Friedrich Botho and Karl Ludwig Joint Coinage D **Obverse:** Crowned arms **Reverse:** Stag left before column **Note:** Prev. C# 32b.

Date	Mintage	VG	F	VF	XF	Unc
1766 EFR	—	20.00	40.00	80.00	200	—

KM# 304 1/6 THALER

Silver **Ruler:** Karl Ludwig and Heinrich Christian Friedrich Joint Coinage E **Obverse:** Crowned arms divide date, value below **Reverse:** Stag left before column **Note:** Reichs 1/6 Thaler. Previous C# 49a.

Date	Mintage	VG	F	VF	XF	Unc
1768 EFR	—	12.00	28.00	60.00	170	—
1770 EFR	—	12.00	28.00	60.00	170	—
1777 EFR	—	12.00	28.00	60.00	170	—
1790 EFR	—	12.00	28.00	60.00	170	—

KM# 326 1/6 THALER

Silver **Ruler:** Karl Ludwig and Heinrich Christian Friedrich Joint Coinage E **Obverse:** 4-line inscription, date and mintmaster's initial below **Obv. Legend:** CARL. LUDW. U. H. CHRIST. FRIED. GRAF. Z. STOLB. **Obv. Inscription:** VI/EINEN/THALER/FEIN SILB. **Reverse:** Stag left in front of column **Rev. Legend:** GOTT SEEGNE U. ERHALTE UNSERE BERGWERCKE

Date	Mintage	VG	F	VF	XF	Unc
1796 Z	—	22.00	45.00	80.00	125	—

KM# 201 8 GROSCHEN (1/3 Thaler)

Silver **Ruler:** Jost Christian and Christof Ludwig II Joint Coinage B **Obverse:** 4-line inscription, mintmaster's initials divide date below **Obv. Legend:** IOST. CHRIST. U. CHRISTO. LUD. GRAF. Z. STOLB. K. R. W. U. H. **Obv. Inscription:** VIII/GUTE/GROSCH/N.D.L. FUS. **Reverse:** Stag left in front of column **Rev. Legend:** GOTT SEEGNE UND ERHALTE UNSERE BERGWERCKE.

Date	Mintage	VG	F	VF	XF	Unc
1739 IIG	—	50.00	90.00	160	250	—

KM# 133 12 MARIENGROSCHEN (1/3 Thaler)

Silver **Ruler:** Christof Friedrich and Jost Christian Joint Coinage A **Obverse:** 4-line inscription, mintmaster's initials divide date below **Obv. Legend:** CHRISTO. FRID. U. IOST. CHRISTI. GEB. GR. ZU. ST. K. R. W. U. H. **Obv. Inscription:** XII/MARIEN/ GROSCH:/FEIN. SILBER. **Reverse:** Stag left in front of column **Rev. Legend:** GOTT SEEGNE UND ERHALTE UNSERE BERGWERCKE. **Note:** Varieties exist

Date	Mintage	VG	F	VF	XF	Unc
1707 IIG	—	35.00	65.00	120	200	—
1708 IIG	—	35.00	65.00	120	200	—
1709 IIG	—	35.00	65.00	120	200	—
1710 IIG	—	35.00	65.00	120	200	—
1712 IIG	—	35.00	65.00	120	200	—
1714 IIG	—	35.00	65.00	120	200	—
1715 IIG	—	35.00	65.00	120	200	—
1716 IIG	—	35.00	65.00	120	200	—
1718 IIG	—	35.00	65.00	120	200	—
1720 IIG	—	35.00	65.00	120	200	—
1721 IIG	—	35.00	65.00	120	200	—
1722 IIG	—	35.00	65.00	120	200	—
1723 IIG	—	35.00	65.00	120	200	—
1724 IIG	—	35.00	65.00	120	200	—
1725 IIG	—	35.00	65.00	120	200	—
1726 IIG	—	35.00	65.00	120	200	—
1727 IIG	—	35.00	65.00	120	200	—

KM# 207 12 MARIENGROSCHEN (1/3 Thaler)

Silver **Ruler:** Jost Christian and Christof Ludwig II Joint Coinage B **Obverse:** 4-line inscription, mintmaster's initials divide date below **Obv. Legend:** IOST. CHRISTI. U. CHRISTO. LUD. GRAF Z. STOLB. K. R. W. U. H. **Obv. Inscription:** XVI/GUTE/ GROSCH/ N.D.L FUS. **Reverse:** Stag left in front of column **Rev. Legend:** GOTT SEEGNE U. ERHALTE UNSERE BERGWERCKE. **Note:** Dav# 1005.

Date	Mintage	VG	F	VF	XF	Unc
1739 IIG	—	75.00	140	240	400	—

KM# 149 1/3 THALER (1/2 Gulden)

Silver **Ruler:** Christof Friedrich and Jost Christian Joint Coinage A **Obverse:** Crowned 11-fold arms divide date and mintmaster's initials, value 1/3 in oval divides FEIN — SILB: below **Obv. Legend:** CHRISTO. FRID. U. IOST. CHRISTI. GEBR. GR. Z. ST. K. R. W. U. H. **Reverse:** Stag left in front of column **Rev. Legend:** GOTT SEEGNE UND ERHALTE UNSERE BERGWERCKE **Note:** Varieties exist.

Date	Mintage	VG	F	VF	XF	Unc
1715 IIG	—	30.00	55.00	100	165	—
1716 IIG	—	30.00	55.00	100	165	—
1718 IIG	—	30.00	55.00	100	165	—
1719 IIG	—	30.00	55.00	100	165	—
1720 IIG	—	30.00	55.00	100	165	—
1721 IIG	—	30.00	55.00	100	165	—
1722 IIG	—	30.00	55.00	100	165	—
1723 IIG	—	30.00	55.00	100	165	—
1726 IIG	—	30.00	55.00	100	165	—
1731 IIG	—	30.00	55.00	100	165	—
1732 IIG	—	30.00	55.00	100	165	—
1733 IIG	—	30.00	55.00	100	165	—
1735 IIG	—	30.00	55.00	100	165	—
1736 IIG	—	30.00	55.00	100	165	—
1737 IIG	—	30.00	55.00	100	165	—
1738 IIG	—	30.00	55.00	100	165	—

KM# 163 1/3 THALER (1/2 Gulden)

Silver **Ruler:** Christof Friedrich and Jost Christian Joint Coinage A **Subject:** Bicentennial of the Reformation **Obverse:** Stag left in front of column **Obv. Legend:** GOTT SEEGNE UND ERHALTE UNSERE BERGWERCKE **Reverse:** 7-line inscription with year in chronogram, value 1/3 in oval below divides mintmaster's initials **Rev. Inscription:** DAS/WORT SIE/SOLLEN KLAR/ LASSEN STAHN:/VND REIN DANK/FERNER HABEN/DEN. 31. OCTOB.

Date	Mintage	VG	F	VF	XF	Unc
1717 IIG	—	35.00	65.00	120	185	—

KM# 203 1/3 THALER (1/2 Gulden)

Silver **Ruler:** Jost Christian and Christof Ludwig II Joint Coinage B **Obverse:** Crowned 11-fold arms divide date and mintmaster's initials, value 1/3 in oval below divides FEIN — SILB: **Obv. Legend:** IOST. CHRISTI. U. CHRISTO. LUD. GRAF. Z. STOLB. K. R. W. U. H. **Reverse:** Stag left in front of column **Rev. Legend:** GOTT SEEGNE UND ERHALTE UNSERE BERGWERCKE

Date	Mintage	VG	F	VF	XF	Unc
1739 IIG	—	60.00	110	200	315	—

KM# 204 1/3 THALER (1/2 Gulden)

Silver **Ruler:** Jost Christian and Christof Ludwig II Joint Coinage B **Obverse:** Crowned 11-fold arms divide date and mintmaster's initials, value 1/3 in oval below divides N.D.L. — FUS: **Obv. Legend:** IOST. CHRISTI. U. CHRISTO. LUD. GRAF. Z. STOLB. K. R. W. U. H. **Reverse:** Stag left in front of column **Rev. Legend:** GOTT SEEGNE UND ERHALTE UNSERE BERGWERCKE

Date	Mintage	VG	F	VF	XF	Unc
1739 IIG	—	45.00	80.00	200	350	—

KM# 220 1/3 THALER (1/2 Gulden)

Silver **Ruler:** Christof Ludwig II and Friedrich Botho Joint Coinage C **Obverse:** Crowned arms **Obv. Legend:** CHRIST • LUDEWIG • U • FRIED • BOTHO • GR • Z • STOLB • R • R • ... **Reverse:** Stag left in front of column **Note:** Previous C# 12.

Date	Mintage	VG	F	VF	XF	Unc
1740 IIG	—	65.00	90.00	155	285	—
1742 IIG	—	65.00	90.00	155	285	—
1743 IIG	—	65.00	90.00	155	285	—
1744 IIG	—	65.00	90.00	155	285	—
1745 IIG	—	65.00	90.00	155	285	—
1746 IIG	—	65.00	90.00	155	285	—
1747 IIG	—	65.00	90.00	155	285	—
1748 IIG	—	65.00	90.00	155	285	—
1749 IIG	—	65.00	90.00	155	285	—
1750 IEVC	—	65.00	90.00	155	285	—
1752 IEVC	—	65.00	90.00	155	285	—
1753 IEVC	—	65.00	90.00	155	285	—
1754 IEVC	—	65.00	90.00	155	285	—
1755 IEVC	—	65.00	90.00	155	285	—
1756 IEVC	—	65.00	90.00	155	285	—
1758 IEVC	—	65.00	90.00	155	285	—

KM# 265 1/3 THALER (1/2 Gulden)

9.5400 g., Silver **Ruler:** Friedrich Botho and Karl Ludwig Joint Coinage D **Countermark:** 1/3 and X over L **Obverse:** Manifold arms, three ornate helmets above, mintmaster's initial in cartouche below **Obv. Legend:** FRID. BOTHO. U. CARL LUDW. GR. Z. ST. K. R. W. U. H. **Reverse:** Stag left in front of column, date at end of legend **Rev. Legend:** LXXX. EINE FEINE MARCK **Note:** Klippe of 1/6 Taler, KM# 263, revalued with countermarks.

Date	Mintage	VG	F	VF	XF	Unc
1763 C Rare	—	—	—	—	—	—

KM# 264 1/3 THALER (1/2 Gulden)

Silver **Ruler:** Friedrich Botho and Karl Ludwig Joint Coinage D **Obverse:** Crowned arms, C below **Reverse:** Stag left before column with S in base in inner circle; date in exergue **Note:** Previous C#12A.

Date	Mintage	VG	F	VF	XF	Unc
1763 C	—	18.00	35.00	85.00	200	—

KM# 273 1/3 THALER (1/2 Gulden)

Silver **Ruler:** Friedrich Botho and Karl Ludwig Joint Coinage D **Obverse:** Crowned oval manifold arms between two branches, value 1/3 in cartouche below **Obv. Legend:** FRID • BOTHO • U • CARL • LUDW • GR • Z • STOLB • R • R • W • U • H **Reverse:** Stag left in front of column with S in base in inner circle; mintmaster's initial in exergue, date at end of legend **Rev. Legend:** .XL. EINE FEINE MARCK NACH DEM CONV. FUSS. **Note:** Previous C# A50.

Date	Mintage	VG	F	VF	XF	Unc
1764 C	—	18.00	35.00	85.00	200	—
1766 C	—	18.00	35.00	85.00	200	—

KM# 328 1/3 THALER (1/2 Gulden)

Silver **Ruler:** Karl Ludwig and Heinrich Christian Friedrich Joint Coinage E **Obverse:** Manifold arms divide date and mintmaster's initials, 3 ornate helmets above, value 1/3 in oval below divides FEIN — SILB. **Obv. Legend:** CARL LUDW. U. H. CHR. FRIED. GR. Z.STOLB. **Reverse:** Stag left in front of column **Rev. Legend:** GOTT SEEGNE U. ERHALTE UNSERE BERGWERCKE

Date	Mintage	VG	F	VF	XF	Unc
1796 EHAZ	—	45.00	85.00	160	225	—

KM# 306 1/3 THALER

Silver **Ruler:** Karl Ludwig and Heinrich Christian Friedrich Joint Coinage E **Obverse:** Crowned arms divide date, value below **Reverse:** Stag left before column **Note:** Previous C# 50.

Date	Mintage	VG	F	VF	XF	Unc
1768 EFR	—	45.00	75.00	125	260	—
1770 EFR	—	45.00	75.00	125	260	—
1777 EFR	—	45.00	75.00	125	260	—
1790 EFR	—	45.00	75.00	125	260	—

KM# 267 1/2 THALER

Silver **Ruler:** Karl Ludwig and Heinrich Christian Friedrich Joint Coinage E **Obverse:** Crowned oval arms, C below **Reverse:** Stag left before column with S in base, in inner circle; date in exergue **Note:** Previous C# 35.

Date	Mintage	VG	F	VF	XF	Unc
1763 C	—	80.00	150	300	500	—

KM# 206 16 GROSCHEN (2/3 Thaler)

Silver **Ruler:** Christof Friedrich and Jost Christian Joint Coinage A **Obverse:** 4-line inscription, mintmaster's initials divide date below **Obv. Legend:** CHRISTO. FRID. U. IOST. CHRISTI. GEBR. GR. Z. ST. K. R. W. U. H. **Obv. Inscription:** XVI/GUTE/GROSCH/N.D.L FUS. **Reverse:** Stag left in front of column **Rev. Legend:** GOTT SEEGNE U. ERHALTE UNSERE BERGWERCKE. **Note:** Dav# 1001.

Date	Mintage	VG	F	VF	XF	Unc
1737 IIG	—	60.00	100	200	325	—

KM# 151 2/3 THALER (Gulden)

Silver **Ruler:** Christof Friedrich and Jost Christian Joint Coinage A **Obverse:** Crowned 11-fold arms divide date and mintmaster's initials, value 2/3 in oval below divides FEIN — SILB: **Obv. Legend:** CHRISTO: FRID: U. IOST. CHRISTI: GEBR. GR. Z. ST. K. R. W. U. H. **Reverse:** Stag left in front of column **Rev. Legend:** GOTT SEEGNE U. ERHALTE UNSERE BERGWERCKE. **Note:** Varieties exist. Dav# 997.

Date	Mintage	VG	F	VF	XF	Unc
1715 IIG	—	40.00	75.00	145	240	—
1716 IIG	—	40.00	75.00	145	240	—
1717 IIG	—	40.00	75.00	145	240	—
1718 IIG	—	40.00	75.00	145	240	—
1719 IIG	—	40.00	75.00	145	240	—
1720 IIG	—	40.00	75.00	145	240	—
1721 IIG	—	40.00	75.00	145	240	—
1722 IIG	—	40.00	75.00	145	240	—
1723 IIG	—	40.00	75.00	145	240	—
1724 IIG	—	40.00	75.00	145	240	—
1726 IIG	—	40.00	75.00	145	240	—
1727 IIG	—	40.00	75.00	145	240	—
1729 IIG	—	40.00	75.00	145	240	—
1730 IIG	—	40.00	75.00	145	240	—
1731 IIG	—	40.00	75.00	145	240	—
1733 IIG	—	40.00	75.00	145	240	—
1734 IIG	—	40.00	75.00	145	240	—
1735 IIG	—	40.00	75.00	145	240	—
1736 IIG	—	40.00	75.00	145	240	—
1737 IIG	—	40.00	75.00	145	240	—
1738 IIG	—	40.00	75.00	145	240	—

KM# 165 2/3 THALER (Gulden)

Silver **Ruler:** Christof Friedrich and Jost Christian Joint Coinage A **Subject:** Bicentennial of the Reformation **Obverse:** Stag left in front of column **Obv. Legend:** GOTT SEEGNE U. ERHALTE UNSERE BERGWERCKE **Reverse:** 8-line inscription with year in chronogram, value 2/3 in oval at bottom divides mintmaster's initials **Rev. Inscription:** HERR GOTT/ZEBAOTH TRÖSTE/UNS LAS UNS/LEBEN SO WOLLEN/WIR DEINEN NAH:/MEN ANRVFFEN/PSALM. 80. U. 1. 9/DEN. 31. OCTOB. **Note:** Dav# 998.

Date	Mintage	VG	F	VF	XF	Unc
1717 IIG	—	60.00	110	200	325	—

KM# 183 2/3 THALER (Gulden)

Silver **Ruler:** Christof Friedrich and Jost Christian Joint Coinage A **Subject:** Bicentennial of the Augsburg Confession **Obverse:** Stag left in front of column **Obv. Legend:** GOTT SEEGNE U. ERHALTE UNSERE BERGWERCKE **Reverse:** 8-line inscription with year in chronogram, value 2/3 in oval below divides mintmaster's initials **Rev. Inscription:** WOHL/DENEN DIE/SEINE ZEVGNISSE/HALTEN DIE IHN/VON GANZEN HERZEN/SVCHEN/PS. CXIX. V. 2./DEN. 25 IVNII. **Note:** Dav# 999.

Date	Mintage	VG	F	VF	XF	Unc
1730 IIG	—	50.00	95.00	180	275	—

KM# 197 2/3 THALER (Gulden)

Silver **Ruler:** Jost Christian and Christof Ludwig II Joint Coinage B **Obverse:** 11-fold arms divide date and mintmaster's initials, value 2/3 in oval below divides FEIN — SILB: **Obv. Legend:** IOST. CHRISTI. U. CHRISTO. LUD. GRAF. Z. STOLB. K. R. W. U. H. **Reverse:** Stag left in front of column **Rev. Legend:** GOTT SEEGNE U. ERHALT UNSERE BERGWERCKE **Note:** Varieties exist. Dav# 1002.

Date	Mintage	VG	F	VF	XF	Unc
1738 IIG	—	40.00	75.00	140	220	—
1739 IIG	—	40.00	75.00	140	220	—

KM# 211 2/3 THALER (Gulden)

Silver **Ruler:** Christof Ludwig II and Friedrich Botho Joint Coinage C **Obverse:** Crowned manifold arms divide date and mintmaster's initials, value 2/3 in oval divides FEIN— SILB: below **Obv. Legend:** CHRIST • LUDEWIG • U • FRIED • BOTHO • GR • Z • STOLB • R • R • W • U • H **Reverse:** Stag left in front of column **Note:** Dav# 1006. Previous C# 13.

Date	Mintage	VG	F	VF	XF	Unc
1739 IIG	—	45.00	75.00	145	260	—
1740 IIG	—	45.00	75.00	145	260	—
1741 IIG	—	45.00	75.00	145	260	—
1742 IIG	—	45.00	75.00	145	260	—
1743 IIG	—	45.00	75.00	145	260	—
1744 IIG	—	45.00	75.00	145	260	—
1745 IIG	—	45.00	75.00	145	260	—
1746 IIG	—	45.00	75.00	145	260	—
1747 IIG	—	45.00	75.00	145	260	—
1748 IIG	—	45.00	75.00	145	260	—
1749 IIG	—	45.00	75.00	145	260	—
1750 IEVC	—	45.00	75.00	145	260	—
1751 IEVC	—	45.00	75.00	145	260	—
1752 IEVC	—	45.00	75.00	145	260	—
1753 IEVC	—	45.00	75.00	145	260	—
1754 IEVC	—	45.00	75.00	145	260	—

KM# 212 2/3 THALER (Gulden)

Silver **Ruler:** Jost Christian and Christof Ludwig II Joint Coinage B **Obverse:** 11-fold arms divide date and mintmaster's initials, value 2/3 in oval below divides N.D.L — FUS. **Obv. Legend:** IOST. CHRISTI. U. CHRISTO. LUD. GRAF. Z. STOLB. K .R. W. U. H. **Reverse:** Stag left in front of column **Rev. Legend:** GOTT SEEGNE U. ERHALTE UNSERE BERGWERCKE **Note:** Dav# 1003.

Date	Mintage	VG	F	VF	XF	Unc
1739 IIG	—	50.00	90.00	160	250	—

KM# 251 2/3 THALER (Gulden)

Silver **Ruler:** Friedrich Botho and Karl Ludwig Joint Coinage D **Obverse:** Crowned 11-fold arms divide date and mintmaster's initials, value 2/3 in oval divides FEIN — SILB. **Obv. Legend:** FRIED. BOTHO. U. CARL. LUDW: GR: Z. STOLB. K. R. W. U. H. **Reverse:** Stag left in front of column **Rev. Legend:** GOTT SEEGNE U. ERHALTE UNSERE BERGWERCKE.

Date	Mintage	VG	F	VF	XF	Unc
1762 IEVC	—	30.00	50.00	100	175	—

KM# 275 2/3 THALER (Gulden)

Silver **Ruler:** Friedrich Botho and Karl Ludwig Joint Coinage D **Obverse:** Crowned oval manifold arms in baroque frame, value 2/3 in cartouche below **Obv. Legend:** FRID • BOTHO • U • CARL • LUDW • GR • Z • STOLB • K • R • W • U • H • **Reverse:** Stag left in front of column with S in base in inner circle; C in exergue, date at end of legend **Rev. Legend:** XX. EINE FEINE MARCK NACH DEM CONV. FUSS. **Note:** Previous C# 37 and 37.1.

Date	Mintage	VG	F	VF	XF	Unc
1764 C	—	40.00	65.00	120	250	—

KM# 277 2/3 THALER (Gulden)

Silver **Ruler:** Friedrich Botho and Karl Ludwig Joint Coinage D **Obverse:** Crowned oval arms, value and T below **Reverse:** Stag left in front of column **Note:** Previous C# 37.2.

Date	Mintage	VG	F	VF	XF	Unc
1764 T	—	40.00	65.00	120	250	—

KM# 296 2/3 THALER (Gulden)

Silver **Ruler:** Christof Ludwig II and Friedrich Botho Joint Coinage C **Obverse:** Crowned square arms divide date, value below **Reverse:** Stag left before column **Note:** Previous C# A52.

Date	Mintage	VG	F	VF	XF	Unc
1766 EFR	—	50.00	90.00	165	350	—

KM# 308 2/3 THALER (Gulden)

Silver **Ruler:** Karl Ludwig and Heinrich Christian Friedrich Joint Coinage E **Obverse:** Crowned manifold arms divide date and mintmaster's initials, value 2/3 in oval below divides FEIN — SILB: **Obv. Legend:** CARL • LUDW • U • H • CHRIST • FRIED • GR • Z: STOLB • R • R • W • U • H • **Reverse:** Stag left in front of column **Rev. Legend:** GOTT SEEGNE U. ERHALTE UNSERE BERGWERCKE **Note:** Reichs 2/3 Thaler. Previous C# 52.

Date	Mintage	VG	F	VF	XF	Unc
1768 EFR	—	30.00	60.00	100	175	—
1770 EFR	—	30.00	60.00	100	175	—
1777 EFR	—	35.00	75.00	125	200	—
1782 EFR	—	60.00	120	200	325	—
1788 EFR	—	30.00	60.00	100	175	—
1790 EFR	—	42.00	80.00	135	225	—
1793 EHAZ	—	45.00	90.00	150	250	—

KM# 330 2/3 THALER (Gulden)

Pewter **Ruler:** Karl Ludwig and Heinrich Christian Friedrich Joint Coinage E **Obverse:** Helmeted arms divide date, value below **Obv. Legend:** CARL • LUDW • U • H • CHR • FRIED • GR • Z • STOLB • **Reverse:** Stag left in front of column **Rev. Legend:** GOTT SEEGNE U. ERHALTE UNSERE BERGWERCKE **Note:** Previous C# 53.

Date	Mintage	VG	F	VF	XF	Unc
1796 EHAZ	—	30.00	65.00	120	200	—

KM# 117 24 MARIENGROSCHEN (2/3 Thaler)

Silver **Ruler:** Christof Friedrich and Jost Christian Joint Coinage A **Obverse:** 4-line inscription, mintmaster's initials divide date below **Obv. Legend:** CHRIST. FRID. U. IOST. CHRISTI. GEB. G. ZU. ST. K. R. W. U. H. **Obv. Inscription:** XXIIII/MARIEN/GROSCH/V. FEIN. SILB:. **Reverse:** Stag to left in front of column **Rev. Legend:** GOTT SEEGNE UND ERHALTE UNSERE BERGWERCKE.

Date	Mintage	VG	F	VF	XF	Unc
1706 IIG	—	45.00	85.00	150	240	—
1707 IIG	—	45.00	85.00	150	240	—

KM# 134 24 MARIENGROSCHEN (2/3 Thaler)

Silver **Ruler:** Christof Friedrich and Jost Christian Joint Coinage A **Obverse:** 4-line inscription, mintmaster's initials divide date below **Obv. Legend:** CHRISTO. FRID. U. IOST. CHRISTI. GEB(R). G(R). ZU. ST. K. R. W. U. H(ON). **Obv. Inscription:** XXIV/MARIEN/GROSCH/FEIN SILBER. **Reverse:** Stag left in front of column **Rev. Legend:** GOTT SEEGNE U. ERHALTE UNSERE BERGWERCKE. **Note:** Varieties exist. Dav# 1000.

Date	Mintage	VG	F	VF	XF	Unc
1707 IIG	—	25.00	50.00	100	175	—
1708 IIG	—	25.00	50.00	100	175	—
1709 IIG	—	25.00	50.00	100	175	—
1710 IIG	—	25.00	50.00	100	175	—
1711 IIG	—	25.00	50.00	100	175	—
1712 IIG	—	25.00	50.00	100	175	—
1713 IIG	—	25.00	50.00	100	175	—
1714 IIG	—	25.00	50.00	100	175	—
1715 IIG	—	25.00	50.00	100	175	—
1716 IIG	—	25.00	50.00	100	175	—
1717 IIG	—	25.00	50.00	100	175	—
1718 IIG	—	25.00	50.00	100	175	—
1719 IIG	—	25.00	50.00	100	175	—
1720 IIG	—	25.00	50.00	100	175	—
1721 IIG	—	25.00	50.00	100	175	—
1722 IIG	—	25.00	50.00	100	175	—
1723 IIG	—	25.00	50.00	100	175	—
1724 IIG	—	25.00	50.00	100	175	—
1725 IIG	—	25.00	50.00	100	175	—
1726 IIG	—	25.00	50.00	100	175	—
1727 IIG	—	25.00	50.00	100	175	—
1728 IIG	—	25.00	50.00	100	175	—
1733 IIG	—	25.00	50.00	100	175	—
1734 IIG	—	25.00	50.00	100	175	—
1735 IIG	—	25.00	50.00	100	175	—
1736 IIG	—	25.00	50.00	100	175	—
1737 IIG	—	25.00	50.00	100	175	—
1738 IIG	—	25.00	50.00	100	175	—

KM# 195 24 MARIENGROSCHEN (2/3 Thaler)

Silver **Ruler:** Jost Christian and Christof Ludwig II Joint Coinage B **Obverse:** 4-line inscription, mintmaster's initials divide date below **Obv. Legend:** IOST. CHRISTI. U. CHRISTO. LUD. GRAF Z. STOLB. K. R. W. U. H. **Obv. Inscription:** XXIV/MARIEN/GROSCH/FEIN SILBER. **Reverse:** Stag left in front of column **Rev. Legend:** GOTT SEEGNE U. ERHALTE UNSERE BERGWERCKE. **Note:** Varieties exist. Dav# 1004.

Date	Mintage	VG	F	VF	XF	Unc
1738 IIG	—	35.00	65.00	120	200	—
1739 IIG	—	35.00	65.00	120	200	—

KM# 286 24 MARIENGROSCHEN (2/3 Thaler)

Silver **Ruler:** Friedrich Botho and Karl Ludwig Joint Coinage D **Obverse:** Crowned 11-fold arms in baroque frame divide date and mintmaster's initials, value 2/3 in cartouche below divides FEIN — SILB. **Obv. Legend:** FRIED. BOTHO. U. CARL LUDW: GR: Z, STOLB. K. R. W. U. H. **Reverse:** Stag left in front of column **Rev. Legend:** GOTT SEEGNE U. ERHALTE UNSERE BERGWERCKE.

Date	Mintage	VG	F	VF	XF	Unc
1765 IEVC	—	30.00	50.00	100	175	—

KM# 294 24 MARIENGROSCHEN (2/3 Thaler)

Silver **Ruler:** Friedrich Botho and Karl Ludwig Joint Coinage D **Obverse:** 4-line inscription, mintmaster's initials and date below **Obv. Legend:** FRIED. BOTHO. V. CARL. LVDEW. GR. Z. STOLB. K. R. W. V. H. **Obv. Inscription:** XXIV/MARIEN/ GROSCH:/FEIN SILBER. **Reverse:** Stag left in front of column **Rev. Legend:** GOTT SEEGNE V. ERHALTE VNSERE BERGWERCKE. **Note:** Previous C# 23a.

Date	Mintage	VG	F	VF	XF	Unc
1766 EFR	—	75.00	150	350	500	—

KM# 315 24 MARIENGROSCHEN (2/3 Thaler)

Silver **Ruler:** Karl Ludwig and Heinrich Christian Friedrich Joint Coinage E **Obverse:** 4-line inscription, mintmaster's initials and date below **Obv. Legend:** CARL. LVDV. V. H. CHRISTI. FRIED. GR. V. STOLB. K. R. W. V. H. **Obv. Inscription:** XXIV/MARIEN/ GROSCH:/FEIN SILBER. **Reverse:** Stag left in front of column **Rev. Legend:** GOTT SEEGNE V. ERHALTE VNSERE BERGWERCKE.

Date	Mintage	VG	F	VF	XF	Unc
1777 EFR	—	60.00	100	250	400	—
1790 EFR	—	60.00	100	250	400	—

KM# 269 24 MARIENGROSCHEN

Silver **Ruler:** Friedrich Botho and Karl Ludwig Joint Coinage D **Obverse:** 4-line inscription, mintmaster's initials and date below **Obv. Legend:** FRIED. BOTHO. V. CARL. LVDEW. GR. Z. STOLB. K. R. W. V. H. **Obv. Inscription:** XXIV/MARIEN/ GROSCH./FEIN SILBER **Reverse:** Stag left in front of column **Rev. Legend:** GOTT SEEGNE V. ERHALTE VNSERE BERGWERCKE **Note:** Previous C# 23.

Date	Mintage	VG	F	VF	XF	Unc
1763 IEVC	—	25.00	45.00	85.00	175	—

KM# 113 THALER

Silver **Ruler:** Christof Friedrich and Jost Christian Joint Coinage A **Obverse:** Manifold arms divide date and mintmaster's initials, 3 ornate helmets above **Obv. Legend:** CHRISTOPH FRIDRICH UND I(G)GOST CRISTIAN GEB: GRAF: ZU STOLB: **Reverse:** Stag left in front of column **Rev. Legend:** GOTT SEEGNE UND ERHALTE UNSERE BERGWERCKE * **Note:** Dav# 2794 and 2794A.

Date	Mintage	VG	F	VF	XF	Unc
1705 IIG	—	250	500	850	1,450	—

KM# 119 THALER

Silver **Ruler:** Christof Friedrich and Jost Christian Joint Coinage A **Obverse:** Ornate manifold arms, mintmaster's initials divided below, 3 ornate helmets above with date divided among crests **Obv. Legend:** CHRIST: FRID: U: IOST: CHRIST: GEB: G: ZU: ST: K: R: W: U: H: H: E: M: B: A: L: U: C: **Reverse:** Stag left in front of column **Rev. Legend:** GOTT SEEGNE UND ERHALTE UNSERE BERGWERCKE * **Note:** Dav# 2795.

Date	Mintage	VG	F	VF	XF	Unc
1706 IIG	—	200	400	750	1,150	—

KM# 120 THALER

Silver **Ruler:** Christof Friedrich and Jost Christian Joint Coinage A **Obverse:** Ornate manifold arms, mintmaster's initials divided below, 3 ornate helmets above with date divided among crests **Obv. Legend:** CHRIST: FRID: U: IOST: CHRIST: GEB: G: Z: ST: K: R: W: U: H: H: Z: E: M: B: A: L: U: C **Reverse:** Stag left in front of column **Rev. Legend:** GOTT SEEGNE UND ERHALTE UNSERE BERGWERCKE * **Note:** Dav# 2797.

Date	Mintage	VG	F	VF	XF	Unc
1706 IIG	—	200	400	700	1,150	—
1707 IIG	—	200	400	700	1,150	—

KM# 153 THALER

Silver **Ruler:** Christof Friedrich and Jost Christian Joint Coinage A **Obverse:** Conjoined busts of C. Friedrich and J. Christian right **Obv. Legend:** CHRISTO • FRID • & IOST • CHRISTI • FR • COM • D • STOLB • K • R • W • & H • * **Reverse:** Stag above mining scene, date in Roman numerals below **Rev. Legend:** SPES NESCIA FALLI, below; MDCCXV./I.I.G. **Note:** Dav# 2798.

Date	Mintage	VG	F	VF	XF	Unc
1715 CW//IIG	—	450	800	1,350	2,250	—

KM# 154 THALER

Silver **Ruler:** Christof Friedrich and Jost Christian Joint Coinage A **Obverse:** Two busts to right **Obv. Legend:** CHRISTO. FRID. & IOST. CHRISTI. FR. COM. D. STOLB. K. R. W. & H. **Reverse:** Landscape with castle in left background, 3-line inscription with Roman numeral date in exergue **Rev. Legend:** CVNCTANDO RESTITVIT REM **Rev. Inscription:** FRVCT9 FODINÆ STOLB:- /STRASBERGENSIS/MDCCXXII. **Note:** Mule of obverse of KM#153 and reverse of KM# 177. Dav# 2803B.

Date	Mintage	VG	F	VF	XF	Unc
(1715)//1722 CW//IIG	—	—	—	—	—	—

KM# 167 THALER

Silver **Ruler:** Christof Friedrich and Jost Christian Joint Coinage A **Obverse:** Conjoined busts right **Obv. Legend:** CHRISTO • FRID • & IOST • CHRISTI • FR • COM • D • STOLB • K • R • W • & H • * **Reverse:** Man raising bucket, date in exergue **Rev. Legend:** WIR FEYREN IEZT EIN IUBELIAHR • DAS BERGWERCK GIBT DIE MUNTZE DAR *, IUBI/LEUM on bucket, en exergue; DEN 31 OCTOBRIS/*1717*/I•I•G• **Note:** Dav# 2799.

Date	Mintage	VG	F	VF	XF	Unc
1717 CW//IIG	—	450	800	1,350	2,250	—

KM# 171 THALER

Silver **Ruler:** Christof Friedrich and Jost Christian Joint Coinage A **Obverse:** Conjoined busts right **Obv. Legend:** CHRISTO • FRID • & IOST • CHRISTI • FR • COM • D • STOLB • K • R • W • & H • * **Reverse:** Rays falling on clasped hands **Note:** Dav# 2800.

Date	Mintage	VG	F	VF	XF	Unc
1719 CW//IIG	—	150	300	550	900	—

KM# 172 THALER

Silver **Ruler:** Christof Friedrich and Jost Christian Joint Coinage A **Obverse:** Different helmets and ornamentation **Obv. Legend:** CHRIST • FRID • U • IOST • CHRIST • GEB • G • Z • ST • K • R • W • U • H • H • Z • E • M • B • A • L • U • C • **Reverse:** Stag left before column **Rev. Legend:** GOTT SEEGNE U. ERHALTE UNSERE BERGWERCKE **Note:** Dav# 2802.

Date	Mintage	VG	F	VF	XF	Unc
1719 IIG	—	200	400	700	1,150	—
1721 IIG	—	200	400	700	1,150	—
1723 IIG	—	200	400	700	1,150	—
1734 IIG	—	200	400	700	1,150	—

KM# 173 THALER

Silver **Ruler:** Christof Friedrich and Jost Christian Joint Coinage A **Obverse:** Rays from above shining down on clasped hands, 2-line inscription in exergue, year in chronogram in legend **Obv. Legend:** VI VNITA CONCORDIA FRATRVM FORTIOR **Obv. Inscription:** D. VI. IULII./I.I.G. **Reverse:** Stag left in front of column **Rev. Legend:** GOTT SEEGNE U. ERHALTE UNSERE BERGWERCKE **Note:** Mule of reverse of KM# 171 with reverse of KM# 172.

Date	Mintage	VG	F	VF	XF	Unc
1719 IIG	—	—	—	—	—	—

KM# 178 THALER

Silver **Ruler:** Christof Friedrich and Jost Christian Joint Coinage A **Obverse:** Stag left in front of column, MDCIIC in exergue **Obv. Legend:** CHRISTO. FRID. ET IOST. — CHRISTI. COM. STOLB. ET H —CONCORDIA FRATRVM **Reverse:** Man raisting bucket in mine shaft labled IUBI/LEUM, 3-line inscription with date and mintmaster's initials **Rev. Legend:** WIR FEYREN IEZT EIN IUBELIAHR. DAS BERGWERCK GIVT DIE MUNTZE DAR **Rev. Inscription:** DEN 31 OCTOBRIS/1717/I.I.G. **Note:** Mule of obverse of KM# 177 with reverse of KM# 167.

Date	Mintage	VG	F	VF	XF	Unc
(1722)//1717 W//IIG	—	—	—	—	—	—

KM# 179 THALER

Silver **Ruler:** Christof Friedrich and Jost Christian Joint Coinage A **Obverse:** Stag left in front of column, MDCIIC in exergue **Obv. Legend:** CHRISTO. FRID. ET IOST. — CHRISTI. COM. STOLB. ET H — CONCORDIA FRATRVM. **Reverse:** Stag left in front of column **Rev. Legend:** GOTT SEEGNE U. ERHALTE UNSERE BERGWERCKE. **Note:** Mule of obverse of KM# 177 with reverse of 24 Mariengroschen KM# 172.

Date	Mintage	VG	F	VF	XF	Unc
(1722)//(1712) W	—	—	—	—	—	—

KM# 177 THALER

Silver **Ruler:** Christof Friedrich and Jost Christian Joint Coinage A **Obverse:** Stag left before column **Obv. Legend:** CHRISTO • FRID • ET IOST • - CHRISTI • COM. STOLB • ET H * CONCORDIA FRATRVM *, S/MDCIIC • below stag **Reverse:** Castle in landscape, Roman numeral date **Rev. Legend:** CVNCTANDO RESTITVIT REM •, in exergue; FRVCT9 FODINÆ STOLB:- /STRASBERGENSIS•/ MDCCXXII•/I•I•G• **Note:** Varieties exist. Dav# 2803.

Date	Mintage	VG	F	VF	XF	Unc
ND(1722) W//IIG	—	450	900	1,650	2,750	—

KM# 185 THALER

Silver **Ruler:** Christof Friedrich and Jost Christian Joint Coinage A **Subject:** Bicentennial of the Augsburg Confession **Obverse:** FIAT LVX over open book with THESES/1517 on pages, WITTENBERG and STOLBERG/IVBILABAT below **Obv. Legend:** CHRISTO • FRID • & IOST CHRISTI • FRATR • ET COM • ST • K • R • W • ET H • **Reverse:** ET FIEBAT over open book with AVGVSTANA/CONFESSIO/15.30 and BIBLIA SACRA., AVGSBVRG. and STOLBERG./IVBILAT below **Rev. Legend:** DOM. IN EPST. MUNZ. BRAIB. AIGM. LOHR. ET CLET. and I.I.(1730)G. **Note:** Dav# 2804.

Date	Mintage	VG	F	VF	XF	Unc
1730 IIG	—	225	450	800	1,350	—

KM# 234 THALER

Silver **Ruler:** Christof Ludwig II and Friedrich Botho Joint Coinage C **Obverse:** Helmeted arms, date above **Reverse:** Stag left in front of column **Note:** Species Thaler. Dav# 2805. Previous C# 15.

Date	Mintage	VG	F	VF	XF	Unc
1746 IIG	—	450	950	1,750	3,200	—

KM# 271 THALER

Silver **Ruler:** Friedrich Botho and Karl Ludwig Joint Coinage D **Obverse:** Crowned oval arms in sprays and garlands; C below **Reverse:** Stag left before column with S in base, date below **Note:** Dav. #2806. Previous C# 39.

Date	Mintage	VG	F	VF	XF	Unc
1763 C	—	—	—	—	—	—

KM# 279 THALER

Silver **Ruler:** Friedrich Botho and Karl Ludwig Joint Coinage D **Obverse:** Crowned ornamental arms in garlands; C below **Obv. Legend:** FRIEDRICH BOTHO U • CARL LUDWIG GR • Z • STOLB • K • R • W • U • H * **Reverse:** Stag left before column with S in base, without inner circle **Rev. Legend:** X. EINE FEINE MARCK NAACH DEM CONVENT: FUSS. 1764 **Note:** Dav# 2807.

Date	Mintage	VG	F	VF	XF	Unc
1764 C	—	75.00	200	300	450	—

KM# 280 THALER

Silver **Ruler:** Friedrich Botho and Karl Ludwig Joint Coinage D **Obverse:** Crowned ornate arms with garlands **Obv. Legend:** FRIEDRICH BOTHO U • CARL LUDWIG GR • Z • STOLB • K • R • W • U • H * **Reverse:** Stag left before column **Rev. Legend:** X. EINE FEINE MARCK NACH DEM CONVENT: FUSS • 1764 **Note:** Dav# 2808. Previous C# 40.

Date	Mintage	VG	F	VF	XF	Unc
1764 C	—	75.00	200	300	450	—

KM# 187 1-1/4 THALER

Silver **Ruler:** Christof Friedrich and Jost Christian Joint Coinage A **Countermark:** 1 1/4 **Obverse:** Crowned 11-fold arms divide date and mintmaster's initials, value 2/3 in oval below divides FEIN — SILB: **Obv. Legend:** CHRISTO: FRID: U. IOST. CHRISTI: GEBR. GR. Z. ST. K. R. W. U. **Reverse:** Stag left in front of column **Rev. Legend:** GOTT SEEGNE U. ERHALTE UNSERE BERGWERCKE. **Note:** Klippe. Dies of 2/3 Taler, KM# 151, with countermark revalue punched over oval with 2/3.

Date	Mintage	VG	F	VF	XF	Unc
1735 IIG Rare	—	—	—	—	—	—

KM# 332 1-1/3 THALER

Silver **Ruler:** Karl Ludwig and Heinrich Christian Friedrich Joint Coinage E **Obverse:** Manifold arms divide date and mintmaster's initials, value 1 1/3 in oval below divides FEIN — SILB. **Obv. Legend:** CARL LUDW • U • H • CHRIST • FRIED • GRAF • Z • STOLB •, FEIN (11/2) SILB• below shield **Reverse:** Stag left in front of column **Rev. Legend:** GOTT SEEGNE U • ERHALTE UNSERE BERGWERCKE **Note:** Dav. #2809. Previous C# 54.

Date	Mintage	VG	F	VF	XF	Unc
1796 EHAZ	—	250	650	1,250	2,000	—

KM# 136 2 THALER

Silver **Ruler:** Christof Friedrich and Jost Christian Joint Coinage A **Obverse:** Helmeted arms within circle **Reverse:** Stag left before column **Note:** Dav# 2796. Similar to 1 Thaler, Dav. #2797.

Date	Mintage	VG	F	VF	XF	Unc
1707 IIG Rare	—	—	—	—	—	—

KM# 175 2 THALER

Silver **Ruler:** Christof Friedrich and Jost Christian Joint Coinage A **Obverse:** Helmeted arms within circle **Reverse:** Stag left before column **Note:** Dav# 2801. Similar to 1 Thaler, Dav. #2802.

Date	Mintage	VG	F	VF	XF	Unc
1719 IIG	—	1,500	2,500	4,000	6,000	—
1723 IIG	—	1,500	2,500	4,000	6,000	—

JOINT COINAGE

Stolberg-Stolberg / Stolberg-Rossla

KM# 1 24 MARIENGROSCHEN

13.0000 g., Silver, 34.8 mm. **Ruler:** Christof Friedrich **Obverse:** Value date and legend **Reverse:** Stag and pillar **Edge:** Plain

Date	Mintage	F	VF	XF	Unc
1717IIG	—	50.00	90.00	185	—

KM# 209 24 MARIENGROSCHEN

Silver **Ruler:** Christof Ludwig II and Friedrich Botho Joint Coinage C **Obverse:** 4-line inscription, mintmaster's initials divide date below **Obv. Legend:** CHRIST • LUDEWIG • U • FRIED • BOTHO • GR • Z • STOLB • K • R • W • U • H • **Obv. Inscription:** XXIV/MARIEN/GROSCH./FEIN SILBER **Reverse:** Stag left before column **Rev. Legend:** GOTT SEEGNE U. ERHALTE. VNSERE BERGWERCKE **Note:** Dav# 1007. Previous C# 14.

Date	Mintage	VG	F	VF	XF	Unc
1739 IIG	—	30.00	50.00	90.00	185	—
1740 IIG	—	30.00	50.00	90.00	185	—
1741 IIG	—	30.00	50.00	90.00	185	—
1742 IIG	—	30.00	50.00	90.00	185	—
1743 IIG	—	30.00	50.00	90.00	185	—
1744 IIG	—	30.00	50.00	90.00	185	—
1745 IIG	—	30.00	50.00	90.00	185	—
1746 IIG	—	30.00	50.00	90.00	185	—
1747 IIG	—	30.00	50.00	90.00	185	—
1750 IEVC	—	30.00	50.00	90.00	185	—
1751 IEVC	—	30.00	50.00	90.00	185	—
1753 IEVC	—	30.00	50.00	90.00	185	—
1754 IEVC	—	30.00	50.00	90.00	185	—
1755 IEVC	—	30.00	50.00	90.00	185	—

TRADE COINAGE

KM# 240 1/32 DUCAT

0.1091 g., 0.9860 Gold 0.0035 oz. AGW **Ruler:** Christof Ludwig II **Obverse:** CL monogram **Reverse:** Stag **Note:** Prev. C# 1.

Date	Mintage	VG	F	VF	XF	Unc
ND(1759)	—	50.00	100	200	300	—

KM# 241 1/16 DUCAT

0.2188 g., 0.9860 Gold 0.0069 oz. AGW **Ruler:** Christof Ludwig II **Obverse:** CL monogram **Reverse:** Stag **Note:** Previous C# 2.

Date	Mintage	VG	F	VF	XF	Unc
ND(1759)	—	50.00	100	225	350	—

KM# 109 1/8 DUCAT

0.4375 g., 0.9860 Gold 0.0139 oz. AGW **Ruler:** Christof Friedrich **Obverse:** CF monogram **Reverse:** Stag in front of column **Note:** Fr# 3330.

Date	Mintage	VG	F	VF	XF	Unc
ND(1704)	—	50.00	75.00	175	275	—

KM# 214 1/8 DUCAT

0.4375 g., 0.9860 Gold 0.0139 oz. AGW **Ruler:** Christof Ludwig II and Friedrich Botho Joint Coinage C **Obverse:** Stag in front of column **Reverse:** Crowned shield of arms **Note:** Previous C# 17.

Date	Mintage	VG	F	VF	XF	Unc
ND(1739)	—	50.00	100	225	400	—

KM# 242 1/8 DUCAT

0.4375 g., 0.9860 Gold 0.0139 oz. AGW **Ruler:** Christof Ludwig II **Obverse:** Crowned monogram **Reverse:** Stag in front of column **Note:** Previous C# 3.

Date	Mintage	VG	F	VF	XF	Unc
ND(1759)	—	50.00	75.00	175	275	—

KM# 111 1/4 DUCAT

0.8750 g., 0.9860 Gold 0.0277 oz. AGW **Ruler:** Christof Friedrich **Obverse:** Crowned CF monogram **Reverse:** Stag left before column **Note:** Fr# 3329.

Date	Mintage	VG	F	VF	XF	Unc
ND(1704)	—	90.00	175	350	550	—

KM# 122 1/4 DUCAT

0.8750 g., 0.9860 Gold 0.0277 oz. AGW **Ruler:** Christof Friedrich and Jost Christian Joint Coinage A **Obverse:** Stag in front of column **Reverse:** Crowned shield of arms **Note:** Fr# 3326.

Date	Mintage	VG	F	VF	XF	Unc
1706 IEVC	—	100	200	425	700	—

KM# 216 1/4 DUCAT

0.8750 g., 0.9860 Gold 0.0277 oz. AGW **Ruler:** Christof Ludwig II and Friedrich Botho Joint Coinage C **Obverse:** Stag in front of column **Note:** Previous C# 18.

Date	Mintage	VG	F	VF	XF	Unc
ND(1739)	—	75.00	135	275	500	—

KM# 243 1/4 DUCAT

0.8750 g., 0.9860 Gold 0.0277 oz. AGW **Ruler:** Christof Friedrich **Obverse:** Crowned CF monogram **Reverse:** Stag in front of column **Note:** Previous C# 4.

Date	Mintage	VG	F	VF	XF	Unc
ND(1759)	—	75.00	125	225	400	—

KM# 156 1/2 DUCAT

1.7500 g., 0.9860 Gold 0.0555 oz. AGW **Ruler:** Christof Friedrich **Obverse:** Crowned CF monogram **Reverse:** Stag left before column, date below **Note:** Fr# 3328.

Date	Mintage	VG	F	VF	XF	Unc
1715	—	100	225	400	700	—

KM# 231 1/2 DUCAT

1.7500 g., 0.9860 Gold 0.0555 oz. AGW **Ruler:** Christof Ludwig II and Friedrich Botho Joint Coinage C **Obverse:** Stag left in front of column **Reverse:** Crowned arms divide date **Note:** Previous C# 19.

Date	Mintage	VG	F	VF	XF	Unc
1745 IIG	—	100	185	375	650	—
1748 IIG	—	100	185	375	650	—
1750 IEVC	—	100	185	375	650	—

KM# 253 1/2 DUCAT

1.7500 g., 0.9860 Gold 0.0555 oz. AGW **Ruler:** Friedrich Botho and Karl Ludwig Joint Coinage D **Obverse:** Stag left in front of column **Reverse:** Crowned arms divide date **Note:** Previous C# 41.

Date	Mintage	VG	F	VF	XF	Unc
1762 IEVC	—	200	400	900	1,500	—

KM# 292 1/2 DUCAT

1.7500 g., 0.9860 Gold 0.0555 oz. AGW **Ruler:** Friedrich Botho and Karl Ludwig Joint Coinage D **Obverse:** Helmeted arms divide date **Reverse:** Stag left before column with S in base, without inner circle **Note:** Previous C# 41a.

Date	Mintage	VG	F	VF	XF	Unc
1766 EFR	—	200	400	900	1,500	—

KM# 312 1/2 DUCAT

1.7500 g., 0.9860 Gold 0.0555 oz. AGW **Ruler:** Karl Ludwig and Heinrich Christian Friedrich Joint Coinage E **Reverse:** Stag left before column **Note:** Previous C# 56a.

Date	Mintage	VG	F	VF	XF	Unc
1770 EFR	—	200	400	900	1,500	—

KM# 124 DUCAT

3.5000 g., 0.9860 Gold 0.1109 oz. AGW **Ruler:** Christof Friedrich and Jost Christian Joint Coinage A **Obverse:** Stag left in front of column **Obv. Legend:** CHRIST: FRIED: &. IOST: CHRISTI: FRA: &. CO: ST. K: R: WE: & H:. **Reverse:** 11-fold arms divide mintmaster's initials at bottom, 3 ornate helmets above with date divided between crests **Rev. Legend:** DOM: IN. EPST: MUN: BR: AI: LOHR: &. CLET. **Note:** Fr# 3325. Struck from same dies as 1/6 Thaler, KM# 115.

Date	Mintage	VG	F	VF	XF	Unc
1706 IIG	—	200	400	900	1,600	—
1723 IIG	—	150	300	700	1,200	—
1725 IIG	—	150	300	700	1,200	—
1734 IIG	—	150	300	700	1,200	—

KM# 169 DUCAT

3.5000 g., 0.9860 Gold 0.1109 oz. AGW **Ruler:** Christof Friedrich and Jost Christian Joint Coinage A **Subject:** Bicentennial of the Reformation **Obverse:** Martin Luther; date in chronogram **Reverse:** 7-line inscription, mintmaster's initials at bottom **Note:** Fr# 3327.

Date	Mintage	VG	F	VF	XF	Unc
ND(1717)	—	150	300	700	1,200	—

KM# 222 DUCAT

3.5000 g., 0.9860 Gold 0.1109 oz. AGW **Ruler:** Christof Ludwig II and Friedrich Botho Joint Coinage C **Obverse:** Stag left in front of column **Reverse:** Helmeted ornate arms **Note:** Previous C# 20.

Date	Mintage	VG	F	VF	XF	Unc
1740 IIG	—	175	350	800	1,350	—
1742 IIG	—	175	350	800	1,350	—
1743 IIG	—	175	350	800	1,350	—
1748 IIG	—	175	350	800	1,350	—
1750 IEVC	—	175	350	800	1,350	—
1757 IEVC	—	175	350	800	1,350	—

KM# 244 DUCAT

3.5000 g., 0.9860 Gold 0.1109 oz. AGW **Ruler:** Christof Ludwig II and Friedrich Botho Joint Coinage C **Obverse:** Stag left in front of column **Reverse:** Helmeted arms **Note:** Previous C# 20.1.

Date	Mintage	VG	F	VF	XF	Unc
1759 IEVC	—	300	600	1,200	2,000	—

KM# 254 DUCAT

3.5000 g., 0.9860 Gold 0.1109 oz. AGW **Ruler:** Friedrich Botho and Karl Ludwig Joint Coinage D **Obverse:** Stag left in front of column **Obv. Legend:** FRID • BOTHO • & CAR • LUD • COM • STOLB • R • R • W • & H **Reverse:** Helmeted arms **Note:** Previous C# 42.

Date	Mintage	VG	F	VF	XF	Unc
1762 IEVC	—	200	450	1,000	2,000	—
1764 IEVC	—	200	450	1,000	2,000	—
1766 EFR	—	200	450	1,000	2,000	—

KM# 282 DUCAT

3.5000 g., 0.9860 Gold 0.1109 oz. AGW **Ruler:** Friedrich Botho and Karl Ludwig Joint Coinage D **Obverse:** Small stag left before column with S in base, with inner circle **Reverse:** Helmeted arms, date in outer legend **Note:** Previous C# 42.1.

Date	Mintage	VG	F	VF	XF	Unc
1764 IEVC	—	200	450	1,000	2,000	—
1766 EFR	—	200	450	1,000	2,000	—

KM# 310 DUCAT

3.5000 g., 0.9860 Gold 0.1109 oz. AGW **Ruler:** Karl Ludwig and Heinrich Christian Friedrich Joint Coinage E **Obverse:** Stag left in front of column **Reverse:** Manifold arms, 3 ornate helmets above, date divided among crests **Note:** Previous C# 57.

Date	Mintage	VG	F	VF	XF	Unc
1768 EFR	—	200	450	1,000	2,000	—
1770 EFR	—	200	450	1,000	2,000	—

KM# 316 DUCAT

3.5000 g., 0.9860 Gold 0.1109 oz. AGW **Ruler:** Karl Ludwig **Obverse:** EFR below arms **Note:** Previous C# 57a.

Date	Mintage	VG	F	VF	XF	Unc
1788 EFR	—	200	450	1,000	2,000	—

KM# 335 DUCAT

3.5000 g., 0.9860 Gold 0.1109 oz. AGW **Ruler:** Karl Ludwig **Obverse:** Bust left; SENIOR DOMUS in field **Reverse:** Z below arms **Note:** Previous C# 45.

Date	Mintage	VG	F	VF	XF	Unc
1796 EHAZ	—	250	500	1,200	2,200	—

KM# 181 2 DUCAT

7.0000 g., 0.9860 Gold 0.2219 oz. AGW **Ruler:** Christof Friedrich and Jost Christian Joint Coinage A **Obverse:** Stag in front of column **Reverse:** Crowned arms **Note:** Fr# 3324.

Date	Mintage	VG	F	VF	XF	Unc
1725 IIG	—	750	1,450	2,750	4,500	—

KM# 226 2 DUCAT

7.0000 g., 0.9860 Gold 0.2219 oz. AGW **Ruler:** Christof Ludwig II and Friedrich Botho Joint Coinage C **Obverse:** Stag left in front of column **Obv. Legend:** CHRIST • LUDEWIG • & FRIED • BOTHO • CO • STOLB • R • R • W • & H **Reverse:** Helmeted ornate arms **Note:** Previous C# 21.

Date	Mintage	VG	F	VF	XF	Unc
1743 IIG	—	850	1,650	3,000	5,000	—

KM# 284 2 DUCAT

7.0000 g., 0.9860 Gold 0.2219 oz. AGW **Ruler:** Friedrich Botho and Karl Ludwig Joint Coinage D **Obverse:** Stag left in front of column **Reverse:** Manifold arms, 3 ornate helmets above **Note:** Previous C# 43.

Date	Mintage	VG	F	VF	XF	Unc
1764 IEVC	—	1,850	3,000	5,000	7,500	—

KM# 228 4 DUCAT

14.0000 g., 0.9860 Gold 0.4438 oz. AGW **Ruler:** Christof Ludwig II and Friedrich Botho Joint Coinage C **Obverse:** Stag left in front of column **Reverse:** Arms topped by three ornate helmets **Note:** Struck with 2 Ducat dies, KM# 226.

Date	Mintage	VG	F	VF	XF	Unc
1743 IIG Rare	—	—	—	—	—	—

JOINT TRADE COINAGE

Stolberg-Stolberg / Stolberg-Rossla

KM# 318 DUCAT

3.5000 g., 0.9860 Gold 0.1109 oz. AGW **Ruler:** Karl Ludwig and Heinrich Christian Friedrich Joint Coinage E **Obverse:** EHAZ below arms **Note:** Previous C# 57b.

Date	Mintage	VG	F	VF	XF	Unc
1793 EHAZ	—	200	450	1,000	2,000	—

KM# 334 DUCAT

3.5000 g., 0.9860 Gold 0.1109 oz. AGW **Ruler:** Karl Ludwig **Obverse:** Bust to left **Reverse:** Helmeted arms, date in legend, arms divide EH - AZ **Note:** Previous C# 57c.

Date	Mintage	VG	F	VF	XF	Unc
1796 EHAZ	—	200	450	1,000	2,000	—

PATTERNS

Including off metal strikes

KM#	Date	Mintage	Identification	Mkt Val
Pn2		—	1/8 Ducat. Silver.	—
Pn3		—	1/4 Ducat. Silver.Crowned CF monogram	—
Pn4		—	1/4 Ducat. Silver. C4	—
Pn5	1715	—	1/2 Ducat. Silver. FR.#2987	—
Pn6	1759	—	Ducat. Copper. C20	—

STOLBERG-WERNIGERODE

The castle of Wernigerode is situated across the Harz Mountains to the north of Stolberg castle, some 12 miles (20 km) west-southwest of Halberstadt. An early division of the old Stolberg line in 1538 resulted in a separate line in Wernigerode. A second division in 1572 established Stolberg-Ortenberg and Stolberg-Schwarza (Wernigerode) and the latter was divided further into 1876 divided further into the senior branch of Stolberg-Wernigerode and the junior branch of Stolberg-Stolberg.Once again, Stolberg-Wernigerode was the foundation of three separate lines at Gedern, Schwarza and Wernigerode in 1710. The first two fell extinct within a century, but Stolberg-Wernigerode lasted into the 20th century.

RULERS

Ernst von Stolberg-Wernigerode-Ilsenburg, ...1672-1710 and Ludwig Christian, 1672-1710
Christian Ernst I, 1710-1771
Heinrich Ernst II, 1771-1778
Christian Friedrich, 1778-1824

COUNTSHIP

REGULAR COINAGE

KM# 50 1/8 THALER

Silver **Ruler:** Ernst von Ilsenburg **Subject:** Death of Ernst **Obverse:** Wigged and armored bust to left **Obv. Legend:** ERNEST9 COM. IN STOLB. K. R. W. & H. D. I. E. M. B. A. L & C. **Reverse:** 9-line inscription with Roman numeral dates and mintmaster's initials at bottom **Rev. Inscription:** NATVS/ ILSENBVRGI/XXV. MART./MDCL./DEFVNCTVS/ IBIDEM/D. IX. NOV./MDCCX./I.I.G. **Note:** Friedrich 1391.

Date	Mintage	VG	F	VF	XF	Unc
1710 IIG	—	100	200	375	700	—

KM# 51 1/4 THALER

Silver **Ruler:** Ernst von Ilsenburg **Subject:** Death of Ernst **Obverse:** Stag leaping to left looking back at column falling in its direction, legend curved above **Obv. Legend:** IN CASU TERROR. **Reverse:** 10-line inscription with Roman numeral date, mintmaster's initials below **Rev. Inscription:** MEMORIÆ/ERNESTI/COMIT. IN STOLB./KON. ROCHEF. WERNIG/ET HOHNSTEIN/NATI ILSENB./XXV. MARTII 1650./DENATI IBID/D. IX. NOVEM./ MDCCX. **Note:** Previous KM# 1.

Date	Mintage	VG	F	VF	XF	Unc
1710 IIG	—	150	250	450	800	—

KM# 61 1/4 THALER

Silver **Ruler:** Christian Ernst I **Obverse:** Stag left in circle **Obv. Legend:** CHRISTIANUS. ERNESTUS. COMES. IN STOLBERG. K. R. W. ET. H. **Reverse:** Manifold arms, 3 ornate helmets above, date divided among crests, mintmaster's initials divided below **Rev. Legend:** DYNASTA. IN. EPST. MUNZ. BRAIB. AIGM. LOHRA. ET. KLETTENB. **Note:** Previous C# 3.

Date	Mintage	VG	F	VF	XF	Unc
1724 IIG	—	40.00	65.00	125	250	—
1725 IIG	—	40.00	65.00	125	250	—

KM# 53 1/2 THALER

Silver **Ruler:** Ernst von Ilsenburg **Subject:** Death of Ernst **Obverse:** Wigged and armored bust right **Obv. Legend:** ERNEST9 COM. IN STOLB. K. R. WERN. & HOHN. DN. IN E. M. B. A. L. & C. **Reverse:** 15-line inscription with dates, mintmaster's initials below **Rev. Inscription:** NATVS/ILSENBURGI/A. 1650. D. 25. MART./REGIMEN CAPESSIVIT/A. 1672 EODEMQ. ANNO/SOPHIAM DOROTHEAM/SCHWARZBVRGICAM/MATRIMONIO SIBI IUNXIT./OBIIT ILSENBURGI/D. 9. NOV. A. 1710./PATRI DESIDERATISSIMO/EXTENERRIMO AFFECTV/HOC CONSECRAT/FILIA UNICA/SVPERSTE **Note:** Previous KM# 2.

Date	Mintage	VG	F	VF	XF	Unc
1710 CW//IIG	—	175	275	550	1,000	—

KM# 63 1/2 THALER

Silver **Ruler:** Christian Ernst I **Obverse:** Stag left in circle **Obv. Legend:** CHRISTIANUS. ERNESTUS. COMES. IN STOLBERG. K. R. W. ET. H. **Reverse:** Manifold arms, 3 ornate helmets above, date divided among crests, mintmaster's initials divided below **Rev. Legend:** DYNASTA. IN. EPST. MUNZ. BRAIB. AIGM. LOHRA. ET. KLETTENB. **Note:** Previous C# 5.

Date	Mintage	VG	F	VF	XF	Unc
1724 IIG	—	180	280	500	850	—
1725 IIG	—	180	280	500	850	—

KM# 70 1/2 THALER

Silver **Ruler:** Christian Ernst I **Obverse:** Stag left in circle **Obv. Legend:** CHRISTIANUS. ERNESTUS. COMES. IN STOLBERG. K. R. W. ET. H. **Reverse:** Crowned arms divide date and mintmaster's initials, chain of order around **Rev. Legend:** DYNASTA. IN. EPST. MUNZ. BRAIB. — AIGM. LOHRA ET KLETTENB. **Note:** Previous C# 7.

Date	Mintage	VG	F	VF	XF	Unc
1738 IIG	—	100	180	360	600	—

KM# 71 1/2 THALER

Silver **Ruler:** Christian Ernst I **Obverse:** Stag left in circle **Reverse:** Crowned arms divide mintmaster's initials, date below, chain of order around **Rev. Legend:** CHRISTIANUS. ERNESTUS. COMES. IN STOLBERG. K. R. W. ET. H. **Note:** Previous C# 8.

Date	Mintage	VG	F	VF	XF	Unc
1741 IIG	—	175	350	600	1,000	—

KM# 75 1/2 THALER

Silver **Ruler:** Christian Ernst I **Obverse:** Stag left in circle, date in exergue **Obv. Legend:** CHRISTIANUS. ERNESTUS. COMES. IN STOLBERG. K. R. W. ET. H. **Reverse:** Crowned manifold arms divide mintmaster's initials, all in chain of order **Rev. Legend:** DYNASTA. IN. EPST. MUNZ. BRAIB. — AIGM. LOHRA ET KLETTENB. **Note:** Previous C# 9.

Date	Mintage	VG	F	VF	XF	Unc
1747 IIG Rare	—	—	—	—	—	—

KM# 55 THALER

Silver **Ruler:** Ernst von Ilsenburg **Subject:** Death of Ernst **Obverse:** Wigged and armored bust right **Obv. Legend:** ERNEST, COM • IN STOLB • K • R • WERN • & HOHN • DN • IN E • M • B • A • L • & C • **Reverse:** Fifteen-line inscription with Roman numeral dates, mintmaster's initials below **Rev. Inscription:** NATVS/ILSENBURGI/XXV. MART. MDCL./REGIMEN CAPESSIVIT/MDCLXXII. EODEMQ. ANO/SOPHIAM DOROTHEAM/SCHWARZBVRGICAM/MATRIMONIO SIBI IUNXIT./OBIIT ILSENBURGI/D. EX. NOV. MDCCX./PATRI DESIDERATISSIMO/EXTENERRIMO AFFECTV/HOC CONSECRAT/FILIA UNICA/SVPERSTES. **Note:** Dav# 2790.

Date	Mintage	VG	F	VF	XF	Unc
1710 CW//IIG	—	300	550	900	1,500	—

KM# 65 THALER

Silver **Ruler:** Christian Ernst I **Obverse:** Stag left in circle **Obv. Legend:** CHRISTIANUS • ERNESTUS • COMES • IN • STOLBERG • K • R • W • ET • H • **Reverse:** Ornate manifold arms, 3 ornate helmets above, date divided among crests, mintmaster's initials divided below **Rev. Legend:** DYNASTA IN EPST • MUNZ • BRAIB • AIGM • LOHRA • ET • KLETTENBERG **Note:** Dav# 2791. Previous C# 10.

Date	Mintage	VG	F	VF	XF	Unc
1724 IIG	—	175	350	600	1,000	—

KM# 66 THALER

Silver **Ruler:** Christian Ernst I **Obverse:** Stag left in circle **Obv. Legend:** CHRISTIANUS • ERNESTUS • COMES • IN • STOLBERG • K • R • W • ET • H • **Reverse:** Large manifold arms, 3 ornate helmets above, date divided among crests, mintmaster's initials divided below **Rev. Legend:** DYNASTA IN EPST • MUNZ • BRAIB • AIGM • LOHRA • ET • KLETTENBERG **Note:** Dav# 2791A. Previous C# 10a.

Date	Mintage	VG	F	VF	XF	Unc
1725 IIG	—	175	350	600	1,000	—

KM# 81 THALER

Silver **Ruler:** Ernst von Ilsenburg **Subject:** 50th Anniversary of Reign **Note:** Octagonal klippe from Thaler dies, KM# 80.

Date	Mintage	VG	F	VF	XF	Unc
1760 IEVC	—	—	—	—	—	—

KM# 77 THALER

Silver **Ruler:** Christian Ernst I **Subject:** 50th Year of Reign **Obverse:** Armored bust to right in circle, date at end of legend **Obv. Legend:** CHRISTIAN • ERNST • GRAF • ZU • STOLBERG • K • R • W • U • H • HERR • Z • E • M • B • A • L • u • C **Reverse:** A round altar with smoke rising, set in landscape with buildings in background, 5-line inscription with date and mintmaster's initials in exergue **Rev. Legend:** GOTT SEY GEBENEDEYT • FÜR DIESE SELTNE ZEIT **Rev. Inscription:** NACH FÜNFZIGIÄHRIG• REGIER•/ZU WERNIGERODE/SEIT DEM 9 NOV•/1710•/I•B•H• **Note:** Dav# 2792. Previous C# 11.

Date	Mintage	F	VF	XF	Unc
1760 IBH	—	350	600	1,000	1,650

KM# 78 THALER

Silver **Ruler:** Christian Ernst I **Subject:** 50th Year of Reign **Obverse:** Armored bust to right in circle, date at end of legend **Obv. Legend:** CHRISTIAN • ERNST • GRAF • ZU • STOLBERG • K • R • W • U • H • HERR • Z • E • M • B • A • L • u • C **Reverse:** A round altar with smoke rising, set in landscape with buildings in background, 5-line inscription with additional inscription FEIN. SILB. **Rev. Legend:** GOTT SEY GEBENEDEYT • FÜR DIESE SELTNE ZEIT **Rev. Inscription:** NACH FÜNFZIGIÄHRIG• REGIER•/ZU WERNIGERODE/SEIT DEM 9 NOV•/1710•/I•B•H• **Note:** Dav# 2792A. Previous C# 11a.

Date	Mintage	F	VF	XF	Unc
1760 IBH	—	350	600	1,000	1,650

KM# 79 THALER

Silver **Ruler:** Christian Ernst I **Subject:** 50th Year of Reign **Obverse:** Large ornate manifold arms, 3 ornate helmets above, chain of order suspended in curve below, date at end of legend, mintmaster's initials at lower right **Obv. Legend:** CHRISTIAN • ERNST • GRAF • ZU • STOLBERG • K • R • W • U • H • HERR • Z • E • M • B • A • L • U • C **Reverse:** A round altar with smoke rising, set in landscape with buildings in background, 4-line inscription with date in exergue **Rev. Legend:** GOTT SEY GEBENEDEYT • FÜR DIESE SELTNE ZEIT • **Rev. Inscription:** NACH FÜNFZIGIÄHRIG• REGIER•/ZU WERNIGERODE/SEIT DEM 9 NOV•/1710• **Note:** Dav# 2793. Previous C# 12.

Date	Mintage	F	VF	XF	Unc
1760 IEVC	—	2,000	3,500	5,500	—

KM# 80 THALER

Silver **Ruler:** Christian Ernst I **Subject:** 50th Year of Reign **Obverse:** Modified arms **Note:** Dav# 2793A. Previous C# 12a.

Date	Mintage	F	VF	XF	Unc
1760 IVEC	—	2,000	3,500	5,500	—

KM# 57 2 THALER

Silver **Ruler:** Ernst von Ilsenburg **Subject:** Death of Ernst **Obverse:** Stag prancing to right on river bank, castle on hill in left background, legend curving over scene **Obv. Legend:** SALVTIS RIPAM TENEO **Reverse:** 18-line inscription with Roman numeral dates and mintmaster's initials at bottom **Rev. Inscription:** MEMORIAE/ERNESTI/COMIT. STOLB. KOENIGST./ROCHEF. WERNIG. ET. HOHNST./DN. IN. EPST. MUNZENB. BREUB./AIGM. LOHRA. ET. CLETTENBERG/ NATI. ILSENBURG./D. XXV. MARTII. A. MDCL./REGIMEN. ADEPTI. A. MDCLXXII./ **Note:** Dav# 2789.

Date	Mintage	VG	F	VF	XF	Unc
1710 IIG	—	2,000	3,500	5,500	8,500	—

TRADE COINAGE

KM# 59 DUCAT

3.5000 g., 0.9860 Gold 0.1109 oz. AGW **Ruler:** Ernst von Ilsenburg **Subject:** Death of Ernst **Obverse:** Wigged and armored bust to right **Obv. Legend:** ERNEST9 COM. IN STOLB. K. R. W. & H. D. I. E. M. B. A. L & C. **Reverse:** 9-line inscription with Roman numeral dates and mintmaster's initials at bottom **Rev. Inscription:** NATVS/ILSENBVRGI/XXV. MART./MDCL./DEFVNCTVS/IBIDEM/D. IX. NOV./MDCCX./I.I.G. **Note:** Struck from 1/8 Thaler dies, KM# 50. Fr# 3355. Previous KM# 5.

Date	Mintage	VG	F	VF	XF	Unc
1710 IIG	—	500	1,000	2,150	3,500	—

KM# 68 DUCAT

3.5000 g., 0.9860 Gold 0.1109 oz. AGW **Ruler:** Christian Ernst I **Obverse:** Bust right **Obv. Legend:** CHRISTIANUS ERNESTUS COM STOLB. K. R. W. ET H. **Reverse:** Ornate shield of manifold arms, crown above, chain of order around, date at top over crown, mintmaster's initials below **Rev. Legend:** DOM. IN. EPST. MUNZ. BR — AIB. AIGM. LOHR. ET. CLE. **Note:** Fr# 3356. Previous C# 14.

Date	Mintage	VG	F	VF	XF	Unc
1730 CW//IIG	—	300	650	1,350	2,250	—
1733 CW//IIG	—	300	650	1,350	2,250	—

KM# 73 DUCAT

3.5000 g., 0.9860 Gold 0.1109 oz. AGW **Ruler:** Christian Ernst I **Obverse:** Stag left **Obv. Legend:** CHRISTIANUS ERNESTUS COM. STOLB. K. R. W. U. H. **Reverse:** Ornate shield of manifold arms, crown above, chain of order around, date at top over crown, mintmaster's initials below **Rev. Legend:** DOM. IN. EPST. MUNZ. BR — AIB. AIGM. LOHR. ET. CLE. **Note:** Fr# 3357. Previous C# 15.

Date	Mintage	VG	F	VF	XF	Unc
1742 IIG	—	250	600	1,200	2,000	—
1759 IEVC	—	250	600	1,200	2,000	—

KM# 85 DUCAT

3.5000 g., 0.9860 Gold 0.1109 oz. AGW **Ruler:** Christian Ernst I **Obverse:** Bust right **Reverse:** Stag left, date below **Note:** Fr# 3360. Previous C# 16.

Date	Mintage	VG	F	VF	XF	Unc
1768 EFR	—	250	600	1,250	2,200	—

KM# 87 DUCAT

3.5000 g., 0.9860 Gold 0.1109 oz. AGW **Ruler:** Heinrich Ernst II **Obverse:** Head right **Obv. Legend:** HENR. ERNST GR. Z. STOLB. K. R. WERN. u. H. HR. Z. E. M. B. A. L u K. **Reverse:** Stag left, date in exergue **Note:** Fr# 3361. Previous C# 20.

Date	Mintage	F	VF	XF	Unc
1778	—	375	750	1,400	3,000

KM# 88 DUCAT

3.5000 g., 0.9860 Gold 0.1109 oz. AGW **Ruler:** Christian Friedrich **Obverse:** Stag to left **Obv. Legend:** CHRISTIAN FRIDR: GRAF ZU STOLBERG WERNIGERODE **Reverse:** 3-line inscription with date on large memorial tablet **Rev. Inscription:** I/DUCATEN/(date) **Note:** Fr# 3362. Previous C# 24.

Date	Mintage	F	VF	XF	Unc
1784	—	350	700	1,300	3,000
1795	—	350	700	1,300	3,000

KM# 83 12 DUCAT

41.7000 g., 0.9860 Gold 1.3219 oz. AGW **Ruler:** Christian Ernst I **Subject:** 50th Year of Reign **Obverse:** Armored bust to right in circle, date at end of legend **Obv. Legend:** CHRISTIAN • ERNST • GRAF • ZU • STOLBERG • K • R • W • U • H • HERR • Z • E • M • B • A • L • u • C **Reverse:** A round altar with smoke rising, set in landscape with buildings in background, 5-line inscription with date and mintmaster's initials in exergue **Rev. Inscription:** NACH FÜNFZIGIÄHRIG• REGIER•/ZU WERNIGERODE/SEIT DEM 9 NOV•/1710•/I•B•H• **Note:** Fr# 3358. Struck from Thaler dies, KM# 77.

Date	Mintage	VG	F	VF	XF	Unc
1760 IBH Rare	—	—	—	—	—	—

PATTERNS

Including off metal strikes

KM#	Date	Mintage	Identification	Mkt Val
Pn1	1760	—	Thaler. Iron. KM# 77.	—
Pn2	1760	—	Thaler. Lead.KM# 77.	—
Pn3	1760	—	Thaler. Lead. KM# 79.	—
Pn4	1778	—	Ducat. Silver.KM# 87.	—
Pn5	1784	—	Ducat. Silver. KM# 88.	—
Pn6	1795	—	Ducat. Silver. KM# 88.	—

STOLBERG-WERNIGERODE-GEDERN

Gedern

As a cadet line of the senior house of Stolberg, Gedern was created by the division of Stolberg-Wernigerode in 1710. The count was raised to the rank of prince in 1742, but the line fell extinct in 1804 after only two generations. The lands and titles then reverted to Stolberg-Wernigerode. The castle of Gedern is located in the Wetterau some 20 miles (34 km) northeast of Friedberg.

RULERS

Friedrich Karl, 1710-1767
Karl Heinrich, 1767-1804

PRINCIPALITY

TRADE COINAGE

KM# 1 DUCAT

3.5000 g., 0.9860 Gold 0.1109 oz. AGW **Ruler:** Friedrich Karl **Obverse:** Head right **Reverse:** Stag left in front of column with S in base

Date	Mintage	VG	F	VF	XF	Unc
1719	—	300	700	1,450	2,500	—

STRALSUND

The town of Stralsund, founded about the year 1200 on the mainland opposite the island of Rügen in the Baltic Sea, obtained the rights of a Germanic city in 1234. Stralsund later joined the Hanseatic League and remained strong enough to maintain its independence from the dukes of Pomerania, who struck coins in that place during the 13th century. In 1325, the city purchased the right to coin its own money from the duke and began a series which continued until 1763. The city fell under the rule of Sweden from 1637 until 1815, then passed to Prussia along with the rest of Swedish Pomerania.

RULER

Swedish, 1637-1815

MONEYERS' INITIALS

Initials	Date	Name
HIH (b) battle axe	1662-1705	Heinrich Johann Hille
ICH	1705-09	Johann Christian Hille
LDS	1763	Ludwig Detoff Sodeman

SWEDISH ADMINISTRATION

REGULAR COINAGE

KM# 58 WITTEN (1/192 Thaler)

Silver **Obverse:** City arms above cross **Reverse:** Value

Date	Mintage	VG	F	VF	XF	Unc
1706 HIH	—	12.50	25.00	50.00	100	—
1706 ICH	—	12.50	25.00	50.00	100	—
1708 ICH	—	15.00	30.00	60.00	120	—

KM# 84 WITTEN (1/192 Thaler)

Billon **Obverse:** Crowned arrowhead, date above **Reverse:** Value

Date	Mintage	VG	F	VF	XF	Unc
1763 LDS	—	6.00	12.00	25.00	50.00	—

KM# 85 SECHSLING (1/96 Thaler)

Billon **Obverse:** Crowned arrowhead, date above **Reverse:** Value

Date	Mintage	VG	F	VF	XF	Unc
1763 LDS	—	10.00	20.00	40.00	90.00	—

KM# 80 1/96 THALER (Sechsling)

Silver **Obverse:** City arms above ICH and cross **Reverse:** Value within inner circle

Date	Mintage	VG	F	VF	XF	Unc
1706 ICH	—	20.00	40.00	70.00	135	—

KM# 81 1/96 THALER (Sechsling)

Silver **Obverse:** City arms above cross **Reverse:** Value above ICH

Date	Mintage	VG	F	VF	XF	Unc
1706 ICH	—	20.00	40.00	70.00	135	—

KM# 83 1/48 THALER (Schilling)

Silver **Obverse:** Arrowhead above cross in circle, date in legend **Obv. Legend:** STRALSUND (date). **Reverse:** 4-line inscription **Rev. Legend:** SCHILLING STUCK **Rev. Inscription:** 48/EINEN/ REICHS/DALER.

Date	Mintage	VG	F	VF	XF	Unc
1715 B#171	—	22.00	45.00	80.00	130	—

KM# 82 16 SCHILLING (1/6 Thaler)

Silver **Obverse:** Stralsund city arms **Obv. Legend:** STRALSUND **Reverse:** Value above date

Date	Mintage	VG	F	VF	XF	Unc
1715	—	20.00	40.00	70.00	135	—

KM# 76 2/3 THALER (1 Gulden)

Silver **Obverse:** City arms above value in inner circle, small letters **Reverse:** Narrow moline cross with trefoils in inner circle

Date	Mintage	VG	F	VF	XF	Unc
1707 ICH	—	65.00	125	250	480	—

KM# 77 2/3 THALER (1 Gulden)

Silver **Obverse:** Larger legends **Obv. Legend:** MONETA NOVA STRALSUNDENSIS **Reverse:** Larger legends **Rev. Legend:** ...SALVA NOS DEUS

Date	Mintage	VG	F	VF	XF	Unc
1707 ICH	—	80.00	165	320	600	—

KM# 78 2/3 THALER (1 Gulden)

Silver **Obverse:** City arms in shield **Obv. Legend:** MONETA • NOVA • STRALSUNDENSIS • **Reverse:** Cross within ornate circle with 4 fleur de lis **Rev. Legend:** ...SALVA NOS DEUS

Date	Mintage	VG	F	VF	XF	Unc
1707 ICH	—	80.00	165	320	600	—

STRASSBURG

The capital and principal city of Alsace, Strassburg is located very near the Rhine, 55 miles (92 km) southeast of Saarbrucken. It was an early Celtic settlement, then the Roman town of Argentoratum, from which is derived its name as found on many of Strassburg's coins. The first mention of a bishopric existing in the place dates from the 6th century. The city was both home to the bishops and the site of an imperial mint, the latter which functioned from the 9th to the 11th centuries. The bishops had received the right to coin their own money in 873, but it was not until Strassburg was made a free imperial city in the early 13th century that the townspeople came into conflict with them. When bishop Walter von Hohengeroldseck (1260-1263) tried to reassert authority over the town, the populace rose up and soundly defeated him at the Battle of Oberhausbergen in 1262. The power of the bishopric never recovered, then the city grew in importance and Strassburg city received the mint right in 1334, even though coins were struck in its name locally beginning in 1296.Strassburg's coinage continued until beyond the annexation of the city in 1681, whereas issues by the bishops continued until 1773. The bishopric was finally secularized and annexed by France in 1789.

RULERS

Wilhelm Egon, Fürst von Fürstenberg, 1682-1704
Armand Gaston, Fürst von Rohan-Soubise, 1704-1749, cardinal 1712
Armand, Fürst von Rohan-Soubise, 1749-1756
Ludwig Constantin, Fürst von Rohan-Guemené, 1756-1779
Ludwig Renatus, Fürst von Rohan-Guemené, 1779-1803

BISHOPRIC

REGULAR COINAGE

C# 1 KREUZER

Copper **Ruler:** Ludwig Constantin, Furst von Rohan-Guemene **Obverse:** Cardinal's hat above crowned 5-fold arms within mantle **Obv. Legend:** LUD • CARD • DE ROHAN • D • G • EPUS • ET • PS • ARGENT • **Reverse:** Value, date within cartouche

Date	Mintage	VG	F	VF	XF	Unc
1773 G	—	10.00	20.00	40.00	100	—

C# 4 5 KREUZER

Billon **Ruler:** Ludwig Constantin, Furst von Rohan-Guemene **Obverse:** Cardinal's hat above crowned 5-fold arms within mantle **Obv. Legend:** LUD • CARD • DE: ROHAN • D • G • EPUS • ET • PS • ARGENT • **Reverse:** Oval arms within cartouche, value framed below **Rev. Legend:** MONETA NOVA EPISCOPATUS ARGENTINENSIS

Date	Mintage	VG	F	VF	XF	Unc
1773 G	—	20.00	35.00	75.00	125	—

C# 8 10 KREUZER

Silver **Ruler:** Ludwig Constantin, Furst von Rohan-Guemene **Obverse:** Cardinal's hat above crowned 5-fold arms within mantle **Obv. Legend:** LUD • CARD • DE ROHAN • D • G • EPUS • ET • PS • ARGENT • **Reverse:** Oval arms within cartouche, framed value below **Rev. Legend:** MONETA NOVA EPISCOPATUS ARGENTINENSIS

Date	Mintage	VG	F	VF	XF	Unc
1773 G	—	30.00	50.00	90.00	175	—

C# 12 20 KREUZER

Silver **Ruler:** Ludwig Constantin, Furst von Rohan-Guemene **Obverse:** Cardinal's hat above crowned 5-fold arms within mantle **Obv. Legend:** LUD • CARD • DEROHAN • D • G • EPUS • ET • PS • ARGENT • 1773 • **Reverse:** Oval arms within cartouche, framed value below **Rev. Legend:** MONETA NOVA EPISCOPATUS ARGENTINENSIS

Date	Mintage	VG	F	VF	XF	Unc
1773 G	—	35.00	65.00	115	235	—

C# 6 1/12 THALER

Silver **Ruler:** Ludwig Constantin, Furst von Rohan-Guemene **Obverse:** Bust right divides value **Obv. Legend:** LUD • CONST • D • G • EPUS • ET • PPS • ARG • **Reverse:** Cardinal's hat above crowned arms within mantle **Rev. Legend:** SIT NOMEN DOMINI BENEDICTUM

Date	Mintage	VG	F	VF	XF	Unc
1759 JG	—	25.00	45.00	75.00	145	—

C# 10 1/6 THALER

Silver **Ruler:** Ludwig Constantin, Furst von Rohan-Guemene **Obverse:** Bust right divides date **Obv. Legend:** LUD • CONST • D • G • EPUS • ET • PPS • ARGENT... **Reverse:** Cardinal's hat above crowned arms within mantle **Rev. Legend:** SIT NOMEN DOMINI BENEDICTUM

Date	Mintage	VG	F	VF	XF	Unc
1759 JG	—	40.00	65.00	115	225	—

C# 16 1/4 THALER

Silver **Ruler:** Ludwig Constantin, Furst von Rohan-Guemene **Subject:** Ludwig Constantine **Obverse:** Bust right **Obv. Legend:** LUD • CONST • D • G • EPUS • ET • PPS • ARGENTILANAL **Reverse:** Cardinal's hat above crowned arms within mantle **Rev. Legend:** SIT NOMEN DOMINI BENEDICTUM

Date	Mintage	VG	F	VF	XF	Unc
1759 JG	—	90.00	170	275	450	—
1760 JG	—	90.00	170	275	450	—

C# 14 1/4 THALER

Silver **Ruler:** Ludwig Constantin, Furst von Rohan-Guemene **Obverse:** Bust right **Reverse:** Cardinal's hat above crowned arms within mantle **Note:** Similar to 1/2 Thaler, C#16.

Date	Mintage	VG	F	VF	XF	Unc
1759 JG	—	—	—	—	—	—

C# 18 THALER

Silver **Ruler:** Ludwig Constantin, Furst von Rohan-Guemene **Obverse:** Bust right with dog and J.G. below **Obv. Legend:** LUD • CONST • D • G • EPUS • ET PPS • ARGENTI • LAN • AL • **Reverse:** Cardinal's hat above crowned arms within mantle **Rev. Legend:** SIT NOMEN DOMINI - BENEDICTUM * **Note:** Dav. #2810.

Date	Mintage	VG	F	VF	XF	Unc
1759 JG	—	400	850	1,650	2,500	—
1760 JG	—	400	850	1,650	2,500	—

FR# 242 1/2 PISTOLE

Gold **Ruler:** Ludwig Constantin, Furst von Rohan-Guemene **Obverse:** Bust right **Reverse:** Crowned oval mantled arms, cardinal hat above

Date	Mintage	VG	F	VF	XF	Unc
1759	—	1,500	2,500	4,750	8,000	—

FR# 241 PISTOLE

Gold **Ruler:** Ludwig Constantin, Furst von Rohan-Guemene **Obverse:** Bust right **Reverse:** Crowned oval mantled arms, cardinal hat above

Date	Mintage	VG	F	VF	XF	Unc
1759	—	1,200	2,200	4,000	7,000	—

FR# 240 2 PISTOLEN

Gold **Ruler:** Armand, Furst von Rohan-Soubise **Obverse:** Bust right **Reverse:** Crowned oval mantled arms, cardinal hat above

Date	Mintage	VG	F	VF	XF	Unc
1759 Rare	—	—	—	—	—	—

SWABIAN CIRCLE

An area in Swabia maintained as an imperial administrative district from 1500 to 1806. Constance and Württemberg were the usual administrators over this occasional coin issuer.

IMPERIAL CIRCLE

TRADE COINAGE

FR# A3371 DUCAT

3.5000 g., 0.9860 Gold 0.1109 oz. AGW **Obverse:** Cross added to lower part of shield

Date	Mintage	VG	F	VF	XF	Unc
1737	—	450	900	2,000	4,000	—

FR# 3371 DUCAT

3.5000 g., 0.9860 Gold 0.1109 oz. AGW **Mint:** Augsburg **Obverse:** Lion arms within cartouche **Reverse:** 2 Shields; one with crown and one with mitre

Date	Mintage	VG	F	VF	XF	Unc
1737 FB	—	500	1,000	2,250	4,500	—

TEUTONIC ORDER

Deutscher Orden

The Order of Knights was founded during the Third Crusade in 1198. They acquired considerable territory by conquest from the heathen Prussians in the late 13th and early 14th centuries. The seat of the Grand Master moved from Acre to Venice and in 1309 to Marienburg, Prussia. The Teutonic Order began striking coins in the late 13th century. In 1355 permission was granted to strike hellers at Mergentheim. However, the bulk of the Order's coinage until 1525 was schillings and half schoters minted in and for Prussia. In 1809 the Order was suppressed and Mergentheim was annexed to Württemberg.

RULERS

Ludwig Franz von Pfalz-Neuburg, 1694-1732
Clemens August von Bayern, 1732-1761
Karl Alexander of Lorraine, 1761-1780.
Max Franz of Austria, 1780-1801

ARMS

Grand Master: Cross, shield w/eagle in ctr., shield is often w/double outline.
Later versions include family and territorial arms in angles of cross.
Order Arms: Long cross superimposed, usually on empty shield, sometimes w/eagle in ctr.

MINT OFFICIALS' INITIALS

Initials	Date	Name
GFN	1689-1724	Georg Friedrich Nürnberger, mintmaster in Nürnberg
LPH	1678-1701	Leonhard Paul Haller, mintmaster in Neisse (Breslau)
SS	1701-17	Siegmund Strasser, warden in Breslau
CGL	1746-55	Carl Gottlieb Laufer, mintmaster in Nürnberg
W(W)E or WE/W	1765-77	Weber, warden and Eberhard, mintmaster in Wertheim

ORDER OF KNIGHTS

REGULAR COINAGE

C# 15 KREUZER

Billon **Ruler:** Karl Alexander von Lorraine **Obverse:** Crowned order arms in sprays **Reverse:** Value above date separates W.E.

Date	Mintage	VG	F	VF	XF	Unc
1776 W(W)E	—	15.00	25.00	50.00	100	—

C# 17 2-1/2 KREUZER

Billon **Ruler:** Karl Alexander von Lorraine **Obverse:** Crowned oval arms between two palm fronds **Reverse:** Six-line inscription with date, mint officials' initials **Rev. Inscription:** 2 1/2 Kr:/NACH DEM/CONVENS:/FUS./1776/W(W)E **Note:** Varieties exist.

Date	Mintage	VG	F	VF	XF	Unc
1776 W(W)E	—	20.00	40.00	70.00	150	—

C# 5 3 KREUZER

Silver **Ruler:** Clemens August von Bayern **Subject:** Death of the Grand Master **Obverse:** Crowned and mantled oval four-fold arms with central shield **Reverse:** Nine-line inscription with dates **Rev. Inscription:** NATVS/17.AVG:1700./ELECTVS/IN SUPR:ADM:PRUSS./ET M:MAG:O:T:/17.IUL:1732./ DEFUNCTUS/6.FEBR:1761./R:I:P:

Date	Mintage	VG	F	VF	XF	Unc
1761	—	20.00	40.00	70.00	150	—

C# 19 5 KREUZER

Billon **Ruler:** Karl Alexander von Lorraine **Obverse:** Crowned oval arms between two palm fronds **Obv. Legend:** S.A.B.E.-O.T.M.M. **Reverse:** Four-line inscription with date in cartouche **Rev. Inscription:** 240/EINE FEINE/MARCK/(date) **Note:** Convention 5 Kreuzer.

Date	Mintage	VG	F	VF	XF	Unc
1776 WE//W	—	22.00	45.00	80.00	150	—
1776 WE	—	22.00	45.00	80.00	150	—

C# 21 10 KREUZER

Silver **Ruler:** Karl Alexander von Lorraine **Subject:** Death of the Grand Master **Obverse:** Crowned complex arms with eagle supporters **Reverse:** Inscription

Date	Mintage	VG	F	VF	XF	Unc
1780	800	25.00	50.00	85.00	175	—

C# 23 20 KREUZER

Silver **Ruler:** Karl Alexander von Lorraine **Obverse:** Armored bust right **Reverse:** Crowned complex arms within branches, value below **Note:** Convention 20 Kreuzer.

Date	Mintage	VG	F	VF	XF	Unc
1776 W(W)E	—	35.00	75.00	175	280	—

C# 9 1/4 THALER

Silver **Ruler:** Clemens August von Bayern **Subject:** Death of the Grand Master **Obverse:** Complex arms within crowned mantle **Reverse:** Inscription

Date	Mintage	VG	F	VF	XF	Unc
1761	—	45.00	90.00	175	350	—

C# 25 1/4 THALER

Silver **Ruler:** Karl Alexander von Lorraine **Subject:** Death of the Grand Master **Obverse:** Crowned complex arms with eagle supporters **Obv. Legend:** C • A • D • G • S • A • B • G • O • T • A • E • P • G • E • ... **Reverse:** Inscription with value below **Note:** Convention 1/4 Thaler.

Date	Mintage	VG	F	VF	XF	Unc
1780	400	50.00	100	180	365	—

C# 13 1/2 THALER

Silver **Ruler:** Clemens August von Bayern **Obverse:** Crowned monogram divides date within branches **Obv. Legend:** CLEM • AUG • D • G • AR • EPIS • & EL • .... **Reverse:** Crowned woman standing at center **Rev. Legend:** ....PATRONA ORDINIS TEUTONICI •

Date	Mintage	VG	F	VF	XF	Unc
1750 CGL	—	125	275	600	1,100	—

C# 27 1/2 THALER

Silver **Ruler:** Karl Alexander von Lorraine **Obverse:** Bust right **Obv. Legend:** D • G • CAROL • ALE • - DUX • .... **Reverse:** Crowned complex arms with eagle supporters **Note:** Convention 1/2 Thaler.

Date	Mintage	VG	F	VF	XF	Unc
1776 W(W)E	—	100	200	400	800	—
1776 W(W)E	—	100	200	350	700	—

C# 29 THALER

Silver **Ruler:** Karl Alexander von Lorraine **Obverse:** Bust right **Obv. Legend:** D • G • CAROL • ALE • - DUX LOTH • ET BAR • **Reverse:** Crowned and supported arms, value in exergue **Rev. Legend:** SUP • ADM • BOR • ET ORD • TEUT • MAGN • MAG • 1776, X. EINE F. MARCK/W (W) E below **Note:** Convention Thaler. Dav. #2813.

Date	Mintage	F	VF	XF	Unc
1776 W(W)E	—	150	300	750	1,400

C# 30 2 THALER

Silver **Ruler:** Karl Alexander von Lorraine **Note:** Convention 2 Thaler. Struck with Thaler dies, C#29. Dav. #2812.

Date	Mintage	VG	F	VF	XF	Unc
1776 W(W)G	—	300	700	1,750	3,000	—

TRADE COINAGE

FR# 3389 DUCAT

3.5000 g., 0.9860 Gold 0.1109 oz. AGW **Ruler:** Ludwig Franz von Pfalz-Neuburg **Obverse:** Armored bust right **Reverse:** Cruciform arms

Date	Mintage	VG	F	VF	XF	Unc
1699 LPH	—	350	800	1,650	2,750	—
1701 LPH	—	350	800	1,650	2,750	—
1701	—	350	800	1,650	2,750	—

C# 32 DUCAT

3.5000 g., 0.9860 Gold 0.1109 oz. AGW **Ruler:** Karl Alexander von Lorraine **Obverse:** Armored bust right **Reverse:** Crowned arms

Date	Mintage	VG	F	VF	XF	Unc
1765	—	600	1,200	2,500	4,000	—

PATTERNS

Including off metal strikes

KM#	Date	Mintage	Identification	Mkt Val
Pn1	1765	—	Thaler. Tin. Karl Alexander.	—
Pn2	1770	—	Ducat. Copper. Karl Alexander and Maximilian.	70.00
Pn3	1770	—	Ducat. Silver. Karl Alexander and Maximilian. Weight of 1/12 Thaler.	120
Pn4	1770	—	Ducat. Silver. Karl Alexander and Maximilian. Weight of 1/6 Thaler.	200
Pn5	1770	—	Ducat. Gold. Karl Alexander and Maximilian.	—
Pn6	1770	—	15 Ducat. Silver. Karl Alexander and Maximilian. Weight of 1 1/4 Thaler.	500
Pn7	1770	—	15 Ducat. Gold. Karl Alexander and Maximilian.	—

THURN AND TAXIS

Founded by the family of an Italian noble of the late 13th century, Thurn and Taxis eventually had holdings in Flanders, Hungary, Spain and Bohemia. They became postmaster for the empire and in the 19th century operated a postal system for all German States too small to operate their own. The castle of Taxis is 26 miles northeast of Ulm.

RULER

Anselm Franz, 1714-1739

PRINCIPALITY

TRADE COINAGE

FR# 3391 DUCAT

3.5000 g., 0.9860 Gold 0.1109 oz. AGW **Ruler:** Anselm Franz **Obverse:** Bust right **Reverse:** Crowned and mantled arms, date below

Date	Mintage	Good	VG	F	VF	XF
1734	—	—	700	1,450	2,750	4,500

TRIER

ARCHBISHOPRIC

The city of Trier, located on the Mosel River just a few miles from the border with Luxembourg, was an important place from Roman times up to the modern era. Tradition holds that the Emperor Claudius founded the city as Augusta Trevirorum (imperial city of the Treviri, a Belgian tribe of that locale). Even today, Trier contains more Roman antiquities than any other city in northern Europe and was one of the earliest centers of Christianity north of the Alps. Some parts of the 4th century basilica built by Valentinian I (364-75) are extant in the present cathedral, which dates from the 11th to 13th centuries. Trier was the western capital of the Roman Empire until it was taken by the Franks in 464. A bishopric was established there at the dawn of the Middle Ages and was raised to an archbishopric under Bishop Hetto (814-47). The earliest archiepiscopal coinage dates from the end of the 10th century. The importance of Trier grew during the High Middle Ages as the city became one of the ecclesiastic electorates of the German Empire under Baldwin of Luxembourg (1307-54). That lofty status was confirmed by the Golden Bull of 1356, which permanently established the seven electorates of the Empire. The wealth, power and prestige of the archbishops continued through the Late Middle Ages and withstood the Protestant Reformation in the 16th century. The economy of Trier was severely circumscribed by the hyper-inflation of the early period of the Thirty Years' War, and the city never regained its former position. Trier was taken by the French in 1794 and the last archbishop fled from his domains. In 1802, the archbishopric was secularized and divided between Nassau and France, but Prussia obtained most of Trier's territory in 1815, following the conclusion of the Napoleonic Wars.

RULERS

Johann Hugo von Orsbeck, 1676-1711
Karl Josef of Lorraine, 1711-1715
Franz Ludwig von Pfalz-Neuburg, 1716-1729
Franz Georg von Schönborn-Puckheim, 1729-1756
Johann Philipp von Walderdorff, 1756-1768
Clemens Wenzel, Prinz von Sachsen, Archbishop, 1768-1794

MINT OFFICIALS' INITIALS

Initials	Date	Name
DF	1746-52	Daniel Fritsch
EG, G	1750-75 1765-69	Elias Gervais, die-cutter in Neuwied Die-cutter in Coblenz
GG	1698-1734	Gerhardt Godt
GM	1763-94	Gotthard Martinengo
MG	1769	Martinengo & Gervais
NM	1756-63	Nikolaus Martinengo
S	1744-99	Anton Schaffer, die-cutter and mintmaster in Manheim
SC	1765-73	Schnabel, mintmaster, and Clotz, warden in Gunzburg
St	1765-89	August Friedrich Stieler, engraver in Mainz
St	?-1794	Friedrich Stieler, die-cutter in Mainz
VL, V.LON	1727-64	Franz Anton van Lon, die-cutter
W	1734-46	(encountered w/crossed staffs)

ARMS

Cross, usually displayed in conjunction with the family arms of the archbishop

REFERENCES

N = **Alfred Noss,** *Die Münzen von Trier*, v. I, pt. 2, *Beschreibung der Münzen 1307-1556.* **Bonn, 1916.**

S = **Friedrich von Schrötter,** *Die Münzen von Trier*, v. II, *Beschreibung der neuzeitlichen Münzen 1556-1794.* **Bonn, 1908.**

Sch = **Wolfgang Schulten,** *Deutsche Münzen aus der Zeit Karls V.* **Frankfurt am Main, 1974.**

REGULAR COINAGE

KM# 257 PFENNIG

Copper **Ruler:** Franz Georg von Schoenborn-Puckheim **Obverse:** Crowned script FGC monogram **Reverse:** Value, date

Date	Mintage	VG	F	VF	XF	Unc
1748 DF	—	5.00	10.00	20.00	40.00	—
1749 DF	—	5.00	10.00	20.00	40.00	—
1750 DF	—	5.00	10.00	20.00	40.00	—

KM# 270 PFENNIG

Copper **Ruler:** Johann Philipp von Walderdorf **Obverse:** Crowned JPC monogram **Reverse:** Value and date

Date	Mintage	VG	F	VF	XF	Unc
1757 NM	—	4.00	8.00	16.00	35.00	—
1758 NM	—	4.00	8.00	16.00	35.00	—
1761 NM	—	4.00	8.00	16.00	35.00	—
1762 NM	—	4.00	8.00	16.00	35.00	—

KM# 341 PFENNIG

Copper **Ruler:** Clemens Wenzel, Archbishop **Obverse:** CWC monogram **Reverse:** Value above date, G.M. below

Date	Mintage	VG	F	VF	XF	Unc
1789 GM	—	3.00	6.00	12.00	25.00	—

KM# 166 2 PFENNIG (1/2 Kreuzer)

Billon **Obverse:** Shield of arms divides G G, elector's hat above **Reverse:** Value

Date	Mintage	VG	F	VF	XF	Unc
ND GG	—	30.00	60.00	80.00	150	—

KM# 232 2 PFENNIG (1/2 Kreuzer)

Billon **Ruler:** Franz Ludwig von Pfalz-Neuburg **Obverse:** Crowned arms divide date

Date	Mintage	VG	F	VF	XF	Unc
1723	—	15.00	30.00	60.00	120	—

KM# 240.1 2 PFENNIG (1/2 Kreuzer)

Billon **Obverse:** Value: 2/PFENNIG, crowned FGC monogram, date divided above **Reverse:** Crowned arms

Date	Mintage	VG	F	VF	XF	Unc
1730 GG	—	5.00	10.00	20.00	40.00	—
1731 GG	—	5.00	10.00	20.00	40.00	—

KM# 240.2 2 PFENNIG (1/2 Kreuzer)

Billon **Ruler:** Franz Georg von Schoenborn-Puckheim **Obverse:** Value: 2 PFEN **Reverse:** Arms in palm branches

Date	Mintage	VG	F	VF	XF	Unc
1731 GG	—	5.00	10.00	20.00	40.00	—

KM# 240.3 2 PFENNIG (1/2 Kreuzer)

Billon **Ruler:** Franz Georg von Schoenborn-Puckheim **Obverse:** Value: 2 PFENNIG

Date	Mintage	VG	F	VF	XF	Unc
1732 GG	—	5.00	10.00	20.00	40.00	—
1733 GG	—	5.00	10.00	20.00	40.00	—
1740	—	5.00	10.00	20.00	40.00	—
1745 DF	—	5.00	10.00	20.00	40.00	—
1746	—	5.00	10.00	20.00	40.00	—
1747	—	5.00	10.00	20.00	40.00	—

KM# 240.4 2 PFENNIG (1/2 Kreuzer)

Billon **Ruler:** Franz Georg von Schoenborn-Puckheim **Obverse:** Value: II PFENNIG

Date	Mintage	VG	F	VF	XF	Unc
1743	—	5.00	10.00	20.00	40.00	—

KM# 258 2 PFENNIG (1/2 Kreuzer)

Copper **Ruler:** Franz Georg von Schoenborn-Puckheim **Obverse:** Crowned script FGC monogram **Reverse:** Value, date

Date	Mintage	VG	F	VF	XF	Unc
1748 DF	—	5.00	10.00	20.00	40.00	—
1749 DF	—	5.00	10.00	20.00	40.00	—
1750 DF	—	5.00	10.00	20.00	40.00	—

KM# 271 2 PFENNIG (1/2 Kreuzer)

Copper **Ruler:** Johann Philipp von Walderdorf **Obverse:** Crowned JPC monogram **Reverse:** Value and date

Date	Mintage	VG	F	VF	XF	Unc
1757 NM	—	3.00	6.00	10.00	25.00	—
1758 NM	—	3.00	6.00	10.00	25.00	—
1760 NM	—	3.00	6.00	10.00	25.00	—
1761 NM	—	3.00	6.00	10.00	25.00	—
1762 NM	—	3.00	6.00	10.00	25.00	—

KM# 342 2 PFENNIG (1/2 Kreuzer)

Copper **Ruler:** Clemens Wenzel, Archbishop **Obverse:** CWC monogram **Reverse:** Value above date; G. M. below

Date	Mintage	VG	F	VF	XF	Unc
1789 GM	—	3.00	6.00	10.00	25.00	—

KM# 301 3 PFENNING

Copper **Ruler:** Johann Philipp von Walderdorf **Obverse:** Crowned JPC monogram **Reverse:** Value and date

Date	Mintage	VG	F	VF	XF	Unc
1761 NM	—	10.00	20.00	40.00	70.00	—

KM# 259 4 PFENNIG (1/2 Albus)

Copper **Ruler:** Franz Georg von Schoenborn-Puckheim **Obverse:** Crowned script FGC monogram **Reverse:** Value, date

Date	Mintage	VG	F	VF	XF	Unc
1748 DF	—	5.00	12.00	22.00	50.00	—
1750 DF	—	5.00	12.00	22.00	50.00	—

KM# 272 4 PFENNIG (1/2 Albus)

Copper **Ruler:** Johann Philipp von Walderdorf **Obverse:** Crowned JPC monogram **Reverse:** Value and date

Date	Mintage	VG	F	VF	XF	Unc
1757 NM	—	5.00	12.00	25.00	60.00	—
1758 NM	—	5.00	12.00	25.00	60.00	—
1759 NM	—	5.00	12.00	25.00	60.00	—
1760 NM	—	5.00	12.00	25.00	60.00	—
1761 NM	—	5.00	12.00	25.00	60.00	—
1764 NM	—	5.00	12.00	25.00	60.00	—

KM# 343 4 PFENNIG (1/2 Albus)

Copper **Ruler:** Clemens Wenzel, Archbishop **Obverse:** CWC monogram **Reverse:** Value above date, G.M. below

Date	Mintage	VG	F	VF	XF	Unc
1789 GM	—	5.00	12.00	25.00	45.00	—

KM# 302 6 PFENNING

Copper **Ruler:** Johann Philipp von Walderdorf **Obverse:** Crowned JPC monogram **Reverse:** Value and date

Date	Mintage	VG	F	VF	XF	Unc
1761 NM	—	20.00	40.00	75.00	160	—

KM# 186 1/2 PETERMENGER

Billon **Ruler:** Johann Hugo von Orsbeck **Obverse:** Date above arms **Reverse:** Value: 1/2/PETER/MENGEN

Date	Mintage	VG	F	VF	XF	Unc
1701 GG	—	7.00	13.00	25.00	50.00	—
1702 GG	—	7.00	13.00	25.00	50.00	—
1703 GG	—	7.00	13.00	25.00	50.00	—
1704 GG	—	7.00	13.00	25.00	50.00	—

KM# 207 1/2 PETERMENGER

Billon **Ruler:** Karl Josef of Lorraine **Obverse:** Crowned arms on Maltese cross **Reverse:** Value: 1/2/PETER/MENGEN/1715

Date	Mintage	VG	F	VF	XF	Unc
1715 GG	—	7.00	13.00	25.00	50.00	—

KM# 227 1/2 PETERMENGER

Billon **Ruler:** Franz Ludwig von Pfalz-Neuburg **Obverse:** Flat-topped shield of Trier, date above **Reverse:** Value: 1/2/PETER/MENGEN

Date	Mintage	VG	F	VF	XF	Unc
1722 GG	—	12.00	25.00	50.00	100	—

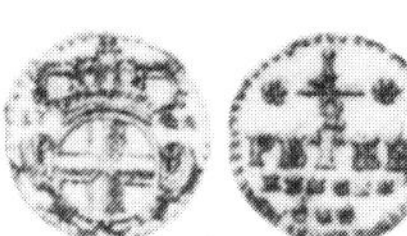

KM# 228 1/2 PETERMENGER

Billon **Ruler:** Franz Ludwig von Pfalz-Neuburg **Obverse:** Crowned oval arms in palm branches, date divided by crown **Reverse:** Value

Date	Mintage	VG	F	VF	XF	Unc
1722 GG	—	12.00	25.00	50.00	100	—

KM# 229 1/2 PETERMENGER

Billon **Ruler:** Franz Ludwig von Pfalz-Neuburg **Obverse:** Crowned round arms divide date

Date	Mintage	VG	F	VF	XF	Unc
1722 GG	—	10.00	16.00	25.00	60.00	—
1723 GG	—	10.00	16.00	25.00	60.00	—
1724 GG	—	10.00	16.00	25.00	60.00	—
1725 GG	—	10.00	16.00	25.00	60.00	—

KM# 256 1/2 PETERMENGER

Billon **Ruler:** Franz Georg von Schoenborn-Puckheim **Obverse:** Crowned arms within cartouche **Reverse:** Value, date

Date	Mintage	VG	F	VF	XF	Unc
1746 DF	—	4.00	8.00	15.00	30.00	—
1747 DF	—	4.00	8.00	15.00	30.00	—
1748 DF	—	4.00	8.00	15.00	30.00	—
1749 DF	—	4.00	8.00	15.00	30.00	—
1750 DF	—	4.00	8.00	15.00	30.00	—
1751 DF	—	4.00	8.00	15.00	30.00	—

KM# 281 PETERMENGER

Silver **Ruler:** Johann Philipp von Walderdorf **Obverse:** Crowned arms **Reverse:** St. Peter with book and keys

Date	Mintage	VG	F	VF	XF	Unc
1758 NM	—	10.00	20.00	40.00	75.00	—
1759 NM	—	9.00	18.00	35.00	65.00	—
1760 NM	—	9.00	18.00	35.00	65.00	—
1761 NM	—	9.00	18.00	35.00	65.00	—
1762 NM	—	9.00	18.00	35.00	65.00	—
1764 GM	—	10.00	20.00	45.00	80.00	—

KM# 190 3 PETERMENGER (3 Albus)

Silver **Ruler:** Johann Hugo von Orsbeck **Obverse:** Crowned arms divide date **Reverse:** Value in palm branches

Date	Mintage	VG	F	VF	XF	Unc
1703 GG	—	15.00	25.00	50.00	100	—

KM# 191 3 PETERMENGER (3 Albus)

Silver **Ruler:** Johann Hugo von Orsbeck **Obverse:** Shield of arms topped by elector's cap divides date **Reverse:** Bust of St. Peter with key and book in clouds, value below in inner circle

Date	Mintage	VG	F	VF	XF	Unc
1705 GG	—	7.00	14.00	28.00	60.00	—
1706 GG	—	7.00	14.00	28.00	60.00	—
1707 GG	—	7.00	14.00	28.00	60.00	—
1708 GG	—	7.00	14.00	28.00	60.00	—
1709 GG	—	7.00	14.00	28.00	60.00	—

KM# 201 3 PETERMENGER (3 Albus)

Silver **Obverse:** Crowned arms on Maltese cross **Reverse:** Bust of St. Peter with key and book in clouds, value below in inner circle, date divided at top

Date	Mintage	VG	F	VF	XF	Unc
1711 GG	—	10.00	20.00	35.00	65.00	—

KM# 205 3 PETERMENGER (3 Albus)

Silver **Ruler:** Karl Josef of Lorraine **Obverse:** Crowned round arms on Maltese cross **Reverse:** St. Peter with key and book in clouds, value below, circle surrounds all, date divided above

Date	Mintage	VG	F	VF	XF	Unc
1712 GG	—	7.00	14.00	25.00	55.00	—
1713 GG	—	7.00	14.00	25.00	55.00	—
1714 GG	—	7.00	14.00	25.00	55.00	—
1715 GG	—	7.00	14.00	25.00	55.00	—

KM# 290 3 PETERMENGER (3 Albus)

Silver **Ruler:** Johann Philipp von Walderdorf **Obverse:** Crowned arms in branches divide date in inner circle **Reverse:** St. Peter with book and keys in inner circle, value below

Date	Mintage	VG	F	VF	XF	Unc
1760 NM	—	15.00	30.00	60.00	100	—
1762 NM	—	15.00	30.00	60.00	100	—

KM# 303 10 PFENNIG (Kreuzer)

Copper **Ruler:** Johann Philipp von Walderdorf **Obverse:** Crowned JPC monogram **Reverse:** Value and date with LAND MUNZ

Date	Mintage	VG	F	VF	XF	Unc
1761 NM	—	12.00	25.00	50.00	100	—

KM# 351 10 PFENNIG (Kreuzer)

Billon **Ruler:** Clemens Wenzel, Archbishop **Obverse:** CWC monogram **Reverse:** Value above date

Date	Mintage	VG	F	VF	XF	Unc
1794 GM	—	7.00	15.00	30.00	60.00	—

KM# 241.1 KREUZER

Billon **Ruler:** Franz Georg von Schoenborn-Puckheim **Obverse:** Crowned monogram **Reverse:** Crowned arms

Date	Mintage	VG	F	VF	XF	Unc
1730 GG	—	8.00	16.00	35.00	65.00	—
1731 GG	—	8.00	16.00	35.00	65.00	—

KM# 241.2 KREUZER

Billon **Ruler:** Franz Georg von Schoenborn-Puckheim **Obverse:** Crowned monogram divides date above horizontal base line **Reverse:** Crowned arms

Date	Mintage	Good	VG	F	VF	XF
1732 GG	—	—	7.00	12.00	25.00	50.00

KM# 241.3 KREUZER

Billon **Ruler:** Franz Georg von Schoenborn-Puckheim **Obverse:** Crowned monogram **Reverse:** Crowned arms

Date	Mintage	Good	VG	F	VF	XF
1734 GG	—	—	7.00	12.00	25.00	50.00
1743 W	—	—	7.00	12.00	25.00	50.00
1744 W	—	—	7.00	12.00	25.00	50.00
1745 W	—	—	7.00	12.00	25.00	50.00

KM# 291 5 KREUZER

Billon **Ruler:** Johann Philipp von Walderdorf **Obverse:** Crowned complex arms divide date **Reverse:** St. Peter with book and keys in inner circle, value below **Note:** Convention 5 Kreuzer.

Date	Mintage	VG	F	VF	XF	Unc
1760 NM	—	10.00	22.00	55.00	120	—
1761 NM	—	10.00	22.00	55.00	120	—

KM# 306 5 KREUZER

Billon **Ruler:** Johann Philipp von Walderdorf **Obverse:** Crowned JPC monogram on pedestal **Reverse:** Electoral hat above pedestal with rosette below **Rev. Legend:** EINE MAREK FEIN SILBER

Date	Mintage	VG	F	VF	XF	Unc
1761 NM	—	10.00	22.00	45.00	100	—
1762 NM	—	10.00	22.00	45.00	100	—
1762 GM	—	10.00	22.00	45.00	100	—
1763 GM	—	9.00	18.00	40.00	100	—
1764 GM	—	9.00	18.00	40.00	100	—

KM# 307 5 KREUZER

Billon **Ruler:** Johann Philipp von Walderdorf **Obverse:** Crowned arms

Date	Mintage	VG	F	VF	XF	Unc
1763	—	10.00	22.00	45.00	100	—

KM# 309 5 KREUZER

Billon **Ruler:** Johann Philipp von Walderdorf **Obverse:** St. Peter **Reverse:** Value and date

Date	Mintage	VG	F	VF	XF	Unc
1765 G-GM	—	15.00	30.00	55.00	125	—

KM# A291 10 KREUZER

Silver **Ruler:** Johann Philipp von Walderdorf **Obverse:** Bust right **Reverse:** Crowned arms with lion supporters, date divided at top, value in exergue

Date	Mintage	VG	F	VF	XF	Unc
1760 NM	—	25.00	50.00	125	250	—

KM# 292 10 KREUZER

Silver **Ruler:** Johann Philipp von Walderdorf **Reverse:** "120 EINE..." around outer border

Date	Mintage	VG	F	VF	XF	Unc
1760 VL-NM	—	20.00	40.00	80.00	175	—
1761 VL-NM	—	20.00	40.00	80.00	175	—
1761 V. LON-NM	—	20.00	40.00	80.00	175	—
1761 LON-NM	—	20.00	40.00	80.00	175	—
1762 LON-GM	—	15.00	30.00	60.00	125	—
1762 GM	—	15.00	30.00	60.00	125	—
1762 EG	—	15.00	30.00	60.00	125	—

KM# 320 10 KREUZER

Silver **Ruler:** Johann Philipp von Walderdorf **Obverse:** Bust right within branches of palm and laurel **Reverse:** Crowned arms on pedestal with value

Date	Mintage	VG	F	VF	XF	Unc
1763 GM	—	15.00	30.00	60.00	125	—
1764 GM	—	15.00	30.00	60.00	125	—
1764 EG	—	15.00	30.00	60.00	125	—
1765 EG	—	15.00	30.00	60.00	125	—
ND GM	—	15.00	30.00	60.00	125	—

KM# 245 10 KREUZER (1/2 Kopfstuck)

Silver **Ruler:** Franz Georg von Schoenborn-Puckheim **Obverse:** Crowned arms **Reverse:** Value, date

Date	Mintage	VG	F	VF	XF	Unc
1734	—	95.00	140	250	425	—
1734 gg	—	95.00	140	250	425	—

KM# 293 20 KREUZER

Silver **Ruler:** Johann Philipp von Walderdorf **Obverse:** Bust right **Reverse:** Crowned arms with lion supporters, date divided at top, value in exergue

Date	Mintage	VG	F	VF	XF	Unc
1760 VL-NM	—	100	200	350	750	—

KM# 294 20 KREUZER

Silver **Ruler:** Johann Philipp von Walderdorf **Obverse:** Bust right within branches of palm and laurel **Reverse:** Crowned arms on pedestal with value

Date	Mintage	VG	F	VF	XF	Unc
1760 VL-NM	—	25.00	65.00	130	275	—
1761 V.LON-NM	—	25.00	65.00	130	275	—
1762 V.LON-NM	—	25.00	60.00	120	275	—
1763 V.LON-GM	—	25.00	60.00	120	275	—
1765 EG-GM	—	25.00	60.00	120	275	—

KM# 317 20 KREUZER

Silver **Ruler:** Clemens Wenzel, Archbishop **Obverse:** Crowned arms above value **Reverse:** Value and date within cartouche

Date	Mintage	VG	F	VF	XF	Unc
1769 EG-MG/GM	—	22.00	55.00	120	225	—

KM# 316 20 KREUZER

Silver **Ruler:** Clemens Wenzel, Archbishop **Obverse:** Bust right within branches of palm and laurel **Reverse:** Crowned arms on pedestal with value **Note:** Convention 20 Kreuzer.

Date	Mintage	VG	F	VF	XF	Unc
1769 EG-MG	—	25.00	60.00	130	300	—

KM# 327 20 KREUZER

Silver **Ruler:** Clemens Wenzel, Archbishop

Date	Mintage	VG	F	VF	XF	Unc
1771 GM	—	20.00	50.00	100	200	—

KM# 246 20 KREUZER (Kopfstuck)

Silver **Ruler:** Franz Georg von Schoenborn-Puckheim **Obverse:** Four shields around oval center shield, sword and crozier at top **Reverse:** Value and date within cartouche

Date	Mintage	VG	F	VF	XF	Unc
1734 GG	—	60.00	100	175	300	—

KM# 295 30 KREUZER

Silver **Ruler:** Johann Philipp von Walderdorf **Obverse:** Bust right **Reverse:** Crowned arms above value

Date	Mintage	VG	F	VF	XF	Unc
1760 V. LON-NM	—	70.00	140	280	525	—
1762 V. LON-NM	—	50.00	100	200	450	—

KM# 344 ALBUS (New Standard)

Billon **Ruler:** Clemens Wenzel, Archbishop **Obverse:** CWC monogram **Reverse:** Value above date

Date	Mintage	VG	F	VF	XF	Unc
1789 GM	—	10.00	20.00	40.00	80.00	—
1790 GM	—	10.00	20.00	40.00	80.00	—
1791 GM	—	10.00	20.00	40.00	80.00	—

KM# 345 3 ALBUS

Billon **Ruler:** Clemens Wenzel, Archbishop **Obverse:** Arms **Reverse:** Value and date

Date	Mintage	VG	F	VF	XF	Unc
1789 GM	—	12.00	25.00	50.00	90.00	—
1790 GM	—	12.00	25.00	50.00	90.00	—
1791 GM	—	12.00	25.00	50.00	90.00	—
1793 GM	—	12.00	25.00	50.00	90.00	—

KM# 202 1/32 THALER

Silver **Ruler:** Karl Josef of Lorraine **Subject:** Death of the Archbishop **Obverse:** Crown above three shields of arms, two above one, double border legend **Reverse:** 8-line inscription above palm branches

Date	Mintage	VG	F	VF	XF	Unc
1711	—	80.00	160	350	600	—

KM# 208 1/32 THALER

Silver **Ruler:** Karl Josef of Lorraine **Subject:** Death of the Archbishop **Obverse:** Crowned and supported arms in double border legend **Reverse:** 10-line inscription

Date	Mintage	VG	F	VF	XF	Unc
1715	—	60.00	120	250	400	—

KM# 209 1/32 THALER

Silver **Ruler:** Karl Josef of Lorraine **Subject:** Death of the Archbishop **Obverse:** Crowned arms on Maltese cross, date divided at top **Reverse:** 10-line inscription

Date	Mintage	VG	F	VF	XF	Unc
1715	—	60.00	120	250	400	—

KM# 210 1/32 THALER

Silver **Ruler:** Karl Josef of Lorraine **Obverse:** St. Peter with key and book in clouds in inner circle **Reverse:** Crowned facing figure of St. Helena, date in exergue **Note:** Sede Vacante Issue

Date	Mintage	VG	F	VF	XF	Unc
1715	—	45.00	90.00	185	300	—

KM# 266 1/32 THALER

Silver **Ruler:** Johann Philipp von Walderdorf **Subject:** Death of the Archbishop **Obverse:** Crowned complex arms with supporters **Reverse:** Inscription **Note:** Species 1/16 Thaler.

Date	Mintage	VG	F	VF	XF	Unc
1756	—	100	260	450	700	—

KM# 265 1/32 THALER

Silver **Ruler:** Johann Philipp von Walderdorf **Subject:** Death of the Archbishop **Obverse:** Crowned arms supported by two lions **Reverse:** 10-line inscription, date **Note:** Species 1/32 Thaler.

Date	Mintage	VG	F	VF	XF	Unc
1756	—	90.00	225	350	600	—

KM# 311 1/32 THALER

Silver **Ruler:** Clemens Wenzel, Archbishop **Subject:** Death of the Archbishop **Obverse:** Crowned arms with lion supporters **Reverse:** 14-line inscription

Date	Mintage	VG	F	VF	XF	Unc
1768	—	25.00	60.00	150	300	—

KM# 312 1/32 THALER

Silver **Ruler:** Johann Philipp von Walderdorf **Subject:** Death of the Archbishop **Obverse:** Crowned complex arms with supporters **Reverse:** Inscription

Date	Mintage	VG	F	VF	XF	Unc
1768	—	30.00	60.00	120	250	—

KM# 267 1/8 THALER

Silver **Ruler:** Johann Philipp von Walderdorf **Subject:** Death of the Archbishop **Obverse:** Crowned complex arms with supporters **Reverse:** Inscription **Note:** Species 1/8 Thaler.

Date	Mintage	VG	F	VF	XF	Unc
1756	—	125	325	500	750	—

KM# 313 1/8 THALER

Silver **Ruler:** Clemens Wenzel, Archbishop **Subject:** Death of the Archbishop **Obverse:** Crowned arms with supporters **Reverse:** Inscription

Date	Mintage	VG	F	VF	XF	Unc
1768	—	40.00	80.00	160	325	—

KM# 192 1/6 THALER

Silver **Ruler:** Johann Hugo von Orsbeck **Obverse:** Crowned shield divides date **Obv. Legend:** IOAN • HVGO • D • G • ARCH • TREV • S • R • I • A E L **Reverse:** Value within inner circle **Rev. Inscription:** MONETA • NOUA • ARGENTA •

Date	Mintage	VG	F	VF	XF	Unc
1705	—	30.00	50.00	100	200	—

KM# 273 1/6 THALER

Silver **Ruler:** Johann Philipp von Walderdorf **Obverse:** Crowned JPC monogram **Reverse:** Value

Date	Mintage	VG	F	VF	XF	Unc
1757 NM	—	20.00	40.00	80.00	225	—
1758 NM	—	25.00	50.00	100	250	—

KM# 274 1/6 THALER

Silver **Ruler:** Johann Philipp von Walderdorf **Obverse:** "100 EINE... " around outer border **Reverse:** Value, date

Date	Mintage	VG	F	VF	XF	Unc
1757 NM	—	30.00	60.00	120	235	—

KM# 275 1/6 THALER

Silver **Ruler:** Johann Philipp von Walderdorf **Obverse:** Crowned monogram **Reverse:** Value, date

Date	Mintage	VG	F	VF	XF	Unc
1757 NM	—	30.00	60.00	120	325	—

KM# 276 1/6 THALER

Silver **Ruler:** Franz Georg von Schoenborn-Puckheim **Obverse:** Bust right **Reverse:** "100 EINE... " around outer border

Date	Mintage	VG	F	VF	XF	Unc
1757 NM	—	70.00	140	280	500	—

KM# 277 1/6 THALER

Silver **Ruler:** Johann Philipp von Walderdorf **Obverse:** Bust right **Reverse:** Without legend around outer border

Date	Mintage	VG	F	VF	XF	Unc
1757 NM	—	70.00	140	250	400	—

KM# 203 1/4 THALER

Silver **Ruler:** Karl Josef of Lorraine **Subject:** Death of the Archbishop **Obverse:** Crown above three shields of arms, two above one, double border legend **Reverse:** 8-line inscription above palm branches

Date	Mintage	VG	F	VF	XF	Unc
1711	—	120	250	500	1,000	—

KM# 211 1/4 THALER

Silver **Ruler:** Karl Josef of Lorraine **Subject:** Death of the Archbishop **Obverse:** Crowned and supported arms in double border legend **Reverse:** 10-line inscription

Date	Mintage	VG	F	VF	XF	Unc
1715	—	150	300	600	1,200	—

KM# 212 1/4 THALER

Silver **Ruler:** Karl Josef of Lorraine **Subject:** Death of the Archbishop **Obverse:** Crowned arms on Maltese cross, date divided at top **Reverse:** 11-line inscription

Date	Mintage	VG	F	VF	XF	Unc
1715	—	135	285	550	1,100	—

KM# 213 1/4 THALER

Silver **Ruler:** Karl Josef of Lorraine **Obverse:** St. Peter with key and book in clouds in inner circle **Reverse:** Crowned facing figure of St. Helena, date in exergue **Note:** Sede Vacante Issue.

Date	Mintage	VG	F	VF	XF	Unc
1715	—	80.00	160	325	600	—

KM# 296 1/2 THALER

Silver **Obverse:** Bust right **Reverse:** Supported arms

Date	Mintage	VG	F	VF	XF	Unc
1760 V. LON-NM	—	90.00	185	365	850	—
1761 V. LON-NM	—	85.00	175	350	800	—
1762 V. LON-NM	—	85.00	175	350	800	—
1763 V. LON-NM	—	85.00	175	350	800	—
1765 EG-GM	—	85.00	175	350	800	—

KM# 214 1/2 THALER

Silver **Ruler:** Karl Josef of Lorraine **Subject:** Death of the Archbishop **Obverse:** Crowned and supported arms in double border legend **Reverse:** 10-line inscription

Date	Mintage	VG	F	VF	XF	Unc
1715	—	200	450	1,150	1,750	—

KM# 215 1/2 THALER

Silver **Ruler:** Karl Josef of Lorraine **Subject:** Death of the Archbishop **Obverse:** Crowned arms on Maltese cross, date divided at top **Reverse:** 13-line inscription

Date	Mintage	VG	F	VF	XF	Unc
1715	—	200	450	1,150	1,750	—

KM# 216 1/2 THALER

Silver **Ruler:** Karl Josef of Lorraine **Obverse:** St. Peter with key and book in clouds in innner circle **Obv. Legend:** TREVIRENSE - CAPITVLVM - METROPOLITANVM **Reverse:** Crowned facing figure of St. Helena, date in exergue **Note:** Sede Vacante Issue.

Date	Mintage	VG	F	VF	XF	Unc
1715	—	200	450	1,150	1,750	—

KM# 230 1/2 THALER

Silver **Ruler:** Franz Ludwig von Pfalz-Neuburg **Obverse:** Bust right **Obv. Legend:** FRAN • LUD • D • G • AR • ... **Reverse:** Arms within crowned mantle

Date	Mintage	VG	F	VF	XF	Unc
1722	—	350	750	1,500	3,000	—
1729	—	350	750	1,500	3,000	—

KM# 268 1/2 THALER

Silver **Ruler:** Johann Philipp von Walderdorf **Subject:** Death of the Archbishop **Obverse:** Crowned arms with supporters **Reverse:** Inscription **Note:** Species 1/2 Thaler

Date	Mintage	VG	F	VF	XF	Unc
1756	—	175	375	950	1,500	—

KM# 269 1/2 THALER

Silver **Ruler:** Johann Philipp von Walderdorf **Subject:** Vilmar Mining **Obverse:** Bust right **Obv. Legend:** IOAN • PHIL • D • G • A • EP • TREVIR • S • R • I • PR • EL • ADMI • PRUM • P • P • **Reverse:** Crowned arms with supporters, value below **Rev. Legend:** EX FODINIS VILLMARIENSIBUS... **Note:** Convention 1/2 Thaler

Date	Mintage	VG	F	VF	XF	Unc
1756 V. LON	—	200	400	800	1,700	—
1757 V. LON-NM	—	150	325	650	1,500	—
1761 V. LON-NM	—	150	325	650	1,500	—

KM# 304 1/2 THALER

Silver **Ruler:** Johann Philipp von Walderdorf **Subject:** Berncastel Mining **Rev. Legend:** EX FODINIS BERNCASTELIANIS 1761

Date	Mintage	VG	F	VF	XF	Unc
1761 V. LON-NM	—	250	600	1,250	3,000	—
1762 NM	—	250	600	1,250	3,000	—

KM# 314 1/2 THALER

Silver **Ruler:** Clemens Wenzel, Archbishop **Subject:** Death of the Archbishop **Obverse:** Crowned arms with supporters **Reverse:** Inscription

Date	Mintage	VG	F	VF	XF	Unc
1768	—	200	400	1,000	1,600	—

KM# 325 1/2 THALER

Silver **Ruler:** Clemens Wenzel, Archbishop **Obverse:** Bust right **Obv. Legend:** D: G: CLEM • WENC • A • E • TR • S • R • I • .... **Reverse:** Order cross below arms with crowned arms at center

Date	Mintage	VG	F	VF	XF	Unc
1770 EG-GM	—	175	275	450	800	—

KM# 330 1/2 THALER

Silver **Ruler:** Clemens Wenzel, Archbishop **Obverse:** Bust right **Obv. Legend:** CLEM • WENC • D • G • A • EP • TREV • S • R • I • A • C • & EL **Reverse:** Order cross below arms with crowned arms at center **Rev. Legend:** ...P • P • - CO - AD • ELVANG

Date	Mintage	VG	F	VF	XF	Unc
1773 St-GM	—	150	300	500	1,000	—

KM# 331 1/2 THALER

Silver **Ruler:** Clemens Wenzel, Archbishop **Obverse:** Bust right **Obv. Legend:** CLEM • WENC • D • G • A • EPISC • TREV • S • R • I • A • C • & EL • **Reverse:** Order cross below arms with crowned shield at center **Rev. Legend:** EPISC • AUG • A • P • P • - CO - AD • ELVAC • 1773 •

Date	Mintage	VG	F	VF	XF	Unc
1773 SC	—	150	300	600	1,150	—

KM# 206 2/3 THALER

Silver **Ruler:** Karl Josef of Lorraine **Obverse:** Bust of Archbishop right in inner circle **Reverse:** Crown above three shields of arms, one above two, date in legend

Date	Mintage	VG	F	VF	XF	Unc
1714 GG	—	175	325	1,000	2,000	—

KM# 167 THALER

Silver **Reverse:** Large elector's cap above three shields of arms, two above on in inner circle **Note:** Dav. #2815.

Date	Mintage	VG	F	VF	XF	Unc
ND	—	750	1,500	3,000	5,000	—

KM# 168 THALER

Silver **Ruler:** Johann Hugo von Orsbeck **Obverse:** Bust right **Obv. Legend:** IOAN • HVGO • D • G • ARCH • TREC • S • R • I • PER • GALL • ET • REG • ARELAT * **Reverse:** Flat elector's hat **Rev. Legend:** ARCHIC • ET • PRINC • EL • EPIS • SPIR • ADMR • PRVM • PRAEP • WEISS * **Note:** Dav. #2817.

Date	Mintage	VG	F	VF	XF	Unc
ND	—	750	1,500	3,000	5,000	—

KM# 169 THALER

Silver **Ruler:** Johann Hugo von Orsbeck **Obverse:** Bust right **Obv. Legend:** IOAN • HUGO • D • G • ARCH • TREV • S • R • I • PER • GALL • ET • REG • AREIAT * **Reverse:** Palm branches below arms **Rev. Legend:** ARCHIC • ET • PRINC • EL • EPIS • SPIR • ADMR • PRVM • PRÆP • WEISS **Note:** Dav. #2818.

Date	Mintage	VG	F	VF	XF	Unc
ND	—	700	1,250	2,750	4,500	—

KM# 187 THALER

Silver **Ruler:** Johann Hugo von Orsbeck **Obverse:** Bust of Archbishop right **Obv. Legend:** IOAN • PHIL • D • G • AR • EP • TREVIR • S • R • I • PRIN • EL • ADMI • PRUM • PP •, V. LON below **Reverse:** Elector's cap above three shields of arms **Note:** Varieties exist. Dav. #2829

Date	Mintage	VG	F	VF	XF	Unc
1701	—	750	1,500	3,000	6,000	—
1702	—	750	1,500	3,000	6,000	—

KM# 204 THALER

Silver **Ruler:** Karl Josef of Lorraine **Subject:** Death of the Archbishop **Obverse:** Elector's cap above three shields of arms, two above one, double border legend **Obv. Legend:** IOAN. HVGO. D.G. ARCHITREV. S.R.I. PER • GALL • ET • REG • AREIAT •, in inner row; ARCHIC • ET • PRINC • EL • EPIS • SPIR • ADMR • PRVMPRÆP • WEISS • **Reverse:** 8-line inscription above palm branches **Rev. Inscription:** * NATVS */13 • IAN: 1634/ELECT • IN • COAD • TREV: 7/IAN • 1672 IN • EPIS:/SPEI: 16 • IVLY • 1675/SVCCESSIT • IN • ELECT •/1676 • I • IVNY •/OBYT • 1711: 6: IAN • **Note:** Dav. #2822.

Date	Mintage	VG	F	VF	XF	Unc
1711	—	400	1,000	2,000	3,500	—

KM# 217 THALER

Silver **Ruler:** Karl Josef of Lorraine **Subject:** Death of the Archbishop **Obverse:** Crowned and supported arms in double border legend, titles of Karl **Reverse:** 10-line inscription **Note:** Dav. #2823.

Date	Mintage	VG	F	VF	XF	Unc
1715	—	550	1,100	2,000	3,000	—

KM# 218 THALER

Silver **Ruler:** Karl Josef of Lorraine **Subject:** Death of the Archbishop **Obverse:** Crowned complex arms with supporters, date divided above **Obv. Legend:** DOMINUS PROVIDEBIT below **Reverse:** 15-line inscription **Note:** Dav. #2824.

Date	Mintage	VG	F	VF	XF	Unc
1715	—	400	1,000	2,000	3,500	—

KM# 219 THALER

Silver **Ruler:** Karl Josef of Lorraine **Obverse:** St. Paul with key and book in clouds in inner circle **Obv. Legend:** CAPITVLVM METROPOLITANVM TREVIRENSE **Reverse:** Crowned facing figure of St. Helena, date in exergue **Rev. Legend:** SANCTA HELENA FVNDATRIX ECCLESIÆ, in exergue; SEDE VACANTE/ANNO 1715 **Note:** Sede vacante issue. Dav. #2825.

Date	Mintage	VG	F	VF	XF	Unc
1715	—	700	1,450	2,750	5,000	—

KM# 231 THALER

Silver **Ruler:** Franz Ludwig von Pfalz-Neuburg **Obverse:** Bust right **Reverse:** Crowned and supported arms, date divided at bottom of shield **Note:** Dav. #2826.

Date	Mintage	VG	F	VF	XF	Unc
1722	—	1,000	2,000	3,500	5,500	—

KM# 278 THALER

Silver **Ruler:** Johann Philipp von Walderdorf **Obverse:** Bust right **Obv. Legend:** IOAN • PHILIP • D • G • AR • EP • & EL • TREVIR • ADMI • PRVM • PP., V. LON. F. 1757 below **Reverse:** Elector's cap above arms with supporters, value below **Rev. Legend:** EINE MARCK FEIN SILBER **Note:** Dav. #2827.

Date	Mintage	F	VF	XF	Unc
1757 V. LON-NM	—	125	250	500	1,200

KM# 299 THALER

Silver **Ruler:** Johann Philipp von Walderdorf **Obverse:** Bust right **Obv. Legend:** IOAN • PHIL • D • G • AR • EP. TREVIR • S • R • I • PR • EL • ADMI • PRUM • PP • **Reverse:** Elector's cap above arms with supporters, value and date below **Rev. Legend:** 10/EINE MARCK FEIN/SILBER/date

Date	Mintage	F	VF	XF	Unc
1760 V. LON//NM	—	125	250	600	1,200
1761	—	125	250	600	1,200

KM# 297 THALER

Silver **Ruler:** Johann Philipp von Walderdorf **Obverse:** Bust right **Obv. Legend:** IOAN • PHIL • D • G • AR • EP • TREVIR • S • R • I • PRIN • EL • ADMI • PRUM • PP •, V. LON below **Reverse:** Elector's cap above arms with supporters, value and date below **Rev. Legend:** 10/EINE MARCK FEIN/SILBER/date/N•M• **Note:** Dav. #2828.

Date	Mintage	F	VF	XF	Unc
1760	—	125	250	550	1,200
1761 V. LON//NM	—	125	250	550	1,200

KM# 298 THALER

Silver **Ruler:** Johann Philipp von Walderdorf **Obverse:** Bust right **Obv. Legend:** IOAN • PHIL • D • G • AR • EP • TREVIR • S • R • I • PRIN • EL • ADMI • PRUM • PP **Reverse:** Value all in one line **Rev. Legend:** 10/EINE MARCK FEIN SILBER/ date **Note:** Dav. #2828A.

Date	Mintage	F	VF	XF	Unc
1760 V. LON-NM	—	125	250	600	1,200

KM# 305.1 THALER

Silver **Ruler:** Johann Philipp von Walderdorf **Obverse:** Bust right **Obv. Legend:** IOAN • PHIL • D • G • AR • EP • TREVIR • S • R • I • PRIN • EL • ADMI • PRUM • PP • **Reverse:** Elector's cap above arms with supporters, value and date below **Rev. Legend:** 10/EINE MARCK FEIN/SILBER/date **Note:** Dav. #2829.

Date	Mintage	F	VF	XF	Unc
1762 V. LON//NM	—	175	375	700	1,250
1763 GM	—	175	375	700	1,250

KM# 305.2 THALER

Silver **Ruler:** Johann Philipp von Walderdorf **Obverse:** Bust right **Obv. Legend:** ... S. R. I. PRINC... **Reverse:** Elector's cap above arms with supporters, value and date below **Note:** Dav. #2829A.

Date	Mintage	F	VF	XF	Unc
1762 V. LON//NM	—	175	375	700	1,250

KM# 308 THALER

Silver **Ruler:** Johann Philipp von Walderdorf **Obverse:** Cloaked bust right **Obv. Legend:** IOAN • PHIL • D • G • AR • EP • TREV • S • R • I • PR • EL • EP • WORM • ADMI • PRUM • PP • **Reverse:** Elector's cap above arms with supporters, value and date below **Rev. Legend:** EINE MARK - FEIN SILBER **Note:** Dav. #2830.

Date	Mintage	F	VF	XF	Unc
1764 V. LON//GM	—	175	375	700	1,250

KM# A309 THALER

Silver **Ruler:** Johann Philipp von Walderdorf **Obverse:** Cloaked bust right **Reverse:** Elector's cap above complex arms with supporters, value and date below **Note:** Mule. Dav. #2830A.

Date	Mintage	F	VF	XF	Unc
1764 EG//GM	—	175	375	700	1,250

KM# 315 THALER

Silver **Ruler:** Johann Philipp von Walderdorf **Obverse:** Cloaked bust right **Obv. Legend:** IOAN • PHIL • D: G • A • E • TREV • S • R • I • P • EL • E • WORM • A • PR • PP • **Reverse:** Elector's cap above complex arms **Rev. Legend:** 10 EINE MARK FEIN SILBER 1765 **Note:** Dav. #2831.

Date	Mintage	F	VF	XF	Unc
1765 EG//GM	—	150	300	650	1,200

KM# 318 THALER

Silver **Ruler:** Clemens Wenzel, Archbishop **Obverse:** Bust right **Obv. Legend:** D: G: CLEMENS WENC • A • E • T • S • R • I • P • G • & R • A • A • C • & P • E • **Reverse:** Elector's cap above arms with supporters, crowned shield at center **Rev. Legend:** EP. FRIS. & RATISB: AD. PRUM: PP: COAD: AUG., G - M/ X EINE FEINE MARC below **Note:** Convetnion Thaler. Dav. #2832.

Date	Mintage	F	VF	XF	Unc
1768 EG//GM	—	1,500	2,500	4,000	6,000

KM# A320 THALER

Silver **Ruler:** Clemens Wenzel, Archbishop **Obverse:** Bust left **Obv. Legend:** D • G • CLEM • WENC • A • EP • TREV • S • R • I • P • GAL • & R • AR • E • L • A • CANC • & P • EL • EP • AUG • ADM • PRVM • P • P * **Reverse:** Elector's cap above arms, Order cross below, sword and crozier behind **Rev. Legend:** REG • PR • POL • - ET - LITH • - SAXON • DUX •, X • EINE MARK FEINS • /1769 below **Note:** Dav. #2833.

Date	Mintage	F	VF	XF	Unc
1769	—	150	350	650	1,250

KM# 328.1 THALER

Silver **Ruler:** Clemens Wenzel, Archbishop **Obverse:** Bust right **Obv. Legend:** CLEM • WENC • D • G • A • EP • TREV • S • R • I • A • C • & EL • **Reverse:** Elector's cap above arms, order cross below, sword and crozier behind **Rev. Legend:** EPIS C • AVG • A • P • P • - COAD • ELV • 1771, G - M/10 • EIN - MARC F below **Note:** Dav. #2834.

Date	Mintage	F	VF	XF	Unc
1771/0 GM	—	150	350	600	1,100
1771 GM	—	150	350	600	1,100

KM# 328.2 THALER

Silver **Ruler:** Clemens Wenzel, Archbishop **Obverse:** Bust right **Obv. Legend:** CLEM • WENC • D • G • A • EP • TREV • S • R • I • A • C • & EL • **Reverse:** Elector's cap above arms, order cross below, sword and crozier behind **Rev. Legend:** EPIS C • AVG • A • P • P • - COAD • ELV • 1771, G - M/10 • EIN - MARC F below **Note:** Dav. #2834A.

Date	Mintage	F	VF	XF	Unc
1771 SC	—	150	350	600	1,250

KM# 332 THALER

Silver **Ruler:** Clemens Wenzel, Archbishop **Obverse:** Draped bust right **Obv. Legend:** CLEM • WENC • D • G • A • EPISC • TREV • S • R • I • A • C • & EL • **Reverse:** Elector's cap above arms, order cross divides value below, sword and crozier behind **Rev. Legend:** EPISCOP • AUG • A • - P • P • - CO • - ELVANG • 1773, X• EINE - MARK F•/S• - C• **Note:** Dav. #2835.

Date	Mintage	F	VF	XF	Unc
1773 SC	—	200	400	750	1,500

KM# 333 THALER

Silver **Ruler:** Clemens Wenzel, Archbishop **Obverse:** Draped bust right **Obv. Legend:** CLEM • WENC • D • G • A • EP • TREV • S • R • I • A • C • & EL • **Reverse:** Elector's cap above arms, order cross divides date and value below, sword and crozier behind **Rev. Legend:** EPISC • AVG • A • - P • P • - CO - AD • ELVANG, X • EINE - MARK F •/17 - 73/G• - M• **Note:** Dav. #2836.

Date	Mintage	F	VF	XF	Unc
1773 St//GM	—	200	400	750	1,250

KM# 352.2 THALER

Silver **Ruler:** Clemens Wenzel, Archbishop **Obverse:** Small bust right **Reverse:** Crowned arms at center of arms within mantle, elector's cap above **Note:** Dav. #2837A.

Date	Mintage	F	VF	XF	Unc
ND(1794) GM Rare	—	—	—	—	—

KM# 352.1 THALER

Silver **Ruler:** Clemens Wenzel, Archbishop **Obverse:** Large bust right **Obv. Legend:** CLEM • WENC • D: G: A • EP • & EL • TREV • EP • AVG • P • PR • ELV • ADM • PRVM • P • P • R • POL • D • SAX • **Reverse:** Date in chronogram **Rev. Legend:** EX VASIS ARGENTEIS IN VSVM PATRIAE SINE CENSIBVS DATIS ACLERO ET PRIVATIS *, X. EINE MARK FEIN below arms **Note:** Contribution Thaler. Dav. #2837.

Date	Mintage	F	VF	XF	Unc
ND(1794) S-GM	—	150	350	550	1,000

KM# 170 2 THALER

Silver **Ruler:** Johann Hugo von Orsbeck **Obverse:** Bust right **Obv. Legend:** IOAN • HVGO • D • G • ARCH • TREV • S • R • I • PER • GALL • ET • REG • ARELAT * **Reverse:** Large elector's cap above three shields of arms, two above, one in inner circle **Rev. Legend:** ARCHIC • ET • PRINC • EL • EPIS • SPIR • ADMR • PRVM • PRAEP • WEISS * **Note:** Dav. #2814

Date	Mintage	VG	F	VF	XF	Unc
ND	—	1,750	3,000	6,000	10,000	—

KM# 172 2 THALER

Silver **Ruler:** Johann Hugo von Orsbeck **Obverse:** Bust right **Obv. Legend:** IOAN • HUGO • D • G • ARCH • TREV • S • R • I • PER • GALL • ET • REG • AREIAT • **Reverse:** Palm branches below arms **Rev. Legend:** ARCHIC • ET • PRINC • EL • EPIS • SPIR • ADMR • PRVMPRAEP • WEISS • **Note:** Dav. #2818

Date	Mintage	VG	F	VF	XF	Unc
ND	—	1,750	3,000	6,500	10,000	—

KM# 171 2 THALER

Silver **Ruler:** Johann Hugo von Orsbeck **Obverse:** Bust right **Reverse:** Flat elector's hat **Note:** Similar to 1 Thaler KM#168. Dav. #2816.

Date	Mintage	VG	F	VF	XF	Unc
ND	—	1,750	3,000	6,000	10,000	—

KM# 188 2 THALER

Silver **Ruler:** Johann Hugo von Orsbeck **Obverse:** Bust of Archbishop right **Reverse:** Helmeted arms, date divided at bottom **Note:** Struck with 1 Thaler dies, KM#187. Dav. #2820.

Date	Mintage	VG	F	VF	XF	Unc
1701	—	2,000	3,500	6,500	10,000	—

TRADE COINAGE

KM# 165 GOLDGULDEN

3.5000 g., 0.9860 Gold 0.1109 oz. AGW **Ruler:** Johann Hugo von Orsbeck **Obverse:** Bust of St. Peter, value below **Reverse:** Three shields of arms **Note:** Fr#3471.

Date	Mintage	VG	F	VF	XF	Unc
1701	—	1,000	2,000	4,000	6,500	—

KM# 225 DUCAT

3.5000 g., 0.9860 Gold 0.1109 oz. AGW **Ruler:** Franz Ludwig von Pfalz-Neuburg **Obverse:** Bust right **Reverse:** Crowned arms **Note:** Fr#3472.

Date	Mintage	VG	F	VF	XF	Unc
1720	—	450	1,000	2,500	5,000	—
1722	—	450	1,000	2,500	5,000	—

KM# 226 DUCAT

3.5000 g., 0.9860 Gold 0.1109 oz. AGW **Ruler:** Franz Ludwig von Pfalz-Neuburg **Obverse:** Bust right **Obv. Legend:** D • G • FRAN • LUD • - ARCH • TREV • PR • Æl • **Reverse:** Lion in reins held by hand from above, date below **Rev. Legend:** DEO - DUCE • **Note:** Fr#3473.

Date	Mintage	VG	F	VF	XF	Unc
1721	—	400	800	1,800	3,000	—

KM# 247 DUCAT

3.5000 g., 0.9860 Gold 0.1109 oz. AGW **Ruler:** Franz Georg von Schoenborn-Puckheim **Obverse:** Bust right **Reverse:** Crowned arms with lion supporters **Note:** Fr#3475.

Date	Mintage	VG	F	VF	XF	Unc
1735 V. LON	—	600	1,200	3,000	6,000	—
1750 V. LON	—	600	1,200	3,000	6,000	—
1752 V. LON	—	600	1,200	3,000	6,000	—
1752 V. LON-DF	—	600	1,200	3,000	6,000	—

KM# 279 DUCAT

3.5000 g., 0.9860 Gold 0.1109 oz. AGW **Ruler:** Johann Philipp von Walderdorf **Obverse:** Draped bust right **Reverse:** Date in chronogram

Date	Mintage	VG	F	VF	XF	Unc
ND(1757) V. LON	—	1,500	3,000	5,000	7,500	—

KM# 280 DUCAT

3.5000 g., 0.9860 Gold 0.1109 oz. AGW **Ruler:** Johann Philipp von Walderdorf **Reverse:** Crowned arms **Rev. Legend:** VNIONE MIRIFICA... **Note:** Fr#3476.

Date	Mintage	VG	F	VF	XF	Unc
1759	—	1,200	2,500	4,500	7,500	—

KM# 300 DUCAT

3.5000 g., 0.9860 Gold 0.1109 oz. AGW **Ruler:** Johann Philipp von Walderdorf **Reverse:** Without VNIONE MIRIFICA... in legend **Note:** Fr#3477.

Date	Mintage	VG	F	VF	XF	Unc
1760 V. LON-NM	—	1,000	2,000	3,500	6,000	—
1761 NM	—	1,000	2,000	3,500	6,000	—
1762 NM	—	1,000	2,000	3,500	6,000	—

KM# 326 DUCAT

3.5000 g., 0.9860 Gold 0.1109 oz. AGW **Ruler:** Clemens Wenzel, Archbishop **Obverse:** Draped bust right **Obv. Legend:** CLEM • WENC • D • G • A • EP • TREV • S • R • I • A • C • & EL • **Reverse:** Elector's cap above arms, Order cross below **Rev. Legend:** EPISC • AUG • A • P • P • - CO AD • ELV • 1770 • **Note:** Fr#3478.

Date	Mintage	F	VF	XF	Unc
1770	—	1,000	2,000	3,500	5,000

KM# 189 2 DUCAT

7.0000 g., 0.9860 Gold 0.2219 oz. AGW **Ruler:** Johann Hugo von Orsbeck **Obverse:** Bust right **Reverse:** Crowned arms **Note:** Fr#3467.

Date	Mintage	VG	F	VF	XF	Unc
1703	—	2,000	3,500	6,500	11,000	—

KM# 248 2 DUCAT

7.0000 g., 0.9860 Gold 0.2219 oz. AGW **Ruler:** Franz Georg von Schoenborn-Puckheim **Obverse:** Bust right **Reverse:** Crowned arms with lion supporters **Note:** Fr#3474.

Date	Mintage	VG	F	VF	XF	Unc
1735	—	2,000	3,500	7,000	12,500	—
1745	—	2,000	3,500	7,000	12,500	—
1750 V. LON	—	2,000	3,500	7,000	12,500	—
1752 V. LON-DF	—	2,000	3,500	7,000	12,500	—

KM# 282 2 DUCAT

7.0000 g., 0.9860 Gold 0.2219 oz. AGW **Ruler:** Johann Philipp von Walderdorf **Obverse:** Bust right **Reverse:** Crowned arms, date in chronogram

Date	Mintage	VG	F	VF	XF	Unc
1759	—	1,750	2,750	6,000	10,000	—

PATTERNS

Including off metal strikes

KM#	Date	Mintage	Identification	Mkt Val
Pn7	1703	—	3 Petermenger. Gold.	4,500
Pn8	1715	—	1/4 Thaler. Gold. Sede Vacante	12,000
Pn9	1749	—	2 Pfennig. Silver. KM#258	150
Pn10	1750	—	1/2 Petermenger. Gold. KM#256	3,500
Pn11	1773	—	1/2 Thaler. Copper. KM#331	550
Pn12	1773	—	1/2 Thaler. Gold. KM#331	5,000

ULM

A free city on the Danube located about 60 miles southeast of Stuttgart, Ulm is known from documents to have existed at least from the mid-9th century. During the 11th century, Ulm rose to prominence as the chief urban center of Swabia. The city was granted the distinction of a free imperial city in 1155. The right to mint its own coinage was given to the city in 1398. After a period of jointly issued coins with the cities of Ravensburg and Überlingen, Ulm struck a long series on its own beginning in 1546. Local city coinage ended in 1773, but it was not until 1803 that its free status ended, at which time Ulm became part of Bavaria. Ulm passed permanently to Württemberg in 1809.

MINT MARKS

G - Günzburg

MINT OFFICIALS' INITIALS

Initials	Date	Name
M	1671-1704	Johann Bartholomäus Müller
	1702	Georg Kolb
	1731	Jacob Sedelmaier
IT/T	1740-69	Jonas Peter Thiebaud, die-cutter in Augsburg
FH	1760-66	Frings, mintwarden and Johann Christian Hohleisen, mintmaster in Augsburg

ARMS

2-fold, divided horizontally, upper half usually shaded with cross-hatching or other pattern.

FREE CITY

REGULAR COINAGE

KM# 118 HELLER

Copper **Obverse:** City arms in circle of dots **Note:** Uniface. Varieties exist.

Date	Mintage	VG	F	VF	XF	Unc
ND(mid-18 c)	—	5.00	10.00	18.00	35.00	—

KM# 128 HELLER

Copper **Obverse:** Oval city arms **Note:** Uniface. Prev. C#1.

Date	Mintage	VG	F	VF	XF	Unc
ND(1772)	—	8.00	16.00	32.00	60.00	—

KM# 132 HELLER

Copper **Obverse:** City arms in rounded shield, annulet ornaments around **Note:** Prev. C#2.

Date	Mintage	VG	F	VF	XF	Unc
ND(1780)	—	8.00	16.00	32.00	60.00	—

KM# 116 1/2 KREUZER

Billon **Obverse:** City arms in cartouche **Note:** Uniface. Prev. C#2.5.

Date	Mintage	VG	F	VF	XF	Unc
ND	—	8.00	16.00	32.00	60.00	—

KM# 81 KREUZER

Silver **Obverse:** Shield of round city arms in baroque frame, lower half of arms ornamented **Reverse:** Crowned imperial eagle, 'I' in orb on breast

Date	Mintage	VG	F	VF	XF	Unc
ND(1701-3)	—	10.00	20.00	35.00	70.00	—

KM# 125 KREUZER

Billon **Obverse:** Crowned imperial eagle with 1 in oval on breast **Reverse:** City arms in cartouche, value, date **Note:** Previous C#7.

Date	Mintage	VG	F	VF	XF	Unc
1767 FH	255,000	9.00	18.00	35.00	70.00	—
1768 FH	47,000	9.00	18.00	35.00	70.00	—

KM# 124 KREUZER

Billon **Obverse:** Crowned city arms in ornamented shield, mintmaster's initials below, date at end of legend **Obv. Legend:** ULM KREVZER (date). **Reverse:** Crowned imperial eagle, '1' in orb on breast **Note:** Varieties exist.

Date	Mintage	VG	F	VF	XF	Unc
1767 T/FH	—	8.00	16.00	40.00	80.00	—
1768 T/FH	—	8.00	16.00	40.00	80.00	—

KM# 130 KREUZER

Copper **Obverse:** Arms within cartouche **Obv. Legend:** • ULM • **Reverse:** Value, date **Note:** Previous C#3.

Date	Mintage	VG	F	VF	XF	Unc
1772 G	—	10.00	20.00	40.00	75.00	—
1773 G	—	10.00	20.00	40.00	75.00	—

KM# 120 3-1/2 KREUZER-2-1/2 KREUZER

Billon **Obverse:** ULM above city arms, value: III 1/2 K. city standard, date **Reverse:** Crowned imperial eagle, 2-1/2K. imperial standard **Note:** Prev. C#9.

Date	Mintage	VG	F	VF	XF	Unc
1758	19,000	35.00	70.00	140	225	—

KM# 126 5 KREUZER

Billon **Obverse:** Crowned city arms in cartouche, date **Reverse:** Crowned imperial eagle on pedestal, value **Note:** Convention 5 Kreuzer. Prev. C#13.

Date	Mintage	VG	F	VF	XF	Unc
1767 FH	31,000	30.00	50.00	90.00	175	—

KM# 122 7 KREUZER-5 KREUZER

Billon **Obverse:** City arms, value and date **Reverse:** Imperial eagle, value below **Note:** Similar to 3 1/2 Kreuzer, KM#120, but with value: VII K. city standard and 5 K. imperial standard. Prev. C#11.

Date	Mintage	VG	F	VF	XF	Unc
1758	22,000	35.00	70.00	140	225	—

TRADE COINAGE

KM# 105 1/2 DUCAT

1.7500 g., 0.9860 Gold 0.0555 oz. AGW **Subject:** Bicentennial of the Reformation **Obverse:** City arms divide date **Obv. Legend:** * VLM * **Reverse:** Legend **Note:** Fr#3487.

Date	Mintage	VG	F	VF	XF	Unc
1717	—	300	600	1,100	1,800	—

KM# 109 1/2 DUCAT

1.7500 g., 0.9860 Gold 0.0555 oz. AGW **Subject:** Bicentennial of the Augsburg Confession **Obverse:** City arms divide date **Reverse:** "Eye of God" above open book with date **Note:** Fr#3490.

Date	Mintage	VG	F	VF	XF	Unc
1730	—	250	500	900	1,600	—

KM# 103 DUCAT

3.5000 g., 0.9860 Gold 0.1109 oz. AGW **Obverse:** Arms within cartouche, inner circle surrounds **Obv. Legend:** IOSEPH,• D • - G • R • I • S • A • T • F • **Reverse:** Laureate bust right **Rev. Legend:** MONETA • AVREA • REIPVBL • VLMANS • MDCCV **Note:** Fr#3483.

Date	Mintage	VG	F	VF	XF	Unc
1705 Rare	—	—	—	—	—	—

KM# 107 DUCAT

3.5000 g., 0.9860 Gold 0.1109 oz. AGW **Subject:** Bicentennial of the Reformation **Obverse:** City arms divide date **Reverse:** Inscription within wreath **Note:** Fr#3486.

Date	Mintage	VG	F	VF	XF	Unc
1717	—	350	650	1,400	2,500	—

KM# 111 DUCAT

7.0000 g., 0.9860 Gold 0.2219 oz. AGW **Subject:** Bicentennial of the Augsburg Confession **Obverse:** Ornate city arms **Reverse:** Inscription on altar **Note:** Fr#3488.

Date	Mintage	VG	F	VF	XF	Unc
1730	—	1,200	2,500	5,000	7,500	—

KM# 112 DUCAT

3.5000 g., 0.9860 Gold 0.1109 oz. AGW **Subject:** Bicentennial of the Augsburg Confession **Obverse:** City arms **Obv. Legend:** • M • IVN * VINISCHES • IVE.... **Reverse:** "Eye of God" above open book **Note:** Varieties exist. Fr#3489.

Date	Mintage	VG	F	VF	XF	Unc
1730	—	300	650	1,400	2,500	—

KM# 114 DUCAT

3.5000 g., 0.9860 Gold 0.1109 oz. AGW **Obverse:** City arms **Obv. Legend:** CAROLUS • D • G • R • .... **Reverse:** Bust right **Note:** Fr#3491.

Date	Mintage	VG	F	VF	XF	Unc
1742 IT	—	600	1,500	3,000	5,000	—

SIEGE COINAGE

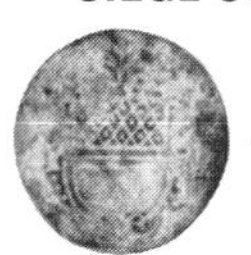

KM# 31 KREUZER

Silver **Obverse:** Shield of squarish city arms in baroque frame **Reverse:** Crowned imperial eagle, '1' in orb on breast **Note:** Prev. KM#99.

Date	Mintage	VG	F	VF	XF	Unc
ND(ca1704)	—	24.00	40.00	75.00	120	—

KM# 87 2 KREUZER

Silver **Obverse:** Ornamented city arms **Obv. Legend:** MONETA. ARG. REIP. ULMENSIS. **Reverse:** Crowned imperial eagle, '2' in orb on breast, date at end of legend **Rev. Legend:** DA. PACEM. NOBIS. DOMINE. (date). **Note:** Prev. KM#32.

Date	Mintage	VG	F	VF	XF	Unc
1703	—	165	275	475	750	—

KM# 88 4 KREUZER (Batzen)

Silver **Obverse:** Ornamented city arms. **Obv. Legend:** MONETA. ARG. REIP. ULMENSIS. **Reverse:** Crowned imperial eagle, '4' in orb on breast, date at end of legend **Rev. Legend:** DA. PACEM. NOBIS. DOMINE. (date). **Note:** Prev. KM#33.

Date	Mintage	VG	F	VF	XF	Unc
1703	—	100	175	300	475	—

KM# 90 GULDEN

Silver **Obverse:** City arms in ornamented shield, angel's head and wings above **Obv. Legend:** MONETA. ARGENT. REIP. ULMENSIS. **Reverse:** Crowned imperial eagle with orb on breast, date at end of legend **Rev. Legend:** DA • PACEM • NOBIS • DOMINE • 1704 • **Note:** Klippe. Prev. KM#34.

Date	Mintage	VG	F	VF	XF	Unc
1704	—	100	175	275	400	—

KM# 91 GULDEN

Tin **Obverse:** City arms **Reverse:** Imperial eagle with orb on breast **Note:** Prev. KM#34a.

Date	Mintage	VG	F	VF	XF	Unc
1704	—	—	—	—	—	—

KM# 92 GULDEN

Silver **Note:** Weight of 1/4Thaler. Klippe. Prev. KM#35.

Date	Mintage	VG	F	VF	XF	Unc
1704	—	—	—	275	400	—

KM# 93 GULDEN

Copper **Obverse:** City arms **Reverse:** Imperial eagle with orb on breast **Note:** Similar to KM#90, but round. Prev. KM#36.

Date	Mintage	VG	F	VF	XF	Unc
1704	—	—	—	—	—	—

KM# 94 GULDEN

Silver **Obverse:** Cherub facing left above arms **Reverse:** Imperial eagle with orb on breast **Note:** Prev.KM#37.

Date	Mintage	VG	F	VF	XF	Unc
1704	—	100	175	300	475	—

KM# 95 GULDEN

Silver **Obverse:** City arms, cherub above **Reverse:** Imperial eagle with orb on breast **Note:** Prev. KM#38.

Date	Mintage	VG	F	VF	XF	Unc
1704	—	100	175	275	400	—

KM# 96 GOLDGULDEN

3.5000 g., 0.9860 Gold 0.1109 oz. AGW **Obverse:** City arms within baroque frame **Reverse:** Legend, date **Note:** Prev. KM#39.

Date	Mintage	VG	F	VF	XF	Unc
1704	—	500	1,250	2,500	3,500	—

KM# 97 GOLDGULDEN

3.5000 g., 0.9860 Gold 0.1109 oz. AGW **Obverse:** City arms within baroque frame **Reverse:** Legend, date **Shape:** 4-Sided **Note:** Klippe. Prev. KM#40.

Date	Mintage	VG	F	VF	XF	Unc
1704	—	1,250	3,000	6,000	8,000	—

KM# 41 6 GOLDGULDEN

21.0000 g., 0.9860 Gold 0.6657 oz. AGW **Note:** Klippe.

Date	Mintage	VG	F	VF	XF	Unc
1704 Rare	—	—	—	—	—	—

PATTERNS

Including off metal strikes

KM#	Date	Mintage	Identification	Mkt Val
Pn3	1717	—	1/2 Ducat. Silver. KM#105.	75.00
Pn4	1717	—	Ducat. Silver. KM#107.	150
Pn5	1730	—	Ducat. Silver. KM#112.	150
Pn6	1730	—	2 Ducat. Silver. KM#111.	150
Pn7	(1772)	—	Heller. Gold. Oval city arms. KM#128.	1,200

WALDECK

The former Countship of Waldeck was located in the western part of the German Empire, bordered by the Landgraviate of Hesse-Cassel on the east and south, the Duchy of Westphalia on the west and the Bishopric of Paderborn on the north. Arolsen was the seat of the counts and they traced their line of descent from a branch of the counts of Schwalenberg beginning in the early 11th century. Waldeck underwent several divisions over the centuries, the first such significant occurrence having taken place in 1474 with the establishment of Waldeck-Wildungen and Waldeck-Eisenberg. The latter was further divided into Waldeck-Eisenberg and Waldeck-Neu-Landau in 1539, but the former inherited Wildungen when the elder branch of the family became extinct in 1598. The line at Neu-Landau failed after two generations and reverted to Eisenberg the previous year (1597). A new line at Wildungen was established from Eisenberg in 1598 as well, but this, too, fell extinct in 1692, only ten years after the count having been raised to the rank of prince.

Waldeck-Eisenberg had received the Countship of Pyrmont in 1625 and became known as Waldeck-Pyrmont (see) upon the permanent unification of the two countships in 1668.

RULERS

Waldeck-Eisenberg

Friedrich Anton Ulrich, 1706-28; as Prince 1712
Christian Philipp, Jan.-May 1728
Karl August Friedrich, 1728-63
Friedrich, 1763-1812

MINT OFFICIALS' INITIALS

Initials	Date	Name
IB	1732-44	Jeremias Bunsen, mintmaster
PS	1765-1806	Philipp Steinmetz, mintmaster

ARMS

6-pointed (early) or 8-pointed (later) star.

COUNTY / PRINCIPALITY

REGULAR COINAGE

C# 1 PFENNIG

Copper **Ruler:** Karl August Friedrich **Obverse:** Crowned double-C monogram **Reverse:** Value in cartouche, date

Date	Mintage	VG	F	VF	XF	Unc
1730	—	7.00	12.00	25.00	50.00	—
1758	—	7.00	12.00	25.00	50.00	—
1759	—	7.00	12.00	25.00	50.00	—
1761	—	7.00	12.00	25.00	50.00	—

C# 2 2 PFENNIG

Copper **Ruler:** Karl August Friedrich **Obverse:** Crowned double-C monogram **Reverse:** Value in cartouche, date

Date	Mintage	VG	F	VF	XF	Unc
1730	—	7.00	12.00	25.00	50.00	—

C# 3 2 PFENNIG

Copper **Ruler:** Karl August Friedrich **Reverse:** Value, date without cartouche

Date	Mintage	VG	F	VF	XF	Unc
1751	—	7.00	12.00	25.00	50.00	—
1754	—	7.00	12.00	25.00	50.00	—
1755	—	7.00	12.00	25.00	50.00	—
1757	—	7.00	12.00	25.00	50.00	—
1759	—	7.00	12.00	25.00	50.00	—

C# 4 3 PFENNIG

Copper **Ruler:** Karl August Friedrich **Obverse:** Crowned monogram **Reverse:** Value within ornate circle **Note:** Similar to 4 Pfennig, C#6.

Date	Mintage	VG	F	VF	XF	Unc
1730	—	7.00	12.00	25.00	50.00	—

C# 5 3 PFENNIG

Copper **Ruler:** Karl August Friedrich **Reverse:** Value, date without cartouche

Date	Mintage	VG	F	VF	XF	Unc
1751	—	7.00	12.00	25.00	50.00	—
1755	—	7.00	12.00	25.00	50.00	—
1758	—	7.00	12.00	25.00	50.00	—
1759	—	7.00	12.00	25.00	50.00	—
1760	—	7.00	12.00	25.00	50.00	—
1761	—	7.00	12.00	25.00	50.00	—

C# 6 4 PFENNIG

Copper **Ruler:** Karl August Friedrich **Obverse:** Crowned monogram **Reverse:** Value within ornate circle

Date	Mintage	VG	F	VF	XF	Unc
1730	—	12.00	25.00	50.00	90.00	—

C# 8 4 PFENNIG

Billon **Ruler:** Karl August Friedrich **Obverse:** Crowned double-C monogram **Reverse:** Value, date

Date	Mintage	VG	F	VF	XF	Unc
1740 IB	—	15.00	30.00	60.00	100	—
1741 IB	—	7.00	14.00	28.00	60.00	—
1744 IB	—	7.00	14.00	28.00	60.00	—

C# 7 6 PFENNIG

Copper **Ruler:** Karl August Friedrich **Obverse:** Crowned intertwined 'CC' monogram **Obv. Legend:** FURSTL. WALDECK. LANDMUNTZ **Reverse:** Value 'VI' within ornamented circle **Rev. Legend:** ANNO.DOMINI.(date)

Date	Mintage	VG	F	VF	XF	Unc
1730	—	8.00	16.00	32.00	65.00	—

C# 12.1 6 PFENNIG

Billon **Ruler:** Karl August Friedrich **Obverse:** Crowned double-C monogram **Reverse:** Value, date **Rev. Legend:** F: WALDECK: LANDMUNTZ

Date	Mintage	VG	F	VF	XF	Unc
1740 IB	—	12.00	25.00	50.00	100	—
1744 IB	—	12.00	25.00	50.00	100	—

C# 12.2 6 PFENNIG

Billon **Ruler:** Karl August Friedrich **Obverse:** Crowned monogram **Reverse:** Value, date **Rev. Legend:** FURSTL: WEALDECK: LANDMUNTZ

Date	Mintage	VG	F	VF	XF	Unc
1750	—	12.00	25.00	50.00	100	—
1752	—	12.00	25.00	50.00	100	—
1755	—	12.00	25.00	50.00	100	—

C# 9 KREUZER

Billon **Ruler:** Karl August Friedrich **Obverse:** Crowned monogram **Reverse:** Value within ornate circle **Note:** Similar to 6 Pfennig, C#7.

Date	Mintage	VG	F	VF	XF	Unc
1730	—	—	—	—	—	—

Note: Reported, not confirmed

C# 16 1/24 THALER

Billon **Ruler:** Karl August Friedrich **Obverse:** Crowned arms in cartouche **Reverse:** Value, date

Date	Mintage	VG	F	VF	XF	Unc
1732	—	60.00	120	250	400	—
1737	—	60.00	120	250	400	—

C# 19 1/12 THALER

Silver **Ruler:** Karl August Friedrich **Obverse:** Crowned arms **Reverse:** Value within inner circle

Date	Mintage	VG	F	VF	XF	Unc
1732	—	90.00	150	300	500	—
1737	—	90.00	150	300	500	—

C# 23 2/3 THALER

Silver **Ruler:** Karl August Friedrich **Obverse:** Armored bust right **Obv. Legend:** CAROLUS • D: G: - FR: WALD ECC • **Reverse:** Crowned arms above value **Note:** Varieties exist. Dav.#1026-7.

Date	Mintage	VG	F	VF	XF	Unc
1733 IB	—	100	220	450	750	—
1734 IB	—	90.00	200	400	700	—

C# 26 2/3 THALER

Silver **Ruler:** Karl August Friedrich **Obverse:** Head left **Obv. Legend:** CAROL • D • G • P • WALD • C • P • E • R • **Reverse:** Crowned arms **Rev. Legend:** ARDUA AD - GLORIAM VIA • **Note:** Dav.#1028.

Date	Mintage	VG	F	VF	XF	Unc
1752	—	100	225	460	775	—

C# 28 THALER

Silver **Ruler:** Georg Friedrich of Wildungen **Obverse:** Bust right **Obv. Legend:** CAROL: AUG: FRID: D: G: PR: WALD: C: P: E: R: **Reverse:** Crowned arms, date divided below **Rev. Legend:** ARDUA AD GLORIAM VIA **Note:** Species Thaler. Dav. #2838.

Date	Mintage	VG	F	VF	XF	Unc
1741	—	400	900	1,600	2,500	—

C# 29 THALER

Silver **Ruler:** Georg Friedrich of Wildungen **Obverse:** Armored bust left **Obv. Legend:** CAROL • D • G • P • WALD • C • P • E • R • **Reverse:** Crowned arms, date below **Rev. Legend:** ARDUA AD GLORIAM VIA • **Note:** Dav. #2839.

Date	Mintage	VG	F	VF	XF	Unc
1752	—	275	650	1,200	2,000	—

TRADE COINAGE

C# 36 1/4 CAROLIN

2.4250 g., 0.7700 Gold 0.0600 oz. AGW **Ruler:** Karl August Friedrich **Obverse:** Bust right **Reverse:** Cruciform double C monograms with arms at center

Date	Mintage	VG	F	VF	XF	Unc
1735	—	500	900	1,750	2,750	—

C# 37 1/2 CAROLIN (5 Gulden)

4.8500 g., 0.7700 Gold 0.1201 oz. AGW **Ruler:** Karl August Friedrich **Obverse:** Head right **Reverse:** Crowned arms and monograms

Date	Mintage	VG	F	VF	XF	Unc
1734	—	500	1,100	2,500	4,000	—

C# 38 1/2 CAROLIN (5 Gulden)

4.8500 g., 0.7700 Gold 0.1201 oz. AGW **Ruler:** Karl August Friedrich **Reverse:** Cruciform double C monograms with arms at center

Date	Mintage	VG	F	VF	XF	Unc
1735	—	450	900	2,000	3,500	—

C# 39 CAROLIN (10 Gulden)

9.7000 g., 0.7700 Gold 0.2401 oz. AGW **Ruler:** Karl August Friedrich **Obverse:** Head right **Reverse:** Cruciform double D monograms with arms at center

Date	Mintage	VG	F	VF	XF	Unc
1734	—	800	1,250	3,000	5,000	—

C# 40 CAROLIN (10 Gulden)

9.7000 g., 0.7700 Gold 0.2401 oz. AGW **Ruler:** Karl August Friedrich **Reverse:** Crowned arms

Date	Mintage	VG	F	VF	XF	Unc
1734	—	800	1,250	3,000	5,000	—

C# 41 CAROLIN (10 Gulden)

9.7000 g., 0.7700 Gold 0.2401 oz. AGW **Ruler:** Karl August Friedrich **Obverse:** Head left **Obv. Legend:** CAROL • D • G • P • WALD • C • P • E • R • **Reverse:** Crowned arms, date below **Rev. Legend:** ARDUA AD GLORIAM VIA •

Date	Mintage	VG	F	VF	XF	Unc
1750	—	700	1,350	3,000	5,000	—

C# 30 1/4 DUCAT

0.8750 g., 0.9860 Gold 0.0277 oz. AGW **Ruler:** Karl August Friedrich **Obverse:** Head right **Reverse:** Star within crowned cartouche

Date	Mintage	VG	F	VF	XF	Unc
1741	—	100	175	400	650	—
1760	—	100	175	400	650	—
1761	—	100	175	400	650	—

C# 31 1/2 DUCAT

1.7500 g., 0.9860 Gold 0.0555 oz. AGW **Ruler:** Karl August Friedrich **Obverse:** Head right **Reverse:** Crowned arms

Date	Mintage	VG	F	VF	XF	Unc
1736	—	300	650	1,450	2,500	—

C# 32.1 DUCAT

3.5000 g., 0.9860 Gold 0.1109 oz. AGW **Ruler:** Karl August Friedrich **Obverse:** Bust right **Obv. Legend:** CAR • AUG • FR • D • G • ... **Reverse:** Crowned complex arms with city arms at center divide date

Date	Mintage	VG	F	VF	XF	Unc
1731	—	500	1,000	2,000	3,500	—
1732	—	500	1,000	2,000	3,500	—

C# 32.2 DUCAT

3.5000 g., 0.9860 Gold 0.1109 oz. AGW **Ruler:** Karl August Friedrich **Obverse:** Bust right **Reverse:** Crowned complex arms with city arms at center divide date

Date	Mintage	VG	F	VF	XF	Unc
1736	—	500	1,000	2,000	3,500	—

C# 32.3 DUCAT

3.5000 g., 0.9860 Gold 0.1109 oz. AGW **Ruler:** Karl August Friedrich **Obverse:** Head right **Reverse:** Crowned ornate arms, date below

Date	Mintage	VG	F	VF	XF	Unc
1742	—	500	1,000	2,000	3,500	—

C# 32.4 DUCAT

3.5000 g., 0.9860 Gold 0.1109 oz. AGW **Ruler:** Karl August Friedrich **Obverse:** Head left **Reverse:** Crowned complex arms

Date	Mintage	VG	F	VF	XF	Unc
1750	—	300	800	1,600	3,000	—

C# 33 DUCAT

3.5000 g., 0.9860 Gold 0.1109 oz. AGW **Ruler:** Karl August Friedrich **Obverse:** Bust right

Date	Mintage	VG	F	VF	XF	Unc
1762	—	550	1,100	2,200	3,750	—

C# 34 DUCAT

3.5000 g., 0.9860 Gold 0.1109 oz. AGW **Ruler:** Karl August Friedrich **Obverse:** Bust right **Obv. Legend:** CAROL • D • G • P • WALD • C • ... **Reverse:** Crowned complex arms with city arms at center

Date	Mintage	VG	F	VF	XF	Unc
1762	—	650	1,250	2,500	4,250	—

C# 35 2 DUCAT

7.0000 g., 0.9860 Gold 0.2219 oz. AGW **Ruler:** Karl August Friedrich **Obverse:** Head left **Obv. Legend:** CAROL • D • G • P • WALD • - C • P • E • R • **Reverse:** Crowned complex arms with city arms at center, date below **Rev. Legend:** ARDUA AD - GLORIAM VIA •

Date	Mintage	VG	F	VF	XF	Unc
1750	—	1,200	2,500	4,500	7,500	—

C# 41.5 10 DUCAT

35.0000 g., 0.9860 Gold 1.1095 oz. AGW **Ruler:** Karl August Friedrich **Obverse:** Bust left **Reverse:** Crowned complex arms with city arms at center, date below **Note:** Similar to 1 Thaler, C#29.

Date	Mintage	VG	F	VF	XF	Unc
1752 Rare	—	—	—	—	—	—

PATTERNS

Including off metal strikes

KM#	Date	Mintage	Identification	Mkt Val
Pn1	1730	—	6 Pfennig. Silver. C#7.	—

WALDECK-PYRMONT

RULER

Friedrich Karl August in Waldeck, 1763-1812

MINTMASTERS' INITIALS

AW - Albert Welle

FW, F*w, W, .W. - Friedrich Welle

PRINCIPALITY

REGULAR COINAGE

C# 42 PFENNIG

Copper **Ruler:** Friedrich Karl August in Waldeck **Obverse:** Crowned F **Reverse:** Value above date

Date	Mintage	VG	F	VF	XF	Unc
1773 PS	—	4.00	8.00	16.00	35.00	—
1781 PS	—	4.00	8.00	16.00	35.00	—
1797 PS	—	4.00	8.00	16.00	35.00	—
1799 PS	—	4.00	8.00	16.00	35.00	—

C# 42a PFENNIG

Copper **Ruler:** Friedrich Karl August in Waldeck **Obverse:** Crowned F **Obv. Legend:** FURSTL: WALDECK: L: MUNZ **Reverse:** Value, date

Date	Mintage	VG	F	VF	XF	Unc
1780 PS	—	4.00	8.00	16.00	35.00	—
1783 PS	—	4.00	8.00	16.00	35.00	—
1795 PS	—	4.00	8.00	16.00	35.00	—
1796 PS	—	4.00	8.00	16.00	35.00	—

C# 43 PFENNIG

Copper **Ruler:** Friedrich Karl August in Waldeck **Obverse:** Crowned arms **Reverse:** Value, date

Date	Mintage	VG	F	VF	XF	Unc
1781	—	4.00	8.00	16.00	35.00	—
1786	—	4.00	8.00	16.00	35.00	—
1799	—	4.00	8.00	16.00	35.00	—

C# 44a 3 PFENNIG

Copper **Ruler:** Friedrich Karl August in Waldeck **Obverse:** Crowned F monogram **Obv. Legend:** FURSTL. WALDECK SCH. MUNZ **Reverse:** Value **Rev. Legend:** III PFENNIGE

Date	Mintage	F	VF	XF	Unc
1781 PS	—	7.00	15.00	45.00	160

C# 45 3 PFENNIG

Copper **Ruler:** Friedrich Karl August in Waldeck **Obverse:** Crowned star arms

Date	Mintage	F	VF	XF	Unc
1781 PS	—	7.00	15.00	45.00	165

C# 44 3 PFENNIG

Copper **Ruler:** Friedrich Karl August in Waldeck **Obverse:** Crowned F within legend **Reverse:** Value above date

Date	Mintage	VG	F	VF	XF	Unc
1781 PS	—	5.00	10.00	20.00	45.00	—

C# 44b 3 PFENNIG

Copper **Ruler:** Friedrich Karl August in Waldeck **Obverse:** Crowned F, without legend

Date	Mintage	VG	F	VF	XF	Unc
1797	—	5.00	10.00	20.00	45.00	—
1798	—	5.00	10.00	20.00	45.00	—

C# 50 10 KREUZER

Silver **Ruler:** Friedrich Karl August in Waldeck **Obverse:** Crowned arms **Reverse:** Value within cartouche

Date	Mintage	VG	F	VF	XF	Unc
1763	—	22.00	45.00	90.00	200	—

C# 57 THALER

28.0600 g., 0.8330 Silver 0.7515 oz. ASW **Ruler:** Friedrich Karl August in Waldeck **Obverse:** Head right **Obv. Legend:** FRIED. D. G. PR. WALD. C. P. E. R. **Reverse:** Arms within Order chain and crowned mantle **Rev. Legend:** VIRTUTE VIAM - DIMETIAR. 1781, 10.EINE FEINE MARK **Note:** Dav. #2840.

Date	Mintage	VG	F	VF	XF	Unc
1781 PS	—	300	600	1,000	1,550	—

TRADE COINAGE

C# 61 DUCAT

3.5000 g., 0.9860 Gold 0.1109 oz. AGW **Ruler:** Friedrich Karl August in Waldeck **Obverse:** Bust right **Reverse:** Crowned and mantled arms

Date	Mintage	VG	F	VF	XF	Unc
1781 PS	—	700	1,500	3,000	5,000	—
1782 PS Rare	—	—	—	—	—	—

WERDEN & HELMSTAEDT

Abbeys

Bishop Ludger of Münster (791-809) founded the monasteries of Werden and Helmstedt early in his tenure as bishop. Werden is located on the River Ruhr six miles (10 kilometers) south of Essen, whereas Helmstedt is situated 20 miles (34 kilometers) east of Braunschweig in Niedersachsen. The abbot obtained the right to mint coins at Werden and at Lüdinghausen from Emperor Otto II (973-83) in 974, but the earliest known coins of the two monasteries date from the 11th century. A small, but fairly steady, stream of issues were produced from the 16th century through the middle of the 18th century. In 1803, Werden and Helmstedt were secularized and their fifty square miles of territory were annexed to Prussia.

RULERS

Ferdinand von Erwitte, 1670-1706

Cölestin von Geismar, 1707-1719

Theodor Thier, 1719-1727

Simon von Bischoping (Bischopinck), 1727-1728

Benedict von Geismar, 1728-1757

Anselm von Sonius, 1757-1774

Johann VI Hellersberg, 1775-1780

Bernhard II Birnbaum, 1780-1797

Beda Cornelius Savels, 1797-1803

MINT OFFICIAL'S INITIALS

Initials	Date	Name
HK	1723-1735	Heinrich Koppers, mintmaster in Cologne

Arms: (early type) – two crossed crosiers.

(later type) – two crossed crosiers in small shield superimposed on cross in larger shield

Imperial eagle - sometimes included to signify that the abbeys had imperial support and sanction.

CROSS REFERENCES:

G = Hermann Grote, "Die Münzen der Abtei Werden," ***Münzstudien***, v. 3 (1862- 63), pp. 411-445.

S = Hugo Frhr. Von Saurma-Jeltsch, **Die Saurmasche Münzsammlung deutscher, schweizerischer und polnischer Gepräge von etwa dem Beginn der Groschenzeit bis zur Kipperperiode**, Berlin, 1892.

Sch = Wolfgang Schulten, **Deutsche Münzen aus der Zeit Karls V.**, Frankfurt am Main, 1974.

ABBEY

REGULAR COINAGE

KM# 64 1/12 THALER (Doppelgroschen)

Silver, 24 mm. **Ruler:** Theodor Thier **Obverse:** Four-fold arms with central shield of early arms of Werden and Helmstedt superimposed on cross, in oval baroque frame, mitre above, crossed croziers and sword behind arms **Obv. Legend:** THEODORUS D.G. SAC. ROM, IMP. **Reverse:** 5-line inscription with date, in circle **Rev. Legend:** ABBAS. WERDINENSIS ET HELMSTADIENSIS. **Rev. Inscription:** 12/EINEN/REICHS/ THALER/ (date) **Note:** Ref. G# 55.

Date	Mintage	VG	F	VF	XF	Unc
1724 HK	—	35.00	80.00	160	300	—

KM# 68 1/12 THALER (Doppelgroschen)

Silver, 24 mm. **Ruler:** Benedict von Geismar **Obverse:** Six-fold arms with round central shield of Geismar arms (2-fold, upper half of eagle above wheel), all in oval baroque frame, mitre above, crozier and sword crossed behind **Obv. Legend:** BENEDICTUS - D G. SAC. ROM. IMP. **Reverse:** 5-line inscription with date **Rev. Legend:** ABBAS. WERDINENSIS &. HELMSTADIENSIS. **Rev. Inscription:** 12/EINEN/REICHS/THALER/(date). **Note:** Ref. G# 59.

Date	Mintage	VG	F	VF	XF	Unc
1730	—	25.00	50.00	100	225	—

KM# 65 6 MARIENGROSCHEN (1/6 Thaler)

Silver, 26 mm. **Ruler:** Theodor Thier **Obverse:** Four-fold arms with central shield of early arms of Werden and Helmstedt superimposed on cross, in oval baroque frame, mitre above, crossed croziers and sword behind arms **Obv. Legend:** THEODORUS. D.G. SAC. ROM. IMP. **Reverse:** 4-line inscription with date, in circle **Rev. Legend:** ABBAS. WERDINENSIS ET HELMSTADIENSIS. **Rev. Inscription:** VI/MARIEN/GROS/(date). **Note:** Ref. G# 54.

Date	Mintage	VG	F	VF	XF	Unc
1724 HK	—	100	200	375	600	—

KM# 69 6 MARIENGROSCHEN (1/6 Thaler)

Silver, 26 mm. **Ruler:** Benedict von Geismar **Obverse:** Six-fold arms with round central shield of Geismar arms (2-fold, upper half of eagle above wheel), all in oval baroque frame, mitre above, crozier and sword crossed behind **Obv. Legend:** BENEDICTUS - D G. SAC. ROM. IMP. **Reverse:** 4-line inscription with date **Rev. Legend:** ABBAS. WERDINENSIS &. HELMSTADIENSIS. **Rev. Inscription:** VI/MARIEN/GROS/(date) **Note:** Ref. G# 58.

Date	Mintage	VG	F	VF	XF	Unc
1730	—	50.00	100	175	400	—

KM# 66 THALER

Silver, 42 mm. **Ruler:** Theodor Thier **Obverse:** Four-fold arms with central shield of early Werden and Helmstedt arms superimposed on cross, in oval baroque frame, mitre above, crossed croziers and sword behind arms, date at end of legend. **Obv. Legend:** THEODORUS D • G • SAC • ROM • IMP • ABBAS WERDINENSIS ET HELMSTADIENSIS **Reverse:** Figure of saint in cloud with S. LVDGERE in band above, view of Werden monastery below. **Rev. Legend:** RESPICE DE COELO ET VISITA VINEAM ISTAM, ET PERFICE EAM, QUAM PLANTIAVIT DEXTERA TUA. PS. 79. **Note:** Dav. #2841, G# 53; prev. C#7.

Date	Mintage	Good	VG	F	VF	XF
1724 HK	—	—	750	1,500	2,500	4,000

KM# 70 THALER

Silver, 42 mm. **Ruler:** Benedict von Geismar **Obverse:** Six-fold arms with round central shield of Geismar arms (2-fold, upper half of eagle above wheel), all in oval baroque frame, 3 ornate helmets above, mitre on middle helmet. **Obv. Legend:** BENEDICTVS • D • G • S • R • I • ABBAS • WERDINENSIS • & • HELMSTADIENSIS. **Reverse:** Full-length facing figure of St. Ludger standing between two geese divides date **Rev. Legend:** S • LVDGERVS • FVNDATOR • WERDINENSIS **Note:** Dav. #2842, G#56; prev. C#8.

Date	Mintage	Good	VG	F	VF	XF
1730 HK	—	—	400	800	1,600	2,650

KM# 71 THALER

Silver, 42 mm. **Ruler:** Benedict von Geismar **Obverse:** Ornately-shaped shield of 6-fold arms with central shield of Geismar arms (2-fold, upper half of eagle above whell), 3 ornate helmets above, mitre on middle helmet **Obv. Legend:** BENEDICTVS • D • G • S • R • I • ABBAS • WERDINENSIS • & HELMSTADIENSIS • **Reverse:** Full-length facing figure of St. Ludger standing between 2 geese divides date **Rev. Legend:** S•LVDGERVS•FVNDATOR•WERDINENSIS **Note:** Dav. #2843, G#57; prev. C#9.

Date	Mintage	Good	VG	F	VF	XF
1745	—	—	400	800	1,600	2,650

KM# 72 THALER

Silver, 43 mm. **Ruler:** Anselm von Sonius **Obverse:** Ornately-shaped shield of 6-fold arms with central shield of Sonius arms (sunburst), 3 ornate helmets above, mitre on middle helmet, date at end of legend **Obv. Legend:** ANSELMVS D • G • S • R • I • ABBAS WERDINENSIS • & • HELMSTAD: **Reverse:** Saint in clouds above the two abbeys **Rev. Legend:** S. LUDGERUS. FUNDATOR ABATIARUM WERDINENSIS. &. HELMSTAD. **Note:** Dav. #2844, G#60; prev. C#10.

Date	Mintage	Good	VG	F	VF	XF
1765	—	—	350	700	1,500	2,550

PATTERNS

Including off metal strikes

KM#	Date	Mintage	Identification	Mkt Val
Pn2	1724	—	Thaler. Copper. 42 mm.	—

WIED-NEUWIED

The county of Wied was located in western Germany near Coblenz. In 1698 the house divided into the branches of Neuwied and Runkel. Neuweid was located northwest of Coblenz and consisted of 3 unjoined properties. It was mediatized during Napoleonic times but there were claimants for many years after.

RULER

(Johann) Friedrich Alexander, 1737-1791

MINT OFFICIALS' INITIALS

Initials	Date	Name
D, DOB	1748-52	Wilhelm Dobicht
ICS	1757-64	Johann Conrad Stocklet
QF	1752-57	Quirin Fritsch

MONETARY SYSTEM

12 Pfennig = 3 Kreuzer = 1 Groschen

60 Stuber = 24 Groschen = 1 Thaler

COUNTY

REGULAR COINAGE

C# 2 PFENNIG

Copper **Ruler:** Friedrich Alexander **Obverse:** Crowned FFAW monogram **Reverse:** Value and date

Date	Mintage	VG	F	VF	XF	Unc
1753	—	175	325	650	—	—

C# 9 2 PFENNIG

Billon **Ruler:** Friedrich Alexander **Obverse:** Peacock in crowned cartouche **Reverse:** Value and date

Date	Mintage	VG	F	VF	XF	Unc
1751	1,014	175	325	650	—	—

C# 10 3 PFENNIG

Billon **Ruler:** Friedrich Alexander **Obverse:** Peacock in crowned cartouche **Reverse:** Value and date

Date	Mintage	VG	F	VF	XF	Unc
1751	632	250	450	850	—	—

C# A3 3 PFENNIG

Copper **Ruler:** Friedrich Alexander **Obverse:** Crowned FFAW monogram **Reverse:** Value and date

Date	Mintage	VG	F	VF	XF	Unc
1753	—	225	425	800	—	—

C# 12 4 PFENNIG

Billon **Ruler:** Friedrich Alexander **Obverse:** Peacock in crowned cartouche **Reverse:** Value and date

Date	Mintage	VG	F	VF	XF	Unc
1751	486	250	475	900	—	—

C# 3 1/4 STUBER

Copper **Ruler:** Friedrich Alexander **Obverse:** Crowned FFAW monogram **Reverse:** Windlass in cartouche, date divided below **Note:** Varieties exist for the 1748 date.

Date	Mintage	VG	F	VF	XF	Unc
1748	—	5.00	10.00	20.00	40.00	—
1749	—	5.00	10.00	20.00	40.00	—
1750	—	5.00	10.00	20.00	40.00	—

C# 4 1/4 STUBER

Copper **Ruler:** Friedrich Alexander **Obverse:** Crowned FFA monogram **Reverse:** Value and date in inner circle

Date	Mintage	VG	F	VF	XF	Unc
1749	—	20.00	40.00	80.00	160	—
1751	—	20.00	40.00	80.00	160	—

C# 5 1/4 STUBER

Copper **Ruler:** Friedrich Alexander **Obverse:** Crowned FFAW monogram **Reverse:** Windlass and Roman numeral date in cartouche

Date	Mintage	VG	F	VF	XF	Unc
1749 RN	—	15.00	30.00	65.00	125	—

C# 6 1/4 STUBER

Copper **Ruler:** Friedrich Alexander **Obverse:** Mining scene in inner circle **Reverse:** Value in cartouche, date below

Date	Mintage	VG	F	VF	XF	Unc
1750	—	16.00	35.00	70.00	150	—

C# 7 1/4 STUBER

Copper **Ruler:** Friedrich Alexander **Obverse:** Mining scene **Reverse:** Date in legend

Date	Mintage	VG	F	VF	XF	Unc
1752	—	8.00	16.00	35.00	75.00	—

C# 14 1/2 STUBER

Billon **Ruler:** Friedrich Alexander **Obverse:** Peacock in crowned cartouche **Reverse:** Value, date

Date	Mintage	VG	F	VF	XF	Unc
1752	—	30.00	60.00	125	275	—

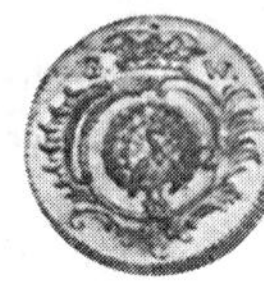

C# 16 STUBER

Billon **Ruler:** Friedrich Alexander **Obverse:** Peacock in crowned cartouche **Reverse:** Value, date

Date	Mintage	VG	F	VF	XF	Unc
1751	—	25.00	50.00	120	265	—
1752	—	25.00	50.00	120	265	—

C# 18 2 STUBER

Billon **Ruler:** Friedrich Alexander **Obverse:** Peacock in crowned cartouche **Reverse:** Value, date

Date	Mintage	VG	F	VF	XF	Unc
1752	—	25.00	50.00	120	265	—

C# 26 3 STUBER

Billon **Ruler:** Friedrich Alexander **Obverse:** Crowned four-fold arms **Reverse:** Value, date within cartouche

Date	Mintage	VG	F	VF	XF	Unc
1752	—	20.00	45.00	85.00	200	—
1753	—	20.00	45.00	85.00	200	—
1754	—	20.00	45.00	85.00	200	—

C# 27 4 STUBER

Billon **Ruler:** Friedrich Alexander **Obverse:** Crowned four-fold arms **Reverse:** Value, date within cartouche

Date	Mintage	VG	F	VF	XF	Unc
1752	—	50.00	100	200	450	—

C# 28 4 STUBER

Billon **Ruler:** Friedrich Alexander **Obverse:** Armored bust right **Obv. Legend:** FRID • ALEX • - COM • WEDAE **Reverse:** Value, date within cartouche

Date	Mintage	VG	F	VF	XF	Unc
1752	—	150	300	450	1,000	—

C# 15 KREUZER

Billon **Ruler:** Friedrich Alexander **Obverse:** Armored bust right **Reverse:** Crowned peacock arms

Date	Mintage	VG	F	VF	XF	Unc
1751	15,000	100	200	300	500	—

C# A16 2 KREUZER

Billon **Ruler:** Friedrich Alexander **Obverse:** Armored bust right **Reverse:** Peacock in crowned cartouche

Date	Mintage	VG	F	VF	XF	Unc
1751 Rare	2,103	—	—	—	—	—

C# B16 3 KREUZER

Billon **Ruler:** Friedrich Alexander **Obverse:** Armored bust right **Reverse:** Peacock in crowned cartouche

Date	Mintage	VG	F	VF	XF	Unc
1749	—	150	250	375	650	—
Note: Varieties exist of 1749						
1750	—	100	200	350	600	—
1751	—	150	250	375	650	—

C# 22 3 KREUZER

Billon **Ruler:** Friedrich Alexander **Obverse:** Peacock in crowned cartouche **Reverse:** Value in cartouche, date below

Date	Mintage	VG	F	VF	XF	Unc
1751	—	75.00	150	300	600	—

C# 24 4 KREUZER

Billon **Ruler:** Friedrich Alexander **Obverse:** Crowned shields, G-W above **Reverse:** Value within baroque frame

Date	Mintage	VG	F	VF	XF	Unc
1753	—	125	250	450	800	—

C# 34 12 KREUZER

Billon **Ruler:** Friedrich Alexander **Obverse:** Crowned shields, G-W above **Reverse:** Value within baroque frame

Date	Mintage	VG	F	VF	XF	Unc
1754 QF	—	50.00	100	200	350	—
1755 QF	—	50.00	100	200	350	—
1757	—	50.00	100	200	350	—

C# 42 30 KREUZER

Silver **Ruler:** Friedrich Alexander **Obverse:** Large armored bust right **Obv. Legend:** FRID • ALEX • C • W • D • R • ET .... **Reverse:** Crowned complex arms, value below

Date	Mintage	VG	F	VF	XF	Unc
1755	—	300	600	1,200	2,000	—

C# 42a 30 KREUZER

Silver **Ruler:** Friedrich Alexander **Obverse:** Small armored bust right **Reverse:** Crowned complex arms, value below

Date	Mintage	VG	F	VF	XF	Unc
1755	—	300	600	1,200	2,000	—

C# 36 1/4 GULDEN

Silver **Ruler:** Friedrich Alexander **Obverse:** Armored bust right **Obv. Legend:** FRID • ALEX •... **Reverse:** City view

Date	Mintage	VG	F	VF	XF	Unc
1753	—	50.00	100	200	400	—

C# 32 1/12 THALER

Billon **Ruler:** Friedrich Alexander **Obverse:** Armored bust right **Obv. Legend:** FRID • ALEX • COM • WEDAE **Reverse:** Value, date **Note:** Varieties exist.

Date	Mintage	VG	F	VF	XF	Unc
1752	—	450	900	1,750	2,750	—
1755	—	450	900	1,750	2,750	—
1756	—	400	850	1,600	2,500	—
1757	—	450	900	1,750	2,750	—

C# 38 1/6 THALER

Silver **Ruler:** Friedrich Alexander **Obverse:** Armored bust right **Obv. Legend:** FR • ID • ALEX • COM • WEDAE **Reverse:** Value, date

Date	Mintage	VG	F	VF	XF	Unc
1752	—	25.00	50.00	100	200	—
1756	—	25.00	50.00	100	200	—

C# 37 1/6 THALER

Silver **Ruler:** Friedrich Alexander **Obverse:** Crowned FFAW monogram **Obv. Legend:** G•Z•W•-R•U•I• **Reverse:** Value, date

Date	Mintage	VG	F	VF	XF	Unc
1756 ICS	—	20.00	40.00	80.00	185	—
1757 ICS	—	20.00	40.00	80.00	185	—

C# 40 1/3 THALER

Silver **Ruler:** Friedrich Alexander **Obverse:** Armored bust right **Obv. Legend:** FRID • ALEX • COMES • WEDAE R • ET I • **Reverse:** City view

Date	Mintage	VG	F	VF	XF	Unc
1752 DOB-QF	—	70.00	140	275	450	—

C# 43 1/3 THALER

Silver **Ruler:** Friedrich Alexander **Subject:** Wedding of Friedrich Karl to Maria Louise Wilhelmine **Obverse:** Inscription within branches **Reverse:** City view of Neuwied

Date	Mintage	VG	F	VF	XF	Unc
1766	—	55.00	110	235	375	—

TRADE COINAGE

C# 44 GOLDGULDEN

3.5000 g., 0.9860 Gold 0.1109 oz. AGW **Ruler:** Friedrich Alexander **Obverse:** Armored bust right **Obv. Legend:** FRID • ALEX • COM • WEDAE **Reverse:** Peacock in crowned cartouche

Date	Mintage	VG	F	VF	XF	Unc
1751	—	900	1,400	3,000	5,000	—

C# 45 DUCAT

3.5000 g., 0.9860 Gold 0.1109 oz. AGW **Ruler:** Friedrich Alexander **Obverse:** Large armored bust right **Reverse:** All-seeing eye above tree

Date	Mintage	VG	F	VF	XF	Unc
1744 M	—	600	1,000	1,500	2,500	—

C# 46 DUCAT

3.5000 g., 0.9860 Gold 0.1109 oz. AGW **Ruler:** Friedrich Alexander **Obverse:** Armored bust right **Obv. Legend:** FRID • ALEX • COM • WEDAE **Reverse:** Peacock in crowned cartouche, date below in Arabic numerals

Date	Mintage	VG	F	VF	XF	Unc
1751	—	1,650	3,000	5,000	8,500	—

C# 47 2 DUCAT

7.0000 g., 0.9860 Gold 0.2219 oz. AGW **Ruler:** Friedrich Alexander **Obverse:** Armored bust right **Reverse:** City view of Neuwied

Date	Mintage	VG	F	VF	XF	Unc
1752	—	2,500	4,500	7,500	12,500	—

C# 48 ALEX D'OR (5 Thaler)

6.6500 g., 0.9000 Gold 0.1924 oz. AGW **Ruler:** Friedrich Alexander **Obverse:** Armored bust right **Reverse:** Peacock in crowned cartouche, date below

Date	Mintage	VG	F	VF	XF	Unc
1752 D	—	2,000	3,500	5,500	9,500	—

TOKEN COINAGE

KM# Tn1 1/2 STUBER

Copper **Obverse:** Mine name LOUISENGLUCK in cartouche, date below **Reverse:** Standing figure of miner facing **Note:** Mining Thaler.

Date	Mintage	VG	F	VF	XF	Unc
1749	—	100	200	300	475	—

PATTERNS

Including off metal strikes

KM#	Date	Mintage	Identification	Mkt Val
Pn1	1751	—	Ducat. Copper. C#46.	250
Pn2	1752	—	1/3 Thaler. Gold. C#40.	12,000

WIED-RUNKEL

After the division of Wied in 1698, Runkel was made up of 3 unjoined properties. The largest of these was east of Coblenz and the other 2 were north of Coblenz and adjoined Wied-Neuwied. Wied-Runkel was mediatized in the Napoleonic era but had claimants long after.

RULERS

Johann Ludwig Adolph, 1706-1762
Christian Ludwig, 1762-1791

MONETARY SYSTEM

12 Pfennig = 3 Kreuzer = 1 Groschen
60 Stuber = 24 Groschen = 1 Reichstaler

PRINCIPALITY

REGULAR COINAGE

C# 1 PFENNING

Copper **Ruler:** Johann Ludwig Adolph **Obverse:** Crowned GW monogram **Reverse:** Value and date

Date	Mintage	VG	F	VF	XF	Unc
1751	—	15.00	30.00	70.00	150	—
1752	—	15.00	30.00	70.00	150	—

C# 2 PFENNING

Copper **Ruler:** Johann Ludwig Adolph **Reverse:** Value as 1 GUTER PFENNIG

Date	Mintage	VG	F	VF	XF	Unc
1752	—	25.00	50.00	100	200	—

C# 3 1/4 STUBER

Copper **Ruler:** Johann Ludwig Adolph **Obverse:** Crowned GW monogram **Reverse:** Value, date

Date	Mintage	VG	F	VF	XF	Unc
1751	—	6.00	12.00	25.00	55.00	—
1752	—	6.00	12.00	25.00	55.00	—
1753	—	6.00	12.00	25.00	55.00	—
1754	—	6.00	12.00	25.00	55.00	—
1755	—	6.00	12.00	25.00	55.00	—
1756	—	6.00	12.00	25.00	55.00	—
1757	—	6.00	12.00	25.00	55.00	—
1758	—	6.00	12.00	25.00	55.00	—

C# 19 1/4 STUBER

Copper **Ruler:** Christian Ludwig **Obverse:** CL monogram **Reverse:** Value above date in cartouche

Date	Mintage	VG	F	VF	XF	Unc
1777 Rare	—	—	—	—	—	—

C# 10 2 STUBER

Billon **Ruler:** Johann Ludwig Adolph **Obverse:** Crowned GW monogram **Reverse:** Value, date

Date	Mintage	VG	F	VF	XF	Unc
1758	—	35.00	70.00	140	325	—

C# 11 2 STUBER

Billon **Ruler:** Johann Ludwig Adolph **Obverse:** Peacock in crowned cartouche **Reverse:** Value, date

Date	Mintage	VG	F	VF	XF	Unc
1758	—	25.00	55.00	120	275	—

C# 5 KREUZER

Billon **Ruler:** Johann Ludwig Adolph **Obverse:** Bust right **Obv. Legend:** IOH • LUD • ADOL • .... **Reverse:** Value within frame

Date	Mintage	VG	F	VF	XF	Unc
1758	—	100	200	300	500	—

C# 7 KREUZER

Billon **Ruler:** Johann Ludwig Adolph **Obverse:** Bust right **Reverse:** Crown above 2 shields of arms

Date	Mintage	VG	F	VF	XF	Unc
1758 Rare	—	—	—	—	—	—

C# 12 3 KREUZER

Billon **Ruler:** Johann Ludwig Adolph **Obverse:** Bust right **Obv. Legend:** IOH • LUD • ADOL • ... **Reverse:** Crown above 2 shields, value below

Date	Mintage	VG	F	VF	XF	Unc
1758	—	100	200	300	500	—

C# 14 4 KREUZER

Billon **Ruler:** Johann Ludwig Adolph **Obverse:** Crown separates G-W above 3 shields **Reverse:** Value within cartouche

Date	Mintage	VG	F	VF	XF	Unc
1758	—	200	400	650	1,000	—

C# 30 5 KREUZER

Billon **Ruler:** Christian Ludwig **Obverse:** Crowned 4-fold arms **Reverse:** Crowned GW monogram on pedestal, branches at sides

Date	Mintage	VG	F	VF	XF	Unc
1764	—	300	500	800	1,200	—
ND	—	300	500	800	1,200	—

C# 16 6 KREUZER

Billon **Ruler:** Johann Ludwig Adolph **Obverse:** Bust right **Obv. Legend:** IOH • LUD • ADOL • ... **Reverse:** Crown above 2 shields of arms

Date	Mintage	VG	F	VF	XF	Unc
1758	—	185	375	600	1,200	—

C# 18 1/6 THALER

Silver **Ruler:** Johann Ludwig Adolph **Obverse:** Crowned JLA monogram **Reverse:** Value and date

Date	Mintage	VG	F	VF	XF	Unc
1758	—	25.00	50.00	100	200	—

C# 20 THALER

Silver **Ruler:** Christian Ludwig **Subject:** Wedding of Count Christian Ludwig and Charlotte Sophie **Obverse:** Busts facing each other **Obv. Legend:** CHRIST: LUD: COM: WED: ISENB. & CRICH: * CHARL: SOPH: AUG: COM: SAYN & WITG: * **Reverse:** Mountain view with RUNCKEL below **Rev. Legend:** * IN MEMORIAM FELICISSIMI MATRIMONII XXIII IUN. MDCCLXII **Note:** Dav. #2845.

Date	Mintage	VG	F	VF	XF	Unc
1762	—	600	1,350	2,600	4,000	—

WIEDENBRUCK

The parish church of St. Aegidius in Wiedenbrück was home to a seminary from 1259 until 1810. It was closely tied to the bishopric of Osnabrück (which see). However, the town is located on the upper Ems River, next to Rheda and about 55 miles (90 kilometers) south-southeast of Osnabrück. At various times, Wiedenbrück served as a mint site for the bishops, but it also issued a series of coins for local use from 1596 to 1716.

MINT OFFICIAL

AS = unknown, ca. 1716

ARMS OR SYMBOL OF TOWN

The wheel of Osnabrück, showing the close association it had with that city and bishopric.

PROVINCIAL TOWN

TOWN COINAGE

KM# 34 PFENNIG

Copper **Obverse:** Wheel of Osnabrück **Obv. Legend:** MO. CIVI WIDENBRVG. **Reverse:** Large 'I' in center, date in legend **Rev. Legend:** ANNO (date).

Date	Mintage	Good	VG	F	VF	XF
1707	—	18.00	40.00	75.00	120	—

KM# 36 1-1/2 PFENNIG

Copper **Obverse:** Wheel of Osnabrück **Obv. Legend:** MO. CIVI. WIDENBG. **Reverse:** 'I' over I—I, date in legend **Rev. Legend:** ANNO DNI (date). **Note:** Varieties exist.

Date	Mintage	VG	F	VF	XF	Unc
1707	—	25.00	55.00	115	185	—

KM# 38 3 PFENNIG

Copper **Obverse:** Wheel in ornamented circle, date in legend **Obv. Legend:** ANNO DOMINI (date). **Rev. Legend:** WIDENBRVCK STADT MVNTZ. **Rev. Inscription:** III/PFENN.

Date	Mintage	VG	F	VF	XF	Unc
1710	—	30.00	65.00	130	200	—
1716 AR	—	30.00	65.00	130	200	—

KM# 40 4 PFENNIG

Copper **Obverse:** Wheel in ornamented circle, date in legend **Obv. Legend:** ANNO DOMINI (date). **Rev. Legend:** WIDENBRVCK STADT MVNTZ. **Rev. Inscription:** IIII/PFENN.

Date	Mintage	VG	F	VF	XF	Unc
1710	—	30.00	65.00	130	200	—
1716 AR	—	30.00	65.00	130	200	—

WISMAR

A seaport on the Baltic, the city of Wismar is said to have obtained municipal rights from Mecklenburg in 1229. It was an important member of the Hanseatic League in the 13th and 14th centuries. Their coinage began at the end of the 13th century and terminated in 1854. They belonged to Sweden from 1648 to 1803. A special plate money was struck by the Swedes in 1715 when the town was under siege. In 1803, Sweden sold Wismar to Mecklenburg-Schwerin. The transaction was confirmed in 1815.

RULERS

Swedish, 1648-1803
Friedrich Franz I, 1785-1837

MINT OFFICIALS' INITIALS

Initials	Date	Name
IM	1685-1702	Johann Memmies, mintmaster in Rostock
	1715	Christoffer Franck, mintmaster
IG	1715-41	Johann (Joachim Dietrich) Gade, mintmaster
	Ca. 1720	Hanss Joachim Witte, warden
	1721	Samuel Christopher Gussmer, warden
	1722	Friedrich Andrews, warden
	1723	Gottfried Schröder, warden
	1724	Niclauss Dähn, warden
F, CF, CAF	1734-62	Caspar August Falck (Falk), mintmaster
	1743-44	Johann Friedrich Rahm, mintmaster
FL	1799	Friedrich Lautersack (Laftersack), mintmaster in Rostock

ARMS

2-fold arms divided vertically, half of bull's head of Mecklenburg on left, four alternating light and dark horizontal bars on right. In coin designs, the darker bars are usually designated by cross-hatching or other filler. Some designs show only the four-bar arms in a shield and these are designated "single Wismar arms."

SWEDISH ADMINISTRATION

REGULAR COINAGE

KM# 2 3 PFENNIG

Copper **Obverse:** Shield **Reverse:** Value, date

Date	Mintage	VG	F	VF	XF	Unc
1721 IG	—	4.00	8.00	16.00	35.00	—
1724 IG	—	4.00	8.00	16.00	35.00	—
1727 IG	—	4.00	8.00	16.00	35.00	—
1730 IG	—	6.00	12.00	25.00	50.00	—
1731 CAF	—	4.00	8.00	16.00	35.00	—
1733 CAF	—	4.00	8.00	16.00	35.00	—
1738 IG	—	4.00	8.00	16.00	35.00	—
1740 IG	—	4.00	8.00	16.00	35.00	—
1743 CF	—	4.00	8.00	16.00	35.00	—
1744 CF	—	4.00	8.00	16.00	35.00	—

C# 1 3 PFENNIG

Copper **Obverse:** Shield in inner circle **Reverse:** Value and date in shield

Date	Mintage	VG	F	VF	XF	Unc
1746 F	—	4.00	8.00	16.00	35.00	—
1749 F	—	4.00	8.00	16.00	35.00	—
1749 I	—	5.00	7.50	15.00	30.00	—
1751 F	—	3.50	7.00	15.00	35.00	—
1755 F	—	3.50	7.00	15.00	35.00	—
1759 F	—	3.50	7.00	15.00	35.00	—
1761 F	—	3.50	7.00	15.00	35.00	—

C# 1a 3 PFENNIG

Copper **Obverse:** Shield without inner circle **Obv. Legend:** MONETA NOVA WISMARIENSIS **Reverse:** Value, date within frame

Date	Mintage	VG	F	VF	XF	Unc
1751 F	—	3.50	7.00	15.00	35.00	—
1755 F	—	3.50	7.00	15.00	35.00	—
1799 FL	—	3.50	7.00	15.00	35.00	—

C# 1b 3 PFENNIG

Silver **Obverse:** Shield of arms **Reverse:** Value, date

Date	Mintage	VG	F	VF	XF	Unc
1799 FL	—	200	300	500	750	—

C# 1c 3 PFENNIG

Copper **Obverse:** Shield of arms **Obv. Legend:** MONETA NOVA WISMARIENSIS **Reverse:** Value, date within cartouche **Shape:** Square **Note:** Klippe.

Date	Mintage	VG	F	VF	XF	Unc
1799 FL	—	300	500	800	1,200	—

C# 2 6 PFENNIG

Copper **Obverse:** Shield **Obv. Legend:** MONETA NOVA WISMARIENSIS **Reverse:** Value, date

Date	Mintage	VG	F	VF	XF	Unc
1762 F	—	8.00	16.00	32.00	65.00	—

COUNTERMARKED COINAGE

Siege of 1715

KM# 18 1/48 THALER

Silver **Countermark:** Wismar coat of arms and N W **Note:** Countermark on Wismar 1/48 Thaler.

CM Date	Host Date	Good	VG	F	VF	XF
ND(1715)	ND(1692)	—	40.00	75.00	125	200

KM# 19 1/24 THALER

Silver **Countermark:** Wismar coat of arms and N W **Note:** Countermark on Mecklenburg 2 Schillings or Wismar 1/24 Thaler.

CM Date	Host Date	Good	VG	F	VF	XF
ND	ND(1692)	—	50.00	90.00	150	250

KM# 20 1/6 THALER

Silver **Countermark:** Wismar coat of arms and N W **Note:** Countermark on Mecklenburg 1/6 Thaler.

CM Date	Host Date	Good	VG	F	VF	XF
ND	ND(1692) Rare	—	—	—	—	—

SIEGE COINAGE

Siege of 1715

KM# 1 3 PFENNIG

Copper **Obverse:** Shield in inner circle **Reverse:** Value and date

Date	Mintage	VG	F	VF	XF	Unc
1715 IG	—	10.00	20.00	40.00	80.00	—

KM# 22 4 SCHILLING

Gun Metal **Obverse:** Value, WISMAR in wreath, date in corners **Shape:** Square

Date	Mintage	VG	F	VF	XF	Unc
1715 Rare	—	—	—	—	—	—

KM# 23 8 SCHILLING

Gun Metal **Obverse:** Value, WISMAR in wreath, date in corners **Shape:** Square

Date	Mintage	VG	F	VF	XF	Unc
1715	—	500	1,000	1,700	2,400	—

KM# 24 16 SCHILLING

Gun Metal, 90 mm. **Obverse:** Value, WISMAR in wreath, date in corners **Note:** Illustration reduced.

Date	Mintage	VG	F	VF	XF	Unc
1715	—	1,000	1,650	2,500	3,500	—

KM# 25 32 SCHILLING

Gun Metal **Obverse:** Value, WISMAR in wreath, date in corners

Date	Mintage	VG	F	VF	XF	Unc
1715 Rare	—	—	—	—	—	—

KM# 26 4 MARK

Gun Metal **Obverse:** Value in wreath, date in corners

Date	Mintage	VG	F	VF	XF	Unc
1715 Rare	—	—	—	—	—	—

KM# 27 8 MARK

Gun Metal **Obverse:** Value in wreath, date in corners

Date	Mintage	VG	F	VF	XF	Unc
1715 Rare	—	—	—	—	—	—

TRADE COINAGE

FR# 3530 DUCAT

3.5000 g., 0.9860 Gold 0.1109 oz. AGW **Obverse:** Crowned imperial eagle **Reverse:** Shield

Date	Mintage	VG	F	VF	XF	Unc
1743	—	450	900	1,800	3,000	—

PATTERNS

Including off metal strikes

KM#	Date	Mintage	Identification	Mkt Val
Pn1	1743	—	Ducat. Copper. Fr. 3530.	—

KM#	Date	Mintage	Identification	Mkt Val
Pn2	1799	—	3 Pfennig. Silver. . C#1a.	1,000

WORMS

The site of present-day Worms, located on the Rhine River 25 miles south of Mainz, was occupied before the Roman advance into Germany. An imperial mint was established in the town in the late 9th century and operated through the end of the 11th century. Worms was created a free imperial city in 1156 and obtained the mint right, separate from the bishopric, in 1234. However, most of the city's coinage was produced during the 17th century, with a few commemoratives having been struck also in the early18th century. French forces burned the city to the ground in 1689 and Worms was very slow to recover. It was annexed to France in 1801, but passed along with the episcopal lands to Hesse-Darmstadt in 1815.

RULERS

Franz Ludwig, Graf von Pfalz-Neuburg, 1694-1732
Franz Georg, Graf von Schönborn, 1732-1756
Johann Friedrich Karl, Graf von Ostein, 1756-1763
Johann Philipp, Graf von Walderdorff, 1763-1768
Emmerich Joseph, Graf von Breidbach-Bürresheim, 1768-1774
Friedrich Karl Joseph, Graf von Erthal, 1774-1802

FREE IMPERIAL CITY

REGULAR COINAGE

KM# 141 1/2 THALER

Silver **Subject:** Bicentennial of the Reformation **Obverse:** Crowned imperial eagle above city view, in margin around top SUB CAESARIS UMBRA, 4-line inscription with Roman numeral below date **Reverse:** Key of Worms, 8-pointed star to right, SERVA above, radiant Eye of God at top, around lower margin HANC PURAM ERECTAM

Date	Mintage	Good	VG	F	VF	XF
1717 BIB	—	—	225	475	800	1,500

KM# 135 THALER

Silver **Subject:** Dedication of the New City Hall **Obverse:** 2 Dragons with city arms above the city **Obv. Legend:** • LIBERA • WORMATIA • SACRI • ROMANI • IMPERII • FIDELIS • FILIA • ** **Reverse:** City Hall, date in chronogram **Rev. Legend:** SO SETZT MICH GOTT NUN AN DEN ORT WO LUTHER EH BEKANNT SEIN WORT *

Date	Mintage	Good	VG	F	VF	XF
1709 IL	—	—	600	1,100	1,750	3,000

TRADE COINAGE

C# 142 DUCAT

Gold **Subject:** Bicentennial of the Reformation **Obverse:** Similar to 1/2 Thaler, KM#141, date divided near top **Reverse:** Five-line inscription, around VERBVM DOMINI MANET IN AETERNVM, mintmaster's initials

Date	Mintage	F	VF	XF	Unc
1717 BIB Rare	—	—	—	—	—

PATTERNS

Including off metal strikes

KM#	Date	Mintage	Identification	Mkt Val
Pn4	1717	—	Ducat. Silver. KM#142.	320

WURTTEMBERG

Located in South Germany, between Baden and Bavaria, Württemberg obtained the mint right in 1374. In 1495 the rulers became dukes. In 1802 the duke exchanged some of his land on the Rhine with France for territories nearer his capital city. Napoleon elevated the duke to the status of elector in 1803 and made him a king in 1806. The kingdom joined the German Empire in 1871and endured until the king abdicated in 1918.

RULERS

Friedrich I, 1593-1608
Eberhard Ludwig, 1693-1733
Karl Alexander, 1733-1737
With Karl Rudolf von Neuenstadt
As Regent, 1737-1738
With Karl Friedrich von Oels
As Regent, 1738-1744
Karl Eugen, Duke, 1744-1793
Ludwig Eugen, 1793-1795
Friedrich I Eugen, 1795-1797
Friedrich, as Duke Friedrich II, 1797-1803

MINT MARKS

C, CT - Christophstal Mint
F - Freudenstadt Mint
S - Stuttgart Mint
T - Tubingen Mint

MINT OFFICIALS' INITIALS

Stuttgart Mint

Initials	Date	Name
ARW/W	1748-84	Adam Rudolf Werner, die-cutter
B	(d.1756)	Konrad Burer, die-cutter in Augsburg
CH, ICH	1783-1813	Johann Christian Heuglin
CS/S	1734-38	Christoph Schmelz, die-cutter
DFH, DH, FH, H	1760-94	Daniel Friedrich Heuglin, warden
FB/IFB	1734-38	Johann Friedrich Breuer
IGB	1786-97	Johann gottfried Betulius, die-cutter
IIW/wheel	1681-1702	Johann Jakob Wagner
ILW, LW, W	1798-1837	Johann Ludwig Wagner, die-cuttere
IPR, PR, R	1746-72	Johann Peter Rasp
IT/T	1734	Jonas Thiebaud, die-cutter in Augsburg
M/*	1731-35	Christian Ernst Muller, die-cutter in Nüremberg
PHM/*	1694-1707	Philipp Heinrich Muller, die-cutter
S/VS	1744-73	Veit Schrempf, die-cutter
SS	1744-45	Simon Schnell
	1748-54	Warden
	1746-48	Warden
(c) = Crossed wheat stalk	1702-21	Johann David Baur
(d) = bird	1721-26	Jakob Marcell Finck
	1694-1707	Johann Christoph Pfaffenhauser, warden
	1705-14	Johann David Daniel der Jungere, die-cutter
	1707-25	Christian Thill, warden
	?-1708	Martin Heuglin, warden
	1725-48	Christoph Heinrich Muller, warden
	1730-33	Johann Konrad Kaltschmid
	1734-35	Jeremias Daniel, die-cutter
	1738-44	Carb
	1741-?	Johann David Daniel, die-cutter
	1786-?	Johann Martin Buckle, die-cutter in Karlsruhe

ARMS

Württemberg: 3 stag antlers arranged vertically.
Teck (duchy): Field of lozenges (diamond shapes).
Mompelgart (principality): 2 fish standing on tails.

DUCHY

REGULAR COINAGE

KM# 256 PFENNIG

Silver **Ruler:** Eberhard Ludwig **Obverse:** Oval Wurttemberg arms in baroque frame, ELH above **Note:** Uniface; weight varies 0.24-0.39 grams

Date	Mintage	VG	F	VF	XF	Unc
ND(1693-1733)	—	7.00	15.00	32.00	55.00	—

KM# 327 PFENNIG

Silver **Ruler:** Karl Alexander **Obverse:** CAH above arms **Note:** Weight varies 0.33-0.36 grams

Date	Mintage	VG	F	VF	XF	Unc
ND(1733-1737)	—	12.00	30.00	60.00	95.00	—

KM# 353 PFENNIG

Silver **Ruler:** Karl Alexander with Karl Friedrich von Oels as Regent **Obverse:** CFH above arms **Note:** Weight varies 0.31-0.32 grams

Date	Mintage	VG	F	VF	XF	Unc
ND(1738-1744)	—	18.00	40.00	75.00	115	—

KM# 354 PFENNIG

Copper **Ruler:** Karl Alexander with Karl Friedrich von Oels as Regent **Obverse:** CH above shield with antlers **Note:** Uniface

Date	Mintage	VG	F	VF	XF	Unc
ND	—	6.00	12.00	28.00	50.00	—

KM# 257 1/6 KREUZER

Copper **Ruler:** Eberhard Ludwig **Obverse:** Squarish shield of arms **Note:** Weight varies 0.45-.070 grams

Date	Mintage	VG	F	VF	XF	Unc
ND(1693-1733)	—	—	—	—	—	—

KM# 270 1/2 KREUZER (4 Pfennig)

Silver **Ruler:** Eberhard Ludwig **Obverse:** Round Wurttemberg arms in baroque frame, value 1/2 divides date above **Note:** Weight varies 0.23-0.50 grams

Date	Mintage	VG	F	VF	XF	Unc
1701	—	5.00	12.00	25.00	45.00	—
1701	—	5.00	12.00	25.00	45.00	—
1702	—	5.00	12.00	25.00	45.00	—
1703	—	5.00	12.00	25.00	45.00	—
1704	—	5.00	12.00	25.00	45.00	—
1705	—	5.00	12.00	25.00	45.00	—
1708	—	5.00	12.00	25.00	45.00	—
1709	—	5.00	12.00	25.00	45.00	—
1710	—	5.00	12.00	25.00	45.00	—
1712	—	5.00	12.00	25.00	45.00	—
1714	—	5.00	12.00	25.00	45.00	—
1719	—	5.00	12.00	25.00	45.00	—
1721	—	5.00	12.00	25.00	45.00	—
1723	—	5.00	12.00	25.00	45.00	—
1724	—	5.00	12.00	25.00	45.00	—
1725	—	5.00	12.00	25.00	45.00	—
1726	—	5.00	12.00	25.00	45.00	—
1727	—	5.00	12.00	25.00	45.00	—
1728	—	5.00	12.00	25.00	45.00	—
1729	—	5.00	12.00	25.00	45.00	—
1731	—	5.00	12.00	25.00	45.00	—
1732	—	5.00	12.00	25.00	45.00	—
1733	—	5.00	12.00	25.00	45.00	—

KM# 340 1/2 KREUZER (4 Pfennig)

Silver **Ruler:** Karl Alexander **Note:** Weight varies 0.29-0.33 grams.

Date	Mintage	VG	F	VF	XF	Unc
1735	—	12.00	30.00	60.00	100	—
1736	—	12.00	30.00	60.00	100	—

KM# 365 1/2 KREUZER (4 Pfennig)

Silver **Ruler:** Karl Alexander with Karl Friedrich von Oels as Regent **Obverse:** Oval arms **Note:** Weight varies 0.32-0.44 grams

Date	Mintage	VG	F	VF	XF	Unc
1740	—	5.00	12.00	25.00	45.00	—
1741	—	5.00	12.00	25.00	45.00	—
1742	—	5.00	12.00	25.00	45.00	—
1743	—	5.00	12.00	25.00	45.00	—

KM# 372 1/2 KREUZER (4 Pfennig)

Billon **Ruler:** Karl Eugen, Duke **Obverse:** Crowned arms **Note:** Uniface.

Date	Mintage	VG	F	VF	XF	Unc
1744	—	7.00	16.00	32.00	75.00	—
1745	—	7.00	16.00	32.00	75.00	—
1746	—	7.00	16.00	32.00	75.00	—
1747	—	7.00	16.00	32.00	75.00	—
1748	—	7.00	16.00	32.00	75.00	—
1750	—	7.00	16.00	32.00	75.00	—

KM# 395 1/2 KREUZER (4 Pfennig)

Billon **Ruler:** Karl Eugen, Duke **Obverse:** Crowned shield of arms in palm branches. Crown divides date **Reverse:** Fraction **Note:** Uniface.

Date	Mintage	VG	F	VF	XF	Unc
1758	—	7.00	16.00	32.00	75.00	—

KM# 420 1/2 KREUZER (4 Pfennig)

Billon **Ruler:** Karl Eugen, Duke **Obverse:** 3 antlers in round shield **Reverse:** 1/2 above date

Date	Mintage	VG	F	VF	XF	Unc
1766	—	7.00	16.00	32.00	75.00	—

KM# 424 1/2 KREUZER (4 Pfennig)

Billon **Ruler:** Karl Eugen, Duke **Obverse:** Crowned round arms **Reverse:** Fraction

Date	Mintage	VG	F	VF	XF	Unc
1769	—	7.00	16.00	32.00	75.00	—
1774	—	7.00	16.00	32.00	75.00	—
1775	—	7.00	16.00	32.00	75.00	—
1787	—	7.00	16.00	32.00	75.00	—

KM# 448 1/2 KREUZER (4 Pfennig)

Billon **Ruler:** Karl Eugen, Duke **Reverse:** Fraction and date

Date	Mintage	VG	F	VF	XF	Unc
1791	—	7.00	16.00	32.00	75.00	—

KM# 450 1/2 KREUZER (4 Pfennig)

Billon **Ruler:** Ludwig Eugen **Obverse:** Crowned arms **Reverse:** Fraction

Date	Mintage	VG	F	VF	XF	Unc
1794	—	15.00	35.00	65.00	150	—

KM# 459 1/2 KREUZER (4 Pfennig)

Billon **Ruler:** Friedrich as Duke Friedrich II **Obverse:** Crowned monogram and date **Reverse:** Fraction

Date	Mintage	F	VF	XF	Unc
1798	—	14.00	28.00	85.00	250

KM# 258 KREUZER

Silver **Ruler:** Eberhard Ludwig **Obverse:** Date above divided arms within shield **Reverse:** IK above 2-fold arms on shield within inner circle **Note:** Weight varies 0.43-0.71 grams. Varieties exist.

Date	Mintage	VG	F	VF	XF	Unc
1705 (c)	—	7.00	15.00	30.00	60.00	—
1706 (c)	—	7.00	15.00	30.00	60.00	—
1707 (c)	—	7.00	15.00	30.00	60.00	—

KM# 288 KREUZER

Silver **Ruler:** Eberhard Ludwig **Mint:** Stuttgart **Obverse:** 3 small shields of arms, 2 above 1, date divided by lower shield **Reverse:** Oval 2-fold arms in baroque frame, IK above **Note:** Weight varies 0.40-0.83 grams. Varieties exist.

Date	Mintage	VG	F	VF	XF	Unc
1707 (c)	—	8.00	16.00	32.00	60.00	—
1708 (c)	—	5.00	12.00	25.00	50.00	—
1709 (c)	—	5.00	12.00	25.00	50.00	—
1710 (c)	—	5.00	12.00	25.00	50.00	—
1711 (c)	—	5.00	12.00	25.00	50.00	—
1712 (c)	—	5.00	12.00	25.00	50.00	—
1713 (c)	—	5.00	12.00	25.00	50.00	—
1715 (c)	—	5.00	12.00	25.00	50.00	—
1718 (c)	—	5.00	12.00	25.00	50.00	—
1722 (d)	—	5.00	12.00	25.00	50.00	—
1723 (d)	—	5.00	12.00	25.00	50.00	—
1724 (d)	—	5.00	12.00	25.00	50.00	—
1725 (d)	—	5.00	12.00	25.00	50.00	—
1726 (d)	—	5.00	12.00	25.00	50.00	—

KM# 306 KREUZER

Silver **Ruler:** Eberhard Ludwig **Obverse:** Shield of arms of Württemberg and Teck dividied vertically, date above **Reverse:** L.M. in laurel wreath **Rev. Legend:** I/KREU/ZER **Note:** Weight varies 0.48-0.69 grams. Varieties exist.

Date	Mintage	VG	F	VF	XF	Unc
1726	—	8.00	16.00	32.00	60.00	—
1727	—	8.00	16.00	32.00	60.00	—
1731	—	8.00	16.00	32.00	60.00	—

KM# 323 KREUZER

Silver **Ruler:** Eberhard Ludwig **Obverse:** Crowned 4-fold arms with central shield of Württemberg arms **Reverse:** Value and date in laurel wreath **Rev. Legend:** I/KREU/ZER/LM **Note:** Weight varies 0.48-0.73 grams. Varieties exist.

Date	Mintage	VG	F	VF	XF	Unc
1732	—	15.00	35.00	70.00	140	—
1733	—	15.00	35.00	70.00	140	—

KM# 331 KREUZER

Silver **Ruler:** Karl Alexander **Obverse:** Crowned and mantled 4-fold arms with central shield of Württemberg **Reverse:** Value and date in laurel wreath **Rev. Legend:** I K:/WURTEMB/ LAND/MUNZ **Note:** Weight varies 0.44-0.70 grams. Varieties exist.

Date	Mintage	VG	F	VF	XF	Unc
1734	—	12.00	30.00	60.00	100	—
1735	—	12.00	30.00	60.00	100	—
1736	—	12.00	30.00	60.00	100	—

KM# 369 KREUZER

Silver **Ruler:** Karl Alexander with Karl Friedrich von Oels as Regent **Obverse:** Ornately-shaped shield of Württemberg on left, Teck on right **Reverse:** Value and date in laurel wreath **Rev. Legend:** I.K./WURTE.B/LAND/MUNZ **Note:** Weight varies 0.50-0.69 grams. Varieties exist.

Date	Mintage	VG	F	VF	XF	Unc
1741	—	10.00	20.00	40.00	75.00	—

KM# 370 KREUZER

Silver **Ruler:** Karl Alexander with Karl Friedrich von Oels as Regent **Obverse:** Oval arms of Teck in baroque frame **Reverse:** Adjacent oval arms of Württemberg on left and pagan's head on right, value: IK above, date below **Note:** Weight varies 0.45-0.72 grams. Varieties exist.

Date	Mintage	VG	F	VF	XF	Unc
1742	—	10.00	20.00	40.00	75.00	—

KM# 371 KREUZER

Silver **Ruler:** Karl Alexander with Karl Friedrich von Oels as Regent **Obverse:** 2 adjacent shields of arms, crown above **Reverse:** 3 small oval arms, 2 above 1, value: IK above, date divided below **Note:** Weight varies 0.50-0.77 grams. Varieties exist.

Date	Mintage	VG	F	VF	XF	Unc
1743	—	5.00	12.00	25.00	50.00	—

KM# A373 KREUZER

Silver **Ruler:** Karl Eugen, Duke **Obverse:** Crowned monogram in chain of order, flanked by two branches, divides date **Reverse:** Crowned shield of Württemberg arms in baroque frame between two branches, value 1 — K divided above

Date	Mintage	VG	F	VF	XF	Unc
1744	—	12.00	25.00	60.00	115	—
1745	—	12.00	25.00	60.00	115	—

KM# B373 KREUZER

Silver **Ruler:** Karl Eugen, Duke **Obverse:** Crowned monogram divides value I — KR., date in exergue **Reverse:** Crowned oval Württemberg arms between two branches

Date	Mintage	VG	F	VF	XF	Unc
1746	—	15.00	30.00	75.00	125	—

KM# 373 KREUZER

Billon **Ruler:** Karl Eugen, Duke **Obverse:** Bust to right **Reverse:** Crowned Württemberg arms in baroque frame divide 1 — K, date in exergue **Note:** Varieties exist.

Date	Mintage	VG	F	VF	XF	Unc
1746	—	6.00	14.00	30.00	60.00	—
1747	—	6.00	14.00	30.00	60.00	—
1748	—	6.00	14.00	30.00	60.00	—
1749	—	6.00	14.00	30.00	60.00	—
1750	—	6.00	14.00	30.00	60.00	—
1758	—	6.00	14.00	30.00	60.00	—

KM# 396 KREUZER

Billon **Ruler:** Karl Eugen, Duke **Obverse:** Bust right **Obv. Legend:** CAROLUS D G ... **Reverse:** Crowned arms divide value, date below

Date	Mintage	VG	F	VF	XF	Unc
1758	—	8.00	16.00	35.00	70.00	—

KM# 397 KREUZER

Billon **Ruler:** Karl Eugen, Duke **Obverse:** Bust right **Obv. Legend:** CAROLVS D: G: DVX WURT: **Reverse:** Crowned ornate shield, value below

Date	Mintage	VG	F	VF	XF	Unc
1758	—	4.50	9.00	20.00	40.00	—
1766	—	4.50	9.00	20.00	40.00	—
1767	—	4.50	9.00	20.00	40.00	—
1769	—	4.50	9.00	20.00	40.00	—
1770	—	4.50	9.00	20.00	40.00	—
1772	—	4.50	9.00	20.00	40.00	—
1783	—	4.50	9.00	20.00	40.00	—
1784	—	4.50	9.00	20.00	40.00	—
1785	—	4.50	9.00	20.00	40.00	—
1786	—	4.50	9.00	20.00	40.00	—

KM# A398 KREUZER

Billon **Obverse:** Mature bust of Karl Eugene right **Reverse:** Crowned shield in sprays, value below

Date	Mintage	VG	F	VF	XF	Unc
1787	—	4.50	9.00	20.00	40.00	—
1788	—	4.50	9.00	20.00	40.00	—
1789	—	4.50	9.00	20.00	40.00	—
1790	—	4.50	9.00	20.00	40.00	—
1791	—	4.50	9.00	20.00	40.00	—
1792	—	4.50	9.00	20.00	40.00	—

KM# 451 KREUZER

Billon **Ruler:** Ludwig Eugen **Reverse:** Arms

Date	Mintage	VG	F	VF	XF	Unc
1794	—	8.00	16.00	35.00	80.00	—

KM# 456 KREUZER

Billon **Ruler:** Friedrich I Eugen **Obverse:** Crowned circular shield, branches and date below **Reverse:** Value above branches

Date	Mintage	VG	F	VF	XF	Unc
1796	—	12.00	25.00	50.00	120	—

KM# 460 KREUZER

Billon **Ruler:** Friedrich as Duke Friedrich II **Obverse:** Crowned F II **Reverse:** Value above branches

Date	Mintage	F	VF	XF	Unc
1798	—	12.00	25.00	50.00	150

KM# 467 KREUZER

Billon **Ruler:** Friedrich as Duke Friedrich II **Obverse:** Crowned FII **Reverse:** Value, branches reach middle of coin

Date	Mintage	F	VF	XF	Unc
1799	—	10.00	20.00	45.00	150
1800	—	10.00	20.00	45.00	150

KM# 259 2 KREUZER (Halbbatzen)

Silver **Ruler:** Eberhard Ludwig **Obverse:** Titles of Eberhard Ludwig **Note:** Weight varies 0.91-1.26 grams.

Date	Mintage	VG	F	VF	XF	Unc
1701	—	10.00	22.00	40.00	65.00	—
1704 (c)	—	10.00	22.00	40.00	65.00	—
1705 (c)	—	10.00	22.00	40.00	65.00	—

KM# 294 2 KREUZER (Halbbatzen)

1.1000 g., Silver **Ruler:** Eberhard Ludwig **Obverse:** 3 Shields, lower one divides date, all within circle **Reverse:** Oval 2-fold arms in baroque frame

Date	Mintage	VG	F	VF	XF	Unc
1708 (c)	—	12.00	30.00	60.00	100	—

KM# 307 2-1/2 KREUZER

Billon **Ruler:** Eberhard Ludwig **Obverse:** Crowned round 4-fold arms with central shield of Württemberg in baroque frame **Reverse:** Value and date in laurel wreath **Rev. Legend:** II. 1/2.WURTEMB/LAND/MUNZ

Date	Mintage	VG	F	VF	XF	Unc
1726	—	16.00	35.00	70.00	125	—

KM# 308 2-1/2 KREUZER

Billon **Ruler:** Eberhard Ludwig **Reverse:** Value 2-1/2 K

Date	Mintage	VG	F	VF	XF	Unc
1726	—	16.00	35.00	70.00	125	—
1727	—	16.00	35.00	70.00	125	—

KM# 324 2-1/2 KREUZER

Billon **Ruler:** Eberhard Ludwig **Obverse:** Chain of Order of the Hunt around arms **Reverse:** Value, date within frame **Note:** Weight varies 0.92-1.05 grams.

Date	Mintage	VG	F	VF	XF	Unc
1732	—	16.00	35.00	70.00	125	—
1733	—	16.00	35.00	70.00	125	—

KM# 332 2-1/2 KREUZER

Billon **Ruler:** Karl Alexander **Obverse:** Crowned and mantled 4-fold arms with central shield of Württemberg and Order of the Golden Fleece around **Reverse:** Value and date **Rev. Legend:** 2-1/2 K/WURTEMB/LAND/MUNZ **Note:** Weight varies 0.76-1.08 grams.

Date	Mintage	VG	F	VF	XF	Unc
1734	—	22.00	50.00	100	165	—
1735	—	22.00	50.00	100	165	—
1736	—	22.00	50.00	100	165	—

KM# 380 3 KREUZER (Groschen)

Billon **Ruler:** Karl Eugen, Duke **Obverse:** Double C monogram **Reverse:** Arms, value: III

Date	Mintage	VG	F	VF	XF	Unc
1746	—	12.00	25.00	55.00	120	—

KM# 381 3 KREUZER (Groschen)

Billon **Ruler:** Karl Eugen, Duke **Reverse:** Value: 3K

Date	Mintage	VG	F	VF	XF	Unc
1746	—	12.00	25.00	55.00	120	—

KM# 382 3 KREUZER (Groschen)

Billon **Ruler:** Karl Eugen, Duke **Reverse:** Value: 3 **Rev. Legend:** WÜRTEMBERG LAND MUNZ

Date	Mintage	VG	F	VF	XF	Unc
1746	—	12.00	25.00	55.00	120	—

KM# 391 3 KREUZER (Groschen)

Billon **Ruler:** Karl Eugen, Duke **Obverse:** Bust right **Reverse:** 4-panelled arms

Date	Mintage	VG	F	VF	XF	Unc
1747	—	10.00	20.00	45.00	100	—
1748	—	10.00	20.00	45.00	100	—
1749	—	10.00	20.00	45.00	100	—

KM# 398 3 KREUZER (Groschen)

Billon **Ruler:** Karl Eugen, Duke **Reverse:** Legend without WURTEMBERG, value: 3K

Date	Mintage	VG	F	VF	XF	Unc
1758	—	6.00	12.00	25.00	50.00	—

KM# 461 3 KREUZER (Groschen)

1.3500 g., 0.3330 Silver 0.0145 oz. ASW **Ruler:** Friedrich as Duke Friedrich II **Obverse:** Crowned F II monogram above 3 within rectangular border **Reverse:** Crowned arms within branches, date divided below

Date	Mintage	F	VF	XF	Unc
1798	—	25.00	45.00	100	300

KM# 468 3 KREUZER (Groschen)

1.3500 g., 0.3330 Silver 0.0145 oz. ASW **Ruler:** Friedrich as Duke Friedrich II **Obverse:** Crowned monogram, value below **Reverse:** Crowned arms above branches dividing date below

Date	Mintage	F	VF	XF	Unc
1799	—	16.00	35.00	85.00	250

KM# 475 3 KREUZER (Groschen)

1.3500 g., 0.3330 Silver 0.0145 oz. ASW **Ruler:** Friedrich as Duke Friedrich II **Reverse:** W dividing date

Date	Mintage	F	VF	XF	Unc
1800	—	16.00	35.00	85.00	250

KM# 476 3 KREUZER (Groschen)

1.3500 g., 0.3330 Silver 0.0145 oz. ASW **Ruler:** Friedrich as Duke Friedrich II **Obverse:** 3 between round clasps **Reverse:** Date not divided

Date	Mintage	F	VF	XF	Unc
1800	—	16.00	35.00	85.00	250

KM# 260 4 KREUZER (Batzen)

Silver **Ruler:** Eberhard Ludwig **Obverse:** Value above 3 shields, date divided by lower shield **Reverse:** Crowned arms within baroque frame **Note:** Weight varies 1.62-2.53 grams.

Date	Mintage	VG	F	VF	XF	Unc
1701	—	16.00	35.00	75.00	140	—
1702	—	16.00	35.00	75.00	140	—
1703	—	16.00	35.00	75.00	140	—
1705	—	16.00	35.00	75.00	140	—

KM# 295 4 KREUZER (Batzen)

Silver **Ruler:** Eberhard Ludwig **Obverse:** Value above 3 shields, date divided by lower shield **Reverse:** Crowned arms

Date	Mintage	VG	F	VF	XF	Unc
1708 (c)	—	12.00	30.00	60.00	110	—
1715 (c)	—	12.00	30.00	60.00	110	—
1718 (c)	—	12.00	30.00	60.00	110	—

KM# 410 4 KREUZER (Batzen)

Billon **Ruler:** Karl Eugen, Duke **Obverse:** Value above 3 shields, branches below **Reverse:** Date above 2-fold arms on shield

Date	Mintage	VG	F	VF	XF	Unc
1760	—	35.00	75.00	125	250	—

KM# 309 5 KREUZER

Silver **Ruler:** Eberhard Ludwig **Obverse:** Crowned round 4-fold arms with central shield of Württemberg in baroque frame **Reverse:** Value and date in laurel wreath **Rev. Legend:** V K/WURTEMB/LAND/MUNZ

Date	Mintage	VG	F	VF	XF	Unc
1726	—	16.00	35.00	70.00	130	—
1727	—	16.00	35.00	70.00	130	—
1728	—	16.00	35.00	70.00	130	—
1729	—	16.00	35.00	70.00	130	—
1730	—	16.00	35.00	70.00	130	—
1731	—	16.00	35.00	70.00	130	—

KM# 315 5 KREUZER

Silver **Ruler:** Eberhard Ludwig **Obverse:** Chain of Order of the Hunt around arms **Reverse:** Value, date within branches **Note:** Weight varies 1.90-2.44 grams.

Date	Mintage	VG	F	VF	XF	Unc
1731	—	16.00	35.00	70.00	130	—
1732	—	16.00	35.00	70.00	130	—
1733	—	16.00	35.00	70.00	130	—

KM# 325 5 KREUZER

Silver **Ruler:** Eberhard Ludwig **Obverse:** Date at bottom **Obv. Legend:** CUM DEO - ET DIE **Reverse:** Value, date within branches

Date	Mintage	VG	F	VF	XF	Unc
1732	—	35.00	80.00	160	275	—

KM# 333 5 KREUZER

Silver **Ruler:** Karl Alexander **Obverse:** Order collar around arms within crowned mantle **Reverse:** Value, date within branches **Note:** Weight varies 1.56-2.15 grams.

Date	Mintage	VG	F	VF	XF	Unc
1734	—	22.00	45.00	85.00	165	—
1735	—	22.00	45.00	85.00	165	—
1735 FB	—	22.00	45.00	85.00	165	—
1736	—	22.00	45.00	85.00	165	—

KM# 421 5 KREUZER

Billon **Ruler:** Karl Eugen, Duke **Obverse:** Crowned arms in branches, date below **Reverse:** Legend iin cartouche **Rev. Legend:** 240/EINE FEINE/MARK **Note:** Convention 5 Kreuzer.

Date	Mintage	VG	F	VF	XF	Unc
1767	—	25.00	50.00	100	250	—

KM# 425 5 KREUZER

Billon **Ruler:** Karl Eugen, Duke **Obverse:** Bust right **Obv. Legend:** CAROLVS D: G: DVX WURT: **Reverse:** Arms and date

Date	Mintage	VG	F	VF	XF	Unc
1769	—	20.00	45.00	90.00	240	—

KM# 445 5 KREUZER

Billon **Ruler:** Karl Eugen, Duke **Obverse:** Bust right **Obv. Legend:** CAROL D: G: - DVX WIRT: & T • **Reverse:** Crowned arms within baroque frame, date below

Date	Mintage	VG	F	VF	XF	Unc
1790	—	18.00	35.00	70.00	185	—

KM# 383 6 KREUZER

Billon **Ruler:** Karl Eugen, Duke **Obverse:** Crowned monogram **Reverse:** Crowned arms within baroque frame

Date	Mintage	VG	F	VF	XF	Unc
1746	—	35.00	75.00	150	300	—

KM# 384 6 KREUZER

Billon **Ruler:** Karl Eugen, Duke **Obverse:** Crowned monogram above value **Reverse:** Crowned complex arms within baroque frame

Date	Mintage	VG	F	VF	XF	Unc
1746	—	25.00	50.00	100	250	—

KM# 385 6 KREUZER

Billon **Ruler:** Karl Eugen, Duke **Obverse:** Armored bust right **Obv. Legend:** CAROLVS D • G • - DVX WURT: & T • **Reverse:** Crowned arms, value below

Date	Mintage	VG	F	VF	XF	Unc
1746	—	12.00	25.00	50.00	100	—
1747	—	12.00	25.00	50.00	100	—
1748	—	12.00	25.00	50.00	100	—
1749	—	12.00	25.00	50.00	100	—
1750	—	12.00	25.00	50.00	100	—

KM# 399 6 KREUZER

Billon **Ruler:** Karl Eugen, Duke **Obverse:** Bust right **Obv. Legend:** CAROLVS D: G: - DVX WURT: & T **Reverse:** Crowned complex arms, date divided below

Date	Mintage	VG	F	VF	XF	Unc
1758	—	7.00	15.00	30.00	60.00	—
1759	—	7.00	15.00	30.00	60.00	—

KM# 469 6 KREUZER

2.7000 g., 0.3330 Silver 0.0289 oz. ASW **Ruler:** Friedrich as Duke Friedrich II **Obverse:** Crowned monogram, value below **Reverse:** Crowned arms above date

Date	Mintage	F	VF	XF	Unc
1799	—	50.00	100	225	500

KM# 310 10 KREUZER

Silver **Ruler:** Eberhard Ludwig **Obverse:** Bust right **Reverse:** Crowned oval 4-fold arms with central shield of Wurttemberg, value (10) at bottom divides date

Date	Mintage	VG	F	VF	XF	Unc
1726 Rare	—	—	—	—	—	—

KM# 415 10 KREUZER

Billon **Ruler:** Karl Eugen, Duke **Obverse:** Bust right within wreath **Obv. Legend:** CAROLVS D • - G • DVX WURT • **Reverse:** Arms and date **Rev. Legend:** PROVIDE ET - CONSTANTER **Note:** Convention 10 Kreuzer.

Date	Mintage	VG	F	VF	XF	Unc
1763	—	15.00	30.00	60.00	125	—
1764	—	15.00	30.00	60.00	125	—
1765	—	15.00	30.00	60.00	125	—
1767	—	15.00	30.00	60.00	125	—
1768	—	15.00	30.00	60.00	125	—

KM# 446 10 KREUZER

Billon **Ruler:** Karl Eugen, Duke **Obverse:** Bust right within wreath **Obv. Legend:** CAROLVS • D • G • DVX • WIRTEMB • **Reverse:** Crowned arms within baroque frame, value below **Rev. Legend:** PROVIDE ET - CONSTANTER

Date	Mintage	VG	F	VF	XF	Unc
1790	—	25.00	50.00	100	250	—

KM# 470 10 KREUZER

3.9000 g., 0.5000 Silver 0.0627 oz. ASW **Obverse:** Bust left **Reverse:** Crowned arms with chain **Rev. Legend:** CUM DEO-ET. IURE

Date	Mintage	F	VF	XF	Unc
1799	—	125	250	425	800

KM# 400 12 KREUZER (Dreibatzner)

Billon **Ruler:** Karl Eugen, Duke **Obverse:** Head right **Obv. Legend:** CAROLVS D: - G: DVX WURT: **Reverse:** Crowned complex arms, value divides date below

Date	Mintage	VG	F	VF	XF	Unc
1758	—	40.00	80.00	175	350	—

KM# 401 12 KREUZER (Dreibatzner)

Billon **Ruler:** Karl Eugen, Duke **Obverse:** Armored bust right **Reverse:** Crowned complex arms, value divides date below

Date	Mintage	VG	F	VF	XF	Unc
1758	—	40.00	80.00	175	350	—

KM# 386 15 KREUZER (1/4 Gulden)

Billon **Obverse:** Crowned monogram within sprigs **Reverse:** Crowned arms divides date **Rev. Legend:** PROVIDE ET - CONSTANTER

Date	Mintage	VG	F	VF	XF	Unc
1746	—	25.00	50.00	110	225	—

KM# 387 15 KREUZER (1/4 Gulden)

Billon **Ruler:** Karl Eugen, Duke **Obverse:** Crowned double C monogram with date below **Reverse:** Crowned arms in branches with value below

Date	Mintage	VG	F	VF	XF	Unc
1746 R	—	25.00	50.00	110	225	—

KM# 388 15 KREUZER (1/4 Gulden)

Billon **Ruler:** Karl Eugen, Duke **Obverse:** Armored bust right **Obv. Legend:** CAROLVS D. - G. DVX WURT. **Reverse:** Crowned arms within baroque frame, value below

Date	Mintage	VG	F	VF	XF	Unc
1746	—	12.50	25.00	50.00	100	—
1747	—	12.50	25.00	50.00	100	—
1748	—	12.50	25.00	50.00	100	—
1749	—	12.50	25.00	50.00	100	—
1750	—	12.50	25.00	50.00	100	—
1758	—	12.50	25.00	50.00	100	—
1759	—	12.50	25.00	50.00	100	—
1760	—	12.50	25.00	50.00	100	—

KM# 402 20 KREUZER

Silver **Ruler:** Karl Eugen, Duke **Obverse:** Bust right within laurel branch wreath **Obv. Legend:** CAROLVS D: - G: DVX WURT: **Reverse:** Crowned complex arms in branches, pedestal with value below **Rev. Legend:** PROVIDE ET - CONSTANTER

Date	Mintage	VG	F	VF	XF	Unc
1758	—	15.00	30.00	60.00	120	—
1759	—	15.00	30.00	60.00	120	—

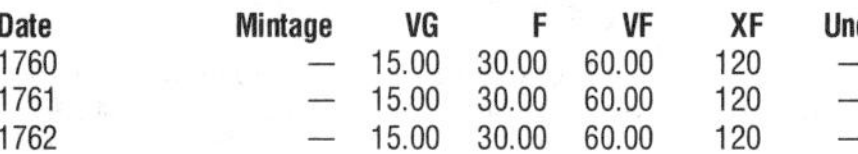

Date	Mintage	VG	F	VF	XF	Unc
1760	—	15.00	30.00	60.00	120	—
1761	—	15.00	30.00	60.00	120	—
1762	—	15.00	30.00	60.00	120	—

KM# 416 20 KREUZER

6.6800 g., 0.5830 Silver 0.1252 oz. ASW **Ruler:** Karl Eugen, Duke **Obverse:** Bust right within laurel wreath **Obv. Legend:** CAROLVS • D - G • DVX • WURT • **Reverse:** Crowned arms in baroque frame, value below **Rev. Legend:** PROVIDE ET - CONSTANTER • **Note:** Convention 20 Kreuzer.

Date	Mintage	VG	F	VF	XF	Unc
1763	—	15.00	30.00	60.00	120	—
1764	—	15.00	30.00	60.00	120	—

KM# 418 20 KREUZER

6.6800 g., 0.5830 Silver 0.1252 oz. ASW **Ruler:** Karl Eugen, Duke **Obverse:** Bust right within laurel wreath **Obv. Legend:** CAROLVS • D - G • DVX • WURT • **Reverse:** Similar to KM#419 but without Order collar chain **Rev. Legend:** PROVIDE ET - CONSTANTER •

Date	Mintage	VG	F	VF	XF	Unc
1765	—	—	—	—	—	—

KM# 419 20 KREUZER

6.6800 g., 0.5830 Silver 0.1252 oz. ASW **Ruler:** Karl Eugen, Duke **Obverse:** Bust right within laurel wreath **Obv. Inscription:** CAROLVS D • - G • DVX • WURT **Reverse:** Crowned arms within baroque frame and Order collar, value below **Rev. Legend:** PROVIDE ET - CONSTANTER

Date	Mintage	VG	F	VF	XF	Unc
1765	—	15.00	30.00	70.00	140	—
1766	—	15.00	30.00	70.00	140	—
1767	—	15.00	30.00	70.00	140	—
1768	—	15.00	30.00	70.00	140	—

KM# 432 20 KREUZER

6.6800 g., 0.5830 Silver 0.1252 oz. ASW **Ruler:** Karl Eugen, Duke **Reverse:** Crowned arms

Date	Mintage	VG	F	VF	XF	Unc
1768	—	15.00	30.00	70.00	140	—
1772	—	15.00	30.00	70.00	140	—
1774	—	15.00	30.00	70.00	140	—

KM# 426 20 KREUZER

6.6800 g., 0.5830 Silver 0.1252 oz. ASW **Ruler:** Karl Eugen, Duke **Obverse:** Bust right within rhombus **Obv. Legend:** CAROLVS - D: G: DVX - WURTEM - BERG & T **Reverse:** Crowned arms in baroque frame within rhombus **Rev. Legend:** PROVIDE - ET CON - STANTER

Date	Mintage	VG	F	VF	XF	Unc
1769	—	18.00	35.00	75.00	150	—

KM# 430 20 KREUZER

6.6800 g., 0.5830 Silver 0.1252 oz. ASW **Ruler:** Karl Eugen, Duke **Obverse:** Bust right, value below within rhombus **Obv. Legend:** CAROLVS - D: G: DVX - WURTEM - BERG & T **Reverse:** Crowned arms in baroque frame within rhombus **Rev. Legend:** PROVIDE - ET CON - STANTER

Date	Mintage	VG	F	VF	XF	Unc
1770	—	15.00	30.00	70.00	140	—

KM# 431 20 KREUZER

6.6800 g., 0.5830 Silver 0.1252 oz. ASW **Ruler:** Karl Eugen, Duke **Obverse:** Bust right within laurel wreath **Reverse:** Crowned arms within Order collar, value divides date below

Date	Mintage	VG	F	VF	XF	Unc
1775	—	12.00	25.00	60.00	130	—

KM# 457 20 KREUZER

6.6800 g., 0.5830 Silver 0.1252 oz. ASW **Ruler:** Friedrich I Eugen **Obverse:** Head right **Reverse:** Crowned arms within Order collar

Date	Mintage	VG	F	VF	XF	Unc
1796	—	40.00	80.00	145	275	—

KM# 462 20 KREUZER

6.6800 g., 0.5830 Silver 0.1252 oz. ASW **Ruler:** Friedrich as Duke Friedrich II **Obverse:** Armored bust left **Obv. Legend:** FRIDERICUS • II • D • G • DUX WIRTEMB & T **Reverse:** Crowned complex arms within Order collar, value below

Date	Mintage	F	VF	XF	Unc
1798 W	—	100	175	350	600

KM# 463 20 KREUZER

6.6800 g., 0.5830 Silver 0.1252 oz. ASW **Ruler:** Friedrich as Duke Friedrich II **Obverse:** Armored bust left **Obv. Legend:** FRIDERICUS II • D • G • DUX WIRTEMB • & T • **Reverse:** (20) below date, divided legend

Date	Mintage	F	VF	XF	Unc
1798	—	75.00	150	300	600
1799	—	65.00	125	275	575

KM# 317 30 KREUZER (1/2 Gulden)

Silver **Ruler:** Eberhard Ludwig **Obverse:** Bust right, value 30 below **Reverse:** Crowned ornately-shaped 4-fold arms with central shield of Wurttemberg in Chain of Order of the Hunt, date divided below

Date	Mintage	VG	F	VF	XF	Unc
1731	—	45.00	100	200	350	—

KM# 318 30 KREUZER (1/2 Gulden)

Silver **Ruler:** Eberhard Ludwig **Obverse:** Armored bust right **Obv. Legend:** EBER: LUD: D • - G • DUX WUR • T • **Reverse:** Value in legend **Rev. Legend:** 30 KREUTZER-LANDMUNZ **Note:** Varieties exist.

Date	Mintage	VG	F	VF	XF	Unc
1731 *	—	40.00	90.00	180	285	—
1732 *	—	40.00	90.00	180	285	—
1733	—	40.00	90.00	180	285	—

KM# 319 30 KREUZER (1/2 Gulden)

Silver **Ruler:** Eberhard Ludwig **Obverse:** Armored bust right **Obv. Legend:** EBER: LUD: D • - G • DUX ... **Reverse:** Oval arms **Note:** Varieties exist.

Date	Mintage	VG	F	VF	XF	Unc
1731 *	—	40.00	90.00	180	285	—
1732 *	—	40.00	90.00	180	285	—
1733 *	—	40.00	90.00	180	285	—
1733	—	40.00	90.00	180	285	—

KM# 316 30 KREUZER (1/2 Gulden)

Silver **Ruler:** Eberhard Ludwig **Obverse:** Bust right **Reverse:** Crowned oval 4-fold arms with central shield of Wurttemberg, value: 30 at bottom divides date **Note:** Weight varies 6.29-7.56 grams.

Date	Mintage	VG	F	VF	XF	Unc
1731	—	45.00	100	200	350	—

KM# 334 30 KREUZER (1/2 Gulden)

Silver **Ruler:** Karl Alexander **Obverse:** Draped bust right **Obv. Legend:** CAROL: ALEX: - D G DUX WURT & T **Reverse:** Order of Golden Fleece around arms **Note:** Weight varies 5.83-10.27 grams.

Date	Mintage	VG	F	VF	XF	Unc
1734 FB	—	45.00	100	200	350	—
1734 M	—	45.00	100	200	350	—
1734 S	—	45.00	100	200	350	—
1734 S/FB	—	45.00	100	200	350	—
1734 T	—	45.00	100	200	350	—
1735	—	45.00	100	200	350	—
1735 FB	—	45.00	100	200	350	—
1735 M/FB	—	45.00	100	200	350	—
1735 S/FB	—	45.00	100	200	350	—
1736 FB	—	45.00	100	200	350	—

KM# 389 30 KREUZER (1/2 Gulden)

8.5100 g., Silver **Ruler:** Karl Eugen, Duke **Obverse:** Bust right **Reverse:** Crowned arms, value below

Date	Mintage	VG	F	VF	XF	Unc
1746	—	65.00	145	300	500	—

KM# 422 1/48 THALER

Billon **Ruler:** Karl Eugen, Duke **Obverse:** Crowned arms, date below **Reverse:** Value within cartouche **Note:** Convention 1/48 Thaler.

Date	Mintage	VG	F	VF	XF	Unc
1767	—	6.00	12.00	25.00	50.00	—
1769	—	6.00	12.00	25.00	50.00	—
1770	—	6.00	12.00	25.00	50.00	—
1772	—	6.00	12.00	25.00	50.00	—
1775	—	6.00	12.00	25.00	50.00	—
1776	—	6.00	12.00	25.00	50.00	—
1779	—	6.00	12.00	25.00	50.00	—
1781	—	6.00	12.00	25.00	50.00	—
1782	—	6.00	12.00	25.00	50.00	—
1783	—	6.00	12.00	25.00	50.00	—
1784	—	6.00	12.00	25.00	50.00	—
1785	—	6.00	12.00	25.00	50.00	—
1787	—	6.00	12.00	25.00	50.00	—
1788	—	6.00	12.00	25.00	50.00	—
1789	—	6.00	12.00	25.00	50.00	—
1790	—	6.00	12.00	25.00	50.00	—
1791	—	6.00	12.00	25.00	50.00	—
1792	—	6.00	12.00	25.00	50.00	—

KM# A422 1/48 THALER

Billon **Mint:** Stuttgart **Obverse:** Mantled bust right **Obv. Legend:** CAROLVS D: - G: DVX WURT. **Reverse:** Crowned oval arms between palm and laurel branches, date below **Rev. Legend:** 48 EIN CONVENTIONS THALER **Note:** Weight varies: 1.07-1.09 g.

Date	Mintage	VG	F	VF	XF	Unc
1769	—	8.00	15.00	32.00	65.00	—

KM# 452 1/48 THALER

Billon **Ruler:** Ludwig Eugen

Date	Mintage	VG	F	VF	XF	Unc
1794	—	6.00	12.00	25.00	50.00	—

KM# 458 1/48 THALER

Billon **Ruler:** Friedrich I Eugen

Date	Mintage	VG	F	VF	XF	Unc
1796	—	6.00	12.00	25.00	50.00	—

KM# 403 1/6 THALER

4.4000 g., Silver **Ruler:** Karl Eugen, Duke **Obverse:** Armored bust right **Obv. Legend:** CAROLVS D: G: - DVX • WURT... **Reverse:** Value, date

Date	Mintage	VG	F	VF	XF	Unc
1758	—	25.00	60.00	120	250	—

KM# 404 1/6 THALER

4.4000 g., Silver **Ruler:** Karl Eugen, Duke **Obverse:** Crowned monogram **Reverse:** Value, date

Date	Mintage	VG	F	VF	XF	Unc
1758 R	—	30.00	70.00	140	300	—

KM# 289 1/4 THALER

7.2900 g., Silver **Ruler:** Eberhard Ludwig **Obverse:** Draped bust right **Obv. Legend:** EBERH • LUD • D • G • DUX • WURTEMB • **Reverse:** Arms have central shield of Wurttemberg **Rev. Inscription:** * CUM DEO ET DIE *

Date	Mintage	VG	F	VF	XF	Unc
1707 */(c)	—	90.00	200	400	650	—

KM# 357 1/4 THALER

7.3900 g., Silver **Ruler:** Karl Alexander with Karl Friedrich von Oels as Regent **Reverse:** Crowned and mantled oval 4-fold arms with central shield of Württemberg, value: 1/4 in oval below divides date

Date	Mintage	VG	F	VF	XF	Unc
1739 B	—	175	400	800	1,350	—

KM# 374 1/4 THALER

7.2500 g., Silver **Obverse:** Armored bust right **Obv. Legend:** CAROL • D • G • DVX: WURTEMB & TEC • **Reverse:** Crowned arms witin baroque frame **Rev. Legend:** PROVIDE & CONSTANTER

Date	Mintage	VG	F	VF	XF	Unc
1744 SS	—	100	200	400	900	—

KM# 345 1/3 THALER

10.0300 g., Silver **Ruler:** Karl Alexander with Karl Rudolf von Neuenstadt as Regent **Obverse:** Karl Rudolf **Obv. Legend:** CAR: RUD: D: G: D: WUR: & T: .... **Reverse:** Crowned oval 4-fold arms with central shield of Württemberg, value: 1/3 in oval below divides date

Date	Mintage	VG	F	VF	XF	Unc
1737 FB	—	200	450	850	1,400	—

KM# 405 1/3 THALER

6.2000 g., Silver **Ruler:** Karl Eugen, Duke **Obverse:** Bust right **Reverse:** Crowned arms, value divides date below

Date	Mintage	VG	F	VF	XF	Unc
1759	—	100	220	450	1,000	—

KM# 290 1/2 THALER

14.5700 g., Silver **Ruler:** Eberhard Ludwig **Obverse:** Draped bust right **Obv. Legend:** EBERH • LUD • D • G • - DUX • WURTEMB • **Reverse:** Helmeted arms **Rev. Legend:** CUM DEO ET DIE

Date	Mintage	VG	F	VF	XF	Unc
1707 */(c)	—	135	300	600	1,000	—

KM# 347 1/2 THALER

Silver **Reverse:** Arms in baroque frame without mantle

Date	Mintage	VG	F	VF	XF	Unc
1737 FB	—	325	725	1,450	2,200	—

KM# 346 1/2 THALER

Silver **Ruler:** Karl Alexander with Karl Rudolf von Neuenstadt as Regent **Obverse:** Karl Rudolf **Obv. Legend:** CAR: RUD: D: G: D: WURT: & T: C: M: .... **Reverse:** Crowned and mantled oval 4-fold arms with central shield of Württemberg, date at bottom **Note:** Weight varies 14.05-14.42 grams.

Date	Mintage	VG	F	VF	XF	Unc
1737 IFB	—	325	725	1,450	2,200	—

KM# 358 1/2 THALER

14.6900 g., Silver **Ruler:** Karl Alexander with Karl Friedrich von Oels as Regent **Obverse:** Armored bust right **Obv. Legend:** CAROL • FRID • D • G • DVX • WURT • TEC • & O • A • & T • **Reverse:** Without value shown

Date	Mintage	VG	F	VF	XF	Unc
1739 B	—	300	650	1,200	2,000	—

KM# 366 1/2 THALER

Silver **Ruler:** Karl Alexander with Karl Friedrich von Oels as Regent **Obverse:** Armored bust right **Obv. Legend:** CAROL • FRID • DVX • WURT • TEC • ET OLS • A • D • M • I • ET TVTOR • **Reverse:** St. Christopher with Christ child in field, shield at left **Note:** Weight varies 14.50-14.59 grams.

Date	Mintage	VG	F	VF	XF	Unc
1740 T/IT	—	225	525	1,000	1,750	—

KM# 375 1/2 THALER

14.5000 g., Silver **Ruler:** Karl Eugen, Duke **Obverse:** Armored bust right **Obv. Legend:** CAROLVS. D. G. DVX. - WURTEMB. & TEC. **Reverse:** Order cross divides date below **Rev. Legend:** PROVIDE ET. - CONSTANTER

Date	Mintage	VG	F	VF	XF	Unc
1744 SS	—	235	550	1,100	1,850	—

KM# 379 1/2 THALER

14.5000 g., Silver **Ruler:** Karl Eugen, Duke **Obverse:** Armored bust right **Obv. Legend:** CAROLVS • D • G • DVX - WURTEMB • & TEC • **Reverse:** Different shield ornamentation **Rev. Legend:** PROVIDE ET. - CONSTANTER.

Date	Mintage	VG	F	VF	XF	Unc
1745 SS	—	235	550	1,100	1,850	—

KM# 406 2/3 THALER

12.8000 g., Silver **Ruler:** Karl Eugen, Duke **Obverse:** Armored bust right **Obv. Legend:** CAROLVS D: G: DVX WURT: & T: **Reverse:** Crowned arms above value **Rev. Legend:** PROVIDE ET CONSTANTER •

Date	Mintage	VG	F	VF	XF	Unc
1759	—	200	300	450	1,000	—

KM# 286 THALER

Silver **Ruler:** Eberhard Ludwig **Obverse:** Draped bust right **Obv. Legend:** EBERH. LUD.. **Reverse:** Helmeted arms, date below, CUM DEO ET DIE above **Note:** Dav. #2848.

Date	Mintage	VG	F	VF	XF	Unc
1706 */C Rare	—	—	—	—	—	—

KM# 291 THALER

Silver **Ruler:** Eberhard Ludwig **Obverse:** Draped bust right **Obv. Legend:** EBERH • LUD • D • G • DUX • WURTEMB • **Reverse:** Different shaped arms **Rev. Legend:** * CUM DEO ET DIE * **Note:** Dav. #2849.

Date	Mintage	VG	F	VF	XF	Unc
1707 */C	—	450	900	1,650	2,750	—

KM# 312 THALER

Silver **Ruler:** Eberhard Ludwig **Obverse:** Draped bust right **Obv. Legend:** EBERH • LUD • D • G • DUX • WURTEMB • **Reverse:** Helmeted arms, inner legend **Rev. Legend:** * CUM DEO ET DIE *, VON GEWACHSENEN SILBER AUS DER FUNDGR. 3. K. STERN **Note:** Dav. #2850.

Date	Mintage	VG	F	VF	XF	Unc
1728 *	780	450	900	1,650	2,750	—

KM# 348 THALER

Silver **Ruler:** Karl Alexander with Karl Rudolf von Neuenstadt as Regent **Obverse:** Bust right, date below **Obv. Legend:** CAR: RUDOL: D: G: D: WURT: & T: C: M: ADMINIS: & TUTOR • **Reverse:** Crowned and mantled arms divide initials **Rev. Legend:** SALUTI - PUBLICÆ, below; * AD LEGEM IMPERII * **Note:** Dav. #2851.

Date	Mintage	VG	F	VF	XF	Unc
1737 IFB	—	400	750	1,250	2,000	—

KM# 349 THALER

Silver **Ruler:** Karl Alexander with Karl Rudolf von Neuenstadt as Regent **Obverse:** Armored bust right **Obv. Legend:** CAR: RUDOL: D: G: D: WURT: & T: C: M: ADMINIST • & TUTOR **Reverse:** Without initials **Rev. Legend:** SALUTI - PUBLICÆ, below; * AD LEGEM IMPERII * **Note:** Dav. #2851A.

Date	Mintage	VG	F	VF	XF	Unc
1737	—	400	750	1,250	2,000	—

KM# 359 THALER

Silver **Ruler:** Karl Alexander with Karl Friedrich von Oels as Regent **Obverse:** Bust right, B below **Obv. Legend:** CAROL • FRID • D • G • DVX • WÜRTEM • TEC • & ÖLS • ADMI • & TVT • **Reverse:** Crowned and mantled arms, date divided below **Rev. Legend:** CEV. FERT. DIVINA. VOLVNTAS, below; AD LEGEM 17 - 39 IMPERII **Note:** Dav. #2853.

Date	Mintage	VG	F	VF	XF	Unc
1739 B	—	450	900	1,650	2,750	—

KM# 367 THALER

Silver **Ruler:** Karl Alexander with Karl Friedrich von Oels as Regent **Obverse:** Bust right, IT below **Obv. Legend:** CAROL • FRID • DUX WURT • TEC • ET OLS • ADMI • ET TVTOR • **Reverse:** St. Christopher with Christ child in field, shield at left **Rev. Legend:** R. THALER AVS DEM BERG WERCK, in exergue; ZV. CHRISTOPHS/THAL. **Note:** Dav. #2855.

Date	Mintage	VG	F	VF	XF	Unc
1740 IT	—	850	1,500	2,500	4,000	—

KM# 376 THALER

Silver **Ruler:** Karl Eugen, Duke **Obverse:** Bust right **Obv. Legend:** CAROLVS D • G • - DVX WURT: & T: **Reverse:** Arms within Order chain, date below **Rev. Legend:** PROVIDE • ET • - CONSTANTER • **Note:** Dav. #2857. Convention Thaler.

Date	Mintage	VG	F	VF	XF	Unc
1744 SS	—	300	600	1,200	2,000	—

KM# 392 THALER

Silver **Ruler:** Karl Eugen, Duke **Obverse:** Armored bust right **Obv. Legend:** CAROLVS D: G: - DVX • WURT: & T: **Reverse:** Order collar below arms **Rev. Legend:** PROVIDE • ET • CONSTANTER • **Note:** Dav. #2858.

Date	Mintage	VG	F	VF	XF	Unc
1748 VS-PR	—	250	450	900	1,500	—

KM# 407 THALER

Silver **Ruler:** Karl Eugen, Duke **Obverse:** Order sash over right shoulder **Obv. Legend:** CAROLVS D: G: - DVX WURT: & T: **Reverse:** Helmeted arms divide date below **Rev. Legend:** PROVIDE ET CONSTANTER • **Note:** Dav. #2859.

Date	Mintage	VG	F	VF	XF	Unc
1759 R	—	150	300	600	900	—

KM# 408 THALER

Silver **Ruler:** Karl Eugen, Duke **Obverse:** Order sash over left shoulder **Obv. Legend:** CAROLVS D: G: - DVX WURT: & T: **Reverse:** Helmeted arms divide date below **Rev. Legend:** PROVIDE ET CONSTANTER **Note:** Dav. #2859A.

Date	Mintage	VG	F	VF	XF	Unc
1759 R	—	150	300	600	900	—

KM# 411 THALER

Silver **Ruler:** Karl Eugen, Duke **Obverse:** Armored bust right **Obv. Legend:** CAROLVS D: G: - DVX WURT: & T: **Reverse:** Crowned arms within branches, value below **Rev. Legend:** PROVIDE ET CONSTANTER **Note:** Dav. #2860.

Date	Mintage	VG	F	VF	XF	Unc
1760	—	100	200	350	700	—

KM# 412 THALER

Silver **Ruler:** Karl Eugen, Duke **Obverse:** Armored bust right **Obv. Legend:** CAROLVS D: G: - DVX WURT: & T: **Reverse:** Straight date divided by oval arms **Rev. Legend:** PROVIDE ET - CONSTANTER, P - R and 10 AUF EINE - FEINE MARC below **Note:** Dav. #2861.

Date	Mintage	VG	F	VF	XF	Unc
1760 PR	—	100	200	350	700	—

KM# 413 THALER

Silver **Ruler:** Karl Eugen, Duke **Obverse:** Armored bust right **Obv. Legend:** CAROLVS D: G: - DVX • WURT: & T: **Reverse:** Curved date divided by oval arms **Rev. Legend:** PROVIDE ET CONSTANTER, 10 AUF EINE - FEINE MARC below **Note:** Dav. #2862.

Date	Mintage	VG	F	VF	XF	Unc
1761 PR	—	100	200	350	700	—

KM# 414 THALER

Silver **Ruler:** Karl Eugen, Duke **Obverse:** Armored bust right **Obv. Legend:** CAROLVS D: G: - DVX WURT: & T: **Reverse:** Order cross below arms **Rev. Legend:** PROVIDE ET - CONSTANTER, below; 10 AUF EINE - FEINE MARC **Note:** Dav. #2863.

Date	Mintage	VG	F	VF	XF	Unc
1762	—	100	200	400	800	—
1763	—	100	200	400	800	—

KM# 417 THALER

Silver **Obverse:** Armored bust right **Obv. Legend:** CAROLVS D: G: - DVX WURT: & T: **Reverse:** Crowned shield in sprays **Rev. Legend:** PROVIDE ET - CONSTANTER, 10 AUF EINE - FEINE MARC **Note:** Dav. #2864.

Date	Mintage	VG	F	VF	XF	Unc
1764	—	125	250	500	900	—
1765	—	125	250	500	900	—
1766	—	125	250	500	900	—

KM# 423 THALER

Silver **Ruler:** Karl Eugen, Duke **Obverse:** Armored busts right **Obv. Legend:** CAROLVS D: G: - DVX WURT: & T • **Reverse:** Crowned complex arms with supporters, Order cross, date and value below **Rev. Legend:** PROVIDE ET - CONSTANTER, below; 1768/10 EINE FEINE MARCK• **Note:** Dav. #2865.

Date	Mintage	VG	F	VF	XF	Unc
1768	—	200	450	900	1,400	—

KM# 427 THALER

Silver **Ruler:** Karl Eugen, Duke **Obverse:** Armored bust right **Obv. Legend:** CAROLVS D: G: - DVX WURT: & T: **Reverse:** Crowned arms in baroque frame, date and value below **Rev. Legend:** • PROVIDE ET - CONSTANTER, date and 10. EINE FEINE MARC. below **Note:** Dav. #2866.

Date	Mintage	VG	F	VF	XF	Unc
1769	—	100	200	450	850	—
1776	—	100	200	450	850	—

KM# 433 THALER

Silver **Ruler:** Karl Eugen, Duke **Obverse:** Bust right with W on arm **Obv. Legend:** CAROLVS D: G: - DVX WURT: & TEC • **Reverse:** Crowned oval arms within Order collar, date divided below **Rev. Legend:** PROVIDE ET - CONSTANTER, 10 EINE FEINE MARC. **Note:** Dav. #2867.

Date	Mintage	VG	F	VF	XF	Unc
1777 DFH	—	100	200	450	850	—
1779 DFH	—	100	200	450	850	—

KM# 434 THALER

Silver **Ruler:** Karl Eugen, Duke **Obverse:** Armored bust right **Obv. Legend:** CAROLVS D: G: - DVX WURT: & TEC • **Reverse:** Crowned arms in Order collar, date divided below **Rev. Legend:** • PROVIDE ET - CONSTANTER, 10. EINE FEINE MARC. **Note:** Dav. #2868.

Date	Mintage	VG	F	VF	XF	Unc
1779 DFH	—	100	250	500	900	—

KM# 440 THALER

Silver **Ruler:** Karl Eugen, Duke **Obverse:** Armored bust right with Order collar **Obv. Legend:** CAROLVS D: G: - DVX • WURT: & TEC • **Reverse:** Crowned arms within branches, date divided above **Rev. Legend:** PROVIDE ET - CONSTANTER, .D.F.H./10. EINE FEINE MARC. below **Note:** Dav. #2869.

Date	Mintage	VG	F	VF	XF	Unc
1780 DFH	—	100	200	400	750	—

KM# 441 THALER

Silver **Ruler:** Karl Eugen, Duke **Obverse:** Armored bust right **Obv. Legend:** CAROLVS D: G: - DVX WURT: & TEC • **Reverse:** Order collar around arms **Rev. Legend:** PROVIDE ET - CONSTANTER., .D.F.H./10.EINE FEINE MARC. below **Note:** Dav. #2870.

Date	Mintage	VG	F	VF	XF	Unc
1781 DH	—	100	200	350	700	—

KM# 442 THALER

Silver **Ruler:** Karl Eugen, Duke **Obverse:** Armored bust right with Order cross **Obv. Legend:** CAROLVS • D: G: - DVX WURT: & TEC • **Reverse:** Crowned arms within branches, value below **Rev. Legend:** PROVIDE ET - CONSTANTER,D.F.H. - I.C.H./10 EINE FEINE MARC below **Note:** Dav. #2871.

Date	Mintage	VG	F	VF	XF	Unc
1784 DFH-ICH	—	100	200	350	700	—

KM# 453 THALER

Silver **Ruler:** Ludwig Eugen **Obverse:** Bust right **Obv. Legend:** LUDOV • EUGEN • D • G • DUX • WIRTEMB • & T • **Reverse:** Arms within Order collar, cross divides date below **Rev. Legend:** PRO MAXIMA DEI GLORIA ET BONO PUBLICO **Note:** Dav. #2872.

Date	Mintage	VG	F	VF	XF	Unc
1794 FH-CH	—	175	400	800	1,350	—

KM# 455 THALER

Silver **Ruler:** Friedrich I Eugen **Subject:** 300 Years of Duchy **Obverse:** Bust left, BETULIUS on the arm **Obv. Legend:** FRID. EVG. D. G. DVX WIRTEMB. ET T. **Reverse:** Double Order collar **Rev. Legend:** AD NORMAM - CONVENTIONIS, in exergue; TERT - DUCAT/SECULAR **Note:** Dav. #2873.

Date	Mintage	VG	F	VF	XF	Unc
1795 REGI	—	150	350	700	1,250	—

KM# 464 THALER

28.0600 g., 0.8330 Silver 0.7515 oz. ASW **Ruler:** Friedrich as Duke Friedrich II **Obverse:** Armored bust left **Note:** Dav. #2875.

Date	Mintage	F	VF	XF	Unc
1798	—	250	500	1,100	2,300

KM# 465 THALER

28.0600 g., 0.8330 Silver 0.7515 oz. ASW **Ruler:** Friedrich as Duke Friedrich II **Obverse:** Armored bust left **Obv. Legend:** FRIDERICUS II • D • G • DUX • WIRTEMB • & T **Reverse:** Crown divides legend **Rev. Legend:** CUM DEO - ET IURE. AD NORMAM - CONVENTION **Note:** Dav. #2876.

Date	Mintage	F	VF	XF	Unc
1798 W	—	250	500	1,100	2,300

KM# 287 2 THALER

Silver **Ruler:** Eberhard Ludwig **Obverse:** Bust right **Obv. Legend:** EBERH. LUD. D-G **Reverse:** Helmeted arms, date divided below **Note:** Dav. #2847.

Date	Mintage	VG	F	VF	XF	Unc
1706 */(c) Rare	—	—	—	—	—	—

KM# 360 2 THALER

Silver **Ruler:** Karl Alexander with Karl Friedrich von Oels as Regent **Obverse:** Armored bust right **Reverse:** Crowned and mantled arms, date divided below **Note:** Dav. #2852. Similar to 1 Thaler, KM#359.

Date	Mintage	VG	F	VF	XF	Unc
1739 B Rare	—	—	—	—	—	—

KM# 368 2 THALER

Silver **Ruler:** Karl Alexander with Karl Friedrich von Oels as Regent **Obverse:** Crowned monogram, branches below **Reverse:** Crowned complex arms, value below **Note:** Dav. #2854. Similar to 1 Thaler, KM#367.

Date	Mintage	VG	F	VF	XF	Unc
1740 IT Rare	—	—	—	—	—	—

KM# 377 2 THALER

58.8000 g., Silver **Ruler:** Karl Eugen, Duke **Obverse:** Armored bust right **Reverse:** Crowned arms in Order collar and branches, date below **Note:** Dav. #2856.

Date	Mintage	VG	F	VF	XF	Unc
1744 SS Rare	—	—	—	—	—	—

KM# 466 2 THALER

50.0000 g., 0.8330 Silver 1.3390 oz. ASW **Ruler:** Friedrich as Duke Friedrich II **Obverse:** Armored bust left **Note:** Dav. #2874. Similar to 1 Thaler, KM#464.

Date	Mintage	F	VF	XF	Unc
1798	—	350	700	1,500	3,200

TRADE COINAGE

KM# 300 GOLDGULDEN

3.5000 g., 0.9860 Gold 0.1109 oz. AGW **Ruler:** Eberhard Ludwig **Obverse:** Equestrian figure left **Reverse:** Helmeted arms

Date	Mintage	VG	F	VF	XF	Unc
ND(1712)	—	500	1,000	2,000	3,500	—

KM# 301 GOLDGULDEN

3.5000 g., 0.9860 Gold 0.1109 oz. AGW **Ruler:** Eberhard Ludwig **Subject:** Groundbreaking for the Palace Chapel at Ludwigsburg **Obverse:** Groundplan of chapel, inscription around and another below, with date **Reverse:** Inscription

Date	Mintage	VG	F	VF	XF	Unc
1716 Rare	—	—	—	—	—	—

KM# 305 GOLDGULDEN

3.5000 g., 0.9860 Gold 0.1109 oz. AGW **Ruler:** Eberhard Ludwig **Subject:** Oath of Fealty for Mompelgart **Obverse:** Bust right **Reverse:** Memorial inscription with date

Date	Mintage	VG	F	VF	XF	Unc
1723 Rare	—	—	—	—	—	—

KM# 320 1/4 CAROLIN

2.4250 g., 0.7700 Gold 0.0600 oz. AGW **Ruler:** Eberhard Ludwig **Obverse:** Armored bust right **Reverse:** Crowned arms **Rev. Legend:** * CUM DEO - ET DIE *

Date	Mintage	VG	F	VF	XF	Unc
1731	—	125	250	450	900	—
1732	—	125	250	450	900	—
1733	—	125	250	450	900	—

KM# 335.1 1/4 CAROLIN

2.4250 g., 0.7700 Gold 0.0600 oz. AGW **Ruler:** Karl Alexander **Obverse:** Armored bust right **Obv. Legend:** CAROL: ALEXAND: - D • G • DUX WUR & T • **Reverse:** Crowned and mantled arms, date divided at bottom **Rev. Legend:** * PER ARDVA - VIRTUS *

Date	Mintage	VG	F	VF	XF	Unc
1734 M-FB	—	125	250	500	1,000	—
1735 M-FB	—	125	250	500	1,000	—

KM# 342.1 1/4 CAROLIN

2.4250 g., 0.7700 Gold 0.0600 oz. AGW **Ruler:** Karl Alexander **Obverse:** Draped armored bust **Obv. Legend:** CAROL ALEX.. **Reverse:** Legend extends past mantle knot

Date	Mintage	VG	F	VF	XF	Unc
1735 FB	—	125	250	500	1,000	—
1736 FB	—	125	250	500	1,000	—

KM# 342.2 1/4 CAROLIN

2.4250 g., 0.7700 Gold 0.0600 oz. AGW **Ruler:** Karl Alexander **Obverse:** Revised draped armored bust **Reverse:** Legends ends at mantle knot

Date	Mintage	VG	F	VF	XF	Unc
1736 FB	—	125	250	500	1,000	—

KM# 321 1/2 CAROLIN

4.8500 g., 0.7700 Gold 0.1201 oz. AGW **Ruler:** Eberhard Ludwig **Obverse:** Bust right **Obv. Legend:** EBER: LUD: D • - G • DUX WUR: & T • **Reverse:** Crowned arms within Order collar **Rev. Legend:** * CUM DEO - ET DIE *

Date	Mintage	VG	F	VF	XF	Unc
1731	—	150	300	650	1,200	—
1732	—	150	300	650	1,200	—
1733	—	150	300	650	1,200	—

KM# 336 1/2 CAROLIN

4.8500 g., 0.7700 Gold 0.1201 oz. AGW **Ruler:** Karl Alexander **Obverse:** Armored bust right **Obv. Legend:** CAROL: ALEX: - D: G: ... **Reverse:** Crowned and mantled arms, date divided at bottom **Rev. Legend:** * PER ARDVA - VIRTVS *

Date	Mintage	VG	F	VF	XF	Unc
1734 M-FB	—	150	300	650	1,200	—
1734 S	—	150	300	650	1,200	—
1735 S-FB	—	150	300	650	1,200	—
1735 M-FB	—	150	300	650	1,200	—
1735 FB	—	150	300	650	1,200	—
1736 FB	—	150	300	650	1,200	—

KM# 322 CAROLIN

9.7000 g., 0.7700 Gold 0.2401 oz. AGW **Ruler:** Eberhard Ludwig **Obverse:** Small armored bust right **Obv. Legend:** EBER: LUD: D • - G • DUX • WUR & T • **Reverse:** Order collar around arms **Rev. Legend:** * CUM DEO - ET DIE • *

Date	Mintage	VG	F	VF	XF	Unc
1731	—	350	750	1,350	2,250	—
1732	—	350	750	1,350	2,250	—

KM# 328 CAROLIN

9.7000 g., 0.7700 Gold 0.2401 oz. AGW **Ruler:** Eberhard Ludwig **Obverse:** Large armored bust right **Obv. Legend:** EBER: LVD: D • - G • DUX WUR: & T • **Reverse:** Order chain divides date below **Rev. Legend:** * CUM DEO - ET DIE • *

Date	Mintage	VG	F	VF	XF	Unc
1733	—	350	750	1,350	2,250	—

KM# 337 CAROLIN

9.7000 g., 0.7700 Gold 0.2401 oz. AGW **Ruler:** Karl Alexander **Obverse:** Armored bust right **Obv. Legend:** CAROL: ALEX.... **Reverse:** Crowned oval arms in cartouche, date in legend at right **Rev. Legend:** PER ARDUA - VIRTUS •

Date	Mintage	VG	F	VF	XF	Unc
1734 T	—	300	650	1,250	2,000	—

KM# 338 CAROLIN

9.7000 g., 0.7700 Gold 0.2401 oz. AGW **Ruler:** Karl Alexander **Obverse:** Armored bust right **Obv. Legend:** CAROL • ALEX - D • G • DUX • WUR • & T • **Reverse:** Order collar surrounds arms within crowned mantle **Rev. Legend:** PER ARDUA - VIRTUS

Date	Mintage	VG	F	VF	XF	Unc
1734 S-FB	—	300	650	1,250	2,000	—
1734 T-FB	—	300	650	1,250	2,000	—

KM# 339 CAROLIN

9.7000 g., 0.7700 Gold 0.2401 oz. AGW **Ruler:** Karl Alexander **Obverse:** Armored bust right **Obv. Legend:** CAROL: ALEX: - D: G • DVX WUR & T **Reverse:** Order collarm surrounds arms within crowned mantle **Rev. Legend:** PER ARDUA - VIRTUS

Date	Mintage	VG	F	VF	XF	Unc
1734 S-FB	—	400	800	1,400	2,250	—
1735 S-FB	—	400	800	1,400	2,250	—
1735 M-FB	—	400	800	1,400	2,250	—
1736 FB	—	400	800	1,400	2,250	—

KM# 350 1/4 DUCAT

0.8750 g., 0.9860 Gold 0.0277 oz. AGW **Ruler:** Karl Alexander with Karl Rudolf von Neuenstadt as Regent **Obverse:** Armored bust right **Obv. Legend:** CAR: RUD: D: WUR: ... **Reverse:** Crowned arms within baroque frame, value below

Date	Mintage	VG	F	VF	XF	Unc
ND	—	250	500	900	1,500	—

KM# 355 1/4 DUCAT

0.8750 g., 0.9860 Gold 0.0277 oz. AGW **Obverse:** Karl Friedrich **Reverse:** Arms within baroque frame, value below

Date	Mintage	VG	F	VF	XF	Unc
ND	—	175	350	700	1,250	—

KM# 251 1/2 DUCAT

1.7500 g., 0.9860 Gold 0.0555 oz. AGW **Ruler:** Eberhard Ludwig **Obverse:** Armored bust right **Reverse:** Crowned arms

Date	Mintage	VG	F	VF	XF	Unc
ND	—	375	750	1,350	2,250	—

KM# 329 1/2 DUCAT

1.7500 g., 0.9860 Gold 0.0555 oz. AGW **Ruler:** Karl Alexander **Obverse:** Head right **Obv. Legend:** CAROL • ALEX • D • G • DUX • WUR • **Reverse:** Oval arms above value

Date	Mintage	VG	F	VF	XF	Unc
ND	—	250	550	1,150	2,000	—

KM# 351 1/2 DUCAT

1.7500 g., 0.9860 Gold 0.0555 oz. AGW **Ruler:** Karl Alexander with Karl Rudolf von Neuenstadt as Regent **Obverse:** Bust right **Obv. Legend:** CAR: RUD: DUX WURT... **Reverse:** Crowned arms, framed value below

Date	Mintage	VG	F	VF	XF	Unc
ND	—	250	550	1,150	2,000	—

KM# 356 1/2 DUCAT

1.7500 g., 0.9860 Gold 0.0555 oz. AGW **Ruler:** Karl Alexander with Karl Friedrich von Oels as Regent **Obverse:** Karl Friedrich

Date	Mintage	VG	F	VF	XF	Unc
ND	—	250	550	1,150	2,000	—

KM# 326 DUCAT

3.5000 g., 0.9860 Gold 0.1109 oz. AGW **Ruler:** Eberhard Ludwig **Obverse:** Laureate bust right **Obv. Legend:** EBERH: LUD: - D: G: DUX WURT • **Reverse:** Helmeted arms **Rev. Legend:** * CUM DEO - ET DIE *

Date	Mintage	VG	F	VF	XF	Unc
1732 M	—	300	600	1,450	2,400	—
1733 M	—	300	600	1,450	2,400	—
ND	—	300	600	1,450	2,400	—

KM# 330 DUCAT

3.5000 g., 0.9860 Gold 0.1109 oz. AGW **Ruler:** Karl Alexander **Obverse:** Armored bust right

Date	Mintage	VG	F	VF	XF	Unc
1733	—	400	800	1,750	3,250	—

KM# 341 DUCAT

3.5000 g., 0.9860 Gold 0.1109 oz. AGW **Ruler:** Karl Alexander **Obverse:** Armored bust right **Reverse:** Arms within crowned mantle

Date	Mintage	VG	F	VF	XF	Unc
1735	—	350	700	1,600	3,000	—
1735 FB	—	350	700	1,600	3,000	—
ND	—	350	700	1,600	3,000	—

KM# 343 DUCAT

3.5000 g., 0.9860 Gold 0.1109 oz. AGW **Ruler:** Karl Alexander **Obverse:** Small bust right **Obv. Legend:** CAROL: ALEXAND: D G DUX WIR & T **Reverse:** Crowned shields in cruciform with monogram at angles

Date	Mintage	VG	F	VF	XF	Unc
1736	—	700	1,500	2,750	4,500	—

KM# 344 DUCAT

3.5000 g., 0.9860 Gold 0.1109 oz. AGW **Ruler:** Karl Alexander **Obverse:** Large bust right **Obv. Legend:** CAROL • ALEX • - D: G • DUX • WUR & T **Reverse:** Crowned shields in cruciform with monogram in angles

Date	Mintage	VG	F	VF	XF	Unc
1736	—	700	1,500	2,750	4,500	—

KM# 352 DUCAT

3.5000 g., 0.9860 Gold 0.1109 oz. AGW **Ruler:** Karl Alexander with Karl Rudolf von Neuenstadt as Regent **Obverse:** Armored bust right **Reverse:** Crowned arms in baroque frame

Date	Mintage	VG	F	VF	XF	Unc
1737	—	700	1,500	2,750	4,500	—

KM# 361 DUCAT

3.5000 g., 0.9860 Gold 0.1109 oz. AGW **Ruler:** Karl Alexander with Karl Friedrich von Oels as Regent **Obverse:** Karl Friedrich **Obv. Legend:** CAROL • FRID • D • G • DVX • WURTEM • YEC • & • OLS • A • & • T • **Reverse:** Crowned and mantled arms, date divided below **Rev. Legend:** CEV • FERT • DIVINA • VOLVNIAS ...

Date	Mintage	VG	F	VF	XF	Unc
1739	—	700	1,500	2,750	4,500	—
1742	—	700	1,500	2,750	4,500	—

KM# 378 DUCAT

3.5000 g., 0.9860 Gold 0.1109 oz. AGW **Ruler:** Karl Eugen, Duke **Obverse:** Bust right **Obv. Legend:** CAROLVS D: G: - DVX • WURT & T • **Reverse:** Arms in baroque frame, date below **Rev. Legend:** PROVIDE ET • - CONSTANTER

Date	Mintage	VG	F	VF	XF	Unc
ND S-R	—	350	750	1,650	2,850	—
1744 SS	—	350	750	1,650	2,850	—
1744 SS	—	350	750	1,650	2,850	—
1747 PR	—	350	750	1,650	2,850	—
1748 S-R	—	350	750	1,650	2,850	—
1749 S-R	—	350	750	1,650	2,850	—
1750 S-R	—	350	750	1,650	2,850	—
1762	—	350	750	1,650	2,850	—

KM# 390 DUCAT

3.5000 g., 0.9860 Gold 0.1109 oz. AGW **Ruler:** Karl Eugen, Duke **Reverse:** Helmeted arms

Date	Mintage	VG	F	VF	XF	Unc
1746 PR	—	500	1,000	2,000	3,500	—

KM# 393 DUCAT

3.5000 g., 0.9860 Gold 0.1109 oz. AGW **Ruler:** Karl Eugen, Duke **Subject:** Wedding Commemorative **Obverse:** Crowned shielded monogram within branches, date below **Reverse:** Radiant sun above altar

Date	Mintage	VG	F	VF	XF	Unc
1749 IPR	—	350	700	1,500	2,500	—

KM# 447 DUCAT

3.5000 g., 0.9860 Gold 0.1109 oz. AGW **Ruler:** Karl Eugen, Duke **Obverse:** Head right **Obv. Legend:** CAROLVS • D • G • DVX • WIRT & T • **Reverse:** Crowned arms and date **Rev. Legend:** PROVIDE ET - CONSTANTER

Date	Mintage	F	VF	XF	Unc
1790 FH-CH	—	900	1,750	3,500	6,000

KM# 449 DUCAT

3.5000 g., 0.9860 Gold 0.1109 oz. AGW **Ruler:** Karl Eugen, Duke **Obverse:** Head right **Obv. Legend:** CAROLUS D • - G • DUX WIRTEMB • **Reverse:** Order cross divides date below arms **Rev. Legend:** PROVIDE ET - CONSTANTER •

Date	Mintage	F	VF	XF	Unc
1791 FH-CH	—	700	1,350	2,750	4,500

KM# 454 DUCAT

3.5000 g., 0.9860 Gold 0.1109 oz. AGW **Ruler:** Ludwig Eugen **Obverse:** Draped bust right **Obv. Legend:** LUDOV • EUGEN • D • G • DUX WIRTEMB & T **Reverse:** Crowned arms within Order collar, date divided below **Rev. Legend:** PROMAXIMA LEIG....

Date	Mintage	F	VF	XF	Unc
1794 FH-CH	—	650	1,500	3,000	5,000

KM# 269 2 DUCAT

7.0000 g., 0.9860 Gold 0.2219 oz. AGW **Ruler:** Eberhard Ludwig **Obverse:** Armored bust right **Reverse:** Crowned arms in palm branches, date divided at bottom

Date	Mintage	VG	F	VF	XF	Unc
1706 (c) Rare	—	—	—	—	—	—

KM# 278 2 DUCAT

7.0000 g., 0.9860 Gold 0.2219 oz. AGW **Ruler:** Eberhard Ludwig **Obverse:** Armored draped bust right **Obv. Legend:** EBERH: LUD: D: - G: DUX WURTEMB: **Reverse:** Helmeted arms **Rev. Legend:** * CUM DEO ET DIE *

Date	Mintage	VG	F	VF	XF	Unc
1707 (c)	—	600	1,250	3,000	5,000	—
ND (c)	—	600	1,250	3,000	5,000	—

KM# 311 3 DUCAT

10.5000 g., 0.9860 Gold 0.3328 oz. AGW **Subject:** Marriage of Karl Alexander and Marie Augusta von Thurn and Taxis **Obverse:** Bust of Karl Alexander left **Reverse:** Bust of Marie Augusta right

Date	Mintage	VG	F	VF	XF	Unc
ND(1727)	—	2,000	3,500	5,500	8,000	—

KM# 280 4 DUCAT

14.0000 g., 0.9860 Gold 0.4438 oz. AGW **Ruler:** Eberhard Ludwig **Obverse:** Armored bust right **Reverse:** Arms topped by 3 helmets, date divided at bottom

Date	Mintage	VG	F	VF	XF	Unc
1707 (c) Rare	—	—	—	—	—	—
1707 Rare	—	—	—	—	—	—
1707 */(c) Rare	—	—	—	—	—	—

KM# 292 6 DUCAT

21.0000 g., 0.9860 Gold 0.6657 oz. AGW **Ruler:** Eberhard Ludwig **Obverse:** Bust right **Obv. Legend:** EBERH • LUD • D • - G • DUX • WURTEMB • **Reverse:** Helmeted arms **Rev. Legend:** CUM DEO ET DIE * **Note:** Struck with 1 Thaler dies, KM#291.

Date	Mintage	VG	F	VF	XF	Unc
1707 */(c) Rare	—	—	—	—	—	—

KM# 285 10 DUCAT

34.6200 g., 0.9860 Gold 1.0974 oz. AGW **Ruler:** Eberhard Ludwig **Obverse:** Bust right, date below, where present **Reverse:** Hand from clouds holding imperial banner, legend above **Rev. Legend:** PRO DEO ET IMPERIO

Date	Mintage	VG	F	VF	XF	Unc
1701 Rare	—	—	—	—	—	—
ND Rare	—	—	—	—	—	—

PATTERNS

Including off metal strikes

KM#	Date	Mintage	Identification	Mkt Val
Pn9	ND1701	—	10 Ducat. Silver.KM#285.	—
Pn10	ND(1701)	—	10 Ducat. Silver. KM#285.	—
Pn11	ND(1701)	—	20 Ducat. Silver. KM#162.	—
Pn12	ND1706	—	Thaler. Lead.. KM#286.	—
Pn13	ND1706	—	Thaler. Tin. KM#286.	—
Pn14	ND1716	—	Goldgulden. Silver. KM#301.	100
Pn15	ND1723	—	Goldgulden. Silver. KM#305.	150
Pn16	ND1726	—	10 Kreuzer. Lead. KM#310.	—
Pn17	ND(1727)	—	3 Ducat. Silver. KM#311.	375
Pn18	ND1739	—	Thaler. Pewter. KM#359.	—
Pn19	ND1740	—	Thaler. Lead. KM#367.	—
Pn20	ND1740	—	Thaler. Iron. KM#367.	—
Pn21	ND(1740)	—	Thaler. Silver. 27.2000 g.	—
Pn22	ND1741	—	1/2 Kreuzer. Copper. KM#365.	—
Pn23	ND	—	1/2 Gulden. Aluminum.	—
Pn24	ND1798	—	Thaler. Zinc.	—
Pn25	ND1798	—	Thaler. Tin.	—

KM#	Date	Mintage	Identification	Mkt Val
Pn26	ND1798	—	Thaler. Silver.	—

WURTTEMBERG-OELS

In 1647, Sylvius Nimrod, the elder son of Duke Julius Friedrich of Württemberg-Weiltingen, married Elisabeth Maria, the only child of the last duke of Münsterberg-Öls in Silesia, Karl Friedrich. The duchy of Öls thus passed to the control of a cadet line of the dukes of Württemberg until nearly the end of the 18th century.

The three surviving sons of Sylvius Nimrod lived under the regency of their mother until 1672, as he had died while they were still young, but then they divided their territory and titles. They established the branches of Württemberg-Öls, Württemberg-Öls-Bernstadt and Württemberg-Öls-Juliusburg. The elder line of Württemberg-Öls became extinct after only one generation and the two younger brothers divided those lands as well. When Bernstadt and Juliusburg died out in 1742 and 1745 respectively, all the Öls territories were reconstituted in the remaining member of the family, Karl Christian Erdmann, nephew of the last Bernstadt duke. He died childless in 1792 and Öls passed to Brunswick-Wolfenbüttel by virtue of his marriage to Friederike, daughter of Friedrich August of that duchy.

RULERS

Christian Ulrich von Bernstadt, 1664-1704
Karl von Juliusburg und Bernstadt, 1684-1745
Karl Friedrich, 1704-1744 (died 1761)
Karl Christian Erdmann, 1744-1792

MINT OFFICIALS' INITIALS AND SYMBOLS

Initials	Date	Name
IN	1672-1705	Johann Neidhardt, die-cutter in Öls
CVL	1700-1717	Christian von Loh, warden in Öls
K	1776-1803	Anton König, die-cutter in Breslau
IGH	Ca.1768-1792 (died 1808)	Johann Gottlieb Held, die-cutter in Breslau

Arms: Württemberg – refer to that state for pertinent arms.

Silesia – eagle with crescent horizontally on breast.

Öls - eagle.

CROSS REFERENCES:

F&S = **Ferdinand Friedensburg and Hans Seger,** *Schlesiens Münzen und Medaillen der neueren Zeit*, **Breslau, 1901.** [reprint Frankfurt/Main, 1976].

J&M = **Norbert Jaschke and Fritz P. Maercker,** *Schlesische Münzen und Medaillen,* **Ihringen, 1985.**

B&E = **Christian Binder and Julius Ebner,** *Württembergische Münz- und Medaillen-Kunde,* **vol. 2, Stuttgart, 1912.**

DUCHY

REGULAR COINAGE

KM# 58 GROESCHL (3 Pfennig)

0.7600 g., Silver, 16 mm. **Ruler:** Christian Ulrich in Bernstadt **Obverse:** Oval 4-fold arms with central shield of Öls in baroque frame supported by mermaid at right, princely hat divides date above, value '3' in oval at bottom **Reverse:** Silesian eagle in oval baroque frame, mintmaster's initials below, where present **Note:** Varieties exist.

Date	Mintage	VG	F	VF	XF	Unc
1691 F&S#2399	—	4.00	10.00	15.00	40.00	—
1694 LL F&S#2401	—	4.00	10.00	15.00	40.00	—
1695 F&S#2403	—	4.00	10.00	15.00	40.00	—
1696 LL F&S#2408	—	4.00	10.00	15.00	40.00	—
1696 F&S#2409	—	4.00	10.00	15.00	40.00	—
1697 LL F&S#2411	—	4.00	10.00	15.00	40.00	—
1698 LL F&S#2414	—	4.00	10.00	15.00	40.00	—
1698 T F&S#2415	—	4.00	10.00	15.00	40.00	—
1699 LL F&S#2416	—	4.00	10.00	15.00	40.00	—
1700 CVL F&S#2420	—	4.00	10.00	15.00	40.00	—
1701 CVL F&S#2424	—	4.00	10.00	15.00	40.00	—
1702 CVL F&S#2428	—	4.00	10.00	15.00	40.00	—
1703 CVL F&S#2431	—	4.00	10.00	15.00	40.00	—
1704 CVL F&S#2432	—	4.00	10.00	15.00	40.00	—

KM# 75 GROESCHL (3 Pfennig)

0.7600 g., Silver, 16 mm. **Ruler:** Karl Friedrich **Obverse:** Oval 4-fold arms with central shield of Öls in baroque frame supported by mermaid at right, princely hat divides date above, value '3' in oval at bottom **Reverse:** Silesian eagle in oval baroque frame, mintmaster's initials below

Date	Mintage	VG	F	VF	XF	Unc
1705 CVL F&S#2457	—	8.00	15.00	30.00	65.00	—
1716 CVL F&S#2470	—	8.00	15.00	30.00	65.00	—

KM# 74 KREUZER

0.7500 g., Silver, 17 mm. **Ruler:** Karl in Juliusburg and Bernstadt **Obverse:** Bust to right, value (1) below **Obv. Legend:** D.G. CAROL. DUX. - WURT. T. I. S. O. B. **Reverse:** Silesian eagle in oval baroque frame, princely hat divides date above **Rev. Legend:** COM. MONTB. DOM. I. HEID(ENH). (&) MED.

Date	Mintage	VG	F	VF	XF	Unc
1704 CVL F&S#2450	—	7.00	12.00	25.00	60.00	—

KM# 61 3 KREUZER (Groschen)

1.4500 g., Silver, 21 mm. **Ruler:** Christian Ulrich in Bernstadt **Obverse:** Bust to right, value (3) below **Obv. Legend:** (D.G.) CHRIST. (U)(V)LR(IC). (—) (D.G.) DUX. (—) W(URT). T. I. S. O. (&) B. **Reverse:** Silesian eagle in circle, princely hat divides date in margin at top **Rev. Legend:** COM(ES). MON(T)(B). DOM. I. HEID(ENH). (STE)(R)(N)(B). & M(ED)(ZB). **Note:** Varieties exist. Weight varies 1.45-1.62g.

Date	Mintage	VG	F	VF	XF	Unc
1695 LL F&S#2402	—	6.00	12.00	25.00	60.00	—
1696 LL F&S#2406	—	6.00	12.00	25.00	60.00	—
1698 LL F&S#2413	—	6.00	12.00	25.00	60.00	—
1701 CVL F&S#2423	—	6.00	12.00	25.00	60.00	—
1702 CVL F&S#2427	—	6.00	12.00	25.00	60.00	—

KM# 76 3 KREUZER (Groschen)

1.7600 g., Silver, 21 mm. **Ruler:** Karl in Juliusburg and Bernstadt **Obverse:** Bust to right, value (3) below **Obv. Legend:** D. G. CAR(O)L. DUX. — W(URT). T. I. S. O. (&) B. **Reverse:** Silesian eagle in circle, princely hat divides date in margin at top **Rev. Legend:** COM. MON(T). DOM. I. HEID. STER. (&) M(ED). **Note:** Varieties exist.

Date	Mintage	VG	F	VF	XF	Unc
1705 CVL F&S#2453	—	7.00	15.00	30.00	65.00	—
1708 CVL F&S#2454	—	7.00	15.00	30.00	65.00	—

KM# 79 3 KREUZER (Groschen)

1.5600 g., Silver, 21 mm. **Ruler:** Karl Friedrich **Obverse:** Bust to right, value (3) below **Obv. Legend:** D. G. CAR(OL). FRID. (—) DUX. (—) W. T. I. S. O(LS). (&) B. **Reverse:** Silesian eagle in circle, princely hat divides date in margin at top **Rev. Legend:** COM. MON(T)(B). DOM. I. HEID. ST(ER). (&) M. **Note:** Varieties exist.

Date	Mintage	VG	F	VF	XF	Unc
1708 CVL F&S#2459	—	7.00	15.00	30.00	65.00	—
1709 CVL F&S#2460	—	7.00	15.00	30.00	65.00	—

KM# 77 6 KREUZER

2.6600 g., Silver, 26 mm. **Ruler:** Karl in Juliusburg and Bernstadt **Obverse:** Bust to right, value (VI) below **Obv. Legend:** D. G. CAROLUS. DUX. WURT. T. I. S. OLS. & B. **Reverse:** Silesian eagle in oval baroque frame, princely hat divides date at top in margin **Rev. Legend:** COM. MON(T)(B). D(OM). I. HEID. STERN. & M. **Note:** Varieties exist.

Date	Mintage	VG	F	VF	XF	Unc
1705 CVL F&S#2452	—	22.00	40.00	80.00	135	—
1712 CVL F&S#2455	—	22.00	40.00	80.00	135	—

KM# 80 6 KREUZER

Silver, 26 mm. **Ruler:** Karl Friedrich **Obverse:** Bust right, value (VI) below **Obv. Legend:** D.G. CAR(OL)(9). FRID. DUX. - W(U)(Ü)RT(EM). T. I. S. OLS. (&) B. **Reverse:** Silesian eagle in oval baroque frame, princely hat divides date at top in margin **Rev. Legend:** COM. MON(T)(B). DOM. I. HEID(ENH). ST(ER)(N)(B). & M(E)(T)(Z). **Note:** Weight varies: 2.71-2.90g. Varieties exist.

Date	Mintage	VG	F	VF	XF	Unc
1708 CVL J&M#167	—	10.00	20.00	40.00	75.00	—
1712 CVL F&S#2462	—	10.00	20.00	40.00	75.00	—
1713 CVL F&S#2464	—	10.00	20.00	40.00	75.00	—
1714 CVL F&S#2466	—	10.00	20.00	40.00	75.00	—
1715 CVL F&S#2467	—	10.00	20.00	40.00	75.00	—
1716 CVL F&S#2469	—	10.00	20.00	40.00	75.00	—

KM# 73 THALER

Silver **Ruler:** Christian Ulrich in Bernstadt **Obverse:** Armored bust right **Obv. Legend:** D.G. CHRIST. ULR DUX - WURT. T. I. S. O. B. **Reverse:** Helmeted arms, date divided above, initials below **Rev. Legend:** COM • MONTB • DOM • I • HEID • STERNB: & MED: **Note:** Dav#2877.

Date	Mintage	F	VF	XF	Unc
1702 CVL	—	325	650	1,200	2,000

KM# 84 THALER

Silver **Ruler:** Karl Friedrich **Obverse:** Large bust right **Obv. Legend:** D: G: CAROL9 • FRIDR: - DUX • - W: T: I • S: OLS • & B: **Reverse:** Helmeted arms, date divided above, initials below **Rev. Legend:** COM: MONB: DOM: IN: HEID: STERNB: M: & A: **Note:** Dav#2878. Varieties exist.

Date	Mintage	F	VF	XF	Unc
1716 CVL	—	225	450	800	1,500
1717 CVL	—	225	450	800	1,500

KM# 85 THALER

Silver **Ruler:** Karl Friedrich **Obverse:** Small bust right **Obv. Legend:** D: G: CAROL9 • FRIDR: - DUX • - W: T: I • S: OLS • & B: **Reverse:** Helmeted arms **Rev. Legend:** COM: MONB: DOM: IN: HEID: STERNB: M: & A: **Note:** Dav#2878A.

Date	Mintage	F	VF	XF	Unc
1717	—	225	450	800	1,500

KM# 87 THALER

Silver **Ruler:** Karl Christian Erdmann **Obverse:** Bust right with K at bottom of bust **Obv. Legend:** CAROL • CHRIST • ERDM • DUX WURTEMB • OLSN • & BEROLST • **Reverse:** Crowned and mantled arms, date below **Rev. Legend:** EIN REICHS THALER **Note:** Dav.#2879; previous Cr#1.1.

Date	Mintage	F	VF	XF	Unc
1785 K//B	—	135	275	500	850

KM# 88 THALER

Silver **Ruler:** Karl Christian Erdmann **Obverse:** Without K on bust **Obv. Legend:** CAROL•CHRIST•ERDM•DUX WURTEMB • OLSN. & BEROLST • **Reverse:** Crowned and mantled arms with date below **Rev. Legend:** EIN REICHS THALER **Note:** Varieties exist. Dav#2879A; previous Cr#1.2.

Date	Mintage	F	VF	XF	Unc
1785 B	—	135	275	500	850

TRADE COINAGE

KM# 81 1/4 DUCAT

0.8750 g., 0.9860 Gold 0.0277 oz. AGW **Ruler:** Karl Friedrich **Obverse:** Shield of arms **Reverse:** Crowned CF monogram **Note:** Fr#3287.

Date	Mintage	VG	F	VF	XF	Unc
1708	—	135	275	550	950	—

KM# 83 1/4 DUCAT

0.8750 g., 0.9860 Gold 0.0277 oz. AGW **Ruler:** Karl Friedrich **Obverse:** Bust right **Reverse:** Shield of arms **Note:** Fr#3286.

Date	Mintage	VG	F	VF	XF	Unc
1711	—	135	275	550	950	—

KM# 43 DUCAT

3.5000 g., 0.9860 Gold 0.1109 oz. AGW **Ruler:** Christian Ulrich in Bernstadt **Obverse:** Bust right in inner circle **Reverse:** Arms topped by 4 helmets in inner circle, date divided near top **Note:** Fr#3276.

Date	Mintage	VG	F	VF	XF	Unc
1701	—	500	1,000	2,000	3,500	—
1703	—	500	1,000	2,000	3,500	—

KM# 78 DUCAT

3.5000 g., 0.9860 Gold 0.1109 oz. AGW **Ruler:** Karl in Juliusburg and Bernstadt **Obverse:** Bust right in inner circle **Reverse:** Shield of arms in inner circle **Note:** Fr#3285.

Date	Mintage	VG	F	VF	XF	Unc
1705 CVL	—	700	1,500	3,000	5,000	—

KM# 82 DUCAT

3.5000 g., 0.9860 Gold 0.1109 oz. AGW **Ruler:** Karl Friedrich **Obverse:** Bust right in inner circle **Note:** Fr#3285.

Date	Mintage	VG	F	VF	XF	Unc
1708 CVL	—	600	1,350	2,750	4,500	—
1711 CVL	—	600	1,350	2,750	4,500	—
1713 CVL	—	600	1,350	2,750	4,500	—
1714 CVL	—	600	1,350	2,750	4,500	—

KM# 72 2 DUCAT

7.0000 g., 0.9860 Gold .2219 AGW 0.2219 oz. AGW **Ruler:** Christian Ulrich in Bernstadt **Obverse:** Bust to right **Obv. Legend:** D. G. CHRIST. ULR. — DUX. W. T. I. S. O. et B. **Reverse:** Ornate 4-fold arms with central shield of Öls, 4 helmets above, date divided in margin at upper left and right **Rev. Legend:** COM. MONTB. DOM. HEID. &. MED. **Note:** F&S#2421, B&E#153; struck on thick flan from Ducat dies, KM#43.

Date	Mintage	VG	F	VF	XF	Unc
1701 Rare	—	—	—	—	—	—

WURZBURG

BISHOPRIC

The Bishopric, located in Franconia, was established in 741. The mint right was obtained in the 11th century. The first coins were struck c. 1040. In 1441 the bishops were confirmed as dukes. In 1802 the area was secularized and granted to Bavaria. It was made a grand duchy in 1806 but the 1815 Congress of Vienna returned it to Bavaria.

RULERS

Johann Philipp II, Frhr. von Greiffenklau-Vollraths, 1699-1719
Johann Philipp Franz, Graf von Schönborn,
Christoph Franz von Hutten, 1724-1729
Friedrich Karl Graf von Schönborn, 1729-1746
Anselm Franz, Graf von Ingelheim, 1746-1749
Karl Philipp, Frhr. von Greiffenklau-Vollraths, 1749-1754
Adam Friedrich von Seinsheim, 1755-1779
Franz Ludwig von Erthal, 1779-1795
Georg Karl, Freiherr von Fechenbach, Bishop, 1795-1802

MINT MARKS

F - Fürth
N - Nürnberg
W - Würzburg

MINT OFFICIALS' INITIALS

Initials	Date	Name
BN	1754	Bischof and Neumeister
FHP	1762-90	Franz Hermann Prange, warden
GN	1754-62	Georg Neumeister, warden
I.L.OE	1740-87	Johann Leonhard Oexlein, die-cutter and medailleur
INM	1762-90	Johann Nikolaus Martinengo
L, Loos	1742-66	Georg Friedrica Loos, die-cutter
MP	1762-94	Martinengo & Prange
PB	1754-61	Philipp Bischof
V	(d. 1740)	Georg Wilhelm Vestner, die-cutter in Nürnberg
V.Lon	1727-64	Franz Anton Van Lon, die-cutter
VESTNER	(d. 1754)	Andreas Vestner, die-cutter in Nürnberg
WF	1746-48	Wilhelm Fehr or Feser
WGBN	1754	Wurzberg Mint & Bishof and Neumeister
	1746-51	Salomon Auerbach, die-cutter

MONETARY SYSTEM

3 Drier (Kortling) = 1 Shillinger
7 Shillinger = 15 Kreuzer
28 Shillinger = 1 Guter Gulden
44-4/5 Shillinger = 1 Convention Thaler

REGULAR COINAGE

KM# 270 3 HELLER

Silver **Ruler:** Christoph Franz von Hutten **Obverse:** Lower arms of Hutten **Note:** Uniface. Varieties exist

Date	Mintage	VG	F	VF	XF	Unc
1724	—	4.00	8.00	15.00	26.00	—
1725	—	4.00	8.00	15.00	26.00	—
1728	—	4.00	8.00	15.00	26.00	—
1729	—	4.00	8.00	15.00	26.00	—

KM# 306 3 HELLER

Silver **Ruler:** Friedrich Karl Graf von Schonborn **Obverse:** Lower arms of Schonborn

Date	Mintage	VG	F	VF	XF	Unc
173Z	—	6.00	12.00	25.00	45.00	—
1737	—	6.00	12.00	25.00	45.00	—

KM# 315 3 HELLER

Silver **Ruler:** Anselm Franz, Graf von Ingelheim **Obverse:** Lower arms of Ingelheim

Date	Mintage	VG	F	VF	XF	Unc
1746	—	6.00	12.00	25.00	45.00	—
1747	—	6.00	12.00	25.00	45.00	—
1748	—	6.00	12.00	25.00	45.00	—
ND	—	6.00	12.00	25.00	45.00	—

KM# 349 3 HELLER

Billon **Ruler:** Adam Friedrich von Seinsheim **Obverse:** Value in orb **Note:** Uniface

Date	Mintage	VG	F	VF	XF	Unc
1759	—	7.00	14.00	28.00	50.00	—
1760	—	7.00	14.00	28.00	50.00	—
1761	—	7.00	14.00	28.00	50.00	—
1762	—	7.00	14.00	28.00	50.00	—
1763	—	7.00	14.00	28.00	50.00	—

KM# 336 1/2 PFENNING

Copper **Ruler:** Karl Philipp von Greifenklau **Obverse:** Crowned monogram **Reverse:** Value, legend and date **Rev. Legend:** 1/2/WIRZBURG/PFENNING

Date	Mintage	Good	VG	F	VF	XF
1751	—	—	4.00	8.00	16.00	30.00

KM# 335 1/2 PFENNING

Copper **Ruler:** Karl Philipp von Greifenklau **Obverse:** Crowned CP monogram **Reverse:** Value: 1/2 /PFENNING/date in ornament

Date	Mintage	VG	F	VF	XF	Unc
1751 Rare	—	—	—	—	—	—

KM# 355 1/2 PFENNING

Copper **Obverse:** AFF monogram **Obv. Legend:** WIRZBURG SCHEIDE ... **Reverse:** Value, date

Date	Mintage	VG	F	VF	XF	Unc
1760	—	5.00	10.00	20.00	40.00	—
1761	—	5.00	10.00	20.00	40.00	—

KM# 367.1 1/2 PFENNING

Copper **Ruler:** Adam Friedrich von Seinsheim **Obverse:** Two shields, crown above **Reverse:** Value

Date	Mintage	VG	F	VF	XF	Unc
1761	—	3.00	6.00	12.00	25.00	—
1762	—	3.00	6.00	12.00	25.00	—
1763	—	3.00	6.00	12.00	25.00	—
1764	—	3.00	6.00	12.00	25.00	—

KM# 367.2 1/2 PFENNING

Copper **Ruler:** Franz Ludwig von Erthal **Obverse:** Large shields **Reverse:** Value

Date	Mintage	VG	F	VF	XF	Unc
ND (1779-95)	—	3.00	6.00	12.00	25.00	—

KM# 212 1/84 GULDEN (Kortling)

Silver **Ruler:** Johann Philipp II von Greifenklau-Vollraths **Obverse:** Lower arms of Greifenklau **Reverse:** Value on imperial orb within rhombus **Note:** Varieties exist.

Date	Mintage	VG	F	VF	XF	Unc
1713	—	5.00	10.00	20.00	40.00	—
1715F	—	5.00	10.00	20.00	40.00	—
1716	—	5.00	10.00	20.00	40.00	—
1717	—	5.00	10.00	20.00	40.00	—
1718	—	5.00	10.00	20.00	40.00	—
1719F	—	5.00	10.00	20.00	40.00	—

KM# 271 1/84 GULDEN (Kortling)

Silver **Ruler:** Christoph Franz von Hutten **Obverse:** Lower arms of Hutton **Reverse:** Value on imperial orb within rhombus **Note:** Varieties exist.

Date	Mintage	VG	F	VF	XF	Unc
1724F	—	4.00	8.00	15.00	30.00	—
1725F	—	4.00	8.00	15.00	30.00	—
1726F	—	4.00	8.00	15.00	30.00	—
1727F	—	4.00	8.00	15.00	30.00	—
1728F	—	4.00	8.00	15.00	30.00	—
1729F	—	4.00	8.00	15.00	30.00	—

KM# 320 1/84 GULDEN (Kortling)

Silver **Ruler:** Anselm Franz, Graf von Ingelheim **Obverse:** Lower arms of Ingelheim **Reverse:** Value on imperial orb within rhombus

Date	Mintage	VG	F	VF	XF	Unc
1748F	—	7.00	15.00	30.00	50.00	—

KM# 337 1/84 GULDEN (Kortling)

Billon **Ruler:** Karl Philipp von Greifenklau **Obverse:** Crowned oval arms between two branches, date **Reverse:** Value, 84 on imperial orb in rhombus

Date	Mintage	VG	F	VF	XF	Unc
1751	—	5.00	10.00	20.00	40.00	—

KM# 376 1/84 GULDEN (Kortling)

Billon **Ruler:** Adam Friedrich von Seinsheim **Obverse:** Crown above two shields **Reverse:** Value on imperial orb within rhombus

Date	Mintage	VG	F	VF	XF	Unc
1764	—	4.00	8.00	15.00	30.00	—

KM# 437 1/84 GULDEN (Kortling)

Billon **Ruler:** Franz Ludwig von Erthal **Obverse:** Crown above two shields, date below **Reverse:** Value on imperial orb within rhombus

Date	Mintage	VG	F	VF	XF	Unc
1794	—	7.00	15.00	30.00	50.00	—

KM# 442 1/84 GULDEN (Kortling)

Billon **Ruler:** Georg Karl, Freiherr von Fechenbach, Bishop **Obverse:** Crowned arms within branches **Reverse:** Value on imperial orb within rhombus

Date	Mintage	F	VF	XF	Unc
1795	—	5.00	10.00	25.00	70.00
1796	—	—	—	—	—

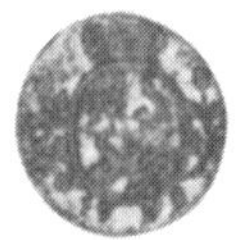

KM# 458 1/84 GULDEN (Kortling)

Billon **Ruler:** Georg Karl, Freiherr von Fechenbach, Bishop **Obverse:** Crowned arms within branches **Reverse:** Value on imperial orb within rhombus

Date	Mintage	F	VF	XF	Unc
1796	—	4.00	8.00	20.00	60.00
1797	—	4.00	8.00	20.00	60.00
1798	—	4.00	8.00	20.00	60.00
1799	—	4.00	8.00	20.00	60.00
1800	—	4.00	8.00	20.00	60.00

KM# 213 SCHILLING (8 Pfennig)

Silver **Ruler:** Johann Philipp II von Greifenklau-Vollraths **Obverse:** Lower arms of Greifenklau **Reverse:** Value on imperial orb within rhombus **Note:** Varieties exist.

Date	Mintage	VG	F	VF	XF	Unc
1701	—	10.00	20.00	45.00	85.00	—
1703	—	10.00	20.00	45.00	85.00	—
1704	—	10.00	20.00	45.00	85.00	—
1705	—	10.00	20.00	45.00	85.00	—
1706	—	10.00	20.00	45.00	85.00	—

KM# 286 SCHILLING (8 Pfennig)

Silver **Ruler:** Christoph Franz von Hutten **Obverse:** Four-fold arms of Wurzburg and hutten in two joined ovals within baroque frame, crown above, date at bottom **Reverse:** St. Kilian standing

Date	Mintage	VG	F	VF	XF	Unc
1726	—	22.00	50.00	100	185	—

KM# 317 SCHILLING (6 Neue Pfennige)

Silver **Ruler:** Anselm Franz, Graf von Ingelheim **Obverse:** Crowned oval four-fold arms with central shield of Ingelheim **Reverse:** St. Kilian divides date

Date	Mintage	VG	F	VF	XF	Unc
1746	—	7.00	16.00	32.00	60.00	—
1747	—	7.00	16.00	32.00	60.00	—
1748	—	7.00	16.00	32.00	60.00	—

KM# 316 SCHILLING (6 Neue Pfennige)

Silver **Obverse:** Crowned round two-fold arms of Wurzburg, date divided at bottom **Reverse:** St. Kilian **Note:** Sede vacante issue.

Date	Mintage	VG	F	VF	XF	Unc
1746	—	38.00	70.00	140	230	—

KM# 318 SCHILLING (6 Neue Pfennige)

Silver **Ruler:** Anselm Franz, Graf von Ingelheim **Obverse:** Crowned oval two-fold arms of Wurzburg, arms of Ingelheim lower in front **Obv. Legend:** ANS.FRANC.D.G.EP.H.S.R.I.P.F.O.D. **Reverse:** St. Kilian standing divides date **Rev. Legend:** SANCTUS.-KILIANUS

Date	Mintage	VG	F	VF	XF	Unc
1747	—	12.00	25.00	50.00	85.00	—

KM# 338 SCHILLING (6 Neue Pfennige)

Billon **Ruler:** Karl Philipp von Greifenklau **Obverse:** Crowned oval three-fold arms **Reverse:** St. Kilian divides date

Date	Mintage	VG	F	VF	XF	Unc
1751 Rare	—	—	—	—	—	—

KM# 339 SCHILLING (6 Neue Pfennige)

Billon **Ruler:** Karl Philipp von Greifenklau **Obverse:** Four-fold arms **Reverse:** St. Kilian standing divides date

Date	Mintage	VG	F	VF	XF	Unc
1751	—	6.00	12.00	25.00	50.00	—

KM# 374 SCHILLING (6 Neue Pfennige)

Billon **Ruler:** Adam Friedrich von Seinsheim **Obverse:** Arms **Reverse:** Madonna

Date	Mintage	VG	F	VF	XF	Unc
1763	—	7.00	15.00	30.00	75.00	—

KM# 438 SCHILLING (6 Neue Pfennige)

Billon **Ruler:** Franz Ludwig von Erthal **Obverse:** Crowned arms within Order collar **Obv. Legend:** FRANC • LUD • D • G • ... **Reverse:** St. Kilian standing divides date

Date	Mintage	VG	F	VF	XF	Unc
1794	—	5.00	10.00	20.00	40.00	—
1795	—	5.00	10.00	20.00	40.00	—

KM# 443 SCHILLING (6 Neue Pfennige)

Billon **Ruler:** Georg Karl, Freiherr von Fechenbach, Bishop **Obverse:** Crowned arms **Obv. Legend:** GEORG. CAROL. D. G... **Reverse:** St. Kilian divides date

Date	Mintage	VG	F	VF	XF	Unc
1795	—	3.00	7.00	15.00	30.00	—
1796	—	3.00	7.00	15.00	30.00	—

KM# 340 1/4 KREUZER

Copper **Ruler:** Karl Philipp von Greifenklau **Obverse:** Crowned arms within branches **Reverse:** Value, date

Date	Mintage	VG	F	VF	XF	Unc
1752	—	3.00	6.00	12.00	25.00	—
1753	—	3.00	6.00	12.00	25.00	—

KM# 370 1/2 KREUZER

Copper **Ruler:** Adam Friedrich von Seinsheim **Obverse:** Crown above two shields within frame **Reverse:** Value within cartouche

Date	Mintage	VG	F	VF	XF	Unc
1762	—	4.00	8.00	16.00	35.00	—
ND	—	4.00	8.00	16.00	35.00	—

KM# 341 KREUZER

Copper **Obverse:** Crowned two-fold arms within branches **Reverse:** Value, date **Note:** Similar to 1/4 Kreuzer, KM#340.

Date	Mintage	VG	F	VF	XF	Unc
1752	—	10.00	20.00	35.00	65.00	—
1753	—	10.00	20.00	35.00	65.00	—

KM# 239 2 KREUZER (1/2 Batzen)

Silver **Ruler:** Johann Philipp II von Greifenklau-Vollraths **Obverse:** Crowned round four-fold arms of Wurzburg and Greifenklau, value 2 in oval at bottom divides date **Reverse:** Madonna and child

Date	Mintage	VG	F	VF	XF	Unc
1704	—	12.00	30.00	60.00	95.00	—
1706	—	12.00	30.00	60.00	95.00	—

KM# 240 2 KREUZER (1/2 Batzen)

Silver **Ruler:** Johann Philipp II von Greifenklau-Vollraths **Obverse:** Three helmets above four-fold arms divide date **Reverse:** St. Kilian, 2 in shield below

Date	Mintage	VG	F	VF	XF	Unc
1704	—	12.00	30.00	60.00	95.00	—
1706	—	12.00	30.00	60.00	95.00	—

KM# 377 2 KREUZER (1/2 Batzen)

Billon **Ruler:** Adam Friedrich von Seinsheim **Obverse:** AF monogram **Reverse:** Arms

Date	Mintage	VG	F	VF	XF	Unc
1764	—	15.00	35.00	70.00	125	—
1765	—	15.00	35.00	70.00	125	—

KM# 260 3 KREUZER (Groschen)

Silver **Ruler:** Johann Philipp II von Greifenklau-Vollraths **Subject:** Death of Johann Philipp II **Obverse:** Crowned and supported round four-fold arms of Wurzburg and Greifenklau, inscriptions in two ribbons above **Reverse:** Six-line inscription with dates, value: 3 on imperial orb below **Note:** Varieties exist.

Date	Mintage	VG	F	VF	XF	Unc
1719	—	18.00	40.00	70.00	125	—

KM# 272 3 KREUZER (Groschen)

Silver **Ruler:** Johann Philipp Franz, Graf von Schonborn **Subject:** Death of Johann Philipp Franz **Obverse:** Crowned and mantled oval ten-fold arms with central shield of Schonborn **Reverse:** Nine-line inscription with dates, value: 3 on imperial orb divides bottom line **Note:** Varieties exist.

Date	Mintage	VG	F	VF	XF	Unc
1724	—	12.00	25.00	50.00	95.00	—

KM# 293 3 KREUZER (Groschen)

Silver **Ruler:** Christoph Franz von Hutten **Subject:** Death of Christian Franz **Obverse:** Crowned and mantled oval four-fold arms of Wurzburg and Hutten **Reverse:** Inscription **Note:** Varieties exist.

Date	Mintage	VG	F	VF	XF	Unc
1729	—	20.00	40.00	80.00	140	—

KM# 324 3 KREUZER (Groschen)

Silver, 25 mm. **Ruler:** Friedrich Karl Graf von Schonborn **Subject:** Death of Friedrich Karl **Obverse:** Crowned and mantled complex arms **Reverse:** Inscription

Date	Mintage	VG	F	VF	XF	Unc
1746	—	20.00	35.00	65.00	130	—

KM# 325 3 KREUZER (Groschen)

Silver **Ruler:** Anselm Franz, Graf von Ingelheim **Subject:** Death of Anselm Franz **Obverse:** Crowned and mantled oval four-fold arms with central shield of Ingelheim **Reverse:** Nine-line inscription with dates, value: 3 on imperial orb divides bottom line **Note:** Varieties exist.

Date	Mintage	VG	F	VF	XF	Unc
1749	—	10.00	20.00	35.00	70.00	—

KM# 342 3 KREUZER (Groschen)

Silver **Ruler:** Karl Philipp von Greifenklau **Subject:** Death of Karl Philipp **Obverse:** Crowned complex arms **Reverse:** Inscription

Date	Mintage	VG	F	VF	XF	Unc
1754	—	15.00	28.00	55.00	110	—

KM# 410 3 KREUZER (Groschen)

Billon **Ruler:** Adam Friedrich von Seinsheim **Subject:** Death of Anselm Friedrich **Obverse:** Crowned and mantled arms **Reverse:** Inscription

Date	Mintage	VG	F	VF	XF	Unc
1779	—	10.00	20.00	40.00	80.00	—

KM# 444 3 KREUZER (Groschen)

Silver, 21 mm. **Ruler:** Franz Ludwig von Erthal **Subject:** Death of Franz Ludwig **Obverse:** Crowned arms **Obv. Legend:** ...F. OR. DUX... **Reverse:** Nine-line inscription

Date	Mintage	VG	F	VF	XF	Unc
1795	—	7.00	15.00	30.00	60.00	—

KM# 445 3 KREUZER (Groschen)

Silver **Ruler:** Franz Ludwig von Erthal **Subject:** Death of Franz Ludwig **Obverse:** Crowned arms **Obv. Legend:** ...F. O. DUX... **Reverse:** Inscription

Date	Mintage	VG	F	VF	XF	Unc
1795	—	5.00	10.00	20.00	40.00	—

KM# 446 3 KREUZER (Groschen)

Silver **Reverse:** Inscription: MARZ instead of MERZ in fifth line

Date	Mintage	VG	F	VF	XF	Unc
1795	—	—	—	—	—	—

KM# 241 4 KREUZER (Batzen)

Silver **Ruler:** Johann Philipp II von Greifenklau-Vollraths **Obverse:** Three helmets above four-fold arms divide date **Reverse:** St. Kilian, 4 in shield below

Date	Mintage	VG	F	VF	XF	Unc
1704	—	18.00	40.00	80.00	135	—
1705	—	18.00	40.00	80.00	135	—
ND	—	18.00	40.00	80.00	135	—

KM# 244 4 KREUZER (Batzen)

Silver **Ruler:** Johann Philipp II von Greifenklau-Vollraths **Obverse:** Crowned round four-fold arms of Wurzburg and Greiffenklau, in oval at bottom divide date **Reverse:** Madonna and child

Date	Mintage	VG	F	VF	XF	Unc
1706	—	18.00	40.00	80.00	135	—

KM# 245 4 KREUZER (Batzen)

Silver **Ruler:** Johann Philipp II von Greifenklau-Vollraths **Obverse:** Date divided above arms

Date	Mintage	VG	F	VF	XF	Unc
1706	—	12.00	30.00	60.00	95.00	—

KM# 321 4 KREUZER (Batzen)

Silver **Ruler:** Anselm Franz, Graf von Ingelheim **Obverse:** Crowned and mantled four-fold arms with center shield of Ingelheim, value: 4 below **Reverse:** Madonna and child on crescent, date divided below

Date	Mintage	VG	F	VF	XF	Unc
1748	—	8.00	18.00	32.00	55.00	—

KM# 372 4 KREUZER (Batzen)

Billon **Ruler:** Adam Friedrich von Seinsheim **Obverse:** Arms **Reverse:** Madonna

Date	Mintage	VG	F	VF	XF	Unc
1763	—	6.00	12.00	25.00	50.00	—

KM# 322 5 KREUZER

Silver **Ruler:** Anselm Franz, Graf von Ingelheim **Obverse:** Crowned and mantled four-fold arms with center shield of Ingelheim, V at bottom **Reverse:** Madonna and child on crescent, date divided below

Date	Mintage	VG	F	VF	XF	Unc
1748 WF	—	7.00	15.00	28.00	50.00	—

KM# 378 5 KREUZER

Billon **Ruler:** Adam Friedrich von Seinsheim **Obverse:** Crowned complex arms **Reverse:** Crowned monogram **Note:** Convention 5 Kreuzer.

Date	Mintage	VG	F	VF	XF	Unc
1764	—	10.00	20.00	40.00	90.00	—
1765	—	10.00	20.00	40.00	90.00	—

KM# 389 5 KREUZER

Copper **Ruler:** Adam Friedrich von Seinsheim **Note:** Klippe.

Date	Mintage	VG	F	VF	XF	Unc
1765	—	20.00	40.00	70.00	150	—

KM# 290 6 KREUZER

Silver **Ruler:** Christoph Franz von Hutten **Obverse:** Three helmets above oval four-fold arms of Wurzburg and Hutten, value: 6.K in cartouche at bottom divides date **Reverse:** Crowned and mantled oval with ornate CF monogram

Date	Mintage	VG	F	VF	XF	Unc
1728	—	35.00	60.00	120	200	—

KM# 357 10 KREUZER

Silver **Ruler:** Adam Friedrich von Seinsheim **Obverse:** Bust right **Reverse:** Standing Madonna holding child

Date	Mintage	VG	F	VF	XF	Unc
1760 NB	—	75.00	125	200	350	—
1762 NB	—	—	—	—	—	—
1762	—	—	—	—	—	—

KM# 356 10 KREUZER

Silver **Ruler:** Adam Friedrich von Seinsheim **Obverse:** Bust right **Reverse:** Arms **Note:** Convention 10 Kreuzer.

Date	Mintage	VG	F	VF	XF	Unc
1760 OE/GN PB	—	15.00	30.00	60.00	125	—

KM# 373 10 KREUZER

Silver **Ruler:** Adam Friedrich von Seinsheim **Obverse:** Bust right within branches **Obv. Legend:** AD • FRI • D • G • EP • BAM • - ET WIR • S • R • I • P • F • O • D • **Reverse:** Crowned arms

Date	Mintage	VG	F	VF	XF	Unc
1763 R MP	—	10.00	20.00	40.00	90.00	—
1763 L MP	—	10.00	20.00	40.00	90.00	—
1764 R MP	—	10.00	20.00	40.00	90.00	—
1764 L MP	—	10.00	20.00	40.00	90.00	—
1765 R MP	—	10.00	20.00	40.00	90.00	—
1766 R MP	—	10.00	20.00	40.00	90.00	—
1767 R MP	—	10.00	20.00	40.00	90.00	—

KM# 281 15 KREUZER (1/4 Gulden)

Silver **Ruler:** Christoph Franz von Hutten **Obverse:** Bust right **Reverse:** Three helmets above oval four-fold arms of Wurzburg and Hutten, value: XV in cartouche divides date

Date	Mintage	VG	F	VF	XF	Unc
1725 N	—	50.00	90.00	160	245	—

KM# 287 15 KREUZER (1/4 Gulden)

Silver **Ruler:** Christoph Franz von Hutten **Obverse:** Three helmets above oval four-fold arms of Wurzburg and Hutten **Reverse:** Crowned and mantled oval with ornate CF monogram, date divided at bottom, without value

Date	Mintage	VG	F	VF	XF	Unc
1726	—	45.00	85.00	155	240	—

KM# 368 20 KREUZER

Silver **Ruler:** Adam Friedrich von Seinsheim **Obverse:** Bust right **Reverse:** Crowned arms

Date	Mintage	F	VF	XF	Unc
1760 OE GN P B	—	20.00	40.00	80.00	160
1762 F(N)S	—	20.00	40.00	80.00	160
1762 NB	—	20.00	40.00	80.00	160

KM# 358 20 KREUZER

Silver **Ruler:** Adam Friedrich von Seinsheim **Obverse:** Bust right **Obv. Legend:** AD • FRI • D • G • EP • BAM • ET WIR • S • R • I • P • F • O • D • **Reverse:** Standing Madonna holding child **Note:** Convention 20 Kreuzer.

Date	Mintage	F	VF	XF	Unc
1760	—	10.00	16.00	32.00	75.00
1763 MP	—	10.00	16.00	32.00	75.00
1764	—	10.00	16.00	32.00	75.00

KM# 369 20 KREUZER

Silver **Ruler:** Adam Friedrich von Seinsheim **Obverse:** Crowned arms **Reverse:** Value and date

Date	Mintage	F	VF	XF	Unc
1761 NB	—	10.00	16.00	32.00	75.00
1762 NB	—	10.00	16.00	32.00	75.00

KM# 371 20 KREUZER

Silver **Ruler:** Adam Friedrich von Seinsheim **Obverse:** Armored bust right **Obv. Legend:** AD • FRI • D • G • EP • BAM • ET WIR • S • R • I • P • F • O • D • **Reverse:** Crowned arms on pedestal with value

Date	Mintage	F	VF	XF	Unc
1762 LOOS MP	—	6.00	10.00	20.00	60.00
1762 MP	—	6.00	10.00	20.00	60.00
1762 OE FS	—	6.00	10.00	20.00	60.00
1763 MP	—	6.00	10.00	20.00	60.00
1763 V. LON MP	—	6.00	10.00	20.00	60.00
1763 L MP	—	6.00	10.00	20.00	60.00
1763 LOOS MP	—	6.00	10.00	20.00	60.00
1764 L MP	—	6.00	10.00	20.00	60.00
1765 L MP	—	6.00	10.00	20.00	60.00
1769 RF MP	—	6.00	10.00	20.00	60.00
1773 R MP	—	6.00	10.00	20.00	60.00
1774 RF MP	—	6.00	10.00	20.00	60.00
1776 RF MP	—	6.00	10.00	20.00	60.00
1777 RF MP	—	6.00	10.00	20.00	60.00

KM# 379 20 KREUZER

Silver **Ruler:** Adam Friedrich von Seinsheim **Obverse:** Bust in wreath **Reverse:** Arms on pedestal

Date	Mintage	F	VF	XF	Unc
1764 L MP	—	12.00	20.00	40.00	100
1765 L MP	—	12.00	20.00	40.00	100
1766 MP	—	12.00	20.00	40.00	100
1767 R MP	—	12.00	20.00	40.00	100
1768 MP	—	12.00	20.00	40.00	100
1768 R MP	—	12.00	20.00	40.00	100
1769 MP	—	12.00	20.00	40.00	100
1769 R MP	—	12.00	20.00	40.00	100
1770 MP	—	12.00	20.00	40.00	100

KM# 411 20 KREUZER

Silver **Obverse:** Bust with ermine mantle **Reverse:** Crowned and mantled round arms

Date	Mintage	VG	F	VF	XF	Unc
1779	—	85.00	135	200	400	—

Note: Supposedly removed from circulation at the insistence of the Bishop's brother, the Elector of Mainz; He contended that ermine mantles were to be worn only by electors

KM# 420 20 KREUZER

Silver **Ruler:** Franz Ludwig von Erthal **Obverse:** Draped bust right **Obv. Legend:** FRANC • LUD • D • G • EP • BAM • ET WIR • S • R • I • P • F • O • DUX • **Reverse:** Arms within crowned mantle, value below **Note:** Varieties exist.

Date	Mintage	VG	F	VF	XF	Unc
1780 RF MP	—	25.00	45.00	90.00	180	—
1783 RF MP	—	25.00	45.00	90.00	180	—
1784 G MP	—	25.00	45.00	90.00	180	—
1784 RF MP	—	25.00	45.00	90.00	180	—
1784 OE MP	—	25.00	45.00	90.00	180	—

KM# 422 20 KREUZER

Silver **Ruler:** Franz Ludwig von Erthal **Obverse:** Draped bust right **Obv. Legend:** FRANC • LUD • D • G • EP • BAM • ET WIR • S • R • I • P • F • O • DUX • **Reverse:** Saint on pedestal with value **Note:** Varieties exist.

Date	Mintage	VG	F	VF	XF	Unc
1785 RF MP	—	20.00	35.00	65.00	140	—
1786 RF MP	—	20.00	35.00	65.00	140	—
1787 RF MP	—	20.00	35.00	65.00	140	—
1787 G MP	—	20.00	35.00	65.00	140	—
1790 RF MP	—	20.00	35.00	65.00	140	—

KM# 431 20 KREUZER

Silver **Ruler:** Franz Ludwig von Erthal **Obverse:** Draped bust right **Obv. Legend:** FRANC • LUD • D • G • .... **Reverse:** Arms within crowned mantle **Note:** Varieties exist.

Date	Mintage	VG	F	VF	XF	Unc
1788 MP	—	20.00	35.00	65.00	140	—
1789 MP	—	20.00	35.00	65.00	140	—
1790 MP	—	20.00	35.00	65.00	140	—
1791 MP	—	20.00	35.00	65.00	140	—
1791 RF MP	—	20.00	35.00	65.00	140	—

Date	Mintage	VG	F	VF	XF	Unc
1791 G MP	—	20.00	35.00	65.00	140	—
1791 GF MP	—	20.00	35.00	65.00	140	—

KM# 448 20 KREUZER

Silver **Ruler:** Georg Karl, Freiherr von Fechenbach, Bishop **Obverse:** Arms within crowned mantle **Obv. Legend:** GEORG • CAROL • D • G • EP • WIR • S • R • I • PR • FR • OR • DUX • **Reverse:** Value and date within branches **Rev. Legend:** PRO PATRIA/LX/EINE FEINE/MARK/1795/MM/20 **Note:** Varieties exist.

Date	Mintage	VG	F	VF	XF	Unc
1795 MM	—	30.00	50.00	100	200	—

KM# 450 20 KREUZER

Silver **Ruler:** Georg Karl, Freiherr von Fechenbach, Bishop **Obverse:** Bust right **Reverse:** Value and date within branches **Note:** Varieties exist.

Date	Mintage	VG	F	VF	XF	Unc
1795 MM	—	35.00	60.00	120	235	—

KM# 451 20 KREUZER

Silver **Ruler:** Georg Karl, Freiherr von Fechenbach, Bishop **Obverse:** Bust right **Reverse:** Madonna

Date	Mintage	VG	F	VF	XF	Unc
1795 RF MM	—	25.00	40.00	65.00	185	—

KM# 452 20 KREUZER

Silver **Ruler:** Georg Karl, Freiherr von Fechenbach, Bishop **Obverse:** Bust right **Obv. Legend:** GEORG • CAROL • D • G • EP • WIRC • S • R • I • P • F • O • DUX • **Reverse:** Three saints on pedestals, value in center one, date below

Date	Mintage	VG	F	VF	XF	Unc
1795 MM	—	35.00	50.00	75.00	225	—

KM# 447 20 KREUZER

Silver **Obverse:** Arms within crowned mantle **Reverse:** Value, date within branches

Date	Mintage	VG	F	VF	XF	Unc
1795 MM	—	30.00	50.00	100	200	—

KM# 449 20 KREUZER

Silver **Ruler:** Georg Karl, Freiherr von Fechenbach, Bishop **Obverse:** Bust right **Obv. Legend:** GEORG • CAROL • D • G • EP • WIR • S • R • I • PR • FR • OR • DUX • **Reverse:** Arms within Order collar **Rev. Legend:** PRO - PATRIA, below; 10 EINE FEINE - MARCK date

Date	Mintage	VG	F	VF	XF	Unc
1795 RF MM	—	35.00	50.00	100	200	—

KM# 459 20 KREUZER

Silver **Ruler:** Georg Karl, Freiherr von Fechenbach, Bishop **Obverse:** Bust right **Obv. Legend:** GEORG • CAROL • D • G • EP • WIRC • • S • R • I • PR • FR • O • DUX • **Reverse:** Crowned 2-fold arms within Order collar, value below

Date	Mintage	VG	F	VF	XF	Unc
1796 MM	—	25.00	40.00	65.00	185	—

KM# 255 1/8 THALER

Silver **Ruler:** Johann Philipp II von Greifenklau-Vollraths **Obverse:** Bust right **Reverse:** Three helmets above oval four-fold arms, date divided below

Date	Mintage	VG	F	VF	XF	Unc
1718	—	150	325	600	950	—

KM# 222 1/4 THALER

Silver **Ruler:** Johann Philipp II von Greifenklau-Vollraths **Obverse:** Bust right **Reverse:** Three helmets above oval four-fold arms, tiny date divided at bottom

Date	Mintage	VG	F	VF	XF	Unc
1702	—	150	325	600	1,000	—
1718	—	150	325	600	1,000	—

KM# 246 1/4 THALER

Silver **Ruler:** Johann Philipp II von Greifenklau-Vollraths **Obverse:** Bust right **Reverse:** Madonna and child above four-fold arms, tiny date divided at left and right

Date	Mintage	VG	F	VF	XF	Unc
1707	—	200	450	800	1,325	—

KM# 291 1/4 THALER

Silver **Ruler:** Christoph Franz von Hutten **Obverse:** Three helmets above oval four-fold arms of Wurzburg and Hutten, value: 1/4 in cartouche at bottom divides date **Reverse:** Crowned and mantled oval with ornate F monogram

Date	Mintage	VG	F	VF	XF	Unc
1728	—	120	250	500	925	—

KM# 292 1/4 THALER

Silver **Ruler:** Christoph Franz von Hutten **Obverse:** Bust right **Reverse:** Crowned and mantled oval four-fold arms of Wurzburg and Hutten, value: 1/4 in cartouche at bottom

Date	Mintage	VG	F	VF	XF	Unc
ND	—	150	325	600	1,000	—

KM# 223 1/2 THALER

Silver **Ruler:** Johann Philipp II von Greifenklau-Vollraths **Obverse:** Bust right **Reverse:** Crowned and supported oval four-fold arms, large fir tree above and behind, small date at bottom

Date	Mintage	VG	F	VF	XF	Unc
1702	—	220	450	800	1,300	—

KM# 224 1/2 THALER

Silver **Ruler:** Johann Philipp II von Greifenklau-Vollraths **Obverse:** Bust right **Reverse:** Crowned and mantled oval four-fold arms, tiny date divided at bottom

Date	Mintage	VG	F	VF	XF	Unc
1702	—	300	525	1,000	1,650	—

KM# 225 1/2 THALER

Silver **Ruler:** Johann Philipp II von Greifenklau-Vollraths **Obverse:** Bust right **Reverse:** Three saints on pedestals, date in chronogram

Date	Mintage	VG	F	VF	XF	Unc
1702	—	—	—	—	—	—

KM# 226 1/2 THALER

Silver **Ruler:** Johann Philipp II von Greifenklau-Vollraths **Obverse:** Bust right **Obv. Legend:** IOAN • PHILIP • D • G • EP • HERB • S • R • I • PR • FR • OR • DVX • **Reverse:** Three helmets above round four-fold arms, date divided below

Date	Mintage	VG	F	VF	XF	Unc
1702	—	220	450	800	1,300	—

KM# 247 1/2 THALER

Silver **Ruler:** Johann Philipp II von Greifenklau-Vollraths **Reverse:** Madonna and child above four-fold arms, tiny date divided at left and right

Date	Mintage	VG	F	VF	XF	Unc
1707	—	350	650	1,200	1,850	—

KM# 282 1/2 THALER

Silver **Ruler:** Christoph Franz von Hutten **Obverse:** Bust right **Obv. Legend:** CHRISTOPH: FRANC: D: G: EP: HERB: S: R: I: PR: FR: OR: DVX **Reverse:** Crowned and mantled oval four-fold arms of Wurzburg and Hutten, date divided at lower left and right of arms

Date	Mintage	VG	F	VF	XF	Unc
1725	—	150	325	600	1,000	—

KM# 288 1/2 THALER

Silver **Ruler:** Christoph Franz von Hutten **Obverse:** Three helmets above oval four-fold arms of Wurzburg and Hutten, without value **Obv. Legend:** CHRISTOPH • FRANC • D • G • EP • HERB • S • R • I • PR • FR • OR • DVX • **Reverse:** Crowned and mantled oval with ornate CF monogram, date at bottom

Date	Mintage	VG	F	VF	XF	Unc
1726	—	80.00	150	300	650	—

KM# 343 1/2 THALER

Silver **Ruler:** Karl Philipp von Greifenklau **Obverse:** Bust right **Reverse:** Crowned oval arms in baroque frame, value, date **Note:** Convention 1/2 Thaler.

Date	Mintage	VG	F	VF	XF	Unc
1754 I.L. OE-WG-BN	—	—	475	800	1,650	—

KM# 359 1/2 THALER

Silver **Ruler:** Adam Friedrich von Seinsheim **Obverse:** Bust right **Reverse:** Crowned and mantled arms

Date	Mintage	F	VF	XF	Unc
1760 GN-PB	—	120	200	375	650

KM# A369 1/2 THALER

Silver **Ruler:** Adam Friedrich von Seinsheim **Obverse:** Bust right **Reverse:** Madonna standing facing with child **Rev. Legend:** PATRONA - FRANCONIAE

Date	Mintage	F	VF	XF	Unc
1761 GN-PB	—	80.00	125	220	500

KM# 383 1/2 THALER

Silver **Ruler:** Adam Friedrich von Seinsheim **Obverse:** Bust right **Obv. Legend:** AD • FRI • D • G • EP • BAM • ET WIR • S • R • I • P • F • O • DUX • **Reverse:** Crowned arms with supporters

Date	Mintage	F	VF	XF	Unc
1764 INM-FHP	—	100	150	275	550
1765 INM-FHP	—	100	150	275	550

KM# 390 1/2 THALER

Silver **Ruler:** Adam Friedrich von Seinsheim **Obverse:** Bust right **Obv. Legend:** AD • FRI • D • G • EP • BAM • ET WIR • S • R • I • P • F • O • DUX • **Reverse:** Madonna and child **Rev. Legend:** PATRONA FRANCONIAE

Date	Mintage	F	VF	XF	Unc
1765 MP	—	80.00	15.00	220	500

KM# 221 THALER

Silver **Ruler:** Johann Philipp II von Greifenklau-Vollraths **Obverse:** Legend, date, bust right **Obv. Legend:** IOAN. PHILIP... **Reverse:** Helmeted arms **Note:** Dav. #2880

Date	Mintage	F	VF	XF	Unc
1701	—	800	1,250	2,000	3,500

KM# 227 THALER

Silver **Ruler:** Johann Philipp II von Greifenklau-Vollraths **Obverse:** Draped bust right **Obv. Legend:** IOAN • PHILIP • D • G • EP • HERB • S • R • I • PR • FR • OR • DVX • **Reverse:** Three saints on pedestalS **Rev. Legend:** HAC MAGNA TRIADE PATROCINANTE • **Note:** Dav. #2881.

Date	Mintage	F	VF	XF	Unc
1702	—	175	350	750	1,400

KM# 228 THALER

Silver **Ruler:** Johann Philipp II von Greifenklau-Vollraths **Obverse:** Draped bust right **Obv. Legend:** IOAN • PHILIP • D • G • EP • HERB • S • R • I • PR • FR • OR • DVX • **Reverse:** Crowned and mantled arms, date below **Rev. Legend:** ADIVTORIVM NOSTRVM IN NOMINE DOMINI **Note:** Dav. #2882.

Date	Mintage	F	VF	XF	Unc
1702	—	175	350	750	1,400

KM# 229 THALER

Silver **Ruler:** Johann Philipp II von Greifenklau-Vollraths **Obverse:** Bust right **Obv. Legend:** IOAN • PHILIP • D • G • EP • HERB • S • R • I • PR • FR • OR • DVX • **Reverse:** Tree above crowned and supported arms, date below **Rev. Legend:** SEMPER - IDEM • **Note:** Dav. #2883.

Date	Mintage	F	VF	XF	Unc
1702	—	175	350	750	1,400

KM# 230 THALER

Silver **Ruler:** Johann Philipp II von Greifenklau-Vollraths **Reverse:** Helmeted arms with divided date below **Note:** Dav. #2884.

Date	Mintage	F	VF	XF	Unc
1702	—	175	350	750	1,400
1707	—	175	350	750	1,400

KM# 248 THALER

Silver **Ruler:** Johann Philipp II von Greifenklau-Vollraths **Obverse:** Slightly larger bust **Reverse:** Madonna and child on cloud in rays, date divided below **Note:** Dav. #2885.

Date	Mintage	F	VF	XF	Unc
1707	—	275	550	1,000	1,750

KM# 283 THALER

Silver **Ruler:** Christoph Franz von Hutten **Obverse:** Bust right **Obv. Legend:** CHRISTOPH: FRANC: D. G. EP: HERB: S. R. I. PR: FR: OR: DVX. **Reverse:** Helmeted arms, date below **Rev. Legend:** MISERICORDIAS DOMINI IN ÆTERNVM CANTABO **Note:** Dav. #2886.

Date	Mintage	F	VF	XF	Unc
1725N	—	200	400	800	1,500
1726	—	200	400	800	1,500
1727	—	200	400	800	1,500
1728	—	200	400	800	1,500

KM# 345 THALER

Silver **Ruler:** Karl Philipp von Greifenklau **Reverse:** Undivided value ... MARCK **Note:** Dav. #2888.

Date	Mintage	F	VF	XF	Unc
1754 ILOE-WG-BN	—	450	850	1,650	2,600

KM# 344 THALER

Silver **Ruler:** Karl Philipp von Greifenklau **Obverse:** Draped bust right **Obv. Legend:** CAROL: PHILIPP: D: G: EP: HER: B: S: R: I: PR: FR: OR: DVX: **Reverse:** Crowned 4-fold arms within baroque frame divides date, value below **Rev. Legend:** 10 EINE - FEINE MAR. **Note:** Convention Thaler. Varieties exist. Dav. #2887.

Date	Mintage	F	VF	XF	Unc
1754 I.L. OE-WG-BN	—	400	800	1,600	2,500

KM# 363 THALER

Silver **Ruler:** Adam Friedrich von Seinsheim **Obverse:** Without OEXLEIN below bust **Note:** Dav. #2891A.

Date	Mintage	F	VF	XF	Unc
1760 GN-PB	—	300	600	1,250	2,500

KM# 365 THALER

Silver **Ruler:** Adam Friedrich von Seinsheim **Obv. Legend:** ADAM FRIDERIC... **Note:** Dav. #2892A.

Date	Mintage	F	VF	XF	Unc
1760 GN-PB	—	125	200	350	850

KM# 360 THALER

Silver **Ruler:** Adam Friedrich von Seinsheim **Obverse:** Bust right **Reverse:** Eleven-line inscription: date in chronogram **Note:** Dav. #2889.

Date	Mintage	F	VF	XF	Unc
1760	—	500	1,000	2,000	3,000

KM# 361 THALER

Silver **Ruler:** Adam Friedrich von Seinsheim **Reverse:** Crowned, mantled arms into legend **Note:** Dav. #2890.

Date	Mintage	F	VF	XF	Unc
1760 GN-PB	—	250	500	1,000	2,000

KM# 362 THALER

Silver **Ruler:** Adam Friedrich von Seinsheim **Obverse:** OEXLEIN below bust **Reverse:** Smaller arms within legend **Note:** Dav. #2891.

Date	Mintage	F	VF	XF	Unc
1760 GN-PB	—	250	500	1,000	2,000

KM# 364 THALER

Silver **Ruler:** Adam Friedrich von Seinsheim **Obverse:** Bust right **Obv. Legend:** AD • FRIDER • D • G • EP • BAM • ET WIRCEB • S • R • I • PR • FR • OR • DVX, OEXLEIN below **Reverse:** Madonna with child divides date **Rev. Legend:** PATRONA - FRANCONIÆ, X. EINE (W) F. MARK/G.N. - P.B. below **Note:** Dav. #2892.

Date	Mintage	F	VF	XF	Unc
1760 GN-PB	—	125	200	350	850

KM# 366 THALER

Silver **Ruler:** Karl Philipp von Greifenklau **Obv. Legend:** ADAM FRIDER... **Note:** Dav. #2892B.

Date	Mintage	F	VF	XF	Unc
1760 GN-PB	—	125	200	350	850

KM# 380 THALER

Silver **Ruler:** Adam Friedrich von Seinsheim **Obverse:** G.F. LOOS. F. below bust right **Obv. Legend:** ADAM • FRID • D • G • EP • BAM • ET WIRC •, S • R • I • PRIN • FR • OR • DUX • **Reverse:** Crowned arms with supporters **Rev. Legend:** 10 EINE FEINE - MARCK • 1763, I•N•M• * F•H•P• at bottom **Note:** Dav. #2893.

Date	Mintage	F	VF	XF	Unc
1763 INM-FHP	—	75.00	125	250	650

KM# 381 THALER

Silver **Ruler:** Adam Friedrich von Seinsheim **Obverse:** V. LON F. below bust **Note:** Dav. #2893A.

Date	Mintage	F	VF	XF	Unc
1763 INM-FHP	—	75.00	125	250	650

KM# 375 THALER

Silver **Ruler:** Adam Friedrich von Seinsheim **Obverse:** G.F. LOOS. F. below bust **Reverse:** Seated Madonna holding child **Note:** Dav. #2894.

Date	Mintage	F	VF	XF	Unc
1763 MP	—	500	1,000	2,000	4,000

KM# 382 THALER

Silver **Ruler:** Adam Friedrich von Seinsheim **Obverse:** Draped bust right **Obv. Legend:** ADAM • FRID • D • G • EP • BAM • ET WIRC • S • R • I • PR • FR • OR • DVX **Reverse:** Madonna and child **Rev. Legend:** PATRONA - FRANCONIAE, 10 EINE FEINE - MARCK date **Note:** Dav. #2894A.

Date	Mintage	F	VF	XF	Unc
1763 MP	—	65.00	100	200	500
1764 MP	—	65.00	100	200	500

KM# 385 THALER

Silver **Ruler:** Adam Friedrich von Seinsheim **Obverse:** Bust right **Obv. Legend:** ADAM • FRID • D • G • EP • BAM • ET WIRC • S • R • I • PRIN • FR • OR • DUX • **Reverse:** Crowned 4-fold arms with supporters **Rev. Legend:** PATRONA - FRANCONIAE, 10 EINE FEINE - MARCK date **Note:** Dav. #2896.

Date	Mintage	F	VF	XF	Unc
1764 INM-FHP	—	75.00	125	250	650

KM# 387 THALER

Silver **Ruler:** Adam Friedrich von Seinsheim **Obverse:** G.F. LOOS F. below bust **Note:** Dav. #2897.

Date	Mintage	F	VF	XF	Unc
1764 MP	—	65.00	100	200	500

KM# 386 THALER

Silver **Ruler:** Adam Friedrich von Seinsheim **Obverse:** LOOS below bust **Obv. Legend:** AD • FRI • D • G • EP • BAM • ET • WIR • S • R • I • P • F • O • DUX • **Reverse:** Madonna and child **Rev. Legend:** PATRONA - FRANCONIAE, 10 EINE FEINE - MARCK date **Note:** Dav. #2897A.

Date	Mintage	F	VF	XF	Unc
1764 MP	—	65.00	100	200	500

KM# 384 THALER

Silver **Ruler:** Adam Friedrich von Seinsheim **Obverse:** Bust right **Obv. Legend:** AD. FRI. D.G. EP. BAM. ET WIR. S. R. I. P. F. O. DUX **Reverse:** Crowned arms with supporters, 'W' below in frame **Rev. Legend:** PATRONA - FRANCONIAE, 10 EINE FEINE - MARCK date **Note:** Dav. #2895.

Date	Mintage	F	VF	XF	Unc
1764 INM-FHP	—	75.00	125	250	650

KM# 391 THALER

Silver **Ruler:** Adam Friedrich von Seinsheim **Obverse:** L below bust **Note:** Dav. #2896A.

Date	Mintage	F	VF	XF	Unc
1765 INM-FHP	—	65.00	100	200	500

KM# 393 THALER

Silver **Ruler:** Adam Friedrich von Seinsheim **Obverse:** LOOS below bust **Note:** Dav. #2898.

Date	Mintage	F	VF	XF	Unc
1765 MP	—	65.00	100	200	500
1766 MP	—	65.00	100	200	500

KM# 394 THALER

Silver **Ruler:** Adam Friedrich von Seinsheim **Obverse:** G.F. LOOS F. below bust **Note:** Dav. #2898A.

Date	Mintage	F	VF	XF	Unc
1765 MP	—	65.00	100	200	500
1766 MP	—	65.00	100	200	500

KM# 395 THALER

Silver **Ruler:** Adam Friedrich von Seinsheim **Obverse:** L below bust **Note:** Dav. #2898B.

Date	Mintage	F	VF	XF	Unc
1765 MP	—	65.00	100	200	500

KM# 392 THALER

Silver **Ruler:** Adam Friedrich von Seinsheim **Obverse:** Draped bust right **Obv. Legend:** AD • FRI • D • G • EP • BAM • ET • WIR • S • R • I • PR • FR • OR • DUX • **Reverse:** Madonna and child **Rev. Legend:** PATRONA - FRANCONIAE, 10 EINE FEINE - MARCK date **Note:** Dav. #2899.

Date	Mintage	F	VF	XF	Unc
1765 MP	—	65.00	100	200	500

KM# 396 THALER

Silver **Ruler:** Adam Friedrich von Seinsheim **Note:** Dav. #2900.

Date	Mintage	F	VF	XF	Unc
1766 MP	—	650	1,000	1,800	3,500

KM# 397 THALER

Silver **Ruler:** Adam Friedrich von Seinsheim **Obverse:** L below bust **Reverse:** Crowned arms with supporters, 'W' in frame below **Note:** Dav. #2901.

Date	Mintage	F	VF	XF	Unc
1767 MP	—	75.00	125	250	650
1769 MP	—	75.00	125	250	650
1770 MP	—	75.00	125	250	650

KM# 398 THALER

Silver **Obverse:** R.F. below bust **Obv. Legend:** AD • FRI • D • G • EP - BAM • ET WIR • S • R • I • PR • FR • OR • DUX. **Reverse:** Crowned and supported arms, W in cartouche below **Rev. Legend:** 10 EINE FEINE - MARCK. date **Note:** Dav. #2901A.

Date	Mintage	F	VF	XF	Unc
1769 MP	—	75.00	125	250	650
1770 MP	—	75.00	125	250	650
1771 MP	—	75.00	125	250	650
1772 MP	—	75.00	125	250	650
1773 MP	—	75.00	125	250	650

KM# 407 THALER

Silver **Ruler:** Adam Friedrich von Seinsheim **Obverse:** R.F. below bust **Obv. Legend:** AD • FRI • D • G • EP • BAM • ET • WIR • S • R • I • PR • FR • OR • DUX • **Reverse:** Crowned arms with supporters, "W" in frame below **Rev. Legend:** 10 EINE FEINE - MARCK **Note:** Dav. #2901B.

Date	Mintage	F	VF	XF	Unc
1773 INM-FHP	—	75.00	125	250	650
1774 INM-FHP	—	75.00	125	250	650
1777 INM-FHP	—	75.00	125	250	650

KM# 406 THALER

Silver **Ruler:** Adam Friedrich von Seinsheim **Note:** Varieties exist. Dav. #2902.

Date	Mintage	F	VF	XF	Unc
1773 MP	—	80.00	140	275	600
1775 MP	—	80.00	140	275	600
1776 MP	—	80.00	140	275	600
1779 MP	—	80.00	140	275	600

KM# 413 THALER

Silver **Ruler:** Franz Ludwig von Erthal **Note:** Dav. #2904.

Date	Mintage	F	VF	XF	Unc
1779 MP	—	75.00	125	250	525
1781 MP	—	75.00	125	250	525
1784 MP	—	75.00	125	250	525

KM# 412 THALER

Silver **Ruler:** Franz Ludwig von Erthal **Obverse:** Bust right **Obv. Legend:** FRANC • LUDOV • D • G • EP • WIRC • S • R • I • PR • FR • OR • DUX • **Reverse:** Arms within crowned mantle **Rev. Legend:** 10 • EINE FEINE - MARCK **Note:** Dav. #2903.

Date	Mintage	F	VF	XF	Unc
1779 MP	—	100	150	285	750

KM# 423 THALER

Silver **Ruler:** Franz Ludwig von Erthal **Note:** Dav. #2905.

Date	Mintage	F	VF	XF	Unc
1785 MP	—	75.00	125	250	650

KM# 426 THALER

Silver **Ruler:** Franz Ludwig von Erthal **Obverse:** Draped bust right **Obv. Legend:** FRANC • LUDOV • D • G • EP • BAMB • ET • WIRC • S • R • I • PR • FR • OR • DUX • **Reverse:** Cherub with book and globe divides date, value below **Rev. Legend:** MERCES LABORUM, in exergue; X. EINE FEINE/MARCK **Note:** Dav. #2907.

Date	Mintage	F	VF	XF	Unc
1786 MP	—	100	150	300	700
1787 MP	—	100	150	300	700
1791 MP	—	100	150	300	700

KM# 425 THALER

Silver **Ruler:** Franz Ludwig von Erthal **Obverse:** Draped bust right **Obv. Legend:** FRANC ? LUDOV ? D ? G ? EP ? BAMB ? ET ? WIRC ? S ? R ? I ? PR ? FR ? OR ? DUX ? **Reverse:** Madonna with child **Rev. Legend:** PATRONA - FRANCONI?, below; 10 E ? FEINE - MARK **Note:** Dav. #2908.

Date	Mintage	F	VF	XF	Unc
1786 MP	—	80.00	125	250	525

KM# 435 THALER

Silver **Ruler:** Franz Ludwig von Erthal **Obverse:** G.F. below bust **Obv. Legend:** FRANC • LUDOV • D • G • EP • BAMB • ET • WIRC • S • R • I • PR • FR • OR • DUX • **Reverse:** Saint on pedestal divides date, value in exergue **Rev. Legend:** * S • KILIANUS • FRAN - CORUM. APOSTOLUS, below; X • EINE • FEINE/MARCK **Note:** Dav. #2909.

Date	Mintage	F	VF	XF	Unc
1790 MP	—	125	200	350	800

KM# 439 THALER

Silver **Ruler:** Franz Ludwig von Erthal **Obverse:** R.F. below bust **Obv. Legend:** FRANC • LUDOV • D • G • EP • BAMB • ET • WIRC • S • R • I • PR • FR • OR • DUX • **Reverse:** Cherub with book and globe divides date, value below **Rev. Legend:** MERCES LABORUM, below; X • EINE FEINE/MARCK **Note:** Dav. #2910.

Date	Mintage	F	VF	XF	Unc
1794 MP	—	125	200	350	800

KM# 440 THALER

Silver **Ruler:** Franz Ludwig von Erthal **Reverse:** Value and date in sprays; PRO PATRIA above **Note:** Contribution Thaler. Dav. #2911.

Date	Mintage	F	VF	XF	Unc
1794 MM	—	125	200	350	800
1795 MM	—	125	200	350	800

KM# 441 THALER

Silver **Ruler:** Franz Ludwig von Erthal **Obverse:** Crowned and mantled arms: W below **Obv. Legend:** FRANC • LUD • D • G • EP • BAMB • - ET • WIRC • S • R • I • PR • FR • OR • DUX • **Reverse:** Value and date within laurel wreath **Rev. Legend:** PRO PATRIA, in wreath; X/EINE FEINE/MARK/date **Note:** Contribution Thaler. Dav. #2912.

Date	Mintage	F	VF	XF	Unc
1794 MM	—	175	385	800	1,600
1795 MM	—	175	385	800	1,600

KM# 453 THALER

Silver **Ruler:** Georg Karl, Freiherr von Fechenbach, Bishop **Obverse:** Bust right **Obv. Legend:** GEORG • CAROL • D • G • EP • WIRC • S • R • I • PR • FR • OR • DUX • **Reverse:** Crowned arms divide M M **Rev. Legend:** PRO PATRIA, below; X • EINE FEINE MARCK 1795 **Note:** Contribution Thaler. Dav. #2913.

Date	Mintage	F	VF	XF	Unc
1795 MM	—	100	150	325	750

KM# 454 THALER

Silver **Ruler:** Georg Karl, Freiherr von Fechenbach, Bishop **Obverse:** Bust right **Obv. Legend:** GEORG • CAROL • D • G • EP • WIRC • S • R • I • PR • FR • OR • DUX • **Reverse:** Value and date in laurel wreath **Rev. Legend:** PRO PATRIA, in wreath; * X */EINEFEINE/MARK/1795 **Note:** Contribution Thaler. Dav. #2914.

Date	Mintage	F	VF	XF	Unc
1795 MM	—	150	250	550	1,100

KM# 455 THALER

Silver **Reverse:** Value: X, EINE FEINE MARCK, date in sprays **Note:** Contribution Thaler. Dav. #2915.

Date	Mintage	F	VF	XF	Unc
1795 MM	—	175	300	600	1,200

KM# 427 2 THALER

Silver **Ruler:** Franz Ludwig von Erthal **Note:** Convention 2 Thaler. Prize Double Thalers. Dav. #2906.

Date	Mintage	F	VF	XF	Unc
1786 MP	—	400	800	1,200	2,200
1787 MP	—	400	800	1,200	2,200
1791 MP	—	400	800	1,200	2,200

TRADE COINAGE

KM# 294 GOLDGULDEN

3.2500 g., 0.7700 Gold 0.0805 oz. AGW **Obverse:** Arms **Reverse:** Franconia standing with lion at side

Date	Mintage	VG	F	VF	XF	Unc
1729	—	275	600	1,250	2,250	—

KM# 326 GOLDGULDEN

3.2500 g., 0.7700 Gold 0.0805 oz. AGW **Ruler:** Karl Philipp von Greifenklau **Obverse:** Bust right **Obv. Legend:** CAROLUS • PHILIPP • D • G • .... **Reverse:** Crowned and helmeted arms **Rev. Legend:** SINCERE FORTITER ET CONSTANTER

Date	Mintage	VG	F	VF	XF	Unc
ND(1749)	—	300	650	1,600	2,800	—

KM# 327 GOLDGULDEN

3.2500 g., 0.7700 Gold 0.0805 oz. AGW **Obverse:** Arms topped by three helmets **Reverse:** Griffon

Date	Mintage	VG	F	VF	XF	Unc
ND(1749)	—	400	900	1,600	2,800	—

KM# 346 GOLDGULDEN

3.2500 g., 0.7700 Gold 0.0805 oz. AGW **Ruler:** Karl Philipp von Greifenklau **Subject:** Homage of Wurzburg **Obverse:** Bust right

Date	Mintage	F	VF	XF	Unc
1755	—	375	650	1,250	2,500

KM# 347 GOLDGULDEN

3.2500 g., 0.7700 Gold 0.0805 oz. AGW **Ruler:** Adam Friedrich von Seinsheim **Obverse:** Angel above arms **Obv. Legend:** ADAM • FRID • D • G • EP • .... **Reverse:** Three female figures

Date	Mintage	F	VF	XF	Unc
ND(1755)	—	275	550	1,150	2,250

KM# 388 GOLDGULDEN

3.2500 g., 0.7700 Gold 0.0805 oz. AGW **Ruler:** Adam Friedrich von Seinsheim **Subject:** Peace of Hubertusburg **Obverse:** Bust right **Reverse:** Franconia standing

Date	Mintage	F	VF	XF	Unc
1764	—	400	800	1,650	2,750

KM# 408 GOLDGULDEN

3.2500 g., 0.7700 Gold 0.0805 oz. AGW **Ruler:** Adam Friedrich von Seinsheim **Obverse:** Bust right **Obv. Legend:** AD • FRI • D • G • EP • BAM • ET WIR • S • R • I • P • F • O • DUX • **Reverse:** Tree above arms, date below

Date	Mintage	F	VF	XF	Unc
1773	—	275	550	1,100	2,000
1774	—	275	550	1,100	2,000
1777	—	275	550	1,100	2,000
1778	—	275	550	1,100	2,000

KM# 414 GOLDGULDEN

3.2500 g., 0.7700 Gold 0.0805 oz. AGW **Ruler:** Franz Ludwig von Erthal **Obverse:** Bust right **Reverse:** Tree above arms, date below

Date	Mintage	F	VF	XF	Unc
1779	—	275	550	1,000	1,850

KM# 428 GOLDGULDEN

3.2500 g., 0.7700 Gold 0.0805 oz. AGW **Ruler:** Franz Ludwig von Erthal **Obverse:** Bust right **Reverse:** Standing saint divides date

Date	Mintage	F	VF	XF	Unc
1786	—	350	700	1,500	2,500

KM# 429 GOLDGULDEN

3.2500 g., 0.7700 Gold 0.0805 oz. AGW **Ruler:** Franz Ludwig von Erthal **Obverse:** Bust right **Obv. Legend:** FRANC • LUD • D • G • EP • BAM • ET WIR • S • R • I • P • F • O • DUX • **Reverse:** Helmeted arms divide date

Date	Mintage	F	VF	XF	Unc
1786	—	275	550	1,100	2,000

Date	Mintage	F	VF	XF	Unc
1791	—	275	550	1,100	2,000
1794	—	275	550	1,100	2,000

KM# 436 GOLDGULDEN

3.2500 g., 0.7700 Gold 0.0805 oz. AGW **Ruler:** Franz Ludwig von Erthal **Obverse:** Bust right; arms at shoulder **Reverse:** St. Burkhard standing dividing date; value in exergue

Date	Mintage	F	VF	XF	Unc
1790	—	300	600	1,200	2,200

KM# 457 GOLDGULDEN

3.2500 g., 0.7700 Gold 0.0805 oz. AGW **Obverse:** Arms **Reverse:** Palm tree

Date	Mintage	F	VF	XF	Unc
1795	—	300	600	1,250	2,250

KM# 460 GOLDGULDEN

3.2500 g., 0.7700 Gold 0.0805 oz. AGW **Ruler:** Georg Karl, Freiherr von Fechenbach, Bishop **Obverse:** Bust left **Reverse:** City view

Date	Mintage	F	VF	XF	Unc
1798	—	450	850	1,650	2,750

KM# 295 2 GOLDGULDEN

6.5000 g., 0.7700 Gold 0.1609 oz. AGW **Obverse:** Arms **Reverse:** Franconia standing with lion at side

Date	Mintage	VG	F	VF	XF	Unc
1729	—	1,500	2,500	4,500	7,500	—

KM# 430 2 GOLDGULDEN

3.5000 g., 0.9860 Gold 0.1109 oz. AGW **Ruler:** Franz Ludwig von Erthal **Obverse:** Bust right **Obv. Legend:** FRANC • LUD • D • G • EP • BAR • ETWIR • S • R • I • P • F • O • DUX • **Reverse:** St. Kilianus

Date	Mintage	F	VF	XF	Unc
1786	—	500	1,000	2,000	3,000

KM# 309 1/4 CAROLIN (2-1/2 Gulden)

2.4250 g., 0.7700 Gold 0.0600 oz. AGW **Ruler:** Friedrich Karl Graf von Schonborn **Obverse:** Bust right **Obv. Legend:** FRID • CAR • D • G • EP • .... **Reverse:** Arms within crowned mantle

Date	Mintage	VG	F	VF	XF	Unc
1735	—	175	375	750	1,450	—
1736	—	175	375	750	1,450	—

KM# 314 1/4 CAROLIN (2-1/2 Gulden)

2.4250 g., 0.7700 Gold 0.0600 oz. AGW **Ruler:** Friedrich Karl Graf von Schonborn **Reverse:** Crowned and mantled oval with FC monogram

Date	Mintage	VG	F	VF	XF	Unc
1736	—	175	375	750	1,450	—

KM# 310 1/2 CAROLIN (5 Gulden)

4.8500 g., 0.7700 Gold 0.1201 oz. AGW **Ruler:** Friedrich Karl Graf von Schonborn **Obverse:** Bust right **Reverse:** Crowned arms below crowned mantle

Date	Mintage	VG	F	VF	XF	Unc
1735	—	275	600	1,250	2,250	—

KM# 311 1/2 CAROLIN (5 Gulden)

4.8500 g., 0.7700 Gold 0.1201 oz. AGW **Ruler:** Friedrich Karl Graf von Schonborn **Reverse:** Crowned and mantled oval with FC monogram

Date	Mintage	VG	F	VF	XF	Unc
1735	—	275	600	1,250	2,250	—
1736	—	275	600	1,250	2,250	—

KM# 312 CAROLIN (10 Gulden)

9.7000 g., 0.7700 Gold 0.2401 oz. AGW **Ruler:** Friedrich Karl Graf von Schonborn **Obverse:** Bust right **Reverse:** Crowned arms below crowned mantle

Date	Mintage	VG	F	VF	XF	Unc
1735	—	400	700	1,650	3,250	—
1736	—	400	700	1,650	3,250	—

KM# 313 CAROLIN (10 Gulden)

9.7000 g., 0.7700 Gold 0.2401 oz. AGW **Ruler:** Friedrich Karl Graf von Schonborn **Reverse:** Crowned and mantled oval with FC monogram

Date	Mintage	VG	F	VF	XF	Unc
1735	—	400	700	1,650	3,250	—
1736	—	400	700	1,650	3,250	—

KM# 456 CAROLIN (10 Gulden)

9.7000 g., 0.7700 Gold 0.2401 oz. AGW **Obverse:** Bust **Reverse:** Arms

Date	Mintage	F	VF	XF	Unc
1795	—	900	1,500	3,000	5,000

KM# 273 1/2 DUCAT

1.7500 g., 0.9860 Gold 0.0555 oz. AGW **Obverse:** Crowned arms **Reverse:** Sword with ribbon

Date	Mintage	VG	F	VF	XF	Unc
ND(1724)	—	75.00	150	300	500	—

KM# 296 1/2 DUCAT

1.7500 g., 0.9860 Gold 0.0555 oz. AGW **Ruler:** Friedrich Karl Graf von Schonborn **Obverse:** Arms **Reverse:** Crowned and mantled oval with FC monogram

Date	Mintage	VG	F	VF	XF	Unc
1729	—	150	300	600	1,000	—

KM# 194 DUCAT

3.5000 g., 0.9860 Gold 0.1109 oz. AGW **Obverse:** Bust of Johann Gottfried II right **Reverse:** Five ornate helmets above oval 4-fold arms

Date	Mintage	VG	F	VF	XF	Unc
ND	—	850	1,650	3,000	5,000	—

KM# 220 DUCAT

3.5000 g., 0.9860 Gold 0.1109 oz. AGW **Ruler:** Johann Philipp II von Greifenklau-Vollraths **Obverse:** Bust right **Reverse:** Arms topped by three helmets

Date	Mintage	VG	F	VF	XF	Unc
1701	—	350	800	1,500	2,500	—
1702	—	350	800	1,500	2,500	—

KM# 231 DUCAT

3.5000 g., 0.9860 Gold 0.1109 oz. AGW **Ruler:** Johann Philipp II von Greifenklau-Vollraths **Reverse:** Three saints, date in chronogram

Date	Mintage	VG	F	VF	XF	Unc
1702	—	450	900	1,850	3,000	—

KM# 237 DUCAT

3.5000 g., 0.9860 Gold 0.1109 oz. AGW **Ruler:** Johann Philipp II von Greifenklau-Vollraths **Reverse:** Tree with arms at base, Roman numeral date below

Date	Mintage	VG	F	VF	XF	Unc
1703	—	500	1,000	2,000	3,000	—

KM# 256 DUCAT

3.5000 g., 0.9860 Gold 0.1109 oz. AGW **Ruler:** Johann Philipp II von Greifenklau-Vollraths **Obverse:** Bust right **Reverse:** Crowned and mantled oval four-fold arms, date divided at bottom

Date	Mintage	VG	F	VF	XF	Unc
1718	—	500	1,000	2,000	3,500	—

KM# 263 DUCAT

3.5000 g., 0.9860 Gold 0.1109 oz. AGW **Ruler:** Johann Philipp Franz, Graf von Schonborn **Obverse:** Bust right **Reverse:** Crowned oval arms of Schonborn in wreath **Rev. Legend:** FIRMA IN DE - VM FIDVCIA

Date	Mintage	VG	F	VF	XF	Unc
ND	—	450	950	2,000	3,250	—

KM# 264 DUCAT

3.5000 g., 0.9860 Gold 0.1109 oz. AGW **Ruler:** Johann Philipp Franz, Graf von Schonborn **Obverse:** Bust right **Reverse:** Arms in cartouche

Date	Mintage	VG	F	VF	XF	Unc
ND(1719)	—	550	1,150	2,250	3,750	—

KM# 274 DUCAT

3.5000 g., 0.9860 Gold 0.1109 oz. AGW **Obverse:** Helmeted arms **Obv. Legend:** D. G. EL. EP... **Reverse:** St. Christopher

Date	Mintage	VG	F	VF	XF	Unc
ND(1724)	—	175	325	650	1,150	—

KM# 275 DUCAT

3.5000 g., 0.9860 Gold 0.1109 oz. AGW **Obverse:** Arms topped by three helmets **Reverse:** View of harbor with ships

Date	Mintage	VG	F	VF	XF	Unc
ND(1724)	—	500	1,000	2,000	3,500	—

KM# 276 DUCAT

3.5000 g., 0.9860 Gold 0.1109 oz. AGW **Obverse:** Helmeted arms **Obv. Legend:** D. G. EP... **Reverse:** St. Christopher

Date	Mintage	VG	F	VF	XF	Unc
ND(1724)	—	125	250	600	1,000	—

KM# 284 DUCAT

3.5000 g., 0.9860 Gold 0.1109 oz. AGW **Ruler:** Christoph Franz von Hutten **Obverse:** Crowned and mantled oval four-fold arms of Wurzburg and Hutten **Reverse:** DA / ET ACCIPE / ET / IUSTIFICA ANIMAM / TUAM / MDCCXXV

Date	Mintage	VG	F	VF	XF	Unc
1725	—	400	800	1,500	2,500	—

KM# 285.1 DUCAT

3.5000 g., 0.9860 Gold 0.1109 oz. AGW **Ruler:** Christoph Franz von Hutten **Obverse:** Arms **Reverse:** Crowned and mantled CF monogram

Date	Mintage	VG	F	VF	XF	Unc
1725	—	200	450	950	1,850	—

KM# 285.2 DUCAT

3.5000 g., 0.9860 Gold 0.1109 oz. AGW **Ruler:** Christoph Franz von Hutten **Obverse:** Helmeted arms **Reverse:** Crowned and mantled oval with CF monogram

Date	Mintage	VG	F	VF	XF	Unc
1727	—	200	450	950	1,850	—
1728	—	200	450	950	1,850	—

KM# 297 DUCAT

3.5000 g., 0.9860 Gold 0.1109 oz. AGW **Ruler:** Friedrich Karl Graf von Schonborn **Obverse:** Helmeted arms **Reverse:** Monogram within crowned mantle

Date	Mintage	VG	F	VF	XF	Unc
1729	—	175	350	750	1,450	—
1730	—	225	450	1,000	1,850	—
1731	—	—	—	—	—	—

KM# 305 DUCAT

3.5000 g., 0.9860 Gold 0.1109 oz. AGW **Ruler:** Friedrich Karl Graf von Schonborn **Obverse:** Bust right **Reverse:** Crowned and mantled oval eight-fold arms with center shield of Schonborn, date divided at top

Date	Mintage	VG	F	VF	XF	Unc
1731	—	200	500	1,000	2,000	—

KM# 307 DUCAT

3.5000 g., 0.9860 Gold 0.1109 oz. AGW **Ruler:** Friedrich Karl Graf von Schonborn **Reverse:** Ornately-shaped arms, almost square

Date	Mintage	VG	F	VF	XF	Unc
1732	—	175	375	850	1,750	—
1733	—	175	375	850	1,750	—

KM# 308 DUCAT

3.5000 g., 0.9860 Gold 0.1109 oz. AGW **Ruler:** Friedrich Karl Graf von Schonborn **Reverse:** Crowned ten-fold arms with center shield of Schonborn, supported by two lions

Date	Mintage	VG	F	VF	XF	Unc
ND	—	350	700	1,500	2,750	—

KM# 319 DUCAT

3.5000 g., 0.9860 Gold 0.1109 oz. AGW **Ruler:** Anselm Franz, Graf von Ingelheim **Subject:** Consecration of the Bishop **Obverse:** Angel with crozier followed by lambs **Reverse:** Seven-line inscription **Note:** Date in chronogram.

Date	Mintage	VG	F	VF	XF	Unc
1747	—	250	550	1,250	2,250	—

KM# 323 DUCAT

3.5000 g., 0.9860 Gold 0.1109 oz. AGW **Ruler:** Anselm Franz, Graf von Ingelheim **Obverse:** Bust right **Reverse:** Crowned and mantled four-fold arms with center shield of Ingelheim, date divided below

Date	Mintage	VG	F	VF	XF	Unc
1748	—	750	1,250	1,750	3,500	—

KM# 348 DUCAT

3.5000 g., 0.9860 Gold 0.1109 oz. AGW **Ruler:** Adam Friedrich von Seinsheim **Obverse:** Bust right **Obv. Legend:** AD • FRI • D • G • .... **Reverse:** Crowned arms, without legend

Date	Mintage	F	VF	XF	Unc
1755	—	450	900	1,500	2,300
1762	—	450	900	1,500	2,300
1765	—	450	900	1,500	2,300
1768	—	450	900	1,500	2,300
1770	—	450	900	1,500	2,300
1772	—	450	900	1,500	2,300

KM# 405 DUCAT

3.5000 g., 0.9860 Gold 0.1109 oz. AGW **Ruler:** Adam Friedrich von Seinsheim **Obverse:** Bust right in rhombus **Reverse:** Arms in rhombus

Date	Mintage	F	VF	XF	Unc
1772	—	300	600	1,200	2,000

KM# 409 DUCAT

3.5000 g., 0.9860 Gold 0.1109 oz. AGW **Ruler:** Adam Friedrich von Seinsheim **Obverse:** Bust right in rhombus **Reverse:** Madonna and child facing in rhombus

Date	Mintage	F	VF	XF	Unc
1773	—	250	400	800	1,200
1774	—	250	400	800	1,200
1776	—	250	400	800	1,200
1777	—	250	400	800	1,200
1778	—	250	400	800	1,200
1779	—	250	400	800	1,200

KM# 421 DUCAT

3.5000 g., 0.9860 Gold 0.1109 oz. AGW **Ruler:** Franz Ludwig von Erthal **Obverse:** Draped bust right **Obv. Legend:** FRANC • LUD • D • G • EP • BAR • ET WIR • S • R • I • P • F • O • DUX • **Reverse:** Crowned and mantled arms **Rev. Legend:** DUCATUS DUCIS - FRANCORUM • 1780 •

Date	Mintage	F	VF	XF	Unc
1780	—	300	600	1,350	2,250
1781	—	300	600	1,350	2,250
1782	—	300	600	1,350	2,250
1783	—	300	600	1,350	2,250

KM# 424 DUCAT

3.5000 g., 0.9860 Gold 0.1109 oz. AGW **Ruler:** Franz Ludwig von Erthal **Obverse:** Draped bust right **Obv. Legend:** FRANC • LUD • D • G • EP • BAR • ET WIR • S • R • I • P • F • O • DUX • **Reverse:** Three saints on pedestals, arms in center foreground

Date	Mintage	F	VF	XF	Unc
1785	—	200	400	800	1,600

KM# 238 2 DUCAT

7.0000 g., 0.9860 Gold 0.2219 oz. AGW **Ruler:** Johann Philipp II von Greifenklau-Vollraths **Obverse:** Bust right **Reverse:** Fir tree, Roman numeral date below

Date	Mintage	VG	F	VF	XF	Unc
1703	—	850	1,750	3,500	6,000	—

KM# 242 2 DUCAT

7.0000 g., 0.9860 Gold 0.2219 oz. AGW **Ruler:** Johann Philipp II von Greifenklau-Vollraths **Obverse:** Bust right **Reverse:** Arms topped by three helmets

Date	Mintage	VG	F	VF	XF	Unc
1705	—	700	1,500	3,250	5,500	—

KM# 243 2 DUCAT

7.0000 g., 0.9860 Gold 0.2219 oz. AGW **Ruler:** Johann Philipp II von Greifenklau-Vollraths **Reverse:** Crowned and mantled arms

Date	Mintage	VG	F	VF	XF	Unc
1705	—	700	1,500	3,250	5,500	—

KM# 249 2 DUCAT

7.0000 g., 0.9860 Gold 0.2219 oz. AGW **Ruler:** Johann Philipp II von Greifenklau-Vollraths **Obverse:** Armored bust right **Obv. Legend:** JOAN • PHILIP • D • G • EP • HERB • S • R • I • PR • FR • OR • DVX • **Reverse:** Arms below Madonna and child

Date	Mintage	VG	F	VF	XF	Unc
1707	—	400	700	1,600	2,800	—

KM# 265 2 DUCAT

7.0000 g., 0.9860 Gold 0.2219 oz. AGW **Ruler:** Johann Philipp Franz, Graf von Schonborn **Obverse:** Bust right **Reverse:** Lion holding sword and scales, city view in background

Date	Mintage	VG	F	VF	XF	Unc
ND(1719)	—	1,000	2,000	4,500	7,000	—

KM# 266 2 DUCAT

7.0000 g., 0.9860 Gold 0.2219 oz. AGW **Ruler:** Johann Philipp Franz, Graf von Schonborn **Reverse:** Without city view

Date	Mintage	VG	F	VF	XF	Unc
ND(1719)	—	1,250	2,500	5,000	8,000	—

KM# 267 2 DUCAT

7.0000 g., 0.9860 Gold 0.2219 oz. AGW **Subject:** Election of the Bishop **Reverse:** Crowned and mantled arms

Date	Mintage	VG	F	VF	XF	Unc
1719	—	2,000	3,500	6,000	9,000	—
ND	—	2,000	3,500	6,000	9,000	—

KM# 268 2 DUCAT

7.0000 g., 0.9860 Gold 0.2219 oz. AGW **Ruler:** Christoph Franz von Hutten **Obverse:** Helmeted arms **Obv. Legend:** CHRISTOPH • FRANC • D • G • .... **Reverse:** City view back of standing figure

Date	Mintage	VG	F	VF	XF	Unc
ND(1724)	—	500	1,000	2,000	3,500	—

KM# 277 2 DUCAT

7.0000 g., 0.9860 Gold 0.2219 oz. AGW **Ruler:** Christoph Franz von Hutten **Obverse:** Bust right

Date	Mintage	VG	F	VF	XF	Unc
ND	—	300	600	1,300	2,500	—

KM# 298 2 DUCAT

7.0000 g., 0.9860 Gold 0.2219 oz. AGW **Ruler:** Friedrich Karl Graf von Schonborn **Obverse:** Crowned and mantled eight-fold arms with center shield of Schonborn **Reverse:** Franconia standing at right, Schonborn lion at left holding episcopal arms, date in chronogram

Date	Mintage	VG	F	VF	XF	Unc
1729	—	850	1,750	3,250	5,500	—

KM# 299 2 DUCAT

7.0000 g., 0.9860 Gold 0.2219 oz. AGW **Ruler:** Friedrich Karl Graf von Schonborn **Obverse:** Bust right **Reverse:** Helmeted arms

Date	Mintage	VG	F	VF	XF	Unc
1729	—	500	1,000	2,500	4,000	—
1730	—	500	1,000	2,500	4,000	—
1731	—	500	1,000	2,500	4,000	—

KM# 233 3 DUCAT

10.5000 g., 0.9860 Gold 0.3328 oz. AGW **Ruler:** Johann Philipp II von Greifenklau-Vollraths **Obverse:** Bust right **Reverse:** Two saints on pedestals, chronogram date

Date	Mintage	VG	F	VF	XF	Unc
1702 Rare	—	—	—	—	—	—

KM# 250 3 DUCAT

10.5000 g., 0.9860 Gold 0.3328 oz. AGW **Ruler:** Johann Philipp II von Greifenklau-Vollraths **Obverse:** Bust right **Reverse:** Madonna and child above crowned arms flanked by cherubs

Date	Mintage	VG	F	VF	XF	Unc
1707	—	700	1,500	3,000	5,000	—

KM# 289 3 DUCAT

10.5000 g., 0.9860 Gold 0.3328 oz. AGW **Ruler:** Christoph Franz von Hutten **Obverse:** Three helmets above mantled oval four-fold arms of Wurzburg and Hutten **Reverse:** Crowned and mantled ornate CF monogram, date below

Date	Mintage	VG	F	VF	XF	Unc
1726 Rare	—	—	—	—	—	—

KM# 257 4 DUCAT

14.0000 g., 0.9860 Gold 0.4438 oz. AGW **Ruler:** Johann Philipp II von Greifenklau-Vollraths **Obverse:** Bust right **Reverse:** Three helmets above oval four-fold arms, tiny date divided at bottom

Date	Mintage	VG	F	VF	XF	Unc
1718	—	5,000	8,000	10,000	12,000	—

KM# 258 4 DUCAT

14.0000 g., 0.9860 Gold 0.4438 oz. AGW **Ruler:** Friedrich Karl Graf von Schonborn **Obverse:** Bust right **Reverse:** Crowned and supported oval arms, four helmets behind

Date	Mintage	VG	F	VF	XF	Unc
ND	—	5,000	8,000	10,000	12,000	—

KM# 234 5 DUCAT

17.5000 g., 0.9860 Gold 0.5547 oz. AGW **Ruler:** Johann Philipp II von Greifenklau-Vollraths **Obverse:** Bust right **Reverse:** Crowned and supported oval four-fold arms, large fir tree above and behind, small date below

Date	Mintage	VG	F	VF	XF	Unc
1702	—	5,000	8,000	10,000	12,000	—

KM# 235 5 DUCAT

17.5000 g., 0.9860 Gold 0.5547 oz. AGW **Ruler:** Johann Philipp II von Greifenklau-Vollraths **Reverse:** Three helmets above round four-fold arms, date divided below **Note:** Struck with 1/2 Thaler dies, KM#226.

Date	Mintage	VG	F	VF	XF	Unc
1702	—	4,000	5,500	7,200	10,000	—

KM# A250 5 DUCAT

17.5000 g., 0.9860 Gold 0.5547 oz. AGW **Ruler:** Johann Philipp II von Greifenklau-Vollraths **Reverse:** Madonna and child above four-fold arms, tiny date divided at left and right

Date	Mintage	VG	F	VF	XF	Unc
1707	—	5,000	8,000	10,000	12,000	—

KM# 278 5 DUCAT

17.5000 g., 0.9860 Gold 0.5547 oz. AGW **Ruler:** Christoph Franz von Hutten **Obverse:** Three helmets above crowned and mantled oval four-fold arms of Wurzburg and Hutten **Reverse:** Bust right **Rev. Legend:** LAEFIFICA ANIMAM SERVI TVI

Date	Mintage	VG	F	VF	XF	Unc
ND V	—	5,000	8,000	10,000	12,000	—

KM# 279 5 DUCAT

17.5000 g., 0.9860 Gold 0.5547 oz. AGW **Ruler:** Christoph Franz von Hutten **Obverse:** Bust right **Reverse:** Crowned and mantled oval four-fold arms of Wurzburg and Hutten

Date	Mintage	VG	F	VF	XF	Unc
ND V	—	5,000	8,000	10,000	12,000	—

KM# 280 5 DUCAT

17.5000 g., 0.9860 Gold 0.5547 oz. AGW **Reverse:** Figure of Franconia seated at left holding pennant, beehive in center and swarm of bees at right

Date	Mintage	VG	F	VF	XF	Unc
ND V	—	6,000	9,000	11,000	13,500	—

KM# 328 6 DUCAT

21.0000 g., 0.9860 Gold 0.6657 oz. AGW **Subject:** Consecration of Bishop **Obverse:** Bust right **Reverse:** Oval arms on throne, inscription

Date	Mintage	VG	F	VF	XF	Unc
1749 VESTNER Rare	—	—	—	—	—	—

KM# 259 7-1/2 DUCAT

0.9860 Gold **Obverse:** Bust of Friedrich Franz right **Reverse:** Crown and supported oval arms, four helmets behind

Date	Mintage	VG	F	VF	XF	Unc
ND	—	5,000	7,500	9,000	12,000	—

KM# 236 10 DUCAT

35.0000 g., 0.9860 Gold 1.1095 oz. AGW **Ruler:** Johann Gottfried II von Guttenberg **Obverse:** Bust right **Reverse:** Tree above crowned and supported arms, date below **Note:** Similar to 1 Thaler, KM#229.

Date	Mintage	VG	F	VF	XF	Unc
1702	—	8,000	12,000	16,000	20,000	—

KM# 251 10 DUCAT

35.0000 g., 0.9860 Gold 1.1095 oz. AGW **Ruler:** Johann Philipp II von Greifenklau-Vollraths **Obverse:** Slightly larger bust **Obv. Legend:** JOAN • PHILIP • D • G • EP • .... **Reverse:** Madonna and child on cloud in rays, date divided below

Date	Mintage	VG	F	VF	XF	Unc
1707	—	8,000	12,000	16,000	20,000	—

KM# 329 10 DUCAT

35.0000 g., 0.9860 Gold 1.1095 oz. AGW **Subject:** Consecration of Bishop **Obverse:** Bust right **Reverse:** Oval arms on throne, inscription

Date	Mintage	VG	F	VF	XF	Unc
1749 Vestner Rare	—	—	—	—	—	—

KM# 330 12 DUCAT

42.0000 g., 0.9860 Gold 1.3314 oz. AGW **Subject:** Consecration of Bishop **Obverse:** Bust right **Reverse:** Oval arms on throne, inscription

Date	Mintage	VG	F	VF	XF	Unc
1749 VESTNER Rare	—	—	—	—	—	—

PATTERNS

Including off metal strikes

KM#	Date	Mintage	Identification	Mkt Val
Pn9	1706	—	4 Kreuzer. Gold. Weight of 1 Ducat, KM#244.	—
Pn10	1713	—	Schilling. Copper. KM#44	—
Pn11	173Z	—	3 Heller. Copper. KM#306	—
Pn12	1747	—	Ducat. Silver. KM#319	—
Pn13	1748	—	Ducat. Silver. KM#319	—
Pn14	1749	—	6 Ducat. Silver. KM#328	375
Pn15	1749	—	10 Ducat. Copper. KM#329	—
Pn16	1749	—	10 Ducat. Silver. KM#329	—
Pn17	1759	—	3 Heller. Gold. KM#349	—
Pn18	1795	—	3 Kreuzer. Copper. KM#444	—

GOLD COAST

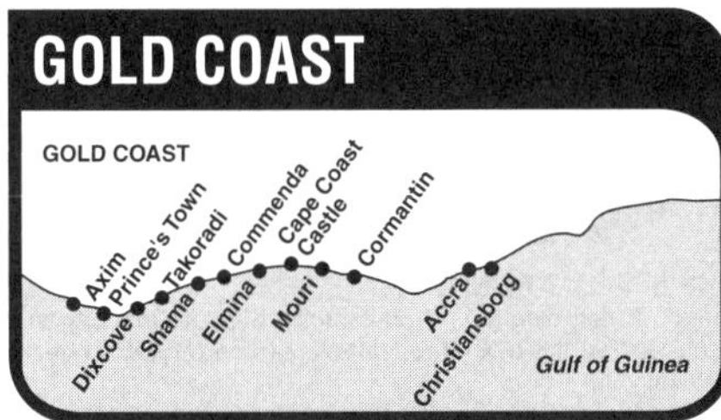

The Gold Coast, a region of Northwest Africa along the Gulf of Guinea, was first visited by Portuguese traders in 1470, and through the 17th century was used by various European powers -England, Denmark, Holland, Germany - as a center for their slave trade. Britain achieved control of the Gold Coast in 1821, and established the colony of Gold Coast in1874. In 1901 Britain annexed the neighboring Ashanti Kingdom in the same year a northern region known as the Northern Territories became a British protectorate. Part of the former German colony of Togoland was mandated to Britain by the League of Nations and administered as part of the Gold Coast.

The state of Ghana, comprising the Gold Coast and British Togoland, obtained independence on March 6, 1957, becoming the first Negro African colony to do so.

RULERS

British

MONETARY SYSTEM

8 Tackow = 1 Ackey

BRITISH OUTPOST

TOKEN COINAGE

KM# Tn1 TACKOE

1.9437 g., 0.9250 Silver 0.0578 oz. ASW **Obv:** Crowned monogram **Rev:** Arms **Note:** Prev. KM#1.

Date	Mintage	F	VF	XF	Unc	BU
1796	5,760	65.00	125	200	375	—
1796 Proof	—	Value: 475				

KM# Tn1a TACKOE

0.8900 Silver **Obv:** Crowned monogram **Rev:** Arms **Note:** Prev. KM#1a.

Date	Mintage	F	VF	XF	Unc	BU
1796(1801)	6,400	110	225	300	650	—

KM# Tn2 1/4 ACKEY

3.8875 g., 0.9250 Silver 0.1156 oz. ASW **Obv:** Crowned monogram **Rev:** Arms **Rev. Legend:** PARLIMENT (error) **Note:** Prev. KM#2.

Date	Mintage	F	VF	XF	Unc	BU
1796 (1801)	2,880	125	250	375	750	—
1796 (1801) Proof	—	Value: 1,000				

KM# Tn3 1/4 ACKEY

0.8900 Silver **Obv:** Crowned monogram **Rev:** Arms with garnishments **Rev. Legend:** PARLIAMENT **Note:** Prev. KM#3.

Date	Mintage	F	VF	XF	Unc	BU
1796(1801)	3,200	125	250	350	700	—
1796(1801) Proof	—	Value: 950				

KM# Tn4 1/2 ACKEY

7.7750 g., 0.9250 Silver 0.2312 oz. ASW **Obv:** Crowned monogram **Rev:** Arms with garnishments **Rev. Legend:** PARLIMENT (error) **Note:** Prev. KM#4.

Date	Mintage	F	VF	XF	Unc	BU
1796	2,160	100	200	400	650	—
1796 Proof	—	Value: 850				

KM# Tn5 1/2 ACKEY

7.0900 g., 0.8900 Silver 0.2029 oz. ASW **Rev. Legend:** PARLIAMENT **Note:** Prev. KM#5.

Date	Mintage	F	VF	XF	Unc	BU
1796(1801)	2,400	200	400	650	950	—
1796(1801) Proof	—	Value: 1,250				

KM# Tn6 ACKEY

15.5500 g., 0.9250 Silver 0.4624 oz. ASW **Obv:** Crowned monogram within branches **Rev:** Arms with supporters **Rev. Legend:** PARLIMENT (error) **Note:** Prev. KM#6.

Date	Mintage	F	VF	XF	Unc	BU
1796	1,080	375	650	1,250	2,250	—
1796 Proof	—	Value: 3,000				

KM# Tn7 ACKEY

0.8900 Silver **Obv:** Crowned monogram within branches **Rev:** Arms with supporters **Rev. Legend:** PARLIAMENT **Note:** Prev. KM#7.

Date	Mintage	F	VF	XF	Unc	BU
1796(1801)	1,200,000	400	800	1,400	2,900	—
1796(1801) Proof	—	Value: 3,250				

PATTERNS

Including off metal strikes

KM#	Date	Mintage	Identification	Mkt Val
Pn1	1796	—	Tackoe. Bronzed-Copper. KM1.	375
Pn2	1796	—	Tackoe. Copper-Gilt. KM1.	500
Pn3	1796	—	1/4 Ackey. Bronzed-Copper. KM3	400
Pn4	1796	—	1/4 Ackey. Copper-Gilt. KM3	650
Pn5	1796	—	1/2 Ackey. Copper. KM5	—
Pn6	1796	—	1/2 Ackey. Copper-Gilt. KM5	—
Pn7	1796	—	Ackey. Bronzed-Copper. KM7	300
Pn8	1796	—	Ackey. Copper-Gilt. KM7	950

GREAT BRITAIN

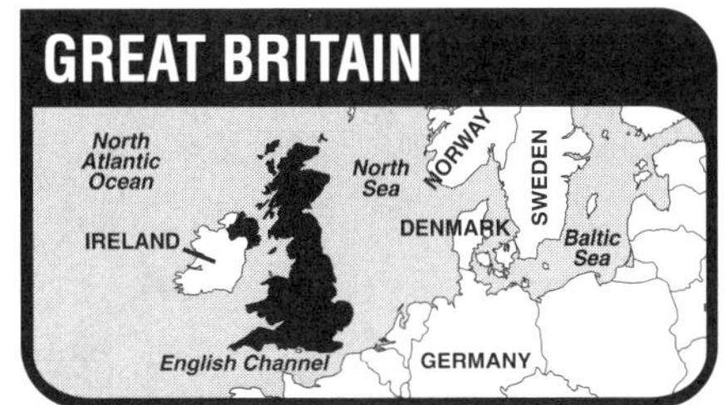

The United Kingdom of Great Britain and Northern Ireland, located off the northwest coast of the European continent, has an area of 94,227 sq. mi. (244,820 sq. km.) and a population of 54 million. Capital: London. The economy is based on industrial activity and trading. Machinery, motor vehicles, chemicals, and textile yarns and fabrics are exported.

After the departure of the Romans, who brought Britain into a more active relationship with Europe, it fell prey to invaders from Scandinavia and the Low Countries who drove the original Britons into Scotland and Wales, and established a profusion of kingdoms that finally united in the 11th century under the Danish King Canute. Norman rule, following the conquest of 1066, stimulated the development of those institutions, which have since distinguished British life. Henry VIII (1509-47) turned Britain from continental adventuring and faced it to the sea - a decision that made Britain a world power during the reign of Elizabeth I (1558-1603). Strengthened by the Industrial Revolution and the defeat of Napoleon, 19th century Britain turned to the remote parts of the world and established a colonial empire of such extent and prosperity that the world has never seen its like. World Wars I and II sealed the fate of the Empire and relegated Britain to a lesser role in world affairs by draining her resources and inaugurating a worldwide movement toward national self-determination in her former colonies.

By the mid 20th century, most of the territories formerly comprising the British Empire had gained independence, and the empire had evolved into the Commonwealth of Nations, an association of equal and autonomous states, which enjoy special trade interests. The Commonwealth is presently composed of 50 member nations, including the United Kingdom. All recognize the British monarch as head of the Commonwealth. Sixteen continue to recognize the British monarch as Head of State. They are: United Kingdom, Antigua and Barbuda, Australia, Bahamas, Barbados, Belize, Canada, Grenada, Jamaica, New Zealand, Papua New Guinea, St. Christopher & Nevis, Saint Lucia, Saint Vincent and the Grenadines, Solomon Islands, and Tuvalu. Elizabeth II is personally, and separately, the Queen of the sovereign, independent countries just mentioned. There is no other British connection between the several individual, national sovereignties, except that they are each represented by High Commissioners instead of ambassadors in each others countries.

RULERS

William III, 1694-1702
Anne, 1702-1714
George I, 1714-1727
George II, 1727-1760
George III, 1760-1820

Mint Marks

Under Anne
E, E* - Edinburgh, 1707-09

MONETARY SYSTEM

(Until 1970)

4 Farthings = 1 Penny
12 Pence = 1 Shilling
2 Shillings = 1 Florin
5 Shillings = 1 Crown
20 Shillings = 1 Pound (Sovereign)
21 Shillings = 1 Guinea

NOTE: Proofs exist for many dates of British coins in the 19th and early 20th centuries and for virtually all coins between 1926 and 1964. Those not specifically listed here are extremely rare.

KINGDOM

Resumed

POUND COINAGE

KM# 537 FARTHING

Copper **Ruler:** Anne **Obv:** Bust left **Obv. Legend:** ANNA DEI - GRATIA **Rev:** Brittania seated left **Rev. Legend:** BRITAN - NIA **Note:** Not released for general circulation.

Date	Mintage	VG	F	VF	XF	Unc
1714	—	75.00	200	350	750	—

KM# 548 FARTHING

Copper **Ruler:** George I **Obv:** Laureate bust right **Obv. Legend:** GEORGIVS - • - REX • **Rev:** Brittania seated left **Rev. Legend:** BRITA - N - NIA • **Note:** "Dump" issue, small planchet.

Date	Mintage	VG	F	VF	XF	Unc
1717	—	35.00	110	275	600	—

KM# 556 FARTHING

Copper **Ruler:** George I **Obv:** Laureate bust right **Obv. Legend:** GEORGIVS • - REX • **Rev:** Brittania seated left **Rev. Legend:** BRITA - N - NIA • **Note:** Larger planchet. Varieties exist.

Date	Mintage	VG	F	VF	XF	Unc
1719	—	10.00	25.00	95.00	350	—
1720	—	10.00	25.00	85.00	300	—
1721/0	—	15.00	30.00	80.00	275	—
1721	—	10.00	25.00	85.00	300	—
1722	—	10.00	25.00	90.00	350	—
1723	—	10.00	25.00	90.00	350	—
1724	—	10.00	25.00	90.00	350	—

KM# 556a FARTHING

Silver **Ruler:** George II **Obv:** Laureate bust right **Rev:** Brittania seated left

Date	Mintage	VG	F	VF	XF	Unc
1719 Proof	—	—	—	—	—	—

KM# 572 FARTHING

Copper **Ruler:** George II **Obv:** Laureate bust left **Obv. Legend:** GEORGIVS • - II • REX • **Rev:** Brittania seated left **Rev. Legend:** BRITAN - NIA •

Date	Mintage	VG	F	VF	XF	Unc
1730	—	6.00	12.50	35.00	175	—
1731	—	6.00	12.50	40.00	175	—
1732	—	7.00	15.00	40.00	175	—
1733	—	6.00	12.00	35.00	175	—
1734	—	7.00	15.00	40.00	175	—
1734	—	9.00	18.00	70.00	225	—
Note: Obverse without periods						
1735/55	—	10.00	20.00	75.00	225	—
1735	—	4.00	10.00	30.00	150	—
1736	—	5.00	12.50	35.00	150	—
1737 Small date	—	4.00	10.00	30.00	150	—
1737 Large date	—	4.00	10.00	35.00	150	—
1739	—	4.00	10.00	30.00	175	—

KM# 572a FARTHING

Silver **Ruler:** George II **Obv:** Laureate bust left **Rev:** Brittania seated left

Date	Mintage	VG	F	VF	XF	Unc
1730 Proof	—	—	—	—	—	2,250

KM# 581.1 FARTHING

Copper **Ruler:** George II **Obv:** Older laureate head left **Obv. Legend:** GEORGIUS • - II • REX • **Rev:** Brittania seated left **Rev. Legend:** BRITAN - NIA •

Date	Mintage	VG	F	VF	XF	Unc
1741	—	5.00	12.00	40.00	150	—
1744	—	4.00	10.00	40.00	150	—

KM# 581.2 FARTHING

Copper **Ruler:** George II **Obv:** Laureate head left **Obv. Legend:** GEORGIVS • - II • REX • **Rev:** Brittania seated left **Rev. Legend:** BRITAN - NIA •

Date	Mintage	VG	F	VF	XF	Unc
1746	—	4.00	10.00	35.00	100	—
1749	—	6.00	12.50	40.00	125	—
1750	—	6.00	12.50	40.00	150	—
1754/0	—	10.00	20.00	65.00	225	—
1754	—	4.00	6.00	26.00	85.00	—

KM# 602 FARTHING

Copper **Ruler:** George III **Obv:** Laureate bust right **Obv. Legend:** GEORGIVS • - III • REX • **Rev:** Brittania seated left **Rev. Legend:** BRITAN - NIA • **Note:** Contemporary counterfeits are quite common.

Date	Mintage	F	VF	XF	Unc	BU
1771	—	20.00	50.00	125	400	—
1771 Proof	—	—	—	—	500	—
1773	—	9.00	22.00	85.00	250	—
1774	—	10.00	25.00	85.00	250	—
1775	—	12.00	28.00	95.00	200	—

KM# 646 FARTHING

Copper **Ruler:** George III **Obv:** Laureate bust right **Obv. Legend:** GEORGIUS III DEI GRATIA REX **Rev:** Brittania seated left **Rev. Legend:** BRITANNIA

Date	Mintage	F	VF	XF	Unc	BU
1799	—	4.00	8.00	35.00	85.00	—
1799 Proof	—	—	—	—	250	—

KM# 646a FARTHING

Gilt Copper **Ruler:** George III **Obv:** Laureate bust right **Rev:** Brittania seated left

Date	Mintage	F	VF	XF	Unc	BU
1799 Proof	—	—	—	—	350	—

KM# 646b FARTHING

Bronzed Copper **Ruler:** George III **Obv:** Laureate bust right **Rev:** Brittania seated left

Date	Mintage	F	VF	XF	Unc	BU
1799 Proof	—	—	—	—	250	—

KM# 503 1/2 PENNY

Copper **Ruler:** William III **Obv:** Laureate head right **Rev:** Britannia seated left with right hand near knee, date in exergue **Note:** Varieties exist.

Date	Mintage	VG	F	VF	XF	Unc
1701	—	10.00	25.00	125	750	—

KM# 549 1/2 PENNY

Copper **Ruler:** George I **Obv:** Laureate bust right **Obv. Legend:** GEORGIVS • REX • **Rev:** Brittania seated left, right hand near knee **Rev. Legend:** BRITAN - NIA • **Note:** "Dump" issue.

Date	Mintage	VG	F	VF	XF	Unc
1717	—	10.00	27.00	175	550	—
1717 Proof	—	—	—	—	—	850
1718	—	9.00	28.00	150	550	—
1719	—	—	—	—	—	—

KM# 557 1/2 PENNY

Copper **Ruler:** George I **Obv:** Laureate bust right **Obv. Legend:** GEORGIVS • REX • **Rev:** Brittania seated left, right hand near knee **Rev. Legend:** BRITAN - NIA • **Note:** Varieties exist.

Date	Mintage	VG	F	VF	XF	Unc
1719	—	10.00	30.00	100	500	—
1720	—	10.00	20.00	100	450	—
1721/0	—	15.00	35.00	100	500	—
1721	—	10.00	25.00	100	500	—
1722	—	10.00	25.00	100	—	—
1723	—	8.00	22.00	100	500	—
1724	—	8.00	22.00	100	400	—

KM# 566 1/2 PENNY

Copper **Ruler:** George II **Obv:** Laureate bust left **Obv. Legend:** GEORGIVS • - II • REX • **Rev:** Brittania seated left **Rev. Legend:** BRITAN - NIA •

Date	Mintage	VG	F	VF	XF	Unc
1729	—	6.00	15.00	60.00	225	—
1729 Proof	—	—	—	—	—	725
1730	—	5.00	13.00	55.00	175	—
1730 GEOGIVS	—	8.00	22.00	90.00	225	—
1731	—	5.00	13.00	55.00	175	—
1732	—	5.00	16.00	55.00	175	—
1733	—	5.00	16.00	55.00	175	—
1734/3	—	10.00	25.00	100	200	—
1734	—	5.00	13.00	55.00	175	—
1735	—	5.00	16.00	55.00	175	—
1736	—	6.00	16.00	55.00	175	—
1737	—	6.00	16.00	55.00	175	—
1738	—	5.00	16.00	55.00	175	—
1739	—	5.00	16.00	55.00	175	—

KM# 579.1 1/2 PENNY

Copper **Ruler:** George II **Obv:** Older laureate head left **Obv. Legend:** GEORGIVS • - II • REX • **Rev:** Brittania seated left **Rev. Legend:** BRITAN - NIA •

Date	Mintage	VG	F	VF	XF	Unc
1740	—	4.00	10.00	45.00	150	—
1742/0	—	8.00	20.00	75.00	200	—
1742	—	4.00	10.00	55.00	150	—
1743	—	4.00	10.00	55.00	150	—
1744	—	4.00	10.00	55.00	150	—
1745	—	4.00	10.00	55.00	150	—

KM# 579.2 1/2 PENNY

Copper **Ruler:** George II **Obv:** Laureate bust left **Obv. Legend:** GEORGIUS • - II • REX • **Rev:** Brittania seated left **Rev. Legend:** BRITAN - NIA •

Date	Mintage	VG	F	VF	XF	Unc
1746	—	4.00	10.00	55.00	150	—
1747	—	4.00	10.00	55.00	150	—
1748	—	3.00	8.00	55.00	150	—
1749	—	3.00	8.00	55.00	150	—
1750	—	3.50	9.00	55.00	150	—
1751	—	3.50	9.00	55.00	150	—
1752	—	3.50	9.00	55.00	150	—
1753	—	3.50	9.00	55.00	150	—
1754	—	3.50	9.00	55.00	150	—

KM# 601 1/2 PENNY

Copper **Ruler:** George III **Obv:** Laureate bust right **Obv. Legend:** GEORGIVS • - III • REX • **Rev:** Brittania seated left **Rev. Legend:** BRITAN - NIA • **Note:** Contemporary counterfeits, especially of 1775, are very common. The counterfeits vary in quality, but most are somewhat smalle, thinner, and more crudely designed the the genuine.

Date	Mintage	F	VF	XF	Unc	BU
1770	—	10.00	40.00	125	450	—
1770 Proof	—	—	—	—	600	—
1771	—	8.00	35.00	125	400	—
Note: Die varieties exist						
1772	—	8.00	35.00	125	400	—
1772 GEORIVS (error)	—	30.00	80.00	225	450	—
1773	—	8.00	35.00	125	400	—
1774	—	15.00	40.00	125	400	—
1775	—	8.00	35.00	125	450	—

KM# 647 1/2 PENNY

12.1900 g., Copper, 30.20 mm. **Ruler:** George III **Obv:** Laureate bust right **Obv. Legend:** GEORGIUS III DEI GRATIA REX **Rev:** Brittania seated left **Rev. Legend:** BRITANNIA

Date	Mintage	F	VF	XF	Unc	BU
1799	—	4.00	10.00	40.00	100	—
Note: With five incuse gunports						
1799	—	4.00	10.00	40.00	110	—
Note: With six relief gunports						
1799	—	5.00	14.00	50.00	125	—
Note: With nine relief gunports						
1799	—	5.00	14.00	50.00	120	—
Note: Plain hull						
1799	—	5.00	14.00	50.00	125	—
Note: Raised line along hull						
1799 Proof	—	—	—	—	250	—

KM# 647a 1/2 PENNY

Bronzed Copper **Ruler:** George III **Obv:** Laureate bust right **Rev:** Brittania seated left

Date	Mintage	F	VF	XF	Unc	BU
1799 Proof	—	—	—	—	400	—

KM# 499 PENNY

Silver **Ruler:** William III **Obv:** Laureate head right **Rev:** Crowned Roman numeral I, crown divides date **Note:** Varieties exist.

Date	Mintage	VG	F	VF	XF	Unc
1701	—	9.00	18.00	35.00	100	—

KM# 512 PENNY

Silver **Ruler:** Anne **Obv:** Bust left **Rev:** Crowned Roman numeral I, crown divides date

Date	Mintage	VG	F	VF	XF	Unc
1703	—	9.00	18.00	35.00	80.00	—
1705	—	8.00	17.00	30.00	70.00	—
1706	—	8.00	17.00	30.00	—	—
1708	—	9.00	18.00	35.00	100	—
1709	—	8.00	17.00	30.00	75.00	—
1710	—	10.00	22.00	50.00	100	—
1713/0	—	8.00	18.00	35.00	80.00	—
1713	—	8.00	18.00	35.00	65.00	—

KM# 544 PENNY

0.5017 g., 0.9250 Silver 0.0149 oz. ASW **Ruler:** George I **Obv:** Laureate bust right **Rev:** Crowned Roman numeral I, crown divides date

Date	Mintage	VG	F	VF	XF	Unc
1716	—	5.00	8.00	21.00	50.00	—
1716 Prooflike	—	—	—	—	—	60.00
1718	—	5.00	8.00	21.00	50.00	—
1718 Prooflike	—	—	—	—	—	60.00
1720	—	5.00	8.00	21.00	50.00	—
1720 Prooflike	—	—	—	—	—	60.00
1723	—	5.00	8.00	22.00	50.00	—
1723 Prooflike	—	—	—	—	—	60.00
1725	—	5.00	8.00	21.00	50.00	—
1725 Prooflike	—	—	—	—	—	60.00
1726	—	6.00	10.00	27.00	55.00	—
1726 Prooflike	—	—	—	—	—	60.00
1727	—	7.00	12.00	40.00	75.00	—
1727 Prooflike	—	—	—	—	—	60.00

KM# 567 PENNY

0.5017 g., 0.9250 Silver 0.0149 oz. ASW **Ruler:** George II **Obv:** Young laureate head left **Obv. Legend:** GEORGIVS • II • - DEI GRATIA • **Rev:** Crowned Roman numeral I, crown divides date

Date	Mintage	VG	F	VF	XF	Unc
1729	—	5.00	8.00	20.00	35.00	—
1729 Prooflike	—	—	—	—	—	45.00
1731	—	5.00	7.00	17.00	40.00	—
1731 Prooflike	—	—	—	—	—	50.00
1732	—	5.00	7.00	17.00	40.00	—
1732 Prooflike	—	—	—	—	—	50.00
1735	—	5.00	8.00	21.00	50.00	—
1735 Prooflike	—	—	—	—	—	50.00
1737	—	5.00	8.00	20.00	45.00	—
1737 Prooflike	—	—	—	—	—	50.00
1739	—	5.00	7.00	17.00	40.00	—
1739 Prooflike	—	—	—	—	—	50.00
1740/30	—	7.00	12.00	22.50	50.00	—
1740	—	5.00	7.00	17.00	40.00	—
1740 Prooflike	—	—	—	—	—	50.00
1743/0	—	7.00	12.00	22.50	50.00	—
1743	—	5.00	7.00	17.00	40.00	—
1743 Prooflike	—	—	—	—	—	50.00
1746/3	—	5.00	8.00	21.00	45.00	—
1746	—	5.00	7.00	17.00	40.00	—
1746 Prooflike	—	—	—	17.00	—	50.00
1750	—	5.00	7.00	17.00	40.00	—
1752/0	—	5.00	8.00	21.00	45.00	—
1752	—	5.00	7.00	17.00	40.00	—
1753/2	—	6.00	8.00	21.00	45.00	—
1753	—	5.00	7.00	17.00	40.00	—
1754	—	4.50	6.00	17.00	40.00	—
1755	—	4.50	6.00	17.00	40.00	—
1756	—	4.50	6.00	17.00	40.00	—
1757	—	4.50	6.00	17.00	40.00	—
1758	—	4.50	6.00	17.00	40.00	—
1759	—	4.50	6.00	17.00	40.00	—
1760	—	5.00	7.00	21.00	45.00	—
1760 Prooflike	—	—	—	—	—	50.00

KM# 594 PENNY

0.5017 g., 0.9250 Silver 0.0149 oz. ASW **Ruler:** George III **Obv:** Head right **Obv. Legend:** GEORGIVS • III • DEI • GRATIA • **Rev:** Crowned Roman numeral I

Date	Mintage	F	VF	XF	Unc	BU
1763	—	6.50	17.50	30.00	50.00	—
1763 Prooflike	—	—	—	—	60.00	—
1763 Proof; rare	—	—	—	—	—	—
1765 Rare	—	—	—	—	—	—
1766	—	6.50	15.00	25.00	40.00	—
1766 Prooflike	—	—	—	—	60.00	—
1770	—	6.50	10.00	18.00	35.00	—
1770 Prooflike	—	—	—	—	—	—
1772	—	6.50	15.00	25.00	40.00	—
1772 Prooflike	—	—	—	—	60.00	—
1776	—	6.50	15.00	25.00	40.00	—
1779	—	6.50	15.00	25.00	40.00	—
1780	—	6.50	17.50	30.00	50.00	—
1780 Prooflike	—	—	—	—	60.00	—
1781	—	6.50	10.00	18.00	35.00	—
1784	—	6.50	10.00	18.00	35.00	—
1784 Prooflike	—	—	—	—	60.00	—
1786	—	6.50	10.00	18.00	35.00	—
1786 Prooflike	—	—	—	—	60.00	—

KM# 610 PENNY

0.5017 g., 0.9250 Silver 0.0149 oz. ASW **Ruler:** George III **Obv:** Older bust right **Rev:** Crowned value

Date	Mintage	F	VF	XF	Unc	BU
1792	—	10.00	25.00	45.00	70.00	—
1792 Prooflike	—	—	—	—	80.00	—

KM# 614 PENNY

0.5017 g., 0.9250 Silver 0.0149 oz. ASW **Ruler:** George III **Obv:** Bust right **Rev:** Crowned value

Date	Mintage	F	VF	XF	Unc	BU
1795	—	7.00	10.00	25.00	45.00	—
1795 Prooflike	—	—	—	—	50.00	—
1800	—	5.00	8.00	20.00	40.00	—
1800 Prooflike	—	—	—	—	50.00	—

KM# 618 PENNY

Copper **Ruler:** George III **Obv:** Laureate bust right **Obv. Legend:** GEORGIUS III • D : G • REX • **Rev:** Brittania seated left **Rev. Legend:** BRITANNIA •

Date	Mintage	F	VF	XF	Unc	BU
1797	—	8.00	35.00	150	450	—
1797 Proof	—	—	—	—	350	—

KM# 618a PENNY

Gilt Copper **Ruler:** George III **Obv:** Laureate bust right **Rev:** Brittania seated left

Date	Mintage	F	VF	XF	Unc	BU
1797 Proof	—	—	—	—	850	—

KM# 500.2 2 PENCE

Silver **Ruler:** William III **Obv:** Laureate bust right **Rev:** Crown smaller and lower

Date	Mintage	VG	F	VF	XF	Unc
1701	—	9.00	18.00	35.00	95.00	—

KM# 513 2 PENCE

Silver **Ruler:** Anne **Obv:** Bust left **Obv. Legend:** ANNA DEI - GRATIA **Rev:** Crown above value **Note:** Varieties exist.

Date	Mintage	VG	F	VF	XF	Unc
1703	—	7.00	11.00	27.00	75.00	—
1704	—	7.00	10.00	21.00	50.00	—
1704 Prooflike	—	—	—	—	—	60.00
1705	—	7.00	10.00	21.00	55.00	—
1706	—	7.00	10.00	22.00	65.00	—
1707	—	7.00	10.00	22.00	65.00	—
1707 Proof-like	—	—	—	—	—	60.00
1708	—	7.00	10.00	21.00	50.00	—
1709	—	7.00	10.00	27.00	70.00	—
1710	—	7.00	10.00	21.00	50.00	—
1713	—	7.00	10.00	21.00	50.00	—

KM# 550 2 PENCE

1.0033 g., 0.9250 Silver 0.0298 oz. ASW **Ruler:** George I **Obv:** Laureate bust right **Rev:** Crown above value **Note:** Varieties exist.

Date	Mintage	VG	F	VF	XF	Unc
1717	—	7.00	10.00	21.00	50.00	—
1717 Prooflike	—	—	—	—	—	70.00
1721	—	7.00	10.00	19.00	40.00	—
1721 Prooflike	—	—	—	—	—	70.00
1723	—	7.00	10.00	26.00	65.00	—
1723 Prooflike	—	—	—	—	—	70.00
1726	—	7.00	10.00	19.00	40.00	—
1726 Prooflike	—	—	—	—	—	70.00
1727	—	7.00	10.00	22.00	55.00	—
1727 Prooflike	—	—	—	—	—	70.00

KM# 568 2 PENCE

1.0033 g., 0.9250 Silver 0.0298 oz. ASW **Ruler:** George II **Obv:** Young head left **Rev:** Crown above value

Date	Mintage	VG	F	VF	XF	Unc
1729	—	7.00	10.00	19.00	40.00	—
1729 Prooflike	—	—	—	—	—	60.00
1731	—	7.00	10.00	19.00	40.00	—
1731 Prooflike	—	—	—	—	—	60.00
1732	—	7.00	10.00	19.00	35.00	—
1732 Prooflike	—	—	—	—	—	60.00
1735	—	7.00	10.00	19.00	35.00	—
1735 Prooflike	—	—	—	—	—	60.00
1737	—	7.00	10.00	19.00	35.00	—
1737 Prooflike	—	—	—	—	—	60.00
1739	—	7.00	10.00	19.00	40.00	—
1739 Prooflike	—	—	—	—	—	60.00
1740	—	7.00	10.00	22.00	55.00	—
1740 Prooflike	—	—	—	—	—	60.00
1743/0	—	7.00	10.00	19.00	45.00	—
1743	—	7.00	10.00	19.00	35.00	—
1743 Prooflike	—	—	—	—	—	60.00
1746	—	7.00	10.00	19.00	35.00	—
1746 Prooflike	—	—	—	—	—	60.00
1756	—	7.00	10.00	20.00	35.00	—
1759	—	7.00	10.00	20.00	35.00	—
1760	—	7.00	10.00	20.00	35.00	—
1760 Prooflike	—	—	—	—	—	60.00

KM# 595 2 PENCE

1.0033 g., 0.9250 Silver 0.0298 oz. ASW **Ruler:** George III **Obv:** Laureate bust right **Obv. Legend:** GEORGIVS • III • DEI • GRATIA • **Rev:** Crown above value

Date	Mintage	F	VF	XF	Unc	BU
1763	—	8.00	20.00	27.50	45.00	—
1763 Prooflike	—	—	—	—	50.00	—
1763 Proof	—	—	—	—	1,250	—
1765 10-20 pieces	—	150	300	800	—	—
1766	—	8.00	12.00	22.50	40.00	—
1766 Prooflike	—	—	—	—	50.00	—
1772/62	—	8.50	13.50	27.50	45.00	—
1772	—	8.00	12.00	22.50	40.00	—
1772 Prooflike	—	—	—	—	50.00	—
1776	—	8.00	12.00	22.50	40.00	—
1780	—	8.00	12.00	22.50	40.00	—
1780 Prooflike	—	—	—	—	50.00	—
1784	—	8.00	12.00	22.50	40.00	—
1784 Prooflike	—	—	—	—	50.00	—
1786	—	8.00	12.00	22.50	40.00	—
1786 Prooflike	—	—	—	—	50.00	—

KM# 611 2 PENCE

1.0033 g., 0.9250 Silver 0.0298 oz. ASW **Ruler:** George III

Date	Mintage	F	VF	XF	Unc	BU
1792	—	10.00	22.00	45.00	75.00	—
1792 Prooflike	—	—	—	—	80.00	—

KM# 615 2 PENCE

1.0033 g., 0.9250 Silver 0.0298 oz. ASW **Ruler:** George III **Obv:** Bust right **Obv. Legend:** GEORGIVS • III • DEI • GRATIA • **Rev:** Crown above value

Date	Mintage	F	VF	XF	Unc	BU
1795	—	8.00	12.00	25.00	45.00	—
1795 Prooflike	—	—	—	—	50.00	—
1800	—	7.00	11.00	20.00	40.00	—
1800 Prooflike	—	—	—	—	50.00	—

KM# 619 2 PENCE

Copper **Ruler:** George III **Obv:** Laureate head right **Obv. Legend:** GEORGIUS III • D : G • REX • **Rev:** Brittania seated left **Rev. Legend:** BRITANNIA •

Date	Mintage	F	VF	XF	Unc	BU
1797	722,000	17.00	70.00	250	500	—
1797 Proof	Inc. above	—	—	—	650	—

KM# 501 3 PENCE

Silver **Ruler:** William III **Obv:** Laureate bust right **Rev:** Crowned 3, crown divides date **Note:** Varieties exist.

Date	Mintage	VG	F	VF	XF	Unc
1701	—	9.00	18.00	38.00	100	—

KM# 514 3 PENCE

Silver **Ruler:** Anne **Obv:** Bust left **Obv. Legend:** ANNA • DEI • - GRATIA • **Rev:** Crown above value divides date **Note:** Varieties exist.

Date	Mintage	VG	F	VF	XF	Unc
1703	—	7.50	13.00	30.00	90.00	—
1704	—	7.00	10.00	25.00	80.00	—
1704 Prooflike	—	—	—	—	—	95.00
1705	—	7.00	10.00	25.00	80.00	—
1706	—	7.00	10.00	23.00	60.00	—
1707	—	7.00	10.00	23.00	60.00	—
1707 Prooflike	—	—	—	—	—	95.00
1708/7	—	9.00	15.00	35.00	75.00	—
1708	—	7.00	10.00	23.00	65.00	—
1709	—	7.00	10.00	23.00	60.00	—
1710	—	7.00	10.00	23.00	60.00	—
1713	—	7.00	10.00	23.00	60.00	—

KM# 551 3 PENCE

1.5050 g., 0.9250 Silver 0.0448 oz. ASW **Ruler:** George I **Obv:** Laureate bust right **Obv. Legend:** GEORGIVS • DEI • GRA • **Rev:** Crowned value

Date	Mintage	VG	F	VF	XF	Unc
1717	—	8.00	14.00	35.00	90.00	—
1717 Prooflike	—	—	—	—	—	125
1721	—	9.00	16.00	37.00	90.00	—
1721 Prooflike	—	—	—	—	—	125
1723	—	10.00	18.00	37.00	90.00	—
1723 Prooflike	—	—	—	—	—	125
1727	—	10.00	18.00	37.00	100	—
1727 Prooflike	—	—	—	—	—	125

KM# 569 3 PENCE

1.5050 g., 0.9250 Silver 0.0448 oz. ASW **Ruler:** George II **Obv:** Young head left **Obv. Legend:** GEORGIVS • II • DEI • GRATIA • **Rev:** Crowned value

Date	Mintage	VG	F	VF	XF	Unc
1729	—	6.50	10.00	22.00	60.00	—
1729 Prooflike	—	—	—	—	—	65.00
1731	—	6.50	10.00	22.00	55.00	—
1731 Prooflike	—	—	—	—	—	65.00
1732	—	6.50	10.00	22.00	55.00	—
1732 Prooflike	—	—	—	—	—	65.00
1735	—	6.50	10.00	22.00	55.00	—
1735 Prooflike	—	—	—	—	—	65.00
1737	—	6.50	10.00	20.00	50.00	—
1737 Prooflike	—	—	—	—	—	65.00
1739	—	6.50	10.00	20.00	50.00	—
1739 Prooflike	—	—	—	—	—	65.00
1740	—	6.50	10.00	20.00	50.00	—
1740 Prooflike	—	—	—	—	—	65.00
1743	—	6.50	10.00	20.00	50.00	—
1743 Prooflike	—	—	—	—	—	65.00
1746/3	—	7.00	12.00	25.00	60.00	—
1746	—	6.50	10.00	20.00	50.00	—
1746 Prooflike	—	—	—	—	—	65.00
1760	—	6.50	10.00	20.00	50.00	—
1760 Prooflike	—	—	—	—	—	65.00

KM# 591 3 PENCE

1.5050 g., 0.9250 Silver 0.0448 oz. ASW **Ruler:** George III **Obv:** Laureate bust right **Obv. Legend:** GEORGIVS • III • DEI • GRATIA • **Rev:** Crown above value divides date **Rev. Legend:** MAG • BRI • FR • ET • HIB • REX •

Date	Mintage	F	VF	XF	Unc	BU
1762	—	5.00	10.00	27.00	60.00	—
1763	—	5.00	10.00	27.00	60.00	—
1763 Proof-like	—	—	—	—	65.00	—
1763 Proof; rare	—	—	—	—	—	—
1765 10-20 pieces	—	150	300	750	—	—
1766	—	8.00	17.00	35.00	60.00	—
1766 Prooflike	—	—	—	—	65.00	—
1770	—	8.00	17.00	35.00	60.00	—
1772/0	—	10.00	20.00	40.00	70.00	—
1772	—	8.00	16.00	35.00	60.00	—
1772 Prooflike	—	—	—	—	65.00	—
1780	—	8.00	16.00	35.00	60.00	—
1780 Prooflike	—	—	—	—	65.00	—
1784	—	8.00	17.00	35.00	60.00	—
1784 Prooflike	—	—	—	—	65.00	—
1786	—	8.00	16.00	35.00	60.00	—
1786 Prooflike	—	—	—	—	65.00	—

KM# 612 3 PENCE

1.5050 g., 0.9250 Silver 0.0448 oz. ASW **Ruler:** George III **Obv:** Bust right **Obv. Legend:** GEORGIVS III DEI GRATIA **Rev:** Crowned value **Rev. Legend:** MAG • BRI • FR • ET • HIB • REX •

Date	Mintage	F	VF	XF	Unc	BU
1792	—	12.50	30.00	65.00	125	—
1792 Prooflike	—	—	—	—	150	—

KM# 616 3 PENCE

1.5050 g., 0.9250 Silver 0.0448 oz. ASW **Ruler:** George III **Obv:** Bust right **Obv. Legend:** GEORGIVS III DEI GRATIA **Rev:** Crowned value **Rev. Legend:** MAG • BRI • FR ET • HIB • REX •

Date	Mintage	F	VF	XF	Unc	BU
1795	—	8.00	16.00	35.00	80.00	—
1795 Prooflike	—	—	—	—	85.00	—
1800	—	8.00	16.00	35.00	60.00	—
1800 Prooflike	—	—	—	—	85.00	—

KM# 495 4 PENCE (Groat)
Silver **Ruler:** William III **Obv:** Laureate bust right **Rev:** Crown above value divides date

Date	Mintage	VG	F	VF	XF	Unc
1701	—	10.00	20.00	40.00	125	—
1702	—	9.00	18.00	35.00	100	—
1702 Prooflike	—	—	—	—	—	150

KM# 515 4 PENCE (Groat)
Silver **Ruler:** Anne **Obv:** Bust left **Obv. Legend:** ANNA • DEI • - GRATIA • **Rev:** Crown above value divides date **Rev. Legend:** MAG • BR • VR • ET • HIB • REG •

Date	Mintage	VG	F	VF	XF	Unc
1703	—	8.00	13.00	27.00	70.00	—
1704	—	7.00	10.00	23.00	60.00	—
1704 Prooflike	—	—	—	—	—	—
1705	—	8.00	13.00	30.00	70.00	—
1706	—	7.00	10.00	23.00	60.00	—
1708	—	7.00	10.00	23.00	60.00	—
1709	—	7.00	10.00	23.00	60.00	—
1710	—	7.00	10.00	23.00	60.00	—
1713	—	7.00	10.00	23.00	60.00	—

KM# 552 4 PENCE (Groat)
2.0067 g., 0.9250 Silver 0.0597 oz. ASW **Ruler:** George I **Obv:** Laureate bust right **Obv. Legend:** GEORGIVS • - DEI • GRA • **Rev. Legend:** MAG • BRI • FR • ET • HIB • REX •

Date	Mintage	VG	F	VF	XF	Unc
1717	—	9.00	14.00	30.00	80.00	—
1717 Prooflike	—	—	—	—	—	125
1721	—	9.00	14.00	30.00	80.00	—
1721 Prooflike	—	—	—	—	—	125
1723	—	9.00	14.00	30.00	80.00	—
1723 Prooflike	—	—	—	—	—	125
1727	—	10.00	18.00	35.00	100	—
1727 Prooflike	—	—	—	—	—	125

KM# 570 4 PENCE (Groat)
2.0067 g., 0.9250 Silver 0.0597 oz. ASW **Ruler:** George II **Obv:** Young head left **Obv. Legend:** GEORGIVS • II • - DEI • GRATIA • **Rev:** Crown above value divides date **Rev. Legend:** MAG • BRI • FR • ET • HIB • REX •

Date	Mintage	VG	F	VF	XF	Unc
1729	—	7.00	10.00	25.00	60.00	—
1729 Prooflike	—	—	—	—	—	65.00
1731	—	7.00	10.00	25.00	60.00	—
1731 Prooflike	—	—	—	—	—	65.00
1732	—	7.00	10.00	23.00	60.00	—
1732 Prooflike	—	—	—	—	—	65.00
1735	—	7.00	10.00	23.00	60.00	—
1735 Prooflike	—	—	—	—	—	65.00
1737	—	7.00	10.00	23.00	60.00	—
1737 Prooflike	—	—	—	—	—	65.00
1739	—	7.00	10.00	23.00	60.00	—
1739 Prooflike	—	—	—	—	—	65.00
1740	—	7.00	10.00	23.00	60.00	—
1740 Prooflike	—	—	—	—	—	65.00
1743/0	—	10.00	15.00	55.00	125	—
1743	—	7.00	10.00	23.00	60.00	—
1743 Prooflike	—	—	—	—	—	65.00
1746	—	7.00	10.00	22.50	55.00	—
1746 Prooflike	—	—	—	—	—	65.00
1760	—	7.00	10.00	23.00	55.00	—
1760 Prooflike	—	—	—	—	—	65.00

KM# 596.1 4 PENCE (Groat)
2.0067 g., 0.9250 Silver 0.0597 oz. ASW **Ruler:** George III **Obv:** Young head right **Obv. Legend:** GEORGIVS • III • DEI • GRATIA • **Rev:** Crown above value divides date **Rev. Legend:** MAG • BRI • FR • ET • HIB • REX •

Date	Mintage	F	VF	XF	Unc	BU
1763	—	10.00	15.00	30.00	70.00	—
1763 Prooflike	—	—	—	—	90.00	—
1763 Proof; rare	—	—	—	—	—	—
1765 10-20 pieces	—	200	350	800	—	—
1766	—	12.00	18.00	35.00	85.00	—
1766 Prooflike	—	—	—	—	90.00	—
1770	—	12.00	18.00	35.00	85.00	—
1772/0	—	12.00	18.00	40.00	100	—
1772	—	12.00	18.00	35.00	85.00	—
1772 Prooflike	—	—	—	—	90.00	—
1776	—	12.00	17.00	35.00	85.00	—
1780	—	12.00	17.00	35.00	85.00	—
1780 Prooflike	—	—	—	—	90.00	—
1784	—	12.00	18.00	35.00	85.00	—
1784 Prooflike	—	—	—	—	90.00	—
1786	—	12.00	20.00	40.00	95.00	—
1786 Prooflike	—	—	—	—	90.00	—

KM# 596.2 4 PENCE (Groat)
2.0067 g., 0.9250 Silver 0.0597 oz. ASW **Ruler:** George III **Obv:** Larger lettering **Rev:** Crown above value divides date

Date	Mintage	F	VF	XF	Unc	BU
1786	—	9.00	20.00	50.00	100	—

KM# 613 4 PENCE (Groat)
2.0067 g., 0.9250 Silver 0.0597 oz. ASW **Ruler:** George III **Obv:** Armored bust right **Rev:** Small crown above thin numerals

Date	Mintage	F	VF	XF	Unc	BU
1792	—	15.00	30.00	60.00	100	—
1792 Prooflike	—	—	—	—	125	—

KM# 617 4 PENCE (Groat)
2.0067 g., 0.9250 Silver 0.0597 oz. ASW **Ruler:** George III **Obv:** Bust right **Obv. Legend:** GEORGIVS III DEI GRATIA **Rev:** Crowned value **Rev. Legend:** MAG • BRI • FR - ET • HIB • REX

Date	Mintage	F	VF	XF	Unc	BU
1795	—	8.00	15.00	35.00	85.00	—
1795 Prooflike	—	—	—	—	90.00	—
1800	—	6.50	15.00	30.00	75.00	—
1800 Prooflike	—	—	—	—	90.00	—

KM# 496.1 6 PENCE
Silver **Ruler:** William III **Obv:** Third bust right **Rev:** Cruciform crowned arms, crown divides date, large crown **Note:** Varieties exist.

Date	Mintage	VG	F	VF	XF	Unc
1701	—	10.00	20.00	55.00	200	—

KM# 516.1 6 PENCE
Silver **Ruler:** Anne **Obv:** Bust left, VIGO below **Rev:** Cruciform crowned arms, crown divides date **Note:** Struck from silver seized at Vigo Bay, Spain.

Date	Mintage	VG	F	VF	XF	Unc
1703	—	17.00	35.00	80.00	250	—

KM# 516.2 6 PENCE
Silver **Ruler:** Anne **Obv:** Without VIGO below bust **Rev:** Cruciform crowned arms

Date	Mintage	VG	F	VF	XF	Unc
1705	—	22.00	45.00	150	400	—

KM# 516.3 6 PENCE
Silver **Ruler:** Anne **Obv:** Bust left **Rev:** Cruciform crowned arms with early shield plumes in angles, crown divides date

Date	Mintage	VG	F	VF	XF	Unc
1705	—	15.00	35.00	100	300	—

KM# 516.4 6 PENCE
Silver **Ruler:** Anne **Obv:** Bust left **Rev:** Late shields

Date	Mintage	VG	F	VF	XF	Unc
1705	—	20.00	45.00	100	300	—

KM# 516.5 6 PENCE
Silver **Ruler:** Anne **Obv:** Bust left **Rev:** Roses and plumes in angles

Date	Mintage	VG	F	VF	XF	Unc
1705	—	20.00	45.00	125	300	—
1707	—	13.00	30.00	100	250	—

KM# 522.1 6 PENCE
Silver **Ruler:** Anne **Rev:** English and Scottish shield halved **Note:** Varieties exist.

Date	Mintage	VG	F	VF	XF	Unc
1707	—	13.00	21.00	55.00	175	—
1708	—	16.00	27.00	70.00	200	—
1711	—	10.00	16.00	50.00	150	—

KM# 522.2 6 PENCE
Silver **Ruler:** Anne **Obv:** W/E (Edinburgh) below bust **Rev:** English and Scottish shield halved **Note:** Varieties exist.

Date	Mintage	VG	F	VF	XF	Unc
1707	—	10.00	20.00	70.00	225	—
1707 Proof	—	—	—	—	—	2,000
Note: Plain edge						
1708/7	—	25.00	50.00	100	400	—
1708	—	17.50	35.00	65.00	225	—

KM# 522.3 6 PENCE
Silver **Ruler:** Anne **Obv:** E with star below bust **Rev:** English and Scottish shield halved

Date	Mintage	VG	F	VF	XF	Unc
1708/7	—	22.00	45.00	100	400	—
1708	—	20.00	40.00	90.00	350	—

KM# 530.1 6 PENCE
Silver **Ruler:** Anne **Obv:** Cruder (EDINBURGH) bust wtih E and star **Rev:** English and Scottish shield halved

Date	Mintage	VG	F	VF	XF	Unc
1708	—	22.00	45.00	100	350	—

KM# 530.2 6 PENCE
Silver **Ruler:** Anne **Obv:** Without E and star below bust **Obv. Legend:** ANNA • DEI • - GRATIA • **Rev:** Plumes in angles of cruciform arms. English and Scottish shield halved **Rev. Legend:** MAG • - BRI • FR - ET • HIB - REG •

Date	Mintage	VG	F	VF	XF	Unc
1707	—	10.00	18.00	55.00	175	—
1708	—	12.00	20.00	60.00	200	—

KM# 530.3 6 PENCE
Silver **Ruler:** Anne **Rev:** Roses and plumes in angles of cruciform arms. English and Scottish shield halved

Date	Mintage	VG	F	VF	XF	Unc
1710	—	20.00	35.00	100	250	—

KM# 553.1 6 PENCE
3.0100 g., 0.9250 Silver 0.0895 oz. ASW **Ruler:** George I **Obv:** Laureate bust right **Rev:** Shields in cruciform **Note:** Varieties exist.

Date	Mintage	VG	F	VF	XF	Unc
1717	—	22.00	45.00	150	400	—
1717 Proof	—	—	—	—	—	1,500
Note: Plain edge						
1720/17	—	22.00	45.00	150	400	—

KM# 553.2 6 PENCE
3.0100 g., 0.9250 Silver 0.0895 oz. ASW **Ruler:** George I **Obv:** Laureate bust right **Obv. Legend:** GEORGIVS • D • G • M • BR • ... **Rev:** SSC in angles of cruciform arms **Note:** Varieties exist. Struck from silver supplied by South Sea Company.

Date	Mintage	VG	F	VF	XF	Unc
1723	—	11.00	21.00	65.00	200	—

KM# 553.3 6 PENCE
3.0100 g., 0.9250 Silver 0.0895 oz. ASW **Ruler:** George I **Obv:** Laureate bust right **Rev:** Small roses and plumes in angles of cruciform arms

Date	Mintage	VG	F	VF	XF	Unc
1726	—	17.00	35.00	125	350	—

KM# 564.1 6 PENCE
3.0100 g., 0.9250 Silver 0.0895 oz. ASW **Ruler:** George II **Obv:** Laureate bust left **Obv. Legend:** GEORGIVS • II • - DEI • GRATIA • **Rev:** Without emblems between shields

Date	Mintage	VG	F	VF	XF	Unc
1728	—	28.00	55.00	175	400	—
1728 Plain edge; Proof	—	—	—	—	—	1,500

KM# 564.2 6 PENCE

3.0100 g., 0.9250 Silver 0.0895 oz. ASW **Ruler:** George II **Obv:** Laureate bust left **Obv. Legend:** GEORGIVS • II • - DEI • GRATIA • **Rev:** Plumes between shields

Date	Mintage	VG	F	VF	XF	Unc
1728	—	21.00	45.00	125	300	—

KM# 564.3 6 PENCE

3.0100 g., 0.9250 Silver 0.0895 oz. ASW **Ruler:** George II **Obv:** Laureate bust left **Obv. Legend:** GEORGIVS • II • - DEI • GRATIA • **Rev:** Roses and plumes between shields

Date	Mintage	VG	F	VF	XF	Unc
1728	—	11.00	23.00	85.00	250	—
1731	—	11.00	23.00	85.00	250	—
1732	—	11.00	23.00	85.00	250	—
1734	—	20.00	40.00	100	300	—
1735	—	20.00	40.00	100	300	—
1736	—	17.00	35.00	100	250	—

KM# 564.4 6 PENCE

3.0100 g., 0.9250 Silver 0.0895 oz. ASW **Ruler:** George II **Obv:** Laureate bust left **Obv. Legend:** GEORGIVS • II • - DEI • GRATIA • **Rev:** Roses between shields

Date	Mintage	VG	F	VF	XF	Unc
1739	—	11.00	23.00	75.00	225	—
1741	—	11.00	23.00	80.00	200	—

KM# 582.1 6 PENCE

3.0100 g., 0.9250 Silver 0.0895 oz. ASW **Ruler:** George II **Obv:** Older laureate head left **Obv. Legend:** GEORGIVS • II • - DEI • GRATIA • **Rev:** Roses between shields

Date	Mintage	VG	F	VF	XF	Unc
1743	—	11.00	22.00	80.00	225	—
1745/3	—	20.00	35.00	100	300	—
1745	—	14.00	27.00	85.00	225	—

KM# 582.2 6 PENCE

3.0100 g., 0.9250 Silver 0.0895 oz. ASW **Ruler:** George II **Obv:** Older laureate head left **Obv. Legend:** GEORGIVS • II • - DEI • GRATIA • **Rev:** Shields in cruciform

Date	Mintage	VG	F	VF	XF	Unc
1746 Proof	—	—	—	—	—	800
1750	—	17.00	35.00	100	250	—
1751	—	22.00	45.00	125	350	—
1757	—	6.00	10.00	19.00	60.00	—
1758/7	—	8.00	15.00	28.00	70.00	—
1758	—	6.00	10.00	26.00	60.00	—

KM# 582.3 6 PENCE

3.0100 g., 0.9250 Silver 0.0895 oz. ASW **Ruler:** George II **Obv:** Older head left; LIMA below bust **Obv. Legend:** GEORGIVS • II • - DEI • GRATIA • **Rev:** Shields in cruciform **Note:** Struck from Spanish silver seized from Lima, Peru.

Date	Mintage	VG	F	VF	XF	Unc
1745	—	9.00	17.00	60.00	150	—
1746	—	9.00	15.00	60.00	150	—

KM# 606.1 6 PENCE

3.0100 g., 0.9250 Silver 0.0895 oz. ASW **Ruler:** George III **Obv:** Bust right **Obv. Legend:** GEORGIVS • III • DEI • GRATIA • **Rev:** Shields in cruciform, crowns in angles

Date	Mintage	F	VF	XF	Unc	BU
1787	—	10.00	20.00	45.00	80.00	—
1787 Proof; plain edge	—	—	—	—	500	—

KM# 606.2 6 PENCE

3.0100 g., 0.9250 Silver 0.0895 oz. ASW **Ruler:** George III **Obv:** Bust right **Obv. Legend:** GEORGIVS • III • DEI • GRATIA • **Rev:** Hearts in Hanoverian shield

Date	Mintage	F	VF	XF	Unc	BU
1787	—	10.00	20.00	45.00	80.00	—

KM# 504.1 SHILLING

Silver **Ruler:** William III **Obv:** Fifth bust (hair high) **Note:** Varieties exist.

Date	Mintage	VG	F	VF	XF	Unc
1701	—	22.00	55.00	150	400	—

KM# 504.2 SHILLING

Silver **Ruler:** William III **Rev:** Plumes in angles

Date	Mintage	VG	F	VF	XF	Unc
1701	—	35.00	100	250	900	—

KM# 509.1 SHILLING

Silver **Ruler:** Anne **Obv:** First bust (long ties) left **Rev:** Crowned cruciform arms, date divided at top

Date	Mintage	VG	F	VF	XF	Unc
1702	—	30.00	60.00	200	500	—

KM# 509.2 SHILLING

Silver **Ruler:** Anne **Obv:** Bust left **Rev:** Plumes in angles

Date	Mintage	VG	F	VF	XF	Unc
1702	—	40.00	75.00	250	550	—

KM# 509.3 SHILLING

Silver **Ruler:** Anne **Obv:** First bust with VIGO below **Obv. Legend:** ANNA • DEI • - GRATIA • **Rev:** Crowned shields in cruciform **Rev. Legend:** MAG - BR • FRA - ET • HIB - REG • **Note:** Struck from silver seized at Vigo Bay, Spain.

Date	Mintage	VG	F	VF	XF	Unc
1702	—	30.00	55.00	175	450	—

KM# 517.1 SHILLING

Silver **Ruler:** Anne **Obv:** Second bust (short ties), VIGO below **Obv. Legend:** ANNA • DEI • - GRATIA • **Rev:** Crowned shield in cruciform **Rev. Legend:** MAG - BR • FRA - ET • HIB - REG •

Date	Mintage	VG	F	VF	XF	Unc
1703	—	27.00	55.00	175	400	—

KM# 517.2 SHILLING

Silver **Ruler:** Anne **Obv:** Without VIGO below **Rev:** Crowned shields in cruciform

Date	Mintage	VG	F	VF	XF	Unc
1704	—	160	425	950	—	—
1705	—	35.00	70.00	225	550	—

KM# 517.3 SHILLING

Silver **Ruler:** Anne **Obv:** Bust left **Obv. Legend:** ANNA • DEI • - GRATIA • **Rev:** Plumes in angles **Rev. Legend:** MAG - BR • FRA - ET • HIB - REG •

Date	Mintage	VG	F	VF	XF	Unc
1704	—	35.00	70.00	250	600	—
1705	—	30.00	60.00	200	500	—

KM# 517.4 SHILLING

Silver **Ruler:** Anne **Obv:** Bust left **Rev:** Roses and plumes in angles

Date	Mintage	VG	F	VF	XF	Unc
1705	—	25.00	55.00	200	450	—
1707	—	30.00	60.00	200	450	—

KM# 517.5 SHILLING

Silver **Ruler:** Anne **Obv:** E (Edinburgh) below bust **Rev:** English and Scottish shield halved **Note:** Varieties exist.

Date	Mintage	VG	F	VF	XF	Unc
1707	—	15.00	30.00	95.00	350	—
1707 Plain edge; Proof; rare	—	—	—	—	—	—
1708	—	40.00	80.00	200	550	—

KM# 517.6 SHILLING

Silver **Ruler:** Anne **Obv:** W/E and star below bust **Rev:** English and Scottish shield halved

Date	Mintage	VG	F	VF	XF	Unc
1707	—	30.00	75.00	225	500	—
1708/7	—	30.00	75.00	225	500	—
1708	—	24.00	50.00	150	400	—

KM# 517.7 SHILLING
Silver **Ruler:** Anne **Obv:** Without E below bust **Rev:** English and Scottish shield halved

Date	Mintage	VG	F	VF	XF	Unc
1708	—	40.00	85.00	300	650	—

KM# 523.1 SHILLING
Silver **Ruler:** Anne **Obv:** Third bust left **Obv. Legend:** ANNA • DEI • - GRATIA • **Rev:** Crowned shield in cruciform **Rev. Legend:** MAG - BR • FRA - ET • HIB - REG •

Date	Mintage	VG	F	VF	XF	Unc
1707	—	11.00	22.00	100	300	—
1708	—	12.00	24.00	65.00	250	—
1709	—	17.50	35.00	80.00	300	—
1711	—	60.00	125	350	800	—

KM# 523.2 SHILLING
Silver **Ruler:** Anne **Obv:** Bust left **Rev:** Plumes in angles

Date	Mintage	VG	F	VF	XF	Unc
1707	—	19.00	40.00	125	400	—
1708	—	19.00	40.00	100	350	—

KM# 523.3 SHILLING
Silver **Ruler:** Anne **Obv:** E below bust **Rev:** Shields in cruciform **Note:** Varieties exist.

Date	Mintage	VG	F	VF	XF	Unc
1707	—	13.00	28.00	90.00	350	—
1708/7	—	35.00	75.00	200	550	—
1708	—	28.00	60.00	200	500	—

KM# 523.4 SHILLING
Silver **Ruler:** Anne **Obv:** Bust left **Rev:** Roses and plumes in angles

Date	Mintage	VG	F	VF	XF	Unc
1708	—	28.00	60.00	200	450	—
1710	—	17.00	35.00	100	300	—

KM# 524.1 SHILLING
Silver **Ruler:** Anne **Obv:** EDINBURGH bust left with E and star below bust **Rev:** Crowned cruciform arms, date divided at top

Date	Mintage	VG	F	VF	XF	Unc
1707 Rare	—	—	—	—	—	—
1708	—	30.00	75.00	175	450	—
1709	—	35.00	75.00	160	375	—

KM# 524.2 SHILLING
Silver **Ruler:** Anne **Obv:** E without star below bust **Rev:** Crowned arms in cruciform **Note:** Possibly a filled die variety.

Date	Mintage	VG	F	VF	XF	Unc
1709 Rare	—	—	—	—	—	—

KM# 533.1 SHILLING
Silver **Ruler:** Anne **Obv:** Fourth bust, (poorer style, more waves) left **Rev:** Roses and plumes in angles

Date	Mintage	VG	F	VF	XF	Unc
1710	—	22.00	45.00	150	400	—
1712	—	12.00	26.00	90.00	250	—
1713/2	—	17.00	35.00	100	300	—
1714	—	13.00	28.00	100	250	—

KM# 533.2 SHILLING
Silver **Ruler:** Anne **Obv:** Bust left **Rev:** Plain angles

Date	Mintage	VG	F	VF	XF	Unc
1710 Plain edge; Proof; Rare	—	—	—	—	—	—
1711	—	10.00	19.00	65.00	200	—

KM# 539.1 SHILLING
6.0200 g., 0.9250 Silver 0.1790 oz. ASW **Ruler:** George I **Obv:** First bust (two-ended ties) right **Obv. Legend:** GEORGIVS • III • D • G • M • BR • FR • ET • HIB • REX • F • D • **Rev:** Crowned cruciform arms and roses and plumes in angles **Rev. Legend:** BRVN - ET • L • DVX - S • R • I • A • TH - ET • EL •

Date	Mintage	VG	F	VF	XF	Unc
1715	—	17.00	35.00	100	350	—
1716	—	35.00	85.00	250	700	—
1717	—	15.00	40.00	100	400	—
1718	—	17.00	35.00	100	350	—
1719	—	40.00	95.00	225	650	—
1720	—	17.00	35.00	100	400	—
1720/18	—	17.00	35.00	100	400	—
1721/19	—	17.00	35.00	100	450	—
1721/0	—	17.00	35.00	100	400	—
1721	—	17.00	35.00	100	400	—
1722	—	15.00	35.00	100	400	—
1723	—	25.00	55.00	145	450	—

KM# 539.2 SHILLING
6.0200 g., 0.9250 Silver 0.1790 oz. ASW **Ruler:** George I **Obv:** First laureate bust right **Obv. Legend:** GEORGIVS • D • G • M • BR • FR • ET • HIB • REX • F • D • **Rev:** Plain field in angles in cruciform arms **Rev. Legend:** BRVN - ET • L • DVX - S • R • I • A • TH - ET • EL • **Note:** Varieties exist.

Date	Mintage	VG	F	VF	XF	Unc
1720	—	13.00	30.00	100	350	—
1721	—	60.00	150	350	850	—

KM# 539.3 SHILLING
6.0200 g., 0.9250 Silver 0.1790 oz. ASW **Ruler:** George I **Obv:** First laureate bust right **Obv. Legend:** GEORGIVS • D • G • M • BR • FR•ET • HIB • REX • F • D • **Rev:** SS, C in opposed angles of cruciform arms **Rev. Legend:** BRVN - ET • L • DVX - S • R • I • A • TH - ET • EL • **Note:** Varieties exist. Struck from silver supplied by the South Sea Company.

Date	Mintage	VG	F	VF	XF	Unc
1723	—	12.50	25.00	60.00	250	—

KM# 558.1 SHILLING
6.0200 g., 0.9250 Silver 0.1790 oz. ASW **Ruler:** George I **Obv:** Second laureate bust right with loop in tie **Obv. Legend:** GEORGIVS•D•G•M•BR•FR•ET•HIB•REX•F•D• **Rev:** SS, C in opposed angles of cruciform arms **Rev. Legend:** BRVN•ET•L•DVS-S•R•I•A•TH•ET•EL• **Note:** Varieties exist.

Date	Mintage	VG	F	VF	XF	Unc
1723	—	17.00	35.00	100	400	—

KM# 558.2 SHILLING
6.0200 g., 0.9250 Silver 0.1790 oz. ASW **Ruler:** George I **Obv:** Second laureate bust right **Rev:** Roses and plumes in opposed angles of cruciform arms

Date	Mintage	VG	F	VF	XF	Unc
1723	—	25.00	50.00	125	350	—
1724	—	25.00	50.00	125	350	—
1725	—	25.00	50.00	125	350	—
1726	—	200	400	1,000	1,800	—
1727	—	200	400	1,000	1,800	—

KM# 558.3 SHILLING
6.0200 g., 0.9250 Silver 0.1790 oz. ASW **Ruler:** George I **Obv:** Second laureate bust right with loop in tie, W.C.C. below **Obv. Legend:** GEORGIVS • D • G • M • BR • FR • ET • HIB • REX • F • D • **Rev:** Interlocked C's, plumes in opposed angles of cruciform arms **Rev. Legend:** BRVN - ET • L • DVX - S • R• I • A • TH - ET • EL • **Note:** Struck from silver supplied by Welsh Copper Company.

Date	Mintage	VG	F	VF	XF	Unc
1723	—	100	250	600	1,850	—
1724	—	100	250	650	1,900	—
1725	—	125	300	700	2,000	—
1726	—	125	300	700	1,950	—

KM# 561.1 SHILLING
6.0200 g., 0.9250 Silver 0.1790 oz. ASW **Ruler:** George II **Obv:** Young bust left, small letters **Obv. Legend:** GEORGIVS • II • - DEI • GRATIA • **Rev:** Cruciform arms with roses and plumes between shields, small letters

Date	Mintage	VG	F	VF	XF	Unc
1727	—	20.00	40.00	125	400	—
1728	—	27.00	65.00	175	500	—
1729	—	30.00	70.00	175	500	—
1731	—	22.00	45.00	125	400	—
1732	—	27.50	55.00	150	500	—

KM# 561.2 SHILLING
6.0200 g., 0.9250 Silver 0.1790 oz. ASW **Ruler:** George II **Obv:** Laureate bust left **Obv. Legend:** GEORGIVS • II • - DEI • GRATIA • **Rev:** Plumes between shields

Date	Mintage	VG	F	VF	XF	Unc
1727	—	35.00	70.00	250	600	—
1731	—	50.00	100	300	850	—

KM# 561.3 SHILLING
6.0200 g., 0.9250 Silver 0.1790 oz. ASW **Ruler:** George II **Obv:** Laureate bust left **Rev:** Without emblems between shields

Date	Mintage	VG	F	VF	XF	Unc
1728	—	60.00	125	350	750	—

KM# 561.4 SHILLING
6.0200 g., 0.9250 Silver 0.1790 oz. ASW **Ruler:** George II **Obv:** Laureate bust left **Rev:** Roses between shields

Date	Mintage	VG	F	VF	XF	Unc
1739	—	15.00	22.00	95.00	300	—
1741	—	16.00	23.00	100	300	—

KM# 561.5 SHILLING
6.0200 g., 0.9250 Silver 0.1790 oz. ASW **Ruler:** George II **Obv:** Large letters **Rev:** Large letters

Date	Mintage	VG	F	VF	XF	Unc
1734	—	18.00	35.00	100	350	—
1735	—	18.00	35.00	100	350	—
1736/5	—	35.00	65.00	150	450	—
1736	—	18.00	35.00	100	350	—
1737	—	18.00	35.00	100	400	—

KM# 583.1 SHILLING

6.0200 g., 0.9250 Silver 0.1790 oz. ASW **Ruler:** George II **Obv:** Older laureate head left **Obv. Legend:** GEORGIVS • II • DEI • GRATIA • **Rev:** Crowned arms in cruciform, roses at angles **Rev. Legend:** F • D • B • - ET • L • D • S • R • I • - A • T • ET • E • - M • B • F • ET • - H • REX •

Date	Mintage	VG	F	VF	XF	Unc
1743/1	—	25.00	50.00	100	250	—
1743	—	11.00	22.00	65.00	250	—
1745/3	—	20.00	40.00	150	375	—
1745	—	17.00	35.00	95.00	300	—
1747	—	12.00	30.00	75.00	250	—

KM# 583.2 SHILLING

6.0200 g., 0.9250 Silver 0.1790 oz. ASW **Ruler:** George II **Obv:** LIMA below bust **Obv. Legend:** GEORGIUS • II • - DEI • GRATIA • **Rev:** Crowned shields in cruciform **Rev. Legend:** F • D • B • - ET • L • D • S • R • I • - A • T • ET • E • - M • B • F • ET • - H • REX • **Note:** Struck from Spanish silver siezed at Lima, Peru.

Date	Mintage	VG	F	VF	XF	Unc
1745	—	10.00	20.00	60.00	250	—
1746/5	—	50.00	100	225	600	—
1746	—	45.00	90.00	175	550	—

KM# 583.3 SHILLING

6.0200 g., 0.9250 Silver 0.1790 oz. ASW **Ruler:** George II **Obv:** Without LIMA below bust **Obv. Legend:** GEORGIVS • II • - DEI • GRATIA • **Rev:** Crowned shields in cruciform **Rev. Legend:** F • D • B • - ET • L • D • S • R • I • - A • T • ET • E • - M • B • F • ET • - H • REX •

Date	Mintage	VG	F	VF	XF	Unc
1746 Proof	—	—	—	—	—	850
1750/40	—	20.00	35.00	100	400	—
1750/6	—	27.00	50.00	125	450	—
1750	—	20.00	35.00	100	400	—
1751	—	30.00	65.00	175	500	—
1758	—	8.00	13.00	30.00	65.00	—

KM# 597 SHILLING

6.0200 g., 0.9250 Silver 0.1790 oz. ASW **Ruler:** George III **Obv:** Laureate bust right **Obv. Legend:** GEORGIVS • III • - DEI • GRATIA • **Rev:** Crowned shields in cruciform **Rev. Legend:** F • D • B • - ET • L • D • S • R • I • - A • T • ET • E • - M • B • F • ET • - H • REX •

Date	Mintage	F	VF	XF	Unc	BU
1763	—	225	350	650	1,000	—

KM# 607.1 SHILLING

6.0200 g., 0.9250 Silver 0.1790 oz. ASW **Ruler:** George III **Obv:** Armored laureate bust right **Obv. Legend:** GEORGIVS • III • - DEI • GRATIA • **Rev:** Without hearts in Hanoverian shield **Rev. Legend:** F • D • B • ET • L • D • S • R • I • A • T • ET • E • - M • B • F • ET • H • REX •

Date	Mintage	F	VF	XF	Unc	BU
1787	—	13.00	25.00	60.00	125	—
1787 Without stops at date	—	20.00	50.00	100	200	—
1787 Without stops on obverse	—	175	450	850	1,300	—
1787 Without stop above head	—	19.00	40.00	85.00	175	—
1787 Proof	—	—	—	—	650	—
1787 Plain edge; Proof	—	—	—	—	650	—

KM# 607.2 SHILLING

6.0200 g., 0.9250 Silver 0.1790 oz. ASW **Ruler:** George III **Obv:** Armored laureate bust right **Obv. Legend:** GEORGIVS • III • - DEI • GRATIA • **Rev:** Hearts in Hanoverian shield **Rev. Legend:** F•D•B•ET•L•D•S•R•I•A•T•ET•E•-M•B•F•ET•H•REX•

Date	Mintage	F	VF	XF	Unc	BU
1787	—	13.00	25.00	60.00	125	—

KM# 607.3 SHILLING

6.0200 g., 0.9250 Silver 0.1790 oz. ASW **Ruler:** George III **Obv:** Armored laureate bust right **Rev:** Shields in cruciform **Note:** Known as "Dorrien and Magens Shilling" struck for merchants. Fewer than 20 pieces are known to exist today.

Date	Mintage	F	VF	XF	Unc	BU
1798 Without stops above head	—	—	3,000	5,000	8,000	—

KM# 492.2 1/2 CROWN

Silver **Ruler:** William III **Obv:** Laureate bust right **Rev:** Crowned cruciform arms **Note:** Varieties exist.

Date	Mintage	VG	F	VF	XF	Unc
1701	—	22.00	45.00	275	650	—

KM# 492.3 1/2 CROWN

Silver **Ruler:** William III **Obv:** Elephant and castle below bust **Rev:** Crowned shields in cruciform **Note:** Struck from gold mined in Guinea, now Ghana.

Date	Mintage	VG	F	VF	XF	Unc
1701	—	1,000	1,700	—	—	—

KM# 492.4 1/2 CROWN

Silver **Ruler:** William III **Obv:** Laureate bust right **Obv. Legend:** GVLIELMVS - III DEI GRA **Rev:** Plumes in angles **Rev. Legend:** MAG - BR • FRA - ET • HIB -...

Date	Mintage	VG	F	VF	XF	Unc
1701	—	75.00	150	450	1,500	—

KM# 518.1 1/2 CROWN

Silver **Ruler:** Anne **Obv:** Bust left **Rev:** Crowned cruciform arms, date divided at top

Date	Mintage	VG	F	VF	XF	Unc
1703	—	250	550	1,400	—	—

KM# 518.2 1/2 CROWN

Silver **Ruler:** Anne **Obv:** VIGO below bust **Obv. Legend:** ANNA • DEI • - GRATIA • **Rev:** Crowned shields in cruciform **Rev. Legend:** MAG - BR • FRA - ET • HIB - REG • **Note:** Struck from silver seized at Vigo Bay, Spain.

Date	Mintage	VG	F	VF	XF	Unc
1703	—	45.00	100	250	800	—

KM# 518.3 1/2 CROWN

Silver **Ruler:** Anne **Obv:** Bust left **Obv. Legend:** ANNA • DEI • - GRATIA • **Rev:** Plumes in angles **Rev. Legend:** MAG - BR • FRA - ET • HIB • - REG •

Date	Mintage	VG	F	VF	XF	Unc
1704	—	70.00	150	450	1,000	—
1705	—	45.00	100	300	1,000	—

KM# 518.4 1/2 CROWN

Silver **Ruler:** Anne **Obv:** Bust left **Rev:** Roses and plumes in alternate angles

Date	Mintage	VG	F	VF	XF	Unc
1706	—	35.00	75.00	200	700	—
1707	—	27.00	55.00	200	700	—

KM# 525.1 1/2 CROWN

Silver **Ruler:** Anne **Obv:** Bust left **Obv. Legend:** ANNA • DEI • - GRATIA • **Rev:** English and Scottish shield halved **Rev. Legend:** MAG - BRI • FR - ET • HIB - • REG •

Date	Mintage	VG	F	VF	XF	Unc
1707	—	21.00	40.00	150	500	—
1708	—	21.00	40.00	150	500	—
1709	—	21.00	40.00	175	550	—
1713	—	27.00	55.00	200	600	—

KM# 525.2 1/2 CROWN

Silver **Ruler:** Anne **Obv:** E below bust **Rev:** English and Scottish shield halved

Date	Mintage	VG	F	VF	XF	Unc
1707	—	22.00	40.00	150	600	—
1707 Proof	—	—	—	—	—	7,500
1708	—	22.00	40.00	175	650	—
1709	—	150	300	650	1,200	—

KM# 525.3 1/2 CROWN

Silver **Ruler:** Anne **Obv:** Bust left **Obv. Legend:** ANNA • DEI • - GRATIA • **Rev:** Plumes in angles **Rev. Legend:** MAG - BRI • FR - ET • HIB - • REG •

Date	Mintage	VG	F	VF	XF	Unc
1708	—	35.00	70.00	225	800	—

KM# 525.4 1/2 CROWN

Silver **Ruler:** Anne **Obv:** Bust left **Rev:** Roses and plumes in alternate angles

Date	Mintage	VG	F	VF	XF	Unc
1710	—	35.00	65.00	225	650	—
1712	—	19.00	40.00	175	550	—
1713	—	30.00	60.00	225	650	—
1714/3	—	50.00	100	300	900	—
1714	—	19.00	40.00	200	600	—

KM# 540.1 1/2 CROWN

15.0501 g., 0.9250 Silver 0.4476 oz. ASW **Ruler:** George I **Obv:** Laureate bust right **Obv. Legend:** GEORGIVS • D • G • M • BR • FR • ET • HIB • REX • F • D • **Rev:** Crowned shields in cruciform, roses and plumes in alternate angles **Rev. Legend:** BRVN - ET • L • DVX - S • R • ... **Note:** Varieties exist.

Date	Mintage	VG	F	VF	XF	Unc
1715	—	45.00	100	350	1,600	—
1717	—	45.00	100	350	1,700	—
1720/17	—	45.00	100	350	1,600	—
1720	—	125	250	675	2,100	—

KM# 540.2 1/2 CROWN

15.0501 g., 0.9250 Silver 0.4476 oz. ASW **Ruler:** George I **Obv:** Laureate bust right **Obv. Legend:** GEORGIVS • D • G • M • BR • FR • ET • HIB • REX • F • D • **Rev:** C and SS in alternating angle **Rev. Legend:** BRVN - ET • L • DVX - S • R • I • ... **Note:** Silver supplied by the South Sea Company.

Date	Mintage	VG	F	VF	XF	Unc
1723	—	45.00	100	350	1,250	—

KM# 540.3 1/2 CROWN

15.0501 g., 0.9250 Silver 0.4476 oz. ASW **Ruler:** George I **Obv:** Laureate bust right **Rev:** Small roses and plumes in alternate angles

Date	Mintage	VG	F	VF	XF	Unc
1726	—	800	1,750	3,000	8,000	—

KM# 574.1 1/2 CROWN

0.9250 Silver **Ruler:** George II **Obv:** Laureate bust left **Obv. Legend:** GEORGIVS • II • - DEI • GRATIA • **Rev:** Roses and plumes in angles **Rev. Legend:** F • D • B • - ET • L • D • S • R • I • - A • T • ET • E • - M • B • F • ET • - H • REX •

Date	Mintage	VG	F	VF	XF	Unc
1731	—	35.00	75.00	225	750	—
1732	—	35.00	75.00	225	750	—
1734	—	40.00	80.00	250	750	—
1735	—	40.00	80.00	250	750	—
1736	—	45.00	95.00	250	950	—

KM# 574.2 1/2 CROWN

0.9250 Silver **Ruler:** George II **Obv:** Laureate bust left **Obv. Legend:** GEORGIVS • II • - DEI • GRATIA • **Rev:** Roses in angles **Rev. Legend:** F • D • B • - ET • L • D • S • R • I • - A • T • ET • E • - M • B • F • ET • - H • REX •

Date	Mintage	VG	F	VF	XF	Unc
1739	—	25.00	55.00	175	600	—
1741/39	—	50.00	110	275	750	—
1741	—	30.00	65.00	200	650	—

KM# 574.3 1/2 CROWN

0.9250 Silver **Ruler:** George II **Obv:** Large lettering **Rev:** Shields in cruciform

Date	Mintage	VG	F	VF	XF	Unc
1741/39	—	30.00	70.00	225	700	—
1741	—	35.00	75.00	225	750	—

KM# 584.1 1/2 CROWN

0.9250 Silver **Ruler:** George II **Obv:** Older laureate head left **Obv. Legend:** GEORGIUS • II • - DEI • GRATIA • **Rev:** Roses in angles **Rev. Legend:** F • D • B • - ET • L • D • S • R • I • - A • T • ET • E • - M • B • F • ET • - H • REX •

Date	Mintage	VG	F	VF	XF	Unc
1743	—	27.00	50.00	150	550	—
1745/3	—	65.00	135	315	700	—
1745	—	24.00	45.00	125	600	—

KM# 584.3 1/2 CROWN

0.9250 Silver **Ruler:** George II **Obv:** LIMA below bust **Obv. Legend:** GEORGIUS • II • - DEI • GRATIA • **Rev:** Shields in cruciform **Rev. Legend:** F • D • B • - ET • L • D • S • R • I • - A • T • ET • E • - M • B • F • ET • - H • REX • **Note:** Struck from Spanish silver seized at Lima, Peru.

Date	Mintage	VG	F	VF	XF	Unc
1745	—	24.00	40.00	100	550	—
1746/5	—	25.00	55.00	120	450	—
1746	—	24.00	40.00	100	400	—

KM# 584.2 1/2 CROWN

0.9250 Silver **Ruler:** George II **Obv:** Laureate bust left **Obv. Legend:** GEORGIVS • II • - DEI • GRATIA • **Rev:** Without emblems between shields **Rev. Legend:** F • D • B • - ET • L • D • S • R • I • - A • T • ET • E • - M • B • F • ET • - H • REX •

Date	Mintage	VG	F	VF	XF	Unc
1746 Proof	—	—	—	—	—	1,500
1750	—	40.00	80.00	300	900	—
1751	—	45.00	90.00	350	1,100	—

KM# 519.1 CROWN

Silver **Ruler:** Anne **Obv:** VIGO below bust **Obv. Legend:** ANNA • DEI • - GRATIA • **Rev:** Crowned shields in cruciform **Rev. Legend:** MAG - BR • FRA - ET HIB - REG • **Note:** Struck from silver seized at Vigo Bay, Spain. Dav. #1338.

Date	Mintage	VG	F	VF	XF	Unc
1703	—	100	200	600	2,000	—

KM# 519.2 CROWN

Silver **Ruler:** Anne **Obv:** Without VIGO below bust **Obv. Legend:** ANNA • DEI • - GRATIA • **Rev:** Crowned shields in cruciform, plumes in angles **Rev. Legend:** MAG - BRI • FRA - ET • HIB - REG **Note:** Dav. #1339.

Date	Mintage	VG	F	VF	XF	Unc
1705	—	175	350	1,250	3,000	—

KM# 519.3 CROWN

Silver **Ruler:** Anne **Obv:** Bust left **Obv. Legend:** ANNA • DEI • - GRATIA • **Rev:** Roses and plumes in alternating angles **Rev. Legend:** MAG - BR • FRA - ET • HIB - REG • **Note:** Dav. #1340.

Date	Mintage	VG	F	VF	XF	Unc
1706	—	85.00	175	450	1,600	—
1707	—	85.00	175	425	1,600	—

KM# 526.1 CROWN

Silver **Ruler:** Anne **Obv:** Right bust (wider) of Anne left, W/E below bust **Rev:** English and Scottish shield halved **Note:** Dav. #1342

Date	Mintage	VG	F	VF	XF	Unc
1707	—	50.00	100	250	1,200	—
1708/7	—	65.00	125	350	1,500	—
1708	—	65.00	125	300	1,400	—

KM# 526.2 CROWN

Silver **Ruler:** Anne **Obv:** Without E below bust **Obv. Legend:** ANNA • DEI • - GRATIA • **Rev:** English and Scottish shield halved **Rev. Legend:** MAG - BRI FR - ET • HIB - REG • **Note:** Dav. #1342A.

Date	Mintage	VG	F	VF	XF	Unc
1707	—	50.00	100	350	1,250	—
1708	—	60.00	125	400	1,300	—

KM# 526.3 CROWN

Silver **Ruler:** Anne **Rev:** Plumes in angles **Note:** Varieties exist. Dav. #1343.

Date	Mintage	VG	F	VF	XF	Unc
1708	—	95.00	200	400	1,500	—

KM# 536 CROWN

Silver **Ruler:** Anne **Obv:** Third bust (narrow curls) left **Obv. Legend:** ANNA • DEI - GRATIA • **Rev:** Crowned shields in cruciform, roses and plumes in alternating angles **Rev. Legend:** MAG - BRI • FR - ET • HIB - REG • **Note:** Dav. #1344.

Date	Mintage	VG	F	VF	XF	Unc
1713	—	75.00	175	400	1,500	—

KM# 545.1 CROWN

30.1002 g., 0.9250 Silver 0.8951 oz. ASW **Ruler:** George I **Obv:** Laureate bust right **Obv. Legend:** GEORGIVS D • G • M • BR • FR • ET • HIB • REX • F • D • **Rev:** Roses and plumes in alternating angles **Rev. Legend:** BRVN - ET • L • DVX - S • R • I • A • TH - ET • EL • **Note:** Dav. #1345.

Date	Mintage	VG	F	VF	XF	Unc
1716	—	150	225	500	2,400	—
1718/6	—	160	300	650	2,400	—
1720/18	—	160	300	650	2,400	—
1720	—	180	350	675	2,500	—
1726	—	200	350	750	2,900	—

KM# 545.2 CROWN

30.1002 g., 0.9250 Silver 0.8951 oz. ASW **Ruler:** George I **Obv:** Laureate bust right **Obv. Legend:** GEORGIVS D • G • M • BR • FR • ET • HIB • REX • F • D • **Rev:** C and SS in alternating angles **Rev. Legend:** BRVN - ET • L • DVX - S • R • I • A • TH - ET • EL • - **Note:** Struck from silver supplied by the South Sea Company. Dav. #1346.

Date	Mintage	VG	F	VF	XF	Unc
1723	—	135	225	600	1,750	—

KM# 575.1 CROWN

30.1002 g., 0.9250 Silver 0.8951 oz. ASW **Ruler:** George II **Obv:** Laureate bust left **Obv. Legend:** GEORGIVS • II • - DEI • GRATIA • **Rev:** Roses and plumes between shields **Rev. Legend:** F • D • B • - ET • L • D • S • R • I • - A • T • ET • E • - M • B • F • ET • - H • REX • **Note:** Dav. #1347.

Date	Mintage	VG	F	VF	XF	Unc
1732	—	125	175	450	1,300	—
1732 Proof	—	—	—	—	—	5,000

Date	Mintage	VG	F	VF	XF	Unc
1734	—	135	225	550	1,600	—
1735	—	150	225	500	1,250	—
1736	—	150	225	500	1,250	—

KM# 575.2 CROWN

30.1002 g., 0.9250 Silver 0.8951 oz. ASW **Ruler:** George II **Obv:** Laureate bust left **Obv. Legend:** GEORGIVS • II • - DEI • GRATIA • **Rev:** Roses between shields **Rev. Legend:** F • D • B • - ET • L • D • S • R • I • - A • T • ET • E • - M • B • F • ET • - H • REX • **Note:** Dav. #1348.

Date	Mintage	VG	F	VF	XF	Unc
1739	—	125	175	450	900	—
1741	—	125	175	450	900	—

KM# 585.1 CROWN

30.1002 g., 0.9250 Silver 0.8951 oz. ASW **Ruler:** George II **Obv:** Older bust left **Obv. Legend:** GEORGIUS • II • - DEI • GRATIA • **Rev:** Roses in angles **Rev. Legend:** F • D • B • - ET • L • D • S • R • I • - A • T • ET • E • - M • B • F • ET - H • REX • **Note:** Dav. #1349.

Date	Mintage	VG	F	VF	XF	Unc
1743	—	125	175	400	900	—

KM# 585.2 CROWN

30.1002 g., 0.9250 Silver 0.8951 oz. ASW **Ruler:** George II **Obv:** Laureate bust left **Obv. Legend:** GEORGIVS • II • - DEI • GRATIA • **Rev:** Without emblems between shields **Rev. Legend:** F • D • B • - ET • L • D • S • R • I • - A • T • ET • E • - M • B • F • ET - H • REX • **Note:** Dav. #1351.

Date	Mintage	VG	F	VF	XF	Unc
1746 Proof	—	—	—	—	—	3,000
1750	—	150	250	500	1,500	—
1751	—	175	300	600	1,700	—

KM# 585.3 CROWN

30.1002 g., 0.9250 Silver 0.8951 oz. ASW **Ruler:** George II **Obv:** LIMA below bust **Obv. Legend:** GEORGIVS • II • - DEI • GRATIA • **Rev:** Crowned shields in cruciform **Rev. Legend:** F • D • B - ET • L • D • S • R • I - A • T • ET • E • - M • B • F • ET - H • REX • **Note:** Struck from Spanish silver seized at Lima, Peru. Dav. #1350.

Date	Mintage	VG	F	VF	XF	Unc
1746	—	150	225	500	1,300	—

GUINEA COINAGE

KM# 555 1/4 GUINEA

2.0875 g., 0.9170 Gold 0.0615 oz. AGW **Ruler:** George I **Obv:** Laureate head right **Obv. Legend:** GEORGIVS • D • G • M • BR • FR • ET • HIB • REX • F • D • **Rev:** Crowned shields in cruciform, sceptres at angles

Date	Mintage	VG	F	VF	XF	Unc
1718	—	70.00	125	250	500	—

KM# 592 1/4 GUINEA

2.0875 g., 0.9170 Gold 0.0615 oz. AGW **Ruler:** George III **Obv:** Laureate head right **Obv. Legend:** GEORGIVS • III • DEI • GRATIA • **Rev:** Crowned 4-fold arms

Date	Mintage	F	VF	XF	Unc	BU
1762	—	65.00	125	250	500	—

KM# 620 1/3 GUINEA

2.7834 g., 0.9170 Gold 0.0821 oz. AGW **Ruler:** George III **Obv:** Laureate head right **Obv. Legend:** GEORGIVS II DEI GRATIA • **Rev:** Crown **Rev. Legend:** MAG • BRI • FR • ET • HIB • REX •

Date	Mintage	F	VF	XF	Unc	BU
1797	—	70.00	125	200	300	—
1798	—	70.00	125	200	300	—
1799	—	105	125	300	475	—
1800	—	70.00	100	200	300	—

KM# 487.3 1/2 GUINEA

4.1750 g., 0.9170 Gold 0.1231 oz. AGW **Ruler:** William III **Obv:** Head right **Obv. Legend:** GVLIELMVS • III • DEI • GRA • **Rev:** Crowned shields in cruciform, sceptres at angles **Rev. Legend:** MAG - BR • FRA - ET • HIB • - REX

Date	Mintage	VG	F	VF	XF	Unc
1701	—	150	250	600	2,200	—

KM# 510.1 1/2 GUINEA

4.1750 g., 0.9170 Gold 0.1231 oz. AGW **Ruler:** Anne **Obv:** Bust left **Rev:** Crowned cruciform arms with scepters in angles, date divided at top

Date	Mintage	VG	F	VF	XF	Unc
1702	—	200	500	1,300	3,000	—
1705	—	200	500	1,300	3,000	—

KM# 510.2 1/2 GUINEA

4.1750 g., 0.9170 Gold 0.1231 oz. AGW **Ruler:** Anne **Obv:** VIGO below bust **Rev:** Crowned shields in cruciform, sceptres at angles **Note:** Struck from gold seized at Vigo Bay, Spain.

Date	Mintage	VG	F	VF	XF	Unc
1703	—	—	—	13,000	—	—

KM# 527 1/2 GUINEA

4.1750 g., 0.9170 Gold 0.1231 oz. AGW **Ruler:** Anne **Obv:** Bust left **Obv. Legend:** ANNA • DEI • - GRATIA • **Rev:** English and Scottish shields halved **Rev. Legend:** MAG - BRI • FR - ET • HIB - REG •

Date	Mintage	VG	F	VF	XF	Unc
1707	—	175	300	700	1,900	—
1708	—	225	330	800	2,000	—
1709	—	175	300	650	1,800	—
1710	—	175	300	650	1,800	—
1711	—	175	300	475	1,800	—
1712	—	175	300	650	1,800	—
1713	—	175	300	650	1,800	—
1714	—	175	300	650	1,800	—

KM# 541.1 1/2 GUINEA

4.1750 g., 0.9170 Gold 0.1231 oz. AGW **Ruler:** George I **Obv:** Laureate head right **Obv. Legend:** GEORGIVS • D • G • M • BR • FR • ET • HIB • REX • F • D • **Rev:** Crowned shields in cruciform, sceptres at angles **Rev. Legend:** BRVN - ET • L • DVX - S • R • I • A • TH - ET • EL •

Date	Mintage	VG	F	VF	XF	Unc
1715	—	150	225	500	1,250	—
1717	—	150	225	500	1,250	—
1718	—	150	225	500	1,250	—
1719	—	150	225	500	1,250	—
1720	—	175	275	500	1,250	—
1721 Rare	—	—	—	—	—	—
1722	—	150	225	500	1,250	—
1723 Rare	—	—	—	—	—	—
1724	—	150	225	500	1,250	—

KM# 541.2 1/2 GUINEA

4.1750 g., 0.9170 Gold 0.1231 oz. AGW **Ruler:** George I **Obv:** Elephant and castle below head **Rev:** Crowned shields in cruciform, sceptres at angles **Note:** Struck from gold mined in Guinea, now Ghana.

Date	Mintage	VG	F	VF	XF	Unc
1721	—	325	675	1,700	—	—

KM# 560 1/2 GUINEA

4.1750 g., 0.9170 Gold 0.1231 oz. AGW **Ruler:** George I **Obv:** Laureate head right **Obv. Legend:** GEORGIVS • D • G • M • BR • FR • ET • HIB • REX • F • D • **Rev:** Crowned shields in cruciform, sceptres at angles **Rev. Legend:** BRVN - ET • L • DVX - S • R • I • A • TH - ET • EL •

Date	Mintage	VG	F	VF	XF	Unc
1725	—	125	200	500	1,200	—
1726	—	125	200	500	1,200	—
1727	—	125	200	500	1,200	—

KM# 565.1 1/2 GUINEA

4.1750 g., 0.9170 Gold 0.1231 oz. AGW **Ruler:** George II **Obv:** Laureate head left **Obv. Legend:** GEORGIVS • II • - DEI • GRATIA • **Rev:** Crowned 4-fold arms **Rev. Legend:** F • D • B • ET • L • D • S • R • I • A • T • ET • E • - M • B • F • ET • H • REX •

Date	Mintage	VG	F	VF	XF	Unc
1728	—	175	250	500	1,500	—
1729	—	175	300	550	1,500	—
1730 Rare	—	—	—	—	—	—
1731	—	200	300	725	2,500	—
1732	—	200	300	550	1,500	—
1734	—	175	250	550	1,500	—
1736	—	175	250	550	1,500	—
1737 Rare	—	—	—	—	—	—
1738	—	175	250	550	1,500	—
1739	—	175	250	550	1,500	—

KM# 565.2 1/2 GUINEA

4.1750 g., 0.9170 Gold 0.1231 oz. AGW **Ruler:** George II **Obv:** E.I.C. below head **Rev:** Crowned 4-fold arms **Note:** Struck from gold supplied by the East India Company.

Date	Mintage	VG	F	VF	XF	Unc
1729	—	225	400	1,000	2,800	—
1730	—	250	600	1,200	3,000	—
1731 Rare	—	—	—	—	—	—
1732 Rare	—	—	—	—	—	—
1739 Rare	—	—	—	—	—	—

KM# 580.1 1/2 GUINEA

4.1750 g., 0.9170 Gold 0.1231 oz. AGW **Ruler:** George II **Obv:** Intermediate laureate head left **Obv. Legend:** GEORGIUS • II • - DEI • GRATIA • **Rev:** Crowned 4-fold arms **Rev. Legend:** F • D • B • ET • L • D • S • R • I • A • T • ET • E • - M • B • F • ET • H • REX •

Date	Mintage	VG	F	VF	XF	Unc
1740	—	225	400	650	2,400	—
1743 Unique	—	—	—	—	—	—
1745	—	225	400	650	2,400	—
1746	—	200	250	550	1,800	—

KM# 580.2 1/2 GUINEA

4.1750 g., 0.9170 Gold 0.1231 oz. AGW **Ruler:** George II **Obv:** LIMA below laureate head left **Obv. Legend:** GEORGIUS • II • - DEI • GRATIA • **Rev:** Crowned 4-fold arms **Rev. Legend:** F • D • B • ET • L • D • S • R • I • A • T • ET • E • - M • B • F • ET • H • REX • **Note:** Struck from gold seized at Lima, Peru.

Date	Mintage	VG	F	VF	XF	Unc
1745	—	350	750	1,900	2,800	—

KM# 587 1/2 GUINEA

4.1750 g., 0.9170 Gold 0.1231 oz. AGW **Ruler:** George II **Obv:** Old laureate head left **Obv. Legend:** GEORGIVS • II • DEI • GRATIA • **Rev:** Crowned 4-fold arms **Rev. Legend:** F • D • B • ET • L • D • S • R • I • A • T • ET • E • - M • B • F • ET • H • REX •

Date	Mintage	VG	F	VF	XF	Unc
1747	—	150	225	500	1,600	—
1748	—	150	175	450	1,300	—
1749 Rare	—	—	—	—	—	—
1750	—	175	225	500	1,400	—
1751	—	175	225	500	1,400	—
1752	—	175	225	500	1,400	—
1753	—	150	175	450	1,300	—
1755	—	150	175	450	1,300	—
1756	—	150	175	450	1,300	—
1758	—	150	175	450	1,300	—
1759	—	150	175	400	1,250	—
1760	—	150	175	400	1,250	—

KM# 593 1/2 GUINEA

4.1750 g., 0.9170 Gold 0.1231 oz. AGW **Ruler:** George III **Obv:** Young head right **Rev:** Crowned arms

Date	Mintage	F	VF	XF	Unc	BU
1762	—	550	1,150	2,400	9,000	—
1763	—	775	1,400	3,250	12,500	—

KM# 599 1/2 GUINEA

4.1750 g., 0.9170 Gold 0.1231 oz. AGW **Ruler:** George III **Obv:** Redesigned head right **Obv. Legend:** GEORGIVS • III • DEI • GRATIA • **Rev:** Crowned 4-fold arms **Rev. Legend:** F • D • B • ET • L • D • S • R • I • A • T • ET • E • - M • B • F • ET • H • REX •

Date	Mintage	F	VF	XF	Unc	BU
1764	—	225	450	900	1,700	—
1764 Proof	—	—	—	—	6,000	—
1765	—	325	600	1,650	3,500	—
1766	—	250	450	1,100	2,200	—
1768	—	225	450	1,000	2,200	—
1769	—	225	450	950	1,900	—
1772 Rare	—	—	—	—	—	—
1773	—	250	450	1,000	2,100	—
1774	—	275	550	1,700	3,500	—

KM# 603 1/2 GUINEA

4.1750 g., 0.9170 Gold 0.1231 oz. AGW **Ruler:** George III **Obv:** New head, top of laurel breaks legend **Obv. Legend:** GEORGIVS • III • - DEI • GRATIA • **Rev:** Crowned 4-fold arms **Rev. Legend:** F•D•B•ET•L•D•S•R•I•A•T•ET•E•-M•B•F•ET•H•REX•

Date	Mintage	F	VF	XF	Unc	BU
1774 Rare	—	—	—	—	—	—
1775	—	450	1,100	2,500	4,500	—

KM# 605 1/2 GUINEA

4.1750 g., 0.9170 Gold 0.1231 oz. AGW **Ruler:** George III **Obv:** Smaller head, laurel wreath ends below legend **Obv. Legend:** GEORGIVS • III • DEI • GRATIA • **Rev:** Crowned 4-fold arms **Rev. Legend:** F • D • B • ET • L • D • S • R • I • A • T • ET • E • - M • B • F • ET • H • REX •

Date	Mintage	F	VF	XF	Unc	BU
1775	—	150	250	550	950	—
1775 Proof	—	—	—	—	5,500	—
1776	—	150	250	550	950	—
1777	—	150	250	550	950	—
1778	—	150	250	600	950	—
1779	—	150	250	650	1,100	—
1781	—	150	250	600	900	—
1783	—	600	1,400	—	—	—
1784	—	150	250	550	950	—
1785	—	150	250	550	950	—
1786	—	150	250	550	950	—

KM# 608 1/2 GUINEA

4.1750 g., 0.9170 Gold 0.1231 oz. AGW **Ruler:** George III **Obv:** Laureate head right **Obv. Legend:** GEORGIVS III DEI GRATIA • **Rev:** Crowned 4-fold spade arms **Rev. Legend:** F • D • B • ET • L • D • S • R • I • A • T • ET • E • - M • B • F • ET • H • REX •

Date	Mintage	F	VF	XF	Unc	BU
1787	—	150	175	350	700	—
1787 Proof	—	—	—	—	2,400	—
1788	—	150	175	350	700	—
1789	—	150	200	450	750	—
1790	—	150	175	475	600	—
1791	—	150	175	475	600	—
1792 Rare	—	—	—	—	—	—
1793	—	150	175	475	600	—
1794	—	150	175	475	600	—
1795	—	150	175	450	750	—
1796	—	150	175	475	600	—
1797	—	150	175	475	600	—
1798	—	150	175	475	600	—
1800	—	150	375	950	1,750	—

KM# 498.2 GUINEA

8.3500 g., 0.9170 Gold 0.2462 oz. AGW **Ruler:** William III **Obv:** Elephant and castle below bust **Rev:** Crowned shields in cruciform, sceptres at angles **Note:** Struck from gold mined in Guinea, now Ghana.

Date	Mintage	VG	F	VF	XF	Unc
1701	—	300	750	1,350	3,750	—

KM# 498.1 GUINEA

8.3500 g., 0.9170 Gold 0.2462 oz. AGW **Ruler:** William III **Obv:** Laureate head right **Obv. Legend:** GVLIELMVS • - III • DEI • GRA • **Rev:** Crowned shields in cruciform, sceptres at angles **Rev. Legend:** MAG - BR • FRA - ET • HIB - REX •

Date	Mintage	VG	F	VF	XF	Unc
1701	—	175	250	1,100	2,450	—

KM# 506 GUINEA

8.3500 g., 0.9170 Gold 0.2462 oz. AGW **Ruler:** William III **Obv:** Type III laureate bust right

Date	Mintage	VG	F	VF	XF	Unc
1701	—	325	700	1,400	3,500	—

KM# 511.1 GUINEA

8.3500 g., 0.9170 Gold 0.2462 oz. AGW **Ruler:** Anne **Obv:** Bust left **Obv. Legend:** ANNA • DEI • - GRATIA • **Rev:** Crowned shields in cruciform, sceptres at angles **Rev. Legend:** MAG - BR FRA - ET • HIB - REG •

Date	Mintage	VG	F	VF	XF	Unc
1702	—	225	500	1,750	3,250	—
1705	—	225	500	1,750	3,250	—
1706	—	225	500	1,750	3,250	—
1707	—	225	500	1,750	3,250	—

KM# 511.2 GUINEA

8.3500 g., 0.9170 Gold 0.2462 oz. AGW **Ruler:** Anne **Obv:** VIGO below bust **Rev:** Crowned shields in cruciform, sceptres at angles **Note:** Struck from gold seized at Vigo Bay, Spain.

Date	Mintage	VG	F	VF	XF	Unc
1703 Rare	—	—	—	—	—	—

KM# 528.2 GUINEA

8.3500 g., 0.9170 Gold 0.2462 oz. AGW **Ruler:** Anne **Obv:** Elephant and castle below bust **Rev:** English and Scottish shield halved **Note:** Struck from gold mined in Guinea, now Ghana.

Date	Mintage	VG	F	VF	XF	Unc
1707 Rare	—	300	600	1,250	—	—

KM# 528.1 GUINEA

8.3500 g., 0.9170 Gold 0.2462 oz. AGW **Ruler:** Anne **Obv:** First bust left, elephant and castle below **Obv. Legend:** ANNA • DEI • - GRATIA • **Rev:** English and Scottish shield halved **Rev. Legend:** MAG - BRI • FR - ET • HIB - REG •

Date	Mintage	VG	F	VF	XF	Unc
1707	—	175	350	750	2,500	—
1708 Rare	—	—	—	—	—	—

KM# 529.1 GUINEA

8.3500 g., 0.9170 Gold 0.2462 oz. AGW **Ruler:** Anne **Obv:** Second bust left **Rev:** English and Scottish shield halved

Date	Mintage	VG	F	VF	XF	Unc
1707 Rare	—	—	—	—	—	—
1708	—	175	325	1,000	2,100	—
1709	—	175	325	1,000	2,100	—

KM# 529.2 GUINEA

8.3500 g., 0.9170 Gold 0.2462 oz. AGW **Ruler:** Anne **Obv:** Second bust left, elephant and castle below **Obv. Legend:** ANNA • DEI • - GRATIA • **Rev:** English and Scottish shield halved **Rev. Legend:** MAG - BRI • FR - ET • HIB - REG • **Note:** Struck from gold mined in Guinea, now Ghana.

Date	Mintage	VG	F	VF	XF	Unc
1708	—	350	700	1,750	5,000	—
1709	—	350	700	1,750	5,000	—

KM# 534 GUINEA

8.3500 g., 0.9170 Gold 0.2462 oz. AGW **Ruler:** Anne **Obv:** Third bust left **Obv. Legend:** ANNA • DEI • - GRATIA • **Rev:** Crowned shields in cruciform, sceptres at angles **Rev. Legend:** MAG - BRI • FR - ET • HIB - REG •

Date	Mintage	VG	F	VF	XF	Unc
1710	—	175	300	750	2,100	—
1711	—	175	300	750	2,100	—
1712	—	175	300	750	2,100	—
1713	—	175	300	750	2,100	—
1714	—	175	300	750	2,100	—

KM# 538 GUINEA

8.3500 g., 0.9170 Gold 0.2462 oz. AGW **Ruler:** George I **Obv:** Laureate head right **Obv. Legend:** GEORGIVS • D • G • MAG • BR • FR • ET • HIB • REX • F • D • **Rev:** Title of prince elector **Rev. Legend:** BRVN • ET - L • DVX - S • R • I • A • TH - ET • EL •

Date	Mintage	VG	F	VF	XF	Unc
1714	—	450	950	1,800	3,250	—

KM# 542 GUINEA

8.3500 g., 0.9170 Gold 0.2462 oz. AGW **Ruler:** George I **Obv:** Tie in hair with two ends **Obv. Legend:** GEORGIVS • D • G • M • BR • FR • ET • HIB • REX • F • D • **Rev:** Crowned shields in cruciform, sceptres at angles **Rev. Legend:** BRVN - ET • L • DVX - S • R • I • A • TH - ET • EL •

Date	Mintage	VG	F	VF	XF	Unc
1715	—	175	350	950	2,300	—

KM# 543 GUINEA

8.3500 g., 0.9170 Gold 0.2462 oz. AGW **Ruler:** George I **Obv:** Without hair below truncation **Obv. Legend:** GEORGIVS • D • G • M • BR • FR • ET • HIB • REX • F • D • **Rev:** Crowned shields in cruciform, sceptres at angles **Rev. Legend:** BRVN - ET • L • DVX - S • R • I • A • TH - ET • EL •

Date	Mintage	VG	F	VF	XF	Unc
1715	—	175	350	950	2,100	—
1716	—	175	350	950	2,100	—

KM# 546.1 GUINEA

8.3500 g., 0.9170 Gold 0.2462 oz. AGW **Ruler:** George I **Obv:** Tie in hair with loop and one end **Obv. Legend:** GEORGIVS • D • G • M • BR • FR ET • HIB REX FD **Rev:** Crowned shields in cruciform, sceptres at angles **Rev. Legend:** BRVN - ET • L • DVX - S • R • I • A • TH - ET • EL •

Date	Mintage	VG	F	VF	XF	Unc
1716	—	175	400	850	2,300	—
1717	—	175	400	850	2,300	—
1718 Rare	—	—	—	—	—	—
1719	—	175	400	850	2,300	—
1720	—	175	400	850	2,300	—
1721	—	175	400	850	2,300	—
1722	—	175	400	850	2,300	—
1723	—	175	400	850	2,300	—

KM# 546.2 GUINEA

8.3500 g., 0.9170 Gold 0.2462 oz. AGW **Ruler:** George I **Obv:** Elephant and castle below bust **Rev:** Crowned shields in cruciform, sceptres at angles **Note:** Struck from gold mined in Guinea, now Ghana.

Date	Mintage	VG	F	VF	XF	Unc
1721 Rare	—	—	—	—	—	—
1722 Rare	—	—	—	—	—	—

KM# 559.1 GUINEA

8.3500 g., 0.9170 Gold 0.2462 oz. AGW **Ruler:** George I **Obv:** Older laureate head **Obv. Legend:** GEORGIVS • D • G • M • BR • FR • ET • HIB • REX • F • D • **Rev:** Crowned shields in cruciform, sceptres at angles **Rev. Legend:** BRVN - ET • L • DVX - S • R • I • A • TH - ET • EL •

Date	Mintage	VG	F	VF	XF	Unc
1723	—	175	400	850	2,100	—
1724	—	175	400	850	2,100	—
1725	—	175	400	850	2,100	—
1726	—	175	400	850	2,100	—
1727	—	175	400	1,000	2,500	—

KM# 559.2 GUINEA

8.3500 g., 0.9170 Gold 0.2462 oz. AGW **Ruler:** George I **Obv:** Elephant and castle below head **Obv. Legend:** GEORGIVS • D • G • M • BR • FR • ET • HIB • REX • F • D • **Rev:** Crowned shields in cruciform, sceptres at angles **Rev. Legend:** BRVN - ET • L • DVX • - S • R • I • A • TH - ET • EL • **Note:** Struck from gold mined in Guinea, now Ghana.

Date	Mintage	VG	F	VF	XF	Unc
1726 Rare	—	350	900	3,250	—	—

KM# 562 GUINEA

8.3500 g., 0.9170 Gold 0.2462 oz. AGW **Ruler:** George II **Obv:** Young laureate head left **Obv. Legend:** GEORGIVS • II • - DEI • GRATIA **Rev:** Crowned 4-fold arms **Rev. Legend:** F • D • B • ET • L • D • S • R • I • A • T • ET • E • - M • B • F • ET • H • REX •

Date	Mintage	VG	F	VF	XF	Unc
1727	—	300	600	1,750	3,250	—

KM# 563 GUINEA

8.3500 g., 0.9170 Gold 0.2462 oz. AGW **Ruler:** George II **Obv:** Large letters **Rev:** Large letters, smaller shield

Date	Mintage	VG	F	VF	XF	Unc
1727	—	225	500	1,250	2,300	—
1728	—	225	500	1,250	2,300	—

KM# 573.2 GUINEA

8.3500 g., 0.9170 Gold 0.2462 oz. AGW **Ruler:** George II **Obv:** E.I.C. below head **Rev:** Crowned 4-fold arms **Note:** Struck from gold mined in Guinea, now Ghana, and supplied by the East India Company.

Date	Mintage	VG	F	VF	XF	Unc
1729	—	225	525	1,150	2,500	—
1731	—	175	400	900	2,500	—
1732	—	175	400	850	2,100	—

KM# 573.1 GUINEA

8.3500 g., 0.9170 Gold 0.2462 oz. AGW **Ruler:** George II **Obv:** Narrow laureate head left **Obv. Legend:** GEORGIVS • II • - DEI • GRATIA • **Rev:** Crowned 4-fold arms **Rev. Legend:** F • D • B • ET • L • D • S • R • I • A • T • ET • E • - M • B • F • ET • H • REX •

Date	Mintage	VG	F	VF	XF	Unc
1730	—	250	400	900	2,300	—
1731	—	225	300	750	2,200	—
1732	—	250	400	800	2,300	—

KM# 573.3 GUINEA

8.3500 g., 0.9170 Gold 0.2462 oz. AGW **Ruler:** George II **Obv:** Large letters **Obv. Legend:** GEORGIVS II - DEI GRATIA **Rev:** Small letters **Rev. Legend:** F • D • B • ET • L • D • S • R • I • A • T • ET • E • - M • B • F • ET • H • REX •

Date	Mintage	VG	F	VF	XF	Unc
1732 Rare	—	—	—	—	—	—
1733	—	200	300	750	2,000	—
1734	—	200	300	750	2,000	—
1735	—	200	300	750	2,000	—
1736	—	200	300	750	2,000	—
1737	—	200	300	850	2,500	—
1738	—	200	300	850	2,500	—

KM# 573.4 GUINEA

8.3500 g., 0.9170 Gold 0.2462 oz. AGW **Ruler:** George II **Obv:** E.I.C. below head **Rev:** Crowned 4-fold arms **Note:** Struck from gold supplied by the East India Company.

Date	Mintage	VG	F	VF	XF	Unc
1732	—	250	550	1,400	2,600	—

KM# 577.1 GUINEA

8.3500 g., 0.9170 Gold 0.2462 oz. AGW **Ruler:** George II **Obv:** Intermediate head **Obv. Legend:** GEORGIUS • II • - DEI • GRATIA • **Rev:** Crowned 4-fold arms **Rev. Legend:** F • D • B • ET • L • D • S • R • I • A • T • ET • E • - M • B • F • ET • H • REX •

Date	Mintage	VG	F	VF	XF	Unc
1739	—	175	250	600	2,400	—
1740	—	175	300	700	1,800	—
1741/39	—	175	300	750	1,800	—
1743	—	—	—	2,250	3,250	—

KM# 577.2 GUINEA

8.3500 g., 0.9170 Gold 0.2462 oz. AGW **Ruler:** George II **Obv:** E.I.C. below "Intermediate" head **Rev:** Crowned 4-fold arms **Note:** Struck from gold supplied by the East India Company.

Date	Mintage	VG	F	VF	XF	Unc
1739	—	250	550	1,100	2,900	—

KM# 577.3 GUINEA

8.3500 g., 0.9170 Gold 0.2462 oz. AGW **Ruler:** George II **Obv:** Large letters **Rev:** Crowned 4-fold arms

Date	Mintage	VG	F	VF	XF	Unc
1745	—	200	300	850	2,250	—
1746	—	200	300	650	1,700	—

KM# 577.4 GUINEA

8.3500 g., 0.9170 Gold 0.2462 oz. AGW **Ruler:** George II **Obv:** LIMA below head **Obv. Legend:** GEORGIUS • II • - DEI • GRATIA • **Rev:** Crowned 4-fold arms **Rev. Legend:** F • D • B • ET • L • D • S • R • I • A • T • ET • E • - M • B • F • ET • H • REX • **Note:** Struck from gold seized at Lima, Peru.

Date	Mintage	VG	F	VF	XF	Unc
1745	—	350	800	1,500	3,500	—

KM# 588 GUINEA

8.3500 g., 0.9170 Gold 0.2462 oz. AGW **Ruler:** George II **Obv:** Older laureate head left **Obv. Legend:** GEORGIVS • II • DEI • GRATIA • **Rev:** Crowned 4-fold arms **Rev. Legend:** F • D • B • ET • L • D • S • R • I • A • T • ET • E • - M • B • F • ET • H • REX •

Date	Mintage	VG	F	VF	XF	Unc
1747	—	200	250	600	1,600	—
1748	—	200	250	600	1,500	—
1749	—	200	250	600	1,500	—
1750	—	200	250	600	1,600	—
1751	—	200	250	600	1,500	—
1752	—	200	250	600	1,500	—
1753	—	200	250	600	1,500	—
1755	—	200	275	650	1,600	—
1756	—	200	250	600	1,500	—
1758	—	—	250	600	1,500	—
1759	—	200	225	550	1,500	—
1760	—	200	250	600	1,500	—

KM# 590 GUINEA

8.3500 g., 0.9170 Gold 0.2462 oz. AGW **Ruler:** George III **Obv:** Laureate head right **Obv. Legend:** GEORGIVS • III • DEI • GRATIA • **Rev:** Crowned 4-fold arms **Rev. Legend:** F • D • B • ET • L • D • S • R • I • A • T • ET • E • - M • B • F • ET • H • REX • **Note:** First issue.

Date	Mintage	F	VF	XF	Unc	BU
1761	—	600	1,500	3,000	6,500	—

KM# 598 GUINEA

8.3500 g., 0.9170 Gold 0.2462 oz. AGW **Ruler:** George III **Note:** Second issue.

Date	Mintage	F	VF	XF	Unc	BU
1763	—	450	1,200	3,600	6,500	—
1764	—	350	950	2,750	6,000	—

KM# 600 GUINEA

8.3500 g., 0.9170 Gold 0.2462 oz. AGW **Ruler:** George III **Obv:** Laureate head right **Obv. Legend:** GEORGIVS • III - DEI • GRATIA • **Rev:** Crowned 4-fold arms **Rev. Legend:** F • D • B • ET • L • D • S • R • I • A • T • ET • E • - M • B • F • ET • H • REX • **Note:** Third issue.

Date	Mintage	F	VF	XF	Unc	BU
1765	—	200	450	1,000	3,500	—
1766	—	200	400	950	3,000	—
1767	—	200	450	1,000	3,500	—
1768	—	200	400	950	3,000	—
1769	—	200	400	950	3,000	—
1770	—	200	450	1,000	3,500	—
1771	—	200	400	950	3,000	—
1772	—	200	400	950	3,000	—
1773	—	200	400	950	3,000	—

KM# 604 GUINEA

8.3500 g., 0.9170 Gold 0.2462 oz. AGW **Ruler:** George III **Obv:** Laureate head right **Obv. Legend:** GEORGIVS • III - DEI • GRATIA • **Rev:** Crowned 4-fold arms **Rev. Legend:** F • D • B • ET • L • D • S • R • I • A • T • ET • E • - M • B • F • ET • H • REX • **Note:** Fourth issue.

Date	Mintage	F	VF	XF	Unc	BU
1774	—	175	250	600	1,250	—
1774 Proof	—	—	—	—	3,000	—
1775	—	175	250	600	1,250	—
1776	—	175	250	600	1,250	—
1777	—	175	250	600	1,250	—
1778	—	175	250	600	1,400	—
1779	—	175	250	600	1,250	—
1781	—	175	250	600	1,250	—
1782	—	175	250	600	1,250	—
1783	—	175	250	600	1,250	—
1784	—	175	250	600	1,250	—
1785	—	175	250	600	1,250	—
1786	—	175	250	600	1,250	—

KM# 609 GUINEA

8.3500 g., 0.9170 Gold 0.2462 oz. AGW **Ruler:** George III **Obv:** Laureate head right **Obv. Legend:** GEORGIVS III DEI GRATIA • **Rev:** Crowned 4-fold spade arms **Rev. Legend:** F • D • B • ET • L • D • S • R • I • A • T • ET • E • - M • B • F • ET • H • REX •

Date	Mintage	F	VF	XF	Unc	BU
1787	—	175	250	450	850	—
1787 1 Proof	—	—	—	—	4,250	—
1788	—	175	250	450	850	—
1789	—	175	250	450	850	—
1790	—	175	250	450	850	—
1791	—	175	250	450	850	—
1792	—	175	250	450	850	—
1793	—	175	250	450	850	—
1794	—	175	250	450	850	—
1795	—	175	250	700	1,400	—
1796	—	200	300	750	1,400	—
1797	—	200	300	700	1,300	—
1798	—	175	250	450	850	—
1799	—	200	350	800	1,300	—

KM# 507 2 GUINEAS

16.7000 g., 0.9170 Gold 0.4923 oz. AGW **Ruler:** William III **Obv:** Laureate head right **Obv. Legend:** GVLIELMVS • - III • DEI • GRA • **Rev:** Crowned cruciform arms with sceptres in angles, date divided at top **Rev. Legend:** MAG - BR • FRA - • ET • HIB - REX •

Date	Mintage	VG	F	VF	XF	Unc
1701	—	475	1,150	2,500	5,000	—

KM# 531 2 GUINEAS

16.7000 g., 0.9170 Gold 0.4923 oz. AGW **Ruler:** Anne **Obv:** Bust left **Obv. Legend:** ANNA DEI - GRATIA • **Rev:** English and Scottish shield halved **Rev. Legend:** MAG - BRI • FR - ET • HIB - REG •

Date	Mintage	VG	F	VF	XF	Unc
1709	—	350	850	2,000	3,500	—
1711	—	350	850	2,000	3,500	—
1713	—	350	850	2,000	3,500	—
1714	—	350	850	2,000	3,500	—

KM# 554 2 GUINEAS

16.7000 g., 0.9170 Gold 0.4923 oz. AGW **Ruler:** George I **Obv:** Laureate head right **Obv. Legend:** GEORGIUS • D • G • M • BR • FR • ET • HIB • REX • F • D • **Rev:** Crowned shields in cruciform, sceptres at angles **Rev. Legend:** BRVN - ET • L • DVX - S • R • I • A • TH - ET • EL •

Date	Mintage	VG	F	VF	XF	Unc
1717	—	375	850	2,250	5,000	—
1720	—	375	850	2,250	5,000	—
1726	—	375	850	2,250	5,000	—

KM# 576 2 GUINEAS

16.7000 g., 0.9170 Gold 0.4923 oz. AGW **Ruler:** George II **Obv:** Young laureate head left **Obv. Legend:** GEORGIVS • II • - DEI • GRATIA • **Rev:** Crowned 4-fold arms **Rev. Legend:** F • D • B • ET • L • D • S • R • I • A • T • ET • E • - M • B • F • ET • H • REX •

Date	Mintage	VG	F	VF	XF	Unc
1734/3	—	550	1,100	3,250	6,500	—
1735	—	350	500	1,100	2,500	—
1738	—	350	425	750	1,800	—
1739	—	350	425	825	1,800	—

KM# 578 2 GUINEAS

16.7000 g., 0.9170 Gold 0.4923 oz. AGW **Ruler:** George II **Obv:** Intermediate head **Obv. Legend:** GEORGIUS • II • - DEI • GRATIA • **Rev:** Crowned 4-fold arms **Rev. Legend:** F • D • B • ET • L • D • S • R • I • A • T • ET • E • - M • B • F • ET • H • REX •

Date	Mintage	VG	F	VF	XF	Unc
1739	—	350	425	750	1,500	—
1740/39	—	—	—	—	—	—
1740	—	350	425	775	1,500	—

KM# 589 2 GUINEAS

16.7000 g., 0.9170 Gold 0.4923 oz. AGW **Ruler:** George II **Obv:** Older head left

Date	Mintage	VG	F	VF	XF	Unc
1748	—	350	500	1,100	2,800	—
1753	—	350	575	1,800	3,250	—

KM# 508 5 GUINEAS

41.7500 g., 0.9170 Gold 1.2308 oz. AGW **Ruler:** William III **Obv:** Laureate head right **Obv. Legend:** GVLIELMVS • - III • DEI • GRA • **Rev:** Crowned shields in cruciform, sceptres at angles **Rev. Legend:** MAG - BR • FRA - ET • HIB - REX •

Date	Mintage	VG	F	VF	XF	Unc
1701	—	1,000	1,600	3,000	8,000	—

KM# 520.1 5 GUINEAS

41.7500 g., 0.9170 Gold 1.2308 oz. AGW **Ruler:** Anne **Obv:** Bust left, VIGO below bust **Obv. Legend:** ANNA • DEI • - GRATIA • **Rev:** Crowned shields in cruciform, sceptres at angles **Rev. Legend:** MAG - BR • FRA - ET • HIB - REG • **Note:** Struck from gold seized at Vigo Bay, Spain.

Date	Mintage	VG	F	VF	XF	Unc
1703	—	—	—	50,000	85,000	—

KM# 520.2 5 GUINEAS
41.7500 g., 0.9170 Gold 1.2308 oz. AGW **Ruler:** Anne **Obv:** Without VIGO below bust **Obv. Legend:** ANNA • DEI • - GRATIA • **Rev:** Crowned shields in cruciform, sceptres at angles **Rev. Legend:** MAG - BR • FRA - ET • HIB - REG •

Date	Mintage	VG	F	VF	XF	Unc
1705	—	1,000	2,000	4,000	9,000	—
1706	—	1,000	2,000	4,000	9,000	—

KM# 521 5 GUINEAS
41.7500 g., 0.9170 Gold 1.2308 oz. AGW **Ruler:** Anne **Obv:** Bust left **Obv. Legend:** ANNA • DEI • - GRATIA • **Rev:** English and Scottish shield halved **Rev. Legend:** MAG - BRI • FR • - ET • HIB - REG •

Date	Mintage	VG	F	VF	XF	Unc
1706	—	1,100	1,800	3,500	9,000	—

KM# 532 5 GUINEAS
41.7500 g., 0.9170 Gold 1.2308 oz. AGW **Ruler:** Anne **Obv:** Bust left **Obv. Legend:** ANNA • DEI • - GRATIA • **Rev:** Taller shields, English and Scottish shield halved **Rev. Legend:** MAG - BRI • FR - ET • HIB - REG •

Date	Mintage	VG	F	VF	XF	Unc
1709	—	1,100	1,800	3,500	9,000	—

KM# 535 5 GUINEAS
41.7500 g., 0.9170 Gold 1.2308 oz. AGW **Ruler:** Anne **Obv:** Last bust left **Obv. Legend:** ANNA • DEI • - GRATIA • **Rev:** Crowned shields in cruciform, sceptres at angles **Rev. Legend:** MAG - BRI • FR - ET • HIB - REG •

Date	Mintage	VG	F	VF	XF	Unc
1711	—	1,100	1,800	3,500	9,000	—
1713	—	1,100	1,800	3,500	9,000	—
1714	—	1,100	1,800	3,500	9,000	—

KM# 547 5 GUINEAS
41.7500 g., 0.9170 Gold 1.2308 oz. AGW **Ruler:** George I **Obv:** Laureate head right **Obv. Legend:** GEORGIVS • D • G • M • BR • FR • ET • HIB • REX • F • D • **Rev:** Crowned shields in cruciform, sceptres at angles **Rev. Legend:** BRVN - ET • L • DVX • - S • R • I • A • TH • ET • EL •

Date	Mintage	VG	F	VF	XF	Unc
1716	—	950	2,100	4,500	12,000	—
1717	—	950	2,100	4,500	12,000	—
1720	—	950	2,100	4,500	12,000	—
1726	—	950	2,100	4,500	12,000	—

KM# 571.1 5 GUINEAS
41.7500 g., 0.9170 Gold 1.2308 oz. AGW **Ruler:** George II **Obv:** Laureate head left **Obv. Legend:** GEORGIVS • II • - DEI • GRATIA • **Rev:** Crowned 4-fold arms **Rev. Legend:** F • D • B • ET • L • D • S • R • I • A • T • ET • E • - M • B • F • ET • H • REX •

Date	Mintage	VG	F	VF	XF	Unc
1729	—	1,100	1,900	3,000	7,500	—
1731	—	1,100	1,900	3,500	10,500	—
1735	—	1,100	1,900	3,000	7,500	—
1738	—	1,100	1,900	3,000	7,500	—
1741	—	1,100	1,900	3,000	7,500	—

KM# 571.2 5 GUINEAS
41.7500 g., 0.9170 Gold 1.2308 oz. AGW **Ruler:** George II **Obv:** E.I.C. below head **Obv. Legend:** GEORGIVS • II • - DEI • GRATIA • **Rev:** Crowned 4-fold arms **Rev. Legend:** F • D • B • ET • L • D • S • R • I • A • T • ET • E • - M • B • F • ET • H • REX • **Note:** Struck from gold supplied by the East India Company.

Date	Mintage	VG	F	VF	XF	Unc
1729	—	1,000	1,800	3,500	8,000	—

KM# 586.1 5 GUINEAS
41.7500 g., 0.9170 Gold 1.2308 oz. AGW **Ruler:** George II **Obv:** LIMA below head **Obv. Legend:** GEORGIVS • II • - DEI • GRATIA • **Rev:** Crowned 4-fold arms **Rev. Legend:** F • D • B • ET • L • D • S • R • I • A • T • ET • E • - M • B • F • ET • H • REX • **Note:** Struck from gold seized at Lima, Peru.

Date	Mintage	VG	F	VF	XF	Unc
1746	—	1,000	1,800	3,500	8,000	—

KM# 586.2 5 GUINEAS
41.7500 g., 0.9170 Gold 1.2308 oz. AGW **Ruler:** George II **Obv:** Laureate head left **Obv. Legend:** GEORGIVS • II • - DEI • GRATIA • **Rev:** Crowned 4-fold arms **Rev. Legend:** F • D • B • ET • L • D • S • R • I • A • T • ET • E • - M • B • F • ET • H • REX •

Date	Mintage	VG	F	VF	XF	Unc
1748	—	1,000	1,700	3,000	6,500	—
1753	—	1,000	1,700	3,000	6,500	—

COUNTERMARKED COINAGE

Bank of England

Emergency issue consisting of foreign silver coins, usually Spanish Colonial, having a bust of George III within an oval (1797) or octagonal (1840) frame. Countermarked 8 Reales circulated at 4 Shillings 9 Pence in 1797 and 5 Shillings in 1804. The puncheons used for countermarking foreign coins for this series were available for many years afterward, especially the oval die and apparently a number of foreign coins other than Spanish or Spanish Colonial 8 Reales were countermarked for collectors.

KM# B622 1/2 DOLLAR
Silver **Ruler:** George III **Countermark:** Type I **Note:** Countermark on Mexico City 4 Reales, KM#97.2a.

CM Date	Host Date	Good	VG	F	VF	XF
ND(1797)	1785-89FM	—	—	—	—	—

KM# C622 1/2 DOLLAR
0.9030 Silver **Ruler:** George III **Issuer:** Bank of England **Countermark:** Type I **Note:** Countermark on Guatemala 4 Reales, KM#17.

CM Date	Host Date	Good	VG	F	VF	XF
ND(1797)	1754-60	—	—	—	—	—

KM# A622 1/2 DOLLAR

Silver **Issuer:** Bank of England **Countermark:** Type I **Note:** Countermark on Bolivia (Potosi) 4 Reales, KM#54.

CM Date	Host Date	Good	VG	F	VF	XF
ND(1797)	1773-89	—	—	—	—	—

KM# 622.1 1/2 DOLLAR

Silver **Issuer:** Bank of England **Countermark:** Type I **Note:** Countermark on various Spanish (Madrid) 4 Reales. Prev. KM#622.

CM Date	Host Date	Good	VG	F	VF	XF
ND(1797)	1772-88	35.00	60.00	100	250	550

KM# 622.2 1/2 DOLLAR

Silver **Ruler:** George III **Issuer:** Bank of England **Countermark:** Type I **Note:** Countermark on Spanish (Seville Mint) 4 Reales, KM#413.2.

CM Date	Host Date	Good	VG	F	VF	XF
ND(1797)	1772-88	75.00	125	200	400	750

KM# 641 DOLLAR

0.9030 Silver, 38.2 mm. **Countermark:** Type I **Note:** Countermark on Mexico City 8 Reales, KM#108.

CM Date	Host Date	Good	VG	F	VF	XF
ND(1797)	1790	—	65.00	100	150	325

KM# 623 DOLLAR (5 Shillings)

Silver **Issuer:** Bank of England **Countermark:** Type I **Note:** Countermark on Bolivia (Potosi) 8 Reales, KM#50.

CM Date	Host Date	Good	VG	F	VF	XF
ND(1797)	1767-70 Rare	—	—	—	—	—

KM# 624 DOLLAR (5 Shillings)

Silver **Issuer:** Bank of England **Countermark:** Type I **Note:** Countermark on Bolivia (Potosi) 8 Reales, KM#55.

CM Date	Host Date	Good	VG	F	VF	XF
ND(1797)	1773-89	—	80.00	125	300	550

KM# 625 DOLLAR (5 Shillings)

Silver **Issuer:** Bank of England **Countermark:** Type I **Note:** Countermark on Bolivia (Potosi) 8 Reales, KM#64.

CM Date	Host Date	Good	VG	F	VF	XF
ND(1797)	1789-91	—	80.00	125	300	550

KM# 626 DOLLAR (5 Shillings)

Silver **Issuer:** Bank of England **Countermark:** Type I **Note:** Countermark on Bolivia (Potosi) 8 Reales, KM#73.1.

CM Date	Host Date	Good	VG	F	VF	XF
ND(1797)	1791-1808	—	80.00	125	300	550

KM# 627 DOLLAR (5 Shillings)

Silver **Issuer:** Bank of England **Countermark:** Type I **Note:** Countermark on Chile (Santiago) 8 Reales, KM#51.

CM Date	Host Date	Good	VG	F	VF	XF
ND(1797)	1791-1808	—	225	425	850	1,100

KM# 628 DOLLAR (5 Shillings)

Silver **Issuer:** Bank of England **Countermark:** Type I **Note:** Countermark on France 1 ECU, C#78.

CM Date	Host Date	Good	VG	F	VF	XF
ND(1797)	1774-92	—	—	—	—	—

KM# 629 DOLLAR (5 Shillings)

Silver **Issuer:** Bank of England **Countermark:** Type I **Note:** Countermark on Guatemala 8 Reales, KM#53.

CM Date	Host Date	Good	VG	F	VF	XF
ND(1797)	1790-1808	—	200	350	750	1,100

KM# 630 DOLLAR (5 Shillings)

Silver **Issuer:** Bank of England **Countermark:** Type I **Note:** Countermark on Mexico 8 Reales, KM#104.

CM Date	Host Date	Good	VG	F	VF	XF
ND(1797)	1747-60 Rare	—	—	—	—	—

KM# 631 DOLLAR (5 Shillings)

Silver **Issuer:** Bank of England **Countermark:** Type I **Note:** Countermark on Mexico 8 Reales, KM#105.

CM Date	Host Date	Good	VG	F	VF	XF
ND(1797)	1760-71 Rare	—	—	—	—	—

KM# 632 DOLLAR (5 Shillings)

Silver **Issuer:** Bank of England **Countermark:** Type I **Note:** Countermark on Mexico 8 Reales, KM#106.

CM Date	Host Date	Good	VG	F	VF	XF
ND(1797)	1772-89	—	65.00	100	250	450

KM# 633 DOLLAR (5 Shillings)
Silver **Issuer:** Bank of England **Countermark:** Type I **Note:** Countermark on Mexico 8 Reales, KM#107.

CM Date	Host Date	Good	VG	F	VF	XF
ND(1797)	1789-90	—	80.00	125	250	450

KM# 634 DOLLAR (5 Shillings)
Silver **Issuer:** Bank of England **Countermark:** Type I **Note:** Countermark on Mexico 8 Reales, KM#109.

CM Date	Host Date	Good	VG	F	VF	XF
ND(1797)	1791-1808	—	65.00	100	250	450

KM# 635 DOLLAR (5 Shillings)
Silver **Issuer:** Bank of England **Countermark:** Type I **Note:** Countermark on Peru (Lima) 8 Reales, C#35.

CM Date	Host Date	Good	VG	F	VF	XF
ND(1797)	1760-72 Rare	—	—	—	—	—

KM# 636 DOLLAR (5 Shillings)
Silver **Issuer:** Bank of England **Countermark:** Type I **Note:** Countermark on Peru (Lima) 8 Reales, C#45.

CM Date	Host Date	Good	VG	F	VF	XF
ND(1797)	1772-89	—	80.00	125	300	550

KM# 637 DOLLAR (5 Shillings)
Silver **Issuer:** Bank of England **Countermark:** Type I **Note:** Countermark on Peru (Lima) 8 Reales, C#69.

CM Date	Host Date	Good	VG	F	VF	XF
ND(1797)	1789-91	—	75.00	125	300	500

KM# 638 DOLLAR (5 Shillings)
Silver **Issuer:** Bank of England **Countermark:** Type I **Note:** Countermark on Peru (Lima) 8 Reales, C#76.

CM Date	Host Date	Good	VG	F	VF	XF
ND(1797)	1791-1808	—	80.00	125	300	550

KM# 639 DOLLAR (5 Shillings)
Silver **Issuer:** Bank of England **Countermark:** Type I **Note:** Countermark on Spanish 8 Reales, C#40.

CM Date	Host Date	Good	VG	F	VF	XF
ND(1797)	1772-88	—	85.00	150	450	900

KM# 640 DOLLAR (5 Shillings)
Silver **Issuer:** Bank of England **Countermark:** Type I **Note:** Countermark on Spanish 8 Reales, C#71.

CM Date	Host Date	Good	VG	F	VF	XF
ND(1797)	1788-1808	—	85.00	150	450	900

COUNTERMARKED COINAGE

English Tradesmen

During the last half of the 18th century and the early years of the 19th century, the gold coinage predominated in Great Britain and the limited issues of silver coins between the years 1758 and 1816 did little to relieve the shortage of smaller denominations. During the 1790s a partial solution to the problem began to be offered by private tradesmen through the countermarking of foreign dollars, chiefly Spanish Colonial issues from the Americas, with a punch validating them for local circulation and redemption. The majority of these tradesmens countermarked issues circulated in Scotland; in England two cotton mills, two colleries, and a merchant also countermarked foreign silver coins.

KM# 642 4 SHILLING 6 PENCE
0.9030 Silver **Issuer:** English Tradesmen **Countermark:** CARK COTTON WORKS 1787//FOUR SHILLINGS and SIX PENCE **Note:** Countermark on Spanish Colonial 8 Reales. 1787 indicates the company's founding, not the date of issue.

CM Date	Host Date	Good	VG	F	VF	XF
ND(1790s)	17xx	—	—	500	800	—

KM# A645 5 SHILLING
0.9030 Silver **Issuer:** Undetermined **Countermark:** CBCo in rectangle **Note:** Countermark on Lima 8 Reales.

CM Date	Host Date	Good	VG	F	VF	XF
ND	1790 Rare	—	—	—	—	—

KM# 645 5 SHILLING
0.9030 Silver **Issuer:** English Tradesmen **Countermark:** Crowned "&" **Note:** "Revolution Mill, East Retford, Nottinghamshire" countermark on Spanish Colonial 8 Reales. False punches have been used on genuine host coins.

CM Date	Host Date	Good	VG	F	VF	XF
ND(1790s)	17xx	—	—	400	750	—

TRADESMENS' TOKEN COINAGE

18th Century English

The late 1700s witnessed a severe shortage of small change. Regal coppers were last struck in 1775. Coins in circulation were badly worn and accompanied by many counterfeits. In 1787 Matthew Boulton produced the first token issue for the Parys Mines Co. Gaining popularity these were followed by many issues by merchants, manufacturers, shopkeepers, workhouse officials, etc. for general circulation. Mules, without an issuers name or address, advertising tokens without an expressed value, and political and collector types saw little or no legitimate circulation. The most common denomination was the 1/2 penny, with farthings and one penny tokens also being issued. Illustrated is a 1/2 penny token of Coventry depicting Lady Godiva. These can be found listed in British Tokens and Their Values by P. Seaby and M. Bussell.

KM# TTn1 1/2 PENNY
Copper

Date	Mintage	Good	VG	F	VF	XF
1792	—	—	—	—	—	—

PATTERNS

Including off metal strikes

KM#	Date	Mintage	Identification	Mkt Val
Pn33	1702	—	Guinea. Anne	—

KM#	Date	Mintage	Identification	Mkt Val
PnA34	ND(ca. 1707)	—	1/2 Penny. Anne	—

KM#	Date	Mintage	Identification	Mkt Val
PnB34	1713	—	Farthing. Gold. Anne	—
PnC34	1715	—	1/2 Crown. Silver. George I.	—
PnD34	1717	—	Farthing. Silver. KM#548	—
PnE34	1717	—	1/2 Penny. Silver. KM#549	1,400
PnF34	1718	—	Farthing. Silver. KM#548	—
PnG34	1718	—	1/2 Penny. Silver. KM#549	—
PnH34	1722	—	1/2 Penny. Brass. KM#557	—
Pn34	1727	—	Guinea. Gold. George I, head right.	—
Pn35	1727	—	Guinea. Gold. George II, first head.	—

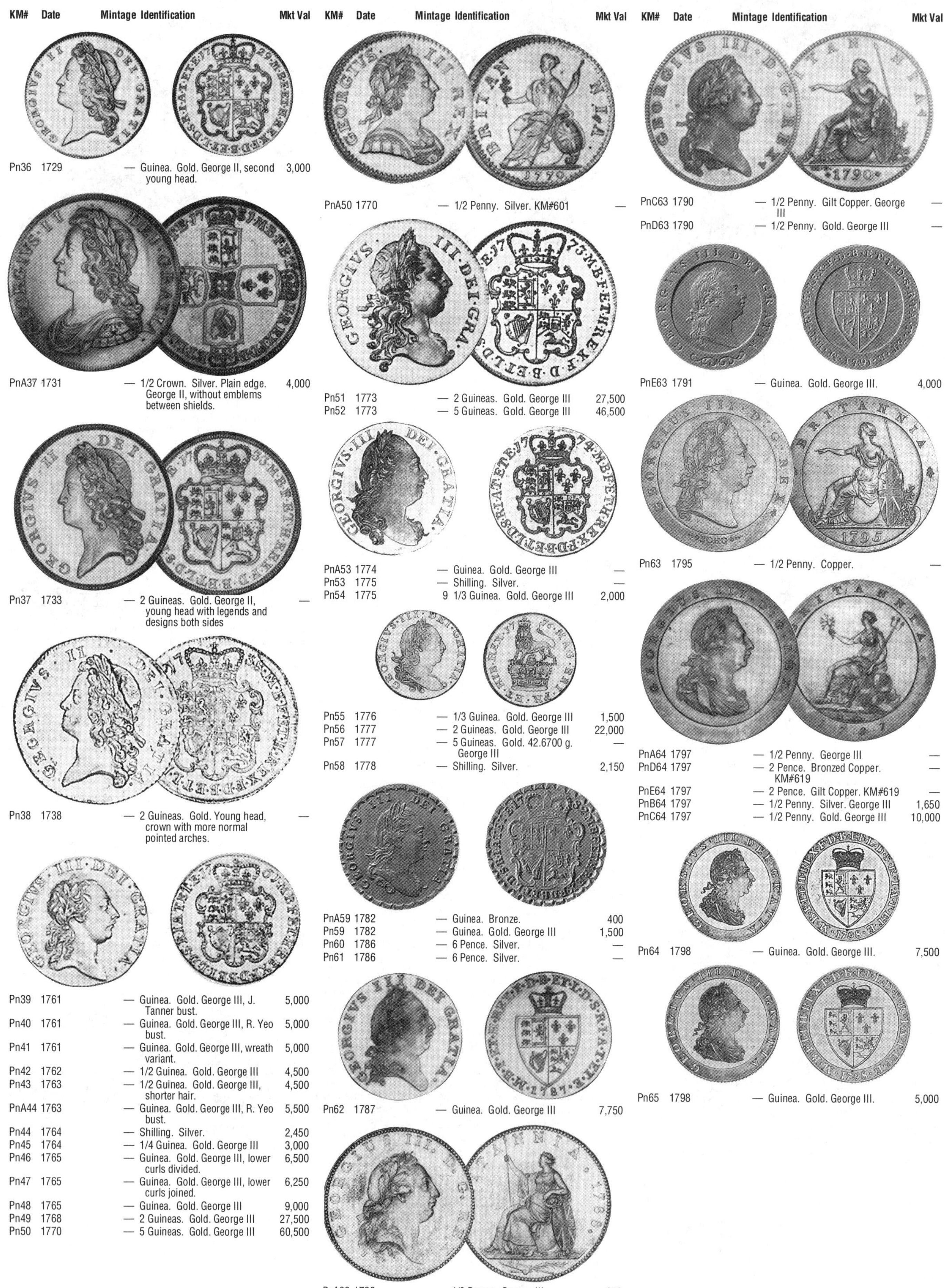

KM#	Date	Mintage	Identification	Mkt Val
Pn36	1729	—	Guinea. Gold. George II, second young head.	3,000
PnA37	1731	—	1/2 Crown. Silver. Plain edge. George II, without emblems between shields.	4,000
Pn37	1733	—	2 Guineas. Gold. George II, young head with legends and designs both sides	—
Pn38	1738	—	2 Guineas. Gold. Young head, crown with more normal pointed arches.	—
Pn39	1761	—	Guinea. Gold. George III, J. Tanner bust.	5,000
Pn40	1761	—	Guinea. Gold. George III, R. Yeo bust.	5,000
Pn41	1761	—	Guinea. Gold. George III, wreath variant.	5,000
Pn42	1762	—	1/2 Guinea. Gold. George III	4,500
Pn43	1763	—	1/2 Guinea. Gold. George III, shorter hair.	4,500
PnA44	1763	—	Guinea. Gold. George III, R. Yeo bust.	5,500
Pn44	1764	—	Shilling. Silver.	2,450
Pn45	1764	—	1/4 Guinea. Gold. George III	3,000
Pn46	1765	—	Guinea. Gold. George III, lower curls divided.	6,500
Pn47	1765	—	Guinea. Gold. George III, lower curls joined.	6,250
Pn48	1765	—	Guinea. Gold. George III	9,000
Pn49	1768	—	2 Guineas. Gold. George III	27,500
Pn50	1770	—	5 Guineas. Gold. George III	60,500
PnA50	1770	—	1/2 Penny. Silver. KM#601	—
Pn51	1773	—	2 Guineas. Gold. George III	27,500
Pn52	1773	—	5 Guineas. Gold. George III	46,500
PnA53	1774	—	Guinea. Gold. George III	—
Pn53	1775	—	Shilling. Silver.	—
Pn54	1775	9	1/3 Guinea. Gold. George III	2,000
Pn55	1776	—	1/3 Guinea. Gold. George III	1,500
Pn56	1777	—	2 Guineas. Gold. George III	22,000
Pn57	1777	—	5 Guineas. Gold. 42.6700 g. George III	—
Pn58	1778	—	Shilling. Silver.	2,150
PnA59	1782	—	Guinea. Bronze.	400
Pn59	1782	—	Guinea. Gold. George III	1,500
Pn60	1786	—	6 Pence. Silver.	—
Pn61	1786	—	6 Pence. Silver.	—
Pn62	1787	—	Guinea. Gold. George III	7,750
PnA63	1788	—	1/2 Penny. George III	250
PnB63	1788	—	1/2 Penny. Silver. George III	600
PnC63	1790	—	1/2 Penny. Gilt Copper. George III	—
PnD63	1790	—	1/2 Penny. Gold. George III	—
PnE63	1791	—	Guinea. Gold. George III.	4,000
Pn63	1795	—	1/2 Penny. Copper.	—
PnA64	1797	—	1/2 Penny. George III	—
PnD64	1797	—	2 Pence. Bronzed Copper. KM#619	—
PnE64	1797	—	2 Pence. Gilt Copper. KM#619	—
PnB64	1797	—	1/2 Penny. Silver. George III	1,650
PnC64	1797	—	1/2 Penny. Gold. George III	10,000
Pn64	1798	—	Guinea. Gold. George III.	7,500
Pn65	1798	—	Guinea. Gold. George III.	5,000

KM#	Date	Mintage	Identification	Mkt Val
PnF64	1798	—	Dollar. White Metal. George III.	—
PnG64	1798	—	Dollar. Copper. George III.	—

KM#	Date	Mintage	Identification	Mkt Val
Pn63B	1798	—	Farthing. Gilt Copper. George III	—

MAUNDY SETS

KM#	Date	Mintage	Identification	Issue Price	Mkt Val
MDS33	1701 (4)	—	KM#495, 499, 500.2, 501	—	350
MDS34	1703 (4)	—	KM#512-515	—	350
MDS35	1705 (4)	—	KM#512-515	—	350
MDS36	1706 (4)	—	KM#512-515	—	225
MDS37	1708 (4)	—	KM#512-515	—	350
MDS38	1709 (4)	—	KM#512-515	—	275
MDS39	1710 (4)	—	KM#512-515	—	350
MDS40	1713 (4)	—	KM#512-515	—	225
MDS41	1723 (4)	—	KM#544, 550-552	—	350
MDS42	1727 (4)	—	KM#544, 550-552	—	325
MDS43	1729 (4)	—	KM#567-570	—	300
MDS44	1731 (4)	—	KM#567-570	—	300
MDS45	1732 (4)	—	KM#567-570	—	200
MDS46	1735 (4)	—	KM#567-570	—	200
MDS47	1737 (4)	—	KM#567-570	—	200
MDS48	1739 (4)	—	KM#567-570	—	200
MDS49	1740 (4)	—	KM#567-570	—	200
MDS50	1743 (4)	—	KM#567-570	—	300
MDS51	1746 (4)	—	KM#567-570	—	200
MDS52	1760 (4)	—	KM#567-570	—	300
MDS53	1763 (4)	—	KM#591, 594-596.1	—	225
MDS55	1766 (4)	—	KM#591, 594-596.1	—	225
MDS56	1772 (4)	—	KM#591, 594-596.1	—	225
MDS57	1780 (4)	—	KM#591, 594-596.1	—	225
MDS58	1784 (4)	—	KM#591, 594-596.1	—	225
MDS59	1786 (4)	—	KM#591, 594-596.1	—	225
MDS60	1792 (4)	—	KM#610-613	—	375
MDS61	1795 (4)	—	KM#614-617	—	200
MDS62	1800 (4)	—	KM#614-617	—	350

GRENADA

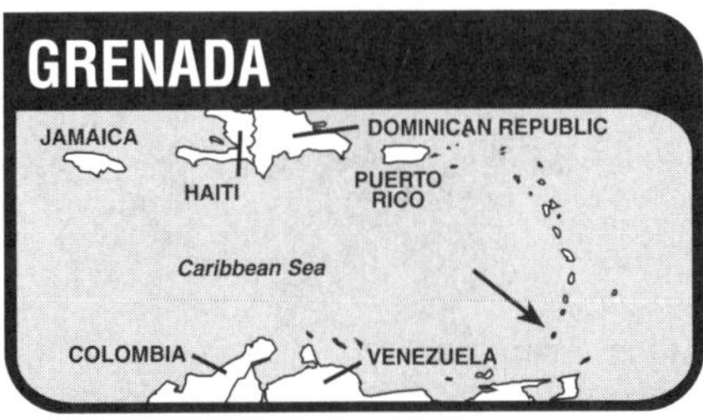

The State of Grenada, located in the Windward Islands of the Caribbean Sea 90 miles (145 km.) north of Trinidad, has (with Carriacou and Petit Martinique) an area of 133 sq. mi. (344 sq. km.) and a population of 94,000. Capital: St.George's. Grenada is the smallest independent nation in the Western Hemisphere. The economy is based on agriculture and tourism. Sugar, coconuts, nutmeg, cocoa and bananas are exported.

Columbus discovered Grenada in 1498 during his third voyage to the Americas. Spain failed to colonize the island, and in 1627 granted it to the British who sold it to the French who colonized it in 1650. Grenada was captured by the British in 1763, retaken by the French in 1779, and finally ceded to the British in 1783. In 1958 Grenada joined the Federation of the West Indies, which was dissolved in 1962. In 1967 it became an internally self-governing British associated state. Full independence was attained on Feb. 4, 1974. Grenada is a member of the Commonwealth of Nations. The prime minister is the Head of Government. Elizabeth II is Head of State as Queen of Grenada.

The early coinage of Grenada consists of cut and countermarked pieces of Spanish or Spanish Colonial Reales, which were valued at 11 Bits. In 1787 8 Reales coins were cut into 11 triangular pieces and countermarked with an incuse G. Later in 1814 large denomination cut pieces were issued being 1/2, 1/3 or 1/6 cuts and countermarked with a TR, incuse G and a number 6, 4,2, or 1 indicating the value in bitts.

RULERS

British

MONETARY SYSTEM

1789-1798
1 Bit = 9 Pence
11 Bits = 8 Shillings 3 Pence
= 1 Dollar
1798-1840
12 Bits = 9 Shillings = 1 Dollar

BRITISH COLONY

NECESSITY COINAGE

KM# 1 BIT (9 Pence)

Silver **Countermark:** Incuse "G" **Note:** Countermark on 1/11th of Spanish or Spanish Colonial 8 Reales.

Date	Mintage	Good	VG	F	VF	XF
ND(c. 1787)	—	85.00	175	300	525	—

KM# 2 66 SHILLING

Gold **Note:** 11.5-11.79 g. Brazilian or Portuguese 6400 Reis forged or authentic weighing at least 9.33 g were plugged with gold to raise the weight to a legal specification of 11.66 g. A margin of error among goldsmiths gave rise to slight variances. The plug was countermarked with the goldsmiths script initials IW, WS or JR. Three "G" countermarks are also spaced along the edge to prevent clipping.

Date	Mintage	Good	VG	F	VF	XF
ND(1798)	—	—	—	7,500	10,000	—

KM# 3 66 SHILLING

Gold **Note:** 11.5-11.79 g. A heavier 6400 Reis coin originally weighing 13.21 g or more, not needing the center plug to raise the weight but with the three "G" countermarks along the edge. Unfortunately this measure still allowed for some clipping as all known examples fall into the weight range of KM#2.

Date	Mintage	Good	VG	F	VF	XF
ND(1798)	—	—	—	4,500	6,500	—

GUADELOUPE

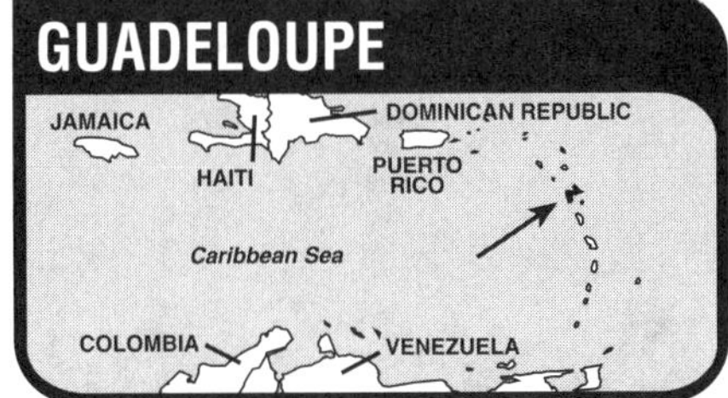

The French Overseas Department of Guadeloupe, located in the Leeward Islands of the West Indies about300 miles (493 km.) southeast of Puerto Rico, has an area of 687 sq. mi. (1,780 sq. km.) and a population of 306,000. Actually it is two islands separated by a narrow salt water stream: volcanic Basse-Terre to the west and the flatter limestone formation of Grande-Terre to the east. Capital: Basse-Terre, on the island of that name. The principal industries are agriculture, the distillation of liquors, and tourism. Sugar, bananas, and rum are exported.

Guadeloupe was discovered by Columbus in 1493 and settled in 1635 by two Frenchmen, L'Olive and Duplessis, who took possession in the name of the French Company of the Islands of America. When repeated efforts by private companies to colonize the island failed, it was relinquished to the French crown in 1674, and established as a dependency of Martinique. The British occupied the island on two occasions, 1759-63 and 1810-16, before it passed permanently to France. A colony until 1946 Guadeloupe was then made an overseas territory of the French Union. In 1958 it voted to become an Overseas Department within the new French Community.

The well-known R.F. in garland oval countermark of the French Government is only legitimate if on a French Colonies 12 deniers dated 1767A, KM#6. Two other similar but incuse RF countermarks are on cut pieces in the values of 1 and 4 escalins. Contemporary and modern counterfeits are known of both these types.

RULERS

French, until 1759, 1763-1810, 1816-
British, 1759-1763, 1810-1816

MONETARY SYSTEM

3 Deniers = 1 Liard
4 Liards = 1 Sol (Sous)
20 Sols = 1 Livre
6 Livres = 1 Ecu

NOTE: During the British Occupation period the Spanish and Spanish Colonial 8 Reales equaled 10 Livres.

FRENCH OCCUPATION

COUNTERMARKED COINAGE

KM# 1 3 SOLS 9 DENIERS

Bronze **Countermark:** RF in garland oval **Note:** Countermark on French Colonial 12 Deniers, C#4.

CM Date	Host Date	Good	VG	F	VF	XF
ND(1793)	1767A	15.00	30.00	45.00	75.00	250

GUATEMALA

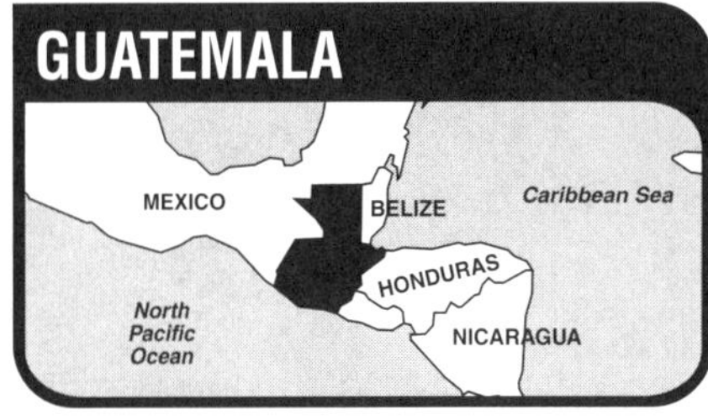

The Republic of Guatemala, the northernmost of the five Central American republics, has an area of 42,042 sq. mi. (108,890 sq. km.) and a population of 10.7 million. Capital: Guatemala City. The economy of Guatemala is heavily dependent on agriculture, however, the country is rich in nickel resources which are being developed. Coffee, cotton and bananas are exported.

Guatemala, once the site of an ancient Mayan civilization, was conquered by Pedro de Alvarado, the resourceful lieutenant of Cortes who undertook the conquest from Mexico. Cruel but strategically skillful, he progressed rapidly along the Pacific coastal lowlands to the highland plain of Quetzaltenango where the decisive battle for Guatemala was fought. After routing the Indian forces, he established the city of Guatemala in 1524. The Spanish Captaincy-General of Guatemala included all Central America but Panama. Guatemala declared its independence of Spain in 1821 and was absorbed into the Mexican empire of Augustin Iturbide (1822-23). From1823 to 1839 Guatemala was a constituent state of the Central American Republic. Upon dissolution of that confederation, Guatemala proclaimed itself an independent republic. Like El Salvador, Guatemala suffered from internal strife between right-wing, US-backed military government and leftist indigenous peoples from ca. 1954 to ca. 1997.

RULERS

Spanish until 1821

MINT MARKS

Antigua, the old capital city of Santiago de los Caballeros, including the mint, was destroyed by a volcanic eruption and earthquake in 1773. A new mint and capital city was established in Nueva Guatemala City. Coin production recommenced in late 1776 using the NG mint mark.

G or G-G - Guatemala until 1776, 1878-1889
H - Heaton, Birmingham
NG - Nueva Grenada - Guatemala, 1777-1829, 1992

ASSAYER'S INITIALS

J, 1733-1759, Jose de Leon y Losa
P, 1759-1785, Pedro Sanchez de Guzman
M, 1785-1822, Manuel Eusebio Sanchez

SPANISH COLONY

COLONIAL COB COINAGE

KM# 2 1/2 REAL

1.6917 g., 0.9170 Silver 0.0499 oz. ASW **Ruler:** Philip V **Obv:** Crowned arms **Rev:** Crowned hemispheres between pillars

Date	Mintage	Good	VG	F	VF	XF
ND(1733-1747) J Date off flan	—	15.00	25.00	35.00	50.00	—
1733 J Denomination as 1/2; Rare	—	—	—	—	—	—
1733 J Denomination as +	—	50.00	75.00	110	150	—
1734 J	—	50.00	75.00	100	150	—
1735 J	—	50.00	75.00	100	150	—
1736 J	—	50.00	75.00	100	150	—
1737/6 J	—	50.00	75.00	100	150	—
1737 J	—	50.00	75.00	100	150	—
1738 J	—	50.00	75.00	100	150	—
1739 J	—	50.00	75.00	100	150	—
1740 J	—	50.00	75.00	100	150	—
1741/40	—	50.00	75.00	100	150	—
1741 J	—	50.00	75.00	100	150	—
1742 J	—	50.00	75.00	100	150	—
1743 J	—	50.00	75.00	100	150	—
1744 J	—	90.00	150	225	375	—
1745 J	—	90.00	150	225	375	—
1746 J	—	90.00	150	225	375	—
1747 J Rare	—	—	—	—	—	—

KM# 8 1/2 REAL

1.6917 g., 0.9170 Silver 0.0499 oz. ASW **Ruler:** Ferdinand VI **Obv:** Crowned arms **Obv. Legend:** FERD. VI D.G... **Rev:** Crowned hemispheres between pillars

Date	Mintage	Good	VG	F	VF	XF
ND(1747-1753) J Date off flan	—	12.50	22.50	30.00	45.00	—
1747 J	—	45.00	70.00	100	135	—
1748 J	—	45.00	70.00	100	135	—
1749 J	—	45.00	70.00	100	135	—
1750 J	—	45.00	70.00	100	135	—
1751 J	—	45.00	70.00	100	135	—
1752 J	—	45.00	70.00	100	135	—
1753 J	—	35.00	60.00	90.00	120	—

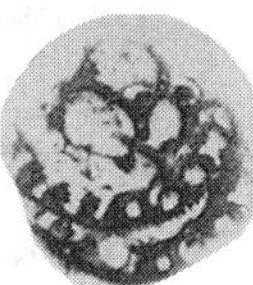

KM# 3 REAL

3.3834 g., 0.9170 Silver 0.0997 oz. ASW **Ruler:** Philip V **Obv:** Crowned arms **Rev:** Crowned hemispheres

Date	Mintage	Good	VG	F	VF	XF
ND(1733-1746) J Date off flan	—	7.00	10.00	15.00	25.00	—
1733 J	—	75.00	100	150	200	—
1734 J	—	20.00	40.00	60.00	90.00	—
1735 J	—	20.00	40.00	60.00	90.00	—
1736 J	—	20.00	40.00	60.00	90.00	—
1737 J	—	20.00	40.00	60.00	90.00	—
1738 J	—	20.00	40.00	60.00	90.00	—
1739 J	—	20.00	40.00	60.00	90.00	—
1740 J	—	20.00	40.00	60.00	90.00	—
1741 J	—	20.00	40.00	60.00	90.00	—
1742 J	—	20.00	40.00	60.00	90.00	—
1743/2 J	—	20.00	40.00	60.00	90.00	—
1743 J	—	20.00	40.00	60.00	90.00	—
1744 J	—	25.00	45.00	70.00	100	—
1745 J	—	25.00	45.00	70.00	100	—
1746 J	—	25.00	45.00	70.00	100	—

KM# 9 REAL

3.3834 g., 0.9170 Silver 0.0997 oz. ASW **Ruler:** Ferdinand VI **Obv:** Crowned arms **Obv. Legend:** FERD VI D.G... **Rev:** Crowned hemispheres between pillars

Date	Mintage	Good	VG	F	VF	XF
ND(1747-1753) J Date off flan	—	7.00	10.00	15.00	25.00	—
1747 J	—	20.00	40.00	60.00	90.00	—
1748 J	—	20.00	40.00	60.00	90.00	—
1749 J	—	20.00	40.00	60.00	90.00	—
1750 J	—	20.00	40.00	60.00	90.00	—
1751 J	—	20.00	40.00	60.00	90.00	—
1752 J	—	20.00	40.00	60.00	90.00	—
1753 J	—	15.00	30.00	50.00	75.00	—

KM# 4 2 REALES

6.7668 g., 0.9170 Silver 0.1995 oz. ASW **Ruler:** Philip V **Rev:** Crowned hemispheres

Date	Mintage	Good	VG	F	VF	XF
ND(1733-1746) Date off flan	—	10.00	15.00	22.50	35.00	—
1733 J	—	90.00	125	200	350	—
1734 J	—	30.00	50.00	70.00	100	—
1735 J	—	30.00	50.00	70.00	100	—
1736 J	—	30.00	50.00	70.00	100	—
1737 J	—	30.00	50.00	70.00	100	—
1738 J	—	30.00	50.00	70.00	100	—
1739 J	—	30.00	50.00	70.00	100	—
1740 J	—	30.00	50.00	70.00	100	—
1741 J	—	30.00	50.00	70.00	100	—
1742 J	—	30.00	50.00	70.00	100	—
1743 J	—	30.00	50.00	70.00	100	—
1744 J	—	35.00	55.00	75.00	110	—
1745 J	—	35.00	55.00	75.00	110	—
1746 J	—	35.00	55.00	75.00	110	—

KM# 10 2 REALES

6.7668 g., 0.9170 Silver 0.1995 oz. ASW **Ruler:** Ferdinand VI **Obv:** Crowned arms **Rev:** Crowned hemispheres

Date	Mintage	Good	VG	F	VF	XF
ND(1747-1753) J Date off flan	—	10.00	15.00	22.50	35.00	—
1747 J	—	30.00	50.00	70.00	100	—
1748 J	—	30.00	50.00	70.00	100	—
1749 J	—	30.00	50.00	70.00	100	—
1750 J	—	30.00	50.00	70.00	100	—
1751 J	—	30.00	50.00	70.00	100	—
1752 J	—	30.00	50.00	70.00	100	—
1753 J	—	25.00	45.00	60.00	90.00	—

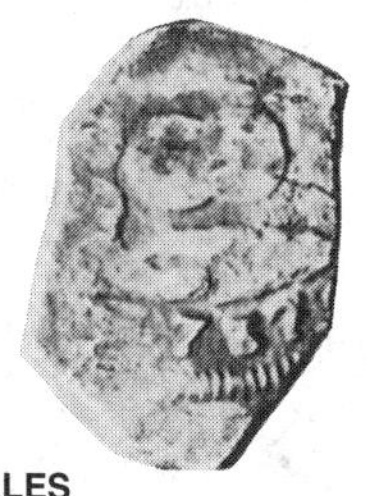

KM# 5 4 REALES

13.5337 g., 0.9170 Silver 0.3990 oz. ASW **Ruler:** Philip V **Rev:** Crowned hemispheres

Date	Mintage	Good	VG	F	VF	XF
ND(1733-1746) J Date off flan	—	50.00	75.00	100	125	—
1733 J Rare	—	—	—	—	—	—
1734 J	—	75.00	125	200	275	—
1735 J	—	75.00	125	200	275	—
1736 J	—	75.00	125	200	275	—
1737 J	—	75.00	125	200	275	—
1738 J	—	75.00	125	200	275	—
1739 J	—	75.00	125	200	275	—
1740 J	—	75.00	125	200	275	—
1741 J	—	75.00	125	200	275	—
1742 J Rare	—	—	—	—	—	—
1743 J	—	75.00	125	200	275	—
1744 J	—	75.00	125	200	275	—
1745 J	—	75.00	125	200	275	—
1746 J	—	75.00	125	200	275	—

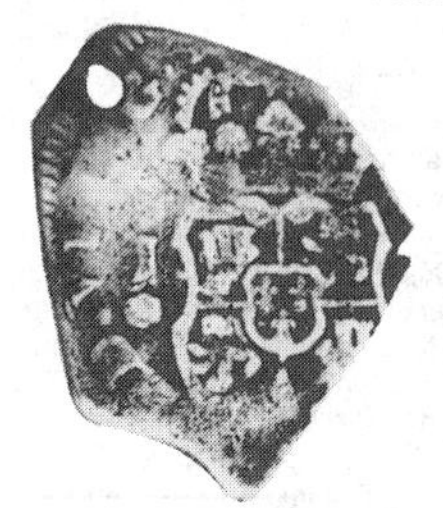

KM# 11 4 REALES

13.5337 g., 0.9170 Silver 0.3990 oz. ASW **Ruler:** Ferdinand VI **Obv:** Crowned arms **Rev:** Crowned hemispheres between pillars

Date	Mintage	Good	VG	F	VF	XF
ND(1747-53) Date off flan	—	50.00	75.00	100	125	—
1748 J	—	100	175	240	325	—
1747 J	—	100	175	240	325	—
1749 J	—	150	225	280	400	—
1750 J	—	100	175	240	325	—
1751 J	—	100	175	240	325	—
1752/1 J	—	100	175	240	325	—
1752 J	—	100	175	240	325	—
1753 J	—	70.00	100	100	250	—

KM# 6 8 REALES

27.0674 g., 0.9170 Silver 0.7980 oz. ASW **Ruler:** Philip V **Obv:** Crowned arms **Rev:** Crowned hemispheres between pillars

Date	Mintage	Good	VG	F	VF	XF
ND(1733-1746) J Date off flan	—	70.00	100	125	150	—
1733 J	—	750	1,350	2,000	2,750	—
1734 J	—	90.00	125	225	325	—
1735 J	—	90.00	125	225	325	—
1736 J	—	90.00	125	225	325	—
1737 J	—	100	175	275	375	—
1738 J	—	100	175	275	375	—
1739 J	—	100	175	275	375	—
1740/39 J	—	100	175	275	375	—
1740 J	—	100	175	275	375	—
1741 J	—	100	175	275	375	—
1742 J	—	100	175	275	375	—
1743/37 J	—	100	175	275	375	—
1743 J	—	100	175	275	375	—
1744 J Rare	—	—	—	—	—	—
1745 J Rare	—	—	—	—	—	—
1746 J Rare	—	—	—	—	—	—

KM# 12 8 REALES

27.0674 g., 0.9170 Silver 0.7980 oz. ASW **Ruler:** Ferdinand VI **Obv:** Crowned arms **Rev:** Crowned hemispheres between pillars **Note:** Often the coins below will be encountered with a countermark consisting of the sun behind a mountain or above several mountain peaks. These countermarks were used during the existence of the Central American Republic (1823-1847) and were added in the period 1838-1841. (refer to listings following Provisional Coinage).

Date	Mintage	Good	VG	F	VF	XF
ND(1747-1753) J Date off flan	—	70.00	100	125	150	—
1747 J	—	100	175	275	375	—
1748 J	—	100	175	275	375	—
1749 J	—	100	175	275	375	—
1749/7 J	—	100	175	275	375	—
1750 J	—	100	175	275	375	—
1751 J	—	100	175	275	375	—
1752/1 J	—	100	175	275	375	—
1752 J	—	100	175	275	375	—
1753 J	—	100	175	275	375	—

KM# A6 ESCUDO

3.3834 g., 0.9170 Gold 0.0997 oz. AGW **Ruler:** Ferdinand VI **Obv:** Small bust, date below **Rev:** Crowned arms

Date	Mintage	Good	VG	F	VF	XF
1751G J Rare	—	—	—	—	—	—

KM# 7 8 ESCUDOS

27.0674 g., 0.9170 Gold 0.7980 oz. AGW **Ruler:** Philip V **Obv:** Bust, date below **Rev:** Crowned arms

Date	Mintage	Good	VG	F	VF	XF
1733 J Unique	—	—	—	—	—	—
1734 J Unique	—	—	—	—	—	—
1737 J Rare	—	—	—	—	—	—
1740 J Rare	—	—	—	—	—	—
1741/0 J Unique	—	—	—	—	—	—
1741 J Rare	—	—	—	—	—	—
1742 J Rare	—	—	—	—	—	—
1743 J Rare	—	—	—	—	—	—
1745 J Rare	—	—	—	—	—	—

KM# A13 8 ESCUDOS

27.0674 g., 0.9170 Gold 0.7980 oz. AGW **Ruler:** Ferdinand VI **Obv:** Bust right **Rev:** Crowned arms within Order chain

Date	Mintage	Good	VG	F	VF	XF
1750 J 2 known; Rare	—	—	—	—	—	—

Note: Superior ANA sale 8-75 VF realized $37,000

Date	Mintage	Good	VG	F	VF	XF
1752/1 J Rare	—	—	—	—	—	—

COLONIAL MILLED COINAGE

KM# 59 1/4 REAL

0.8458 g., 0.8960 Silver 0.0244 oz. ASW **Ruler:** Charles IV **Obv:** Castle **Rev:** Lion

Date	Mintage	VG	F	VF	XF	Unc
1796G	—	20.00	35.00	50.00	70.00	—
1797G	—	20.00	35.00	50.00	70.00	—
1798G	—	20.00	35.00	50.00	70.00	—
1799G	—	20.00	35.00	50.00	70.00	—
1800G	—	20.00	35.00	50.00	70.00	—
1801G	—	20.00	35.00	50.00	70.00	—
1802G	—	20.00	35.00	50.00	70.00	—
1803G	—	20.00	35.00	50.00	70.00	—
1804G	—	20.00	35.00	50.00	70.00	—
1805G	—	30.00	50.00	70.00	100	—
1806G	—	30.00	50.00	70.00	100	—
1807G	—	20.00	35.00	50.00	70.00	—

KM# 15 1/2 REAL

1.6917 g., 0.9170 Silver 0.0499 oz. ASW **Ruler:** Ferdinand VI **Obv:** Crowned arms **Obv. Legend:** FERD • VI • D • G • HISP ET IND • R • **Rev:** Crowned hemispheres between pillars **Note:** These coins are often found clipped to proper weight.

Date	Mintage	VG	F	VF	XF	Unc
1754G	—	30.00	60.00	110	200	—
1755/4G	—	30.00	60.00	110	200	—
1755G	—	30.00	60.00	110	200	—
1756/5G	—	30.00	60.00	110	200	—
1756G	—	30.00	60.00	110	200	—
1757G	—	20.00	40.00	90.00	160	—
1758G	—	20.00	40.00	90.00	160	—
1759G	—	20.00	40.00	90.00	160	—
1760G	—	25.00	50.00	100	180	—

KM# 23 1/2 REAL

1.6917 g., 0.9170 Silver 0.0499 oz. ASW **Ruler:** Charles III **Obv:** Crowned arms **Obv. Legend:** CARO • III • D • G • HISP • ETIND • R • **Rev:** Crowned hemispheres between pillars **Rev. Legend:** VTRA QUE VNUM

Date	Mintage	VG	F	VF	XF	Unc
1760G	—	25.00	50.00	100	180	—
1761G	—	25.00	50.00	100	180	—
1762G	—	25.00	50.00	100	180	—
1763G	—	25.00	50.00	100	180	—
1764G	—	25.00	50.00	100	180	—
1765G	—	25.00	50.00	100	180	—
1766G	—	25.00	50.00	100	180	—
1767G	—	25.00	50.00	100	180	—
1768G	—	25.00	50.00	100	180	—
1769G	—	25.00	50.00	100	180	—
1770G	—	25.00	50.00	100	180	—
1771G	—	25.00	50.00	100	180	—

KM# 32.1 1/2 REAL

1.6921 g., 0.9030 Silver 0.0491 oz. ASW **Ruler:** Charles III **Obv:** Bust right **Rev:** Arms, pillars

Date	Mintage	VG	F	VF	XF	Unc
1772G P	—	15.00	30.00	75.00	110	—
1773G P	—	15.00	30.00	75.00	110	—
1776G P	—	15.00	30.00	75.00	110	—

KM# 32.2 1/2 REAL

1.6921 g., 0.9030 Silver 0.0491 oz. ASW **Ruler:** Charles III

Date	Mintage	VG	F	VF	XF	Unc
1779NG	—	50.00	80.00	140	250	—
1780NG P	—	15.00	30.00	70.00	100	—
1781NG P	—	15.00	30.00	70.00	100	—
1782NG P	—	15.00	30.00	70.00	100	—
1783NG P	—	15.00	30.00	70.00	100	—
1785NG M	—	15.00	30.00	70.00	100	—

KM# 32.2a 1/2 REAL

1.6921 g., 0.8960 Silver 0.0487 oz. ASW **Ruler:** Charles III

Date	Mintage	VG	F	VF	XF	Unc
1786NG M	—	15.00	30.00	70.00	100	—
1787NG M	—	15.00	30.00	70.00	100	—

KM# 41 1/2 REAL

1.6921 g., 0.8960 Silver 0.0487 oz. ASW **Ruler:** Charles IV **Obv:** Bust right **Obv. Legend:** CAROLVS IV...

Date	Mintage	VG	F	VF	XF	Unc
1789NG M	—	20.00	40.00	90.00	150	—
1789NG M IV/III	—	—	—	—	—	—
1790NG M	—	20.00	40.00	90.00	150	—

KM# 50 1/2 REAL

1.6921 g., 0.8960 Silver 0.0487 oz. ASW **Ruler:** Charles IV **Obv:** Bust right **Obv. Legend:** CAROLUS • IIII • - DEI • GRATIA • **Rev:** Arms, pillar **Rev. Legend:** HISPAN • ET • IND • R • A • G • M •

Date	Mintage	VG	F	VF	XF	Unc
1791NG M	—	30.00	60.00	110	200	—

Note: 1791NG M has a different bust than later dates of this type

Date	Mintage	VG	F	VF	XF	Unc
1792NG M	—	15.00	30.00	75.00	120	—
1793NG M	—	15.00	30.00	75.00	120	—
1794NG M	—	15.00	30.00	75.00	120	—
1795NG M	—	30.00	60.00	110	200	—
1796NG M	—	15.00	30.00	75.00	120	—
1797NG M	—	50.00	100	200	350	—
1798NG M	—	15.00	30.00	75.00	120	—
1799NG M	—	75.00	150	300	500	—
1800NG M	—	40.00	90.00	180	300	—
1801NG M	—	15.00	30.00	75.00	120	—
1802NG M	—	15.00	30.00	75.00	120	—
1803NG M	—	15.00	30.00	75.00	120	—
1804NG M	—	15.00	30.00	75.00	120	—
1805NG M	—	15.00	30.00	75.00	120	—
1806NG M	—	30.00	60.00	110	200	—
1807NG M	—	30.00	60.00	110	200	—

KM# 16 REAL

3.3834 g., 0.9170 Silver 0.0997 oz. ASW **Ruler:** Ferdinand VI **Obv:** Crowned arms **Obv. Legend:** FERD VI D.G... **Rev:** Crowned hemispheres between pillars

Date	Mintage	VG	F	VF	XF	Unc
1754G J	—	40.00	90.00	180	300	—
1755G J	—	40.00	90.00	180	300	—
1756G J	—	40.00	90.00	180	300	—
1757G J	—	35.00	80.00	150	250	—
1758G J	—	35.00	80.00	150	250	—
1758G J E in REX retrograde	—	40.00	90.00	180	300	—
1759G P	—	35.00	80.00	150	250	—
1760G P	—	40.00	90.00	180	300	—

KM# 24 REAL

3.3834 g., 0.9170 Silver 0.0997 oz. ASW **Ruler:** Charles III **Obv:** Crowned arms **Obv. Legend:** CAROLUS III... **Rev:** Crowned hemispheres between pillars

Date	Mintage	VG	F	VF	XF	Unc
1760G P	—	40.00	90.00	180	300	—
1761G P	—	40.00	90.00	180	300	—
1762G P	—	40.00	90.00	180	300	—
1763G P	—	40.00	90.00	180	300	—
1764G P	—	40.00	90.00	180	300	—
1765G P	—	40.00	90.00	180	300	—
1766G P	—	40.00	90.00	180	300	—
1767G P	—	40.00	90.00	180	300	—
1768G P	—	40.00	90.00	180	300	—
1769G P	—	40.00	90.00	180	300	—
1770G P	—	40.00	90.00	180	300	—
1771G P	—	40.00	90.00	180	300	—

KM# 33.1 REAL

3.3834 g., 0.9030 Silver 0.0982 oz. ASW **Ruler:** Charles III **Obv:** Bust right **Rev:** Crowned hemispheres between pillars

Date	Mintage	VG	F	VF	XF	Unc
1772G P	—	35.00	80.00	150	250	—
1773G P	—	35.00	80.00	150	250	—
1776G P	—	35.00	80.00	150	250	—

KM# 33.2 REAL

3.3834 g., 0.9030 Silver 0.0982 oz. ASW **Ruler:** Charles III **Obv:** Bust right **Rev:** Crowned hemispheres between pillars

Date	Mintage	VG	F	VF	XF	Unc
1779NG P	—	35.00	85.00	175	350	—
1780NG P	—	15.00	40.00	80.00	150	—
1781NG P	—	15.00	40.00	80.00	150	—
1782NG P	—	15.00	40.00	80.00	150	—
1783NG P	—	15.00	40.00	80.00	150	—
1785NG M	—	15.00	40.00	80.00	150	—

KM# 33.2a REAL

3.3834 g., 0.8960 Silver 0.0975 oz. ASW **Ruler:** Charles III **Obv:** Bust right **Rev:** Crowned hemispheres between pillars

Date	Mintage	VG	F	VF	XF	Unc
1786NG M	—	15.00	40.00	80.00	150	—
1787NG M	—	15.00	40.00	80.00	150	—

KM# 42 REAL

3.3834 g., 0.8960 Silver 0.0975 oz. ASW **Ruler:** Charles IV **Obv:** Bust right **Obv. Legend:** CAROLUS IIII...

Date	Mintage	VG	F	VF	XF	Unc
1789NG M IV/III	—	20.00	40.00	75.00	150	—
1789NG M	—	20.00	40.00	75.00	150	—
1790/89NG M	—	30.00	50.00	110	200	—
1790NG M	—	30.00	50.00	110	200	—

KM# 54 REAL

3.3834 g., 0.8960 Silver 0.0975 oz. ASW **Ruler:** Charles IV **Obv:** Bust right **Rev:** Crown above quartered arms with pillars flanking

Date	Mintage	VG	F	VF	XF	Unc
1790NG M	—	30.00	50.00	110	200	—
1791NG M	—	15.00	30.00	75.00	120	—
1792NG M	—	15.00	30.00	75.00	120	—
1793NG M	—	15.00	30.00	75.00	120	—
1794NG M	—	15.00	30.00	75.00	120	—
1795NG M	—	15.00	30.00	75.00	120	—
1796NG M	—	15.00	30.00	75.00	120	—
1797NG M	—	15.00	30.00	75.00	120	—
1798NG M	—	15.00	30.00	75.00	120	—
1799NG M	—	15.00	30.00	75.00	120	—
1800NG M	—	15.00	30.00	75.00	120	—

KM# 20 2 REALES

6.7668 g., 0.9170 Silver 0.1995 oz. ASW **Ruler:** Ferdinand VI **Obv:** Crowned arms **Obv. Legend:** * FERD • VI • D • G • HISP • ET • IND • R * **Rev:** Crowned hemispheres between pillars **Rev. Legend:** VTRA QUE VNUM

Date	Mintage	VG	F	VF	XF	Unc
1754G J Spanish 5; Rare	—	—	—	—	—	—
1755G J	—	40.00	80.00	150	250	—
1756G J	—	40.00	80.00	150	250	—
1757G J	—	30.00	50.00	110	200	—
1758G J	—	30.00	50.00	110	200	—
1759G P	—	30.00	50.00	110	200	—
1759G P	—	40.00	80.00	150	250	—

Note: Retrograde D in D.G. on reverse

Date	Mintage	VG	F	VF	XF	Unc
1760G P	—	40.00	80.00	150	250	—

KM# 25 2 REALES

6.7668 g., 0.9170 Silver 0.1995 oz. ASW **Ruler:** Charles III **Obv:** Crowned arms **Obv. Legend:** CAR • III • D • G • HISP • ET IND • R • **Rev:** Crowned hemispheres between pillars **Rev. Legend:** * VTRA QUE VNUM *

Date	Mintage	VG	F	VF	XF	Unc
1760G P Rare	—	—	—	—	—	—
1761G P	—	40.00	80.00	150	250	—
1761G P CAR (without O)	—	—	—	—	—	—
1762G P	—	45.00	90.00	180	300	—
1763G P	—	40.00	80.00	150	250	—
1764G P	—	40.00	80.00	150	250	—
1765G P Rare	—	—	—	—	—	—
1766G P Rare	—	—	—	—	—	—
1767G P	—	40.00	80.00	150	250	—
1768G P	—	40.00	80.00	150	250	—
1769G P	—	40.00	80.00	150	250	—
1770G P	—	40.00	80.00	150	250	—
1771G P	—	40.00	80.00	150	250	—

KM# 34.1 2 REALES
6.7668 g., 0.9030 Silver 0.1964 oz. ASW **Ruler:** Charles III **Obv:** Bust right **Obv. Legend:** CAROLUS • III • - DEI • GRATIA • **Rev:** Crowned arms between pillars **Rev. Legend:** HISPAN • ET • IND • REX • ...

Date	Mintage	VG	F	VF	XF	Unc
1772G P	—	45.00	90.00	180	300	—
Note: Two bust varieties exist dated 1772						
1773G P	—	45.00	90.00	180	300	—
1776G P	—	45.00	90.00	180	300	—

KM# 34.2 2 REALES
6.7668 g., 0.9030 Silver 0.1964 oz. ASW **Ruler:** Charles III **Obv:** Bust right **Rev:** Crowned arms between pillars

Date	Mintage	VG	F	VF	XF	Unc
1779NG P	—	45.00	90.00	180	300	—
1780NG P	—	20.00	40.00	80.00	150	—
1781NG P	—	20.00	40.00	80.00	150	—
1782NG P	—	20.00	40.00	80.00	150	—
1783NG P	—	20.00	40.00	80.00	150	—
1785NG M	—	20.00	40.00	80.00	150	—

KM# 34.2a 2 REALES
6.7668 g., 0.8960 Silver 0.1949 oz. ASW **Ruler:** Charles III **Obv:** Bust right **Rev:** Crowned arms between pillars

Date	Mintage	VG	F	VF	XF	Unc
1786NG M	—	20.00	40.00	80.00	150	—
1787NG M	—	20.00	40.00	80.00	150	—

KM# 43 2 REALES
6.7668 g., 0.8960 Silver 0.1949 oz. ASW **Ruler:** Charles IV **Obv:** Bust right **Obv. Legend:** CAROLUS IV...

Date	Mintage	VG	F	VF	XF	Unc
1789NG M	—	25.00	40.00	75.00	130	—
1789NG M IV/III	—	25.00	40.00	80.00	150	—
1790NG M	—	25.00	40.00	75.00	130	—

KM# 51 2 REALES
6.7668 g., 0.8960 Silver 0.1949 oz. ASW **Ruler:** Charles IV **Obv:** Draped laureate bust right **Obv. Legend:** CAROLUS • IIII • - DEI • GRATIA • **Rev:** Crown above quartered arms with pillars flanking **Rev. Legend:** • HISPAN • ET • IND • REX • NG • ...

Date	Mintage	VG	F	VF	XF	Unc
1790NG M	—	17.50	30.00	45.00	60.00	—
1791NG M	—	17.50	30.00	45.00	60.00	—
1792NG M	—	17.50	30.00	45.00	60.00	—
1793NG M	—	17.50	30.00	45.00	60.00	—
1794NG M	—	17.50	30.00	45.00	60.00	—
1795/4NG M	—	17.50	30.00	45.00	60.00	—
1795NG M	—	17.50	30.00	45.00	60.00	—
1796NG M	—	17.50	30.00	45.00	60.00	—
1797NG M	—	17.50	30.00	45.00	60.00	—
1798NG M	—	17.50	30.00	45.00	60.00	—
1799NG M	—	17.50	30.00	45.00	60.00	—
1800NG M	—	17.50	30.00	45.00	60.00	—

KM# 17.1 4 REALES
13.5337 g., 0.9170 Silver 0.3990 oz. ASW **Ruler:** Ferdinand VI **Obv:** Crowned arms **Obv. Legend:** FERDIND • VI • D • G • HISPAN • ET IND • REX **Rev:** Crowned hemispheres between pillars **Rev. Legend:** VTRA QUE - VNUM

Date	Mintage	VG	F	VF	XF	Unc
1754G J Arabic 5	—	200	300	500	800	—
1754G J Spanish 5	—	150	250	350	500	—
1755G J	—	150	250	350	500	—
1756/5G J Rare	—	—	—	—	—	—
1756G J	—	150	250	350	500	—
1757G J	—	150	250	350	500	—
1758G J	—	150	250	350	500	—
1759G P/J Rare	—	—	—	—	—	—
1759G P	—	150	250	350	500	—
1760G P	—	150	250	350	500	—

KM# 17.2 4 REALES
13.5337 g., 0.9170 Silver 0.3990 oz. ASW **Ruler:** Ferdinand VI **Obv:** Crowned arms **Rev:** Small legend

Date	Mintage	VG	F	VF	XF	Unc
1758G J	—	155	220	455	750	—

KM# 26 4 REALES
13.5337 g., 0.9170 Silver 0.3990 oz. ASW **Ruler:** Charles III **Obv:** Crowned arms **Obv. Legend:** CAROLUS • III • D • G • HISPAN • ET IND • REX **Rev:** Crowned hemispheres between pillars **Rev. Legend:** VTRA QUE VNUM

Date	Mintage	VG	F	VF	XF	Unc
1760G P	—	200	300	450	1,000	—
1761G P	—	200	325	525	850	—
1762G P	—	200	325	525	850	—
1763G P	—	200	325	525	850	—
1764G P	—	200	325	525	850	—
1765G P	—	200	325	525	850	—
1766G P	—	200	325	525	850	—
1767G P	—	200	325	525	850	—
1768G P	—	200	325	525	850	—
1769G P	—	200	325	525	850	—
1770G P	—	200	325	525	850	—
1771G P	—	200	325	525	850	—

KM# 35.1 4 REALES
13.5337 g., 0.9030 Silver 0.3929 oz. ASW **Ruler:** Charles III **Obv:** Bust right **Obv. Legend:** CAROLUS • III • - DEI • GRATIA • **Rev:** Crowned arms between pillars **Rev. Legend:** • HISPAN • ET IND • REX • ...

Date	Mintage	VG	F	VF	XF	Unc
1772G P	—	125	250	400	750	—
1773G P	—	125	250	400	750	—
1776G P	—	125	250	400	750	—

KM# 35.2 4 REALES
13.5337 g., 0.9030 Silver 0.3929 oz. ASW **Ruler:** Charles III **Obv:** Bust right **Rev:** Crowned arms between pillars

Date	Mintage	VG	F	VF	XF	Unc
1777NG P	—	125	250	400	750	—
1778NG P	—	125	250	400	750	—
1779NG P	—	125	250	400	750	—
1780NG P	—	125	250	400	750	—
1781NG P	—	150	300	450	950	—
1782NG P	—	150	300	450	950	—
1783NG P	—	200	350	550	1,200	—
1785NG P	—	125	250	400	750	—

KM# 35.2a 4 REALES
13.5337 g., 0.8960 Silver 0.3898 oz. ASW **Ruler:** Charles III **Obv:** Bust right **Rev:** Crowned arms between pillars

Date	Mintage	VG	F	VF	XF	Unc
1787NG M	—	125	250	400	750	—

KM# 44 4 REALES
13.5337 g., 0.8960 Silver 0.3898 oz. ASW **Ruler:** Charles IV **Obv:** Bust right **Obv. Legend:** CAROLUS • IV • - DEI • GRATIA • **Rev:** Crowned arms between pillars **Rev. Legend:** • HISPAN • ET IND • REX • ...

Date	Mintage	VG	F	VF	XF	Unc
1789NG M	—	175	275	400	700	—
1790NG M	—	175	275	400	700	—

KM# 52 4 REALES
13.5337 g., 0.8960 Silver 0.3898 oz. ASW **Ruler:** Charles IV **Obv:** Draped laureate bust right **Obv. Legend:** CAROLUS • IIII • - DEI • GRATIA • **Rev:** Crowned arms between pillars **Rev. Legend:** • HISPAN • ET IND • REX • ...

Date	Mintage	VG	F	VF	XF	Unc
1790NG M	—	150	250	400	900	—
1791NG M	—	75.00	150	250	400	—
1792NG M	—	75.00	150	250	400	—
1793NG M	—	50.00	100	200	350	—
1794NG M	—	50.00	150	250	400	—
1795NG M	—	75.00	150	250	400	—
1796NG M	—	50.00	100	200	350	—
1797NG M	—	75.00	150	250	400	—
1798NG M	—	75.00	150	250	400	—
1799NG M	—	75.00	150	250	400	—
1800NG M	—	75.00	150	250	400	—

KM# 18 8 REALES
27.0674 g., 0.9170 Silver 0.7980 oz. ASW **Ruler:** Ferdinand VI **Obv:** Crowned arms **Obv. Legend:** FERDIND • VI • D • G • HISPAN • ET IND • REX **Rev:** Crowned hemispheres between pillars **Rev. Legend:** VTRA QUE VNUM

Date	Mintage	VG	F	VF	XF	Unc
1754G J Arabic 5	—	700	1,200	2,000	3,000	—
1754G J Spanish 5	—	350	500	750	1,000	—
1755G J Small J	—	350	500	750	1,000	—
1755G J Large J	—	350	500	750	1,000	—
1756/5G J Rare	—	—	—	—	—	—
1756G J	—	350	500	750	1,000	—
1757G J	—	350	500	750	1,000	—
1757G J	—	350	500	750	1,000	—
Note: Reverse without points in legend						
1758G J	—	350	500	750	1,000	—
1759G P	—	200	300	500	700	—
1760G P	—	350	500	800	1,100	—

KM# 27.1 8 REALES

27.0674 g., 0.9170 Silver 0.7980 oz. ASW **Ruler:** Charles III **Obv:** Crowned arms **Obv. Legend:** CAROLUS • III • D • G • HISPAN • ET IND • REX **Rev:** Crowned hemispheres between pillars **Rev. Legend:** VTRA QUE VNUM **Note:** Large planchet. Varieties in hemispheres and pillars exist.

Date	Mintage	VG	F	VF	XF	Unc
1760G P	—	500	1,000	2,500	4,000	—
1761G P	—	200	300	500	750	—
1762G P	—	200	300	500	750	—
1763G P	—	200	300	500	750	—
1764G P	—	350	750	1,250	2,500	—
1765G P	—	1,200	2,000	3,750	—	—
1766G P	—	200	300	500	750	—
1767G P	—	200	300	500	750	—
1768G P	—	200	300	500	750	—

Note: 4 varieties of crowns have been recorded for 1768

Date	Mintage	VG	F	VF	XF	Unc
1769G P	—	175	250	400	600	—

KM# 27.2 8 REALES

27.0674 g., 0.9170 Silver 0.7980 oz. ASW **Ruler:** Charles III **Obv:** Crowned arms **Rev:** Crowned hemispheres between pillars **Note:** Small planchet.

Date	Mintage	VG	F	VF	XF	Unc
1769G P	—	300	400	600	850	—

Note: S over retrograde S

Date	Mintage	VG	F	VF	XF	Unc
1770G P	—	200	300	500	750	—
1771G P	—	200	300	500	750	—

KM# 36.1 8 REALES

27.0674 g., 0.9030 Silver 0.7858 oz. ASW **Ruler:** Charles III **Obv:** Laureate bust right **Rev:** Crowned arms between pillars

Date	Mintage	VG	F	VF	XF	Unc
1772G P	—	400	550	800	1,250	—
1773G P	—	650	900	1,200	2,000	—

KM# 36.2 8 REALES

27.0674 g., 0.9030 Silver 0.7858 oz. ASW **Ruler:** Charles III **Obv:** Laureate bust right **Obv. Legend:** CAROLUS • III • - DEI • GRATIA • **Rev:** Crowned arms between pillars **Rev. Legend:** • HISPAN • ET IND • REX • ...

Date	Mintage	VG	F	VF	XF	Unc
1776NG P	—	750	1,500	2,500	3,500	—
1776NG P (NG/GN)	—	1,000	2,000	3,500	5,000	—
1777NG P	—	200	300	500	750	—
1778NG P	—	200	300	500	750	—
1779NG P	—	250	450	650	1,000	—
1780NG P	—	650	900	1,200	2,000	—
1781NG P	—	450	675	900	1,500	—
1782NG P	—	700	1,350	1,800	3,000	—
1783NG P	—	400	800	1,100	1,750	—
1785NG M	—	250	450	650	1,000	—

KM# 36.2a 8 REALES

27.0674 g., 0.8960 Silver 0.7797 oz. ASW **Ruler:** Charles III **Obv:** Laureate bust right **Rev:** Crowned arms between pillars

Date	Mintage	VG	F	VF	XF	Unc
1786NG M	—	650	900	1,200	2,000	—
1787NG M	—	250	450	650	1,000	—

KM# 45 8 REALES

27.0674 g., 0.8960 Silver 0.7797 oz. ASW **Ruler:** Charles IV **Obv:** Laureate bust right **Obv. Legend:** • CAROLUS • IV • - DEI • GRATIA • **Rev:** Crowned arms between pillars **Rev. Legend:** • HISPAN • ET IND • REX • ...

Date	Mintage	VG	F	VF	XF	Unc
1789NG M	—	250	400	600	850	—
1790/89NG M	—	250	450	650	950	—
1790NG M	—	250	450	650	950	—

KM# 53 8 REALES

27.0674 g., 0.8960 Silver 0.7797 oz. ASW **Ruler:** Charles IV **Obv:** Draped laureate bust right **Obv. Legend:** • CAROLUS • IIII • - DEI • GRATIA • **Rev:** Crowned arms between pillars **Rev. Legend:** • HISPAN • ET IND • REX • ...

Date	Mintage	VG	F	VF	XF	Unc
1790NG M	—	700	1,000	1,300	2,250	—
1791NG M	—	100	300	500	650	—
1792NG M	—	60.00	140	240	375	—
1793NG M	—	60.00	140	260	375	—
1794NG M	—	60.00	140	240	375	—
1795/4NG M	—	—	—	—	—	—
1795NG M	—	55.00	100	200	350	—
1796NG M	—	55.00	100	200	350	—
1797/6NG M	—	75.00	200	275	425	—
1797NG M	—	55.00	150	225	350	—
1798NG M	—	55.00	100	200	350	—
1799NG M	—	60.00	150	225	375	—
1800NG M	—	55.00	100	200	350	—

KM# 22.1 ESCUDO

3.3834 g., 0.9170 Gold 0.0997 oz. AGW **Ruler:** Ferdinand VI **Obv:** Small bust, date **Obv. Legend:** FERDIND VI DG HISPAN ET IND REX **Rev:** Crowned arms **Rev. Legend:** NOMINA MAGNA SEQUOR

Date	Mintage	VG	F	VF	XF	Unc
1755G J	—	600	1,250	2,500	5,000	—

KM# 22.2 ESCUDO

3.3834 g., 0.9170 Gold 0.0997 oz. AGW **Ruler:** Ferdinand VI **Obv:** Larger bust **Rev:** Crowned arms

Date	Mintage	VG	F	VF	XF	Unc
1757G J	—	600	1,250	2,500	5,000	—

KM# 29 ESCUDO

3.3834 g., 0.9170 Gold 0.0997 oz. AGW **Ruler:** Charles III **Obv:** Young bust right **Rev:** Crowned arms **Rev. Legend:** IN UTROQ FELIX

Date	Mintage	VG	F	VF	XF	Unc
1765G Rare	—	—	—	—	—	—
1770G Rare	—	—	—	—	—	—

KM# 37 ESCUDO

3.3834 g., 0.9010 Gold 0.0980 oz. AGW **Ruler:** Charles III **Obv:** Bust right; older, standard bust **Rev:** Crowned arms within collar of the Order of the Golden Fleece

Date	Mintage	VG	F	VF	XF	Unc
1778NG P	—	500	1,000	1,750	3,250	—
1783NG P	—	500	1,000	1,750	3,250	—
1785NG M	—	600	1,250	2,000	4,000	—

KM# 46 ESCUDO

3.3834 g., 0.8750 Gold 0.0952 oz. AGW **Ruler:** Charles IV **Obv:** Bust right **Obv. Legend:** CAROL • IV • D • G • ... **Rev:** Crowned arms within Order collar **Rev. Legend:** IN • UTROQ • FELIX • ...

Date	Mintage	VG	F	VF	XF	Unc
1789NG M	—	250	500	1,000	1,500	—
1790NG M	—	300	550	1,100	1,750	—

KM# 55 ESCUDO

3.3834 g., 0.8750 Gold 0.0952 oz. AGW **Ruler:** Charles IV **Obv:** Armored bust right **Obv. Legend:** CAROL • IIII • D • G • - HISP • ET IND • R • **Rev:** Crowned arms within Order collar **Rev. Legend:** IN • UTROQ • FELIX • ...

Date	Mintage	VG	F	VF	XF	Unc
1794NG M	—	225	500	850	1,250	—
1797NG M	—	225	500	850	1,250	—

KM# 38 2 ESCUDOS

6.7668 g., 0.9010 Gold 0.1960 oz. AGW **Ruler:** Charles III **Obv:** Bust right **Obv. Legend:** CAROL • III • D • G • - HISP • ET IND • R • **Rev:** Crowned arms within collar of the Order of the Golden Fleece **Rev. Legend:** IN • UTROQ • FELIX • - AUSPICE • DEO •

Date	Mintage	VG	F	VF	XF	Unc
1783NG P	—	600	1,250	2,000	4,000	—
1785NG M	—	600	1,250	2,000	4,000	—

KM# 47 2 ESCUDOS

6.7668 g., 0.8750 Gold 0.1904 oz. AGW **Ruler:** Charles IV **Obv:** Bust right **Obv. Legend:** CAROL IV...

Date	Mintage	VG	F	VF	XF	Unc
1789NG M	—	500	1,100	1,900	3,750	—
1790NG M	—	700	1,400	2,200	4,250	—

KM# 56 2 ESCUDOS

6.7668 g., 0.8750 Gold 0.1904 oz. AGW **Ruler:** Charles IV **Obv:** Armored bust right **Obv. Legend:** CAROL • IIII • D • G • - HISP • ET IND • R • **Rev:** Crowned arms within Order collar **Rev. Legend:** IN • UTROQ • FELIX • AUSPICE • DEO •

Date	Mintage	VG	F	VF	XF	Unc
1794NG M	—	450	900	1,600	3,000	—
1797NG M	—	500	1,100	1,850	3,500	—

KM# A19 4 ESCUDOS

13.5337 g., 0.9170 Gold 0.3990 oz. AGW **Ruler:** Ferdinand VI **Obv:** Bust right **Rev:** Crowned arms within collar of the Order of the Golden Fleece **Rev. Legend:** NOMINA MAGNA SEQUOR

Date	Mintage	VG	F	VF	XF	Unc
1755G J Rare	—	—	—	—	—	—

KM# 30 4 ESCUDOS

13.5337 g., 0.9170 Gold 0.3990 oz. AGW **Ruler:** Charles III **Obv:** Young bust right **Rev:** Crowned arms within collar of the Order of the Golden Fleece **Rev. Legend:** IN VTROQ FELIX ANSPICE DEO

Date	Mintage	VG	F	VF	XF	Unc
1765G P Rare	—	—	—	—	—	—

KM# 39 4 ESCUDOS

13.5337 g., 0.9010 Gold 0.3920 oz. AGW **Ruler:** Charles III **Obv:** Older, standard bust

Date	Mintage	VG	F	VF	XF	Unc
1778NG P	—	750	1,500	3,000	5,500	—
1781NG P	—	750	1,500	3,000	5,500	—
1783NG P	—	750	1,500	3,000	5,500	—

KM# 48 4 ESCUDOS
13.5337 g., 0.8750 Gold 0.3807 oz. AGW **Ruler:** Charles IV **Obv:** Armored bust right **Obv. Legend:** CAROL • IV • D • G • - HISP • ET IND • R • **Rev:** Crowned arms within Order collar **Rev. Legend:** IN • UTROQ • FELIX • AUSPICE • DEO •

Date	Mintage	VG	F	VF	XF	Unc
1789NG M	—	1,250	2,750	4,500	7,500	—

KM# 57 4 ESCUDOS
13.5337 g., 0.8750 Gold 0.3807 oz. AGW **Ruler:** Charles IV

Date	Mintage	VG	F	VF	XF	Unc
1794NG M	—	1,000	2,000	3,750	6,500	—
1797NG M	—	1,000	2,000	3,750	6,500	—

KM# 19 8 ESCUDOS
27.0674 g., 0.9170 Gold 0.7980 oz. AGW **Ruler:** Ferdinand VI **Obv:** Armored bust right **Obv. Legend:** FERDIND • VI • D • G • HISPAN • ET IND • REX **Rev:** Crowned arms within collar of the Order of the Golden Fleece **Rev. Legend:** NOMINA MAGNA SEQUOR

Date	Mintage	VG	F	VF	XF	Unc
1754G J	—	—	10,000	15,000	25,000	—
1755G J	—	—	10,000	15,000	25,000	—

KM# 21 8 ESCUDOS
27.0674 g., 0.9170 Gold 0.7980 oz. AGW **Ruler:** Ferdinand VI **Obv:** Armored bust right **Obv. Legend:** FERDIND • VI • D • G • HISPAN • ET IND • REX **Rev:** Crowned arms within Order collar **Rev. Legend:** NOMINA MAGNA SEQUOR

Date	Mintage	VG	F	VF	XF	Unc
1757G J	—	—	9,000	14,000	25,000	—

KM# 28 8 ESCUDOS
27.0674 g., 0.9170 Gold 0.7980 oz. AGW **Ruler:** Charles III **Obv:** Unique bust of Ferdinand VII, legend of Charles III **Rev:** Crowned arms within collar of the Order of the Golden Fleece

Date	Mintage	VG	F	VF	XF	Unc
1761G J Rare	—	—	—	—	—	—

KM# 31 8 ESCUDOS
27.0674 g., 0.9170 Gold 0.7980 oz. AGW **Ruler:** Charles III **Obv:** Young bust right **Obv. Legend:** CAROLUS • III • D • G • - HISP • ET • IND • REX • **Rev:** Crowned arms within Order collar **Rev. Legend:** IN • UTROQ • FELIX • AUSPICE • DEO •

Date	Mintage	VG	F	VF	XF	Unc
1765G Rare	—	—	—	—	—	—
1768G	—	—	7,000	12,000	20,000	—
1770G Rare	—	—	—	—	—	—

KM# 40 8 ESCUDOS
27.0674 g., 0.9010 Gold 0.7841 oz. AGW **Ruler:** Charles III **Obv:** Older, standard bust right **Obv. Legend:** CAROL • III • D • G • - HISP • ET IND • R • **Rev:** Crowned arms within Order collar **Rev. Legend:** IN • UTROQ • FELIX • AUSPICE • DEO •

Date	Mintage	VG	F	VF	XF	Unc
1778NG P	—	—	2,500	4,500	8,500	—
1781NG P	—	—	3,500	5,500	12,500	—
1783NG P	—	—	3,500	5,500	12,500	—
1785NG M	—	—	4,500	6,500	15,500	—

KM# 49 8 ESCUDOS
27.0674 g., 0.9010 Gold 0.7841 oz. AGW **Ruler:** Charles IV **Obv:** Armored bust right **Obv. Legend:** CAROL • IV • D • G • - HISP • ET IND • R • **Rev:** Crowned arms within Order collar **Rev. Legend:** IN • UTROQ • FELIX • AUSPICE • DEO •

Date	Mintage	VG	F	VF	XF	Unc
1789NG M	—	—	2,500	4,500	8,500	—
1790NG M	—	—	4,000	6,500	15,500	—

KM# 58 8 ESCUDOS
27.0674 g., 0.8750 Gold 0.7614 oz. AGW **Ruler:** Charles IV **Obv:** Armored bust right **Obv. Legend:** CAROL • IIII • D • G • - HISP • ET IND • R • **Rev:** Crowned arms within order collar **Rev. Legend:** IN • UTROQ • FELIX • AUSPICE • DEO •

Date	Mintage	VG	F	VF	XF	Unc
1794NG M	—	—	2,000	4,500	7,500	—
1797NG M	—	—	2,000	4,500	7,500	—

HAITI

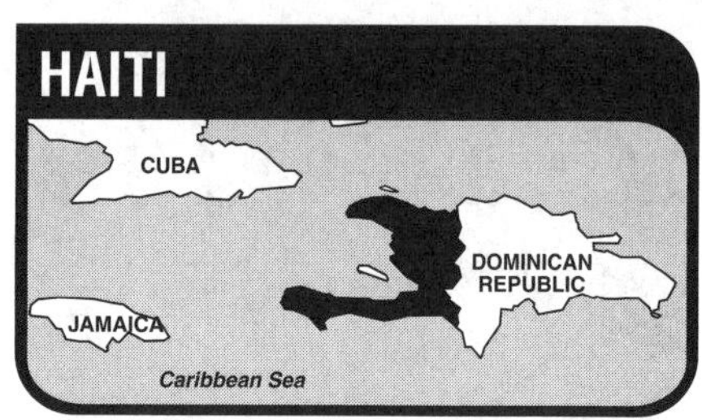

The Republic of Haiti, which occupies the western one-third of the island of Hispaniola in the Caribbean Sea between Puerto Rico and Cuba, has an area of 10,714 sq. mi. (27,750 sq. km.) and a population of 6.5 million. Capital: Port-au-Prince. The economy is based on agriculture; but light manufacturing and tourism are increasingly important. Coffee, bauxite, sugar, essential oils and handicrafts are exported.

Columbus discovered Hispaniola in 1492. Spain colonized the island, making Santo Domingo the base for exploration of the Western Hemisphere. The area that is now Haiti was ceded to France by Spain in 1697. Slaves brought from Africa to work the coffee and sugar cane plantations made it one of the richest colonies of the French Empire. A slave revolt in the 1790's led to the establishment of the Republic of Haiti in1804, making it the oldest Black republic in the world and the second oldest republic (after the United States) in the Western Hemisphere.

The French language is used on Haitian coins although it is spoken by only about 10% of the populace. A form of Creole is the language of the Haitians.

RULERS
French, until 1804

REVOLUTIONARY GOVERNMENT
1798 - 1802

COLONIAL COINAGE

KM# 21 1/2 ESCALIN
Silver **Ruler:** Toussaint L'Ouverture **Obv:** Standing figure facing, flanked by fasces and liberty cap on pole **Rev:** Written value

Date	Mintage	VG	F	VF	XF	Unc
ND(1802)	—	250	400	900	1,850	—

TOWN OF LE CAP

(Old Cap Francois)

Port city on the northern coast of Haiti. Under a French edict of July 13, 1781 various Spanish-American and other circulating silver coins were to be counterstamped with a crowned anchor and C for the island. These were made at the capitol and the pieces given values of 1 Escalin and 1/2 Escalin.

In 1792, a decree from the local Governor authorized the countermarking of Spanish American, French, and English copper coins. An L.C. mark was designated for use in the capital city of Le Cap, while an S:D. mark was to be used for general circulation on the entire island.

Type I - 1791
Crowned anchor with C

Type II - 1792
Anchor with C

MONETARY SYSTEM
15 Sols = 1 Escalin (1 Real)

FRENCH PROTECTORATE

COUNTERMARKED COINAGE

Type I - 1791

KM# 7.2 1/2 ESCALIN
1.0700 g., Silver **Countermark:** Type I **Note:** Countermark struck on Potosi 1 Real size cob.

CM Date	Host Date	Good	VG	F	VF	XF
ND(1791)	(1701-73)	200	375	550	850	—

KM# 7.1 1/2 ESCALIN

0.9300 g., Silver **Countermark:** Type I **Note:** Countermark struck on Potosi 1/2 Real size cob.

CM Date	Host Date	Good	VG	F	VF	XF
ND(1791)	(1701-73)	175	300	450	750	—

KM# 8.1 ESCALIN

2.3600 g., Silver **Countermark:** Type I **Note:** Countermark struck on center of Lima or Potosi 2 Real size cob.

CM Date	Host Date	Good	VG	F	VF	XF
ND(1791)	(1701-52)	175	300	450	700	—

KM# 8.2 ESCALIN

3.3800 g., Silver **Counterstamp:** Type I **Note:** Counterstamp struck on Lima 1 Real cob.

CM Date	Host Date	Good	VG	F	VF	XF
ND(1791)	(1701-52)	185	325	500	800	—

COUNTERMARKED COINAGE

Type II - 1792

KM# 9 ESCALIN

2.8000 g., Silver **Counterstamp:** Type II **Note:** Counterstamp struck on Angola 2 Macutas, KM#13.

CM Date	Host Date	Good	VG	F	VF	XF
ND(1791)	1762	175	300	450	700	—
ND(1792)	1763	175	300	450	700	—

HEJAZ

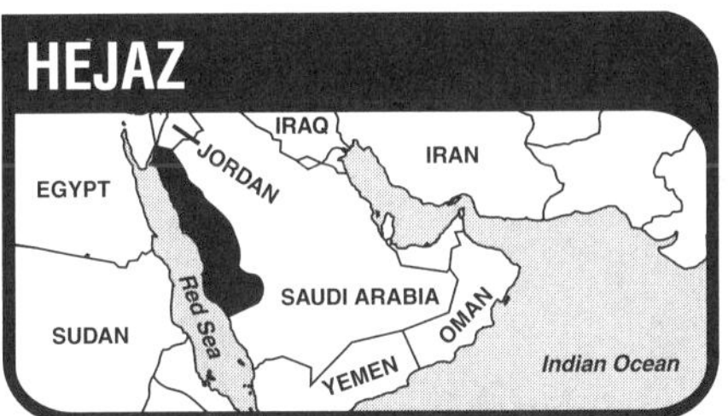

Hejaz, a province of Saudi Arabia and a former vilayet of the Ottoman Empire, occupies an 800-mile long (1,287km.) coastal strip between Nejd and the Red Sea. The province was a Turkish dependency until freed in World War I. Husain Ibn Ali, Amir of Mecca, opposed the Turkish control and, with the aid of Lawrence of Arabia, wrested much of Hejaz from the Turks and in 1916 assumed the title of King of Hejaz. Abd Al-Aziz Bin Sa'ud, of Nejd conquered Hejaz in 1925, and in 1926 combined it and Nejd into a single kingdom.

TITLES

Hal-Hejaz

MECCA

Mecca, the metropolis of Islam and the capital of Hejaz, is located inland from the Red Sea due east of the port of Jidda. A center of non-political commercial, cultural and religious activities, Mecca remained virtually independent until 1259. Two centuries of Egyptian rule were followed by four centuries of Turkish rule which lasted until the Arab revolts which extinguished pretensions to sovereignty over any part of the Arabian peninsula.

MINT NAME

Makkah, Mecca

KINGDOM

COUNTERMARKED COINAGE

Minor Coins

Following the defeat of the Ottomans in 1916, Turkish 10, 20 and 40 Para coins of Muhammed V and 40 Para coins of Muhammed VI were countermarked al-Hejaz in Arabic. The countermark was applied to the obverse side effacing the Ottoman Sultan's toughra, and thus refuting Turkish rule in Hejaz.

Countermarks on the reverse are rare errors. The 10 Para of Muhammed V and 10 and 20 Para (billon) of Abdul Mejid and Mahmud II exist with a smaller, 6-milimeter countermark. These are probably unofficial. Other host coins are considered controversial.

KM# 2 10 PARA

Nickel **Countermark:** Hejaz **Obv:** Reshat **Note:** Large countermark on Turkey 10 Para, KM#760. Accession date: 1327.

CM Date	Host Date	Good	VG	F	VF	XF
ND(AH1327)	AH1327//7 Rare	—	—	—	—	—
ND(AH1327)	AH1327//7 Rare	—	—	—	—	—
ND(1327)	AH1327//2-7 Rare	—	—	—	—	—
ND(1327)	AH1327//2-7 Rare	—	—	—	—	—

KM# 3 20 PARA

Nickel **Countermark:** "Hejaz" **Note:** Countermark on Turkey 20 Para, KM#761. Accession date: 1327.

CM Date	Host Date	Good	VG	F	VF	XF
ND(1327)	AH1327//2	5.00	9.00	20.00	40.00	—
ND(1327)	AH1327//2	5.00	9.00	20.00	40.00	—
ND(1327)	AH1327//3	4.00	7.00	15.00	30.00	—
ND(1327)	AH1327//3	4.00	7.00	15.00	30.00	—
ND(1327)	AH1327//4	3.00	6.00	12.00	25.00	—
ND(1327)	AH1327//4	3.00	6.00	12.00	25.00	—
ND(1327)	AH1327//5	3.00	6.00	12.00	25.00	—
ND(1327)	AH1327//5	3.00	6.00	12.00	25.00	—
ND(1327)	AH1327//6	3.00	6.00	12.00	25.00	—
ND(1327)	AH1327//6	3.00	6.00	12.00	25.00	—
ND(1327)	AH1327//x p.y. obliterated	2.00	5.00	10.00	20.00	—
ND(1327)	AH1327//x p.y. obliterated	2.00	5.00	10.00	20.00	—

KM# 4 40 PARA

Nickel **Countermark:** "Hejaz" **Obv:** El Ghazi **Note:** Countermark on Turkey 40 Para, KM#766. Accession date: 1327.

CM Date	Host Date	Good	VG	F	VF	XF
ND(1327)	AH1327//3	6.00	10.00	20.00	40.00	—
ND(1327)	AH1327//3	6.00	10.00	20.00	40.00	—
ND(1327)	AH1327//4	3.00	6.00	12.00	25.00	—
ND(1327)	AH1327//4	3.00	6.00	12.00	25.00	—
ND(1327)	AH1327//5	3.00	6.00	12.00	25.00	—
ND(1327)	AH1327//5	3.00	6.00	12.00	25.00	—
ND(1327)	AH1327//x p.y. obliterated	2.00	5.00	10.00	20.00	—
ND(1327)	AH1327//x p.y. obliterated	2.00	5.00	10.00	20.00	—

KM# 5 40 PARA

Copper-Nickel **Countermark:** "Hejaz" **Note:** Countermark on Turkey 40 Para, KM#779. Accession date: 1327.

CM Date	Host Date	Good	VG	F	VF	XF
ND(1327)	AH1327//8	4.00	6.00	12.00	25.00	—
ND(1327)	AH1327//8	4.00	6.00	12.00	25.00	—
ND(1327)	AH1327//9	20.00	30.00	75.00	150	—
ND(1327)	AH1327//9	20.00	30.00	75.00	150	—
ND(1327)	AH1327//x p.y. obliterated	3.00	6.00	10.00	20.00	—
ND(1327)	AH1327//x p.y. obliterated	3.00	6.00	10.00	20.00	—

KM# 6 40 PARA

Copper-Nickel **Countermark:** "Hejaz" **Note:** Countermark on Turkey 40 Para, KM#828. Accession date: 1336.

CM Date	Host Date	Good	VG	F	VF	XF
ND(1326)	AH1336//4	50.00	75.00	150	250	—
ND(1326)	AH1336//4	50.00	75.00	150	250	—
ND(1326)	AH1336//x	40.00	50.00	100	200	—
ND(1326)	AH1336//x	40.00	50.00	100	200	—

COUNTERMARKED COINAGE

Silver Coins

Silver coins of various sizes were also countermarked al-Hejaz. The most common host coins include the Maria Theresa Thaler of Austria, and 5, 10, and 20 Kurush or Qirsh of Turkey and Egypt. The countermark occurs in various sizes and styles of script. These countermarks may have been applied by local silversmiths to discourage re-exportation of the badly needed hard currency and silver of known fineness.

Some crown-sized examples exist with both the al-Hejaz and Nejd countermarks. The authenticity of the silver countermarked coins has long been discussed, and it is likely that most were privately produced. Other host coins are considered controversial.

KM# 10 5 PIASTRES

Silver **Countermark:** "Hejaz" **Note:** Countermark on Turkey 5 Kurush, KM#750. Accession date: 1327.

CM Date	Host Date	Good	VG	F	VF	XF
(1916-20)	ND(AH1327//1-7)	100	125	200	400	—
(1916-20)	ND(AH1327//1-7)	100	125	200	400	—

KM# 11 5 PIASTRES

Silver **Countermark:** "Hejaz" **Note:** Countermark on Turkey 5 Kurush, KM#771. Accession date: 1327.

CM Date	Host Date	Good	VG	F	VF	XF
(1916-20)	ND(AH1327//7-9)	100	125	200	400	—
(1916-20)	ND(AH1327//7-9)	100	125	200	400	—

KM# 12 5 PIASTRES

Silver **Countermark:** "Hejaz" **Note:** Countermark on Egypt 5 Qirsh, KM#308. Accession date: 1327.

CM Date	Host Date	Good	VG	F	VF	XF
(1916-20)	ND(AH1327// 2H-4H, 6H)	100	125	200	400	—
(1916-20)	ND(AH1327// 2H-4H, 6H)	100	125	200	400	—

KM# 13 10 PIASTRES

Silver **Countermark:** "Hejaz" **Note:** Countermark on Turkey 10 Kurush, KM#751. Accession date: 1327.

CM Date	Host Date	Good	VG	F	VF	XF
(1916-20)	ND(AH1327//1-7)	125	200	300	500	—
(1916-20)	ND(AH1327//1-7)	125	200	300	500	—

KM# 14 10 PIASTRES

Silver **Countermark:** "Hejaz" **Note:** Countermark on Turkey 10 Kurush, KM#772. Accession date: 1327.

CM Date	Host Date	Good	VG	F	VF	XF
(1916-20)	ND(AH1327//7-10)	125	200	300	500	—
(1916-20)	ND(AH1327//7-10)	125	200	300	500	—

KM# 15 10 PIASTRES

Silver **Countermark:** "Hejaz" **Note:** Countermark on Egypt 10 Qirsh, KM#309. Accession date: 1327.

CM Date	Host Date	Good	VG	F	VF	XF
(1916-20)	ND(AH1327// 2H-4H, 6H)	125	200	300	500	—
(1916-20)	ND(AH1327// 2H-4H, 6H)	125	200	300	500	—

KM# 16 20 PIASTRES

Silver **Countermark:** "Hejaz" **Note:** Countermark on Egypt 20 Qirsh, KM#310. Accession date: 1327.

CM Date	Host Date	Good	VG	F	VF	XF
(1916-20)	ND(AH1327// 2H-4H, 6H)	125	200	300	500	—
(1916-20)	ND(AH1327// 2H-4H, 6H)	125	200	300	500	—

KM# 17 20 PIASTRES

Silver **Countermark:** "Hejaz" **Note:** Countermark on Turkey 20 Kurush, KM#780. Accession date: 1327.

CM Date	Host Date	Good	VG	F	VF	XF
(1916-20)	ND(AH1327//8-10)	125	200	300	500	—
(1916-20)	ND(AH1327//8-10)	125	200	300	500	—

KM# 18 20 PIASTRES

Silver **Countermark:** "Hejaz" **Note:** Countermark on Austria Maria Theresa Thaler, KM#T1. Accession date: 1327.

CM Date	Host Date	Good	VG	F	VF	XF
ND(1916-20)	1780	100	150	250	400	—
ND(1916-20)	1780	100	150	250	400	—

REGULAR COINAGE

All the regular coins of Hejaz bear the accessional date AH1334 of Al-Husain Ibn Ali, plus the regnal year. Many of the bronze coins occur with a light silver wash mostly on thicker specimens. A variety of planchet thicknesses exist.

KM# 21 1/8 PIASTRE

Bronze, 12-13 mm. **Note:** Reeded and plain edge varieties exist. Size varies.

Date	Mintage	Good	VG	F	VF	XF
AH1334//5	—	—	125	200	300	600
AH1334//5	—	—	125	200	300	600

KM# 22 1/4 PIASTRE

1.1400 g., Bronze, 16 mm. **Note:** Reeded and plain edge varieties exist.

Date	Mintage	Good	VG	F	VF	XF
AH1334//5	—	—	8.00	15.00	35.00	65.00
AH1334//5	—	—	8.00	15.00	35.00	65.00
AH1334//6/5	—	—	75.00	300	600	1,200
AH1334//6/5	—	—	75.00	300	600	1,200
AH1334//6	—	—	400	750	1,500	2,500
AH1334//6	—	—	400	750	1,500	2,500

KM# 25 1/4 PIASTRE

Bronze, 17 mm. **Edge:** Plain

Date	Mintage	Good	VG	F	VF	XF
AH1334//8	—	—	10.00	20.00	40.00	75.00
AH1334//8	—	—	10.00	20.00	40.00	75.00

KM# 23 1/2 PIASTRE

Bronze, 18-19 mm. **Note:** Reeded and plain edge varieties exist. Size varies.

Date	Mintage	Good	VG	F	VF	XF
AH1334//5	—	—	10.00	20.00	35.00	75.00
AH1334//5	—	—	10.00	20.00	35.00	75.00

KM# 26 1/2 PIASTRE

3.1400 g., Bronze, 19 mm. **Note:** Similar to 1/4 Piastre, KM#25. Most known specimens were overstruck as "Hejaz & Nejd" KM#1.

Date	Mintage	Good	VG	F	VF	XF
AH1334//8 Rare	—	—	—	—	—	—
AH1334//8 Rare	—	—	—	—	—	—

KM# 24 PIASTRE

Bronze, 21-22 mm. **Edge:** Reeded **Note:** Size varies.

Date	Mintage	Good	VG	F	VF	XF
AH1334//5	—	—	10.00	20.00	40.00	75.00
AH1334//5	—	—	10.00	20.00	40.00	75.00
AH1334//6/5	—	—	100	200	400	750
AH1334//6/5	—	—	100	200	400	750

KM# 27 PIASTRE

Bronze, 21 mm. **Edge:** Plain

Date	Mintage	Good	VG	F	VF	XF
AH1334//8	—	—	60.00	125	200	325
AH1334//8	—	—	60.00	125	200	325

KM# 28 5 PIASTRES

6.1000 g., 0.9170 Silver .1798 oz. ASW, 24 mm.

Date	Mintage	Good	VG	F	VF	XF
AH1334//8	—	—	50.00	90.00	175	300
AH1334//8	—	—	50.00	90.00	175	300

KM# 29 10 PIASTRES

12.0500 g., 0.9170 Silver .3552 oz. ASW, 28 mm.

Date	Mintage	Good	VG	F	VF	XF
AH1334//8	—	—	250	400	750	1,200
AH1334//8	—	—	250	400	750	1,200

KM# 30 20 PIASTRES (1 Riyal)

24.1000 g., 0.9170 Silver .7105 oz. ASW, 37 mm.

Date	Mintage	Good	VG	F	VF	XF
AH1334//8	—	—	40.00	75.00	125	200
AH1334//8	—	—	40.00	75.00	125	200
AH1334//9	—	—	125	200	300	500
AH1334//9	—	—	125	200	300	500

KM# 31 DINAR HASHIMI

Gold

Date	Mintage	VG	F	VF	XF	Unc
AH1334-8	—	—	250	400	600	1,000
AH1334-8	—	—	250	400	600	1,000
AH1334-8	—	—	250	400	600	1,000

PATTERNS

Including off metal strikes

KM#	Date	Mintage	Identification	Mkt Val
Pn1	AH1340//1	—	20 Piastres. Bronze. Struck at the Heaton Mint (not to be confused with the modern copies listed in Unusual World Coins; struck in various metals, including bronze, nickel and silver).	—
pnA1	AH1340/1	—	10 Piastres. Bronze. Struck at the Heaton Mint.	—

HUNGARY

The Republic of Hungary, located in central Europe, has an area of 35,929 sq. mi. (93,030 sq. km.) and a population of 10.7 million. Capital: Budapest. The economy is based on agriculture, bauxite and a rapidly expanding industrial sector. Machinery, chemicals, iron and steel, and fruits and vegetables are exported.

The ancient kingdom of Hungary, founded by the Magyars in the 9th century, achieved its greatest extension in the mid-14th century when its dominions touched the Baltic, Black and Mediterranean Seas. After suffering repeated Turkish invasions, Hungary accepted Habsburg rule to escape Turkish occupation, regaining independence in 1867 with the Emperor of Austria as king of a dual Austro-Hungarian monarchy.

After World War I, Hungary lost 2/3 of its territory and 1/2 of its population and underwent a period of drastic political revision. The short-lived republic of 1918 was followed by a chaotic interval of communist rule, 1919, and the restoration of the monarchy in 1920 with Admiral Horthy as regent of the kingdom. Although a German ally in World War II, Hungary was occupied by German troops who imposed a pro-Nazi dictatorship, 1944. Soviet armies drove out the Germans in 1945 and assisted the communist minority in seizing power. A revised constitution published on Aug. 20, 1949, established Hungary as a People's Republic' of the Soviet type. On October 23, 1989, Hungary was proclaimed the Republic of Hungary.

RULER

Austrian

MINT MARKS

A, CA, WI - Vienna (Becs)
B, K, KB - Kremnitz (Kormoczbanya)
BP - Budapest
CH - Pressburg (Pozsony)
CM - Kaschau (Kassa)
(c) - castle - Pressburg
(d) - double trefoil - Pressburg
G, GN, NB - Nagybanya
(g) - GC script monogram - Pressburg
GYF - Karlsburg (Gyulafehervar)
HA - Hall
(L) - ICB monogram - Pressburg
(r) - rampant lion left - Pressburg
S - Schmollnitz (Szomolnok)

LEGEND VARIETIES

X: After 1750, during the reign of Maria Theresa, crossed staves which appear as an "X" were placed after the date denoting her reign over the Austrian Netherlands.

MINT OFFICIALS' INITIALS

Kremnitz Mint

Initials	Date	Name
D, PD	1763-80	Josef Paschal von Damiani
EVM	1748-74	Edler von Munzburg
EVM-D	1763-80	Edler von Munzburg and J.P. von Damiani
K, SK	1774-80	Sigismund A. Klemmer von Klemmersberg
SK-PD	1774-80	Sigismund A. Klemmer von Klemmersberg and J.P. von Damiani

Nagybanya Mint

Initials	Date	Name
B, IB	1765-80	Josef Brunner
FL, L	1765-71	Franz anton Lechner
IB-FL	1765-71	Josef Brunner and Fr. A. Lochner
IB-IV, B-V	1772-80	Josef Brunner and Josef Vischer
ICB	1698-1728	J.C. Block
IV, V	1772-80	Josef Vischer

Pressburg Mint

Initials	Date	Name
B	1717-18	
CSH	1705-90	Christoph Sigmund Hunger
IGS	1712, 1715	Johann George Seidlitz
PW	1709-21	Paul Wodrich
Seidlitz	1705, 1707-10	Johann George Seidlitz

MONETARY SYSTEM

Until 1857

2 Poltura = 3 Krajczar
60 Krajczar = 1 Forint (Gulden)
2 Forint = 1 Convention Thaler

KINGDOM

STANDARD COINAGE

KM# 173 OBULUS

Billon **Ruler:** Leopold I **Obv:** Crowned arms divide K-B **Rev:** Madonna and child divide date **Note:** Varieties exist

Date	Mintage	VG	F	VF	XF	Unc
1701KB	—	8.00	16.00	35.00	75.00	—
1703KB	—	8.00	16.00	35.00	75.00	—
1705KB	—	8.00	16.00	35.00	75.00	—

KM# 243 DUARIUS

Billon **Ruler:** Leopold I **Obv:** Crowned arms divide K-B **Rev:** Madonna and child above value and date

Date	Mintage	VG	F	VF	XF	Unc
1700KB	—	10.00	20.00	40.00	80.00	—
1701KB	—	10.00	20.00	40.00	80.00	—

KM# 254 DUARIUS

Billon **Ruler:** Leopold I **Obv:** Crowned arms **Obv. Legend:** LEOP • D • G • R • ... **Rev:** Child on left, value and date

Date	Mintage	VG	F	VF	XF	Unc
1702KB	—	8.00	16.00	35.00	75.00	—
1703KB	—	8.00	16.00	35.00	75.00	—
1704KB	—	8.00	16.00	35.00	75.00	—
1705KB	—	8.00	16.00	35.00	75.00	—

KM# 278 DUARIUS

Billon **Ruler:** Joseph I **Note:** Posthumous issue.

Date	Mintage	VG	F	VF	XF	Unc
1707	—	8.00	16.00	35.00	75.00	—

KM# 304 DUARIUS

Billon **Ruler:** Karl VI

Date	Mintage	VG	F	VF	XF	Unc
1724	—	8.00	16.00	35.00	75.00	—

KM# 221 DENAR

Silver **Ruler:** Leopold I **Obv:** Crowned arms divid N-B in inner circle **Rev:** Madonna and child in inner circle, date in legend

Date	Mintage	VG	F	VF	XF	Unc
1701NB	—	6.00	15.00	30.00	50.00	—
1702NB	—	6.00	15.00	30.00	50.00	—

KM# 255 DENAR

Silver **Ruler:** Leopold I **Obv:** Without inner circle **Rev:** Without inner circle, date in legend **Note:** Varieties exist.

Date	Mintage	VG	F	VF	XF	Unc
1702	—	3.00	6.00	12.00	25.00	—
1703	—	3.00	6.00	12.00	25.00	—

KM# 312 DENAR

Billon **Ruler:** Karl VI **Obv:** Crowned arms divide K-B **Rev:** Madonna and child, date in legend

Date	Mintage	VG	F	VF	XF	Unc
1733	—	5.00	10.00	20.00	40.00	—
1733KB	—	—	—	—	—	—
1734	—	5.00	10.00	20.00	40.00	—
1734KB	—	—	—	—	—	—
1740	183,000	4.00	8.00	16.00	35.00	—
1740KB	—	—	—	—	—	—
1741KB	94,000	4.00	8.00	30.00	70.00	—
1742	73,000	4.00	8.00	30.00	70.00	—
1743	64,000	4.00	8.00	30.00	70.00	—
1745KB	—	5.00	10.00	40.00	80.00	—

KM# 340 DENAR

Billon **Ruler:** Maria Theresia **Obv:** Crowned arms **Obv. Legend:** M • THER • D • G • I • G • HU(N) • B • R • **Rev:** Madonna and child, date in legend **Rev. Legend:** PATRONA • HUNG

Date	Mintage	VG	F	VF	XF	Unc
1746KB	1,590,000	2.50	5.00	25.00	50.00	—
1747KB	82,000	2.50	5.00	25.00	50.00	—
1750KB	825,000	2.50	5.00	25.00	50.00	—
1751KB	456,000	2.50	5.00	25.00	50.00	—
1752KB	2,851,000	2.50	5.00	25.00	50.00	—

KM# 362.1 DENAR

0.5200 g., 0.1490 Silver 0.0025 oz. ASW **Ruler:** Franz I **Rev:** Rays behind Madonna

Date	Mintage	VG	F	VF	XF	Unc
1753	606,000	2.00	4.00	20.00	45.00	—
1754	601,000	2.00	4.00	20.00	45.00	—
1755	543,000	2.00	4.00	20.00	45.00	—
1756	2,041,999	2.00	4.00	20.00	45.00	—
1757	162,000	2.00	4.00	20.00	45.00	—
1758	197,000	2.00	4.00	20.00	45.00	—
1759	153,000	2.00	4.00	20.00	45.00	—
1760	37,000	2.00	4.00	20.00	45.00	—

KM# 362.2 DENAR

0.5200 g., 0.1490 Silver 0.0025 oz. ASW **Ruler:** Franz I

Date	Mintage	VG	F	VF	XF	Unc
1756	73,000	8.00	16.00	20.00	35.00	—

KM# 375.1 DENAR

Copper **Ruler:** Maria Theresia **Obv:** Crowned arms in ornamental cartouche, open crown **Obv. Legend:** M • THERESIA • D • G • .... **Rev:** Radiant Madonna and child **Rev. Legend:** PATRONA • HUNGARIÆ •

Date	Mintage	VG	F	VF	XF	Unc
1760	1,089,000	5.00	10.00	60.00	120	—
1761	97,000	5.00	10.00	60.00	120	—
1763	6,300	—	—	—	—	—

KM# 375.2 DENAR

Copper **Ruler:** Maria Theresia **Obv:** Closed crown **Obv. Legend:** M • THERESIA • D • G • ... **Rev:** Radiant Madonna and child **Rev. Legend:** PATRONA • HUNGARIAE • **Note:** Variations in thickness of planchets exist.

Date	Mintage	VG	F	VF	XF	Unc
1763	14,179,000	4.00	8.00	20.00	45.00	—
1765	—	4.00	8.00	20.00	45.00	—
1766	63,000	4.00	8.00	20.00	45.00	—

KM# 383 DENAR

Copper **Ruler:** Joseph II **Obv:** Crowned arms **Obv. Legend:** M • THERESIA • D • G • ... **Rev:** Radiant Madonna and child **Rev. Legend:** PATRONA • HUNGARIAE • **Note:** Without mint mark. Also referred to as 1/2 Denar.

Date	Mintage	VG	F	VF	XF	Unc
1767	196,000	3.00	6.00	15.00	40.00	—
1768	450,000	3.00	6.00	15.00	40.00	—
1769	411,000	3.00	6.00	15.00	40.00	—
1770	313,000	3.00	6.00	15.00	40.00	—
1771	509,000	3.00	6.00	15.00	40.00	—

KM# 326 10 DENARE

2.3700 g., 0.5280 Silver 0.0402 oz. ASW **Ruler:** Maria Theresia **Obv:** Bust right **Obv. Legend:** M • THE • D • G • ... **Rev:** Madonna and child

Date	Mintage	VG	F	VF	XF	Unc
1741	9,409	5.00	30.00	60.00	120	—
Note: 1741 dated coin is 1-2mm smaller						
1742	7,435	5.00	30.00	60.00	120	—
1743	6,404	5.00	30.00	60.00	120	—
1744	—	5.00	30.00	60.00	120	—
1745	—	5.00	30.00	60.00	120	—

KM# 232 POLTURA

Copper **Ruler:** Leopold I **Obv:** Monogram divides date **Rev:** Crowned value within branches **Note:** Without mint mark. City issue. Varieties exist.

Date	Mintage	VG	F	VF	XF	Unc
1701	1,196,000	6.00	12.50	26.00	55.00	—
1702	126,000	6.00	12.50	26.00	55.00	—
1703	2,106,000	6.00	12.50	26.00	55.00	—

KM# 245.1 POLTURA

Silver **Ruler:** Leopold I **Obv:** Laureate bust right in inner circle, initials on truncation **Obv. Legend:** LEOPOLD • D • G • ... **Rev:** Madonna and child above value and date

Date	Mintage	VG	F	VF	XF	Unc
1701NB ICB	—	10.00	17.50	30.00	60.00	—
1703NB ICB	—	10.00	17.50	30.00	60.00	—

KM# 252.1 POLTURA

Silver **Ruler:** Leopold I **Obv:** Without inner circle

Date	Mintage	VG	F	VF	XF	Unc
1701 ICB	—	10.00	17.50	30.00	60.00	—
1702 ICB	—	10.00	17.50	30.00	60.00	—
1703 ICB	—	10.00	17.50	30.00	60.00	—

KM# 245.2 POLTURA

Silver **Ruler:** Leopold I **Obv:** Without ICB **Rev:** Madonna and child above value and date

Date	Mintage	VG	F	VF	XF	Unc
1703	—	10.00	17.50	30.00	60.00	—

KM# 252.2 POLTURA

Silver **Ruler:** Joseph I **Obv:** Bust right **Obv. Legend:** IOSEPH • D • G • R • .... **Rev:** Madonna and child divide PH above value and date

Date	Mintage	VG	F	VF	XF	Unc
1706KB	—	—	—	—	—	—
1709KB	3,013,000	—	—	—	—	—
1710KB	—	—	—	—	—	—
1711KB PH	—	7.00	15.00	25.00	50.00	—

KM# 294.2 POLTURA

Silver **Ruler:** Karl VI **Obv:** Laureate bust right **Rev:** Madonna and child above value and date **Note:** Without mint mark.

Date	Mintage	VG	F	VF	XF	Unc
1711 PH	—	6.00	12.00	22.00	45.00	—
1715 PH	—	6.00	12.00	22.00	45.00	—
1716 PH	—	6.00	12.00	22.00	45.00	—
1717 PH	—	6.00	12.00	22.00	45.00	—
1718 PH	—	6.00	12.00	22.00	45.00	—
1719 PH	—	6.00	12.00	22.00	45.00	—
1720 PH	—	6.00	12.00	22.00	45.00	—
1721 PH	—	6.00	12.00	22.00	45.00	—
1722 PH	—	6.00	12.00	22.00	45.00	—
1723 PH	—	6.00	12.00	22.00	45.00	—
1724 PH	—	6.00	12.00	22.00	45.00	—
1726 PH	—	6.00	12.00	22.00	45.00	—
1728 PH	—	6.00	12.00	22.00	45.00	—
1729 PH	—	6.00	12.00	22.00	45.00	—
1730 PH	—	6.00	12.00	22.00	45.00	—
1731 PH	—	6.00	12.00	22.00	45.00	—

KM# 294.1 POLTURA

Silver **Ruler:** Karl VI **Obv:** Laureate bust right in inner circle **Rev:** Madonna and child divide N-B, value and date below

Date	Mintage	VG	F	VF	XF	Unc
1714NB	—	7.00	15.00	25.00	50.00	—
1716NB	—	7.00	15.00	25.00	50.00	—
1725NB	—	7.00	15.00	25.00	50.00	—

KM# 299 POLTURA

Silver **Ruler:** Karl VI **Obv:** Without inner circle **Rev:** Madonna and child divide P-H, value and date and N-B below

Date	Mintage	VG	F	VF	XF	Unc
1716NB	—	7.00	15.00	25.00	50.00	—
1730NB	—	7.00	15.00	25.00	50.00	—
1734NB	—	7.00	15.00	25.00	50.00	—
1735NB	—	7.00	15.00	25.00	50.00	—
1738NB	—	7.00	15.00	25.00	50.00	—
1739NB	—	7.00	15.00	25.00	50.00	—
1740NB	—	7.00	15.00	25.00	50.00	—

KM# 323 POLTURA

Silver **Ruler:** Karl VI **Obv:** Bust right **Rev:** Madonna and child

Date	Mintage	VG	F	VF	XF	Unc
1736	—	—	—	—	—	—

KM# 350 POLTURA

1.4400 g., 0.1950 Silver 0.0090 oz. ASW **Ruler:** Maria Theresia **Obv:** Bust right **Obv. Legend:** M • THERES • D • G • .... **Rev:** Crowned arms above value

Date	Mintage	VG	F	VF	XF	Unc
1747 MS	14,000	10.00	17.50	30.00	60.00	—

KM# 341 POLTURA

1.4400 g., 0.1950 Silver 0.0090 oz. ASW **Ruler:** Maria Theresia **Obv:** Bust right **Obv. Legend:** M • THER • D • G • R • I • ... **Rev:** Crowned arms above value

Date	Mintage	VG	F	VF	XF	Unc
1747 PH	12,000	10.00	17.50	30.00	60.00	—

KM# 346.1 POLTURA

0.9700 g., 0.2420 Silver 0.0075 oz. ASW **Ruler:** Maria Theresia **Obv:** Bust right **Obv. Legend:** M • THER • D • G • R • I • ... **Rev:** Madonna and child divide date, value below **Note:** Varieties exist.

Date	Mintage	VG	F	VF	XF	Unc
1748 PH	67,000	7.50	12.50	17.50	30.00	—
1750 PH	444,000	7.50	12.50	17.50	30.00	—
1751 PH	438,000	7.50	12.50	17.50	30.00	—
1751	Inc. above	—	—	—	—	—
1752 PH	610,000	7.50	12.50	17.50	30.00	—
1752	Inc. above	—	—	—	—	—
1754 PH	175,000	4.00	7.50	15.00	30.00	—
1756 PH	975,000	2.50	5.00	10.00	20.00	—
1758 PH	79,000	4.00	7.50	15.00	30.00	—
1759 PH	92,000	4.00	7.50	15.00	30.00	—

KM# 346.2 POLTURA

0.9700 g., 0.2420 Silver 0.0075 oz. ASW **Ruler:** Maria Theresia **Obv:** Bust right **Rev:** Madonna and child above value

Date	Mintage	VG	F	VF	XF	Unc
1752WI PH	184,000	2.50	5.00	10.00	20.00	—

KM# 359 POLTURA

0.9700 g., 0.2420 Silver 0.0075 oz. ASW **Ruler:** Maria Theresia **Rev:** Larger Madonna

Date	Mintage	VG	F	VF	XF	Unc
1752HA PH	997,000	2.50	5.00	10.00	20.00	—
1753HA PH	272,000	2.50	5.00	10.00	20.00	—
1754HA PH	56,000	2.50	5.00	10.00	20.00	—
1755HA PH	—	7.50	12.50	17.50	35.00	—
1756HA PH	—	7.50	12.50	17.50	35.00	—

KM# 377.2 POLTURA

Copper **Ruler:** Maria Theresia **Obv:** Bust right **Rev:** Madonna and child

Date	Mintage	VG	F	VF	XF	Unc
1763 PH-KM Rosette below bust	—	15.00	25.00	45.00	75.00	—
1763 PH-KM Without rosette	—	15.00	25.00	45.00	75.00	—

KM# 377.3 POLTURA

Copper **Ruler:** Maria Theresia **Obv:** Bust right **Rev:** Madonna and child

Date	Mintage	VG	F	VF	XF	Unc
1763S PH-KM	—	6.00	12.50	17.50	30.00	—

KM# 377.1 POLTURA

Copper **Ruler:** Maria Theresia **Obv:** Bust right **Obv. Legend:** M • THERES • D • G • R • .... **Rev:** Madonna and child **Note:** Varieties in legend position exist.

Date	Mintage	VG	F	VF	XF	Unc
1763KB PH-KM	1,668,000	3.00	7.50	15.00	30.00	—
1764KB PH-KM	4,772,000	3.00	7.50	15.00	30.00	—
1765KB PH-KM	3,967,000	3.00	7.50	15.00	30.00	—
1766KB PH-KM	2,091,000	3.00	7.50	15.00	30.00	—

KM# 391 POLTURA

Copper **Ruler:** Maria Theresia **Obv:** Veiled bust right **Obv. Legend:** M • THERESIA • D • G • R • .... **Rev:** Madonna and child **Rev. Legend:** PATRONA • REGNI • HUNGARIÆ •

Date	Mintage	VG	F	VF	XF	Unc
1775	—	10.00	20.00	50.00	120	—

KM# 256 3 POLTUREN

Copper **Ruler:** Leopold I **Obv:** Crowned L in branches **Rev:** SC monogram divides date **Note:** Schemnitz issue.

Date	Mintage	VG	F	VF	XF	Unc
1701	—	20.00	40.00	80.00	150	—
1702	—	20.00	40.00	80.00	150	—

KM# 271 10 POLTUREN

Copper **Rev:** Inscription: PRO/NECESSITATE above value in cartouche

Date	Mintage	VG	F	VF	XF	Unc
1705	Inc. above	45.00	90.00	175	350	—

KM# 269 10 POLTUREN

Copper **Ruler:** Leopold I **Note:** Leopoldstadt issue. Similar to KM#270.

Date	Mintage	VG	F	VF	XF	Unc
1705	6,956,000	35.00	75.00	150	300	—

KM# 270 10 POLTUREN

Copper **Ruler:** Leopold I **Note:** Reduced size.

Date	Mintage	VG	F	VF	XF	Unc
1705	Inc. above	30.00	70.00	140	280	—

KM# 253 KRAJCZAR

Silver **Ruler:** Leopold I **Obv:** Without inner circle **Rev:** Without inner circle, Madonna and child without rays **Note:** Varieties exist.

Date	Mintage	VG	F	VF	XF	Unc
1701NB	—	3.50	7.50	15.00	30.00	—
1703NB	—	3.50	7.50	15.00	30.00	—

KM# 258 KRAJCZAR

Silver **Ruler:** Leopold I **Rev:** Radiant Madonna, date in legend **Note:** Varieties exist.

Date	Mintage	VG	F	VF	XF	Unc
1703	—	3.50	7.50	15.00	30.00	—

KM# 293 KRAJCZAR

Silver **Ruler:** Karl VI **Obv:** Laureate bust right, value below **Rev:** Radiant Madonna and child divide N-B in inner circle, date divided at top **Note:** Varieties exist.

Date	Mintage	VG	F	VF	XF	Unc
1713	—	3.50	7.50	15.00	35.00	—
1714	—	3.50	7.50	15.00	35.00	—
1716	—	3.50	7.50	15.00	35.00	—
1717	—	3.50	7.50	15.00	35.00	—
1718	—	3.50	7.50	15.00	35.00	—
1721	—	3.50	7.50	15.00	35.00	—
1723	—	3.50	7.50	15.00	35.00	—
1724	—	3.50	7.50	15.00	35.00	—

KM# 363.3 KRAJCZAR

0.8000 g., 0.1950 Silver 0.0050 oz. ASW **Ruler:** Karl VI **Obv:** Bust right **Rev:** Radiant Madonna and child **Note:** Without mint mark.

Date	Mintage	VG	F	VF	XF	Unc
1721	—	3.50	7.50	15.00	35.00	—
1724	—	3.50	7.50	15.00	35.00	—

KM# 363.1 KRAJCZAR

0.8000 g., 0.1950 Silver 0.0050 oz. ASW **Ruler:** Maria Theresia **Obv:** Bust right **Obv. Legend:** M • THER • D • G • R ... **Rev:** Radiant Madonna and child **Rev. Legend:** PATRONA • HUNG • 1758

Date	Mintage	VG	F	VF	XF	Unc
1753KB	—	2.50	5.00	20.00	40.00	—
1756KB	1,084,000	2.50	5.00	20.00	40.00	—
1757KB	63,000	2.50	5.00	20.00	40.00	—
1758KB	455,000	2.50	5.00	20.00	40.00	—
1759KB	266,000	2.50	5.00	20.00	40.00	—
1760KB	212,000	2.50	5.00	20.00	40.00	—
1760HB Error	—	3.50	6.00	30.00	50.00	—

KM# 363.2 KRAJCZAR

0.8000 g., 0.1950 Silver 0.0050 oz. ASW **Ruler:** Maria Theresia **Obv:** Bust right **Rev:** Madonna and child

Date	Mintage	VG	F	VF	XF	Unc
1758NB	57,000	2.50	5.00	30.00	50.00	—

KM# 200 3 KRAJCZAR (Groschen)

Silver **Ruler:** Leopold I **Obv:** Bust right in inner circle **Obv. Legend:** LEOPOLDVS • D • G • .... **Rev:** Radiant Madonna and child divide N-B in inner circle, date in legend **Note:** Varieties exist.

Date	Mintage	VG	F	VF	XF	Unc
1703NB	—	7.00	15.00	30.00	60.00	—

KM# 225 3 KRAJCZAR (Groschen)

Silver **Ruler:** Leopold I **Obv:** Bust right in inner circle **Obv. Legend:** LEOPOLD • D • G • R • .... **Rev:** Date divided at top **Note:** Varieties exist.

Date	Mintage	VG	F	VF	XF	Unc
1703NB	—	7.00	15.00	30.00	60.00	—

KM# 236 3 KRAJCZAR (Groschen)

Silver **Ruler:** Leopold I **Obv:** Bust right within inner circle **Obv. Legend:** LEOPOLD • D • G • .... **Rev:** Radiant Madonna and child divides C-M in inner circle, date in legend **Note:** Varieties exist.

Date	Mintage	VG	F	VF	XF	Unc
1704CM	—	7.00	15.00	30.00	60.00	—

KM# 272 3 KRAJCZAR (Groschen)

Silver **Ruler:** Joseph I **Obv:** Bust right within inner circle **Obv. Legend:** IOSEPHVS: D: G • R • .... **Rev:** Madonna and child **Note:** Varieties exist.

Date	Mintage	VG	F	VF	XF	Unc
1705CH	—	5.00	10.00	20.00	40.00	—
1706CH	—	5.00	10.00	20.00	40.00	—
1707CH	—	5.00	10.00	20.00	40.00	—
1708CH	—	5.00	10.00	20.00	40.00	—
1709CH	—	5.00	10.00	20.00	40.00	—
1709CH PW	—	5.00	10.00	20.00	40.00	—
1710CH PW	—	5.00	10.00	20.00	40.00	—
1711CH PW	—	5.00	10.00	20.00	40.00	—

KM# 282.1 3 KRAJCZAR (Groschen)

Silver **Ruler:** Joseph I **Obv:** Laureate bust right in inner circle, value below **Rev:** Radiant Madonna and child divide K-B in inner circle

Date	Mintage	VG	F	VF	XF	Unc
1709KB	—	5.00	10.00	20.00	40.00	—
1711KB	—	5.00	10.00	20.00	40.00	—

KM# 282.2 3 KRAJCZAR (Groschen)

Silver **Ruler:** Joseph I **Obv:** Laureate bust right **Rev:** Madonna and child **Note:** Without mint mark.

Date	Mintage	VG	F	VF	XF	Unc
1710	—	5.00	10.00	20.00	40.00	—

KM# 286 3 KRAJCZAR (Groschen)

Silver **Ruler:** Karl VI **Obv:** Laureate bust right, value below **Rev:** Radiant Madonna and child in inner circle, date divided at top **Note:** Varieties exist.

Date	Mintage	VG	F	VF	XF	Unc
1712CH	—	6.00	12.00	25.00	50.00	—
1713CH	—	6.00	12.00	25.00	50.00	—
1715CH	—	6.00	12.00	25.00	50.00	—
1716CH	—	6.00	12.00	25.00	50.00	—
1717CH	—	6.00	12.00	25.00	50.00	—
1718CH	—	6.00	12.00	25.00	50.00	—
1720CH	—	6.00	12.00	25.00	50.00	—
1721CH	—	6.00	12.00	25.00	50.00	—

KM# 295 3 KRAJCZAR (Groschen)

Silver **Ruler:** Karl VI **Obv:** Laureate bust right in inner circle, value below **Rev:** Radiant Madonna and child divides N-B in inner circle, date divided at top

Date	Mintage	VG	F	VF	XF	Unc
1714NB	—	12.50	22.50	45.00	90.00	—

KM# 298 3 KRAJCZAR (Groschen)

Silver **Ruler:** Karl VI **Obv:** Without inner circle **Rev:** Without inner circle

Date	Mintage	VG	F	VF	XF	Unc
1715	—	12.50	22.50	45.00	90.00	—

KM# 342.1 3 KRAJCZAR (Groschen)
1.6800 g., 0.3590 Silver 0.0194 oz. ASW **Ruler:** Maria Theresia **Obv:** Bust right **Obv. Legend:** M • THER • D • G • R • I • ... **Rev:** Radiant Madonna and child **Rev. Legend:** PATRONA • HUNGARIAE •

Date	Mintage	VG	F	VF	XF	Unc
1747	6,668	7.50	15.00	35.00	65.00	—
1748	—	7.50	15.00	35.00	65.00	—
1751	26,000	10.00	20.00	35.00	75.00	—
1752	13,000	10.00	20.00	35.00	75.00	—
1753	30,000	10.00	20.00	35.00	75.00	—
1754	13,000	10.00	20.00	35.00	75.00	—
1755	35,000	10.00	20.00	35.00	75.00	—
1756	32,000	10.00	20.00	35.00	75.00	—

KM# 342.2 3 KRAJCZAR (Groschen)
1.6800 g., 0.3590 Silver 0.0194 oz. ASW **Ruler:** Maria Theresia **Obv:** Cross after date **Rev:** Radiant Madonna and child

Date	Mintage	VG	F	VF	XF	Unc
1749NB	19,000	15.00	25.00	50.00	100	—
1750NB	13,000	—	—	—	—	—
1752NB	18,000	15.00	25.00	50.00	100	—
1753NB	12,000	—	—	—	—	—

KM# 367.1 3 KRAJCZAR (Groschen)
1.6800 g., 0.3590 Silver 0.0194 oz. ASW **Ruler:** Maria Theresia **Obv:** Simple drapes **Obv. Legend:** M • THER • D • G • R • I • ... **Rev:** Radiant Madonna and child, value below **Rev. Legend:** PATRONA • REGNI • HUNGARIÆ •

Date	Mintage	VG	F	VF	XF	Unc
1757KB	30,000	6.00	12.00	25.00	50.00	—
1758KB	92,000	5.00	10.00	20.00	45.00	—
1759KB	94,000	5.00	10.00	20.00	45.00	—
1760KB	121,000	5.00	10.00	20.00	45.00	—
1761KB	107,000	5.00	10.00	20.00	45.00	—
1762KB	57,000	5.00	10.00	20.00	45.00	—
1764KB	118,000	5.00	10.00	20.00	45.00	—
1765KB	92,000	5.00	10.00	20.00	45.00	—

KM# 367.2 3 KRAJCZAR (Groschen)
1.6800 g., 0.3590 Silver 0.0194 oz. ASW **Ruler:** Maria Theresia **Obv:** Bust right **Rev:** Radiant Madonna and child

Date	Mintage	VG	F	VF	XF	Unc
1757NB	15,000	—	—	—	—	—
1758NB	17,000	—	—	—	—	—
1759NB	14,000	—	—	—	—	—
1760NB	22,000	—	—	—	—	—
1764NB	100,000	12.50	22.50	45.00	120	—
1765NB	39,000	—	—	—	—	—

KM# 380 3 KRAJCZAR (Groschen)
1.7000 g., 0.3440 Silver 0.0188 oz. ASW **Ruler:** Maria Theresia **Obv:** Similar to KM#393, legend ends... B.C.T. **Rev:** Madonna and child

Date	Mintage	VG	F	VF	XF	Unc
1766B EVM-D	74,000	6.00	8.00	30.00	60.00	—
1767B EVM-D	61,000	6.00	8.00	30.00	60.00	—
1768B EVM-D	45,000	6.00	8.00	30.00	60.00	—
1769B EVM-D	—	6.00	8.00	30.00	60.00	—
1770B EVM-D	—	6.00	8.00	30.00	60.00	—
1771B EVM-D	—	6.00	8.00	30.00	60.00	—
1773B EVM-D	—	6.00	8.00	30.00	60.00	—

KM# 392 3 KRAJCZAR (Groschen)
1.7000 g., 0.3440 Silver 0.0188 oz. ASW **Ruler:** Maria Theresia **Obv:** Pleats in veil **Obv. Legend:** M • THERES • D • G • ... **Rev:** Radiant Madonna and child **Rev. Legend:** PATRONA • REGNI • HUNGARIÆ •

Date	Mintage	VG	F	VF	XF	Unc
1778	—	4.00	8.00	16.00	35.00	—
1779	—	3.00	6.00	12.50	30.00	—
1779	—	3.00	6.00	12.50	30.00	—

KM# 393 3 KRAJCZAR (Groschen)
1.7000 g., 0.3440 Silver 0.0188 oz. ASW **Ruler:** Maria Theresia **Obv:** Without pleats in veil **Obv. Legend:** M • THERES • D • G • ... **Rev:** Radiant Madonna and child **Rev. Legend:** PATRONA • REGNI • HUNGARIÆ •

Date	Mintage	VG	F	VF	XF	Unc
1779NB IB-IV	—	6.00	10.00	20.00	40.00	—
1779NB B-V	—	6.00	10.00	20.00	40.00	—

KM# 190 6 KRAJCZAR
Silver **Ruler:** Leopold I **Obv:** Bust right in inner circle **Obv. Legend:** LEOPOLDVS • D • G • R • ... **Rev:** Radiant Madonna and child divide N-B in inner circle **Rev. Legend:** PATRONA • HUNGARIÆ • **Note:** Varieties exist.

Date	Mintage	VG	F	VF	XF	Unc
1701NB	—	8.00	18.00	35.00	70.00	—

KM# 302.2 6 KRAJCZAR
Silver **Ruler:** Leopold I **Note:** Without mint mark.

Date	Mintage	VG	F	VF	XF	Unc
1701	—	7.50	15.00	30.00	60.00	—

KM# 302.1 6 KRAJCZAR
Silver **Ruler:** Karl VI **Obv:** Laureate bust right in inner circle, value below **Rev:** Radiant Madonna and child divide K-B in inner circle, date in legend

Date	Mintage	VG	F	VF	XF	Unc
1718KB Rare	—	—	—	—	—	—

KM# 343 6 KRAJCZAR
3.2900 g., 0.4380 Silver 0.0463 oz. ASW **Ruler:** Maria Theresia **Obv:** Bust right **Rev:** Madonna and child, value below

Date	Mintage	VG	F	VF	XF	Unc
1747	8,146	50.00	100	200	400	—

KM# 355 7 KRAJCZAR
3.2500 g., 0.4200 Silver 0.0439 oz. ASW **Ruler:** Maria Theresia **Obv:** Bust right **Obv. Legend:** M • THER • D • G • R • IMP • ... **Rev:** Radiant Madonna and child **Rev. Legend:** PATRONA • REGNI • HUNGARIÆ •

Date	Mintage	VG	F	VF	XF	Unc
1751KB	26,000	15.00	22.50	45.00	90.00	—
1752KB	14,000	10.00	20.00	40.00	80.00	—
1754KB	22,000	7.50	15.00	30.00	60.00	—
1755KB	27,000	6.00	12.50	25.00	50.00	—
1757KB	38,000	6.00	12.50	25.00	50.00	—
1758KB	55,000	6.00	12.50	25.00	50.00	—
1759KB	—	6.00	12.50	25.00	50.00	—
1760KB	186,000	15.00	22.50	45.00	90.00	—
1763KB	523,000	5.00	10.00	20.00	40.00	—
1764KB	958,000	4.00	8.00	16.00	32.00	—
1765KB	1,629,000	4.00	8.00	16.00	32.00	—

KM# 369 7 KRAJCZAR
3.2500 g., 0.4200 Silver 0.0439 oz. ASW **Obv:** Bust with armor over shoulder

Date	Mintage	VG	F	VF	XF	Unc
1759	—	65.00	125	250	450	—

KM# 365 10 KRAJCZAR
3.9000 g., 0.5000 Silver 0.0627 oz. ASW **Ruler:** Maria Theresia **Obv:** Bust right within palm and laurel wreath **Obv. Legend:** M • THERESIA • D • G • R • - IMP • ... **Rev:** Radiant Madonna and child atop pedestal with value **Rev. Legend:** PATRONA • REGNI • - HUNGARIÆ • date

Date	Mintage	VG	F	VF	XF	Unc
1755	23,000	5.00	10.00	20.00	40.00	—
1758	30,000	5.00	10.00	20.00	40.00	—
1759	17,000	5.00	10.00	20.00	40.00	—
1760/59	26,000	7.50	15.00	30.00	50.00	—
1760	Inc. above	5.00	10.00	20.00	40.00	—
1764	477,000	3.50	7.50	15.00	30.00	—
1765	14,000	3.50	7.50	15.00	30.00	—
1766	581,000	3.50	7.50	15.00	30.00	—
1767	247,000	3.50	7.50	15.00	30.00	—

KM# 387 10 KRAJCZAR
3.9000 g., 0.5000 Silver 0.0627 oz. ASW **Ruler:** Maria Theresia **Obv:** Veiled head right **Rev:** Madonna and child above value

Date	Mintage	VG	F	VF	XF	Unc
1768B	—	—	—	—	—	—
1769B EVM-D	142,000	85.00	150	275	500	—

KM# 330.1 15 KRAJCZAR
6.4000 g., 0.5630 Silver 0.1158 oz. ASW **Ruler:** Maria Theresia **Obv:** Bust right **Rev:** Radiant Madonna and child

Date	Mintage	VG	F	VF	XF	Unc
1742KB	179,000	3.50	7.00	14.00	25.00	—

KM# 330.2 15 KRAJCZAR
6.4000 g., 0.5630 Silver 0.1158 oz. ASW **Ruler:** Maria Theresia **Obv:** Bust right **Obv. Legend:** M • THERES • D • G • - REG: HU: BO: A: A: **Rev:** Half length Madonna **Rev. Legend:** PATRONA • REG • - HUNGA :

Date	Mintage	VG	F	VF	XF	Unc
1743	—	3.50	7.00	14.00	25.00	—
1744	—	3.50	7.00	14.00	25.00	—

KM# 332 15 KRAJCZAR
6.4000 g., 0.5630 Silver 0.1158 oz. ASW **Ruler:** Maria Theresia **Obv:** Bust with earring **Rev:** Half-length Madonna

Date	Mintage	VG	F	VF	XF	Unc
1743NB	—	4.00	8.00	16.00	35.00	—
1744NB	—	4.00	8.00	16.00	35.00	—

KM# 335 15 KRAJCZAR
6.4000 g., 0.5630 Silver 0.1158 oz. ASW **Ruler:** Maria Theresia **Obv:** Bust right without earring **Obv. Legend:** M: THERES: D: G: REG: .... **Rev:** Half-length Madonna **Rev. Legend:** PATRONA • REG • - HUNGA:

Date	Mintage	VG	F	VF	XF	Unc
1744KB	—	5.00	10.00	14.00	25.00	—
1745KB	—	5.00	10.00	14.00	25.00	—

KM# 338 15 KRAJCZAR
6.4000 g., 0.5630 Silver 0.1158 oz. ASW **Ruler:** Maria Theresia **Obv:** Bust with earring **Rev:** Full-length Madonna with rays behind

Date	Mintage	VG	F	VF	XF	Unc
1745NB	—	6.00	12.00	25.00	50.00	—

KM# 339.1 15 KRAJCZAR
6.4000 g., 0.5630 Silver 0.1158 oz. ASW **Ruler:** Maria Theresia **Obv:** Legend ends BCT **Rev:** Full-length Madonna

Date	Mintage	VG	F	VF	XF	Unc
1746KB	—	5.00	10.00	20.00	45.00	—

KM# 339.2 15 KRAJCZAR
6.4000 g., 0.5630 Silver 0.1158 oz. ASW **Ruler:** Maria Theresia

Date	Mintage	VG	F	VF	XF	Unc
1746NB	—	7.50	15.00	25.00	55.00	—

KM# 344 15 KRAJCZAR
6.4000 g., 0.5630 Silver 0.1158 oz. ASW **Ruler:** Maria Theresia **Rev:** Half-length Madonna, rays behind

Date	Mintage	VG	F	VF	XF	Unc
1747KB	—	6.00	12.00	16.00	30.00	—
1748KB	—	6.00	12.00	16.00	30.00	—
1749KB	—	6.00	12.00	16.00	30.00	—
1750KB	—	6.00	12.00	16.00	30.00	—

KM# 345 15 KRAJCZAR

6.4000 g., 0.5630 Silver 0.1158 oz. ASW **Ruler:** Maria Theresia **Obv:** Bust right **Obv. Legend:** M • THER • D • G • R • I • ... **Rev:** Radiant Madonna and child **Rev. Legend:** PATRONA REGNI HUNGARIÆ

Date	Mintage	VG	F	VF	XF	Unc
1747	—	5.00	10.00	20.00	45.00	—
1748	—	5.00	10.00	20.00	45.00	—
1749	—	5.00	10.00	20.00	45.00	—
1750	—	5.00	10.00	20.00	45.00	—

KM# 356.2 17 KRAJCZAR

6.1200 g., 0.5420 Silver 0.1066 oz. ASW **Ruler:** Maria Theresia **Obv:** Bust right **Rev:** Radiant Madonna and child

Date	Mintage	VG	F	VF	XF	Unc
1751NB	49,000	10.00	20.00	40.00	80.00	—
1752NB	127,000	10.00	20.00	40.00	80.00	—
1753NB	251,000	10.00	20.00	40.00	80.00	—
1754NB	284,000	10.00	16.00	35.00	75.00	—
1755NB	204,000	10.00	16.00	35.00	75.00	—
1761NB	47,000	—	—	—	—	—
1762NB	431,000	10.00	25.00	50.00	100	—
1763NB	587,000	10.00	25.00	50.00	100	—
1764NB	632,000	10.00	15.00	30.00	65.00	—
1765NB	538,000	10.00	16.00	35.00	75.00	—
1766NB	460,000	—	—	—	—	—

KM# 356.1 17 KRAJCZAR

6.1200 g., 0.5420 Silver 0.1066 oz. ASW **Ruler:** Maria Theresia **Obv:** Crowned bust right **Obv. Legend:** M • THER • D: G: R • I • .... **Rev:** Radiant Madonna and child **Rev. Legend:** PATRONA REGNI - HUNGARIÆ • **Note:** Varieties in dress embroidery exist.

Date	Mintage	VG	F	VF	XF	Unc
1751KB	1,833,000	7.50	15.00	25.00	50.00	—
1752KB	1,759,000	7.50	15.00	25.00	50.00	—
1753KB	1,486,000	7.50	15.00	25.00	50.00	—
1754KB	1,849,000	7.50	15.00	25.00	50.00	—
1755KB	1,307,000	7.50	15.00	25.00	50.00	—
1756KB	1,117,000	7.50	15.00	25.00	50.00	—
1757KB	944,000	7.50	15.00	25.00	50.00	—
1758KB	1,074,000	7.50	15.00	25.00	50.00	—
1759KB	946,000	7.50	15.00	25.00	50.00	—
1760KB	1,071,000	7.50	15.00	25.00	50.00	—
1761KB	1,765,000	7.50	15.00	25.00	50.00	—
1762KB	4,092,000	7.50	15.00	25.00	50.00	—
1763KB	542,000	7.50	15.00	25.00	50.00	—
1764KB	1,178,000	7.50	15.00	25.00	50.00	—
1765KB	1,795,000	7.50	15.00	25.00	50.00	—

KM# 366.1 20 KRAJCZAR

6.6800 g., 0.5830 Silver 0.1252 oz. ASW **Ruler:** Maria Theresia **Obv:** Bust right within palm and laurel wreath **Rev:** Radiant Madonna and child atop pedestal with value **Note:** Similar to KM#365.

Date	Mintage	VG	F	VF	XF	Unc
1755KB	32,000	3.00	6.00	12.50	30.00	—
1758KB	13,000	5.00	7.50	15.00	35.00	—
1759KB	91,000	3.00	6.00	12.50	30.00	—
1760KB	36,000	5.00	7.50	15.00	35.00	—
1761KB	71,000	3.00	6.00	12.50	30.00	—
1763KB	3,534,000	3.00	6.00	12.50	30.00	—
1764KB	2,211,000	3.00	6.00	12.50	30.00	—
1765KB	—	3.00	6.00	12.50	30.00	—

KM# 366.2 20 KRAJCZAR

6.6800 g., 0.5830 Silver 0.1252 oz. ASW **Ruler:** Maria Theresia **Obv:** Bust right within palm and laurel wreath **Rev:** Radiant Madonna and child atop pedestal

Date	Mintage	VG	F	VF	XF	Unc
1757NB	230,000	5.00	10.00	20.00	40.00	—
1758NB	227,000	3.50	7.50	15.00	35.00	—
1759NB	257,000	3.50	7.50	15.00	35.00	—
1760NB	225,000	3.50	7.50	15.00	35.00	—
1761NB	229,000	3.50	7.50	15.00	35.00	—
1763NB	—	5.00	10.00	20.00	40.00	—
1765NB	—	3.50	7.50	15.00	35.00	—

KM# 381.1 20 KRAJCZAR

6.6800 g., 0.5830 Silver 0.1252 oz. ASW **Ruler:** Maria Theresia **Obv:** Veiled bust right within wreath of branches **Rev:** Radiant Madonna and child **Note:** Similar to KM#390.

Date	Mintage	VG	F	VF	XF	Unc
1766B EVM-D	1,471,000	2.50	5.50	11.50	22.00	—
1767B EVM-D	2,132,000	3.50	7.00	12.50	25.00	—
1768B EVM-D	1,488,000	2.50	5.50	11.50	22.00	—
1769B EVM-D	—	2.50	5.50	11.50	22.00	—
1770B EVM-D	—	2.50	5.50	11.50	22.00	—
1771B EVM-D	—	2.50	5.50	11.50	22.00	—
1772B EVM-D	—	2.50	5.50	11.50	22.00	—
1773B EVM-D	—	2.50	5.50	11.50	22.00	—
1774B EVM-D	—	2.50	5.50	11.50	22.00	—

KM# 381.2 20 KRAJCZAR

6.6800 g., 0.5830 Silver 0.1252 oz. ASW **Ruler:** Maria Theresia **Obv:** Bust right within palm and laurel wreath **Obv. Legend:** M • THERESIA • D • G • R • IMP • .... **Rev:** Radiant Madonna and child **Rev. Legend:** PATRONA REGNI - HUNGARIÆ • **Note:** Without mint mark.

Date	Mintage	VG	F	VF	XF	Unc
1766 IB-FL	—	5.00	10.00	20.00	40.00	—
1767 IB-FL	323,000	5.00	10.00	20.00	40.00	—
1768 IB-FL	355,000	3.50	7.00	14.00	28.00	—
1769 IB-FL	—	3.50	7.00	14.00	28.00	—
1770 IB-FL	—	3.00	6.00	12.00	25.00	—
1771 IB-FL	—	3.50	7.00	14.00	28.00	—
1771 IB-IV//N-B	—	7.00	14.00	28.00	55.00	—
1771 IB-FL//N-B N-B on reverse	—	7.00	14.00	28.00	55.00	—
1773 IB-IV	—	3.50	7.00	14.00	28.00	—
1774 IB-IV	—	3.50	7.00	14.00	28.00	—
1775 IB-IV	—	3.50	7.00	14.00	28.00	—
1776 IB-IV	—	3.50	7.00	14.00	28.00	—
1777 IB-IV	—	3.50	7.00	14.00	28.00	—
1778 IB-IV	—	3.00	6.00	12.00	25.00	—
1779 IB-IV	—	3.00	6.00	12.00	25.00	—
1779 B-V	—	4.00	8.00	16.00	35.00	—
1780 IB-IV	—	3.00	6.00	12.00	25.00	—

KM# 381.3 20 KRAJCZAR

6.6800 g., 0.5830 Silver 0.1252 oz. ASW **Ruler:** Maria Theresia **Obv:** Bust right within wreath **Rev:** Radiant Madonna and child

Date	Mintage	VG	F	VF	XF	Unc
1768NB	—	5.00	10.00	20.00	40.00	—
1769NB IB-IV	—	5.00	10.00	20.00	40.00	—
1775NB IB-IV	—	5.00	10.00	20.00	40.00	—
1776NB IB-IV	—	5.00	10.00	20.00	40.00	—
1777NB IB-IV	—	5.00	10.00	20.00	40.00	—

KM# 381.4 20 KRAJCZAR

6.6800 g., 0.5830 Silver 0.1252 oz. ASW **Ruler:** Maria Theresia **Obv:** Bust right within wreath **Rev:** Radiant Madonna and child

Date	Mintage	VG	F	VF	XF	Unc
1773G IB-IV	—	3.50	7.00	14.00	28.00	—
1773G IB-IV//N-B	—	7.00	14.00	28.00	55.00	—

KM# 390 20 KRAJCZAR

6.6800 g., 0.5830 Silver 0.1252 oz. ASW **Ruler:** Maria Theresia **Obv:** Veil hangs straight without folds **Obv. Legend:** M • THERESIA • D • G • R • IMP • ... **Rev:** Radiant Madonna and child **Rev. Legend:** PATRONA • REGNI • - HUNGARIÆ •

Date	Mintage	VG	F	VF	XF	Unc
1774 SK-PD	—	3.00	6.00	12.00	25.00	—
1775 SK-PD	—	3.00	6.00	12.00	25.00	—
1776 SK-PD	—	3.00	6.00	12.00	25.00	—
1777 SK-PD	—	3.00	6.00	12.00	25.00	—
1778 SK-PD	—	3.00	6.00	12.00	25.00	—
1779 SK-PD	—	3.00	6.00	12.00	25.00	—
1780 SK-PD	—	3.00	6.00	12.00	25.00	—

KM# 319 30 KRAJCZAR

2.6600 g., 0.5000 Silver 0.0428 oz. ASW **Ruler:** Karl VI **Obv:** Bust right **Obv. Legend:** CAROL • VI • D • G • R • I... **Rev:** Radiant Madonna and child **Rev. Legend:** PATRONA • REGNI - HUNGARIÆ • **Note:** Charles VI

Date	Mintage	VG	F	VF	XF	Unc
1739KB	—	25.00	45.00	90.00	200	—
1740KB	—	25.00	45.00	90.00	200	—

KM# 331 30 KRAJCZAR

7.2000 g., 0.8750 Silver 0.2025 oz. ASW **Ruler:** Maria Theresia **Obv:** Young bust right **Obv. Legend:** MA: THERESIA - D: G: REG: HU: BO **Rev:** Standing Madonna and child, value below **Rev. Legend:** PATRONA REGNA - HUNGARIÆ

Date	Mintage	VG	F	VF	XF	Unc
1742	—	75.00	125	225	475	—

KM# 347 30 KRAJCZAR

7.0300 g., 0.8330 Silver 0.1883 oz. ASW **Ruler:** Maria Theresia **Obv:** Bust right, value in diamond **Obv. Legend:** MARIA THERESA... **Rev:** Madonna and child in diamond

Date	Mintage	VG	F	VF	XF	Unc
1748NB	31,000	35.00	75.00	150	275	—
1750NB	75,000	40.00	80.00	160	300	—

KM# 357.2 30 KRAJCZAR

7.0300 g., 0.8330 Silver 0.1883 oz. ASW **Ruler:** Maria Theresia **Note:** Legend varieties exist.

Date	Mintage	VG	F	VF	XF	Unc
1750KB	—	—	—	—	—	—
1751KB	—	15.00	32.00	70.00	150	—
1752KB	13,000	15.00	32.00	70.00	150	—
1753KB	10,092	15.00	32.00	70.00	150	—
1754KB	8,025	15.00	32.00	70.00	150	—
1755KB	11,000	15.00	32.00	70.00	150	—
1756KB	13,000	15.00	32.00	70.00	150	—
1757KB	13,000	15.00	32.00	70.00	150	—
1758	7,737	15.00	32.00	70.00	150	—

KM# 357.1 30 KRAJCZAR

7.0300 g., 0.8330 Silver 0.1883 oz. ASW **Ruler:** Maria Theresia **Obv:** Bust right **Rev:** Madonna and child **Note:** Similar to KM347 but cross after date.

Date	Mintage	VG	F	VF	XF	Unc
1751	110,000	10.00	25.00	50.00	125	—
1752	8,518	20.00	45.00	90.00	180	—

KM# 368 30 KRAJCZAR

7.0300 g., 0.8330 Silver 0.1883 oz. ASW **Ruler:** Maria Theresia **Obv:** Smaller bust with short hair

Date	Mintage	VG	F	VF	XF	Unc
1758	Inc. above	17.50	35.00	80.00	160	—
1759	6,857	15.00	32.00	70.00	150	—
1760	4,687	15.00	32.00	70.00	150	—
1761	6,069	15.00	32.00	70.00	150	—
1762	2,339	15.00	32.00	70.00	150	—
1763	54,000	15.00	30.00	60.00	135	—
1764	6,888	15.00	32.00	70.00	150	—
1765	57,000	15.00	30.00	60.00	135	—

KM# 368a 30 KRAJCZAR

7.0200 g., 0.8330 Silver 0.1880 oz. ASW **Ruler:** Maria Theresia

Date	Mintage	VG	F	VF	XF	Unc
1766 EVM-D	3,538	15.00	32.00	70.00	150	—

KM# 384.1 30 KRAJCZAR

7.0200 g., 0.8330 Silver 0.1880 oz. ASW **Ruler:** Maria Theresia **Obv:** Crowned arms with angel supporters within rhombus **Obv. Legend:** M • THER • - D: G • R • IMP • - HU • BO • R • - A • A • D • B • C • T • **Rev:** Radiant Madonna and child within rhombus **Rev. Legend:** S: MARIA • - MATER • DEI • - PATRONA • - HUNG •

Date	Mintage	VG	F	VF	XF	Unc
1768K EVM-D	2,842	15.00	32.00	70.00	165	—
1769K EVM-D	3,521	12.00	25.00	50.00	125	—
1770K EVM-D	—	12.00	25.00	50.00	125	—
1771K EVM-D	—	15.00	32.00	70.00	165	—
1772K EVM-D	—	15.00	32.00	70.00	165	—

KM# 384.2 30 KRAJCZAR

7.0200 g., 0.8330 Silver 0.1880 oz. ASW **Ruler:** Maria Theresia **Obv:** Crowned arms with angel supporters within rhombus **Rev:** Radiant Madonna and child within rhombus

Date	Mintage	VG	F	VF	XF	Unc
1768B EVM-D	—	20.00	40.00	80.00	175	—

KM# 228 1/4 THALER

Silver **Ruler:** Leopold I **Obv:** Laureate bust right flanked by arms and Madonna, value below, all in rhombus **Obv. Legend:** LEOPOLD • - D: G:... **Rev:** Crowned imperial eagle in rhombus, date in legend **Rev. Legend:** ARCHID • - AVST • DVX • ... **Note:** Varieties exist.

Date	Mintage	VG	F	VF	XF	Unc
1701KB	—	12.00	25.00	50.00	100	—
1702KB	—	—	—	—	—	—
1703KB	—	12.00	25.00	50.00	100	—
1704KB	—	12.00	25.00	50.00	100	—

KM# 250 1/4 THALER

Silver **Ruler:** Leopold I **Obv:** Crowned arms and Madonna and child added at sides of bust **Rev:** Crowned imperial eagle divides N-B in rhombus, date divided at top **Note:** Varieties exist.

Date	Mintage	VG	F	VF	XF	Unc
1700NB	—	12.00	25.00	50.00	100	—
1701NB	—	12.00	25.00	50.00	100	—
1702NB	—	12.00	25.00	50.00	100	—

KM# 259 1/4 THALER

Silver **Ruler:** Leopold I **Rev:** Date in legend **Note:** Varieties exist.

Date	Mintage	VG	F	VF	XF	Unc
1703	—	18.00	35.00	70.00	145	—

KM# 296.1 1/4 THALER

Silver **Ruler:** Karl VI **Obv:** Armored bust right divides arms and Madonna within rhombus, value below **Obv. Legend:** CAROL VI • D • G • R • IMP • .... **Rev:** Crowned shield of arms in Order chain on eagle's breast within rhombus **Rev. Legend:** ARCHIDV • AVS • DVX • BV • MA • ...

Date	Mintage	VG	F	VF	XF	Unc
ND	—	12.00	25.00	50.00	100	—
1714	—	12.00	25.00	50.00	100	—
1715	—	12.00	25.00	50.00	100	—
1716	—	10.00	20.00	40.00	80.00	—
1717	—	10.00	20.00	40.00	80.00	—

KM# 296.2 1/4 THALER

Silver **Ruler:** Karl VI **Obv:** Armored bust right divides arms and Madonna within rhombus, value below **Obv. Legend:** CAROL • VI • D • G • RO • IMP • ... **Rev:** Oval arms in Order chain on eagle's breast within rhombus **Rev. Legend:** ARCHID • AVS • DVX • BV • ... **Note:** Varieties exist.

Date	Mintage	VG	F	VF	XF	Unc
1718	—	10.00	20.00	40.00	80.00	—
1719	—	10.00	20.00	40.00	80.00	—
1720	—	10.00	20.00	40.00	80.00	—
1721	—	10.00	20.00	40.00	80.00	—
1722	—	10.00	20.00	40.00	80.00	—
1723	—	10.00	20.00	40.00	80.00	—
1724	—	12.00	25.00	50.00	100	—
1725	—	10.00	20.00	40.00	80.00	—
1726	—	12.00	25.00	50.00	100	—

KM# 305 1/4 THALER

Silver **Ruler:** Karl VI **Obv:** Bust right within rhombus **Obv. Legend:** CAROL • VI • D • G • R • IMP • ... **Rev:** Arms in Order chain on eagle's breast within rhombus **Rev. Legend:** ARCHID: AUS: D: G: M: ... **Note:** Varieties exist.

Date	Mintage	VG	F	VF	XF	Unc
1727	—	10.00	20.00	40.00	80.00	—
1728	—	10.00	20.00	40.00	80.00	—
1729	—	10.00	20.00	40.00	80.00	—
1730	—	10.00	20.00	40.00	80.00	—
1731	—	10.00	20.00	40.00	80.00	—
1732	—	10.00	20.00	40.00	80.00	—
1733	—	10.00	20.00	40.00	80.00	—
1734	—	10.00	20.00	40.00	80.00	—
1735	—	10.00	20.00	40.00	80.00	—
1736	—	10.00	20.00	40.00	80.00	—
1737	—	10.00	20.00	40.00	80.00	—
1738	—	10.00	20.00	40.00	80.00	—
1739	—	10.00	20.00	40.00	80.00	—
1740	—	10.00	20.00	40.00	80.00	—

KM# 251 1/2 THALER

Silver **Ruler:** Leopold I **Obv:** Armored bust right **Obv. Legend:** LEOPOLD: - D: G: R: I: S: A: GER: - HV: BO: REX: **Rev:** Crowned arms within Order chain on eagle's breast **Rev. Legend:** ARCHID: AV: DVX: BV: MAR: MOR:... **Note:** Varieties exist.

Date	Mintage	VG	F	VF	XF	Unc
1701KB	—	30.00	60.00	120	220	—
1702KB	—	30.00	60.00	120	220	—
1703KB	—	30.00	60.00	120	220	—
1704KB	—	30.00	60.00	120	220	—

KM# 260 1/2 THALER

Silver **Ruler:** Leopold I **Obv:** Bust right **Obv. Legend:** LEOPOLD - D • G • R • I • S • A • GER • HV • - BOHEM • REX • **Rev:** Arms within Order chain on eagle's breast **Rev. Legend:** ARCHID • AVST • DVX • BV...

Date	Mintage	VG	F	VF	XF	Unc
1703NB	—	40.00	80.00	150	300	—

KM# 280 1/2 THALER

Silver **Ruler:** Joseph I **Obv:** Armored bust right **Obv. Legend:** IOSEPHUS - D: G: R: I: S: A: G: H: - B: REX: **Rev:** Crowned arms on eagle's breast **Rev. Legend:** ARCHID: AV: DVX: BV: MAR:... **Note:** Joseph I

Date	Mintage	VG	F	VF	XF	Unc
1708KB	—	25.00	55.00	110	180	—
1709KB	—	25.00	55.00	110	180	—

KM# 281 1/2 THALER

Silver **Ruler:** Joseph I **Obv:** Draped bust right **Obv. Legend:** IOSEPHUS • - D: G: R: I: S: A: G: - H: B: REX • **Rev:** Crowned arms on eagle's breast **Rev. Legend:** ARCHID: AV: DVX • BV: MAR:.. **Note:** Varieties exist.

Date	Mintage	VG	F	VF	XF	Unc
1708	—	25.00	55.00	110	180	—
1709	—	25.00	55.00	110	180	—
1710/00	—	25.00	55.00	110	180	—
1710	—	25.00	55.00	110	180	—
1711/00	—	25.00	55.00	110	180	—
1711	—	25.00	55.00	110	180	—

KM# 287 1/2 THALER

Silver **Ruler:** Karl VI **Obv:** Bust right **Obv. Legend:** CAR • VI • G • R • I • S • - A • G • - HI • HU • B • REX **Rev:** Arms within Order chain on eagle's breast **Note:** Varieties exist.

Date	Mintage	VG	F	VF	XF	Unc
1712	—	22.50	50.00	80.00	125	—
1713	—	22.50	50.00	80.00	125	—
1714	—	22.50	50.00	80.00	125	—
1715	—	22.50	50.00	80.00	125	—
1716	—	22.50	50.00	80.00	125	—
1717	—	22.50	50.00	80.00	125	—
1718	—	22.50	50.00	80.00	125	—

KM# 303 1/2 THALER
Silver **Ruler:** Karl VI **Obv:** Armored bust right **Obv. Legend:** CAR • VI • D • G • R • I • S • - A • G... **Rev:** Arms within Order chain on eagle's breast **Rev. Legend:** ARCHID • AV • D • EV... **Note:** Varieties exist.

Date	Mintage	VG	F	VF	XF	Unc
1719	—	22.50	50.00	80.00	125	—
1720	—	22.50	50.00	80.00	125	—
1721	—	22.50	50.00	80.00	125	—
1722	1,204	22.50	50.00	80.00	125	—
1723	—	22.50	50.00	80.00	125	—
1724KB	—	22.50	50.00	80.00	125	—
1724BK Error	—	—	—	—	—	—
1725	—	22.50	50.00	80.00	125	—
1726	—	22.50	50.00	80.00	125	—
1727	—	22.50	50.00	80.00	125	—
1728	—	22.50	50.00	80.00	125	—
1729	—	22.50	50.00	80.00	125	—
1730	—	22.50	50.00	80.00	125	—
1731	—	22.50	50.00	80.00	125	—
1732	—	22.50	50.00	80.00	125	—

KM# 313 1/2 THALER
Silver **Ruler:** Karl VI **Obv:** Legend begins at lower left **Obv. Legend:** CAR • VI • D: G: R: I: .... **Rev:** Arms within Order chain on eagle's breast **Rev. Legend:** ARCHID: AU: D: BU... **Note:** Varieties exist.

Date	Mintage	VG	F	VF	XF	Unc
1733	—	22.50	50.00	80.00	125	—
1734	—	22.50	50.00	80.00	125	—
1735	—	22.50	50.00	80.00	125	—
1736	—	22.50	50.00	80.00	125	—
1737	—	22.50	50.00	80.00	125	—
1738	—	22.50	50.00	80.00	125	—
1739	12,000	22.50	50.00	80.00	125	—
1740	56,000	22.50	50.00	80.00	125	—

KM# 314 1/2 THALER
Silver **Ruler:** Karl VI **Rev:** Seated Madonna and child with crowned arms right, date in legend

Date	Mintage	VG	F	VF	XF	Unc
1735 Rare	—	—	—	—	—	—

KM# 320 1/2 THALER
Silver **Ruler:** Karl VI **Rev:** Crowned imperial eagle, date in legend

Date	Mintage	VG	F	VF	XF	Unc
1739	—	25.00	60.00	120	180	—

KM# 327.1 1/2 THALER
14.4100 g., 0.8750 Silver 0.4054 oz. ASW **Ruler:** Maria Theresia **Obv:** Bust right **Obv. Legend:** MA: THERESIA: - D: G: REG: HUN: BO: **Rev:** Radiant Madonna and child **Rev. Legend:** S: MARIA MATER DEI...

Date	Mintage	VG	F	VF	XF	Unc
1741KB	37,000	22.50	50.00	75.00	110	—
1742KB	43,000	22.50	50.00	75.00	110	—
1743KB	27,000	22.50	50.00	75.00	110	—
1744KB	29,000	22.50	50.00	75.00	110	—

KM# 327.2 1/2 THALER
14.4100 g., 0.8750 Silver 0.4054 oz. ASW **Ruler:** Maria Theresia **Obv:** Legend ends ... HU: BO **Rev:** Radiant Madonna and child

Date	Mintage	VG	F	VF	XF	Unc
1743	Inc. above	50.00	125	175	250	—
1744	Inc. above	50.00	125	175	250	—

KM# 336.1 1/2 THALER
14.4100 g., 0.8750 Silver 0.4054 oz. ASW **Ruler:** Maria Theresia **Obv:** Bust right **Obv. Legend:** MA: THERESIA: - D: G: REG: HU: BO: **Rev:** Radiant Madonna and child **Rev. Legend:** S: MARIA MATER DEI...

Date	Mintage	VG	F	VF	XF	Unc
1744	Inc. above	—	—	—	—	—
1745	24,000	22.50	50.00	75.00	120	—

KM# 336.2 1/2 THALER
14.4100 g., 0.8750 Silver 0.4054 oz. ASW **Ruler:** Maria Theresia **Obv:** Bust right **Obv. Legend:** M: THER: D: G: R: I: - G: H: B: R: A: A: D: B: C: T: **Rev:** Radiant Madonna and child **Rev. Legend:** S: MARIA MATER DEI...

Date	Mintage	VG	F	VF	XF	Unc
1746	—	22.50	50.00	75.00	110	—
1747	—	22.50	50.00	75.00	110	—

KM# 348 1/2 THALER
14.4100 g., 0.8750 Silver 0.4054 oz. ASW **Ruler:** Maria Theresia **Obv:** Bust right **Obv. Legend:** M • THER • G • G • R • IMP • ... **Rev:** Radiant Madonna and child **Rev. Legend:** S• MARIA MATER DEI - PATRONA HUNG •

Date	Mintage	VG	F	VF	XF	Unc
1748	—	25.00	55.00	85.00	125	—
1749	—	25.00	55.00	85.00	125	—
1750	—	25.00	55.00	85.00	125	—
1751	—	25.00	55.00	85.00	125	—
1752	46,000	25.00	55.00	85.00	125	—

KM# 364 1/2 THALER
14.4100 g., 0.8750 Silver 0.4054 oz. ASW **Ruler:** Maria Theresia **Obv:** Bust right **Rev:** Radiant Madonna and child **Note:** Mule.

Date	Mintage	VG	F	VF	XF	Unc
1753	50,000	22.50	50.00	75.00	110	—
1754	41,000	22.50	50.00	75.00	110	—
1755	49,000	22.50	50.00	75.00	110	—
1756	46,000	22.50	50.00	75.00	110	—
1757	40,000	22.50	50.00	75.00	110	—
1758	37,000	22.50	50.00	75.00	110	—

KM# 370 1/2 THALER
14.4100 g., 0.8750 Silver 0.4054 oz. ASW **Ruler:** Maria Theresia **Obv:** Bust right **Obv. Legend:** M • THER • D: G • R • IMP • - GE • HU • BO • R • A • A • D • B • C • T • **Rev:** Radiant Madonna and child **Rev. Inscription:** S • MARIA • MATER • DEI...

Date	Mintage	VG	F	VF	XF	Unc
1759	37,000	22.50	50.00	75.00	110	—
1760	25,000	22.50	50.00	75.00	110	—
1761	34,000	22.50	50.00	75.00	110	—
1762	14,000	22.50	50.00	75.00	110	—
1763	90,000	22.50	50.00	75.00	110	—
1764	3,070	22.50	50.00	75.00	110	—
1765	25,000	22.50	50.00	75.00	110	—

KM# 370a 1/2 THALER
14.0300 g., 0.8330 Silver 0.3757 oz. ASW **Ruler:** Maria Theresia **Obv:** Bust right **Rev:** Radiant Madonna and child

Date	Mintage	VG	F	VF	XF	Unc
1766 EVM-D	13,000	22.50	55.00	75.00	110	—

KM# 385.1 1/2 THALER
14.0300 g., 0.8330 Silver 0.3757 oz. ASW **Ruler:** Maria Theresia **Obv:** Angels holding crown above arms **Obv. Legend:** M • THER • D • G • R • IMP • - HU • BO • R • A • A • D • B• C • T • **Rev:** Radiant Madonna and child **Rev. Legend:** S • MARIA MATER DEI...

Date	Mintage	VG	F	VF	XF	Unc
1767K EVM-D	7,016	20.00	35.00	50.00	75.00	—
1768K EVM-D	—	20.00	35.00	50.00	75.00	—
1769K EVM-D	12,000	20.00	35.00	50.00	75.00	—
1770K EVM-D	—	20.00	35.00	50.00	75.00	—
1771K EVM-D	—	20.00	35.00	50.00	75.00	—
1772K EVM-D	—	20.00	35.00	50.00	75.00	—
1775K SK-PD	—	20.00	35.00	50.00	75.00	—
1776K SK-PD	—	20.00	35.00	50.00	75.00	—

KM# 385.2 1/2 THALER
14.0300 g., 0.8330 Silver 0.3757 oz. ASW **Ruler:** Maria Theresia **Obv:** Angels holding crown above arms **Rev:** Radiant Madonna and child

Date	Mintage	VG	F	VF	XF	Unc
1778B SK-PD	—	20.00	35.00	50.00	75.00	—
1779B SK-PD	—	20.00	35.00	50.00	75.00	—
1780B SK-PD	—	20.00	35.00	50.00	75.00	—

KM# 398.1 1/2 THALER
14.0300 g., 0.8330 Silver 0.3757 oz. ASW **Ruler:** Joseph II **Obv:** Sitting angels **Obv. Legend:** IOS. II. D. G. R. IMP... **Rev:** Radiant Madonna and child

Date	Mintage	VG	F	VF	XF	Unc
1782A	—	25.00	55.00	85.00	125	—

KM# 398.2 1/2 THALER

14.0300 g., 0.8330 Silver 0.3757 oz. ASW **Ruler:** Joseph II **Obv:** Angels holding crown above arms **Obv. Legend:** IOS • II • D • G • R • IMP • S • A... **Rev:** Radiant Madonna and child **Rev. Legend:** S• MARIA MATER DEI...

Date	Mintage	VG	F	VF	XF	Unc
1782B	—	15.00	30.00	45.00	70.00	—
1783B	—	15.00	30.00	45.00	70.00	—
1785B	—	15.00	30.00	45.00	70.00	—
1786B	—	15.00	30.00	45.00	70.00	—
1789B	—	15.00	30.00	45.00	70.00	—

KM# 399 1/2 THALER

14.0300 g., 0.8330 Silver 0.3757 oz. ASW **Ruler:** Joseph II **Obv:** Flying angels with crown **Obv. Legend:** IOS • II • D • - G • R • IMP • S • A... **Rev:** Radiant Madonna and child **Rev. Legend:** S • MARIA MATER DEI...

Date	Mintage	VG	F	VF	XF	Unc
1785A	—	12.00	25.00	40.00	65.00	—
1786A	—	12.00	25.00	40.00	65.00	—
1787A	—	12.00	25.00	40.00	65.00	—
1788A	—	12.00	25.00	40.00	65.00	—
1789A	—	12.00	25.00	40.00	65.00	—
1790A	—	12.00	25.00	40.00	65.00	—

KM# 405 1/2 THALER

14.0300 g., 0.8330 Silver 0.3757 oz. ASW **Ruler:** Leopold II **Obv:** Angels with crown above arms **Obv. Legend:** LEOP • II • D • - G • R • IMP... **Rev:** Radiant Madonna and child **Rev. Legend:** S • MARIA MATER DEI...

Date	Mintage	F	VF	XF	Unc	BU
1790	—	160	400	600	950	—
1791	—	140	350	475	725	—
1792	—	140	350	475	725	—

KM# 408 1/2 THALER

14.0300 g., 0.8330 Silver 0.3757 oz. ASW **Ruler:** Franz II **Obv:** Angels holding crown above arms **Obv. Legend:** FRANC • II • - D • G • R • I... **Rev:** Radiant Madonna and child **Rev. Legend:** S • MARIA MATER DEI...

Date	Mintage	F	VF	XF	Unc	BU
1792	—	140	350	475	725	—
1793	—	75.00	175	325	550	—
1794	—	100	200	400	600	—

KM# 214.9 THALER

Silver **Ruler:** Leopold I **Obv:** Laureate bust right **Obv. Legend:** LEOPOLDUS - D: G: ROM: IMP: S: A: - CE: HV: BO: R: **Rev:** Crown divides date at top **Rev. Legend:** ARCHIDVX • AVS: DVX... **Note:** Dav. #3265.

Date	Mintage	VG	F	VF	XF	Unc
1700KB	337,000	60.00	110	175	300	—
1701KB	287,000	60.00	110	175	300	—
1702KB	225,000	60.00	110	175	300	—

KM# 257 THALER

Silver **Ruler:** Leopold I **Obv:** Laureate bust right **Obv. Legend:** LEOPOLDVS • - D • G • RO • I • S • AVG • GER • - HV • BO • REX • **Rev:** Arms within Order chain on eagle's breast **Rev. Legend:** ARCHIDVX • AVS • DVX • BVR • MAR... **Note:** Dav. #1005.

Date	Mintage	VG	F	VF	XF	Unc
1702NB ICB	—	100	200	350	650	—
1703NB	—	100	200	350	650	—

KM# 261 THALER

Silver **Ruler:** Leopold I **Obv:** Laureate bust right **Obv. Legend:** LEOPOLD: - D: G: R: I: S: A: GER: HVN: - BO: REX: **Rev:** Arms on eagle's breast **Note:** This type was restruck between 1704 and 1708 with 1703 date. Dav. #1004.

Date	Mintage	VG	F	VF	XF	Unc
1703KB	814,000	50.00	100	175	325	—

KM# 273.1 THALER

Silver **Ruler:** Joseph I **Obv:** Armored bust right **Obv. Legend:** IOSEPHUS - D • G • R • I • S • AV • GE • - HV • B • REX • **Rev:** Crowned shield on imperial eagle **Rev. Legend:** ARCHID • AV • DV • BV... **Note:** Dav. #1022.

Date	Mintage	VG	F	VF	XF	Unc
1705CH	—	250	400	700	1,150	—
1706CH	—	250	400	700	1,150	—

KM# 273.2 THALER

Silver **Ruler:** Joseph I **Obv:** Armored bust right **Obv. Legend:** IOSEPHUS - D • G • R • I • S • AV • GE • - HV • B • REX **Rev:** Crowned oval shield on imperial eagle **Rev. Legend:** ARCHID • AV • DV • BV... **Note:** Varieties exist. Dav. #1023.

Date	Mintage	VG	F	VF	XF	Unc
1705 IGS	—	250	400	700	1,150	—
1706 IGS//CSH	—	250	400	700	1,150	—
1707 IGS//CSH	—	250	400	700	1,150	—
1708 IGS//CSH	—	250	400	700	1,150	—
1710 P-W	—	250	400	700	1,150	—
1711 IGS//P-W	—	250	400	700	1,150	—

KM# 283 THALER

Silver **Ruler:** Joseph I **Rev:** Crowned imperial eagle in inner circle, date in legend **Note:** Dav. #1019.

Date	Mintage	VG	F	VF	XF	Unc
1709KB	49,000	75.00	150	300	550	—

KM# 284 THALER

Silver **Ruler:** Joseph I **Obv:** Without inner circle **Note:** Dav. #1020.

Date	Mintage	VG	F	VF	XF	Unc
1709	Inc. above	75.00	150	300	550	—

KM# 285 THALER

Silver **Ruler:** Joseph I **Obv:** Different laureate bust right **Rev:** Without inner circle **Note:** Dav. #1021.

Date	Mintage	VG	F	VF	XF	Unc
1711	—	250	450	800	1,500	—

KM# 288.1 THALER

Silver **Ruler:** Karl VI **Obv:** Draped laureate bust right **Obv. Legend:** CAR: VI: D: G: R: I: S: - A: G: - HI: HU: B: REX: **Rev:** ARCHID: AVS: D: BU:... **Note:** Dav. #1057.

Date	Mintage	VG	F	VF	XF	Unc
1712	—	200	350	650	1,250	—
1715	—	150	250	400	750	—

KM# 289 THALER

Silver **Ruler:** Karl VI **Obv:** Laureate bust right **Obv. Legend:** CAROLUS • VI - D: G • R • I • S • A • GER • HISP • HUN • - BOH • REX **Rev:** Arms in Order chain on eagle's breast **Rev. Legend:** • ARCHID AV • DV • BV ... **Note:** Dav. #1063.

Date	Mintage	VG	F	VF	XF	Unc
1712CH IGS//P-W	—	125	225	375	700	—
1715CH IGS//P-W	—	100	200	350	650	—

KM# 288.2 THALER

Silver **Ruler:** Karl VI **Obv:** Modified bust right **Rev:** Arms on eagle's breast **Note:** Dav. #1058.

Date	Mintage	VG	F	VF	XF	Unc
1715	—	125	225	375	700	—

KM# 300 THALER

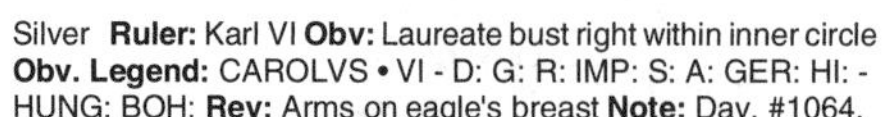

Silver **Ruler:** Karl VI **Obv:** Laureate bust right within inner circle **Obv. Legend:** CAROLVS • VI - D: G: R: IMP: S: A: GER: HI: - HUNG: BOH: **Rev:** Arms on eagle's breast **Note:** Dav. #1064.

Date	Mintage	VG	F	VF	XF	Unc
1717 C-H, P-W	—	100	200	350	650	—
1718 C-H, P-W	—	100	200	350	650	—

KM# 301 THALER

Silver **Ruler:** Karl VI **Obv:** Without inner circle **Obv. Legend:** CAR • VI • D • G • R • I • S • - A • G • - HI • HV • B • REX **Rev:** Arms within Order chain on eagle's breast **Rev. Legend:** ARCHID • AV • D • BV... **Note:** Varieties exist. Dav. #1059.

Date	Mintage	VG	F	VF	XF	Unc
1717KB	—	30.00	60.00	110	160	—
1718KB	—	30.00	60.00	110	160	—
1719KB	—	30.00	60.00	110	160	—
1720KB	—	30.00	60.00	110	160	—
1721KB	—	30.00	60.00	110	160	—
1722KB	—	30.00	60.00	110	160	—
1723KB	—	30.00	60.00	110	160	—
1724KB	—	30.00	60.00	110	160	—
1725KB	—	30.00	60.00	110	160	—
1726KB	—	30.00	60.00	110	160	—
1727KB	—	30.00	60.00	110	160	—
1728KB	—	30.00	60.00	110	160	—
1729KB	—	30.00	60.00	110	160	—
1730KB	—	30.00	60.00	110	160	—

KM# 310.1 THALER

Silver **Ruler:** Karl VI **Obv:** Armored laureate bust right **Obv. Legend:** CAR: VI • D: G: R: I: - S: A: G: HI: H: B: REX: **Rev:** Arms within Order chain on eagle's breast **Rev. Legend:** ARCHID: AU: D: BU: M:... **Note:** Dav. #1060.

Date	Mintage	VG	F	VF	XF	Unc
1730KB	—	30.00	60.00	110	160	—
1731KB	—	30.00	60.00	110	160	—
1732KB	—	30.00	60.00	110	160	—
1733KB	—	30.00	60.00	110	160	—
1734KB	—	30.00	60.00	110	160	—
1735KB	—	30.00	60.00	110	160	—

KM# 310.2 THALER

Silver **Ruler:** Karl VI **Obv:** Modified bust **Obv. Legend:** CAR • VI • D • G • R • I • - S • A • G • HI • H • B • REX • **Rev:** Arms within Order chain on eagle's breast **Rev. Legend:** ARCHID: AU: D: BU: M:... **Note:** Varieties exist. Dav. #1062.

Date	Mintage	VG	F	VF	XF	Unc
1736KB	—	30.00	60.00	110	160	—
1737KB	—	30.00	60.00	110	160	—
1738KB	—	30.00	60.00	110	160	—
1739KB	309,000	30.00	60.00	110	160	—
1740KB	262,000	30.00	60.00	110	160	—

KM# 328.1 THALER

28.8200 g., 0.8750 Silver 0.8107 oz. ASW **Ruler:** Maria Theresia **Obv:** MA. THERESA... Similar to KM#328.3 **Obv. Legend:** MAR. THERESIA• -D:G: REG. HUNG. BOH: **Rev:** Similar to KM#328.3; legend ends: HUNG **Rev. Legend:** S: MARIA MATER DEI - PATRONA HUNG: **Note:** Dav. #1125.

Date	Mintage	F	VF	XF	Unc	BU
1741KB	620,000	45.00	85.00	150	350	—

KM# 328.2 THALER

28.8200 g., 0.8750 Silver 0.8107 oz. ASW **Ruler:** Maria Theresia **Obv:** Bust right **Obv. Legend:** MAR • THERESIA • - D: G: REG: HUNG: BO **Rev:** Radiant Madonna and child **Rev. Legend:** S: MARIA MATER DEI - PATRONA HUNG: **Note:** Dav. #1125A.

Date	Mintage	F	VF	XF	Unc	BU
1741KB	Inc. above	45.00	85.00	135	300	—
1742KB	879,000	45.00	85.00	135	300	—

KM# 328.3 THALER

28.8200 g., 0.8750 Silver 0.8107 oz. ASW **Ruler:** Maria Theresia **Obv:** Bust right with two curls hanging in back **Obv. Legend:** MA • THERESIA • - D: G: REG: HUN: BO **Rev:** Radiant Madonna and child **Rev. Legend:** S: MARIA MATER DEI - PATRONA HUNG **Note:** Dav. #1125B.

Date	Mintage	F	VF	XF	Unc	BU
1741KB	Inc. above	45.00	85.00	135	300	—
1742KB	Inc. above	45.00	85.00	135	300	—

KM# 328.4 THALER

28.8200 g., 0.8750 Silver 0.8107 oz. ASW **Ruler:** Maria Theresia **Obv:** Bust right **Rev:** Radiant Madonna and child **Note:** Dav. #1126.

Date	Mintage	F	VF	XF	Unc	BU
1743	654,000	45.00	85.00	135	300	—
1744	847,000	45.00	85.00	135	300	—

KM# 333 THALER

28.8200 g., 0.8750 Silver 0.8107 oz. ASW **Ruler:** Maria Theresia **Obv:** Modified hair style **Obv. Legend:** M: THERES: - D: G: REG: HU: BO: **Rev:** Radiant Madonna and child **Rev. Legend:** S • MARIA • MATER • DEI... **Note:** Dav. #1127.

Date	Mintage	F	VF	XF	Unc	BU
1743 O	Inc. above	45.00	85.00	135	300	—
1744 O	Inc. above	45.00	85.00	135	300	—

KM# 337.1 THALER

28.8200 g., 0.8750 Silver 0.8107 oz. ASW **Ruler:** Maria Theresia **Obv:** Smaller bust **Obv. Legend:** M: THERES: - D: G: REG: HU: BO: **Rev:** Radiant Madonna and child **Rev. Legend:** S • MARIA • MATER • DEI... **Note:** Dav. #1128.

Date	Mintage	F	VF	XF	Unc	BU
1744	Inc. above	45.00	85.00	135	300	—
1745	875,000	45.00	85.00	135	300	—

KM# 337.2 THALER

28.8200 g., 0.8750 Silver 0.8107 oz. ASW **Ruler:** Maria Theresia **Obv:** Bust with décolletage right **Obv. Legend:** M. THER... **Rev:** Radiant Madonna and child **Note:** Dav. #1129.

Date	Mintage	F	VF	XF	Unc	BU
1746	—	45.00	85.00	135	300	—
1747	—	45.00	85.00	135	300	—
1748	6,170	45.00	85.00	135	300	—

KM# 349.1 THALER

28.8200 g., 0.8750 Silver 0.8107 oz. ASW **Ruler:** Maria Theresia **Obv:** Bust with décolletage right **Obv. Legend:** M • THER • D • G • R • - I • G • H • B • R • A • A • D • B • C • T • **Rev:** Larger shield below Madonna **Rev. Legend:** S • MARIA • MATER • DEI... **Note:** Dav. #1130.

Date	Mintage	F	VF	XF	Unc	BU
1749	—	45.00	80.00	130	300	—
1750	—	45.00	80.00	130	300	—
1751	—	45.00	80.00	130	300	—
1752	263,000	45.00	80.00	130	300	—

KM# 349.2 THALER

28.8200 g., 0.8750 Silver 0.8107 oz. ASW **Ruler:** Maria Theresia **Obv:** Bust with décolletage right **Rev:** Radiant Madonna and child **Note:** Dav. #1131.

Date	Mintage	F	VF	XF	Unc	BU
1751 • X •	—	45.00	80.00	130	300	—

KM# 358.1 THALER

28.8200 g., 0.8750 Silver 0.8107 oz. ASW **Ruler:** Maria Theresia **Obv:** Younger bust right **Obv. Legend:** M • THER • D: G • R • IMP • - GE • HU • BO • R • A • A • D • B • C • T • **Rev:** Radiant Madonna and child **Rev. Legend:** S • MARIA • MATER • DEI... **Note:** Dav. #1132.

Date	Mintage	F	VF	XF	Unc	BU
1751 •X•	335,000	45.00	80.00	130	300	—
1751 •X•	335,000	45.00	80.00	130	300	—
1752 •X•	263,000	45.00	80.00	130	300	—
1753 •X•	279,000	45.00	80.00	130	300	—
1754 •X•	262,000	45.00	80.00	130	300	—
1755 •X•	262,000	45.00	80.00	130	300	—
1756 •X•	264,000	45.00	80.00	130	300	—
1757 •X•	266,000	45.00	80.00	130	300	—
1758 •X•	212,000	45.00	80.00	130	300	—
1759 •X•	271,000	45.00	80.00	130	300	—
1760 •X•	157,000	50.00	90.00	150	325	—
1761 •X•	254,000	50.00	90.00	150	325	—
1762 •X•	85,000	50.00	90.00	150	325	—
1763 •X•	—	50.00	90.00	150	325	—
1764 •X•	—	50.00	90.00	150	325	—
1765 •X•	79,000	50.00	90.00	150	325	—

KM# 349.3 THALER

28.8200 g., 0.8750 Silver 0.8107 oz. ASW **Ruler:** Maria Theresia **Obv:** Modified drapery

Date	Mintage	F	VF	XF	Unc	BU
1752 •X•	Inc. above	45.00	80.00	130	300	—

KM# 358.2 THALER

28.8200 g., 0.8750 Silver 0.8107 oz. ASW **Ruler:** Maria Theresia **Obv:** Bust right **Rev:** Radiant Madonna and child **Note:** Dav. #1135.

Date	Mintage	F	VF	XF	Unc	BU
1763NB Reported, not confirmed	—	—	—	—	—	—

KM# 378 THALER

28.0600 g., 0.8330 Silver 0.7515 oz. ASW **Ruler:** Maria Theresia **Obv:** Decorative gown

Date	Mintage	F	VF	XF	Unc	BU
1763KB •X•	—	50.00	90.00	150	325	—
1764KB •X•	—	50.00	90.00	150	325	—

KM# 358.3 THALER

28.8200 g., 0.8750 Silver 0.8107 oz. ASW **Ruler:** Maria Theresia **Obv:** Bust right **Rev:** Radiant Madonna and child

Date	Mintage	F	VF	XF	Unc	BU
1766K •X•	58,000	50.00	90.00	150	325	—

KM# 386.1 THALER

28.0600 g., 0.8330 Silver 0.7515 oz. ASW **Ruler:** Maria Theresia **Obv:** Crowned arms with angel supporters **Obv. Legend:** M • THER • D • G • R • IMP • - HU • BO • R • A • A • D • B • C • T • **Rev:** Madonna and child **Rev. Legend:** S • MARIA • MATER • DEI... **Note:** Dav. #1133.

Date	Mintage	F	VF	XF	Unc	BU
1767K •X•	25,000	25.00	45.00	100	180	—
1767K •X• EVM-D	Inc. above	25.00	45.00	100	180	—
1768K •X• EVM-D	43,000	25.00	45.00	100	180	—
1769K •X• EVM-D	44,000	25.00	45.00	100	180	—
1770K •X• EVM-D	—	25.00	45.00	100	180	—
1771K •X• EVM-D	—	25.00	45.00	100	180	—
1772K •X• EVM-D	—	25.00	45.00	100	180	—
1773K •X•	—	25.00	45.00	100	180	—
1775K •X• SK-PD	—	25.00	45.00	100	180	—
1776K •X• SK-PD	—	25.00	45.00	100	180	—

KM# 386.2 THALER

28.0600 g., 0.8330 Silver 0.7515 oz. ASW **Ruler:** Maria Theresia **Obv:** Angels holding crown above arms **Obv. Legend:** M • THER • D • G • R • IMP • - HU • BO • R • A • A • D • B • C • T • **Rev:** Radiant Madonna and child **Rev. Legend:** S • MARIA MATER DEI... **Note:** Dav. #1133A.

Date	Mintage	F	VF	XF	Unc	BU
1777B •X• SK-PD	—	25.00	45.00	80.00	180	—
1778B •X• SK-PD	—	25.00	45.00	80.00	180	—
1779B •X• SK-PD	—	25.00	45.00	80.00	180	—
1780B •X• SK-PD	—	25.00	45.00	80.00	180	—

KM# 388 THALER
28.0600 g., 0.8330 Silver 0.7515 oz. ASW **Ruler:** Maria Theresia **Obv:** Veiled bust **Rev:** Crowned eagle with crowned shields on breast **Note:** Dav. #1134.

Date	Mintage	F	VF	XF	Unc	BU
1780 •X• B//SK-PD	—	—	—	—	—	—
1780 •X• B//SK-PD	—	—	—	—	—	—

KM# 395.1 THALER
28.0600 g., 0.8330 Silver 0.7515 oz. ASW **Ruler:** Joseph II **Obv:** Angels holding crown above arms **Obv. Legend:** IOS • II • D • G • R • IMP • S • A • - G • H • B • REX • A • A • D • B • & • L • **Rev:** Radiant Madonna and child **Rev. Legend:** S • MARIA MATER DEI - PATRONA HUNG **Note:** Dav. #1168B.

Date	Mintage	F	VF	XF	Unc	BU
1781 •X•	—	35.00	65.00	110	200	—
1782 •X•	—	35.00	65.00	110	200	—
1783 •X•	—	35.00	65.00	110	200	—

KM# 395.2 THALER
28.0600 g., 0.8330 Silver 0.7515 oz. ASW **Ruler:** Joseph II **Obv:** Angels holding crown above arms **Obv. Legend:** IOS. II. D. G. R. I. S. A... **Rev:** Radiant Madonna and child **Note:** Dav. #1168A.

Date	Mintage	F	VF	XF	Unc	BU
1783A •X•	—	35.00	65.00	110	200	—
1785A •X•	—	35.00	65.00	110	200	—

KM# 400.1 THALER
28.0600 g., 0.8330 Silver 0.7515 oz. ASW **Ruler:** Joseph II **Obv:** Flying angels holding crown above arms **Note:** Dav. #1169A.

Date	Mintage	F	VF	XF	Unc	BU
1785	—	45.00	75.00	120	225	—
1786	—	45.00	75.00	120	225	—
1789	—	45.00	75.00	120	225	—

KM# 400.2 THALER
28.0600 g., 0.8330 Silver 0.7515 oz. ASW **Ruler:** Joseph II **Note:** Dav. #1169B.

Date	Mintage	F	VF	XF	Unc	BU
1786B	—	75.00	125	175	300	—

KM# 406.1 THALER
28.0600 g., 0.8330 Silver 0.7515 oz. ASW **Ruler:** Leopold II **Obv:** Flying angels holding crown above arms **Obv. Legend:** LEOP. II. D. - G. HV. BO... **Rev:** Madonna **Rev. Legend:** S MARIA MATER DEI - PATRONA HUNG **Note:** Dav. #1172.

Date	Mintage	F	VF	XF	Unc	BU
1790A	—	375	750	1,100	1,400	—

KM# 406.2 THALER
28.0600 g., 0.8330 Silver 0.7515 oz. ASW **Ruler:** Leopold II **Obv:** Angels holding crown above arms **Obv. Legend:** LEOP. II. D. G. R. IMP... **Rev:** Radiant Madonna and child **Note:** Dav. #1174.

Date	Mintage	F	VF	XF	Unc	BU
1790	—	325	650	1,250	1,800	—
1791	—	325	650	1,250	1,800	—

KM# 409.1 THALER
28.0600 g., 0.8330 Silver 0.7515 oz. ASW **Ruler:** Franz II **Obv:** Crowned arms wtih angels **Obv. Legend:** FRANC D. G. **Rev:** Madonna with child **Note:** Dav. #1177.

Date	Mintage	F	VF	XF	Unc	BU
1792	—	275	550	900	1,400	—

KM# 409.2 THALER
28.0600 g., 0.8330 Silver 0.7515 oz. ASW **Ruler:** Franz II **Obv:** Crowned arms with angels **Obv. Legend:** FRANC II. D. G... **Rev:** Madonna and child **Note:** Dav. #1179.

Date	Mintage	F	VF	XF	Unc	BU
1792	—	325	600	1,200	1,600	—

KM# 325 2 THALER
Silver **Ruler:** Karl VI **Obv:** Large laureate bust right, legend begins at lower left **Rev:** Crowned imperial eagle, date in legend **Note:** Dav. #1061.

Date	Mintage	VG	F	VF	XF	Unc
1740 KB Rare	—	—	—	—	—	—

REVOLUTIONARY COINAGE

Malcontents

Hungary was discontented with the Habsburg Monarchy. Its opportunity to break free came when the emperor, due to his involvement in the War of the Spanish Succession, withdrew nearly all his troops. There was an immediate rebellion and Francis Rakoczy II, elected prince by the diet in 1704, became the leader. Even though the armies were large in number, they were ill-equipped and without artillery. After defeating the French at Blenheim, the emperor sent an army into Hungary and badly defeated Rakoczy in 1705. Two Rakoczyian diets deposed the Habsburgs in 1707 and formed an interim government with Rakoczy at its head until a national king could be elected. Joseph I, who succeeded Leopold as emperor, refused to come to terms with his subjects even though he was strongly urged to do so by his allies.

In 1708 Rakoczy was defeated again very decisively even though a guerilla war still went on. Joseph died in 1711 and was succeeded by his brother Charles VI who restored peace on the basis of a general amnesty.

RULER
Ferenc Rakoczi II, 1703-1711

MINT MARKS
CM, MC = Kassa (Kosice)
KB = Kormoczbanya (Kremnica)
MM = Munkacs (Mukachevo)
N-B = Nagybanya

KM# 274 DENAR
Copper **Obv:** Crowned arms divide mint mark **Rev:** DENARIUS divides date

Date	Mintage	VG	F	VF	XF	Unc
1705CM	—	5.00	10.00	25.00	40.00	—

KM# 262 POLTURA
Copper **Obv:** Crowned arms **Obv. Legend:** MONETA. NOVA. ARGEN. REG. HUNG **Rev:** Madonna and child divide P-H, POLTURA above **Note:** Varieties exist.

Date	Mintage	VG	F	VF	XF	Unc
1703NB	—	7.50	15.00	25.00	50.00	—
1704NB	—	7.50	15.00	25.00	50.00	—

KM# 263.1 POLTURA
Copper **Ruler:** Leopold I **Obv:** Crowned arms **Obv. Legend:** POLTURA **Rev:** Madonna and child **Rev. Legend:** PATRONA • HVNGARIÆ

Date	Mintage	VG	F	VF	XF	Unc
1704KB	—	4.50	9.00	17.50	35.00	—
1705KB	—	4.50	9.00	17.50	35.00	—
1706KB	—	4.50	9.00	17.50	35.00	—
1707KB	—	4.50	9.00	17.50	35.00	—

KM# 263.2 POLTURA
Copper **Obv:** Crowned arms **Rev:** Madonna and child

Date	Mintage	VG	F	VF	XF	Unc
1705NB	—	5.00	10.00	20.00	40.00	—

KM# 263.3 POLTURA
Copper **Obv:** Crowned arms **Rev:** Madonna and child

Date	Mintage	VG	F	VF	XF	Unc
1705CM	—	4.50	9.00	18.50	37.50	—
1706CM	—	4.50	9.00	18.50	37.50	—
1707CM	—	4.50	9.00	18.50	37.50	—

KM# 263.4 POLTURA
Copper **Obv:** Crowned arms **Rev:** Madonna and child **Note:** Without mint mark.

Date	Mintage	VG	F	VF	XF	Unc
1705	—	3.50	7.50	16.00	32.50	—
1706	—	3.50	7.50	16.00	32.50	—
1707	—	3.50	7.50	16.00	32.50	—

KM# 263.5 POLTURA
Copper **Obv:** Crowned arms **Rev:** Madonna and child

Date	Mintage	VG	F	VF	XF	Unc
1706MM	—	4.50	9.00	18.50	37.50	—
1707MM	—	4.50	9.00	18.50	37.50	—

KM# 263.6 POLTURA
Copper **Obv:** Crowned arms **Rev:** Madonna and child

Date	Mintage	VG	F	VF	XF	Unc
1707MC	—	7.50	15.00	30.00	60.00	—

KM# 277.1 4 POLTURA
Copper **Obv:** Crowned arms **Obv. Legend:** MONETA. NOVA. 1706 **Rev:** Madonna and child above value: IV in cartouche

Date	Mintage	VG	F	VF	XF	Unc
1706C Rare	—	—	—	—	—	—

KM# 277.2 4 POLTURA
Copper **Obv:** Crowned arms divide date, 4 in cartouche below **Rev:** Madonna and child **Note:** Without mint mark.

Date	Mintage	VG	F	VF	XF	Unc
1707 Rare	—	—	—	—	—	—

KM# 264.1 10 POLTURA

Copper **Obv:** Crowned arms divide date **Rev:** Value within cartouche **Rev. Legend:** PRO/LIBERTATE **Note:** Without mint mark.

Date	Mintage	VG	F	VF	XF	Unc
1704	—	5.00	10.00	20.00	45.00	—
1705	—	5.00	10.00	20.00	45.00	—
1706	—	5.00	10.00	20.00	45.00	—
1707	—	5.00	10.00	20.00	45.00	—

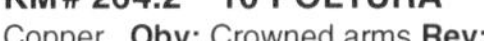

KM# 264.2 10 POLTURA

Copper **Obv:** Crowned arms **Rev:** Value

Date	Mintage	VG	F	VF	XF	Unc
1705NB	—	10.00	20.00	40.00	80.00	—

KM# 264.3 10 POLTURA

Copper **Obv:** Crowned arms **Rev:** Value

Date	Mintage	VG	F	VF	XF	Unc
1705CM	—	6.50	12.50	25.00	50.00	—
1706CM	—	6.50	12.50	25.00	50.00	—

KM# 264.4 10 POLTURA

Copper **Obv:** Crowned arms **Rev:** Value

Date	Mintage	VG	F	VF	XF	Unc
1706MM	—	9.00	18.00	35.00	75.00	—

KM# 275.1 20 POLTURA

Copper **Obv:** Crowned arms **Rev:** Value **Note:** Similar to 10 Poltura, KM#264 but arms divide mint mark.

Date	Mintage	VG	F	VF	XF	Unc
1705CM	—	10.00	20.00	40.00	80.00	—

KM# 275.2 20 POLTURA

Copper **Obv:** Crowned arms **Rev:** Value **Note:** Without mint mark.

Date	Mintage	VG	F	VF	XF	Unc
1705	—	10.00	20.00	40.00	80.00	—
1706	—	10.00	20.00	40.00	80.00	—

KM# 265.1 1/2 THALER

Silver **Obv:** Crowned arms **Obv. Legend:** ...MO NO: ARG: **Rev:** Madonna and child **Rev. Legend:** PATRONA • HUNGARIÆ •

Date	Mintage	VG	F	VF	XF	Unc
1704KB	—	40.00	80.00	140	250	—
1705KB	—	40.00	80.00	140	250	—
1706KB	—	40.00	80.00	140	250	—
1707KB	—	40.00	80.00	140	250	—

KM# 265.2 1/2 THALER

Silver **Obv:** Crowned arms **Rev:** Madonna and child

Date	Mintage	VG	F	VF	XF	Unc
1706MM	—	65.00	135	240	450	—

KM# 266 DUCAT

3.5000 g., 0.9860 Gold 0.1109 oz. AGW **Obv:** Crowned arms **Rev:** Madonna and child

Date	Mintage	VG	F	VF	XF	Unc
1704KB	—	300	500	1,000	1,650	—
1705KB	—	300	550	1,150	1,850	—
1707KB	—	300	550	1,150	1,850	—

KM# 266A DUCAT

3.5000 g., 0.9860 Gold 0.1109 oz. AGW **Obv:** Crowned arms **Rev:** Madonna and child

Date	Mintage	VG	F	VF	XF	Unc
1704NB	—	300	600	1,250	2,200	—
1705NB	—	300	600	1,250	2,200	—

KM# 279 DUCAT

3.5000 g., 0.9860 Gold 0.1109 oz. AGW **Obv:** Crowned arms in floral cartouche, without inner circle **Rev:** Radiant Madonna and child divide mint mark, without inner circle

Date	Mintage	VG	F	VF	XF	Unc
1707	—	300	600	1,250	2,200	—

TRADE COINAGE

KM# 321 1/12 DUCAT

0.2916 g., 0.9860 Gold 0.0092 oz. AGW **Ruler:** Karl VI **Obv:** Laureate head right, value at shoulder **Rev:** Madonna and child above arms and mint mark

Date	Mintage	VG	F	VF	XF	Unc
1739NB	—	50.00	100	200	250	—

KM# 322 1/8 DUCAT

0.4375 g., 0.9860 Gold 0.0139 oz. AGW **Ruler:** Karl VI **Obv:** Laureate head right, value at shoulder **Rev:** Madonna and child in inner circle above arms

Date	Mintage	VG	F	VF	XF	Unc
1739NB	—	50.00	100	200	300	—

KM# 376 1/8 DUCAT

0.4375 g., 0.9860 Gold 0.0139 oz. AGW **Ruler:** Maria Theresia **Obv:** Bust right **Rev:** Imperial eagle

Date	Mintage	F	VF	XF	Unc	BU
1761	—	75.00	125	175	250	—

KM# A284 1/6 DUCAT

0.5833 g., 0.9860 Gold 0.0185 oz. AGW **Ruler:** Joseph I **Obv:** Laureate bust right, value at shoulder **Rev:** Madonna and child divide mint mark above arms **Note:** Prev. KM#284.

Date	Mintage	VG	F	VF	XF	Unc
1711KB	—	100	150	275	450	—

KM# A289 1/6 DUCAT

0.5833 g., 0.9860 Gold 0.0185 oz. AGW **Ruler:** Karl VI **Obv:** Laureate bust right, value at shoulder **Rev:** Madonna and child divide mint mark above arms **Note:** Prev. KM#289.

Date	Mintage	VG	F	VF	XF	Unc
1712CH PW	—	125	200	350	650	—

KM# 307.1 1/6 DUCAT

0.5833 g., 0.9860 Gold 0.0185 oz. AGW **Ruler:** Karl VI

Date	Mintage	VG	F	VF	XF	Unc
1728NB	—	75.00	125	200	350	—
1730NB	—	75.00	125	200	350	—
1740NB	—	75.00	125	200	350	—

KM# 307.2 1/6 DUCAT

0.5833 g., 0.9860 Gold 0.0185 oz. AGW **Ruler:** Karl VI **Note:** Thick, struck from 1/2 Ducat dies.

Date	Mintage	VG	F	VF	XF	Unc
1739	—	75.00	125	225	450	—

KM# 360 1/6 DUCAT

0.5833 g., 0.9860 Gold 0.0185 oz. AGW **Ruler:** Maria Theresia **Obv:** Bust right **Rev:** Imperial eagle

Date	Mintage	F	VF	XF	Unc	BU
1752	—	125	225	425	700	—

KM# A281 1/4 DUCAT

0.8750 g., 0.9860 Gold 0.0277 oz. AGW **Ruler:** Joseph I **Obv:** Joseph standing divides mint mark in inner circle **Rev:** Radiant Madonna and child in inner circle, arms below **Note:** Previous KM#281.

Date	Mintage	VG	F	VF	XF	Unc
1710CH PW	—	125	200	500	800	—
1711CH PW	—	125	200	500	800	—

KM# A280 1/4 DUCAT

0.8750 g., 0.9860 Gold 0.0277 oz. AGW **Ruler:** Karl VI **Obv:** Laureate head right **Rev:** Radiant Madonna and child above arms **Note:** Prev. KM#280.

Date	Mintage	VG	F	VF	XF	Unc
1710KB	—	125	200	450	750	—
1711KB	—	125	200	450	750	—

KM# 290 1/4 DUCAT

0.8750 g., 0.9860 Gold 0.0277 oz. AGW **Ruler:** Karl VI **Obv:** Charles VI standing divides mint mark in inner circle

Date	Mintage	VG	F	VF	XF	Unc
1712 PW	—	125	250	550	900	—

KM# 311 1/4 DUCAT

0.8750 g., 0.9860 Gold 0.0277 oz. AGW **Ruler:** Karl VI **Obv:** Charles VI standing divides mint mark **Rev:** Madonna and child above arms, legend starts at upper right

Date	Mintage	VG	F	VF	XF	Unc
1730NB	—	100	150	200	350	—
1735NB	—	100	150	200	350	—
1737NB	—	100	150	200	350	—

KM# 318 1/4 DUCAT

0.8750 g., 0.9860 Gold 0.0277 oz. AGW **Ruler:** Karl VI **Obv:** Standing figure **Rev:** Legend starts at lower left

Date	Mintage	VG	F	VF	XF	Unc
1738	—	75.00	125	175	325	—
1740	—	75.00	125	175	325	—

KM# 361 1/4 DUCAT

0.8750 g., 0.9860 Gold 0.0277 oz. AGW **Ruler:** Maria Theresia **Obv:** Bust right **Rev:** Madonna and child above arms

Date	Mintage	F	VF	XF	Unc	BU
1752	—	125	200	500	800	—
1755	—	125	200	500	800	—

KM# 409 1/2 DUCAT

1.7500 g., 0.9860 Gold 0.0555 oz. AGW, 19.3 mm. **Ruler:** Franz II **Obv:** Bust right **Obv. Legend:** FRANC • II • D•G • R•I•S•A• GE • HV • BO • REX **Rev:** Imperial eagle with Hungarian crown on chest **Rev. Legend:** ARCH • A • D • BVRG• - LOTH • M • D • H • **Note:** Fr. #370.

Date	Mintage	F	VF	XF	Unc	BU
1796	—	550	900	1,500	—	—

KM# 151 DUCAT

3.5000 g., 0.9860 Gold 0.1109 oz. AGW **Ruler:** Leopold I **Obv:** Leopold standing right divides mint mark in inner circle **Obv. Legend:** LEOPOLD: D: G: R - S: A: G: H: B: R E X **Rev:** Madonna with child at right **Rev. Legend:** • AR • AV • DV • BV • M • - MOCO • TY • date

Date	Mintage	VG	F	VF	XF	Unc
1701K-B	—	125	225	350	550	—
1702K-B	—	125	225	350	550	—
1703K-B	—	125	225	350	550	—
1704K-B	—	125	225	350	550	—

KM# 247 DUCAT

3.5000 g., 0.9860 Gold 0.1109 oz. AGW **Ruler:** Leopold I **Obv:** Initials below Leopold standing

Date	Mintage	VG	F	VF	XF	Unc
1701NB	—	200	400	750	1,250	—
1702NB	—	200	400	750	1,250	—
1703NB	—	200	400	750	1,250	—

KM# A214.2 DUCAT

3.5000 g., 0.9860 Gold 0.1109 oz. AGW **Ruler:** Leopold I **Obv:** Leopold standing right in inner circle, I below feet **Rev:** Madonna and child divide mint mark **Note:** Prev. KM#214.2.

Date	Mintage	VG	F	VF	XF	Unc
1702N-B	—	200	400	750	1,250	—

KM# A214.3 DUCAT

3.5000 g., 0.9860 Gold 0.1109 oz. AGW **Ruler:** Leopold I **Obv:** Leopold standing **Rev:** Madonna and child divide date at top **Note:** Prev. KM#214.3.

Date	Mintage	VG	F	VF	XF	Unc
1703 S	—	200	400	750	1,250	—

KM# 267 DUCAT

3.5000 g., 0.9860 Gold 0.1109 oz. AGW **Ruler:** Joseph I **Obv:** Joseph standing left of table in inner circle **Rev:** Madonna and child in radiant oval in inner circle

Date	Mintage	VG	F	VF	XF	Unc
1705C SH	—	400	800	1,500	2,500	—

KM# 268 DUCAT

3.5000 g., 0.9860 Gold 0.1109 oz. AGW **Ruler:** Joseph I **Obv:** Joseph standing facing 1/2 left divides mint mark in inner circle **Rev:** Madonna and child in radiant oval in inner circle, three shields below

Date	Mintage	VG	F	VF	XF	Unc
1705CH CSH	—	400	800	1,500	2,500	—
1706CH CSH	—	400	800	1,500	2,500	—
1707CH CSH	—	400	800	1,500	2,500	—
1708CH CSH	—	400	800	1,500	2,500	—

KM# A272 DUCAT

3.5000 g., 0.9860 Gold 0.1109 oz. AGW **Ruler:** Joseph I **Obv:** Joseph standing right divides mint mark in inner circle **Obv. Legend:** IOSEPH • D: G: R: I: S: ... **Rev:** Radiant Madonna and child in inner circle, crowned arms below **Rev. Legend:** AR: AV: DV: BV: BV: M - MOCO: TY: date **Note:** Prev. KM#272.

Date	Mintage	VG	F	VF	XF	Unc
1708K-B	—	325	650	1,200	2,000	—
1709K-B	—	325	650	1,200	2,000	—

KM# 276 DUCAT

3.5000 g., 0.9860 Gold 0.1109 oz. AGW **Ruler:** Joseph I **Obv:** Standing figure **Obv. Legend:** IOSEPHVS: D: G: R: I: S: ... **Rev:** Radiant Madonna and child

Date	Mintage	VG	F	VF	XF	Unc
1709CH PW	—	400	800	1,500	2,500	—
1710CH PW	—	400	800	1,500	2,500	—
1711CH PW	—	400	800	1,500	2,500	—

KM# 282 DUCAT

3.5000 g., 0.9860 Gold 0.1109 oz. AGW **Ruler:** Karl VI **Obv:** Standing figure **Obv. Legend:** CAROLVS • VI • D: G: - R: I: S: A: G: H: H: B: R: **Rev:** Madonna and child in radiant oval, crowned arms below **Rev. Legend:** PATRONA • REGN • - HUNGARIÆ •

Date	Mintage	VG	F	VF	XF	Unc
1710K-B	—	325	650	1,200	2,000	—
1711K-B	—	325	650	1,200	2,000	—

KM# 291 DUCAT

3.5000 g., 0.9860 Gold 0.1109 oz. AGW **Ruler:** Karl VI **Obv:** Standing figure **Obv. Legend:** CAROLUS • VI • D: G: - R: I: S: A: G: H: H: B: R: **Rev:** Radiant Madonna and child **Rev. Legend:** PATRONA • REGNI - HVNGARIÆ • date

Date	Mintage	VG	F	VF	XF	Unc
1712K-B	—	125	150	250	350	—
1713K-B	—	125	150	250	350	—
1714K-B	—	125	150	250	350	—
1715K-B	—	125	150	250	350	—
1716K-B	—	125	150	250	350	—
1717K-B	—	125	150	250	350	—
1718K-B	—	125	150	250	350	—
1719K-B	37,000	125	150	250	350	—
1720K-B	—	125	150	250	350	—
1721K-B	40,000	125	150	250	350	—
1722K-B	—	125	150	250	350	—
1723K-B	—	125	150	250	350	—
1724K-B	—	125	150	250	350	—
1725K-B	—	125	150	250	350	—
1726K-B	—	125	150	250	350	—
1727K-B	—	125	150	250	350	—
1728K-B	—	125	150	250	350	—
1729K-B	—	125	150	250	350	—
1730K-B	—	125	150	250	350	—

KM# 292 DUCAT

3.5000 g., 0.9860 Gold 0.1109 oz. AGW **Ruler:** Karl VI **Obv:** Standing figure **Rev:** Madonna and child in radiant oval in inner circle, three shields below

Date	Mintage	VG	F	VF	XF	Unc
1712 PW	—	400	800	1,500	2,500	—
1714 PW	—	400	800	1,500	2,500	—
1716 PW	—	400	800	1,500	2,500	—
1718 PW	—	400	800	1,500	2,500	—

KM# 297 DUCAT

3.5000 g., 0.9860 Gold 0.1109 oz. AGW **Ruler:** Karl VI **Obv:** Legends starts at upper right **Rev:** Madonna and child in radiant oval, date divided at top, crowned arms at bottom

Date	Mintage	VG	F	VF	XF	Unc
1714NB	—	125	175	325	550	—
1716NB	—	125	175	325	550	—
1717NB	—	125	175	325	550	—
1718NB	—	125	175	325	550	—
1719NB	—	125	175	325	550	—
1720NB	—	125	175	325	550	—
1721NB	—	125	175	325	550	—
1722NB	—	125	175	325	550	—
1723NB	—	125	175	325	550	—
1724NB	—	125	175	325	550	—
1725NB	—	125	175	325	550	—
1726NB	—	125	175	325	550	—

KM# 306.1 DUCAT

3.5000 g., 0.9860 Gold 0.1109 oz. AGW **Ruler:** Karl VI **Obv:** Legends starts at lower left **Obv. Legend:** CAROL • VI • D • G • R • I... **Rev:** Radiant Madonna and child **Rev. Legend:** S • IMMAC • V • MAR • MAT - DEI • HUNGAR • PAT • date

Date	Mintage	VG	F	VF	XF	Unc
1727N-B	—	125	175	300	500	—
1728N-B	—	125	175	300	500	—
1729N-B	—	125	175	300	500	—
1730N-B	—	125	175	300	500	—
1731N-B	—	125	175	300	500	—
1732N-B	—	125	175	300	500	—
1733N-B	—	125	175	300	500	—
1735N-B	—	125	175	300	500	—

KM# 306.2 DUCAT

3.5000 g., 0.9860 Gold 0.1109 oz. AGW **Ruler:** Karl VI **Obv:** Standing figure **Obv. Legend:** CAROL • VI • D: G: R: I:... **Rev:** Radiant Madonna and child **Rev. Legend:** PATRONA • REGNI - HUNGARIÆ • date

Date	Mintage	VG	F	VF	XF	Unc
1731K-B	106,000	125	150	250	350	—
1732K-B	—	125	150	250	350	—
1733K-B	—	125	150	250	350	—
1734K-B	—	125	150	250	350	—
1735K-B	—	125	150	250	350	—
1736K-B	—	125	150	250	350	—
1737K-B	—	125	150	250	350	—
1738K-B	—	125	150	250	350	—
1739K-B	—	125	150	250	350	—
1740K-B	—	125	150	250	350	—

KM# 306.3 DUCAT

3.5000 g., 0.9860 Gold 0.1109 oz. AGW **Ruler:** Karl VI **Obv:** Legend starts at upper right **Rev:** Radiant Madonna and child

Date	Mintage	VG	F	VF	XF	Unc
1732N-B	—	125	175	300	500	—
1734N-B	—	125	175	300	500	—

KM# 315 DUCAT

3.5000 g., 0.9860 Gold 0.1109 oz. AGW **Ruler:** Karl VI **Obv:** Laureate head right, mint mark in oval below head

Date	Mintage	VG	F	VF	XF	Unc
1735N-B	—	125	200	350	600	—

KM# 316 DUCAT

3.5000 g., 0.9860 Gold 0.1109 oz. AGW **Ruler:** Karl VI **Rev:** Radiant Madonna and child divide mint mark

Date	Mintage	VG	F	VF	XF	Unc
1736N-B	—	125	200	350	600	—

KM# 317 DUCAT

3.5000 g., 0.9860 Gold 0.1109 oz. AGW **Ruler:** Karl VI **Rev:** Crowned arms at bottom divide mint mark

Date	Mintage	VG	F	VF	XF	Unc
1736N-B	—	125	150	250	400	—
1737N-B	—	125	150	250	400	—
1738N-B	—	125	150	250	400	—
1739N-B	—	125	150	250	400	—
1740N-B	—	125	150	250	400	—

KM# 334 DUCAT

3.5000 g., 0.9860 Gold 0.1109 oz. AGW **Ruler:** Maria Theresia **Obv:** Bust right **Obv. Legend:** M • THERES • D • G • R • - IMP .... **Rev:** Madonna and child above arms **Rev. Legend:** PATRONA • REGNI • - HUNGARIÆ •

Date	Mintage	F	VF	XF	Unc	BU
1741N-B	8,646	—	—	—	—	—
1742N-B	8,762	—	—	—	—	—
1743N-B	6,533	125	200	300	550	—
1744N-B	8,615	—	—	—	—	—
1745N-B	8,532	125	200	300	500	—
1746N-B	7,046	—	—	—	—	—
1747N-B	7,390	125	200	300	500	—
1748N-B	7,947	125	200	300	500	—
1749N-B	9,670	—	—	—	—	—
1750N-B	13,000	125	200	300	500	—
1751N-B	16,000	125	200	300	500	—
1752N-B	15,000	125	200	300	500	—
1753N-B	17,000	125	200	300	500	—
1754N-B	18,000	125	200	300	500	—
1755N-B	23,000	125	200	300	500	—
1756N-B	25,000	125	200	300	500	—
1757N-B	22,000	125	200	300	500	—
1758N-B	27,000	—	—	—	—	—
1759N-B	30,000	125	200	300	500	—
1760N-B	22,000	125	200	300	500	—
1761N-B	27,000	125	200	300	500	—
1762N-B	27,000	125	200	300	500	—
1763N-B	26,000	125	200	300	500	—
1764N-B	31,000	125	200	300	500	—
1765N-B	33,000	125	200	300	500	—

KM# 329.1 DUCAT

3.5000 g., 0.9860 Gold 0.1109 oz. AGW **Ruler:** Maria Theresia **Obv:** Standing figure **Obv. Legend:** MA • THERESIA • - D: G: REG: MU: BO: **Rev:** Radiant Madonna and child **Rev. Legend:** PATRONA • REGNI • - HUNGARIÆ •

Date	Mintage	F	VF	XF	Unc	BU
1741K-B	238,000	125	175	275	450	—
1742K-B	616,000	125	175	275	450	—
1743K-B	604,000	125	175	275	450	—
1744K-B	205,000	125	175	275	450	—
1745K-B	170,000	125	175	275	450	—

KM# 329.2 DUCAT

3.5000 g., 0.9860 Gold 0.1109 oz. AGW **Ruler:** Maria Theresia **Obv:** Standing figure **Obv. Legend:** M • THER • D • G • R • I • - G • H • B • R • A • A • D • B • C • T • **Rev:** Radiant Madonna and child **Rev. Legend:** PATRONA REGNI - HUNGARIÆ • date

Date	Mintage	F	VF	XF	Unc	BU
1746K-B	177,000	125	175	275	450	—
1747K-B	150,000	125	175	275	450	—
1748K-B	106,000	125	175	275	450	—
1749K-B	148,000	125	175	275	450	—
1750K-B	132,000	125	175	275	450	—
1751K-B	154,000	125	175	275	450	—
1752K-B	144,000	125	175	275	450	—
1753K-B	136,000	125	175	275	450	—
1754K-B	147,000	125	175	275	450	—
1755K-B	145,000	125	175	275	450	—
1756K-B	292,000	125	175	275	450	—
1757K-B	153,000	125	175	275	450	—
1758K-B	129,000	125	175	275	450	—
1759K-B	144,000	125	175	275	450	—
1760K-B	127,000	125	175	275	450	—
1761K-B	145,000	125	175	275	450	—
1762K-B	137,000	125	175	275	450	—
1763K-B	121,000	125	175	275	450	—
1764K-B	178,000	125	175	275	450	—
1765K-B	80,000	125	175	275	450	—

KM# 329.3 DUCAT

3.5000 g., 0.9860 Gold 0.1109 oz. AGW **Ruler:** Maria Theresia **Obv:** Standing figure **Obv. Legend:** M • THER • D • G • R • I • - G • H • B • R • A • A • D • B • C • T • **Rev:** Radiant Madonna and child **Rev. Inscription:** PATRONA • REGNI • - HUNGARIÆ • date

Date	Mintage	F	VF	XF	Unc	BU
1765 KBII/KD	882,000	125	175	275	450	—

KM# 382 DUCAT

3.5000 g., 0.9860 Gold 0.1109 oz. AGW **Ruler:** Maria Theresia **Obv:** Veiled head right **Rev:** Madonna and child

Date	Mintage	F	VF	XF	Unc	BU
1766 B-L	29,000	125	200	300	500	—
1767 B-L	29,000	125	200	300	500	—
1768 B-L	27,000	125	200	300	500	—
1769 B-L	—	125	200	300	500	—
1770 B-L	—	125	200	300	500	—
1771 B-L	—	125	200	300	500	—
1774 B-V	—	125	200	300	500	—
1775 B-V	—	125	200	300	500	—
1779 IB-IV	—	125	200	300	500	—
1779 B-V	—	125	200	300	500	—
1780 IB-IV	—	125	200	300	500	—

KM# 396 DUCAT

3.5000 g., 0.9860 Gold 0.1109 oz. AGW **Ruler:** Joseph II **Obv:** Joseph I standing right **Obv. Legend:** IOS. II. D. G. R. I. S. A. - G. H. B. R. A. A. D. B. ET. L. **Rev:** Madonna **Rev. Legend:** PATRONA REGNI HVNGARIAE

Date	Mintage	F	VF	XF	Unc	BU
1781	—	125	200	300	500	—
1782	—	125	200	300	500	—
1783	—	125	200	300	500	—
1784	—	125	200	300	500	—
1785/4	—	125	200	300	500	—
1785	—	125	200	300	500	—

KM# 407.1 DUCAT

3.5000 g., 0.9860 Gold 0.1109 oz. AGW **Ruler:** Leopold II **Obv:** Leopold I standing right **Obv. Legend:** LEOP. II. D. G. HV. BO. GA. - L. R. A. A. D. B. ET. L. M. D. H. **Rev:** Madonna **Rev. Legend:** S. MARIA MATER DEI-PATRONA HVNG.

Date	Mintage	F	VF	XF	Unc	BU
1790	—	150	250	400	600	—

KM# 407.2 DUCAT

3.5000 g., 0.9860 Gold 0.1109 oz. AGW **Ruler:** Leopold II **Obv:** Standing figure **Obv. Legend:** LEOP • II • D • G • R • I • S • ... **Rev:** Radiant Madonna and child **Rev. Legend:** S • MARIA MATER DEI - PATRONA HVNG • date

Date	Mintage	F	VF	XF	Unc	BU
1791	—	150	225	375	650	—
1792	—	150	225	375	650	—

KM# 410 DUCAT

3.5000 g., 0.9860 Gold 0.1109 oz. AGW **Ruler:** Franz II **Obv:** Standing figure **Obv. Legend:** FRANC • II • D • G • R • I • S • A... **Rev:** Radiant Madonna and child **Rev. Legend:** S • MARIA MATER DEI - PATRONA HVNG • date

Date	Mintage	F	VF	XF	Unc	BU
1792	—	110	150	200	350	—
1793	—	110	150	200	350	—
1794	—	110	150	200	350	—
1795	—	110	150	200	350	—
1796	—	110	150	200	350	—
1797	—	110	150	200	350	—
1798	—	110	150	200	350	—
1799	—	110	150	200	350	—

KM# 277 2 DUCAT

7.0000 g., 0.9860 Gold 0.2219 oz. AGW **Ruler:** Joseph I **Obv:** Joseph standing right divides mint mark **Rev:** Madonna and child in radiant oval, crowned arms below

Date	Mintage	VG	F	VF	XF	Unc
1709K-B	—	1,200	2,250	4,000	6,500	—

KM# 379 2 DUCAT

6.9800 g., 0.9900 Gold 0.2222 oz. AGW **Ruler:** Maria Theresia **Obv:** Standing woman **Obv. Legend:** M • THER • D: G • R • I • - G • H • B • R • A • A • D • B • C • T • **Rev:** Radiant Madonna and child **Rev. Legend:** PATRONA • REGNI • - HUNGARIÆ • date

Date	Mintage	VG	F	VF	XF	Unc
1763	—	150	250	350	600	—
1764	40,000	150	250	350	600	—
1765	26,000	150	250	350	600	—
1765 KB/KD	712,000	150	250	350	600	—

KM# 397 2 DUCAT

6.9800 g., 0.9900 Gold 0.2222 oz. AGW **Ruler:** Joseph II **Obv:** Standing figure **Obv. Legend:** IOS • II • D • G • R • I • S • A • G • H • B • R • A • A • D • B • ET • L • **Rev:** Radiant Madonna and child **Rev. Legend:** PATRONA REGNI HUNGARIÆ • **Note:** Without mint mark

Date	Mintage	VG	F	VF	XF	Unc
1781	39,000	150	250	350	600	—
1782	45,000	150	250	350	600	—
1783 Rare	35,000	—	—	—	—	—
1784/3	31,000	150	250	350	600	—
1784 Rare	Inc. above	—	—	—	—	—
1785	42,000	150	250	350	600	—
1786	58,000	150	250	350	600	—
1787	20,000	175	300	450	700	—

KM# A215 3 DUCAT

10.5000 g., 0.9860 Gold 0.3328 oz. AGW **Ruler:** Leopold I **Note:** Struck with 1/2 Thaler dies, KM#260.

Date	Mintage	VG	F	VF	XF	Unc
1703NB	—	900	1,800	3,250	5,500	—

KM# B215 4 DUCAT

14.0000 g., 0.9860 Gold 0.4438 oz. AGW **Ruler:** Leopold I **Obv:** Bust right **Rev:** Crowned imperial eagle **Note:** Klippe. Struck with 1/2 Thaler dies, KM#260.

Date	Mintage	VG	F	VF	XF	Unc
1703NB	—	1,500	2,500	4,500	7,500	—

KM# A257 5 DUCAT

17.5000 g., 0.9860 Gold 0.5547 oz. AGW **Ruler:** Leopold I **Obv:** Bust right **Rev:** Crowned imperial eagle in inner circle, crown divides date at top **Note:** Previous KM#257.

Date	Mintage	VG	F	VF	XF	Unc
1703NB	—	1,200	2,000	4,000	6,500	—

KM# 248 5 DUCAT

17.5000 g., 0.9860 Gold 0.5547 oz. AGW **Ruler:** Leopold I **Obv:** Bust right **Rev:** Crowned imperial eagle **Note:** Struck with 1/2 Thaler dies, KM#251.

Date	Mintage	VG	F	VF	XF	Unc
1703KB	—	2,500	4,000	6,500	10,000	—

KM# A319 5 DUCAT

17.5000 g., 0.9860 Gold 0.5547 oz. AGW **Ruler:** Karl VI **Rev:** Crowned imperial eagle, date in legend **Note:** Struck with 1/2 Thaler dies, KM#320.

Date	Mintage	VG	F	VF	XF	Unc
1739 Rare	—	—	—	—	—	—

KM# A253 10 DUCAT

35.0000 g., 0.9860 Gold 1.1095 oz. AGW **Ruler:** Leopold I **Note:** Struck with 1 Thaler dies, KM#257. Prev. KM#253.

Date	Mintage	VG	F	VF	XF	Unc
1703NB	—	—	—	6,500	10,000	—

KM# A278 10 DUCAT

35.0000 g., 0.9860 Gold 1.1095 oz. AGW **Ruler:** Joseph I **Rev:** Crowned imperial eagle in inner circle, date in legend **Note:** Struck with 1 Thaler dies, KM#283.

Date	Mintage	VG	F	VF	XF	Unc
1709KB Rare	—	—	—	—	—	—

COUNTERMARKED COINAGE

KM# 268.2 10 POLTURA

Copper **Countermark:** Madonna and child in oval **Note:** Countermark on obverse. Varieties of shield exist.

CM Date	Host Date	Good	VG	F	VF	XF
ND1706-11	1704	—	15.00	25.00	50.00	100
ND1706-11	1705	—	15.00	25.00	50.00	100
ND1706-11	1706	—	15.00	25.00	50.00	100

KM# 268.3 10 POLTURA

Copper **Countermark:** Madonna and child in oval **Note:** Countermark on obverse of KM#264.2.

CM Date	Host Date	Good	VG	F	VF	XF
ND1706-11	1705NB	—	35.00	45.00	75.00	160

KM# 268.4 10 POLTURA

Copper **Countermark:** Madonna and child in oval **Note:** Countermark on obverse of KM#264.3.

CM Date	Host Date	Good	VG	F	VF	XF
ND1706-11	1705CM	—	15.00	25.00	50.00	100
ND1706-11	1706CM	—	15.00	25.00	50.00	100

KM# 268.5 10 POLTURA

Copper **Countermark:** Madonna and child in oval **Note:** Countermark on obverse and reverse of KM#264.3.

CM Date	Host Date	Good	VG	F	VF	XF
ND1706-11	1706	—	25.00	35.00	65.00	135

KM# 268.6 10 POLTURA

Copper **Countermark:** Madonna and child in oval **Note:** Countermark on obverse of KM#264.4.

CM Date	Host Date	Good	VG	F	VF	XF
ND1706-11	1706MM	—	25.00	40.00	70.00	145

KM# 268.7 10 POLTURA

Copper **Countermark:** Madonna and child in oval **Note:** Countermark on obverse and reverse of KM#264.4.

CM Date	Host Date	Good	VG	F	VF	XF
ND1706-11	1706	—	35.00	50.00	90.00	185

KM# 268.1 10 POLTURA

Copper **Countermark:** Madonna and child in oval **Note:** Without mint mark. Countermark on obverse and reverse.

CM Date	Host Date	Good	VG	F	VF	XF
ND1706-11	1704	—	20.00	30.00	60.00	120
ND1706-11	1705	—	20.00	30.00	60.00	120
ND1706-11	1706	—	20.00	30.00	60.00	120

KM# 276.2 20 POLTURA

Copper **Countermark:** Madonna and child in oval **Note:** Countermark on obverse and reverse of KM#275.1.

CM Date	Host Date	Good	VG	F	VF	XF
ND1706-11	1705	—	20.00	30.00	60.00	120

KM# 276.4 20 POLTURA

Copper **Countermark:** Madonna and child in oval **Note:** Countermark on obverse and reverse of KM#275.2.

CM Date	Host Date	Good	VG	F	VF	XF
ND1706-11	1705	—	20.00	30.00	60.00	120

KM# 276.1 20 POLTURA

Copper **Countermark:** Madonna and child in oval **Note:** Countermark on obverse of KM#275.1.

CM Date	Host Date	Good	VG	F	VF	XF
ND1706-11	1705	—	20.00	30.00	60.00	120

KM# 276.3 20 POLTURA

Copper **Countermark:** Madonna and child in oval **Note:** Without mint mark. Countermark on obverse of KM#275.2.

CM Date	Host Date	Good	VG	F	VF	XF
ND1706-11	1705	—	20.00	30.00	60.00	120

PATTERNS

Including off metal strikes

KM#	Date	Mintage	Identification	Mkt Val
Pn73	1703K-B	—	Krajczar. Gold. KM#173	400
Pn77	1723KB	—	Ducat. Copper. KM#291	150
Pn78	1723NB	—	Ducat. Copper. KM#297	150
Pn80	1740 K-B	—	30 Krajczar. Gold. KM#319. Weight of 5 Ducat.	—
Pn81	1742	—	1/2 Thaler. Copper.	—
Pn82	1751	—	Thaler. Pewter.	—
Pn83	1753	—	Ducat. Silver.	—
Pn84	1754	—	Denar. Gold. KM#362.1	—
Pn85	1756	—	Thaler. Pewter.	—
Pn86	1759	—	Poltura. Copper. KM#346	—
Pn87	1760	—	Denar. Copper. KM#375. Madonna without rays.	—
Pn88	1761	—	Poltura. Copper. KM#346	—
Pn89	1761	—	Poltura. Copper. KM#346	—
Pn90	1770	—	30 Kreuzer. Pewter.	—
Pn91	1779	—	Poltura. Copper.	—
Pn92	1779	—	3 Kreuzer. Copper.	—
Pn93	1788B	—	Hungrish. Copper. Crowned arms. Value.	—
Pn94	1788A	—	Denarius. Copper. With wreath.	—
Pn95	1788	—	Denarius. Copper. Without wreath.	—
Pn96	ND	—	20 Kreuzer. Bust right with 13 stars around. Madonna above 20.	—

PIEFORTS

KM#	Date	Mintage	Identification	Mkt Val
P18	1766	—	Denar. KM#375	—

TRIAL STRIKES

KM#	Date	Mintage	Identification	Mkt Val
TS-A1	1704	—	10 Poltura. Lead. KM#269.	—
TS-A1a	1704	—	10 Poltura. Silver. KM#269.	—
TS-A1b	1704	—	10 Poltura. Gold. KM#269.	—
TS-A2	1706	—	10 Poltura. Silver. KM#269.	—
TS1	1742KB	—	1/2 Thaler. Copper. KM#327.	—
TS2	1743NB	—	15 Krajczar. Gold. KM#332.	—
TS3	1751KB	—	Thaler. Lead. KM#349.	—
TS4	1752W-I	—	Poltura. Copper. KM#346.3.	—
TS5	1753KB	—	Ducat. Silver. KM#329	—
TS6	1754KB	—	Denar. Gold. KM#362.1.	—
TS8	1756KB	—	Thaler. Lead. KM#358.	—
TS7	1770 OEVM-D/K	—	30 Krajczar. Lead. KM#384.	—
TS9	1779 SK-PD	—	3 Krajczar. Copper. KM#392.	—

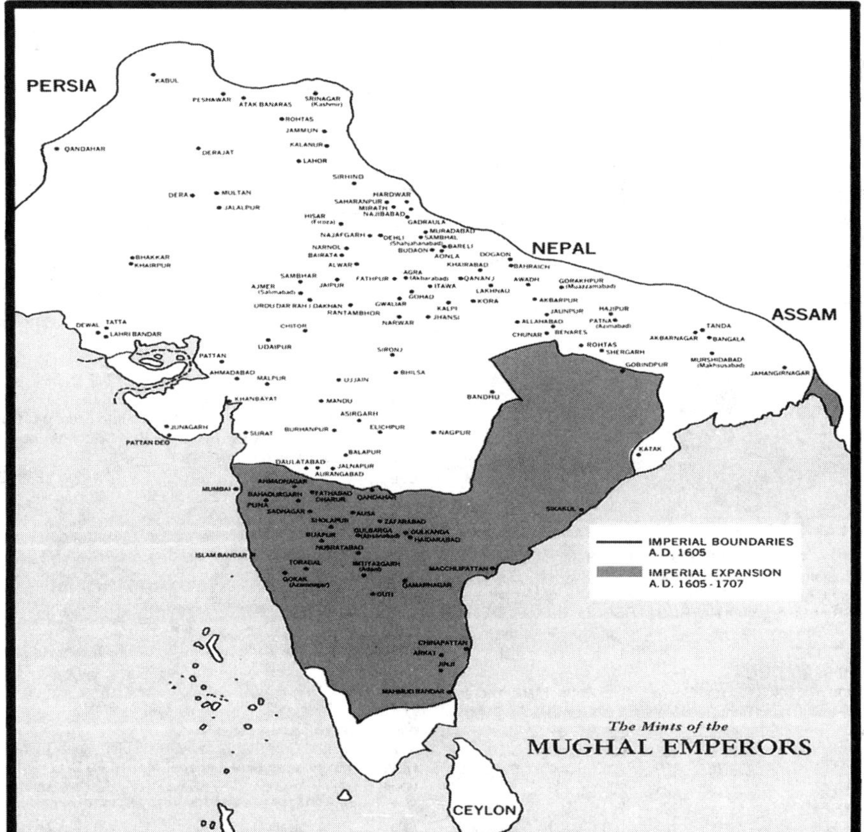

The Lodi Sultanate of Delhi was conquered by Zahir-ud-din Muhammad Babur, a Chagatai Turk descended from Tamerlane, in 1525AD. His son, Nasir-ud-din Muham-mad Humayun, lost the new empire in a series of battles with the Bihari Afghan Sher Shah, who founded the short-lived Suri dynasty. Humayun, with the assistance of the Emperor of Persia, recovered his kingdom from Sher Shah's successors in 1555AD. He did not long enjoy the fruits of victory for his fatal fall down his library steps brought his teenage son Jalal-ud-din Muhammad Akbar to the throne in the following year. During Akbar's long reign of a half century, the Mughal Empire was firmly established throughout much of North India. Under Akbar's son and grandson, the emperors Nur-ud-din Muhammad Jahangir and Shihab-ud-din Muhammad Shah Jahan, the state reached its apogee and art, culture and commerce flourished.

One of the major achievements of the Mughal government was the establishment of a universal silver currency, based on the rupee, a coin of 11.6 grams and as close to pure silver content as the metallurgy of the time was capable of attaining. Supplementary coins were the copper dam and gold mohur. The values of these coin denominations were nominally fixed at 40 dams to 1 rupee, and 8 rupees to 1 mohur; however, market forces determined actual exchange rates.

The maximum expansion of the geographical area under direct Mughal rule was achieved during the reign of Aurangzeb Alamgir. By his death in 1707AD, the whole peninsula, with minor exceptions, the whole subcontinent of India owed fealty to the Mughal emperor.

Aurangzeb's wars, lasting decades, upset the stability and prosperity of the kingdom. The internal dissension and rebellion which resulted brought the eclipse of the empire in succeeding reigns. The Mughal monetary system, especially the silver rupee, supplanted most local currencies throughout India. The number of Mughal mints rose sharply and direct central control declined, so that by the time of the emperor Shah Alam II, many nominally Mughal mints served independent states. The common element in all these coinage issues was the presence of the Mughal emperor's name and titles on the obverse. In the following listings no attempt has been made to solve the problem of separating Mughal from Princely State coins by historical criteria: all Mughal-style coins are considered products of the Mughal empire until the death of Muhammad Shah in 1784AD; thereafter all coins are considered Princely State issues unless there is evidence of the mint being under ever-diminishing Imperial control.

EMPERORS

اورنگ زیب عالم گیر

Aurangzeb Alamgir, Muhayyi-ud-din, AH1068-1118/1658-1707AD

Azam Shah, in Gujarat and Malwa, AH1118-1119/1707AD

Kam Bakhsh, in Deccan, AH1119-1120/1707-1708AD

شاه عالم بهادر

Shah Alam Bahadur, AH1119-1124/1707-1712AD

Azim-ush-Shan, in Bengal, AH1124/1712AD

جهاندار شاه

Jahandar Shah, AH1124/1712AD

Farrukhsiyar, AH1124-1131/1713-1719AD

لطف الله محمد شاه

Nikusiyar, AH1131/1719AD

رفیع الدرجات

Rafi-ud-Darjat, AH1131/1719AD

شاه جهان

Shah Jahan II, Rafi-ud-Daula AH1131/1719AD

محمد ابراهیم

Muhammad Ibrahim, in Delhi, AH1132-1133/1720AD

محمد شاه

Muhammad Shah, AH1131-1161/1719-1748AD

احمد شاه بهادر

Ahmad Shah Bahadur, AH1161-1167/AH1748-1754AD

عزیز الدین عالمگیر

Alamgir II, Aziz-ud-din, AH1167-1173/1754-1759AD

شاه جهان

Shah Jahan III, AH1173-1174/1759-1760AD

بیدار بخت

Bedar Bakht, Muhammad, in Delhi and Gujarat, AH1202-1203/1788AD

اکبر شاه

Akbar Shah AH1203/1788AD

شاه عالم

Shah Alam II, AH1174-1202/1759-1788AD and AH1203-1221/1789-1806AD

MINT NAMES

ادوني

Adoni
(Imtiyazgarh)

ادواني

Advani

اگره

Agra
(Akbarabad)

The city and fort of Agra or Akbarabad fell to the Jats of Bharatpur after the battle of Panipat in 1761AD. For issues dated AH1175-1186/1761-1773AD see Indian Princely States, Bharatpur. A succession of governors from 1773AD controlled Agra nominally as officers of the Mughal emperor but actually for themselves and, after 1785, for the Maratha Peshwa.

احمداباد

Ahmadabad

Mint marks:

Obverse and reverse

Reverse

Obverse and reverse

Reverse

Obverse and reverse

احمدنگر

Ahmadnagar

احسن اباد

Ahsanabad
(Gulbarga)

اجمير

Ajmer
(Salimabad)

اجمير سليم اباد

Ajmer Salimabad

اكبراباد

Akbarabad
(Agra)

اكبرنگر

Akbarnagar

اكبرپور

Akbarpur
(Tanda)

اكبرپور تانده

Akbarpur Tanda

اخترنگر

Akhtarnagar (Awadh)

عالمگيرنگر

Alamgirnagar

عالم گيرپور

Alamgirpur
(Bhilsa)

Alinagar
(Calcutta)

الله اباد

Allahabad
(Ilahabad)

At the accession of Shah Alam II the city and fortress of Allahabad were in the possession of the Nawab-Vizier of Awadh. From 1765 to 1771 (AH1179-1185) the Mughal emperor was in residence in Allahabad; subsequently it was seized by the East India Company and sold to Awadh once more in 1773 (AH1187). For issues AH1173-1178/1759-1765AD and AH1187-1195/1773-1781AD see Indian Princely States, Awadh.

الوار

Alwar
Mint marks:

Reverse

East India Company

Reverse

Reverse

انحيروالا پتن

Anhirwala Pattan

انوله

Anwala
(Anola)

اركات

Arkat

Asadnagar

اصف اباد

Asafabad
(Bareli)

اصف اباد بريلي

Asafabad Bareli

اسير

Asir

اتك

Atak

اتك بنارس

Atak Banaras

اورنگ اباد

Aurangabad
(Khujista Bunyad)

اورنگ نگر

Aurangnagar

اوسا

Ausa

اوده

Awadh, Oudh
(Khitta)

اعظم نگر

Azamnagar
(Gokak)

اعظم نگر بنکاپور

Azamnagar Bankapur

اعظم نگر گوکاك

Azamnagar Gokak

عظیم اباد

Azimabad
(Patna)

Azimabad or Patna was lost by Shah Alam II to the East India Company in 1765AD. For subsequent issues of the Patna Mint in the mint-name Murshidabad, see India, British, Bengal Presidency.

بهادرگره

Bahadurgarh
Mint mark

Reverse

بهرایچ بهریچ

Bahraich

بیراتة

Bairata

بهکّر بهکهر

Bakkar
(Bhakkar)

بالاپور

Balapur

بلخ

Balkh

بلونت نگر

Balwantnagar
(Jhansi)

بنده ملواري

Banda Malwari
(Maratha)

بندرشاهي

Bandar Shahi

بندحو

Bandhu

بنگالة

Bangala

بنکپ بنکاپور

Bankapur

بارامتي برامتي

Baramati

بريلي

Bareli
(Asafabad)

بروچ

Baroch
(sometimes Bairata)

برار

Berar

بهکّر

Bhakhar

بهروچ

Bharoch

بهیلسة

Bhilsa
(Alamgirpur)

بیجاپور

Bijapur

بیکانیر

Bikaner

بداون

Budaon

برهان اباد

Burhanabad

برهانپور

Burhanpur

چیناپتن

Chinapattan

چیتور

Chitor
(Akbarpur)

چنار

Chunar

دولت اباد دولتاباد

Daulatabad
(Deogir)

دهلي

Dehli
(Shahjahanabad)

دیوگیر

Deogir
(Daulatabad)

دیرجات

Derajat

دیول بندر

Dewal Bandar

دلشاداباد

Dilshadabad

دوگاون

Dogaon

ایلچپور

Elichpur

فرخنده بنیاد

Farkhanda Bunyad
(Haidarabad)

فرخ اباد

Farrukhabad
(Ahmadnagar)

فتح اباد دهرور

Fathabad Dharur

فتحنگر

Fathnagar

فتحپور

Fathpur

فیروزگره

Firozgarh

فیروزنگر

Firoznagar

گدرولة

Gadraula

گجیکوتا

Gajjikota

گوبندپور

Gobindpur

گوهد

Gohad

گوکاك

Gokak
(Azamnagar)

گوکل گره

Gokulgarh

گورکپور

Gorakpur (Muazzamabad)
Mint marks

گلبرگة

Gulbarga (Ahsanabad)

گلکندة

Gulkanda

گلشن اباد
Gulshanabad (Nasik)

گوتي
Guti

گواليار
Gwalior

هافظاباد
Hafizabad

حيدراباد
Haidarabad
(Farkhanda Bunyad)

حجيپور
Hajipur

هاردوار
Hardwar
(Tirath)

A mint of the Mughal governor of Saharanpur.

هاتهرس
Hathras

Hathras, near Aligarh, was in the control of the Nawab – Vizier of Awadh until 1782AD. For issues before AH1196/24, see India Princely State, Awadh.

حصار
Hisar
(Firoza)

حصار فيروزة
Hisar Firoza

هوكري
Hukeri

امتيازگره
Imtiyazgarh
(Adoni)

اسلام اباد
Islamabad
(Mathura)

اسلام بندر
Islam Bandar
(Rajapur)

اسلام نگر
Islamnagar

اتاوه اتاوا
Itawa

جبّالپور
Jabbalpore

جهانگيرنگر
Jahangirnagar
(Dacca)
Mint mark

The city of Jahangirnagar (modern Dhakka, or Dacca) during the reign of Shah Alam II remained a mint city under the control of the Nawab of Bengal, Siraj ad-daulah, until the British took over administration of the province in 1765AD (AH1178/9). The date and style of this coin type suggest the last issue of the Mughals from this city.

جي پور
Jaipur
(Sawai)

جلال نگر
Jalalnagar

جلالپور
Jalalpur

جليسار
Jalesar

جالندر جلّندر
Jallandar

جالنة پور
Jalnapur

جونپور
Jaunpur

جنجي
Jinji

جودهپور
Jodhpur

جونة گره
Junagarh

كابل
Kabul

كالانور
Kalanur

كلكته
Kalkatta

كلپي
Kalpi

قنوج
Kanauj
(Qanauj)

كمبايت
Kanbayat
(Khambayat)

كنجي
Kanji

كانكرتي
Kankurti

كراراباد
Kararabad

كريم اباد
Karimabad

كرناتك
Karnatak

كرپا
Karpa

كشمير
Kashmir
(Srinagar)

كتك
Katak

كتك بنارس
Katak Banaras

خيراباد
Khairabad

خيرنگر
Khairnagar

خيرپور
Khairpur

كمنبايت
Khambayat
(Kanbayat)

خجسته بنياد
Khujista Bunyad
(Aurangabad)

كويلكونده
Koilkunda

كولاپور كلاپور
Kolapur

كورا
Kora
Mint mark

Shah Alam II received Kora from Awadh in AH1178/1765AD, and lost it to the East India company in AH1184/1771AD when he moved to Delhi.

لاهور
Lahore

لهري بندر
Lahri Bandar

لكهنو
Lakhnau

مچهلي پتن
Machhlipattan

مدنكوت
Madankot

مهه اندرپور
Mahindurpur
(Mahe Indrapur)

محمودبندر
Mahmud Bandar

ميلاپور
Mailapur

مخصوص اباد
Makhsusabad
(Murshidabad)

ملك نگر
Maliknagar

مالپور
Malpur

مندو
Mandu

مانگره
Mangarh
(Manghar)

مانكپور
Manikpur

متهره
Mathura
(Islamabad)

ميرتا ميرتة
Mirath
(Mirtha)

معظم اباد
Muazzamabad
(Gorakhpur)

محمداباد
Muhammadabad
(Udaipur)

محمداباد بنارس
Muhammadabad Banaras

مجاحداباد
Mujahidabad

ملهر
Mulher

ملتان
Multan

منبي
Mumbai

مهنگير
Mungir

Coins were struck during the conflict between Mir Kasim, Nawab of Bengal and the East India Company. Mungir (Monghyr) was the temporary residence and headquarters of the Nawab.

مراداباد
Muradabad

مرشداباد
Murshidabad
(Makhsusabad)
Mint mark

Bengal, including the mint-town of Murshidabad, was lost by Shah Alam II to the East India Company in 1765AD. For coins later than AH1179, regnal yr. 5, see India, British, Bengal Presidency.

نجيباباد
Najibadad

نارنول
Narnol

نرور
Narwar

نصيراباد
Nasirabad

نصرت اباد
Nusratabad
(Fathpur)

نصرت گره
Nusratgarh

پرينده پرنده
Parenda

پرنالا (قلع)
Parnala
(Qila)

پتنة
Patna
(Azimabad)

پتن
Pattan
(Anhirwala)

پتن ديو
Pattan Deo

پشاور
Peshawar

پهونده
Phonda

پونامالي
Punamali

پونچ
Punch

مرتضاباد
Murtazabad

مظفرگره
Muzaffargarh
Mint marks

NOTE: The placing of Muzaffargarh under Khetri has been discontinued as recent research has shown that no rupees had ever been struck there.

ناگور
Nagor

پونه
Pune
(Muhiabad, Poona)

پوربندر
Purbandar

پرينده
Purenda

قمرنگر
Qamarnagar

قنوج
Qanauj
(Shahgarh Qanauj)

قندهار
Qandahar

راجاپور
Rajapur
(Islam Bandar)

رنتهور
Ranthambhor

رنتهور
Ranthor

رحتاس رهتاس
Rohtas
(Ruhtas)

سعدنگر
Sadnagar
(see Asadnagar)

سهارنپور
Saharanpur

سرهند سهرند
Sahrind
(Sarhind)

سيمور
Saimur

سليم اباد
Salimabad
(Ajmer)

سنبل
Sambhal

سانبهر
Sambhar

سنگمنر
Sangamner

سارنگپور
Sarangpur

سرهند سهرند
Sarhind
(Sahrind)
Mint marks

ستارا
Satara

شاه اباد قنوج
Shahabad Qanauj

شاه اباد قنوج
Shahgarh Qanauj

شاه جهان اباد
Shahjahanabad
(Dehli)
Mint marks

Obverse

Reverse

NOTE: The size of the Shahjahanabad rupees of Shah Alam II was subject to a wide variance. The early issues tended to be normal size for the hammered coinage (about 22mm). As the power of the emperor waned, the flan size of the Shahjahanabad rupees waxed, reflecting the increasingly ceremonial role of the coinage. The later coins should not be confused with the Nazarana (presentation) coins, which always show a full border design around the legend.

شكولا
Shakola

شيرگره
Shergarh

شيركوت
Sherkot

شيرپور
Sherpur

شولاپور
Sholapur

سيكاكل
Sikakul

سكندره
Sikandarah

سند
Sind

سرونج
Sironj

سيتاپور
Sitapur

سرينگر
Srinagar
(Kashmir)

سورت
Surat

The Nawab of Surat continued to issue coins in the name of his nominal Mughal suzerain Shah Alam II until the British took over Surat and its mint in 1800AD (AH1214/5), Shah Alam's 43rd regnal year. These coin types of the Nawab of Surat were replicated by the British East India Company in Surat using privy mark #1 and the frozen regnal year 46 of Shah Alam II, see Bombay Presidency types KM#209.1, 210.1, 211.1, 212.1 and 214.

تدپتري
Tadpatri

تانده
Tanda
(Akbarpur)

تراپتري
Tarpatri

تته
Tatta

تورگل توراگال
Toragal

اوديپور اديپور
Udaipur
(Muhammadabad)

ادگير
Udgir

Ujjain

Ujjainpur

Umarkot
(in Sind)

Urdu

Urdu Dar Rah-i-Dakhan

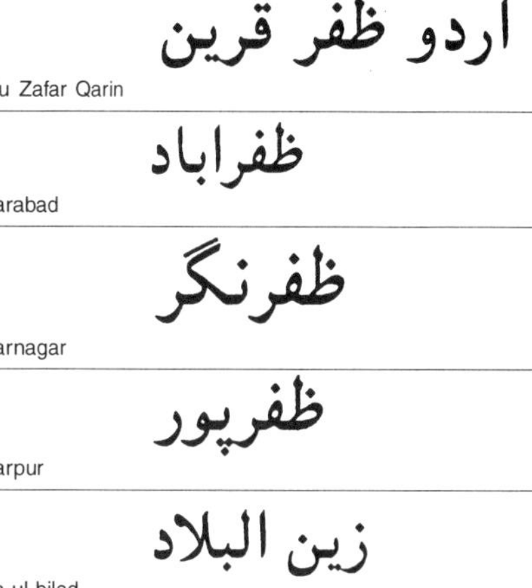

Urdu Zafar Qarin

Zafarabad

Zafarnagar

Zafarpur

Zain-ul-bilad
(Ahmadabad)

MINT EPITHETS

Mughal mintnames were often accompanied by honorific epithets. Quite often the epithet is visible on the flan when the mintname is absent or cut; in such cases the epithet is the best identification for the coin's mint of issue.

I. Geographical Terms:

بلدات
Baldat
City - Agra, Allahabad, Burhanpur, Bikanir, Sirhind, Ujjain

بندر
Bandar
Port - Dewal, Lahri

داخل
Dakhil
Breach (in Fort) - Chitor

خطة
Khitta
District - Awadh, Kalpi, Kashmir, Lakhnau

قصبة
Qasba
Town - Panipat, Sherkot

قلعة قلع
Qila
Fort - Agra, Alwar, Gwalior, Punch

قلع
Qila (var.)
Fort - Agra, Alwar, Gwalior, Punch

قلعة مقام
Qila Muqam
Fort Residence - Gwalior

قطة
Qita
District - Bareli

سركار
Sarkar
County - Lakhnau

شهر
Shahr
City - Anhirwala Pattan

سوبة
Suba
Province - Awadh

ترتة

Tirtha
Shrine - Hardwar

II. Poetic Allusion:

بلدات فخيرة

Baldat-i-Fakhira
Splendid City - Burhanpur

بندر مبارك

Bandar-i-Mubarak
Blessed Port - Surat

دار الامان

Dar-ul-Aman
Seat of Safety - Agra, Jammun, Multan, Sirhind

دار البركات

Dar-ul-Barakat
Seat of Blessings - Nagor

دار الفتح

Dar-ul-Fath
Seat of Conquest - Ujjain

دار الاسلام

Dar-ul-Islam
Seat of Islam - Dogaon, Mandisor

دار الجهاد

Dar-ul-Jihad
Seat of Holy War - Haidarabad

دار الخير

Dar-ul-Khair
Seat of Welfare - Ajmer

دار الخلافة

Dar-ul-Khilafat
Capital (Seat of Caliphate) - Agra, Ahmadabad, Akbarabad, Akbarpur Tanda, Awadh, Bahraich, Daulatabad, Dogaon, Gorakhpur, Gwalior, Jaunpur,
Lahore, Lakhnau, Malpur, Shahgarh Qanauj, Shahjahanabad

دار المنصور

Dar-ul-Mansur
Seat of the Victorious - Ajmer, Jodhpur

دار الملك

Dar-ul-Mulk
Capital (Seat of the Kingdom) - Dehli, Fathpur, Kabul

دار السلام

Dar-us-Salam
Seat of Peace - Dogaon

دار السرور

Dar-us-Sarur
Seat of Delight - Burhanpur, Saharanpur

دارالسلطنت

Dar-us-Sultanat
Seat of Sovereignty - Ahmadabad, Burhanpur, Fathpur, Kora, Lahore

دار الظفر

Dar-uz-Zafar
Seat of Victory - Advani, Bijapur

دار الضرب

Dar-uz-Zarb
Seat of the Mint - Jaunpur, Kalpi, Patna

فرخنده بنياد

Farkhanda Bunyad
Of Auspicious Foundation - Haidarabad

حضرت

Hazrat
Venerable - Dehli

خجستة بنياد

Khujista Bunyad
Of Fortunate Foundation - Aurangabad

مستقر الخلافة

Mustaqir-ul-Khilafat
Abode of the Caliphate - Akbarabad, Ajmer

مستقر الملك

Mustaqir-ul-Mulk
Abode of the Kingdom - Akbarabad, Azimabad

سواي

Sawai-
1/4 (A Notch Better) - Jaipur

زين البلاد

Zain-ul-Bilad
Beauty of Cities - Ahmadabad

DATING

The Mughal coins were dated both in the Hejira era and in the regnal era of each emperor. The four-digit Hejira year usually was shown on the obverse, with the one or two-digit regnal (jalus) year on the reverse. Since the regnal and calendar years did not coincide, it was common for two different regnal years to appear on the coins produced during any calendar year. The first jalus year of each reign was usually written as a word, *ahd,* rather than as a numeral.

An exception to the foregoing is that the date on certain coins struck in the Islamic millenial year AH1000 is sometimes represented by the Arabic word *Alf,* meaning,"one thousand". This device was especially used by the Urdu Zafar Qarin Mint.

THE ILAHI ERA

In his 29th regnal year Akbar determined to use a regnal era based on solar years in his administration, instead of the Hejira or Era of the Hegira based on lunar years. The new dating system appeared on the coins the same year, and continued until Akbar's death in Year 50. Mints gradually changed their usage from AH to Ilahi, although some did not convert. During the Ilahi period, many of the mints included the Persian month names as well as year of issue. Use of Ilahi dates continued into the reign of Shah Jahan.

Synchronization of Ilahi, Hejira and AD Eras:

Ilahi	Hejira	AD
Ilahi 30	AH993/4	1585/6
Ilahi 31	AH994/5	1586/7
Ilahi 32	AH995/6	1587/8
Ilahi 33	AH996/7	1588/9
Ilahi 34	AH997/8	1589/90
Ilahi 35	AH998/9	1590/1
Ilahi 36	AH999/1000	1591/2
Ilahi 37	AH1000	1592/3
Ilahi 38	AH1001/2	1593/4
Ilahi 39	AH1002/3	1594/5
Ilahi 40	AH1003/4	1595/6
Ilahi 41	1004/5	1596/7
Ilahi 42	1005/6	1597/8
Ilahi 43	1006/7	1598/9
Ilahi 44	1007/8	1599/1600
Ilahi 45	1008/9	1600/1
Ilahi 46	1009/10	1601/2
Ilahi 47	1010/11	1602/3
Ilahi 48	1011/12	1603/4
Ilahi 49	1012/13	1604/5
Ilahi 50	1013/14	1605/6
Ilahi 51	1014/15	1606/7

Ilahi months:

فروردين

(1) Farwardin

ارديبهشت

(2) Ardibihisht

خرداد

(3) Khurdad

تير

(4) Tir

امرداد

(5) Amardad

شهريور

(6) Shahrewar

مهر

(7) Mihr

آبان

(8) Aban

آذر

(9) Azar

دى

(10) Di

بهمن

(11) Bahman

اسفندارمز

(12) Isfandarmuz

STANDARD COIN PATTERN

The Mughal Rupees and Mohurs from the time of Aurangzeb (d.1707AD), generally followed a standard pattern of layout.

Obverse:

Inscription, (read right to left, bottom to top) 'Auspicious coin of the fighter of infidels, the emperor of Shah Alam'.

Reverse:

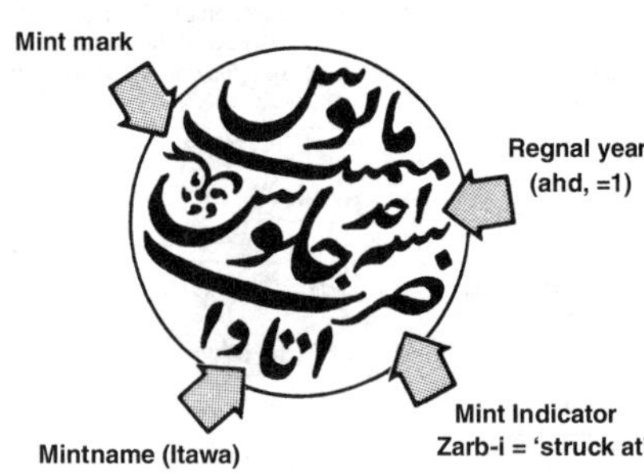

Inscription, (read right to left, bottom to top) 'Struck in Itawa in the Year One of the accession associated with prosperity'.

There are many variations of this layout, especially as to the poetic couplet containing the ruler's name on the obverse. In general however the provincial mints and independent state mints used the simple standard pattern.

MOHUR

First general issue in gold, the mohur with Hejira dating. All mohurs during Akbar's first thirty years (and some thereafter) carried the Kalima on the obverse and his name and titles on the reverse. They maintained the same weight standard, around 11 grams. Planchets were regularly round except for the rare lozenge-shaped "mehrabi" and some square types after AH987. There was much variety in borders and ornamentation, and some in royal titulature.

Largesse Coinage

Nisar

The nisar, literally scattering coins, were lightweight silver and gold coins minted especially as largesse money to be scattered amongst the crowd during festival processions and such-like state occasions. The coins were struck to 1/32 rupee, 1/16 rupee, 1/8 rupee, 1/4 rupee and 1/2 rupee weights. To better economize, they were very thin with wide flans, appearing more generous than was the case. All coins bore the name nisar, and the different weights should not be considered separate denominations, since this was ceremonial and not circulating currency. The 1/4 rupee weight is encountered more frequently while specimens struck in the other weights remain quite rare.

EMPIRE

Muhayyi-ud-din Aurangzeb Alamgir
AH1068-1118 / 1658-1707AD

HAMMERED COINAGE

Mint: Narnol
KM# 280.2 1/8 PAISA
Copper **Note:** Weight varies 1.9 - 2.2 grams.

Date	Mintage	Good	VG	F	VF	XF
ND(1658-1707)	—	2.50	6.00	12.00	20.00	—

Mint: Haidarabad
KM# 281.3 1/4 PAISA
Copper **Note:** Weight varies 3.90-4.05 grams.

Date	Mintage	Good	VG	F	VF	XF
ND(1658-1707)	—	5.50	11.00	18.00	30.00	—

Mint: Haidarabad
KM# 282.3 1/4 PAISA
Copper **Note:**

Date	Mintage	Good	VG	F	VF	XF
AH112x	—	5.50	11.00	18.00	30.00	—

Mint: Surat
KM# 282.2 1/4 PAISA
Copper **Note:** Weight varies 3.90-4.05 grams.

Date	Mintage	Good	VG	F	VF	XF
ND(1658-1707)	—	5.50	11.00	18.00	30.00	—

Mint: Bijapur
KM# 283.7 1/2 PAISA
Copper **Note:** Weight varies 6.15-7.05 grams.

Date	Mintage	Good	VG	F	VF	XF
AHxxxx//x	—	—	—	—	—	—

Mint: Elichpur
KM# 283.9 1/2 PAISA
Copper **Note:** Weight varies 6.15-7.05 grams.

Date	Mintage	Good	VG	F	VF	XF
AH1113//xx	—	—	—	—	—	—

Mint: Haidarabad (Farkhanda Bunyad)
KM# 283.1 1/2 PAISA
Copper **Note:** Weight varies 6.15-7.05 grams.

Date	Mintage	Good	VG	F	VF	XF
AH1114//4x	—	4.00	8.50	14.00	20.00	—

Mint: Macchlipattan
KM# 283.2 1/2 PAISA
Copper **Obv:** Inscription **Rev:** Inscription **Note:** Weight varies 6.15-7.05 grams.

Date	Mintage	Good	VG	F	VF	XF
AH1113//xx	—	5.50	11.00	25.00	40.00	—
AH1114//47	—	5.50	11.00	25.00	40.00	—
AH117/50	—	5.50	11.00	25.00	40.00	—
AH1118//50	—	5.50	11.00	25.00	40.00	—
AH1118//51	—	5.50	11.00	25.00	40.00	—

Mint: Mailapur
KM# 283.5 1/2 PAISA
Copper **Note:** Weight varies 6.15-7.05 grams.

Date	Mintage	Good	VG	F	VF	XF
AH1116//4x Rare	—	—	—	—	—	—

Mint: Sholapur
KM# 283.4 1/2 PAISA
Copper **Note:** Weight varies 6.15-7.05 grams.

Date	Mintage	Good	VG	F	VF	XF
ND(1658-1707)	—	2.75	5.50	12.00	20.00	—

Mint: Akbarnagar
KM# 285.27 PAISA
Copper **Note:** Weight varies 12.3 - 14.1 grams.

Date	Mintage	Good	VG	F	VF	XF
AHxxxx//49	—	—	—	—	—	—

Mint: Banaras
KM# 285.25 PAISA
Copper **Note:** Weight varies 12.30-14.10 grams.

Date	Mintage	Good	VG	F	VF	XF
ND(1658-1707)	—	—	—	—	—	—

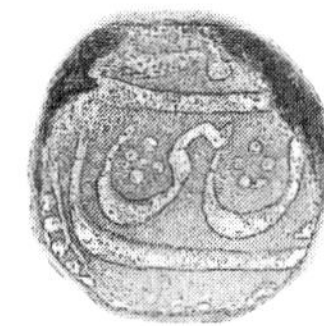

Mint: Bijapur
KM# 285.21 PAISA
Copper **Note:** Weight varies 12.3 - 14.1 grams.

Date	Mintage	Good	VG	F	VF	XF
ND(1658-1707)	—	5.50	11.00	18.00	30.00	—

Mint: Chinapattan
KM# 285.23 PAISA
Copper **Note:** Weight varies 12.3 - 14.1 grams.

Date	Mintage	Good	VG	F	VF	XF
ND(1658-1707)	—	5.50	11.00	20.00	35.00	—

Mint: Elichpur
KM# 285.17 PAISA
Copper **Note:** Weight varies 12.30-14.10 grams.

Date	Mintage	Good	VG	F	VF	XF
AH111x//48	—	5.50	11.00	20.00	35.00	—

Mint: Haidarabad (Farkhanda Bunyad)
KM# 285.3 PAISA
Copper **Note:** Weight varies 12.3 - 14.1 grams.

Date	Mintage	Good	VG	F	VF	XF
AH1113//46	—	2.75	5.50	9.00	15.00	—
AH1116//49	—	2.75	5.50	9.00	15.00	—

Mint: Lahore
KM# 285.5 PAISA
Copper **Note:** Weight varies 12.30-14.10 grams.

Date	Mintage	Good	VG	F	VF	XF
AH111x//49	—	2.75	5.50	9.00	15.00	—

Mint: Macchlipattan
KM# 285.6 PAISA
Copper **Obv:** Inscription, date **Rev:** Inscription **Note:** Weight varies 12.30-14.10 grams.

Date	Mintage	Good	VG	F	VF	XF
AH1113//45	—	2.25	4.50	12.00	25.00	—
AH1114//46	—	2.25	4.50	12.00	25.00	—
AH111x//47	—	2.25	4.50	12.00	25.00	—
AH1115//48	—	2.25	4.50	12.00	25.00	—
AH1116//49	—	2.25	4.50	12.00	25.00	—
AH1117//49	—	2.25	4.50	12.00	25.00	—
AH1118//50	—	2.25	4.50	12.00	25.00	—

Mint: Murshidabad
KM# 285.16 PAISA
Copper **Note:** Weight varies 12.30-14.10 grams.

Date	Mintage	Good	VG	F	VF	XF
AH111x//49	—	5.50	11.00	18.00	30.00	—

Mint: Patna
KM# 285.28 PAISA
Copper **Note:** Weight varies 12.3 - 14.1 grams.

Date	Mintage	Good	VG	F	VF	XF
AHxxxx//x	—	—	—	—	—	—

Mint: Surat
KM# 285.11 PAISA
Copper **Obv:** Inscription **Rev:** Inscription **Note:** Weight varies 12.30-14.10 grams.

Date	Mintage	Good	VG	F	VF	XF
AH1115//4x	—	2.75	5.50	9.00	15.00	—

Mint: Burhanpur
KM# A292.1 1/8 RUPEE
1.4300 g., Silver **Obv:** Couplet legend. **Shape:** Square. **Note:**

Date	Mintage	Good	VG	F	VF	XF
ND(1658-1707)	—	—	—	—	—	—

Mint: Bijapur
KM# 292.2 1/8 RUPEE
Silver **Obv:** Inscription, star, date **Rev:** Inscription, star **Note:** Weight varies 1.38-1.45 grams.

Date	Mintage	Good	VG	F	VF	XF
AH1114//4x	—	8.00	20.00	45.00	85.00	135

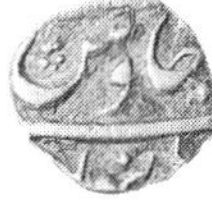

Mint: Burhanpur
KM# 292.4 1/8 RUPEE
Silver **Obv:** Inscription **Rev:** Inscription **Note:** Weight varies 1.38-1.45 grams.

Date	Mintage	Good	VG	F	VF	XF
ND	—	—	20.00	45.00	85.00	135

Mint: Ujjain
KM# 292.5 1/8 RUPEE
1.4300 g., Silver **Obv:** Inscription **Rev:** Inscription **Note:** Weight varies 1.38-1.45 grams.

Date	Mintage	Good	VG	F	VF	XF
ND	—	8.00	20.00	45.00	85.00	135

Mint: Burhanpur
KM# A293.1 1/4 RUPEE
2.8610 g., Silver **Obv:** Inscription **Rev:** Inscription **Shape:** Square **Note:** Weight varies: 2.75-2.90 grams.

Date	Mintage	Good	VG	F	VF	XF
ND Rare	—	—	—	—	—	—

Mint: Bareli
KM# 293.10 1/4 RUPEE
Silver **Note:** Weight varies 2.75-2.90 grams.

Date	Mintage	Good	VG	F	VF	XF
AH1117//49	—	—	—	—	—	—

Mint: Machhilipattan Bandar
KM# 293.4 1/4 RUPEE
Silver **Note:** Weight varies 2.75-2.90 grams.

Date	Mintage	Good	VG	F	VF	XF
AH1113//xx	—	6.00	15.00	35.00	75.00	125

Mint: Surat
KM# 293.17 1/4 RUPEE
2.8610 g., Silver **Note:** Weight varies 2.75-2.90 grams.

Date	Mintage	Good	VG	F	VF	XF
AH1114	—	—	—	—	—	—

Mint: Ujjain
KM# 293.5 1/4 RUPEE
Silver **Obv:** Inscription **Rev. Inscription:** Dar-ul Fath **Note:** Weight varies 2.75-2.90 grams.

Date	Mintage	Good	VG	F	VF	XF
AH111x//5x	—	6.00	15.00	35.00	75.00	125

Mint: Ahmadabad
KM# 294.1 1/2 RUPEE
Silver **Note:** Weight varies: 5.50-5.80 grams.

Date	Mintage	Good	VG	F	VF	XF
AH1117//50	—	10.00	15.00	35.00	75.00	150
AH1118//50	—	10.00	15.00	35.00	75.00	135

Mint: Ahmadanagar
KM# 294.18 1/2 RUPEE
Silver **Note:** Weight varies 5.50-5.80 grams.

Date	Mintage	Good	VG	F	VF	XF
AH1116//4x	—	—	—	—	—	—

Mint: Azimabad
KM# 294.8 1/2 RUPEE
Silver **Note:** Weight varies 5.50-5.80 grams.

Date	Mintage	Good	VG	F	VF	XF
AH1118//50	—	10.00	25.00	50.00	90.00	150

Mint: Bijapur
KM# 294.19 1/2 RUPEE
Silver **Obv:** Inscription **Rev. Inscription:** Dav uz Zafar **Note:** Weight varies 5.50-5.80 grams.

Date	Mintage	Good	VG	F	VF	XF
AH1113//45	—	—	—	—	—	—

Mint: Haidarabad
KM# 294.9 1/2 RUPEE
Silver **Note:** Weight varies 5.50-5.80 grams. This is a Nizam coin.

Date	Mintage	Good	VG	F	VF	XF
AH1113//45	—	10.00	25.00	50.00	90.00	150
AH1115//48	—	10.00	25.00	50.00	90.00	150

Mint: Kambayat
KM# 294.20 1/2 RUPEE
Silver **Note:** Weight varies 5.50-5.80 grams.

Date	Mintage	Good	VG	F	VF	XF
AH1113//45	—	—	—	—	—	—

Mint: Nusratabad
KM# 294.17 1/2 RUPEE
Silver **Note:** Weight varies 5.50-5.80 grams.

Date	Mintage	Good	VG	F	VF	XF
AH1113//45	—	—	—	—	—	—
AH1115//48	—	—	—	—	—	—

Mint: Surat
KM# 294.6 1/2 RUPEE
Silver **Rev:** Without mint epithet **Note:** Weight varies 5.50-5.80 grams.

Date	Mintage	Good	VG	F	VF	XF
AH1113//46	—	2.50	6.00	12.00	20.00	30.00
AH1113//45	—	2.50	6.00	12.00	20.00	30.00
AH1114//46	—	2.50	6.00	12.00	20.00	30.00
AH1114//47	—	2.50	6.00	12.00	20.00	30.00
AH1115//47	—	2.50	6.00	12.00	20.00	30.00
AH1115//48	—	2.50	6.00	12.00	20.00	30.00
AH1116//48	—	2.50	6.00	12.00	20.00	30.00
AH1117//49	—	2.50	6.00	12.00	20.00	30.00
AH1118//50	—	2.50	6.00	12.00	20.00	30.00
AH1118//51	—	2.50	6.00	12.00	20.00	30.00

Mint: Zafarabad
KM# 294.23 1/2 RUPEE
Silver **Note:** Weight varies 5.50-5.80 grams.

Date	Mintage	Good	VG	F	VF	XF
AH1114//46	—	—	—	—	—	—

Mint: Ahmadabad
KM# 300.2 RUPEE
Silver **Obv:** Poetic couplet **Rev:** Inscription **Note:** Weight varies 11.00-11.60 grams.

Date	Mintage	Good	VG	F	VF	XF
AH1116//xx	—	—	5.00	10.00	17.50	27.50
AH1117//49	—	—	5.00	10.00	17.50	27.50
AH1117//50	—	—	5.00	10.00	17.50	27.50
AH1118//50	—	—	5.00	10.00	17.50	27.50
AH1118//51	—	—	5.00	10.00	17.50	27.50
AH1119//51	—	—	5.00	10.00	17.50	27.50

Mint: Ahmadanagar
KM# 300.3 RUPEE
Silver **Note:** Weight varies 11.00-11.60 grams.

Date	Mintage	Good	VG	F	VF	XF
AH1115//48	—	5.00	7.00	10.00	17.50	27.50
AH1115//47	—	5.00	7.00	10.00	17.50	27.50
AH1116//48	—	5.00	7.00	10.00	17.50	27.50
AH1116//49	—	5.00	7.00	10.00	17.50	27.50
AH1117//49	—	5.00	7.00	10.00	17.50	27.50
AH1117//50	—	5.00	7.00	10.00	17.50	27.50
AH1118//50	—	5.00	7.00	10.00	17.50	27.50
AH1118//51	—	5.00	7.00	10.00	17.50	27.50

Mint: Ahsanabad
KM# 300.4 RUPEE
Silver **Note:** Weight varies 11.00-11.60 grams.

Date	Mintage	Good	VG	F	VF	XF
AH1113//45	—	5.00	8.00	12.00	20.00	32.50
AH1113//46	—	5.00	8.00	12.00	20.00	32.50
AH1115//47	—	5.00	8.00	12.00	20.00	32.50
AH1115//48	—	5.00	8.00	12.00	20.00	32.50
AH1116//48	—	5.00	8.00	12.00	20.00	32.50
AH1116//49	—	5.00	8.00	12.00	20.00	32.50
AH1117//50	—	5.00	8.00	12.00	20.00	32.50
AH1118//51	—	5.00	8.00	12.00	20.00	32.50

Mint: Ajmer
KM# 300.5 RUPEE
Silver **Obv:** Inscription, date **Rev. Inscription:** Dar-ul-Khair **Note:** Weight varies 11.00-11.60 grams.

Date	Mintage	Good	VG	F	VF	XF
AH1112//45	—	5.00	8.00	12.00	20.00	32.50
AH1113//xx	—	5.00	8.00	12.00	20.00	32.50
AH1114//46	—	5.00	8.00	12.00	20.00	32.50
AH1114//47	—	5.00	8.00	12.00	20.00	32.50
AH1115//47	—	5.00	8.00	12.00	20.00	32.50
AH1115//48	—	5.00	8.00	12.00	20.00	32.50
AH1116//48	—	5.00	8.00	12.00	20.00	32.50
AH1116//49	—	5.00	8.00	12.00	20.00	32.50
AH1117//49	—	5.00	8.00	12.00	20.00	32.50
AH1117//50	—	5.00	8.00	12.00	20.00	32.50
AH1118//50	—	5.00	8.00	12.00	20.00	32.50
AH1118//51	—	5.00	8.00	12.00	20.00	32.50

Mint: Akbarabad
KM# 300.6 RUPEE
Silver **Obv:** Mustagir-ul-Khirafa **Rev. Inscription:** Inscription **Note:** Weight varies 11.00-11.60 grams.

Date	Mintage	Good	VG	F	VF	XF
AH1113//xx	—	5.00	7.00	10.00	17.50	27.50
AH1114//46	—	5.00	7.00	10.00	17.50	27.50
AH1114//47	—	5.00	7.00	10.00	17.50	27.50
AH1115//47	—	5.00	7.00	10.00	17.50	27.50
AH1115//48	—	5.00	7.00	10.00	17.50	27.50
AH1116//48	—	5.00	7.00	10.00	17.50	27.50
AH1116//49	—	5.00	7.00	10.00	17.50	27.50
AH1117//49	—	5.00	7.00	10.00	17.50	27.50
AH1117//50	—	5.00	7.00	10.00	17.50	27.50
AH1118//50	—	5.00	7.00	10.00	17.50	27.50
AH1118//51	—	5.00	7.00	10.00	17.50	27.50
AH-//51	—	5.00	7.00	10.00	17.50	27.50

Mint: Akbarnagar
KM# 300.100 RUPEE
11.4440 g., Silver **Note:** "Badr" couplet

Date	Mintage	Good	VG	F	VF	XF
AH1113//45	—	—	—	—	—	—

Mint: Akbarnagar
KM# 300.7 RUPEE
Silver **Note:** "Mihr" couplet; Weight varies 11.00-11.60 grams.

Date	Mintage	Good	VG	F	VF	XF
AH1113//46	—	5.00	7.00	10.00	17.50	27.50
AH1113//xx	—	5.00	7.00	10.00	17.50	27.50
AH1114//46	—	5.00	7.00	10.00	17.50	27.50
AH1114//47	—	5.00	7.00	10.00	17.50	27.50
AH1115//47	—	5.00	7.00	10.00	17.50	27.50
AH1115//48	—	5.00	7.00	10.00	17.50	27.50
AH1116//48	—	5.00	7.00	10.00	17.50	27.50
AH1116//49	—	5.00	7.00	10.00	17.50	27.50
AH1117//49	—	5.00	7.00	10.00	17.50	27.50
AH1117//50	—	5.00	7.00	10.00	17.50	27.50
AH1118//50	—	5.00	7.00	10.00	17.50	27.50
AH1118//51	—	5.00	7.00	10.00	17.50	27.50

Mint: Alamgirpur
KM# 300.10 RUPEE
Silver **Rev:** Mint name at bottom **Note:** Weight varies 11.00-11.60 grams.

Date	Mintage	Good	VG	F	VF	XF
AH1113//45	—	5.00	8.00	13.50	22.50	35.00
AH111x//47	—	5.00	8.00	13.50	22.50	35.00
AHxxxx//48	—	5.00	8.00	13.50	22.50	35.00
AH111x//51	—	5.00	8.00	13.50	22.50	35.00

Mint: Allahabad
KM# 300.12 RUPEE
Silver **Obv:** Inscription **Rev:** "badr" couplets, mint name at bottom **Note:** Weight varies 11.00-11.60 grams.

Date	Mintage	Good	VG	F	VF	XF
AH111x//45	—	5.00	7.00	10.00	17.50	27.50
AH1115//48	—	5.00	7.00	10.00	17.50	27.50

Mint: Azamnagar
KM# 300.15 RUPEE
Silver **Note:** Weight varies 11.00-11.60 grams.

Date	Mintage	Good	VG	F	VF	XF
AH1117//48 (sic)	—	7.00	18.00	25.00	35.00	50.00
xxxx//49	—	7.00	—	—	—	—
AH111x//50	—	7.00	18.00	25.00	35.00	50.00

Mint: Azimabad
KM# 300.16 RUPEE
Silver **Note:** Weight varies 11.00-11.60 grams. For earlier issues see Patna, KM#300.71.

Date	Mintage	Good	VG	F	VF	XF
AH1117//50	—	5.00	8.00	13.50	22.50	35.00
AH1118//50	—	5.00	8.00	13.50	22.50	35.00
AH1118//51	—	5.00	8.00	13.50	22.50	35.00
AH1119//51	—	5.00	8.00	13.50	22.50	35.00

Mint: Bankapur
KM# 300.18 RUPEE
Silver **Note:** Weight varies 11.00-11.60 grams.

Date	Mintage	Good	VG	F	VF	XF
AHxxxx//44	—	8.00	20.00	30.00	45.00	75.00
AH1113//4x	—	8.00	20.00	30.00	45.00	75.00
AH1114//4x	—	8.00	20.00	30.00	45.00	75.00

Mint: Bareli
KM# 300.19 RUPEE

Silver **Obv:** Inscription, date **Rev:** Inscription **Note:** Weight varies 11.00-11.60 grams.

Date	Mintage	Good	VG	F	VF	XF
AH1113//45	—	5.00	7.00	10.00	17.50	27.50
AH1113//46	—	5.00	7.00	10.00	17.50	27.50
AH1114//4x	—	5.00	7.00	10.00	17.50	27.50
AH1114//47	—	5.00	7.00	10.00	17.50	27.50
AH1115//47	—	5.00	7.00	10.00	17.50	27.50
AH1115//48	—	5.00	7.00	10.00	17.50	27.50
AH1116//48	—	5.00	7.00	10.00	17.50	27.50
AH1116//49	—	5.00	7.00	10.00	17.50	27.50
AH1117//49	—	5.00	7.00	10.00	17.50	27.50
AH1117//50	—	5.00	7.00	10.00	17.50	27.50
AH1118//50	—	5.00	7.00	10.00	17.50	27.50
AH1118//51	—	5.00	7.00	10.00	17.50	27.50
AH1119//51	—	5.00	7.00	10.00	17.50	27.50

Mint: Bhakkar
KM# 300.20 RUPEE

Silver **Note:** Weight varies 11.00-11.60 grams.

Date	Mintage	Good	VG	F	VF	XF
AH1118//50	—	5.50	8.00	15.00	25.00	40.00

Mint: Bijapur
KM# 300.23 RUPEE

Silver **Obv:** Inscription **Rev. Inscription:** Dar-uz-Zafar **Note:** Weight varies 11.00-11.60 grams. Mint name exist in various arrangements.

Date	Mintage	Good	VG	F	VF	XF
AH1113//45	—	5.00	7.00	10.00	17.50	27.50
AH111x//46	—	5.00	7.00	10.00	17.50	27.50
AH1114//47	—	5.00	7.00	10.00	17.50	27.50
AH1115//47	—	5.00	7.00	10.00	17.50	27.50
AH1115//48	—	5.00	7.00	10.00	17.50	27.50
AH1116//48	—	5.00	7.00	10.00	17.50	27.50
AH1116//49	—	5.00	7.00	10.00	17.50	27.50
AH1117//49	—	5.00	7.00	10.00	17.50	27.50
AH1117//50	—	5.00	7.00	10.00	17.50	27.50
AH1118//50	—	5.00	7.00	10.00	17.50	27.50
AH1118//51	—	5.00	7.00	10.00	17.50	27.50

Mint: Burhanpur
KM# 300.24 RUPEE

Silver **Note:** "Badr" couplet; Weight varies 11.00-11.60 grams.

Date	Mintage	Good	VG	F	VF	XF
AH1113//45	—	5.00	7.00	10.00	17.50	27.50
AH1114//46	—	5.00	7.00	10.00	17.50	27.50
AH1114//47	—	5.00	7.00	10.00	17.50	27.50
AH1115//47	—	5.00	7.00	10.00	17.50	27.50
AH1115//48	—	5.00	7.00	10.00	17.50	27.50
AH1116//48	—	5.00	7.00	10.00	17.50	27.50
AH1116//49	—	5.00	7.00	10.00	17.50	27.50
AH1117//49	—	5.00	7.00	10.00	17.50	27.50
AH1117//50	—	5.00	7.00	10.00	17.50	27.50
AH1118//50	—	5.00	7.00	10.00	17.50	27.50
AH1118//51	—	5.00	7.00	10.00	17.50	27.50

Mint: Burhanpur
KM# 300.105 RUPEE

11.4440 g., Silver **Note:** "Mihr" couplet.

Date	Mintage	Good	VG	F	VF	XF
AH1115//47	—	—	—	—	—	—

Mint: Dicholi
KM# 300.106 RUPEE

Silver **Note:** Weight varies 11.00-11.60 grams.

Date	Mintage	Good	VG	F	VF	XF
AHxxxx//49	—	—	—	—	—	—

Mint: Elichpur
KM# 300.26 RUPEE

Silver **Note:** Weight varies 11.00-11.60 grams.

Date	Mintage	Good	VG	F	VF	XF
AH1117//49	—	5.00	8.00	16.00	28.00	45.00

Mint: Haidarabad
KM# 300.31 RUPEE

Silver **Obv:** Inscription **Rev. Inscription:** Dar-ul-Jihad **Note:** Weight varies 11.00-11.60 grams.

Date	Mintage	Good	VG	F	VF	XF
AH1113//45	—	5.00	7.50	12.00	20.00	30.00
AH1114//46	—	5.00	7.50	12.00	20.00	30.00
AH1114//47	—	5.00	7.50	12.00	20.00	30.00
AH1115//47	—	5.00	7.50	12.00	20.00	30.00
AH1115//48	—	5.00	7.50	12.00	20.00	30.00
AH1116//48	—	5.00	7.50	12.00	20.00	30.00
AH1116//49	—	5.00	7.50	12.00	20.00	30.00
AH1117//49	—	5.00	7.50	12.00	20.00	30.00
AH1117//50	—	5.00	7.50	12.00	20.00	30.00
AH1118//50	—	5.00	7.50	12.00	20.00	30.00

Mint: Haidarabad
KM# 300.32 RUPEE

Silver **Obv:** Inscription **Rev:** Inscription, without mint epithet **Note:** Weight varies 11.00-11.60 grams.

Date	Mintage	Good	VG	F	VF	XF
AH1118//51	—	—	7.50	15.00	25.00	40.00

Mint: Hukeri
KM# 300.33 RUPEE

Silver **Note:** Weight varies 11.00-11.60 grams.

Date	Mintage	Good	VG	F	VF	XF
AH1110//49 (sic)	—	—	—	—	—	—
AH111x//49 Rare	—	—	—	—	—	—

Mint: Islamnagar
KM# 300.38 RUPEE

Silver **Note:** Weight varies 11.00-11.60 grams.

Date	Mintage	Good	VG	F	VF	XF
AH1116//48 Rare	—	—	—	—	—	—
AH1116//49 Rare	—	—	—	—	—	—
AH1118//50 Rare	—	—	—	—	—	—
AH1118//51 Rare	—	—	—	—	—	—

Mint: Itawa
KM# 300.39 RUPEE

Silver **Obv:** Inscription **Rev:** Inscription **Note:** Weight varies 11.00-11.60 grams.

Date	Mintage	Good	VG	F	VF	XF
AH1113//45	—	5.00	7.00	10.00	17.50	27.50
AH1113//46	—	5.00	7.00	10.00	17.50	27.50
AH1114//46	—	5.00	7.00	10.00	17.50	27.50
AH1114//47	—	5.00	7.00	10.00	17.50	27.50
AH1115//47	—	5.00	7.00	10.00	17.50	27.50
AH1115//48	—	5.00	7.00	10.00	17.50	27.50
AH1116//48	—	5.00	7.00	10.00	17.50	27.50
AH1116//49	—	5.00	7.00	10.00	17.50	27.50
AH1117//49	—	5.00	7.00	10.00	17.50	27.50
AH1117//50	—	5.00	7.00	10.00	17.50	27.50
AH1118//50	—	5.00	7.00	10.00	17.50	27.50
AH1118//51	—	5.00	7.00	10.00	17.50	27.50

Mint: Jahangirnagar
KM# 300.108 RUPEE

11.4440 g., Silver **Rev:** Mint name at bottom **Note:** "Mihr" couplet.

Date	Mintage	Good	VG	F	VF	XF
AH1113//45	—	—	—	—	—	—

Mint: Jahangirnagar
KM# 300.40 RUPEE

Silver **Obv:** Inscription **Rev:** Inscription **Note:** Weight varies 11.00-11.60 grams.

Date	Mintage	Good	VG	F	VF	XF
AH1113//4x	—	5.00	7.00	10.00	17.50	27.50
AH1114//46	—	5.00	7.00	10.00	17.50	27.50
AH1115//47	—	5.00	7.00	10.00	17.50	27.50
AH1118//51	—	5.00	7.00	10.00	17.50	27.50

Mint: Junagadh
KM# 300.43 RUPEE

Silver **Note:** Weight varies 11.00-11.60 grams.

Date	Mintage	Good	VG	F	VF	XF
AH1113//4x	—	5.00	7.00	10.00	17.50	27.50
AH1114//46	—	5.00	7.00	10.00	17.50	27.50
AH1114//47	—	5.00	7.00	10.00	17.50	27.50
AH1115//47	—	5.00	7.00	10.00	17.50	27.50
AH1115//48	—	5.00	7.00	10.00	17.50	27.50
AH1116//48	—	5.00	7.00	10.00	17.50	27.50
AH1116//49	—	5.00	7.00	10.00	17.50	27.50
AH1117//49	—	5.00	7.00	10.00	17.50	27.50
AH1117//50	—	5.00	7.00	10.00	17.50	27.50
AH1118//50	—	5.00	7.00	10.00	17.50	27.50
AH1118//51	—	5.00	7.00	10.00	17.50	27.50
AH1119//51	—	5.00	7.00	10.00	17.50	27.50

Mint: Kabul
KM# 300.45 RUPEE

Silver **Obv:** Inscription **Rev. Inscription:** Dar-ul-Mulk and mint name **Note:** Weight varies 11.00-11.60 grams.

Date	Mintage	Good	VG	F	VF	XF
AH1114//xx	—	5.00	7.50	12.00	20.00	30.00
AH1115//47	—	5.00	7.50	12.00	20.00	30.00
AH1115//48	—	5.00	7.50	12.00	20.00	30.00
AH1116//48	—	5.00	7.50	12.00	20.00	30.00
AH1116//49	—	5.00	7.50	12.00	20.00	30.00
AH1117//49	—	5.00	7.50	12.00	20.00	30.00
AH1118//xx	—	5.00	7.50	12.00	20.00	30.00

Mint: Kanji
KM# 300.46 RUPEE

Silver **Note:** Weight varies: 11.00-11.60 grams.

Date	Mintage	Good	VG	F	VF	XF
AH11xx//45	—	6.00	15.00	28.00	45.00	65.00

Mint: Kashmir
KM# 300.48 RUPEE

Silver **Obv:** Couplet in three lines **Note:** Weight varies 11.00-11.60 grams.

Date	Mintage	Good	VG	F	VF	XF
AH111x//46	—	5.50	9.00	18.50	32.50	50.00
AH1115//4x	—	5.50	9.00	18.50	32.50	50.00
AH1116//48	—	5.50	9.00	18.50	32.50	50.00
AH1116//49	—	5.50	9.00	18.50	32.50	50.00
AH1117//49	—	5.50	9.00	18.50	32.50	50.00
AH1117//50	—	5.50	9.00	18.50	32.50	50.00

Mint: Kashmir
KM# 300.96 RUPEE

Silver **Obv:** Couplet in four lines **Rev:** Inscription **Note:** Weight varies 11.00-11.60 grams.

Date	Mintage	Good	VG	F	VF	XF
AH1117//49	—	—	8.00	20.00	35.00	60.00
AH1117//50	—	—	8.00	20.00	35.00	60.00
AH1118//50	—	—	8.00	20.00	35.00	60.00

Mint: Katak
KM# 300.50 RUPEE

Silver **Obv:** Inscription **Rev:** Mint name at bottom **Note:** "Badr" couplet; Weight varies 11.00-11.60 grams.

Date	Mintage	Good	VG	F	VF	XF
AH1112//45	—	5.00	7.50	12.00	20.00	30.00
AH1113//45	—	5.00	7.50	12.00	20.00	30.00
AH1113//46	—	5.00	7.50	12.00	20.00	30.00
AH1114//47	—	5.00	7.50	12.00	20.00	30.00
AH1116//49	—	5.00	7.50	12.00	20.00	30.00
AH1117//49	—	5.00	7.50	12.00	20.00	30.00
AH1117//50	—	5.00	7.50	12.00	20.00	30.00
AH1118//50	—	5.00	7.50	12.00	20.00	30.00
AH1118//51	—	5.00	7.50	12.00	20.00	30.00

Mint: Khambayat
KM# 300.51 RUPEE

Silver **Obv:** Inscription **Rev:** Mint name at bottom **Note:** "Badr" couplet; Weight varies 11.00-11.60 grams.

Date	Mintage	Good	VG	F	VF	XF
AH1113//4x	—	5.00	7.00	10.00	17.50	27.50
AH1114//46	—	5.00	7.00	10.00	17.50	27.50
AH1114//47	—	5.00	7.00	10.00	17.50	27.50
AH1115//47	—	5.00	7.00	10.00	17.50	27.50
AH1115//48	—	5.00	7.00	10.00	17.50	27.50
AH1116//48	—	5.00	7.00	10.00	17.50	27.50
AH1116//49	—	5.00	7.00	10.00	17.50	27.50
AH1117//49	—	5.00	7.00	10.00	17.50	27.50
AH1117//50	—	5.00	7.00	10.00	17.50	27.50
AH1118//50	—	5.00	7.00	10.00	17.50	27.50
AH1118//51	—	5.00	7.00	10.00	17.50	27.50

Mint: Khujista Bunyad
KM# 300.52 RUPEE

Silver **Obv:** Inscription **Rev:** Inscription **Note:** Weight varies 11.00-11.60 grams.

Date	Mintage	Good	VG	F	VF	XF
AH1113//46	—	5.00	7.50	12.00	20.00	30.00
AH1115//47	—	5.00	7.50	12.00	20.00	30.00

Date	Mintage	Good	VG	F	VF	XF
AH1115//48	—	5.00	7.50	12.00	20.00	30.00
AH1116//48	—	5.00	7.50	12.00	20.00	30.00
AH1116//49	—	5.00	7.50	12.00	20.00	30.00
AH1117//49	—	5.00	7.50	12.00	20.00	30.00
AH1117//50	—	5.00	7.50	12.00	20.00	30.00
AH1118//50	—	5.00	7.50	12.00	20.00	30.00
AH1118//51	—	5.00	7.50	12.00	20.00	30.00

Mint: Lahore
KM# 300.53 RUPEE

Silver **Obv:** Inscription **Rev. Inscription:** Dar-us-Sultanat and mint name **Note:** "Badr couplet"; Weight varies 11.00-11.60 grams.

Date	Mintage	Good	VG	F	VF	XF
AH1113//4x	—	5.00	7.00	10.00	17.50	27.50
AH1114//46	—	5.00	7.00	10.00	17.50	27.50
AH1114//47	—	5.00	7.00	10.00	17.50	27.50
AH1115//47	—	5.00	7.00	10.00	17.50	27.50
AH1115//48	—	5.00	7.00	10.00	17.50	27.50
AH1116//48	—	5.00	7.00	10.00	17.50	27.50
AH1116//49	—	5.00	7.00	10.00	17.50	27.50
AH1117//49	—	5.00	7.00	10.00	17.50	27.50
AH1117//50	—	5.00	7.00	10.00	17.50	27.50
AH1118//50	—	5.00	7.00	10.00	17.50	27.50
AH1118//51	—	5.00	7.00	10.00	17.50	27.50

Mint: Lakhnau
KM# 300.54 RUPEE

Silver **Obv:** Inscription **Rev:** Inscription **Note:** Weight varies 11.00-11.60 grams.

Date	Mintage	Good	VG	F	VF	XF
AH1113//46	—	5.00	7.00	10.00	17.50	27.50
AH1114//46	—	5.00	7.00	10.00	17.50	27.50
AH1114//47	—	5.00	7.00	10.00	17.50	27.50
AH1115//47	—	5.00	7.00	10.00	17.50	27.50
AH111x//48	—	5.00	7.00	10.00	17.50	27.50
AH1116//49	—	5.00	7.00	10.00	17.50	27.50
AH111x//50	—	5.00	7.00	10.00	17.50	27.50
AH111x//51	—	5.00	7.00	10.00	17.50	27.50

Mint: Macchlipattan
KM# 300.55 RUPEE

Silver **Note:** Weight varies 11.00-11.60 grams.

Date	Mintage	Good	VG	F	VF	XF
AH1113//45	—	5.00	8.00	16.00	28.00	40.00
AH1115//47	—	5.00	8.00	16.00	28.00	40.00
AH1115//48	—	5.00	8.00	16.00	28.00	40.00
AH1116//48	—	5.00	8.00	16.00	28.00	40.00
AH1116//49	—	5.00	8.00	16.00	28.00	40.00
AH1117//49	—	5.00	8.00	16.00	28.00	40.00
AH1117//50	—	5.00	8.00	16.00	28.00	40.00
AH1118//50	—	5.00	8.00	16.00	28.00	40.00
AH1118//51	—	5.00	8.00	16.00	28.00	40.00

Mint: Mahmud Bandar
KM# 300.56 RUPEE

Silver **Note:** Weight varies 11.00-11.60 grams.

Date	Mintage	Good	VG	F	VF	XF
AH1119//51 Rare	—	—	—	—	—	—

Mint: Mailapur
KM# 300.57 RUPEE

Silver **Note:** Weight varies 11.00-11.60 grams.

Date	Mintage	Good	VG	F	VF	XF
AH1114//47	—	6.00	16.00	32.00	55.00	80.00
AH1118//50	—	6.00	16.00	32.00	55.00	80.00
AH1118//51	—	6.00	16.00	32.00	55.00	80.00

Mint: Makhsusabad
KM# 300.58 RUPEE

Silver **Obv:** Inscription, date **Rev:** Inscription **Note:** Weight varies 11.00-11.60 grams. For later isues see Murshidabad, KM#300.65.

Date	Mintage	Good	VG	F	VF	XF
AH1115//48	—	5.50	14.00	28.50	48.00	75.00
AH1116//48	—	5.50	14.00	28.50	48.00	75.00
AH1116//49	—	5.50	14.00	28.50	48.00	75.00

Mint: Multan
KM# 300.63 RUPEE

Silver **Obv:** Inscription **Rev:** Inscription, without mint epithet, mint name at bottom **Note:** Weight varies 11.00-11.60 grams.

Date	Mintage	Good	VG	F	VF	XF
AH1114//47	—	5.00	7.00	10.00	17.50	27.50
AH1115//47	—	5.00	7.00	10.00	17.50	27.50
AH1115//48	—	5.00	7.00	10.00	17.50	27.50
AH1116//48	—	5.00	7.00	10.00	17.50	27.50
AH1116//49	—	5.00	7.00	10.00	17.50	27.50
AH1117//49	—	5.00	7.00	10.00	17.50	27.50
AH1117//50	—	5.00	7.00	10.00	17.50	27.50
AH1118//50	—	5.00	7.00	10.00	17.50	27.50
AH1118//51	—	5.00	7.00	10.00	17.50	27.50
AH1119//51	—	5.00	7.00	10.00	17.50	27.50

Mint: Murshidabad
KM# 300.65 RUPEE

Silver **Note:** Weight varies 11.00-11.60 grams. For earlier issues see Makhsusabad, KM#300.58.

Date	Mintage	Good	VG	F	VF	XF
AH1116//48	—	5.00	7.00	13.50	22.50	32.50
AH1116//49	—	5.00	7.00	13.50	22.50	32.50
AH1117//49	—	5.00	7.00	13.50	22.50	32.50
AH1117//50	—	5.00	7.00	13.50	22.50	32.50
AH1118//50	—	5.00	7.00	13.50	22.50	32.50
AH1118//51	—	5.00	7.00	13.50	22.50	32.50

Mint: Nusratabad
KM# 300.68 RUPEE

Silver **Note:** Weight varies 11.00-11.60 grams.

Date	Mintage	Good	VG	F	VF	XF
AH1114//47	—	5.50	9.00	18.00	30.00	45.00
AH1115//47	—	5.50	9.00	18.00	30.00	45.00
AH111x//48	—	5.50	9.00	18.00	30.00	45.00
AHxxxx//48	—	5.50	9.00	18.00	30.00	45.00
AH111x//49	—	5.50	9.00	18.00	30.00	45.00
AH111x//50	—	5.50	9.00	18.00	30.00	45.00
AH1118//51	—	5.50	9.00	18.00	30.00	45.00

Mint: Parenda
KM# 300.70 RUPEE

Silver **Note:** Weight varies 11.00-11.60 grams.

Date	Mintage	Good	VG	F	VF	XF
AH1116//48	—	5.50	11.00	22.00	35.00	50.00
AH1116//49	—	5.50	11.00	22.00	35.00	50.00
AH1117//49	—	5.50	11.00	22.00	35.00	50.00
AH1117//50	—	5.50	11.00	22.00	35.00	50.00
AH1118//50	—	5.50	11.00	22.00	35.00	50.00
AH1118//51	—	5.50	11.00	22.00	35.00	50.00

Mint: Patna
KM# 300.71 RUPEE

Silver **Note:** Weight varies 11.00-11.60 grams. For later issues see Azimabad, KM#300.16.

Date	Mintage	Good	VG	F	VF	XF
AH1113//45	—	5.00	7.00	10.00	17.50	27.50
AH1113//46	—	5.00	7.00	10.00	17.50	27.50
AH1114//46	—	5.00	7.00	10.00	17.50	27.50
AH1114//47	—	5.00	7.00	10.00	17.50	27.50
AH1115//47	—	5.00	7.00	10.00	17.50	27.50
AH1115//48	—	5.00	7.00	10.00	17.50	27.50
AH1116//48	—	5.00	7.00	10.00	17.50	27.50
AH1116//49	—	5.00	7.00	10.00	17.50	27.50
AH1117//49	—	5.00	7.00	10.00	17.50	27.50

Mint: Pune
KM# 300.74 RUPEE

Silver **Rev:** Without mint epithet; mint name at bottom **Note:** Weight varies: 11.00-11.60 grams.

Date	Mintage	Good	VG	F	VF	XF
AH111x/45 Rare	—	—	—	—	—	—

Mint: Sahrind
KM# 300.78 RUPEE

Silver **Obv:** Inscription, date **Rev:** Inscription **Note:** Weight varies 11.00-11.60 grams.

Date	Mintage	Good	VG	F	VF	XF
AH1113//45	—	5.00	7.00	10.00	17.50	27.50
AH1115//47	—	5.00	7.00	10.00	17.50	27.50
AH1115//48	—	5.00	7.00	10.00	17.50	27.50
AH1116//48	—	5.00	7.00	10.00	17.50	27.50
AH1116//49	—	5.00	7.00	10.00	17.50	27.50
AH1117//49	—	5.00	7.00	10.00	17.50	27.50
AH1117//50	—	5.00	7.00	10.00	17.50	27.50

Mint: Sangamner
KM# 300.80 RUPEE

Silver **Note:** Weight varies 11.00-11.60 grams.

Date	Mintage	Good	VG	F	VF	XF
AH1116//48 Rare	—	—	—	—	—	—
AH1118//50 Rare	—	—	—	—	—	—

Mint: Shahjahanabad
KM# 300.81 RUPEE

Silver **Obv:** Inscription **Rev. Inscription:** Dar-ul-Khilafat and mint name **Note:** "Badr" couplet; Weight varies 11.00-11.60 grams.

Date	Mintage	Good	VG	F	VF	XF
AH1113//4x	—	5.00	7.00	10.00	17.50	27.50
AH1114//46	—	5.00	7.00	10.00	17.50	27.50
AH1114//47	—	5.00	7.00	10.00	17.50	27.50
AH1115//47	—	5.00	7.00	10.00	17.50	27.50
AH1115//48	—	5.00	7.00	10.00	17.50	27.50
AH1116//48	—	5.00	7.00	10.00	17.50	27.50
AH1116//49	—	5.00	7.00	10.00	17.50	27.50
AH1117//49	—	5.00	7.00	10.00	17.50	27.50
AH1117//50	—	5.00	7.00	10.00	17.50	27.50
AH1118//50	—	5.00	7.00	10.00	17.50	27.50
AH1118//51	—	5.00	7.00	10.00	17.50	27.50
AH1119//51	—	5.00	7.00	10.00	17.50	27.50

Mint: Sholapur
KM# 300.82 RUPEE

Silver **Note:** Weight varies 11.00-11.60 grams.

Date	Mintage	Good	VG	F	VF	XF
AH1113//46	—	5.00	7.00	10.00	17.50	27.50
AH1114//46	—	5.00	7.00	10.00	17.50	27.50
AH1114//47	—	5.00	7.00	10.00	17.50	27.50
AH1115//47	—	5.00	7.00	10.00	17.50	27.50
AH1115//48	—	5.00	7.00	10.00	17.50	27.50
AH1116//48	—	5.00	7.00	10.00	17.50	27.50
AH1116//49	—	5.00	7.00	10.00	17.50	27.50
AH1117//49	—	5.00	7.00	10.00	17.50	27.50
AH1117//50	—	5.00	7.00	10.00	17.50	27.50
AH1118//50	—	5.00	7.00	10.00	17.50	27.50
AH1118//51	—	5.00	7.00	10.00	17.50	27.50

Mint: Surat
KM# 300.86 RUPEE

Silver **Obv:** Inscription **Rev:** Inscription, without mint epithet **Note:** Weight varies 11.00-11.60 grams.

Date	Mintage	Good	VG	F	VF	XF
AH1113//46	—	5.00	7.00	10.00	17.50	27.50
AH1114//46	—	5.00	7.00	10.00	17.50	27.50
AH1114//47	—	5.00	7.00	10.00	17.50	27.50
AH1115//47	—	5.00	7.00	10.00	17.50	27.50
AH1115//48	—	5.00	7.00	10.00	17.50	27.50
AH1116//48	—	5.00	7.00	10.00	17.50	27.50
AH1116//49	—	5.00	7.00	10.00	17.50	27.50
AH1117//49	—	5.00	7.00	10.00	17.50	27.50
AH1117//50	—	5.00	7.00	10.00	17.50	27.50
AH1118//50	—	5.00	7.00	10.00	17.50	27.50
AH1118//51	—	5.00	7.00	10.00	17.50	27.50

Mint: Tatta
KM# 300.87 RUPEE

Silver **Note:** "Badr" couplet; Weight varies 11.00-11.60 grams.

Date	Mintage	Good	VG	F	VF	XF
AH1113//4x	—	5.00	7.00	10.00	17.50	27.50
AH1114//46	—	5.00	7.00	10.00	17.50	27.50
AH1115//47	—	5.00	7.00	10.00	17.50	27.50
AH1115//48	—	5.00	7.00	10.00	17.50	27.50
AH1116//48	—	5.00	7.00	10.00	17.50	27.50
AH1117//49	—	5.00	7.00	10.00	17.50	27.50
AH1117//5	—	5.00	7.00	10.00	17.50	27.50
AH1118//50	—	5.00	7.00	10.00	17.50	27.50
AH1118//51	—	5.00	7.00	10.00	17.50	27.50
AH1119//51	—	5.00	7.00	10.00	17.50	27.50

Mint: Toragal
KM# 300.88 RUPEE

Silver **Note:** Weight varies 11.00-11.60 grams.

Date	Mintage	Good	VG	F	VF	XF
AH1110//50 (sic)	—	—	—	—	—	—
AH1118//50 Rare	—	—	—	—	—	—

Mint: Ujjain
KM# 300.90 RUPEE
Silver **Rev:** "Dar al-Fath" and mint name at top **Note:** "Dar-ul-Fath". Weight varies: 11.00-11.60 grams.

Date	Mintage	Good	VG	F	VF	XF
AH1115//48	—	5.00	8.00	13.50	22.50	35.00

Mint: Ujjain
KM# 300.91 RUPEE
Silver **Rev:** "Dar alFath" and mint name at bottom **Note:** Weight varies 11.00-11.60 grams.

Date	Mintage	Good	VG	F	VF	XF
AH1113//4x	—	5.00	7.50	13.50	22.50	35.00
AH1114//46	—	5.00	7.50	13.50	22.50	35.00
AH1114//47	—	5.00	7.50	13.50	22.50	35.00
AH1115//47	—	5.00	7.50	13.50	22.50	35.00
AH1115//48	—	5.00	7.50	13.50	22.50	35.00
AH1116//48	—	5.00	7.50	13.50	22.50	35.00
AH1116//49	—	5.00	7.50	13.50	22.50	35.00
AH1117//49	—	5.00	7.50	13.50	22.50	35.00

Mint: Zafarabad
KM# 300.93 RUPEE
Silver **Obv:** Inscription **Rev:** Inscription **Note:** "Badr" couplet; Weight varies 11.00-11.60 grams.

Date	Mintage	Good	VG	F	VF	XF
AH1113//xx	—	5.50	9.00	18.00	30.00	50.00
AH1115//48	—	5.50	9.00	18.00	30.00	50.00
AH1116//48	—	5.50	9.00	18.00	30.00	50.00
AH1116//49	—	5.50	9.00	18.00	30.00	50.00
AH1117//49	—	5.50	9.00	18.00	30.00	50.00
AH1118//51	—	5.50	9.00	18.00	30.00	50.00

Mint: Zafarabad
KM# 300.116 RUPEE
11.4440 g., Silver **Note:** "Mihr" couplet.

Date	Mintage	Good	VG	F	VF	XF
AH1113//45	—	—	—	—	—	—

Mint: Ahmadabad
KM# 315.1 MOHUR
Gold **Note:** Weight varies: 10.80-11.00 grams.

Date	Mintage	Good	VG	F	VF	XF
AH1113//45	—	235	265	325	425	550

Mint: Ahsanabad
KM# 315.3 MOHUR
Gold **Obv:** Inscription **Rev:** Inscription **Note:** Weight varies 10.80-11 grams.

Date	Mintage	Good	VG	F	VF	XF
AH1113//45	—	235	265	335	425	550
AH1113//46	—	235	265	335	425	550
AH1114//46	—	235	265	335	425	550
AH1114//47	—	235	265	335	425	550
AH1115//47	—	235	265	335	425	550
AH1115//48	—	235	265	335	425	550
AH1116//48	—	235	265	335	425	550
AH1117//50	—	235	265	335	425	550
AH1118//50	—	235	265	335	425	550

Mint: Akbarabad
KM# 315.52 MOHUR
Gold **Obv:** Inscription **Rev. Inscription:** Mustagir al-Khilafat **Note:** Weight varies 10.80-11.00 grams.

Date	Mintage	Good	VG	F	VF	XF
AH1114//46	—	235	265	325	400	500
AH1119//51	—	235	265	325	400	500
AH1117//50	—	235	265	325	400	500

Mint: Akbarnagar
KM# 315.51 MOHUR
Gold **Note:** Weight varies 10.80-11.00 grams.

Date	Mintage	Good	VG	F	VF	XF
AH1115//47 Rare	—	—	—	—	—	—
AH111x//48 Rare	—	—	—	—	—	—

Mint: Azimabad
KM# 315.12 MOHUR
Gold **Note:** Weight varies 10.80-11 grams.

Date	Mintage	Good	VG	F	VF	XF
AH1117//50	—	235	265	325	400	500
AH1118//5	—	235	265	325	400	500

Mint: Bareli
KM# 315.13 MOHUR
Gold **Note:** Weight varies 10.80-11 grams.

Date	Mintage	Good	VG	F	VF	XF
AH1113//45	—	—	250	300	375	500

Mint: Macchlipattan
KM# 315.56 MOHUR
Gold **Note:** Weight varies 10.80-11 grams.

Date	Mintage	Good	VG	F	VF	XF
AH1114//46	—	—	—	—	—	—

Mint: Murshidabad
KM# 315.37 MOHUR
Gold **Note:** Weight varies 10.80-11 grams.

Date	Mintage	Good	VG	F	VF	XF
AH1116//48	—	235	265	325	400	500
AH1116//49	—	235	265	325	400	500
AH1118//51	—	235	265	325	400	500

Mint: Purenda
KM# 315.41 MOHUR
Gold **Note:** Weight varies 10.80-11 grams.

Date	Mintage	Good	VG	F	VF	XF
AH1117//50 Rare	—	—	—	—	—	—
AH1118//51 Rare	—	—	—	—	—	—

Mint: Surat
KM# 315.58 MOHUR
Gold **Note:** Weight varies: 10.8-11 grams.

Date	Mintage	Good	VG	F	VF	XF
AH1113//46	—	235	265	325	400	500
AH1114//xx	—	235	265	325	400	500
AH1115//47	—	235	265	325	400	500

HAMMERED COINAGE

Largesse Issues

Mint: Allahabad
KM# B306.4 NISAR
Silver **Obv. Inscription:** "Alamgir Bad Shah" **Note:** Weight varies 0.60-0.70 grams.

Date	Mintage	Good	VG	F	VF	XF
AH1117//49	—	—	—	—	—	—

Mint: Bijapur
KM# B306.5 NISAR
Silver **Obv. Inscription:** "Nisar 'Alamgir" **Note:** Weight varies 0.60-0.70 grams.

Date	Mintage	Good	VG	F	VF	XF
AH1114//46	—	—	—	—	—	—

Mint: Shahjahanabad
KM# B306.8 NISAR
Silver **Obv. Inscription:** "Nisar 'Alamgir Bad Shah" **Rev:** Mint **Rev. Inscription:** "dar al-Khilafa" **Note:** Weight varies 0.60-0.70 grams.

Date	Mintage	Good	VG	F	VF	XF
AHxxxx//x	—	—	—	—	—	—

Mint: Bijapur
KM# C306.5 NISAR
Silver **Obv. Inscription:** "Alamgir..." **Note:** Weight varies 1.1 - 1.5 grams.

Date	Mintage	Good	VG	F	VF	XF
AHxxxx//x	—	—	—	—	—	—

Mint: Ahmadanagar
KM# D306.2 NISAR
Silver **Obv. Inscription:** "Nisar 'Alamgir Bad Shah Ghazi" **Note:** Weight varies 2.5-2.9 grams.

Date	Mintage	Good	VG	F	VF	XF
AH1118//5x	—	—	—	—	—	—

Mint: Akbarabad
KM# D306.3 NISAR
Silver **Obv. Inscription:** "Nisar 'Alamgir Bad Shah Ghazi" **Rev:** Mint name **Rev. Inscription:** "Jalus Maimanat Manus" **Note:** Weight varies 2.5 - 2.9 grams.

Date	Mintage	Good	VG	F	VF	XF
AHxxxx//x	—	—	—	—	—	—

Mint: Itawa
KM# D306.9 NISAR
Silver **Note:** Weight varies 2.5-2.9 grams.

Date	Mintage	Good	VG	F	VF	XF
AH1097//29	—	—	—	—	—	—
AH1114//47	—	—	—	—	—	—

Mint: Ahmadnagar
KM# 306.3 NISAR
Silver **Note:**

Date	Mintage	Good	VG	F	VF	XF
AH1118//5x	—	22.00	55.00	90.00	150	250

Mint: Itawa
KM# 306.9 NISAR
Silver **Note:** Weight varies: 0.35-2.90 grams.

Date	Mintage	Good	VG	F	VF	XF
AH1112//4x	—	—	—	—	—	—
AH111x//47	—	—	—	—	—	—

Mint: Lahore
KM# 306.6 NISAR
Silver **Note:** Weight varies: 5.60-5.80 grams (1/2 Rupee weight).

Date	Mintage	Good	VG	F	VF	XF
AHxxxx//26	—	16.00	40.00	65.00	110	180
AHxxxx//35	—	16.00	40.00	65.00	110	180
AH1112//45	—	16.00	40.00	65.00	110	180

HAMMERED COINAGE (RESUMED)

Mint: Ahmadanagar
KM# 315.2 MOHUR
Gold **Note:** Weight varies 10.80-11.00 grams.

Date	Mintage	Good	VG	F	VF	XF
AH1115//48	—	235	265	325	425	550
AH1116//xx	—	235	265	325	425	550
AH1118//51	—	235	265	325	425	550
AH1118//50	—	235	265	325	425	550

Mint: Ajmir
KM# 315.4 MOHUR
Gold **Note:** Weight varies: 10.80-11.00 grams.

Date	Mintage	Good	VG	F	VF	XF
AHxxxx//x	—	—	135	225	325	475

Mint: Akbarabad
KM# 315.6 MOHUR
Gold **Obv:** Inscription **Rev. Inscription:** Mustagir-ul-Mulk **Note:** Weight varies 10.80-11.00 grams.

Date	Mintage	Good	VG	F	VF	XF
AH1114//46	—	235	265	325	400	500
AH1117//50	—	235	265	325	400	500
AH1119//51	—	235	265	325	400	500

Mint: Allahabad
KM# 315.9 MOHUR
Gold **Obv:** Inscription **Rev:** Inscription, mint name below **Note:** Weight varies 10.80-11.00 grams.

Date	Mintage	Good	VG	F	VF	XF
AH1113//45	—	235	265	325	400	500
AH1113//46	—	235	265	325	400	500
AH1114//46	—	235	265	325	400	500

Mint: Bijapur
KM# 315.15 MOHUR
Gold **Obv:** Inscription **Rev. Inscription:** Dar-uz-Zafar **Note:** Arrangement of the mint name varies. Weight varies 10.80-11.00 grams.

Date	Mintage	Good	VG	F	VF	XF
AH1113//45	—	235	265	325	400	500
AH1114//4x	—	235	265	325	400	500
AH1115//48	—	235	265	325	400	500
AH1116//49	—	235	265	325	400	500
AH1118//50	—	235	265	325	400	500
AH1118//51	—	235	265	325	400	500

Mint: Burhanpur
KM# 315.16 MOHUR
Gold **Note:** Weight varies 10.80-11 grams.

Date	Mintage	Good	VG	F	VF	XF
AH1114//47	—	235	265	325	400	500
AH1115//47	—	235	265	325	400	500
AH1115//48	—	235	265	325	400	500
AH1117//49	—	235	265	325	400	500
AH1117//50	—	235	265	325	400	500

Mint: Haidarabad
KM# 315.20 MOHUR
Gold **Obv:** Inscription **Rev. Inscription:** Dar-ul-Jihad, mint name **Note:** Weight varies 10.80-11.00 grams.

Date	Mintage	Good	VG	F	VF	XF
AH1113//45	—	235	265	325	400	500
AH1113//46	—	235	265	325	400	500
AH1114//46	—	235	265	325	400	500
AH1114//47	—	235	265	325	400	500
AH1112/45	—	235	265	325	400	500
AH1115//47	—	235	265	325	400	500
AH1115//48	—	235	265	325	400	500
AH1116//48	—	235	265	325	400	500
AH1118//50	—	235	265	325	400	500

Mint: Hukeri
KM# 315.54 MOHUR
Gold **Note:** Weight varies: 10.80-11.00 grams.

Date	Mintage	Good	VG	F	VF	XF
AHxxxx//49	—	—	—	—	—	—

Mint: Itawa
KM# 315.22 MOHUR
Gold **Note:** Weight varies 10.80-11.00 grams.

Date	Mintage	Good	VG	F	VF	XF
AH1116//49	—	235	265	300	350	500
AH1117//49	—	235	265	300	350	500
AH1117//50	—	235	265	300	350	500
AH1118//50	—	235	265	300	350	500

Mint: Jahangirnagar
KM# 315.23 MOHUR
Gold **Note:** Weight varies: 10.80-11.00 grams.

Date	Mintage	Good	VG	F	VF	XF
AH1114//47	—	235	265	325	425	550

Mint: Kabul
KM# 315.25 MOHUR
Gold **Obv:** Inscription **Rev. Inscription:** Dar-ul-Mulk, mint name **Note:** "Mihr" couplet; Weight varies 10.8 - 11 grams.

Date	Mintage	Good	VG	F	VF	XF
AH1114//46	—	235	265	325	425	550
AH1119//51	—	235	265	325	425	550

Mint: Katak
KM# 315.29 MOHUR
Gold **Note:** Weight varies: 10.80-11.00 grams.

Date	Mintage	Good	VG	F	VF	XF
AHxxxx//44	—	250	350	500	700	1,000
AH1117//50	—	250	350	500	700	1,000

Mint: Khujista Bunyad
KM# 315.30 MOHUR
Gold **Note:** Weight varies 10.80-11.00 grams.

Date	Mintage	Good	VG	F	VF	XF
AH1113//45	—	235	265	325	400	500
AH1115//47	—	235	265	325	400	500
AH111x//48	—	235	265	325	400	500
AH1116//4x	—	235	265	325	400	500
AH1117//49	—	235	265	325	400	500

Mint: Lahore
KM# 315.31 MOHUR
Gold **Obv:** Inscription **Rev. Inscription:** Dar-us-Sultanat **Note:** Weight varies 10.80-11.00 grams.

Date	Mintage	Good	VG	F	VF	XF
AH1114//46	—	235	265	325	400	500
AH1114//47	—	235	265	325	400	500
AH1115//48	—	235	265	325	400	500
AH1116//48	—	235	265	325	400	500
AH1118//50	—	235	265	325	400	500

Mint: Multan
KM# 315.36 MOHUR
Gold **Obv:** Inscription **Rev:** Inscription, without mint epithet, mint name at bottom **Note:** Weight varies 10.80 - 11.00 grams.

Date	Mintage	Good	VG	F	VF	XF
AH1115//47	—	235	265	325	400	500

Date	Mintage	Good	VG	F	VF	XF
AH1117//4x	—	235	265	325	400	500
AH1119//51	—	235	265	325	400	500

Mint: Nusratabad
KM# 315.39 MOHUR
Gold **Note:** Weight varies 10.80 - 11.00 grams.

Date	Mintage	Good	VG	F	VF	XF
AH1101//34	—	235	275	350	475	650
AHxxxx//38	—	235	275	350	475	650
AH11xx//42	—	235	275	350	475	650
AH1114//46	—	235	275	350	475	650
AH111x//50	—	235	275	350	475	650

Mint: Patna
KM# 315.40 MOHUR
Gold **Note:** Struck at Patna. Weight varies: 10.80-11.00 grams.

Date	Mintage	Good	VG	F	VF	XF
AH1113//45	—	235	275	300	375	500

Mint: Shahjahanabad
KM# 315.42 MOHUR
Gold **Obv:** Inscription **Rev. Inscription:** Dar-ul-Khilafat, mint name **Note:** "Badr" couplet; Weight varies 10.80 - 11.00 grams.

Date	Mintage	Good	VG	F	VF	XF
AH1114//47	—	235	265	300	350	425
AH1115//47	—	235	265	300	350	425
AH1116//48	—	235	265	300	350	425
AH1116//49	—	235	265	300	350	425
AH1117//49	—	235	265	300	350	425
AH1117//50	—	235	265	300	350	425
AH1118//51	—	235	265	300	350	425
AH1119//51	—	235	265	300	350	425

Mint: Sholapur
KM# 315.43 MOHUR
Gold **Note:** Weight varies: 10.80-11.00 grams.

Date	Mintage	Good	VG	F	VF	XF
AH1113//46	—	235	265	325	400	500
AH1114//4x	—	235	265	325	400	500
AH1115//47	—	235	265	325	400	500
AH1116//48	—	235	265	325	400	500
AH1118//50	—	235	265	325	400	500

Mint: Surat
KM# 315.45 MOHUR
Gold **Note:** Without mint epithet. Weight varies: 10.80-11.00 grams.

Date	Mintage	Good	VG	F	VF	XF
AH1113//45	—	235	265	325	400	500

Mint: Tatta
KM# 315.46 MOHUR
Gold **Obv:** Inscription **Rev:** Inscription **Note:** "Mihr" couplet; Weight varies 10.80 to 11.00 grams.

Date	Mintage	Good	VG	F	VF	XF
AH1113//46	—	235	265	300	400	500

Mint: Ujjain
KM# 315.48 MOHUR
Gold **Obv:** Inscription **Rev. Inscription:** Dar-ul-Fath **Note:** Weight varies 10.80 - 11.00 grams.

Date	Mintage	Good	VG	F	VF	XF
AH1115//48	—	235	265	325	400	500

Mint: Zafarabad
KM# 315.49 MOHUR
Gold **Note:** Weight varies 10.80 - 11.00 grams.

Date	Mintage	Good	VG	F	VF	XF
AH1113//45	—	235	275	335	425	550
AH1114//47	—	235	275	335	425	550
AH1115//47	—	235	275	335	425	550
AH1116//48	—	235	275	335	425	550
AH1118//51	—	235	275	335	425	550

Azam Shah

In Gujarat - Khandesh - Malwa, AH1118-1119 / 1707AD

HAMMERED COINAGE

Mint: Haidarabad
KM# 328.1 1/8 RUPEE
Silver **Note:** Weight varies 1.38-1.45 grams.

Date	Mintage	Good	VG	F	VF	XF
AHxxxx//x Rare	—	—	—	—	—	—

Mint: Khujista Bunyad
KM# 330.2 1/2 RUPEE
Silver **Obv:** Inscription, date **Rev:** Inscription **Note:** Weight varies 5.50-5.80 grams.

Date	Mintage	Good	VG	F	VF	XF
AH1119//1 (Ahad) Rare	—	—	—	—	—	—

Mint: Surat
KM# 330.1 1/2 RUPEE
Silver **Note:** Weight varies 5.50-5.80 grams.

Date	Mintage	Good	VG	F	VF	XF
AH1119//1 (Ahad) Rare	—	—	—	—	—	—

Mint: Ahmadabad
KM# 332.1 RUPEE
Silver **Obv:** Inscription **Rev:** Inscription **Note:** Weight varies 11.00-11.60 grams.

Date	Mintage	Good	VG	F	VF	XF
AH1118//1 (Ahad)	—	50.00	125	250	350	500
AH1119//1 (Ahad)	—	50.00	125	250	350	500

Mint: Ahmadanagar
KM# 332.2 RUPEE
11.4440 g., Silver **Note:** Weight varies 11.00-11.60 grams.

Date	Mintage	Good	VG	F	VF	XF
AH1118//1 (Ahad)	—	50.00	125	250	350	500
AH1119//1 (Ahad)	—	50.00	125	250	350	500

Mint: Alamgirpur
KM# 332.7 RUPEE
Silver **Note:** Weight varies 11.00-11.60 grams.

Date	Mintage	Good	VG	F	VF	XF
AHxxxx//1 (Ahad)	—	—	—	—	—	—

Mint: Burhanpur
KM# 332.3 RUPEE
Silver **Obv:** Inscription, date **Rev:** Inscription **Note:** Weight varies 11.00-11.60 grams.

Date	Mintage	Good	VG	F	VF	XF
AH1118//1 (Ahad)	—	45.00	110	220	320	450
AH1119//1 (Ahad)	—	45.00	110	220	320	450

Mint: Haidarabad
KM# 332.8 RUPEE
Silver **Obv:** Inscription **Rev. Inscription:** Dar-ul-Jihad **Note:** Weight varies 11.00-11.60 grams.

Date	Mintage	Good	VG	F	VF	XF
AH1119//1 (Ahad) Rare	—	—	—	—	—	—

Mint: Junagarh
KM# 332.9 RUPEE
Silver **Note:** Weight varies 11.00-11.60 grams.

Date	Mintage	Good	VG	F	VF	XF
AH1119//1 (Ahad) Rare	—	—	—	—	—	—

Mint: Khujista Bunyad
KM# 332.4 RUPEE
Silver **Obv:** Inscription, date **Rev:** Inscription **Note:** Weight varies 11.00-11.60 grams.

Date	Mintage	Good	VG	F	VF	XF
AH1118//1 (Ahad)	—	45.00	110	220	320	450
AH1119//1 (Ahad)	—	45.00	110	220	320	450

Mint: Surat
KM# 332.5 RUPEE
Silver **Obv:** Inscription **Rev:** Inscription **Note:** Weight varies 11.00-11.60 grams.

Date	Mintage	Good	VG	F	VF	XF
AH1119//1 (Ahad)	—	45.00	110	220	320	450

Mint: Ujjain
KM# 332.6 RUPEE
Silver **Obv:** Inscription **Rev. Inscription:** Dar-ul-Fath **Note:** Weight varies 11.00-11.60 grams.

Date	Mintage	Good	VG	F	VF	XF
AH1119//1 (Ahad)	—	50.00	125	250	350	500

Mint: Ahmadanagar
KM# 334.1 MOHUR
Gold **Note:** Weight varies: 10.80-11.00 grams.

Date	Mintage	Good	VG	F	VF	XF
AH1118//1 (Ahad)	—	250	350	600	1,000	1,500
AH1119//1 (Ahad)	—	250	350	600	1,000	1,500

Mint: Alamgirpur
KM# 334.2 MOHUR
Gold **Note:** Weight varies 10.80-11.00 grams.

Date	Mintage	Good	VG	F	VF	XF
AH111x//1 (Ahad) Rare	—	—	—	—	—	—

Mint: Asir
KM# 334.3 MOHUR
Gold **Note:** Weight varies 10.80-11.00 grams.

Date	Mintage	Good	VG	F	VF	XF
AH111x//1 (Ahad) Rare	—	—	—	—	—	—

Mint: Burhanpur
KM# 334.4 MOHUR
Gold **Note:** Weight varies 10.80-11.00 grams.

Date	Mintage	Good	VG	F	VF	XF
AH1119//1 (Ahad)	—	250	400	700	1,000	1,500

Mint: Haidarabad
KM# 334.7 MOHUR
Gold **Rev:** Mint epithet: "Dar-ul-Jihad" **Note:** Weight varies 10.80-11.00 grams.

Date	Mintage	Good	VG	F	VF	XF
AH1119//1 (Ahad)	—	250	400	800	1,250	2,000

Mint: Khujista Bunyad
KM# 334.5 MOHUR
Gold **Obv:** Inscription **Rev:** Inscription **Note:** Weight varies 10.80-11.00 grams.

Date	Mintage	Good	VG	F	VF	XF
AH1118//1 (Ahad)	—	250	400	800	1,250	2,000
AH1119//1 (Ahad)	—	250	400	800	1,250	2,000

Mint: Surat
KM# 334.6 MOHUR
Gold **Note:** Weight varies 10.80-11.00 grams.

Date	Mintage	Good	VG	F	VF	XF
AH1119//1 (Ahad)	—	—	1,250	2,250	3,500	5,000

Kam Bakhsh

In Deccan AH1119-1120 / 1707-1708AD

HAMMERED COINAGE

Mint: Bijapur
KM# 335 PAISA
14.0000 g., Copper **Note:**

Date	Mintage	Good	VG	F	VF	XF
AH1120//x Rare	—	—	—	—	—	—

Mint: Ahsanabad
KM# 336.1 RUPEE
Silver **Note:** Weight varies 11.00-11.60 grams.

Date	Mintage	Good	VG	F	VF	XF
AH1119//1 (Ahad)	—	50.00	125	250	425	600

Mint: Bijapur
KM# 336.2 RUPEE
Silver **Obv:** Inscription **Rev. Inscription:** Dar uz-Zafar **Note:** Weight varies 11.00-11.60 grams.

Date	Mintage	Good	VG	F	VF	XF
AH1119//1 (Ahad)	—	50.00	125	250	425	600
AH1120//2	—	50.00	125	250	425	600

Mint: Gokak
KM# 336.4 RUPEE
Silver **Note:** Weight varies 11.00-11.60 grams.

Date	Mintage	Good	VG	F	VF	XF
AH11xx//1 (Ahad) Rare	—	—	—	—	—	—

Mint: Gulbarga
KM# 336.3 RUPEE
Silver **Note:** Weight varies 11.00-11.60 grams.

Date	Mintage	Good	VG	F	VF	XF
AH1120//2	—	50.00	125	250	425	600

Mint: Haidarabad
KM# 336.5 RUPEE
Silver **Obv:** Inscription, date **Rev. Inscription:** Dar ul-Jihad **Note:** Weight varies 11.00-11.60 grams.

Date	Mintage	Good	VG	F	VF	XF
AH1120//2	—	50.00	125	250	425	600

Mint: Imtiyazgarh
KM# 336.9 RUPEE
Silver **Note:** Weight varies 11.00-11.60 grams.

Date	Mintage	Good	VG	F	VF	XF
AHxxxx//1 (Ahad)	—	—	—	—	—	—

Mint: Nusratabad
KM# 336.6 RUPEE
Silver **Note:** Weight varies 11.00-11.60 grams.

Date	Mintage	Good	VG	F	VF	XF
AH1120//1 (Ahad) Rare	—	—	—	—	—	—
AH11xx//2 Rare	—	—	—	—	—	—

Mint: Surat
KM# 336.8 RUPEE
Silver **Note:** Weight varies 11.00-11.60 grams.

Date	Mintage	Good	VG	F	VF	XF
AH111x//1 (Ahad)	—	—	—	—	—	—

Mint: Toragal
KM# 336.7 RUPEE
Silver **Note:** Weight varies 11.00-11.60 grams.

Date	Mintage	Good	VG	F	VF	XF
AH111x//1 (Ahad) Rare	—	—	—	—	—	—

Mint: Bijapur
KM# 338.1 MOHUR
Gold **Rev:** Mint epithet: "Dar-uz-Zafar" **Note:** Weight varies 10.60-10.90 grams.

Date	Mintage	Good	VG	F	VF	XF
AH1119//1 (Ahad)	—	250	425	700	1,000	1,400

Mint: Haidarabad
KM# 338.2 MOHUR
Gold **Obv:** Inscription, date **Rev. Inscription:** Dar ul-Jihad **Note:** Weight varies 10.80-11.00 grams.

Date	Mintage	Good	VG	F	VF	XF
AH1119//1 (Ahad)	—	250	350	600	1,000	1,500
AH1120//2	—	250	350	600	1,000	1,500

Mint: Nusratabad
KM# 338.3 MOHUR
Gold **Note:** Weight varies 10.80-11.00 grams.

Date	Mintage	Good	VG	F	VF	XF
AH11xx//x Rare	—	—	—	—	—	—

Shah Alam Bahadur

AH1119-1124 / 1707-1712AD

HAMMERED COINAGE

Mint: Bijapur
KM# A339.1 1/2 PAISA
Copper **Note:** Type A339. Weight varies: 10.10-11.40 grams.

Date	Mintage	Good	VG	F	VF	XF
AHxxxx//x	—	—	—	—	—	—

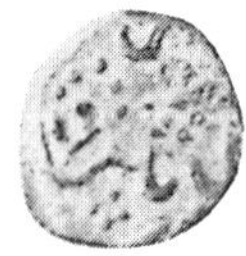 

Mint: Macchlipattan
KM# A339.2 1/2 PAISA
Copper **Note:** Weight varies: 10.10-11.40 grams.

Date	Mintage	Good	VG	F	VF	XF
AH1120//2	—	—	—	—	—	—
AH1124//6	—	—	—	—	—	—

Mint: Sholapur
KM# A339.3 1/2 PAISA
Copper **Note:** Weight varies: 10.10-11.40 grams.

Date	Mintage	Good	VG	F	VF	XF
AHxxxx//1 (Ahad)	—	—	—	—	—	—
AHxxxx//2	—	—	—	—	—	—
AHxxxx//4	—	—	—	—	—	—

Mint: Allahabad
KM# 339.1 1/2 DAM
Copper **Note:**

Date	Mintage	Good	VG	F	VF	XF
AHxxxx//x	—	5.50	11.00	18.00	30.00	—

Mint: Muhammadabad
KM# 339.2 1/2 DAM
Copper **Note:**

Date	Mintage	Good	VG	F	VF	XF
AHxxxx//x	—	5.50	11.00	18.00	30.00	—

Mint: Bijapur
KM# 340.4 PAISA
Copper **Obv:** Inscription, date **Rev. Inscription:** Dar-uz-Zatar **Note:** Weight varies 12.90-13.80 grams.

Date	Mintage	Good	VG	F	VF	XF
AHxx24//x	—	5.50	11.00	18.00	30.00	—

Mint: Hyderabad
KM# 340.2 PAISA
Copper **Rev:** Mint epithet Dar-al-Jihad **Note:** Weight varies 12.90-13.80 grams.

Date	Mintage	Good	VG	F	VF	XF
AH1119//x	—	5.50	11.00	18.00	30.00	—
AH112x//4	—	5.50	11.00	18.00	30.00	—
AH112x//6	—	5.50	11.00	18.00	30.00	—

Mint: Macchlipattan
KM# 340.1 PAISA
Copper **Note:** Weight varies 12.90-13.80 grams.

Date	Mintage	Good	VG	F	VF	XF
AH1119//1	—	5.50	11.00	18.00	30.00	—
AH1119//2	—	5.50	11.00	18.00	30.00	—
AH1120//2	—	5.50	11.00	18.00	30.00	—
AH1121//3	—	5.50	11.00	18.00	30.00	—
AH1122//4	—	5.50	11.00	18.00	30.00	—
AH1123//5	—	5.50	11.00	18.00	30.00	—
AH1124//5 (sic)	—	5.50	11.00	18.00	30.00	—

Mint: Sholapur
KM# 340.3 PAISA

Copper **Note:** Weight varies 12.90-13.80 grams.

Date	Mintage	Good	VG	F	VF	XF
ND//x	—	5.50	11.00	18.00	30.00	—
AHxxxx//3	—	5.50	11.00	18.00	30.00	—

Mint: Ahmadabad
KM# A341.1 1/2 DAM

Copper **Note:** Weight varies 12.90-13.80 grams.

Date	Mintage	Good	VG	F	VF	XF
ND//x	—	—	—	—	—	—
AH1124//x	—	—	—	—	—	—

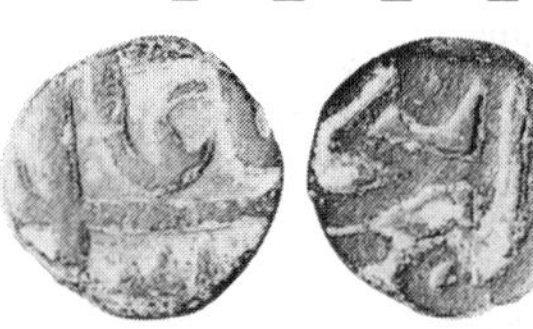

Mint: Elichpur
KM# A341.2 1/2 DAM

9.5000 g., Copper **Note:** Weight varies 12.90-13.80 grams.

Date	Mintage	Good	VG	F	VF	XF
AHxxxx//x	—	—	—	—	—	—

Mint: Firoznagar
KM# A341.3 1/2 DAM

Copper **Note:** Weight varies 12.90-13.80 grams.

Date	Mintage	Good	VG	F	VF	XF
ND//x	—	—	—	—	—	—
AH1123//x	—	—	—	—	—	—

Mint: Muhammadabad
KM# A341.5 1/2 DAM

Copper **Rev:** Mint epithet Dar-al-Fulus **Note:** Weight varies 12.90-13.80 grams.

Date	Mintage	Good	VG	F	VF	XF
AH(11)24//x	—	—	—	—	—	—

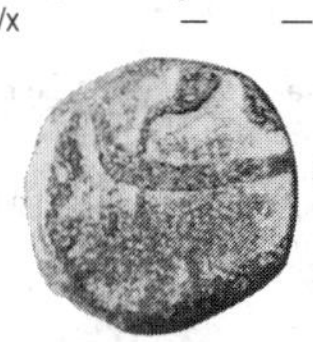

Mint: Surat
KM# A341.4 1/2 DAM

10.0000 g., Copper **Note:** Weight varies 12.90-13.80 grams.

Date	Mintage	Good	VG	F	VF	XF
ND//x	—	—	—	—	—	—

Mint: Ahmadabad
KM# 341.4 DAM

Copper **Note:** Weight varies: 19.7-20.2 grams.

Date	Mintage	Good	VG	F	VF	XF
AH1121//x	—	5.50	11.00	18.00	30.00	—

Mint: Elichpur
KM# 341.1 DAM

Copper **Note:** Weight varies: 19.7-20.2 grams.

Date	Mintage	Good	VG	F	VF	XF
AH1120//x	—	5.50	11.00	18.00	30.00	—
AH1121//3	—	5.50	11.00	18.00	30.00	—
AH1121//4	—	5.50	11.00	18.00	30.00	—
AH1122//4	—	5.50	11.00	18.00	30.00	—

Mint: Shahjahanabad
KM# 341.5 DAM

Copper **Note:** Weight varies: 19.7-20.2 grams.

Date	Mintage	Good	VG	F	VF	XF
AH1124//6 (sic)	—	—	—	—	—	—

Note: Retrograde 6 as 2

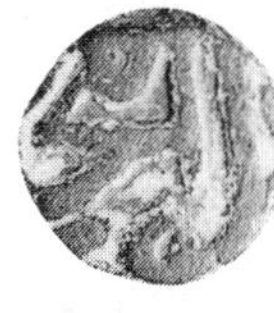

Mint: Jahangirnagar
KM# 341.2 PAISA

Copper **Note:** Weight varies: 12.90-13.80 grams.

Date	Mintage	Good	VG	F	VF	XF
AHxxxx//1 (Ahad) Rare	—	—	—	—	—	—

Mint: Sholapur
KM# 341.3 PAISA

Copper **Note:** Weight varies: 12.90-13.80 grams.

Date	Mintage	Good	VG	F	VF	XF
AHxxxx//2 Rare	—	—	—	—	—	—
AHxxxx//4 Rare	—	—	—	—	—	—
AHxxxx//5 Rare	—	—	—	—	—	—
AHxxxx//6 Rare	—	—	—	—	—	—

Mint: Surat
KM# 341.6 PAISA

Copper **Note:** Weight varies: 12.90-13.80 grams.

Date	Mintage	Good	VG	F	VF	XF
ND1120//x Rare	—	—	—	—	—	—
AH1121//x Rare	—	—	—	—	—	—

Mint: Akbarnagar
KM# A342 DAM

Copper **Note:** Weight varies: 19.7-20.2 grams.

Date	Mintage	Good	VG	F	VF	XF
AH1119//1 (Ahad)	—	—	—	—	—	—

Mint: Shahjahanabad
KM# 342.1 1/8 RUPEE

Silver **Note:** Weight varies 1.38-1.45 grams.

Date	Mintage	Good	VG	F	VF	XF
AH1124//5 (sic)	—	3.50	9.00	18.00	30.00	45.00

Mint: Macchlipattan
KM# A343 1/4 RUPEE

Silver **Note:** Weight varies 2.75-2.90 grams.

Date	Mintage	Good	VG	F	VF	XF
AH1120//2	—	4.00	10.00	20.00	35.00	50.00

Mint: Khambayat
KM# 343.2 1/2 RUPEE

Silver **Note:** Weight varies 5.50-5.80 grams.

Date	Mintage	Good	VG	F	VF	XF
AHxxxx//3	—	5.00	12.50	25.00	42.00	60.00

Mint: Surat
KM# 343.1 1/2 RUPEE

Silver **Note:** Weight varies 5.50-5.80 grams.

Date	Mintage	Good	VG	F	VF	XF
AHxxxx//1 (Ahad)	—	5.00	12.50	25.00	42.00	60.00
AH1123//x	—	—	12.50	25.00	42.00	60.00

Mint: Azimabad
KM# 344.1 RUPEE

Silver **Obv. Inscription:** Muazzam, the Second Alamgir **Rev:** Inscription **Note:** Weight varies 11.00-11.60 grams.

Date	Mintage	Good	VG	F	VF	XF
AHxxxx//1 (Ahad)	—	25.00	60.00	125	210	300

Mint: Murshidabad
KM# 344.2 RUPEE

Silver **Obv:** Inscription is a pre-accession name "Muazzam, the Second Alamgir" **Note:** Weight varies 11.00-11.60 grams.

Date	Mintage	Good	VG	F	VF	XF
AHxxxx//1 (Ahad) Rare	—	—	—	—	—	—

Mint: Multan
KM# 344A.1 RUPEE

Silver **Obv:** Inscription, date **Rev. Inscription:** Hami-Din Shah Alam **Note:** Weight varies 11.00-11.60 grams.

Date	Mintage	Good	VG	F	VF	XF
AH1119//1 (Ahad)	—	25.00	60.00	125	210	300

Mint: Tatta
KM# 345.1 RUPEE

Silver **Obv:** Inscription is a pre-accession name "Muazzam, the Second Shah Jahan" **Rev:** Inscription **Note:** Weight varies 11.00-11.60 grams.

Date	Mintage	Good	VG	F	VF	XF
AH1119//1 (Ahad) Rare	—	—	—	—	—	—

Mint: Akbarabad
KM# 346.1 RUPEE

Silver **Obv. Inscription:** Bahadur Shah, the second Alamgir **Rev. Inscription:** Mustagir-ul-Khilafat **Note:** Weight varies 11.00-11.60 grams.

Date	Mintage	Good	VG	F	VF	XF
AH1119//1 (Ahad)	—	10.00	25.00	50.00	85.00	125

Mint: Ajmer
KM# 347.24 RUPEE

Silver **Obv. Inscription:** Sikka I Shah Alam Badshah Ghazi **Rev:** Inscription **Note:** Weight varies 11.00-11.60 grams.

Date	Mintage	Good	VG	F	VF	XF
AH1119//1 (Ahad)	—	10.00	25.00	50.00	85.00	125

Mint: Ajmer
KM# 347.23 RUPEE

Silver **Obv:** Inscription **Rev. Inscription:** Mustagir-ul-Khilafat **Note:** Weight varies 11.00-11.60 grams.

Date	Mintage	Good	VG	F	VF	XF
AH1119//1 (Ahad)	—	8.00	20.00	40.00	65.00	95.00

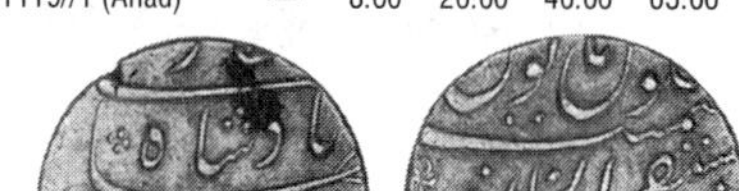

Mint: Akbarabad
KM# 347.1 RUPEE

Silver **Obv:** Inscription **Rev. Inscription:** Mustagir-ul-Khilafat **Note:** Weight varies 11.00-11.60 grams.

Date	Mintage	Good	VG	F	VF	XF
AH1119//1 (Ahad)	—	5.00	7.50	12.00	20.00	30.00
AH11xx//2	—	5.00	7.50	12.00	20.00	30.00
AH11xx//4	—	5.00	7.50	12.00	20.00	30.00

Mint: Akbarnagar
KM# 347.2 RUPEE

Silver **Obv:** Inscription **Rev:** Inscription **Note:** Weight varies 11.00-11.60 grams.

Date	Mintage	Good	VG	F	VF	XF
AH1119//1 (Ahad)	—	5.50	12.00	20.00	32.50	50.00
AH1120//2	—	5.50	12.00	20.00	32.50	50.00
AH1121//3	—	5.50	12.00	20.00	32.50	50.00
AH1123//5	—	5.50	12.00	20.00	32.50	50.00
AH(11)24//6	—	5.50	12.00	20.00	32.50	50.00

Mint: Allahabad
KM# 347.3 RUPEE

Silver **Note:** Weight varies 11.00-11.60 grams.

Date	Mintage	Good	VG	F	VF	XF
AH1120//3	—	5.00	8.00	16.00	26.00	40.00
AH1122//4	—	5.00	8.00	16.00	26.00	40.00

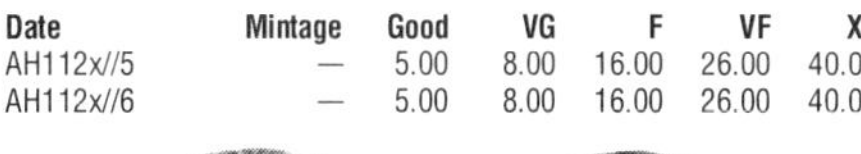

Date	Mintage	Good	VG	F	VF	XF
AH112x//5	—	5.00	8.00	16.00	26.00	40.00
AH112x//6	—	5.00	8.00	16.00	26.00	40.00

Mint: Azimabad
KM# 347.4 RUPEE
Silver **Obv:** Inscription, date below **Rev:** Inscription **Note:** Weight varies 11.00-11.60 grams.

Date	Mintage	Good	VG	F	VF	XF
AH1119//1 (Ahad)	—	5.00	7.50	12.00	20.00	30.00
AH1120//2	—	5.00	7.50	12.00	20.00	30.00
AH1120//3	—	5.00	7.50	12.00	20.00	30.00
AH1121//3	—	5.00	7.50	12.00	20.00	30.00
AH1121//4	—	5.00	7.50	12.00	20.00	30.00
AH1122//5	—	5.00	7.50	12.00	20.00	30.00
AH1124//6	—	5.00	7.50	12.00	20.00	30.00

Mint: Bankapur
KM# 347.5 RUPEE
Silver **Note:** Weight varies 11.00-11.60 grams.

Date	Mintage	Good	VG	F	VF	XF
AH1122//4 Rare	—	—	—	—	—	—

Mint: Bareli
KM# 347.6 RUPEE
Silver **Obv:** Inscription, date below **Rev:** Inscription **Note:** Weight varies 11.00-11.60 grams.

Date	Mintage	Good	VG	F	VF	XF
AH1119//1 (Ahad)	—	5.00	7.50	12.00	20.00	30.00
AH1119//2	—	5.00	7.50	12.00	20.00	30.00
AH1120//2	—	5.00	7.50	12.00	20.00	30.00
AH1120//3	—	5.00	7.50	12.00	20.00	30.00
AH1121//3	—	5.00	7.50	12.00	20.00	30.00
AH1121//4	—	5.00	7.50	12.00	20.00	30.00
AH1122//4	—	5.00	7.50	12.00	20.00	30.00

Mint: Imtiyazgarh
KM# 347.25 RUPEE
Silver **Note:** Weight varies 11.00-11.60 grams.

Date	Mintage	Good	VG	F	VF	XF
AHxxxx//4	—	—	—	—	—	—
AH11xx//6	—	—	—	—	—	—

Mint: Itawa
KM# 347.8 RUPEE
Silver **Obv:** Inscription, date below **Rev:** Inscription **Note:** Weight varies 11.00-11.60 grams.

Date	Mintage	Good	VG	F	VF	XF
AH1119//1 (Ahad)	—	5.00	7.50	12.00	20.00	30.00
AH1119//2	—	5.00	7.50	12.00	20.00	30.00
AH1120//2	—	5.00	7.50	12.00	20.00	30.00
AH1120//3	—	5.00	7.50	12.00	20.00	30.00
AH1121//3	—	5.00	7.50	12.00	20.00	30.00
AH1121//4	—	5.00	7.50	12.00	20.00	30.00
AH1122//4	—	5.00	7.50	12.00	20.00	30.00
AH1122//5	—	5.00	7.50	12.00	20.00	30.00
AH1123//5	—	5.00	7.50	12.00	20.00	30.00

Mint: Jahangirnagar
KM# 347.9 RUPEE
Silver **Note:** Weight varies 11.00-11.60 grams.

Date	Mintage	Good	VG	F	VF	XF
AH11xx//1 (Ahad)	—	5.00	7.50	12.00	20.00	30.00
AH11xx//2	—	5.00	7.50	12.00	20.00	30.00
AH1120//3	—	5.00	7.50	12.00	20.00	30.00
AH112x//4	—	5.00	7.50	12.00	20.00	30.00
AH112x//5	—	5.00	7.50	12.00	20.00	30.00

Mint: Kanbayat
KM# 347.10 RUPEE
Silver **Note:** Weight varies 11.00-11.60 grams.

Date	Mintage	Good	VG	F	VF	XF
AH1119//1 (Ahad)	—	6.00	12.50	25.00	42.00	60.00

Mint: Karimabad
KM# 347.11 RUPEE
Silver **Obv:** Inscription **Rev:** Inscription **Note:** Weight varies 11.00-11.60 grams.

Date	Mintage	Good	VG	F	VF	XF
AH1120//2	—	6.00	12.50	25.00	40.00	60.00
AH11xx//3	—	6.00	12.50	25.00	40.00	60.00
AH1123//5	—	6.00	12.50	25.00	40.00	60.00

Mint: Katak
KM# 347.12 RUPEE
11.4440 g., Silver **Note:** Weight varies 11.00-11.60 grams.

Date	Mintage	Good	VG	F	VF	XF
AH11xx//2	—	5.00	10.00	20.00	35.00	50.00
AH112x//3	—	5.00	10.00	20.00	35.00	50.00
AH1122//4	—	5.00	10.00	20.00	35.00	50.00

Mint: Lahore
KM# 347.13 RUPEE
Silver **Obv:** Inscription, date, 5-petal flower **Rev. Inscription:** Dar-us-Sultanat **Note:** Weight varies 11.00-11.60 grams.

Date	Mintage	Good	VG	F	VF	XF
AH1119//1 (Ahad)	—	5.00	7.50	12.00	20.00	30.00
AH1119//2	—	5.00	7.50	12.00	20.00	30.00
AH1120//2	—	5.00	7.50	12.00	20.00	30.00
AH1120//3	—	5.00	7.50	12.00	20.00	30.00
AH1121//3	—	5.00	7.50	12.00	20.00	30.00
AH1121//4	—	5.00	7.50	12.00	20.00	30.00
AH1122//4	—	5.00	7.50	12.00	20.00	30.00
AH1123//5	—	5.00	7.50	12.00	20.00	30.00

Mint: Lakhnau
KM# 347.14 RUPEE
Silver **Note:** Weight varies 11.00-11.60 grams.

Date	Mintage	Good	VG	F	VF	XF
AH1119//1 (Ahad)	—	5.00	7.50	12.00	20.00	30.00
AHxxxx//2	—	5.00	7.50	12.00	20.00	30.00
AHxxxx//3	—	5.00	7.50	12.00	20.00	30.00
AHxxxx//4	—	5.00	7.50	12.00	20.00	30.00

Mint: Multan
KM# 347.15 RUPEE
Silver **Note:** Weight varies 11.00-11.60 grams.

Date	Mintage	Good	VG	F	VF	XF
AH1119//1 (Ahad)	—	6.00	12.50	25.00	40.00	60.00
AH1119//2	—	6.00	12.50	25.00	40.00	60.00
AH1120//2	—	6.00	12.50	25.00	40.00	60.00
AH1120//3	—	6.00	12.50	25.00	40.00	60.00
AH1121//3	—	6.00	12.50	25.00	40.00	60.00

Mint: Murshidabad
KM# 347.21 RUPEE
11.4440 g., Silver **Obv:** Inscription **Rev:** Inscription **Note:** Weight varies 11.00-11.60 grams.

Date	Mintage	Good	VG	F	VF	XF
AHxxxx//1 (Ahad)	—	—	—	—	—	—
AHxxxx//2	—	—	—	—	—	—

Mint: Peshawar
KM# 347.16 RUPEE
Silver **Note:** Weight varies 11.00-11.60 grams.

Date	Mintage	Good	VG	F	VF	XF
AH1121//3	—	6.00	12.00	20.00	35.00	50.00
AH1121//4	—	6.00	12.00	20.00	35.00	50.00

Mint: Sahrind
KM# 347.17 RUPEE
11.4440 g., Silver **Note:** Weight varies 11.00-11.60 grams.

Date	Mintage	Good	VG	F	VF	XF
AH1119//1 (Ahad)	—	5.00	7.50	12.00	20.00	30.00
AH1119//2	—	5.00	7.50	12.00	20.00	30.00
AH1120//2	—	5.00	7.50	12.00	20.00	30.00
AH1120//3	—	5.00	7.50	12.00	20.00	30.00
AH1121//3	—	5.00	7.50	12.00	20.00	30.00
AH112x//4	—	5.00	7.50	12.00	20.00	30.00
AHxxxx//13	—	5.00	7.50	12.00	20.00	30.00

Mint: Shahabad Qanauj
KM# 347.22 RUPEE
11.4440 g., Silver **Note:** Weight varies 11.00-11.60 grams.

Date	Mintage	Good	VG	F	VF	XF
AHxxxx//1 (Ahad)	—	6.00	12.50	25.00	42.00	60.00

Mint: Shahjahanabad
KM# 347.18 RUPEE
Silver **Obv:** Inscription, date **Rev. Inscription:** Dar-ul-Khilafat **Note:** Weight varies 11.00-11.60 grams.

Date	Mintage	Good	VG	F	VF	XF
AH1119//1 (Ahad)	—	5.00	7.50	12.00	20.00	30.00
AH1119//2	—	5.00	7.50	12.00	20.00	30.00
AH1120//2	—	5.00	7.50	12.00	20.00	30.00
AH1120//3	—	5.00	7.50	12.00	20.00	30.00
AH1121//3	—	5.00	7.50	12.00	20.00	30.00
AH1121//4	—	5.00	7.50	12.00	20.00	30.00
AH1122//4	—	5.00	7.50	12.00	20.00	30.00
AH1122//5	—	5.00	7.50	12.00	20.00	30.00
AH1123//5	—	5.00	7.50	12.00	20.00	30.00
AH1123//6	—	5.00	7.50	12.00	20.00	30.00

Mint: Tatta
KM# 347.19 RUPEE
Silver **Note:** Weight varies 11.00-11.60 grams.

Date	Mintage	Good	VG	F	VF	XF
AHxxxx//2	—	5.00	8.00	16.00	26.00	40.00
AH1121//3	—	5.00	8.00	16.00	26.00	40.00
AH1122//x	—	5.00	8.00	16.00	26.00	40.00
AHxxxx//5	—	5.00	8.00	16.00	26.00	40.00

Mint: Ujjain
KM# 347.20 RUPEE
Silver **Obv:** Inscription **Rev. Inscription:** Dar-ul-Fath **Note:** Weight varies 11.00-11.60 grams.

Date	Mintage	Good	VG	F	VF	XF
AHxxxx//x	—	5.00	7.50	12.00	20.00	30.00

Mint: Haidarabad
KM# A348.37 RUPEE
Silver **Obv:** Inscription **Rev. Inscription:** Dar-ul-Jihud **Note:** Weight varies 11.00-11.60 grams.

Date	Mintage	Good	VG	F	VF	XF
AH1119//1 (Ahad) Rare	—	—	—	—	—	—

Mint: Ahmadabad
KM# 348.1 RUPEE

Silver **Obv. Inscription:** Sikka Mubarak-I-Shah Alam Bahadur Badshah Ghazi **Rev:** Inscription **Note:** Weight varies 11.00-11.60 grams.

Date	Mintage	Good	VG	F	VF	XF
AH1119//1 (Ahad)	—	5.00	7.50	12.00	20.00	30.00
AH1119//2	—	5.00	7.50	12.00	20.00	30.00
AH1120//2	—	5.00	7.50	12.00	20.00	30.00
AH1120//3	—	5.00	7.50	12.00	20.00	30.00
AH1121//3	—	5.00	7.50	12.00	20.00	30.00
AH1121//4	—	5.00	7.50	12.00	20.00	30.00
AH1122//4	—	5.00	7.50	12.00	20.00	30.00
AH1122//5	—	5.00	7.50	12.00	20.00	30.00
AH1123//5	—	5.00	7.50	12.00	20.00	30.00

Mint: Ahmadanagar
KM# 348.2 RUPEE

11.4440 g., Silver **Note:** Weight varies 11.00-11.60 grams.

Date	Mintage	Good	VG	F	VF	XF
AHxxxx//2	—	5.00	8.00	16.00	26.00	40.00
AH1120//3	—	5.00	8.00	16.00	26.00	40.00
AH1121//3	—	5.00	8.00	16.00	26.00	40.00
AH1121//4	—	5.00	8.00	16.00	26.00	40.00
AH1122//4	—	5.00	8.00	16.00	26.00	40.00
AH1122//5	—	5.00	8.00	16.00	26.00	40.00
AH1123//5	—	5.00	8.00	16.00	26.00	40.00

Mint: Ahsanabad
KM# 348.3 RUPEE

Silver **Note:** Weight varies 11.00-11.60 grams.

Date	Mintage	Good	VG	F	VF	XF
AH1119//1 (Ahad)	—	6.00	12.50	25.00	40.00	60.00
AH1122//4	—	6.00	12.50	25.00	40.00	60.00
AH1123//x	—	6.00	12.50	25.00	40.00	60.00

Mint: Ajmer
KM# 348.4 RUPEE

Silver **Obv:** Inscription **Rev. Inscription:** Mustagir-ul-Khilafat **Note:** Weight varies 11.00-11.60 grams.

Date	Mintage	Good	VG	F	VF	XF
AH1119//1 (Ahad)	—	5.00	8.00	16.00	26.00	40.00
AHxxxx//2	—	5.00	8.00	16.00	26.00	40.00
AHxxxx//3	—	5.00	8.00	16.00	26.00	40.00
AH112x//4	—	5.00	8.00	16.00	26.00	40.00
AH1123//x	—	5.00	8.00	16.00	26.00	40.00

Mint: Akbarabad
KM# 348.5 RUPEE

Silver **Obv:** Inscription, date **Rev. Inscription:** Mustagir-ul-Khilafat **Note:** Weight varies 11.00-11.60 grams.

Date	Mintage	Good	VG	F	VF	XF
AH1119//1 (Ahad)	—	5.00	7.50	12.00	20.00	30.00

Mint: Akbarabad
KM# 348.6 RUPEE

Silver **Obv:** Inscription **Rev. Inscription:** Mustagir-ul-Mulk **Note:** Weight varies 11.00-11.60 grams.

Date	Mintage	Good	VG	F	VF	XF
AH1119//1 (Ahad)	—	5.00	7.50	12.00	20.00	30.00
AH1119//2	—	5.00	7.50	12.00	20.00	30.00
AH1120//2	—	5.00	7.50	12.00	20.00	30.00
AH1120//3	—	5.00	7.50	12.00	20.00	30.00
AH1121//3	—	5.00	7.50	12.00	20.00	30.00
AH1121//4	—	5.00	7.50	12.00	20.00	30.00
AH1122//4	—	5.00	7.50	12.00	20.00	30.00
AH112x//5	—	5.00	7.50	12.00	20.00	30.00

Mint: Akbarnagar
KM# 348.7 RUPEE

Silver **Note:** Weight varies 11.00-11.60 grams.

Date	Mintage	Good	VG	F	VF	XF
AHxxxx//2	—	5.00	8.00	16.00	28.00	40.00

Mint: Alamgirpur
KM# 348.8 RUPEE

Silver **Note:** Weight varies 11.00-11.60 grams.

Date	Mintage	Good	VG	F	VF	XF
AH1120//3	—	6.00	12.50	20.00	32.50	50.00
AH1121//3	—	6.00	12.50	20.00	32.50	50.00
AH1123//x	—	6.00	12.50	20.00	32.50	50.00

Mint: Arkat
KM# 348.9 RUPEE

Silver **Note:** Weight varies 11.00-11.60 grams.

Date	Mintage	Good	VG	F	VF	XF
AH1120//2	—	8.00	20.00	40.00	65.00	100
AH1120//3	—	8.00	20.00	40.00	65.00	100
AH1121//3	—	8.00	20.00	40.00	65.00	100
AH1121//4	—	8.00	20.00	40.00	65.00	100
AH1122//4	—	8.00	20.00	40.00	65.00	100
AH1122//5	—	8.00	20.00	40.00	65.00	100
AH1122//6	—	8.00	20.00	40.00	65.00	100

Mint: Ausa
KM# 348.10 RUPEE

Silver **Note:** Weight varies 11.00-11.60 grams.

Date	Mintage	Good	VG	F	VF	XF
AHxxxx//3	—	8.00	20.00	40.00	65.00	100
AHxxxx//4	—	8.00	20.00	40.00	65.00	100
AH1122//5	—	8.00	20.00	40.00	65.00	100

Mint: Azamnagar
KM# 348.11 RUPEE

Silver **Note:** Weight varies 11.00-11.60 grams.

Date	Mintage	Good	VG	F	VF	XF
AHxxxx//2 Rare	—	—	—	—	—	—

Mint: Bahadargarh
KM# 348.12 RUPEE

Silver **Note:** Weight varies 11.00-11.60 grams.

Date	Mintage	Good	VG	F	VF	XF
AH1123//6 Rare	—	—	—	—	—	—

Mint: Baramati
KM# 348.37 RUPEE

Silver **Note:** Weight varies 11.00-11.60 grams.

Date	Mintage	Good	VG	F	VF	XF
AH1123//x Rare	—	—	—	—	—	—

Mint: Bijapur
KM# 348.13 RUPEE

Silver **Obv:** Inscription **Rev. Inscription:** Dar-uz-Zafar **Note:** Weight varies 11.00-11.60 grams.

Date	Mintage	Good	VG	F	VF	XF
AHxxxx//2	—	5.00	8.00	16.00	26.00	40.00
AH1121//4	—	5.00	8.00	16.00	26.00	40.00

Mint: Burhanpur
KM# 348.14 RUPEE

Silver **Obv:** Inscription **Rev. Inscription:** Dar-us-Sarur **Note:** Weight varies 11.00-11.60 grams.

Date	Mintage	Good	VG	F	VF	XF
AH1119//1 (Ahad)	—	5.00	7.50	12.00	20.00	30.00
AH1119//2	—	5.00	7.50	12.00	20.00	30.00
AH1120//2	—	5.00	7.50	12.00	20.00	30.00
AH1120//3	—	5.00	7.50	12.00	20.00	30.00
AH1121//3	—	5.00	7.50	12.00	20.00	30.00
AH1122//4	—	5.00	7.50	12.00	20.00	30.00
AH1122//4	—	5.00	7.50	12.00	20.00	30.00
AH1123//5	—	5.00	7.50	12.00	20.00	30.00
AH1123//5	—	5.00	7.50	12.00	20.00	30.00
AH11(24)//6	—	5.00	7.50	12.00	20.00	30.00

Mint: Elichpur
KM# 348.15 RUPEE

Silver **Note:** Weight varies 11.00-11.60 grams.

Date	Mintage	Good	VG	F	VF	XF
AH1119//1 (Ahad)	—	9.00	22.50	35.00	50.00	75.00
AH1122//5	—	9.00	22.50	35.00	50.00	75.00
AH1123//5	—	9.00	22.50	35.00	50.00	75.00
AH1123//6	—	9.00	22.50	35.00	50.00	75.00
AH1123//6	—	9.00	22.50	35.00	50.00	75.00

Mint: Firozgarh
KM# 348.16 RUPEE

Silver **Note:** Weight varies 11.00-11.60 grams.

Date	Mintage	Good	VG	F	VF	XF
AH1121//3	—	9.00	22.50	35.00	50.00	75.00
AH1122//4	—	9.00	22.50	35.00	50.00	75.00
AH1122//5	—	9.00	22.50	35.00	50.00	75.00
AH1123//5	—	9.00	22.50	35.00	50.00	75.00

Mint: Firoznagar
KM# 348.17 RUPEE

Silver **Obv:** Inscription, stars and date **Rev:** Inscription **Note:** Weight varies 11.00-11.60 grams.

Date	Mintage	Good	VG	F	VF	XF
AH1122//4	—	9.00	22.50	35.00	50.00	75.00
AH1122//5	—	9.00	22.50	35.00	50.00	75.00
AH1123//5	—	9.00	22.50	35.00	50.00	75.00
AH1124//6	—	9.00	22.50	35.00	50.00	75.00

Mint: Guti
KM# 348.18 RUPEE

Silver **Note:** Weight varies 11.00-11.60 grams.

Date	Mintage	Good	VG	F	VF	XF
AHxxxx//5 Rare	—	—	—	—	—	—

Mint: Haidarabad
KM# 348.19 RUPEE

Silver **Obv:** Inscription **Rev. Inscription:** Farkhanda Bunyad **Note:** Weight varies 11.00-11.60 grams.

Date	Mintage	Good	VG	F	VF	XF
AH1120//2	—	5.00	7.50	12.00	20.00	30.00
AH1120//3	—	5.00	7.50	12.00	20.00	30.00
AH1121//3	—	5.00	7.50	12.00	20.00	30.00
AH1121//4	—	5.00	7.50	12.00	20.00	30.00
AH1122//4	—	5.00	7.50	12.00	20.00	30.00
AH1122//5	—	5.00	7.50	12.00	20.00	30.00
AH1123//5	—	5.00	7.50	12.00	20.00	30.00

Mint: Imtiyazgarh
KM# 348.20 RUPEE

Silver **Note:** Weight varies 11.00-11.60 grams.

Date	Mintage	Good	VG	F	VF	XF
AH1122//4 Rare	—	—	—	—	—	—

Mint: Junagarh
KM# 348.21 RUPEE

Silver **Obv:** Inscription **Rev:** Inscription **Note:** Weight varies 11.00-11.60 grams.

Date	Mintage	Good	VG	F	VF	XF
AH1119//1 (Ahad)	—	5.00	8.00	16.00	26.00	40.00
AH1119//2	—	5.00	8.00	16.00	26.00	40.00
AH1120//2	—	5.00	8.00	16.00	26.00	40.00
AH1120//3	—	5.00	8.00	16.00	26.00	40.00
AH1121//3	—	5.00	8.00	16.00	26.00	40.00

Mint: Kabul
KM# 348.22 RUPEE

Silver **Obv:** Inscription **Rev. Inscription:** Dar-ul-Mulk **Note:** Weight varies 11.00-11.60 grams.

Date	Mintage	Good	VG	F	VF	XF
AH1120//2	—	5.00	8.00	16.00	26.00	40.00
AH1120//3	—	5.00	8.00	16.00	26.00	40.00
AH1121//3	—	5.00	8.00	16.00	26.00	40.00
AH1121//4	—	5.00	8.00	16.00	26.00	40.00
AH1122//4	—	5.00	8.00	16.00	26.00	40.00
AH1122//5	—	5.00	8.00	16.00	26.00	40.00
AH1123//5	—	5.00	8.00	16.00	26.00	40.00

Mint: Kanbayat
KM# 348.23 RUPEE

Silver **Note:** Weight varies 11.00-11.60 grams.

Date	Mintage	Good	VG	F	VF	XF
AHxxxx//1 (Ahad)	—	5.00	7.50	12.00	20.00	30.00
AHxxxx//2	—	5.00	7.50	12.00	20.00	30.00
AHxxxx//3	—	5.00	7.50	12.00	20.00	30.00
AHxxxx//4	—	5.00	7.50	12.00	20.00	30.00
AHxxxx//5	—	5.00	7.50	12.00	20.00	30.00

Mint: Kashmir
KM# 348.24 RUPEE
Silver **Obv:** Inscription **Rev:** Inscription **Note:** Weight varies 11.00-11.60 grams.

Date	Mintage	Good	VG	F	VF	XF
AH1120//2	—	6.00	15.00	25.00	35.00	50.00
AH1122//4	—	6.00	15.00	25.00	35.00	50.00
AH1123//5	—	6.00	15.00	25.00	35.00	50.00

Mint: Khujista Bunyad
KM# 348.25 RUPEE
Silver **Obv:** Inscription, date **Rev:** Inscription **Note:** Weight varies 11.00-11.60 grams.

Date	Mintage	Good	VG	F	VF	XF
AH1119//1 (Ahad)	—	5.00	7.50	12.00	20.00	30.00
AH1119//2	—	5.00	7.50	12.00	20.00	30.00
AH1120//2	—	5.00	7.50	12.00	20.00	30.00
AH1120//3	—	5.00	7.50	12.00	20.00	30.00
AH1121//3	—	5.00	7.50	12.00	20.00	30.00
AH1121//4	—	5.00	7.50	12.00	20.00	30.00
AH1122//4	—	5.00	7.50	12.00	20.00	30.00
AH1122//5	—	5.00	7.50	12.00	20.00	30.00
AH1123//5	—	5.00	7.50	12.00	20.00	30.00
AH1123//6	—	5.00	7.50	12.00	20.00	30.00
AH1124//6	—	5.00	7.50	12.00	20.00	30.00

Mint: Mahmud Bandar
KM# 348.26 RUPEE
Silver **Note:** Weight varies 11.00-11.60 grams.

Date	Mintage	Good	VG	F	VF	XF
AH1121//3 Rare	—	—	—	—	—	—

Mint: Mailapur
KM# 348.27 RUPEE
Silver **Note:** Weight varies 11.00-11.60 grams.

Date	Mintage	Good	VG	F	VF	XF
AH1120//2 Rare	—	—	—	—	—	—
AH1122//4 Rare	—	—	—	—	—	—

Mint: Muhammadabad
KM# 348.28 RUPEE
Silver **Note:** Weight varies 11.00-11.60 grams.

Date	Mintage	Good	VG	F	VF	XF
AHxxxx//1 (Ahad)	—	6.00	12.50	25.00	42.00	60.00
AH1119//2	—	6.00	12.50	25.00	42.00	60.00
AH1120//2	—	6.00	12.50	25.00	42.00	60.00
AH1120//3	—	6.00	12.50	25.00	42.00	60.00
AH1121//3	—	6.00	12.50	25.00	42.00	60.00
AH1121//4	—	6.00	12.50	25.00	42.00	60.00
AH1122//4	—	6.00	12.50	25.00	42.00	60.00
AH1124//6	—	6.00	12.50	25.00	42.00	60.00

Mint: Narnol
KM# 348.29 RUPEE
Silver **Note:** Weight varies 11.00-11.60 grams.

Date	Mintage	Good	VG	F	VF	XF
AH1121//3	—	5.00	8.00	16.00	26.00	40.00
AH1122//4	—	5.00	8.00	16.00	26.00	40.00

Mint: Nusratabad
KM# 348.30 RUPEE
Silver **Note:** Weight varies 11.00-11.60 grams.

Date	Mintage	Good	VG	F	VF	XF
AH1122//4	—	6.00	12.50	25.00	42.00	60.00

Mint: Parenda
KM# 348.31 RUPEE
Silver **Note:** Weight varies 11.00-11.60 grams.

Date	Mintage	Good	VG	F	VF	XF
AH1120//2	—	6.00	12.50	25.00	42.00	60.00
AH1121//3	—	6.00	12.50	25.00	42.00	60.00

Date	Mintage	Good	VG	F	VF	XF
AH1122//4	—	6.00	12.50	25.00	42.00	60.00
AH1123//5	—	6.00	12.50	25.00	42.00	60.00

Mint: Sholapur
KM# 348.32 RUPEE
Silver **Note:** Weight varies 11.00-11.60 grams.

Date	Mintage	Good	VG	F	VF	XF
AHxxxx//2	—	6.00	12.50	25.00	42.00	60.00
AH1122//4	—	6.00	12.50	25.00	42.00	60.00
AH1122//5	—	6.00	12.50	25.00	42.00	60.00
AH1123//5	—	6.00	12.50	25.00	42.00	60.00

Mint: Sikakul
KM# 348.33 RUPEE
11.4440 g., Silver **Note:** Weight varies 11.00-11.60 grams.

Date	Mintage	Good	VG	F	VF	XF
AHxxxx//1 (Ahad) Rare	—	—	—	—	—	—
AHxxxx//4 Rare	—	—	—	—	—	—

Mint: Surat
KM# 348.34 RUPEE
Silver **Obv:** Inscription **Rev:** Inscription **Note:** Weight varies 11.00-11.60 grams.

Date	Mintage	Good	VG	F	VF	XF
AH1119//1 (Ahad)	—	5.00	7.50	12.00	20.00	30.00
AH1119//2	—	5.00	7.50	12.00	20.00	30.00
AH1120//2	—	5.00	7.50	12.00	20.00	30.00
AH1120//3	—	5.00	7.50	12.00	20.00	30.00
AH1121//3	—	5.00	7.50	12.00	20.00	30.00
AH1121//4	—	5.00	7.50	12.00	20.00	30.00
AH1122//4	—	5.00	7.50	12.00	20.00	30.00
AH1122//5	—	5.00	7.50	12.00	20.00	30.00
AH1123//5	—	5.00	7.50	12.00	20.00	30.00
AH1123//6	—	5.00	7.50	12.00	20.00	30.00
AH1124//6	—	5.00	7.50	12.00	20.00	30.00

Mint: Toragal
KM# 348.35 RUPEE
Silver **Obv:** Inscription, date **Rev:** Inscription, beaded flowers **Note:** Weight varies 11.00-11.60 grams.

Date	Mintage	Good	VG	F	VF	XF
AH1120//x Rare	—	—	—	—	—	—
AH1123//4 Rare	—	—	—	—	—	—
AH1123//x Rare	—	—	—	—	—	—

Mint: Ujjain
KM# 348.36 RUPEE
Silver **Obv:** Inscription **Rev. Inscription:** Dar-ul-Fath **Note:** Weight varies 11.00-11.60 grams.

Date	Mintage	Good	VG	F	VF	XF
AH1119//1 (Ahad)	—	5.00	7.50	12.00	20.00	30.00
AH1120//2	—	5.00	7.50	12.00	20.00	30.00
AH1121//3	—	5.00	7.50	12.00	20.00	30.00
AH112x//5	—	5.00	7.50	12.00	20.00	30.00

Mint: Akbarnagar
KM# 349.1 HEAVY RUPEE
Silver **Note:** Weight varies 13.40-13.70 grams.

Date	Mintage	Good	VG	F	VF	XF
AH1123//5	—	—	—	—	—	—

Mint: Azimabad
KM# 349.2 HEAVY RUPEE
Silver **Note:** Weight varies 13.40-13.70 grams.

Date	Mintage	Good	VG	F	VF	XF
AH1123//5	—	—	—	—	—	—

Mint: Lahore
KM# 349.3 HEAVY RUPEE
Silver **Note:** Weight varies 13.40-13.70 grams.

Date	Mintage	Good	VG	F	VF	XF
AH1123//5	—	—	—	—	—	—

Mint: Shahjahanabad
KM# 349.4 HEAVY RUPEE
Silver **Note:** Weight varies 13.40-13.70 grams.

Date	Mintage	Good	VG	F	VF	XF
AH1123//5	—	—	—	—	—	—

Mint: Karimabad
KM# A350 HEAVY NAZARANA RUPEE
Silver **Note:** Weight varies 13.40-13.70 grams.

Date	Mintage	Good	VG	F	VF	XF
AH1123//5	—	—	—	—	—	—

Mint: Azimabad
KM# 350.1 MOHUR
Gold **Obv. Inscription:** Muazzqm, the Second Alamgir **Rev:** Inscription **Note:** Weight varies 10.60-10.90 grams.

Date	Mintage	Good	VG	F	VF	XF
AHxxxx//1 (Ahad) Rare	—	—	—	—	—	—

Mint: Akbarabad
KM# 351.1 MOHUR
Gold **Note:** Without epithet. Weight varies 10.60-10.90 grams.

Date	Mintage	Good	VG	F	VF	XF
AH1119 Shawwal Rare	—	—	—	—	—	—

Note: Shawwal = first month.

Mint: Akbarabad
KM# 352.1 MOHUR
Gold **Obv. Inscription:** Bahadur Shah, the second Alamgir **Rev. Inscription:** Mustagir-ul-Khilafat **Note:** Type 352. Weight varies 10.60-10.90 grams.

Date	Mintage	Good	VG	F	VF	XF
AH1119//1 (Ahad)	—	—	250	325	425	550

Mint: Allahabad
KM# 354.6 MOHUR
Gold **Obv. Inscription:** Sikka-I-Shah Alam Badshah Ghazi **Rev:** Inscription, date **Note:** Weight varies 10.60-10.90 grams.

Date	Mintage	Good	VG	F	VF	XF
AH1119//1 (Ahad)	—	235	265	325	375	450
AH1122//4	—	235	265	325	375	450

Mint: Itawa
KM# 354.1 MOHUR
Gold **Obv:** Inscription, date **Rev:** Inscription **Note:** Weight varies 10.60-10.90 grams.

Date	Mintage	Good	VG	F	VF	XF
AH1120//2	—	235	265	325	375	450
AH1121//3	—	235	265	325	375	450

Mint: Lahore
KM# 354.2 MOHUR
Gold **Obv:** Inscription, date **Rev. Inscription:** Dar-us-Sultanat **Note:** Weight varies 10.60-10.90 grams.

Date	Mintage	Good	VG	F	VF	XF
AH1120//2	—	235	265	325	375	450
AH1124//6	—	235	265	325	375	450

Mint: Multan
KM# 354.3 MOHUR
Gold **Note:** Weight varies 10.60-10.90 grams.

Date	Mintage	Good	VG	F	VF	XF
AH1119//1 (Ahad)	—	235	265	325	425	550
AH1121//3	—	235	265	325	425	550

Mint: Shahjahanabad
KM# 354.4 MOHUR
Gold **Obv:** Inscription **Rev. Inscription:** Dar-ul-Khilafat **Note:** Weight varies 10.60-10.90 grams.

Date	Mintage	Good	VG	F	VF	XF
AH1119//1 (Ahad)	—	235	265	325	375	450
AH1119//2	—	235	265	325	375	450

Date	Mintage	Good	VG	F	VF	XF
AH1120//2	—	235	265	325	375	450
AH1120//3	—	235	265	325	375	450
AH1121//3	—	235	265	325	375	450

Mint: Tatta
KM# 354.5 MOHUR
Gold **Note:** Weight varies 10.60-10.90 grams.

Date	Mintage	Good	VG	F	VF	XF
ND//x	—	235	265	325	375	450

Mint: Kabul
KM# A356.19 MOHUR
Gold **Obv:** Inscription **Rev. Inscription:** Dar-ul-Mulk **Note:** Weight varies 10.60-10.90 grams.

Date	Mintage	Good	VG	F	VF	XF
AH1120//x Rare	—	—	—	—	—	—
AH1123//x Rare	—	—	—	—	—	—

Mint: Akbarabad
KM# 356.1 MOHUR
Gold **Obv. Inscription:** Sikka Mubarak-I-Shah Alam Bahadur Badshah Ghazi **Rev. Inscription:** Mustagir-ul-Khilafat **Note:** Weight varies 10.60-10.90 grams.

Date	Mintage	Good	VG	F	VF	XF
AH1119//1 (Ahad)	—	235	265	235	375	450

Mint: Akbarabad
KM# 356.2 MOHUR
Gold **Obv:** Inscription **Rev. Inscription:** Mustagir-ul-Mulk **Note:** Weight varies 10.60-10.90 grams.

Date	Mintage	Good	VG	F	VF	XF
AH11xx//2	—	235	265	325	375	450
AHxxxx//3	—	235	265	325	375	450
AHxxxx//4	—	235	265	325	375	450
AH1123//5	—	235	265	325	375	450
AH112x//6	—	235	265	325	375	450

Mint: Arkat
KM# 356.18 MOHUR
Gold **Note:** Weight varies 10.60-10.90 grams.

Date	Mintage	Good	VG	F	VF	XF
AH1120//2	—	250	350	500	700	1,000

Mint: Azimabad
KM# 356.19 MOHUR
Gold **Note:** Weight varies 10.60-10.90 grams.

Date	Mintage	Good	VG	F	VF	XF
AH1119//1 (Ahad)	—	—	—	—	—	—

Mint: Burhanpur
KM# 356.3 MOHUR
Gold **Rev:** Mint epithet: "Dar-us-Sarur" **Note:** Weight varies 10.60-10.90 grams.

Date	Mintage	Good	VG	F	VF	XF
AHxxxx//1 (Ahad)	—	235	265	310	375	450
AH1120//2	—	235	265	310	375	450
AH112x//4	—	235	265	310	375	450
AH112x//5	—	235	265	310	375	450
11xx//14	—	235	265	310	375	450

Mint: Elichpur
KM# 356.21 MOHUR
Gold **Note:** Weight varies 10.60-10.90 grams.

Date	Mintage	Good	VG	F	VF	XF
AH1124//6 Rare	—	—	—	—	—	—

Mint: Firozgarh
KM# 356.4 MOHUR
Gold **Note:** Weight varies 10.60-10.90 grams.

Date	Mintage	Good	VG	F	VF	XF
AH112x//3	—	235	265	335	425	550
AH1122//x	—	235	265	335	425	550

Mint: Haidarabad
KM# 356.5 MOHUR
Gold **Obv:** Inscription **Rev. Inscription:** Dar-ul-Jihad **Note:** Weight varies 10.60-10.90 grams.

Date	Mintage	Good	VG	F	VF	XF
AH1120//x	—	235	265	310	375	450

Mint: Haidarabad
KM# 356.6 MOHUR
Gold **Obv:** Inscription **Rev. Inscription:** Farkhanda Bunyad **Note:** Weight varies 10.60-10.90 grams.

Date	Mintage	Good	VG	F	VF	XF
AH1122//5	—	235	265	310	375	450
AH1123//5	—	235	265	310	375	450

Mint: Khujista Bunyad
KM# 356.7 MOHUR
Gold **Obv:** Inscription, date **Rev:** Inscription **Note:** Weight varies 10.60-10.90 grams.

Date	Mintage	Good	VG	F	VF	XF
AH1119//1 (Ahad)	—	235	265	310	375	450
AH1119//2	—	235	265	310	375	450
AH1120//2	—	235	265	310	375	450
AH1120//3	—	235	265	310	375	450
AH1121//3	—	235	265	310	375	450
AH1121//4	—	235	265	310	375	450
AH1123//5	—	235	265	310	375	450
AH1124//6	—	235	265	310	375	450

Mint: Mailapur
KM# 356.8 MOHUR
Gold **Note:** Weight varies 10.60-10.90 grams.

Date	Mintage	Good	VG	F	VF	XF
AH1121//2 (sic) Rare	—	—	—	—	—	—

Mint: Muhammadabad
KM# 356.9 MOHUR
Gold **Note:** Weight varies 10.60-10.90 grams.

Date	Mintage	Good	VG	F	VF	XF
AHxxxx//1 (Ahad)	—	235	265	335	425	550

Mint: Nusratabad
KM# 356.22 MOHUR
Gold **Note:** Weight varies 10.60-10.90 grams.

Date	Mintage	Good	VG	F	VF	XF
AH1122//4 Rare	—	—	—	—	—	—

Mint: Parenda
KM# 356.10 MOHUR
Gold **Note:** Weight varies 10.60-10.90 grams.

Date	Mintage	Good	VG	F	VF	XF
AH1122//4	—	235	265	335	425	550

Mint: Peshawar
KM# 356.11 MOHUR
Gold **Obv:** Inscription, date **Rev:** Inscription **Note:** Weight varies 10.60-10.90 grams.

Date	Mintage	Good	VG	F	VF	XF
AH1120//2	—	235	265	325	400	500
AH1121//3	—	235	265	325	400	500

Mint: Shahjahanabad
KM# 356.12 MOHUR
Gold **Obv:** Inscription **Rev. Inscription:** Dar-ul-Khilafat **Note:** Weight varies 10.60-10.90 grams.

Date	Mintage	Good	VG	F	VF	XF
AH1122//4	—	235	265	310	375	450
AH1122//5	—	235	265	310	375	450
AH1123//5	—	235	265	310	375	450

Mint: Sholapur
KM# 356.13 MOHUR
Gold **Note:** Weight varies 10.60-10.90 grams.

Date	Mintage	Good	VG	F	VF	XF
AH1121//x	—	235	265	310	375	450

Mint: Sikakul
KM# 356.23 MOHUR
Gold **Note:** Weight varies 10.60-10.90 grams.

Date	Mintage	Good	VG	F	VF	XF
AH112x//4	—	—	—	—	—	—

Mint: Surat
KM# 356.14 MOHUR
Gold **Obv:** Inscription **Rev:** Inscription **Note:** Weight varies 10.60-10.90 grams.

Date	Mintage	Good	VG	F	VF	XF
AH1119//x	—	235	265	310	375	450

Mint: Toragal
KM# 356.15 MOHUR
Gold **Note:** Weight varies 10.60-10.90 grams.

Date	Mintage	Good	VG	F	VF	XF
AHxxxx//4 Rare	—	—	—	—	—	—

Mint: Ujjain
KM# 356.16 MOHUR
Gold **Obv:** Inscription **Rev. Inscription:** Dar-ul-Fath **Note:** Weight varies 10.60-10.90 grams.

Date	Mintage	Good	VG	F	VF	XF
AH1122//x	—	235	265	310	375	450

Mint: Akbarabad
KM# 357.1 NAZARANA MOHUR
Gold **Obv:** Inscription, date **Rev:** Inscription **Note:** Weight varies: 11.80-12.00 grams.

Date	Mintage	Good	VG	F	VF	XF
AH1123//5 Rare	—	—	—	—	—	—

Azim-ush-Shan

In Bengal, AH1124 / 1712AD

HAMMERED COINAGE

Mint: Jahangirnagar
KM# 358.1 RUPEE
Silver **Obv:** Inscription, date **Rev:** Inscription **Note:** Weight varies 11.00-11.60 grams.

Date	Mintage	Good	VG	F	VF	XF
AH1124//1 (Ahad) Rare	—	—	—	—	—	—

Mint: Katak
KM# 358.2 RUPEE
Silver **Note:** Weight varies 11.00-11.60 grams.

Date	Mintage	Good	VG	F	VF	XF
AH1124//1 (Ahad) Rare	—	—	—	—	—	—

Jahandar Shah

AH1124 / 1712-1713AD

HAMMERED COINAGE

Largesse Issues

Mint: Shahjahanabad
KM# 366.1 NISAR
1.4600 g., Silver **Obv:** Inscription **Rev. Inscription:** Dar-ul-Khilafat **Note:**

Date	Mintage	Good	VG	F	VF	XF
AH1124//1 (Ahad) Rare	—	—	—	—	—	—

Mint: Shahjahanabad
KM# 367.1 NISAR
2.9200 g., Silver **Obv:** Inscription, date **Rev. Inscription:** Dar-ul-Khilafat **Note:**

Date	Mintage	Good	VG	F	VF	XF
AH1124//1 (Ahad) Rare	—	—	—	—	—	—

HAMMERED COINAGE

Mint: Ahmadabad
KM# 360.1 PAISA
Copper **Obv:** Inscription **Rev:** Inscription **Note:** Weight varies 12.90-13.80 grams.

Date	Mintage	Good	VG	F	VF	XF
AH1124//1 (Ahad)	—	20.00	40.00	65.00	95.00	—

Mint: Bahadarqarh
KM# 360.2 PAISA
Copper **Note:** Weight varies 12.90-13.80 grams.

Date	Mintage	Good	VG	F	VF	XF
AH1124//1 (Ahad) Rare	—	—	—	—	—	—

Mint: Bijapur
KM# 360.3 PAISA
Copper **Note:** Weight varies 12.90-13.80 grams.

Date	Mintage	Good	VG	F	VF	XF
AH1124//1 (Ahad) Rare	—	—	—	—	—	—

Mint: Farkhanda Bunyad
KM# 360.4 PAISA
Copper **Note:** Weight varies 12.90-13.80 grams.

Date	Mintage	Good	VG	F	VF	XF
AH1124//1 (Ahad)	—	20.00	40.00	65.00	95.00	—

Mint: Kabul
KM# 360.5 PAISA
Copper **Note:** Weight varies 12.90-13.80 grams.

Date	Mintage	Good	VG	F	VF	XF
AH1124//1 (Ahad) Rare	—	—	—	—	—	—

Mint: Muzzamabad
KM# 360.6 PAISA
Copper **Note:** Weight varies 12.90-13.80 grams.

Date	Mintage	Good	VG	F	VF	XF
AH1124//1 (Ahad) Rare	—	—	—	—	—	—

Mint: Surat
KM# 360.7 PAISA
Copper **Note:** Weight varies 12.90-13.80 grams.

Date	Mintage	Good	VG	F	VF	XF
AH1124//1 (Ahad)	—	20.00	40.00	65.00	95.00	—

Mint: Surat
KM# 361.1 1/4 RUPEE
Silver **Note:** Weight varies 2.75-2.90 grams.

Date	Mintage	Good	VG	F	VF	XF
AHxxxx//1 (Ahad) Rare	—	—	—	—	—	—

Mint: Burhanpur
KM# 362.2 1/2 RUPEE
Silver **Obv:** Inscription **Rev:** Inscription **Note:** Weight varies 5.50-5.80 grams.

Date	Mintage	Good	VG	F	VF	XF
AHxxxx//1 (Ahad)	—	—	—	—	—	—

Mint: Kashmir
KM# 362.3 1/2 RUPEE
Silver **Note:** Weight varies 5.50-5.80 grams.

Date	Mintage	Good	VG	F	VF	XF
AHxxxx//1 (Ahad)	—	—	—	—	—	—

Mint: Multan
KM# 362.4 1/2 RUPEE
Silver **Note:** Weight varies 5.50-5.80 grams.

Date	Mintage	Good	VG	F	VF	XF
AH1124//1 (Ahad)	—	—	—	—	—	—

Mint: Surat
KM# 362.1 1/2 RUPEE
Silver **Note:** Weight varies 5.50-5.80 grams.

Date	Mintage	Good	VG	F	VF	XF
AH1124//1 (Ahad) Rare	—	—	—	—	—	—

Mint: Akbarnagar
KM# 362A.1 1/2 RUPEE
Silver **Obv:** Inscription **Rev:** Inscription **Note:** Weight varies 5.50-5.80 grams.

Date	Mintage	Good	VG	F	VF	XF
AH1124//1 (Ahad) Rare	—	—	—	—	—	—

Mint: Surat
KM# 362A.2 1/2 RUPEE
Silver **Note:** Weight varies 5.50-5.80 grams.

Date	Mintage	Good	VG	F	VF	XF
AH1124//1 (Ahad) Rare	—	—	—	—	—	—

Mint: Ahmadabad
KM# 363.1 RUPEE
Silver **Obv. Inscription:** Abu Fath Jahandar Shah Ghazi **Rev:** Inscription **Note:** Weight varies 11.00-11.60 grams.

Date	Mintage	Good	VG	F	VF	XF
AH1124//1 (Ahad)	—	5.00	10.00	20.00	35.00	50.00

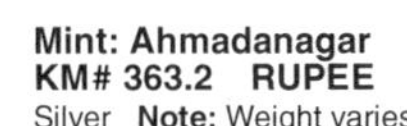

Mint: Ahmadanagar
KM# 363.2 RUPEE
Silver **Note:** Weight varies 11.00-11.60 grams.

Date	Mintage	Good	VG	F	VF	XF
AH1124//1 (Ahad)	—	6.00	12.50	25.00	42.50	60.00

Mint: Akbarabad
KM# 363.3 RUPEE
Silver **Obv:** Inscription **Rev. Inscription:** Mustagir-ul-Mulk **Note:** Weight varies 11.00-11.60 grams.

Date	Mintage	Good	VG	F	VF	XF
AH1124//1 (Ahad)	—	5.00	10.00	20.00	35.00	50.00

Mint: Akbarnagar
KM# 363.3a RUPEE
Silver **Note:**

Date	Mintage	Good	VG	F	VF	XF
AH(11)24//1 (Ahad)	—	—	—	—	—	—

Mint: Akbarpur
KM# 363.4 RUPEE
Silver **Note:** Weight varies 11.00-11.60 grams.

Date	Mintage	Good	VG	F	VF	XF
AH1124//1 (Ahad)	—	6.50	15.00	30.00	50.00	70.00

Mint: Alamgirpur
KM# 363.27 RUPEE
Silver **Note:** Weight varies 11.00-11.60 grams.

Date	Mintage	Good	VG	F	VF	XF
AHxxxx//1 (Ahad)	—	—	—	—	—	—

Mint: Allahabad
KM# 363.25 RUPEE
Silver **Note:** Weight varies 11.00-11.60 grams.

Date	Mintage	Good	VG	F	VF	XF
AH1124//1 (Ahad)	—	—	—	—	—	—

Mint: Arkat
KM# 363.5 RUPEE
Silver **Note:** Weight varies 11.00-11.60 grams.

Date	Mintage	Good	VG	F	VF	XF
AH1124//1 (Ahad)	—	12.00	30.00	60.00	100	160

Mint: Ausa
KM# 363.6 RUPEE
Silver **Note:** Weight varies 11.00-11.60 grams.

Date	Mintage	Good	VG	F	VF	XF
AH1124//1 (Ahad) Rare	—	—	—	—	—	—

Mint: Bahadarqarh
KM# 363.7 RUPEE
Silver **Obv:** Inscription **Rev:** Inscription **Note:** Weight varies 11.00-11.60 grams.

Date	Mintage	Good	VG	F	VF	XF
AH1124//1 (Ahad)	—	40.00	100	200	325	450

Mint: Baramati
KM# 363.28 RUPEE
Silver **Note:** Weight varies 11.00-11.60 grams.

Date	Mintage	Good	VG	F	VF	XF
AHxxxx//1 (Ahad)	—	—	—	—	—	—

Mint: Bijapur
KM# 363.8 RUPEE
Silver **Obv:** Inscription **Rev. Inscription:** Dar-uz-Zafar **Note:** Weight varies 11.00-11.60 grams.

Date	Mintage	Good	VG	F	VF	XF
AH1124//1 (Ahad)	—	6.00	12.50	25.00	42.00	60.00

Mint: Burhanpur
KM# 363.9 RUPEE
Silver **Obv:** Inscription **Rev. Inscription:** Dar-us-Sarur **Note:** Weight varies 11.00-11.60 grams.

Date	Mintage	Good	VG	F	VF	XF
AH1124//1 (Ahad)	—	5.00	10.00	20.00	35.00	50.00

Mint: Elichpur
KM# 363.10 RUPEE
Silver **Note:** Weight varies 11.00-11.60 grams.

Date	Mintage	Good	VG	F	VF	XF
AH1124//1 (Ahad)	—	10.00	25.00	50.00	85.00	120

Mint: Fathabad Dharur
KM# 363.11 RUPEE
Silver **Note:** Weight varies 11.00-11.60 grams.

Date	Mintage	Good	VG	F	VF	XF
AH1124//1 (Ahad) Rare	—	—	—	—	—	—

Mint: Firozgarh
KM# 363.24 RUPEE
Silver **Note:** Weight varies 11.00-11.60 grams.

Date	Mintage	Good	VG	F	VF	XF
AH1125//1 (Ahad)	—	8.00	21.00	42.00	70.00	100

Mint: Gwalior
KM# 363.12 RUPEE
Silver **Note:** Weight varies 11.00-11.60 grams.

Date	Mintage	Good	VG	F	VF	XF
AH1124//1 (Ahad)	—	5.00	10.00	20.00	35.00	50.00

Mint: Haidarabad
KM# 363.13 RUPEE
Silver **Obv:** Inscription **Rev. Inscription:** Farkhanda Bunyad **Note:** Weight varies 11.00-11.60 grams.

Date	Mintage	Good	VG	F	VF	XF
AH1124//1 (Ahad)	—	6.00	12.50	25.00	42.00	60.00

Mint: Itawa
KM# 363.14 RUPEE
Silver **Obv:** Inscription, date **Rev:** Inscription **Note:** Weight varies 11.00-11.60 grams.

Date	Mintage	Good	VG	F	VF	XF
AH1124//1 (Ahad)	—	5.00	10.00	20.00	35.00	50.00

Mint: Kashmir
KM# 363.26 RUPEE
Silver **Note:** Weight varies 11.00-11.60 grams.

Date	Mintage	Good	VG	F	VF	XF
AH1124//1 (Ahad)	—	20.00	50.00	85.00	120	180

Mint: Khambayat
KM# 363.15 RUPEE
Silver **Note:** Weight varies 11.00-11.60 grams.

Date	Mintage	Good	VG	F	VF	XF
AH1124//1 (Ahad)	—	5.00	10.00	20.00	35.00	50.00

Mint: Khujista Bunyad
KM# 363.16 RUPEE
Silver **Note:** Weight varies 11.00-11.60 grams.

Date	Mintage	Good	VG	F	VF	XF
AH1124//1 (Ahad)	—	6.00	12.50	25.00	42.00	60.00

Mint: Lahore
KM# 363.17 RUPEE
Silver **Obv:** Inscription **Rev. Inscription:** Dar-us-Sultanat **Note:** Weight varies 11.00-11.60 grams.

Date	Mintage	Good	VG	F	VF	XF
AH1124//1 (Ahad)	—	5.00	10.00	20.00	35.00	50.00

Mint: Muazzamabad
KM# 363.29 RUPEE
Silver **Note:** Weight varies 11.00-11.60 grams.

Date	Mintage	Good	VG	F	VF	XF
AH1124//1 (Ahad)	—	—	—	—	—	—

Mint: Muhammadabad
KM# 363.30 RUPEE
Silver **Note:** Weight varies 11.00-11.60 grams.

Date	Mintage	Good	VG	F	VF	XF
AH1124//1 (Ahad)	—	—	—	—	—	—

Mint: Murtazabad
KM# 363.31 RUPEE
Silver **Note:** Weight varies 11.00-11.60 grams.

Date	Mintage	Good	VG	F	VF	XF
AHxxxx//1 (Ahad)	—	—	—	—	—	—

Mint: Nusratabad
KM# 363.32 RUPEE
11.4440 g., Silver **Note:**

Date	Mintage	Good	VG	F	VF	XF
AH1124//1	—	—	—	—	—	—

Mint: Parenda
KM# 363.18 RUPEE
Silver **Note:** Weight varies 11.00-11.60 grams.

Date	Mintage	Good	VG	F	VF	XF
AH1124//1 (Ahad)	—	10.00	25.00	50.00	85.00	120
AH1125//1 (Ahad)	—	10.00	25.00	50.00	85.00	120

Mint: Peshawar
KM# 363.19 RUPEE
Silver **Note:** Weight varies 11.00-11.60 grams.

Date	Mintage	Good	VG	F	VF	XF
AH1124//1 (Ahad) Rare	—	—	—	—	—	—

Mint: Qamarnagar
KM# 363.20 RUPEE
Silver **Note:** Weight varies 11.00-11.60 grams.

Date	Mintage	Good	VG	F	VF	XF
AH1124//1 (Ahad) Rare	—	—	—	—	—	—

Mint: Shahjahanabad
KM# 363.21 RUPEE
Silver **Obv:** Inscription **Rev. Inscription:** Dar-ul-Khilafat **Note:** Weight varies 11.00-11.60 grams.

Date	Mintage	Good	VG	F	VF	XF
AH1124//1 (Ahad)	—	5.00	10.00	20.00	35.00	50.00

Mint: Sholapur
KM# 363.33 RUPEE
Silver **Note:** Weight varies 11.00-11.60 grams.

Date	Mintage	Good	VG	F	VF	XF
AH1124//1 (Ahad)	—	—	—	—	—	—

Mint: Sikakul
KM# 363.34 RUPEE
Silver **Note:** Weight varies 11.00-11.60 grams.

Date	Mintage	Good	VG	F	VF	XF
AHxxxx//1 (Ahad)	—	—	—	—	—	—

Mint: Surat
KM# 363.22 RUPEE
Silver **Note:** Weight varies 11.00-11.60 grams.

Date	Mintage	Good	VG	F	VF	XF
AH1124//1 (Ahad)	—	5.00	10.00	20.00	35.00	50.00

Mint: Ujjain
KM# 363.23 RUPEE
Silver **Note:** Weight varies 11.00-11.60 grams.

Date	Mintage	Good	VG	F	VF	XF
AH1124//1 (Ahad)	—	5.00	10.00	20.00	35.00	50.00

Mint: Ahmadanagar
KM# 364.1 RUPEE
Silver **Obv. Inscription:** Sahib Qiran Jahandar Shah Badshah-i-Jahan **Rev:** Inscription **Note:** Weight varies 11.00-11.60 grams.

Date	Mintage	Good	VG	F	VF	XF
AH1124//1 (Ahad)	—	6.00	12.50	25.00	42.00	60.00

Mint: Ajmer
KM# 364.2 RUPEE
Silver **Obv:** Inscription **Rev. Inscription:** Mustagir-ul-Khilafat **Note:** Weight varies 11.00-11.60 grams.

Date	Mintage	Good	VG	F	VF	XF
AH1124//1 (Ahad)	—	6.00	12.50	25.00	42.00	60.00

Mint: Akbarabad
KM# 364.3 RUPEE
Silver **Obv:** Inscription **Rev. Inscription:** Mustagir-ul-Mulk **Note:** Weight varies 11.00-11.60 grams.

Date	Mintage	Good	VG	F	VF	XF
AH1124//1 (Ahad)	—	5.00	10.00	20.00	35.00	50.00

Mint: Akbarnagar
KM# 364.23 RUPEE
Silver **Note:** Weight varies 11.00-11.60 grams.

Date	Mintage	Good	VG	F	VF	XF
AH1124//1	—	6.50	14.00	28.00	45.00	65.00

Mint: Alamgirpur
KM# 364.25 RUPEE
Silver **Note:** Weight varies 11.00-11.60 grams.

Date	Mintage	Good	VG	F	VF	XF
AHxxxx//1 (Ahad)	—	—	—	—	—	—

Mint: Allahabad
KM# 364.26 RUPEE
Silver **Note:** Weight varies 11.00-11.60 grams.

Date	Mintage	Good	VG	F	VF	XF
AH1124//1 (Ahad)	—	—	—	—	—	—

Mint: Arkat
KM# 364.4 RUPEE
Silver **Note:** Weight varies 11.00-11.60 grams.

Date	Mintage	Good	VG	F	VF	XF
AH1124//1 (Ahad)	—	—	30.00	60.00	100	160

Mint: Azamnagar Gokak
KM# 364.5 RUPEE
Silver **Note:** Weight varies 11.00-11.60 grams.

Date	Mintage	Good	VG	F	VF	XF
AH1124//1 (Ahad)	—	8.00	21.00	42.00	70.00	100
AH1126//x (sic)	—	8.00	21.00	42.00	70.00	100

Mint: Bahadarqarh
KM# 364.6 RUPEE
Silver **Note:** Weight varies 11.00-11.60 grams.

Date	Mintage	Good	VG	F	VF	XF
AH1124//1 (Ahad) Rare	—	—	—	—	—	—

Mint: Bankapur
KM# 364.27 RUPEE
Silver **Note:** Weight varies 11.00-11.60 grams.

Date	Mintage	Good	VG	F	VF	XF
AH1124//1 (Ahad)	—	—	—	—	—	—

Mint: Bareli
KM# 364.7 RUPEE
Silver **Note:** Weight varies 11.00-11.60 grams.

Date	Mintage	Good	VG	F	VF	XF
AH1124//1 (Ahad)	—	5.00	10.00	20.00	35.00	50.00

Mint: Bhakkar
KM# 364.24 RUPEE
Silver **Note:** Weight varies 11.00-11.60 grams.

Date	Mintage	Good	VG	F	VF	XF
AH1124//1 (Ahad) Rare	—	—	—	—	—	—

Mint: Burhanpur
KM# 364.8 RUPEE
Silver **Obv:** Inscription **Rev. Inscription:** Dar-us-Sarur **Note:** Weight varies 11.00-11.60 grams.

Date	Mintage	Good	VG	F	VF	XF
AH1124//1 (Ahad)	—	5.00	10.00	20.00	35.00	50.00

Mint: Gwalior
KM# 364.10 RUPEE
Silver **Note:** Weight varies 11.00-11.60 grams.

Date	Mintage	Good	VG	F	VF	XF
AH1124//1 (Ahad)	—	5.00	10.00	20.00	35.00	50.00

Mint: Haidarabad
KM# 364.11 RUPEE
Silver **Obv:** Inscription **Rev. Inscription:** Farkhanda Bunyad **Note:** Weight varies 11.00-11.60 grams.

Date	Mintage	Good	VG	F	VF	XF
AH1124//1 (Ahad)	—	6.00	12.50	25.00	42.00	60.00

Mint: Itawa
KM# 364.12 RUPEE
Silver **Obv:** Inscription, date **Rev:** Inscription **Note:** Weight varies 11.00-11.60 grams.

Date	Mintage	Good	VG	F	VF	XF
AH1124//1 (Ahad)	—	5.00	10.00	20.00	35.00	50.00

Mint: Jahangirnagar
KM# 364.30 RUPEE
Silver **Note:** Weight varies 11.00-11.60 grams.

Date	Mintage	Good	VG	F	VF	XF
AH1124//1 (Ahad)	—	7.00	17.50	35.00	60.00	85.00

Mint: Kabul
KM# 364.31 RUPEE
Silver **Obv:** Inscription **Rev. Inscription:** Dar-ul-Mulk **Note:** Weight varies 11.00-11.60 grams.

Date	Mintage	Good	VG	F	VF	XF
AHxxxx//1 (Ahad)	—	7.00	17.50	35.00	60.00	85.00

Mint: Katak
KM# 364.28 RUPEE
Silver **Note:** Weight varies 11.00-11.60 grams.

Date	Mintage	Good	VG	F	VF	XF
AHxxxx//1 (Ahad)	—	—	—	—	—	—

Mint: Khujista Bunyad
KM# 364.13 RUPEE
Silver **Note:** Weight varies 11.00-11.60 grams.

Date	Mintage	Good	VG	F	VF	XF
AH1124//1 (Ahad)	—	6.00	12.50	25.00	42.00	60.00

Mint: Lahore
KM# 364.14 RUPEE
Silver **Obv:** Inscription **Rev. Inscription:** Dar-us-Sultanat **Note:** Weight varies 11.00-11.60 grams.

Date	Mintage	Good	VG	F	VF	XF
AH1124//1 (Ahad)	—	5.00	10.00	20.00	35.00	50.00

Mint: Lakhnau
KM# 364.15 RUPEE
Silver **Obv:** Inscription, date **Rev:** Inscription **Note:** Weight varies 11.00-11.60 grams.

Date	Mintage	Good	VG	F	VF	XF
AH1124//1 (Ahad)	—	6.00	12.50	25.00	42.00	60.00

Mint: Multan
KM# 364.32 RUPEE
Silver **Note:** Weight varies 11.00-11.60 grams.

Date	Mintage	Good	VG	F	VF	XF
AH1124//1 (Ahad)	—	6.50	14.00	28.00	45.00	65.00

Mint: Murshidabad
KM# 364.22 RUPEE
Silver **Obv:** Inscription, date **Rev:** Inscription **Note:** Weight varies 11.00-11.60 grams.

Date	Mintage	Good	VG	F	VF	XF
AH1124//1 (Ahad)	—	6.00	12.50	25.00	42.00	60.00

Mint: Sahrind
KM# 364.16 RUPEE
Silver **Note:** Weight varies 11.00-11.60 grams.

Date	Mintage	Good	VG	F	VF	XF
AH1124//1 (Ahad)	—	6.00	12.50	25.00	42.00	60.00

Mint: Shahjahanabad
KM# 364.17 RUPEE
Silver **Note:** Weight varies 11.00-11.60 grams.

Date	Mintage	Good	VG	F	VF	XF
AH1124//1 (Ahad)	—	5.00	10.00	20.00	35.00	50.00

Mint: Sikakul
KM# 364.18 RUPEE
Silver **Note:** Weight varies 11.00-11.60 grams.

Date	Mintage	Good	VG	F	VF	XF
AH1124//1 (Ahad) Rare	—	—	—	—	—	—

Mint: Surat
KM# 364.19 RUPEE
Silver **Obv:** Inscription **Rev:** Inscription **Note:** Weight varies 11.00-11.60 grams.

Date	Mintage	Good	VG	F	VF	XF
AH1124//1 (Ahad)	—	5.00	10.00	20.00	35.00	50.00

Mint: Tatta
KM# 364.20 RUPEE
Silver **Note:** Weight varies 11.00-11.60 grams.

Date	Mintage	Good	VG	F	VF	XF
AH1124//1 (Ahad)	—	7.00	17.50	35.00	60.00	85.00
AH1125//1 (Ahad)	—	7.00	17.50	35.00	60.00	85.00

Mint: Ujjain
KM# 364.29 RUPEE
Silver **Obv:** Inscription **Rev. Inscription:** Dar-ul-Fath **Note:** Weight varies 11.00-11.60 grams.

Date	Mintage	Good	VG	F	VF	XF
AH1124//1 (Ahad)	—	—	—	—	—	—

Mint: Aurangabad
KM# 365.2 RUPEE
Silver **Note:** Weight varies 11.00-11.60 grams.

Date	Mintage	Good	VG	F	VF	XF
AH1124//1 (Ahad)	—	—	14.00	28.00	45.00	65.00

Mint: Kararabad
KM# 365.5 RUPEE
Silver **Note:** Weight varies 11.00-11.60 grams.

Date	Mintage	Good	VG	F	VF	XF
AH1124//1 (Ahad) Rare	—	—	—	—	—	—

Mint: Mumbai
KM# 365.7 RUPEE
Silver **Note:** Weight varies 11.00-11.60 grams.

Date	Mintage	Good	VG	F	VF	XF
AH1124//1 (Ahad)	—	17.50	42.50	85.00	140	200

Mint: Akbarabad
KM# 368.1 MOHUR
Gold **Obv:** Inscription **Rev. Inscription:** Mustagir-ul-Mulk **Note:** Weight varies 10.60-10.90 grams. Similar to Rupee, type 363.

Date	Mintage	Good	VG	F	VF	XF
AH1124//1 (Ahad)	—	235	275	350	475	650

Mint: Burhanpur
KM# 368.2 MOHUR
Gold **Obv:** Inscription **Rev. Inscription:** Dar-us-Sarur **Note:** Weight varies 10.60-10.90 grams.

Date	Mintage	Good	VG	F	VF	XF
AH1124//1 (Ahad)	—	235	275	350	475	650

Mint: Elichpur
KM# 368.10 MOHUR
Gold **Note:** Weight varies 10.60-10.90 grams.

Date	Mintage	Good	VG	F	VF	XF
AHxxxx//1 (Ahad) Rare	—	—	—	—	—	—

Mint: Gulbarga
KM# 368.3 MOHUR
Gold **Note:** Weight varies 10.60-10.90 grams.

Date	Mintage	Good	VG	F	VF	XF
AH1124//1 (Ahad)	—	235	275	350	475	650

Mint: Gwalior
KM# 368.8 MOHUR
Gold **Note:** Weight varies 10.60-10.90 grams.

Date	Mintage	Good	VG	F	VF	XF
AH1124//1 (Ahad)	—	—	175	300	450	650

Mint: Itawa
KM# 368.4 MOHUR
Gold **Note:** Weight varies 10.60-10.90 grams.

Date	Mintage	Good	VG	F	VF	XF
AH1124//1 (Ahad)	—	235	275	350	475	650

Mint: Khujista Bunyad
KM# 368.5 MOHUR
Gold **Note:** Weight varies 10.60-10.90 grams.

Date	Mintage	Good	VG	F	VF	XF
AH1124//1 (Ahad)	—	235	275	350	475	650

Mint: Shahjahanabad
KM# 368.6 MOHUR
Gold **Obv:** Inscription, date **Rev:** Inscription **Note:** Weight varies 10.60-10.90 grams.

Date	Mintage	Good	VG	F	VF	XF
AH1124//1 (Ahad)	—	235	275	365	525	750

Mint: Surat
KM# 368.7 MOHUR
Gold **Note:** Weight varies 10.60-10.90 grams.

Date	Mintage	Good	VG	F	VF	XF
AH1124//1 (Ahad)	—	235	275	350	475	650

Mint: Toragal
KM# 368.9 MOHUR
Gold **Note:** Weight varies 10.60-10.90 grams.

Date	Mintage	Good	VG	F	VF	XF
AH1124//1 (Ahad)	—	—	—	—	—	—

Mint: Allahabad
KM# 369.6 MOHUR
Gold **Obv:** Inscription, date **Rev:** Inscription **Note:** Weight varies 10.60-10.90 grams. Similar to Rupee, type 364.

Date	Mintage	Good	VG	F	VF	XF
AH1124//1 (Ahad)	—	—	—	—	—	—

Mint: Bareli
KM# 369.1 MOHUR
Gold **Note:** Weight varies 10.60-10.90 grams.

Date	Mintage	Good	VG	F	VF	XF
AH1124//1 (Ahad)	—	—	250	350	475	650

Mint: Gwalior
KM# 369.7 MOHUR
Gold **Note:** Weight varies 10.60-10.90 grams.

Date	Mintage	Good	VG	F	VF	XF
AH1124//1 (Ahad)	—	—	—	—	—	—

Mint: Haidarabad (Farkhanda Bunyad)
KM# 369.8 MOHUR
Gold **Obv:** Inscription **Rev. Inscription:** Farkhanda Bunyad **Note:** Weight varies 10.60-10.90 grams.

Date	Mintage	Good	VG	F	VF	XF
AH1124//1 (Ahad)	—	—	—	—	—	—

Mint: Khujista Bunyad
KM# 369.2 MOHUR
Gold **Note:** Weight varies 10.60-10.90 grams.

Date	Mintage	Good	VG	F	VF	XF
AH1124//1 (Ahad)	—	—	250	350	475	650

Mint: Lahore
KM# 369.3 MOHUR
Gold **Note:** Weight varies 10.60-10.90 grams.

Date	Mintage	Good	VG	F	VF	XF
AH1124//1 (Ahad)	—	235	275	350	475	650

Mint: Shahjahanabad
KM# 369.5 MOHUR
Gold **Note:** Weight varies 10.60-10.90 grams.

Date	Mintage	Good	VG	F	VF	XF
AH1124//1 (Ahad)	—	—	250	365	525	750

Mint: Surat
KM# 369.4 MOHUR
Gold **Note:** Weight varies 10.60-10.90 grams.

Date	Mintage	Good	VG	F	VF	XF
AH1124//1 (Ahad)	—	235	275	350	475	650

Farrukhsiyar

AH1124-1131 / 1713-1719AD

The silver and gold coins of Farrukhsiyar all display the same obverse poetic couplet. However, there are many varieties of word arrangement on the flan. While many of these have a radically different appearance, they are simply too numerous to list as independent varieties. Some collectors may wish to distinguish between these; they are referred to the museum catalogues of Mughal coins.

HAMMERED COINAGE

Mint: Ahmadabad
KM# 370.1 1/2 PAISA
Copper **Obv:** Inscription **Rev:** Inscription, flower **Note:** Weight varies 4.85-5.55 grams.

Date	Mintage	Good	VG	F	VF	XF
AHxxxx//2 Rare	—	—	—	—	—	—

Mint: Akbarabad
KM# 370.2 1/2 PAISA
Copper **Note:** Weight varies 4.85-5.55 grams.

Date	Mintage	Good	VG	F	VF	XF
AHxxxx//3 Rare	—	—	—	—	—	—

Mint: Bijapur
KM# 370.3 1/2 PAISA
Copper **Obv:** Inscription **Rev:** Inscription **Note:** Weight varies 4.85-5.55 grams.

Date	Mintage	Good	VG	F	VF	XF
AHxxxx//2 Rare	—	—	—	—	—	—

Mint: Macchlipattan
KM# 371.2 1/2 PAISA
Copper **Note:** Type 371. Weight varies 4.85-5.55 grams.

Date	Mintage	Good	VG	F	VF	XF
AH1126//x	—	—	—	—	—	—
AH1129//5	—	—	—	—	—	—
AH1130//7	—	—	—	—	—	—
AH1131//8	—	—	—	—	—	—

Mint: Purenda
KM# 371.1 1/2 PAISA
Copper **Obv:** Inscription **Rev:** Inscription **Note:** Weight varies 4.85-5.55 grams.

Date	Mintage	Good	VG	F	VF	XF
ND//x Rare	—	—	—	—	—	—

Mint: Ahmadabad
KM# 372.7 PAISA
Copper **Obv:** Inscription, date **Rev:** Inscription **Note:** Weight varies 12.80-13.80 grams.

Date	Mintage	Good	VG	F	VF	XF
AH1125//2	—	—	—	—	—	—

Mint: Ahmadanagar
KM# 372.3 PAISA
Copper **Note:** Weight varies 12.90-13.80 grams.

Date	Mintage	Good	VG	F	VF	XF
AH1127//x	—	15.00	36.00	60.00	100	—

Mint: Akbarabad
KM# 372.12 PAISA
Copper **Note:** Weight varies 12.90-13.80 grams.

Date	Mintage	Good	VG	F	VF	XF
AH1126//x	—	—	—	—	—	—

Mint: Ausa
KM# 372.5 PAISA
Copper **Note:** Weight varies 12.90-13.80 grams.

Date	Mintage	Good	VG	F	VF	XF
ND//x Rare	—	—	—	—	—	—

Mint: Bahadarqarh
KM# 372.8 PAISA
Copper **Obv:** Inscription **Rev:** Inscription **Note:** Weight varies 12.90-13.80 grams.

Date	Mintage	Good	VG	F	VF	XF
ND//x	—	—	—	—	—	—

Mint: Bijapur
KM# 372.9 PAISA
Copper **Obv:** Inscription **Rev. Inscription:** Dar-uz-Zafar **Note:** Weight varies: 12.90-13.80 grams.

Date	Mintage	Good	VG	F	VF	XF
AH112x//3	—	—	—	—	—	—
AH1130//-	—	—	—	—	—	—

Mint: Elichpur
KM# 372.4 PAISA
Copper **Note:** Weight varies 12.90-13.80 grams.

Date	Mintage	Good	VG	F	VF	XF
AH1127//x	—	18.00	36.00	60.00	100	—

Mint: Khambayat
KM# 372.10 PAISA
Copper **Note:** Weight varies 12.90-13.80 grams.

Date	Mintage	Good	VG	F	VF	XF
AHxxxx//1 (Ahad)	—	—	—	—	—	—
AH1126//3	—	—	—	—	—	—

Mint: Macchlipattan
KM# 372.2 PAISA
Copper **Obv:** Inscription, date **Rev:** Inscription **Note:** Weight varies 12.90 - 13.80 grams.

Date	Mintage	Good	VG	F	VF	XF
AH1124//1 (Ahad)	—	15.00	36.00	60.00	100	—
AH1125//2	—	15.00	36.00	60.00	100	—
AH1127//3	—	15.00	36.00	60.00	100	—
AH1128//5	—	15.00	36.00	60.00	100	—
AH1129//6	—	15.00	36.00	60.00	100	—
AH1130//6	—	15.00	36.00	60.00	100	—
AH1131//8	—	15.00	36.00	60.00	100	—

Mint: Muhammadabad
KM# 372.11 PAISA
Copper **Obv:** Inscription **Rev:** Inscription **Note:** Weight varies 12.90-13.80 grams.

Date	Mintage	Good	VG	F	VF	XF
ND//x	—	—	—	—	—	—

Mint: Purenda
KM# 372.1 PAISA
Copper **Obv:** Inscription **Rev:** Inscription, date **Note:** Weight varies 12.90-13.80 grams.

Date	Mintage	Good	VG	F	VF	XF
AH1124//1 (Ahad) Rare	—	—	—	—	—	—
AH1125//x Rare	—	—	—	—	—	—
AH1126//x Rare	—	—	—	—	—	—

Mint: Surat
KM# 372.6 PAISA
Copper **Note:** Weight varies 12.90-13.80 grams.

Date	Mintage	Good	VG	F	VF	XF
ND//x	—	18.00	36.00	60.00	100	—

Mint: Burhanpur
KM# A373.1 1/16 RUPEE
Silver **Obv:** Inscription **Rev. Inscription:** Dar-us-Sarur **Note:** Weight varies 0.69-0.77 grams.

Date	Mintage	Good	VG	F	VF	XF
AHxxxx//x	—	—	—	—	—	—

Mint: Burhanpur
KM# 373.1 1/8 RUPEE
Silver **Note:** Weight varies 1.38-1.45 grams.

Date	Mintage	Good	VG	F	VF	XF
AH1127//4 Rare	—	—	—	—	—	—

Mint: Shahjahanabad
KM# 373.2 1/8 RUPEE
Silver **Obv:** Inscription **Rev. Inscription:** Dar-ul-Khilafat **Note:** Weight varies 1.38-1.45 grams.

Date	Mintage	Good	VG	F	VF	XF
AHxxxx//5	—	—	—	—	—	—

Mint: Ujjain
KM# 373.3 1/8 RUPEE
Silver **Obv:** Inscription **Rev. Inscription:** Dar-ul-Fath **Note:** Weight varies 1.38-1.45 grams.

Date	Mintage	Good	VG	F	VF	XF
AHxxxx//x	—	—	—	—	—	—

Mint: Burhanpur
KM# 374.5 1/4 RUPEE
Silver **Rev:** Mint epithet: "Dar-us-Sarur" **Note:** Weight varies: 2.75-2.90 grams.

Date	Mintage	Good	VG	F	VF	XF
AH1129//6	—	—	—	—	—	—

Mint: Khujista Bunyad
KM# 374.6 1/4 RUPEE
2.8610 g., Silver **Note:**

Date	Mintage	Good	VG	F	VF	XF
AHxxxx//6	—	—	—	—	—	—

Mint: Murshidabad
KM# 374.3 1/4 RUPEE
Silver **Note:** Weight varies 2.75-2.90 grams.

Date	Mintage	Good	VG	F	VF	XF
AHxxxx//7 Rare	—	—	—	—	—	—

Mint: Shahjahanabad
KM# 374.4 1/4 RUPEE
Silver **Note:** Weight varies 2.75-2.90 grams.

Date	Mintage	Good	VG	F	VF	XF
AHxxxx//5 Rare	—	—	—	—	—	—

Mint: Surat
KM# 374.2 1/4 RUPEE
Silver **Note:** Weight varies 2.75-2.90 grams.

Date	Mintage	Good	VG	F	VF	XF
AHxxxx//4 Rare	—	—	—	—	—	—

Mint: Ujjain
KM# 374.7 1/4 RUPEE
Silver **Obv:** Inscription **Rev. Inscription:** Dar-ul-Fath **Note:** Weight varies 2.75-2.90 grams.

Date	Mintage	Good	VG	F	VF	XF
AHxxxx//x	—	—	—	—	—	—

Mint: Aurangnagar
KM# 375.10 1/2 RUPEE
Silver **Note:** Weight varies 5.50-5.80 grams.

Date	Mintage	Good	VG	F	VF	XF
AHxxxx//7	—	—	—	—	—	—

Mint: Azimabad
KM# 375.1 1/2 RUPEE
Silver **Obv:** Inscription **Rev. Inscription:** Mustagir-ul-Mulk **Note:** Weight varies 5.50-5.80 grams.

Date	Mintage	Good	VG	F	VF	XF
AHxxxx//5 Rare	—	—	—	—	—	—
AHxxxx//6 Rare	—	—	—	—	—	—
AHxxxx//7 Rare	—	—	—	—	—	—
AH1131//8 Rare	—	—	—	—	—	—

Mint: Azimabad
KM# 375.11 1/2 RUPEE
Silver **Rev:** Without epithet **Note:** Weight varies 5.50-5.80 grams.

Date	Mintage	Good	VG	F	VF	XF
AH1125//2	—	—	—	—	—	—

Mint: Burhanpur
KM# 375.7 1/2 RUPEE
Silver **Note:** Weight varies 5.50-5.80 grams.

Date	Mintage	Good	VG	F	VF	XF
AHxxxx//6	—	—	—	—	—	—

Mint: Farrukhabad
KM# 375.5 1/2 RUPEE
Silver **Obv:** Inscription **Rev:** Inscription **Note:** Weight varies 5.50-5.80 grams.

Date	Mintage	Good	VG	F	VF	XF
AHxxxx//6	—	8.00	20.00	40.00	70.00	100
AHxxxx//7	—	8.00	20.00	40.00	70.00	100

Mint: Junagarh
KM# 375.12 1/2 RUPEE
Silver **Note:** Weight varies 5.50-5.80 grams.

Date	Mintage	Good	VG	F	VF	XF
AHxxxx//x	—	—	—	—	—	—

Mint: Kambayat
KM# 375.6 1/2 RUPEE
Silver **Obv:** Inscription **Rev:** Inscription **Note:** Weight varies 5.50-5.80 grams.

Date	Mintage	Good	VG	F	VF	XF
AHxxxx//1 (Ahad)	—	8.00	20.00	40.00	70.00	100
AH11xx//3	—	8.00	20.00	40.00	70.00	100

Mint: Lahore
KM# 375.8 1/2 RUPEE
Silver **Note:** Weight varies 5.50-5.80 grams.

Date	Mintage	Good	VG	F	VF	XF
AHxxxx//6	—	—	—	—	—	—

Mint: Murshidabad
KM# 375.4 1/2 RUPEE
Silver **Obv:** Inscription **Rev:** Inscription **Note:** Weight varies 5.50-5.80 grams.

Date	Mintage	Good	VG	F	VF	XF
AH1130//7 Rare	—	—	—	—	—	—

Mint: Shahjahanabad
KM# 375.9 1/2 RUPEE
Silver **Note:** Weight varies 5.50-5.80 grams.

Date	Mintage	Good	VG	F	VF	XF
AH1129//x	—	—	—	—	—	—

Mint: Surat
KM# 375.2 1/2 RUPEE
Silver **Note:** Weight varies 5.50-5.80 grams.

Date	Mintage	Good	VG	F	VF	XF
AHxxxx//1 (Ahad)	—	12.00	30.00	50.00	90.00	150
AHxxxx//3	—	12.00	30.00	50.00	90.00	150

Date	Mintage	Good	VG	F	VF	XF
AHxxxx//4	—	12.00	30.00	50.00	90.00	150
AH1128//5	—	12.00	15.00	25.00	45.00	75.00
AHxxxx//6	—	12.00	30.00	50.00	90.00	150
AHxxxx//7	—	12.00	30.00	50.00	90.00	150

Mint: Tatta
KM# 376.1 RUPEE
Silver **Obv. Inscription:** Sahib Qiran Salis **Rev:** Inscription **Note:** Weight varies 11.00-11.60 grams.

Date	Mintage	Good	VG	F	VF	XF
AH1125//1 (Ahad) Rare	—	—	—	—	—	—
AH1124//1 (Ahad) Rare	—	—	—	—	—	—

Mint: Ahmadabad
KM# 377.1 RUPEE
Silver **Obv. Inscription:** Badshah **Rev:** Inscription **Note:** Weight varies 11.00-11.60 grams.

Date	Mintage	Good	VG	F	VF	XF
AH112x//1 (Ahad)	—	5.00	8.00	13.00	20.00	30.00
AH1125//2	—	5.00	8.00	13.00	20.00	30.00
AH1126//2	—	5.00	8.00	13.00	20.00	30.00
AH1126//3	—	5.00	8.00	13.00	20.00	30.00
AH1127//3	—	5.00	8.00	13.00	20.00	30.00
AH1127//4	—	5.00	8.00	13.00	20.00	30.00
AH1128//4	—	5.00	8.00	13.00	20.00	30.00
AH1128//5	—	5.00	8.00	13.00	20.00	30.00
AH1129//5	—	5.00	8.00	13.00	20.00	30.00
AH1129//6	—	5.00	8.00	13.00	20.00	30.00
AH1130//6	—	5.00	8.00	13.00	20.00	30.00
AH1130//7	—	5.00	8.00	13.00	20.00	30.00
AH1131//7	—	5.00	8.00	13.00	20.00	30.00
AH1131//8	—	5.00	8.00	13.00	20.00	30.00

Mint: Ahmadanagar
KM# 377.2 RUPEE
Silver **Note:** Weight varies 11.00-11.60 grams.

Date	Mintage	Good	VG	F	VF	XF
AH1125//x	—	6.00	10.00	20.00	35.00	50.00
AH1126//2	—	6.00	10.00	20.00	35.00	50.00
AH1126//3	—	6.00	10.00	20.00	35.00	50.00
AH1127//3	—	6.00	10.00	20.00	35.00	50.00
AH1127//4	—	6.00	10.00	20.00	35.00	50.00
AH1128//4	—	6.00	10.00	20.00	35.00	50.00
AH1128//5	—	6.00	10.00	20.00	35.00	50.00
AH1129//x	—	6.00	10.00	20.00	35.00	50.00

Mint: Ahsanabad
KM# 377.71 RUPEE
Silver **Note:** Weight varies 11.00-11.60 grams.

Date	Mintage	Good	VG	F	VF	XF
AHxxxx//1 (Ahad)	—	—	—	—	—	—

Mint: Ajmer
KM# 377.3 RUPEE
Silver **Obv:** Inscription **Rev. Inscription:** Mustagir-ul-Khilafat **Note:** Weight varies 11.00-11.60 grams.

Date	Mintage	Good	VG	F	VF	XF
AHxxxx//1 (Ahad)	—	5.00	8.00	13.00	20.00	30.00
AHxxxx//2	—	5.00	8.00	13.00	20.00	30.00
AHxxxx//3	—	5.00	8.00	13.00	20.00	30.00
AHxxxx//4	—	5.00	8.00	13.00	20.00	30.00
AHxxxx//5	—	5.00	8.00	13.00	20.00	30.00
AHxxxx//6	—	5.00	8.00	13.00	20.00	30.00

Mint: Ajmer
KM# 377.4 RUPEE
Silver **Obv:** Inscription **Rev. Legend:** Dar-ul-Khair **Note:** Weight varies 11.00-11.60 grams.

Date	Mintage	Good	VG	F	VF	XF
AHxxxx//6	—	5.00	7.00	12.00	20.00	30.00
AH1130//7	—	5.00	7.00	12.00	20.00	30.00

Mint: Akbarabad
KM# 377.5 RUPEE
Silver **Obv:** Inscription **Rev. Inscription:** Mustagir-ul-Mulk **Note:** Weight varies 11.00-11.60 grams.

Date	Mintage	Good	VG	F	VF	XF
AH1124//1 (Ahad)	—	5.00	8.00	13.00	20.00	30.00
AH1125//2	—	5.00	8.00	13.00	20.00	30.00
AH1126//2	—	5.00	8.00	13.00	20.00	30.00
AH1126//3	—	5.00	8.00	13.00	20.00	30.00
AH1127//3	—	5.00	8.00	13.00	20.00	30.00
AH1127//4	—	5.00	8.00	13.00	20.00	30.00
AH1128//4	—	5.00	8.00	13.00	20.00	30.00
AH1128//5	—	5.00	8.00	13.00	20.00	30.00

Mint: Akbarabad
KM# 377.6 RUPEE
Silver **Obv:** Inscription **Rev. Inscription:** Mustagir-ul-Mulk **Note:** Weight varies 11.00-11.60 grams.

Date	Mintage	Good	VG	F	VF	XF
AH11xx//4	—	5.00	7.00	10.00	17.00	25.00
AH1129//5	—	5.00	7.00	10.00	17.00	25.00
AH1129//6	—	5.00	7.00	10.00	17.00	25.00
AH1130//6	—	5.00	7.00	10.00	17.00	25.00
AH1130//7	—	5.00	7.00	10.00	17.00	25.00

Mint: Akbarnagar
KM# 377.7 RUPEE
Silver **Note:** Weight varies 11.00-11.60 grams.

Date	Mintage	Good	VG	F	VF	XF
AHxxxx//3	—	5.50	11.00	18.00	30.00	45.00
AHxxxx//4	—	5.50	11.00	18.00	30.00	45.00
AHxxxx//6	—	5.50	11.00	18.00	30.00	45.00
AHxxxx//7	—	5.50	11.00	18.00	30.00	45.00

Mint: Alamgirpur
KM# 377.8 RUPEE
Silver **Note:** Weight varies 11.00-11.60 grams.

Date	Mintage	Good	VG	F	VF	XF
AHxxxx//2	—	6.50	13.00	22.00	35.00	50.00
AHxxxx//3	—	6.50	13.00	22.00	35.00	50.00
AHxxxx//7	—	6.50	13.00	22.00	35.00	50.00

Mint: Allahabad
KM# 377.9 RUPEE
Silver **Note:** Weight varies 11.00-11.60 grams.

Date	Mintage	Good	VG	F	VF	XF
AH1125//2	—	5.00	9.00	15.00	25.00	35.00
AH1126//2	—	5.00	9.00	15.00	25.00	35.00
AH1126//3	—	5.00	9.00	15.00	25.00	35.00
AH1127//3	—	5.00	9.00	15.00	25.00	35.00
AH1128//5	—	5.00	9.00	15.00	25.00	35.00
AH1130//7	—	5.00	9.00	15.00	25.00	35.00

Mint: Arkat
KM# 377.10 RUPEE
Silver **Obv:** Inscription, date **Rev:** Inscription **Note:** Weight varies 11.00-11.60 grams.

Date	Mintage	Good	VG	F	VF	XF
AH1124//1 (Ahad)	—	8.00	21.50	36.00	60.00	85.00
AH1125//1 (Ahad)	—	8.00	21.50	36.00	60.00	85.00
AH1125//2	—	8.00	21.50	36.00	60.00	85.00
AH1126//2	—	8.00	21.50	36.00	60.00	85.00
AH1126//3	—	8.00	21.50	36.00	60.00	85.00
AH1127//3	—	8.00	21.50	36.00	60.00	85.00
AH1127//4	—	8.00	21.50	36.00	60.00	85.00
AH1128//4	—	8.00	21.50	36.00	60.00	85.00
AH1128//5	—	8.00	21.50	36.00	60.00	85.00
AH1129//5	—	8.00	21.50	36.00	60.00	85.00
AH1129//6	—	8.00	21.50	36.00	60.00	85.00
AH1130//6	—	8.00	21.50	36.00	60.00	85.00
AH1130//7	—	8.00	21.50	36.00	60.00	85.00
AH1131//7	—	8.00	21.50	36.00	60.00	85.00
AH1131//8	—	8.00	21.50	36.00	60.00	85.00

Mint: Aurangnagar
KM# 377.11 RUPEE
Silver **Obv:** Inscription **Rev:** Inscription **Note:** Weight varies 11.00-11.60 grams.

Date	Mintage	Good	VG	F	VF	XF
AHxxxx//2	—	8.00	21.50	36.00	60.00	85.00
AHxxxx//3	—	8.00	21.50	36.00	60.00	85.00
AHxxxx//4	—	8.00	21.50	36.00	60.00	85.00
AHxxxx//7	—	8.00	21.50	36.00	60.00	85.00

Mint: Azamnagar
KM# 377.12 RUPEE
Silver **Obv:** Inscription **Rev:** Inscription **Note:** Without epithet. Weight varies 11.00-11.60 grams.

Date	Mintage	Good	VG	F	VF	XF
AHxxxx//6	—	7.00	18.00	30.00	50.00	70.00

Mint: Azimabad
KM# 377.13 RUPEE
Silver **Obv:** Inscription **Rev:** Inscription **Note:** Weight varies 11.00-11.60 grams.

Date	Mintage	Good	VG	F	VF	XF
AH1124//1 (Ahad)	—	5.00	7.00	12.00	20.00	30.00
AH1125//1 (Ahad)	—	5.00	7.00	12.00	20.00	30.00
AH1125//2	—	5.00	7.00	12.00	20.00	30.00
AH1126//2	—	5.00	7.00	12.00	20.00	30.00
AH1126//3	—	5.00	7.00	12.00	20.00	30.00

Mint: Azimabad
KM# 377.14 RUPEE
11.4440 g., Silver **Obv:** Inscription **Rev. Inscription:** Mustagir-ul-Mulk **Note:** Without epithet. Weight varies 11.00-11.60 grams.

Date	Mintage	Good	VG	F	VF	XF
AH1126//3	—	5.00	8.00	13.00	22.00	35.00
AH(11)27//4	—	5.00	8.00	13.00	22.00	35.00
AH1128//4	—	5.00	8.00	13.00	22.00	35.00
AH1128//5	—	5.00	8.00	13.00	22.00	35.00
AH1129//6	—	5.00	8.00	13.00	22.00	35.00
AHxxxx//7	—	5.00	8.00	13.00	22.00	35.00
AH1131//8	—	5.00	8.00	13.00	22.00	35.00

Mint: Bahadarqarh
KM# 377.15 RUPEE

Silver **Note:** Weight varies 11.00-11.60 grams.

Date	Mintage	Good	VG	F	VF	XF
AHxxxx//1 Rare	—	—	—	—	—	—
AHxxxx//2 Rare	—	—	—	—	—	—
AHxxxx//3 Rare	—	—	—	—	—	—
AHxxxx//4 Rare	—	—	—	—	—	—

Mint: Banda Maluari
KM# 377.72 RUPEE

Silver **Note:** Weight varies 11.00-11.60 grams.

Date	Mintage	Good	VG	F	VF	XF
AHxxxx//x	—	—	—	—	—	—

Mint: Bankapur
KM# 377.16 RUPEE

Silver **Note:** Weight varies 11.00-11.60 grams.

Date	Mintage	Good	VG	F	VF	XF
AHxxxx//1 (Ahad) Rare	—	—	—	—	—	—
AH1126//3 Rare	—	—	—	—	—	—
AH1127//x Rare	—	—	—	—	—	—
AHxxxx//4 Rare	—	—	—	—	—	—
AHxxxx//5 Rare	—	—	—	—	—	—
AH1129//6 Rare	—	—	—	—	—	—
AH1130//7 Rare	—	—	—	—	—	—

Mint: Baramati
KM# 377.17 RUPEE

Silver **Note:** Weight varies 11.00-11.60 grams.

Date	Mintage	Good	VG	F	VF	XF
AH1125//x Rare	—	—	—	—	—	—

Mint: Bareli
KM# 377.18 RUPEE

Silver **Obv:** Inscription **Rev:** Inscription **Note:** Weight varies 11.00-11.60 grams.

Date	Mintage	Good	VG	F	VF	XF
AH1124//1 (Ahad)	—	5.00	7.00	12.00	20.00	30.00
AH1125//1 (Ahad)	—	5.00	7.00	12.00	20.00	30.00
AH1125//2	—	5.00	7.00	12.00	20.00	30.00
AH1126//2	—	5.00	7.00	12.00	20.00	30.00
AH1126//3	—	5.00	7.00	12.00	20.00	30.00
AH1127//3	—	5.00	7.00	12.00	20.00	30.00
AH1127//4	—	5.00	7.00	12.00	20.00	30.00
AH1128//4	—	5.00	7.00	12.00	20.00	30.00
AH1128//5	—	5.00	7.00	12.00	20.00	30.00
AH1129//5	—	5.00	7.00	12.00	20.00	30.00
AH1129//6	—	5.00	7.00	12.00	20.00	30.00
AH1130//6	—	5.00	7.00	12.00	20.00	30.00
AH1130//7	—	5.00	7.00	12.00	20.00	30.00
AH1131//7	—	5.00	7.00	12.00	20.00	30.00
AH113x//8	—	5.00	7.00	12.00	20.00	30.00

Mint: Bhakkar
KM# 377.19 RUPEE

Silver **Note:** Weight varies 11.00-11.60 grams.

Date	Mintage	Good	VG	F	VF	XF
ND//x	—	—	12.00	20.00	35.00	50.00

Mint: Bidrur
KM# 377.20 RUPEE

Silver **Note:** Weight varies 11.00-11.60 grams.

Date	Mintage	Good	VG	F	VF	XF
AH1129//6 Rare	—	—	—	—	—	—
AH1130//7 Rare	—	—	—	—	—	—
AH1130//8 Rare	—	—	—	—	—	—

Mint: Bijapur
KM# 377.21 RUPEE

Silver **Obv:** Inscription **Rev. Inscription:** Dar-uz-Zafar **Note:** Weight varies 11.00-11.60 grams.

Date	Mintage	Good	VG	F	VF	XF
AH1124//1 (Ahad) Rare	—	—	—	—	—	—
AHxxxx//4 Rare	—	—	—	—	—	—
AHxxxx//5 Rare	—	—	—	—	—	—

Mint: Burhanpur
KM# 377.22 RUPEE

Silver **Obv:** Inscription **Rev. Inscription:** Dar-us-Sarur **Note:** Weight varies 11.00-11.60 grams.

Date	Mintage	Good	VG	F	VF	XF
AH1125//1 (Ahad)	—	5.00	7.00	12.00	20.00	30.00
AH1125//2	—	5.00	7.00	12.00	20.00	30.00
AH1126//2	—	5.00	7.00	12.00	20.00	30.00
AH1126//3	—	5.00	7.00	12.00	20.00	30.00
AH1127//3	—	5.00	7.00	12.00	20.00	30.00
AH1127//4	—	5.00	7.00	12.00	20.00	30.00
AH1128//4	—	5.00	7.00	12.00	20.00	30.00
AH1128//5	—	5.00	7.00	12.00	20.00	30.00
AH1129//5	—	5.00	7.00	12.00	20.00	30.00
AH1129//6	—	5.00	7.00	12.00	20.00	30.00
AH1130//6	—	5.00	7.00	12.00	20.00	30.00
AH1130//7	—	5.00	7.00	12.00	20.00	30.00
AH1131//7	—	5.00	7.00	12.00	20.00	30.00
AH1131//8	—	5.00	7.00	12.00	20.00	30.00

Mint: Elichpur
KM# 377.24 RUPEE

Silver **Note:** Weight varies 11.00-11.60 grams.

Date	Mintage	Good	VG	F	VF	XF
AH1125//1 (Ahad)	—	6.00	12.00	20.00	35.00	50.00
AH1125//2	—	6.00	12.00	20.00	35.00	50.00
AH1126//2	—	6.00	12.00	20.00	35.00	50.00
AH1126//3	—	6.00	12.00	20.00	35.00	50.00
AH1127//4	—	6.00	12.00	20.00	35.00	50.00
AH1129//6	—	6.00	12.00	20.00	35.00	50.00
AH1130//7	—	6.00	12.00	20.00	35.00	50.00

Mint: Farrukhabad
KM# 377.25 RUPEE

Silver **Obv:** Inscription **Rev:** Inscription **Note:** Formerly Ahmadnagar. Weight varies 11.00-11.60 grams.

Date	Mintage	Good	VG	F	VF	XF
AH1127//4	—	5.00	9.00	15.00	25.00	35.00
AHxxxx//5	—	5.00	9.00	15.00	25.00	35.00
AH1129//6	—	5.00	9.00	15.00	25.00	35.00
AH1130//6	—	5.00	9.00	15.00	25.00	35.00
AH1130//7	—	5.00	9.00	15.00	25.00	35.00
AH1131//7	—	5.00	9.00	15.00	25.00	35.00

Mint: Farrukhnagar
KM# 377.64 RUPEE

11.4440 g., Silver **Note:** Weight varies 11.00-11.60 grams.

Date	Mintage	Good	VG	F	VF	XF
ND//x Rare	—	—	—	—	—	—

Mint: Fathabad Dharur
KM# 377.26 RUPEE

Silver **Obv:** Inscription **Rev:** Inscription **Note:** Weight varies 11.00-11.60 grams.

Date	Mintage	Good	VG	F	VF	XF
AHxxxx//	—	50.00	120	200	325	450
AH1126//3	—	50.00	120	200	325	450
AH1127//x	—	50.00	120	200	325	450
AHxxxx//6	—	50.00	120	200	325	450

Mint: Firozgarh
KM# 377.74 RUPEE

Silver **Note:** Weight varies 11.00-11.60 grams.

Date	Mintage	Good	VG	F	VF	XF
ND(1713-1719)	—	—	—	—	—	—

Mint: Firoznagar
KM# 377.75 RUPEE

Silver **Note:** Weight varies 11.00-11.60 grams.

Date	Mintage	Good	VG	F	VF	XF
AH1125//2	—	—	—	—	—	—

Mint: Gokak
KM# 377.27 RUPEE

Silver **Note:** Weight varies 11.00-11.60 grams.

Date	Mintage	Good	VG	F	VF	XF
AH1125//2 Rare	—	—	—	—	—	—
AH1125//6 Rare	—	—	—	—	—	—

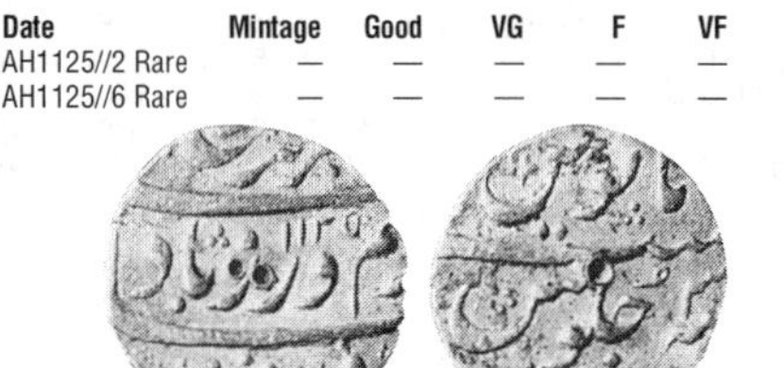

Mint: Gulshanabad
KM# 377.28 RUPEE

Silver **Obv:** Inscription **Rev:** Inscription **Note:** Weight varies 11.00-11.60 grams.

Date	Mintage	Good	VG	F	VF	XF
AH1125//2	—	45.00	110	180	300	425
AH1125//3	—	45.00	110	180	300	425
AH1127//3	—	45.00	110	180	300	425

Mint: Guty
KM# 377.29 RUPEE

Silver **Note:** Weight varies 11.00-11.60 grams.

Date	Mintage	Good	VG	F	VF	XF
AH1125//4 Rare	—	—	—	—	—	—
AHxxxx//4 Rare	—	—	—	—	—	—

Mint: Gwalior
KM# 377.30 RUPEE

Silver **Obv:** Inscription **Rev:** Inscription **Note:** Weight varies 11.00-11.60 grams.

Date	Mintage	Good	VG	F	VF	XF
AH1125//1 (Ahad)	—	5.00	7.00	10.00	16.50	25.00
AH1125//2	—	5.00	7.00	10.00	16.50	25.00
AH1126//2	—	5.00	7.00	10.00	16.50	25.00
AH1126//3	—	5.00	7.00	10.00	16.50	25.00
AH1127//3	—	5.00	7.00	10.00	16.50	25.00
AH1127//4	—	5.00	7.00	10.00	16.50	25.00
AH1128//4	—	5.00	7.00	10.00	16.50	25.00
AH1128//5	—	5.00	7.00	10.00	16.50	25.00
AH1129//5	—	5.00	7.00	10.00	16.50	25.00
AH1129//6	—	5.00	7.00	10.00	16.50	25.00
AH1130//6	—	5.00	7.00	10.00	16.50	25.00
AH1130//7	—	5.00	7.00	10.00	16.50	25.00
AH1131//7	—	5.00	7.00	10.00	16.50	25.00
AH1131//8	—	5.00	7.00	10.00	16.50	25.00

Mint: Haidarabad (Farkhanda Bunyad)
KM# 377.31 RUPEE

Silver **Obv:** Inscription **Rev. Inscription:** Farkhanda Bunyad **Note:** Weight varies 11.00-11.60 grams.

Date	Mintage	Good	VG	F	VF	XF
AH1127//3	—	5.00	8.00	13.00	22.00	30.00
AH1128//5	—	5.00	8.00	13.00	22.00	30.00
AH1129//6	—	5.00	8.00	13.00	22.00	30.00
AH1130//7	—	5.00	8.00	13.00	22.00	30.00

Mint: Imtiyazgarh
KM# 377.32 RUPEE

Silver **Note:** Weight varies 11.00-11.60 grams.

Date	Mintage	Good	VG	F	VF	XF
AH1124//x Rare	—	—	—	—	—	—
AHxxxx//7 Rare	—	—	—	—	—	—

Mint: Islamabad
KM# 377.33 RUPEE

Silver **Obv:** Inscription **Rev:** Mint name at bottom **Note:** Weight varies 11.00-11.60 grams.

Date	Mintage	Good	VG	F	VF	XF
AHxxxx//3	—	6.00	12.00	20.00	35.00	50.00
AHxxxx//4	—	6.00	12.00	20.00	35.00	50.00

Date	Mintage	Good	VG	F	VF	XF
AH1128//5	—	6.00	12.00	20.00	35.00	50.00
AHxxxx//6	—	6.00	12.00	20.00	35.00	50.00
AH1130//7	—	6.00	12.00	20.00	35.00	50.00

Mint: Itawa
KM# 377.34 RUPEE

Silver **Obv:** Inscription, date **Rev:** Inscription **Note:** Weight varies 11.00-11.60 grams.

Date	Mintage	Good	VG	F	VF	XF
AH1124//1 (Ahad)	—	5.00	7.00	10.00	16.50	25.00
AH1125//1 (Ahad)	—	5.00	7.00	10.00	16.50	25.00
AH1125//2	—	5.00	7.00	10.00	16.50	25.00
AH1126//2	—	5.00	7.00	10.00	16.50	25.00
AH1126//3	—	5.00	7.00	10.00	16.50	25.00
AH1127//3	—	5.00	7.00	10.00	16.50	25.00
AH1127//4	—	5.00	7.00	10.00	16.50	25.00
AH1128//4	—	5.00	7.00	10.00	16.50	25.00
AH1128//5	—	5.00	7.00	10.00	16.50	25.00
AH1129//5	—	5.00	7.00	10.00	16.50	25.00
AH1129//6	—	5.00	7.00	10.00	16.50	25.00
AH1130//6	—	5.00	7.00	10.00	16.50	25.00
AH1130//7	—	5.00	7.00	10.00	16.50	25.00
AH1131//7	—	5.00	7.00	10.00	16.50	25.00
AH1131//8	—	5.00	7.00	10.00	16.50	25.00

Mint: Jahangirnagar
KM# 377.35 RUPEE

Silver **Note:** Weight varies 11.00-11.60 grams.

Date	Mintage	Good	VG	F	VF	XF
AH1124//1 (Ahad)	—	6.00	12.50	20.00	32.50	50.00
AH1125//2	—	6.00	12.50	20.00	32.50	50.00
AHxxxx//4	—	6.00	12.50	20.00	32.50	50.00
AHxxxx//3	—	6.00	12.50	20.00	32.50	50.00
AH1129//6	—	6.00	12.50	20.00	32.50	50.00
AH1130//7	—	6.00	12.50	20.00	32.50	50.00

Mint: Junagarh
KM# 377.36 RUPEE

Silver **Note:** Weight varies 11.00-11.60 grams.

Date	Mintage	Good	VG	F	VF	XF
AHxxxx//4	—	6.00	12.50	20.00	32.50	50.00
AH1129//6	—	6.00	12.50	20.00	32.50	50.00
AH1130//6	—	6.00	12.50	20.00	32.50	50.00
AH1130//7	—	6.00	12.50	20.00	32.50	50.00
AH1131//7	—	6.00	12.50	20.00	32.50	50.00

Mint: Kabul
KM# 377.37 RUPEE

Silver **Obv:** Inscription **Rev. Legend:** Dar-ul-Mulk **Note:** Weight varies 11.00-11.60 grams.

Date	Mintage	Good	VG	F	VF	XF
AH1125//2	—	10.00	25.00	35.00	55.00	70.00
AH1127//x	—	10.00	25.00	35.00	55.00	70.00

Mint: Kanbayat
KM# 377.41 RUPEE

Silver **Obv:** Inscription **Rev:** Inscription **Note:** Weight varies 11.00-11.60 grams.

Date	Mintage	Good	VG	F	VF	XF
AH1124//1 (Ahad)	—	5.00	7.00	10.00	16.50	25.00
AH1125//1 (Ahad)	—	5.00	7.00	10.00	16.50	25.00
AH1125//2	—	5.00	7.00	10.00	16.50	25.00
AH1126//3	—	5.00	7.00	10.00	16.50	25.00
AHxxxx//4	—	5.00	7.00	10.00	16.50	25.00
AH1128//5	—	5.00	7.00	10.00	16.50	25.00
AH1129//6	—	5.00	7.00	10.00	16.50	25.00
AH1130//7	—	5.00	7.00	10.00	16.50	25.00
AH1131//7	—	5.00	7.00	10.00	16.50	25.00
AH1131//8	—	5.00	7.00	10.00	16.50	25.00

Mint: Kankurti
KM# 377.38 RUPEE

Silver **Note:** Weight varies 11.00-11.60 grams.

Date	Mintage	Good	VG	F	VF	XF
AH112x//5 Rare	—	—	—	—	—	—
AH1129//6 Rare	—	—	—	—	—	—
AHxxxx//7 Rare	—	—	—	—	—	—

Mint: Kararabad
KM# 377.39 RUPEE

Silver **Note:** Weight varies 11.00-11.60 grams.

Date	Mintage	Good	VG	F	VF	XF
AHxxxx//7 Rare	—	—	—	—	—	—

Mint: Kashmir
KM# 377.68 RUPEE

Silver **Obv:** Inscription, date **Rev:** Inscription **Note:** Weight varies 11.00-11.60 grams.

Date	Mintage	Good	VG	F	VF	XF
AHxxxx//1 (Ahad)	—	—	—	—	—	—
AH1129//6	—	—	—	—	—	—

Mint: Katak
KM# 377.40 RUPEE

Silver **Note:** Weight varies 11.00-11.60 grams.

Date	Mintage	Good	VG	F	VF	XF
AH1125//2	—	5.50	11.00	18.00	30.00	45.00
AH1126//2	—	5.50	11.00	18.00	30.00	45.00
AH1126//3	—	5.50	11.00	18.00	30.00	45.00
AH1128//5	—	5.50	11.00	18.00	30.00	45.00

Mint: Khujista Bunyad
KM# 377.42 RUPEE

Silver **Obv:** Inscription **Rev:** Inscription **Note:** Weight varies 11.00-11.60 grams.

Date	Mintage	Good	VG	F	VF	XF
AH1125//1 (Ahad)	—	5.00	8.00	13.00	25.00	35.00
AH1126//2	—	5.00	8.00	13.00	25.00	35.00
AH1125//2	—	5.00	8.00	13.00	25.00	35.00
AH(11)26//3	—	5.00	8.00	13.00	25.00	35.00
AH1128//5	—	5.00	8.00	13.00	25.00	35.00
AH1129//6	—	5.00	8.00	13.00	25.00	35.00
AH1130//7	—	5.00	8.00	13.00	25.00	35.00

Mint: Kolapur
KM# 377.77 RUPEE

Silver **Note:** Weight varies 11.00-11.60 grams.

Date	Mintage	Good	VG	F	VF	XF
ND(1713-1719)	—	—	—	—	—	—

Mint: Lahore
KM# 377.43 RUPEE

Silver **Obv:** Inscription, date **Rev. Inscription:** Dar-us-Sultanat **Note:** Weight varies 11.00-11.60 grams.

Date	Mintage	Good	VG	F	VF	XF
AH1125//1 (Ahad)	—	5.00	7.00	10.00	16.50	25.00
AH1125//2	—	5.00	7.00	10.00	16.50	25.00
AH1126//2	—	5.00	7.00	10.00	16.50	25.00
AH1126//3	—	5.00	7.00	10.00	16.50	25.00
AH1127//3	—	5.00	7.00	10.00	16.50	25.00
AH1127//4	—	5.00	7.00	10.00	16.50	25.00
AH1128//4	—	5.00	7.00	10.00	16.50	25.00
AH1128//5	—	5.00	7.00	10.00	16.50	25.00
AH1129//5	—	5.00	7.00	10.00	16.50	25.00
AH1129//6	—	5.00	7.00	10.00	16.50	25.00
AH1130//6	—	5.00	7.00	10.00	16.50	25.00
AH1130//7	—	5.00	7.00	10.00	16.50	25.00
AH1131//7	—	5.00	7.00	10.00	16.50	25.00
AH1131//8	—	5.00	7.00	10.00	16.50	25.00

Mint: Lakhnau
KM# 377.44 RUPEE

Silver **Note:** Weight varies 11.00-11.60 grams.

Date	Mintage	Good	VG	F	VF	XF
AH1134//1 (Ahad) Error for 1124	—	5.00	7.00	10.00	16.50	25.00
AH1124//1 (Ahad)	—	5.00	7.00	10.00	16.50	25.00

Date	Mintage	Good	VG	F	VF	XF
AH1125//1 (Ahad)	—	5.00	7.00	10.00	16.50	25.00
AH1125//2	—	5.00	7.00	10.00	16.50	25.00
AH1126//2	—	5.00	7.00	10.00	16.50	25.00
AH1126//3	—	5.00	7.00	10.00	16.50	25.00
AH1127//3	—	5.00	7.00	10.00	16.50	25.00
AH1127//4	—	5.00	7.00	10.00	16.50	25.00
AH1128//4	—	5.00	7.00	10.00	16.50	25.00
AH1128//5	—	5.00	7.00	10.00	16.50	25.00
AH1129//5	—	5.00	7.00	10.00	16.50	25.00
AH1129//6	—	5.00	7.00	10.00	16.50	25.00
AH1130//6	—	5.00	7.00	10.00	16.50	25.00
AH1130//7	—	5.00	7.00	10.00	16.50	25.00

Mint: Macchlipattan
KM# 377.45 RUPEE

Silver **Note:** Weight varies 11.00-11.60 grams.

Date	Mintage	Good	VG	F	VF	XF
AH1125//x	—	10.00	25.00	42.00	70.00	100
AH1128//5	—	10.00	25.00	42.00	70.00	100
AH1129//6	—	10.00	25.00	42.00	70.00	100
AH1130//6	—	10.00	25.00	42.00	70.00	100

Mint: Muazzamabad
KM# 377.46 RUPEE

Silver **Obv:** Inscription, date **Rev:** Inscription **Note:** Weight varies 11.00-11.60 grams.

Date	Mintage	Good	VG	F	VF	XF
AH11xx//2	—	5.50	11.00	18.00	30.00	45.00
AH1127//4	—	5.50	11.00	18.00	30.00	45.00
AH1129//x	—	5.50	11.00	18.00	30.00	45.00
AH113x//7	—	5.50	11.00	18.00	30.00	45.00

Mint: Muhammadabad
KM# 377.78 RUPEE

Silver **Note:** Weight varies 11.00-11.60 grams.

Date	Mintage	Good	VG	F	VF	XF
AHxxxx//1 (Ahad)	—	—	—	—	—	—

Mint: Muhammadabad Banaras
KM# 377.69 RUPEE

Silver **Note:** Weight varies 11.00-11.60 grams.

Date	Mintage	Good	VG	F	VF	XF
AHxxxx//3	—	—	—	—	—	—

Mint: Multan
KM# 377.47 RUPEE

Silver **Obv:** Inscription within circle **Rev:** Inscription within circle **Note:** Weight varies 11.00-11.60 grams.

Date	Mintage	Good	VG	F	VF	XF
AH1125//1 (Ahad)	—	5.00	7.00	10.00	16.50	25.00
AH1125//2	—	5.00	7.00	10.00	16.50	25.00
AH1126//2	—	5.00	7.00	10.00	16.50	25.00
AH1126//3	—	5.00	7.00	10.00	16.50	25.00
AH1127//3	—	5.00	7.00	10.00	16.50	25.00
AH1127//4	—	5.00	7.00	10.00	16.50	25.00
AH1129//5	—	5.00	7.00	10.00	16.50	25.00
AH1129//6	—	5.00	7.00	10.00	16.50	25.00
AH1130//6	—	5.00	7.00	10.00	16.50	25.00

Date	Mintage	Good	VG	F	VF	XF
AH1130//7	—	5.00	7.00	10.00	16.50	25.00
AH1131//7	—	5.00	7.00	10.00	16.50	25.00
AH1131//8	—	5.00	7.00	10.00	16.50	25.00

Mint: Murshidabad
KM# 377.49 RUPEE
Silver **Note:** Weight varies 11.00-11.60 grams.

Date	Mintage	Good	VG	F	VF	XF
AH1125//2	—	5.00	9.00	15.00	25.00	37.50
AH1126//2	—	5.00	9.00	15.00	25.00	37.50
AH1126//3	—	5.00	9.00	15.00	25.00	37.50
AH1127//3	—	5.00	9.00	15.00	25.00	37.50
AH1127//4	—	5.00	9.00	15.00	25.00	37.50
AH1128//4	—	5.00	9.00	15.00	25.00	37.50
AH1128//5	—	5.00	9.00	15.00	25.00	37.50
AH1129//5	—	5.00	9.00	15.00	25.00	37.50
AH1129//6	—	5.00	9.00	15.00	25.00	37.50
AH1130//6	—	5.00	9.00	15.00	25.00	37.50
AH1130//7	—	5.00	9.00	15.00	25.00	37.50
AH1131//7	—	5.00	9.00	15.00	25.00	37.50
AH1131//8	—	5.00	9.00	15.00	25.00	37.50

Mint: Murtazabad
KM# 377.79 RUPEE
Silver **Note:** Weight varies 11.00-11.60 grams.

Date	Mintage	Good	VG	F	VF	XF
AH1127//4	—	—	—	—	—	—

Mint: Nusratabad
KM# 377.80 RUPEE
Silver **Note:** Weight varies 11.00-11.60 grams.

Date	Mintage	Good	VG	F	VF	XF
AHxxxx//4	—	—	—	—	—	—

Mint: Nusratgarh
KM# 377.50 RUPEE
Silver **Note:** Weight varies 11.00-11.60 grams.

Date	Mintage	Good	VG	F	VF	XF
ND//x Rare	—	—	—	—	—	—

Mint: Parenda
KM# 377.52 RUPEE
Silver **Obv:** Inscription **Rev:** Inscription **Note:** Weight varies 11.00-11.60 grams.

Date	Mintage	Good	VG	F	VF	XF
AH1124//1 (Ahad)	—	32.00	80.00	135	275	325
AH1125//1 (Ahad)	—	32.00	80.00	135	275	325
AH1126//6 sic)	—	32.00	80.00	135	275	325

Mint: Parnala
KM# 377.81 RUPEE
Silver **Note:** Weight varies 11.00-11.60 grams.

Date	Mintage	Good	VG	F	VF	XF
AHxxxx//3	—	—	—	—	—	—

Mint: Parnala
KM# 377.82 RUPEE
Silver **Note:** Weight varies 11.00-11.60 grams.

Date	Mintage	Good	VG	F	VF	XF
AH1124//x	—	—	—	—	—	—

Mint: Peshawar
KM# 377.51 RUPEE
Silver **Note:** Weight varies 11.00-11.60 grams.

Date	Mintage	Good	VG	F	VF	XF
AH1125//2 Rare	—	—	—	—	—	—
AHxxxx//5 Rare	—	—	—	—	—	—
AH1130//7 Rare	—	—	—	—	—	—
AH1131//8 Rare	—	—	—	—	—	—

Mint: Qamarnagar
KM# 377.65 RUPEE
Silver **Note:** Weight varies 11.00-11.60 grams.

Date	Mintage	Good	VG	F	VF	XF
AH1126//3	—	—	—	—	—	—
AH1128//5	—	—	—	—	—	—

Mint: Qandahar
KM# 377.66 RUPEE
Silver **Note:** Weight varies 11.00-11.60 grams.

Date	Mintage	Good	VG	F	VF	XF
AHxxxx//1 (Ahad)	—	—	—	—	—	—

Mint: Sadnagar
KM# 377.53 RUPEE
Silver **Note:** Weight varies 11.00-11.60 grams.

Date	Mintage	Good	VG	F	VF	XF
AHxxxx//5 Rare	—	—	—	—	—	—

Mint: Sahrind
KM# 377.54 RUPEE
Silver **Note:** Weight varies 11.00-11.60 grams.

Date	Mintage	Good	VG	F	VF	XF
AH1125//2	—	5.00	9.00	15.00	25.00	37.50
AH1126//3	—	5.00	9.00	15.00	25.00	37.50
AH1127//4	—	5.00	9.00	15.00	25.00	37.50
AH(11)29//5	—	5.00	9.00	15.00	25.00	37.50
AH1129//6	—	5.00	9.00	15.00	25.00	37.50
AH1130//6	—	5.00	9.00	15.00	25.00	37.50
AH11(31)//8	—	5.00	9.00	15.00	25.00	37.50

Mint: Shahjahanabad
KM# 377.55 RUPEE
Silver **Obv:** Inscription, date **Rev. Inscription:** Dar-ul-Khilafat **Note:** Weight varies 11.00-11.60 grams.

Date	Mintage	Good	VG	F	VF	XF
AH1125//1 (Ahad)	—	5.00	7.00	10.00	16.50	25.00
AH1125//2	—	5.00	7.00	10.00	16.50	25.00
AH1126//2	—	5.00	7.00	10.00	16.50	25.00
AH1126//3	—	5.00	7.00	10.00	16.50	25.00
AH1127//3	—	5.00	7.00	10.00	16.50	25.00
AH1127//4	—	5.00	7.00	10.00	16.50	25.00
AH1128//4	—	5.00	7.00	10.00	16.50	25.00
AH1128//5	—	5.00	7.00	10.00	16.50	25.00
AH1129//5	—	5.00	7.00	10.00	16.50	25.00
AH1129//6	—	5.00	7.00	10.00	16.50	25.00
AH1130//6	—	5.00	7.00	10.00	16.50	25.00
AH1130//7	—	5.00	7.00	10.00	16.50	25.00
AH1131//7	—	5.00	7.00	10.00	16.50	25.00
AH1131//8	—	5.00	7.00	10.00	16.50	25.00

Mint: Shakola
KM# 377.83 RUPEE
Silver **Note:** Weight varies 11.00-11.60 grams.

Date	Mintage	Good	VG	F	VF	XF
AHxxxx//2	—	—	—	—	—	—
AH1127//4	—	—	—	—	—	—
AH1129//6	—	—	—	—	—	—

Mint: Sholapur
KM# 377.56 RUPEE
Silver **Note:** Weight varies 11.00-11.60 grams.

Date	Mintage	Good	VG	F	VF	XF
AH1125//2	—	5.50	11.00	18.00	30.00	45.00
AH1126//2	—	5.50	11.00	18.00	30.00	45.00
AHxxxx//7	—	5.50	11.00	18.00	30.00	45.00

Mint: Sikakul
KM# 377.57 RUPEE
Silver **Note:** Weight varies 11.00-11.60 grams.

Date	Mintage	Good	VG	F	VF	XF
AHxxxx//4 Rare	—	—	—	—	—	—
AH1130//7 Rare	—	—	—	—	—	—
AH1131//8 Rare	—	—	—	—	—	—

Mint: Sironj
KM# 377.58 RUPEE
Silver **Note:** Weight varies 11.00-11.60 grams.

Date	Mintage	Good	VG	F	VF	XF
AHxxxx//7	—	5.50	11.00	18.00	30.00	45.00

Mint: Surat
KM# 377.59 RUPEE
Silver **Obv:** Inscription **Rev:** Inscription **Note:** Weight varies 11.00-11.60 grams.

Date	Mintage	Good	VG	F	VF	XF
AH1125//1 (Ahad)	—	5.00	7.00	10.00	16.50	25.00
AH1125//2	—	5.00	7.00	10.00	16.50	25.00
AH1126//2	—	5.00	7.00	10.00	16.50	25.00
AH1126//3	—	5.00	7.00	10.00	16.50	25.00
AH1127//3	—	5.00	7.00	10.00	16.50	25.00
AH1127//4	—	5.00	7.00	10.00	16.50	25.00
AH1128//4	—	5.00	7.00	10.00	16.50	25.00
AH1128//5	—	5.00	7.00	10.00	16.50	25.00
AH1129//5	—	5.00	7.00	10.00	16.50	25.00
AH1129//6	—	5.00	7.00	10.00	16.50	25.00
AH1130//6	—	5.00	7.00	10.00	16.50	25.00
AH1130//7	—	5.00	7.00	10.00	16.50	25.00
AH1131//7	—	5.00	7.00	10.00	16.50	25.00
AH1131//8	—	5.00	7.00	10.00	16.50	25.00

Mint: Tatta
KM# 377.60 RUPEE
Silver **Obv:** Inscription **Rev:** Mint name at bottom **Note:** Weight varies 11.00-11.60 grams.

Date	Mintage	Good	VG	F	VF	XF
AH1125//1 (Ahad)	—	5.00	7.00	10.00	16.50	25.00
AH1125//2	—	5.00	7.00	10.00	16.50	25.00
AH1126//2	—	5.00	7.00	10.00	16.50	25.00
AH1126//3	—	5.00	7.00	10.00	16.50	25.00
AH1127//3	—	5.00	7.00	10.00	16.50	25.00
AH1127//4	—	5.00	7.00	10.00	16.50	25.00
AH1128//4	—	5.00	7.00	10.00	16.50	25.00
AH1128//5	—	5.00	7.00	10.00	16.50	25.00
AH1129//5	—	5.00	7.00	10.00	16.50	25.00
AH1129//6	—	5.00	7.00	10.00	16.50	25.00
AH1130//6	—	5.00	7.00	10.00	16.50	25.00
AH1130//7	—	5.00	7.00	10.00	16.50	25.00

Mint: Tatta
KM# 377.70 RUPEE
Silver **Obv:** Inscription **Rev:** Inscription, mint name above **Note:** Weight varies 11.00-11.60 grams.

Date	Mintage	Good	VG	F	VF	XF
AH1131//8 Rare	—	—	—	—	—	—

Mint: Toragal
KM# 377.61 RUPEE
Silver **Note:** Weight varies 11.00-11.60 grams.

Date	Mintage	Good	VG	F	VF	XF
AHxxxx//1 (Ahad) Rare	—	—	—	—	—	—
AHxxxx//2 Rare	—	—	—	—	—	—
AHxxxx//3 Rare	—	—	—	—	—	—
AHxxxx//4 Rare	—	—	—	—	—	—
AHxxxx//7 Rare	—	—	—	—	—	—

Mint: Udgir
KM# 377.62 RUPEE
Silver **Note:** Weight varies 11.00-11.60 grams.

Date	Mintage	Good	VG	F	VF	XF
AHxxxx//1 (Ahad) Rare	—	—	—	—	—	—

Mint: Ujjain
KM# 377.63 RUPEE
Silver **Obv:** Inscription, date **Rev. Inscription:** Dar-ul-Fath **Note:** Weight varies 11.00-11.60 grams.

Date	Mintage	Good	VG	F	VF	XF
AH1125//2	—	5.00	7.00	10.00	16.50	25.00
AHxxxx//3	—	5.00	7.00	10.00	16.50	25.00
AH1128//6	—	5.00	7.00	10.00	16.50	25.00
AH1129//6	—	5.00	7.00	10.00	16.50	25.00

Date	Mintage	Good	VG	F	VF	XF
AH1130//7	—	5.00	7.00	10.00	16.50	25.00
AH1131//8	—	5.00	7.00	10.00	16.50	25.00

Mint: Lahore
KM# 378.1 LEGAL DIRHAM
2.7200 g., Silver **Obv:** Inscription, date **Rev:** Inscription **Note:**

Date	Mintage	Good	VG	F	VF	XF
AH1129//6 Rare	—	—	—	—	—	—

Mint: Ganjikot
KM# 380.1 1/2 PAGODA
Gold **Note:** Weight varies 1.35-1.45 grams.

Date	Mintage	Good	VG	F	VF	XF
AHxxxx//5 Rare	—	—	—	—	—	—

Mint:
KM# 380.2 1/2 PAGODA
Gold **Note:** Weight varies 1.35-1.45 grams.

Date	Mintage	Good	VG	F	VF	XF
AH1125//x Rare	—	—	—	—	—	—

Mint: Ganjikot
KM# 385.1 PAGODA
Gold **Note:** Weight varies 2.65-2.75 grams.

Date	Mintage	Good	VG	F	VF	XF
AHxxxx//x Rare	—	—	—	—	—	—

Mint: Guty
KM# 385.2 PAGODA
Gold **Note:** Weight varies 2.65-2.75 grams.

Date	Mintage	Good	VG	F	VF	XF
AH1128//5 Rare	—	—	—	—	—	—

Mint: Imtiyazgarh
KM# 385.3 PAGODA
Gold **Note:** Weight varies 2.65-2.75 grams.

Date	Mintage	Good	VG	F	VF	XF
AHxxxx//3 Rare	—	—	—	—	—	—

Mint: Tadpatri
KM# 385.4 PAGODA
Gold **Note:** Weight varies 2.65-2.75 grams.

Date	Mintage	Good	VG	F	VF	XF
AHxxxx//x Rare	—	—	—	—	—	—

Mint: Sira
KM# 386.1 FANAM
Gold **Note:** Weight varies 0.33-0.40 grams.

Date	Mintage	Good	VG	F	VF	XF
ND//x	—	—	—	—	—	—

Mint: Ahmadabad
KM# 390.36 MOHUR
Gold **Note:**

Date	Mintage	Good	VG	F	VF	XF
AHxxxx//7	—	—	—	—	—	—
AH1131//8	—	—	—	—	—	—

Mint: Ahmadanagar
KM# 390.37 MOHUR
Gold **Note:**

Date	Mintage	Good	VG	F	VF	XF
ND(1713-1719)	—	—	—	—	—	—

Mint: Ajmer
KM# 390.2 MOHUR
Gold **Obv:** Inscription **Rev. Inscription:** Dar-ul-Khair **Note:**

Date	Mintage	Good	VG	F	VF	XF
AHxxxx//x	—	—	150	225	275	350

Mint: Ajmer
KM# 390.1 MOHUR
Gold **Obv:** Inscription, date **Rev. Inscription:** Mustagir-ul-Mulk **Note:** Weight varies 10.80-11.00 grams.

Date	Mintage	Good	VG	F	VF	XF
AHxxxx//x	—	235	265	310	375	450

Mint: Akbarabad
KM# 390.3 MOHUR
Gold **Obv:** Inscription **Rev. Inscription:** Mustagir-ul-Mulk **Note:**

Date	Mintage	Good	VG	F	VF	XF
AH1124//1	—	235	265	310	375	450
AH1125//1 (Ahad)	—	235	265	310	375	450
AHxxxx//3	—	235	265	310	375	450
AH1128//5	—	235	265	310	375	450
AH1130//7	—	235	265	310	375	450

Mint: Akbarabad
KM# 390.4 MOHUR
Gold **Obv:** Inscription **Rev. Inscription:** Mustagir-ul-Khilafat **Note:**

Date	Mintage	Good	VG	F	VF	XF
AHxxxx//6	—	235	265	310	375	450
AH1130//7	—	235	265	310	375	450

Mint: Allahabad
KM# 390.5 MOHUR
Gold **Note:** Weight varies 10.80-11.00 grams.

Date	Mintage	Good	VG	F	VF	XF
AH1130//7	—	235	265	325	425	550
AH1131//7	—	235	265	325	425	550

Mint: Arkat
KM# 390.6 MOHUR
Gold **Note:** Weight varies 10.90-11.00 grams.

Date	Mintage	Good	VG	F	VF	XF
AHxxxx//5	—	235	265	325	425	550

Mint: Asadnagar
KM# 390.28 MOHUR
Gold **Note:** Weight varies 10.80-11.00 grams.

Date	Mintage	Good	VG	F	VF	XF
AHxxxx//5 Rare	—	—	—	—	—	—

Mint: Azimabad
KM# 390.7 MOHUR
Gold **Obv:** Inscription **Rev:** Inscription **Note:** Weight varies 10.80-11.00 grams.

Date	Mintage	Good	VG	F	VF	XF
AHxxxx//1 (Ahad)	—	235	265	310	375	450
AHxxxx//2	—	235	265	310	375	450
AH1128//5	—	235	265	310	375	450

Mint: Azimabad
KM# 390.8 MOHUR
Gold **Obv:** Inscription **Rev. Inscription:** Mustagir-ul-Mulk **Note:** Weight varies 10.80-11.00 grams.

Date	Mintage	Good	VG	F	VF	XF
AH1129//5	—	235	265	310	375	450

Mint: Bareli
KM# 390.9 MOHUR
Gold **Note:** Weight varies 10.80-11.00 grams.

Date	Mintage	Good	VG	F	VF	XF
AH1127//3	—	235	265	310	375	450

Mint: Bijapur
KM# 390.10 MOHUR
Gold **Obv:** Inscription **Rev. Inscription:** Dar-uz-Zafar **Note:** Weight varies 10.80-11.00 grams.

Date	Mintage	Good	VG	F	VF	XF
AHxxxx//7	—	235	265	310	375	450

Mint: Burhanpur
KM# 390.11 MOHUR
Gold **Obv:** Inscription **Rev. Inscription:** Dar-us-Sarur **Note:** Weight varies 10.80-11.00 grams.

Date	Mintage	Good	VG	F	VF	XF
AHxxxx//4	—	235	265	310	375	450
AHxxxx//6	—	235	265	310	375	450
AHxxxx//7	—	235	265	310	375	450

Mint: Elichpur
KM# 390.12 MOHUR
Gold **Note:** Weight varies 10.80-11.00 grams.

Date	Mintage	Good	VG	F	VF	XF
AH1126//3	—	235	265	325	400	500

Mint: Farrukhabad
KM# 390.13 MOHUR
Gold **Note:** Weight varies 10.80-11.00 grams.

Date	Mintage	Good	VG	F	VF	XF
AHxxxx//6 Rare	—	—	—	—	—	—

Mint: Fathabad Dharur
KM# 390.38 MOHUR
Gold **Note:** Weight varies 10.80-11.00 grams.

Date	Mintage	Good	VG	F	VF	XF
AHxxxx//3	—	—	—	—	—	—

Mint: Firozgarh
KM# 390.14 MOHUR
Gold **Note:** Weight varies 10.80-11.00 grams.

Date	Mintage	Good	VG	F	VF	XF
AHxxxx//3 Rare	—	—	—	—	—	—

Mint: Haidarabad (Farkhanda Bunyad)
KM# 390.15 MOHUR
Gold **Obv:** Inscription **Rev. Inscription:** Farkhanda Bunyad **Note:** Weight varies 10.80-11.00 grams.

Date	Mintage	Good	VG	F	VF	XF
AH1125//1 (Ahad)	—	235	265	325	400	500

Mint: Islamabad
KM# 390.16 MOHUR
Gold **Obv:** Inscription **Rev:** Inscription **Note:** Weight varies 10.80-11.00 grams.

Date	Mintage	Good	VG	F	VF	XF
AHxxxx//7	—	235	265	310	375	450

Mint: Itawa
KM# 390.17 MOHUR
Gold **Note:** Weight varies 10.80-11.00 grams.

Date	Mintage	Good	VG	F	VF	XF
AH1128//4	—	235	265	310	375	450
AH1128//5	—	235	265	310	375	450
AH1130//7	—	235	265	310	375	450

Mint: Jahangirnagar
KM# 390.39 MOHUR
Gold **Note:** Weight varies 10.80-11.00 grams.

Date	Mintage	Good	VG	F	VF	XF
AHxxxx//7	—	250	325	425	575	850

Mint: Kanbayat
KM# 390.35 MOHUR
Gold **Note:** Weight varies 10.80-11.00 grams.

Date	Mintage	Good	VG	F	VF	XF
AHxxxx//8	—	—	—	—	—	—

Mint: Kashmir
KM# 390.18 MOHUR
Gold **Note:** Weight varies 10.80-11.00 grams.

Date	Mintage	Good	VG	F	VF	XF
AH1127//x	—	235	275	325	425	550
AH1130//7	—	235	275	325	425	550

Mint: Khujista Bunyad
KM# 390.19 MOHUR
Gold **Obv:** Inscription **Rev:** Inscription **Note:** Weight varies 10.80-11.00 grams.

Date	Mintage	Good	VG	F	VF	XF
AH1125//1 (Ahad)	—	235	265	310	375	450
AH1125//2	—	235	265	310	375	450
AH1126//3	—	235	265	310	375	450
AH1127//4	—	235	265	310	375	450
AH1128//4	—	235	265	310	375	450
AH1128//5	—	235	265	310	375	450
AH1129//5	—	235	265	310	375	450
AH1129//6	—	235	265	310	375	450
AH1130//6	—	235	265	310	375	450
AH1130//7	—	235	265	310	375	450
AH1131//7	—	235	265	310	375	450

Mint: Lahore
KM# 390.20 MOHUR
Gold **Obv:** Inscription **Rev. Inscription:** Dar-us-Sultanat **Note:** Weight varies 10.80-11.00 grams.

Date	Mintage	Good	VG	F	VF	XF
AH1127//4	—	235	265	310	375	450
AH1128//5	—	235	265	310	375	450
AH1129//5	—	235	265	310	375	450
AH1130//7	—	235	265	310	375	450
AH1131//7	—	235	265	310	375	450
AH1131//8	—	235	265	310	375	450

Mint: Macchlipattan
KM# 390.21 MOHUR
Gold **Note:** Weight varies 10.80-11.00 grams.

Date	Mintage	Good	VG	F	VF	XF
AHxxxx//x	—	235	275	335	465	600

Mint: Muazzamabad
KM# 390.22 MOHUR
Gold **Note:** Weight varies 10.80-11.00 grams.

Date	Mintage	Good	VG	F	VF	XF
AH112x//4	—	235	265	325	400	500
AH1128//5	—	235	265	325	400	500
AHxxxx//7	—	235	265	325	400	500

Mint: Multan
KM# 390.23 MOHUR
Gold **Note:** Weight varies 10.80-11.00 grams.

Date	Mintage	Good	VG	F	VF	XF
AH1130//7	—	235	265	310	375	450

Mint: Murshidabad
KM# 390.24 MOHUR
Gold **Note:** Weight varies 10.80-11.00 grams.

Date	Mintage	Good	VG	F	VF	XF
AHxxxx//1 (Ahad)	—	235	265	310	375	450
AH1127//4	—	235	265	310	375	450

Mint: Patna
KM# 390.25 MOHUR
Gold **Note:** Weight varies 10.80-11.00 grams.

Date	Mintage	Good	VG	F	VF	XF
AH1130//7	—	235	265	310	375	450

Mint: Peshawar
KM# 390.26 MOHUR
Gold **Note:** Weight varies 10.80-11.00 grams.

Date	Mintage	Good	VG	F	VF	XF
AH1131//8	—	235	275	325	400	500

Mint: Purenda
KM# 390.27 MOHUR
Gold **Note:** Weight varies 10.80-11.00 grams.

Date	Mintage	Good	VG	F	VF	XF
AHxxxx//5 Rare	—	—	—	—	—	—

Mint: Sahrind
KM# 390.29 MOHUR
Gold **Note:** Weight varies 10.80-11.00 grams.

Date	Mintage	Good	VG	F	VF	XF
AHxxxx//x	—	235	265	310	375	450

Mint: Shahjahanabad
KM# 390.30 MOHUR
Gold **Obv:** Inscription **Rev:** Inscription **Note:** Weight varies 10.80-11.00 grams.

Date	Mintage	Good	VG	F	VF	XF
AH1124//1 (Ahad)	—	235	265	310	375	450
AH1125//1 (Ahad)	—	235	265	310	375	450
AH1125//2	—	235	265	310	375	450
AH1126//2	—	235	265	310	375	450
AH1126//3	—	235	265	310	375	450
AH1127//3	—	235	265	310	375	450
AH1127//4	—	235	265	310	375	450
AH1128//4	—	235	265	310	375	450
AH1130//7	—	235	265	310	375	450
AH1131//7	—	235	265	310	375	450

Mint: Shakola
KM# 390.40 MOHUR
Gold **Note:** Weight varies 10.80-11.00 grams.

Date	Mintage	Good	VG	F	VF	XF
AHxxxx//x	—	—	—	—	—	—

Mint: Sikakul
KM# 390.31 MOHUR
Gold **Note:** Weight varies 10.80-11.00 grams.

Date	Mintage	Good	VG	F	VF	XF
AHxxxx//x Rare	—	—	—	—	—	—

Mint: Surat
KM# 390.32 MOHUR
Gold **Note:** Weight varies 10.80-11.00 grams.

Date	Mintage	Good	VG	F	VF	XF
AHxxxx//1 (Ahad)	—	235	265	310	375	450
AHxxxx//2	—	235	265	310	375	450
AHxxxx//4	—	235	265	310	375	450
AHxxxx//6	—	235	265	310	375	450

Mint: Toragal
KM# 390.33 MOHUR
Gold **Note:** Weight varies 10.80-11.00 grams.

Date	Mintage	Good	VG	F	VF	XF
AHxxxx//3 Rare	—	—	—	—	—	—
AHxxxx//5 Rare	—	—	—	—	—	—

Mint: Ujjain
KM# 390.34 MOHUR
Gold **Obv:** Inscription **Rev. Inscription:** Dar-ul-Fath **Note:** Weight varies 10.80-11.00 grams.

Date	Mintage	Good	VG	F	VF	XF
AHxxxx//x	—	235	265	310	375	450

LARGESSE COINAGE

Mint: Shahjahanabad
KM# A379.1 NISAR
0.7000 g., Silver **Obv:** Inscription **Rev. Inscription:** Dar-ul-Khilafat

Date	Mintage	Good	VG	F	VF	XF
AHxxxx//4	—	—	—	—	—	—

Mint: Shahjahanabad
KM# B379.1 NISAR
1.4000 g., Silver **Obv:** Inscription **Rev. Inscription:** Dar-ul-Khilafat

Date	Mintage	Good	VG	F	VF	XF
AH1129//6	—	—	—	—	—	—
AH1130//x	—	—	—	—	—	—

Mint: Akbarabad
KM# 379.2 NISAR
2.8500 g., Silver

Date	Mintage	Good	VG	F	VF	XF
AH1125//2	—	—	—	—	—	—

Mint: Shahjahanabad
KM# 379.1 NISAR
2.8500 g., Silver

Date	Mintage	Good	VG	F	VF	XF
AHxxxx//5 Rare	—	—	—	—	—	—
AH1129//6 Rare	—	—	—	—	—	—
AH1130//3 Rare	—	—	—	—	—	—

Rafi-ud-Darjat
AH1131 / 1719AD

HAMMERED COINAGE

Mint: Kabul
KM# 401.1 PAISA
14.0000 g., Copper **Obv:** Inscription **Rev:** Inscription **Note:** Weight varies 12.90-13.80 grams.

Date	Mintage	Good	VG	F	VF	XF
AH1131//1 (Ahad)	—	35.00	60.00	100	175	—

Mint: Peshawar
KM# 401.3 PAISA
14.0000 g., Copper **Note:** Weight varies 12.90-13.80 grams.

Date	Mintage	Good	VG	F	VF	XF
AH1131//1 (Ahad) Rare	—	—	—	—	—	—

Mint: Surat
KM# 401.2 PAISA
14.0000 g., Copper **Note:** Weight varies 12.90 - 13.80 grams.

Date	Mintage	Good	VG	F	VF	XF
AH1131//1 (Ahad)	—	35.00	60.00	100	175	—

Mint: Shahjahanabad
KM# 404.1 1/2 RUPEE
5.7220 g., Silver **Obv:** Inscription **Rev:** Inscription **Note:** Weight varies 5.50-5.80 grams.

Date	Mintage	Good	VG	F	VF	XF
AH11xx//1 (Ahad)	—	20.00	50.00	80.00	150	200

Mint: Ahmadabad
KM# 405.1 RUPEE
Silver **Obv:** Inscription, date **Rev. Inscription:** Zain-ul-Bilad **Note:** Weight varies 11.00-11.60 grams.

Date	Mintage	Good	VG	F	VF	XF
AH1131//1 (Ahad)	—	8.00	20.00	40.00	75.00	120

Mint: Ahmadabad
KM# 405.25 RUPEE
Silver **Note:** Without epithet. Weight varies 11.00-11.60 grams.

Date	Mintage	Good	VG	F	VF	XF
AH1131//1 (Ahad)	—	10.00	25.00	50.00	85.00	120

Mint: Ajmir
KM# 405.2 RUPEE
Silver **Obv:** Inscription **Rev. Inscription:** Dar-ul-Khair **Note:** Weight varies 11.00-11.60 grams.

Date	Mintage	Good	VG	F	VF	XF
AH1131//1 (Ahad)	—	12.00	30.00	60.00	100	150

Mint: Akbarabad
KM# 405.3 RUPEE
Silver **Obv:** Inscription **Rev. Inscription:** Mustagar-ul-Khilafat **Note:** Weight varies 11.00-11.60 grams.

Date	Mintage	Good	VG	F	VF	XF
AH1131//1 (Ahad)	—	7.00	17.50	35.00	60.00	85.00

Mint: Bankapur
KM# 405.4 RUPEE
Silver **Note:** Weight varies 11.00-11.60 grams.

Date	Mintage	Good	VG	F	VF	XF
AH1131//1 (Ahad) Rare	—	—	—	—	—	—

Mint: Bareli
KM# 405.5 RUPEE
Silver **Note:** Weight varies 11.00-11.60 grams.

Date	Mintage	Good	VG	F	VF	XF
AH1131//1 (Ahad)	—	10.00	25.00	50.00	85.00	120

Mint: Burhanpur
KM# 405.6 RUPEE
Silver **Obv:** Inscription **Rev. Inscription:** Dar-us-Sarur **Note:** Weight varies 11.00-11.60 grams.

Date	Mintage	Good	VG	F	VF	XF
AH1131//1 (Ahad)	—	10.00	25.00	50.00	85.00	120

Mint: Gwalior
KM# 405.7 RUPEE
Silver **Note:** Weight varies 11.00-11.60 grams.

Date	Mintage	Good	VG	F	VF	XF
AH1131//1 (Ahad)	—	10.00	25.00	50.00	85.00	120

Mint: Itawa
KM# 405.8 RUPEE
Silver **Note:** Weight varies 11.00-11.60 grams.

Date	Mintage	Good	VG	F	VF	XF
AH1131//1 (Ahad)	—	7.00	17.50	35.00	60.00	85.00

Mint: Jahangirnagar
KM# 405.23 RUPEE
Silver **Note:** Weight varies 11.00-11.60 grams.

Date	Mintage	Good	VG	F	VF	XF
AH1131//1 (Ahad) Rare	—	—	—	—	—	—

Mint: Junagarh
KM# 405.26 RUPEE
Silver **Note:** Weight varies 11.00-11.60 grams.

Date	Mintage	Good	VG	F	VF	XF
AH11(31)//1 (Ahad) Rare	—	—	—	—	—	—

Mint: Kabul
KM# 405.9 RUPEE
Silver **Note:** Weight varies 11.00-11.60 grams.

Date	Mintage	Good	VG	F	VF	XF
AH1131//1 (Ahad) Rare	—	—	—	—	—	—

Mint: Khambayat
KM# 405.10 RUPEE
Silver **Note:** Weight varies 11.00-11.60 grams.

Date	Mintage	Good	VG	F	VF	XF
AH1131//1 (Ahad)	—	7.00	17.50	35.00	60.00	85.00

Mint: Khujista Bunyad
KM# 405.11 RUPEE
Silver **Note:** Weight varies 11.00-11.60 grams.

Date	Mintage	Good	VG	F	VF	XF
AH1131//1 (Ahad)	—	10.00	25.00	50.00	85.00	120

Mint: Kora
KM# 405.12 RUPEE
Silver **Note:** Weight varies 11.00-11.60 grams.

Date	Mintage	Good	VG	F	VF	XF
AH1131//1 (Ahad) Rare	—	—	—	—	—	—

Mint: Lahore
KM# 405.13 RUPEE
Silver **Obv:** Inscription **Rev. Inscription:** Dar-us-Sultanat **Note:** Weight varies 11.00-11.60 grams.

Date	Mintage	Good	VG	F	VF	XF
AH1131//1 (Ahad)	—	7.00	17.50	35.00	60.00	85.00

Mint: Lakhnau
KM# 405.14 RUPEE
Silver **Note:** Weight varies 11.00-11.60 grams.

Date	Mintage	Good	VG	F	VF	XF
AH1131//1 (Ahad)	—	10.00	25.00	50.00	85.00	120

Mint: Multan
KM# 405.15 RUPEE
Silver **Obv:** Inscription **Rev:** Inscription, date **Note:** Weight varies 11.00-11.60 grams.

Date	Mintage	Good	VG	F	VF	XF
AH1131//1 (Ahad)	—	10.00	25.00	50.00	85.00	120

Mint: Murshidabad
KM# 405.16 RUPEE
Silver **Obv:** Inscription, date **Rev:** Inscription **Note:** Weight varies 11.00-11.60 grams.

Date	Mintage	Good	VG	F	VF	XF
AH1131//1 (Ahad) Rare	—	—	—	—	—	—

Mint: Patna
KM# 405.17 RUPEE
Silver **Note:** Weight varies 11.00-11.60 grams.

Date	Mintage	Good	VG	F	VF	XF
AH1131//1 (Ahad) Rare	—	—	—	—	—	—

Mint: Sahrind
KM# 405.18 RUPEE
Silver **Note:** Weight varies 11.00-11.60 grams.

Date	Mintage	Good	VG	F	VF	XF
AH1131//1 (Ahad) Rare	—	—	—	—	—	—

Mint: Shahjahanabad
KM# 405.19 RUPEE
Silver **Obv:** Inscription **Rev. Inscription:** Dar-ul-Khilafat **Note:** Weight varies 11.00-11.60 grams.

Date	Mintage	Good	VG	F	VF	XF
AH1131//1 (Ahad)	—	7.00	17.50	35.00	60.00	85.00

Mint: Sikakul
KM# 405.20 RUPEE
Silver **Note:** Weight varies 11.00-11.60 grams.

Date	Mintage	Good	VG	F	VF	XF
AH1131//1 (Ahad) Rare	—	—	—	—	—	—

Mint: Surat
KM# 405.21 RUPEE
Silver **Note:** Weight varies 11.00-11.60 grams.

Date	Mintage	Good	VG	F	VF	XF
AH1131//1 (Ahad)	—	7.00	17.50	35.00	60.00	85.00

Mint: Tatta
KM# 405.24 RUPEE
Silver **Note:** Weight varies 11.00-11.60 grams.

Date	Mintage	Good	VG	F	VF	XF
AH1131//1 (Ahad) Rare	—	—	—	—	—	—

Mint: Ujjain
KM# 405.22 RUPEE
Silver **Note:** Weight varies 11.00-11.60 grams.

Date	Mintage	Good	VG	F	VF	XF
AH1131//1 (Ahad)	—	12.00	30.00	60.00	100	150

Mint: Ahmadabad
KM# 408.1 MOHUR
Gold **Obv:** Inscription **Rev. Inscription:** Zain-ul-Bilad **Note:** Weight varies: 10.55-10.90 grams.

Date	Mintage	Good	VG	F	VF	XF
AH1131//1 (Ahad) Rare	—	—	—	—	—	—

Mint: Akbarabad
KM# 408.2 MOHUR
Gold **Obv:** Inscription **Rev. Inscription:** Mustagir-ul-Khilafat **Note:** Weight varies 10.55-10.90 grams.

Date	Mintage	Good	VG	F	VF	XF
AH1131//1 (Ahad)	—	250	375	600	1,000	1,500

Mint: Burhanpur
KM# 408.11 MOHUR
Gold **Rev:** Mint epithet: "Dar-as-Sarur" **Note:** Weight varies 10.55-10.90 grams.

Date	Mintage	Good	VG	F	VF	XF
AH1131//1 (Ahad)	—	—	—	—	—	—

Mint: Kabul
KM# 408.3 MOHUR
Gold **Note:** Weight varies 10.55-10.90 grams.

Date	Mintage	Good	VG	F	VF	XF
AH1131//1 (Ahad) Rare	—	—	—	—	—	—

Mint: Khujista Bunyad
KM# 408.4 MOHUR
Gold **Note:** Weight varies 10.55-10.90 grams.

Date	Mintage	Good	VG	F	VF	XF
AH1131//1 (Ahad)	—	250	375	600	1,100	1,500

Mint: Lahore
KM# 408.5 MOHUR
Gold **Obv:** Inscription **Rev. Inscription:** Dar-us-Sultanat **Note:** Weight varies 10.55-10.90 grams.

Date	Mintage	Good	VG	F	VF	XF
AH1131//1 (Ahad)	—	250	375	600	1,000	1,500

Mint: Muazzamabad
KM# 408.6 MOHUR
Gold **Note:** Weight varies 10.55-10.90 grams.

Date	Mintage	Good	VG	F	VF	XF
AH1131//1 (Ahad) Rare	—	—	—	—	—	—

Mint: Multan
KM# 408.7 MOHUR
Gold **Note:** Weight varies 10.55-10.90 grams.

Date	Mintage	Good	VG	F	VF	XF
AH1131//1 (Ahad) Rare	—	—	—	—	—	—

Mint: Peshawar
KM# 408.8 MOHUR
Gold **Note:** Weight varies 10.55-10.90 grams.

Date	Mintage	Good	VG	F	VF	XF
AH1131//1 (Ahad) Rare	—	—	—	—	—	—

Mint: Shahjahanabad
KM# 408.9 MOHUR
Gold **Obv:** Inscription **Rev. Inscription:** Dar-ul-Khilafat **Note:** Weight varies 10.55-10.90 grams.

Date	Mintage	Good	VG	F	VF	XF
AH1131//1 (Ahad)	—	250	375	600	1,000	1,500

Mint: Surat
KM# 408.10 MOHUR
Gold **Note:** Weight varies 10.55-10.90 grams.

Date	Mintage	Good	VG	F	VF	XF
AH1131//1 (Ahad)	—	250	400	750	1,200	1,500

Mint: Ujjain
KM# 408.12 MOHUR
Gold **Note:** Weight varies 10.55-10.90 grams.

Date	Mintage	Good	VG	F	VF	XF
AH1131//1 (Ahad) Rare	—	—	—	—	—	—

Shah Jahan II, Rafi-ud-Daula

AH1131 / 1719AD

HAMMERED COINAGE

Mint: Akbarabad
KM# 411.1 DAM
Copper **Obv:** Inscription **Rev:** Inscription **Note:** Weight varies 19.70-20.20 grams.

Date	Mintage	Good	VG	F	VF	XF
AH1131//1 (Ahad)	—	5.00	10.00	17.50	25.00	—

Mint: Surat
KM# 411.2 DAM
Copper **Note:** Weight varies 19.70-20.20 grams.

Date	Mintage	Good	VG	F	VF	XF
AH1131//1 (Ahad)	—	5.00	10.00	17.50	25.00	—

Mint: Lahore
KM# 412.1 1/2 RUPEE
Silver **Note:** Weight varies 5.50-5.80 grams.

Date	Mintage	Good	VG	F	VF	XF
AH1131//1 (Ahad) Rare	—	—	—	—	—	—

Mint: Surat
KM# 412.2 1/2 RUPEE
Silver **Note:** Weight varies 5.50-5.80 grams.

Date	Mintage	Good	VG	F	VF	XF
AHxxxx//1 (Ahad) Rare	—	—	—	—	—	—

Mint: Peshawar
KM# 413.2 RUPEE
Silver **Note:** Weight varies 11.00-11.60 grams.

Date	Mintage	Good	VG	F	VF	XF
AH1131//1 (Ahad) Rare	—	—	—	—	—	—

Mint: Sikakul
KM# 413.1 RUPEE
Silver **Obv. Inscription:** Sahib Qiran **Rev:** Inscription **Note:** Weight varies 11.00-11.60 grams.

Date	Mintage	Good	VG	F	VF	XF
AH1131//1 (Ahad) Rare	—	—	—	—	—	—

Mint: Tatta
KM# 413.3 RUPEE
Silver **Obv. Legend:** SAHIB QIRAN **Note:** Weight varies 11.00-11.60 grams. Varieties exist with dates in different positions.

Date	Mintage	Good	VG	F	VF	XF
AH1131 (Ahad) Rare	—	—	—	—	—	—

Mint: Ahmadabad
KM# 415.1 RUPEE
Silver **Obv:** Inscription **Rev:** Inscription **Note:** Weight varies 11.00-11.60 grams.

Date	Mintage	Good	VG	F	VF	XF
AH1131//1 (Ahad)	—	12.00	27.50	55.00	90.00	130

Mint: Ajmir
KM# 415.2 RUPEE
Silver **Rev:** Mint epithet: Dar-ul-Khair **Note:** Weight varies 11.00-11.60 grams.

Date	Mintage	Good	VG	F	VF	XF
AH1131//1 (Ahad)	—	12.00	27.50	55.00	90.00	130

Mint: Akbarabad
KM# 415.3 RUPEE
Silver **Obv:** Inscription **Rev. Inscription:** Mustagir-ul-Khilafat **Note:** Weight varies 11.00-11.60 grams.

Date	Mintage	Good	VG	F	VF	XF
AH1131//1 (Ahad)	—	10.00	25.00	50.00	85.00	120

Mint: Akbarnagar
KM# 415.26 RUPEE
Silver **Note:** Weight varies 11.00-11.60 grams.

Date	Mintage	Good	VG	F	VF	XF
AH1131//1 (Ahad) Rare	—	—	—	—	—	—

Mint: Arkat
KM# 415.4 RUPEE
Silver **Note:** Weight varies 11.00-11.60 grams.

Date	Mintage	Good	VG	F	VF	XF
AH1131//1 (Ahad) Rare	—	—	—	—	—	—

Mint: Azimabad
KM# 415.5 RUPEE
Silver **Note:** Weight varies 11.00-11.60 grams.

Date	Mintage	Good	VG	F	VF	XF
AH1131//1 (Ahad)	—	12.00	27.50	55.00	90.00	125

Mint: Bahadarqarh
KM# 415.6 RUPEE
11.4440 g., Silver **Note:** Weight varies 11.00-11.60 grams.

Date	Mintage	Good	VG	F	VF	XF
AH1131//1 (Ahad) Rare	—	—	—	—	—	—

Mint: Bareli
KM# 415.7 RUPEE
Silver **Note:** Weight varies 11.00-11.60 grams.

Date	Mintage	Good	VG	F	VF	XF
AH1131//1 (Ahad)	—	10.00	25.00	50.00	85.00	120

Mint: Burhanpur
KM# 415.8 RUPEE
Silver **Obv:** Inscription **Rev. Inscription:** Dar-us-Sarur **Note:** Weight varies 11.00-11.60 grams.

Date	Mintage	Good	VG	F	VF	XF
AH1131//1 (Ahad)	—	10.00	25.00	50.00	85.00	120

Mint: Gwalior
KM# 415.9 RUPEE
Silver **Obv:** Inscription **Rev:** Inscription **Note:** Weight varies 11.00-11.60 grams.

Date	Mintage	Good	VG	F	VF	XF
AH1131//1 (Ahad)	—	10.00	25.00	50.00	85.00	120

Mint: Islamabad
KM# 415.10 RUPEE
Silver **Note:** Weight varies 11.00-11.60 grams.

Date	Mintage	Good	VG	F	VF	XF
AH1131//1 (Ahad)	—	15.00	35.00	60.00	100	140

Mint: Itawa
KM# 415.11 RUPEE
Silver **Note:** Weight varies 11.00-11.60 grams.

Date	Mintage	Good	VG	F	VF	XF
AH1131//1 (Ahad)	—	10.00	25.00	50.00	85.00	120

Mint: Jahangirnagar
KM# 415.27 RUPEE
Silver **Note:** Weight varies 11.00-11.60 grams.

Date	Mintage	Good	VG	F	VF	XF
AH1131//1 (Ahad) Rare	—	—	—	—	—	—

Mint: Junagarh
KM# 415.12 RUPEE
Silver **Note:** Weight varies 11.00-11.60 grams.

Date	Mintage	Good	VG	F	VF	XF
AH1131//1 (Ahad)	—	15.00	35.00	60.00	100	140

Mint: Katak
KM# 415.28 RUPEE
Silver **Note:** Weight varies 11.00-11.60 grams.

Date	Mintage	Good	VG	F	VF	XF
AH1131//1 (Ahad)	—	—	—	—	—	—

Mint: Khambayat
KM# 415.13 RUPEE
Silver **Note:** Weight varies 11.00-11.60 grams.

Date	Mintage	Good	VG	F	VF	XF
AH1131//1 (Ahad)	—	11.50	27.50	55.00	90.00	130

Mint: Khujista Bunyad
KM# 415.14 RUPEE
Silver **Note:** Weight varies 11.00-11.60 grams.

Date	Mintage	Good	VG	F	VF	XF
AH1131//1 (Ahad)	—	11.50	27.50	55.00	90.00	130

Mint: Kora
KM# 415.15 RUPEE
Silver **Note:** Weight varies 11.00-11.60 grams.

Date	Mintage	Good	VG	F	VF	XF
AH1131//1 (Ahad)	—	11.50	27.50	55.00	90.00	130

Mint: Lahore
KM# 415.16 RUPEE
Silver **Obv:** Inscription, date **Rev. Inscription:** Dar-us-Sultanat **Note:** Weight varies 11.00-11.60 grams.

Date	Mintage	Good	VG	F	VF	XF
AH1131//1 (Ahad)	—	10.00	25.00	50.00	85.00	120

Mint: Lakhnau
KM# 415.17 RUPEE
Silver **Note:** Weight varies 11.00-11.60 grams.

Date	Mintage	Good	VG	F	VF	XF
AH1131//1 (Ahad)	—	11.50	27.50	55.00	90.00	130

Mint: Macchlipattan
KM# 415.18 RUPEE
Silver **Note:** Weight varies 11.00-11.60 grams.

Date	Mintage	Good	VG	F	VF	XF
AH1131//1 (Ahad) Rare	—	—	—	—	—	—

Mint: Muhammadabad
KM# 415.29 RUPEE
Silver **Note:** Weight varies 11.00-11.60 grams.

Date	Mintage	Good	VG	F	VF	XF
AH1132//1 (Ahad)	—	—	—	—	—	—

Mint: Multan
KM# 415.19 RUPEE
Silver **Note:** Weight varies 11.00-11.60 grams.

Date	Mintage	Good	VG	F	VF	XF
AH1131//1 (Ahad) Rare	—	—	—	—	—	—

Mint: Murshidabad
KM# 415.21 RUPEE
Silver **Obv:** Inscription **Rev:** Inscription **Note:** Weight varies 11.00-11.60 grams.

Date	Mintage	Good	VG	F	VF	XF
AH1131//1 (Ahad)	—	12.00	30.00	60.00	100	140

Mint: Sahrind
KM# 415.22 RUPEE
Silver **Note:** Weight varies 11.00-11.60 grams.

Date	Mintage	Good	VG	F	VF	XF
AH1131//1 (Ahad)	—	11.50	27.50	55.00	90.00	130

Mint: Shahjahanabad
KM# 415.23 RUPEE
Silver **Obv:** Inscription **Rev. Inscription:** Dar-ul-Khilafat **Note:** Weight varies 11.00-11.60 grams.

Date	Mintage	Good	VG	F	VF	XF
AH1131//1 (Ahad)	—	10.00	25.00	50.00	85.00	125

Mint: Sikakul
KM# 415.30 RUPEE
Silver **Note:** Weight varies 11.00-11.60 grams.

Date	Mintage	Good	VG	F	VF	XF
AH1131//1 (Ahad)	—	—	—	—	—	—

Mint: Surat
KM# 415.24 RUPEE
Silver **Obv:** Inscription **Rev:** Inscription **Note:** Weight varies 11.00-11.60 grams.

Date	Mintage	Good	VG	F	VF	XF
AH1131//1 (Ahad)	—	10.00	25.00	50.00	85.00	125

Mint: Tatta
KM# 415.25 RUPEE
Silver **Obv. Legend:** PAD-I SHAH GHAZI **Note:** Weight varies 11.00-11.60 grams.

Date	Mintage	Good	VG	F	VF	XF
AH1131//1 (Ahad) Rare	—	—	—	—	—	—

Mint: Ujjain
KM# A415.26 RUPEE
Silver **Obv:** Inscription **Rev. Inscription:** Dar-ul-Fath **Note:** Weight varies 11.00-11.60 grams.

Date	Mintage	Good	VG	F	VF	XF
AH1131//1 (Ahad) Rare	—	—	—	—	—	—

Mint: Allahabad
KM# 417.1 MOHUR
Gold **Obv. Inscription:** Sahib Qiran **Rev:** Inscription **Note:** Weight varies 10.55-10.85 grams.

Date	Mintage	Good	VG	F	VF	XF
AH1131//1 (Ahad) Rare	—	—	—	—	—	—

Mint: Akbarabad
KM# 418.1 MOHUR
Gold **Obv:** Inscription, date **Rev. Inscription:** Mustagir-ul-Khilafat **Note:** Weight varies 10.55-10.85 grams.

Date	Mintage	Good	VG	F	VF	XF
AH1131//1 (Ahad)	—	225	325	700	1,200	1,800

Mint: Arkat
KM# 418.2 MOHUR
Gold **Note:** Weight varies 10.55-10.85 grams.

Date	Mintage	Good	VG	F	VF	XF
AH1131//1 (Ahad) Rare	—	—	—	—	—	—

Mint: Burhanpur
KM# 418.3 MOHUR
Gold **Obv:** Inscription **Rev. Inscription:** Dar-us-Sarur **Note:** Weight varies 10.55-10.85 grams.

Date	Mintage	Good	VG	F	VF	XF
AH1131//1 (Ahad)	—	225	325	700	1,200	1,800

Mint: Haidarabad
KM# 418.4 MOHUR
Gold **Note:** Weight varies 10.55-10.85 grams.

Date	Mintage	Good	VG	F	VF	XF
AH1131//1 (Ahad)	—	225	325	700	1,200	1,800

Mint: Khujista Bunyad
KM# 418.5 MOHUR
Gold **Note:** Weight varies 10.55-10.85 grams.

Date	Mintage	Good	VG	F	VF	XF
AH1131//1 (Ahad)	—	225	325	700	1,200	1,800

Mint: Lahore
KM# 418.6 MOHUR
Gold **Obv:** Inscription **Rev. Inscription:** Dar-us-Sultanat **Note:** Weight varies 10.55-10.85 grams.

Date	Mintage	Good	VG	F	VF	XF
AH1131//1 (Ahad)	—	225	325	700	1,200	1,800

Mint: Shahjahanabad
KM# 418.7 MOHUR
Gold **Obv:** Inscription **Rev. Inscription:** Dar-ul-Khilafat **Note:** Weight varies 10.55-10.85 grams.

Date	Mintage	Good	VG	F	VF	XF
AH1131//1 (Ahad)	—	225	325	700	1,200	1,800

Mint: Surat
KM# 418.8 MOHUR
Gold **Note:** Weight varies 10.55-10.85 grams.

Date	Mintage	Good	VG	F	VF	XF
AH1131//1 (Ahad)	—	225	325	700	1,200	1,800

Mint: Ujjain
KM# 418.9 MOHUR
Gold **Obv:** Inscription **Rev. Inscription:** Dar-ul-Fath **Note:** Weight varies 10.55-10.85 grams.

Date	Mintage	Good	VG	F	VF	XF
AH1131//1 (Ahad)	—	225	325	700	1,200	1,800

Muhammad Shah
AH1131-1161 / 1719-1748AD

HAMMERED COINAGE

Mint: Ahmadabad
KM# 364.33 RUPEE
Silver **Obv:** Sahib Qiran Jahandar Shah Badshah-i-Jahan **Note:** Weight varies 11.00 - 11.60 grams.

Date	Mintage	Good	VG	F	VF	XF
AH1124//1	—	—	10.00	20.00	35.00	50.00

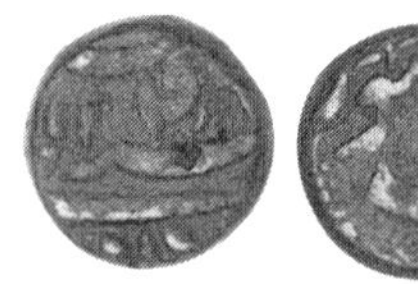

Mint: Burhanpur
KM# 429.3 1/2 DAM
6.3000 g., Copper **Obv:** Inscription **Rev:** Inscription **Note:**

Date	Mintage	Good	VG	F	VF	XF
AH1149//x	—	10.00	20.00	35.00	50.00	—

Mint: Hafizabad
KM# 429.2 1/2 DAM
6.3000 g., Copper **Obv:** Inscription **Rev:** Inscription **Note:**

Date	Mintage	Good	VG	F	VF	XF
ND//x	—	—	—	—	—	—

Mint: Macchlipattan
KM# 429.1 1/2 DAM
Copper **Obv:** Inscription **Rev:** Inscription **Note:** Weight varies 7.50-9.60 grams.

Date	Mintage	Good	VG	F	VF	XF
AH1133//2	—	10.00	20.00	35.00	50.00	—
AH1135//5	—	10.00	20.00	35.00	50.00	—
AH1136//6	—	10.00	20.00	35.00	50.00	—
AH1141//11	—	10.00	20.00	35.00	50.00	—
AH1144//14	—	10.00	20.00	35.00	50.00	—
AH1147//17	—	10.00	20.00	35.00	50.00	—
AH1148//18	—	10.00	20.00	35.00	50.00	—
AH1152//22	—	10.00	20.00	35.00	50.00	—
AH1161//31	—	—	20.00	35.00	50.00	—

Mint: Bakkar
KM# A430.2 DAM
Copper **Note:** Weight varies 17.36-19.31 grams.

Date	Mintage	Good	VG	F	VF	XF
AH1138//7	—	5.00	10.00	18.00	30.00	—
AH1145//15	—	5.00	10.00	18.00	30.00	—
AH1146//15	—	5.00	10.00	18.00	30.00	—
AH1146//16	—	5.00	10.00	18.00	30.00	—
AH1147//16	—	5.00	10.00	18.00	30.00	—
AH1147//17	—	5.00	10.00	18.00	30.00	—
AH1160//30	—	5.00	10.00	18.00	30.00	—

Mint: Elichpur
KM# A430.1 DAM
Copper **Note:** Weight varies 17.36-19.31 grams.

Date	Mintage	Good	VG	F	VF	XF
AH1136//x	—	2.25	4.50	7.50	12.00	—
AH113x//8	—	2.25	4.50	7.50	12.00	—
AH1139//9	—	2.25	4.50	7.50	12.00	—
AH1145//15	—	2.25	4.50	7.50	12.00	—

Mint: Aurangnagar
KM# 430.9 PAISA
Copper **Note:** Weight varies 13.00-13.87 grams.

Date	Mintage	Good	VG	F	VF	XF
ND(1719-48)	—	5.00	10.00	18.00	30.00	—

Mint: Azimabad
KM# 430.11 PAISA
Copper **Note:** Weight varies 13.00-13.87 grams.

Date	Mintage	Good	VG	F	VF	XF
AH114x//11 (Ahad)	—	—	—	—	—	—

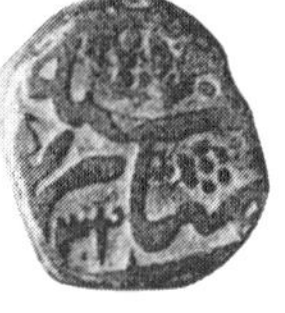

Mint: Haidarabad
KM# 430.12 PAISA
Copper **Note:** Weight varies 13.00-13.87 grams.

Date	Mintage	Good	VG	F	VF	XF
AH1132//x Rare	—	—	—	—	—	—

Mint: Kabul
KM# 430.3 PAISA
Copper **Note:** Weight varies 13.00-13.87 grams.

Date	Mintage	Good	VG	F	VF	XF
ND//x	—	6.00	12.00	20.00	35.00	—

Mint: Kashmir
KM# 430.4 PAISA
Copper **Note:** Weight varies 13.00-13.87 grams.

Date	Mintage	Good	VG	F	VF	XF
AHxxxx//11	—	5.00	10.00	18.50	30.00	—
AH1150//xx	—	5.00	10.00	18.50	30.00	—

Mint: Khambayat
KM# 430.13 PAISA
Copper **Obv:** Inscription **Rev:** Inscription **Note:** Weight varies 13.00-13.87 grams.

Date	Mintage	Good	VG	F	VF	XF
AH11xx//11	—	—	—	—	—	—

Mint: Macchlipattan
KM# 430.5 PAISA
Copper **Note:** Weight varies 13.00-13.87 grams.

Date	Mintage	Good	VG	F	VF	XF
AH1131//1 (Ahad)	—	7.50	15.00	25.00	40.00	—
AH1132//1 (Ahad)	—	7.50	15.00	25.00	40.00	—
AH1135//4	—	7.50	15.00	25.00	40.00	—
AH1139//x	—	7.50	15.00	25.00	40.00	—
AH1140//10	—	7.50	15.00	25.00	40.00	—
AH1141//10	—	7.50	15.00	25.00	40.00	—
AH1141//11	—	7.50	15.00	25.00	40.00	—
AH1142//11	—	7.50	15.00	25.00	40.00	—
AH1143//1x	—	7.50	15.00	25.00	40.00	—
AH1150//xx	—	7.50	15.00	25.00	40.00	—
AH1158//28	—	7.50	15.00	25.00	40.00	—

Mint: Multan
KM# 430.6 PAISA
Copper **Note:** Weight varies 13.00-13.87 grams.

Date	Mintage	Good	VG	F	VF	XF
AH1133//3	—	5.00	10.00	18.50	30.00	—
AH1143//13	—	5.00	10.00	18.50	30.00	—

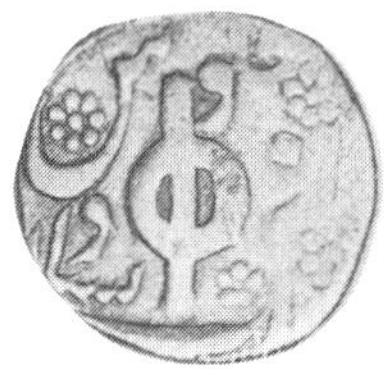

Mint: Peshawar
KM# 430.10 PAISA
Copper **Obv:** Beaded flowers, thick upright rod through circle **Rev:** Inscription **Note:** Weight varies 13.00-13.87 grams.

Date	Mintage	Good	VG	F	VF	XF
ND//x	—	50.00	75.00	125	200	—

Mint: Shahjahanabad
KM# 430.8 PAISA
Copper **Note:** Weight varies 13.00-13.87 grams.

Date	Mintage	Good	VG	F	VF	XF
AH1159//29 Rare	—	—	—	—	—	—

Mint: Surat
KM# 430.7 PAISA
Copper **Note:** Weight varies 13.00-13.87 grams.

Date	Mintage	Good	VG	F	VF	XF
ND1140//10	—	3.50	7.00	12.00	20.00	—
AH1143//13	—	3.50	7.00	12.00	20.00	—

Mint: Khujista Bunyad
KM# A431 1/32 RUPEE
Silver **Note:** Weight varies 0.34-0.36 grams.

Date	Mintage	Good	VG	F	VF	XF
AHxxxx//2	—	—	—	—	—	—
AHxxxx//7	—	—	—	—	—	—
AHxxxx//9	—	—	—	—	—	—
AHxxxx//11	—	—	—	—	—	—
AHxxxx//20	—	—	—	—	—	—
AH1151//xx	—	—	—	—	—	—
AH1157//xx	—	—	—	—	—	—

Mint: Burhanpur
KM# B431.4 1/16 RUPEE
Silver **Obv:** Inscription **Rev. Inscription:** Dar-us-Sarur **Note:** Weight varies 1.38-1.45 grams.

Date	Mintage	Good	VG	F	VF	XF
AHxxxx//x	—	—	—	—	—	—

Mint: Khujista Bunyad
KM# B431.3 1/16 RUPEE
Silver **Note:** Weight varies 0.68-0.72 grams.

Date	Mintage	Good	VG	F	VF	XF
AHxxxx//27	—	—	—	—	—	—

Mint: Macchlipattan
KM# B431.1 1/16 RUPEE
Silver **Note:** Weight varies 0.68-0.72 grams.

Date	Mintage	Good	VG	F	VF	XF
AH1135//5 Rare	—	—	—	—	—	—
AH1157//xx Rare	—	—	—	—	—	—

Mint: Murshidabad
KM# B431.2 1/16 RUPEE
0.7150 g., Silver **Note:** Weight varies 0.68-0.72 grams.

Date	Mintage	Good	VG	F	VF	XF
AHxxxx//14	—	—	—	—	—	—

Mint: Ujjain
KM# B431.5 1/8 RUPEE
Silver **Obv:** Inscription **Rev. Inscription:** Dar-ul-Fath **Note:** Weight varies 1.38-1.45 grams.

Date	Mintage	Good	VG	F	VF	XF
AHxxxx//x	—	—	—	—	—	—

Mint: Akbarabad
KM# C431.1 1/8 RUPEE
Silver **Obv:** Inscription **Rev. Inscription:** Mustagir-ul-Khilafat **Note:** Weight varies 1.38-1.45 grams.

Date	Mintage	Good	VG	F	VF	XF
AHxxxx//4	—	—	—	—	—	—
AHxxxx//8	—	—	—	—	—	—
AHxxxx//29	—	—	—	—	—	—

Mint: Burhanpur
KM# C431.4 1/8 RUPEE
Silver **Obv:** Inscription **Rev. Inscription:** Dar-us-Sarur **Note:** Weight varies 1.38-1.45 grams.

Date	Mintage	Good	VG	F	VF	XF
AHxxxx//27	—	—	—	—	—	—
AHxxxx//30	—	—	—	—	—	—

Mint: Macchlipattan
KM# C431.2 1/8 RUPEE
Silver **Note:** Weight varies 1.38-1.45 grams.

Date	Mintage	Good	VG	F	VF	XF
AH1138//8 Rare	—	—	—	—	—	—
AH1140//9 Rare	—	—	—	—	—	—
AH1147//16 Rare	—	—	—	—	—	—

Mint: Murshidabad
KM# C431.3 1/8 RUPEE
Silver **Note:** Weight varies 1.38-1.45 grams.

Date	Mintage	Good	VG	F	VF	XF
AH1133//2 Rare	—	—	—	—	—	—
AHxxxx//4 Rare	—	—	—	—	—	—
AH11xx//25 Rare	—	—	—	—	—	—
AHxxxx//30 Rare	—	—	—	—	—	—

Mint: Ujjain
KM# C431.5 1/8 RUPEE
Silver **Obv:** Inscription **Rev. Inscription:** Dar-ul-Fath **Note:** Weight varies 1.38-1.45 grams.

Date	Mintage	Good	VG	F	VF	XF
AHxxxx//x	—	—	—	—	—	—

Mint: Akbarabad
KM# 431.7 1/4 RUPEE
Silver **Obv:** Inscription **Rev. Inscription:** Mustagir-ul-Khilafat **Note:** Weight varies 2.75-2.90 grams.

Date	Mintage	Good	VG	F	VF	XF
AH1146//xx	—	—	—	—	—	—

Mint: Akhtarnagar
KM# 431.8 1/4 RUPEE
Silver **Note:** Weight varies 2.75-2.90 grams.

Date	Mintage	Good	VG	F	VF	XF
AH1141//11	—	—	—	—	—	—
AHxxxx//12	—	—	—	—	—	—

Mint: Burhanpur
KM# 431.2 1/4 RUPEE
Silver **Obv. Inscription:** Badshah Ghazi **Rev. Inscription:** Dar-ul-Sarur **Note:** Weight varies 2.75-2.90 grams.

Date	Mintage	Good	VG	F	VF	XF
AHxxxx//2	—	—	—	—	—	—
AHxxxx//9	—	—	—	—	—	—

Mint: Haidarabad (Farkhanda Bunyad)
KM# 431.9 1/4 RUPEE
Silver **Obv:** Inscription **Rev. Inscription:** Farkhanda Bunyad **Note:** Weight varies 2.75-2.90 grams.

Date	Mintage	Good	VG	F	VF	XF
AHxxxx//x	—	—	—	—	—	—

Mint: Islamabad
KM# 431.10 1/4 RUPEE
Silver **Note:** Weight varies 2.75-2.90 grams.

Date	Mintage	Good	VG	F	VF	XF
AHxxxx//15	—	—	—	—	—	—

Mint: Khujista Bunyad
KM# 431.11 1/4 RUPEE
Silver **Note:** Weight varies 2.75-2.90 grams.

Date	Mintage	Good	VG	F	VF	XF
AHxxxx//15	—	—	—	—	—	—

Mint: Kora
KM# 431.12 1/4 RUPEE
Silver **Note:** Weight varies 2.75-2.90 grams.

Date	Mintage	Good	VG	F	VF	XF
AHxxxx//6	—	—	—	—	—	—

Mint: Macchlipattan
KM# 431.6 1/4 RUPEE
Silver **Note:** Weight varies 2.75-2.90 grams.

Date	Mintage	Good	VG	F	VF	XF
AH1138//8	—	—	—	—	—	—
AH1159//29	—	—	—	—	—	—

Mint: Murshidabad
KM# 431.3 1/4 RUPEE
Silver **Note:** Weight varies 2.75-2.90 grams.

Date	Mintage	Good	VG	F	VF	XF
AHxxxx//8	—	—	—	—	—	—
AHxxxx//10	—	—	—	—	—	—
AHxxxx//16	—	—	—	—	—	—
AHxxxx//17	—	—	—	—	—	—
AHxxxx//24	—	—	—	—	—	—

Mint: Shahabad Qanauj
KM# 431.13 1/4 RUPEE
Silver **Note:** Weight varies 2.75-2.90 grams.

Date	Mintage	Good	VG	F	VF	XF
AHxxxx//20	—	—	—	—	—	—

Mint: Surat
KM# 431.5 1/4 RUPEE
Silver **Note:** Weight varies 2.75-2.90 grams.

Date	Mintage	Good	VG	F	VF	XF
AHxxxx//5	—	—	—	—	—	—

Mint: Ujjain
KM# 431.4 1/4 RUPEE
Silver **Obv:** Inscription **Rev. Inscription:** Dar-ul-Fath **Note:** Weight varies 2.75-2.90 grams.

Date	Mintage	Good	VG	F	VF	XF
ND//x	—	—	—	—	—	—
AH1138//8	—	—	—	—	—	—

Mint: Shahjahanabad
KM# 432.1 1/4 RUPEE
Silver **Obv:** Inscription **Rev. Inscription:** Dar-ul-Khilafat **Note:** Weight varies 2.75-2.90 grams.

Date	Mintage	Good	VG	F	VF	XF
AHxxxx//14 Rare	—	—	—	—	—	—
AHxxxx//18 Rare	—	—	—	—	—	—
AHxxxx//24 Rare	—	—	—	—	—	—
AHxxxx//26 Rare	—	—	—	—	—	—

Mint: Surat
KM# A433.1 1/2 RUPEE
Silver **Obv. Inscription:** Ba-Lutfullah Badshahi Zaman **Rev:** Inscription **Note:** Weight varies 5.50-5.80 grams.

Date	Mintage	Good	VG	F	VF	XF
AHxxxx//1 (Ahad)	—	35.00	90.00	180	300	450
AHxxxx//2	—	35.00	90.00	180	300	450
AHxxxx//3	—	35.00	90.00	180	300	450
AHxxxx//6	—	35.00	90.00	180	300	450
AHxxxx//11	—	35.00	90.00	180	300	450
AHxxxx//26	—	35.00	90.00	180	300	450

Mint: Burhanpur
KM# B433.1 1/2 RUPEE
Silver **Obv. Inscription:** Abul Fateh Nazir-Ud-Din **Rev:** Inscription **Note:** Weight varies 5.50-5.80 grams.

Date	Mintage	Good	VG	F	VF	XF
AHxxxx//1 (Ahad) Rare	—	—	—	—	—	—

Mint: Ahmadabad
KM# 433.1 1/2 RUPEE
Silver **Obv:** Inscription **Rev:** Inscription **Note:** Weight varies 5.50-5.80 grams.

Date	Mintage	Good	VG	F	VF	XF
AH11xx//1 (Ahad) Rare	—	—	—	—	—	—
AHxxxx//9 Rare	—	—	—	—	—	—
AHxxxx//12 Rare	—	—	—	—	—	—
AHxxxx//13 Rare	—	—	—	—	—	—
AHxxxx//14 Rare	—	—	—	—	—	—
AHxxxx//16 Rare	—	—	—	—	—	—

Mint: Akbarabad
KM# 433.7 1/2 RUPEE
Silver **Obv:** Inscription **Rev. Inscription:** Mustagir-ul-Mulk **Note:** Weight varies 5.50-5.80 grams.

Date	Mintage	Good	VG	F	VF	XF
AH115x//23	—	—	—	—	—	—

Mint: Arkat
KM# 433.10 1/2 RUPEE
Silver **Note:** Weight varies 5.50-5.80 grams.

Date	Mintage	Good	VG	F	VF	XF
AH115x//xx	—	—	—	—	—	—

Mint: Azimabad
KM# 433.11 1/2 RUPEE
Silver **Note:** Weight varies 5.50-5.80 grams.

Date	Mintage	Good	VG	F	VF	XF
AHxxxx//3	—	—	—	—	—	—
AHxxxx//5	—	—	—	—	—	—

Mint: Gwalior
KM# 433.5 1/2 RUPEE
Silver **Note:** Weight varies 5.50-5.80 grams.

Date	Mintage	Good	VG	F	VF	XF
AH11xx//24	—	—	—	—	—	—

Mint: Itawa
KM# 433.13 1/2 RUPEE
Silver **Note:** Weight varies 5.50-5.80 grams.

Date	Mintage	Good	VG	F	VF	XF
AHxxxx//2	—	—	—	—	—	—

Mint: Khambayat
KM# 433.3 1/2 RUPEE
Silver **Note:** Weight varies 5.50-5.80 grams.

Date	Mintage	Good	VG	F	VF	XF
AHxxxx//5	—	—	—	—	—	—
AHxxxx//14	—	—	—	—	—	—
AHxxxx//16	—	—	—	—	—	—
AHxxxx//29	—	—	—	—	—	—
AHxxxx//31	—	—	—	—	—	—

Mint: Kora
KM# 433.6 1/2 RUPEE
Silver **Obv:** Inscription **Rev:** Inscription **Note:** Weight varies 5.50-5.80 grams.

Date	Mintage	Good	VG	F	VF	XF
AHxxxx//4	—	—	—	—	—	—
AH114x//10	—	—	—	—	—	—
AH115x//20	—	—	—	—	—	—

Mint: Lahore
KM# 433.14 1/2 RUPEE

Silver **Obv:** Inscription **Rev. Legend:** Dar-us-Sultanat **Note:** Weight varies 5.50-5.80 grams.

Date	Mintage	Good	VG	F	VF	XF
AH115x//22	—	—	—	—	—	—

Mint: Macchlipattan
KM# 433.15 1/2 RUPEE

Silver **Note:** Weight varies 5.5-5.80 grams.

Date	Mintage	Good	VG	F	VF	XF
AH1145//15	—	—	—	—	—	—

Mint: Muhammadabad Banaras
KM# 433.12 1/2 RUPEE

Silver **Note:** Weight varies 5.50-5.80 grams.

Date	Mintage	Good	VG	F	VF	XF
AHxxxx//18	—	—	—	—	—	—

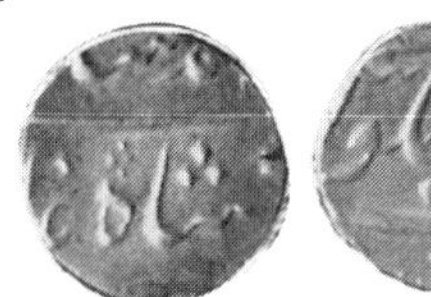

Mint: Murshidabad
KM# 433.8 1/2 RUPEE

Silver **Obv:** Inscription **Rev:** Inscription **Note:** Weight varies 5.50-5.80 grams.

Date	Mintage	Good	VG	F	VF	XF
AHxxxx//12	—	—	—	—	—	—
AHxxxx//17	—	—	—	—	—	—
AHxxxx//29	—	—	—	—	—	—

Mint: Shahabad Qanauj
KM# 433.9 1/2 RUPEE

Silver **Obv:** Inscription, date **Rev:** Inscription **Note:** Weight varies 5.50-5.80 grams.

Date	Mintage	Good	VG	F	VF	XF
AH1153//2x	—	—	—	—	—	—
AH1153//3	—	—	—	—	—	—
AH1154//2x	—	—	—	—	—	—
AH115x//26	—	—	—	—	—	—

Mint: Surat
KM# 433.4 1/2 RUPEE

Silver **Obv:** Inscription **Rev:** Inscription **Note:** Weight varies 5.50-5.80 grams.

Date	Mintage	Good	VG	F	VF	XF
AHxxxx//1 (Ahad)	—	6.00	15.00	30.00	50.00	75.00
AHxxxx//2	—	6.00	15.00	30.00	50.00	75.00
AH113x//3	—	6.00	15.00	30.00	50.00	75.00
AH11xx//4	—	6.00	15.00	30.00	50.00	75.00
AH11xx//5	—	6.00	15.00	30.00	50.00	75.00
AH11xx//8	—	6.00	15.00	30.00	50.00	75.00
AH11xx//9	—	6.00	15.00	30.00	50.00	75.00
AH114x//10	—	6.00	15.00	30.00	50.00	75.00
AH11xx//12	—	6.00	15.00	30.00	50.00	75.00
AH11xx//15	—	6.00	15.00	30.00	50.00	75.00
AH11xx//17	—	6.00	15.00	30.00	50.00	75.00
AH11xx//18	—	6.00	15.00	30.00	50.00	75.00
AH11xx//19	—	6.00	15.00	30.00	50.00	75.00
AH11xx//20	—	6.00	15.00	30.00	50.00	75.00
AH11xx//24	—	6.00	15.00	30.00	50.00	75.00
AH11xx//25	—	6.00	15.00	30.00	50.00	75.00
AH11xx//26	—	6.00	15.00	30.00	50.00	75.00
AH11xx//27	—	6.00	15.00	30.00	50.00	75.00
AH11xx//3x	—	6.00	15.00	30.00	50.00	75.00

Mint: Farrukhabad
KM# A434.2 1/2 RUPEE

Silver **Note:** Weight varies 5.50-5.80 grams.

Date	Mintage	Good	VG	F	VF	XF
AH1154//24	—	—	—	—	—	—
AH115x//28	—	—	—	—	—	—

Mint: Shahjahanabad
KM# A434.1 1/2 RUPEE

Silver **Obv. Inscription:** Sahib Qiran Sani, Second Lord of the Conjunction **Rev:** Inscription **Note:** Weight varies 5.50-5.80 grams.

Date	Mintage	Good	VG	F	VF	XF
AH114x//10	—	—	—	—	—	—
AHxxxx//16	—	—	—	—	—	—
AHxxxx//23	—	—	—	—	—	—
AHxxxx//25	—	—	—	—	—	—

Mint: Azamnagar
KM# 434.1 RUPEE

Silver **Obv. Inscription:** Ba-Luft-ullah Badshah-i-Zaman, By Favour of God, Emperor of the Age **Rev:** Inscription **Note:** Weight varies 11.00-11.60 grams.

Date	Mintage	Good	VG	F	VF	XF
AH1132//2	—	5.00	7.50	12.00	20.00	30.00
Note: For later issues in the name of Muhammad Shah see Princely States listings.						
AHxxxx//6	—	5.00	7.50	12.00	20.00	30.00

Mint: Azamnagar
KM# 434.5 RUPEE

Silver **Note:** Weight varies 11.00-11.60 grams.

Date	Mintage	Good	VG	F	VF	XF
AHxxxx//6	—	—	—	—	—	—

Mint: Azamnagar
KM# 434.6 RUPEE

Silver **Note:** Weight varies 11.00-11.60 grams.

Date	Mintage	Good	VG	F	VF	XF
ND(1719-1748)	—	—	—	—	—	—

Mint: Bankapur
KM# 434.7 RUPEE

Silver **Note:** Weight varies 11.00-11.60 grams.

Date	Mintage	Good	VG	F	VF	XF
ND(1719-1748)	—	—	—	—	—	—

Mint: Bijapur
KM# 434.8 RUPEE

Silver **Note:** Weight varies 11.00-11.60 grams.

Date	Mintage	Good	VG	F	VF	XF
ND(1719-1748)	—	—	—	—	—	—

Mint: Fathabad Dharur
KM# 434.9 RUPEE

Silver **Note:** Weight varies 11.00-11.60 grams.

Date	Mintage	Good	VG	F	VF	XF
AHxxxx//3	—	—	—	—	—	—

Mint: Gulshanabad
KM# 434.2 RUPEE

Silver **Note:** Weight varies 11.00-11.60 grams.

Date	Mintage	Good	VG	F	VF	XF
AH1133//3	—	10.00	25.00	50.00	85.00	125

Mint: Malnapur
KM# 434.3 RUPEE

Silver **Note:** Weight varies 11.00-11.60 grams.

Date	Mintage	Good	VG	F	VF	XF
AHxxxx//2 Rare	—	—	—	—	—	—

Mint: Surat
KM# 434.4 RUPEE

Silver **Note:** Weight varies 11.00-11.60 grams.

Date	Mintage	Good	VG	F	VF	XF
AH1131//1 (Ahad)	—	—	37.50	75.00	125	180
AH1132//1 (Ahad)	—	—	37.50	75.00	125	180

Mint: Bhakkar
KM# 435.1 RUPEE

Silver **Obv. Inscription:** Az-Fazl-ullah Badshah-i-Jahan, By Grace of God, Emperor of the World **Rev:** Inscription **Note:** Weight varies 11.00-11.60 grams.

Date	Mintage	Good	VG	F	VF	XF
AH1151//20 Rare	—	—	—	—	—	—
AH1151//21 Rare	—	—	—	—	—	—
AH1152//21 Rare	—	—	—	—	—	—
AH1152//22 Rare	—	—	—	—	—	—
AH1153//22 Rare	—	—	—	—	—	—

Mint: Multan
KM# 435.2 RUPEE

Silver **Note:** Weight varies 11.00-11.60 grams.

Date	Mintage	Good	VG	F	VF	XF
AH1131//1 (Ahad) Rare	—	—	—	—	—	—

Mint: Burhanpur
KM# A436.1 RUPEE

Silver **Obv. Inscription:** Abul Fateh Nasir-ud-Din **Rev:** Inscription **Note:** Weight varies 11.00-11.60 grams.

Date	Mintage	Good	VG	F	VF	XF
AHxxxx//1 (Ahad) Rare	—	—	—	—	—	—

Mint: Jahangirnagar
KM# A436.2 RUPEE

Silver **Note:** Weight varies 11.00-11.60 grams.

Date	Mintage	Good	VG	F	VF	XF
AHxxxx//1 (Ahad) Rare	—	—	—	—	—	—

Mint: Murshidabad
KM# A436.3 RUPEE

Silver **Note:** Weight varies 11.00-11.60 grams.

Date	Mintage	Good	VG	F	VF	XF
AH1131//1 (Ahad) Rare	—	—	—	—	—	—

Mint: Ahmadabad
KM# 436.1 RUPEE

Silver **Obv. Inscription:** Badshah Ghazi, The Emperor, Conqueror of Infidels **Rev:** Inscription **Note:** Weight varies 11.00-11.60 grams.

Date	Mintage	Good	VG	F	VF	XF
AH1131//1 (Ahad)	—	5.00	6.50	9.00	14.00	20.00
AH11xx//4	—	5.00	6.50	9.00	14.00	20.00
AH11xx//7	—	5.00	6.50	9.00	14.00	20.00
AH1138//8	—	5.00	6.50	9.00	14.00	20.00
AH1139//8	—	5.00	6.50	9.00	14.00	20.00
AH1139//9	—	5.00	6.50	9.00	14.00	20.00
AH1140//9	—	5.00	6.50	9.00	14.00	20.00
AH1140//10	—	5.00	6.50	9.00	14.00	20.00
AH1141//10	—	5.00	6.50	9.00	14.00	20.00
AH1141//11	—	5.00	6.50	9.00	14.00	20.00
AH1142//11	—	5.00	6.50	9.00	14.00	20.00
AH1142//12	—	5.00	6.50	9.00	14.00	20.00
AH1143//12	—	5.00	6.50	9.00	14.00	20.00
AH1143//13	—	5.00	6.50	9.00	14.00	20.00
AH1144//13	—	5.00	6.50	9.00	14.00	20.00
AH1144//14	—	5.00	6.50	9.00	14.00	20.00
AH1145//14	—	5.00	6.50	9.00	14.00	20.00
AH11xx//15	—	5.00	6.50	9.00	14.00	20.00
AH11xx//16	—	5.00	6.50	9.00	14.00	20.00
AHxxxx//17	—	5.00	6.50	9.00	14.00	20.00
AH1148//18	—	5.00	6.50	9.00	14.00	20.00
AH1150//20	—	5.00	6.50	9.00	14.00	20.00
AHxxxx//22	—	5.00	6.50	9.00	14.00	20.00
AH115x//23	—	5.00	6.50	9.00	14.00	20.00
AHxxxx//25	—	5.00	6.50	9.00	14.00	20.00
AH11xx//26	—	5.00	6.50	9.00	14.00	20.00
AH11xx//27	—	5.00	6.50	9.00	14.00	20.00
AH1159//29	—	5.00	6.50	9.00	14.00	20.00
AH1160//30	—	5.00	6.50	9.00	14.00	20.00

Mint: Ahmadanagar
KM# 436.68 RUPEE

Silver **Note:** Weight varies 11.00-11.60 grams.

Date	Mintage	Good	VG	F	VF	XF
AHxxxx//20	—	—	—	—	—	—

Mint: Ajmer
KM# 436.2 RUPEE
Silver **Obv:** Inscription **Rev. Inscription:** Dar-ul-Khair **Note:** Weight varies 11.00-11.60 grams.

Date	Mintage	Good	VG	F	VF	XF
AH1131//1 (Ahad)	—	5.00	7.00	10.00	16.50	25.00
AH1132//1 (Ahad)	—	5.00	7.00	10.00	16.50	25.00
AHxxxx//2	—	5.00	7.00	10.00	16.50	25.00
AHxxxx//3	—	5.00	7.00	10.00	16.50	25.00
AH11xx//4	—	5.00	7.00	10.00	16.50	25.00
AH1135//5	—	5.00	7.00	10.00	16.50	25.00
AHxxxx//7	—	5.00	7.00	10.00	16.50	25.00
AH11xx//8	—	5.00	7.00	10.00	16.50	25.00
AH1141//11	—	5.00	7.00	10.00	16.50	25.00
AH1145//14	—	5.00	7.00	10.00	16.50	25.00
AH11xx//16	—	5.00	7.00	10.00	16.50	25.00
AHxxxx//17	—	5.00	7.00	10.00	16.50	25.00
AHxxxx//19	—	5.00	7.00	10.00	16.50	25.00
AH1150//20	—	5.00	7.00	10.00	16.50	25.00
AH1151//21	—	5.00	7.00	10.00	16.50	25.00
AH1155//25	—	5.00	7.00	10.00	16.50	25.00
AH11xx//26	—	5.00	7.00	10.00	16.50	25.00
AH1159//29	—	5.00	7.00	10.00	16.50	25.00
AH1160//30	—	5.00	7.00	10.00	16.50	25.00
AH116x//31	—	5.00	7.00	10.00	16.50	25.00

Mint: Akbarabad
KM# 436.3 RUPEE
Silver **Obv:** Inscription, date **Rev. Inscription:** Mustagir-ul-Khilafat **Note:** Weight varies 11.00-11.60 grams.

Date	Mintage	Good	VG	F	VF	XF
AH1131//1 (Ahad)	—	5.00	6.50	8.50	14.00	20.00
AH1132//1 (Ahad)	—	5.00	6.50	8.50	14.00	20.00
AH1132//2	—	5.00	6.50	8.50	14.00	20.00
AH1133//2	—	5.00	6.50	8.50	14.00	20.00
AH1133//3	—	5.00	6.50	8.50	14.00	20.00
AH1134//3	—	5.00	6.50	8.50	14.00	20.00
AH1134//4	—	5.00	6.50	8.50	14.00	20.00
AH1135//4	—	5.00	6.50	8.50	14.00	20.00
AH1135//5	—	5.00	6.50	8.50	14.00	20.00
AH1136//5	—	5.00	6.50	8.50	14.00	20.00
AH1137//5	—	5.00	6.50	8.50	14.00	20.00
AH1136//6	—	5.00	6.50	8.50	14.00	20.00
AH1137//6	—	5.00	6.50	8.50	14.00	20.00
AH1137//7	—	5.00	6.50	8.50	14.00	20.00
AH1138//7	—	5.00	6.50	8.50	14.00	20.00
AH1138//8	—	5.00	6.50	8.50	14.00	20.00
AH1139//8	—	5.00	6.50	8.50	14.00	20.00
AH1139//9	—	5.00	6.50	8.50	14.00	20.00
AH1140//9	—	5.00	6.50	8.50	14.00	20.00
AH1140//10	—	5.00	6.50	8.50	14.00	20.00
AH1141//10	—	5.00	6.50	8.50	14.00	20.00
AH1141//11	—	5.00	6.50	8.50	14.00	20.00
AH1142//11	—	5.00	6.50	8.50	14.00	20.00
AH1142//12	—	5.00	6.50	8.50	14.00	20.00
AH1143//12	—	5.00	6.50	8.50	14.00	20.00
AH1143//13	—	5.00	6.50	8.50	14.00	20.00
AH1144//13	—	5.00	6.50	8.50	14.00	20.00
AH1144//14	—	5.00	6.50	8.50	14.00	20.00
AH1145//14	—	5.00	6.50	8.50	14.00	20.00
AH1145//15	—	5.00	6.50	8.50	14.00	20.00
AH1146//15	—	5.00	6.50	8.50	14.00	20.00
AH1146//16	—	5.00	6.50	8.50	14.00	20.00
AH1147//16	—	5.00	6.50	8.50	14.00	20.00
AH1147//17	—	5.00	6.50	8.50	14.00	20.00
AH1148//17	—	5.00	6.50	8.50	14.00	20.00
AH1148//18	—	5.00	6.50	8.50	14.00	20.00
AH1149//18	—	5.00	6.50	8.50	14.00	20.00
AH1149//19	—	5.00	6.50	8.50	14.00	20.00
AH1150//19	—	5.00	6.50	8.50	14.00	20.00
AH1150//20	—	5.00	6.50	8.50	14.00	20.00
AH1151//20	—	5.00	6.50	8.50	14.00	20.00
AH1151//21	—	5.00	6.50	8.50	14.00	20.00
AH1152//21	—	5.00	6.50	8.50	14.00	20.00
AH1152//22	—	5.00	6.50	8.50	14.00	20.00
AH1153//22	—	5.00	6.50	8.50	14.00	20.00
AH1153//23	—	5.00	6.50	8.50	14.00	20.00
AH1154//23	—	5.00	6.50	8.50	14.00	20.00
AH1154//24	—	5.00	6.50	8.50	14.00	20.00
AH1155//24	—	5.00	6.50	8.50	14.00	20.00
AH1155//25	—	5.00	6.50	8.50	14.00	20.00
AH1156//25	—	5.00	6.50	8.50	14.00	20.00
AH1156//26	—	5.00	6.50	8.50	14.00	20.00
AH1157//26	—	5.00	6.50	8.50	14.00	20.00
AH1157//27	—	5.00	6.50	8.50	14.00	20.00
AH1158//27	—	5.00	6.50	8.50	14.00	20.00
AH1158//28	—	5.00	6.50	8.50	14.00	20.00
AH1159//28	—	5.00	6.50	8.50	14.00	20.00
AH1159//29	—	5.00	6.50	8.50	14.00	20.00
AH1160//29	—	5.00	6.50	8.50	14.00	20.00
AH1160//30	—	5.00	6.50	8.50	14.00	20.00

Mint: Akbarnagar
KM# 436.4 RUPEE
Silver **Obv:** Inscription **Rev:** Inscription **Note:** Weight varies 11.00-11.60 grams.

Date	Mintage	Good	VG	F	VF	XF
AH1131//1 (Ahad)	—	5.00	7.00	10.00	16.50	25.00
AHxxxx//2	—	5.00	7.00	10.00	16.50	25.00
AHxxxx//5	—	5.00	7.00	10.00	16.50	25.00
AHxxxx//12	—	5.00	7.00	10.00	16.50	25.00
AHxxxx//14	—	5.00	7.00	10.00	16.50	25.00
AHxxxx//15	—	5.00	7.00	10.00	16.50	25.00
AHxxxx//18	—	5.00	7.00	10.00	16.50	25.00
AHxxxx//25	—	5.00	7.00	10.00	16.50	25.00
AH116(0)//29	—	5.00	7.00	10.00	16.50	25.00

Mint: Akhtarnagar
KM# 436.11 RUPEE
Silver **Obv:** Inscription, date **Rev:** Inscription **Note:** Weight varies 11.00-11.60 grams.

Date	Mintage	Good	VG	F	VF	XF
AH1135//5	—	5.50	10.00	16.50	27.50	45.00
AH1136//5	—	5.50	10.00	16.50	27.50	45.00
AH1136//6	—	5.50	10.00	16.50	27.50	45.00
AH1137//6	—	5.50	10.00	16.50	27.50	45.00
AH1137//7	—	5.50	10.00	16.50	27.50	45.00
AH1138//8	—	5.50	10.00	16.50	27.50	45.00
AH1140//9	—	5.50	10.00	16.50	27.50	45.00
AH1140//10	—	5.50	10.00	16.50	27.50	45.00
AH1141//10	—	5.50	10.00	16.50	27.50	45.00
AH1141//11	—	5.50	10.00	16.50	27.50	45.00
AH1142//11	—	5.50	10.00	16.50	27.50	45.00
AH1142//12	—	5.50	10.00	16.50	27.50	45.00
AH1143//12	—	5.50	10.00	16.50	27.50	45.00
AH1143//13	—	5.50	10.00	16.50	27.50	45.00
AH1144//13	—	5.50	10.00	16.50	27.50	45.00
AH1144//14	—	5.50	10.00	16.50	27.50	45.00
AH114x//12	—	5.50	10.00	16.50	27.50	45.00
AH1145//15	—	5.50	10.00	16.50	27.50	45.00
AH1150//20	—	5.50	10.00	16.50	27.50	45.00

Mint: Alamgirpur
KM# 436.5 RUPEE
Silver **Note:** Weight varies 11.00-11.60 grams.

Date	Mintage	Good	VG	F	VF	XF
AHxxxx//1 (Ahad) Rare	—	—	—	—	—	—
AHxxxx//5 Rare	—	—	—	—	—	—
AHxxxx//16 Rare	—	—	—	—	—	—

Mint: Allahabad
KM# 436.6 RUPEE
Silver **Obv:** Inscription, date **Rev:** Inscription **Note:** Weight varies 11.00-11.60 grams.

Date	Mintage	Good	VG	F	VF	XF
AH1135//4	—	5.00	6.50	8.50	14.00	20.00
AH1135//5	—	5.00	6.50	8.50	14.00	20.00
AH1136//5	—	5.00	6.50	8.50	14.00	20.00
AH1136//6	—	5.00	6.50	8.50	14.00	20.00
AH11xx//7	—	5.00	6.50	8.50	14.00	20.00
AH1138//8	—	5.00	6.50	8.50	14.00	20.00
AH1139//9	—	5.00	6.50	8.50	14.00	20.00
AH1140//9	—	5.00	6.50	8.50	14.00	20.00
AH1140//10	—	5.00	6.50	8.50	14.00	20.00
AH1141//10	—	5.00	6.50	8.50	14.00	20.00
AH1141//11	—	5.00	6.50	8.50	14.00	20.00
AH1141//11	—	5.00	6.50	8.50	14.00	20.00
AH1142//11	—	5.00	6.50	8.50	14.00	20.00
AH1142//12	—	5.00	6.50	8.50	14.00	20.00
AH1143//12	—	5.00	6.50	8.50	14.00	20.00
AH1143//13	—	5.00	6.50	8.50	14.00	20.00
AH1144//13	—	5.00	6.50	8.50	14.00	20.00
AH1144//14	—	5.00	6.50	8.50	14.00	20.00

Date	Mintage	Good	VG	F	VF	XF
AH1145//14	—	5.00	6.50	8.50	14.00	20.00
AH1145//15	—	5.00	6.50	8.50	14.00	20.00
AH1146//15	—	5.00	6.50	8.50	14.00	20.00
AH1146//16	—	5.00	6.50	8.50	14.00	20.00
AH1147//16	—	5.00	6.50	8.50	14.00	20.00
AH1147//17	—	5.00	6.50	8.50	14.00	20.00
AH1148//17	—	5.00	6.50	8.50	14.00	20.00
AH1148//18	—	5.00	6.50	8.50	14.00	20.00
AH1149//18	—	5.00	6.50	8.50	14.00	20.00
AH1149//19	—	5.00	6.50	8.50	14.00	20.00
AH1150//19	—	5.00	6.50	8.50	14.00	20.00
AH1150//20	—	5.00	6.50	8.50	14.00	20.00
AH1151//20	—	5.00	6.50	8.50	14.00	20.00
AH1151//21	—	5.00	6.50	8.50	14.00	20.00
AH1152//21	—	5.00	6.50	8.50	14.00	20.00
AH1152//22	—	5.00	6.50	8.50	14.00	20.00
AH1153//22	—	5.00	6.50	8.50	14.00	20.00
AH1153//23	—	5.00	6.50	8.50	14.00	20.00
AH1154//23	—	5.00	6.50	8.50	14.00	20.00
AH1154//24	—	5.00	6.50	8.50	14.00	20.00
AH1155//24	—	5.00	6.50	8.50	14.00	20.00
AH1155//25	—	5.00	6.50	8.50	14.00	20.00
AH1156//25	—	5.00	6.50	8.50	14.00	20.00
AH1156//26	—	5.00	6.50	8.50	14.00	20.00
AH1157//26	—	5.00	6.50	8.50	14.00	20.00
AH1157//27	—	5.00	6.50	8.50	14.00	20.00
AH1158//27	—	5.00	6.50	8.50	14.00	20.00
AH1158//28	—	5.00	6.50	8.50	14.00	20.00
AH116x//30	—	5.00	6.50	8.50	14.00	20.00
AH116(1)//31	—	5.00	6.50	8.50	14.00	20.00

Mint: Arkat
KM# 436.7 RUPEE
Silver **Obv:** Inscription **Rev:** Inscription **Note:** Weight varies 11.00-11.60 grams. Varieties exist.

Date	Mintage	Good	VG	F	VF	XF
AH1132//1 (Ahad)	—	8.00	20.00	40.00	65.00	95.00
AH113x//2	—	8.00	20.00	40.00	65.00	95.00
AH11xx//3	—	8.00	20.00	40.00	65.00	95.00
AHxxxx//4	—	8.00	20.00	40.00	65.00	95.00
AH1135//5	—	8.00	20.00	40.00	65.00	95.00
AH1137//7	—	8.00	20.00	40.00	65.00	95.00
AH1138//8	—	8.00	20.00	40.00	65.00	95.00
AH11xx//9	—	8.00	20.00	40.00	65.00	95.00
AH11xx//10	—	8.00	20.00	40.00	65.00	95.00
AH11xx//11	—	8.00	20.00	40.00	65.00	95.00
AH11xx//12	—	8.00	20.00	40.00	65.00	95.00
AH11xx//13	—	8.00	20.00	40.00	65.00	95.00
AH11xx//14	—	8.00	20.00	40.00	65.00	95.00
AH11xx//15	—	8.00	20.00	40.00	65.00	95.00
AH11xx//16	—	8.00	20.00	40.00	65.00	95.00
AH11xx//18	—	8.00	20.00	40.00	65.00	95.00
AH11xx//19	—	8.00	20.00	40.00	65.00	95.00
AH11xx//20	—	8.00	20.00	40.00	65.00	95.00
AH115x//21	—	8.00	20.00	40.00	65.00	95.00
AH11xx//22	—	8.00	20.00	40.00	65.00	95.00
AH11xx//23	—	8.00	20.00	40.00	65.00	95.00
AH11xx//24	—	8.00	20.00	40.00	65.00	95.00
AH11xx//25	—	8.00	20.00	40.00	65.00	95.00
AH11xx//26	—	8.00	20.00	40.00	65.00	95.00
AH11xx//27	—	8.00	20.00	40.00	65.00	95.00
AH11xx//28	—	8.00	20.00	40.00	65.00	95.00
AH11xx//29	—	8.00	20.00	40.00	65.00	95.00
AH11xx//30	—	8.00	20.00	40.00	65.00	95.00

Mint: Atak
KM# 436.8 RUPEE
Silver **Note:** Weight varies 11.00-11.60 grams.

Date	Mintage	Good	VG	F	VF	XF
AH1154//24 Rare	—	—	—	—	—	—
AH1156//25 Rare	—	—	—	—	—	—
AH1157//27 Rare	—	—	—	—	—	—
AH1158//27 Rare	—	—	—	—	—	—
AH1158//28 Rare	—	—	—	—	—	—

Mint: Aurangnagar
KM# 436.9 RUPEE
Silver **Note:** Weight varies 11.00-11.60 grams.

Date	Mintage	Good	VG	F	VF	XF
AH11xx//2 Rare	—	—	—	—	—	—
AH11xx//3 Rare	—	—	—	—	—	—
AH1114//4 Error for 1134 Rare	—	—	—	—	—	—
AH11xx//19 Rare	—	—	—	—	—	—
AH1160//30 Rare	—	—	—	—	—	—

Mint: Ausa
KM# 436.10 RUPEE
Silver **Note:** Weight varies 11.00-11.60 grams.

Date	Mintage	Good	VG	F	VF	XF
AH11xx//3	—	8.00	20.00	40.00	65.00	95.00
AH11xx//7	—	8.00	20.00	40.00	65.00	95.00

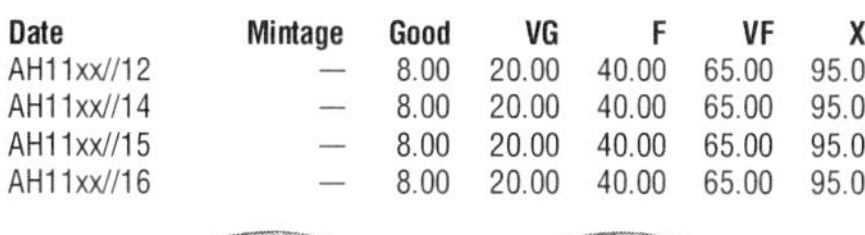

Date	Mintage	Good	VG	F	VF	XF
AH11xx//12	—	8.00	20.00	40.00	65.00	95.00
AH11xx//14	—	8.00	20.00	40.00	65.00	95.00
AH11xx//15	—	8.00	20.00	40.00	65.00	95.00
AH11xx//16	—	8.00	20.00	40.00	65.00	95.00

Mint: Azimabad
KM# 436.12 RUPEE

Silver **Obv:** Inscription **Rev:** Inscription **Note:** Weight varies 11.00-11.60 grams.

Date	Mintage	Good	VG	F	VF	XF
AH1131//1 (Ahad)	—	5.00	8.00	16.00	28.00	40.00
AH1132//1 (Ahad)	—	5.00	8.00	16.00	28.00	40.00
AH1132//2	—	5.00	8.00	16.00	28.00	40.00
AH1133//2	—	5.00	8.00	16.00	28.00	40.00
AH1133//3	—	5.00	8.00	16.00	28.00	40.00
AH1134//3	—	5.00	8.00	16.00	28.00	40.00
AH1134//4	—	5.00	8.00	16.00	28.00	40.00
AH1135//4	—	5.00	8.00	16.00	28.00	40.00
AH113x//5	—	5.00	8.00	16.00	28.00	40.00
AH11xx//6	—	5.00	8.00	16.00	28.00	40.00
AH11xx//7	—	5.00	8.00	16.00	28.00	40.00
AH11xx//8	—	5.00	8.00	16.00	28.00	40.00
AH11xx//9	—	5.00	8.00	16.00	28.00	40.00
AH1140//10	—	5.00	8.00	16.00	28.00	40.00
AH11xx//11	—	5.00	8.00	16.00	28.00	40.00
AH11xx//12	—	5.00	8.00	16.00	28.00	40.00
AH11xx//13	—	5.00	8.00	16.00	28.00	40.00
AH11xx//14	—	5.00	8.00	16.00	28.00	40.00
AH11xx//15	—	5.00	8.00	16.00	28.00	40.00
AH11xx//16	—	5.00	8.00	16.00	28.00	40.00
AH11xx//18	—	5.00	8.00	16.00	28.00	40.00
AH1149//19	—	5.00	8.00	16.00	28.00	40.00
AH1150//19	—	5.00	8.00	16.00	28.00	40.00
AH1150//20	—	5.00	8.00	16.00	28.00	40.00
AH1151//20	—	5.00	8.00	16.00	28.00	40.00
AH1151//21	—	5.00	8.00	16.00	28.00	40.00
AH1152//21	—	5.00	8.00	16.00	28.00	40.00
AH1152//22	—	5.00	8.00	16.00	28.00	40.00
AH1153//22	—	5.00	8.00	16.00	28.00	40.00
AH1153//23	—	5.00	8.00	16.00	28.00	40.00
AH1154//23	—	5.00	8.00	16.00	28.00	40.00
AH1154//24	—	5.00	8.00	16.00	28.00	40.00
AH1155//24	—	5.00	8.00	16.00	28.00	40.00
AH1155//25	—	5.00	8.00	16.00	28.00	40.00
AH1156//25	—	5.00	8.00	16.00	28.00	40.00
AH1156//26	—	5.00	8.00	16.00	28.00	40.00
AH1157//26	—	5.00	8.00	16.00	28.00	40.00
AH1157//27	—	5.00	8.00	16.00	28.00	40.00
AH1158//27	—	5.00	8.00	16.00	28.00	40.00
AH1158//28	—	5.00	8.00	16.00	28.00	40.00
AH1159//29	—	5.00	8.00	16.00	28.00	40.00
AH1159//29	—	5.00	8.00	16.00	28.00	40.00
AH1160//29	—	5.00	8.00	16.00	28.00	40.00
AH1160//30	—	5.00	8.00	16.00	28.00	40.00
AH116(1)//31	—	5.00	8.00	16.00	28.00	40.00

Mint: Bahadarqarh
KM# 436.13 RUPEE

Silver **Note:** Weight varies 11.00-11.60 grams.

Date	Mintage	Good	VG	F	VF	XF
AH1132//2 Rare	—	—	—	—	—	—
AH1138//9 (sic) Rare	—	—	—	—	—	—

Mint: Balwantnagar
KM# 436.14 RUPEE

Silver **Obv:** Inscription **Rev:** Inscription, mint marks **Note:** Weight varies 11.00-11.60 grams.

Date	Mintage	Good	VG	F	VF	XF
AHxxxx//5	—	5.00	10.00	20.00	32.50	50.00
AH1157//2x	—	5.00	10.00	20.00	32.50	50.00
AH1158//28	—	5.00	10.00	20.00	32.50	50.00
AH1159//28	—	5.00	10.00	20.00	32.50	50.00
AH1159//29	—	5.00	10.00	20.00	32.50	50.00
AH1160//29	—	5.00	10.00	20.00	32.50	50.00
AH1160//30	—	5.00	10.00	20.00	32.50	50.00
AH1161//30	—	5.00	10.00	20.00	32.50	50.00
AH1161//31	—	5.00	10.00	20.00	32.50	50.00

Mint: Bankapur
KM# 436.16 RUPEE

Silver **Note:** Weight varies 11.00-11.60 grams.

Date	Mintage	Good	VG	F	VF	XF
AH113x//1 (Ahad) Rare	—	—	—	—	—	—
AH1132//2 Rare	—	—	—	—	—	—
AH11xx//3 Rare	—	—	—	—	—	—
AH11xx//4 Rare	—	—	—	—	—	—

Mint: Baramati
KM# 436.17 RUPEE

Silver **Note:** Weight varies 11.00-11.60 grams.

Date	Mintage	Good	VG	F	VF	XF
AHxxxx//7 Rare	—	—	—	—	—	—
AH1148//1x Rare	—	—	—	—	—	—
AH1148//xx	—	—	—	—	—	—

Mint: Bareli
KM# 436.18 RUPEE

Silver **Obv:** Inscription **Rev:** Inscription **Note:** Two different reverse inscriptions. Weight varies 11.00-11.60 grams. Varieties exist.

Date	Mintage	Good	VG	F	VF	XF
AH1132//1 (Ahad)	—	5.00	6.50	8.50	14.00	20.00
AH11xx//2	—	5.00	6.50	8.50	14.00	20.00
AH11xx//3	—	5.00	6.50	8.50	14.00	20.00
AH11xx//4	—	5.00	6.50	8.50	14.00	20.00
AH1135//5	—	5.00	6.50	8.50	14.00	20.00
AH11xx//6	—	5.00	6.50	8.50	14.00	20.00
AH113x//7	—	5.00	6.50	8.50	14.00	20.00
AH11xx//8	—	5.00	6.50	8.50	14.00	20.00
AH11xx//9	—	5.00	6.50	8.50	14.00	20.00
AH11xx//10	—	5.00	6.50	8.50	14.00	20.00
AH11xx//11	—	5.00	6.50	8.50	14.00	20.00
AH11xx//12	—	5.00	6.50	8.50	14.00	20.00
AH11xx//13	—	5.00	6.50	8.50	14.00	20.00
AH114x//14	—	5.00	6.50	8.50	14.00	20.00
AH11xx//15	—	5.00	6.50	8.50	14.00	20.00
AH11xx//16	—	5.00	6.50	8.50	14.00	20.00
AH11xx//17	—	5.00	6.50	8.50	14.00	20.00
AH1149//19	—	5.00	6.50	8.50	14.00	20.00
AH1150//19	—	5.00	6.50	8.50	14.00	20.00
AH1150//20	—	5.00	6.50	8.50	14.00	20.00
AH1151//20	—	5.00	6.50	8.50	14.00	20.00
AH1151//21	—	5.00	6.50	8.50	14.00	20.00
AH1152//21	—	5.00	6.50	8.50	14.00	20.00
AH1152//22	—	5.00	6.50	8.50	14.00	20.00
AH1153//22	—	5.00	6.50	8.50	14.00	20.00
AH1153//23	—	5.00	6.50	8.50	14.00	20.00
AH1154//23	—	5.00	6.50	8.50	14.00	20.00
AH1154//24	—	5.00	6.50	8.50	14.00	20.00
AH1155//24	—	5.00	6.50	8.50	14.00	20.00
AH1155//25	—	5.00	6.50	8.50	14.00	20.00
AH1156//25	—	5.00	6.50	8.50	14.00	20.00
AH1156//26	—	5.00	6.50	8.50	14.00	20.00
AH1157//26	—	5.00	6.50	8.50	14.00	20.00
AH1157//27	—	5.00	6.50	8.50	14.00	20.00
AH1158//27	—	5.00	6.50	8.50	14.00	20.00
AH1158//28	—	5.00	6.50	8.50	14.00	20.00
AH1159//28	—	5.00	6.50	8.50	14.00	20.00
AH1159//29	—	5.00	6.50	8.50	14.00	20.00
AH1160//29	—	5.00	6.50	8.50	14.00	20.00
AH1160//30	—	5.00	6.50	8.50	14.00	20.00
AH1161//30	—	5.00	6.50	8.50	14.00	20.00
AH116(1)//31	—	5.00	6.50	8.50	14.00	20.00

Mint: Bidrur
KM# 436.19 RUPEE

Silver **Note:** Weight varies 11.00-11.60 grams.

Date	Mintage	Good	VG	F	VF	XF
AHxxxx//4 Rare	—	—	—	—	—	—
AHxxxx//15 Rare	—	—	—	—	—	—
AHxxxx//18 Rare	—	—	—	—	—	—

Date	Mintage	Good	VG	F	VF	XF
AHxxxx//20 Rare	—	—	—	—	—	—
AHxxxx//21 Rare	—	—	—	—	—	—
AHxxxx//22 Rare	—	—	—	—	—	—
AHxxxx//25 Rare	—	—	—	—	—	—

Mint: Bijapur
KM# 436.20 RUPEE

Silver **Obv:** Inscription **Rev. Inscription:** Dar-uz-Zafar **Note:** Weight varies 11.00-11.60 grams.

Date	Mintage	Good	VG	F	VF	XF
AHxxxx//3 Rare	—	—	—	—	—	—
AHxxxx//10 Rare	—	—	—	—	—	—

Mint: Burhanpur
KM# 436.21 RUPEE

Silver **Obv:** Inscription **Rev. Inscription:** Dar-us-Sarur **Note:** Weight varies 11.00-11.60 grams.

Date	Mintage	Good	VG	F	VF	XF
AH1131//1 (Ahad)	—	5.00	8.00	16.00	28.00	40.00
AH1132//1 (Ahad)	—	5.00	8.00	16.00	28.00	40.00
AH1132//2	—	5.00	8.00	16.00	28.00	40.00
AH1133//2	—	5.00	8.00	16.00	28.00	40.00
AH1133//3	—	5.00	8.00	16.00	28.00	40.00
AH1134//3	—	5.00	8.00	16.00	28.00	40.00
AH1134//4	—	5.00	8.00	16.00	28.00	40.00
AH1135//4	—	5.00	8.00	16.00	28.00	40.00
AH1135//5	—	5.00	8.00	16.00	28.00	40.00
AH1136//5	—	5.00	8.00	16.00	28.00	40.00
AH1136//6	—	5.00	8.00	16.00	28.00	40.00
AH1137//6	—	5.00	8.00	16.00	28.00	40.00
AH1137//7	—	—	8.00	16.00	28.00	40.00
AH1138//7	—	5.00	8.00	16.00	28.00	40.00
AH1138//8	—	5.00	8.00	16.00	28.00	40.00
AH1139//8	—	5.00	8.00	16.00	28.00	40.00
AH1139//9	—	5.00	8.00	16.00	28.00	40.00
AH1140//10	—	5.00	8.00	16.00	28.00	40.00
AH1143//13	—	5.00	8.00	16.00	28.00	40.00
AH11xx//14	—	5.00	8.00	16.00	28.00	40.00
AH11xx//16	—	5.00	8.00	16.00	28.00	40.00
AH11xx//17	—	5.00	8.00	16.00	28.00	40.00
AH11xx//18	—	5.00	8.00	16.00	28.00	40.00
AH11xx//19	—	5.00	8.00	16.00	28.00	40.00
AH11xx//20	—	5.00	8.00	16.00	28.00	40.00
AH11xx//21	—	5.00	8.00	16.00	28.00	40.00
AH11xx//22	—	5.00	8.00	16.00	28.00	40.00
AH11xx//24	—	5.00	8.00	16.00	28.00	40.00
AH1158//27	—	5.00	8.00	16.00	28.00	40.00
AH1158//28	—	5.00	8.00	16.00	28.00	40.00
AH1160//30	—	5.00	8.00	16.00	28.00	40.00
AH1161//30	—	5.00	8.00	16.00	28.00	40.00

Mint: Derajat
KM# 436.23 RUPEE

Silver **Obv:** Inscription, date **Rev:** Inscription **Note:** Weight varies 11.00-11.60 grams.

Date	Mintage	Good	VG	F	VF	XF
AH1160//30 Rare	—	—	—	—	—	—

Mint: Dilshadabad
KM# 436.67 RUPEE

Silver **Note:** Weight varies 11.00-11.60 grams. Nizam coin.

Date	Mintage	Good	VG	F	VF	XF
ND//x Rare	—	—	—	—	—	—

Mint: Elichpur
KM# 436.24 RUPEE

Silver **Note:** Weight varies 11.00-11.60 grams.

Date	Mintage	Good	VG	F	VF	XF
AH113x//6	—	6.00	11.00	18.00	30.00	50.00
AH1138 (sic)//9	—	6.00	11.00	18.00	30.00	50.00
AH1147//17	—	6.00	11.00	18.00	30.00	50.00
AH11xx//29	—	6.00	11.00	18.00	30.00	50.00

Mint: Firozgarh
KM# 436.64 RUPEE

Silver **Note:** Weight varies 11.00-11.60 grams.

Date	Mintage	Good	VG	F	VF	XF
AH11xx//7 Rare	—	—	—	—	—	—
AH1147//x Rare	—	—	—	—	—	—

Mint: Firoznagar
KM# 436.71 RUPEE
Silver **Note:**

Date	Mintage	Good	VG	F	VF	XF
AH1143//12 Rare	—	—	—	—	—	—
AH114x//13 Rare	—	—	—	—	—	—
AH11xx//15 Rare	—	—	—	—	—	—

Mint: Gwalior
KM# 436.25 RUPEE
Silver **Obv:** Inscription **Rev:** Inscription **Note:** Weight varies 11.00-11.60 grams.

Date	Mintage	Good	VG	F	VF	XF
AH1132//1 (Ahad)	—	5.00	6.50	8.50	14.00	20.00
AH1132//2	—	5.00	6.50	8.50	14.00	20.00
AH1133//2	—	5.00	6.50	8.50	14.00	20.00
AH1133//3	—	5.00	6.50	8.50	14.00	20.00
AH1134//3	—	5.00	6.50	8.50	14.00	20.00
AH1134//4	—	5.00	6.50	8.50	14.00	20.00
AH1135//4	—	5.00	6.50	8.50	14.00	20.00
AH1135//5	—	5.00	6.50	8.50	14.00	20.00
AH1136//5	—	5.00	6.50	8.50	14.00	20.00
AH1136//6	—	5.00	6.50	8.50	14.00	20.00
AH1137//6	—	5.00	6.50	8.50	14.00	20.00
AH1137//7	—	5.00	6.50	8.50	14.00	20.00
AH1138//7	—	5.00	6.50	8.50	14.00	20.00
AH1138//8	—	5.00	6.50	8.50	14.00	20.00
AH1139//8	—	5.00	6.50	8.50	14.00	20.00
AH1139//9	—	5.00	6.50	8.50	14.00	20.00
AH1140//10	—	5.00	6.50	8.50	14.00	20.00
AH1141//10	—	5.00	6.50	8.50	14.00	20.00
AH1141//11	—	5.00	6.50	8.50	14.00	20.00
AH1142//11	—	5.00	6.50	8.50	14.00	20.00
AH1142//12	—	5.00	6.50	8.50	14.00	20.00
AH1143//12	—	5.00	6.50	8.50	14.00	20.00
AH1143//13	—	5.00	6.50	8.50	14.00	20.00
AH1144//13	—	5.00	6.50	8.50	14.00	20.00
AH1144//14	—	5.00	6.50	8.50	14.00	20.00
AH1145//14	—	5.00	6.50	8.50	14.00	20.00
AH1145//15	—	5.00	6.50	8.50	14.00	20.00
AH1146//15	—	5.00	6.50	8.50	14.00	20.00
AH1146//16	—	5.00	6.50	8.50	14.00	20.00
AH1147//16	—	5.00	6.50	8.50	14.00	20.00
AH1147//17	—	5.00	6.50	8.50	14.00	20.00
AH1148//17	—	5.00	6.50	8.50	14.00	20.00
AH1148//18	—	5.00	6.50	8.50	14.00	20.00
AH1149//18	—	5.00	6.50	8.50	14.00	20.00
AH1149//19	—	5.00	6.50	8.50	14.00	20.00
AH1150//19	—	5.00	6.50	8.50	14.00	20.00
AH1150//20	—	5.00	6.50	8.50	14.00	20.00
AH1151//20	—	5.00	6.50	8.50	14.00	20.00
AH1151//21	—	5.00	6.50	8.50	14.00	20.00
AH1152//21	—	5.00	6.50	8.50	14.00	20.00
AH1152//22	—	5.00	6.50	8.50	14.00	20.00
AH1153//22	—	5.00	6.50	8.50	14.00	20.00
AH1153//23	—	5.00	6.50	8.50	14.00	20.00
AH1154//23	—	5.00	6.50	8.50	14.00	20.00
AH1154//24	—	5.00	6.50	8.50	14.00	20.00
AH1155//24	—	5.00	6.50	8.50	14.00	20.00
AH1155//25	—	5.00	6.50	8.50	14.00	20.00
AH1158//28	—	5.00	6.50	8.50	14.00	20.00
AH1159//29	—	5.00	6.50	8.50	14.00	20.00

Mint: Haidarabad (Farkhanda Bunyad)
KM# 436.26 RUPEE
Silver **Obv:** Inscription **Rev. Legend:** Farkhanda Bunyad **Note:** Weight varies 11.00-11.60 grams.

Date	Mintage	Good	VG	F	VF	XF
AH11xx//3	—	5.00	7.00	10.00	16.50	25.00
AH11xx//10	—	5.00	7.00	10.00	16.50	25.00
AH11xx//11	—	5.00	7.00	10.00	16.50	25.00
AH11xx//12	—	5.00	7.00	10.00	16.50	25.00
AH11xx//13	—	5.00	7.00	10.00	16.50	25.00
AH1149//xx	—	5.00	7.00	10.00	16.50	25.00
AH115(9)//29	—	5.00	7.00	10.00	16.50	25.00

Mint: Imtiyazgarh
KM# 436.27 RUPEE
Silver **Obv:** Inscription **Rev:** Inscription **Note:** Weight varies 11.00-11.60 grams.

Date	Mintage	Good	VG	F	VF	XF
AHxxxx//2 Rare	—	—	—	—	—	—
AH1133//3 Rare	—	—	—	—	—	—

Mint: Islamabad
KM# 436.28 RUPEE
Silver **Note:** Weight varies 11.00-11.60 grams.

Date	Mintage	Good	VG	F	VF	XF
AH11xx//3	—	5.00	7.50	15.00	25.00	37.50
AH1138//8	—	5.00	7.50	15.00	25.00	37.50
AH11xx//9	—	5.00	7.50	15.00	25.00	37.50
AH11xx//14	—	5.00	7.50	15.00	25.00	37.50
AH11xx//15	—	5.00	7.50	15.00	25.00	37.50
AH11xx//16	—	5.00	7.50	15.00	25.00	37.50
AH11xx//17	—	5.00	7.50	15.00	25.00	37.50
AH11xx//18	—	5.00	7.50	15.00	25.00	37.50
AH11xx//19	—	5.00	7.50	15.00	25.00	37.50
AH1152//22	—	5.00	7.50	15.00	25.00	37.50
AH1155//25	—	5.00	7.50	15.00	25.00	37.50
AH1156//26	—	5.00	7.50	15.00	25.00	37.50
AH1157//26	—	5.00	7.50	15.00	25.00	37.50
AH1157//27	—	5.00	7.50	15.00	25.00	37.50
AH1158//27	—	5.00	7.50	15.00	25.00	37.50
AH1158//28	—	5.00	7.50	15.00	25.00	37.50
AH115x//28	—	5.00	7.50	15.00	25.00	37.50
AH1159//28	—	5.00	7.50	15.00	25.00	37.50

Mint: Itawa
KM# 436.29 RUPEE
Silver **Obv:** Inscription **Rev:** Inscription **Note:** Weight varies 11.00-11.60 grams.

Date	Mintage	Good	VG	F	VF	XF
AH1131//1 (Ahad)	—	5.00	6.50	8.50	14.00	20.00
AH1132//2	—	5.00	6.50	8.50	14.00	20.00
AH1133//3	—	5.00	6.50	8.50	14.00	20.00
AH1134//4	—	5.00	6.50	8.50	14.00	20.00
AH1135//5	—	5.00	6.50	8.50	14.00	20.00
AH113x//6	—	—	4.50	8.50	14.00	20.00
AH113x//7	—	—	4.50	8.50	14.00	20.00
AH1138//8	—	5.00	6.50	8.50	14.00	20.00
AH1139//9	—	5.00	6.50	8.50	14.00	20.00
AH11xx//11	—	5.00	6.50	8.50	14.00	20.00
AH11xx//13	—	5.00	6.50	8.50	14.00	20.00
AH1144//14	—	5.00	6.50	8.50	14.00	20.00
AH11xx//15	—	5.00	6.50	8.50	14.00	20.00
AH11xx//16	—	5.00	6.50	8.50	14.00	20.00
AH11xx//17	—	5.00	6.50	8.50	14.00	20.00
AH11xx//18	—	5.00	6.50	8.50	14.00	20.00
AH1149//19	—	5.00	6.50	8.50	14.00	20.00
AH11xx//20	—	5.00	6.50	8.50	14.00	20.00
AH1152//22	—	5.00	6.50	8.50	14.00	20.00
AH11xx//24	—	5.00	6.50	8.50	14.00	20.00
AH1155//25	—	5.00	6.50	8.50	14.00	20.00
AH1156//26	—	5.00	6.50	8.50	14.00	20.00
AH1157//26	—	5.00	6.50	8.50	14.00	20.00
AH1158//27	—	5.00	6.50	8.50	14.00	20.00
AH1159//29	—	5.00	6.50	8.50	14.00	20.00

Mint: Jahangirnagar
KM# 436.30 RUPEE
Silver **Note:** Weight varies 11.00-11.60 grams.

Date	Mintage	Good	VG	F	VF	XF
AH11xx//2	—	5.00	7.00	10.00	16.50	25.00
AH1134//4	—	5.00	7.00	10.00	16.50	25.00
AH1145//15	—	5.00	7.00	10.00	16.50	25.00
AH114x//16	—	5.00	7.00	10.00	16.50	25.00
AH1155//25	—	5.00	7.00	10.00	16.50	25.00
AH1157//27	—	5.00	7.00	10.00	16.50	25.00

Mint: Jaipur
KM# 436.31 RUPEE
Silver **Obv:** Inscription **Rev. Inscription:** Sawai **Note:** Weight varies 11.00-11.60 grams.

Date	Mintage	Good	VG	F	VF	XF
AH1153//23	—	5.00	7.00	10.00	16.50	25.00
AH1156//25	—	5.00	7.00	10.00	16.50	25.00
AH1157//27	—	5.00	7.00	10.00	16.50	25.00
AH1158//28	—	5.00	7.00	10.00	16.50	25.00
AH1159//29	—	5.00	7.00	10.00	16.50	25.00
AH1161//31	—	5.00	7.00	10.00	16.50	25.00
AH1160//30	—	5.00	7.00	10.00	16.50	25.00

Mint: Junagarh
KM# 436.32 RUPEE
Silver **Note:** Weight varies 11.00-11.60 grams.

Date	Mintage	Good	VG	F	VF	XF
AH1132//1 (Ahad) Rare	—	—	—	—	—	—
AHxxxx//2 Rare	—	—	—	—	—	—
AHxxxx//5 Rare	—	—	—	—	—	—

Mint: Kabul
KM# 436.33 RUPEE
Silver **Note:** Weight varies 11.00-11.60 grams.

Date	Mintage	Good	VG	F	VF	XF
AH1135//1 (Ahad) Rare	—	—	—	—	—	—
AHxxxx//14 Rare	—	—	—	—	—	—

Mint: Kanbayat
KM# 436.34 RUPEE
Silver **Obv:** Inscription **Rev:** Inscription **Note:** Weight varies 11.00-11.60 grams.

Date	Mintage	Good	VG	F	VF	XF
AH1131//1 (Ahad)	—	5.00	6.50	8.50	14.00	20.00
AH1132//1 (Ahad)	—	5.00	6.50	8.50	14.00	20.00
AH1132//2	—	5.00	6.50	8.50	14.00	20.00
AH1133//2	—	5.00	6.50	8.50	14.00	20.00
AH113x//3	—	5.00	6.50	8.50	14.00	20.00
AH1135//5	—	5.00	6.50	8.50	14.00	20.00
AH1137//6	—	5.00	6.50	8.50	14.00	20.00
AH1137//7	—	5.00	6.50	8.50	14.00	20.00
AH1138//8	—	5.00	6.50	8.50	14.00	20.00
AH11xx//10	—	5.00	6.50	8.50	14.00	20.00
AH11xx//11	—	5.00	6.50	8.50	14.00	20.00
AH11xx//12	—	5.00	6.50	8.50	14.00	20.00
AH1143//13	—	5.00	6.50	8.50	14.00	20.00
AH1144//14	—	5.00	6.50	8.50	14.00	20.00
AH1145//15	—	5.00	6.50	8.50	14.00	20.00
AH11xx//17	—	5.00	6.50	8.50	14.00	20.00
AH11xx//21	—	5.00	6.50	8.50	14.00	20.00
AH1155//25	—	5.00	6.50	8.50	14.00	20.00
AH115x//26	—	5.00	6.50	8.50	14.00	20.00
AH1159//29	—	5.00	6.50	8.50	14.00	20.00
AH11xx//30	—	5.00	6.50	8.50	14.00	20.00
AH1161//31	—	5.00	6.50	8.50	14.00	20.00

Mint: Kankurti
KM# 436.35 RUPEE
Silver **Obv:** Inscription **Rev:** Inscription **Note:** Weight varies 11.00-11.60 grams.

Date	Mintage	Good	VG	F	VF	XF
AH1139//9 Rare	—	—	—	—	—	—

Date	Mintage	Good	VG	F	VF	XF
AH1142//11 Rare	—	—	—	—	—	—
AH1149//xx Rare	—	—	—	—	—	—

Mint: Kashmir
KM# 436.36 RUPEE
Silver **Obv:** Inscription **Rev:** Inscription **Note:** Weight varies 11.00-11.60 grams.

Date	Mintage	Good	VG	F	VF	XF
AH1131//1 (Ahad)	—	6.00	15.00	25.00	35.00	47.50
AH1133//3	—	6.00	15.00	25.00	35.00	47.50
AH113x//4	—	6.00	15.00	25.00	35.00	47.50
AH1136//x	—	6.00	15.00	25.00	35.00	47.50
AHxxxx//8	—	6.00	15.00	25.00	35.00	47.50
AH11xx//14	—	6.00	15.00	25.00	35.00	47.50
AH1148//1x	—	6.00	15.00	25.00	35.00	47.50
AH11xx//17	—	6.00	15.00	25.00	35.00	47.50
AH11xx//18	—	6.00	15.00	25.00	35.00	47.50
AH11xx//27	—	6.00	15.00	25.00	35.00	47.50
AH1159//29	—	—	15.00	25.00	35.00	47.50
AH1160//30	—	—	15.00	25.00	35.00	47.50

Mint: Katak
KM# 436.37 RUPEE
Silver **Note:** Weight varies 11.00-11.60 grams.

Date	Mintage	Good	VG	F	VF	XF
AH113x//1 (Ahad) Rare	—	—	—	—	—	—
AH1136//6 Rare	—	—	—	—	—	—
AH1154//24 Rare	—	—	—	—	—	—

Mint: Khujista Bunyad
KM# 436.38 RUPEE
Silver **Note:** Weight varies 11.00-11.60 grams.

Date	Mintage	Good	VG	F	VF	XF
AH1132//2	—	5.00	6.50	8.50	14.00	20.00
AH1134//4	—	5.00	6.50	8.50	14.00	20.00
AH1135//5	—	5.00	6.50	8.50	14.00	20.00
AH11xx//6	—	5.00	6.50	8.50	14.00	20.00
AH11xx//7	—	5.00	6.50	8.50	14.00	20.00
AH11xx//9	—	5.00	6.50	8.50	14.00	20.00
AH11xx//20	—	5.00	6.50	8.50	14.00	20.00
AH11xx//21	—	5.00	6.50	8.50	14.00	20.00

Mint: Kora
KM# 436.39 RUPEE
Silver **Obv:** Inscription, date **Rev:** Inscription **Note:** Weight varies 11.00-11.60 grams.

Date	Mintage	Good	VG	F	VF	XF
AH1132//2	—	5.00	7.00	10.00	16.50	25.00
AH11xx//3	—	5.00	7.00	10.00	16.50	25.00
AH1135//4	—	5.00	7.00	10.00	16.50	25.00
AH1135//5	—	5.00	7.00	10.00	16.50	25.00
AH1137//6	—	5.00	7.00	10.00	16.50	25.00
AH11xx//8	—	5.00	7.00	10.00	16.50	25.00
AH1140//10	—	5.00	7.00	10.00	16.50	25.00
AH1141//11	—	5.00	7.00	10.00	16.50	25.00
AH1142//11	—	5.00	7.00	10.00	16.50	25.00
AH1142//12	—	5.00	7.00	10.00	16.50	25.00
AH1142//13	—	5.00	7.00	10.00	16.50	25.00
AH1144//14	—	5.00	7.00	10.00	16.50	25.00
AH1145//14	—	5.00	7.00	10.00	16.50	25.00
AH1146//15	—	5.00	7.00	10.00	16.50	25.00
AH1147//16	—	5.00	7.00	10.00	16.50	25.00
AH1147//17	—	5.00	7.00	10.00	16.50	25.00
AH1149//18	—	5.00	7.00	10.00	16.50	25.00
AH1149//19	—	5.00	7.00	10.00	16.50	25.00
AH11xx//22	—	5.00	7.00	10.00	16.50	25.00
AH115x//24	—	5.00	7.00	10.00	16.50	25.00
AH115x//26	—	5.00	7.00	10.00	16.50	25.00
AH11xx//28	—	5.00	7.00	10.00	16.50	25.00
AH11xx//29	—	5.00	7.00	10.00	16.50	25.00
AH11xx//30	—	5.00	7.00	10.00	16.50	25.00

Mint: Lahore
KM# 436.40 RUPEE
Silver **Obv:** Inscription **Rev. Legend:** Dar-us-Sultanat **Note:** Coins dated AH1131/1-1132/2 have mint name in one line in second row of inscription. Later dates have the mint name at the top. Weight varies 11.00-11.60 grams.

Date	Mintage	Good	VG	F	VF	XF
AH1131//1 (Ahad)	—	5.00	6.50	8.50	14.00	20.00
AH1132//1 (Ahad)	—	5.00	6.50	8.50	14.00	20.00
AH1132//2	—	5.00	6.50	8.50	14.00	20.00
AH11xx/3	—	5.00	6.50	8.50	14.00	20.00
AH1134//4	—	5.00	6.50	8.50	14.00	20.00
AH1135//5	—	5.00	6.50	8.50	14.00	20.00
AH1136//5	—	5.00	6.50	8.50	14.00	20.00
AH11xx//6	—	5.00	6.50	8.50	14.00	20.00
AH1137//7	—	5.00	6.50	8.50	14.00	20.00
AH1138//7	—	5.00	6.50	8.50	14.00	20.00
AH11xx//8	—	5.00	6.50	8.50	14.00	20.00
AH1139//9	—	5.00	6.50	8.50	14.00	20.00
AH11xx//10	—	5.00	6.50	8.50	14.00	20.00
AH11xx//11	—	5.00	6.50	8.50	14.00	20.00
AH11xx//12	—	5.00	6.50	8.50	14.00	20.00
AH11xx//13	—	5.00	6.50	8.50	14.00	20.00
AH11xx//14	—	5.00	6.50	8.50	14.00	20.00
AH11xx//15	—	5.00	6.50	8.50	14.00	20.00
AH11xx//16	—	5.00	6.50	8.50	14.00	20.00
AH11xx//17	—	5.00	6.50	8.50	14.00	20.00
AH1148//18	—	5.00	6.50	8.50	14.00	20.00
AH1149//19	—	5.00	6.50	8.50	14.00	20.00
AH11xx//20	—	5.00	6.50	8.50	14.00	20.00
AH11xx//21	—	5.00	6.50	8.50	14.00	20.00
AH11xx//22	—	5.00	6.50	8.50	14.00	20.00
AH1153//23	—	5.00	6.50	8.50	14.00	20.00
AH1154//24	—	5.00	6.50	8.50	14.00	20.00
AH1155//25	—	5.00	6.50	8.50	14.00	20.00
AH11xx//26	—	5.00	6.50	8.50	14.00	20.00
AH1157//27	—	5.00	6.50	8.50	14.00	20.00
AH1159//28	—	5.00	6.50	8.50	14.00	20.00
AH11xx//29	—	5.00	6.50	8.50	14.00	20.00
AH11xx//30	—	—	6.50	8.50	14.00	20.00
AH1161//31	—	5.00	6.50	8.50	14.00	20.00

Mint: Lahore
KM# 436.65 RUPEE
Silver **Obv. Inscription:** Emperors name, with Badadur **Rev. Inscription:** Dar-us-Sultanat **Note:** Weight varies 11.00-11.60 grams.

Date	Mintage	Good	VG	F	VF	XF
AHxxxx//2	—	5.00	6.50	8.50	11.50	15.00

Mint: Lakhnau
KM# 436.41 RUPEE
Silver **Note:** Weight varies 11.00-11.60 grams.

Date	Mintage	Good	VG	F	VF	XF
AH1132//1 (Ahad)	—	5.00	6.50	8.50	14.00	20.00
AH1132//2	—	5.00	6.50	8.50	14.00	20.00
AH1133//2	—	5.00	6.50	8.50	14.00	20.00
AH1133//3	—	5.00	6.50	8.50	14.00	20.00
AH1134//3	—	5.00	6.50	8.50	14.00	20.00
AH1134//4	—	5.00	6.50	8.50	14.00	20.00
AH1135//4	—	5.00	6.50	8.50	14.00	20.00
AH1135//5	—	5.00	6.50	8.50	14.00	20.00

Mint: Macchlipattan
KM# 436.42 RUPEE
Silver **Obv:** Inscription, date **Rev:** Inscription **Note:** Weight varies 11.00-11.60 grams.

Date	Mintage	Good	VG	F	VF	XF
AH1133//2 Rare	—	—	—	—	—	—
AH1133//3 Rare	—	—	—	—	—	—
AH1134//3 Rare	—	—	—	—	—	—
AH1134//4 Rare	—	—	—	—	—	—
AH1135//4 Rare	—	—	—	—	—	—
AH1135//5 Rare	—	—	—	—	—	—
AH1136//5 Rare	—	—	—	—	—	—
AH1138//8 Rare	—	—	—	—	—	—
AH1142//12 Rare	—	—	—	—	—	—
AH1143//13 Rare	—	—	—	—	—	—
AH1145//15 Rare	—	—	—	—	—	—
AH1147//16 Rare	—	—	—	—	—	—
AH1147//17 Rare	—	—	—	—	—	—
AH1150//20 Rare	—	—	—	—	—	—
AH1156//25 Rare	—	—	—	—	—	—
AH1156//26 Rare	—	—	—	—	—	—
AH1159//29 Rare	—	—	—	—	—	—
AH1160//29 Rare	—	—	—	—	—	—
AH1160//30 Rare	—	—	—	—	—	—
AH1161//30 Rare	—	—	—	—	—	—

Mint: Muazzamabad
KM# 436.43 RUPEE
Silver **Note:** Weight varies 11.00-11.60 grams.

Date	Mintage	Good	VG	F	VF	XF
AH1139//9 Rare	—	—	—	—	—	—

Mint: Muhammadabad Banaras
KM# 436.15 RUPEE
Silver **Obv:** Inscription **Rev. Inscription:** Muhammadabad above, Banaras below **Note:** Weight varies 11.00-11.60 grams.

Date	Mintage	Good	VG	F	VF	XF
AH1146//15	—	5.00	6.50	8.50	14.00	20.00
AH1146//16	—	5.00	6.50	8.50	14.00	20.00
AH1147//16	—	5.00	6.50	8.50	14.00	20.00
AH1147//17	—	5.00	6.50	8.50	14.00	20.00
AH1148//17	—	5.00	6.50	8.50	14.00	20.00
AH1148//18	—	5.00	6.50	8.50	14.00	20.00
AH1149//18	—	5.00	6.50	8.50	14.00	20.00
AH1149//19	—	5.00	6.50	8.50	14.00	20.00
AH1150//19	—	5.00	6.50	8.50	14.00	20.00
AH1150//20	—	5.00	6.50	8.50	14.00	20.00
AH1151//20	—	5.00	6.50	8.50	14.00	20.00
AH1151//21	—	5.00	6.50	8.50	14.00	20.00
AH1152//21	—	5.00	6.50	8.50	14.00	20.00
AH1152//22	—	5.00	6.50	8.50	14.00	20.00
AH1153//22	—	5.00	6.50	8.50	14.00	20.00
AH1153//23	—	5.00	6.50	8.50	14.00	20.00
AH1154//23	—	5.00	6.50	8.50	14.00	20.00
AH1154//24	—	5.00	6.50	8.50	14.00	20.00
AH1155//24	—	5.00	6.50	8.50	14.00	20.00
AH1155//25	—	5.00	6.50	8.50	14.00	20.00
AH1156//25	—	5.00	6.50	8.50	14.00	20.00
AH1156//26	—	5.00	6.50	8.50	14.00	20.00
AH1157//26	—	5.00	6.50	8.50	14.00	20.00
AH1157//27	—	5.00	6.50	8.50	14.00	20.00
AH1158//27	—	5.00	6.50	8.50	14.00	20.00
AH1158//28	—	5.00	6.50	8.50	14.00	20.00
AH1159//28	—	5.00	6.50	8.50	14.00	20.00
AH1159//29	—	5.00	6.50	8.50	14.00	20.00
AH1160//29	—	5.00	6.50	8.50	14.00	20.00
AH1160//30	—	5.00	6.50	8.50	14.00	20.00
AH1161//30	—	5.00	6.50	8.50	14.00	20.00
AH1161//31	—	5.00	6.50	8.50	14.00	20.00

Mint: Multan
KM# 436.44 RUPEE
Silver **Obv:** Inscription **Rev:** Inscription **Note:** Weight varies 11.00-11.60 grams.

Date	Mintage	Good	VG	F	VF	XF
AH1132//1 (Ahad)	—	5.00	6.50	8.50	14.00	20.00
AH1132//2	—	5.00	6.50	8.50	14.00	20.00
AH1133//3	—	5.00	6.50	8.50	14.00	20.00
AH1135//5	—	5.00	6.50	8.50	14.00	20.00
AH11xx//6	—	5.00	6.50	8.50	14.00	20.00
AH11xx//7	—	5.00	6.50	8.50	14.00	20.00
AH1140//10	—	5.00	6.50	8.50	14.00	20.00
AH1144//14	—	5.00	6.50	8.50	14.00	20.00
AH1145//14	—	5.00	6.50	8.50	14.00	20.00
AH1145//15	—	5.00	6.50	8.50	14.00	20.00
AH1147//17	—	5.00	6.50	8.50	14.00	20.00
AH1148//17	—	5.00	6.50	8.50	14.00	20.00
AH1148//18	—	5.00	6.50	8.50	14.00	20.00
AH1149//18	—	5.00	6.50	8.50	14.00	20.00
AH1149//19	—	5.00	6.50	8.50	14.00	20.00

Date	Mintage	Good	VG	F	VF	XF
AH1150//20	—	5.00	6.50	8.50	14.00	20.00
AH1151//21	—	5.00	6.50	8.50	14.00	20.00
AH1152//21	—	5.00	6.50	8.50	14.00	20.00
AH1152//22	—	5.00	6.50	8.50	14.00	20.00
AH1153//22	—	5.00	6.50	8.50	14.00	20.00
AH1153//23	—	5.00	6.50	8.50	14.00	20.00
AH1154//23	—	5.00	6.50	8.50	14.00	20.00
AH1154//24	—	5.00	6.50	8.50	14.00	20.00
AH1155//24	—	5.00	6.50	8.50	14.00	20.00
AH1155//25	—	5.00	6.50	8.50	14.00	20.00
AH1156//25	—	5.00	6.50	8.50	14.00	20.00
AH1156//26	—	5.00	6.50	8.50	14.00	20.00
AH1157//26	—	5.00	6.50	8.50	14.00	20.00
AH1157//27	—	5.00	6.50	8.50	14.00	20.00
AH1158//27	—	5.00	6.50	8.50	14.00	20.00
AH1158//28	—	5.00	6.50	8.50	14.00	20.00
AH1159//28	—	5.00	6.50	8.50	14.00	20.00
AH1159//29	—	5.00	6.50	8.50	14.00	20.00
AH1160//29	—	5.00	6.50	8.50	14.00	20.00
AH1160//30	—	5.00	6.50	8.50	14.00	20.00
AH1161//30	—	5.00	6.50	8.50	14.00	20.00
AH1161//31	—	5.00	6.50	8.50	14.00	20.00

Mint: Murshidabad
KM# 436.46 RUPEE
Silver **Obv:** Inscription, date **Rev:** Inscription **Note:** Weight varies 11.00-11.60 grams.

Date	Mintage	Good	VG	F	VF	XF
AH11xx//2	—	5.00	6.50	9.00	15.00	25.00
AH1134//3	—	5.00	6.50	9.00	15.00	25.00
AH11xx//4	—	5.00	6.50	9.00	15.00	25.00
AH11xx//5	—	5.00	6.50	9.00	15.00	25.00
AH11xx//8	—	5.00	6.50	9.00	15.00	25.00
AH11xx//10	—	5.00	6.50	9.00	15.00	25.00
AH11xx//12	—	5.00	6.50	9.00	15.00	25.00
AH11xx//13	—	5.00	6.50	9.00	15.00	25.00
AH11xx//14	—	5.00	6.50	9.00	15.00	25.00
AH11xx//15	—	5.00	6.50	9.00	15.00	25.00
AH1147//17	—	5.00	6.50	9.00	15.00	25.00
AH114x//18	—	5.00	6.50	9.00	15.00	25.00
AH1149//19	—	5.00	6.50	9.00	15.00	25.00
AH11xx//20	—	5.00	6.50	9.00	15.00	25.00
AH11xx//21	—	5.00	6.50	9.00	15.00	25.00
AH11xx//22	—	5.00	6.50	9.00	15.00	25.00
AH11xx//23	—	5.00	6.50	9.00	15.00	25.00
AH11xx//24	—	5.00	6.50	9.00	15.00	25.00
AH11xx//25	—	5.00	6.50	9.00	15.00	25.00
AH11xx//26	—	5.00	6.50	9.00	15.00	25.00
AH1157//27	—	5.00	6.50	9.00	15.00	25.00
AH1159//28	—	5.00	6.50	9.00	15.00	25.00
AH1160//29	—	5.00	6.50	9.00	15.00	25.00
AH116x//30	—	5.00	6.50	9.00	15.00	25.00

Mint: Najibabad
KM# 436.47 RUPEE
Silver **Note:** Weight varies 11.00-11.60 grams.

Date	Mintage	Good	VG	F	VF	XF
AH1139//6 (sic) Rare	—	—	—	—	—	—

Mint: Narwar
KM# 436.66 RUPEE
Silver **Note:** Weight varies 11.00-11.60 grams.

Date	Mintage	Good	VG	F	VF	XF
AH116x//30 Rare	—	—	—	—	—	—
AH1161//31 Rare	—	—	—	—	—	—

Mint: Nusratabad
KM# 436.48 RUPEE
Silver **Note:** Weight varies 11.00-11.60 grams.

Date	Mintage	Good	VG	F	VF	XF
AH113x//x Rare	—	—	—	—	—	—
AH11xx//12 Rare	—	—	—	—	—	—
AHxxxx//21 Rare	—	—	—	—	—	—

Mint: Parenda
KM# 436.49 RUPEE
Silver **Note:** Weight varies 11.00-11.60 grams.

Date	Mintage	Good	VG	F	VF	XF
AHxxxx//1 Rare	—	—	—	—	—	—
AHxxxx//10 Rare	—	—	—	—	—	—
AHxxxx//16 Rare	—	—	—	—	—	—

Mint: Peshawar
KM# 436.50 RUPEE
Silver **Note:** Weight varies 11.00-11.60 grams.

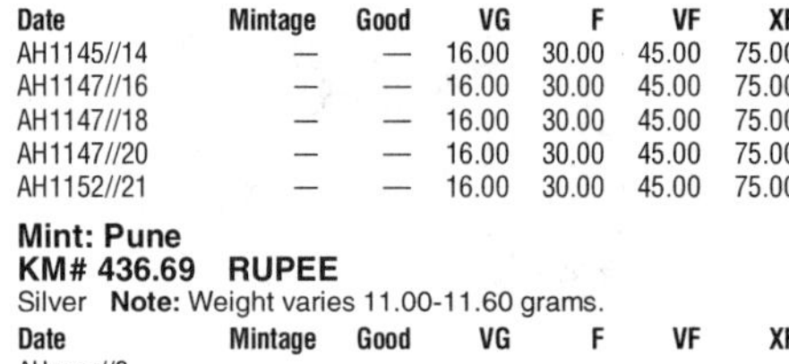

Date	Mintage	Good	VG	F	VF	XF
AH11xx//1 (Ahad)	—	—	16.00	30.00	45.00	75.00
AH11xx//2	—	—	16.00	30.00	45.00	75.00
AH11xx//4	—	—	16.00	30.00	45.00	75.00
AH1136//6	—	—	16.00	30.00	45.00	75.00
AH11xx//7	—	—	16.00	30.00	45.00	75.00
AH1144//14	—	—	16.00	30.00	45.00	75.00
AH1145//14	—	—	16.00	30.00	45.00	75.00
AH1147//16	—	—	16.00	30.00	45.00	75.00
AH1147//18	—	—	16.00	30.00	45.00	75.00
AH1147//20	—	—	16.00	30.00	45.00	75.00
AH1152//21	—	—	16.00	30.00	45.00	75.00

Mint: Pune
KM# 436.69 RUPEE
Silver **Note:** Weight varies 11.00-11.60 grams.

Date	Mintage	Good	VG	F	VF	XF
AHxxxx//2	—	—	—	—	—	—
AHxxxx//19	—	—	—	—	—	—
AHxxxx//20	—	—	—	—	—	—

Mint: Qamarnagar
KM# 436.51 RUPEE
Silver **Obv:** Inscription **Rev:** Inscription **Note:** Weight varies 11.00-11.60 grams.

Date	Mintage	Good	VG	F	VF	XF
AH1132//1 (Ahad) Rare	—	—	—	—	—	—
AH11xx//11 Rare	—	—	—	—	—	—
AH1143//13 Rare	—	—	—	—	—	—
AH1147//17 Rare	—	—	—	—	—	—
AH(11)51//20 Rare	—	—	—	—	—	—
AH1150//20 Rare	—	—	—	—	—	—
AH1151//12 (sic) Error for 21 Rare	—	—	—	—	—	—

Mint: Qandahar
KM# 436.53 RUPEE
Silver **Note:** Weight varies 11.00-11.60 grams.

Date	Mintage	Good	VG	F	VF	XF
AH1155//xx Rare	—	—	—	—	—	—
AH1159//30 Rare	—	—	—	—	—	—

Mint: Rajapur
KM# 436.70 RUPEE
Silver **Note:** Weight varies 11.00-11.60 grams.

Date	Mintage	Good	VG	F	VF	XF
AH1148//xx	—	—	—	—	—	—

Mint: Sahrind
KM# 436.54 RUPEE
Silver **Obv:** Inscription **Rev:** Inscription **Note:** Weight varies 11.00-11.60 grams.

Date	Mintage	Good	VG	F	VF	XF
AH11xx//1 (Ahad)	—	5.00	6.50	8.50	14.00	20.00
AH1134//3	—	5.00	6.50	8.50	14.00	20.00
AH1134//4	—	5.00	6.50	8.50	14.00	20.00
AH11xx//5	—	5.00	6.50	8.50	14.00	20.00
AH11xx//6	—	5.00	6.50	8.50	14.00	20.00
AH11xx//10	—	5.00	6.50	8.50	14.00	20.00
AH11xx//12	—	5.00	6.50	8.50	14.00	20.00
AH11xx//13	—	5.00	6.50	8.50	14.00	20.00
AH1146//15	—	5.00	6.50	8.50	14.00	20.00
AH1146//16	—	5.00	6.50	8.50	14.00	20.00
AH1147//16	—	5.00	6.50	8.50	14.00	20.00
AH1147//17	—	5.00	6.50	8.50	14.00	20.00
AH11xx//18	—	5.00	6.50	8.50	14.00	20.00
AH11xx//20	—	5.00	6.50	8.50	14.00	20.00
AH11xx//21	—	5.00	6.50	8.50	14.00	20.00
AH1154//24	—	5.00	6.50	8.50	14.00	20.00
AH1156//26	—	5.00	6.50	8.50	14.00	20.00
AH1158//28	—	5.00	6.50	8.50	14.00	20.00
AH11xx//29	—	5.00	6.50	8.50	14.00	20.00
AH11xx//30	—	5.00	6.50	8.50	14.00	20.00

Mint: Satara
KM# 436.55 RUPEE
Silver **Note:** Weight varies 11.00-11.60 grams.

Date	Mintage	Good	VG	F	VF	XF
AH1146//x Rare	—	—	—	—	—	—

Mint: Shahabad Qanauj
KM# 436.52 RUPEE
Silver **Obv:** Inscription **Rev:** Inscription **Note:** Weight varies 11.00-11.60 grams.

Date	Mintage	Good	VG	F	VF	XF
AH11xx//4	—	6.00	11.00	18.00	30.00	50.00
AH11xx//5	—	6.00	11.00	18.00	30.00	50.00
AH1138//7	—	6.00	11.00	18.00	30.00	50.00
AH11xx//8	—	6.00	11.00	18.00	30.00	50.00
AH1139//9	—	6.00	11.00	18.00	30.00	50.00
AH1140//9	—	6.00	11.00	18.00	30.00	50.00
AH1140//10	—	6.00	11.00	18.00	30.00	50.00
AH1141//10	—	6.00	11.00	18.00	30.00	50.00
AH1141//11	—	6.00	11.00	18.00	30.00	50.00
AH1142//11	—	6.00	11.00	18.00	30.00	50.00
AH1142//12	—	6.00	11.00	18.00	30.00	50.00
AH1143//12	—	6.00	11.00	18.00	30.00	50.00
AH1143//13	—	6.00	11.00	18.00	30.00	50.00
AH1144//13	—	6.00	11.00	18.00	30.00	50.00
AH1144//14	—	6.00	11.00	18.00	30.00	50.00
AH1145//14	—	6.00	11.00	18.00	30.00	50.00
AH1145//15	—	6.00	11.00	18.00	30.00	50.00
AH1146//15	—	6.00	11.00	18.00	30.00	50.00
AH1146//16	—	6.00	11.00	18.00	30.00	50.00
AH1147//16	—	6.00	11.00	18.00	30.00	50.00
AH1147//17	—	6.00	11.00	18.00	30.00	50.00
AH1148//17	—	6.00	11.00	18.00	30.00	50.00
AH1148//18	—	6.00	11.00	18.00	30.00	50.00
AH1149//18	—	6.00	11.00	18.00	30.00	50.00
AH1149//19	—	6.00	11.00	18.00	30.00	50.00
AH1150//19	—	6.00	11.00	18.00	30.00	50.00
AH1150//20	—	6.00	11.00	18.00	30.00	50.00
AH1151//20	—	6.00	11.00	18.00	30.00	50.00
AH1151//21	—	6.00	11.00	18.00	30.00	50.00
AH1152//21	—	6.00	11.00	18.00	30.00	50.00
AH1152//22	—	6.00	11.00	18.00	30.00	50.00
AH1153//22	—	6.00	11.00	18.00	30.00	50.00
AH1153//23	—	6.00	11.00	18.00	30.00	50.00
AH1154//23	—	6.00	11.00	18.00	30.00	50.00
AH1154//24	—	6.00	11.00	18.00	30.00	50.00
AH1155//24	—	6.00	11.00	18.00	30.00	50.00
AH1155//25	—	6.00	11.00	18.00	30.00	50.00
AH1156//25	—	6.00	11.00	18.00	30.00	50.00
AH1156//26	—	6.00	11.00	18.00	30.00	50.00
AH1157//26	—	6.00	11.00	18.00	30.00	50.00
AH1157//27	—	6.00	11.00	18.00	30.00	50.00
AH1159//29	—	6.00	11.00	18.00	30.00	50.00

Mint: Shahjahanabad
KM# 436.56 RUPEE
Silver **Obv:** Inscription **Rev. Inscription:** Dar-ul-Khilifat **Note:** Weight varies 11.00-11.60 grams.

Date	Mintage	Good	VG	F	VF	XF
AH1131//1 (Ahad)	—	5.00	10.00	18.00	30.00	50.00
AH1132//1 (Ahad)	—	5.00	10.00	18.00	30.00	50.00
AH1132//2	—	5.00	10.00	18.00	30.00	50.00
AH1133//2	—	5.00	10.00	18.00	30.00	50.00

Mint: Sholapur
KM# 436.57 RUPEE
Silver **Obv:** Inscription, date **Rev:** Inscription **Note:** Weight varies 11.00-11.60 grams.

Date	Mintage	Good	VG	F	VF	XF
AH1132//2	—	5.00	10.00	20.00	35.00	50.00
AH1148//28	—	5.00	10.00	20.00	35.00	50.00

Mint: Sikakul
KM# 436.58 RUPEE
Silver **Note:** Weight varies 11.00-11.60 grams.

Date	Mintage	Good	VG	F	VF	XF
AH1131//1 (Ahad) Rare	—	—	—	—	—	—
AH1139//9 Rare	—	—	—	—	—	—
AH11xx//11 Rare	—	—	—	—	—	—
AH11xx//13 Rare	—	—	—	—	—	—

Mint: Sironj
KM# 436.59 RUPEE

Silver **Obv:** Inscription **Rev:** Inscription **Note:** Weight varies 11.00-11.60 grams.

Date	Mintage	Good	VG	F	VF	XF
AH1131//1 (Ahad)	—	6.50	11.00	20.00	35.00	60.00
AH11xx//2	—	6.50	11.00	20.00	35.00	60.00
AH113x//3	—	6.50	11.00	20.00	35.00	60.00
AH11xx//5	—	6.50	11.00	20.00	35.00	60.00
AH11xx//8	—	6.50	11.00	20.00	35.00	60.00
AH11xx//13	—	6.50	11.00	20.00	35.00	60.00
AH1152//22	—	6.50	11.00	20.00	35.00	60.00
AH1159//29	—	6.50	11.00	20.00	35.00	60.00

Mint: Surat
KM# 436.60 RUPEE

Silver **Note:** Weight varies 11.00-11.60 grams.

Date	Mintage	Good	VG	F	VF	XF
AH1131//1 (Ahad)	—	5.00	6.50	9.00	15.00	25.00
AH1132//1 (Ahad)	—	5.00	6.50	9.00	15.00	25.00
AH1133//2	—	5.00	6.50	9.00	15.00	25.00
AH1132//2	—	5.00	6.50	9.00	15.00	25.00
AH1133//3	—	5.00	6.50	9.00	15.00	25.00
AH1134//4	—	5.00	6.50	9.00	15.00	25.00
AH11xx//9	—	5.00	6.50	9.00	15.00	25.00
AH1140//10	—	5.00	6.50	9.00	15.00	25.00
AH11xx//13	—	5.00	6.50	9.00	15.00	25.00
AH11xx//14	—	5.00	6.50	9.00	15.00	25.00
AH1145//15	—	5.00	6.50	9.00	15.00	25.00
AH11XX//16	—	5.00	6.50	9.00	15.00	25.00
AH11xx//17	—	5.00	6.50	9.00	15.00	25.00
AH11xx/18	—	5.00	6.50	9.00	15.00	25.00
AH11xx//19	—	5.00	6.50	9.00	15.00	25.00
AH11xx//20	—	5.00	6.50	9.00	15.00	25.00
AH11xx//21	—	5.00	6.50	9.00	15.00	25.00
AH1153//22	—	5.00	6.50	9.00	15.00	25.00
AH11xx//24	—	5.00	6.50	9.00	15.00	25.00
AH115x//26	—	5.00	6.50	9.00	15.00	25.00
AH1157//28	—	5.00	6.50	9.00	15.00	25.00
AH11xx//29	—	5.00	6.50	9.00	15.00	25.00
AH11xx//30	—	5.00	6.50	9.00	15.00	25.00
AH11xx//31	—	5.00	6.50	9.00	15.00	25.00

Mint: Tatta
KM# 436.61 RUPEE

Silver **Obv:** Inscription, date **Rev:** Inscription **Note:** Weight varies 11.00-11.60 grams.

Date	Mintage	Good	VG	F	VF	XF
AH1132//1 (Ahad)	—	6.00	15.00	30.00	50.00	85.00
AH1132//2	—	6.00	15.00	30.00	50.00	85.00
AH1133//2	—	6.00	15.00	30.00	50.00	85.00
AH1133//3	—	6.00	15.00	30.00	50.00	85.00
AH1134//3	—	6.00	15.00	30.00	50.00	85.00
AH1137//7	—	6.00	15.00	30.00	50.00	85.00
AH113x//8	—	6.00	15.00	30.00	50.00	85.00
AH1140//xx	—	6.00	15.00	30.00	50.00	85.00
AH1142//xx	—	6.00	15.00	30.00	50.00	85.00
AH1144//xx	—	6.00	15.00	30.00	50.00	85.00
AH1149//xx	—	6.00	15.00	30.00	50.00	85.00

Mint: Ujjain
KM# 436.62 RUPEE

Silver **Obv:** Inscription **Rev. Inscription:** Dar-ul-Fath **Note:** Weight varies 11.00-11.60 grams.

Date	Mintage	Good	VG	F	VF	XF
AHxxxx//1 (Ahad)	—	5.00	8.00	12.00	18.00	30.00
AHxxxx//2	—	5.00	8.00	12.00	18.00	30.00
AHxxxx//3	—	5.00	8.00	12.00	18.00	30.00
AHxxxx//4	—	5.00	8.00	12.00	18.00	30.00
AHxxxx//8	—	5.00	8.00	12.00	18.00	30.00
AHxxxx//9	—	5.00	8.00	12.00	18.00	30.00
AH11xx//11	—	5.00	8.00	12.00	18.00	30.00
AHxxxx//12	—	5.00	8.00	12.00	18.00	30.00
AHxxxx//13	—	5.00	8.00	12.00	18.00	30.00
AHxxxx//15	—	5.00	8.00	12.00	18.00	30.00
AHxxxx//17	—	5.00	8.00	12.00	18.00	30.00
AHxxxx//18	—	5.00	8.00	12.00	18.00	30.00
AHxxxx//20	—	5.00	8.00	12.00	18.00	30.00
AHxxxx//24	—	5.00	8.00	12.00	18.00	30.00

Mint: Zain-ul-Bilad
KM# 436.63 RUPEE

Silver **Obv:** Inscription, date **Rev:** Inscription **Note:** Also see Ahmadabad. Weight varies 11.00-11.60 grams.

Date	Mintage	Good	VG	F	VF	XF
AH1135//4 Rare	—	—	—	—	—	—
AH1135//5 Rare	—	—	—	—	—	—
AH1136//5 Rare	—	—	—	—	—	—
AH1136//6 Rare	—	—	—	—	—	—
AH1137//6 Rare	—	—	—	—	—	—
AH1137//7 Rare	—	—	—	—	—	—

Mint: Akbarabad
KM# 437.1 RUPEE

Silver **Obv. Inscription:** Sahib Giran Sani, Second Lord of the Conjunction **Rev. Inscription:** Mustaqir-ul-Khilafat **Note:** Weight varies 11.00-11.60 grams.

Date	Mintage	Good	VG	F	VF	XF
AH1132//1 (Ahad)	—	5.00	8.00	16.00	28.00	40.00
AH1132//2	—	5.00	8.00	16.00	28.00	40.00

Mint: Akhtarnagar
KM# 437.2 RUPEE

Silver **Note:** Weight varies 11.00-11.60 grams.

Date	Mintage	Good	VG	F	VF	XF
AH1158//27	—	—	8.00	16.00	28.00	40.00
AH1158//28	—	—	8.00	16.00	28.00	40.00

Mint: Farrukhabad
KM# 437.3 RUPEE

Silver **Obv:** Inscription **Rev:** Inscription **Note:** Weight varies 11.00-11.60 grams.

Date	Mintage	Good	VG	F	VF	XF
AH1152//22	—	5.00	6.50	8.50	14.00	20.00
AH1153//22	—	5.00	6.50	8.50	14.00	20.00
AH1153//23	—	5.00	6.50	8.50	14.00	20.00
AH1154//23	—	5.00	6.50	8.50	14.00	20.00
AH1154//24	—	5.00	6.50	8.50	14.00	20.00
AH1155//24	—	5.00	6.50	8.50	14.00	20.00
AH1155//25	—	5.00	6.50	8.50	14.00	20.00
AH1156//25	—	5.00	6.50	8.50	14.00	20.00
AH1156//26	—	5.00	6.50	8.50	14.00	20.00
AH1157//26	—	5.00	6.50	8.50	14.00	20.00
AH1157//27	—	5.00	6.50	8.50	14.00	20.00
AH1158//27	—	5.00	6.50	8.50	14.00	20.00
AH1158//28	—	5.00	6.50	8.50	14.00	20.00
AH1159//28	—	5.00	6.50	8.50	14.00	20.00
AH1159//29	—	5.00	6.50	8.50	14.00	20.00
AH1160//29	—	5.00	6.50	8.50	14.00	20.00
AH1160//30	—	5.00	6.50	8.50	14.00	20.00
AH1161//30	—	5.00	6.50	8.50	14.00	20.00
AH1161//31	—	5.00	6.50	8.50	14.00	20.00

Mint: Shahjahanabad
KM# 437.4 RUPEE

Silver **Obv:** Inscription **Rev. Inscription:** Dar-ul-Khilafat **Note:** Weight varies 11.00-11.60 grams.

Date	Mintage	Good	VG	F	VF	XF
AH1133//2	—	5.00	6.50	8.50	11.50	16.50
AH1133//3	—	5.00	6.50	8.50	11.50	16.50
AH1134//3	—	5.00	6.50	8.50	11.50	16.50
AH1134//4	—	5.00	6.50	8.50	11.50	16.50
AH1135//4	—	5.00	6.50	8.50	11.50	16.50
AH1135//5	—	5.00	6.50	8.50	11.50	16.50
AH1136//5	—	5.00	6.50	8.50	11.50	16.50
AH1136//6	—	5.00	6.50	8.50	11.50	16.50
AH1137//6	—	5.00	6.50	8.50	11.50	16.50
AH1137//7	—	5.00	6.50	8.50	11.50	16.50
AH1138//7	—	5.00	6.50	8.50	11.50	16.50
AH1138//8	—	5.00	6.50	8.50	11.50	16.50
AH1139//8	—	5.00	6.50	8.50	11.50	16.50
AH1139//9	—	5.00	6.50	8.50	11.50	16.50
AH1140//9	—	5.00	6.50	8.50	11.50	16.50
AH1140//10	—	5.00	6.50	8.50	11.50	16.50
AH1141//10	—	5.00	6.50	8.50	11.50	16.50
AH1141//11	—	5.00	6.50	8.50	11.50	16.50
AH1142//11	—	5.00	6.50	8.50	11.50	16.50
AH1142//12	—	5.00	6.50	8.50	11.50	16.50
AH1143//12	—	5.00	6.50	8.50	11.50	16.50
AH1143//13	—	5.00	6.50	8.50	11.50	16.50
AH1144//13	—	5.00	6.50	8.50	11.50	16.50
AH1144//14	—	5.00	6.50	8.50	11.50	16.50
AH1145//14	—	5.00	6.50	8.50	11.50	16.50
AH1145//15	—	5.00	6.50	8.50	11.50	16.50
AH1146//15	—	5.00	6.50	8.50	11.50	16.50
AH1146//16	—	5.00	6.50	8.50	11.50	16.50
AH1147//16	—	5.00	6.50	8.50	11.50	16.50
AH1147//17	—	5.00	6.50	8.50	11.50	16.50
AH1148//17	—	5.00	6.50	8.50	11.50	16.50
AH1148//18	—	5.00	6.50	8.50	11.50	16.50
AH1149//18	—	5.00	6.50	8.50	11.50	16.50
AH1149//19	—	5.00	6.50	8.50	11.50	16.50
AH1150//19	—	5.00	6.50	8.50	11.50	16.50
AH1150//20	—	5.00	6.50	8.50	11.50	16.50
AH1151//20	—	5.00	6.50	8.50	11.50	16.50
AH1151//21	—	5.00	6.50	8.50	11.50	16.50
AH1152//21	—	5.00	6.50	8.50	11.50	16.50
AH1152//22	—	5.00	6.50	8.50	11.50	16.50
AH1153//22	—	5.00	6.50	8.50	11.50	16.50
AH1153//23	—	5.00	6.50	8.50	11.50	16.50
AH1154//23	—	5.00	6.50	8.50	11.50	16.50
AH1154//24	—	5.00	6.50	8.50	11.50	16.50
AH1155//24	—	5.00	6.50	8.50	11.50	16.50
AH1155//25	—	5.00	6.50	8.50	11.50	16.50
AH1156//25	—	—	6.50	8.50	11.50	16.50
AH1156//26	—	5.00	6.50	8.50	11.50	16.50
AH1157//26	—	5.00	6.50	8.50	11.50	16.50
AH1157//27	—	5.00	6.50	8.50	11.50	16.50
AH1158//27	—	5.00	6.50	8.50	11.50	16.50
AH1158//28	—	5.00	6.50	8.50	11.50	16.50
AH1159//28	—	5.00	6.50	8.50	11.50	16.50
AH1159//29	—	5.00	6.50	8.50	11.50	16.50
AH1160//29	—	5.00	6.50	8.50	11.50	16.50
AH1160//30	—	5.00	6.50	8.50	11.50	16.50
AH1161//30	—	5.00	6.50	8.50	11.50	16.50
AH1161//31	—	5.00	6.50	8.50	11.50	16.50

Mint: Shahjahanabad
KM# A438 RUPEE

Silver **Obv:** Inscription **Rev. Inscription:** Dar-ul-Khilafat **Shape:** Square **Note:** Weight varies 11.00-11.60 grams.

Date	Mintage	Good	VG	F	VF	XF
AH1154//24	—	—	—	—	—	—

Mint: Jaipur
KM# B438.1 NAZARANA RUPEE

Silver **Obv:** Inscription **Rev. Legend:** Sawai **Note:** Weight varies 11.00-11.60 grams.

Date	Mintage	Good	VG	F	VF	XF
AH1159//29	—	—	—	—	—	—

Mint: Shahjahanabad
KM# C438.1 1/4 MOHUR

Gold **Note:** Weight varies 2.67-2.72 grams.

Date	Mintage	Good	VG	F	VF	XF
AHxxxx//21	—	—	—	—	—	—

Mint: Shahjahanabad
KM# D438.1 1/2 MOHUR

Gold **Obv:** Inscription **Rev. Inscription:** Dar-ul-Khilifat **Note:** Weight varies 5.35-5.45 grams.

Date	Mintage	Good	VG	F	VF	XF
AHxxxx//11 Rare	—	—	—	—	—	—
AHxxxx//12 Rare	—	—	—	—	—	—
AH1152//22 Rare	—	—	—	—	—	—
AH11xx//30 Rare	—	—	—	—	—	—

Mint: Sind
KM# D438.2 1/2 MOHUR
Gold **Note:** Weight varies 5.35-5.45 grams.

Date	Mintage	Good	VG	F	VF	XF
AHxxxx//12 Rare	—	—	—	—	—	—

Mint: Surat
KM# E438.1 MOHUR
Gold **Obv. Inscription:** Ba-luf-ullah Badshah-i-Zaman **Rev:** Inscription **Note:** Weight varies 10.70-10.90 grams.

Date	Mintage	Good	VG	F	VF	XF
AH1131//1 (Ahad)	—	—	600	850	1,000	1,500

Mint: Burhanpur
KM# F438.1 MOHUR
Gold **Note:** Weight varies 10.70-10.90 grams.

Date	Mintage	Good	VG	F	VF	XF
AHxxxx//1 (Ahad)	—	—	—	—	—	—

Mint: Ahmadabad
KM# 438.26 MOHUR
Gold **Obv. Inscription:** Badshah Ghazi **Rev:** Inscription **Note:** Weight varies 10.70-10.90 grams.

Date	Mintage	Good	VG	F	VF	XF
AHxxxx//10	—	—	—	—	—	—
AHxxxx//12	—	—	—	—	—	—
AHxxxx//15	—	—	—	—	—	—
AHxxxx//16	—	—	—	—	—	—
AHxxxx//29	—	—	—	—	—	—

Mint: Ahmadanagar
KM# 438.1 MOHUR
Gold **Note:** Weight varies 10.70-10.90 grams.

Date	Mintage	Good	VG	F	VF	XF
AHxxxx//9	—	235	265	310	375	450

Mint: Akbarabad
KM# 438.2 MOHUR
Gold **Obv:** Inscription **Rev. Inscription:** Mustagir-ul-Khilifat **Note:** Weight varies 10.70-10.90 grams.

Date	Mintage	Good	VG	F	VF	XF
AH11xx//1 (Ahad)	—	235	265	310	375	450
AH1136//5	—	235	265	310	375	450
AH11xx//14	—	235	265	310	375	450
AH11xx//17	—	235	265	310	375	450
AH1149//19	—	235	265	310	375	450
AH115x//25	—	235	265	310	375	450
AH11xx//29	—	2,354	265	310	375	450
AH1160//30	—	235	265	310	375	450

Mint: Akhtarnagar
KM# 438.4 MOHUR
Gold **Obv:** Inscription, date **Rev:** Inscription **Note:** Weight varies 10.70-10.90 grams.

Date	Mintage	Good	VG	F	VF	XF
AHxxxx//11	—	—	235	265	325	425
AH114x//13	—	—	235	265	325	425

Mint: Allahabad
KM# 438.3 MOHUR
Gold **Note:** Weight varies 10.70-10.90 grams.

Date	Mintage	Good	VG	F	VF	XF
AH1138//8	—	—	235	265	325	425

Mint: Azimabad
KM# 438.30 MOHUR
Gold **Note:** Weight varies 10.70-10.90 grams.

Date	Mintage	Good	VG	F	VF	XF
AH1134//4	—	—	—	—	—	—

Mint: Burhanpur
KM# 438.6 MOHUR
Gold **Obv:** Inscription **Rev. Legend:** Dar-us-Sarur **Note:** Weight varies 10.70-10.90 grams.

Date	Mintage	Good	VG	F	VF	XF
AHxxxx//3	—	235	265	310	375	450
AHxxxx//7	—	235	265	310	375	450
AH1152//22	—	235	265	310	375	450

Mint: Gwalior
KM# 438.7 MOHUR
Gold **Note:** Weight varies 10.70-10.90 grams.

Date	Mintage	Good	VG	F	VF	XF
AHxxxx//17	—	235	265	310	375	450

Mint: Haidarabad (Farkhanda Bunyad)
KM# 438.8 MOHUR
Gold **Obv:** Inscription **Rev. Legend:** Farkhanda Bunyad **Note:** Weight varies 10.70-10.90 grams.

Date	Mintage	Good	VG	F	VF	XF
AH1138//8	—	235	265	310	375	450
AH11xx//10	—	235	265	310	375	450
AH11xx//15	—	235	265	310	375	450
AH11xx//19	—	235	265	310	375	450

Mint: Islamabad
KM# 438.9 MOHUR
Gold **Note:** Weight varies 10.70-10.90 grams.

Date	Mintage	Good	VG	F	VF	XF
AH1134//3	—	235	265	310	375	450
AH114x//11	—	235	265	310	375	450
AH1151//21	—	235	265	310	375	450
AH1152//2x	—	235	265	310	375	450
AH115x//22	—	235	265	310	375	450
AH1155//25	—	235	265	310	375	450

Mint: Itawa
KM# 438.10 MOHUR
Gold **Note:** Weight varies 10.70-10.90 grams.

Date	Mintage	Good	VG	F	VF	XF
AH1139//8	—	235	265	325	400	500
AH1139//9	—	235	265	325	400	500
AH1140//9	—	235	265	325	400	500
AH1140//10	—	235	265	325	400	500
AH1145//15	—	235	265	325	400	500
AH11xx//21	—	235	265	325	400	500
AH11xx//24	—	235	265	325	400	500
AH1156//26	—	235	265	325	400	500

Mint: Kabul
KM# 438.11 MOHUR
Gold **Note:** Weight varies 10.70-10.90 grams.

Date	Mintage	Good	VG	F	VF	XF
AH1137//x Rare	—	—	—	—	—	—

Mint: Kanbayat
KM# 438.28 MOHUR
Gold **Note:** Weight varies 10.70-10.90 grams.

Date	Mintage	Good	VG	F	VF	XF
AHxxxx//18	—	235	325	425	575	850

Mint: Katak
KM# 438.12 MOHUR
Gold **Note:** Weight varies 10.70-10.90 grams.

Date	Mintage	Good	VG	F	VF	XF
AH1135//4 Rare	—	—	—	—	—	—

Mint: Khujista Bunyad
KM# 438.13 MOHUR
Gold **Obv:** Inscription **Rev:** Inscription **Note:** Weight varies 10.70-10.90 grams.

Date	Mintage	Good	VG	F	VF	XF
AH1131//1 (Ahad)	—	235	265	310	375	450
AH113x//2	—	235	265	310	375	450
AH1132//1	—	235	265	310	375	450
AH1133//3	—	235	265	310	375	450
AH11xx//4	—	235	265	310	375	450
AH11xx//7	—	235	265	310	375	450
AH11xx//10	—	—	265	310	375	450
AH11xx//11	—	235	265	310	375	450
AH11xx//13	—	235	265	310	375	450
AH1149//19	—	235	265	310	375	450

Mint: Kora
KM# 438.14 MOHUR
Gold **Obv:** Inscription, date **Rev:** Inscription **Note:** Weight varies 10.70-10.90 grams.

Date	Mintage	Good	VG	F	VF	XF
AH11xx//2	—	235	265	310	375	450
AH1140//10	—	235	265	310	375	450
AH1144//14	—	235	265	310	375	450
AH114x//18	—	235	265	310	375	450

Mint: Lahore
KM# 438.15 MOHUR
Gold **Obv:** Inscription **Rev. Inscription:** Dar-us-Sultanat **Note:** Weight varies 10.70-10.90 grams.

Date	Mintage	Good	VG	F	VF	XF
AH1138//8	—	235	265	310	375	450
AH11xx//11	—	235	265	310	375	450
AH11xx//17	—	235	265	310	375	450
AH11xx//21	—	235	265	310	375	450
AH1154//24	—	235	265	310	375	450
AH1155//25	—	235	265	310	375	450
AH1156//26	—	235	265	310	375	450
AH1158//28	—	235	265	310	375	450
AH116x//30	—	235	265	310	375	450
AH1161//31	—	235	265	310	375	450

Mint: Macchlipattan
KM# 438.27 MOHUR
Gold **Note:** Weight varies 10.70-10.90 grams.

Date	Mintage	Good	VG	F	VF	XF
AH1150//19	—	235	265	325	400	500

Mint: Muazzamabad
KM# 438.16 MOHUR
Gold **Note:** Weight varies 10.70-10.90 grams.

Date	Mintage	Good	VG	F	VF	XF
AH1132//2	—	235	275	350	475	650
AH113x//4	—	235	275	350	475	650
AH1135//5	—	235	275	350	475	650
AH11xx//6	—	235	275	350	475	650
AH11xx//11	—	235	275	350	475	650
AH1144//15	—	235	275	350	475	650
AH115x//21	—	235	275	350	475	650

Mint: Muhammadabad Banaras
KM# 438.5 MOHUR
Gold **Note:** Weight varies 10.70-10.90 grams.

Date	Mintage	Good	VG	F	VF	XF
AHxxxx//5	—	235	265	310	375	450
AHxxxx//20	—	235	265	310	375	450
AHxxxx//25	—	235	265	310	375	450
AHxxxx//30	—	235	265	310	375	450

Mint: Multan
KM# 438.17 MOHUR
Gold **Obv:** Inscription **Rev:** Inscription **Note:** Weight varies 10.70-10.90 grams.

Date	Mintage	Good	VG	F	VF	XF
AH1152//21	—	—	235	265	325	425
AH1157//26	—	—	235	265	325	425
AH1157//26	—	—	235	265	325	425

Mint: Murshidabad
KM# 438.18 MOHUR
Gold **Note:** Weight varies 10.70-10.90 grams.

Date	Mintage	Good	VG	F	VF	XF
AHxxxx//23	—	235	265	310	375	450

Mint: Peshawar
KM# 438.19 MOHUR
Gold **Note:** Weight varies 10.70-10.90 grams.

Date	Mintage	Good	VG	F	VF	XF
AHxxxx//21 Rare	—	—	—	—	—	—

Mint: Qanauj
KM# 438.20 MOHUR
Gold **Note:** Weight varies 10.70-10.90 grams.

Date	Mintage	Good	VG	F	VF	XF
AH1144//13	—	235	265	325	400	500
AH114x//14	—	235	265	325	400	500

Mint: Sahrind
KM# 438.21 MOHUR
Gold **Obv:** Inscription **Rev:** Inscription **Note:** Weight varies 10.70-10.90 grams.

Date	Mintage	Good	VG	F	VF	XF
AHxxxx//10	—	235	265	310	375	450
AH1147//17	—	235	265	310	375	450
AH1153//23	—	235	265	310	375	450

Mint: Shahjahanabad
KM# 438.22 MOHUR
Gold **Obv:** Inscription **Rev. Inscription:** Dar-ul-Khilifat **Note:** Weight varies 10.70-10.90 grams.

Date	Mintage	Good	VG	F	VF	XF
AH1131//1 (Ahad)	—	235	265	310	375	450

Mint: Surat
KM# 438.23 MOHUR
Gold **Note:** Weight varies 10.70-10.90 grams.

Date	Mintage	Good	VG	F	VF	XF
AHxxxx//13	—	235	265	310	375	450
AHxxxx//15	—	235	265	310	375	450
AHxxxx//17	—	235	265	310	375	450
AHxxxx//21	—	235	265	310	375	450

Mint: Tatta
KM# 438.24 MOHUR
Gold **Note:** Weight varies 10.70-10.90 grams.

Date	Mintage	Good	VG	F	VF	XF
AH1135//4	—	235	265	310	375	450

Mint: Ujjain
KM# 438.25 MOHUR
Gold **Obv:** Inscription **Rev. Inscription:** Dar-ul-Fath **Note:** Weight varies 10.70-10.90 grams.

Date	Mintage	Good	VG	F	VF	XF
AHxxxx//20	—	235	265	310	375	450
AHxxxx//24	—	235	265	310	375	450

Mint: Akbarabad
KM# 439.1 MOHUR
Gold **Obv. Inscription:** Sahib Qiran Sani **Rev. Inscription:** Mustagir-ul-Khilifat **Note:** Weight varies 10.70-10.90 grams.

Date	Mintage	Good	VG	F	VF	XF
AHxxxx//2	—	—	235	265	325	425

Mint: Aurangabad
KM# 439.2 MOHUR
Gold **Obv:** Inscription **Rev:** Inscription **Note:** Weight varies 10.70-10.90 grams.

Date	Mintage	Good	VG	F	VF	XF
AHxxxx//8	—	235	265	310	375	450
AHxxxx//12	—	235	265	310	375	450

Mint: Farrukhabad
KM# 439.3 MOHUR
Gold **Note:** Weight varies 10.70-10.90 grams.

Date	Mintage	Good	VG	F	VF	XF
AH1155//25	—	—	235	265	325	425

Mint: Shahjahanabad
KM# 439.4 MOHUR
Gold **Obv:** Inscription **Rev. Inscription:** Dar-ul-Khilifat **Note:** Weight varies 10.70-10.90 grams.

Date	Mintage	Good	VG	F	VF	XF
AH1133//3	—	235	265	310	375	450
AH1134//3	—	235	265	310	375	450
AH1134//4	—	235	265	310	375	450
AH1135//4	—	235	265	310	375	450
AH1135//5	—	235	265	310	375	450
AH1136//5	—	235	265	310	375	450
AH1136//6	—	235	265	310	375	450
AH1137//6	—	235	265	310	375	450
AH1137//7	—	235	265	310	375	450
AH1138//7	—	235	265	310	375	450
AH1138//8	—	235	265	310	375	450
AH1139//8	—	235	265	310	375	450
AH1139//9	—	235	265	310	375	450
AH1140//9	—	235	265	310	375	450
AH1140//10	—	235	265	310	375	450
AH1141//10	—	235	265	310	375	450
AH1141//11	—	235	265	310	375	450
AH1142//11	—	235	265	310	375	450
AH1142//12	—	235	265	310	375	450
AH1143//12	—	235	265	310	375	450
AH1143//13	—	235	265	310	375	450
AH1144//13	—	235	265	310	375	450
AH1144//14	—	235	265	310	375	450
AH1145//14	—	235	265	310	375	450
AH1145//15	—	235	265	310	375	450
AH1146//15	—	235	265	310	375	450
AH1146//16	—	235	265	310	375	450
AH1147//16	—	235	265	310	375	450
AH1147//17	—	235	265	310	375	450
AH1148//17	—	235	265	310	375	450
AH1148//18	—	235	265	310	375	450
AH1149//18	—	235	265	310	375	450
AH1149//19	—	235	265	310	375	450
AH1150//19	—	235	265	310	375	450
AH1150//20	—	235	265	310	375	450
AH1151//20	—	235	265	310	375	450
AH1151//21	—	235	265	310	375	450
AH1152//21	—	235	265	310	375	450
AH1152//22	—	235	265	310	375	450
AH1153//22	—	235	265	310	375	450
AH1153//23	—	235	265	310	375	450
AH115x//25	—	235	265	310	375	450
AH1156//26	—	235	265	310	375	450
AH115x//29	—	235	265	310	375	450
AH11xx//30	—	235	265	310	375	450

Mint: Sind
KM# 439.5 MOHUR
Gold **Note:** Weight varies 10.70-10.90 grams.

Date	Mintage	Good	VG	F	VF	XF
AHxxxx//12 Rare	—	—	—	—	—	—

Mint: Kashmir
KM# A440.1 MOHUR
Gold **Obv. Inscription:** Inscription is arranged in toughra **Rev. Inscription:** Inscription with small triple circle and 4 foliated marginal areas **Note:** Prev. KM#439A.1. Weight varies 10.70-10.90 grams.

Date	Mintage	Good	VG	F	VF	XF
AH1151//21 Rare	—	—	—	—	—	—
AH1154//24 Rare	—	—	—	—	—	—

Mint: Guti
KM# D440.1 1/2 PAGODA
1.3500 g., Gold **Note:**

Date	Mintage	Good	VG	F	VF	XF
AH1146//x Rare	—	—	—	—	—	—

Mint: Balapur
KM# C440.2 FANAM
Gold **Note:** Weight varies 0.33-0.40 grams.

Date	Mintage	Good	VG	F	VF	XF
ND//x	—	—	—	—	—	—

Mint: Kurpa
KM# C440.1 FANAM
Gold **Note:** Weight varies 0.33-0.40 grams.

Date	Mintage	Good	VG	F	VF	XF
ND//x	—	—	—	—	—	—

Mint: Shahjahanabad
KM# B440.1 NAZARANA MOHUR
Gold **Obv:** Inscription **Rev. Legend:** Dar-ul-Khilifat **Note:** Weight varies 10.70-10.90 grams.

Date	Mintage	Good	VG	F	VF	XF
AH1142//11 Rare	—	—	—	—	—	—
AH1158//27 Rare	—	—	—	—	—	—
AH1160//29 Rare	—	—	—	—	—	—

Mint: Ganjikot
KM# E440.3 PAGODA
1.3500 g., Gold **Note:**

Date	Mintage	Good	VG	F	VF	XF
AH1153//xx Rare	—	—	—	—	—	—

Mint: Guti
KM# E440.2 PAGODA
Gold **Note:** Weight varies 2.65-2.75 grams.

Date	Mintage	Good	VG	F	VF	XF
AH1168//x (sic) Rare	—	—	—	—	—	—

Mint: Imtiyazgarh
KM# E440.1 PAGODA
Gold **Note:** Weight varies 2.65-2.75 grams.

Date	Mintage	Good	VG	F	VF	XF
ND Rare	—	—	—	—	—	—
AH11xx//1 (Ahad) Rare	—	—	—	—	—	—
AH11xx//2 Rare	—	—	—	—	—	—
AH11xx//3 Rare	—	—	—	—	—	—
AH11xx//8 Rare	—	—	—	—	—	—
AH11xx//12 Rare	—	—	—	—	—	—
AH1161//31 Rare	—	—	—	—	—	—

Mint: Mumbai
KM# 436.45 RUPEE
Silver **Obv:** Inscription **Rev:** Inscription **Note:** Weight varies 11.00-11.60 grams.

Date	Mintage	Good	VG	F	VF	XF
AHxxxx//9	—	—	—	—	—	—
AHxxxx//14	—	—	—	—	—	—
AH1148//18	—	—	—	—	—	—

Mint: Shahjahanabad
KM# B438.2 NAZARANA RUPEE
Silver **Note:** Weight varies 11.00-11.60 grams.

Date	Mintage	Good	VG	F	VF	XF
AH1135//5	—	—	—	—	—	—
AH1158//27	—	—	—	—	—	—

Muhammad Ibrahim
In Delhi, AH1132-1133 / 1720AD
HAMMERED COINAGE

Mint: Shahjahanabad
KM# 426.1 RUPEE
11.4440 g., Silver **Obv:** Inscription **Rev. Inscription:** Dar-ul-Khilafat **Note:** Weight varies 11.00-11.60 grams.

Date	Mintage	Good	VG	F	VF	XF
AH1132//1 (Ahad)	—	—	250	420	500	600
AH1133//1 (Ahad)	—	—	250	420	500	600

Mint: Shahjahanabad
KM# 428.1 MOHUR
Gold **Obv:** Inscription **Rev. Legend:** Dar-ul-Khilifat **Note:** Weight varies 10.60-10.90 grams. Type 428.

Date	Mintage	Good	VG	F	VF	XF
AH1132//1 (Ahad)	—	—	275	500	850	1,200

Ahmad Shah Bahadur
AH1161-1167 / 1748-1754AD
HAMMERED COINAGE

Mint: Macchlipattan
KM# A440 1/2 DAM
6.6000 g., Copper **Note:**

Date	Mintage	Good	VG	F	VF	XF
AH116x	—	—	—	—	—	85.00

Mint: Lahore
KM# 440.1 DAM
Copper **Note:** Weight varies 12.30-13.60 grams.

Date	Mintage	Good	VG	F	VF	XF
AH1161//x Rare	—	—	—	—	—	—

Mint: Macchlipattan
KM# 440.3 DAM
Copper **Note:** Weight varies 19.70-20.20 grams.

Date	Mintage	Good	VG	F	VF	XF
AH116x//4	—	—	—	—	—	—
AH1166//x	—	—	—	—	—	—

Mint: Peshawar
KM# 440.2 DAM
Copper **Note:** Weight varies 19.70-20.20 grams.

Date	Mintage	Good	VG	F	VF	XF
AH1164//4 Rare	—	—	—	—	—	—

Mint: Burhanpur
KM# 441.1 1/16 RUPEE
Silver **Note:** Weight varies 0.68-0.72 grams.

Date	Mintage	Good	VG	F	VF	XF
AH1162//2 Rare	—	—	—	—	—	—

Mint: Lahore
KM# 442.1 1/8 RUPEE
1.4300 g., Silver **Obv:** Inscription **Rev. Inscription:** Dar-us-Sultanat **Note:** Weight varies 1.38-1.45 grams.

Date	Mintage	Good	VG	F	VF	XF
AHxxxx//3 Rare	—	—	—	—	—	—

Mint: Murshidabad
KM# 443.1 1/4 RUPEE
Silver **Note:** Weight varies 2.75-2.90 grams.

Date	Mintage	Good	VG	F	VF	XF
AHxxxx//5	—	—	—	—	—	—

Mint: Azimabad
KM# 444.5 1/2 RUPEE
Silver **Note:** Weight varies 5.50-5.80 grams.

Date	Mintage	Good	VG	F	VF	XF
AH1166//6	—	—	—	—	—	—

Mint: Itawa
KM# 444.6 1/2 RUPEE
Silver **Note:** Weight varies 5.50-5.80 grams.

Date	Mintage	Good	VG	F	VF	XF
AHxxxx//4	—	—	—	—	—	—

Mint: Muhammadabad Banaras
KM# 444.1 1/2 RUPEE
Silver **Note:** Weight varies 5.50-5.80 grams.

Date	Mintage	Good	VG	F	VF	XF
AH1165//5	—	—	21.00	42.00	70.00	100

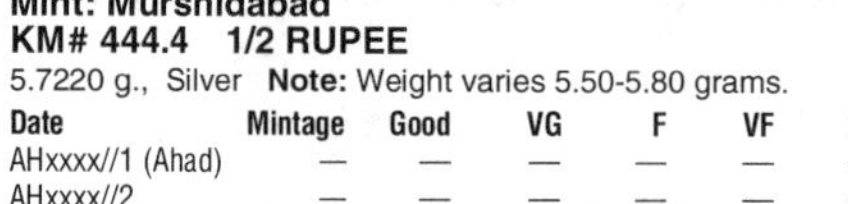

Mint: Murshidabad
KM# 444.4 1/2 RUPEE
5.7220 g., Silver **Note:** Weight varies 5.50-5.80 grams.

Date	Mintage	Good	VG	F	VF	XF
AHxxxx//1 (Ahad)	—	—	—	—	—	—
AHxxxx//2	—	—	—	—	—	—

Mint: Shahjahanabad
KM# 444.2 1/2 RUPEE
Silver **Obv:** Inscription **Rev. Inscription:** Dar-ul-Khilafat **Note:** Weight varies 5.50-5.80 grams.

Date	Mintage	Good	VG	F	VF	XF
AH1164//4	—	18.00	42.50	85.00	140	200
AH1165//4	—	18.00	42.50	85.00	140	200
AH1165//5	—	18.00	42.50	85.00	140	200

Mint: Surat
KM# 444.3 1/2 RUPEE
Silver **Note:** Weight varies 5.50-5.80 grams.

Date	Mintage	Good	VG	F	VF	XF
AHxxxx//1 (Ahad)	—	8.00	21.00	42.00	70.00	100

Mint: Ahmadabad
KM# 446.18 RUPEE
Silver **Obv. Inscription:** Ahmad Shah, Emperor **Rev:** Inscription **Note:** Weight varies 11.00-11.60 grams.

Date	Mintage	Good	VG	F	VF	XF
AH1162//1 (Ahad)	—	6.00	12.50	25.00	42.00	60.00
AH11xx//2	—	6.00	12.50	25.00	42.00	60.00
AH11xx//3	—	6.00	12.50	25.00	42.00	60.00
AH1165//4	—	6.00	12.50	25.00	42.00	60.00

Mint: Ajmir
KM# 446.1 RUPEE
Silver **Obv:** Inscription **Rev. Inscription:** Dar-ul-Khair **Note:** Weight varies 11.00-11.60 grams.

Date	Mintage	Good	VG	F	VF	XF
AH1161//1 (Ahad)	—	5.00	7.00	10.00	16.50	25.00
AH1162//1 (Ahad)	—	5.00	7.00	10.00	16.50	25.00
AH1162//2	—	5.00	7.00	10.00	16.50	25.00
AH1163//2	—	5.00	7.00	10.00	16.50	25.00
AH1163//3	—	5.00	7.00	10.00	16.50	25.00
AH1164//3	—	5.00	7.00	10.00	16.50	25.00
AH1164//4	—	5.00	7.00	10.00	16.50	25.00
AH116x//5	—	5.00	7.00	10.00	16.50	25.00
AH116x//6	—	5.00	7.00	10.00	16.50	25.00
AH1167//7	—	5.00	7.00	10.00	16.50	25.00

Mint: Akbarabad
KM# 446.2 RUPEE
Silver **Obv:** Inscription **Rev. Inscription:** Mustagir-ul-Khilafat **Note:** Weight varies 11.00-11.60 grams.

Date	Mintage	Good	VG	F	VF	XF
AH116x//1 (Ahad)	—	5.00	7.00	10.00	16.50	25.00
AH116x//2	—	5.00	7.00	10.00	16.50	25.00
AH1163//3	—	5.00	7.00	10.00	16.50	25.00
AH1164//3	—	5.00	7.00	10.00	16.50	25.00
AH1164//4	—	5.00	7.00	10.00	16.50	25.00
AH1165//4	—	5.00	7.00	10.00	16.50	25.00
AH1165//5	—	5.00	7.00	10.00	16.50	25.00
AH1166//5	—	5.00	7.00	10.00	16.50	25.00
AH1166//6	—	5.00	7.00	10.00	16.50	25.00
AH1167//6	—	5.00	7.00	10.00	16.50	25.00
AH1167//7	—	5.00	7.00	10.00	16.50	25.00

Mint: Akbarnagar
KM# 446.3 RUPEE
Silver **Note:** Weight varies 11.00-11.60 grams.

Date	Mintage	Good	VG	F	VF	XF
AH1163//3	—	5.00	7.50	15.00	25.00	35.00
AHxxxx//4	—	5.00	7.50	15.00	25.00	35.00
AH1165//5	—	5.00	7.50	15.00	25.00	35.00

Mint: Allahabad
KM# 446.4 RUPEE
Silver **Note:** Weight varies 11.00-11.60 grams.

Date	Mintage	Good	VG	F	VF	XF
AH1161//1 (Ahad)	—	5.00	7.00	13.00	22.00	32.00
AH1162//1 (Ahad)	—	5.00	7.00	13.00	22.00	32.00
AH1162//2	—	5.00	7.00	13.00	22.00	32.00
AH1163//2	—	5.00	7.00	13.00	22.00	32.00
AH1163//3	—	5.00	7.00	13.00	22.00	32.00
AH1164//3	—	5.00	7.00	13.00	22.00	32.00

Date	Mintage	Good	VG	F	VF	XF
AH1164//4	—	5.00	7.00	13.00	22.00	32.00
AH1165//4	—	5.00	7.00	13.00	22.00	32.00
AH1165//5	—	5.00	7.00	13.00	22.00	32.00
AH1166//5	—	5.00	7.00	13.00	22.00	32.00
AH1166//6	—	5.00	7.00	13.00	22.00	32.00

Mint: Aurangnagar
KM# 446.19 RUPEE
Silver **Note:** Weight varies 11.00-11.60 grams.

Date	Mintage	Good	VG	F	VF	XF
AH1161//1 (Ahad)	—	5.00	8.00	16.00	28.00	40.00

Mint: Azimabad
KM# 446.5 RUPEE
Silver **Note:** Weight varies 11.00-11.60 grams.

Date	Mintage	Good	VG	F	VF	XF
AH1161//1 (Ahad)	—	5.00	7.00	13.00	22.00	32.00
AH1162//1 (Ahad)	—	5.00	7.00	13.00	22.00	32.00
AH1162//2	—	5.00	7.00	13.00	22.00	32.00
AH1163//2	—	5.00	7.00	13.00	22.00	32.00
AH116x//4	—	5.00	7.00	13.00	22.00	32.00
AH1165//5	—	5.00	7.00	13.00	22.00	32.00
AH1167//7	—	5.00	7.00	13.00	22.00	32.00

Mint: Balwantnagar
KM# 446.20 RUPEE
Silver **Note:** Weight varies 11.00-11.60 grams.

Date	Mintage	Good	VG	F	VF	XF
AH116x//1 (Ahad)	—	5.00	8.00	16.00	28.00	40.00
AH116x//2	—	5.00	8.00	16.00	28.00	40.00
AH116x//3	—	5.00	8.00	16.00	28.00	40.00
AH1164//4	—	5.00	8.00	16.00	28.00	40.00
AH11xx//5	—	5.00	8.00	16.00	28.00	40.00
AH11xx//6	—	5.00	8.00	16.00	28.00	40.00
AH11XX//7	—	5.00	8.00	16.00	28.00	40.00

Mint: Bareli
KM# 446.21 RUPEE
Silver **Note:** Weight varies 11.00-11.60 grams.

Date	Mintage	Good	VG	F	VF	XF
AH1161//1 (Ahad)	—	5.00	8.00	16.00	28.00	40.00
AH1162//1 (Ahad)	—	5.00	8.00	16.00	28.00	40.00
AH1162//2	—	5.00	8.00	16.00	28.00	40.00
AH1163//2	—	5.00	8.00	16.00	28.00	40.00
AH1163//3	—	5.00	8.00	16.00	28.00	40.00
AH1164//3	—	5.00	8.00	16.00	28.00	40.00
AH1164//4	—	5.00	8.00	16.00	28.00	40.00
AH1165//4	—	5.00	8.00	16.00	28.00	40.00
AH1165//5	—	5.00	8.00	16.00	28.00	40.00
AH1166//5	—	5.00	8.00	16.00	28.00	40.00
AH1166//6	—	5.00	8.00	16.00	28.00	40.00
AH1167//6	—	5.00	8.00	16.00	28.00	40.00

Mint: Bhakkar
KM# 446.7 RUPEE
Silver **Note:** Weight varies 11.00-11.60 grams.

Date	Mintage	Good	VG	F	VF	XF
AH1161//1 (Ahad)	—	5.00	9.00	18.00	30.00	45.00
AH1162//2	—	5.00	9.00	18.00	30.00	45.00

Mint: Broach
KM# 446.40 RUPEE
Silver **Obv:** Inscription **Rev:** Inscription **Note:** Weight varies 11.00-11.60 grams.

Date	Mintage	Good	VG	F	VF	XF
AH1167//x	—	—	—	—	—	—

Mint: Burhanpur
KM# 446.22 RUPEE
Silver **Note:** Weight varies 11.00-11.60 grams.

Date	Mintage	Good	VG	F	VF	XF
AH1161//1 (Ahad)	—	5.00	8.00	16.00	28.00	40.00
AH1162//1 (Ahad)	—	5.00	8.00	16.00	28.00	40.00

Date	Mintage	Good	VG	F	VF	XF
AH1162//2	—	5.00	8.00	16.00	28.00	40.00
AH1163//2	—	5.00	8.00	16.00	28.00	40.00
AH1163//3	—	5.00	8.00	16.00	28.00	40.00
AH1164//3	—	5.00	8.00	16.00	28.00	40.00
AH1164//4	—	5.00	8.00	16.00	28.00	40.00
AH1165//4	—	5.00	8.00	16.00	28.00	40.00
AH1165//5	—	5.00	8.00	16.00	28.00	40.00
AH1166//5	—	5.00	8.00	16.00	28.00	40.00
AH1166//6	—	5.00	8.00	16.00	28.00	40.00
AH1167//6	—	5.00	8.00	16.00	28.00	40.00
AH1167//7	—	5.00	8.00	16.00	28.00	40.00

Mint: Cuttack
KM# 446.38 RUPEE

Silver **Note:** Weight varies 11.00-11.60 grams.

Date	Mintage	Good	VG	F	VF	XF
AHxxxx//1 (Ahad)	—	—	—	—	—	—
AHxxxx//2	—	—	—	—	—	—
AHxxxx//3	—	—	—	—	—	—
AHxxxx//4	—	—	—	—	—	—
AHxxxx//5	—	—	—	—	—	—
AHxxxx//6	—	—	—	—	—	—
AHxxxx//7	—	—	—	—	—	—

Mint: Dera
KM# 446.8 RUPEE

Silver **Obv:** Inscription, date **Rev:** Inscription **Note:** Weight varies 11.00-11.60 grams.

Date	Mintage	Good	VG	F	VF	XF
AH1162//2	—	6.00	15.00	28.00	45.00	65.00
AH1163//2	—	6.00	15.00	28.00	45.00	65.00
AH1163//3	—	6.00	15.00	28.00	45.00	65.00
AH116x//5	—	6.00	15.00	28.00	45.00	65.00
AH1164//x	—	6.00	15.00	28.00	45.00	65.00

Mint: Derajat
KM# 446.9 RUPEE

Silver **Note:** Weight varies 11.00-11.60 grams.

Date	Mintage	Good	VG	F	VF	XF
ND//x Rare	—	—	—	—	—	—

Mint: Farrukhabad
KM# 446.23 RUPEE

Silver **Obv:** Inscription, date **Rev:** Inscription **Note:** Weight varies 11.00-11.60 grams.

Date	Mintage	Good	VG	F	VF	XF
AH1161//1 (Ahad)	—	6.00	13.50	27.50	45.00	65.00
AH1162//1 (Ahad)	—	6.00	13.50	27.50	45.00	65.00
AH1162//2	—	6.00	13.50	27.50	45.00	65.00
AH1163//2	—	6.00	13.50	27.50	45.00	65.00
AH1165//5	—	6.00	13.50	27.50	45.00	65.00
AH1166//5	—	6.00	13.50	27.50	45.00	65.00
AH1166//6	—	6.00	13.50	27.50	45.00	65.00
AH1167//6	—	6.00	13.50	27.50	45.00	65.00
AH1167//7	—	6.00	13.50	27.50	45.00	65.00

Mint: Gwalior
KM# 446.24 RUPEE

Silver **Obv:** Inscription **Rev:** Inscription **Note:** Weight varies 11.00-11.60 grams.

Date	Mintage	Good	VG	F	VF	XF
AH11xx//2	—	5.00	9.00	18.00	30.00	45.00
AH1163//3	—	5.00	9.00	18.00	30.00	45.00
AH11xx//4	—	5.00	9.00	18.00	30.00	45.00
AH116x//5	—	5.00	9.00	18.00	30.00	45.00
AH1167//7	—	5.00	9.00	18.00	30.00	45.00

Mint: Islamabad
KM# 446.25 RUPEE

Silver **Obv:** Inscription **Rev:** Inscription **Note:** Weight varies 11.00-11.60 grams.

Date	Mintage	Good	VG	F	VF	XF
AH1162//2	—	5.00	8.00	16.00	28.00	40.00
AH116x//3	—	5.00	8.00	16.00	28.00	40.00
AH1166//6	—	5.00	8.00	16.00	28.00	40.00

Mint: Itawa
KM# 446.10 RUPEE

Silver **Note:** Weight varies 11.00-11.60 grams.

Date	Mintage	Good	VG	F	VF	XF
AH1163//2	—	5.00	7.00	11.00	18.00	26.00
AH1163//3	—	5.00	7.00	11.00	18.00	26.00
AH116x//5	—	5.00	7.00	11.00	18.00	26.00
AH1166//6	—	5.00	7.00	11.00	18.00	26.00

Mint: Jabbalpore
KM# 446.37 RUPEE

Silver **Note:** Weight varies 11.00-11.60 grams.

Date	Mintage	Good	VG	F	VF	XF
AHxxxx//5	—	—	—	—	—	—

Mint: Jahangirnagar
KM# 446.11 RUPEE

Silver **Note:** Weight varies 11.00-11.60 grams.

Date	Mintage	Good	VG	F	VF	XF
AHxxxx//1 (Ahad)	—	5.00	9.00	18.00	30.00	45.00
AHxxxx//5	—	5.00	9.00	18.00	30.00	45.00
AHxxxx//6	—	5.00	9.00	18.00	30.00	45.00
AHxxxx//7	—	5.00	9.00	18.00	30.00	45.00

Mint: Kalpi
KM# 446.41 RUPEE

Silver **Note:** Weight varies 11.00-11.60 grams.

Date	Mintage	Good	VG	F	VF	XF
AH1163//3	—	6.00	15.00	28.00	45.00	65.00
AHxxxx//4	—	6.00	15.00	28.00	45.00	65.00

Mint: Katak
KM# 446.29 RUPEE

Silver **Note:** Weight varies 11.00-11.60 grams.

Date	Mintage	Good	VG	F	VF	XF
AHxxxx//3	—	5.00	8.00	16.00	28.00	40.00
AHxxxx//5	—	5.00	8.00	16.00	28.00	40.00
AHxxxx//7	—	5.00	8.00	16.00	28.00	40.00
AHxxxx//57 (sic)	—	5.00	8.00	16.00	28.00	40.00

Mint: Khambayat
KM# 446.30 RUPEE

Silver **Obv:** Inscription **Rev:** Inscription **Note:** Weight varies 11.00-11.60 grams.

Date	Mintage	Good	VG	F	VF	XF
AHxxxx//1 (Ahad)	—	8.00	20.00	40.00	65.00	95.00
AHxxxx//2	—	8.00	20.00	40.00	65.00	95.00
AH1163//3	—	8.00	20.00	40.00	65.00	95.00
AHxxxx//4	—	8.00	20.00	40.00	65.00	95.00
AH1164//5	—	8.00	20.00	40.00	65.00	95.00

Mint: Kora
KM# 446.12 RUPEE

Silver **Obv:** Inscription **Rev:** Inscription **Note:** Weight varies 11.00-11.60 grams.

Date	Mintage	Good	VG	F	VF	XF
AH1161//1 (Ahad)	—	5.00	7.50	15.00	25.00	37.50
AH116x//3	—	5.00	7.50	15.00	25.00	37.50
AH1164//4	—	5.00	7.50	15.00	25.00	37.50
AH1166//6	—	5.00	7.50	15.00	25.00	37.50
AHxxxx//8 (sic)	—	5.00	7.50	15.00	25.00	37.50

Mint: Lahore
KM# 446.13 RUPEE

Silver **Obv:** Inscription **Rev. Inscription:** Dar-us-Sultanat **Note:** Weight varies 11.00-11.60 grams.

Date	Mintage	Good	VG	F	VF	XF
AH1161//1	—	5.00	7.00	11.00	18.00	26.00
AH1162//1 (Ahad)	—	5.00	7.00	11.00	18.00	26.00
AH1162//2	—	5.00	7.00	11.00	18.00	26.00
AH1163//2	—	5.00	7.00	11.00	18.00	26.00
AH1163//3	—	5.00	7.00	11.00	18.00	26.00
AH1164//3	—	5.00	7.00	11.00	18.00	26.00
AH1164//4	—	5.00	7.00	11.00	18.00	26.00
AH1165//4	—	5.00	7.00	11.00	18.00	26.00
AH1165//5	—	5.00	7.00	11.00	18.00	26.00
AH1166//5	—	5.00	7.00	11.00	18.00	26.00
AH1166//6	—	5.00	7.00	11.00	18.00	26.00
AH1167//6	—	5.00	7.00	11.00	18.00	26.00
AH1167//7	—	5.00	7.00	11.00	18.00	26.00

Mint: Macchlipattan
KM# 446.31 RUPEE

Silver **Note:** Weight varies 11.00-11.60 grams.

Date	Mintage	Good	VG	F	VF	XF
AHxxxx//3	—	5.00	8.00	16.00	28.00	40.00
AH1164//4	—	5.00	8.00	16.00	28.00	40.00
AH1167//7	—	5.00	8.00	16.00	28.00	40.00

Mint: Maha Indrapur
KM# 446.43 RUPEE

Silver **Note:** Weight varies 11.00-11.60 grams.

Date	Mintage	Good	VG	F	VF	XF
AH1167//7	—	—	—	—	—	—

Mint: Muhammadabad Banaras
KM# 446.6 RUPEE

Silver **Obv:** Inscription **Rev:** Inscription **Note:** Weight varies 11.00-11.60 grams.

Date	Mintage	Good	VG	F	VF	XF
AH1161//1 (Ahad)	—	5.00	7.00	13.00	22.00	32.00
AH1162//1 (Ahad)	—	5.00	7.00	13.00	22.00	32.00
AH1162//2	—	5.00	7.00	13.00	22.00	32.00
AH1163//2	—	5.00	7.00	13.00	22.00	32.00
AH(11)63//3	—	5.00	7.00	13.00	22.00	32.00
AH1164//3	—	5.00	7.00	13.00	22.00	32.00
AH1164//4	—	5.00	7.00	13.00	22.00	32.00
AH1165//4	—	5.00	7.00	13.00	22.00	32.00
AH1165//5	—	5.00	7.00	13.00	22.00	32.00
AH1166//5	—	5.00	7.00	13.00	22.00	32.00
AH1166//6	—	5.00	7.00	13.00	22.00	32.00
AH1167//6	—	5.00	7.00	13.00	22.00	32.00
AH1167//7	—	5.00	7.00	13.00	22.00	32.00

Mint: Multan
KM# 446.14 RUPEE

Silver **Obv:** Inscription, date **Rev:** Inscription **Note:** Weight varies 11.00-11.60 grams.

Date	Mintage	Good	VG	F	VF	XF
AH1161//1 (Ahad)	—	5.00	8.00	15.00	25.00	35.00
AH1162//1 (Ahad)	—	5.00	8.00	15.00	25.00	35.00
AH1162//2	—	5.00	8.00	15.00	25.00	35.00
AH1163//2	—	5.00	8.00	15.00	25.00	35.00
AH1163//3	—	5.00	8.00	15.00	25.00	35.00
AH1164//3	—	5.00	8.00	15.00	25.00	35.00
AH1164//4	—	5.00	8.00	15.00	25.00	35.00
AH1165//4	—	5.00	8.00	15.00	25.00	35.00
AH1165//5	—	5.00	8.00	15.00	25.00	35.00

Mint: Muradabad
KM# 446.32 RUPEE

Silver **Note:** Weight varies 11.00-11.60 grams.

Date	Mintage	Good	VG	F	VF	XF
AH1167//6 Rare	—	—	—	—	—	—
AH1167//7 Rare	—	—	—	—	—	—

Mint: Murshidabad
KM# 446.15 RUPEE
Silver **Obv:** Inscription **Rev:** Inscription **Note:** Weight varies 11.00-11.60 grams.

Date	Mintage	Good	VG	F	VF	XF
AH1161//1 (Ahad)	—	5.00	9.00	18.00	30.00	45.00
AH1162//1 (Ahad)	—	5.00	9.00	18.00	30.00	45.00
AH1162//2	—	5.00	9.00	18.00	30.00	45.00
AH1163//2	—	5.00	9.00	18.00	30.00	45.00
AH1163//3	—	5.00	9.00	18.00	30.00	45.00
AH1164//3	—	5.00	9.00	18.00	30.00	45.00
AH1164//4	—	5.00	9.00	18.00	30.00	45.00
AH1165//4	—	5.00	9.00	18.00	30.00	45.00
AH1165//5	—	5.00	9.00	18.00	30.00	45.00
AH1166//5	—	5.00	9.00	18.00	30.00	45.00
AH1166//6	—	5.00	9.00	18.00	30.00	45.00
AH1167//6	—	5.00	9.00	18.00	30.00	45.00

Mint: Nagor
KM# 446.33 RUPEE
Silver **Obv:** Inscription **Rev. Inscription:** Dar-ul-Barakat **Note:** Weight varies 11.00-11.60 grams.

Date	Mintage	Good	VG	F	VF	XF
AH1163//x	—	5.00	8.00	16.00	28.00	40.00
AH116x//4	—	5.00	8.00	16.00	28.00	40.00

Mint: Narwar
KM# 446.39 RUPEE
Silver **Note:** Weight varies 11.00-11.60 grams.

Date	Mintage	Good	VG	F	VF	XF
AH1161//1 (Ahad) Rare	—	—	—	—	—	—
AH1162//2 Rare	—	—	—	—	—	—
AH1163//3 Rare	—	—	—	—	—	—
AH1164//3 Rare	—	—	—	—	—	—
AH1164//4 Rare	—	—	—	—	—	—
AH116x//5 Rare	—	—	—	—	—	—
AH1165//6 Rare	—	—	—	—	—	—

Mint: Sahrind
KM# 446.16 RUPEE
Silver **Note:** Weight varies 11.00-11.60 grams.

Date	Mintage	Good	VG	F	VF	XF
AH1161//1 (Ahad)	—	5.00	7.00	11.00	18.00	26.00
AH1162//1 (Ahad)	—	5.00	7.00	11.00	18.00	26.00
AH1162//2	—	5.00	7.00	11.00	18.00	26.00
AH1163//2	—	5.00	7.00	11.00	18.00	26.00
AH1163//3	—	5.00	7.00	11.00	18.00	26.00
AH1164//3	—	5.00	7.00	11.00	18.00	26.00
AH1164//4	—	5.00	7.00	11.00	18.00	26.00
AH1165//4	—	5.00	7.00	11.00	18.00	26.00
AH1165//5	—	5.00	7.00	11.00	18.00	26.00
AH1166//5	—	5.00	7.00	11.00	18.00	26.00
AH1166//6	—	5.00	7.00	11.00	18.00	26.00

Mint: Shahabad Qanauj
KM# 446.34 RUPEE
Silver **Note:** Weight varies 11.00-11.60 grams.

Date	Mintage	Good	VG	F	VF	XF
AH1163//3 Rare	—	—	—	—	—	—
AH1164//4 Rare	—	—	—	—	—	—
AH1165//5 Rare	—	—	—	—	—	—
AH1166//5 Rare	—	—	—	—	—	—
AH1167//6 Rare	—	—	—	—	—	—

Mint: Shahjahanabad
KM# 446.17 RUPEE
Silver **Obv:** Inscription **Rev. Inscription:** Dar-ul-Khilafat **Note:** Weight varies 11.00-11.60 grams.

Date	Mintage	Good	VG	F	VF	XF
AH1161//1 (Ahad)	—	5.00	7.00	11.00	18.00	26.00
AH1162//1 (Ahad)	—	5.00	7.00	11.00	18.00	26.00
AH1162//2	—	5.00	7.00	11.00	18.00	26.00
AH1163//2	—	5.00	7.00	11.00	18.00	26.00
AH1163//3	—	5.00	7.00	11.00	18.00	26.00
AH1164//3	—	5.00	7.00	11.00	18.00	26.00
AH1164//4	—	5.00	7.00	11.00	18.00	26.00
AH1165//4	—	5.00	7.00	11.00	18.00	26.00
AH1165//5	—	5.00	7.00	11.00	18.00	26.00
AH1166//5	—	5.00	7.00	11.00	18.00	26.00
AH1166//6	—	5.00	7.00	11.00	18.00	26.00
AH1167//6	—	5.00	7.00	11.00	18.00	26.00
AH1167//7	—	5.00	7.00	11.00	18.00	26.00

Mint: Sironj
KM# 446.35 RUPEE
Silver **Note:** Weight varies 11.00-11.60 grams.

Date	Mintage	Good	VG	F	VF	XF
AHxxxx//1 (Ahad)	—	10.00	25.00	45.00	75.00	125
AHxxxx//3	—	10.00	25.00	45.00	75.00	125

Mint: Surat
KM# 446.36 RUPEE
Silver **Obv:** Inscription **Rev:** Inscription **Note:** Weight varies 11.00-11.60 grams.

Date	Mintage	Good	VG	F	VF	XF
AHxxxx//1 (Ahad)	—	5.00	8.00	16.00	28.00	40.00

Mint: Tatta
KM# 446.42 RUPEE
11.4440 g., Silver **Note:**

Date	Mintage	Good	VG	F	VF	XF
ND(1748-1754)	—	—	—	—	—	—

Mint: Firoznagar
KM# 447.2 RUPEE
Silver **Obv:** Inscription **Rev:** Inscription **Note:** Weight varies 11.00-11.60 grams.

Date	Mintage	Good	VG	F	VF	XF
AH1162//2 Rare	—	—	—	—	—	—

Mint: Imtiyazgarh
KM# 447.3 RUPEE
Silver **Obv:** Inscription, date **Rev:** Inscription **Note:** Weight varies 11.00-11.60 grams.

Date	Mintage	Good	VG	F	VF	XF
NDxxxx//1 (Ahad) Rare	—	—	—	—	—	—

Mint: Kashmir
KM# 447.1 RUPEE
Silver **Obv. Inscription:** Ahmad Shah, Refuge of the World, with couplet **Rev:** Inscription **Note:** Weight varies 11.00-11.60 grams.

Date	Mintage	Good	VG	F	VF	XF
AH1161//1 (Ahad) Rare	—	—	—	—	—	—
AH1162//2 Rare	—	—	—	—	—	—
AH1163//2 Rare	—	—	—	—	—	—
AH1163//3 Rare	—	—	—	—	—	—
AH1164//3 Rare	—	—	—	—	—	—
AH116x//5 Rare	—	—	—	—	—	—
AH1166//6 Rare	—	—	—	—	—	—

Mint: Shahjahanabad
KM# 448.1 NAZARANA RUPEE
Silver **Obv:** Inscription **Rev. Inscription:** Dar-ul-Khilafat **Note:** Weight varies 11.00-11.60 grams.

Date	Mintage	Good	VG	F	VF	XF
AH1167//7 Rare	—	—	—	—	—	—

Mint: Akbarabad
KM# 449.1 MOHUR
Gold **Obv:** Inscription **Rev. Inscription:** Mustagir-ul-Khilafat **Note:** Weight varies 10.80-11.00 grams.

Date	Mintage	Good	VG	F	VF	XF
AHxxxx//2	—	235	265	310	375	450

Mint: Allahabad
KM# 449.2 MOHUR
Gold **Note:** Weight varies 10.80-11.00 grams.

Date	Mintage	Good	VG	F	VF	XF
AHxxxx//3	—	235	265	310	375	450

Mint: Azimabad
KM# 449.3 MOHUR
Gold **Note:** Weight varies 10.80-11.00 grams.

Date	Mintage	Good	VG	F	VF	XF
AH1166//5	—	235	265	310	375	450

Mint: Dera
KM# 449.5 MOHUR
Gold **Obv:** Inscription **Rev:** Inscription **Note:** Weight varies 10.80-11.00 grams.

Date	Mintage	Good	VG	F	VF	XF
AH1162//2 Rare	—	—	—	—	—	—

Mint: Derajat
KM# 449.6 MOHUR
Gold **Note:** Weight varies 10.80-11.00 grams.

Date	Mintage	Good	VG	F	VF	XF
AH1161//1 Rare	—	—	—	—	—	—

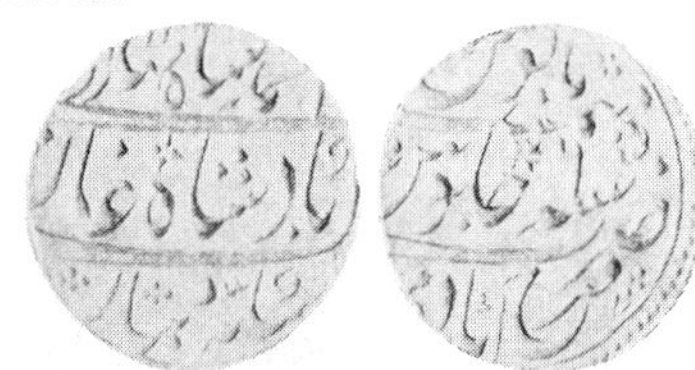

Mint: Farrukhabad
KM# 449.14 MOHUR
Gold **Obv:** Inscription **Rev:** Inscription **Note:** Weight varies 10.80-11.00 grams.

Date	Mintage	Good	VG	F	VF	XF
AH1166//6 Rare	—	—	—	—	—	—

Mint: Itawa
KM# 449.7 MOHUR
Gold **Note:** Weight varies 10.80-11.00 grams.

Date	Mintage	Good	VG	F	VF	XF
ND//x	—	235	265	310	375	450

Mint: Kora
KM# 449.15 MOHUR
Gold **Note:** Weight varies 10.80-11.00 grams.

Date	Mintage	Good	VG	F	VF	XF
AHxxxx//1	—	—	—	—	—	—

Mint: Lahore
KM# 449.8 MOHUR
Gold **Obv:** Inscription **Rev. Inscription:** Dar-us-Sultanat **Note:** Weight varies 10.80-11.00 grams.

Date	Mintage	Good	VG	F	VF	XF
AH1161//1 (Ahad) Rare	—	—	—	—	—	—
AH1165//5 Rare	—	—	—	—	—	—
AH1165//6 Rare	—	—	—	—	—	—
AH1166//5 Rare	—	—	—	—	—	—
AH1166//6 Rare	—	—	—	—	—	—
AH1167//6 Rare	—	—	—	—	—	—

Mint: Muhammadabad Banaras
KM# 449.4 MOHUR
Gold **Note:** Weight varies 10.80-11.00 grams.

Date	Mintage	Good	VG	F	VF	XF
AH1162//2	—	235	265	310	375	450
AH1166//6	—	235	265	310	375	450

Mint: Mujahidabad
KM# 449.9 MOHUR
Gold **Note:** Weight varies 10.80-11.00 grams.

Date	Mintage	Good	VG	F	VF	XF
AH1163//3 Rare	—	—	—	—	—	—

Mint: Multan
KM# 449.10 MOHUR
Gold **Obv:** Inscription **Rev:** Inscription **Note:** Weight varies 10.80-11.00 grams.

Date	Mintage	Good	VG	F	VF	XF
AH1161//1	—	235	275	325	425	550
AH1165//5	—	235	275	325	425	550

Mint: Sahrind
KM# 449.11 MOHUR
Gold **Obv:** Inscription **Rev:** Inscription **Note:** Weight varies 10.80-11.00 grams.

Date	Mintage	Good	VG	F	VF	XF
ND//x	—	235	265	310	375	450
AHxxxx//6	—	235	265	310	375	450

Mint: Shahjahanabad
KM# 449.12 MOHUR
Gold **Obv:** Inscription **Rev. Inscription:** Dar-ul-Khilafat **Note:** Weight varies 10.80-11.00 grams.

Date	Mintage	Good	VG	F	VF	XF
AH1161//1	—	235	265	310	375	450
AH1162//1	—	235	265	310	375	450
AH1162//2	—	235	265	310	375	450
AH1163//2	—	235	265	310	375	450
AH1163//3	—	235	265	310	375	450
AH1164//3	—	235	265	310	375	450
AH1164//4	—	235	265	310	375	450
AH1165//4	—	235	265	310	375	450
AH1165//5	—	235	265	310	375	450
AH1166//5	—	235	265	310	375	450
AH1166//6	—	235	265	310	375	450
AH1167//6	—	235	265	310	375	450
AH1167//7	—	235	265	310	375	450

Mint: Tatta
KM# 449.13 MOHUR
Gold **Note:** Weight varies 10.80-11.00 grams.

Date	Mintage	Good	VG	F	VF	XF
AHxxxx//1 (Ahad)	—	—	—	—	—	—

Mint: Karpa
KM# A450 2 MOHUR
Gold **Shape:** Square **Note:** Weight varies 21.60-22.00 grams. Prev. KM#449a.1.

Date	Mintage	Good	VG	F	VF	XF
AHxxxx//1 (Ahad) Rare	—	—	—	—	—	—

Mint: Karpa
KM# B450.1 FANAM
Gold **Note:** Weight varies: 0.33-0.40 grams. Prev. KM#449C.1.

Date	Mintage	Good	VG	F	VF	XF
ND//x	—	—	—	—	—	—

Mint: Imtiyazgarh
KM# C450.1 PAGODA
Gold **Note:** Weight varies 2.65-2.82 grams; Prev. KM#449B.1.

Date	Mintage	Good	VG	F	VF	XF
ND//x Rare	—	—	—	—	—	—

Mint: Karpa
KM# C450.2 PAGODA
Gold **Note:** Weight varies 2.65-2.82 grams. Prev. KM#449B.2.

Date	Mintage	Good	VG	F	VF	XF
AH11xx//x	—	—	—	—	—	—

Aziz-ud-din Alamgir II

AH1167-1173 / 1754-1759AD

HAMMERED COINAGE

Mint: Jodhpur
KM# 446.28 RUPEE
Silver **Obv:** Inscription **Rev. Inscription:** Dar-ul-Mansur **Note:** Weight varies 11.00-11.60 grams.

Date	Mintage	Good	VG	F	VF	XF
AHxxxx/ //4,5	—	5.00	8.00	16.00	28.00	40.00

Mint: Elichpur
KM# 450.3 DAM
17.6000 g., Copper **Obv:** Inscription **Rev:** Falus **Note:** Weight varies 19.70-20.20 grams. Nizam coin.

Date	Mintage	Good	VG	F	VF	XF
AH1167//x	—	—	—	—	—	—

Mint: Lahore
KM# 450.1 DAM
17.6000 g., Copper **Obv:** Inscription **Rev:** Inscription **Note:** Weight varies 19.70-20.20 grams.

Date	Mintage	Good	VG	F	VF	XF
AH1172//5	—	4.50	9.00	15.00	25.00	—
AH1172//6	—	4.50	9.00	15.00	25.00	—
AH117x//7 (sic)	—	4.50	9.00	15.00	25.00	—

Mint: Macchlipattan
KM# 450.2 DAM
17.6000 g., Copper **Note:** Weight varies 19.70-20.20 grams.

Date	Mintage	Good	VG	F	VF	XF
AH1168//1 (Ahad)	—	4.50	9.00	15.00	25.00	—

Mint: Najibadad
KM# 450.4 DAM
19.0000 g., Copper **Obv:** Inscription **Rev:** Inscription **Note:** Weight varies 19.70-20.20 grams.

Date	Mintage	Good	VG	F	VF	XF
AHxxxx//6	—	—	—	—	—	—

Mint: Akbarabad
KM# 451.2 DAM
Copper **Obv:** Falus **Rev. Inscription:** Mustagir-ul-Khilafat **Note:** Weight varies 11.60-13.60 grams.

Date	Mintage	Good	VG	F	VF	XF
AH1170//x	—	4.50	9.00	15.00	25.00	—

Mint: Elichpur
KM# 451.3 DAM
Copper **Note:** Weight varies 19.70-20.20 grams.

Date	Mintage	Good	VG	F	VF	XF
AH(11)69//4 (sic)	—	4.50	9.00	15.00	25.00	—
AH1170//x	—	4.50	9.00	15.00	25.00	—
AH1172//x	—	4.50	9.00	15.00	25.00	—

Mint: Haidarabad
KM# 451.4 DAM
13.8000 g., Copper **Note:** Weight varies 19.70-20.20 grams.

Date	Mintage	Good	VG	F	VF	XF
AH1167//1 (Ahad)	—	4.50	9.00	15.00	25.00	—

Mint: Shahjahanabad
KM# 451.1 DAM
12.2000 g., Copper **Note:** Weight varies 19.70-20.20 grams.

Date	Mintage	Good	VG	F	VF	XF
AH1168//1 (Ahad)	—	4.50	9.00	15.00	25.00	—
AH1168//2	—	4.50	9.00	15.00	25.00	—
AH1169//2	—	4.50	9.00	15.00	25.00	—
AH1169//3	—	4.50	9.00	15.00	25.00	—
AH1170//3	—	4.50	9.00	15.00	25.00	—
AH1170//4	—	4.50	9.00	15.00	25.00	—

Mint: Kashmir
KM# A452.1 1/16 RUPEE
Silver **Note:** Weight varies 0.68-0.72 grams.

Date	Mintage	Good	VG	F	VF	XF
AHxxxx//2 Rare	—	—	—	—	—	—

Mint: Shahjahanabad
KM# B452.1 1/8 RUPEE
Silver **Note:** Weight varies 1.38-1.45 grams.

Date	Mintage	Good	VG	F	VF	XF
AHxxxx//3 Rare	—	—	—	—	—	—

Mint: Macchlipattan
KM# 452.1 1/4 RUPEE
Silver **Obv:** Inscription, date **Rev:** Inscription **Note:** Weight varies 2.75-2.90 grams.

Date	Mintage	Good	VG	F	VF	XF
AH1169//1 (sic) Rare	—	—	—	—	—	—

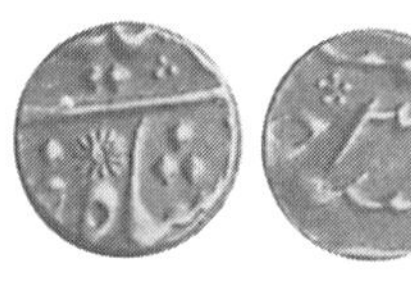

Mint: Murshidabad
KM# 452.2 1/4 RUPEE
Silver **Obv:** Inscription, sun **Rev:** Inscription, beaded flower **Note:** Weight varies 2.75-2.90 grams.

Date	Mintage	Good	VG	F	VF	XF
AHxxxx//2	—	—	—	—	—	—
AHxxxx//3 Rare	—	—	—	—	—	—

Mint: Azimabad
KM# 453.1 1/2 RUPEE
Silver **Obv. Inscription:** Badshah Alamgir **Rev:** Inscription, trident **Note:** Weight varies 5.50-5.80 grams.

Date	Mintage	Good	VG	F	VF	XF
AH1168//2	—	10.00	25.00	50.00	85.00	125
AH1169//3	—	10.00	25.00	50.00	85.00	125
AH11xx//4	—	10.00	25.00	50.00	85.00	125

Mint: Balwantnagar
KM# 453.4 1/2 RUPEE
Silver **Note:** Weight varies 5.50-5.80 grams.

Date	Mintage	Good	VG	F	VF	XF
AHxxxx//2	—	10.00	25.00	50.00	85.00	125

Mint: Muhammadabad Banaras
KM# 453.2 1/2 RUPEE
Silver **Note:** Weight varies 5.50-5.80 grams.

Date	Mintage	Good	VG	F	VF	XF
AHxxxx//5	—	10.00	25.00	50.00	85.00	125
AHxxxx/6	—	10.00	25.00	50.00	85.00	125

Mint: Surat
KM# 453.5 1/2 RUPEE
Silver **Note:** Weight varies 5.50-5.80 grams.

Date	Mintage	Good	VG	F	VF	XF
AHxxxx//2	—	10.00	25.00	50.00	85.00	125

Mint: Murshidabad
KM# 455.1 RUPEE
Silver **Obv:** Inscription within and outside of square **Rev:** Inscription within and outside of square **Note:** Weight varies 5.50-5.80 grams.

Date	Mintage	Good	VG	F	VF	XF
AH1168//2 Rare	—	—	—	—	—	—

Mint: Shahjahanabad
KM# 455.2 RUPEE

Silver **Obv:** Inscription within and outside of square **Rev. Inscription:** Dar-ul-Khilafat **Note:** Weight varies 11.00-11.60 grams.

Date	Mintage	Good	VG	F	VF	XF
AH1168//2	—	—	60.00	120	200	300

Mint: Shahjahanabad
KM# A456.1 NAZARANA RUPEE

Silver **Obv:** Inscription **Rev. Inscription:** Dar-ul-Khilafat **Note:** Weight varies 11.00-11.60 grams.

Date	Mintage	Good	VG	F	VF	XF
AH1168//2	—	—	—	—	—	—

Mint: Shahjahanabad
KM# 456.1 RUPEE

Silver **Obv. Inscription:** Muhammad Azizuddin Alamgir, Badshah Ghazi, May God Protect His Kingdom **Rev. Inscription:** Dar-ul-Khilafat **Note:** Weight varies 11.00-11.60 grams.

Date	Mintage	Good	VG	F	VF	XF
AH1168//2	—	5.00	10.00	20.00	35.00	60.00
AH1169//2	—	5.00	10.00	20.00	35.00	60.00
AH1169//3	—	5.00	10.00	20.00	35.00	60.00
AH1170//3	—	5.00	10.00	20.00	35.00	60.00

Mint: Shahjahanabad
KM# 457.1 RUPEE

Silver **Obv. Inscription:** Azizuddin Alamgir, Badshah Ghazi, coin like the sun and moon **Rev. Inscription:** Dar-ul-Khilafat **Note:** Weight varies 11.00-11.60 grams.

Date	Mintage	Good	VG	F	VF	XF
AH116x//2	—	5.00	9.00	18.00	30.00	45.00
AH1169//3	—	5.00	9.00	18.00	30.00	45.00
AH1170//3	—	5.00	9.00	18.00	30.00	45.00
AH1170//4	—	5.00	9.00	18.00	30.00	45.00
AH1171//4	—	5.00	9.00	18.00	30.00	45.00
AH1171//5	—	5.00	9.00	18.00	30.00	45.00
AH1172//5	—	5.00	9.00	18.00	30.00	45.00
AH1172//6	—	5.00	9.00	18.00	30.00	45.00
AH1173//6	—	5.00	9.00	18.00	30.00	45.00

Mint: Dilshadabad
KM# 458.2 RUPEE

Silver **Obv. Inscription:** Shah Jahan, Badshah Alamgir **Rev:** Inscription **Note:** Siraj ud-Doulah Nowab of Bengal captured Calcutta on June 20, 1756 and renamed it Alinagar. Weight varies 11.00-11.60 grams.

Date	Mintage	Good	VG	F	VF	XF
AH117x//x Rare	—	—	—	—	—	—

Mint: Shahjahanabad
KM# 458.1 RUPEE

Silver **Obv:** Inscription **Rev. Inscription:** Dar-ul-Khilafat **Note:** Weight varies 11.00-11.60 grams.

Date	Mintage	Good	VG	F	VF	XF
AHxxxx//4	—	8.00	20.00	32.50	45.00	70.00

Mint: Balwantnagar
KM# 459.2 RUPEE

Silver **Obv:** Titles "Sahib Qiran Azizuddin Alamgir" **Obv. Inscription:** Sahib Qiran Azizuddin Alamgir **Rev:** Inscription, beaded flower **Note:** Weight varies 11.00-11.60 grams.

Date	Mintage	Good	VG	F	VF	XF
AH1167//1 (Ahad)	—	5.00	8.00	16.00	28.00	40.00
AH1170//4	—	5.00	8.00	16.00	28.00	40.00
AH1171//5	—	5.00	8.00	16.00	28.00	40.00
AH1172//6	—	5.00	8.00	16.00	28.00	40.00

Mint: Muhammadabad Banaras
KM# 459.1 RUPEE

Silver **Note:** Weight varies 11.00-11.60 grams.

Date	Mintage	Good	VG	F	VF	XF
AH1167//1 (Ahad) Rare	—	—	—	—	—	—

Mint: Narwar
KM# 459.3 RUPEE

Silver **Note:** Weight varies 11.00-11.60 grams.

Date	Mintage	Good	VG	F	VF	XF
AH1167//1 (Ahad)	—	10.00	25.00	45.00	75.00	125

Mint: Sironj
KM# 459.4 RUPEE

Silver **Note:** Weight varies 11.00-11.60 grams.

Date	Mintage	Good	VG	F	VF	XF
AH1169//2	—	5.00	8.00	16.00	28.00	40.00

Mint: Ajmir
KM# 460.1 RUPEE

Silver **Obv:** Inscription **Rev. Inscription:** Dar-ul-Khair **Note:** Weight varies 11.00-11.60 grams.

Date	Mintage	Good	VG	F	VF	XF
AHxxxx//6	—	5.00	8.00	16.00	28.00	40.00

Mint: Akbarabad
KM# 460.2 RUPEE

Silver **Obv:** Inscription **Rev. Inscription:** Mustagir-ul-Khilafat **Note:** Weight varies 11.00-11.60 grams.

Date	Mintage	Good	VG	F	VF	XF
AH1167//1 (Ahad)	—	5.00	7.00	13.00	22.00	32.00
AH1168//1 (Ahad)	—	5.00	7.00	13.00	22.00	32.00
AH1168//2	—	5.00	7.00	13.00	22.00	32.00
AH1169//2	—	5.00	7.00	13.00	22.00	32.00
AH1169//3	—	5.00	7.00	13.00	22.00	32.00
AH1170//3	—	5.00	7.00	13.00	22.00	32.00
AH1170//4	—	5.00	7.00	13.00	22.00	32.00
AH1171//4	—	5.00	7.00	13.00	22.00	32.00
AH1171//5	—	5.00	7.00	13.00	22.00	32.00
AH1172//5	—	5.00	7.00	13.00	22.00	32.00
AH11xx//6	—	5.00	7.00	13.00	22.00	32.00

Mint: Akbarnagar
KM# 460.3 RUPEE

Silver **Note:** Weight varies 11.00-11.60 grams.

Date	Mintage	Good	VG	F	VF	XF
AH1167//1 (Ahad)	—	5.00	7.00	13.00	22.00	32.00

Mint: Alinagar
KM# 460.39 RUPEE

Silver **Obv:** Inscription **Rev:** Inscription **Note:** Siraj ud-Doulah Nowab of Bengal captured Calcutta on June 20, 1756 and renamed it Alinagar. Weight varies 11.00-11.60 grams.

Date	Mintage	Good	VG	F	VF	XF
AH1169//3 Rare	—	—	—	—	—	—

Mint: Allahabad
KM# 460.4 RUPEE

Silver **Note:** Weight varies 11.00-11.60 grams.

Date	Mintage	Good	VG	F	VF	XF
AH1168//1 (Ahad)	—	5.00	7.00	13.00	22.00	32.00
AH1168//2	—	5.00	7.00	13.00	22.00	32.00
AH1169//2	—	5.00	7.00	13.00	22.00	32.00
AH117x//4	—	5.00	7.00	13.00	22.00	32.00
AH117x//5	—	5.00	7.00	13.00	22.00	32.00
AH117x//6	—	5.00	7.00	13.00	22.00	32.00

Mint: Aurangnagar
KM# 460.22 RUPEE

Silver **Note:** Weight varies 11.00-11.60 grams.

Date	Mintage	Good	VG	F	VF	XF
AHxxxx//1 (Ahad) Rare	—	—	—	—	—	—

Mint: Ausa
KM# 460.46 RUPEE

Silver **Obv:** Inscription **Rev:** Inscription **Note:** Weight varies 11.00-11.60 grams.

Date	Mintage	Good	VG	F	VF	XF
AHxxxx//4	—	—	—	—	—	—
AH1174//5	—	—	—	—	—	—

Mint: Azimabad
KM# 460.5 RUPEE

Silver **Note:** Weight varies 11.00-11.60 grams.

Date	Mintage	Good	VG	F	VF	XF
AH1167//1 (Ahad)	—	5.00	6.00	11.50	17.50	25.00
AH1168//1 (Ahad)	—	5.00	6.00	11.50	17.50	25.00
AH1168//2	—	5.00	6.00	11.50	17.50	25.00
AH1169//2	—	5.00	6.00	11.50	17.50	25.00
AH1169//3	—	5.00	6.00	11.50	17.50	25.00
AH1170//3	—	5.00	6.00	11.50	17.50	25.00
AH1170//4	—	5.00	6.00	11.50	17.50	25.00
AH1171//4	—	5.00	6.00	11.50	17.50	25.00
AH1171//5	—	5.00	6.00	11.50	17.50	25.00
AH1172//5	—	5.00	6.00	11.50	17.50	25.00
AH1172//6	—	5.00	6.00	11.50	17.50	25.00
AH1173//6	—	5.00	6.00	11.50	17.50	25.00

Mint: Bareli
KM# 460.23 RUPEE

Silver **Obv:** Inscription **Rev:** Inscription, beaded flower, mint mark below **Note:** Weight varies 11.00-11.60 grams.

Date	Mintage	Good	VG	F	VF	XF
AH116x//1 (Ahad)	—	5.00	8.00	16.00	28.00	40.00
AH1169//2	—	5.00	8.00	16.00	28.00	40.00
AH11xx//3	—	5.00	8.00	16.00	28.00	40.00
AH117x//4	—	5.00	8.00	16.00	28.00	40.00
AH117x//6	—	5.00	8.00	16.00	28.00	40.00

Mint: Broach
KM# 460.24 RUPEE

Silver **Note:** Weight varies 11.00-11.60 grams.

Date	Mintage	Good	VG	F	VF	XF
AH11xx//4	—	6.50	16.00	32.00	55.00	80.00
AH1173//6	—	6.50	16.00	32.00	55.00	80.00

Mint: Burhanpur
KM# 460.25 RUPEE

Silver **Obv:** Inscription, date **Rev:** Inscription **Note:** Weight varies 11.00-11.60 grams.

Date	Mintage	Good	VG	F	VF	XF
AH1168//1 (Ahad)	—	5.00	8.00	16.00	28.00	40.00
AH1169//3	—	5.00	8.00	16.00	28.00	40.00
AH117x//4	—	5.00	8.00	16.00	28.00	40.00

Mint: Dera
KM# 460.7 RUPEE

Silver **Note:** Weight varies 11.00-11.60 grams.

Date	Mintage	Good	VG	F	VF	XF
AH1173//7 (sic)	—	6.50	16.00	32.00	55.00	80.00

Mint: Firozgarh
KM# 460.43 RUPEE
Silver **Note:** Weight varies 11.00-11.60 grams.

Date	Mintage	Good	VG	F	VF	XF
AH117x//4	—	5.00	8.00	16.00	28.00	40.00
AH1172//x	—	5.00	8.00	16.00	28.00	40.00

Mint: Ghulshanabad
KM# 460.27 RUPEE
Silver **Note:** Weight varies 11.00-11.60 grams.

Date	Mintage	Good	VG	F	VF	XF
AH1176//x Error for 1167	—	5.00	8.00	16.00	28.00	40.00

Mint: Gwalior
KM# 460.28 RUPEE
Silver **Obv:** Inscription, mint mark **Rev:** Inscription **Note:** Weight varies 11.00-11.60 grams.

Date	Mintage	Good	VG	F	VF	XF
AH116x//1 (Ahad)	—	5.00	8.00	16.00	28.00	40.00
AH116x//2	—	5.00	8.00	16.00	28.00	40.00
AH1169//3	—	5.00	8.00	16.00	28.00	40.00
AH1170//3	—	5.00	8.00	16.00	28.00	40.00
AH117x//4	—	5.00	8.00	16.00	28.00	40.00
AH117x//5	—	5.00	8.00	16.00	28.00	40.00
AH117x//6	—	5.00	8.00	16.00	28.00	40.00

Mint: Itawa
KM# 460.8 RUPEE
Silver **Obv:** Inscription **Rev:** Inscription **Note:** Weight varies 11.00-11.60 grams.

Date	Mintage	Good	VG	F	VF	XF
AH1168//1 (Ahad)	—	5.00	7.00	13.00	22.00	32.00
AH1169//2	—	5.00	7.00	13.00	22.00	32.00
AH1170//4	—	5.00	7.00	13.00	22.00	32.00

Mint: Jahangirnagar
KM# 460.9 RUPEE
Silver **Note:** Weight varies 11.00-11.60 grams.

Date	Mintage	Good	VG	F	VF	XF
AHxxxx//1 (Ahad)	—	5.00	7.00	13.00	22.00	32.00
AHxxxx//2	—	5.00	7.00	13.00	22.00	32.00
AHxxxx//5	—	5.00	7.00	13.00	22.00	32.00
AHxxxx//6	—	5.00	7.00	13.00	22.00	32.00

Mint: Jodhpur
KM# 460.29 RUPEE
Silver **Obv:** Inscription **Rev. Inscription:** Dar-ul-Mansur **Note:** Weight varies 11.00-11.60 grams.

Date	Mintage	Good	VG	F	VF	XF
AH1170//x	—	6.50	16.00	32.00	55.00	80.00
AH117x//4	—	6.50	16.00	32.00	55.00	80.00
AH117x//5	—	6.50	16.00	32.00	55.00	80.00
AH1173//6	—	6.50	16.00	32.00	55.00	80.00

Mint: Kalpi
KM# 460.30 RUPEE
Silver **Note:** Weight varies 11.00-11.60 grams.

Date	Mintage	Good	VG	F	VF	XF
AH1170//4 Rare	—	—	—	—	—	—

Mint: Kankurti
KM# 460.42 RUPEE
Silver **Note:** Weight varies 11.00-11.60 grams.

Date	Mintage	Good	VG	F	VF	XF
ND//x Rare	—	—	—	—	—	—

Mint: Kashmir
KM# 460.11 RUPEE
Silver **Obv:** Inscription, date **Rev:** Inscription **Note:** Weight varies 11.00-11.60 grams.

Date	Mintage	Good	VG	F	VF	XF
AH1169//2	—	6.50	16.00	32.00	55.00	80.00
AH1170//3	—	6.50	16.00	32.00	55.00	80.00
AH1171//4	—	6.50	16.00	32.00	55.00	80.00
AH1172//5	—	6.50	16.00	32.00	55.00	80.00
AH1173//5 (sic)	—	6.50	16.00	32.00	55.00	80.00

Mint: Kashmir
KM# 460.40 RUPEE
Silver **Obv:** Inscription; Similar to KM# 460 **Rev:** Inscription; Similar to KM# 446 **Note:** Weight varies 11.00-11.60 grams. Mule.

Date	Mintage	Good	VG	F	VF	XF
AHxxxx//8 (sic)	—	5.00	8.00	16.00	28.00	40.00

Mint: Katak
KM# 460.44 RUPEE
Silver **Note:** Weight varies 11.00-11.60 grams.

Date	Mintage	Good	VG	F	VF	XF
AHxxxx//6	—	—	—	—	—	—

Mint: Khambayat
KM# 460.31 RUPEE
Silver **Obv:** Inscription **Rev:** Inscription **Note:** Weight varies 11.00-11.60 grams.

Date	Mintage	Good	VG	F	VF	XF
AH1173//6	—	5.00	8.00	16.00	28.00	40.00

Mint: Khujista Bunyad
KM# 460.32 RUPEE
Silver **Note:** Weight varies 11.00-11.60 grams.

Date	Mintage	Good	VG	F	VF	XF
AHxxxx//x	—	5.00	8.00	16.00	28.00	40.00

Mint: Kora
KM# 460.12 RUPEE
Silver **Note:** Weight varies 11.00-11.60 grams.

Date	Mintage	Good	VG	F	VF	XF
AH11xx//1 (Ahad)	—	5.00	6.00	11.00	17.50	25.00
AH1168//2	—	5.00	6.00	11.00	17.50	—
AH1169//2	—	5.00	6.00	11.00	17.50	—
AH1169//3	—	5.00	6.00	11.00	17.50	—
AH1170//3	—	5.00	6.00	11.00	17.50	—
AH1170//4	—	5.00	6.00	11.00	17.50	—
AH1171//4	—	5.00	6.00	11.00	17.50	—
AH1171//5	—	5.00	6.00	11.00	17.50	—
AH1172//5	—	5.00	6.00	11.00	17.50	—
AH1172//6	—	5.00	6.00	11.00	17.50	—
AH1173//6	—	5.00	6.00	11.00	17.50	—

Mint: Lahore
KM# 460.13 RUPEE
Silver **Obv:** Inscription **Rev. Inscription:** Dar-us-Sultanat **Note:** Weight varies 11.00-11.60 grams.

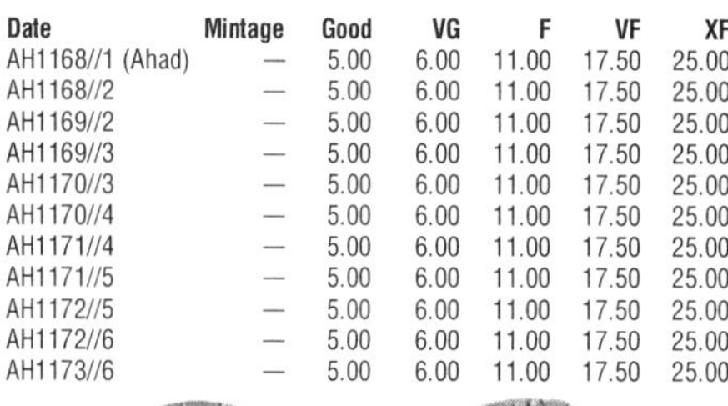

Date	Mintage	Good	VG	F	VF	XF
AH1168//1 (Ahad)	—	5.00	6.00	11.00	17.50	25.00
AH1168//2	—	5.00	6.00	11.00	17.50	25.00
AH1169//2	—	5.00	6.00	11.00	17.50	25.00
AH1169//3	—	5.00	6.00	11.00	17.50	25.00
AH1170//3	—	5.00	6.00	11.00	17.50	25.00
AH1170//4	—	5.00	6.00	11.00	17.50	25.00
AH1171//4	—	5.00	6.00	11.00	17.50	25.00
AH1171//5	—	5.00	6.00	11.00	17.50	25.00
AH1172//5	—	5.00	6.00	11.00	17.50	25.00
AH1172//6	—	5.00	6.00	11.00	17.50	25.00
AH1173//6	—	5.00	6.00	11.00	17.50	25.00

Mint: Maha Indrapur
KM# 460.33 RUPEE
Silver **Obv:** Inscription **Rev:** Inscription **Note:** Weight varies 11.00-11.60 grams.

Date	Mintage	Good	VG	F	VF	XF
AH1170//3	—	13.00	32.50	65.00	110	165
AH11xx//4	—	13.00	32.50	65.00	110	165
AH1172//5	—	13.00	32.50	65.00	110	165
AH117x//6	—	13.00	32.50	65.00	110	165

Mint: Muhammadabad Banaras
KM# 460.6 RUPEE
Silver **Obv:** Inscription, trident **Rev:** Inscription, date, star and cresent **Note:** Weight varies 11.00-11.60 grams.

Date	Mintage	Good	VG	F	VF	XF
AH1168//1 (Ahad)	—	5.00	6.00	11.00	17.50	25.00
AH1168//2	—	5.00	6.00	11.00	17.50	25.00
AH1169//2	—	5.00	6.00	11.00	17.50	25.00
AH1169//3	—	5.00	6.00	11.00	17.50	25.00
AH1170//3	—	5.00	6.00	11.00	17.50	25.00
AH1170//4	—	5.00	6.00	11.00	17.50	25.00
AH1171//4	—	5.00	6.00	11.00	17.50	25.00
AH1171//5	—	5.00	6.00	11.00	17.50	25.00
AH1172//5	—	5.00	6.00	11.00	17.50	25.00
AH1172//6	—	5.00	6.00	11.00	17.50	25.00
AH1173//6	—	5.00	6.00	11.00	17.50	25.00
AH1173//7	—	5.00	6.00	11.00	17.50	25.00

Mint: Multan
KM# 460.14 RUPEE
Silver **Obv:** Inscription **Rev. Inscription:** Dar-ul-Aman **Note:** Weight varies 11.00-11.60 grams.

Date	Mintage	Good	VG	F	VF	XF
AH1173//7(sic)	—	7.00	18.00	35.00	60.00	95.00

Mint: Muradabad
KM# 460.34 RUPEE
Silver **Obv:** Inscription **Rev:** Inscription **Note:** Weight varies 11.00-11.60 grams.

Date	Mintage	Good	VG	F	VF	XF
AH1168//1 (Ahad)	—	5.00	8.00	16.00	28.00	40.00
AH1168//2	—	5.00	8.00	16.00	28.00	40.00
AH1169//2	—	5.00	8.00	16.00	28.00	40.00
AH1169//3	—	5.00	8.00	16.00	28.00	40.00
AH1171//5	—	5.00	8.00	16.00	28.00	40.00
AH1172//5	—	5.00	8.00	16.00	28.00	40.00
AH1172//6	—	5.00	8.00	16.00	28.00	40.00

Mint: Murshidabad
KM# 460.15 RUPEE
Silver **Obv:** Inscription, sun **Rev:** Inscription **Note:** Weight varies 11.00-11.60 grams.

Date	Mintage	Good	VG	F	VF	XF
AH1167//1 (Ahad)	—	5.00	7.00	13.00	22.00	32.00
AH1168//1 (Ahad)	—	5.00	7.00	13.00	22.00	32.00
AH1168//2	—	5.00	7.00	13.00	22.00	32.00
AH1169//2	—	5.00	7.00	13.00	22.00	32.00
AH11xx//3	—	5.00	7.00	13.00	22.00	32.00
AH11xx//5	—	5.00	7.00	13.00	22.00	32.00
AH1173//6	—	5.00	7.00	13.00	22.00	32.00

Mint: Najibabad
KM# 460.35 RUPEE
Silver **Obv:** Inscription, star **Rev:** Inscription **Note:** Weight varies 11.00-11.60 grams.

Date	Mintage	Good	VG	F	VF	XF
AHxxxx//4 Rare	—	6.00	—	—	—	—
AHxxxx//5 Rare	—	6.00	—	—	—	—

Mint: Narwar
KM# 460.37 RUPEE
Silver **Note:** Weight varies 11.00-11.60 grams.

Date	Mintage	Good	VG	F	VF	XF
AH1168//1 (Ahad)	—	6.00	12.00	22.00	35.00	50.00
AH1169//2	—	6.00	12.00	22.00	35.00	50.00
AH1171//5	—	6.00	12.00	22.00	35.00	50.00
AH1173//6	—	6.00	12.00	22.00	35.00	50.00

Mint: Nasirabad
KM# 460.36 RUPEE
Silver **Note:** Weight varies 11.00-11.60 grams.

Date	Mintage	Good	VG	F	VF	XF
AH117x//7 (sic)	—	6.00	15.00	27.00	45.00	65.00

Mint: Nusratabad
KM# 460.48 RUPEE
Silver **Obv:** Inscription **Rev:** Inscription **Note:** Weight varies 11.00-11.60 grams.

Date	Mintage	Good	VG	F	VF	XF
AH1172//x	—	—	—	—	—	—

Mint: Sahrind
KM# 460.16 RUPEE
Silver **Note:** Weight varies 11.00-11.60 grams.

Date	Mintage	Good	VG	F	VF	XF
AH1167//1 (Ahad)	—	5.00	7.00	13.00	22.00	32.00
AH1168//1 (Ahad)	—	5.00	7.00	13.00	22.00	32.00
AH1168//2	—	5.00	7.00	13.00	22.00	32.00
AH1169//2	—	5.00	7.00	13.00	22.00	32.00
AH1169//3	—	5.00	7.00	13.00	22.00	32.00
AH1170//3	—	5.00	7.00	13.00	22.00	32.00
AH1170//4	—	5.00	7.00	13.00	22.00	32.00
AH1171//4	—	5.00	7.00	13.00	22.00	32.00
AH1171//5	—	5.00	7.00	13.00	22.00	32.00
AH1172//5	—	5.00	7.00	13.00	22.00	32.00
AH1172//6	—	5.00	7.00	13.00	22.00	32.00

Mint: Shahabad Qanauj
KM# 460.47 RUPEE
Silver **Note:** Weight varies 11.00-11.60 grams.

Date	Mintage	Good	VG	F	VF	XF
AH1167//1	—	—	—	—	—	—

Mint: Shahjahanabad
KM# 460.17 RUPEE
Silver **Obv:** Inscription, date **Rev. Inscription:** Dar-ul-Khilafat **Note:** Weight varies 11.00-11.60 grams.

Date	Mintage	Good	VG	F	VF	XF
AH1167//1 (Ahad)	—	5.00	6.50	10.00	16.50	25.00
AH1169//3	—	5.00	6.50	10.00	16.50	25.00
AH1170//4	—	5.00	6.50	10.00	16.50	25.00
AH1162//7 (sic)	—	5.00	6.50	10.00	16.50	25.00

Mint: Surat
KM# 460.19 RUPEE
Silver **Obv:** Inscription **Rev:** Inscription **Note:** Weight varies 11.00-11.60 grams.

Date	Mintage	Good	VG	F	VF	XF
AHxxxx//4	—	5.00	8.00	16.00	28.00	40.00
AHxxxx//5	—	5.00	8.00	16.00	28.00	40.00

Mint: Nagor
KM# 461.1 RUPEE
Silver **Obv:** Inscription **Rev. Inscription:** Dar-ul-Barakat **Note:** Weight varies 11.00-11.60 grams.

Date	Mintage	Good	VG	F	VF	XF
AH1170//4	—	—	—	—	—	—
AH117x//5	—	—	—	—	—	—

Mint: Shahjahanabad
KM# 464.1 MOHUR
Gold **Obv:** Inscription within and outside of square **Rev:** Inscription within and outside of square **Rev. Inscription:** Dar-ul-Khilafat **Note:** Weight varies: 10.80-11.00 grams.

Date	Mintage	Good	VG	F	VF	XF
AH1168//2	—	250	350	550	850	1,200

Mint: Shahjahanabad
KM# 465.1 MOHUR
Gold **Obv. Inscription:** Muhammad Azizuddin Alamgir, Badshah Ghazi, may God protect his kingdom **Rev. Inscription:** Dar-ul-Khilafat **Note:** Weight varies: 10.80-11.00 grams.

Date	Mintage	Good	VG	F	VF	XF
AH1168//2	—	235	265	325	400	500
AH1169//2	—	235	265	325	400	500
AH1169//3	—	235	265	325	400	500

Mint: Shahjahanabad
KM# 465A.1 MOHUR
Gold **Obv. Inscription:** Shah Jahan, Badshah Alamgir **Rev. Inscription:** Dar-ul-khilafat **Note:** Weight varies: 10.80-11.00 grams.

Date	Mintage	Good	VG	F	VF	XF
AH1170//4 Rare	—	—	—	—	—	—

Mint: Itawa
KM# 466.2 MOHUR
Gold **Obv. Inscription:** Azizuddin Alamgir, Badshah Ghazi, coin like the sun and moon.... **Rev:** Inscription **Note:** Weight varies: 10.80-11.00 grams.

Date	Mintage	Good	VG	F	VF	XF
AH1170//5 Rare	—	—	—	—	—	—
AH117x//5 Rare	—	—	—	—	—	—

Mint: Shahjahanabad
KM# 466.1 MOHUR
Gold **Obv:** Inscription **Rev. Inscription:** Dar-ul-Khilafat **Note:** Weight varies 10.80-11.00 grams.

Date	Mintage	Good	VG	F	VF	XF
AH1170//4	—	235	265	310	375	450
AH1171//4	—	235	265	310	375	450
AH1171//5	—	235	265	310	375	450
AH1172//5	—	235	265	310	375	450
AH1172//6	—	235	265	310	375	450
AH1173//6	—	235	265	310	375	450

Mint: Sironj
KM# 466.3 MOHUR
Gold **Note:**

Date	Mintage	VG	F	VF	XF	Unc
AH(11)68//2	—	175	300	550	875	—

Mint: Akbarabad
KM# 467.1 MOHUR
Gold **Obv. Inscription:** Badshah Ghazi Alamgir **Rev. Inscription:** Mustagir-ul-Khilafat **Note:** Weight varies: 10.80-11.00 grams.

Date	Mintage	Good	VG	F	VF	XF
AH11xx//1 (Ahad)	—	235	265	310	375	450
AH1169//3	—	235	265	310	375	450
AH1172//6	—	235	265	310	375	450

Mint: Allahabad
KM# 467.2 MOHUR
Gold **Note:** Weight varies: 10.80-11.00 grams.

Date	Mintage	Good	VG	F	VF	XF
ND//x	—	235	265	310	375	450

Mint: Azimabad
KM# 467.3 MOHUR
Gold **Note:** Weight varies: 10.80-11.00 grams.

Date	Mintage	Good	VG	F	VF	XF
AH116x//3	—	235	265	310	375	450
AH1170//3	—	235	265	310	375	450
AH117x//5	—	235	265	310	375	450

Mint: Farrukhabad
KM# 467.13 MOHUR
Gold **Note:** Weight varies: 10.80-11.00 grams.

Date	Mintage	Good	VG	F	VF	XF
AH1167//1 (Ahad)	—	—	—	—	—	—
AH1170//2	—	—	—	—	—	—

Mint: Islamabad
KM# 467.14 MOHUR
Gold **Note:** Weight varies: 10.80-11.00 grams.

Date	Mintage	Good	VG	F	VF	XF
AH1170//3	—	—	—	—	—	—

Mint: Itawa
KM# 467.5 MOHUR
Gold **Note:** Weight varies: 10.80-11.00 grams.

Date	Mintage	Good	VG	F	VF	XF
ND//x	—	—	250	300	375	500

Mint: Kora
KM# 467.6 MOHUR
Gold **Note:** Weight varies: 10.80-11.00 grams.

Date	Mintage	Good	VG	F	VF	XF
ND//x	—	235	265	325	400	500

Mint: Lahore
KM# 467.7 MOHUR
Gold **Obv:** Inscription **Rev. Inscription:** Dar-us-Sultanat **Note:** Weight varies: 10.80-11.00 grams.

Date	Mintage	Good	VG	F	VF	XF
AH1171//5	—	235	265	310	375	450
AH1172//5	—	235	265	310	375	450

Mint: Mahindurpur
KM# 467.12 MOHUR
Gold **Note:** Weight varies: 10.80-11.00 grams.

Date	Mintage	Good	VG	F	VF	XF
AHxxxx//5	—	—	—	—	—	—

Mint: Muhammadabad Banaras
KM# 467.4 MOHUR
Gold **Obv:** Inscription **Rev:** Inscription **Note:** Weight varies: 10.80-11.00 grams.

Date	Mintage	Good	VG	F	VF	XF
AHxxxx//1 (Ahad)	—	235	265	310	375	450
AHxxxx//2	—	235	265	310	375	450
AHxxxx//3	—	235	265	310	375	450
AHxxxx//4	—	235	265	310	375	450

Mint: Multan
KM# 467.8 MOHUR
Gold **Obv:** Inscription **Rev. Inscription:** Dar-ul-Aman **Note:** Weight varies: 10.80-11.00 grams.

Date	Mintage	Good	VG	F	VF	XF
ND//x	—	235	265	325	400	500

Mint: Najibadad
KM# 467.11 MOHUR
Gold **Obv:** Inscription **Rev:** Inscription **Note:** Weight varies: 10.80-11.00 grams.

Date	Mintage	Good	VG	F	VF	XF
AHxxxx//3	—	—	—	—	—	—
AHxxxx//6	—	—	—	—	—	—

Mint: Sahrind
KM# 467.9 MOHUR
Gold **Note:** Weight varies: 10.80-11.00 grams.

Date	Mintage	Good	VG	F	VF	XF
AHxxxx//4	—	235	265	310	375	450

Mint: Shahjahanabad
KM# 467.10 MOHUR
Gold **Obv:** Inscription **Rev. Inscription:** Dar-ul-Khilafat **Note:** Weight varies: 10.80-11.00 grams.

Date	Mintage	Good	VG	F	VF	XF
AH1167//1 (Ahad)	—	235	265	325	425	550

Mint: Guti
KM# 468.2 PAGODA
Gold **Note:** Weight varies 2.65-2.75 grams.

Date	Mintage	Good	VG	F	VF	XF
AH1168//x	—	—	—	—	—	—

Mint: Imtiyazgarh
KM# 468.1 PAGODA
Gold **Obv:** Inscription **Rev:** Inscription **Note:** Weight varies 2.65-2.75 grams.

Date	Mintage	Good	VG	F	VF	XF
ND//x	—	—	—	—	—	—
AHxxxx//3	—	—	—	—	—	—
AHxxxx//7 (sic)	—	—	—	—	—	—

LARGESSE COINAGE

Mint: Akbarabad
KM# 462.1 NISAR
1.3000 g., Silver **Obv:** Inscription **Rev:** Inscription **Note:**

Date	Mintage	Good	VG	F	VF	XF
AH1171//4 Rare	—	—	—	—	—	—

Shah Jahan III

AH1173-1174 / 1759-1760AD

HAMMERED COINAGE

Mint: Shahjahanabad
KM# 469 DAM
Copper **Obv:** Inscription **Rev:** Inscription **Note:** Weight varies 19.70-20.20 grams.

Date	Mintage	Good	VG	F	VF	XF
AH1173//1 Rare	—	—	—	—	—	—

Mint: Ahmadabad
KM# 470.2 1/2 RUPEE
Silver **Obv:** Inscription **Rev:** Inscription **Note:** Weight varies 5.50-5.80 grams.

Date	Mintage	Good	VG	F	VF	XF
AHxxxx//1 (Ahad)	—	—	—	—	—	—

Mint: Azimabad
KM# 470.1 1/2 RUPEE
5.7220 g., Silver **Note:** Weight varies 5.50-5.80 grams.

Date	Mintage	Good	VG	F	VF	XF
AH1173//1 (Ahad) Rare	—	—	—	—	—	—

Mint: Akbarabad
KM# 475.1 RUPEE
Silver **Obv:** Inscription **Rev. Inscription:** Mustagir-ul-Khilafat **Note:** Weight varies 11.00-11.60 grams.

Date	Mintage	Good	VG	F	VF	XF
AH1174//1 (Ahad)	—	11.00	27.50	55.00	90.00	130

Mint: Azimabad
KM# 475.2 RUPEE
Silver **Note:** Weight varies 11.00-11.60 grams.

Date	Mintage	Good	VG	F	VF	XF
AH1173//1 (Ahad)	—	10.00	25.00	50.00	85.00	120
AH1174//1 (Ahad)	—	10.00	25.00	50.00	85.00	120

Mint: Hasanabad
KM# 475.7 RUPEE
Silver **Note:** Weight varies 11.00-11.60 grams.

Date	Mintage	Good	VG	F	VF	XF
AH1174//1 (Ahad)	—	—	—	—	—	—

Mint: Maha Indrapur
KM# 475.8 RUPEE
Silver **Obv:** Inscription **Rev:** Inscription **Note:** Weight varies 11.00-11.60 grams.

Date	Mintage	Good	VG	F	VF	XF
AH1173//1 (Ahad)	—	—	—	—	—	—

Mint: Shahjahanabad
KM# 475.3 RUPEE
Silver **Obv:** Inscription **Rev. Inscription:** Dar-us-Sultanat **Note:** Weight varies 11.00-11.60 grams.

Date	Mintage	Good	VG	F	VF	XF
AH1173//1 (Ahad)	—	15.00	35.00	60.00	100	140
AH1174//1 (Ahad)	—	15.00	35.00	60.00	100	140

Mint: Ahmadnagar-Farrukhabad
KM# 478.5 MOHUR
Gold **Obv:** Inscription **Rev:** Inscription **Note:** Weight varies 10.80-11.00 grams.

Date	Mintage	Good	VG	F	VF	XF
AH1173//1 (Ahad)	—	250	425	700	1,000	1,600
AH1174//1 (Ahad)	—	250	425	700	1,000	1,600

Mint: Akbarabad
KM# 478.1 MOHUR
Gold **Obv:** Inscription **Rev. Inscription:** Mustagir-ul-Khilafat **Note:** Weight varies 10.80-11.00 grams.

Date	Mintage	Good	VG	F	VF	XF
AHxxxx//1 (Ahad)	—	250	375	700	1,200	1,800

Mint: Mahindrapur
KM# 478.4 MOHUR
Gold **Obv:** Inscription **Rev:** Inscription **Note:** Weight varies 10.80-11.00 grams.

Date	Mintage	Good	VG	F	VF	XF
AH(117)3//1 (Ahad)	—	250	400	800	1,250	2,000
AH1174//1 (Ahad)	—	250	400	800	1,250	2,000

Mint: Shahjahanabad
KM# 478.3 MOHUR
Gold **Obv:** Inscription **Rev. Inscription:** Dar-us-Sultanat **Note:** Weight varies 10.80-11.00 grams.

Date	Mintage	Good	VG	F	VF	XF
AH1174//1 (Ahad)	—	250	375	700	1,200	1,800

Shah Alam II

AH1174-1221 / 1759-1806AD

This ruler was deposed from July, AH1202 to March, AH1203 by the Rohilla rebel Ghulam Qadir Khan. He was restored to the throne of Delhi by the Marathas in March, AH1203/1789.

Except for the Delhi Mint, most of the later coins struck in the name of this Emperor were Princely State issues, and can be found in their appropriate place under the States. Earlier issues come from nearly 100 mints, and it is always a problem to determine in what year coins of a particular mint cease to be Mughal and become State issues.

The following mints, for the most part in the Delhi (Shahjahanabad) area, may be considered the nucleus of Mughal mints during Shah Alam's reign. They were located in provinces governed by Mughal functionaries, whose increasing independence is reflected in the growing eccentricity of coin design.

In some cases the distinctive geometric designs and floral devices found on the coins were true mint marks, representative of a single mint. In other instances the mint marks' listed below were temporary privy marks or simply decoration.

Shah Alam II legends were used in some states long after his death, until AH1314/1879AD at Ujjain, for example. This is not the case with true Mughal issues.

Local and Mughal Governors

Akbarabad Mint
Najat Khan Rohilla, AH1186-93/1773-79AD
Muhammad Beg Hamadani, AH1193-98/1779-84AD
Mahadji Sindhia, AH1199-1208/1785-94AD
Ghulam Qadir Rohilla, AH1202-03/1787-88AD
Daulat Rao Sindhia, AH1213-18/1799-1803AD,
(With John and George Hessing in charge)

Gokulgarh Mint
Raja of Rewari
Rohilla Governor
Sindhia Governor

Hardwar Mint
Saharanpur Governor

Hathras Mint
Madhoji Sindhia as Amir-ul-Umara, AH1199-1203, 1203-1209/1784-88, 1788-94AD

Kora Mint
Mirza Najaf Khan

Saharanpur Mint
Ghani Bahadur, AH1203-05/1788-91AD
Bhairon Pant Tantia, AH1206-08/1791-94AD
Sikh Occupation, AH1209-10/1794-94AD
Bapu Sindhia, AH1211-12/1796-98AD
Imam Baksh, AH1213-14/1799AD
General Perron (for Sindhia), AH1215-18/1800-03

GOVERNORS' HAMMERED COINAGE

Mint: Husaingarh
KM# 643 1/2 PAISA

Copper **Issuer:** Mahadji Sindhia. **Obv:** Inscription **Rev:** Inscription **Note:** Uncertain mint. Possibly a mint of the Doab or eastern Rajasthan.

Date	Mintage	Good	VG	F	VF	XF
AH119x//23 Rare	—	—	—	—	—	—

Mint: Shahjahanabad
KM# 699 1/2 PAISA

Copper **Note:** Mint marks are symbols.

Date	Mintage	Good	VG	F	VF	XF
AH1210//38	—	5.00	9.00	13.00	20.00	—

Mint: Ahmadabad
KM# 480 PAISA

Copper **Obv:** Inscription, date **Rev:** Inscription **Note:**

Date	Mintage	Good	VG	F	VF	XF
AH1202//29	—	1.75	3.50	6.00	10.00	—

Mint: Akbarabad
KM# 505 PAISA

Copper **Issuer:** Muhammad Beg Hamadani. **Obv:** Inscription **Rev:** Inscription, date **Note:**

Date	Mintage	Good	VG	F	VF	XF
AH1194//23 (sic)	—	1.75	3.50	6.00	10.00	—
AH1195//23	—	1.75	3.50	6.00	10.00	—

Mint: Akbarabad
KM# 549.1 PAISA

Copper **Issuer:** Daulat Rao Sindhia with John and George Hessing in charge. **Obv:** Inscription **Rev:** JWH **Note:**

Date	Mintage	Good	VG	F	VF	XF
AH1215//43	—	45.00	75.00	100	150	—
AH1216//42 (sic)	—	45.00	75.00	100	150	—
AH12xx//43	—	45.00	75.00	100	150	—
AH1218//xx	—	45.00	75.00	100	150	—

Note: J.W.H. - John William Hessing, Governor of Agra

Mint: Akbarabad
KM# 549.3 PAISA

Copper **Issuer:** Daulat Rao Sindhia with John and George Hessing in charge. **Obv:** Inscription, date **Rev:** Katar **Note:**

Date	Mintage	Good	VG	F	VF	XF
AH1215//xx	—	12.50	25.00	42.00	60.00	—

Mint: Allahabad
KM# 565 PAISA

Copper **Obv:** Inscription **Rev:** Inscription **Note:**

Date	Mintage	Good	VG	F	VF	XF
ND//8	—	3.50	7.50	12.00	20.00	—
AH1210	—	3.50	7.50	12.00	20.00	—

Mint: Bindraban
KM# 603 PAISA

10.2000 g., Copper **Issuer:** East India Company **Obv:** Inscription **Rev:** Inscription **Note:**

Date	Mintage	Good	VG	F	VF	XF
AH1194//xx	—	—	—	—	—	—

Mint: Chhachrauli
KM# 673 PAISA

Copper, 24 mm. **Obv:** Inscription, stars **Rev:** Inscription, additional symbols, chakra, and hexfoil **Rev. Inscription:** Dar-us-Sarur **Note:** Issue of the Governor of Saharanpur

Date	Mintage	Good	VG	F	VF	XF
AH1206//33	—	4.00	6.50	10.00	15.00	—
AH1207//33 (sic)	—	4.00	6.50	10.00	15.00	—
AH1212//39	—	4.00	6.50	10.00	15.00	—
AH1212//40	—	4.00	6.50	10.00	15.00	—
AH1214//41	—	4.00	6.50	10.00	15.00	—
AH1215//42	—	4.00	6.50	10.00	15.00	—
AH12xx//43	—	4.00	6.50	10.00	15.00	—
AH1217//44	—	4.00	6.50	10.00	15.00	—
AH1218//45	—	4.00	6.50	10.00	15.00	—

Mint: Hasanabad
KM# 631 PAISA

Copper **Obv:** Inscription, date **Rev:** Inscription **Note:** Uncertain mint. Possibly a mint of Awadh or Rohilkhand.

Date	Mintage	Good	VG	F	VF	XF
AH1177//x	—	4.50	9.00	15.00	25.00	—

Mint: Husaingarh
KM# 646 PAISA

Copper **Obv:** Inscription **Rev:** Inscription **Note:**

Date	Mintage	Good	VG	F	VF	XF
AH119x//23	—	5.50	11.00	18.00	30.00	—

Mint: Macchlipattan
KM# 655 PAISA

Copper **Obv:** Inscription **Rev:** Inscription, date **Note:** Weight varies 13.20-13.40 grams.

Date	Mintage	Good	VG	F	VF	XF
AH1188//xx	—	—	—	—	—	—
AH1191//xx	—	—	—	—	—	—

Mint: Muazzamabad
KM# 656 PAISA

Copper **Obv:** Inscription **Rev:** Inscription **Note:**

Date	Mintage	Good	VG	F	VF	XF
AH1190	—	6.00	12.00	—	—	—

Mint: Muradabad
KM# 659 PAISA

Copper **Obv:** Inscription **Rev:** Inscription **Note:**

Date	Mintage	Good	VG	F	VF	XF
yr. 2	—	4.00	7.00	12.00	25.00	—
yr. 4	—	4.00	7.00	12.00	25.00	—

Mint: Najafgarh
KM# 667 PAISA

12.0000 g., Copper **Obv:** Inscription **Rev:** Inscription **Note:**

Date	Mintage	Good	VG	F	VF	XF
AH1178//6	—	—	—	—	—	—
AH1192	—	—	—	—	—	—

Mint: Saharanpur
KM# 672 PAISA

Copper, 21 mm. **Obv:** Inscription **Rev. Inscription:** Dar-us-Sarur **Note:** Varieties in additional symbols exist: 3-pronged quatrefoil, vertical and horizontal spray.

Date	Mintage	Good	VG	F	VF	XF
AHxxxx//31	—	4.00	6.50	10.00	15.00	—

Mint: Shahjahanabad
KM# 700 PAISA

Copper **Obv:** Inscription, date **Rev:** Inscription **Note:** Weight varies 11.00-11.60 grams.

Date	Mintage	Good	VG	F	VF	XF
AH1185//12 (Ahad)	—	2.00	3.25	5.00	8.50	—
AH1186//13	—	2.00	3.25	5.00	8.50	—
AH1187//15	—	2.00	3.25	5.00	8.50	—
AH1190//18	—	2.00	3.25	5.00	8.50	—
AH11xx//25	—	2.00	3.25	5.00	8.50	—
AH1198//xx	—	2.00	3.25	5.00	8.50	—
AH1199//27	—	2.00	3.25	5.00	8.50	—
AH1xxx//28	—	2.00	3.25	5.00	8.50	—
AH1205//32	—	2.00	3.25	5.00	8.50	—
AH1206//33	—	2.00	3.25	5.00	8.50	—
AH1206//34	—	2.00	3.25	5.00	8.50	—
AH1207//35	—	2.00	3.25	5.00	8.50	—
AH1208//35	—	2.00	3.25	5.00	8.50	—
AH1209//36	—	2.00	3.25	5.00	8.50	—
AH1207//36 (sic)	—	2.00	3.25	5.00	8.50	—
AH1208//36	—	2.00	3.25	5.00	8.50	—
AH1210//38	—	2.00	3.25	5.00	8.50	—
AH1211//39	—	2.00	3.25	5.00	8.50	—
AH1214//41	—	2.00	3.25	5.00	8.50	—
AH1219//46	—	4.00	6.50	10.00	20.00	—
AH1219//47	—	4.00	6.50	10.00	20.00	—
AH1220//48	—	4.00	6.50	10.00	20.00	—

Mint: Azimabad
KM# 590 1/16 RUPEE
Silver **Issuer:** East India Company **Obv:** Inscription **Rev:** Inscription, mint mark **Note:** Mint mark is a symbol. Weight varies 0.68-0.72 grams.

Date	Mintage	Good	VG	F	VF	XF
AH117x//1	—	5.00	12.50	25.00	42.00	60.00

Mint: Azimabad
KM# 591 1/8 RUPEE
Silver **Issuer:** East India Company **Obv:** Inscription **Rev:** Inscription, trident **Note:** Weight varies 1.38-1.45 grams.

Date	Mintage	Good	VG	F	VF	XF
AH1174//2	—	6.00	15.00	30.00	50.00	70.00

Mint: Murshidabad
KM# 657 1/8 RUPEE
Silver **Note:** Weight varies 1.38-1.45 grams.

Date	Mintage	Good	VG	F	VF	XF
AH117x//4	—	3.50	9.00	15.00	22.00	32.00
AH117x//5	—	3.50	9.00	15.00	22.00	32.00

Mint: Shahjahanabad
KM# 701 1/8 RUPEE
Silver **Obv:** Inscription **Rev:** Inscription, mint mark **Note:** Weight varies 1.38-1.45 grams.

Date	Mintage	Good	VG	F	VF	XF
AHxxxx//7	—	5.00	10.00	20.00	35.00	60.00

Mint: Akbarabad
KM# 510 1/4 RUPEE
Silver **Issuer:** Muhammad Beg Hamadani. **Obv:** Inscription **Rev:** Inscription, fish **Note:** Mint mark is a fish. Weight varies 2.75-2.90 grams.

Date	Mintage	Good	VG	F	VF	XF
AH119x//22	—	1.50	3.50	7.00	12.00	17.00

Mint: Azimabad
KM# A592 1/4 RUPEE
Silver **Issuer:** East India Company **Obv:** Inscription **Rev:** Inscription, mint mark **Note:** Weight varies 2.75-2.90 grams.

Date	Mintage	Good	VG	F	VF	XF
AHxxxx//6	—	—	—	—	—	—

Mint: Shahjahanabad
KM# 702 1/4 RUPEE
Silver **Obv. Inscription:** Hami Din **Rev:** Inscription **Note:** Weight varies 2.75-2.90 grams.

Date	Mintage	Good	VG	F	VF	XF
AH1197//25	—	5.50	14.00	28.00	45.00	75.00

Mint: Shahjahanabad
KM# 703 1/4 RUPEE
Silver **Obv. Inscription:** Sahib Qiran, parasol **Rev:** Inscription **Note:** Weight varies 2.75-2.90 grams.

Date	Mintage	Good	VG	F	VF	XF
AH12xx//33	—	5.50	14.00	28.00	47.50	65.00

Mint: Akbarabad
KM# 552 1/2 RUPEE
Silver **Issuer:** Daulat Rao Sindhia with John and George Hessing in charge. **Obv:** Inscription **Rev:** Inscription, fish **Note:** Weight varies 5.50-5.80 grams.

Date	Mintage	Good	VG	F	VF	XF
AH12xx//40	—	3.25	8.00	16.00	28.00	40.00

Mint: Shahjahanabad
KM# 705 1/2 RUPEE
Silver **Obv. Inscription:** Hami Din, flower symbol **Rev:** Inscription **Note:** Weight varies 5.50-5.80 grams.

Date	Mintage	Good	VG	F	VF	XF
AH1177//5	—	6.00	15.00	30.00	50.00	70.00

Mint: Shahjahanabad
KM# 706 1/2 RUPEE
Silver **Obv. Inscription:** Sahib Qiran **Rev:** Inscription **Note:** Weight varies 5.50-5.80 grams.

Date	Mintage	Good	VG	F	VF	XF
AH12xx//33	—	8.00	17.50	35.00	60.00	100
AH1211//39	—	8.00	17.50	35.00	60.00	100
AH1213//41	—	8.50	20.00	40.00	65.00	110

Mint: Surat
KM# 723 1/2 RUPEE
Silver **Obv:** Privy mark #1 **Rev:** Long stem flower in "S" of "Julus" **Note:** Weight varies 5.50-5.80 grams.

Date	Mintage	Good	VG	F	VF	XF
AHxxxx/19	—	2.50	5.50	11.00	17.50	25.00
AHxxxx//31	—	2.50	5.50	11.00	17.50	25.00

Mint: Ahmadabad
KM# 482 RUPEE
Silver **Obv:** Inscription, beaded flowers **Rev:** Inscription **Note:** Weight varies 11.00-11.60 grams. For coin dated AH1202 Year 29, refer to KM#738.

Date	Mintage	Good	VG	F	VF	XF
AH1201//28	—	5.00	8.00	12.00	20.00	35.00

Mint: Akbarabad
KM# 520 RUPEE
Silver, 23 mm. **Issuer:** Mahadji Sindhia. **Obv:** Inscription, date **Rev:** Inscription, fish **Note:** Mint mark is a symbol. Weight varies 11.00-11.60 grams.

Date	Mintage	Good	VG	F	VF	XF
AH1198//26	—	5.00	8.50	15.00	25.00	40.00
AH1199//26	—	5.00	8.50	15.00	25.00	40.00

Mint: Akbarabad
KM# 530 RUPEE
Silver, 22 mm. **Issuer:** Ghulam Qadir Rohilla. **Obv:** Inscription **Rev:** Inscription **Note:** Mint mark is a symbol. Weight varies 11.00-11.60 grams.

Date	Mintage	Good	VG	F	VF	XF
AH1201//28	—	5.50	10.00	20.00	32.50	55.00

Mint: Akbarabad
KM# 540 RUPEE
Silver **Issuer:** Mahadji Sindhia **Obv:** Inscription, date, star **Rev:** Inscription, fish **Note:** Mint mark is a symbol. Weight varies 11.00-11.60 grams.

Date	Mintage	Good	VG	F	VF	XF
AH1203//30	—	5.00	6.50	13.00	22.00	32.00
AH1207//34	—	5.00	6.50	13.00	22.00	32.00

Mint: Akbarabad
KM# 500 RUPEE
Silver, 22 mm. **Issuer:** Najaf Khan Rohilla. **Obv:** Inscription, symbol at upper left **Rev:** Inscription, symbol at bottom **Note:** Mughal Governor Issue. Mint mark is a symbol. Weight varies 11.00-11.60 grams.

Date	Mintage	Good	VG	F	VF	XF
AH1185//14 (sic)	—	5.00	11.00	18.00	30.00	50.00
AH1186//14	—	5.00	11.00	18.00	30.00	50.00

Mint: Akbarabad
KM# 490 RUPEE
Silver, 25 mm. **Obv:** Inscription **Rev:** Inscription **Note:** Pre-Panipat issue. Without mint mark. Weight varies 11.00-11.60 grams.

Date	Mintage	Good	VG	F	VF	XF
AH1174//1	—	5.00	8.50	15.00	25.00	40.00
AH117x//2	—	5.00	8.50	15.00	25.00	40.00
AH1176//4	—	5.00	8.50	15.00	25.00	40.00
AH1177//5	—	5.00	8.50	15.00	25.00	40.00
AH1178//5	—	5.00	8.50	15.00	25.00	40.00
AH1179//6	—	5.00	8.50	15.00	25.00	40.00
AH1180//7	—	5.00	8.50	15.00	25.00	40.00
AH1181//8	—	5.00	8.50	15.00	25.00	40.00

Mint: Akbarabad
KM# 512 RUPEE
Silver **Issuer:** Muhammad Beg Hamadani. **Obv:** Inscription **Rev:** Inscription, fish **Note:** Weight varies 11.00-11.60 grams.

Date	Mintage	Good	VG	F	VF	XF
AH1192//20	—	5.00	8.00	15.00	25.00	42.50
AH1193//20	—	5.00	8.00	15.00	25.00	42.50
AH1195//23	—	5.00	8.00	15.00	25.00	42.50
AH1196//24	—	5.00	8.00	15.00	25.00	42.50
AH1197//25	—	5.00	8.00	15.00	25.00	42.50
AH1198//25	—	5.00	8.00	15.00	25.00	42.50

Mint: Akbarabad
KM# 554 RUPEE
Silver **Issuer:** Daulat Rao Sindhia with John and George Hessing in charge **Obv:** Inscription, beaded flower **Rev:** Inscription, fish **Note:** Weight varies 11.00-11.60 grams.

Date	Mintage	Good	VG	F	VF	XF
AH12xx//38	—	5.00	7.50	15.00	25.00	40.00
AH12xx//42	—	5.00	7.50	15.00	25.00	40.00

Date	Mintage	Good	VG	F	VF	XF
AH1215//43 (sic)	—	5.00	7.50	15.00	25.00	40.00
AH1217//44	—	5.00	7.50	15.00	25.00	40.00
AH12xx//45	—	5.00	7.50	15.00	25.00	40.00

Mint: Allahabad
KM# 570 RUPEE

Silver **Obv:** Inscription, date **Rev:** Inscription, upright sprig **Note:** Mint mark symbol. Weight varies 11.00-11.60 grams.

Date	Mintage	Good	VG	F	VF	XF
AH1185//13	—	5.00	7.50	15.00	25.00	35.00

Mint: Allahabad
KM# 580 RUPEE

Silver, 23 mm. **Issuer:** East India Company **Obv:** Inscription **Rev:** Inscription, stylized fish **Note:** Weight varies 11.00-11.60 grams.

Date	Mintage	Good	VG	F	VF	XF
AH1198//23 (sic)	—	5.50	9.00	16.50	27.50	45.00

Mint: Allahabad
KM# 583 RUPEE

Silver **Issuer:** East India Company **Obv:** Inscription **Rev:** Inscription without arabic numeral 6 at left of Julus **Note:** Weight varies 11.00-11.60 grams.

Date	Mintage	Good	VG	F	VF	XF
AH1204//26 (sic)	—	5.00	7.00	13.00	21.50	30.00
AH1206//25 (sic)	—	5.00	7.00	12.00	20.00	28.50
AH1206//26 (sic)	—	5.00	7.00	12.00	20.00	28.50

Mint: Allahabad
KM# 585 RUPEE

Silver **Issuer:** East India Company **Obv:** Inscription, sun **Rev:** Inscription, fish **Note:** Weight varies 11.00-11.60 grams.

Date	Mintage	Good	VG	F	VF	XF
AH1206//26	—	5.00	7.00	13.00	22.00	32.50

Mint: Allahabad
KM# 584 RUPEE

Silver **Issuer:** East India Company **Obv:** Inscription, sun, date **Rev:** Inscription, fish **Note:** Weight varies 11.00-11.60 grams.

Date	Mintage	Good	VG	F	VF	XF
AH1207//26 (sic)	—	5.00	7.00	13.00	22.00	32.50

Mint: Allahabad
KM# 586 RUPEE

Silver, 21 mm. **Issuer:** East India Company **Obv:** Inscription, ball and sword **Rev:** Inscription, fish **Note:** Weight varies 11.00-11.60 grams.

Date	Mintage	Good	VG	F	VF	XF
AH1216//26 (sic)	—	5.00	7.00	13.00	22.00	32.50

Mint: Allahabad
KM# 587 RUPEE

Silver **Issuer:** East India Company **Obv:** Inscription, symbol **Rev:** Inscription **Note:** Weight varies 11.00-11.60 grams.

Date	Mintage	Good	VG	F	VF	XF
AH1205//26	—	5.00	7.00	13.00	22.00	32.50

Mint: Allahabad
KM# 588 RUPEE

Silver **Issuer:** East India Company **Obv:** Inscription, sun and sword **Rev:** Inscription, fish **Note:** Weight varies 11.00-11.60 grams.

Date	Mintage	Good	VG	F	VF	XF
AH1210//26 (sic)	—	5.00	7.00	13.00	22.00	32.50

Mint: Allahabad
KM# 709.1 RUPEE

Silver **Obv. Inscription:** Hami Din **Rev:** Inscription **Note:** Weight varies 11.00-11.60 grams.

Date	Mintage	Good	VG	F	VF	XF
AH1174//1	—	5.00	8.00	16.00	28.00	42.00
AH1174//2	—	5.00	8.00	16.00	28.00	42.00
AH1175//2	—	5.00	8.00	16.00	28.00	42.00
AH1175//3	—	5.00	8.00	16.00	28.00	42.00
AH1176//3	—	5.00	8.00	16.00	28.00	42.00
AH1176//4	—	5.00	8.00	16.00	28.00	42.00
AH1177//4	—	5.00	8.00	16.00	28.00	42.00
AH1177//5	—	5.00	8.00	16.00	28.00	42.00
AH1178//5	—	5.00	8.00	16.00	28.00	42.00
AH1178//6	—	5.00	8.00	16.00	28.00	42.00
AH1179//6	—	5.00	8.00	16.00	28.00	42.00
AH1179//7	—	5.00	8.00	16.00	28.00	42.00
AH1180//7	—	5.00	8.00	16.00	28.00	42.00
AH1180//8	—	5.00	8.00	16.00	28.00	42.00
AH1181//8	—	5.00	8.00	16.00	28.00	42.00
AH1181//9	—	5.00	8.00	16.00	28.00	42.00
AH1182//9	—	5.00	8.00	16.00	28.00	42.00
AH1186//14	—	5.00	8.00	16.00	28.00	42.00
AH1187//14	—	5.00	8.00	16.00	28.00	42.00

Mint: Allahabad
KM# 582 RUPEE

Silver **Issuer:** East India Company **Obv:** Inscription, date **Rev:** Arabic numeral 6 at left of Julus, fish mint mark below **Note:** Weight varies: 11.00-11.60 grams.

Date	Mintage	Good	VG	F	VF	XF
AH11xx//25	—	5.00	8.50	15.00	25.00	40.00
AH1199//26	—	5.00	8.50	15.00	25.00	40.00
AH1200//26 (sic)	—	5.00	8.50	15.00	25.00	40.00

Mint: Azimabad
KM# 592 RUPEE

Silver, 21 mm. **Issuer:** East India Company **Obv:** Inscription **Rev:** Inscription, trident **Note:** Weight varies 11.00-11.60 grams.

Date	Mintage	Good	VG	F	VF	XF
AH1174//2	—	8.00	20.00	42.50	70.00	100
AH1175//2	—	8.00	20.00	42.50	70.00	100
AH1175//3	—	8.00	20.00	42.50	70.00	100
AH1176//3	—	8.00	20.00	42.50	70.00	100
AH1176//4	—	8.00	20.00	42.50	70.00	100
AH1177//4	—	8.00	20.00	42.50	70.00	100
AH1177//5	—	8.00	20.00	42.50	70.00	100
AH1178//5	—	8.00	20.00	42.50	70.00	100
AH1178//6	—	8.00	20.00	42.50	70.00	100

Mint: Gohad
KM# 5 RUPEE

Silver **Issuer:** East India Company **Note:** Weight varies 11.00-11.60 grams.

Date	Mintage	Good	VG	F	VF	XF
AH1187//xx	—	8.00	20.00	35.00	55.00	90.00

Mint: Gokulgarh
KM# 620 RUPEE

Silver, 21-23 mm. **Issuer:** Raja of Rewari **Obv:** Inscription **Rev:** Inscription **Note:** Local Governor Issue. Size varies. Weight varies: 11.00-11.60 grams.

Date	Mintage	Good	VG	F	VF	XF
AH1182//10	—	5.00	7.00	13.50	22.50	35.00
AH1183//10	—	5.00	7.00	13.50	22.50	35.00
AH1183//11	—	5.00	7.00	13.50	22.50	35.00
AH1184//11	—	5.00	7.00	13.50	22.50	35.00
AH1184//12	—	5.00	7.00	13.50	22.50	35.00
AH1185//12	—	5.00	7.00	13.50	22.50	35.00
AH1185//13	—	7.00	7.00	13.50	22.50	35.00
AH1186//13	—	5.00	7.00	13.50	22.50	35.00
AH(11)86//14	—	5.00	7.00	13.50	22.50	35.00
AH1187//14	—	5.00	7.00	13.50	22.50	35.00
AH1187//15	—	5.00	7.00	13.50	22.50	35.00
AH1188//15	—	5.00	7.00	13.50	22.50	35.00
AH1188//16	—	5.00	7.00	13.50	22.50	35.00
AH1189//16	—	5.00	7.00	13.50	22.50	35.00
AH1189//17	—	5.00	7.00	13.50	22.50	35.00
AH1190//17	—	5.00	7.00	13.50	22.50	35.00
AH1190//18	—	5.00	7.00	13.50	22.50	35.00
AH1191//18	—	5.00	7.00	13.50	22.50	35.00
AH1191//19	—	5.00	7.00	13.50	22.50	35.00
AH1192//19	—	5.00	7.00	13.50	22.50	35.00
AH1192//20	—	5.00	7.00	13.50	22.50	35.00
AH1193//20	—	5.00	7.00	13.50	22.50	35.00
AH1193//21	—	5.00	7.00	13.50	22.50	35.00
AH1195//22	—	5.00	7.00	13.50	22.50	35.00
AH1194//21	—	5.00	7.00	13.50	22.50	35.00
AH1194//22	—	5.00	7.00	13.50	22.50	35.00
AH1195//23	—	5.00	7.00	13.50	22.50	35.00
AH1196//23	—	5.00	7.00	13.50	22.50	35.00
AH1196//24	—	5.00	7.00	13.50	22.50	35.00
AH1197//24	—	5.00	7.00	13.50	22.50	35.00
AH1197//25	—	5.00	7.00	13.50	22.50	35.00
AH1198//25	—	5.00	7.00	13.50	22.50	35.00
AH1198//26	—	5.00	7.00	13.50	22.50	35.00
AH1199//26	—	5.00	7.00	13.50	22.50	35.00
AH1199//27	—	5.00	7.00	13.50	22.50	35.00
AH1200//27	—	5.00	7.00	13.50	22.50	35.00
AH1200//28	—	5.00	7.00	13.50	22.50	35.00

Mint: Gokulgarh
KM# 622 RUPEE

Silver, 21-23 mm. **Issuer:** Rohilla Governor **Note:** Size varies. Weight varies: 11.00-11.60 grams.

Date	Mintage	Good	VG	F	VF	XF
AH1202//29	—	5.50	10.00	20.00	32.50	55.00
AH1202//30	—	5.50	10.00	20.00	32.50	55.00

Mint: Gokulgarh
KM# 624 RUPEE

Silver, 21-23 mm. **Issuer:** Sindhia Governor **Obv:** Inscription, sword **Rev:** Inscription, mint mark **Note:** Size varies. Weight varies: 11.00-11.60 grams.

Date	Mintage	Good	VG	F	VF	XF
AH1204//31	—	5.00	7.00	13.50	22.50	35.00
AH1202//31 (sic)	—	5.00	7.00	13.50	22.50	35.00
AH1203//31	—	5.00	7.00	13.50	22.50	35.00
AH1204//32	—	5.00	7.00	13.50	22.50	35.00
AH1205//32	—	5.00	7.00	13.50	22.50	35.00
AH1205//33	—	5.00	7.00	13.50	22.50	35.00
AH1206//33	—	5.00	7.00	13.50	22.50	35.00
AH1206//34	—	5.00	7.00	13.50	22.50	35.00
AH1207//34	—	5.00	7.00	13.50	22.50	35.00
AH1207//35	—	5.00	7.00	13.50	22.50	35.00
AH1208//35	—	5.00	7.00	13.50	22.50	35.00
AH1208//36	—	5.00	7.00	13.50	22.50	35.00
AH1209//36	—	5.00	7.00	13.50	22.50	35.00
AH1209//37	—	5.00	7.00	13.50	22.50	35.00
AH1210//37	—	5.00	7.00	13.50	22.50	35.00
AH1210//38	—	5.00	7.00	13.50	22.50	35.00
AH1211//38	—	5.00	7.00	13.50	22.50	35.00
AH1211//39	—	5.00	7.00	13.50	22.50	35.00
AH1212//39	—	5.00	7.00	13.50	22.50	35.00
AH1212//40	—	5.00	7.00	13.50	22.50	35.00
AH1213//40	—	5.00	7.00	13.50	22.50	35.00
AH1213//41	—	5.00	7.00	13.50	22.50	35.00
AH1214//41	—	5.00	7.00	13.50	22.50	35.00
AH1214//42	—	5.00	7.00	13.50	22.50	35.00
AH1215//42	—	5.00	7.00	13.50	22.50	35.00
AH1215//43	—	5.00	7.00	13.50	22.50	35.00

Mint: Hardwar
KM# 630 RUPEE

Silver **Obv:** Inscription **Rev:** Inscription **Note:** Struck at a mint of the Mughal governor of Saharanpur. Weight varies 11.00-11.60 grams.

Date	Mintage	Good	VG	F	VF	XF
AH1205//31 (sic)	—	15.00	35.00	70.00	100	150
AH1212//39	—	15.00	35.00	70.00	100	150
AH1214//41	—	15.00	35.00	70.00	100	150
AH1219//46	—	15.00	35.00	70.00	100	150

Mint: Hasanabad
KM# 634 RUPEE

Silver, 21 mm. **Obv. Inscription:** Badshah Ghazi **Rev:** Inscription, beaded flower **Note:** Weight varies 11.00-11.60 grams.

Date	Mintage	Good	VG	F	VF	XF
AH1174//1 Rare	—	—	—	—	—	—

Mint: Hasanabad
KM# 635 RUPEE

Silver, 21 mm. **Obv. Inscription:** Fazl-I-Hami Din, date **Rev:** Inscription **Note:** Weight varies 11.00-11.60 grams.

Date	Mintage	Good	VG	F	VF	XF
AH1177//5	—	—	—	—	—	—
AH1196//25 (sic) Rare	—	—	—	—	—	—

Mint: Hathras
KM# 640 RUPEE

Silver, 22.5 mm. **Issuer:** Local Governor, Mahadji Sindhia. **Obv:** Inscription **Rev:** Inscription **Note:** Coins dated AH1202/30 and 1203/30 may have been issued by Ghulam Qadir. Weight varies 11.00-11.60 grams.

Date	Mintage	Good	VG	F	VF	XF
AH1197//25	—	6.00	12.50	25.00	42.50	70.00
AH11xx//26	—	6.00	12.50	25.00	42.50	70.00
AH12xx//28	—	6.00	12.50	25.00	42.50	70.00
AH12xx//29	—	6.00	12.50	25.00	42.50	70.00
AH12xx//30	—	6.00	12.50	25.00	42.50	70.00

Mint: Jahangirnagar
KM# 648 RUPEE

Silver **Obv:** Inscription, date **Rev:** Inscription, sun-like symbol **Note:** Weight varies 11.00-11.60 grams.

Date	Mintage	Good	VG	F	VF	XF
AH1178//5	—	5.00	11.00	22.00	38.00	55.00

Mint: Kora
KM# 650 RUPEE

Silver **Issuer:** Local governor, Mirza Najaf Khan **Obv:** Inscription **Rev:** Inscription, mint mark at upper right **Note:** Mint mark is a symbol. Weight varies 11.00-11.60 grams.

Date	Mintage	Good	VG	F	VF	XF
AH11xx//7	—	5.00	7.00	13.00	22.00	32.00
AH11xx//8	—	5.00	7.00	13.00	22.00	32.00
AH11xx//9	—	5.00	7.00	13.00	22.00	32.00
AH11xx//10	—	5.00	7.00	13.00	22.00	32.00

Mint: Kora
KM# 651 RUPEE

Silver **Issuer:** Local governor, Mirza Najaf Khan **Obv:** Inscription, sword, beaded flower, cross **Rev:** Inscription, mint mark at upper right **Note:** Weight varies 11.00-11.60 grams.

Date	Mintage	Good	VG	F	VF	XF
AH11xx//11	—	5.00	7.00	13.00	22.00	32.00
AH11xx//12	—	5.00	7.00	13.00	22.00	32.00

Mint: Mungir
KM# 661 RUPEE

Silver **Note:** Weight varies 11.00-11.60 grams.

Date	Mintage	Good	VG	F	VF	XF
AH1176//4 Rare	—	—	—	—	—	—

Mint: Murshidabad
KM# 660 RUPEE

Silver **Note:** Mint mark is a cinquefoil. Weight varies 11.00-11.60 grams.

Date	Mintage	Good	VG	F	VF	XF
AH1175//2	—	5.00	9.00	18.00	30.00	45.00
AH1176//3	—	5.00	9.00	18.00	30.00	45.00
AH1177//5	—	5.00	9.00	18.00	30.00	45.00
AH1178//5	—	5.00	9.00	18.00	30.00	45.00
AH1179	—	5.00	9.00	18.00	30.00	45.00

Mint: Muzaffargarh
KM# 669 RUPEE

Silver, 21.5 mm. **Obv:** Inscription, mint mark, date **Obv. Inscription:** Sahib Qiran **Rev:** Inscription, mint mark, beaded flower at left **Note:** Prev. KM#2.

Date	Mintage	Good	VG	F	VF	XF
AH1202//30	—	5.50	11.50	18.00	30.00	50.00
AH1208//35	—	5.50	11.50	18.00	30.00	50.00
AH1209//36	—	5.50	11.50	18.00	30.00	50.00
AH1209//37	—	5.50	11.50	18.00	30.00	50.00
AH1209//38 (sic)	—	5.50	11.50	18.00	30.00	50.00
AH1209//39 (sic)	—	5.50	11.50	18.00	30.00	50.00
AH1211//39	—	5.50	11.50	18.00	30.00	50.00
AH1211//40 (sic)	—	5.50	11.50	18.00	30.00	50.00
AH1212//40	—	5.50	11.50	18.00	30.00	50.00
AH1212//41 (sic)	—	5.50	11.50	18.00	30.00	50.00
AH1213//41	—	5.50	11.50	18.00	30.00	50.00
AH1214//42	—	5.50	11.50	18.00	30.00	50.00
AH121x//43	—	5.50	11.50	18.00	30.00	50.00
AH12xx//44	—	5.50	11.50	18.00	30.00	50.00
AH12xx//45	—	5.50	11.50	18.00	30.00	50.00
AH1218//46	—	5.50	11.50	18.00	30.00	50.00
AH12xx//47	—	5.50	11.50	18.00	30.00	50.00

Mint: Muzaffargarh
KM# 668 RUPEE

Silver **Obv. Inscription:** Fazl-I-Hami Din **Rev:** Inscription **Note:** Weight varies 11.00-11.60 grams.

Date	Mintage	Good	VG	F	VF	XF
AH1197//25	—	7.00	15.00	27.50	45.00	75.00
AH1198//26	—	7.00	15.00	27.50	45.00	75.00
AH1199//27	—	7.00	15.00	27.50	45.00	75.00
AH1201//29	—	7.00	15.00	27.50	45.00	75.00

Mint: Saharanpur
KM# 675 RUPEE

11.4440 g., Silver, 20.5 mm. **Obv:** Inscription, date, beaded flowers **Rev:** Inscription, mint marks **Rev. Inscription:** Dar-ul-Khilafat **Note:** Mint epithet: "Dar-ul-Khilafat".

Date	Mintage	Good	VG	F	VF	XF
AH1204//31	—	5.00	9.00	18.00	30.00	45.00
AH1205//33	—	5.00	9.00	18.00	30.00	45.00
AH1207//34	—	5.00	9.00	18.00	30.00	45.00
AH1211//38	—	5.00	9.00	18.00	30.00	45.00
AH1212//40	—	5.00	9.00	18.00	30.00	45.00
AH1214//41	—	5.00	9.00	18.00	30.00	45.00
AH1215//42	—	5.00	9.00	18.00	30.00	45.00
AH1216//43	—	5.00	9.00	18.00	30.00	45.00
AH1217//44	—	5.00	9.00	18.00	30.00	45.00
AH1218/7//43 (sic)	—	5.00	9.00	18.00	30.00	45.00
AH1218//45	—	5.00	9.00	18.00	30.00	45.00

Mint: Saharanpur
KM# 680 RUPEE

Silver **Obv:** Inscription **Rev. Inscription:** Dar-us-Sarur **Note:** Weight varies 11.00-11.60 grams. Originally believed by some authorities to have been struck by the Sikhs, but now it's felt it was issued under the Maratha Administration. Other authorities insist Saran Singh gave this rupee to the Sikhs.

Date	Mintage	Good	VG	F	VF	XF
AH1210//37	—	—	15.00	30.00	50.00	70.00

Mint: Shahjahanabad
KM# 709.2 RUPEE

Silver **Obv:** Parasol, inscription **Rev:** Inscription **Note:** Weight varies 11.00-11.60 grams.

Date	Mintage	Good	VG	F	VF	XF
AH1186//x	—	5.50	12.00	20.00	32.50	55.00
AH1195//23	—	5.50	12.00	20.00	32.50	55.00
AH(1)196//23	—	5.50	12.00	20.00	32.50	55.00
AH1196//24	—	5.50	12.00	20.00	32.50	55.00
AH1197//25	—	5.50	12.00	20.00	32.50	55.00
AH1199//27	—	5.50	12.00	—	32.50	—
AH1201//29	—	5.50	12.00	20.00	32.50	55.00

Mint: Shahjahanabad
KM# 710 RUPEE

Silver **Obv:** Inscription, parasol, date **Obv. Inscription:** Sahib Qiran **Rev:** Inscription, mint mark **Note:** Weight varies 11.00-11.60 grams.

Date	Mintage	Good	VG	F	VF	XF
AH1202//30	—	6.00	11.50	18.00	30.00	50.00
AH1203//31	—	6.00	11.50	18.00	30.00	50.00
AH1204//31	—	6.00	11.50	18.00	30.00	50.00
AH1204//32	—	6.00	11.50	18.00	30.00	50.00
AH1205//32	—	6.00	11.50	18.00	30.00	50.00
AH1205//33	—	6.00	11.50	18.00	30.00	50.00
AH1206//33	—	6.00	11.50	18.00	30.00	50.00
AH1206//34	—	6.00	11.50	18.00	30.00	50.00
AH1207//34	—	6.00	11.50	18.00	30.00	50.00

Date	Mintage	Good	VG	F	VF	XF
AH1207//35	—	6.00	11.50	18.00	30.00	50.00
AH1208//35	—	6.00	11.50	18.00	30.00	50.00
AH1208//36	—	6.00	11.50	18.00	30.00	50.00
AH1209//36	—	6.00	11.50	18.00	30.00	50.00
AH1209//37	—	6.00	11.50	18.00	30.00	50.00
AH1210//37	—	6.00	11.50	18.00	30.00	50.00
AH1210//38	—	6.00	11.50	18.00	30.00	50.00
AH1211//38	—	6.00	11.50	18.00	30.00	50.00
AH1211//39	—	6.00	11.50	18.00	30.00	50.00
AH1212//39	—	6.00	11.50	18.00	30.00	50.00
AH1212//40	—	6.00	11.50	18.00	30.00	50.00
AH1213//40	—	6.00	11.50	18.00	30.00	50.00
AH1213//41	—	6.00	11.50	18.00	30.00	50.00

Mint: Surat
KM# 724 RUPEE

Silver **Obv:** Privy mark #1 **Note:** Weight varies 11.00-11.60 grams.

Date	Mintage	Good	VG	F	VF	XF
AHxxxx//1 (Ahad)	—	5.00	10.00	18.50	30.00	50.00
AH1189//19	—	5.00	10.00	18.50	30.00	50.00
AHxxxx//23	—	5.00	10.00	18.50	30.00	50.00
AHxxxx//30	—	5.00	10.00	18.50	30.00	50.00
AH1212//38	—	5.00	10.00	18.50	30.00	50.00
AH1205//32	—	5.00	10.00	18.50	30.00	50.00
AHxxxx//44	—	—	35.00	60.00	90.00	135

Mint: Zebabad
KM# A725 RUPEE

Silver **Note:** Weight varies 11.00-11.60 grams.

Date	Mintage	Good	VG	F	VF	XF
AH12xx//34	—	—	—	—	—	—
AH121x//39	—	—	—	—	—	—
AH1214//40 (sic)	—	—	—	—	—	—

Mint: Akbarabad
KM# 492 NAZARANA RUPEE

Silver **Obv:** Inscription **Rev:** Inscription **Note:** Pre-Panipat issue. Weight varies 11.00-11.60 grams.

Date	Mintage	Good	VG	F	VF	XF
AH1174//1	—	15.00	37.50	75.00	125	175

Mint: Azimabad
KM# 593 NAZARANA RUPEE

Silver **Issuer:** East India Company **Obv:** Inscription, date **Rev:** Inscription, trident at lower left **Note:** Weight varies 11.00-11.60 grams.

Date	Mintage	Good	VG	F	VF	XF
AH1174//2	—	—	—	—	—	—

Mint: Shahjahanabad
KM# 716 NAZARANA RUPEE

Silver, 29-36 mm. **Note:** Size varies. Similar to KM#709. Weight varies: 11.00-11.60 grams.

Date	Mintage	Good	VG	F	VF	XF
AH1174//2	—	50.00	100	200	275	400

Mint: Shahjahanabad
KM# 717 NAZARANA RUPEE

Silver **Obv:** Inscription, parasol **Rev:** Inscription **Note:** Weight varies 11.00-11.60 grams.

Date	Mintage	Good	VG	F	VF	XF
AH1202//30	—	50.00	100	200	275	400
AH1208//36	—	50.00	100	200	275	400
AH1209//37	—	50.00	100	200	275	400

Mint: Surat
KM# 726 2 RUPEES

Silver **Obv:** Inscription, flower **Rev:** Inscription **Note:** Weight varies 11.00-11.60 grams.

Date	Mintage	Good	VG	F	VF	XF
AH118x//16	—	—	—	—	—	—

Mint: Ahmadabad
KM# 484 MOHUR

Gold, 19 mm. **Note:** Weight varies 10.70-11.40 grams.

Date	Mintage	Good	VG	F	VF	XF
AH1202//29	—	235	265	310	375	450

Mint: Murshidabad
KM# 663 MOHUR

Silver **Obv:** Inscription **Rev:** Inscription **Note:** Weight varies 10.70-10.90 grams.

Date	Mintage	Good	VG	F	VF	XF
AH1176//3	—	235	265	310	375	450
AH1177//5	—	235	265	310	375	450

Mint: Shahjahanabad
KM# 719 MOHUR

Gold **Obv. Inscription:** Hami Din **Rev:** Inscription **Note:** Weight varies 10.70-10.90 grams.

Date	Mintage	Good	VG	F	VF	XF
AH1174//2	—	235	265	310	375	450
AH1175//2	—	235	265	310	375	450
AH1175//3	—	235	265	310	375	450
AH1176//3	—	235	265	310	375	450
AH1180//8	—	235	265	310	375	450
AH1192//19	—	235	265	310	375	450
AH1197//24	—	235	265	310	375	450
AH1197//25	—	235	265	310	375	450
AH1201//29	—	235	265	310	375	450

Mint: Shahjahanabad
KM# 720 MOHUR

Gold **Obv. Inscription:** Sahib Qiran, parasol **Rev:** Inscription **Note:** Weight varies 10.70-10.90 grams.

Date	Mintage	Good	VG	F	VF	XF
AH1202//30	—	235	265	310	375	450
AH1204//31	—	235	265	310	375	450
AH1205//32	—	235	265	310	375	450
AH1206//33	—	235	265	310	375	450
AH1206//34	—	235	265	310	375	450

ANONYMOUS COINAGE

Mint: Without Mint Name
KM# 730 FALUS

Copper **Note:** Weight varies 14.70-21.50 grams.

Date	Mintage	VG	F	VF	XF	Unc
AH1202//xx	—	16.50	25.00	40.00	—	—

Mint: Without Mint Name
KM# 731 FALUS

Copper **Note:** Weight varies 14.70-21.50 grams. Mint unknown.

Date	Mintage	VG	F	VF	XF	Unc
AH1202//30 Retrograde	—	16.50	25.00	40.00	—	—

Mint: Without Mint Name
KM# 732 FALUS

Copper **Note:** Weight varies 14.70-21.50 grams. Mint unknown.

Date	Mintage	VG	F	VF	XF	Unc
AH1202//30	—	16.50	25.00	40.00	—	—

Mint: Without Mint Name
KM# 734 FALUS

Copper **Note:** Weight varies 14.70-21.50 grams. Mint unknown.

Date	Mintage	VG	F	VF	XF	Unc
AH1211//xx	—	16.50	25.00	40.00	—	—

Note: These anonymous copper coins, attributed to the region of Shah Alam II on the basis of their daring, have been found in Northwest India, especially in the Punjab. They may have been issued by one of the autonomous princely states.

Mint: Zebabad
KM# 733 FALUS

Copper, 24 mm. **Note:** Weight varies 14.70-21.50 grams.

Date	Mintage	VG	F	VF	XF	Unc
AH1204//31 Retrograde	—	16.50	25.00	40.00	—	—
AH1205//31 (sic) Retrograde	—	16.50	25.00	40.00	—	—

Bedar Bakht

AH1202-1203 / 1788AD

Bedar Bakht, a son of the late Mughal Emperor Ahmad Shah, was a puppet king placed on the Mughal throne by the Rohilla rebel Ghulam Qadir Khan in August AH1202/1788AD after deposing Shah Alam II. The latter was subsequently tortured and blinded by Ghulam Qadir Khan. Bedar Bakht reigned in name only for a little over two months and was replaced by a cousin, Muhammad Akbar Shah, a son of the deposed emperor Shah Alam II.

Ahmadabad Mint

This mintname does not refer to the Gujarat city of that name, but is either an epithet for Saharanpur, Ghulam Qadir's stronghold, or another city in the Delhi vicinity.

HAMMERED COINAGE

Mint: Mohammadabad
KM# 740 PAISA

Copper **Note:** Weight varies 12.90-13.80 grams.

Date	Mintage	Good	VG	F	VF	XF
AH1203//1	—	30.00	55.00	75.00	120	—

Mint: Ahmadabad
KM# 738 RUPEE

Silver **Obv:** Inscription **Rev:** Inscription **Note:** Weight varies 11.00-11.60 grams. Issued by Bedar Bakht at the beginning of his rebellion before placing his own name on coinage, at Saharanpur which took the name Ahmadabad during the reign of Bedar Bakht (not the Ahmedebad in Gujarat).

Date	Mintage	Good	VG	F	VF	XF
AH1202//29	—	25.00	62.50	135	225	335

Mint: Mohammadabad
KM# 742 RUPEE
Silver **Note:** Weight varies 11.00-11.60 grams.

Date	Mintage	Good	VG	F	VF	XF
AH1202//1 Rare	—	—	—	—	—	—
AH1203//1 Rare	—	—	—	—	—	—

Mint: Shahjahanabad
KM# 750 RUPEE
Silver **Obv:** Inscription, date **Rev:** Inscription **Note:** Weight varies 11.00-11.60 grams.

Date	Mintage	Good	VG	F	VF	XF
AH1202//1 Rare	—	—	—	—	—	—

Mint: Mohammadabad
KM# 744 MOHUR
Gold **Obv:** Inscription, mint mark **Rev:** Inscription **Note:** Weight varies 10.70-11.40 grams.

Date	Mintage	Good	VG	F	VF	XF
AH1202//1 Rare	—	—	—	—	—	—
AH1203//1 Rare	—	—	—	—	—	—

Mint: Shahjahanabad
KM# 752 MOHUR
Gold **Obv:** Inscription **Rev:** Inscription **Note:** Weight varies 10.70-11.40 grams.

Date	Mintage	Good	VG	F	VF	XF
AH1202//1	—	275	600	900	1,250	1,750

Muhammad Akbar Shah II
AH1203 / 1788AD

On his retreat to Saharanpur following the Maratha occupation of Delhi in October 1788AD, the Rohilla rebel Ghulam Qadir Khan deposed Bedar Bakht and substituted his cousin Muhammad Akbar, Shah Alam's favorite son, to rule nominally in exile. After

Ghulam Qadir's capture and execution by the Marathas in March 1789AD, they restored the pathetic Shah Alam II to the Mughal throne at Delhi to reign as a puppet king. Akbar Shah II's only known coins were issued from the temporary capital at Saharanpur.

HAMMERED COINAGE

Mint: Saharanpur
KM# 760 RUPEE
Silver **Obv:** Inscription **Rev:** Inscription **Note:** Weight varies 11.00-11.60 grams.

Date	Mintage	Good	VG	F	VF	XF
AH1203//1	—	275	600	1,000	1,250	1,750

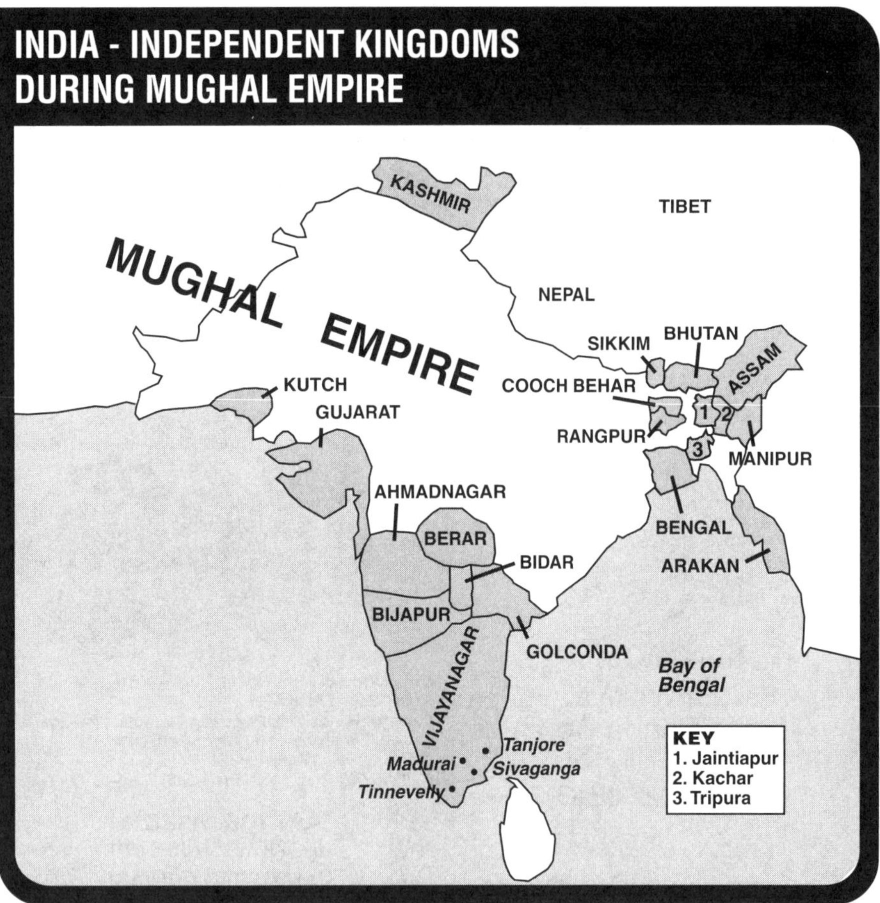

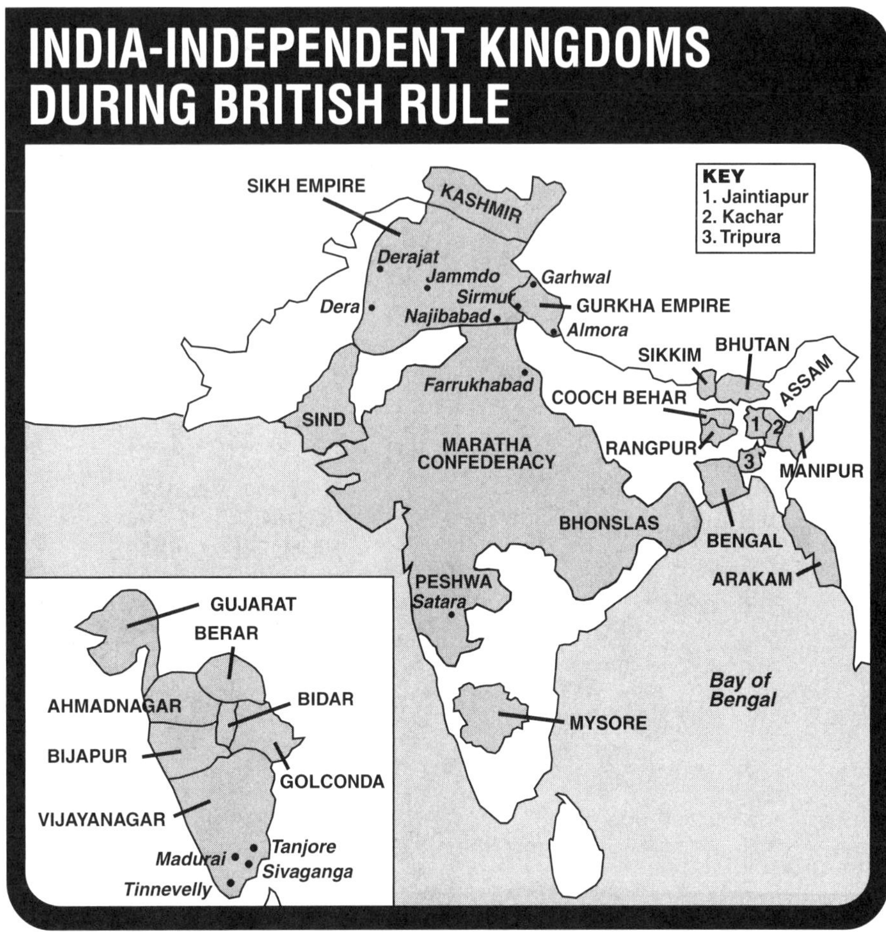

ARAKAN

A coastal region of Burma on the Bay of Bengal. The Buddhist Arakanese trace their history back 4500 years.

Arakan surrendered to the Burmese King Bodawpaya in 1784 and coins were issued by the king's governor in Arakan, bearing the following inscription: Amarapura, Kingdom of the Lord of Many White Elephants.

RULERS

Kalamandat, BE1059-1072/1697-1710AD
Sanda Wizaya, Maha Danda Bo, BE1072-1093/1710-1731AD
Sanda Thuriya, BE1093-1097/1731-1738AD
Narapawara, BE1097-1098/1735-1736AD
Sanda Wizala, BE1098-1099/1736-1737AD
Madarit Raza, BE1099-1104/1737-1742AD
Nara Apaya, BE1104-1123/1742-1761AD
Sanda Parma, BE1123-1126/1761-1764AD
Apaya Maha Raza, BE1126-1135/1764-1773AD
Sanda Thumana, BE1135-1139/1773-1777AD
Sanda Wimala, BE1139/1777AD
Thaditha Dhammarit, BE1139-1144/1777-1782AD
Maha Thamada, BE1144-1146/1782-1784AD
Amarapura Lord, Bodawpaya, BE1146/1784AD

KINGDOM

Sanda Wizaya, Maha Danda Bo

BE1072-93/1710-31AD

HAMMERED COINAGE

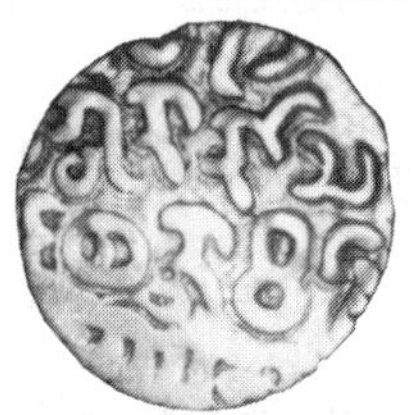
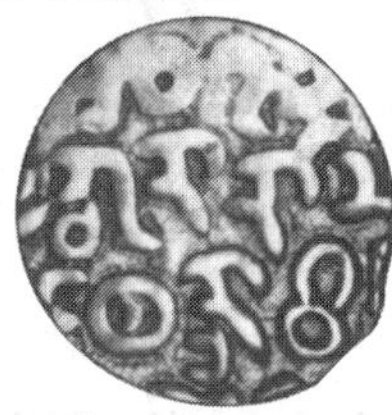

Mint: Without Mint Name
KM# 17 TANKAH
Silver **Obv:** Inscription **Rev:** Inscription **Note:** Weight varies: 8.84-10.20 grams.

Date	Mintage	Good	VG	F	VF	XF
BE1072 (1710)	—	12.50	20.00	30.00	45.00	—
BE1075 (1713)	—	12.50	20.00	30.00	45.00	—

Sanda Thuriya

BE1093-97/1731-38AD

HAMMERED COINAGE

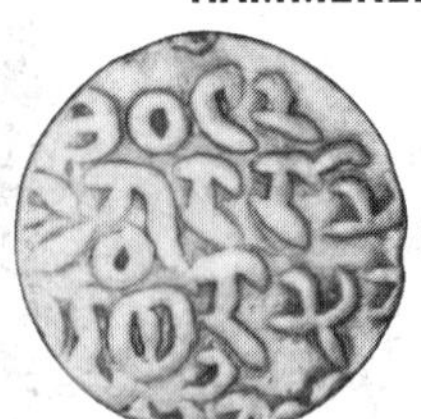
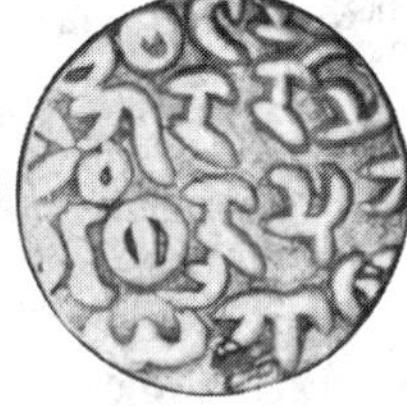

Mint: Without Mint Name
KM# 18 TANKAH
Silver **Obv:** Inscription **Rev:** Inscription **Note:** Weight varies: 9.50-10.21 grams.

Date	Mintage	Good	VG	F	VF	XF
BE1093 (1731)	—	20.00	32.50	50.00	75.00	—

Narapawara

BE1097-98/1735-36AD

HAMMERED COINAGE

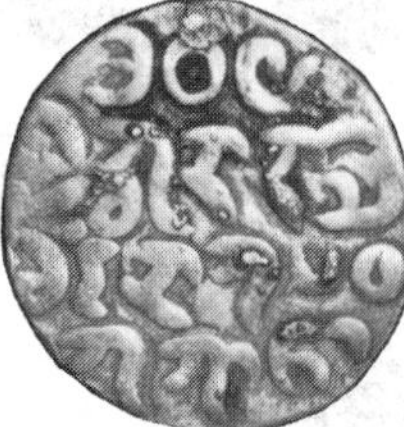
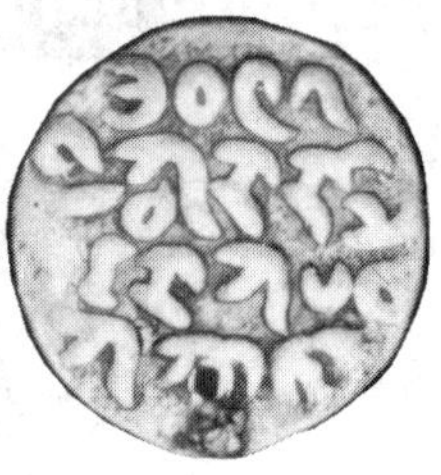

Mint: Without Mint Name
KM# 19.1 TANKAH
Silver **Obv:** Inscription **Rev:** Inscription **Note:** Weight varies: 9.4-10.97 grams.

Date	Mintage	Good	VG	F	VF	XF
BE1097 (1735)	—	20.00	32.50	50.00	75.00	—

Mint: Without Mint Name
KM# 19.2 TANKAH
Silver **Obv:** Inscription **Rev:** Inscription **Note:** Weight varies: 9.40-10.97 grams. Horizontal line added on obverse.

Date	Mintage	Good	VG	F	VF	XF
BE1097 (1735)	—	20.00	32.50	50.00	75.00	—

Sanda Wizala

BE1098-99/1736-37AD

HAMMERED COINAGE

Mint: Without Mint Name
KM# 20 TANKAH
9.9500 g., Silver **Obv:** Inscription **Rev:** Inscription

Date	Mintage	Good	VG	F	VF	XF
BE1098 (1736)	—	40.00	60.00	90.00	130	—

Madarit Raza

BE1099-1104/1737-42AD

HAMMERED COINAGE

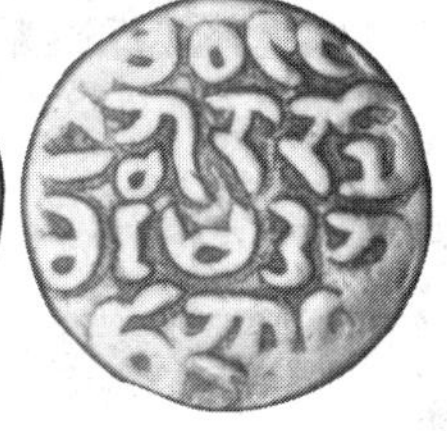

Mint: Without Mint Name
KM# 21 TANKAH
Silver **Obv:** Inscription **Rev:** Inscription **Note:** Weight varies: 9.32-9.97 grams.

Date	Mintage	Good	VG	F	VF	XF
BE1099 (1737)	—	40.00	60.00	90.00	130	—

Nara Apaya

BE1104-23/1742-61AD

HAMMERED COINAGE

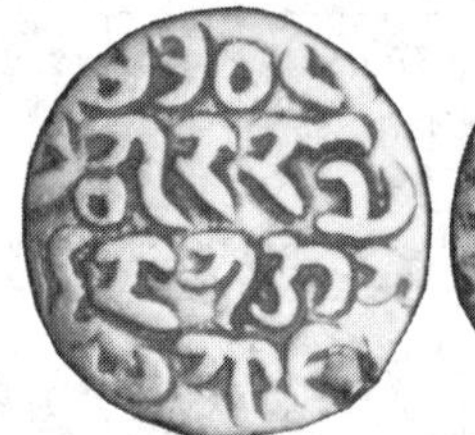

Mint: Without Mint Name
KM# 22 TANKAH
Silver **Obv:** Inscription **Rev:** Inscription **Note:** Weight varies: 9.53-10.58 grams.

Date	Mintage	Good	VG	F	VF	XF
BE1104 (1742)	—	25.00	35.00	50.00	75.00	—

Sanda Parma

BE1123-26/1761-64AD

HAMMERED COINAGE

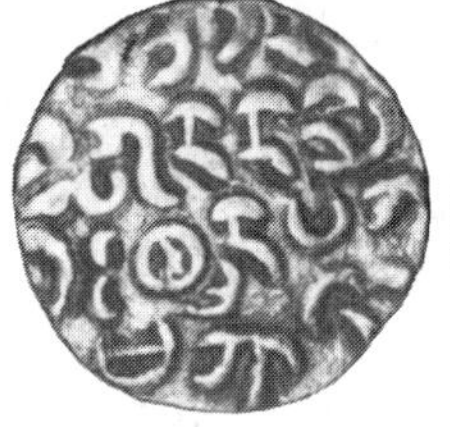
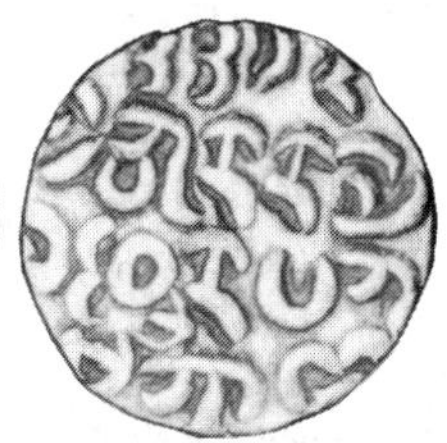

Mint: Without Mint Name
KM# 23 TANKAH
Silver **Obv:** Inscription **Rev:** Inscription **Note:** Weight varies: 8.92-10.08 grams.

Date	Mintage	Good	VG	F	VF	XF
BE1123 (1761)	—	25.00	35.00	50.00	75.00	—

Apaya Maha Raza

BE1126-35/1764-73AD

HAMMERED COINAGE

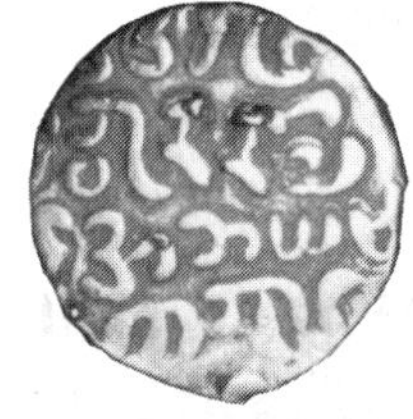

Mint: Without Mint Name
KM# 24 TANKAH
Silver **Obv:** Inscription **Rev:** Inscription **Note:** Weight varies: 6.17-10.36 grams.

Date	Mintage	Good	VG	F	VF	XF
BE1126 (1764)	—	25.00	35.00	50.00	75.00	—

Sanda Thumana

BE1135-39/1773-77AD

HAMMERED COINAGE

Mint: Without Mint Name
KM# 25 TANKAH
Silver **Obv:** Inscription **Rev:** Inscription **Note:** Weight varies: 8.90-10.16 grams.

Date	Mintage	Good	VG	F	VF	XF
BE1135 (1773)	—	40.00	60.00	90.00	130	—

Thaditha Dhammarit Raja

BE1139-44/1777-82AD

HAMMERED COINAGE

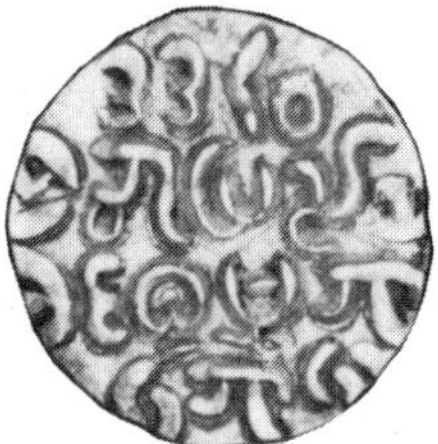
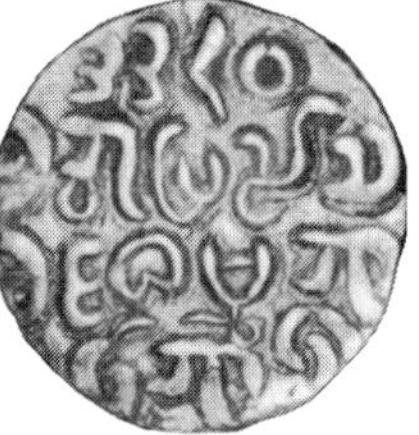

Mint: Without Mint Name
KM# 26 TANKAH
Silver **Obv:** Inscription **Rev:** Inscription **Note:** Weight varies: 9.84-10.13 grams.

Date	Mintage	Good	VG	F	VF	XF
BE1140 (1778)	—	20.00	30.00	45.00	65.00	—

Maha Thamada Raza

BE1144-46/1782-84AD

HAMMERED COINAGE

Mint: Without Mint Name
KM# 27 TANKAH

Silver **Obv:** Inscription **Rev:** Inscription **Note:** Weight varies: 9.87-10.19 grams.

Date	Mintage	Good	VG	F	VF	XF
BE1144 (1782)	—	25.00	35.00	50.00	75.00	—

BURMESE OCCUPATION

Amarapura Lord, Bodawpaya

BE1146/1784AD

HAMMERED COINAGE

Mint: Without Mint Name
KM# 28.1 TANKAH

Silver **Obv:** Inscription within cord borders **Rev:** Inscription within cord borders **Note:** Weight varies: 8.97-10.71 grams.

Date	Mintage	Good	VG	F	VF	XF
BE1146 (1784)	—	30.00	50.00	75.00	100	—

Mint: Without Mint Name
KM# 28.2 TANKAH

Silver **Obv:** Inscription within segmented dotted border **Rev:** Inscription within segmented dotted border **Note:** Weight varies: 8.97-10.71 grams.

Date	Mintage	Good	VG	F	VF	XF
BE1146 (1784)	—	30.00	50.00	75.00	100	—

Mint: Without Mint Name
KM# 28.3 TANKAH

Silver **Obv:** Inscription within beaded circle **Rev:** Inscription within beaded circle **Note:** Weight varies: 8.97-10.71 grams.

Date	Mintage	Good	VG	F	VF	XF
BE1146 (1784)	—	25.00	35.00	50.00	75.00	—

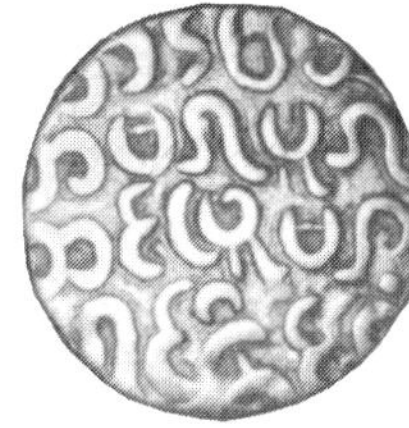
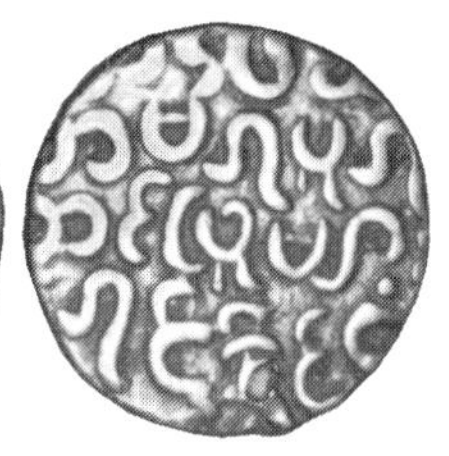

Mint: Without Mint Name
KM# 29 TANKAH

Silver **Obv:** Inscription **Rev:** Inscription **Note:** Weight varies: 9.03-10.80 grams.

Date	Mintage	Good	VG	F	VF	XF
BE1146 (1784)	—	25.00	35.00	50.00	75.00	—

Mint: Without Mint Name
KM# 30 TANKAH

10.1100 g., Gold **Obv:** Inscription within corded border **Rev:** Inscription within corded border **Note:** Reverse as obverse.

Date	Mintage	VG	F	VF	XF	Unc
BE1146 (1784) Rare	—	—	—	—	—	—

ASSAM

It was in the 13th century that a tribal leader called Sukapha, with about 9,000 followers, left their traditional home in the Shan States of Northern Burma, and carved out the Ahom Kingdom in upper Assam.

The Ahom Kingdom gradually increased in power and extent over the following centuries, particularly during the reign of King Suhungmung (1497-1539). This king also took on a Hindu title, Svarga Narayan, which shows the increasing influence of the Brahmins over the court. Although several of the other Hindu states in north-east India started a silver coinage during the 16th century, it was not until the mid-17th century that the Ahoms first struck coin.

From the time of Kusain Shah's invasion of Cooch Behar in 1494AD the Muslims had cast acquisitive eyes towards the valley of the Brahmaputra, but the Ahoms managed to preserve their independence. In 1661 Aurangzeb's governor in Bengal, Mir Jumla, made a determined effort to bring Assam under Mughal rule. Cooch Behar was annexed without difficulty, and in March 1662 Mir Jumla occupied Gargaon, the Ahom capital, without opposition. However, during the rainy season the Muslim forces suffered severely from disease, lack of food and from the occasional attacks from the Ahom forces, who had tactically withdrawn from the capital together with the king. After the end of the monsoon a supply line was opened with Bengal again, but morale in the Muslim army was low, so Mir Jumla was forced to agree to peach terms somewhat less onerous than the Mughals liked to impose on subjugated states. The Ahoms agreed to pay tribute, but the Ahom kingdom remained entirely independent of Mughal control, and never again did a Muslim army venture into upper Assam.

During the eighteenth century the kingdom became weakened with civil war, culminating in the expulsion of Gaurinatha Simha from his capital in 1787 by the Moamarias. The British helped Gaurinatha regain his kingdom in 1794, but otherwise took little interest in the affairs of Assam. The end of the Ahom Kingdom was not due to intervention from Bengal, but from Burma.

RULERS

Ruler's names, where present on the coins, usually appear on the obverse (dated) side, starting either at the end of the first line, after *Shri*, or in the second line. Most of the Ahom rulers after the adoption of Hinduism in about 1500AD had both an Ahom and a Hindu name.

HINDU NAME **AHOM NAME**

Rudra Simha — Sukhrungpha
রুদ্র সিংহ
SE1618-1636/1696-1714/AD

Shiva Simha — Sutanpha
শিব সিংহ
SE1636-1666/1714-1744AD

Queens of Shiva Simha
Queen Phuleshvari or
প্রমথেশ্বরী
Queen Pramatheshvari
ফুলেশ্বরী
SE1639-1653/1717-1731AD

Queen Ambika Devi
অম্বিকাদেবী
SE1654-1660/1732-1738AD

Queen Sarvveshvari
সর্ব্বেশ্বরী
SE1661-1666/1739-1744AD

Pramatta Simha — Sunenpha
প্রমত্তসিংহ
SE1666-1673/1744-1751AD

Rajesvara Simha — Surempha
রাজেশ্বরসিংহ
SE1673-1691/1751-1769AD

Lakshmi Simha — Sunyeopha
লক্ষ্মীসিংহ
SE1691-1702/1769-1780AD

Gaurinatha Simha — Suhitpangpha
গৌরীনাথসিংহ
SE1702-1717/1780-1795AD

Kamalesvara Simha — Suklingpha
কমলেশ্বরসিংহ
SE1717-1733/1795-1811AD

COINAGE

It is frequently stated that coins were first struck in Assam during the reign of King Suklenmung (1539-1552), but this is merely due to a misreading of the Ahom legend on the coins of King Supungmung (1663-70). The earliest Ahom coins known, therefore, were struck during the reign of King Jayadhvaja Simha (1648-1663).

Although the inscription and general design of these first coins of the Ahom Kingdom were copied from the coins of Cooch Behar, the octagonal shape was entirely Ahom, and according to tradition was chosen because of the belief that the Ahom country was eight sided. Apart from the unique shape, the coins were of similar fabric and weight standard to the Mughul rupee.

The earliest coins had inscriptions in Sanskrit using the Bengali script, but the retreat of the Mughul army under Mir Jumla in 1663 seems to have led to a revival of Ahom nationalism that may account for the fact that most of the coins struck between 1663 and 1696 had inscriptions in the old Ahom script, with invocations to Ahom deities.

Up to this time all the coins, following normal practice in Northeast India, were merely dated to the coronation year of the ruler, but Rudra Simha (1696-1714) instituted the practice of dating coins to the year of issue. This ruler was a fervent Hindu, and reinstated Sanskrit inscriptions on the coins. After this the Ahom script was used on a few rare ceremonial issues.

The majority of coins issued were of silver, with binary subdivions down to a fraction of 1/32nd rupee. Cowrie shells were used for small change. Gold coins were struck throughout the period, often using the same dies as were used for the silver coins. A few copper coins were struck during the reign of Brajanatha Simha (1818-19), but these are very rare.

NUMERALS

The early coinage is usually dated in the Saka era using Bengali numerals while later issues use modified numerals called Assamese.

MINT NAMES

گرگاو
Gargaon

رنگپور
Rangpur

REGNAL YEARS

Some of the earliest dated coins have the regnal years in written characters. These listings will have the numerical regnal years in parenthesis in the following listings.

Written	Numeric	Symbol
RAITYEO	13	
PLEKNGI	15	
KAPSAN	21	
KHUCHNGI for KHUTNGI	27	
RAISAN	33	
KATKEU	36	
RAISINGA	43	

KINGDOM

Rudra Simha (Sukhrungpha)

SE1618-1636 / 1696-1714AD

HAMMERED COINAGE

Mint: Without Mint Name
KM# 40 RUPEE
Silver **Obv:** Inscription **Rev:** Inscription **Note:** Weight varies: 10.70-11.60 grams.

Date	Mintage	VG	F	VF	XF	Unc
SE1623 (1701)	—	5.00	8.00	15.00	22.50	—
SE1624 (1702)	—	6.50	11.50	20.00	30.00	—
SE1625 (1703)	—	5.00	8.00	15.00	22.50	—
SE1626 (1704)	—	5.00	8.00	15.00	22.50	—
SE1627 (1705)	—	5.00	8.00	15.00	22.50	—
SE1628 (1706)	—	6.50	11.50	20.00	30.00	—
SE1629 (1707)	—	8.00	14.50	25.00	40.00	—
SE1630 (1708)	—	5.00	8.00	15.00	22.50	—
SE1631 (1709)	—	5.00	8.00	15.00	22.50	—
SE1632 (1710)	—	5.00	8.00	15.00	22.20	—
SE1633 (1711)	—	5.00	8.00	15.00	22.50	—
SE1634 (1712)	—	5.00	8.00	15.00	22.50	—
SE1635 (1713)	—	5.00	8.00	15.00	22.50	—
SE1636 (1714)	—	5.00	8.00	15.00	22.50	—

Mint: Without Mint Name
KM# 45 MOHUR
Gold **Obv:** Inscription **Rev:** Inscription **Note:** Weight varies: 10.70-11.40 grams.

Date	Mintage	VG	F	VF	XF	Unc
SE1630 (1708)	—	175	300	500	800	—

Shiva Simha (Sutanpha)

SE1637-1666/1715-1744AD

HAMMERED COINAGE

Mint: Without Mint Name
KM# 47 1/4 RUPEE
Silver **Note:** Weight varies: 2.68-2.90 grams.

Date	Mintage	VG	F	VF	XF	Unc
SE1637 (1715)	—	10.00	16.50	26.50	40.00	—
SE1643 (1721)	—	10.00	16.50	26.50	40.00	—

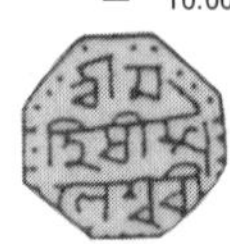

Mint: Without Mint Name
KM# 56 1/4 RUPEE
Silver **Obv. Inscription:** Queen Phulesvari **Rev:** Inscription **Note:** Weight varies: 2.68-2.90 grams.

Date	Mintage	VG	F	VF	XF	Unc
SE1646 (1724)	—	10.00	16.50	26.50	37.50	—

Mint: Without Mint Name
KM# 57 1/4 RUPEE
Silver **Obv. Inscription:** Queen Phulesvari **Rev:** Inscription **Note:** Weight varies: 2.68-2.90 grams.

Date	Mintage	VG	F	VF	XF	Unc
ND(1715-44) (1715)	—	12.50	21.50	35.00	65.00	—

Mint: Without Mint Name
KM# 69 1/4 RUPEE
Silver **Obv. Inscription:** Queen Pramathesvari **Rev:** Inscription **Note:** Weight varies: 2.68-2.90 grams.

Date	Mintage	VG	F	VF	XF	Unc
ND(1715-44) (1715)	—	8.00	13.50	22.50	35.00	—

Mint: Without Mint Name
KM# 85 1/4 RUPEE
Silver **Obv. Inscription:** Queen Ambika **Rev:** Inscription **Note:** Weight varies: 2.68-2.90 grams.

Date	Mintage	VG	F	VF	XF	Unc
ND//19 (1734)	—	8.00	13.50	22.50	35.00	—
ND//20 (1735)	—	8.00	13.50	22.50	35.00	—
ND//23 (1738)	—	8.00	13.50	22.50	35.00	—

Mint: Without Mint Name
KM# 86 1/4 RUPEE
Silver **Obv. Inscription:** Queen Ambika **Rev:** Animal **Note:** Weight varies: 2.68-2.90 grams.

Date	Mintage	VG	F	VF	XF	Unc
ND//24 (1739)	—	10.00	16.50	26.50	40.00	—

Mint: Without Mint Name
KM# 108 1/4 RUPEE
Silver **Obv. Inscription:** Queen Sarvvesvari **Rev:** Inscription **Note:** Weight varies: 2.68-2.90 grams.

Date	Mintage	VG	F	VF	XF	Unc
ND//25 (1740)	—	5.00	7.50	13.50	18.50	—
ND//26 (1741)	—	5.00	7.50	13.50	18.50	—
ND//27 (1742)	—	3.25	5.00	8.50	12.50	—
ND//28 (1743)	—	3.25	5.00	8.50	12.50	—
ND//29 (1744)	—	3.25	5.00	8.50	12.50	—
ND//30 (1745)	—	3.25	5.00	8.50	12.50	—
ND//31 (1746)	—	3.25	5.00	8.50	12.50	—

Mint: Without Mint Name
KM# 100 1/4 RUPEE
Silver **Obv:** Inscription **Rev:** Inscription **Note:** Without queen's name. Weight varies: 2.68-2.90 grams.

Date	Mintage	VG	F	VF	XF	Unc
SE1660//24 (1738)	—	10.00	16.50	26.50	40.00	—
SE1660//25 (1738)	—	10.00	16.50	26.50	40.00	—

Mint: Without Mint Name
KM# 49 1/2 RUPEE
Silver **Obv:** Inscription **Rev:** Inscription **Note:** Weight varies: 5.35-5.80 grams.

Date	Mintage	VG	F	VF	XF	Unc
ND(1715-44)	—	3.50	6.00	10.00	15.00	—

Mint: Without Mint Name
KM# 59 1/2 RUPEE
Silver **Obv. Inscription:** Queen Phulesvari **Rev:** Inscription **Note:** Weight varies: 5.35-5.80 grams.

Date	Mintage	VG	F	VF	XF	Unc
ND(1715-44)	—	12.50	21.50	35.00	65.00	—

Mint: Without Mint Name
KM# 71 1/2 RUPEE
Silver **Obv. Inscription:** Queen Pramathesvari **Note:** Weight varies: 5.35-5.80 grams.

Date	Mintage	VG	F	VF	XF	Unc
ND(1715-44)	—	10.00	16.50	26.50	40.00	—

Mint: Without Mint Name
KM# 88 1/2 RUPEE
Silver **Obv. Inscription:** Queen Ambika **Note:** Weight varies: 5.35-5.80 grams.

Date	Mintage	VG	F	VF	XF	Unc
ND//19 (1734)	—	10.00	16.50	26.50	40.00	—
ND//23 (1738)	—	10.00	16.50	26.50	40.00	—

Mint: Without Mint Name
KM# 89 1/2 RUPEE
Silver **Obv:** Animal **Obv. Inscription:** Queen Ambika **Note:** Weight varies: 5.35-5.80 grams.

Date	Mintage	VG	F	VF	XF	Unc
ND//24 (1735)	—	12.50	21.50	35.00	65.00	—

Mint: Without Mint Name
KM# 110 1/2 RUPEE
Silver **Obv. Inscription:** Queen Sarvvesvari **Rev:** Inscription **Note:** Weight varies: 5.35-5.80 grams.

Date	Mintage	VG	F	VF	XF	Unc
ND//25 (1740)	—	5.00	7.50	13.50	18.50	—
ND//26 (1741)	—	5.00	7.50	13.50	18.50	—
ND//27 (1742)	—	3.50	6.00	10.00	15.00	—
ND//28 (1743)	—	3.50	6.00	10.00	15.00	—
ND//29 (1744)	—	3.50	6.00	10.00	15.00	—
ND//30 (1745)	—	3.50	6.00	10.00	15.00	—
ND//31 (1746)	—	3.50	6.00	10.00	15.00	—

Mint: Without Mint Name
KM# 81 1/2 RUPEE
Silver **Obv:** Inscription **Rev:** Inscription **Note:** Without queen's name. Weight varies: 5.35-5.80 grams.

Date	Mintage	VG	F	VF	XF	Unc
ND//18 (1730)	—	12.50	21.50	35.00	65.00	—

Mint: Without Mint Name
KM# 102 1/2 RUPEE
Silver **Note:** Without queen's name. Weight varies: 5.35-5.80 grams.

Date	Mintage	VG	F	VF	XF	Unc
ND//24 (1740)	—	10.00	18.50	30.00	55.00	—
ND//25 (1740)	—	10.00	18.50	30.00	55.00	—

Mint: Without Mint Name
KM# 51 RUPEE
Silver **Obv:** Inscription **Rev:** Inscription **Note:** Weight varies: 10.70-11.60 grams.

Date	Mintage	VG	F	VF	XF	Unc
SE1637 (1715)	—	5.00	8.00	15.00	22.50	—
SE1638 (1716)	—	5.00	8.00	15.00	22.50	—
SE1639 (1717)	—	6.50	11.50	20.00	30.00	—
SE1640 (1718)	—	6.50	11.50	20.00	30.00	—
SE1641 (1719)	—	5.00	8.00	15.00	22.50	—
SE1642 (1720)	—	5.00	8.00	15.00	22.50	—
SE1643 (1721)	—	5.00	8.00	15.00	22.50	—
SE1644 (1722)	—	5.00	8.00	15.00	22.50	—
SE1645 (1723)	—	5.00	8.00	15.00	22.50	—
SE1646 (1724)	—	5.00	8.00	15.00	22.50	—

Mint: Without Mint Name
KM# 61 RUPEE
Silver **Obv. Inscription:** Queen Phulesvari **Rev:** Inscription **Note:** Weight varies: 10.70-11.60 grams.

Date	Mintage	VG	F	VF	XF	Unc
SE1646 (1724)	—	5.00	9.00	16.00	25.00	—
SE1647 (1725)	—	5.00	9.00	16.00	25.00	—

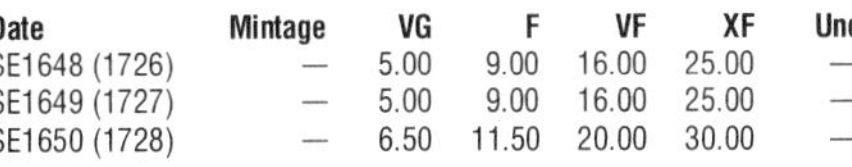

Date	Mintage	VG	F	VF	XF	Unc
SE1648 (1726)	—	5.00	9.00	16.00	25.00	—
SE1649 (1727)	—	5.00	9.00	16.00	25.00	—
SE1650 (1728)	—	6.50	11.50	20.00	30.00	—

Mint: Without Mint Name
KM# 62 RUPEE
Silver **Obv. Inscription:** Queen Phulesvari **Rev:** Inscription, beaded flowers **Note:** Weight varies: 10.70-11.60 grams.

Date	Mintage	VG	F	VF	XF	Unc
SE1646 (1724)	—	16.50	28.50	50.00	90.00	—

Mint: Without Mint Name
KM# 73 RUPEE
Silver **Obv. Inscription:** Queen Pramathesvari **Rev:** Inscription **Note:** Weight varies: 10.70-11.60 grams.

Date	Mintage	VG	F	VF	XF	Unc
SE1648 (1726)	—	5.00	8.00	15.00	22.50	—
SE1649 (1727)	—	5.00	8.00	15.00	22.50	—
SE1650 (1728)	—	5.00	8.00	15.00	22.50	—
SE1651 (1729)	—	5.00	8.00	15.00	22.50	—
SE1652 (1730)	—	5.00	8.00	15.00	22.50	—
SE1653 (1731)	—	5.00	8.00	15.00	22.50	—

Mint: Without Mint Name
KM# 83 RUPEE
Silver **Obv:** Inscription, without Queen's name **Rev:** Inscription **Note:** Weight varies: 10.70-11.60 grams.

Date	Mintage	VG	F	VF	XF	Unc
SE1654//18 (1732)	—	6.50	10.50	17.50	25.00	—

Mint: Without Mint Name
KM# 91 RUPEE
Silver **Obv. Inscription:** Queen Ambika, lion right **Rev:** Inscription **Note:** Weight varies: 10.70-11.60 grams.

Date	Mintage	VG	F	VF	XF	Unc
SE1654//19 (1732)	—	5.00	8.00	15.00	22.50	—
SE1655//19 (1733)	—	5.00	8.00	15.00	22.50	—
SE1655//20 (1733)	—	5.00	8.00	15.00	22.50	—
SE1656//20 (1734)	—	5.00	8.00	15.00	22.50	—
SE1657//21 (1735)	—	5.00	8.00	15.00	22.50	—
SE1658//22 (1736)	—	5.00	8.00	15.00	22.50	—

Mint: Without Mint Name
KM# 92 RUPEE
Silver **Obv. Inscription:** Queen Ambika, lion left **Rev:** Inscription **Note:** Weight varies: 10.70-11.60 grams.

Date	Mintage	VG	F	VF	XF	Unc
SE1658//23 (1736)	—	5.00	8.00	15.00	22.50	—

Mint: Without Mint Name
KM# 93 RUPEE
Silver **Obv. Inscription:** Queen Ambika, lion left **Rev:** Lion left **Note:** Weight varies: 10.70-11.60 grams.

Date	Mintage	VG	F	VF	XF	Unc
SE1658//23 (1736)	—	6.50	11.50	20.00	30.00	—

Mint: Without Mint Name
KM# 94 RUPEE
Silver **Obv. Inscription:** Queen Ambika, lion left **Rev:** Lion right **Note:** Weight varies: 10.70-11.60 grams.

Date	Mintage	VG	F	VF	XF	Unc
SE1659//24 (1737)	—	6.50	11.50	20.00	30.00	—

Mint: Without Mint Name
KM# 104 RUPEE
Silver **Obv:** Inscription, without Queen's name **Rev:** Inscription **Note:** Weight varies: 10.70-11.60 grams.

Date	Mintage	VG	F	VF	XF	Unc
SE1660//24 (1738)	—	6.50	10.50	17.50	25.00	—
SE1660//25 (1738)	—	6.50	10.50	17.50	25.00	—
SE1661//25 (1739)	—	10.00	16.50	26.50	40.00	—

Mint: Without Mint Name
KM# 112 RUPEE
Silver **Obv. Inscription:** Queen Sarvvesvari **Rev:** Inscription, lion left **Note:** Weight varies: 10.70-11.60 grams.

Date	Mintage	VG	F	VF	XF	Unc
SE1661//25 (1739)	—	5.00	8.00	15.00	22.50	—
SE1661//26 (1739)	—	5.00	8.00	15.00	22.50	—
SE1662//27 (1740)	—	5.00	8.00	15.00	22.50	—
SE1663//27 (1741)	—	5.00	8.00	15.00	22.50	—
SE1664//28 (1742)	—	5.00	8.00	15.00	22.50	—
SE1664//29 (1742)	—	5.00	8.00	15.00	22.50	—
SE1665//29 (1743)	—	3.50	6.50	11.00	18.00	—
SE1665//30 (1743)	—	3.50	6.50	11.00	18.00	—
SE1665//31 (1743)	—	5.00	8.00	15.00	22.50	—
SE1666//30 (1744)	—	3.50	6.50	11.00	18.00	—
SE1666//31 (1744)	—	3.50	6.50	11.00	18.00	—

Mint: Gargaon
KM# 75 RUPEE
Silver **Obv. Inscription:** Queen Pramathesvari **Rev:** Inscription, date **Note:** Weight varies: 10.70-11.60 grams.

Date	Mintage	VG	F	VF	XF	Unc
SE1651//15 (1729)	—	18.50	35.00	60.00	100	—

Mint: Rangpur
KM# 74 RUPEE
Silver **Obv. Inscription:** Queen Pramathesvari **Rev:** Inscription **Note:** Weight varies: 10.70-11.60 grams.

Date	Mintage	VG	F	VF	XF	Unc
SE1649//14 (1727)	—	80.00	140	245	375	—

Mint: Rangpur
KM# 90 RUPEE
Silver **Obv. Inscription:** Queen Ambika **Rev:** Lion right, inscription **Note:** Square. Weight varies: 10.70-11.60 grams.

Date	Mintage	VG	F	VF	XF	Unc
SE1654//19 (1732)	—	100	150	300	500	—

Mint: Without Mint Name
KM# 64 1/4 MOHUR
Gold **Obv. Inscription:** Queen Phulesvari **Note:** Weight varies: 2.68-2.85 grams.

Date	Mintage	VG	F	VF	XF	Unc
ND(1715-44)	—	90.00	175	300	500	—

Mint: Without Mint Name
KM# 77 1/4 MOHUR
Gold **Obv. Inscription:** Queen Pramathesvari **Note:** Weight varies: 2.68-2.85 grams.

Date	Mintage	VG	F	VF	XF	Unc
ND(1715-44)	—	90.00	175	300	500	—

Mint: Without Mint Name
KM# 53 1/4 MOHUR
Gold **Note:** Weight varies: 2.68-2.85 grams.

Date	Mintage	VG	F	VF	XF	Unc
SE1643 (1721)	—	90.00	175	300	500	—

Mint: Without Mint Name
KM# 96 1/4 MOHUR
Gold **Obv. Inscription:** Queen Ambika **Note:** Weight varies: 2.68-2.85 grams.

Date	Mintage	VG	F	VF	XF	Unc
ND//20 (1736)	—	90.00	175	300	500	—

Mint: Without Mint Name
KM# 106 1/4 MOHUR
Gold **Obv:** Inscription, without Queen's name **Rev:** Inscription **Note:** Weight varies: 2.68-2.85 grams.

Date	Mintage	VG	F	VF	XF	Unc
SE1660//25 (1738)	—	90.00	175	300	500	—

Mint: Without Mint Name
KM# 114 1/4 MOHUR
Gold **Obv. Inscription:** Queen Sarvvesvari **Note:** Weight varies: 2.68-2.85 grams.

Date	Mintage	VG	F	VF	XF	Unc
ND//28 (1743)	—	90.00	175	300	500	—

Mint: Without Mint Name
KM# 66 MOHUR
Gold **Obv. Inscription:** Queen Phulesvari **Note:** Similar to Rupee, KM#61. Weight varies: 10.70-11.40 grams.

Date	Mintage	VG	F	VF	XF	Unc
SE1646 (1724)	—	175	300	500	800	—

Mint: Without Mint Name
KM# 79 MOHUR
Gold **Obv. Inscription:** Queen Pramathesvari **Rev:** Inscription **Note:** Similar to Rupee, KM#73. Weight varies: 10.70-11.40 grams.

Date	Mintage	VG	F	VF	XF	Unc
SE1650 (1728)	—	175	300	500	800	—
SE1651 (1729)	—	175	300	500	800	—

Mint: Without Mint Name
KM# 55 MOHUR
Gold **Obv:** Inscription **Rev:** Inscription **Note:** Weight varies: 10.70-11.00 grams.

Date	Mintage	VG	F	VF	XF	Unc
SE1637 (1715)	—	175	300	500	800	—

Mint: Without Mint Name
KM# 67 MOHUR
Gold **Obv. Inscription:** Queen Phulesvari **Rev:** Inscription **Note:** Weight varies: 10.70-11.40 grams.

Date	Mintage	VG	F	VF	XF	Unc
SE1646 (1724)	—	175	300	500	800	—

Mint: Without Mint Name
KM# 98 MOHUR
Gold **Obv. Inscription:** Queen Ambika **Rev:** Inscription **Note:** Weight varies: 10.70-11.40 grams.

Date	Mintage	VG	F	VF	XF	Unc
SE1655//19 (1733)	—	150	275	450	750	—
SE1655//20 (1733)	—	150	275	450	750	—
SE1658//22 (1736)	—	150	275	450	750	—

Mint: Without Mint Name
KM# 116 MOHUR
Gold **Obv. Inscription:** Queen Sarvvesvari **Note:** Weight varies: 10.70-11.40 grams.

Date	Mintage	VG	F	VF	XF	Unc
SE1665//30 (1743)	—	150	275	450	750	—

Pramatta Simha (Sunenpha)
SE1666-1673 / 1744-1751AD
HAMMERED COINAGE

Mint: Without Mint Name
KM# 118 1/4 RUPEE
Silver **Obv:** Inscription **Rev:** Inscription **Note:** Weight varies: 2.68-2.90 grams.

Date	Mintage	VG	F	VF	XF	Unc
SE1667 (1745)	—	3.25	5.00	8.50	12.50	—
SE1668 (1746)	—	3.25	5.00	8.50	12.50	—
SE1669 (1747)	—	3.25	5.00	8.50	12.50	—
SE1670 (1748)	—	3.25	5.00	8.50	12.50	—
SE1671 (1749)	—	3.25	5.00	8.50	12.50	—
SE1672 (1750)	—	3.25	5.00	8.50	12.50	—
SE1673 (1751)	—	3.25	5.00	8.50	12.50	—

Mint: Without Mint Name
KM# 120 1/2 RUPEE
Silver **Obv:** Inscription **Rev:** Inscription **Note:** Weight varies: 5.35-5.80 grams.

Date	Mintage	VG	F	VF	XF	Unc
ND(1744-51)	—	2.50	4.00	7.00	10.00	—

Mint: Without Mint Name
KM# 122 RUPEE
Silver **Obv:** Inscription **Rev:** Inscription **Note:** Weight varies: 10.70-11.60 grams.

Date	Mintage	VG	F	VF	XF	Unc
SE1667 (1745)	—	4.00	7.00	13.00	20.00	—
SE1668 (1746)	—	4.00	7.00	13.00	20.00	—
SE1669 (1747)	—	4.00	7.00	13.00	20.00	—
SE1670 (1748)	—	4.00	7.00	13.00	20.00	—
SE1671 (1749)	—	4.00	7.00	13.00	20.00	—
SE1672 (1750)	—	4.00	7.00	13.00	20.00	—
SE1673 (1751)	—	4.00	7.00	13.00	20.00	—

Mint: Without Mint Name
KM# 123 RUPEE
Silver **Obv:** Inscription **Rev:** Inscription **Note:** Weight varies: 10.70-11.60 grams.

Date	Mintage	VG	F	VF	XF	Unc
ND//(36) (1744)	—	45.00	85.00	145	220	—

Mint: Without Mint Name
KM# 125 1/4 MOHUR
Gold **Note:** Weight varies: 2.68-2.85 grams.

Date	Mintage	VG	F	VF	XF	Unc
SE1667 (1745)	—	65.00	120	200	350	—
SE1669 (1747)	—	65.00	120	200	350	—
SE1671 (1749)	—	65.00	120	200	350	—
SE1672 (1750)	—	65.00	120	200	350	—

Mint: Without Mint Name
KM# 127 1/2 MOHUR
Gold **Note:** Weight varies: 5.35-5.70 grams.

Date	Mintage	VG	F	VF	XF	Unc
ND(1744-51)	—	90.00	175	300	500	—

Mint: Without Mint Name
KM# 128 MOHUR
Gold **Obv:** Inscription **Rev:** Inscription **Note:** Weight varies: 10.70-11.40 grams.

Date	Mintage	VG	F	VF	XF	Unc
SE1667 (1745)	—	125	250	400	650	—
SE1669 (1747)	—	125	250	400	650	—

Rajesvara Simha (Suprempha)
SE1673-1691 / 1751-1769AD
HAMMERED COINAGE

Mint: Without Mint Name
KM# 130 1/16 RUPEE
Silver, 10 mm. **Note:** Type I - Bengali inscriptions. Octagonal. Weight varies: 0.67-0.72 grams.

Date	Mintage	VG	F	VF	XF	Unc
ND(1751-69)	—	3.00	4.00	6.00	9.00	—

Mint: Without Mint Name
KM# A132 1/8 RUPEE
Silver **Obv. Inscription:** Sri Sri Ra-jesvara **Rev. Inscription:** Simha / Nrpasya **Shape:** Octagonal **Note:** Weight varies 1.34-1.45 grams. Nagari inscriptions.

Date	Mintage	Good	VG	F	VF	XF
ND(1751-69)	—	—	—	—	—	—

Mint: Without Mint Name
KM# 131 1/8 RUPEE
Silver **Obv:** Bengali inscription **Rev:** Bengali inscription **Shape:** Octagonal **Note:** Type I - Bengali inscriptions. Weight varies: 1.34-1.45 grams.

Date	Mintage	VG	F	VF	XF	Unc
ND(1751-69)	—	2.50	3.50	5.00	7.50	—

Mint: Without Mint Name
KM# A131 1/8 RUPEE
1.4000 g., Silver **Shape:** Octagonal **Note:** Type II - Deva Nagari inscriptions.

Date	Mintage	VG	F	VF	XF	Unc
ND(1751-69)	—	—	—	—	—	—

Mint: Without Mint Name
KM# 153 1/4 RUPEE
Silver **Obv:** Persian inscription **Rev:** Persian inscription **Shape:** Square **Note:** Type III - Persian inscriptions. Weight varies: 2.68-2.90 grams.

Date	Mintage	VG	F	VF	XF	Unc
ND(1751-69)	—	27.50	45.00	75.00	125	—

Mint: Without Mint Name
KM# 132 1/4 RUPEE
Silver **Obv:** Bengali inscription **Rev:** Bengali inscription **Shape:** Octagonal **Note:** Type I - Bengali inscriptions. Weight varies: 2.68-2.90 grams.

Date	Mintage	VG	F	VF	XF	Unc
SE1674 (1752)	—	3.50	4.50	6.50	10.00	—
SE1675 (1753)	—	3.50	4.50	6.50	10.00	—
SE1676 (1754)	—	3.50	4.50	6.50	10.00	—
SE1677 (1755)	—	3.50	4.50	6.50	10.00	—
SE1678 (1756)	—	3.50	4.50	6.50	10.00	—
SE1679 (1757)	—	3.50	4.50	6.50	10.00	—
SE1680 (1758)	—	3.50	4.50	6.50	10.00	—
SE1681 (1759)	—	3.50	4.50	6.50	10.00	—
SE1682 (1760)	—	3.50	4.50	6.50	10.00	—
SE1683 (1761)	—	3.50	4.50	6.50	10.00	—
SE1684 (1762)	—	3.50	4.50	6.50	10.00	—
SE1685 (1763)	—	3.50	4.50	6.50	10.00	—
SE1686 (1764)	—	3.50	4.50	6.50	10.00	—
SE1687 (1765)	—	3.50	4.50	6.50	10.00	—
SE1688 (1766)	—	3.50	4.50	6.50	10.00	—
SE1689 (1767)	—	3.50	4.50	6.50	10.00	—
SE1690 (1768)	—	3.50	4.50	6.50	10.00	—

Mint: Without Mint Name
KM# 132A 1/4 RUPEE
Silver **Obv:** Inscription **Rev:** Inscription **Shape:** Square **Note:** Type I - Bengali inscriptions. Weight varies: 2.68-2.90 grams.

Date	Mintage	VG	F	VF	XF	Unc
SE1689 (1767)	—	25.00	35.00	65.00	100	—

Mint: Without Mint Name
KM# 143 1/4 RUPEE
Silver **Obv:** Deva Nagari inscription **Rev:** Deva Negari inscription **Note:** Type II - Deva Nagari inscriptions. Weight varies: 2.68-2.90 grams.

Date	Mintage	VG	F	VF	XF	Unc
SE1681 (1759)	—	9.00	15.00	25.00	40.00	—

Mint: Without Mint Name
KM# 133 1/2 RUPEE
Silver **Obv:** Inscription **Rev:** Inscription **Shape:** Octagonal **Note:** Type I - Bengali inscriptions. Weight varies: 5.35-5.80 grams.

Date	Mintage	VG	F	VF	XF	Unc
ND(1751-69)	—	BV	4.50	6.00	10.00	—

Mint: Without Mint Name
KM# 133A 1/2 RUPEE
Silver **Obv:** Inscription **Rev:** Inscription **Shape:** Square **Note:** Type I - Bengali inscriptions. Weight varies: 5.35-5.80 grams.

Date	Mintage	VG	F	VF	XF	Unc
ND(1751-69)	—	35.00	50.00	85.00	150	—

Mint: Without Mint Name
KM# 144 1/2 RUPEE
Silver **Shape:** Octagonal **Note:** Type II - Deva Nagari inscriptions. Weight varies: 5.35-5.80 grams.

Date	Mintage	VG	F	VF	XF	Unc
ND(1751-69)	—	11.50	18.50	30.00	50.00	—

Mint: Without Mint Name
KM# 134 RUPEE
Silver **Obv:** Inscription, lion left at bottom **Rev:** Inscription **Shape:** Octagonal **Note:** Type I - Bengali inscriptions. Weight varies: 10.70-11.60 grams.

Date	Mintage	VG	F	VF	XF	Unc
SE1674 (1752)	—	BV	8.50	11.50	17.50	—
SE1675 (1753)	—	BV	8.50	11.50	17.50	—
SE1676 (1754)	—	BV	8.50	11.50	17.50	—
SE1677 (1755)	—	BV	8.50	11.50	17.50	—
SE1678 (1756)	—	BV	8.50	11.50	17.50	—
SE1679 (1757)	—	BV	8.50	11.50	17.50	—
SE1680 (1758)	—	BV	8.50	11.50	17.50	—
SE1681 (1759)	—	BV	8.50	11.50	17.50	—
SE1682 (1760)	—	BV	8.50	11.50	17.50	—
SE1683 (1761)	—	BV	8.50	11.50	17.50	—
SE1684 (1762)	—	BV	8.50	11.50	17.50	—
SE1685 (1763)	—	BV	8.50	11.50	17.50	—
SE1686 (1764)	—	BV	8.50	11.50	17.50	—
SE1687 (1765)	—	BV	8.50	11.50	17.50	—
SE1688 (1766)	—	BV	8.50	11.50	17.50	—
SE1689 (1767)	—	BV	8.50	11.50	17.50	—
SE1690 (1768)	—	BV	8.50	11.50	17.50	—

Mint: Without Mint Name
KM# 135 RUPEE
Silver **Obv:** Inscription, lion right at bottom **Rev:** Inscription **Shape:** Octagonal **Note:** Type I - Bengali inscriptions. Weight varies: 10.70-11.60 grams.

Date	Mintage	VG	F	VF	XF	Unc
SE1690 (1768)	—	BV	8.50	11.50	17.50	—

Mint: Without Mint Name
KM# 145 RUPEE
Silver **Obv:** Inscription **Rev:** Inscription **Shape:** Octagonal **Note:** Type II - Deva Nagari inscriptions. Weight varies: 10.70-11.60 grams.

Date	Mintage	VG	F	VF	XF	Unc
SE1675 (1753)	—	20.00	32.50	55.00	90.00	—

Mint: Without Mint Name
KM# 167 RUPEE
Silver **Shape:** Octagonal **Note:** Type III - Ahom inscriptions. Weight varies: 10.70-11.60 grams.

Date	Mintage	VG	F	VF	XF	Unc
ND (1751) Rare	—	—	—	—	—	—

Mint: Rangpur
KM# 155 RUPEE
Silver **Obv:** Inscription **Rev:** Inscription **Shape:** Square **Note:** Type III - Persian inscriptions. Weight varies: 10.70-11.60 grams.

Date	Mintage	VG	F	VF	XF	Unc
SE1674 (1752)	—	27.50	45.00	75.00	125	—

Mint: Rangpur
KM# 156 RUPEE
Silver **Obv:** Inscription **Rev:** Inscription **Shape:** Octagonal **Note:** Type III - Persian inscriptions. Weight varies: 10.70-11.60 grams.

Date	Mintage	VG	F	VF	XF	Unc
SE1685 (1763)	—	20.00	32.50	55.00	90.00	—

Mint: Without Mint Name
KM# 136 1/16 MOHUR
Gold, 10 mm. **Obv:** Inscription **Rev:** Inscription **Shape:** Octagonal **Note:** Type I - Bengali inscriptions. Weight varies: 0.67-0.71 grams.

Date	Mintage	VG	F	VF	XF	Unc
ND(1751-69)	—	27.50	45.00	75.00	125	—

Mint: Without Mint Name
KM# 137 1/8 MOHUR
Gold **Obv:** Inscription **Rev:** Inscription **Shape:** Octagonal **Note:** Type I - Bengali inscriptions. Weight varies: 1.34-1.42 grams.

Date	Mintage	VG	F	VF	XF	Unc
ND(1751-69)	—	35.00	65.00	120	200	—

Mint: Without Mint Name
KM# 138 1/8 MOHUR
Gold **Shape:** Square **Note:** Type I - Bengali inscriptions. Weight varies: 1.34-1.42 grams.

Date	Mintage	VG	F	VF	XF	Unc
ND(1751-69)	—	70.00	100	150	250	—

Mint: Without Mint Name
KM# 159 1/4 MOHUR
Gold **Obv:** Inscription **Rev:** Inscription **Shape:** Square **Note:** Type III - Persian inscriptions. Weight varies: 2.68-2.85 grams.

Date	Mintage	VG	F	VF	XF	Unc
ND(1751-69)	—	150	220	350	550	—

Mint: Without Mint Name
KM# 139 1/4 MOHUR
Gold, 13 mm. **Shape:** Octagonal **Note:** Type I - Bengali inscriptions. Weight varies: 2.68-2.85 grams.

Date	Mintage	VG	F	VF	XF	Unc
SE1674 (1752)	—	60.00	90.00	150	250	—
SE1675 (1753)	—	60.00	90.00	150	250	—
SE1676 (1754)	—	60.00	90.00	150	250	—
SE1677 (1755)	—	60.00	90.00	150	250	—
SE1678 (1756)	—	60.00	90.00	150	250	—
SE1680 (1758)	—	60.00	90.00	150	250	—
SE1681 (1759)	—	60.00	90.00	150	250	—
SE1683 (1761)	—	60.00	90.00	150	250	—
SE1688 (1766)	—	60.00	90.00	150	250	—

Mint: Without Mint Name
KM# 140 1/4 MOHUR
Gold **Shape:** Square **Note:** Type I - Bengali inscriptions. Weight varies: 2.68-2.85 grams.

Date	Mintage	VG	F	VF	XF	Unc
SE1678 (1756)	—	120	200	350	—	—

Mint: Without Mint Name
KM# 141 1/2 MOHUR
Gold **Shape:** Octagonal **Note:** Type I - Bengali inscriptions. Weight varies: 5.35-5.70 grams.

Date	Mintage	VG	F	VF	XF	Unc
ND(1751-69)	—	80.00	150	250	400	—

Mint: Without Mint Name
KM# 142 MOHUR
Gold, 20 mm. **Shape:** Octagonal **Note:** Type I - Bengali inscriptions. Weight varies: 10.70-11.40 grams.

Date	Mintage	VG	F	VF	XF	Unc
SE1674 (1752)	—	150	225	375	600	—
SE1678 (1756)	—	150	225	375	600	—
SE1681 (1759)	—	150	225	375	600	—
SE1684 (1762)	—	150	225	375	600	—
SE1688 (1766)	—	150	225	375	600	—
SE1689 (1767)	—	150	225	375	600	—
SE1690 (1768)	—	150	225	375	600	—

Mint: Without Mint Name
KM# 150 MOHUR
Gold **Shape:** Octagonal **Note:** Type II - Deva Nagari inscriptions. Weight varies: 10.70-11.40 grams.

Date	Mintage	VG	F	VF	XF	Unc
SE1675 (1753)	—	225	350	600	1,000	—

Mint: Without Mint Name
KM# 172 MOHUR
Gold **Obv:** Inscription **Rev:** Inscription, lion left at bottom **Shape:** Octagonal **Note:** Type III - Ahom inscriptions. Weight varies: 10.70-11.40 grams.

Date	Mintage	VG	F	VF	XF	Unc
ND (1751)	—	500	900	1,500	2,500	—

Mint: Without Mint Name
KM# 161 MOHUR
Gold **Shape:** Square **Note:** Type III - Persian inscriptions. Weight varies: 10.70-11.40 grams.

Date	Mintage	VG	F	VF	XF	Unc
SE1674 (1752)	—	250	450	750	1,250	—

Mint: Without Mint Name
KM# 162 MOHUR
Gold **Shape:** Octagonal **Note:** Type III - Persian inscriptions. Weight varies: 10.70-11.40 grams.

Date	Mintage	VG	F	VF	XF	Unc
SE1685 (1763)	—	250	450	750	1,250	—

Lakshmi Simha (Ramakanta Simha)

SE1691 / 1769AD

HAMMERED COINAGE

Mint: Without Mint Name
KM# 173 1-1/2 RUPEE
16.8000 g., Silver **Obv:** Inscription **Rev:** Inscription

Date	Mintage	VG	F	VF	XF	Unc
SE1691 (1769) Rare	—	—	—	—	—	—

Lakshmi Simha (Sunyeopha)

SE1691-1702 / 1769-1780AD

HAMMERED COINAGE

Mint: Without Mint Name
KM# 174 1/16 RUPEE
Silver **Obv:** Inscription **Rev:** Inscription **Note:** Weight varies: 0.67-0.72 grams.

Date	Mintage	VG	F	VF	XF	Unc
ND(1769-80)	—	3.50	5.00	7.50	11.50	—

Mint: Without Mint Name
KM# 175 1/8 RUPEE
Silver **Obv:** Inscription **Rev:** Inscription **Note:** Weight varies: 1.34-1.45 grams.

Date	Mintage	VG	F	VF	XF	Unc
ND(1769-80)	—	3.50	5.00	7.50	11.50	—

Mint: Without Mint Name
KM# 176 1/4 RUPEE
Silver **Obv:** Inscription **Rev:** Inscription **Note:** Weight varies: 2.68-2.90 grams.

Date	Mintage	VG	F	VF	XF	Unc
SE1692 (1770)	—	3.50	4.50	6.50	10.00	—
SE1693 (1771)	—	3.50	4.50	6.50	10.00	—
SE1694 (1772)	—	3.50	4.50	6.50	10.00	—
SE1695 (1773)	—	3.50	4.50	6.50	10.00	—
SE1696 (1774)	—	3.50	4.50	6.50	10.00	—
SE1697 (1775)	—	3.50	4.50	6.50	10.00	—
SE1698 (1776)	—	3.50	4.50	6.50	10.00	—
SE1699 (1777)	—	3.50	4.50	6.50	10.00	—
SE1700 (1778)	—	3.50	4.50	6.50	10.00	—
SE1701 (1779)	—	3.50	4.50	6.50	10.00	—
SE1702 (1780)	—	3.50	4.50	6.50	10.00	—

Mint: Without Mint Name
KM# 177 1/2 RUPEE
Silver **Obv:** Inscription **Rev. Inscription:** Hari Hara **Note:** Weight varies: 5.35-5.80 grams.

Date	Mintage	VG	F	VF	XF	Unc
ND(1769-80)	—	6.50	10.50	17.50	25.00	—

Mint: Without Mint Name
KM# 178 1/2 RUPEE
Silver **Obv:** Inscription **Rev. Inscription:** Hari Gauri **Note:** Weight varies: 5.35-5.80 grams.

Date	Mintage	VG	F	VF	XF	Unc
ND(1769-80)	—	4.25	7.00	10.00	16.50	—

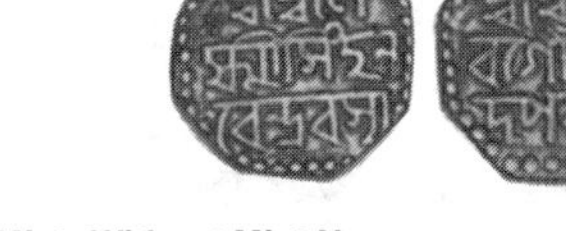

Mint: Without Mint Name
KM# 179 1/2 RUPEE
Silver **Obv:** Inscription **Rev:** Inscription **Note:** Weight varies: 5.35-5.80 grams.

Date	Mintage	VG	F	VF	XF	Unc
ND(1769-80)	—	3.75	6.00	8.50	12.50	—

Mint: Without Mint Name
KM# 180 1/2 RUPEE
Silver **Obv:** Inscription **Rev:** Inscription **Note:** Weight varies: 5.35-5.80 grams.

Date	Mintage	VG	F	VF	XF	Unc
ND//1 (1773)	—	3.75	6.00	8.50	12.50	—

Mint: Without Mint Name
KM# 181 RUPEE
Silver **Obv:** Inscription **Rev. Inscription:** Hari Hara... **Note:** Weight varies: 10.70-11.60 grams.

Date	Mintage	VG	F	VF	XF	Unc
SE1692 (1770)	—	12.50	15.50	20.00	30.00	—

Mint: Without Mint Name
KM# 182 RUPEE
Silver **Obv:** Inscription **Rev. Inscription:** Hari Gauri... **Note:** Weight varies: 10.70-11.60 grams.

Date	Mintage	VG	F	VF	XF	Unc
SE1692 (1770)	—	4.25	7.50	11.50	20.00	—
SE1693 (1771)	—	4.25	7.50	11.50	20.00	—
SE1694 (1772)	—	4.25	7.50	11.50	20.00	—
SE1695 (1773)	—	4.25	7.50	11.50	20.00	—
SE1696 (1774)	—	4.25	7.50	11.50	20.00	—
SE1697 (1775)	—	4.25	7.50	11.50	20.00	—
SE1698 (1776)	—	4.25	7.50	11.50	20.00	—
SE1699 (1777)	—	4.25	7.50	11.50	20.00	—
SE1700 (1778)	—	4.25	7.50	11.50	20.00	—
SE1701 (1779)	—	4.25	7.50	11.50	20.00	—

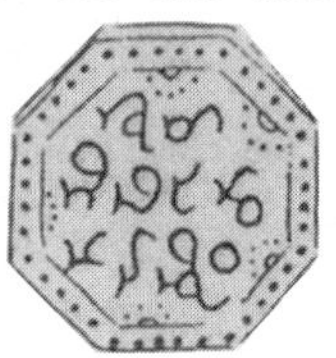

Mint: Without Mint Name
KM# 182B RUPEE
Silver **Obv:** Inscription **Rev:** Inscription **Note:** Weight varies: 10.70-11.60 grams. Similar to KM#182, but Ahom script.

Date	Mintage	VG	F	VF	XF	Unc
ND//1 (1769)	—	75.00	100	200	300	—

Mint: Without Mint Name
KM# 182A RUPEE
Silver **Obv:** Inscription **Rev:** Inscription **Note:** Weight varies: 10.70-11.60 grams. Similar to KM#182, but square flan.

Date	Mintage	VG	F	VF	XF	Unc
SE1693 (1771)	—	75.00	100	200	300	—

Mint: Without Mint Name
KM# 183 1/16 MOHUR
Gold **Note:** Weight varies: 0.67-0.71 grams.

Date	Mintage	VG	F	VF	XF	Unc
ND(1769-80)	—	25.00	40.00	75.00	125	—

Mint: Without Mint Name
KM# 184 1/8 MOHUR
Gold **Note:** Weight varies: 1.34-1.42 grams.

Date	Mintage	VG	F	VF	XF	Unc
ND(1769-80)	—	35.00	65.00	120	200	—

Mint: Without Mint Name
KM# 186 1/4 MOHUR
Gold **Obv:** Inscription **Rev:** Inscription **Note:** Square. Weight varies: 2.68-2.85 grams.

Date	Mintage	VG	F	VF	XF	Unc
SE1692 (1770)	—	100	200	350	550	—

Mint: Without Mint Name
KM# 185 1/4 MOHUR
Gold **Note:** Weight varies: 2.68-2.85 grams.

Date	Mintage	VG	F	VF	XF	Unc
SE1692 (1770)	—	55.00	90.00	150	250	—
SE1693 (1771)	—	55.00	90.00	150	250	—
SE1694 (1772)	—	55.00	90.00	150	250	—
SE1695 (1773)	—	55.00	90.00	150	250	—
SE1696 (1774)	—	55.00	90.00	150	250	—
SE1697 (1775)	—	55.00	90.00	150	250	—
SE1702 (1780)	—	55.00	90.00	150	250	—

Mint: Without Mint Name
KM# 187 1/2 MOHUR
Gold **Note:** Weight varies: 5.35-5.70 grams.

Date	Mintage	VG	F	VF	XF	Unc
ND(1769-80)	—	80.00	150	250	400	—

Mint: Without Mint Name
KM# 188 MOHUR
Gold **Note:** 10.70-11.40 grams.

Date	Mintage	VG	F	VF	XF	Unc
SE1692 (1770)	—	165	225	375	600	—
SE1693 (1771)	—	165	225	375	600	—
SE1694 (1772)	—	165	225	375	600	—
SE1698 (1776)	—	165	225	375	600	—
SE1701 (1779)	—	165	225	375	600	—

Gaurinatha Simha (Suhitpanpha)

SE1702-1718 / 1780-1796AD

HAMMERED COINAGE

Mint: Without Mint Name
KM# 190 1/32 RUPEE
Silver **Obv:** Inscription **Rev:** Inscription **Note:** Weight varies: 0.34-0.36 grams.

Date	Mintage	VG	F	VF	XF	Unc
ND(1780-96)	—	4.00	5.00	7.00	10.00	—

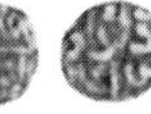

Mint: Without Mint Name
KM# 191 1/32 RUPEE
Silver **Obv:** Inscription **Rev:** Inscription **Note:** Weight varies: 0.34-0.36 grams.

Date	Mintage	VG	F	VF	XF	Unc
ND(1780-96)	—	5.00	6.00	8.50	12.50	—

Mint: Without Mint Name
KM# 192 1/16 RUPEE
Silver **Obv:** Inscription **Rev:** Type 1 **Note:** Weight varies: 0.67-0.72 grams.

Date	Mintage	VG	F	VF	XF	Unc
ND(1780-96)	—	4.00	5.50	7.50	11.50	—

Mint: Without Mint Name
KM# 193 1/16 RUPEE
Silver **Obv:** Inscription **Rev:** Type 2 **Note:** Weight varies: 0.67-0.72 grams.

Date	Mintage	VG	F	VF	XF	Unc
ND(1780-96)	—	4.00	5.50	7.50	11.50	—

Mint: Without Mint Name
KM# 194 1/16 RUPEE
Silver **Rev:** Letter "Na" below legend **Note:** Weight varies: 0.67-0.72 grams.

Date	Mintage	VG	F	VF	XF	Unc
ND(1780-96)	—	7.50	10.00	14.00	20.00	—

Mint: Without Mint Name
KM# 195 1/8 RUPEE
Silver **Obv:** Inscription **Rev:** Inscription **Note:** Variety 1. Weight varies: 1.34-1.45 grams.

Date	Mintage	VG	F	VF	XF	Unc
ND(1780-96)	—	4.00	5.50	7.50	11.50	—

Mint: Without Mint Name
KM# 196 1/8 RUPEE
Silver **Obv:** Inscription **Rev:** Inscription **Note:** Variety 2. Weight varies: 1.34-1.45 grams.

Date	Mintage	VG	F	VF	XF	Unc
ND(1780-96)	—	4.00	5.50	7.50	11.50	—

Mint: Without Mint Name
KM# 197 1/8 RUPEE
Silver **Obv:** Inscription **Rev:** Letter "Na" below inscription **Note:** Weight varies: 1.34-1.45 grams.

Date	Mintage	VG	F	VF	XF	Unc
ND(1780-96)	—	7.50	10.00	14.00	20.00	—

Mint: Without Mint Name
KM# 203 1/4 RUPEE
Silver **Obv:** Inscription **Rev:** Inscription **Note:** Square flan. Weight varies: 2.68-2.90 grams.

Date	Mintage	VG	F	VF	XF	Unc
SE1705 (1783)	—	22.50	30.00	37.50	50.00	—

Mint: Without Mint Name
KM# 198 1/4 RUPEE
Silver **Obv:** Inscription **Rev:** Inscription **Note:** Weight varies: 2.68-2.90 grams.

Date	Mintage	VG	F	VF	XF	Unc
SE1703 (1781)	—	5.00	7.00	10.00	15.00	—
SE1704 (1782)	—	5.00	7.00	10.00	15.00	—
SE1705 (1783)	—	5.00	7.00	10.00	15.00	—
SE1706//5 (1784)	—	3.50	5.00	7.00	10.00	—
SE1707//6 (1785)	—	3.50	5.00	7.00	10.00	—
SE1708//7 (1786)	—	3.50	5.00	7.00	10.00	—
SE1708 (1786)	—	5.00	7.00	10.00	15.00	—
SE1709//8 (1787)	—	5.00	7.00	10.00	15.00	—
SE1711 (1789)	—	10.00	12.50	17.50	25.00	—
SE1712//11 (1790)	—	10.00	12.50	17.50	25.00	—
SE1712 (1790)	—	10.00	12.50	17.50	25.00	—
SE1713 (1791)	—	10.00	12.50	17.50	25.00	—
SE1714 (1792)	—	10.00	12.50	17.50	25.00	—
SE1715//14 (1793)	—	10.00	12.50	17.50	25.00	—
SE1716 (1794)	—	3.50	5.00	7.00	10.00	—
SE1717 (1795)	—	3.50	5.00	7.00	10.00	—

Mint: Without Mint Name
KM# 199 1/4 RUPEE
Silver **Obv:** Inscription **Rev:** Regnal year below inscription **Note:** Weight varies: 2.68-2.90 grams.

Date	Mintage	VG	F	VF	XF	Unc
SE1716//1 (1794)	—	5.00	7.00	10.00	15.00	—
SE1717//16 (1795)	—	5.00	7.00	10.00	15.00	—

Mint: Without Mint Name
KM# 200 1/4 RUPEE
Silver **Obv:** Inscription **Rev:** Regnal year below inscription **Note:** Weight varies: 2.68-2.90 grams.

Date	Mintage	VG	F	VF	XF	Unc
SE1716//1 (1794)	—	5.00	7.00	10.00	15.00	—
SE1717//1 (1795)	—	5.00	7.00	10.00	15.00	—

Mint: Without Mint Name
KM# 201 1/4 RUPEE
Silver **Obv:** Regnal year 1 below inscription **Rev:** Regnal year 16 below inscription **Note:** Weight varies: 2.68-2.90 grams.

Date	Mintage	VG	F	VF	XF	Unc
SE1717//1/16 (1795)	—	5.00	7.00	10.00	15.00	—

Mint: Without Mint Name
KM# 202 1/4 RUPEE
Silver **Rev:** Letter "Di" below legend **Note:** Weight varies: 2.68-2.90 grams.

Date	Mintage	VG	F	VF	XF	Unc
SE1717 (1795)	—	7.50	10.00	14.00	20.00	—

Mint: Without Mint Name
KM# 211 1/2 RUPEE
Silver **Rev:** Letter "Na" below legend

Date	Mintage	VG	F	VF	XF	Unc
ND(1780-96)	—	5.00	8.00	14.00	20.00	—

Mint: Without Mint Name
KM# 212 1/2 RUPEE
Silver **Obv:** Letter "Na" below legend **Rev:** Letter "Na" below legend

Date	Mintage	VG	F	VF	XF	Unc
ND(1780-96)	—	5.00	8.00	14.00	20.00	—

Mint: Without Mint Name
KM# 213 1/2 RUPEE
Silver **Obv:** Letter "Na" below inscription **Rev:** Letter "Ha" below inscription

Date	Mintage	VG	F	VF	XF	Unc
ND(1780-96)	—	5.00	8.00	14.00	20.00	—

Mint: Without Mint Name
KM# 204 1/2 RUPEE
Silver **Obv:** Inscription **Rev:** Inscription **Note:** Legend varieties are known. Without regnal year. Weight varies: 5.35-5.80 grams.

Date	Mintage	VG	F	VF	XF	Unc
ND(1780-96)	—	3.50	5.00	7.00	10.00	—

Mint: Without Mint Name
KM# 208 1/2 RUPEE
Silver **Obv:** Letter "Di" below legend **Note:** Weight varies: 5.35-5.80 grams.

Date	Mintage	VG	F	VF	XF	Unc
ND(1780-96)	—	5.00	8.00	14.00	20.00	—

Mint: Without Mint Name
KM# 209 1/2 RUPEE
Silver **Rev:** Letter "Ha" below legend **Note:** Weight varies: 5.35-5.80 grams.

Date	Mintage	VG	F	VF	XF	Unc
ND(1780-96)	—	5.00	8.00	14.00	20.00	—

Mint: Without Mint Name
KM# 210 1/2 RUPEE
Silver **Obv:** Letter "Na" below legend **Note:** Weight varies: 5.35-5.80 grams.

Date	Mintage	VG	F	VF	XF	Unc
ND(1780-96)	—	5.00	8.00	14.00	20.00	—

Mint: Without Mint Name
KM# 205 1/2 RUPEE
Silver **Obv:** Inscription **Rev:** Inscription **Note:** Regnal year. Weight varies: 5.35-5.80 grams.

Date	Mintage	VG	F	VF	XF	Unc
ND//5 (1784)	—	5.00	7.50	9.00	12.50	—
Note: Two legend varieties of regnal year 5 are known						
ND//6 (1785)	—	5.00	7.50	9.00	12.50	—
ND//7 (1786)	—	3.50	6.00	9.00	13.50	—
ND//8 (1787)	—	3.50	6.00	9.00	13.50	—
ND//12 (1791)	—	8.00	14.00	20.00	30.00	—
ND//13 (1792)	—	8.00	14.00	20.00	30.00	—
ND//14 (1793)	—	8.00	14.00	20.00	30.00	—
ND//15 (1794)	—	8.00	14.00	20.00	30.00	—
ND//16 (1795)	—	3.50	6.00	9.00	13.50	—

Mint: Without Mint Name
KM# 206 1/2 RUPEE
Silver **Obv:** Regnal year 1 below legend **Note:** Weight varies: 5.35-5.80 grams.

Date	Mintage	VG	F	VF	XF	Unc
ND//1 (1780)	—	5.00	8.00	14.00	20.00	—

Mint: Without Mint Name
KM# 207 1/2 RUPEE
Silver **Obv:** Inscription **Rev:** Regnal year 1 below inscription **Note:** Weight varies: 5.35-5.80 grams.

Date	Mintage	VG	F	VF	XF	Unc
ND//1 (1780)	—	3.50	6.00	7.50	12.50	—

Mint: Without Mint Name
KM# 214 RUPEE
Silver **Obv:** Inscription **Rev:** Inscription **Note:** Weight varies: 10.70-11.60 grams.

Date	Mintage	VG	F	VF	XF	Unc
SE1703 (1781)	—	7.50	13.50	20.00	35.00	—

Mint: Without Mint Name
KM# 215 RUPEE
Silver **Obv:** Inscription, lion left **Rev:** Inscription **Note:** Weight varies: 10.70-11.60 grams.

Date	Mintage	VG	F	VF	XF	Unc
SE1703 (1781)	—	5.50	9.50	15.00	25.00	—
SE1704 (1782)	—	5.50	9.50	15.00	25.00	—
SE1705 (1783)	—	5.00	8.50	14.00	22.50	—
SE1706//5 (1784)	—	5.00	8.50	14.00	22.50	—

Mint: Without Mint Name
KM# 216 RUPEE
Silver **Obv:** Inscription, lion left at bottom **Rev:** Inscription **Note:** Weight varies: 10.70-11.60 grams.

Date	Mintage	VG	F	VF	XF	Unc
SE1706//5 (1784)	—	6.00	11.00	16.50	27.50	—

Mint: Without Mint Name
KM# 217 RUPEE
Silver **Obv:** Inscription **Rev:** Inscription, lion right **Note:** Weight varies: 10.70-11.60 grams.

Date	Mintage	VG	F	VF	XF	Unc
SE1706//5 (1784)	—	6.50	11.50	18.50	30.00	—

Mint: Without Mint Name
KM# 218 RUPEE
Silver **Obv:** Inscription **Rev:** Inscription **Note:** Weight varies: 10.70-11.60 grams.

Date	Mintage	VG	F	VF	XF	Unc
SE1707//6 (1785)	—	5.50	8.50	14.00	22.50	—
SE1708//7 (1786)	—	5.50	8.50	14.00	22.50	—
SE1709//8 (1787)	—	5.50	8.50	14.00	22.50	—
SE1711 (1789)	—	11.00	18.50	26.50	40.00	—
SE1712//11 (1790)	—	—	—	—	—	—
SE1713//12 (1791)	—	11.00	18.50	26.50	40.00	—
SE1715//14 (1793)	—	11.00	18.50	26.50	40.00	—
SE1716 (1794)	—	5.50	9.50	15.00	25.00	—
SE1716//1 (1794)	—	5.50	9.50	15.00	25.00	—
SE1717 (1795)	—	5.50	9.50	15.00	25.00	—
SE1717//16 (1795)	—	5.50	9.50	15.00	25.00	—

Mint: Without Mint Name
KM# 219 RUPEE
Silver **Rev:** Regnal year below legend **Note:** Weight varies: 10.70-11.60 grams.

Date	Mintage	VG	F	VF	XF	Unc
SE1716//1 (1794)	—	7.50	13.50	20.00	32.50	—

Mint: Without Mint Name
KM# 220 RUPEE
Silver **Obv:** Letter "Di" below legend **Note:** Weight varies: 10.70-11.60 grams.

Date	Mintage	VG	F	VF	XF	Unc
SE1716 (1794)	—	7.50	13.50	20.00	32.50	—
SE1717 (1795)	—	7.50	13.50	20.00	32.50	—

Mint: Without Mint Name
KM# 221 RUPEE
Silver **Obv:** Inscription **Rev:** Letter "Ha" below inscription **Note:** Weight varies: 10.70-11.60 grams.

Date	Mintage	VG	F	VF	XF	Unc
SE1716 (1794)	—	6.50	12.00	18.50	30.00	—

Mint: Without Mint Name
KM# 222 RUPEE
Silver **Rev:** Letter "Na" below legend **Note:** Weight varies: 10.70-11.60 grams.

Date	Mintage	VG	F	VF	XF	Unc
SE1716 (1794)	—	6.50	12.00	18.50	30.00	—

Mint: Without Mint Name
KM# 223 RUPEE
Silver **Rev:** 68 below legend **Note:** Weight varies: 10.370-11.60 grams.

Date	Mintage	VG	F	VF	XF	Unc
SE1716 (1794)	—	6.50	12.00	18.50	30.00	—

Mint: Without Mint Name
KM# 224 1/32 MOHUR
Gold **Note:** Weight varies: 0.34-0.35 grams.

Date	Mintage	VG	F	VF	XF	Unc
ND(1780-96)	—	20.00	35.00	60.00	90.00	—

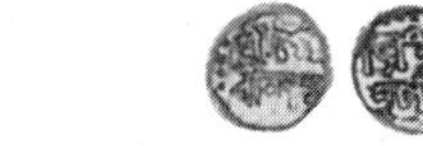

Mint: Without Mint Name
KM# 225 1/16 MOHUR
Gold **Obv:** Inscription **Rev:** Inscription **Note:** Weight varies: 0.67-0.71 grams.

Date	Mintage	VG	F	VF	XF	Unc
ND(1780-96)	—	20.00	35.00	60.00	100	—

Mint: Without Mint Name
KM# 226 1/8 MOHUR
Gold **Obv:** Inscription **Rev:** Inscription **Note:** Weight varies: 1.34-1.42 grams.

Date	Mintage	VG	F	VF	XF	Unc
ND(1780-96)	—	30.00	50.00	90.00	165	—

Mint: Without Mint Name
KM# 227 1/4 MOHUR
Gold **Obv:** Inscription **Rev:** Inscription **Note:** Weight varies: 2.68-2.85 grams.

Date	Mintage	VG	F	VF	XF	Unc
SE1703 (1781)	—	55.00	80.00	135	225	—
SE1706//5 (1784)	—	55.00	80.00	135	225	—
SE1707//6 (1785)	—	55.00	80.00	135	225	—
SE1711 (1789)	—	60.00	80.00	135	225	—
SE1712//11 (1790)	—	55.00	80.00	135	225	—
SE1716 (1794)	—	55.00	80.00	135	225	—

Mint: Without Mint Name
KM# 228 1/2 MOHUR
Gold **Note:** Weight varies: 5.35-5.70 grams.

Date	Mintage	VG	F	VF	XF	Unc
ND(1780-96)	—	75.00	125	225	375	—
ND//13(1792)	—	75.00	125	225	375	—

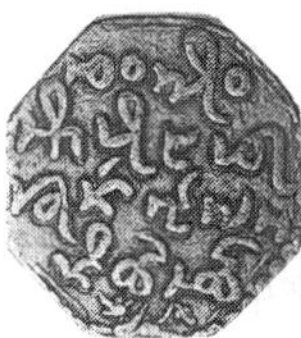

Mint: Without Mint Name
KM# 233 MOHUR
Gold **Obv:** Inscription **Rev:** Inscription **Note:** Ahom inscriptions. Weight varies: 10.70-11.40 grams.

Date	Mintage	VG	F	VF	XF	Unc
SE1715//13 (1793)	—	700	1,000	1,500	2,500	—

Mint: Without Mint Name
KM# 229 MOHUR
Gold **Obv:** Inscription **Rev:** Inscription **Note:** Weight varies: 10.70-11.40 grams.

Date	Mintage	VG	F	VF	XF	Unc
SE1703 (1781)	—	165	210	325	550	—
SE1705 (1783)	—	165	210	325	550	—

Mint: Without Mint Name
KM# 230 MOHUR
Gold **Note:** Weight varies: 10.70-11.40 grams.

Date	Mintage	VG	F	VF	XF	Unc
SE1706//5 (1784)	—	165	210	325	550	—

Mint: Without Mint Name
KM# 231 MOHUR
Gold **Obv:** Inscription **Rev:** Inscription **Note:** Weight varies: 10.70-11.40 grams.

Date	Mintage	VG	F	VF	XF	Unc
SE1707//6 (1785)	—	165	210	325	550	—
SE1709//8 (1787)	—	165	210	325	550	—
SE1711 (1789)	—	165	210	325	550	—
SE1712//11 (1790)	—	165	210	325	550	—
SE1716 (1794)	—	165	210	325	550	—
SE1716//15 (1794)	—	165	210	325	550	—

Mint: Without Mint Name
KM# 232 MOHUR
Gold **Rev:** Regnal year below legend **Note:** Weight varies: 10.70-11.40 grams.

Date	Mintage	VG	F	VF	XF	Unc
SE1716 (1794)	—	165	210	325	550	—

Sarvvananda Simha
SE1715-1717 / 1793-1795AD

HAMMERED COINAGE
Matak Rebel Issues

In Bengmars, east of Rangpur

Mint: Without Mint Name
KM# 300 1/16 RUPEE
Silver **Note:** Weight varies: 0.67-0.72 grams.

Date	Mintage	VG	F	VF	XF	Unc
ND (1793)	—	10.00	13.50	18.50	27.50	—

Mint: Without Mint Name
KM# 301 1/8 RUPEE
Silver **Obv:** Inscription **Rev:** Inscription **Note:** Weight varies: 0.34-0.36 grams.

Date	Mintage	VG	F	VF	XF	Unc
ND (1793)	—	12.50	16.50	21.50	30.00	—

Mint: Without Mint Name
KM# 302 1/4 RUPEE
Silver **Note:** Weight varies: 2.68-2.90 grams.

Date	Mintage	VG	F	VF	XF	Unc
SE1715 (1793)	—	15.00	18.50	25.00	35.00	—
SE1716 (1794)	—	15.00	18.50	25.00	35.00	—

Mint: Without Mint Name
KM# 304 1/2 RUPEE
Silver **Obv. Inscription:** Variety 2 **Rev. Inscription:** Krishna Pada ...

Date	Mintage	VG	F	VF	XF	Unc
ND (1793)	—	20.00	27.50	37.50	50.00	—

Mint: Without Mint Name
KM# 305 1/2 RUPEE
Silver **Obv. Legend:** Variety 3 **Rev. Legend:** "Krishna Madhu"...

Date	Mintage	VG	F	VF	XF	Unc
ND (1793)	—	20.00	27.50	37.50	50.00	—

Mint: Without Mint Name
KM# 306 1/2 RUPEE
Silver **Obv. Inscription:** Variety 4 **Rev. Inscription:** Krishna Charana...

Date	Mintage	VG	F	VF	XF	Unc
ND (1793)	—	20.00	27.50	37.50	50.00	—

Mint: Without Mint Name
KM# 303 1/2 RUPEE
Silver **Obv. Legend:** Variety 1 **Rev:** Inscription **Note:** Weight varies: 5.35-5.80 grams.

Date	Mintage	VG	F	VF	XF	Unc
ND (1793)	—	20.00	27.50	37.50	50.00	—

Mint: Without Mint Name
KM# 308 RUPEE
Silver **Obv. Inscription:** Variety 2 **Rev:** Inscription

Date	Mintage	VG	F	VF	XF	Unc
SE1716 (1794)	—	20.00	27.50	35.00	50.00	—

Mint: Without Mint Name
KM# 309 RUPEE
Silver **Obv. Inscription:** Variety 3 **Rev:** Inscription

Date	Mintage	VG	F	VF	XF	Unc
SE1716 (1794)	—	20.00	27.50	35.00	50.00	—
SE1717 (1795)	—	20.00	27.50	35.00	50.00	—

Mint: Without Mint Name
KM# 307 RUPEE
Silver **Obv. Legend:** Variety 1 **Note:** Weight varies: 10.70-11.60 grams.

Date	Mintage	VG	F	VF	XF	Unc
SE1715 (1793)	—	20.00	27.50	37.50	50.00	—

Mint: Without Mint Name
KM# 312 1/4 MOHUR
Gold **Note:** Weight varies: 2.68-2.85 grams.

Date	Mintage	VG	F	VF	XF	Unc
SE1716 (1794)	—	125	250	400	650	—

Mint: Without Mint Name
KM# 313 1/2 MOHUR
Gold **Obv:** Inscription **Rev:** Inscription **Note:** Weight varies: 5.35-5.70 grams.

Date	Mintage	VG	F	VF	XF	Unc
ND (1793)	—	175	300	500	800	—

Mint: Without Mint Name
KM# 314 MOHUR
Gold **Obv:** Inscription **Rev:** Inscription **Note:** Weight varies: 10.70-11.40 grams.

Date	Mintage	VG	F	VF	XF	Unc
SE1715 (1793)	—	220	400	650	1,000	—

Bharatha Simha
SE1709-1715, 1718-1719 / 1787-1793, 1796-1797AD

HAMMERED COINAGE
Rangpur Rebel Issues

In Ahom, capital of Rangpur, during the exile of the legitimate ruler

Mint: Without Mint Name
KM# 401 1/16 RUPEE
Silver **Note:** Weight varies: 0.67-0.72 grams.

Date	Mintage	VG	F	VF	XF	Unc
ND (1709)	—	10.00	13.50	18.50	26.50	—

Mint: Without Mint Name
KM# 402 1/8 RUPEE
Silver **Note:** Weight varies: 1.34-1.45 grams.

Date	Mintage	VG	F	VF	XF	Unc
ND (1710)	—	12.50	16.50	22.50	30.00	—

Mint: Without Mint Name
KM# 403 1/4 RUPEE
Silver **Obv:** Inscription **Rev:** Inscription **Note:** Weight varies: 2.68-2.90 grams.

Date	Mintage	VG	F	VF	XF	Unc
SE1713 (1791)	—	15.00	20.00	28.50	40.00	—
SE1714 (1792)	—	15.00	20.00	28.50	40.00	—
SE1715 (1793)	—	15.00	20.00	28.50	40.00	—
SE1718 (1796)	—	15.00	20.00	28.50	40.00	—
SE1719 (1797)	—	15.00	20.00	28.50	40.00	—

Mint: Without Mint Name
KM# 404 1/2 RUPEE
Silver **Obv:** Inscription **Rev:** Inscription **Note:** Weight varies: 5.35-5.80 grams.

Date	Mintage	VG	F	VF	XF	Unc
ND (1712)	—	12.50	17.50	23.50	32.50	—

Mint: Without Mint Name
KM# 405 RUPEE
Silver **Obv:** Inscription **Rev:** Inscription **Note:** Weight varies: 10.70-11.60 grams.

Date	Mintage	VG	F	VF	XF	Unc
SE1713 (1791)	—	15.00	20.00	28.50	40.00	—
SE1714 (1792)	—	15.00	20.00	28.50	40.00	—
SE1715 (1793)	—	15.00	20.00	28.50	40.00	—
SE1718 (1796)	—	12.50	20.00	28.50	40.00	—
SE1719 (1797)	—	12.50	20.00	28.50	40.00	—

Mint: Without Mint Name
KM# 408 1/8 MOHUR
Gold **Note:** Weight varies: 1.34-1.42 grams.

Date	Mintage	VG	F	VF	XF	Unc
ND (1713) Rare	—	—	—	—	—	—

Mint: Without Mint Name
KM# 409 1/4 MOHUR
Gold **Note:** Weight varies: 2.68-2.85 grams.

Date	Mintage	VG	F	VF	XF	Unc
SE1713 (1791) Rare	—	—	—	—	—	—

Mint: Without Mint Name
KM# 410 1/2 MOHUR
Gold **Note:** Weight varies: 5.35-5.70 grams.

Date	Mintage	VG	F	VF	XF	Unc
ND (1713) Rare	—	—	—	—	—	—

Kamalesvara Simha
SE1718-1732 / 1796-1810AD

HAMMERED COINAGE

Mint: Without Mint Name
KM# 235 1/8 RUPEE
Silver, 10 mm. **Note:** Octagonal. Weight varies: 1.34-1.45 grams.

Date	Mintage	VG	F	VF	XF	Unc
ND(1796-1810)	—	20.00	30.00	40.00	60.00	—

Mint: Without Mint Name
KM# 237 1/2 RUPEE
Silver **Obv:** Inscription **Rev:** Inscription **Note:** Weight varies: 5.35-5.80 grams.

Date	Mintage	VG	F	VF	XF	Unc
ND(1796-1810)	—	25.00	35.00	45.00	70.00	—

Mint: Without Mint Name
KM# 238 RUPEE
Silver **Obv:** Inscription **Rev:** Inscription **Note:** Weight varies: 10.70-11.60 grams.

Date	Mintage	VG	F	VF	XF	Unc
SE1720 (1798)	—	35.00	45.00	60.00	95.00	—

Mint: Without Mint Name
KM# 241 1/8 MOHUR
Gold **Note:** Octagonal. Weight varies: 1.34-1.42 grams.

Date	Mintage	VG	F	VF	XF	Unc
ND(1796-1810)	—	50.00	90.00	175	275	—

Mint: Without Mint Name
KM# 244 MOHUR
Gold **Note:** Octagonal. 10.70-11.40 grams.

Date	Mintage	VG	F	VF	XF	Unc
SE1720 (1798)	—	225	425	700	1,200	—

COOCH BEHAR

During the 15th century, the area that was to become Cooch Behar was ruled by the powerful Hindu kings of Kamata, who were defeated by Sultan Ala al din Husain, Shah of Bengal in 1494AD. In 1511AD the kingdom of Cooch Behar was established by Chandan, a chieftain of the Koch tribe.

After Lakshmi Narayan's death in 1627, the new ruler Vira Narayan exhibited a certain degree of independence by striking full rupees and retaking the former Eastern Cooch Behar Kingdom from the Mughals. By this time, however, a powerful leader had emerged in Bhutan, and trade was disrupted by wars between Bhutan and Tibet, causing a reduction in the number of coins struck.

The Mughals soon recaptured the eastern territories, but the next ruler, Prana Narayan, was able to reopen trade links with Tibet through Bhutan. In 1661 Prana Narayan was expelled from his capital by the Mughal governor of Bengal, Mir Jumia, and sought refuge in Bhutan. At this time, Mir Jumia struck coins in Cooch Behar in the name of the Mughal Emperor Aurangzeb, but while Mir Jumia was stuck in Assam during the monsoon of 1663, Prana Narayan managed to regain control of his kingdom paying tribute to the Mughal Emperor.

For the next century Cooch Behar was relatively peaceful until there was a dispute over the succession in 1772. After a confusing period during which the Bhutanese installed their own nominated ruler and captured Dhairyendra Narandra, the Chief Minister appealed to the British for assistance. With an eye on the potentially lucrative Tibetan trade, which had increased somewhat in volume since Prithvi Narayan's rise to power in Nepal, the British agreed to support Darendra Narayan, so long as British suzerainty was acknowledged.

Bhutanese copies: Until the 1780's the Bhutanese used to periodically send surplus silver to the mint in Cooch Behar to strike into coin for local use, as Cooch Behar coins circulated widely in Bhutan. After the Cooch Behar mint was closed in 1788 the Bhutanese established their own mints, striking copies of the 1/2 rupees, initially of fine silver with slight differences in design from the original Cooch Behar coins, but later the silver content reduced until they were of pure copper or brass. For these issues see Bhutan listing.

RULERS

Rupa Narayan,
CB185-205/SE1617-37/1695-1715AD

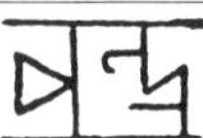

Upendra Narayan,
CB205-254/SE1637-86/1715-64AD

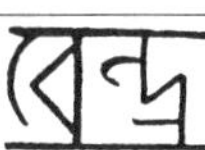

Devendra Narayan,
CB254-256/SE1686-88/1764-66AD

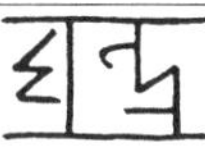

Dhairjendra Narayan,
CB256-261/SE1688-93/1766-72AD

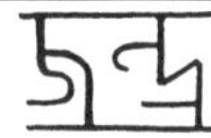

Rajendra Narayan,
CB261-263/SE1693-95/1771-73AD

Darendra Narayan,
CB263-270/SE1695-1702/1772-80AD
CB270-273/SE1702-05/1780-83AD, 2nd reign

Harendra Narayan,
CB273-329/SE1705-61/1783-1839AD

DATING

The coins are dated in either the Saka era (Saka yr. + 78 = AD year) or the Cooch Behar era (CB yr. + 1510 = AD year) calculated from the year of the founding of the kingdom by Chandan in 1511AD. Some coins have dates in both eras, but as the Saka always refers back to the accession year, and the Cooch Behar year seems to show the actual date of striking, the two years seems to show the actual date of striking, the two years do not necessarily correspond to the same AD year.

Unfortunately the dies for the half rupees were usually rather broader than the flans, so the year is only rarely visible.

KINGDOM

Upendra Narayan
CB205-254 / SE1637-1686 / 1715-1764AD

HAMMERED COINAGE

Mint: Without Mint Name
KM# 115 1/2 RUPEE
Silver **Obv:** Inscription **Rev:** Inscription **Note:** Weight varies 5.35 - 5.8 grams.

Date	Mintage	Good	VG	F	VF	XF
ND	—	3.25	5.00	8.50	12.50	—

Devendra Narayan

CB254-256 / SE1686-1688 / 1764-1766AD

HAMMERED COINAGE

Mint: Without Mint Name
KM# 121 1/2 RUPEE
Silver **Obv:** Inscription **Rev:** Inscription **Note:** Weight varies 5.35 - 5.8 grams.

Date	Mintage	Good	VG	F	VF	XF
ND	—	—	5.00	8.00	11.00	15.00

Dhairjendra Narayan

CB256-261, 270-273 / SE1688-1693, 1702-1705 / 1766-1771, 1780-1783AD

HAMMERED COINAGE

Mint: Without Mint Name
KM# 127 1/2 RUPEE
Silver **Obv:** Inscription **Rev:** Inscription **Note:** Weight varies 5.35 - 5.8 grams.

Date	Mintage	Good	VG	F	VF	XF
ND	—	—	6.00	9.00	11.50	16.50

Rajendra Narayan

CB261-263 / SE1693-1695 / 1771-1773AD

HAMMERED COINAGE

Mint: Without Mint Name
KM# 133 1/2 RUPEE
4.7000 g., Silver **Obv:** Inscription **Rev:** Inscription

Date	Mintage	Good	VG	F	VF	XF
ND	—	—	5.00	8.00	11.00	15.00

Darendra Narayan or Harendra Narayan

SE1695-1702 / 1773-1780AD or SE1705-1761 / 1783-1839AD

HAMMERED COINAGE

Mint: Without Mint Name
KM# 141 1/2 RUPEE
4.7000 g., Silver **Obv:** Inscription **Rev:** Inscription

Date	Mintage	Good	VG	F	VF	XF
ND	—	—	5.00	8.00	11.00	15.00

FARRUKHABAD

Farrukhabad, a district in north India, was founded early in the eighteenth century by the Afghan, Mohammed Khan (d.1743), who was governor first of Allahabad and later of Malwa. The subsequent struggles of his sons with Awadh, with the Rohillas and with the Marathas, culminated in Farrukhabad becoming a tributary to Awadh, by which state Farrukhabad was entirely surrounded. In 1801 Farrukhabad was ceded to the British by the Nawab Vizier of Awadh.

For similar coins struck in the name of Ahmad Shah (Durrani) dated AH1174, 1176 refer to Afghanistan, Durrani listings. For later issues with fixed regnal year 45 refer to India-British/Bengal Presidency listings.

BANGASH NAWABS

Muhammad Khan,
AH1126-1156/1714-1743AD
Qaim Khan,
AH1156-1164/1743-1750
Ahmad Khan,
AH1164-1185/1750-1771AD
Muzaffar Jang,
AH1185-1210/1771-1796AD
Amin-ud-Daula,
AH1210-1217/1796-1802AD

MINT NAME

Until AH1167
Farrukhabad
Commencing AH1167
Ahmadnagar-Farrukhabad

NOTE: Catalog numbers were in reference to Craig's basic Mughal listings.

KINGDOM

HAMMERED COINAGE

Mint: Without Mint Name
KM# 28 RUPEE
Silver **Obv. Inscription:** "Shah Alam II" **Rev:** Inscription **Note:** Weight varies: 10.70-11.60 grams.

Date	Mintage	VG	F	VF	XF	Unc
AH1175//1 (1761)	—	8.50	13.50	20.00	35.00	—
AH1175//2 (1761)	—	8.50	13.50	20.00	35.00	—
AH1175//3 (1761)	—	8.50	13.50	20.00	35.00	—
AH1176//3 (1762)	—	8.50	13.50	20.00	35.00	—
AH1177//4 (1763)	—	8.50	13.50	20.00	35.00	—
AH1177//5 (1763)	—	8.50	13.50	20.00	35.00	—
AH1178//5 (1764)	—	8.50	13.50	20.00	35.00	—
AH1179//6 (1765)	—	8.50	13.50	20.00	35.00	—
AH1179//7 (1765)	—	8.50	13.50	20.00	35.00	—
AH1180/7 (1766)	—	8.50	13.50	20.00	35.00	—
AH1183/10 (1769)	—	8.50	13.50	20.00	35.00	—
AH1186/13 (1772)	—	8.50	13.50	20.00	35.00	—
AH1187//15 (1773)	—	8.50	13.50	20.00	35.00	—
AH1189/16 (1775)	—	8.50	13.50	20.00	35.00	—
AH1189//17 (1775)	—	8.50	13.50	20.00	35.00	—
AH1190//18 (1776)	—	8.50	13.50	20.00	35.00	—
AH1192//19 (1778)	—	8.50	13.50	20.00	35.00	—
AH1193//20 (1779)	—	8.50	13.50	20.00	35.00	—
AH1194//21 (1780)	—	8.50	13.50	20.00	35.00	—
AH1195//21 (1780)	—	8.50	13.50	20.00	35.00	—
AH1196//21 (1781)	—	8.50	13.50	20.00	35.00	—
AH1196//22 (1781)	—	8.50	13.50	20.00	35.00	—
AH1196//23 (1781)	—	8.50	13.50	20.00	35.00	—
AH1197//23 (1782)	—	8.50	13.50	20.00	35.00	—
AH1197//24 (1782)	—	8.50	13.50	20.00	35.00	—
AH1198//24 (1783)	—	8.50	13.50	20.00	35.00	—
AH1198//25 (1783)	—	8.50	13.50	20.00	35.00	—
AH1199//27 (1784)	—	8.50	13.50	20.00	35.00	—
AH1200//27 (1785)	—	8.50	13.50	20.00	35.00	—
AH1203//29 (1788)	—	8.50	13.50	20.00	35.00	—
AH1205//31 (1790)	—	8.50	13.50	20.00	35.00	—
AH1206//31 (1791)	—	8.50	13.50	20.00	35.00	—
AH1207//31 (1792)	—	8.50	13.50	20.00	35.00	—
AH1208//31 (1793)	—	8.50	13.50	20.00	35.00	—
AH1209//31 (1794)	—	8.50	13.50	20.00	35.00	—
AH1211//31 (1796)	—	8.50	13.50	20.00	35.00	—
AH1212//31 (1797)	—	8.50	13.50	20.00	35.00	—
AH1212//39 (1797)	—	8.50	13.50	20.00	35.00	—
AH1213//39 (1798)	—	8.50	13.50	20.00	35.00	—
AH1214//39 (1799)	—	8.50	13.50	20.00	35.00	—
AH1215//39 (1800)	—	8.50	13.50	20.00	35.00	—

Mint: Ahmadnagar-Farrukhabad
KM# 12 RUPEE
Silver **Obv. Inscription:** Alamgir (II) **Rev. Inscription:** Ahmadnagar-Farrukhabad

Date	Mintage	VG	F	VF	XF	Unc
AH1169//2 (1756)	—	12.00	20.00	32.50	55.00	—
AH1170//2 (1757)	—	12.00	20.00	32.50	55.00	—
AH1170//3 (1757)	—	12.00	20.00	32.50	55.00	—
AH1170//4 (1757)	—	12.00	20.00	32.50	55.00	—
AH1171//5 (1758)	—	12.00	20.00	32.50	55.00	—
AH1172//5 (1759)	—	12.00	20.00	32.50	55.00	—
AH1172//6 (1759)	—	12.00	20.00	32.50	55.00	—
AH1173//6 (1760)	—	12.00	20.00	32.50	55.00	—

Mint: Ahmadnagar-Farrukhabad
KM# 16 RUPEE
Silver **Obv. Inscription:** Shah Jahan (III) **Rev. Inscription:** Ahmadnagar-Farrukhabad **Note:** Weight varies: 10.70-11.60 grams.

Date	Mintage	VG	F	VF	XF	Unc
AH1173//1 (1760)	—	150	200	300	450	—

Mint: Farrukhabad
KM# 4 RUPEE
Silver **Obv. Inscription:** Alamgir (II) **Rev. Inscription:** Farrukhabad **Note:** Weight varies: 10.70-11.60 grams.

Date	Mintage	VG	F	VF	XF	Unc
AH1168//1(Ahd) (1755)	—	18.00	30.00	50.00	85.00	—
AH1168//2 (1755)	—	18.00	30.00	50.00	85.00	—

Mint: Farrukhabad
KM# 34 MOHUR
Gold **Obv:** Inscription **Rev:** Inscription **Note:** Weight varies: 10.70-11.40 grams.

Date	Mintage	VG	F	VF	XF	Unc
AH1173//1 (1759)	—	150	225	450	600	—
AH1178//6 (1764)	—	150	225	450	600	—
AH1194//21 (1780)	—	150	225	450	600	—
AH1196//23 (1782)	—	150	225	450	600	—
AH1211//31 (1797)	—	150	225	450	600	—
AH1215//39 (1800)	—	150	225	450	600	—

Mint: Farrukhabad
KM# 8 MOHUR
Gold **Obv. Inscription:** Alamgir II **Rev. Inscription:** Farrukhabad **Note:** Weight varies: 10.70-11.60 grams.

Date	Mintage	VG	F	VF	XF	Unc
AH1170//2 (1757)	—	175	300	500	800	—

Mint: Without Mint Name
KM# 26 1/4 RUPEE
Silver **Obv. Inscription:** Shah Alam II **Rev:** Inscription **Note:** Weight varies: 2.68-2.90 grams.

Date	Mintage	VG	F	VF	XF	Unc
AH-//39	—	10.00	15.00	25.00	40.00	—

GURKHA KINGDOM

Almora was the principal town of the Kumaon territory in northern India. It was under the control of the Chand Rajas until the Gurkhas, who had already overrun the Kathmandu Valley in 1768, captured it in 1790.

MINT

المورا

Almora

ALMORA

Chand Rajas

Until 1790AD

HAMMERED COINAGE

Mint: Almora
C# 5 PAISA

Copper **Obv:** Inscription, 2 small crowns **Rev:** Inscription **Note:** Struck in the name of local ruler. Regnal years of Shah Alam II.

Date	Mintage	Good	VG	F	VF	XF
ND//14 (1772)	—	4.50	8.50	13.50	20.00	—
ND//18 (1776)	—	4.50	8.50	13.50	20.00	—
ND//19 (1777)	—	4.50	8.50	13.50	20.00	—
ND//21 (1779)	—	4.50	8.50	13.50	20.00	—
ND//22 (1780)	—	4.50	8.50	13.50	20.00	—
ND//41(sic) (1799)	—	4.50	8.50	13.50	20.00	—

JAINTIAPUR

Farrukhabad, a district in north India, was founded early in the eighteenth century by the Afghan, Mohammed Khan (d.1743), who was governor first of Allahabad and later of Malwa. The subsequent struggles of his sons with Awadh, with the Rohillas and with the Marathas, culminated in Farrukhabad becoming a tributary to Awadh, by which state Farrukhabad was entirely surrounded. In 1801 Farrukhabad was ceded to the British by the Nawab Vizier of Awadh.

For similar coins struck in the name of Ahmad Shah (Durrani) dated AH1174, 1176 refer to Afghanistan, Durrani listings. For later issues with fixed regnal year 45 refer to India-British/Bengal Presidency listings.

BANGASH NAWABS

Muhammad Khan,
AH1126-1156/1714-1743AD
Qaim Khan,
AH1156-1164/1743-1750
Ahmad Khan,
AH1164-1185/1750-1771AD
Muzaffar Jang,
AH1185-1210/1771-1796AD
Amin-ud-Daula,
AH1210-1217/1796-1802AD

MINT NAME

Until AH1167
Farrukhabad
Commencing AH1167
Ahmadnagar-Farrukhabad

NOTE: Catalog numbers were in reference to Craig's basic Mughal listings.

KINGDOM

Ram Simha

SE1625-1630 / 1703-1708AD

HAMMERED COINAGE

Anonymous

Mint: Without Mint Name
KM# 150 RUPEE

9.2000 g., Silver **Obv:** Inscription within square and circle **Rev:** Inscription within circle

Date	Mintage	Good	VG	F	VF	XF
SE1625 (1703)	—	—	60.00	85.00	125	175

Jaya Narayan

SE1630-1653 / 1708-1731AD

HAMMERED COINAGE

Anonymous

Mint: Without Mint Name
KM# 160 RUPEE

9.2000 g., Silver **Obv:** Inscription within circle **Rev:** Inscription within circle

Date	Mintage	Good	VG	F	VF	XF
SE1630 (1708)	—	—	42.50	60.00	85.00	125

Bar Gossain II

SE1653-1692 / 1731-1770AD

HAMMERED COINAGE

Anonymous

Mint: Without Mint Name
KM# 175 1/4 RUPEE

Silver **Obv:** Inscription within circle **Rev:** Inscription within circle **Note:** Weight varies 2.68 - 2.90 grams.

Date	Mintage	Good	VG	F	VF	XF
SE1653 (1731)	—	—	60.00	85.00	125	175

Mint: Without Mint Name
KM# 177 RUPEE

Silver **Obv:** Inscription within circle, with symbols **Rev:** Inscription within circle **Note:** Weight varies 7.1 - 10 grams.

Date	Mintage	Good	VG	F	VF	XF
SE1653 (1731)	—	—	25.00	35.00	50.00	85.00

Chattra Simha

SE1692-1704 / 1770-1782AD

HAMMERED COINAGE

Anonymous

Mint: Without Mint Name
KM# 185 RUPEE

9.4000 g., Silver

Date	Mintage	Good	VG	F	VF	XF
SE1696 (1774)	—	—	25.00	35.00	50.00	85.00

Jatra Narayan

SE1704-1707 / 1782-1785AD

HAMMERED COINAGE

Anonymous

Mint: Without Mint Name
KM# 192 RUPEE

Silver **Obv:** Inscription within circle, with symbols **Rev:** Inscription, date below, within circle **Note:** Weight varies 9 - 10.7 grams.

Date	Mintage	Good	VG	F	VF	XF
SE1704 (1782)	—	—	50.00	70.00	100	150

Vijaya Narayan

SE1707-1712 / 1785-1790AD

HAMMERED COINAGE

Anonymous

Mint: Without Mint Name
KM# 199 RUPEE

9.4000 g., Silver

Date	Mintage	Good	VG	F	VF	XF
SE1707 (1785)	—	—	50.00	70.00	100	150

Ram Simha II

SE1712-1754 / 1790-1832AD

HAMMERED COINAGE

Anonymous

Mint: Without Mint Name
KM# 204 1/4 RUPEE

Silver **Obv:** Inscription within circle **Rev:** Inscription, date within circle **Note:** Weight varies 2.68 - 2.9 grams.

Date	Mintage	Good	VG	F	VF	XF
SE1712 (1790)	—	—	60.00	85.00	125	175

Mint: Without Mint Name
KM# 207 RUPEE

11.0000 g., Silver **Obv:** Inscription **Rev:** Inscription, date **Shape:** Octagonal

Date	Mintage	Good	VG	F	VF	XF
SE1722 (1800)	—	—	85.00	125	175	250

Mint: Without Mint Name
KM# 206 RUPEE

Silver **Obv:** Inscription within circle, with symbols **Rev:** Inscription within circle **Note:** Weight varies 7.3 - 9.2 grams.

Date	Mintage	Good	VG	F	VF	XF
SE1712 (1790)	—	—	25.00	35.00	50.00	85.00

JAMMU

Prior to the 14th century Jammu and Kashmir were ruled by a series of Buddhist and Hindu dynasties. As Islam tightened its hold on the northwest of India, a succession of Muslim sultans occupied Kashmir until Akbar's annexation in 1587, after which it became the summer capital of the emperors of Delhi. With Mughal decline, Kashmir passed into the hands of governors appointed by Ahmad Shah Durrani of Afghanistan. During this last period Jammu remained in the hands of the Dogra Raja Ranjit Dev and his successor Brij Raj Dev. Early in the nineteenth century both Jammu and Kashmir fell into Sikh hands for about twenty-five years until the British asserted their authority after the first Anglo-Sikh War. By the Treaty of Amritsar in 1846 the British established Gulab Singh, a relative of Ranjit Singh, as the ruler of the entire region. In return he was obliged to present a horse, twelve goats and a few Kashmiri shawls annually as tribute - a requirement which was later dropped as being inconvenient! The treaty of 1846 really marked the beginning of Jammu and Kashmir as a modern political entity, and remained in force up to India's independence.

NOTE: Evidently new obverse dies were produced regularly because of the need to change AH dates or mintmarks, but old reverse dies with obsolete regnal years were used until worn out.

For later issues see Indian Princely State, Kashmir.

RULERS

Dogra Rajas

Ranjit Dev, AH1155-1194/VS1799-1837/
1742-1780AD
Brij Raj Dev, AH1195- /VS1838- /1781AD

MINT

جمون

Jammu

دارالامان جمون

Mint name: ***Dar-ul-Aman***

INDEPENDENT KINGDOM

Shah Alam II

AH1173-1221/1753-1806AD

HAMMERED COINAGE

Mint: Jammu
KM# 5.6 RUPEE

Obv: Inscription **Rev:** Inscription, mint name at top **Note:** Struck at Jammu with mint name Dar-ul-Aman.

Date	Mintage	VG	F	VF	XF	Unc
AH1194/22 (1780)	—	20.00	30.00	45.00	75.00	—
AH1195/23 (1780)	—	20.00	30.00	45.00	75.00	—
AH1195/25 (1780)	—	20.00	30.00	45.00	75.00	—
AH1196/24 (1781)	—	20.00	30.00	45.00	75.00	—
AH1197/24 (1782)	—	20.00	30.00	45.00	75.00	—
AH1197/25 (1782)	—	20.00	30.00	45.00	75.00	—
AH1198/25 (1783)	—	20.00	30.00	45.00	75.00	—

Mint: Jammu
KM# 5.2 RUPEE

Silver **Obv:** Inscription **Rev:** Inscription **Note:** Struck at Jammu with mint name Dar-ul-Aman.

Date	Mintage	VG	F	VF	XF	Unc
AH1195/24 (1780)	—	20.00	32.50	55.00	85.00	—
AH1196/24 (1781)	—	20.00	32.50	55.00	85.00	—

Mint: Jammu
KM# 5.3 RUPEE

Silver **Obv:** Inscription, date **Rev:** Inscription, fish **Note:** Struck at Jammu with mint name Dar-ul-Aman.

Date	Mintage	VG	F	VF	XF	Unc
AH1196/24 (1781)	—	20.00	32.50	55.00	85.00	—

Mint: Jammu
KM# 5.4 RUPEE

Silver **Obv:** Inscription, date, mint mark **Rev:** Inscription **Note:** Struck at Jammu with mint name Dar-ul-Aman.

Date	Mintage	VG	F	VF	XF	Unc
AH1197/25 (1782)	—	20.00	32.50	55.00	85.00	—
AH1198/25 (1783)	—	20.00	32.50	55.00	85.00	—

Mint: Jammu
KM# 5.7 RUPEE

Silver **Obv:** Stemmed flower mint mark, inscription, date **Rev:** Inscription **Note:** Struck at Jammu with mint name Dar-ul-Aman.

Date	Mintage	VG	F	VF	XF	Unc
AH1197/25 (1782)	—	20.00	32.50	55.00	85.00	—

Mint: Jammu
KM# 5.5 RUPEE

Silver **Obv:** Katar, date, inscription **Rev:** Inscription **Note:** Struck at Jammu with mint name Dar-ul-Aman.

Date	Mintage	VG	F	VF	XF	Unc
AH1198/26 (1783)	—	20.00	32.50	55.00	85.00	—

Mint: Jammu
KM# 5.1 RUPEE

Silver **Obv:** Inscription **Rev:** Inscription, mint name at bottom **Note:** Struck at Jammu with mint name Dar-ul-Aman. Without mint marks. Weight varies: 10.70-11.60 grams.

Date	Mintage	VG	F	VF	XF	Unc
AH(1193)//21 (1779)	—	20.00	30.00	45.00	75.00	—

Mint: Jammu
KM# 10.1 RUPEE

Silver **Obv:** Inscription, parasol **Rev:** Inscription **Note:** Struck in the name of local ruler Ranjit Dev.

Date	Mintage	VG	F	VF	XF	Unc
VS1841/27 (1784)	—	50.00	85.00	135	200	—
VS1841/28 (1784)	—	50.00	85.00	135	200	—

Mint: Jammu
KM# 10.2 RUPEE

Silver **Obv:** Crude style, inscription **Rev:** Crude style, inscription **Note:** Struck in the name of local ruler Ranjit Dev.

Date	Mintage	VG	F	VF	XF	Unc
VS1841/28 (1784)	—	40.00	55.00	80.00	115	—

KACHAR

The Kacharis are probably the original inhabitants of the Assam Valley, and in the 13th century ruled much of the south bank of the Brahmaputra from their capital at Dimapur.

Around 1530 the Ahoms inflicted several crushing defeats on the Kacharis, Dimapur was sacked, and the Kacharis were forced to retreat further south and set up a new capital at Maibong.

Very little is known about this obscure state, and the only time that coins were struck in any quantity was during the late 16th and early 17th centuries. One coin, indeed, proudly announces the conquest of Sylhet, but the military prowess seems to have been short lived, and the small kingdom was only saved from Muslim domination by its isolation and lack of economic worth.

A few coins were struck during the 18th and 19th centuries, but this was probably merely as a demonstration of independence, rather than for any economic reason.

In 1819, the last Kachari ruler, Govind Chandra was ousted by the Manipuri ruler Chaurajit Simha, and during the Burmese occupation of Manipur and Assam, the Manipuris remained in control of Kachar. In 1824, Govind Chandra was restored to his throne by the British, and ruled under British suzerainty. By all accounts his administration was not a success, and in 1832, soon after Govind Chandra had been murdered, the British took over the administration of the State in "compliance with the frequent and earnestly expressed wishes of the people.

The earliest coins of Kachar were clearly copied from the contemporary coins of Cooch Behar, with weight standard also copied from the Bengali standard. The flans are, however, even broader than those of the Cooch Behar coins, making the coins very distinctive.

A number of spectacular gold and silver coins, purporting to come from Kachar, appeared in Calcutta during the 1960's, but as their authenticity has been doubted, they have been omitted from this listing.

RULERS

A list of the Kings of Kachar has been preserved in local traditions, but is rather unreliable. The following list has been compiled from this traditional list, together with names and dates obtained from other sources, but may not be completely accurate.

Tamradhvaja, SEc.1622-1630/ c.1700-1708AD
Sura Darpa, SE1630-/1708-AD
Harish Chandra, SEc.1643/c.1721AD
Kirti Chandra Narayan, SEc.1658/ c.1736AD
Sandhikari, SEc.1687/c.1765AD
Harish Chandra, SEc.1693/c.1771AD
Lakshmi Chandra Narayan, SE1694-1702/ 1772-1780AD
Krishna Chandra Narayan, SE1712-1735/ c.1790-1813AD

KINGDOM

Tamradhvaja

SE c.1622-1630 / c.1700-1708AD

HAMMERED COINAGE

Mint: Without Mint Name
KM# 132 1/4 RUPEE

Silver **Obv:** Inscription within circle **Rev:** Inscription within circle

Date	Mintage	Good	VG	F	VF	XF
ND(ca.1700-08)	—	32.50	55.00	90.00	125	—

Lakshmi Chandra Narayan

SE1694-1702 / 1772-1780AD

HAMMERED COINAGE

Mint: Without Mint Name
KM# 136 RUPEE

10.4000 g., Silver **Obv:** Inscription **Rev:** Inscription **Shape:** Octagonal

Date	Mintage	Good	VG	F	VF	XF
SE1694 (1772)	—	—	100	150	225	325

Mint: Without Mint Name
KM# 140 MOHUR

11.5000 g., Gold **Obv:** Inscription **Rev:** Inscription **Shape:** Octagonal

Date	Mintage	Good	VG	F	VF	XF
SE1694 (1772)	—	—	500	800	1,300	2,000

KUMAON

KINGDOM

HAMMERED COINAGE

Mint: Almora
C# 5 PAISA
Copper **Note:** During the reign of local rule of the Chand Rajas.

Date	Mintage	Good	VG	F	VF	XF
AH14 (1772)	—	4.50	8.50	13.50	20.00	—
AH18 (1776)	—	4.50	8.50	13.50	20.00	—
AH19 (1777)	—	4.50	8.50	13.50	20.00	—
AH21 (1779)	—	4.50	8.50	13.50	20.00	—
AH22 (1780)	—	4.50	8.50	13.50	20.00	—
AH41 (1799)	—	4.50	8.50	13.50	20.00	—

KUTCH

State located in northwest India, consisting of a peninsula north of the Gulf of Kutch.

The rulers of Kutch were Jareja Rajputs who, coming from Tatta in Sind, conquered Kutch in the 14th or 15th centuries. The capital city of Bhuj is thought to date from the mid-16th century. In 1617, after Akbar's conquest of Gujerat and the fall of the Gujerat sultans, the Kutch ruler, Rao Bharmal I (1586-1632) visited Jahangir and established a relationship which was sufficiently warm as to leave Kutch virtually independent throughout the Mughal period. Early in the 19th century internal disorder and the existence of rival claimants to the throne resulted in British intrusion into the state's affairs. Rao Bharmalji II was deposed in favor of Rao Desalji II who proved much more amenable to the Government of India's wishes. He and his successors continued to rule in a manner considered by the British to be most enlightened and, as a result, Maharao Khengarji III was created a Knight Grand Commander of the Indian Empire. In view of its geographical isolation Kutch came under the direct control of the Central Government at India's independence.

First coinage was struck in 1617AD.

RULERS

राउ श्री प्रागजी

Pragmalji I, 1698-1715AD
Ra-o Sri Pra-g-ji

राउ श्री गोदाउजी

Gohodaji I, 1715-1719AD
Ra-o Sri Go-ho-d-ji

राउ श्री देशलजी

Desalji I, 1719-1752AD
Ra-o Sri De-sh(a)-l-ji

राउ लषपतजी

Lakhpatji, AAH1165-1175/1752-61AD
Ra-o L(a)-sh-p(a)-t-ji

महाराउ श्री लखपतजी

M(a)-ha-ra-o Sri L(a)-kh-p(a)-(t-ji)

राउ श्री गोदाउजी

Gohodaji, AH1175-1192/1761-1778AD
Ra-o Sri-Go-ho-d-ji

राउ श्री रायधणजी

Rayadhanji II, AH1192-1230/1778-1814AD
Ra-o Sri Ra-y(a)-dh(a)-n-ji

MINT

भुज Or بھج

Bhuj **(Devavnagri)** **(Persian)**

NOTE: All coins through Bharmalji II bear a common type, derived from the Gujarati coinage of Muzaffar III (late 16th century AD), and bear a stylized form of the date AH978 (1570AD). The silver issues of Bharmalji. II also have the fictitious date AH1165. The rulers name appears in the Devanagri script on the obverse.

NOTE: Br#'s are in reference to *Coinage of Kutch* by Richard K. Bright.

MONETARY SYSTEM

1/2 Trambiyo = 1 Babukiya
2 Trambiyo = 1 Dokdo
3 Trambiyo = 1 Dhinglo
2 Dhinglo = 1 Dhabu
2 Dhabu = 1 Payalo
2 Payalo = 1 Adlinao
2 Adlina = 1 Kori

KINGDOM

Pragmalji I

AH1110-1127 / 1698-1715AD

HAMMERED COINAGE

Mint: Without Mint Name
KM# 39 DOKDO
Copper **Obv:** Inscription, date **Rev:** Inscription **Note:** Br.#27.

Date	Mintage	Good	VG	F	VF	XF
ND(1698-1715)	—	2.00	3.00	4.50	6.50	—

Mint: Without Mint Name
KM# 40 DHINGLO
11.8000 g., Copper **Obv:** Inscription **Rev:** Inscription, scissors **Note:** Br.#28.

Date	Mintage	Good	VG	F	VF	XF
ND(1698-1715)	—	2.00	3.00	4.50	6.50	—

Mint: Without Mint Name
KM# 43 KORI
4.5000 g., Silver **Obv:** Inscription, date **Rev:** Inscription **Note:** Br.#30.

Date	Mintage	Good	VG	F	VF	XF
AH978 Frozen	—	2.25	5.50	8.00	13.50	20.00

Gohadaji I

AH1127-1132 / 1715-1719AD

HAMMERED COINAGE

Mint: Without Mint Name
KM# 45 KORI
4.5000 g., Silver, 15 mm. **Obv:** Inscription, trident **Rev. Inscription:** Rao Sri Gohodji (Nagari in small characters) **Note:** Br.#35.

Date	Mintage	Good	VG	F	VF	XF
AH978 Frozen; Rare	—	—	—	—	—	—

Desalji I

AH1132-1166 / 1719-1752AD

HAMMERED COINAGE

Mint: Without Mint Name
KM# 47 1/2 TRAMBIYO
1.1000 g., Copper, 8-9 mm. **Obv:** Inscription, trisul **Rev. Inscription:** Rao Sri Deshlji in Nagari **Note:** Br.#A36.

Date	Mintage	Good	VG	F	VF	XF
ND(1719-52)	—	1.50	2.50	3.50	5.50	—

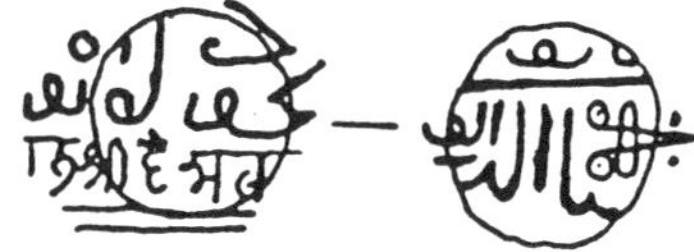

Mint: Without Mint Name
KM# 48 TRAMBIYO
4.5000 g., Copper **Obv:** Inscription, date **Rev:** Inscription, scissors **Note:** Br.#36.

Date	Mintage	Good	VG	F	VF	XF
ND(1719-52)	—	1.75	2.75	4.00	6.00	—

Mint: Without Mint Name
KM# 51 TRAMBIYO
4.5000 g., Copper **Note:** Br.#36a.

Date	Mintage	Good	VG	F	VF	XF
ND(1719-52)	—	1.75	2.75	4.00	6.00	—

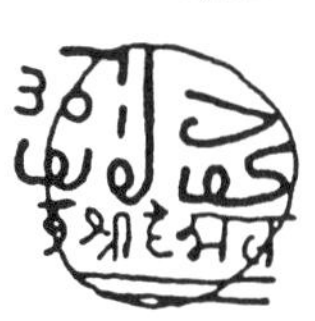

Mint: Without Mint Name
KM# 49 DOKDO
8.7000 g., Copper **Obv:** Inscription, date **Rev:** Inscription, scissors **Note:** Br.#37.

Date	Mintage	Good	VG	F	VF	XF
ND(1719-52)	—	2.00	3.00	4.50	6.50	—

Mint: Without Mint Name
KM# 52 DOKDO
8.7000 g., Copper **Obv:** Persian legend more debased **Note:** Br.#37a.

Date	Mintage	Good	VG	F	VF	XF
ND(1719-52)	—	2.00	3.00	4.50	6.50	—

Mint: Without Mint Name
KM# 50 DHINGLO
Copper **Obv:** Inscription, date **Rev:** Inscription, scissors **Note:** Br.#38. Weight varies: 12.20-12.80 grams.

Date	Mintage	Good	VG	F	VF	XF
ND(1719-52)	—	2.00	3.00	4.50	6.50	—

Mint: Without Mint Name
KM# 53 DHINGLO
Copper **Obv:** Inscription, date **Rev:** Inscription, scissors **Note:** Br.#38a. Weight varies: 12.20-12.80 grams.

Date	Mintage	Good	VG	F	VF	XF
ND(1719-52)	—	2.00	3.00	4.50	6.50	—

Mint: Without Mint Name
KM# 54 1/4 KORI
1.1000 g., Silver, 10-11 mm. **Obv:** Trisul, inscription **Rev:** "Rao Sri Deshlji" in Nagari **Note:** Br.#A39.

Date	Mintage	Good	VG	F	VF	XF
ND(1719-52)	—	2.25	5.50	8.50	13.50	20.00

Mint: Without Mint Name
KM# 55 1/2 KORI
2.2000 g., Silver **Obv:** Inscription, date **Rev:** Inscription **Note:** Br.#39.

Date	Mintage	Good	VG	F	VF	XF
ND(1719-52)	—	2.25	5.50	8.50	13.50	20.00

Mint: Without Mint Name
KM# 56 KORI
4.4000 g., Silver **Obv:** Inscription, trisul **Rev:** Inscription **Note:** Br.#40.

Date	Mintage	Good	VG	F	VF	XF
AH978 Frozen	—	2.00	5.00	7.00	10.00	15.00

Lakhpatji

AH1165-1175 / 1752-1761AD

HAMMERED COINAGE

Mint: Without Mint Name
C# 8 DHINGLO
12.5000 g., Copper

Date	Mintage	Good	VG	F	VF	XF
ND(1752-61)	—	3.00	5.00	7.50	10.00	—

Mint: Without Mint Name
C# 10 1/2 KORI
2.2000 g., Silver **Obv:** Inscription, trisul, date **Rev:** Inscription

Date	Mintage	Good	VG	F	VF	XF
AH1165	—	2.50	6.00	9.00	13.50	20.00

Mint: Without Mint Name
C# 11 KORI
5.0000 g., Silver **Obv:** Inscription, trisul, date **Obv. Inscription:** Ahamad Shah **Rev:** Inscription

Date	Mintage	Good	VG	F	VF	XF
AH1165	—	2.50	6.00	9.00	13.50	20.00

Mint: Without Mint Name
C# 12 KORI
4.4000 g., Silver, 16-18 mm. **Obv. Inscription:** Muzaffar Shah **Rev:** Inscription

Date	Mintage	Good	VG	F	VF	XF
ND(1752-61)	—	4.00	10.00	15.00	21.50	30.00

Gohadaji II

AH1175-1192 / 1761-1778AD

HAMMERED COINAGE

Mint: Without Mint Name
C# 15 1/2 TRAMBIYO
1.1000 g., Copper, 9 mm.

Date	Mintage	Good	VG	F	VF	XF
ND(1761-78) Rare	—	—	—	—	—	—

Mint: Without Mint Name
C# 16 TRAMBIYO
4.5000 g., Copper, 13 mm. **Obv:** Inscription, date **Rev:** Inscription

Date	Mintage	Good	VG	F	VF	XF
ND(1761-78)	—	1.75	2.50	3.50	5.50	—

Mint: Without Mint Name
C# 17 DOKDO
8.5000 g., Copper **Obv:** Inscription, date **Rev:** Inscription, scissors

Date	Mintage	Good	VG	F	VF	XF
ND(1761-78)	—	1.75	2.50	3.50	5.50	—

Mint: Without Mint Name
C# 18 DHINGLO
12.8800 g., Copper **Obv:** Inscription, date **Rev:** Inscription, scissors

Date	Mintage	Good	VG	F	VF	XF
ND(1761-78)	—	1.75	2.50	3.50	5.50	—

Mint: Without Mint Name
C# 20 1/4 KORI
1.1000 g., Silver, 9-11 mm.

Date	Mintage	Good	VG	F	VF	XF
ND(1761-78)	—	2.25	5.50	8.00	13.50	20.00

Mint: Without Mint Name
C# 21 1/2 KORI
2.2000 g., Silver, 12 mm. **Obv:** Inscription, date **Rev:** Inscription, scissors

Date	Mintage	Good	VG	F	VF	XF
ND(1761-78)	—	2.25	5.50	8.00	13.50	20.00

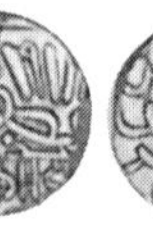

Mint: Without Mint Name
C# 22 KORI
4.4000 g., Silver **Obv:** Inscription, trisul, date **Rev:** Inscription

Date	Mintage	Good	VG	F	VF	XF
ND(1761-78)	—	2.00	5.00	7.00	10.00	15.00

Rayadhanji II

AH1192-1230 / 1778-1814AD

HAMMERED COINAGE

Mint: Without Mint Name
C# 24 1/2 TRAMBIYO
1.7000 g., Copper

Date	Mintage	Good	VG	F	VF	XF
ND(1778-1814)	—	—	—	—	—	—

Mint: Without Mint Name
C# 25 TRAMBIYO
4.1000 g., Copper

Date	Mintage	Good	VG	F	VF	XF
ND(1778-1814)	—	1.50	2.50	3.50	5.50	—

Mint: Without Mint Name
C# 26 DOKDO
7.1000 g., Copper

Date	Mintage	Good	VG	F	VF	XF
ND(1778-1814)	—	1.50	2.50	3.50	5.50	—

Mint: Without Mint Name
C# 27 DHINGLO
12.8000 g., Copper

Date	Mintage	VG	F	VF	XF	Unc
ND(1778-1814)	—	2.75	4.00	6.00	—	—

Mint: Without Mint Name
C# 28 1/4 KORI
1.3000 g., Silver, 7-8 mm.

Date	Mintage	Good	VG	F	VF	XF
ND(1778-1814)	—	2.25	5.50	8.50	13.50	20.00

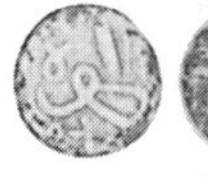

Mint: Without Mint Name
C# 29 1/2 KORI
2.3500 g., Silver

Date	Mintage	Good	VG	F	VF	XF
ND(1778-1814)	—	2.00	5.00	7.00	10.00	15.00

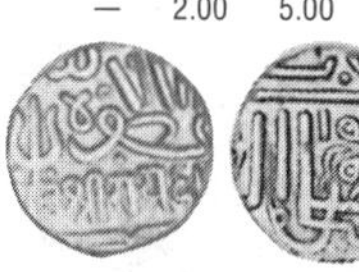

Mint: Without Mint Name
C# 30 KORI
4.5000 g., Silver

Date	Mintage	Good	VG	F	VF	XF
ND(1778-1814)	—	2.00	5.00	7.00	10.00	15.00

Mint: Without Mint Name
C# 30a KORI
4.5000 g., Silver **Note:** Perso-Arabic legends.

Date	Mintage	Good	VG	F	VF	XF
ND(1778-1814)	—	—	—	—	—	—

MADURAI

Nayakas

Located in South India approximately 180 miles north of the southernmost tip. It is noted for its great temple with colonnades and nine massive gate towers (gopuras) adorned with elaborate carvings and enclosing a quadrangle, the "Tank of the Golden Lilies". It was the capital of the Pandya dynasty from 5th century B.C. to the end of the 11th century A.D. It came under Vijayanagar control in the 14th century A.D.; and then under the Nayak dynasty from about the middle of the 16th century to 1735AD when it was taken by the Nawab of the Carnatic. Later, in 1801, it came under the rule of the British East India Company.

KINGDOM

HAMMERED COINAGE

Mint: Without Mint Name
KM# 3 KASU
Obv: Deity standing with right hand raised **Rev:** Legend around trident **Rev. Legend:** MINAKSHI **Note:** Struck in the name of Queen Minakshi (1732-1736AD).

Date	Mintage	Good	VG	F	VF	XF
ND(1732-36)	—	5.00	7.50	13.50	18.50	—

ANONYMOUS HAMMERED COINAGE

Mint: Without Mint Name
KM# 20 KASU
Copper **Obv:** Bull seated right

Date	Mintage	Good	VG	F	VF	XF
ND	—	3.50	5.50	9.00	13.50	—

Mint: Without Mint Name
KM# 4 KASU
Copper **Obv:** Horse to right **Rev. Legend:** MADHURAI in Kanarese **Note:** Weight varies 1.50 - 3.0 grams.

Date	Mintage	Good	VG	F	VF	XF
ND	—	2.50	4.50	7.50	11.50	—

Mint: Without Mint Name
KM# 5 KASU
Copper **Obv:** Lion to right **Rev:** Legend in Tamil **Rev. Legend:** PALANI **Note:** Weight varies 1.50 - 3.0 grams.

Date	Mintage	Good	VG	F	VF	XF
ND	—	2.50	4.50	7.50	—	11.50

Mint: Without Mint Name
KM# 6 KASU
Copper **Obv:** Two deities seated, bird **Rev. Legend:** SRI VIRA **Note:** Weight varies 1.50 - 3.0 grams.

Date	Mintage	Good	VG	F	VF	XF
ND	—	2.50	4.50	7.50	11.50	—

Mint: Without Mint Name
KM# 7 KASU
Copper **Obv:** Two deities reclining **Note:** Weight varies 1.50 - 3.0 grams.

Date	Mintage	Good	VG	F	VF	XF
ND	—	2.50	4.50	7.50	11.50	—

Mint: Without Mint Name
KM# 8 KASU
Copper **Obv:** Two deities seated **Note:** Weight varies 1.50 - 3.0 grams.

Date	Mintage	Good	VG	F	VF	XF
ND	—	2.50	4.50	7.50	11.50	—

Mint: Without Mint Name
KM# 9 KASU
Copper **Obv:** Deity standing to the left of one seated **Note:** Weight varies 1.50 - 3.0 grams.

Date	Mintage	Good	VG	F	VF	XF
ND	—	2.50	4.50	7.50	11.50	—

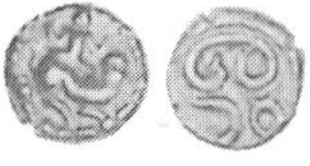

Mint: Without Mint Name
KM# 10 KASU
Copper **Obv:** Stylized deity on horseback to right **Note:** Weight varies 1.50 - 3.0 grams.

Date	Mintage	Good	VG	F	VF	XF
ND	—	3.00	5.00	8.50	12.50	—

Mint: Without Mint Name
KM# 11 KASU
Copper **Obv:** Deity on horseback to right **Note:** Weight varies 1.50 - 3.0 grams.

Date	Mintage	Good	VG	F	VF	XF
ND	—	3.00	5.00	8.50	12.50	—

Mint: Without Mint Name
KM# 12 KASU
Copper **Obv:** Deity standing in square outline **Rev:** Legend in square outline **Rev. Legend:** SRI VIRA **Note:** Weight varies 1.50 - 3.0 grams.

Date	Mintage	Good	VG	F	VF	XF
ND	—	3.50	5.50	9.00	13.50	—

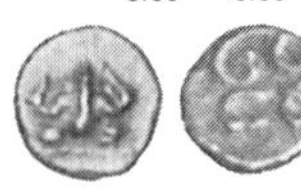

Mint: Without Mint Name
KM# 13 KASU
Copper **Obv:** Ganash seated with an elephant head **Rev. Legend:** SRI VIRA **Note:** Weight varies 1.50 - 3.0 grams.

Date	Mintage	Good	VG	F	VF	XF
ND	—	3.50	5.50	9.00	13.50	—

Mint: Without Mint Name
KM# 14 KASU
Copper **Obv:** Hanuman running to right **Note:** Weight varies 1.50 - 3.0 grams.

Date	Mintage	Good	VG	F	VF	XF
ND	—	3.50	5.50	9.00	13.50	—

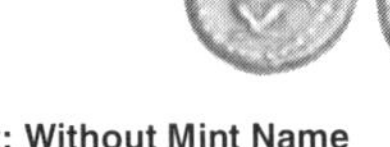

Mint: Without Mint Name
KM# 15 KASU
Copper **Obv:** Hanuman seated in circle of dots **Note:** Weight varies 1.50 - 3.0 grams.

Date	Mintage	Good	VG	F	VF	XF
ND	—	3.50	5.50	9.00	13.50	—

Mint: Without Mint Name
KM# 16 KASU
Copper **Obv:** Similar to KM#14, but crude **Note:** Weight varies 1.50 - 3.0 grams.

Date	Mintage	Good	VG	F	VF	XF
ND	—	2.50	4.50	7.50	11.50	—

Mint: Without Mint Name
KM# 17 KASU
Copper **Obv:** Hanuman seated in circle outlined with dots **Note:** Weight varies 1.50 - 3.0 grams.

Date	Mintage	Good	VG	F	VF	XF
ND	—	3.50	5.50	9.00	13.50	—

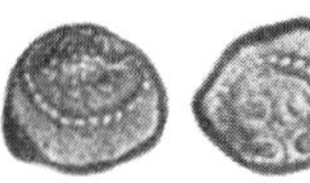

Mint: Without Mint Name
KM# 18 KASU
Copper **Obv:** Fish **Note:** Weight varies 1.50 - 3.0 grams.

Date	Mintage	Good	VG	F	VF	XF
ND	—	3.50	5.50	9.00	13.50	—

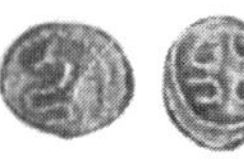

Mint: Without Mint Name
KM# 19 KASU
Copper **Obv:** Serpent **Note:** Weight varies 1.50 - 3.0 grams.

Date	Mintage	Good	VG	F	VF	XF
ND	—	3.50	5.50	9.00	13.50	—

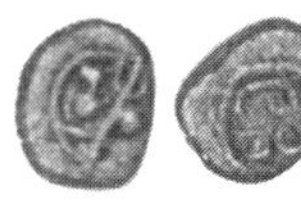

Mint: Without Mint Name
KM# 21 KASU
Copper **Obv:** Horse and trident **Note:** Weight varies 1.50 - 3.0 grams.

Date	Mintage	Good	VG	F	VF	XF
ND	—	3.50	5.50	9.00	13.50	—

Mint: Without Mint Name
KM# 22 KASU
Copper **Obv:** Peacock right **Note:** Weight varies 1.50 - 3.0 grams.

Date	Mintage	Good	VG	F	VF	XF
ND	—	3.50	5.50	9.00	13.50	—

Mint: Without Mint Name
KM# 23 KASU
Copper **Obv:** Elephant right **Note:** Weight varies 1.50 - 3.0 grams.

Date	Mintage	Good	VG	F	VF	XF
ND	—	3.50	5.50	9.00	13.50	—

MANIPUR

Although the Manipuri traditions preserve a long list of kings which purports to go back to the early years of the Christian era, the first ruler whose existence can be verified from more tangible sources was a Naga called Panheiba, who adopted the Hindu religion and took the name of Gharib Niwaz about 1714AD.

Gharib Niwaz seems to have been a powerful ruler, who was successful in the frequent wars with Burma, and hence raised the country from obscurity. He was murdered in 1750, together with his eldest son, and it was during the reign of the latter's son, Gaura Singh, that the British first came into contact with Manipur. After the death of Gharib Niwaz the Burmese had more success with their incursions into Manipur, and by 1761 there was a danger that the capital would be captured, so the Manipuris appealed to the British for military assistance. This was granted, and in 1762 British troops helped the Manipuris drive out the Burmese, and a treaty of alliance was signed. On this occasion 500 meklee gold rupees were sent to the British as part payment for the expenses of this assistance.

Gaura Singh died in 1764 and from then until 1798 his brother Jai Singh heroically defended his country against the Burmese. In the early years of his reign he suffered many setbacks, but for the last ten years of his reign his position was fairly secure. In 1798 Jai Singh abdicated and died the following year. The next 35 years were to see five of his eight sons on the throne, plotting against each other and enlisting Burmese support for their internecine rivalry. After 1812 the Manipuri King was little more than a puppet in the hands of the Burmese, and when the Kings tried to assert their independence they were ousted to become Kings of Kachar.

In 1824, after the 1st Burma war, the Burmese were finally driven out of Manipur and Gambhir Singh, one of the younger sons of Jai Singh, asked for British assistance to regain control of his kingdom. This was granted, and from 1825 until his death in 1834 Gambhir Singh ruled well and restored an element of prosperity to his kingdom. A British resident was stationed in Manipur, but the king ruled his country independently. The British stayed aloof from several palace intrigues and revolutions, and it was only in 1891, after several British Officials had been killed, that the administration was brought under the control of a British Political Agent.

RULERS

Gharib Niwaz, SEc.1636-1672/c.1714-1750AD
Ajit Shah, SE1672-1678/1750-1756AD
Bharat Shah, SE1678-1680/1756-1758AD
Gaura Singh, SE1680-1686/1758-1764AD
Jai Singh, SE1686-1720/1764-1798AD
Labanya Chandra, SE1720-1723/1798-1801AD

COINAGE

The only coins struck in quantity for circulation in Manipur were small bell-metal (circa 74 percent copper, 23 percent tin, 3 percent zinc) coins called"sel". According to local tradition these coins were first struck in the 17th century, but this is doubtful, and it seems likely that the sels were first struck in the second half of the 18th century. Unfortunately few of the sels can be attributed to any particular ruler, as they merely bear a Nagari letter deemed auspicious for the particular reign, and it has not been recorded which letter was deemed auspicious for which ruler.

The value of the sel functioned relative to the rupees which also circulated in Manipur for making large purchases, although Government accounts were kept in sel until 1891. Prior to 1838 the sel was valued at about 900 to the rupee, but after that date it fell in value to around 480 to the rupee, although there were occasional fluctuations. About 1878, speculative hoarding of sel forced the value up to 240 to the rupee, but large numbers of sel were struck at this time, and from then until 1891, when the sel were withdrawn from circulation, their value remained fairly stable at about 400 to the rupee.

During the years after 1714AD some square gold and silver coins were struck, but as few have survived, they were probably only struck in small quantities for ceremonial rather than monetary use.

Apart from the coins mentioned above, some larger bell-metal coins have been attributed to Manipur, but the attribution is still somewhat tentative. Also several other gold coins, two with an image of Krishna playing the flute, have been discovered in Calcutta in recent years, but as their authenticity has been queried, they have not been included in the following listing.

DATING

Most of the silver and gold coins of Manipur are dated in the Saka era (Sake date + 78 = AD date), but at least one coin is dated in the Manipuri "Chandrabda" era, which may be converted to the AD year by adding 788 to the Chandrabda date.

MONETARY SYSTEM

(Until 1838AD)

880 to 960 Sel = 1 Rupee

KINGDOM

Gharib Niwaz

SE c.1636-1672 / c.1714-1750AD

HAMMERED COINAGE

Mint: Without Mint Name
C# 10 UNKNOWN DENOMINATION
Note: Base Silver or Bell-metal, 4.02 grams.

Date	Mintage	Good	VG	F	VF	XF
SE1646 (1724)	—	—	32.50	55.00	90.00	125

Gaura Singh

SE1680-1686 / 1758-1764AD

HAMMERED COINAGE

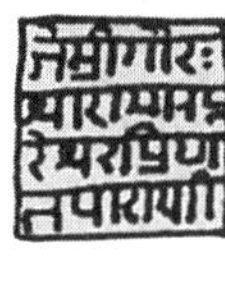

Mint: Without Mint Name
C# 23 RUPEE
Silver **Note:** Weight varies 10.7 - 11.6 grams.

Date	Mintage	Good	VG	F	VF	XF
SE1678 (1756)	—	—	80.00	130	190	250

Mint: Without Mint Name
C# 27 1/4 MOHUR
Gold **Note:** Weight varies: 2.68 - 2.85 grams.

Date	Mintage	Good	VG	F	VF	XF
ND(1758-64) Rare	—	—	—	—	—	—

Mint: Without Mint Name
C# 28 1/2 MOHUR
Gold **Note:** Weight varies: 5.35 - 5.7 grams.

Date	Mintage	Good	VG	F	VF	XF
SE1684 (1762) Rare	—	—	—	—	—	—

Mint: Without Mint Name
C# 29 MOHUR
Gold **Note:** Weight varies: 10.7 - 11.4 Grams.

Date	Mintage	Good	VG	F	VF	XF
SE1678 (1756) Rare	—	—	—	—	—	—
SE1684 (1762) Rare	—	—	—	—	—	—

Jai Singh

SE1686-1720 / 1764-1798AD

HAMMERED COINAGE

Mint: Without Mint Name
C# 32 1/2 RUPEE
Silver **Note:** Weight varies: 5.35 - 5.8 grams.

Date	Mintage	Good	VG	F	VF	XF
ND(1764-98)	—	—	50.00	100	175	250

Mint: Without Mint Name
C# 34 RUPEE
11.5000 g., Silver

Date	Mintage	Good	VG	F	VF	XF
SE1689 (1767)	—	—	75.00	120	200	300

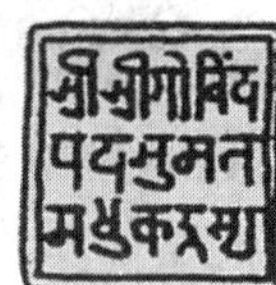

Mint: Without Mint Name
C# 36 MOHUR

Gold **Note:** Weight varies: 10.7 - 11.4 grams.

Date	Mintage	Good	VG	F	VF	XF
SE1694 (1772) Rare	—	—	—	—	—	—

MARATHA CONFEDERACY

The origins of the Marathas are lost in the early history of the remote hill country of the Western Ghats in present-day Maharashtra. By the 15th century they had come into occasional prominence for their resistance to Muslim incursions into their homelands. They were a rugged wiry people who, by the 17th century, had accomodated themselves to the political realities of their times by becoming feudatories, or mercenaries, to the sultans of Bijapur. It is not clear exactly what happened to suddenly thrust the Marathas into the limelight of Indian history in the 17th century. The most likely explanation seems to be that the broad sweep of Aurangzeb's campaigns across the Deccan, his insensitivity towards Hindu sentiment, and the pre-eminence he gave to Islam, all served to politicize a hitherto politically quiescent people. And just as Aurangzeb supplied the occasion, the Marathas found in Sivaji the man

In the 17th century Shahji, the father of Sivaji, was holder of a small fiefdom under the Bijapur sultans. His son, taking advantage of the declining authority of his overlords, seized some of the surrounding territory. Bijapur proved incapable of quelling his insurrection. Drawing encouragement from this experience, Sivaji's forces sacked and plundered the Mughal port of Surat in1664. From this point until his death in 1680 Sivaji maintained a sort of running guerilla war with Aurangzeb. There were no decisive victories for either side but Sivaji left behind him a cohesive and well organized regional alliance in the Western Deccan, a small isolated kingdom in Tanjore and a few pockets of territory on the west coast.

After Sivaji's death the struggle was renewed as Aurangzeb advanced into the Deccan. It was the years after Aurangzeb's death in 1707, which really saw revival as the Maratha confederacy gained a new cohesiveness and its military successes began to make it look as if the Marathas might even become the new masters of India. The revenues of much of the Deccan now flowed into (finished up in) Maratha pockets. Baji Rao I, the Peshwa, pressed as far north as the gates of Delhi and in 1738 he gained control of Malwa. Parts of Gujarat also were in confederacy hands. Bengal was invaded, Orissa annexed (1751), and the territories of the Nizam of Hyderabad and the Carnatic appeared at risk. It was during this period that some of the great Maratha families gained prominence - the Holkars, the Sindhias, the Gaekwars and the Bhonslas - families who later, as the confederacy began to disintegrate and give way to rivalry, would assert their own regional interests at the expense of the alliance.

The turning point for Maratha fortunes was the battle of Panipat on January 14th 1761. Intending to stop the Afghan, Ahmad Shah Abdali (Durrani), in his tracks, the Marathas assembled the greatest army in their history and placed it under the unified command of the Peshwa of Poona. By nightfall the Peshwa's son and heir, Bhao Sahib, and all the leading chiefs, were dead. Maratha losses were said to have been in excess of a hundred thousand men. The Marathas would still remain a force to be reckoned with, they would again cross the Chambel (1767), and they would still give the Nizam's forces a thrashing (1795), but from 1761 onwards internal dissension grew rife and the Maratha Confederacy would never again exhibit sufficient cohesion to be considered a serious contender for the crown of India.

This powerful alliance of Marathi warriors owed nominal allegiance to the Rajas of Satara (descendents of Shivaji) and drew their unity from the leadership of the Peshwa, the hereditary prime minister of the confederation. In the mid-18th century the Marathas were at the apogee of their influence, having hastened the end of effective Mughal power in the Deccan and western India. They successfully checked the intrusions of the Durranis into north India, although the experience left them so militarily exhausted that the dominance in Hindustan passed to other hands.

The great families of the lieutenants of the Peshwa gradually carved out regional power bases and became progressively less responsive to the authority of their formal superiors. The Maratha power, as such, was broken in a series of wars with the East India Company, bitterly fought and very close contests which settled the fate of large sections of India. Broadly speaking, the Marathas may for convenience sake be listed in two categories, the lines which became extinct through British action and those which accommodated the English after defeat and survived to become Princely States. The latter will be found elsewhere in the catalogue; the non-surviving political units are catalogued below.

BHONSLAS

RULERS

Januji, 1753-72AD
Raghoji II, 1788-1816AD

MINTS

بنده ملواري

Banda Malwari (Maratha)

چانده

Chanda

كتك

Cuttack

حنگنهات

Hinganhat

ناگپور

Nagpur

Most coins are imitations of Mughal coins of Ahmad Shah (1748-54AD), more or less barbarized. The Bhonslas mints were closed when the state was abolished in 1854.

PESHWAS

RULERS

Madhoji Rao, 1761-1771AD
Raghunath Rao, 1772-1774AD
Madho Rao, 1774-1795AD
Baji Rao, 1796-1818AD

MINTS AND MINT MARKS

احمداباد

Ahmadabad

One of Maratha Mints from 1757-1800, it was leased to Baroda from 1800-1804, returned during 1804-1806, released to Baroda in 1806, and ceded to Baroda in 1817 (1232AH). In 1818, it was annexed by the East India Company and finally closed in 1835.

Obv: Ankus

Ankus with

Mint symbol on rev. at lower left:

NOTE: Baroda coins of this mint have the Nagari initial of the ruler. British coins have the following mark on rev:

اجمير

Ajmer

A Maratha Mint 1759-1787, taken by Jodhpur 1787-1792, and ruled by Gwalior 1792-1818. Ceded to the British in 1818.

Mint mark:

NOTE: For issues with only 2 dots, see Gwalior.

اورنگ نگر

Aurangnagar

Possibly an issue of the Purandhare Sardars from Nasirabad in Khandesh, ca. AH1170-1205/1757-1790AD.

بگلکوت

Bagalkot

A mint in the Bijapur region. The coins are attributed to the Rastias of Wai, ca. AH1170-1233/1757-1818AD, and are copies of the rupee of Dar-ul-khilafat Shahjahanabad.

بالانگر گدہا

Balanagor Gadha (Mandla)

برهانپور

Burhanpur

چاكن

Chakan

چاندور

Chandor

چكودي

Chikodi

Coins are similar to the Nipani issue, but with the lingam mint mark. Inscribed in the name of the Mughal Emperor Aurangzeb.

چنچور

Chinchwar

Struck by the Patwardans of Miraj, possibly at Poona.

گلشن اباد

Gulshanabad (Nasik)

Reverse: Bow and arrow

Symbols on reverse

Reverse: banner

اتاوه اتاوا

Itawa

Maratha to AH1175/R.Y.3/1762AD; Rohilla until reconquest by Marathas in AH1184/R.Y.12/1771AD. Ceded to Awadh AH1188/R.Y.15/1774AD. For early issues see Rohilkhand.

جلون

Jalaun

Obv symbols and

Rev or

Mint name
Zarb ba Jalaun Hijr

Jhansi
Mint mark on reverse

بلونت نگر

Mint name Balwantnagar

كلپي

Kalpi

Rev:

Symbols

Mint name Kalpi Hijri

كانكرتي

Kankurti

كورا

Kora

Mint mark

Mint name Kora

كنار

Kunar
Mint name Kahar Hijri

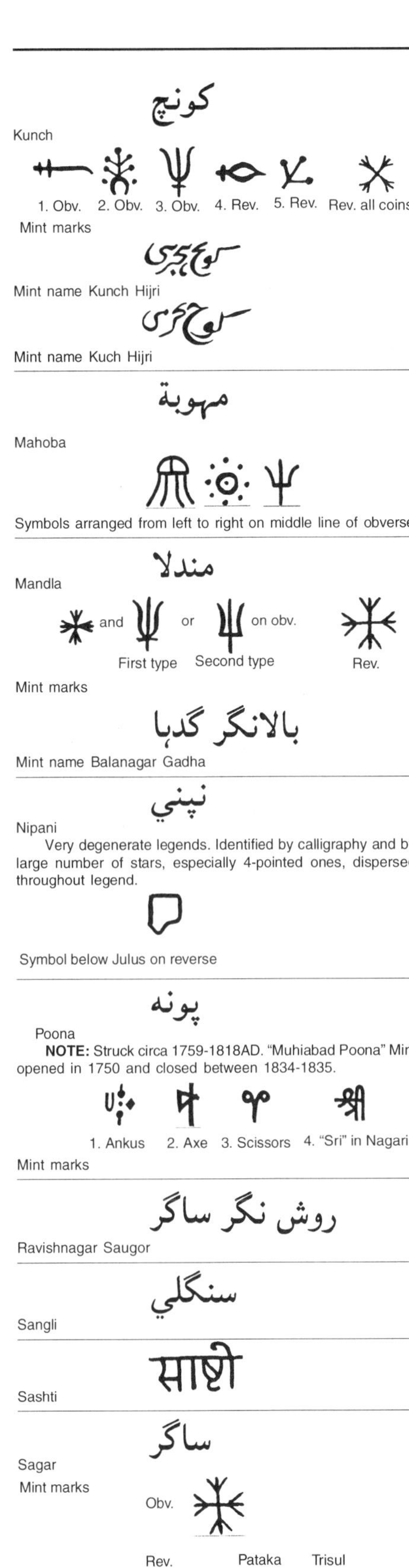

كونچ

Kunch

1. Obv. 2. Obv. 3. Obv. 4. Rev. 5. Rev. Rev. all coins

Mint marks

Mint name Kunch Hijri

Mint name Kuch Hijri

مهوبة

Mahoba

Symbols arranged from left to right on middle line of obverse.

مندلا

Mandla

and or on obv.

First type Second type Rev.

Mint marks

بالانگر گدہا

Mint name Balanagar Gadha

نپني

Nipani

Very degenerate legends. Identified by calligraphy and by large number of stars, especially 4-pointed ones, dispersed throughout legend.

Symbol below Julus on reverse

پونه

Poona

NOTE: Struck circa 1759-1818AD. "Muhiabad Poona" Mint opened in 1750 and closed between 1834-1835.

1. Ankus 2. Axe 3. Scissors 4. "Sri" in Nagari

Mint marks

روش نگر ساگر

Ravishnagar Saugor

سنگلي

Sangli

साष्टी

Sashti

ساگر

Sagar

Mint marks

Obv.

Rev. Pataka Trisul

First type

Second type

روش نگر ساگر

Mint name Ravishnagar Saugar

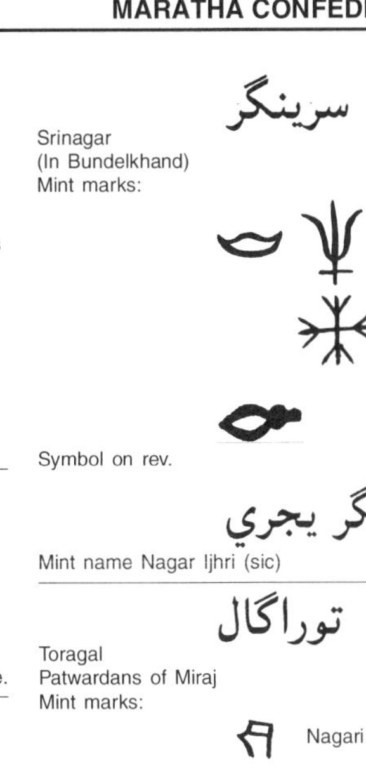

سرینگر

Srinagar
(In Bundelkhand)
Mint marks:

Obv.

Rev.

Symbol on rev.

نگر يجري

Mint name Nagar Ijhri (sic)

تورگل توراگال

Toragal
Patwardans of Miraj
Mint marks:

Nagari Sa — Chhatra

Persian Mim upside down on flan — Trisula

Mint name: Sarkar Tor(gal)

INDEPENDENT KINGDOM

HAMMERED COINAGE

Angria Issues

Mint: Uncertain Mint
KM# 260 1/2 RUPEE
Silver

Date	Mintage	Good	VG	F	VF	XF
ND	—	—	10.00	15.00	20.00	30.00

Mint: Uncertain Mint
KM# 261 RUPEE
Silver

Date	Mintage	Good	VG	F	VF	XF
ND	—	12.50	17.50	25.00	37.50	—

Ali Gauhar

The name of Shah Alam II before his accession

HAMMERED COINAGE

Mint: Poona
KM# 205 PAISA
6.4000 g., Copper **Obv. Inscription:** Ali Gauhar **Rev:** Mint mark #2

Date	Mintage	Good	VG	F	VF	XF
ND	—	2.00	3.00	5.00	7.50	—

Mint: Poona
KM# 206 PAISA
6.4000 g., Copper **Obv. Inscription:** Ali Gauhar **Rev:** Mint mark #3

Date	Mintage	Good	VG	F	VF	XF
ND	—	1.50	2.50	4.00	6.50	—

Mint: Poona
KM# 216 RUPEE
Silver **Note:** Similar to KM#217 with mint mark #3, Samvat dates in Arabic numerals.

Date	Mintage	VG	F	VF	XF	Unc
AH-//2	—	5.00	9.00	15.00	25.00	—
AH-//11	—	5.00	9.00	15.00	25.00	—
AH-//14	—	5.00	9.00	15.00	25.00	—
AH-//15	—	5.00	9.00	15.00	25.00	—
AH//18	—	5.00	9.00	15.00	25.00	—
VS1835	—	5.00	9.00	15.00	25.00	—
VS1841	—	5.00	9.00	15.00	25.00	—

Mint: Poona
KM# 215 RUPEE
Silver **Rev:** Mint mark #2 **Note:** Weight varies 10.70-11.60 grams.

Date	Mintage	VG	F	VF	XF	Unc
AH-//6	—	12.50	15.00	25.00	40.00	—
AH1189	—	12.50	15.00	25.00	40.00	—

Mint: Poona
KM# 218 RUPEE
Silver **Rev:** Mint mark #4, AH dates **Note:** This coin was copied by the local rulers at Kolaba and Wadgaon.

Date	Mintage	VG	F	VF	XF	Unc
AH1206 (1791)	—	7.50	12.50	20.00	35.00	—
AH1211 (1796)	—	7.50	12.50	20.00	35.00	—
ND (1796) Date off flan	—	5.50	9.00	15.00	25.00	—

Chhatrapati Sivaji

HAMMERED COINAGE

Mint: Satara
KM# 263 1/4 PAISA
3.3300 g., Copper **Obv. Inscription:** Chhatrapati Sivaji

Date	Mintage	Good	VG	F	VF	XF
ND	—	1.25	2.00	3.00	4.50	—

Mint: Satara
KM# 264 1/2 PAISA
Copper, 15-17 mm. **Obv. Inscription:** Chhatrapati Sivaji **Note:** Size varies. Weight varies: 7.00-8.50 grams. Early fine style.

Date	Mintage	Good	VG	F	VF	XF
ND	—	1.25	2.00	3.00	4.50	—

Mint: Satara
KM# 265 1/2 PAISA
Copper, 13-16 mm. **Obv. Inscription:** Chhatrapati Sivaji **Note:** Size varies. Weight varies: 7.00-8.50 grams. Later crude style.

Date	Mintage	Good	VG	F	VF	XF
ND	—	1.00	1.50	2.25	3.00	—

Mint: Satara
KM# 266 PAISA
Copper **Obv. Inscription:** Chhatrapati Sivaji **Note:** Weight varies: 14-15 grams. Early fine style.

Date	Mintage	Good	VG	F	VF	XF
ND	—	3.00	4.00	6.00	9.00	—

Mint: Satara
KM# 267 PAISA
Copper **Obv:** Double lines in center **Obv. Inscription:** Chhatrapati Sivaji **Note:** Weight varies: 14-15 grams. Later crude style.

Date	Mintage	Good	VG	F	VF	XF
ND	—	2.00	3.00	4.50	6.00	—

Muhammad Shah

AH1131-61/1719-48AD

HAMMERED COINAGE

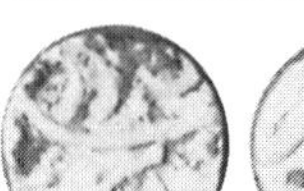

Mint: Dicholi
KM# 152 1/2 RUPEE
Silver **Obv. Inscription:** Muhammad Shah **Rev:** Mint and date

Date	Mintage	VG	F	VF	XF	Unc
ND(1719-48)	—	—	—	—	—	—

Mint: Dicholi
KM# 153 RUPEE
Silver **Obv. Inscription:** Muhammad Shah **Rev:** Mint and date

Date	Mintage	VG	F	VF	XF	Unc
AH-//1 ahd	—	—	—	—	—	—

Mint: Hukeri
KM# 154 RUPEE
Silver **Obv. Inscription:** Muhammad Shah **Rev:** Mint and date

Date	Mintage	VG	F	VF	XF	Unc
ND(1719-48)	—	—	—	—	—	—

Mint: Hukeri
KM# 154.1 RUPEE
Silver **Obv. Inscription:** Muhammad Shah **Rev:** Mint inverted and date

Date	Mintage	VG	F	VF	XF	Unc
ND(1719-48)	—	—	—	—	—	—

Mint: Kankurti
KM# 155 RUPEE
Silver **Note:** Weight varies: 10.70-11.60 grams.

Date	Mintage	VG	F	VF	XF	Unc
AHxxx5 (1719)	—	20.00	35.00	50.00	70.00	—

Mint: Sangli
KM# 225 RUPEE
Silver, 20-21 mm. **Obv. Inscription:** Muhammad Shah **Note:** Size varies. Weight varies: 10.70-11.60 grams. Struck during the reign of local ruler Chintaman Rao, 1799-1851AD long after death of Muhammad Shah. Struck at Sangli Mint.

Date	Mintage	VG	F	VF	XF	Unc
ND(1799-1851)	—	7.50	12.50	18.50	27.50	—

Shah Alam II
AH1173-1221/1759-1806AD
HAMMERED COINAGE

Mint: Jhansi
KM# 134 1/2 PAISA
4.2000 g., Copper **Note:** Weight varies.

Date	Mintage	Good	VG	F	VF	XF
AH-//32	—	—	—	—	—	—

Mint: Sagar
KM# 233 1/2 PAISA
5.8000 g., Copper **Obv. Inscription:** Shah Alam II **Note:** Mint name: Ravishnagar Sagar.

Date	Mintage	Good	VG	F	VF	XF
AH-//36	—	2.00	3.50	6.00	10.00	—

Mint: Ahmadabad
KM# 47 PAISA
Copper **Obv. Inscription:** Shah Alam (II)

Date	Mintage	Good	VG	F	VF	XF
ND(1759-1806)	—	2.50	3.50	5.00	7.50	—

Mint: Ajmer
KM# 65 PAISA
Copper **Obv. Inscription:** Shah Alam (II)

Date	Mintage	Good	VG	F	VF	XF
ND(1759-1806)	—	2.50	4.00	6.00	8.50	—

Mint: Jalaun
KM# 120 PAISA
Copper **Obv:** Symbols **Rev:** Symbols

Date	Mintage	Good	VG	F	VF	XF
AH//53 (1759)	—	2.00	3.50	5.00	8.00	—

Mint: Jhansi
KM# 136 PAISA
Copper, 17-19 mm. **Rev:** Nagari "Dhu" right of Julus **Note:** Size varies.

Date	Mintage	Good	VG	F	VF	XF
AH1204	—	7.50	12.50	18.50	27.50	—

Mint: Mahoba
KM# 185 PAISA
Copper, 22-24 mm. **Obv. Inscription:** Shah Alam (II) **Note:** Symbols arranged from left to right on middle line of obverse. Size varies.

Date	Mintage	Good	VG	F	VF	XF
ND(1759-1806)	—	3.00	4.50	7.50	12.50	—

Mint: Sagar
KM# 234 PAISA
Copper **Obv. Inscription:** Shah Alam (II) **Note:** Mint name: Ravishnagar Sagar.

Date	Mintage	Good	VG	F	VF	XF
AH-//35	—	2.00	3.50	6.00	10.00	—

Mint: Sagar
KM# 235 PAISA
Copper **Obv. Inscription:** Shah Alam (II) **Note:** Mint name: Ravishnagar Sagar.

Date	Mintage	Good	VG	F	VF	XF
AH-//37	—	2.00	3.50	6.00	10.00	—

Mint: Srinagar
KM# 245 PAISA
Copper **Obv. Inscription:** Shah Alam II **Note:** Mint marks are symbols.

Date	Mintage	Good	VG	F	VF	XF
AH//3	—	1.50	2.50	4.00	6.00	—
AH-//5	—	1.50	2.50	4.00	6.00	—

Mint: Srinagar
KM# 246 PAISA
Copper, 14-19 mm. **Obv. Inscription:** Shah Alam (II) **Shape:** Squarish **Note:** Size varies.

Date	Mintage	Good	VG	F	VF	XF
AH//1	—	1.75	3.00	4.50	7.00	—
AH-//5	—	1.75	3.00	4.50	7.00	—

Mint: Jalaun
KM# 121 1/4 RUPEE
Silver

Date	Mintage	VG	F	VF	XF	Unc
AH//55 (1759)	—	9.00	15.00	25.00	40.00	—

Mint: Jhansi
KM# 137 1/4 RUPEE
Silver, 13 mm. **Note:** Weight varies: 2.68-2.90 grams.

Date	Mintage	VG	F	VF	XF	Unc
AH-//5	—	7.50	12.50	20.00	35.00	—
AH-//2x	—	7.50	12.50	20.00	35.00	—
AH1206	—	7.50	12.50	20.00	35.00	—

Mint: Ahmadabad
KM# 49 1/2 RUPEE
Silver **Note:** Mint mark: Ankus and Nagari "Ram".

Date	Mintage	VG	F	VF	XF	Unc
ND(1759-1806)	—	12.00	16.00	22.50	40.00	—

Mint: Ahmadabad
KM# 48 1/2 RUPEE
Silver **Note:** Weight varies: 5.35-5.80 grams. Mint mark: Ankus.

Date	Mintage	VG	F	VF	XF	Unc
ND-//27	—	6.50	11.00	18.00	30.00	—

Mint: Jalaun
KM# 122 1/2 RUPEE
Silver **Note:** Weight varies: 5.35-5.80 grams.

Date	Mintage	VG	F	VF	XF	Unc
AH//16	—	9.00	15.00	25.00	40.00	—
AH//17	—	9.00	15.00	25.00	40.00	—
AH//2x	—	9.00	15.00	25.00	40.00	—

Mint: Jhansi
KM# 138 1/2 RUPEE
Silver **Note:** Weight varies: 5.35-5.80 grams.

Date	Mintage	VG	F	VF	XF	Unc
AH-//5x	—	10.00	20.00	38.00	55.00	—

Mint: Ajmer
KM# 67 RUPEE
Silver, 21 mm. **Note:** Weight varies: 10.70-11.60 grams. Mint mark: Three dots on vertical line.

Date	Mintage	VG	F	VF	XF	Unc
AH1188//1	—	9.00	15.00	25.00	40.00	—
AH1190//1	—	9.00	15.00	25.00	40.00	—
AH1197//24	—	9.00	15.00	25.00	40.00	—
AH1203//31	—	9.00	15.00	25.00	40.00	—

Mint: Ajmer
KM# 66 RUPEE
Silver **Note:** Weight varies: 10.70-11.60 grams. Without mint mark.

Date	Mintage	VG	F	VF	XF	Unc
AH1178//6	—	9.00	15.00	25.00	40.00	—
AH-//10	—	9.00	15.00	25.00	40.00	—

Mint: Athani
KM# 71 RUPEE
Silver **Obv. Inscription:** Shah Alam (II) **Rev:** Similar to KM#70

Date	Mintage	VG	F	VF	XF	Unc
AH1181	—	13.50	20.00	30.00	47.50	—

Mint: Aurangnagar
KM# 75 RUPEE
Silver **Obv. Inscription:** Shah Alam (II) **Rev:** Lingam and Nagari "Mu" **Note:** Weight varies: 10.70-11.60 grams.

Date	Mintage	VG	F	VF	XF	Unc
ND(1759-1806)	—	16.00	32.00	55.00	80.00	—
AH-//16	—	16.00	32.00	55.00	80.00	—
AH1180	—	16.00	32.00	55.00	80.00	—
AH1187//1x	—	16.00	32.00	55.00	80.00	—

Mint: Bagalkot
KM# 84 RUPEE

Silver **Obv. Inscription:** Shah Alam (II) **Note:** Weight varies: 10.70-11.60 grams. Fine fabric. Mint name: Bagalkot.

Date	Mintage	VG	F	VF	XF	Unc
AH-//9	—	10.00	20.00	35.00	50.00	—

Mint: Burhanpur
KM# 90 RUPEE

Silver **Obv. Inscription:** Shah Alam (II) **Note:** Weight varies: 10.70-11.60 grams. For coins struck after AH1192-R.Y.20 (1778AD), see Gwalior.

Date	Mintage	VG	F	VF	XF	Unc
AH1175//1-1193//19	—	10.00	18.00	28.00	45.00	—

Mint: Chakan
KM# 92 RUPEE

Silver **Obv. Inscription:** Shah Alam (II)

Date	Mintage	VG	F	VF	XF	Unc
ND(1759-1806)	—	100	150	200	—	—

Mint: Chandor
KM# 93 RUPEE

Silver **Obv. Inscription:** Shah Alam (II) **Note:** Weight varies: 10.70-11.60 grams. Previously listed under IPS - Indore.

Date	Mintage	VG	F	VF	XF	Unc
AH-//23	—	7.50	13.50	20.00	28.50	—
AH-//24	—	7.50	13.50	20.00	28.50	—
AH-//25	—	7.50	13.50	20.00	28.50	—
AH1195//26	—	7.50	13.50	20.00	28.50	—
AH1196//23	—	7.50	13.50	20.00	28.50	—
Note: With lingam cm on reverse (imitation)						
AH1197	—	7.50	13.50	20.00	28.50	—

Mint: Chinchwar
KM# 100 RUPEE

Silver **Obv. Inscription:** Shah Alam (II) **Rev:** Battle axe **Note:** Weight varies: 10.70-11.60 grams. Struck during the reign of local ruler Puresham Bhau.

Date	Mintage	VG	F	VF	XF	Unc
AH1189	—	18.00	36.00	60.00	85.00	—

Mint: Gulshanabad
KM# 105.2 RUPEE

Silver **Rev:** Crescent above "Julus"

Date	Mintage	VG	F	VF	XF	Unc
AH1184//11	—	7.50	12.50	20.00	35.00	—
AH1186//8	—	7.50	12.50	20.00	35.00	—

Mint: Gulshanabad
KM# 105.1 RUPEE

Silver **Rev:** Bow and arrow **Note:** Weight varies: 10.70-11.60 grams.

Date	Mintage	VG	F	VF	XF	Unc
AH1182//4	—	7.50	12.50	20.00	35.00	—

Mint: Gulshanabad
KM# 106 RUPEE

Silver **Rev:** Symbols **Note:** Weight varies: 10.70-11.60 grams.

Date	Mintage	VG	F	VF	XF	Unc
AH1195//22	—	9.00	15.00	25.00	40.00	—

Mint: Gulshanabad
KM# 110 RUPEE

Silver **Rev:** Banner

Date	Mintage	VG	F	VF	XF	Unc
AH1202 (1787)	—	9.00	15.00	25.00	40.00	—

Mint: Itawa
KM# 116 RUPEE

Silver **Subject:** Second Occupation **Obv:** Trident

Date	Mintage	VG	F	VF	XF	Unc
AH-//12	—	7.50	12.50	20.00	35.00	—
AH-//13	—	7.50	12.50	20.00	35.00	—

Mint: Itawa
KM# 115 RUPEE

Silver **Subject:** First Occupation **Obv. Inscription:** Shah Alam (II) **Note:** Weight varies: 10.70-11.60 grams.

Date	Mintage	VG	F	VF	XF	Unc
AH-//1	—	8.00	13.50	22.50	37.50	—

Mint: Jalaun
KM# 123 RUPEE

Silver **Note:** Fine fabric, normal flan. Weight varies: 10.70-11.60 grams.

Date	Mintage	VG	F	VF	XF	Unc
AH-//46	—	9.00	15.00	25.00	45.00	—

Mint: Jhansi
KM# 141.1 RUPEE

Silver **Rev:** Symbol

Date	Mintage	VG	F	VF	XF	Unc
AH-//28	—	8.00	12.50	22.50	37.50	—

Mint: Jhansi
KM# 142 RUPEE

Silver **Obv:** 2 added

Date	Mintage	VG	F	VF	XF	Unc
AH1204//3X	—	7.00	12.50	20.00	35.00	—
AH-//32	—	7.00	12.50	20.00	35.00	—
AH-//33	—	7.00	12.50	20.00	35.00	—
AH1206//34	—	7.00	12.50	20.00	35.00	—
AH1206//35	—	7.00	12.50	20.00	35.00	—
AH1206//35	—	7.00	12.50	20.00	35.00	—

Mint: Jhansi
KM# 143 RUPEE

Silver **Obv:** 92 added

Date	Mintage	VG	F	VF	XF	Unc
AH1206//34	—	7.50	12.50	20.00	35.00	—
AH-//35	—	7.50	12.50	20.00	35.00	—
AH1209//36	—	7.50	12.50	20.00	35.00	—
AH1210//36	—	7.50	12.50	20.00	35.00	—

Mint: Jhansi
KM# 140 RUPEE

Silver **Note:** Crude fabric. Weight varies: 10.70-11.60 grams.

Date	Mintage	VG	F	VF	XF	Unc
AH1187//15	—	7.50	12.50	20.00	35.00	—
AH1187//16	—	7.50	12.50	20.00	35.00	—
AH1187//17	—	11.50	18.50	18.50	45.00	—
AH1187//18	—	11.50	18.50	28.50	45.00	—
AH1189//16	—	7.50	12.50	20.00	35.00	—
AH1192//20	—	7.50	12.50	20.00	35.00	—
AH1192//21	—	11.50	18.50	28.50	45.00	—
AH1194//22	—	7.50	12.50	20.00	35.00	—
AH(119)6//23	—	7.50	125	20.00	35.00	—
AH1197//24	—	7.50	12.50	20.00	35.00	—
AH1198//25	—	7.50	12.50	20.00	35.00	—
ND-//27	—	7.50	12.50	20.00	35.00	—
AH-//28	—	7.50	12.50	20.00	35.00	—
AH1209//29	—	7.50	12.50	20.00	35.00	—
AH-//30	—	7.50	12.50	20.00	35.00	—
AH-//31	—	7.50	12.50	20.00	35.00	—

Mint: Jhansi
KM# 139 RUPEE

Silver **Note:** Fine fabric. Weight varies: 10.70-11.60 grams.

Date	Mintage	VG	F	VF	XF	Unc
AH(11)68//2	—	9.00	15.00	25.00	40.00	—
AH1174//1	—	9.00	15.00	25.00	40.00	—
AH1174//3	—	9.00	15.00	25.00	40.00	—
AH1175//3	—	9.00	15.00	25.00	40.00	—
AH1175//4	—	9.00	15.00	25.00	40.00	—
AH117x//5	—	9.00	15.00	25.00	40.00	—
AH1180//8	—	9.00	15.00	25.00	40.00	—
AH1181//9	—	9.00	15.00	25.00	40.00	—
AH1182//10	—	11.50	18.50	28.50	45.00	—
AH1183//12	—	11.50	18.50	28.50	45.00	—
AH1183//11	—	9.00	15.00	25.00	40.00	—
AH1184//12	—	9.00	15.00	25.00	40.00	—
AH1185//13	—	9.00	15.00	25.00	40.00	—
AH1185//14	—	11.50	18.50	28.50	45.00	—

Mint: Jhansi
KM# 141.2 RUPEE

Silver **Rev:** Symbol **Note:** With additional symbol.

Date	Mintage	VG	F	VF	XF	Unc
AH-//28	—	8.00	12.50	22.50	37.50	—

Mint: Kalpi
KM# 150 RUPEE

Silver **Obv. Inscription:** Shah Alam (II) **Note:** Weight varies: 10.70-11.60 grams. Mint name: Kalpi Hijri.

Date	Mintage	VG	F	VF	XF	Unc
AH-//22	—	6.50	11.50	18.50	30.00	—
AH1198//25	—	6.50	11.50	18.50	30.00	—
AH-//26	—	6.50	11.50	18.50	30.00	—
AH-//27	—	6.50	11.50	18.50	30.00	—
AH-//28	—	6.50	11.50	18.50	30.00	—
AH-//29	—	6.50	11.50	18.50	30.00	—
AH1201//30	—	6.50	11.50	18.50	30.00	—
AH-//31	—	6.50	11.50	18.50	30.00	—
AH-//32	—	6.50	11.50	18.50	30.00	—
AH-//33	—	6.50	11.50	18.50	30.00	—

Mint: Kora
KM# 161 RUPEE

Silver **Obv:** Lotus and trisula **Obv. Inscription:** Shah Alam (II) **Note:** Mint name: Kora.

Date	Mintage	VG	F	VF	XF	Unc
AH117x//1	—	6.50	11.50	18.50	30.00	—
AH117x//2	—	6.50	11.50	18.50	30.00	—

Mint: Kora
KM# 162 RUPEE

Silver **Obv:** Pataka (banner) and trisula **Obv. Inscription:** Shah Alam (II) **Note:** Mint name: Kora.

Date	Mintage	VG	F	VF	XF	Unc
AH117x//2	—	6.50	11.50	18.50	30.00	—
AH117x//3	—	6.50	11.50	18.50	30.00	—
AH117x//4	—	6.50	11.50	18.50	30.00	—

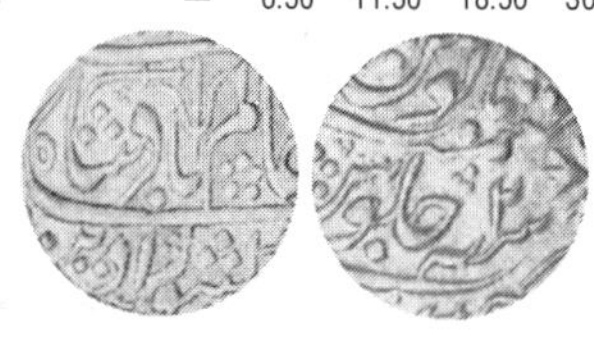

Mint: Kora
KM# 163 RUPEE

Silver **Obv:** Sword left and trisula **Obv. Inscription:** Shah Alam (II) **Note:** Mint name: Kora.

Date	Mintage	VG	F	VF	XF	Unc
AH117x//2	—	6.50	11.50	18.50	30.00	—

Mint: Kora
KM# 164 RUPEE

Silver **Obv:** Sword right and trisula **Obv. Inscription:** Shah Alam (II) **Note:** Mint name: Kora. For later issues of Kora mint from AD1765/AH1178/R.Y. 6, see India, Mughal Empire: Kora.

Date	Mintage	VG	F	VF	XF	Unc
AH117x//2	—	6.50	11.50	18.50	30.00	—

Mint: Kora
KM# 160 RUPEE

Silver **Obv:** Trisula (trident) **Obv. Inscription:** Shah Alam (II) **Note:** Weight varies: 10.70-11.60 grams. Mint name: Kora.

Date	Mintage	VG	F	VF	XF	Unc
AH117x//1	—	6.50	11.50	18.50	30.00	—
AH117x//2	—	6.50	11.50	18.50	30.00	—

Mint: Kunar
KM# 170 RUPEE

Silver **Obv:** Axe head and trisula **Obv. Inscription:** Shah Alam (II) **Note:** Mint name: Kahar Hijri.

Date	Mintage	VG	F	VF	XF	Unc
AH-//22	—	12.50	20.00	35.00	60.00	—

Mint: Kunar
KM# 171 RUPEE

Silver **Obv:** Parasu (axe), axe head and trisula **Obv. Inscription:** Shah Alam (II) **Note:** Mintname: Kahar Hijri. For other issues with mint name Kunar see Jalaun Rupee KM#66.1.

Date	Mintage	VG	F	VF	XF	Unc
AH-//25	—	15.00	21.50	35.00	50.00	—

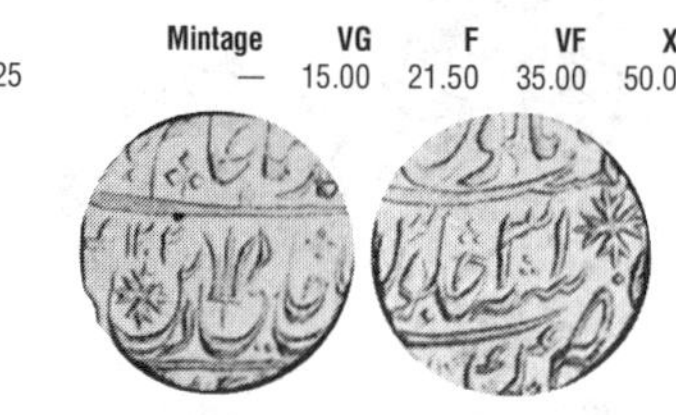

Mint: Mandla
KM# 191 RUPEE

Silver, 20 mm. **Obv:** Second type Trisula **Obv. Inscription:** Shah Alam (II) **Note:** Mint name: Balanagar Gadha.

Date	Mintage	VG	F	VF	XF	Unc
AH-//30	—	7.50	12.50	20.00	35.00	—
AH1202//31	—	7.50	12.50	20.00	35.00	—
AH1205//32	—	7.50	12.50	20.00	35.00	—
AH1207//33	—	7.50	12.50	20.00	35.00	—
AH-//34	—	7.50	12.50	20.00	35.00	—
AH-//35	—	7.50	12.50	20.00	35.00	—
AH-//36	—	7.50	12.50	20.00	35.00	—
AH-//38	—	7.50	12.50	20.00	35.00	—

Mint: Mandla
KM# 190 RUPEE

Silver **Obv:** First type Trisula **Obv. Inscription:** Shah Alam (II) **Note:** Weight varies: 10.70-11.60 grams. Mint name: Balanagar Gadha.

Date	Mintage	VG	F	VF	XF	Unc
AH1198//25	—	7.50	12.50	20.00	35.00	—
AH1199//26	—	7.50	12.50	20.00	35.00	—
AH1200//27	—	7.50	12.50	20.00	35.00	—
AH1201//28	—	7.50	12.50	20.00	35.00	—
AH-//29	—	7.50	12.50	20.00	35.00	—

Mint: Sagar
KM# 238 RUPEE

Silver **Rev:** Pataka and trisul first type **Note:** Weight varies 10.70-11.60 grams. Mint name: Ravishnagar Sagar.

Date	Mintage	VG	F	VF	XF	Unc
AH1198//25	—	9.00	15.00	25.00	40.00	—

Mint: Sagar
KM# 239 RUPEE

Silver **Rev:** Pataka second type, trisul first type **Note:** Weight varies: 10.70-11.60 grams. Mint name: Ravishnagar Sagar.

Date	Mintage	VG	F	VF	XF	Unc
AH1199//26	—	8.00	13.50	21.50	32.50	—
AH-//27	—	8.00	13.50	21.50	32.50	—
AH-//28	—	8.00	13.50	21.50	32.50	—
AH-//29	—	8.00	13.50	21.50	32.50	—
AH1202//30	—	8.00	13.50	21.50	32.50	—

Mint: Srinagar
KM# 247 RUPEE

Silver **Rev:** Asynchronous date in "Sin" of Julus **Note:** Weight varies: 10.70-11.60 grams. Mintname: Nagar Ijhri (sic).

Date	Mintage	VG	F	VF	XF	Unc
AH-//26	—	7.50	12.50	20.00	35.00	—
AH-//27	—	7.50	12.50	20.00	35.00	—
AHxxx2//28	—	7.50	12.50	20.00	35.00	—
AHxx99//29	—	7.50	12.50	20.00	35.00	—

Mint: Srinagar
KM# 248 RUPEE

Silver **Obv:** AH date **Rev:** Quadrafoil in "Sin" of Julus **Note:** Weight varies: 10.70-11.60 grams. Mint name: Nagar Ijhri (sic).

Date	Mintage	VG	F	VF	XF	Unc
AH1206//32	—	7.50	12.50	20.00	35.00	—
AH1206//33	—	7.50	12.50	20.00	35.00	—
AH12012//35 Error	—	7.50	12.50	20.00	35.00	—
AH120x//38	—	7.50	12.50	20.00	35.00	—

Mint: Srinagar
KM# 249 RUPEE

Silver **Note:** Weight varies: 10.70-11.60 grams. Small flan, crude execution. Mint name: Nagar Ijhri (sic).

Date	Mintage	VG	F	VF	XF	Unc
AH-//39 Frozen	—	5.50	9.00	15.00	25.00	—
AH1212//39	—	—	—	—	—	—

Mint: Uncertain Mint
KM# 50 RUPEE

Silver **Note:** Weight varies: 10.70-11.60 grams. Mint mark: Ankus.

Date	Mintage	VG	F	VF	XF	Unc
AH-//5	—	8.50	13.50	20.00	35.00	—
AH-//8	—	8.50	13.50	20.00	35.00	—
AH-//10	—	8.50	13.50	20.00	35.00	—
AH-//11	—	8.50	13.50	20.00	35.00	—
AH118x//12	—	8.50	13.50	20.00	35.00	—
AH-//13	—	8.50	13.50	20.00	35.00	—
AH-//14	—	8.50	13.50	20.00	35.00	—
AH1187//15	—	8.50	13.50	20.00	35.00	—
AH1188//15	—	8.50	13.50	20.00	35.00	—
AH1188//16	—	8.50	13.50	20.00	35.00	—
AH-//17	—	8.50	13.50	20.00	35.00	—
AH1192//20	—	8.50	13.50	20.00	35.00	—
AH119x//21	—	8.50	13.50	20.00	35.00	—
AH1194//22	—	8.50	13.50	20.00	35.00	—
AH119x//23	—	8.50	13.50	20.00	35.00	—
AH1194//24	—	8.50	13.50	20.00	35.00	—
AH1195//22	—	8.50	13.50	20.00	35.00	—
AH1196//24	—	8.50	13.50	20.00	35.00	—
AH1197//24	—	8.50	13.50	20.00	35.00	—
AH-//25	—	8.50	13.50	20.00	35.00	—
AH-//26	—	8.50	13.50	20.00	35.00	—
AH-//27	—	8.50	13.50	20.00	35.00	—
AH-//29	—	8.50	13.50	20.00	35.00	—
AH1205//3X	—	8.50	13.50	20.00	35.00	—
AH1207//33	—	8.50	13.50	20.00	35.00	—
AH1208//34	—	8.50	13.50	20.00	35.00	—
AH-//35	—	8.50	13.50	20.00	35.00	—
AH-//36	—	8.50	13.50	20.00	35.00	—
AH1209	—	8.50	13.50	20.00	35.00	—
AH-//37	—	8.50	13.50	20.00	35.00	—
AH-//38	—	8.50	13.50	20.00	35.00	—

Mint: Ajmer
KM# 68 MOHUR

Gold **Note:** Weight varies: 10.70-11.40 grams. Without mint mark.

Date	Mintage	VG	F	VF	XF	Unc
ND(1759-1806) Rare	—	—	—	—	—	—

Shah Alam II and Latif Khan

AH1173-1221/1759-1806AD

HAMMERED COINAGE

Mint: Uncertain Mint
KM# 51 RUPEE

Silver **Note:** Mint mark: Ankus and Nagari "Ram".

Date	Mintage	VG	F	VF	XF	Unc
ND-//39	—	13.50	18.50	25.00	35.00	—

Shah Jahan III

AH1173-74/1759-60AD

HAMMERED COINAGE

Mint: Ahmadabad
KM# 44 1/2 RUPEE

Silver **Obv. Inscription:** Shah Jahan III **Note:** Weight varies: 5.60-5.80 grams. Mint mark: Ankus.

Date	Mintage	VG	F	VF	XF	Unc
AH117x//1 Rare	—	—	—	—	—	—

Mint: Ahmadabad
KM# 45 RUPEE

Silver **Note:** Weight varies: 10.70-11.60 grams.

Date	Mintage	VG	F	VF	XF	Unc
AH1173//1 ahad	—	40.00	50.00	65.00	90.00	—
AH1174//1	—	40.00	50.00	65.00	90.00	—

Aurangzeb Alamgir

AH1068-1119 / 1658-1707AD

HAMMERED COINAGE

Mint: Nipani
KM# 200 1/4 RUPEE

Silver **Obv. Inscription:** Aurangzeb Alamgir **Note:** Weight varies: 2.68-2.90 grams.

Date	Mintage	VG	F	VF	XF	Unc
ND(1658-1707)	—	7.50	12.50	20.00	35.00	—

Mint: Chikodi
KM# 95 1/2 RUPEE

Silver **Obv. Inscription:** Mughal Emperor Aurangzeb **Note:** Weight varies 5.35-5.80 grams.

Date	Mintage	VG	F	VF	XF	Unc
ND(1658-1707)	—	4.25	8.50	14.00	20.00	—

Mint: Nipani
KM# 201 1/2 RUPEE

Silver, 17-18 mm. **Obv. Inscription:** Aurangzeb Alamgir **Note:** Size varies. Weight varies: 5.35-5.80 grams.

Date	Mintage	VG	F	VF	XF	Unc
ND(1658-1707)	—	8.00	13.50	18.50	30.00	—

Mint: Chikodi
KM# 96 RUPEE

Silver **Obv. Inscription:** Mughal Emperor Aurangzeb **Note:** Weight varies: 10.70-11.60 grams.

Date	Mintage	VG	F	VF	XF	Unc
ND(1658-1707)	—	5.50	11.00	17.50	25.00	—

Mint: Nipani
KM# 202 RUPEE

Silver, 23-24 mm. **Obv. Inscription:** Aurangzeb Alamgir **Note:** Size varies. Weight varies: 10.70-11.60 grams.

Date	Mintage	VG	F	VF	XF	Unc
ND(1658-1707)	—	11.50	18.50	30.00	50.00	—

Ahmad Shah Bahadur

AH1161-1167 / 1748-1754AD

HAMMERED COINAGE

Mint: Ahmadabad
KM# 40 RUPEE

Silver **Obv. Inscription:** Ahmad Shah Bahadur **Note:** Weight varies: 10.70-11.60 grams.

Date	Mintage	VG	F	VF	XF	Unc
AH1165//4	—	12.00	17.50	25.00	35.00	—
AH1166//6	—	12.00	17.50	25.00	35.00	—

Alamgir II

AH1167-1173 / 1754-1759AD

HAMMERED COINAGE

Mint: Ahmadabad
KM# 42 1/2 RUPEE

Silver **Obv. Inscription:** Alamgir II **Note:** Weight varies: 5.60-5.80 grams.

Date	Mintage	VG	F	VF	XF	Unc
AH-//2	—	15.00	20.00	27.50	40.00	—

Mint: Jhansi
KM# 131 1/2 RUPEE

Silver **Obv. Inscription:** Alamgir II **Note:** Weight varies: 5.35-5.80 grams. Mint name: Balwantnagar. Struck from rupee dies on thin planchet.

Date	Mintage	VG	F	VF	XF	Unc
AH1169//3 Rare	—	—	—	—	—	—

Mint: Ahmadabad
KM# 43 RUPEE

Silver **Note:** Weight varies: 10.70-11.60 grams.

Date	Mintage	VG	F	VF	XF	Unc
AH1168//1	—	10.00	15.00	25.00	40.00	—
AH1169//2	—	10.00	15.00	25.00	40.00	—
AH1169//3	—	10.00	15.00	25.00	40.00	—
AH1170//3	—	10.00	15.00	25.00	40.00	—
AH1170//4	—	10.00	15.00	25.00	40.00	—
AH1171//4	—	10.00	15.00	25.00	40.00	—
AH117x//6	—	10.00	15.00	25.00	40.00	—

Mint: Athani
KM# 70 RUPEE

Silver **Obv:** Nagari "Ra" **Obv. Inscription:** Alamgir II **Note:** Weight varies: 10.70-11.60 grams.

Date	Mintage	VG	F	VF	XF	Unc
AH1181 Frozen	—	13.50	20.00	30.00	47.50	—

Mint: Bagalkot
KM# 82 RUPEE

Silver **Obv:** Long-tailed Persian "Wa"

Date	Mintage	VG	F	VF	XF	Unc
AH1172	—	10.00	20.00	35.00	50.00	—
AHxx81	—	10.00	20.00	35.00	50.00	—
AH(11)89//(1)5	—	—	—	—	—	—

Mint: Bagalkot
KM# 80 RUPEE

Silver **Obv. Inscription:** Alamgir II **Note:** Struck during the reign of local ruler Malhar Rao. Mint name: Bijapur.

Date	Mintage	VG	F	VF	XF	Unc
AH1121 False	—	22.50	45.00	75.00	110	—

Mint: Jhansi
KM# 132 RUPEE

Silver **Note:** Weight varies: 10.70-11.60 grams.

Date	Mintage	VG	F	VF	XF	Unc
AH1167//1 Rare	—	—	—	—	—	—
AH1168//2 Rare	—	—	—	—	—	—
AH1170//4 Rare	—	—	—	—	—	—
AH1171//5 Rare	—	—	—	—	—	—
AH1172//6 Rare	—	—	—	—	—	—

Mint: Kunch
KM# 175 RUPEE

Silver **Obv:** Symbols #1, 3 **Obv. Inscription:** Alamgir II **Note:** Mint name: Kunch Hijri.

Date	Mintage	VG	F	VF	XF	Unc
AH-//22	—	8.00	13.50	21.50	37.50	—
AH-//25	—	8.00	13.50	21.50	37.50	—

Mint: Kunch
KM# 176 RUPEE

Silver **Obv:** Symbols #1, #2, #3 **Obv. Inscription:** Alamgir II **Note:** Mint name: Kunch Hijri.

Date	Mintage	VG	F	VF	XF	Unc
AH-//27	—	8.00	13.50	21.50	37.50	—
AH-//28	—	8.00	13.50	21.50	37.50	—

Mint: Kunch
KM# 177 RUPEE

Silver **Obv:** Symbols #1, #2, #3 **Obv. Inscription:** Alamgir III **Rev:** Symbols #4, #5 **Note:** Mint name: Kunch Hijri.

Date	Mintage	VG	F	VF	XF	Unc
AH1203//31	—	7.50	12.50	20.00	35.00	—
AH1208//31 Error	—	7.50	12.50	20.00	35.00	—
AH8121//39 Error	—	7.50	12.50	20.00	35.00	—
AH1203//39 Error	—	7.50	12.50	20.00	35.00	—
AH1213//39	—	7.50	12.50	20.00	35.00	—
AH3121//39 Error	—	7.50	12.50	20.00	35.00	—

Mint: Kunch
KM# 174 RUPEE

Silver **Obv. Inscription:** Alamgir II **Note:** Weight varies: 10.70-11.60 grams. Mint name: Kunch Hijri.

Date	Mintage	VG	F	VF	XF	Unc
AH-//6	—	—	—	—	—	—

Mint: Toragal
KM# 255 RUPEE

Silver **Note:** Weight varies: 10.70-11.60 grams. Mint name: Sarkar Tor(gal). Struck during the reign of local ruler Pureshuram Bhau, 1771-1799AD, long after death of Alamgir II.

Date	Mintage	VG	F	VF	XF	Unc
ND(1771-99)	—	20.00	35.00	60.00	100	—

Anonymous Ruler

HAMMERED COINAGE

Mint: Sashti
KM# 230 PAISA

Copper **Note:** Struck under the Peshwa, 1739-1782.

Date	Mintage	Good	VG	F	VF	XF
AH(11)96	—	6.00	8.50	12.50	20.00	—

BHONSLAS

HAMMERED COINAGE

Mint: Hinganghat
KM# 25 PAISA

9.6500 g., Copper, 19-20 mm. **Note:** Size varies. Anonymous issue.

Date	Mintage	Good	VG	F	VF	XF
ND(1788-1816)	—	2.00	3.00	4.00	5.50	—

Mint: Nagpur
KM# 30 PAISA

Copper, 24 mm. **Note:** Nagpur Mint probably produced varieties of Chanda Mint rupee KM#5. Uniface. "Barakat Nagpur" in recessed area. Anonymous issue.

Date	Mintage	Good	VG	F	VF	XF
ND(1788-1816)	—	3.00	5.00	7.00	10.00	—

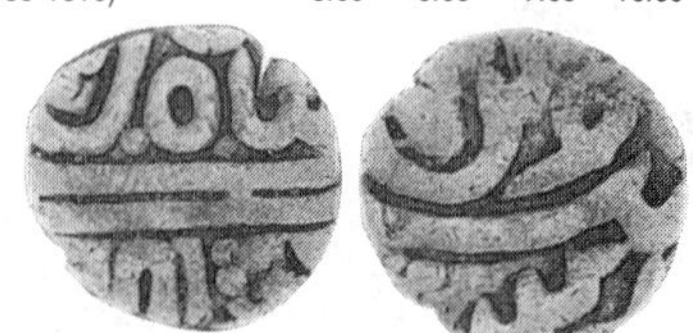

Mint: Hinganghat
KM# 26 2 PAISA

Copper **Note:** Anonymous issue, varieties exist.

Date	Mintage	VG	F	VF	XF	Unc
ND(1788-1816)	—	3.50	4.50	7.00	—	—

Anonymous Ruler

HAMMERED COINAGE

Mint: Katak
KM# 10 PAISA

Copper **Obv. Inscription:** Ahmad Shah Bahadur **Rev:** Symbol of trident, mint marks a and b

Date	Mintage	Good	VG	F	VF	XF
AH(1788-1816)	—	1.50	2.25	3.50	6.50	—

Mint: Uncertain Mint
KM# 35 PAISA

Copper **Note:** Barbarous designs.

Date	Mintage	Good	VG	F	VF	XF
ND-//2x	—	1.25	2.50	3.50	5.00	—

Mint: Katak
KM# 5 RUPEE

Silver **Obv. Inscription:** Ahmad Shah Bahadur **Note:** Weight varies: 10.70-11.60 grams. Mint name Surat, in both barbarous and regular forms.

Date	Mintage	VG	F	VF	XF	Unc
AH-//27	—	9.00	15.00	25.00	40.00	—

PESHWAS

HAMMERED COINAGE

Mint: Sagar
KM# 236 PAISA

Copper **Obv:** Text **Rev:** Symbol **Note:** Mint name: Ravishnagar Sagar.

Date	Mintage	VG	F	VF	XF	Unc
AH1255//55	—	3.50	6.00	10.00	—	—
AH-//38	—	3.50	6.00	10.00	—	—
AH-//55	—	3.50	6.00	10.00	—	—

Mint: Chandor
KM# A93 1/4 RUPEE

Silver **Note:** Weight varies: 2.67-2.87.

Date	Mintage	VG	F	VF	XF	Unc
AH-	—	—	—	—	—	—

Mint: Gulshanabad
KM# 108 1/2 RUPEE

Silver **Note:** Anonymous issue. Weight varies: 5.35-5.80 grams.

Date	Mintage	VG	F	VF	XF	Unc
AH1207 (1793)	—	7.50	12.50	20.00	35.00	—

Mint: Gulshanabad
KM# 109 RUPEE

Silver **Obv:** Text **Rev:** Text **Note:** Anonymous issue. Weight varies: 10.70-11.60 grams.

Date	Mintage	VG	F	VF	XF	Unc
AH1206 (1792)	—	9.00	15.00	25.00	40.00	—
AH1208 (1794)	—	9.00	15.00	25.00	40.00	—
AH1212 (1797)	—	9.00	15.00	25.00	40.00	—

Mint: Poona
KM# 217 RUPEE

Silver **Obv:** Inscription in the name of "Ali Gauhar" (Shah Alam II prior to his accession) **Rev:** Mint mark #3, Fasli date in Nagari numerals **Note:** Anonymous issue. Struck during East India Company administration.

Date	Mintage	VG	F	VF	XF	Unc
FE1207//20 (1792)	—	10.00	16.50	21.50	30.00	—

Mint: Poona
KM# 213 RUPEE

Silver **Obv. Inscription:** Inscription in the name of "Ali Gauhar" (Shah Alam II prior to his accession) **Rev:** Mint mark #1 with regnal year in Persian numerals **Note:** Anonymous issue. Weight varies: 10.70-11.60 grams. Ankusi Rupee. Struck during East India Company administration .

Date	Mintage	VG	F	VF	XF	Unc
ND (1771)	—	7.00	11.00	16.50	25.00	—
ND (1774)	—	7.00	11.00	16.50	25.00	—
ND (1777)	—	7.00	11.00	16.50	25.00	—

Mint: Sagar
KM# 240 RUPEE

Silver **Obv:** Text, mint mark **Rev:** Pataka and trisul both second type **Note:** Anonymous issue. Weight varies: 10.70-11.60 grams. Mint name: Ravishnagar Sagar.

Date	Mintage	VG	F	VF	XF	Unc
AH-//31 (1789)	—	7.00	11.50	17.50	28.50	—
AH-//32 (1790)	—	7.00	11.50	17.50	28.50	—
AH-//33 (1791)	—	7.00	11.50	17.50	28.50	—
AH1207//34 (1792)	—	7.00	11.50	17.50	28.50	—
AH-//35 (1793)	—	7.00	11.50	17.50	28.50	—
AH-//36 (1794)	—	7.00	11.50	17.50	28.50	—
AH-//37 (1795)	—	7.00	11.50	17.50	28.50	—
AH-//38 (1796)	—	7.00	11.50	17.50	28.50	—
AH-//39 (1797)	—	7.00	11.50	17.50	28.50	—
AH-//40 (1798)	—	7.00	11.50	17.50	28.50	—
AH-//41 (1799)	—	7.00	11.50	17.50	28.50	—

MYSORE

Mysore was an old Hindu Kingdom, built on remnants of the Vijayanager Empire. Hindu rulers were in power before Haidar Ali, the first Muslim ruler of Mysore, had come to South India as a military adventurer. Rising from the ranks he eventually became the commander of the army of the Mysore raja. Although he never formally occupied the throne, in 1761 he forced the raja to retire and took the administration of the state into his own hands. Until this time coins of both the Mughals and the Vijayanagar kingdom had been current in the region. Haidar Ali, owing fealty to no one besides himself, issued his own coins in the style of Vijayanagar but bearing his initial in Persian on the reverse. In 1782 Haidar Ali's son, Tipu, succeeded his father and declared himself sultan.

Both Haidar Ali and Tipu Sultan became notorious in British circles for their military adventures across the south of India and for their general dislike of the British presence on the Coromandel Coast. This led to a series of Anglo-Mysore wars in 1780-1784, 1790-1792, and finally in 1799 when Tipu was killed in the breach at Seringapatan. With Tipu gone, the British chose a child of the family that had originally been ousted by Haidar Ali, and installed him upon the masnad (throne) as Krishnaraja Wodeyar III under British protection and control.

NOTE: For later issues see Mysore, Indian Princely States.

HINDU RULERS

Chikkadeva, 1672-1704AD
Kanthirava Narasa II, 1704-1713AD
Dodda Krishna I, 1713-1731AD

Chamaraja, 1731-1734AD
Immadi Krishna II, 1734-1766AD
Devaloy Devaraja, de facto ruler, 1731-1761AD

MUSLIM RULERS

Haidar Ali, AH1174-1197/1761-1782AD
Tipu Sultan, AH1197-1202/1782-1787AD/AM1215-1227/1787-1799AD

DATING

Sultan Tipu used Hijri years on his coins from AH1197 to AH1201. Thereafter he instituted the Mauludi era (AM), which used solar years, 14 years advanced from the Hijri year. They are indicated on the coins by being written in Arabic numerals from right to left, the opposite of normal usage. The Mauludi years were from 1215 to his death in1227. The last four of these were often indicated by letters rather than numbers. Thus Arabic ALIF = Mauludi 1224, BE = 1225, TE = 1226, SE = 1227.

Many blundered dates exist on the copper coins. Two digit regnal years were also written from right to left.

Alif 1 or ا AM1224

Be or ب AM1225

Te or ت AM1226

Se or ث AM1227

Regnal Year		Cyclic Year	Year Hijri	First Day of Year Hijri
1	زكي	37	1197	7th Dec. 1782
2	ازل	38	1198	26th Nov. 1783
3	جلو	39	1199	14th Nov. 1784
4	دلو	40	1200	4th Nov. 1785
				24th Oct. 1786
			Mauludi	Mauludi
5	شا	41	1215	20th March 1787
6	سارا	42	1216	7th April 1788
7	سراب	43	1217	27th March 1789
8	شتا	44	1218	16th March 1790
9	زبرجد	45	1219	4th April 1791
10	سحر	46	1220	23rd March 1792
11	ساحر	47	1221	13th March 1793
12	راسخ	48	1222	1st April 1794
13	شاد	49	1223	21st March 1795
14	حراست	50	1224	8th April 1796
15	ساز	51	1225	29th March 1797
16	شاداب	52	1226	18th March 1798
17	بارش	53	1227	6th April 1799

MINTS

Bahadurpatan
(See Patan Mint)

Balhari بلهاري

Bengalur بنگالور

Dharwar دهاروار

Faiz Hisar فعز حصار

Farrukhi فرخي

Farrukhyab فرخياب حصار

Gooty گوتي

Haidarnagar حيدرنگر

Kalikut كليكوت

Khaliqabad خالق اباد

Khurshed-Sawad خورشيد سواد

Mysore مهيسور مهي سور

Nagar ناگور

Nazarbar نظربار

Patan پتن

Salamabad سلام اباد

Seringapatan(See Patan Mint)

Zafarabad ظفراباد

MONETARY SYSTEM

Rupee

2 Qutb = 1 Akhtar
2 Akhtar = 1 Bahram
2 Bahram = 1 Paisa (Zohra)
2 Paisa = 1 Osmani (Mushtari)
2 Khizri = 1 Kazimi
2 Kazimi = 1 Jafari
2 Jafari = 1 Bagiri
2 Baqiri = 1 Abidi
2 Abidi = 1 Rupee
1 Imami = 1 Rupee
2 Rupees = 1 Faruqi
Pagoda (Sadiqi)
4 Pagodas = 1 Ahmadi

KANARESE NUMERALS

May vary slightly but in general appear as the following.

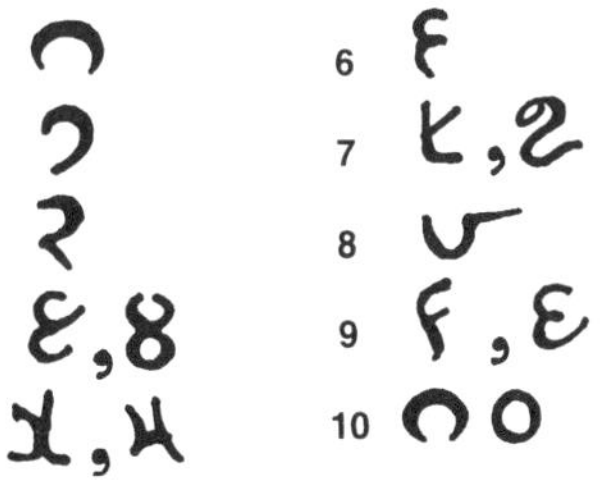

1	೧	6	೬
2	೨	7	೭
3	೩	8	೮
4	೪	9	೯
5	೫	10	೧೦

INDEPENDENT KINGDOM

Anonymous

HAMMERED COINAGE

Mint: Uncertain Mint
KM# A144 1/4 KASU

0.8000 g., Copper **Obv:** Dot above crescent **Rev:** Dots in crossed double lines

Date	Mintage	Good	VG	F	VF	XF
ND	—	3.00	6.00	10.00	16.00	—

Mint: Uncertain Mint
KM# 144 1/2 KASU

1.4800 g., Copper, 10 mm. **Obv:** Elephant left **Rev:** Star or shell

Date	Mintage	Good	VG	F	VF	XF
ND	—	2.50	4.50	7.00	12.00	—

Mint: Uncertain Mint
KM# 146 1/2 KASU

1.4800 g., Copper **Obv:** Elephant left **Rev:** Circles in crossed double lines

Date	Mintage	Good	VG	F	VF	XF
ND	—	2.00	3.00	5.00	8.00	—

Mint: Uncertain Mint
KM# 148 1/2 KASU

1.4800 g., Copper **Obv:** Elephant right

Date	Mintage	Good	VG	F	VF	XF
ND	—	2.00	3.00	5.00	8.00	—

Mint: Uncertain Mint
KM# 164.1 1/2 KASU

1.4800 g., Copper **Obv:** Kanarese #1

Date	Mintage	Good	VG	F	VF	XF
ND	—	2.00	3.00	5.00	8.00	—

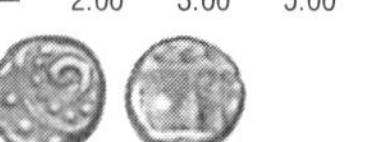

Mint: Uncertain Mint
KM# 164.2 1/2 KASU

1.4800 g., Copper **Obv:** Kanarese #2

Date	Mintage	Good	VG	F	VF	XF
ND	—	2.00	3.00	5.00	8.00	—

Mint: Uncertain Mint
KM# 164.4 1/2 KASU

1.4800 g., Copper **Obv:** Kanarese #4

Date	Mintage	Good	VG	F	VF	XF
ND	—	2.00	3.00	5.00	8.00	—

Mint: Uncertain Mint
KM# 164.6 1/2 KASU

1.4800 g., Copper **Obv:** Kanarese #6

Date	Mintage	Good	VG	F	VF	XF
ND	—	2.00	3.00	5.00	8.00	—

Mint: Uncertain Mint
KM# 164.9 1/2 KASU

1.4800 g., Copper **Obv:** Kanarese #9

Date	Mintage	Good	VG	F	VF	XF
ND	—	2.00	3.00	5.00	8.00	—

Mint: Uncertain Mint
KM# 164.22 1/2 KASU

1.4800 g., Copper **Obv:** Kanarese #22

Date	Mintage	Good	VG	F	VF	XF
ND	—	2.00	3.00	5.00	8.00	—

Mint: Uncertain Mint
KM# 164.23 1/2 KASU

1.4800 g., Copper **Obv:** Kanarese #23

Date	Mintage	Good	VG	F	VF	XF
ND	—	2.00	3.00	5.00	8.00	—

Mint: Uncertain Mint
KM# 164.27 1/2 KASU

1.4800 g., Copper **Obv:** Kanarese #27

Date	Mintage	Good	VG	F	VF	XF
ND	—	2.00	3.00	5.00	8.00	—

Mint: Uncertain Mint
KM# 154 KASU

Copper **Obv:** Elephant left **Rev:** Elephant left **Note:** Mule. Weight varies 2.37-3.11 grams.

Date	Mintage	Good	VG	F	VF	XF
ND	—	4.00	6.50	10.00	15.00	—

Mint: Uncertain Mint
KM# 149.1 KASU
Copper, 12 mm. **Obv:** Elephant right **Rev:** Circles in crossed double lines **Note:** Weight varies 2.37-3.11 grams.

Date	Mintage	Good	VG	F	VF	XF
ND	—	1.00	2.00	3.00	5.00	—

Mint: Uncertain Mint
KM# 149.2 KASU
Copper **Obv:** Smaller elephant **Note:** Weight varies 2.37-3.11 grams.

Date	Mintage	Good	VG	F	VF	XF
ND	—	1.00	2.00	3.00	5.00	—

Mint: Uncertain Mint
KM# 150 KASU
Copper **Obv:** Sword in dotted circle **Rev:** 33 in crossed double lines **Note:** Weight varies 2.37-3.11 grams.

Date	Mintage	Good	VG	F	VF	XF
ND	—	3.00	6.00	10.00	16.00	—

Mint: Uncertain Mint
KM# 151 KASU
Copper **Rev:** Goad **Note:** Weight varies 2.37-3.11 grams.

Date	Mintage	Good	VG	F	VF	XF
ND	—	2.50	4.50	7.00	12.00	—

Mint: Uncertain Mint
KM# 147 KASU
Copper **Obv:** Elephant left **Rev:** W-shaped symbols in crossed double lines **Note:** Weight varies 2.37-3.11 grams.

Date	Mintage	Good	VG	F	VF	XF
ND	—	2.00	3.25	5.00	8.50	—

Mint: Uncertain Mint
KM# 152 KASU
Copper, 12 mm. **Obv:** Sun and moon above elephant **Note:** Weight varies 2.37-3.11 grams.

Date	Mintage	Good	VG	F	VF	XF
ND	—	1.00	1.50	3.00	5.00	—

Mint: Uncertain Mint
KM# 153 KASU
Copper **Obv:** Kanarese #1 above elephant **Rev:** Dots in double lines **Note:** Weight varies 2.37-3.11 grams.

Date	Mintage	Good	VG	F	VF	XF
ND	—	1.00	1.50	3.00	5.00	—

Mint: Uncertain Mint
KM# 155 KASU
Copper, 12 mm. **Obv:** Seated figure of Lakshmi in circle of dots **Rev:** W-shaped symbols in crossed doule lines **Note:** Weight varies 2.37-3.11 grams.

Date	Mintage	Good	VG	F	VF	XF
ND	—	2.00	3.25	5.00	8.50	—

Mint: Uncertain Mint
KM# 156 KASU
Copper, 17 mm. **Obv:** Seated figure of Ganesha facing front **Note:** Weight varies 2.37-3.11 grams.

Date	Mintage	Good	VG	F	VF	XF
ND	—	2.00	3.25	5.00	8.50	—

Mint: Uncertain Mint
KM# 157 KASU
Copper **Obv:** Figure of Hanuman right **Rev:** W shaped symbols in double lines **Note:** Weight varies 2.37-3.11 grams.

Date	Mintage	Good	VG	F	VF	XF
ND	—	2.00	3.25	5.00	8.50	—

Mint: Uncertain Mint
KM# 158 KASU
Copper, 13 mm. **Obv:** Figure of Garuda kneeling left **Note:** Weight varies 2.37-3.11 grams.

Date	Mintage	Good	VG	F	VF	XF
ND	—	2.00	3.25	5.00	8.50	—

Mint: Uncertain Mint
KM# 159 KASU
Copper **Obv:** Bull walking left **Note:** Weight varies 2.37-3.11 grams.

Date	Mintage	Good	VG	F	VF	XF
ND	—	1.00	1.50	2.50	4.00	—

Mint: Uncertain Mint
KM# 160.1 KASU
Copper **Obv:** Lion facing left **Note:** Weight varies 2.37-3.11 grams.

Date	Mintage	Good	VG	F	VF	XF
ND	—	1.00	1.50	2.50	4.00	—

Mint: Uncertain Mint
KM# 160.2 KASU
Copper **Obv:** Lion left, right paw raised **Note:** Weight varies 2.37-3.11 grams.

Date	Mintage	Good	VG	F	VF	XF
ND	—	—	—	—	—	—

Mint: Uncertain Mint
KM# 161 KASU
Copper **Obv:** Horse galloping right in circle of dots **Rev:** Characters between double lines **Note:** Weight varies 2.37-3.11 grams.

Date	Mintage	Good	VG	F	VF	XF
ND	—	2.50	4.00	6.50	10.00	—

Mint: Uncertain Mint
KM# 166 KASU
Copper **Obv:** Horse and rider right **Note:** Weight varies 2.37-3.11 grams.

Date	Mintage	Good	VG	F	VF	XF
ND	—	—	—	—	—	—

Mint: Uncertain Mint
KM# 167 KASU
Copper **Obv:** Horse galloping left **Note:** Weight varies 2.37-3.11 grams.

Date	Mintage	Good	VG	F	VF	XF
ND	—	2.00	3.00	4.50	6.00	—

Mint: Uncertain Mint
KM# 162 KASU
Copper, 14 mm. **Obv:** Peacock right in lined circle **Note:** Weight varies 2.37-3.11 grams.

Date	Mintage	Good	VG	F	VF	XF
ND	—	2.50	4.00	6.50	10.00	—

Mint: Uncertain Mint
KM# A163 KASU
Copper **Obv:** Deer running right **Note:** Weight varies 2.37-3.11 grams.

Date	Mintage	Good	VG	F	VF	XF
ND	—	—	—	—	—	—

Mint: Uncertain Mint
KM# 163 KASU
Copper **Obv:** Bell in circle of dots **Note:** Weight varies 2.37-3.11 grams.

Date	Mintage	Good	VG	F	VF	XF
ND	—	2.00	3.25	5.00	8.50	—

Mint: Uncertain Mint
KM# A168 KASU
Copper **Obv:** Bull reclining facing left **Note:** Weight varies 2.37-3.11 grams.

Date	Mintage	Good	VG	F	VF	XF
ND	—	2.00	3.25	5.00	8.50	—

Mint: Uncertain Mint
KM# 169 KASU
Copper **Obv:** 2 headed eagle facing **Note:** Weight varies 2.37-3.11 grams.

Date	Mintage	Good	VG	F	VF	XF
ND	—	—	—	—	—	—

Mint: Uncertain Mint
KM# 171 KASU
Copper **Obv:** Flower **Note:** Weight varies 2.37-3.11 grams.

Date	Mintage	Good	VG	F	VF	XF
ND	—	—	—	—	—	—

Mint: Uncertain Mint
KM# 165.1 KASU
Copper **Obv:** Kanarese #1 in circle of dots **Note:** Weight varies 2.37-3.11 grams.

Date	Mintage	Good	VG	F	VF	XF
ND	—	1.00	2.00	3.00	5.00	—

Mint: Uncertain Mint
KM# 165.2 KASU
Copper **Obv:** Kanarese #2 in circle of dots **Note:** Weight varies 2.37-3.11 grams.

Date	Mintage	Good	VG	F	VF	XF
ND	—	1.50	2.00	3.00	5.00	—

Mint: Uncertain Mint
KM# 165.3 KASU
Copper **Obv:** Kanarese #3 in circle of dots **Note:** Weight varies 2.37-3.11 grams.

Date	Mintage	Good	VG	F	VF	XF
ND	—	1.50	2.00	3.00	5.00	—

Mint: Uncertain Mint
KM# 165.4 KASU
Copper **Obv:** Kanarese #4 in circle of dots **Note:** Weight varies 2.37-3.11 grams.

Date	Mintage	Good	VG	F	VF	XF
ND	—	1.50	2.00	3.00	5.00	—

Mint: Uncertain Mint
KM# 165.5 KASU
Copper, 14 mm. **Obv:** Kanarese #5 in circle of dots **Note:** Weight varies 2.37-3.11 grams.

Date	Mintage	Good	VG	F	VF	XF
ND	—	1.50	2.00	3.00	5.00	—

Mint: Uncertain Mint
KM# 165.6 KASU
Copper **Obv:** Kanarese #6 in circle of dots **Note:** Weight varies 2.37-3.11 grams.

Date	Mintage	Good	VG	F	VF	XF
ND	—	1.50	2.00	3.00	5.00	—

Mint: Uncertain Mint
KM# 165.7 KASU
Copper **Obv:** Kanarese #7 in circle of dots **Note:** Weight varies 2.37-3.11 grams.

Date	Mintage	Good	VG	F	VF	XF
ND	—	1.50	2.00	3.00	5.00	—

Mint: Uncertain Mint
KM# 165.8 KASU
Copper, 13 mm. **Obv:** Kanarese #8 in circle of dots **Note:** Weight varies 2.37-3.11 grams.

Date	Mintage	Good	VG	F	VF	XF
ND	—	1.50	2.00	3.00	5.00	—

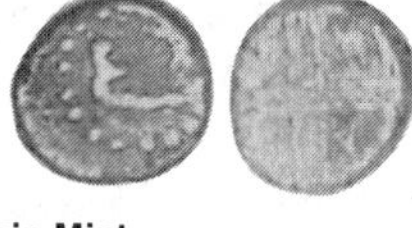

Mint: Uncertain Mint
KM# 165.9 KASU
Copper **Obv:** Kanarese #9 in circle of dots **Note:** Weight varies 2.37-3.11 grams.

Date	Mintage	Good	VG	F	VF	XF
ND	—	1.50	2.00	3.00	5.00	—

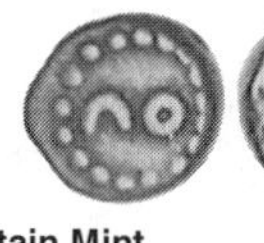

Mint: Uncertain Mint
KM# 165.10 KASU
Copper, 14 mm. **Obv:** Kanarese #10 in circle of dots **Note:** Weight varies 2.37-3.11 grams.

Date	Mintage	Good	VG	F	VF	XF
ND	—	1.50	2.00	3.00	5.00	—

Mint: Uncertain Mint
KM# 165.11 KASU
Copper **Obv:** Kanarese #11 in circle of dots **Note:** Weight varies 2.37-3.11 grams.

Date	Mintage	Good	VG	F	VF	XF
ND	—	1.50	2.00	3.00	5.00	—

Mint: Uncertain Mint
KM# 165.12 KASU
Copper, 13 mm. **Obv:** Kanarese #12 in circle of dots **Note:** Weight varies 2.37-3.11 grams.

Date	Mintage	Good	VG	F	VF	XF
ND	—	1.50	2.00	3.00	5.00	—

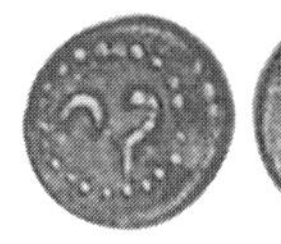

Mint: Uncertain Mint
KM# 165.13 KASU

Copper, 14 mm. **Obv:** Kanarese #13 in circle of dots **Note:** Weight varies 2.37-3.11 grams.

Date	Mintage	Good	VG	F	VF	XF
ND	—	1.50	2.00	3.00	5.00	—

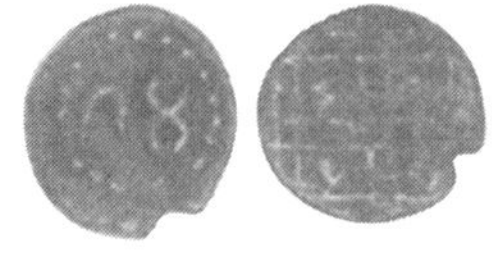

Mint: Uncertain Mint
KM# 165.14 KASU

Copper **Obv:** Kanarese #14 in circle of dots **Note:** Weight varies 2.37-3.11 grams.

Date	Mintage	Good	VG	F	VF	XF
ND	—	1.50	2.00	3.00	5.00	—

Mint: Uncertain Mint
KM# 165.15 KASU

Copper, 14 mm. **Obv:** Kanarese #15 in circle of dots **Note:** Weight varies 2.37-3.11 grams.

Date	Mintage	Good	VG	F	VF	XF
ND	—	1.50	2.00	3.00	5.00	—

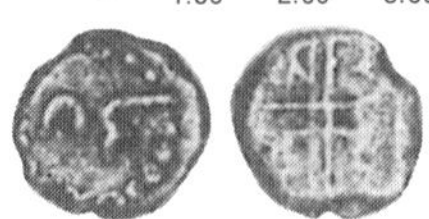

Mint: Uncertain Mint
KM# 165.16 KASU

Copper **Obv:** Kanarese #16 in circle of dots **Note:** Weight varies 2.37-3.11 grams.

Date	Mintage	Good	VG	F	VF	XF
ND	—	1.50	2.00	3.00	5.00	—

Mint: Uncertain Mint
KM# 165.17 KASU

Copper **Obv:** Kanarese #17 in circle of dots **Note:** Weight varies 2.37-3.11 grams.

Date	Mintage	Good	VG	F	VF	XF
ND	—	1.50	2.00	3.00	5.00	—

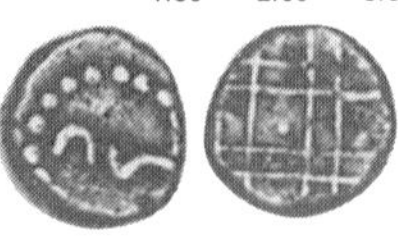

Mint: Uncertain Mint
KM# 165.18 KASU

Copper **Obv:** Kanarese #18 in circle of dots **Note:** Weight varies 2.37-3.11 grams.

Date	Mintage	Good	VG	F	VF	XF
ND	—	1.50	2.00	3.00	5.00	—

Mint: Uncertain Mint
KM# 165.19 KASU

Copper, 13 mm. **Obv:** Kanarese #19 in circle of dots **Note:** Weight varies 2.37-3.11 grams.

Date	Mintage	Good	VG	F	VF	XF
ND	—	1.50	2.00	3.00	5.00	—

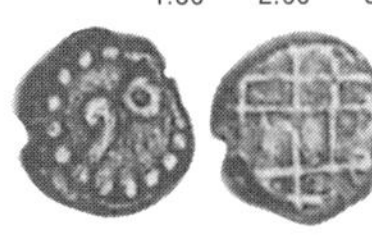

Mint: Uncertain Mint
KM# 165.20 KASU

Copper, 14 mm. **Obv:** Kanarese #20 in circle of dots **Note:** Weight varies 2.37-3.11 grams.

Date	Mintage	Good	VG	F	VF	XF
ND	—	1.50	2.00	3.00	5.00	—

Mint: Uncertain Mint
KM# 165.21 KASU

Copper, 12 mm. **Obv:** Kanarese #21 in circle of dots **Note:** Weight varies 2.37-3.11 grams.

Date	Mintage	Good	VG	F	VF	XF
ND	—	1.50	2.00	3.00	5.00	—

Mint: Uncertain Mint
KM# 165.22 KASU

Copper **Obv:** Kanarese #22 in circle of dots **Note:** Weight varies 2.37-3.11 grams.

Date	Mintage	Good	VG	F	VF	XF
ND	—	1.50	2.00	3.00	5.00	—

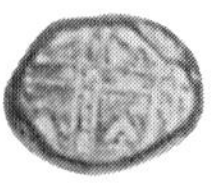

Mint: Uncertain Mint
KM# 165.23 KASU

Copper **Obv:** Kanarese #23 in circle of dots **Note:** Weight varies 2.37-3.11 grams.

Date	Mintage	Good	VG	F	VF	XF
ND	—	1.50	2.00	3.00	5.00	—

Mint: Uncertain Mint
KM# 165.24 KASU

Copper **Obv:** Kanarese #24 in circle of dots **Note:** Weight varies 2.37-3.11 grams.

Date	Mintage	Good	VG	F	VF	XF
ND	—	1.50	2.00	3.00	5.00	—

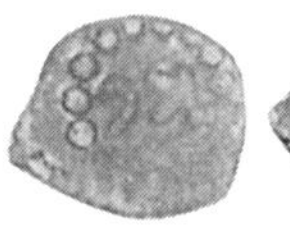

Mint: Uncertain Mint
KM# 165.25 KASU

Copper, 14 mm. **Obv:** Kanarese #25 in circle of dots **Note:** Weight varies 2.37-3.11 grams.

Date	Mintage	Good	VG	F	VF	XF
ND	—	1.50	2.00	3.00	5.00	—

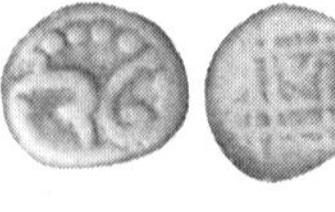

Mint: Uncertain Mint
KM# 165.26 KASU

Copper, 14 mm. **Obv:** Kanarese #26 in circle of dots **Note:** Weight varies 2.37-3.11 grams.

Date	Mintage	Good	VG	F	VF	XF
ND	—	1.50	2.00	3.00	5.00	—

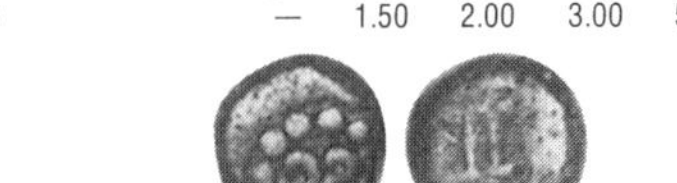

Mint: Uncertain Mint
KM# 165.27 KASU

Copper, 13 mm. **Obv:** Kanarese #27 in circle of dots **Note:** Weight varies 2.37-3.11 grams.

Date	Mintage	Good	VG	F	VF	XF
ND	—	1.50	2.00	3.00	5.00	—

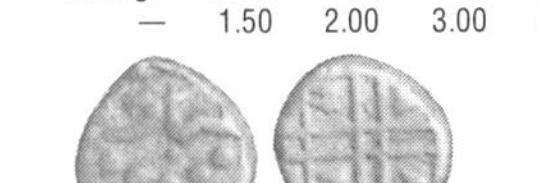

Mint: Uncertain Mint
KM# 165.28 KASU

Copper **Obv:** Kanarese #28 in circle of dots **Note:** Weight varies 2.37-3.11 grams.

Date	Mintage	Good	VG	F	VF	XF
ND	—	1.50	2.00	3.00	5.00	—

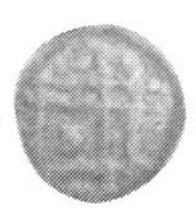

Mint: Uncertain Mint
KM# 165.29 KASU

Copper **Obv:** Kanarese #29 in circle of dots **Note:** Weight varies 2.37-3.11 grams.

Date	Mintage	Good	VG	F	VF	XF
ND	—	1.50	2.00	3.00	5.00	—

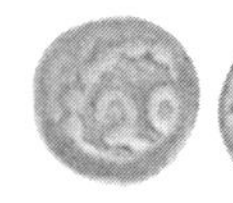

Mint: Uncertain Mint
KM# 165.30 KASU

Copper **Obv:** Kanarese #30 in circle of dots **Note:** Weight varies 2.37-3.11 grams.

Date	Mintage	Good	VG	F	VF	XF
ND	—	1.50	2.00	3.00	5.00	—

Mint: Uncertain Mint
KM# 165.31 KASU

Copper **Obv:** Kanarese #31 in circle of dots **Note:** Weight varies 2.37-3.11 grams.

Date	Mintage	Good	VG	F	VF	XF
ND	—	1.50	2.00	3.00	5.00	—

Mint: Uncertain Mint
KM# 165.32 KASU

Copper **Obv:** Kanarese #32 in circle of dots **Note:** Weight varies 2.37-3.11 grams.

Date	Mintage	Good	VG	F	VF	XF
ND	—	—	—	—	—	—

Mint: Uncertain Mint
KM# 165.33 KASU

Copper **Obv:** Kanarese #33 in circle of dots **Note:** Weight varies 2.37-3.11 grams.

Date	Mintage	Good	VG	F	VF	XF
ND	—	—	—	—	—	—

Mint: Uncertain Mint
KM# A170 KASU

Copper **Obv:** Fish left **Note:** Weight varies 2.37-3.11 grams. Prev. KM#170.

Date	Mintage	Good	VG	F	VF	XF
ND	—	—	—	—	—	—

Mint: Uncertain Mint
KM# A159 KASU

Copper **Obv:** Lion walking left **Note:** Weight varies 2.37-3.11 grams. Struck at Uncertain Mints.

Date	Mintage	Good	VG	F	VF	XF
ND	—	—	—	—	—	—

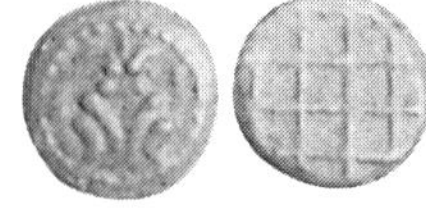

Mint: Uncertain Mint
KM# 168 KASU

Copper **Obv:** Seated beetle facing **Note:** Weight varies: 2.37-3.11 grams.

Date	Mintage	Good	VG	F	VF	XF
ND	—	—	—	—	—	—

Mint: Uncertain Mint
KM# 170 FANAM

Gold **Obv:** Elephant with howdah **Rev:** Crossed lines (anonymous) **Note:** Weight varies: 0.33-0.40 grams.

Date	Mintage	VG	F	VF	XF	Unc
ND	—	8.50	10.00	13.50	20.00	—

Haidar Ali

AH1174-97/1761-82AD

HAMMERED COINAGE

Mint: Uncertain Mint
KM# 20 CASH

Copper **Obv:** Arabic "222" below sun and moon, Kanarese #1-33 **Rev:** Crossed lines

Date	Mintage	Good	VG	F	VF	XF
ND(1761-82)	—	1.50	2.00	3.50	6.00	—

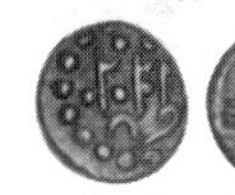
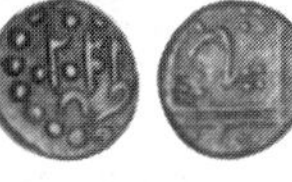

Mint: Uncertain Mint
KM# 21 CASH
Copper **Obv:** Arabic "222" above sun and moon, Kanarese #10, #12

Date	Mintage	Good	VG	F	VF	XF
Yr.10(1771)	—	1.00	1.75	3.00	5.00	—
Yr.12(1773)	—	1.50	2.50	4.00	7.00	—

Mint: Uncertain Mint
KM# 22 1/8 PAISA
1.5300 g., Copper **Obv:** Tiger **Rev:** Battle axe

Date	Mintage	Good	VG	F	VF	XF
ND(1761-82)	—	3.00	5.00	8.00	12.50	—

Mint: Uncertain Mint
KM# 23 1/4 PAISA
3.0500 g., Copper

Date	Mintage	Good	VG	F	VF	XF
ND(1761-82)	—	4.50	8.00	12.00	17.50	—

Mint: Uncertain Mint
KM# 24 1/2 PAISA
6.0300 g., Copper

Date	Mintage	Good	VG	F	VF	XF
ND(1761-82)	—	5.00	9.00	13.00	20.00	—

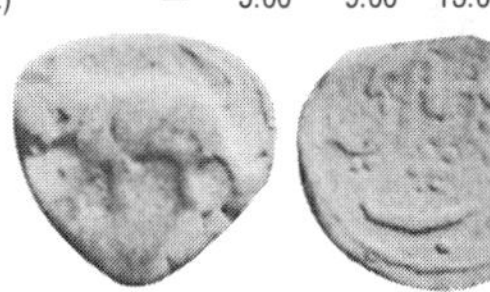

Mint: Balhari
KM# 1 PAISA
Copper **Obv:** Elephant left

Date	Mintage	Good	VG	F	VF	XF
ND(1761-82)	—	10.00	17.50	28.00	47.00	—

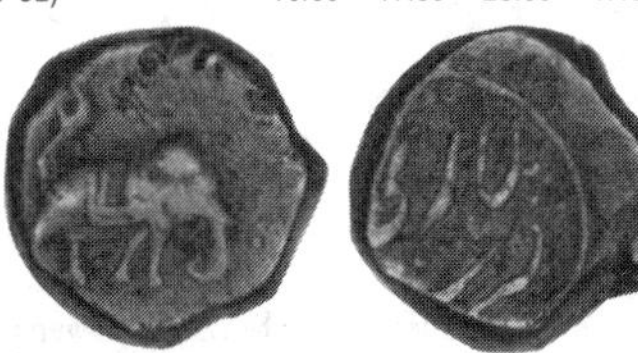

Mint: Balhari
KM# 2 PAISA
Copper **Obv:** Elephant right

Date	Mintage	Good	VG	F	VF	XF
ND(1761-82)	—	8.50	15.00	25.00	45.00	—

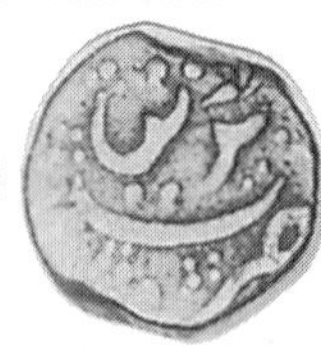

Mint: Gooty
KM# A6 PAISA
Copper **Obv:** Elephant right **Note:** Weight varies: 12.00-12.80 grams.

Date	Mintage	Good	VG	F	VF	XF
ND(1761-82)	—	4.00	6.00	10.00	18.00	—

Mint: Patan
KM# 5.1 PAISA
12.1800 g., Copper

Date	Mintage	Good	VG	F	VF	XF
AH1195	—	3.50	7.00	13.00	25.00	—
AH1196	—	3.50	7.00	13.00	25.00	—
ND(1782-83)	—	3.50	7.00	13.00	25.00	—

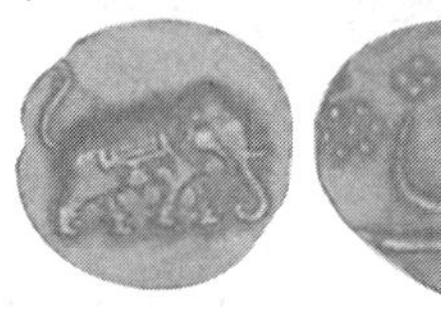

Mint: Patan
KM# 5.2 PAISA
12.1800 g., Copper **Rev:** Rosettes

Date	Mintage	Good	VG	F	VF	XF
ND(1761-82)	—	3.00	6.00	12.00	20.00	—

Mint: Haidarnagar
KM# 4 RUPEE
Silver **Obv. Inscription:** Shah Alam II **Note:** Weight varies: 10.70-11.60 grams.

Date	Mintage	VG	F	VF	XF	Unc
AH1191//14	—	200	400	750	1,250	—
AH1193//16	—	200	400	750	1,250	—
AH1194//17	—	250	475	850	1,350	—

Mint: Haidarnagar
KM# A5 NAZARANA RUPEE
Silver **Obv. Inscription:** Shah Alam II **Note:** Weight varies: 10.70-11.60 grams.

Date	Mintage	VG	F	VF	XF	Unc
AH1176//3	—	300	550	1,000	1,650	—

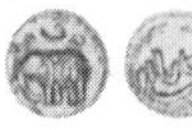

Mint: Balhari
KM# 3 FANAM
Gold **Obv:** Elephant left **Rev:** Mintname **Note:** Weight varies: 0.33-0.40 grams.

Date	Mintage	Good	VG	F	VF	XF
ND(1761-82)	—	8.50	12.50	18.00	30.00	—

Mint: Uncertain Mint
KM# 8 FANAM
Gold **Obv:** God and Goddess **Rev:** Letter "He" (for Haidar) **Note:** Weight varies .33-.40 grams.

Date	Mintage	VG	F	VF	XF	Unc
ND(1761-82)	—	5.50	8.00	12.50	20.00	—

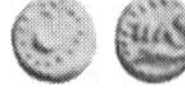

Mint: Uncertain Mint
KM# 9 FANAM
Gold **Obv:** Letter "He" **Rev:** Date **Note:** Weight varies: 0.33-0.40 grams.

Date	Mintage	VG	F	VF	XF	Unc
AH1189	—	10.00	20.00	35.00	60.00	—
AH1196	—	10.00	20.00	35.00	60.00	—

Mint: Uncertain Mint
KM# 11 1/2 PAGODA
1.7000 g., Gold **Obv:** God and Goddess **Rev:** Letter "He"

Date	Mintage	VG	F	VF	XF	Unc
ND(1761-82)	—	27.50	50.00	90.00	150	—

Mint: Uncertain Mint
KM# 12 1/2 PAGODA
1.7000 g., Gold **Obv:** Seated God

Date	Mintage	VG	F	VF	XF	Unc
ND(1761-82)	—	27.50	45.00	75.00	125	—

Mint: Gooty
KM# 7 PAGODA
3.4000 g., Gold **Obv. Inscription:** Muhammad Shah

Date	Mintage	VG	F	VF	XF	Unc
AH1178	—	55.00	85.00	160	275	—
AH1194	—	55.00	85.00	160	275	—
AH1198	—	55.00	85.00	160	275	—

Mint: Uncertain Mint
KM# 15 PAGODA
3.4000 g., Gold **Obv:** God and Goddess **Rev:** Letter "He"

Date	Mintage	VG	F	VF	XF	Unc
ND(1761-82)	—	55.00	85.00	130	185	—

Mint: Haidarnagar
KM# B6 MOHUR
11.6000 g., Gold **Obv. Inscription:** Shah Alam II

Date	Mintage	VG	F	VF	XF	Unc
AH119x Rare	—	—	—	—	—	—

Mint: Patan
KM# 6 MOHUR
Gold **Obv. Inscription:** Shah Alam II **Note:** Weight varies: 10.70-11.40 grams.

Date	Mintage	VG	F	VF	XF	Unc
AH11(91)//14	—	500	900	1,250	1,800	—
AH119X//15	—	500	900	1,250	1,800	—
AH119X//17	—	500	900	1,250	1,800	—
AH1197//20	—	500	900	1,250	1,800	—

Tipu Sultan
AM1215-27/1787-99AD

HAMMERED COINAGE

Mint: Bengalur
KM# 30 1/8 PAISA
1.3000 g., Copper

Date	Mintage	Good	VG	F	VF	XF
AM1216 (1787)	—	10.00	15.00	25.00	40.00	—
AM1217 (1788)	—	10.00	15.00	25.00	40.00	—
AM1218 (1789)	—	10.00	15.00	25.00	40.00	—
AM1219 (1790)	—	10.00	15.00	25.00	40.00	—

Mint: Farrukhyab-Hisar
KM# 60 1/8 PAISA
Copper

Date	Mintage	Good	VG	F	VF	XF
AM1217 (1788)	—	25.00	35.00	60.00	90.00	—

Mint: Nagar
KM# 100.1 1/8 PAISA
Copper **Obv:** Elephant right

Date	Mintage	Good	VG	F	VF	XF
AM1224//1 (1796)	—	11.00	20.00	30.00	50.00	—

Mint: Nagar
KM# 100.2 1/8 PAISA

Copper **Obv:** Persian "Te" above elephant, retrograde date

Date	Mintage	Good	VG	F	VF	XF
AM1226//3 (1798)	—	11.00	20.00	30.00	50.00	—

Mint: Patan
KM# 120.4 1/8 PAISA

1.3000 g., Copper **Obv:** Elephant right **Rev:** Without rosettes

Date	Mintage	Good	VG	F	VF	XF
ND(1782-99)	—	12.00	18.00	30.00	45.00	—

Mint: Patan
KM# 120.3a 1/8 PAISA

Copper **Obv:** Elephant right, Persian "Be" above **Rev:** Inscription at bottom, date at top **Rev. Inscription:** "Patan"

Date	Mintage	Good	VG	F	VF	XF
AM1225//2	—	12.00	18.00	30.00	45.00	—

Mint: Patan
KM# 120.3b 1/8 PAISA

Copper **Obv:** Elephant right, Persian "Te" above **Rev. Inscription:** "Ahktar" at top, "Patan" at bottom

Date	Mintage	Good	VG	F	VF	XF
AM1226//3	—	12.00	18.00	30.00	45.00	—

Mint: Patan
KM# 120.1 1/8 PAISA

1.3000 g., Copper **Obv:** Elephant left **Rev:** "Patan" at upper left

Date	Mintage	Good	VG	F	VF	XF
AM1216 (1787)	—	12.00	18.00	30.00	45.00	—
AM1217 (1788)	—	12.00	18.00	30.00	45.00	—
AM1218 (1789)	—	12.00	18.00	30.00	45.00	—
AM1219 (1790)	—	12.00	18.00	30.00	45.00	—
AM1220 (1791)	—	12.00	18.00	30.00	45.00	—
AM1221 (1792)	—	12.00	18.00	30.00	45.00	—

Mint: Patan
KM# 120.2 1/8 PAISA

1.3000 g., Copper **Obv:** Elephant right **Rev:** "Patan" in center

Date	Mintage	Good	VG	F	VF	XF
AM1221 (1792)	—	12.00	18.00	30.00	45.00	—
AM1222 (1793)	—	12.00	18.00	30.00	45.00	—

Mint: Patan
KM# 120.3 1/8 PAISA

1.3000 g., Copper **Obv:** Persian "Alif" above elephant **Rev:** Retrograde date

Date	Mintage	Good	VG	F	VF	XF
AM1222 (1793)	—	12.00	18.00	30.00	45.00	—
AM1224//1 (1794)	—	12.00	18.00	30.00	45.00	—

Mint: Patan
KM# 120.5 1/8 PAISA

1.3000 g., Copper **Obv:** Elephant left, retrograde date above

Date	Mintage	Good	VG	F	VF	XF
AM1224 (1795)	—	6.50	12.50	20.00	30.00	—

Mint: Salamabad
KM# 130 1/8 PAISA

Copper

Date	Mintage	Good	VG	F	VF	XF
AM1218 (1789)	—	15.00	25.00	40.00	60.00	—

Mint: Bengalur
KM# 31.1 1/4 PAISA

Copper **Obv:** Elephant right **Note:** Weight varies: 2.53-2.72 grams.

Date	Mintage	Good	VG	F	VF	XF
AH1200	—	3.00	4.50	7.50	13.00	—
AM1215	—	3.50	6.00	9.00	15.00	—
AM1216	—	2.50	4.00	7.00	12.00	—
AM1222	—	4.00	6.00	9.00	15.00	—

Mint: Bengalur
KM# 31.2 1/4 PAISA

Copper **Obv:** Elephant left **Note:** Weight varies: 2.53-2.72 grams.

Date	Mintage	Good	VG	F	VF	XF
AM1216 (1787)	—	2.00	3.00	5.00	10.00	—
AM1217 (1788)	—	2.00	3.00	5.00	10.00	—
AM1218 (1789)	—	3.00	4.00	7.00	13.00	—
AM1219 (1790)	—	3.00	4.00	7.00	13.00	—

Mint: Faiz Hisar
KM# 41.1 1/4 PAISA

Copper **Obv:** Elephant left in circle of rosettes **Rev:** Legend in circle of rosettes **Note:** Weight varies 2.72-3.18 grams.

Date	Mintage	Good	VG	F	VF	XF
AM1215 (1786)	—	2.00	3.50	5.00	9.00	—
AM1216 (1787)	—	2.00	3.50	5.00	9.00	—
AM1217 (1788)	—	2.00	3.50	5.00	9.00	—

Mint: Faiz Hisar
KM# 41.4 1/4 PAISA

Copper **Obv:** Persian "Be" above elephant **Note:** Weight varies 2.72-3.18 grams.

Date	Mintage	Good	VG	F	VF	XF
AM1224//2 (1795)	—	2.00	3.00	5.00	9.00	—
AM1225//2 (1796)	—	2.00	3.00	5.00	9.00	—

Mint: Faiz Hisar
KM# 41.5 1/4 PAISA

Copper **Obv:** Persian "Te" above elephant **Note:** Weight varies 2.72-3.18 grams.

Date	Mintage	Good	VG	F	VF	XF
AM1226//3 (1797)	—	2.00	3.00	5.00	9.00	—

Mint: Faiz Hisar
KM# 41.2 1/4 PAISA

Copper **Obv:** Elephant right **Note:** Weight varies: 2.72-3.18 grams.

Date	Mintage	Good	VG	F	VF	XF
AM1222 (1793)	—	3.00	4.50	9.00	18.00	—
AM1223 (1794)	—	3.00	4.50	9.00	18.00	—

Mint: Faiz Hisar
KM# 41.3 1/4 PAISA

Copper **Obv:** Persian "Alif" above elephant **Note:** Weight varies: 2.72-3.18 grams.

Date	Mintage	Good	VG	F	VF	XF
AM1224//1 (1795)	—	2.00	3.00	5.00	9.00	—

Mint: Farrukhi
KM# 51 1/4 PAISA

Copper **Obv:** Corded borders **Rev:** Corded borders

Date	Mintage	Good	VG	F	VF	XF
AM1216 (1787)	—	3.00	5.00	9.00	18.00	—
AM1217 (1788)	—	3.00	5.00	9.00	18.00	—
AM1218 (1789)	—	3.00	5.00	9.00	18.00	—

Mint: Farrukhyab-Hisar
KM# 61.1 1/4 PAISA

Copper

Date	Mintage	Good	VG	F	VF	XF
AM1216 (1787)	—	2.00	3.00	5.00	9.00	—
AM1217 (1788)	—	2.00	3.00	5.00	9.00	—
AM1218 (1789)	—	2.00	3.00	5.00	9.00	—
AM1219 (1790)	—	2.00	3.00	5.00	9.00	—

Mint: Farrukhyab-Hisar
KM# 61.2 1/4 PAISA

Copper **Obv:** Elephant right

Date	Mintage	Good	VG	F	VF	XF
AM1222 (1793)	—	—	—	—	—	—

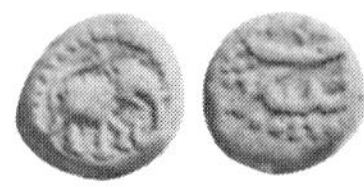

Mint: Kalikut
KM# 71 1/4 PAISA

2.9200 g., Copper

Date	Mintage	Good	VG	F	VF	XF
ND(1782-99)	—	3.50	7.00	13.00	25.00	—

Mint: Khaliqabad
KM# 81.1 1/4 PAISA

Copper **Obv:** Elephant left

Date	Mintage	Good	VG	F	VF	XF
AH1200	—	5.00	8.00	15.00	25.00	—
AM1215	—	2.00	3.50	5.00	9.00	—
AM1216	—	2.00	3.50	5.00	9.00	—
AM1217	—	2.00	3.50	5.00	9.00	—
AM1218	—	2.00	3.50	5.00	9.00	—
AM1225	—	2.00	3.50	5.00	9.00	—

Mint: Khaliqabad
KM# 81.2 1/4 PAISA

Copper **Obv:** Elephant right

Date	Mintage	Good	VG	F	VF	XF
ND(1782-99) (1782)	—	—	—	—	—	—
AM1215 (1786)	—	3.00	5.00	10.00	15.00	—
AM1216 (1787)	—	—	—	—	—	—
AM1217 (1788)	—	—	—	—	—	—
AM1225 (1796)	—	5.00	9.00	15.00	25.00	—

Mint: Nagar
KM# 101.1 1/4 PAISA

2.9200 g., Copper **Obv:** Elephant right

Date	Mintage	Good	VG	F	VF	XF
AH1198	—	2.25	3.50	6.00	10.00	—
AH1200	—	2.25	3.50	6.00	10.00	—

Mint: Nagar
KM# 101.2 1/4 PAISA

2.9200 g., Copper **Obv:** Persian "Alif" above elephant

Date	Mintage	Good	VG	F	VF	XF
AM1224//1 (1796)	—	2.25	3.50	6.00	10.00	—

Mint: Nagar
KM# 101.4 1/4 PAISA

2.9200 g., Copper **Obv:** Persian "Te" above elephant

Date	Mintage	Good	VG	F	VF	XF
AM1226//3 (1798)	—	2.25	3.50	6.00	10.00	—

Mint: Nagar
KM# 101.5 1/4 PAISA

2.9200 g., Copper **Obv:** Elephant left **Rev:** Rosettes

Date	Mintage	Good	VG	F	VF	XF
AM1216 (1787)	—	2.25	3.50	6.00	10.00	—
AM1217 (1788)	—	2.25	3.50	6.00	10.00	—
AM1221 (1789)	—	2.25	3.50	6.00	10.00	—

Mint: Nagar
KM# 101.3 1/4 PAISA
2.9200 g., Copper **Obv:** Persian "Be" above elephant **Note:** Struck at Nagar Mint.

Date	Mintage	Good	VG	F	VF	XF
AM1225//2 (1797)	—	2.25	3.50	6.00	10.00	—

Mint: Nazarbar
KM# 111 1/4 PAISA
Copper

Date	Mintage	Good	VG	F	VF	XF
AM1216 (1787)	—	15.00	25.00	35.00	50.00	—

Mint: Patan
KM# 121.3a 1/4 PAISA
Copper **Obv:** Elephant right, retrograde date above **Rev:** "Akhtar" at top, "Patan" at bottom

Date	Mintage	Good	VG	F	VF	XF
AM1222	—	5.00	7.00	11.00	18.00	—
AM1223	—	5.00	7.00	11.00	18.00	—

Mint: Patan
KM# 121.1 1/4 PAISA
Copper **Obv:** Elephant left **Rev:** Rosettes **Note:** Weight varies: 2.66-2.92 grams.

Date	Mintage	Good	VG	F	VF	XF
AH1198	—	3.00	4.50	7.00	12.00	—
AH1200	—	3.00	4.50	7.00	12.00	—
AH1201	—	3.00	4.50	7.00	12.00	—
AM1215	—	3.00	4.50	7.00	12.00	—
AM1216	—	2.00	3.00	5.00	9.00	—
AM1217	—	3.00	4.50	7.00	12.00	—
AM1218	—	3.00	4.50	7.00	12.00	—

Mint: Patan
KM# 121.4 1/4 PAISA
Copper **Obv:** Elephant right **Rev:** "Patan" at top **Note:** Weight varies: 2.66-2.92 grams.

Date	Mintage	Good	VG	F	VF	XF
AH1200	—	3.00	5.00	8.00	15.00	—
AM1221	—	3.00	4.50	7.00	12.00	—
AM1222	—	2.00	3.00	5.00	9.00	—

Mint: Patan
KM# 121.8 1/4 PAISA
Copper **Rev:** "Patan" at top, without rosettes **Note:** Weight varies: 2.66-2.92 grams.

Date	Mintage	Good	VG	F	VF	XF
ND(1782-99)	—	2.50	4.00	7.00	12.00	—

Mint: Patan
KM# 121.2 1/4 PAISA
Copper **Rev:** Without rosettes **Note:** Weight varies: 2.66-2.92 grams.

Date	Mintage	Good	VG	F	VF	XF
AM1220 (1791)	—	5.00	7.00	11.00	18.00	—
AM1221 (1792)	—	3.00	4.50	7.00	12.00	—

Mint: Patan
KM# 121.3 1/4 PAISA
Copper **Obv:** Retrograde date **Rev:** "Patan" at bottom **Note:** Weight varies: 2.66-2.92 grams.

Date	Mintage	Good	VG	F	VF	XF
AM1222 (1793)	—	3.00	4.50	7.00	12.00	—
AM1223 (1794)	—	3.00	4.50	7.00	12.00	—

Mint: Patan
KM# 121.5 1/4 PAISA
Copper **Rev:** "Patan" at bottom, Persian "Akhtar" at top **Note:** Weight varies: 2.66-2.92 grams.

Date	Mintage	Good	VG	F	VF	XF
AM1222 (1793)	—	3.00	4.50	7.00	12.00	—
AM1224//1 (1795)	—	3.00	4.50	7.00	12.00	—

Mint: Patan
KM# 121.6 1/4 PAISA
Copper **Obv:** Persian "Be" above elephant **Rev:** Retrograde date **Note:** Weight varies: 2.66-2.92 grams.

Date	Mintage	Good	VG	F	VF	XF
AM1225//2 (1796)	—	1.50	2.75	4.50	7.50	—

Mint: Patan
KM# 121.9 1/4 PAISA
Copper **Rev:** Normal date **Note:** Weight varies: 2.66-2.92 grams.

Date	Mintage	Good	VG	F	VF	XF
AM1225//2 (1796)	—	1.50	2.75	4.50	7.50	—

Mint: Patan
KM# 121.7 1/4 PAISA
Copper **Obv:** Persian "Te" above elephant **Rev:** Retrograde date **Note:** Weight varies: 2.66-2.92 grams.

Date	Mintage	Good	VG	F	VF	XF
AM1226//3 (1797)	—	1.50	2.50	4.00	7.50	—

Mint: Patan
KM# 121.10 1/4 PAISA
Copper **Rev:** Normal date **Note:** Weight varies: 2.66-2.92 grams.

Date	Mintage	Good	VG	F	VF	XF
AM1226//3 (1796)	—	1.50	2.50	4.00	7.50	—

Mint: Salamabad
KM# 131 1/4 PAISA
Copper

Date	Mintage	Good	VG	F	VF	XF
AM1216 (1787)	—	30.00	45.00	60.00	80.00	—

Mint: Zafarabad
KM# 141 1/4 PAISA
Copper **Obv:** Retrograde date

Date	Mintage	Good	VG	F	VF	XF
AM1216 (1787)	—	30.00	40.00	55.00	75.00	—

Mint: Bengalur
KM# 32.1 1/2 PAISA
Copper **Obv:** Elephant right **Note:** Weight varies: 5.44-5.77 grams.

Date	Mintage	Good	VG	F	VF	XF
AM1215 (1786)	—	2.50	4.00	7.00	12.00	—
AM1216 (1787)	—	1.75	3.00	5.00	10.00	—
AM1219 (1790)	—	3.00	5.00	9.00	17.00	—

Mint: Bengalur
KM# 32.2 1/2 PAISA
Copper **Obv:** Elephant left **Note:** Weight varies: 5.44-5.77 grams.

Date	Mintage	Good	VG	F	VF	XF
AM1216 (1787)	—	2.00	3.50	6.00	12.00	—
AM1217 (1788)	—	2.00	3.50	6.00	12.00	—
AM1218 (1789)	—	2.00	3.50	6.00	12.00	—
AM1219 (1790)	—	2.00	3.50	6.00	12.00	—
AM1220 (1791)	—	2.00	3.50	6.00	12.00	—

Mint: Faiz Hisar
KM# 42.2 1/2 PAISA
Copper **Obv:** Elephant left within circle of dots **Rev:** Legend within circle of dots **Note:** Weight varies 5.38-5.77 grams.

Date	Mintage	Good	VG	F	VF	XF
AM1216 (1787)	—	2.00	3.50	5.00	12.00	—
AM1217 (1788)	—	2.00	3.50	5.00	12.00	—
AM1218 (1789)	—	2.00	3.50	5.00	12.00	—

Mint: Faiz Hisar
KM# 42.3 1/2 PAISA
Copper **Obv:** Elephant right **Note:** Weight varies 5.38-5.77 grams.

Date	Mintage	Good	VG	F	VF	XF
AM1221 (1792)	—	2.00	3.50	5.00	12.00	—
AM1222 (1793)	—	2.00	3.50	5.00	12.00	—
AM1223 (1794)	—	2.00	3.50	5.00	12.00	—

Mint: Faiz Hisar
KM# 42.4 1/2 PAISA
Copper **Obv:** Persian "Alif" above elephant **Note:** Weight varies 5.38-5.77 grams.

Date	Mintage	Good	VG	F	VF	XF
AM1224//1 (1795)	—	2.00	3.50	5.00	12.00	—

Mint: Faiz Hisar
KM# 42.5 1/2 PAISA
Copper **Obv:** Persian "Be" above elephant **Note:** Weight varies 5.38-5.77 grams.

Date	Mintage	Good	VG	F	VF	XF
AM1225//2 (1795)	—	2.00	3.50	5.00	12.00	—

Mint: Faiz Hisar
KM# 42.6 1/2 PAISA
Copper **Obv:** Persian "Be" and date above elephant **Note:** Weight varies 5.38-5.77 grams.

Date	Mintage	Good	VG	F	VF	XF
AM1225//2 (1796)	—	2.00	3.50	5.00	12.00	—

Mint: Faiz Hisar
KM# 42.7 1/2 PAISA
Copper **Obv:** Persian "Te" and date above elephant **Note:** Weight varies 5.38-5.77 grams.

Date	Mintage	Good	VG	F	VF	XF
AM1226//3 (1797)	—	2.00	3.50	5.00	12.00	—

Mint: Faiz Hisar
KM# 42.1 1/2 PAISA
Copper **Note:** Weight varies: 5.38-5.77 grams.

Date	Mintage	Good	VG	F	VF	XF
AM1215 (1786)	—	2.00	3.50	5.00	12.00	—
AM1216 (1787)	—	2.00	3.50	5.00	12.00	—

Mint: Farrukhi
KM# 52 1/2 PAISA
Copper

Date	Mintage	Good	VG	F	VF	XF
AM1217 (1788)	—	2.50	5.00	9.00	17.00	—
AM1218 (1789)	—	2.50	5.00	9.00	17.00	—

Mint: Farrukhyab-Hisar
KM# 62 1/2 PAISA
Copper **Note:** Weight varies: 5.44-5.77 grams.

Date	Mintage	Good	VG	F	VF	XF
AM1215 (1786)	—	2.00	3.50	7.00	12.00	—
AM1216 (1787)	—	2.00	3.50	7.00	12.00	—
AM1217 (1788)	—	2.00	3.50	7.00	12.00	—
AM1218 (1789)	—	2.00	3.50	7.00	12.00	—
AM1219 (1790)	—	2.00	3.50	7.00	12.00	—

Mint: Khaliqabad
KM# 82 1/2 PAISA
5.3100 g., Copper

Date	Mintage	Good	VG	F	VF	XF
AM1215 (1786)	—	3.00	5.00	10.00	18.00	—
AM1217 (1787)	—	3.00	5.00	10.00	18.00	—
AM1218 (1788)	—	3.00	5.00	10.00	18.00	—

Mint: Khurshed-Sawad
KM# 92 1/2 PAISA
Copper

Date	Mintage	Good	VG	F	VF	XF
AM1217 (1788)	—	6.00	12.00	20.00	30.00	—

Mint: Nagar
KM# 102.1 1/2 PAISA
Copper **Obv:** Elephant right **Note:** Weight varies: 5.18-5.83 grams.

Date	Mintage	Good	VG	F	VF	XF
AH1200	—	2.00	3.00	5.00	10.00	—
AM1215	—	2.00	3.00	5.00	10.00	—

Mint: Nagar
KM# 102.2 1/2 PAISA
Copper **Obv:** Persian "Alif" above elephant **Note:** Weight varies 5.18-5.83 grams.

Date	Mintage	Good	VG	F	VF	XF
AM1224//1 (1796)	—	2.00	3.00	5.00	10.00	—

Mint: Nagar
KM# 102.3 1/2 PAISA
Copper **Obv:** Persian "Be" above elephant **Note:** Weight varies 5.18-5.83 grams.

Date	Mintage	Good	VG	F	VF	XF
AM1225//2 (1797)	—	2.00	3.00	5.00	10.00	—

Mint: Nagar
KM# 102.4 1/2 PAISA
Copper **Obv:** Persian "Te" above elephant **Note:** Weight varies 5.18-5.83 grams.

Date	Mintage	Good	VG	F	VF	XF
AM1226//3 (1798)	—	2.00	3.00	5.00	10.00	—

Mint: Nagar
KM# 102.5 1/2 PAISA
Copper **Obv:** Persian "Se" above elehant **Note:** Weight varies 5.18-5.83 grams.

Date	Mintage	Good	VG	F	VF	XF
AM1227//4 (1799)	—	2.00	3.00	5.00	10.00	—

Mint: Nagar
KM# 102.6 1/2 PAISA
Copper **Obv:** Elephant left **Rev:** Similar to KM#102.1 **Note:** Weight varies 5.18-5.83 grams.

Date	Mintage	Good	VG	F	VF	XF
AM1217 (1788)	—	2.00	3.00	5.00	10.00	—

Mint: Nagar
KM# 102.7 1/2 PAISA
Copper **Note:** Weight varies 5.18-5.83 grams.

Date	Mintage	Good	VG	F	VF	XF
AM1222 (1793)	—	2.00	3.00	5.00	10.00	—

Mint: Nazarbar
KM# 112 1/2 PAISA
5.5100 g., Copper **Obv:** Retrograde date

Date	Mintage	Good	VG	F	VF	XF
AM1216 (1787)	—	15.00	25.00	35.00	50.00	—

Mint: Patan
KM# 122.1 1/2 PAISA
Copper **Obv:** Elephant left **Note:** Weight varies: 5.51-5.77 grams.

Date	Mintage	Good	VG	F	VF	XF
AH1200	—	2.00	3.00	5.00	10.00	—
AH1201	—	2.00	3.00	5.00	10.00	—
AM1215	—	1.50	2.50	4.00	8.00	—
AM1216	—	1.50	2.50	4.00	8.00	—
AM1217	—	1.50	2.50	4.00	8.00	—
AM1218	—	2.00	3.00	5.00	10.00	—
AM1219	—	2.00	3.00	5.00	10.00	—
AM1220	—	1.50	2.50	4.00	8.00	—
AM1221	—	1.50	2.50	4.00	8.00	—
AM1222	—	2.00	3.00	5.00	10.00	—
AM1223	—	2.00	3.00	5.00	10.00	—

Mint: Patan
KM# 122.8 1/2 PAISA
Copper **Rev:** Without rosettes **Note:** Weight varies: 5.51-5.77 grams.

Date	Mintage	Good	VG	F	VF	XF
ND(1782-99)	—	2.00	3.00	5.00	10.00	—

Mint: Patan
KM# 122.2 1/2 PAISA
Copper **Obv:** Elephant right **Rev:** "Patan" at top **Note:** Weight varies: 5.51-5.77 grams.

Date	Mintage	Good	VG	F	VF	XF
AM1220 (1791)	—	2.00	3.00	5.00	10.00	—
AM1221 (1792)	—	1.50	2.50	4.00	8.00	—
AM1222 (1793)	—	1.50	2.50	4.00	8.00	—
AM1223 (1794)	—	1.50	2.50	4.00	8.00	—

Mint: Patan
KM# 122.3 1/2 PAISA
Copper **Rev:** "Patan" in center, Persian "Bahram" at top **Note:** Weight varies: 5.51-5.77 grams.

Date	Mintage	Good	VG	F	VF	XF
AM1221 (1792)	—	2.00	3.00	5.00	10.00	—
AM1222 (1793)	—	2.00	3.00	5.00	10.00	—

Mint: Patan
KM# 122.4 1/2 PAISA
Copper **Rev:** "Patan" at lower left, Persian "Bahram" at top **Note:** Weight varies: 5.51-5.77 grams.

Date	Mintage	Good	VG	F	VF	XF
AM1222 (1793)	—	2.00	3.00	5.00	10.00	—
AM1223 (1794)	—	2.00	3.00	5.00	10.00	—

Mint: Patan
KM# 122.10 1/2 PAISA
Copper **Obv:** Elephant left **Note:** Weight varies: 5.51-5.77 grams.

Date	Mintage	Good	VG	F	VF	XF
AM1222 (1793)	—	2.00	3.00	5.00	10.00	—
AM1223 (1794)	—	2.00	3.00	5.00	10.00	—

Mint: Patan
KM# 122.5 1/2 PAISA
Copper **Obv:** Persian "Alif" at top **Note:** Weight varies: 5.51-5.77 grams.

Date	Mintage	Good	VG	F	VF	XF
AM1224//1 (1795)	—	1.50	2.50	4.00	8.00	—

Mint: Patan
KM# 122.6 1/2 PAISA
Copper **Obv:** Persian "Be" at top **Note:** Weight varies: 5.51-5.77 grams.

Date	Mintage	Good	VG	F	VF	XF
AM1225//2 (1796)	—	1.50	2.50	4.00	8.00	—

Mint: Patan
KM# 122.7 1/2 PAISA
Copper **Obv:** Persian "Te" at top **Note:** Weight varies: 5.51-5.77 grams.

Date	Mintage	Good	VG	F	VF	XF
AM1226//3 (1797)	—	2.00	3.00	5.00	10.00	—

Mint: Salamabad
KM# 132 1/2 PAISA
Copper **Obv:** Retrograde date

Date	Mintage	Good	VG	F	VF	XF
AM1216 (1787)	—	30.00	40.00	55.00	75.00	—
AM1217 (1788)	—	30.00	40.00	55.00	75.00	—
AM1218 (1789)	—	30.00	40.00	55.00	75.00	—

Mint: Zafarabad
KM# 142 1/2 PAISA
Copper **Obv:** Retrograde date **Note:** Weight varies: 5.70-5.96 grams.

Date	Mintage	Good	VG	F	VF	XF
AM1215 (1786)	—	30.00	40.00	55.00	75.00	—
AM1216 (1787)	—	30.00	40.00	55.00	75.00	—
AM1217 (1788)	—	30.00	40.00	55.00	75.00	—
AM1218 (1789)	—	30.00	40.00	55.00	75.00	—

Mint: Bengalur
KM# 33.1 PAISA
10.5600 g., Copper **Obv:** Elephant right

Date	Mintage	Good	VG	F	VF	XF
AH1200	—	6.00	12.00	20.00	35.00	—
AM1215	—	—	—	—	—	—
AM1216	—	6.00	12.00	20.00	35.00	—

Mint: Bengalur
KM# 33.2 PAISA
10.5600 g., Copper **Obv:** Elephant left **Note:** Varieties exist.

Date	Mintage	Good	VG	F	VF	XF
AM1217 (1788)	—	4.00	8.00	15.00	25.00	—
AM1218 (1789)	—	4.00	8.00	15.00	25.00	—
AM1219 (1790)	—	4.00	8.00	15.00	25.00	—

Mint: Faiz Hisar
KM# 43.1 PAISA
Copper **Obv:** Elephant left in circle of rosettes **Rev:** Legend in circle of rosettes **Note:** Weight varies 11.02-11.41 grams.

Date	Mintage	Good	VG	F	VF	XF
AM1215 (1786)	—	2.00	3.50	7.00	15.00	—
AM1216 (1787)	—	2.00	3.50	7.00	15.00	—

Mint: Faiz Hisar
KM# 43.2 PAISA
Copper **Obv:** Elephant left in circle of dots **Rev:** Legend in circle of dots **Note:** Weight varies 11.02-11.41 grams.

Date	Mintage	Good	VG	F	VF	XF
AM1218 (1789)	—	2.00	3.50	7.00	15.00	—

Mint: Faiz Hisar
KM# 43.3 PAISA
Copper **Obv:** Elephant right **Note:** Weight varies 11.02-11.41 grams.

Date	Mintage	Good	VG	F	VF	XF
AM1216 (1786)	—	2.00	3.50	7.00	15.00	—
AM1217 (1787)	—	2.00	3.50	7.00	15.00	—
AM1218 (1788)	—	2.00	3.50	7.00	15.00	—
AM1221 (1792)	—	2.00	3.50	7.00	15.00	—
AM1222 (1793)	—	2.00	3.50	7.00	15.00	—

Mint: Faiz Hisar
KM# 43.4 PAISA
Copper **Obv:** Persian "Alif" above elephant **Note:** Weight varies 11.02-11.41 grams.

Date	Mintage	Good	VG	F	VF	XF
AM1224//1 (1795)	—	2.00	3.50	7.00	15.00	—

Mint: Faiz Hisar
KM# 43.5 PAISA
Copper **Obv:** Persian "Be" above elephant **Note:** Weight varies 11.02-11.41 grams.

Date	Mintage	Good	VG	F	VF	XF
AM1225//2 (1796)	—	2.00	3.50	7.00	15.00	—

Mint: Faiz Hisar
KM# 43.6 PAISA
Copper **Obv:** Persian "Te" above elephant **Note:** Weight varies 11.02-11.41 grams. Struck at Faiz Hisar Mint.

Date	Mintage	Good	VG	F	VF	XF
AM1226//3 (1797)	—	2.00	3.50	7.00	15.00	—

Mint: Farrukhi
KM# 53.1 PAISA
Copper **Obv:** Elephant right in corded border **Note:** Weight varies: 11.15-11.73 grams.

Date	Mintage	Good	VG	F	VF	XF
AM1216 (1787)	—	4.00	7.00	12.00	25.00	—

Mint: Farrukhi
KM# 53.2 PAISA
Copper **Obv:** Elephant left in beaded border **Note:** Weight varies: 11.15-11.73 grams.

Date	Mintage	Good	VG	F	VF	XF
AM1216 (1787)	—	3.00	5.50	11.00	20.00	—
AM1217 (1788)	—	3.00	5.50	11.00	20.00	—
AM1218 (1789)	—	3.00	5.50	11.00	20.00	—
AM1219 (1790)	—	3.00	5.50	11.00	20.00	—

Mint: Farrukhyab-Hisar
KM# 63.1 PAISA
10.5600 g., Copper **Obv:** Elephant left

Date	Mintage	Good	VG	F	VF	XF
AH1201 (1786)	—	3.00	6.00	11.00	20.00	—
AM1215 (1786)	—	3.00	6.00	11.00	20.00	—
AM1216 (1787)	—	3.00	6.00	11.00	20.00	—
AM1217 (1788)	—	3.00	6.00	11.00	20.00	—
AM1218 (1789)	—	3.00	6.00	11.00	20.00	—
AM1219 (1790)	—	3.00	6.00	11.00	20.00	—

Mint: Farrukhyab-Hisar
KM# 63.2 PAISA
10.5600 g., Copper **Obv:** Elephant right

Date	Mintage	Good	VG	F	VF	XF
AM1215 (1786)	—	4.00	7.00	15.00	25.00	—

Mint: Kalikut
KM# 72 PAISA
Copper **Rev:** Date **Note:** Weight varies: 11.21-11.41 grams.

Date	Mintage	Good	VG	F	VF	XF
AH1199	—	—	—	—	—	—

Mint: Kalikut
KM# 73 PAISA

Copper **Obv:** Retrograde date **Note:** Weight varies: 11.21-11.41 grams.

Date	Mintage	Good	VG	F	VF	XF
ND(1782-99)	—	6.00	10.00	18.00	30.00	—
AH1198	—	5.00	8.00	15.00	25.00	—
AH1199	—	5.00	8.00	15.00	25.00	—
AH1200	—	5.00	8.00	15.00	25.00	—
AM1215	—	4.50	7.00	12.00	20.00	—

Mint: Kalikut
KM# A72 PAISA

Copper **Note:** Weight varies: 12.00-12.80 grams.

Date	Mintage	Good	VG	F	VF	XF
AH1198	—	4.00	8.00	15.00	22.00	—

Mint: Khaliqabad
KM# 83 PAISA

Copper

Date	Mintage	Good	VG	F	VF	XF
AM1215 (1786)	—	6.00	11.00	20.00	30.00	—
AM1217 (1788)	—	6.00	11.00	20.00	30.00	—

Mint: Khurshed-Sawad
KM# 93 PAISA

11.1500 g., Copper **Obv:** Retrograde date

Date	Mintage	Good	VG	F	VF	XF
AM1217 (1788)	—	5.00	9.00	15.00	25.00	—
AM1218 (1789)	—	5.00	9.00	15.00	25.00	—

Mint: Nagar
KM# 103.1 PAISA

Copper **Note:** Weight varies: 10.82-12.51 grams.

Date	Mintage	Good	VG	F	VF	XF
AH1197	—	3.00	5.00	9.00	18.00	—
AH1198	—	3.00	5.00	9.00	18.00	—
AH1199	—	3.00	5.00	9.00	18.00	—

Mint: Nagar
KM# 103.2 PAISA

Copper **Obv:** Rosette above elephant's head **Note:** Weight varies: 10.82-12.51 grams.

Date	Mintage	Good	VG	F	VF	XF
AH1197	—	3.00	5.00	9.00	18.00	—

Mint: Nagar
KM# 103.4 PAISA

Copper **Rev:** Date at bottom **Note:** Weight varies 10.82-12.51 grams.

Date	Mintage	Good	VG	F	VF	XF
AM(1)216/1225 (1788)	—	3.00	5.00	9.00	18.00	—
AM1223/1225 (1795)	—	3.00	5.00	9.00	18.00	—

Mint: Nagar
KM# 103.6 PAISA

Copper **Obv:** Persian "Alif" above elephant **Rev:** Retrograde date **Note:** Weight varies 10.82-12.51 grams.

Date	Mintage	Good	VG	F	VF	XF
AM1224//1 (1796)	—	4.00	7.00	12.00	22.00	—

Mint: Nagar
KM# 103.7 PAISA

Copper **Obv:** Persian "Be" above elephant **Note:** Weight varies 10.82-12.51 grams.

Date	Mintage	Good	VG	F	VF	XF
AM1225//2 (1797)	—	4.00	7.00	12.00	22.00	—

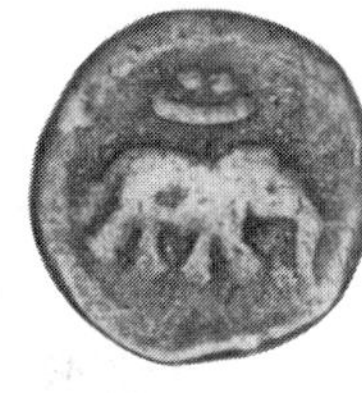

Mint: Nagar
KM# 103.8 PAISA

Copper **Obv:** Persian "Te" above elephant **Note:** Weight varies 10.82-12.51 grams.

Date	Mintage	Good	VG	F	VF	XF
AM1226//3 (1798)	—	4.00	7.00	12.00	22.00	—

Mint: Nagar
KM# 103.9 PAISA

Copper **Obv:** Persian "Se" above elephant **Rev:** Retrograde date **Note:** Weight varies 10.82-12.51 grams.

Date	Mintage	Good	VG	F	VF	XF
AM1227//4 (1799)	—	3.50	6.00	10.00	18.00	—

Mint: Nagar
KM# 103.10 PAISA

Copper **Obv:** Elephant left, retrograde date **Note:** Weight varies 10.82-12.51 grams.

Date	Mintage	Good	VG	F	VF	XF
AM1216 (1787)	—	2.75	5.00	8.00	15.00	—
AM1217 (1788)	—	2.75	5.00	8.00	15.00	—
AM1218 (1789)	—	2.75	5.00	8.00	15.00	—
AM1219 (1790)	—	2.75	5.00	8.00	15.00	—
AM1220 (1791)	—	2.75	5.00	8.00	15.00	—
AM1221 (1792)	—	2.75	5.00	8.00	15.00	—

Mint: Nagar
KM# 103.11 PAISA

Copper **Obv:** Retrograde date **Rev:** "Nagar" at bottom **Note:** Weight varies 10.82-12.51 grams.

Date	Mintage	Good	VG	F	VF	XF
AM1222 (1793)	—	2.75	5.00	8.00	15.00	—
AM1223 (1794)	—	2.75	5.00	8.00	15.00	—

Mint: Nagar
KM# 103.12 PAISA

Copper **Obv:** Persiant "Alif" above elephant, retrograde date **Note:** Weight varies 10.82-12.51 grams.

Date	Mintage	Good	VG	F	VF	XF
AM1224//1 (1796)	—	3.50	6.00	10.00	18.00	—

Mint: Nagar
KM# 103.5 PAISA

Copper **Obv:** Similar to KM#103.3 **Rev:** Similar to KM#103.4 **Note:** Weight varies 10.82-12.51 grams. Struck at Nagar Mint.

Date	Mintage	Good	VG	F	VF	XF
AM1222 (1793)	—	3.00	5.00	9.00	18.00	—
AM1223 (1794)	—	3.00	5.00	9.00	18.00	—

Mint: Nagar
KM# 103.3 PAISA

Copper **Obv:** Date above elephant **Note:** Weight varies: 10.82-12.51 grams.

Date	Mintage	Good	VG	F	VF	XF
AH1200 (1785)	—	3.00	5.00	9.00	18.00	—
AM1215 (1786)	—	3.00	5.00	9.00	18.00	—
AH(1)216 (1787)	—	3.00	5.00	9.00	18.00	—

Mint: Nazarbar
KM# 113 PAISA

Copper **Obv:** Retrograde date

Date	Mintage	Good	VG	F	VF	XF
AM1216 (1787)	—	15.00	25.00	35.00	50.00	—

Mint: Patan
KM# A123 PAISA

Copper **Obv:** Elephant right **Note:** Weight varies: 10.82-12.51 grams.

Date	Mintage	Good	VG	F	VF	XF
AH1195	—	—	—	—	—	—

Mint: Patan
KM# 123.3 PAISA

Copper **Obv:** Elephant right **Rev:** "Patan" at top **Note:** Weight varies: 10.82-12.51 grams.

Date	Mintage	Good	VG	F	VF	XF
AH1200	—	2.50	6.00	12.00	18.00	—
AH1260 Error for 1220	—	2.50	6.00	12.00	18.00	—
AM1221	—	2.50	6.00	12.00	18.00	—
AM1222	—	2.50	6.00	12.00	18.00	—
AM1223	—	2.50	6.00	12.00	18.00	—

Mint: Patan
KM# 123.9 PAISA

Copper **Rev:** Mint name above **Note:** Weight varies: 10.82-12.51 grams.

Date	Mintage	Good	VG	F	VF	XF
ND(1782-99)	—	2.50	6.00	12.00	18.00	—

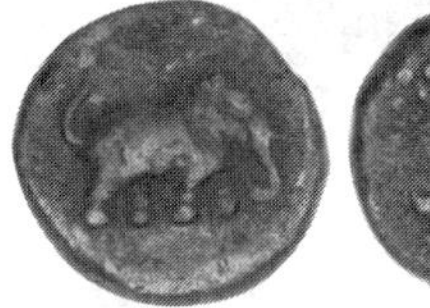
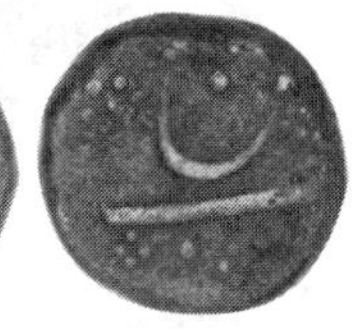

Mint: Patan
KM# 123.12 PAISA

Copper **Rev:** Rosettes **Note:** Weight varies: 10.82-12.51 grams.

Date	Mintage	Good	VG	F	VF	XF
ND(1782-99)	—	—	—	—	—	—

Mint: Patan
KM# 123.1 PAISA

Copper **Obv:** Elephant left **Note:** Weight varies: 10.82-12.51 grams. AM dates from 1216 to 1222 are retrograde.

Date	Mintage	Good	VG	F	VF	XF
AH1192	—	2.50	6.00	12.00	18.00	—
AH1200	—	2.50	6.00	12.00	18.00	—
AH1201	—	2.50	6.00	12.00	18.00	—
AM1215	—	2.00	4.50	9.00	15.00	—

Date	Mintage	Good	VG	F	VF	XF
AM1216	—	2.00	4.50	9.00	15.00	—
AM1217	—	2.00	4.50	9.00	15.00	—
AM1218	—	2.00	4.50	9.00	15.00	—
AM1219	—	2.00	4.50	9.00	15.00	—
AM1220	—	2.00	4.50	9.00	15.00	—
AM1221	—	2.00	4.50	9.00	15.00	—
AM1222	—	2.00	4.50	9.00	15.00	—

Mint: Patan
KM# 123.2 PAISA

Copper **Obv:** Persian legend above elephant **Rev:** Persian "Zahra" at top **Note:** Weight varies: 10.82-12.51 grams.

Date	Mintage	Good	VG	F	VF	XF
AM1221 (1792)	—	2.00	4.50	9.00	15.00	—
AM1222 (1793)	—	2.00	4.50	9.00	15.00	—

Mint: Patan
KM# 123.11 PAISA

Copper **Note:** Weight varies: 10.82-12.51 grams.

Date	Mintage	Good	VG	F	VF	XF
AM1222 (1793)	—	—	—	—	—	—
AM1223 (1794)	—	—	—	—	—	—

Mint: Patan
KM# 123.4 PAISA

Copper **Rev:** "Patan" in center **Note:** Weight varies: 10.82-12.51 grams.

Date	Mintage	Good	VG	F	VF	XF
AM1221 (1792)	—	2.00	4.50	9.00	15.00	—

Mint: Patan
KM# 123.10 PAISA

Copper **Obv:** Only date above elephant, "Zahrah" at top **Rev:** Mint name at top **Note:** Weight varies: 10.82-12.51 grams.

Date	Mintage	Good	VG	F	VF	XF
AM1221 (1792)	—	4.00	8.00	15.00	22.00	—

Mint: Patan
KM# 123.5 PAISA

Copper **Obv:** Retrograde date **Rev:** "Patan" at bottom, "Zahrah" at top **Note:** Weight varies: 10.82-12.51 grams.

Date	Mintage	Good	VG	F	VF	XF
AM1222 (1793)	—	2.00	4.50	9.00	15.00	—
AM1223 (1794)	—	2.00	4.50	9.00	15.00	—

Mint: Patan
KM# 123.6 PAISA

Copper **Obv:** Persian "Alif" above elephant **Rev:** Retrograde date **Note:** Weight varies: 10.82-12.51 grams.

Date	Mintage	Good	VG	F	VF	XF
AM1224//1 (1795)	—	4.00	8.00	15.00	22.00	—

Mint: Patan
KM# 123.7 PAISA

Copper **Obv:** Persian "Be" above elephant **Note:** Weight varies: 10.82-12.51 grams.

Date	Mintage	Good	VG	F	VF	XF
AM1225//2 (1796)	—	4.00	8.00	15.00	22.00	—

Mint: Patan
KM# 123.8 PAISA

Copper **Obv:** Persian "Te" above elephant **Note:** Weight varies: 10.82-12.51 grams.

Date	Mintage	Good	VG	F	VF	XF
AM1226//3 (1797)	—	4.00	8.00	15.00	22.00	—

Mint: Patan
KM# 123.13 PAISA

Copper **Obv:** Persian "Sheen" above elephant **Note:** Weight varies: 10.82-12.51 grams. Struck at Patan Mint (Seringapatan).

Date	Mintage	Good	VG	F	VF	XF
AM1227//4 (1798)	—	4.00	8.00	15.00	22.00	—

Mint: Sakkar Kot
KM# A130 PAISA

Copper **Obv:** Elephant right **Rev:** Date **Note:** Struck at Sakkar Kot Mint.

Date	Mintage	VG	F	VF	XF	Unc
AH1198	—	—	—	—	—	—

Mint: Salamabad
KM# 133 PAISA

Copper **Obv:** Retrograde date

Date	Mintage	Good	VG	F	VF	XF
AM1216 (1787)	—	40.00	55.00	75.00	100	—
AM1217 (1788)	—	40.00	55.00	75.00	100	—
AM1218 (1789)	—	40.00	55.00	75.00	100	—

Mint: Zafarabad
KM# 143 PAISA

Copper **Obv:** Retrograde date

Date	Mintage	Good	VG	F	VF	XF
AM1216 (1787)	—	30.00	40.00	55.00	75.00	—
AM1218 (1788)	—	30.00	40.00	55.00	75.00	—

Mint: Farrukhi
KM# 54 2 PAISA

22.1600 g., Copper

Date	Mintage	Good	VG	F	VF	XF
AM1217//6 (1788)	—	—	—	—	—	—
AM1218 (1789)	—	25.00	40.00	65.00	125	—

Mint: Farrukhyab-Hisar
KM# 64 2 PAISA

Copper

Date	Mintage	Good	VG	F	VF	XF
AM1218 (1789)	—	25.00	40.00	65.00	125	—
AM1219 (1790)	—	25.00	40.00	65.00	125	—

Mint: Nagar
KM# 104.1 2 PAISA

Copper **Obv:** Elephant right **Rev:** Without rosettes **Note:** Weight varies 21.45-22.81 grams.

Date	Mintage	Good	VG	F	VF	XF
AM1218 (1789)	—	18.00	30.00	45.00	90.00	—

Mint: Nagar
KM# 104.2 2 PAISA

Copper **Obv:** Persian "Alif" in flag **Rev:** Rosettes, retrograde date **Note:** Weight varies 21.45-22.81 grams.

Date	Mintage	Good	VG	F	VF	XF
AM1224//1 (1796)	—	18.00	30.00	45.00	90.00	—

Mint: Nagar
KM# 104.4 2 PAISA

Copper **Obv:** Persian "Te" in flag **Rev:** Retrograde date **Note:** Weight varies 21.45-22.81 grams.

Date	Mintage	Good	VG	F	VF	XF
AM1226//3 (1798)	—	18.00	30.00	45.00	90.00	—

Mint: Nagar
KM# 104.5 2 PAISA

Copper **Obv:** Elephant left, retrograde date **Rev:** Without rosettes **Note:** Weight varies 21.45-22.81 grams.

Date	Mintage	Good	VG	F	VF	XF
AM1222 (1793)	—	18.00	30.00	45.00	90.00	—
AM1223 (1794)	—	18.00	30.00	45.00	90.00	—

Mint: Nagar
KM# 104.3 2 PAISA

Copper **Obv:** Persian "Be" in flag **Note:** Weight varies 21.45-22.81 grams. Struck at Nagar Mint.

Date	Mintage	Good	VG	F	VF	XF
AM1225//2 (1797)	—	18.00	30.00	45.00	90.00	—

Mint: Patan
KM# 124.1 2 PAISA

Copper **Obv:** Elephant left with trunk raised **Note:** Weight varies: 21.45-22.81 grams.

Date	Mintage	Good	VG	F	VF	XF
AM1218 (1789)	—	12.00	20.00	35.00	60.00	—
AM1219 (1790)	—	12.00	20.00	35.00	60.00	—
AM1220 (1791)	—	—	—	—	—	—
Note: Reported, not confirmed						
AM1221 (1792)	—	12.00	20.00	35.00	60.00	—

Mint: Patan
KM# 124.2 2 PAISA

Copper **Obv:** Elephant right with trunk raised, retrograde date **Rev:** Legend "Patan" at top left **Note:** Weight varies: 21.45-22.81 grams.

Date	Mintage	Good	VG	F	VF	XF
AM1218 (1789)	—	12.00	20.00	35.00	60.00	—
AM1219 (1790)	—	12.00	20.00	35.00	60.00	—
AM1220 (1791)	—	—	—	—	—	—
Note: Reported, not confirmed						

Mint: Patan
KM# 124.3 2 PAISA

Copper **Obv:** Persian legend above elephant **Rev:** "Patan" in center **Note:** Weight varies: 21.45-22.81 grams.

Date	Mintage	Good	VG	F	VF	XF
AM1221 (1792)	—	12.00	20.00	35.00	60.00	—

Mint: Patan
KM# 124.4 2 PAISA

Copper **Obv:** Persian legend below flag, retrograde date **Note:** Weight varies: 21.45-22.81 grams.

Date	Mintage	Good	VG	F	VF	XF
AM1222 (1793)	—	12.00	20.00	35.00	60.00	—
AM1223 (1794)	—	20.00	35.00	55.00	90.00	—

Mint: Patan
KM# 124.5 2 PAISA
Copper **Obv:** Persian "Alif" in flag **Rev:** Retrograde date **Note:** Weight varies: 21.45-22.81 grams.

Date	Mintage	Good	VG	F	VF	XF
AM1224//1 (1795)	—	12.00	20.00	35.00	60.00	—

Mint: Patan
KM# 124.6 2 PAISA
Copper **Obv:** Persian "Be" in flag **Note:** Weight varies: 21.45-22.81 grams. Struck at Patan Mint (Seringapatan).

Date	Mintage	Good	VG	F	VF	XF
AM1225//2 (1796)	—	17.50	30.00	50.00	80.00	—
AM1226//3 (1811)	—	—	—	—	—	—

Mint: Patan
KM# A125 1/32 RUPEE
Silver **Note:** Weight varies: .34-.36 grams.

Date	Mintage	VG	F	VF	XF	Unc
AM1222//10 (1793) Rare	—	—	—	—	—	—

Mint: Patan
KM# B125 1/16 RUPEE
Silver **Note:** Weight varies: 0.68-0.72 grams.

Date	Mintage	VG	F	VF	XF	Unc
AM1220//10 (1791)	—	45.00	70.00	100	150	—
AM1221//11 (1792)	—	45.00	70.00	100	150	—
AM1222//12 (1793)	—	45.00	70.00	100	150	—
AM1223//13 (1794)	—	45.00	70.00	100	150	—
AM1224//14 (1795)	—	45.00	70.00	100	150	—
AM1225//15 (1796)	—	45.00	70.00	100	150	—
AM1226//16 (1797)	—	45.00	70.00	100	150	—

Mint: Patan
KM# C125 1/8 RUPEE
Silver **Note:** Weight varies: 1.34-1.45 grams.

Date	Mintage	VG	F	VF	XF	Unc
AM1218//8 (1789)	—	30.00	50.00	70.00	100	—
AM1220//10 (1791)	—	30.00	50.00	70.00	100	—
AM1221//11 (1792)	—	30.00	50.00	70.00	100	—
AM1222//12 (1793)	—	30.00	50.00	70.00	100	—
AM1223//13 (1794)	—	30.00	50.00	70.00	100	—
AM1224//14 (1795)	—	30.00	50.00	70.00	100	—
AM1225//15 (1796)	—	30.00	50.00	70.00	100	—
AM1226//16 (1797)	—	30.00	50.00	70.00	100	—

Mint: Patan
KM# D125 1/4 RUPEE
Silver **Note:** Weight varies: 2.68-2.90 grams.

Date	Mintage	VG	F	VF	XF	Unc
AM1216//6 (1787)	—	30.00	50.00	70.00	100	—
AM1217//7 (1788)	—	30.00	50.00	70.00	100	—
AM1218//7 (1789)	—	30.00	50.00	70.00	100	—
AM1218//8 (1789)	—	30.00	50.00	70.00	100	—
AM1219//9 (1790)	—	30.00	50.00	70.00	100	—
AM1221//9 (1791)	—	30.00	50.00	70.00	100	—
AM1221//11 (1792)	—	30.00	50.00	70.00	100	—
AM1222//10 (1793)	—	30.00	50.00	70.00	100	—
AM1224//11 (1795)	—	30.00	50.00	70.00	100	—

Mint: Nagar
KM# 105 1/2 RUPEE
Silver **Note:** Weight varies 5.35-5.80 grams. Struck at Nagar Mint.

Date	Mintage	VG	F	VF	XF	Unc
AM1215 (1786)	—	40.00	65.00	100	150	—

Mint: Patan
KM# 125 1/2 RUPEE
Silver **Note:** Weight varies: 5-35-5.80 grams.

Date	Mintage	VG	F	VF	XF	Unc
AH1200//4 (1785)	—	30.00	50.00	70.00	100	—
AM1215//5 (1786)	—	30.00	50.00	70.00	100	—
AM1216//6 (1787)	—	30.00	50.00	70.00	100	—
AM1217//7 (1788)	—	30.00	50.00	70.00	100	—
AM1218//8 (1789)	—	30.00	50.00	70.00	100	—
AM1219//9 (1790)	—	30.00	50.00	70.00	100	—
AM1220//10 (1791)	—	30.00	50.00	70.00	100	—
AM1221//11 (1792)	—	30.00	50.00	70.00	100	—
AM1222//12 (1793)	—	30.00	50.00	70.00	100	—
AM1224//14 (1795)	—	30.00	50.00	70.00	100	—

Mint: Dharwar
KM# 40 RUPEE
Silver

Date	Mintage	VG	F	VF	XF	Unc
1216	—	—	—	—	—	—

Mint: Farrukhi
KM# 57 RUPEE
Silver

Date	Mintage	VG	F	VF	XF	Unc
AM1217//6 (1788)	—	90.00	150	250	400	—

Mint: Kalikut
KM# 76 RUPEE
Silver **Note:** Weight varies: 10.70-11.60 grams.

Date	Mintage	VG	F	VF	XF	Unc
AM1215//5 (1786)	—	175	350	600	1,000	—

Mint: Khurshed-Sawad
KM# 96 RUPEE
Silver **Note:** Weight varies 10.70-11.60 grams.

Date	Mintage	VG	F	VF	XF	Unc
AM1216//6 (1787)	—	125	275	500	900	—
AM1217//7 (1788)	—	125	275	500	900	—
AM1218//8 (1789)	—	125	275	500	900	—

Mint: Nagar
KM# 106 RUPEE
Silver **Note:** Weight varies 10.70-11.60 grams.

Date	Mintage	VG	F	VF	XF	Unc
AH1200	—	50.00	75.00	110	160	—
AM1216	—	50.00	75.00	110	160	—

Mint: Patan
KM# 126 RUPEE
Silver **Note:** Weight varies: 10.70-11.60 grams.

Date	Mintage	VG	F	VF	XF	Unc
AH1200//4 (1785)	—	15.00	22.50	32.50	50.00	—
AM1216//6 (1787)	—	15.00	22.50	32.50	50.00	—
AM1217//7 (1789)	—	15.00	22.50	32.50	50.00	—
AM1218//8 (1789)	—	15.00	22.50	32.50	50.00	—
AM1219//9 (1790)	—	15.00	22.50	32.50	50.00	—
AM1220//10 (1791)	—	15.00	22.50	32.50	50.00	—
AM1223//13 (1794)	—	15.00	22.50	32.50	50.00	—

Mint: Kalikut
KM# 77 2 RUPEES
Silver **Note:** Weight varies: 21.40-23.20 grams. Dav. #249.

Date	Mintage	VG	F	VF	XF	Unc
AM1215 (1786)	—	400	800	1,500	2,500	—

Mint: Nagar
KM# 107 2 RUPEES
Silver **Note:** Weight varies 21.40-23.20 grams. Dav. #249.

Date	Mintage	VG	F	VF	XF	Unc
AH1200//4	—	150	225	350	500	—
AM1215	—	150	225	350	500	—

Mint: Patan
KM# 127 2 RUPEES
Silver **Note:** Weight varies: 21.40-23.20 grams. Dav. #249.

Date	Mintage	VG	F	VF	XF	Unc
AH1198//2	—	90.00	150	250	400	—
AH1198//3	—	90.00	150	250	400	—
AH1199//3	—	90.00	150	250	400	—
AH1200//4	—	90.00	150	250	400	—
AM1215//5	—	90.00	150	250	400	—
AM1216//6	—	90.00	150	250	400	—

Mint: Patan
KM# 127a 2 RUPEES
Silver **Obv:** Fields without rosettes **Rev:** Fields without rosettes **Note:** Weight varies: 21.40-23.20 grams. Dav. #250.

Date	Mintage	VG	F	VF	XF	Unc
AH1200//4 (1785)	—	90.00	150	250	400	—
AM1216//6 (1787)	—	90.00	150	250	400	—
AM1217//7 (1788)	—	90.00	150	250	400	—
AM1218//8 (1789)	—	90.00	150	250	400	—
AM1219//9 (1790)	—	90.00	150	250	400	—
AM1220//10 (1791)	—	90.00	150	250	400	—

Mint: Farrukhi
KM# 58 FANAM
Gold **Note:** Weight varies: 0.33-0.40 grams.

Date	Mintage	VG	F	VF	XF	Unc
AM1216 (1787)	—	10.00	17.00	22.00	27.50	—
AM1217 (1788)	—	10.00	17.00	22.00	27.50	—
AM1218 (1789)	—	10.00	17.00	22.00	27.50	—

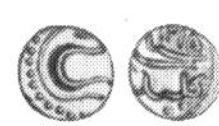

Mint: Kalikut
KM# 78 FANAM
Gold **Note:** Weight varies: 0.33-0.40 grams.

Date	Mintage	VG	F	VF	XF	Unc
AH1198	—	8.00	12.00	18.00	25.00	—
AH1199	—	8.00	12.00	18.00	25.00	—
AH1200	—	8.00	12.00	18.00	25.00	—
AM1215	—	8.00	12.00	18.00	25.00	—

Mint: Khaliqabad
KM# 88 FANAM
Gold **Note:** Weight varies: 0.33-0.40 grams.

Date	Mintage	VG	F	VF	XF	Unc
AM1215 (1786)	—	8.50	12.50	20.00	40.00	—
AM1217 (1788)	—	8.50	12.50	20.00	40.00	—

Mint: Khurshed-Sawad
KM# 98 FANAM
Gold, 7-8 mm. **Note:** Size varies. Weight varies: 0.33-0.40 grams.

Date	Mintage	VG	F	VF	XF	Unc
AM1216 (1787)	—	12.50	18.50	28.00	45.00	—

Mint: Nagar
KM# 108 FANAM
Gold **Note:** Weight varies: 0.33-0.40 grams.

Date	Mintage	VG	F	VF	XF	Unc
AH1197	—	8.50	12.50	17.50	25.00	—
AH1198	—	8.50	12.50	17.50	25.00	—
AH1199	—	8.50	12.50	17.50	25.00	—
AH1200	—	8.50	12.50	17.50	25.00	—
AM1215	—	8.50	12.50	17.50	25.00	—
AM1216	—	8.50	12.50	17.50	25.00	—
AM1217	—	8.50	12.50	17.50	25.00	—
AM1220	—	8.50	12.50	17.50	25.00	—
AM1221	—	8.50	12.50	17.50	25.00	—

Mint: Patan
KM# 128.1 FANAM
Gold **Note:** Weight varies: 0.33-0.40 grams.

Date	Mintage	VG	F	VF	XF	Unc
AH1197	—	8.50	12.00	17.50	25.00	—
AH1198	—	8.50	12.00	17.50	25.00	—
AH1199	—	8.50	12.00	17.50	25.00	—
AH1200	—	8.50	12.00	17.50	25.00	—
AH1201	—	8.50	12.00	17.50	25.00	—
AM1215	—	8.50	12.00	17.50	25.00	—
AM1216	—	8.50	12.00	17.50	25.00	—
AM1217	—	8.50	12.00	17.50	25.00	—
AM1218	—	8.50	12.00	17.50	25.00	—
AM1219	—	8.50	12.00	17.50	25.00	—
AM1220	—	8.50	12.00	17.50	25.00	—
AM1221	—	8.50	12.00	17.50	25.00	—
AM1222	—	8.50	12.00	17.50	25.00	—
AM1223	—	8.50	12.00	17.50	25.00	—

Mint: Dharwar
KM# 99 PAGODA
3.4000 g., Gold

Date	Mintage	VG	F	VF	XF	Unc
AM1216 (1787)	—	100	140	200	300	—
AM1216//6 (1787)	—	100	140	200	300	—

Mint: Farrukhyab-Hisar
KM# 211 PAGODA
3.4000 g., Gold

Date	Mintage	Good	VG	F	VF	XF
ND(1782-99)	—	55.00	70.00	85.00	120	—

Mint: Khurshed-Sawad
KM# 99a PAGODA
3.4000 g., Gold

Date	Mintage	VG	F	VF	XF	Unc
AM1217 (1788)	—	60.00	90.00	130	200	—
AM1218 (1789)	—	60.00	90.00	130	200	—

Mint: Nagar
KM# 109 PAGODA
3.4000 g., Gold

Date	Mintage	VG	F	VF	XF	Unc
AH1198//2	—	50.00	70.00	125	175	—
AH1199//3	—	45.00	60.00	90.00	150	—
AH1200	—	45.00	60.00	90.00	150	—

Mint: Nagar
KM# A110 PAGODA
3.4000 g., Gold

Date	Mintage	VG	F	VF	XF	Unc
AM1215//5 (1786)	—	45.00	60.00	90.00	150	—
AM1216//6 (1787)	—	45.00	60.00	90.00	150	—
AM1217 (1788)	—	45.00	60.00	90.00	150	—

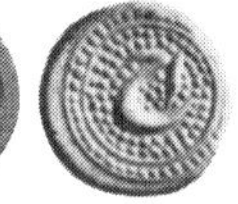

Mint: Patan
KM# 129 PAGODA
3.4000 g., Gold

Date	Mintage	VG	F	VF	XF	Unc
AH1197//1	—	45.00	65.00	90.00	150	—
AH1198//2	—	45.00	65.00	90.00	150	—
AH1200	—	45.00	65.00	90.00	150	—

Mint: Patan
KM# 129a PAGODA
3.4000 g., Gold

Date	Mintage	VG	F	VF	XF	Unc
AM1215//5 (1786)	—	45.00	65.00	90.00	150	—
AM1216//6 (1787)	—	45.00	65.00	90.00	150	—
AM1217//7 (1788)	—	45.00	65.00	90.00	150	—
AM1218//8 (1789)	—	45.00	65.00	90.00	150	—
AM1219//9 (1790)	—	45.00	65.00	90.00	150	—
AM1220//10 (1791)	—	45.00	65.00	90.00	150	—
AM1221//11 (1792)	—	45.00	65.00	90.00	150	—
AM1223//13 (1794)	—	45.00	65.00	90.00	150	—

Mint: Patan
KM# A129 2 PAGODAS
Gold **Note:** Weight varies: 6.80-6.90 grams.

Date	Mintage	VG	F	VF	XF	Unc
AM1216//6 (1787)	—	250	500	950	1,750	—
AM1217//7 (1788)	—	250	500	950	1,750	—
AM1218//8 (1789)	—	250	500	950	1,750	—
AM1219//9 (1790)	—	250	500	950	1,750	—

Mint: Nagar
KM# 110 4 PAGODAS
13.6000 g., Gold

Date	Mintage	VG	F	VF	XF	Unc
AM1216 (1787) Rare	—	—	—	—	—	—

Mint: Patan
KM# B129 4 PAGODAS
13.6000 g., Gold **Note:** KM#B129 is reported as also being struck on the lighter mohur standard of 11.0 grams. Dates of AH1197 and 1199 have been recorded.

Date	Mintage	VG	F	VF	XF	Unc
AH1197//1	—	400	800	1,500	2,500	—
AH1198//2	—	400	800	1,500	2,500	—
AH1199//3	—	400	800	1,500	2,500	—
AH1200//4	—	400	800	1,500	2,500	—
AM1215//5	—	400	800	1,500	2,500	—
AM1217//7	—	400	800	1,500	2,500	—
AM1218//8	—	400	800	1,500	2,500	—
AM1219//9	—	400	800	1,500	2,500	—

Ranadhira Kanthirava-Narasa II

Raja Wodeyar, AH1116-1125 / 1704-1713AD

HAMMERED COINAGE

Mint: Uncertain Mint
KM# 180 FANAM
0.3600 g., Gold **Obv:** Seated figure of Narashimha Avatar of Vishnu **Rev. Legend:** SRI-KAMTH-RAVA **Note:** Struck at Uncertain Mints.

Date	Mintage	VG	F	VF	XF	Unc
ND(1704-13)	—	—	30.00	50.00	85.00	—

Shah Alam II

AH1173-1221/1759-1806AD

HAMMERED COINAGE

Anonymous

Mint: Without Mint Name
KM# A149 KASU
2.4500 g., Copper **Obv:** Elephant right **Rev:** Shah Alam

Date	Mintage	Good	VG	F	VF	XF
ND	—	5.00	7.50	12.00	18.00	—

PUDUKKOTTAI

Pudukota

Raghunatha Raya Tondaiman founded Pudukkottai in 1686 when he defeated the Pallavaraya chiefs of the area. The family came from Tondaimandalam, a small village near Tirupathi, and belonged to the Kallen (or robber) caste. In the late 18th century the Tondaimans aided the British in their struggles against the French in the Carnatic. With British ascendancy, the Pudukkottai rulers were confirmed in their control of the region. This was regularized in 1806 when, subject to a yearly tribute of one elephant, the rajas of Pudukkottai were guaranteed their position. In 1948 the State was merged into the Trichinopoly District.

RULER
Martanda Bhairava, 1886-1928AD

INDEPENDENT KINGDOM

Martanda Bhairava

HAMMERED COINAGE

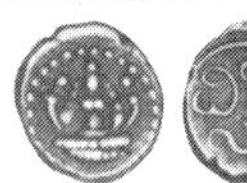

Mint: Without Mint Name
KM# 3.2 AMMAN CASH
1.3000 g., Copper **Obv:** Seated Goddess Brihadamba facing **Rev:** Telugu: Vijaya **Note:** Fine style.

Date	Mintage	Good	VG	F	VF	XF
ND(1550-1750)	—	0.35	0.90	1.50	2.50	4.00

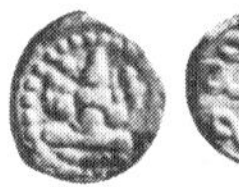

Mint: Without Mint Name
KM# 3.1 AMMAN CASH
1.3000 g., Copper **Obv:** Goddess Brihadamba seated facing **Rev:** Telugu: "Vijaya" **Note:** Crude style.

Date	Mintage	VG	F	VF	XF	Unc
ND(1550-1750)	—	0.90	1.50	2.50	4.00	—

ROHILKHAND

The Nawabs of Rohilkhand were Rohillas who traced their origins to Sardar Daud Khan (d. 1749), an Afghan adventurer. Daud Khan's adopted son, Ali Muhammed, annexed a huge tract of land north of the Ganges between Itawa and the Himalayas, and received the Nawab title from the Mughal emperor.

In 1754 this territory was partitioned among his many sons, who thereafter formed a loose confederacy, alternately given to feuding internally and uniting to meet aggression by the Marathas, Awadh, and Imperial forces in turn. By the end of the century Rohilla power had been crushed by the combined forces of Awadh and the British, leaving only Rampur in Rohilla hands under the sovereignty of Nawab Faizullah Khan. In 1801 Rampur was ceded to the East India Company and in 1950 it was absorbed into Uttar Pradesh.

RULERS

Bareli Mint
Hafiz Rahmat Khan, AH1167-88/1754-74AD
NOTE: For issues struck in the name of Ahmad Shah Durrani, see Afghanistan, Durrani Empire, Bareli.

Bisauli Mint
Abdullah Khan, AH1167-74/1754-61AD
Nasrulla Khan, AH1175-83/1761-70AD
Dunde Khan, AH1184/1770AD
Muhib-ud-daula, AH1184-88/1770-74AD

Itawa Mint
Inayat Khan, AH1176-84/1762-71AD

Muradabad Mint
Hafiz Rahmat Khan, AH1167-88/1754-59AD
NOTE: For issues in the name of Ahmad Shah Durrani, see Afghanistan, Durrani Empire, Muradabad.

Najafgarh Mint
Nawab Najaf Khan, AH1180-96/1766-82AD
Afrasyab Khan, AH1196-98/1782-84AD

Najibabad Mint
Najib Khan alias Najib-ud-daula, AH1166-83/1753-70AD
Zabita Khan, AH1183-88/1770-74AD

This mint city was named for its governor Najib Khan. Its coins begin in the second year of the Mughal Emperor Alamgir II. For issues in the name of Ahmad Shah Durrani, see Afghanistan Durrani Empire, Najibabad.

Rampur Mint

Faizullah Khan, AH1167-1208/1754-1794AD
Muhammad Ali Khan, AH1209-/1794-AD

MINTS

انوله

Mint name: Anwala

اصفنگر

Mint name: Asafnagar

بريلي

Mint name: Bareli

بسولى بسولى

Type I Type II

بسولے بسولي

Mint name: Bisauli

NOTE: The Bisauli mint became inactive after conquest by Awadh AH1888/R.Y. 15/1774AD

اتاوه اتاوا

Mint name: Itawa

مجى بالانگر

Mint name: Mujibalanagar

مراداباد

Mint name: Muradabad

نجف گره

Mint name: Najafgarh

نجيباباد

Mint name: Najibabad

نصرالله نگر

Mint name: Nasrullanagar
The mint of Zabita Khan of Saharanpur

قصبة پاني پت

Mint name: Qasbah Panipat

شاه اباد قنوج

Shahabad Qanauj

مصطفاباد

Mint name: Mustafabad
(tentative attribution)

INDEPENDENT KINGDOM

HAMMERED COINAGE

Mint: Anwala
KM# 10 RUPEE

Silver **Obv. Legend:** "Badshah Ghazi" **Obv. Inscription:** Shah Alam II

Date	Mintage	VG	F	VF	XF	Unc
AH1176/4	—	12.50	16.50	20.00	30.00	—

Mint: Anwala
KM# 16.1 RUPEE

Silver **Obv. Legend:** "Fazl-i-Hami Din" **Obv. Inscription:** Shah Alam II **Rev:** Dot in lilies

Date	Mintage	VG	F	VF	XF	Unc
AH1174/2	—	10.00	12.50	18.50	25.00	—
AH1175/3	—	10.00	12.50	18.50	25.00	—
AH1176/3	—	10.00	12.50	18.50	25.00	—
AH1176/4	—	10.00	12.50	18.50	25.00	—

Mint: Anwala
KM# 16.2 RUPEE

Silver **Obv. Inscription:** Shah Alam II **Rev:** Cluster of cross-like ornaments

Date	Mintage	VG	F	VF	XF	Unc
AH1183/11	—	12.50	17.50	22.50	30.00	—
AH1184/11	—	12.50	17.50	22.50	30.00	—

Mint: Anwala
KM# 16.3 RUPEE

Silver **Obv. Inscription:** Shah Alam II **Rev:** Fish and rosette

Date	Mintage	VG	F	VF	XF	Unc
AH1184/12	—	12.50	20.00	30.00	40.00	—

Mint: Anwala
KM# 16.4 RUPEE

Silver **Obv. Inscription:** Shah Alam II **Rev:** Pretzel shape and rosette **Note:** The Anwala mint became inactive after conquest by Awadh AH1188/R.Y.15/1744AD.

Date	Mintage	VG	F	VF	XF	Unc
AH1185/13	—	12.50	20.00	30.00	40.00	—

Mint: Anwala
KM# 6 RUPEE

Silver **Obv. Inscription:** Shah Alam II **Note:** Weight varies: 10.70-11.60 grams. For issues in the name of Ahmad Shah Durani, see Afghanistan Durrani Empire, Anwala. Anwala is the Persian rendition of the Hindi Anola.

Date	Mintage	VG	F	VF	XF	Unc
AH-/2	—	12.50	20.00	26.50	33.50	—
AH1175/3	—	12.50	20.00	26.50	33.50	—

Mint: Asafnagar
KM# 26 RUPEE

Silver **Obv. Inscription:** Shah Alam II **Note:** Weight varies: 10.70-11.60 grams. For issues of Asafnagar mint dated later than AH1188/R.Y.15, see Awadh.

Date	Mintage	VG	F	VF	XF	Unc
AH-/14	—	16.50	27.50	37.50	50.00	—

Mint: Bareli
KM# 36.5 RUPEE

Silver **Obv. Inscription:** Shah Alam II **Rev:** Danda (mace) and rosettes **Note:** Struck during the reign of local ruler, Hafiz Rahmat Khan, AH1167-88/1754-74A. Weight varies: 10.70-11.60 grams. For issues of Bareli mint later that AH1188/R.Y. 15, see Indian Princely State, Awadh.

Date	Mintage	VG	F	VF	XF	Unc
AH1181/9	—	10.00	15.00	20.00	27.50	—

Mint: Bareli
KM# 36.1 RUPEE

Silver **Obv. Inscription:** Shah Alam II **Rev:** Scimitar **Note:** Struck during the reign of local ruler, Hafiz Rahmat Khan, AH1167-88/1754-74AD. Weight varies: 10.70-11.60 grams.

Date	Mintage	VG	F	VF	XF	Unc
AH1173/2	—	12.50	16.50	22.50	30.00	—

Mint: Bareli
KM# 36.2 RUPEE

Silver **Obv. Inscription:** Shah Alam II **Rev:** Rosettes **Note:** Struck during the reign of local ruler, Hafiz Rahmat Khan, AH1167-88/1754-74AD. Weight varies: 10.70-11.60 grams.

Date	Mintage	VG	F	VF	XF	Unc
AH1174/2	—	9.00	12.50	16.50	22.50	—
AH1174/3	—	9.00	12.50	16.50	22.50	—
AH1175/3	—	9.00	12.50	16.50	22.50	—
AH1177/4	—	9.00	12.50	16.50	22.50	—
AH1183/10	—	9.00	12.50	16.50	22.50	—
AH1184/10	—	9.00	12.50	16.50	22.50	—
AH1184/11	—	9.00	12.50	16.50	22.50	—
AH1184/12	—	9.00	12.50	16.50	22.50	—
AH1185/12	—	9.00	12.50	16.50	22.50	—

Mint: Bareli
KM# 36.3 RUPEE

Silver, 23 mm. **Obv. Inscription:** Shah Alam II **Rev:** Crescent, stars, and rosettes **Note:** Struck during the reign of local ruler, Hafiz Rahmat Khan, AH1167-88/1754-74AD. Weight varies: 10.70-11.60 grams.

Date	Mintage	VG	F	VF	XF	Unc
AH1177/4	—	10.00	15.00	20.00	27.50	—
AH1177/5	—	10.00	15.00	20.00	27.50	—

Mint: Bareli
KM# 36.4 RUPEE

Silver **Obv. Inscription:** Shah Alam II **Rev:** Lamp shade and rosettes **Note:** Struck during the reign of local ruler, Hafiz Rahmat Khan, AH1167-88/1754-74AD. Weight varies: 10.70-11.60 grams.

Date	Mintage	VG	F	VF	XF	Unc
AH1178/5	—	10.00	15.00	20.00	27.50	—

Mint: Bareli
KM# 32 RUPEE

Silver **Obv. Inscription:** Alamgir II **Rev:** Quatrefoil **Note:** Weight varies: 10.70-11.60 grams. Struck during the reign of local ruler, Hafiz Rahmat Khan, AH1167-88/1754-74AD. For issues of Asafnagar mint dated later that AH1188/R.Y.15, see Awadh.

Date	Mintage	VG	F	VF	XF	Unc
AH-//1	—	15.00	25.00	40.00	60.00	—
AH-//2	—	15.00	25.00	40.00	60.00	—
AH1172//6	—	15.00	25.00	40.00	60.00	—

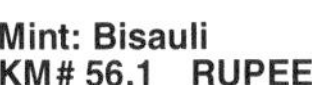

Mint: Bisauli
KM# 56.1 RUPEE

Silver **Obv. Inscription:** Shah Alam II **Note:** Weight varies: 10.70-11.60 grams. Mintname: Type I.

Date	Mintage	VG	F	VF	XF	Unc
AH1182/10	—	14.00	22.50	30.00	40.00	—
AH1186//14	—	14.00	22.50	30.00	40.00	—

Mint: Bisauli
KM# 56.2 RUPEE

Silver **Obv. Inscription:** Shah Alam II **Note:** Weight varies: 10.70-11.60 grams. Mintname: Type II. The Bisauli mint became inactive after conquest by Awadh AH1888/R.Y.15/1774AD.

Date	Mintage	VG	F	VF	XF	Unc
AH1182/10	—	14.00	22.50	30.00	40.00	—
AH1183/11	—	14.00	22.50	30.00	40.00	—
AH1184/11	—	14.00	22.50	30.00	40.00	—

Mint: Itawa
KM# 66 RUPEE

Silver **Obv:** Sword. Inscription: Shah Alam II **Note:** Weight varies: 10.70-11.60 grams. For later issues from Itawa mint dated AH1185//12 and 1186//13, see Maratha Confederacy, Peshwa. For issues dated AH1187//14 and later, see Awadh.

Date	Mintage	VG	F	VF	XF	Unc
AH1173/1	—	12.00	16.00	22.50	35.00	—
AH1176/3	—	10.00	13.50	18.50	28.50	—
AH117x/4	—	10.00	13.50	18.50	28.50	—
AH1179/5	—	10.00	13.50	18.50	28.50	—
AH1180/6	—	10.00	13.50	18.50	28.50	—
AH118x/7	—	10.00	13.50	18.50	28.50	—

Mint: Mujibullanagar
KM# 70 RUPEE

Silver **Obv. Inscription:** Shah Alam II **Note:** For issues in the name of Ahmad Shah Durrani, see Afghanistan, Durrani Empire, Muradabad.

Date	Mintage	VG	F	VF	XF	Unc
AH-/14 Rare	—	—	—	—	—	—

Mint: Muradabad
KM# 76.9 RUPEE

Silver **Obv. Inscription:** Alamgir II **Rev:** Flower **Note:** Struck during the reign of local ruler Hafiz Rahmat Khan, AH1167-88/1754-74AD. Weight varies: 10.70-11.60 grams.

Date	Mintage	VG	F	VF	XF	Unc
AH1170/4	—	10.00	15.00	20.00	27.50	—
AH1171/5	—	10.00	15.00	20.00	27.50	—
AH1172/6	—	10.00	15.00	20.00	27.50	—

Mint: Muradabad
KM# 76.7 RUPEE

Silver **Obv:** "Fazl-i-Hami Din" **Obv. Inscription:** Shah Alam II **Rev:** "Manas Sanah" and crescent **Note:** Struck during the reign of local ruler Hafiz Rahmat Khan, AH1167-88/1754-74AD. Weight varies: 10.70-11.60 grams.

Date	Mintage	VG	F	VF	XF	Unc
AH-/3	—	15.00	22.50	30.00	40.00	—

Mint: Muradabad
KM# 76.2 RUPEE

Silver **Obv. Inscription:** Shah Alam II **Rev:** Legend, quatrefoil, and triskules **Rev. Legend:** "Sanah Jalus" **Note:** Struck during the reign of local ruler Hafiz Rahmat Khan, AH1167-88/1754-74Ad. Weight varies: 10.70-11.60 grams.

Date	Mintage	VG	F	VF	XF	Unc
AH1176/4	—	8.50	13.50	20.00	30.00	—

Mint: Muradabad
KM# 76.3 RUPEE

Silver **Obv. Inscription:** Shah Alam II **Rev:** Legend and sunburst **Rev. Legend:** "Manus Sanah" **Note:** Struck during the reign of local ruler Hafiz Rahmat Khan, AH1167-88/1754-74AD. Weight varies: 10.70-11.60 grams.

Date	Mintage	VG	F	VF	XF	Unc
AH1176/4	—	8.50	13.50	20.00	30.00	—
AH1178/8	—	8.50	13.50	20.00	30.00	—

Mint: Muradabad
KM# 76.5 RUPEE

Silver **Obv. Inscription:** Shah Alam II **Rev:** "Nun" and five dots **Note:** Struck during the reign of local ruler Hafiz Rahmat Khan, AH1167-88/1754-74AD. Weight varies: 10.70-11.60 grams.

Date	Mintage	VG	F	VF	XF	Unc
AH117x/6	—	8.50	13.50	20.00	30.00	—

Mint: Muradabad
KM# 76.4 RUPEE

Silver **Obv. Inscription:** Shah Alam II **Rev:** "Nun" inverted and quatrefoil **Note:** Struck during the reign of local ruler Hafiz Rahmat Khan, AH1167-88/1754-74AD. Weight varies: 10.70-11.60 grams.

Date	Mintage	VG	F	VF	XF	Unc
AH1178/5	—	15.00	25.00	35.00	50.00	—

Mint: Muradabad
KM# 76.6 RUPEE

Silver **Obv. Inscription:** Shah Alam II **Rev:** Normal "Nun" **Note:** Struck during the reign of local ruler Hafiz Rahmat Khan, AH1167-88/1754-74AD. Weight varies: 10.70-11.60 grams.

Date	Mintage	VG	F	VF	XF	Unc
AH1179/7	—	8.50	13.50	20.00	30.00	—
AH1180/7	—	8.50	13.50	20.00	30.00	—
AH1180/8	—	8.50	13.50	20.00	30.00	—
AH1181/9	—	8.50	13.50	20.00	30.00	—
AH1182/10	—	8.50	13.50	20.00	30.00	—

Mint: Muradabad
KM# 76.8 RUPEE

Silver **Obv. Inscription:** Shah Alam II **Rev:** "Nun" and sun **Note:** Struck during the reign of local ruler Hafiz Rahmat Khan, AH1167-88/1754-74AD. Weight varies: 10.70-11.60 grams. For later issues of Muradabad mint dated after AH1188/R.Y.15, see Awadh.

Date	Mintage	VG	F	VF	XF	Unc
AH1186/14	—	8.50	13.50	20.00	30.00	—

Mint: Muradabad
KM# 76.1 RUPEE

Silver **Obv:** Trefoil **Obv. Inscription:** Alamgir II **Rev:** Legend and anchor **Rev. Legend:** "Jalus Sanah" **Note:** Struck during the reign of local ruler Hafiz Rahmat Khan, AH1167-88/1754-74AD. Weight varies:10.70-11.60 grams.

Date	Mintage	VG	F	VF	XF	Unc
AH1168/1	—	10.00	15.00	20.00	27.50	—
AH1168/2	—	10.00	15.00	20.00	27.50	—
AH-/3	—	10.00	15.00	20.00	27.50	—

Mint: Najafgarh
KM# 86 RUPEE

Silver **Obv. Inscription:** Shah Alam II **Note:** Weight varies: 10.70-11.60 grams.

Date	Mintage	VG	F	VF	XF	Unc
AH-/21	—	15.00	22.50	30.00	40.00	—
AH1198/26	—	15.00	22.50	30.00	40.00	—

Mint: Najibabad
KM# 96.1 RUPEE

Silver **Obv. Inscription:** Shah Alam II **Rev:** Without marks

Date	Mintage	VG	F	VF	XF	Unc
AH1174/2	—	10.00	13.50	16.50	22.50	—
AH1175/3	—	10.00	13.50	16.50	22.50	—
AH1176/3	—	10.00	13.50	16.50	22.50	—
AH1176/4	—	10.00	13.50	16.50	22.50	—
AH1177/4	—	10.00	13.50	16.50	22.50	—
AH1177/5	—	10.00	13.50	16.50	22.50	—

Mint: Najibabad
KM# 96.2 RUPEE

Silver **Obv. Inscription:** Shah Alam II

Date	Mintage	VG	F	VF	XF	Unc
AH1177/5	—	10.00	13.50	16.50	22.50	—
AH1178/6	—	10.00	13.50	16.50	22.50	—
AH1179/6	—	10.00	13.50	16.50	22.50	—
AH1179/7	—	10.00	13.50	16.50	22.50	—
AH1180/7	—	10.00	13.50	16.50	22.50	—
AH1180/8	—	10.00	13.50	16.50	22.50	—
AH1181/8	—	10.00	13.50	16.50	22.50	—
AH1181/9	—	10.00	13.50	16.50	22.50	—
AH118x/12	—	10.00	13.50	16.50	22.50	—
AH1187/14	—	10.00	13.50	16.50	22.50	—

Mint: Nasrullanagar
KM# 106 RUPEE

Silver **Obv. Inscription:** Shah Alam II **Note:** Weight varies: 10.70-11.60 grams.

Date	Mintage	VG	F	VF	XF	Unc
AH1181/9	—	35.00	50.00	70.00	100	—
AH1185/13	—	35.00	50.00	70.00	100	—
AH-/14	—	35.00	50.00	70.00	100	—

Mint: Qanauj
KM# 121 RUPEE

Silver **Obv. Inscription:** Alamgir II **Note:** Weight varies: 10.70-11.60 grams.

Date	Mintage	VG	F	VF	XF	Unc
AH116x//2	—	18.50	31.50	42.50	60.00	—
AH1169//3	—	18.50	31.50	42.50	60.00	—
AH-//4	—	18.50	31.50	42.50	60.00	—

Mint: Qasbah Panipat
KM# 116 RUPEE
Silver **Obv. Inscription:** Shah Alam II **Note:** Weight varies: 10.70-11.60 grams.

Date	Mintage	VG	F	VF	XF	Unc
AH1198/25	—	10.00	14.00	20.00	30.00	—

Mint: Rampur
KM# 126.1 RUPEE
Silver **Obv:** Inscription: Shah Alam II **Rev:** Ten-pointed star **Note:** Weight varies: 10.70-11.60 grams.

Date	Mintage	VG	F	VF	XF	Unc
AH1184/11	—	18.50	27.50	37.50	50.00	—
AH1184/12	—	18.50	27.50	37.50	50.00	—
AH1185/12	—	18.50	27.50	37.50	50.00	—

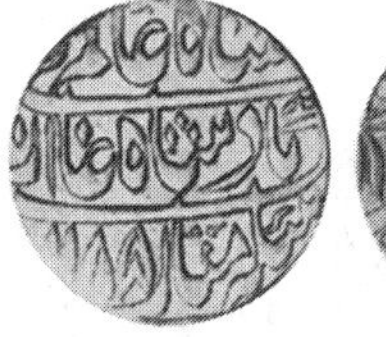

Mint: Rampur
KM# 126.2 RUPEE
Silver **Obv. Inscription:** Shah Alam II **Rev:** Floral symbol and trident quatrefoil **Note:** Weight varies: 10.70-11.60 grams.

Date	Mintage	VG	F	VF	XF	Unc
AH1185/13	—	18.50	27.50	37.50	50.00	—

Mint: Muradabad
KM# A70 PAISA
19.2000 g., Copper **Obv:** Inscription: Alamgir II **Note:** Struck during the reign of local ruler Hafiz Rahmat Khan, AH1167-88/1754-74AD, at the Muradabad Mint.

Date	Mintage	VG	F	VF	XF	Unc
Yr.2	—	—	—	—	—	—

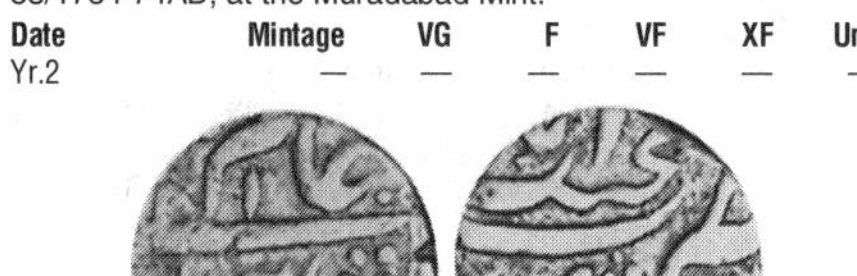

Mint: Najibabad
KM# 91 PAISA
Copper **Obv. Inscription:** Shah Alam II

Date	Mintage	Good	VG	F	VF	XF
AH1176/3	—	2.00	4.00	6.50	10.00	—
AH1176/4	—	2.00	4.00	6.50	10.00	—
AH1177/4	—	2.00	4.00	6.50	10.00	—
AH1177/5	—	2.00	4.00	6.50	10.00	—
AH1178/5	—	2.00	4.00	6.50	10.00	—
AH1178/6	—	2.00	4.00	6.50	10.00	—
AH1179/6	—	2.00	4.00	6.50	10.00	—
AH1179/7	—	2.00	4.00	6.50	10.00	—
AH1180/8	—	2.00	4.00	6.50	10.00	—
AH1181/9	—	2.00	4.00	6.50	10.00	—
AH1182/9	—	2.00	4.00	6.50	10.00	—
AH1182/10	—	2.00	4.00	6.50	10.00	—
AH1183/11	—	2.00	4.00	6.50	10.00	—
AH1184/11	—	2.00	4.00	6.50	10.00	—
AH1185/12	—	2.00	4.00	6.50	10.00	—
AH1185/13	—	2.00	4.00	6.50	10.00	—
AH1186/13	—	2.00	4.00	6.50	10.00	—
AH1187/15	—	2.00	4.00	6.50	10.00	—
AH1188/16	—	2.00	4.00	6.50	10.00	—

Alamgir II

AH1167-1173 / 1754-1759AD

HAMMERED COINAGE

Mint: Anwala
KM# 4 RUPEE
Silver **Obv:** Names and titles of Alamgir II **Rev:** Mint and date

Date	Mintage	VG	F	VF	XF	Unc
AHxxxx/6	—	15.00	25.00	40.00	65.00	—

Zabita Khan

AH1183-1188 / 1770-1774AD

HAMMERED COINAGE

Mint: Najibabad
KM# 100 MOHUR
Gold **Obv. Inscription:** Shah Alam II **Note:** Weight varies: 10.70-11.60 grams. For later issues of the Najibabad mint after AH1188/R.Y.15, see Indian Princely State, Awadh.

Date	Mintage	VG	F	VF	XF	Unc
AH117x/3	—	175	225	375	650	—
AH1177/5	—	175	225	375	650	—
AH1178/5	—	175	225	375	650	—
AH1186/13 (1772)	—	—	—	—	—	—

SIKH EMPIRE

The father of Sikhism, Guru Nanak (1469-1539), was distinguished from almost all others who founded states or empires in India by being a purely religious teacher. Deeply Indian in the basic premises, which underlay even those aspects of his theology which differed from the mainstream, he stressed the unity of God and the universal brotherhood of man. He was totally opposed to the divisions of the caste system and his teaching struggled to attain a practical balance between Hinduism and Islam. His message was a message of reconciliation, first with God, then with man. He exhibited no political ambition.

Guru Nanak was succeeded by nine other gurus of Sikhism. Together they laid the foundations of a religious community in the Punjab, which would, much later, transform itself into the Sikh Empire. Gradually this gentle religion of reconciliation became transformed into a formidable, aggressive military power. It was a metamorphosis, which was, at least partly, thrust upon the Sikh community by Mughal oppression. The fifth guru of Sikhism, Arjun, was executed in 1606 on the order of Jahangir. His successor, Hargobind, was to spend his years in constant struggle against the Mughals, first against Jahangir and later against Shah Jahan. The ninth guru, Tegh Bahadur, was executed by Aurangzeb for refusing to embrace Islam. The stage had been set for a full confrontation with Mughal authority. It was against such a background that Sikhism's tenth guru, Guru Govind Singh (1675-1708), set about organizing the Sikhs into a military power. He gave new discipline to Sikhism. Its adherents were forbidden wine and tobacco and they were required to conform to the 5 outward signs of allegiance - to keep their hair unshaven and to wear short drawers (kuchcha),a comb (kungha), an iron bangle (kara) and a dagger (kirpan).

With Govind Singh's death the Khalsa, the Sikh brotherhood, emerged as the controlling body of Sikhism and the Granth, the official compilation of Govind Singh's teaching, became the "Bible" of Sikhism. At this point the Sikhs took to the hills. It was here, constantly harassed by Mughal forces, that Sikh militarism was forged into an effective weapon and tempered by fire. Gradually the Sikhs emerged from their safe forts in the hills and made their presence felt in the plains of the Punjab. As Nadir Shah retired from Delhi laden with the prizes of war in 1739, the stragglers of his Persian army were cut down by the Sikhs. Similarly, Ahmad Shah Durrani's first intrusion into India (1747-1748) was made the more lively by Sikh sorties into his rear guard. Gradually the Sikhs became both more confident and more effective, and their quite frequent military reversals served only to strengthen their determination and to deepen their sense of identity. Their first notable success came about 1756 when the Sikhs temporarily occupied Lahore and used the Mughal mint to strike their own rupee bearing the inscription: *Coined by the grace of the Khalsa in the country of Ahmad,conquered by Jessa the Kalal.* But the Sikhs were, as yet, most effective as guerrilla bands operating out of the hill country. On Ahmad Shah's fifth expedition into India (1759-1761) the Sikhs reverted to their well-tried role of forming tight mobile units, which could choose both the time and the place of their attacks on the Durrani army. In spite of a serious reverse near Bernala in 1762 at the hands of Ahmad Shah, the Sikhs once again regrouped. In December 1763 they decisively defeated the Durrani governor of Sirhind and occupied the area.

The Sikhs now swept all before them, recapturing Lahore in 1765. The whole tract of land between the Jhelum and the Sutlej was now divided among the Sikh chieftains. At Lahore, and later at Amritsar, the Govind Shahi rupee proclaiming that Guru Govind Singh had received *Deg, Tegh and Fath* (Grace, Power and Victory) from Nanak was struck. The name of the Mughal emperor was pointedly omitted. The Sikhs now subdivided into twelve *misls* "equals", each responsible for its own fate and each conducting its own military adventures into surrounding areas. By 1792 the most prominent chief in the Punjab was Mahan Singh of the Sukerchakia *misl.* His death that same year left the boy destined to become Sikhism's best-known statesman, Ranjit Singh, as his successor. In 1799, Shah Zaman, King of Kabul, confirmed him as the possessor of Lahore.

RULERS

Banda Singh Bahadur, AH1120-1129/1708-1716AD
Khalsa, Military Government, AH1129-1214/1716-1799AD
Ranjit Singh, VS1856-1896/1799-1839AD

MINTS

امبرت سر امرت سر
Amritsar
(Ambratsar)

لاهور
Lahore

ملتان
Multan

پشاور
Peshawar

NOTE: Most coins struck after the accession of Ranjit Singh bear a large leaf on one side, and have Persian or Gurmukhi (Punjabi) legends in the name of Gobind Singh, the tenth and last Guru of the Sikhs, 1675-1708AD. Earlier pieces are similar, but lack the leaf, except the Amritsar Mint where the leaf is present since VS1845.

There is a great variety of coppers, and only representative types are catalogued here; many crude pieces were struck at the official and at unofficial mints, and bear illegible or semi-literate inscriptions. None of the coins bear the name of the Sikh ruler.

EMPIRE

HAMMERED COINAGE

Mint: Jammu
KM# 35 PAISA
Copper

Date	Mintage	Good	VG	F	VF	XF
ND	—	3.50	6.50	11.50	18.50	—

Mint: Multan
KM# 76 PAISA
Copper **Obv. Inscription:** "Guru Gobind Singh" **Note:** Without leaf symbol.

Date	Mintage	Good	VG	F	VF	XF
VS1834 (1777)	—	5.50	9.00	15.00	25.00	—

Mint: Lahore
KM# 62 1/2 RUPEE
Silver, 18 mm. **Obv:** Text **Rev:** Text, date **Note:** Weight varies: 5.50-5.60 grams.

Date	Mintage	VG	F	VF	XF	Unc
VS1828 (1771)	—	18.50	50.00	85.00	130	—
VS1832 (1775)	—	18.50	50.00	85.00	130	—
VS1847 (1790)	—	18.50	50.00	85.00	130	—
VS1858 (1801)	—	18.50	30.00	50.00	85.00	—
VS1864 (1807)	—	18.50	30.00	50.00	85.00	—
VS1889 (1832)	—	18.50	30.00	50.00	85.00	—

Mint: Amritsar
KM# A20.1a RUPEE
Silver **Obv:** Legend differently arranged

Date	Mintage	Good	VG	F	VF	XF
VS1838 (1781)	—	90.00	150	250	350	—
VS1839 (1782)	—	60.00	100	200	300	—
VS1840 (1783)	—	90.00	150	250	350	—

Mint: Amritsar
KM# A20.4 RUPEE
Silver **Rev:** First issue with leaf, date to left

Date	Mintage	VG	F	VF	XF	Unc
VS1845/318 (1788)	—	12.50	20.00	32.50	55.00	—
VS1846/319 (1789)	—	12.50	20.00	32.50	55.00	—
VS1846/320 (1789)	—	12.50	20.00	32.50	55.00	—
VS1847/321 (1790)	—	12.50	20.00	32.50	55.00	—

Mint: Amritsar
KM# A20.3a RUPEE
Silver **Rev:** Without leaf symbol **Note:** Weight varies: 11.20-12.00 grams.

Date	Mintage	VG	F	VF	XF	Unc
VS1844 (1787)	—	80.00	130	275	375	—
VS1845 (1788)	—	80.00	130	275	375	—

Mint: Lahore
KM# 66.1 RUPEE
10.7000 g., Silver, 23mm mm. **Obv. Inscription:** Guru Gobind Singh **Rev:** Leaf to left of date **Note:** Actual VS years. Weight varies: 10.80-11.20 grams.

Date	Mintage	Good	VG	F	VF	XF
VS1855	—	5.00	9.00	15.00	25.00	40.00
VS1856	—	—	8.00	13.50	21.50	35.00
VS1857	—	—	8.00	13.50	21.50	35.00

Mint: Lahore
KM# 64 RUPEE
Silver **Obv:** Persian legend **Obv. Legend:** "Sachcha Shahan" **Obv. Inscription:** "Guru Gobind Singh" **Note:** Weight varies: 10.70-11.30 grams.

Date	Mintage	VG	F	VF	XF	Unc
VS1841 (1784)	—	8.00	13.50	21.50	35.00	—
VS1842 (1785)	—	8.00	13.50	21.50	35.00	—
VS1843 (1786)	—	8.00	13.50	21.50	35.00	—
VS1844 (1787)	—	8.00	13.50	21.50	35.00	—
VS1845 (1788)	—	8.00	13.50	21.50	35.00	—
VS1846 (1789)	—	8.00	13.50	21.50	35.00	—
VS1847 (1790)	—	8.00	13.50	21.50	35.00	—
VS1848 (1791)	—	8.00	13.50	21.50	35.00	—
VS1849 (1792)	—	8.00	13.50	21.50	35.00	—
VS1869 (1792)	—	—	—	250	350	—

Note: Rare variety with flower plant as main mark.

Date	Mintage	VG	F	VF	XF	Unc
VS1850 (1793)	—	8.00	13.50	21.50	35.00	—
VS1851 (1794)	—	8.00	13.50	21.50	35.00	—
VS1852 (1795)	—	8.00	13.50	21.50	35.00	—
VS1853 (1796)	—	8.00	13.50	21.50	35.00	—
VS1854 (1797)	—	8.00	13.50	21.50	35.00	—
VS1855 (1798)	—	8.00	13.50	21.50	35.00	—
VS1856 (1799)	—	10.00	20.00	30.00	50.00	—

Mint: Lahore
KM# A63 RUPEE
Silver **Obv. Inscription:** "Guru Gobind Singh" **Note:** Without leaf symbol. Weight varies: 11.10-11.20 grams. Struck at Lahore Mint.

Date	Mintage	VG	F	VF	XF	Unc
VS1822 (1765)	—	8.00	13.50	35.00	50.00	—
VS1823 (1766)	—	8.00	13.50	35.00	50.00	—
VS1824 (1767)	—	8.00	13.50	35.00	50.00	—
VS1825 (1768)	—	8.00	13.50	35.00	50.00	—
VS1826 (1769)	—	8.00	13.50	35.00	50.00	—
VS1827 (1770)	—	8.00	13.50	35.00	50.00	—
VS1828 (1771)	—	8.00	13.50	35.00	50.00	—
VS1829 (1772)	—	8.00	13.50	35.00	50.00	—
VS1830 (1773)	—	8.00	13.50	35.00	50.00	—
VS1831 (1774)	—	8.00	13.50	35.00	50.00	—
VS1832 (1775)	—	8.00	13.50	35.00	50.00	—
VS1833 (1776)	—	8.00	13.50	35.00	50.00	—
VS1834 (1777)	—	8.00	13.50	35.00	50.00	—
VS1835 (1778)	—	8.00	13.50	35.00	50.00	—
VS1836 (1779)	—	8.00	13.50	35.00	50.00	—
VS1837 (1780)	—	8.00	13.50	35.00	50.00	—
VS1838 (1781)	—	8.00	13.50	35.00	50.00	—
VS1839 (1782)	—	8.00	13.50	35.00	50.00	—

Note: An 1839 rare variety exists with a sword as additional mark

Date	Mintage	VG	F	VF	XF	Unc
VS1840 (1783)	—	8.00	13.50	35.00	50.00	—

Mint: Multan
KM# 83 RUPEE
Silver **Obv:** Inscription: "Guru Gobind Singh" **Rev:** Without leaf **Note:** Weight varies: 10.70-11.60 grams. Struck at Multan Mint.

Date	Mintage	VG	F	VF	XF	Unc
VS1829 (1772)	—	16.50	27.50	45.00	75.00	—
VS1830 (1773)	—	16.50	27.50	45.00	75.00	—
VS1831 (1774)	—	16.50	27.50	45.00	75.00	—
VS1832 (1775)	—	16.50	27.50	45.00	75.00	—
VS1833 (1776)	—	16.50	27.50	45.00	75.00	—
VS1834 (1777)	—	16.50	27.50	45.00	75.00	—
VS1835 (1778)	—	16.50	27.50	45.00	75.00	—
VS1836 (1779)	—	16.50	27.50	45.00	75.00	—

Mint: Lahore
KM# 70 1/2 MOHUR
Gold **Obv. Inscription:** "Guru Gobind Singh"

Date	Mintage	VG	F	VF	XF	Unc
VS1857 (1800) Rare	—	—	—	—	—	—

Banda Singh Bahadur

AH1120-1129 / 1708-1716AD

HAMMERED COINAGE

Mint: Uncertain Mint
KM# 1 RUPEE
11.9600 g., Silver **Obv. Inscription:** "Guru Nanak and Guru Gobind"

Date	Mintage	VG	F	VF	XF	Unc
ND(1711)/2 Rare	—	—	—	—	—	—

Mint: Uncertain Mint
KM# 2 RUPEE
11.9600 g., Silver **Obv. Inscription:** "Guru Nanak and Guru Gobind" **Note:** Crude style and corrupt legends.

Date	Mintage	VG	F	VF	XF	Unc
ND(1712)/3	—	750	1,250	1,750	2,500	—

Khalsa, Military Government

AH1129-1214 / 1716-1799AD

HAMMERED COINAGE

Mint: Amritsar
KM# A20.3 RUPEE
Silver **Obv:** Third legend arrangement **Rev:** Mint name and date

Date	Mintage	VG	F	VF	XF	Unc
VS1841/315 (1784)	—	11.50	18.00	30.00	50.00	—
VS1842/315 (1785)	—	11.50	18.00	30.00	50.00	—
VS1842/316 (1785)	—	11.50	18.00	30.00	50.00	—
VS1843/316 (1786)	—	11.50	18.00	30.00	50.00	—
VS1844/317 (1787)	—	11.50	18.00	30.00	50.00	—
VS1845/318 (1788)	—	11.50	18.00	30.00	50.00	—

Mint: Amritsar
KM# A20.2 RUPEE
Silver **Obv:** Second legend arrangement **Rev:** Katar, leaf **Note:** Weight varies 10.60-11.20 grams.

Date	Mintage	VG	F	VF	XF	Unc
VS1841 (1784)	—	11.50	18.00	30.00	50.00	—
VS1842 (1785)	—	11.50	18.00	30.00	50.00	—
VS1843 (1786)	—	11.50	18.00	30.00	50.00	—
VS1845 (1788)	—	11.50	18.00	30.00	50.00	—
VS1846 (1789)	—	11.50	18.00	30.00	50.00	—
VS1849 (1792)	—	11.50	18.00	30.00	50.00	—
VS1850 (1793)	—	11.50	18.00	30.00	50.00	—
VS1851 (1794)	—	11.50	18.00	30.00	50.00	—
VS1852 (1795)	—	11.50	18.00	30.00	50.00	—
VS1854 (1797)	—	11.50	18.00	30.00	50.00	—

Mint: Amritsar
KM# A20.1 RUPEE
Silver **Obv:** First legend arrangement **Note:** Weight varies: 10.60-11.20 grams.

Date	Mintage	VG	F	VF	XF	Unc
VS1832 (1775)	—	22.50	35.00	50.00	75.00	—
VS1833 (1776)	—	20.00	30.00	45.00	65.00	—
VS1834 (1777)	—	12.50	20.00	45.00	65.00	—
VS1835 (1778)	—	11.50	18.00	45.00	65.00	—
VS1836 (1779)	—	11.50	18.00	45.00	65.00	—
VS1837 (1780)	—	11.50	18.00	45.00	65.00	—
VS1838 (1781)	—	11.50	18.00	45.00	65.00	—
VS1839 (1782)	—	11.50	18.00	45.00	65.00	—

Mint: Anandghar
KM# 30 RUPEE
Silver **Note:** Weight varies: 10.50-11.10 grams. AH dates at top of obverse are usually off the flan. Some specimens dated VS1841 show "ahad" to lower left of reverse, connoting "1", some VS1844 show "4" and VS1846, "6". This feature may occur on all dies.

Date	Mintage	VG	F	VF	XF	Unc
VS1840 (1783)	—	27.50	45.00	75.00	125	—
VS1841 (1784)	—	21.50	35.00	60.00	100	—
VS1842 (1785)	—	21.50	35.00	60.00	100	—
VS1843 (1786)	—	21.50	35.00	60.00	100	—
VS1844 (1787)	—	21.50	35.00	60.00	100	—
VS1845 (1788)	—	21.50	35.00	60.00	100	—

Date	Mintage	VG	F	VF	XF	Unc
VS1846 (1789)	—	21.50	35.00	60.00	100	—
VS1848 (1791)	—	21.50	35.00	60.00	100	—
VS1849 (1792)	—	27.50	45.00	75.00	125	—

Ranjit Singh
VS1856-1896 / 1799-1839AD
HAMMERED COINAGE

Mint: Amritsar
KM# 20.1 RUPEE
Silver **Obv:** Text, beaded flowers **Rev:** Mint name, date, leaf, beaded flowers **Note:** Double lines below dates exist for some 1869, 1870, and 1871 coins and are considered rare. Mint symbols seem to change frequently in this series.

Date	Mintage	VG	F	VF	XF	Unc
VS1846 (1789)	—	7.50	12.50	35.00	55.00	—
VS1847 (1790)	—	7.50	12.50	35.00	55.00	—
VS1848 (1791)	—	7.50	12.50	35.00	55.00	—
VS1849 (1792)	—	7.50	12.50	20.00	32.50	—
VS1850 (1793)	—	7.50	12.50	20.00	32.50	—
VS1851 (1794)	—	7.00	11.00	18.00	30.00	—
VS1852 (1795)	—	7.00	11.00	18.00	30.00	—
VS1853 (1796)	—	7.00	11.00	18.00	30.00	—
VS1854 (1797)	—	7.00	11.00	18.00	30.00	—
VS1855 (1798)	—	7.00	11.00	18.00	30.00	—
VS1856 (1799)	—	7.00	11.00	18.00	30.00	—
VS1857 (1800)	—	7.00	11.00	18.00	30.00	—

SIKH FEUDATORY NAJIBABAD

PROTECTORATE
HAMMERED COINAGE

Mint: Without Mint Name
KM# 131 PAISA
Copper **Obv:** Date

Date	Mintage	Good	VG	F	VF	XF
Yr.21	—	17.50	30.00	45.00	60.00	—
Yr.x4	—	17.50	30.00	45.00	60.00	—

SIVAGANGA

Lords
1743-1801AD

The Lords of Sivaganga, located in southernmost India came under British rule in 1801.

KINGDOM
ANONYMOUS HAMMERED COINAGE

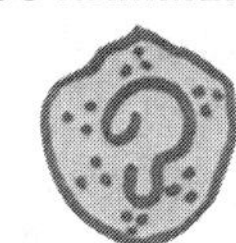

Mint: Without Mint Name
KM# 1 1/2 KASU
0.7500 g., Copper **Obv:** Bull or elephant at left **Rev:** Crude lingam on altar

Date	Mintage	Good	VG	F	VF	XF
ND(1743-1801)	—	1.75	3.00	4.50	7.50	—

Mint: Without Mint Name
KM# 2 KASU
1.5000 g., Copper **Obv:** Vishnu standing **Rev:** Legend within dotted pattern **Rev. Legend:** Vi

Date	Mintage	Good	VG	F	VF	XF
ND(1743-1801)	—	2.00	3.50	5.00	8.00	—

Mint: Without Mint Name
KM# 5 KASU
Copper **Obv:** 2 deitites **Rev:** Crude lingam on altar outlined with dots

Date	Mintage	Good	VG	F	VF	XF
ND(1743-1801)	—	0.75	2.00	3.50	5.00	—

Mint: Without Mint Name
KM# 6.1 2 KASU
Copper **Obv:** 2 deities **Rev:** Crude lingam on altar within dotted circle

Date	Mintage	Good	VG	F	VF	XF
ND(1743-1801)	—	0.75	2.00	3.50	5.00	—

Mint: Without Mint Name
KM# 6.2 2 KASU
Copper **Obv:** 2 deities **Rev:** Crude lingam on altar outlined with dots

Date	Mintage	Good	VG	F	VF	XF
ND(1743-1801)	—	0.75	2.00	3.50	5.00	—

TANJORE

(Thanjavur)
Nayakas

Located approximately 240 miles up the east coast from the southernmost tip of India inland 50 miles on the Cauvery River.

Thanjavur was the capital of the Cholas in the 10th century. The independent state was established here in the 16th century by a governor of Vijayanagar. It came under Madura sovereignty in 1662; was conquered by the Marathas in 1674 who held it until 1799. In 1855 it came under British rule.

INDEPENDENT KINGDOM
HAMMERED COINAGE

Mint: Without Mint Name
KM# 1 1/2 KASU
Copper **Obv:** 2 deities seated **Rev:** Wheel design with 4 spokes **Note:** Weight varies: 0.88-0.91 grams.

Date	Mintage	Good	VG	F	VF	XF
ND	—	1.75	3.00	5.00	8.50	—

Mint: Without Mint Name
KM# 2 KASU
Copper **Obv:** Legend in Tamil **Obv. Legend:** Than javur **Rev:** Four-petalled flower **Note:** Weight varies: 1.76-1.82 grams.

Date	Mintage	Good	VG	F	VF	XF
ND	—	5.00	8.50	15.00	25.00	—

Mint: Without Mint Name
KM# 3 2 KASU
Copper **Obv:** Garuda right **Rev:** Ganesh with head of elephant seated **Note:** Weight varies: 3.5-3.6 grams.

Date	Mintage	Good	VG	F	VF	XF
ND	—	3.00	5.00	8.00	12.00	—

Mint: Without Mint Name
KM# 4 2 KASU
Copper **Obv:** 3 deities standing **Rev:** Deity standing **Note:** Weight varies: 3.5-3.6 grams.

Date	Mintage	Good	VG	F	VF	XF
ND	—	1.75	3.00	5.00	8.50	—

TINNEVELLY

Nayakas

Located approximately 60 miles north of the southernmost tip of India. The Nayakas ruled between the early 17th to late 18th century when they came under British rule.

INDEPENDENT KINGDOM
ANONYMOUS HAMMERED COINAGE

Mint: Without Mint Name
KM# 1 KASU
Copper **Obv:** Venkatesvara standing in archway **Rev:** Conch shell between symbols **Note:** Weight varies: 1.4-1.5 grams.

Date	Mintage	Good	VG	F	VF	XF
ND	—	2.50	4.50	7.50	11.50	—

Mint: Without Mint Name
KM# 2 KASU
Copper **Obv:** 2 deities on horseback **Rev. Legend:** "Sri Vira" **Note:** Weight varies: 1.4-1.5 grams.

Date	Mintage	Good	VG	F	VF	XF
ND	—	2.50	4.50	7.50	11.50	—

Mint: Without Mint Name
KM# 3 2 KASU
Copper **Obv:** Venkatesvara standing in archway **Rev:** Legend to the right of the conch shell **Rev. Legend:** "Sri Vira" **Note:** Weight varies: 2.7-3.2 grams.

Date	Mintage	Good	VG	F	VF	XF
ND	—	6.00	10.00	15.00	22.50	—

Mint: Without Mint Name
KM# 4 2 KASU
Copper **Obv:** Venkatesvara standing in archway **Rev. Legend:** "Sri Vira" **Note:** Weight varies: 2.7-3.2 grams.

Date	Mintage	Good	VG	F	VF	XF
ND	—	2.00	3.50	5.50	8.50	—

TRIPURA

Hill Tipperah

Tripura was a Hindu Kingdom consisting of a strip of the fertile plains east of Bengal, and a large tract of hill territory beyond, which had a reputation for providing wild elephants.

At times when Bengal was weak, Tripura rose to prominence and extended its rule into the plains, but when Bengal was strong the kingdom consisted purely of the hill area, which was virtually impregnable and not of enough economic worth to encourage the Muslims to conquer it. In this way Tripura was able to maintain its full independence until the 19th century.

The origins of the Kingdom are veiled in legend, but the first coins were struck during the reign of Ratna Manikya (1464-89) and copied the weight and fabric of the contemporary issues of the Sultans of Bengal. He also copied the lion design that had appeared on certain rare tangkas of Nasir-ud-din Mahmud Shah I dated AH849 (1445AD). In other respects the designs were purely Hindu, and the lion was retained on most of the later issues as a national emblem.

Tripura rose to a political zenith during the 16th century, while Muslim rule in Bengal was weak, and several coins were struck to commemorate successful military campaigns from Chittagong in the south to Sylhetin the north. These conquests were not sustained, and in the early 17th century the Mughal army was able to inflict severe defeats on Tripura, which was forced to pay tribute.

In about 1733AD all the territory in the plains was annexed by the Mughals, and the Raja merely managed his estate there as a zemindar, although he still retained control as independent King of his hill territory.

The situation remained unchanged when the British took over the administration of Bengal in 1765, and it was only in 1871 that the British appointed an agent in the hills, and began to assist the Maharaja in the administration of his hill territory, which became known as the State of Hill Tipperah.

After the middle of the 18th century, coins were not struck for monetary reasons, but merely for ceremonial use at coronations and other ceremonies, and to keep up the treasured right of coinage.

The coins of Tripura are unusual in that the majority have the name of the King together with that of his Queen, and is the only coinage in the world where this was done consistently.

In common with most other Hindu coinages of northeast India, the coins bear fixed dates. Usually the date used was that of the coronation ceremony, but during the 16th century, coins which were struck with a design commemorating a particular event, bore the date of that event, which can be useful as a historical source, where other written evidence is virtually non-existent.

All modern Tripura coins were presentation pieces, more medallic than monetary in nature. They were struck in very limited numbers and although not intended for local circulation as money, they are often encountered in worn condition.

RULERS

Ratna Manikya II
SE1607-15, c1617-34/
1685-93, c1695-1712AD
Queens of Ratna Manikya II
Queen Satyavati
Queen Bhagavati

Mahendra Manikya
SEc1634-36/c1712-14AD

Dharma Manikya
SEc1636-61/c1714-39AD
Queen of Dharma Manikya
Queen Dharmashila

Mukunde Manikya
Jaya Manikya II
SEc1661-66/c1739-44AD
Queen of Jaya Manikya II
Queen Jasovati

Indra Manikya
SEc1666-69/c1744-47AD

Vijaya Manikya II

Krishna Manikya
SE1682-1705/1760-83AD
Queen of Krishna Manikya
Queen Jahanbi

Rajadhara Manikya
SE1707-26/1785-1804AD

DATING

While the early coinage is dated in the Saka Era (SE) the later issues are dated in the Tripurabda era (TE). Toconvert, TE date plus 590 = AD date. The dates appear to be accession years.

KINGDOM

Mahendra Manikya

SE c.1634-1636 / c.1712-1714AD

HAMMERED COINAGE

Mint: Without Mint Name
KM# 184 1/16 RUPEE
0.6500 g., Silver

Date	Mintage	VG	F	VF	XF	Unc
ND(1712-14)	—	25.00	40.00	75.00	110	—

Mint: Without Mint Name
KM# 186 1/4 RUPEE
Silver

Date	Mintage	VG	F	VF	XF	Unc
SE1634 (1712)	—	45.00	75.00	150	200	—

Mint: Without Mint Name
KM# 188 RUPEE
10.5000 g., Silver

Date	Mintage	VG	F	VF	XF	Unc
SE1634 (1712)	—	80.00	130	225	325	—

Dharma Manikya

SEc1636-1661 / c.1714-1739AD

HAMMERED COINAGE

Mint: Without Mint Name
KM# 193 1/32 RUPEE
Silver

Date	Mintage	VG	F	VF	XF	Unc
ND(1714-39)	—	20.00	30.00	60.00	90.00	—

Mint: Without Mint Name
KM# 194 1/16 RUPEE
0.6500 g., Silver

Date	Mintage	VG	F	VF	XF	Unc
ND(1714-39)	—	12.00	20.00	35.00	55.00	—

Mint: Without Mint Name
KM# 196 1/4 RUPEE
2.6000 g., Silver

Date	Mintage	VG	F	VF	XF	Unc
SE1636 (1714)	—	12.00	20.00	35.00	55.00	—

Mint: Without Mint Name
KM# 197 1/2 RUPEE
5.2000 g., Silver

Date	Mintage	VG	F	VF	XF	Unc
SE1636 (1714)	—	50.00	80.00	150	200	—

Mint: Without Mint Name
KM# 198 RUPEE
10.5000 g., Silver **Rev:** Legend without Queen's name

Date	Mintage	VG	F	VF	XF	Unc
SE1636 (1714)	—	21.50	35.00	50.00	80.00	—

Mint: Without Mint Name
KM# 199 RUPEE
10.5000 g., Silver **Rev. Legend:** "Queen Darmasila..."

Date	Mintage	VG	F	VF	XF	Unc
SE1636 (1714)	—	21.50	35.00	50.00	80.00	—

Mint: Without Mint Name
KM# 203 MOHUR
Gold **Rev:** Queen's name

Date	Mintage	VG	F	VF	XF	Unc
SE1636 (1714)	—	700	1,000	1,500	2,000	—

Jaya Manikya II

SE1661-1666 / c.1739-1744AD

HAMMERED COINAGE

Mint: Without Mint Name
KM# 205 1/16 RUPEE
0.6500 g., Silver

Date	Mintage	VG	F	VF	XF	Unc
ND(1739-44)	—	25.00	40.00	75.00	110	—

Mint: Without Mint Name
KM# 207 1/4 RUPEE
2.6000 g., Silver

Date	Mintage	VG	F	VF	XF	Unc
SE1661 (1739)	—	30.00	50.00	100	160	—

Mint: Without Mint Name
KM# 209 RUPEE
10.5000 g., Silver **Rev. Legend:** "Queen Jasovati..."

Date	Mintage	VG	F	VF	XF	Unc
SE1661 (1739)	—	55.00	90.00	160	225	—

Indra Manikya

SEc.1666-1669 / c.1744-1747AD

HAMMERED COINAGE

Mint: Without Mint Name
KM# 215 1/16 RUPEE
0.6500 g., Silver

Date	Mintage	VG	F	VF	XF	Unc
ND(1744-47)	—	40.00	70.00	150	200	—

Mint: Without Mint Name
KM# 217 1/4 RUPEE
2.6000 g., Silver

Date	Mintage	VG	F	VF	XF	Unc
SE1666 (1744)	—	90.00	150	225	300	—

Mint: Without Mint Name
KM# 219 RUPEE
10.4000 g., Silver **Rev. Legend:** Queen Lakshmivati

Date	Mintage	VG	F	VF	XF	Unc
SE1666 (1744)	—	300	500	750	1,000	—

Krishna Manikya

SE1682-1705 / 1760-1783AD

HAMMERED COINAGE

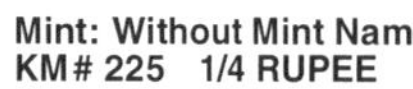

Mint: Without Mint Name
KM# 225 1/4 RUPEE
Silver **Note:** Weight varies: 2.57-2.67 grams.

Date	Mintage	VG	F	VF	XF	Unc
SE1682 (1760)	—	30.00	42.50	55.00	100	—

Mint: Without Mint Name
KM# 226 1/2 RUPEE
Silver **Note:** Weight varies: 5.15-5.35 grams.

Date	Mintage	VG	F	VF	XF	Unc
SE1682 (1760)	—	35.00	50.00	70.00	150	—

Mint: Without Mint Name
KM# 227 RUPEE
Silver **Rev. Legend:** "Krishna Manikya" **Note:** Weight varies: 10.30-10.70 grams.

Date	Mintage	VG	F	VF	XF	Unc
SE1682 (1760)	—	75.00	100	150	200	—

Mint: Without Mint Name
KM# 228 RUPEE
Silver **Rev. Legend:** "Krishna Manikya with Queen Jahnavi"
Note: Weight varies: 10.30-10.70 grams.

Date	Mintage	VG	F	VF	XF	Unc
SE1682 (1760)	—	75.00	100	150	200	—

Mint: Without Mint Name
KM# 231 1/4 MOHUR
Gold

Date	Mintage	VG	F	VF	XF	Unc
SE1682 (1760)	—	150	250	450	800	—

Mint: Without Mint Name
KM# 233 MOHUR
Gold **Rev. Legend:** "Krishna Manikya"

Date	Mintage	VG	F	VF	XF	Unc
SE1682 (1760)	—	700	1,000	1,500	2,000	—

Mint: Without Mint Name
KM# 234 MOHUR
Gold **Rev:** "with Queen Jahnavi"

Date	Mintage	VG	F	VF	XF	Unc
SE1682 (1760)	—	700	1,000	1,500	2,000	—

Rajadhara Manikya
SE1707-1726 / 1785-1804AD
HAMMERED COINAGE

Mint: Without Mint Name
KM# 244 RUPEE
Silver **Note:** Weight varies: 10.30-10.70 grams.

Date	Mintage	VG	F	VF	XF	Unc
SE1707 (1785)	—	75.00	125	175	250	—

Mint: Without Mint Name
KM# 249 MOHUR
Gold

Date	Mintage	VG	F	VF	XF	Unc
SE1707 (1785)	—	700	1,000	1,500	2,000	—

PLAINS TRIPURA

Shah Alam II
AH1173-1221 / 1759-1806AD
HAMMERED COINAGE

Mint: Roshanabad Tripura Mint
KM# 511 NAZARANA RUPEE
Silver **Note:** Weight varies: 10.70-11.60 grams. Struck at Roshanabad Tripura Mint.

Date	Mintage	VG	F	VF	XF	Unc
AH1175//3	—	120	200	350	550	—

VIJAYANAGAR

The Vijayanagar kingdom was founded by two brothers, Harihari and Bukka, from the Telangana region of present day Andhra Pradesh in East Central India. They had previously served the raja of Warangal until they were captured and transported to Delhi where they were reputed to have become converts to Islam. They then revolted and, returning to the Hindu fold, in 1336 founded the kingdom as a bulwark against further Muslim inroads into the South. Vijayanagar (literally, City of Victory) grew into the most remarkable of all the medieval Hindu kingdoms. Some 19 square miles in area, Vijayanage itself - the capital after which the empire was named – sat on the southern bank of the Kristna river, not far from modern Hospet in Mysore State. Contemporary observers compared the city both in size and stature to ancient Rome.

Even to this day, the ruins of this remarkable capital are among the most impressive anywhere in India. Resplendent with intricate stone carving, fine temples and broad public ways, it was a city whose wealth knew no equal in South or Central India. Its sovereignty extended over virtually the whole of South India. The rulers, or rayas, of Vijayanagar were patrons of the arts and under their authority art, architecture and literature flourished. Its Hinduism was eclectic, Vaishnavite in sentiment and vibrant in expression. It was a wealthy city, whose vices were the vices of the rich. Its coinage was predominantly in gold and, like its culture, distinctly South Indian in style.

After the period of the 2 chiefs Harihari (1336-1354) and Bukka (1354-1377), Vijayanagar history fell into 4 periods, viz., the Sangama dynasty (1377-1485), the Saluva dynasty (1486-ca.1503), the Tuluva dynasty(ca. 1503-1570), and the Aravidu (or Karnata) dynasty (1570-ca. 1646). For over 2 centuries the Vijayanagar kingdom was more or less in a constant state of war against the Bahmanis and their successor sultanates in the Deccan. And for those two hundred years Vijayanagar effectively halted Muslim attempts to encroach southwards. This was the empire's golden age as Vijayanagar grew to be the one real center in India for Hindu self-expression within a context of political self-determination. Vassal to none, Vijayanagar held the south of India as a constant rebuke to Muslim expansionism.

Then, in 1565, disaster struck. The sultanates of Ahmadnagar, Bijapur, Bidar and Golkonda combined forces to bring about the destruction of Vijayanagar. Vijayanagar was well equipped for this confrontation, putting perhaps as many as a million men on the field. But, by one of those quirks in the fortunes of war, the Vijayanagar commander, Ramaraja (who was also the regent and controlling noble of the kingdom), was cut off from his troops, dragged down from his elephant, and at once beheaded. His army immediately panicked and their strategy fell apart. This battle, remembered as the battle of Talikota, was followed by a complete rout of the forces of Vijayanagar and by the plunder and destruction of their capital city.

The nominal king, in whose place Ramaraja had ruled, fled to Penukonda. There on this rocky hill further south he re-established the dynasty. Five years later he was overthrown by Tirumala, his brother, and the Karnata dynasty was inaugurated. A few years later the capital was shifted to Chandragiri, under Venkata I. Here, for a while, the truncated kingdom seemed to regain some of its lost vigor. But after Venkata's death even this dynasty disintegrated and the remnants of this once-proud empire were reduced to the status of local chiefs. Yet, in spite of Muslim encroachment into the Deccan, first by the Adil Shahis of Bijapur and the Qutb Shahis of Golkonda, and by the Mughal armies under Aurangzeb, these chieftains continued to exercise a considerable degree of local independence.

But Vijayanagar was gone, and in its passing the brightest star of Hindu art, architecture, philosophy and culture was extinguished. Never again would there rise a Hindu kingdom comparable to Vijayanagar, and never again until Indian Independence, would South India be so free of foreign domination.

RULERS

Aravidu Dynasty

KINGDOM
ANONYMOUS HAMMERED COINAGE
1642-1757AD

Mint: Without Mint Name
KM# 9 PAGODA
3.4000 g., Gold **Obv:** Sri-devi Venkatesvara and Bhu-devi standing

Date	Mintage	VG	F	VF	XF	Unc
ND	—	50.00	65.00	85.00	135	—

Mint: Without Mint Name
KM# 8 PAGODA
3.4000 g., Gold **Obv:** Venkatesvara kneeling **Note:** Uniface.

Date	Mintage	VG	F	VF	XF	Unc
ND	—	50.00	60.00	75.00	125	—

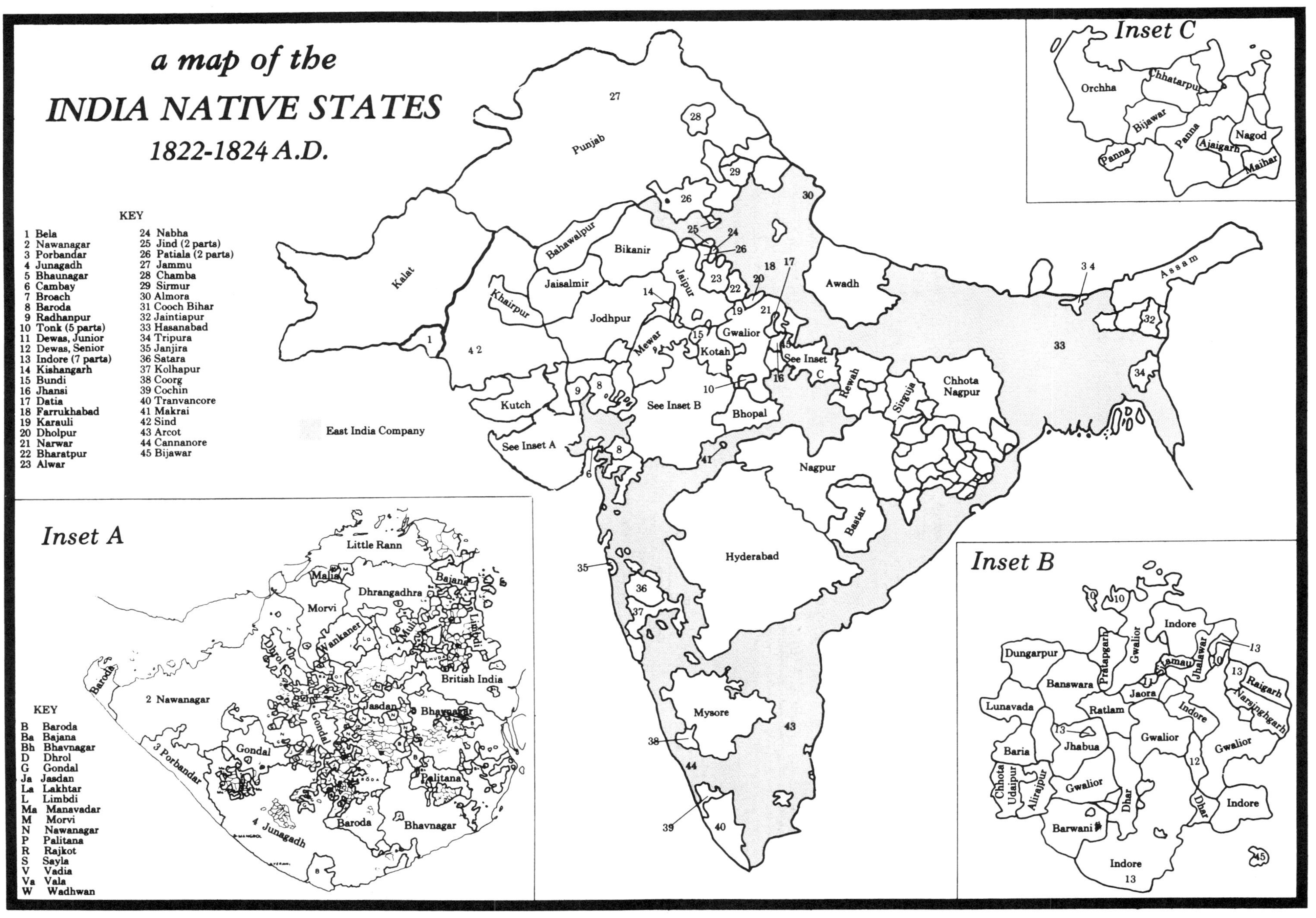
a map of the
INDIA NATIVE STATES
1822-1824 A.D.
KEY
1 Bela
2 Nawanagar
3 Porbandar
4 Junagadh
5 Bhaunagar
6 Cambay
7 Broach
8 Baroda
9 Radhanpur
10 Tonk (5 parts)
11 Dewas, Junior
12 Dewas, Senior
13 Indore (7 parts)
14 Kishangarh
15 Bundi
16 Jhansi
17 Datia
18 Farrukhabad
19 Karauli
20 Dholpur
21 Narwar
22 Bharatpur
23 Alwar
24 Nabha
25 Jind (2 parts)
26 Patiala (2 parts)
27 Jammu
28 Chamba
29 Sirmur
30 Almora
31 Cooch Bihar
32 Jaintiapur
33 Hasanabad
34 Tripura
35 Janjira
36 Satara
37 Kolhapur
38 Coorg
39 Cochin
40 Tranvancore
41 Makrai
42 Sind
43 Arcot
44 Cannanore
45 Bijawar
East India Company
Kalat
Punjab
Bahawalpur
Bikanir
Khairpur
Jaisalmir
Jodhpur
Jaipur
Mewar
Kotah
Gwalior
Awadh
Assam
Kutch
See Inset A
See Inset B
See Inset C
Bhopal
Rewah
Sirguja
Chhota Nagpur
Nagpur
Bastar
Hyderabad
Mysore
Inset A
Little Rann
Malia
Morvi
Dhrangadhra
Bajana
Limbdi
Wankaner
Muli
Dhrol
British India
2 Nawanagar
Baroda
Jasdan
Bhavnagar
Gondal
3 Porbandar
Palitana
4 Junagadh
KEY
B Baroda
Ba Bajana
Bh Bhavnagar
D Dhrol
G Gondal
Ja Jasdan
La Lakhtar
L Limbdi
Ma Manavadar
M Morvi
N Nawanagar
P Palitana
R Rajkot
S Sayla
V Vadia
Va Vala
W Wadhwan
Inset B
Dungarpur
Pratapgarh
Gwalior
Indore
Sitamau
Jhalawar
Raigarh
Narsinghgarh
Banswara
Jaora
Ratlam
Lunavada
Jhabua
Baria
Chhota Udaipur
Alirajpur
Dhar
Barwani
Inset C
Orchha
Chhatarpur
Bijawar
Panna
Ajaigarh
Nagod
Maihar

MONETARY SYSTEMS

In each state, local rates of exchange prevailed. There was no fixed rate between copper, silver or gold coin, but the rates varied in accordance with the values of the metal and by the edict of the local authority.

Within the subcontinent, different regions used distinctive coinage standards. In North India and the Deccan, the silver rupee (11.6 g) and gold mohur (11.0 g) predominated. In Gujarat, the silver kori (4.7 g) and gold kori (6.4 g) were the main currency. In South India the silver fanam (0.7-1.0 g) and gold hun or Pagoda (3.4 g) were current. Copper coins in all parts of India were produced to a myriad of local metrologies with seemingly endless varieties.

NAZARANA ISSUES

Throughout the Indian Princely States listings are Nazarana designations for special full flan strikings of copper, silver and some gold coinage. The purpose of these issues was for presentation to the local monarch to gain favor. For example if one had an audience with one's ruler he would exchange goods, currency notes or the cruder struck circulating coinage for Nazarana pieces which he would present to the ruler as a gift. The borderline between true Nazarana pieces and well struck regular issues is often indistinct. The Nazaranas sometimes circulated alongside the cruder "dump" issues.

PRICING

As the demand for Indian Princely coinage develops, and more dealers handle the material, sale records and price lists enable a firmer basis for pricing most series. For scarcer types adequate sale records are often not available, and prices must be regarded as tentative. Inasmuch as date collectors of Princely States series are few, dates known to be scarce are usually worth little more than common ones. Coins of a dated type, which do not show the full date on their flans should be valued at about 70 per cent of the prices indicated.

DATING

Coins are dated in several eras. Arabic and Devanagari numerals are used in conjunction with the Hejira era (AH), the Vikrama Samvat (VS), Saka Samvat (Saka), Fasli era(FE) Mauludi era (AM), and Malabar era (ME), as well as the Christian era (AD).

GRADING

Copper coins are rarely found in high grade, as they were the workhorse of coinage circulation, and were everywhere used for day-to-day transactions. Moreover, they were carelessly struck and even when 'new', can often only be distinguished from VF coins with difficulty, if at all.

Silver coins were often hoarded and not infrequently, turn up in nearly as-struck condition. The silver coins of Hyderabad (dump coins) are common in high grades, and the rupees of some states are scarcer 'used' than 'new'. Great caution must be exercised in determining the value or scarcity of high grade dump coins.

Dump gold was rarely circulated, and usually occurs in high grades, or is found made into jewelry.

INDEX

Ajmir – Gwalior and Jodhpur

Akbarabad – Bharatpur

Allahabad – Awadh

ALWAR
....Rajgarh

ARCOT
- Arkat
- Kadapa
- Madras
- Madurai
- Nahtarnagar
- Ramnad
- Tanjore
- Tinnevelly
- Trichinopoly

Arkat – Arcot

Asafabad – Awadh

Asafnagar – Awadh

Aurangabad – Hyderabad

AWADH
- Allahabad
- Asafabad
- Asafnagar
- Awadh (Subah)
- Banaras (Muhammadabad)
- Bareli
- Hathras
- Itawa
- Kanauj
- Kora
- Lucknow
- Muradabad
- Najibabad
- Shahabad (Anupnagar)
- Tanda (Muhammadnagar)

BAHAWALPUR
- Bahawalpur
- Khanpur

Banaras – Awadh

Bareli – Awadh

BARODA
- Ahmadabad
- Baroda

BHARATPUR
- Akbarabad
- Bharatpur
- Dig
- Kumber

BHAUNAGAR

Bhinda – Mewar

BHOPAL

BIKANIR

BINDRABAN (Vrindavan)
- Bindraban
- Gokul
- Mathura

BROACH
- See also Gwalior

BUNDI

Burhanpur – Gwalior

CANNANORE

Chanderi – Gwalior

Chandor – Indore

CHHATARPUR

Chitor – Mewar

CIS-SUTLEJ STATES
- Hansi
- Jind
- Kaithal
- Maler Kotla
- Patiala

COCHIN

COORG

Dalipnagar – Datia

DATIA
- Dalipnagar

Daulatabad – Hyderabad

Deogarh – Partabgarh

DHOLPUR
- Gohad

Dig – Bharatpur

DUNGARPUR

East India Company
- See also Awadh, Bareli, Broach, Indore, Kunch and Satara

Gadwal – Hyderabad

Garhakota – Gwalior

GARHWAL (Srinagar)

Gohad – Dholpur

Gokul – Bindraban

GWALIOR
- Ajmir
- Broach
- Burhanpur
- Chanderi
- Gwalior Fort
- Jawad
- Lashkar
- Narwar
- Sipri
- Ujjain

Hansi – Cis-Sutlej States

Hathras – Awadh

HYDERABAD
- Aurangabad (Khujista Bunyad)
- Daulatabad
- Hyderabad (Farkhanda Bunyad)

HYDERABAD FEUDATORIES
- Gadwal
- Kalayani
- Narayanpett

INDORE
- Chandor
- Maheshwar
- Malharnagar

INDORE FEUDATORIES
- Sironj

Itawa – Awadh

JAIPUR
- Jaipur Sawai
- Khetri
- Muzaffargarh
- Madhopur Sawai

JAISALMIR

Jambusar – Baroda

JANJIRA ISLAND

Jawad – Gwalior

Jind – Cis-Sutlej States

JODHPUR (Marwar)
- Ajmir
- Jodhpur
- Merta
- Nagor

JODHPUR FEUDATORIES
- Kuchawan

Kadapa – Arcot

Kaithal – Cis-Sutlej States

Kalayani – Hyderabad

Kanauj – Awadh

KARAULI

Khanpur – Bahawalpur

KISHANGARH

Kora – Awadh

KOTAH

Kuchawan – Jodhpur

Kumber – Bharatpur

KUTCH

LADAKH

Lashkar – Gwalior

Lucknow – Awadh

Madhopur – Jaipur

Madras – Arcot

Madurai – Arcot

Maheshwar – Indore

Maler Kotia – Cis-Sutlej States

Malharnagar – Indore

Mathura – Bindraban

Merta – Jodhpur

MEWAR
- Chitor
- Udaipur

MEWAR LOCAL ISSUES
- Bhilwara
- Chitor
- Umarda

Muradabad – Awadh

MYSORE

Nagor – Jodhpur

Nahtarnagar – Arcot

Najibabad – Awadh
- Awadh, Bharatpur (Pseudo)

Narayanpett – Hyderabad

NARWAR
- See also Gwalior

NAWANAGAR

ORCHHA

PANNA

PARTABGARH (Pratapgarh)
- Deogarh

Patiala – Cis-Sutlej States

Rajgarh – Alwar

Ramnad – Arcot

RATLAM

SELAM (Salem)

Shahabad – Awadh

Sironj – Indore

Srinagar – Garhwal

Tanda – Awadh

Tanjore – Arcot

Tinnevelly – Arcot

TRAVANCORE

Trichinopoly – Arcot

TRIPURA

Udaipur – Mewar

Ujjain – Gwalior

Umarda - Mewar

ALWAR

State located in Rajputana in northwestern India.

Alwar was founded about 1722 by a Rajput chieftain of the Naruka clan, Rao Pratap Singh of Macheri (1740-1791), a descendant of the family, which had ruled Jaipur in the 14th century. Alwar was distinguished by being the first of the Princely States to use coins struck at the Calcutta Mint. These, first issued in 1877, were of the same weight and assay as the Imperial Rupee, and carried the bust of Queen Victoria, Empress of India. Alwar State, having allied itself with East India Company interests in their struggles against the Marathas early in the 19th century, continued to maintain a good relationship with the British right up to Indian Independence in 1947. In May 1949, Alwar was merged into Rajasthan.

LOCAL RULERS

Pratap Singh, AH1186-1206/1772-1791AD
Bakhtawar Singh, AH1206-1230/1791-1815AD

MINT

راج گره

Rajgarh

PRINCELY STATE

HAMMERED COINAGE

KM# 10 RUPEE
Silver **Obverse:** Inscription **Obv. Inscription:** "Shah Alam II" **Reverse:** Inscription **Note:** Weight varies: 11.2-11.4g.

Date	Mintage	Good	VG	F	VF	XF
AH//15 (1773-74)	—	6.00	13.00	22.50	30.00	40.00
AH//16 (1774-75)	—	6.00	13.00	22.50	30.00	40.00
AH//19 (1777-78)	—	6.00	13.00	22.50	30.00	40.00
AH//20 (1778-79)	—	6.00	13.00	22.50	30.00	40.00
AH1195//24 (sic)	—	6.00	13.00	22.50	30.00	40.00
AH//25 (1783-84)	—	6.00	13.00	22.50	30.00	40.00
AH//26 (1784-85)	—	6.00	13.00	22.50	30.00	40.00
AH//30 (1788-89)	—	6.00	13.00	22.50	30.00	40.00
AH//32 (1790-91)	—	6.00	13.00	22.50	30.00	40.00
AH//33 (1791-92)	—	6.00	13.00	22.50	30.00	40.00
AH//35 (1793-94)	—	6.00	13.00	22.50	30.00	40.00
AH//38 (1796-97)	—	6.00	13.00	22.50	30.00	40.00
AH//40 (1798-99)	—	6.00	13.00	22.50	30.00	40.00
AH//41 (1799-1800)	—	6.00	13.00	22.50	30.00	40.00
AH//42 (1800-01)	—	6.00	13.00	22.50	30.00	40.00

Shah Alam II

AH1173-1221 / 1759-1806AD

HAMMERED COINAGE

KM# 5 TAKKA
Copper, 21 mm. **Obv. Inscription:** Shah Alam (II) **Mint:** Rajgarh **Note:** Weight varies: 17.5-18.5g. Mint mark: Fish.

Date	Mintage	Good	VG	F	VF	XF
ND//16 (1774-75)	—	2.50	4.00	6.00	15.00	—
ND//19 (1777-78)	—	2.50	4.00	6.00	15.00	—
ND//20 (1778-79)	—	2.50	4.00	6.00	15.00	—
ND//21 (1779-80)	—	2.50	4.00	6.00	15.00	—
ND//22 (1780)	—	2.50	4.00	6.00	15.00	—
ND//25 (1783-84)	—	2.50	4.00	6.00	15.00	—
ND//27 (1785-86)	—	2.50	4.00	6.00	15.00	—
ND//28 (1786-87)	—	2.50	4.00	6.00	15.00	—
ND//29 (1787-88)	—	2.50	4.00	6.00	15.00	—
AH1202//30	—	2.50	4.00	6.00	15.00	—
AH1202//31 (sic)	—	2.50	4.00	6.00	15.00	—
ND//32 (1790-91)	—	2.50	4.00	6.00	15.00	—
AH1204//33 (sic)	—	2.50	4.00	6.00	15.00	—
AH1205//34 (sic)	—	2.50	4.00	6.00	15.00	—
ND//35 (1793-94)	—	2.50	4.00	6.00	15.00	—
ND//37 (1795-96)	—	2.50	4.00	6.00	15.00	—
ND//40 (1798-99)	—	2.50	4.00	6.00	15.00	—
ND//41 (1799-1800)	—	2.50	4.00	6.00	15.00	—

KM# 10a NAZARANA RUPEE
11.3000 g., Silver **Obv. Inscription:** Shah Alam (II)

Date	Mintage	Good	VG	F	VF	XF
AH1212//37 (sic)	—	—	40.00	60.00	100	200

ARCOT

Arkat

Possession located on the east coast of India between Madras and Calcutta.

The Nawab of Arcot ranked, under British India, as the first noble of the Carnatic. The family was descended from Anwar-al-Din who, in the early part of the 18th century, had received his title as the Nawab of the Carnatic from the Nizam of Hyderabad. In the struggle that took place shortly afterwards along the Coromandel Coast between the English, under Clive, and the French, under Dupleix, Anwar-al-Din's son, Muhammed Ali, allied himself with the British. The French in turn were supported by Chanda Sahib, a rival claimant to the throne of the Carnatic. Although Arcot town fell to the French in 1760 and both town and countryside were ravaged by Haider Ali of Mysore in 1780, the ultimate triumph of British arms ensured Muhammed Ali's success. Muhammed Ali chose to be known as Walajah Nawab of the Carnatic and it is this title that is conspicuous on the coinage. In 1801 Arcot came under direct British administration and the Arcot mint was closed.

It is also convenient to group under Arcot the tiny copper coins of the Nayakas and Poligars of Madurai, Ramnad, Tanjore, Tinnevelly, Trichinopoly and the surrounding areas. These were local chieftains who had, especially since the decline of the great Hindu kingdom of Vijayanagar after 1565, exercised a great measure of autonomy over their fiefdoms. The chieftains themselves were numerous and quite local in authority, and their coinage was typically South Indian in style.

RULERS

Muhammad Ali, AH1165-1209/1751-1795AD
Umdat-ul-Umara, AH1209-1216/1795-1801AD

MINTS

اركات

Arkat

Rupees were coined by the Nawab of Arcot, his subsidiaries, and the English and French East India Companies, all in the mint-name Arkat. The French issues were distinguishable by broad flan and dotted field, and the English by the lotus mint mark and anachronistic use of Alamgir II's legend (see respective sections). The actual issues of Arkat mint were differentiated from other mint products by the four-petal flower or star beside the regnal year on the reverse.

Kadapa

Madras-Tiruvallur

Madurai, Ramnad

نهتر نگر

Nahtarnagar

Tanjore

Tinnevelly

Uncertain

TITLES

والا جاه

Wala Jah

Wala

Wa

PRINCELY STATE

HAMMERED COINAGE

KM# A8 1/4 PAISA
Copper **Mint:** Kadapa

Date	Mintage	Good	VG	F	VF	XF
AH1201 //28	—	3.00	6.00	12.00	25.00	—

KM# A18 PAISA
Copper **Mint:** Kadapa

Date	Mintage	Good	VG	F	VF	XF
//26?	—	5.00	10.00	20.00	45.00	—

Muhammad Ali

AH1165-1209/1751-95AD

HAMMERED COINAGE

KM# 8 1/4 PAISA
Copper **Obv. Inscription:** Shah Alam (II) **Mint:** Arkat **Note:** With the title "Wala" or "Wala Jah".

Date	Mintage	Good	VG	F	VF	XF
AH1183	—	1.50	2.50	3.50	10.00	—
AH1201	—	1.50	2.50	3.50	10.00	—
AH1202	—	1.50	2.50	3.50	10.00	—

KM# 21 1/4 PAISA
Copper **Mint:** Madras-Tiruvalur

Date	Mintage	Good	VG	F	VF	XF
AH1208//35	—	1.50	2.50	3.50	10.00	—
AH1209//36	—	1.50	2.50	3.50	10.00	—

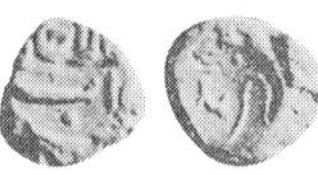

KM# 47 1/4 PAISA
Copper **Obverse:** Mint name **Mint:** Nahtarnagar

Date	Mintage	Good	VG	F	VF	XF
AH1208	—	1.50	3.00	5.00	8.00	—

KM# A1 1/2 PAISA
7.0000 g., Copper **Mint:** Arkat

Date	Mintage	Good	VG	F	VF	XF
AH1142	—	3.50	5.00	8.50	15.00	—

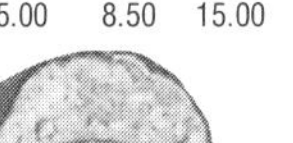

KM# 17 1/2 PAISA
Copper **Mint:** Kadapa

Date	Mintage	Good	VG	F	VF	XF
AH1166//26	—	2.00	3.50	5.00	12.00	—

KM# 18 1/2 PAISA
6.9000 g., Copper **Obv. Inscription:** Shah Alam (II) **Mint:** Kadapa

Date	Mintage	Good	VG	F	VF	XF
AH1166	—	2.00	3.50	5.00	10.00	—
AH1179	—	2.00	3.50	5.00	10.00	—
AH1190	—	2.00	3.50	5.00	10.00	—
AH1195	—	2.00	3.50	5.00	10.00	—

KM# 9 1/2 PAISA
Copper **Obv. Inscription:** Shah Alam (II) **Mint:** Arkat

Date	Mintage	Good	VG	F	VF	XF
AH1200//27 (1785)	—	1.25	2.25	3.00	7.50	—
AH1201//28 (1786)	—	1.25	2.25	3.00	7.50	—
AH1203 (1788)	—	1.25	2.25	3.00	7.50	—
AH1204 (1789)	—	1.25	2.25	3.00	7.50	—
AH1205 (1790)	—	1.25	2.25	3.00	7.50	—
AH1206//30 (1791)	—	1.25	2.25	3.00	7.50	—
AH1206//34 (1791)	—	1.25	2.25	3.00	7.50	—
AH1207//34 (1792)	—	1.25	2.25	3.00	7.50	—

KM# 48 1/2 PAISA
Copper **Mint:** Nahtarnagar

Date	Mintage	Good	VG	F	VF	XF
AH1207	—	4.00	8.00	15.00	22.50	—

KM# 22 1/2 PAISA

Copper **Mint:** Madras-Tiruvalur

Date	Mintage	Good	VG	F	VF	XF
AH1207//34	—	3.00	4.50	6.50	15.00	—
AH1208//35	—	3.00	4.50	6.50	15.00	—
AH1209//36	—	3.00	4.50	6.50	15.00	—

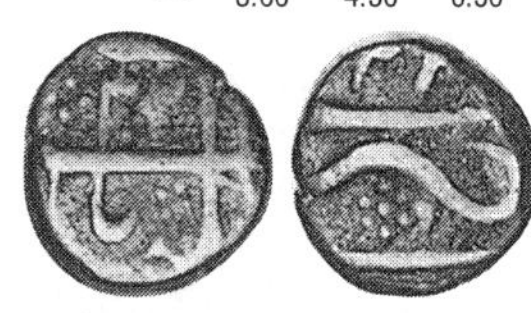

KM# B1 PAISA

13.0000 g., Copper **Mint:** Arkat

Date	Mintage	Good	VG	F	VF	XF
AH1142	—	3.50	5.00	8.50	15.00	—
AH1180 Retrograde	—	—	—	—	—	—

KM# 19 PAISA

13.6000 g., Copper **Obv. Inscription:** Shah Alam (II) **Reverse:** Without "Wala" **Mint:** Kadapa

Date	Mintage	Good	VG	F	VF	XF
AH1175//7	—	2.00	3.50	5.00	10.00	—
AH1182	—	2.00	3.50	5.00	10.00	—
AH1183	—	2.00	3.50	5.00	10.00	—
AH1189	—	2.00	3.50	5.00	10.00	—
AH1190	—	2.00	3.50	5.00	10.00	—
AH1191	—	2.00	3.50	5.00	10.00	—
AH1198	—	2.00	3.50	5.00	10.00	—

KM# 3 PAISA

Copper **Obv. Inscription:** Shah Alam (II) **Mint:** Arkat

Date	Mintage	Good	VG	F	VF	XF
AH1177//4	—	2.00	3.50	5.50	12.00	—
AH1177//5	—	2.00	3.50	5.50	12.00	—

KM# 23 PAISA

Copper **Mint:** Madras-Tiruvalur

Date	Mintage	Good	VG	F	VF	XF
AH1200//27	—	4.50	6.50	9.00	20.00	—
AH1206//34	—	4.50	6.50	9.00	20.00	—
AH1208//35	—	4.50	6.50	9.00	20.00	—

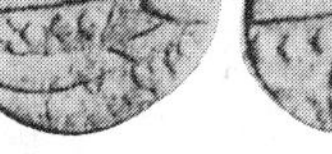

KM# 10 PAISA

Copper **Obv. Inscription:** Shah Alam (II) **Mint:** Arkat

Date	Mintage	Good	VG	F	VF	XF
AH1201//28	—	3.00	4.50	7.50	12.00	—
AH1203	—	3.00	4.50	7.50	12.00	—
AH1206//30	—	3.00	4.50	7.50	12.00	—
AH1208	—	3.00	4.50	7.50	12.00	—

KM# 49 PAISA

Copper **Obv. Inscription:** Wala Jah **Shape:** Octagonal **Mint:** Nahtarnagar

Date	Mintage	Good	VG	F	VF	XF
AH1207	—	6.00	10.00	20.00	30.00	—

KM# 52 1/2 RUPEE

Silver **Obv. Inscription:** Shah Alam (II) **Mint:** Arkat **Note:** Mint mark: Trisul in "S" of "Julus". Weight varies: 5.35-5.80g.

Date	Mintage	Good	VG	F	VF	XF
AH1183//14	—	12.50	30.00	50.00	70.00	100

KM# 50 RUPEE

Silver **Obv. Inscription:** Mohammad Shah **Mint:** Arkat **Note:** Mint mark: Bud or flower above "J" of "Julus". Weight varies: 10.70-11.60 grams.

Date	Mintage	Good	VG	F	VF	XF
AH1147	—	12.50	30.00	50.00	70.00	100
AH-//20	—	12.50	30.00	50.00	70.00	100

KM# 51 RUPEE

Silver **Obverse:** Mint mark: Crescent above Mubarak. **Obv. Inscription:** Mohammad Shah **Mint:** Arkat **Note:** Weight varies: 10.70-11.60 grams.

Date	Mintage	Good	VG	F	VF	XF
AH115x//23	—	12.50	30.00	50.00	70.00	100

KM# 1 RUPEE

Silver **Obv. Inscription:** Ahmad Shah Bahadur **Mint:** Arkat **Note:** Weight varies: 10.70-11.60 grams.

Date	Mintage	VG	F	VF	XF	Unc
AH1162//2	—	—	—	—	—	—
AH116x//4	—	—	—	—	—	—

KM# 2 RUPEE

Silver **Obv. Inscription:** Alamgir (II) **Mint:** Arkat **Note:** Weight varies: 10.70-11.60 grams.

Date	Mintage	VG	F	VF	XF	Unc
AH1168//2 Rare	—	—	—	—	—	—

KM# 53 RUPEE

Silver **Obv. Inscription:** Shah Alam (II) **Mint:** Uncertain Mint **Note:** Weight varies: 10.70-11.60 grams.

Date	Mintage	Good	VG	F	VF	XF
AH1183//14	—	12.50	30.00	50.00	70.00	100

KM# 5 RUPEE

Silver **Obv. Inscription:** Shah Alam (II) **Mint:** Arkat **Note:** Weight varies: 10.70-11.60 grams. Mint mark: 4-petal flower.

Date	Mintage	Good	VG	F	VF	XF
AH1186//10	—	5.00	12.50	21.00	28.50	40.00
AH1188//10	—	5.00	12.50	21.00	28.50	40.00
AH119x//12	—	5.00	12.50	21.00	28.50	40.00
AH1191//14	—	5.00	12.50	21.00	28.50	40.00
AH1191//18	—	5.00	12.50	21.00	28.50	40.00
AH1200//27	—	5.00	12.50	21.00	28.50	40.00
AH1201//28	—	5.00	12.50	21.00	28.50	40.00
AH1203//29	—	5.00	12.50	21.00	28.50	40.00
AH1205//30	—	5.00	12.50	21.00	28.50	40.00

KM# 6 RUPEE

Silver **Obv. Inscription:** Shah Alam (II) **Mint:** Arkat **Note:** Mint marks: 4-petal flower and "Wala".

Date	Mintage	Good	VG	F	VF	XF
AH1206//31	—	6.50	16.50	21.50	27.50	40.00

KM# 4a NAZARANA 1/4 RUPEE

Silver **Obv. Inscription:** Shah Alam (II) **Mint:** Arkat **Note:** Weight varies: 2.65-2.90 grams. Without flower mint mark.

Date	Mintage	Good	VG	F	VF	XF
AH1202//29 Rare	—	—	—	—	—	—

KM# 7 2 RUPEES

Silver **Obv. Inscription:** Shah Alam (II) **Mint:** Arkat

Date	Mintage	Good	VG	F	VF	XF
AH1200//27	—	—	500	700	1,000	1,500

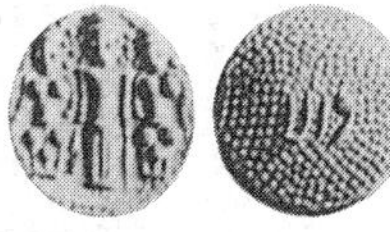

KM# 13 PAGODA

3.0000 g., 0.8000 Gold 0.0772 oz. AGW **Obverse:** 3 Swamis **Obv. Inscription:** Shah Alam (II) **Rev. Inscription:** WALA **Mint:** Arkat

Date	Mintage	VG	F	VF	XF	Unc
ND(1790)	—	80.00	120	180	300	—

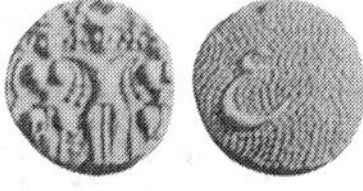

KM# 14 PAGODA

3.0000 g., 0.8000 Gold 0.0772 oz. AGW **Obverse:** 3 Swamis **Obv. Inscription:** Shah Alam (II) **Rev. Inscription:** Arabic "AIN" **Mint:** Arkat

Date	Mintage	VG	F	VF	XF	Unc
ND(1790)	—	80.00	100	130	175	—

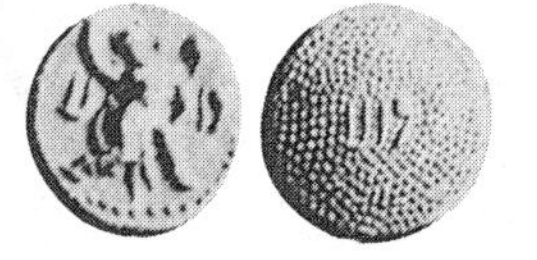

KM# 15 PAGODA

3.0000 g., 0.8000 Gold 0.0772 oz. AGW **Obverse:** Figure between inscription **Obv. Inscription:** Shah Alam (II) **Rev. Inscription:** Wala **Mint:** Arkat

Date	Mintage	VG	F	VF	XF	Unc
ND(1790)	—	160	235	400	700	—

KM# 29 NAYAKA CASH

Copper **Obverse:** Deities, geometric figures, etc. **Reverse:** Crude Wala Jah, without date **Mint:** Madurai **Note:** Struck at Ramnad Mint.

Date	Mintage	Good	VG	F	VF	XF
ND(1751-95)	—	0.60	1.00	1.75	2.50	—

KM# 25 NAYAKA CASH

Copper **Obv. Inscription:** "WALA JAH" **Reverse:** Date **Mint:** Madurai **Note:** Poliyagars. Struck at Ramnad Mint.

Date	Mintage	Good	VG	F	VF	XF
AH1196	—	1.50	2.50	4.00	6.50	—

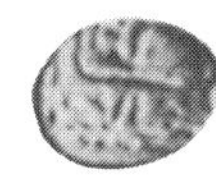

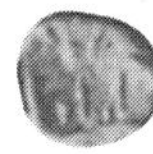

KM# 27 NAYAKA CASH

Copper **Obverse:** Deities, animal figures, etc. **Obv. Inscription:** "WALA JAH" **Reverse:** Date **Mint:** Madurai **Note:** Struck at Ramnad Mint.

Date	Mintage	Good	VG	F	VF	XF
AH1200	—	0.75	1.25	2.75	4.50	—
AH1201	—	0.75	1.25	2.75	4.50	—
AH1202	—	0.75	1.25	2.75	4.50	—
AH1204	—	0.75	1.25	2.75	4.50	—
AH1207	—	0.75	1.25	2.75	4.50	—

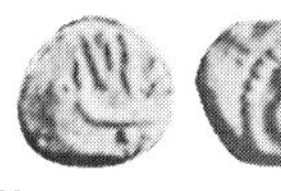

KM# 42 CASH

Copper **Obv. Inscription:** "WALA JAH" **Reverse:** Arabic letter: "Ain". **Mint:** Nahtarnagar

Date	Mintage	Good	VG	F	VF	XF
ND(1751-95)	—	1.50	2.75	4.00	6.00	—

KM# 43 CASH

Copper **Obv. Inscription:** "WALA JAH" **Reverse:** Tamil **Rev. Inscription:** "NAWAB" **Mint:** Nahtarnagar

Date	Mintage	Good	VG	F	VF	XF
ND(1751-95)	—	0.80	1.50	2.50	4.00	—

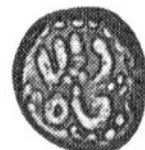

KM# 41 CASH

Copper **Obv. Legend:** "WALA JAH" **Reverse:** Date **Mint:** Nahtarnagar

Date	Mintage	Good	VG	F	VF	XF
AH1181	—	1.50	3.00	5.00	7.00	—
AH1186	—	1.50	3.00	5.00	7.00	—
AH1189	—	1.50	3.00	5.00	7.00	—
AH1195	—	1.50	3.00	5.00	7.00	—
AH1197	—	1.50	3.00	5.00	7.00	—
AH1203	—	1.50	3.00	5.00	7.00	—
AH1206	—	1.50	3.00	5.00	7.00	—

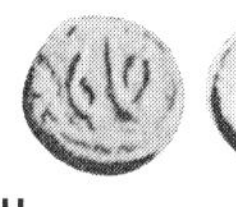

KM# 44 CASH

Copper **Obv. Inscription:** "WALA" **Rev. Inscription:** "JAH" **Mint:** Nahtarnagar

Date	Mintage	Good	VG	F	VF	XF
ND(1792)	—	0.80	1.50	2.50	4.00	—

KM# 31 CASH

Copper **Obverse:** Fish, bull, etc **Reverse:** Tamil letter "Na" **Mint:** Tanjore

Date	Mintage	Good	VG	F	VF	XF
ND(1792)	—	2.00	4.00	5.50	7.50	—

KM# 32 CASH

Copper **Obverse:** Deities, bow and arrow, horse, etc. **Reverse:** Tamil **Rev. Inscription:** "NAWAB" **Mint:** Tanjore

Date	Mintage	Good	VG	F	VF	XF
ND(1792)	—	1.00	1.50	2.75	5.00	—

KM# 35 CASH

Copper **Obv. Legend:** "WALA" **Reverse:** Date **Mint:** Tinnevelly

Date	Mintage	Good	VG	F	VF	XF
AH1207	—	2.00	3.50	5.50	8.50	—

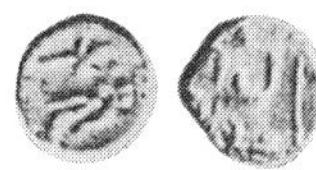

KM# 36 CASH

Copper **Obverse:** Deities, lingam, etc. **Rev. Inscription:** "WALA JAH" **Mint:** Tinnevelly

Date	Mintage	Good	VG	F	VF	XF
ND(1793)	—	1.50	2.75	4.00	6.50	—

KM# 37 CASH

Copper **Obverse:** Sun, moon, bull, lingam, etc. **Reverse:** Tamil **Rev. Inscription:** "KAMPANI" **Mint:** Tinnevelly

Date	Mintage	Good	VG	F	VF	XF
ND(1794)	—	2.00	3.50	6.50	10.00	—

KM# 38 CASH

Copper **Obverse:** Star within dots **Reverse:** Tamil **Rev. Legend:** "NAWABU" **Mint:** Tinnevelly

Date	Mintage	Good	VG	F	VF	XF
ND(1795)	—	1.50	2.75	4.00	6.50	—

Umdat-ul-Umara

AH1209-16/1795-1801AD

HAMMERED COINAGE

KM# 56 1/4 PAISA

Copper **Mint:** Madras-Tiruvalur

Date	Mintage	Good	VG	F	VF	XF
AH1213	—	2.00	4.00	6.00	12.50	—

KM# 57 1/2 PAISA

Copper **Mint:** Madras-Tiruvalur

Date	Mintage	Good	VG	F	VF	XF
AH1213	—	2.50	5.00	7.50	15.00	—

KM# 58 PAISA

Copper **Mint:** Madras-Tiruvalur

Date	Mintage	Good	VG	F	VF	XF
AH1213	—	4.50	7.00	10.00	18.50	—

KM# 54 RUPEE

Silver **Obv. Inscription:** Shah Alam (II) **Mint:** Arkat **Note:** Weight varies: 10.70-11.60 grams. Mint marks: 4-petal flower and "Wa".

Date	Mintage	Good	VG	F	VF	XF
AH1211//3	—	12.50	30.00	50.00	70.00	100
AH1212	—	12.50	30.00	50.00	70.00	100
AH1213	—	12.50	30.00	50.00	70.00	100
AH1214	—	12.50	30.00	50.00	70.00	100

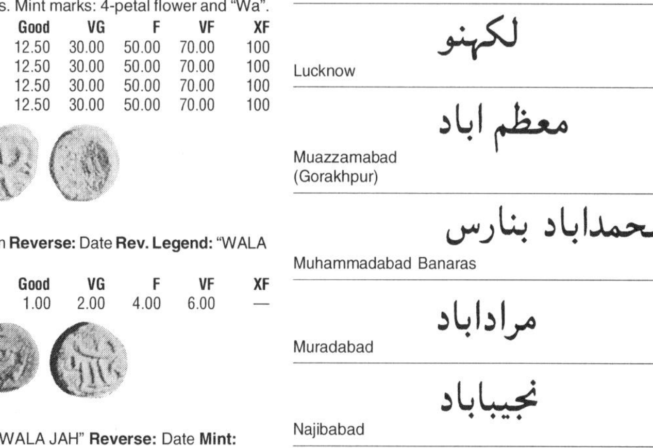

KM# 61 CASH

Copper **Obverse:** Lingam **Reverse:** Date **Rev. Legend:** "WALA JAH" **Mint:** Tinnevelly

Date	Mintage	Good	VG	F	VF	XF
AH1210	—	1.00	2.00	4.00	6.00	—

KM# 63 CASH

Copper **Obv. Legend:** "WALA JAH" **Reverse:** Date **Mint:** Nahtarnagar

Date	Mintage	Good	VG	F	VF	XF
AH1214	—	1.00	2.00	3.50	5.50	—

AWADH

Oudh

Kingdom located in northeastern India. The Nawabs of Awadh traced their origins to Muhammed Amin, a Persian adventurer who had attached himself to the court of Muhammed Shah, the Mughal Emperor, early in the 18th century. In 1720 Muhammed Amin was appointed Mughal Subahdar of Awadh, in which capacity he soon exhibited a considerable measure of independence. Until 1819, after Ghazi-ud-din had been encouraged by the Governor-General, Lord Hastings, to accept the title of King, Muhammed Amim's successors were known simply as the Nawabs of Awadh. The British offer, and Ghazi-ud-din's acceptance of it provided a clear indication of just how far Mughal decline had proceeded. The Mughal Emperor was now little more than a pensioner of the East India Company. Yet the coinage of Ghazi-ud-din immediately after 1819 marks also the hesitation he felt in taking so dramatic, and in the eyes of some of the princes of India, so ungrateful a step.

In 1856 Awadh was annexed by the British on the grounds of internal misrule. The king makers were now also seen as the king breakers. In setting aside the royal house of Awadh, the Muslim princes of India were added to that growing list of those who had come to fear the outcome of British hegemony. And it was here, in Awadh, that the Great Revolt of 1857 found its most fertile soil.

In 1877, Awadh along with Agra was placed under one administrator. It was made part of the United Provinces in 1902.

RULERS

Sa'adat Khan, Subahdar, AH1133-/1720AD--
Shuja-ud-Daula, AH1170-1189/1756-1775AD
Asaf-ud-Dawla, AH1189-1212/1775-1797AD
Wazir Ali, AH1212-1213/1797-1798AD
Sa'adat Ali, AH1213-1230/1798-1814AD

MINTS

Allahabad	الله اباد
Asafabad (Bareli)	اصف اباد
Asafnagar	اصف نگر
Awadh	اوده
Banaras	بنارس
Bareli	بريلي
Hathras	هاتهرس
Itawa	اتاوه اتاوا
Kanauj	قنوج
Kora	كورا
Lucknow	لكهنو
Muazzamabad (Gorakhpur)	معظم اباد
Muhammadabad Banaras	محمداباد بنارس
Muradabad	مراداباد
Najibabad	نجيباباد

شاهاباد

Shahabad

تانده

Tanda

KINGDOM

HAMMERED COINAGE

Mughal Style

KM# 98 FALUS
Copper **Obverse:** Inscription **Obv. Inscription:** "Shah Alam II" **Reverse:** Fish, cresent **Mint:** Lucknow **Note:** Round flan.

Date	Mintage	Good	VG	F	VF	XF
AH-//24	—	1.75	3.00	4.50	12.00	—
AH1208//26	—	1.75	3.00	4.50	12.00	—

KM# 111 PAISA (Various weight standards)
Copper **Obverse:** Crescent **Obv. Inscription:** "Shah Alam II" **Reverse:** Vertical fish **Mint:** Najibabad **Note:** Various weight standards.

Date	Mintage	Good	VG	F	VF	XF
AH11xx//18	—	3.00	4.00	6.00	12.00	—
AH1198//23	—	3.00	4.00	6.00	12.00	—
AH1199//26	—	3.00	4.00	6.00	12.00	—
AH1207//33	—	3.00	4.00	6.00	12.00	—
AH1211//37	—	—	—	—	—	—
AH1212//37	—	3.00	4.00	6.00	12.00	—
AH1212//38	—	3.00	4.00	6.00	12.00	—
AH1212//39	—	3.00	4.00	6.00	12.00	—
AH1212//40	—	3.00	4.00	6.00	12.00	—
AH1214//40	—	3.00	4.00	6.00	12.00	—
AH-//41	—	3.00	4.00	6.00	12.00	—
AH1215//43	—	3.00	4.00	6.00	12.00	—
AH-//42	—	3.00	4.00	6.00	12.00	—

KM# 113 PAISA (Various weight standards)
Copper **Obverse:** Inscription, inverted heart **Obv. Inscription:** "Shah Alam II" **Reverse:** Horizontal fish **Mint:** Najibabad

Date	Mintage	Good	VG	F	VF	XF
AH-//38	—	5.00	7.00	10.00	15.00	—
AH1215//43	—	5.00	7.00	10.00	15.00	—

KM# 100.2 1/8 RUPEE
Silver **Obverse:** Inscription **Obv. Inscription:** "Shah Alam II" **Reverse:** Frozen regnal year, mint mark: Flag and star **Mint:** Lucknow **Note:** Weight varies: 1.34-1.45 grams.

Date	Mintage	Good	VG	F	VF	XF
AH1207//26	—	10.00	25.00	50.00	80.00	120
AH1215//26	—	10.00	25.00	50.00	80.00	120

KM# 116.11 RUPEE
Silver **Obverse:** Inscription **Obv. Inscription:** "Shah Alam II" **Reverse:** Without horizontal fish **Mint:** Najibabad **Note:** Weight varies: 10.70-11.60 grams.

Date	Mintage	Good	VG	F	VF	XF
AH1188//15	—	5.00	12.50	16.50	22.50	32.50
AH1188//16	—	5.00	12.50	16.50	22.50	32.50

Date	Mintage	Good	VG	F	VF	XF
AH1200//28	—	5.00	12.50	16.50	22.50	32.50
AHxxxx//47	—	5.00	12.50	16.50	22.50	32.50

KM# 103.2 RUPEE
Silver **Obverse:** Inscription, star, date **Obv. Inscription:** "Shah Alam II" **Reverse:** Frozen regnal year, mint mark: Flag and star, fish **Mint:** Lucknow **Note:** Weight varies: 10.70-11.60 grams.

Date	Mintage	Good	VG	F	VF	XF
AH1201//26	—	3.00	7.50	12.50	18.50	27.50
AH1202//26	—	3.00	7.50	12.50	18.50	27.50
AH1203//26	—	3.00	7.50	12.50	18.50	27.50
AH1204//26	—	3.00	7.50	12.50	18.50	27.50
AH1205//26	—	3.00	7.50	12.50	18.50	27.50
AH1206//26	—	3.00	7.50	12.50	18.50	27.50
AH1207//26	—	3.00	7.50	12.50	18.50	27.50
AH1208//26	—	3.00	7.50	12.50	18.50	27.50
AH1209//26	—	3.00	7.50	12.50	18.50	27.50
AH1210//26	—	3.00	7.50	12.50	18.50	27.50
AH1211//26	—	3.00	7.50	12.50	18.50	27.50
AH1212//26	—	3.00	7.50	12.50	18.50	27.50
AH1213//26	—	3.00	7.50	12.50	18.50	27.50
AH1214//26	—	3.00	7.50	12.50	18.50	27.50
AH1215//26	—	3.00	7.50	12.50	18.50	27.50

KM# 116.7 RUPEE
Silver **Obverse:** Inscription, date **Obv. Inscription:** "Shah Alam II" **Reverse:** Persian letter "Mim" written as word, bud, fish **Mint:** Najibabad **Note:** Weight varies: 10.70-11.60 grams.

Date	Mintage	Good	VG	F	VF	XF
AH1214//41	—	5.00	12.50	16.50	22.50	32.50
AH1215//42	—	5.00	12.50	16.50	22.50	32.50

KM# 51.6 RUPEE
Silver **Obverse:** Inscription, date **Obv. Inscription:** "Shah Alam II" **Reverse:** Fish, Persian letter "Mim", star-shaped flower, crescent **Mint:** Bareli **Note:** Weight varies: 10.70-11.60 grams.

Date	Mintage	Good	VG	F	VF	XF
AH1215//37 (sic)	—	4.00	10.00	16.50	22.50	32.50

KM# 103.3 RUPEE
Silver **Obverse:** Without AH date **Obv. Inscription:** "Shah Alam II" **Reverse:** Flag, star, date, fish **Mint:** Lucknow **Note:** Weight varies: 10.70-11.60 grams.

Date	Mintage	Good	VG	F	VF	XF
AH-//26	—	5.00	10.00	40.00	75.00	90.00

Muhammed Shah

AH1131-1161 / 1719-1748AD

HAMMERED COINAGE

KM# 80 1/2 RUPEE
Silver **Obv. Inscription:** Muhammed Shah **Mint:** Kanauj **Note:** Mint name: Shahabad Qanauj. Weight varies: 5.35-5.60 grams.

Date	Mintage	Good	VG	F	VF	XF
AH-//26	—	6.50	16.50	23.50	32.50	45.00

Alamgir II

AH1167-1173 / 1754-1759AD

HAMMERED COINAGE

KM# 85 RUPEE
Silver **Obv. Inscription:** Alamgir (II) **Mint:** Kanauj **Note:** Weight varies: 10.70-11.60 grams.

Date	Mintage	VG	F	VF	XF	Unc
AH1167//1 (Ahad)	—	—	—	—	—	—

KM# 86.1 RUPEE
Silver **Obv. Inscription:** Alamgir (II) **Reverse:** Mint mark: Trisula **Mint:** Kanauj **Note:** Weight varies: 10.70-11.60 grams.

Date	Mintage	VG	F	VF	XF	Unc
AH1188//16	—	16.50	23.50	32.50	45.00	—

KM# 86.2 RUPEE
Silver **Obv. Inscription:** Alamgir (II) **Reverse:** Mint mark: Quatrefoil **Mint:** Kanauj **Note:** Weight varies: 10.70-11.60 grams.

Date	Mintage	VG	F	VF	XF	Unc
AH1190//17	—	16.50	23.50	32.50	45.00	—

Shah Alam II

AH1173-1221 / 1759-1806AD

HAMMERED COINAGE

KM# 97 FALUS
Copper **Obv. Inscription:** Shah Alam (II) **Mint:** Lucknow **Note:** Irregular flan.

Date	Mintage	Good	VG	F	VF	XF
AH1213//26	—	0.75	1.50	2.50	4.00	—

KM# 110.1 1/2 PAISA
Copper **Reverse:** Vertical fish **Mint:** Najibabad **Note:** Weight varies: 3.60-3.80 grams. Struck at Najibabad Mint.

Date	Mintage	Good	VG	F	VF	XF
AH-//24	—	2.50	4.00	6.50	10.00	—

KM# 110 1/2 PAISA
Copper **Obv. Inscription:** Shah Alam (II) **Reverse:** Vertical fish **Mint:** Najibabad **Note:** Weight varies: 3.60-3.80 grams.

Date	Mintage	VG	F	VF	XF	Unc
AH-//24	—	2.50	4.00	6.50	10.00	—

KM# 110.2 1/2 PAISA
4.2000 g., Copper, 15.7 mm. **Mint:** Najibabad

Date	Mintage	Good	VG	F	VF	XF
AH(1)206	—	—	—	—	—	—

KM# 40 1/2 PAISA
Copper **Obv. Inscription:** Shah Alam (II) **Mint:** Bareli **Note:** Similar to 1 Paisa, KM#41.

Date	Mintage	Good	VG	F	VF	XF
AH-	—	3.00	6.00	10.00	15.00	—

KM# A106 PAISA
11.8000 g., Copper **Obv. Inscription:** Shah Alam (II) **Mint:** Muazzamabad

Date	Mintage	VG	F	VF	XF	Unc
AH1190	—	3.00	6.00	10.00	15.00	—

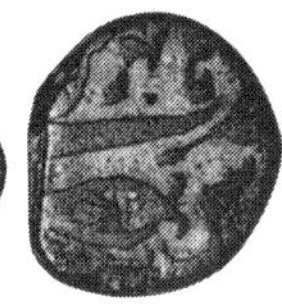

KM# 61 PAISA

Copper **Obv. Inscription:** Shah Alam (II) **Reverse:** Fish **Mint:** Hathras

Date	Mintage	Good	VG	F	VF	XF
ND(1779)	—	6.00	10.00	16.50	25.00	—

KM# 32 PAISA

Copper **Obv. Inscription:** Shah Alam (II) **Reverse:** Horizontal fish **Mint:** Banaras **Note:** Mint name: Muhammadabad Banaras.

Date	Mintage	Good	VG	F	VF	XF
AH121x	—	—	3.00	6.00	10.00	15.00

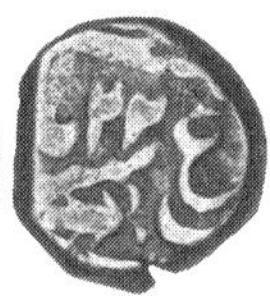

KM# A99 PAISA

Copper **Obv. Inscription:** Shah Alam (II) **Reverse:** Stylized fish **Mint:** Lucknow **Note:** Prev. Bengal Presidency, KM#14.

Date	Mintage	Good	VG	F	VF	XF
AHxxxx//22	—	3.50	6.00	12.00	20.00	—
AHxxxx//25	—	3.50	6.00	12.00	20.00	—
AH1213//26	—	3.50	6.00	12.00	20.00	—

KM# 41 PAISA

Copper **Obverse:** Dagger **Obv. Inscription:** Shah Alam (II) **Reverse:** Fish **Mint:** Bareli

Date	Mintage	Good	VG	F	VF	XF
AH12xx//35	—	3.00	6.00	10.00	15.00	—
AH12xx//37	—	3.00	6.00	10.00	15.00	—

KM# 112 PAISA (Various weight standards)

Copper **Obv. Inscription:** Shah Alam (II) **Reverse:** Stylized dagger **Mint:** Najibabad

Date	Mintage	Good	VG	F	VF	XF
AH1197//24 (1782)	—	3.00	4.00	6.00	8.50	—
AH1197//25 (1782)	—	3.00	4.00	6.00	8.50	—
AH1198//25 (1783)	—	3.00	4.00	6.00	8.50	—
AH-//27 (1785)	—	3.00	4.00	6.00	8.50	—
AH-//29 (1787)	—	3.00	4.00	6.00	8.50	—
AH1202//30 (1787)	—	3.00	4.00	6.00	8.50	—
AH-//31 (1788)	—	3.00	4.00	6.00	8.50	—
AH1205//32 (1789)	—	3.00	4.00	6.00	8.50	—
AH1206//33 (1791)	—	3.00	4.00	6.00	8.50	—
AH121x//36 (1794)	—	3.00	4.00	6.00	8.50	—
AH-//37 (1795)	—	3.00	4.00	6.00	8.50	—
AH1210//38 (1795)	—	3.00	4.00	6.00	8.50	—
AH1212//39 (1797)	—	3.00	4.00	6.00	8.50	—
AH1215//42 (1800)	—	3.00	4.00	6.00	8.50	—

KM# 114 PAISA (Various weight standards)

Copper **Obv. Inscription:** Shah Alam (II) **Reverse:** Sword **Mint:** Najibabad

Date	Mintage	Good	VG	F	VF	XF
AH1214//40 (1799)	—	5.00	7.00	10.00	15.00	—
AH1214//41 (1799)	—	5.00	7.00	10.00	15.00	—

KM# 99 1/16 RUPEE

Silver **Obv. Inscription:** Shah Alam (II) **Reverse:** Fixed regnal year **Mint:** Lucknow **Note:** Weight varies: 0.67-0.72 grams.

Date	Mintage	Good	VG	F	VF	XF
AH1215//26	—	6.50	10.00	15.00	22.50	—

KM# 100.1 1/8 RUPEE

Silver **Obv. Inscription:** Shah Alam (II) **Reverse:** Actual regnal year; mint mark: Parasol **Mint:** Lucknow **Note:** Weight varies: 1.34-1.45 grams.

Date	Mintage	Good	VG	F	VF	XF
AH1195//23	—	6.50	10.00	15.00	22.50	—
AH1196//24	—	6.50	10.00	15.00	22.50	—

KM# 101.1 1/4 RUPEE

Silver **Obv. Inscription:** Shah Alam (II) **Reverse:** Actual regnal year; mint mark: Parasol **Mint:** Lucknow **Note:** Weight varies: 2.68-2.90 grams.

Date	Mintage	Good	VG	F	VF	XF
AH1196//23	—	2.25	5.50	8.00	11.50	17.50

KM# 95 1/2 RUPEE

Silver **Obverse:** Mint mark: Vertical fish **Obv. Inscription:** Shah Alam (II) **Mint:** Kora **Note:** Weight varies: 5.35-5.60 grams.

Date	Mintage	Good	VG	F	VF	XF
AH119x//16	—	3.00	7.50	11.00	16.50	25.00

KM# 102.1 1/2 RUPEE

Silver **Obv. Inscription:** Shah Alam (II) **Reverse:** Actual regnal year; mint mark: Parasol **Mint:** Lucknow **Note:** Weight varies: 5.35-5.80 grams.

Date	Mintage	Good	VG	F	VF	XF
AH1196//23	—	2.50	6.00	9.00	13.50	20.00

KM# 102.3 1/2 RUPEE

Silver **Obverse:** Without AH date **Obv. Inscription:** Shah Alam (II) **Mint:** Lucknow **Note:** Weight varies: 5.38-5.80 grams.

Date	Mintage	Good	VG	F	VF	XF
AH-//26	—	30.00	75.00	135	200	285

KM# 45 1/2 RUPEE

Silver **Obv. Inscription:** Shah Alam (II) **Mint:** Bareli **Note:** Weight varies: 5.35-5.80 grams.

Date	Mintage	Good	VG	F	VF	XF
AH1213//37	—	6.00	15.00	21.50	30.00	40.00

KM# 6.1 RUPEE

Silver **Obv. Legend:** "Shah Alam Badshah" **Mint:** Allahabad **Note:** Weight varies: 10.70-11.60 grams.

Date	Mintage	Good	VG	F	VF	XF
AH1174//1	—	5.00	12.50	18.50	25.00	35.00

KM# 36.1 RUPEE

Silver **Obv. Legend:** "Haft Kishwar" **Obv. Inscription:** Shah Alam (II) **Reverse:** Bud **Mint:** Banaras **Note:** Weight varies: 10.70-11.60 grams.

Date	Mintage	Good	VG	F	VF	XF
AH1174//1	—	4.00	10.00	15.00	22.50	32.50
AH1174//2	—	4.00	10.00	15.00	22.50	32.50

KM# 36.2 RUPEE

Silver **Obv. Legend:** "Shah Alam Badshah" **Obv. Inscription:** Shah Alam (II) **Reverse:** Six-pointed star **Mint:** Banaras **Note:** Weight varies: 10.70-11.60 grams.

Date	Mintage	Good	VG	F	VF	XF
AH1174//2	—	4.00	10.00	15.00	22.50	32.50
AH1175//2	—	4.00	10.00	15.00	22.50	32.50
AH1175//3	—	4.00	10.00	15.00	22.50	32.50
AH1176//3	—	4.00	10.00	15.00	22.50	32.50
AH1176//4	—	4.00	10.00	15.00	22.50	32.50
AH1177//4	—	4.00	10.00	15.00	22.50	32.50
AH1177//5	—	4.00	10.00	15.00	22.50	32.50
AH1178//5	—	4.00	10.00	15.00	22.50	32.50
AH1178//6	—	4.00	10.00	15.00	22.50	32.50
AH1179//6	—	4.00	10.00	15.00	22.50	32.50
AH1179//7	—	4.00	10.00	15.00	22.50	32.50
AH1180//7	—	4.00	10.00	15.00	22.50	32.50
AH1180//8	—	4.00	10.00	15.00	22.50	32.50
AH1181//8	—	4.00	10.00	15.00	22.50	32.50
AH1181//9	—	4.00	10.00	15.00	22.50	32.50
AH1182//9	—	4.00	10.00	15.00	22.50	32.50
AH1182//10	—	4.00	10.00	15.00	22.50	32.50
AH1183//10	—	4.00	10.00	15.00	22.50	32.50
AH1183//11	—	4.00	10.00	15.00	22.50	32.50
AH1184//11	—	4.00	10.00	15.00	22.50	32.50
AH1186//13	—	4.00	10.00	15.00	22.50	32.50
AH-//14	—	4.00	10.00	15.00	22.50	32.50
AH1187//15	—	4.00	10.00	15.00	22.50	32.50
AH1188//15	—	4.00	10.00	15.00	22.50	32.50

KM# 36.4 RUPEE

Silver **Obverse:** Similar to KM#36.1 **Obv. Inscription:** Shah Alam (II) **Reverse:** Comb symbol **Mint:** Banaras **Note:** Weight varies: 10.70-11.60 grams.

Date	Mintage	Good	VG	F	VF	XF
AH-//6	—	5.50	14.00	23.50	32.50	45.00

KM# 36.6 RUPEE

Silver **Obverse:** Similar to KM#36.1 **Obv. Inscription:** Shah Alam (II) **Mint:** Banaras **Note:** Weight varies: 10.70-11.60 grams.

Date	Mintage	Good	VG	F	VF	XF
AH1182//9	—	5.50	14.00	23.50	32.50	45.00

KM# 136.1 RUPEE

Silver **Obverse:** Crosses **Obv. Inscription:** Shah Alam (II) **Mint:** Tanda **Note:** Weight varies: 10.70-11.60 grams.

Date	Mintage	Good	VG	F	VF	XF
AH1184//11	—	6.50	16.50	22.50	32.50	45.00

KM# 136.2 RUPEE

Silver **Obverse:** Pataka **Obv. Inscription:** Shah Alam (II) **Mint:** Tanda **Note:** Weight varies: 10.70-11.60 grams.

Date	Mintage	Good	VG	F	VF	XF
AH1185//11	—	6.50	16.50	22.50	27.50	35.00
AH1185//12	—	6.50	16.50	22.50	27.50	35.00
AH1186//12	—	6.50	16.50	22.50	27.50	35.00
AH-//14	—	6.50	16.50	22.50	27.50	35.00

KM# 36.8 RUPEE

Silver **Reverse:** Sunburst and trident **Mint:** Banaras **Note:** Weight: 10.70-11.60.

Date	Mintage	VG	F	VF	XF	Unc
AH1185//12 (1771)	—	14.00	23.50	32.50	45.00	—

KM# 36.5 RUPEE

Silver **Obverse:** Seven-pointed star **Obv. Inscription:** Shah Alam (II) **Reverse:** Trident **Mint:** Banaras **Note:** Weight varies: 10.70-11.60 grams.

Date	Mintage	Good	VG	F	VF	XF
AH1186//13	—	5.50	14.00	23.50	32.50	45.00

KM# 36.7 RUPEE

Silver **Obv. Inscription:** Shah Alam (II) **Reverse:** Eight-pointed star **Mint:** Banaras **Note:** Weight varies: 10.70-11.60 grams.

Date	Mintage	Good	VG	F	VF	XF
AH1187//15	—	5.50	14.00	23.50	32.50	45.00

KM# 76.1 RUPEE

Silver **Obverse:** Mint mark: umbrella **Obv. Inscription:** Shah Alam (II) **Mint:** Itawa **Note:** Weight varies: 10.70-11.60 grams.

Date	Mintage	Good	VG	F	VF	XF
AH-//15	—	3.50	8.50	13.50	20.00	28.50
AH1189//17	—	3.50	8.50	13.50	20.00	28.50

KM# 96.1 RUPEE

Silver **Obverse:** Mintmark: Vertical fish **Obv. Legend:** "Shah Alam Badshah" **Obv. Inscription:** Shah Alam (II) **Mint:** Kora **Note:** Weight varies: 10.70-11.60 grams.

Date	Mintage	Good	VG	F	VF	XF
AH1188//16	—	2.75	7.00	11.00	16.50	25.00
AH1189//16	—	2.75	7.00	11.00	16.50	25.00
AH1190//17	—	2.75	7.00	11.00	16.50	25.00

KM# 126 RUPEE

Silver **Obv. Inscription:** Shah Alam (II) **Reverse:** Trident **Mint:** Shahabad **Note:** Weight varies: 10.70-11.60 grams.

Date	Mintage	Good	VG	F	VF	XF
AH1188//16	—	7.50	17.50	25.00	35.00	50.00
AH1189//16	—	7.50	17.50	25.00	35.00	50.00
AH1190//17	—	7.50	17.50	25.00	35.00	50.00

KM# 106.1 RUPEE

Silver **Obv. Inscription:** Shah Alam (II) **Reverse:** Star **Mint:** Muradabad **Note:** Weight varies: 10.70-11.60 grams.

Date	Mintage	VG	F	VF	XF	Unc
AH1189//16	—	7.00	11.00	16.50	25.00	—
AH1189//17	—	7.00	11.00	16.50	25.00	—
AH1190//17	—	7.00	11.00	16.50	25.00	—
AH1190//18	—	7.00	11.00	16.50	25.00	—
AH1191//18	—	7.00	11.00	16.50	25.00	—
AH1191//19	—	7.00	11.00	16.50	25.00	—

KM# 36.3 RUPEE

Silver **Obverse:** Star **Obv. Inscription:** Shah Alam (II) **Reverse:** Bud **Mint:** Banaras **Note:** Weight varies: 10.70-11.60 grams.

Date	Mintage	Good	VG	F	VF	XF
AH1189//16	—	5.50	14.00	23.50	32.50	45.00

KM# 46.1 RUPEE

Silver **Obv. Legend:** "Fazl-i-Hami Din" **Obv. Inscription:** Shah Alam (II) **Reverse:** Legend at lower left, without symbols **Rev. Legend:** "Bareli" **Mint:** Bareli **Note:** Weight varies: 10.70-11.60 grams.

Date	Mintage	Good	VG	F	VF	XF
AH1189//17	—	4.00	10.00	16.50	22.50	32.50

KM# 26.1 RUPEE

Silver **Obverse:** Sword **Obv. Inscription:** Shah Alam (II) **Reverse:** Inverted Persian letter "Nun" **Mint:** Asafnagar **Note:** Weight varies: 10.70-11.60 grams.

Date	Mintage	Good	VG	F	VF	XF
AH1189//17	—	8.00	20.00	31.50	42.50	60.00

KM# 26.2 RUPEE

Silver **Obv. Inscription:** Shah Alam (II) **Reverse:** Fish and inverted Persian letter "Nun" **Mint:** Asafnagar **Note:** Weight varies: 10.70-11.60 grams.

Date	Mintage	Good	VG	F	VF	XF
AH1189//17	—	8.00	20.00	31.50	42.50	60.00
AH1190//18	—	8.00	20.00	31.50	42.50	60.00

KM# 6.2 RUPEE

Silver **Obv. Legend:** "Fazl-I-Shah-Alam" **Reverse:** Pataka (banner) **Mint:** Allahabad **Note:** Weight varies: 10.70-11.60 grams.

Date	Mintage	Good	VG	F	VF	XF
AH1190//18	—	5.00	12.50	18.50	25.00	35.00
AH1191//18	—	5.00	12.50	18.50	25.00	35.00
AH1192//18	—	5.00	12.50	18.50	25.00	35.00
AH1192//19	—	5.00	12.50	18.50	25.00	35.00
AH1194//19	—	5.00	12.50	18.50	25.00	35.00

KM# 16.1 RUPEE

Silver **Obv. Inscription:** Shah Alam (II) **Reverse:** Cluster of four crosses, sword **Mint:** Asafabad **Note:** Weight varies: 10.70-11.60 grams.

Date	Mintage	Good	VG	F	VF	XF
AH-//18	—	7.50	17.50	25.00	35.00	50.00

KM# 46.2 RUPEE

Silver **Obv. Inscription:** Shah Alam (II) **Reverse:** Crescent **Mint:** Bareli **Note:** Weight varies: 10.70-11.60 grams.

Date	Mintage	Good	VG	F	VF	XF
AH1190//17	—	4.00	10.00	16.50	22.50	32.50
AH1191//18	—	4.00	10.00	16.50	22.50	32.50
AH1191//19	—	4.00	10.00	16.50	22.50	32.50

KM# 46.3 RUPEE

Silver **Obv. Inscription:** Shah Alam (II) **Reverse:** Fish **Mint:** Bareli **Note:** Weight varies: 10.70-11.60 grams.

Date	Mintage	Good	VG	F	VF	XF
AH1190//18	—	4.00	10.00	16.50	22.50	32.50

KM# 46.4 RUPEE

Silver **Obv. Inscription:** Shah Alam (II) **Reverse:** Danda (mace) **Mint:** Bareli **Note:** Weight varies: 10.70-11.60 grams.

Date	Mintage	Good	VG	F	VF	XF
AH1191//19	—	4.00	10.00	16.50	22.50	32.50
AH1192//19	—	4.00	10.00	16.50	22.50	32.50
AH1194//21	—	4.00	10.00	16.50	22.50	32.50

KM# 16.2 RUPEE

Silver **Obv. Inscription:** Shah Alam (II) **Reverse:** Cluster of four crosses, inverted; Persian letter "Nun" **Mint:** Asafabad **Note:** Weight varies: 10.70-11.60 grams.

Date	Mintage	Good	VG	F	VF	XF
AH1191//18	—	7.50	17.50	25.00	35.00	50.00

KM# 116.1 RUPEE

Silver **Obverse:** Horizontal fish **Obv. Inscription:** Shah Alam (II) **Reverse:** Crude dagger **Mint:** Najibabad **Note:** Weight varies: 10.70-11.60 grams.

Date	Mintage	Good	VG	F	VF	XF
AH1191//19 (1777)	—	5.00	12.50	16.50	22.50	32.50
AH1194//22 (1781)	—	5.00	12.50	16.50	22.50	32.50
AH1196//23 (1783)	—	5.00	12.50	16.50	22.50	32.50
AH1197//24 (1784)	—	5.00	12.50	16.50	22.50	32.50
AH1200//27 (1785)	—	5.00	12.50	16.50	22.50	32.50

KM# 106.2 RUPEE

Silver **Obv. Inscription:** Shah Alam (II) **Reverse:** Clover **Mint:** Muradabad **Note:** Weight varies: 10.70-11.60 grams.

Date	Mintage	Good	VG	F	VF	XF
AH1191//18	—	6.50	16.00	22.50	31.50	40.00

KM# 106.3 RUPEE

Silver **Obv. Inscription:** Shah Alam (II) **Reverse:** Danda (mace) **Mint:** Muradabad **Note:** Weight varies: 10.70-11.60 grams.

Date	Mintage	Good	VG	F	VF	XF
AH1191//19	—	—	7.00	11.00	16.50	25.00
AH1193//21	—	2.75	7.00	11.00	16.50	25.00
AH119x//22	—	2.75	7.00	11.00	16.50	25.00

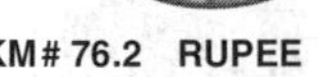

KM# 76.2 RUPEE

Silver **Obverse:** Mint marks: umbrella, pataka **Obv. Inscription:** Shah Alam (II) **Mint:** Itawa **Note:** Weight varies: 10.70-11.60 grams.

Date	Mintage	Good	VG	F	VF	XF
AH1191//18	—	6.00	15.00	21.50	30.00	40.00

KM# 76.3 RUPEE

Silver **Obverse:** Mint marks: umbrella, small fish **Obv. Inscription:** Shah Alam (II) **Mint:** Itawa **Note:** Weight varies: 10.70-11.60 grams.

Date	Mintage	Good	VG	F	VF	XF
AH-//19	—	3.50	8.50	13.50	20.00	28.50

KM# 103.1 RUPEE

Silver **Obv. Inscription:** Shah Alam (II) **Reverse:** Actual regnal year; mint mark: Parasol **Mint:** Lucknow **Note:** Weight varies: 10.70-11.60 grams.

Date	Mintage	Good	VG	F	VF	XF
AH1192//19	—	3.00	7.50	12.50	18.50	27.50
AH-//20	—	3.25	8.00	13.50	20.00	30.00
AH-//22	—	3.00	7.50	12.50	18.50	27.50
AH1198//25	—	3.00	7.50	12.50	18.50	27.50
AH1198//26	—	3.00	7.50	12.50	18.50	27.50

KM# 76.4 RUPEE

Silver **Obverse:** Mint marks: umbrella, stylized fish **Obv. Inscription:** Shah Alam (II) **Mint:** Itawa **Note:** Weight varies: 10.70-11.60 grams.

Date	Mintage	Good	VG	F	VF	XF
AH-//20	—	3.50	8.50	13.50	20.00	28.50
AH-//21	—	3.50	8.50	13.50	20.00	28.50
AH1194//22	—	3.50	8.50	13.50	20.00	28.50
AH-//23	—	3.50	8.50	13.50	20.00	28.50
AH1196//24	—	3.50	8.50	13.50	20.00	28.50
AH1197//25	—	3.50	8.50	13.50	20.00	28.50
AH1198//25	—	3.50	8.50	13.50	20.00	28.50

KM# 116.2 RUPEE

Silver **Obverse:** Crescent **Obv. Inscription:** Shah Alam (II) **Reverse:** Persian letter "Suaad", fish **Mint:** Najibabad **Note:** Weight varies: 10.70-11.60 grams.

Date	Mintage	Good	VG	F	VF	XF
AH1192//20 (1778)	—	5.00	12.50	16.50	22.50	32.50
AH1198//25 (1783)	—	5.00	12.50	16.50	22.50	32.50
AH1199//26 (1784)	—	5.00	12.50	16.50	22.50	32.50

KM# 16.3 RUPEE

Silver **Obv. Inscription:** Shah Alam (II) **Reverse:** Danda (mace) **Mint:** Asafabad **Note:** Weight varies: 10.70-11.60 grams.

Date	Mintage	Good	VG	F	VF	XF
AH119x//19	—	7.50	17.50	25.00	35.00	50.00
AH-//21	—	7.50	17.50	25.00	35.00	50.00

KM# 46.5 RUPEE

Silver **Obv. Inscription:** Shah Alam (II) **Reverse:** Sword **Mint:** Bareli **Note:** Weight varies: 10.70-11.60 grams.

Date	Mintage	Good	VG	F	VF	XF
AH1193//20	—	4.00	10.00	16.50	22.50	32.50
AH1193//21	—	4.00	10.00	16.50	22.50	32.50

KM# 26.3 RUPEE

Silver **Obv. Legend:** "Hami-din Shah Alam" **Obv. Inscription:** Shah Alam (II) **Mint:** Asafnagar **Note:** Weight varies: 10.70-11.60 grams.

Date	Mintage	Good	VG	F	VF	XF
AH1194//21	—	8.00	20.00	31.50	42.50	60.00

KM# 96.2 RUPEE

Silver **Obverse:** Mint mark: Horizontal fish **Obv. Legend:** "Fazl-i-Shah Alam" **Obv. Inscription:** Shah Alam (II) **Mint:** Kora **Note:** Weight varies: 10.70-11.60 grams.

Date	Mintage	Good	VG	F	VF	XF
AH1194//20	—	4.50	11.50	11.00	16.50	25.00

KM# 66 RUPEE

Silver **Obv. Inscription:** Shah Alam (II) **Mint:** Hathras **Note:** Weight varies: 10.70-11.60 grams.

Date	Mintage	VG	F	VF	XF	Unc
AH-//22	—	30.00	45.00	60.00	80.00	—

KM# 116.10 RUPEE

Silver **Reverse:** Symbol and star **Mint:** Najibabad **Note:** Weight varies: 10.70-11.60 grams.

Date	Mintage	Good	VG	F	VF	XF
AH-//22 (1783)	—	4.50	11.50	13.50	17.50	25.00
AH1198//25 (1783)	—	4.50	11.50	13.50	17.50	25.00
AH-//28 (1783)	—	4.50	11.50	13.50	17.50	25.00

KM# 47.1 RUPEE

Silver **Obverse:** Pataka **Obv. Inscription:** Shah Alam (II) **Reverse:** Legend at top, fish **Rev. Legend:** "Bareli" **Mint:** Bareli **Note:** Weight varies: 10.70-11.60 grams.

Date	Mintage	Good	VG	F	VF	XF
AH(1)198//26	—	4.00	10.00	16.50	22.50	32.50
AH1199//26	—	4.00	10.00	16.50	22.50	32.50
AH1199//27	—	4.00	10.00	16.50	22.50	32.50
AH1200//27	—	4.00	10.00	16.50	22.50	32.50
AH1201//27 (sic)	—	4.00	10.00	16.50	22.50	32.50
AH1201//27 (sic)	—	4.00	10.00	16.50	22.50	32.50

KM# 116.12 RUPEE

Silver **Obverse:** Twig **Obv. Inscription:** Shah Alam (II) **Reverse:** Dagger **Mint:** Najibabad **Note:** Weight varies: 10.70-11.60 grams.

Date	Mintage	Good	VG	F	VF	XF
AH1200//27 (1785)	—	5.00	12.50	16.50	22.50	32.50
AH1201//28 (1786)	—	5.00	12.50	16.50	22.50	32.50
AH1203//29 (1788)	—	—	12.50	16.50	22.50	32.50

KM# 76.5 RUPEE

Silver **Obverse:** Mint marks: umbrella, sword **Obv. Inscription:** Shah Alam (II) **Mint:** Itawa **Note:** Weight varies: 10.70-11.60 grams.

Date	Mintage	Good	VG	F	VF	XF
AH-//29	—	6.00	15.00	21.50	30.00	40.00

KM# 47.2 RUPEE

Silver **Obverse:** Cross **Obv. Inscription:** Shah Alam (II) **Reverse:** Fish, Persian letter "Mim" **Mint:** Bareli **Note:** Weight varies: 10.70-11.60 grams.

Date	Mintage	Good	VG	F	VF	XF
AH1202//28 (sic)	—	4.00	10.00	16.50	22.50	32.50
AH1202//29 (sic)	—	4.00	10.00	16.50	22.50	32.50
AH1203//29 (sic)	—	4.00	10.00	16.50	22.50	32.50

KM# 76.6 RUPEE

Silver **Obverse:** Mint marks: umbrella, sword, shamrock **Obv. Inscription:** Shah Alam (II) **Mint:** Itawa **Note:** Weight varies: 10.70-11.60 grams.

Date	Mintage	Good	VG	F	VF	XF
AH-//30	—	4.50	11.50	18.50	24.00	32.50

KM# 76.7 RUPEE

Silver **Obverse:** Mint marks: umbrella, stylized fish, shamrock **Obv. Inscription:** Shah Alam (II) **Mint:** Itawa **Note:** Weight varies: 10.70-11.60 grams.

Date	Mintage	Good	VG	F	VF	XF
AH-//31	—	3.50	8.50	13.50	20.00	28.50
AH-//32	—	3.50	8.50	13.50	20.00	28.50
AH-//33	—	3.50	8.50	13.50	20.00	28.50

KM# 116.3 RUPEE

Silver **Obv. Inscription:** Shah Alam (II) **Reverse:** Persian letters "Mim" and "Ain", fish **Mint:** Najibabad **Note:** Weight varies: 10.70-11.60 grams.

Date	Mintage	Good	VG	F	VF	XF
AH1204//30 (1789)	—	5.00	12.50	16.50	22.50	32.50
AH1205//31 (1790)	—	5.00	12.50	16.50	22.50	32.50
AH1208//34 (1793)	—	5.00	12.50	16.50	22.50	32.50

KM# 48.1 RUPEE

Silver **Obverse:** Cross **Obv. Inscription:** Shah Alam (II) **Reverse:** Legend at top, fish, Persian letters "Mim" and "Ain", trident **Rev. Legend:** "Bareli Qita" **Mint:** Bareli **Note:** Weight varies: 10.70-11.60 grams.

Date	Mintage	Good	VG	F	VF	XF
AH1205//29	—	4.00	10.00	16.50	22.50	32.50
AH1206//29	—	4.00	10.00	16.50	22.50	32.50

KM# 116.4 RUPEE

Silver **Obv. Inscription:** Shah Alam (II) **Reverse:** Persian letters "Mim", bud or halberd, fish **Mint:** Najibabad **Note:** Weight varies: 10.70-11.60 grams.

Date	Mintage	Good	VG	F	VF	XF
AH1206//32	—	5.00	12.50	16.50	22.50	32.50
AH1207//33	—	5.00	12.50	16.50	22.50	32.50
AH1213//40	—	5.00	12.50	16.50	22.50	32.50
AH1214//41	—	5.00	12.50	16.50	22.50	32.50

KM# 48.2 RUPEE

Silver **Obv. Inscription:** Shah Alam (II) **Reverse:** Without trident **Mint:** Bareli **Note:** Weight varies: 10.70-11.60 grams.

Date	Mintage	Good	VG	F	VF	XF
AH1207//29 (sic)	—	4.00	10.00	16.50	22.50	32.50

KM# 49.1 RUPEE

Silver **Obverse:** Cross **Obv. Legend:** "Sahib Qirani" **Obv. Inscription:** Shah Alam (II) **Reverse:** Legend at top, fish, Persian letters "Mim" and "Ain", trident with crescent **Rev. Legend:** "Bareli Qita" **Mint:** Bareli **Note:** Weight varies: 10.70-11.60 grams.

Date	Mintage	Good	VG	F	VF	XF
AH1208//31 (sic)	—	4.00	10.00	16.50	22.50	32.50

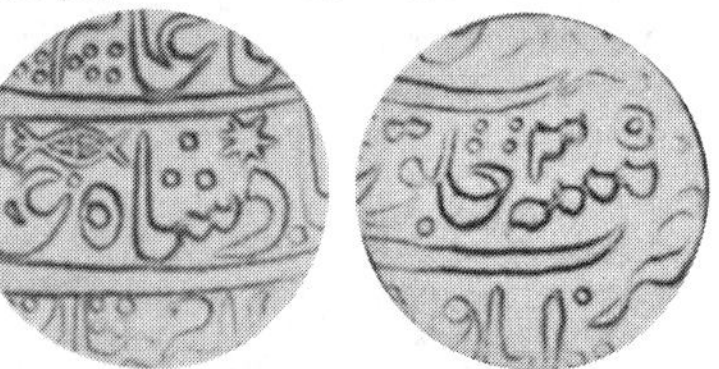

KM# 76.8 RUPEE

Silver **Obverse:** Mint marks: umbrella, stylized fish, star **Obv. Inscription:** Shah Alam (II) **Mint:** Itawa **Note:** Weight varies: 10.70-11.60 grams.

Date	Mintage	Good	VG	F	VF	XF
AH-//35	—	3.50	8.50	13.50	20.00	28.50

KM# 116.13 RUPEE

Silver **Obv. Inscription:** Shah Alam (II) **Reverse:** Eight-pointed star **Mint:** Najibabad **Note:** Weight varies: 10.70-11.60 grams.

Date	Mintage	Good	VG	F	VF	XF
AH1209//35	—	5.00	12.50	16.50	22.50	32.50

KM# 49.2 RUPEE

Silver **Obv. Inscription:** Shah Alam (II) **Reverse:** Fish, Persian letter "Re", star-shaped flower **Mint:** Bareli **Note:** Weight varies: 10.70-11.60 grams.

Date	Mintage	Good	VG	F	VF	XF
AH1209//31 (sic)	—	4.00	10.00	16.50	22.50	32.50
AH1209//35 (sic)	—	4.00	10.00	16.50	22.50	32.50

KM# 49.3 RUPEE

Silver **Obv. Inscription:** Shah Alam (II) **Reverse:** Legend near center **Rev. Legend:** "Bareli Qita" **Mint:** Bareli **Note:** Weight varies: 10.70-11.60 grams.

Date	Mintage	Good	VG	F	VF	XF
AH1209	—	—	—	—	—	—

KM# 50.1 RUPEE

Silver **Obv. Inscription:** Shah Alam (II) **Reverse:** Legend in center, Persian letter "Re", fish, crescent **Rev. Legend:** "Asafabad Bareli" **Mint:** Bareli **Note:** Weight varies: 10.70-11.60 grams.

Date	Mintage	Good	VG	F	VF	XF
AH1209//35 (sic)	—	15.00	37.50	50.00	70.00	100
AH1210//35 (sic)	—	15.00	37.50	50.00	70.00	100

KM# 50.2 RUPEE

Silver **Obv. Inscription:** Shah Alam (II) **Reverse:** Persian letter "Re", fish, swastika **Mint:** Bareli **Note:** Weight varies: 10.70-11.60 grams.

Date	Mintage	Good	VG	F	VF	XF
AH1210//35 (sic)	—	15.00	37.50	50.00	70.00	100

KM# 50.3 RUPEE

Silver **Obv. Inscription:** Shah Alam (II) **Reverse:** Fish, Persian letter "Alif" **Mint:** Bareli **Note:** Weight varies: 10.70-11.60 grams.

Date	Mintage	Good	VG	F	VF	XF
AH1210//35 (sic)	—	15.00	37.50	50.00	70.00	100

KM# 50.4 RUPEE

Silver **Obv. Inscription:** Shah Alam (II) **Reverse:** Fish and symbol **Mint:** Bareli **Note:** Weight varies: 10.70-11.60 grams.

Date	Mintage	Good	VG	F	VF	XF
AH1210//35 (sic)	—	15.00	37.50	50.00	70.00	100

KM# 116.5 RUPEE

Silver **Obv. Inscription:** Shah Alam (II) **Reverse:** Swastika, fish **Mint:** Najibabad **Note:** Weight varies: 10.70-11.60 grams.

Date	Mintage	Good	VG	F	VF	XF
AH1210//36	—	5.00	12.50	16.50	22.50	32.50
AH1211//36	—	5.00	12.50	16.50	22.50	32.50

KM# 117 RUPEE

Silver **Obv. Inscription:** Shah Alam (II) **Reverse:** "Vajra" symbol **Mint:** Najibabad **Note:** Weight varies: 10.70-11.60 grams.

Date	Mintage	Good	VG	F	VF	XF
AH1210//38	—	4.50	11.50	13.50	17.50	25.00

KM# 51.2 RUPEE

Silver **Obv. Inscription:** Shah Alam (II) **Reverse:** Fish, Persian letter "Mim", trident **Rev. Legend:** "Bareli Qita" **Mint:** Bareli **Note:** Weight varies: 10.70-11.60 grams.

Date	Mintage	Good	VG	F	VF	XF
AH1211//37 (sic)	—	4.00	10.00	16.50	22.50	32.50
AH1212//37 (sic)	—	4.00	10.00	16.50	22.50	32.50

KM# 51.1 RUPEE

Silver **Obv. Inscription:** Shah Alam (II) **Reverse:** Legend at top, fish, Persian letter "Alif" **Rev. Legend:** "Bareli Qita" **Mint:** Bareli **Note:** Weight varies: 10.70-11.60 grams.

Date	Mintage	Good	VG	F	VF	XF
AH1211//35 (sic)	—	4.00	10.00	16.50	22.50	32.50
AH1211//36 (sic)	—	4.00	10.00	16.50	22.50	32.50

KM# 116.14 RUPEE

Silver **Obv. Inscription:** Shah Alam (II) **Reverse:** Symbol, bud, and fish **Mint:** Najibabad **Note:** Weight varies: 10.70-11.60 grams.

Date	Mintage	Good	VG	F	VF	XF
AH1211//37 (1796)	—	5.00	12.50	16.50	22.50	32.50
AH1212//37 (1797)	—	5.00	12.50	16.50	22.50	32.50

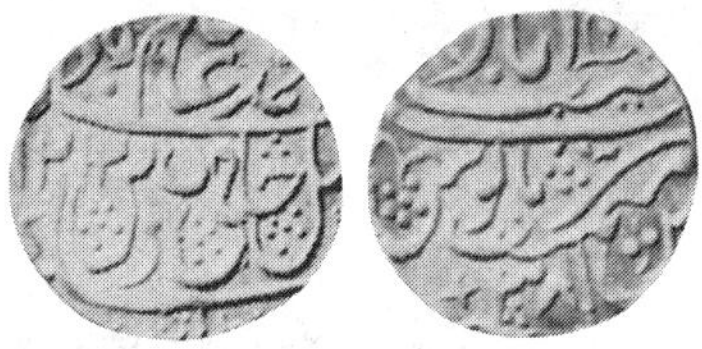

KM# 116.9 RUPEE

Silver **Obv. Inscription:** Shah Alam (II) **Reverse:** Star and symbol **Mint:** Najibabad **Note:** Weight varies: 10.70-11.60 grams.

Date	Mintage	Good	VG	F	VF	XF
AH1212//38 (1797)	—	4.50	11.50	13.50	17.50	25.00
AH1213//40 (1798)	—	4.50	11.50	13.50	17.50	25.00
AH-//41 (1799)	—	4.50	11.50	13.50	17.50	25.00

KM# 51.3 RUPEE

Silver **Obv. Inscription:** Shah Alam (II) **Reverse:** Fish, Persian letters "Mim" and "Nun", dagger **Mint:** Bareli **Note:** Weight varies: 10.70-11.60 grams.

Date	Mintage	Good	VG	F	VF	XF
AH1212//37 (sic)	—	4.00	10.00	16.50	22.50	32.50
AH1213//37 (sic)	—	4.00	10.00	16.50	22.50	32.50

KM# 51.4 RUPEE

Silver **Obv. Inscription:** Shah Alam (II) **Reverse:** Fish, Persian letter "Mim", trident, dagger **Mint:** Bareli **Note:** Weight varies: 10.70-11.60 grams.

Date	Mintage	Good	VG	F	VF	XF
AH1213//37 (sic)	—	4.00	10.00	16.50	22.50	32.50
AH1214//37 (sic)	—	4.00	10.00	16.50	22.50	32.50
AH1215//37 (sic)	—	4.00	10.00	16.50	22.50	32.50

KM# 116.15 RUPEE

Silver **Obv. Inscription:** Shah Alam (II) **Reverse:** Persian letter "Mim", bud, and fish **Mint:** Najibabad **Note:** Weight varies: 10.70-11.60 grams.

Date	Mintage	Good	VG	F	VF	XF
AH1213//40	—	5.00	12.50	16.50	22.50	32.50
AH1214//41	—	5.00	12.50	16.50	22.50	32.50

KM# 116.6 RUPEE
Silver **Obv. Inscription:** Shah Alam (II) **Reverse:** Persian letter "Mim", bud, fish, dagger **Mint:** Najibabad **Note:** Weight varies: 10.70-11.60 grams.

Date	Mintage	Good	VG	F	VF	XF
AH1213//39	—	2.75	7.00	11.00	16.50	25.00

KM# 51.5 RUPEE
Silver **Obv. Inscription:** Shah Alam (II) **Reverse:** Fish, Persian letter "Mim", star-shaped flower, dagger **Mint:** Bareli **Note:** Weight varies: 10.70-11.60 grams.

Date	Mintage	Good	VG	F	VF	XF
AH1215//37 (sic)	—	4.00	10.00	16.50	22.50	32.50

KM# 51.7 RUPEE
Silver **Obv. Inscription:** Shah Alam (II) **Reverse:** Fish, Persian letter "Mim", star-shaped flower, swastika **Mint:** Bareli **Note:** Weight varies: 10.70-11.60 grams.

Date	Mintage	Good	VG	F	VF	XF
AH1215//37 (sic)	—	4.00	10.00	16.50	22.50	32.50

KM# 37 NAZARANA RUPEE
Silver **Obv. Inscription:** Shah Alam (II) **Reverse:** Banner **Mint:** Banaras **Note:** Weight varies: 10.70-11.60 grams.

Date	Mintage	VG	F	VF	XF	Unc
AH1183//11 Rare	—	—	—	—	—	—

KM# 118 DOUBLE RUPEE
Silver **Obv. Inscription:** Shah Alam (II) **Mint:** Najibabad **Note:** Weight varies: 21.40-23.20 grams.

Date	Mintage	Good	VG	F	VF	XF
AH1195//22	—	—	125	175	225	300

KM# 38 MOHUR
Gold **Obv. Inscription:** Shah Alam (II) **Reverse:** Trisul **Mint:** Banaras

Date	Mintage	VG	F	VF	XF	Unc
AH1181//8 Rare	—	—	—	—	—	—

KM# 120 MOHUR
Gold **Obv. Inscription:** Shah Alam (II) **Mint:** Najibabad **Note:** Weight varies: 10.70-11.40 grams.

Date	Mintage	VG	F	VF	XF	Unc
AH(11)91//18	—	220	240	265	350	—
AH-//24	—	220	240	265	350	—
AH-//25	—	220	240	265	350	—
AH-//26	—	220	240	265	350	—

BAHAWALPUR

The Amirs of Bahawalpur established their independence from Afghan control towards the close of the 18th century. In the 1830's the state's independence under British suzerainty became guaranteed by treaty. With the creation of Pakistan in 1947 Bahawalpur, with an area of almost 17,500 square miles, became its premier Princely State. Bahawalpur State, named after its capital, stretched for almost three hundred miles along the left bank of the Sutlej, Panjnad and Indus rivers.

For earlier issues in the names of the Durrani rulers, see Afghanistan.

RULERS
Amirs
Muhammad Bahawal Khan II, AH1186-1224/1772-1809AD

MINTS

بہاولپور
Bahawalpur

خانپور
Khanpur

PRINCELY STATE

ANONYMOUS HAMMERED COINAGE

Y# 1 FALUS
Copper **Obverse:** Bare, upright sprig **Reverse:** Inscription **Shape:** Square, irregular, folded over, or round **Mint:** Bahawalpur **Note:** Contemporary ND imitations exist.

Date	Mintage	Good	VG	F	VF	XF
ND(1790-1864)	—	3.00	5.00	7.00	10.00	—
AH1205	—	3.00	5.00	7.00	10.00	—
AH1206	—	3.00	5.00	7.00	10.00	—
AH1214	—	3.00	5.00	7.00	10.00	—

Muhammad Bahawal Khan II
AH1186-1224 / 1772-1809AD

ANONYMOUS HAMMERED COINAGE

C# 10 FALUS
Copper **Obverse:** Lion left, looking right **Reverse:** Inscription **Mint:** Ahmadpur

Date	Mintage	Good	VG	F	VF	XF
ND(1772-1809)	—	7.50	12.50	20.00	30.00	—

C# 7 FALUS
Copper **Mint:** Khanpur

Date	Mintage	Good	VG	F	VF	XF
ND(1772-1809)	—	10.00	15.00	22.50	35.00	—
AH1197	—	20.00	32.50	50.00	75.00	—

C# 5 FALUS
Copper **Mint:** Khanpur

Date	Mintage	Good	VG	F	VF	XF
AH1194	—	3.50	6.50	10.00	15.00	—
AH1195	—	3.50	6.50	10.00	15.00	—
AH1196	—	3.50	6.50	10.00	15.00	—
AH1197	—	3.50	6.50	10.00	15.00	—
AH1197 Date retrograde	—	3.50	6.50	10.00	15.00	—

BANSWARA

This state in southern Rajputana was founded in 1538 when the state of Dungarpur was divided between 2 sons of the Maharawal, the younger receiving the territory of Banswara with the title also of Maharawal. The rulers of Banswara were Sissodia Rajputs who claimed descent from the powerful Maharanas of Mewar-Udaipur.

Constantly harassed by the Marathas during the 18th Century, Banswara concluded an alliance in 1818 with the British who provided protection from external enemies in exchange for a portion of the state's revenues. In 1935 the state comprised 1,606 square miles with a population of 225,000, a quarter of whom were aboriginal Bhil tribal people.

PRINCELY STATE

ANONYMOUS HAMMERED COINAGE

Ra'ej Series

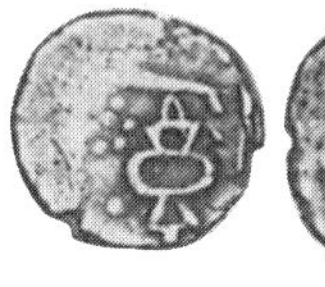 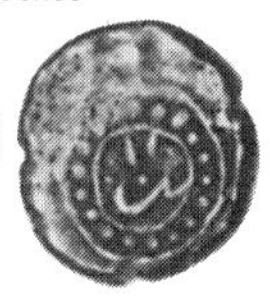

KM# 79 1/2 PAISA
Copper **Obverse:** Water pot **Reverse:** "Ra'ej" in dotted circle

Date	Mintage	Good	VG	F	VF	XF
ND(1778)	—	7.50	10.00	15.00	22.00	—

KM# 30 PAISA
Copper **Note:** Dated in years of Shah Alam II.

Date	Mintage	Good	VG	F	VF	XF
AH1192	—	3.00	4.50	7.00	11.00	—

KM# 31 PAISA
Copper **Note:** Dated in years of Shah Alam II.

Date	Mintage	Good	VG	F	VF	XF
AH1192//20	—	2.00	3.00	4.50	7.50	—

KM# 32 PAISA
Copper **Note:** Dated in years of Shah Alam II.

Date	Mintage	Good	VG	F	VF	XF
AH1197//24	—	2.50	3.50	7.00	11.00	—

KM# 33 PAISA
Copper **Note:** Dated in years of Shah Alam II.

Date	Mintage	Good	VG	F	VF	XF
AH119x//25	—	1.75	2.75	4.00	7.00	—

KM# 34 PAISA
Copper **Note:** Dated in years of Shah Alam II.

Date	Mintage	Good	VG	F	VF	XF
AH1198//26	—	3.00	4.50	7.00	11.00	—

KM# 35 PAISA
Copper **Note:** Dated in years of Shah Alam II.

Date	Mintage	Good	VG	F	VF	XF
AH11xx//27	—	1.75	2.75	4.00	7.00	—

KM# 81 PAISA
Copper **Obverse:** Branch **Note:** Dated in years of Shah Alam II.

Date	Mintage	Good	VG	F	VF	XF
AH120x//30	—	4.00	4.50	5.00	7.00	—

KM# 80 PAISA
Copper **Obverse:** Scimitar **Note:** Dated in years of Shah Alam II. Prev. KM#41.

Date	Mintage	Good	VG	F	VF	XF
AH12xx//30	—	5.00	5.50	6.00	8.00	—

KM# 36 PAISA
Copper **Note:** Dated in years of Shah Alam II.

Date	Mintage	Good	VG	F	VF	XF
AH120x//30	—	1.75	2.75	4.00	7.00	—

KM# 37 PAISA
Copper **Note:** Dated in years of Shah Alam II.

Date	Mintage	Good	VG	F	VF	XF
AH120x//31	—	1.75	2.75	4.00	7.00	—

KM# 38 PAISA
Copper **Note:** Dated in years of Shah Alam II.

Date	Mintage	Good	VG	F	VF	XF
AH120x//34	—	1.75	2.75	4.00	7.00	—

KM# 39 PAISA
Copper **Note:** Dated in years of Shah Alam II.

Date	Mintage	Good	VG	F	VF	XF
ND(1790-93)	—	1.75	2.75	4.00	7.00	—

KM# 40 PAISA
Copper **Obverse:** Leaf **Note:** Dated in years of Shah Alam II.

Date	Mintage	Good	VG	F	VF	XF
ND(1793)	—	1.75	2.75	4.00	7.00	—

KM# 82 PAISA
Copper **Obverse:** Sunface **Note:** Dated in years of Shah Alam II.

Date	Mintage	Good	VG	F	VF	XF
ND(1800)//59	—	3.00	4.00	4.50	6.00	—

KM# 83 PAISA
Copper **Obverse:** Broad axe **Note:** Dated in years of Shah Alam II.

Date	Mintage	Good	VG	F	VF	XF
ND(1800)//59	—	3.50	4.50	5.00	7.00	—

KM# 84 PAISA
Copper **Obverse:** Flower **Note:** Dated in years of Shah Alam II.

Date	Mintage	Good	VG	F	VF	XF
ND(1800)//5x	—	3.50	4.50	5.50	7.50	—

KM# 85 PAISA
Copper **Obverse:** 7-petalled flower **Note:** Dated in years of Shah Alam II.

Date	Mintage	Good	VG	F	VF	XF
ND(1800)	—	—	—	—	—	—

KM# 86 PAISA
Copper **Obverse:** Leaf **Note:** Dated in years of Shah Alam II.

Date	Mintage	Good	VG	F	VF	XF
ND(1777)//20	—	—	—	—	—	—

BARODA

Maratha state located in western India. The ruling line was descended from Damaji, a Maratha soldier, who received the title of "Distinguished Swordsman" in 1721 (hence the scimitar on most Baroda coins). The Baroda title "Gaikwara" comes from "gaikwar" or cow herd, Damaji's father's occupation.

The Maratha rulers of Baroda, the Gaekwar family rose to prominence in the mid-18th century by carving out for themselves a dominion from territories, which were previously under the control of the Poona Marathas, and to a lesser extent, of the Raja of Jodhpur. Chronic internal disputes regarding the succession to the masnad culminated in the intervention of British troops in support of one candidate, Anand Rao Gaekwar, in 1800. Then, in 1802, an agreement with the East India Company released the Baroda princes from their fear of domination by the Maratha Peshwa of Poona but subordinated them to Company interests. Nevertheless, for almost the next century and a half Baroda maintained a good relationship with the British and continued as a major Princely State right up to 1947, when it acceded to the Indian Union.

RULERS
Gaekwars
Govind Rao (first reign), AH1182-1185/1768-1771AD
Sayaji Rao I, AH1185-1192/1771-1778AD
Fatah Singh (regent), AH1192-1204/1778-1789AD
Manaji Rao (regent), AH1204-1208/1789-1793AD
Govind Rao (second reign), AH1208-1215/1793-1800AD
Anand Rao, AH1215-1235/1800-1819AD

MINTS

بروده

Baroda

جمبوسر

Jambusar

پتلاد

Petlad

MINT MARKS
Ahmadabad Mint

म

Ma - Manaji Rao's Shah Alam II coins, Baroda Mint.

आ

A - Anand Rao's Muhammad Akbar II coins, Baroda Mint.

PRINCELY STATE

HAMMERED COINAGE

C# 5 RUPEE
11.5000 g., Silver **Obv. Inscription:** Shah Alam II **Mint:** Jambusar

Date	Mintage	Good	VG	F	VF	XF
AH--//22	—	35.00	90.00	150	225	325

Manaji Rao

Regent: AH1204-1208 / 1789-1793AD

HAMMERED COINAGE

C# 14 1/2 RUPEE
Silver, 15-16 mm. **Mint:** Baroda **Note:** Weight varies: 5.35-5.80 grams. Size varies.

Date	Mintage	VG	F	VF	XF	Unc
ND(1790-91)//2	—	7.00	11.00	16.50	25.00	—
ND(1792-93)//4	—	7.00	11.00	16.50	25.00	—

C# A17 RUPEE
Silver **Mint:** Baroda **Note:** Weight varies: 10.70-11.60 grams.

Date	Mintage	VG	F	VF	XF	Unc
AH--//3	—	8.50	13.50	20.00	28.50	—
AH--//4	—	8.50	13.50	20.00	28.50	—

Anand Rao

AH1215-1235 / 1800-1819AD

HAMMERED COINAGE

C# 19 RUPEE
Silver **Obverse:** Inscription **Obv. Inscription:** Shah Alam (II) **Reverse:** Inscription, mint mark **Mint:** Ahmadabad **Note:** Weight varies: 10.70-11.60 grams. Varities exists with 2 "leaves" attached to ankus.

Date	Mintage	Good	VG	F	VF	XF
ND//3x (1788-98)	—	4.25	6.00	11.00	18.00	28.00
ND//40 (1798-99)	—	2.25	5.50	11.00	18.00	28.00
ND//41(1799-1800)	—	4.25	6.00	11.00	18.00	28.00
ND//5x (1808)	—	4.25	6.00	11.00	18.00	28.00

BHARATPUR

State located in Rajputana in northwest India.

Bharatpur was founded by Balchand, a Jat chieftain who took advantage of Mughal confusion and weakness after the death of Aurangzeb to seize the area. In 1756 the ruler at that time, Suraj Mal, received the title of Raja. Bharatpur became increasingly associated with Maratha ambitions and, in spite of treaty ties to the East India Company, assisted the Maratha Confederacy in their struggles against the British. This gained them few friends in British circles, but the early attempts by the British to force the submission of Bharatpur fortress proved abortive. In 1826 however, the British took the opportunity offered by a bitter internal feud concerning the succession finally to reduce the stronghold. The rival claimant was exiled to Allahabad and Balwant Singh, then a child of seven, was placed on the throne under the supervision of a British Political Agent. From that time onwards Bharatpur came under British control until it acceded to the Indian Union at Independence.

RULERS
Suraj Mal, AH1170-1177/1756-1763AD
Jawahir Singh, AH1177-1182/1764-1768AD
Ratan Singh, AH1182-1183/1768-1769AD
Kehri Singh, AH1183-1190/1769-1776AD
Ranjit Singh, AH1190-1220/1776-1805AD

MINTS

اکبراباد

Akbarabad

Agra or Akbarabad was controlled by the Bharatpur Jats from AH1175-1186/1761-1773AD. For earlier or later issues see Mughal Empire: Akbarabad Mint.

بهرت پور

Bharatpur
Braj Indrapur

Mint marks

مهه اندرپور

Dig
Mahe Indrapur

Mint mark

Sa, = Sanh, "year"

مهه اندرپور

Kumber
Maha Indrapur

Mint mark

Uncertain Mint
Possibly the fortress of Ver (Wair).
Arabic *Wa* = ver?

Mint mark

PRINCELY STATE

HAMMERED COINAGE

KM# 91 PAISA
Copper **Obv. Inscription:** Shah Alam (II) **Mint:** Uncertain Mint **Note:** Mint name unclear. Possibly the fortress of Ver (Wair).

Date	Mintage	Good	VG	F	VF	XF
AH-//27	—	4.00	6.50	10.00	15.00	—

KM# 30 PAISA
Copper **Obv. Inscription:** Shah Alam II **Mint:** Mahe Indrapur

Date	Mintage	Good	VG	F	VF	XF
AH-//13	—	—	—	—	—	—
AH1206/5	—	—	—	—	—	—

KM# 2 PAISA
Bronze **Obv. Inscription:** Shah Alam (II) **Mint:** Akbarabad

Date	Mintage	VG	F	VF	XF	Unc
AH1202	—	—	—	—	—	—

KM# 11 TAKKA

Copper **Obverse:** Inscription **Obv. Inscription:** Shah Alam (II) **Reverse:** Inscription, katar **Mint:** Bharatpur **Note:** Weight varies: 17.50-18.50 grams.

Date	Mintage	Good	VG	F	VF	XF
AH-//4	—	3.00	5.00	10.00	15.00	—
AH-//24	—	3.00	5.00	10.00	15.00	—
AH-//25	—	3.00	5.00	10.00	15.00	—
AH-//29	—	3.00	5.00	10.00	15.00	—
AH-//33	—	3.00	5.00	10.00	15.00	—
AH-//41	—	3.00	5.00	10.00	15.00	—
AH1214//42	—	3.00	5.00	10.00	15.00	—
AH-//44	—	3.00	5.00	10.00	15.00	—
AH-//44	—	3.00	5.00	10.00	15.00	—
AH-//45	—	3.00	5.00	10.00	15.00	—
AH-//48	—	3.00	5.00	10.00	15.00	—
AH1215//49 (sic)	—	3.00	5.00	10.00	15.00	—

KM# A31 TAKKA

18.0000 g., Copper **Reverse:** With mint marks **Mint:** Mahe Indrapur

Date	Mintage	Good	VG	F	VF	XF
AH-//13	—	10.00	15.00	20.00	35.00	—

KM# 31 TAKKA

18.0000 g., Copper **Reverse:** Without mint marks **Mint:** Mahe Indrapur

Date	Mintage	Good	VG	F	VF	XF
AH12xx//35	—	10.00	15.00	25.00	50.00	—
AH-//37	—	10.00	15.00	25.00	50.00	—

KM# 4 1/4 RUPEE

Silver **Obv. Inscription:** Shah Alam (II) **Mint:** Akbarabad **Note:** Weight varies: 2.75-2.80 grams.

Date	Mintage	Good	VG	F	VF	XF
AH-//2	—	10.00	20.00	35.00	50.00	75.00

KM# 5 1/2 RUPEE

Silver **Obv. Inscription:** Shah Alam (II) **Mint:** Akbarabad **Note:** Weight varies: 5.50-5.60 grams.

Date	Mintage	Good	VG	F	VF	XF
AH1181//6 (sic)	—	10.00	20.00	35.00	50.00	75.00

KM# 27 RUPEE

Silver **Obv. Inscription:** Alamgir (II) **Mint:** Mahe Indrapur **Note:** Weight varies: 11.00-11.20 grams.

Date	Mintage	Good	VG	F	VF	XF
AH(11)69//3	—	10.00	20.00	35.00	60.00	100
AH-//4	—	10.00	20.00	35.00	60.00	100
AH-//5	—	10.00	20.00	35.00	60.00	100
AH1172//6	—	10.00	20.00	35.00	60.00	100

KM# 29 RUPEE

Silver **Obv. Inscription:** Shah Jahan III **Mint:** Mahe Indrapur **Note:** Weight varies: 11.00-11.20 grams.

Date	Mintage	Good	VG	F	VF	XF
AH1173//1 (sic)	—	18.50	45.00	90.00	150	225
AH1174//1 (sic)	—	18.50	45.00	90.00	150	225

KM# 36 RUPEE

Silver **Mint:** Mahe Indrapur **Note:** Weight varies: 11.00-11.20 grams.

Date	Mintage	Good	VG	F	VF	XF
AH1175//3	—	5.00	10.00	15.00	25.00	35.00
AH1176//4	—	5.00	10.00	15.00	25.00	35.00
AH1177//4	—	5.00	10.00	15.00	25.00	35.00
AH-//6	—	5.00	10.00	15.00	25.00	35.00
AH1178//5	—	5.00	10.00	15.00	25.00	35.00
AH118x//7	—	5.00	10.00	15.00	25.00	35.00
AH1181//8	—	5.00	10.00	15.00	25.00	35.00

KM# 6 RUPEE

Silver **Obv. Inscription:** Shah Alam (II) **Mint:** Akbarabad **Note:** Weight varies: 11.00-11.20 grams.

Date	Mintage	Good	VG	F	VF	XF
AH1175//2	—	5.00	10.00	15.00	25.00	35.00
AH1175//3	—	5.00	10.00	15.00	25.00	35.00
AH1176//3	—	5.00	10.00	15.00	25.00	35.00
AH1176//4	—	5.00	10.00	15.00	25.00	35.00
AH1177//4	—	5.00	10.00	15.00	25.00	35.00
AH1177//5	—	5.00	10.00	15.00	25.00	35.00
AH1178//5	—	5.00	10.00	15.00	25.00	35.00
AH1179//6	—	5.00	10.00	15.00	25.00	35.00
AH1180//7	—	5.00	10.00	15.00	25.00	35.00
AH1180//8	—	5.00	10.00	15.00	25.00	35.00
AH1181//8	—	5.00	10.00	15.00	25.00	35.00
AH1182//9	—	5.00	10.00	15.00	25.00	35.00
AH1182//10	—	5.00	10.00	15.00	25.00	35.00
AH1184//11	—	5.00	10.00	15.00	25.00	35.00
AH1184//12	—	5.00	10.00	15.00	25.00	35.00
AH1185//14 (sic)	—	5.00	10.00	15.00	25.00	35.00

KM# 46 RUPEE

Silver **Mint:** Mahe Indrapur **Note:** Weight varies: 11.00-11.10 grams.

Date	Mintage	VG	F	VF	XF	Unc
AH1182//9	—	10.00	15.00	25.00	40.00	—
AH1183//10	—	10.00	15.00	25.00	40.00	—

KM# 56 RUPEE

Silver **Mint:** Mahe Indrapur **Note:** Weight varies: 10.70-11.60 grams.

Date	Mintage	Good	VG	F	VF	XF
AH118x//13	—	3.00	10.00	15.00	25.00	40.00
AH1185//14 (sic)	—	3.00	10.00	15.00	25.00	40.00
AH1186//14	—	3.00	10.00	15.00	25.00	40.00
AH1187//15	—	3.00	10.00	15.00	25.00	40.00
AH118x//16	—	3.00	10.00	15.00	25.00	40.00

KM# 26 RUPEE

Silver **Obverse:** Inscription **Reverse:** Inscription, star **Mint:** Braj Indrapur **Note:** Weight varies: 11.00-11.10 grams.

Date	Mintage	Good	VG	F	VF	XF
AH118x//14	—	5.00	10.00	15.00	25.00	40.00
AH12xx//29	—	5.00	10.00	15.00	25.00	40.00
AH-//30	—	5.00	10.00	15.00	25.00	40.00
AH12xx//31	—	5.00	10.00	15.00	25.00	40.00
AH-//32	—	5.00	10.00	15.00	25.00	40.00
AH1206//34	—	5.00	10.00	15.00	25.00	40.00
AH1207//34	—	5.00	10.00	15.00	25.00	40.00
AH12xx//35	—	5.00	10.00	15.00	25.00	40.00
AH1209//37	—	5.00	10.00	15.00	25.00	40.00
AH-//38	—	5.00	10.00	15.00	25.00	40.00
AH-//39	—	5.00	10.00	15.00	25.00	40.00
AH12xx//40	—	5.00	10.00	15.00	25.00	40.00
AH1214//42	—	5.00	10.00	15.00	25.00	40.00
AH1215//43	—	5.00	10.00	15.00	25.00	40.00

KM# 16 RUPEE

Silver **Mint:** Bharatpur **Note:** Weight varies: 11.00-11.10 grams.

Date	Mintage	Good	VG	F	VF	XF
AH1187//14	—	10.00	15.00	25.00	35.00	50.00

KM# 88 RUPEE

Silver **Mint:** Mahe Indrapur **Note:** Weight varies: 10.70-11.60 grams.

Date	Mintage	Good	VG	F	VF	XF
AH120x//29	—	10.00	15.00	25.00	35.00	50.00

KM# 86 RUPEE

Silver **Mint:** Mahe Indrapur **Note:** Weight varies: 10.70-11.60 grams.

Date	Mintage	Good	VG	F	VF	XF
AH1206//34	—	5.00	10.00	15.00	25.00	40.00
AH121x//36	—	5.00	10.00	15.00	25.00	40.00
AH121x//46	—	5.00	10.00	15.00	25.00	40.00

KM# 66 RUPEE

Silver **Obverse:** Inscription **Obv. Inscription:** Shah Alam (II) **Reverse:** Inscription, star **Mint:** Kumber **Note:** Weight varies: 11.00-11.10 grams.

Date	Mintage	Good	VG	F	VF	XF
AH1206//34	—	—	10.00	20.00	35.00	50.00
AH12xx//40	—	—	10.00	20.00	35.00	50.00
AH121x//41	—	—	10.00	20.00	35.00	50.00
AH121x//42	—	—	10.00	20.00	35.00	50.00

KM# 28 MOHUR

Silver **Mint:** Mahe Indrapur

Date	Mintage	VG	F	VF	XF	Unc
AH-//4	—	—	—	—	—	—

KM# 40 MOHUR

Gold, 20 mm. **Mint:** Mahe Indrapur **Note:** Weight varies: 10.70-11.20 grams.

Date	Mintage	VG	F	VF	XF	Unc
AH1175//2	—	220	240	350	600	—
AH-//4	—	220	240	350	600	—

KM# 8 MOHUR

Gold **Obv. Inscription:** "Shah Alam II" **Mint:** Akbarabad **Note:** Weight varies: 10.70-11.40 grams.

Date	Mintage	VG	F	VF	XF	Unc
AH1175//2	—	350	450	550	700	—
AH1175//6 (sic) retrograde "2"	—	350	450	550	700	—

KM# 50 MOHUR

Gold, 22 mm. **Mint:** Mahe Indrapur **Note:** Weight varies: 10.70-11.40 grams.

Date	Mintage	VG	F	VF	XF	Unc
AH1182//9	—	275	350	450	675	—
AH1183//10	—	275	350	450	675	—

KM# 37 NAZARANA RUPEE

Silver **Mint:** Mahe Indrapur **Note:** Weight varies: 11.00-11.20 grams.

Date	Mintage	VG	F	VF	XF	Unc
AH1176//4	—	75.00	125	200	300	—

BHAUNAGAR

State located in northwest India on the west shore of the Gulf of Cambay.

The Thakurs of Bhaunagar, as the rulers were titled, were Gohel Rajputs. They traced their control of the area back to the 13th century. Under the umbrella of British paramountcy, the Thakurs of Bhaunagar were regarded as relatively enlightened rulers. The State was absorbed into Saurashtra in February 1948.

Anonymous Types: Bearing the distinguishing Nagari legend *Bahadur* in addition to the Mughal legends.

MONETARY SYSTEM

2 Trambiyo = 1 Dokda
1-1/2 Dokda = 1 Dhingla

PRINCELY STATE

Thakurs of Bhaunagar

Gohel Rajputs

MUGHAL COINAGE

C# 25 DOKDO

Copper **Obverse:** Inscription **Obv. Inscription:** Shah Alam (II) **Reverse:** Inscription, date

Date	Mintage	Good	VG	F	VF	XF
ND(1759-1806)	—	2.50	4.50	6.50	10.00	—

Thakurs of Bhaunagar

MUGHAL COINAGE

C# 13 1/4 TRAMBIYO

Copper **Obv. Inscription:** Shah Jahan III

Date	Mintage	Good	VG	F	VF	XF
ND(1759-60)	—	2.00	3.25	5.00	8.50	—

C# 14 TRAMBIYO

Copper **Obv. Inscription:** Shah Jahan III

Date	Mintage	Good	VG	F	VF	XF
ND(1759-60)	—	2.50	4.50	6.50	10.00	—

C# 15 DOKDO

Copper **Obv. Inscription:** Shah Jahan III **Reverse:** Without "Sri" scimitar curved up

Date	Mintage	Good	VG	F	VF	XF
ND(1759-60)	—	2.50	4.50	6.50	10.00	—

C# 15.1 DOKDO

Copper **Obv. Inscription:** Shah Jahan III **Reverse:** Without "Sri" scimitar curved down

Date	Mintage	Good	VG	F	VF	XF
ND(1759-60)	—	2.50	4.50	6.50	10.00	—

C# 15a DOKDO

Copper **Obv. Inscription:** Shah Jahan III **Reverse:** Nagari "Sri" added **Note:** "Sri" may be in relief or incuse, right-side-up or inverted.

Date	Mintage	Good	VG	F	VF	XF
ND(1759-60)	—	2.50	4.50	6.50	10.00	—

C# 20 DHINGLO

Copper **Note:** Inscription: Shah Jahan III.

Date	Mintage	Good	VG	F	VF	XF
ND(1756)	—	2.50	4.50	6.50	10.00	—

BHOPAL

Bhopal was the second largest Muslim state located in central India. It was founded in 1723 by Dost Muhammed Khan, an Afghan adventurer of the Mirazi Khel clan, who was in the service of Aurangzeb. After the Emperor's death in 1707 Dost Muhammed asserted his independence. Early in the following century his successors, threatened by the Marathas and subjected to Pindari raids into their territory, sought to cultivate a good relationship with the British. In 1817, at the time of the Maratha and Pindari War, Bhopal signed a treaty with the British East India Company, which placed them squarely under imperial protection and control. After 1897 the British rupee was recognized as the only legal tender.

MINT

بهوپال

Bhopal

PRINCELY STATE

HAMMERED COINAGE

Mughal Series

C# 12 RUPEE

Silver **Obverse:** Inscription **Obv. Inscription:** Shah Alam (II) **Reverse:** Inscription, trident at upper right **Mint:** Bhopal **Note:** Weight varies: 10.70-11.60 grams.

Date	Mintage	Good	VG	F	VF	XF
AH11xx//1	—	10.00	15.00	20.00	35.00	50.00
AH11xx//3	—	10.00	15.00	20.00	35.00	50.00
AH-//17	—	10.00	15.00	20.00	35.00	50.00
AH1191//19	—	10.00	15.00	20.00	35.00	50.00
AH1192//20	—	10.00	15.00	20.00	35.00	50.00
AH1192//25 (sic)	—	10.00	15.00	20.00	35.00	50.00
AH119x//21	—	10.00	15.00	20.00	35.00	50.00
AH119x//24	—	10.00	15.00	20.00	35.00	50.00
AH1198//25	—	10.00	15.00	20.00	35.00	50.00
AH1199//26	—	10.00	15.00	0.20	35.00	50.00
AH1200//28	—	10.00	15.00	20.00	35.00	50.00
AH1201//31 (sic)	—	10.00	15.00	20.00	35.00	50.00
AH1201//30 (sic)	—	10.00	15.00	20.00	35.00	50.00
AH1201//29	—	10.00	15.00	20.00	35.00	50.00
AH1202//30	—	10.00	15.00	20.00	35.00	50.00
AH1203//30	—	10.00	15.00	20.00	35.00	50.00
AH120x//32	—	10.00	15.00	20.00	35.00	50.00
AH1206//33	—	10.00	15.00	20.00	35.00	50.00
AH1206//34	—	10.00	15.00	20.00	35.00	50.00
AH1207//35	—	10.00	15.00	20.00	35.00	50.00
AH1208//30 (sic)	—	10.00	15.00	20.00	35.00	50.00
AH1208//36	—	10.00	15.00	20.00	35.00	50.00
AH1208//37 (sic)	—	10.00	15.00	20.00	35.00	50.00
AH1215//42	—	10.00	15.00	20.00	35.00	50.00

BIKANIR

Bikanir, located in Rajputana was established as a state sometime between 1465 and 1504 by Jodhpur Rathor Rajput named Rao Bikaji. During the period of the Great Mughals Bikanir was intimately linked to Delhi by ties of both loyalty and marriage. Both Akbar and Jahangir contracted marriages with princesses of the Bikanir Rajputs,and the Bikanir nobility rendered outstanding service in the Mughal armies. Bikanir came under British influence in 1817 and after 1947 was incorporated into Rajasthan.

RULERS

Gaj Singh, AH1159-1201/1746-1786AD
Raj Singh, AH1201/1786AD
Partap Singh, AH1201-1204/1786-1788AD
Surat Singh, AH1204-1244/1788-1828AD

MINT

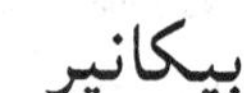

Bikanir

RULER'S SYMBOLS

1. Gaj Singh, AH1159-1202

2. (")

3. Surat Singh, AH1202-1244

4. (")

5. (")

NOTE: The above symbols normally occur in groups on the obverse or reverse of the coins; the various combinations are shown for each series.

PRINCELY STATE

Gaj Singh

AH1159-1201 / 1746-1786AD

MUGHAL COINAGE

KM# 5 PAISA

Copper **Obv. Inscription:** Alamgir (II)

Date	Mintage	Good	VG	F	VF	XF
AH--//36	—	5.00	10.00	15.00	20.00	—

KM# 9 RUPEE

Silver **Obv. Inscription:** Alamgir (II) **Note:** Weight varies: 10.70-11.60 grams. Mint name: Garh Bikanir.

Date	Mintage	VG	F	VF	XF
AH1167 Ahad (1)	—	50.00	100	125	175	250
AH1168 Ahad (1)	—	50.00	100	125	175	—
AH1168//2	—	50.00	100	125	175	250

KM# 10 RUPEE

Silver **Obverse:** Alamgir (II) **Note:** Weight varies: 10.70-11.60 grams. Mint name: Garh Bikanir. Cruder style.

Date	Mintage	Good	VG	F	VF	XF
AH-//2	—	7.50	18.50	26.50	37.50	55.00
AH-//3	—	7.50	18.50	26.50	37.50	55.00
AH-//5	—	7.50	18.50	26.50	37.50	55.00
AH-//6	—	7.50	18.50	26.50	37.50	55.00
AH-//7	—	7.50	18.50	26.50	37.50	55.00
AH-//9	—	7.50	18.50	26.50	37.50	55.00
AH-//10	—	7.50	18.50	26.50	37.50	55.00
AH-//11	—	7.50	18.50	26.50	37.50	55.00
AH-//13	—	7.50	18.50	26.50	37.50	55.00
AH-//15	—	7.50	18.50	26.50	37.50	55.00
AH-//16	—	7.50	18.50	26.50	37.50	55.00
AH-//17	—	7.50	18.50	26.50	37.50	55.00
AH-//21	—	7.50	18.50	26.50	37.50	55.00
AH-//22	—	7.50	18.50	26.50	37.50	55.00
AH-//26	—	7.50	18.50	26.50	37.50	55.00

KM# 12 NAZARANA RUPEE

Silver **Obv. Inscription:** Shah Alam (II) **Note:** Weight varies: 10.70-11.60 grams.

Date	Mintage	Good	VG	F	VF	XF
AH114 Error	—	50.00	75.00	90.00	125	150

KM# 10a NAZARANA RUPEE

Silver **Obv. Inscription:** Alamgir II **Note:** Weight varies: 10.70-11.60 grams. Mint name: Garh Bikanir.

Date	Mintage	Good	VG	F	VF	XF
AH-//2	—	50.00	75.00	90.00	125	150
AH-//6	—	50.00	75.00	90.00	125	150

Surat Singh
AH1204-1244 / 1788-1828AD

MUGHAL COINAGE

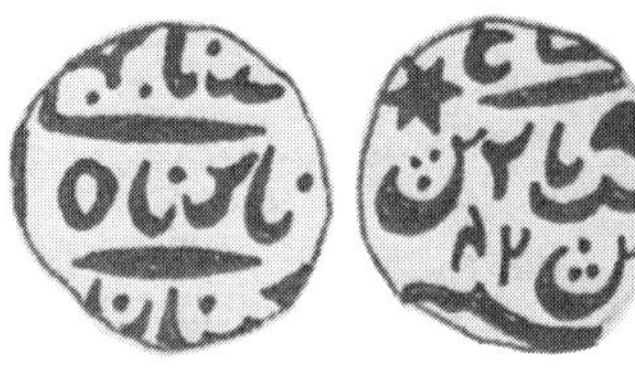

KM# 14 PAISA

Copper **Obverse:** Inscription **Obv. Inscription:** Alamgir (II) **Reverse:** Mark #3 **Note:** Regnal years 28-52 of Shah Alam II. Year 47 is of much cruder fabric.

Date	Mintage	Good	VG	F	VF	XF
AH-//41 (1799)	—	1.50	2.25	3.00	4.00	—
AH-//42 (1801)	—	1.50	2.25	3.00	4.00	—
AH-//47 (1805)	—	1.50	2.25	3.00	4.00	—

KM# 17a NAZARANA RUPEE

Silver, 29 mm. **Obv. Inscription:** Alamgir II **Note:** Weight varies: 10.70-11.60 grams.

Date	Mintage	VG	F	VF	XF	Unc
AH1204	—	75.00	90.00	125	150	—

BINDRABAN

This city, the modern Vrindavan, was not a princely state. The area surrounding the city, including the neighboring city of Mathura, was under Jat control in the mid-18th century, although nominally subject to Awadh. After varying fortunes the area passed to the East India Company in 1803-05 (i.e. AH1217-1220; VS1860-1862). The coins below display symbols of Awadh, Mughals, Delhi and Bhartpur, although it is clear that they were not mints of any of those authorities, especially in the British period.

MINTS AND MINT NAMES

بندربن

Bindraban

مؤمن اباد

Muminabad

شاه جهان اباد

Shahjahanabad

گوکل

Gokul

متهره

Mathura
Islamabad

CITY

HAMMERED COINAGE

KM# 4 PAISA

Copper **Obv. Inscription:** Shah Alam (II) **Reverse:** Trident and Arabic "N" **Mint:** Shahjahanabad

Date	Mintage	Good	VG	F	VF	XF
AH-//27	—	5.00	10.00	15.00	25.00	—
AH1202//30	—	5.00	10.00	15.00	25.00	—

KM# 2 PAISA

Copper **Obv. Inscription:** Shah Alam (II) **Reverse:** Fish left **Mint:** Shahjahanabad

Date	Mintage	Good	VG	F	VF	XF
AH-//32	—	5.00	10.00	15.00	25.00	—

KM# 3 PAISA

Copper **Obv. Inscription:** Shah Alam (II) **Reverse:** Fish right **Mint:** Shahjahanabad

Date	Mintage	Good	VG	F	VF	XF
AH1205//32	—	5.00	10.00	15.00	25.00	—
AH1206//33	—	5.00	10.00	15.00	25.00	—
AH1208//35	—	5.00	10.00	15.00	25.00	—
AH1209//36	—	5.00	10.00	15.00	25.00	—
AH1210//38	—	5.00	10.00	15.00	25.00	—
AH1212//39	—	5.00	10.00	15.00	25.00	—
AH1214//41	—	5.00	10.00	15.00	25.00	—

KM# 5 PAISA

Copper **Obverse:** Inscription, date **Obv. Inscription:** Shah Alam (II) **Reverse:** Fish, small sun below **Mint:** Muminabad

Date	Mintage	Good	VG	F	VF	XF
AH1211//36	—	5.00	10.00	15.00	25.00	—
AH1611 Error for 1211	—	5.00	10.00	15.00	25.00	—
AH1211//40 (sic)	—	5.00	10.00	15.00	25.00	—
AH1212//44	—	5.00	10.00	15.00	25.00	—
AH1212//40	—	5.00	10.00	15.00	25.00	—
AH1212//41	—	5.00	10.00	15.00	25.00	—
AH1212//36 (sic) Error	—	5.00	10.00	15.00	25.00	—
AH121x//(4)3	—	5.00	10.00	15.00	25.00	—

KM# 8a 1/4 RUPEE

Silver **Obv. Inscription:** Shah Alam (II) **Reverse:** Scimitar and katar **Note:** Weight varies: 2.68-2.90 grams.

Date	Mintage	Good	VG	F	VF	XF
AH12xx//44	—	—	15.00	25.00	50.00	75.00

KM# 9a 1/2 RUPEE

Silver **Obv. Inscription:** Shah Alam (II) **Reverse:** Scimitar and dagger **Note:** Weight varies: 5.35-5.80 grams.

Date	Mintage	Good	VG	F	VF	XF
AH12xx//44	—	10.00	15.00	20.00	40.00	60.00

KM# 10.1 RUPEE

Silver **Obv. Inscription:** Shah Alam (II) **Reverse:** Scimitar and trident **Note:** Weight varies: 10.70-11.60 grams.

Date	Mintage	Good	VG	F	VF	XF
AH-//23	—	10.00	20.00	30.00	50.00	75.00
AH-//24	—	10.00	20.00	30.00	50.00	75.00
AH1199//27	—	10.00	20.00	30.00	50.00	75.00

KM# 10.2 RUPEE

Silver **Obv. Inscription:** Shah Alam (II) **Reverse:** Scimitar, dagger, trident, and "Sri" **Note:** Weight varies: 10.70-11.60 grams.

Date	Mintage	Good	VG	F	VF	XF
AH-//23	—	10.00	20.00	30.00	50.00	60.00
AH120(9)//37	—	10.00	20.00	30.00	50.00	60.00

KM# 10.7 RUPEE

Silver **Obv. Inscription:** Shah Alam (II) **Reverse:** Scimitar, swastika, and trident **Note:** Weight varies: 10.70-11.60 grams.

Date	Mintage	Good	VG	F	VF	XF
AH12xx//37	—	10.00	20.00	30.00	50.00	75.00

KM# 10.2a RUPEE

Silver **Reverse:** Scimitar, bow and arrow, "Sri" and trident **Mint:** Bindraban

Date	Mintage	VG	F	VF	XF	Unc
AH-//37	—	—	—	—	—	—

KM# 15 MOHUR

Gold **Obv. Inscription:** "Shah Alam II" **Note:** Weight varies: 10.70-11.40 grams.

Date	Mintage	VG	F	VF	XF	Unc
AH1192//20	—	200	300	450	650	—

LOCAL COINAGE

KM# 35 PAISA

6.0000 g., Copper **Obv. Inscription:** Shah Alam (II) **Mint:** Mathura

Date	Mintage	Good	VG	F	VF	XF
ND(1794)	—	5.00	10.00	15.00	25.00	—

KM# 36 PAISA

6.0000 g., Copper **Obv. Inscription:** Shah Alam (II) **Mint:** Mathura

Date	Mintage	Good	VG	F	VF	XF
AH-//36	—	3.00	8.00	10.00	20.00	—
AH121x//39	—	—	—	—	—	—

KM# 40.1 RUPEE

Silver **Obv. Inscription:** Shah Alam (II) **Reverse:** Scimitar in "Seen" of "Manks" **Mint:** Mathura

Date	Mintage	Good	VG	F	VF	XF
AH-//18	—	10.00	20.00	30.00	50.00	75.00
AH119x//23	—	10.00	20.00	30.00	50.00	75.00
AH1199//26	—	10.00	20.00	30.00	50.00	75.00
AH1202//29	—	10.00	20.00	30.00	50.00	75.00
AH-//30	—	10.00	20.00	30.00	50.00	75.00
AH12xx//34	—	10.00	20.00	30.00	50.00	75.00

KM# 40.2 RUPEE

Silver **Obv. Inscription:** Shah Alam (II) **Reverse:** Scimitar and dagger **Mint:** Mathura

Date	Mintage	Good	VG	F	VF	XF
AH-//35	—	10.00	20.00	30.00	50.00	75.00

KM# 40.3 RUPEE

Silver **Obv. Inscription:** Shah Alam (II) **Reverse:** Scimitar in "Seen" of "Julus" **Mint:** Mathura

Date	Mintage	Good	VG	F	VF	XF
AH-//35	—	10.00	20.00	30.00	50.00	75.00

KM# 20 RUPEE

Silver **Obv. Inscription:** Shah Alam (II) **Reverse:** Flower **Mint:** Gokul **Note:** Weight varies: 10.70-11.60 grams.

Date	Mintage	Good	VG	F	VF	XF
AH-//36	—	11.00	27.50	40.00	52.50	75.00

KM# 21 RUPEE

Silver **Obv. Inscription:** Shah Alam (II) **Reverse:** "Shri" **Mint:** Gokul **Note:** Weight varies: 10.70-11.60 grams.

Date	Mintage	Good	VG	F	VF	XF
AH-//39	—	11.00	27.50	40.00	52.50	75.00

KM# 45 MOHUR

Gold **Obv. Inscription:** "Shah Alam II" **Mint:** Mathura **Note:** Weight varies: 10.70-11.40 grams.

Date	Mintage	VG	F	VF	XF	Unc
AH1182//9	—	350	500	700	1,000	—

BROACH

From very early times Broach, located on the north bank of the Narmada River 30 miles from the Gulf of Cambay, was an important port on the sea route to Europe. It was known as Barakacheva to early Chinese travellers, and as Barygaza to Ptolemy. After the Islamic invasions of India it was incorporated into the Muslim kingdom of Gujerat and remained so until 1572 when it was annexed by Akbar. During the reign of Aurangzeb, Broach first began to experience Maratha incursions. In 1772, it came briefly under British influence before being ceded to Sindhia in 1783. It was returned to the East India Company in 1803 and thereafter remained in British control.

RULERS

Town ruled by Nawabs, AH1150-1186/1736-1772AD
Nek Nam Khan, AH1168-1182/1754-1768AD
Imtya-Ud-Daula, AH1182-1186/1768-1772AD
To British 1772-1783 and 1803 on
To Gwalior 1783-1803

MINT

بروني

Broach

MINT MARKS

Flower (Nawabs)

Cross of St. Stephan (Gwalior and E.I.C.)

PRINCELY STATE

Nek Nam Khan

AH1168-1182 / 1754-1768AD

HAMMERED COINAGE

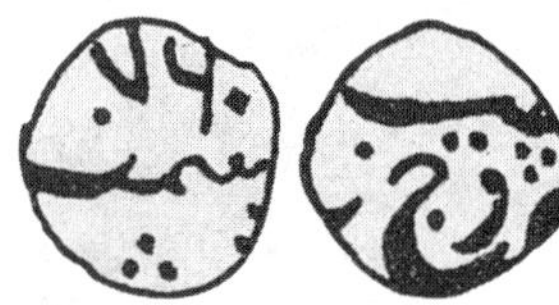

C# 20 PAISA

Copper

Date	Mintage	Good	VG	F	VF	XF
AH1176	—	5.00	8.00	15.00	25.00	—

Imtaya-ud-Daula

AH1182-1186 / 1768-1772AD

HAMMERED COINAGE

C# 25 PAISA

Copper, 17 mm. **Note:** Similar to 1 Rupee, C#36.

Date	Mintage	Good	VG	F	VF	XF
ND(1761-88)	—	5.00	10.00	15.00	25.00	—

C# 34 1/2 RUPEE

Silver **Note:** Weight varies: 5.35-5.80 grams.

Date	Mintage	Good	VG	F	VF	XF
AH-//2x	—	5.00	10.00	15.00	25.00	40.00

C# 35 RUPEE

Silver **Reverse:** Mint mark flower **Note:** Weight varies: 10.70-11.60 grams.

Date	Mintage	Good	VG	F	VF	XF
AH-//3	—	10.00	15.00	20.00	35.00	50.00
AH11xx//4	—	10.00	15.00	20.00	35.00	50.00
AH1172//5	—	10.00	15.00	20.00	35.00	50.00
AH1181//9	—	10.00	15.00	20.00	35.00	50.00

BUNDI

State in Rajputana in northwest India.

Bundi was founded in 1342 by a Chauhan Rajput, Rao Dewa (Deoraj). Until the Maratha defeat early in the 19th century, Bundi was greatly harassed by the forces of Holkar and Sindhia. In 1818 it came under British protection and control and remained so until 1947.In 1948 the State was absorbed into Rajasthan.

RULERS

Ajit Singh, AH1185-1187/ VS1828-1830/1771-1773AD
Bishen Singh, AH1187-1236/ VS1830-1878/1773-1821AD

MINT

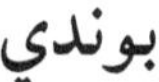

Bundi

Mint name: Bundi

All of the coins of Bundi struck prior to the Mutiny (1857) are in the name of the Mughal emperor and bear the following 2 marks on the reverse, to the left and right of the regnal year, respectively:

 On all Mughal issues

 Only on Muhammad Akbar and Muhammad Bahadur issues

The same symbols appear on the coins of Kotah, but the difference is that the Kotah pieces have the mintname *Kotahurf Nandgaon* and later issues only have *Nandgaon.*

PRINCELY STATE

HAMMERED COINAGE

Mughal Series

C# 5.1 TAKKA

Copper **Obverse:** Inscription **Obv. Inscription:** Shah Alam (II) **Reverse:** Inscription, flower symbol **Note:** Weight varies: 17.50-18.00 grams.

Date	Mintage	Good	VG	F	VF	XF
AH-//2	—	5.00	10.00	15.00	25.00	—
AH-//3	—	5.00	10.00	15.00	25.00	—
AH-//5	—	5.00	10.00	15.00	25.00	—
AH-//11	—	5.00	10.00	15.00	25.00	—
AH-//20	—	5.00	10.00	15.00	25.00	—
AH-//21	—	5.00	10.00	15.00	25.00	—
AH-//22	—	5.00	10.00	15.00	25.00	—
AH-//23	—	5.00	10.00	15.00	25.00	—
AH-//24	—	5.00	10.00	15.00	25.00	—
AH-//25	—	5.00	10.00	15.00	25.00	—
AH-//26	—	5.00	10.00	15.00	25.00	—
AH-//27	—	5.00	10.00	15.00	25.00	—
AH-//28	—	5.00	10.00	15.00	25.00	—
AH-//29	—	5.00	10.00	15.00	25.00	—
AH-//30	—	5.00	10.00	15.00	25.00	—
AH-//31	—	5.00	10.00	15.00	25.00	—
AH-//32	—	5.00	10.00	15.00	25.00	—

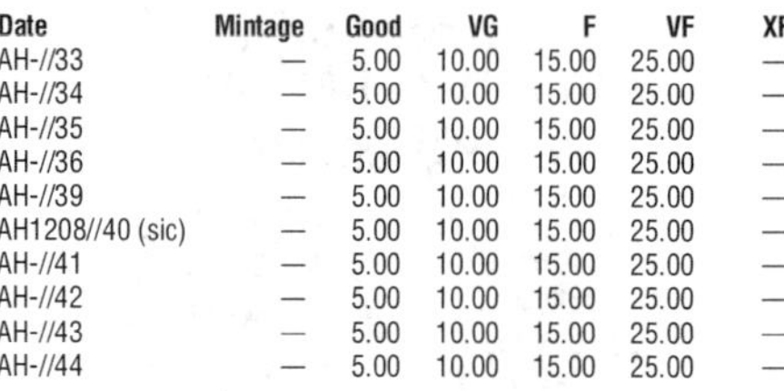

Date	Mintage	Good	VG	F	VF	XF
AH-//33	—	5.00	10.00	15.00	25.00	—
AH-//34	—	5.00	10.00	15.00	25.00	—
AH-//35	—	5.00	10.00	15.00	25.00	—
AH-//36	—	5.00	10.00	15.00	25.00	—
AH-//39	—	5.00	10.00	15.00	25.00	—
AH1208//40 (sic)	—	5.00	10.00	15.00	25.00	—
AH-//41	—	5.00	10.00	15.00	25.00	—
AH-//42	—	5.00	10.00	15.00	25.00	—
AH-//43	—	5.00	10.00	15.00	25.00	—
AH-//44	—	5.00	10.00	15.00	25.00	—

 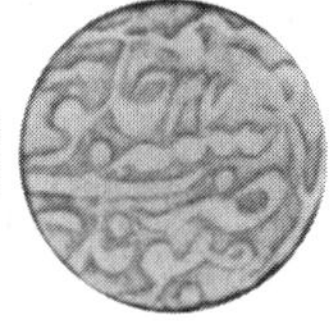

C# 10.1 RUPEE

Silver **Obverse:** Inscription **Obv. Inscription:** Shah Alam (II) **Reverse:** Inscription **Note:** Weight varies: 10.90-11.15 grams.

Date	Mintage	Good	VG	F	VF	XF
AH-// Ahad (1)	—	4.00	10.00	15.00	22.50	35.00
AH-//2	—	4.00	10.00	15.00	22.50	35.00
AH-//3	—	4.00	10.00	15.00	22.50	35.00
AH-//7	—	4.00	10.00	15.00	22.50	35.00
AH-//10	—	4.00	10.00	15.00	22.50	35.00
AH-//12	—	4.00	10.00	15.00	22.50	35.00
AH-//18	—	4.00	10.00	15.00	22.50	35.00
AH-//20	—	4.00	10.00	15.00	22.50	35.00
AH-//21	—	4.00	10.00	15.00	22.50	35.00
AH-//23	—	4.00	10.00	15.00	22.50	35.00
AH-//24	—	4.00	10.00	15.00	22.50	35.00
AH-//25	—	4.00	10.00	15.00	22.50	35.00
AH-//27	—	4.00	10.00	15.00	22.50	35.00
AH-//28	—	4.00	10.00	15.00	22.50	35.00
AH-//29	—	4.00	10.00	15.00	22.50	35.00
AH-//30	—	4.00	10.00	15.00	22.50	35.00
AH-//31	—	4.00	10.00	15.00	22.50	35.00
AH-//32	—	4.00	10.00	15.00	22.50	35.00
AH1204//33 (sic)	—	4.00	10.00	15.00	22.50	35.00
AH-//34	—	4.00	10.00	15.00	22.50	35.00
AH-//37	—	4.00	10.00	15.00	22.50	35.00
AH-//40	—	4.00	10.00	15.00	22.50	35.00
AH-//43	—	5.00	10.00	15.00	22.50	35.00
AH-//44	—	5.00	10.00	15.00	22.50	35.00

C# 10a NAZARANA RUPEE

Silver **Obv. Inscription:** Shah Alam (II) **Shape:** Square **Note:** Weight varies: 11.00-11.10 grams.

Date	Mintage	Good	VG	F	VF	XF
AH-//9	—	20.00	40.00	65.00	85.00	125
AH-//28	—	20.00	40.00	65.00	85.00	125
AH-//37	—	20.00	40.00	65.00	85.00	125
AH-//42	—	20.00	40.00	65.00	85.00	125

C# 14 MOHUR

10.7800 g., Gold **Obv. Inscription:** "Shah Alam II"

Date	Mintage	VG	F	VF	XF	Unc
AH-//39	—	240	350	500	700	—

CANNANORE

Cannanore, on the Malabar Coast in southwest India, was ruled by the Cherakal Rajas. Late in the 18th century it was overrun by Haider Ali, the Muslim ruler of Mysore. Then, in AH1198/1783, Cannanore was captured from Haider Ali's son, Tipu Sultan, by the East India Company. From that time onwards Cannanore was reduced to the status of a British tributary.

RULER

Ali Rajas, Lords of the deep,
AH1122-1231/1710-1815AD

BRITISH TRIBUTARY

HAMMERED COINAGE

KM# 5 1/5 RUPEE

Silver **Obverse:** Inscription **Reverse:** Inscription, date **Note:** Varieties exist. Weight varies: 2.14-2.32 grams.

Date	Mintage	Good	VG	F	VF	XF
AH1121	—	2.35	6.00	9.00	13.50	20.00
AH1122	—	2.35	6.00	9.00	13.50	20.00
AH1123	—	2.35	6.00	9.00	13.50	20.00
AH1124	—	2.35	6.00	9.00	13.50	20.00
AH1132	—	2.35	6.00	9.00	13.50	20.00
AH1134	—	2.35	6.00	9.00	13.50	20.00

Date	Mintage	Good	VG	F	VF	XF
AH1137	—	2.35	6.00	9.00	13.50	20.00
AH1139	—	2.35	5.00	8.50	12.50	18.50
AH1143	—	2.00	5.00	8.50	12.50	18.50
AH1144	—	2.00	5.00	8.50	12.50	18.50
AH1145	—	2.00	5.00	8.50	12.50	18.50
AH1146	—	2.00	5.00	8.50	12.50	18.50
AH1148	—	2.00	5.00	8.50	12.50	18.50
AH1163	—	2.00	5.00	8.50	12.50	18.50
AH1164	—	2.00	5.00	8.50	12.50	18.50
AH1169	—	2.00	5.00	8.50	12.50	18.50
AH1173	—	2.00	5.00	8.50	12.50	18.50
AH1181	—	2.00	5.00	8.50	12.50	18.50
AH1187	—	1.50	4.00	7.00	10.00	15.00
AH1188	—	1.50	4.00	7.00	10.00	15.00
AH1194	—	1.50	4.00	7.00	10.00	15.00
AH1199	—	1.50	4.00	7.00	10.00	15.00

KM# 10 2 FANAMS

Gold, 16 mm. **Note:** Weight varies: 0.70-0.80 grams.

Date	Mintage	Good	VG	F	VF	XF
AH1194	—	—	85.00	125	150	175

CHHATARPUR

Chhatarpur in Bundelkhand was founded about 1785 by a Ponwar Rajput. In 1806 the State accepted a mandate (sanad) from the British and acquiesced to East India Company protection. Sixteen years later in 1822,Chhatarpur came under direct British control.

Mint struck ca. 1816-1882AD, w/frozen date AH1192, (sometimes blundered).

MINT

چترپور

Chhatarpur

Mint mark

PRINCELY STATE

Shah Alam II

AH1173-1221/1759-1806AD

HAMMERED DUMP COINAGE

KM# 2 PAISA

Copper, 15 mm. **Obv. Inscription:** Shah Alam (II)

Date	Mintage	Good	VG	F	VF	XF
ND(1765-81)	—	5.00	10.00	20.00	35.00	—

KM# 5 1/4 RUPEE

Copper **Obv. Inscription:** Shah Alam (II) **Note:** Weight varies 2.68 - 2.90 grams.

Date	Mintage	Good	VG	F	VF	XF
ND/25 (1783-84)	—	5.00	15.00	25.00	40.00	75.00

KM# 21 RUPEE

Silver

Date	Mintage	Good	VG	F	VF	XF
ND(1765-81)	—	5.00	10.00	15.00	25.00	50.00

KM# 15.1 RUPEE

Silver **Obverse:** Trisul **Obv. Inscription:** Shah Alam (II) **Note:** Weight varies 10.7 - 11.6 grams.

Date	Mintage	Good	VG	F	VF	XF
ND//9 (1767-68)	—	3.50	9.00	15.00	21.50	30.00
ND//11 (1769-70)	—	3.50	9.00	15.00	21.50	30.00

KM# 15.2 RUPEE

Silver **Obverse:** Small circle within dotted circle **Obv. Inscription:** Shah Alam (II) **Reverse:** Mint marks cross of St. Stephan, trident below

Date	Mintage	Good	VG	F	VF	XF
ND//10 (1768-69)	—	3.50	9.00	15.00	21.50	30.00

KM# 17 RUPEE

Silver **Obverse:** Chakra **Obv. Inscription:** Shah Alam (II)

Date	Mintage	Good	VG	F	VF	XF
ND//15 (1773-74)	—	3.50	9.00	15.00	21.50	30.00

KM# 20 RUPEE

Silver **Obverse:** Elephant goad

Date	Mintage	Good	VG	F	VF	XF
AH1192	—	3.00	7.50	15.00	21.00	30.00

KM# 19 RUPEE

Silver **Obverse:** Pataka **Obv. Inscription:** Shah Alam (II)

Date	Mintage	Good	VG	F	VF	XF
ND//24 (1782-83)	—	2.75	6.50	11.00	16.50	25.00
AH1192//25 (sic)	—	2.25	5.50	8.00	12.50	18.50
AH1211	—	2.25	5.50	8.00	12.50	18.50

HAMMERED DUMP COINAGE

Uncertain Types

C# 15 RUPEE

Silver **Note:** Types to be determined. Weight varies 10.70-11.60 grams.

Date	Mintage	Good	VG	F	VF	XF
ND//7 (1765-66)	—	3.75	9.50	15.00	21.00	30.00
ND//10 (1768-69)	—	3.75	9.50	15.00	21.00	30.00
ND//11 (1769-70)	—	3.75	9.50	15.00	21.00	30.00
ND//12 (1770-71)	—	3.75	9.50	15.00	21.00	30.00
ND//16 (1774-75)	—	3.75	9.50	15.00	21.00	30.00
ND//17 (1775-76)	—	3.75	9.50	15.00	21.00	30.00
ND//20 (1778-79)	—	3.75	9.50	15.00	21.00	30.00
ND//21 (1779-80)	—	3.75	9.50	15.00	21.00	30.00
ND//22 (1780-81)	—	3.75	9.50	15.00	21.00	30.00

COCHIN

Located on the Malabar Coast, at the southern tip of India.

Although the name Cochin appears to have come into use only at the end of the 15th century, this was a very ancient state whose origins were lost in antiquity. In Roman times there was a steady trade between Cochin and the West, but from that time onward Cochin's history is largely conjecture until the arrival of the Portuguese under Vasco de Gama in the 15th century. In 1663 Cochin came under Dutch occupation and remained so for almost a hundred years until Haider Ali and Tipu Sultan of Mysore overran the region. In 1791, largely to escape the demands of Mysore, the Raja of Cochin placed himself under British protection. In 1809 a second treaty strengthened British control of the State.

In 1949 Cochin merged with Travencore forming the state of Travancore and Cochin which became part of the new state of Kerala in 1956.

See Netherlands possessions in India for similar coins prior to 1795AD.

BRITISH PROTECTORATE

HAMMERED COINAGE

KM# 1 PUTTUN

0.3240 g., Silver **Obverse:** Sun and moon above "lazy J" and dots **Reverse:** Conch shell

Date	Mintage	Good	VG	F	VF	XF
ND(1795-1850)	—	—	4.00	6.00	9.00	13.50

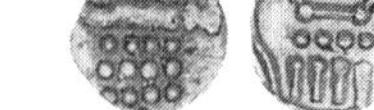

KM# 2 2 PUTTUNS

1.0000 g., Silver **Obverse:** Sun and moon above "lazy J" and dots **Reverse:** Conch shell

Date	Mintage	Good	VG	F	VF	XF
ND(1795-1850)	—	—	6.00	9.00	13.50	20.00

KM# 10 FANAM

Gold **Obverse:** Sun and moon above dots **Reverse:** Conch shell

Date	Mintage	Good	VG	F	VF	XF
ND(1795-1850)	—	—	7.00	11.00	16.50	25.00

COOCH BEHAR

Cooch Behar was relatively peaceful until there was a dispute over the succession in 1772. After a confusing period during which the Bhutanese installed their own nominated ruler and captured Dhairyendra Narandra, the Chief Minister appealed to the British for assistance. With an eye on the potentially lucrative Tibetan trade, which had increased somewhat in volume since Prithvi Narayan's rise to power in Nepal, the British agreed to support Darendra Narayan, so long as British suzerainty was acknowledged.

Over the following decades the British gradually increased their control over the state. After large numbers of debased silver half, or "Narainy" rupees had been struck, the British decided to close the mint, and after that a few coins only were struck at the coronation of each ruler, although it was only in 1866 that the local coins ceased to be legal tender.

RULERS

Nripendra Narayan, CB353-401/SE1785-1833/1863-1911AD
Raja Rajendra Narayan, CB401-403/SE1833-1835/1911-1913AD
Jitendra Narayan, CB403-412/SE1835-1844/1913-1922AD
Jagaddipendra Narayan, CB412-439/SE1844-1871/1922-1949AD

BRITISH PROTECTORATE

Rupa Narayan

SE1617-1637 / 1695-1715AD

STANDARD COINAGE

KM# 109 1/2 RUPEE

Silver

Date	Mintage	Good	VG	F	VF	XF
ND(1695-1715)	—	3.50	6.00	10.00	15.00	—

Upendra Narayan

SE1637-1686 / 1715-1764AD

STANDARD COINAGE

KM# 115 1/2 RUPEE

Silver **Note:** "Pendra" center left on obverse. Weight varies 5.35-5.80 grams.

Date	Mintage	Good	VG	F	VF	XF
ND(1715-64)	—	3.25	5.00	8.50	13.50	—

Devendra Narayan

SE1686-1688 / 1764-1766AD

STANDARD COINAGE

KM# 121 1/2 RUPEE

Silver **Note:** "Vendra" center left on obverse. Weight varies 5.35-5.80 grams.

Date	Mintage	Good	VG	F	VF	XF
ND(1764-66)	—	2.00	5.00	8.00	11.50	16.50

Dhairjendra Narayan

SE1688-1693 / 1766-1772AD

STANDARD COINAGE

KM# 127 1/2 RUPEE

Silver **Note:** "Yendra" center left on obverse. Weight varies 5.35-5.80 grams.

Date	Mintage	VG	F	VF	XF	Unc
ND(1780-83)	—	6.00	9.00	11.50	17.50	—

Rajendra Narayan
SE1693-1695 / 1771-1773AD
STANDARD COINAGE

KM# 133 1/2 RUPEE
4.7000 g., Silver **Note:** "Jendra" center left on obverse.

Date	Mintage	Good	VG	F	VF	XF
ND(1771-73)	—	2.00	5.00	8.00	11.00	16.50

Darendra Narayan// Narendra Narayan
SE1695-1761 / 1773-1839AD
HAMMERED COINAGE
Presentation Issues

KM# 141 1/2 RUPEE
4.7000 g., Silver **Obverse:** Inscription, "Rendra" center left **Reverse:** Inscription **Note:** Ruler names cannot be differentiated.

Date	Mintage	Good	VG	F	VF	XF
ND(1773-1839)	—	2.00	5.00	8.00	11.00	16.50

COORG

Kurg

A landlocked district in Karnataka, located between the districts of South Kanare and Mysore.

The name Coorg is an anglicization of Kodagu which, in turn, is probably derived from Kudu meaning steep or hilly. From the 11th century onward most of Coorg was under the control of the Changalva rajas, although at different times the Changalvas themselves became feudatories to the Cholas, the Hoysalas or to the rulers of Vijayanagar. After the fall of Vijayanagar to the Muslim alliance of the Deccan in the 16th century, Coorg was ruled by a Bednur prince. The State was annexed by the East India Company in 1834, and was administered by the chief commissioner of Mysore from 1881-1947. The coinage, bearing neither ascription nor date, is typically South Indian.

PRINCIPALITY
Chikkvirappa Wodeyar
HAMMERED COINAGE

KM# 1 FANAM
0.3900 g., Silver, 7-8 mm. **Obverse:** Devanagari "Ka" above **Reverse:** Vira Raya **Note:** Similar to KM#2. Size varies.

Date	Mintage	Good	VG	F	VF	XF
ND//10 (1736-66)	—	1.65	4.00	6.00	9.00	15.00

KM# 2 FANAM
0.3800 g., Silver **Obverse:** Devanagari "Ka" above **Reverse:** Vira Raya **Note:** Struck at Mercara.

Date	Mintage	Good	VG	F	VF	XF
ND//20 (1736-66)	—	2.75	7.00	11.00	16.50	25.00

DATIA

State located in north-central India, governed by Maharajas.

Datia was founded in 1735 by Bhagwan Das, son of Narsingh Dev of the Orchha royal house. In 1804 the State concluded its first treaty with the East India Company and thereafter came under British protection and control.

MINT

Dalipnagar

Raja Shahi Series
Frozen date AH1178 and regnal year 6.

On obverse

On reverse.

BRITISH PROTECTORATE
HAMMERED COINAGE
Raja Shahi Series

C# 25 1/4 RUPEE
Silver **Note:** Weight varies 2.68-2.90 grams.

Date	Mintage	Good	VG	F	VF	XF
AH1178//6	—	10.00	15.00	25.00	50.00	75.00

C# 26 1/2 RUPEE
Silver, 14-15 mm. **Note:** Weight varies 5.35-5.80 grams. Size varies.

Date	Mintage	Good	VG	F	VF	XF
AH1178//6	—	5.00	10.00	15.00	35.00	50.00

C# 27 RUPEE
Silver **Note:** Weight varies 10.70-11.60 grams.

Date	Mintage	Good	VG	F	VF	XF
AH1171//6 (Error)	—	5.00	10.00	15.00	25.00	40.00
AH1171//6 (Error)	—	5.00	10.00	15.00	25.00	40.00
AH1177//6	—	5.00	10.00	15.00	25.00	40.00
AH1178//6	—	5.00	10.00	15.00	25.00	40.00
AH(117)8//6	—	5.00	10.00	15.00	25.00	40.00
AH1181//6 (Error)	—	5.00	10.00	15.00	25.00	40.00
AH1182//6 (Error)	—	5.00	10.00	15.00	25.00	40.00
AH8811//6 (Error)	—	5.00	10.00	15.00	25.00	40.00
AH1188//6 (Error)	—	5.00	10.00	15.00	25.00	40.00
AH11782//6 (Error)	—	5.00	10.00	15.00	25.00	40.00
AH1811//6 (Error)	—	5.00	10.00	15.00	25.00	40.00
AH117112//6 (Error)	—	5.00	10.00	15.00	25.00	40.00

HAMMERED COINAGE
Gaja Shahi Series

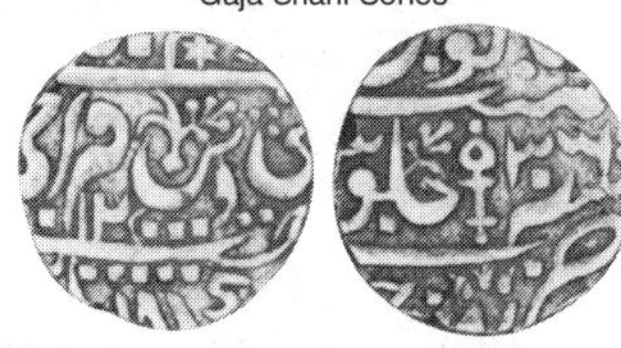

C# 38 RUPEE
Silver **Obverse:** Inscription, mint mark **Reverse:** Inscription, mint mark **Note:** Weight varies 10.70-11.60 grams.

Date	Mintage	Good	VG	F	VF	XF
AH1211//39	—	5.00	10.00	15.00	20.00	25.00
AH1211//43	—	5.00	10.00	15.00	20.00	25.00
AH1214//42	—	5.00	10.00	15.00	20.00	25.00

Shah Alam II
AH1173-1221 / 1759-1806AD
MUGHAL COINAGE

KM# 6 RUPEE
Silver **Obv. Inscription:** Shah Alam (II) **Mint:** Dalipnagar **Note:** Weight varies 10.70-11.60 grams.

Date	Mintage	Good	VG	F	VF	XF
AH1178//6	—	11.00	27.50	40.00	52.50	75.00

KM# 7 RUPEE
Silver **Obverse:** Small sword; Shah Alam (II).. **Obv. Inscription:** Shah Alam (II)

Date	Mintage	Good	VG	F	VF	XF
AH1194//22	—	13.00	32.50	45.00	62.50	85.00

C# 21 TEGH SHAHI PAISA
Copper **Obverse:** Shah Alam (II)..

Date	Mintage	Good	VG	F	VF	XF
ND//1 (1781)	—	3.00	5.00	10.00	15.00	—

DHOLPUR

State located in Rajputana, northwest India.

Dholpur had a varied and turbulent history. From the 8th until the 12th centuries it was ruled by Tonwar Rajputs. Early in the 16th century the entire region came under the Mughals. It was included by Akbar in Agra province. With Mughal decline after 1707, Dholpur experienced many masters until, in 1782, it fell into the hands of Sindhia. In 1803 the territory was captured by the British and in 1805 it was returned to the ranas of Gohad, Bamraolia Jats, from whom it had earlier been wrested by Sindhia. The ranas of Gohad opened the mint which operated until 1857.

RULER

Kirat Singh,
AH1203-1221/1788-1806AD, in Gohad

MINT

Gohad

Mint marks:

On obverse

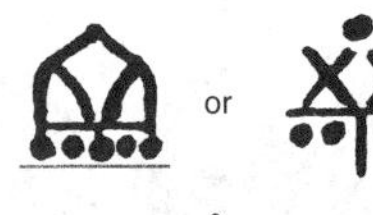

or

On reverse

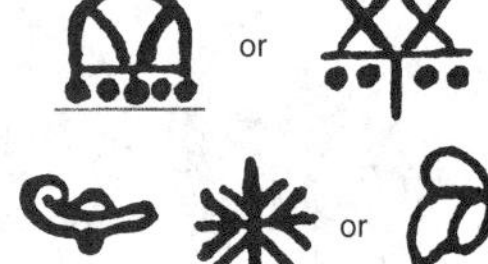

Pistol Star or Leaf

KINGDOM OF GOHAD
HAMMERED COINAGE

C# 2 PAISA
Copper **Obverse:** Pistol **Obv. Inscription:** Shah Alam (II) **Note:** Struck at Gohad Mint.

Date	Mintage	VG	F	VF	XF	Unc
AH1197//25	—	—	—	—	—	—

C# 5.1 RUPEE

11.0000 g., Silver **Obverse:** Inscription, date **Obv. Inscription:** "Shah Alam II" **Reverse:** Pistol, 5-petal flower **Mint:** Gohad

Date	Mintage	Good	VG	F	VF	XF
AH1185//13	—	10.00	25.00	40.00	60.00	85.00
AH1186//14	—	10.00	25.00	40.00	60.00	85.00
AH1188//16	—	10.00	25.00	40.00	60.00	85.00
AH1189//17	—	10.00	25.00	40.00	60.00	85.00
AH1190//18	—	10.00	25.00	40.00	60.00	85.00
AH1191//19	—	10.00	25.00	40.00	60.00	85.00
AH1208//36	—	10.00	25.00	40.00	60.00	85.00

C# 4 RUPEE

11.2400 g., Silver **Obverse:** Inscription **Obv. Inscription:** Shah Alam (II) **Mint:** Gohad

Date	Mintage	VG	F	VF	XF	Unc
AH1187//10	—	—	—	—	—	—

C# 5.2 RUPEE

11.0000 g., Silver **Obv. Inscription:** Shah Alam (II) **Reverse:** Pistol **Mint:** Gohad

Date	Mintage	Good	VG	F	VF	XF
AH1195//23	—	10.00	25.00	40.00	60.00	85.00

GARHWAL

Garhwal was a rugged tract embracing a number of peaks over twenty-three thousand feet in north India. The state dated from the 14th century when a number of local chieftains came under the sway of Ajai Pal. From that time onward his descendants ruled over this Himalayan kingdom until 1803, when the Gurkhas invaded both Garhwal and Kumaon. Shortly afterwards, in the Nepal War of 1814-1816, these States fell under British control and the State was then partially restored to its original ruler.

The Gurkhas captured Almora, the principal town of Kumaon, in 1790 and went on to seize Garhwal and Sirmur in 1803. From then until their definitive defeat at the hands of the East India Company, the Gurkhas issued coins from the Srinagar (Garhwal), Almora (Kumaon) and Nahan (Sirmur) mints.

MINT

Srinagar

KINGDOM

Fath Shah

VS1743-1774 / 1686-1717AD

HAMMERED COINAGE

KM# 2 TIMASHA

Silver **Obv. Inscription:** Farrukhsiyar **Reverse:** Corruption of KM#1 **Note:** Weight varies: 2.56-2.62 grams.

Date	Mintage	Good	VG	F	VF	XF
AH1125//2 Retrograde	—	26.50	65.00	100	150	225
AH1126//2x	—	26.50	65.00	100	150	225

Pradip Shah

VS1774-1829 / 1717-1772AD

HAMMERED COINAGE

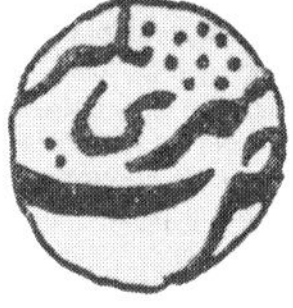

C# 5 TACA

Copper **Obv. Inscription:** Farrukhsiyar

Date	Mintage	Good	VG	F	VF	XF
VS1827	—	3.00	5.00	8.00	12.00	—
VS1829	—	3.00	5.00	8.00	12.00	—
VS1830	—	3.00	5.00	8.00	12.00	—

KM# 3 TIMASHA

Silver **Obverse:** Inscription; Corruption of KM#2 **Obv. Inscription:** Farrukhsiyar **Reverse:** Corruption of KM#2 **Note:** Weight varies: 2.16-2.39 grams.

Date	Mintage	Good	VG	F	VF	XF
AH-//29	—	—	25.00	35.00	45.00	60.00

C# 3 TIMASHA

Silver **Obv. Inscription:** Shah Alam (II)

Date	Mintage	Good	VG	F	VF	XF
ND(1759-72) Rare	—	—	—	—	—	—

C# 10 TIMASHA

Silver **Obv. Inscription:** Shah Alam (II)

Date	Mintage	Good	VG	F	VF	XF
ND-//1 (1759)	—	3.00	5.00	10.00	15.00	20.00
ND//2 (1760-61)	—	3.00	5.00	10.00	15.00	20.00
ND//3 (1761-62)	—	3.00	5.00	10.00	15.00	20.00
ND//4 (1762-63)	—	3.00	5.00	10.00	15.00	20.00
ND//5 (1763-64)	—	3.00	5.00	10.00	15.00	20.00
ND//7 (1765-66)	—	3.00	5.00	10.00	15.00	20.00
ND//8 (1766-67)	—	3.00	5.00	10.00	15.00	20.00
ND//9 (1767-68)	—	3.00	5.00	10.00	15.00	20.00
ND//11 (1769-70)	—	3.00	5.00	10.00	15.00	20.00
ND//12 (1770-71)	—	3.00	5.00	10.00	15.00	20.00
ND//14 (1772-73)	—	3.00	5.00	10.00	15.00	20.00
ND//15 (1773-74)	—	3.00	5.00	10.00	15.00	20.00

C# 10a TIMASHA

Silver **Obv. Inscription:** Shah Alam (II)

Date	Mintage	Good	VG	F	VF	XF
AH1181	—	5.00	10.00	15.00	20.00	30.00
AH1182	—	5.00	10.00	15.00	20.00	30.00

Lallat Shah

VS1829-1838 / 1772-1781AD

HAMMERED COINAGE

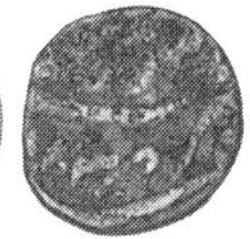

C# 15 TACA

Copper **Obv. Inscription:** Shah Alam (II)

Date	Mintage	Good	VG	F	VF	XF
VS1830	—	5.00	10.00	15.00	25.00	—
VS1831	—	5.00	10.00	15.00	25.00	—
VS1835	—	5.00	10.00	15.00	25.00	—
VS1837	—	5.00	10.00	15.00	25.00	—
VS1838	—	5.00	10.00	15.00	25.00	—

C# 20 TIMASHA

Silver **Obv. Inscription:** Shah Alam (II)

Date	Mintage	Good	VG	F	VF	XF
AH1188/VS1831	—	5.00	10.00	15.00	25.00	50.00
AH1189/VS1832	—	5.00	10.00	15.00	25.00	50.00
AH1xxx/VS1834 Mule	—	5.00	10.00	15.00	25.00	50.00
AH1190/VS1833	—	5.00	10.00	15.00	25.00	50.00
AH1190/VS1833	—	5.00	10.00	15.00	25.00	50.00
AH1191/VS1834	—	5.00	10.00	15.00	25.00	50.00
AH1192/VS1835	—	5.00	10.00	15.00	25.00	50.00
AH1192/VS1836	—	5.00	10.00	15.00	25.00	50.00

C# 20a TIMASHA

Silver **Obv. Inscription:** Shah Alam (II) **Reverse:** Trident replaces AH date

Date	Mintage	Good	VG	F	VF	XF
VS1837	—	5.00	10.00	15.00	25.00	50.00

Parduman Shah

VS1842-1860 / 1785-1803AD

HAMMERED COINAGE

C# 25.1 TACA

Copper **Note:** Error: Mule-doubled.

Date	Mintage	Good	VG	F	VF	XF
ND(1785-1803)	—	—	—	—	—	—

C# 25 TACA

Copper, 16-17 mm. **Reverse:** Katar

Date	Mintage	Good	VG	F	VF	XF
VS1844	—	—	—	—	—	—
VS1845	—	5.00	10.00	15.00	25.00	—
VS1846	—	5.00	10.00	15.00	25.00	—
VS1849	—	5.00	10.00	15.00	25.00	—
VS1853	—	5.00	10.00	15.00	25.00	—
VS1835(sic) Error	—	—	—	—	—	—
VS1855	—	5.00	10.00	15.00	25.00	—
VS1856	—	5.00	10.00	15.00	25.00	—

C# 24 TACA

Copper **Note:** Date error.

Date	Mintage	Good	VG	F	VF	XF
VS1145(1845)	—	5.00	10.00	15.00	25.00	—

GWALIOR

Sindhia

State located in central India. Capital originally was Ujjain (= Daru-l-fath), but was later transferred to Gwalior in 1810. The Gwalior ruling family, the Sindhias, were descendants of the Maratha chief Ranoji Sindhia (d.1750). His youngest son, Mahadji Sindhia (d.1794) was anxious to establish his independence from the overlordship of the Peshwas of Poona. Unable to achieve this alone, it was the Peshwa's crushing defeat by Ahmad Shah Durrani at Panipat in 1761, which helped realize his ambitions. Largely in the interests of sustaining this autonomy, but partly as a result of a defeat at East India Company hands in 1781, Mahadji concluded an alliance with the British in 1782. In 1785, he reinstalled the fallen Mughal Emperor, Shah Alam, on the throne at Dehli. Very early in the 19th century, Gwalior's relationship with the British began to deteriorate, a situation which culminated in the Anglo-Maratha War of 1803. Gwalior's forces under Daulat Rao were defeated. In consequence, and by the terms of the peace treaty which followed, his territory was truncated. In 1818, Gwalior suffered a further loss of land at British hands. In the years that ensued, as the East India Company's possessions became transformed into empire and as the Pax Britannica swept across the subcontinent, the Sindhia family's relationship with their British overlords steadily improved.

RULERS
Jayapa Rao, AH1164-1175/1750-1761AD
Mahadji Rao, AH1175-1209/1761-1794AD
Daulat Rao, AH1209-1243/1794-1827AD

MINTS

اجمير

Ajmir

Mint marks

بسوده

Basoda

With additional mint mark

بروني

Broach

برهانپور

Burhanpur

دار السرور

Dar-as-Surar
Abode of Happiness

Mint mark on reverse

چنديري

Chanderi
Mint name: Kankurti

Mint mark

گواليار

Gwalior Fort

Mint marks:
Copper and silver coins on reverse

Silver coins on obverse

لاشكار

Lashkar

نرور

Narwar

نرور

Sipri
Narwar

اجين دارالفتح

Ujjain, dar ul Fateh

Mint marks — On most issues

On many copper issues

NOTE: None of the coins of Gwalior prior to the beginning of machine-struck coinage in 1889AD bears the name of the Sindhia (ruler of Gwalior), but beginning with the reign of Baija Bao, a Nagari letter is used to indicate the ruler under whom it was struck, as follows:

However, not all the coins bear the initial of the ruler, especially the copper.

The coinage of Gwalior is extremely complicated and not fully understood. Each mint, and there were probably more than twenty in all, maintained its own styles and types, and operated fully independently of every other mint. Hence it is most logical to list the issues of each mint together, rather than attempt to list the coins by reign or denomination. The mints are best identified by the presence of special symbols on the obverse or reverse of the coins, and those symbols are noted whenever possible. Types are listed with designation of reign only when the initial of the ruler appears on the coin; others are assigned a single number for the full duration of their issuance.

Most of the coins of Gwalior are undated, or issued overlong periods of time with frozen dates, in order to discourage the nefarious practice of devaluing coins of older dates (for example, one-year old coins might be devalued 1%, two-year olds 2%, and so forth). Many of the types were struck with frozen dates for several decades, and in many other cases, the dates remained frozen while the ruler's initial changed. The frozen dates may be either AH dates or regnal years, or both.

Regularly dated series often continued over long durations, such as the Ujjain rupees (C#259); the lists of such coins are probably very fragmentary, and many unlisted dates will be discovered. In general, unlisted dates are worth no more than listed dates of the same type.

KINGDOM

HAMMERED COINAGE

KM# 33 PAISA

Copper **Obv. Inscription:** Shah Alam II **Mint:** Broach

Date	Mintage	Good	VG	F	VF	XF
AH1173-1221	—	—	—	—	—	—
ND//3 (1797)	—	2.50	4.50	7.50	12.50	—

KM# 1 PAISA

Copper **Obv. Inscription:** "Shah Alam II" **Mint:** Ajmir

Date	Mintage	Good	VG	F	VF	XF
AH-//6	—	3.00	5.00	8.00	12.50	—
AH1196//24	—	3.00	5.00	8.00	12.50	—

KM# 94 PAISA

Copper **Obverse:** Scimitar and katar **Mint:** Jawad

Date	Mintage	Good	VG	F	VF	XF
ND	—	2.50	4.50	6.50	10.00	—

KM# 95 PAISA

Copper **Obverse:** Leaf and scimitar **Mint:** Jawad

Date	Mintage	Good	VG	F	VF	XF
ND	—	2.50	4.50	6.50	10.00	—

KM# 96 PAISA

Copper **Obverse:** Lotus bud and scimitar **Mint:** Jawad

Date	Mintage	Good	VG	F	VF	XF
ND	—	2.50	4.50	6.50	10.00	—

KM# 97 PAISA

Copper **Obverse:** Scimitar **Mint:** Jawad

Date	Mintage	Good	VG	F	VF	XF
ND	—	2.50	4.50	6.50	10.00	—

KM# 98 PAISA

Copper **Obverse:** Spear and scimitar **Mint:** Jawad

Date	Mintage	Good	VG	F	VF	XF
ND	—	2.50	4.50	6.50	10.00	—

KM# 99 PAISA

Copper **Obverse:** Spear right and scimitar **Reverse:** Star added **Mint:** Jawad

Date	Mintage	Good	VG	F	VF	XF
ND	—	2.50	4.50	6.50	10.00	—

KM# 100 PAISA

Copper **Obverse:** Spear, snake and scimitar **Mint:** Jawad

Date	Mintage	Good	VG	F	VF	XF
ND	—	2.50	4.50	6.50	10.00	—

KM# 101 PAISA

Copper **Obverse:** Spear left above scimitar **Mint:** Jawad

Date	Mintage	Good	VG	F	VF	XF
ND	—	2.50	4.50	6.50	10.00	—

KM# 102 PAISA

Copper **Obverse:** Banner and scimitar **Mint:** Jawad

Date	Mintage	Good	VG	F	VF	XF
VS1840	—	2.50	4.50	6.50	10.00	—

KM# 2 RUPEE

Silver **Obv. Inscription:** "Shah Alam II" **Mint:** Ajmir **Note:** Weight varies 10.70-11.60 grams. Without mint mark.

Date	Mintage	Good	VG	F	VF	XF
ND//1 (1759-60)	—	2.75	6.50	13.00	22.00	32.00
ND//2 (1760-61)	—	2.75	6.50	13.00	22.00	32.00
ND//3 (1761-62)	—	2.75	6.50	13.00	22.00	32.00
ND//4 (1762-63)	—	2.75	6.50	13.00	22.00	32.00
ND//5 (1763-64)	—	2.75	6.50	13.00	22.00	32.00
AH1178//6	—	3.50	9.00	18.00	28.00	40.00
ND//10 (1768-69)	—	2.75	6.50	13.00	22.00	32.00

KM# 3 RUPEE

Silver **Obv. Inscription:** "Shah Alam II" **Reverse:** Mint mark: 3 knots **Mint:** Ajmir

Date	Mintage	Good	VG	F	VF	XF
AH1188//14 (sic)	—	2.75	6.50	13.00	22.00	32.00
AH1189//14 (sic)	—	2.75	6.50	13.00	22.00	32.00
AH1190//14 (sic)	—	2.75	6.50	13.00	22.00	32.00

KM# 4 RUPEE

Silver **Obv. Inscription:** "Shah Alam II" **Reverse:** Mint mark: 2 knots **Mint:** Ajmir

Date	Mintage	Good	VG	F	VF	XF
AH1196//24	—	2.25	5.50	11.00	18.00	28.00
AH1197//24	—	2.25	5.50	11.00	18.00	28.00
AH1198//24 (sic)	—	2.25	5.50	11.00	18.00	28.00
AH1200//26 (sic)	—	2.25	5.50	11.00	18.00	28.00
AH1203//31	—	2.25	5.50	11.00	18.00	28.00

KM# 5 RUPEE

Silver **Obv. Inscription:** "Shah Alam II" **Reverse:** "Shri" to left of regnal year, branch in Persian letter "S" **Mint:** Ajmir

Date	Mintage	Good	VG	F	VF	XF
AH1203//31	—	8.00	20.00	31.50	42.50	60.00

Jayapa Rao

AH1158-1173 / 1745-1759AD

HAMMERED COINAGE

KM# 212 RUPEE

Silver **Obv. Inscription:** Alamgir (II) **Mint:** Ujjain **Note:** Weight varies 10.70-11.60 grams.

Date	Mintage	Good	VG	F	VF	XF
AH11xx//5	—	5.00	12.50	18.50	25.00	35.00
AH11xx//7	—	5.00	12.50	18.50	25.00	35.00
AH1169	—	5.00	12.50	18.50	25.00	35.00

Mahadji Rao

AH1175-1209 / 1761-1794AD

HAMMERED COINAGE

KM# 213.1 PAISA

Copper **Obverse:** Flower **Obv. Inscription:** Shah Alam (II) **Reverse:** Scimitar **Mint:** Ujjain **Note:** Weight varies: 13.5-14 grams.

Date	Mintage	Good	VG	F	VF	XF
ND//15 (1773-74)	—	2.50	4.00	6.50	10.00	—

KM# 54 PAISA

Copper **Obv. Inscription:** Shah Alam (II) **Mint:** Gwalior Fort

Date	Mintage	Good	VG	F	VF	XF
AH1201//29	—	1.25	2.00	3.00	5.00	—

KM# 213.2 PAISA

Copper **Obv. Inscription:** Shah Alam (II) **Reverse:** Spear **Mint:** Ujjain

Date	Mintage	Good	VG	F	VF	XF
AH1205//33	—	1.50	3.00	5.00	7.50	—

KM# 36 PAISA

Copper **Obv. Inscription:** Shah Alam (II) **Mint:** Burhanpur **Note:** Weight varies 19.00-20.00 grams.

Date	Mintage	Good	VG	F	VF	XF
AH1206//32 (sic)	—	3.50	5.50	8.50	13.50	—

KM# 214 1/8 RUPEE

Silver **Obv. Inscription:** Shah Alam (II) **Mint:** Ujjain **Note:** Weight varies 1.34-1.45 grams.

Date	Mintage	Good	VG	F	VF	XF
AH1176//3	—	2.25	5.50	8.00	12.50	18.50

KM# 215 1/4 RUPEE

Silver, 13 mm. **Obv. Inscription:** Shah Alam (II) **Mint:** Ujjain **Note:** Weight varies 2.68-2.90 grams.

Date	Mintage	Good	VG	F	VF	XF
ND//4 (1762-63)	—	2.25	5.50	9.00	13.50	20.00
AH11xx//7	—	2.25	5.50	9.00	13.50	20.00
AH1187//15	—	2.25	5.50	9.00	13.50	20.00
AH1191//19	—	2.25	5.50	9.00	13.50	20.00
AH1193//2x	—	2.25	5.50	9.00	13.50	20.00
AH1197	—	2.25	5.50	9.00	13.50	20.00
AH1200//26	—	2.25	5.50	9.00	13.50	20.00
AH1201//28	—	2.25	5.50	9.00	13.50	20.00
AH1212//36	—	2.25	5.50	9.00	13.50	20.00

KM# 216 1/2 RUPEE

Silver **Obv. Inscription:** Shah Alam (II) **Mint:** Ujjain **Note:** Weight varies 5.35-5.80 grams.

Date	Mintage	Good	VG	F	VF	XF
AH119x//20	—	2.65	6.50	10.00	15.00	22.50
AH1201//30	—	2.65	6.50	10.00	15.00	22.50
ND//31 (1789)	—	2.65	6.50	10.00	15.00	22.50

KM# 55 RUPEE

Silver **Obv. Inscription:** Shah Alam (II) **Mint:** Gwalior Fort **Note:** Weight varies 10.70-11.60 grams.

Date	Mintage	Good	VG	F	VF	XF
AH1174//1	—	3.50	9.00	18.00	28.00	40.00
AH1175//2	—	3.50	9.00	18.00	28.00	40.00
AH1176//4	—	3.50	9.00	18.00	28.00	40.00
AH1177//4	—	3.50	9.00	18.00	28.00	40.00
AH1178//5	—	3.50	9.00	18.00	28.00	40.00
AH1179//6	—	3.50	9.00	18.00	28.00	40.00
AH1179//7	—	3.50	9.00	18.00	28.00	40.00
AH1183//11	—	3.50	9.00	18.00	28.00	40.00
AH1184//12	—	3.50	9.00	18.00	28.00	40.00
AH1185//13	—	3.50	9.00	18.00	28.00	42.50

KM# 217 RUPEE

Silver **Obv. Inscription:** Shah Alam (II) **Reverse:** Without scimitar **Mint:** Ujjain **Note:** Weight varies 10.70-11.60 grams.

Date	Mintage	VG	F	VF	XF	Unc
AH117x//2	—	11.50	17.50	23.50	32.50	—
AH1176//3	—	11.50	17.50	23.50	32.50	—
AH11xx//8	—	11.50	17.50	23.50	32.50	—

KM# 218 RUPEE

Silver **Obv. Inscription:** Shah Alam (II) **Reverse:** Scimitar **Mint:** Ujjain

Date	Mintage	Good	VG	F	VF	XF
AH11xx//8	—	3.50	8.50	13.50	20.00	28.50
AH1187//15	—	3.50	8.50	13.50	20.00	28.50
AH1188	—	3.50	8.50	13.50	20.00	28.50
AH1189//16	—	3.50	8.50	13.50	20.00	28.50
AH1192//19	—	3.50	8.50	13.50	20.00	28.50
AH1193//19 (sic)	—	3.50	8.50	13.50	20.00	28.50
AH1193//20	—	3.50	8.50	13.50	20.00	28.50
AH1194//20 (sic)	—	3.50	8.50	13.50	20.00	28.50
AH1194//21	—	3.50	8.50	13.50	20.00	28.50
AH1195//22	—	3.50	8.50	13.50	20.00	28.50
AH1197//23 (sic)	—	3.50	8.50	13.50	20.00	28.50
AH1198//24 (sic)	—	3.50	8.50	13.50	20.00	28.50
AH1198//25	—	3.50	8.50	13.50	20.00	28.50
AH1199//25 (sic)	—	3.50	8.50	13.50	20.00	28.50
AH1199//26	—	3.50	8.50	13.50	20.00	28.50
AH1200//26 (sic)	—	3.50	8.50	13.50	20.00	28.50
AH1200//27	—	3.50	8.50	13.50	20.00	28.50
AH1201//27 (sic)	—	3.50	8.50	13.50	20.00	28.50
AH1201//30	—	3.50	8.50	13.50	20.00	28.50
AH1201//28	—	3.50	8.50	13.50	20.00	28.50
AH1201//29	—	3.50	8.50	13.50	20.00	28.50
AH1202//31 (sic)	—	3.50	8.50	13.50	20.00	28.50
AH1203//31	—	3.50	8.50	13.50	20.00	28.50
AH1203//32 (sic)	—	3.50	8.50	13.50	20.00	28.50
AH1204//32	—	3.50	8.50	13.50	20.00	28.50
AH1204//33 (sic)	—	3.50	8.50	13.50	20.00	28.50
AH1205//33	—	3.50	8.50	13.50	20.00	28.50
AH1205//34 (sic)	—	3.50	8.50	13.50	20.00	28.50
AH1206//34	—	3.50	8.50	13.50	20.00	28.50
AH1206//35 (sic)	—	3.50	8.50	13.50	20.00	28.50
AH1207//35	—	3.50	8.50	13.50	20.00	28.50
AH1208//36	—	3.50	8.50	13.50	20.00	28.50

KM# 56 RUPEE

Silver **Obverse:** Flower **Obv. Inscription:** Shah Alam (II) **Mint:** Gwalior Fort

Date	Mintage	Good	VG	F	VF	XF
AH1191//19	—	3.00	7.50	15.00	25.00	40.00

KM# 38.1 RUPEE

Copper **Obv. Inscription:** Shah Alam (II) **Mint:** Burhanpur **Note:** Weight varies 10.70-11.60 grams.

Date	Mintage	Good	VG	F	VF	XF
AH1194//2x	—	2.35	6.00	12.00	20.00	28.00
AH1195//2x	—	2.35	6.00	12.00	20.00	28.00
AH1196//23	—	2.35	6.00	12.00	20.00	28.00
AH1197//24	—	2.35	6.00	12.00	20.00	28.00
AH1198//24	—	2.35	6.00	12.00	20.00	28.00
AH1200//26 (sic)	—	2.35	6.00	12.00	20.00	28.00
AH1201//2x	—	2.35	6.00	12.00	20.00	28.00
AH1202	—	2.35	6.00	12.00	20.00	28.00
AH1203//30 (sic)	—	2.35	6.00	12.00	20.00	28.00
AH1204//3x	—	2.35	6.00	12.00	20.00	28.00
AH1205//3x	—	2.35	6.00	12.00	20.00	28.00
AH1206//3x	—	2.35	6.00	12.00	20.00	28.00

KM# 57 RUPEE

Silver **Obverse:** Flower **Obv. Inscription:** Shah Alam (II) **Reverse:** Dagger like stalk **Mint:** Gwalior Fort

Date	Mintage	Good	VG	F	VF	XF
AH1197//25	—	2.75	6.50	13.00	22.00	35.00
AH1200//28	—	2.75	6.50	13.00	22.00	35.00
AH1201//29	—	2.75	6.50	13.00	22.00	35.00
AH1203//31	—	2.75	6.50	13.00	22.00	35.00
AH1204//32	—	2.75	6.50	13.00	22.00	35.00
AH1206//34	—	2.75	6.50	13.00	22.00	35.00

KM# 57.2 RUPEE

Silver **Obv. Inscription:** "Shah Alam II" **Mint:** Gwalior Fort **Note:** Weight varies 10.70-11.60 grams.

Date	Mintage	Good	VG	F	VF	XF
AH1203//31	—	5.00	8.00	13.50	20.00	28.50
AH1210	—	3.25	8.00	13.50	20.00	28.50
AH1212//40	—	3.25	8.00	13.50	20.00	28.50
AH1213//41	—	3.25	8.00	13.50	20.00	28.50
ND//43 (1801-02)	—	8.00	8.00	13.50	20.00	28.50
AH1216//44	—	4.00	8.00	13.50	20.00	28.50
AH1221//58	—	4.00	8.00	13.50	20.00	28.50

KM# 39 MOHUR

11.0200 g., Gold **Obv. Inscription:** Shah Alam (II) **Mint:** Burhanpur

Date	Mintage	VG	F	VF	XF	Unc
AH1195//22	—	—	—	—	—	—

Daulat Rao

AH1209-1243 / 1794-1827AD

HAMMERED COINAGE

KM# 40.2 PAISA

Copper **Obv. Inscription:** "Shah Alam II" **Mint:** Burhanpur **Note:** Full mint name and date.

Date	Mintage	Good	VG	F	VF	XF
AH1206//32 (sic)	—	2.50	4.00	6.50	10.00	—

KM# 220 PAISA

Copper **Obv. Inscription:** "Shah Alam II" **Mint:** Ujjain

Date	Mintage	Good	VG	F	VF	XF
ND(1794-1827)	—	1.50	3.00	5.00	7.50	—

 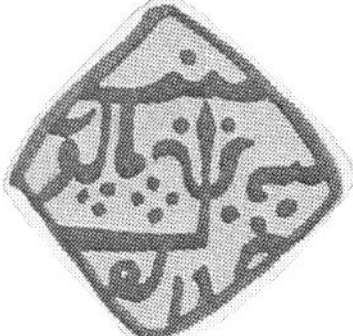

KM# 221 PAISA

Copper **Obv. Inscription:** "Shah Alam II" **Mint:** Ujjain **Note:** Square flan.

Date	Mintage	Good	VG	F	VF	XF
ND(1794-1827)	—	1.50	3.00	5.00	7.50	—

KM# 219 PAISA
Copper **Obv. Inscription:** "Shah Alam II" **Mint:** Ujjain **Note:** Weight varies 12.83-14.00 grams. With continued regnal years of Shah Alam II.

Date	Mintage	Good	VG	F	VF	XF
ND(1794-1827)	—	1.50	3.00	5.00	7.50	—

KM# 117 1/4 RUPEE
Silver **Obv. Inscription:** "Shah Alam II" **Mint:** Lashkar **Note:** Weight varies 2.68-2.90 grams.

Date	Mintage	Good	VG	F	VF	XF
ND(1759-1806)	—	2.35	6.00	9.00	13.50	20.00

KM# A38 1/4 RUPEE
Silver, 15 mm. **Mint:** Burhanpur **Note:** Weight varies 2.68-2.90 grams.

Date	Mintage	Good	VG	F	VF	XF
AH1214	—	10.00	25.00	40.00	60.00	85.00

KM# A34 1/2 RUPEE
Silver **Obv. Inscription:** "Shah Alam II" **Mint:** Broach **Note:** Weight varies 5.35-5.80 grams.

Date	Mintage	Good	VG	F	VF	XF
ND(1759-1806)	—	7.50	15.00	25.00	37.50	—

KM# B38 1/2 RUPEE
Silver, 17 mm. **Mint:** Burhanpur **Note:** Weight varies 5.35-5.70 grams.

Date	Mintage	Good	VG	F	VF	XF
AH1214	—	12.00	30.00	50.00	80.00	120
AH1261	—	12.00	30.00	50.00	80.00	120
AH1274	—	12.00	30.00	50.00	80.00	120

KM# 46 1/2 RUPEE
Silver **Obv. Inscription:** Shah Alam II **Mint:** Chanderi **Note:** Mint name: Kankurti.

Date	Mintage	Good	VG	F	VF	XF
ND	—	—	—	—	—	—

KM# 119 RUPEE
Silver **Obv. Inscription:** "Shah Alam II" **Mint:** Lashkar **Note:** Weight varies 10.70-11.60 grams.

Date	Mintage	Good	VG	F	VF	XF
ND(1759-1806)	—	5.00	10.00	15.00	21.50	30.00

KM# 47 RUPEE
Silver **Obv. Inscription:** "Shah Alam II" **Mint:** Chanderi **Note:** Weight varies 10.70-11.60 grams.

Date	Mintage	Good	VG	F	VF	XF
ND//7 (1760-61)	—	4.00	10.00	13.50	20.00	30.00

KM# 34 RUPEE
Silver **Obv. Inscription:** "Shah Alam II" **Mint:** Broach **Note:** Weight varies 10.70-11.60 grams.

Date	Mintage	Good	VG	F	VF	XF
ND//27 (1785-86)	—	5.00	5.00	10.00	17.50	25.00
ND//23 (1787-88)	—	5.00	5.00	10.00	17.50	25.00
ND//32 (1800-01)	—	5.00	7.00	10.00	17.50	25.00

KM# 205 RUPEE
Silver **Obv. Inscription:** "Shah Alam II" **Mint:** Sipri **Note:** Weight varies 10.70-11.60 grams.

Date	Mintage	Good	VG	F	VF	XF
AH1120//32 (sic)	—	2.75	7.00	14.00	24.00	35.00
AH1130//33 (sic)	—	2.75	7.00	14.00	24.00	35.00
AH1120//33 (sic)	—	2.75	7.00	14.00	24.00	35.00
AH1106//34 (sic)	—	2.75	7.00	14.00	24.00	35.00
AH1106//35 (sic)	—	2.75	7.00	14.00	24.00	35.00
AH1106//37 (sic)	—	2.75	7.00	14.00	24.00	35.00
AH1106//40 (sic)	—	2.75	7.00	14.00	24.00	35.00
AH1106//41 (sic)	—	2.75	7.00	14.00	24.00	35.00
AH1106//43 (sic)	—	4.50	7.00	14.00	24.00	35.00
AH1106//44 (sic)	—	4.50	7.00	14.00	24.00	35.00
AH1106//46 (sic)	—	4.50	7.00	14.00	24.00	35.00
AH1106//47 (sic)	—	4.50	7.00	14.00	24.00	35.00

KM# 38.2 RUPEE
Silver **Obv. Inscription:** "Shah Alam II" **Mint:** Burhanpur **Note:** Weight varies 10.70-11.60 grams.

Date	Mintage	Good	VG	F	VF	XF
AH1209	—	2.35	6.00	12.00	20.00	30.00
AH1210//84 (sic)	—	2.35	6.00	12.00	20.00	30.00
AH1211//3x	—	2.35	6.00	12.00	20.00	30.00
AH1213//3x	—	2.35	6.00	12.00	20.00	30.00
AH1214	—	2.35	6.00	12.00	20.00	30.00
AH1215//4x	—	2.35	6.00	12.00	20.00	30.00

KM# 86 RUPEE
Silver **Obverse:** Cannon left **Obv. Inscription:** "Muhammad Akbar II" **Reverse:** Bhilsa leaf and battle axe **Mint:** Isagarh

Date	Mintage	Good	VG	F	VF	XF
ND-//(1794-1827)	—	5.50	13.50	20.00	27.50	38.00

KM# 88 RUPEE
Silver **Obverse:** Cannon right and snake **Obv. Inscription:** "Muhammad Akbar II" **Reverse:** Bhilsa leaf and battle axe **Mint:** Isagarh

Date	Mintage	Good	VG	F	VF	XF
AH-//(1794-1827)	—	5.50	13.50	20.00	27.50	40.00

KM# 223 RUPEE
Silver **Obverse:** AH date below **Obv. Inscription:** "Shah Alam II" **Mint:** Ujjain **Note:** Weight varies 10.70-11.60 grams.

Date	Mintage	Good	VG	F	VF	XF
AH1208//37 (sic)	—	2.00	5.00	7.00	10.00	15.00
AH1209//38 (sic)	—	2.00	5.00	7.00	10.00	15.00
AH1211//38	—	2.00	5.00	7.00	10.00	15.00
AH1210//39 (sic)	—	2.00	5.00	7.00	10.00	15.00
AH1212//35 (sic)	—	2.00	5.00	7.00	10.00	15.00
AH1212//39	—	2.00	5.00	7.00	10.00	15.00
AH1211//40 (sic)	—	2.00	5.00	7.00	10.00	15.00
AH1212//40	—	2.00	5.00	7.00	10.00	15.00
AH1213//40	—	2.00	5.00	7.00	10.00	15.00
AH1214//41	—	2.00	5.00	7.00	10.00	15.00
AH1215//41 (sic)	—	2.00	5.00	7.00	10.00	15.00
AH1215//42	—	4.25	5.00	7.00	10.00	15.00

KM# 35 NAZARANA RUPEE
Silver **Obv. Inscription:** "Shah Alam II" **Mint:** Broach **Note:** Weight varies 10.70-11.60 grams.

Date	Mintage	Good	VG	F	VF	XF
AH1212//3 Rare	—	—	—	—	—	—

KM# 58 NAZARANA 1/3 MOHUR
Gold, 18 mm. **Obv. Inscription:** "Muhammad Shah" **Mint:** Gwalior Fort **Note:** Weight varies 3.57-3.80 grams.

Date	Mintage	Good	VG	F	VF	XF
AH1130//2 Frozen	—	—	125	165	225	275

KM# A59 MOHUR
Gold **Obv. Inscription:** "Shah Alam II" **Mint:** Gwalior Fort **Note:** Weight varies 10.70-11.40 grams.

Date	Mintage	Good	VG	F	VF	XF
AH1215//42	—	—	250	375	550	800

Jankoji Rao
AH1243-1259 / 1827-1843AD

HAMMERED COINAGE

KM# A19 1/4 RUPEE
Silver **Obv. Inscription:** "Muhammad Akbar II" and "Jankoji Rao" **Mint:** Basoda

Date	Mintage	Good	VG	F	VF	XF
ND(1827-1837)	—	16.00	40.00	65.00	100	150

KM# B19 1/2 RUPEE
Silver **Obv. Inscription:** "Muhammad Akbar II" and "Jankoji Rao" **Mint:** Basoda **Note:** Weight varies 5.35-5.80 grams.

Date	Mintage	Good	VG	F	VF	XF
ND(1827-37)	—	18.00	45.00	80.00	120	175

KM# 211 RUPEE
Silver **Mint:** Daulat Rao **Note:** With regnal years of Shah Alam II

Date	Mintage	Good	VG	F	VF	XF
ND//35 (1824-25)	—	3.50	9.00	18.00	30.00	42.00

Jayaji Rao
AH1259-1304 / 1843-1886AD

HAMMERED COINAGE

KM# 116 1/8 RUPEE
Silver, 12 mm. **Obv. Inscription:** "Shah Alam II" **Mint:** Lashkar **Note:** Weight varies 1.34-1.45 grams.

Date	Mintage	Good	VG	F	VF	XF
ND(1759-1806)	—	2.35	6.00	9.00	13.50	20.00

KM# 118 1/2 RUPEE
Silver, 16 mm. **Obv. Inscription:** "Shah Alam II" **Mint:** Lashkar **Note:** Weight varies 5.35-5.80 grams.

Date	Mintage	Good	VG	F	VF	XF
ND(1759-1806)	—	2.75	7.00	11.00	16.50	30.00

KM# 114 MOHUR
10.8000 g., Gold **Obv. Inscription:** "Muhammad Shah" **Mint:** Lashkar **Note:** Weight varies 10.70-11.40 grams.

Date	Mintage	Good	VG	F	VF	XF
AH1135//2 Frozen	—	—	—	—	—	—

HYDERABAD

Haidarabad

Hyderabad State, the argest Indian State and the last remnant of Mughal suzerainty in South or Central India, traced its foundation to Nizam-ul Mulk, the Mughal viceroy in the Deccan. From about 1724 the first nizam, as the rulers of Hyderabad came to be called, took advantage of Mughal decline in the North to assert an all but ceremonial independence of the emperor. The East India Company defeated Hyderabad's natural enemies, the Muslim rulers of Mysore and the Marathas, with the help of troops furnished under alliances between them and the Nizam. This formed the beginning of a relationship, which persisted for a century and a half until India's Independence. Hyderabad was the premier Princely State, with a population (in 1935) of fourteen and a half million. It was not absorbed into the Indian Union until 1948. Hyderabad City is located beside Golkonda, the citadel of the Qutb Shahi sultans until they were overthrown by Aurangzeb in 1687. A beautifully located city on the bank of the Musi river, the mint epithet was appropriately Farkhanda Bunyad, "of happy foundation".

Hyderabad exercised authority over a number of feudatories or samasthans. Some of these, such as Gadwal and Shorapur, paid tribute to both the Nizam and the Marathas. These feudatories were generally in the hands of local rajas whose ancestry predated the establishment of Hyderabad State. There were also many mints in the State, both private and government. There was little or no standardization of the purity of silver coinage until the 20th century. At least one banker, Pestonji Meherji by name, was distinguished by minting his own coins.

RULERS

Nizam Ali Khan, AH1175-1218/1761-1803AD

MINTS

Aurangabad

Mint mark

خجسته بنياد

Mint name: Khujista Bunyad

دولت اباد   دولتاباد

Daulatabad

Reverse: Persian letter *N*

حيدراباد

Haidarabad

فرخنده بنياد

Mint name: Farkhanda Bunyad

Mint mark

Reverse: Persian letter *N*

NIZAMATE

Nizam Ali Khan

AH1175-1218 / 1761-1803AD

HAMMERED 'DUMP' COINAGE

KM# 11 PAISA

6.7000 g., Copper **Obv. Inscription:** Shah Alam II **Mint:** Daulatabad

Date	Mintage	Good	VG	F	VF	XF
AH1312//40 (error for 1213)	—	6.00	9.00	14.00	20.00	—

KM# 12 2 PAISA

Copper **Obv. Inscription:** Shah Alam II **Mint:** Daulatabad **Note:** Struck at Daulatabad Mint.

Date	Mintage	Good	VG	F	VF	XF
AH1213//40	—	6.50	10.00	17.00	25.00	—

KM# 18 RUPEE

Silver **Obv. Inscription:** Shah Alam II **Mint:** Daulatabad **Note:** Weight varies 10.7 - 11.6 grams; Struck at Daulatabad Mint.

Date	Mintage	Good	VG	F	VF	XF
AH1187//14	—	6.00	15.00	25.00	35.00	50.00
AH1195//2x	—	6.00	15.00	25.00	35.00	50.00
AH1197//24	—	6.00	15.00	25.00	35.00	50.00
AH1199//26	—	6.00	15.00	25.00	35.00	50.00
AH1200//27	—	6.00	15.00	25.00	35.00	50.00

KM# 25.1 RUPEE

Silver **Obv. Inscription:** Shah Alam (II) **Mint:** Haidarabad (Farkhanda Bunyad) **Note:** With Persian "N". Weight varies: 10.7-11.6 grams. Struck at Farkhanda Bunyad Mint.

Date	Mintage	Good	VG	F	VF	XF
AH1193//19 (sic)	—	—	—	—	—	—

KM# 25.2 RUPEE

Silver **Obv. Inscription:** Shah Alam (II) **Mint:** Haidarabad (Farkhanda Bunyad) **Note:** Without Persian "N". Weight varies: 10.7-11.6 grams. Struck at Farkhanda Bunyad Mint.

Date	Mintage	Good	VG	F	VF	XF
AH1193//19 (sic)	—	—	—	—	—	—

HAMMERED COINAGE

KM# 2 PAISA

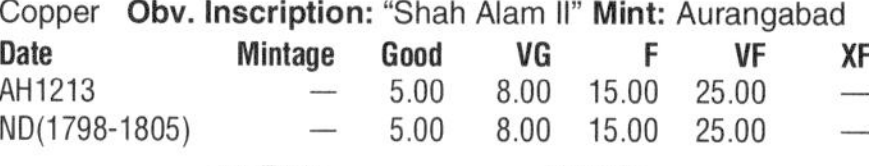

Copper **Obv. Inscription:** "Shah Alam II" **Mint:** Aurangabad

Date	Mintage	Good	VG	F	VF	XF
AH1213	—	5.00	8.00	15.00	25.00	—
ND(1798-1805)	—	5.00	8.00	15.00	25.00	—

KM# 5 RUPEE

Silver **Obv. Inscription:** "Shah Alam II" **Mint:** Aurangabad **Note:** Weight varies: 10.7-11.6 grams.

Date	Mintage	Good	VG	F	VF	XF
AH1176//3	—	—	10.00	17.50	30.00	45.00
AH1177//4	—	—	10.00	17.50	30.00	45.00
AH1178//5	—	—	10.00	17.50	30.00	45.00
AH1179//6	—	—	10.00	17.50	30.00	45.00
AH1182//10	—	—	10.00	17.50	30.00	45.00
AH1187	—	—	10.00	17.50	30.00	45.00
AH1193//19 (sic)	—	—	10.00	17.50	30.00	45.00

HYDERABAD FEUDATORIES-ELICHPUR

PRINCELY STATE

HAMMERED COINAGE

KM# 3 PAISA

Copper **Note:** Weight varies: 15.6-19.6 grams.

Date	Mintage	Good	VG	F	VF	XF
AH1177	—	4.50	7.50	12.50	20.00	—
AH1178//4 (sic)	—	4.50	7.50	12.50	20.00	—
AH(11)78//7 (sic)	—	4.50	7.50	12.50	20.00	—
ND//8 (1766-67)	—	4.50	7.50	12.50	20.00	—
ND	—	4.50	7.50	12.50	20.00	—
ND//15 (1773-74)	—	4.50	7.50	12.50	20.00	—

HYDERABAD FEUDATORIES-FIROZNAGAR

PRINCELY STATE

Shah Alam II

AH1173-1221/1759-1806AD

HAMMERED 'DUMP' COINAGE

KM# 2 RUPEE

Silver **Note:** Possibly restruck in AH1241, bearing that date, but unconfirmed. 10.70-11.60 grams.

Date	Mintage	Good	VG	F	VF	XF
ND//1 (1759)	—	—	50.00	100	150	220

HYDERABAD FEUDATORIES-GADWAL

LOCAL RAJAS

HAMMERED COINAGE

C# 18 1/4 RUPEE

Silver **Note:** Weight varies: 2.6-2.9 grams.

Date	Mintage	Good	VG	F	VF	XF
ND(1771-73)	—	12.00	30.00	45.00	70.00	100

C# 19 1/2 RUPEE

Silver **Note:** Weight varies: 5.35-5.80 grams.

Date	Mintage	Good	VG	F	VF	XF
ND(1771-73)	—	8.00	20.00	30.00	50.00	70.00

C# 20 RUPEE

Silver **Note:** Weight varies 10.7 - 11.6 grams.

Date	Mintage	Good	VG	F	VF	XF
AH1185	—	15.00	37.50	65.00	150	225
AH1186//11	—	15.00	37.50	65.00	150	225

HYDERABAD FEUDATORIES-KALAYANI

Kallian

A town located in north Mysore.

Nawab

Mohammad Shah Khair al-Din

Mint mark

TOWN

(Kallian)

Mohammad Shah Khair al-Din

Nawab

HAMMERED COINAGE

KM# 6 RUPEE

Silver **Reverse:** Persian 'Ha' to right of tiger

Date	Mintage	Good	VG	F	VF	XF
AH1212	—	—	60.00	100	150	220
ND(1797-1812)	—	—	60.00	100	150	220
AH1215	—	—	60.00	100	160	230
AH1226	—	—	60.00	100	150	220

KM# 5 RUPEE

Silver **Reverse:** Without Persian 'Ha' to right of tiger **Note:** Weight varies: 10.7-11.6 grams.

Date	Mintage	Good	VG	F	VF	XF
AH1212	—	—	55.00	90.00	150	220
AH1215	—	—	55.00	90.00	150	220

KM# 9 MOHUR

10.9400 g., Gold **Note:** Similar to 1 Rupee, KM#6.

Date	Mintage	Good	VG	F	VF	XF
AH12xx Rare	—	—	—	—	—	—

HYDERABAD FEUDATORIES-NARAYANPETT

Local Rajas

Dilshadabad on coins.

MINT MARKS

Ti obv. dated AH1186/1186, C#40

क

K rev. dated AH1186/1186, C#40

Go obv. dated AH1186/1252, C#37-40

L rev. dated AH1186/1252, C#37-40

PRINCELY STATE

Shah Alam II

AH1173-1221 / 1759-1806AD

HAMMERED COINAGE

C# 34 PAISA

Copper **Obv. Inscription:** Shah Alam (II) **Mint:** Dilshadabad

Date	Mintage	Good	VG	F	VF	XF
AH1202	—	5.00	10.00	15.00	25.00	—

C# 37 1/8 RUPEE

Silver **Obv. Inscription:** Shah Alam (II) **Mint:** Dilshadabad **Note:** Weight varies 1.34 - 1.45 grams.

Date	Mintage	Good	VG	F	VF	XF
AH1186//1252	—	—	12.00	20.00	30.00	45.00

C# 38 1/4 RUPEE

Silver, 13 mm. **Obv. Inscription:** Shah Alam (II) **Mint:** Dilshadabad **Note:** Weight varies 2.68 - 2.9 grams.

Date	Mintage	Good	VG	F	VF	XF
AH1186//1252	—	—	12.00	20.00	30.00	45.00

C# 39 1/2 RUPEE

Silver, 16 mm. **Obv. Inscription:** Shah Alam (II) **Mint:** Dilshadabad **Note:** Weight varies 5.35-5.8 grams.

Date	Mintage	Good	VG	F	VF	XF
AH1186//1252	—	—	20.00	32.00	50.00	70.00

C# 40 RUPEE

Silver **Obv. Inscription:** Shah Alam (II) **Mint:** Dilshadabad **Note:** Weight varies: 10.7-11.6 grams.

Date	Mintage	Good	VG	F	VF	XF
AH1186//1186	—	—	15.00	30.00	50.00	75.00
AH1186//1239	—	—	15.00	30.00	50.00	75.00
AH1186//1245	—	—	15.00	30.00	50.00	75.00
AH1186//1246	—	—	15.00	30.00	50.00	75.00
AH1186//1251	—	—	15.00	30.00	50.00	75.00
AH1186//1252	—	—	15.00	30.00	50.00	75.00
AH1186//1254	—	—	15.00	30.00	50.00	75.00

INDORE

The Holkars were one of the three dominant Maratha powers (with the Peshwas and Sindhias), with major landholdings in Central India.

Indore State originated in 1728 with a grant of land north of the Narbada river by the Maratha Peshwa of Poona to Malhar Rao Holkar, a cavalry commander in his service. After Holkar's death (ca.1765) his daughter-in-law, Ahalya Bai, assumed the position of Queen Regent. Together with Tukoji Rao she effectively ruled the State until her death thirty years later. But it was left to Tukoji's son, Jaswant Rao, to challenge the dominance of the Poona Marathas in the Maratha Confederacy, eventually defeating the Peshwa's army in 1802. But at this point the fortunes of the Holkars suffered a serious reverse. Although Jaswant Rao had initially defeated a small British force under Col. William Monson, he was badly beaten by a contingent under Lord Lake. As a result Holkar was forced to cede a considerable portion of his territory and from this time until India's independence in 1947, the residual State of Indore was obliged to accept British protection.

For more detailed data on the Indore series, see *A Study of Holkar State Coinage*, by P.K.Sethi, S.K. Bhatt and R. Holkar (1976).

HOLKAR RULERS

Malhar Rao I, AH1141-1179/1728-1765AD
Ahalya Bai, AH1179-1210/1765-1795AD
Tukoji Rao I, AH1210-1212/1795-1797AD
Kashi Rao, AH1212-1213/1797-1798AD
Jaswant Rao, SE1719-1734/AH1213-1226/1798-1811AD

HONORIFIC TITLE

Bahadur

REGNAL YEARS

In reference to:
Alamgir II, Year 1/AH1167-1168
Shah Alam II, Year 1/AH1173-1174
Malhar Rao I, as Subehdar, Year 1/AH1170-1171

MINTS

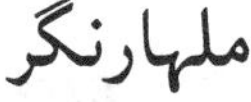

Chandor
In operation from 1773 to the early 1800's.

جعفراباد عرف چاندور

Mint name: J'afarabad 'urf Chandor

Maheshwar (see Malharnagar)
In operation from 1767 to 1803.
Distinctive marks

Bilva Leaf
Silver

Lingam - Yoni
Copper and Silver

ملهارنگر

Malharnagar
Located in capital, Indore City. In operation regularly from 1768 to 1878.
Distinctive marks

Bilva Leaf
Copper

Sunface
Copper and Silver

سرونج

Sironj

NOTE: According to Sethi, Bhatt and Holkar, the coins of both the Maheshwar and Malharnagar Mints bear the mint name "Malharnagar" in honor of Malhar Rao I, founder of the state. They can only be distinguished by their distinctive mint marks, as noted below.

MUGHAL ISSUES

In the name of Shah Alam II
AH1173-1221/1759-1806AD

Until AH1296/1880AD all coinage of Indore was struck in the name of Shah Alam II, with the exception of a few rare special or nazarana issues. The coinage of the individual rulers, until 1880AD, cannot be told apart except by the date, as no change of type was made for more than a century.

BRITISH PROTECTORATE

HAMMERED COINAGE

KM# 60 1/2 PAISA

3.8000 g., Copper **Obv. Inscription:** Shah Alam (II) **Mint:** Malharnagar

Date	Mintage	Good	VG	F	VF	XF
ND(1790-95)	—	5.00	7.50	10.00	13.50	—
ND//32 (1790-91)	—	5.00	7.50	10.00	13.50	—
AH1209	—	5.00	7.50	10.00	13.50	—

KM# A61.1 PAISA

7.1500 g., Copper **Obverse:** Katar **Obv. Inscription:** Shah Alam (II) **Reverse:** 3 dots in sun face **Mint:** Malharnagar

Date	Mintage	Good	VG	F	VF	XF
ND//30 (1787-88)	—	2.00	4.00	6.50	10.00	—

KM# A61.2 PAISA

7.1500 g., Copper **Obv. Inscription:** Shah Alam (II) **Reverse:** 4 dots in sun face **Mint:** Malharnagar

Date	Mintage	Good	VG	F	VF	XF
ND(1796)	—	6.00	10.00	14.00	20.00	—

KM# A51 1/8 ANNA

Copper **Reverse:** Lingam in frame **Mint:** Maheshwar

Date	Mintage	Good	VG	F	VF	XF
ND(1787-88)	—	—	—	—	—	—

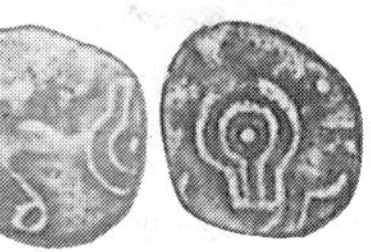

KM# B51 1/8 ANNA

Copper **Obverse:** Lingam **Reverse:** Lingam **Mint:** Maheshwar

Date	Mintage	Good	VG	F	VF	XF
ND(1788-89)	—	5.00	10.00	17.50	25.00	—

KM# 51 1/4 ANNA

8.7000 g., Copper **Reverse:** Lingam and fly whisk **Mint:** Maheshwar

Date	Mintage	Good	VG	F	VF	XF
AH1202	—	2.00	2.75	3.50	5.00	—
AH1203	—	2.00	2.75	3.50	5.00	—
AH1204	—	2.00	2.75	3.50	5.00	—

KM# 52 1/4 ANNA

7.3000 g., Copper **Reverse:** Lingam **Mint:** Maheshwar

Date	Mintage	Good	VG	F	VF	XF
AH1203	—	2.00	2.75	3.50	5.00	—
AH1207	—	2.00	2.75	3.50	5.00	—

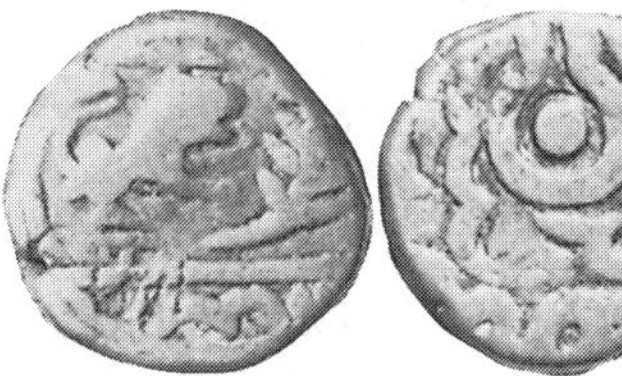

KM# A53 1/2 ANNA

Copper **Obverse:** Lion right, palm branch **Reverse:** Lingam **Mint:** Maheshwar **Note:** Weight varies: 13.50-16.50 grams.

Date	Mintage	Good	VG	F	VF	XF
AH(11)94	—	—	—	—	—	—

KM# B53 1/2 ANNA

Copper **Reverse:** Leaves **Mint:** Maheshwar **Note:** Weight varies: 13.50-16.50 grams.

Date	Mintage	Good	VG	F	VF	XF
ND(1785-86)	—	—	—	—	—	—

KM# C53 1/2 ANNA

Copper **Reverse:** Lingam with snake around **Mint:** Maheshwar **Note:** Weight varies: 13.50-16.50 grams.

Date	Mintage	Good	VG	F	VF	XF
ND(1786-87)	—	—	—	—	—	—

KM# 53 1/2 ANNA

Copper **Reverse:** Leaves and lingam **Mint:** Maheshwar **Note:** Weight varies: 13.50-16.50 grams.

Date	Mintage	Good	VG	F	VF	XF
AH1202	—	2.50	3.25	4.00	6.00	—

KM# B54 1/2 ANNA

Copper **Obverse:** Sun face **Reverse:** Lingam **Mint:** Maheshwar

Date	Mintage	Good	VG	F	VF	XF
ND(1202)	—	—	—	—	—	—

KM# 54 1/2 ANNA

Copper **Reverse:** Lingam and fly whisk **Mint:** Maheshwar **Note:** Weight varies: 13.50-16.50 grams.

Date	Mintage	Good	VG	F	VF	XF
AH1203	—	2.50	3.25	4.00	6.00	—

KM# 90.1 1/2 ANNA

Copper **Rev. Legend:** Bilva leaf and dagger **Mint:** Uncertain Mint

Date	Mintage	Good	VG	F	VF	XF
AH1203	—	3.50	4.50	5.50	7.50	—

KM# 90.2 1/2 ANNA

Copper **Rev. Legend:** Lingam and fly whisk **Mint:** Uncertain Mint

Date	Mintage	Good	VG	F	VF	XF
AH1207	—	3.50	4.50	5.50	7.50	—

KM# A54 1/2 ANNA

Copper **Obverse:** Fly whisk and trident **Reverse:** Lingam **Mint:** Maheshwar **Note:** Weight varies: 13.50-16.50 grams. Square flan.

Date	Mintage	Good	VG	F	VF	XF
ND//4x (1798-99)	—	—	—	—	—	—

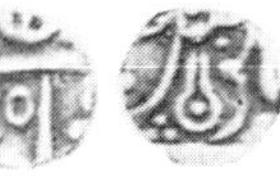

KM# 55 1/8 RUPEE

Silver **Obv. Inscription:** Shah Alam (II) **Reverse:** Bilva leaf and lingam **Mint:** Maheshwar **Note:** Weight varies: 1.34-1.45 grams.

Date	Mintage	VG	F	VF	XF	Unc
AH1205	—	7.00	11.00	16.50	25.00	—

KM# 1 1/4 RUPEE

Silver **Obv. Inscription:** Shah Alam (II) **Mint:** Chandor **Note:** Weight varies 2.68-2.90 grams.

Date	Mintage	Good	VG	F	VF	XF
ND(1773)	—	3.50	8.50	13.50	20.00	32.50

KM# 56.1 1/4 RUPEE

Silver **Obv. Inscription:** Shah Alam (II) **Reverse:** Lingam **Mint:** Maheshwar **Note:** Weight varies: 2.68-2.90 grams.

Date	Mintage	Good	VG	F	VF	XF
AH1185//15 (sic)	—	—	8.50	13.50	20.00	28.50

KM# 56.2 1/4 RUPEE

Silver **Obv. Inscription:** "Shah Alam II" **Reverse:** Bilva leaf and lingam **Mint:** Maheshwar **Note:** Weight varies: 2.68-2.90 grams.

Date	Mintage	Good	VG	F	VF	XF
AH1202	—	5.00	12.50	20.00	30.00	50.00
AH1203	—	5.00	12.50	20.00	30.00	50.00
AH1204	—	5.00	12.50	20.00	30.00	50.00
AH1205	—	5.00	12.50	20.00	30.00	50.00
AH1211//38	—	5.00	12.50	20.00	30.00	50.00
AH1215	—	5.00	12.50	20.00	30.00	50.00

KM# 72 1/4 RUPEE

Silver **Obv. Inscription:** "Shah Alam II" **Reverse:** Sun face **Mint:** Malharnagar **Note:** Weight varies 2.68-2.90 grams.

Date	Mintage	Good	VG	F	VF	XF
AH1214	—	1.20	3.00	5.00	7.00	12.00

KM# 2 1/2 RUPEE

Silver **Obv. Inscription:** Shah Alam (II) **Mint:** Chandor **Note:** Weight varies 5.35-5.80 grams.

Date	Mintage	Good	VG	F	VF	XF
ND(1774)	—	3.50	8.00	13.50	20.00	32.50

KM# 57.1 1/2 RUPEE

Silver **Obv. Inscription:** Shah Alam (II) **Reverse:** Lingam **Mint:** Maheshwar **Note:** Weight varies: 5.35-5.80 grams.

Date	Mintage	Good	VG	F	VF	XF
AH1192//2x	—	5.00	12.50	18.50	25.00	35.00
AH1197//24	—	5.00	12.50	18.50	25.00	35.00

KM# 57.2 1/2 RUPEE

Silver **Obv. Inscription:** "Shah Alam II" **Reverse:** Bilva leaf and lingam **Mint:** Maheshwar **Note:** Weight varies: 5.35-5.80 grams.

Date	Mintage	Good	VG	F	VF	XF
AH1202	—	6.00	15.00	25.00	40.00	60.00
AH1203//3x	—	6.00	15.00	25.00	40.00	60.00
AH1205	—	6.00	15.00	25.00	40.00	60.00
AH1207	—	6.00	15.00	25.00	40.00	60.00
AH1211//38	—	6.00	15.00	25.00	40.00	60.00

KM# 69 RUPEE

Silver **Obv. Inscription:** Shah Alam (II) **Reverse:** Sunface **Mint:** Malharnagar **Note:** Weight varies: 10.70-11.60 grams.

Date	Mintage	Good	VG	F	VF	XF
AH1174//7 (sic) Rare	—	—	—	—	—	—

KM# 58.1 RUPEE

Silver **Obv. Inscription:** Shah Alam (II) **Reverse:** Lingam **Mint:** Maheshwar **Note:** Weight varies: 10.70-11.60 grams.

Date	Mintage	Good	VG	F	VF	XF
AH1180//11 (sic)	—	10.00	25.00	37.50	50.00	75.00
AH1181//11 (sic)	—	6.00	15.00	21.50	30.00	45.00
AH1185//15 (sic)	—	3.00	7.50	11.00	16.50	25.00
AH1186//15 (sic)	—	3.00	7.50	11.00	16.50	25.00
AH1186//16 (sic)	—	3.00	7.50	11.00	16.50	25.00
AH1186//17 (sic)	—	3.00	7.50	11.00	16.50	25.00
AH1190//18 (sic)	—	3.00	7.50	11.00	16.50	25.00
AH1190//19 (sic)	—	3.00	7.50	11.00	16.50	25.00
AH1191//19	—	3.00	7.50	11.00	16.50	25.00
AH1191//20 (sic)	—	3.00	7.50	12.00	17.50	25.00
AH1191//21 (sic)	—	3.00	7.50	12.00	17.50	25.00
AH1190//20 (sic)	—	3.00	7.50	11.00	16.50	25.00
AH1192//22 (sic)	—	3.00	7.50	12.00	17.50	25.00
AH1193//23 (sic)	—	3.00	7.50	12.00	17.50	25.00
AH1194//24 (sic)	—	3.00	7.50	12.00	17.50	25.00
AH1197//24	—	3.00	7.50	12.00	17.50	25.00
AH1198//25	—	3.00	7.50	12.00	17.50	25.00
AH1197//25	—	3.00	7.50	12.00	17.50	25.00

KM# 3.1 RUPEE

Silver **Obv. Inscription:** Shah Alam (II) **Mint:** Chandor

Date	Mintage	Good	VG	F	VF	XF
ND//13 (1771-72)	—	3.50	8.50	13.50	22.50	37.50
AH1194	—	3.50	8.50	13.50	22.50	37.50
ND//66 (1780-81) Error for 22	—	4.00	10.00	15.00	25.00	40.00
AH1196//23	—	3.50	8.50	13.50	22.50	37.50
ND//25 (1783-84)	—	3.50	8.50	13.50	22.50	37.50
AH1199//24 (sic)	—	3.50	8.50	13.50	22.50	37.50
ND//27 (1785-86)	—	3.50	8.50	13.50	22.50	37.50
ND//28 (1786-87)	—	3.50	8.50	13.50	22.50	37.50

KM# 76 RUPEE

Silver **Obv. Inscription:** "Shah Alam II" **Reverse:** Sun face **Mint:** Malharnagar **Note:** Weight varies: 10.70-11.60 grams.

Date	Mintage	Good	VG	F	VF	XF
AH1185//15 (sic)	—	2.00	5.00	7.50	11.50	18.50
AH1186//15 (sic)	—	2.00	5.00	7.50	11.50	18.50
AH1186//16 (sic)	—	2.00	5.00	7.50	11.50	18.50
AH1187//17 (sic)	—	2.00	5.00	7.50	11.50	18.50
AH1190//18 (sic)	—	2.00	5.00	7.50	11.50	18.50
AH1195	—	2.00	5.00	7.50	11.50	18.50
AH1197//24	—	2.00	5.00	7.50	11.50	18.50
AH1198//25	—	2.00	5.00	7.50	11.50	18.50
AH1199//26	—	2.00	5.00	7.50	11.50	18.50
AH1200//27	—	2.00	5.00	7.50	11.50	18.50
AH1201//28	—	2.00	5.00	7.50	11.50	18.50
AH1202//29	—	2.00	5.00	7.50	11.50	18.50
AH1201//29	—	2.00	5.00	7.50	11.50	18.50
AH1203//30	—	2.00	5.00	7.50	11.50	18.50
AH1204//32	—	2.00	5.00	7.50	11.50	18.50
AH1205//32	—	2.00	5.00	7.50	11.50	18.50
AH1206//33	—	2.00	5.00	7.50	11.50	18.50
AH1207//35	—	2.00	5.00	7.50	11.50	18.50
AH1208	—	2.00	5.00	7.50	11.50	18.50
AH1209	—	2.00	5.00	7.50	11.50	18.50
AH1210	—	2.00	5.00	7.50	11.50	18.50
AH1211	—	2.00	5.00	7.50	11.50	18.50
AH1212	—	2.00	5.00	7.50	11.50	18.50
AH1213//4x	—	2.00	5.00	7.50	11.50	18.50
AH1214	—	2.00	5.00	7.50	11.50	18.50
AH1215//42	—	4.25	6.00	7.50	11.50	18.50

KM# 58.2 RUPEE

Silver **Obv. Inscription:** "Shah Alam II" **Reverse:** Bilva leaf and lingam **Mint:** Maheshwar **Note:** Weight varies: 10.70-11.60 grams.

Date	Mintage	Good	VG	F	VF	XF
AH1202//29	—	3.50	6.00	10.00	14.00	20.00
AH1201//28	—	3.50	6.00	10.00	14.00	20.00
AH1203//31	—	3.50	6.00	10.00	14.00	20.00
AH1205//33	—	3.50	6.00	10.00	14.00	20.00
AH1207//35	—	3.50	6.00	10.00	14.00	20.00
AH1208//35	—	3.50	6.00	10.00	14.00	20.00
AH1209//3x	—	3.50	6.00	10.00	14.00	20.00
AH1211//38	—	3.50	6.00	10.00	14.00	20.00
AH1215//42	—	4.50	7.00	10.00	14.00	20.00

KM# 58.3 RUPEE

Silver **Obv. Inscription:** Shah Alam (II) **Reverse:** Dagger **Mint:** Maheshwar **Note:** Weight varies: 10.70-11.60 grams.

Date	Mintage	Good	VG	F	VF	XF
AH1198	—	—	10.00	15.00	25.00	40.00

Ahalya Bai

AH1179-1210 / 1765-1795AD

HAMMERED COINAGE

C# 51 1/4 ANNA

Copper **Obverse:** Star, inscription **Obv. Inscription:** Shah Alam II **Reverse:** Leaf, trident **Mint:** Uncertain Mint

Date	Mintage	Good	VG	F	VF	XF
AH1197//24	—	—	—	—	—	—

INDORE FEUDATORY

PRINCELY STATE

HAMMERED COINAGE

KM# 102 MOHUR

10.8300 g., Gold

Date	Mintage	Good	VG	F	VF	XF
AH1168	—	—	—	—	—	—

Alamgir II

HAMMERED COINAGE

KM# 100 RUPEE

Silver **Obv. Inscription:** Alamgir (II) **Mint:** Sironj **Note:** Weight varies: 10.7-11.6 grams.

Date	Mintage	Good	VG	F	VF	XF
AH1167//1	—	—	25.00	40.00	85.00	175
AH1168//1	—	—	25.00	40.00	85.00	175
AH1169//1	—	—	45.00	65.00	125	275

KM# A101 MOHUR

Gold **Mint:** Sironj

Date	Mintage	VG	F	VF	XF	Unc
AH1168//2	—	400	650	1,000	1,350	—

Shah Alam

HAMMERED COINAGE

KM# 111 RUPEE

Silver **Obv. Inscription:** Shah Alam (II) **Mint:** Sironj **Note:** Weight varies: 10.7-11.6 grams.

Date	Mintage	Good	VG	F	VF	XF
AH11xx//7	—	8.00	20.00	35.00	50.00	70.00
AH1172//10	—	8.00	20.00	35.00	50.00	70.00
AH1184//12	—	8.00	20.00	35.00	50.00	70.00
AH1185//12	—	8.00	20.00	35.00	50.00	70.00
AH1187	—	8.00	20.00	35.00	50.00	70.00
AH1188//16	—	8.00	20.00	35.00	50.00	70.00
AH1189//16	—	8.00	20.00	35.00	50.00	70.00
AH119x//20	—	8.00	20.00	35.00	50.00	70.00
AH1194//21	—	8.00	20.00	35.00	50.00	70.00

Date	Mintage	Good	VG	F	VF	XF
AH1195	—	8.00	20.00	35.00	50.00	70.00
AH1199//24	—	8.00	20.00	35.00	50.00	70.00
AH1199//25	—	8.00	20.00	35.00	50.00	70.00
AH1200//27	—	8.00	20.00	35.00	50.00	70.00

JAIPUR

Tradition has it that the region of Jaipur, located in northwest India, once belonged to an ancient Kachwaha Rajput dynasty which claimed descent from Kush, one of the sons of Rama, King of Ayodhya. But the Princely State of Jaipur originated in the 12th century. Comparatively small in size, the State remained largely unnoticed until after the 16th century when the Jaipur royal house became famous for its military skills and thereafter supplied the Mughals with some of their more distinguished generals. The city of Jaipur was founded about 1728 by Maharaja Jai Singh II who was well known for his knowledge of mathematics and astronomy. The late 18th and early 19th centuries were difficult times for Jaipur. They were marked by internal rivalry, exacerbated by Maratha or Pindari incursions. In 1818 this culminated with a treaty whereby Jaipur came under British protection and oversight.

RULERS

Sawai Jai Singh, AH1111-1156/1699-1743AD
Isvari Singh, AH1156-1174/1743-1760AD
Madho Singh, AH1174-1192/1760-1778AD
Pratap Singh, AH1192-1218/1778-1803AD

All coins struck prior to AH1274/1857AD are in the name of the Mughal emperor. The corresponding AH date is listed in ( ) with each regnal year. Some overlapping of AH dates with regnal years will be found. Partial dates and recorded full dates are represented by partial ( ) or without ( ).

Beginning in 1857AD, coins were struck jointly in the names and corresponding AD dates of the British sovereign and the names and regnal years of the Maharajas of Jaipur.

The coins ordinarily bear both the AH date before 1857 or the AD date after 1857, as well as the regnal year, but as it is found only at the extreme right of the obverse die, it is almost never visible on the regular coinage but generally legible on the Nazarana coins which were struck utilizing the entire dies.

The listing of regnal years is very incomplete and many more years will turn up. In general, unlisted years are usually worth no more than years listed.

MINT NAMES

Coins were struck at two mints, which bear the following characteristic marks on the reverse:

سواي جيپور

Sawai Jaipur

سواي مادهوپور

Sawai Madhopur

NOTE: *Sawai* is merely an honorific title accorded each of the two cities.

MINT MARKS

Jhar

Leaf

Whisk

PRINCELY STATE

HAMMERED COINAGE

KM# A4 PAISA

18.1000 g., Copper **Obverse:** Leaf symbol **Obv. Inscription:** "Ahmad Shah Bahadur" **Mint:** Sawai Jaipur **Note:** Weight varies: 10.70-11.60 grams.

Date	Mintage	Good	VG	F	VF	XF
ND//4 (1750-51)	—	5.00	10.00	15.00	25.00	—

KM# 15 PAISA

Copper **Obv. Inscription:** "Alamgir II" **Mint:** Sawai Jaipur

Date	Mintage	VG	F	VF	XF	Unc
ND//4 (1750-51)	—	5.00	10.00	15.00	25.00	—
ND//5 (1751-52)	—	5.00	10.00	15.00	25.00	—
ND//6 (1752)	—	5.00	10.00	15.00	25.00	—

KM# 28 PAISA

Copper, 26 mm. **Obv. Inscription:** "Shah Alam II" **Mint:** Sawai Jaipur

Date	Mintage	Good	VG	F	VF	XF
ND//1 (1759-60)	—	—	—	—	—	—
ND//4 (1762-63)	—	—	—	—	—	—
ND//5 (1763-64)	—	—	—	—	—	—

KM# 29 PAISA

Copper **Obv. Inscription:** "Shah Alam II" **Mint:** Sawai Jaipur

Date	Mintage	Good	VG	F	VF	XF
ND//4 (1762-63)	—	3.00	5.00	10.00	15.00	—
ND//8 (1763-64)	—	3.00	5.00	10.00	15.00	—
ND//12 (1770-71)	—	3.00	5.00	10.00	15.00	—
ND//13 (1771-72)	—	3.00	5.00	10.00	15.00	—
ND//14 (1772-73)	—	3.00	5.00	10.00	15.00	—
ND//15 (1773-74)	—	3.00	5.00	10.00	15.00	—
ND//16 (1774-75)	—	3.00	5.00	10.00	15.00	—
ND//17 (1775-76)	—	3.00	5.00	10.00	15.00	—
ND//18 (1776-77)	—	3.00	5.00	10.00	15.00	—
ND//19 (1777-78)	—	3.00	5.00	10.00	15.00	—
AH1195//22	—	3.00	5.00	10.00	15.00	—

KM# 32 PAISA

Copper **Obv. Inscription:** "Shah Alam II" **Reverse:** Cross **Mint:** Sawai Jaipur **Note:** For crude degenerate copies of KM#32, see Kishangarh.

Date	Mintage	Good	VG	F	VF	XF
ND//20 (1778-79)	—	5.00	10.00	15.00	25.00	—
ND//21 (1779-80)	—	5.00	10.00	15.00	25.00	—
ND//22 (1780)	—	5.00	10.00	15.00	25.00	—
ND//23 (1781-82)	—	5.00	10.00	15.00	25.00	—
ND//24 (1782-83)	—	5.00	10.00	15.00	25.00	—
ND//25 (1783-84)	—	5.00	10.00	15.00	25.00	—

KM# 58 PAISA

Copper **Obv. Inscription:** "Shah Alam II" **Mint:** Sawai Madhopur

Date	Mintage	Good	VG	F	VF	XF
ND//25 (1783-84)	—	5.00	10.00	15.00	25.00	—
ND//32 (1790-91)	—	5.00	10.00	15.00	25.00	—
ND//33 (1791-92)	—	5.00	10.00	15.00	25.00	—
ND//36 (1794-95)	—	5.00	10.00	15.00	25.00	—
ND//37 (1795-96)	—	5.00	10.00	15.00	25.00	—
ND//42 (1800-01)	—	5.00	10.00	15.00	25.00	—

KM# 34 PAISA

Copper **Obv. Inscription:** "Shah Alam II" **Reverse:** Three-lobed flower **Mint:** Sawai Jaipur

Date	Mintage	Good	VG	F	VF	XF
ND//25 (1783-84)	—	5.00	10.00	15.00	25.00	—

KM# 35 PAISA

Copper **Obv. Inscription:** "Shah Alam II" **Reverse:** Three-lobed leaf **Mint:** Sawai Jaipur

Date	Mintage	Good	VG	F	VF	XF
ND//26 (1784-85)	—	5.00	10.00	15.00	25.00	—

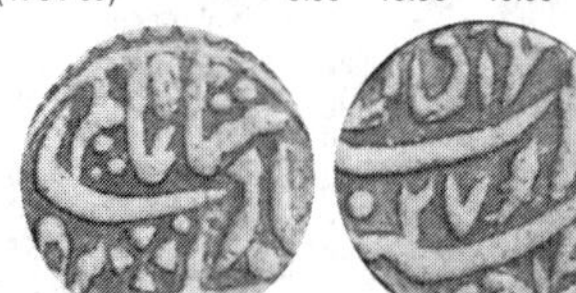

KM# 36 PAISA

Copper **Obv. Inscription:** "Shah Alam II" **Reverse:** Fish **Mint:** Sawai Jaipur

Date	Mintage	Good	VG	F	VF	XF
ND//26 (1784-85)	—	5.00	10.00	15.00	25.00	—
ND//27 (1785-86)	—	5.00	10.00	15.00	25.00	—
ND//28 (1786-87)	—	5.00	10.00	15.00	25.00	—
ND//29 (1787-88)	—	5.00	10.00	15.00	25.00	—
ND//30 (1788-89)	—	5.00	10.00	15.00	25.00	—
ND//31 (1789)	—	5.00	10.00	15.00	25.00	—
ND//37 (1795-96)	—	5.00	10.00	15.00	25.00	—

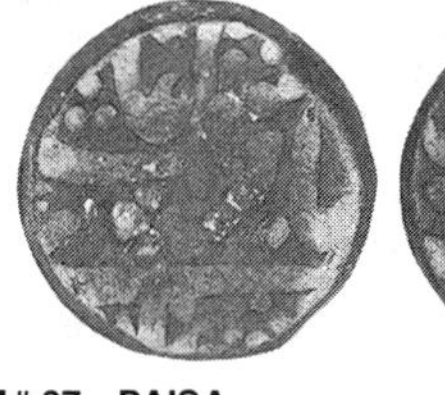

KM# 37 PAISA

Copper, 26 mm. **Obv. Inscription:** "Shah Alam II" **Reverse:** Fish and leaf **Mint:** Sawai Jaipur

Date	Mintage	Good	VG	F	VF	XF
ND//30 (1788-89)	—	5.00	10.00	15.00	25.00	—
ND//31 (1789)	—	5.00	10.00	15.00	25.00	—
ND//32 (1790-91)	—	5.00	10.00	15.00	25.00	—
ND//33 (1791-92)	—	5.00	10.00	15.00	25.00	—
ND//34 (1792-93)	—	5.00	10.00	15.00	25.00	—
ND//35 (1793-94)	—	5.00	10.00	15.00	25.00	—

KM# 30 NAZARANA PAISA

Copper **Obv. Inscription:** "Shah Alam II" **Reverse:** Jhar at right **Mint:** Sawai Jaipur

Date	Mintage	Good	VG	F	VF	XF
AH1190//18	—	30.00	50.00	75.00	90.00	—

KM# 33 NAZARANA PAISA

Copper **Obv. Inscription:** "Shah Alam II" **Reverse:** Cross **Mint:** Sawai Jaipur

Date	Mintage	Good	VG	F	VF	XF
ND//23 (1781-82)	—	30.00	50.00	75.00	90.00	—

KM# 38 NAZARANA PAISA

Copper **Obv. Inscription:** "Shah Alam II" **Reverse:** Leaf and fish **Mint:** Sawai Jaipur

Date	Mintage	Good	VG	F	VF	XF
ND//33 (1791-92)	—	30.00	50.00	75.00	90.00	—
ND//34 (1792-93)	—	30.00	50.00	75.00	90.00	—

KM# 2 1/4 RUPEE

Silver **Obv. Inscription:** Ahmad Shah Bahadur **Mint:** Sawai Jaipur **Note:** Weight varies: 2.67-2.90 grams.

Date	Mintage	Good	VG	F	VF	XF
AH116x//3	—	5.00	10.00	15.00	35.00	50.00

KM# 44 1/4 RUPEE

Silver **Obv. Inscription:** Shah Alam (II) **Mint:** Sawai Jaipur **Note:** Mint mark: Flower. Weight varies: 2.67-2.90 grams.

Date	Mintage	Good	VG	F	VF	XF
ND//15 (1773-74)	—	4.50	11.50	18.50	30.00	45.00
ND//18 (1776-77)	—	4.50	11.50	18.50	30.00	45.00

KM# 45 1/4 RUPEE

Silver **Obv. Inscription:** Shah Alam (II) **Mint:** Sawai Jaipur **Note:** Mint mark: Jhar. Weight varies: 2.67-2.90 grams.

Date	Mintage	Good	VG	F	VF	XF
ND//19 (1777-78)	—	5.00	12.50	20.00	35.00	60.00

KM# 3 1/2 RUPEE

Silver **Obv. Inscription:** Muhammad Shah **Mint:** Sawai Jaipur **Note:** Weight varies: 5.35-5.80 grams.

Date	Mintage	Good	VG	F	VF	XF
AH1159//29	—	5.50	13.50	22.50	32.50	45.00

KM# 47 1/2 RUPEE

Silver **Obv. Inscription:** Shah Alam (II) **Mint:** Sawai Jaipur **Note:** Mint mark: Flower. Weight varies: 5.35-5.80 grams.

Date	Mintage	Good	VG	F	VF	XF
ND//15 (1773-74)	—	4.50	11.50	18.50	30.00	50.00

KM# 48 1/2 RUPEE

Silver **Obv. Inscription:** Shah Alam (II) **Mint:** Sawai Jaipur **Note:** Mint mark: Jhar. Weight varies: 5.35-5.80 grams.

Date	Mintage	Good	VG	F	VF	XF
ND//16 (1774-75)	—	5.00	12.50	20.00	35.00	60.00

KM# 4 RUPEE

Silver **Obv. Inscription:** Muhammad Shah **Mint:** Sawai Jaipur **Note:** Weight varies: 10.70-11.60 grams.

Date	Mintage	Good	VG	F	VF	XF
AH1153//23	—	5.00	13.00	21.50	30.00	40.00
AH1155//24	—	5.00	13.00	21.50	30.00	40.00
AH1156//25	—	5.00	13.00	21.50	30.00	40.00
AH1155//25	—	5.00	13.00	21.50	30.00	40.00
AH1156//26	—	5.00	13.00	21.50	30.00	40.00
AH115x//27	—	5.00	13.00	21.50	30.00	40.00
AH1158//28	—	5.00	13.00	21.50	30.00	40.00
AH1159//29	—	5.00	13.00	21.50	30.00	40.00
AH11xx//30	—	5.00	13.00	21.50	30.00	40.00
AH116(1)//31	—	5.00	13.00	21.50	30.00	40.00

KM# 8 RUPEE

Silver, 21 mm. **Obv. Inscription:** "Ahmad Shah Bahadur" **Mint:** Sawai Jaipur **Note:** Weight varies: 10.70-11.60 grams.

Date	Mintage	Good	VG	F	VF	XF
AH1161//1	—	4.75	11.50	17.50	23.50	32.50
AH1162//1	—	4.75	11.50	17.50	23.50	32.50
AH1162//2	—	4.75	11.50	17.50	23.50	32.50
AH1163//3	—	4.75	11.50	17.50	23.50	32.50
AH1164//4	—	4.75	11.50	17.50	23.50	32.50
AH1165//5	—	4.75	11.50	17.50	23.50	32.50
AH1167//6	—	4.75	11.50	17.50	23.50	32.50

KM# 21 RUPEE

Silver **Obv. Inscription:** "Alamgir II" **Mint:** Sawai Jaipur **Note:** Weight varies: 10.70-11.60 grams.

Date	Mintage	Good	VG	F	VF	XF
ND//1 (1748)	—	4.00	10.00	15.00	21.00	30.00
ND//2 (1748-49)	—	4.00	10.00	15.00	21.00	30.00
ND//3 (1749-50)	—	4.00	10.00	15.00	21.00	30.00
ND//4 (1750-51)	—	4.00	10.00	15.00	21.00	30.00
ND//5 (1751-52)	—	4.00	10.00	15.00	21.00	30.00
ND//6 (1752-53)	—	4.00	10.00	15.00	21.00	30.00

KM# 63 RUPEE

Silver **Obv. Inscription:** "Shah Alam II" **Mint:** Sawai Madhopur **Note:** Weight varies: 10.70-11.60 grams.

Date	Mintage	Good	VG	F	VF	XF
ND//7 (1765-66)	—	2.75	6.50	10.00	15.00	22.50
ND//13 (1771-72)	—	2.75	6.50	10.00	15.00	22.50
ND//14 (1772-73)	—	2.75	6.50	10.00	15.00	22.50
ND//21 (1779-80)	—	2.75	6.50	10.00	15.00	22.50
ND//27 (1785-86)	—	2.75	6.50	10.00	15.00	22.50
ND//28 (1786-87)	—	2.75	6.50	10.00	15.00	22.50
AH1203//31	—	2.75	6.50	10.00	15.00	22.50
ND//33 (1791-92)	—	2.75	6.50	10.00	15.00	22.50
ND//38 (1796-97)	—	2.75	6.50	10.00	15.00	22.50
ND//41 (1799-1800)	—	2.75	6.50	10.00	15.00	22.50

KM# 9 NAZARANA RUPEE

Silver **Obv. Inscription:** "Ahmad Shah Bahadur" **Mint:** Sawai Jaipur **Note:** Weight varies: 10.70-11.60 grams.

Date	Mintage	Good	VG	F	VF	XF
AH1166//6	—	—	55.00	90.00	125	175
AH1167//7	—	—	55.00	90.00	125	175

KM# 64 NAZARANA RUPEE

Silver **Obv. Inscription:** Shah Alam (II) **Mint:** Sawai Madhopur **Note:** Weight varies: 10.70-11.60 grams.

Date	Mintage	Good	VG	F	VF	XF
AH1178//6	—	—	45.00	70.00	100	140
AH1181//12 (sic)	—	—	45.00	70.00	100	140
AH1186//10 (sic)	—	—	45.00	70.00	100	140
AH1186//12 (sic)	—	—	45.00	70.00	100	140

KM# 13 MOHUR

Gold **Obv. Inscription:** "Ahmad Shah Bahadur" **Mint:** Sawai Jaipur **Note:** Weight varies: 10.70-11.40 grams.

Date	Mintage	Good	VG	F	VF	XF
ND(1748-54)	—	—	—	—	—	—

Note: Reported, not confirmed

KM# 25 MOHUR

Gold **Obv. Inscription:** "Alamgir II" **Mint:** Sawai Jaipur **Note:** Weight varies: 10.70-11.40 grams.

Date	Mintage	Good	VG	F	VF	XF
AH1169//3	—	—	250	280	325	400
ND//4 (1757-58)	—	—	250	280	325	400
AH117x//6	—	—	250	280	325	400

KM# 55 MOHUR

Gold **Obv. Inscription:** "Shah Alam II" **Mint:** Sawai Jaipur **Note:** Weight varies: 10.70-11.40 grams.

Date	Mintage	Good	VG	F	VF	XF
ND//15 (1773-74)	—	—	135	160	225	325
AH11xx//25	—	—	135	160	225	325
AH121x//44	—	—	225	250	275	325

HAMMERED COINAGE

Mughal Style

KM# 39 PAISA

Copper **Obv. Inscription:** "Shah Alam II" **Reverse:** Large Jhar **Mint:** Sawai Jaipur

Date	Mintage	Good	VG	F	VF	XF
ND//35 (1793-94)	—	5.00	10.00	15.00	25.00	—
ND//36 (1794-95)	—	5.00	10.00	15.00	25.00	—
ND//37 (1795-96)	—	5.00	10.00	15.00	25.00	—
ND//38 (1796-97)	—	5.00	10.00	15.00	25.00	—
ND//39 (1797-98)	—	5.00	10.00	15.00	25.00	—
ND//40 (1798-99)	—	5.00	10.00	15.00	25.00	—
ND//41 (1799-1800)	—	5.00	10.00	15.00	25.00	—

KM# 40 NAZARANA PAISA

Copper **Obv. Inscription:** "Shah Alam II" **Reverse:** Large Jhar **Mint:** Sawai Jaipur

Date	Mintage	Good	VG	F	VF	XF
ND//37 (1795-96)	—	30.00	50.00	75.00	90.00	—
ND//38 (1796-97)	—	30.00	50.00	75.00	90.00	—
ND//39 (1797-98)	—	30.00	50.00	75.00	90.00	—

KM# 61 1/4 RUPEE

Silver **Obv. Inscription:** Shah Alam (II) **Mint:** Sawai Madhopur **Note:** Weight varies: 2.67-2.90 grams.

Date	Mintage	Good	VG	F	VF	XF
ND//5 (1763-64)	—	5.00	10.00	15.00	20.00	30.00
ND//12 (1770-71)	—	5.00	10.00	15.00	20.00	30.00
ND//14 (1772-73)	—	5.00	10.00	15.00	20.00	30.00

KM# 62 1/2 RUPEE

Silver **Obv. Inscription:** Shah Alam (II) **Mint:** Sawai Madhopur **Note:** Weight varies: 5.35-5.80 grams.

Date	Mintage	Good	VG	F	VF	XF
ND//13 (1771-72)	—	5.00	10.00	15.00	20.00	30.00

KM# 50 RUPEE

Silver **Obv. Inscription:** "Shah Alam II" **Mint:** Sawai Jaipur **Note:** Mint mark: Jhar. Weight varies: 10.70-11.60 grams.

Date	Mintage	Good	VG	F	VF	XF
ND//17 (1775-76)	—	2.25	5.50	8.00	12.50	18.50
ND//20 (1778-79)	—	2.25	5.50	8.00	12.50	18.50
ND//24 (1782-83)	—	2.25	5.50	8.00	12.50	18.50
ND//25 (1783-84)	—	2.25	5.50	8.00	12.50	18.50
AH1198//26	—	2.25	5.50	8.00	12.50	18.50
AH1199//26	—	2.25	5.50	8.00	12.50	18.50
ND//28 (1786-87)	—	2.25	5.50	8.00	12.50	18.50
ND//32 (1790-91)	—	2.25	5.50	8.00	12.50	18.50
ND//33 (1791-92)	—	2.25	5.50	8.00	12.50	18.50
ND//34 (1792-93)	—	2.25	5.50	8.00	12.50	18.50
AH1209//37	—	2.25	5.50	8.00	12.50	18.50
ND//38 (1796-97)	—	2.25	5.50	8.00	12.50	18.50
ND//39 (1797-98)	—	2.25	5.50	8.00	12.50	18.50
ND//40 (1798-99)	—	2.25	5.50	8.00	12.50	18.50
ND//41 (1799-1800)	—	2.25	5.50	8.00	12.50	18.50

KM# 66 NAZARANA 1/4 RUPEE

Silver, 18.4 mm. **Obv. Inscription:** Shah Alam (II) **Mint:** Sawai Madhopur **Note:** Weight varies: 10.70-11.60 grams.

Date	Mintage	Good	VG	F	VF	XF
AH1192//25 (sic)	—	—	—	—	—	—

KM# 51 NAZARANA RUPEE

Silver, 35 mm. **Obv. Inscription:** "Shah Alam II" **Mint:** Sawai Jaipur **Note:** Large flan. Weight varies: 10.70-11.60 grams.

Date	Mintage	Good	VG	F	VF	XF
AH1176//3	—	21.50	42.50	70.00	100	150
AH1178//6	—	21.50	42.50	70.00	100	150
AH1182//10	—	21.50	42.50	70.00	100	150
AH1192//19	—	21.50	42.50	70.00	100	150
AH1207//33 (sic)	—	21.50	42.50	70.00	100	150
AH1206//34	—	21.50	42.50	70.00	100	150
AH1208//34 (sic)	—	21.50	42.50	70.00	100	150
AH1214//40 (sic)	—	21.50	42.50	70.00	100	150

JAISALMIR

Although the ruling Rajputs (or rawals) of this desert territory, located in northwest India traced their ancestry back to pre-Asokan times, the State of Jaisalmir was founded by Deoraj, the first rawal, only in the 10th century. Jaisalmir city was established by

Rawal Jaisal, after whom both the city and the State were named. Like Jaipur, Jaisalmir reached its zenith in Mughal times, after being forced to acknowledge the supremacy of Delhi in the time of the Emperor Shah Jahan. With Mughal disintegration, Jaisalmir also fell upon hard times and most of its outlying provinces were lost. The state came under British protection in 1818, and on March 30th, 1949 it was merged into Rajasthan.

RULERS

Budh Singh, AH1119-1135/1707-1721AD
Tej Singh, AH1135-1136/1721-1722AD
Sawai Singh, AH1136/1722AD
Akhey Singh, AH1136-1176/1722-1762AD
Mulraj Singh, AH1176-1235/1762-1819AD

MINT

Jaisalmir

PRINCELY STATE

ANONYMOUS HAMMERED COINAGE

Mughal Style

KM# 7 1/8 RUPEE

1.3655 g., Silver **Series:** Akhey Shahi **Obv. Inscription:** "Muhammad Shah" **Note:** Struck 1756-1860AD. Prev. C#7.

Date	Mintage	Good	VG	F	VF	XF
AH1153//22 Frozen	—	—	15.00	25.00	35.00	50.00

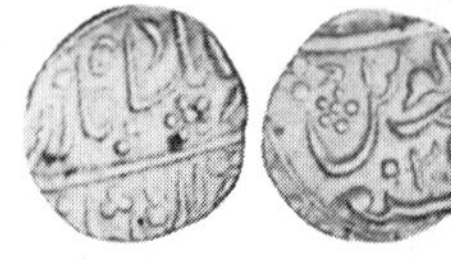

KM# 8 1/4 RUPEE

2.4310 g., Silver **Series:** Akhey Shahi **Obverse:** Gujarati "105" (inverted) above "n" in "qiran" **Obv. Inscription:** "Muhammad Shah" **Note:** Struck 1756-1860AD. Prev. C#8.

Date	Mintage	Good	VG	F	VF	XF
AH1153//22 Frozen	—	—	10.00	15.00	20.00	35.00

KM# 9 1/2 RUPEE

5.4620 g., Silver **Series:** Akhey Shahi **Obverse:** Gujarati "106" above "n" in "qiran" **Obv. Inscription:** "Muhammad Shah" **Note:** Struck 1756-1860AD. Prev. C#9.

Date	Mintage	Good	VG	F	VF	XF
AH1153//22 Frozen	—	—	10.00	15.00	20.00	35.00

KM# 5.1 RUPEE

10.9240 g., Silver **Series:** Akhey Shahi **Obv. Inscription:** "Muhammad Shah" **Note:** Struck 1756-1860AD.

Date	Mintage	Good	VG	F	VF	XF
AH1152//22 Frozen	—	—	12.00	20.00	30.00	45.00
AH1153//22 Frozen	—	—	9.00	15.00	21.50	30.00
AH1155//25	—	—	—	—	—	—

KM# 5.2 RUPEE

10.9240 g., Silver **Series:** Ahkey Shahi **Obv. Inscription:** "Muhammad Shah" **Reverse:** Swastika at lower right

Date	Mintage	Good	VG	F	VF	XF
AH1153//22 Frozen	—	8.00	12.00	20.00	30.00	40.00

KM# 10.1 RUPEE

10.9240 g., Silver **Series:** Akhey Shahi **Obverse:** Gujarati "I" (inverted) above "n" in "giran" **Obv. Inscription:** "Muhammad Shah" **Note:** Struck 1756-1860AD.

Date	Mintage	Good	VG	F	VF	XF
AH1153// Frozen	—	—	—	—	—	—

KM# 10.2 RUPEE

10.9240 g., Silver **Series:** Akhey Shahi **Obverse:** Gujarati "15" (inverted) above "n" in "giran" **Obv. Inscription:** "Muhammad Shah" **Note:** Struck 1756-1860AD.

Date	Mintage	Good	VG	F	VF	XF
AH1153//22 Frozen	—	—	—	—	—	—

KM# 10.3 RUPEE

10.9240 g., Silver **Obverse:** Gujarati "106" above "n" in "giran" **Obv. Inscription:** "Muhammad Shah" **Note:** Struck 1756-1860AD.

Date	Mintage	Good	VG	F	VF	XF
AH1150//22 Frozen	—	—	—	—	—	—

KM# 10.4 RUPEE

10.9240 g., Silver **Series:** Ahkey Shahi **Obverse:** Gujarati "601" above "n" in "giran" **Obv. Inscription:** "Muhammad Shah" **Note:** Struck 1756-1860AD.

Date	Mintage	Good	VG	F	VF	XF
AH115-//22 Frozen	—	10.00	15.00	25.00	35.00	50.00

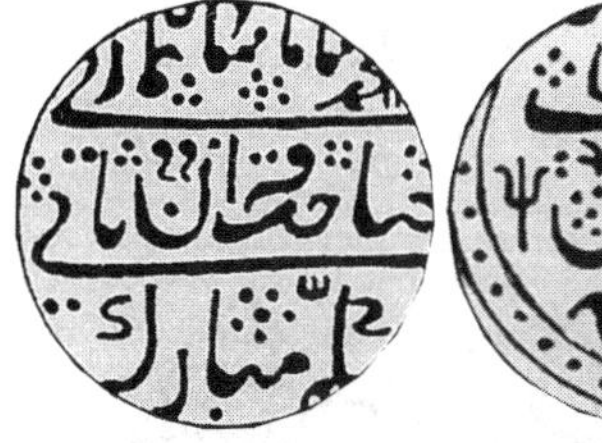

KM# 11 RUPEE

10.9240 g., Silver **Series:** Akhey Shahi **Obverse:** Gujarati "11" above "n" in "giran" **Obv. Inscription:** "Muhammad Shah" **Reverse:** Trisul at left **Note:** Struck 1756-1860AD.

Date	Mintage	Good	VG	F	VF	XF
AH1153//22 Frozen, Rare	—	—	—	—	—	—

KM# 14.1 RUPEE

10.9240 g., Silver **Series:** Akhey Shahi **Obverse:** Gujarati "1" above "n" in "giran" **Obv. Inscription:** "Muhammad Shah" **Reverse:** Swastika at bottom right **Note:** Struck 1756-1860AD.

Date	Mintage	Good	VG	F	VF	XF
AH1153//22 Frozen	—	—	—	—	—	—

KM# 14.2 RUPEE

10.9240 g., Silver **Series:** Akhey Shahi **Obverse:** Gujarati "107" above "n" in "giran" **Obv. Inscription:** "Muhammad Shah" **Reverse:** Swastika at bottom right

Date	Mintage	Good	VG	F	VF	XF
AH1153//22 Frozen	—	—	—	—	—	—

KM# 14.3 RUPEE

10.9240 g., Silver **Series:** Akhey Shahi **Obverse:** Persian "801" (108 retrograde) above "n" in "giran" **Obv. Inscription:** "Muhammad Shah" **Reverse:** Swastika at lower right **Note:** Struck 1756-1860AD.

Date	Mintage	Good	VG	F	VF	XF
AH1153/22 Frozen	—	—	—	—	—	—

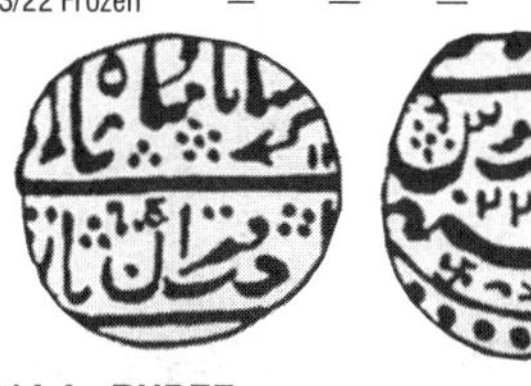

KM# 14.4 RUPEE

10.9240 g., Silver **Series:** Akhey Shahi **Obverse:** Gujarati "106" above "n" in "giran" **Obv. Inscription:** "Muhammad Shah" **Reverse:** Swastika at lower left **Note:** Struck 1756-1860AD.

Date	Mintage	Good	VG	F	VF	XF
AH1153//22 Frozen	—	—	—	—	—	—

KM# 5a NAZARANA RUPEE

10.9240 g., Silver **Series:** Akhey Shahi **Obv. Inscription:** "Muhammad Shah" **Shape:** Square **Note:** Struck 1756-1860AD.

Date	Mintage	Good	VG	F	VF	XF
AH1153//22 Frozen	—	—	—	—	—	—

KM# 5aa NAZARANA RUPEE

10.9240 g., Silver, 29 mm. **Series:** Akhey Shahi **Obv. Inscription:** Muhammad Shah **Note:** C#10a; Struck 1756-1860AD.

Date	Mintage	Good	VG	F	VF	XF
AH1153//22 Frozen	—	—	45.00	75.00	110	150

KM# 10a NAZARANA RUPEE

10.9240 g., Silver, 31 mm. **Series:** Akhey Shahi **Obverse:** Gujarati "1" above "n" in "giran" **Obv. Inscription:** Muhammad Shah **Reverse:** Swastika at bottom right **Note:** Struck 1756-1860AD.

Date	Mintage	Good	VG	F	VF	XF
AH1153//22 Frozen	—	—	—	—	—	—

KM# 4 1/2 NAZARANA RUPEE

5.4620 g., Silver **Series:** Akhey Shahi **Obv. Inscription:** Muhammad Shah **Shape:** Square **Note:** Struck 1756-1860AD.

Date	Mintage	Good	VG	F	VF	XF
AH1153//22 Frozen	—	20.00	40.00	65.00	100	—

KM# 15 NAZARANA 2-1/2 RUPEE
28.0000 g., Silver **Series:** Akhey Shahi **Obverse:** Persian "801" (108 retrograde) above "n" in "giran" **Obv. Inscription:** Muhammad Shah **Reverse:** Swastika at bottom right **Shape:** Square

Date	Mintage	Good	VG	F	VF	XF
AH1153//22 Frozen; Rare	—	—	—	—	—	—

JANJIRA ISLAND

Island near Bombay. Dynasty of Nawabs dates from 1489AD.

The origin of the nawabs of Janjira is obscure. They were Sidi or Abyssinian Muslims whose ancestors, serving as admirals to the Muslim rulers of the Deccan, had been granted jagirs (revenue-producing land tenures) under the Adil Shahi sultans of Bijapur. In 1870, Janjira came under direct British rule. Until 1924 the nawabs of Janjira also exercised suzerainty over Jafarabad on the Kathiawar peninsular.

PRINCELY STATE

Sidi Ibrahim Khan II

First Reign: AH1204-1206 / 1789-1792AD

HAMMERED COINAGE

KM# 5 PAISA
Copper

Date	Mintage	Good	VG	F	VF	XF
ND(1789)	—	10.00	15.00	25.00	35.00	20.00

JAORA

Ghafar Khan (d.1825), the first Nawab of Jaora, was brother-in-law to Amir Khan, the Pindari leader. Jaora was subordinate to Indore, having been granted control of the territory in central India in return for the maintenance of a body of cavalry and, later, of foot soldiers which were to be made available to Indore when required. The nawabs of Jaora maintained a good relationship with the British which, after 1818, left them in control of the area independently of Indore. In August 1948 Jaora was absorbed into Madhya Pradesh.

MINT

جاوره

Jaora

PRINCELY STATE

HAMMERED COINAGE

KM# 1 PAISA
Copper **Mint:** Jaora

Date	Mintage	Good	VG	F	VF	XF
ND-//15	—	—	—	—	—	—

JIND

State located in the southern Punjab and north Haryana States.

The ruling princes belonged to the same Jat family as the maharajas of Patiala. Like them, they traced their ancestry back to Baryam, a revenue collector under Babur (1526). The state was founded by Gajpat Singh after he took part in the Sikh uprising against the Afghan governor of Sirhind in 1763. One of Gajpat Singh's daughters became the mother of Ranjit Singh.

RULERS

Gaipat Singh, 1764-1786AD
Bhag Singh, 1786-1819AD

NOTE: These are believed to have been struck for Gaipat Singh, Sangat Singh and Sarup Singh and are not distinguishable.

BRITISH PROTECTORATE

Gajpat Singh

HAMMERED COINAGE

KM# 1 RUPEE
Silver, 16-18 mm. **Note:** Weight varies: 10.70-11.60 grams. Size varies.

Date	Mintage	Good	VG	F	VF	XF
ND/4(1764-86) Frozen	—	10.00	25.00	75.00	125	175

KM# 2 MOHUR
Gold, 16-18 mm. **Note:** Weight varies: 10.70-11.40 grams. Size varies.

Date	Mintage	Good	VG	F	VF	XF
ND/(4)(1764-86) Frozen	—	—	225	240	300	450

Bhag Singh

VS1843-1892 / 1786-1819AD

HAMMERED COINAGE

KM# 3 RUPEE
Silver, 16-18 mm. **Note:** Weight varies: 10.70-11.60 grams. Size varies. Uniface.

Date	Mintage	Good	VG	F	VF	XF
ND(1786-1819)	—	10.00	25.00	75.00	125	175

JODHPUR

Jodhpur, also known as Marwar, located in northwest India, was the largest Princely State in the Rajputana Agency. Its population in 1941 exceeded two and a half million. The "Maharajadhirajas" ("Great Kings of Kings") of Jodhpur were Rathor Rajputs who claimed an extremely ancient ancestry from Rama, king of Ayodhya. With the collapse of the Rathor rulers of Kanauj in 1194 the family entered Marwar where they laid the foundation of the new state. The city of Jodhpur was built by Rao Jodha in 1459, and the city and the state were named after him. In 1561 the Mughal Emperor Akbar invaded Jodhpur, forcing its submission. In 1679 Emperor Aurangzeb sacked the city, an experience which stimulated the Rajput royal house to forge a new unity among themselves in order to extricate themselves from Mughal hegemony. Internal dissension once again asserted itself and Rajput unity, which had both benefited from and accelerated Mughal decline, fell apart before the Marathas. In 1818 Jodhpur came under British protection and control and after Indian independence in 1947 the State was merged into Rajasthan. Jodhpur is best known for its particular style of riding breeches (jodpurs) which became very popular in the West in the late 19th century.

RULERS

The issues of the first four rulers before 1858AD bearing both the AH and VS dates as well as the regnal years, are rarely actual dates and years, but were "frozen" and used for many years without change, and were often quite indiscriminately applied. Mismatched regnal years and dates are frequently encountered, as well as blundered dates of all sorts. Dates lying outside the reigns of the rulers named on coins (after 1858AD) were often used. Thus the date or regnal year may not represent the actual dating of the coin.

Coinage of the first four rulers (until 1858AD) is not distinguished by reign, but by type of inscription, mint, and pseudo-date.

Bijay Singh, AH1166-1207/1752-1793AD
Bhim Singh, AH1207-1218/1792-1803AD

MINTS

اجمير

Ajmer

دار الخير

Dar-al-Khair

جودهپور

Jodhpur (Jodpur)

Operative between AH1175/1761AD – VS2002/1945AD. There are a number of mules of late Jodhpur types struck in 1945 and later for collectors.

دار المنصور

Dar-al-Mansur

ميرتا ميرتة

Balot Merta
(City of Merta)

ناگور

Nagor

Operative until AH1289/1872AD.

دار البركات

Dar-al-Barkat

MINT MARKS

Before 1858AD

Nagor

Usually on obverse

KINGDOM

HAMMERED COINAGE

KM# A172 PAISA
Copper **Mint:** Nagor **Note:** Weight varies 15-22 grams. Square countermark "Barkat Nagore" struck over anonymous Mughal Falus, KM#730.

Date	Mintage	Good	VG	F	VF	XF
ND(1751)	—	5.00	10.00	15.00	20.00	—

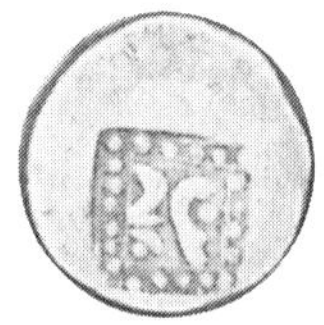

KM# 172 PAISA
Copper **Mint:** Nagor **Note:** Weight varies 15.00-18.00 grams.

Date	Mintage	Good	VG	F	VF	XF
ND(1751)	—	5.00	10.00	15.00	20.00	—

KM# 11 PAISA
Copper **Mint:** Jodhpur

Date	Mintage	Good	VG	F	VF	XF
ND(1792)	—	3.00	5.00	10.00	20.00	—

KM# 12.2 TAKKA (2 Paisas)
18.0000 g., Copper **Series:** Dhabu Shahi **Obverse:** Large legends **Reverse:** Large legends **Mint:** Jodhpur

Date	Mintage	Good	VG	F	VF	XF
AHxx92	—	3.00	5.00	10.00	20.00	—
AH1192	—	3.00	5.00	10.00	20.00	—
AH1205//35 (sic)	—	3.00	5.00	10.00	20.00	—

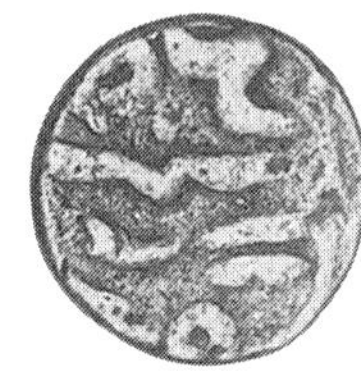

KM# 12.1 TAKKA (2 Paisas)
18.0000 g., Copper **Series:** Dhabu Shahi **Mint:** Jodhpur **Note:** Medium legends.

Date	Mintage	Good	VG	F	VF	XF
AH1192	—	3.00	5.00	10.00	20.00	—

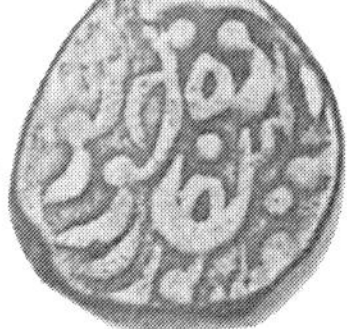

KM# 12.3 TAKKA (2 Paisas)

18.0000 g., Copper **Series:** Dhabu Shahi **Obverse:** "Ki" at top **Mint:** Jodhpur

Date	Mintage	Good	VG	F	VF	XF
ND(1790)	—	3.00	5.00	10.00	20.00	—

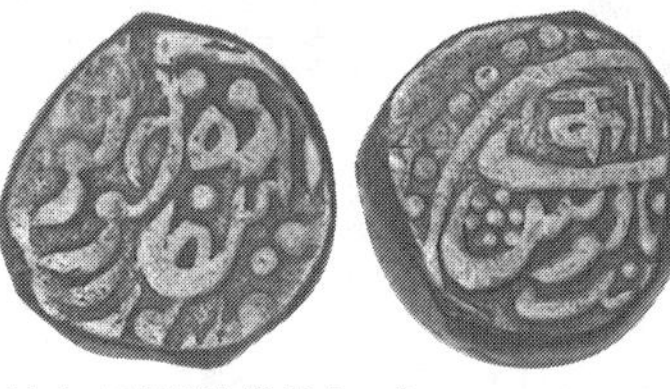

KM# 14.1 TAKKA (2 Paisas)
18.0000 g., Copper **Series:** Bhim Shahi **Obverse:** Nagari "K" at top **Mint:** Jodhpur

Date	Mintage	Good	VG	F	VF	XF
AHxxxx	—	—	—	—	—	—

KM# 13 TAKKA (2 Paisas)
18.0000 g., Copper **Series:** Dhabu Shahi **Mint:** Jodhpur **Note:** Small legends.

Date	Mintage	Good	VG	F	VF	XF
AH1205//35 (sic)	—	5.00	10.00	15.00	20.00	—

KM# 5 1/2 RUPEE
5.0000 g., Silver **Obv. Inscription:** "Shah Alam II" **Mint:** Ajmer

Date	Mintage	Good	VG	F	VF	XF
AH1203//31	—	10.00	15.00	25.00	35.00	50.00

KM# 17 1/2 RUPEE
Silver **Series:** Bijai Shahi **Obverse:** Sword **Obv. Inscription:** "Shah Alam II" **Mint:** Jodhpur **Note:** Weight varies 5.35-5.80 grams.

Date	Mintage	Good	VG	F	VF	XF
AH1203//31	—	—	15.00	25.00	35.00	50.00

KM# 176 RUPEE
Silver **Obv. Inscription:** "Alamgir II" **Mint:** Nagor **Note:** Weight varies 11.20-11.35 grams.

Date	Mintage	Good	VG	F	VF	XF
AH1167//1	—	11.50	28.50	47.50	65.00	90.00
AH1168//1	—	13.00	32.50	52.50	75.00	110
AH1169//3	—	11.50	28.50	47.50	65.00	90.00
AH1170//3	—	11.50	28.50	47.50	65.00	90.00
AH1170//4	—	11.50	28.50	47.50	65.00	90.00
AH1172//4 (sic)	—	11.50	28.50	47.50	65.00	90.00
AH1172//5	—	11.50	28.50	47.50	65.00	90.00
AH1173//6	—	11.50	28.50	47.50	65.00	90.00
AH1174//6	—	11.50	28.50	47.50	65.00	90.00
AH1176//6 (sic)	—	11.50	28.50	47.50	65.00	90.00
AH1184//9	—	11.50	28.50	47.50	65.00	90.00

Note: Posthumous issue

KM# 18 RUPEE
11.3000 g., Silver **Series:** Bijai Shahi **Obverse:** Various styles of swords **Obv. Inscription:** "Shah Alam II" **Mint:** Jodhpur

Date	Mintage	Good	VG	F	VF	XF
ND//14 (1772-73)	—	2.75	6.50	10.00	15.00	22.50
AH1192//20	—	2.75	6.50	10.00	15.00	22.50
AH1197//25	—	2.75	6.50	10.00	15.00	22.50
AH1199//26	—	2.75	6.50	10.00	15.00	22.50
AH1204	—	2.75	6.50	10.00	15.00	22.50
AH1205//33	—	2.75	6.50	10.00	15.00	22.50
AH1201//33 (sic)	—	2.75	6.50	10.00	15.00	22.50
AH1203//33 (sic)	—	2.75	6.50	10.00	15.00	22.50
AH1206//xx	—	2.75	6.50	10.00	15.00	22.50
AH1206//36	—	2.75	6.50	10.00	15.00	22.50
AH1209//36	—	2.75	6.50	10.00	15.00	22.50
AH1212//40	—	2.75	6.50	10.00	15.00	22.50
AH1213//41	—	2.75	6.50	10.00	15.00	22.50
AH1212//42 (sic)	—	2.75	6.50	10.00	15.00	22.50
AH1215//42	—	4.25	6.50	10.00	15.00	22.50

KM# 166 RUPEE
Silver **Obv. Inscription:** "Shah Alam II" **Mint:** Merta **Note:** Weight varies 10.70-11.60 grams.

Date	Mintage	Good	VG	F	VF	XF
AH1188	—	5.00	12.50	21.50	30.00	40.00
AH1201//28	—	5.00	12.50	21.50	30.00	40.00
AH1201//29	—	5.00	12.50	21.50	30.00	40.00
AH1202//30	—	5.00	12.50	21.50	30.00	40.00
AH1203//31	—	5.00	12.50	21.50	30.00	40.00
AH1203//32 (sic)	—	5.00	12.50	21.50	30.00	40.00
AH1203//33 (sic)	—	5.00	12.50	21.50	30.00	40.00
AH1206//35 (sic)	—	5.00	12.50	21.50	30.00	40.00
AH1207//36 (sic)	—	5.00	12.50	21.50	30.00	40.00
AH1209//37	—	5.00	12.50	21.50	30.00	40.00

KM# 177.1 RUPEE
Silver **Obv. Inscription:** "Shah Alam II" **Reverse:** "Nagore" at top **Mint:** Nagor **Note:** Weight varies 11.20-11.30 grams.

Date	Mintage	Good	VG	F	VF	XF
AH1190//18	—	6.00	15.00	25.00	40.00	60.00
AH1191	—	6.00	15.00	25.00	40.00	60.00
AH1193//19 (sic)	—	6.00	15.00	25.00	40.00	60.00
AH1194	—	6.00	15.00	25.00	40.00	60.00
AH1197//24	—	6.00	15.00	25.00	40.00	60.00
AH1196//26 (sic)	—	6.00	15.00	25.00	40.00	60.00
AH1200//28	—	6.00	15.00	25.00	40.00	60.00
AH1201//28	—	6.00	15.00	25.00	40.00	60.00
AH1203	—	6.00	15.00	25.00	40.00	60.00
AH1204//33	—	6.00	15.00	25.00	40.00	60.00
AH1215	—	6.00	15.00	25.00	40.00	60.00

KM# 6 RUPEE
Silver **Obv. Inscription:** "Shah Alam II" **Reverse:** Nagari "Sri" and Jhar **Mint:** Ajmer **Note:** Weight varies 10.80-11.90 grams. See also Gwalior-Ajmir and Kuchaman Mint listings.

Date	Mintage	Good	VG	F	VF	XF
AH1203//31	—	10.00	15.00	20.00	30.00	45.00

KM# 177a RUPEE
Silver **Obverse:** Sword **Mint:** Nagor **Note:** Weight varies 11.20-11.30 grams.

Date	Mintage	VG	F	VF	XF	Unc
AH1215//42	—	—	—	—	—	—

KM# 22 NAZARANA RUPEE
11.3000 g., Silver **Series:** Bijai Shahi **Obv. Inscription:** "Shah Alam II" **Mint:** Jodhpur **Note:** Round flan. Size varies 32-33mm.

Date	Mintage	Good	VG	F	VF	XF
AH1209//36	—	—	60.00	85.00	120	170

JODHPUR FEUDATORY - KUCHAWAN

Kuchaman was a semi-independent feudatory. The Thakur of Kuchaman, an Udawat Rajput, was the only feudatory of Jodhpur permitted to strike his own coinage.

Refer also to Gwalior-Ajmir Mint and Maratha Confederacy-Ajmir Mint.

KUCHAWAN

Shah Alam II

AH1173-1221 / 1759-1806AD

HAMMERED COINAGE

KM# 274 1/4 RUPEE
2.7000 g., Silver, 13 mm. **Series:** Bopushahi

Date	Mintage	Good	VG	F	VF	XF
AH1203//31	—	2.75	7.00	11.00	16.50	25.00

KM# 275 1/2 RUPEE
Silver, 16-17 mm. **Note:** Weight varies: 5.3-5.4 grams. Size varies.

Date	Mintage	Good	VG	F	VF	XF
AH1203//31	—	3.00	7.50	12.50	18.50	27.50

KM# 276 RUPEE
Silver **Note:** Weight varies: 10.5-10.9 grams.

Date	Mintage	Good	VG	F	VF	XF
AH1203//31	—	2.75	6.50	10.00	15.00	22.50

KAITHAL

A town located in Haryana in northwest India. The jat rajas of this small feudatory were descended from the elder branch of the Patiala royal family.

RULERS
Desu Singh, 1767-1787AD
Lal Singh, 1781-1819AD

Identifying marks

PRINCELY STATE

HAMMERED COINAGE

KM# 10 RUPEE
Silver **Obv. Inscription:** Shah Alam (II) **Note:** Weight varies: 10.70-11.60 grams.

Date	Mintage	Good	VG	F	VF	XF
ND(1767-1819)	—	15.00	25.00	35.00	50.00	75.00

KM# 11 MOHUR
10.7000 g., Gold, 14 mm. **Obv. Inscription:** Shah Alam (II)

Date	Mintage	Good	VG	F	VF	XF
ND(1767-1819)	—	—	600	900	1,400	2,000

KALSIA

A Sikh state located in the Punjab.

MINT

چحچرولي

Chhachrauli

BRITISH PROTECTORATE

HAMMERED COINAGE

KM# 32 PAISA

Copper **Obverse:** Dagger mint mark **Reverse:** Quatrefoil and sword

Date	Mintage	Good	VG	F	VF	XF
AH1214/41 (1799)	—	15.00	25.00	40.00	60.00	—
AH1215//41 (sic) (1800)	—	15.00	25.00	40.00	60.00	—
AH1215/42 (1800)	—	15.00	25.00	40.00	60.00	—
AH1216//41 (sic) (1801) Error	—	15.00	25.00	40.00	60.00	—
AH1218//44 (sic) (1803)	—	15.00	25.00	40.00	60.00	—

KARAULI

State located in Rajputana, northwest India.

Karauli was established in the 11th century by Jadon Rajputs, of the same stock as the royal house of Jaisalmir. They are thought to have migrated to Rajasthan from the Mathura region some years earlier. The state passed successively under Mughal and Maratha suzerainty before coming under British authority in 1817.

The Maharajas of Karauli first struck coins in the reign of Manak Pal.

RULER

Manak Pal, AH1186-1233/1772-1817AD

MINT

كرولي and करौली

Karauli

MINT NAME

سواي جيپور

Sawai Jaipur

MINT MARKS

Katar jhar on reverse

KINGDOM, BRITISH PROTECTORATE

HAMMERED COINAGE

Mughal Style

KM# 11 TAKKA (2 Paise)

Copper **Obv. Inscription:** "Shah Alam II" **Note:** Weight varies 17.35-17.8 grams; similar to one Rupee, KM#16.

Date	Mintage	Good	VG	F	VF	XF
ND//25 (1783-84)	—	3.00	6.00	10.00	16.50	—
ND//26 (1784-85)	—	3.00	6.00	10.00	16.50	—
ND//30 (1788-89)	—	3.00	6.00	10.00	16.50	—
ND//33 (1791-92)	—	3.00	6.00	10.00	16.50	—
ND//38 (1796-97)	—	3.00	6.00	10.00	16.50	—

KM# 16 RUPEE

Silver **Obv. Inscription:** "Shah Alam II" **Note:** Weight varies: 10.8-11.2 grams.

Date	Mintage	Good	VG	F	VF	XF
AH1197//24	—	8.00	20.00	31.50	42.50	60.00
ND//28 (1786-87)	—	8.00	20.00	31.50	42.50	60.00
ND//29 (1787-88)	—	8.00	20.00	31.50	42.50	60.00
ND//30 (1788-89)	—	8.00	20.00	31.50	42.50	60.00
ND//40 (1798-99)	—	8.00	20.00	31.50	42.50	60.00
ND//41 (1799-1800)	—	8.00	20.00	31.50	42.50	60.00
ND//42 (1800-01)	—	8.00	20.00	31.50	42.50	60.00

KISHANGARH

The maharajas of Kishangarh, a small state in northwest India, in the vicinity of Ajmer, belonged to the Rathor Rajputs. The town of Kishangarh, which gave its name to the state, was founded in 1611 and was itself named after Kishen Singh, the first ruler. The maharajas succeeded in reaching terms with Akbar in the late 16th century, and again in 1818 with the British. In 1949 the state was merged into Rajasthan.

RULERS

Birad Singh, VS1838-1845/1781-1788AD
Pratap Sinah, VS1845-1854/1788-1797AD
Kalyan Singh, VS1854-1889/1797-1832AD

MINT

Kishangarh

MINT MARK

Symbol on reverse: Jhar

KINGDOM

HAMMERED COINAGE

Mughal Style

C# 4 1/4 PAISA

Copper **Obv. Inscription:** "Shah Alam II" **Mint:** Kishangarh **Note:** Weight varies 3.5-3.6 grams.

Date	Mintage	Good	VG	F	VF	XF
AH1199//25	—	3.50	6.00	10.00	16.50	—

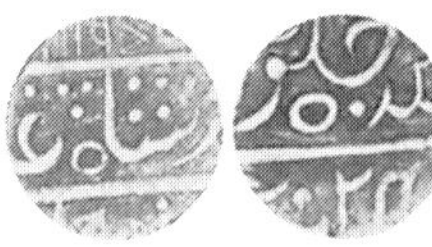

C# 8 1/4 RUPEE

Silver **Obv. Inscription:** "Shah Alam II" **Mint:** Kishangarh **Note:** Weight varies 2.68-2.9 grams.

Date	Mintage	Good	VG	F	VF	XF
AH1198//24	—	—	12.50	18.50	25.00	35.00

C# 10.2 RUPEE

Silver **Obv. Inscription:** "Shah Alam II" **Reverse:** Flowers **Mint:** Kishangarh **Note:** Weight varies 10.6-10.95 grams.

Date	Mintage	Good	VG	F	VF	XF
AH1197//24	—	—	16.50	23.50	32.50	45.00
AH1198//24	—	—	16.50	23.50	32.50	45.00

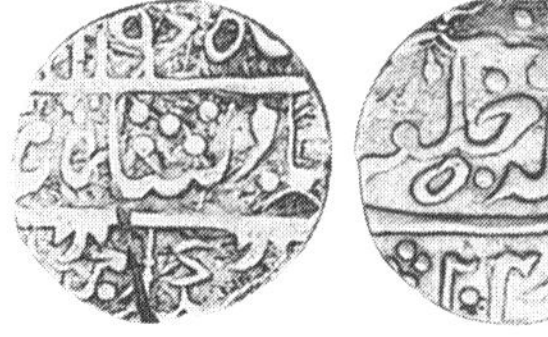

C# 10.1 RUPEE

Silver **Obv. Inscription:** "Shah Alam II" **Reverse:** Jhar **Mint:** Kishangarh **Note:** Weight varies 10.75-10.85 grams.

Date	Mintage	Good	VG	F	VF	XF
AH1197//24	—	—	13.50	20.00	27.50	37.50
AH1198//24	—	—	13.50	20.00	27.50	37.50
AH1198//25	—	—	13.50	20.00	27.50	37.50
AH1199//24	—	—	13.50	20.00	27.50	37.50

C# 17 MOHUR

Gold **Obv. Inscription:** "Shah Alam II" **Mint:** Kishangarh **Note:** Weight varies 10.9-11.0 grams.

Date	Mintage	Good	VG	F	VF	XF
ND//24 (1782)	—	—	185	300	600	1,000

KOLHAPUR

Maratha state is located in southwest India between Goa and Bombay.

The maharajas of Kolhapur traced their origins and ancestry to Raja Ram, son of Shivaji, the founder of the Maratha kingdom, and to his courageous wife Tarabai, who officiated as regent on behalf of her son after Raja Ram's death in 1698. Kolhapur's existence as a separate state dates from about 1730 when a family quarrel left Sambaji, the great-grandson of Sivaji, as the first raja of Kolhapur. In recognition of their special eminence among the Maratha chieftains, the rulers of Kolhapur bore the honorific title of "Chhatrapati Maharaja". Between 1811 and 1862 Kolhapur concluded a series of treaties and agreements with the British whereby the state came increasingly under British protection and control.

The mint closed ca. 1850AD.

MINT

Mint name: A'zamnagar Gokak, Pseudo

BRITISH PROTECTORATE

HAMMERED COINAGE

Mughal Style

C# 14 1/4 RUPEE

Silver, 12 mm. **Obv. Inscription:** "Muhammad Shah" **Note:** Weight varies 2.68-2.90 grams.

Date	Mintage	Good	VG	F	VF	XF
ND(1759-1839)	—	5.00	12.50	20.00	30.00	50.00

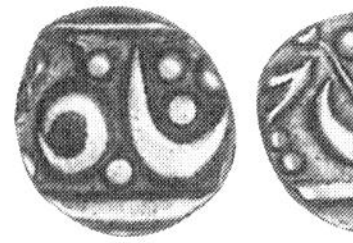

C# 15 1/2 RUPEE

Silver, 15 mm. **Obv. Inscription:** "Muhammad Shah" **Note:** Weight varies 5.35-5.80 grams.

Date	Mintage	Good	VG	F	VF	XF
ND(1759-1839)	—	5.00	12.50	20.00	30.00	50.00

C# 16 RUPEE

Silver **Obv. Inscription:** "Muhammad Shah" **Note:** Weight varies 10.70-11.60 grams.

Date	Mintage	Good	VG	F	VF	XF
ND(1759-1839)	—	4.50	9.00	15.00	25.00	42.50

KOTAH

Kotah State, located in northwest India was subdivided out of Bundi early in the 17th century when it was given to a younger son of the Bundi raja by the Mughal emperor. The ruler, or maharao, was a Chauhan Rajput. During the years of Maratha ascendancy Kotah fell on hard times, especially from the depredations of Holkar. In 1817 the State came under treaty with the British.

MINT

نندگانو

Mint name: *Nandgaon*

نندگانو عرف كوته

Kotah urf Nandgaon
or *Nandgaon urf Kotah* on earliest issues.

MINT MARKS

Mint mark #1 appears beneath #4 on most Kotah coins, and serves to distinguish coins of Kotah from similar issues of Bundi in the pre-Victoria period.

C#28 has mint mark #2 on obv., #1, 3 and 4 on rev. All later issues have #1 on obv., #1, 5 and 4 on rev.

BRITISH PROTECTORATE

HAMMERED COINAGE

Mughal Style

C# 20 TAKKA

Copper **Obv. Inscription:** "Shah Alam II" **Note:** Weight varies 17.5-18.5 grams.

Date	Mintage	Good	VG	F	VF	XF
ND//23 (1781-82)	—	3.00	4.00	5.50	8.00	—
ND//25 (1783-84)	—	3.00	4.00	5.50	8.00	—
ND//28 (1786-87)	—	3.00	4.00	5.50	8.00	—
ND//30 (1788-89)	—	3.00	4.00	5.50	8.00	—
ND//39 (1797-98)	—	3.00	4.00	5.50	8.00	—
ND//41 (1798-99)	—	3.00	4.00	5.50	8.00	—

C# 10 RUPEE

11.3500 g., Silver **Obv. Inscription:** "Alamgir (II) Badshah Ghazi..." **Edge:** Plain

Date	Mintage	Good	VG	F	VF	XF
ND//6 (1752-53)	—	—	—	—	—	—

C# 28.1 RUPEE

Silver **Obv. Inscription:** Shah Alam (II) **Reverse:** Flower mint mark in front of regnal year **Note:** Struck at Kotah urf Nandgaon; weight varies 11.05-11.2 grams.

Date	Mintage	Good	VG	F	VF	XF
AH118x//5	—	3.50	8.50	13.50	20.00	28.50
ND//7 (1765-66)	—	3.50	8.50	13.50	20.00	28.50
ND//8 (1766-67)	—	3.50	8.50	13.50	20.00	28.50
ND//9 (1767-68)	—	3.50	8.50	13.50	20.00	28.50

C# 28.2 RUPEE

Silver **Obv. Inscription:** Shah Alam (II) **Reverse:** Flower mint mark in front of regnal year **Note:** Struck at Kotah urfNandgaon; weight varies 11.05-11.20 grams.

Date	Mintage	Good	VG	F	VF	XF
ND//10 (1769)	—	3.50	8.50	13.50	20.00	28.50

C# 28.3 RUPEE

Silver **Obv. Inscription:** "Shah Alam II" **Reverse:** Flower mint mark in front of regnal year **Mint:** Nandgaon **Note:** Weight varies 11.05-11.20 grams.

Date	Mintage	Good	VG	F	VF	XF
ND//24 (1782-83)	—	3.50	8.50	13.50	20.00	28.50
AH1199//25 (sic)	—	3.50	8.50	13.50	20.00	28.50
ND//26 (1784-85)	—	3.50	8.50	13.50	20.00	28.50
ND//27 (1785-86)	—	3.50	8.50	13.50	20.00	28.50
ND//28 (1786-87)	—	3.50	8.50	13.50	20.00	28.50
ND//29 (1787-88)	—	3.50	8.50	13.50	20.00	28.50
ND//30 (1788-89)	—	3.50	8.50	13.50	20.00	28.50
ND//31 (1789)	—	3.50	8.50	13.50	20.00	28.50
ND//32 (1790-91)	—	3.50	8.50	13.50	20.00	28.50
ND//33 (1791-92)	—	3.50	8.50	13.50	20.00	28.50
ND//34 (1792-93)	—	3.50	8.50	13.50	20.00	28.50
ND//35 (1793-94)	—	3.50	8.50	13.50	20.00	28.50
ND//36 (1794-95)	—	3.50	8.50	13.50	20.00	28.50
ND//37 (1795-96)	—	3.50	8.50	13.50	20.00	28.50
ND//38 (1796-97)	—	3.50	8.50	13.50	20.00	28.50
ND//41 (1799-1800)	—	3.50	8.50	13.50	20.00	28.50
ND//42 (1800-01)	—	4.50	8.50	13.50	20.00	28.50

LADAKH

Ladakh, a district in northern India, contained the western Himalayas and the valley of the upper Indus river. Area: 45,762 sq. mi. Capital: Leh.

In 1639, the Moghuls marched on Ladakh and defeated them near Karpu. The King Sen-ge-rnam-rgyal promised to pay tribute, if allowed to return home, but never did. In 1665, the Moghul governor of Kashmir demanded the acceptance of Moghul suzerainty under threat of invasion. Knowing the strength of Aurangzeb, King Deb-Idan-rnam-rgyal sent a tribute of gold ashraphis, rupees and other precious objects. It is probable that coins were struck for this occasion in the name of Aurangzeb but no such coins have yet been discovered.

For the next century no further mention is made of coins until in 1781 it is recorded that a Muslim goldsmith from Leh was hired to strike Ladakhi coins called ja'u.

The obverse of the first Ladakhi timashas or ja'u is a close copy of the Farrukhsiyar inscription of the early Garhwali timashas even including the regnal year at the bottom. The reverse has a clearly written Zarb Tibet at the bottom and dots at the top. At the center are crescents and an illegible inscription.

On some of the early Ladakh coins Hejira dates appear which coincide with the period when the Garhwal mint was closed and trade was diverted from Garhwal to Ladakh. No other Ladakh coins of this first issue have been discovered with a literate date. Between 1781 and 1803 it is likely that a considerable number of ja'u were struck. Most specimens were of good silver but later issues were very debased because of the scarcity of silver.

The next type of coin has a different obverse with the Muslim title of the King of Ladakh clearly inscribed as well as the number 14 at the lower left. This issue may have been prompted to demonstrate Ladakhi independence and is the only ja'u to bear a date.

The most remarkable of all Ladakhi coins has a fully legible inscription on the obverse in smaller writing and is enclosed in a circle with no regnal year. The reverse legend refers to the prime minister as well as the title of the king and is the only Ladakhi coin to do so and is very rare.

The appearance of Mahmud Shah on the obverse of the next type coin is thought to acknowledge suzeraintу of the ruler of Kashmir. There is a plain circle surrounded by a border of dots. The reverse reverts to the earlier designs but has a finer style with thicker writing.

The next change in type took place after the conquest of Ladakh by Gulab Singh and the Dogra army in 1835.After a crushing defeat of the Dogra army in Tibet, the Ladakhis tried to shake off the Dogra supremacy but the rebellion was crushed. Ladakh was now firmly incorporated within the Empire of Jammu and the monarchy was abolished. Until 1845, Gulab Singh acknowledged Sikh suzerainty but ruled Ladakh as a part of Jammu.

After the defeat of the Sikhs by the British, Gulab Singh offered to pay the war indemnities to the British in exchange for being made independent ruler of Jammu and Kashmir.

Two types of ja'u were struck during the period of the Dogra domination. One combined the tiger knife and Mahmud Shah design and the other the tiger knife and Raja Gulab Singh in Nagari script.

Between 1867 and 1870 an issue of copper coins was made for Ladakh for local use and in 1871 a small issue of ja'u was made. Neither of these coins seemed to have much commercial impact in Ladakh and their issue was suspended after 1871. No special currency was struck in or for Ladakh after this.

KINGDOM

HAMMERED COINAGE

KM# 1.3 JA'U

Silver **Obverse:** Rosettes at bottom

Date	Mintage	Good	VG	F	VF	XF
ND(1771-1815)	—	5.00	10.00	15.00	25.00	—

KM# 2 JA'U

Silver **Obverse:** Square around "Siyar" of Farrukhsiyar

Date	Mintage	Good	VG	F	VF	XF
ND(1771-1815)	—	35.00	60.00	90.00	125	—

KM# 1.1 JA'U

Silver **Obverse:** Without date **Reverse:** Top legend "Butan" and bottom legend "Zarb Tibet"

Date	Mintage	Good	VG	F	VF	XF
ND(1771-1815)	—	5.00	10.00	15.00	25.00	—

KM# 1.2 JA'U

Silver **Obverse:** Date

Date	Mintage	Good	VG	F	VF	XF
AH1185	—	8.50	15.00	25.00	35.00	—
AH114x (sic)	—	7.50	12.50	20.00	30.00	—
AH1186	—	8.50	15.00	25.00	35.00	—

MALER KOTLA

State located in the Punjab in northwest India, founded by the Maler Kotla family who were Sherwani Afghans who had travelled to India from Kabul in 1467 as officials of the Delhi emperors.

Coins are rupees of Ahmad Shah Durrani, and except for the last ruler, contain the chief's initial on the reverse. The chiefs were called Ra'is until 1821, Nawabs thereafter.

For similar issues see Jind, Nabha and Patiala.

RULERS

Umar Khan, AH1182-1192/1768-1778AD

Identifying marks on reverse

Asadullah Khan, AH1192-1197/1778-1782AD

Identifying marks on reverse

PRINCELY STATE

Umar Khan

AH1182-1192 / 1768-1778AD

HAMMERED COINAGE

C# 5 RUPEE

Silver, 17 mm. **Note:** 10.70-11.60 grams.

Date	Mintage	Good	VG	F	VF	XF
ND/4 (1768-78) Frozen	—	4.75	12.00	20.00	27.50	37.50

Asadullah Khan

AH1192-1197 / 1778-1782AD

HAMMERED COINAGE

C# 10 RUPEE

Silver, 17 mm. **Note:** 10.70-11.60 grams.

Date	Mintage	Good	VG	F	VF	XF
ND/4 (1778-82) Frozen	—	4.00	10.00	16.50	25.00	35.00

MEWAR

State located in Rajputana, northwest India. Capital:Udaipur.

The rulers of Mewar were universally regarded as the highest ranking Rajput house in India. The maharana of Mewar was looked upon as the representative of Rama, the ancient king of Ayodhya - and the family who were Sesodia Rajputs of the Gehlot clan, traced its descent through Rama to Kanak Sen who ruled in the 2nd century. The clan is believed to have migrated to Chitor from Gujarat sometime in the 8th century.

None of the indigenous rulers of India resisted the Muslim invasions into India with greater tenacity than the Rajputs of Mewar. It was their proud boast that they had never permitted a daughter to go into the Mughal harem. Three times the fortress and town of Chitor had fallen to Muslim invaders, to Alauddin Khilji (1303), to Bahadur Shah of Gujarat (1534) and to Akbar (1568). Each time Chitor gradually recovered but the last was the most traumatic experience of all. Rather than to submit to the Mughal onslaught, the women burned themselves on funeral pyres in a fearful rite called jauhar, and the men fell on the swords of the invaders.

After the sacking of Chitor the rana, Udai Singh, retired to the Aravali hills where he founded Udaipur, the capital after 1570. Udai Singh's son, Partab, refused to submit to the Mughal and recovered most of the territory lost in 1568. In the early 19th century Mewar suffered much at the hands of Marathas - Holkar, Sindhia and the Pindaris - until, in 1818, the State came under British supervision. In April 1948 Mewar was merged into Rajasthan and the maharana became governor Maharaj pramukh of the new province.

RULERS

Jai Singh II, AH1168-1175/1753-1760AD
Ari Singh II, AH1175-1187/1760-1772AD
Hammir Singh II, AH1187-1192/1772-1777AD
Bhim Singh, AH1192-1244/1777-1828AD

MINTS

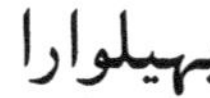

Bhilwara

Struck at Bhilwara Mint between ca. 1760 to the middle of the 19th century with fictitious mint epithet: *Dar al-Khilafat Shahjahanabad.*

Mint mark

jhar

चितोड़

Chitor

Struck at Chitor Mint between ca. 1760 to the middle of the 19th century with fictitious mint epithet: *Dar al-Khilafat Shahjahanabad.*

Mint marks

 and flag  on obverse

चित्रकूट

Chitarkot

उदयपुर

Udaipur

and ★ on obverse

Mint mark

Old Chandori Series

Ordered by Bhim Singh, and struck at the Udaipur Mint until 1842AD. Recalled by Swarup Shah.

 on obverse  on reverse

 on obverse

Symbol

Struck at the Udaipur mint between ca. 1780 to the middle of the 19th century with fictitious mint epithet: *Dar al-Khilafat Shahjahanabad.*

NOTE: All Mewar coinage is struck without ruler's name, and is largely undated. Certain types were generally struck over several reigns.

BRITISH PROTECTORATE

HAMMERED COINAGE

C# 2.5 PAISA

Copper **Obverse:** Symbol vertical **Obv. Inscription:** "Shah Alam (II)" **Mint:** Bhilwara

Date	Mintage	Good	VG	F	VF	XF
ND//4 (1760-1806)	—	3.00	5.00	7.50	11.50	—

Note: Known as the old Bhilwari Paisa, struck between 1780 and 1800AD

C# 3.1 PAISA

Copper **Obverse:** Leaf **Obv. Inscription:** "Shah Alam (II)" **Mint:** Bhilwara

Date	Mintage	Good	VG	F	VF	XF
ND(1760-1806)	—	1.50	2.50	4.00	6.50	—

C# 3.2 PAISA

Copper **Obverse:** Symbol oblique **Obv. Inscription:** "Shah Alam II" **Mint:** Bhilwara

Date	Mintage	Good	VG	F	VF	XF
ND//5 (1760-1806)	—	1.50	2.50	4.00	6.50	—
ND//12 (1760-1806)	—	1.50	2.50	4.00	6.50	—

Note: Known as the new Bhilwari Paisa, struck between about 1795 and 1845

C# 5 PAISA

Copper **Obverse:** Symbol **Obv. Inscription:** "Shah Alam II" **Reverse:** Legend **Mint:** Bhilwara

Date	Mintage	Good	VG	F	VF	XF
ND(1760-1806)	—	1.50	2.50	4.00	6.50	—

C# 1.1 PAISA

Copper **Obverse:** Pennant **Obv. Inscription:** "Shah Alam II" **Reverse:** Trident **Mint:** Chitor

Date	Mintage	Good	VG	F	VF	XF
ND(1760-1806)	—	1.50	2.50	4.00	6.50	—

C# 1.2 PAISA

Copper **Obverse:** Palm frond **Obv. Inscription:** "Shah Alam II" **Mint:** Chitor

Date	Mintage	Good	VG	F	VF	XF
ND(1760-1806)	—	1.50	2.50	4.00	6.50	—

C# 27 PAISA

Copper **Obv. Inscription:** "Alamgir II" **Mint:** Udaipur **Note:** Weight varies 10.00-10.20 grams.

Date	Mintage	Good	VG	F	VF	XF
ND(1780-1850)	—	—	—	—	—	—

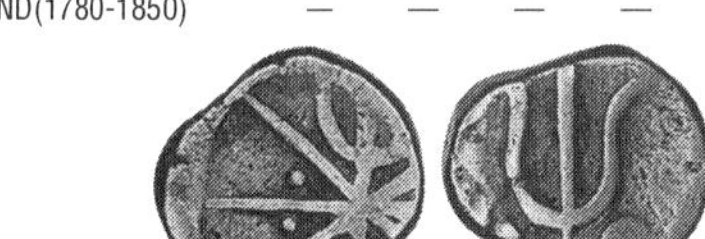

C# 2.1 2 PIES

Copper **Obv. Inscription:** "Shah Alam II" **Mint:** Chitor

Date	Mintage	Good	VG	F	VF	XF
ND(1760-1806)	—	0.45	0.75	1.25	1.75	—

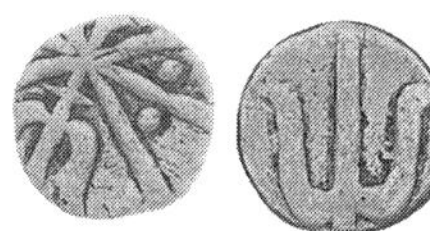

C# 2.2 2 PIES

Copper **Obv. Inscription:** "Shah Alam II" **Mint:** Chitor

Date	Mintage	Good	VG	F	VF	XF
ND(1760-1806)	—	0.60	1.00	1.40	2.00	—

C# 2.3 2 PIES

Copper **Obverse:** Pennant **Obv. Inscription:** "Shah Alam II" **Reverse:** Trident **Mint:** Chitor

Date	Mintage	Good	VG	F	VF	XF
ND(1760-1806)	—	1.50	2.50	4.00	6.50	—

Note: Struck by local coppersmiths

C# 22 1/16 RUPEE

0.7000 g., Silver **Obv. Inscription:** "Alamgir II" **Mint:** Chitor

Date	Mintage	Good	VG	F	VF	XF
ND(1760-1850)	—	3.00	7.50	12.50	20.00	30.00

C# 23 1/8 RUPEE

1.3000 g., Silver **Obv. Inscription:** "Alamgir II" **Mint:** Chitor

Date	Mintage	Good	VG	F	VF	XF
ND(1760-1850)	—	3.00	7.50	12.50	20.00	30.00

C# 24 1/4 RUPEE

Silver **Obv. Inscription:** "Alamgir II" **Mint:** Chitor **Note:** Weight varies 2.60-2.70 grams.

Date	Mintage	Good	VG	F	VF	XF
ND(1760-1850)	—	2.50	6.00	10.00	15.00	25.00

C# 30 1/4 RUPEE

2.7000 g., Silver **Obv. Inscription:** "Alamgir II" **Mint:** Udaipur

Date	Mintage	Good	VG	F	VF	XF
ND(1780-1850)	—	3.00	7.50	12.50	20.00	30.00

C# 25 1/2 RUPEE

Silver **Obv. Inscription:** "Alamgir II" **Mint:** Chitor **Note:** Weight varies 5.30-5.40 grams.

Date	Mintage	Good	VG	F	VF	XF
ND(1760-1850)	—	2.50	6.00	10.00	15.00	25.00

C# 43 1/2 RUPEE

Silver **Obv. Inscription:** "Alamgir II" **Mint:** Udaipur **Note:** Weight varies 5.35-5.80 grams.

Date	Mintage	Good	VG	F	VF	XF
ND(1777-1842)	—	2.75	7.00	11.00	16.50	25.00

C# 31 1/2 RUPEE

5.4000 g., Silver **Obv. Inscription:** "Alamgir II" **Mint:** Udaipur

Date	Mintage	Good	VG	F	VF	XF
ND(1780-1850)	—	3.00	7.50	12.50	20.00	30.00

C# 26 RUPEE

Silver **Obv. Inscription:** "Alamgir II" **Mint:** Chitor **Note:** Weight varies 10.70-11.10 grams.

Date	Mintage	Good	VG	F	VF	XF
ND(1760-1850)	—	4.25	5.00	7.00	10.00	15.00
AH1180	—	4.00	10.00	20.00	30.00	45.00

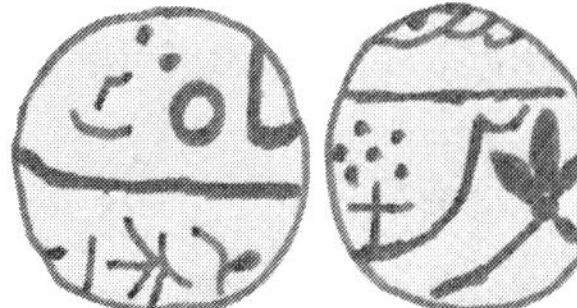

C# 44 RUPEE

Silver **Obv. Inscription:** "Alamgir II" **Mint:** Udaipur **Note:** Weight varies 10.90-11.00 grams.

Date	Mintage	Good	VG	F	VF	XF
ND(1777-1842)	—	4.25	7.00	11.00	16.50	25.00

C# 32 RUPEE

11.8000 g., Silver **Obv. Inscription:** "Alamgir II" **Mint:** Udaipur

Date	Mintage	Good	VG	F	VF	XF
ND(1780-1850)	—	4.25	6.00	8.00	12.50	18.50

C# A27 NAZARANA RUPEE

Silver **Obv. Inscription:** "Alamgir II Shah" **Mint:** Chitor **Note:** Weight varies 10.70-11.10 grams.

Date	Mintage	Good	VG	F	VF	XF
ND(1760-1850)	—	—	—	—	—	—

Fatteh Singh

VS1941-1986 / 1884-1929AD

HAMMERED COINAGE

C# 38 RUPEE

Silver **Mint:** Bhilwara **Note:** Weight varies: 10.70-11.10 grams.

Date	Mintage	Good	VG	F	VF	XF
AH-//1	—	4.00	10.00	20.00	30.00	45.00
ND//1 (1760-1850)	—	5.00	10.00	20.00	30.00	45.00
ND//2 (1760-1850)	—	5.00	10.00	20.00	30.00	45.00
ND//3 (1760-1850)	—	5.00	10.00	20.00	30.00	45.00
ND//4 (1760-1850)	—	5.00	10.00	20.00	30.00	45.00
ND//5 (1760-1850)	—	5.00	10.00	20.00	30.00	45.00
ND//6 (1760-1850)	—	5.00	10.00	20.00	30.00	45.00
ND//7 (1760-1850)	—	5.00	10.00	20.00	30.00	45.00
ND//8 (1760-1850)	—	5.00	10.00	20.00	30.00	45.00

MYSORE

Large state in Southern India. Governed until 1761AD by various Hindu dynasties, then by Haider Ali and Tipu Sultan.

In 1831, Krishnaraja being deposed for mal-administration and pensioned off, the administration of Mysore State then came directly under the British. The coinage of Mysore ceased in 1843. After the Great Revolt of 1857, the policy of eliminating Indian princes was discontinued and as a result, Mysore was returned in 1881 to the control of an adopted son of Krishnaraja Wodeyar. The Wodeyars continued to hold the State until 1947 although they did not issue coins. In November 1956 modern Mysore was inaugurated as a linguistic state within the Indian Union.

NOTE: For earlier issues see Mysore, Independent Kingdoms during British rule.

RULER

Dewan Purnaiya, regent AH1214-1225/1799-1810AD

MINTS

مهيسور مهي سور

Mysore

ناگور

Nagar

MONETARY SYSTEM

2 Fanams = 1 Anna
4 Annas = 1 Pavali
4 Pavalis = 1 Rupee

BRITISH PROTECTORATE

ANONYMOUS HAMMERED COINAGE

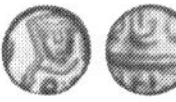

C# 199 1/6 PAVALI

Silver **Obv. Inscription:** "Shah Alam II" **Mint:** Mysore **Note:** Weight varies 0.45-0.48 grams.

Date	Mintage	Good	VG	F	VF	XF
ND(1799-1810)	—	2.25	5.50	11.00	18.00	25.00

C# 200 1/3 PAVALI

Silver **Obverse:** Dancing figure (Chamundi) **Obv. Inscription:** "Shah Alam II" **Mint:** Mysore **Note:** Weight varies 0.89-0.96 grams.

Date	Mintage	VG	F	VF	XF	Unc
ND(1799-1810)	—	12.50	25.00	42.00	70.00	—

C# 201 2/3 PAVALI

Silver **Obverse:** Dancing figure (Chamundi) **Obv. Inscription:** "Shah Alam II" **Mint:** Mysore **Note:** Weight varies: 1.78-1.92 grams.

Date	Mintage	Good	VG	F	VF	XF
ND(1799-1810)	—	5.00	12.50	25.00	42.00	70.00

C# 206 1/2 RUPEE

Silver **Obv. Inscription:** "Shah Alam II" **Mint:** Mysore **Note:** Weight varies 5.35-5.80 grams.

Date	Mintage	Good	VG	F	VF	XF
ND//35 (1793-94)	—	6.00	15.00	25.00	40.00	60.00
ND//39 (1797-98)	—	6.00	15.00	25.00	40.00	60.00

C# 207 RUPEE

Silver **Obv. Inscription:** "Shah Alam II" **Mint:** Mysore **Note:** Weight varies 10.70-11.60 grams.

Date	Mintage	Good	VG	F	VF	XF
AH1214//39 (sic)	—	5.00	7.50	12.50	20.00	30.00
AH1215//39 (sic)	—	5.00	7.50	12.50	20.00	30.00

C# 212 FANAM

Gold **Subject:** Narasimha **Obv. Inscription:** "Shah Alam II" **Mint:** Mysore **Note:** Weight varies: 0.33-0.40 grams.

Date	Mintage	Good	VG	F	VF	XF
ND(1799-1810)	—	—	7.50	10.00	20.00	30.00

Dewan Purnaiya
AH1214-1225 / 1799-1810AD

A Sardula (mythical tiger) is illustrated on all of Dewan Purnaiya's coins.

HAMMERED COINAGE

C# 185 6-1/4 CASH

Copper **Obverse:** Sardula (mythical tiger) **Reverse:** Without value, with Mysore **Mint:** Mysore

Date	Mintage	Good	VG	F	VF	XF
ND(1799-1810)	—	4.00	6.50	10.00	16.00	—

C# 185a 6-1/4 CASH

Copper **Obverse:** Sardula (mythical tiger) **Reverse:** Without value or Mysore **Mint:** Mysore

Date	Mintage	Good	VG	F	VF	XF
ND(1799-1810)	—	5.00	10.00	15.00	20.00	—

C# 185b 6-1/4 CASH

Copper **Obverse:** Sardula (mythical tiger) **Reverse:** Value in English, with Mysore **Mint:** Mysore

Date	Mintage	Good	VG	F	VF	XF
ND(1799-1810)	—	3.00	5.50	9.00	14.00	—
ND(1799-1810) CASH retrograde	—	4.00	6.50	10.00	16.00	—

C# 186 12-1/2 CASH

Copper **Obverse:** Sardula (mythical tiger) **Mint:** Mysore

Date	Mintage	Good	VG	F	VF	XF
ND(1799-1810)	—	7.00	12.00	18.00	28.00	—

C# 187 25 CASH

Copper **Obverse:** Sardula (mythical tiger) **Reverse:** English legend often blundered **Mint:** Mysore

Date	Mintage	Good	VG	F	VF	XF
ND(1799-1810)	—	10.00	15.00	25.00	50.00	—

C# 189 75 CASH

23.5900 g., Copper **Obverse:** Sardula (mythical tiger) **Mint:** Mysore

Date	Mintage	Good	VG	F	VF	XF
ND(1799-1810)	—	—	—	—	—	—

Note: Silver coinage of Dewan Purnaiya is identical to that of Krishna Raja Wodeyar and they are all listed together following these copper issues

NABHA

Cis-Sutlej state located in the Punjab in northwest India and founded in the 18th century.

The ancestry of these rulers was identical to that of Jind. Until 1845 Nabha's history closely paralleled that of Patiala. At this point, however, the raja sided with the Sikhs. It was left to his son to make amends to the British in 1847 after the first Sikh war (1845-46). Their independence became somewhat circumscribed and in 1849 the Punjab was annexed and the states were merged into the new province of British India.

RULERS

Bharpur Singh, VS1903-1920/1846-1863AD
Identifying Marks:

On reverse

Hira Singh, VS1928-1968/1871-19
Identifying Marks:

On reverse

MINTS

سرکار نابهہ

Sarkar Nabha

PRINCELY STATE

Jaswant Singh
VS1840-1897 / 1783-1840AD

HAMMERED COINAGE

C# 20.1 RUPEE

Silver **Obv. Inscription:** Ahmad Shah Durrani **Reverse:** Cross-like symbol below "Sin"

Date	Mintage	Good	VG	F	VF	XF
ND(1782-1840)	—	11.00	—	—	70.00	100

NARWAR

Narwar was a tiny state in western Malwa with a population of about four thousand (ca.1900). The ruling chiefs were Jhala Rajputs. In AH1220/1805AD it came under Gwalior.

For later issues see Gwalior - Narwar Mint listings.

RULERS

Mahadji Rao, AH1175-1209/1761-1794AD
Daulat Rao, AH1209-1243/1794-1827AD

MNT MARKS

Katar — or — on reverse (Copper)

Bhilsa leaf — on reverse (Silver)

PRINCELY STATE

HAMMERED COINAGE

KM# A20 1/2 PAISA

3.3700 g., Copper **Obverse:** Inscription **Reverse:** Horizontal katar **Obverse Inscription:** Shah Alam (II) **Note:** Struck during the reign of local ruler Daulat Rao, AH1209-43/1794-1827AD.

Date	Mintage	Good	VG	F	VF	XF
AH1205//3x	—	1.75	3.00	5.00	8.00	—
AH1206//3x	—	1.75	3.00	5.00	8.00	—
AH1207//35	—	1.75	3.00	5.00	8.00	—
AH1207//46	—	1.75	3.00	5.00	8.00	—
AH1208//46	—	1.75	3.00	5.00	8.00	—
AH1210//4x	—	1.75	3.00	5.00	8.00	—
AH1211//43	—	1.75	3.00	5.00	8.00	—
AH1215//35	—	1.75	3.00	5.00	8.00	—

KM# 22 1/2 PAISA

3.3700 g., Copper **Obv. Inscription:** "Shah Alam II" **Reverse:** Vertical katar **Note:** Struck during the reign of local ruler Daulat Rao, AH1209-43/1794-1827AD.

Date	Mintage	Good	VG	F	VF	XF
AH1215//43	—	1.75	3.00	5.00	8.00	—
AH1215//42	—	1.75	3.00	5.00	8.00	—
AH1216//43	—	1.75	3.00	5.00	8.00	—
AH1216//44	—	1.75	3.00	5.00	8.00	—
AH1216//45	—	1.75	3.00	5.00	8.00	—
AH1217//44	—	1.75	3.00	5.00	8.00	—
AH1217//45	—	1.75	3.00	5.00	8.00	—
AH1217//46	—	1.75	3.00	5.00	8.00	—
AH1219//46	—	1.75	3.00	5.00	8.00	—

KM# 24 1/4 RUPEE

Silver **Obv. Inscription:** Shah Alam (II) **Note:** Weight varies: 2.68-2.90 grams. Struck during the reign of local ruler Daulat Rao, AH1209-43/1794-1827AD.

Date	Mintage	VG	F	VF	XF	Unc
AH1207//3x	—	6.50	10.00	15.00	22.50	—

KM# 10 1/2 RUPEE

Silver **Obv. Inscription:** Shah Alam (II) **Note:** Weight varies: 5.35-5.80 grams. Struck during the reign of local ruler Mahadji Rao, AH1175-1209/1761-94AD.

Date	Mintage	VG	F	VF	XF	Unc
ND(1761-94)	—	15.00	25.00	35.00	50.00	—

KM# 16 RUPEE

Silver **Obv. Inscription:** Shah Alam (II) **Note:** Weight varies: 10.70-11.60 grams. Struck during the reign of local ruler Mahadji Rao, AH1175-1209/1761-94AD.

Date	Mintage	VG	F	VF	XF	Unc
AH1174//1	—	20.00	35.00	50.00	75.00	—
AH-//2	—	20.00	35.00	50.00	75.00	—

Date	Mintage	VG	F	VF	XF	Unc
AH1176//4	—	20.00	35.00	50.00	75.00	—
AH1177//2	—	20.00	35.00	50.00	75.00	—
AH1177//5	—	20.00	35.00	50.00	75.00	—
AH(117)8//5	—	20.00	35.00	50.00	75.00	—
AH1179//6	—	20.00	35.00	50.00	75.00	—
AH1185//13	—	20.00	35.00	50.00	75.00	—
AH1188//14	—	20.00	35.00	50.00	75.00	—
AH(119)4//21	—	20.00	35.00	50.00	75.00	—
AH1195//22	—	20.00	35.00	50.00	75.00	—

KM# 17 RUPEE
Silver **Obv. Inscription:** Shah Alam (II) **Reverse:** Katar **Note:** Weight varies: 10.70-11.60 grams. Struck during the reign of local ruler Mahadji Rao, AH1175-1209/1761-94AD.

Date	Mintage	VG	F	VF	XF	Unc
AH1179//6	—	14.00	27.50	45.00	65.00	—

KM# 20 RUPEE
Silver **Obv. Inscription:** Shah Alam (II) **Reverse:** Lotus bud and quatrefoil **Note:** Weight varies: 10.70-11.60 grams. Struck during the reign of local ruler Mahadji Rao, AH1175-1209/1761-94AD.

Date	Mintage	VG	F	VF	XF	Unc
AH1192//23	—	6.50	11.00	16.50	25.00	—
AH1195//25	—	6.50	11.00	16.50	25.00	—
AH1201//29	—	8.00	13.50	20.00	28.50	—
AH1202//30	—	6.50	11.00	16.50	25.00	—
AH1202//31	—	6.50	11.00	16.50	25.00	—
AH1203//31	—	6.50	11.00	16.50	25.00	—
AH1205//32	—	6.50	11.00	16.50	25.00	—
AH1205//33	—	6.50	11.00	16.50	25.00	—
AH1206//34	—	6.50	11.00	16.50	25.00	—
AH1207//35	—	6.50	11.00	16.50	25.00	—

KM# 19 RUPEE
Silver **Obv. Inscription:** Shah Alam (II) **Reverse:** Flag and quatrefoil **Note:** Weight varies: 10.70-11.60 grams. Struck during the reign of local ruler Mahadji Rao, AH1175-1209/1761-94AD.

Date	Mintage	VG	F	VF	XF	Unc
AH1197//27	—	14.00	23.50	32.50	45.00	—

Mahadji Rao
AH1175-1209/1761-94AD

HAMMERED COINAGE

KM# 18 RUPEE
Silver **Obv. Inscription:** Shah Alam (II) **Reverse:** Floral symbols **Note:** Weight varies: 10.70-11.60 grams.

Date	Mintage	VG	F	VF	XF	Unc
AH1189//16	—	14.00	23.50	32.50	45.00	—
AH1190//17	—	14.00	23.50	32.50	45.00	—
AH1191//18	—	14.00	23.50	32.50	45.00	—
AH1192//24	—	14.00	23.50	32.50	45.00	—
AH1196//24	—	14.00	23.50	32.50	45.00	—

NAWANAGAR

(Navanagar)

State located on the Kathiawar peninsula, west-central India.

The rulers, or jams, of Kutch were Jareja Rajputs who had entered the Kathiawar peninsular from Kutch and dispossessed the ancient family of Jathwas. Nawanagar was founded about 1535 by Jam Raval, who was possibly the elder brother of the Jam of Kutch. The great fort of Nawanagar was built by Jam Jasaji (d. 1814). The state became tributary to the Gaekwar family and, in the 19th century, also to the British. In 1948 the state was merged into Saurashtra.

MONETARY SYSTEM

2 Trambiyo = 1 Dokda
3 Trambiyo = 1 Dhinglo
8 Dokda = 1 Kori

Early Types: Stylized imitations of the coins of Muzaffar III of Gujarat (156-173AD), dated AH978 (= 1570AD), were struck from the end of the 16th century until the early part of the reign of Vibhaji. These show a steady degradation of style over the nearly 300 years of issue, but no types can be dated to specific rulers. The former attribution of these coins to Ranmalji II (1820-1852AD) is incorrect. All are inscribed Sri Jamji, title of all rulers of Nawanagar.

Varieties in this series are the rule, not the exception. These include legend style, small marks in the field such as a crescent, Katar (dagger), etc., and weight ranges.

BRITISH PROTECTORATE

HAMMERED COINAGE

Crude Style; ca. 1570 - 1850AD

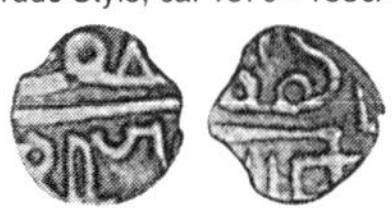

KM# 1 TRAMBIYO
Copper **Note:** Weight varies: 3.2-4 grams.

Date	Mintage	Good	VG	F	VF	XF
AH(9)78 frozen	—	2.00	3.00	5.00	10.00	—

KM# 2 DOKDO
Copper **Note:** Weight varies 7-8 grams, but earlier issues weigh up to 9.3 grams.

Date	Mintage	Good	VG	F	VF	XF
AH(9)78 frozen	—	2.00	3.00	5.00	10.00	—

KM# 3 DHINGLO (1-1/2 Dokda)
Copper **Note:** Weight varies 10.5-12.5 grams.

Date	Mintage	Good	VG	F	VF	XF
AH(9)78 frozen	—	2.00	3.00	5.00	10.00	—

KM# 4 1/2 KORI
Silver **Note:** Weight varies 2.3-2.4 grams.

Date	Mintage	Good	VG	F	VF	XF
AH(9)78 frozen	—	2.00	3.00	5.00	10.00	—

KM# 5 KORI
Silver **Note:** Weight varies 4.6-4.8 grams.

Date	Mintage	Good	VG	F	VF	XF
AH(9)78 frozen	—	2.00	3.00	5.00	10.00	—

ORCHHA

State located in north-central India.

Orchha, the oldest and highest ranking of all the Bundela States, was founded by Rudra Pratap, a Garhwar Rajput, early in the 16th century. During the years of Mughal expansion, Orchha came under the supervision of Delhi. A few years later Jujhar Singh (1626-1635) rebelled but was defeated and dispossessed. Shah Jahan installed his brother as ruler in 1641. In the 18th century, as the Marathas took control of the region, only Orchha from among the Bundela States was not totally subjugated by the Peshwa. In the 19th century Orchha came under British protection.

The Orchha coinage was called Gaja Shahi because of the gaja or mace which was its symbol.

RULER

Vikramajit Mahendra, AH1211-1233/1796-1817AD

MINT MARKS

1 

Reverse

(This is the symbol most characteristic of Orchha's coinage and is copied on the Datia imitations)

2 

Obverse, most common

3 

Obverse, less common

On reverse:

Marks #4 through #10 are found in addition to Mark#1.

The Datia copies can only be distinguished by the mint-marks, other than #1, which is common to both series for the list of Datia marks, see listings under that state.

There seems to be no correspondence between AH dates on the obverse and regnal years on the reverse.

BRITISH PROTECTORATE

Vikramajit Mahendra
AH1211-1233 / 1796-1817AD

HAMMERED COINAGE

C# 24 1/2 PAISA
Silver, 16 mm. **Obv. Inscription:** "Shah Alam II"

Date	Mintage	Good	VG	F	VF	XF
AH(12)32 (1816-17)	—	3.00	5.00	10.00	15.00	—
AH(12)33 (1817-18)	—	3.00	5.00	10.00	15.00	—

C# 25 PAISA
Copper **Obv. Inscription:** "Shah Alam II"

Date	Mintage	Good	VG	F	VF	XF
AH120x//35	—	5.00	10.00	15.00	25.00	—
AH121x//40	—	5.00	10.00	15.00	25.00	—
AH1211//41	—	5.00	10.00	15.00	25.00	—
AH1212//4x	—	5.00	10.00	15.00	25.00	—
AH1214//4x	—	5.00	10.00	15.00	25.00	—

C# 29 1/8 RUPEE
Silver **Obv. Inscription:** Shah Alam (II) **Note:** Weight varies 1.34-1.45 grams.

Date	Mintage	Good	VG	F	VF	XF
AH-//3x	—	10.00	16.50	25.00	35.00	—
AH-//45 (1233)	—	—	10.00	16.50	25.00	35.00

C# 30 1/4 RUPEE
Silver, 12 mm. **Obv. Inscription:** Shah Alam (II) **Note:** Weight varies 2.68-2.90 grams.

Date	Mintage	Good	VG	F	VF	XF
AH1211	—	10.00	16.50	25.00	35.00	—

C# 31 1/2 RUPEE

Silver **Obv. Inscription:** Shah Alam (II) **Note:** Weight varies: 5.35-5.8 grams.

Date	Mintage	Good	VG	F	VF	XF
AH1211//42	—	15.00	25.00	40.00	60.00	—
AH1212//40	—	15.00	25.00	40.00	60.00	—
AH1214//45	—	15.00	25.00	40.00	60.00	—
AH1215//42	—	15.00	25.00	40.00	60.00	—

C# 32 RUPEE

Silver **Obv. Inscription:** Shah Alam (II) **Note:** Weight varies 10.7-11.6 grams.

Date	Mintage	Good	VG	F	VF	XF
AH1211//39	—	6.00	10.00	14.00	20.00	—
AH1211//41	—	6.00	10.00	14.00	20.00	—
AH1211//43	—	6.00	10.00	14.00	20.00	—
AH1212//45	—	6.00	10.00	14.00	20.00	—
AH1213//42	—	6.00	10.00	14.00	20.00	—
AH1214//40	—	6.00	10.00	14.00	20.00	—
AH1214//42	—	6.00	10.00	14.00	20.00	—
AH1214//43	—	6.00	10.00	14.00	20.00	—
AH1214//44	—	6.00	10.00	14.00	20.00	—
AH1214//45	—	6.00	10.00	14.00	20.00	—
AH1214//46	—	6.00	10.00	14.00	20.00	—
AH1215//43	—	6.00	10.00	14.00	20.00	—

KM# 33 NAZARANA 2 RUPEE

21.8300 g., Silver, 31 mm. **Obverse:** 3-line inscription with Mughal ruler's titles **Obv. Inscription:** Shah Alam II **Reverse:** 3-line inscription with mint and date **Mint:** Orchha

Date	Mintage	VG	F	VF	XF	Unc
AH1214/45 1 known	—	—	—	—	—	—

PANNA

State located in central India.

The ruling family of Panna was descended from Rudra Pratap, founder of the Orchha royal house. Rudra Pratap's great grandson, Champat Rai, declared his independence of both Orchha and the Mughals. Champat Rai's son, Maharaja Chhatrasal, greatly extended the principality when he acquired extensive tracts of land elsewhere in Bundelkhand. In 1807 the Panna chief Kishor Singh obtained a sanad from the British, and thereafter came under British supervision.

MINT MARK

Kukureti

Hanuman (monkey god) running

PRINCELY STATE

Shah Alam II

AH1173-1221 / 1759-1806AD

HAMMERED COINAGE

KM# 10 PAISA

Copper **Obverse:** Hanuman running **Obv. Inscription:** Shah Alam (II)

Date	Mintage	Good	VG	F	VF	XF
AH-//24	—	7.00	12.00	17.00	—	25.00

PARTABGARH

Pratapgarh

The rulers of Partabgarh, a state located in northwest India, the maharawals, were Sesodia Rajputs who are believed to have migrated in 1553 from Mewar, where their ancestors once ruled. Arriving in the area they seized control from the local Bhil chieftains but it was not until the early 18th century that Partabgarh town was founded by Maharawal Partab Singh. Partabgarh was tributary to Holkar until 1818 when, with the collapse of the Maratha states, the state came under British protection. The state was then managed through the Rajputana Agency until, in April 1948, it was merged into Rajasthan.

RULERS

Salim Singh, AH1167-1189/1753-1775 AD
Sawant Singh, AH1189-1241/1775-1825AD

MINT

دیوگره

Deogarh

BRITISH PROTECTORATE

Sawant Singh

AH1189-1241 / 1775-1825AD

HAMMERED COINAGE

KM# 10 1/8 RUPEE

1.3000 g., Silver, 11 mm.

Date	Mintage	Good	VG	F	VF	XF
AH1199/29	—	—	3.50	6.00	9.00	14.00

KM# 5 1/4 RUPEE

Silver **Obv. Inscription:** Shah Alam (II) **Note:** Second type with frozen date "AH1199" and regnal date "yr.26"; weight varies 2.72 - 2.82 grams. Prev. KM#3.

Date	Mintage	Good	VG	F	VF	XF
AH1199//26	—	—	7.50	12.50	18.50	27.50

KM# 11 1/4 RUPEE

2.6500 g., Silver

Date	Mintage	Good	VG	F	VF	XF
AH1199/29	—	2.00	5.00	7.00	10.00	16.00

KM# 2 1/2 RUPEE

Silver **Obv. Inscription:** "Shah Alam (II)" **Note:** Weight varies 5.4-5.6 grams. Prev. KM#4.

Date	Mintage	Good	VG	F	VF	XF
AH1189//16	—	—	7.00	11.00	16.50	25.00
AH1193//20	—	—	7.00	11.00	16.50	25.00
AH1197//2x	—	—	7.00	11.00	16.50	25.00
AH1198//25	—	—	7.00	11.00	16.50	25.00

KM# 6 1/2 RUPEE

Silver **Obv. Inscription:** Shah Alam (II) **Note:** Second type with frozen date "AH1199" and regnal date "yr.26". Weight varies: 5.4-5.6 grams. Prev. KM#7.

Date	Mintage	Good	VG	F	VF	XF
AH1199//26	—	—	7.00	11.00	16.50	25.00

KM# 12 1/2 RUPEE

5.3000 g., Silver

Date	Mintage	Good	VG	F	VF	XF
AH1199/29	—	2.25	3.50	6.00	9.00	14.00

KM# 3 RUPEE

Silver **Obv. Inscription:** Shah Alam (II) **Note:** Weight varies: 10.9-11.3 grams. Prev. KM#5.

Date	Mintage	Good	VG	F	VF	XF
AH1184//11	—	—	11.50	17.50	23.50	32.50
AH1185//12	—	—	11.50	17.50	23.50	32.50
AH1186//13	—	—	11.50	17.50	23.50	32.50
AH1187//14	—	—	11.50	17.50	23.50	32.50
AH1189//16	—	—	11.50	17.50	23.50	32.50
AH1190//17	—	—	11.50	17.50	23.50	32.50
AH1191//18	—	—	11.50	17.50	23.50	32.50
AH1192//19	—	—	11.50	17.50	23.50	32.50
AH1192//20	—	—	11.50	17.50	23.50	32.50
AH1193//20	—	—	11.50	17.50	23.50	32.50
AH1193//21	—	—	11.50	17.50	23.50	32.50
AH1195//22	—	—	11.50	17.50	23.50	32.50
AH1196//23	—	—	11.50	17.50	23.50	32.50
AH1196//24	—	—	11.50	17.50	23.50	32.50
AH1197//24	—	—	11.50	17.50	23.50	32.50
AH1198//25	—	—	11.50	17.50	23.50	32.50

KM# 7 RUPEE

10.7000 g., Silver **Obv. Inscription:** Shah Alam (II) **Note:** Second type with frozen date "AH1199" and regnal date "yr.26".

Date	Mintage	Good	VG	F	VF	XF
AH1199//26	—	—	11.50	17.50	23.50	32.50

KM# 13 RUPEE

10.7000 g., Silver, 19-20 mm. **Note:** Size varies.

Date	Mintage	Good	VG	F	VF	XF
AH1199/29	—	4.25	5.00	7.00	10.00	16.00

KM# 4 NAZARANA RUPEE

Silver **Obv. Inscription:** Shah Alam (II) **Shape:** Square **Note:** Weight varies: 10.9-11.3 grams. Prev. KM#6.

Date	Mintage	Good	VG	F	VF	XF
AH1193//20	—	—	40.00	70.00	90.00	120

KM# 14 NAZARANA RUPEE

10.8500 g., Silver **Shape:** Square

Date	Mintage	Good	VG	F	VF	XF
AH1199/29	—	17.50	35.00	60.00	85.00	125

PATIALA

State located in the Punjab in northwest India. In the mid-18th century the Raja was given his title and mint right by Ahmad Shah Durrani of Afghanistan, whose coin he copied.

The rulers became Maharajas in 1810AD. The maharaja of Patiala was also recognized as the leader of the Phulkean tribe. Unlike others, Patiala's Sikh rulers had never hesitated to seek British assistance at those times when they felt threatened by their co-religionist neighbors. In 1857, Patiala's forces were immediately made available on the side of the British.

RULERS

Amar Singh, AH1179-96/1765-81AD

Identifying marks on reverse.

Sahib Singh, AH1196-1229/1781-1813AD

Identifying marks on reverse.

MINT

سرهند سهرند

Sirhind (Sahrind)

PRINCELY STATE

Amar Singh

AH1179-1196 / 1765-1781AD

HAMMERED COINAGE

C# 10 RUPEE

Silver **Obv. Inscription:** Ahmad Shah Durrani **Note:** 11.10-11.20 grams.

Date	Mintage	Good	VG	F	VF	XF
ND/4 (1765-81) Frozen	—	8.00	20.00	31.50	42.50	60.00

Sahib Singh

AH1196-1229 / 1781-1813AD

HAMMERED COINAGE

C# 20 RUPEE

Silver **Obverse:** Similar to 1 Rupee, C#10 **Obv. Inscription:** Ahmad Shah Durrani **Note:** Weight varies: 11.10-11.20 grams.

Date	Mintage	Good	VG	F	VF	XF
ND(1781-1813)	—	7.00	17.50	25.00	35.00	50.00

RATLAM

State located northwest of Indore in Madhya Pradesh.

The rajas of Ratlam were Rathor Rajputs, descendants of the younger branch of the Jodhpur ruling family. Ratlam became the premier Rajput state in western Malwa. The founder, Ratan Singh, received the territory as a grant from Shah Jahan in 1631. Before Maratha collapse some 15% of the state's annual revenue went to Sindhia as tribute. Under British protection it was supervised by the Central India Agency and in 1948 Ratlam became a district of Madhya Bharat.

MINT

رتلام

Ratlam

BRITISH PROTECTORATE

Uncertain Ruler

HAMMERED COINAGE

KM# 15 PAISA

Copper **Obverse:** Katar **Reverse:** Sword

Date	Mintage	Good	VG	F	VF	XF
ND(c.1780-1806)	—	5.00	10.00	18.00	25.00	—

KM# 21 PAISA
Copper **Obverse:** "Ra'ej" retrograde in dotted circle **Reverse:** Spade symbol

Date	Mintage	Good	VG	F	VF	XF
ND(1785-89)	—	6.50	12.00	20.00	30.00	—

KM# 20 PAISA
Copper **Obverse:** "Ra'ej" in dotted circle right of "jalus"

Date	Mintage	Good	VG	F	VF	XF
ND//25 (1783-84)	—	5.00	10.00	18.00	25.00	—

Shah Alam II
AH1173-1221 / 1759-1806AD
HAMMERED COINAGE

KM# 10 PAISA
11.1000 g., Copper **Obverse:** "Ratlam" below "Ra'ej" in dotted circle

Date	Mintage	Good	VG	F	VF	XF
ND(1759-1806)//2x	—	6.50	12.00	20.00	30.00	—

KM# 5 PAISA
11.1000 g., Copper **Obv. Inscription:** "Ratlam" below "Shah Alam" **Note:** Struck at Ratlam.

Date	Mintage	Good	VG	F	VF	XF
ND(1759-1806)	—	5.00	10.00	18.00	25.00	—

SELAM
PRINCELY STATE
HAMMERED COINAGE

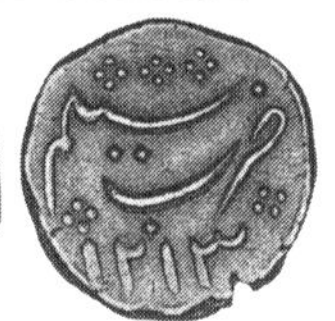

KM# 5 PAISA
6.4000 g., Copper

Date	Mintage	Good	VG	F	VF	XF
AH1213	—	25.00	50.00	75.00	150	—

TRAVANCORE

State located in extreme southwest India. A mint was established in ME965/1789-1790AD.

The region of Travancore had a lengthy history before being annexed by the Vijayanagar kingdom. With Vijayanagar's defeat at the battle of Talikota in 1565, Travancore passed under Muslim control until the late 18th century, when it merged as a state in its own right under Raja Martanda Varma. At this time the raja allied himself with British interests as a protection against the Muslim dynasty of Mysore. In 1795 the raja of Travancore officially accepted a subsidiary alliance with the East India Company, and remained within the orbit of British influence from then until India's independence.

RULER
Bala Rama Varma I, ME973-986/1798-1810AD

MONETARY SYSTEM
16 Cash (Kasu) = 1 Chuckram
4 Chuckram = 1 Fanam
2 Fanams = 1 Anantaraya
7 Fanams = 1 Rupee
52-1/2 Fanam = 1 Pagoda

DATING
ME dates are of the Malabar Era. Add 824 or 825 to the ME date for the AD date. (i.e., ME1112 plus 824-825 = 1936-1937AD).

KINGDOM
HAMMERED COINAGE

KM# 1 CHUCKRAM
Silver **Obverse:** Left and right angles with dots at bottom

Date	Mintage	Good	VG	F	VF	XF
ND(1600-1847)	—	1.00	2.50	5.00	8.00	12.00

Bala Rama Varma I
ME973-986 / 1798-1810AD
HAMMERED COINAGE

KM# 2 1/2 ANANTARAYA (Fanam)
Gold

Date	Mintage	Good	VG	F	VF	XF
ND(1790-1830)	—	—	6.00	9.00	14.00	25.00

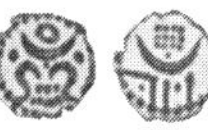

KM# 3 ANANTARAYA (2 Fanam)
Gold

Date	Mintage	Good	VG	F	VF	XF
ND(1790-1860)	—	—	10.00	15.00	21.50	40.00

Note: For similar coins with leaf sprays on the obverse, see KM#23 in the 19th century listings

EUROPEAN INFLUENCES IN INDIA

Danish India or Tranquebar is a town and former Danish colony on the southeast coast of India. In Danish times, 1620-1845, it was a factory site and seaport operated by the Danish Asiatic Company. Tranquebar and the other Danish settlements in India were sold to the British East India Company in 1845.

RULER
Danish, until 1845

ADMINISTRATION OF TRANQUEBAR
Danish East India Company (DOC)
1670-1729
Danish Crown
1729-1732
Frederick IV, 1699-1730
Christian VI, 1730-1746
Danish Asiatic Company (DOC)
1732-1777
Danish Crown
1777-Oct. 1845
British Occupation May, 1801-Aug., 1802

MONETARY SYSTEM
80 Kas (Cash) = Royaliner (Fano or
8 Royaliner = 1 Rupee
18 Royaliner = 1 Speciesdaler

DANISH COLONY
HAMMERED COINAGE

KM# 122 CASH
Copper **Ruler:** Frederik IV **Issuer:** Danish East India Company **Obverse:** Crowned double F4 monogram **Reverse:** Crowned DOC monogram

Date	Mintage	Good	VG	F	VF	XF
ND	—	7.00	11.00	25.00	55.00	—

KM# 123.1 CASH
Copper **Ruler:** Frederik IV **Issuer:** Danish East India Company **Obverse:** Crowned F4 monogram using one vertical for both **Reverse:** Crowned DOC monogram **Note:** Weight varies: 0.40-1.65 grams.

Date	Mintage	Good	VG	F	VF	XF
ND	—	3.00	5.00	10.00	25.00	—

KM# 123.2 CASH
Copper **Ruler:** Frederik IV **Issuer:** Danish East India Company **Reverse:** Inverted DOC monogram

Date	Mintage		VG	F	VF	XF
	—	—	—	—	—	—

KM# 124 CASH
Copper **Ruler:** Frederik IV **Issuer:** Danish East India Company **Obverse:** Crowned F4 monogram **Reverse:** Crowned DOC monogram **Note:** Weight varies: 0.40-1.65 grams.

Date	Mintage	Good	VG	F	VF	XF
ND	—	8.00	12.00	25.00	60.00	—

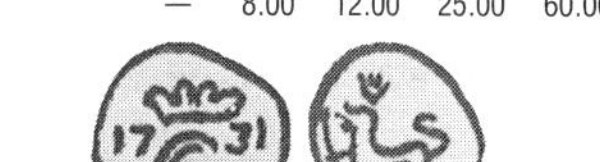

KM# 130 CASH
0.8000 g., Copper **Ruler:** Christian VI **Issuer:** Danish Royal Colony **Obverse:** Crowned C6 monogram divides date **Reverse:** Norse lion on battle axe to left

Date	Mintage	Good	VG	F	VF	XF
1731	—	12.00	25.00	50.00	100	—
1732	—	12.00	20.00	50.00	100	—

KM# 131 CASH

0.8000 g., Copper **Ruler:** Christian VI **Issuer:** Danish Royal Colony **Obverse:** Crowned C6 monogram, C and 6 separate **Reverse:** Crowned DAC monogram

Date	Mintage	Good	VG	F	VF	XF
ND	—	7.00	10.00	25.00	50.00	—

KM# A133 CASH

0.8000 g., Copper **Ruler:** Christian VI **Issuer:** Danish Royal Colony **Obverse:** Crowned C6 monogram **Reverse:** DAC monogram without crown

Date	Mintage	Good	VG	F	VF	XF
ND	—	—	—	—	—	—

KM# 133 CASH

0.8000 g., Copper **Ruler:** Christian VI **Issuer:** Danish Royal Colony **Obverse:** C6 monogram **Reverse:** DAC monogram

Date	Mintage	Good	VG	F	VF	XF
ND	—	7.00	11.00	25.00	45.00	—

KM# 134 CASH

0.8000 g., Copper **Ruler:** Christian VI **Issuer:** Danish Royal Colony **Obverse:** C6 monogram **Reverse:** T B ligate

Date	Mintage	Good	VG	F	VF	XF
ND	—	6.50	10.00	24.00	45.00	—

KM# 132 CASH

0.8000 g., Copper **Ruler:** Christian VI **Issuer:** Danish Royal Colony **Obverse:** Crowned C6 monogram, C and 6 entwined **Reverse:** Crowned DAC monogram **Note:** Varieties exist.

Date	Mintage	Good	VG	F	VF	XF
ND	—	4.00	6.00	13.00	30.00	—

KM# 143 CASH

0.6000 g., Copper **Ruler:** Frederik V **Issuer:** Danish Asiatic Company **Obverse:** Crowned F5 monogram, block F **Reverse:** Crowned DAC monogram divides date, 1 below

Date	Mintage	Good	VG	F	VF	XF
1761	—	50.00	100	200	400	—

KM# 150 CASH

0.6000 g., Copper **Ruler:** Christian VII **Issuer:** Danish Royal Colony **Obverse:** Crowned C7 monogram **Reverse:** Crowned DAC monogram between date, 1 below

Date	Mintage	Good	VG	F	VF	XF
1767	—	25.00	40.00	75.00	150	—
1768	—	25.00	40.00	75.00	150	—
1770	—	30.00	45.00	85.00	185	—
1777 Rare	—	—	—	—	—	—
1780	—	25.00	40.00	70.00	80.00	150

KM# A135 2 CASH

1.6000 g., Copper **Ruler:** Frederik IV **Issuer:** Danish East India Company **Obverse:** Crowned double F4 monogram **Reverse:** DOC monogram, 2 KAS below

Date	Mintage	Good	VG	F	VF	XF
ND	—	10.00	15.00	33.00	65.00	—

KM# 135 2 CASH

1.6000 g., Copper **Ruler:** Christian VI **Issuer:** Danish Royal Colony **Obverse:** Crowned C6 monogram, C and 6 separate **Reverse:** Crowned DAC monogram, 2 below

Date	Mintage	Good	VG	F	VF	XF
ND	—	11.00	17.00	45.00	85.00	—

KM# 136 2 CASH

1.6000 g., Copper **Ruler:** Christian VI **Issuer:** Danish Royal Colony **Obverse:** Crowned C6 monogram, C and 6 entwined **Reverse:** Crowned DAC monogram, 2 below

Date	Mintage	Good	VG	F	VF	XF
ND	—	7.00	10.00	25.00	55.00	—

KM# 137 2 CASH

1.6000 g., Copper **Ruler:** Christian VI **Issuer:** Danish Royal Colony **Obverse:** C6 monogram **Reverse:** DAC monogram, 2 KAS below

Date	Mintage	Good	VG	F	VF	XF
ND Rare	—	—	—	—	—	—

KM# 144 2 CASH

1.2000 g., Copper **Ruler:** Frederik V **Issuer:** Danish Asiatic Company **Obverse:** Crowned F5 monogram, block F **Reverse:** Crowned DAC monogram divides date, 2 below

Date	Mintage	Good	VG	F	VF	XF
1761	—	15.00	22.00	55.00	130	—

KM# 152 2 CASH

1.2000 g., Copper **Ruler:** Christian VII **Issuer:** Danish Royal Colony **Obverse:** Crowned C7 monogram **Reverse:** Crowned DAC monogram between date, 2 below

Date	Mintage	Good	VG	F	VF	XF
1767	—	25.00	40.00	75.00	150	—
1768	—	20.00	35.00	65.00	130	—
1770	—	20.00	35.00	65.00	130	—
1777	—	—	100	200	400	—

KM# 153.1 2 CASH

1.2000 g., Copper **Ruler:** Christian VII **Reverse:** Without crown above DAC monogram

Date	Mintage	Good	VG	F	VF	XF
1770 Rare	—	—	—	—	—	—

KM# 153.2 2 CASH

1.2000 g., Copper **Ruler:** Christian VII **Issuer:** Danish Royal Colony **Reverse:** Retrograde 2

Date	Mintage	Good	VG	F	VF	XF
1780 Rare	—	—	—	—	—	—

KM# 126.1 4 CASH

4.8000 g., Copper **Ruler:** Frederik IV **Issuer:** Danish East India Company **Obverse:** Crowned double F4 monogram **Reverse:** DOC monogram, 4 KAS below

KM# 138.2 4 CASH

3.2000 g., Copper **Ruler:** Christian VI **Issuer:** Danish Royal Colony **Obverse:** Crowned C6 monogram, C and 6 entwined **Reverse:** Crowned DAC monogram, 4 below between dots

Date	Mintage	Good	VG	F	VF	XF
ND	—	7.00	10.00	20.00	45.00	—

KM# 139 4 CASH

3.2000 g., Copper **Ruler:** Christian VI **Issuer:** Danish Royal Colony **Obverse:** Crowned retrograde C6 monogram **Reverse:** Crowned DAC monogram **Note:** Varieties exist.

Date	Mintage	Good	VG	F	VF	XF
ND	—	25.00	40.00	90.00	150	—

KM# 145 4 CASH

2.4000 g., Copper **Ruler:** Frederik V **Issuer:** Danish Asiatic Company **Obverse:** Crowned F5 monogram, block F **Reverse:** Crowned DAC monogram divides date, 4 below

Date	Mintage	Good	VG	F	VF	XF
1761	—	10.00	15.00	33.00	80.00	—
1763	—	5.00	8.00	17.00	45.00	—

KM# 154.1 4 CASH

2.4000 g., Copper **Ruler:** Christian VII **Issuer:** Danish Royal Colony **Obverse:** Crowned C7 monogram **Reverse:** Crowned DAC monogram between date, 4 below

Date	Mintage	Good	VG	F	VF	XF
1767	—	7.00	12.00	30.00	50.00	—
1768	—	6.00	10.00	30.00	50.00	—
1770	—	5.00	7.00	15.00	35.00	—
1777	—	6.00	10.00	30.00	50.00	—

KM# 154.2 4 CASH

2.4000 g., Copper **Ruler:** Christian VII **Issuer:** Danish Royal Colony **Reverse:** Second 7 in date retrograde

Date	Mintage	Good	VG	F	VF	XF
1770	—	8.00	13.00	35.00	60.00	—

KM# 155 4 CASH

2.4000 g., Copper **Ruler:** Christian VII **Issuer:** Danish Royal Colony **Obverse:** Crowned C7 monogram **Reverse:** Value and date

Date	Mintage	Good	VG	F	VF	XF
1782	—	6.00	10.00	20.00	50.00	—
1786	—	6.00	10.00	20.00	50.00	—
1787	—	6.00	10.00	20.00	50.00	—
1788	—	6.00	10.00	20.00	50.00	—
1790	—	5.00	7.00	15.00	35.00	—
1797	—	5.50	8.00	18.00	45.00	—

KM# 156 4 CASH

Date	Mintage	Good	VG	F	VF	XF
ND	—	60.00	100	220	425	—

KM# 126.2 4 CASH

4.8000 g., Copper **Ruler:** Frederik IV **Issuer:** Danish East India Company **Reverse:** 4 CAS below monogram

Date	Mintage	Good	VG	F	VF	XF
ND Rare	—	—	—	—	—	—

KM# 138.1 4 CASH

3.2000 g., Copper **Ruler:** Christian VI **Issuer:** Danish Royal Colony **Obverse:** Crowned C6 monogram, C and 6 separate **Reverse:** Crowned DAC monogram, 4 below between dots **Note:** Varieties exist.

Date	Mintage	Good	VG	F	VF	XF
ND	—	5.00	7.50	16.00	35.00	—

2.4000 g., Copper **Ruler:** Christian VII **Issuer:** Danish Royal Colony **Obverse:** Crowned C7 monogram **Reverse:** R between date

Date	Mintage	Good	VG	F	VF	XF
1786	—	8.00	13.00	30.00	60.00	—

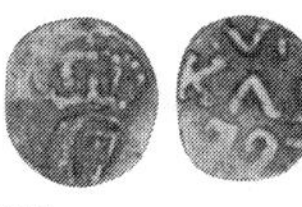

KM# 157 4 CASH

2.4000 g., Copper **Ruler:** Christian VII **Issuer:** Danish Royal Colony **Obverse:** Crowned C7 monogram **Reverse:** Value VI for IV

Date	Mintage	Good	VG	F	VF	XF
1797	—	10.00	15.00	35.00	65.00	—
1799	—	10.00	15.00	30.00	65.00	—
1800	—	7.00	10.00	25.00	50.00	—

KM# 127 10 CASH

10.0000 g., Copper **Ruler:** Frederik IV **Issuer:** Danish East India Company **Obverse:** Crowned double F4 monogram **Reverse:** Crowned DAC monogram, 10 and Kass below

Date	Mintage	Good	VG	F	VF	XF
ND	—	100	200	500	900	—

KM# 163 10 CASH

Copper **Ruler:** Christian VII **Issuer:** Danish Royal Colony **Obverse:** Crowned double C7 monogram **Reverse:** Crowned DAC monogram, value 10 below date

Date	Mintage	Good	VG	F	VF	XF
1768	—	60.00	90.00	250	650	—

KM# 164 10 CASH

Copper **Ruler:** Christian VII **Issuer:** Danish Royal Colony **Obverse:** Crowned monogram **Reverse:** Value appears X.KAS above date, crowned DAC monogram above

Date	Mintage	Good	VG	F	VF	XF
1768	—	30.00	42.00	90.00	250	—
1770	—	20.00	40.00	75.00	220	—
1777	—	20.00	35.00	70.00	200	—

KM# 165 10 CASH

Copper **Ruler:** Christian VII **Issuer:** Danish Royal Colony **Obverse:** Crowned C7 **Reverse:** Value appears .X./.KAS. on two lines

Date	Mintage	Good	VG	F	VF	XF
1782	—	25.00	40.00	75.00	200	—
1786	—	25.00	40.00	75.00	200	—
1788	—	25.00	40.00	75.00	200	—
1790	—	25.00	40.00	75.00	200	—

KM# 128 ROYALIN

1.5500 g., Silver **Ruler:** Frederik IV **Issuer:** Danish East India Company **Obverse:** Crowned F4 monogram divides date **Reverse:** Crowned Norse lion on battle axe to left

Date	Mintage	Good	VG	F	VF	XF
1730	—	100	200	600	1,200	—

KM# 140 ROYALIN

Silver **Ruler:** Christian VI **Issuer:** Danish Royal Colony
Obverse: Crowned C6 monogram divides date **Reverse:** Crowned Norse lion on battle axe to left

Date	Mintage	Good	VG	F	VF	XF
1731	—	150	350	700	1,400	—

KM# 146 ROYALIN

Silver **Ruler:** Frederik V **Issuer:** Danish Asiatic Company
Obverse: Crowned F5 monogram **Reverse:** Arms divide date, value at top

Date	Mintage	Good	VG	F	VF	XF
1755	—	60.00	100	190	350	—

KM# 147 ROYALIN

Silver **Ruler:** Frederik V **Issuer:** Danish Asiatic Company
Obverse: Crowned F5 monogram, block F **Reverse:** Arms divide date, value at top

Date	Mintage	Good	VG	F	VF	XF
1756	—	30.00	50.00	100	200	—
1762	—	60.00	110	220	400	—
1763 Rare	—	—	—	—	—	—
1764	—	60.00	140	300	600	—
1765	—	50.00	100	210	375	—
1766	—	60.00	140	300	600	—

KM# 168 ROYALIN

Silver **Ruler:** Christian VII **Issuer:** Danish Royal Colony
Obverse: Crowned C7 monogram **Reverse:** Value, arms with lion between date

Date	Mintage	VG	F	VF	XF	Unc
1767	—	30.00	50.00	100	200	—
1768 Rare	—	—	—	—	—	—
1769	—	35.00	60.00	120	250	—
1770	—	60.00	130	260	400	—
1771	—	30.00	50.00	100	200	—
1772 Rare	—	—	—	—	—	—
1773	—	15.00	30.00	60.00	120	—
1774	—	20.00	30.00	75.00	135	—
1775	—	30.00	60.00	120	250	—
1776	—	15.00	25.00	50.00	100	—
1779	—	20.00	40.00	100	200	—
1780	—	15.00	25.00	60.00	120	—
1781	—	14.00	20.00	55.00	100	—
1783	—	20.00	30.00	80.00	150	—
1784	—	50.00	75.00	185	320	—
1786	—	20.00	30.00	70.00	140	—
1787	—	20.00	30.00	70.00	140	—
1788	—	50.00	75.00	185	320	—
1789	—	20.00	30.00	80.00	150	—
1791 Rare	—	—	—	—	—	—
1792	—	20.00	30.00	80.00	150	—
1793	—	50.00	75.00	185	320	—
1794	—	20.00	30.00	80.00	150	—
1795	—	20.00	30.00	80.00	150	—
1796	—	20.00	30.00	80.00	150	—
1797	—	20.00	30.00	80.00	150	—
1799	—	35.00	55.00	120	220	—

KM# 169 ROYALIN

Silver **Ruler:** Christian VII **Issuer:** Danish Royal Colony
Obverse: Crowned C7 monogram **Reverse:** Value, arms with lion between date

Date	Mintage	VG	F	VF	XF	Unc
1786R Rare	—	—	—	—	—	—

KM# 142 2 ROYALINER (2 Fano, 2 Fanams)

Silver **Ruler:** Christian VI **Issuer:** Danish Royal Colony
Obverse: Crowned C6 monogram divides date **Reverse:** Crowned Norse lion on battle axe to left

Date	Mintage	Good	VG	F	VF	XF
1731	—	250	400	700	1,400	—

KM# 141 2 ROYALINER (2 Fano, 2 Fanams)

Silver **Ruler:** Christian VI **Issuer:** Danish East India Company
Obverse: Crowned F4 monogram divides date **Reverse:** Crowned Norse lion on battle axe to left **Note:** Posthumous issue.

Date	Mintage	Good	VG	F	VF	XF
1731	—	250	450	900	1,800	—

KM# 148 2 ROYALINER (2 Fano, 2 Fanams)

Silver **Ruler:** Frederik V **Issuer:** Danish Asiatic Company
Obverse: Crowned F5 monogram **Reverse:** Arms divide date, value at top

Date	Mintage	Good	VG	F	VF	XF
1755	—	100	170	300	500	—

KM# 149 2 ROYALINER (2 Fano, 2 Fanams)

Silver **Ruler:** Frederik V **Issuer:** Danish Asiatic Company
Obverse: Crowned F5 monogram, block F **Reverse:** Arms divide date, value at top

Date	Mintage	Good	VG	F	VF	XF
1756	—	50.00	100	235	425	—
1762	—	125	200	375	700	—
1764 Rare	—	—	—	—	—	—
1765	—	125	200	375	700	—
1766 Rare	—	—	—	—	—	—

KM# 171 2 ROYALINER (2 Fano, 2 Fanams)

Silver **Ruler:** Christian VII **Issuer:** Danish Royal Colony
Obverse: Crowned C7 monogram **Reverse:** Arms divides date, value above

Date	Mintage	VG	F	VF	XF	Unc
1767	—	60.00	100	200	400	—
1768	—	60.00	100	220	430	—
1769 Rare	—	—	—	—	—	—
1770	—	80.00	125	300	500	—
1771	—	60.00	100	200	400	—
1772	—	80.00	125	300	500	—
1773	—	20.00	35.00	70.00	120	—
1774	—	20.00	35.00	70.00	120	—
1775	—	20.00	40.00	80.00	140	—
1776	—	20.00	35.00	70.00	120	—
1779	—	50.00	100	200	400	—
1780	—	20.00	35.00	70.00	120	—
1781	—	20.00	30.00	60.00	100	—
1783	—	15.00	30.00	60.00	120	—
1784	—	15.00	30.00	60.00	120	—
1786	—	20.00	50.00	100	180	—
1787	—	15.00	30.00	60.00	120	—
1788	—	15.00	30.00	60.00	120	—
1789	—	30.00	60.00	130	250	—
1792	—	30.00	60.00	150	300	—
1793	—	85.00	130	300	500	—
1794	—	30.00	70.00	130	250	—
1795	—	15.00	30.00	60.00	120	—
1796	—	15.00	30.00	60.00	120	—
1797	—	15.00	30.00	60.00	120	—
1799	—	45.00	70.00	185	340	—

KM# 172 2 ROYALINER (2 Fano, 2 Fanams)

Silver **Ruler:** Christian VII **Issuer:** Danish Royal Colony
Obverse: Crowned C7 monogram **Reverse:** Arms divides date, value above

Date	Mintage	VG	F	VF	XF	Unc
1786R	—	200	300	500	1,000	—

KM# 174 PAGODE (Pagoda)

Gold **Ruler:** Christian VII **Issuer:** Danish Royal Colony
Obverse: Crowned C7 monogram in oval on granulated field
Reverse: Indian diety

Date	Mintage	VG	F	VF	XF	Unc
ND(1789)	—	2,500	3,500	5,000	10,000	—

TRIAL STRIKES

KM#	Date	Mintage	Identification	Mkt Val
TS1	ND1756	—	Royalin. Billon. Counterstamp on Danish 1 Skilling.	675
TS2	ND1756	—	Royalin. Billon. Counterstamp on Danish 2 Skilling.	—
TS3	ND1756	—	Royalin. Tin.	—
TS4	ND	—	Royalin. Tin.	—
TS5	ND1756	—	Royalin. Silver.	500
TS6	ND	—	Royalin. Silver.	675
TS7	ND1756	—	Royalin. Gold..	—
TS8	ND	—	Royalin. Gold.	1,500
TS9	ND1756	—	2 Royaliner. Billon. Counterstamp on Danish 2 Skilling.	2,000
TS10	ND	—	2 Royaliner. Tin.	—
TS11	ND1756	—	2 Royaliner. Silver. Thin planchet.	500
TS12	ND1756	—	2 Royaliner. Silver. Thick planchet.	—
TS13	ND	—	2 Royaliner. Silver.	700
TS14	ND1756	—	2 Royaliner. Gold.	4,000
TS15	ND	—	2 Royaliner. Gold.	1,700

INDIA-FRENCH

It was not until 1664, during the reign of Louis XIV, that the Compagnie des Indes Orientales was formed for the purpose of obtaining holdings on the subcontinent of India. Between 1666 and 1721, French settlements were established at Arcot, Mahe, Surat, Pondichery, Masulipatam, Karikal, Yanam, Murshidabad, Chandernagore, Balasore and Calicut. War with Britain reduced the French holdings to Chandernagore, Pondichery, Karikal, Yanam and Mahe. Chandernagore voted in 1949 to join India and became part of the Republic of India in 1950. Pondichery, Karikal, Yanam and Mahe formed the Pondichery union territory and joined the republic of India in 1954.

RULER

French, until 1954

MINTS

اركات

Arcot (Arkat)
Mint mark:

Crescent

A crescent moon mint mark is found to left of the regnal year for those struck at the Pondichery Mint. For listings of similar coins with lotus mint mark refer to India-British-Madras Presidency.

Masulipatnam

Mint mark
Trident

مرشداباد

Murshidabad
(Moxoudabat)

In 1738, Dupleix, then the governor of Chandernagor obtained coining rights. These issues are very similar to the late issues of the Mughals. For later issues refer to India-British-Bengal Presidency.

Mint mark
Jasmine Flower

پهلچري

Pondichery

A city south of Madras on the southeast coast which became the site of the French Mint from 1700 to 1841. Pondichery was settled by the French in 1683. It became their main Indian possession even though it was occupied by the Dutch in 1693-1698 and several times by the British from 1761-1816.

سورت

Surat

The French silver coins struck similar to late Mughal issues in two different periods. See also India-British, Bombay Presidency.

MONETARY SYSTEM

Cache Kas or Cash
Doudou = 4 Caches
Biche = 1 Pice
2 Royalins = 1 Fanon Pondichery
5 Heavy Fanons = 1 Rupee Mahe
64 Biches = 1 Rupee

NOTE: The undated coinage was struck ca. 1720 well into the early 19th century.

ARCOT

HAMMERED COINAGE

KM# A28 1/32 RUPEE

0.3600 g., Silver **Ruler:** Shah Alam II **Mint:** Murshidabad
Obverse: Persian - Shah Alam (II) couplet **Reverse:** Persian - Julus (formula), mint name

Date	Mintage	VG	F	VF	XF	Unc
AH1183 //0	—	125	225	375	500	—

KM# B28 1/16 RUPEE

0.7200 g., Silver **Ruler:** Shah Alam II **Mint:** Murshidabad
Obverse: Persian - Shah Alam (II) couplet **Reverse:** Persian - Julus (formula), mint name

Date	Mintage	VG	F	VF	XF	Unc
AH1183 //0	—	125	225	375	500	—

KM# 13 1/4 RUPEE

2.8000 g., Silver **Ruler:** Shah Alam II **Mint:** Arkat **Obverse:** Persian - Shah Alam II couplet **Reverse:** Persian - Julus (formula), mint name **Note:** Similar coins with crescent mint mark were also issued by Mysore Sate, using the latter mint name.

Date	Mintage	Good	VG	F	VF	XF
AHxxxx//45	—	—	35.00	70.00	100	160
AH1184//10	—	—	21.50	42.00	85.00	120

KM# 3 1/4 RUPEE

2.8100 g., Silver **Ruler:** Muhammad Shah **Mint:** Arkat **Obverse:** Persian - Muhammad Shah, regal title **Reverse:** Persian - Julus (formula), mint name

Date	Mintage	VG	F	VF	XF	Unc
AH1149 //19 (1737)	—	80.00	135	225	325	—

KM# 25 1/4 RUPEE

2.8000 g., Silver **Ruler:** Muhammad Shah **Mint:** Murshidabad **Obverse:** Persian - Muhammed Shah **Reverse:** Persian - Julus (formula), mint name

Date	Mintage	VG	F	VF	XF	Unc
AH1151 //21	—	20.00	30.00	100	140	—
AH115x //24	—	20.00	30.00	100	140	—

KM# 6 1/4 RUPEE

2.8000 g., Silver **Ruler:** Ahmad Shah Bahadur **Mint:** Arkat **Obverse:** Persian - Ahmad Shah Bahadur **Reverse:** Persian - Julus (formula), mint name

Date	Mintage	VG	F	VF	XF	Unc
AH1163 //3	—	90.00	150	225	325	—
AH1165 //5	—	90.00	150	225	325	—

KM# 10 1/4 RUPEE

2.8000 g., Silver **Ruler:** Alamgir II **Mint:** Arkat **Obverse:** Persian - Alamgir (II) **Reverse:** Persian - Julus (formula), mint name

Date	Mintage	VG	F	VF	XF	Unc
AH1168 //1	—	60.00	120	175	250	—
AH1169 //3	—	30.00	60.00	85.00	125	—
AH1171 //4	—	30.00	60.00	85.00	125	—

KM# 28 1/4 RUPEE

2.8000 g., Silver **Ruler:** Shah Alam II **Mint:** Murshidabad **Obverse:** Persian - Shah Alam (II) couplet **Reverse:** Persian - Julus (formula), mint name

Date	Mintage	VG	F	VF	XF	Unc
AH1183 //10	—	15.00	25.00	65.00	100	—
AH1184 //11	—	15.00	25.00	65.00	100	—
AH1185 //12	—	15.00	25.00	65.00	100	—

KM# 4 1/2 RUPEE

5.6300 g., Silver **Ruler:** Muhammad Shah **Mint:** Arkat **Obverse:** Persian - Muhammad Shah **Reverse:** Persian - Julus (formula), mint name

Date	Mintage	VG	F	VF	XF	Unc
AH1149 //19	—	90.00	150	240	350	—

KM# 26 1/2 RUPEE

5.8000 g., Silver **Ruler:** Muhammad Shah **Mint:** Murshidabad **Obverse:** Persian - Muhammed Shah **Reverse:** Persian - Julus (formula), mint name

Date	Mintage	VG	F	VF	XF	Unc
AH1151 //21	—	20.00	30.00	100	140	—

KM# 7 1/2 RUPEE

5.6000 g., Silver **Ruler:** Ahmad Shah Bahadur **Mint:** Arkat **Obverse:** Persian - Ahmad Shah Bahadur **Reverse:** Persian - Julus (formula), mint name

Date	Mintage	VG	F	VF	XF	Unc
AH116x //3	—	90.00	150	225	325	—

KM# 11 1/2 RUPEE

5.7000 g., Silver **Ruler:** Alamgir II **Mint:** Arkat **Obverse:** Persian - Alamgir (II) **Reverse:** Persian - Julus (formula), mint name

Date	Mintage	VG	F	VF	XF	Unc
AH1167 //1	—	30.00	60.00	85.00	125	—
AH1168 //0	—	60.00	120	175	250	—

KM# 29 1/2 RUPEE

5.8000 g., Silver **Ruler:** Shah Alam II **Mint:** Murshidabad **Obverse:** Persian - Shah Alam (II) couplet **Reverse:** Persian - Julus (formula), mint name

Date	Mintage	VG	F	VF	XF	Unc
AH1183 //10	—	18.50	30.00	70.00	115	—
AH1184 //11	—	18.50	30.00	70.00	115	—
AH1185 //12	—	18.50	30.00	70.00	115	—

KM# 14 1/2 RUPEE

5.7000 g., Silver **Ruler:** Shah Alam II **Mint:** Arcot **Obverse:** Persian - Shah Alam II couplet **Reverse:** Persian - Julus (formula), mint name

Date	Mintage	Good	VG	F	VF	XF
AH1184//10	—	12.50	25.00	45.00	90.00	130
AH1198//32(sic)	—	12.50	25.00	45.00	90.00	130
AH1205//32(sic)	—	12.50	25.00	45.00	90.00	130

KM# 5 RUPEE

11.2600 g., Silver **Ruler:** Muhammad Shah **Mint:** Arkat **Obverse:** Persian - Muhammad Shah **Reverse:** Persian - Julus (formula), mint name

Date	Mintage	VG	F	VF	XF	Unc
AH1149 //19	—	25.00	45.00	75.00	125	—
AH1153 //23	—	25.00	45.00	75.00	125	—
AH115x //24	—	25.00	45.00	75.00	125	—
AH1155 //25	—	25.00	45.00	75.00	125	—
AH1156 //26	—	25.00	45.00	75.00	125	—
AH1159 //29	—	25.00	45.00	75.00	125	—
AH116x //30	—	17.50	30.00	45.00	75.00	—

KM# 27 RUPEE

11.6000 g., Silver **Ruler:** Muhammad Shah **Mint:** Murshidabad **Obverse:** Persian - Muhammed Shah **Reverse:** Persian - Julus (formula), mint name

Date	Mintage	VG	F	VF	XF	Unc
AH1151//21	—	30.00	45.00	100	150	—
AH1152//22	—	30.00	45.00	100	150	—

KM# 20 RUPEE

11.4000 g., Silver **Ruler:** Ahmad Shah Bahadur **Mint:** *Machhlipatan* **Obverse:** Persian- Ahmad Shah Bahadur **Reverse:** Persian - Julus (formula), mint name **Note:** Mint mark: Trident.

Date	Mintage	VG	F	VF	XF	Unc
AH- //2 Trisul (Trident)	—	50.00	80.00	200	275	—
AH- //4 Trisul (Trident)	—	50.00	80.00	200	275	—

KM# 8 RUPEE

11.5000 g., Silver **Ruler:** Ahmad Shah Bahadur **Mint:** Arkat **Obverse:** Persian - Ahmad Shah Bahadur **Reverse:** Persian - Julus (formula), mint name

Date	Mintage	VG	F	VF	XF	Unc
AH1161 //1	—	18.50	35.00	60.00	85.00	—
AH1162 //2	—	18.50	35.00	60.00	85.00	—
AH1163 //3	—	18.50	35.00	60.00	85.00	—
AH1164 //4	—	18.50	35.00	60.00	85.00	—
AH1165 //5	—	18.50	35.00	60.00	85.00	—
AH1166 //6	—	18.50	35.00	60.00	85.00	—
AH1167 //7	—	18.50	35.00	60.00	85.00	—

KM# 12 RUPEE

11.4000 g., Silver **Ruler:** Alamgir II **Mint:** Arkat **Obverse:** Persian - Alamgir (II) **Reverse:** Persian - Julus (formula), mint name

Date	Mintage	VG	F	VF	XF	Unc
AH1167 ////1 Ahad	—	20.00	42.50	85.00	120	—
AH116x //2	—	20.00	42.50	85.00	120	—
AH11xx //3	—	20.00	42.50	85.00	120	—
AH1171 //4	—	20.00	42.50	85.00	120	—
AH117x //5	—	20.00	42.00	85.00	120	—

KM# 21 RUPEE

Silver **Ruler:** Alamgir II **Mint:** *Machhlipatan* **Obverse:** Persian - Alamgir (II) **Reverse:** Persian - Julus (formula), mint name **Note:** Mint mark: Trident.

Date	Mintage	VG	F	VF	XF	Unc
AH- //1 Trisul (Trident)	—	55.00	90.00	225	300	—
AH- //6 Trisul (Trident)	—	55.00	90.00	225	300	—

KM# 15 RUPEE

11.4000 g., Silver **Ruler:** Shah Alam II **Mint:** Arcot **Obverse:** Persian-Shah Alam(II) couplet **Obv. Inscription:** "Shah Alam II" **Reverse:** Persian-Julus (formula), mint name

Date	Mintage	Good	VG	F	VF	XF
AH1177//4	—	5.00	12.50	20.00	30.00	50.00
AH1178//5	—	5.00	12.50	20.00	30.00	50.00
AH1181//7	—	5.00	12.50	20.00	30.00	50.00
AH1182//8	—	5.00	12.50	20.00	30.00	50.00
AH1183//8	—	5.00	12.50	20.00	30.00	50.00
AH1183//9	—	5.00	12.50	20.00	30.00	50.00
AH1184//10	—	5.00	12.50	20.00	30.00	50.00
AH1185//10	—	5.00	12.50	20.00	30.00	50.00
AH1186//11	—	5.00	12.50	20.00	30.00	50.00
AH1187//12	—	5.00	12.50	20.00	30.00	50.00
AH1188//13	—	5.00	12.50	20.00	30.00	50.00
AH1189//14	—	5.00	12.50	20.00	30.00	50.00
AH(11)89//15	—	5.00	12.50	20.00	30.00	50.00
AH1190//15	—	5.00	12.50	20.00	30.00	50.00
AH1191//16	—	5.00	12.50	20.00	30.00	50.00
AH1191//17	—	5.00	12.50	20.00	30.00	50.00
AH1197//22	—	5.00	12.50	20.00	30.00	50.00
AH1198//32(sic)	—	5.00	12.50	20.00	30.00	50.00
AH1199//24	—	5.00	12.50	20.00	30.00	50.00
AH1200//25	—	5.00	12.50	20.00	30.00	50.00
AH1201//26	—	5.00	12.50	20.00	30.00	50.00
AH1202//27	—	5.00	12.50	20.00	30.00	50.00
AH1203//27	—	5.00	12.50	20.00	30.00	50.00
AH1204//29	—	5.00	12.50	20.00	30.00	50.00
AH1205//30	—	5.00	12.50	20.00	30.00	50.00
AH1206//31	—	5.00	12.50	20.00	30.00	50.00
AH1207//32	—	5.00	12.50	20.00	30.00	50.00
AH1208//34	—	5.00	12.50	20.00	30.00	50.00

KM# 30 RUPEE

11.6000 g., Silver **Ruler:** Shah Alam II **Mint:** Murshidabad **Obverse:** Persian - Shah Alam (II) couplet **Reverse:** Persian - Julus (formula), mint name **Note:** For other years refer to India-British-Bengal Presidency.

Date	Mintage	VG	F	VF	XF	Unc
AH1183 //10	—	22.50	37.50	75.00	125	—
AH1184 //11	—	22.50	37.50	75.00	125	—
AH1185 //12	—	22.50	37.50	75.00	125	—

KM# 9 NAZARANA RUPEE

11.5000 g., Silver **Ruler:** Ahmad Shah Bahadur **Mint:** Arkat **Obverse:** Persian - Ahmad Shah Bahadur **Reverse:** Persian - Julus (formula), mint name

Date	Mintage	VG	F	VF	XF	Unc
AH1164 //4	—	—	300	530	800	—

KM# 16 NAZARANA RUPEE
11.4000 g., Silver, 32-33 mm. **Ruler:** Shah Alam II **Mint:** Arcot **Obverse:** Persian - Shah Alam II couplet **Reverse:** Persian - Julius (formula), mint name **Note:** Size varies.

Date	Mintage	VG	F	VF	XF	Unc
AH1178//5	—	150	250	450	750	—
AH1181//6	—	150	250	450	750	—
AH1183//9	—	150	250	450	750	—
AH1184//10	—	150	250	450	750	—
AH1185//10	—	150	250	450	750	—
AH1185//11	—	150	250	450	750	—
AH1198//32(sic)	—	150	250	450	750	—
AH1199//24	—	150	250	450	750	—

KM# 17.1 NAZARANA 2 RUPEES
22.5000 g., Silver **Ruler:** Shah Alam II **Mint:** Arkat **Obverse:** Persian - Shah Alam (II) couplet **Reverse:** Persian - Julus (formula), mint name **Edge:** Reeded

Date	Mintage	VG	F	VF	XF	Unc
AH1181 //6	—	—	550	1,000	1,750	—

KM# 17.2 NAZARANA 2 RUPEES
22.5000 g., Silver **Ruler:** Shah Alam II **Mint:** Arkat **Obverse:** Persian - Shah Alam (II) couplet **Reverse:** Persian - Julus (formula), mint name **Edge:** Plain

Date	Mintage	VG	F	VF	XF	Unc
AH1181 //6	—	—	550	1,000	1,750	—

KM# 2 MOHUR
Gold **Ruler:** Muhammad Shah **Mint:** Arkat **Obverse:** Persian - Muhammad Shah **Reverse:** Persian - Julus (formula), mint name

Date	Mintage	VG	F	VF	XF	Unc
AH1150/20 //20 Rare	—	—	—	—	—	—

KM# A6 PAISA
10.1400 g., Copper **Ruler:** Ahmad Shah Bahadur **Mint:** Arkat **Obverse:** Persian - Ahmad Shah Bahadur **Reverse:** Persian - Julus (formula), mint name

Date	Mintage	VG	F	VF	XF	Unc
AH- //2	—	10.00	16.50	22.00	—	—

KM# 23 ANNA
0.6000 g., Silver **Ruler:** Muhammad Shah **Mint:** Murshidabad **Obverse:** Persian - Muhammed Shah **Reverse:** Persian - Julus (formula), mint name

Date	Mintage	VG	F	VF	XF	Unc
AH- //21	—	—	—	—	—	—

KARIKAL

A town south of Pondichery on the southeast coast. It was ceded to France in 1739. Coins listed here were struck at the Pondichery Mint.

HAMMERED COINAGE

KM# 58 CACHE
1.2000 g., Copper **Obverse:** Tamil - ka/reik/kal **Reverse:** Tamil - Puda/Tche/ri

Date	Mintage	Good	VG	F	VF	XF
ND(1740)	—	4.00	6.50	14.00	25.00	—

KM# 59 1/2 DOUDOU
3.0000 g., Copper, 12-13 mm. **Obverse:** Tamil - ka/reik/kal **Reverse:** Tamil - Puda/Tche/ri **Note:** Size varies.

Date	Mintage	Good	VG	F	VF	XF
ND(1740)	—	6.00	10.00	17.50	30.00	—

KM# 60 DOUDOU
3.2000 g., Copper **Obverse:** Tamil - ka/reik/kal **Reverse:** Tamil - Puda/Tche/ri

Date	Mintage	Good	VG	F	VF	XF
ND(1740)	—	6.00	10.00	17.50	30.00	—

MAHE

A town south of Tellicherry on the southwest coast. It was ceded to France in 1726. Coins listed here were struck at the Pondichery Mint.

HAMMERED COINAGE

KM# 66 FANON (1/5 Rupee)
Silver **Mint:** *Bhultcheri* **Obverse:** Persian - Frans/campangi **Reverse:** Persian - mint name

Date	Mintage	VG	F	VF	XF	Unc
1731	—	15.00	21.50	30.00	40.00	—
1732	—	15.00	21.50	30.00	40.00	—
1733	—	15.00	21.50	30.00	40.00	—
1734	—	15.00	21.50	30.00	40.00	—
1735	—	15.00	21.50	30.00	40.00	—

KM# 67 FANON (1/5 Rupee)
Silver **Mint:** *Bhultcheri* **Obverse:** Persian - Frans/campangi **Reverse:** Persian - mint name

Date	Mintage	VG	F	VF	XF	Unc
1738P	—	13.50	20.00	27.50	37.50	—
1743P	—	13.50	20.00	27.50	37.50	—
1744P	—	13.50	20.00	27.50	37.50	—
1749P	—	13.50	20.00	27.50	37.50	—
1750P	—	13.50	20.00	27.50	37.50	—
1751P	—	13.50	20.00	27.50	37.50	—
1752P	—	13.50	20.00	27.50	37.50	—
1753P	—	13.50	20.00	27.50	37.50	—
1754P	—	13.50	20.00	27.50	37.50	—
1755P	—	13.50	20.00	27.50	37.50	—
1766P	—	13.50	20.00	27.50	37.50	—
1767P	—	13.50	20.00	27.50	37.50	—
1768P	—	13.50	20.00	27.50	37.50	—
1771P	—	13.50	20.00	27.50	37.50	—
1774P	—	13.50	20.00	27.50	37.50	—
1775P	—	13.50	20.00	27.50	37.50	—
1776P	—	13.50	20.00	27.50	37.50	—
1777P	—	13.50	20.00	27.50	37.50	—
1778P	—	13.50	20.00	27.50	37.50	—
1782P	—	13.50	20.00	27.50	37.50	—
1788P	—	13.50	20.00	27.50	37.50	—
1792P	—	13.50	20.00	27.50	37.50	—

KM# 63 1/4 BICHE
1.4000 g., Bronze **Obverse:** 5 fleur-de-lis **Reverse:** Date

Date	Mintage	Good	VG	F	VF	XF
1752	—	12.50	20.00	35.00	60.00	—
1753	—	12.50	20.00	35.00	60.00	—
1767	—	12.50	20.00	35.00	60.00	—
1769	—	12.50	20.00	35.00	60.00	—

KM# 64 1/2 BICHE
3.5000 g., Bronze **Obverse:** 5 fleur-de-lis **Reverse:** Date

Date	Mintage	Good	VG	F	VF	XF
1730	—	7.50	13.50	22.50	30.00	—
1731	—	8.50	16.50	25.00	35.00	—
1743	—	6.50	13.50	22.50	30.00	—
1752	—	6.50	13.50	22.50	30.00	—
1753	—	6.50	13.50	22.50	30.00	—
1769	—	6.50	13.50	22.50	30.00	—
1785	—	6.50	13.50	22.50	30.00	—

KM# 65 BICHE
6.3500 g., Bronze **Obverse:** 5 fleur-de-lis **Reverse:** Date

Date	Mintage	Good	VG	F	VF	XF
1730	—	8.00	13.50	30.00	45.00	—
1731	—	7.50	11.50	20.00	27.50	—
1736	—	7.50	11.50	20.00	27.50	—
1740	—	7.50	11.50	20.00	27.50	—
1750	—	7.50	11.50	20.00	27.50	—
1752	—	7.50	11.50	20.00	27.50	—
1753	—	7.50	11.50	20.00	27.50	—
1755	—	7.50	11.50	20.00	27.50	—
1756	—	7.50	11.50	20.00	27.50	—
1767	—	8.00	13.50	25.00	40.00	—
1769	—	8.00	13.50	25.00	40.00	—
1785	—	6.50	11.50	17.50	25.00	—
1787	—	6.50	11.50	17.50	25.00	—
1790	—	6.50	10.00	15.00	25.00	—

PONDICHERY

Dutch Occupation

HAMMERED COINAGE

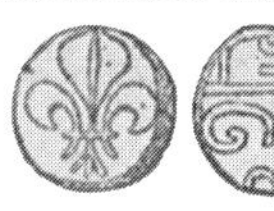

KM# 33 CACHE
1.6000 g., Bronze **Mint:** Tamil - *Pudu/tche/ri* **Obverse:** Fleur-de-lis

Date	Mintage	Good	VG	F	VF	XF
ND(1720-1835)	—	3.50	6.50	13.50	25.00	—

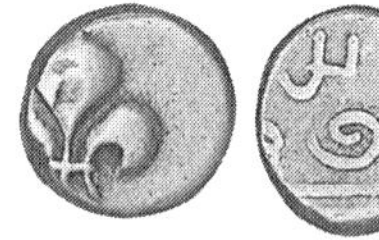

KM# 34 1/2 DOUDOU
Bronze, 13-15 mm. **Mint:** Tamil - *Pudu/tche/ri* **Obverse:** Fleur-de-lis **Note:** Weight varies: 2.00-2.50 grams. Size varies.

Date	Mintage	Good	VG	F	VF	XF
ND(1720-1835)	—	2.00	3.00	6.00	15.00	—

KM# 35 DOUDOU
4.2000 g., Copper **Mint:** Tamil - *Pudu/tche/ri* **Obverse:** Fleur-de-lis

Date	Mintage	Good	VG	F	VF	XF
ND(1720-1835)	—	2.00	3.00	5.00	12.00	—

KM# 37 1/2 FANON
Silver **Obverse:** Small pearled crown **Reverse:** 5 fleur-de-lis **Note:** Weight varies 0.50-0.70 grams.

Date	Mintage	VG	F	VF	XF	Unc
ND(1715-20)	—	10.00	17.50	35.00	60.00	—

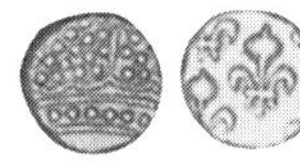

KM# 39 1/2 FANON
Silver **Obverse:** Large pearley crown **Reverse:** 5 Fleur-de-lis **Note:** Weight varies 0.50-0.70 grams.

Date	Mintage	Good	VG	F	VF	XF
ND(1720-1837)	—	5.00	10.00	15.00	25.00	40.00

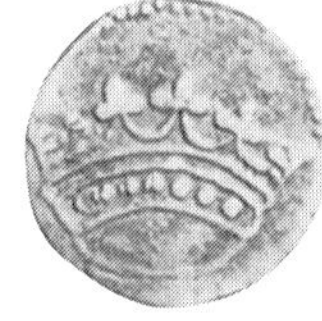

KM# 36 1/2 FANON
Bronze, 19-20 mm. **Obverse:** Crown **Reverse:** 10 small Fleur-de-lis **Note:** Size varies.

Date	Mintage	Good	VG	F	VF	XF
ND(1723)	—	25.00	50.00	100	175	—

KM# 41 FANON
Silver **Obverse:** Small pearled crowned **Reverse:** 5 fleur-de-lis

Date	Mintage	VG	F	VF	XF	Unc
ND(1715-1720)	—	25.00	45.00	125	200	—

KM# A41 FANON
2.5000 g., 0.9480 Silver 0.0762 oz. ASW **Obverse:** Crowned Lis **Reverse:** Lis in center of outlined cross

Date	Mintage	VG	F	VF	XF	Unc
ND(1720)	—	40.00	65.00	175	250	—

KM# 42 FANON
Bronze **Obverse:** Crown **Reverse:** 9 fleur-de-lis

Date	Mintage	Good	VG	F	VF	XF
ND(1723)	—	20.00	40.00	100	175	—

KM# 43 FANON

1.6000 g., Silver **Obverse:** Crown **Reverse:** 5 fleur-de-lis

Date	Mintage	VG	F	VF	XF	Unc
ND(1750)	—	15.00	25.00	80.00	140	—

KM# 44 FANON

Silver **Obverse:** Pearled crown **Reverse:** 5 fleur-de-lis **Note:** Weight varies 1.50-1.60 grams.

Date	Mintage	VG	F	VF	XF	Unc
ND(1760)	—	10.00	15.00	28.00	45.00	—

KM# 49 2 FANON

3.0000 g., Silver, 14-15 mm. **Obverse:** Ornamented crown **Reverse:** 5 fleur-de-lis **Note:** Size varies.

Date	Mintage	Good	VG	F	VF	XF
ND(1720-1837)	—	8.50	16.50	28.50	45.00	75.00

KM# 46 2 FANON

0.9480 Silver **Obverse:** Crowned lis **Reverse:** Lis in center of outlined cross **Note:** Weight varies 5.00-6.00 grams.

Date	Mintage	VG	F	VF	XF	Unc
ND(1720)	—	75.00	125	200	325	—

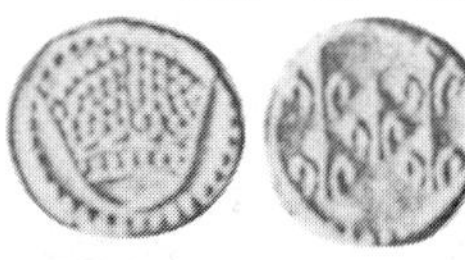

KM# 48 2 FANON

3.0000 g., Silver, 15-16 mm. **Obverse:** Pearled crown **Reverse:** 5 fleur-de-lis **Note:** Size varies.

Date	Mintage	Good	VG	F	VF	XF
ND(1720-1837)	—	8.50	16.50	28.50	45.00	75.00

KM# 47 2 FANON

3.0000 g., Silver, 18-20 mm. **Obverse:** Ornamented crown **Reverse:** 5 fleur-de-lis **Note:** Size varies.

Date	Mintage	VG	F	VF	XF	Unc
ND(1770)	—	55.00	75.00	100	250	—

KM# 50 PAGODA

3.4000 g., Gold **Obverse:** Deity Kali **Reverse:** Crescent in granular field

Date	Mintage	VG	F	VF	XF	Unc
ND(1715-74)	—	125	175	275	375	—

YANAON

Located on the Golconda coast northeast of Mazulipatam. This pagoda was struck at the Pondichery Mint.

HAMMERED COINAGE

KM# 72 RUPEE

11.4000 g., Silver **Ruler:** Ahmad Shah Bahadur **Mint:** Surat **Obverse:** Persian - Ahmad Shah Bahadur **Reverse:** Persian - Julus (formula), mint name

Date	Mintage	VG	F	VF	XF	Unc
AH- //2	—	55.00	85.00	175	250	—

KM# 74 RUPEE

11.4000 g., Silver **Ruler:** Alamgir II **Mint:** Surat **Obverse:** Persian - Alamgir (II) **Reverse:** Persian - Julus (formula), mint name

Date	Mintage	VG	F	VF	XF	Unc
AH- //2	—	55.00	85.00	175	250	—

KM# 69 PAGODA

3.4000 g., Gold **Mint:** Pondichery **Obverse:** 3 figures with Vishu in center **Reverse:** Crescent in granular field

Date	Mintage	VG	F	VF	XF	Unc
ND(1715-1774)	—	100	175	300	400	—

PATTERNS

Including off metal strikes

KM#	Date	Mintage	Identification	Mkt Val
Pn1	ND(1720-1835)	—	Doudou. Bronze. 4.4000 g.	—

INDIA-DUTCH

The Netherlands, operating as the United East India Company of the Netherlands, were the real successors to the Portuguese in India. They maintained a number of thriving establishments on the subcontinent until 1795, when Robert Clive, founder of the empire of British India, completed Britain's conquest of Bengal. Thereafter the Dutch holdings were gradually ceded to Britain, the most important to numismatics being Cochin, ceded in 1814; Negapatnam, ceded in 1784; Pulicat, ceded in 1824; and Tuticorin, ceded in 1795.

MINTS

Cochin

Cochin, which is located on the west coast in South India, was acquired from Portugal in 1663. Even though the British occupied it in 1795 it wasn't ceded to them until 1814. Later issues are referenced with Indian Princely States - Cochin.

Jagganthapur

Masulipatnam

A Dutch trading station since 1605AD. The gold coins were struck on the old South Indian standards, mainly to pay the rent to the local ruler. Taken over by the French in 1751AD.

Negapatnam

Taken from the Portuguese in 1658AD. Mint right established in 1662. VOC - head-office of the Coromandel (Southeast Indian coast) from 1690AD to the British takeover in 1784AD.

Pulicat

VOC head office of the Coromandel (South East Indian coast) from its establishment in 1610-1690 and after 1784. Fortress Gelria was the first company mint in India. It was a British possession from 1781-1784, 1795-1818 and finally ceded to Great Britain in 1824.

Tuticorin

MONETARY SYSTEM

80 Cash = 1 Silver Fanam
6 Stuivers = 1 Silver Fanam
24 Gold Fanam = 1 Pagoda

MINT MARKS

NOTE: On Princely style coins the Dutch East India Company often used the mint mark: Lazy J (possibly a Kris: Malay knife).

MONETARY SYSTEM

(1724-1795)

8 Bazaruk = 1 Duit
4 Duiten = 1 Stuiver
8 Silver Fanams = 1 Stuiver

COLONY

HAMMERED COINAGE

KM# 2 BAZARUK

Tin **Mint:** Cochin **Obverse:** VOC monogram **Reverse:** Cauri shell

Date	Mintage	Good	VG	F	VF	XF
ND(1663-1724)	—	—	—	—	—	—

KM# 3 BAZARUK

Tin **Mint:** Cochin **Obverse:** 8/VOC monogram **Reverse:** Oval shield **Note:** 1/8 Duit.

Date	Mintage	Good	VG	F	VF	XF
ND(1724-95)	—	—	—	—	—	—

KM# 4 1/2 RASI

Copper **Mint:** Cochin **Note:** Struck for trade with Muscat. Weight varies 5.42-5.89 grams. Similar to 1 Rasi, KM#5.

Date	Mintage	Good	VG	F	VF	XF
ND	—	20.00	35.00	75.00	150	—

KM# 5 RASI

Copper **Mint:** Cochin **Note:** Weight varies 10.84-11.79 grams. Struck for trade with Muscat.

Date	Mintage	Good	VG	F	VF	XF
ND	—	5.00	10.00	20.00	40.00	—

KM# 9 1/2 RUPEE

Silver **Mint:** Jagganthapur

Date	Mintage	VG	F	VF	XF	Unc
NDYr.28	—	—	—	—	—	—

KM# 40 FANAM

Gold **Mint:** Pulicat **Obverse:** Degenerated Kali **Reverse:** Similar to 1 Cash, KM#35; Arabic legend **Rev. Legend:** "In the name of Sultan Abd'allah"

Date	Mintage	VG	F	VF	XF	Unc
ND(1646-1781) Rare	—	—	—	—	—	—

KM# 6 FANAM

Gold **Mint:** Cochin **Reverse:** Lazy "J" above OC/three rows of four dots each

Date	Mintage	VG	F	VF	XF	Unc
ND(1740-80)	—	25.00	35.00	50.00	80.00	—

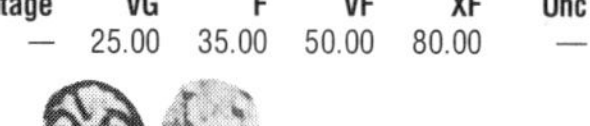

KM# 7 FANAM

Silver **Mint:** Cochin

Date	Mintage	VG	F	VF	XF	Unc
ND(1782-91)	—	10.00	15.00	20.00	35.00	—

KM# 8 FANAM

Silver **Mint:** Cochin

Date	Mintage	VG	F	VF	XF	Unc
ND	—	10.00	15.00	20.00	35.00	—

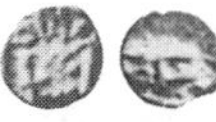

KM# 48 FANAM

Gold **Mint:** Tuticorin **Obverse:** Degenerated Kali **Reverse:** Degenerated Nagari legend "Rama Raya"

Date	Mintage	VG	F	VF	XF	Unc
ND(1785-92)	—	20.00	35.00	75.00	150	—

Note: Similar coins were struck at Negapatnam, KM#31, the difference is in the shape of the letter "Ra"

KM# 10 PAGODA

Gold **Mint:** Masulipatnam **Obverse:** Facing figures of three gods with two pointed crowns **Reverse:** Granular dots

Date	Mintage	VG	F	VF	XF	Unc
ND(1646-1747) Rare	—	—	—	—	—	—

Note: Copied by the British (Madras KM#3a) and the Nawab of Arcot (KM#13)

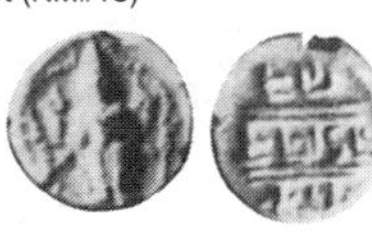

KM# 41 PAGODA

Gold **Mint:** Pulicat **Obverse:** Facing figure of God Ganesh **Reverse:** Three-line Nagari inscription

Date	Mintage	VG	F	VF	XF	Unc
ND(1646-1781) Unique	—	—	—	—	—	—

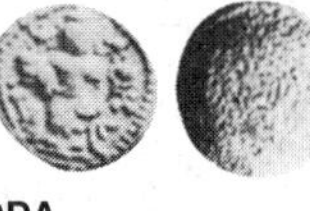

KM# 21 PAGODA

Gold **Mint:** Negapatnam **Obverse:** Facing god, lazy "J" at right **Reverse:** Granulated

Date	Mintage	VG	F	VF	XF	Unc
ND(1662-1749) Rare	—	—	—	—	—	—

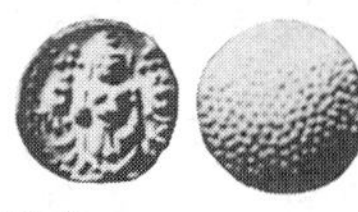

KM# 22 PAGODA

Gold **Mint:** Negapatnam **Obverse:** Degenerated Vishnu, lazy "J" **Reverse:** Granulated

Date	Mintage	VG	F	VF	XF	Unc
ND(1747-84)	—	60.00	70.00	85.00	100	—

Note: Pagodas with devices on reverse were struck in Tranquebar KM#174, Madras KM#303, Pondichery KM#129, Arcot KM#14, and Mysore KM#15; Three main varieties exist of the above coin: gold contents of .800 (1747-67), .769 (1767-81) and .675 (1781-84); For similar coins without lazy J see Tuticorn

KM# 49 PAGODA

0.6250 Gold **Mint:** Tuticorin **Obverse:** Degenerated Vinshnu, without lazy "J" at three-o'clock **Reverse:** Granulated

Date	Mintage	VG	F	VF	XF	Unc
ND(1784-94)	7,100	20.00	35.00	75.00	150	—

Note: From 1784-85, Tuticorin coins were struck at Colombo where they also circulated

KM# 44 CASH

Copper **Mint:** Pulicat **Obverse:** P/VOC monogram **Reverse:** Legend, date around G (elria) **Rev. Legend:** PALCATE **Note:** Third Series.

Date	Mintage	VG	F	VF	XF	Unc
1743	—	25.00	40.00	50.00	75.00	—

Note: Struck between 1740-1790, although 1743 is the only confirmed date; Many varieties in spelling

KM# 45 2 CASH

Copper **Mint:** Pulicat **Obverse:** P/VOC monogram **Reverse:** Legend, date around G (elria) **Rev. Legend:** PALCATE **Note:** Third Series.

Date	Mintage	VG	F	VF	XF	Unc
1780	—	30.00	45.00	70.00	100	—

INDIA-PORTUGUESE

Vasco da Gama, the Portuguese explorer, first visited India in 1498. Portugal seized control of a number of islands and small enclaves on the west coast of India, and for the next hundred years enjoyed a monopoly on trade. With the arrival of powerful Dutch and English fleets in the first half of the 17th century, Portuguese power in the area declined until virtually all of India that remained under Portuguese control were the west coast enclaves of Goa, Damao and Diu. They were forcibly annexed by India in 1962.

RULER

Portuguese, until 1961

IDENTIFICATION

The undated coppers are best identified by the shape of the coat of arms.

Maria I – somewhat triangular shield (Baroque style)

Joao VI, as Regent: oval shield

DENOMINATION

The denomination of most copper coins appears in numerals on the reverse, though 30 Reis is often given as "1/2 T", and 60 Reis as "T" (T = Tanga). The silver coins have the denomination in words, usually on the obverse until 1850, then on the reverse.

BACAIM

(Bessein)

Located less than 30 miles north of Bombay on the Gulf of Cambay. In 1611 the Portuguese opened a mint at Bacaim. The greatest minting activity was between 1678 and 1697. Many issues for Bacaim were in conjunction with other Portuguese settlements. The British took Bacaim in 1780.

MINT MARK

B - Bacain

MONETARY SYSTEM

375 Bazarucos = 1 Pardao

2 Pardaos = 1 Rupia

COLONY

HAMMERED COINAGE

KM# 3 2 BAZARUCOS

4.4000 g., Tin **Obverse:** Crude arms divide BB **Reverse:** Crude divided concentric circles

Date	Mintage	Good	VG	F	VF	XF
ND(1706-50)	—	15.00	30.00	50.00	100	—

KM# 2 2 BAZARUCOS

4.4000 g., Tin **Ruler:** John V **Obverse:** Crowned arms divide BB **Reverse:** Divided concentric circles

Date	Mintage	VG	F	VF	XF	Unc
ND(1706-50)	—	35.00	60.00	125	—	—

KM# 7 5 BAZARUCOS

Tin **Ruler:** Jose (Joseph) I

Date	Mintage	Good	VG	F	VF	XF
1770	—	15.00	30.00	50.00	100	—

KM# 9 5 BAZARUCOS

Tin **Reverse:** Maltese cross with date in angles

Date	Mintage	Good	VG	F	VF	XF
1777	—	—	—	—	—	—

Note: Reported, not confirmed

KM# 8 10 BAZARUCOS

Tin **Ruler:** Jose (Joseph) I **Obverse:** Crowned arms **Reverse:** Maltese cross divides date

Date	Mintage	Good	VG	F	VF	XF
1770	—	16.50	32.00	55.00	110	—

KM# 6 PARDAO

Silver **Ruler:** Jose (Joseph) I **Obverse:** Crowned arms **Reverse:** Designed cross divides date

Date	Mintage	Good	VG	F	VF	XF
1766	—	55.00	90.00	150	225	—

KM# 5 RUPIA

Silver **Ruler:** Jose (Joseph) I **Obverse:** Crowned arms **Reverse:** Designed cross divides date

Date	Mintage	Good	VG	F	VF	XF
1759	—	35.00	60.00	100	165	—
1764	—	40.00	65.00	110	175	—
1765	—	45.00	75.00	120	185	—
1766	—	55.00	90.00	150	225	—
1771	—	45.00	72.50	120	200	—

DAMAO

(Daman)

A city located 100 miles north of Bombay. It was captured by the Portuguese in 1559. A mint was opened in Damao in 1611. This mint continued in operation until 1854. While important to early Portuguese trade, Damao dwindled as time passed. It was annexed to India in 1962.

MONETARY SYSTEM

375 Bazacucos = 300 Reis

300 Reis = 1 Pardao

60 Reis = 1 Tanga

2 Pardao (Xerafins) = 1 Rupia

COLONY

CAST COINAGE

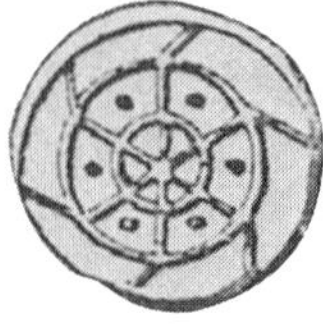

KM# 7 2 BAZARUCOS

3.2000 g., Tin **Ruler:** John V **Obverse:** Crowned arms divide DA **Reverse:** Divided concentric circles

Date	Mintage	Good	VG	F	VF	XF
ND(1706-50)	—	15.00	30.00	50.00	100	—

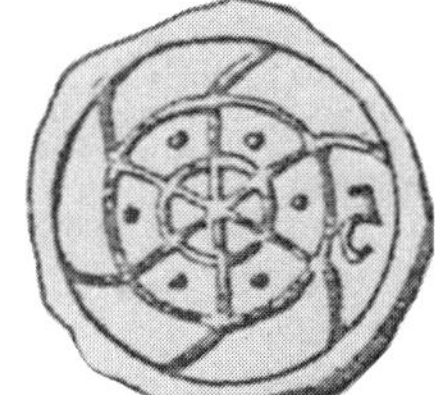

KM# 8 5 BAZARUCOS

5.1000 g., Tin **Ruler:** John V **Obverse:** Crowned arms divide DA **Reverse:** Divided concentric circle, retrograde 5 at right

Date	Mintage	Good	VG	F	VF	XF
ND(1706-50)	—	20.00	40.00	70.00	150	—

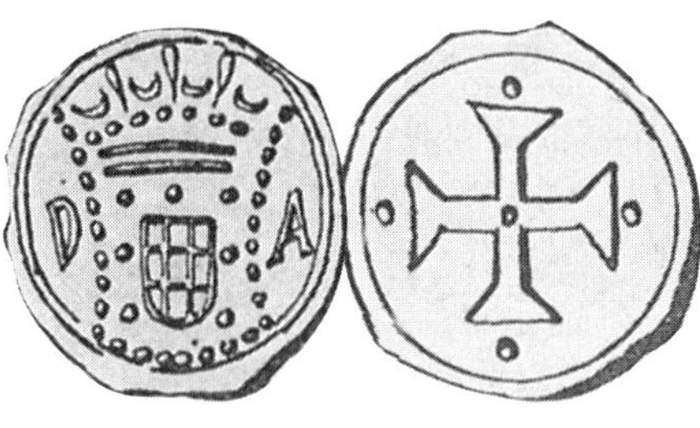

KM# 9 5 BAZARUCOS

5.1000 g., Tin **Obverse:** Crowned arms divides DA **Reverse:** Maltese cross

Date	Mintage	Good	VG	F	VF	XF
ND	—	10.00	20.00	35.00	70.00	—

KM# 18 5 BAZARUCOS

5.1000 g., Tin **Ruler:** Jose (Joseph) I **Obverse:** Crowned arms divides JA **Reverse:** Maltese cross divides date

Date	Mintage	Good	VG	F	VF	XF
1770	—	10.00	20.00	40.00	80.00	—

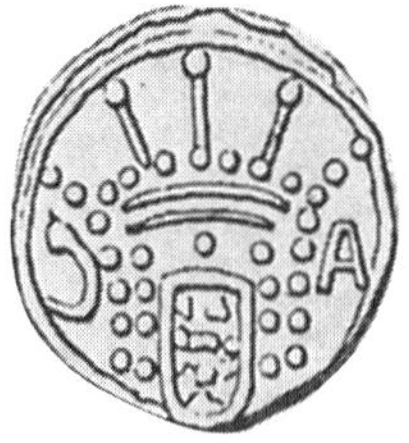

KM# 20 5 BAZARUCOS

5.1000 g., Tin **Ruler:** Jose (Joseph) I **Obverse:** Crowned arms divides JA **Reverse:** Maltese cross divides date in angles

Date	Mintage	Good	VG	F	VF	XF
1775	—	12.00	25.00	50.00	100	—

KM# 10 10 BAZARUCOS

19.8000 g., Tin **Ruler:** John V **Obverse:** Crowned arms divide DA **Reverse:** Divided concentric circles

Date	Mintage	Good	VG	F	VF	XF
ND(1706-50)	—	15.00	30.00	60.00	125	—

KM# 11 10 BAZARUCOS

19.5900 g., Tin **Ruler:** John V **Obverse:** Crowned arms divide DB **Reverse:** Divided concentric circles **Note:** For Damao and Bacaim.

Date	Mintage	Good	VG	F	VF	XF
ND(1706-50)	—	40.00	80.00	150	300	—

KM# 12 10 BAZARUCOS

21.7100 g., Tin **Ruler:** John V **Obverse:** Crowned arms divide DC **Reverse:** Divided concentric circles **Note:** For Damao and Chaul.

Date	Mintage	Good	VG	F	VF	XF
ND(1706-50)	—	70.00	130	250	500	—

KM# A18 10 BAZARUCOS

18.9500 g., Tin **Ruler:** John V **Subject:** For Bacaim and Diu **Obverse:** Crowned arms divide DB in plain circle **Reverse:** Numerals of date in angles of cross in plain circle

Date	Mintage	Good	VG	F	VF	XF
1723	—	75.00	125	250	500	—
1734	—	100	175	325	650	—

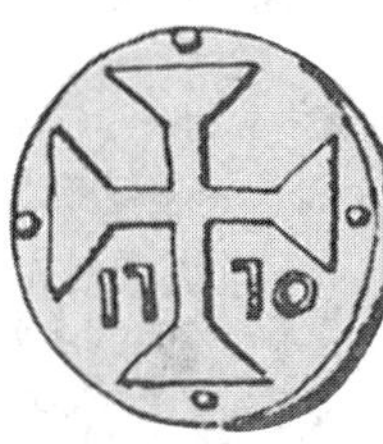

KM# 19 10 BAZARUCOS
9.5000 g., Tin **Ruler:** Jose (Joseph) I **Obverse:** Crowned arms divides AO **Reverse:** Maltese cross divides date

Date	Mintage	Good	VG	F	VF	XF
1770	—	12.00	25.00	50.00	100	—

HAMMERED COINAGE

KM# 14 10 REIS
8.0000 g., Copper **Ruler:** John V **Obverse:** Crowned I V in branches, date below **Reverse:** Three crossed arrows pointing downward between DB, value below

Date	Mintage	Good	VG	F	VF	XF
1735	—	50.00	100	200	400	—

KM# 15 20 REIS
18.0000 g., Copper **Ruler:** John V **Obverse:** Crowned I V in branches, date below **Reverse:** Three crossed arrows pointing downward between DB, value below

Date	Mintage	Good	VG	F	VF	XF
1735	—	40.00	80.00	175	350	—

KM# 13 2 XERAFINS
1.5300 g., Gold **Ruler:** Jose (Joseph) I

Date	Mintage	Good	VG	F	VF	XF
ND	—	550	900	1,550	2,250	—

KM# 16 5 XERAFINS
2.8700 g., Gold **Ruler:** Jose (Joseph) I **Obverse:** Crowned arms **Reverse:** Designed cross divides date

Date	Mintage	Good	VG	F	VF	XF
1755	—	600	1,000	1,850	2,750	—

KM# 17 5 XERAFINS
Gold **Ruler:** Jose (Joseph) I **Obverse:** Crowned arms **Reverse:** Designed cross **Note:** Weight varies: 5.69-5.70 grams.

Date	Mintage	Good	VG	F	VF	XF
1755	—	750	1,200	2,250	3,250	—

DIU

A district in Western India formerly belonging to Portugal. It is 170 miles northwest of Bombay on the Kathiawar peninsula. The Portuguese settled here and built a fort in 1535. A mint was opened in 1685 and was closed in 1859. As with Damao, the importance of Diu diminished with the passage of time. It was annexed to India in 1962.

MONETARY SYSTEM
750 Bazarucos = 600 Reis
40 Atia = 10 Tanga = 1 Rupia

COLONY

CAST COINAGE

KM# 48 3 BAZARUCOS
2.4000 g., Tin **Ruler:** Joao, as Prince Regent **Obverse:** Crowned arms **Reverse:** Maltese cross divides date in angles

Date	Mintage	Good	VG	F	VF	XF
1799	—	12.00	25.00	45.00	90.00	—
1800	—	10.00	17.50	27.50	45.00	—

KM# 35 5 BAZARUCOS
4.1000 g., Tin **Ruler:** Jose (Joseph) I **Obverse:** Crowned arms **Reverse:** Maltese cross divides date in angles

Date	Mintage	Good	VG	F	VF	XF
1765	—	6.00	12.00	25.00	50.00	—
1768	—	7.00	15.00	30.00	60.00	—
1777	—	5.00	10.00	20.00	40.00	—

KM# 44 5 BAZARUCOS
Lead Or Tin **Ruler:** Maria I **Obverse:** Crude crowned arms **Reverse:** Maltese cross divides date in angles

Date	Mintage	Good	VG	F	VF	XF
1799	—	10.00	20.00	40.00	80.00	—
1800	—	6.00	12.00	25.00	45.00	—

KM# 28 10 BAZARUCOS
8.0000 g., Tin **Ruler:** John V **Obverse:** Crowned arms divide OD (retrograde) in plain circle **Reverse:** Numerals of date in angles of cross

Date	Mintage	Good	VG	F	VF	XF
1748	—	18.00	35.00	70.00	120	—

KM# 39 10 BAZARUCOS
8.7000 g., Tin **Ruler:** Jose (Joseph) I **Note:** Similar to 5 Bazarucos, KM#35.

Date	Mintage	Good	VG	F	VF	XF
1777	—	10.00	20.00	35.00	55.00	—

KM# 45 10 BAZARUCOS
Lead Or Tin **Ruler:** Joao, as Prince Regent **Obverse:** Arms **Reverse:** Maltese cross divides date in angles

Date	Mintage	Good	VG	F	VF	XF
1799	—	10.00	20.00	35.00	70.00	—
1800	—	9.00	17.50	27.50	45.00	—

KM# 30 20 BAZARUCOS
16.0000 g., Tin **Ruler:** John V **Obverse:** Crowned arms divide DO **Reverse:** Maltese cross divides date in angles

Date	Mintage	Good	VG	F	VF	XF
1748	—	25.00	50.00	80.00	125	—

KM# 36 20 BAZARUCOS
Tin **Ruler:** Jose (Joseph) I **Obverse:** Crowned arms **Reverse:** Maltese cross divides date in angles **Note:** Weight varies: 4.00-16.50 grams.

Date	Mintage	Good	VG	F	VF	XF
1765	—	8.50	16.00	32.50	55.00	—
1768	—	8.50	16.00	32.50	55.00	—
1771	—	8.50	16.00	32.50	55.00	—
1777	—	8.50	16.00	32.50	55.00	—

KM# 47 20 BAZARUCOS
Tin **Ruler:** Maria I **Obverse:** Crude crowned arms **Reverse:** Maltese cross divides date in angles **Note:** Weight varies: 14.00-16.50 grams.

Date	Mintage	Good	VG	F	VF	XF
1799	—	12.00	25.00	50.00	90.00	—
1800	—	10.00	20.00	40.00	70.00	—

HAMMERED COINAGE

KM# 25 5 BAZARUCOS
4.6000 g., Copper **Ruler:** John V **Obverse:** Crowned large arms divide retrograde OD in plain circle **Reverse:** Maltese cross divides date in angles

Date	Mintage	Good	VG	F	VF	XF
1745	—	6.50	12.50	27.50	55.00	—
1748	—	6.00	12.00	25.00	50.00	—

KM# 26 5 BAZARUCOS
3.6000 g., Copper **Ruler:** John V **Obverse:** Crowned medium arms divide DO in plain circle **Reverse:** Maltese cross divides date in angles

Date	Mintage	Good	VG	F	VF	XF
1748	—	6.00	12.00	25.00	50.00	—

KM# 18 10 BAZARUCOS
18.9500 g., Tin **Subject:** John V **Obverse:** Crowned arms divide DB in plain circle **Reverse:** Numerals of date in angles of cross in plain circle **Note:** For Bacaim and Diu. Varieties in crown and arms.

Date	Mintage	Good	VG	F	VF	XF
1723	—	75.00	125	250	500	—
1734	—	100	175	325	650	—

KM# 31 1/8 ATIA
1.5000 g., Copper **Ruler:** John V **Obverse:** Crowned arms in plain circle **Reverse:** Maltese cross divides date in angles

Date	Mintage	Good	VG	F	VF	XF
1750	—	7.50	14.50	25.00	50.00	—

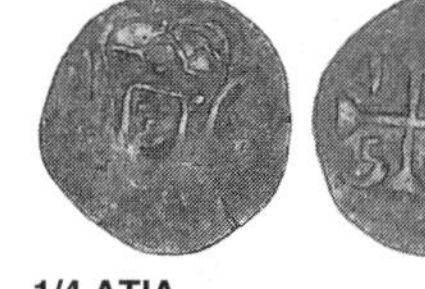

KM# 32 1/4 ATIA
3.0000 g., Copper **Ruler:** John V **Obverse:** Crowned arms divide DO in plain circle **Reverse:** Maltese cross divides date in angles

Date	Mintage	Good	VG	F	VF	XF
1750	—	10.00	20.00	35.00	60.00	—

KM# 40 1/4 ATIA
Copper **Ruler:** Maria I and Pedro III

Date	Mintage	Good	VG	F	VF	XF
1778	—	12.00	25.00	40.00	70.00	—

KM# 16 1/2 ATIA (1/8 Tanga)
4.0000 g., Copper **Ruler:** John V **Obverse:** Arms divide DO **Reverse:** Numerals of date in angles of cross potent

Date	Mintage	Good	VG	F	VF	XF
1721 Rare	—	—	—	—	—	—

KM# 27 1/2 ATIA (1/8 Tanga)
4.6000 g., Copper **Ruler:** John V **Obverse:** Crowned arms divide DO in plain circle **Reverse:** Maltese cross divides date in angles within circle

Date	Mintage	Good	VG	F	VF	XF
1748	—	8.00	16.00	35.00	70.00	—

KM# 33 1/2 ATIA (1/8 Tanga)

5.0000 g., Copper **Ruler:** John V **Obverse:** Crowned arms divide DO in plain circle **Reverse:** Maltese cross divides date in angles

Date	Mintage	Good	VG	F	VF	XF
1750	—	7.00	15.00	30.00	65.00	—

KM# 37 1/2 ATIA (1/8 Tanga)

5.0000 g., Copper **Ruler:** Jose (Joseph) I **Obverse:** Crowned arms **Reverse:** Maltese cross divides date in angles within circle **Note:** Weight varies: 4.20-4.90 grams.

Date	Mintage	Good	VG	F	VF	XF
1767	—	6.00	12.00	28.00	55.00	—
1768	—	5.00	10.00	20.00	40.00	—

KM# 41 1/2 ATIA (1/8 Tanga)

5.0000 g., Copper **Ruler:** Maria I and Pedro III **Obverse:** Crowned arms **Reverse:** Maltese cross within circle

Date	Mintage	Good	VG	F	VF	XF
1778	—	6.00	12.00	25.00	50.00	—
1780	—	5.00	10.00	20.00	40.00	—
1785	—	5.00	10.00	20.00	40.00	—
1787	—	5.00	10.00	20.00	40.00	—
1789	—	7.00	15.00	30.00	60.00	—
1799	—	7.00	15.00	30.00	60.00	—

KM# 17 ATIA (1/4 Tanga)

7.3000 g., Copper **Ruler:** John V **Obverse:** Arms divide DO **Reverse:** Numerals of date in angles of cross potent

Date	Mintage	Good	VG	F	VF	XF
1721 Rare	—	—	—	—	—	—

KM# 29 ATIA (1/4 Tanga)

9.0000 g., Copper **Ruler:** John V **Obverse:** Crowned arms divide DO in plain circle **Reverse:** Maltese cross divides date in angles within circle

Date	Mintage	Good	VG	F	VF	XF
1748	—	10.00	20.00	35.00	70.00	—

KM# 34 ATIA (1/4 Tanga)

9.0000 g., Copper **Ruler:** John V **Obverse:** Crowned arms **Reverse:** Maltese cross divides date in angles, 4 below

Date	Mintage	Good	VG	F	VF	XF
1750	—	5.00	10.00	20.00	40.00	—

KM# 38 ATIA (1/4 Tanga)

Copper **Ruler:** Jose (Joseph) I **Obverse:** Crowned arms divides DO **Reverse:** Maltese cross divides date in angles within circle **Note:** Weight varies: 9.00-9.20 grams.

Date	Mintage	Good	VG	F	VF	XF
1764	—	—	—	—	—	—
1766	—	—	—	—	—	—
1767	—	6.50	12.50	223	45.00	—
1768	—	5.00	8.00	15.00	30.00	—
1777	—	6.50	12.50	22.50	45.00	—

KM# 42 ATIA (1/4 Tanga)

Copper **Ruler:** Maria I and Pedro III **Obverse:** Crowned arms **Reverse:** Maltese cross divides date in angles within circle

Date	Mintage	Good	VG	F	VF	XF
1778	—	3.00	6.00	12.00	20.00	—
1789	—	3.00	6.00	12.00	20.00	—

KM# 46 ATIA (1/4 Tanga)

Copper Or Tin **Ruler:** Joao, as Prince Regent **Obverse:** Crowned arms divides JO **Reverse:** Maltese cross divides date in angles

Date	Mintage	Good	VG	F	VF	XF
1799	—	2.00	5.00	10.00	20.00	—

KM# 4 1/2 XERAFIM

5.8900 g., Silver **Ruler:** Peter II **Obverse:** Crude crowned arms in branches **Reverse:** Voided floreated cross

Date	Mintage	Good	VG	F	VF	XF
ND(1683-1706)	—	80.00	160	285	425	—

KM# 21 1/2 XERAFIM

5.1800 g., Silver **Ruler:** John V **Obverse:** Arms in branches **Reverse:** Numerals of date in angles of ornamented cross

Date	Mintage	Good	VG	F	VF	XF
1736	—	150	275	550	1,000	—
1738	—	150	275	550	1,000	—

KM# 5 XERAFIM

11.4700 g., Silver **Ruler:** Peter II **Obverse:** Crowned arms in branches **Reverse:** Voided floreated cross

Date	Mintage	Good	VG	F	VF	XF
ND(1683-1706)	—	65.00	125	225	350	—

KM# 8 XERAFIM

10.6300 g., Silver **Ruler:** Peter II **Obverse:** Crowned arms divide DO within circle **Reverse:** Numerals of date in angles of cross within circle

Date	Mintage	Good	VG	F	VF	XF
1706	—	65.00	135	235	425	—

KM# 13 XERAFIM

10.3500 g., Silver **Ruler:** John V **Obverse:** Crowned arms divide DO in within circle **Reverse:** Numerals of date in angles of cross

Date	Mintage	Good	VG	F	VF	XF
1707	—	80.00	160	270	500	—
1710	—	90.00	180	300	550	—
1711	—	80.00	160	270	500	—
1712	—	75.00	150	250	480	—
1713	—	70.00	140	230	460	—
1716	—	75.00	150	250	480	—
1719	—	70.00	140	230	460	—

KM# 14 XERAFIM

0.5600 g., Gold **Ruler:** John V **Obverse:** Arms **Reverse:** Numerals of date in angles of cross

Date	Mintage	Good	VG	F	VF	XF
1717	—	600	1,000	1,850	3,000	—

KM# 20 XERAFIM

11.9000 g., Silver **Obverse:** Crowned arms divide DO in plain circle **Reverse:** Numerals of date in angles of ornamented cross

Date	Mintage	Good	VG	F	VF	XF
1729	—	60.00	120	225	435	—
1731	—	50.00	90.00	165	350	—
1735	—	40.00	75.00	150	300	—
1736	—	40.00	75.00	150	300	—
1737	—	45.00	85.00	160	350	—
1738	—	45.00	85.00	160	350	—
1739	—	40.00	75.00	150	300	—

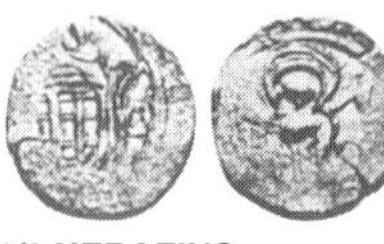

KM# A15 2-1/2 XERAFINS

1.4000 g., Gold **Ruler:** John V **Obverse:** Crowned arms divide DO within circle **Reverse:** Standing figure of St. Thomas divide dates

Date	Mintage	Good	VG	F	VF	XF
1730	—	750	1,400	2,350	3,800	—

KM# 15.1 5 XERAFINS

2.8700 g., Gold **Ruler:** John V **Obverse:** Crowned arms with grate design **Reverse:** St. Thomas facing divides date

Date	Mintage	Good	VG	F	VF	XF
1718	—	750	1,200	2,000	3,500	—
1719	—	800	1,250	2,200	4,000	—
1721	—	850	1,350	2,400	4,500	—
1726	—	850	1,350	2,400	4,500	—
1727	—	750	1,200	2,000	3,500	—
1728	—	850	1,350	2,400	4,500	—

KM# 15.2 5 XERAFINS

2.8700 g., Gold **Ruler:** John V **Obverse:** Crowned arms with dot design divides DO **Reverse:** St. Thomas facing divides date

Date	Mintage	Good	VG	F	VF	XF
1721	—	850	1,350	2,400	4,500	—
1723	—	850	1,350	2,400	4,500	—
1726	—	850	1,350	2,400	4,500	—

KM# 19 1/2 PARDAO

2.6200 g., Silver **Ruler:** John V **Obverse:** Arms **Reverse:** Maltese cross divides date in angles

Date	Mintage	Good	VG	F	VF	XF
1726-4	—	125	250	500	900	—
1726	—	125	250	500	900	—

KM# 22 1/2 PARDAO

2.9700 g., Silver **Ruler:** John V **Obverse:** Crowned arms **Reverse:** Numerals of date in angles of voided cross

Date	Mintage	Good	VG	F	VF	XF
1741	—	45.00	90.00	165	325	—
1744	—	50.00	100	175	350	—
1749	—	45.00	90.00	165	325	—

KM# 23 PARDAO

5.7700 g., Silver **Ruler:** John V **Obverse:** Crowned arms **Reverse:** Numerals of date in angles of ornamented voided cross

Date	Mintage	Good	VG	F	VF	XF
1741	—	60.00	120	250	500	—
1744	—	60.00	120	250	500	—
1749	—	60.00	120	250	500	—

KM# A24 RUPIA (600 Reis)

11.0000 g., Silver **Ruler:** John V **Obverse:** Cross of St. Thomas with DO

Date	Mintage	Good	VG	F	VF	XF
1728	—	—	—	—	—	—
1729	—	—	—	—	—	—

KM# 24 RUPIA (600 Reis)

11.0000 g., Silver **Ruler:** Jose (Joseph) I **Obverse:** Crowned arms **Reverse:** Numerals of date in angles of ornamented cross

Date	Mintage	Good	VG	F	VF	XF
1741	—	25.00	50.00	100	165	—
1744	—	25.00	50.00	100	165	—
1747	—	25.00	50.00	100	165	—
1749	—	27.50	55.00	110	175	—
1750	—	27.50	55.00	110	175	—
1766	—	25.00	50.00	100	165	—

KM# 43 RUPIA (600 Reis)

10.6300 g., Silver **Ruler:** Maria I and Pedro III **Obverse:** Accolated bust of Maria and Pedro **Reverse:** Crowned arms

Date	Mintage	Good	VG	F	VF	XF
1781	—	65.00	125	250	400	—

GOA

Goa was the capitol of Portuguese India and is located 250 miles south of Bombay on the west coast of India. It was taken by Albuquerque in 1510. A mint was established immediately and operated until closed by the British in 1869. Later coins were struck at Calcutta and Bombay. Goa was annexed by India in 1962.

MONETARY SYSTEM

375 Bazarucos = 300 Reis
240 Reis = 1 Pardao
2 Xerafim = 1 Rupia

NOTE: The silver Xerafim was equal to the silver Pardao, but the gold Xerafim varied according to fluctuations in the gold/silver ratio.

COLONY

CAST COINAGE

KM# 80 BAZARUCO

2.6900 g., Tin **Ruler:** John V **Obverse:** Crowned arms divide GA in plain circle **Reverse:** Latin cross with floreate bottom in plain circle

Date	Mintage	Good	VG	F	VF	XF
ND(1706-50)	—	12.00	25.00	45.00	85.00	—

KM# 81 1-1/2 REALS (Roda)

2.6000 g., Tin **Ruler:** John V **Obverse:** Crowned arms divide GA within circle **Reverse:** Divided concentric circles **Note:** "Roda" is Portuguese for "wheel" and is used in reference to any coin with a wheel design.

Date	Mintage	Good	VG	F	VF	XF
ND(1706-50)	—	12.50	25.00	50.00	100	—

KM# 82 2 BAZARUCOS

3.9600 g., Tin **Ruler:** John V **Obverse:** Crowned arms divide GA **Reverse:** Cross on mound divides star and 2

Date	Mintage	Good	VG	F	VF	XF
ND(1706-50)	—	18.00	35.00	70.00	150	—

KM# 101 2 BAZARUCOS

2.6000 g., Tin **Ruler:** John V **Obverse:** Crowned arms divide GA **Reverse:** Cross divides date at top, star, and 2

Date	Mintage	Good	VG	F	VF	XF
1722	—	15.00	30.00	60.00	135	—

KM# 102 2-1/2 BAZARUCOS

3.3000 g., Tin **Ruler:** John V **Obverse:** Crowned arms divide GA **Reverse:** I S divided by date, value below

Date	Mintage	Good	VG	F	VF	XF
1722	—	12.50	25.00	45.00	90.00	—

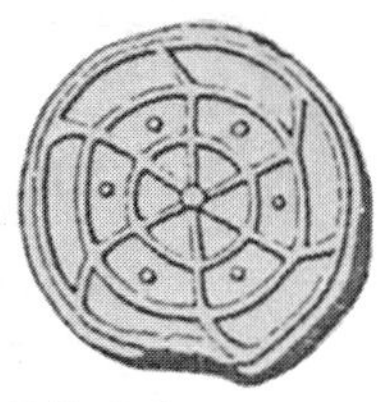

KM# 83 5 BAZARUCOS (3 Rodas)

5.2800 g., Tin **Ruler:** John V **Obverse:** Crowned arms divide GA **Reverse:** Divided concentric circles

Date	Mintage	Good	VG	F	VF	XF
ND(1706-50)	—	12.50	25.00	50.00	100	—

KM# 84 5 BAZARUCOS (3 Rodas)

6.7700 g., Tin **Ruler:** John V **Obverse:** Crowned arms divide GA **Reverse:** Cross on mound divides star and 5

Date	Mintage	Good	VG	F	VF	XF
ND(1706-50)	—	10.00	20.00	40.00	80.00	—

KM# 103 5 BAZARUCOS (3 Rodas)

6.6000 g., Tin **Ruler:** John V **Obverse:** Crowned arms divide GA **Reverse:** Cross divides date at top and star and 5 at bottom

Date	Mintage	Good	VG	F	VF	XF
1722	—	12.50	22.50	45.00	90.00	—

KM# 136 5 BAZARUCOS (3 Rodas)

4.1000 g., Tin **Ruler:** Jose (Joseph) I **Obverse:** Crowned arms divide GA **Reverse:** Value, date within wreath

Date	Mintage	Good	VG	F	VF	XF
1760	—	12.50	22.50	45.00	90.00	—

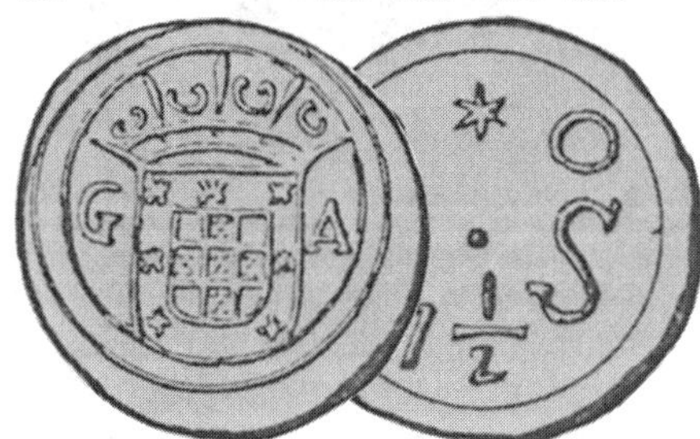

KM# 85 7-1/2 BAZARUCOS

13.6000 g., Tin **Ruler:** John V **Obverse:** Crowned arms divide GA **Reverse:** Letters I and S topped by O, star above, value below

Date	Mintage	Good	VG	F	VF	XF
ND(1706-50)	—	20.00	45.00	100	200	—

KM# 86 7-1/2 BAZARUCOS

12.3000 g., Tin **Ruler:** John V **Obverse:** Crowned arms divide GA **Reverse:** Letters I and S topped by O divided by value, star above

Date	Mintage	Good	VG	F	VF	XF
ND(1706-50)	—	15.00	35.00	85.00	175	—

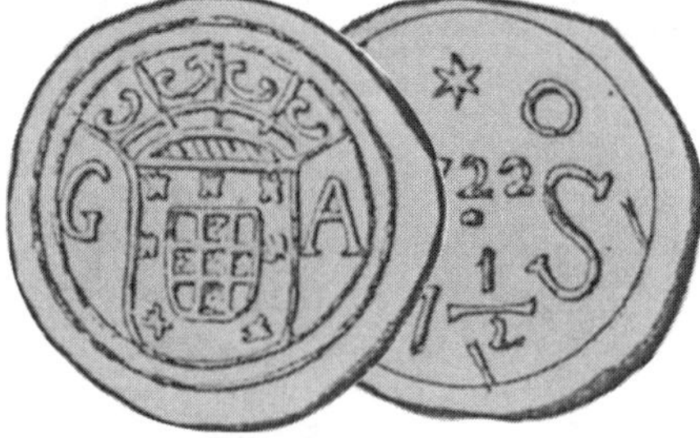

KM# 104 7-1/2 BAZARUCOS

9.0000 g., Tin **Ruler:** John V **Obverse:** Crowned arms divide GA **Reverse:** Letters I and S topped by O divided by date, star above, value below

Date	Mintage	Good	VG	F	VF	XF
1722	—	12.50	25.00	75.00	165	—

KM# 105 7-1/2 BAZARUCOS

10.6000 g., Tin **Ruler:** John V **Obverse:** Crowned arms divide GA **Reverse:** Letters I and S topped by O divided by value, star and date above

Date	Mintage	Good	VG	F	VF	XF
1722	—	20.00	45.00	100	200	—

KM# 87 10 BAZARUCOS

11.6000 g., Tin **Ruler:** John V **Obverse:** Crowned arms divide GA within circle **Reverse:** I at left, 10 at right, O above, all within circle

Date	Mintage	Good	VG	F	VF	XF
ND(1706-50)	—	18.00	40.00	90.00	185	—

KM# 106 10 BAZARUCOS

9.6000 g., Tin **Ruler:** John V **Obverse:** Crowned arms divide GA **Reverse:** I topped by O at left, date above 10 at right

Date	Mintage	Good	VG	F	VF	XF
1722	—	18.00	40.00	90.00	185	—

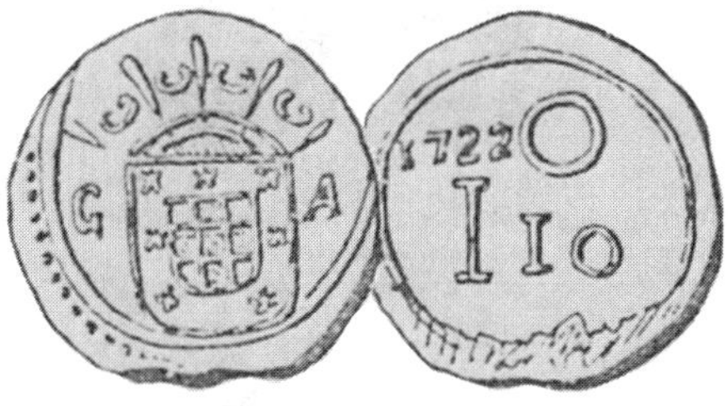

KM# 107 10 BAZARUCOS

8.9000 g., Tin **Ruler:** John V **Obverse:** Crowned arms divide GA **Reverse:** Date above I at left, O above 10 at right, all within circle

Date	Mintage	Good	VG	F	VF	XF
1722	—	15.00	35.00	85.00	175	—

KM# 137.1 10 BAZARUCOS

8.2000 g., Tin **Ruler:** Jose (Joseph) I **Obverse:** Crowned arms divide GA **Reverse:** Value, date within wreath

Date	Mintage	Good	VG	F	VF	XF
1760	—	10.00	20.00	60.00	125	—

KM# 137.2 10 BAZARUCOS

6.8000 g., Tin **Ruler:** Jose (Joseph) I **Obverse:** Crowned arms divide GA **Reverse:** Value, date within wreath

Date	Mintage	Good	VG	F	VF	XF
1769	—	10.00	20.00	60.00	125	—

KM# 88 15 BAZARUCOS

15.3000 g., Tin **Ruler:** John V **Obverse:** Crowned arms divide GA within circle **Reverse:** I topped by O at left, value at right

Date	Mintage	Good	VG	F	VF	XF
ND(1706-50)	—	25.00	55.00	125	250	—

KM# 89 15 BAZARUCOS

19.0000 g., Tin **Ruler:** John V **Obverse:** Crowned arms divide GA within circle **Reverse:** Divided concentric circles with value above

Date	Mintage	Good	VG	F	VF	XF
ND(1706-50)	—	40.00	100	225	450	—

KM# 90 15 BAZARUCOS

20.0000 g., Tin **Ruler:** John V **Obverse:** Crowned arms divide GA within circle **Reverse:** Divided concentric circles

Date	Mintage	Good	VG	F	VF	XF
ND(1706-50)	—	50.00	120	250	500	—

KM# 138.1 15 BAZARUCOS

Tin **Ruler:** Jose (Joseph) I **Obverse:** Crowned arms divide GA **Reverse:** Value, date within wreath **Note:** Weight varies: 12.00-13.70 grams.

Date	Mintage	Good	VG	F	VF	XF
1760	—	12.00	25.00	65.00	135	—

KM# 138.2 15 BAZARUCOS

11.6000 g., Tin **Ruler:** Jose (Joseph) I **Obverse:** Crowned arms divide GA **Reverse:** Value, date within wreath

Date	Mintage	Good	VG	F	VF	XF
1769	—	10.00	20.00	60.00	125	—

KM# 151 2 REIS

2.2000 g., Tin **Ruler:** Jose (Joseph) I **Obverse:** Crowned arms divide GA within circle **Reverse:** II

Date	Mintage	Good	VG	F	VF	XF
ND(1769)	—	20.00	40.00	90.00	200	—

KM# 152 4 REIS

Tin **Ruler:** Jose (Joseph) I **Obverse:** Crowned arms divide GA **Reverse:** IV, date within thin wreath

Date	Mintage	Good	VG	F	VF	XF
1769	—	12.50	25.00	50.00	125	—

KM# 153 6 REIS

8.6000 g., Tin **Ruler:** Jose (Joseph) I **Obverse:** Crowned arms divide GA **Reverse:** VI, date within thin wreath

Date	Mintage	Good	VG	F	VF	XF
1769	—	12.50	25.00	50.00	125	—

KM# 154 12 REIS

Tin **Ruler:** Jose (Joseph) I **Obverse:** Crowned arms divide GA **Reverse:** XII, date within thin wreath

Date	Mintage	Good	VG	F	VF	XF
1769	—	12.50	25.00	50.00	125	—

HAMMERED COINAGE

KM# 165 1-1/2 REIS

Copper **Ruler:** Maria I and Pedro III **Obverse:** Crowned shield **Reverse:** Denomination

Date	Mintage	Good	VG	F	VF	XF
ND	—	18.00	35.00	75.00	150	—

KM# 143 2 REIS

1.2000 g., Copper **Ruler:** Jose (Joseph) I **Obverse:** Crowned arms **Reverse:** Value, date

Date	Mintage	Good	VG	F	VF	XF
1763	—	25.00	50.00	100	225	—

KM# 166 3 REIS

Copper **Ruler:** Maria I and Pedro III **Note:** Similar to 6 Reis, KM#168.

Date	Mintage	Good	VG	F	VF	XF
ND	—	10.00	20.00	40.00	80.00	—

KM# 167 4-1/2 REIS

Copper **Ruler:** Maria I and Pedro III **Note:** Similar to 6 Reis, KM#168.

Date	Mintage	Good	VG	F	VF	XF
ND	—	8.50	15.00	35.00	75.00	—

KM# 95 5 REIS

4.5000 g., Copper **Ruler:** John V **Obverse:** Crowned I V monograms; date below **Reverse:** Value in wreath

Date	Mintage	Good	VG	F	VF	XF
1711	—	15.00	30.00	60.00	160	—
1712	—	15.00	30.00	60.00	160	—
1715	—	18.00	35.00	70.00	175	—

KM# 156 5 REIS

3.3000 g., Copper **Ruler:** Jose (Joseph) I **Obverse:** Crowned arms **Reverse:** Value, date

Date	Mintage	Good	VG	F	VF	XF
1774	—	12.50	25.00	50.00	125	—

KM# 139 6 REIS

Copper **Ruler:** Jose (Joseph) I **Obverse:** Crowned arms **Reverse:** Value, date **Note:** Weight varies: 3.70-4.30 grams.

Date	Mintage	Good	VG	F	VF	XF
1762	—	10.00	20.00	35.00	90.00	—
1764	—	12.00	25.00	45.00	100	—
1768	—	10.00	20.00	35.00	90.00	—

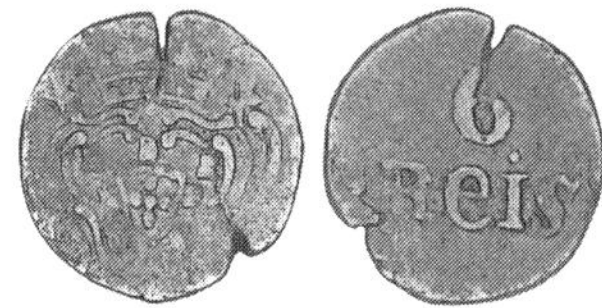

KM# 168 6 REIS

Copper **Ruler:** Maria I and Pedro III **Obverse:** Crowned arms **Reverse:** Value, date **Note:** Weight varies: 3.70-4.30 grams.

Date	Mintage	Good	VG	F	VF	XF
ND	—	6.00	10.00	20.00	40.00	—

KM# 96 7-1/2 REIS

6.6000 g., Copper **Ruler:** John V **Obverse:** Crowned IV monogram; date below **Reverse:** Value in wreath

Date	Mintage	Good	VG	F	VF	XF
1711	—	15.00	30.00	60.00	145	—
1715	—	20.00	40.00	80.00	185	—

KM# A119 10 REIS

Copper **Ruler:** Jose (Joseph) I **Obverse:** Crowned arms **Reverse:** Value

Date	Mintage	Good	VG	F	VF	XF
ND	—	12.50	25.00	50.00	125	—

KM# 157 10 REIS

Copper **Ruler:** Jose (Joseph) I **Obverse:** Crowned arms **Reverse:** value, date within wreath

Date	Mintage	Good	VG	F	VF	XF
1774	—	10.00	20.00	40.00	90.00	—

KM# 120 12 REIS

Copper **Ruler:** Jose (Joseph) I **Obverse:** Crowned arms **Reverse:** Value within wreath

Date	Mintage	Good	VG	F	VF	XF
ND	—	15.00	30.00	60.00	135	—

KM# 140 12 REIS

Copper **Ruler:** Jose (Joseph) I **Obverse:** Crowned arms **Reverse:** Value, date within wreath

Date	Mintage	Good	VG	F	VF	XF
1762	—	7.50	15.00	32.00	65.00	—
1767	—	7.50	15.00	32.00	65.00	—
1768	—	7.50	15.00	32.00	65.00	—
1769	—	7.50	15.00	32.00	65.00	—

KM# 169 12 REIS

Copper **Ruler:** Maria I and Pedro III **Note:** Similar to 6 Reis, KM#168.

Date	Mintage	Good	VG	F	VF	XF
ND	—	6.00	10.00	27.50	50.00	—

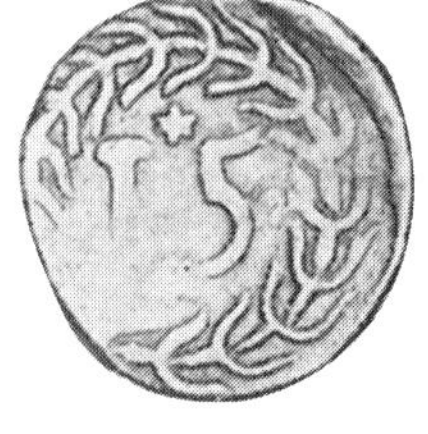

KM# 91 15 REIS

15.1800 g., Copper **Ruler:** John V **Obverse:** Crowned I V monogram **Reverse:** Value within wreath, star above and below value

Date	Mintage	Good	VG	F	VF	XF
1717	—	25.00	50.00	120	250	—

KM# 121 20 REIS

Copper **Ruler:** Jose (Joseph) I **Obverse:** Crowned arms **Reverse:** Star above value within wreath

Date	Mintage	Good	VG	F	VF	XF
ND	—	10.00	20.00	40.00	85.00	—

KM# 155 20 REIS

Copper **Ruler:** Jose (Joseph) I **Obverse:** Crowned arms **Reverse:** Value, date within wreath

Date	Mintage	Good	VG	F	VF	XF
1770	—	9.00	18.00	35.00	75.00	—
1772	—	9.00	18.00	35.00	75.00	—
1774	—	9.00	18.00	35.00	75.00	—

KM# 170 20 REIS

Copper **Ruler:** Maria I and Pedro III **Note:** Similar to 6 Reis, KM#161.

Date	Mintage	Good	VG	F	VF	XF
ND	—	6.00	10.00	25.00	—	—

KM# 196 20 REIS

Copper **Ruler:** Maria I **Obverse:** Crowned arms **Reverse:** Star above value, date within wreath

Date	Mintage	Good	VG	F	VF	XF
1787	—	8.00	—	30.00	60.00	—

KM# 108 1/2 TANGA (30 Reis)

0.5700 g., Silver **Ruler:** John V **Obverse:** Crown between branches, date below **Reverse:** Value in wreath **Note:** Varieties exist.

Date	Mintage	Good	VG	F	VF	XF
1726	—	30.00	60.00	175	350	—
ND(1727)	—	20.00	40.00	150	325	—

KM# 118.1 1/2 TANGA (30 Reis)

0.6000 g., Silver **Ruler:** John V **Obverse:** Head right, date below **Reverse:** Crown above date

Date	Mintage	Good	VG	F	VF	XF
1740	—	16.00	32.00	75.00	165	—
1741	—	20.00	40.00	80.00	175	—
1742	—	20.00	40.00	80.00	175	—
1744	—	16.00	32.00	75.00	165	—
1745	—	20.00	40.00	80.00	175	—
1750	—	20.00	40.00	80.00	175	—
1751	—	20.00	40.00	80.00	175	—

KM# 118.2 1/2 TANGA (30 Reis)

0.5800 g., Silver **Ruler:** John V **Obverse:** Head right **Reverse:** Crown above retrograde value

Date	Mintage	Good	VG	F	VF	XF
1742	—	20.00	40.00	80.00	175	—

KM# 122 1/2 TANGA (30 Reis)

Copper **Ruler:** Jose (Joseph) I **Obverse:** Crowned arms **Reverse:** Stars above value within wreath

Date	Mintage	Good	VG	F	VF	XF
ND	—	10.00	20.00	40.00	80.00	—

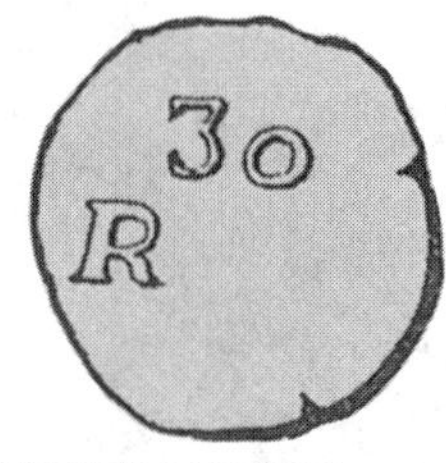

KM# 123 1/2 TANGA (30 Reis)

Copper **Reverse:** Value

Date	Mintage	Good	VG	F	VF	XF
ND	—	15.00	30.00	65.00	150	—

KM# 124 1/2 TANGA (30 Reis)

Copper **Ruler:** Jose (Joseph) I **Note:** Varieties exist.

Date	Mintage	Good	VG	F	VF	XF
ND	—	25.00	50.00	110	220	—
1751	—	20.00	40.00	100	200	—
1755	—	20.00	40.00	100	200	—
1756	—	20.00	40.00	100	200	—
1761	—	30.00	60.00	120	240	—
1764	—	20.00	40.00	100	200	—

KM# 135 1/2 TANGA (30 Reis)

Copper **Ruler:** Jose (Joseph) I **Obverse:** Crowned arms **Reverse:** Value, stars and date within wreath

Date	Mintage	Good	VG	F	VF	XF
1759	—	12.00	25.00	50.00	125	—
1762	—	12.00	25.00	50.00	125	—
1764	—	12.00	25.00	50.00	125	—
1766	—	12.00	25.00	50.00	125	—
1768	—	12.00	25.00	50.00	125	—
1769	—	12.00	25.00	50.00	125	—
1770	—	12.00	25.00	50.00	125	—
1771	—	10.00	20.00	45.00	100	—
1773	—	10.00	20.00	45.00	100	—
1774	—	10.00	20.00	45.00	100	—
1776	—	10.00	20.00	45.00	100	—

KM# 171 1/2 TANGA (30 Reis)

Copper **Ruler:** Maria I and Pedro III **Note:** Similar to 6 Reis, KM#168.

Date	Mintage	Good	VG	F	VF	XF
ND	—	6.00	10.00	25.00	50.00	—

KM# 172 1/2 TANGA (30 Reis)

0.6000 g., Silver **Obverse:** Bust of Maria in veil **Reverse:** Arms in irregular shield

Date	Mintage	Good	VG	F	VF	XF
ND	—	100	200	300	650	—

KM# 193 1/2 TANGA (30 Reis)

0.6000 g., Silver **Ruler:** Maria I and Pedro III

Date	Mintage	Good	VG	F	VF	XF
1784 Rare	—	—	—	—	—	—

KM# 197 1/2 TANGA (30 Reis)

Copper **Ruler:** Maria I **Reverse:** Date below value 30 in wreath

Date	Mintage	Good	VG	F	VF	XF
1787	—	100	200	300	650	—

KM# 92 TANGA (60 Reis)

1.9800 g., Silver **Ruler:** John V **Obverse:** Crowned arms in circle **Reverse:** Dots in angles of cross in circle

Date	Mintage	Good	VG	F	VF	XF
ND(1706-50)	—	25.00	50.00	125	250	—

KM# 93 TANGA (60 Reis)

1.9800 g., Silver **Ruler:** John V **Obverse:** Crown above value 60 in circle **Reverse:** Small crosses in angles of maltese cross in circle

Date	Mintage	Good	VG	F	VF	XF
ND(1706-50)	—	25.00	50.00	125	250	—

KM# 94 TANGA (60 Reis)

1.1900 g., Silver **Ruler:** John V **Obverse:** Head right **Reverse:** Crown above value

Date	Mintage	Good	VG	F	VF	XF
ND(1706-50)	—	25.00	50.00	125	250	—

KM# 109 TANGA (60 Reis)

1.1500 g., Silver **Ruler:** John V **Obverse:** Crown above branches, date below **Reverse:** Value 60 in wreath

Date	Mintage	Good	VG	F	VF	XF
1726	—	25.00	50.00	125	250	—
1727	—	20.00	40.00	—	200	—

KM# 115 TANGA (60 Reis)

1.1600 g., Silver **Ruler:** John V **Obverse:** Crowned arms **Reverse:** Cross divides date in angles

Date	Mintage	Good	VG	F	VF	XF
1729	—	17.50	35.00	80.00	165	—
1730	—	17.50	35.00	80.00	165	—
1733	—	20.00	40.00	90.00	175	—
1738	—	15.00	30.00	70.00	155	—

KM# 116 TANGA (60 Reis)

1.3500 g., Silver **Ruler:** John V **Obverse:** Value 60 in wreath **Reverse:** Numerals of date in angles of cross

Date	Mintage	Good	VG	F	VF	XF
1733	—	20.00	40.00	100	200	—

KM# 119 TANGA (60 Reis)

1.2000 g., Silver **Ruler:** John V **Obverse:** Head right, date below **Reverse:** Crown above value 60 in circle

Date	Mintage	Good	VG	F	VF	XF
1740	—	16.00	32.00	75.00	165	—
1741	—	15.00	30.00	60.00	150	—
1744	—	16.00	32.00	75.00	165	—
1745	—	16.00	32.00	75.00	165	—
1747	—	20.00	40.00	80.00	175	—
1748	—	15.00	30.00	60.00	150	—
1749	—	15.00	30.00	60.00	150	—
1750	—	16.00	32.00	75.00	165	—
1751	—	16.00	32.00	75.00	165	—

KM# 125 TANGA (60 Reis)

Copper **Ruler:** Jose (Joseph) I **Obverse:** Crowned arms **Reverse:** Star above value within wreath

Date	Mintage	Good	VG	F	VF	XF
ND	—	10.00	20.00	40.00	100	—

KM# 126 TANGA (60 Reis)

Copper **Obverse:** Crowned arms **Reverse:** Value

Date	Mintage	Good	VG	F	VF	XF
ND	—	15.00	30.00	55.00	125	—

KM# 127 TANGA (60 Reis)

Silver **Obverse:** Crowned arms **Reverse:** Maltese cross

Date	Mintage	Good	VG	F	VF	XF
ND	—	25.00	50.00	125	250	—

KM# 128 TANGA (60 Reis)

Silver **Obverse:** Crown above value **Reverse:** Maltese cross

Date	Mintage	Good	VG	F	VF	XF
ND	—	25.00	50.00	125	250	—

KM# 130.2 TANGA (60 Reis)

Silver **Ruler:** Jose (Joseph) I **Obverse:** Head right **Reverse:** Value stated "06", crown above

Date	Mintage	Good	VG	F	VF	XF
1751	—	20.00	35.00	70.00	165	—

KM# 130.1 TANGA (60 Reis)

Silver **Ruler:** Jose (Joseph) I **Obverse:** Head right **Reverse:** Crown above value **Note:** Varieties exist.

Date	Mintage	Good	VG	F	VF	XF
1751	—	20.00	30.00	65.00	160	—
1754	—	15.00	25.00	45.00	150	—
1755	—	20.00	30.00	65.00	160	—
1756	—	25.00	40.00	90.00	200	—
1760	—	20.00	35.00	70.00	165	—
1761	—	25.00	40.00	90.00	200	—

KM# 134 TANGA (60 Reis)

Silver **Ruler:** Jose (Joseph) I **Obverse:** Head right **Reverse:** Crowned arms

Date	Mintage	Good	VG	F	VF	XF
1756	—	35.00	60.00	125	275	—

KM# 173 TANGA (60 Reis)

Ruler: Maria I and Pedro III **Note:** Similar to 6 Reis, KM#168.

Date	Mintage	Good	VG	F	VF	XF
ND	—	35.00	60.00	100	200	—

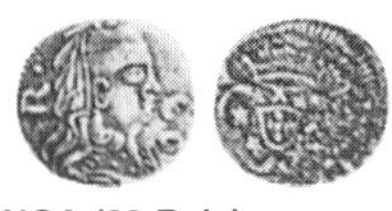

KM# 174 TANGA (60 Reis)

1.1000 g., Silver **Obverse:** Head right, with widow's veil **Reverse:** Crowned arms

Date	Mintage	Good	VG	F	VF	XF
ND	—	40.00	80.00	160	300	—

KM# 198 TANGA (60 Reis)

Copper **Ruler:** Maria I and Pedro III **Obverse:** Crowned arms **Reverse:** Star above value within wreath

Date	Mintage	Good	VG	F	VF	XF
1781	—	15.00	30.00	65.00	145	—
1787	—	15.00	30.00	65.00	145	—

KM# 194 TANGA (60 Reis)

1.1000 g., Silver **Ruler:** Maria I and Pedro III **Obverse:** Conjoined heads, right **Reverse:** Crowned arms

Date	Mintage	Good	VG	F	VF	XF
1784	—	45.00	90.00	180	350	—
1785	—	45.00	90.00	180	350	—

KM# 110 1/2 PARDAO (150 Reis)

Silver **Ruler:** John V **Obverse:** Bust right, date below **Reverse:** Crowned arms divide GA **Note:** 2.80-2.95 grams.

Date	Mintage	Good	VG	F	VF	XF
1726	—	40.00	80.00	200	400	—
1727	—	30.00	65.00	175	375	—
1728	—	30.00	65.00	175	375	—

KM# 113 1/2 PARDAO (150 Reis)

Silver **Ruler:** John V **Obverse:** Head right, date below **Reverse:** Crowned arms **Note:** Weight varies: 2.80-2.95 grams. Varieties exist.

Date	Mintage	Good	VG	F	VF	XF
1728	—	40.00	80.00	130	250	—
1729	—	35.00	70.00	120	225	—
1731	—	35.00	70.00	120	225	—
1732	—	35.00	70.00	120	225	—
1734	—	35.00	70.00	120	225	—
1735	—	35.00	70.00	120	225	—
1738	—	35.00	70.00	120	225	—
1739	—	35.00	70.00	120	225	—
1740	—	30.00	65.00	110	210	—
1741	—	30.00	65.00	110	210	—
1742	—	30.00	65.00	110	210	—
1743	—	30.00	65.00	110	210	—
1744	—	35.00	60.00	120	225	—
1745	—	35.00	70.00	100	200	—
1746	—	35.00	70.00	120	225	—
1747	—	35.00	70.00	120	225	—
1748	—	35.00	70.00	120	225	—
1749	—	30.00	60.00	100	200	—
1750	—	35.00	70.00	120	225	—

KM# 133 1/2 PARDAO (150 Reis)

Silver **Ruler:** Jose (Joseph) I **Obverse:** Head right, date below **Reverse:** Crowned arms **Note:** Weight varies: 2.80-2.95 grams. Varieties exist.

Date	Mintage	Good	VG	F	VF	XF
1752	—	30.00	60.00	120	230	—
1753	—	30.00	60.00	120	230	—
1755	—	40.00	75.00	125	250	—
1760	—	40.00	75.00	125	250	—
1761	—	45.00	85.00	135	265	—
1762	—	40.00	75.00	125	250	—
1764	—	40.00	75.00	125	250	—

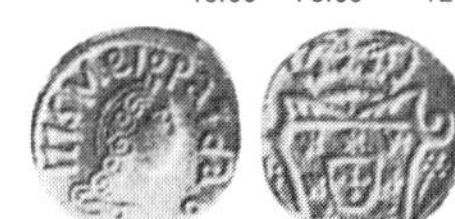

KM# 158 1/2 PARDAO (150 Reis)

Silver **Ruler:** Jose (Joseph) I **Obverse:** Head right **Reverse:** Crowned arms **Note:** Weight varies: 2.80-2.95 grams. Varieties exist.

Date	Mintage	Good	VG	F	VF	XF
1775	—	15.00	30.00	60.00	150	—
1776	—	15.00	30.00	60.00	150	—
1777	—	30.00	50.00	85.00	175	—

KM# 181 1/2 PARDAO (150 Reis)

Silver **Ruler:** Maria I and Pedro III **Obverse:** Bust right **Reverse:** Crowned arms **Note:** Weight varies: 2.80-2.95 grams. Value: MEIO PARDAO.

Date	Mintage	Good	VG	F	VF	XF
1777	—	20.00	40.00	75.00	160	—
1780	—	20.00	40.00	75.00	160	—

KM# 182 1/2 PARDAO (150 Reis)

Silver **Ruler:** Maria I and Pedro III **Obverse:** Head right **Reverse:** Crowned arms **Note:** Weight varies: 2.80-2.95 grams.

Date	Mintage	Good	VG	F	VF	XF
1781	—	25.00	50.00	110	225	—

KM# 189 1/2 PARDAO (150 Reis)

Silver **Ruler:** Maria I and Pedro III **Obverse:** Conjoined heads right, date below **Reverse:** Crowned arms **Note:** Weight varies: 2.80-2.95 grams.

Date	Mintage	Good	VG	F	VF	XF
1782	—	20.00	40.00	85.00	175	—
1784	—	20.00	40.00	85.00	175	—
1785	—	20.00	40.00	85.00	175	—
1786	—	20.00	40.00	85.00	175	—

KM# 188 1/2 PARDAO (150 Reis)

Silver **Ruler:** Maria I and Pedro III **Note:** Weight varies: 2.80-2.95 grams. Value: 150 R.

Date	Mintage	Good	VG	F	VF	XF
1782	—	25.00	50.00	110	225	—

KM# 199 1/2 PARDAO (150 Reis)

Silver **Ruler:** Maria I **Obverse:** Head right **Reverse:** Crowned arms **Note:** Weight varies: 2.80-2.95 grams.

Date	Mintage	Good	VG	F	VF	XF
1787	—	20.00	40.00	85.00	175	—
1788	—	20.00	40.00	85.00	175	—
1790	—	20.00	40.00	85.00	175	—
1791	—	20.00	40.00	85.00	175	—
1793	—	20.00	40.00	85.00	175	—
1794	—	20.00	40.00	85.00	175	—

KM# 203 1/2 PARDAO (150 Reis)

Silver **Ruler:** Maria I **Obverse:** Value: 150 R **Note:** Weight varies: 2.80-2.95 grams.

Date	Mintage	Good	VG	F	VF	XF
1796	—	20.00	40.00	85.00	175	—
1797	—	20.00	40.00	85.00	175	—

KM# 206 1/2 PARDAO (150 Reis)

Silver **Ruler:** Maria I **Obverse:** Head right, value: 150 REIS **Reverse:** Crowned arms **Note:** Weight varies: 2.80-2.95 grams.

Date	Mintage	Good	VG	F	VF	XF
1798	—	20.00	40.00	85.00	175	—
1799	—	20.00	40.00	85.00	175	—

KM# 111 PARDAO (300 Reis)

Silver **Ruler:** John V **Obverse:** Head right, date below **Reverse:** Crowned arms **Note:** Weight varies: 5.84-5.95 grams. Varieties exist.

Date	Mintage	Good	VG	F	VF	XF
1726	—	60.00	125	275	500	—
1728	—	45.00	100	220	400	—
1730	—	35.00	80.00	200	375	—
1732	—	55.00	110	245	450	—
1733	—	35.00	80.00	200	375	—
1737	—	30.00	70.00	175	350	—
1739	—	30.00	60.00	150	300	—
1740	—	30.00	70.00	175	350	—
1741	—	30.00	60.00	150	300	—
1742	—	30.00	65.00	160	325	—
1744	—	30.00	60.00	150	300	—
1745	—	30.00	60.00	150	300	—
1746	—	30.00	60.00	150	300	—
1747	—	30.00	70.00	175	350	—
1748	—	55.00	110	220	400	—
1749	—	30.00	60.00	150	300	—
1750	—	30.00	70.00	175	350	—
1751	—	30.00	70.00	175	350	—

KM# 131 PARDAO (300 Reis)

Silver **Ruler:** Jose (Joseph) I **Obverse:** Head right, date below **Obv. Legend:** JOZE... **Reverse:** Crowned arms **Note:** Weight varies: 5.84-5.95 grams. Varieties exist.

Date	Mintage	Good	VG	F	VF	XF
1751	—	55.00	110	245	450	—
1752	—	55.00	110	245	450	—
1753	—	45.00	100	220	400	—
1754	—	45.00	100	225	425	—
1755	—	45.00	100	230	435	—
1756	—	45.00	100	230	435	—
1761	—	60.00	115	255	475	—
1762	—	55.00	110	245	450	—
1763	—	55.00	110	245	450	—
1764	—	45.00	100	430	435	—

KM# 159 PARDAO (300 Reis)

Silver **Ruler:** Jose (Joseph) I **Obverse:** Head right, date **Reverse:** Crowned arms **Note:** Weight varies: 5.84-5.95 grams.

Date	Mintage	Good	VG	F	VF	XF
1775	—	20.00	45.00	90.00	185	—
1776	—	15.00	35.00	80.00	175	—

KM# 179 PARDAO (300 Reis)

Silver **Ruler:** Maria I and Pedro III **Note:** Weight varies: 5.84-5.95 grams.

Date	Mintage	Good	VG	F	VF	XF
1779	—	25.00	50.00	100	200	—
1780	—	25.00	50.00	100	200	—

KM# 183 PARDAO (300 Reis)

Silver **Ruler:** Maria I and Pedro III **Obverse:** Head right, date **Reverse:** Crowned arms **Note:** Weight varies: 5.84-5.95 grams.

Date	Mintage	Good	VG	F	VF	XF
1781	—	30.00	60.00	150	300	—
1782	—	30.00	60.00	150	300	—

KM# 190 PARDAO (300 Reis)

Silver **Ruler:** Maria I and Pedro III **Obverse:** Similar to KM#195 **Reverse:** Arms **Note:** Weight varies: 5.84-5.95 grams.

Date	Mintage	Good	VG	F	VF	XF
1782	—	12.50	25.00	60.00	150	—
1783	—	12.50	25.00	60.00	150	—

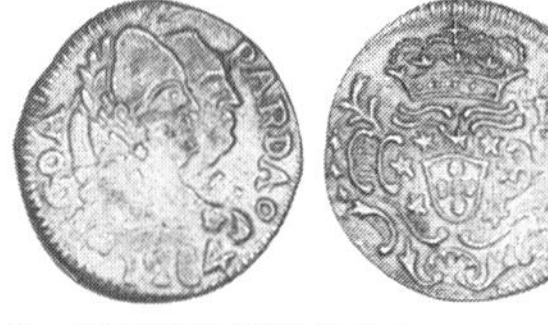

KM# 195 PARDAO (300 Reis)

Silver **Ruler:** Maria I and Pedro III **Obverse:** Conjoined heads right, date below **Reverse:** Crowned arms **Note:** Weight varies: 5.84-5.95 grams.

Date	Mintage	Good	VG	F	VF	XF
1784	—	10.00	20.00	45.00	100	—
1785	—	10.00	20.00	45.00	100	—
1786	—	10.00	20.00	45.00	100	—
1787	—	10.00	20.00	45.00	100	—

KM# 200 PARDAO (300 Reis)

Silver **Ruler:** Maria I **Note:** Weight varies: 5.84-5.95 grams. Similar to 60 Reis, KM#174.

Date	Mintage	Good	VG	F	VF	XF
1787	—	20.00	40.00	90.00	200	—
1789	—	20.00	40.00	90.00	200	—
1791	—	20.00	40.00	90.00	200	—
1792	—	20.00	40.00	90.00	200	—
1793	—	20.00	40.00	90.00	200	—

KM# 204 PARDAO (300 Reis)

Silver **Ruler:** Maria I **Obverse:** Head right, date below **Reverse:** Crowned arms **Note:** Weight varies 5.84-5.95 grams.

Date	Mintage	Good	VG	F	VF	XF
1796	—	10.00	20.00	55.00	135	—
1797	—	10.00	20.00	55.00	135	—
1798	—	10.00	20.00	55.00	135	—
1799	—	10.00	20.00	55.00	135	—
1800	—	10.00	20.00	55.00	135	—

KM# 97 XERAFIM

0.5700 g., Gold **Ruler:** John V **Obverse:** Crowned arms divide GA **Reverse:** Numerals of date in angles of cross

Date	Mintage	Good	VG	F	VF	XF
ND(1714)	—	125	250	425	750	—
1715	—	125	275	450	775	—
1716	—	125	275	450	775	—
1717	—	150	300	500	850	—
1718	—	125	250	425	750	—
1721	—	125	250	425	750	—
1728	—	125	250	425	750	—

KM# 117 XERAFIM

11.8000 g., Silver **Ruler:** John V **Obverse:** Crowned arms **Reverse:** Maltese cross divides date in angles

Date	Mintage	Good	VG	F	VF	XF
1737	—	50.00	125	250	400	—
1740	—	35.00	100	185	350	—

KM# 129 XERAFIM

Gold **Ruler:** Jose (Joseph) I **Obverse:** Crown **Reverse:** Designed cross **Note:** Weight varies: 0.40-0.41 grams.

Date	Mintage	Good	VG	F	VF	XF
ND(1766)	—	200	400	700	1,150	—

KM# 112 RUPIA

11.8000 g., Silver **Ruler:** John V **Obverse:** Head right, date below **Reverse:** Crowned arms **Note:** Varieties exist.

Date	Mintage	Good	VG	F	VF	XF
1726	—	70.00	140	275	500	—
1727	—	70.00	140	275	500	—
1728	—	40.00	85.00	175	350	—
1729	—	40.00	85.00	175	350	—
1730	—	40.00	85.00	175	350	—
1732	—	30.00	70.00	150	300	—
1733	—	30.00	70.00	150	300	—
1734	—	30.00	70.00	150	300	—
1735	—	30.00	70.00	150	300	—
1737	—	30.00	70.00	150	300	—
1740	—	22.50	45.00	100	225	—
1741	—	30.00	70.00	150	300	—
1742	—	25.00	60.00	120	250	—
1743	—	25.00	60.00	120	250	—
1744	—	30.00	70.00	150	300	—
1745	—	30.00	70.00	150	300	—
1746	—	25.00	60.00	120	250	—
1747	—	25.00	60.00	120	250	—
1748	—	22.50	45.00	100	225	—
1749	—	25.00	60.00	120	250	—
1750	—	25.00	60.00	120	250	—
1751 Posthumous	—	22.50	45.00	100	225	—
1752 Posthumous	—	30.00	70.00	150	300	—

KM# 132 RUPIA

11.8000 g., Silver **Ruler:** Jose (Joseph) I **Obverse:** Head right, date below **Reverse:** Crowned arms **Note:** Varieties exist.

Date	Mintage	Good	VG	F	VF	XF
1751	—	40.00	85.00	175	350	—
1752	—	40.00	85.00	175	350	—
1753	—	40.00	85.00	175	350	—
1755	—	40.00	85.00	175	350	—
1756	—	50.00	100	200	400	—
1757	—	45.00	90.00	185	375	—
1761	—	45.00	90.00	185	375	—
1762	—	45.00	90.00	185	375	—

KM# 160 RUPIA

11.8000 g., Silver **Ruler:** Jose (Joseph) I **Obverse:** Bust right **Reverse:** Crowned arms **Note:** Varieties exist.

Date	Mintage	Good	VG	F	VF	XF
1775	—	25.00	45.00	90.00	200	—
1776	—	25.00	45.00	90.00	200	—
1777	—	25.00	45.00	90.00	200	—

KM# 175 RUPIA

11.8000 g., Silver **Ruler:** Maria I and Pedro III

Date	Mintage	Good	VG	F	VF	XF
1778	—	20.00	45.00	100	225	—
1779	—	20.00	45.00	100	225	—
1780	—	20.00	45.00	100	225	—
1781	—	20.00	45.00	100	225	—

KM# 185 RUPIA

11.8000 g., Silver **Ruler:** Maria I and Pedro III **Obverse:** Similar to KM#91 **Reverse:** Similar to KM#184

Date	Mintage	Good	VG	F	VF	XF
1781	—	20.00	40.00	85.00	175	—
1782	—	20.00	40.00	85.00	175	—

KM# 184 RUPIA

11.8000 g., Silver **Ruler:** Maria I and Pedro III **Obverse:** Head right, date **Reverse:** Crowned arms **Note:** Posthumous issue of Joseph I.

Date	Mintage	Good	VG	F	VF	XF
1781	—	30.00	55.00	120	250	—

KM# 191 RUPIA

11.8000 g., Silver **Ruler:** Maria I and Pedro III **Obverse:** Conjoined heads, right, date below **Reverse:** Crowned arms

Date	Mintage	Good	VG	F	VF	XF
1782	—	12.50	20.00	35.00	65.00	—
1783	—	12.50	20.00	35.00	65.00	—
1784	—	12.50	20.00	35.00	65.00	—
1785	—	12.50	20.00	35.00	65.00	—
1786	—	12.50	20.00	35.00	65.00	—
1786	—	16.50	27.50	45.00	80.00	—
Note: Inverted A for V in RVPIA						
1787	—	12.50	20.00	35.00	65.00	—
1787	—	16.50	27.50	45.00	80.00	—
Note: Inverted A for V in RVPIA						

KM# 201 RUPIA

11.8000 g., Silver **Ruler:** Maria I **Obverse:** Bust right **Reverse:** Crowned arms

Date	Mintage	Good	VG	F	VF	XF
1787	—	16.50	27.50	45.00	80.00	—
1788	—	16.50	27.50	45.00	80.00	—
1789	—	16.50	27.50	45.00	80.00	—
1790	—	16.50	27.50	45.00	80.00	—
1791	—	16.50	27.50	45.00	80.00	—
1792	—	16.50	27.50	45.00	80.00	—
1793	—	16.50	27.50	45.00	80.00	—
1794	—	16.50	27.50	45.00	80.00	—
1795	—	16.50	27.50	45.00	80.00	—

KM# 205 RUPIA

11.8000 g., Silver **Ruler:** Maria I **Obverse:** Head right **Reverse:** Crowned arms **Note:** Several varieties exist.

Date	Mintage	Good	VG	F	VF	XF
1796	—	11.50	18.50	30.00	50.00	—
1797	—	11.50	18.50	30.00	50.00	—
1798	—	11.50	18.50	30.00	50.00	—
1799	—	11.50	18.50	30.00	50.00	—
1800	—	11.50	18.50	30.00	50.00	—

KM# 141 2 XERAFINS

0.8100 g., Gold **Ruler:** Jose (Joseph) I **Obverse:** Crowned arms **Reverse:** Cross divides date

Date	Mintage	Good	VG	F	VF	XF
1762	—	350	650	1,150	1,850	—

KM# 146 2 XERAFINS

0.8100 g., Gold **Ruler:** Jose (Joseph) I **Obverse:** Crowned arms **Reverse:** Cross divides value and date

Date	Mintage	Good	VG	F	VF	XF
1766	—	250	400	650	1,150	—
1772	—	250	400	650	1,150	—

KM# 147.1 2 XERAFINS

0.8100 g., Gold **Ruler:** Jose (Joseph) I **Obverse:** Crown without bottom loop **Reverse:** Cross

Date	Mintage	Good	VG	F	VF	XF
1766	—	250	425	725	1,200	—

KM# 147.2 2 XERAFINS

0.8100 g., Gold **Ruler:** Jose (Joseph) I **Obverse:** Crown with bottom loop **Reverse:** Cross divides date

Date	Mintage	Good	VG	F	VF	XF
1766	—	200	350	650	1,000	—
1767	—	225	425	725	1,200	—
1768	—	200	350	650	1,000	—
1769	—	250	450	750	1,250	—
1772	—	200	350	650	1,000	—
1774	—	250	450	750	1,250	—

KM# 161 2 XERAFINS

0.8100 g., Gold **Ruler:** Jose (Joseph) I **Obverse:** Crown above star **Reverse:** Cross

Date	Mintage	Good	VG	F	VF	XF
1775	—	300	500	900	1,500	—

KM# 176 2 XERAFINS

0.8100 g., Gold **Ruler:** Maria I and Pedro III **Obverse:** Crowned arms **Reverse:** Value and date in angles of cross

Date	Mintage	Good	VG	F	VF	XF
1778	—	350	650	1,250	2,000	—
1786	—	350	650	1,250	2,000	—

KM# 207 2 XERAFINS

0.8100 g., Gold **Ruler:** Maria I

Date	Mintage	Good	VG	F	VF	XF
1799	—	250	450	750	1,250	—

KM# 98 2-1/2 XERAFINS

1.4000 g., Gold **Ruler:** John V **Obverse:** Crowned arms divide GA in circle **Reverse:** Standing figure of St. Thomas divides date

Date	Mintage	Good	VG	F	VF	XF
1714	—	300	600	1,000	1,850	—
1715	—	300	600	1,000	1,850	—
1716	—	300	600	1,000	1,850	—
1717	—	300	600	1,000	1,850	—
1720	—	350	650	1,250	2,000	—
ND	—	200	400	800	1,500	—

KM# 144 4 XERAFINS

1.6300 g., Gold **Ruler:** Jose (Joseph) I **Obverse:** Crowned arms **Reverse:** Cross divides date

Date	Mintage	Good	VG	F	VF	XF
1763	—	450	900	1,500	2,500	—
1764	—	450	900	1,500	2,500	—
1765	—	450	900	1,500	2,500	—

KM# 148 4 XERAFINS

1.6300 g., Gold **Ruler:** Jose (Joseph) I **Obverse:** Crowned arms **Reverse:** Cross divides date

Date	Mintage	Good	VG	F	VF	XF
1765	—	175	350	600	1,000	—
1766	—	175	350	600	1,000	—
1768	—	250	450	750	1,250	—
1769	—	300	500	900	1,500	—
1771	—	350	600	1,000	1,650	—
1774	—	250	450	750	1,250	—

KM# 162 4 XERAFINS

1.6300 g., Gold **Ruler:** Jose (Joseph) I **Obverse:** Crowned arms **Reverse:** Cross divides date

Date	Mintage	Good	VG	F	VF	XF
1775	—	350	600	1,000	1,650	—

KM# 177 4 XERAFINS

1.6300 g., Gold **Ruler:** Maria I and Pedro III **Obverse:** Crowned arms **Reverse:** Value and date in angles of cross

Date	Mintage	Good	VG	F	VF	XF
1778	—	—	—	—	—	—
Note: Reported, not confirmed						

KM# 202 4 XERAFINS

1.6300 g., Gold **Ruler:** Maria I **Obverse:** Crowned arms **Reverse:** Cross divides value and date

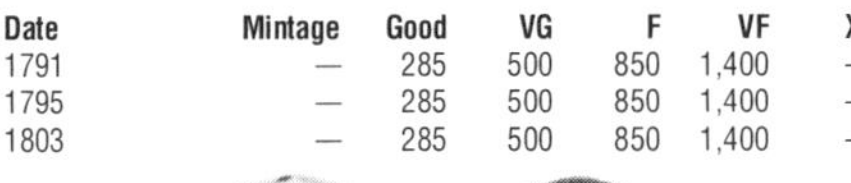

Date	Mintage	Good	VG	F	VF	XF
1791	—	285	500	850	1,400	—
1795	—	285	500	850	1,400	—
1803	—	285	500	850	1,400	—

KM# 99 5 XERAFINS
2.8000 g., Gold **Ruler:** John V **Obverse:** Crowned arms **Reverse:** Standing figure of St. Thomas left divides date

Date	Mintage	Good	VG	F	VF	XF
1714	—	350	750	1,500	3,000	—
1715	—	350	750	1,500	3,000	—
1716	—	350	750	1,500	3,000	—
1717	—	350	750	1,500	3,000	—
1718	—	350	750	1,500	3,000	—
1720	—	350	750	1,500	3,000	—

KM# 145 8 XERAFINS
3.2500 g., Gold **Ruler:** Jose (Joseph) I **Obverse:** Crowned arms **Reverse:** Cross divides date

Date	Mintage	Good	VG	F	VF	XF
1763	—	500	900	1,350	2,000	—

KM# 149 8 XERAFINS
3.2500 g., Gold **Ruler:** Jose (Joseph) I **Obverse:** Crowned arms **Reverse:** Cross divides date, value in angles

Date	Mintage	Good	VG	F	VF	XF
1766	—	300	550	950	1,600	—
1768	—	300	550	950	1,600	—
1769	—	300	550	950	1,600	—
1771	—	300	550	950	1,600	—
1773	—	300	550	950	1,600	—

KM# 163 8 XERAFINS
3.2500 g., Gold **Ruler:** Jose (Joseph) I **Obverse:** Crowned arms **Reverse:** Cross divides date

Date	Mintage	Good	VG	F	VF	XF
1775	—	350	600	1,000	1,650	—

KM# 178 8 XERAFINS
3.2500 g., Gold **Ruler:** Maria I and Pedro III **Obverse:** Crowned arms **Reverse:** Value and date in angles of cross

Date	Mintage	Good	VG	F	VF	XF
1778	—	500	900	1,350	2,000	—

KM# 192.1 8 XERAFINS
3.2500 g., Gold **Ruler:** Maria I and Pedro III

Date	Mintage	Good	VG	F	VF	XF
1782	—	450	800	1,250	1,850	—
1784	—	450	800	1,250	1,850	—
1787	—	450	800	1,250	1,850	—

KM# 192.2 8 XERAFINS
3.2500 g., Gold **Ruler:** Maria I **Obverse:** Crowned round arms **Reverse:** Cross divides value and date

Date	Mintage	Good	VG	F	VF	XF
1788	—	450	800	1,250	1,850	—
1791	—	450	800	1,250	1,850	—
1793	—	450	800	1,250	1,850	—
1794	—	450	800	1,250	1,850	—
1795	—	450	800	1,250	1,850	—

KM# 100 10 XERAFINS
5.6000 g., Gold **Ruler:** John V **Obverse:** Crowned arms divide GA in circle **Reverse:** Standing figure of St. Thomas left divides date

Date	Mintage	Good	VG	F	VF	XF
1714	—	1,000	1,750	3,000	5,000	—

KM# 114 10 XERAFINS
5.7000 g., Gold **Ruler:** John V **Obverse:** Crowned arms **Reverse:** Cross divides date

Date	Mintage	Good	VG	F	VF	XF
1728	—	600	1,000	1,750	3,000	—
1729	—	600	1,000	1,750	3,000	—
1732	—	600	1,000	1,750	3,000	—
1737	—	600	1,000	1,750	3,000	—

KM# 142 12 XERAFINS
4.8700 g., Gold **Ruler:** Jose (Joseph) I **Obverse:** Crowned arms **Reverse:** Cross divides date

Date	Mintage	Good	VG	F	VF	XF
1762	—	350	550	950	1,600	—
1763	—	300	500	800	1,350	—
1764	—	300	500	800	1,350	—
1765	—	350	550	950	1,600	—

KM# 150 12 XERAFINS
4.8700 g., Gold **Obverse:** Crowned arms **Reverse:** Cross divides value and date

Date	Mintage	Good	VG	F	VF	XF
1766	—	300	500	800	1,350	—
1767	—	300	500	800	1,350	—
1768	—	500	500	800	1,350	—
1769	—	300	500	800	1,350	—
1770	—	300	500	800	1,350	—
1771	—	300	500	800	1,350	—
1772	—	300	500	800	1,350	—
1773	—	300	500	800	1,350	—
1774	—	300	500	800	1,350	—
1775	—	300	500	800	1,350	—
1776	—	300	500	800	1,350	—
1781	—	300	500	800	1,350	—
Note: Value 11x (error for 12x)						
1781	—	300	500	800	1,350	—
1782	—	300	500	800	1,350	—

KM# 164 12 XERAFINS
4.8700 g., Gold **Obverse:** Crowned arms **Reverse:** Cross divides date

Date	Mintage	Good	VG	F	VF	XF
1775	—	300	500	800	1,350	—
1776	—	300	500	800	1,350	—
1777	—	300	500	800	1,350	—
1778	—	300	500	800	1,350	—
1780	—	300	500	800	1,350	—

KM# 180 12 XERAFINS
4.8700 g., Gold **Ruler:** Maria I and Pedro III **Obverse:** Crowned arms **Reverse:** Cross divides date and value

Date	Mintage	Good	VG	F	VF	XF
1779	—	500	900	1,500	2,000	—

KM# 187 12 XERAFINS
4.8700 g., Gold **Ruler:** Maria I **Obverse:** Crowned arms **Reverse:** Cross divides value and date

Date	Mintage	Good	VG	F	VF	XF
1781	—	300	500	800	1,350	—
1782	—	300	500	800	1,350	—
1783	—	300	500	800	1,350	—
1784	—	300	500	800	1,350	—
1785	—	300	500	800	1,350	—
1786	—	300	500	800	1,350	—
1787	—	300	500	800	1,350	—
1788	—	300	500	800	1,350	—
1789	—	300	500	750	1,300	—
1790	—	300	500	750	1,300	—
1791	—	300	500	750	1,300	—
1792	—	300	500	800	1,500	—
1793	—	250	450	750	1,300	—
1794	—	250	450	750	1,300	—
1795	—	250	450	800	1,300	—
1796	—	250	450	750	1,300	—
1797	—	250	450	750	1,300	—
1799	—	250	450	750	1,300	—
1800	—	250	450	750	1,300	—

INDIA-BRITISH

BENGAL PRESIDENCY

East India Company
(Until 1835)

In 1633 a group of 8 Englishmen obtained a permit to trade in Bengal from the Nawab of Orissa. Shortly thereafter trading factories were established at Balasore and Hariharpur. Although greater trading privileges were granted to the East India Company by the Emperor Shah Jahan in 1634, by 1642 the 2 original factories were abandoned.

In 1651, through an English surgeon named Broughton, a permit was acquired to trade at Bengal. Hugli was the first location, followed by Kasimbazar, Balasore and Patna (the last 3 in 1653). Calcutta became of increasing importance in this area and on December 20, 1699 Calcutta was declared a presidency and renamed Fort William.

During these times there were many conflicts with the Nawab, both diplomatic and military, and the ultimate outcome was the intervention of Clive and the restoration of Calcutta as an important trading center.

During the earlier trading times in Bengal most of the monies used were imported rupees from the Madras factory. These were primarily of the Arcot type. After Clive's victory one of the concessions in the peace treaty was the right to make Mughal type coinage. The Nawab gave specific details as to what form the coinage should take.

In 1765 Emperor Shah Alam gave the East India Company possessions in Bengal, Orissa and Bihar. This made the company nominally responsible only to the Emperor.

In 1777 the "Frozen Year 19" (of Shah Alam) rupees were made at Calcutta and were continued until 1835. The Arcot rupees were discontinued at Calcutta about 1777.

MINTS

علي نگر كلكته

Alinagar Kalkatah (Calcutta)

عظيم اباد

Azimabad (Patna)

بنارس

Banaras
(Banares, Varanasi)

NOTE: Coins of similar dates with different legends are listed in Indian Princely States, Awadh under Lucknow Mint, with fixed regnal year 26.

كلكته

Calcutta (Kalkatah)

جهانگيرنگر

Jahangirnagar

مرشداباد

Murshidabad

پتنة

Patna

NOTE: For further information refer to *The Coins of the Commonwealth of Nations* Part 4, India -Volume 1: *East India Company Presidency Series* ca.1642-1835 by F. Pridmore (Spink & Son Ltd.).

MONETARY SYSTEM
3 Pies = 1 Pice (Paisa)

BRITISH COLONY

HAMMERED COINAGE

KM# 15 PICE
10.0600 g., Copper **Issuer:** East India Company **Mint:** Muhammadabad Banaras **Obverse:** Darogah's mark of stylized fish **Obv. Inscription:** Persian-falus, Shah Alam (II) **Rev. Inscription:** Persian mint name

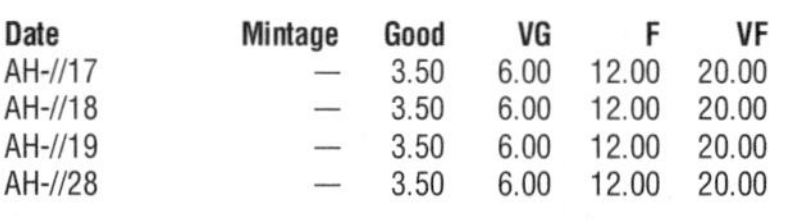

Date	Mintage	Good	VG	F	VF	XF
AH-//17	—	3.50	6.00	12.00	20.00	—
AH-//18	—	3.50	6.00	12.00	20.00	—
AH-//19	—	3.50	6.00	12.00	20.00	—
AH-//28	—	3.50	6.00	12.00	20.00	—

KM# 16 PICE

10.0600 g., Copper **Issuer:** East India Company **Mint:** Muhammadabad Banaras **Obverse:** Trisul (trident) symbol **Obv. Inscription:** "falus..Shah Alam II" **Reverse:** Trisul (trident) symbol, Persian mint name

Date	Mintage	Good	VG	F	VF	XF
AH-//28	—	2.00	5.00	10.00	20.00	—
AH-//35	—	2.00	5.00	10.00	20.00	—
AH-//42	—	2.00	5.00	10.00	20.00	—

KM# 17 1/2 ANNA

14.4500 g., Copper **Issuer:** East India Company **Mint:** Kalkattah **Obverse:** Inscription **Obv. Inscription:** Persian-Shah Alam (II) Badshah **Reverse:** Inscription **Rev. Inscription:** Persian mint name, value 1/10 of 5 Annas **Note:** P#190.

Date	Mintage	Good	VG	F	VF	XF
AH1188	—	15.00	25.00	45.00	100	—

KM# 18 ANNA

28.2800 g., Copper **Issuer:** East India Company **Mint:** Kalkattah **Obverse:** Inscription **Obv. Inscription:** Persian-Shah Alam (II) Badshah **Reverse:** Inscription **Rev. Inscription:** Persian mint name, value 1 Anna

Date	Mintage	Good	VG	F	VF	XF
AH1177	—	65.00	100	150	225	—
AH1188	—	—	—	—	—	—

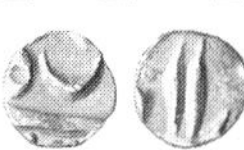

KM# A80 1/64 RUPEE

Silver **Mint:** Murshidabad

Date	Mintage	F	VF	XF	Unc
AH-//11	—	—	—	—	—

KM# 4 1/16 RUPEE

Silver **Issuer:** East India Company **Mint:** A'linagar Kalkattah **Obv. Inscription:** Persian-Alamgir (II) **Rev. Inscription:** Persian-julus (formula), mint name **Note:** Weight varies: 0.67-0.73 grams.

Date	Mintage	VG	F	VF	XF	Unc
AH117x//5	—	50.00	100	200	300	—
AH-//6	—	50.00	100	200	300	—

KM# 80.1 1/16 RUPEE

0.7300 g., Silver **Mint:** Murshidabad **Obverse:** Inscription **Obv. Inscription:** Shah Alam (II) Badshah, couplet **Reverse:** Inscription **Rev. Inscription:** Persian-julus (forumula), mint name

Date	Mintage	VG	F	VF	XF	Unc
AH-//6	—	15.00	35.00	75.00	125	—
AH-//8	—	15.00	35.00	75.00	125	—
AH-//9	—	15.00	35.00	75.00	125	—
AH-//10	—	15.00	35.00	75.00	125	—

KM# 80.2 1/16 RUPEE

0.7300 g., Silver **Mint:** Murshidabad **Obv. Inscription:** Shah Alam (II) Badshah, couplet **Rev. Inscription:** Persian-julus (formula), mint name

Date	Mintage	VG	F	VF	XF	Unc
AH-//11	—	15.00	35.00	75.00	125	—
AH-//12	—	15.00	35.00	75.00	125	—
AH-//15	—	15.00	35.00	75.00	125	—

KM# 80.3 1/16 RUPEE

0.7300 g., Silver **Mint:** Murshidabad **Obv. Inscription:** Shah Alam II) Badshah, couplet **Rev. Inscription:** Persian-julus (formula), mintname

Date	Mintage	VG	F	VF	XF	Unc
AH-//19	—	15.00	35.00	75.00	125	—

KM# 32 1/16 RUPEE

Silver **Issuer:** East India Company **Mint:** Muhammadabad Banaras **Obverse:** Darogah's marks and stylized fish with "antenna" within Persian inscription, couplet **Obv. Inscription:** "Shah Alam II Badshah" **Reverse:** Darogah's mark of flower, Persian-julus (formula), mint name **Note:** Weight varies: 0.67-0.73 grams. A transitional type.

Date	Mintage	Good	VG	F	VF	XF
AH1193//17-20	—	10.00	25.00	6,060	100	175
AH119x//17-21	—	10.00	25.00	60.00	100	175

KM# 5 1/8 RUPEE

Silver **Issuer:** East India Company **Mint:** Kalkattah **Obverse:** Inscription **Obv. Inscription:** Persian-Alamgir (II) **Reverse:** Inscription **Rev. Inscription:** Persian-julus (formula) mint name **Note:** Weight varies 1.34-1.45 grams.

Date	Mintage	VG	F	VF	XF	Unc
AH117x//4	—	40.00	100	200	300	—
AH117x//5	—	40.00	100	200	300	—

KM# 81.1 1/8 RUPEE

1.4500 g., Silver **Mint:** Murshidabad **Obverse:** Inscription **Obv. Inscription:** Shah Alam (II) Badshah, couplet **Reverse:** Inscription **Rev. Inscription:** Persian-julus (formula), mint name

Date	Mintage	VG	F	VF	XF	Unc
AH-//7	—	10.00	25.00	50.00	100	—
AH-//8	—	10.00	25.00	50.00	100	—
AH-//9	—	10.00	25.00	50.00	100	—

KM# 81.2 1/8 RUPEE

1.4500 g., Silver **Mint:** Murshidabad **Obv. Inscription:** Shah ALam (II) Badshah, couplet **Rev. Inscription:** Persian-julus (formula), mint mame

Date	Mintage	VG	F	VF	XF	Unc
AH-//11	—	10.00	25.00	50.00	100	—
AH-//12	—	10.00	25.00	50.00	100	—
AH-//15	—	10.00	25.00	50.00	100	—

KM# 81.3 1/8 RUPEE

1.4500 g., Silver **Mint:** Murshidabad **Obv. Inscription:** Shah Alam (II) Badshah, couplet **Rev. Inscription:** Persian-julus (formula), mint name

Date	Mintage	VG	F	VF	XF	Unc
AH-//19	—	10.00	25.00	50.00	100	—

KM# 33 1/8 RUPEE

Silver **Issuer:** East India Company **Mint:** Muhammadabad Banaras **Obverse:** Darogah's marks and stylized fish within Persian inscription, couplet **Obv. Inscription:** "Shah Alam II Badshah" **Reverse:** Darogah's mark of flower, Persian-julus (formula), mint name

Date	Mintage	Good	VG	F	VF	XF
AH1193//17-20	—	15.00	40.00	100	200	300
AH119x//17-24	—	15.00	40.00	100	200	300
AH120x//17-30	—	15.00	40.00	100	200	300

KM# 6 1/4 RUPEE

Silver **Issuer:** East India Company **Mint:** Kalkattah **Obverse:** Inscription **Obv. Inscription:** Persian-Alamgir (II) **Reverse:** Inscription **Rev. Inscription:** Persian-julus (formula), mint name **Note:** Weight varies 2.68-2.91 grams.

Date	Mintage	VG	F	VF	XF	Unc
AH117x//4	—	100	200	400	600	—

KM# 82.1 1/4 RUPEE

2.9000 g., Silver **Mint:** Murshidabad **Obv. Inscription:** Shah Alam (II) Badshah, couplet **Rev. Inscription:** Persian-julus (formula), mint name

Date	Mintage	VG	F	VF	XF	Unc
AH-//4	—	10.00	35.00	75.00	125	—
AH-//5	—	10.00	35.00	75.00	125	—
AH-//7	—	10.00	35.00	75.00	125	—
AH-//9	—	10.00	35.00	75.00	125	—

KM# 82.2 1/4 RUPEE

2.9000 g., Silver **Mint:** Murshidabad **Obv. Inscription:** Shah Alam (II) Badshah, couplet **Rev. Inscription:** Persian-julus (formula), mint name

Date	Mintage	VG	F	VF	XF	Unc
AH-//11	—	10.00	35.00	75.00	125	—
AH-//12	—	10.00	35.00	75.00	125	—
AH-//15	—	10.00	35.00	75.00	125	—

KM# 82.3 1/4 RUPEE

2.9000 g., Silver **Mint:** Murshidabad **Obverse:** Inscription **Obv. Inscription:** Shah Alam (II) Badshah, couplet **Reverse:** Inscription **Rev. Inscription:** Persian-julus (formula), mint name

Date	Mintage	VG	F	VF	XF	Unc
AH-//19	—	7.50	15.00	25.00	50.00	—

KM# 7 1/2 RUPEE

Silver **Issuer:** East India Company **Mint:** Kalkattah **Obv. Inscription:** Persian-Alamgir (II) **Rev. Inscription:** Persian-julus (formula) mint name **Note:** Weight varies 5.35-5.82 grams.

Date	Mintage	VG	F	VF	XF	Unc
AH1171//4	—	200	400	750	1,000	—

KM# 83.1 1/2 RUPEE

5.8000 g., Silver **Mint:** Murshidabad **Obv. Inscription:** Persian-Shah Alam (II) Badshah, couplet **Rev. Inscription:** Persian-julus (formula), mint name

Date	Mintage	VG	F	VF	XF	Unc
AH1181//8	—	25.00	100	200	300	—
AH1181//8	—	35.00	75.00	125	250	—

KM# 83.2 1/2 RUPEE

5.8000 g., Silver **Mint:** Murshidabad **Obv. Inscription:** Persian-Shah Alam (II) Badshah, couplet **Rev. Inscription:** Persian-julus (formula), mint name

Date	Mintage	VG	F	VF	XF	Unc
AH11xx//11	—	25.00	100	200	300	—
AH11xx//12	—	25.00	100	200	300	—

KM# 83.3 1/2 RUPEE

5.8000 g., Silver **Mint:** Murshidabad **Obverse:** Inscription **Obv. Inscription:** Persian-Shah Alam (II) Badshah, couplet **Reverse:** Inscription **Rev. Inscription:** Persian-julus (formula), mint name

Date	Mintage	VG	F	VF	XF	Unc
AH119x//19	—	25.00	100	200	300	—

KM# 37 1/2 RUPEE

Silver **Issuer:** East India Company **Mint:** Banaras **Obverse:** Darogah's marks of stylized fish within Persian inscription, couplet **Obv. Inscription:** "Shah Alam II Badshah" **Reverse:** Darogah's mark of flower, Persian-julus (formula), mint name **Note:** Weight varies: 5.35-5.82 grams.

Date	Mintage	Good	VG	F	VF	XF
AH1193//17-20	—	60.00	150	300	650	950

KM# 8.1 RUPEE

Silver **Issuer:** East India Company **Mint:** Kalkattah **Obv. Inscription:** Persian-Alamgir (II) regal title **Rev. Inscription:** Persian-julus (formula), mint name **Note:** Weight varies 10.70-11.60 grams.

Date	Mintage	VG	F	VF	XF	Unc
AH1170//4 Rare	—	—	—	—	—	—

KM# 8.2 RUPEE

Silver **Issuer:** East India Company **Mint:** Kalkattah **Obverse:** Inscription **Obv. Inscription:** Persian-Alamgir (II) regal title **Reverse:** Inscription **Rev. Inscription:** Persian-julus (formula), mint name **Note:** Weight varies 10.70-11.60 grams.

Date	Mintage	VG	F	VF	XF	Unc
AH1171//4	—	250	450	750	1,000	—
AH1171//5	—	250	450	750	1,000	—
AH1172//5	—	250	450	750	1,000	—
AH-//6	—	250	450	750	1,000	—

KM# 19 RUPEE

Silver **Issuer:** East India Company **Mint:** Azimabad **Obverse:** Inscription **Obv. Inscription:** Persian-Shah Alam (II) Badshah, couplet **Reverse:** Inscription **Rev. Inscription:** Persian-julus (formula), mint name **Note:** Weight varies 10.70-11.60 grams. Mint mark: Trident. For earlier Rupee issues refer to Mughal listings.

Date	Mintage	VG	F	VF	XF	Unc
AH1179//7	—	35.00	75.00	125	250	—
AH1180//8	—	35.00	75.00	125	250	—
AH1181//9	—	35.00	75.00	125	250	—
AH1182//9	—	35.00	75.00	125	250	—
AH1182//10	—	35.00	75.00	125	250	—
AH1183//11	—	35.00	75.00	125	250	—

KM# 84.1 RUPEE

11.6000 g., Silver **Mint:** Murshidabad **Obverse:** Inscription **Obv. Inscription:** Persian-Shah Alam (II) Badshah, couplet **Reverse:** Inscription **Rev. Inscription:** Persian-julus (formula), mint name **Note:** Mint mark: Star or radiant sun.

Date	Mintage	VG	F	VF	XF	Unc
AH1179//5	—	15.00	35.00	75.00	125	—
AH1179//7	—	10.00	20.00	35.00	75.00	—
AH1180//7	—	10.00	20.00	35.00	75.00	—
AH1180//8	—	10.00	20.00	35.00	75.00	—
AH1181//8	—	10.00	20.00	35.00	75.00	—
AH1181//9	—	10.00	20.00	35.00	75.00	—
AH1182//9	—	10.00	20.00	35.00	75.00	—
AH1182//10	—	10.00	20.00	35.00	75.00	—
AH1183//10	—	10.00	20.00	35.00	75.00	—

KM# 84.2 RUPEE

11.6000 g., Silver **Mint:** Murshidabad **Obverse:** Inscription **Obv. Inscription:** Persian-Shah Alam (II) Badshah, couplet **Reverse:** Inscription **Rev. Inscription:** Persian-julus (formula), mint name **Note:** Mint mark: Crescent.

Date	Mintage	Good	VG	F	VF	XF
AH1183//10	—	5.00	10.00	20.00	35.00	75.00
AH1183//11	—	2.50	6.00	10.00	20.00	50.00
AH1184//11	—	2.50	6.00	10.00	20.00	50.00
AH1185//12	—	2.50	6.00	10.00	20.00	50.00
AH1185//11	—	2.50	6.00	10.00	20.00	50.00
AH1186//12 frozen	—	2.50	6.00	10.00	20.00	50.00
AH1187//12 frozen	—	2.50	6.00	10.00	20.00	50.00
AH1187//15 frozen	—	2.50	6.00	10.00	20.00	50.00
AH1188//12 frozen	—	2.50	6.00	10.00	20.00	50.00
AH1189//12 frozen	—	2.50	6.00	10.00	20.00	50.00
AH1189//15 frozen	—	2.50	6.00	10.00	20.00	50.00
AH1190//15 frozen	—	2.50	6.00	10.00	20.00	50.00
AH1191//19	—	2.50	6.00	10.00	20.00	50.00
AH1190//19 frozen	—	2.50	6.00	10.00	20.00	50.00
AH1192//19	—	2.50	6.00	10.00	20.00	50.00
AH1193//19 forzen	—	2.50	6.00	10.00	20.00	50.00
AH1194//19 frozen	—	2.50	6.00	10.00	20.00	50.00
AH1195//19 frozen	—	2.50	6.00	10.00	20.00	50.00
AH1196//19 frozen	—	2.50	6.00	10.00	20.00	50.00
AH1197//19 frozen	—	2.50	6.00	10.00	20.00	50.00
AH1198//19 frozen	—	2.50	6.00	10.00	20.00	50.00
AH1199//19 frozen	—	2.50	6.00	10.00	20.00	50.00
AH1201//19 frozen	—	2.50	6.00	10.00	20.00	50.00
AH1200//19 frozen	—	2.50	6.00	10.00	20.00	50.00
AH1202//19 frozen	—	2.50	6.00	10.00	20.00	50.00
AH1203//19 frozen	—	2.50	6.00	10.00	20.00	50.00
AH1204//19 frozen	—	2.50	6.00	10.00	20.00	50.00

KM# 20 RUPEE

Silver **Issuer:** East India Company **Mint:** Azimabad **Obverse:** Inscription **Reverse:** Inscription **Note:** Weight varies 10.70-11.60 grams. Mint mark: flower bud.

Date	Mintage	VG	F	VF	XF	Unc
AH1183//11	—	50.00	125	250	350	—
AH118x//15 Rare	—	—	—	—	—	—

KM# 40.1 RUPEE

11.3300 g., Silver **Issuer:** East India Company **Mint:** Muhammadabad Banaras **Obverse:** Darogah's marks and stylized fish within Persian inscription, couplet **Obv. Inscription:** "Shah Alam II Badshah" **Reverse:** Darogah's mark of flower, Persian-julus (formula), mint name **Note:** Prev. KM#40.

Date	Mintage	Good	VG	F	VF	XF
AH1190//17	—	5.50	14.00	23.50	32.50	45.00
AH1191//17	—	5.50	14.00	23.50	32.50	45.00
AH1192//17	—	5.50	14.00	23.50	32.50	45.00
AH1193//17-20	—	5.50	14.00	23.50	32.50	45.00
AH1193//17-21	—	5.50	14.00	23.50	32.50	45.00
AH1194//17-22	—	5.50	14.00	23.50	32.50	45.00
AH1194//17-21	—	5.50	14.00	23.50	32.50	45.00
AH1195//17-22	—	5.50	14.00	23.50	32.50	45.00
AH1195//17-23	—	5.50	14.00	23.50	32.50	45.00
AH1196//17-24	—	5.50	14.00	23.50	32.50	45.00
AH1197//17-25	—	5.50	14.00	23.50	32.50	45.00
AH1198//17-26	—	5.50	14.00	23.50	32.50	45.00
AH1199//17-26	—	5.50	14.00	23.50	32.50	45.00
AH1199//17-27	—	5.50	14.00	23.50	32.50	45.00
AH1200//17-27	—	5.50	14.00	23.50	32.50	45.00
AH1201//17-29	—	5.50	14.00	23.50	32.50	45.00
AH1202//17-28 **Note:** Error	—	6.00	15.00	25.00	35.00	50.00
AH1201//17-28	—	5.50	14.00	23.50	32.50	45.00
AH1202//17-29	—	5.50	14.00	23.50	32.50	45.00
AH1202//17-30	—	5.50	14.00	23.50	32.50	45.00
AH1203//17-30	—	5.50	14.00	23.50	32.50	45.00
AH1203//17-31	—	5.50	14.00	23.50	32.50	45.00
AH1204//17-32	—	5.50	14.00	23.50	32.50	45.00
AH1205//17-33	—	5.50	14.00	23.50	32.50	45.00
AH1206//17-33	—	5.50	14.00	23.50	32.50	45.00
AH1206//17-34	—	5.50	14.00	23.50	32.50	45.00
AH1207//17-34	—	5.50	14.00	23.50	32.50	45.00
AH1207//17-35	—	5.50	14.00	23.50	32.50	45.00
AH1208//17-35	—	5.50	14.00	23.50	32.50	45.00
AH1208//17-36	—	5.50	14.00	23.50	32.50	45.00
AH1209//17-36	—	5.50	14.00	23.50	32.50	45.00
AH1209//17-37	—	5.50	14.00	23.50	32.50	45.00
AH1210//17-37	—	5.50	14.00	23.50	32.50	45.00
AH1210//17-38	—	5.50	14.00	23.50	32.50	45.00
AH1211//17-38	—	5.50	14.00	23.50	32.50	45.00
AH1211//17-39	—	5.50	14.00	23.50	32.50	45.00
AH1212//17-39	—	5.50	14.00	23.50	32.50	45.00
AH1212//17-40	—	5.50	14.00	23.50	32.50	45.00
AH1213//17-33 **Note:** Error	—	6.00	15.00	25.00	35.00	50.00
AH1213//17-40	—	5.50	14.00	23.50	25.00	45.00
AH1213//17-41	—	5.50	14.00	23.50	25.00	45.00
AH1214//17-41	—	5.50	14.00	23.50	25.00	45.00
AH1214//17-42	—	5.50	14.00	23.50	25.00	45.00
AH1215//17-42	—	5.50	14.00	23.50	25.00	45.00

KM# 21 NAZARANA RUPEE

11.6400 g., Silver **Issuer:** East India Company **Mint:** Kalkattah **Obverse:** Inscription **Obv. Inscription:** Persian-Shah Alam (II) Badshah, couplet **Reverse:** Inscription **Rev. Inscription:** Persian-julus (formula), mint name

Date	Mintage	VG	F	VF	XF	Unc
AH1175//3 Rare	—	—	—	—	—	—
AH1176//4 Rare	—	—	—	—	—	—

KM# 22 NAZARANA RUPEE

11.6400 g., Silver **Issuer:** East India Company **Mint:** Jahangirnagar **Obverse:** Inscription **Obv. Inscription:** Persian-Shah Alam (II) Badshah, couplet **Reverse:** Inscription **Rev. Inscription:** Persian-julus (formula), mint name

Date	Mintage	VG	F	VF	XF	Unc
AH1183//10	—	—	—	—	—	—

KM# 43.1 NAZARANA RUPEE

11.6400 g., Silver **Issuer:** East India Company **Mint:** Muhammadabad Banaras **Obverse:** Inscription **Obv. Inscription:** Persian-Shah Alam (II) Badshah, couplet **Reverse:** Inscription **Rev. Inscription:** Persian-julus (formula), mint name **Note:** Full flan in dotted border.

Date	Mintage	VG	F	VF	XF	Unc
AH1201//17-29	—	100	200	350	600	—

KM# 43.2 NAZARANA RUPEE

11.6400 g., Silver **Issuer:** East India Company **Mint:** Muhammadabad Banaras **Obv. Inscription:** Persian-Shah Alam (II) Badshah, couplet **Rev. Inscription:** Persian-julus (formula), mint name **Note:** Flan without dotted border.

Date	Mintage	VG	F	VF	XF	Unc
AH1207//17-35	—	100	200	350	600	—

KM# 23 1/16 MOHUR

0.7700 g., Gold **Mint:** Azimabad **Obv. Inscription:** Persian-Shah Alam (II) Badshah, couplet **Rev. Inscription:** Persian-julus (formula), mint name

Date	Mintage	VG	F	VF	XF	Unc
AH1182//10 Rare	—	—	—	—	—	—

KM# 87 1/16 MOHUR

0.7700 g., Gold, 11 mm. **Mint:** Murshidabad **Obverse:** Inscription **Obv. Inscription:** Persian-Shah Alam (II) Badshah, fine style **Reverse:** Inscription **Rev. Inscription:** Persian-sanat, mint name, fine style

Date	Mintage	VG	F	VF	XF	Unc
AH1182//10	—	65.00	125	250	400	—
AH1183//10 Frozen	—	65.00	125	250	400	—
AH1202//19 Frozen	—	45.00	75.00	150	300	—
AH1203//19 Frozen	—	45.00	75.00	150	300	—

KM# 88 1/16 MOHUR

0.7700 g., Gold **Mint:** Murshidabad **Obverse:** Inscription **Obv. Inscription:** Shah Alam (II) Badshah, large style **Reverse:** Inscription **Rev. Inscription:** Julus, Zarb, mint name, large style

Date	Mintage	VG	F	VF	XF	Unc
AH118x//15	—	—	—	—	—	—

KM# A89 1/8 MOHUR

1.5000 g., Gold **Mint:** Murshidabad **Obv. Inscription:** Shah Alam (II) Badshah, crude style **Rev. Inscription:** Julus, Zark, mint name, (Calcutta), large style **Note:** Mint mark: Large C.

Date	Mintage	VG	F	VF	XF	Unc
AH1180//7	—	—	—	—	—	—

KM# 89 1/8 MOHUR

1.5000 g., Gold, 14 mm. **Mint:** Murshidabad **Obverse:** Inscription **Obv. Inscription:** Persian-Shah Alam (II) Badshah, fine style **Reverse:** Inscription **Rev. Inscription:** Sanat, Zarb, mint name, fine style

Date	Mintage	VG	F	VF	XF	Unc
AH1182//10	—	90.00	150	275	450	—
AH1183//10 Frozen	—	90.00	150	275	450	—
AH1200//19 Frozen	—	—	—	—	—	—
AH1202//19 Frozen	—	60.00	100	200	350	—
AH1203//19 Frozen	—	60.00	100	200	350	—

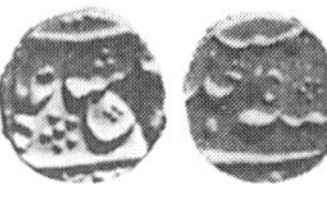

KM# 90 1/8 MOHUR

1.5000 g., Gold **Mint:** Murshidabad **Obverse:** Inscription **Obv. Inscription:** Shah Alam (II) Badshah, large style **Reverse:** Inscription **Rev. Inscription:** Julus, Zarb, mint name, (Calcutta), large style

Date	Mintage	VG	F	VF	XF	Unc
AH118x//15 Rare	—	—	—	—	—	—

KM# 10 1/4 MOHUR

2.8000 g., Gold **Mint:** Kalkattah **Obv. Inscription:** Persian-Alamgir (II) regal title **Rev. Inscription:** Persian-julus (formula), mint name

Date	Mintage	VG	F	VF	XF	Unc
AH1171//5 Rare	—	—	—	—	—	—
AH1172//6 Rare	—	—	—	—	—	—

KM# A91 1/4 MOHUR

3.0900 g., Gold **Mint:** Calcutta **Obv. Inscription:** Shah Alam (II) Badshah, large style **Rev. Inscription:** Julus, Zarb, mint name, large style **Note:** Mint mark: Large "C".

Date	Mintage	VG	F	VF	XF	Unc
AH1180//7	—	—	—	—	—	—

KM# 91 1/4 MOHUR

3.0900 g., Gold **Mint:** Murshidabad **Obverse:** Inscription **Obv. Inscription:** Shah Alam (II) Badshah, couplet, fine style **Reverse:** Inscription **Rev. Inscription:** Julus (formula), mint name

Date	Mintage	VG	F	VF	XF	Unc
AH1182//10	—	120	200	450	800	—
AH1202//19 Frozen	—	120	200	450	800	—
AH1203//19 Frozen	—	120	200	450	800	—

KM# 11 1/2 MOHUR

5.5000 g., Gold **Mint:** Kalkattah **Obv. Inscription:** Persian-Alamgir (II) **Rev. Inscription:** Persian-julus (formula), mint name

Date	Mintage	VG	F	VF	XF	Unc
AH1171//5 Rare	—	—	—	—	—	—
AH1172//6 Rare	—	—	—	—	—	—

KM# 93 1/2 MOHUR

6.1800 g., Gold **Mint:** Calcutta **Obv. Inscription:** Persian-Shah Alam (II) Badshah, couplet, large style **Rev. Inscription:** Persian-julus (formula), mint name, large style

Date	Mintage	VG	F	VF	XF	Unc
AH1179//7	—	750	1,250	1,850	2,500	—
AH1180//8	—	750	1,250	1,850	2,500	—
AH1181//9	—	750	1,250	1,850	2,500	—
AH1182//10	—	750	1,250	1,850	2,500	—

KM# A92 1/2 MOHUR

6.1800 g., Gold **Mint:** Calcutta **Note:** Mint mark: Large "C".

Date	Mintage	VG	F	VF	XF	Unc
AH1180//7	—	—	—	—	—	—

KM# 92 1/2 MOHUR

6.1800 g., Gold **Mint:** Calcutta **Obverse:** Inscription **Obv. Inscription:** Persian-Shah Alam (II) Badshah, couplet, fine style **Reverse:** Inscription **Rev. Inscription:** Persian-julus (formula), mint name, fine style

Date	Mintage	VG	F	VF	XF	Unc
AH1182//10	—	300	500	750	1,250	—
AH1183//11	—	300	500	750	1,250	—

KM# 12.1 MOHUR

Gold **Mint:** A'linagar Kalkattah **Obv. Inscription:** Persian-ALamgir (III) **Rev. Inscription:** Persian-julus (formula), mint name

Date	Mintage	VG	F	VF	XF	Unc
AH-//4 Rare	—	—	—	—	—	—

KM# 12.2 MOHUR

Gold **Mint:** Kalkattah **Obverse:** Inscription **Reverse:** Inscription

Date	Mintage	VG	F	VF	XF	Unc
AH1171//5 Rare	—	—	—	—	—	—
AH1174//6 Error; Rare	—	—	—	—	—	—

KM# 95 MOHUR

12.3600 g., Gold **Mint:** Calcutta **Obv. Inscription:** Persian-Shah Alam (II) Badshah, couplet, large style **Rev. Inscription:** Persian-julus (formula), mint name, large style

Date	Mintage	VG	F	VF	XF	Unc
AH1179//7	—	750	1,250	1,850	2,500	—
AH1180//8	—	750	1,250	1,850	2,500	—
AH1181//9	—	750	1,250	1,850	2,500	—
AH1182//10	—	750	1,250	1,850	2,500	—

KM# 94.1 MOHUR

12.3600 g., Gold, 25-26 mm. **Mint:** Calcutta **Obverse:** Persian-Shah Alam (II) Badshah, couplet, fine style **Reverse:** Persian-julus (formula), mint name, fine style **Note:** Size varies.

Date	Mintage	VG	F	VF	XF	Unc
AH1182//10	—	300	500	900	1,500	—
AH1183//10	—	300	500	900	1,500	—
AH1185//12	—	300	500	900	1,500	—
AH1186//12 Frozen	—	300	500	900	1,500	—
AH1187//15	—	300	500	900	1,500	—
AH1188//12	—	300	500	900	1,500	—
AH1189//12	—	300	500	900	1,500	—
AH1189//15	—	300	500	900	1,500	—
AH1190//15	—	300	500	900	1,500	—
AH1194//19 Frozen	—	300	500	900	1,500	—
AH1195//19 Frozen	—	300	500	900	1,500	—
AH1196//19 Frozen	—	300	500	900	1,500	—
AH1197//19 Frozen	—	300	500	900	1,500	—
AH1198//19 Frozen	—	300	500	900	1,500	—
AH1199//19 Frozen	—	300	500	900	1,500	—
AH1200//19 Frozen	—	300	500	900	1,500	—
AH1201//19 Frozen	—	300	500	900	1,500	—
AH1202//19 Frozen	—	300	500	900	1,500	—

KM# 94.2 MOHUR

12.3600 g., Gold, 21-22 mm. **Mint:** Calcutta **Obverse:** Persian-Shah Alam (11) Badshah, couplet, fine style **Reverse:** Persian-julus (formula), mint name, fine style **Note:** Struck at Calcutta Mint. Mint name: Murshidabad. Reduced size varies.

Date	Mintage	VG	F	VF	XF	Unc
AH1183//11	—	300	500	900	1,500	—
AH1184//11	—	300	500	900	1,500	—

KM# A95 MOHUR

12.3600 g., Gold **Mint:** Calcutta **Obverse:** Persian inscription, couplet **Obv. Inscription:** Shah Alam (II) Badshsh **Reverse:** Persian inscription, julus (formula), mint name, fine style **Note:** Mule - old obverse die, reverse KM#94.1. Mint name: Murshidabad.

Date	Mintage	VG	F	VF	XF	Unc
AH1188//12	—	—	—	—	—	—
AH1189//12	—	—	—	—	—	—

KM# 13 MOHUR

Gold **Mint:** Muhammadabad Banaras **Obverse:** Inscription **Obv. Inscription:** Persian-Shah Alam (II) Badshah, couplet **Reverse:** Inscription **Rev. Inscription:** Persian-julus (formula), mint name

Date	Mintage	VG	F	VF	XF	Unc
AH11xx//24 Rare	—	—	—	—	—	—

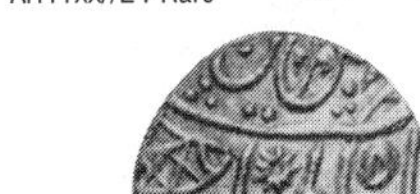

KM# 31 MOHUR

Gold **Mint:** Muhammadabad Banaras **Obverse:** Inscription **Obv. Inscription:** Persian-Shah Alam (II) Badshah, couplet **Reverse:** Inscription **Rev. Inscription:** Persian-julus (formula), mint name **Note:** Mint mark: stylized fish, sunburst//flowers.

Date	Mintage	Good	VG	F	VF	XF
AH1199//17-26	—	135	225	500	1,150	1,750
AH1202//17-29	—	135	225	500	1,150	1,750
AH1202//30	—	135	225	500	1,150	1,750
AH1201//17-29	—	135	225	500	1,150	1,750
AH1203//32	—	135	225	500	1,150	1,750
AH1203//31	—	135	225	500	1,150	1,750
AH1204//32	—	135	225	500	1,150	1,750
AH1209//37	—	135	225	500	1,150	1,750
AH1213//41	—	135	225	500	1,150	1,750

DUMP TOKEN COINAGE

KM# Tn1 ANNA

Copper **Mint:** Azimabad **Obv. Inscription:** Patna Post, value **Rev. Inscription:** Persian-Azimabad dak ani

Date	Mintage	Good	VG	F	VF	XF
1774	—	50.00	75.00	110	—	—

KM# Tn2 2 ANNAS

Copper **Mint:** Azimabad **Obv. Inscription:** Patna Post, value **Rev. Inscription:** Persian-Azimabad dak do ani

Date	Mintage	Good	VG	F	VF	XF
1774	—	65.00	100	150	—	—

MILLED COINAGE

KM# 50 1/2 PICE

5.8200 g., Copper, 23-24 mm. **Obverse:** Inscription **Obv. Inscription:** Persian-Shah Alam (II), Badshah, julus **Reverse:** Inscription **Rev. Inscription:** Value in Bangali, Persian and Hindi **Edge:** Plain **Note:** Size varies.

Date	Mintage	VG	F	VF	XF	Unc
AH-//37	—	4.50	9.00	15.00	25.00	—

KM# 51 1/2 PICE

4.3600 g., Copper **Obv. Inscription:** Persian-Shah Alam (II), Badshah julus **Rev. Inscription:** Value in Bangali, Persian and Hindi **Edge:** Plain

Date	Mintage	VG	F	VF	XF	Unc
AH-//37	—	3.50	6.00	10.00	16.00	—

KM# 25 PICE

6.2000 g., Copper **Mint:** Calcutta

Date	Mintage	VG	F	VF	XF	Unc
AH-//37	—	10.00	20.00	30.00	50.00	—
AH-//37 Proof	—	Value: 90.00				

KM# 52 PICE

11.6400 g., Copper, 29-30 mm. **Obverse:** Inscription **Obv. Inscription:** Persian-Shah Alam (II) Badsahah julus **Reverse:** Inscription **Rev. Inscription:** Value in Bengali, Persian and Hindi **Edge:** Plain **Note:** Size varies.

Date	Mintage	VG	F	VF	XF	Unc
AH-//37	—	5.50	11.50	18.50	30.00	—

KM# 53 PICE

8.7300 g., Copper, 27-30 mm. **Obv. Inscription:** Persian-Shah Alam (II) Badshah julus **Rev. Inscription:** Value in Bengali, Persian and Hindi **Edge:** Plain **Note:** Size varies.

Date	Mintage	VG	F	VF	XF	Unc
AH-//37	—	2.00	3.50	6.00	10.00	—

KM# 120 1/16 ANNA

1.8100 g., Copper, 15.8 mm. **Mint:** Falta **Obverse:** Inscription **Obv. Inscription:** Persian-Shah Alam (II) Badshah, couplet **Reverse:** Inscription **Rev. Inscription:** Persian-julus (formula), mint name **Edge:** Plain

Date	Mintage	VG	F	VF	XF	Unc
AH1195//22	—	2.50	4.00	8.00	15.00	—
AH1195//22 Proof	—	—	—	—	65.00	—

KM# 121 1/16 ANNA

1.8100 g., Copper **Mint:** Falta **Obverse:** Inscription **Obv. Inscription:** Persian-Shah Alam (II) Badshah, couplet **Reverse:** Inscription **Rev. Inscription:** Persian-julus (formula), mint name **Edge:** Plain

Date	Mintage	VG	F	VF	XF	Unc
AH1195//22	—	2.50	4.00	8.00	15.00	—

KM# 122 1/8 ANNA

3.6400 g., Copper, 19.6 mm. **Mint:** Falta **Obverse:** Inscription **Obv. Inscription:** Persian-Shah Alam (II) Badshah, couplet **Reverse:** Inscription **Rev. Inscription:** Persian-julus (formula), mint name **Edge:** Plain

Date	Mintage	VG	F	VF	XF	Unc
AH1195//22	—	3.00	4.50	10.00	18.00	—
AH1195//22 Proof	—	Value: 70.00				

KM# 123 1/8 ANNA

3.6400 g., Copper, 18.3 mm. **Mint:** Falta **Obverse:** Inscription **Obv. Inscription:** Persian-Shah Alam (II) Badshah, couplet **Reverse:** Inscription **Rev. Inscription:** Persian-julus (formula), mint name **Edge:** Plain

Date	Mintage	VG	F	VF	XF	Unc
AH1195//22	—	2.50	4.00	8.00	15.00	—

KM# 124 1/4 ANNA

7.2700 g., Copper, 23.7 mm. **Mint:** Falta **Obv. Inscription:** Persian-Shah Alam (II) Badshah, couplet **Rev. Inscription:** Persian-julus (formula), mint name **Edge:** Plain

Date	Mintage	VG	F	VF	XF	Unc
AH1195//22	—	3.00	5.00	12.50	25.00	—
AH1195//22 Proof	—	Value: 75.00				

KM# 125 1/4 ANNA

7.2700 g., Copper, 22.8 mm. **Mint:** Falta **Obv. Inscription:** Persian-Shah Alam (II) Badshah, couplet **Rev. Inscription:** Persian-julus (formula), mint name **Edge:** Plain

Date	Mintage	VG	F	VF	XF	Unc
AH1195//22	—	3.00	5.00	12.50	25.00	—

KM# 126 1/2 ANNA

14.5400 g., Copper, 26 mm. **Mint:** Falta **Obverse:** Inscription **Obv. Inscription:** Persian-Shah Alam (II) Badshah, couplet **Reverse:** Inscription **Rev. Inscription:** Persian-julus (formula), mint name **Edge:** Plain

Date	Mintage	VG	F	VF	XF	Unc
AH1195//22	—	3.50	6.00	11.00	23.00	—
AH1195//22 Proof	—	Value: 85.00				

KM# 127 1/2 ANNA

14.5400 g., Copper, 26 mm. **Mint:** Falta **Obverse:** Inscription **Obv. Inscription:** Persian-Shah Alam (II) Badshah, couplet **Reverse:** Inscription **Rev. Inscription:** Persian-julus (formula), mint name **Edge:** Plain

Date	Mintage	VG	F	VF	XF	Unc
AH1195//22	—	3.50	6.00	11.00	23.00	—

KM# 96.1 1/4 RUPEE

2.9000 g., Silver **Mint:** Murshidabad **Obv. Inscription:** Shah Alam (II) Badshah, couplet **Rev. Inscription:** Persian-sanat (year, mint name) **Edge:** Oblique milling **Note:** Prev. KM#96. Struck at Calcutta Mint, 1793-1818.

Date	Mintage	F	VF	XF	Unc
AH1204//19 Frozen	—	2.00	5.00	15.00	25.00
AH1204//19 Proof; Frozen	—	Value: 300			

KM# 96.2 1/4 RUPEE

2.9000 g., Silver **Mint:** Murshidabad **Obv. Inscription:** Shah Alam (II) Badshah, couplet **Rev. Inscription:** Persian-sanat (year, mint name) **Edge:** Oblique milling **Note:** Struck at Dacca Mint, 1793-1797.

Date	Mintage	F	VF	XF	Unc
AH1204//19 Frozen	—	3.00	10.00	30.00	50.00

KM# 96.3 1/4 RUPEE

2.9000 g., Silver **Mint:** Murshidabad **Obv. Inscription:** Shah Alam (II) Badshah, couplet **Rev. Inscription:** Persian-sanat (year, mint name) **Edge:** Oblique milling **Note:** Struck at Murshidabad Mint, 1793-1797.

Date	Mintage	F	VF	XF	Unc
AH1204//19 Frozen	—	1.50	5.00	15.00	25.00

KM# 96.4 1/4 RUPEE

2.9000 g., Silver **Mint:** Murshidabad **Obv. Inscription:** Shah Alam (II) Badshah, couplet **Rev. Inscription:** Persian-sanat (year, mint name) **Edge:** Oblique milling **Note:** Struck at Patna Mint, 1793-1797.

Date	Mintage	F	VF	XF	Unc
AH1204//19 Frozen	—	3.00	10.00	30.00	50.00

KM# 97.2 1/2 RUPEE

5.8000 g., Silver **Mint:** Dacca **Obverse:** Persian inscription, couplet **Obv. Inscription:** "Shah Alam II Badshah" **Reverse:** Persian-julus (formula), mint name **Note:** Privy mark in center of first circle.

Date	Mintage	Good	VG	F	VF	XF
ND-//19 Frozen	—	2.25	4.00	7.50	25.00	75.00

KM# 97.3 1/2 RUPEE

5.8000 g., Silver **Mint:** Murshidabad **Obverse:** Persian inscription, couplet **Obv. Inscription:** "Shah Alam II Badshah" **Reverse:** Persian-julus (formula), mint name **Note:** Privy mark in center of second circle.

Date	Mintage	Good	VG	F	VF	XF
ND-//19 Frozen	—	2.25	4.00	7.50	25.00	75.00

KM# 97.4 1/2 RUPEE

5.8000 g., Silver **Mint:** Patna **Obverse:** Persian inscription, couplet **Obv. Inscription:** "Shah Alam II Badshah" **Reverse:** Persian - julus (formula), mint name **Rev. Inscription:** "Murshidabad" **Note:** Privy mark in center of third dot group.

Date	Mintage	Good	VG	F	VF	XF
ND-//19 Frozen	—	2.25	4.00	7.50	25.00	75.00
ND-//19 Proof; Frozen	—	Value: 400				

KM# 97.1 1/2 RUPEE

5.8000 g., Silver **Obverse:** Persian inscription, couplet **Obv. Inscription:** "Shah Alam II Badshah" **Reverse:** Milling: Persian-julus (formula), mint name **Edge:** Oblique **Note:** Struck at Calcutta Dacca, Murshidabad, Patna Mint. Privy mark - top line. Mint mark: 6 petalled rosette.

Date	Mintage	Good	VG	F	VF	XF
AH-//19 Frozen	—	—	BV	2.50	8.50	25.00

KM# 85 RUPEE

11.6000 g., Silver **Mint:** Murshidabad **Obverse:** KM#84 **Obv. Inscription:** Persian-Shah Alam (II) Badshah, couplet **Reverse:** KM#86 **Rev. Inscription:** Persian-julus (formula), mint name **Note:** Mule.

Date	Mintage	VG	F	VF	XF	Unc
AH1190 (sic)//19	—	—	—	—	—	—

KM# 98.2 RUPEE

11.6000 g., Silver **Mint:** Murshidabad **Obverse:** Persian inscription, couplet **Obv. Inscription:** Shah Alam (II) Badshah **Reverse:** Persian-julus (formula), mint name **Note:** Narrow, fine stroke border. Struck at Calcutta, Dacca, Murshidabad mints.

Date	Mintage	F	VF	XF	Unc
AH1202//19 Frozen	—	27.50	55.00	90.00	—

KM# 106 RUPEE

11.6000 g., Silver **Mint:** Calcutta **Obverse:** Inscription **Obv. Inscription:** Persian-Shah Alam (II) Badshah, couplet **Reverse:** Inscription **Rev. Inscription:** Persian-julus (formula), mint name **Edge:** Oblique milling **Note:** Broad dentilated border. Mint name: Murshidabad.

Date	Mintage	F	VF	XF	Unc
AH1202//19 Frozen	—	45.00	90.00	150	250

KM# 86 RUPEE

11.6000 g., Silver **Mint:** Murshidabad **Obverse:** Inscription **Obv. Inscription:** Persian-Shah Alam (II) Badshah, couplet **Reverse:** Inscription **Rev. Inscription:** Persian-julus (formula), mint name **Note:** Large flan.

Date	Mintage	F	VF	XF	Unc
AH1205//19 Frozen	—	30.00	60.00	125	250

KM# 98.1 RUPEE

11.6000 g., Silver **Mint:** Calcutta **Obv. Inscription:** Persian-Shah Alam (II) Badshah, couplet **Rev. Inscription:** Persian-julus (formula), mint name **Note:** Struck at Calcutta, Dacca, Murshidabad Mints.

Date	Mintage	F	VF	XF	Unc
AH1202//19 Frozen	—	13.50	27.50	45.00	75.00

KM# 99 RUPEE

11.6000 g., Silver **Mint:** Calcutta **Obverse:** Inscription **Obv. Inscription:** Persian-Shah Alam (II) Badshah, couplet **Reverse:** Inscription **Rev. Inscription:** Persian-julus (formula), mint name **Edge:** Oblique **Note:** Privy mark - top line. Struck at Calcutta, Darra, Murshidabad, Patna Mint.

Date	Mintage	F	VF	XF	Unc
AH-//19	—	15.00	25.00	45.00	90.00

KM# 99.2 RUPEE

11.6000 g., Silver **Mint:** Dacca **Obv. Inscription:** Persian-Shah Alam (II) Badshah, couplet **Rev. Inscription:** Persian-julus (formula), mintname **Note:** Privy mark - center of second circle. Struck at Dacca Mint.

Date	Mintage	F	VF	XF	Unc
AH-//19	—	—	—	—	—

KM# 99.3 RUPEE

11.6000 g., Silver **Mint:** Murshidabad **Obv. Inscription:** Persian-Shah Alam (II) Badshah, couplet **Rev. Inscription:** Persian-julus (formula), mintname **Note:** Privy mark - center of second circle.

Date	Mintage	F	VF	XF	Unc
AH-//19	—	—	—	—	—

KM# 99.4 RUPEE

11.6000 g., Silver **Mint:** Patna **Obv. Inscription:** Persian-Shah Alam (II) Badshah, couplet **Rev. Inscription:** Persian-julus (formula), mintname **Note:** Privy mark - center of third dot group.

Date	Mintage	F	VF	XF	Unc
AH-//19	—	—	—	—	—

KM# 100 1/4 MOHUR
3.0900 g., 0.9960 Gold 0.0989 oz. AGW **Mint:** Murshidabad **Obverse:** Inscription **Obv. Inscription:** "Shah Alam II Badshah" **Reverse:** Sanat, mint name **Edge:** Oblique milling

Date	Mintage	Good	VG	F	VF	XF
AH1204//19 Frozen	—	—	BV	65.00	80.00	150

KM# 101 1/2 MOHUR
6.1800 g., 0.9960 Gold 0.1979 oz. AGW **Mint:** Calcutta **Obverse:** Persian inscription, couplet **Obv. Inscription:** "Shah Alam II Badshah" **Reverse:** Persian-julus (formula), mint name Murshidabad **Edge:** Oblique milling

Date	Mintage	VG	F	VF	XF	Unc
AH1202//19	—	BV	125	200	350	—

KM# A94 MOHUR
12.3600 g., Gold **Mint:** Calcutta **Obverse:** Inscription **Obv. Inscription:** Persian-Shah Alam (II) Badshah, couplet **Reverse:** Inscription **Rev. Inscription:** Persian-julus (formula), mint name **Note:** Mint mark: Large "C".

Date	Mintage	VG	F	VF	XF	Unc
AH1180//8	—	—	—	5,000	—	—

KM# 102 MOHUR
12.3600 g., Gold **Mint:** Calcutta **Obverse:** Inscription **Obv. Inscription:** Persian-Shah Alam (II) Badshah, couplet **Reverse:** Inscription **Rev. Inscription:** Persian-julus (formula), mint name **Edge:** Oblique

Date	Mintage	VG	F	VF	XF	Unc
AH1202//19	—	—	200	300	500	—

KM# 103.1 MOHUR
12.3600 g., 0.9960 Gold 0.3958 oz. AGW **Mint:** Calcutta **Obverse:** Persian inscription, couplet **Obv. Inscription:** "Shah Alam II Badshah" **Reverse:** Persian-julus (formula), mint name Murshidabad **Edge:** Oblique milling

Date	Mintage	VG	F	VF	XF	Unc
AH1202//19	—	—	BV	250	275	350

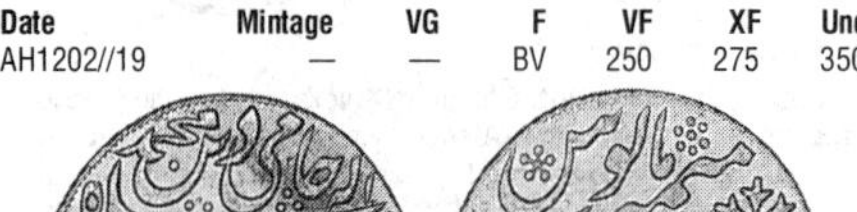

KM# 103.2 MOHUR
12.3600 g., 0.9960 Gold 0.3958 oz. AGW **Mint:** Murshidabad **Obverse:** Persian inscription, couplet **Obv. Inscription:** "Shah Alam II Badshah" **Reverse:** Persian-julus (formula), mint name Murshidabad **Edge:** Oblique milling **Note:** Prev. KM#103.

Date	Mintage	VG	F	VF	XF	Unc
AH1202//19 Rare	—	—	—	—	—	—

TRIAL STRIKES

KM# TS2 PICE
1.4500 g., Copper, 15 mm. **Reverse:** Scales, Persian-Adil (Justice) **Shape:** Hexagonal **Note:** P#367.

Date	Mintage	F	VF	XF	Unc
ND(1792)	—	—	—	—	—

KM# TS1 PICE
1.4500 g., Copper, 15 mm. **Obverse:** U.E.I.Co. bale mark **Shape:** Hexagonal **Note:** Prid.#366.

Date	Mintage	F	VF	XF	Unc
1792	—	—	—	—	—

PATTERNS

Including off metal strikes

Due to extensive revisions and new information, the following section in part is listed by Pridmore(P#) numbers. These are in reference to The Coins of the Commonwealth of Nations, Part 4, India - Volume I: East India Company Presidency Series ca. 1642-1835, by F. Pridmore (Spink and Son, Ltd.).

KM#	Date	Mintage	Identification	Mkt Val
PnA1	1180//8	—	Nazarana Rupee. Silver. KM#84.1.	—

KM#	Date	Mintage	Identification	Mkt Val
Pn1	1182//10	—	Rupee. Silver. P#343.	—
PnA2	1183//11	—	Nazarana Rupee. Silver. P#109.	—
PnB2	1184//11	—	Nazarana Rupee. Silver. KM#84.1.	—
Pn2	1185//13	—	Rupee. Silver. P#344.	2,000
PnA3	-//19	—	Rupee. Copper.	—

KM#	Date	Mintage	Identification	Mkt Val
Pn3	1190//19 frozen	—	Nazarana Rupee. Silver. P#345.	—

KM#	Date	Mintage	Identification	Mkt Val
Pn4	1194//22	—	Falus. Copper. P#351.	—

KM#	Date	Mintage	Identification	Mkt Val
Pn5	1195//22	—	Falus. Copper. P#352.	—
Pn6	1198//26	—	1/8 Rupee. Silver. P#350.	—

KM#	Date	Mintage	Identification	Mkt Val
Pn7	1198//26	—	1/4 Rupee. Silver. P#349.	—
Pn8	1198//26	—	Rupee. Silver. P#347.	—

KM#	Date	Mintage	Identification	Mkt Val
Pn9	1198//26	—	2 Rupees. Silver. P#346.	3,000
Pn10	1792	—	1/2 Pice. Copper. P#368.	—
Pn11	1792	—	Pice. Copper. P#365.	600
Pn12	(1793)	—	1/4 Rupee. Silver. Plain edge. P#357.	—
Pn12a	(1793)	—	1/4 Rupee. Silver. Oblique edge. P#360.	—
Pn13	(1793)	—	1/2 Rupee. Silver. Plain edge. P#356.	—
Pn13a	(1793)	—	1/2 Rupee. Silver. Oblique edge. P#359.	—

KM#	Date	Mintage	Identification	Mkt Val
Pn14	(1793)	—	Rupee. Silver. Plain edge. P#355.	—
Pn14a	(1793)	—	Rupee. Silver. Oblique edge. P#358.	—
Pn15	1793	—	1/48 Rupee. Copper. Lettered edge. P#369.	500
Pn15a	1793	—	1/48 Rupee. Copper. Plain edge. P#370.	500

KM#	Date	Mintage	Identification	Mkt Val
Pn16	1793	—	1/48 Rupee. Copper. P#371.	—
Pn17	1794	—	1/48 Rupee. Copper. P#372.	850
Pn18	1794	—	1/48 Rupee. Copper. P#373.	—

KM#	Date	Mintage	Identification	Mkt Val
Pn19	(1795)	—	Pice. Copper. Plain edge. P#380.	—
Pn19a	(1795)	—	Pice. Copper. Milled edge. P#381.	—
Pn19b	(1795)	—	Pice. Copper Gilt. Plain edge. P#382.	—
Pn19c	(1795)	—	Pice. Pewter. . P#383.	—

BOMBAY PRESIDENCY

Following a naval victory over the Portuguese on December 24, 1612 negotiations were started that developed into the opening of the first East India Company factory in Surat in 1613. Silver coins for the New World as well as various other foreign coins were used in early trade. Within the decade the Mughal mint at Surat was melting all of these foreign coins and re-minting them as various denominations of Mughal coinage.

Bombay became an English holding as part of the dowry of Catherine of Braganza, Princess of Portugal when she was betrothed to Charles II of England. Also included in the dowry was Tangier and $500,000. With this acquisition the trading center of the Indian West Coast moved from Surat to Bombay.

Possession of Bombay Island took place on February 8, 1665 and by 1672 the East India Company had a mint in Bombay to serve their trading interests. European designed coins were struck here until 1717. Experimental issues of Mughal style rupees with regnal years pertaining to the reigns of James II and William and Mary were made in 1693-94.

From 1717 to 1778 the Mughal style Bombay rupee was the principal coin of the West India trade, although bulk foreign coins were used for striking rupees at Surat.

After the East India Company took over the city of Surat in 1800 they slowed the mint production and finally transferred all activity to Mumbai in 1815.

MINTS

منبي

Bombay (Mumbai)

سورت

Surat

تلجري تالچري

Tellicherry

MONETARY SYSTEM

3 Pies = 1 Pice (Paisa)
11 Tinnys (Bujruk) = 1 Copperoon (Pice)
48 Copperoons = 1 Anglina (Rupee)

BRITISH COLONY

CAST COINAGE

KM# 155 TINNY (Bujruk)
1.6500 g., Cast Tin **Obverse:** U.E.I.Co. bale mark **Reverse:** Date

Date	Mintage	Good	VG	F	VF	XF
1716	—	150	200	250	300	—

KM# 170 1/4 PICE
3.4800 g., Cast Tin **Obverse:** U.E.I.Co. bale mark **Rev. Inscription:** 1/4 Pice

Date	Mintage	Good	VG	F	VF	XF
ND(1757)	—	150	200	250	300	—

KM# 169 1/2 PICE
6.8000 g., Cast Tin, 27 mm. **Obverse:** Large crown with "Bomb" below **Reverse:** Inscription **Rev. Inscription:** Auspicio/Regis ET/Senatus/Angliae **Note:** P247.

Date	Mintage	Good	VG	F	VF	XF
ND(1754)	—	100	200	300	400	—

KM# 171 1/2 PICE
6.9500 g., Cast Tin **Obverse:** U.E.I. Co. Bale mark **Reverse:** 1/2 Pice **Note:** P248.

Date	Mintage	Good	VG	F	VF	XF
ND(1757)	—	150	200	250	300	—

KM# 156.1 PICE
13.6000 g., Cast Tin, 32-34 mm. **Obverse:** Large crown, "BOMB" below **Reverse:** Inscription **Rev. Inscription:** AUSPICIO/REGIS ET/SENATUS/ANGLIAE **Note:** Size varies. P241-P245.

Date	Mintage	Good	VG	F	VF	XF
1717	—	15.00	25.00	40.00	65.00	—
1741	—	15.00	25.00	40.00	65.00	—
1743	—	—	—	—	—	—
1747	—	—	—	—	—	—
1771	—	—	—	—	—	—

KM# 156.2 PICE
13.6000 g., Cast Tin **Reverse:** Ornament below "ANGLIAE"

Date	Mintage	Good	VG	F	VF	XF
ND(1754)	—	10.00	20.00	35.00	60.00	—

KM# 157.1 2 PICE (8 Reas = Nim (1/2) Anna)
27.2100 g., Cast Tin **Obverse:** Large crown divides G-R, "BOMB" below **Reverse:** Inscription **Rev. Inscription:** AUSPICIO/REGIS ET/SENATUS/ANGLIAE **Note:** P230-P239.

Date	Mintage	Good	VG	F	VF	XF
1717	—	17.50	27.50	42.50	62.50	—
1718	—	17.50	27.50	42.50	62.50	—
1732	—	17.50	27.50	42.50	62.50	—
1733	—	17.50	27.50	42.50	62.50	—
1741	—	17.50	27.50	42.50	62.50	—
1742	—	17.50	27.50	42.50	62.50	—
1743	—	17.50	27.50	42.50	62.50	—
1748	—	17.50	27.50	42.50	62.50	—
ND(1754)	—	17.50	27.50	42.50	62.50	—
1761	—	17.50	27.50	42.50	62.50	—
1771	—	17.50	27.50	42.50	62.50	—
1771 SENATUT	—	—	—	—	—	—

KM# 157.2 2 PICE (8 Reas = Nim (1/2) Anna)
27.2100 g., Cast Tin **Note:** P240.

Date	Mintage	Good	VG	F	VF	XF
ND(1754)	—	15.00	25.00	40.00	60.00	—

HAMMERED COINAGE

KM# 187 1/4 PICE
Copper **Obverse:** U.E.I.Co. bale mark **Reverse:** 1/4

Date	Mintage	Good	VG	F	VF	XF
ND(1773)	—	7.50	13.50	20.00	30.00	—

KM# 172 1/2 PICE
6.7500 g., Copper **Obverse:** Large crown, 2 stars above, 1 below **Reverse:** Inscription **Rev. Inscription:** Company motto in four lines

Date	Mintage	Good	VG	F	VF	XF
ND(1704-16)	—	10.00	18.50	28.50	40.00	—

KM# 151 1/2 PICE
Copper, 12 mm. **Obverse:** Center of U.E.I. Co. Bale mark **Reverse:** Date **Note:** Weight varies 1.62-1.08 g. For previously listed 1/2 Piece, KM#152, dated 1714, with lion reverse, refer to St. Helena.

Date	Mintage	Good	VG	F	VF	XF
1710	—	7.50	13.50	20.00	30.00	—
1712	—	—	13.50	20.00	30.00	—
1726	—	7.50	13.50	20.00	30.00	—
1741	—	7.50	13.50	20.00	30.00	—
1753	—	7.50	13.50	20.00	30.00	—
1759	—	7.50	13.50	20.00	30.00	—
1785	—	7.50	13.50	20.00	30.00	—

KM# 164 1/2 PICE
2.6300 g., Copper, 15 mm. **Obverse:** U.E.I. Co. Bale mark **Reverse:** 1/2

Date	Mintage	Good	VG	F	VF	XF
ND(1723)	—	10.00	18.50	28.50	40.00	—

KM# A173 1/2 PICE
Copper **Obverse:** Very large crown divides G-R at top, "BOMB" below

Date	Mintage	Good	VG	F	VF	XF
ND(1728-49)	—	10.00	18.50	28.50	40.00	—

KM# 173 1/2 PICE
Copper **Obverse:** Large crown divides G-R at top, "BOMB" below **Reverse:** Inscription **Note:** Weight varies 3.23-4.40 grams.

Date	Mintage	Good	VG	F	VF	XF
ND(1728-49)	—	10.00	18.50	28.50	40.00	—

KM# 151a 1/2 PICE
1.3700 g., Copper, 8.9 mm. **Obverse:** Center of U.E.I.Co. bale mark **Reverse:** Date

Date	Mintage	Good	VG	F	VF	XF
(1)786	—	7.50	13.50	20.00	30.00	—

KM# 149 PICE
13.6500 g., Copper **Obverse:** Large crown, 2 stars above, 1 below **Reverse:** Inscription **Rev. Inscription:** AUSPICIO/REGIS ET/SENATUS/ANGLIU with ornaments above and below

Date	Mintage	Good	VG	F	VF	XF
ND(1704-16)	—	20.00	35.00	45.00	65.00	—

KM# 150 PICE
Copper, 15.7 mm. **Obverse:** U.E.I. Co. Bale mark **Reverse:** Date **Note:** Weight varies 3.17-5.96 grams. For previously listed 1 Pice, KM#153, date 1714, with lion refer to St. Helena.

Date	Mintage	Good	VG	F	VF	XF
1705	—	7.50	13.50	20.00	35.00	—
1729	—	7.50	13.50	20.00	35.00	—
1731	—	7.50	13.50	20.00	35.00	—
1732	—	7.50	13.50	20.00	35.00	—
1734	—	7.50	13.50	20.00	35.00	—
1739	—	7.50	13.50	20.00	35.00	—
1742	—	7.50	13.50	20.00	35.00	—
1743	—	7.50	13.50	20.00	35.00	—
1747	—	—	—	—	—	—
1752	—	7.50	13.50	20.00	35.00	—
1773	—	—	—	—	—	—
1779	—	7.50	13.50	20.00	35.00	—

KM# A165 PICE
Bronze **Obverse:** Very large crown divides G-R at top, "BOMB" below **Reverse:** Inscription **Rev. Inscription:** AUSPICIO/REGIS ET/SENATUS/ANGLIAE **Note:** Size varies 16-18 mm

Date	Mintage	Good	VG	F	VF	XF
ND(1728-49)	—	—	—	—	—	—

KM# 165 PICE
Copper **Obverse:** Large crown divides G-R at top, "BOMB" below **Reverse:** Inscription **Rev. Inscription:** AUSPICIO/REGIS ET/SENATUS/ANGLIAE with ornaments above and below **Note:** Weight varies 8.55-8.87 grams. P104.

Date	Mintage	Good	VG	F	VF	XF
1728	—	12.50	20.00	30.00	42.50	—
173x	—	12.50	20.00	30.00	42.50	—

KM# 167 PICE
Copper **Obverse:** Large crown divides G-R at top, "BOMB" below **Reverse:** Inscription **Rev. Inscription:** AUSPICIO/REGIS ET/SENATUS/ANGLIAE with ornaments above and below **Note:** Weight varies 5.90-6.10 grams.

Date	Mintage	Good	VG	F	VF	XF
1749	—	12.50	20.00	30.00	42.50	—

KM# 188 PICE
5.1300 g., Copper **Obverse:** U.E.I. Co. Bale mark **Reverse:** Inscription **Rev. Inscription:** 1/PICE/BOMB/1773 in 4 lines

Date	Mintage	Good	VG	F	VF	XF
1773	—	10.00	18.50	28.50	40.00	—
1775	—	10.00	18.50	28.50	40.00	—

KM# 166 2 PICE (8 Reas = Nim (1/2) Anna)
17.8200 g., Copper **Mint:** Mumbai **Obverse:** Large crown divides G-R at top, "BOMB" below **Reverse:** Inscription **Rev. Inscription:** AUSPICIO/REGIS ET/SENATUS/ANGLIAE **Note:** Weight varies 3.17-5.96 grams. For previously listed 2 Pice, KM#154, date 1714, with lion refer to St. Helena.

Date	Mintage	Good	VG	F	VF	XF
1728	—	12.50	20.00	30.00	42.50	—
1730	—	12.50	20.00	30.00	42.50	—
1733	—	12.50	20.00	30.00	42.50	—
1735	—	12.50	20.00	30.00	42.50	—
1737	—	12.50	20.00	30.00	42.50	—

KM# 189 2 PICE (8 Reas = Nim (1/2) Anna)

10.2800 g., Copper **Mint:** Bombay **Obverse:** Large crown divides G-R at top, "BOMB" below **Reverse:** U.E.I. Co. Bale mark

Date	Mintage	Good	VG	F	VF	XF
1773	—	10.00	18.50	28.50	40.00	—

KM# 161 1/12 RUPEE

Silver **Mint:** Mumbai **Obverse:** Inscription **Obv. Inscription:** Persian-Muhammad Shah couplet **Reverse:** Inscription **Rev. Inscription:** Persian-julus (formula), mint name

Date	Mintage	VG	F	VF	XF	Unc
AH1138//8	—	15.00	25.00	35.00	50.00	—

KM# 271 1/5 RUPEE

Silver **Mint:** Mumbai **Obverse:** Inscription **Reverse:** Ano of Muhammad Shah

Date	Mintage	VG	F	VF	XF	Unc
AH-//1	—	3.50	7.50	15.00	35.00	—
AH-//2	—	3.50	7.50	15.00	35.00	—
AH1133//3	—	3.50	7.50	15.00	35.00	—
AH1135//5	—	3.50	7.50	15.00	35.00	—
AH-//8	—	3.50	7.50	15.00	35.00	—
AH1139//9	—	3.50	7.50	15.00	35.00	—
AH-//11	—	3.50	7.50	15.00	35.00	—
AH-//12	—	3.50	7.50	15.00	35.00	—
AH-//13	—	3.50	7.50	15.00	35.00	—
AH-//21	—	3.50	7.50	15.00	35.00	—
AH1124//24	—	3.50	7.50	15.00	35.00	—
AH-//25	—	3.50	7.50	15.00	35.00	—

KM# 270 1/5 RUPEE

Silver **Mint:** Mumbai **Obverse:** Persian inscription **Obv. Inscription:** Sha(h) (Jahan II) (Bad) Shah **Reverse:** Inscription **Rev. Inscription:** Persian-julus (formula), mint name **Note:** Weight varies 2.20-2.29 grams.

Date	Mintage	VG	F	VF	XF	Unc
AH(11)31//1	—	30.00	50.00	80.00	110	—

KM# 275 1/5 RUPEE

Silver **Mint:** Mumbai **Obverse:** Inscription **Reverse:** Inscription

Date	Mintage	VG	F	VF	XF	Unc
AH-//2	—	7.50	12.50	20.00	30.00	—

KM# 274 1/5 RUPEE

Silver **Mint:** Cannanore **Obverse:** Inscription **Reverse:** Inscription

Date	Mintage	VG	F	VF	XF	Unc
AH-//9	—	7.50	12.50	20.00	30.00	—

KM# 273 1/5 RUPEE

Silver **Mint:** Mumbai **Obverse:** Character "5" inverted, cruder legends **Reverse:** Inscription

Date	Mintage	VG	F	VF	XF	Unc
ND(1730-96)	—	2.50	5.00	10.00	20.00	—

KM# 272 1/5 RUPEE

Silver **Mint:** Mumbai **Subject:** Posthumous Issue **Obverse:** Inscription **Reverse:** Inscription **Rev. Inscription:** Persian-julus (formula), mint name

Date	Mintage	VG	F	VF	XF	Unc
AH1188//9	—	3.50	7.50	15.00	30.00	—

KM# 269 1/5 RUPEE

Silver **Mint:** Mumbai **Obverse:** Persian inscription, couplet **Obv. Inscription:** Alamgir (II)

Date	Mintage	VG	F	VF	XF	Unc
AH1214//2	—	3.50	7.50	15.00	35.00	—

KM# 276 1/5 RUPEE

2.3200 g., Silver **Mint:** Tellicherry **Obverse:** Inscription **Obv. Inscription:** T99, Persian-Sikkanishin (government coin), date **Reverse:** Inscription **Rev. Inscription:** Persian-Zarb, mint name, julus

Date	Mintage	VG	F	VF	XF	Unc
AH1214//(17)99	—	2.50	4.50	8.50	13.50	—

KM# 174 1/4 RUPEE

2.8800 g., Silver **Obverse:** Inscription **Obv. Inscription:** Persian-Alamgir (II) couplet **Reverse:** Crescent privy mark **Rev. Inscription:** Persian-julus (formula), mint name

Date	Mintage	VG	F	VF	XF	Unc
AH1188//9 Frozen	—	5.00	15.00	30.00	50.00	—
AH-//10 Frozen	—	5.00	15.00	30.00	50.00	—

KM# 210.1 1/4 RUPEE

2.8800 g., Silver **Mint:** Surat **Obverse:** Persian inscription, couplet **Obv. Inscription:** "Shah Alam II Badshah" **Reverse:** Persian-julus (formula), mint name **Note:** Privy mark #1.

Date	Mintage	Good	VG	F	VF	XF
AH-//46	—	1.25	2.00	5.00	10.00	15.00

KM# 210.2 1/4 RUPEE

2.8800 g., Silver **Mint:** Mumbai **Obverse:** Persian inscription, couplet **Obv. Inscription:** "Shah Alam II Badshah" **Reverse:** Persian-julus (formula), mint name **Note:** Privy mark #7.

Date	Mintage	Good	VG	F	VF	XF
AH-//46	—	1.25	2.00	5.00	10.00	15.00

KM# 159 1/2 RUPEE

Silver **Mint:** Mumbai **Obv. Inscription:** Persian-Shah Jahan (II) couplet **Rev. Inscription:** Persian-julus (formula), mintname **Note:** Struck at Mumbai (Bombay) Mint. Weight varies 5.66-5.73 grams.

Date	Mintage	VG	F	VF	XF	Unc
AH1131//1(1719)	—	30.00	60.00	90.00	150	—

KM# 162 1/2 RUPEE

5.8000 g., Silver **Mint:** Mumbai **Obverse:** Inscription **Obv. Inscription:** Persian-Muhammad Shah, couplet **Reverse:** Inscription **Rev. Inscription:** Persian-julus (formula), mint name

Date	Mintage	VG	F	VF	XF	Unc
AH1134//4(1722)	—	25.00	50.00	75.00	125	—
AH1147//17(1734)	—	25.00	50.00	75.00	125	—
AH1151//21(1738)	—	25.00	50.00	75.00	125	—

KM# 175 1/2 RUPEE

5.8000 g., Silver **Mint:** Mumbai **Obverse:** Inscription **Obv. Inscription:** Persian-Alamgir (II) couplet **Reverse:** Inscription **Rev. Inscription:** Persian-julus (formula), mint name

Date	Mintage	VG	F	VF	XF	Unc
AH1169//2(1756)	—	15.00	25.00	50.00	100	—
AH1170//3(1757)	—	15.00	25.00	50.00	100	—
AH1172//5(1759)	—	15.00	25.00	50.00	100	—

KM# A177 1/2 RUPEE

5.7200 g., Silver **Mint:** Surat **Note:** Prev. India, Mughal Empire, 1/2 Rupee KM#470.3

Date	Mintage	VG	F	VF	XF	Unc
AHxxxx//1 Ahad	—	—	—	—	—	—

KM# 177 1/2 RUPEE

5.8000 g., Silver **Mint:** Mumbai **Obv. Inscription:** Persian-Alamgir (II), couplet **Reverse:** Crescent privy mark **Rev. Inscription:** Persian-julus (formula), mint name **Note:** Posthumous issue. Similar to 1 Rupee, KM#178. Date AH1188/9 is reported, not confirmed for KM#177.

Date	Mintage	VG	F	VF	XF	Unc
AH1176//9(1774)	—	15.00	25.00	50.00	100	—

KM# 211.1 1/2 RUPEE

5.7600 g., Silver **Mint:** Surat **Obverse:** Persian inscription, couplet **Obv. Inscription:** "Shah Alam II Badshah" **Reverse:** Persian-julus (formula), mint name **Note:** Privy mark #1.

Date	Mintage	Good	VG	F	VF	XF
AH-//46	—	2.25	4.00	8.00	15.00	25.00

KM# 211.2 1/2 RUPEE

5.7600 g., Silver **Mint:** Mumbai **Obverse:** Persian inscription, couplet **Obv. Inscription:** "Shah Alam II Badshah" **Reverse:** Persian-julus (formula), mint name **Note:** Privy mark #6. For listings of coins with regnal year 52 see India-French.

Date	Mintage	Good	VG	F	VF	XF
AH-//46	—	2.25	4.00	8.00	15.00	25.00

KM# 158 RUPEE

Silver **Obverse:** Inscription **Obv. Inscription:** Persian-Farrukh Siyar, couplet **Reverse:** Inscription **Rev. Inscription:** Persian-julus (formula), mint name **Note:** Weight varies 10.70-11.60 grams.

Date	Mintage	VG	F	VF	XF	Unc
AH1126//2	—	25.00	50.00	100	200	—
AH1129//6	—	15.00	35.00	75.00	125	—
AH1130//7	—	15.00	35.00	75.00	125	—

KM# 160 RUPEE

Silver **Obverse:** Inscription **Obv. Inscription:** Persian-Shah Jahan (II), couplet **Reverse:** Inscription **Rev. Inscription:** Persian-julus (formula), mint name

Date	Mintage	VG	F	VF	XF	Unc
AH1131//1 (Ahad)	—	35.00	75.00	150	250	—

KM# 163 RUPEE

11.6000 g., Silver **Mint:** Mumbai **Obverse:** Inscription **Obv. Inscription:** Persian-Muhammad Shah, couplet **Reverse:** Inscription **Rev. Inscription:** Persian-julus (formula), mint name

Date	Mintage	VG	F	VF	XF	Unc
AH1132//2	—	15.00	40.00	75.00	125	—
AH11xx//3	—	25.00	50.00	100	200	—
AH1134//4	—	15.00	40.00	75.00	125	—
AH1135//5	—	15.00	40.00	75.00	125	—
AH1136//6	—	15.00	40.00	75.00	125	—

Date	Mintage	VG	F	VF	XF	Unc
AH1136//7	—	15.00	40.00	75.00	125	—
AH1137//7	—	15.00	40.00	75.00	125	—
AH1138//8	—	15.00	40.00	75.00	125	—
AH1139//9	—	15.00	40.00	75.00	125	—
AH1141//11	—	15.00	40.00	75.00	125	—
AH1142//12	—	15.00	40.00	75.00	125	—
AH1144//14	—	15.00	40.00	75.00	125	—
AH1145//15	—	15.00	40.00	75.00	125	—
AH1146//16	—	15.00	40.00	75.00	125	—
AH1147//17	—	15.00	40.00	75.00	125	—
AH1148//18	—	15.00	40.00	75.00	125	—
AH1149//19	—	15.00	40.00	75.00	125	—
AH1150//19	—	15.00	40.00	75.00	125	—
AH1151//21	—	15.00	40.00	75.00	125	—
AH1152//22	—	15.00	40.00	75.00	125	—
AH1155//25	—	15.00	40.00	75.00	125	—
AH1156//26	—	15.00	40.00	75.00	125	—
AH1157//27	—	15.00	40.00	75.00	125	—
AH1159//29	—	15.00	40.00	75.00	125	—
AH11xx//30	—	15.00	40.00	75.00	125	—
AH1161//31	—	15.00	40.00	75.00	125	—

KM# 168 RUPEE

11.6000 g., Silver **Obverse:** Inscription **Obv. Inscription:** Persian-Ahmad Shah Bahadur, couplet **Reverse:** Inscription **Rev. Inscription:** Persian-julus (formula), mint name

Date	Mintage	VG	F	VF	XF	Unc
AH-//3	—	10.00	25.00	50.00	100	—
AH1165//4	—	10.00	25.00	50.00	100	—
AH1166//5	—	10.00	25.00	50.00	100	—
AH1167//6	—	10.00	25.00	50.00	100	—

KM# 176 RUPEE

11.6000 g., Silver **Obverse:** Inscription **Obv. Inscription:** Persian-Alamgir (II), couplet **Reverse:** Inscription **Rev. Inscription:** Persian-julus (formula), mint name **Note:** P67-P70.

Date	Mintage	VG	F	VF	XF	Unc
AH1169//2(1756)	—	15.00	35.00	75.00	125	—
AH1170//2 frozen(1757)	—	15.00	35.00	75.00	125	—
AH1173//5 frozen(1760)	—	15.00	35.00	75.00	125	—

KM# A178 RUPEE

11.4400 g., Silver **Mint:** Surat **Note:** Prev. India Mughal Empire, 1 Rupee, KM#475.4.

Date	Mintage	VG	F	VF	XF	Unc
AHxxxx//1 Rare	—	—	—	—	—	—

KM# 178 RUPEE

11.6000 g., Silver **Mint:** Mumbai **Obverse:** Inscription **Obv. Inscription:** Persian-Shah Alam (II) Badshah, couplet **Reverse:** Inscription **Rev. Inscription:** Persian-julus (formula), mint name **Note:** Posthumous issue. Privy mark: Crescent.

Date	Mintage	VG	F	VF	XF	Unc
AH1188//6 Frozen	—	7.50	15.00	25.00	75.00	—
AH1188//9 Frozen	—	7.50	15.00	25.00	75.00	—

KM# 212.1 RUPEE

11.5900 g., Silver **Mint:** Surat **Obv. Inscription:** Shah Alam II Badshah **Reverse:** Persian-julus (formula), mint name **Note:** Privy mark #1.

Date	Mintage	Good	VG	F	VF	XF
AH-//46	—	4.50	7.00	10.00	15.00	25.00

KM# 212.2 RUPEE

11.5900 g., Silver **Mint:** Mumbai **Obv. Inscription:** Shah Alam II Badshah **Reverse:** Persian-julus (formula), mint name **Note:** Privy mark #6. For coins with regnal years 51-54 see India-French listings.

Date	Mintage	Good	VG	F	VF	XF
AH-//46	—	4.50	7.00	10.00	15.00	25.00

KM# 179 1/15 MOHUR (Gold Rupee)

0.7600 g., Gold **Mint:** Mumbai **Obverse:** Inscription **Obv. Inscription:** Persian-Shah Alam (II) Badshah, couplet **Reverse:** Inscription **Rev. Inscription:** Persian-julus (formula), mint name **Note:** Posthumous issue.

Date	Mintage	VG	F	VF	XF	Unc
AH1188//9(1774)	—	—	100	250	375	—

KM# 213 1/15 MOHUR (Gold Rupee)

0.7700 g., Gold **Mint:** Surat **Obverse:** Persian inscription, couplet **Obv. Inscription:** "Shah Alam II Badshah" **Reverse:** Persian-julus (formula), mint name **Note:** Size varies 7-8mm.

Date	Mintage	Good	VG	F	VF	XF
AH-//46	—	—	27.50	45.00	75.00	135

KM# 184 1/4 MOHUR

2.7400 g., Gold **Mint:** Mumbai **Obverse:** E.I. Co. arms **Obv. Legend:** ENGLISH EAST INDIA COMPANY **Reverse:** Ornamentation above and below **Rev. Inscription:** BOMBAY/1765 **Note:** English style.

Date	Mintage	VG	F	VF	XF	Unc
1765	—	2,000	3,500	6,500	10,000	—

KM# 180 1/4 MOHUR

3.8400 g., Gold **Mint:** Mumbai **Obverse:** Inscription **Obv. Inscription:** Persian-Alamgir (II), couplet **Reverse:** Inscription **Rev. Inscription:** Persian-julus (formula), mint name **Note:** Posthumous issue.

Date	Mintage	VG	F	VF	XF	Unc
AH1188//9	—	—	—	—	—	—

KM# 185 1/2 MOHUR

5.4800 g., Gold **Mint:** Mumbai **Obverse:** E.I. Co. arms **Obv. Legend:** ENGLISH EAST INDIA COMPANY **Reverse:** Ornamentation above and below **Rev. Inscription:** BOMBAY/1765 **Note:** English style.

Date	Mintage	VG	F	VF	XF	Unc
1765	—	3,000	5,000	8,000	120,000	—

KM# 181 1/2 MOHUR

5.7700 g., Gold **Mint:** Mumbai **Obv. Inscription:** Persian-Alamgir (II) couplet **Rev. Inscription:** Persian-julus (formula), mint name **Note:** Posthumous issue.

Date	Mintage	VG	F	VF	XF	Unc
AH1188//9	—	—	—	—	—	—

KM# 182 MOHUR

11.5500 g., Gold **Mint:** Mumbai **Obverse:** Inscription **Obv. Inscription:** Persian-Alamgir (II) couplet **Reverse:** Inscription **Rev. Inscription:** Persian-julus (formula), mint name **Note:** Posthumous issue.

Date	Mintage	VG	F	VF	XF	Unc
AH1188//9	—	200	300	450	650	—

KM# 186 MOHUR (15 Rupees)

10.9500 g., Gold **Mint:** Mumbai **Obverse:** E.I. Co. arms **Obv. Legend:** ENGLISH EAST INDIA COMPANY **Reverse:** Ornamentation above and below **Rev. Inscription:** BOMBAY/1765 **Note:** English style.

Date	Mintage	VG	F	VF	XF	Unc
1765	—	4,250	7,000	10,000	18,000	—

KM# 183 MOHUR (15 Rupees)

10.9500 g., Gold **Obverse:** Inscription **Obv. Inscription:** Persian-Alamgir (II) couplet **Reverse:** Inscription **Rev. Inscription:** BOMBAY/1770/15 Rups, ornamentation above and below **Note:** Posthumous issue.

Date	Mintage	VG	F	VF	XF	Unc
1770	—	2,750	4,500	6,500	9,500	—

MILLED COINAGE

KM# 192 1/2 PICE

6.7500 g., Copper, 20 mm. **Obverse:** U.E.I. Co. bale mark **Reverse:** Scales, Persian-Adil (just)

Date	Mintage	VG	F	VF	XF	Unc
1791	—	1.25	2.50	5.00	10.00	—
1791 Proof	—	Value: 70.00				
1794	—	1.25	2.50	5.00	10.00	—
1794 Proof	—	Value: 70.00				

KM# 192a 1/2 PICE

5.3100 g., Copper **Note:** Gilt.

Date	Mintage	VG	F	VF	XF	Unc
1791 Proof	—	Value: 125				
1794 Proof	—	Value: 125				

KM# 193 PICE

6.4700 g., Copper, 25.4 mm. **Mint:** Bombay **Obverse:** U.E.I. Co. Bale mark **Reverse:** Scales, Persian-Adil (just) **Edge:** Plain

Date	Mintage	VG	F	VF	XF	Unc
1791	—	1.50	3.00	6.00	12.00	—
1791 Proof	—	Value: 80.00				
1794	—	1.50	3.00	6.00	12.00	—
1794 Proof	—	Value: 80.00				

KM# 193a PICE

10.6200 g., Copper **Mint:** Bombay **Edge:** Plain **Note:** Gilt.

Date	Mintage	VG	F	VF	XF	Unc
1791 Proof	—	Value: 135				
1794 Proof	—	Value: 135				

KM# 195 1-1/2 PICE (6 Reas)

9.7100 g., Copper, 29 mm. **Obverse:** U.E.I. Co. Bale mark **Reverse:** Large scales Persian-Adil (just) **Edge:** Oblique milling

Date	Mintage	VG	F	VF	XF	Unc
1791	—	3.00	6.00	10.00	20.00	—
1791 Proof	—	Value: 125				
1794 Proof	—	Value: 125				

KM# 195a 1-1/2 PICE (6 Reas)

9.7100 g., Copper Gilt

Date	Mintage	VG	F	VF	XF	Unc
1791 Proof	—	Value: 175				

KM# 194 1-1/2 PICE (6 Reas)

9.7100 g., Copper **Reverse:** Small scales, vertical milling

Date	Mintage	VG	F	VF	XF	Unc
1791 Proof	—	Value: 200				

KM# 196 2 PICE (8 Reas = Nim (1/2) Anna)

12.9500 g., Copper, 30.5 mm. **Obverse:** U.E.I. Co Bale mark **Reverse:** Scales, Persian-Adil (just)

Date	Mintage	VG	F	VF	XF	Unc
1791	—	2.50	3.50	7.50	15.00	—
1791 Proof	—	Value: 120				
1794	—	2.50	3.50	7.50	15.00	—
1794 Proof	—	Value: 120				

KM# 196a 2 PICE (8 Reas = Nim (1/2) Anna)

12.9500 g., Copper Gilt, 30.5 mm.

Date	Mintage	VG	F	VF	XF	Unc
1791 Proof	—	Value: 175				
1794 Proof	—	Value: 175				

COUNTERMARKED COINAGE

KM# 190 PICE

Copper **Mint:** Bombay **Countermark:** BOMB/1788 in beaded rectangle on various native dump coins

CM Date	Host Date	Good	VG	F	VF	XF
ND	1788 Large date; Rare	—	—	—	—	—
1788	1788 Large date, Rare	—	—	—	—	—

KM# 191 PICE

Copper **Mint:** Bombay **Countermark:** BOMB/1788 in beaded rectangle on various native dump coins

CM Date	Host Date	Good	VG	F	VF	XF
1788	1788 Small date, Rare	—	—	—	—	—

PATTERNS

Including off metal strikes

KM#	Date	Mintage	Identification	Mkt Val
Pn5	1791	—	1-1/2 Pice. Copper. 9.7100 g.. Vertical milling edge. KM#124.	—

MADRAS PRESIDENCY

English trade was begun on the east coast of India in 1611. The first factory was at Mazulipatam and was maintained intermittently until modern times.

Madras was founded in 1639 and Fort St. George was made the chief factory on the east coast in 1641. A mint was established at Fort St. George where coins of the style of Vijayanagar were struck.

The Madras mint began minting copper coins after the renovation. In 1689 silver fanams were authorized to be struck by the new Board of Directors.

In 1692 the Mughal Emperor Aurangzeb gave permission for Mughal type rupees to be struck at Madras. These circulated locally and were also sent to Bengal. The chief competition for the Madras coins were the Arcot rupees. Some of the bulk coins from Madras were sent to the Nawabs mint to be made into Arcot rupees.

In 1742 the East India Company applied for and received permission to make their own Arcot rupees. Coining operations ceased in Madras in 1869.

MONETARY SYSTEM

1 Dudu = 10 Cash
8 Dudu = 1 Fanam
36 Fanam = 1 Pagoda (1688-1802)
3-1/2 Rupees = 1 Pagoda

MINTS

اركات

Arcot

مچهلي پتن

Masulipatnam (Machilipatnam)

BRITISH COLONY

HAMMERED COINAGE

KM# 365 CASH

Copper **Obverse:** Bale mark with E E I C **Reverse:** Standing deity

Date	Mintage	Good	VG	F	VF	XF
ND(1701)	—	—	—	—	—	—

KM# 301 CASH

0.8800 g., Copper, 8.0 mm. **Obverse:** Bale mark with date divided between upper and lower halves

Date	Mintage	Good	VG	F	VF	XF
1702	—	7.00	13.00	22.00	35.00	—
1705	—	7.00	13.00	22.00	35.00	—

KM# 302 CASH

1.2000 g., Copper, 8-10 mm. **Obverse:** E.I. Co. bale mark **Reverse:** Date in beaded circle **Note:** Size varies.

Date	Mintage	Good	VG	F	VF	XF
173(0)	—	—	—	—	—	—
1731	—	5.00	9.00	15.00	25.00	—
1733	—	5.00	9.00	15.00	25.00	—
1734	—	5.00	9.00	15.00	25.00	—
1736	—	5.00	9.00	15.00	25.00	—
1737 IEC (retrograde)	—	5.00	9.00	15.00	25.00	—
1739	—	5.00	9.00	15.00	25.00	—
1748	—	5.00	9.00	15.00	25.00	—
1752	—	5.00	9.00	15.00	25.00	—

KM# 378 CASH

Copper **Obverse:** Tamil inscription - Sri (Honorable) **Reverse:** Tamil inscription - Kumpini (company) **Note:** Struck at Tegnapatam (Fort St. David) Mint.

Date	Mintage	Good	VG	F	VF	XF
ND(ca.1740)	—	—	—	—	—	—

KM# 379 CASH

Copper **Obverse:** Star **Reverse:** Tamil inscription - Kumpini (company) **Note:** Struck at Tegnapatam (Fort St. David) Mint.

Date	Mintage	Good	VG	F	VF	XF
ND(ca.1741)	—	—	—	—	—	—

KM# 311 CASH

Copper, 9.5-10.5 mm. **Obverse:** Inverted heart shield with "G V E I" **Reverse:** Double lined square **Rev. Inscription:** Persian, date **Note:** Weight varies 0.97-1.23 grams. Size varies.

Date	Mintage	Good	VG	F	VF	XF
AH-//VII(1211)	—	3.00	6.00	10.00	15.00	—

KM# 312 CASH

Copper

Date	Mintage	Good	VG	F	VF	XF
AH1212	—	3.00	6.00	10.00	15.00	—

KM# 313 CASH

Copper **Obverse:** Inverted heartshield wtih "V E I G" **Note:** Many varieties exist.

Date	Mintage	Good	VG	F	VF	XF
ND	—	3.00	6.00	10.00	15.00	—

KM# 290 1/2 DUDU (5 Cash)

4.4300 g., Copper **Obverse:** Bale mark with CC/E or GC/E **Reverse:** Date in 2 lines

Date	Mintage	Good	VG	F	VF	XF
1705	—	7.00	11.00	22.00	35.00	—
1726	—	7.00	11.00	22.00	35.00	—

KM# 305 1/2 DUDU (5 Cash)

4.4300 g., Copper

Date	Mintage	Good	VG	F	VF	XF
1755	—	5.00	8.00	18.00	30.00	—
1777	—	5.00	8.00	18.00	30.00	—
1784	—	5.00	8.00	18.00	30.00	—
1786	—	5.00	8.00	18.00	30.00	—

KM# 291 DUDU (10 Cash)

Copper, 16.9 mm. **Obverse:** Bale mark with CC/E or GC/E **Reverse:** Date with wavy lines above and below **Note:** Weight varies 8.21-8.35 grams.

Date	Mintage	Good	VG	F	VF	XF
1702	—	3.50	9.00	15.00	25.00	—
1703	—	3.50	9.00	15.00	25.00	—
1706	—	3.50	9.00	15.00	25.00	—
1709	—	3.50	9.00	15.00	25.00	—
1716	—	3.50	9.00	15.00	25.00	—
1720	—	—	9.00	15.00	25.00	—
1722	—	3.50	9.00	15.00	25.00	—
1726	—	3.50	9.00	15.00	25.00	—
1739	—	3.50	9.00	15.00	25.00	—
1741	—	3.50	9.00	15.00	25.00	—
1744	—	3.50	9.00	15.00	25.00	—
1748	—	3.50	9.00	15.00	25.00	—

KM# 306 DUDU (10 Cash)

Copper **Obverse:** Bale mark with CC/E **Reverse:** Date with wavy lines above and below **Note:** Weight varies 8.21-8.35 grams.

Date	Mintage	Good	VG	F	VF	XF
1755	—	2.00	4.00	10.00	15.00	—
1756	—	2.00	4.00	10.00	15.00	—
1761	—	2.00	4.00	10.00	15.00	—
1765	—	—	—	—	—	—
Note: Reported, not confirmed						
1768	—	2.00	4.00	10.00	15.00	—
1769	—	2.00	4.00	10.00	15.00	—
1774	—	2.00	4.00	10.00	15.00	—
1777	—	—	—	—	—	—
Note: Reported, not confirmed						
1780	—	—	—	—	—	—
Note: Reported, not confirmed						
1784	—	2.00	4.00	10.00	15.00	—
1786	—	2.00	4.00	10.00	15.00	—
1787	—	—	—	—	—	—
Note: Reported, not confirmed						
1788	—	—	—	—	—	—
Note: Reported, not confirmed						
1789	—	—	—	—	—	—
Note: Reported, not confirmed						
1790	—	—	—	—	—	—
Note: Reported, not confirmed						
1795	—	2.00	4.00	10.00	15.00	—
1796	—	2.00	4.00	10.00	15.00	—
1798	—	—	—	—	—	—
Note: Reported, not confirmed						
1800	—	2.00	4.00	10.00	15.00	—

KM# 385 1/2 DUB

Copper, 16 mm. **Mint:** *Machhlipatan* **Rev. Inscription:** Sanat julus mubarak **Note:** Wight varies 6.60-6.90 grams. Prid#302.

Date	Mintage	Good	VG	F	VF	XF
AH1175-1222	—	5.00	9.00	13.50	20.00	—

KM# 386 DUB

Copper, 20 mm. **Mint:** *Machhlipatan* **Rev. Inscription:** Sanat julus mubarak **Note:** Prid#301. Weight varies 13.00-14.00 grams.

Date	Mintage	Good	VG	F	VF	XF
AH1175-1222	—	5.50	11.50	21.50	35.00	—

KM# 297 1/2 FANAM

0.5100 g., Silver **Obverse:** Large deity Vishnu **Reverse:** Bead at left and right of interlocked C's **Note:** P17.

Date	Mintage	Good	VG	F	VF	XF
ND(1690-1763)	—	8.00	20.00	50.00	100	—

KM# 298 FANAM

1.0300 g., Silver **Obverse:** Large deity Vishnu **Reverse:** Bead at left and right of interlocked C's **Note:** P16.

Date	Mintage	VG	F	VF	XF	Unc
ND(1690-1763)	—	8.00	20.00	50.00	125	—

KM# 294.1 FANAM

Silver, 11.6 mm. **Obverse:** Bale mark with CC/E **Reverse:** Large Persian inscription **Rev. Inscription:** In griz / Kmpny

Date	Mintage	Good	VG	F	VF	XF
ND(1704)	—	—	—	—	—	—

KM# 294.2 FANAM

Silver **Obverse:** Bale mark with CC/E **Reverse:** Small Persian inscription **Rev. Inscription:** In Griz / Kmpny

Date	Mintage	Good	VG	F	VF	XF
ND(1704)	—	—	—	—	—	—

KM# 307 FANAM

0.9100 g., Silver **Obverse:** Large deity Vishnu **Note:** Prid#19.

Date	Mintage	Good	VG	F	VF	XF
ND(1764-1807)	—	1.50	3.00	7.00	17.50	40.00

KM# 296 2 FANAM

2.4600 g., Silver **Obverse:** Large deity Vishnu **Reverse:** Bead at left and right of interlocked C's

Date	Mintage	VG	F	VF	XF	Unc
ND(1690-1763)	—	8.00	20.00	40.00	100	—

KM# 299 2 FANAM

2.0700 g., Silver **Reverse:** Without bead at left and right

Date	Mintage	VG	F	VF	XF	Unc
ND(ca. 1750s)	—	6.50	16.00	40.00	80.00	—

KM# 308 2 FANAM

1.8300 g., Silver

Date	Mintage	Good	VG	F	VF	XF
ND(1764-1807)	—	1.50	4.00	10.00	25.00	50.00

KM# 380 1/16 RUPEE

0.7300 g., Silver, 8.8 mm. **Mint:** Arcot **Obverse:** Couplet **Obv. Inscription:** "Alamgir II" **Reverse:** Julus (formula), mint name **Note:** Struck at Calcutta, Dacca, Madras, Murshidabad Mint. Mint name: Arkat (Arcot). The regnal year 6 was a frozen date struck until 1809. Prid#145.

Date	Mintage	Good	VG	F	VF	XF
ND-//6 Frozen	—	4.00	10.00	15.00	35.00	75.00

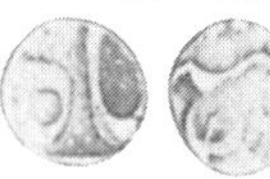

KM# 381 1/8 RUPEE

1.4200 g., Silver, 11 mm. **Obverse:** Inscription and couplet **Obv. Inscription:** "Alamgir II" **Reverse:** Julus (formula), mint name **Note:** Struck at Calcutta, Dacca, Madras, Murshidabad Mint. Mint name: Arcot. The regnal year 6 was a frozen date struck until 1809. Prid#144.

Date	Mintage	Good	VG	F	VF	XF
ND-//6 Frozen	—	4.00	10.00	15.00	35.00	75.00

KM# C302 1/4 RUPEE

2.8610 g., Silver **Mint:** Chinapattan **Obverse:** Couplet **Obv. Legend:** FARRUKHSIYAR **Reverse:** Legend in Persian **Rev. Legend:** julus **Note:** Prev. KM#374.1.

Date	Mintage	VG	F	VF	XF	Unc
AH1128//5	—	150	275	400	—	—
AH1130 Rare	—	150	275	400	—	—

KM# F302 1/4 RUPEE

2.8610 g., Silver **Mint:** Chinapattan **Obverse:** Legend in Persian **Obv. Legend:** MUHAMMAD SHAH **Reverse:** Legend in Persian **Rev. Legend:** julus **Note:** Prev. KM#431.1.

Date	Mintage	VG	F	VF	XF	Unc
ND(1719-48) Rare	—	—	—	—	—	—

KM# 382 1/4 RUPEE

Silver, 15.5 mm. **Obverse:** Inscription, couplet **Obv. Inscription:** "Alamgir II" **Reverse:** Julus (formula) mint name **Note:** Weight varies 2.81-2.86 grams. Struck at Calcutta, Dacca, Madras, Murshidabad Mint. Mint name: Arcot. Prid#143.

Date	Mintage	Good	VG	F	VF	XF
ND-//6 Frozen	—	5.00	10.00	25.00	50.00	100

KM# 388 1/4 RUPEE

Silver **Mint:** *Machhlipatan* **Obverse:** Inscription **Obv. Inscription:** Alamgir (II) couplet **Reverse:** Inscription **Rev. Inscription:** Julus (formula) mint name **Note:** Mint name: Machhilipatan. P299, P300.

Date	Mintage	VG	F	VF	XF	Unc
AH1200//(27)	—	15.00	45.00	75.00	150	—
AH1210//(37)	—	15.00	45.00	75.00	150	—

KM# D302 1/2 RUPEE

5.7220 g., Silver **Mint:** Chinapattan **Obverse:** Couplet, legend in Persian **Obv. Legend:** FARRUKHSIYAR **Reverse:** Legend in Persian **Rev. Legend:** julus **Note:** Prev. KM#375.3.

Date	Mintage	VG	F	VF	XF	Unc
AH1129//6 Rare	—	—	—	—	—	—

KM# 375 1/2 RUPEE

5.7200 g., Silver, 17 mm. **Mint:** Arcot **Obv. Inscription:** Ahmad Shah Bahadur, couplet **Rev. Inscription:** Julus (formula), mint name **Note:** Struck at Arcot Mint. Mint name: Arcot. P141.

Date	Mintage	VG	F	VF	XF	Unc
ND(1748)	—	—	—	—	—	—

KM# 383 1/2 RUPEE

5.7200 g., Silver **Obv. Inscription:** Alamgir (II), couplet **Rev. Inscription:** Julus (formula), mint name **Note:** Struck at Calcutta, Dacca, Madras, Murshidabad Mint. Mint name: Arcot. Similar to 1/2 Rupee, KM#389 without AH. P142.

Date	Mintage	VG	F	VF	XF	Unc
ND-//6 Frozen	—	10.00	25.00	65.00	100	—

KM# 389 1/2 RUPEE

5.6400 g., Silver **Mint:** *Machhlipatan* **Obverse:** Inscription **Obv. Inscription:** Alamgir (II) couplet **Reverse:** Inscription **Rev. Inscription:** Julus (formula), mint name **Note:** Mint name: Machhilipatan. P296-P298.

Date	Mintage	VG	F	VF	XF	Unc
AH118x//x	—	—	—	—	—	—
AH1198//(21)	—	35.00	75.00	150	300	—
AH1199//2(2)	—	35.00	75.00	150	300	—
AH1204//(27)	—	35.00	75.00	150	300	—

KM# A289 RUPEE

11.5900 g., Silver **Obverse:** Legend in Persian **Obv. Legend:** AURANGZEG ALAMGIR **Reverse:** Legend in Persian **Rev. Legend:** julus **Note:** Struck at Chinapattan Mint. Prev. KM#300.25.

Date	Mintage	Good	VG	F	VF	XF
AH1112//45	—	3.25	8.00	16.00	28.00	45.00
AH1113//45	—	3.25	8.00	16.00	28.00	45.00
AH111x//46	—	3.25	8.00	16.00	28.00	45.00
AH1114//47	—	3.25	8.00	16.00	28.00	45.00
AH111x//48	—	3.25	8.00	16.00	28.00	45.00
AH111x//49	—	3.25	8.00	16.00	28.00	45.00
AH111x//50	—	3.25	8.00	16.00	28.00	45.00
AH111x//51	—	3.25	8.00	16.00	28.00	45.00

KM# A302 RUPEE

11.5700 g., Silver, 23.4 mm. **Mint:** Chinapattan **Obverse:** Legend in Persian **Obv. Legend:** SHAH ALAM BAHADUR **Reverse:** Legend in Persian **Rev. Legend:** julus **Note:** Prev. KM#347.7.

Date	Mintage	Good	VG	F	VF	XF
AH1119//1	—	8.00	20.00	40.00	65.00	95.00
AH1119//2	—	8.00	20.00	40.00	65.00	95.00
AH1120//2	—	8.00	20.00	40.00	65.00	95.00
AH1120//3	—	8.00	20.00	40.00	65.00	95.00
AH1121//3	—	8.00	20.00	40.00	65.00	95.00
AH1121//4	—	8.00	20.00	40.00	65.00	95.00
AH1122//4	—	8.00	20.00	40.00	65.00	95.00
AH1122//5	—	8.00	20.00	40.00	65.00	95.00
AH1123//5	—	8.00	20.00	40.00	65.00	95.00
AH1123//6	—	8.00	20.00	40.00	65.00	95.00
AH1124//6	—	8.00	20.00	40.00	65.00	95.00

KM# B302 RUPEE

11.5700 g., Silver **Obverse:** Couplet, legend in Persian **Obv. Legend:** JAHANDAR SHAH **Reverse:** Legend in Persian **Rev. Legend:** julus **Note:** Prev. KM#364.9.

Date	Mintage	VG	F	VF	XF	Unc
AH1124//1	—	30.00	60.00	100	160	—

KM# E302 RUPEE

11.5700 g., Silver **Mint:** Chinapattan **Obverse:** Couplet, legend in Persian **Obv. Legend:** FARRUHHSIYAR **Reverse:** Legend in Persian **Rev. Legend:** julus **Note:** Prev. KM#377.23.

Date	Mintage	Good	VG	F	VF	XF
AH1125//2	—	4.00	10.00	16.00	28.00	40.00
AH1126//2	—	4.00	10.00	16.00	28.00	40.00
AH1126//3	—	4.00	10.00	16.00	28.00	40.00
AH1128//5	—	4.00	10.00	16.00	28.00	40.00
AH1129//5	—	4.00	10.00	16.00	28.00	40.00
AH1129//6	—	4.00	10.00	16.00	28.00	40.00
AH1130//6	—	4.00	10.00	16.00	28.00	40.00
AH1130//7	—	4.00	10.00	16.00	28.00	40.00

KM# G302 RUPEE

11.5700 g., Silver **Obverse:** Legend in Persian **Obv. Legend:** MUHAMMAD SHAH **Reverse:** Legend in Persian **Rev. Legend:** julus **Note:** Struck at Chinapattan Mint. Prev. KM#436.22.

Date	Mintage	Good	VG	F	VF	XF
AHxxxx//4	—	4.00	10.00	20.00	32.50	50.00
AHxxxx//7	—	4.00	10.00	20.00	32.50	50.00
AHxxxx//8	—	4.00	10.00	20.00	32.50	50.00
AHxxxx//9	—	4.00	10.00	20.00	32.50	50.00
AHxxxx//11	—	4.00	10.00	20.00	32.50	50.00

Rev: *Ahad* (Regnal year 1)

Rev: 2 (Regnal year)

KM# 376 RUPEE

11.4300 g., Silver **Mint:** Arcot **Obverse:** Inscription **Obv. Inscription:** Ahmad Shah Bahadur couplet **Reverse:** Inscription **Rev. Inscription:** Julus (formula), mint name **Note:** Mint name: Arkat (Arcot). P135-P137.

Date	Mintage	VG	F	VF	XF	Unc
AH-//(1) (Ahad)	—	7.50	25.00	50.00	100	—
AH-//2	—	7.50	25.00	50.00	100	—
AH-//3	—	7.50	25.00	50.00	100	—
AH-//4	—	7.50	25.00	50.00	100	—

KM# 384 RUPEE

11.4300 g., Silver **Mint:** Arcot **Obverse:** Inscription **Obv. Inscription:** Alamgir (II), couplet **Reverse:** Inscription **Rev. Inscription:** Julus (formula), mint name **Note:** P138-P140. Year 6 was struck at Calcutta, Dacca, Madras, Murshidabad.

Date	Mintage	VG	F	VF	XF	Unc
AH-//2	—	7.50	25.00	50.00	100	—
AH-//3	—	7.50	25.00	50.00	100	—
AH-//4	—	7.50	25.00	50.00	75.00	—
AH-//5	—	7.50	25.00	50.00	75.00	—
AH-//6 Frozen	—	5.00	7.50	12.50	25.00	—

KM# 390 RUPEE

11.4300 g., Silver, 21.2 mm. **Mint:** *Machhlipatan* **Obverse:** Inscription **Obv. Inscription:** Alamgir (II), regal title **Reverse:** Inscription **Rev. Inscription:** Julus (formula), mint name **Note:** P292-P295.

Date	Mintage	VG	F	VF	XF	Unc
AH1195//2x	—	50.00	100	200	400	—
AH1197//24	—	50.00	100	200	400	—
AH1199//2x	—	50.00	100	200	400	—
AH1205//(32)	—	35.00	50.00	150	350	—
AH1211//(38)	—	35.00	50.00	150	350	—
AH1212//(39)	—	35.00	50.00	150	350	—
AH1213//(40)	—	35.00	50.00	150	350	—

KM# 391 2 RUPEES
22.5500 g., Silver, 32.4 mm. **Mint:** *Machhlipatan* **Obverse:** Inscription **Obv. Inscription:** Alamgir (II), regal title **Reverse:** Inscription **Rev. Inscription:** Julus (formula), mint name **Edge:** Plain **Note:** Mint name: Machhlipatan (Masulipatnam). P291. Prev. catalogued in British Museum Catalog (#145) as a double rupee. It is believed the above is a specimen strike.

Date	Mintage	VG	F	VF	XF	Unc
AH1194//2 Rare	—	—	—	—	—	—

KM# B289 MOHUR
11.0100 g., Gold **Mint:** Chinapattan **Obverse:** Couplet, legend in Persian **Obv. Legend:** AURANGZEB ALAMGIR **Reverse:** Legend in Persian **Rev. Legend:** julus

Date	Mintage	VG	F	VF	XF	Unc
AH1114//47 Rare	—	—	—	—	—	—

HAMMERED COINAGE

Pagoda Series

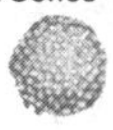

KM# A288 1/4 PAGODA
0.8370 g., Gold **Mint:** Madras **Obverse:** Single standing deity Vishnu **Reverse:** Granulated **Note:** Single swami type.

Date	Mintage	VG	F	VF	XF	Unc
ND(c.1678-1740)	—	—	—	—	—	—

KM# A280 1/4 PAGODA
0.8500 g., Gold, 7.5 mm. **Mint:** Fort St. George **Obverse:** Three full swami **Reverse:** Granulated **Note:** P5. A possible jewelry item struck later.

Date	Mintage	VG	F	VF	XF	Unc
ND(1691-1740)	—	—	—	—	—	—

KM# B280 1/2 PAGODA
1.7250 g., Gold, 9.3 mm. **Mint:** Fort St. George **Obverse:** 3 full swami **Reverse:** Granulated **Note:** P4. A possible jewelry item struck later

Date	Mintage	VG	F	VF	XF	Unc
ND(1691-1740)	—	—	—	—	—	—

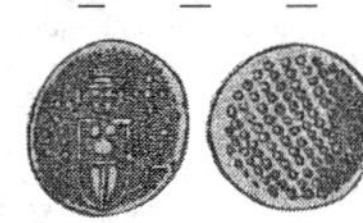

KM# 288 PAGODA
3.4300 g., Gold **Mint:** Fort St. George **Obverse:** Single standing deity Vishnu **Reverse:** Granulated **Note:** Struck at Madras Mint. P2.

Date	Mintage	VG	F	VF	XF	Unc
ND(c.1678-1740)	—	60.00	90.00	110	160	—

KM# 289 PAGODA
3.4000 g., Gold **Mint:** Fort St. George **Obverse:** 3 full length dieties **Reverse:** Granulated **Note:** Struck at Madras Mint. P3A.

Date	Mintage	VG	F	VF	XF	Unc
ND(c.1691-1740)	—	60.00	100	135	175	—

KM# 304 PAGODA
3.4300 g., Gold, 12-14 mm. **Mint:** Fort St. George **Obverse:** Three 1/2 figure deities (3 Swami Pagoda) **Reverse:** Granulated **Note:** Size varies. Prid#3B.

Date	Mintage	Good	VG	F	VF	XF
ND(1740-1807)	—	BV	75.00	125	175	275

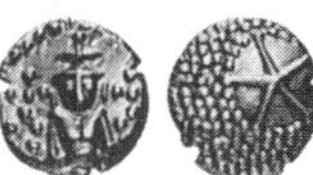

KM# 303 PAGODA
Gold, 10-11 mm. **Mint:** Fort St. George **Obverse:** "Star Pagoda" diety Vishnu **Reverse:** Star in center, granulations around **Note:** Size varies. Prid#9, Prid#10.

Date	Mintage	Good	VG	F	VF	XF
ND(1740-1807)	—	BV	75.00	125	175	275

MILLED COINAGE

KM# 310 V (5) CASH
4.4300 g., Copper **Obverse:** Solid line above denomination

Date	Mintage	Good	VG	F	VF	XF
ND(1790-1800)	—	—	—	—	—	—

KM# 392b 1/96 RUPEE (1/2 Dub)
Gold **Obverse:** Crowned and supported arms **Rev. Legend:** UNITED EAST INDIA COMPANY

Date	Mintage	F	VF	XF	Unc
1794 Proof; Rare	—	—	—	—	—

KM# 393 1/96 RUPEE (1/2 Dub)
Copper **Obverse:** KM#397 **Reverse:** KM#392 **Note:** Mule.

Date	Mintage	F	VF	XF	Unc
1794 Proof	—	Value: 100			

KM# 392c 1/96 RUPEE (1/2 Dub)
Bronze **Note:** P320.

Date	Mintage	F	VF	XF	Unc
1794 Proof	—	Value: 85.00			

KM# 392a 1/96 RUPEE (1/2 Dub)
Copper Gilt **Note:** P321.

Date	Mintage	F	VF	XF	Unc
1794 Proof	—	—	—	—	—

KM# 392 1/96 RUPEE (1/2 Dub)
6.6700 g., Copper, 24.5 mm. **Mint:** Soho **Obverse:** E.I. Co. arms **Obv. Legend:** AUSPICIO REGIS ET SENATUS ANGLIAE UNITED EAST INDIA COMPANY **Reverse:** Bale mark **Rev. Legend:** ENGLISH UNITED EAST INDIA COMPANY (incuse) **Edge:** Lettered **Note:** Struck at Soho, Birmingham Mint. P319, P320.

Date	Mintage	F	VF	XF	Unc
1794	—	2.50	5.00	10.00	20.00
1794 Proof	—	Value: 85.00			

KM# 397 1/96 RUPEE (1/2 Dub)
6.6700 g., Copper, 24.5 mm. **Obverse:** E.I. Co. arms **Obv. Legend:** AUSPICIO REGIS ET SENATUS ANGLIAE UNITED EAST INDIA COMPANY **Reverse:** Bale mark **Rev. Legend:** ENGLISH UNITED EAST INDIA COMPANY (incuse) **Note:** P323, P324.

Date	Mintage	F	VF	XF	Unc
1797	—	2.50	5.00	10.00	20.00
1797 Proof	—	Value: 85.00			

KM# 397a 1/96 RUPEE (1/2 Dub)
Bronze **Note:** P324.

Date	Mintage	F	VF	XF	Unc
1797 Proof	—	Value: 85.00			

KM# 397b 1/96 RUPEE (1/2 Dub)
Copper Gilt **Note:** P325.

Date	Mintage	F	VF	XF	Unc
1797 Proof	—	—	—	—	—

KM# 397c 1/96 RUPEE (1/2 Dub)
7.6000 g., Silver, 17.7 mm. **Note:** P326.

Date	Mintage	F	VF	XF	Unc
1797 Proof	—	—	—	—	—

KM# 394a 1/48 RUPEE (Dub)
Bronze

Date	Mintage	F	VF	XF	Unc
1794 Proof	—	Value: 100			

KM# 394b 1/48 RUPEE (Dub)
Copper Gilt

Date	Mintage	F	VF	XF	Unc
1794 Proof	—	—	—	—	—

KM# 396 1/48 RUPEE (Dub)
13.3400 g., Copper **Edge:** Plain (error) **Note:** P313.

Date	Mintage	F	VF	XF	Unc
1794	—	—	—	—	—

KM# 395 1/48 RUPEE (Dub)
13.3400 g., Copper, 31.0 mm. **Subject:** Mule **Obverse:** KM#398 **Reverse:** KM#394 **Note:** P314.

Date	Mintage	F	VF	XF	Unc
1794 Proof	—	Value: 125			

KM# 394 1/48 RUPEE (Dub)
13.3400 g., Copper, 31.0 mm. **Mint:** Soho **Obverse:** E.I. Co. arms **Obv. Legend:** AUSPICIO REGIS T SENATUS ANGLIAE UNITED EAST INDIA COMPANY **Reverse:** Bale mark **Rev. Legend:** ENGLISH UNITED EAST INDIA COMPANY (incuse) **Note:** Struck at Soho, Birmingham Mint. P310, P311.

Date	Mintage	F	VF	XF	Unc
1794	—	3.50	6.50	12.50	25.00
1794 Proof	—	Value: 100			

KM# 398 1/48 RUPEE (Dub)
13.3400 g., Copper **Obverse:** E.I. Co. arms **Obv. Legend:** AUSPICIO REGIS ET SENATUS ANGLIAE UNITED EAST INDIA COMPANY **Reverse:** Bale mark **Rev. Legend:** ENGLISH UNITED EAST INDIA COMPANY (incuse) **Note:** P316, P317

Date	Mintage	F	VF	XF	Unc
1797	—	3.50	6.50	12.50	25.00
1797 Proof	—	Value: 100			

KM# 398a 1/48 RUPEE (Dub)
Copper Gilt **Note:** P318.

Date	Mintage	F	VF	XF	Unc
1797 Proof	—	—	—	—	—

KM# 398c 1/48 RUPEE (Dub)
Bronze

Date	Mintage	F	VF	XF	Unc
1797 Proof	—	Value: 100			

KM# 398b 1/48 RUPEE (Dub)
Gold **Obverse:** Crowned and supported arms **Rev. Legend:** UNITED EAST INDIA COMPANY

Date	Mintage	F	VF	XF	Unc
1797 Proof; Rare	—	—	—	—	—

PATTERNS

Including off metal strikes

KM#	Date	Mintage	Identification	Mkt Val
Pn1	1798	—	5 Cash. Copper. . Prid#341.	—

IRAN

The Islamic Republic of Iran, located between the Caspian Sea and the Persian Gulf in southwestern Asia, has an area of 636,296 sq. mi. (1,648,000 sq. km.) and a population of 40 million. Capital: Tehran. Although predominantly an agricultural state, Iran depends heavily on oil for foreign exchange. Crude oil, carpets and agricultural products are exported.

Iran (historically known as Persia until 1931AD) is one of the world's most ancient and resilient nations. Strategically astride the lower land gate to Asia, it has been conqueror and conquered, sovereign nation and vassal state, ever emerging from its periods of glory or travail with its culture and political individuality intact. Iran (Persia) was a powerful empire under Cyrus the Great (600-529 B.C.), its borders extending from the Indus to the Nile. It has also been conquered by the predatory empires of antique and recent times - Assyrian, Medean, Macedonian, Seljuq, Turk, Mongol - and more recently been coveted by Russia, the Third Reich and Great Britain. Revolts against the absolute power of the Persian shahs resulted in the establishment of a constitutional monarchy in1906.

With 4,000 troops, Reza Khan marched on the capital arriving in Tehran in the early morning of Feb. 22,1921. The government was taken over with hardly a shot and Zia ad-Din was set up as premier, but the real power was with Reza Khan, although he was officially only the minister of war. In 1923, Reza Khan appointed himself prime minister and summoned the "majlis." Who eventually gave him military powers and he became independent of the shah's authority. In 1925 Reza Khan Pahlavi was elected Shah of Persia. A few weeks later his eldest son, Shahpur Mohammed Reza was appointed Crown Prince and was crowned on April 25, 1926.

In 1931 the Kingdom of Persia became known as the Kingdom of Iran. In 1979 the monarchy was toppled and an Islamic Republic proclaimed.

MINT EPITHET

دار الخلافة

Dar al-Khilafat

RULERS

Safavid Dynasty

حسين

Husayn I, AH1105-1135/1694-1722AD

طهماسب ثاني

Tahmasp II, AH1135-1145/1722-1732AD

Malik Mahmud, rebel at Mashhad, AH1137-38/1724-25AD

Abbas III, AH1145-1148/1732-1736AD

Sam Mirza, In Tabriz only, AH1160/1747AD

حسين

Sulayman II, AH1163/1750AD

Isma'il III, AH1163-69/1750-56AD

Safavid Dynasty Rebel

Sayyid Ahmed, rebel at Kirman, AH1138-41/1725-28AD

Hotaki Dynasty

محمود

Mahmud, AH1135-1137/1722-1725AD

اشرف

Ashraf, AH1137-1142/1725-1729AD

Azad Khan, AH1163-1170/1750-1757AD

Afsharid Dynasty

نادر

Nadir Shah as Viceroy in the East, AH1142-48/1729-35AD
As King, AH1148-1160/1736-1747AD

Adil Shah (Ali), AH1160-1161/1747-1748AD

Jumada II – Dhu'l-Hijja, AH1161/1748AD

Amir Arslan Khan at Tabriz, AH1161/1748AD

ابراهيم

Ibrahim, AH1161-1162/1748-1749AD

Shahrukh, Viceroy at Herat, AH1151-60/1739-47AD
King of Iran AH1161-63/1748-49AD
2nd Reign AH1163/1750AD (first quarter)
3rd Reign AH1168-1210/1755-1796AD

Nadir Mirza, AH1210-1218/1796-1803AD

Zand Dynasty

Karim Khan, AH1172-1193/1759-1779AD
NOTE: Used "Ya Karim", an invocation.

Abul-Fath Khan (Zand), AH1193/1779AD

Sadiq Khan (Zand), AH1193-1196/1779-1782AD
NOTE: Used "Ya Karim", an invocation.

Ali Murad Khan (Zand), AH1193-1199/1779-1785AD
NOTE: Used "Ya Ali", an invocation.

Ja'far Khan (Zand),AH1199-1203/1785-1789AD
NOTE: Used "Ya Imman Jafar as-Sadiq", an invocation.

Sayyid Murad at Shiraz, AH1203-04/1789-90AD

Luft'Ali Khan, AH1203-1209/1789-1794AD

Zand Dynasty Rebels

Taqi Khan Bafqi at Yazd, AH1199-1201/1785-87AD

Hedayat Khan at Rasht, AH1199-1200/1785-86AD

Abu'l-Hasan Beglerbeg in Kirman, AH1193-1206/1779-91AD

Isma'il Khan at Hamadan and Qazvin, AH1200/1785AD

Qajar Dynasty

محمد حسن

Mohammed Hasan Khan, AH1163-1172/1750-1759AD

Agha Muhammad Khan, AH1193-1211/1779-1797AD
Crowned, AH1210/1796AD
NOTE: Used "Ya Muhammad", an invocation.

بابا خان

Baba Khan (Fath'ali before coronation)
AH1211-1212/1797-1798AD

Fath'Ali Shah, AH1212-1250/1797-1834AD

MINT NAMES

Abu Shahr (Bushire) — ابو شهر

Ardebil (Ardabil) — اردبيل

Ahmadabad	احمداباد
Astarabad (Iran)	استراباد
Azimabad	عظيم اباد
Bandar Abbas	بندر عباس
Bandar Abu Shahr	بندرابو شهر
Basra (al-Basrah, Iraq)	البصرة
Behbahan (Bihbihan)	بهبهان
Bahkar (Afghanistan)	بهكر
Borujerd	بروجرد
Darband	دربند
Dezful	دزفول
Eravan (Iravan, Armenia)	ايروان
Fouman	فومان
Ganjeh (Ganja, Azerbaijan)	كنجه
Gilan	كيلان
Hamadan	همدان
Herat, (Afghanistan)	هراة هرات
Huwayza	حويزة
Isfahan (Esfahan)	اصفهان
Jelou (Army Mint)	ابرقوه
Kashan	كاشان
Kirman (Kerman)	كرمان
Kirmanshahan (Kermanshah)	كرمانشاهان
Khoy (Khoi, Khuy)	خوى
Lahijan	لاهيجان
Lahore (Afghanistan)	لاهور
Maragheh	مراغه
Mashhad (Meshad Iman Rida)	مشهد
Mazandaran	مازندران
Muhammadabad Banaras	محمداباد بنارس
Multan	ملتان
Murshidabad	مرشداباد
Nahawand	نهاوند
Nakhjawan (Azerbaijan)	نخجوان
Naseri	ناصري
Nukhwi	نخوى
Panahabad (Azerbaijan)	پناه اباد
Peshawar (Afghanistan)	بشاور
Qandahar (Kandahar, Afghanistan)	قندهار
Qazvin	قزوين
Qomm (Kumm, Qumm)	قم
Ra'nash (Ramhurmuz)	رعنش
Rasht	رشت
Rekab (Rikab)	ركاب
Reza'iyeh (Army Mint)	رضائية
Sahrind	سرهند سهرند
Sarakhs	سرخس
Sari	ساري
Sawuj Balagh	ساوج بلاق
Shamakha (Shemakhi, Shimakhi, Azerbaijan)	شماخه
Shikarpur	شكارپور
Shiraz	شيراز
Shirwan (Azerbaijan)	شيروان
Shushtar	شوشتر
Simnan (Semnan)	سمنان
Sind (Afghanistan)	سند
Sultanabad	سلطاناباد
Tabaristan (Tabarestan, region N.W. of Iran)	طبرستان
Tabriz	تبريز
Tatta	تته
Tehran	طهران
Tiflis (Georgia)	تفليس
Tuyserkan	توى سركان
Urumi (Reza'iyeh)	ارومى
Yazd	يزد
Zanjan	زنجان

MONETARY SYSTEM

1797-98 (AH 1211-12)

50 Dinars = 1 Shahi
15 Shahis = 1 Rupee (?)
12 Rupees and 2 Shahis = 1 Toman
200 Dinars = 1 Abbasi

NOTE: The Shahi was a fixed unit, first coined in AD1501, equal to 50 Dinars. The Toman, introduced as a unit of account about AH1240 (1824AD), was always fixed at 10,000 Dinars. The value of the Rupee for this period is not known with certainty.

1798-1825 (AH 1212-1241)

1250 Dinars = 1 Riyal
8 Riyals = 1 Toman

SILVER and GOLD COINAGE

The precious metal monetary system of Qajar Persia prior to the reforms of 1878 was the direct descendant of the Mongol system introduced by Ghazan Mahmud in 1297AD, and was the last example of a medieval Islamic coinage. It is not a modern system, and cannot be understood as such. It is not possible to list types, dates, and mints as for other countries, both because of the nature of the coinage, and because very little research has been done on the series. The following comments should help elucidate its nature.

STANDARDS: The weight of the primary silver and gold coins was set by law and was expressed in terms of the Mesqal (about 4.61 g) and the Nokhod (24 Nokhod = 1 Mesqal). The primary silver coin was the Rupee from AH1211-1212, the Riyal from AH1212-1241, and the Gheran from AH1241-1344. The standard gold coin was the Toman. Currently the price of gold is quoted in Mesqals.

DENOMINATIONS: In addition to the primary denominations, noted in the last paragraph, fractional pieces were coined, valued at one-eighth, one-fourth, and one-half the primary denomination, usually in much smaller quantities. These were ordinarily struck from the same dies as the larger pieces, sometimes on broad, thin flans, sometimes on thick, dumpy flans. On the smaller coins, the denomination can best be determined only by weighing the coin. The denomination is almost never expressed on the coin!

DEVALUATIONS: From time to time, the standard for silver and gold was reduced, and the old coin recalled and replaced with lighter coin, the difference going to the government coffers. The effect was that of a devaluation of the primary silver and gold coins, or inversely regarded, an increase in the price of silver and gold. The durations of each standard varied from about 2 to 20 years. The standards are given for each ruler, as the denomination can only be determined when the standard is known.

LIGHTWEIGHT AND ALLOYED PIECES: Most of the smaller denomination coins were issued at lighter weights than those prescribed by law, with the difference going to the pockets of the mintmasters. Other mints, notably Hamadan, added excessive amounts of alloy to the coins, and some mintmasters lost their heads as a result. Discrepancies in weight of as much as 15 percent and more are observed, with the result that it is often quite impossible to determine the denomination of a coin!

OVERSIZE COINS: Occasionally, multiples of the primary denominations were produced, usually on special occasions for presentation by the Shah to his favorites. These coins' did not circulate (except as bullion), and were usually worn as ornaments. They were the NCLT's' of their day.

MINTS & EPITHETS: Qajar coinage was struck at 34 mints (plus at least a dozen others striking only copper Falus), which are listed previously, with drawings of the mint names in Persian, as they appear on the coins. However, the Persian script admits of infinite variation and stylistic whimsy, so the forms given are only guides, and not absolute. Only a knowledge of the script will assure correct reading. In addition to the city name, most mint names were given identifying epithets, which occasionally appear in lieu of the mint name, particularly at Iravan and Mashhad.

TYPES: There were no types in the modern sense, but the arrangement of the legends and the ornamental borders were frequently changed. These changes do not coincide with changes in standards, and cannot be used to determine the mint, which must be found by actually reading the reverse inscriptions. The following listings are arranged first by ruler, with various standards explained. Then, the coins are listed by denomination within each reign. For each denomination, one or more pieces, when available, are illustrated, with the mint and date noted beneath each photo. For each type, a date range is given, but this range indicates the years during which the particular type was current, and does not imply that every year of the interval is known on actual coins. Because dates were carelessly engraved, and old dies were used until they wore out or broke, we occasionally find coins of a particular type dated before or after the indicated interval. Such coins command no premium. No attempt has been made to determine which mints actually exist for which types.

KINGDOM

Anonymous

HAMMERED COINAGE

Mint: Without Mint Name
KM# A21 FALUS
16.0000 g., Copper, 35 mm. **Obv:** Lion walking right **Rev:** Mint, date

Date	Mintage	Good	VG	F	VF	XF
AH1122 Isfahan	—	30.00	60.00	100	150	—

Mint: Abu Shahr
KM# 1 FALUS
Copper **Obv:** Sun face

Date	Mintage	Good	VG	F	VF	XF
AH1214	—	9.00	15.00	25.00	45.00	—

Mint: Bandar
KM# 8 FALUS
Copper **Obv:** Lion **Rev:** Inscription

Date	Mintage	Good	VG	F	VF	XF
AH1211	—	11.50	18.50	30.00	50.00	—

Mint:
KM# 9 FALUS
Copper **Obv:** Lion attacking stag **Rev:** Inscription

Date	Mintage	Good	VG	F	VF	XF
ND	—	9.00	15.00	25.00	45.00	—

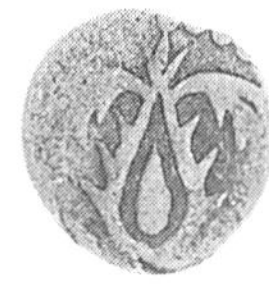 

Mint: Dezful
KM# 12 FALUS
Copper **Obv:** Lyre bird **Rev:** Inscription

Date	Mintage	Good	VG	F	VF	XF
ND	—	6.50	11.50	18.50	30.00	—

Mint: Dezful
KM# 13 FALUS
Copper **Obv:** Fish

Date	Mintage	Good	VG	F	VF	XF
ND	—	7.50	12.50	20.00	35.00	—

Mint: Dezful
KM# 14 FALUS
Copper **Obv:** Bull **Rev:** Legend **Rev. Legend:** "Farahabad"

Date	Mintage	Good	VG	F	VF	XF
ND	—	11.50	18.50	30.00	50.00	—

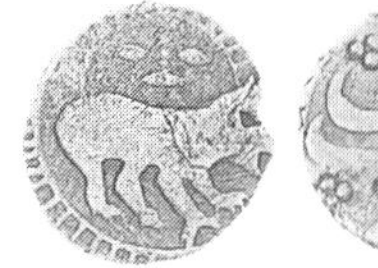 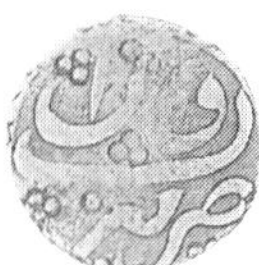

Mint: Eravan
KM# 20 FALUS
Copper **Obv:** Lion and sun **Rev:** Inscription

Date	Mintage	Good	VG	F	VF	XF
AH1204	—	9.00	15.00	25.00	40.00	—

Mint: Gilan
KM# 61 FALUS
Copper **Obv:** Rider on camel right

Date	Mintage	Good	VG	F	VF	XF
ND	—	11.50	18.50	30.00	50.00	—

 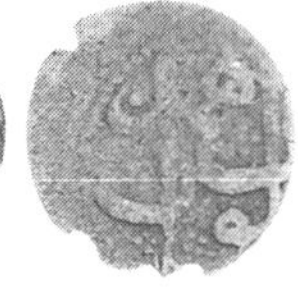

Mint: Hamadan
KM# 17 FALUS
Copper **Obv:** Lion attacking wolf **Rev:** Inscription

Date	Mintage	Good	VG	F	VF	XF
ND	—	7.50	12.50	20.00	35.00	—

Mint: Kashan
KM# 22 FALUS
Copper **Obv:** Boar **Rev:** Inscription

Date	Mintage	Good	VG	F	VF	XF
AH1206	—	9.00	15.00	25.00	40.00	—

Mint: Kashan
KM# 23.1 FALUS
Copper **Obv:** Small sunface **Rev:** Inscription

Date	Mintage	Good	VG	F	VF	XF
ND	—	7.50	12.50	20.00	35.00	—

Mint: Kashan
KM# 23.2 FALUS
Copper **Obv:** Large sun face **Rev:** Inscription

Date	Mintage	Good	VG	F	VF	XF
AH1139	—	7.50	12.50	20.00	35.00	—

Mint: Khoy
KM# 25 FALUS
Copper **Obv:** Lion and sun **Rev:** Inscription within circle

Date	Mintage	Good	VG	F	VF	XF
AH1189	—	9.00	15.00	25.00	45.00	—
AH1191	—	9.00	15.00	25.00	45.00	—

Mint: Khoy
KM# A26 FALUS
Copper **Obv:** Two fish **Rev:** Inscription

Date	Mintage	Good	VG	F	VF	XF
AH1193	—	9.00	15.00	25.00	45.00	—

Mint: Lahijan
KM# 30 FALUS
Copper **Obv:** Peacock **Rev:** Inscription within square

Date	Mintage	Good	VG	F	VF	XF
ND	—	11.50	18.50	30.00	50.00	—

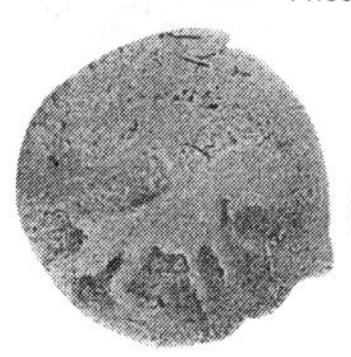

Mint: Lahijan
KM# A30 FALUS
Copper **Obv:** Lion and sun **Rev:** Inscription

Date	Mintage	Good	VG	F	VF	XF
AH1203	—	7.50	12.50	20.00	32.50	—

Mint: Mazandaran
KM# 33 FALUS
Copper **Obv:** Peacock **Rev:** Inscription

Date	Mintage	Good	VG	F	VF	XF
AH1167	—	9.00	15.00	25.00	45.00	—

Mint:
KM# 65 FALUS
Copper **Obv:** Peacock left

Date	Mintage	Good	VG	F	VF	XF
AH1198	—	9.00	15.00	25.00	45.00	—

Mint: Qandahar
KM# 90 FALUS
Copper **Obv:** Stag left **Rev:** Inscription

Date	Mintage	Good	VG	F	VF	XF
ND	—	9.00	15.00	25.00	40.00	—

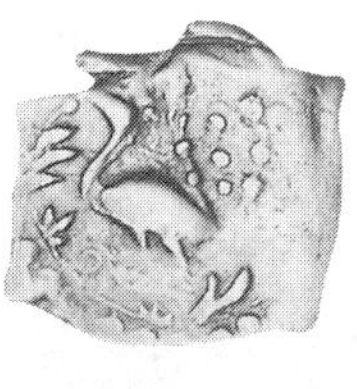

Mint: Qandahar
KM# 91.1 FALUS
Copper **Obv:** Peacock left **Rev:** Inscription

Date	Mintage	Good	VG	F	VF	XF
ND	—	9.00	15.00	25.00	40.00	—

Mint: Qandahar
KM# 91.2 FALUS
Copper **Obv:** Peacock left **Rev:** Inscription

Date	Mintage	Good	VG	F	VF	XF
ND	—	9.00	15.00	25.00	40.00	—

Mint: Qandahar
KM# 92 FALUS
Copper **Obv:** Two fish around six-pointed star in circle **Rev:** Inscription within circle

Date	Mintage	Good	VG	F	VF	XF
ND	—	9.00	15.00	25.00	40.00	—

Mint: Sari
KM# 38 FALUS
Copper **Obv:** Sun face **Rev:** Inscription

Date	Mintage	Good	VG	F	VF	XF
ND	—	7.50	12.50	20.00	35.00	—

Mint: Sari
KM# 66 FALUS
Copper **Obv:** Bird right

Date	Mintage	Good	VG	F	VF	XF
ND	—	7.50	12.50	20.00	35.00	—

Mint: Shushtar
KM# 42 FALUS
Copper **Obv:** Inscription **Rev:** Inscription **Note:** Inscriptions only.

Date	Mintage	Good	VG	F	VF	XF
ND	—	6.50	11.50	18.50	30.00	—

Mint: Sultanabad
KM# 43 FALUS
Copper **Obv:** Lion and sun **Rev:** Inscription within wreath

Date	Mintage	Good	VG	F	VF	XF
ND	—	8.00	13.50	21.50	35.00	—

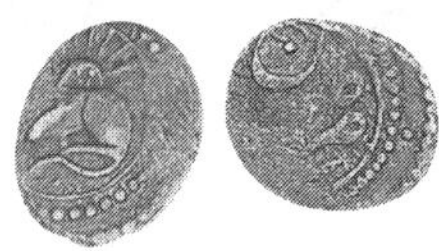

Mint: Tabaristan
KM# 95 FALUS
Copper **Obv:** Lion and sun **Rev:** Inscription

Date	Mintage	Good	VG	F	VF	XF
ND	—	6.50	11.50	18.50	30.00	—

Mint: Tabaristan
KM# 96 FALUS
12.0000 g., Copper **Obv:** Peacock left **Rev:** Inscription within circle

Date	Mintage	Good	VG	F	VF	XF
ND	—	21.50	35.00	60.00	100	—

Mint: Tabaristan
KM# 97 FALUS
3.4000 g., Copper **Obv:** Inverted retrograde "RD" above bull moose, sturgeon fish below **Rev:** Inscription

Date	Mintage	Good	VG	F	VF	XF
ND	—	18.50	30.00	50.00	85.00	—

Mint: Tabriz
KM# 106 FALUS
Copper **Obv:** Lion right and sun

Date	Mintage	Good	VG	F	VF	XF
AH1126	—	11.00	18.00	30.00	50.00	—

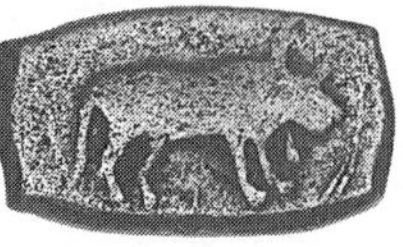

Mint: Tabriz
KM# A106 FALUS
Copper **Obv:** Brahma bull right **Rev:** Inscription

Date	Mintage	Good	VG	F	VF	XF
AH1116	—	9.00	15.00	25.00	40.00	—

Mint: Tabriz
KM# 107 FALUS
Copper **Obv:** Brahma bull left **Rev:** Inscription

Date	Mintage	Good	VG	F	VF	XF
AH1133	—	15.00	25.00	40.00	65.00	—

Mint: Tabriz
KM# A108 FALUS
Copper **Obv:** Brahma bull right

Date	Mintage	Good	VG	F	VF	XF
AH1134	—	11.50	18.50	30.00	50.00	—

Mint: Tabriz
KM# 109 FALUS
Copper **Obv:** Lion right and sun **Rev:** Inscription, date

Date	Mintage	Good	VG	F	VF	XF
AH1136	—	9.00	15.00	25.00	40.00	—

Mint: Tabriz
KM# 110 FALUS
Copper **Obv:** Lion left and sun

Date	Mintage	Good	VG	F	VF	XF
AH117x	—	11.50	18.50	30.00	50.00	—

Mint: Tabriz
KM# 111 FALUS
Copper **Obv:** Lion right and sun

Date	Mintage	Good	VG	F	VF	XF
AH(1)17x	—	11.50	18.50	30.00	50.00	—

Mint: Tabriz
KM# 113 FALUS
Copper **Obv:** Brahma bull right, fish below **Rev:** Inscription within circle

Date	Mintage	Good	VG	F	VF	XF
AH1202	—	11.50	18.50	30.00	50.00	—

Note: Coin originally struck round, but shaped for ornamental purposes.

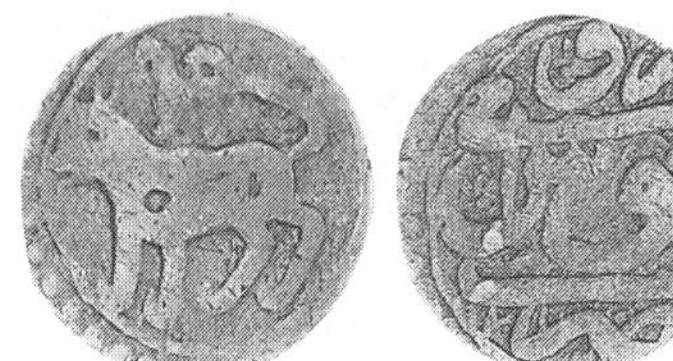

Mint: Urumi
KM# 50 FALUS
Copper **Obv:** Lion with fancy tail **Rev:** Inscription

Date	Mintage	Good	VG	F	VF	XF
AH1210	—	9.00	15.00	25.00	50.00	—

Mint: Urumi
KM# 51 FALUS
Copper **Obv:** Scorpion

Date	Mintage	Good	VG	F	VF	XF
AHxxxx	—	11.50	18.50	30.00	50.00	—

Mint: Urumi
KM# 52 FALUS
Copper **Obv:** Small bird **Rev:** Inscription within circle

Date	Mintage	Good	VG	F	VF	XF
AH120x	—	9.00	15.00	25.00	50.00	—

Mint: Yazd
KM# 53 FALUS
Copper **Obv:** Man riding beast **Rev:** Inscription

Date	Mintage	Good	VG	F	VF	XF
AH1188	—	9.00	15.00	25.00	40.00	—

Mint: Yazd
KM# 54 FALUS
Copper **Obv:** Lion and sun **Rev:** Inscription

Date	Mintage	Good	VG	F	VF	XF
ND	—	7.50	12.50	20.00	35.00	—

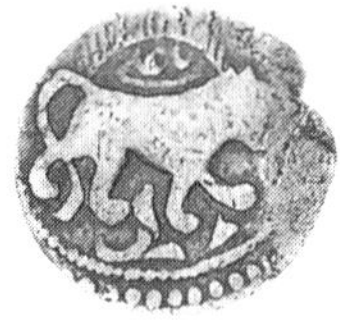

Mint: Yazd
KM# A54 FALUS
Copper **Obv:** Lion right **Rev:** Inscription

Date	Mintage	Good	VG	F	VF	XF
ND	—	7.50	12.50	20.00	35.00	—

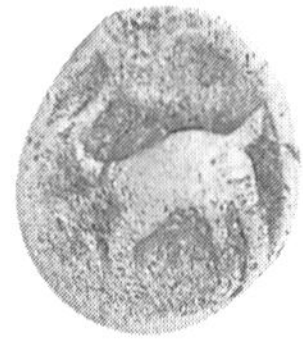
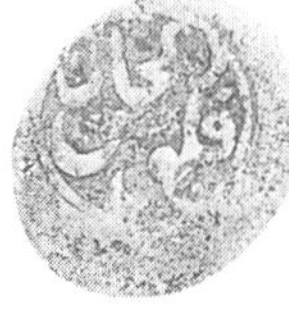

Mint: Zanjan
KM# 55 FALUS
Copper **Obv:** Deer **Rev:** Inscription

Date	Mintage	Good	VG	F	VF	XF
ND	—	11.50	18.50	30.00	50.00	—

HAMMERED COINAGE

Mint: Bhakkar
KM# 356 FALUS
Copper

Date	Mintage	VG	F	VF	XF	Unc
AH1156	—	18.00	30.00	50.00	—	—
AH1158	—	18.00	30.00	50.00	—	—

Mint: Peshawar
KM# 357 FALUS
Copper **Note:** Previous Afghanistan, KM# A685.

Date	Mintage	VG	F	VF	XF	Unc
AH1157	—	20.00	35.00	60.00	—	—
AH1160	—	20.00	35.00	60.00	—	—

Mint: Sind
KM# 358 FALUS
Copper

Date	Mintage	Good	VG	F	VF	XF
ND(1735-47)	—	9.00	18.00	30.00	50.00	—

Husayn I

AH1105-1135 / 1694-1722AD

Husayn, son of Sulayman I, was enthroned on 14 Dhu'l-Hijja 1105 (August 6, 1694), and abdicated under pressure from the Afghan invaders on 11 Muharram 1135 (October 23, 1722). He was murdered by his Afghan mentors in AH1142 (1729AD). He is sometimes known as Husayn I, to distinguish him from a pretender who set himself up in the mid-18th century, but struck no coins.

Silver types for this reign:

A. Obverse couplet, *zad za toufiq-e haqq be-chehre-ye zar / seeke-ye soltan Hosein-e din-parvar*, "Upon the face of precious metal, by the grace of God, was imprinted the stamp of Sultan Husayn, the nurturer of the religion". Used AH1105-1107 only. Struck to the 1925 nokhod standard in use since AH1054.

B. Obverse couplet, *gasht saheb-e sekke az toufiq-e rab ol-mashreqein / dar jahan kalb-e amir ol-mo'menin soltan Hosayn*, "In this world, the dog of the commander of the believers (i.e., Ali ibn Abi Talib), Sultan Husayn, became master of the die, by the grace of the Lord of the Two Easts". Used AH1107-1123.

NOTE: Because the mint is normal at the bottom of the die and the date near the top, specimens with date and mint of Types A and B are relatively scarce, especially for the smaller denominations.

C. Obverse, mint and date, plus the formula *bande-ye shah-e velayat Hosein* (cf. Type D of Abbas I). Struck to the standard of 1800 nokhod (abbasi = 6.91 g).

D. As Type C, but to the standard of 1400 nokhod (abbasi = 5.34 g). During the siege of Isfahan, in AH1134 (1721-22AD), the Isfahan abbasi was reduced to the 1200 nokhod standard (abbasi = 4.61 g). The 1400 standard was retained at all other mints.

E. Obverse, mint and date, plus the formula *kalb-e astan-e Ali Hosein*, "Husayn, the dog on the doorstep of Ali". Used only at Mashhad. Struck in AH1123 to the 1800 nokhod standard and from AH1130-1137 to the 1400 standard. Issues of AH1135-1137 were orderd by Shah Mahmud Sistani, who later in AH1137-1138, struck coins in his own name.

As in the previous reign, there are a great variety of presentation pieces, few of which have been published. Only a small number are listed here. Most are extremely rare.

HAMMERED COINAGE

Mint: Without Mint Name
KM# 256 SHAHI
1.8400 g., Silver **Note:** Type B.

Date	Mintage	VG	F	VF	XF	Unc
AH1108	—	10.00	25.00	35.00	50.00	—
AH1109	—	8.00	20.00	30.00	40.00	—
AH1110	—	10.00	25.00	35.00	50.00	—
AH1110	—	8.00	20.00	30.00	40.00	—
AH1112	—	8.00	20.00	30.00	40.00	—
AH1116	—	8.00	20.00	30.00	40.00	—
AH1116	—	10.00	25.00	35.00	50.00	—
AH1118	—	10.00	25.00	35.00	50.00	—
AH1118	—	10.00	25.00	35.00	50.00	—
AH1118	—	10.00	25.00	35.00	50.00	—
ND	—	3.50	7.50	12.50	20.00	—

Note: Date and/or mint missing

Mint: Eravan
KM# 274.1 SHAHI
Silver **Shape:** Rectangular **Note:** Type C (normal variant).

Date	Mintage	F	VF	XF	Unc
ND	—	50.00	70.00	100	—

Note: Central lozenge containing date and mint

Date	Mintage	F	VF	XF	Unc
ND	—	50.00	70.00	100	—

Note: Plain

Mint: Eravan
KM# 267.1 SHAHI
1.7300 g., Silver **Note:** Type C (normal variant). Round flan.

Date	Mintage	F	VF	XF	Unc
AH1124	—	25.00	35.00	45.00	—
AH1125	—	25.00	35.00	45.00	—
AH1126	—	25.00	35.00	45.00	—
AH1129	—	25.00	35.00	45.00	—
ND	—	10.00	15.00	20.00	—

Note: Date and/or mint missing

Mint: Eravan
KM# 280.1 SHAHI
1.3400 g., Silver **Note:** Type D.

Date	Mintage	F	VF	XF	Unc
AH1134	—	20.00	30.00	40.00	—
ND	—	7.50	11.00	15.00	—

Note: Date and/or mint missing

Mint: Ganjah
KM# 280.2 SHAHI
1.3400 g., Silver **Note:** Type D.

Date	Mintage	F	VF	XF	Unc
AH1131	—	20.00	30.00	40.00	—
AH1131	—	20.00	30.00	40.00	—

Mint: Ganjah
KM# 256.2 SHAHI
1.8400 g., Silver **Note:** Type B.

Date	Mintage	VG	F	VF	XF	Unc
AH1110	—	10.00	25.00	35.00	50.00	—
AH1118	—	10.00	25.00	35.00	50.00	—

Mint: Isfahan
KM# 263 SHAHI
1.7300 g., Silver **Note:** Type C (early variant).

Date	Mintage	F	VF	XF	Unc
AH1117	—	20.00	30.00	40.00	—
AH1119	—	20.00	30.00	40.00	—
AH1120	—	20.00	30.00	40.00	—

Mint: Isfahan
KM# 274.2 SHAHI
Silver **Note:** Type C (normal variant). Rectangular flan, central lozenge containing date and mint.

Date	Mintage	F	VF	XF	Unc
ND	—	65.00	90.00	125	—

Mint: Isfahan
KM# 267.2 SHAHI
1.7300 g., Silver **Note:** Type C (normal variant). Round flan.

Date	Mintage	F	VF	XF	Unc
AH1123	—	25.00	35.00	45.00	—
AH1124	—	25.00	35.00	45.00	—
AH1126	—	25.00	35.00	45.00	—
AH1128	—	25.00	35.00	45.00	—

Mint: Isfahan
KM# 280.3 SHAHI
1.3400 g., Silver **Note:** Type D.

Date	Mintage	F	VF	XF	Unc
AH1131	—	17.50	25.00	35.00	—
AH1132	—	15.00	20.00	30.00	—
AH1133	—	17.50	25.00	35.00	—

Mint: Isfahan
KM# 256.3 SHAHI
1.8400 g., Silver **Note:** Type B.

Date	Mintage	VG	F	VF	XF	Unc
AH1109	—	8.00	20.00	30.00	40.00	—
AH1110	—	8.00	20.00	30.00	40.00	—
AH1112	—	8.00	20.00	30.00	40.00	—
AH1116	—	8.00	20.00	30.00	40.00	—

Mint: Kashan
KM# 280.4 SHAHI
1.3400 g., Silver **Note:** Type D.

Date	Mintage	F	VF	XF	Unc
AH1130	—	20.00	30.00	40.00	—

Mint: Mashhad
KM# 290 SHAHI
Silver **Note:** Type E.

Date	Mintage	F	VF	XF	Unc
AHxxxx	—	30.00	40.00	55.00	—

Mint: Nakhchawan
KM# 256.4 SHAHI
1.8400 g., Silver **Note:** Struck at Nakhchawan.

Date	Mintage	F	VF	XF	Unc
AH1118	—	25.00	35.00	50.00	—

Mint: Nakhjavan
KM# 280.5 SHAHI
1.3400 g., Silver **Note:** Type D.

Date	Mintage	F	VF	XF	Unc
AH1130	—	25.00	35.00	45.00	—
AH1131	—	15.00	20.00	30.00	—

Mint: Qazvin
KM# 280.6 SHAHI
1.3400 g., Silver **Note:** Type D.

Date	Mintage	F	VF	XF	Unc
AH1131	—	20.00	30.00	40.00	—

Mint: Rasht
KM# 280.7 SHAHI
1.3400 g., Silver **Note:** Type D.

Date	Mintage	F	VF	XF	Unc
AH1131	—	15.00	20.00	30.00	—

Mint: Tabriz
KM# 267.3 SHAHI
1.7300 g., Silver **Note:** Type C(normal variant). Round flan.

Date	Mintage	F	VF	XF	Unc
AH1125	—	25.00	35.00	45.00	—
AH1129	—	25.00	35.00	45.00	—

Mint: Tabriz
KM# 280.8 SHAHI
1.3400 g., Silver **Note:** Type D.

Date	Mintage	F	VF	XF	Unc
AH1131	—	25.00	35.00	45.00	—
AH1134	—	15.00	20.00	30.00	—

Mint: Tiflis
KM# 256.5 SHAHI

1.8400 g., Silver **Note:** Struck at Tiflis.

Date	Mintage	F	VF	XF	Unc
AH1116	—	25.00	35.00	50.00	—
AH1118	—	25.00	35.00	50.00	—

Mint: Tiflis
KM# 274.3 SHAHI

Silver **Note:** Type C (normal variant).

Date	Mintage	F	VF	XF	Unc
AH1127	—	50.00	70.00	100	—

Mint: Tiflis
KM# 267.4 SHAHI

1.7300 g., Silver **Note:** Type C (normal variant). Round flan.

Date	Mintage	F	VF	XF	Unc
AH1128	—	35.00	50.00	70.00	—

Mint: Tiflis
KM# 280.9 SHAHI

1.3400 g., Silver **Note:** Type D.

Date	Mintage	F	VF	XF	Unc
AH1131	—	17.50	25.00	35.00	—
AH1132	—	20.00	30.00	40.00	—

Mint: Eravan
KM# 268.1 2 SHAHI

3.4500 g., Silver **Obv:** Inscription **Rev:** Inscription, date within circle **Note:** Type C (normal variant).

Date	Mintage	F	VF	XF	Unc
AH1123	—	30.00	40.00	50.00	—
AH1126	—	30.00	40.00	50.00	—
ND	—	10.00	15.00	20.00	—

Note: Date and/or mint missing

Mint: Eravan
KM# 275.1 2 SHAHI

3.4500 g., Silver **Obv:** Inscription **Rev:** Inscription **Shape:** Rectangular **Note:** Type C (normal variant).

Date	Mintage	F	VF	XF	Unc
AH1128	—	50.00	70.00	90.00	—
AH1129	—	50.00	75.00	100	—

Note: Mint and date in central cartouche

Date	Mintage	F	VF	XF	Unc
ND	—	20.00	30.00	40.00	—

Note: Date and/or mint missing

Mint: Eravan
KM# 281.1 2 SHAHI

2.6800 g., Silver **Obv:** Inscription **Rev:** Inscription **Note:** Type D.

Date	Mintage	F	VF	XF	Unc
AH1131	—	15.00	20.00	28.50	—
ND	—	7.50	11.00	15.00	—

Note: Date and/or mint missing

Mint: Ganjah
KM# 281.2 2 SHAHI

2.6800 g., Silver **Obv:** Inscription **Rev:** Inscription **Note:** Type D.

Date	Mintage	F	VF	XF	Unc
AH1134	—	20.00	30.00	45.00	—

Mint: Isfahan
KM# 264 2 SHAHI

3.4500 g., Silver **Note:** Type C (early variant).

Date	Mintage	F	VF	XF	Unc
AH1117	—	40.00	50.00	65.00	—
AH1119	—	40.00	50.00	65.00	—

Mint: Isfahan
KM# 275.2 2 SHAHI

3.4500 g., Silver **Note:** Type C (normal variant).

Date	Mintage	F	VF	XF	Unc
AH1127	—	50.00	70.00	90.00	—

Note: Plain obverse field

Mint: Isfahan
KM# 268.2 2 SHAHI

3.4500 g., Silver **Obv:** Inscription **Rev:** Inscription, date within circle **Note:** Type C (normal variant).

Date	Mintage	F	VF	XF	Unc
AH1123	—	30.00	40.00	50.00	—
AH1128	—	30.00	40.00	50.00	—

Mint: Isfahan
KM# 281.3 2 SHAHI

2.6800 g., Silver **Obv:** Inscription **Rev:** Inscription **Note:** Type D.

Date	Mintage	F	VF	XF	Unc
AH1130	—	12.50	16.50	25.00	—
AH1131	—	12.50	16.50	25.00	—
AH1132	—	12.50	16.50	25.00	—
AH1133	—	12.50	16.50	25.00	—
AH1134	—	12.50	16.50	25.00	—

Mint: Kashan
KM# 281.4 2 SHAHI

2.6800 g., Silver **Obv:** Inscription **Rev:** Inscription **Note:** Type D.

Date	Mintage	F	VF	XF	Unc
AH1130	—	12.50	16.50	25.00	—

Mint: Nakhjavan
KM# 281.5 2 SHAHI

2.6800 g., Silver **Obv:** Inscription **Rev:** Inscription **Note:** Type D.

Date	Mintage	F	VF	XF	Unc
AH1130	—	15.00	20.00	28.50	—
AH1131	—	—	—	—	—
AH1132	—	12.50	16.50	25.00	—

Mint: Qazvin
KM# 281.6 2 SHAHI

2.6800 g., Silver **Obv:** Inscription **Rev:** Inscription **Note:** Type D.

Date	Mintage	F	VF	XF	Unc
AH1131	—	12.50	16.50	25.00	—

Mint: Tabriz
KM# 268.3 2 SHAHI

3.4500 g., Silver **Obv:** Inscription **Rev:** Inscription, date within circle **Note:** Type C (normal variant).

Date	Mintage	F	VF	XF	Unc
AH1125	—	25.00	35.00	45.00	—
AH1128	—	25.00	35.00	45.00	—
AH1129	—	25.00	35.00	45.00	—

Mint: Tabriz
KM# 275.3 2 SHAHI

3.4500 g., Silver **Obv:** Inscription **Rev:** Inscription **Note:** Type C (normal variant).

Date	Mintage	F	VF	XF	Unc
AH1126	—	50.00	70.00	90.00	—

Note: Plain obverse field

Date	Mintage	F	VF	XF	Unc
AH1129	—	50.00	75.00	100	—

Note: Mint and date in central cartouche

Mint: Tabriz
KM# 281.7 2 SHAHI

2.6800 g., Silver **Obv:** Inscription **Rev:** Inscription **Note:** Type D.

Date	Mintage	F	VF	XF	Unc
AH1130	—	12.50	16.50	25.00	—
AH1132	—	12.50	16.50	25.00	—

Mint: Tiflis
KM# 275.4 2 SHAHI

3.4500 g., Silver **Obv:** Inscription **Rev:** Inscription **Note:** Type C (normal variant).

Date	Mintage	F	VF	XF	Unc
AH1127	—	40.00	60.00	80.00	—

Note: Plain obverse field

Date	Mintage	F	VF	XF	Unc
AH1128	—	40.00	60.00	80.00	—

Note: Plain obverse field

Mint: Tiflis
KM# 281.8 2 SHAHI

2.6800 g., Silver **Obv:** Inscription **Rev:** Inscription **Note:** Type D.

Date	Mintage	F	VF	XF	Unc
AH1130	—	20.00	30.00	45.00	—
AH1131	—	15.00	20.00	28.50	—
AH1132	—	15.00	20.00	28.50	—
AH1134	—	20.00	30.00	45.00	—

Mint: Eravan
KM# 269 ABBASI

6.9100 g., Silver **Note:** Type C (normal version).

Date	Mintage	F	VF	XF	Unc
AH1123	—	12.50	20.00	30.00	—
AH1124	—	9.00	15.00	25.00	—
AH1125	—	9.00	15.00	25.00	—
AH1126	—	9.00	15.00	25.00	—
ND	—	4.50	6.00	12.50	—

Note: Date and/or mint missing

Mint: Eravan
KM# 282.1 ABBASI

5.3700 g., Silver **Obv:** Inscription **Rev:** Inscription **Note:** Type D. Reduced full weight. Varieties exist.

Date	Mintage	F	VF	XF	Unc
AH1130	—	5.00	8.00	15.00	—
AH1131	—	5.00	8.00	15.00	—
AH1132	—	5.00	10.00	17.00	—
AH1133	—	5.00	10.00	17.00	—
AH1134	—	6.00	10.00	17.50	—
ND	—	4.00	5.00	8.50	—

Note: Date and/or mint missing

Mint: Ganjah
KM# 269.2 ABBASI

6.9100 g., Silver **Note:** Type C (normal version).

Date	Mintage	F	VF	XF	Unc
AH1123	—	9.00	15.00	25.00	—

Mint: Ganjah
KM# 282.2 ABBASI

5.3700 g., Silver **Obv:** Inscription **Rev:** Inscription **Note:** Type D. Reduced full weight. Varieties exist.

Date	Mintage	F	VF	XF	Unc
AH1132	—	5.00	12.00	20.00	—
AH1133	—	6.00	12.00	20.00	—
AH1134	—	6.00	10.00	17.50	—

Mint: Isfahan
KM# 265 ABBASI

7.3900 g., Silver **Note:** Type C (early version).

Date	Mintage	F	VF	XF	Unc
AH1117	—	20.00	30.00	45.00	—
AH1120	—	20.00	30.00	45.00	—

Mint: Isfahan
KM# 269.3 ABBASI

6.9100 g., Silver **Note:** Type C (normal version).

Date	Mintage	F	VF	XF	Unc
AH1123	—	25.00	35.00	45.00	—
AH1124	—	9.00	15.00	25.00	—
AH1126	—	9.00	15.00	25.00	—

Mint: Isfahan
KM# 282.3 ABBASI

5.3700 g., Silver **Obv:** Inscription **Rev:** Inscription **Note:** Type D. Reduced full weight. Varieties exist.

Date	Mintage	F	VF	XF	Unc
AH1129	—	10.00	14.00	25.00	—
AH1130	—	5.00	8.00	15.00	—
AH1131	—	5.00	8.00	15.00	—
AH1132	—	5.00	8.00	15.00	—
AH1133	—	5.00	8.00	15.00	—
AH1134	—	6.00	10.00	17.50	—

Mint: Isfahan
KM# 282.2a ABBASI

4.6200 g., Silver **Note:** Type D. Reduced weight. Struck during the Afghan siege of Isfahan. Distinguishable from full-weight abbasis only by weight. Coins dated AH1133 must have been struck in AH1134 with old dies.

Date	Mintage	F	VF	XF	Unc
AH1133	—	15.00	20.00	27.50	—
AH1134	—	12.50	17.50	27.50	—

Mint: Kashan
KM# 282.4 ABBASI

5.3700 g., Silver **Obv:** Inscription **Rev:** Inscription **Note:** Type D. Reduced full weight. Varieties exist.

Date	Mintage	F	VF	XF	Unc
AH1130	—	10.00	14.00	25.00	—
AH1131	—	15.00	20.00	30.00	—
AH1134	—	15.00	20.00	30.00	—

Mint: Mashhad
KM# 314 ABBASI

5.4000 g., Silver **Note:** Type D.

Date	Mintage	F	VF	XF	Unc
AH1136	—	10.00	17.50	25.00	—
AH1137	—	10.00	17.50	25.00	—

Note: Coins struck in his name at Mashhad after his deposal at Isfahan

Mint: Mashhad
KM# 282.5 ABBASI

5.3700 g., Silver **Obv:** Inscription **Rev:** Inscription **Note:** Type D. Reduced full weight. Varieties exist.

Date	Mintage	F	VF	XF	Unc
AH1134	—	10.00	17.50	25.00	—
AH1137	—	15.00	25.00	35.00	—

Mint: Mashhad
KM# 291 ABBASI
6.9100 g., Silver **Note:** Type E.

Date	Mintage	F	VF	XF	Unc
AH1123	—	25.00	37.50	50.00	—

Mint: Mashhad
KM# 291a ABBASI
5.3400 g., Silver **Note:** Type E. Reduced weight.

Date	Mintage	F	VF	XF	Unc
AH1130	—	10.00	14.00	22.50	—
AH1131	—	10.00	14.00	22.50	—
AH1132	—	10.00	14.00	22.50	—
AH1133	—	10.00	14.00	22.50	—
AH1135	—	12.50	17.50	27.50	—
AH1136	—	12.50	17.50	27.50	—
AHxxxx	—	5.00	6.50	12.50	—

Mint: Nakhjavan
KM# 282.6 ABBASI
5.3700 g., Silver **Obv:** Inscription **Rev:** Inscription **Note:** Type D. Reduced full weight. Varieties exist.

Date	Mintage	F	VF	XF	Unc
AH1130	—	5.00	12.00	20.00	—
AH1131	—	5.00	12.00	20.00	—
AH1132	—	5.00	12.00	20.00	—
AH1133	—	5.00	12.00	20.00	—
AH1134	—	6.00	15.00	20.00	—

Mint: Qazvin
KM# 282.7 ABBASI
5.3700 g., Silver **Obv:** Inscription **Rev:** Inscription **Note:** Type D. Reduced full weight. Varieties exist.

Date	Mintage	F	VF	XF	Unc
AH1130	—	5.00	8.00	15.00	—
AH1131	—	5.00	8.00	15.00	—

Note: Some types of Qazvin AH1131 are struck in ornate designs, and are worth from two to five times more than ordinary sorts.

Date	Mintage	F	VF	XF	Unc
AH1132	—	5.00	8.00	15.00	—
AH1133	—	5.00	8.00	15.00	—

Mint: Rasht
KM# 282.8 ABBASI
5.3700 g., Silver **Obv:** Inscription **Rev:** Inscription **Note:** Type D. Reduced full weight. Varieties exist.

Date	Mintage	F	VF	XF	Unc
AH1131	—	5.00	8.00	15.00	—
AH1132	—	5.00	8.00	15.00	—
AH1133	—	5.00	8.00	15.00	—

Mint: Shiraz
KM# 282.9 ABBASI
5.3700 g., Silver **Obv:** Inscription **Rev:** Inscription **Note:** Type D. Reduced full weight. Varieties exist.

Date	Mintage	F	VF	XF	Unc
AH1129	—	5.00	8.00	15.00	—
AH1130	—	15.00	20.00	30.00	—
AH1132	—	15.00	20.00	30.00	—

Mint: Tabriz
KM# 269.4 ABBASI
6.9100 g., Silver **Note:** Type C (normal version).

Date	Mintage	F	VF	XF	Unc
AH1123	—	9.00	15.00	25.00	—
AH1124	—	9.00	15.00	25.00	—
AH1125	—	9.00	15.00	25.00	—
AH1126	—	9.00	15.00	25.00	—
AH1127	—	15.00	22.50	30.00	—

Mint: Tabriz
KM# 282.10 ABBASI
5.3700 g., Silver **Obv:** Inscription **Rev:** Inscription **Note:** Type D. Reduced full weight. Varieties exist.

Date	Mintage	F	VF	XF	Unc
AH1130	—	5.00	8.00	15.00	—
AH1131	—	5.00	8.00	15.00	—
AH1132	—	5.00	8.00	15.00	—
AH1133	—	5.00	8.00	15.00	—
AH1134	—	5.00	8.00	15.00	—
AH1135	—	10.00	15.00	25.00	—
AH1136	—	12.50	20.00	30.00	—

Note: The Tabriz AH1136 is probably struck from dies prepared in the previous year with the new date.

Mint: Tabriz
KM# A265 ABBASI
5.1200 g., Silver **Obv:** Tughra of Ottoman Sultan Ahmed III, AH1115-43/1703-30AD. **Rev. Inscription:** Struck in Tabriz 1115. **Note:** Issued during Ottoman occupation of northwestern Iran AH1135-48/1722-35AD. Struck to the weight standard of Husayn's Type D coinage.

Date	Mintage	VG	F	VF	XF	Unc
AH1115	—	45.00	75.00	125	225	—

Mint: Tiflis
KM# 269.5 ABBASI
6.9100 g., Silver **Note:** Type C (normal version).

Date	Mintage	F	VF	XF	Unc
AH1123	—	9.00	15.00	25.00	—

Mint: Tiflis
KM# 282.11 ABBASI
5.3700 g., Silver **Obv:** Inscription **Rev:** Inscription **Note:** Type D. Reduced full weight. Varieties exist.

Date	Mintage	F	VF	XF	Unc
AH1130	—	5.00	8.00	15.00	—
AH1131	—	5.00	15.00	25.00	—
AH1132	—	5.00	15.00	25.00	—
AH1133	—	5.00	8.00	15.00	—
AH1134	—	6.00	10.00	17.50	—

Mint: Without Mint Name
KM# 258 ABBASI
7.3900 g., Silver **Note:** Type B. Coins are known of this type dated AH1123. All coins AH1120 and later are scarce.

Date	Mintage	F	VF	XF	Unc
ND	—	5.00	7.00	15.00	—

Note: Date and/or mint missing

Mint: Eravan
KM# 258.1 ABBASI
9.2400 g., Silver **Note:** Type B.

Date	Mintage	VG	F	VF	XF	Unc
AH1108	—	4.00	10.00	15.00	25.00	—
AH1109	—	4.00	10.00	15.00	25.00	—
AH1110	—	4.00	10.00	15.00	25.00	—
AH1111	—	4.00	10.00	15.00	25.00	—
AH1112	—	4.00	10.00	15.00	25.00	—
AH1113	—	4.00	10.00	15.00	25.00	—
AH1115	—	4.00	10.00	15.00	25.00	—
AH1117	—	4.00	10.00	15.00	25.00	—
AH1118	—	4.00	10.00	15.00	25.00	—
AH1119	—	4.00	10.00	15.00	25.00	—

Mint: Ganjah
KM# 258.2 ABBASI
9.2400 g., Silver **Note:** Type B.

Date	Mintage	VG	F	VF	XF	Unc
AH1107	—	5.00	12.50	17.50	27.50	—
AH1108	—	5.00	12.50	17.50	27.50	—
AH1110	—	5.00	12.50	17.50	27.50	—
AH1111	—	5.00	12.50	17.50	27.50	—
AH1112	—	5.00	12.50	17.50	27.50	—
AH1115	—	5.00	12.50	17.50	27.50	—
AH1116	—	5.00	12.50	17.50	27.50	—
AH1120	—	5.00	12.50	17.50	27.50	—
AH1121	—	6.00	15.00	20.00	30.00	—

Mint: Herat
KM# 258.3 ABBASI
9.2400 g., Silver **Note:** Type B.

Date	Mintage	F	VF	XF	Unc
AH1122	—	30.00	45.00	60.00	—

Mint: Isfahan
KM# 258.4 ABBASI
9.2400 g., Silver **Note:** Type B.

Date	Mintage	VG	F	VF	XF	Unc
AH1107	—	4.00	10.00	15.00	25.00	—
AH1108	—	4.00	10.00	15.00	25.00	—
AH1109	—	4.00	10.00	15.00	25.00	—
AH1111	—	4.00	10.00	15.00	25.00	—
AH1112	—	4.00	10.00	15.00	25.00	—
AH1113	—	4.00	10.00	15.00	25.00	—
AH1114	—	4.00	10.00	15.00	25.00	—
AH1118	—	4.00	10.00	15.00	25.00	—

Mint: Nakhchawan
KM# 258.5 ABBASI
9.2400 g., Silver **Note:** Type B.

Date	Mintage	VG	F	VF	XF	Unc
AH1107	—	6.00	15.00	25.00	35.00	—
AH1108	—	6.00	15.00	25.00	35.00	—
AH1110	—	6.00	15.00	25.00	35.00	—
AH1111	—	6.00	15.00	25.00	35.00	—
AH1115	—	6.00	15.00	25.00	35.00	—

Mint: Rasht
KM# 258.6 ABBASI
9.2400 g., Silver **Note:** Type B.

Date	Mintage	VG	F	VF	XF	Unc
AH1109	—	6.00	15.00	25.00	35.00	—
AH1113	—	6.00	15.00	25.00	35.00	—

Mint: Tabriz
KM# 258.7 ABBASI
9.2400 g., Silver **Note:** Type B.

Date	Mintage	VG	F	VF	XF	Unc
AH1108	—	4.00	10.00	15.00	25.00	—
AH1110	—	4.00	10.00	15.00	25.00	—
AH1114	—	4.00	10.00	15.00	25.00	—
AH1117	—	4.00	10.00	15.00	25.00	—
AH1118	—	4.00	10.00	15.00	25.00	—
AH1120	—	5.00	12.50	17.50	27.50	—

Mint: Tiflis
KM# 258.8 ABBASI
9.2400 g., Silver **Note:** Type B.

Date	Mintage	VG	F	VF	XF	Unc
AH1107	—	4.00	10.00	15.00	25.00	—
AH1108	—	4.00	10.00	15.00	25.00	—
AH1109	—	4.00	10.00	15.00	25.00	—
AH1110	—	4.00	10.00	15.00	25.00	—
AH1111	—	4.00	10.00	15.00	25.00	—
AH1112	—	4.00	10.00	15.00	25.00	—
AH1113	—	4.00	10.00	15.00	25.00	—
AH1114	—	4.00	10.00	15.00	25.00	—
AH1115	—	4.00	10.00	15.00	25.00	—
AH1116	—	4.00	10.00	15.00	25.00	—
AH1117	—	4.00	10.00	15.00	25.00	—
AH1118	—	4.00	10.00	15.00	25.00	—
AH1119	—	4.00	10.00	15.00	25.00	—
AH1120	—	5.00	12.50	17.50	27.50	—
AH1121	—	6.00	15.00	20.00	30.00	—

Mint: Eravan
KM# 276.1 5 SHAHI
8.6400 g., Silver **Shape:** Rectangular **Note:** Type C. Rectangular flan, plain field obverse.

Date	Mintage	F	VF	XF	Unc
AH1123	—	25.00	35.00	45.00	—
AH1124	—	25.00	35.00	45.00	—
AH1125	—	30.00	40.00	50.00	—
AH1126	—	25.00	35.00	45.00	—
AH1127	—	25.00	35.00	45.00	—
AH1128	—	25.00	35.00	45.00	—
ND	—	—	—	—	—

Note: Date and/or mint missing

Mint: Eravan
KM# A276.1 5 SHAHI
8.6400 g., Silver **Obv:** Inscription within beaded circle **Rev:** Inscription, date within circle **Note:** Type C. Similar mint and date in central cartouche obverse.

Date	Mintage	F	VF	XF	Unc
AH1130	—	35.00	45.00	60.00	—

Mint: Isfahan
KM# 276.2 5 SHAHI
8.6400 g., Silver **Shape:** Rectangular **Note:** Type C. Plain field obverse.

Date	Mintage	F	VF	XF	Unc
AH1126	—	30.00	40.00	50.00	—
AH1127	—	30.00	40.00	50.00	—
AH1128	—	30.00	40.00	50.00	—

Mint: Isfahan
KM# 259.3 5 SHAHI
9.2400 g., Silver **Note:** Type B.

Date	Mintage	VG	F	VF	XF	Unc
AH1107	—	8.00	20.00	35.00	50.00	—
AH1113	—	20.00	40.00	60.00	90.00	—
AH1114	—	20.00	40.00	60.00	90.00	—
AH1115	—	20.00	40.00	60.00	90.00	—

Mint: Isfahan
KM# A276.2 5 SHAHI
8.6400 g., Silver **Obv:** Inscription within beaded circle **Rev:** Inscription, date within circle **Note:** Type C. Similar mint and date in central cartouche obverse.

Date	Mintage	VG	F	VF	XF	Unc
AH1126	—	12.00	30.00	40.00	50.00	—

Mint: Tabriz
KM# 276.3 5 SHAHI
8.6400 g., Silver **Note:** Type C. Plain field obverse.

Date	Mintage	F	VF	XF	Unc
AH1123	—	25.00	35.00	45.00	—
AH1124	—	25.00	35.00	45.00	—
AH1126	—	25.00	35.00	45.00	—
AH1127	—	25.00	35.00	45.00	—
AH1128	—	25.00	35.00	45.00	—

Mint: Tabriz
KM# A276.3 5 SHAHI
8.6400 g., Silver **Obv:** Inscription within beaded circle **Rev:** Inscription, date within circle **Note:** Type C. Similar mint and date in central cartouche obverse.

Date	Mintage	F	VF	XF	Unc
AH1128	—	35.00	45.00	60.00	—
AH1129	—	22.50	32.50	45.00	—
AH1130	—	35.00	45.00	60.00	—

Mint: Tiflis
KM# 276.4 5 SHAHI
8.6400 g., Silver **Shape:** Rectangular **Note:** Type C. Plain field obverse.

Date	Mintage	F	VF	XF	Unc
AH1126	—	30.00	40.00	50.00	—
AH1127	—	30.00	40.00	50.00	—

Mint: Tiflis
KM# A276.4 5 SHAHI
8.6400 g., Silver **Obv:** Inscription within beaded circle **Rev:** Inscription, date within circle **Note:** Type C. Similar mint and date in central cartouche obverse.

Date	Mintage	F	VF	XF	Unc
AH1129	—	30.00	40.00	55.00	—
AH1130	—	35.00	45.00	60.00	—

Mint: Isfahan
KM# 285 2-1/2 ABBASI
Silver **Obv:** Name and titles in Arabic, as on 16th century Safavid coins **Note:** Special type. About 14.00 grams. Denomination may be 8 shahis to second standard (13.82 grams in theory).

Date	Mintage	F	VF	XF	Unc
AHxxxx	—	400	650	1,200	—

Mint: Isfahan
KM# 260 2-1/2 ABBASI
17.3800 g., Silver **Shape:** Round **Note:** Type B.

Date	Mintage	F	VF	XF	Unc
AH1115	—	250	300	500	—

Mint: Isfahan
KM# 270 2-1/2 ABBASI
17.3800 g., Silver **Obv:** Inscription **Rev:** Inscription, date within circle **Note:** Type C.

Date	Mintage	F	VF	XF	Unc
AH1123	—	150	200	300	—

Mint: Isfahan
KM# 271 5 ABBASI
26.7000 g., Silver **Note:** Type C.

Date	Mintage	F	VF	XF	Unc
AH1123 Rare	—	—	—	—	—

Mint: Isfahan
KM# 283.1 5 ABBASI
26.7000 g., Silver **Note:** Type D variety. Shah Sultan Husayn in center obverse, long Arabic titles around in field.

Date	Mintage	F	VF	XF	Unc
AH1132 Rare	—	—	—	—	—

Mint: Qazvin
KM# 283.2 5 ABBASI
26.7000 g., Silver **Note:** Type D variety. Shah Sultan Husayn in center obverse, long Arabic titles around in field.

Date	Mintage	F	VF	XF	Unc
AH1131	—	—	—	—	—

Mint: Isfahan
KM# 284 10 ABBASI
53.4000 g., Silver **Obv:** Inscription within circle **Rev:** Inscription **Note:** Type D variety.

Date	Mintage	F	VF	XF	Unc
AH1118 Rare	—	—	—	—	—
AH1132 Rare	—	—	—	—	—

Mint: Isfahan
KM# 287.1 ASHRAFI
3.5000 g., Gold **Obv:** Inscription, date within beaded circle **Rev:** Inscription within circle **Note:** Type D variety. Coins prior to AH1129 have date and calligraphy as Type C silver. Later dates resemble Type D silver coins.

Date	Mintage	F	VF	XF	Unc
AH1127	—	120	150	200	—
AH1128	—	120	150	200	—
AH1129	—	150	200	275	—
Note: Extra outer marginal inscription obverse					
AH1130	—	110	140	200	—
AH1133	—	110	140	200	—
AH1134	—	90.00	115	175	—
ND	—	55.00	65.00	100	—
Note: Date and/or mint missing					

Mint: Kashan
KM# 287.2 ASHRAFI
3.5000 g., Gold **Obv:** Inscription, date within beaded circle **Rev:** Inscription within circle **Note:** Type D variety. Coins prior to AH1129 have date and calligraphy as Type C silver. Later dates resemble Type D silver coins.

Date	Mintage	F	VF	XF	Unc
AH1130	—	120	150	200	—

Mint: Mashhad
KM# 287.3 ASHRAFI
3.8000 g., Gold **Obv:** Inscription, date within beaded circle **Rev:** Inscription within circle **Note:** Type D variety. Coins prior to AH1129 have date and calligraphy as Type C silver. Later dates resemble Type D silver coins.

Date	Mintage	F	VF	XF	Unc
AH1134	—	120	150	200	—

Mint: Qazvin
KM# 287.4 ASHRAFI
3.5000 g., Gold **Obv:** Inscription, date within beaded circle **Rev:** Inscription within circle **Note:** Type D variety. Coins prior to AH1129 have date and calligraphy as Type C silver. Later dates resemble Type D silver coins.

Date	Mintage	F	VF	XF	Unc
AH1130	—	120	150	200	—
AH1132	—	120	150	200	—

Shah Mahmud
AH1135-1137 / 1722-1725AD

Types for this reign:

A. Couplet obverse, with mint & date. Reverse has the Sunni Kalima.

Sekkeh zad as mashreq-e Iran cho qors-e aftab Shah Mahmud-e Jahangir-e siyadat-ansab.

"From the east of Iran, Shah Mahmud, the world- conqueror of Sayyid descent, has struck coin like (i.e., as brilliant as) the solar disk."

B. As type A, but a different couplet:

Foru ravad be-zamin mah o aftab-e monir za reshk-e sekke-ye Mahmud Shah-e alamgir.

"The moon and the shining sun shall set, out of envy of the coin of Mahmud Shah the world conqueror."

C. As type A, but a different couplet:

Cho mehr o mah zar-e shahanshahi mahmud-e alam shod keh naqd-e qalbash az feyz-e Khoda az ghash mossalam shod.

"Like the sun and the moon, the imperial precious metal is praised throughout the world, for the currency of his (Mahmud's) heart has, by the benevolence of God, been cleansed of impurity." (There are numerous puns in this distich that do not survive translation).

D. As type A, but different couplet:

Din-e Haqqra sekkeh bar zar kard az hokm-e Elah Aqebat Mahmud bashad Padshah-e din-e Khoda.

"At God's command, he struck coin in precious metal for the sake of the True Religion. In the end, Mahmud shall be king in accordance with God's Religion." The second part may also be translated, "In the end, the King of the Religion of God (i.e., Ali ibn Abi Talib) shall be praised," meaning that the Shiite sect shall ultimately prevail. The use of puns and word plays in Persian poetry is renowned. As a result, most of the elegance and humor of such verse is lost in translation.

E. As type A, but only a half-couplet, still only tentatively read:

Be Mahmud-e arshad dad Khoda Shahi.

"To Mahmud, the Elder, did God grant kingship." There appears to be one additional word, still not deciphered, in this text.

HAMMERED COINAGE

Mint: Isfahan
KM# 321 2 SHAHI
2.3000 g., Silver **Note:** Type A.

Date	Mintage	F	VF	XF	Unc
AH1135	—	50.00	75.00	100	—

Mint: Isfahan
KM# 330 2 SHAHI
2.3000 g., Silver **Note:** Type E.

Date	Mintage	F	VF	XF	Unc
AH1137 Rare	—	—	—	—	—

Mint: Isfahan
KM# 322 ABBASI
4.6000 g., Silver **Obv:** Inscription, date within beaded circle **Rev:** Inscription **Note:** Type A.

Date	Mintage	F	VF	XF	Unc
AH1135	—	25.00	40.00	70.00	—
AH1137	—	30.00	45.00	80.00	—

Note: Coins dated AH1137 are believed to be coins of AH1135 with broken "5"

Mint: Isfahan
KM# 324 ABBASI
4.6000 g., Silver **Note:** Type B.

Date	Mintage	F	VF	XF	Unc
AH1135	—	25.00	40.00	70.00	—

Mint: Isfahan
KM# 326.1 5 SHAHI
Silver **Obv:** Inscription **Rev:** Inscription **Note:** Type C. 7.30-7.40 grams.

Date	Mintage	F	VF	XF	Unc
AH1135	—	30.00	50.00	75.00	—
AH1136	—	30.00	50.00	75.00	—

Mint: Isfahan
KM# 327 5 SHAHI
Silver **Note:** Type D.

Date	Mintage	F	VF	XF	Unc
AH1136	—	40.00	75.00	110	—

Mint: Kashan
KM# 326.2 5 SHAHI
Silver **Obv:** Inscription **Rev:** Inscription **Note:** Type C. Weight varies 7.30-7.40 grams.

Date	Mintage	F	VF	XF	Unc
AH1136	—	40.00	75.00	110	—

Mint: Isfahan
KM# A327 2 ABBASI
9.2000 g., Silver **Note:** Type A. Denomination uncertain. Known only from damaged specimens. Rectangular flan.

Date	Mintage	F	VF	XF	Unc
ND Rare	—	—	—	—	—

Note: Date off flan

Mint: Isfahan
KM# 328 RUPI
14.6000 g., Silver **Obv:** Inscription, date within flower design **Rev:** Inscription **Note:** Type D.

Date	Mintage	F	VF	XF	Unc
AH1135	—	300	500	800	—
AH1136	—	300	500	800	—

Mint: Qandahar
KM# 323 RUPI
11.5000 g., Silver **Obv:** Inscription **Rev:** Inscription **Note:** Type A.

Date	Mintage	F	VF	XF	Unc
AH1135	—	60.00	100	160	—
ND	—	35.00	60.00	100	—

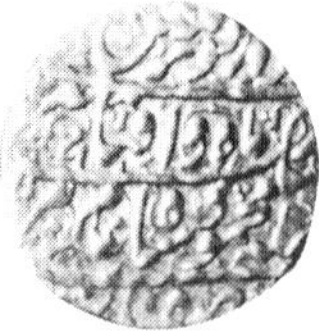

Mint: Isfahan
KM# 325.1 ASHRAFI
Gold **Obv:** Inscription **Rev:** Inscription **Note:** Type B. Weight varies 3.50-3.55 grams.

Date	Mintage	F	VF	XF	Unc
AH1135	—	150	200	350	—
AH1136	—	150	200	350	—

Mint: Isfahan
KM# 329 ASHRAFI
Gold **Note:** Type D. Weight varies: 3.50-3.55 grams.

Date	Mintage	F	VF	XF	Unc
AH1137	—	175	225	300	—

Mint: Kashan
KM# 325.2 ASHRAFI
Gold **Obv:** Inscription **Note:** Type B. Weight varies 3.50-3.55 grams.

Date	Mintage	F	VF	XF	Unc
AH1136	—	175	250	425	—

Tahmasp II

AH1135-1145 / 1722-1732AD

Types for this reign:

A. Obverse couplet, together with mint and date, the mint in the bottom line, the date in various locations in the field. Reverse has the Shiite formula, usually with the names of the 12 Imams in a circular marginal legend around.

Be-giti sekke-ye sahebqerani Zad az toufiq-e haqq Tahmasp-e thani

"By the grace of God, Tahmasp the Second struck the sahebqerani coin throughout the world."

B. Obverse simple inscription, with mint below, and date in field. Reverse as type A, always with the names of the Imams. Used only at Yazd Mint.

Tahmasp-e Ghazi Bande-ye Shah-e Velayat

"Tahmasp the Second, servant of the king of the Velayat (i.e., Ali ibn Abi Talib)".

C. Obverse simple inscription, mint and date below. Reverse as type A, but without names of the Imams. Used only at Kirman Mint.

Gholam-e Shah-e Din Tahmasp-e Thani

"Tahmasp the Second, servant of the king of faith"

Again a reference to Tahmasp's Shiite belief, as the "king of faith" is yet another epithet of Ali ibn Abi Talib.

D. Obverse couplet, with mint and date below as usual. Reverse as type A, with the names of the Imams.

Sekkeh zad Tahmasp-e Thani bar zar-e kamel-'ayyar La fata illa 'Ali la seyf ella Zolfegar

"Tahmasp the Second struck coin in precious metal of full alloy. There is no other warrior like Ali (ibn Abi Talib), no other sword like Zolfeqar (the legendary sword used by Ali ibn Abi Talib)".

HAMMERED COINAGE

Mint: Tabriz
KM# 300 PUL
0.6700 g., Silver **Obv:** Inscription **Rev:** Inscription **Note:** Type A.

Date	Mintage	F	VF	XF	Unc
AH1143	—	40.00	60.00	80.00	—

Mint: Astarabad
KM# 301.1 SHAHI
1.3500 g., Silver **Obv:** Inscription **Rev:** Inscription **Note:** Type A.

Date	Mintage	F	VF	XF	Unc
AH1141	—	25.00	40.00	60.00	—

Mint: Ganjah
KM# 301.2 SHAHI
1.3500 g., Silver **Obv:** Inscription **Rev:** Inscription **Note:** Type A.

Date	Mintage	F	VF	XF	Unc
AH1135	—	10.00	20.00	30.00	—

Mint: Isfahan
KM# 301.3 SHAHI
1.3500 g., Silver **Obv:** Inscription **Rev:** Inscription **Note:** Type A.

Date	Mintage	F	VF	XF	Unc
AH1142	—	20.00	30.00	45.00	—
AH1143	—	25.00	40.00	55.00	—

Mint: Mashhad
KM# 301.4 SHAHI
1.3500 g., Silver **Obv:** Inscription **Rev:** Inscription **Note:** Type A.

Date	Mintage	F	VF	XF	Unc
AH1139	—	17.50	27.50	40.00	—

Mint: Mazandaran
KM# 301.5 SHAHI
1.3500 g., Silver **Obv:** Inscription **Rev:** Inscription **Note:** Type A.

Date	Mintage	F	VF	XF	Unc
AH1139	—	20.00	35.00	50.00	—

Mint: Nakhjavan
KM# 301.6 SHAHI
1.3500 g., Silver **Obv:** Inscription **Rev:** Inscription **Note:** Type A.

Date	Mintage	F	VF	XF	Unc
AH1135	—	10.00	20.00	30.00	—

Mint: Qazvin
KM# 301.7 SHAHI
1.3500 g., Silver **Obv:** Inscription **Rev:** Inscription **Note:** Type A.

Date	Mintage	F	VF	XF	Unc
AH1135	—	30.00	45.00	60.00	—

Mint: Tabriz
KM# 301.8 SHAHI
1.3500 g., Silver **Obv:** Inscription **Rev:** Inscription **Note:** Type A.

Date	Mintage	F	VF	XF	Unc
AH1135	—	30.00	45.00	60.00	—
AH1136	—	12.50	22.50	35.00	—
AH1143	—	10.00	20.00	30.00	—
AH1144	—	10.00	20.00	30.00	—

Note: A shahi of Isfahan AH1144 is known as a gold off-metal strike (rare)

Mint: Tehran
KM# 301.9 SHAHI
1.3500 g., Silver **Obv:** Inscription **Rev:** Inscription **Note:** Type A.

Date	Mintage	F	VF	XF	Unc
AH1137	—	25.00	45.00	65.00	—

Mint: Isfahan
KM# 302.1 2 SHAHI
2.7000 g., Silver **Note:** Type A.

Date	Mintage	F	VF	XF	Unc
AH1142	—	20.00	35.00	50.00	—
AH1143	—	20.00	35.00	50.00	—

Mint: Kashan
KM# 302.2 2 SHAHI
2.7000 g., Silver **Note:** Type A.

Date	Mintage	F	VF	XF	Unc
AH1135	—	30.00	45.00	60.00	—

Mint: Lahijan
KM# 302.3 2 SHAHI
2.7000 g., Silver **Note:** Type A.

Date	Mintage	F	VF	XF	Unc
AH1139	—	30.00	45.00	60.00	—

Mint: Mazandaran
KM# 302.4 2 SHAHI
2.7000 g., Silver **Note:** Type A.

Date	Mintage	F	VF	XF	Unc
AH1138	—	25.00	40.00	55.00	—
AH1139	—	25.00	40.00	55.00	—

Mint: Nakhjavan
KM# 302.5 2 SHAHI
2.7000 g., Silver **Note:** Type A.

Date	Mintage	F	VF	XF	Unc
AH1135	—	35.00	50.00	70.00	—

Mint: Tabriz
KM# 302.6 2 SHAHI
2.7000 g., Silver **Note:** Type A.

Date	Mintage	F	VF	XF	Unc
AH1135	—	15.00	25.00	35.00	—
AH1136	—	15.00	25.00	35.00	—
AH1137	—	20.00	30.00	40.00	—
AH1143	—	15.00	25.00	35.00	—

Mint: Astarabad
KM# 303.1 ABBASI
5.4000 g., Silver **Obv:** Inscription **Rev:** Inscription **Note:** Type A.

Date	Mintage	F	VF	XF	Unc
AH1139	—	30.00	45.00	65.00	—

Mint: Eravan
KM# 303.2 ABBASI
5.4000 g., Silver **Obv:** Inscription **Rev:** Inscription **Note:** Type A.

Date	Mintage	F	VF	XF	Unc
AH1135	—	20.00	35.00	50.00	—

Mint: Ganjah
KM# 303.3 ABBASI
5.4000 g., Silver **Obv:** Inscription **Rev:** Inscription **Note:** Type A.

Date	Mintage	F	VF	XF	Unc
AH1135	—	25.00	40.00	55.00	—
AH1136	—	25.00	40.00	55.00	—

Mint: Isfahan
KM# 303.4 ABBASI
5.4000 g., Silver **Obv:** Inscription **Rev:** Inscription **Note:** Type A.

Date	Mintage	F	VF	XF	Unc
AH1142	—	8.00	14.00	22.50	—
AH1143	—	8.00	14.00	22.50	—
AH1144	—	8.00	14.00	22.50	—
AH1145	—	15.00	25.00	35.00	—

Mint: Kashan
KM# 303.5 ABBASI
5.4000 g., Silver **Obv:** Inscription **Rev:** Inscription **Note:** Type A.

Date	Mintage	F	VF	XF	Unc
AH1135	—	25.00	40.00	55.00	—

Mint: Kirman
KM# 303.6 ABBASI
5.4000 g., Silver **Obv:** Inscription **Rev:** Inscription **Note:** Type A.

Date	Mintage	F	VF	XF	Unc
AH1142	—	30.00	45.00	65.00	—

Mint: Kirman
KM# 309 ABBASI
5.4000 g., Silver **Note:** Type C.

Date	Mintage	F	VF	XF	Unc
AH1135	—	30.00	45.00	65.00	—

Mint: Lahijan
KM# 303.7 ABBASI
5.4000 g., Silver **Obv:** Inscription **Rev:** Inscription **Note:** Type A.

Date	Mintage	F	VF	XF	Unc
AH1137	—	10.00	17.50	30.00	—
AH1138	—	10.00	17.50	27.50	—
AH1139	—	10.00	17.50	27.50	—

Mint: Mashhad
KM# 303.8 ABBASI
5.4000 g., Silver **Obv:** Inscription **Rev:** Inscription **Note:** Type A.

Date	Mintage	F	VF	XF	Unc
AH1139	—	10.00	16.00	25.00	—
AH1140	—	10.00	16.00	25.00	—
AH1141	—	10.00	16.00	25.00	—
AH1142	—	12.50	20.00	30.00	—

Mint: Mazandaran
KM# 303.9 ABBASI
5.4000 g., Silver **Obv:** Inscription **Rev:** Inscription **Note:** Type A.

Date	Mintage	F	VF	XF	Unc
AH1138	—	15.00	25.00	35.00	—
AH1140	—	15.00	25.00	35.00	—
AH1141	—	12.50	20.00	30.00	—
AH1142	—	12.50	20.00	30.00	—
AH1143	—	15.00	25.00	35.00	—

Mint: Nakhjavan
KM# 303.10 ABBASI
5.4000 g., Silver **Obv:** Inscription **Rev:** Inscription **Note:** Type A.

Date	Mintage	F	VF	XF	Unc
AH1135	—	25.00	40.00	55.00	—
AH1137	—	30.00	45.00	65.00	—

Mint: Qazvin
KM# 303.11 ABBASI
5.4000 g., Silver **Obv:** Inscription **Rev:** Inscription **Note:** Type A.

Date	Mintage	F	VF	XF	Unc
AH1135	—	8.00	14.00	22.50	—
AH1142	—	10.00	17.50	25.00	—
AH1143	—	10.00	17.50	25.00	—

Mint: Qomm
KM# 303.12 ABBASI
5.4000 g., Silver **Obv:** Inscription **Rev:** Inscription **Note:** Type A.

Date	Mintage	F	VF	XF	Unc
AH1136	—	15.00	25.00	35.00	—
AH1144	—	30.00	45.00	65.00	—

Mint: Rasht
KM# 303.13 ABBASI
5.4000 g., Silver **Obv:** Inscription **Rev:** Inscription **Note:** Type A.

Date	Mintage	F	VF	XF	Unc
AH1135	—	17.50	30.00	45.00	—
AH1136	—	25.00	40.00	55.00	—
AH1137	—	17.50	30.00	45.00	—
AH1139	—	15.00	25.00	35.00	—

Mint: Shiraz
KM# 303.14 ABBASI
5.4000 g., Silver **Obv:** Inscription **Rev:** Inscription **Note:** Type A.

Date	Mintage	F	VF	XF	Unc
AH1136	—	20.00	35.00	50.00	—
AH1142	—	15.00	25.00	35.00	—
AH1143	—	15.00	25.00	35.00	—

Date	Mintage	F	VF	XF	Unc
AH1144	—	15.00	25.00	35.00	—
AH1145	—	15.00	25.00	35.00	—

Mint: Tabriz
KM# 303.15 ABBASI

5.4000 g., Silver **Obv:** Inscription **Rev:** Inscription **Note:** Type A. Coins of Tabriz are reported with the date AH1134, possibly an error, possibly a misreading of AH1136.

Date	Mintage	F	VF	XF	Unc
AH1153 Error for 1135	—	—	—	—	—
AH1135	—	6.00	10.00	20.00	—
AH1136	—	8.00	14.00	22.50	—
AH1137	—	8.00	14.00	22.50	—
AH1138	—	15.00	25.00	37.50	—
AH1142	—	20.00	30.00	40.00	—
AH1143	—	6.00	10.00	17.50	—
AH1144	—	6.00	10.00	17.50	—

Mint: Tehran
KM# 303.16 ABBASI

5.4000 g., Silver **Obv:** Inscription **Rev:** Inscription **Note:** Type A.

Date	Mintage	F	VF	XF	Unc
AH1137	—	25.00	40.00	55.00	—
AH1143	—	25.00	40.00	55.00	—
AH1144	—	25.00	40.00	55.00	—

Mint: Yazd
KM# 303.17 ABBASI

5.4000 g., Silver **Obv:** Inscription **Rev:** Inscription **Note:** Type A.

Date	Mintage	F	VF	XF	Unc
AH1137	—	25.00	40.00	55.00	—

Mint: Yazd
KM# 308 ABBASI

5.4000 g., Silver **Note:** Type B.

Date	Mintage	F	VF	XF	Unc
AH1135	—	35.00	50.00	70.00	—

Mint: Isfahan
KM# 304.1 2-1/2 ABBASI

13.5000 g., Silver **Note:** Type A.

Date	Mintage	F	VF	XF	Unc
AH1142 Rare	—	—	—	—	—
AH1144 Rare	—	—	—	—	—

Mint: Tabriz
KM# 304.2 2-1/2 ABBASI

13.5000 g., Silver **Note:** Type A.

Date	Mintage	F	VF	XF	Unc
AH1135	—	150	200	—	—

Mint: Isfahan
KM# 305 5 ABBASI

27.0000 g., Silver **Obv:** Inscription **Rev:** Inscription **Note:** Type A.

Date	Mintage	F	VF	XF	Unc
AH1142	—	150	250	400	—

Mint: Kirman
KM# 310 5 ABBASI

27.0000 g., Silver **Obv:** Inscription **Rev:** Inscription **Note:** Type D.

Date	Mintage	F	VF	XF	Unc
AH1135 Rare	—	—	—	—	—

Mint: Astarabad
KM# 306.1 ASHRAFI

Gold **Obv:** Inscription **Rev:** Inscription **Note:** Type D. Weight varies 3.50-3.55 grams.

Date	Mintage	F	VF	XF	Unc
AH1141	—	200	250	325	—

Mint: Ganjah
KM# 306.2 ASHRAFI

Gold **Obv:** Inscription **Rev:** Inscriptin **Note:** Type D. Weight varies 3.5-3.55 grams.

Date	Mintage	F	VF	XF	Unc
AH1135 Rare	—	—	—	—	—

Mint: Isfahan
KM# 306.3 ASHRAFI

Gold **Obv:** Inscription **Rev:** Inscription **Note:** Type D. Weight varies 3.50-3.55 grams.

Date	Mintage	F	VF	XF	Unc
AH1142	—	100	140	175	—
AH1143	—	100	140	175	—
AH1144	—	100	140	175	—

Mint: Mashhad
KM# 306.4 ASHRAFI

Gold **Obv:** Inscription **Rev:** Inscription **Note:** Type D. Weight varies 3.50-3.55 grams.

Date	Mintage	F	VF	XF	Unc
AH1139	—	125	160	200	—
AH1140	—	125	160	200	—

Mint: Nakhjavan
KM# 306.5 ASHRAFI

Gold **Obv:** Inscription **Rev:** Inscription **Note:** Type D. Weight varies 3.50-3.55 grams.

Date	Mintage	F	VF	XF	Unc
AH1135 Rare	—	—	—	—	—

Mint: Qazvín
KM# 306.6 ASHRAFI

Gold **Obv:** Inscription **Rev:** Inscription **Note:** Type D. Weight varies 3.50-3.55 grams.

Date	Mintage	F	VF	XF	Unc
AH1135	—	150	200	250	—
AH1142	—	125	160	200	—
AH1144	—	125	160	200	—

Mint: Qomm
KM# 306.7 ASHRAFI

Gold **Obv:** Inscription **Rev:** Inscription **Note:** Type D. Weight varies 3.50-3.55 grams.

Date	Mintage	F	VF	XF	Unc
AH1144	—	200	250	325	—

Mint: Shiraz
KM# 306.8 ASHRAFI

Gold **Obv:** Inscription **Rev:** Inscription **Note:** Type D. Weight varies 3.50-3.55 grams.

Date	Mintage	F	VF	XF	Unc
AH1143	—	125	160	200	—

Mint: Tabriz
KM# 306.9 ASHRAFI

Gold **Obv:** Inscription **Rev:** Inscription **Note:** Type D. Weight varies 3.50-3.55 grams.

Date	Mintage	F	VF	XF	Unc
AH1136	—	125	160	200	—
AH1143	—	100	140	175	—

Mint: Tabriz
KM# 307 10 ASHRAFI

Gold **Note:** Type D. Weight varies: 35.00-36.00 grams.

Date	Mintage	F	VF	XF	Unc
AH1135 Rare	—	—	—	—	—

Malik Mahmud at Mashhad

AH1137-1138 / 1724-1725AD

HAMMERED COINAGE

Mint: Mashhad
KM# 317 ABBASI

5.4000 g., Silver **Note:** Type D.

Date	Mintage	F	VF	XF	Unc
AH1137	—	150	200	250	—
AH1138	—	150	200	250	—

Ashraf

AH1137-1142 / 1725-1729AD

Types for this reign:

A. Obverse couplet, with mint below. Reverse, Sunni Kalima, together with date.

Be-Ashrafi athar-e nam-e anjenab rasid Sharaf za sekke-ye Ashraf bar aftab rasid.

"As the name of that noble person (Ashraf) was traced upon the ashrafi (coin), from the coin of Ashraf, (his) honor surpassed (that of) the sun".

B. Similar to type A, but a different couplet:

Khor o mah chun tala o noqreh az feyzash monavvar shod Sharaf bar aftab az name-e Ashraf sekkeh bar zar shod.

"The sun and moon, like gold and silver, were illuminated by his (Ashraf's) generosity. From the name Ashraf, coin in precious metal gained honor above (that of) the sun.

C. Similar to type A, but different couplet. The accessional year 1137 is normally added to the reverse, with the actual year of issue appearing on the obverse.

Az altaf-e Shah Ashraf-e haqq-shenas be-zar naqsh shod sekke-ye Char Yar.

"Courtesy of the rights-respecting Shah Ashraf, the coin of the Four Friends was struck in precious metal." The Four Friends are the four caliphs who followed the death of the Prophet Muhammad, who are honored by Sunnis in their sectarian opposition to the Shiites. This difficult couplet contains numerous untranslatable puns.

D. Obverse couplet, with date below. Reverse, short inscription as on the Mughal coinage, including the mint, its epithetical designation, and the accessional date of Shah Ashraf. Obverse couplet:

Dast-zad bar jalalaho bovad gonah Dad-e Taghyir-e sekke-ye Ashraf Shah.

"The crime of counterfeiting the coin of Ashraf Shah would be (tantamount to) an offence the Glorious." The last part could equally well be translated as "an attack against his glory," either the Glory of God or the glory of Ashraf Shah. All these meanings are intended in the Persian text. Still other puns can be found in this distich. The reverse inscription is:

Jolus-e meymanat-ma nus-e Dar os-Saltanat Isfahan 1137.

"1137, (year of) the auspicious enthronement, at the Abode of the Sultanate, Isfahan".

HAMMERED COINAGE

Mint: Isfahan
KM# 340 SHAHI

1.1500 g., Silver **Note:** Type C undetermined. Surviving examples show portions of couplet, which appears to be different from couplets on types A through D.

Date	Mintage	F	VF	XF	Unc
AHxxxx Date off flan	—	50.00	75.00	100	—

Mint: Isfahan
KM# 337 2 SHAHI

3.0000 g., Silver **Note:** Type C. Rectangular. Probably based on the heavy shahi of 1.35 grams, as the coins of type B, rather than on the shahi of 1.15 grams, as the round silver abbasi of type C.

Date	Mintage	F	VF	XF	Unc
AH1138	—	60.00	100	150	—

Mint: Isfahan
KM# 338.1 ABBASI

4.6000 g., Silver **Obv:** Inscription **Rev:** Inscription **Note:** Type C.

Date	Mintage	F	VF	XF	Unc
AH1138	—	25.00	45.00	65.00	—
AH1139	—	25.00	45.00	65.00	—
AH1141	—	25.00	45.00	65.00	—

Mint: Isfahan
KM# 339 ABBASI

4.6000 g., Silver **Obv:** Inscription **Rev:** Dated AH1137, inscription **Note:** Type D.

Date	Mintage	F	VF	XF	Unc
AH1140//1137	—	20.00	35.00	55.00	—
AH1340//1137	—	40.00	60.00	80.00	—
AH1141//1137	—	20.00	35.00	55.00	—

Mint: Qazvin
KM# 338.2 ABBASI

4.6000 g., Silver **Obv:** Inscription **Rev:** Inscription **Note:** Type C.

Date	Mintage	F	VF	XF	Unc
AH1139	—	30.00	55.00	75.00	—

Mint: Shiraz
KM# 338.3 ABBASI

4.6000 g., Silver **Obv:** Inscription **Rev:** Inscription **Note:** Type C.

Date	Mintage	F	VF	XF	Unc
AH1142	—	50.00	80.00	100	—

Mint: Isfahan
KM# 336 5 SHAHI
Silver **Obv:** Inscription **Rev:** Inscription **Note:** Type B. Weight varies: 7.00-7.20 grams. Denominations may be 6 shahi.

Date	Mintage	F	VF	XF	Unc
AH1137	—	50.00	75.00	100	—
AH1138	—	50.00	75.00	100	—

Mint: Isfahan
KM# 335.1 ASHRAFI
Silver **Obv:** Inscription **Rev:** Inscription **Note:** Type A.

Date	Mintage	F	VF	XF	Unc
AH1137	—	150	200	350	—
AH1139	—	150	200	350	—
AH1140	—	150	200	350	—

Mint: Qazvin
KM# 335.2 ASHRAFI
Silver **Obv:** Inscription **Rev:** Inscription **Note:** Type A.

Date	Mintage	F	VF	XF	Unc
AH1139	—	175	240	450	—

Sultan Ahmad

AH1138-1141 / 1726-1728AD

HAMMERED COINAGE

Mint: Kirman
KM# 319 ABBASI
5.4000 g., Silver **Note:** Type D.

Date	Mintage	F	VF	XF	Unc
AH113x	—	150	200	250	—

Nadir Shah

AH1142-1148 / 1729-1735AD

As viceroy in the eastern provinces.

Nadir Shah was the commanding general and engineer of the defeat of the Afghans under Shah Ashraf at Isfahan in AH1142/1729. He was granted autonomy in Khorasan in reward for that service. Other provinces were later added to his vice-regency.

There is only one type, with the following couplet on the obverse, the Shiite formula on the reverse.

Az Khorasan sekkeh bar zar shod be-toufiq-e Khoda Nosrat o emdad-e Shah-e Din Ali-ye Musa Reza.

"From Khorasan, the coin of precious metal became, by the grace of God, succor and reinforcements for the King of the Religion, Ali, son of Musa, (known as) Reza."

The reference is to the 8th Imam of the Twelver sect of Shiites.

HAMMERED COINAGE

Mint: Mazandaran
KM# 350 PUL
0.6800 g., Silver **Note:** Type A.

Date	Mintage	F	VF	XF	Unc
AH114x	—	30.00	55.00	85.00	—

Mint: Mashhad
KM# 351 SHAHI
1.3500 g., Silver **Note:** Type A.

Date	Mintage	F	VF	XF	Unc
AH1143	—	20.00	35.00	50.00	—

Mint: Herat
KM# A352.1 2 SHAHI
2.7000 g., Silver **Note:** Type A.

Date	Mintage	F	VF	XF	Unc
AH1146	—	45.00	70.00	100	—

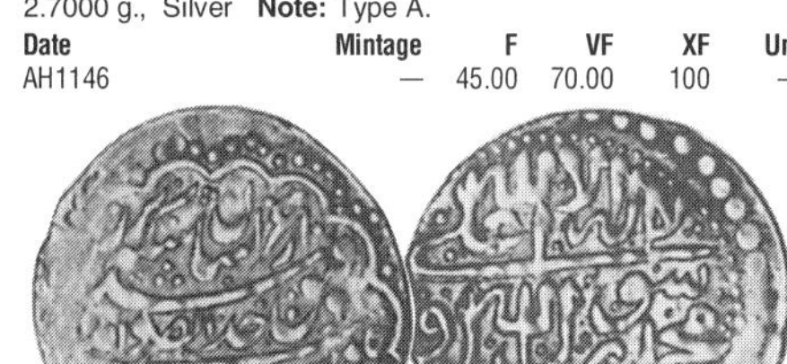

Mint: Herat
KM# 352.1 ABBASI
5.4000 g., Silver **Obv:** Inscription **Rev:** Inscription **Note:** Type A. Varieties exist.

Date	Mintage	F	VF	XF	Unc
AH1146	—	30.00	50.00	80.00	—

Mint: Mashhad
KM# 352.3 ABBASI
5.4000 g., Silver **Obv:** Inscription **Rev:** Inscription **Note:** Type A. Varieties exist.

Date	Mintage	F	VF	XF	Unc
AH1143	—	6.00	10.00	20.00	—
AH1144	—	6.00	10.00	20.00	—
AH1145	—	6.00	10.00	20.00	—
AH1146	—	6.00	10.00	20.00	—
AH1147	—	6.00	10.00	20.00	—
AH1148	—	6.00	10.00	20.00	—

Mint: Qazvin
KM# 369.6 ABBASI
5.4000 g., Silver **Obv:** Inscription **Rev:** Inscription within flower design **Note:** Type B.

Date	Mintage	F	VF	XF	Unc
AH1149	—	25.00	40.00	65.00	—

Mint: Mashhad
KM# 353 ASHRAFI
3.5000 g., Gold **Note:** Type A.

Date	Mintage	F	VF	XF	Unc
AH1146	—	125	175	225	—
AH1148	—	125	175	225	—

Shah Abbas III

AH1145-1148 / 1732-1736AD

HAMMERED COINAGE

Mint: Eravan
KM# 344.1 SHAHI
1.3500 g., Silver **Note:** Type A.

Date	Mintage	F	VF	XF	Unc
AH1148	—	50.00	75.00	100	—

Mint: Isfahan
KM# 344.2 SHAHI
1.3500 g., Silver **Note:** Type A.

Date	Mintage	F	VF	XF	Unc
ND	—	15.00	25.00	37.50	—

Mint: Qazvin
KM# 344.3 SHAHI
1.3500 g., Silver **Note:** Type A.

Date	Mintage	F	VF	XF	Unc
AH1145	—	20.00	35.00	50.00	—

Mint: Rasht
KM# 344.4 SHAHI
103500.0000 g., Silver **Note:** Type A.

Date	Mintage	F	VF	XF	Unc
AH1145	—	30.00	45.00	65.00	—

Mint: Qazvin
KM# 345.1 2 SHAHI
2.7000 g., Silver **Note:** Type A.

Date	Mintage	F	VF	XF	Unc
AH1145	—	30.00	50.00	75.00	—

Mint: Tiflis
KM# 345.2 2 SHAHI
2.7000 g., Silver **Note:** Type A.

Date	Mintage	F	VF	XF	Unc
AH1148	—	50.00	80.00	125	—

Mint: Eravan
KM# 346.1 ABBASI
5.4000 g., Silver **Obv:** Inscription **Rev:** Inscription **Note:** Type A.

Date	Mintage	F	VF	XF	Unc
AH1148	—	50.00	75.00	100	—

Mint: Isfahan
KM# 346.2 ABBASI
5.4000 g., Silver **Obv:** Inscription **Rev:** Inscription **Note:** Type A.

Date	Mintage	F	VF	XF	Unc
AH1145	—	17.50	27.50	40.00	—
AH1146	—	17.50	27.50	40.00	—
AH1147	—	17.50	27.50	40.00	—

Mint: Maragheh
KM# 346.3 ABBASI
5.4000 g., Silver **Obv:** Inscription **Rev:** Inscription **Note:** Type A.

Date	Mintage	F	VF	XF	Unc
AH1146	—	40.00	65.00	90.00	—

Mint: Nakhjavan
KM# 346.4 ABBASI
5.4000 g., Silver **Obv:** Inscription **Rev:** Inscription **Note:** Type A.

Date	Mintage	F	VF	XF	Unc
AH1148	—	40.00	65.00	90.00	—

Mint: Qazvin
KM# 346.5 ABBASI
5.4000 g., Silver **Obv:** Inscription **Rev:** Inscription **Note:** Type A.

Date	Mintage	F	VF	XF	Unc
AH1145	—	20.00	35.00	50.00	—
AH1147	—	20.00	35.00	50.00	—

Mint: Rasht
KM# 346.6 ABBASI
5.4000 g., Silver **Obv:** Inscription **Rev:** Inscription **Note:** Type A.

Date	Mintage	F	VF	XF	Unc
AH0012	—	25.00	40.00	60.00	—

Mint: Shiraz
KM# 346.7 ABBASI
5.4000 g., Silver **Obv:** Inscription **Rev:** Inscription **Note:** Type A.

Date	Mintage	F	VF	XF	Unc
AH1145	—	25.00	40.00	60.00	—
AH1146	—	20.00	35.00	50.00	—
AH1147	—	20.00	35.00	50.00	—
AH1148	—	20.00	35.00	50.00	—

Mint: Shushtar
KM# 346.8 ABBASI
5.4000 g., Silver **Obv:** Inscription **Rev:** Inscription **Note:** Type A.

Date	Mintage	F	VF	XF	Unc
AH1145	—	35.00	55.00	80.00	—
AH1146	—	35.00	55.00	80.00	—

Mint: Tabriz
KM# 346.9 ABBASI
5.4000 g., Silver **Obv:** Inscription **Rev:** Inscription **Note:** Type A.

Date	Mintage	F	VF	XF	Unc
AH1145	—	20.00	35.00	50.00	—
AH1146	—	20.00	35.00	50.00	—
AH1147	—	20.00	35.00	50.00	—
AH1148	—	20.00	35.00	50.00	—

Mint: Tehran
KM# 346.10 ABBASI
5.4000 g., Silver **Obv:** Inscription **Rev:** Inscription **Note:** Type A.

Date	Mintage	F	VF	XF	Unc
AH1145	—	35.00	55.00	80.00	—
AH1148	—	35.00	55.00	80.00	—

Mint: Tiflis
KM# 346.11 ABBASI
5.4000 g., Silver **Obv:** Inscription **Rev:** Inscription **Note:** Type A.

Date	Mintage	F	VF	XF	Unc
AH1148	—	40.00	65.00	100	—

Mint: Shiraz
KM# 347 5 ABBASI
27.0000 g., Silver **Note:** Type A.

Date	Mintage	F	VF	XF	Unc
AH1145	—	250	350	600	—

Mint: Isfahan
KM# 348.1 ASHRAFI
3.5000 g., Gold **Obv:** Inscription **Rev:** Inscription **Note:** Type A.

Date	Mintage	F	VF	XF	Unc
AH1145	—	110	170	235	—
AH1148	—	110	170	235	—

Mint: Maragheh
KM# 348.2 ASHRAFI
3.5000 g., Gold **Obv:** Inscription **Rev:** Inscription **Note:** Type A.

Date	Mintage	F	VF	XF	Unc
AH1146 Rare	—	—	—	—	—

Mint: Qazvin
KM# 348.3 ASHRAFI
3.5000 g., Gold **Obv:** Inscription **Rev:** Inscription **Note:** Type A.

Date	Mintage	F	VF	XF	Unc
AH1145	—	125	185	250	—

Mint: Tabriz
KM# 348.4 ASHRAFI
3.5000 g., Gold **Obv:** Inscription **Rev:** Inscription **Note:** Type A.

Date	Mintage	F	VF	XF	Unc
AH1146	—	125	185	250	—

Mint: Tiflis
KM# 348.5 ASHRAFI
3.5000 g., Gold **Obv:** Inscription **Rev:** Inscription **Note:** Type A.

Date	Mintage	F	VF	XF	Unc
AH1148	—	200	300	450	—

Nadir Shah

AH1148-1160 / 1736-1747AD

Types for this reign:

A. (Toughra type) Couplet on obverse, as below, sometimes, with mint & date. Reverse chronogram in the form of a toughra, usually with the date below, and with mint when mint not on obverse.

Sekkeh bar zar kard nam-e saltanat-ra dar jahan Nader-e Iran-zamin o Khosrov-e Giti-setan.

"The Nadir of the land of Iran, the Caesar who seizes the world, coin in precious metal broadcast the name of this sultanate (throughout) the world." Nadir means "rare" "unparalleled," whence the pun. The reverse chronogram, in Arabic, is as follows:

Be-tarikh-e al-khayr fi ma waqa.

"In the year, what has happened is good." According to the abjad system of date reckoning, the total values of the letters in this expression 1148.

B. (Julus type). Obverse couplet as type A, with mint and date below. Reverse has the same chronogram, not in the form of a toughra, within a circular border, with several additional words:

Tarikh-e jolus-e meymanat-ma'nus-e al-khayr fi ma waqa'.

"In the year of the auspicious enthronement, 'what has happened good." The year AH1148 is often cited on the reverse, with the actual date of issue on the obverse.

C. Obverse *al-soltan Nader* and reverse the benediction *khalad Allah mulkahu.*

"May God prolong his kingship," together with mint and date.

D.1 Couplet obverse, with the same reverse as type C (usually without the benediction).

Hast Soltan bar salatin-e jahan Shah-e Shahan Nader-e sahebqeran.

"The shah of shahs, Nadir, the sahebqeran, is sultan over the sultans of the world."

D.2 Same as D.1 but with benediction *khalad Allah mulkahu* added to reverse (used only in Afghanistan and India).

E. Inscriptional obverse. Reverse as Type F. *Sekke-ye mobarak-e padshah-e ghazi Nader Shah,* Fortunate coin of the victorious shah Nader shah.

F. couplet obverse. Reverse as the standard jolus reverse of the 18th century of the Mughal Empire, with mint and regnal year. *Dadeh zib-e tazeh-ye ru bar mehr o mah / as sekke-ye Nader Shah-e giti-panah,* Given beauth fresh of face on the sun and moon, By the die of Nadir Shah, the asylum of the World.

OCCUPATION COINAGE

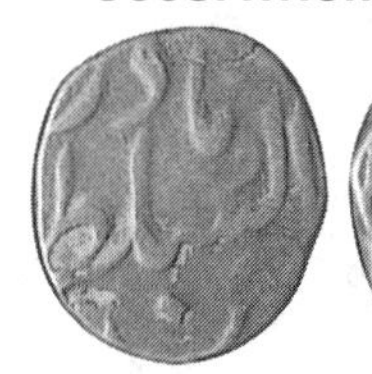

Mint: Najibabad
KM# 391 FALUS

Copper Or Bronze **Note:** Prev. Afghanistan, KM#A685.

Date	Mintage	Good	VG	F	VF	XF
AH1160 (1747)	—	—	—	—	—	—

Mint: Bhakkar
KM# 393 RUPI

Silver **Note:** Weight varies: 11.00-11.60 g. Prev. Afghanistan KM#A280.

Date	Mintage	VG	F	VF	XF	Unc
AH1155 (1742)	—	35.00	50.00	80.00	125	—
AH1156 (1743)	—	35.00	50.00	80.00	125	—
AH1158 (1745)	—	35.00	50.00	80.00	125	—

Mint: Derajat
KM# 394 RUPI

Silver **Note:** Weight varies: 11.20-11.40 g. Prev. Afghanistan KM#336.

Date	Mintage	VG	F	VF	XF	Unc
AH1159 (1746)	—	35.00	50.00	80.00	125	—
AH1160 (1747)	—	35.00	50.00	80.00	125	—

Mint: Najibabad
KM# 395 RUPI

Silver **Note:** Weight varies: 11.20-11.40 g. Prev. Afghanistan KM#685.

Date	Mintage	VG	F	VF	XF	Unc
AH1153 (1740)	—	35.00	50.00	80.00	125	—
AH1160 (1747)	—	35.00	50.00	80.00	125	—

Mint: Peshawar
KM# 396 RUPI

Silver **Note:** Prev. Afghanistan KM#685.

Date	Mintage	VG	F	VF	XF	Unc
AH1153 (1740)	—	35.00	50.00	80.00	125	—

Mint: Shahjahanabad
KM# 397 RUPI

Silver **Note:** Weight varies: 11.00-11.60 g. Prev. Afghanistan KM#A759.

Date	Mintage	VG	F	VF	XF	Unc
AH1151 (1738)	—	45.00	100	150	200	—

Mint: Sind
KM# 398 RUPI

Silver

Date	Mintage	VG	F	VF	XF	Unc
ND(1735-47)	—	35.00	50.00	80.00	125	—

HAMMERED COINAGE

Mint: Murshidabad
KM# A385 1/16 RUPI

0.7100 g., Silver **Note:** Type F.

Date	Mintage	Good	VG	F	VF	XF
AH1152	—	40.00	100	200	350	—

Mint: Murshidabad
KM# D385 1/2 RUPI

5.7500 g., Silver **Note:** Type F.

Date	Mintage	Good	VG	F	VF	XF
AH1152	—	40.00	100	200	350	—

Mint: Murshidabad
KM# B385 1/8 RUPI

1.4300 g., Silver **Note:** Type F.

Date	Mintage	Good	VG	F	VF	XF
AH1152	—	40.00	100	200	350	—

Mint: Kabul
KM# 359 FALUS

12.0000 g., Copper **Note:** Type A.

Date	Mintage	VG	F	VF	XF	Unc
AH1159	—	30.00	50.00	80.00	—	—

Mint: Shiraz
KM# 366 PUL

0.6500 g., Silver **Note:** Type B.

Date	Mintage	F	VF	XF	Unc
AHxxxx	—	20.00	30.00	40.00	—

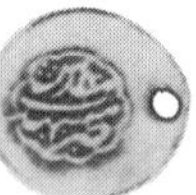

Mint: Darband
KM# 383.1 SHAHI

1.1500 g., Silver **Obv:** Inscription **Rev:** Inscription within flower design **Note:** Type D.

Date	Mintage	F	VF	XF	Unc
AH1154	—	30.00	50.00	75.00	—

Mint: Ganjah
KM# 383.2 SHAHI

1.1500 g., Silver **Obv:** Inscription, hole at right **Rev:** Inscription within flower design, hole at right **Note:** Type D.

Date	Mintage	F	VF	XF	Unc
AH1154	—	15.00	25.00	40.00	—

Mint: Isfahan
KM# 360.1 SHAHI

1.3500 g., Silver **Note:** Type A.

Date	Mintage	F	VF	XF	Unc
AH1149	—	35.00	60.00	100	—

Mint: Isfahan
KM# 367.1 SHAHI

1.3500 g., Silver **Note:** Type B.

Date	Mintage	F	VF	XF	Unc
AH1148	—	10.00	17.50	30.00	—

Mint: Isfahan
KM# 373.1 SHAHI

1.1500 g., Silver **Obv:** Inscription **Rev:** Inscription within beaded circle **Note:** Type C.

Date	Mintage	F	VF	XF	Unc
AH1150	—	30.00	50.00	75.00	—

Mint: Isfahan
KM# 383.3 SHAHI

1.1500 g., Silver **Obv:** Inscription, hole at right **Rev:** Inscription within flower design, hole at right **Note:** Type D.

Date	Mintage	F	VF	XF	Unc
AH1154	—	20.00	32.50	50.00	—
AH1156	—	20.00	30.00	50.00	—
AH1157	—	20.00	30.00	50.00	—
AH1158	—	15.00	25.00	40.00	—
AH1159	—	10.00	18.50	32.50	—

Mint: Mashhad
KM# 373.2 SHAHI

1.1500 g., Silver **Obv:** Inscription **Rev:** Inscription within beaded circle **Note:** Type C.

Date	Mintage	F	VF	XF	Unc
AH1150	—	10.00	20.00	35.00	—
AH1151	—	10.00	20.00	35.00	—
AH1152	—	10.00	20.00	35.00	—

Mint: Mashhad
KM# 383.4 SHAHI

1.1500 g., Silver **Obv:** Inscription, hole at right **Rev:** Inscription within flower design, hole at right **Note:** Type D.

Date	Mintage	F	VF	XF	Unc
ND	—	20.00	32.50	50.00	—
AH1152	—	15.00	25.00	40.00	—
AH1154	—	15.00	25.00	40.00	—
AH1156	—	20.00	30.00	50.00	—

Mint: Qazvin
KM# 367.2 SHAHI

1.3500 g., Silver **Note:** Type B.

Date	Mintage	F	VF	XF	Unc
AHxxxx	—	30.00	50.00	75.00	—

Mint: Rasht
KM# 360.2 SHAHI

1.3500 g., Silver **Note:** Type A.

Date	Mintage	F	VF	XF	Unc
AH114x	—	25.00	42.50	60.00	—

Mint: Shamakha
KM# 367.3 SHAHI

1.3500 g., Silver **Note:** Type B.

Date	Mintage	F	VF	XF	Unc
AH1149	—	20.00	35.00	50.00	—

Mint: Shiraz
KM# 373.3 SHAHI

1.1500 g., Silver **Obv:** Inscription **Rev:** Inscription within beaded circle **Note:** Type C.

Date	Mintage	F	VF	XF	Unc
AH1151	—	20.00	35.00	55.00	—

Mint: Tabriz
KM# 367.4 SHAHI

1.3500 g., Silver **Note:** Type B.

Date	Mintage	F	VF	XF	Unc
AH1149	—	35.00	60.00	90.00	—

Mint: Tabriz
KM# 373.4 SHAHI

1.1500 g., Silver **Obv:** Inscription **Rev:** Inscription within beaded circle **Note:** Type C.

Date	Mintage	F	VF	XF	Unc
AH1150	—	25.00	40.00	60.00	—
AH1151	—	25.00	40.00	60.00	—

Mint: Tabriz
KM# 383.5 SHAHI

1.1500 g., Silver **Obv:** Inscription, hole at right **Rev:** Inscription within flower design, hole at right **Note:** Type D.

Date	Mintage	F	VF	XF	Unc
AH1152	—	15.00	25.00	40.00	—
AH1153	—	50.00	75.00	125	—
AH1154	—	15.00	25.00	40.00	—
AH1155	—	20.00	32.50	50.00	—
AH1156	—	15.00	25.00	40.00	—
AH1157	—	15.00	25.00	40.00	—
AH1158	—	15.00	25.00	40.00	—

Mint: Tiflis
KM# 367.5 SHAHI

1.3500 g., Silver **Note:** Type B.

Date	Mintage	F	VF	XF	Unc
AH1149	—	50.00	75.00	100	—

Mint: Tiflis
KM# 373.5 SHAHI

1.1500 g., Silver **Obv:** Inscription **Rev:** Inscription within beaded circle **Note:** Type C.

Date	Mintage	F	VF	XF	Unc
AH1152	—	30.00	50.00	75.00	—

Mint: Ahmadabad
KM# 384.1 2 SHAHI

2.3000 g., Silver **Note:** Type D

Date	Mintage	VG	F	VF	XF	Unc
AH1152 Rare	—	—	—	—	—	—

Mint: Bukhara
KM# 374 2 SHAHI

2.3000 g., Silver **Obv:** Inscription **Rev:** Inscription, date **Note:** Type C.

Date	Mintage	F	VF	XF	Unc
AH1153	—	75.00	125	200	—

Mint: Eravan
KM# 361 2 SHAHI

2.7000 g., Silver **Obv:** Inscription **Rev:** Toughra type design **Note:** Type A.

Date	Mintage	F	VF	XF	Unc
AH1148	—	50.00	75.00	100	—

Mint: Ganjah
KM# 368.1 2 SHAHI

2.7000 g., Silver **Note:** Type B.

Date	Mintage	F	VF	XF	Unc
AH1150	—	50.00	75.00	100	—

Mint: Isfahan
KM# 384 2 SHAHI

2.3000 g., Silver **Obv:** Inscription **Rev:** Inscription within small circle **Note:** Type D.

Date	Mintage	F	VF	XF	Unc
AH1157	—	40.00	65.00	100	—

Mint: Isfahan
KM# 384.2 2 SHAHI

2.3000 g., Silver **Note:** Type D

Date	Mintage	Good	VG	F	VF	XF
AH1157	—	8.00	20.00	40.00	65.00	100

Mint: Mazandaran
KM# A352.2 2 SHAHI

2.7000 g., Silver **Note:** Type A. Varieties exist.

Date	Mintage	F	VF	XF	Unc
AH1144	—	40.00	65.00	90.00	—
AH1148	—	40.00	65.00	90.00	—

Mint: Shamakha
KM# 368.2 2 SHAHI

2.7000 g., Silver **Note:** Type B.

Date	Mintage	F	VF	XF	Unc
AH1149	—	50.00	75.00	100	—

Mint: Tabriz
KM# 368.3 2 SHAHI

2.7000 g., Silver **Note:** Type B.

Date	Mintage	F	VF	XF	Unc
AH1150	—	30.00	50.00	70.00	—

Mint: Tiflis
KM# 368.4 2 SHAHI

2.7000 g., Silver **Note:** Type B.

Date	Mintage	F	VF	XF	Unc
AH1149	—	35.00	55.00	80.00	—
AH1150	—	35.00	55.00	80.00	—

Mint: Eravan
KM# 362.1 ABBASI

5.4000 g., Silver **Obv:** Toughra type design in center **Rev:** Inscription **Note:** Type A.

Date	Mintage	F	VF	XF	Unc
AH1148	—	25.00	40.00	60.00	—

Mint: Ganjah
KM# 369.1 ABBASI

5.4000 g., Silver **Obv:** Inscription **Rev:** Inscription within flower design **Note:** Type B.

Date	Mintage	F	VF	XF	Unc
AH1150	—	40.00	65.00	90.00	—

Mint: Ganjah
KM# 375.1 ABBASI

4.6000 g., Silver **Note:** Type C.

Date	Mintage	F	VF	XF	Unc
AH1151 Rare	—	—	—	—	—

Mint: Isfahan
KM# 362.2 ABBASI

5.4000 g., Silver **Obv:** Toughra type design in center **Rev:** Inscription **Note:** Type A.

Date	Mintage	F	VF	XF	Unc
AH1148	—	25.00	40.00	60.00	—

Mint: Isfahan
KM# 369.2 ABBASI

5.4000 g., Silver **Obv:** Inscription **Rev:** Inscription within flower design **Note:** Type B.

Date	Mintage	F	VF	XF	Unc
AH1149	—	17.50	25.00	40.00	—

Mint: Kirman
KM# 362.3 ABBASI

5.4000 g., Silver **Obv:** Toughra type design in center **Rev:** Inscription **Note:** Type A.

Date	Mintage	F	VF	XF	Unc
AH1148	—	30.00	45.00	70.00	—

Mint: Kirman
KM# 352.2 ABBASI

5.4000 g., Silver **Obv:** Inscription **Rev:** Inscription **Note:** Type A. Varieties exist.

Date	Mintage	F	VF	XF	Unc
AHxxxx	—	25.00	40.00	65.00	—

Mint: Mashhad
KM# 362.4 ABBASI

5.4000 g., Silver **Obv:** Toughra type design in center **Rev:** Inscription **Note:** Type A.

Date	Mintage	F	VF	XF	Unc
AH1148	—	50.00	75.00	100	—
AH1149	—	30.00	45.00	70.00	—
AH1150	—	25.00	40.00	60.00	—

Mint: Mashhad
KM# 369.3 ABBASI

5.4000 g., Silver **Obv:** Inscription **Rev:** Inscription within flower design **Note:** Type B.

Date	Mintage	F	VF	XF	Unc
AH1150	—	20.00	30.00	45.00	—

Mint: Mazandaran
KM# 352.4 ABBASI

5.4000 g., Silver **Obv:** Inscription **Rev:** Inscription **Note:** Type A. Varieties exist.

Date	Mintage	F	VF	XF	Unc
AH1143	—	20.00	35.00	55.00	—
AH1144	—	10.00	20.00	30.00	—
AH1146	—	12.50	20.00	30.00	—
AH1148	—	12.50	20.00	30.00	—

Mint: Mazandaran
KM# 369.4 ABBASI

5.4000 g., Silver **Obv:** Inscription **Rev:** Inscription within flower design **Note:** Type B.

Date	Mintage	F	VF	XF	Unc
AH1148	—	30.00	50.00	75.00	—
AH1149	—	30.00	50.00	75.00	—

Mint: Nakhjavan
KM# 362.5 ABBASI

5.4000 g., Silver **Obv:** Toughra type design in center **Rev:** Inscription **Note:** Type A.

Date	Mintage	F	VF	XF	Unc
AH1148	—	30.00	45.00	70.00	—
AH1149	—	25.00	40.00	60.00	—

Mint: Nakhjavan
KM# 369.5 ABBASI

5.4000 g., Silver **Obv:** Inscription **Rev:** Inscription within flower design **Note:** Type B.

Date	Mintage	F	VF	XF	Unc
AH1149	—	40.00	65.00	90.00	—

Mint: Qazvin
KM# 362.6 ABBASI

5.4000 g., Silver **Obv:** Toughra type design in center **Rev:** Inscription **Note:** Type A.

Date	Mintage	F	VF	XF	Unc
AH1148	—	50.00	75.00	100	—
AH1149	—	35.00	55.00	75.00	—

Mint: Rasht
KM# 352.5 ABBASI

5.4000 g., Silver **Obv:** Inscription **Rev:** Inscription **Note:** Type A. Varieties exist.

Date	Mintage	F	VF	XF	Unc
AH1147	—	15.00	25.00	40.00	—
AH1148	—	15.00	25.00	40.00	—

Mint: Shiraz
KM# 362.7 ABBASI

5.4000 g., Silver **Obv:** Toughra type design in center **Rev:** Inscription **Note:** Type A.

Date	Mintage	F	VF	XF	Unc
AH1148	—	25.00	40.00	65.00	—
AH1149	—	25.00	40.00	60.00	—

Mint: Shiraz
KM# 369.7 ABBASI

5.4000 g., Silver **Obv:** Inscription **Rev:** Inscription within flower design **Note:** Type B.

Date	Mintage	F	VF	XF	Unc
AH1149	—	20.00	30.00	45.00	—

Mint: Simnan
KM# 352.6 ABBASI

5.4000 g., Silver **Obv:** Inscription **Rev:** Inscription **Note:** Type A. Varieties exist.

Date	Mintage	F	VF	XF	Unc
AH1142	—	—	—	—	—
Note: Reported, not confirmed					
AH1144	—	20.00	30.00	45.00	—

Mint: Tabriz
KM# 369.8 ABBASI

5.4000 g., Silver **Obv:** Inscription **Rev:** Inscription within flower design **Note:** Type B.

Date	Mintage	F	VF	XF	Unc
AH1149	—	25.00	40.00	60.00	—
AH1150	—	25.00	40.00	60.00	—

Mint: Tiflis
KM# 362.8 ABBASI

5.4000 g., Silver **Obv:** Toughra type design in center **Rev:** Inscription **Note:** Type A.

Date	Mintage	F	VF	XF	Unc
AH1148	—	50.00	75.00	100	—
AH1149	—	50.00	75.00	100	—

Mint: Tiflis
KM# 369.9 ABBASI

5.4000 g., Silver **Obv:** Inscription **Rev:** Inscription within flower design **Note:** Type B.

Date	Mintage	F	VF	XF	Unc
AH1149	—	20.00	30.00	45.00	—
AH1150	—	20.00	30.00	45.00	—
AH1151	—	20.00	30.00	45.00	—

Mint: Tiflis
KM# 375.2 ABBASI

4.6000 g., Silver **Note:** Type C.

Date	Mintage	F	VF	XF	Unc
AH1151 Rare	—	—	—	—	—

Mint: Yazd
KM# 352.7 ABBASI

5.4000 g., Silver **Obv:** Inscription **Rev:** Inscription **Note:** Type A. Varieties exist.

Date	Mintage	F	VF	XF	Unc
AH1144	—	40.00	65.00	100	—

Mint: Isfahan
KM# 376.1 6 SHAHI

6.9000 g., Silver **Obv:** Inscription **Rev:** Inscription within small circle in center **Note:** Type C.

Date	Mintage	F	VF	XF	Unc
AH1150	—	4.00	7.00	12.50	—
AH1151	—	4.00	7.00	12.50	—
AH1152	—	4.00	7.00	12.50	—

Mint: Mashhad
KM# 376.2 6 SHAHI

6.9000 g., Silver **Obv:** Inscription **Rev:** Inscription within small circle in center **Note:** Type C.

Date	Mintage	F	VF	XF	Unc
AH1150	—	4.00	7.00	12.50	—

Date	Mintage	F	VF	XF	Unc
AH1151	—	4.00	7.00	12.50	—
AH1152	—	5.00	8.50	15.00	—

Mint: Qandahar
KM# 376.4 6 SHAHI
6.9000 g., Silver **Obv:** Inscription **Rev:** Inscription within small circle in center **Note:** Type C.

Date	Mintage	F	VF	XF	Unc
AH1150	—	10.00	17.50	30.00	—
AH1151	—	—	—	—	—

Note: Reported, not confirmed

Mint: Shiraz
KM# 376.5 6 SHAHI
6.9000 g., Silver **Obv:** Inscription **Rev:** Inscription within small circle in center **Note:** Type C.

Date	Mintage	F	VF	XF	Unc
AH1150	—	5.00	8.50	15.00	—
AH1151	—	5.00	8.50	15.00	—

Mint: Tabriz
KM# 376.6 6 SHAHI
6.9000 g., Silver **Obv:** Inscription **Rev:** Inscription within small circle in center **Note:** Type C.

Date	Mintage	F	VF	XF	Unc
AH1150	—	4.00	7.00	12.50	—
AH1151	—	4.00	7.00	12.50	—
AH1152	—	4.00	7.00	12.50	—

Mint: Tiflis
KM# 376.7 6 SHAHI
6.9000 g., Silver **Obv:** Inscription **Rev:** Inscription within small circle in center **Note:** Type C.

Date	Mintage	F	VF	XF	Unc
AH1150	—	5.00	8.50	15.00	—
AH1151	—	5.00	8.50	15.00	—
AH1152	—	5.00	8.50	15.00	—

Mint: Ahmadabad
KM# 385A.1 RUPI
11.5000 g., Silver **Rev. Inscription:** "Khalad Allah Mulkahu" added **Note:** Type D.2

Date	Mintage	Good	VG	F	VF	XF
AH1152	—	30.00	—	75.00	150	250

Mint: Azimabad
KM# 385B RUPI
11.5000 g., Silver **Note:** Type E.

Date	Mintage	Good	VG	F	VF	XF
AH1151 Rare	—	—	—	—	—	—

Mint: Bhakkar
KM# 385A.2 RUPI
11.5000 g., Silver **Rev. Inscription:** "Khalad Allah Mulkahu" added **Note:** Type D. Previous Afghanistan KM# A280.

Date	Mintage	Good	VG	F	VF	XF
AH1153	—	6.00	15.00	30.00	50.00	75.00
AH1154	—	6.00	15.00	30.00	50.00	75.00
AH1155	—	6.00	15.00	30.00	50.00	75.00
AH1156	—	6.00	15.00	30.00	50.00	75.00
AH1157	—	6.00	15.00	30.00	50.00	75.00
AH1158	—	6.00	15.00	30.00	50.00	75.00
AH1159	—	6.00	15.00	30.00	50.00	75.00
AH1160	—	6.00	15.00	30.00	50.00	75.00

Mint: Derajat
KM# 385A.3 RUPI
11.5000 g., Silver **Rev. Inscription:** "Khalad Allah Mulkahu" added **Note:** Type D.2. Prev. Afghanistan KM# 336.

Date	Mintage	Good	VG	F	VF	XF
AH1158	—	18.00	45.00	90.00	150	225
AH1159	—	12.00	30.00	60.00	100	150
AH1160	—	12.00	30.00	60.00	100	150

Mint: Kabul
KM# 385A.4 RUPI
11.5000 g., Silver **Rev. Inscription:** "Khalad Allah Mulkahu" added **Note:** Type D.2. AH1159 mintname is Qabul while AH1158 and 1160 are Kabul.

Date	Mintage	Good	VG	F	VF	XF
AH1157	—	18.00	45.00	90.00	150	225
AH1158	—	18.00	45.00	90.00	150	225
AH1159	—	25.00	60.00	120	200	300

Mint: Lahore
KM# 385A.5 RUPI
11.5000 g., Silver **Rev. Inscription:** "Khalad Allah Mulkahu" added **Note:** Type D.2

Date	Mintage	Good	VG	F	VF	XF
AH1152 Rare	—	—	—	—	—	—

Mint: Multan
KM# 385A.6 RUPI
11.5000 g., Silver **Rev. Inscription:** "Khalad Allah Mulkahu" and "Dar al-Amân" **Note:** Type D.2

Date	Mintage	Good	VG	F	VF	XF
AH1152	—	25.00	62.50	135	225	335

Mint: Murshidabad
KM# 385C.2 RUPI
11.5000 g., Silver **Note:** Type F.

Date	Mintage	Good	VG	F	VF	XF
AH1151	—	60.00	150	300	500	—
AH1152	—	60.00	150	300	500	—

Mint: Peshawar
KM# 385A.7 RUPI
11.5000 g., Silver **Rev. Inscription:** "Khalad Allah Mulkahu" **Note:** Type D.2. Prev. Afghanistan KM# 685.

Date	Mintage	Good	VG	F	VF	XF
AH1153	—	8.00	20.00	40.00	65.00	100
AH1154	—	9.00	24.00	48.00	80.00	120
AH1155	—	9.00	24.00	48.00	80.00	120
AH1157	—	8.00	20.00	40.00	65.00	100
AH1158	—	8.00	20.00	40.00	65.00	100
AH1159	—	8.00	20.00	40.00	65.00	100
AH1160	—	8.00	20.00	40.00	65.00	100

Mint: Sahrind
KM# 385A.8 RUPI
11.5000 g., Silver **Rev. Inscription:** "Khalad Allah Mulkahu" and "Dar al-Âman" **Note:** Type D.2

Date	Mintage	Good	VG	F	VF	XF
AH1152	—	18.00	45.00	90.00	150	225

Mint: Shahjahanabad
KM# 385A.9 RUPI
11.5000 g., Silver **Rev. Inscription:** "Khalad Allah Mulkahu" and "Dar al-Khilafa" **Note:** Type D.2. Prev. Afghanistan KM# A759.

Date	Mintage	Good	VG	F	VF	XF
AH1151	—	12.00	30.00	60.00	100	150
AH1152	—	12.00	30.00	60.00	100	150

Mint: Shikarpur
KM# 385A.10 RUPI
11.5000 g., Silver **Rev. Inscription:** "Khalad Allah Mulkahu" **Note:** Type D.2

Date	Mintage	Good	VG	F	VF	XF
AH1155 Rare	—	—	—	—	—	—

Mint: Sind
KM# A385.10 RUPI
11.5000 g., Silver **Note:** Type D.1

Date	Mintage	Good	VG	F	VF	XF
ND(1740-47) Date off flan	—	9.00	22.50	45.00	75.00	110
AH1153	—	15.00	37.50	75.00	125	180
AH1155	—	15.00	37.50	75.00	125	180
AH1156	—	18.00	45.00	90.00	150	225
AH1157	—	15.00	37.50	75.00	125	180
AH1158	—	18.00	45.00	90.00	150	225
AH1160	—	20.00	50.00	100	175	260

Mint: Tatta
KM# 385A.11 RUPI
11.5000 g., Silver **Rev. Inscription:** "Khalad Allah Mulkahu" **Note:** Type D.2

Date	Mintage	Good	VG	F	VF	XF
ND(1738-47)	—	25.00	67.50	135	225	335

Mint: Bahkar
KM# 385.1 RUPI
11.5000 g., Silver **Obv:** Inscription **Rev:** Inscription, date within small circle at upper right **Note:** Type D.

Date	Mintage	F	VF	XF	Unc
AH1159	—	—	—	—	—

Mint: Daghistan
KM# 385.2 RUPI
11.5000 g., Silver **Obv:** Inscription **Rev:** Inscription, date within small circle at upper right **Note:** Type D.

Date	Mintage	F	VF	XF	Unc
AH1154	—	100	150	250	—

Mint: Darband
KM# 385.3 RUPI
11.5000 g., Silver **Obv:** Inscription **Rev:** Inscription, date within small circle at upper right **Note:** Type D.

Date	Mintage	F	VF	XF	Unc
AH1154	—	75.00	125	200	—

Mint: Ganjah
KM# 385.4 RUPI
11.5000 g., Silver **Obv:** Inscription **Rev:** Inscription, date within small circle at upper right **Note:** Type D.

Date	Mintage	F	VF	XF	Unc
AH1154	—	40.00	60.00	90.00	—

Mint: Isfahan
KM# 385.5 RUPI
11.5000 g., Silver **Obv:** Inscription **Rev:** Inscription, date within small circle at upper right **Note:** Type D.

Date	Mintage	F	VF	XF	Unc
AH1151	—	15.00	25.00	40.00	—
AH1152	—	8.00	12.50	20.00	—
AH1153	—	8.00	12.50	20.00	—
AH1154	—	8.00	12.50	20.00	—
AH1155	—	8.00	12.50	20.00	—
AH1156	—	8.00	12.50	20.00	—
AH1157	—	8.00	12.50	20.00	—
AH1158	—	8.00	12.50	20.00	—
AH1159	—	8.00	12.50	20.00	—
AH1160	—	8.00	12.50	20.00	—

Mint: Kabul
KM# 385.6 RUPI
11.5000 g., Silver **Obv:** Inscription **Rev:** Inscription, date within small circle at upper right **Note:** Type D.

Date	Mintage	F	VF	XF	Unc
AH1157	—	80.00	125	180	—
AH1160	—	80.00	125	180	—

Mint: Mashhad
KM# 385.7 RUPI
11.5000 g., Silver **Obv:** Inscription **Rev:** Inscription, date within small circle at upper right **Note:** Type D.

Date	Mintage	F	VF	XF	Unc
ND	—	8.00	12.50	20.00	—
AH1151	—	15.00	25.00	40.00	—
AH1152	—	10.00	15.00	25.00	—
AH1153	—	10.00	15.00	25.00	—
AH1154	—	10.00	15.00	25.00	—
AH1155	—	10.00	15.00	25.00	—
AH1156	—	10.00	15.00	25.00	—
AH1157	—	10.00	15.00	25.00	—
AH1158	—	12.50	20.00	30.00	—
AH1159	—	15.00	25.00	40.00	—
AH1160	—	15.00	25.00	40.00	—

Mint: Muhammadabad Banaras
KM# 385C.1 RUPI
11.5000 g., Silver **Note:** Type F.

Date	Mintage	Good	VG	F	VF	XF
AH115x	—	60.00	150	300	500	—

Mint: Nadirabad
KM# 385.8 RUPI
11.5000 g., Silver **Obv:** Inscription **Rev:** Inscription, date within small circle at upper right **Note:** Type D.

Date	Mintage	F	VF	XF	Unc
AH1153	—	45.00	70.00	110	—

Mint: Qazvin
KM# 385.9 RUPI
11.5000 g., Silver **Obv:** Inscription **Rev:** Inscription, date within small circle at upper right **Note:** Type D.

Date	Mintage	F	VF	XF	Unc
AH1153	—	30.00	50.00	75.00	—

Mint: Shiraz
KM# 385.10 RUPI
11.5000 g., Silver **Obv:** Inscription **Rev:** Inscription, date within small circle at upper right **Note:** Type D.

Date	Mintage	F	VF	XF	Unc
AH1152	—	20.00	32.50	50.00	—
AH1153	—	20.00	32.50	50.00	—

Mint: Tabriz
KM# 385.11 RUPI
11.5000 g., Silver **Obv:** Inscription **Rev:** Inscription, date within small circle at upper right **Note:** Type D.

Date	Mintage	F	VF	XF	Unc
AH1152	—	8.00	12.50	20.00	—
AH1153	—	8.00	12.50	20.00	—
AH1154	—	8.00	12.50	20.00	—
AH1155	—	8.00	12.50	20.00	—
AH1156	—	8.00	12.50	20.00	—
AH1157	—	8.00	12.50	20.00	—
AH1158	—	8.00	12.50	20.00	—
AH1159	—	8.00	12.50	20.00	—
AH1160	—	8.00	12.50	20.00	—

Mint: Tiflis
KM# 385.12 RUPI
11.5000 g., Silver **Obv:** Inscription **Rev:** Inscription, date within small circle at upper right **Note:** Type D.

Date	Mintage	F	VF	XF	Unc
AH1152	—	20.00	32.50	50.00	—
AH1159	—	25.00	40.00	60.00	—

Mint: Kabul
KM# 377.1 2 RUPI
23.0000 g., Silver **Obv:** Inscription within beaded circle **Rev:** Inscription **Note:** Type C.

Date	Mintage	F	VF	XF	Unc
AHxxxx	—	75.00	125	200	—

Mint: Lahore
KM# 377.2 2 RUPI
23.0000 g., Silver **Obv:** Inscription within beaded circle **Rev:** Inscription **Note:** Type C.

Date	Mintage	F	VF	XF	Unc
AH1152	—	75.00	125	200	—

Mint: Mashhad
KM# 377.3 2 RUPI
23.0000 g., Silver **Obv:** Inscription within beaded circle **Rev:** Inscription **Note:** Type C.

Date	Mintage	F	VF	XF	Unc
AH1151	—	60.00	90.00	140	—

Mint: Multan
KM# 385D 2 RUPI
23.0000 g., Silver **Rev. Inscription:** "Dar al-Amân **Note:** Type D.2

Date	Mintage	Good	VG	F	VF	XF
AH1152 Rare	—	—	—	—	—	—

Mint: Nadirabad
KM# 377.4 2 RUPI
23.0000 g., Silver **Obv:** Inscription within beaded circle **Rev:** Inscription **Note:** Type C.

Date	Mintage	F	VF	XF	Unc
AH1151	—	30.00	50.00	85.00	—

Mint: Peshawar
KM# 377.6 2 RUPI
23.0000 g., Silver **Obv:** Inscription within beaded circle **Rev:** Inscription **Note:** Type C.

Date	Mintage	F	VF	XF	Unc
AH1151	—	75.00	125	200	—

Mint: Qandahar
KM# 377.5 2 RUPI
23.0000 g., Silver **Obv:** Inscription within beaded circle **Rev:** Inscription **Note:** Type C.

Date	Mintage	F	VF	XF	Unc
AH1150	—	25.00	40.00	70.00	—
AH1151	—	35.00	60.00	100	—

Mint: Isfahan
KM# 363.1 ASHRAFI
3.5000 g., Gold **Obv:** Inscription **Rev:** Inscription within center circle **Note:** Type A.

Date	Mintage	F	VF	XF	Unc
AH1148	—	150	200	275	—

Mint: Isfahan
KM# 378.1 ASHRAFI
3.5000 g., Gold **Obv:** Inscription within small circle in center **Rev:** Inscription **Note:** Type C.

Date	Mintage	F	VF	XF	Unc
AH1151	—	150	200	250	—
AH1152	—	175	225	300	—

Mint: Isfahan
KM# 388.1 ASHRAFI
3.5000 g., Gold **Note:** Type D.

Date	Mintage	F	VF	XF	Unc
AH1152	—	150	225	325	—
AH1159	—	—	—	—	—

Note: Reported, not confirmed

Mint: Mashhad
KM# 363.2 ASHRAFI
3.5000 g., Gold **Obv:** Inscription **Rev:** Inscription within center circle **Note:** Type A.

Date	Mintage	F	VF	XF	Unc
AH1149	—	150	200	275	—
AH1150	—	150	200	275	—

Mint: Mashhad
KM# 378.2 ASHRAFI
3.5000 g., Gold **Obv:** Inscription within small circle in center **Rev:** Inscription **Note:** Type C.

Date	Mintage	F	VF	XF	Unc
AH1150	—	150	200	250	—
AH1151	—	150	200	250	—

Mint: Mashhad
KM# 388.2 ASHRAFI
3.5000 g., Gold **Note:** Type D.

Date	Mintage	F	VF	XF	Unc
ND	—	125	160	225	—

Mint: Shiraz
KM# 363.3 ASHRAFI
3.5000 g., Gold **Obv:** Inscription **Rev:** Inscription within center circle **Note:** Type A.

Date	Mintage	F	VF	XF	Unc
AH1149	—	150	200	275	—

Mint: Shiraz
KM# 370 ASHRAFI
3.5000 g., Gold **Note:** Type B.

Date	Mintage	F	VF	XF	Unc
AH1150	—	150	200	250	—

Mint: Shiraz
KM# 378.3 ASHRAFI
3.5000 g., Gold **Obv:** Inscription within small circle in center **Rev:** Inscription **Note:** Type C.

Date	Mintage	F	VF	XF	Unc
AH1151	—	175	225	300	—

Mint: Tabriz
KM# 363.4 ASHRAFI
3.5000 g., Gold **Obv:** Inscription **Rev:** Inscription within center circle **Note:** Type A.

Date	Mintage	F	VF	XF	Unc
AH1149	—	150	200	275	—

Mint: Tabriz
KM# 378.4 ASHRAFI
3.5000 g., Gold **Obv:** Inscription within small circle in center **Rev:** Inscription **Note:** Type C.

Date	Mintage	F	VF	XF	Unc
AH1151	—	175	225	300	—

Mint: Tiflis
KM# 378.5 ASHRAFI
3.5000 g., Gold **Obv:** Inscription within small circle in center **Rev:** Inscription **Note:** Type C.

Date	Mintage	F	VF	XF	Unc
AH1152	—	175	225	300	—

Mint: Bahkar
KM# 390.1 ASHRAFI
11.0000 g., Gold **Note:** Type D.2

Date	Mintage	Good	VG	F	VF	XF
AH1158 Rare	—	—	—	—	—	—

Mint: Derajat
KM# 390.2 ASHRAFI
11.0000 g., Gold **Note:** Type D.2

Date	Mintage	Good	VG	F	VF	XF
AH1159	—	—	425	850	1,250	—
AH1160	—	—	425	850	1,250	—

Mint: Isfahan
KM# 389.1 ASHRAFI
11.0000 g., Gold **Obv:** Inscription **Rev:** Inscription within small circle in center **Note:** Type D.

Date	Mintage	F	VF	XF	Unc
AH1153	—	150	200	300	—
AH1154	—	150	200	300	—
AH1156	—	150	200	300	—
AH1157	—	150	200	300	—
AH1158	—	150	200	300	—
AH1159	—	150	200	300	—
AH1160	—	150	200	300	—

Mint: Kabul
KM# 390.3 ASHRAFI
11.0000 g., Gold **Note:** Type D.2

Date	Mintage	Good	VG	F	VF	XF
AH1157	—	—	225	450	650	—
AH1160	—	—	225	450	650	—

Mint: Mashhad
KM# 379.1 ASHRAFI
11.0000 g., Gold **Note:** Type C.

Date	Mintage	F	VF	XF	Unc
AH1150	—	250	350	550	—

Mint: Mashhad
KM# 389.2 ASHRAFI
11.0000 g., Gold **Obv:** Inscription **Rev:** Inscription within small circle in center **Note:** Type D.

Date	Mintage	F	VF	XF	Unc
AH1156	—	150	200	300	—
AH1157	—	175	225	340	—

Mint: Peshawar
KM# 390.4 ASHRAFI
11.0000 g., Gold **Note:** Type D.2

Date	Mintage	Good	VG	F	VF	XF
AH1154	—	—	350	700	1,000	—
AH1155	—	—	350	700	1,000	—
AH1157	—	—	350	700	1,000	—
AH1159	—	—	350	700	1,000	—

Mint: Shiraz
KM# 379.2 ASHRAFI
11.0000 g., Gold **Note:** Type C.

Date	Mintage	F	VF	XF	Unc
AH1151	—	—	—	—	—

Note: Reported, not confirmed

Mint: Sind
KM# 389.4 ASHRAFI
11.0000 g., Gold **Note:** Type D.1

Date	Mintage	Good	VG	F	VF	XF
ND(1738-47)	—	—	265	525	750	—

Mint: Tabriz
KM# 389.3 ASHRAFI
11.0000 g., Gold **Obv:** Inscription **Rev:** Inscription within small circle in center **Note:** Type D.

Date	Mintage	F	VF	XF	Unc
AH1154	—	150	200	300	—
AH1157	—	150	200	300	—
AH1158	—	150	200	300	—

Mint: Without Mint Name
KM# 386 1/12 MOHUR
0.9000 g., Gold **Note:** Type D.

Date	Mintage	F	VF	XF	Unc
AH1158 Isfahan	—	125	160	225	—

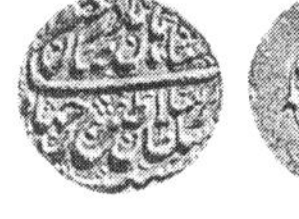

Mint: Isfahan
KM# 387 1/6 MOHUR
1.8300 g., Gold **Obv:** Inscription **Rev:** Inscription within small circle in center **Note:** Type D.

Date	Mintage	F	VF	XF	Unc
AH115x	—	100	150	200	—

Shahrukh, Viceroy at Herat
AH1151-1160 / 1739-1747AD

Type for this ruler:

A. Couplet, divided on the two faces of the coin, with the date added to obverse or reverse field.

Amr shod az shah-e shahan Nader-e Sahebqeran Sekke yabad az Harat az Shahrokh nam o neshan.

"It was ordered by the king of kings, Nadir, the Sahebqiran, that the coin of Herat should bear the name and sign of Shahrukh."

HAMMERED COINAGE

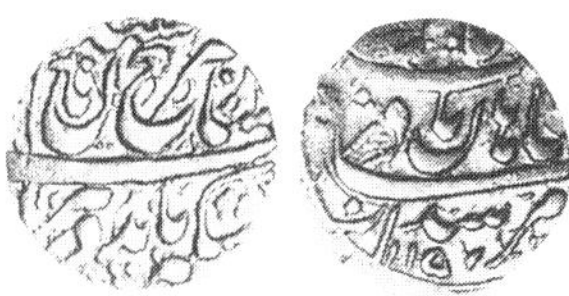

Mint: Herat
KM# 431 RUPI
11.5000 g., Silver **Obv:** Inscription **Rev:** Inscription **Note:** Type A.

Date	Mintage	F	VF	XF	Unc
ND	—	15.00	25.00	45.00	—
AH1153	—	25.00	40.00	65.00	—
AH1155	—	25.00	40.00	65.00	—
AH1157	—	25.00	40.00	65.00	—
AH1159	—	25.00	40.00	65.00	—

Adel Shah (Ali)
AH1160-1161 / 1747-1748AD

Types for this reign:

A. Obverse short couplet, as below, with mint below, and date, if any, somewhere in the field. Reverse, the Shiite formula, sometimes with the names of the 12 Imams in a surrounding marginal legend.

Gasht rayej be-hokm-e Lam-Yazli Sekke-ye Saltanat be-nam-e Ali.

"By the order of the Eternal One, the coin of the sultanate has become current in the name of Ali." Ali was another name of Adel Shah.

On some examples, the word *be-hokm-e* is replaced by *be-amr-e*, with the same meaning.

B. Obverse long couplet, with mint and date below. Reverse, the Shiite formula.

Za ba'd-e dorr-e douran-e edalat sekke bar zar shod Be-nam-e shah-e din Soltan Ali alam monavvar shod.

"After the pearl of the age of justice (i.e., Nadir Shah), coin was struck in precious metal. In the name of the king of the faith, Sultan Ali, the world was illuminated." This difficult passage is replete with wordplays lost in translation. Sultan Ali here refers simultaneously to Adel Shah himself, to Ali ibn Abi Talib, and to the eighth Shiite Imam (to whom the evocation on type C).

C. Obverse evocation of the eighth Imam, *Ya 'Ali ebn-e Musa al-Reza,* O Ali, son of Musa, al-Reza." Reverse as type A. Type C in anonymous, and many have been struck largely during the interregnum of a couple months that followed the overthrow of Adel Shah.

HAMMERED COINAGE

Mint: Isfahan
KM# 401.1 SHAHI
1.1500 g., Silver **Note:** Type A.

Date	Mintage	F	VF	XF	Unc
AHxxxx	—	20.00	40.00	65.00	—

Mint: Mashhad
KM# 401.2 SHAHI
1.1500 g., Silver **Note:** Type A.

Date	Mintage	F	VF	XF	Unc
AH1160	—	25.00	45.00	75.00	—

Mint: Mazandaran
KM# 401.3 SHAHI
1.1500 g., Silver **Note:** Type A.

Date	Mintage	F	VF	XF	Unc
AH1161	—	25.00	45.00	75.00	—

Mint: Qazvin
KM# 401.4 SHAHI
1.1500 g., Silver **Note:** Type A.

Date	Mintage	F	VF	XF	Unc
AH1160	—	25.00	45.00	75.00	—

Mint: Herat
KM# 402.1 ABBASI
4.6000 g., Silver **Obv:** Inscription **Rev:** Inscription **Note:** Type A.

Date	Mintage	F	VF	XF	Unc
AH1160	—	15.00	25.00	40.00	—

Mint: Isfahan
KM# 402.2 ABBASI
4.6000 g., Silver **Obv:** Inscription **Rev:** Inscription **Note:** Type A.

Date	Mintage	F	VF	XF	Unc
AH1160	—	6.00	10.00	16.00	—
AH1161	—	6.00	10.00	16.00	—

Mint: Isfahan
KM# 407.1 ABBASI
4.6000 g., Silver **Note:** Type C.

Date	Mintage	F	VF	XF	Unc
AH1160	—	20.00	35.00	50.00	—
AH1161	—	8.00	14.00	22.50	—

Mint: Mashhad
KM# 402.3 ABBASI
4.6000 g., Silver **Obv:** Inscription **Rev:** Inscription **Note:** Type A.

Date	Mintage	F	VF	XF	Unc
AH1160	—	7.00	11.50	18.00	—
AH1161	—	7.00	11.50	18.00	—

Mint: Mazandaran
KM# 405 ABBASI
4.6000 g., Silver **Obv:** Inscription **Rev:** Inscription **Note:** Type B.

Date	Mintage	F	VF	XF	Unc
AH1161	—	30.00	50.00	80.00	—

Mint: Qazvin
KM# 402.4 ABBASI
4.6000 g., Silver **Obv:** Inscription **Rev:** Inscription **Note:** Type A.

Date	Mintage	F	VF	XF	Unc
AH1160	—	6.00	10.00	16.00	—
AH1161	—	6.00	10.00	16.00	—

Mint: Qazvin
KM# 407.2 ABBASI
4.6000 g., Silver **Note:** Type C.

Date	Mintage	F	VF	XF	Unc
AH1161	—	6.00	10.00	17.50	—

Mint: Rasht
KM# 407.3 ABBASI
4.6000 g., Silver **Note:** Type C.

Date	Mintage	F	VF	XF	Unc
AH1161	—	20.00	35.00	50.00	—
AH1163 (sic)	—	25.00	45.00	75.00	—

Mint: Shiraz
KM# 402.5 ABBASI
4.6000 g., Silver **Obv:** Inscription **Rev:** Inscription **Note:** Type A.

Date	Mintage	F	VF	XF	Unc
AH1160	—	7.00	11.50	18.00	—
AH1161	—	6.00	10.00	16.00	—

Mint: Tabriz
KM# 402.6 ABBASI
4.6000 g., Silver **Obv:** Inscription **Rev:** Inscription **Note:** Type A.

Date	Mintage	F	VF	XF	Unc
AH1160	—	8.00	12.50	20.00	—
AH1161	—	10.00	16.00	25.00	—

Mint: Tabriz
KM# 407.4 ABBASI
4.6000 g., Silver **Note:** Type C.

Date	Mintage	F	VF	XF	Unc
AH1161	—	25.00	45.00	75.00	—

Mint: Herat
KM# 403.1 RUPI
11.5000 g., Silver **Note:** Type A.

Date	Mintage	F	VF	XF	Unc
AH1160	—	15.00	25.00	40.00	—
AH1161	—	15.00	25.00	40.00	—

Mint: Herat
KM# 408.1 RUPI
11.5000 g., Silver **Obv:** Inscription **Rev:** Inscription **Note:** Type C.

Date	Mintage	F	VF	XF	Unc
AH1160 Herat	—	45.00	70.00	125	—

Mint: Kirman
KM# 408.2 RUPI
11.5000 g., Silver **Obv:** Inscription **Rev:** Inscription **Note:** Type C.

Date	Mintage	F	VF	XF	Unc
AH1161	—	35.00	60.00	100	—
AH1162	—	40.00	70.00	120	—

Mint: Mashhad
KM# 403.2 RUPI
11.5000 g., Silver **Note:** Type A.

Date	Mintage	F	VF	XF	Unc
AH1161	—	15.00	25.00	40.00	—

Mint: Mashhad
KM# 408.4 RUPI
11.5000 g., Silver **Note:** Type C. With this type, the Shiite formula is arranged with the last words "Ali Wali Allah" in a central circle. The rest of the formula is written around in a circle.

Date	Mintage	F	VF	XF	Unc
AH1161	—	8.00	14.00	25.00	—

Mint: Mazandaran
KM# 403.3 RUPI
11.5000 g., Silver **Note:** Type A.

Date	Mintage	F	VF	XF	Unc
AH1161	—	22.50	35.00	50.00	—

Mint: Mazandaran
KM# 406 RUPI
11.5000 g., Silver **Obv:** Inscription **Rev:** Inscription **Note:** Type B.

Date	Mintage	F	VF	XF	Unc
AH1161	—	40.00	75.00	125	—

Mint: Rasht
KM# 408.3 RUPI
11.5000 g., Silver **Obv:** Inscription **Rev:** Inscription **Note:** Type C.

Date	Mintage	F	VF	XF	Unc
AH1160	—	20.00	35.00	50.00	—
AH1161	—	10.00	16.00	27.50	—
AH1162	—	10.00	16.00	27.50	—

Mint: Herat
KM# 404.1 2 RUPI
23.0000 g., Silver **Obv:** Inscription within circle in center **Rev:** Inscription **Note:** Type A. With this type, the Shiite formula is arranged with the last words "Ali Wali Allah" in a central circle. The rest of the formula is written around in a circle.

Date	Mintage	F	VF	XF	Unc
AH1161 Herat	—	60.00	100	150	—

Mint: Mashhad
KM# A404.2 2 RUPI
11.5000 g., Silver **Obv:** Inscription **Rev:** Inscription **Note:** Type A. Formula similar to 1 Rupi, KM#408.2.

Date	Mintage	F	VF	XF	Unc
AH1161	—	15.00	25.00	45.00	—

Mint: Mashhad
KM# 404.2 2 RUPI
23.0000 g., Silver **Obv:** Inscription within circle in center **Rev:** Inscription **Note:** Type A. With this type, the Shiite formula is arranged with the last words "Ali Wali Allah" in a central circle. The rest of the formula is written around in a circle.

Date	Mintage	F	VF	XF	Unc
AH1160	—	45.00	75.00	125	—

Mint: Mashhad
KM# 410 2 RUPI
11.5000 g., Silver **Obv:** Inscription **Rev:** Inscription **Note:** Type C.

Date	Mintage	F	VF	XF	Unc
AH1161	—	100	150	200	—

Mint: Isfahan
KM# 411 MOHUR
11.0000 g., Gold **Note:** Type C.

Date	Mintage	F	VF	XF	Unc
AH1161 Rare	—	—	—	—	—

Sam Mirza
AH1160 / 1747AD

Types for this reign:

A. Obverse title and name of the ruler, *Bande-ye shah-e velayat Sam ebn-e Soltan Hoseyn,* plus mint and date. Reverse, Shiite formula.

B. Obverse couplet. Reverse, the Shiite formula in central circle, the names of the 12 Imams around.

Sekkeh zad bar zar be-giti chun tolu-e neyreyn Vareth-e molk-e Soleyman Sam ebn-e Soltan Hoseyn.

"Heir to the kingdom of Solomon, Sam, son of Sultan, Husayn, has struck coin in precious metal in the world, like the rise of the two brilliances (i.e., the sun and the moon)."

HAMMERED COINAGE

Mint: Tabriz
KM# 427 SHAHI
1.1500 g., Silver **Note:** Type A.

Date	Mintage	F	VF	XF	Unc
AH1160	—	50.00	90.00	150	—

Mint: Tabriz
KM# 429 ABBASI
4.6000 g., Silver **Obv:** Inscription **Rev:** Inscription **Note:** Type B.

Date	Mintage	F	VF	XF	Unc
AH1160	—	65.00	110	200	—

Mint: Tabriz
KM# 428 5 SHAHI
5.7500 g., Silver **Obv:** Inscription **Rev:** Inscription **Note:** Type A. Rectangular flan.

Date	Mintage	F	VF	XF	Unc
AH1160	—	100	175	275	—

Amir Arslan Khan at Tabriz
AH1161 / 1748AD
HAMMERED COINAGE

Mint: Tabriz
KM# 418 SHAHI
1.1500 g., Silver **Note:** Type A.

Date	Mintage	F	VF	XF	Unc
AH1161	—	35.00	60.00	100	—

Mint: Tabriz
KM# 419 ABBASI
4.6000 g., Silver **Obv:** Inscription **Rev:** Inscription **Note:** Type A.

Date	Mintage	F	VF	XF	Unc
AH1161	—	20.00	35.00	65.00	—
AH1162	—	40.00	70.00	110	—

Mint: Tabriz
KM# 420 ASHRAFI
3.5000 g., Gold **Note:** Type A.

Date	Mintage	F	VF	XF	Unc
AH1161 Rare	—	—	—	—	—

Ibrahim

AH1161-1162 / 1748-1749AD

Types for this reign:

A. Obverse couplet, reverse mint and date, the mint usual with its epithet.

Sekke-ye sahebqerani zad be-toufiq-e Allah Hamcho khorshid-e jahan-afruz Ebrahim Shah.

"Like the world-illuminating sun, Irbahim Shah has struck, by God's favor, the Sahebqirani coin."

B. As type A, but with a different couplet:

Beneshast cho aftab naqsh-e zar o sim Ta yaft sharaf za sekke-ye Ebrahim.

"The image of gold and silver remained like the sun not yet risen, until it received the honor of the stamp of Ibrahim."

D. Obverse, the name *al-Sultan Ebrahim.* Reverse, the benediction *khalad Allah mulkahu* as on Nadir Shah's type C, together with the mint and date. Struck only at Astarabad & Ganja.

HAMMERED COINAGE

Mint: Ganjah
KM# 421.1 SHAHI
1.1500 g., Silver **Note:** Type D.

Date	Mintage	F	VF	XF	Unc
AH1162 Ganja	—	30.00	50.00	75.00	—

Mint: Tabriz
KM# A415 SHAHI
1.1500 g., Silver **Note:** Type B.

Date	Mintage	F	VF	XF	Unc
AH1161	—	40.00	70.00	115	—

Mint: Tabriz
KM# 421.2 SHAHI
1.1500 g., Silver **Note:** Type D.

Date	Mintage	F	VF	XF	Unc
AH1162	—	25.00	40.00	60.00	—

Mint: Tiflis
KM# 421.3 SHAHI
1.1500 g., Silver **Note:** Type D.

Date	Mintage	F	VF	XF	Unc
AH1162	—	25.00	40.00	60.00	—

Mint: Tabriz
KM# 415 2 SHAHI
2.3000 g., Silver **Note:** Type B.

Date	Mintage	F	VF	XF	Unc
AH1162	—	40.00	70.00	115	—

Mint: Astarabad
KM# 413.1 ABBASI
4.6000 g., Silver **Obv:** Inscription **Rev:** Inscription within circle in center **Note:** Type A.

Date	Mintage	F	VF	XF	Unc
AH116x Astarabad	—	30.00	45.00	70.00	—

Mint: Astarabad
KM# 416.1 ABBASI
4.6000 g., Silver **Note:** Type B.

Date	Mintage	F	VF	XF	Unc
AHxxxx	—	30.00	45.00	70.00	—

Mint: Ganjah
KM# 413.2 ABBASI
4.6000 g., Silver **Obv:** Inscription **Rev:** Inscription within circle in center **Note:** Type A.

Date	Mintage	F	VF	XF	Unc
AH1162	—	40.00	65.00	100	—

Mint: Shiraz
KM# 413.3 ABBASI
4.6000 g., Silver **Obv:** Inscription **Rev:** Inscription within circle in center **Note:** Type A.

Date	Mintage	F	VF	XF	Unc
AH1162	—	50.00	80.00	125	—

Mint: Tiflis
KM# 416.2 ABBASI
4.6000 g., Silver **Note:** Type B.

Date	Mintage	F	VF	XF	Unc
AH1161	—	40.00	70.00	115	—
AH1162	—	40.00	70.00	115	—

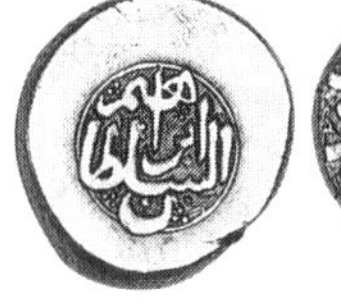

Mint: Astarabad
KM# 422 6 SHAHI
6.9000 g., Silver **Obv:** Inscription within circle **Rev:** Inscription **Note:** Type D.

Date	Mintage	F	VF	XF	Unc
AH1161	—	40.00	70.00	115	—
AH1162	—	40.00	70.00	115	—
ND	—	25.00	45.00	75.00	—

Mint: Mazandaran
KM# 414.1 3 ABBASI
13.8000 g., Silver **Obv:** Inscription **Rev:** Inscription within circle **Note:** Type A.

Date	Mintage	F	VF	XF	Unc
ND	—	75.00	125	200	—

Mint: Qazvin
KM# 414.2 3 ABBASI
13.8000 g., Silver **Obv:** Inscription **Rev:** Inscription within circle **Note:** Type A.

Date	Mintage	F	VF	XF	Unc
AH1160 (sic)	—	60.00	90.00	140	—
AH1161	—	50.00	80.00	125	—
AH1162	—	50.00	80.00	125	—

Mint: Rasht
KM# 414.3 3 ABBASI
13.8000 g., Silver **Obv:** Inscription **Rev:** Inscription within circle **Note:** Type A.

Date	Mintage	F	VF	XF	Unc
AH1161	—	60.00	100	150	—
AH1162	—	60.00	100	150	—

Mint: Shiraz
KM# 414.4 3 ABBASI
13.8000 g., Silver **Obv:** Inscription **Rev:** Inscription within circle **Note:** Type A.

Date	Mintage	F	VF	XF	Unc
AH1162	—	75.00	125	200	—

Mint: Tabriz
KM# 414.5 3 ABBASI
13.8000 g., Silver **Obv:** Inscription **Rev:** Inscription within circle **Note:** Type A.

Date	Mintage	F	VF	XF	Unc
AH1161	—	50.00	80.00	125	—
AH1162	—	50.00	80.00	125	—

Mint: Tiflis
KM# 414.6 3 ABBASI
13.8000 g., Silver **Obv:** Inscription **Rev:** Inscription within circle **Note:** Type A.

Date	Mintage	F	VF	XF	Unc
AH1162	—	60.00	100	150	—

Mint: Tabriz
KM# 417 ASHRAFI
3.5000 g., Gold **Note:** Type B.

Date	Mintage	F	VF	XF	Unc
AH1162 Rare	—	—	—	—	—

Mint: Ganjah
KM# 423 1/4 MOHUR
2.7500 g., Gold **Note:** Type D.

Date	Mintage	F	VF	XF	Unc
AH1162 Rare	—	—	—	—	—

Shahrukh, King of Iran

AH1161-1163 / 1748-1749AD

Type for this ruler's 1st reign:

B. Obverse, couplet as below. Reverse mint and date, usually with the mint epithet as well.

Sekke zad dar jahan be-hokm-e Khoda Shahrokh kalb-e astan-e Reza.

"Shahrukh, the dog at the doorstep of Reza, struck coin in the world by God's command". The reference to the "dog" is self-effacing, and refers to the idea that Shahrukh is devoted to Reza, the eighth Imam, whose tomb is at Mashhad, Shahrukh's capital. This type was struck at various northwestern mints as late as AH1170.

C. Obverse, the name *al-Sultan Shahrokh.* Reverse, the benediction, mint and date, as on Nadir Shah's type C.

HAMMERED COINAGE

Mint: Ganjah
KM# 432.1 SHAHI
1.1500 g., Silver **Note:** Type B.

Date	Mintage	F	VF	XF	Unc
AH1164 Ganja	—	30.00	50.00	85.00	—
AH1166 Ganja	—	30.00	50.00	85.00	—

Mint: Herat
KM# 430 SHAHI
1.1500 g., Silver **Note:** Type A.

Date	Mintage	F	VF	XF	Unc
AHxxxx	—	25.00	40.00	65.00	—

Mint: Mashhad
KM# 435.1 SHAHI
1.1500 g., Silver **Obv:** Inscription **Rev:** Inscription **Note:** Type C.

Date	Mintage	F	VF	XF	Unc
AH1162	—	30.00	50.00	85.00	—

Mint: Mazandaran
KM# 435.2 SHAHI
1.1500 g., Silver **Obv:** Inscription **Rev:** Inscription **Note:** Type C.

Date	Mintage	F	VF	XF	Unc
AH1162	—	30.00	50.00	85.00	—

Mint: Tabriz
KM# 432.2 SHAHI
1.1500 g., Silver **Note:** Type B.

Date	Mintage	F	VF	XF	Unc
AH1162	—	22.50	35.00	60.00	—

Mint: Eravan
KM# 433.1 ABBASI
4.6000 g., Silver **Obv:** Inscription **Rev:** Inscription **Note:** Type B.

Date	Mintage	F	VF	XF	Unc
AH1163	—	50.00	85.00	135	—

Mint: Ganjah
KM# 433.2 ABBASI
4.6000 g., Silver **Obv:** Inscription **Rev:** Inscription **Note:** Type B.

Date	Mintage	F	VF	XF	Unc
AH1162	—	20.00	32.50	50.00	—
AH1163	—	20.00	32.50	50.00	—
AH1164	—	25.00	40.00	65.00	—
AH1165	—	20.00	32.50	50.00	—
AH1166	—	25.00	40.00	65.00	—
AH1167	—	30.00	50.00	80.00	—
AH1168	—	25.00	40.00	65.00	—

Mint: Qazvin
KM# 433.3 ABBASI
4.6000 g., Silver **Obv:** Inscription **Rev:** Inscription **Note:** Type B.

Date	Mintage	F	VF	XF	Unc
AH1162	—	8.00	13.50	20.00	—

Mint: Shiraz
KM# 433.4 ABBASI
4.6000 g., Silver **Obv:** Inscription **Rev:** Inscription **Note:** Type B.

Date	Mintage	F	VF	XF	Unc
AH1162	—	6.00	10.00	16.00	—
AH1163	—	8.00	13.50	20.00	—

Mint: Tabriz
KM# 433.5 ABBASI
4.6000 g., Silver **Obv:** Inscription **Rev:** Inscription **Note:** Type B.

Date	Mintage	F	VF	XF	Unc
AH1162	—	10.00	17.50	27.50	—
AH1163	—	10.00	17.50	27.50	—
AH1164	—	20.00	35.00	55.00	—
AH1165	—	20.00	35.00	55.00	—
AH1166	—	20.00	35.00	55.00	—

Mint: Tiflis
KM# 433.6 ABBASI
4.6000 g., Silver **Obv:** Inscription **Rev:** Inscription **Note:** Type B.

Date	Mintage	F	VF	XF	Unc
AH1162	—	20.00	35.00	55.00	—
AH1163	—	20.00	35.00	55.00	—
AH1164	—	20.00	35.00	55.00	—
AH1169	—	22.50	35.00	55.00	—
AH1170	—	30.00	50.00	80.00	—

Mint: Astarabad
KM# 436.1 6 SHAHI
6.9000 g., Silver **Note:** Type C.

Date	Mintage	F	VF	XF	Unc
AH1162 Astarabad	—	40.00	65.00	110	—

Mint: Mashhad
KM# 436.2 6 SHAHI
6.9000 g., Silver **Note:** Type C.

Date	Mintage	F	VF	XF	Unc
AH1161	—	40.00	65.00	110	—
AH1162	—	40.00	65.00	110	—

Mint: Eravan
KM# 434.1 RUPI
11.5000 g., Silver **Obv:** Inscription **Rev:** Inscription within flower design **Note:** Type B.

Date	Mintage	F	VF	XF	Unc
AH1161	—	50.00	85.00	135	—

Mint: Herat
KM# 434.2 RUPI
11.5000 g., Silver **Obv:** Inscription **Rev:** Inscription within flower design **Note:** Type B.

Date	Mintage	F	VF	XF	Unc
AH1161	—	20.00	35.00	55.00	—
AH1162	—	20.00	35.00	55.00	—

Mint: Mashhad
KM# 434.3 RUPI
11.5000 g., Silver **Obv:** Inscription **Rev:** Inscription within flower design **Note:** Type B.

Date	Mintage	F	VF	XF	Unc
AH1161	—	12.50	20.00	35.00	—
AH1162	—	12.50	20.00	35.00	—

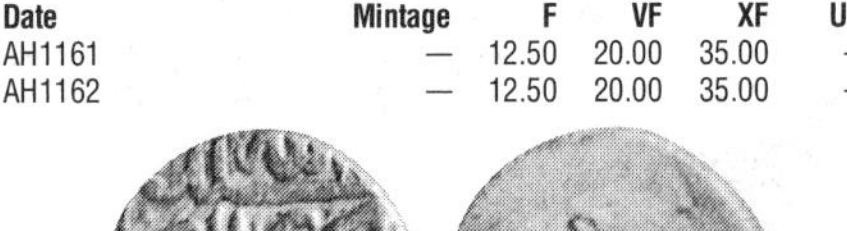

Mint: Mazandaran
KM# 437.1 RUPI
11.5000 g., Silver **Obv:** Inscription **Rev:** Inscription **Note:** Type C.

Date	Mintage	F	VF	XF	Unc
AH1162 Astarabad	—	50.00	85.00	140	—

Mint: Mazandaran
KM# 437.2 RUPI
11.5000 g., Silver **Obv:** Inscription **Rev:** Inscription **Note:** Type C.

Date	Mintage	F	VF	XF	Unc
AH1162	—	40.00	70.00	110	—

Mint: Qazvin
KM# 434.4 RUPI
11.5000 g., Silver **Obv:** Inscription **Rev:** Inscription within flower design **Note:** Type B.

Date	Mintage	F	VF	XF	Unc
AH1160 (sic)	—	20.00	35.00	55.00	—
AH1161	—	15.00	25.00	40.00	—
AH1163	—	15.00	25.00	40.00	—

Mint: Rasht
KM# 434.5 RUPI
11.5000 g., Silver **Obv:** Inscription **Rev:** Inscription within flower design **Note:** Type B.

Date	Mintage	F	VF	XF	Unc
AH1161	—	—	—	—	—
AH1162	—	12.50	20.00	35.00	—
AH1163	—	15.00	25.00	40.00	—

Mint: Rasht
KM# 437.3 RUPI
11.5000 g., Silver **Obv:** Inscription **Rev:** Inscription **Note:** Type C.

Date	Mintage	F	VF	XF	Unc
AH1162	—	50.00	85.00	140	—

Mint: Shiraz
KM# 434.6 RUPI
11.5000 g., Silver **Obv:** Inscription **Rev:** Inscription within flower design **Note:** Type B.

Date	Mintage	F	VF	XF	Unc
AH1162	—	30.00	45.00	75.00	—

Mint: Mashhad
KM# 438 2 RUPI
23.0000 g., Silver **Obv:** Inscription within center circle **Rev:** Inscription within circle **Note:** Type C.

Date	Mintage	F	VF	XF	Unc
AH1161	—	20.00	40.00	75.00	—
AH1162	—	20.00	40.00	75.00	—
AH1163	—	30.00	50.00	85.00	—

Mint: Mashhad
KM# 439 1/2 ASHRAFI
1.7300 g., Gold **Note:** Type C.

Date	Mintage	F	VF	XF	Unc
AH1161 Rare	—	—	—	—	—

Mint: Mashhad
KM# A435 ASHRAFI
3.5000 g., Gold **Note:** Type B.

Date	Mintage	F	VF	XF	Unc
ND	—	115	150	200	—

Mint: Mashhad
KM# 440 MOHUR
11.0000 g., Gold **Obv:** Inscription **Rev:** Inscription within center circle **Note:** Type C.

Date	Mintage	F	VF	XF	Unc
AH1162	—	200	250	325	—
AH1163	—	175	225	275	—

Mint: Mashhad
KM# 444 MOHUR
11.0000 g., Gold **Obv:** Inscription **Rev:** Inscription within small circle **Note:** Type D.

Date	Mintage	F	VF	XF	Unc
AH1163	—	185	275	400	—

Azad Khan
AH1163-1170 / 1750-1757AD

Types for this reign:

A. Obverse couplet. Reverse, mint & date, usually with the mint epithet.

Ta ke azad dar jahan bashad Sekke-ye Saheb Zaman bashad.

"So long as Azad is in the world, there shall be the coin of the Master of Time." The Master of Time, Saheb, oz-Zaman, refers to the 12th Imam, who is believed to have disappeared in the 9th century, and will reappear as the Messiah at the end of time.

B. Same obverse couplet, with mint & date below. Reverse, the Sunni kalima.

C. Obverse couplet. Reverse, mint & date, usually with the mint epithet.

Ta zar o sim dar jahan bashad Sekke-ye Saheb oz-Zaman bashad.

"So long as gold and silver are in the world, there shall be the coin of the Master of Time." Note that there is no reference to Azad by name in this couplet.

D. Same obverse as C, but mint & date below obverse. Reverse, Shiite formula, with the names of the 12 Imams. Used at Qazvin only.

E. Obverse, *Ya Saheb oz-Zaman*, "O Master of Time." Reverse, mint and date, with mint epithet. Used only for the shahi.

F. Obverse, *Udrikni ya Saheb oz-Zaman*, "Give me succor, O Master of Time." Reverse, mint, date, and mint epithet. Used only for the shahi.

G. Obverse couplet, mint and date below. Reverse Shiite formula (?).

Sim o zar anche dar jahan bashad Sekke-ye Saheb oz-Zaman bashad.

"Whatever silver and gold is in the world, shall be (minted into) the coin of the Master of Time." The attribution of this type to Azad Khan is tentative. Used only at Kirman.

H. Obverse, the Sunni Kalima. Reverse, *Ya saheb oz-zaman* above date and mint.

HAMMERED COINAGE

Mint: Isfahan
KM# 471 SHAHI
1.1500 g., Silver **Note:** Type A.

Date	Mintage	F	VF	XF	Unc
AH1167	—	30.00	50.00	85.00	—
AH1168	—	30.00	50.00	85.00	—

Mint: Isfahan
KM# 485.1 SHAHI
1.1500 g., Silver **Obv:** Inscription **Rev:** Inscription **Note:** Type E.

Date	Mintage	F	VF	XF	Unc
AH1167	—	25.00	40.00	70.00	—
AH1168	—	25.00	40.00	70.00	—
AH1170	—	25.00	40.00	70.00	—

Mint: Isfahan
KM# 486 SHAHI
1.1500 g., Silver **Obv:** Inscription **Rev:** Inscription **Note:** Type F.

Date	Mintage	F	VF	XF	Unc
AH1169	—	35.00	60.00	100	—

Mint: Rasht
KM# 488 SHAHI
1.1500 g., Silver **Note:** Type H.

Date	Mintage	F	VF	XF	Unc
AH1170	—	50.00	75.00	100	—

Mint: Shiraz
KM# 485.2 SHAHI
1.1500 g., Silver **Obv:** Inscription **Rev:** Inscription **Note:** Type E.

Date	Mintage	F	VF	XF	Unc
AH1167	—	40.00	70.00	100	—

Mint: Tabriz
KM# 479 SHAHI
1.1500 g., Silver **Note:** Type C.

Date	Mintage	F	VF	XF	Unc
AH1168	—	30.00	55.00	90.00	—

Mint: Tabriz
KM# 475 2 SHAHI
2.3000 g., Silver **Note:** Type B.

Date	Mintage	F	VF	XF	Unc
AH1169	—	50.00	85.00	140	—

Mint: Isfahan
KM# 480.1 ABBASI
4.6000 g., Silver **Obv:** Inscription **Rev:** Inscription within flower design **Note:** Type C.

Date	Mintage	F	VF	XF	Unc
AH1170	—	35.00	60.00	90.00	—

Mint: Kashan
KM# 472 ABBASI
4.6000 g., Silver **Note:** Type A.

Date	Mintage	F	VF	XF	Unc
AH1170	—	35.00	60.00	100	—

Mint: Qazvin
KM# 476.1 ABBASI
4.6000 g., Silver **Obv:** Inscription **Rev:** Inscription **Note:** Type B.

Date	Mintage	F	VF	XF	Unc
AH1167	—	30.00	50.00	85.00	—
AH1168	—	30.00	50.00	85.00	—

Mint: Qazvin
KM# 484 ABBASI
4.6000 g., Silver **Obv:** Inscription **Rev:** Inscription **Note:** Type D.

Date	Mintage	F	VF	XF	Unc
AH1167	—	20.00	35.00	55.00	—
AH1168	—	20.00	35.00	55.00	—

Mint: Tabriz
KM# 476.2 ABBASI
4.6000 g., Silver **Obv:** Inscription **Rev:** Inscription **Note:** Type B.

Date	Mintage	F	VF	XF	Unc
AH1168	—	35.00	55.00	90.00	—
AH1169	—	35.00	55.00	90.00	—

Mint: Tabriz
KM# 480.2 ABBASI
4.6000 g., Silver **Obv:** Inscription **Rev:** Inscription within flower design **Note:** Type C.

Date	Mintage	F	VF	XF	Unc
AH1167	—	50.00	100	150	—
AH1168	—	—	—	—	—

Note: Reported, not confirmed

Mint: Isfahan
KM# 473.1 RUPI
11.5000 g., Silver **Note:** Type A.

Date	Mintage	F	VF	XF	Unc
AH1170	—	40.00	70.00	110	—

Mint: Isfahan
KM# 481.1 RUPI
11.5000 g., Silver **Obv:** Inscription **Rev:** Inscription within circle **Note:** Type C.

Date	Mintage	F	VF	XF	Unc
AH1167	—	30.00	50.00	80.00	—
AH1168	—	—	—	—	—

Mint: Kashan
KM# 473.2 RUPI
11.5000 g., Silver **Note:** Type A.

Date	Mintage	F	VF	XF	Unc
AH1170	—	45.00	80.00	125	—

Mint: Kirman
KM# 481.2 RUPI
11.5000 g., Silver **Obv:** Inscription **Rev:** Inscription within circle **Note:** Type C.

Date	Mintage	F	VF	XF	Unc
ND	—	50.00	80.00	125	—

Mint: Kirman
KM# 487 RUPI
11.5000 g., Silver **Note:** Type G.

Date	Mintage	F	VF	XF	Unc
ND	—	50.00	80.00	125	—

Mint: Tabriz
KM# 477 1/12 MOHUR
0.9000 g., Gold **Note:** Type B.

Date	Mintage	F	VF	XF	Unc
AH1169 Rare	—	—	—	—	—

Mint: Isfahan
KM# 482 1/3 MOHUR
3.6500 g., Gold **Obv:** Inscription **Rev:** Inscription within flower design **Note:** Type C.

Date	Mintage	F	VF	XF	Unc
AH1167	—	150	250	375	—

Mint: Isfahan
KM# 474 MOHUR
11.0000 g., Gold **Obv:** Inscription **Rev:** Inscription within flower design **Note:** Type A.

Date	Mintage	F	VF	XF	Unc
AH1168	—	300	400	550	—
AH1170	—	350	500	650	—

Mint: Isfahan
KM# 483.1 MOHUR
11.0000 g., Gold **Obv:** Inscription **Rev:** Inscription within flower design **Note:** Type C.

Date	Mintage	F	VF	XF	Unc
AH1167	—	225	300	450	—
AH1168	—	225	300	450	—

Mint: Shiraz
KM# 483.2 MOHUR
11.0000 g., Gold **Obv:** Inscription **Rev:** Inscription within flower design **Note:** Type C.

Date	Mintage	F	VF	XF	Unc
AH1167	—	280	400	600	—

Mint: Tabriz
KM# 478 MOHUR
11.0000 g., Gold **Note:** Type B.

Date	Mintage	F	VF	XF	Unc
AH1169	—	400	500	650	—

Muhammad Hasan Khan

AH1163-1172 / 1750-1759AD

Until AH1168, his coins are in the name of Isma'il III, and are listed under that ruler; from AH1168-1172, he struck anonymous coinage.

Types for this reign:

A. Obverse couplet, with mint and date. Reverse, the Shiite formula, usually within a small central cartouche surrounded by a broad blank margin.

Be-zar sekkeh az meymanat zad qaza Be-nam-e 'Ali ebn-e Musa or-Reza.

"Fate has auspiciously struck coin in precious metal, in the name of Ali Reza, son of Musa, (i.e., the 8th Imam)".

B. Obverse evocation of the 8th Imam, *Ya 'Ali ebn-e Musa or-Reza.* Reverse, mint. Date usually on obverse. Used for the shahi only.

C. Obverse couplet, with mint and date. Reverse as type A.

Shod za yomn-e din-e haqq rayej be-toufiq-e Khoda Sekke-ye eqbal bar nam-e 'Ali ebn-e Musa ar-Reza.

"Because of the flourishing of the true religion, the coin of prosperity has become current, by God's grace, in the name of Ali Reza, son of Musa."

HAMMERED COINAGE

Mint: Isfahan
KM# 507.1 SHAHI
1.1500 g., Silver **Note:** Type B.

Date	Mintage	F	VF	XF	Unc
AH1170	—	20.00	35.00	70.00	—
AH1171	—	20.00	35.00	70.00	—

Mint: Mazandaran
KM# 507.2 SHAHI
1.1500 g., Silver **Note:** Type B.

Date	Mintage	F	VF	XF	Unc
AH1168	—	25.00	45.00	85.00	—

Mint: Tabriz
KM# 501 SHAHI
1.1500 g., Silver **Note:** Type A.

Date	Mintage	F	VF	XF	Unc
AH1171	—	35.00	55.00	90.00	—

Mint: Isfahan
KM# 502.1 2 SHAHI
2.3000 g., Silver **Note:** Type A.

Date	Mintage	F	VF	XF	Unc
AH1171 Isfahan	—	50.00	80.00	120	—

Mint: Mazandaran
KM# 502.2 2 SHAHI
2.3000 g., Silver **Note:** Type A.

Date	Mintage	F	VF	XF	Unc
AH1171	—	40.00	70.00	110	—

Mint: Rasht
KM# 502.3 2 SHAHI
2.3000 g., Silver **Note:** Type A.

Date	Mintage	F	VF	XF	Unc
ND	—	35.00	55.00	80.00	—

Mint: Eravan
KM# 503.1 ABBASI
4.6000 g., Silver **Note:** Type A.

Date	Mintage	F	VF	XF	Unc
AH1171	—	60.00	100	150	—

Mint: Isfahan
KM# 503.2 ABBASI
4.6000 g., Silver **Note:** Type A.

Date	Mintage	F	VF	XF	Unc
AH1171	—	40.00	65.00	110	—

Mint: Kashan
KM# 503.3 ABBASI
4.6000 g., Silver **Note:** Type A.

Date	Mintage	F	VF	XF	Unc
AH1169	—	35.00	60.00	100	—

Mint: Mazandaran
KM# 503.4 ABBASI
4.6000 g., Silver **Note:** Type A.

Date	Mintage	F	VF	XF	Unc
AH1170	—	40.00	65.00	110	—

Mint: Tabriz
KM# 503.5 ABBASI
4.6000 g., Silver **Note:** Type A.

Date	Mintage	F	VF	XF	Unc
AH1170	—	40.00	65.00	110	—
AH1171	—	40.00	65.00	110	—
AH1172	—	40.00	65.00	110	—

Mint: Isfahan
KM# 504.1 RUPI
11.5000 g., Silver **Note:** Type A.

Date	Mintage	F	VF	XF	Unc
AH1171	—	40.00	70.00	115	—

Mint: Kashan
KM# 504.2 RUPI
11.5000 g., Silver **Note:** Type A.

Date	Mintage	F	VF	XF	Unc
AH1170	—	40.00	70.00	115	—
AH1171	—	40.00	70.00	115	—
AH1174 Posthumous	—	50.00	85.00	140	—

Mint: Mazandaran
KM# 504.3 RUPI
11.5000 g., Silver **Note:** Type A.

Date	Mintage	F	VF	XF	Unc
AH1168	—	30.00	55.00	90.00	—
AH1169	—	25.00	50.00	80.00	—
AH1170	—	40.00	40.00	115	—
AH1171	—	40.00	60.00	175	—

Mint: Qazvin
KM# 504.4 RUPI
11.5000 g., Silver **Note:** Type A.

Date	Mintage	F	VF	XF	Unc
AH1169	—	40.00	70.00	115	—
AH1170	—	22.50	70.00	70.00	—

Mint: Qomm
KM# 504.5 RUPI
11.5000 g., Silver **Note:** Type A.

Date	Mintage	F	VF	XF	Unc
AH1171	—	45.00	110	135	—

Mint: Rasht
KM# 504.6 RUPI
11.5000 g., Silver **Note:** Type A.

Date	Mintage	F	VF	XF	Unc
AH1168	—	35.00	60.00	100	—
AH1169	—	25.00	50.00	80.00	—

Date	Mintage	F	VF	XF	Unc
AH1170	—	40.00	40.00	115	—
AH1171	—	40.00	80.00	115	—

Mint: Rasht
KM# 504.8 RUPI

11.5000 g., Silver **Note:** Type A.

Date	Mintage	F	VF	XF	Unc
AH1172	—	45.00	70.00	135	—

Mint: Rasht
KM# 508 RUPI

11.5000 g., Silver **Note:** Type C.

Date	Mintage	F	VF	XF	Unc
AH1168	—	50.00	85.00	140	—

Mint: Tabriz
KM# 504.7 RUPI

11.5000 g., Silver **Note:** Type A.

Date	Mintage	F	VF	XF	Unc
AH1170	—	22.50	40.00	70.00	—
AH1171	—	22.50	70.00	70.00	—

Mint: Isfahan
KM# 505.1 1/4 MOHUR

2.7500 g., Gold **Note:** Type A.

Date	Mintage	F	VF	XF	Unc
AH1169(?)	—	175	275	400	—

Mint: Tabriz
KM# 505.2 1/4 MOHUR

2.7500 g., Gold **Note:** Type A.

Date	Mintage	F	VF	XF	Unc
AH1170	—	150	250	350	—
AH1171	—	150	250	350	—
AH1173 Posthumous	—	175	275	400	—

Mint: Isfahan
KM# 506.1 MOHUR

11.0000 g., Gold **Note:** Type A.

Date	Mintage	F	VF	XF	Unc
AH1169 Rare	—	—	—	—	—

Mint: Yazd
KM# 506.2 MOHUR

11.0000 g., Gold **Note:** Type A.

Date	Mintage	F	VF	XF	Unc
AH1170 Rare	—	—	—	—	—

Shah Isma'il III

AH1163-1169 / 1750-1756AD

Types for this reign:

A. Obverse, *Bande-ye shah-e velayat Esma'il*, "Servant of the king of the Velayat, Isma'il," with mint below, date somewhere in field. Reverse, Shiite formula, without the names of the Imams, in a small central cartouche with broad blank margin around.

B. Obverse as type A. Reverse, Shiite formula, with the names of the 12 Imams around.

C. Obverse as type A, but without mint name. Reverse, mint and epithet in cartouche. Date usually on obverse.

D. Obverse, name of ruler, *al-Soltan Esma'il*. Reverse, benediction, mint & date as on Nadir Shah's type C.

Hammered Coinage

Mint: Astarabad
KM# 465.1 SHAHI

1.1500 g., Silver **Note:** Type D.

Date	Mintage	F	VF	XF	Unc
AH1166	—	30.00	50.00	80.00	—

Mint: Isfahan
KM# 464.1 SHAHI

1.1500 g., Silver **Obv:** Inscription **Rev:** Inscription **Note:** Type C.

Date	Mintage	F	VF	XF	Unc
AH1165	—	40.00	70.00	110	—

Mint: Mazandaran
KM# 462.1 SHAHI

1.1500 g., Silver **Obv:** Inscription **Rev:** Inscription **Note:** Type B.

Date	Mintage	F	VF	XF	Unc
AH1166	—	—	—	—	—

Mint: Mazandaran
KM# 464.2 SHAHI

1.1500 g., Silver **Obv:** Inscription **Rev:** Inscription **Note:** Type C.

Date	Mintage	F	VF	XF	Unc
AH116x	—	25.00	45.00	75.00	—

Mint: Mazandaran
KM# 465.2 SHAHI

1.1500 g., Silver **Note:** Type D.

Date	Mintage	F	VF	XF	Unc
AH1166	—	30.00	—	80.00	—

Mint: Shiraz
KM# 462.2 SHAHI

1.1500 g., Silver **Obv:** Inscription **Rev:** Inscription **Note:** Type B.

Date	Mintage	F	VF	XF	Unc
AH1163	—	40.00	70.00	110	—

Mint: Mazandaran
KM# 466 2 SHAHI

2.3000 g., Silver **Note:** Type D.

Date	Mintage	F	VF	XF	Unc
AH1167	—	50.00	85.00	140	—

Mint: Isfahan
KM# 463.1 ABBASI

4.6000 g., Silver **Obv:** Inscription **Rev:** Inscription **Note:** Type B.

Date	Mintage	F	VF	XF	Unc
AH1163	—	50.00	80.00	125	—

Mint: Qazvin
KM# 463.2 ABBASI

4.6000 g., Silver **Obv:** Inscription **Rev:** Inscription **Note:** Type B.

Date	Mintage	F	VF	XF	Unc
AH1163	—	50.00	80.00	125	—

Mint: Rasht
KM# 463.3 ABBASI

4.6000 g., Silver **Obv:** Inscription **Rev:** Inscription **Note:** Type B.

Date	Mintage	F	VF	XF	Unc
AH1163	—	—	—	—	—
Note: Reported, not confirmed					
AH1164	—	50.00	80.00	125	—

Mint: Shiraz
KM# 463.4 ABBASI

4.6000 g., Silver **Obv:** Inscription **Rev:** Inscription **Note:** Type B.

Date	Mintage	F	VF	XF	Unc
AH1163	—	50.00	80.00	125	—

Mint: Astarabad
KM# 467.1 6 SHAHI

6.9000 g., Silver **Note:** Type D.

Date	Mintage	F	VF	XF	Unc
AH1166	—	40.00	60.00	90.00	—
AH1167	—	40.00	60.00	90.00	—

Mint: Mazandaran
KM# 467.2 6 SHAHI

6.9000 g., Silver **Note:** Type D.

Date	Mintage	F	VF	XF	Unc
AH1166	—	30.00	50.00	80.00	—
AH1167	—	30.00	50.00	80.00	—

Mint: Mazandaran
KM# 461.1 RUPI

11.5000 g., Silver **Obv:** Inscription within circle **Rev:** Inscription within beaded circle **Note:** Type A.

Date	Mintage	F	VF	XF	Unc
AH1166	—	40.00	65.00	100	—
AH1167	—	35.00	55.00	90.00	—
AH1168	—	50.00	85.00	140	—

Mint: Rasht
KM# 461.2 RUPI

11.5000 g., Silver **Obv:** Inscription within circle **Rev:** Inscription within beaded circle **Note:** Type A.

Date	Mintage	F	VF	XF	Unc
AH1166	—	35.00	55.00	90.00	—
AH1167	—	35.00	55.00	90.00	—
AH1168	—	45.00	80.00	130	—

Shah Sulayman II

AH1163 / 1750AD

Types for the reign:

A. Obverse couplet, with mint & date. Reverse, Shiite formula, with names of the twelve Imams around.

Zad az lotf-e Haqq sekke-ye kamrani Shah-e 'adl-gostar Soleyman-e Thani.

"By the grace of God, the justice-dispensing shah, Sulayman the Second, struck the coin of prosperity."

B. Obverse, the ruler's name, *al-Soltan Soleyman*. Reverse, benediction, mint and date as on Nadir Shah's type C.

HAMMERED COINAGE

Mint: Mazandaran
KM# 451 ABBASI

4.6000 g., Silver **Obv:** Inscription **Rev:** Inscription **Note:** Type A.

Date	Mintage	F	VF	XF	Unc
AH1163	—	100	175	275	—

Mint: Mazandaran
KM# 455 6 SHAHI

6.9000 g., Silver **Obv:** Inscription **Rev:** Inscription **Note:** Type B.

Date	Mintage	F	VF	XF	Unc
AH1163	—	125	185	275	—

Mint: Mashhad
KM# 452 2 RUPI

23.0000 g., Silver **Note:** Type A.

Date	Mintage	F	VF	XF	Unc
AH1163 Rare	—	—	—	—	—

Mint: Mashhad
KM# 453 3 RUPI

34.5000 g., Silver **Note:** Type A.

Date	Mintage	F	VF	XF	Unc
AH1163 Rare	—	—	—	—	—

Mint: Mashhad
KM# 454 2 MOHURS

22.0000 g., Gold **Obv:** Inscription **Rev:** Inscription **Note:** Type A.

Date	Mintage	F	VF	XF	Unc
AH1163	—	700	900	1,250	—

Shahrukh, 2nd Reign

AH1163-1168 / 1750-1755AD

Type for this ruler's 2nd reign:

D. Couplet obverse, with reverse as on type B. Struck only at Mashhad and Rasht.

Dou-bareh doulat-e Iran gereft az sar javani-ra Be-nam-e Shahrokh zad sekke-ye sahebqerani-ra.

"Once again, the state of Iran has taken on youthful vigor, for Sahebqirani coin has been struck in the name of Shahrukh."

HAMMERED COINAGE

Mint: Mashhad
KM# 441 SHAHI
1.1500 g., Silver **Note:** Type D.

Date	Mintage	F	VF	XF	Unc
AH1165	—	30.00	50.00	90.00	—

Mint: Mashhad
KM# 446 SHAHI
1.1500 g., Silver **Note:** Type E.

Date	Mintage	F	VF	XF	Unc
ND	—	30.00	50.00	90.00	—

Mint: Isfahan
KM# 442.1 RUPI
11.5000 g., Silver **Obv:** Inscription **Rev:** Inscription within design **Note:** Type D.

Date	Mintage	F	VF	XF	Unc
AH1163	—	45.00	75.00	115	—

Mint: Mashhad
KM# 442.2 RUPI
11.5000 g., Silver **Obv:** Inscription **Rev:** Inscription within design **Note:** Type D.

Date	Mintage	F	VF	XF	Unc
AH1163	—	—	—	—	—
AH1168	—	30.00	50.00	80.00	—

Mint: Rasht
KM# 442.3 RUPI
11.5000 g., Silver **Obv:** Inscription **Rev:** Inscription within design **Note:** Type D.

Date	Mintage	F	VF	XF	Unc
AH1163	—	35.00	55.00	80.00	—
AH1164	—	35.00	55.00	80.00	—

Mint: Mashhad
KM# 443 ASHRAFI
3.5000 g., Gold **Obv:** Inscription **Rev:** Inscription within small circle **Note:** Type D.

Date	Mintage	F	VF	XF	Unc
ND	—	85.00	120	160	—
AH1164	—	100	130	175	—
AH1165	—	100	130	175	—

Karim Khan

AH1166-1193 / 1753-1779AD

All coinage of this ruler is, strictly speaking, anonymous. Most is identified by the evocation *Ya Karim*, which may be translated either as "O Karim" or as "O Generous One," Karim being one of the many names of God. In the type descriptions, this phrase is noted as the ruler's evocation.

Types for this reign:

A. Obverse couplet, with mint below, date somewhere in field. Reverse, the Shiite formula.

Shod aftab o mah zar o sim dar jahan Az sekke-ye Emam be-haqq Saheb oz-Zaman

"The sun and moon have become gold and silver throughout the world, from the coin of the Imam, indeed the Master of Time."

B. Same obverse couplet, but without mint. Reverse, mint and date, usually with epithet, usually in ornamental cartouche in larger field. The date may appear on either obverse or reverse, more frequently on reverse.

B*. As type B, but the ruler's evocation *Ya Karim* added to the obverse field in miniscule letters.

C. As type B, but the ruler's evocation is added at the top of the reverse, above the mint and date. The date may appear on obverse, on reverse, on both faces, or twice on the reverse.

D. Obverse, the Shiite formula. Reverse, mint, date, and ruler's evocation as on type C.

E. Obverse as type B. Reverse, mint and date, with epithet, in central area, with the Shiite kalima around.Used only at Qazvin.

F. Obverse, exactly as type A. Reverse, the ruler's evocation, together with the usual benedication, *khalad Allah mulkahu*, "May God perpetuate his kingship.

In addition, there are several local types used by mints at Ganja, Iravan, Nukhwi, Shemakhi, and Tiflis by local rulers. These are listed in Caucasia, under Russia.

HAMMERED COINAGE

Mint: Ganjah
KM# 521.1 SHAHI
1.1500 g., Silver **Note:** Type C.

Date	Mintage	F	VF	XF	Unc
AH1182	—	20.00	40.00	65.00	—
AH1183	—	20.00	40.00	65.00	—
AH1184	—	20.00	40.00	65.00	—
AH1186	—	20.00	40.00	65.00	—

Mint: Isfahan
KM# 514.1 SHAHI
1.1500 g., Silver **Note:** Type B.

Date	Mintage	F	VF	XF	Unc
AH1166	—	30.00	50.00	75.00	—

Mint: Kashan
KM# 521.2 SHAHI
1.1500 g., Silver **Note:** Type C.

Date	Mintage	F	VF	XF	Unc
AH1191	—	20.00	40.00	70.00	—

Mint: Rasht
KM# 521.3 SHAHI
1.1500 g., Silver **Note:** Type C.

Date	Mintage	F	VF	XF	Unc
AH1189	—	25.00	45.00	75.00	—

Mint: Shiraz
KM# 514.2 SHAHI
1.1500 g., Silver **Note:** Type B.

Date	Mintage	F	VF	XF	Unc
AH1170	—	30.00	50.00	75.00	—
AH1178	—	25.00	40.00	60.00	—

Mint: Shiraz
KM# 521.4 SHAHI
1.1500 g., Silver **Note:** Type C.

Date	Mintage	F	VF	XF	Unc
AH1184	—	20.00	35.00	60.00	—
AH1189	—	20.00	35.00	60.00	—
AH1192	—	20.00	35.00	60.00	—
AH1193	—	20.00	35.00	60.00	—

Mint: Tabriz
KM# 527 SHAHI
1.1500 g., Silver **Note:** Type D.

Date	Mintage	F	VF	XF	Unc
AH1182	—	17.50	30.00	50.00	—
AH1184	—	17.50	30.00	50.00	—
AH1186	—	17.50	30.00	50.00	—
AH1187	—	17.50	30.00	50.00	—
AH1188	—	17.50	30.00	50.00	—

Mint: Astarabad
KM# 511.1 ABBASI
4.6000 g., Silver **Obv:** Inscription **Rev:** Inscription **Note:** Type A.

Date	Mintage	F	VF	XF	Unc
ND	—	25.00	45.00	70.00	—

Mint: Astarabad
KM# 515.1 ABBASI
4.6000 g., Silver **Obv:** Inscription **Rev:** Inscription **Note:** Type B.

Date	Mintage	F	VF	XF	Unc
AH1177	—	20.00	35.00	50.00	—

Mint: Astarabad
KM# 522.1 ABBASI
4.6000 g., Silver **Obv:** Inscription **Rev:** Inscription **Note:** Type C.

Date	Mintage	F	VF	XF	Unc
AH1177	—	15.00	25.00	40.00	—

Mint: Basra
KM# 528.1 ABBASI
4.6000 g., Silver **Obv:** Inscription **Rev:** Inscription **Note:** Type D.

Date	Mintage	F	VF	XF	Unc
ND	—	75.00	125	200	—

Mint: Eravan
KM# 522.2 ABBASI
4.6000 g., Silver **Obv:** Inscription **Rev:** Inscription **Note:** Type C.

Date	Mintage	F	VF	XF	Unc
ND	—	30.00	55.00	85.00	—

Mint: Eravan
KM# 528.2 ABBASI
4.6000 g., Silver **Obv:** Inscription **Rev:** Inscription **Note:** Type D.

Date	Mintage	F	VF	XF	Unc
ND	—	50.00	85.00	140	—
AH1179	—	60.00	100	150	—

Mint: Ganjah
KM# 522.3 ABBASI
4.6000 g., Silver **Obv:** Inscription **Rev:** Inscription **Note:** Type C.

Date	Mintage	F	VF	XF	Unc
AH1182	—	20.00	35.00	50.00	—
AH1183	—	20.00	35.00	50.00	—
AH1184	—	20.00	35.00	50.00	—
AH1185	—	20.00	35.00	50.00	—
AH1186	—	20.00	35.00	50.00	—
AH1187	—	20.00	35.00	50.00	—
AH1188	—	20.00	35.00	50.00	—
AH1189	—	20.00	35.00	50.00	—

Mint: Isfahan
KM# 511.2 ABBASI
4.6000 g., Silver **Obv:** Inscription **Rev:** Inscription **Note:** Type A.

Date	Mintage	F	VF	XF	Unc
AH1166	—	40.00	70.00	110	—

Mint: Isfahan
KM# 515a.1 ABBASI
4.6000 g., Silver **Obv:** "Ya Karim" added in field **Note:** Type B.

Date	Mintage	F	VF	XF	Unc
AH1175	—	10.00	17.50	27.50	—

Mint: Isfahan
KM# 515.2 ABBASI
4.6000 g., Silver **Obv:** Inscription **Rev:** Inscription **Note:** Type B.

Date	Mintage	F	VF	XF	Unc
AH(11)75	—	9.00	16.00	25.00	—

Mint: Isfahan
KM# 522.4 ABBASI
4.6000 g., Silver **Obv:** Inscription **Rev:** Inscription **Note:** Type C.

Date	Mintage	F	VF	XF	Unc
AH1173	—	10.00	17.50	27.50	—
AH1175	—	7.00	12.50	20.00	—
AH1176	—	7.00	12.50	20.00	—
AH1177	—	7.00	12.50	20.00	—
AH1178	—	7.00	12.50	20.00	—
AH1179	—	7.00	12.50	20.00	—
AH1180	—	7.00	12.50	20.00	—
AH1181	—	8.50	15.00	24.00	—

Mint: Kashan
KM# 515.3 ABBASI
4.6000 g., Silver **Obv:** Inscription **Rev:** Inscription **Note:** Type B.

Date	Mintage	F	VF	XF	Unc
AH1172	—	15.00	25.00	40.00	—
AH1173	—	10.00	17.50	27.50	—
AH1174	—	7.00	12.50	20.00	—
AH1175	—	7.00	12.50	20.00	—
AH1176	—	7.00	12.50	20.00	—
AH1177	—	8.50	15.00	25.00	—

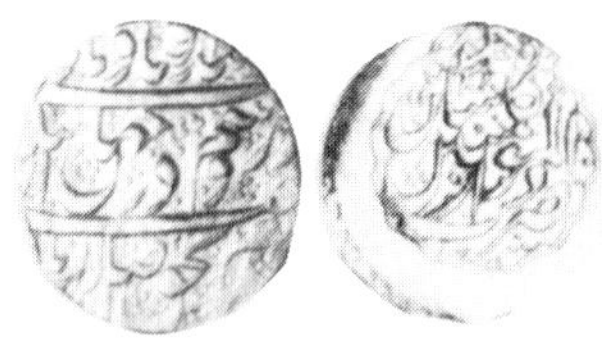

Mint: Kashan
KM# 522.5 ABBASI
4.6000 g., Silver **Obv:** Inscription **Rev:** Inscription **Note:** Type C.

Date	Mintage	F	VF	XF	Unc
AH1177	—	10.00	17.50	27.50	—
AH1178	—	7.00	12.50	20.00	—
AH1179	—	8.00	14.00	22.50	—
AH1180	—	8.00	14.00	22.50	—
AH1181	—	8.00	14.00	22.50	—
AH1182	—	10.00	17.50	27.50	—
AH1189	—	15.00	22.50	35.00	—

Mint: Khoy
KM# 522.6 ABBASI
4.6000 g., Silver **Obv:** Inscription **Rev:** Inscription **Note:** Type C.

Date	Mintage	F	VF	XF	Unc
AH1189	—	50.00	80.00	125	—
AH1190	—	50.00	80.00	125	—

Mint: Kirman
KM# 522.7 ABBASI
4.6000 g., Silver **Obv:** Inscription **Rev:** Inscription **Note:** Type C.

Date	Mintage	F	VF	XF	Unc
ND	—	15.00	25.00	40.00	—
AH1180	—	17.50	27.50	40.00	—
AH1182	—	17.50	27.50	40.00	—

Mint: Mazandaran
KM# 534 ABBASI
4.6000 g., Silver **Obv:** Type A **Rev:** Type C, without epithet **Note:** Miscellaneous type. Mule.

Date	Mintage	F	VF	XF	Unc
AH1187	—	30.00	50.00	75.00	—
ND	—	22.50	35.00	60.00	—

Mint: Mazandaran
KM# 511.3 ABBASI
4.6000 g., Silver **Obv:** Inscription **Rev:** Inscription **Note:** Type A.

Date	Mintage	F	VF	XF	Unc
AH1175	—	30.00	50.00	85.00	—

Mint: Mazandaran
KM# 515.4 ABBASI
4.6000 g., Silver **Obv:** Inscription **Rev:** Inscription **Note:** Type B.

Date	Mintage	F	VF	XF	Unc
AH1178	—	25.00	50.00	80.00	—
AH1187 (sic)	—	25.00	50.00	80.00	—

Mint: Mazandaran
KM# 522.8 ABBASI
4.6000 g., Silver **Obv:** Inscription **Rev:** Inscription **Note:** Type C.

Date	Mintage	F	VF	XF	Unc
AH1177	—	10.00	17.50	27.50	—
AH1180	—	10.00	17.50	27.50	—

Date	Mintage	F	VF	XF	Unc
AH1181	—	10.00	17.50	27.50	—
AH1182	—	10.00	17.50	27.50	—
AH1186	—	12.50	20.00	32.50	—
AH1187	—	12.50	20.00	32.50	—
AH1189	—	12.50	20.00	32.50	—
AH1192	—	12.50	20.00	32.50	—
AH1193	—	12.50	20.00	32.50	—

Mint: Mazandaran
KM# 533 ABBASI

4.6000 g., Silver **Note:** Type F.

Date	Mintage	F	VF	XF	Unc
AH1178	—	20.00	35.00	55.00	—
AH1179	—	25.00	40.00	65.00	—

Mint: Mazandaran
KM# A533 ABBASI

Silver **Obv:** Type A **Rev:** Inscription and date in teardrop cartouche **Rev. Inscription:** "Ya Karim" **Note:**

Date	Mintage	Good	VG	F	VF	XF
AH1180	—	—	—	—	—	—

Mint: Nakhjavan
KM# 522.9 ABBASI

4.6000 g., Silver **Obv:** Inscription **Rev:** Inscription **Note:** Type C.

Date	Mintage	F	VF	XF	Unc
AH1181	—	40.00	65.00	100	—
AH1182	—	40.00	65.00	100	—
AH1183	—	40.00	65.00	100	—

Mint: Qazvin
KM# 522.10 ABBASI

4.6000 g., Silver **Obv:** Inscription **Rev:** Inscription **Note:** Type C.

Date	Mintage	F	VF	XF	Unc
AH1177	—	10.00	17.50	27.50	—
AH1178	—	10.00	17.50	27.50	—
AH1179	—	10.00	17.50	27.50	—
AH1180	—	10.00	17.50	27.50	—
AH1181	—	10.00	17.50	27.50	—
AH1182	—	10.00	17.50	27.50	—
AH1183	—	10.00	17.50	27.50	—
AH1185	—	12.50	20.00	32.50	—
AH1186	—	10.00	17.50	27.50	—

Mint: Qazvin
KM# 528.3 ABBASI

4.6000 g., Silver **Obv:** Inscription **Rev:** Inscription **Note:** Type D.

Date	Mintage	F	VF	XF	Unc
AH1175	—	12.50	20.00	32.50	—
AH1176	—	12.50	20.00	32.50	—

Mint: Qazvin
KM# 532 ABBASI

4.6000 g., Silver **Obv:** Inscription within circle **Rev:** Inscription **Note:** Type E.

Date	Mintage	F	VF	XF	Unc
AH1170 (sic)	—	25.00	40.00	60.00	—
Note: Error, struck AH1174-75					
AH1172	—	15.00	25.00	37.50	—
AH1173	—	10.00	18.00	27.50	—
AH1174	—	10.00	18.00	27.50	—
AH1176	—	13.50	22.50	35.00	—

Mint: Qazvín
KM# 511.4 ABBASI

4.6000 g., Silver **Obv:** Inscription **Rev:** Inscription **Note:** Type A.

Date	Mintage	F	VF	XF	Unc
AH1166	—	40.00	70.00	110	—
AH1167	—	40.00	70.00	110	—

Mint: Qomm
KM# 515.5 ABBASI

4.6000 g., Silver **Obv:** Inscription **Rev:** Inscription **Note:** Type B.

Date	Mintage	F	VF	XF	Unc
AH1171	—	40.00	75.00	110	—

Mint: Rasht
KM# 511a ABBASI

4.6000 g., Silver **Obv:** Inscription **Obv. Legend:** "Ya Karim" added **Rev:** Inscription **Note:** Type A.

Date	Mintage	F	VF	XF	Unc
AH1175	—	10.00	16.00	27.50	—
AH1176	—	10.00	16.00	27.50	—
AH1177	—	10.00	16.00	27.50	—
AH1178	—	10.00	16.00	27.50	—
ND	—	6.00	10.00	17.50	—

Mint: Rasht
KM# 511b ABBASI

4.6000 g., Silver **Obv:** Type A **Rev:** Similar to type C **Note:** Type A. Mule.

Date	Mintage	F	VF	XF	Unc
AH1181	—	25.00	45.00	80.00	—

Mint: Rasht
KM# 515.6 ABBASI

4.6000 g., Silver **Obv:** Inscription **Rev:** Inscription **Note:** Type B.

Date	Mintage	F	VF	XF	Unc
AH1175	—	15.00	25.00	40.00	—

Mint: Rasht
KM# 522.11 ABBASI

4.6000 g., Silver **Obv:** Inscription **Rev:** Inscription **Note:** Type C.

Date	Mintage	F	VF	XF	Unc
AH1181	—	15.00	25.00	40.00	—
AH1182	—	10.00	17.50	27.50	—
AH1188	—	—	—	—	—
Note: Reported, not confirmed					

Mint: Rekab
KM# 515.7 ABBASI

4.6000 g., Silver **Obv:** Inscription **Rev:** Inscription **Note:** Type B.

Date	Mintage	F	VF	XF	Unc
AH1173	—	17.50	30.00	45.00	—
AH1174	—	15.00	25.00	40.00	—

Mint: Rekab
KM# A529 ABBASI

4.6000 g., Silver **Rev:** Without evocative "Ya Karim" **Note:** Type D.

Date	Mintage	F	VF	XF	Unc
AH1174	—	15.00	25.00	37.50	—

Mint: Rekab
KM# 528.4 ABBASI

4.6000 g., Silver **Obv:** Inscription **Rev:** Inscription **Note:** Type D.

Date	Mintage	F	VF	XF	Unc
AH1175	—	15.00	25.00	37.50	—
AH1176	—	15.00	25.00	37.50	—
AH1177	—	15.00	25.00	37.50	—
AH1178	—	12.50	20.00	32.50	—
AH1182	—	25.00	40.00	65.00	—

Mint: Shiraz
KM# 511.5 ABBASI

4.6000 g., Silver **Obv:** Inscription **Rev:** Inscription **Note:** Type A.

Date	Mintage	F	VF	XF	Unc
AH1166	—	40.00	70.00	110	—
AH1173	—	25.00	45.00	70.00	—

Mint: Shiraz
KM# 515.8 ABBASI

4.6000 g., Silver **Obv:** Inscription **Rev:** Inscription **Note:** Type B.

Date	Mintage	F	VF	XF	Unc
AH1173	—	9.00	16.00	25.00	—
AH1174	—	9.00	16.00	25.00	—
AH1175	—	9.00	16.00	25.00	—
AH1176	—	7.00	10.00	17.50	—
AH1177	—	7.00	10.00	17.50	—
AH1178	—	7.00	10.00	17.50	—

Mint: Shiraz
KM# 515a.2 ABBASI

4.6000 g., Silver **Obv:** "Ya Karim" added in field **Note:** Type B.

Date	Mintage	F	VF	XF	Unc
AH1173	—	10.00	17.50	27.50	—
AH1174	—	10.00	17.50	27.50	—
AH1175	—	10.00	17.50	27.50	—

Mint: Shiraz
KM# 522.12 ABBASI

4.6000 g., Silver **Obv:** Inscription **Rev:** Inscription **Note:** Type C.

Date	Mintage	F	VF	XF	Unc
AH1179	—	7.00	10.00	17.50	—
AH1180	—	8.50	12.50	20.00	—
AH1181	—	8.50	12.50	20.00	—
AH1188	—	12.50	20.00	30.00	—

Mint: Tabriz
KM# 522.13 ABBASI

4.6000 g., Silver **Obv:** Inscription **Rev:** Inscription **Note:** Type C.

Date	Mintage	F	VF	XF	Unc
AH1179	—	12.50	20.00	30.00	—
AH1181	—	9.00	15.00	22.50	—
AH1182	—	9.00	15.00	22.50	—
AH1183	—	9.00	15.00	22.50	—
AH1184	—	9.00	15.00	22.50	—
AH1185	—	9.00	15.00	22.50	—
AH1186	—	9.00	15.00	22.50	—
AH1187	—	12.50	20.00	30.00	—
AH1189	—	12.50	20.00	30.00	—

Mint: Tabriz
KM# 528.5 ABBASI

4.6000 g., Silver **Obv:** Inscription **Rev:** Inscription **Note:** Type D.

Date	Mintage	F	VF	XF	Unc
AH1174	—	—	—	—	—
Note: Reported, not confirmed					
AH1175	—	12.50	20.00	35.00	—
AH1177	—	12.50	20.00	35.00	—
AH1178	—	12.50	20.00	35.00	—

Mint: Tehran
KM# 522.14 ABBASI

4.6000 g., Silver **Obv:** Inscription **Rev:** Inscription **Note:** Type C.

Date	Mintage	F	VF	XF	Unc
AH1178	—	20.00	35.00	55.00	—
AH1179	—	20.00	35.00	55.00	—
AH1180	—	20.00	35.00	55.00	—
AH1181	—	20.00	35.00	55.00	—

Mint: Yazd
KM# 515.9 ABBASI

4.6000 g., Silver **Obv:** Inscription **Rev:** Inscription **Note:** Type B.

Date	Mintage	F	VF	XF	Unc
AH1178	—	15.00	25.00	40.00	—

Mint: Yazd
KM# 522.15 ABBASI

4.6000 g., Silver **Obv:** Inscription **Rev:** Inscription **Note:** Type C.

Date	Mintage	F	VF	XF	Unc
AH1179	—	9.00	15.00	22.50	—
AH1180	—	9.00	15.00	22.50	—
AH1181	—	9.00	15.00	22.50	—
AH1182	—	11.00	17.50	27.50	—
AH1186	—	15.00	22.50	35.00	—
AH1187	—	12.50	20.00	30.00	—

Mint: Mazandaran
KM# A512 6 SHAHI

6.9000 g., Silver **Obv:** Type A **Rev:** "Ya Karim" and date in fancy cartouche **Note:** Type A - variation.

Date	Mintage	F	VF	XF	Unc
AH1174	—	50.00	85.00	140	—

Mint: Rasht
KM# 516 6 SHAHI

6.9000 g., Silver **Obv:** Inscription **Rev:** Inscription within small circle **Note:** Type A - variation.

Date	Mintage	F	VF	XF	Unc
AH1174	—	50.00	85.00	140	—

Mint: Basra
KM# 529 2 ABBASI

9.2000 g., Silver **Note:** Type D.

Date	Mintage	F	VF	XF	Unc
AH1190	—	100	175	250	—

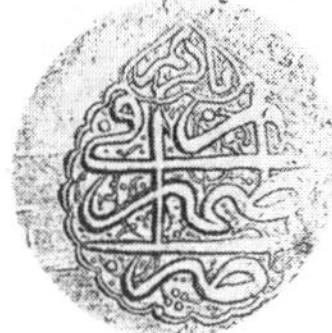

Mint: Eravan
KM# 523.1 2 ABBASI

9.2000 g., Silver **Obv:** Inscription **Rev:** Inscription within flower design **Note:** Type C.

Date	Mintage	F	VF	XF	Unc
ND	—	45.00	80.00	125	—

Mint: Isfahan
KM# 523.2 2 ABBASI

9.2000 g., Silver **Obv:** Inscription **Rev:** Inscription within flower design **Note:** Type C.

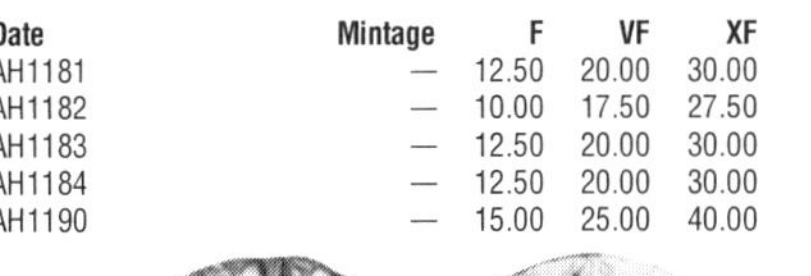

Date	Mintage	F	VF	XF	Unc
AH1181	—	12.50	20.00	30.00	—
AH1182	—	10.00	17.50	27.50	—
AH1183	—	12.50	20.00	30.00	—
AH1184	—	12.50	20.00	30.00	—
AH1190	—	15.00	25.00	40.00	—

Mint: Kashan
KM# 523.3 2 ABBASI
9.2000 g., Silver **Obv:** Inscription **Rev:** Inscription within flower design **Note:** Type C.

Date	Mintage	F	VF	XF	Unc
AH1182	—	12.50	20.00	30.00	—
AH1183	—	12.50	20.00	30.00	—
AH1184	—	12.50	20.00	30.00	—
AH1185	—	12.50	20.00	30.00	—
AH1186	—	11.50	17.50	27.50	—
AH1187	—	12.50	20.00	30.00	—
AH1188	—	12.50	20.00	30.00	—
AH1189	—	12.50	20.00	30.00	—
AH1190	—	12.50	20.00	30.00	—
AH1191	—	15.00	25.00	37.50	—
AH1192	—	15.00	25.00	37.50	—

Mint: Kirman
KM# 523.4 2 ABBASI
9.2000 g., Silver **Obv:** Inscription **Rev:** Inscription within flower design **Note:** Type C.

Date	Mintage	F	VF	XF	Unc
AH1180	—	30.00	50.00	75.00	—
AH1182	—	30.00	50.00	75.00	—
AH1186	—	30.00	50.00	75.00	—
AH1187//1188	—	30.00	50.00	75.00	—
AH1187//1189	—	30.00	50.00	75.00	—

Mint: Mazandaran
KM# 523.5 2 ABBASI
9.2000 g., Silver **Obv:** Inscription **Rev:** Inscription within flower design **Note:** Type C.

Date	Mintage	F	VF	XF	Unc
AH1180	—	15.00	25.00	37.50	—
AH1181	—	10.00	17.50	27.50	—
AH1182	—	10.00	17.50	27.50	—
AH1183	—	10.00	17.50	27.50	—
AH1184	—	10.00	17.50	27.50	—
AH1185	—	10.00	17.50	27.50	—
AH1186	—	10.00	17.50	27.50	—
AH1187	—	10.00	17.50	27.50	—
AH1188	—	12.50	20.00	30.00	—
AH1189	—	12.50	20.00	30.00	—
AH1190	—	12.50	20.00	30.00	—
AH1192	—	15.00	25.00	37.50	—

Mint: Qazvin
KM# 523.6 2 ABBASI
9.2000 g., Silver **Obv:** Inscription **Rev:** Inscription within flower design **Note:** Type C.

Date	Mintage	F	VF	XF	Unc
AH1180	—	14.00	22.50	35.00	—
AH1182	—	14.00	22.50	35.00	—
AH1183	—	14.00	22.50	35.00	—
AH1185	—	14.00	22.50	35.00	—
AH1186	—	14.00	22.50	35.00	—
AH1187	—	14.00	22.50	35.00	—
AH1188	—	14.00	22.50	35.00	—
AH1192	—	20.00	35.00	50.00	—

Mint: Rasht
KM# 523.7 2 ABBASI
9.2000 g., Silver **Obv:** Inscription **Rev:** Inscription within flower design **Note:** Type C.

Date	Mintage	F	VF	XF	Unc
AH1180	—	12.50	20.00	30.00	—
AH1182	—	10.00	17.50	27.50	—
AH1183	—	10.00	17.50	27.50	—
AH1184	—	10.00	17.50	27.50	—
AH1185	—	10.00	17.50	27.50	—
AH1186	—	12.50	20.00	30.00	—
AH1187	—	12.50	20.00	30.00	—
AH1188	—	12.50	20.00	30.00	—
AH1189	—	12.50	20.00	30.00	—
AH1190	—	12.50	20.00	30.00	—
AH1193	—	15.00	25.00	40.00	—

Mint: Shiraz
KM# 523.8 2 ABBASI
9.2000 g., Silver **Obv:** Inscription **Rev:** Inscription within flower design **Note:** Type C.

Date	Mintage	F	VF	XF	Unc
AH1180	—	17.50	30.00	50.00	—
AH1181	—	10.00	17.50	27.50	—
AH1182	—	10.00	17.50	27.50	—
AH1183	—	12.50	20.00	30.00	—
AH1193	—	15.00	25.00	40.00	—

Mint: Tabriz
KM# 523.9 2 ABBASI
9.2000 g., Silver **Obv:** Inscription **Rev:** Inscription within flower design **Note:** Type C.

Date	Mintage	F	VF	XF	Unc
AH1182	—	12.50	20.00	30.00	—
AH1183	—	12.50	20.00	30.00	—
AH1186	—	12.50	20.00	30.00	—
AH1187	—	12.50	20.00	30.00	—
AH1188	—	12.50	20.00	30.00	—

Mint: Tehran
KM# 523.10 2 ABBASI
9.2000 g., Silver **Obv:** Inscription **Rev:** Inscription within flower design **Note:** Type C.

Date	Mintage	F	VF	XF	Unc
AH1182	—	30.00	50.00	80.00	—
AH1186	—	30.00	50.00	80.00	—

Mint: Yazd
KM# 523.11 2 ABBASI
9.2000 g., Silver **Obv:** Inscription **Rev:** Inscription within flower design **Note:** Type C.

Date	Mintage	F	VF	XF	Unc
AH1182	—	20.00	35.00	55.00	—
AH1186	—	20.00	35.00	55.00	—
AH1189	—	20.00	35.00	55.00	—

Mint: Astarabad
KM# 512.1 RUPI
11.5000 g., Silver **Obv:** Inscription **Rev:** Inscription within circle **Note:** Type A.

Date	Mintage	F	VF	XF	Unc
AH1172	—	40.00	70.00	115	—
AH1173	—	40.00	70.00	115	—

Mint: Isfahan
KM# 512a RUPI
11.5000 g., Silver **Rev:** Mint and date **Note:** Type A.

Date	Mintage	F	VF	XF	Unc
AH1166	—	50.00	100	150	—

Mint: Isfahan
KM# 517.1 RUPI
11.5000 g., Silver **Obv:** Inscription **Rev:** Inscription **Note:** Type B.

Date	Mintage	F	VF	XF	Unc
AH1166	—	35.00	60.00	90.00	—
AH1169	—	35.00	60.00	100	—

Mint: Isfahan
KM# 524.1 RUPI
11.5000 g., Silver **Note:** Type C.

Date	Mintage	F	VF	XF	Unc
AH1190	—	25.00	45.00	75.00	—
AH1192	—	25.00	45.00	75.00	—

Mint: Kashan
KM# 517.2 RUPI
11.5000 g., Silver **Obv:** Inscription **Rev:** Inscription **Note:** Type B.

Date	Mintage	F	VF	XF	Unc
AH1171	—	45.00	75.00	120	—

Mint: Kirman
KM# 517.3 RUPI
11.5000 g., Silver **Obv:** Inscription **Rev:** Inscription **Note:** Type B.

Date	Mintage	F	VF	XF	Unc
AH1174	—	55.00	90.00	150	—

Mint: Mazandaran
KM# 512.2 RUPI
11.5000 g., Silver **Obv:** Inscription **Rev:** Inscription within circle **Note:** Type A.

Date	Mintage	F	VF	XF	Unc
AH1172	—	25.00	45.00	75.00	—
AH1173	—	25.00	45.00	75.00	—
AH1175	—	25.00	45.00	75.00	—

Note: Coins of Mazandaran dated AH1175 have sometimes been misread as AH1170

Mint: Qazvin
KM# 517.4 RUPI
11.5000 g., Silver **Obv:** Inscription **Rev:** Inscription **Note:** Type B.

Date	Mintage	F	VF	XF	Unc
AH1171	—	45.00	75.00	120	—
AH1173	—	45.00	75.00	120	—

Mint: Rasht
KM# 512.3 RUPI
Silver **Obv:** Inscription **Rev:** Inscription within circle **Note:** Type A.

Date	Mintage	F	VF	XF	Unc
AH1172	—	30.00	50.00	85.00	—
AH1173	—	30.00	50.00	85.00	—

Mint: Shiraz
KM# 517.5 RUPI
11.5000 g., Silver **Obv:** Inscription **Rev:** Inscription **Note:** Type B.

Date	Mintage	F	VF	XF	Unc
AH1168	—	35.00	60.00	90.00	—
AH1169	—	35.00	60.00	90.00	—
AH1170	—	30.00	50.00	80.00	—
AH1171	—	35.00	60.00	90.00	—
AH1172	—	30.00	50.00	80.00	—
AH1172/6	—	—	—	—	—
AH1173	—	40.00	65.00	100	—

Mint: Shiraz
KM# 524.2 RUPI
11.5000 g., Silver **Note:** Type C.

Date	Mintage	F	VF	XF	Unc
AH1193	—	25.00	45.00	75.00	—

Mint: Yazd
KM# A525 1/8 MOHUR
1.3800 g., Gold **Note:** Type C.

Date	Mintage	F	VF	XF	Unc
AH1186	—	100	160	220	—

Mint: Astarabad
KM# 530.1 1/4 MOHUR
2.7500 g., Gold **Obv:** Inscription within circle **Rev:** Inscription **Note:** Type D.

Date	Mintage	F	VF	XF	Unc
AH1184	—	100	175	250	—

Mint: Basra
KM# 530.2 1/4 MOHUR
2.7500 g., Gold **Obv:** Inscription within circle **Rev:** Inscription **Note:** Type D.

Date	Mintage	F	VF	XF	Unc
AH1191	—	300	500	750	—

Mint: Isfahan
KM# 518.1 1/4 MOHUR
2.7500 g., Gold **Obv:** Inscription **Rev:** Inscription within beaded circle **Note:** Type B.

Date	Mintage	F	VF	XF	Unc
AH1169	—	80.00	150	200	—
AH1171	—	80.00	150	200	—
AH1172	—	80.00	150	200	—

Mint: Isfahan
KM# 525.1 1/4 MOHUR
2.7500 g., Gold **Obv:** Inscription **Rev:** Inscription within flower design **Note:** Type C.

Date	Mintage	F	VF	XF	Unc
AH1172	—	70.00	110	140	—
AH1177	—	70.00	110	140	—
AH1178	—	70.00	110	140	—
AH1179	—	70.00	110	140	—
AH1183	—	70.00	110	140	—
AH1187	—	70.00	110	140	—

Mint: Kashan
KM# 518.2 1/4 MOHUR
2.7500 g., Gold **Obv:** Inscription **Rev:** Inscription within beaded circle **Note:** Type B.

Date	Mintage	F	VF	XF	Unc
AH1174	—	90.00	165	225	—

Mint: Kashan
KM# 525.2 1/4 MOHUR
2.7500 g., Gold **Obv:** Inscription **Rev:** Inscription within flower design **Note:** Type C.

Date	Mintage	F	VF	XF	Unc
AH1178	—	70.00	110	140	—
AH1179	—	70.00	110	140	—
AH1180	—	70.00	110	140	—
AH1182	—	70.00	110	140	—
AH1184	—	60.00	90.00	130	—
AH1185	—	60.00	90.00	130	—
AH1186	—	60.00	90.00	130	—
AH1187	—	60.00	90.00	130	—
AH1188	—	60.00	90.00	130	—
AH1189	—	70.00	110	140	—
AH1190	—	55.00	80.00	125	—
AH1191	—	60.00	90.00	130	—
AH1192	—	60.00	90.00	130	—

Mint: Khoy
KM# 525.3 1/4 MOHUR
2.7500 g., Gold **Obv:** Inscription **Rev:** Inscription within flower design **Note:** Type C.

Date	Mintage	F	VF	XF	Unc
AH1190	—	75.00	125	175	—
AH1191	—	75.00	125	175	—
AH1192	—	75.00	125	175	—
AH1193	—	75.00	125	175	—

Mint: Khoy
KM# 530.4 1/4 MOHUR
2.7500 g., Gold **Obv:** Inscription within circle **Rev:** Inscription **Note:** Type D.

Date	Mintage	F	VF	XF	Unc
AH1189	—	100	150	200	—

Mint: Kirman
KM# 530.3 1/4 MOHUR
2.7500 g., Gold **Obv:** Inscription within circle **Rev:** Inscription **Note:** Type D.

Date	Mintage	F	VF	XF	Unc
AH1180	—	100	130	175	—

Mint: Mazandaran
KM# 525.4 1/4 MOHUR
2.7500 g., Gold **Obv:** Inscription **Rev:** Inscription within flower design **Note:** Type C.

Date	Mintage	F	VF	XF	Unc
AH1189	—	—	—	—	—
Note: Reported, not confirmed					
AH1190	—	—	—	—	—
Note: Reported, not confirmed					
AH1191	—	70.00	115	140	—

Mint: Qazvin
KM# 525.5 1/4 MOHUR
2.7500 g., Gold **Obv:** Inscription **Rev:** Inscription within flower design **Note:** Type C.

Date	Mintage	F	VF	XF	Unc
AH1177	—	60.00	90.00	130	—
AH1178	—	60.00	90.00	130	—
AH1179	—	60.00	90.00	130	—
AH1181	—	60.00	90.00	130	—
AH1182	—	60.00	90.00	130	—
AH1183	—	60.00	90.00	130	—
AH1184	—	60.00	90.00	130	—
AH1186	—	55.00	80.00	125	—
AH1187	—	55.00	80.00	125	—
AH1190	—	55.00	80.00	125	—
AH1191	—	60.00	90.00	130	—
AH1192	—	60.00	90.00	130	—

Mint: Rasht
KM# 525.6 1/4 MOHUR
2.7500 g., Gold **Obv:** Inscription **Rev:** Inscription within flower design **Note:** Type C.

Date	Mintage	F	VF	XF	Unc
AH1183	—	70.00	110	145	—
AH1186	—	70.00	110	145	—

Mint: Rekab
KM# 518.3 1/4 MOHUR
2.7500 g., Gold **Obv:** Inscription **Rev:** Inscription within beaded circle **Note:** Type B.

Date	Mintage	F	VF	XF	Unc
AH1174	—	100	165	225	—

Mint: Rekab
KM# 530.5 1/4 MOHUR
2.7500 g., Gold **Obv:** Inscription within circle **Rev:** Inscription **Note:** Type D.

Date	Mintage	F	VF	XF	Unc
AH1176	—	80.00	120	160	—
AH1177	—	80.00	120	180	—
AH1178	—	70.00	110	160	—

Mint: Shiraz
KM# 518.4 1/4 MOHUR
2.7500 g., Gold **Obv:** Inscription **Rev:** Inscription within beaded circle **Note:** Type B.

Date	Mintage	F	VF	XF	Unc
AH1169	—	80.00	150	200	—

Mint: Shiraz
KM# 525.7 1/4 MOHUR
2.7500 g., Gold **Obv:** Inscription **Rev:** Inscription within flower design **Note:** Type C.

Date	Mintage	F	VF	XF	Unc
AH1193	—	75.00	120	160	—

Mint: Shiraz
KM# 530.6 1/4 MOHUR
2.7500 g., Gold **Obv:** Inscription within circle **Rev:** Inscription **Note:** Type D.

Date	Mintage	F	VF	XF	Unc
AH1179	—	80.00	120	160	—
AH1193	—	—	—	—	—

Mint: Tabriz
KM# 530.7 1/4 MOHUR
2.7500 g., Gold **Obv:** Inscription within circle **Rev:** Inscription **Note:** Type D.

Date	Mintage	F	VF	XF	Unc
AH1178	—	70.00	110	145	—
AH1180	—	70.00	110	145	—
AH1181	—	70.00	110	145	—
AH1182	—	70.00	110	145	—
AH1184	—	70.00	110	145	—
AH1185	—	70.00	110	145	—
AH1186	—	70.00	110	145	—
AH1187	—	70.00	110	145	—
AH1188	—	70.00	110	145	—
AH1189	—	70.00	110	145	—
AH1190	—	70.00	110	145	—
AH1191	—	70.00	110	145	—

Mint: Tehran
KM# 525.8 1/4 MOHUR
2.7500 g., Gold **Obv:** Inscription **Rev:** Inscription within flower design **Note:** Type C.

Date	Mintage	F	VF	XF	Unc
AH1181	—	100	160	225	—
AH1182	—	100	160	225	—

Mint: Yazd
KM# 525.9 1/4 MOHUR
2.7500 g., Gold **Obv:** Inscription **Rev:** Inscription within flower design **Note:** Type C.

Date	Mintage	F	VF	XF	Unc
AH1179	—	70.00	110	140	—
AH1180	—	70.00	110	140	—
AH1181	—	70.00	110	140	—
AH1186	—	60.00	90.00	130	—
AH1187	—	55.00	80.00	120	—
AH1188	—	55.00	80.00	120	—
AH1189	—	55.00	80.00	120	—
AH1190	—	55.00	80.00	120	—
AH1191	—	55.00	80.00	120	—
AH1192	—	55.00	80.00	120	—
AH1193	—	55.00	80.00	120	—

Mint: Basra
KM# 531.1 1/2 MOHUR
5.5000 g., Gold **Obv:** Evocation "Ya Karim" added **Rev:** Inscription within circle **Note:** Type D.

Date	Mintage	F	VF	XF	Unc
AH1190	—	350	500	650	—

Mint: Rasht
KM# 526 1/2 MOHUR
5.5000 g., Gold **Obv:** Evocation "Ya Karim" added **Rev:** Inscription **Note:** Type C.

Date	Mintage	F	VF	XF	Unc
AH1185	—	100	175	225	—
AH1188	—	80.00	125	175	—
AH1189	—	80.00	125	175	—
AH1190	—	80.00	110	150	—
AH1191	—	80.00	110	150	—
AH1192	—	80.00	125	175	—
AH1193	—	80.00	125	175	—

Mint: Shiraz
KM# 519 1/2 MOHUR
5.5000 g., Gold **Obv:** Evocation "Ya Karim" added **Note:** Type B.

Date	Mintage	F	VF	XF	Unc
AH1176	—	300	450	650	—

Mint: Shiraz
KM# 531.2 1/2 MOHUR
5.5000 g., Gold **Obv:** Evocation "Ya Karim" added **Rev:** Inscription within circle **Note:** Type D.

Date	Mintage	F	VF	XF	Unc
AH1184	—	90.00	140	200	—
AH1186	—	90.00	140	200	—
AH1187	—	90.00	140	200	—
AH1192	—	90.00	140	200	—
AH1193	—	90.00	140	200	—

Mint: Tabriz
KM# 531.3 1/2 MOHUR
5.5000 g., Gold **Obv:** Evocation "Ya Karim" added **Rev:** Inscription within circle **Note:** Type D.

Date	Mintage	F	VF	XF	Unc
AH1184	—	110	160	225	—
AH1187	—	110	160	225	—

Mint: Isfahan
KM# 520.1 MOHUR
11.0000 g., Gold **Obv:** Inscription **Rev:** Inscription within flower design **Note:** Type B.

Date	Mintage	F	VF	XF	Unc
AH1169	—	400	650	900	—

Mint: Jelou
KM# 520.2 MOHUR
11.0000 g., Gold **Obv:** Inscription **Rev:** Inscription within flower design **Note:** Type B.

Date	Mintage	F	VF	XF	Unc
AH1172 Rare	—	—	—	—	—

Mint: Mazandaran
KM# 513 MOHUR
11.0000 g., Gold **Rev:** Mint and date in small cartouche **Note:** Type B.

Date	Mintage	F	VF	XF	Unc
AH1176 Rare	—	—	—	—	—

Mint: Shiraz
KM# 520a MOHUR
11.0000 g., Gold **Obv:** Inscription **Obv. Legend:** "Ya Karim" added **Rev:** Inscription within design **Note:** Type B.

Date	Mintage	F	VF	XF	Unc
AH1174	—	450	700	1,000	—
AH1175	—	450	700	1,000	—

Mint: Shiraz
KM# 520.3 MOHUR
11.0000 g., Gold **Obv:** Inscription **Rev:** Inscription within flower design **Note:** Type B.

Date	Mintage	F	VF	XF	Unc
AH1171	—	400	650	900	—

Mint: Shiraz
KM# A532 MOHUR
11.0000 g., Gold **Note:** Type C.

Date	Mintage	F	VF	XF	Unc
AH1178	—	450	700	1,000	—

Shahrukh, 3rd Reign
AH1168-1210 / 1755-1796AD

Types for this ruler's 3rd Reign:

E. As B, but a different couplet. Struck only at Mashhad.

Sekkeh zad az sa'y-e nader-e thani sahebqeran. Kalb-e soltan-e Khorasan Shahrokh shah-e jahan.

"The dog of the sultan of Khorasan (i.e., the 8th Imam), Shahrukh, king of the world, has struck coin, by the efforts of Nadir, the second Sahebqiran." However, the puns and word plays enable various nuances of meaning that cannot be captured in translation.

F. Unread couplet obverse. Reverse as type E.

HAMMERED COINAGE

Mint: Mashhad
KM# 447 RUPI
11.5000 g., Silver **Obv:** Inscription **Rev:** Inscription within cartouche **Note:** Type E.

Date	Mintage	F	VF	XF	Unc
AH1186	—	50.00	80.00	135	—
AH1187	—	25.00	42.50	75.00	—
AH1189	—	25.00	42.50	75.00	—
AH1193	—	35.00	55.00	90.00	—
AH1195	—	35.00	55.00	90.00	—
AH1197	—	40.00	65.00	100	—

Note: Coins of AH1197 have not been re-examined and may be type F rather than type E

Mint: Mashhad
KM# 449 RUPI
11.5000 g., Silver **Note:** Type F.

Date	Mintage	F	VF	XF	Unc
AH1198	—	70.00	100	150	—

Mint: Mashhad
KM# 448 MOHUR
11.0000 g., Gold **Note:** Type E.

Date	Mintage	F	VF	XF	Unc
AH1186	—	250	350	500	—

Abu'l Fath Khan
AH1193 / 1779AD

Types for this reign:

A. (Couplet Type) As type C of Karim Khan, but evocation *Abu'l-Fath.*

B. (Kalima Type) As type D of Karim Khan, but evocation *Abu'l-Fath.*

HAMMERED COINAGE

Mint: Shiraz
KM# 541 SHAHI
1.1500 g., Silver **Obv:** Inscription **Rev:** Inscription **Note:** Type A.

Date	Mintage	F	VF	XF	Unc
AH1193	—	60.00	110	175	—

Mint: Without Mint Name
KM# 542 RUPI
11.5000 g., Silver **Note:** Type A. Mint unknown.

Date	Mintage	F	VF	XF	Unc
AH1193 Rare	—	—	—	—	—

Mint: Isfahan
KM# 544.1 1/4 MOHUR
2.7500 g., Gold **Note:** Type B.

Date	Mintage	F	VF	XF	Unc
AH1193	—	275	450	650	—

Mint: Shiraz
KM# 543.1 1/4 MOHUR
2.7500 g., Gold **Obv:** Inscription **Rev:** Inscription within design **Note:** Type A.

Date	Mintage	F	VF	XF	Unc
AH1193	—	—	—	—	—

Note: Reported, not confirmed

Mint: Shiraz
KM# 544.2 1/4 MOHUR
2.7500 g., Gold **Note:** Type B.

Date	Mintage	F	VF	XF	Unc
AH1193	—	275	450	650	—

Mint: Yazd
KM# 543.2 1/4 MOHUR
2.7500 g., Gold **Obv:** Inscription **Rev:** Inscription within design **Note:** Type A.

Date	Mintage	F	VF	XF	Unc
AH1193	—	275	450	650	—

Agha Muhammad Khan
AH1193-1211 / 1779-97AD

Types for this reign:

A. Obverse couplet. Reverse, mint & date, normally withthe mint epithet.

Be-zar sekkeh az meymanat zad qaza Be-nam-e 'Ali ebn-e Musa or-Reza.

"Fate has auspiciously struck coin in precious metal, in the name of Ali, son of Musa, Reza (i.e., the 8th Imam)." (Same couplet as type A of Muhammad Hasan Khan Qajar)

B1. Obverse couplet. Reverse, mint, date, usually the epithet, and the evocation *Ya Mohammad,* "O Muhammad".

Be-zar o sim ta neshan bashad Sekke-ye Saheb oz-Zaman bashad.

"So long as there shall be a stamp upon gold and silver, there shall be coin of the Master of Time".

B2. As B1, but variant of the couplet:

Ta zar o sim-ra neshan bashad Sekke-ye Saheb oz-Zaman bashad.

"So long as gold and silver shall have a design, there shall be coin of the Master of Time".

B3. As B1, but variant of the couplet:

Ta zar o sim dar jahan bashad Sekke-ye Saheb oz-Zaman bashad.

"So long as there is gold and silver in the world, there shall be coin of the Master of Time".

C. Obverse couplet. Reverse, mint, date, epithet and evocation as on type B.

Shod aftab o mah zar o sim dar jahan Az sekke-ye Emam be-haqq Saheb oz-Zaman.

"The sun and moon have become gold and silver throughout the world, from the coin of the Imam, indeed the Master of Time." This is the same couplet found on most types of Karim Khan Zand and the later Zands. The type is distinguished by the evocation.

C*. As type C, but without the evocation. These are coins of the rebellion of Ahmad Khan Donboli in Azerbayjan, but are traditionally, though somewhat incorrectly, assigned to Agha Muhammad Khan.

D. Obverse, the Shiite formula. Reverse, mint, date, epithet and evocation as on type B.

E. Obverse, within ornate border, the evocation *Ya Ali Vali Allah*, "O Ali, Friend of God". Reverse, mint and date (no epithet), with evocation, *Ya Mohammad.*

NOTE: The coinage of Agha Muhammad Khan is not well understood. The types are clear, but the denominations are tentative. In all probability, there were multiple monetary systems in use in different parts of Iran during his turbulent reign. However, there is at present no clear correlation between type, mint, and denomination. The silver coinage is particularly confused. The schema offered here is tentative. The rupi is believed to have been equal to 10 shahis, with a weight of 11.5 grams. It was gradually replaced after AH1204 with a riyal, weighing 12.67 grams, but reckoned as 20 shahis, thus incorporating a significant devaluation of the shahi. A large number of coins, particularly in gold, have been published without mention of type or denomination. These have been disregarded in the following listings, which are thus quite incomplete.

HAMMERED COINAGE

Mint: Isfahan
KM# 608.1 SHAHI
1.1500 g., Silver **Note:** Type B. Types B1, B2, and B3 are indicated here, with the variant noted after the name of the mint.

Date	Mintage	F	VF	XF	Unc
AH1204 (B1)	—	25.00	40.00	65.00	—

Mint: Isfahan
KM# 629.1 SHAHI
1.1500 g., Silver **Note:** Type D.

Date	Mintage	F	VF	XF	Unc
AH1211	—	40.00	65.00	100	—

Mint: Khoy
KM# 629.2 SHAHI
1.1500 g., Silver **Note:** Type D.

Date	Mintage	F	VF	XF	Unc
AH1210	—	40.00	65.00	100	—

Mint: Shiraz
KM# 608.2 SHAHI
1.1500 g., Silver **Note:** Type B. Types B1, B2 and B3 are indicated here, with the variant noted after the date.

Date	Mintage	F	VF	XF	Unc
AH1207 (B3)	—	25.00	40.00	65.00	—
AH1209 (B3)	—	25.00	40.00	65.00	—

Mint: Rasht
KM# A601 2 SHAHI
Silver **Obv:** Type C **Rev:** Mint **Note:**

Date	Mintage	Good	VG	F	VF	XF
ND	—	—	—	—	—	—

Mint: Astarabad
KM# 601 ABBASI
4.6000 g., Silver **Note:** Type A.

Date	Mintage	F	VF	XF	Unc
ND	—	35.00	60.00	90.00	—

Mint: Isfahan
KM# 609.1 ABBASI
4.6000 g., Silver **Note:** Type B.

Date	Mintage	F	VF	XF	Unc
AH1207 (B2?)	—	25.00	40.00	65.00	—
AH1208 (B1)	—	25.00	40.00	65.00	—
AH1208 (B2)	—	25.00	40.00	65.00	—

Mint: Kashan
KM# 609.2 ABBASI
4.6000 g., Silver **Note:** Type B.

Date	Mintage	F	VF	XF	Unc
AH1203 (B3)	—	40.00	65.00	100	—

Mint: Rasht
KM# 621.1 ABBASI
4.6000 g., Silver **Note:** Type C.

Date	Mintage	F	VF	XF	Unc
AH1202	—	30.00	50.00	80.00	—

Date	Mintage	F	VF	XF	Unc
AH1210	—	30.00	50.00	80.00	—
AH1201 Error for 1210	—	30.00	50.00	80.00	—

Mint: Shiraz
KM# 609.3 ABBASI
4.6000 g., Silver **Note:** Type B.

Date	Mintage	F	VF	XF	Unc
AH1206 (B3)	—	30.00	50.00	80.00	—
AH1207 (B3)	—	30.00	50.00	80.00	—

Mint: Yazd
KM# 621.2 ABBASI
4.6000 g., Silver **Note:** Type C.

Date	Mintage	F	VF	XF	Unc
AH1204 (?)	—	50.00	85.00	125	—

Mint: Astarabad
KM# 602.1 2 ABBASI
9.2000 g., Silver **Note:** Type A.

Date	Mintage	F	VF	XF	Unc
AH1200	—	40.00	65.00	100	—
ND	—	40.00	65.00	100	—

Mint: Isfahan
KM# 602.2 2 ABBASI
9.2000 g., Silver **Note:** Type A.

Date	Mintage	F	VF	XF	Unc
AH1199	—	40.00	65.00	100	—

Mint: Mazandaran
KM# 602.3 2 ABBASI
9.2000 g., Silver **Note:** Type A.

Date	Mintage	F	VF	XF	Unc
AH1194	—	30.00	45.00	75.00	—
AH1195	—	30.00	45.00	75.00	—
AH1196	—	30.00	45.00	75.00	—
AH1198	—	30.00	45.00	75.00	—

Mint: Mazandaran
KM# 611 2 ABBASI
9.2000 g., Silver **Note:** Type B.

Date	Mintage	F	VF	XF	Unc
AH1201 (B1)	—	40.00	65.00	100	—

Mint: Isfahan
KM# 603.1 RUPI
11.5000 g., Silver **Note:** Type A.

Date	Mintage	F	VF	XF	Unc
AH1199	—	70.00	100	150	—

Mint: Isfahan
KM# 612.1 RUPI
11.5000 g., Silver **Note:** Type B.

Date	Mintage	F	VF	XF	Unc
AH1204 (B1)	—	30.00	65.00	70.00	—

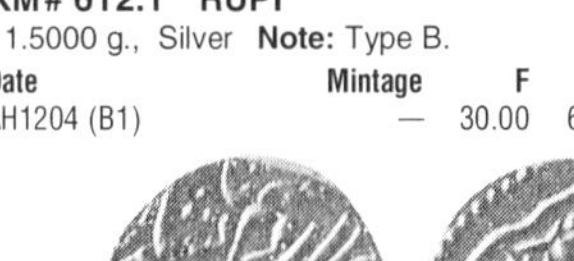

Mint: Isfahan
KM# 612a RUPI
8.9000 g., Silver **Note:** Type B. Reduced standard. Believed to be an imitation struck in the Durrani lands (modern Afghanistan or Pakistan). Most specimens are struck from substantially debased metal.

Date	Mintage	F	VF	XF	Unc
AH1206 (B1)	—	10.00	17.50	27.50	—
ND (B1)	—	10.00	17.50	27.50	—

Mint: Isfahan
KM# 622.1 RUPI
11.0000 g., Silver **Note:** Type C.

Date	Mintage	F	VF	XF	Unc
AH1201	—	25.00	40.00	65.00	—

Mint: Kashan
KM# 603.2 RUPI
11.5000 g., Silver **Note:** Type A.

Date	Mintage	F	VF	XF	Unc
AH1195 (sic)	—	80.00	125	200	—
AH1200	—	80.00	125	200	—

Mint: Khoy
KM# 622.2 RUPI
11.0000 g., Silver **Note:** Type C.

Date	Mintage	F	VF	XF	Unc
AH1199	—	50.00	85.00	130	—

Mint: Mashhad
KM# 622.3 RUPI
11.0000 g., Silver **Note:** Type C.

Date	Mintage	F	VF	XF	Unc
AH1211	—	50.00	85.00	130	—

Note: 30,000 pieces were struck in Mashhad in AH1211, as tribute to the conqueror Qajar army, who occupied the city for several weeks at the beginning of that year

Mint: Qazvín
KM# 612.2 RUPI
11.5000 g., Silver **Note:** Type B.

Date	Mintage	F	VF	XF	Unc
AH1204 (B2)	—	40.00	45.00	100	—

Mint: Shiraz
KM# 612.3 RUPI
11.5000 g., Silver **Note:** Type B.

Date	Mintage	F	VF	XF	Unc
AH1207 (B3)	—	40.00	45.00	100	—
AH1209 (B3)	—	40.00	45.00	100	—

Mint: Shiraz
KM# 630 RUPI
11.5000 g., Silver **Note:** Type D.

Date	Mintage	F	VF	XF	Unc
AH1209	—	30.00	50.00	80.00	—
AH1211	—	30.00	50.00	80.00	—

Mint: Tabriz
KM# 622.4 RUPI
11.0000 g., Silver **Note:** Type C.

Date	Mintage	F	VF	XF	Unc
AH1212	—	40.00	60.00	85.00	—

Mint: Isfahan
KM# 610.1 5 ABBASI
5.7500 g., Silver **Note:** Type B.

Date	Mintage	F	VF	XF	Unc
AH1201 (B1)	—	30.00	45.00	75.00	—

Note: Probably error for 1210

Date	Mintage	F	VF	XF	Unc
AH1210 (B1)	—	30.00	45.00	75.00	—
AH1211 (B1)	—	25.00	40.00	665	—

Mint: Kashan
KM# 610.2 5 ABBASI
5.7500 g., Silver **Note:** Type B.

Date	Mintage	F	VF	XF	Unc
AH1211 (B2)	—	40.00	65.00	100	—

Mint: Tehran
KM# 610.3 5 ABBASI
5.7500 g., Silver **Note:** Type B.

Date	Mintage	F	VF	XF	Unc
AH1210 (B1)	—	40.00	65.00	100	—

Mint: Tabriz
KM# 631 1/2 RIAL
6.3300 g., Silver **Note:** Type D.

Date	Mintage	F	VF	XF	Unc
AH1211	—	35.00	60.00	90.00	—

Mint: Ganjah
KM# 632.1 RIAL
12.6700 g., Silver **Note:** Type D.

Date	Mintage	F	VF	XF	Unc
AH1204	—	65.00	100	160	—

Mint: Ganjah
KM# 638 RIAL
12.6700 g., Silver **Note:** Type E.

Date	Mintage	F	VF	XF	Unc
AH1208	—	65.00	100	160	—
AH1210	—	65.00	100	160	—
AH1211	—	65.00	100	160	—
AH1212	—	65.00	100	160	—

Mint: Isfahan
KM# 613.1 RIAL
12.6700 g., Silver **Note:** Type B.

Date	Mintage	F	VF	XF	Unc
AH1206 (B1)	—	40.00	65.00	100	—

Mint: Kashan
KM# 623.1 RIAL
12.6700 g., Silver **Note:** Type C.

Date	Mintage	F	VF	XF	Unc
AH1209	—	35.00	55.00	90.00	—
AH1210	—	35.00	55.00	90.00	—

Mint: Khoy
KM# 623.2 RIAL
12.6700 g., Silver **Note:** Type C.

Date	Mintage	F	VF	XF	Unc
AH1204 (C*)	—	50.00	85.00	125	—
AH1205 (C*)	—	50.00	85.00	125	—
AH1206	—	40.00	65.00	100	—
AH1207	—	40.00	65.00	100	—
AH1208	—	40.00	65.00	100	—
AH1209	—	—	—	—	—

Note: Reported, not confirmed

Mint: Khoy
KM# 632.2 RIAL
12.6700 g., Silver **Note:** Type D.

Date	Mintage	F	VF	XF	Unc
AH1210	—	35.00	65.00	100	—
AH1211	—	35.00	65.00	100	—
AH1212	—	40.00	70.00	100	—

Mint: Mazandaran
KM# 623.3 RIAL
12.6700 g., Silver **Note:** Type C.

Date	Mintage	F	VF	XF	Unc
ND	—	35.00	55.00	80.00	—

Mint: Qazvin
KM# 623.4 RIAL
12.6700 g., Silver **Note:** Type C.

Date	Mintage	F	VF	XF	Unc
AH1207	—	30.00	45.00	70.00	—
AH1208	—	30.00	45.00	70.00	—
AH1209	—	30.00	45.00	70.00	—
AH1210	—	30.00	45.00	70.00	—
AH1211	—	30.00	45.00	70.00	—

Mint: Rasht
KM# 623.5 RIAL
12.6700 g., Silver **Note:** Type C.

Date	Mintage	F	VF	XF	Unc
AH1210	—	35.00	55.00	80.00	—
AH1211	—	35.00	55.00	80.00	—

Mint: Shiraz
KM# 613.2 RIAL
12.6700 g., Silver **Note:** Type B.

Date	Mintage	F	VF	XF	Unc
AH1208 (B3)	—	40.00	65.00	100	—

Mint: Tabriz
KM# 623.6 RIAL
12.6700 g., Silver **Note:** Type C.

Date	Mintage	F	VF	XF	Unc
AH1204 (C*)	—	40.00	70.00	110	—
AH1205 (C*)	—	40.00	70.00	110	—
AH1206	—	25.00	40.00	60.00	—
AH1207	—	25.00	40.00	60.00	—
AH1208	—	25.00	40.00	65.00	—
AH1209	—	25.00	40.00	65.00	—

Mint: Tabriz
KM# 632.3 RIAL
12.6700 g., Silver **Note:** Type D.

Date	Mintage	F	VF	XF	Unc
AH1211	—	40.00	70.00	100	—

Mint: Tehran
KM# 613.3 RIAL
12.6700 g., Silver **Note:** Type B.

Date	Mintage	F	VF	XF	Unc
AH1210 (B2)	—	50.00	85.00	140	—

Note: The riyal of Tehran AH1210 has the month Muhrarram

Mint: Urumi
KM# 623.7 RIAL
12.6700 g., Silver **Note:** Type C.

Date	Mintage	F	VF	XF	Unc
AH1204 (C*)	—	60.00	100	175	—

Mint: Yazd
KM# 613.4 RIAL
12.6700 g., Silver **Note:** Type B.

Date	Mintage	F	VF	XF	Unc
AH1210 (B1)	—	50.00	85.00	140	—

Mint: Yazd
KM# 632.4 RIAL
12.6700 g., Silver **Note:** Type D.

Date	Mintage	F	VF	XF	Unc
AH1211	—	50.00	85.00	125	—

Mint: Isfahan
KM# 624a.1 1/4 TOMAN
2.8800 g., Gold **Note:** Type C.

Date	Mintage	F	VF	XF	Unc
AH1204	—	90.00	135	185	—

Mint: Kashan
KM# 624a.2 1/4 TOMAN
2.8800 g., Gold **Note:** Type C.

Date	Mintage	F	VF	XF	Unc
AH1203	—	100	150	225	—
AH1205	—	85.00	110	150	—

Mint: Khoy
KM# 625 1/4 TOMAN
2.0500 g., Gold **Note:** Type C.

Date	Mintage	F	VF	XF	Unc
AH1208	—	125	180	260	—

Mint: Mazandaran
KM# 624a.3 1/4 TOMAN
2.8800 g., Gold **Note:** Type C.

Date	Mintage	F	VF	XF	Unc
AH1204	—	100	150	225	—

Mint: Rasht
KM# 624 1/4 TOMAN
3.2000 g., Gold **Note:** Type C.

Date	Mintage	F	VF	XF	Unc
AH1201	—	80.00	100	140	—

Mint: Rasht
KM# 624a.4 1/4 TOMAN
2.8800 g., Gold **Note:** Type C.

Date	Mintage	F	VF	XF	Unc
AH1202	—	70.00	90.00	125	—
AH1203	—	70.00	90.00	125	—
AH1204	—	70.00	90.00	125	—
AH1205	—	70.00	90.00	125	—

Mint: Isfahan
KM# 615.1 1/2 TOMAN
4.1000 g., Gold **Note:** Type B.

Date	Mintage	F	VF	XF	Unc
AH1204 (B1)	—	90.00	135	185	—

Mint: Kashan
KM# 615.2 1/2 TOMAN
4.1000 g., Gold **Note:** Type B.

Date	Mintage	F	VF	XF	Unc
AH1209 (B2)	—	80.00	125	170	—

Mint: Kashan
KM# 626.1 1/2 TOMAN
4.1000 g., Gold **Note:** Type C.

Date	Mintage	F	VF	XF	Unc
AH1205	—	100	130	175	—

Mint: Khoy
KM# 633.1 1/2 TOMAN
4.1000 g., Gold **Note:** Type D.

Date	Mintage	F	VF	XF	Unc
AH1211	—	85.00	120	175	—

Mint: Rasht
KM# 626.2 1/2 TOMAN
4.1000 g., Gold **Note:** Type C.

Date	Mintage	F	VF	XF	Unc
AH1206	—	75.00	100	135	—
AH1207	—	75.00	100	135	—
AH1208	—	75.00	100	135	—
AH1209	—	90.00	125	175	—

Mint: Shiraz
KM# 615.3 1/2 TOMAN
4.1000 g., Gold **Note:** Type B.

Date	Mintage	F	VF	XF	Unc
AH1206	—	100	145	185	—
AH1209 (B3)	—	100	145	200	—

Mint: Tabriz
KM# 633.2 1/2 TOMAN
4.1000 g., Gold **Note:** Type D.

Date	Mintage	F	VF	XF	Unc
AH1211	—	100	140	225	—
AH1212	—	85.00	120	175	—

Mint: Tehran
KM# 633.3 1/2 TOMAN
4.1000 g., Gold **Note:** Type D.

Date	Mintage	F	VF	XF	Unc
AH1211	—	85.00	120	175	—

Mint: Tehran
KM# 617 2 TOMAN
16.4000 g., Gold **Note:** Type B.

Date	Mintage	F	VF	XF	Unc
AH1209 (B1); Rare	—	—	—	—	—

Mint: Tehran
KM# 643.2 10 TOMAN
81.0000 g., Gold **Note:** Type B. Similar to type D.

Date	Mintage	F	VF	XF	Unc
AH1210 Rare	—	—	—	—	—
AH1211 Rare	—	—	—	—	—

Mint: Astarabad
KM# 604.1 1/4 MOHUR
2.7500 g., Gold **Note:** Type A.

Date	Mintage	F	VF	XF	Unc
AH1198	—	100	150	200	—

Mint: Kashan
KM# 604.2 1/4 MOHUR
2.7500 g., Gold **Note:** Type A.

Date	Mintage	F	VF	XF	Unc
AH1200	—	100	140	185	—
AH1201	—	100	140	185	—

Mint: Mazandaran
KM# 604.3 1/4 MOHUR
2.7500 g., Gold **Note:** Type A.

Date	Mintage	F	VF	XF	Unc
AH1195	—	90.00	130	180	—
AH1197	—	90.00	130	180	—
AH1199	—	90.00	130	180	—

PRESENTATION COINAGE

Mint: Isfahan
KM# 643.1 10 TOMAN
81.0000 g., Gold **Note:** Type B. Similar to type D.

Date	Mintage	F	VF	XF	Unc
AH1210 Rare	—	—	—	—	—

Mint: Tehran
KM# 645 20 TOMAN
162.0000 g., Gold **Obv:** Peacock in full splendor **Rev:** Mint, date, and epithet **Note:** Type B.

Date	Mintage	F	VF	XF	Unc
AH1210 Rare	—	—	—	—	—

Mint: Tehran
KM# 646 20 TOMAN
162.0000 g., Gold **Obv:** Lion left with tail upraised, sun rising behind **Note:** Type B.

Date	Mintage	F	VF	XF	Unc
AH1210 Rare	—	—	—	—	—

Mint: Tehran
KM# 644 20 TOMAN
162.0000 g., Gold **Note:** Type B. Similar to type D.

Date	Mintage	F	VF	XF	Unc
AH1210 Rare	—	—	—	—	—

Mint: Tehran
KM# 647 50 TOMAN
402.0000 g., Gold **Note:** Type B. Similar to type D but with ornate outer margins. Square.

Date	Mintage	F	VF	XF	Unc
AH1210 Rare	—	—	—	—	—

Sadiq Khan

AH1193-1196 / 1779-1781AD

Types for this reign:

All coins of this reign bear the evocation *Ya Karim* as used by Karim Khan. Coins dated AH1193 may belong to either Karim Khan or Sadiq Khan, and are listed under Karim Khan.

A. (Couplet Type) Identical to type C of Karim Khan, including the evocation *Ya Karim.*

B. (Kalima Type) Identical to type D of Karim Khan, with evocation as last.

HAMMERED COINAGE

Mint: Tabriz
KM# 553 SHAHI
1.1500 g., Silver **Obv:** Inscription within circle **Rev:** Inscriptionn within design **Note:** Type B.

Date	Mintage	F	VF	XF	Unc
AH1194	—	40.00	65.00	110	—
AH1195	—	40.00	65.00	110	—

Mint: Yazd
KM# 547 SHAHI
1.1500 g., Silver **Note:** Type A.

Date	Mintage	F	VF	XF	Unc
AH1195	—	40.00	70.00	110	—

Mint: Mazandaran
KM# 548 ABBASI
4.6000 g., Silver **Note:** Type A.

Date	Mintage	F	VF	XF	Unc
AH1194	—	30.00	50.00	85.00	—

Mint: Mazandaran
KM# 549 2 ABBASI
9.2000 g., Silver **Obv:** Inscription **Rev:** Inscription **Note:** Type A.

Date	Mintage	F	VF	XF	Unc
AH1194	—	35.00	60.00	100	—

Mint: Isfahan
KM# 550.1 RUPI
11.5000 g., Silver **Obv:** Inscription **Rev:** Inscription, date **Note:** Type A.

Date	Mintage	F	VF	XF	Unc
AH1194	—	35.00	60.00	100	—
AH1195	—	35.00	60.00	100	—
AH1196	—	35.00	60.00	100	—

Mint: Isfahan
KM# A551 RUPI
11.5000 g., Silver **Rev:** "Ya Karim" omitted from legend **Note:** Type A.

Date	Mintage	F	VF	XF	Unc
AH1195	—	45.00	75.00	115	—

Mint: Kashan
KM# 550.2 RUPI
11.5000 g., Silver **Obv:** Inscription **Rev:** Inscription, date **Note:** Type A.

Date	Mintage	F	VF	XF	Unc
AH1194	—	40.00	65.00	100	—
AH1195	—	40.00	65.00	100	—
AH1196	—	40.00	65.00	100	—

Mint: Khoy
KM# 550.3 RUPI
11.5000 g., Silver **Obv:** Inscription **Rev:** Inscription, date **Note:** Type A.

Date	Mintage	F	VF	XF	Unc
AH1195	—	50.00	80.00	145	—

Mint: Shiraz
KM# 550.4 RUPI
11.5000 g., Silver **Obv:** Inscription **Rev:** Inscription, date **Note:** Type A.

Date	Mintage	F	VF	XF	Unc
AH1193	—	40.00	65.00	100	—
AH1194	—	35.00	60.00	100	—
AH1195	—	35.00	60.00	100	—
AH1196	—	40.00	65.00	100	—

Mint: Kirman
KM# 554 1/8 MOHUR
1.3800 g., Gold **Note:** Type B.

Date	Mintage	F	VF	XF	Unc
AH1195	—	150	200	275	—

Mint: Kashan
KM# 551.1 1/4 MOHUR
2.7500 g., Gold **Obv:** Inscription, date within small circle **Rev:** Inscription **Note:** Type A.

Date	Mintage	F	VF	XF	Unc
AH1195	—	100	140	200	—
AH1196	—	100	140	200	—
AH1197 (sic)	—	100	140	200	—

Mint: Khoy
KM# 551.2 1/4 MOHUR
2.7500 g., Gold **Obv:** Inscription, date within small circle **Rev:** Inscription **Note:** Type A.

Date	Mintage	F	VF	XF	Unc
AH1194	—	100	150	225	—
AH1195	—	100	150	225	—

Mint: Kirman
KM# 551.3 1/4 MOHUR
2.7500 g., Gold **Obv:** Inscription, date within small circle **Rev:** Inscription **Note:** Type A.

Date	Mintage	F	VF	XF	Unc
AH1196	—	110	165	250	—

Mint: Qazvin
KM# 551.4 1/4 MOHUR
2.7500 g., Gold **Obv:** Inscription, date within small circle **Rev:** Inscription **Note:** Type A.

Date	Mintage	F	VF	XF	Unc
AH1194	—	100	140	200	—
AH1195	—	110	165	250	—

Mint: Yazd
KM# 551.5 1/4 MOHUR
2.7500 g., Gold **Obv:** Inscription, date within small circle **Rev:** Inscription **Note:** Type A.

Date	Mintage	F	VF	XF	Unc
AH1194	—	100	140	200	—
AH1195	—	100	140	200	—
AH1196	—	100	140	200	—

Mint: Shiraz
KM# A552 1/2 MOHUR
5.5000 g., Gold **Note:** Type B.

Date	Mintage	F	VF	XF	Unc
AH1195	—	150	200	275	—

Mint: Shiraz
KM# 552 MOHUR
11.0000 g., Gold **Obv:** Inscription **Rev:** Inscription within circle **Note:** Type A.

Date	Mintage	F	VF	XF	Unc
AH1194	—	500	950	1,000	—
AH1195	—	500	750	1,000	—

Ali Murad Khan

AH1196-1199 / 1781-1785AD

Types for this reign:

A. (Couplet Type) As type C of Karim Khan, but evocation *Ya Ali.*

B. (Kalima Type) As type D of Karim Khan, but evocation *Ya Ali.*

HAMMERED COINAGE

Mint: Isfahan
KM# 557.1 SHAHI
1.1500 g., Silver **Obv:** Inscription **Rev:** Inscription **Note:** Type A.

Date	Mintage	F	VF	XF	Unc
AH1197	—	20.00	35.00	60.00	—
AH1198	—	20.00	35.00	60.00	—

Mint: Shiraz
KM# 557.2 SHAHI
1.1500 g., Silver **Obv:** Inscription **Rev:** Inscription **Note:** Type A.

Date	Mintage	F	VF	XF	Unc
AH1198	—	30.00	50.00	80.00	—

Mint: Rasht
KM# 558 1/3 RUPI
3.8300 g., Silver **Obv:** Inscription **Rev:** Inscription within design **Note:** Type A.

Date	Mintage	F	VF	XF	Unc
AH1196	—	30.00	50.00	80.00	—
AH1197	—	30.00	50.00	80.00	—
AH1198	—	35.00	55.00	90.00	—
AH1199	—	30.00	50.00	80.00	—

Mint: Mazandaran
KM# 559 2 ABBASI
9.2000 g., Silver **Note:** Type A. Retrograde date known on specimens.

Date	Mintage	F	VF	XF	Unc
AH1197	—	50.00	80.00	120	—

Mint: Isfahan
KM# 560.1 RUPI
11.5000 g., Silver **Obv:** Inscription **Rev:** Inscription **Note:** Type A.

Date	Mintage	F	VF	XF	Unc
AH1194	—	40.00	60.00	100	—
AH1196	—	30.00	45.00	70.00	—
AH1197	—	30.00	45.00	70.00	—
AH1198	—	30.00	45.00	70.00	—

Mint: Kashan
KM# 560.2 RUPI
11.5000 g., Silver **Obv:** Inscription **Rev:** Inscription **Note:** Type A.

Date	Mintage	F	VF	XF	Unc
AH1196	—	35.00	55.00	85.00	—
AH1198	—	35.00	55.00	85.00	—

Mint: Qazvin
KM# 560.3 RUPI
11.5000 g., Silver **Obv:** Inscription **Rev:** Inscription **Note:** Type A.

Date	Mintage	F	VF	XF	Unc
AH1198	—	40.00	65.00	90.00	—

Mint: Shiraz
KM# 560.4 RUPI
11.5000 g., Silver **Obv:** Inscription **Rev:** Inscription **Note:** Type A.

Date	Mintage	F	VF	XF	Unc
AH1196	—	30.00	50.00	75.00	—
AH1197	—	30.00	50.00	75.00	—
AH1198	—	30.00	50.00	75.00	—

Mint: Kashan
KM# 561.1 1/4 MOHUR
2.7500 g., Gold **Obv:** Inscription **Rev:** Inscription within design **Note:** Type A.

Date	Mintage	F	VF	XF	Unc
AH1197	—	100	140	180	—
AH1198	—	100	140	180	—
AH1199	—	100	140	180	—

Mint: Mazandaran
KM# 561.2 1/4 MOHUR
2.7500 g., Gold **Obv:** Inscription **Rev:** Inscription within design **Note:** Type A.

Date	Mintage	F	VF	XF	Unc
AH1198	—	120	175	225	—

Mint: Qazvin
KM# 561.3 1/4 MOHUR
2.7500 g., Gold **Obv:** Inscription **Rev:** Inscription within design **Note:** Type A.

Date	Mintage	F	VF	XF	Unc
AH1198	—	105	145	200	—

Mint: Rasht
KM# 561.4 1/4 MOHUR
2.7500 g., Gold **Obv:** Inscription **Rev:** Inscription within design **Note:** Type A.

Date	Mintage	F	VF	XF	Unc
AH1196	—	90.00	130	170	—
AH1197	—	90.00	130	170	—
AH1198	—	90.00	130	170	—
AH1199	—	90.00	130	170	—

Mint: Yazd
KM# 561.5 1/4 MOHUR
2.7500 g., Gold **Obv:** Inscription **Rev:** Inscription within design **Note:** Type A.

Date	Mintage	F	VF	XF	Unc
AH1197	—	90.00	130	170	—
AH1198	—	90.00	130	170	—
AH1199	—	—	—	—	—

Note: Reported, not confirmed

Mint: Shiraz
KM# 564 MOHUR
11.0000 g., Gold **Obv:** Inscription **Rev:** Inscription **Note:** Type B.

Date	Mintage	F	VF	XF	Unc
AH1197	—	400	550	750	—
AH1198	—	400	550	750	—

Hedayat Khan

AH1199-1200 / 1785-1786AD

Type for this reign:

A. (Kalima Type) As type D of Karim Khan, including the evocation *Ya Karim*. The only type known for reign.

HAMMERED COINAGE

Mint: Rasht
KM# 570 1/3 RUPI
3.8300 g., Silver **Note:** Type A.

Date	Mintage	F	VF	XF	Unc
AH1200	—	60.00	90.00	140	—

Mint: Rasht
KM# 571 1/4 MOHUR
2.7500 g., Gold **Rev:** Invocation "Ya Allah" instead of "Ya Karim" **Note:** Type A.

Date	Mintage	F	VF	XF	Unc
AH1200	—	200	250	325	—

Isma'il Khan

AH1200 / 1785AD

Type for this reign:

A. (Couplet Type) As type C of Karim Khan or type A of Ali Morad, but without evocation. The only type known for reign.

HAMMERED COINAGE

Mint: Qazvin
KM# 573 1/4 MOHUR
2.7500 g., Gold **Note:** Type A.

Date	Mintage	F	VF	XF	Unc
AH1200	—	175	275	375	—
AH1201 (sic)	—	150	240	300	—

Ja'far Khan

AH1199-1203 / 1785-1789AD

Type for this reign:

A. Obverse evocation, *Ya Emam Ja'far Sadeq*, "O Imam Ja'far Sadeq." Reverse: Mint, mint epithet, and date. The only type known for reign.

NOTE: Ja'far was murdered on 25 Rabi II AH1203/23 January 1789, but coins were struck posthumously in his name at Shiraz by the partisans of Lutf Ali Khan in AH1204 and AH1205.

HAMMERED COINAGE

Mint: Isfahan
KM# 576.1 SHAHI
1.1000 g., Silver **Obv:** Inscription **Rev:** Inscription **Note:** Type A.

Date	Mintage	F	VF	XF	Unc
AH1199	—	50.00	85.00	140	—

Mint: Shiraz
KM# 576.2 SHAHI
1.1000 g., Silver **Obv:** Inscription **Rev:** Inscription **Note:** Type A.

Date	Mintage	F	VF	XF	Unc
AH1199	—	40.00	70.00	110	—
AH1202	—	40.00	70.00	110	—

 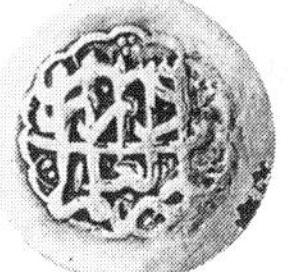

Mint: Shiraz
KM# 577 ABBASI
4.6000 g., Silver **Obv:** Inscription **Rev:** Inscription within flower design **Note:** Type A.

Date	Mintage	F	VF	XF	Unc
AH1200	—	60.00	100	160	—
AH1201	—	60.00	100	160	—
AH1205 (sic)	—	75.00	125	185	—

Mint: Isfahan
KM# 578.1 RUPI
11.5000 g., Silver **Obv:** Inscription **Rev:** Inscription within circle **Note:** Type A.

Date	Mintage	F	VF	XF	Unc
AH1199	—	75.00	125	200	—

Mint: Shiraz
KM# 578.2 RUPI
11.5000 g., Silver **Obv:** Inscription **Rev:** Inscription within circle **Note:** Type A.

Date	Mintage	F	VF	XF	Unc
AH1199	—	60.00	100	160	—
AH1200	—	60.00	100	160	—
AH1201	—	60.00	100	160	—
AH1202	—	75.00	125	200	—
AH1203	—	75.00	125	200	—
AH1204	—	75.00	125	200	—

Mint: Shiraz
KM# 579 1/4 MOHUR
2.7500 g., Gold **Note:** Type A.

Date	Mintage	F	VF	XF	Unc
AH1201	—	300	475	750	—
AH1203	—	300	475	750	—

Mint: Shiraz
KM# 580 MOHUR
11.0000 g., Gold **Note:** Type A.

Date	Mintage	F	VF	XF	Unc
AH1199	—	400	600	1,000	—
AH1200	—	400	600	1,000	—
AH1201	—	400	600	1,000	—
AH1202	—	400	600	1,000	—

Taqi Khan Bafqi

AH1199-1201 / 1785-1787AD

Types for this reign:

A. (Couplet Type) As type C of Karim Khan or type A of Ali Morad, but without evocation. The only type known for reign.

HAMMERED COINAGE

Mint: Yazd
KM# A567 RUPI
Silver **Obv:** Inscription **Rev:** Inscription within design **Note:** Type A.

Date	Mintage	F	VF	XF	Unc
AH1199 Rare	—	—	—	—	—

Mint: Yazd
KM# 567 1/4 MOHUR
2.7500 g., Gold **Note:** Type A.

Date	Mintage	F	VF	XF	Unc
AH1199	—	160	225	300	—

Lutf Ali Khan

AH1203-1209 / 1789-1794AD

Types for this reign:

A. As Type D of Karim Khan, including invocation *Ya Karim*.

B. Obverse inscription, *Sekkeh bar zar gasht din-e Ja'far az Lutf-e "Ali*, "By the grace of Ali, the religion of Ja'far (i.e., Twelver Shiism) became the golden coin of the realm." Reverse, mint and epithet, with date and evocation, *Lutf 'Ali*.

NOTE: A third type is said to exist, similar to type C of Karim Khan, but with evocation *Lutf 'Ali*. No specimen has been confirmed, though the Shiraz gold coin of undetermined denomination reported by Markov is probably of this type.

HAMMERED COINAGE

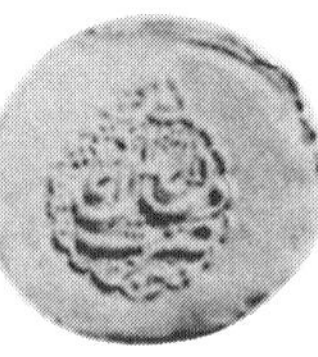

Mint: Kirman
KM# 587 1/4 TOMAN
Gold **Note:** Type A. Approx. 2.7 grams.

Date	Mintage	F	VF	XF	Unc
AH1204	—	200	300	475	—
AH1205	—	200	300	475	—
AH1206	—	200	300	475	—

Mint: Kirman
KM# 588 1/4 TOMAN
2.0500 g., Gold **Note:** Type B.

Date	Mintage	F	VF	XF	Unc
AH1207	—	200	300	475	—
Note: It is not known whether AH1207 is KM#587 or KM#588					
AH1208	—	200	300	475	—

Sayyid Murad

AH1203-1204 / 1789-1790AD

Type for this reign:

A. (Couplet Type) As type C of Karim Khan, with evocation Sayyid Murad.

HAMMERED COINAGE

Mint: Shiraz
KM# 583 SHAHI
1.1500 g., Silver **Note:** Type A.

Date	Mintage	F	VF	XF	Unc
AH1203	—	125	200	300	—

Mint: Shiraz
KM# 584 RUPI
11.5000 g., Silver **Note:** Type A.

Date	Mintage	F	VF	XF	Unc
AH1203	—	200	300	400	—

Baba Khan

AH1211-1212 / 1797 -1798AD

(Fath ali before coronation.)

Baba Khan was the name used by Fath'ali Shah for about 3 months prior to his official julus, or coronation. Mint premiums as for Fath'ali Shah. All known coins of Baba Khan are dated AH1212. They fall into two standards, the first based on a Rupee of 60 Nokhod (= 11.50 g), the second on a Riyal of 54 Nokhod (= 10.40 g).

Types for this reign:

A. Obverse name and benediction, *al-mulk lillah al-Sultan Baba Khan* ("the kingdom is God's, Sultan Baba Khan"). Reverse, mint (sometimes with epithet) & date, with pious evocation above, *al-izzat lillah*, "God's is the glory".

B. Similar to type A, but without the pious evocation above the reverse. Sometimes undated. Type B coins almost always have the mint with its epithet.

C. Obverse, the Shiite formula. Reverse, mint, usually with epithet, and date. Above, in smaller letters, *Baba*

HAMMERED COINAGE

Mint: Isfahan
KM# 654.1 SHAHI SEFID
1.1500 g., Silver **Note:** Type B.

Date	Mintage	F	VF	XF	Unc
ND(1211-12)	—	40.00	65.00	100	—
AH1212	—	40.00	65.00	100	—

Mint: Kashan
KM# 654.2 SHAHI SEFID
1.1500 g., Silver **Note:** Type B.

Date	Mintage	F	VF	XF	Unc
AH1212	—	45.00	75.00	120	—

Mint: Without Mint Name
KM# 659.1 1/2 RIAL
5.7500 g., Silver **Note:** Type C.

Date	Mintage	F	VF	XF	Unc
AH1211	—	50.00	80.00	125	—
AH1212	—	50.00	80.00	125	—

Mint: Shiraz
KM# 659.2 1/2 RIAL
5.7500 g., Silver **Note:** Type C.

Date	Mintage	F	VF	XF	Unc
AH1212	—	35.00	60.00	100	—

Mint: Astarabad
KM# 655.1 RIAL
11.5000 g., Silver **Note:** Type B.

Date	Mintage	F	VF	XF	Unc
AH1212	—	80.00	120	200	—
ND	—	75.00	110	180	—

Mint: Isfahan
KM# 655.2 RIAL
11.5000 g., Silver **Note:** Type B.

Date	Mintage	F	VF	XF	Unc
AH1212	—	60.00	90.00	125	—

Mint: Kashan
KM# 660.1 RIAL
11.5000 g., Silver **Note:** Type C.

Date	Mintage	F	VF	XF	Unc
AH1212	—	70.00	120	185	—

Mint: Khoy
KM# 655.3 RIAL
11.5000 g., Silver **Note:** Type B.

Date	Mintage	F	VF	XF	Unc
AH1212	—	75.00	110	160	—

Mint: Maragheh
KM# 651 RIAL
11.5000 g., Silver **Note:** Type A.

Date	Mintage	F	VF	XF	Unc
AH1212	—	80.00	125	200	—

Mint: Mazandaran
KM# 655.4 RIAL
11.5000 g., Silver **Note:** Type B.

Date	Mintage	F	VF	XF	Unc
AH1211	—	75.00	110	160	—
Note: Some examples of Mazandaran AH1211 have					

Mint: Rasht
KM# 660.2 RIAL
11.5000 g., Silver **Note:** Type C.

Date	Mintage	F	VF	XF	Unc
AH1212	—	70.00	120	185	—

Mint: Shiraz
KM# 655.5 RIAL
11.5000 g., Silver **Note:** Type B.

Date	Mintage	F	VF	XF	Unc
AH1212	—	60.00	90.00	125	—

Mint: Tabriz
KM# 655.6 RIAL
11.5000 g., Silver **Note:** Type B.

Date	Mintage	F	VF	XF	Unc
AH1212	—	60.00	90.00	125	—

Mint: Tehran
KM# 660.3 RIAL
11.5000 g., Silver **Note:** Type C.

Date	Mintage	F	VF	XF	Unc
AH1212	—	50.00	85.00	130	—

Mint: Tehran
KM# 662 1/2 TOMAN
Gold **Note:** Type C. Approx. 3.4 grams.

Date	Mintage	F	VF	XF	Unc
AH1212 Rare	—	—	—	—	—

Fath Ali Shah

AH1212-1250 / 1797-1834AD

Fath Ali Khan succeeded his uncle, Agha Muhammad Shah, upon the latter's death on 16 June 1797, striking coins with the nickname Baba Khan. His formal enthronement took place three months later, on 15 or 16 September 1797, at which time he received the name Fath Ali Shah. His coin types are distinguished both by inscription, calligraphy, and weight standard. As the silver and gold weight standards were not altered simultaneously, the type sequences for silver and gold differ.

Note: All coins of this and succeeding reigns for hammered coinage bear the mint & date on the reverse, the mint usually with its distinguishing epithet. Only the obverse is noted in the type descriptions.

Coinage Standards of Fath Ali Shah

NOTE: Prices for silver coins are for average strikes, with some weakness or unevenness. Poorly struck coins are worth less, well-struck and well-centered coins can be worth from 25-100% more, depending on eye appeal and ornateness of design. Gold coins are generally better struck, but really attractive strikes or fancy designs also command a premium.

NOTE: Coins without legible date are worth about half the price of the cheapest date of the mint & type. Coins without legible mint are of little value. This and the previous note apply to coins of the later rulers Muhammad Shah and Nasir al-Din Shah as well as those of Fath Ali Shah.

Silver Types:

CO (Coronation Type). Obverse, double legend: *Amadeh az Fath-e 'Ali sekke be-zar-e shahi*, "From Fath Ali came the die to the royal precious metals." Standard for the rial (=1250 dinars) was 11.52 g.

A. Obverse, name of ruler with title *al-sultan*. Standard for the rial was 10.36 g.

B. Obverse, name of ruler with the expanded title *al-sultan, ibn al-sulan*, "Sultan, son of the sultan." Plain backgrounds with rather thick calligraphy. Same standard as Type A.

C. Obverse, as Type B, but with floriated backgrounds and finer calligraphy. Same standard as Types A and B.

D. Obverse, as Type C, similar backgrounds & calligraphy, but standard reduced to 9.21 g for the rial.

E. Obverse, new form of the royal protocol, *Fath 'Ali Shah Qajar Khusro-ve Sahebqeran*, "Fath Ali Shah Qajar, Caesar, Sahebqeran (i.e., possessor of an auspicious conjunction)." The rial was abandoned except at Mashhad and replaced by a qiran (kran) of 1000 dinars weighing 6.91 g.

F. Obverse, as Type E but the final portion of the protocol is *Khosro-ve Keshvarsetan*, "World-conquering Caesar." Same standard as type, with which it is contemporary (1246-1250). All Type F silver coins are probably mules with obverse dies intended for the gold. There are also a number of local types, which have not been assigned type letters and are listed following the regular imperial types.

Gold Types:

R. Same as silver Type CO (Coronation Type). Standard for the toman (=10,000 dinars) is 6.14 g.

S. Inscriptions as Type A (Type S.1) or as Type B (Type S.2) same standard as Type R.

T. Inscriptions as Type B (Type T.1) or as Type C (Type T.2), based on a toman of 5.76 g. (No examples of Type T.2 with mint & date are confirmed at the present time.)

U. Inscriptions as Type C, based on a toman of 5.37 g.

V. Inscriptions as Type C, based on a toman of 4.80 g.

W. Inscriptions as Type C or D, based on a toman of 4.61 g (one mithqal weight).

X. Inscriptions as Type E (*sahebqeran* type), based on a toman of 4.61 g.

Y. Inscriptions as Type F (*keshvarsetan* type), based on a toman of 3.45 g.

HAMMERED COINAGE

Riyal Standard

Mint: Khoy
KM# 668 1/12 RIAL

0.8700 g., Silver **Note:** Type A. Riyal standard.

Date	Mintage	F	VF	XF	Unc
AH1214(?) Khuy	—	35.00	45.00	60.00	—
AH1214(?)	—	35.00	45.00	60.00	—

Note: All known specimens lack a clear date

Mint: Mazandaran
KM# 691 1/12 RIAL

0.8600 g., Silver **Note:** Type D.

Date	Mintage	F	VF	XF	Unc
AHxxxx	—	35.00	50.00	65.00	—

Mint: Tehran
KM# 670 1/6 RIAL

1.7300 g., Silver **Note:** Type A. Some authorities regard this coin as a 4/25 rial, equal to four shahis (1.66 grams). Final determination will require the study of many more specimens.

Date	Mintage	F	VF	XF	Unc
AH1213	—	30.00	45.00	60.00	—

Mint: Yazd
KM# 671 1/5 RIAL

2.0700 g., Silver **Note:** Type A.

Date	Mintage	F	VF	XF	Unc
AHxxxx	—	20.00	27.50	35.00	—

Note: Not yet attested with legible date; Such a specimen would be worth about double the price shown

Mint: Tehran
KM# 672.1 1/4 RIAL

2.5900 g., Silver **Note:** Type A.

Date	Mintage	F	VF	XF	Unc
AH1213	—	25.00	35.00	50.00	—

Mint: Yazd
KM# 672.2 1/4 RIAL

2.5900 g., Silver **Note:** Type A.

Date	Mintage	F	VF	XF	Unc
ND	—	25.00	35.00	50.00	—

Mint: Isfahan
KM# 686 1/3 RIAL

3.4500 g., Silver **Note:** Type C. Struck on rectangular flan.

Date	Mintage	F	VF	XF	Unc
AHxxxx	—	60.00	75.00	100	—

Mint: Kirman
KM# 673.2 1/2 RIAL

5.1800 g., Silver **Note:** Type A.

Date	Mintage	VG	F	VF	XF	Unc
AH1214	—	15.00	35.00	47.50	65.00	—

Mint: Rasht
KM# 664 1/2 RIAL

5.7600 g., Silver **Note:** Type CO.

Date	Mintage	F	VF	XF	Unc
AH1212	—	80.00	100	150	—

Mint: Rasht
KM# 673.5 1/2 RIAL

5.1800 g., Silver **Note:** Type A.

Date	Mintage	VG	F	VF	XF	Unc
AH1213	—	10.00	25.00	35.00	50.00	—

Mint: Tehran
KM# 673.6 1/2 RIAL

5.1800 g., Silver **Note:** Type A.

Date	Mintage	F	VF	XF	Unc
AH1213	—	25.00	35.00	50.00	—

Mint: Astarabad
KM# 674.1 RIAL

10.3600 g., Silver **Note:** Type A.

Date	Mintage	F	VF	XF	Unc
AH1213	—	12.50	20.00	30.00	—
AH1214	—	12.50	20.00	30.00	—
AH1215	—	12.50	20.00	30.00	—
AH1216	—	12.50	20.00	30.00	—

Mint: Isfahan
KM# 674.3 RIAL

10.3600 g., Silver **Note:** Type A.

Date	Mintage	F	VF	XF	Unc
AH1213	—	10.00	15.00	25.00	—
AH1214	—	10.00	15.00	25.00	—
AH1215	—	10.00	15.00	25.00	—
AH1216	—	10.00	15.00	25.00	—

Mint: Isfahan
KM# 665.1 RIAL

11.5200 g., Silver **Note:** Type CO.

Date	Mintage	F	VF	XF	Unc
AH1213	—	75.00	100	150	—

Mint: Kashan
KM# 674.4 RIAL

10.3600 g., Silver **Note:** Type A.

Date	Mintage	F	VF	XF	Unc
AH1213	—	15.00	22.50	35.00	—
AH1215	—	12.50	20.00	30.00	—
AH1216	—	12.50	20.00	30.00	—

Mint: Kashan
KM# 665.2 RIAL

11.5200 g., Silver **Note:** Type CO.

Date	Mintage	F	VF	XF	Unc
AH1212	—	80.00	115	175	—

Mint: Khoy
KM# 674.5 RIAL

10.3600 g., Silver **Note:** Type A.

Date	Mintage	F	VF	XF	Unc
AH1214	—	17.50	27.50	40.00	—
AH1215	—	17.50	27.50	40.00	—
AH1216	—	17.50	27.50	40.00	—
AH1217	—	17.50	27.50	40.00	—

Mint: Khoy
KM# 665.3 RIAL

11.5200 g., Silver **Note:** Type CO.

Date	Mintage	F	VF	XF	Unc
AH1213	—	80.00	115	175	—

Mint: Kirman
KM# 674.6 RIAL

10.3600 g., Silver **Note:** Type A.

Date	Mintage	F	VF	XF	Unc
AH1214	—	22.50	35.00	50.00	—
AH1216	—	22.50	35.00	50.00	—

Mint: Kirmanshahan
KM# 674.7 RIAL

10.3600 g., Silver **Note:** Type A.

Date	Mintage	F	VF	XF	Unc
AH1215	—	17.50	27.50	40.00	—
AH1216	—	15.00	25.00	35.00	—

Mint: Lahijan
KM# 674.8 RIAL

10.3600 g., Silver **Note:** Type A.

Date	Mintage	F	VF	XF	Unc
AH1213	—	45.00	70.00	100	—
AH1215	—	40.00	60.00	90.00	—
AH1216	—	40.00	60.00	90.00	—

Mint: Maragheh
KM# 674.9 RIAL

10.3600 g., Silver **Note:** Type A.

Date	Mintage	F	VF	XF	Unc
AH1215	—	50.00	75.00	110	—

Mint: Mazandaran
KM# 674.10 RIAL

10.3600 g., Silver **Note:** Type A.

Date	Mintage	F	VF	XF	Unc
AH1213	—	12.50	20.00	30.00	—
AH1214	—	12.50	20.00	30.00	—
AH1215	—	12.50	20.00	30.00	—
AH1216	—	12.50	20.00	30.00	—

Mint: Qazvin
KM# 674.11 RIAL

10.3600 g., Silver **Note:** Type A.

Date	Mintage	F	VF	XF	Unc
AH1213	—	10.00	15.00	25.00	—
AH1216	—	10.00	15.00	25.00	—

Mint: Qazvin
KM# 665.4 RIAL

11.5200 g., Silver **Note:** Type CO.

Date	Mintage	F	VF	XF	Unc
AH1212	—	80.00	115	175	—
AH1213	—	80.00	115	175	—

Mint: Rasht
KM# 674.12 RIAL

10.3600 g., Silver **Note:** Type A.

Date	Mintage	F	VF	XF	Unc
AH1213	—	10.00	15.00	25.00	—
AH1216	—	10.00	15.00	25.00	—
AH1217	—	12.50	18.50	26.50	—

Mint: Rekab
KM# 674.13 RIAL

10.3600 g., Silver **Note:** Type A.

Date	Mintage	F	VF	XF	Unc
AH1213	—	35.00	55.00	80.00	—

Mint: Shiraz
KM# 674.14 RIAL

10.3600 g., Silver **Note:** Type A.

Date	Mintage	F	VF	XF	Unc
AH1213	—	10.00	15.00	25.00	—
AH1214	—	10.00	15.00	25.00	—
AH1215	—	10.00	15.00	25.00	—
AH1216	—	10.00	15.00	25.00	—

Mint: Simnan
KM# 674.15 RIAL

10.3600 g., Silver **Note:** Type A.

Date	Mintage	F	VF	XF	Unc
AH12xx (1213)	—	50.00	75.00	110	—
AH1214	—	50.00	75.00	110	—

Mint: Tabriz
KM# 674.16 RIAL

10.3600 g., Silver **Note:** Type A.

Date	Mintage	F	VF	XF	Unc
AH1213	—	10.00	15.00	25.00	—
AH1214	—	10.00	15.00	25.00	—
AH1215	—	10.00	15.00	25.00	—
AH1216	—	10.00	15.00	25.00	—
AH1217	—	10.00	15.00	25.00	—
AH1218	—	12.50	20.00	30.00	—
AH1219	—	12.50	20.00	30.00	—

Mint: Tabriz
KM# 665.5 RIAL

11.5200 g., Silver **Note:** Type CO.

Date	Mintage	F	VF	XF	Unc
AH1212	—	80.00	115	175	—

Mint: Tehran
KM# 674.17 RIAL

10.3600 g., Silver **Note:** Type A.

Date	Mintage	F	VF	XF	Unc
AH1213	—	10.00	15.00	25.00	—
AH1214	—	10.00	15.00	25.00	—
AH1215	—	10.00	15.00	25.00	—
AH1216	—	10.00	15.00	25.00	—

Mint: Tehran
KM# 665.6 RIAL
11.5200 g., Silver **Note:** Type CO.

Date	Mintage	F	VF	XF	Unc
AH1212	—	55.00	80.00	135	—

Mint: Yazd
KM# 674.18 RIAL
10.3600 g., Silver **Note:** Type A.

Date	Mintage	F	VF	XF	Unc
AH1213	—	11.50	17.50	27.50	—
AH1214	—	10.00	15.00	25.00	—
AH1216	—	10.00	15.00	25.00	—

Mint: Tabriz
KM# A690 3 RIALS
28.4900 g., Silver **Note:** Type D.

Date	Mintage	F	VF	XF	Unc
AH1213 Rare	—	—	—	—	—

HAMMERED COINAGE

Gold Toman Issues

Mint: Isfahan
KM# 736.1 1/2 TOMAN
3.0700 g., Gold **Note:** Type R.

Date	Mintage	F	VF	XF	Unc
AH1213	—	200	250	300	—

Mint: Rasht
KM# 736.2 1/2 TOMAN
3.0700 g., Gold **Note:** Type R.

Date	Mintage	F	VF	XF	Unc
AH1212	—	200	250	300	—

Mint: Tabriz
KM# 736.3 1/2 TOMAN
3.0700 g., Gold **Note:** Type R.

Date	Mintage	F	VF	XF	Unc
AH1212	—	200	250	300	—

Mint: Tehran
KM# 736.4 1/2 TOMAN
3.0700 g., Gold **Note:** Type R.

Date	Mintage	F	VF	XF	Unc
AH1213	—	200	250	300	—

Mint: Isfahan
KM# 739.1 TOMAN
6.1400 g., Gold **Note:** Type S.

Date	Mintage	F	VF	XF	Unc
AH1213	—	125	160	225	—
AH1217	—	200	250	325	—

Mint: Khoy
KM# 739.2 TOMAN
6.1400 g., Gold **Note:** Type S.

Date	Mintage	F	VF	XF	Unc
AH1215	—	200	250	325	—
AHxxxx	—	150	185	225	—

Mint: Lahijan
KM# 739.3 TOMAN
6.1400 g., Gold **Note:** Type S.

Date	Mintage	F	VF	XF	Unc
AH1213	—	200	250	300	—

Mint: Mazandaran
KM# 739.4 TOMAN
6.1400 g., Gold **Note:** Type S.

Date	Mintage	F	VF	XF	Unc
AH1213	—	200	250	300	—

Mint: Rasht
KM# 739.5 TOMAN
6.1400 g., Gold **Note:** Type S.

Date	Mintage	F	VF	XF	Unc
AH1213	—	100	140	200	—

Mint: Rekab
KM# 739.6 TOMAN
6.1400 g., Gold **Note:** Type S.

Date	Mintage	F	VF	XF	Unc
AH1213	—	200	250	300	—

Mint: Shiraz
KM# 739.7 TOMAN
6.1400 g., Gold **Note:** Type S.

Date	Mintage	F	VF	XF	Unc
AH1213	—	175	225	275	—

Mint: Tabriz
KM# 739.8 TOMAN
6.1400 g., Gold **Note:** Type S.

Date	Mintage	F	VF	XF	Unc
AH1214	—	175	225	275	—

Mint: Tehran
KM# 739.9 TOMAN
6.1400 g., Gold **Note:** Type S.

Date	Mintage	F	VF	XF	Unc
AH1213	—	175	225	275	—
AH1216	—	175	225	275	—

Mint: Yazd
KM# 739.10 TOMAN
6.1400 g., Gold **Note:** Type S.

Date	Mintage	F	VF	XF	Unc
AH1213	—	175	225	275	—
AH1214	—	175	225	275	—
AH1219	—	200	250	325	—

IRAQ

The Republic of Iraq, historically known as Mesopotamia, is located in the Near East and is bordered by Kuwait, Iran, Turkey, Syria, Jordan and Saudi Arabia. It has area of 167,925 sq. mi. (434,920 sq. km.) and a population of 14 million. Capital: Baghdad. The economy of Iraq is based on agriculture and petroleum. Crude oil accounted for 94 percent of the exports before the war with Iran began in 1980.

Mesopotamia was the site of a number of flourishing civilizations of antiquity - Sumeria, Assyria, Babylonia, Parthia, Persia and the Biblical cities of Ur, Ninevehand and Babylon. Desired because of its favored location, which embraced the fertile alluvial plains of the Tigris and Euphrates Rivers, Mesopotamia - 'land between the rivers'- was conquered by Cyrus the Great of Persia, Alexander of Macedonia and by Arabs who made the legendary city of Baghdad the capital of the ruling caliphate. Suleiman the Magnificent conquered Mesopotamia for Turkey in1534, and it formed part of the Ottoman Empire until 1623, and from 1638 to 1917. Great Britain, given a League of Nations mandate over the territory in 1920, recognized Iraq as a kingdom in 1922. Iraq became an independent constitutional monarchy presided over by the Hashemite family, direct descendants of the prophet Mohammed, in 1932. In 1958, the army-led revolution of July 14 overthrew the monarchy and proclaimed a republic.

RULER
Ottoman, until 1917

MESOPOTAMIA

MONETARY SYSTEM
40 Para = 1 Piastre (Kurus)

MINT NAME

Baghdad بغداد

al-Basrah (Basra) البصرة

al-Hille الحلة

Mahmud I
1730-1754AD

HAMMERED COINAGE

KM# 39 5 PARA
Copper **Obv:** Toughra **Rev:** Mint name

Date	Mintage	Good	VG	F	VF	XF
AH1143 (1730)	—	—	50.00	80.00	150	225

KM# 39a 5 PARA
2.6400 g., Silver **Obv:** Toughra **Rev:** Duriba fi Baghdad, date

Date	Mintage	Good	VG	F	VF	XF
AH1143 (1730)	—	—	75.00	150	225	385

Mustafa III
1751-1773AD

HAMMERED COINAGE

KM# 42 PARA
Copper **Obv:** Toughra **Rev:** Duriba fi Baghdad

Date	Mintage	Good	VG	F	VF	XF
ND (1751)	—	12.00	20.00	35.00	55.00	—
AH(11)78 (1764)	—	12.00	20.00	35.00	55.00	—

Abdul Hamid I
1773-1789AD

HAMMERED COINAGE

KM# 45 5 PARA
2.1000 g., Billon **Note:** Similar to 10 Para, KM#48.1

Date	Mintage	Good	VG	F	VF	XF
AH1187//9 //9 (1780) Rare	—	—	—	—	—	—

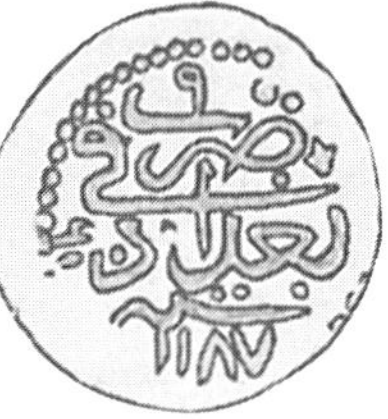

KM# 48.1 10 PARA
4.4000 g., Billon

Date	Mintage	Good	VG	F	VF	XF
AH1187//95 (1780) Rare	—	—	—	—	—	—

KM# 48.2 10 PARA
2.1800 g., Billon

Date	Mintage	Good	VG	F	VF	XF
AH1187//9 (1780) Rare	—	—	—	—	—	—

IRELAND REPUBLIC

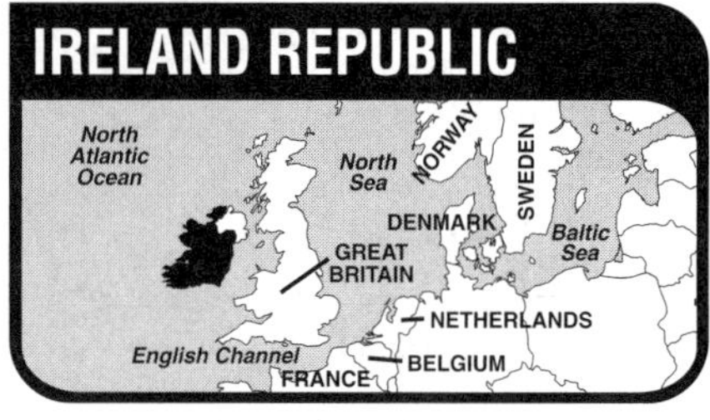

Ireland, the island located in the Atlantic Ocean west of Great Britain, was settled by a race of tall, red-haired Celts from Gaul about 400 BC. They assimilated the native Erainn and Picts and established a Gaelic civilization. After the arrival of St. Patrick in 432 AD, Ireland evolved into a center of Latin learning, which sent missionaries to Europe and possibly North America. In 1154, Pope Adrian IV gave all of Ireland to English King Henry II to administer as a Papal fief. Because of the enactment of anti-Catholic laws and the awarding of vast tracts of Irish land to Protestant absentee landowners, English control did not become reasonably absolute until 1800 when England and Ireland became the "United Kingdom of Great Britain and Ireland". Religious freedom was restored to the Irish in 1829, but agitation for political autonomy continued until the Irish Free State was established as a Dominion on Dec. 6, 1921 while Northern Ireland remained under the British rule.

RULER
British to 1921

MONETARY SYSTEM
4 Farthings = 1 Penny
12 Pence = 1 Shilling
5 Shillings = 1 Crown

UNITED KINGDOM

STANDARD COINAGE

KM# 115 FARTHING
Copper **Obv. Legend:** ends: ...:D:G:REX. **Rev:** Harp at left

Date	Mintage	VG	F	VF	XF	Unc
1722.	—	75.00	200	700	1,500	5,000

KM# 118 FARTHING
Copper **Obv. Legend:** ends: ...:D:G:REX. **Rev:** Harp at right

Date	Mintage	VG	F	VF	XF	Unc
1723.	—	25.00	50.00	150	525	1,400

KM# 119 FARTHING
Copper **Obv. Legend:** ends: ...:DEI • GRATIA • REX • **Rev:** Harp at right

Date	Mintage	VG	F	VF	XF	Unc
1723.	—	15.00	25.00	75.00	350	1,500
1724.	—	30.00	60.00	200	700	2,000
1724	—	30.00	60.00	200	800	3,500

KM# 119a FARTHING
Silver **Obv. Legend:** ends: ...:DEI • GRATIA • REX • **Rev:** Harp at right

Date	Mintage	VG	F	VF	XF	Unc
1723.	—	Value: 5,000				
1724. Proof, Rare	—	—	—	—	—	—
1724 Proof, Rare	—	—	—	—	—	—

KM# 126 FARTHING
Copper **Obv. Legend:** Small letters **Rev. Legend:** Small letters

Date	Mintage	F	VF	XF	Unc	BU
1737	—	9.00	55.00	150	400	—
1737 Proof	—	Value: 1,200				
1738	—	5.00	45.00	125	300	—

KM# 126a FARTHING
Silver **Obv. Legend:** Small letters **Rev. Legend:** Small letters

Date	Mintage	F	VF	XF	Unc	BU
1737 Proof	—	Value: 5,000				

KM# 131 FARTHING
Copper **Obv. Legend:** Large letters **Rev. Legend:** Large letters

Date	Mintage	F	VF	XF	Unc	BU
1744	—	5.00	45.00	120	300	—

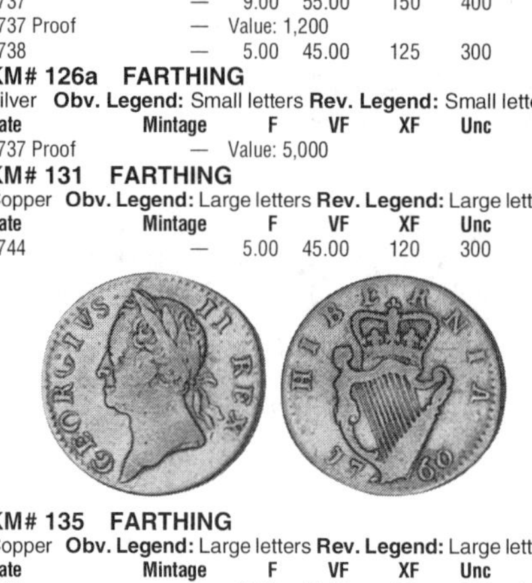

KM# 135 FARTHING
Copper **Obv. Legend:** Large letters **Rev. Legend:** Large letters

Date	Mintage	F	VF	XF	Unc	BU
1760	—	10.00	75.00	200	500	1,000

KM# 116 1/2 PENNY
Copper **Rev:** Harp at left

Date	Mintage	VG	F	VF	XF	Unc
1722	—	50.00	100	300	900	2,000
1722 Proof	—	Value: 2,000				

KM# 116a 1/2 PENNY
Silver **Rev:** Harp at left

Date	Mintage	VG	F	VF	XF	Unc
1722 Proof, Rare	—	Value: 27,000				

KM# 117.1 1/2 PENNY
Copper **Rev:** Harp at right **Note:** Many varieties exist, especially of the 1723.

Date	Mintage	VG	F	VF	XF	Unc
1722.	—	15.00	100	500	750	1,200
1722. Proof	—	Value: 2,200				
1722. Second 2 inverted, Rare	—	—	—	—	—	—
1723/2.	—	25.00	50.00	225	625	2,000
1723.	—	12.50	25.00	100	300	1,000
1723. Proof	—	Value: 2,000				

KM# 117.1a 1/2 PENNY
Silver **Rev:** Harp at right

Date	Mintage	VG	F	VF	XF	Unc
1723. Proof, Rare	—	—	—	—	—	—

KM# 117.2 1/2 PENNY
Copper **Obv. Legend:** R's are altered B's **Rev:** Harp at right

Date	Mintage	VG	F	VF	XF	Unc
1723.	—	20.00	40.00	100	300	—

KM# 117.3 1/2 PENNY
Copper **Rev:** Star in legend

Date	Mintage	VG	F	VF	XF	Unc
1723. Rare	—	—	—	—	—	—

KM# 117.4 1/2 PENNY
Copper **Rev:** Without dot before HIBERNIA

Date	Mintage	VG	F	VF	XF	Unc
1723.	—	25.00	50.00	120	420	—
1723. Proof	—	Value: 2,350				

KM# 120 1/2 PENNY
Copper **Rev:** Legend divided

Date	Mintage	VG	F	VF	XF	Unc
1724.	—	15.00	30.00	100	350	—

KM# 121 1/2 PENNY
Copper **Obv:** Legend continuous **Rev:** Legend divided

Date	Mintage	VG	F	VF	XF	Unc
1724.	—	15.00	75.00	300	900	3,000
1724	—	15.00	65.00	200	600	2,500

KM# 121a 1/2 PENNY
Silver **Obv:** Legend continuous **Rev:** Legend divided

Date	Mintage	VG	F	VF	XF	Unc
1724. Proof, Rare	—	—	—	—	—	—

KM# 125 1/2 PENNY
Copper **Obv:** Small letters **Rev:** Small letters

Date	Mintage	F	VF	XF	Unc	BU
1736	—	10.00	75.00	250	600	—
1736 Proof	—	Value: 800				
1737	—	10.00	75.00	250	600	—
1738	—	7.50	50.00	200	500	—

KM# 125a 1/2 PENNY
Silver **Obv:** Small letters **Rev:** Small letters

Date	Mintage	F	VF	XF	Unc	BU
1736 Proof	—	Value: 4,000				

KM# 130.1 1/2 PENNY
Copper **Obv:** Large letters **Rev:** Large letters

Date	Mintage	F	VF	XF	Unc	BU
1741	—	10.00	55.00	125	250	—
1742	—	10.00	55.00	125	250	—
1743	—	20.00	75.00	150	350	—
1744/3	—	15.00	75.00	150	350	—
1744	—	15.00	75.00	150	350	—
1746	—	15.00	75.00	150	350	—

KM# 130.2 1/2 PENNY
Copper **Obv:** Large letters **Obv. Legend:** GEORGIVS. . . **Rev:** Large letters **Note:** No genuine 1755 1/2 Penny is known to exist, all know examples are counterfeit.

Date	Mintage	F	VF	XF	Unc	BU
1747	—	5.00	30.00	100	300	—
1748	—	5.00	30.00	100	300	—
1749	—	5.00	30.00	100	300	—
1750	—	5.00	30.00	100	300	—
1751	—	5.00	30.00	100	300	—
1752	—	5.00	30.00	100	300	—
1753	—	8.00	35.00	110	350	—

KM# 136 1/2 PENNY
Copper

Date	Mintage	F	VF	XF	Unc	BU
1760	—	6.00	30.00	150	500	2,000

KM# 137 1/2 PENNY

Copper **Obv:** Type I, short bust

Date	Mintage	F	VF	XF	Unc	BU
1766	—	3.50	30.00	200	500	—
1769	—	3.50	30.00	200	500	—

KM# 138 1/2 PENNY

5.4500 g., Copper, 26 mm. **Obv:** Type 2, long bust

Date	Mintage	F	VF	XF	Unc	BU
1769	—	3.50	30.00	200	500	—

KM# 140 1/2 PENNY

Copper **Obv:** Type 3, long hair

Date	Mintage	F	VF	XF	Unc	BU
1775	—	5.00	35.00	110	300	—
1775 Proof	—	Value: 800				
1776	—	15.00	80.00	300	900	—
1781	—	3.50	30.00	100	400	—
1782	—	3.50	30.00	100	400	—
1782 Proof	—	Value: 600				

TRADESMEN'S TOKEN COINAGE

Various token issues exist which include the following: VOCE POPULI with HIBERNIA reverse of the 1760s, many varieties of imitation regal harp Halfpennies of the 18th Century, genuine trade tokens issued by various merchants between 1789-1804, lead tokens ca. 1780-1820, silver issues including countermarked foreign coins ca. 1804, copper tokens ca. 1805-1830 followed by the Farthing tokens of 1830-1856. These are found listed in Seabys Coins and Tokens of Ireland, 1970 edition.

KM# TTN1 1/2 PENNY

Copper **Note:** 'VOCE POPULI' 1/2 penny token of 1760.

Date	Mintage	F	VF	XF	Unc	BU
1760	—	—	—	—	—	—

KM# TTN2 1/2 PENNY

Copper **Obv:** Seated Brittania right, leaning on anchor **Rev:** Square design above date **Note:** Dublin 1/2 Penny token of 1795.

Date	Mintage	F	VF	XF	Unc	BU
1795	—	—	—	—	—	—

PATTERNS

Including off metal strikes

KM#	Date	Mintage	Identification	Mkt Val
Pn18	1722	—	1/2 Penny. Copper. Head. Hibernia seated with rocks at right.	10,000
Pn19	1724	—	Farthing. Copper. Head. Hibernia seated with rocks at right.	—
Pn20	1724	—	Farthing. Silver.	—
Pn21	1724	—	Farthing. Copper. Hibernia leaning on harp at right. Knot holding crossed trident and sceptre.	—
Pn22	1724	—	1/2 Penny. Copper. Head. Hibernia with harp at right.	—
Pn23	1724	—	1/2 Penny. Bell Metal.	—
Pn24	1724	—	1/2 Penny. Copper. Head. Knot holding crossed trident and sceptre.	22,000
Pn25	1742	—	1/2 Penny. Copper. Head. Crowned harp.	—
Pn27	1773	—	1/2 Penny. Copper. Head right. Crowned harp.	—
PNA27	1773	—	1/2 Penny. Copper. Head right, more curls in hair and larger bow. Crowned harp.	—

KM#	Date	Mintage	Identification	Mkt Val
Pn28	1774	5	1/2 Penny. Copper.	1,000

KM#	Date	Mintage	Identification	Mkt Val
Pn29	1775	—	1/2 Penny. Silvered Copper. KM140.	1,150

KM#	Date	Mintage	Identification	Mkt Val
Pn30	1789	—	Penny. Bronze. Bust right. Hibernia and Britannia clasping hands.	1,000
Pn31	1799	11	Penny. Bronze. Women shaking hands, Mossops pattern, unfinished.	1,250
Pn32	1799	6	Penny. Bronze. Women shaking hands, Mossops pattern, finsihed.	1,750

ISLE DE BOURBON

Isles de France et de Bourbon, (later called Mauritius and Reunion) are located in the Indian Ocean about 500 miles east of Madagascar, were administered by France as a single colony. They utilized a common currency issue. Ownership of the isle passed to Great Britain in 1814. Isle de Bourbon, renamed Reunion in 1793, remained a French possession and is now an Overseas Department.

RULER

French, until 1810

MONETARY SYSTEM

20 Sols (Sous) = 1 Livre

FRENCH COLONY

STANDARD COINAGE

KM# 2 3 SOLS

Billon **Obv:** Crown above 3 fleur de lis's **Obv. Legend:** LOUIS XVI • R • DE... **Rev:** Value, date **Rev. Legend:** DE BOURBON...

Date	Mintage	Good	VG	F	VF	XF
1781A	6,700,000	12.00	32.00	70.00	175	400

KM# 1 3 SOUS

Billon **Obv:** Crown above 3 fleur de lis's **Obv. Legend:** LOUIS XVI • R • DE.... **Rev:** Value, date within circle **Rev. Legend:** DE BOURBON...

Date	Mintage	Good	VG	F	VF	XF
1779A	1,900,000	7.00	18.00	45.00	100	300
1780A	130,000	10.00	30.00	70.00	175	375

PATTERNS

Including off metal strikes

KM#	Date	Mintage	Identification	Mkt Val
Pn1	1780A	—	2 Sols. Billon.	1,600

ISLE OF MAN

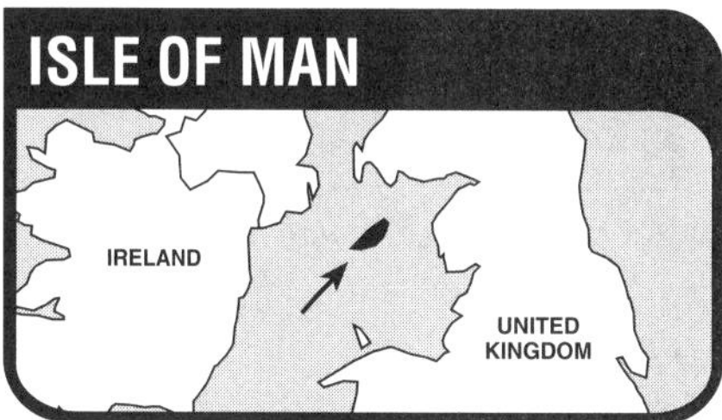

The Isle of Man, a dependency of the British Crown located in the Irish Sea equidistant from Ireland, Scotland and England, has an area of 227 sq. mi. (588 sq. km.) and a population of 68,000. Capital: Douglas. Agriculture, dairy farming, fishing and tourism are the chief industries.

The prevalence of prehistoric artifacts and monuments on the island give evidence that its' mild, almost sub-tropical climate was enjoyed by mankind before the dawn of history. Vikings came to the Isle of Man during the 9th century and remained until ejected by the Scottish in 1266. The island came under the protection of the British Crown in 1288, and in 1406 was granted, in perpetuity, to the earls of Derby, from whom it was inherited, 1736, by the Duke of Atholl. The British Crown purchased the rights and title in 1765; the remaining privileges of the Atholl family were transferred to the crown in 1829. The Isle of Man is ruled by its own legislative council and the House of Keys, one of the oldest legislative assemblies in the world. Acts of Parliament passed in London do not affect the island unless it is specifically mentioned.

RULERS

James Murray, Duke of Atholl, 1736-1765
British Commencing 1765

MONETARY SYSTEM

14 Pence (Manx) = 1 Shilling
5 Shillings = 1 Crown
20 Shillings = 1 Pound

BRITISH DEPENDENCY

STANDARD COINAGE

KM# 1 1/2 PENNY

Copper **Obv:** Eagle and child **Rev:** Triskeles

Date	Mintage	F	VF	XF	Unc	BU
1709 Rare	90,000	25.00	60.00	150	—	—

KM# 3 1/2 PENNY

Copper **Obv:** Eagle and child **Obv. Legend:** SANS • CHANGER **Rev:** Triskeles divide ID **Rev. Legend:** QUOCUNQUE • IECERIS • STABIT •

Date	Mintage	F	VF	XF	Unc	BU
1733 Proof	—	Value: 550				
1733	96,000	15.00	45.00	175	350	—

KM# 3a 1/2 PENNY
Bronze

Date	Mintage	F	VF	XF	Unc	BU
1733 Proof	—	Value: 550				
1733	60,000	15.00	45.00	175	350	—

KM# 3b.1 1/2 PENNY
Bath Metal **Obv:** Plain cap of maintenance

Date	Mintage	F	VF	XF	Unc	BU
1733 Rare	60,000	10.00	30.00	150	—	—

KM# 3b.2 1/2 PENNY
Bath Metal **Obv:** Frosted cap of maintenance

Date	Mintage	F	VF	XF	Unc	BU
1733 Rare	Inc. above	10.00	40.00	180	—	—

KM# 4b.1 1/2 PENNY
Silver **Obv:** Plain cap of maintenance

Date	Mintage	F	VF	XF	Unc	BU
1733 Proof	—	Value: 600				

KM# 4b.2 1/2 PENNY
Silver **Obv:** Frosted cap of maintenance

Date	Mintage	F	VF	XF	Unc	BU
1733 Proof	—	Value: 600				

KM# 6 1/2 PENNY
Copper **Obv:** Crowned *DA* monogram above date **Rev:** Triskeles **Rev. Legend:** QUOCUNQUE • IECERIS • STABIT •

Date	Mintage	F	VF	XF	Unc	BU
1758	72,000	10.00	40.00	125	275	—
1758 Proof; Rare	—	—	—	—	—	—

KM# 8 1/2 PENNY
Copper **Obv:** Head right **Obv. Legend:** GEORGIVS III DEI GRATIA • **Rev:** Triskeles **Rev. Legend:** QUOCUNQVE IECERIS • STABIT

Date	Mintage	F	VF	XF	Unc	BU
1786	—	7.50	30.00	100	220	—
Note: Engrailed edge						
1786	—	30.00	100	300	450	—
Note: Plain edge						
1786 Proof	—	Value: 350				
Note: Engrailed edge						
1786 Proof	—	Value: 800				
Note: Plain edge						

KM# 8a 1/2 PENNY
Bronze

Date	Mintage	F	VF	XF	Unc	BU
1786 Proof	—	Value: 400				

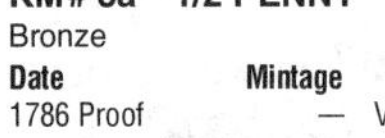

KM# 10 1/2 PENNY
Copper **Obv:** Bust right within circle **Obv. Legend:** GEORGIVS III • D:G • REX • **Rev:** Triskeles within circle **Rev. Legend:** QVOCVNQVE IECERIS STABIT

Date	Mintage	F	VF	XF	Unc	BU
1798	—	5.00	30.00	100	220	—
1798 Proof	—	Value: 300				
1813	—	10.00	35.00	80.00	200	—
1813 Proof	—	Value: 300				

KM# 10a 1/2 PENNY
Copper-Gilt **Obv:** Bust right within circle **Rev:** Triskeles within circle

Date	Mintage	F	VF	XF	Unc	BU
1798 Proof; Rare	—	—	—	—	—	—
1813 Proof; Rare	—	—	—	—	—	—

KM# 10b 1/2 PENNY
Bronze **Obv:** Bust right within circle **Rev:** Triskeles within circle

Date	Mintage	F	VF	XF	Unc	BU
1798 Proof	—	Value: 350				
1813 Proof	—	Value: 350				

KM# 2 PENNY
Copper **Obv:** Eagle and child **Obv. Legend:** SANS CHANGER **Rev:** Triskeles **Rev. Legend:** QVOCVNQVE • GESSERIS • STABIT

Date	Mintage	F	VF	XF	Unc	BU
1709 Proof; Rare	90,000	—	—	—	—	—

KM# 2a PENNY
Brass

Date	Mintage	F	VF	XF	Unc	BU
1709 Rare	—	25.00	80.00	185	—	—

KM# 2b PENNY
Silver

Date	Mintage	F	VF	XF	Unc	BU
1709 Proof; Rare	—	—	—	—	—	—

KM# 5 PENNY
Copper **Obv:** Eagle and child **Obv. Legend:** SANS • CHANGER **Rev:** Triskeles divide ID **Rev. Legend:** QUOCUNQUE • IECERIS • STABIT •

Date	Mintage	F	VF	XF	Unc	BU
1733	72,000	25.00	60.00	125	285	—

KM# 5a PENNY
Bronze

Date	Mintage	F	VF	XF	Unc	BU
1733	60,000	25.00	60.00	125	285	—
1733 Proof	—	Value: 450				

KM# 5b PENNY
Bath Metal

Date	Mintage	F	VF	XF	Unc	BU
1733 Rare	60,000	7.50	25.00	150	—	—

KM# 5c PENNY
Brass

Date	Mintage	F	VF	XF	Unc	BU
1733 Rare	—	20.00	60.00	250	—	—

KM# 5d.1 PENNY
Silver **Obv:** Plain cap of maintenance

Date	Mintage	F	VF	XF	Unc	BU
1733 Proof	—	Value: 550				

KM# 5d.2 PENNY
Silver **Obv:** Frosted cap of maintenance

Date	Mintage	F	VF	XF	Unc	BU
1733 Proof	—	Value: 600				

KM# 5.1 PENNY
Copper **Obv. Legend:** QUOCUNQUE...

Date	Mintage	F	VF	XF	Unc	BU
1733 Rare	—	15.00	50.00	225	—	—

KM# 7 PENNY
Copper **Obv:** Crowned DA monogram above date **Rev:** Triskeles **Rev. Legend:** QUOCUNQUE • IECERIS • STABIT •

Date	Mintage	F	VF	XF	Unc	BU
1758	60,000	5.00	35.00	125	285	—
1758 Proof; Rare	—	—	—	—	—	—

KM# 7a PENNY
Silver

Date	Mintage	F	VF	XF	Unc	BU
1758 Proof	—	Value: 800				

KM# 9.1 PENNY
Copper **Obv:** Head right **Obv. Legend:** GEORGIVS III DEI GRATIA • **Rev:** Triskeles **Rev. Legend:** QVOCVNQVE IECERIS • STABIT **Edge:** Engrailed

Date	Mintage	F	VF	XF	Unc	BU
1786	—	10.00	35.00	100	225	—
1786 Proof	—	Value: 375				

KM# 9.2 PENNY
Copper **Obv:** 3 laurel leaves point to left of numerals III **Edge:** Plain

Date	Mintage	F	VF	XF	Unc	BU
1786 Proof	—	Value: 850				

KM# 11 PENNY
Copper **Obv:** Bust right within circle **Obv. Legend:** GEORGIVS III. D:G. REX. 1813 **Rev:** Triskeles within circle **Rev. Legend:** STABIT QVOCVNQVE IECERIS

Date	Mintage	F	VF	XF	Unc	BU
1798	—	8.00	35.00	100	225	—
1798 Proof	—	Value: 350				
1813	—	8.00	35.00	100	225	—
1813 Proof	—	Value: 350				

KM# 11a PENNY
Bronze **Obv:** Bust right within circle **Rev:** Triskeles within circle

Date	Mintage	F	VF	XF	Unc	BU
1798 Proof	—	Value: 1,250				
1813 Proof; Rare	—	—	—	—	—	—

KM# 11b PENNY
Silver

Date	Mintage	F	VF	XF	Unc	BU
1798 Proof; Rare	—	—	—	—	—	—

PATTERNS
Including off metal strikes

KM#	Date	Mintage	Identification	Mkt Val
Pn1	1721	—	1/2 Penny. Bronze.	—
Pn2	1721	—	Penny. Bronze.	—
Pn3	1722	—	Penny. Copper.	—
Pn4	1722	—	Penny. Silver.	—
Pn5	1723	—	1/2 Penny. Copper.	600

KM#	Date	Mintage	Identification	Mkt Val
Pn6	1723	—	1/2 Penny. Bronze.	—
Pn7	1723	—	1/2 Penny. Bronze. Struck on penny flan.	300
Pn8	1723	—	1/2 Penny. Bronze. Thick flan.	—
Pn9	1723	—	1/2 Penny. Princess Metal.	—
Pn10	1723	—	1/2 Penny. Silver. Engrailed edge.	150
Pn11	1723	—	1/2 Penny. Silver. Thick flan.	—
Pn12	1723	—	1/2 Penny. Silver. Thin flan.	—
Pn13	1723	—	Penny. Copper.	250
Pn14	1723	—	Penny. Bronze.	—
Pn15	1723	—	Penny. Princess Metal center.	—
Pn16	1723	—	Penny. Silver.	450

Note: The William Wood patterns of 1721-32 are extremely rare. The values indicated reflect prices realized for examples of various grades offered in the Spink R.J. Ford sale of 10-90

KM#	Date	Mintage	Identification	Mkt Val
Pn17	1724	—	Penny. Copper.	—
Pn18	1725	—	Penny. Silver.	9,120
PnA19	1732	—	Penny. Bronze. 9.3500 g.	875
Pn19	1732	—	Penny. Bronze. 10.9000 g.	630

PIEFORTS

KM#	Date	Mintage	Identification	Mkt Val
P1	1733	—	Penny. Bronze. KM5a	—
P2	1733	—	Penny. Bath Metal. KM5b.	—
P3	1758	—	1/2 Penny. Copper.	—

a map of the ITALIAN STATES
SWITZERLAND
SAVOY
Chambery
PIEDMONT
Cisterna
Carmagnola
FRANCE
LOMBARDY
Milan
Vercelli
Passerano
Tassarolo
Arquata
Campi
Genoa
Belgioioso
PARMA
MODENA
VENETIA
Porcia
Gazzoldo
Bologna
Forli
Pesaro
Fosdinovo
Massa Di Lunigiana
Leghorn
Orciano
Siena
Ancona
Gubbio
Camerino
TUSCANY
CORSICA
Castro
PAPAL STATES
Vasto
KINGDOM
OF THE TWO
SICILIES
SARDINIA
Belmonte
San Georgio
Reggio
Ventimiglia
SICILY

ALESSANDRIA

RULER
Carlo Emanuele III, 1730-1773

CITY

SIEGE COINAGE

Issue of the Sardinian defenders

C# 1 10 SOLDI
Billon **Ruler:** Carlo Emanuele III **Obv:** Crowned imperial eagle **Rev:** Inscription, date within wreath **Rev. Inscription:** BLOC ARCIS ALEX ...

Date	Mintage	Good	VG	F	VF	XF
1746	—	—	—	200	375	750

PATTERNS

Including off metal strikes

KM#	Date	Mintage	Identification	Mkt Val
Pn1	1746	—	10 Soldi. Silver. C#1.	—

BELGIOJOSO

The county of Belgiojoso was located in Lombardy and was ruled by the Bariano family. Count Antonio assumed the title in 1769, was created a prince and given the coinage right.

RULER
Antonio I, 1769-1779

PRINCIPALITY

STANDARD COINAGE

C# 1 SCUDO
Silver **Ruler:** Antonio I **Obv:** Armored bust, right **Obv. Legend:** ANTONIUS.... **Rev:** Crowned mantled arms with supporters **Rev. Legend:** COMES.... **Note:** Dav. #1356.

Date	Mintage	Good	VG	F	VF	XF
1769	—	—	150	250	450	750

TRADE COINAGE

C# 2 DUCAT
3.5000 g., 0.9860 Gold 0.1109 oz. AGW **Ruler:** Antonio I **Obv:** Armored bust, right **Obv. Legend:** ANTON • I • BARBIANI... **Rev:** Crowned flagged arms with supporters **Rev. Legend:** COMCUNIIETL...

Date	Mintage	Good	VG	F	VF	XF
1769	—	—	400	900	2,000	4,500

BELMONTE

RULER
Anthony Pignatelli

PRINCIPALITY

STANDARD COINAGE

FR# 79 ZECCHINO
3.5000 g., 0.9860 Gold 0.1109 oz. AGW **Ruler:** Anthony Pignatelli **Obv:** Head of Anthony Pignatelli right **Rev:** Crowned and mantled arms

Date	Mintage	Good	VG	F	VF	XF
1733	—	—	1,200	3,000	6,000	9,500
1738	—	—	1,200	3,000	6,000	9,500

CAGLIARI

RULERS
Philip V of Spain
Charles III of Spain (Pretender)

CITY

STANDARD COINAGE

KM# 1 2-1/2 REALES
Silver **Ruler:** Charles III **Obv:** Crowned bust right separates 12 and 6, date in exergue **Rev:** Short ornate cross within circle

Date	Mintage	Good	VG	F	VF	XF
1709	—	75.00	150	300	700	1,450
1710	—	65.00	125	250	550	1,200
1711	—	65.00	125	250	550	1,200

FR# 145 SCUDO D'ORO
3.5000 g., 0.9860 Gold 0.1109 oz. AGW **Ruler:** Philip V **Obv:** Crowned ornate arms within beaded circle **Rev:** Short ornate cross within beaded circle

Date	Mintage	Good	VG	F	VF	XF
1701	—	—	200	450	900	1,800
1702	—	—	200	450	900	1,800
1703	—	—	250	550	1,000	2,000

FR# 146 SCUDO D'ORO
3.5000 g., 0.9860 Gold 0.1109 oz. AGW **Ruler:** Charles III **Obv:** Crowned ornate arms within beaded circle **Rev:** Short ornate cross within beaded circle

Date	Mintage	Good	VG	F	VF	XF
1710	—	—	300	500	1,000	2,000
1711	—	—	300	500	1,000	2,000
1712	—	—	350	600	1,150	2,250

CASALE MONFERRATO

Casale, a city in Piedmont in the province of Alessandria, was the capital of the duchy of Monferrato. It was founded by the Romans and ruled in Renaissance times by the Visconti and Paleologa families. Federico III Gonzaga of Mantua married the Paleologus heiress Marghereta, and the duchy passed to the Nevers branch of the Gonzaga family. Famous sieges of the city occurred in 1628 and 1630. Eventually it passes to Savoy around 1700.

RULERS
Ferdinand Carlo Gonzaga, 1665-1708

CITY

STANDARD COINAGE

KM# 86 MADONNINA
Silver **Obv:** Madonna and child **Rev:** 20 stars **Note:** 1.05-1.34 grams.

Date	Mintage	VG	F	VF	XF	Unc
1706	—	20.00	40.00	75.00	150	—

CASTIGLIONE DEI GATTI

RULERS
Hercules and Cornelius Pepoli
Alessandro and Sicinius Pepoli, 1703-1713

COUNTSHIP

TRADE COINAGE

FR# 208 DUCAT
3.5000 g., 0.9860 Gold 0.1109 oz. AGW **Ruler:** Alessandro and Sicinius Pepoli **Obv:** 5-line inscription on ornamental tablet **Obv. Legend:** ALEXANDER ET... **Rev:** Eagle with crowned arms on breast

Date	Mintage	Good	VG	F	VF	XF
ND	—	—	2,000	4,000	8,000	13,000

CISALPINE REPUBLIC

Transpadane Republic, a revolutionary state founded in northern Italy by Napoleon, came into being at Milan, Lombardy, in July 1797. It was subsequently enlarged by the addition of the Cispadine Republic and territory from the Venetian hinterlands and the Swiss Cantons of the Valtellina. It collapsed upon the conquest of Italy by an Austro-Russian army, but was restored by Napoleon in 1800.

MONETARY SYSTEM
20 Soldi = 1 Lira
6 Lire = 1 Scudo

REVOLUTIONARY STATE

STANDARD COINAGE

C# 2 SCUDO DI LIRE SEI (Scudo of 6 Lire)
23.1300 g., 0.8960 Silver 0.6663 oz. ASW **Obv:** Seated and standing figures **Rev:** Value, inscription within wreath **Rev. Inscription:** SCUDO DI LIRE SEI 27 • PRATILE ANNOVIII **Note:** Dav. #199.

Date	Mintage	Good	VG	F	VF	XF
(1800)VIII	150,000	—	65.00	120	175	300

CISPADINE REPUBLIC

A short-lived revolutionary state comprising the northern Italian districts of Reggio nell'Emilia, Modena and Bologna, was formed in Oct. 1796. In July 1797 it merged into the Cisalpine Republic.

REVOLUTIONARY STATE

STANDARD COINAGE

C# 1 20 LIRE
5.4690 g., 0.9170 Gold 0.1612 oz. AGW **Obv:** Flags, quiver **Rev:** Madonna with child

Date	Mintage	Good	VG	F	VF	XF
1797 Rare	—	—	—	—	—	—

PATTERNS

Including off metal strikes

KM#	Date	Mintage	Identification	Mkt Val
Pn1	1797	—	4 Baiocchi. Copper.	—

KM#	Date	Mintage	Identification	Mkt Val
Pn2	1797	—	Doppia. Lead. Quiver with arrows over crossed banners. REPUBLICA • CISPADANA • ANNO • PRIM. Madonna and Child in clouds. Bell.. PRESIDIVM • ET • DECVS • BONONIA •. Very rare.	—

CORSICA

Napoleon's Island birthplace in the Mediterranean. Mostly under the control of Genoa until 1762 when it became a Republic under General Pasquale Paoli which lasted 6years. The island then came under the control of France.

RULERS

Theodor, Baron Neuhof as King - 1736
General Pasquale Paoli - 1762-1768

MONETARY SYSTEM

12 Denari = 1 Soldo
20 Soldi = 1 Lira

REPUBLIC

STANDARD COINAGE

C# 4 8 DENARI

Billon **Obv:** Crowned arms with mermaid supporters **Rev:** Value and date in wreath

Date	Mintage	VG	F	VF	XF	Unc
1762	—	12.50	18.50	28.50	45.00	—
1763	—	12.50	18.50	28.50	45.00	—
1764	—	12.50	18.50	28.50	45.00	—
1765	—	12.50	18.50	28.50	45.00	—
1766	—	12.50	18.50	28.50	45.00	—
1767	—	12.50	18.50	28.50	45.00	—
1768	—	12.50	18.50	28.50	45.00	—

C# 5 SOLDO

Billon **Ruler:** General Pasquale Paoli **Obv:** Hat on pole within ornate design **Rev:** Value, date within ornate design

Date	Mintage	VG	F	VF	XF	Unc
1768	—	22.50	35.00	50.00	75.00	—

C# 6 2 SOLDI

Billon **Ruler:** General Pasquale Paoli **Obv:** Crowned arms with mermaid supporters **Rev:** Value, date within ornate design

Date	Mintage	VG	F	VF	XF	Unc
1762	—	12.50	20.00	32.50	50.00	—
1763	—	12.50	20.00	32.50	50.00	—
1764	—	12.50	20.00	32.50	50.00	—
1765	—	12.50	20.00	32.50	50.00	—
1766	—	12.50	20.00	32.50	50.00	—
1767	—	12.50	20.00	32.50	50.00	—
1768	—	12.50	20.00	32.50	50.00	—

C# 1 2-1/2 SOLDI

Copper **Ruler:** Theodor, Baron Neuhof as King **Obv:** Crowned TR in branches, date divided below **Rev:** Value in inner circle

Date	Mintage	VG	F	VF	XF	Unc
1736	—	30.00	50.00	75.00	150	—

C# 7 4 SOLDI

Billon **Ruler:** General Pasquale Paoli **Obv:** Crowned arms with mermaid supporters **Rev:** Value, date within wreath

Date	Mintage	VG	F	VF	XF	Unc
1762	—	9.00	15.00	22.50	35.00	—
1763	—	9.00	15.00	22.50	35.00	—
1764	—	9.00	15.00	22.50	35.00	—
1765	—	9.00	15.00	22.50	35.00	—
1766	—	9.00	15.00	22.50	35.00	—
1767	—	9.00	15.00	22.50	35.00	—
1768	—	9.00	15.00	22.50	35.00	—

C# 2 5 SOLDI

Copper **Ruler:** Theodor, Baron Neuhof as King **Obv:** Crowned TR in branches, date divided below **Rev:** Value in inner circle

Date	Mintage	VG	F	VF	XF	Unc
1736	—	25.00	50.00	75.00	150	—

C# 8 10 SOLDI

Silver **Ruler:** General Pasquale Paoli **Obv:** Crowned arms with mermaid supporters **Rev:** Value and date in wreath

Date	Mintage	VG	F	VF	XF	Unc
1762	—	22.50	35.00	50.00	75.00	—
1763	—	22.50	35.00	50.00	75.00	—
1764	—	22.50	35.00	50.00	75.00	—

C# 9 20 SOLDI

Silver **Ruler:** General Pasquale Paoli **Obv:** Crowned arms with mermaid supporters **Rev:** Value and date in wreath

Date	Mintage	VG	F	VF	XF	Unc
1762	—	20.00	30.00	45.00	85.00	—
1763	—	20.00	30.00	45.00	85.00	—
1764	—	20.00	30.00	45.00	85.00	—
1765	—	20.00	30.00	45.00	85.00	—
1766	—	20.00	30.00	45.00	85.00	—
1767	—	20.00	30.00	45.00	85.00	—
1768	—	20.00	30.00	45.00	85.00	—

GENOA

A seaport in Liguria, Genoa was a dominant republic and colonial power in the Middle Ages. In 1798 Napoleon remodeled it into the Ligurian Republic, and in 1805 it was incorporated in the Kingdom of Napoleon. Following a brief restoration of the republic, it was absorbed by the Kingdom of Sardinia in 1815.

MONETARY SYSTEM

12 Denari = 1 Soldo
20 Soldi = 10 Parpagliola = 5 Cavallotti = 1 Lira (Madonnina)

REPUBLIC

STANDARD COINAGE

KM# 77 MINUTO

Copper **Obv:** Bust of Madonna and child **Obv. Legend:** E R E **Rev:** Cross **Rev. Legend:** D G R G

Date	Mintage	Good	VG	F	VF	XF
ND(1638-1752)	—	8.00	16.00	28.00	55.00	—

KM# 161 4 DENARI

Billon **Obv:** Bust of Madonna and child **Rev:** Cross

Date	Mintage	Good	VG	F	VF	XF
1700 OM	—	—	—	—	—	—
1719 FMS	—	—	—	—	—	—
1721 FMS	—	—	—	—	—	—

KM# 205 4 DENARI

Billon **Obv:** Crowned shield **Rev:** Ram's head

Date	Mintage	Good	VG	F	VF	XF
1740	—	—	—	—	—	—

KM# 115 8 DENARI

Billon **Obv:** Three stars surround shield **Rev:** Bust of Madonna and child

Date	Mintage	Good	VG	F	VF	XF
1719 FMS	—	7.00	15.00	25.00	55.00	—
1724 FMS	—	7.00	15.00	25.00	55.00	—
1725 FMS	—	7.00	15.00	25.00	55.00	—
1726 FMS	—	7.00	15.00	25.00	55.00	—
1727 FMS	—	7.00	15.00	25.00	55.00	—
1736 OM	—	7.00	15.00	25.00	55.00	—
1742 OM	—	7.00	15.00	25.00	55.00	—

KM# 167.1 2 SOLDI (Parapagliola)

Billon **Obv:** Crowned shield **Obv. Legend:** DVX ET GVB REIP GENV **Rev:** Bust of Mary, 2 below **Rev. Legend:** ET REGE EOS

Date	Mintage	Good	VG	F	VF	XF
1710 FMS	—	10.00	20.00	35.00	70.00	—

KM# 167.2 2 SOLDI (Parapagliola)

Billon **Obv:** S 2 below shield

Date	Mintage	Good	VG	F	VF	XF
1710 FMS	—	8.00	16.00	32.00	65.00	—
1711 FMS	—	8.00	16.00	32.00	65.00	—
1718 FMS	—	8.00	16.00	32.00	65.00	—
1719 FMS	—	8.00	16.00	32.00	65.00	—
1720 FMS	—	8.00	16.00	32.00	65.00	—
1721 FMS	—	8.00	16.00	32.00	65.00	—
1722 FMS	—	8.00	16.00	32.00	65.00	—
1723 FMS	—	8.00	16.00	32.00	65.00	—
1724 FMS	—	8.00	16.00	32.00	65.00	—
1725 FMS	—	8.00	16.00	32.00	65.00	—
1735 OM	—	8.00	16.00	32.00	65.00	—
1736 OM	—	8.00	16.00	32.00	65.00	—
1739 OM	—	8.00	16.00	32.00	65.00	—
1743 OM	—	8.00	16.00	32.00	65.00	—
1745 OM	—	8.00	16.00	32.00	65.00	—

KM# 195 4 SOLDI (Cavalotto)

Billon **Obv:** Cross with S4 in angles **Rev:** St. George **Note:** Weight varies: 3.8-4 grams.

Date	Mintage	Good	VG	F	VF	XF
1736 OM	—	15.00	30.00	65.00	120	—
1737 OM	—	15.00	30.00	65.00	120	—
1743 OM	—	15.00	30.00	65.00	120	—
1745 OM	—	15.00	30.00	65.00	120	—
1746 OM	—	15.00	30.00	65.00	120	—
1747 OM	—	15.00	30.00	65.00	120	—

KM# 182 12 SOLDI

Silver **Obv:** Two crowned shields, S 12 **Rev:** St. George slaying dragon **Note:** Weight varies: 2.9-3.10 grams.

Date	Mintage	VG	F	VF	XF	Unc
1722 FMS	—	—	—	—	—	—
1723 FMS	—	—	—	—	—	—
1724 FMS	—	—	—	—	—	—

KM# 147 20 SOLDI (Lira)

6.3000 g., Silver **Obv:** Crowned shield **Rev:** St. John, 20 below

Date	Mintage	VG	F	VF	XF	Unc
1709	—	16.00	32.00	65.00	135	—
1710	—	16.00	32.00	65.00	135	—

KM# 207 20 SOLDI (Madonnia)

Silver **Obv:** Griffins support crowned shield **Rev:** Mary as the Immaculate Conception

Date	Mintage	VG	F	VF	XF	Unc
1745 OM	—	—	—	—	—	—
1746 OM	—	—	—	—	—	—
1747 OM	—	—	—	—	—	—

KM# 183 24 SOLDI

Silver **Obv:** Two crowned shields **Obv. Legend:** DVX ET GVB REIP GENV **Rev:** St. George slaying dragon **Rev. Legend:** EX PROBAITATE ROGVR **Note:** Weight varies: 5.6-5.9 grams.

Date	Mintage	VG	F	VF	XF	Unc
1722 FMS	—	—	—	—	—	—
1723 FMS	—	—	—	—	—	—
1724 FMS	—	—	—	—	—	—
1725 FMS	—	—	—	—	—	—

KM# 173 6/8 LIRE

Silver **Obv:** Crowned arms divide denomination **Obv. Legend:** DVX ET GVB REIP GENV **Rev:** Madonna and child in clouds **Rev. Legend:** ET REGE EOS **Note:** Weight varies: 2.6-2.8 grams.

Date	Mintage	VG	F	VF	XF	Unc
1719 FMS	—	—	—	—	—	—
1720 FMS	—	—	—	—	—	—

KM# 208 6/8 LIRE

Silver **Obv:** Griffins support crowned arms **Rev:** Mary as the Immaculate Conception divides denomination

Date	Mintage	VG	F	VF	XF	Unc
1745 OM	—	—	—	—	—	—
1746 OM	—	—	—	—	—	—

KM# 148 2 LIRE

10.0000 g., Silver **Obv:** Griffins support crowned shield **Rev:** St. John

Date	Mintage	VG	F	VF	XF	Unc
1709 FMS	—	28.00	50.00	90.00	170	—
1712 FMS	—	28.00	50.00	90.00	170	—

KM# 196 5 LIRE

Silver **Obv:** Griffins flank two crowned shields **Rev:** Madonna and Jesus in clouds

Date	Mintage	VG	F	VF	XF	Unc
1736 OM	—	—	—	—	—	—

KM# 170 8 REALI

25.0000 g., Silver **Obv:** Crowned and supported arms above sprays **Rev:** Clasped hands, fasces and cornucopia behind **Note:** Dav. #1367.

Date	Mintage	VG	F	VF	XF	Unc
1715 FMS Rare	—	—	—	—	—	—

KM# 80 1/4 SCUDO (Stretto)

Silver **Obv:** Cross **Rev:** Madonna and child **Note:** Weight varies: 8.70-9.50 grams.

Date	Mintage	VG	F	VF	XF	Unc
1717 FMS	—	—	—	—	—	—

KM# 81.1 1/2 SCUDO (Stretto)

Silver **Obv:** Cross **Rev:** Madonna and child **Note:** Weight varies: 18.4-18.6 grams.

Date	Mintage	VG	F	VF	XF	Unc
1704 IBM	—	55.00	110	200	385	—
1705 IBM	—	55.00	110	200	385	—
1713 FMS	—	55.00	110	200	385	—
1715 FMS	—	55.00	110	200	385	—
1717 FMS	—	55.00	110	200	385	—
1721 FMS	—	55.00	110	200	385	—

KM# 81.2 1/2 SCUDO (Largo)

Silver **Note:** Weight varies: 18.4-18.6 grams.

Date	Mintage	VG	F	VF	XF	Unc
1702 IBM	—	60.00	120	220	400	—
1704 IBM	—	60.00	120	220	400	—
1712 FMS	—	60.00	120	220	400	—
1714 FMS	—	60.00	120	220	400	—
1715 FMS	—	60.00	120	220	400	—
1717 FMS	—	60.00	120	220	400	—
1721 FMS	—	60.00	120	220	400	—

KM# 79 SCUDO (Stretto)

Silver **Obv:** Cross with four stars in angles **Rev:** Virgin and child on cloud **Note:** Dav. #3901.

Date	Mintage	VG	F	VF	XF	Unc
1701 IBM	—	65.00	125	200	400	—
1702 IBM	—	65.00	125	200	400	—
1704 IBM	—	65.00	125	200	400	—
1705 IBM	—	65.00	125	200	400	—
1712 FMS	—	65.00	125	200	400	—
1713 FMS	—	65.00	125	200	400	—
1714 FMS	—	65.00	125	200	400	—
1715 FMS	—	65.00	125	200	400	—
1717 FMS	—	65.00	125	200	400	—
1719 FMS	—	65.00	125	200	400	—
1721 FMS	—	65.00	125	200	400	—
1725 FMS	—	65.00	125	200	400	—

KM# 113 SCUDO (Largo)

38.0000 g., Silver **Obv:** Ornate cross with cherub heads and wings in angles **Obv. Legend:** GVBERNATORES * REIP * GENV + DVX * ET * **Rev:** Madonna and child on cloud, two cherubs above **Rev. Legend:** * ET * REGE *.... **Note:** Dav. #LS555.

Date	Mintage	VG	F	VF	XF	Unc
1702 IBM	—	300	500	800	1,350	—
1704 IBM	—	300	500	800	1,350	—
1705 IBM	—	300	500	800	1,350	—
1712 FMS	—	300	500	800	1,350	—
1713 FMS	—	300	500	800	1,350	—
1714 FMS	—	300	500	800	1,350	—
1715 FMS	—	300	500	800	1,350	—
1719 FMS	—	300	500	800	1,350	—

KM# 82 2 SCUDI

76.0000 g., Silver **Obv:** Ornate cross with cherub heads and wings in angles **Rev:** Madonna and child on cloud, two cherubs above **Note:** Dav. #LS553.

Date	Mintage	VG	F	VF	XF	Unc
1702 IBM	—	250	400	750	1,250	—
1704 IBM	—	250	400	750	1,250	—
1705 IBM	—	250	400	750	1,250	—
1712 FMS	—	250	400	750	1,250	—
1713 FMS	—	250	400	750	1,250	—
1714 FMS	—	250	400	750	1,250	—
1715 FMS	—	250	400	750	1,250	—
1717 FMS	—	250	400	750	1,250	—
1719 FMS	—	250	400	750	1,250	—

KM# 83 3 SCUDI

114.0000 g., Silver **Note:** Similar to 2 Scudi, Dav. #1364. Dav. #1363, #LS552.

Date	Mintage	VG	F	VF	XF	Unc
1712 FMS	—	650	1,250	2,000	3,250	—
1713 FMS	—	650	1,250	2,000	3,250	—
1715 FMS	—	650	1,250	2,000	3,250	—
1717 FMS	—	650	1,250	2,000	3,250	—
1719 FMS	—	650	1,250	2,000	3,250	—
1725 FMS	—	650	1,250	2,000	3,250	—

KM# 84 4 SCUDI

152.0000 g., Silver **Note:** Similar to 2 Scudi, Dav. #1364. Dav. #1362, #LS551.

Date	Mintage	VG	F	VF	XF	Unc
1705 IBM	—	1,000	2,000	3,500	6,000	—
1706 IBI	—	1,000	2,000	3,500	6,000	—
1712 FMS	—	1,000	2,000	3,500	6,000	—
1713 FMS	—	1,000	2,000	3,500	6,000	—
1715 FMS	—	1,000	2,000	3,500	6,000	—
1719 FMS	—	1,000	2,000	3,500	6,000	—

KM# 158 6 SCUDI

230.0000 g., Silver **Note:** Similar to 2 Scudi, Dav. #1364. Dav. #1361, #LS549.

Date	Mintage	VG	F	VF	XF	Unc
1705 IBM Rare	—	—	—	—	—	—
1711 FMS Rare	—	—	—	—	—	—
1712 FMS Rare	—	—	—	—	—	—
1715 FMS Rare	—	—	—	—	—	—

KM# 169 10 SCUDI

382.0000 g., Silver **Note:** Similar to 2 Scudi, Dav. #1364. Dav. #1360, #LS548.

Date	Mintage	VG	F	VF	XF	Unc
1712 FMS Rare	—	—	—	—	—	—

KM# 106 1/4 DOPPIA

1.7500 g., 0.9860 Gold 0.0555 oz. AGW **Obv:** Madonna and child on cloud in stars, date in legend **Rev:** Ornate cross

Date	Mintage	VG	F	VF	XF	Unc
1721	—	250	400	700	1,200	—

KM# 90 1/2 DOPPIA

3.5000 g., 0.9860 Gold 0.1109 oz. AGW **Obv:** Madonna and child on cloud in stars, date in legend **Rev:** Ornate cross in inner circle

Date	Mintage	VG	F	VF	XF	Unc
1709 OM	—	275	400	600	900	—
1710 FMS	—	275	400	600	900	—
1711 FMS	—	275	400	600	900	—
1714 FMS	—	275	400	600	900	—
1717 FMS	—	275	400	600	900	—
1720 FMS	—	275	400	600	900	—
1721 FMS	—	275	400	600	900	—
1722 FMS	—	275	400	600	900	—
1725 FMS	—	275	400	600	900	—
1728 FMS	—	275	400	600	900	—
1731 OM	—	275	400	600	900	—
1735 OM	—	275	400	600	900	—
1736 OM	—	275	400	600	900	—
1747 OM	—	275	400	600	900	—
1749	—	275	400	600	900	—

KM# 99 DOPPIA (2 Scudi)
7.0000 g., 0.9860 Gold 0.2219 oz. AGW **Obv:** Madonna and child on cloud

Date	Mintage	VG	F	VF	XF	Unc
1714 FMS	—	400	800	1,750	2,800	—
1720 FMS	—	400	800	1,750	2,800	—
1721	—	400	800	1,750	2,800	—

KM# 85 2 DOPPIE
14.0000 g., 0.9860 Gold 0.4438 oz. AGW **Obv:** Madonna and child on cloud

Date	Mintage	VG	F	VF	XF	Unc
1714 FMS	—	1,200	2,400	4,000	6,500	—
1720 FMS	—	1,200	2,400	4,000	6,500	—
1721 FMS	—	1,200	2,400	4,000	6,500	—
1722 FMS	—	1,200	2,400	4,000	6,500	—

KM# 180 4 DOPPIE (Quadrupia)
28.0000 g., 0.9860 Gold 0.8876 oz. AGW **Obv:** Ornate cross in inner circle **Rev:** Madonna and child on cloud in stars, date in legend

Date	Mintage	VG	F	VF	XF	Unc
1720 FMS	—	2,000	3,000	6,000	10,000	—

KM# 87 25 DOPPIE
175.0000 g., 0.9860 Gold 5.5474 oz. AGW **Obv:** Madonna and child on cloud

Date	Mintage	VG	F	VF	XF	Unc
1714 FMS Rare	—	—	—	—	—	—

REFORM COINAGE

KM# 220 DENARO
Copper **Obv:** Value **Rev:** Cross

Date	Mintage	VG	F	VF	XF	Unc
ND(1752)	—	5.00	10.00	20.00	45.00	—

KM# 221 2 DENARI
Copper **Obv:** Value **Rev:** Cross

Date	Mintage	VG	F	VF	XF	Unc
ND(1752)	—	5.00	10.00	20.00	45.00	—

KM# 222 3 DENARI
Copper **Obv:** Value **Rev:** Cross

Date	Mintage	VG	F	VF	XF	Unc
ND(1752)	—	5.00	10.00	20.00	45.00	—

KM# 223 QUATTRO (4) DENARI
Copper **Obv:** Half figure of Madonna **Rev:** Value (D-4) in angles of cross

Date	Mintage	VG	F	VF	XF	Unc
ND(1752)	—	7.50	15.00	30.00	70.00	—

KM# 235 QUATTRO (4) DENARI
Billon **Obv:** Crowned oval arms **Rev:** Value, date within sprig and laurel wreath

Date	Mintage	Good	VG	F	VF	XF
1767	—	1.50	2.75	5.50	12.00	—
1768	—	1.50	2.75	5.50	12.00	—
1772	—	1.50	2.75	5.50	12.00	—
1773	—	1.50	2.75	5.50	12.00	—
1777	—	1.50	2.75	5.50	12.00	—
1780	—	1.50	2.75	5.50	12.00	—
1781	—	1.50	2.75	5.50	12.00	—
1783	—	1.50	2.75	5.50	12.00	—
1793	—	1.50	2.75	5.50	12.00	—

KM# 258 QUATTRO (4) DENARI
Billon **Rev:** Value: QUATTRO

Date	Mintage	Good	VG	F	VF	XF
1794	—	1.25	2.50	5.00	10.00	—
1795	—	1.25	2.50	5.00	10.00	—
1796	—	1.25	2.50	5.00	10.00	—
1797	—	1.25	2.50	5.00	10.00	—

KM# 185 8 DENARI
Billon **Obv:** Crowned arms in cartouche **Rev:** Madonna

Date	Mintage	VG	F	VF	XF	Unc
1724	—	4.00	10.00	20.00	35.00	—
1725	—	4.00	10.00	20.00	35.00	—
1726	—	4.00	10.00	20.00	35.00	—
1727	—	4.00	10.00	20.00	35.00	—
1742	—	4.00	10.00	20.00	35.00	—
1756	—	4.00	10.00	20.00	35.00	—

KM# 236 8 DENARI
Billon **Obv:** Crowned arms **Obv. Legend:** DUX • ET • GUB-REIP • GENU • **Rev:** Madonna and child **Rev. Legend:** ET REGE EOS

Date	Mintage	Good	VG	F	VF	XF
1767	—	1.50	2.75	5.50	12.50	—
1768	—	1.50	2.75	5.50	12.50	—
1772	—	1.50	2.75	5.50	12.50	—
1773	—	1.50	2.75	5.50	12.50	—
1774	—	1.50	2.75	5.50	12.50	—
1780	—	1.50	2.75	5.50	12.50	—
1782	—	1.50	2.75	5.50	12.50	—
1793	—	1.50	2.75	5.50	12.50	—
1794	—	1.50	2.75	5.50	12.50	—
1795	—	1.50	2.75	5.50	12.50	—
1796	—	1.50	2.75	5.50	12.50	—

KM# 199 2 SOLDI
Billon **Obv:** Crowned arms in cartouche **Rev:** Madonna

Date	Mintage	VG	F	VF	XF	Unc
1739	—	2.50	5.00	15.00	30.00	—
1743	—	2.50	5.00	15.00	30.00	—
1745	—	2.50	5.00	15.00	30.00	—
1748	—	2.50	5.00	15.00	30.00	—
1749	—	2.50	5.00	15.00	30.00	—

KM# 197 4 SOLDI
Billon **Obv:** Crowned arms in cartouche **Rev:** St. George and dragon

Date	Mintage	VG	F	VF	XF	Unc
1736	—	2.50	5.00	15.00	30.00	—
1737	—	2.50	5.00	15.00	30.00	—
1743	—	2.50	5.00	15.00	30.00	—
1745	—	2.50	5.00	15.00	30.00	—
1746	—	2.50	5.00	15.00	30.00	—
1748	—	2.50	5.00	15.00	30.00	—
1749	—	2.50	5.00	15.00	30.00	—
1756	—	2.50	5.00	15.00	30.00	—

KM# 246 CINQUE (5) SOLDI
Billon **Obv:** St. George and dragon without legend **Rev:** Value, date

Date	Mintage	VG	F	VF	XF	Unc
1792	—	4.00	8.00	15.00	35.00	—

KM# 252 CINQUE (5) SOLDI
Billon **Obv:** Figure, DUX ET G.R. GEN around **Rev:** Value, date

Date	Mintage	Good	VG	F	VF	XF
1793	—	2.00	4.00	7.00	18.00	—
1794	—	2.00	4.00	7.00	18.00	—

KM# 247.1 10 SOLDI
Billon **Obv:** Arms **Obv. Legend:** DUX • ET • GUB-REIP • GENU • **Rev:** Value, date in wreath

Date	Mintage	Good	VG	F	VF	XF
1792	—	3.00	5.00	10.00	22.00	—

KM# 247.2 10 SOLDI
Billon **Obv:** Crowned arms **Obv. Legend:** DUX • ET • GUB REIP • GEN • U • **Rev:** Value, date within wreath **Rev. Legend:** SOLDI / DIECI (10)

Date	Mintage	Good	VG	F	VF	XF
1792	—	2.50	4.50	12.00	22.00	—
1793	—	2.50	4.50	12.00	22.00	—
1794	—	2.50	4.50	12.00	22.00	—
1796	—	2.50	4.50	12.00	22.00	—
1797	—	2.50	4.50	12.00	22.00	—

KM# 209 1/3 LIRA
Silver **Obv:** Crowned arms in cartouche **Rev:** The Annunciation

Date	Mintage	VG	F	VF	XF	Unc
1745	—	15.00	35.00	75.00	150	—
1746	—	15.00	35.00	75.00	150	—

KM# 210 1/2 LIRA
Silver **Obv:** Crowned arms in cartouche **Rev:** The Annunciation

Date	Mintage	VG	F	VF	XF	Unc
1745	—	20.00	40.00	80.00	175	—
1746	—	20.00	40.00	80.00	175	—

KM# 211 LIRA
Silver **Obv:** Crowned arms in cartouche **Rev:** The Annunciation

Date	Mintage	VG	F	VF	XF	Unc
1745	—	22.00	45.00	90.00	185	—
1746	—	22.00	45.00	90.00	185	—
1747	—	22.00	45.00	90.00	185	—
1748	—	22.00	45.00	90.00	185	—
1749	—	22.00	45.00	90.00	185	—

KM# 211a LIRA
4.1600 g., 0.8890 Silver 0.1189 oz. ASW **Obv:** Crowned arms with supporters on mantle above value **Obv. Legend:** DUX • ET • GUB REIP • GENU • **Rev:** Standing St. holding staff with banner **Rev. Legend:** NON • SURREXIT • MAJOR

Date	Mintage	VG	F	VF	XF	Unc
1793	—	5.00	10.00	20.00	45.00	—
1794	—	5.00	10.00	20.00	45.00	—
1795	—	5.00	10.00	20.00	45.00	—

KM# 213 2 LIRE
10.0000 g., Silver **Obv:** Griffins support crowned arms **Rev:** Mary as the Immaculate Conception

Date	Mintage	VG	F	VF	XF	Unc
1747 OM	—	—	—	—	—	—

KM# 212 2 LIRE
Silver **Obv:** Crowned arms in cartouche **Rev:** The Annunciation

Date	Mintage	VG	F	VF	XF	Unc
1747	—	22.00	45.00	90.00	185	—

KM# A244 2 LIRE
Silver **Obv:** Crowned arms with griffon supporters, value divided below **Rev:** John the Baptist standing facing with banner in left hand, date in legend

Date	Mintage	VG	F	VF	XF	Unc
1792	—	25.00	50.00	100	200	—
1793	—	25.00	50.00	100	200	—

KM# 244 2 LIRE
8.3200 g., 0.8890 Silver 0.2378 oz. ASW **Obv:** Crowned arms with supporters on mantle above lion head and value **Obv. Legend:** DUX • ET • GUB REIP • GENU • **Rev:** Standing St. holding staff with banner **Rev. Legend:** NON • SURREXIT • MAJOR •

Date	Mintage	VG	F	VF	XF	Unc
1793	—	15.00	28.00	50.00	90.00	—
1794	—	15.00	28.00	50.00	90.00	—
1795	—	15.00	28.00	50.00	90.00	—
1796	—	15.00	28.00	50.00	90.00	—

KM# A248 4 LIRE
Silver **Obv:** Crowned arms with supporters, value divided below **Obv. Legend:** DUX • ET • GUB REIP • GEN • **Rev:** John the Baptist holding staff with banner **Rev. Legend:** NON SURREXIT MAJOR

Date	Mintage	VG	F	VF	XF	Unc
1792	—	35.00	75.00	125	250	—
1793	—	35.00	75.00	125	250	—

KM# 248 4 LIRE
16.6400 g., 0.8890 Silver 0.4756 oz. ASW **Obv:** Crowned arms with supporters on mantle above lion head and value **Obv. Legend:** DUX • ET • GUB REIP... **Rev:** Standing St. holding staff with banner **Rev. Legend:** NON • SURREXIT MAJOR •

Date	Mintage	VG	F	VF	XF	Unc
1793	—	20.00	40.00	70.00	145	—
1794	—	20.00	40.00	70.00	145	—
1795	—	20.00	40.00	70.00	145	—
1796	—	20.00	40.00	70.00	145	—
1797	—	20.00	40.00	70.00	145	—

KM# 198 5 LIRE
Silver **Obv:** Crowned and supported arms, value: L5 below **Rev:** Madonna and child on cloud **Note:** Dav. #1368.

Date	Mintage	VG	F	VF	XF	Unc
1736 Rare	—	—	—	—	—	—

KM# A249 8 LIRE
Silver **Obv:** Crowned arms with supporters, value divided below **Obv. Legend:** DUX • ET • GUB REIP • GEN • **Rev:** John the Baptist holding staff with banner, date in legend **Rev. Legend:** NON SURREXIT REIP MAJOR **Note:** Dav. #1369.

Date	Mintage	VG	F	VF	XF	Unc
1792	—	75.00	150	225	400	—
1793	—	75.00	150	225	400	—

KM# 249 8 LIRE
33.2700 g., 0.8890 Silver 0.9509 oz. ASW **Obv:** Crowned arms with supporters on mantle above lion head and value **Obv. Legend:** DUX • ET • GUB REIP • GENU • **Rev:** Standing St. holding staff with banner **Rev. Legend:** NON • SURREXIT • MAJOR • **Note:** Dav. #1370.

Date	Mintage	VG	F	VF	XF	Unc
1793	—	65.00	95.00	150	250	—
1794	—	65.00	95.00	150	250	—
1795	—	65.00	95.00	150	250	—
1796	—	65.00	95.00	150	250	—
1797	—	65.00	95.00	150	250	—

KM# 254 12 LIRE
3.1510 g., 0.9090 Gold 0.0921 oz. AGW **Obv:** Crowned arms with supporters on mantle **Obv. Legend:** DUX • ET • GUB REIP • GENU **Rev:** Madonna and child above value **Rev. Legend:** ET • REGE • EOS •

Date	Mintage	VG	F	VF	XF	Unc
1793	—	400	700	1,500	3,500	—
1794	—	400	700	1,500	3,500	—
1795	—	400	700	1,500	3,500	—

KM# 225 12-1/2 LIRE
0.9090 Gold **Obv:** Crowned arms with griffon supporters **Rev:** Madonna and child on cloud, date in legend

Date	Mintage	VG	F	VF	XF	Unc
1758	—	1,000	3,000	6,000	10,000	—
1759	—	1,000	3,000	6,000	10,000	—
1760	—	1,000	3,000	6,000	10,000	—
1763	—	1,000	3,000	6,000	10,000	—
1764	—	1,000	3,000	6,000	10,000	—
1765	—	1,000	3,000	6,000	10,000	—
1766	—	1,000	3,000	6,000	10,000	—
1767	—	1,000	3,000	6,000	10,000	—

KM# 255 24 LIRE
0.9090 Gold **Obv:** Crowned arms with supporters on mantle above lion head **Obv. Legend:** DUX • ET • GUB REIP • GENU **Rev:** Madonna and child above value **Rev. Legend:** ET • REGE • EOS • **Note:** Weight varies: 6.28-6.31 grams.

Date	Mintage	VG	F	VF	XF	Unc
1793	—	400	650	1,000	2,000	—
1795	—	400	650	1,000	2,000	—

KM# 226 25 LIRE
0.9090 Gold **Obv:** Crowned arms with griffin supporters **Rev:** Madonna and child on cloud, date in legend

Date	Mintage	VG	F	VF	XF	Unc
1758	—	1,000	2,000	4,500	9,000	—
1759	—	1,000	2,000	4,500	9,000	—
1760	—	1,000	2,000	4,500	9,000	—
1763	—	1,000	2,000	4,500	9,000	—
1764	—	1,000	2,000	4,500	9,000	—
1765	—	1,000	2,000	4,500	9,000	—
1766	—	1,000	2,000	4,500	9,000	—
1767	—	1,000	2,000	4,500	9,000	—

KM# A245 48 LIRE
0.9090 Gold **Obv:** Crowned arms with supporters **Obv. Legend:** DUX • ET • GUB-REIP • GENU **Rev:** Seated Madonna with child on cloud **Rev. Legend:** ET • REGE • EOS • **Note:** Weight varies: 12.54-12.63 grams. Similar to 96 Lire, KM#24.1.

Date	Mintage	VG	F	VF	XF	Unc
1792	—	325	650	1,100	1,850	—
1793	—	325	650	1,100	1,850	—

KM# 245 48 LIRE
0.9090 Gold **Obv:** Crowned arms with supporters on mantle **Obv. Legend:** DUX • ET • GUB REIP • GENU • **Rev:** Madonna and child above value **Rev. Legend:** ET • REGE • EOS •

Date	Mintage	VG	F	VF	XF	Unc
1793	—	325	650	1,100	1,850	—
1794	—	325	650	1,100	1,850	—
1795	—	325	650	1,100	1,850	—
1796	—	325	650	1,100	1,850	—
1797	—	325	650	1,100	1,850	—

KM# 227 50 LIRE
0.9090 Gold **Obv:** Crowned arms with supporters **Obv. Legend:** DUX • ET • GUB REIP • GENU • **Rev:** Madonna and child **Rev. Legend:** ET • REGE • EOS •

Date	Mintage	VG	F	VF	XF	Unc
1758	—	1,600	2,400	4,000	7,500	—
1759	—	1,600	2,400	4,000	7,500	—
1760	—	1,600	2,400	4,000	7,500	—
1762	—	1,600	2,400	4,000	7,500	—
1763	—	1,600	2,400	4,000	7,500	—
1764	—	1,600	2,400	4,000	7,500	—
1767	—	1,600	2,400	4,000	7,500	—

KM# A251 96 LIRE
0.9090 Gold **Obv:** Crowned arms with supporters **Obv. Inscription:** DUX • ET • GUB REIP • GENU • **Rev:** Madonna and child, divided value below **Rev. Legend:** ET • REGE • EOS • **Note:** Weight varies: 24.96-25.47 grams.

Date	Mintage	VG	F	VF	XF	Unc
1792	—	375	425	600	1,500	—
1793	—	375	425	600	1,500	—

KM# 251 96 LIRE
0.9090 Gold **Obv:** Crowned arms with supporters on mantle above lion head **Obv. Legend:** DUX • ET • GUB REIP • GENU • **Rev:** Madonna and child above value **Rev. Legend:** ET • REGE • EOS •

Date	Mintage	VG	F	VF	XF	Unc
1793	—	375	425	600	1,500	—
1795	—	375	425	600	1,500	—
1796	—	375	425	600	1,500	—
1797	—	375	425	600	1,500	—

KM# 228 100 LIRE
0.9090 Gold **Obv:** Crowned arms with supporters **Obv. Legend:** DUX • ET • GUB REIP • GENU • **Rev:** Madonna and child **Rev. Legend:** ET • REGE • EOS •

Date	Mintage	VG	F	VF	XF	Unc
1758	—	3,000	6,000	12,000	20,000	—
1760	—	3,000	6,000	12,000	20,000	—
1761	—	3,000	6,000	12,000	20,000	—
1762	—	3,000	6,000	12,000	20,000	—

Date	Mintage	VG	F	VF	XF	Unc
1763	—	3,000	6,000	12,000	20,000	—
1764	—	3,000	6,000	12,000	20,000	—
1767	—	3,000	6,000	12,000	20,000	—

TRADE COINAGE

KM# 184 1/2 ZECCHINO

1.7500 g., 0.9860 Gold 0.0555 oz. AGW **Obv:** Crowned arms **Rev:** St. George on horseback slaying dragon

Date	Mintage	VG	F	VF	XF	Unc
1723 FMS Rare	—	—	—	—	—	—

KM# 186 1/2 ZECCHINO

1.7500 g., 0.9860 Gold 0.0555 oz. AGW **Rev:** St. John standing

Date	Mintage	VG	F	VF	XF	Unc
1724 FMS	—	400	600	900	1,800	—
1734 OM	—	400	600	900	1,800	—
1735 OM	—	400	600	900	1,800	—
1736 OM	—	400	600	900	1,800	—

KM# 171 ZECCHINO

3.5000 g., 0.9860 Gold 0.1109 oz. AGW **Obv:** Crowned arms **Rev:** St. George on horseback slaying dragon

Date	Mintage	VG	F	VF	XF	Unc
1718 FMS	—	1,000	2,000	4,500	9,000	—
1721 FMS	—	1,000	2,000	4,500	9,000	—
1722 FMS	—	1,000	2,000	4,500	9,000	—
1723 FMS	—	1,000	2,000	4,500	9,000	—

KM# 187 ZECCHINO

3.5000 g., 0.9860 Gold 0.1109 oz. AGW **Obv:** Crowned ornate arms **Rev:** St. John holding staff with banner

Date	Mintage	VG	F	VF	XF	Unc
1724 FMS	—	200	300	600	1,000	—
1727 FMS	—	200	300	600	1,000	—
1729 FMS	—	200	300	600	1,000	—
1730 OM	—	200	300	600	1,000	—
1731 OM	—	200	300	600	1,000	—
1732 OM	—	200	300	600	1,000	—
1733 OM	—	200	300	600	1,000	—
1734 OM	—	200	300	600	1,000	—
1735 OM	—	200	300	600	1,000	—
1736 OM	—	200	300	600	1,000	—
1737 OM	—	200	300	600	1,000	—
1739 OM	—	200	300	600	1,000	—

LIGURIAN REPUBLIC

1798-1805

STANDARD COINAGE

KM# 261 10 SOLDI

Billon **Obv:** Ornate oval shield, liberty cap above **Obv. Legend:** REPUBLICA LIGURE • ANNO • 1 • **Rev:** Value, date within wreath

Date	Mintage	VG	F	VF	XF	Unc
1798//I	—	15.00	35.00	60.00	125	—
1799//II	—	15.00	35.00	60.00	125	—

KM# 263 LIRA

4.1600 g., 0.8890 Silver 0.1189 oz. ASW **Obv:** Shield within wreath, value below, liberty cap above **Obv. Legend:** REPUBLICA LIGURE • ANNO • 1 • **Rev:** Conjoined standing figures, liberty cap on pole, date below **Rev. Legend:** LIBERTA ' EGUAGLIANZA

Date	Mintage	VG	F	VF	XF	Unc
1798//1	—	25.00	45.00	75.00	125	—

KM# 264 2 LIRE

8.3200 g., 0.8890 Silver 0.2378 oz. ASW **Obv:** Shield within wreath, value below, liberty cap above **Obv. Legend:** REPUBLICA • LIGURE • ANNO • 1 • **Rev:** Conjoined standing figures, liberty cap on pole, date below **Rev. Legend:** LIBERTA ' EGUAGLIANZA

Date	Mintage	VG	F	VF	XF	Unc
1798	—	125	200	300	600	—

KM# 265 4 LIRE

16.6400 g., 0.8890 Silver 0.4756 oz. ASW **Obv:** Shield within wreath, liberty cap above, value below **Obv. Legend:** REPUBLICA • LIGURE • ANNO • 1 • **Rev:** Conjoined standing figures, liberty cap on pole, date below **Rev. Legend:** LIBERTA ' EGUAGLIANZA

Date	Mintage	VG	F	VF	XF	Unc
1798//I	—	30.00	65.00	150	300	—
1799//II	—	30.00	65.00	150	300	—

KM# 266.1 8 LIRE

33.2700 g., 0.8890 Silver 0.9509 oz. ASW **Obv:** Shield within wreath, liberty cap above, value below **Obv. Legend:** REPUBLICA • LIGURE • ANNO • 1 • **Rev:** Conjoined standing figures, liberty cap on pole, date below **Rev. Legend:** LIBERTA ' EGUAGLIANZA **Note:** Dav. #1371.

Date	Mintage	VG	F	VF	XF	Unc
1798//I	—	90.00	150	250	425	—
1799//II	—	90.00	150	250	425	—

KM# 267 12 LIRE

3.1515 g., 0.9170 Gold 0.0929 oz. AGW **Obv:** Liguria seated **Rev:** Fasces within wreath

Date	Mintage	VG	F	VF	XF	Unc
1798//I	—	1,000	2,000	3,250	4,500	—

KM# 268 24 LIRE

6.3030 g., 0.9170 Gold 0.1858 oz. AGW **Obv:** Seated crowned female left, with shield and spear, value below **Obv. Legend:** REPUBLICA LIGURE • ANNO • 1 • **Rev:** Fasces with liberty cap within wreath **Rev. Legend:** NELL'UNIONE LA • FORZA

Date	Mintage	F	VF	XF	Unc	BU
1798//I	—	475	1,000	2,000	3,600	—

KM# 269 48 LIRE

12.6070 g., 0.9090 Gold 0.3684 oz. AGW **Obv:** Seated crowned female left, with shield and spear, value below **Obv. Legend:** REPUBLICA LIGURE • AN • VII • **Rev:** Fasces with liberty cap within wreath, date below **Rev. Legend:** NELL'UNIONE LA • FORZA

Date	Mintage	F	VF	XF	Unc	BU
1798//I	—	400	575	1,000	2,500	—
1798//1	—	400	575	1,000	2,500	—
1801//IV	—	400	575	1,000	2,500	—
1804//VII	—	400	575	1,000	2,500	—

KM# 270 96 LIRE

25.2140 g., 0.9170 Gold 0.7433 oz. AGW **Obv:** Seated crowned female left, with shield and spear, value below **Obv. Legend:** REPUBLICA • LIGURE • AN • IV **Rev:** Fasces with liberty cap within wreath, date below **Rev. Legend:** NELL 'UNIONE LA FORZA

Date	Mintage	F	VF	XF	Unc	BU
1798//I	—	500	800	1,450	3,500	—

GORIZIA

Goricia, Gorz

A city in Venetia, passed to Maximilian I of Austria in 1500, and became the holding of Charles, son of Austrian emperor Ferdinand I in 1564.

RULER

Franz II (Austria) 1792-1835

MINT MARKS

A, W - Wien - Vienna
F, H, HA - Hall
G - Graz
G - Nagybanya
H - Gunzburg
K - Kremnitz
O - Oravitza
S - Schmollnitz

MONETARY SYSTEM

20 Soldi = 1 Lira

CITY

STANDARD COINAGE

C# 1 1/2 SOLDO

Copper **Ruler:** Maria Theresa **Obv:** Crowned arms **Rev:** Value and date in cartouche

Date	Mintage	VG	F	VF	XF	Unc
1733	—	2.00	4.00	10.00	20.00	—
1741	—	2.00	3.00	9.00	18.00	—
1743	—	2.00	4.00	10.00	20.00	—
1744	—	2.00	4.00	10.00	20.00	—
1747	—	2.00	4.00	10.00	20.00	—
1761G	—	2.00	4.00	10.00	20.00	—
1762G	—	2.00	3.00	9.00	18.00	—

C# 1.1 1/2 SOLDO

Copper **Ruler:** Maria Theresa **Note:** Without mint mark.

Date	Mintage	VG	F	VF	XF	Unc
1763	—	2.00	3.00	9.00	18.00	—
1764	—	2.00	3.00	9.00	18.00	—
1766	—	2.00	4.00	10.00	20.00	—
1767	—	2.00	4.00	10.00	20.00	—
1768	—	2.00	3.00	9.00	18.00	—

C# 3 1/2 SOLDO

Copper **Ruler:** Joseph II **Obv:** Crowned arms **Rev:** Value and date in cartouche

Date	Mintage	VG	F	VF	XF	Unc
1783F	—	2.00	3.00	8.00	16.00	—
1785F	—	2.00	3.00	8.00	16.00	—
1788F	—	2.00	3.00	8.00	16.00	—
1789F	—	2.00	3.00	8.00	16.00	—
1790F	—	2.00	3.00	8.00	16.00	—
1793F	—	2.00	3.00	8.00	16.00	—

C# 3.1 1/2 SOLDO

Copper **Ruler:** Joseph II

Date	Mintage	VG	F	VF	XF	Unc
1783O	—	3.00	5.00	10.00	20.00	—

C# 3.2 1/2 SOLDO

Copper **Ruler:** Joseph II

Date	Mintage	VG	F	VF	XF	Unc
1788K	—	3.00	5.00	10.00	20.00	—
1789K	—	3.00	5.00	10.00	20.00	—

C# 5.1 1/2 SOLDO

Copper **Ruler:** Leopold II

Date	Mintage	VG	F	VF	XF	Unc
1791A	—	4.00	8.50	17.50	35.00	—

C# 5.2 1/2 SOLDO

Copper **Ruler:** Leopold II

Date	Mintage	VG	F	VF	XF	Unc
1791F	—	6.00	11.50	22.50	45.00	—

C# 7 1/2 SOLDO

Copper **Ruler:** Franz II **Obv:** Crowned arms **Rev:** Value, date within cartouche

Date	Mintage	VG	F	VF	XF	Unc
1792F	—	2.50	4.50	12.00	30.00	—
1793F	—	2.50	4.50	12.00	30.00	—
1794F	—	2.50	4.50	12.00	30.00	—
1799F Rare	—	—	—	—	—	—

C# 2 SOLDO

5.1400 g., Copper, 26.5 mm. **Ruler:** Maria Theresa **Obv:** Crowned arms **Rev:** Value, date within cartouche **Edge:** Plain

Date	Mintage	VG	F	VF	XF	Unc
1733	—	3.00	6.50	15.00	30.00	—
1734	—	3.00	6.50	15.00	30.00	—
1741	—	3.00	6.50	15.00	30.00	—
1742	—	3.00	6.50	15.00	30.00	—
1743	—	3.00	6.50	15.00	30.00	—
1744	—	3.00	6.50	15.00	30.00	—
1745	—	3.00	6.50	15.00	30.00	—
1747	—	3.00	6.50	15.00	30.00	—
1760G	—	3.00	6.50	15.00	30.00	—
1761G	—	3.00	6.50	15.00	30.00	—
1762G	—	3.00	6.50	15.00	30.00	—
1763G	—	3.00	6.50	15.00	30.00	—
1764G	—	3.00	6.50	15.00	30.00	—
1765G	—	3.00	6.50	15.00	30.00	—
1766G	—	3.00	6.50	15.00	30.00	—
1767G	—	3.00	6.50	15.00	30.00	—
1768G	—	2.00	4.00	8.00	20.00	—
1769G	—	2.00	4.00	8.00	20.00	—
1770G	—	3.00	6.50	15.00	30.00	—

C# 2.3 SOLDO

Copper **Ruler:** Maria Theresa

Date	Mintage	VG	F	VF	XF	Unc
1748W	—	3.00	6.50	15.00	30.00	—
1749W	—	3.00	6.50	12.50	25.00	—
1750W	—	3.00	6.50	15.00	30.00	—
1753W	—	3.00	6.50	12.50	25.00	—
1754W	—	3.00	6.50	15.00	30.00	—
1755W	—	3.00	6.50	12.50	25.00	—
1757W	—	3.00	6.50	15.00	30.00	—
1758W	—	3.00	6.50	15.00	30.00	—
1759W	—	3.00	6.50	12.50	25.00	—

C# 2.2 SOLDO

Copper **Ruler:** Maria Theresa **Note:** Without mint mark.

Date	Mintage	VG	F	VF	XF	Unc
1760	—	3.00	6.50	15.00	30.00	—
1763	—	3.00	6.50	15.00	30.00	—
1764	—	3.00	6.50	25.00	50.00	—

C# 2.1 SOLDO

Copper **Ruler:** Maria Theresa **Rev:** Rosette below cartouche

Date	Mintage	VG	F	VF	XF	Unc
1762G	—	3.00	6.00	15.00	30.00	—
1763G	—	3.00	6.50	15.00	30.00	—
1765G	—	3.00	6.50	15.00	30.00	—
1766G	—	3.00	6.50	15.00	30.00	—
1767G	—	3.00	6.50	15.00	30.00	—
1768G	—	3.00	6.50	15.00	30.00	—
1769G	—	3.00	6.50	15.00	30.00	—

C# 2.4 SOLDO

Copper **Ruler:** Maria Theresa

Date	Mintage	VG	F	VF	XF	Unc
1763H	—	3.00	6.50	12.50	25.00	—
1764H	—	3.00	6.50	12.50	25.00	—
1766H	—	3.00	6.50	15.00	30.00	—
1767H	—	3.00	6.50	10.00	20.00	—
1768H	—	3.00	6.50	15.00	30.00	—
1769H	—	3.00	6.50	9.00	18.50	—
1770H	—	3.00	6.50	10.00	20.00	—

C# 4.1 SOLDO

Copper **Ruler:** Joseph II **Obv:** Crowned arms **Rev:** Value and date in cartouche

Date	Mintage	VG	F	VF	XF	Unc
1783F	—	2.50	5.00	10.00	20.00	—
Note: Varieties exist for 1783-dated coins.						
1785F	—	2.50	5.00	10.00	20.00	—
1786F	—	2.50	5.00	10.00	20.00	—
1787F	—	3.50	7.00	15.00	30.00	—
1788F	—	2.50	5.00	10.00	20.00	—
1789F	—	2.50	5.00	10.00	20.00	—
1790F	—	2.50	5.00	10.00	20.00	—

C# 4.2 SOLDO

Copper **Ruler:** Joseph II **Note:** Varieties exist.

Date	Mintage	VG	F	VF	XF	Unc
1788K	—	3.00	7.00	12.00	22.00	—

C# 4.3 SOLDO

Copper **Ruler:** Joseph II

Date	Mintage	VG	F	VF	XF	Unc
1790H	—	2.50	5.00	10.00	20.00	—

C# 6.1 SOLDO

Copper **Ruler:** Leopold II

Date	Mintage	VG	F	VF	XF	Unc
1791A Rare	—	—	—	—	—	—

C# 6.2 SOLDO

Copper **Ruler:** Leopold II

Date	Mintage	VG	F	VF	XF	Unc
1791F	—	6.00	12.50	25.00	50.00	—

C# 8.1 SOLDO

Copper **Ruler:** Leopold II **Obv:** Crowned arms **Rev:** Value, date within cartouche

Date	Mintage	VG	F	VF	XF	Unc
1792F	—	6.00	12.00	25.00	50.00	—
1793F	—	3.50	7.00	15.00	30.00	—
1794F	—	3.50	7.00	15.00	30.00	—
1795F	—	3.50	7.00	15.00	30.00	—
1796F	—	3.50	7.00	15.00	30.00	—
1797F	—	3.00	6.00	12.00	25.00	—
1798F	—	3.00	6.00	12.00	25.00	—
1799F	—	3.00	6.00	12.00	25.00	—
1800F	—	4.00	8.00	16.50	35.00	—

C# 8.2 SOLDO

Copper **Ruler:** Leopold II

Date	Mintage	VG	F	VF	XF	Unc
1794K	—	—	—	—	—	—

C# 8.3 SOLDO

Copper **Ruler:** Franz II

Date	Mintage	VG	F	VF	XF	Unc
1796G	—	—	—	—	—	—

C# 8.4 SOLDO

Copper **Ruler:** Franz II

Date	Mintage	VG	F	VF	XF	Unc
1798H	—	3.00	6.00	12.00	25.00	—
1799H	—	3.00	6.00	12.00	25.00	—
Note: Varieties exist for 1799-dated coins						
1800H	—	3.00	6.00	12.00	25.00	—

C# 9.1 2 SOLDI

Copper **Ruler:** Franz II **Obv:** Crowned arms **Rev:** Value, date within cartouche **Note:** Without mint mark.

Date	Mintage	VG	F	VF	XF	Unc
1799 Rare	—	—	—	—	—	—

C# 9.2 2 SOLDI

Copper **Ruler:** Franz II **Obv:** Crowned arms **Rev:** Value, date

Date	Mintage	VG	F	VF	XF	Unc
1799F	—	3.00	6.00	12.00	27.50	—

C# 9.3 2 SOLDI

Copper **Ruler:** Franz II

Date	Mintage	VG	F	VF	XF	Unc
1799H	—	10.00	20.00	35.00	65.00	—

C# 9.4 2 SOLDI

Copper **Ruler:** Franz II

Date	Mintage	VG	F	VF	XF	Unc
1799K	—	2.50	5.00	10.00	22.00	—

C# 9.5 2 SOLDI

Copper **Ruler:** Franz II

Date	Mintage	VG	F	VF	XF	Unc
1799S	—	2.50	5.00	10.00	22.00	—

GUASTALLA

Located in Emilia on the southern bank of the Po River in the modern province of Reggio. Guastalla was ruled by the Torelli family from 1403, and in 1539, was sold to Ferranti Gonzaga by the last female descendant of the line. It became a duchy in 1621, but, was united with Parma and Piacenza in 1748 and subsequently followed their history.

RULERS

Guiseppe Maria Gonzaga, 1729-1746

DUCHY

STANDARD COINAGE

DAV# 1372 DUCATO (16 Lire)

Silver **Ruler:** Guiseppe Maria Gonzaga **Obv:** Legend, bust right **Obv. Legend:** IOS • MA • GON • GVAS **Rev:** Man in armor stepping on devil, date below

Date	Mintage	VG	F	VF	XF	Unc
1732 Rare	—	—	—	—	—	—

LIVORNO

Livorno (Leghorn), a city on the Tyrrhenian Sea in western Tuscany, had a mint at which the Medici dukes struck coins with the mark LIBVRNI.

RULERS

Cosimo III Medici, 1670-1723

Giovanni Gastone Medici, 1723-1737

DUCHY

STANDARD COINAGE

KM# 15.3 PEZZA DELLA ROSA

Silver **Ruler:** Cosimo III Medici **Obv:** Crowned arms of Medici break legend **Obv. Legend:** COSMVS • III • D • G • M • DVX • ETRVRIAE • **Rev:** Rosebush **Rev. Legend:** GRATIA... **Note:** Dav. #1499.

Date	Mintage	VG	F	VF	XF	Unc
1701	—	125	250	400	650	—
1703	—	100	200	350	600	—
1703/1	—	125	250	400	650	—
1706	—	125	250	400	650	—

KM# 15.4 PEZZA DELLA ROSA

Silver **Ruler:** Cosimo III Medici **Obv:** Higher, narrower crown **Obv. Legend:** COSMVS • IIID • G • M • DVX• ETRVRIAE • **Rev:** Rosebush **Rev. Legend:** GRATIA... **Note:** Dav. #1501.

Date	Mintage	VG	F	VF	XF	Unc
1706	—	100	225	375	650	—
1707	—	100	200	350	600	—
1713	—	100	200	350	600	—
1716	—	100	200	350	600	—
1718	—	100	200	350	600	—

KM# 46 PEZZA DELLA ROSA

Silver **Ruler:** Giovanni Gastone Medici **Obv:** Crowned arms of Medici, IOAN **Note:** Dav. #1503.

Date	Mintage	VG	F	VF	XF	Unc
1726	—	175	350	700	1,200	—

KM# 16.5 TOLLERO

27.0000 g., Silver **Ruler:** Cosimo III Medici **Obv:** Crowned armored bust, right **Obv. Legend:** COSMVS • III • D • G • MAG • DVX • ETRVRIAE • VI • **Rev:** Port of Livorno within roped circle **Rev. Legend:** ET PATET ET FAVET **Note:** Dav. #1498.

Date	Mintage	VG	F	VF	XF	Unc
1701	—	85.00	175	300	500	—
1702	—	85.00	175	300	500	—
1703	—	85.00	175	300	500	—
1704	—	85.00	175	300	500	—

KM# 35 TOLLERO

27.0000 g., Silver **Ruler:** Cosimo III Medici **Obv:** Uncrowned bust right **Obv. Legend:** COSMVS • III • D • G • MAG • DVX • ETRVRIAE • VI • **Rev:** Fortress (at Livorno) below crown **Rev. Legend:** ET PATET ET FAVET **Note:** Dav. #1500.

Date	Mintage	VG	F	VF	XF	Unc
1707	—	100	200	350	600	—
1708	—	100	200	350	600	—
1710	—	100	200	350	600	—
1711	—	100	200	350	600	—
1712	—	100	200	350	600	—
1717	—	100	200	350	600	—
1720	—	100	200	350	600	—
1722	—	100	200	350	600	—
1723	—	100	200	350	600	—

KM# 45 TOLLERO

27.0000 g., Silver **Ruler:** Giovanni Gastone Medici **Obv:** Bust right **Obv. Legend:** IOAN • GASTO • I • D • G • MAG • DVX • ETRVR • VII • **Rev:** Fortress (at Livorno) below crown **Rev. Legend:** ET PATET ET FAVET **Note:** Dav. #1502.

Date	Mintage	VG	F	VF	XF	Unc
1723	—	250	500	900	1,500	—
1724	—	250	500	900	1,500	—
1725	—	250	500	900	1,500	—
1726	—	250	500	900	1,500	—

KM# 41 1/2 PEZZA D'ORO

3.4000 g., Gold **Ruler:** Cosimo III Medici **Obv:** Crowned arms of Medici **Rev:** Rosebush

Date	Mintage	VG	F	VF	XF	Unc
1718	—	900	1,600	3,250	6,500	—
1720	—	900	1,600	3,250	6,500	—

KM# 40 PEZZA D'ORO

6.9000 g., Gold **Ruler:** Cosimo III Medici **Obv:** Crowned arms of Medici **Obv. Legend:** COSMVS • III • D • G • M • DVX.... **Rev:** Rosebush **Rev. Legend:** GRATIA • OBVIA • VLTIO.... **Note:** Fr. #466.

Date	Mintage	VG	F	VF	XF	Unc
1717	—	500	1,000	2,000	3,500	—
1718	—	500	1,000	2,000	3,500	—
1721	—	500	1,000	2,000	3,500	—

KM# 42 2 PEZZA D'ORO

13.5000 g., Gold **Ruler:** Cosimo III Medici **Obv:** Crowned arms of Medici **Rev:** Rosebush

Date	Mintage	VG	F	VF	XF	Unc
1718 Rare	—	—	—	—	—	—

LUCCA

Luca, Lucensis

Lucca and Piombino

A town in Tuscany and the residence of a marquis, was nominally a fief but managed to maintain a *de facto* independence until awarded by Napoleon to his sister Elisa in 1805. In 1814 it was occupied by the Neapolitans, from 1817 to 1847 it was a duchy of the queen of Etruria, after which it became a division of Tuscany.

Republic, 1369-1799

Principality, 1805-1814

Lucca, Duchy, 1817-1847

RULERS

Felix Bacciocchi and Elisa (Bonaparte), 1805-1814

Maria Luisa di Borbone, Duchess, 1817-1824

Carlo Lodovico di Borbone, Duke, 1824-1847

MONETARY SYSTEM

2 Quattrini = 1 Duetto

3 Quattrini = 1 Soldo

12 Soldi = 6 Bolognini = 2 Grossi = 1 Barbone

25 Soldi = 1 Santa Croce

2 Scudi D'oro = 1 Doppia

REPUBLIC

STANDARD COINAGE

KM# 52 1/2 SOLDO

Copper **Obv:** Crowned city arms **Rev:** Value and date in cartouche

Date	Mintage	VG	F	VF	XF	Unc
1733	—	3.00	6.00	15.00	25.00	—
1734	—	3.00	6.00	15.00	25.00	—
1736	—	3.00	6.00	15.00	25.00	—
1756	—	3.00	6.00	15.00	25.00	—
1790	—	3.00	6.00	15.00	25.00	—

KM# 52.2 1/2 SOLDO

Copper **Obv:** Crowned arms to left of rampant spotted leopard, date below **Note:** The date range for this coin is 1733-1790. Varieties exist.

Date	Mintage	VG	F	VF	XF	Unc
1735	—	3.00	6.00	15.00	25.00	—

KM# 42 PANTERINO

Copper **Obv:** Oval republic arms **Rev:** City arms **Note:** Weight varies: 0.60-1.00 grams.

Date	Mintage	VG	F	VF	XF	Unc
1715	—	4.00	8.00	15.00	25.00	—
1716	—	4.00	8.00	15.00	25.00	—
1718	—	4.00	8.00	15.00	25.00	—

KM# 30 GROSSETTO

Billon **Obv:** Arms in cartouche **Obv. Legend:** OTTO **Rev:** St. Peter **Note:** Weight varies: 0.80-1.52 grams.

Date	Mintage	VG	F	VF	XF	Unc
1705	—	7.00	12.00	22.00	40.00	—

KM# 40 DUETTO (2 Quattrino)

1.5000 g., Billon **Obv:** LVCA cruciform around center rosette, date at bottom **Obv. Legend:** CARLO L.O.D.I.D. ... **Rev:** St. Peter standing

Date	Mintage	VG	F	VF	XF	Unc
1754	—	7.00	12.00	20.00	35.00	—
1757	—	7.00	12.00	20.00	35.00	—

KM# 63 DUETTO (2 Quattrino)

1.5000 g., Billon **Countermark:** City arms held by panther

Date	Mintage	VG	F	VF	XF	Unc
1754	—	7.00	12.00	20.00	35.00	—

KM# 67 DUETTO (2 Quattrino)

1.5000 g., Billon **Rev:** St. Peter walking right **Note:** C#2a.

Date	Mintage	VG	F	VF	XF	Unc
1757	—	7.00	12.00	20.00	35.00	—
1758	—	7.00	12.00	20.00	35.00	—
1760	—	7.00	12.00	20.00	35.00	—
1789	—	7.00	12.00	20.00	35.00	—
1790	—	7.00	12.00	20.00	35.00	—

KM# 64 SOLDO

Billon **Obv:** Crowned republic arms **Rev:** Facing figure of St. Paul with mitre and crozier

Date	Mintage	VG	F	VF	XF	Unc
1754	—	7.00	12.00	22.00	38.00	—
1755	—	7.00	12.00	22.00	38.00	—
1756	—	7.00	12.00	22.00	38.00	—
1757	—	7.00	12.00	22.00	38.00	—
1758	—	7.00	12.00	22.00	38.00	—

KM# 65 SOLDO

Billon **Rev:** City arms held by panther

Date	Mintage	VG	F	VF	XF	Unc
1754	—	7.00	12.00	22.00	38.00	—
1755	—	7.00	12.00	22.00	38.00	—
1758	—	7.00	12.00	22.00	38.00	—

KM# 47 MEZZO (1/2) GROSSO

Billon **Obv:** Crowned arms of the republic **Rev:** Crowned arms of the city, date below

Date	Mintage	VG	F	VF	XF	Unc
1717	—	40.00	80.00	150	—	—
1768	—	22.50	50.00	75.00	100	—

KM# 51 GROSSO

1.5700 g., 0.7010 Silver 0.0354 oz. ASW **Obv:** Crowned arms **Obv. Legend:** RES • PUB... **Rev:** Crowned St. Vultus **Rev. Legend:** VULTUS...

Date	Mintage	VG	F	VF	XF	Unc
1732	—	10.00	20.00	60.00	100	—
1733	—	10.00	20.00	60.00	100	—
1735	—	10.00	20.00	60.00	100	—
1766	—	10.00	20.00	60.00	100	—

KM# 34 BARBONE (Grosso - 12 Soldi)
Silver **Obv:** Crowned arms with supporters **Rev:** Justice seated **Note:** Weight varies: 2.94-3.11 grams.

Date	Mintage	VG	F	VF	XF	Unc
1716	—	25.00	50.00	120	200	—
1717	—	25.00	50.00	120	200	—
1718	—	25.00	50.00	120	200	—
1719	—	25.00	50.00	120	200	—
1725	—	25.00	50.00	120	200	—

KM# 45 BARBONE (Grosso of 3)
1.2600 g., Silver **Obv:** L-V-C-A in Latin characters **Rev:** Bust of St. Vultus

Date	Mintage	VG	F	VF	XF	Unc
1715	—	15.00	30.00	90.00	150	—
1716	—	15.00	30.00	90.00	150	—
1721	—	15.00	30.00	90.00	150	—
1725	—	15.00	30.00	90.00	150	—

KM# 46 BARBONE (Grosso of 6)
3.0000 g., Silver **Obv:** L-V-C-A in Gothic script

Date	Mintage	VG	F	VF	XF	Unc
1715	—	25.00	50.00	120	200	—
1717	—	25.00	50.00	120	200	—
1718	—	25.00	50.00	120	200	—
1721	—	25.00	50.00	120	200	—
1725	—	25.00	50.00	120	200	—
1726	—	25.00	50.00	120	200	—

KM# 50.1 BARBONE (2 Grossi)
2.7500 g., 0.7430 Silver 0.0657 oz. ASW **Obv:** Crowned republic arms **Obv. Legend:** Ends with ... LVCENS **Rev:** Seated figure of Justice

Date	Mintage	VG	F	VF	XF	Unc
1731	—	20.00	40.00	90.00	150	—
1732	—	20.00	40.00	90.00	150	—
1733	—	20.00	40.00	90.00	150	—
1736	—	20.00	40.00	90.00	150	—
1737	—	20.00	40.00	90.00	150	—
1751	—	20.00	40.00	90.00	150	—
1757	—	20.00	40.00	90.00	150	—

KM# 61 BARBONE (2 Grossi)
2.7500 g., 0.7430 Silver 0.0657 oz. ASW **Obv:** Crowned city arms **Rev:** Bust of St. Vultus

Date	Mintage	VG	F	VF	XF	Unc
1751	—	20.00	40.00	90.00	150	—

KM# 50.2 BARBONE (2 Grossi)
2.7500 g., 0.7430 Silver 0.0657 oz. ASW **Obv. Legend:** Ends with ... LVCENSI

Date	Mintage	VG	F	VF	XF	Unc
1757	—	20.00	40.00	90.00	150	—

KM# 48 BOLOGNINO (2 Soldi)
Billon **Obv:** City arms held by panther, branch at left has 9 leaves, date below **Rev:** Facing figure of St. Peter holding keys

Date	Mintage	VG	F	VF	XF	Unc
1717	—	—	—	—	—	—
1790	—	15.00	30.00	45.00	65.00	—

KM# 16 SANTACROCE (25 Soldi)
8.6400 g., 0.8950 Silver 0.2486 oz. ASW **Obv:** Crowned republic arms, date below **Obv. Legend:** LUCENSIS • RESPUBLICA **Rev:** St. Vultus on cross **Rev. Legend:** ...VULTUS •

Date	Mintage	VG	F	VF	XF	Unc
1734	—	50.00	100	150	250	—
1735	—	50.00	100	150	250	—
1742	—	50.00	100	150	250	—
1748	—	50.00	100	150	250	—
1756	—	50.00	100	150	250	—

KM# 53 SCUDO
26.5200 g., 0.9160 Silver 0.7810 oz. ASW **Obv:** Crowned ornamental republic arms in branches, date below **Obv. Legend:** LUCENSIS RESPUBLICA **Rev:** Standing figure beside equestrian **Rev. Legend:** SANCTUS... **Note:** Varieties exist. Dav. #1373.

Date	Mintage	VG	F	VF	XF	Unc
1735	—	40.00	60.00	80.00	150	—
1737	—	40.00	60.00	80.00	150	—
1741	—	40.00	60.00	80.00	150	—
1742	—	40.00	60.00	80.00	150	—
1743	—	40.00	60.00	80.00	150	—
1744	—	40.00	60.00	80.00	150	—
1747	—	40.00	60.00	80.00	150	—
1749	—	40.00	60.00	80.00	150	—
1750	—	40.00	60.00	80.00	150	—

KM# 60 SCUDO
26.5200 g., 0.9160 Silver 0.7810 oz. ASW **Obv:** Different shield with garlands at sides **Obv. Legend:** LUCENSIS RESPUBLICA **Rev:** Standing figure beside equestrian **Rev. Legend:** SANCTU... **Note:** Dav. #1374.

Date	Mintage	VG	F	VF	XF	Unc
1750	—	35.00	50.00	80.00	150	—
1751	—	35.00	50.00	80.00	150	—
1752	—	35.00	50.00	80.00	150	—
1754	—	35.00	50.00	80.00	150	—

KM# 62 SCUDO
26.5200 g., 0.9160 Silver 0.7810 oz. ASW **Obv:** Crowned republic arms with supporters **Obv. Legend:** LUCENSIS RESPUBLICA **Rev:** Standing figure beside equestrian **Rev. Legend:** SANCT... **Note:** Dav. #1375.

Date	Mintage	VG	F	VF	XF	Unc
1753	—	40.00	60.00	100	200	—

KM# 66 SCUDO
26.5200 g., 0.9160 Silver 0.7810 oz. ASW **Obv:** Crowned republic arms with supporters **Obv. Legend:** LUCENSIS RESPUBLICA **Rev:** Standing figure beside equestrian **Rev. Legend:** SANCT... **Note:** Dav. #1376.

Date	Mintage	VG	F	VF	XF	Unc
1754	—	35.00	50.00	75.00	150	—
1755	—	35.00	50.00	75.00	150	—
1756	—	35.00	50.00	75.00	150	—

KM# 56 1/2 DOPPIA
3.5000 g., 0.9860 Gold 0.1109 oz. AGW **Obv:** Republic arms within circle **Rev:** Crowned bust facing, date below

Date	Mintage	VG	F	VF	XF	Unc
1749	—	200	450	700	1,500	—
ND	—	200	450	700	1,500	—

KM# 57.1 DOPPIA
7.0000 g., 0.9860 Gold 0.2219 oz. AGW **Obv:** Crowned republic arms **Obv. Legend:** LUCENSIS RESPUBLICA **Rev:** St. Vultus, facing **Rev. Legend:** VULTVS SANCTVS

Date	Mintage	VG	F	VF	XF	Unc
1749	—	200	450	800	1,750	—

KM# 57.2 DOPPIA
7.0000 g., 0.9860 Gold 0.2219 oz. AGW **Obv:** Modified crowned arms **Obv. Legend:** LUCENSIS RESPUBLICA **Rev:** Portrait altered **Rev. Legend:** VULTVS SANCTVS

Date	Mintage	VG	F	VF	XF	Unc
1750	—	200	450	800	1,750	—

KM# 68 DOPPIA
7.0000 g., 0.9860 Gold 0.2219 oz. AGW **Obv:** Crowned ornamental republic arms **Rev:** St. Paul seated facing left

Date	Mintage	VG	F	VF	XF	Unc
1758	—	1,250	2,500	5,000	8,500	—

KM# 55 2 DOPPIE
14.0000 g., 0.9860 Gold 0.4438 oz. AGW **Obv:** Crowned republic arms **Rev:** Facing bust of St. Vultus

Date	Mintage	VG	F	VF	XF	Unc
1748	—	400	800	3,000	5,000	—

REFORM COINAGE

4 Denari = 1 Quattrino; 3 Quattrini = 1 Soldo; 20 Soldi = 1 Lira

C# 4a BOLOGNINO (2 Soldi)
3.0700 g., 0.2000 Silver 0.0197 oz. ASW **Obv:** Branch with six leaves

Date	Mintage	F	VF	XF	Unc	BU
1790(1835) Restrike	—	20.00	32.00	70.00	—	—

MANTUA

Mantova

A city of Lombardy, was taken by the Lombards in 568 and became a fief of the princely Italian Gonzaga family in 1328. It was stormed and sacked by the Austrians in 1630. Besieged by Napoleon in June 1796, it held until February of 1797. After forming part of the Cisalpine and Italian Republics it fell again to Austria in 1799. It was restored to the French in 1801, but reverted to Austria again as part of the Kingdom of Lombardy-Venetia, 1814-1866.

RULERS

Ferdinando Carlo Gonzaga Nevers, 1665-1707
w/Maria Isabella as regent, 1665-1707
Austrian, 1708-1797
Charles VI, Emperor of Austria, 1711-1740
Maria Teresa, 1740-1780
Cisalpine Republic, 1797-1802

MONETARY SYSTEM

6 Denari = 1 Sesino
2 Sesini = 1 Soldo
20 Soldi = 1 Lira
12 Lire = 1 Tallero

MINT

Mantua

MINTMASTERS' INITIALS

CT - Carol Torre
GM, GMF - Gaspare Molo

DUCHY

Gonzaga Family

STANDARD COINAGE

KM# 436 20 SOLDI

Silver **Ruler:** Ferdinando Carlo Gonzaga Nevers with Maria Isabella as Regent **Obv:** Bust of Ferdinand Carol right **Rev:** War trophies **Note:** Weight varies: 1.59-1.63 grams.

Date	Mintage	VG	F	VF	XF	Unc
1701	—	15.00	30.00	50.00	90.00	—
1702	—	15.00	30.00	50.00	90.00	—

KM# 438 40 SOLDI (2 Lire)

Silver **Ruler:** Ferdinando Carlo Gonzaga Nevers with Maria Isabella as Regent **Obv:** Bust right **Obv. Legend:** FERD • CAR • D • G • DVX • MANT • M • **Rev:** War trophies **Rev. Legend:** CONVENIENTIA CVIQVE **Note:** Weight varies: 3.07-3.40 grams.

Date	Mintage	VG	F	VF	XF	Unc
1701	—	25.00	50.00	90.00	200	—
1702	—	25.00	50.00	90.00	200	—
1703	—	25.00	50.00	90.00	200	—
1704	—	25.00	50.00	90.00	200	—
1706	—	25.00	50.00	90.00	200	—

KM# 439 80 SOLDI (1/2 Ducatone)

Silver **Ruler:** Ferdinando Carlo Gonzaga Nevers with Maria Isabella as Regent **Obv:** Bust right **Obv. Legend:** FERD • CAR • D • G • DVX • MANT • M • **Rev:** War trophies **Rev. Legend:** CONVENIENTIA CVIQVE **Note:** Weight varies: 6.16-6.60 grams.

Date	Mintage	VG	F	VF	XF	Unc
1701	—	35.00	70.00	120	275	—
1702	—	35.00	70.00	120	275	—
1706	—	35.00	70.00	120	275	—

KM# 440 1/2 SCUDO (60 Soldi = 1/2 Tallero)

Silver **Ruler:** Ferdinando Carlo Gonzaga Nevers with Maria Isabella as Regent **Obv:** Bust of Ferdinand Carol right **Rev:** War trophies **Note:** Weight varies: 12.60-12.80 grams.

Date	Mintage	VG	F	VF	XF	Unc
1701	—	75.00	150	300	750	—
1702	—	75.00	150	300	750	—

KM# 442 SCUDO

Silver **Obv:** Bust right **Obv. Legend:** FERD • CARD • G • DVX • ... **Rev:** War trophies **Rev. Legend:** CONVENIENTIA CVIQVE **Note:** Weight varies: 24.98-25.85 grams. Dav. #1377.

Date	Mintage	VG	F	VF	XF	Unc
1703	—	125	225	475	1,200	—
1706	—	125	225	475	1,200	—
1706 FER. D. Error	—	125	225	475	1,200	—
1707	—	125	225	475	1,200	—

KM# 481 2 TALLERO

Silver **Obv:** Bust right **Obv. Legend:** CAROL: VI: D: G:... **Rev:** Crowned double eagle with Latin cross for Mantua on breast **Note:** Dav. #1378A.

Date	Mintage	VG	F	VF	XF	Unc
1736 Rare	—	—	—	—	—	—

KM# 393 2 DOPPIE

0.9860 Gold **Ruler:** Ferdinando Carlo Gonzaga Nevers with Maria Isabella as Regent **Obv:** Bust of Ferdinand Carol right in inner circle **Rev:** Crowned arms in inner circle **Note:** Weight varies: 12.80-12.95 grams. Actual gold weight varies: .4058-.4105 ounces.

Date	Mintage	VG	F	VF	XF	Unc
ND(1668-1707) Rare	—	—	—	—	—	—

AUSTRIAN ADMINISTRATION

STANDARD COINAGE

KM# 467 SESINO (1/6 soldi)

Copper **Obv:** Value: SESINO/DI•MAN•/TOVA in cartouche **Rev:** Crowned cross in branches, date below

Date	Mintage	VG	F	VF	XF	Unc
1732	—	2.50	6.00	16.00	40.00	—
1733	—	2.50	6.00	16.00	40.00	—
1736	—	2.50	6.00	16.00	40.00	—
1738	—	2.50	6.00	16.00	40.00	—
ND	—	2.50	6.00	16.00	40.00	—

KM# 490 SESINO (1/6 soldi)

Copper **Obv:** Value in cartouche **Rev:** Crowned cross in cartouche over date

Date	Mintage	VG	F	VF	XF	Unc
1750	—	3.50	9.00	20.00	50.00	—
1754	—	3.50	9.00	20.00	50.00	—
1755	—	3.50	9.00	20.00	50.00	—
1756	—	3.50	9.00	20.00	50.00	—
1757	—	3.50	9.00	20.00	50.00	—
1758	—	3.50	9.00	20.00	50.00	—

KM# 461 1/2 SOLDO

Copper **Obv:** Crowned shield **Obv. Legend:** FRAN • II • D • G • ... **Rev:** Value, date

Date	Mintage	VG	F	VF	XF	Unc
1793	—	20.00	45.00	90.00	200	—

KM# 463 SOLDO

Copper **Obv:** Radiant sun face **Obv. Legend:** CAR • IMP • DVX • ... **Rev:** Value, inscription

Date	Mintage	VG	F	VF	XF	Unc
1731	—	3.50	8.50	20.00	50.00	—
1732	—	3.50	8.50	20.00	50.00	—
1734	—	3.50	8.50	20.00	50.00	—
1736	—	3.50	8.50	20.00	50.00	—
ND	—	3.50	8.50	20.00	50.00	—

KM# 492 SOLDO

Copper **Obv:** Radiant sun face **Rev:** Value

Date	Mintage	VG	F	VF	XF	Unc
1750	—	4.50	12.00	28.00	60.00	—
1754	—	4.50	12.00	28.00	60.00	—
1755	—	4.50	12.00	28.00	60.00	—
1756	—	4.50	12.00	28.00	60.00	—
1757	—	4.50	12.00	28.00	60.00	—
1758	—	4.50	12.00	28.00	60.00	—

KM# 469 SOLDONE (2 Soldi)

Copper **Obv:** Crowned ornate arms **Obv. Legend:** CAR • VI • ROM • ... **Rev:** Value, date within ornate design

Date	Mintage	VG	F	VF	XF	Unc
1732	—	9.00	20.00	45.00	110	—

KM# 471 SOLDONE (2 Soldi)

Copper **Obv:** Legend begins at lower left

Date	Mintage	VG	F	VF	XF	Unc
1732	—	9.00	20.00	45.00	110	—

KM# 473 SOLDONE (2 Soldi)

Copper **Rev:** Value: SLODONE (error)

Date	Mintage	VG	F	VF	XF	Unc
1732	—	12.00	25.00	60.00	145	—

KM# 494 SOLDONE (2 Soldi)

Copper **Obv:** Crowned Austrian arms in cartouche **Rev:** Value and date in cartouche

Date	Mintage	VG	F	VF	XF	Unc
1750	—	10.00	22.00	50.00	120	—
1754	—	10.00	22.00	50.00	120	—
1755	—	10.00	22.00	50.00	120	—
1757	—	10.00	22.00	50.00	120	—
1758	—	10.00	22.00	50.00	120	—

KM# 475 5 SOLDI

Silver **Obv:** Bust of Charles VI right, date below **Rev:** Crowned imperial eagle, value divided below

Date	Mintage	VG	F	VF	XF	Unc
1732	—	15.00	37.50	100	250	—
1733	—	15.00	37.50	100	250	—
1736	—	15.00	37.50	100	250	—

KM# 496 5 SOLDI

Silver **Obv:** Bust of Maria Theresa right, value below S.5. **Rev:** Arms on breast of crowned imperial eagle, date below

Date	Mintage	VG	F	VF	XF	Unc
1750	—	10.00	25.00	60.00	150	—
1754	—	10.00	25.00	60.00	150	—
1755	—	10.00	25.00	60.00	150	—

KM# 500 5 SOLDI

Silver **Obv:** Value: S.V.

Date	Mintage	VG	F	VF	XF	Unc
1756	—	12.00	28.00	65.00	170	—
1757	—	10.00	25.00	60.00	150	—

KM# 477 10 SOLDI

Silver **Obv:** Bust of Charles VI right, value below **Rev:** Crowned imperial eagle, date in legend

Date	Mintage	VG	F	VF	XF	Unc
1732	—	25.00	60.00	140	275	—
1733	—	25.00	60.00	140	275	—
1734	—	25.00	60.00	140	275	—
1735	—	25.00	60.00	140	275	—
1736	—	25.00	60.00	140	275	—

KM# 498 10 SOLDI

Silver **Obv:** Bust of Maria Theresa right, value below S. 10. **Rev:** Arms on breast of crowned imperial eagle, date below

Date	Mintage	VG	F	VF	XF	Unc
1750	—	20.00	50.00	110	220	—
1754	—	20.00	50.00	110	220	—
1755	—	20.00	50.00	110	220	—
1756	—	20.00	50.00	110	220	—

KM# 502 10 SOLDI

Silver **Obv:** Value: S.X.

Date	Mintage	VG	F	VF	XF	Unc
1757	—	25.00	60.00	140	275	—

KM# 450 20 SOLDI

Silver **Obv:** Bust of Charles VI right, value below **Rev:** Crowned imperial eagle, date in legend

Date	Mintage	VG	F	VF	XF	Unc
1714	—	20.00	45.00	100	200	—
1732	—	20.00	45.00	100	200	—
1733	—	20.00	45.00	100	200	—
1734	—	20.00	45.00	100	200	—
1735	—	20.00	45.00	100	200	—
1736	—	20.00	45.00	100	200	—

KM# 485 20 SOLDI

Silver **Obv:** Bust of Maria Theresa right, value below S. 20., legend begins at upper right **Rev:** Arms on breast of crowned imperial eagle, date below, legend begins at upper right

Date	Mintage	VG	F	VF	XF	Unc
1750	—	25.00	50.00	120	300	—
1754	—	25.00	50.00	120	300	—

KM# 487 20 SOLDI

Silver **Rev:** Legend begins at lower left

Date	Mintage	VG	F	VF	XF	Unc
1754	—	35.00	75.00	160	350	—

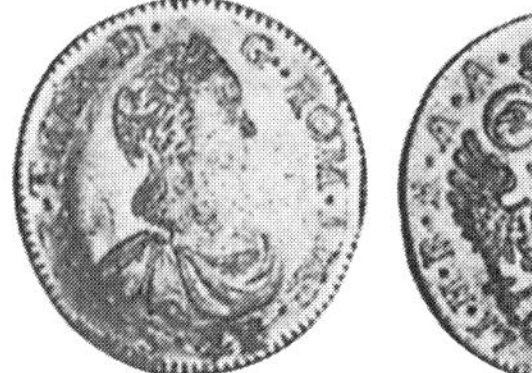

KM# 489 20 SOLDI

Silver **Obv:** Bust right, value S. XX. below **Rev:** Crowned double-headed eagle

Date	Mintage	VG	F	VF	XF	Unc
1755	—	22.00	45.00	100	280	—
1756	—	22.00	45.00	100	280	—
1757	—	22.00	45.00	100	280	—

KM# 504 40 SOLDI

Silver **Obv:** Bust of Maria Theresa right, value below **Rev:** Arms on breast of crowned imperial eagle, date below

Date	Mintage	VG	F	VF	XF	Unc
1757	—	45.00	100	220	450	—
1758	—	45.00	100	220	450	—

KM# 506 60 SOLDI

Silver **Obv:** Bust of Maria Theresa right, value below **Rev:** Arms on breast of crowned imperial eagle, date below

Date	Mintage	VG	F	VF	XF	Unc
1757	—	100	250	375	600	—
1758	—	100	250	375	600	—

KM# 531 MEZZA (1/2) LIRA

3.1000 g., 0.5520 Silver 0.0550 oz. ASW **Obv:** Crowned arms **Obv. Legend:** LEOP • II • D • G • R • I • S • A • ... **Rev:** Value, date within wreath

Date	Mintage	VG	F	VF	XF	Unc
1791	—	30.00	75.00	150	375	—

KM# 527 UNA (1) LIRA

6.2500 g., 0.5520 Silver 0.1109 oz. ASW **Obv:** Crowned arms **Obv. Legend:** Ends: ...MANT **Rev:** Value, date within wreath

Date	Mintage	VG	F	VF	XF	Unc
1791	—	35.00	85.00	175	425	—

KM# 529 UNA (1) LIRA

6.2500 g., 0.5520 Silver 0.1109 oz. ASW **Obv. Legend:** Ends: ...MAN

Date	Mintage	VG	F	VF	XF	Unc
1791	—	35.00	85.00	175	425	—

KM# 515 3 LIRE

Silver **Obv:** Veiled bust of Maria Theresa right **Rev:** Crowned arms in branches, value below

Date	Mintage	VG	F	VF	XF	Unc
1779	—	60.00	150	300	600	—

KM# 465 1/2 TALLERO (6 Lire)

Silver **Subject:** Charles VI **Note:** Similar to Tallero, KM#111.

Date	Mintage	VG	F	VF	XF	Unc
1732	—	300	600	1,000	1,800	—
1733	—	300	600	1,000	1,800	—
1736	—	300	600	1,000	1,800	—

KM# 479 TALLERO (12 Lire)

Silver **Subject:** Charles VI **Obv:** Bust right **Obv. Legend:** CAROL • VI • D: G: R: I: S: A: .... **Rev:** Crowned double eagle **Rev. Legend:** ARCH: AUST: DUX: BU: ET • MANTU... **Note:** Dav. #1378.

Date	Mintage	VG	F	VF	XF	Unc
1733	—	1,000	2,000	3,250	5,500	—
1736	—	1,000	2,000	3,250	5,500	—

SIEGE COINAGE

1796

KM# 533 20 SOLDI

Silver **Obv:** Crowned shield **Rev:** Value, date below designs within wreath

Date	Mintage	VG	F	VF	XF	Unc
1796	—	225	375	650	1,200	—
1796 Error	—	275	450	800	1,500	—

Note: Retrograde S in SOLDI

SIEGE COINAGE

1799

Issues of the French defenders

KM# 535 UN (1) SOLDO

Cast Bell Metal **Obv:** Fasces with liberty cap within sprigs **Rev:** Value

Date	Mintage	VG	F	VF	XF	Unc
ND//7 (1799)	—	18.00	35.00	65.00	145	—

KM# 537 V (5) SOLDI

Silver **Obv:** Fasces with liberty cap **Rev:** Value

Date	Mintage	VG	F	VF	XF	Unc
ND//VII (1799)	—	30.00	60.00	110	200	—

KM# 539 X (10) SOLDI

Silver **Note:** Similar to 5 Soldi, C#32.

Date	Mintage	VG	F	VF	XF	Unc
ND//VII (1799)	—	40.00	70.00	150	250	—

MASSA-CARRARA

A small state in Tuscany, a territorial division consisting of the western part of the center of the Italian peninsula, attained the ranking of a principality in 1568 and of a duchy in 1663. The minting privilege was granted to the Marquis of Massa in 1559

RULER

Austrian until 1796

MONETARY SYSTEM

3 Quattrini = 1 Soldo

20 Soldi = 1 Lira

DUCHY

STANDARD COINAGE

C# 1 QUATTRINO

Copper **Obv:** Crowned arms within legend **Rev:** Value above date

Date	Mintage	Good	VG	F	VF	XF
1792	—	—	20.00	35.00	65.00	150

C# 2 2 SOLDI

Copper **Obv:** Crowned shield **Obv. Legend:** NAR • BEATRIX • ARCHID • ... **Rev:** Value, date **Rev. Legend:** DUX • MASSAE •

Date	Mintage	Good	VG	F	VF	XF
1792	—	—	20.00	40.00	75.00	200

C# 3 4 SOLDI

Billon **Note:** Similar to Due (2) Soldi, C#2.

Date	Mintage	Good	VG	F	VF	XF
1792	—	—	25.00	50.00	90.00	225

C# 4 10 SOLDI

Billon **Note:** Similar to Due (2) Soldi, C#2.

Date	Mintage	Good	VG	F	VF	XF
1792	—	—	25.00	55.00	100	240

MILAN

A city in Lombardy, was ruled by the Lombards before falling to the Franks in 774. It was a dependency of the Spanish Crown from 1535 until the War of the Spanish Succession in 1714. Then it was handed over to Austria who ruled over it until the Napoleonic campaign of 1796 and then became part of the Cisalpine Republic in 1797. In 1802 it became part of the Italian Republic and was part of the Kingdom of Napoleon from 1805 to 1814. From 1814 it was incorporated within Lombardy-Venetia, again under Austrian rule. The Lombard campaign of 1859 restored Milan under the Kingdom of Italy.

RULERS

Spanish, until 1714

Austrian, 1714-1796

French, 1796-1814

MINT MARKS

M - Milan

S - Schmollnitz

W - Vienna

None - Milan

MONETARY SYSTEM

2 Denari = 1 Sestino

2 Sestini = 1 Quattrini

2 Sesini = 1 Soldo

20 Soldi = 1 Lira

6 Lire = 1 Scudo

SPANISH ADMINISTRATION

STANDARD COINAGE

DAV# 1379 FILIPPO

Silver **Obv:** Bust right, date below **Obv. Legend:** PHILIPPVS • V • REX • ... **Rev:** Crowned arms **Rev. Legend:** DVX • ...

Date	Mintage	VG	F	VF	XF	Unc
1702	—	150	250	400	700	—

DAV# 1380 FILIPPO

Silver **Obv:** Bust of Charles right, date below

Date	Mintage	VG	F	VF	XF	Unc
1707	—	250	350	600	1,000	—
1708	—	275	375	650	1,150	—

AUSTRIAN ADMINISTRATION

STANDARD COINAGE

C# 12 1/8 FILIPPO

0.9580 Silver **Obv:** Bust of Maria Theresa right **Rev:** Crowned arms in branches, date below

Date	Mintage	VG	F	VF	XF	Unc
1741	—	75.00	150	300	500	—
1744	—	75.00	150	300	500	—

C# 13 1/4 FILIPPO

0.9580 Silver **Obv:** Bust of Maria Theresa right **Rev:** Crowned arms in branches, date below

Date	Mintage	VG	F	VF	XF	Unc
1741	—	85.00	175	350	450	—
1744	—	85.00	175	350	450	—

C# 14 1/2 FILIPPO

0.9580 Silver **Obv:** Bust of Maria Theresa right **Rev:** Crowned arms in branches, date below

Date	Mintage	VG	F	VF	XF	Unc
1741	—	100	200	375	500	—
1744	—	100	200	375	500	—
1749	—	100	200	375	500	—

C# 14a 1/2 FILIPPO

0.9580 Silver **Note:** Similar to 1 Filippo, C#15 but half thickness.

Date	Mintage	VG	F	VF	XF	Unc
1741	—	125	225	400	550	—

DAV# 1382 FILIPPO

Silver **Obv:** Bust right, date below **Rev:** Crowned arms

Date	Mintage	VG	F	VF	XF	Unc
1719	—	325	550	950	1,600	—
1720	—	325	550	950	1,600	—
1726	—	325	550	950	1,600	—
1728	—	325	550	950	1,600	—
1729	—	325	550	950	1,600	—
1730	—	325	550	950	1,600	—
1731	—	325	550	950	1,600	—
1733	—	325	550	950	1,600	—
1736	—	325	550	950	1,600	—

C# 15 FILIPPO

0.9580 Silver **Obv:** Bust right **Obv. Legend:** MARIA • THERESA • D • G • REG • ... **Rev:** Crowned arms in branches, date below

Date	Mintage	VG	F	VF	XF	Unc
1741	—	275	375	650	1,150	—
1743	—	275	375	650	1,150	—
1744	—	275	375	650	1,150	—
1749	—	275	375	650	1,150	—

DAV# 1381 2 FILIPPI

Silver **Note:** Similar to 1 Filippo, Dav. #1382, but double thickness.

Date	Mintage	VG	F	VF	XF	Unc
1736 Rare	—	—	—	—	—	—

C# 16 2 FILIPPI

0.9580 Silver **Note:** Similar to 1 Filippo C#15, but double thickness. Dav. #1383.

Date	Mintage	VG	F	VF	XF	Unc
1741	—	450	750	1,100	1,750	—
1744	—	450	750	1,100	1,750	—

REFORM COINAGE

C# 1 SESTINO

Copper **Obv:** Crowned arms **Rev:** Value, date

Date	Mintage	VG	F	VF	XF	Unc
1777	—	3.00	5.00	9.00	25.00	—
1779	—	3.00	5.00	9.00	25.00	—

Note: Varieties in letter size exist for 1779

C# 2 QUATTRINO

Copper **Obv:** Bust of Maria Theresa right **Rev:** Crowned arms

Date	Mintage	VG	F	VF	XF	Unc
1750	—	15.00	30.00	65.00	100	—

C# 4 QUATTRINO

Copper **Obv:** Crowned arms **Obv. Legend:** M • THER • D • G • R • I • H • B • R • A • A • D • MED • **Rev:** Value, date

Date	Mintage	VG	F	VF	XF	Unc
1776	—	4.00	7.00	15.00	45.00	—
1777	—	4.00	7.00	15.00	45.00	—
1779	—	4.00	7.00	15.00	45.00	—

C# 5 QUATTRINO

Copper **Obv:** Bust of Maria Theresa **Rev:** Crowned arms

Date	Mintage	VG	F	VF	XF	Unc
ND	—	15.00	30.00	65.00	100	—

C# 9 MEZZO (1/2) SOLDO

Copper **Obv:** Crowned arms **Obv. Legend:** M • THER • D • G • R • I • H • B • R • A • A • D • MED • **Rev:** Value, date within wreath

Date	Mintage	VG	F	VF	XF	Unc
1776	—	10.00	20.00	40.00	85.00	—
1777/000	—	3.00	5.50	10.00	30.00	—
Note: Varieties in letter size exist for 1777						
1777	—	2.50	4.50	8.00	25.00	—
Note: Varieties in letter size exist for 1777						
1779	—	2.50	4.50	8.00	25.00	—

C# 10 SOLDO

Copper **Obv:** Veiled bust right **Obv. Legend:** M • THERESIA • D • G • R • I • .... **Rev:** Value, date within wreath

Date	Mintage	VG	F	VF	XF	Unc
1777	—	6.00	12.00	30.00	60.00	—
1777S	—	2.50	4.50	13.50	45.00	—
1777W	—	2.50	4.50	12.00	35.00	—
1779	—	6.00	12.00	30.00	60.00	—
1779S	—	2.50	4.50	13.50	45.00	—
1779W	—	2.50	4.50	12.00	35.00	—

C# 11 6 QUATTRINI

Copper **Obv:** Veiled bust of Maria Theresa right **Rev:** Value and date in branches

Date	Mintage	VG	F	VF	XF	Unc
1776	—	30.00	75.00	185	300	—

C# 17 PARPAGLIOLA (2-1/2) SOLDI

Silver **Obv:** Bust of Maria Theresa right **Rev:** MLNI/DUX and date in cartouche

Date	Mintage	VG	F	VF	XF	Unc
1749	—	25.00	45.00	75.00	175	—
1750	—	25.00	45.00	75.00	175	—
1758	—	25.00	45.00	75.00	175	—
1768	—	25.00	45.00	75.00	175	—

C# 18 5 SOLDI

Silver **Obv:** Bust right **Obv. Legend:** M • TH • D • G • I • R • ... **Rev:** MLNI DUX and date within ornate design

Date	Mintage	VG	F	VF	XF	Unc
1749	—	5.00	10.00	30.00	120	—
1750	—	5.00	10.00	28.00	110	—
1756	—	5.00	10.00	30.00	120	—
1758	—	5.00	10.00	28.00	100	—
1762	—	5.00	10.00	30.00	120	—
1763	—	5.00	10.00	28.00	100	—

C# 31 5 SOLDI

1.5500 g., 0.5520 Silver 0.0275 oz. ASW **Obv:** Crowned arms **Obv. Legend:** M • THER • D • G • .... **Rev:** Value within wreath, divided date below

Date	Mintage	VG	F	VF	XF	Unc
1778	—	10.00	25.00	60.00	110	—
1779	—	10.00	25.00	50.00	100	—
1780	—	10.00	25.00	50.00	100	—

C# 41 5 SOLDI

1.5500 g., 0.5520 Silver 0.0275 oz. ASW **Obv:** Crowned arms **Rev:** Value within wreath, divided date below

Date	Mintage	VG	F	VF	XF	Unc
1780	—	10.00	15.00	30.00	70.00	—
1781	—	10.00	15.00	40.00	90.00	—
1784	—	10.00	15.00	30.00	70.00	—
1787	—	10.00	15.00	30.00	70.00	—

C# 33 MEZZA (1/2) LIRA

3.1000 g., 0.5520 Silver 0.0550 oz. ASW **Note:** Similar to 6 Lire, C#36.

Date	Mintage	VG	F	VF	XF	Unc
1778	—	25.00	50.00	100	225	—
1779	—	25.00	50.00	100	225	—
1780	—	25.00	50.00	100	225	—

C# 42 MEZZA (1/2) LIRA

3.1000 g., 0.5520 Silver 0.0550 oz. ASW **Subject:** Joseph II **Obv:** Bust right **Obv. Legend:** IOSEPH • II • D • G • R • IMP • S • AUG • ... **Rev:** Crowned arms within sprigs

Date	Mintage	VG	F	VF	XF	Unc
1781	—	20.00	40.00	90.00	200	—
1782	—	20.00	40.00	90.00	200	—
1783/2	—	20.00	40.00	90.00	200	—
1783	—	20.00	40.00	90.00	200	—
1784	—	20.00	40.00	90.00	200	—
1785	—	20.00	40.00	90.00	200	—
1786	—	20.00	40.00	90.00	200	—
1787	—	20.00	40.00	90.00	200	—

C# 20 10 SOLDI

Silver **Obv:** Bust right **Rev:** Crowned shield

Date	Mintage	VG	F	VF	XF	Unc
1762	—	20.00	45.00	90.00	225	—
1767	—	20.00	45.00	90.00	225	—

C# 21 10 SOLDI

Silver **Rev:** Value: 10

Date	Mintage	VG	F	VF	XF	Unc
1766	—	40.00	75.00	150	300	—

Note: Some authorities believe this to be a pattern

C# 22 10 SOLDI

Silver **Obv:** Veiled bust of Maria Theresa right **Rev:** Biscia in branches, value below

Date	Mintage	VG	F	VF	XF	Unc
1771	—	20.00	45.00	85.00	200	—
1774	—	20.00	45.00	85.00	200	—

C# 22a 10 SOLDI

Silver **Rev:** Crowned arms, value below

Date	Mintage	VG	F	VF	XF	Unc
1773	—	35.00	65.00	125	250	—

C# 34 UNA (1) LIRA

6.2500 g., 0.5520 Silver 0.1109 oz. ASW **Note:** Similar to 6 Lire, C#36.

Date	Mintage	VG	F	VF	XF	Unc
1778	—	40.00	80.00	165	375	—
1779	—	35.00	75.00	150	360	—
1780	—	40.00	80.00	165	375	—

C# 43 UNA (1) LIRA

6.2500 g., 0.5520 Silver 0.1109 oz. ASW **Subject:** Joseph II **Obv:** Laureate head right **Obv. Legend:** IOSEPH • II • D • G • .... **Rev:** Crowned oval shield within sprigs **Rev. Legend:** MEDIOLANI ET....

Date	Mintage	VG	F	VF	XF	Unc
1781	—	30.00	60.00	125	300	—
1782	—	30.00	60.00	125	300	—
1783	—	30.00	60.00	125	300	—
1784	—	30.00	65.00	135	325	—
1785	—	30.00	65.00	135	325	—
1786	—	30.00	60.00	125	300	—
1787	—	30.00	60.00	125	300	—
1790	—	30.00	65.00	135	325	—

C# 52 UNA (1) LIRA

6.2500 g., 0.5520 Silver 0.1109 oz. ASW **Subject:** Leopold II **Obv:** Laureate head right **Obv. Legend:** LEOP • II • D • G • .... **Rev:** Crowned oval shield within sprigs **Rev. Legend:** MEDIOLANI ET MANT • DUX ...

Date	Mintage	VG	F	VF	XF	Unc
1790M	—	50.00	100	200	385	—
1791M	—	50.00	100	200	385	—

C# 23 20 SOLDI

Center Composition: Silver **Obv:** Laureate head right **Obv. Legend:** CAROLVS • VI • IMP • ET • HIS • REX **Rev:** Value, date within crowned ornate shield, XX below

Date	Mintage	VG	F	VF	XF	Unc
1722	—	40.00	80.00	150	350	—

C# 24 20 SOLDI

Silver **Obv:** Laureate head right **Obv. Legend:** MA • THERE • D • G • IMP • ... **Rev:** Crowned shield with garland

Date	Mintage	VG	F	VF	XF	Unc
1762	—	25.00	50.00	100	235	—
1767	—	25.00	50.00	100	235	—

C# 24.5 20 SOLDI

Silver **Obv:** Veiled head right **Obv. Legend:** M • THERES • D • G • R • IMP • ... **Rev:** Crowned oval shield within sprigs, XX below

Date	Mintage	VG	F	VF	XF	Unc
1771	—	30.00	55.00	110	245	—
1773	—	30.00	60.00	125	260	—
1774	—	30.00	60.00	125	260	—

C# 58 30 SOLDI

7.3600 g., 0.6890 Silver 0.1630 oz. ASW **Subject:** Francis II **Obv:** Laureate head right **Obv. Legend:** FRANC • II • D • G • R • ... **Rev:** Crowned pointed shield **Rev. Legend:** MEDIOLANI • DUX •

Date	Mintage	VG	F	VF	XF	Unc
1794	—	35.00	75.00	150	265	—
1794 MEDILANI Error	—	75.00	125	225	375	—
1795	—	45.00	100	180	300	—
1796	—	35.00	75.00	150	265	—
1799	—	35.00	75.00	150	265	—
1800	—	35.00	75.00	150	265	—

C# 35 3 LIRE

11.5500 g., 0.8960 Silver 0.3327 oz. ASW **Subject:** Maria Theresa **Obv:** Veiled bust right **Obv. Legend:** M • THERESIA • D • G • R • ... **Rev:** Crowned oval shield within sprigs **Rev. Legend:** MEDIOLANI • DUX • 1778

Date	Mintage	VG	F	VF	XF	Unc
1777	—	45.00	90.00	150	300	—
1778	—	45.00	90.00	150	300	—
1779	—	45.00	90.00	150	300	—
1780	—	45.00	90.00	150	300	—

C# 44 3 LIRE

11.5500 g., 0.8960 Silver 0.3327 oz. ASW **Subject:** Joseph II **Obv:** Laureate head right **Obv. Legend:** IOSEPH • II • D • G • R • IMP • S • AUG • ... **Rev:** Crowned oval shield within sprigs **Rev. Legend:** ...MANT • DUX 1785

Date	Mintage	VG	F	VF	XF	Unc
1781	—	30.00	50.00	80.00	175	—
1782	—	30.00	50.00	90.00	185	—
1783	—	30.00	50.00	90.00	185	—
1784	—	30.00	50.00	90.00	185	—
1785	—	30.00	50.00	90.00	185	—
1786	—	30.00	50.00	90.00	185	—

C# 48 1/2 CROCIONE (1/2 Kronenthaler)

14.7200 g., 0.8730 Silver 0.4131 oz. ASW **Subject:** Joseph II **Obv:** Laureate head right **Obv. Legend:** IOSEPH • II • D • G • R • I • .... **Rev:** Crowns within cross-like design **Rev. Legend:** ARCH • AVST • DVX • BVRG • LOTH • ...

Date	Mintage	VG	F	VF	XF	Unc
1786M	—	15.00	25.00	45.00	100	—
1787M	—	15.00	25.00	45.00	100	—
1788M	—	15.00	25.00	45.00	100	—
1789M	—	15.00	25.00	45.00	100	—
1790M	—	15.00	25.00	45.00	100	—

C# 53 1/2 CROCIONE (1/2 Kronenthaler)

14.7200 g., 0.8730 Silver 0.4131 oz. ASW **Subject:** Leopold II **Obv:** Laureate head right **Obv. Legend:** LEOPOLD • II • D • G • R • I • ... **Rev:** Crowns within cross-like design **Rev. Legend:** ARCH • AVST • DVX • ...

Date	Mintage	VG	F	VF	XF	Unc
1791M	—	15.00	30.00	50.00	110	—

C# 36 6 LIRE

23.1000 g., 0.8960 Silver 0.6654 oz. ASW **Obv:** Veiled bust right **Obv. Legend:** M • THERESIA • D • G • ... **Rev:** Crowned 4-fold arms within sprigs **Rev. Legend:** MEDIOLANI DUX • **Note:** Dav. #1386.

Date	Mintage	VG	F	VF	XF	Unc
1778	—	75.00	125	225	400	—
1779	—	75.00	125	225	400	—
1780	—	75.00	125	225	400	—

C# 45 6 LIRE

23.1000 g., 0.8960 Silver 0.6654 oz. ASW **Subject:** Joseph II **Obv:** Laureate head right **Obv. Legend:** IOSEPH • II • D • G • R • IMP • ... **Rev:** Crowned 4-fold arms within sprigs **Rev. Legend:** MEDIOLANI ET MANT • DUX 1786 **Note:** Dav. #1387.

Date	Mintage	VG	F	VF	XF	Unc
1781 LB	—	60.00	100	165	300	—
1782 LB	—	60.00	100	165	300	—
1783 LB	—	60.00	100	165	300	—
1784 LB	—	60.00	100	165	300	—
1785 LB	—	60.00	100	165	300	—
1786 LB	—	60.00	100	165	300	—

C# 49 CROCIONE (Kronenthaler)

29.4400 g., 0.8730 Silver 0.8263 oz. ASW **Subject:** Joseph II **Obv:** Laureate head right **Obv. Legend:** IOSEPH • II • D • G • ... **Rev:** Crowns within cross-like design **Rev. Legend:** ARCH • AVST • DVX • BVRG • ... **Note:** Dav. #1388.

Date	Mintage	VG	F	VF	XF	Unc
1786M	—	30.00	45.00	90.00	180	—
1787M	—	30.00	45.00	90.00	180	—
1788M	—	30.00	45.00	90.00	180	—
1789M	—	30.00	45.00	90.00	180	—
1790M	—	30.00	45.00	90.00	180	—

C# 54 CROCIONE (Kronenthaler)

29.4400 g., 0.8730 Silver 0.8263 oz. ASW **Subject:** Leopold II **Obv:** Laureate head right **Obv. Legend:** LEOPOLD • II • D • G • R • ... **Rev:** Crowns within cross-like design **Rev. Legend:** ARCH • AVST • DVX • BVRG • ... **Note:** Dav. #1389.

Date	Mintage	VG	F	VF	XF	Unc
1791M	—	30.00	45.00	90.00	180	—
1792M	—	30.00	45.00	90.00	180	—

C# 59.1 CROCIONE (Kronenthaler)

29.4400 g., 0.8730 Silver 0.8263 oz. ASW **Subject:** Francis II **Obv:** Laureate head right **Obv. Legend:** FRANCISC • II • D • G • R • ... **Rev:** Crowns within angles of designed cross **Rev. Legend:** ARCH • AVST • DVX • BVRG • LOTH • BARB • COM • FLAN • ... **Note:** Dav. #1390.

Date	Mintage	VG	F	VF	XF	Unc
1792M	—	25.00	40.00	80.00	165	—
1793M	—	25.00	40.00	80.00	165	—
1794M	—	25.00	40.00	80.00	165	—
1795M	—	25.00	40.00	80.00	165	—
1796M	—	25.00	40.00	80.00	165	—
1799M	—	25.00	40.00	80.00	165	—
1800M	—	25.00	40.00	80.00	165	—

C# 59.2 CROCIONE (Kronenthaler)

29.4400 g., 0.8730 Silver 0.8263 oz. ASW **Edge Lettering:** IVSTITIA ET FIDE

Date	Mintage	VG	F	VF	XF	Unc
1799M	—	30.00	50.00	110	220	—
1800M	—	30.00	50.00	110	220	—

C# 55 1/4 SOVRANO

2.7650 g., 0.9190 Gold 0.0817 oz. AGW **Obv:** Leopold II **Rev:** Crowned arms

Date	Mintage	VG	F	VF	XF	Unc
1791M	—	450	700	2,000	4,000	—

FR# 730 SCUDO D'ORO

3.5000 g., 0.9860 Gold 0.1109 oz. AGW **Obv:** Laureate bust of Charles VI right **Rev:** Crowned imperial eagle with arms on breast, date divided below

Date	Mintage	VG	F	VF	XF	Unc
1723M	—	3,000	5,000	8,500	13,500	—
1724M	—	3,000	5,000	8,500	13,500	—

C# 37 ZECCHINO

3.4900 g., 0.9860 Gold 0.1106 oz. AGW **Obv:** Veiled bust of Maria Theresa **Rev:** Standing figure of St. Ambrose

Date	Mintage	VG	F	VF	XF	Unc
ND Rare	—	—	—	—	—	—

C# 38 ZECCHINO

3.4900 g., 0.9860 Gold 0.1106 oz. AGW **Obv:** Veiled bust right **Obv. Legend:** M • THERESIA • D • G • ... **Rev:** Crowned oval shield within sprigs **Rev. Legend:** MEDIOLANI DUX •

Date	Mintage	VG	F	VF	XF	Unc
1778	—	250	350	600	1,400	—
1779	—	250	350	600	1,400	—
1780	—	250	350	600	1,400	—

C# 46 ZECCHINO

3.4900 g., 0.9860 Gold 0.1106 oz. AGW **Obv:** Laureate head right **Obv. Legend:** IOSEPH • II • D • G • ... **Rev:** Crowned oval shield within sprigs **Rev. Legend:** MEDIOLANI ET MANT • DUX **Note:** Similar to 1/2 Lira, C#42.

Date	Mintage	VG	F	VF	XF	Unc
1781	—	150	250	400	900	—
1782	—	150	250	400	900	—
1783	—	150	250	400	900	—
1784	—	150	250	400	900	—
1785	—	150	250	400	900	—
1786	—	150	250	400	900	—
1787	—	150	250	400	900	—
1788	—	150	250	400	900	—

C# 50 1/2 SOVRANO

Gold **Subject:** Joseph II **Obv:** Laureate head right **Obv. Legend:** IOSEPH • II • D • G • ... **Rev:** Crowned oval shield within Order chain **Rev. Legend:** ARCH • AVST • DVX • BVRG • ...

Date	Mintage	F	VF	XF	Unc	BU
1787M	—	175	250	450	750	—
1788M	—	175	300	525	900	—
1789M	—	200	400	600	1,100	—
1790M	—	200	400	600	1,100	—

C# 56 1/2 SOVRANO

5.5700 g., 0.9190 Gold 0.1646 oz. AGW **Subject:** Leopold II **Obv:** Laureate head right **Obv. Inscription:** LEOPOLD • II • D • G • ... **Rev:** Crowned oval shield within Order chain **Rev. Inscription:** ARCH • AVST • DVX • BVRG • ...

Date	Mintage	F	VF	XF	Unc	BU
1790M	—	300	900	1,800	3,000	—
1791M	—	250	500	1,200	2,000	—
1792M	—	300	700	1,700	3,000	—

C# 56a 1/2 SOVRANO

5.5700 g., 0.9190 Gold 0.1646 oz. AGW **Rev:** Larger crowned arms

Date	Mintage	F	VF	XF	Unc	BU
1791M	—	300	700	1,700	3,000	—

C# 60 1/2 SOVRANO

5.5700 g., 0.9190 Gold 0.1646 oz. AGW **Obv:** Francis II **Rev:** Crowned arms

Date	Mintage	F	VF	XF	Unc	BU
1800	—	700	1,800	4,000	9,000	—

Note: For similar coins with other mint marks refer to Austrian Netherlands

FR# 729 2 SCUDI D'ORO

7.0000 g., 0.9860 Gold 0.2219 oz. AGW **Obv:** Laureate bust right **Obv. Legend:** CAROLVS • VI • IMP • ET • HISP • **Rev:** Crowned arms, date below

Date	Mintage	VG	F	VF	XF	Unc
1720	—	4,000	6,000	10,000	17,000	—

Note: Bowers and Merena Guia sale 3-89 XF 1720 realized $16,500

Date	Mintage	VG	F	VF	XF	Unc
1724 Rare	—	—	—	—	—	—

Note: Superior Pipito Sale 12-87 XF 1724 realized $19,525

C# 39 DOPPIA

6.3000 g., 0.9100 Gold 0.1843 oz. AGW **Obv:** Veiled bust right **Obv. Legend:** M • THERESIA • D • G • ... **Rev:** Crowned oval shield within sprigs **Rev. Legend:** MEDIOLANI DUX •

Date	Mintage	VG	F	VF	XF	Unc
1778	—	250	400	700	1,600	—
1779	—	250	400	700	1,600	—
1780	—	250	400	700	1,600	—

C# 47 DOPPIA

6.3000 g., 0.9100 Gold 0.1843 oz. AGW **Obv:** Laureate head right **Obv. Legend:** IOSEPH • II • D • G • ... **Rev:** Crowned shield within sprigs **Rev. Inscription:** MEDIOLANI ET MANT • DUX

Date	Mintage	VG	F	VF	XF	Unc
1781	—	175	325	650	1,500	—
1782	—	175	325	650	1,500	—
1783	—	175	325	650	1,500	—
1784	—	175	325	650	1,500	—

C# 51 SOVRANO

Gold **Obv:** Laureate head right **Obv. Legend:** IOSEPH • II • D • G • ... **Rev:** Crowned oval shield within order chain **Rev. Legend:** ARCH • AVST • DVX • BVRG • LOTH • BR • AB • COM • FLAN • 1787 •

Date	Mintage	VG	F	VF	XF	Unc
1786M	—	250	325	500	850	—
1787M	—	250	325	500	850	—
1788M	—	250	325	500	850	—
1789M	—	250	325	500	850	—
1790M	—	250	325	500	850	—

C# 57 SOVRANO

11.1400 g., 0.9190 Gold 0.3291 oz. AGW **Subject:** Leopold II **Obv:** Laureate head right **Obv. Legend:** LEOPOLD • II • D • G • R • ... **Rev:** Crowned oval shield within Order chain **Rev. Legend:** ARCH • AVST • DVX • BVRG • LOTH • BRAB • COM • FLAN • 1792 •

Date	Mintage	F	VF	XF	Unc	BU
1790M	—	500	1,200	2,000	4,000	—
1791M	—	600	1,500	2,500	5,000	—
1792M	—	600	1,500	2,200	5,000	—

C# 61 SOVRANO

11.0600 g., 0.9190 Gold 0.3268 oz. AGW **Obv. Legend:** FRANC • II • D • G...

Date	Mintage	F	VF	XF	Unc	BU
1792M	—	250	600	1,600	3,000	—
1793M	—	250	600	1,600	3,000	—

C# 61a SOVRANO

11.0600 g., 0.9190 Gold 0.3268 oz. AGW **Obv:** Laureate head right **Obv. Legend:** FRANCISC • II • D • G • ... **Rev:** Crowned oval shield within Order chain **Rev. Legend:** ARCH • AVST • DVX • BVRG • LOTH • BRAB • COM • FLAN • 1800 •

Date	Mintage	F	VF	XF	Unc	BU
1793M	—	350	800	1,800	3,500	—
1794M	—	250	500	1,000	2,000	—
1795M	—	250	500	1,000	2,000	—
1796M	—	250	500	1,000	2,000	—
1799M	—	400	900	2,000	4,000	—
1800M	—	250	500	1,000	2,250	—

Note: For similar coins with other mint marks refer to Austrian Netherlands

C# 40 2 DOPPIE

12.6000 g., 0.9100 Gold 0.3686 oz. AGW **Obv:** Veiled bust right **Obv. Legend:** M • THERESIA • D • G • ... **Rev:** Crowned oval shield within sprigs **Rev. Legend:** MEDIOLANI DUX •

Date	Mintage	VG	F	VF	XF	Unc
1778	—	400	1,000	2,000	4,000	—
1779	—	400	1,000	2,000	4,000	—

FR# 731 12 SCUDI D'ORO

39.7100 g., Gold **Subject:** Charles VI

Date	Mintage	VG	F	VF	XF	Unc
ND(1711-40) Rare	—	—	—	—	—	—

Note: Superior Pipito Sale 12-87 VF realized $50,600

PATTERNS

Including off metal strikes

KM#	Date	Mintage	Identification	Mkt Val
Pn1	1777	—	Scudo. Silver. Maria Theresa right. DUX, date at left of arms. Dav. #1385.	—

MODENA

Mutina

The ancient Mutina is a territorial division of Italy fronting on the Adriatic Sea between Venetia and Marches which became Roman in 215-212 B.C. Ravaged by Attila and Lombard attacks, it was rebuilt in the 9th century. Obizzo d'Este became its lord in 1288 and it was constituted a duchy in favor of Borso d'Este in 1452.Modena was included in the Napoleonic complex from 1796 to 1813, after which it was governed by the House of Austria-Este. Modena began coining in the 13th century and ceased in 1796.

RULERS

Rinaldo D'Este, 1694-1737
Francesco III d'Este, 1737-1780
Ercole (Hercules) III d'Este 1780-1796

MONETARY SYSTEM

12 Denari = 2 Sesini = 1 Soldo
20 Bolognini = 10 Muraglioli = 4 Giorgini = 3 Capellone = 1 Lira
3 Small Scudi = 1 Tallero

DUCHY

STANDARD COINAGE

C# 13 QVATTRO (4) DENARI

Copper **Obv:** Crowned lily **Rev:** Value

Date	Mintage	VG	F	VF	XF	Unc
ND	—	5.00	10.00	20.00	40.00	—

C# 1 SESINO

Copper **Obv:** Bust of Francesco right, without legend **Rev:** Crowned shield

Date	Mintage	VG	F	VF	XF	Unc
ND	—	10.00	20.00	40.00	75.00	—

C# 2 UN (VN = 1) SOLDO

Copper **Obv:** Fleur-de-lys **Rev:** Value

Date	Mintage	VG	F	VF	XF	Unc
ND	—	6.00	12.00	25.00	50.00	—

C# 14 UN (VN = 1) SOLDO

Copper **Obv:** Date within wreath **Rev:** Value within wreath **Note:** Varieties exist.

Date	Mintage	VG	F	VF	XF	Unc
1783	—	4.50	9.00	18.00	35.00	—
1784	—	4.50	9.00	18.00	35.00	—

C# 3 UN (VN = 1) BOLOGNINO

Copper **Obv:** Displayed d'Este eagle **Rev:** Value

Date	Mintage	VG	F	VF	XF	Unc
ND	—	6.00	12.00	25.00	50.00	—

C# 15 UN (VN = 1) BOLOGNINO

Copper **Obv:** d'Este eagle **Rev:** Value

Date	Mintage	VG	F	VF	XF	Unc
1783	—	4.50	9.00	18.00	35.00	—
1784	—	4.50	9.00	18.00	35.00	—

C# 4 DUE (2) BOLOGNINI (Muragliolo)

Billon **Obv:** Crowned arms **Rev:** Value over date

Date	Mintage	VG	F	VF	XF	Unc
1740	—	5.00	10.00	20.00	40.00	—
1741	—	5.00	10.00	20.00	40.00	—
1747	—	5.00	10.00	20.00	40.00	—

C# 16 DUE (2) BOLOGNINI (Muragliolo)

Billon **Obv:** Eagle **Rev:** Value

Date	Mintage	VG	F	VF	XF	Unc
1783	—	8.00	16.00	30.00	50.00	—
1784	—	8.00	16.00	30.00	50.00	—

C# 5 4 BOLOGNINI

Billon **Obv:** Bust of Francesco right **Rev:** Crowned eagle

Date	Mintage	VG	F	VF	XF	Unc
1739	—	12.00	25.00	45.00	85.00	—
1740	—	12.00	25.00	45.00	85.00	—

C# 6 5 SOLDI (Giorgino)

Billon **Obv:** Crowned eagle **Rev:** Saint standing

Date	Mintage	VG	F	VF	XF	Unc
1740	—	6.00	12.00	25.00	50.00	—
1741	—	6.00	12.00	25.00	50.00	—
1742	—	6.00	12.00	25.00	50.00	—
1750	—	6.00	12.00	25.00	50.00	—
1762	—	6.00	12.00	25.00	50.00	—

C# 7 6 BOLOGNINI 8 DENARI (Capellone)

Billon **Obv:** Bust of Francesco right **Rev:** Value and date

Date	Mintage	VG	F	VF	XF	Unc
1750	—	6.00	12.00	25.00	50.00	—
1751	—	6.00	12.00	25.00	50.00	—

C# 8 10 SOLDI (1/2 Lira)

Billon **Obv:** Crowned eagle **Note:** Similar to Scudo, C#12.

Date	Mintage	VG	F	VF	XF	Unc
1738	—	15.00	30.00	55.00	100	—

C# 9 LIRA

Billon **Obv:** Crowned eagle **Note:** Similar to Scudo, C#12.

Date	Mintage	VG	F	VF	XF	Unc
1738	—	20.00	40.00	85.00	200	—
1739	—	20.00	40.00	85.00	200	—

C# 11 2 LIRE

Billon **Obv:** Crowned eagle **Note:** Similar to Scudo, C#12.

Date	Mintage	VG	F	VF	XF	Unc
1738	—	30.00	60.00	120	275	—

C# 12.1 SCUDO

Silver **Ruler:** Francesco III d'Este **Obv:** Armored bust right **Obv. Legend:** FRANCISCUS • III • MUT • REG • MIR • DUX • **Rev:** Crowned ornate shield **Rev. Legend:** VETERIS MONU - MENTUM DECORIS **Note:** Dav. #1392.

Date	Mintage	VG	F	VF	XF	Unc
1739	—	150	300	500	1,000	—

C# 12.2 SCUDO

Silver **Ruler:** Francesco III d'Este **Rev. Legend:** VETERIS MONVME - NTVM ... **Note:** Dav#1392A.

Date	Mintage	VG	F	VF	XF	Unc
1739	—	—	—	—	—	—

C# 17 SCUDO

9.2310 g., 0.9100 Silver 0.2701 oz. ASW **Ruler:** Ercole (Hercules) III d'Este **Obv:** Bust left **Obv. Legend:** HERCVLES • III • D • G • .... **Rev:** Crowned shield in Order chain **Rev. Legend:** PROXIMA SOLI •

Date	Mintage	VG	F	VF	XF	Unc
1782	—	40.00	70.00	110	250	—
1783	—	40.00	70.00	110	250	—

C# 18 2 SCUDI

18.4620 g., 0.9100 Silver 0.5401 oz. ASW **Ruler:** Ercole (Hercules) III d'Este **Obv:** Bust left **Obv. Legend:** HERCVLES • III • D • G • .... **Rev:** Crowned shield in Order chain **Rev. Legend:** PROXIMA SOLI •

Date	Mintage	VG	F	VF	XF	Unc
1782	—	50.00	90.00	150	200	—
1783	—	50.00	90.00	150	200	—

C# 19.1 3 SCUDI

27.6930 g., 0.9100 Silver 0.8102 oz. ASW **Ruler:** Ercole (Hercules) III d'Este **Obv:** Bust left **Obv. Legend:** HERCVLES • III • D • G • .... **Rev:** Crowned shield in Order chain **Rev. Legend:** PROXIMA SOLI • **Note:** Dav. #1393.

Date	Mintage	VG	F	VF	XF	Unc
1782	—	75.00	150	225	375	—

C# 19.2 3 SCUDI

27.6930 g., 0.9100 Silver 0.8102 oz. ASW **Ruler:** Ercole (Hercules) III d'Este **Rev:** Date below arms **Note:** Dav#1393A.

Date	Mintage	VG	F	VF	XF	Unc
1783	—	75.00	150	225	375	—

C# 1394 TALLERO (Levant)

25.8100 g., 0.9100 Silver 0.7551 oz. ASW **Ruler:** Ercole (Hercules) III d'Este **Obv:** Bust left **Obv. Legend:** HERCVLES • III • D • G • .... **Rev:** Crowned, flagged shield **Rev. Legend:** DEXTERA • DOMINI • EXALTAVIT • ME • 1796

Date	Mintage	VG	F	VF	XF	Unc
1795	—	100	160	275	500	—
1796	—	100	160	275	500	—

C# 20.2 TALLERO (Levant)

25.8100 g., 0.9100 Silver 0.7551 oz. ASW **Ruler:** Ercole (Hercules) III d'Este **Obv. Legend:** Ends with ... MIR • EC • DVX • **Note:** Dav#1394A.

Date	Mintage	VG	F	VF	XF	Unc
1795	—	100	160	275	500	—
1796	—	100	160	275	500	—

DAV# 1391 DUCATO

Silver **Ruler:** Rinaldo d'Este **Obv:** Bust right, date below **Obv. Legend:** RAYNALDVS • I • MVT • REG • E (C OR R) • D • XI • MI • I • **Rev:** St. Gontard kneeling left **Rev. Legend:** PROTECTOR • NOSTE(R) ASPICE :

Date	Mintage	VG	F	VF	XF	Unc
1719	—	200	400	750	1,250	—
1720	—	200	400	750	1,250	—
1721	—	200	400	750	1,250	—

NAPLES & SICILY

Two Sicilies

Consisting of Sicily and the south of Italy, Naples & Sicily came into being in 1130. It passed under Spanish control in 1502; Naples was conquered by Austria in 1707. In 1733 Don Carlos of Spain was recognized as king. From then until becoming part of the United Kingdom of Italy, Naples and Sicily, together and separately, were contested for by Spain, Austria, France, and the republican and monarchial factions of Italy.

RULERS

Bourbon

Charles VI, 1707-1734
Carlo III, 1734-1759
Ferdinando IV, 1759-1799 (1st reign)
Ferdinando IV, 1799-1805 (2nd reign)
1815-1816 (restored in Naples)
1816-1825 (as King of the Two Sicilies)
Neapolitan Republic, 1799

MINT OFFICIALS' INITIALS

Initials	Date	Name
AG	1683-1714	Andrea Giovane
CC	1759	Cesare Coppola
FB	1734, 1736-43	Francesco Maria Berio
GB	1716-30	Giuseppe Basile
GV	1730	Geronimo Vespoli
MF	1715, 1730-34	Don Mattia de Franco
MM	1744-59	Marchese Vincenzo Maria Mazzara
VM	1731-33	Virgilio Martenise

ASSAYERS' INITIALS

Initial	Date	Name
A	1730-47	Francesco Antonio Ariani
C	1776	G. Batt Cangiano
R	1744	Giovanni Russo

ENGRAVERS' INITIALS

Usually found on the obverse below the portrait.

Initial	Date	Name
BP	1769-98	Bernhard Perger
FA	1766	Ferdinando Aveta
GG	1730-34, 1736-55, 1763	Giovanni de Gennard
IA, IA monogram	1754	Ingnazio Aveta
MM	1751	Domenico Maria Mazzara

MONETARY SYSTEM

(Until 1813)

6 Cavalli = 1 Tornese
240 Tornese = 120 Grana = 12 Carlini= 6 Tari = 1 Piastra
5 Grana = 1 Cinquina
100 Grana = 1 Ducato (Tallero)

KINGDOM

Bourbon Rule

STANDARD COINAGE

C# 64 PIASTRA OF 120 GRANA

25.4830 g., 0.9170 Silver 0.7513 oz. ASW **Ruler:** Ferdinando IV 1st reign **Obv:** Bust right **Obv. Legend:** FERDINAN • IV • D • G • SICILIAR • ET HIER • REX • **Rev:** Crowned, oval ornate shield, divides initials **Rev. Legend:** HISPANIAR • INFANS **Note:** Dav. #1401.

Date	Mintage	VG	F	VF	XF	Unc
1766 FA-CC	—	50.00	100	200	400	—

C# 66a PIASTRA OF 120 GRANA

27.2650 g., 0.8330 Silver 0.7302 oz. ASW **Ruler:** Ferdinando IV 1st reign **Obv:** Bust right **Obv. Legend:** FERDINAN • IV • D • G • SICILIAR • ET • HIE • REX **Rev:** Crowned shield with garland divides initials **Rev. Legend:** HISPANIAR - INFANS **Note:** Dav. #1406.

Date	Mintage	VG	F	VF	XF	Unc
1786 P//C-C	—	25.00	35.00	50.00	100	—
1786 BP//C-C	—	25.00	35.00	50.00	100	—
1787 DP//C-C	—	25.00	35.00	50.00	100	—
1788 DP//C-C	—	25.00	35.00	50.00	100	—
1788 P//C-C	—	25.00	35.00	50.00	100	—
1788 C-C	—	25.00	35.00	50.00	100	—
1788 BP//C-C	—	25.00	35.00	50.00	100	—
1789 P//C-C	—	25.00	35.00	50.00	100	—
1790 P//C-C	—	25.00	35.00	50.00	100	—
1790 P//M, R-C	—	25.00	35.00	50.00	100	—
1790 P//M, A-P	—	25.00	35.00	50.00	100	—
1791 P//C-C	—	25.00	35.00	50.00	100	—
1791 P//M, A-P	—	25.00	35.00	50.00	100	—
1791 P//A-P	—	25.00	35.00	50.00	100	—
1792 P//C-C	—	25.00	35.00	50.00	100	—
1792 P//M, A-P	—	25.00	35.00	50.00	100	—
1793 P//C-C	—	25.00	35.00	50.00	100	—
1793 P//M, A-P	—	25.00	35.00	50.00	100	—
1794 P//C-C	—	25.00	35.00	50.00	100	—
1794 P//M, A-P	—	25.00	35.00	50.00	100	—

C# 68 PIASTRA OF 120 GRANA
27.5320 g., 0.8330 Silver 0.7373 oz. ASW **Ruler:** Ferdinando IV 1st reign **Obv:** Conjoined busts right **Obv. Legend:** FERDINANDVS IV • ET M • CAROLINA VNDIQ • FELICES **Rev:** World globe divides date below radiant sun **Rev. Legend:** SOLI REDVCI **Note:** Varieties exist. Dav. #1408.

Date	Mintage	VG	F	VF	XF	Unc
1791 P-AP	—	50.00	100	150	250	—
1791 P-AP, M	—	50.00	100	150	250	—

C# 66b PIASTRA OF 120 GRANA
27.2650 g., 0.8330 Silver 0.7302 oz. ASW **Ruler:** Ferdinando IV 1st reign **Obv:** Head right **Obv. Legend:** FERDINAN • IV • D • G • SICILIAR • ET • HIE • REX **Rev:** Crowned shield with garland divides initials **Rev. Legend:** HISPANIAR INFANS **Note:** Dav. #1409.

Date	Mintage	VG	F	VF	XF	Unc
1795 P//A-P	—	35.00	50.00	70.00	150	—
1795 P//M, A-P	—	35.00	50.00	70.00	150	—
1796 P//A-P	—	35.00	50.00	70.00	150	—
1796 P//M, A-P	—	35.00	50.00	70.00	150	—
1798 P//A-P	—	35.00	50.00	70.00	150	—
1798 P//M, A-P	—	35.00	50.00	70.00	150	—
1799 P//M, A-P	—	35.00	50.00	70.00	150	—
1800 P//M, A-P	—	35.00	50.00	70.00	150	—

C# 75 6 DUCATI
8.7980 g., 0.9060 Gold 0.2563 oz. AGW **Ruler:** Ferdinando IV 1st reign **Obv:** Bust right **Obv. Legend:** FERDINAND • IV • D • G • ... **Rev:** Crowned shield divides initials **Rev. Legend:** HISPANIAR • INFANS • 1761 •

Date	Mintage	VG	F	VF	XF	Unc
1759 C-C R	—	125	200	275	350	—
1760 C-C R	—	125	200	275	350	—
1761 IA//C-C R	—	125	200	275	350	—
1762 IA//C-C R	—	125	200	275	350	—
1763 IA//C-C R	—	125	200	275	350	—
1763 DG//C-C R	—	125	200	275	350	—
1764 IA//C-C R	—	125	200	275	350	—
1765 DG//C-C R	—	125	200	275	350	—
1765 G//C-C R	—	125	200	275	350	—
1766 DG//C-C R	—	125	200	275	350	—
1767 DG//C-C R	—	125	200	275	350	—
1768 DG//C-C R	—	125	200	275	350	—

C# 76 6 DUCATI
8.7980 g., 0.9060 Gold 0.2563 oz. AGW **Ruler:** Ferdinando IV 1st reign **Obv:** Bust right **Obv. Legend:** FERDINAN • IV • D • G • SICIL • ... **Rev:** Crowned oval shield within sprays **Rev. Legend:** HISPANIAR • INFANS

Date	Mintage	VG	F	VF	XF	Unc
1768 BP//CC R	—	125	200	250	325	—
1768 CC R	—	125	200	250	325	—
1768 CC	—	125	200	250	325	—
1769 CC	—	125	200	250	325	—
1770 BP//CC R	—	125	200	250	325	—
1771 BP//CC R	—	125	200	250	325	—
1772 BP//CC R	—	125	200	250	325	—
1773 BP//CC R	—	125	200	250	325	—
1774 BP//CC R	—	125	200	250	325	—
1775 BP//CC R	—	125	200	250	325	—
1776 BP//CC C	—	125	200	250	325	—
1777 BP//CC C	—	125	200	250	325	—
1777 BP//CC	—	125	200	250	325	—
1778 BP//CC C	—	125	200	250	325	—
1780 BP//CC C Rare	—	—	—	—	—	—
1781 BP//CC C Rare	—	—	—	—	—	—

KINGDOM OF NAPLES

Spanish Rule

STANDARD COINAGE

C# 1 3 CAVALLI
Copper **Ruler:** Carlo III **Obv:** Bust right **Obv. Legend:** CAR • D • G • ... **Rev:** 3 in cartouche, date below

Date	Mintage	VG	F	VF	XF	Unc
1755	—	3.00	6.00	12.00	25.00	—
1756	—	3.00	6.00	12.00	25.00	—
1757	—	3.00	6.00	12.00	25.00	—

C# 29 3 CAVALLI
Copper **Ruler:** Ferdinando IV 1st reign **Obv:** Head right **Obv. Legend:** FERDINAN • IV • SICIL • REX • **Rev:** Maltese cross divides C3, date below

Date	Mintage	VG	F	VF	XF	Unc
1788 P	—	2.50	5.00	10.00	22.50	—
1789 P	—	2.50	5.00	10.00	22.50	—
1790 P	—	2.50	5.00	10.00	22.50	—
1791 P	—	2.50	5.00	10.00	22.50	—
1792 P	—	2.50	5.00	10.00	22.50	—

C# 2 4 CAVALLI
Copper **Ruler:** Carlo III **Obv:** Bust right **Rev:** 4 in cartouche, date below`

Date	Mintage	VG	F	VF	XF	Unc
1751	—	3.00	6.00	12.00	25.00	—
1752	—	3.00	6.00	12.00	25.00	—
1753	—	3.00	6.00	12.00	25.00	—
1754	—	3.00	6.00	12.00	25.00	—
1755	—	3.00	6.00	12.00	25.00	—
1756	—	3.00	6.00	12.00	25.00	—
1757	—	3.00	6.00	12.00	25.00	—

C# 31 4 CAVALLI
Copper **Ruler:** Ferdinando IV 1st reign **Obv:** Head right **Obv. Legend:** FERDINAN • IV • SICIL • REX • **Rev:** Grape cluster divides C4, date below

Date	Mintage	VG	F	VF	XF	Unc
1788 P	—	4.00	7.00	14.00	30.00	—
1789 P	—	4.00	7.00	14.00	30.00	—
1790 P	—	4.00	7.00	14.00	30.00	—
1791 P	—	4.00	7.00	14.00	30.00	—
1792 P	—	4.00	7.00	14.00	30.00	—

C# 2.5 TORNESE (6 Cavalli)
Copper **Ruler:** Carlo III **Obv:** Bust right **Rev:** HILA/RI/TAS, date below

Date	Mintage	VG	F	VF	XF	Unc
1754	—	3.50	7.00	14.00	30.00	—
1755	—	3.50	7.00	14.00	30.00	—
1756	—	3.50	7.00	14.00	30.00	—
1757	—	3.50	7.00	14.00	30.00	—

C# 33 TORNESE (6 Cavalli)
Copper **Ruler:** Ferdinando IV 1st reign **Obv:** Head right **Obv. Legend:** FERDINAN • IV • SICIL • REX • **Rev:** Value, date within thin wreath

Date	Mintage	VG	F	VF	XF	Unc
1788 P	—	3.50	7.00	14.00	35.00	—
1789 P	—	3.50	7.00	14.00	35.00	—
1790 P	—	3.50	7.00	14.00	35.00	—
1791 P	—	3.50	7.00	14.00	35.00	—
1792/1 P	—	4.00	8.00	16.00	40.00	—
1792 P	—	3.50	7.00	14.00	35.00	—

C# 3 9 CAVALLI
Copper **Ruler:** Carlo III **Obv:** Bust right **Rev:** 9 in cartouche, date below

Date	Mintage	VG	F	VF	XF	Unc
1756	—	6.00	12.00	25.00	50.00	—
1757	—	6.00	12.00	25.00	50.00	—

C# 37 9 CAVALLI
Copper **Ruler:** Ferdinando IV 1st reign **Obv:** Bust right **Obv. Legend:** FERDINAN • IV • SICIL • REX • **Rev:** Short towered building divides C.9, date below

Date	Mintage	VG	F	VF	XF	Unc
1788 P	—	5.00	10.00	20.00	40.00	—
1789 P	—	5.00	10.00	20.00	40.00	—
1790 P	—	5.00	10.00	20.00	40.00	—
1791 P	—	5.00	10.00	20.00	40.00	—
1792 P	—	5.00	10.00	20.00	40.00	—

C# 5 GRANO (12 Cavalli)
Copper **Ruler:** Carlo III **Obv:** Bust right **Rev:** HILA/RI/TAS, date below

Date	Mintage	VG	F	VF	XF	Unc
1756	—	6.00	12.00	25.00	50.00	—
1757	—	6.00	12.00	25.00	50.00	—

C# 39 GRANO (12 Cavalli)
Copper **Ruler:** Ferdinando IV 1st reign **Obv:** Bust right **Obv. Legend:** FERDINAN • IV • SICILIAR • REX • **Rev:** Inscription, value, date within thin wreath

Date	Mintage	VG	F	VF	XF	Unc
1788 CC	—	3.50	8.00	16.00	40.00	—
1789 CC	—	3.50	8.00	16.00	40.00	—
1790 CC	—	3.50	8.00	16.00	40.00	—
1791 CC	—	3.50	8.00	16.00	40.00	—
1791 AP	—	3.50	8.00	16.00	40.00	—
1792 CC	—	3.50	8.00	16.00	40.00	—
1792 AP	—	3.00	8.00	16.00	40.00	—
1793 CC	—	3.50	8.00	16.00	40.00	—
1797 AP	—	9.00	18.00	30.00	60.00	—
1798 AP	—	16.00	30.00	50.00	110	—

C# 7 3 TORNESI

Copper **Ruler:** Carlo III **Obv:** Bust right **Rev:** Inscription: PUBLICA/LAETI/TIA, date below

Date	Mintage	VG	F	VF	XF	Unc
1756	—	7.00	15.00	30.00	60.00	—
1757	—	7.00	15.00	30.00	60.00	—

C# 8 3 TORNESI

Copper **Ruler:** Ferdinando IV 1st reign **Obv:** Head right **Rev:** Inscription within wreath **Rev. Inscription:** PUBLI/CA/LETI/TIA

Date	Mintage	VG	F	VF	XF	Unc
1778 Rare	—	—	—	—	—	—
1779 Rare	—	—	—	—	—	—

C# 43 3 TORNESI

Copper **Ruler:** Ferdinando IV 1st reign **Obv:** Bust right **Obv. Legend:** FERDINAN IV SICIL ET HIER REX **Rev:** Crown above inscription, date within wreath

Date	Mintage	VG	F	VF	XF	Unc
1788 P	—	7.00	15.00	30.00	60.00	—
1789 P	—	7.00	15.00	30.00	60.00	—
1790 P	—	7.00	15.00	30.00	60.00	—
1791 P	—	7.00	15.00	30.00	60.00	—
1792 P	—	7.00	15.00	30.00	60.00	—
1793 P	—	7.00	15.00	30.00	60.00	—

C# 10 5 GRANI

Silver **Ruler:** Carlo III **Obv:** Bust right **Rev:** 5 in cartouche, date below

Date	Mintage	VG	F	VF	XF	Unc
1735	—	5.00	10.00	20.00	40.00	—

C# 13 5 GRANI

Silver **Ruler:** Carlo III **Obv:** Bust right **Obv. Legend:** CAR • D • G • ... **Rev:** Figure of Abundantia seated, date in exergue

Date	Mintage	VG	F	VF	XF	Unc
1755 IA MM	—	5.00	10.00	20.00	35.00	—
1756 IA MM	—	5.00	10.00	20.00	35.00	—
1757 IA MM	—	5.00	10.00	20.00	35.00	—
1758 IA MMR	—	5.00	10.00	20.00	35.00	—
1759 IA CCR	—	5.00	10.00	20.00	35.00	—

C# 45a 5 TORNESI

Copper, 30 mm. **Ruler:** Ferdinando IV 1st reign **Obv:** Shield within wreath **Rev:** Crown above divides R.C., T.5. and date below

Date	Mintage	VG	F	VF	XF	Unc
1755 IA MMR	—	5.00	10.00	22.00	50.00	—
1756 IA MMR	—	5.00	10.00	22.00	50.00	—
1798 P//R G	—	5.00	9.00	25.00	60.00	—

C# 45 5 TORNESI

Copper, 26-27 mm. **Ruler:** Ferdinando IV 1st reign **Obv:** Shield within wreath **Rev:** Crown above divides R.C., T.5. and date below **Note:** Size varies.

Date	Mintage	VG	F	VF	XF	Unc
1797 P//R G	—	5.00	9.00	20.00	45.00	—
1798 P//R G	—	8.50	14.00	25.00	60.00	—

C# 49 8 TORNESI

Copper **Ruler:** Ferdinando IV 1st reign **Obv:** Head right **Obv. Legend:** FERDIN • IV • D • G • SICIL • ET HIE • REX • **Rev:** Value, date

Date	Mintage	VG	F	VF	XF	Unc
1796 P//R G	—	6.50	12.50	25.00	55.00	—
1797 P//R G	—	6.50	12.50	25.00	55.00	—

C# 51 10 TORNESI

Copper **Ruler:** Ferdinando IV 1st reign **Obv:** Laureate head right **Obv. Legend:** FERDINAN • IV • SICILIAR • REX • **Rev:** Crown above value and date

Date	Mintage	VG	F	VF	XF	Unc
1798 P//R G	—	7.00	15.00	30.00	75.00	—

C# 15 CARLINO

Silver **Ruler:** Carlo III **Obv:** Bust right **Rev:** Cross at center with date below

Date	Mintage	VG	F	VF	XF	Unc
1755 DeG MMR	—	6.00	12.00	25.00	50.00	—

C# 53 CARLINO

2.2940 g., 0.8330 Silver 0.0614 oz. ASW **Ruler:** Ferdinando IV 1st reign **Obv:** Laureate head right **Obv. Legend:** FERDINAN • IV • SICIL • REX • **Rev:** Radiant cross, date below **Rev. Legend:** IN HOC SIGNO VINCES

Date	Mintage	VG	F	VF	XF	Unc
1788 P//C C	—	6.00	10.00	15.00	35.00	—
1791 P//A P	—	6.00	10.00	15.00	35.00	—
1792 P//A P	—	6.00	10.00	15.00	35.00	—
1794 P//A P	—	6.00	10.00	15.00	35.00	—
1795 P//A P	—	6.00	10.00	15.00	35.00	—
1798 P//A P	—	6.00	10.00	15.00	35.00	—

C# 55 20 GRANA

5.5440 g., 0.8330 Silver 0.1485 oz. ASW **Ruler:** Ferdinando IV 1st reign **Obv:** Head right **Rev:** Crowned arms, value below

Date	Mintage	VG	F	VF	XF	Unc
1788 P//C C	—	8.00	10.00	20.00	40.00	—
1789 P//C C	—	8.00	10.00	20.00	40.00	—
1790 P//C C	—	8.00	10.00	20.00	40.00	—

C# 57 20 GRANA

5.5440 g., 0.8330 Silver 0.1485 oz. ASW **Ruler:** Ferdinando IV 1st reign **Obv:** Head right **Obv. Legend:** FERDINAN • IV • SICILIAR • ... **Rev:** Crown within wreath, date in legend **Rev. Legend:** A • P • HISPANIAR • INFANS 1796

Date	Mintage	VG	F	VF	XF	Unc
1790 P//C C	—	8.00	10.00	20.00	40.00	—
1792 P//C C	—	8.00	10.00	20.00	40.00	—
1793 P//C C	—	8.00	10.00	20.00	40.00	—
1794 P//C C	—	8.00	10.00	20.00	40.00	—
1795 P//A P	—	8.00	10.00	20.00	40.00	—
1796 P//A P	—	8.00	10.00	20.00	40.00	—
1798 P//A P	—	8.00	10.00	20.00	40.00	—

C# 59 50 GRANA

11.3500 g., 0.8330 Silver 0.3040 oz. ASW **Ruler:** Ferdinando IV 1st reign **Obv:** Head right **Rev:** Crowned arms, value in exergue

Date	Mintage	VG	F	VF	XF	Unc
1784 BP	—	20.00	60.00	100	185	—
1785 BP	—	15.00	50.00	80.00	155	—

C# 19 60 GRANA

Silver **Ruler:** Carlo III **Obv:** Crowned shield **Obv. Legend:** CAR : D : G : REX ... **Rev:** Seated river god, volcano behind **Rev. Legend:** ...PRINCEPS •

Date	Mintage	VG	F	VF	XF	Unc
1734 FBA//DeG	—	15.00	30.00	60.00	120	—
1735 FBA//DeG	—	15.00	30.00	60.00	120	—
1736 FBA//DeG	—	15.00	30.00	60.00	120	—
1747 MM-A//DeG	—	15.00	30.00	60.00	120	—
1748 MMR D'G	—	15.00	30.00	60.00	120	—
1749 MM-R//D-G	—	15.00	30.00	60.00	120	—

C# 21 60 GRANA

Silver **Ruler:** Carlo III **Subject:** Birth of Prince Philip **Obv:** Accolated busts of Carlo and Maria Amalia right **Rev:** Woman seated holding child, monograms at sides, date in exergue

Date	Mintage	VG	F	VF	XF	Unc
1747	—	—	25.00	50.00	100	—

C# 22 60 GRANA

Silver **Ruler:** Carlo III **Obv:** Bust right **Obv. Legend:** CAR • D • G • UTR • SIC • ET NIER • REX • **Rev:** Crowned shield divides initials **Rev. Legend:** HISPANIAR • INFANS •

Date	Mintage	VG	F	VF	XF	Unc
1750 DeG MMR	—	20.00	40.00	80.00	175	—
1752 DeG MMR	—	20.00	40.00	80.00	175	—
1753 DeG MMR	—	20.00	40.00	80.00	175	—
1754 DeG MMR	—	20.00	40.00	80.00	175	—

C# 60 60 GRANA

12.7410 g., 0.9170 Silver 0.3756 oz. ASW **Ruler:** Ferdinando IV 1st reign **Obv:** Young, small bust right **Obv. Legend:** FERDINAND • IV • D • G • ... **Rev. Legend:** HISPANIAR • ...

Date	Mintage	VG	F	VF	XF	Unc
1760 IA//C C	—	50.00	100	250	600	—

C# 61 60 GRANA

13.7660 g., 0.8330 Silver 0.3687 oz. ASW **Ruler:** Ferdinando IV 1st reign **Obv:** Bust right **Obv. Legend:** FERDINAN • IV • D • G • ... **Rev:** Crowned shield with garland divides initials **Rev. Legend:** HISPANIAR ...

Date	Mintage	VG	F	VF	XF	Unc
1785 BP//C C	—	20.00	40.00	80.00	150	—
1786 BP//C C	—	20.00	40.00	80.00	150	—
1788 BP//C C	—	20.00	40.00	80.00	150	—

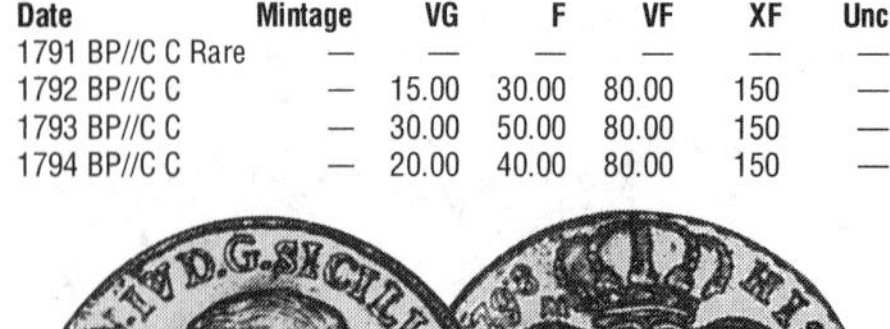

Date	Mintage	VG	F	VF	XF	Unc
1791 BP//C C Rare	—	—	—	—	—	—
1792 BP//C C	—	15.00	30.00	80.00	150	—
1793 BP//C C	—	30.00	50.00	80.00	150	—
1794 BP//C C	—	20.00	40.00	80.00	150	—

C# 61a 60 GRANA

13.7660 g., 0.8330 Silver 0.3687 oz. ASW **Ruler:** Ferdinando IV 1st reign **Obv:** Head right **Obv. Legend:** FERDINAN • IV • D • G • ... **Rev:** Crowned shield with garland divides initials **Rev. Legend:** HISPANIAR ...

Date	Mintage	VG	F	VF	XF	Unc
1796 BP//A P	—	15.00	30.00	80.00	150	—
1798 BP//A P	—	15.00	30.00	60.00	100	—

DAV# 1396 PIASTRA OF 120 GRANA

Silver **Ruler:** Charles VI **Obv:** Bust right **Rev:** Crowned arms, date, and value: L120 below

Date	Mintage	VG	F	VF	XF	Unc
1731	—	150	250	400	700	—
1733	—	150	250	400	700	—

C# 23 PIASTRA OF 120 GRANA

Silver **Obv:** Crowned shield divides initials **Obv. Legend:** CAR : D : G : REX • NEA • HISP : INFANS • & (c) **Rev:** Seated river god, volcano behind **Rev. Legend:** DE SOCIO PRINCEPS **Note:** Dav. #1397.

Date	Mintage	VG	F	VF	XF	Unc
1734 FBA DeG	—	20.00	40.00	60.00	135	—
1735 FBA GH	—	20.00	40.00	60.00	135	—
1736 FBA DeG	—	20.00	40.00	60.00	135	—
1747 MMA DeG	—	20.00	40.00	60.00	135	—

C# 24 PIASTRA OF 120 GRANA

Silver **Ruler:** Carlo III **Subject:** Birth of Prince Philip **Obv:** Conjoined busts right **Obv. Legend:** CAR • UTR • SIC • REX • - & MAR • AMAL • REG • **Rev:** Seated female with child **Rev. Legend:** FIRMATA SECURITAS **Note:** Dav. #1398.

Date	Mintage	VG	F	VF	XF	Unc
1747 MMR	—	50.00	75.00	150	300	—

C# 23a PIASTRA OF 120 GRANA

Silver **Ruler:** Carlo III **Obv:** Crowned shield with MV and MM monograms at sides **Obv. Legend:** CAR : D : G : REX NEA • HISP : INFANS & co. **Rev:** Seated river god, volcano behind, date below **Rev. Legend:** DE SOCIO PRINCEPS **Note:** Dav. #1399.

Date	Mintage	VG	F	VF	XF	Unc
1748 MMR D'G	—	20.00	40.00	60.00	135	—
1749 MMR D'G	—	20.00	40.00	60.00	135	—

C# 25 PIASTRA OF 120 GRANA

Silver **Ruler:** Carlo III **Obv:** Bust right **Obv. Legend:** CAR • D • G • UTR • SIC • ET HIER • REX **Rev:** Crowned shield divides monograms **Rev. Legend:** HISPANIAR • INFANS • **Note:** Dav. #1400.

Date	Mintage	VG	F	VF	XF	Unc
1750 DeG//MM-R	—	25.00	50.00	100	150	—
1752 DeG//MM-R	—	25.00	50.00	100	150	—
1753 DeG//MM-R	—	25.00	50.00	100	150	—
1754/3 DeG//MM-R	—	25.00	50.00	100	150	—
1754 DeG//MM-R	—	25.00	50.00	100	150	—

C# 64a PIASTRA OF 120 GRANA

25.4830 g., 0.9170 Silver 0.7513 oz. ASW **Ruler:** Ferdinando IV 1st reign **Obv:** Smaller youthful bust right **Note:** Dav. #1402.

Date	Mintage	VG	F	VF	XF	Unc
1767 FA-CC	—	50.00	100	200	375	—

C# 65 PIASTRA OF 120 GRANA

25.4830 g., 0.9170 Silver 0.7513 oz. ASW **Ruler:** Ferdinando IV 1st reign **Subject:** Birth of Princess Maria Theresa **Obv:** Conjoined busts right **Obv. Legend:** FERDINANDDVS REX MARIA CAROLINA REGINA **Rev:** Seated female with child **Rev. Legend:** FECUNDITAS / M • THERESIA • NATA / (BELOW) NON • IVNI • B • P • (AT LEFT) R • (AT RIGHT) **Note:** Dav. #1403.

Date	Mintage	VG	F	VF	XF	Unc
1772 CC-BP	—	50.00	100	200	400	—

C# 66 PIASTRA OF 120 GRANA

27.2650 g., 0.8330 Silver 0.7302 oz. ASW **Ruler:** Ferdinando IV 1st reign **Obv:** Head right **Rev:** Crowned plain arms over value **Note:** Dav. #1405.

Date	Mintage	VG	F	VF	XF	Unc
1784 P//C-C	—	50.00	75.00	125	250	—
1785 BP//C-C	—	50.00	75.00	125	250	—

C# 67 PIASTRA OF 120 GRANA

27.5320 g., 0.8330 Silver 0.7373 oz. ASW **Ruler:** Ferdinando IV 1st reign **Obv:** Conjoined busts right **Obv. Legend:** FERDINANDVS IV • ET MARIA CAROLINA **Rev:** Standing and kneeling figure, volcano behind **Rev. Legend:** PRO FAVSIO PP • REDITV V • S • - A • P • / M (AT RIGHT) 1791 (BELOW) **Note:** Dav. #1407.

Date	Mintage	VG	F	VF	XF	Unc
1791 AP	—	50.00	100	150	250	—
1791 DP-AP, M	—	50.00	100	150	250	—

DAV# 1395 DUCATO

Silver **Ruler:** Charles VI **Obv:** Bust right **Obv. Legend:** • CAR • VI • D • G • ... **Rev:** Crowned arms, date divided below **Rev. Legend:** SICI • REX • HISP • VTRI •

Date	Mintage	VG	F	VF	XF	Unc
1715	—	125	200	350	550	—

C# 63 DUCATO (100 Grani)

22.5000 g., 0.8330 Silver 0.6026 oz. ASW **Ruler:** Ferdinando IV 1st reign **Obv:** Head right **Rev:** Crowned arms in sprays, value below **Note:** Dav. #1404.

Date	Mintage	VG	F	VF	XF	Unc
1784 CC	—	30.00	50.00	100	200	—
1785 CC	—	30.00	50.00	75.00	125	—

C# 26 2 DUCATI

7.0000 g., 0.9860 Gold 0.2219 oz. AGW **Ruler:** Carlo III **Obv:** Bust right **Obv. Legend:** CAR • D • G • ... **Rev:** Crowned shield **Rev. Legend:** HISPANIAR • INFANS •

Date	Mintage	VG	F	VF	XF	Unc
1749 DG//MM-R	—	125	150	325	600	—
1750 DG//MM-R	—	125	150	325	600	—
1751 DG//MM-R	—	125	150	325	600	—
1752 DG//MM-R	—	125	150	325	600	—
1753 DG//MM-R	—	125	150	325	600	—
1754 DG//MM-R	—	125	150	325	600	—
1755 DG//MM-R	—	125	150	325	600	—

C# 69 2 DUCATI

2.9320 g., 0.9060 Gold 0.0854 oz. AGW **Ruler:** Ferdinando IV 1st reign **Obv:** Young bust right **Obv. Legend:** FERDINAND • IV • D • G • ... **Rev:** Crowned shield above value **Rev. Legend:** HISPANIAR • INFANS • **Note:** Fr. #848.

Date	Mintage	VG	F	VF	XF	Unc
1762 CC R IA	—	150	200	325	475	—

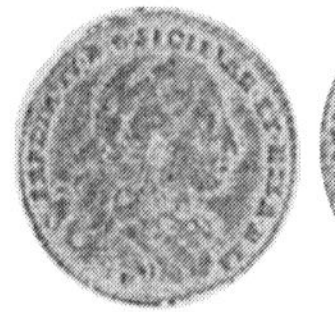
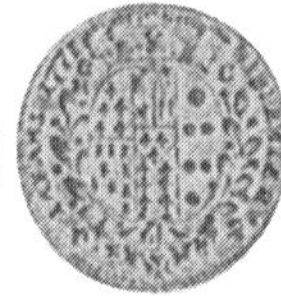

C# 71 2 DUCATI

2.9320 g., 0.9060 Gold 0.0854 oz. AGW **Ruler:** Ferdinando IV 1st reign **Obv:** Older bust right **Obv. Legend:** FERDINAN • IV • D • G • ... **Rev:** Crowned arms in sprays over value **Rev. Legend:** HISPANIAR INFANS

Date	Mintage	VG	F	VF	XF	Unc
1771 CC R P	—	125	150	175	300	—

C# 27 4 DUCATI

5.8650 g., 0.9060 Gold 0.1708 oz. AGW **Ruler:** Carlo III **Obv:** Head right **Rev:** Crowned arms, date in legend, value below

Date	Mintage	VG	F	VF	XF	Unc
1744 MM R DG	—	100	175	300	550	—
1749 MM R DG	—	100	175	300	550	—
1750 MM R DG	—	100	175	300	550	—
1751 MM R DG	—	100	175	300	550	—
1752 MM R DG	—	100	175	300	550	—
1753 MM R DG	—	100	175	300	550	—
1754 MM R DG	—	100	175	300	550	—
1755 MM R DG	—	100	175	300	550	—

C# 73 4 DUCATI

5.8650 g., 0.9060 Gold 0.1708 oz. AGW **Ruler:** Ferdinando IV 1st reign **Obv:** Bust right **Obv. Legend:** FERDINAND • IV • D • G • ... **Rev:** Crowned arms above value **Rev. Legend:** HISPANIAR • INFANS • 1768 •

Date	Mintage	VG	F	VF	XF	Unc
1760 CC R	—	100	175	300	450	—
1761 IA//CC R	—	100	175	300	450	—
1762 IA//CC R	—	100	175	300	450	—
1763 IA//CC R	—	100	175	300	450	—
1764 IA//CC R	—	100	175	300	450	—
1764 DG//CC R	—	100	175	300	450	—
1764 G//CC R	—	100	175	300	450	—
1764 CC R	—	100	175	300	450	—
1765 DG//CC R	—	100	175	300	450	—
1767 DG//CC R	—	100	175	300	450	—
1768 DG//CC R	—	100	175	300	450	—

C# 74 4 DUCATI

5.8650 g., 0.9060 Gold 0.1708 oz. AGW **Ruler:** Ferdinando IV 1st reign **Obv:** Older bust right **Obv. Legend:** FERDINAN • IV • D • G • SICIL • ... **Rev:** Crowned oval ornate shield **Rev. Legend:** HISPANIAR INFANS (N's are backwards)

Date	Mintage	VG	F	VF	XF	Unc
1769 P//C-C R	—	100	175	300	450	—
1770 P//C-C R	—	100	175	300	450	—
1772 P//C-C R	—	100	175	300	450	—
1774 P//C-C R	—	100	175	300	450	—
1776 P//C-C C B	—	100	175	300	450	—

C# 28 6 DUCATI

8.7980 g., 0.9060 Gold 0.2563 oz. AGW **Ruler:** Carlo III **Obv:** Bust right **Obv. Legend:** CAR • D • G • VTR • SIC • ... **Rev:** Crowned shield divides initials **Rev. Legend:** HISPANIAR INFANS

Date	Mintage	VG	F	VF	XF	Unc
1749 DG//MM R	—	125	200	375	650	—
1750 DG//MM R	—	125	200	375	650	—
1751 DG//MM R	—	125	200	375	650	—
1752 DG//MM R	—	125	200	375	650	—
1753 DG//MM R	—	125	200	375	650	—
1754 DG//MM R	—	125	200	375	650	—
1755 DG//MM R	—	125	200	375	650	—

C# 28a 6 DUCATI

8.7980 g., 0.9060 Gold 0.2563 oz. AGW **Ruler:** Carlo III **Obv:** Bust right **Obv. Legend:** CAR.D.G. SIC... **Rev:** Crowned shield divides initials

Date	Mintage	VG	F	VF	XF	Unc
1752	—	—	—	—	—	—

Note: Reported, not confirmed

C# 76a 6 DUCATI

8.7980 g., 0.9060 Gold 0.2563 oz. AGW **Ruler:** Ferdinando IV 1st reign **Obv:** Old bust right **Obv. Legend:** FERDINAN.IV... **Rev:** Crowned, oval shield within sprays **Rev. Legend:** INFANS...

Date	Mintage	VG	F	VF	XF	Unc
1783 BP-CC C BP	—	500	1,000	2,000	3,000	—
1784 BP-CC C BP	—	500	1,000	2,000	3,000	—
1785 BP-CC C BP	—	500	1,000	2,000	3,000	—

NEAPOLITAN REPUBLIC

Parthenopean Republic

STANDARD COINAGE

C# 81 QVATTRO (4) TORNESI

Copper **Obv:** Fasces, liberty cap above **Obv. Legend:** REPUBLICA NAPOLITANA **Rev:** Value within wreath **Note:** Two varieties exist.

Date	Mintage	VG	F	VF	XF	Unc
Anno 7 (1799)	—	5.00	15.00	30.00	75.00	—

C# 82.1 SEI (6) TORNESI

Copper **Obv:** Fasces **Rev:** TORNESI

Date	Mintage	VG	F	VF	XF	Unc
Anno 7 (1799)	—	5.00	15.00	35.00	85.00	—

C# 82.2 SEI (6) TORNESI

Copper **Obv:** Fasces **Rev:** TORNESI Z. N.

Date	Mintage	VG	F	VF	XF	Unc
Anno 7 (1799)	—	5.00	15.00	35.00	85.00	—

C# 83 SEI (6) CARLINI

13.7500 g., 0.8330 Silver 0.3682 oz. ASW **Obv:** Liberty standing **Rev:** Value

Date	Mintage	VG	F	VF	XF	Unc
Anno 7 (1799)	—	30.00	50.00	125	200	—

C# 84.1 DODICI (12) CARLINI

27.5300 g., 0.8330 Silver 0.7373 oz. ASW **Obv:** Liberty standing **Obv. Legend:** ...NAPOLITAN **Rev:** Value **Note:** Dav. #1410A.

Date	Mintage	VG	F	VF	XF	Unc
Anno 7 (1799)	—	50.00	100	175	350	—

C# 84.2 DODICI (12) CARLINI

27.5300 g., 0.8330 Silver 0.7373 oz. ASW **Obv:** Standing female holding pole with liberty cap **Obv. Legend:** REPUBLICA NAPOLITANA **Rev:** "CAR LINI DODI CI" within wreath **Rev. Legend:** ANNO SETTIMO DELLA LIBERTA **Note:** Dav. #1410.

Date	Mintage	VG	F	VF	XF	Unc
Anno 7 (1799)	—	60.00	125	200	450	—

KINGDOM OF NAPLES

Bourbon Rule

STANDARD COINAGE

C# 94.5 VN (1) GRANO

Copper **Obv:** Head of Ferdinand IV right **Rev:** Value within wreath

Date	Mintage	VG	F	VF	XF	Unc
1800 Rare	—	—	—	—	—	—

C# 95 4 TORNESI

Copper **Obv:** Head of Ferdinand IV right **Rev:** Value

Date	Mintage	VG	F	VF	XF	Unc
1799 RC	—	6.50	12.50	27.50	60.00	—
1800 AP	—	6.50	12.50	27.50	60.00	—

C# 96 6 TORNESI

Copper **Ruler:** Ferdinando IV 2nd reign **Obv:** Head right **Obv. Legend:** FERDINAN • IV • SICIL • ET HIE • REX **Rev:** Value above date

Date	Mintage	VG	F	VF	XF	Unc
1799 R C	—	6.00	12.00	28.00	60.00	—
1799 A P	—	6.00	12.00	28.00	60.00	—
1800 R C	—	6.00	12.00	28.00	60.00	—
1800 A P	—	6.00	12.00	28.00	60.00	—

C# 98 120 GRANA

27.5000 g., 0.8330 Silver 0.7365 oz. ASW **Ruler:** Ferdinando IV 2nd reign **Obv:** Head right **Obv. Legend:** FERDINAN IV D • G • SICILIAR ET HIE REX **Rev:** Crowned shield **Rev. Legend:** HISPANIAR INFANS **Note:** Dav. #1409.

Date	Mintage	VG	F	VF	XF	Unc
1799 P-AP	—	25.00	45.00	100	225	—
1800 P-AP	—	25.00	45.00	100	225	—

ORBETELLO

Reali Presidii

A small commune in southwestern Tuscany, which was a possession of the kingdom of Naples and Sicily until 1808.

RULER
Ferdinand IV, 1759-1808

MONETARY SYSTEM
60 Quattrini = 1 Lira

COMMUNE

STANDARD COINAGE

C# 1 QUATTRINO

Billon **Ruler:** Ferdinand IV **Obv:** Bust right **Obv. Legend:** FERDIN • IV • ... **Rev:** Crown above divides initials above inscription, date

Date	Mintage	Good	VG	F	VF	XF
1782	—	—	7.00	12.50	25.00	55.00
1791	—	—	7.00	12.50	25.00	55.00
1798	—	—	7.00	12.50	25.00	55.00

C# 2 2 QUATTRINI

Billon **Ruler:** Ferdinand IV **Obv:** Bust right **Rev:** Value

Date	Mintage	Good	VG	F	VF	XF
1782	—	—	7.00	12.50	25.00	55.00
1791	—	—	7.00	12.50	25.00	55.00
1798	—	—	7.00	12.50	25.00	55.00

C# 3 4 QUATTRINI

Billon **Ruler:** Ferdinand IV **Obv:** Bust right **Obv. Legend:** FERDINANDVS • IV • D • G • SICILIAR • REX • **Rev:** Crown divides initials above inscription, divided date within wreath

Date	Mintage	Good	VG	F	VF	XF
1782	—	—	9.00	17.50	37.50	75.00
1791	—	—	9.00	17.50	37.50	75.00
1798	—	—	9.00	17.50	37.50	75.00

OREZZO

A French adventurer seized this Genovese territory and proclaimed himself king for a reign of eight months.

RULER
Teodoro I, 1736

KINGDOM

STANDARD COINAGE

KM# 5 2-1/2 SOLDI

Copper **Ruler:** Teodoro I **Obv:** Crowned T + R within sprigs, date below **Rev:** SDI/DVE/M within beaded circle **Rev. Legend:** PBCO *RO *CE *PRO *BO * **Note:** Weight varies: 2.02-2.58 grams.

Date	Mintage	Good	VG	F	VF	XF
1736 Rare	—	—	—	—	—	—

KM# 6 5 SOLDI

Copper **Ruler:** Teodoro I **Obv:** Crowned T.R within sprigs, divided date below **Rev:** SOLDI/CINQE within beaded circle **Rev. Legend:** RO • CE • PRO BONO PVBLICO • **Note:** Weight varies: 3.17-3.94 grams.

Date	Mintage	Good	VG	F	VF	XF
1736 Rare	—	—	—	—	—	—

KM# 7 1/2 SCUDO

Silver **Ruler:** Teodoro I **Obv:** Crown above 3 links, head right within beaded circle **Rev:** Madonna separates date within beaded circle **Note:** Weight varies: 10.41-14.20 grams.

Date	Mintage	Good	VG	F	VF	XF
1736	—	—	4,000	6,000	—	—

PAPAL STATES

During many centuries prior to the formation of the unified Kingdom of Italy, when Italy was divided into numerous independent papal and ducal states, the Popes held temporal sovereignty over an area in central Italy comprising some 17,000 sq. mi. (44,030 sq. km.) including the city of Rome. At the time of the general unification of Italy under the Kingdom of Sardinia, 1861, the papal dominions beyond Rome were acquired by that kingdom diminishing the Pope's sovereignty to Rome and its environs. In 1870, while France's opposition to papal dispossession was neutralized by its war with Prussia, the Italian army seized weakly defended Rome and made it the capital of Italy, thereby abrogating the last vestige of papal temporal power. In 1871, the Italian Parliament enacted the Law of Guarantees, which guaranteed a special status for the Vatican area, and spiritual freedom and a generous income for the Pope. Pope Pius IX and his successors adamantly refused to acknowledge the validity of these laws and voluntarily "imprisoned" themselves in the Vatican. The impasse between State and Church lasted until the signing of the Lateran Treaty, Feb. 11, 1929, by which Italy recognized the sovereignty and independence of the new Vatican City state.

PONTIFFS
lClement XI, 1700-1721
Sede Vacante, 1721
Innocent XIII, 1721-1724
Sede Vacante, 1724
Benedict XIII, 1724-1730
Sede Vacante, 1730
Clement XII, 1730-1740
Sede Vacante, 1740
Benedict XIV, 1740-1758
Sede Vacante, 1758
Clement XIII, 1758-1769
Sede Vacante, Feb. 2-May 19, 1769
Clement XIV, 1769-1774
Sede Vacante, Sept. 22, 1774-Feb. 15, 1775
Pius VI (Sextus), 1775-1799
Pius VII, 1800-1823

MINT MARKS
B - Bologna
R – Rome

NOTE: For similar coins dated 1775-1797 with and without "B" mint mark, see Papal City States, Bologna.

MONETARY SYSTEM

(Until 1860)

5 Quattrini = 1 Baiocco
5 Baiocchi = 1 Grosso
6 Grossi = 4 Carlini = 3 Giulio =
3 Paoli = 1 Testone.
14 Carlini = 1 Piastre
100 Baiocchi = 1 Scudo
10 Testone = Doppia

PAPACY

STANDARD COINAGE

KM# 884 QUATTRINO

Copper **Ruler:** Clement XII **Obv:** Papal arms **Rev:** Value within wreath

Date	Mintage	Good	VG	F	VF	XF
1738-IX	—	5.00	10.00	17.50	25.00	45.00
1740-I	—	5.00	10.00	20.00	30.00	50.00
1742-I	—	5.00	10.00	20.00	30.00	50.00
1742-II	—	5.00	10.00	20.00	30.00	50.00

KM# 883 QUATTRINO

Copper **Ruler:** Clement XII **Obv:** Papal arms **Rev:** Value, date **Rev. Legend:** QVAT / TRINO / ROM

Date	Mintage	Good	VG	F	VF	XF
1738-VIII (1738)	—	5.00	10.00	17.50	25.00	45.00
1738-IX (1738)	—	5.00	10.00	17.50	25.00	45.00

KM# 1171 QUATTRINO

Copper **Ruler:** Benedict XIV **Obv:** Papal arms **Obv. Inscription:** BENED • XIV • PON • M • A • XI **Rev:** Holy Door **Rev. Legend:** QVATRINO ROMANO **Note:** Holy year issue.

Date	Mintage	Good	VG	F	VF	XF
1750-IX	—	6.00	15.00	25.00	38.00	50.00

KM# 1174 QUATTRINO

Copper **Ruler:** Benedict XIV **Obv:** Papal arms **Obv. Legend:** BENED • XIV • ... **Rev:** Value **Rev. Legend:** QVATRINO / ROMANO

Date	Mintage	Good	VG	F	VF	XF
1751-XII	—	4.00	8.00	20.00	30.00	40.00
1751-XIV	—	4.00	8.00	20.00	30.00	40.00
1752-XII	—	4.00	8.00	20.00	30.00	40.00

KM# 1176 QUATTRINO

Copper **Ruler:** Benedict XIV **Obv:** Papal arms **Obv. Legend:** BENED • XIV • ... **Rev:** Value, date within rope wreath **Rev. Legend:** QVATRI / NO / ROMANO

Date	Mintage	Good	VG	F	VF	XF
1752-XII	—	5.00	10.00	22.00	35.00	55.00
1754-XV	—	5.00	10.00	22.00	35.00	55.00
1755-XVI	—	5.00	10.00	22.00	35.00	55.00

KM# 1177.1 QUATTRINO

Copper **Ruler:** Benedict XIV **Obv:** Papal arms **Obv. Legend:** BENED • XIV • ... **Rev:** Qvatrino / Romano, date with star above and below within cartouche

Date	Mintage	Good	VG	F	VF	XF
1752-XII	—	5.00	10.00	20.00	30.00	50.00

KM# 1177.2 QUATTRINO

Copper **Ruler:** Benedict XIV **Obv:** Papal arms **Rev:** Qvatrino / Romano, date with star above and below, within cartouche

Date	Mintage	Good	VG	F	VF	XF
1752	—	5.00	10.00	22.00	38.00	55.00

KM# 1182.1 QUATTRINO

Copper **Ruler:** Clement XIII **Obv:** Papal arms **Obv. Legend:** CLEM • XIII **Rev:** Qvatri / No / Romano, date within chain wreath

Date	Mintage	Good	VG	F	VF	XF
1758-I	—	5.00	10.00	22.00	38.00	55.00

KM# 1182.2 QUATTRINO

Copper **Ruler:** Clement XIII **Obv:** Papal arms **Obv. Legend:** CLEM • XIII • ... **Rev:** QVATRI / NO / ROMANO within rope wreath

Date	Mintage	Good	VG	F	VF	XF
ND-I (1759)	—	5.00	10.00	22.00	38.00	55.00

KM# 1223 QUATTRINO

Copper **Ruler:** Pius VI **Obv:** Papal, oval arms **Obv. Legend:** PIV... **Rev:** Value within wreath **Rev. Legend:** QVATRI NO ROMANO

Date	Mintage	Good	VG	F	VF	XF
1783-IX	—	4.00	7.50	12.50	20.00	35.00
1784-IX	—	4.00	7.50	12.50	20.00	35.00
1784-X	—	4.00	7.50	12.50	20.00	35.00
1785-X	—	4.00	7.50	12.50	20.00	35.00
1785-XI	—	4.00	7.50	12.50	20.00	35.00
1786-XII	—	4.00	7.50	12.50	20.00	35.00
1787-XII	—	4.00	7.50	12.50	20.00	35.00

KM# 1242 QUATTRINO

Copper **Ruler:** Pius VI **Obv:** Papal, oval arms **Rev:** Value

Date	Mintage	Good	VG	F	VF	XF
1797-XXIII	—	5.00	10.00	20.00	30.00	50.00
1798-XXIII	—	5.00	10.00	20.00	30.00	50.00

KM# 886 MEZZO (1/2) BAIOCCO

Copper **Ruler:** Clement XII **Rev:** Value in laurel or fleur wreath

Date	Mintage	Good	VG	F	VF	XF
1738-IX	—	3.00	7.00	15.00	30.00	50.00

KM# 900.1 MEZZO (1/2) BAIOCCO

Copper **Ruler:** Clement XII **Rev:** Value in plain field

Date	Mintage	Good	VG	F	VF	XF
1738-VIII	—	3.00	7.00	15.00	30.00	50.00
1738-IX	—	3.00	7.00	15.00	30.00	50.00

KM# 900.2 MEZZO (1/2) BAIOCCO

Copper **Ruler:** Clement XII **Rev:** Value in palm wreath

Date	Mintage	Good	VG	F	VF	XF
1738-IX	—	3.00	7.00	15.00	30.00	50.00

KM# 885 MEZZO (1/2) BAIOCCO

Copper **Ruler:** Clement XIII **Rev:** Value in cartouche **Rev. Legend:** MEZZO / BAIOCCO / ROM

Date	Mintage	Good	VG	F	VF	XF
1738-VIII	—	5.00	10.00	20.00	32.00	50.00
1739-IX	—	5.00	10.00	20.00	32.00	50.00

KM# 1153 MEZZO (1/2) BAIOCCO

Copper **Ruler:** Benedict XIV **Obv:** Papal arms **Obv. Legend:** BENED • XIV • ... **Rev:** MEZZO / BAIOCCO / ROM •, date within wreath **Note:** Varieties exist.

Date	Mintage	Good	VG	F	VF	XF
1740-I	—	6.00	10.00	16.00	35.00	55.00
1741-I	—	6.00	10.00	16.00	35.00	55.00
1742-I	—	6.00	10.00	16.00	35.00	55.00
1742-II	—	6.00	10.00	16.00	35.00	55.00
1751-XII	—	6.00	10.00	16.00	35.00	55.00
1755-XV	—	6.00	10.00	16.00	35.00	55.00

KM# 1157 MEZZO (1/2) BAIOCCO

Copper **Ruler:** Benedict XIV **Obv:** Papal arms **Obv. Legend:** BEN • XIV • P • M • A • I • **Rev:** MEZZO / BAIOCCO / ROM, date within wreath

Date	Mintage	Good	VG	F	VF	XF
1741-I	—	6.00	10.00	16.00	35.00	55.00

KM# 1158 MEZZO (1/2) BAIOCCO

Copper **Ruler:** Benedict XIV **Obv:** Papal arms **Obv. Legend:** BENEDICT • XIV • ... **Rev:** MEZZO / BAIOCCO / ROM, date within cartouche

Date	Mintage	Good	VG	F	VF	XF
1742-II	—	6.00	10.00	16.00	35.00	55.00

KM# 1172 MEZZO (1/2) BAIOCCO

Copper **Ruler:** Benedict XIV **Obv:** Papal arms **Rev:** Holy door **Note:** Holy year issue.

Date	Mintage	Good	VG	F	VF	XF
1750-X	—	7.50	12.50	25.00	40.00	60.00
1750-XI	—	7.50	12.50	25.00	40.00	60.00
1750-XII	—	7.50	12.50	25.00	40.00	60.00

KM# 1173 MEZZO (1/2) BAIOCCO

Copper **Ruler:** Benedict XIV **Obv:** Papal arms **Rev:** Holy door open with rays **Note:** Holy year issue.

Date	Mintage	Good	VG	F	VF	XF
1750-X	—	7.50	12.50	25.00	40.00	60.00

KM# 1181 MEZZO (1/2) BAIOCCO

Copper **Ruler:** Benedict XIV **Obv:** Papal arms **Obv. Legend:** BENED • XIV • ... **Rev:** MEZZO / BAIOCCO / ROM, date within wreath

Date	Mintage	Good	VG	F	VF	XF
1755-XV	—	7.50	18.50	25.00	38.00	60.00

KM# 1183.1 MEZZO (1/2) BAIOCCO

Copper **Ruler:** Clement XIII **Obv:** Papal arms **Obv. Legend:** CLEM • XIII • ... **Rev:** MEZZO / BAIOCCO / ROM within wreath

Date	Mintage	Good	VG	F	VF	XF
ND(1758)-I	—	5.00	10.00	20.00	35.00	55.00

KM# 1183.2 MEZZO (1/2) BAIOCCO

Copper **Ruler:** Clement XIII **Obv:** Papal arms **Obv. Legend:** CLEM • XIII • ... **Rev:** MEZZO / BAIOCCO / ROM, date within wreath

Date	Mintage	Good	VG	F	VF	XF
1758-I	—	5.00	10.00	20.00	35.00	55.00

KM# 1188 MEZZO (1/2) BAIOCCO

Copper **Ruler:** Clement XIII **Obv:** Papal arms **Obv. Legend:** CLEM • XIII • ... **Rev:** MEZZO / BAIOCCO / ROM, date within wreath

Date	Mintage	Good	VG	F	VF	XF
1759-I	—	5.00	10.00	20.00	35.00	55.00
.1759.-I	—	5.00	10.00	20.00	35.00	55.00

KM# 1224 MEZZO (1/2) BAIOCCO

Copper **Ruler:** Pius VI **Obv:** Papal, oval arms **Obv. Legend:** PIVS... **Rev:** MEZZO / BAIOCCO / ROMANO within wreath

Date	Mintage	Good	VG	F	VF	XF
1783-IX	—	3.00	7.00	15.00	30.00	50.00
1784-X	—	3.00	7.00	15.00	30.00	50.00

KM# 1227 MEZZO (1/2) BAIOCCO

Copper **Ruler:** Pius VI **Obv:** Papal arms within circle **Rev:** MEZZO / BAIOCCO / ROMANO within wreath, with stars above, within circle

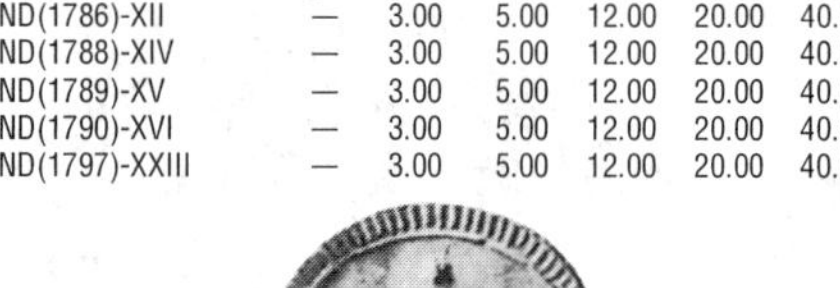

Date	Mintage	Good	VG	F	VF	XF
ND(1786)-XII	—	3.00	5.00	12.00	20.00	40.00
ND(1788)-XIV	—	3.00	5.00	12.00	20.00	40.00
ND(1789)-XV	—	3.00	5.00	12.00	20.00	40.00
ND(1790)-XVI	—	3.00	5.00	12.00	20.00	40.00
ND(1797)-XXIII	—	3.00	5.00	12.00	20.00	40.00

KM# 1243 MEZZO (1/2) BAIOCCO

Copper **Ruler:** Pius VI **Obv:** Papal arms **Rev:** Date and star within circle **Rev. Inscription:** MEZZO / BAIOCCO / ROMANO

Date	Mintage	Good	VG	F	VF	XF
1797-XXIII	—	5.00	10.00	20.00	35.00	55.00

KM# 920 BAIOCCO

Copper **Ruler:** Clement XII **Obv:** Papal arms **Rev:** Value in cartouche **Rev. Legend:** VN BAIOCCO ROM

Date	Mintage	Good	VG	F	VF	XF
1740-X	—	5.00	12.00	25.00	40.00	70.00

KM# 1154 BAIOCCO

Copper **Ruler:** Benedict XIV **Obv:** Papal arms **Obv. Legend:** BENED • XIV • ... **Rev:** VN BAIOCCO ROM, date within cartouche **Note:** Varieties exist.

Date	Mintage	Good	VG	F	VF	XF
1740-I	—	5.00	12.00	25.00	40.00	70.00
1741-I	—	5.00	12.00	25.00	40.00	70.00
1742-II	—	5.00	12.00	25.00	40.00	70.00
1742-III	—	5.00	12.00	25.00	40.00	70.00
1743	—	5.00	12.00	25.00	40.00	70.00
ND	—	5.00	12.00	25.00	40.00	70.00

KM# 1155.3 BAIOCCO

Copper **Ruler:** Benedict XIV **Obv:** Papal arms **Obv. Legend:** BEND • XIV • PONT • MAX • **Rev:** VN BAIOCCO ROM within wreath

Date	Mintage	Good	VG	F	VF	XF
ND	—	6.00	17.00	25.00	40.00	70.00

KM# 1156 BAIOCCO

Copper **Ruler:** Benedict XIV **Obv:** Papal arms **Obv. Legend:** BENEDIC • XIV • P • M • **Rev:** VN BAIOCCO ROM within wreath

Date	Mintage	Good	VG	F	VF	XF
ND	—	6.00	15.00	25.00	40.00	70.00

KM# 1155.1 BAIOCCO

Copper **Ruler:** Benedict XIV **Obv:** Papal arms **Obv. Legend:** BENED • XIV • ... **Rev:** VN BAIOCCO ROM within wreath

Date	Mintage	Good	VG	F	VF	XF
ND (1744)	—	6.00	15.00	25.00	40.00	70.00

KM# 1155.2 BAIOCCO

Copper **Ruler:** Benedict XIV **Obv:** Papal arms **Obv. Legend:** BENED • XIV PONTMAX **Rev:** VN BAIOCCO ROM within wreath

Date	Mintage	Good	VG	F	VF	XF
ND (1744)	—	6.00	15.00	25.00	40.00	70.00

KM# 1175 BAIOCCO

Copper **Ruler:** Benedict XIV **Obv:** Papal arms **Obv. Legend:** BENED • XIV PON • M • A • XVI **Rev:** VN BAIOCCO ROMANO, date within wreath **Note:** Varieties exist.

Date	Mintage	Good	VG	F	VF	XF
1751-XII	—	6.00	15.00	25.00	40.00	70.00
1752-XII	—	6.00	15.00	25.00	40.00	70.00
1756-XVI	—	6.00	15.00	25.00	40.00	70.00

KM# 1178 BAIOCCO

Copper **Ruler:** Benedict XIV **Obv:** Papal arms **Obv. Legend:** BENED • XIV PON • M • A • XII • **Rev:** VN BAIOCCO ROMANO, date in cartouche

Date	Mintage	Good	VG	F	VF	XF
1752-XII	—	6.00	15.00	25.00	40.00	70.00

KM# 1184 BAIOCCO

Copper **Ruler:** Clement XIII **Obv:** Papal arms **Obv. Legend:** CLEM • XIII **Rev:** VN BAIOCCO ROMANO within circle

Date	Mintage	Good	VG	F	VF	XF
1758-I	—	6.00	15.00	25.00	50.00	70.00
1759-I	—	6.00	15.00	25.00	50.00	70.00

KM# 1185 BAIOCCO

Billon **Ruler:** Clement XIII **Obv:** Seated figure below radiant sun **Rev:** Value

Date	Mintage	Good	VG	F	VF	XF
ND(1758-69)	—	8.00	20.00	35.00	55.00	70.00

KM# 1191 BAIOCCO

Copper **Ruler:** Clement XIII **Obv:** Papal arms **Rev:** Value within wreath

Date	Mintage	Good	VG	F	VF	XF
ND(1760)-III	—	6.00	15.00	25.00	50.00	70.00

KM# 1221 BAIOCCO

Billon **Ruler:** Pius VI **Obv:** Crossed keys **Rev:** Value above star within circle

Date	Mintage	Good	VG	F	VF	XF
1780	—	6.00	15.00	25.00	45.00	70.00
1782	—	6.00	15.00	25.00	45.00	70.00
1783	—	6.00	15.00	25.00	45.00	70.00

KM# 1222 BAIOCCO

Copper **Ruler:** Pius VI **Obv:** Papal oval arms **Rev:** Value within wreath

Date	Mintage	Good	VG	F	VF	XF
ND(1782)-VIII	—	3.50	8.50	15.00	30.00	50.00
ND(1783)-IX	—	3.50	8.50	15.00	30.00	50.00
ND(1785)-XI	—	3.50	8.50	15.00	30.00	50.00
ND(1787)-XIII	—	3.50	8.50	15.00	30.00	50.00
ND(1789)-XV	—	3.50	8.50	15.00	30.00	50.00
ND(1790)-XVI	—	3.50	8.50	15.00	30.00	50.00
ND(1791)-XVII	—	3.50	8.50	15.00	30.00	50.00
ND(1793)-XIX	—	3.50	8.50	15.00	30.00	50.00
ND(1794)-XX	—	3.50	8.50	15.00	30.00	50.00

KM# 1228 BAIOCCO

Copper **Ruler:** Pius VI

Date	Mintage	Good	VG	F	VF	XF
1783	—	6.00	15.00	25.00	40.00	70.00

KM# 1225 BAIOCCO

Copper **Ruler:** Pius VI **Obv:** Papal arms within circle **Obv. Legend:** PIVS... **Rev:** Value within circle **Rev. Legend:** VN BAIOCCO ROMANO

Date	Mintage	Good	VG	F	VF	XF
ND(1797)-XXIII	—	5.00	12.00	20.00	30.00	60.00

KM# 1246 BAIOCCO

Copper **Ruler:** Pius VII **Obv:** Legend around Papal arms within circle **Obv. Legend:** PIUS VII... **Rev:** VN BAIOCCO ROMANO within wreath and circle

Date	Mintage	VG	F	VF	XF	Unc
MDCCC (1800)-IR	—	12.00	20.00	30.00	60.00	—
MDCCCI (1801)-IR	—	12.00	25.00	45.00	75.00	—

KM# 921 2 BAIOCCHI (Muraiola)

Billon **Ruler:** Clement XII **Obv:** Crossed keys **Rev:** Value **Rev. Legend:** DVE / BAIOC / CHI

Date	Mintage	Good	VG	F	VF	XF
1740-X	—	6.00	15.00	25.00	40.00	70.00

KM# 1159 2 BAIOCCHI (Muraiola)

Billon **Ruler:** Benedict XIV **Obv:** Crossed keys above date **Obv. Legend:** BE NED XIV **Rev:** Written value

Date	Mintage	Good	VG	F	VF	XF
1746	—	6.00	15.00	30.00	45.00	75.00
1747	—	6.00	15.00	30.00	45.00	75.00
1748	—	6.00	15.00	30.00	45.00	75.00
1749	—	6.00	15.00	30.00	45.00	75.00

KM# 1160 2 BAIOCCHI (Muraiola)

Billon **Ruler:** Clement XIII **Obv:** Seated figure below radiant sun **Rev:** Written value

Date	Mintage	Good	VG	F	VF	XF
ND(1758-69)	—	10.00	22.00	40.00	60.00	85.00

KM# 1205 2 BAIOCCHI (Muraiola)

Billon **Ruler:** Clement XIV **Obv:** Crossed keys above date **Obv. Legend:** CLE MENS XIV **Rev:** Written value

Date	Mintage	Good	VG	F	VF	XF
1771	—	10.00	28.00	45.00	50.00	100

KM# 1220 2 BAIOCCHI (Muraiola)

Billon **Ruler:** Pius VI **Obv:** Crossed keys above date **Obv. Legend:** PIVS... **Rev:** Written value

Date	Mintage	Good	VG	F	VF	XF
1777	—	4.00	12.00	25.00	40.00	60.00
1778	—	4.00	12.00	25.00	40.00	60.00
1794	—	4.00	12.00	25.00	40.00	60.00
1796	—	4.00	12.00	25.00	40.00	60.00

KM# 1226.1 2 BAIOCCHI (Muraiola)

Copper **Ruler:** Pius VI **Obv:** Papal arms **Obv. Legend:** PIVS • SEXTVS • ... **Rev:** Written value within wreath

Date	Mintage	Good	VG	F	VF	XF
ND(1785)-XI	—	3.00	12.00	25.00	45.00	60.00
ND(1786)-XII	—	3.00	12.00	25.00	45.00	60.00
ND(1787)-XIII	—	3.00	12.00	25.00	45.00	60.00
ND(1788)-XIV	—	3.00	12.00	25.00	45.00	60.00
ND(1789)-XV	—	3.00	12.00	25.00	45.00	60.00
ND(1790)-XVI	—	3.00	12.00	25.00	45.00	60.00
ND(1791)-XVII	—	3.00	12.00	25.00	45.00	60.00
ND(1792)-XVIII	—	3.00	12.00	25.00	45.00	60.00
ND(1793)-XIX	—	3.00	12.00	25.00	45.00	60.00
ND(1794)-XX	—	3.00	12.00	25.00	45.00	60.00
ND(1795)-XXI	—	3.00	12.00	25.00	45.00	60.00
ND(1797)-XXIII	—	3.00	12.00	25.00	45.00	60.00

KM# 1226.2 2 BAIOCCHI (Muraiola)

Copper **Ruler:** Pius VI

Date	Mintage	Good	VG	F	VF	XF
1797-XXIII	—	3.50	12.50	25.00	45.00	60.00

KM# 674 1/2 GROSSO

Silver **Ruler:** Clement XI **Obv:** Papal arms **Rev:** Inscription **Rev. Inscription:** INOPIARE / SIT / SVPPLE : / MENTVM

Date	Mintage	Good	VG	F	VF	XF
ND(1705)-V	—	—	10.00	20.00	35.00	60.00

KM# 679 1/2 GROSSO

Silver **Ruler:** Clement XI **Obv:** Arms **Rev. Inscription:** PAVPERI / PORRIGE / MANVM

Date	Mintage	Good	VG	F	VF	XF
ND(1706)-VI	—	—	10.00	20.00	35.00	60.00

KM# 704 1/2 GROSSO

Silver **Ruler:** Clement XI **Obv:** Arms **Rev:** Inscription in laurel wreath **Rev. Inscription:** NEQUE / DIVITIAS

Date	Mintage	Good	VG	F	VF	XF
ND(1708)-VII	—	—	10.00	20.00	35.00	60.00

KM# 711 1/2 GROSSO

Silver **Ruler:** Clement XI **Obv:** Arms **Rev:** Inscription with floral ornaments

Date	Mintage	Good	VG	F	VF	XF
ND(1709)-IX	—	—	10.00	20.00	35.00	60.00

KM# 712 1/2 GROSSO

Silver **Ruler:** Clement XI **Rev:** Inscription in cartouche

Date	Mintage	Good	VG	F	VF	XF
ND(1709)-IX	—	—	10.00	20.00	35.00	60.00

KM# 713 1/2 GROSSO

Silver **Ruler:** Clement XI **Obv:** Arms **Rev:** Bust of St. Peter right

Date	Mintage	Good	VG	F	VF	XF
ND(1709)-IX	—	—	12.00	25.00	45.00	75.00

KM# 735 1/2 GROSSO

Silver **Ruler:** Clement XI **Rev. Inscription:** DA ET ACCIPE

Date	Mintage	Good	VG	F	VF	XF
ND(1710)-X	—	—	10.00	20.00	35.00	60.00

KM# 745 1/2 GROSSO

Silver **Ruler:** Clement XI **Obv:** Arms **Rev:** Inscription in cartouche **Rev. Inscription:** CONSER / VATAE / PEREVNT

Date	Mintage	Good	VG	F	VF	XF
ND(1712)-XII	—	—	10.00	20.00	35.00	60.00

KM# 746 1/2 GROSSO

Silver **Ruler:** Clement XI **Obv:** Arms **Rev. Inscription:** MODI / CVM / IVSTO

Date	Mintage	Good	VG	F	VF	XF
ND(1712)-XII	—	—	10.00	20.00	35.00	60.00
ND(1713)-XIII	—	—	10.00	20.00	35.00	60.00
ND(1714)-XIV	—	—	10.00	20.00	35.00	60.00

KM# 759 1/2 GROSSO

Silver **Ruler:** Clement XI **Obv:** Papal arms **Rev:** Inscription **Rev. Inscription:** NOCET / MINVS

Date	Mintage	Good	VG	F	VF	XF
ND(1715)-XV	—	—	10.00	20.00	35.00	60.00

KM# 777 1/2 GROSSO

Silver **Ruler:** Innocent XIII **Obv:** Arms **Rev:** Inscription in cartouche **Rev. Inscription:** SATIS / AD / NOCEN / DVM

Date	Mintage	Good	VG	F	VF	XF
ND(1721-24)	—	—	15.00	30.00	55.00	90.00

KM# 776 1/2 GROSSO

Silver **Ruler:** Innocent XIII **Obv:** Arms **Rev:** Inscription in cartouche **Rev. Inscription:** SACROSAN / BASILICAE / LATERAN / POSSESS / 1721 **Note:** Lateran issue.

Date	Mintage	Good	VG	F	VF	XF
1721	—	—	15.00	30.00	55.00	90.00

KM# 787 1/2 GROSSO

Silver **Ruler:** Innocent XIII **Obv:** Arms **Rev:** Inscription in cartouche **Rev. Inscription:** CHARI / TAS / FLVIT

Date	Mintage	Good	VG	F	VF	XF
ND(1722)-II	—	—	15.00	30.00	55.00	90.00

KM# 791 1/2 GROSSO

Silver **Ruler:** Innocent XIII **Obv:** Arms **Rev:** Inscription in cartouche **Rev. Inscription:** IN / EGENOS / 1723

Date	Mintage	Good	VG	F	VF	XF
1723-II	—	—	15.00	30.00	55.00	90.00

KM# 793 1/2 GROSSO

Silver **Ruler:** Benedict XIII **Obv:** Tiara over crossed keys **Rev:** Inscription in cartouche **Rev. Inscription:** PRO / TE / EXORABIT

Date	Mintage	Good	VG	F	VF	XF
1724-I	—	—	14.00	28.00	50.00	85.00

KM# 805 1/2 GROSSO

Silver **Ruler:** Benedict XIII **Obv:** Arms **Rev:** Holy door **Note:** Holy Year Issue.

Date	Mintage	Good	VG	F	VF	XF
1725	—	—	18.00	35.00	65.00	110

KM# 813 1/2 GROSSO

Silver **Ruler:** Benedict XIII **Obv:** Arms **Rev:** Inscription in cartouche **Rev. Inscription:** PETENTI / TRIBVE

Date	Mintage	Good	VG	F	VF	XF
1726-III	—	—	14.00	28.00	50.00	85.00

KM# 816 1/2 GROSSO

Silver **Ruler:** Benedict XIII **Obv:** Arms **Rev:** Inscription in cartouche **Rev. Inscription:** SOLATI / VM / MISERIS

Date	Mintage	Good	VG	F	VF	XF
ND(1727)-IV	—	—	14.00	28.00	50.00	85.00

KM# 817 1/2 GROSSO

Silver **Ruler:** Benedict XIII **Obv:** Arms **Rev:** Inscription in cartouche **Rev. Inscription:** SERITE / IN / CHARI / TATE

Date	Mintage	Good	VG	F	VF	XF
ND(1728)-V	—	—	14.00	28.00	50.00	85.00

KM# 831 1/2 GROSSO

Silver **Ruler:** Clement XII **Obv:** Arms **Rev:** Inscription in cartouche **Rev. Inscription:** VT / SALVI / FIANT

Date	Mintage	Good	VG	F	VF	XF
ND(1730-40)	—	—	10.00	20.00	35.00	60.00

KM# 830 1/2 GROSSO

Silver **Ruler:** Clement XII **Obv:** Arms **Rev:** Inscription in cartouche **Rev. Inscription:** ET / MORIEN / TVR IN SITI **Note:** Reform weight.

Date	Mintage	Good	VG	F	VF	XF
ND(1730-40)	—	—	12.00	22.00	40.00	65.00

KM# 902 1/2 GROSSO

Silver **Ruler:** Clement XII **Obv:** Arms **Rev:** Inscription in cartouche **Rev. Inscription:** NON EST / PAX

Date	Mintage	Good	VG	F	VF	XF
ND(1739)-IX	—	—	12.00	22.00	40.00	65.00

KM# 903 1/2 GROSSO

Silver **Ruler:** Clement XII **Obv:** Arms **Rev. Inscription:** BENE / FAC / HVMILI

Date	Mintage	Good	VG	F	VF	XF
ND(1739)-IX	—	—	12.00	22.00	40.00	65.00
ND(1740)-X	—	—	12.00	22.00	40.00	65.00

KM# 922 1/2 GROSSO

Silver **Ruler:** Benedict XIV **Obv:** Papal arms **Rev:** Inscription within cartouche

Date	Mintage	Good	VG	F	VF	XF
ND(1740)-I	—	—	10.00	20.00	35.00	60.00

KM# 923 1/2 GROSSO

Silver **Ruler:** Benedict XIV **Obv:** Papal arms **Rev:** Inscription within cartouche **Rev. Inscription:** BEATI / AVPERES

Date	Mintage	Good	VG	F	VF	XF
ND(1740)-I	—	—	8.00	15.00	25.00	40.00
ND(1742)-III	—	—	8.00	15.00	25.00	40.00
ND(1747)-VIII	—	—	8.00	15.00	25.00	40.00

KM# 965 1/2 GROSSO

Silver **Ruler:** Benedict XIV **Obv:** Papal arms **Obv. Legend:** BEN • XIV • ... **Rev:** Holy Door **Note:** Holy Year issue.

Date	Mintage	Good	VG	F	VF	XF
1750-XI	—	—	9.00	20.00	35.00	55.00
1750-XII	—	—	9.00	20.00	35.00	55.00

KM# 966 1/2 GROSSO

Silver **Ruler:** Benedict XIV **Obv:** Papal arms **Obv. Legend:** BEN • XIV • ... **Rev:** Holy Door open with rays **Note:** Holy Year issue.

Date	Mintage	Good	VG	F	VF	XF
1750-VIIII	—	—	10.00	22.00	38.00	60.00
1750-IVB	—	—	10.00	22.00	38.00	60.00

KM# 975 1/2 GROSSO

Silver **Ruler:** Benedict XIV **Obv:** Papal arms **Rev:** Inscription and date within cartouche

Date	Mintage	Good	VG	F	VF	XF
1757-XVIII	—	—	15.00	25.00	45.00	75.00

KM# 995 1/2 GROSSO

Silver **Ruler:** Clement XIII **Obv:** Papal arms **Rev:** Inscription, date in oval cartouche **Rev. Inscription:** VAE • VOBIS / DIVITIBVS

Date	Mintage	Good	VG	F	VF	XF
1760-III	—	—	5.00	12.00	22.00	40.00
1761-IV	—	—	5.00	12.00	22.00	40.00
1762-IV	—	—	6.00	12.00	22.00	40.00

KM# 1237 2-1/2 BAIOCCHI

Copper **Ruler:** Pius VI **Obv:** Star above written value and date within circle **Rev:** St. Peter looking upwards **Rev. Legend:** PRINCEPS APOST •

Date	Mintage	Good	VG	F	VF	XF
1795	—	15.00	25.00	40.00	90.00	—

KM# 1239 2-1/2 BAIOCCHI

Copper **Ruler:** Pius VI **Obv:** Stars above written value and date **Rev:** St. Peter looking backwards **Rev. Legend:** APOST PRINCEPS •

Date	Mintage	Good	VG	F	VF	XF
1796	—	15.00	25.00	50.00	100	—

KM# 1240 2-1/2 BAIOCCHI

Copper **Ruler:** Pius VI **Obv:** Stars above written value and date within circle **Rev:** St. Peter left **Rev. Legend:** S • P • APOSTOLORUM PRINCEPS

Date	Mintage	Good	VG	F	VF	XF
1796	—	10.00	22.00	38.00	70.00	110
1797	—	10.00	22.00	38.00	70.00	110

KM# 1244 2-1/2 BAIOCCHI

Copper **Ruler:** Pius VI **Obv:** Stars above written value and date within circle **Rev:** St. Peter left **Rev. Legend:** PAPOSTOLORUM PRINC •

Date	Mintage	Good	VG	F	VF	XF
1797	—	10.00	22.00	38.00	70.00	110

KM# 1161 4 BAIOCCHI

Billon **Ruler:** Benedict XIV **Obv:** Crossed keys above divided date **Obv. Legend:** BE NED XIV **Rev:** Written value

Date	Mintage	Good	VG	F	VF	XF
1747	—	7.50	18.00	30.00	45.00	70.00
1748	—	7.50	18.00	30.00	45.00	70.00

KM# 1162 4 BAIOCCHI

Billon **Ruler:** Clement XIII **Obv:** Seated figure below radiant sun **Rev:** Written value

Date	Mintage	Good	VG	F	VF	XF
ND(1758-69)	—	15.00	30.00	40.00	75.00	125

KM# 1206 4 BAIOCCHI

Billon **Ruler:** Clement XIV **Obv:** Crossed keys above date **Obv. Legend:** CLE MENS XIV **Rev:** Written value

Date	Mintage	Good	VG	F	VF	XF
1771	—	12.50	27.50	40.00	75.00	125

KM# 1211 4 BAIOCCHI

Billon **Ruler:** Pius VI **Obv:** Crossed keys above divided date **Obv. Legend:** PIVS SEX TVS **Rev:** Written value

Date	Mintage	Good	VG	F	VF	XF
1777	—	10.00	22.00	38.00	60.00	95.00
1793	—	10.00	22.00	38.00	60.00	95.00
1794	—	10.00	22.00	38.00	60.00	95.00

KM# 635 GROSSO

Silver **Ruler:** Clement XI **Obv:** Papal arms **Rev:** Inscription in cartouche **Rev. Inscription:** DEDIT / PAVPE / RIBVS

Date	Mintage	VG	F	VF	XF	Unc
ND(1700-21)	—	10.00	22.00	38.00	60.00	95.00

KM# 636 GROSSO

Silver **Ruler:** Clement XI **Obv:** Papal arms **Rev:** Inscription in cartouche **Rev. Inscription:** ESVRI / ENTEM / NE / DESPRE / XERIS

Date	Mintage	VG	F	VF	XF	Unc
ND(1700-21)	—	10.00	22.00	38.00	60.00	95.00

KM# 637 GROSSO

Silver **Ruler:** Clement XI **Obv:** Papal arms **Rev:** Inscription without cartouche

Date	Mintage	VG	F	VF	XF	Unc
ND(1700-21)	—	10.00	22.00	38.00	60.00	95.00

KM# 714 GROSSO

Silver **Ruler:** Clement XI **Obv:** Papal arms **Rev:** Inscription in cartouche **Rev. Inscription:** DEDIT / PAVPE / RIBVS

Date	Mintage	VG	F	VF	XF	Unc
ND(1700-21)	—	10.00	22.00	38.00	60.00	95.00

KM# 657 GROSSO

Silver **Ruler:** Clement XI **Obv:** Papal arms **Rev:** Inscription within laurel wreath **Rev. Inscription:** PAVPERI/PORRIGE/MANVM/TVAM

Date	Mintage	VG	F	VF	XF	Unc
ND(1701)-II	—	10.00	22.00	38.00	60.00	95.00
ND	—	10.00	22.00	38.00	60.00	95.00

KM# 658 GROSSO

Silver **Ruler:** Clement XI **Obv:** Papal arms **Rev:** Inscription in cartouche

Date	Mintage	VG	F	VF	XF	Unc
ND(1701)-II	—	10.00	22.00	38.00	60.00	95.00

KM# 638 GROSSO

Silver **Ruler:** Clement XI **Obv:** Papal arms **Rev:** Inscription in cartouche **Rev. Inscription:** SACRS / BASILIC / LATERANEN / POSSESS / MDCCI **Note:** Lateran Issue.

Date	Mintage	VG	F	VF	XF	Unc
MDCCI	—	12.00	22.00	40.00	65.00	100

KM# 659 GROSSO

Silver **Ruler:** Clement XI **Obv:** Papal arms **Rev:** Inscription in cartouche **Rev. Inscription:** SACRS / BASILIC / LATERANEN / POSSESS **Note:** Lateran Issue.

Date	Mintage	VG	F	VF	XF	Unc
MDCCI	—	14.00	28.00	50.00	85.00	110

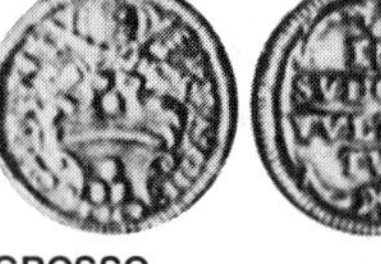

KM# 660 GROSSO

Silver **Ruler:** Clement XI **Obv:** Papal arms **Rev:** Inscription in cartouche **Rev. Inscription:** IN / SVDORE / VVLIVS / TVI

Date	Mintage	VG	F	VF	XF	Unc
ND(1703)-IIII	—	10.00	22.00	38.00	60.00	95.00
ND(1704)-V	—	—	—	—	—	—

KM# 675 GROSSO

Silver **Ruler:** Clement XI **Obv:** Papal arms **Rev:** Inscription in cartouche **Rev. Inscription:** VIDEANT / PAVPERES ET / LATENTVR

Date	Mintage	VG	F	VF	XF	Unc
ND(1705)-VI	—	10.00	22.00	38.00	60.00	95.00

KM# 680 GROSSO

Silver **Ruler:** Clement XI **Obv:** Papal arms **Rev:** Bust of St. Paul right

Date	Mintage	VG	F	VF	XF	Unc
ND(1706)-VII	—	12.00	25.00	45.00	75.00	110
ND(1708)-IX	—	12.00	25.00	45.00	75.00	110

KM# 691 GROSSO

Silver **Ruler:** Clement XI **Obv:** Papal arms **Rev:** Inscription in cartouche **Rev. Inscription:** PAVPERI / PORRIGE / MANVM

Date	Mintage	VG	F	VF	XF	Unc
ND(1707)-VIII	—	10.00	22.00	38.00	60.00	95.00

KM# 724 GROSSO

Silver **Ruler:** Clement XI **Obv:** Papal arms **Rev:** Bust of St. Paul left radiant

Date	Mintage	VG	F	VF	XF	Unc
ND(1708)-IX	—	12.00	25.00	45.00	75.00	110

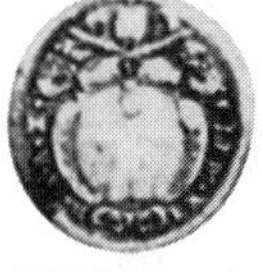

KM# 705 GROSSO

Silver **Ruler:** Clement XI **Obv:** Papal arms **Rev:** Inscription in cartouche **Rev. Inscription:** DATE / ET / DABITVR

Date	Mintage	VG	F	VF	XF	Unc
ND(1709)-X	—	10.00	22.00	38.00	60.00	95.00
ND(1710)-XI	—	10.00	20.00	38.00	60.00	95.00
ND(1711)-XII	—	10.00	20.00	38.00	60.00	95.00
ND(1712)-XIII	—	10.00	20.00	38.00	60.00	95.00

KM# 740 GROSSO

Silver **Ruler:** Clement XI **Obv:** Papal arms **Rev:** Inscription in cartouche **Rev. Inscription:** MANVM / SVAM / APERVIT / INOPI

Date	Mintage	VG	F	VF	XF	Unc
ND(1711)-XII	—	10.00	22.00	38.00	60.00	95.00

KM# 751 GROSSO

Silver **Ruler:** Clement XI **Obv:** Papal arms **Rev:** Inscription in cartouche **Rev. Inscription:** NOLI / COR / APPONERE

Date	Mintage	VG	F	VF	XF	Unc
ND(1713)-XIV	—	10.00	22.00	38.00	60.00	95.00

KM# 754 GROSSO

Silver **Ruler:** Clement XI **Obv:** Papal arms **Rev:** Bust of St. Paul left

Date	Mintage	VG	F	VF	XF	Unc
ND(1714)-XV	—	12.00	25.00	45.00	75.00	110

KM# 760 GROSSO

Silver **Ruler:** Clement XI **Obv:** Papal arms **Rev:** Bust of St. Paul, left

Date	Mintage	VG	F	VF	XF	Unc
ND(1715)-XVI	—	12.00	25.00	45.00	75.00	110

KM# 779 GROSSO

Silver **Ruler:** Innocent XIII **Obv:** Papal arms **Rev:** Inscription in cartouche **Rev. Inscription:** ERIGIT / ELISOS

Date	Mintage	VG	F	VF	XF	Unc
ND(1721)-I	—	20.00	40.00	75.00	125	200
ND(1722)-II	—	20.00	40.00	75.00	125	200
1723-III	—	20.00	40.00	75.00	125	200

KM# 778 GROSSO

Silver **Ruler:** Innocent XIII **Obv:** Papal arms **Rev:** Inscription in cartouche **Rev. Inscription:** SACROSAN / BASILICAE / LATERAN / POSSESS **Note:** Lateran Issue.

Date	Mintage	VG	F	VF	XF	Unc
1721	—	35.00	70.00	125	200	250

KM# 794 GROSSO

Silver **Ruler:** Innocent XIII **Obv:** Tiara over crossed keys **Rev:** Inscription **Rev. Inscription:** SACROSAN / BASILICAE / LATERAN / POSSESS / 1724

Date	Mintage	VG	F	VF	XF	Unc
1724	—	20.00	40.00	70.00	120	200

KM# 795 GROSSO

Silver **Ruler:** Innocent XIII **Obv:** Papal arms **Rev:** Inscription in cartouche **Rev. Inscription:** IVVAT / ET / NOCET

Date	Mintage	VG	F	VF	XF	Unc
ND(1724)-IIII	—	20.00	40.00	70.00	120	200

KM# 808 GROSSO

Silver **Ruler:** Innocent XIII **Obv:** Papal arms **Rev:** Inscription in cartouche **Rev. Inscription:** PRODERIT IN TEMPORE

Date	Mintage	VG	F	VF	XF	Unc
ND(1725)-V	—	20.00	40.00	70.00	120	200

KM# 807 GROSSO

Silver **Ruler:** Benedict XIII **Obv:** Papal arms **Rev:** Holy door **Note:** Holy Year Issue.

Date	Mintage	VG	F	VF	XF	Unc
MDCCXXV (1725)	—	35.00	70.00	125	200	325

KM# 814 GROSSO

Silver **Ruler:** Benedict XIII **Obv:** Papal arms **Rev:** Inscription in cartouche **Rev. Inscription:** BENE / FAC / HVMILI

Date	Mintage	VG	F	VF	XF	Unc
1726	—	20.00	40.00	70.00	120	200

KM# 815 GROSSO

Silver **Ruler:** Benedict XIII **Obv:** Papal arms **Rev:** Inscription in cartouche **Rev. Inscription:** DANE / NOCEAT

Date	Mintage	VG	F	VF	XF	Unc
ND(1726)-VI	—	20.00	40.00	70.00	120	200

KM# 832 GROSSO

Silver **Ruler:** Clement XII **Obv:** Papal arms **Rev:** Inscription in cartouche **Rev. Inscription:** SACROSANC / BASILICAE / LATERANEN / POSSESSIO **Note:** Lateran Issue.

Date	Mintage	VG	F	VF	XF	Unc
1730	—	15.00	30.00	55.00	90.00	125

KM# 833 GROSSO

Silver **Ruler:** Clement XII **Obv:** Papal arms **Rev:** Inscription in cartouche **Rev. Inscription:** VANVM / EST / VOBIS **Note:** Reform weight.

Date	Mintage	VG	F	VF	XF	Unc
ND(1730-40)	—	12.00	22.00	40.00	65.00	90.00

KM# 843 GROSSO

Silver **Ruler:** Clement XII **Obv:** Papal arms **Rev:** Inscription in cartouche **Rev. Inscription:** PAVPERI / PORRIGE

Date	Mintage	VG	F	VF	XF	Unc
1732-III	—	10.00	22.00	38.00	60.00	95.00
1733-IV	—	10.00	22.00	38.00	60.00	95.00

KM# 856 GROSSO

Silver **Ruler:** Clement XII **Rev:** Bust of St. Peter left

Date	Mintage	VG	F	VF	XF	Unc
ND(1735)-V	—	15.00	30.00	55.00	90.00	125

KM# 857 GROSSO

Silver **Ruler:** Clement XII **Rev:** Bust of St. Paul right

Date	Mintage	VG	F	VF	XF	Unc
1735-V	—	15.00	30.00	55.00	90.00	125

KM# 870 GROSSO

Silver **Ruler:** Clement XII **Obv:** Papal arms **Rev:** Inscription in palm wreath **Rev. Inscription:** IN CIBOS / PAVPER / VM

Date	Mintage	VG	F	VF	XF	Unc
1736-VI	—	10.00	22.00	38.00	60.00	95.00
1737-VII	—	10.00	22.00	38.00	60.00	95.00
1738-VIII	—	10.00	22.00	38.00	60.00	95.00
1738-IX	—	10.00	22.00	38.00	60.00	95.00

KM# 871 GROSSO

Silver **Ruler:** Clement XII **Obv:** Papal arms **Rev:** Inscription in cartouche **Rev. Inscription:** TOLLE / ET / PROIICE

Date	Mintage	VG	F	VF	XF	Unc
1736-VII	—	10.00	22.00	38.00	60.00	95.00
1737-VII	—	10.00	22.00	38.00	60.00	95.00

KM# 881 GROSSO

Silver **Ruler:** Clement XII **Obv:** Papal arms **Rev:** Inscription in laurel wreath

Date	Mintage	VG	F	VF	XF	Unc
1737-VIII	—	12.00	22.00	40.00	65.00	90.00

KM# 904 GROSSO

Silver **Ruler:** Clement XII **Obv:** Papal arms **Rev:** Inscription in cartouche **Rev. Inscription:** IN VIA / VIRTVTIS

Date	Mintage	VG	F	VF	XF	Unc
1739-IX	—	12.00	22.00	40.00	65.00	90.00

KM# 905 GROSSO

Silver **Ruler:** Clement XII **Obv:** Papal arms **Rev:** Inscription in cartouche **Rev. Inscription:** HABETIS / PAVPERES

Date	Mintage	VG	F	VF	XF	Unc
1739-IX	—	12.00	22.00	40.00	65.00	90.00
1739-X	—	12.00	22.00	40.00	65.00	90.00

KM# 906 GROSSO

Silver **Ruler:** Clement XII **Obv:** Papal arms **Rev:** Inscription in cartouche **Rev. Inscription:** PAVPERI / PORRIGE / MANVM

Date	Mintage	VG	F	VF	XF	Unc
ND(1739)-X	—	15.00	30.00	55.00	90.00	125

KM# 907 GROSSO

Silver **Ruler:** Clement XII **Obv:** Papal arms **Rev:** Inscription in cartouche **Rev. Inscription:** IMPLETI / ILLVSIO / NIBVS

Date	Mintage	VG	F	VF	XF	Unc
1739-X	—	15.00	30.00	55.00	90.00	125

KM# 928 GROSSO

Silver **Ruler:** Benedict XIV **Obv:** Papal arms **Rev:** St. Peter left **Rev. Legend:** S • PETRVS...

Date	Mintage	VG	F	VF	XF	Unc
ND(1740)-I	—	8.00	13.00	30.00	45.00	70.00
ND(1741)-II	—	8.00	13.00	30.00	45.00	70.00

KM# 926 GROSSO

Silver **Ruler:** Benedict XIV **Obv:** Papal arms **Rev:** Inscription in cartouche **Note:** Varieties exist.

Date	Mintage	VG	F	VF	XF	Unc
1740-I	—	6.00	12.50	25.00	40.00	70.00
ND(1740)-I	—	6.00	12.50	25.00	40.00	70.00
1741-I	—	6.00	12.50	25.00	40.00	70.00
1741-I	—	6.00	12.50	25.00	40.00	70.00

KM# 927 GROSSO

Silver **Ruler:** Benedict XIV **Obv:** Papal arms **Rev:** St. Peter right **Note:** Varieties exist.

Date	Mintage	VG	F	VF	XF	Unc
ND(1740)-I	—	8.00	13.00	30.00	45.00	70.00
ND(1742)-III	—	8.00	13.00	30.00	45.00	70.00
ND(1743)-IV	—	8.00	13.00	30.00	40.00	70.00
ND(1744)-V	—	8.00	13.00	30.00	45.00	70.00
ND(1745)-VI	—	8.00	13.00	30.00	45.00	70.00
ND(1746)-VII	—	8.00	13.00	30.00	45.00	70.00
ND(1747)-VIII	—	8.00	13.00	30.00	45.00	70.00

KM# 924 GROSSO

Silver **Obv:** Arms of Cardinal Annibale Albant **Rev:** Radiant dove **Note:** Sede Vacante Issue.

Date	Mintage	VG	F	VF	XF	Unc
MDCCXL (1740)	—	20.00	40.00	75.00	125	200

KM# 806 GROSSO

Silver **Ruler:** Benedict XIII **Obv:** Tiara over crossed keys **Rev:** Holy door **Note:** Holy Year Issue.

Date	Mintage	VG	F	VF	XF	Unc
MDCCXXV (1740)	—	35.00	70.00	125	200	300

KM# 925 GROSSO

Silver **Ruler:** Benedict XIV **Rev:** Radiant dove, clouds below

Date	Mintage	VG	F	VF	XF	Unc
MDCCXL (1740)	—	20.00	40.00	75.00	125	200

KM# 941 GROSSO

Silver **Ruler:** Benedict XIV **Obv:** Papal arms **Rev:** Inscription, date within wreath **Rev. Inscription:** SACROSAN / BASILICAE / LATERANEN / POSSESS **Note:** Lateran Issue.

Date	Mintage	VG	F	VF	XF	Unc
1741-I	—	15.00	30.00	55.00	90.00	125

KM# 944 GROSSO

Silver **Ruler:** Benedict XIV **Obv:** Papal arms **Rev:** Inscription, date within cartouche **Rev. Inscription:** DISPERSIT / DEDIT / PAVPERIBVS

Date	Mintage	VG	F	VF	XF	Unc
ND(1741)-II	—	8.00	15.00	30.00	45.00	70.00
1742-III	—	8.00	15.00	30.00	45.00	70.00
1743-III	—	8.00	15.00	30.00	45.00	70.00

KM# 945 GROSSO

Silver **Ruler:** Benedict XIV **Obv:** Papal arms **Rev:** Inscription within wreath **Rev. Inscription:** EDENT / PAVPERES / ET SATVR / ABVNTVR

Date	Mintage	VG	F	VF	XF	Unc
ND(1741)-II	—	12.50	25.00	45.00	70.00	110
ND(1742)-III	—	12.50	25.00	45.00	70.00	110

KM# 948 GROSSO

Silver **Ruler:** Benedict XIV **Obv:** Papal arms **Rev:** Inscription within wreath **Rev. Inscription:** NOVIT / IVSTVS /CAVSAM /PAVPERVM

Date	Mintage	VG	F	VF	XF	Unc
ND(1742)-III	—	10.00	22.00	38.00	60.00	95.00
ND(1743)-IV	—	10.00	22.00	38.00	60.00	95.00

KM# 949 GROSSO

Silver **Ruler:** Benedict XIV **Obv:** Papal arms **Rev:** Inscription within wreath **Rev. Inscription:** OCVLI / ELVS / IN / PAVPEREM

Date	Mintage	VG	F	VF	XF	Unc
1743-III	—	8.00	15.00	30.00	45.00	70.00
1743-IV	—	8.00	15.00	30.00	45.00	70.00
1743-IIII	—	8.00	15.00	30.00	45.00	70.00
1743-V	—	8.00	15.00	30.00	45.00	70.00
1744-V	—	8.00	15.00	30.00	45.00	70.00
ND(1744)-IV	—	8.00	15.00	30.00	45.00	70.00

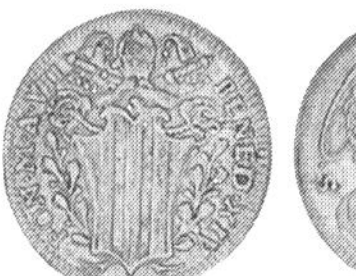

KM# 950 GROSSO

Silver **Ruler:** Benedict XIV **Obv:** Papal arms within sprigs **Rev:** St. Paul right

Date	Mintage	VG	F	VF	XF	Unc
ND(1744)-IV	—	8.00	15.00	30.00	45.00	70.00
ND(1745)-V	—	8.00	15.00	30.00	45.00	70.00
ND(1746)-VI	—	8.00	15.00	30.00	45.00	70.00
ND(1747)-VII	—	8.00	15.00	30.00	45.00	70.00
ND(1748)-VIII	—	8.00	15.00	30.00	45.00	70.00

KM# 951 GROSSO

Silver **Ruler:** Benedict XIV **Obv:** Papal arms within sprigs **Obv. Legend:** BENED • XIV • PON • ... **Rev:** Madonna **Rev. Inscription:** MACULA NON EST IN TE

Date	Mintage	VG	F	VF	XF	Unc
ND(1747)-VII	—	10.00	22.00	38.00	60.00	95.00
ND(1748)-VIII	—	10.00	22.00	38.00	60.00	95.00

KM# 953 GROSSO

Silver **Ruler:** Benedict XIV **Obv:** Papal arms within sprigs **Rev:** St. Peter **Rev. Inscription:** TIBI DABO CLAVES REGNI

Date	Mintage	VG	F	VF	XF	Unc
1748	—	12.50	25.00	45.00	70.00	110

KM# 955 GROSSO

Silver **Ruler:** Benedict XIV **Obv:** Papal arms **Rev:** Inscription in arched lines within cartouche

Date	Mintage	VG	F	VF	XF	Unc
1748-IX	—	8.00	15.00	30.00	45.00	70.00
1749-IX	—	8.00	15.00	30.00	45.00	70.00

KM# 954 GROSSO

Silver **Ruler:** Benedict XIV **Obv:** Papal arms **Rev:** Inscription in cartouche **Rev. Inscription:** VT / ALAT / EOS / IN . FAME

Date	Mintage	VG	F	VF	XF	Unc
ND(1749)-IX	—	8.00	15.00	30.00	45.00	70.00
ND(1750)-X	—	8.00	15.00	30.00	45.00	70.00

KM# 940 GROSSO

Silver **Ruler:** Benedict XIV **Obv:** Papal arms **Rev:** St. Peter 3/4 left looking upwards

Date	Mintage	VG	F	VF	XF	Unc
ND(1749)-X	—	8.00	15.00	30.00	45.00	70.00

KM# 968 GROSSO

Silver **Ruler:** Benedict XIV **Obv:** Papal arms **Rev:** Holy Door divides date **Note:** Holy Year issue.

Date	Mintage	VG	F	VF	XF	Unc
1750-XI	—	12.50	25.00	45.00	70.00	110
1750-XII	—	12.50	25.00	45.00	70.00	110

KM# 967 GROSSO

Silver **Ruler:** Benedict XIV **Obv:** Papal arms **Rev:** Holy Door divides date **Note:** Holy Year issue.

Date	Mintage	VG	F	VF	XF	Unc
1750-X (1750)	—	12.50	25.00	45.00	70.00	110
1750-XI (1750)	—	12.50	25.00	45.00	70.00	110

KM# 969 GROSSO

Silver **Ruler:** Benedict XIV **Obv:** Papal arms **Rev:** Madonna

Date	Mintage	VG	F	VF	XF	Unc
ND(1751)-XII	—	8.00	15.00	30.00	45.00	70.00
ND(1752)-XIII	—	8.00	15.00	30.00	45.00	70.00
ND(1753)-XIV	—	8.00	15.00	30.00	45.00	70.00
ND(1754)-XV	—	8.00	15.00	30.00	45.00	70.00
ND(1755)-XVI	—	8.00	15.00	30.00	45.00	70.00

KM# 977 GROSSO

Silver **Ruler:** Benedict XIV **Obv:** Papal arms **Rev:** Inscription in cartouche **Rev. Inscription:** SACROSAN : / BASILIE : / LATERAN : / POSSESS

Date	Mintage	VG	F	VF	XF	Unc
1758-I	—	8.00	15.00	30.00	45.00	70.00

KM# 978 GROSSO

Silver **Ruler:** Clement XIII **Obv:** Papal arms **Rev:** Inscription, date in cartouche **Rev. Inscription:** DA / PAVPERI

Date	Mintage	VG	F	VF	XF	Unc
1758-I	—	8.00	15.00	30.00	45.00	70.00

KM# 976 GROSSO

Silver **Obv:** Cardinal arms **Rev:** Radiant dove above date **Note:** Sede Vacante issue.

Date	Mintage	VG	F	VF	XF	Unc
1758	—	25.00	45.00	75.00	100	150

KM# 996 GROSSO

Silver **Ruler:** Clement XIII **Obv:** Papal arms **Rev:** Inscription, date in cartouche **Rev. Inscription:** MISERICORS / ET / JVSTVS

Date	Mintage	VG	F	VF	XF	Unc
1760-II	—	8.00	15.00	30.00	45.00	70.00

KM# 1002 GROSSO

Silver **Ruler:** Clement XIII **Obv:** Papal arms **Rev:** Inscription, date in cartouche **Rev. Inscription:** VTERE / QVASI . HOMO / FRVGI

Date	Mintage	VG	F	VF	XF	Unc
1762-IV	—	8.00	12.50	30.00	45.00	70.00

KM# 1003 GROSSO

Silver **Ruler:** Clement XIII **Obv:** Papal arms **Rev:** Inscription, date within wreath **Rev. Inscription:** VTERE / QVASI . HOMO / FRVGI

Date	Mintage	VG	F	VF	XF	Unc
1763-V	—	7.50	15.00	30.00	45.00	70.00
1764-VII	—	7.50	15.00	30.00	45.00	70.00
1765-VIII	—	7.50	15.00	30.00	45.00	70.00
1767-IX	—	7.50	15.00	30.00	45.00	70.00

KM# 1005 GROSSO

Silver **Ruler:** Clement XIV **Obv:** Papal arms **Rev:** Inscription, date in cartouche **Rev. Inscription:** FIAT . PAX / IN / VIRTVTE / TVA

Date	Mintage	VG	F	VF	XF	Unc
1769-I	—	7.50	15.00	30.00	45.00	70.00
1771-III	—	7.50	15.00	30.00	45.00	70.00
1772-III	—	7.50	15.00	30.00	45.00	70.00
1773-IV	—	7.50	15.00	30.00	45.00	70.00
1774-V	—	7.50	15.00	30.00	45.00	70.00

KM# 1025 GROSSO

1.3210 g., 0.9170 Silver 0.0389 oz. ASW **Ruler:** Pius VI **Obv:** Papal arms **Rev:** Holy Door **Note:** Holy Year Issue.

Date	Mintage	VG	F	VF	XF	Unc
1775-I	—	15.00	30.00	55.00	90.00	125

KM# 1033 GROSSO

1.3210 g., 0.9170 Silver 0.0389 oz. ASW **Ruler:** Pius VI **Obv:** Papal arms **Rev:** Star above inscription and date within wreath

Date	Mintage	VG	F	VF	XF	Unc
1777-III	—	5.00	10.00	17.50	30.00	50.00
1778-III	—	5.00	10.00	17.50	30.00	50.00
1778-IV	—	5.00	10.00	17.50	30.00	50.00
1783-VIII	—	5.00	10.00	17.50	30.00	50.00

KM# 1047 GROSSO

1.3210 g., 0.9170 Silver 0.0389 oz. ASW **Ruler:** Pius VI **Obv:** Papal arms **Rev:** Star above inscription within wreath

Date	Mintage	VG	F	VF	XF	Unc
1784-X	—	5.00	10.00	17.50	30.00	50.00
1786-XXI	—	5.00	10.00	17.50	30.00	50.00
1787-XIII	—	5.00	10.00	17.50	30.00	50.00

KM# 1245 5 BAIOCCHI

Copper **Ruler:** Pius VI **Obv:** Value, star above, all within circle **Rev:** Madonna

Date	Mintage	Good	VG	F	VF	XF
1797-XXIII	—	15.00	30.00	55.00	90.00	—
1799-XXIII	—	15.00	30.00	55.00	90.00	—

KM# 1165 CARLINO

Billon **Ruler:** Benedict XIV **Obv:** Papal arms **Rev:** Value, date within cartouche

Date	Mintage	Good	VG	F	VF	XF
1747-VIII	—	5.00	15.00	22.00	38.00	—
1748-VIII	—	5.00	15.00	22.00	38.00	—
1749-VIII	—	5.00	15.00	22.00	38.00	—
1749-IX	—	5.00	15.00	22.00	38.00	—
1749-X	—	5.00	15.00	22.00	38.00	—

Date	Mintage	Good	VG	F	VF	XF
1750-X	—	5.00	15.00	22.00	38.00	—
1750-XI	—	5.00	15.00	22.00	38.00	—
1751-XI	—	5.00	15.00	22.00	38.00	—

KM# 1207 CARLINO

Billon **Ruler:** Clement XIV **Obv:** Papal arms **Rev:** Value, date in cartouche

Date	Mintage	Good	VG	F	VF	XF
1771-III	—	6.00	18.00	27.50	45.00	—

KM# 1212.1 CARLINO

Billon **Ruler:** Pius VI **Obv:** Crown above crossed keys **Rev:** Value, date in cartouche with garland

Date	Mintage	Good	VG	F	VF	XF
1777-III	—	5.00	16.50	25.00	42.00	—
1780-VI	—	4.00	15.00	22.50	40.00	—
1792-XVII	—	4.00	15.00	22.50	40.00	—
1794-XX	—	4.00	15.00	22.50	40.00	—
1796-XXII	—	4.00	15.00	22.50	40.00	—

KM# 1212.2 CARLINO

Billon **Ruler:** Pius VI **Rev:** Inscription without ROMANO

Date	Mintage	Good	VG	F	VF	XF
1777-III	—	20.00	40.00	75.00	120	—

KM# 1235 OTTO (8) BAIOCCHI

Billon **Ruler:** Pius VI **Obv:** Crossed keys **Obv. Legend:** PIVS SEX TVS **Rev:** Value **Rev. Legend:** OTTO BAIOC CHI

Date	Mintage	Good	VG	F	VF	XF
1793	—	7.50	18.00	30.00	45.00	—

KM# A660 GIULIO

Silver **Ruler:** Clement XI **Obv:** Papal arms **Rev:** Inscription in cartouche **Rev. Inscription:** BASILICA / LATERANE / NOLITE / COR / APPONERE **Note:** Lateran Issue.

Date	Mintage	VG	F	VF	XF	Unc
MDCCI-I (1701)	—	22.00	45.00	85.00	140	225

KM# B660 GIULIO

Silver **Ruler:** Clement XI **Obv:** Arms **Rev. Inscription:** BASILIC / LATERANEN / POSSESS / MDCCI **Note:** Lateran Issue.

Date	Mintage	VG	F	VF	XF	Unc
NDMDCCI-I (1701)	—	22.00	45.00	85.00	140	225

KM# 661 GIULIO

Silver **Ruler:** Clement XI **Obv:** Papal arms **Rev:** Inscription **Rev. Inscription:** SI / AFFLVANT / NOLITE / COR / APPONERE

Date	Mintage	VG	F	VF	XF	Unc
1702-II	—	22.00	45.00	85.00	140	225
1703-II	—	22.00	45.00	85.00	140	225

KM# 668 GIULIO

Silver **Ruler:** Clement XI **Obv:** Papal arms **Rev:** Inscription **Rev. Inscription:** NOLI / LABORARE / VT / DITERIS / 1704

Date	Mintage	VG	F	VF	XF	Unc
1704-IIII	—	22.00	45.00	85.00	140	225

KM# 669 GIULIO

Silver **Ruler:** Clement XI **Obv:** Papal arms **Rev:** Inscription in cartouche **Rev. Inscription:** NON / CONCVPISCES / ARGENTVM

Date	Mintage	VG	F	VF	XF	Unc
ND(1704)-IV	—	22.00	45.00	85.00	140	225
ND(1705)-V	—	22.00	45.00	85.00	140	225
ND(1706)-VI	—	22.00	45.00	85.00	140	225
ND(1707)-VII	—	22.00	45.00	85.00	140	225
ND(1708)-VIII	—	22.00	45.00	85.00	140	225
ND(1709)-IX	—	22.00	45.00	85.00	140	225

KM# 692 GIULIO

Silver **Ruler:** Clement XI **Obv:** Papal arms **Rev:** St. Francis kneeling receiving the stigmata

Date	Mintage	VG	F	VF	XF	Unc
ND(1705)-V	—	35.00	75.00	135	225	350

KM# 693 GIULIO

Silver **Ruler:** Clement XI **Obv:** Papal arms **Rev:** Kneeling Holy Mother Church, left, in prayer

Date	Mintage	VG	F	VF	XF	Unc
1707-VII	—	50.00	95.00	175	285	400

KM# 715 GIULIO

Silver **Ruler:** Clement XI **Obv:** Papal arms **Rev:** Inscription in laurel wreath **Rev. Inscription:** NON / CONCVPISCES / ARGENTVM

Date	Mintage	VG	F	VF	XF	Unc
ND(1709)-IX	—	22.00	45.00	85.00	140	225

KM# 736 GIULIO

Silver **Ruler:** Clement XI **Obv:** Papal arms **Rev:** Inscription **Rev. Inscription:** DELICTA / OPERIT / CHARITAS **Note:** Varieties with serif exist.

Date	Mintage	VG	F	VF	XF	Unc
ND(1710)-X	—	22.00	45.00	85.00	140	225

KM# 747 GIULIO

Silver **Ruler:** Clement XI **Obv:** Papal arms **Rev:** Inscription in cartouche **Rev. Inscription:** REDDE / PROXIMO / IN TEMPORE / SVO

Date	Mintage	VG	F	VF	XF	Unc
ND(1712)-XII	—	22.00	45.00	85.00	140	225

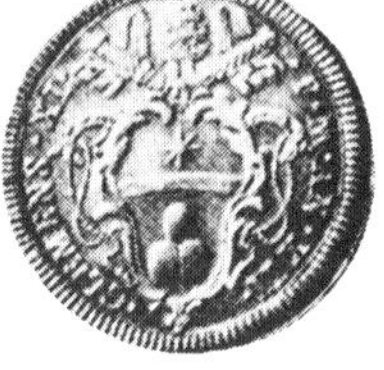

KM# 748 GIULIO

Silver **Ruler:** Clement XI **Obv:** Capped bust right **Obv. Legend:** CLEMENS * XI PONT * M * **Rev:** Papal arms

Date	Mintage	VG	F	VF	XF	Unc
ND(1712)-XII	—	50.00	95.00	175	285	400

KM# 755 GIULIO

Silver **Ruler:** Clement XI **Obv:** Papal arms **Rev:** St. Peter seated right

Date	Mintage	VG	F	VF	XF	Unc
ND(1714)-XIV	—	25.00	50.00	90.00	150	240

KM# 756 GIULIO

Silver **Ruler:** Clement XI **Obv:** Papal arms **Rev:** St. Paul standing

Date	Mintage	VG	F	VF	XF	Unc
ND(1714)-XIV	—	25.00	50.00	90.00	150	240
ND(1715)-XV	—	25.00	50.00	90.00	150	240

KM# 766 GIULIO

Silver **Ruler:** Clement XI **Obv:** Papal arms **Rev:** St. Peter standing

Date	Mintage	VG	F	VF	XF	Unc
ND(1717)-XVII	—	22.00	45.00	85.00	140	240

KM# 781 GIULIO

Silver **Ruler:** Clement XI **Rev. Inscription:** SACROSAN / BASILICAE / LATERAN / POSSESS **Note:** Lateran Issue.

Date	Mintage	VG	F	VF	XF	Unc
1721	—	60.00	125	225	375	—

KM# 780 GIULIO

Silver **Ruler:** Innocent XIII **Obv:** Papal arms **Rev:** Inscription in cartouche **Rev. Inscription:** BEATVS / QVI / INTELLEGIT / SVPER / EGENVM

Date	Mintage	VG	F	VF	XF	Unc
ND(1721-30)	—	50.00	100	200	325	—

KM# 788 GIULIO

Silver **Ruler:** Innocent XIII **Rev. Inscription:** QVI / ACERVAT / ALIIS / CONGREGAT

Date	Mintage	VG	F	VF	XF	Unc
ND(1722)-II	—	50.00	100	200	325	—

KM# 798 GIULIO

Silver **Ruler:** Innocent XIII **Obv:** Papal arms **Rev:** Inscription in cartouche **Rev. Inscription:** CORONAT • TE / IN / MISERICORDIA

Date	Mintage	VG	F	VF	XF	Unc
1724-I	—	50.00	100	185	300	—

KM# 797 GIULIO

Silver **Ruler:** Benedict XIII **Obv:** Papal arms **Obv. Legend:** BENEDICTVS • XIII • P • M • A • I • **Rev:** Inscription, date in cartouche **Rev. Inscription:** SACROSAN / BASILICAE / LATERAN / POSSESS **Note:** Lateran Issue.

Date	Mintage	VG	F	VF	XF	Unc
1724	—	50.00	100	200	325	—

KM# 796 GIULIO

Silver **Obv:** Arms of Cardinal Annibale Albani **Rev:** Radiant dove **Note:** Sede Vacante Issue.

Date	Mintage	VG	F	VF	XF	Unc
MDCCXXIV	—	85.00	165	300	500	—

KM# 818 GIULIO

Silver **Ruler:** Benedict XIII **Obv:** Papal arms **Rev:** Inscription in cartouche **Rev. Inscription:** IN / CHARITATE / MVLTIPLI / CABITVR

Date	Mintage	VG	F	VF	XF	Unc
1728-V	—	50.00	100	185	300	—
ND-VI	—	50.00	100	185	300	—

KM# 809 GIULIO

Silver **Ruler:** Benedict XIII **Obv:** Papal arms **Rev:** Holy Door with pilgrims **Note:** Holy Year Issue.

Date	Mintage	VG	F	VF	XF	Unc
MDCCXXV-I	—	50.00	100	200	325	—

KM# 836 GIULIO

Silver **Ruler:** Benedict XIII **Obv:** Cappd bust right **Rev:** Inscription in cartouche **Rev. Inscription:** SACROSANC / BAISILCAE / LATERANEN / POSSESSIO **Note:** Lateran Issue.

Date	Mintage	VG	F	VF	XF	Unc
MDCCXXX Rare	—	—	—	—	—	—

KM# 837 GIULIO

Silver **Ruler:** Benedict XIII **Obv:** Papal arms **Note:** Lateran Issue.

Date	Mintage	VG	F	VF	XF	Unc
MDCCXXX	—	35.00	70.00	125	200	—

KM# 835 GIULIO

Silver **Ruler:** Clement XII **Obv:** Papal arms **Obv. Legend:** CLEMENS • XII • ... **Rev:** Inscription, divided date in cartouche **Rev. Inscription:** DIADEMA / SPECIEI / DE MANV / DOMININI

Date	Mintage	VG	F	VF	XF	Unc
1730	—	40.00	85.00	150	250	—

KM# 834 GIULIO

Silver **Obv:** Arms of Cardinal Annibale Albani **Rev:** Radiant dove **Note:** Sede Vacante Issue.

Date	Mintage	VG	F	VF	XF	Unc
MDCCXXX	—	50.00	100	200	325	—

KM# 841 GIULIO

Silver **Ruler:** Clement XII **Obv:** Papal arms **Obv. Legend:** CLEM • XII • ... **Rev:** Inscription in cartouche **Rev. Inscription:** VAE • VOBIIS / QVI /SATVRATI / ESTIS

Date	Mintage	VG	F	VF	XF	Unc
ND(1731)-II	—	22.00	45.00	85.00	140	225
ND(1732)-III	—	22.00	45.00	85.00	140	225

KM# 846 GIULIO

Silver **Ruler:** Clement XII **Obv:** Papal arms **Rev:** Inscription within laurel wreath

Date	Mintage	VG	F	VF	XF	Unc
ND(1734)-V	—	25.00	50.00	90.00	150	240

KM# 847 GIULIO

Silver **Ruler:** Clement XII **Obv:** Capped bust right **Rev:** Inscription in laurel wreath

Date	Mintage	VG	F	VF	XF	Unc
ND(1734)-V	—	25.00	50.00	90.00	150	240

KM# 848 GIULIO

Silver **Ruler:** Clement XII **Obv:** Papal arms **Rev:** Inscription in palm wreath

Date	Mintage	VG	F	VF	XF	Unc
ND(1734)-V	—	25.00	50.00	90.00	150	240
ND(1735)-VI	—	25.00	50.00	90.00	150	240
ND(1736)-VII	—	25.00	50.00	90.00	150	240

KM# 849 GIULIO

Silver **Ruler:** Clement XII **Obv:** Papal arms **Rev:** Inscription in cartouche

Date	Mintage	VG	F	VF	XF	Unc
ND(1734)-V	—	25.00	50.00	90.00	150	240
ND(1735)-VI	—	25.00	50.00	90.00	150	240
ND(1736)-VII	—	25.00	50.00	90.00	150	240

KM# 850 GIULIO

Silver **Ruler:** Clement XII **Obv:** Papal arms **Rev:** Inscription in cartouche **Rev. Inscription:** ABVNDET / IN / GLORIAM / DEI

Date	Mintage	VG	F	VF	XF	Unc
ND(1734)-IV	—	25.00	50.00	90.00	150	240
1735-V	—	25.00	50.00	90.00	150	240
ND(1736)-VI	—	25.00	50.00	90.00	150	240

KM# 851 GIULIO

Silver **Ruler:** Clement XII **Obv:** Papal arms **Rev:** Palm wreath replaces cartouche

Date	Mintage	VG	F	VF	XF	Unc
ND(1734)-IV	—	32.00	65.00	110	200	325

KM# 858 GIULIO

Silver **Ruler:** Clement XII **Obv:** Capped bust right **Rev:** Inscription within ornamental wreath **Rev. Inscription:** AAA / FF / RESTITVTVM / COMMERC

Date	Mintage	VG	F	VF	XF	Unc
1735-V	—	35.00	70.00	125	200	350
ND(1735)-V	—	35.00	70.00	125	200	350

KM# 859 GIULIO

Silver **Ruler:** Clement XII **Obv:** Papal arms **Rev:** Inscription in ornamental wreath

Date	Mintage	VG	F	VF	XF	Unc
1735-V	—	20.00	40.00	75.00	125	250
1735-VI	—	20.00	40.00	75.00	125	250

KM# 860 GIULIO

Silver **Ruler:** Clement XII **Obv:** Capped bust right **Rev:** Inscription in palm wreath

Date	Mintage	VG	F	VF	XF	Unc
ND(1735)-VI	—	25.00	50.00	90.00	150	240

KM# 861 GIULIO

Silver **Ruler:** Clement XII **Obv:** Capped bust right **Rev:** Inscription in cartouche

Date	Mintage	VG	F	VF	XF	Unc
ND(1735)-VI	—	25.00	50.00	90.00	150	240

KM# 882 GIULIO

Silver **Ruler:** Clement XII **Obv:** Papal arms **Rev:** Inscription in cartouche **Rev. Inscription:** ABVNDET / IN / GLORIAM / DEI **Note:** Reform weight.

Date	Mintage	VG	F	VF	XF	Unc
1735-IV	—	22.00	45.00	80.00	135	225
ND(1737)-VI	—	22.00	45.00	80.00	135	225

KM# 972 GIULIO

Silver **Ruler:** Benedict XIV **Obv:** Papal arms **Obv. Legend:** BENEDICT • XIV • ... **Rev:** Inscription in cartouche

Date	Mintage	VG	F	VF	XF	Unc
MDCCXLI (1741)	—	20.00	40.00	75.00	125	250

KM# 942 GIULIO

Silver **Ruler:** Benedict XIV **Obv:** Papal arms **Rev:** Inscription in cartouche **Rev. Inscription:** SACROSANC / BASILICAE / LATERANEN / POSSESSIO **Note:** Lateran Issue.

Date	Mintage	VG	F	VF	XF	Unc
MDCCXLI-I (1741)	—	20.00	40.00	75.00	125	250

KM# 929 GIULIO

Silver **Ruler:** Benedict XIV **Obv:** Arms of Cardinal Annibale Albani **Rev:** Radiant dove **Note:** Sede Vacante Issue.

Date	Mintage	VG	F	VF	XF	Unc
MDCCXL (1741)	—	135	275	500	850	—

KM# 997 GIULIO

Silver **Ruler:** Clement XIII **Obv:** Papal arms **Obv. Legend:** CLEM • XIII • ... **Rev:** Radiant seated figure facing right

Date	Mintage	VG	F	VF	XF	Unc
1760-III	—	10.00	20.00	30.00	50.00	100

KM# 1000 GIULIO

Silver **Ruler:** Clement XIII **Obv:** Papal arms **Rev:** Inscription in palms **Rev. Inscription:** THESAVRIZATE / IN / COELIS

Date	Mintage	VG	F	VF	XF	Unc
1761-III	—	10.00	20.00	30.00	50.00	100
1761-IV	—	10.00	20.00	30.00	50.00	100

KM# 1004 GIULIO

Silver **Ruler:** Clement XIII **Obv:** Papal arms **Obv. Legend:** CLEN • XIII • PONT • .... **Rev:** Inscription, divided date in wreath

Date	Mintage	VG	F	VF	XF	Unc
1763-V	—	6.00	15.00	25.00	45.00	90.00
1763-VI	—	6.00	15.00	25.00	45.00	90.00
1764-VI	—	6.00	15.00	25.00	45.00	90.00
1764-VII	—	6.00	15.00	25.00	45.00	90.00
1765-VIII	—	6.00	15.00	25.00	45.00	90.00

KM# 1006 GIULIO

Silver **Obv:** Cardinal arms **Rev:** Radiant dove **Note:** Sede Vacante Issue.

Date	Mintage	VG	F	VF	XF	Unc
MDCCLXIX (1774)	—	17.50	35.00	60.00	90.00	175

KM# 1022 GIULIO

Silver **Obv:** Cardinal arms **Obv. Legend:** SEDE • VACAN • TE • MDCCL XXIV **Rev:** Radiant dove **Note:** Sede Vacante Issue.

Date	Mintage	VG	F	VF	XF	Unc
MDCCLXXIV (1774)	—	17.50	35.00	60.00	90.00	175

KM# 1026 GIULIO

0.9170 Silver **Ruler:** Pius VI **Obv:** Papal arms **Obv. Legend:** PIVS • VI • ... **Rev:** Holy Door open with rays **Note:** Holy Year issue.

Date	Mintage	VG	F	VF	XF	Unc
1775-I	—	12.50	25.00	50.00	80.00	165

KM# 1252 DODICI (12) BAIOCCHI

Billon **Ruler:** Pius VI **Obv:** Crossed keys above divided date **Obv. Legend:** PIVS SEX TVS **Rev:** Written value

Date	Mintage	VG	F	VF	XF	Unc
1793	—	38.00	75.00	120	240	—

KM# 1164.1 DUE (2) CARLINI

Billon **Ruler:** Benedict XIV **Obv:** Papal arms **Obv. Legend:** BENED • XIV • ... **Rev:** Inscription, date in curved lines in carcouche and sprigs **Rev. Inscription:** DVE CARLINI ROMANI

Date	Mintage	VG	F	VF	XF	Unc
1747-VIII	—	20.00	35.00	60.00	90.00	—
1748-VIII	—	20.00	35.00	60.00	90.00	—
1749-VIII	—	20.00	35.00	60.00	90.00	—

KM# 1164.2 DUE (2) CARLINI

Billon **Ruler:** Benedict XIV **Obv:** Papal arms **Obv. Legend:** BENED • XIV • ... **Rev:** Inscription, date in cartouche **Rev. Inscription:** DVE CARLINI ROMANI

Date	Mintage	Good	VG	F	VF	XF
1749-IX	—	7.50	18.00	30.00	48.00	75.00
1749-X	—	7.50	18.00	30.00	48.00	75.00
1750-X	—	7.50	18.00	30.00	48.00	75.00
1751-X	—	7.50	18.00	30.00	48.00	75.00
1752-X	—	7.50	18.00	30.00	48.00	75.00
1752-XII	—	7.50	18.00	30.00	48.00	75.00

KM# 1215 DUE (2) CARLINI

Billon **Ruler:** Pius VI **Obv:** Crown above crossed keys **Obv. Legend:** PIVS • SEX • ... **Rev:** Inscription, date in cartouche with garland **Rev. Inscription:** DVE CARLINI ROMANI

Date	Mintage	Good	VG	F	VF	XF
1777-III	—	8.00	25.00	35.00	45.00	90.00
1780-VI	—	8.00	22.00	35.00	45.00	90.00
1780-VII	—	8.00	22.00	35.00	45.00	90.00
1781-VI	—	8.00	22.00	35.00	45.00	90.00
1781-VIII	—	8.00	22.00	35.00	45.00	90.00
ND(1784)-X	—	8.00	22.00	35.00	45.00	90.00

Date	Mintage	Good	VG	F	VF	XF
ND(1785)-XI	—	8.00	22.00	35.00	45.00	90.00
1794-XX	—	8.00	22.00	35.00	45.00	90.00
1795-XX	—	8.00	22.00	35.00	45.00	90.00
1796-XXI	—	8.00	22.00	35.00	45.00	90.00
1796-XXII	—	8.00	22.00	35.00	45.00	90.00

KM# 974 DOPPIO (2) GIULIO (1/5 Scudo)

Silver **Ruler:** Benedict XIV **Obv:** Bust right **Obv. Legend:** BEN • XIV • PON • M • A • XVI • **Rev:** Radiant seated female **Rev. Legend:** MDCC LVI

Date	Mintage	VG	F	VF	XF	Unc
MDCCLIII-XIV	—	20.00	40.00	75.00	120	—
MDCCLIV-XIV	—	20.00	40.00	75.00	120	—
MDCCLIV-XV	—	20.00	40.00	75.00	120	—
MDCCLV-XV	—	20.00	40.00	75.00	120	—
MDCCLV-XVI	—	20.00	40.00	75.00	120	—
MDCCLVI-XVI	—	20.00	40.00	75.00	120	—
MDCCLVI-XVII	—	20.00	40.00	75.00	120	—
MDCCLVII-XVII	—	20.00	40.00	75.00	120	—

KM# 980 DOPPIO (2) GIULIO (1/5 Scudo)

Silver **Ruler:** Clement XIII **Obv:** Crown within crossed keys above inscription, date in cartouche **Obv. Legend:** CLEM • XIII • PONT • M • A • I • **Obv. Inscription:** SACRO SAN : / BASILIE : / LATERAN : / POSSESS **Rev:** Holy Mother Church, seated

Date	Mintage	VG	F	VF	XF	Unc
1758-I	—	10.00	22.50	35.00	60.00	—

KM# 981 DOPPIO (2) GIULIO (1/5 Scudo)

Silver **Ruler:** Clement XIII **Obv:** Papal arms **Obv. Legend:** CLEMENS • XIII • PONT • M • AN • II • **Rev:** Holy Mother Church, seated

Date	Mintage	VG	F	VF	XF	Unc
1758-I	—	8.00	22.00	35.00	60.00	—
1759-II	—	8.00	22.00	35.00	60.00	—
1766-X	—	8.00	22.00	35.00	60.00	—
1767-X	—	8.00	22.00	35.00	60.00	—
1769-XI	—	8.00	22.00	35.00	60.00	—

KM# 979 DOPPIO (2) GIULIO (1/5 Scudo)

Silver **Obv:** Cardinal arms **Rev:** Radiant dove **Note:** Sede Vacante Issue.

Date	Mintage	VG	F	VF	XF	Unc
MDCCLVIII (1758)	—	40.00	70.00	125	200	—

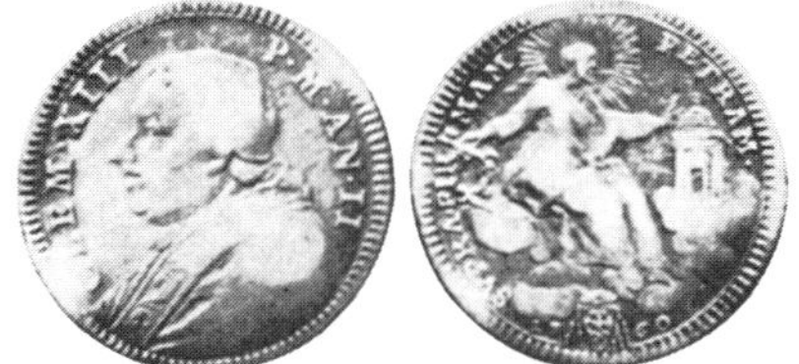

KM# 998 DOPPIO (2) GIULIO (1/5 Scudo)

Silver **Ruler:** Clement XIII **Obv:** Bust left **Obv. Legend:** CLEM • XIII **Rev:** Radiant seated figure, right **Rev. Legend:** PETRAM • ...

Date	Mintage	VG	F	VF	XF	Unc
1760-II	—	8.00	22.00	35.00	60.00	—
1761-III	—	8.00	22.00	35.00	60.00	—
1762-V	—	8.00	22.00	35.00	60.00	—
1765-VIII	—	8.00	22.00	35.00	60.00	—
1766-VIII	—	8.00	22.00	35.00	60.00	—

KM# 1009 DOPPIO (2) GIULIO (1/5 Scudo)

Silver **Ruler:** Clement XIV **Obv:** Papal arms **Obv. Legend:** CLEMENS • XIV • ... **Rev:** Holy Mother Church, seated

Date	Mintage	VG	F	VF	XF	Unc
1769-I	—	8.00	22.00	36.00	60.00	—
1771-II	—	8.00	22.00	36.00	60.00	—
1772-III	—	8.00	22.00	36.00	60.00	—
1772-IV	—	8.00	22.00	36.00	60.00	—
1773-V	—	8.00	22.00	36.00	60.00	—

KM# 1008 DOPPIO (2) GIULIO (1/5 Scudo)

Silver **Ruler:** Clement XIV **Obv:** Crown within crossed keys above inscription in cartouche **Obv. Legend:** CLEM • XIV • ... **Obv. Inscription:** SACROSAN : / BASILIC : / LATERAN : / POSSESS **Rev:** Holy Mother Church, seated **Note:** Lateran Issue.

Date	Mintage	VG	F	VF	XF	Unc
1769-I	—	15.00	25.00	45.00	75.00	—

KM# 1007 DOPPIO (2) GIULIO (1/5 Scudo)

Silver **Obv:** Cardinal arms **Obv. Legend:** SEDE • VACAN • TE • ... **Rev:** Radiant dove **Note:** Sede Vacante Issue.

Date	Mintage	VG	F	VF	XF	Unc
MDCCLXIX (1769)	—	15.00	25.00	45.00	70.00	—

KM# 1023 DOPPIO (2) GIULIO (1/5 Scudo)

Silver **Obv:** Cardinal arms **Obv. Legend:** SEDE • VACAN • TE • ... **Rev:** Radiant dove **Note:** Sede Vacante Issue.

Date	Mintage	VG	F	VF	XF	Unc
MDCCLXXIV (1773)	—	15.00	25.00	45.00	75.00	—

KM# 1028 DOPPIO (2) GIULIO (1/5 Scudo)

5.2850 g., 0.9170 Silver 0.1558 oz. ASW **Ruler:** Pius VI **Obv:** Papal arms **Obv. Legend:** PIVS • VI • PONT • ... **Rev:** Radiant seated figure, facing

Date	Mintage	VG	F	VF	XF	Unc
1775-I (1775)	—	15.00	25.00	40.00	75.00	—

KM# 1027 DOPPIO (2) GIULIO (1/5 Scudo)

5.2850 g., 0.9170 Silver 0.1558 oz. ASW **Ruler:** Pius VI **Obv:** Crown within crossed keys above inscription in cartouche **Obv. Legend:** PIVS • VI • PONT • ... **Rev:** Radiant seated figure, facing **Note:** Lateran Issue.

Date	Mintage	VG	F	VF	XF	Unc
1775-I	—	20.00	40.00	75.00	110	—

KM# 1030 DOPPIO (2) GIULIO (1/5 Scudo)

5.2850 g., 0.9170 Silver 0.1558 oz. ASW **Ruler:** Pius VI **Obv:** Bust right **Obv. Legend:** PIVS • VI • PONT • M • A • II • **Rev:** Holy Mother Church, seated

Date	Mintage	VG	F	VF	XF	Unc
1776-II	—	12.50	27.50	45.00	80.00	—
1777-II	—	12.50	27.50	45.00	80.00	—

KM# 1034 DOPPIO (2) GIULIO (1/5 Scudo)

5.2850 g., 0.9170 Silver 0.1558 oz. ASW **Ruler:** Pius VI **Obv:** Bust right **Obv. Legend:** PIVS • SEXTVS • PONT • ... **Rev:** Holy Mother Church, seated

Date	Mintage	VG	F	VF	XF	Unc
1777-IV	—	8.00	20.00	40.00	50.00	—
1778-IV	—	8.00	20.00	40.00	50.00	—
1779-IV	—	8.00	20.00	40.00	50.00	—
1779-V	—	8.00	20.00	40.00	50.00	—
1780-V	—	8.00	20.00	40.00	50.00	—
1780-VI	—	8.00	20.00	40.00	50.00	—
1780-VII	—	8.00	20.00	40.00	50.00	—
1781-VII	—	8.00	20.00	40.00	50.00	—
1782-VII	—	8.00	20.00	40.00	50.00	—
1782-VIII	—	8.00	20.00	40.00	50.00	—
1783-IX	—	8.00	20.00	40.00	50.00	—
1784-IX	—	8.00	20.00	40.00	50.00	—
1784-X	—	8.00	20.00	40.00	50.00	—

KM# 1045 DOPPIO (2) GIULIO (1/5 Scudo)

5.2850 g., 0.9170 Silver 0.1558 oz. ASW **Ruler:** Pius VI **Obv:** Papal arms **Obv. Legend:** PIVS • SEX PONT • M • A • X U I **Rev:** Holy Mother Church, seated

Date	Mintage	VG	F	VF	XF	Unc
1783-IX	—	7.50	18.00	34.00	50.00	—
1784-IX	—	7.50	18.00	34.00	50.00	—
1784-X	—	7.50	18.00	34.00	50.00	—
1786-XIII	—	7.50	18.00	34.00	50.00	—
1787-XIII	—	7.50	18.00	34.00	50.00	—
1788-XIV	—	7.50	18.00	34.00	50.00	—
1790-XV	—	7.50	18.00	34.00	50.00	—
1790-XVI	—	7.50	18.00	34.00	50.00	—
1792-XVIII	—	7.50	18.00	34.00	50.00	—
1796-XXII	—	7.50	18.00	34.00	50.00	—

KM# 1238 VENTICINQUE (25) BAIOCCHI

Billon **Ruler:** Pius VI **Obv:** Crown above crossed keys **Obv. Legend:** PIVS • SEX • TVS • ... **Rev:** Inscription, date in cartouche **Rev. Inscription:** VENTICIN / QVE / BAIOCCHI

Date	Mintage	Good	VG	F	VF	XF
1795-XX	—	12.00	25.00	38.00	60.00	—
1795-XXI	—	12.00	25.00	38.00	60.00	—
1796-XXI	—	12.00	25.00	38.00	60.00	—
1796-XXII	—	12.00	25.00	38.00	60.00	—

KM# 662 TESTONE (30 Baiocchi)
Silver **Ruler:** Clement XI **Obv:** Papal arms **Obv. Legend:** PONT • M • A • II • CLEMENS • XI **Rev:** Table with bags of coins within circle **Rev. Legend:** * I M P E R A T • A V T • S E R V I T *

Date	Mintage	VG	F	VF	XF	Unc
1702-II	—	80.00	165	300	500	—
1703-III	—	80.00	165	300	500	—

KM# 670 TESTONE (30 Baiocchi)
Silver **Ruler:** Clement XI **Obv:** Papal arms **Obv. Legend:** P O N T • M • A • N • I V C L E M E N S • X I **Rev:** Inscription, date in cartouche **Rev. Inscription:** FOENERATVR / DIMINO QVI / MISERETVR / PAVPERIS

Date	Mintage	VG	F	VF	XF	Unc
1704-IV	—	35.00	75.00	135	225	—

KM# 676 TESTONE (30 Baiocchi)
Silver **Ruler:** Clement XI **Obv:** Papal arms **Obv. Legend:** CLEMENS • XI • PONT • ... **Rev:** Ducal Palace at Urbino

Date	Mintage	VG	F	VF	XF	Unc
ND(1705)-V	—	100	200	350	575	—

KM# 694 TESTONE (30 Baiocchi)
Silver **Ruler:** Clement XI **Obv:** Papal arms **Obv. Legend:** CLEMENS • XI • ... **Rev:** Inscription in cartouche **Rev. Inscription:** QVI / MISERETVR / PAVPERI / BEATVS • ERIT

Date	Mintage	VG	F	VF	XF	Unc
ND(1705)-V	—	35.00	75.00	135	225	—
ND(1706)-VI	—	35.00	75.00	135	225	—
ND(1707)-VII	—	35.00	75.00	135	225	—
ND(1708)-VIII	—	35.00	75.00	135	225	—
ND(1709)-VIIII	—	35.00	75.00	135	225	—

KM# 696 TESTONE (30 Baiocchi)
Silver **Ruler:** Clement XI **Obv:** Papal arms

Date	Mintage	VG	F	VF	XF	Unc
MDCCVII-VII	—	60.00	125	225	375	—

KM# 697 TESTONE (30 Baiocchi)
Silver **Ruler:** Clement XI **Obv:** Capped bust left **Obv. Legend:** CLEMENS * XI * P * M * A * V • I * **Rev:** Three Graces standing in the campidoglio **Rev. Legend:** ...DIGNIS • VICTORIAM

Date	Mintage	VG	F	VF	XF	Unc
ND(1707)-VI	—	75.00	150	275	450	—

KM# 698 TESTONE (30 Baiocchi)
Silver **Ruler:** Clement XI **Obv:** Papal arms

Date	Mintage	VG	F	VF	XF	Unc
ND(1707)-VI	—	70.00	135	250	400	—

KM# 695 TESTONE (30 Baiocchi)
Silver **Ruler:** Benedict XIV **Obv:** Capped bust left **Rev:** Madonna standing with child

Date	Mintage	VG	F	VF	XF	Unc
MDCCVII-VI	—	70.00	135	250	400	—

KM# 706 TESTONE (30 Baiocchi)
Silver **Ruler:** Clement XI **Obv:** Papal arms **Rev:** Legend in laurel wreath

Date	Mintage	VG	F	VF	XF	Unc
ND(1708)-VIII	—	40.00	80.00	140	235	—

KM# 707 TESTONE (30 Baiocchi)
Silver **Ruler:** Clement XI **Obv:** Papal arms **Rev:** St. Joseph and child

Date	Mintage	VG	F	VF	XF	Unc
ND(1708)-VII	—	50.00	100	185	300	—

KM# 708 TESTONE (30 Baiocchi)
Silver **Ruler:** Clement XI **Obv:** Papal arms **Obv. Legend:** CLEMENS * XI * * P * M * AN * VIII • **Rev:** Charity standing with 3 children **Rev. Legend:** ... * PRO * DIO *

Date	Mintage	VG	F	VF	XF	Unc
ND(1708)-VIII	—	40.00	85.00	150	250	—

KM# 737 TESTONE (30 Baiocchi)
Silver **Ruler:** Clement XI **Obv:** Papal arms **Obv. Legend:** * CLEMENS * XI * ... **Rev:** Inscription in cartouche **Rev. Inscription:** NE / OBLIVISCARIS / PAVPERVM

Date	Mintage	VG	F	VF	XF	Unc
ND(1710)-X	—	35.00	75.00	135	225	—

KM# 741 TESTONE (30 Baiocchi)
Silver **Ruler:** Clement XI **Obv:** Papal arms **Rev:** Inscription in cartouche **Rev. Inscription:** MVLTOS / PERDIDIT / ARGENTVM

Date	Mintage	VG	F	VF	XF	Unc
ND(1711)-XI	—	35.00	75.00	135	225	—
ND(1712)-XII	—	35.00	75.00	135	225	—
ND(1713)-XIII	—	35.00	75.00	135	225	—

KM# 767 TESTONE (30 Baiocchi)
Silver **Ruler:** Clement XI **Obv:** Papal arms **Rev:** St. Peter standing

Date	Mintage	VG	F	VF	XF	Unc
ND(1717)-XVII	—	45.00	95.00	175	285	—

KM# 783 TESTONE (30 Baiocchi)
Silver **Ruler:** Innocent XIII **Obv:** Papal arms **Rev:** Inscription in cartouche **Rev. Inscription:** NVLLVS / ARGENTO / COLOR EST / AVARIS

Date	Mintage	VG	F	VF	XF	Unc
ND(1721)-I	—	100	200	350	575	—

KM# 782 TESTONE (30 Baiocchi)
Silver **Obv:** Arms of Cardinal Annibale Albani **Rev:** Radiant dove **Note:** Sede Vacante Issue.

Date	Mintage	VG	F	VF	XF	Unc
MDCCXXI (1721)	—	200	350	600	1,000	—

KM# 789 TESTONE (30 Baiocchi)
Silver **Ruler:** Innocent XIII **Obv:** Papal arms **Obv. Legend:** INNOC * XIII ... **Rev:** Inscription in cartouche **Rev. Inscription:** CONTEMPTA / PECVNIA / DITAT

Date	Mintage	VG	F	VF	XF	Unc
ND(1722)-II	—	100	200	350	575	—

KM# 799 TESTONE (30 Baiocchi)
Silver **Obv:** Arms of Cardinal Annibale Albani **Rev:** Radiant dove **Note:** Sede Vacante Issue.

Date	Mintage	VG	F	VF	XF	Unc
MDCCXXIV (1724)	—	120	225	400	650	—

KM# 864 TESTONE (30 Baiocchi)
Silver **Ruler:** Benedict XIII **Obv:** Capped bust right **Rev:** St. Andrew Corsini receiving mitre from angel **Rev. Legend:** PRAESIDIVM ET DECVS

Date	Mintage	VG	F	VF	XF	Unc
MDCCXXV (1725)	—	60.00	125	225	400	—

KM# 810 TESTONE (30 Baiocchi)
Silver **Ruler:** Benedict XIII **Obv:** Papal arms **Rev:** Holy door with pilgrims at left **Note:** Holy Year issue.

Date	Mintage	VG	F	VF	XF	Unc
ND(1725)-I	—	800	1,500	2,500	4,250	—

KM# 819 TESTONE (30 Baiocchi)
Silver **Ruler:** Benedict XIII **Obv:** Papal arms **Rev:** Inscription in cartouche **Rev. Inscription:** FOENERATVR / DIMINO • QVI / MISERETVR / PAVPERIS

Date	Mintage	VG	F	VF	XF	Unc
ND(1729)-V	—	120	225	400	650	—

KM# 838 TESTONE (30 Baiocchi)
Silver **Obv:** Arms of Cardinal Annibale Albani **Rev:** Radiant dove **Note:** Sede Vacante Issue.

Date	Mintage	VG	F	VF	XF	Unc
ND(1730)	—	70.00	135	250	400	—

KM# 845 TESTONE (30 Baiocchi)
Silver **Ruler:** Clement XII **Obv:** Papal arms **Obv. Legend:** CLEM : XII P • M • AN • IV **Rev:** Inscription in cartouche **Rev. Inscription:** POPVLIS / IMMVNI / EMPORIO / DONATIS

Date	Mintage	VG	F	VF	XF	Unc
ND(1733)-IV	—	30.00	60.00	125	200	—
ND(1734)-V	—	30.00	60.00	125	200	—

KM# 853 TESTONE (30 Baiocchi)
Silver **Ruler:** Clement XII **Obv:** Capped bust right **Obv. Legend:** CLEMENS XII • P • M • AN • V **Rev:** Papal arms

Date	Mintage	VG	F	VF	XF	Unc
ND(1734)-V	—	60.00	125	225	375	—

KM# 844 TESTONE (30 Baiocchi)
Silver **Ruler:** Clement XII **Obv:** Papal arms **Obv. Legend:** C L E M E N S • X I I • ... **Rev:** Inscription in cartouche **Rev. Inscription:** NE • FORRE / OFFENDICVLVM / FIAT

Date	Mintage	VG	F	VF	XF	Unc
MDCCXXXIIII-III (1734)	—	30.00	60.00	125	200	—

KM# 852 TESTONE (30 Baiocchi)

Silver **Ruler:** Clement XII **Obv:** Papal arms **Obv. Legend:** CLEM • XII • ... **Rev:** Inscription in cartouche **Rev. Inscription:** QVAERITE / VT / ABVNDETIS

Date	Mintage	VG	F	VF	XF	Unc
MDCCXXXIV-IIII (1734)	—	30.00	60.00	125	200	—
MDCCXXXIV-V (1734)	—	30.00	60.00	125	200	—

KM# 862 TESTONE (30 Baiocchi)

Silver **Ruler:** Clement XII **Obv:** Papal arms **Obv. Legend:** CLEMENS • XII • ... **Rev:** Inscription in cartouche **Rev. Inscription:** URBE / NOBILITATA

Date	Mintage	VG	F	VF	XF	Unc
MDCCXXXV-V (1735)	—	30.00	60.00	125	200	—
MDCCXXXV (1735)	—	30.00	60.00	125	200	—

KM# 863 TESTONE (30 Baiocchi)

Silver **Ruler:** Clement XII **Rev:** Inscription within palm wreath

Date	Mintage	VG	F	VF	XF	Unc
MDCCXXXV-V (1735)	—	30.00	60.00	125	200	—
MDCCXXXV-VI (1735)	—	30.00	60.00	125	200	—

KM# 865 TESTONE (30 Baiocchi)

Silver **Ruler:** Clement XII **Obv:** Capped bust right **Rev:** St. Andrew Corsini receiving mitre from angel **Rev. Legend:** GENVSALTO A SANGVINE

Date	Mintage	VG	F	VF	XF	Unc
MDCCXXXV-V (1735)	—	50.00	100	185	300	—
MDCCXXXVI-VI (1736)	—	50.00	100	185	300	—

KM# 872 TESTONE (30 Baiocchi)

Silver **Ruler:** Clement XII **Obv:** Papal arms

Date	Mintage	VG	F	VF	XF	Unc
MDCCXXXVI-VI (1736)	—	50.00	100	185	300	—

KM# 873 TESTONE (30 Baiocchi)

Silver **Ruler:** Clement XII **Obv:** Papal arms

Date	Mintage	VG	F	VF	XF	Unc
MDCCXXXVI-VI (1736)	—	50.00	100	185	300	—

KM# 874 TESTONE (30 Baiocchi)

Silver **Ruler:** Clement XII **Obv:** Papal arms **Rev:** Fortune seated left **Rev. Legend:** ...TAS • VIARVM • REDVX

Date	Mintage	VG	F	VF	XF	Unc
MDCCXXXVI (1736)	—	65.00	120	200	325	—

KM# 875 TESTONE (30 Baiocchi)

Silver **Ruler:** Clement XII **Obv:** Capped bust right **Obv. Legend:** C L E M E N S X I I • P : M : A N : V I I * **Rev:** Fortune seated left **Rev. Legend:** ...TAS • VIARVM • REDVR

Date	Mintage	VG	F	VF	XF	Unc
MDCCXXXVI-VII (1736)	—	85.00	150	250	425	—

KM# 878 TESTONE (30 Baiocchi)

Silver **Ruler:** Clement XII **Obv:** Papal arms

Date	Mintage	VG	F	VF	XF	Unc
1736	—	30.00	60.00	125	200	—

KM# 876 TESTONE (30 Baiocchi)

Silver **Ruler:** Clement XII **Obv:** Capped bust right **Rev:** Inscription within palm wreath **Rev. Inscription:** DABIS / DISCERNERE / INTERMALVM

Date	Mintage	VG	F	VF	XF	Unc
ND(1736)-VI	—	40.00	80.00	150	250	—

KM# 877 TESTONE (30 Baiocchi)

Silver **Ruler:** Clement XII **Obv:** Papal arms

Date	Mintage	VG	F	VF	XF	Unc
ND(1736)-VI	—	30.00	60.00	125	200	—
ND(1736)-VII	—	30.00	60.00	125	200	—

KM# 952 TESTONE (30 Baiocchi)

7.9280 g., 0.9170 Silver 0.2337 oz. ASW **Ruler:** Benedict XIV **Obv:** Papal arms **Rev:** St. Peter and St. Paul standing

Date	Mintage	VG	F	VF	XF	Unc
MDCCXLVI-VI (1756)	—	75.00	125	200	300	—

KM# 1001 TESTONE (30 Baiocchi)

7.9280 g., 0.9170 Silver 0.2337 oz. ASW **Ruler:** Clement XIII **Obv:** Papal arms **Obv. Legend:** CLEMENS • XIII • ... **Rev:** St. Peter and St. Paul standing, radiant dove above, temple between

Date	Mintage	VG	F	VF	XF	Unc
MDCCLXI-IV (1761)	—	15.00	30.00	65.00	125	—
MDCCLXIII-VI (1763)	—	15.00	30.00	65.00	125	—
MDCCLXVII-IX (1767)	—	15.00	30.00	65.00	125	—
MDCCLXVII-X (1767)	—	15.00	30.00	65.00	125	—

KM# 1020 TESTONE (30 Baiocchi)

7.9280 g., 0.9170 Silver 0.2337 oz. ASW **Ruler:** Clement XIV **Obv:** Papal arms **Obv. Legend:** CLEMENS • XIV ... **Rev:** St. Peter and St. Paul standing, radiant dove above

Date	Mintage	VG	F	VF	XF	Unc
MDCCLXX-II (1770)	—	20.00	40.00	85.00	150	—
1773-V	—	—	—	—	—	—

KM# 1021 TESTONE (30 Baiocchi)

7.9280 g., 0.9170 Silver 0.2337 oz. ASW **Ruler:** Clement XIV **Obv:** Papal arms **Obv. Legend:** C L E M E N S • X I V ... **Rev:** St. Peter and Paul standing, radiant dove above **Rev. Legend:** ... S • P A V L V S

Date	Mintage	VG	F	VF	XF	Unc
1773-V	—	20.00	40.00	85.00	150	—

KM# 1048 TESTONE (30 Baiocchi)

7.9280 g., 0.9170 Silver 0.2337 oz. ASW **Ruler:** Pius VI **Obv:** Papal arms **Obv. Legend:** P I V S • REXTVS • PON • ... **Rev:** St. Peter and Paul, standing

Date	Mintage	VG	F	VF	XF	Unc
1785-XI	—	17.50	35.00	60.00	100	—
1786-XI	—	17.50	35.00	60.00	100	—
1786-XII	—	17.50	35.00	60.00	100	—
1790-XV	—	17.50	35.00	60.00	100	—
1790-XVI	—	17.50	35.00	60.00	100	—
1796-XXII	—	17.50	35.00	60.00	100	—

KM# 663 1/2 PIASTRE

Silver **Ruler:** Clement XI **Obv:** Arms of Clement XI supported by angel **Obv. Legend:** CLEMENS • XI • ... **Rev:** St. Crescentius on horseback, right, spearing dragon **Rev. Legend:** S • CRESCENTIN ...

Date	Mintage	VG	F	VF	XF	Unc
1702-II	—	85.00	185	300	500	—
1703-III	—	85.00	185	300	500	—
1704-IIII	—	85.00	185	300	500	—

KM# 681 1/2 PIASTRE

Silver **Ruler:** Clement XI **Obv:** Papal arms **Obv. Legend:** CLEMENS • XI PONT • M • A • V • **Rev:** View of Urbino

Date	Mintage	VG	F	VF	XF	Unc
MDCCV-V (1705)	—	125	250	400	650	—

KM# 682 1/2 PIASTRE

Silver **Ruler:** Clement XI **Obv:** Capped bust right **Obv. Legend:** CLEMENS XI • ... **Rev:** View of the Port of Ripetta

Date	Mintage	VG	F	VF	XF	Unc
1706-VI	—	175	345	575	950	—

KM# 699 1/2 PIASTRE

Silver **Ruler:** Clement XI **Obv:** Papal arms **Rev:** Tobias and Angel

Date	Mintage	VG	F	VF	XF	Unc
ND(1707)-VII	—	85.00	185	300	500	—

KM# 709 1/2 PIASTRE

Silver **Ruler:** Clement XI **Obv:** Papal arms **Obv. Legend:** CLEMENS * XI * * P * M * A N * VIII * **Rev:** Inscription in cartouche **Rev. Inscription:** FIAT PAX / IN VIRTVTE / TVA

Date	Mintage	VG	F	VF	XF	Unc
ND(1708)-VIII	—	85.00	185	300	500	—
ND(1708)-VIIII	—	85.00	185	300	500	—

KM# 742 1/2 PIASTRE

Silver **Ruler:** Clement XI **Obv:** Capped bust left **Obv. Legend:** CLEMENS * XI * * P * M * A N * XI **Rev:** Pantheon **Rev. Legend:** ... COREM • DOMVS • TV Æ •

Date	Mintage	VG	F	VF	XF	Unc
ND(1711)-XI	—	200	400	650	1,150	—

KM# 761 1/2 PIASTRE

Silver **Ruler:** Clement XI **Obv:** Papal arms **Obv. Legend:** CLEMENS * XI * * P * M * ... **Rev:** Inscription in cartouche **Rev. Inscription:** ÆRVGO ANIMI / CVRA PECVLII

Date	Mintage	VG	F	VF	XF	Unc
MDCCXV-XV (1715)	—	85.00	185	300	500	—

KM# 784 1/2 PIASTRE

Silver **Ruler:** Innocent XIII **Obv:** Papal arms **Obv. Legend:** INNOC • XIII • ... **Rev:** 2 reapers

Date	Mintage	VG	F	VF	XF	Unc
ND(1721)-I	—	165	300	500	825	—
ND(1722)-II	—	165	300	500	825	—

KM# 801 1/2 PIASTRE

Silver **Ruler:** Clement XII **Obv:** Papal arms **Obv. Legend:** CLEMENS • XII • ... **Rev:** Inscription in cartouche

Date	Mintage	VG	F	VF	XF	Unc
ND(1724)-IV	—	75.00	150	250	450	—
ND(1725)-V	—	75.00	150	250	450	—

KM# 800 1/2 PIASTRE

Silver **Obv:** Arms of Cardinal Annibale Albanti **Rev:** Radiant dove **Note:** Sede Vacante Issue.

Date	Mintage	VG	F	VF	XF	Unc
MDCCXXIV (1724)	—	325	575	975	1,650	—
ND (1724)	—	325	575	975	1,650	—

KM# 879 1/2 PIASTRE

Silver **Ruler:** Clement XII **Subject:** Restoration of St. John of Florentines **Obv:** Capped bust right **Obv. Legend:** CLEMENS XII • P : M : A : VII **Rev:** Facade of St. John of Florentines in Rome **Rev. Legend:** ... C V S P A T R I Æ

Date	Mintage	VG	F	VF	XF	Unc
MDCCXXXVI-VII (1734)	—	165	300	500	825	—

KM# 946 1/2 PIASTRE

Silver **Ruler:** Benedict XIV **Obv:** Capped bust right **Rev:** St. Peter standing, Hospital of the Holy Spirit in background

Date	Mintage	VG	F	VF	XF	Unc
MDCCXLII-III (1742)	—	135	275	450	750	—

KM# 947 1/2 PIASTRE

Silver **Ruler:** Benedict XIV **Rev:** St. Peter standing

Date	Mintage	VG	F	VF	XF	Unc
MDCCXLII-III (1742)	—	125	250	400	650	—

KM# 664 PIASTRA (Scudo of 80 Bolognini)

Silver **Ruler:** Clement XI **Subject:** Church of S. Maria in Trastevere - portico addition **Obv:** Capped bust left **Obv. Legend:** CLEMENS • XI • PONT ... **Rev:** Madonna and child enthroned between two angels, Pope Innocent II kneeling below **Note:** Dav. #1429.

Date	Mintage	VG	F	VF	XF	Unc
1702-II	—	400	650	1,000	1,600	—

KM# 665 PIASTRA (Scudo of 80 Bolognini)

Silver **Ruler:** Clement XI **Obv:** Capped bust left **Obv. Legend:** CLEMENS • XI • PONT ... **Rev:** St. Clement seated on clouds **Note:** Dav. #1430.

Date	Mintage	VG	F	VF	XF	Unc
1702-II	—	750	1,350	2,200	3,650	—

KM# 667 PIASTRA (Scudo of 80 Bolognini)

Silver **Ruler:** Clement XI **Obv:** Papal arms **Rev:** Church of St. Theodore Al Palatino **Note:** Dav. #1431.

Date	Mintage	VG	F	VF	XF	Unc
1703-III	—	450	725	1,200	1,900	—

KM# 671 PIASTRA (Scudo of 80 Bolognini)

Silver **Ruler:** Clement XI **Obv:** Papal arms **Obv. Legend:** CLEMENS • XI • PONT • M • AN • IV **Rev:** Presentation of Jesus at the temple **Note:** Dav. #1432.

Date	Mintage	VG	F	VF	XF	Unc
1704-VI	—	400	650	1,100	1,750	—

KM# 672 PIASTRA (Scudo of 80 Bolognini)
Silver **Ruler:** Clement XI **Obv:** Capped bust left **Obv. Legend:** CLEMENS • XI • PONT MAX • A • VI **Rev:** Pope enthroned right in Church of S. Maria Maggiore **Note:** Dav. #1433.

Date	Mintage	VG	F	VF	XF	Unc
ND(1704)-VI	—	500	700	1,250	2,000	—

KM# 673 PIASTRA (Scudo of 80 Bolognini)
Silver **Ruler:** Clement XI **Obv:** Papal arms within wreath **Obv. Legend:** C L E M E N S • XI • PONT • M • A • V I • **Rev:** Papal audience **Note:** Dav. #1434.

Date	Mintage	VG	F	VF	XF	Unc
ND(1704)-VI	—	400	650	1,100	1,750	—

KM# 677 PIASTRA (Scudo of 80 Bolognini)
Silver **Ruler:** Clement XI **Obv:** Papal arms within FEISTOONS **Obv. Legend:** * CLEMENS * XI * * P * M * ANN * VI * **Rev:** Papal audience **Note:** Dav. #1435.

Date	Mintage	VG	F	VF	XF	Unc
ND(1705)-V	—	400	650	1,100	1,750	—

KM# 683 PIASTRA (Scudo of 80 Bolognini)
Silver **Ruler:** Clement XI **Obv:** Capped bust left **Obv. Legend:** CLEMENS • XIP M • AN • VI **Rev:** St. Peter in ship, right two seraphim above **Note:** Dav. #1436.

Date	Mintage	VG	F	VF	XF	Unc
ND(1706)-VI	—	750	1,350	2,200	3,100	—

KM# 700 PIASTRA (Scudo of 80 Bolognini)
Silver **Ruler:** Clement XI **Obv:** Capped bust left **Obv. Legend:** CLEMENS • XI •• P • M • AN • VII **Rev:** St. Clement kneeling left before Angus Dei, Peace standing **Note:** Dav. #1437.

Date	Mintage	VG	F	VF	XF	Unc
MDCCVII-VII (1707)	—	450	725	1,250	1,900	—

KM# 710 PIASTRA (Scudo of 80 Bolognini)
Silver **Ruler:** Clement XI **Obv:** Papal arms, legend starts at upper right **Obv. Legend:** CLEMENS • XI • P • M • ANN • VII **Rev:** Inscription in cartouche **Rev. Inscription:** FIAT PAX / IN VIRTVTE / TVA **Note:** Dav. #1438.

Date	Mintage	VG	F	VF	XF	Unc
ND(1708)-VII	—	400	650	1,000	1,600	—

KM# 716 PIASTRA (Scudo of 80 Bolognini)
Silver **Ruler:** Clement XI **Obv:** Papal arms, legend starts at lower left **Note:** Dav. #1441.

Date	Mintage	VG	F	VF	XF	Unc
ND(1709)-IX	—	400	650	1,000	1,600	—

KM# 743 PIASTRA (Scudo of 80 Bolognini)
Silver **Ruler:** Clement XI **Subject:** Construction of Bridge at Civita Castellana **Obv:** Papal arms **Obv. Legend:** CLEMENS * XI * ... **Rev:** Bridge of Civita Castellana **Note:** Dav. #1443.

Date	Mintage	VG	F	VF	XF	Unc
ND(1711)-XI	—	500	700	1,250	2,000	—

KM# 752 PIASTRA (Scudo of 80 Bolognini)
Silver **Ruler:** Clement XI **Obv:** Papal arms **Obv. Legend:** * CLEMENS * XIP * M * AN * XIII * **Rev:** Fountain of Piazza del Pantheon shown within Piazza **Note:** Dav. #1445.

Date	Mintage	VG	F	VF	XF	Unc
ND(1713)-XIII	—	400	650	1,000	1,750	—

KM# 753 PIASTRA (Scudo of 80 Bolognini)

Silver **Ruler:** Clement XI **Obv:** Papal arms **Obv. Legend:** * CLEMENS * XI - P * M * AN * XIII * **Rev:** Fountain of Piazza del Pantheon without Piazza **Note:** Dav. #1446.

Date	Mintage	VG	F	VF	XF	Unc
ND(1713)-XIII	—	400	650	1,000	1,750	—

KM# 762 PIASTRA (Scudo of 80 Bolognini)

Silver **Ruler:** Clement XI **Obv:** Capped bust left **Obv. Legend:** CLEMENS•XI••P•M•AN•XV **Rev:** Papal arms **Note:** Dav. #1447.

Date	Mintage	VG	F	VF	XF	Unc
ND(1715)-XV	—	500	700	1,250	2,000	—

KM# 763 PIASTRA (Scudo of 80 Bolognini)

Silver **Ruler:** Clement XI **Obv:** Capped bust right **Obv. Legend:** C L E M E N S * * X I * P * M * A * X V **Rev:** Papal arms **Note:** Dav. #1448.

Date	Mintage	VG	F	VF	XF	Unc
ND(1715)-XV (1715)	—	400	650	1,000	1,750	—

KM# 802 PIASTRA (Scudo of 80 Bolognini)

Silver **Obv:** Arms of Cardinal Annibale Albani **Obv. Legend:** SEDE • VACANTE • **Rev:** Radiant dove **Note:** Sede Vacante Issue. Dav. #1453.

Date	Mintage	VG	F	VF	XF	Unc
MDCCXXIV (1724)	—	1,000	1,800	3,000	5,000	—
ND (1724)	—	1,000	1,800	3,000	5,000	—

KM# 842 PIASTRA (Scudo of 80 Bolognini)

Silver **Ruler:** Clement XII **Obv:** Capped bust right **Rev:** Abundance and Justice seated **Note:** Dav. #1455.

Date	Mintage	VG	F	VF	XF	Unc
MDCCXXXI (1731)	—	3,000	5,500	9,000	—	—

KM# 930 PIASTRA (Scudo of 80 Bolognini)

Silver **Obv:** Arms of Cardinal Annibale Albani **Rev:** Radiant dove among clouds **Note:** Sede Vacante Issue. Dav. #1456.

Date	Mintage	VG	F	VF	XF	Unc
MDCCXL (1740)	—	950	1,650	2,800	2,650	—

KM# 1236.1 SESSANTA (60) BAIOCCHI

Billon

Date	Mintage	Good	VG	F	VF	XF
1769-XXII (sic)	—	75.00	125	150	200	—
1793-XXI (sic)	—	75.00	125	150	200	—

KM# 1236.2 SESSANTA (60) BAIOCCHI

Billon **Ruler:** Pius VI **Obv:** Papal arms **Obv. Legend:** PIVS SEXTVS PONT MAXIMVS ANNO XXII **Rev:** Stars above written value, date, all within circle

Date	Mintage	Good	VG	F	VF	XF
1795-XXI	—	40.00	75.00	110	150	—
1796-XXII	—	35.00	60.00	100	150	—
1797-XXII	—	35.00	60.00	100	150	—
1797-XXIII	—	35.00	60.00	100	150	—
1799-XXV	—	35.00	60.00	100	150	—

KM# 1179 1/2 SCUDO

Silver **Obv:** Capped bust, right **Obv. Legend:** BENED • XIV • PONT • ... **Rev:** Holy Mother Church, seated

Date	Mintage	Good	VG	F	VF	XF
MDCCLIII-XIV	—	35.00	70.00	125	225	—
MDCCLIV-XIV	—	35.00	70.00	125	225	—
MDCCLIV-XV	—	35.00	70.00	125	225	—

KM# 1186 1/2 SCUDO

Silver **Obv:** Cardinal arms **Obv. Legend:** SEDE • VACAN TE • M D ... **Rev:** Radiant dove above small cardinal arms with garland **Note:** Sede Vacante Issue.

Date	Mintage	Good	VG	F	VF	XF
MDCCLVIII (1758)	—	100	200	300	600	—

KM# 1189 1/2 SCUDO

Silver **Ruler:** Clement XIII **Obv:** Papal arms **Obv. Legend:** CLEMENS • XIII... **Rev:** Holy Mother Church, seated

Date	Mintage	Good	VG	F	VF	XF
1759-I	—	75.00	100	150	200	—

KM# 1200 1/2 SCUDO

Silver **Ruler:** Clement XIII **Obv:** Capped bust, left **Obv. Legend:** CLEMENS • XIII... **Rev:** Radiant seated figure, facing right

Date	Mintage	Good	VG	F	VF	XF
1760-III	—	75.00	125	200	350	—

KM# 1208 1/2 SCUDO

Silver **Ruler:** Clement XIV **Obv:** Papal arms **Obv. Legend:** CLEMENS • XIV... **Rev:** Holy Mother Church, seated

Date	Mintage	Good	VG	F	VF	XF
1773-IV	—	35.00	70.00	125	225	—

KM# 1210 1/2 SCUDO

13.2140 g., 0.9170 Silver 0.3896 oz. ASW **Ruler:** Pius VI **Obv:** Papal arms **Obv. Legend:** PIVS • VI • PONT ... **Rev:** Holy Mother Church, seated

Date	Mintage	Good	VG	F	VF	XF
1775-I	—	25.00	45.00	125	225	—
1775-II	—	25.00	45.00	125	225	—

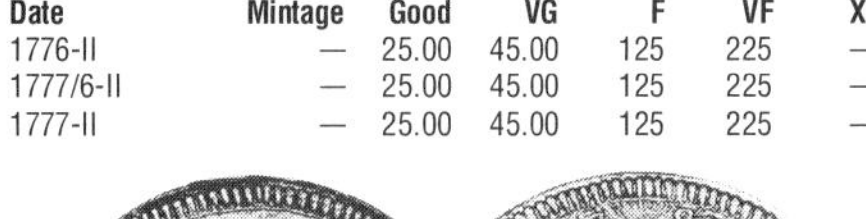

Date	Mintage	Good	VG	F	VF	XF
1776-II	—	25.00	45.00	125	225	—
1777/6-II	—	25.00	45.00	125	225	—
1777-II	—	25.00	45.00	125	225	—

KM# 1213 1/2 SCUDO

13.2140 g., 0.9170 Silver 0.3896 oz. ASW **Ruler:** Pius VI **Obv:** Bust right **Obv. Legend:** PIVS • SEXTVS • ... **Rev:** Holy Mother Church, seated **Rev. Legend:** AVXILIVM • DE • SANCTO

Date	Mintage	Good	VG	F	VF	XF
1777-III	—	30.00	60.00	100	200	—

KM# 1214 1/2 SCUDO

13.2140 g., 0.9170 Silver 0.3896 oz. ASW **Ruler:** Pius VI **Obv:** Papal arms **Obv. Legend:** PIVS • SEXTVS ... **Rev:** Holy Mother Church, seated **Rev. Legend:** AVXILIVM • DE • SANCTO

Date	Mintage	Good	VG	F	VF	XF
1778-IV	—	30.00	60.00	100	175	—
1778-V	—	30.00	60.00	100	175	—
1779-V	—	30.00	60.00	100	175	—
1780-V	—	30.00	60.00	100	175	—
1780-VI	—	30.00	60.00	100	175	—
1785-XI	—	30.00	60.00	100	175	—
1796-XXII	—	30.00	60.00	100	175	—

KM# 1209 1/2 SCUDO

Silver **Ruler:** Pius VI **Obv:** Cardinal arms **Obv. Legend:** SEDE • VACANTE • MDCCLXXIV **Rev:** Radiant dove **Rev. Legend:** ...MEN * CORDIVM * ... **Note:** Sede Vacante Issue.

Date	Mintage	Good	VG	F	VF	XF
MDCCLXXIV (1794)	—	30.00	60.00	175	300	—

KM# 1247 1/2 SCUDO

13.2500 g., 0.9170 Silver 0.3906 oz. ASW **Ruler:** Pius VII **Obv:** Papal arms **Obv. Legend:** PIVS ... **Rev:** Seated female in clouds holding keys and church

Date	Mintage	VG	F	VF	XF	Unc
1800-IR	—	90.00	135	240	—	—

KM# 1180 SCUDO

Silver **Ruler:** Benedict XIV **Obv:** Bust right **Obv. Legend:** ... PONT • MAX • AN • XIV • **Rev:** Holy Mother Church, seated **Rev. Legend:** MDCCLIII **Note:** Dav. #1459.

Date	Mintage	Good	VG	F	VF	XF
MDCCLIII-XIV (1753)	—	85.00	150	250	375	—
MDCCLIV-XV (1754)	—	85.00	150	250	375	—

KM# 1187 SCUDO

Silver **Obv:** Cardinal arms **Obv. Legend:** SEDE • VACANTE • MDCCLVIII **Rev:** Radiant dove **Rev. Legend:** ... VLT • SPIRAT • **Note:** Sede Vacante Issue.

Date	Mintage	Good	VG	F	VF	XF
MDCCLVIII (1758)	—	180	325	450	900	—

KM# 1190 SCUDO

Silver **Ruler:** Clement XIII **Obv:** Papal arms **Obv. Legend:** CLEMENT • XIII ... **Rev:** Holy Mother Church, seated **Rev. Legend:** ...TRAM **Note:** Dav. #1463.

Date	Mintage	Good	VG	F	VF	XF
1759-I	—	175	350	650	1,250	—

KM# 1216.1 SCUDO

26.4280 g., 0.9170 Silver 0.7791 oz. ASW **Ruler:** Pius VI **Obv:** Papal arms **Obv. Legend:** PIUS • SEXTUS ... **Rev:** Holy Mother Church, seated **Rev. Legend:** AUXILIUM DE SANCTO **Note:** Dav. #1471.

Date	Mintage	Good	VG	F	VF	XF
1780-VI	—	50.00	100	150	250	—

KM# 1216.2 SCUDO

26.4280 g., 0.9170 Silver 0.7791 oz. ASW **Ruler:** Pius VI **Rev. Legend:** AVXILIVM **Note:** For similar coins with A mint mark refer to Papal City States - Ancona.

Date	Mintage	Good	VG	F	VF	XF
1780-VI	—	50.00	100	150	250	—

KM# 1248.2 SCUDO

26.4280 g., 0.9170 Silver 0.7791 oz. ASW **Ruler:** Pius VII **Rev. Legend:** PIUS VII

Date	Mintage	Good	VG	F	VF	XF
1800-IR	—	40.00	85.00	150	250	—

KM# 1248.1 SCUDO

26.4280 g., 0.9170 Silver 0.7791 oz. ASW **Ruler:** Pius VII **Rev. Legend:** PIVS VII **Note:** Dav. #1479.

Date	Mintage	Good	VG	F	VF	XF
1800-IR	—	40.00	85.00	150	250	—

KM# 684 1/2 SCUDO D'ORO
1.7500 g., 0.9860 Gold 0.0555 oz. AGW **Ruler:** Clement XI **Obv:** Papal arms **Rev:** Bust of St. Peter left

Date	Mintage	VG	F	VF	XF	Unc
1706-XVII	—	650	1,250	2,500	3,750	—

KM# 685 1/2 SCUDO D'ORO
1.7500 g., 0.9860 Gold 0.0555 oz. AGW **Ruler:** Clement XI **Obv:** 3 stony points rising from the sea

Date	Mintage	VG	F	VF	XF	Unc
1706	—	650	1,250	2,500	3,750	—

KM# 686 1/2 SCUDO D'ORO
1.7500 g., 0.9860 Gold 0.0555 oz. AGW **Ruler:** Clement XI **Obv:** Papal arms **Rev:** Legend in cartouche **Rev. Legend:** NON / IN . AVA / RITIAM

Date	Mintage	VG	F	VF	XF	Unc
ND (1706)	—	400	600	1,250	1,750	—

KM# 717 1/2 SCUDO D'ORO
1.7500 g., 0.9860 Gold 0.0555 oz. AGW **Ruler:** Clement XI **Rev:** Head of St. Peter right

Date	Mintage	VG	F	VF	XF	Unc
ND(1709)-IX	—	400	600	1,250	1,750	—

KM# 768 1/2 SCUDO D'ORO
1.7500 g., 0.9860 Gold 0.0555 oz. AGW **Ruler:** Clement XI **Obv:** Bust right **Rev:** Bust of St. Peter left

Date	Mintage	VG	F	VF	XF	Unc
ND(1717)-XVII	—	400	600	1,250	1,750	—

KM# 769 1/2 SCUDO D'ORO
1.7500 g., 0.9860 Gold 0.0555 oz. AGW **Ruler:** Clement XI **Rev:** Bust of St. Peter 1/2 right

Date	Mintage	VG	F	VF	XF	Unc
ND(1717)-XVII	—	400	600	1,250	1,750	—

KM# 803 1/2 SCUDO D'ORO
1.7500 g., 0.9860 Gold 0.0555 oz. AGW **Ruler:** Innocent XIII **Obv:** Papal arms **Rev:** Crowned eagle with wings spread of Conti arms

Date	Mintage	VG	F	VF	XF	Unc
ND(1724)-III	—	650	1,250	2,150	3,750	—

KM# 919 1/2 SCUDO ROMANO
Gold **Ruler:** Clement XII **Obv:** Inscription below tiara and crossed keys **Obv. Inscription:** CLEM / XII **Rev:** Bust of St. Peter right

Date	Mintage	VG	F	VF	XF	Unc
ND (1739)	—	450	800	1,400	2,000	—

KM# 937 1/2 SCUDO ROMANO
Gold **Obv:** Inscription in branches below, ceremonial umbrella above crossed keys **Obv. Inscription:** SEDE / VAC **Note:** Sede Vacante Issue.

Date	Mintage	VG	F	VF	XF	Unc
1740	—	350	650	800	1,250	—

KM# 939 1/2 SCUDO ROMANO (1/2 Scudo)
Gold **Ruler:** Benedict XIV **Obv:** Crown above crossed keys and ruler's title **Obv. Inscription:** BEN / XIV **Rev:** Bust right

Date	Mintage	VG	F	VF	XF	Unc
1740	—	200	300	450	850	—
1741	—	200	300	450	850	—
1742	—	100	250	350	500	—
1751	—	100	250	350	500	—
ND	—	100	250	350	500	—

KM# 973 1/2 SCUDO ROMANO (1/2 Scudo)
Gold **Ruler:** Benedict XIV **Obv:** Papal arms **Rev:** Head right

Date	Mintage	VG	F	VF	XF	Unc
MDCCLI (1751)	—	250	350	500	700	—

KM# 666 SCUDO D'ORO
3.5000 g., 0.9860 Gold 0.1109 oz. AGW **Ruler:** Clement XI **Obv:** Papal arms **Rev:** Large head of St. Paul right

Date	Mintage	VG	F	VF	XF	Unc
ND(1702)-II	—	350	650	950	1,600	—
ND(1703)-III	—	350	650	950	1,600	—

KM# 678 SCUDO D'ORO
3.5000 g., 0.9860 Gold 0.1109 oz. AGW **Ruler:** Clement XI **Rev:** Head of St. Paul right

Date	Mintage	VG	F	VF	XF	Unc
ND(1705)-V	—	350	650	950	1,600	—

KM# 687 SCUDO D'ORO
3.5000 g., 0.9860 Gold 0.1109 oz. AGW **Ruler:** Clement XI **Rev:** Anchor upright on sea, date in exergue

Date	Mintage	VG	F	VF	XF	Unc
1706-VI	—	450	900	1,800	2,850	—

KM# 718 SCUDO D'ORO
3.5000 g., 0.9860 Gold 0.1109 oz. AGW **Ruler:** Clement XI **Rev:** Head of St. Peter left

Date	Mintage	VG	F	VF	XF	Unc
ND(1709)-IX	—	350	650	950	1,600	—

KM# 719 SCUDO D'ORO
3.5000 g., 0.9860 Gold 0.1109 oz. AGW **Ruler:** Clement XI **Rev:** Radiant head of St. Peter left

Date	Mintage	VG	F	VF	XF	Unc
ND(1709)-IX	—	350	650	950	1,600	—

KM# 720 SCUDO D'ORO
3.5000 g., 0.9860 Gold 0.1109 oz. AGW **Ruler:** Clement XI **Obv:** Oval Papal arms

Date	Mintage	VG	F	VF	XF	Unc
ND(1709)-IX	—	350	650	950	1,600	—

KM# 738 SCUDO D'ORO
3.5000 g., 0.9860 Gold 0.1109 oz. AGW **Ruler:** Clement XI **Obv:** Bust right **Rev:** Papal arms

Date	Mintage	VG	F	VF	XF	Unc
ND(1710)-X	—	500	1,000	2,000	3,250	—

KM# 744 SCUDO D'ORO
3.5000 g., 0.9860 Gold 0.1109 oz. AGW **Ruler:** Clement XI **Obv:** Papal arms **Rev:** Inscription in cartouche and branches **Rev. Inscription:** DIVITAE / NON / PRODE / RVNT

Date	Mintage	VG	F	VF	XF	Unc
ND(1711)-XI	—	350	650	950	1,600	—

KM# 749 SCUDO D'ORO
3.5000 g., 0.9860 Gold 0.1109 oz. AGW **Ruler:** Clement XI **Rev:** Inscription in cartouche **Rev. Inscription:** FERRO / NOCEN / TIVS / AVRVM

Date	Mintage	VG	F	VF	XF	Unc
ND(1712)-XII	—	350	650	950	1,600	—

KM# 757 SCUDO D'ORO
3.5000 g., 0.9860 Gold 0.1109 oz. AGW **Ruler:** Clement XI **Rev:** Inscription in cartouche **Rev. Inscription:** IN / SVDORE / VVLTVS / TVI

Date	Mintage	VG	F	VF	XF	Unc
ND(1714)-XIV	—	350	650	950	1,600	—

KM# 764 SCUDO D'ORO
3.5000 g., 0.9860 Gold 0.1109 oz. AGW **Ruler:** Clement XI **Rev:** Inscription in cartouche **Rev. Inscription:** AVRI / IMPERIO / NE / PARITO

Date	Mintage	VG	F	VF	XF	Unc
ND(1715)-XV	—	400	675	1,000	1,800	—

KM# 765 SCUDO D'ORO
3.5000 g., 0.9860 Gold 0.1109 oz. AGW **Ruler:** Clement XI **Rev:** Bow and arrow pointing up

Date	Mintage	VG	F	VF	XF	Unc
1716-XVI	—	450	900	1,800	2,850	—

KM# 770 SCUDO D'ORO
3.5000 g., 0.9860 Gold 0.1109 oz. AGW **Ruler:** Clement XI **Rev:** Inscription in cartouche **Rev. Inscription:** VT / FACIANT / IVSTITIAS . ET / ELEEMOSYN

Date	Mintage	VG	F	VF	XF	Unc
ND(1717)-XVIII	—	350	650	950	1,600	—

KM# 771 SCUDO D'ORO
3.5000 g., 0.9860 Gold 0.1109 oz. AGW **Ruler:** Clement XI **Obv:** Papal arms **Rev:** Faith standing left

Date	Mintage	VG	F	VF	XF	Unc
ND(1718)-XVIII	—	350	650	950	1,600	—

KM# 775 SCUDO D'ORO
3.5000 g., 0.9860 Gold 0.1109 oz. AGW **Ruler:** Clement XI **Rev:** Olive tree

Date	Mintage	VG	F	VF	XF	Unc
ND(1720)-XX	—	450	900	1,800	2,850	—

KM# 785 SCUDO D'ORO
3.5000 g., 0.9860 Gold 0.1109 oz. AGW **Obv:** Arms of Cardinal Annibale Albani **Rev:** Radiant and flaming dove, date in exergue **Note:** Sede Vacante Issue.

Date	Mintage	VG	F	VF	XF	Unc
MDCCXXI (1721)	—	1,000	2,000	3,750	6,250	—

KM# 790 SCUDO D'ORO
3.5000 g., 0.9860 Gold 0.1109 oz. AGW **Ruler:** Innocent XIII **Obv:** Papal arms **Obv. Legend:** INNOCENT • XIII • ... **Rev:** Inscription in cartouche **Rev. Inscription:** SECTA / MINI / CHARITA / TEM

Date	Mintage	VG	F	VF	XF	Unc
ND(1722)-II	—	600	1,200	2,200	3,500	—

KM# 792 SCUDO D'ORO
3.5000 g., 0.9860 Gold 0.1109 oz. AGW **Ruler:** Innocent XIII **Obv:** Capped bust right **Obv. Legend:** INNOC • XIII • ... **Rev:** Crowned eagle with wings spread of Conti arms

Date	Mintage	VG	F	VF	XF	Unc
ND(1723)-III	—	675	1,350	2,500	4,000	—

KM# 804 SCUDO D'ORO
3.5000 g., 0.9860 Gold 0.1109 oz. AGW **Ruler:** Innocent XIII **Obv:** Arms of Cardinal Annibale Albani **Rev:** Radiant and flaming dove

Date	Mintage	VG	F	VF	XF	Unc
1724	—	1,350	2,750	5,000	8,500	—

KM# 811 SCUDO D'ORO
3.5000 g., 0.9860 Gold 0.1109 oz. AGW **Ruler:** Benedict XIII **Obv:** Papal arms **Rev:** Ceremony of opening the Holy Door **Note:** Holy Year Issue.

Date	Mintage	VG	F	VF	XF	Unc
MDCCXXV-II (1725)	—	675	1,350	2,500	4,000	—

KM# 854 SCUDO D'ORO
3.5000 g., 0.9860 Gold 0.1109 oz. AGW **Ruler:** Clement XII **Obv:** Papal arms **Rev:** Inscription with date below in cartouche with straight sides **Rev. Inscription:** LVMEN / RECTIS

Date	Mintage	VG	F	VF	XF	Unc
1734-V	—	250	350	500	750	—

KM# 866 SCUDO D'ORO
3.5000 g., 0.9860 Gold 0.1109 oz. AGW **Ruler:** Clement XII **Rev:** Inscription as above, cartouche with arched side, sea shell at top

Date	Mintage	VG	F	VF	XF	Unc
1735-V	—	250	350	500	750	—

KM# 867 SCUDO D'ORO
3.5000 g., 0.9860 Gold 0.1109 oz. AGW **Ruler:** Clement XII **Rev:** Inscription and cartouche as above, cherub face at top

Date	Mintage	VG	F	VF	XF	Unc
1735-V	—	250	350	500	750	—

KM# 868 SCUDO D'ORO
3.5000 g., 0.9860 Gold 0.1109 oz. AGW **Ruler:** Clement XII **Obv:** Oval Papal arms **Rev:** Inscription date in cartouche **Rev. Inscription:** LABOR / ADDITVS

Date	Mintage	VG	F	VF	XF	Unc
1735-VI	—	250	350	500	750	—

KM# 869 SCUDO D'ORO
3.5000 g., 0.9860 Gold 0.1109 oz. AGW **Ruler:** Clement XII **Obv:** Bust right

Date	Mintage	VG	F	VF	XF	Unc
1735-VI	—	350	650	800	1,250	—

KM# 880 SCUDO D'ORO
3.5000 g., 0.9860 Gold 0.1109 oz. AGW **Ruler:** Clement XII **Rev:** Inscription date in wreath **Rev. Inscription:** LABOR / ADDITVS

Date	Mintage	VG	F	VF	XF	Unc
1736-VI	—	350	650	800	1,250	—

KM# 887 SCUDO D'ORO
3.5000 g., 0.9860 Gold 0.1109 oz. AGW **Ruler:** Clement XII **Obv:** Capped bust right **Obv. Legend:** CLEM : XII • P • M • A • IX **Rev:** Inscription, date within wreath **Rev. Inscription:** DE.LVTO / FAECIS

Date	Mintage	VG	F	VF	XF	Unc
1738-VIII	—	250	350	500	750	—
1738-IX	—	250	350	500	750	—

KM# 688 DOPPIA (2) SCUDO D'ORO
7.0000 g., 0.9860 Gold 0.2219 oz. AGW **Ruler:** Clement XI **Obv:** Papal arms on globe **Rev. Inscription:** QVI . AVRVM * DILIGIT / NON . IVSTI / FICABITVR

Date	Mintage	VG	F	VF	XF	Unc
ND(1706)-VI	—	1,150	2,200	4,000	6,500	—

KM# 701 DOPPIA (2) SCUDO D'ORO
7.0000 g., 0.9860 Gold 0.2219 oz. AGW **Ruler:** Clement XI **Obv:** Papal arms **Rev:** St. Francis kneeling left receiving the stigmata

Date	Mintage	VG	F	VF	XF	Unc
ND(1707)-VII	—	1,350	2,750	5,000	8,000	—

KM# 721 DOPPIA (2) SCUDO D'ORO
7.0000 g., 0.9860 Gold 0.2219 oz. AGW **Ruler:** Clement XI **Obv:** Ornate Papal arms **Rev:** Radiant St. Francis

Date	Mintage	VG	F	VF	XF	Unc
ND(1709)-IX	—	1,350	2,750	5,000	8,000	—

KM# 739 DOPPIA (2) SCUDO D'ORO
7.0000 g., 0.9860 Gold 0.2219 oz. AGW **Ruler:** Clement XI **Obv:** Bust left **Obv. Legend:** CLEMENS • XI • P • M • ... **Rev:** Inscription in cartouche **Rev. Inscription:** REDDE / PROXIMO / IN • TEMPORE / SVO

Date	Mintage	VG	F	VF	XF	Unc
ND(1710)-X	—	1,150	2,200	4,000	6,500	—

KM# 750 DOPPIA (2) SCUDO D'ORO
7.0000 g., 0.9860 Gold 0.2219 oz. AGW **Ruler:** Clement XI **Obv:** Papal arms **Rev:** Inscription date in cartouche **Rev. Inscription:** FERRO / NOCENTIVS / AVRVM

Date	Mintage	VG	F	VF	XF	Unc
1712-XII	—	1,150	2,200	4,000	6,500	—

KM# 758 DOPPIA (2) SCUDO D'ORO
7.0000 g., 0.9860 Gold 0.2219 oz. AGW **Ruler:** Clement XI **Obv:** Bust left **Rev. Inscription:** FOENVS / PECVNIAE / FVNVS / EST / ANIMAE

Date	Mintage	VG	F	VF	XF	Unc
ND(1714)-XIV	—	1,150	2,200	4,000	6,500	—

KM# 786 DOPPIA (2) SCUDO D'ORO
7.0000 g., 0.9860 Gold 0.2219 oz. AGW **Obv:** Arms of Cardinal Annibale Albani **Rev:** Radiant and flaming dove **Note:** Sede Vacante Issue.

Date	Mintage	VG	F	VF	XF	Unc
ND(1721)	—	—	—	7,500	—	—

KM# 812 DOPPIA (2) SCUDO D'ORO
7.0000 g., 0.9860 Gold 0.2219 oz. AGW **Ruler:** Benedict XIII **Obv:** Papal arms **Rev:** Ceremony of opening the Holy Door **Note:** Holy Year Issue.

Date	Mintage	VG	F	VF	XF	Unc
MDCCXXV-II (1725)	—	1,650	3,250	6,000	9,000	—

KM# 839 DOPPIA (2) SCUDO D'ORO
7.0000 g., 0.9860 Gold 0.2219 oz. AGW **Obv:** Arms of Cardinal Annibale Albani **Rev:** Radiant and flaming dove **Note:** Sede Vacante Issue.

Date	Mintage	VG	F	VF	XF	Unc
MDCCXXX (1730)	—	—	—	6,000	—	—

KM# 690 QUADRUPLA (4) SCUDO D'ORO
14.0000 g., 0.9860 Gold 0.4438 oz. AGW **Ruler:** Clement XI **Obv:** Bust right **Rev:** Piety (left) at altar attempting to drive away Discord (right), date in exergue

Date	Mintage	VG	F	VF	XF	Unc
1706-VI Rare	—	—	—	—	—	—

KM# 689 QUADRUPLA (4) SCUDO D'ORO
14.0000 g., 0.9860 Gold 0.4438 oz. AGW **Ruler:** Clement XI **Obv:** Papal arms **Rev:** Madonna with child standing, date in exergue

Date	Mintage	VG	F	VF	XF	Unc
MDCCVI-VI (1706)	—	3,000	6,000	9,500	14,500	—

KM# 703 QUADRUPLA (4) SCUDO D'ORO
14.0000 g., 0.9860 Gold 0.4438 oz. AGW **Ruler:** Clement XI **Rev:** The 3 Graces standing before a temple

Date	Mintage	VG	F	VF	XF	Unc
ND(1707)-VII Rare	—	—	—	—	—	—

KM# 702 QUADRUPLA (4) SCUDO D'ORO
14.0000 g., 0.9860 Gold 0.4438 oz. AGW **Ruler:** Clement XI **Obv:** Papal arms **Rev:** Charity standing with children

Date	Mintage	VG	F	VF	XF	Unc
ND(1707)-VII	—	3,000	6,000	9,500	14,500	—

KM# 223 MEZZO (1/2) ZECCHINO
1.7260 g., 0.9980 Gold 0.0554 oz. AGW **Ruler:** Clement XII **Obv:** Holy Mother Church seated in clouds **Rev:** Papal arms

Date	Mintage	VG	F	VF	XF	Unc
1739	—	250	350	500	750	—

KM# 931 MEZZO (1/2) ZECCHINO
1.7260 g., 0.9980 Gold 0.0554 oz. AGW **Obv:** Cardinal arms of Annibale Albani **Rev:** Radiant Holy Mother Church, seated **Note:** Sede Vacante Issue.

Date	Mintage	VG	F	VF	XF	Unc
1740	—	275	375	600	900	—

KM# 932 MEZZO (1/2) ZECCHINO
1.7260 g., 0.9980 Gold 0.0554 oz. AGW **Ruler:** Benedict XIV **Obv:** Radiant Holy Mother Church, seated **Rev:** Papal arms **Rev. Legend:** DEDIT PIGNVS

Date	Mintage	VG	F	VF	XF	Unc
1740	—	250	350	600	750	—
1741	—	250	350	500	750	—

KM# 933 MEZZO (1/2) ZECCHINO
1.7260 g., 0.9980 Gold 0.0554 oz. AGW **Ruler:** Benedict XIV **Obv:** Radiant Holy Mother Church, seated **Rev:** Papal arms **Rev. Legend:** REPENTE DE CAELO **Note:** Varieties exist in shield shape.

Date	Mintage	VG	F	VF	XF	Unc
1740-I	—	200	300	400	500	750
1741	—	200	300	400	500	750
1743	—	200	300	400	500	750
1746	—	200	300	400	500	750
1747	—	200	300	400	500	750
1749-IX	—	200	300	400	500	750
1750-IVB.	—	200	300	400	500	750
1751-XI	—	200	300	400	500	750
1751-BEN.XVI. Error	—	275	325	500	600	850
1753-XIII	—	200	300	400	500	750
1755-XV	—	200	300	400	500	750
1756-XVI	—	200	300	400	500	750

KM# 970 MEZZO (1/2) ZECCHINO
1.7260 g., 0.9980 Gold 0.0554 oz. AGW **Ruler:** Benedict XIV **Obv:** Radiant Holy Mother Church, seated **Obv. Legend:** BEN • XIV • P M A • IVB **Rev:** Papal arms **Note:** Holy Year Issue.

Date	Mintage	VG	F	VF	XF	Unc
1750	—	275	375	600	900	—

KM# 982 MEZZO (1/2) ZECCHINO
1.7260 g., 0.9980 Gold 0.0554 oz. AGW **Ruler:** Clement XIII **Obv:** Papal arms **Obv. Legend:** CLEMENS XIII **Rev:** Radiant Holy Mother Church, seated

Date	Mintage	VG	F	VF	XF	Unc
1758-I	—	200	300	400	500	750
1767-IX	—	200	300	400	500	750

KM# 1010 MEZZO (1/2) ZECCHINO
1.7260 g., 0.9980 Gold 0.0554 oz. AGW **Ruler:** Clement XIV **Obv:** Papal arms **Obv. Legend:** CLEMENS • XIV ... **Rev:** Radiant Holy Mother Church, seated

Date	Mintage	VG	F	VF	XF	Unc
1769-I	—	225	325	450	600	850
1769-II	—	225	325	450	600	850

KM# 1241 MEZZO (1/2) ZECCHINO
1.7260 g., 0.9980 Gold 0.0554 oz. AGW **Ruler:** Pius VI **Obv:** Papal oval arms **Obv. Legend:** PIVS • SEXTVS • ... **Rev:** Radiant Holy Mother Church, seated

Date	Mintage	VG	F	VF	XF	Unc
1796-XXII	—	250	350	500	750	—
1797-XXII	—	—	—	—	—	—

KM# 820 ZECCHINO
3.4520 g., 0.9980 Gold 0.1108 oz. AGW **Ruler:** Benedict XIII **Obv:** Holy Mother Church seated in clouds **Rev:** Rose with buds and stem, value above, date in exergue

Date	Mintage	VG	F	VF	XF	Unc
1729	—	750	1,500	2,500	3,500	—

KM# 840 ZECCHINO
3.4520 g., 0.9980 Gold 0.1108 oz. AGW **Rev:** Arms of Cardinal Annibale Albani **Note:** Sede Vacante issue.

Date	Mintage	VG	F	VF	XF	Unc
1730	—	800	1,600	2,750	4,000	—

KM# 888 ZECCHINO
3.4520 g., 0.9980 Gold 0.1108 oz. AGW **Ruler:** Clement XII **Obv:** Holy Mother Church, seated **Obv. Legend:** CLEMENS • XII ... **Rev:** Radiant dove above Papal arms **Note:** Slight variations in shield shape.

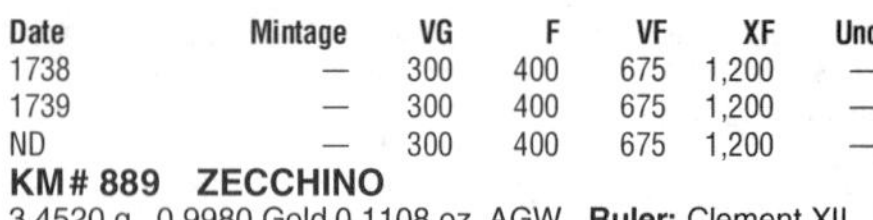

Date	Mintage	VG	F	VF	XF	Unc
1738	—	300	400	675	1,200	—
1739	—	300	400	675	1,200	—
ND	—	300	400	675	1,200	—

KM# 889 ZECCHINO

3.4520 g., 0.9980 Gold 0.1108 oz. AGW **Ruler:** Clement XII **Obv:** Papal arms, value at sides

Date	Mintage	VG	F	VF	XF	Unc
ND (1739) Rare	—	—	—	—	—	—

KM# 935 ZECCHINO

3.4520 g., 0.9980 Gold 0.1108 oz. AGW **Ruler:** Benedict XIV **Obv:** Radiant Holy Mother Church, seated **Obv. Legend:** BEN • XIV • P • M • ... **Rev:** Radiant dove above Papal arms **Rev. Legend:** DEDIT-DIGNVS

Date	Mintage	VG	F	VF	XF	Unc
1740-I	—	225	325	450	600	850

KM# 934 ZECCHINO

3.4520 g., 0.9980 Gold 0.1108 oz. AGW **Obv:** Radiant Holy Mother Church, seated **Obv. Legend:** SEDE VACAN 1740 **Rev:** Radiant dove above Cardinal arms **Note:** Sede Vacante issue. Varieties in size of Church figure and shield shape.

Date	Mintage	VG	F	VF	XF	Unc
1740	—	300	400	625	1,200	—

KM# 936 ZECCHINO

3.4520 g., 0.9980 Gold 0.1108 oz. AGW **Obv:** Radiant Holy Mother Church, seated **Rev:** Radiant dove above Papal arms

Date	Mintage	VG	F	VF	XF	Unc
1740-I	—	225	325	450	600	850

KM# 943 ZECCHINO

3.4520 g., 0.9980 Gold 0.1108 oz. AGW **Ruler:** Benedict XIV **Obv:** Radiant Holy Mother Church, seated **Obv. Legend:** BEN • XIV • P • M • ... **Rev:** Radiant dove above Papal arms **Rev. Legend:** REPENTE DE CAELO **Note:** Varieties of shield shape.

Date	Mintage	VG	F	VF	XF	Unc
1741-I	—	225	325	450	600	850
1741-II	—	225	325	450	600	850
1742	—	225	325	450	600	850
1743	—	225	325	450	600	850
1744	—	225	325	450	600	850
1745	—	225	325	450	600	850
1746	—	225	325	450	600	850
1747	—	225	325	450	600	850
1748-IX	—	225	325	450	600	850
1749-IX	—	225	325	450	600	850
1751-XI	—	225	325	450	600	850
1752-XII	—	225	325	450	600	850
1752-XIII	—	225	325	450	600	850
1753-XIII	—	225	325	450	600	850
1753-XIV	—	225	325	450	600	850
1754-XIV	—	225	325	450	600	850
1754-XV	—	225	325	450	600	850
1755-XVI	—	225	325	450	600	850
1756-XVI	—	225	325	450	600	850
1756-XVII	—	225	325	450	600	850

KM# 971 ZECCHINO

3.4520 g., 0.9980 Gold 0.1108 oz. AGW **Ruler:** Benedict XIV **Obv:** Radiant Holy Mother Church, seated **Obv. Legend:** BEN • XIV • P • M • A • IVB **Rev:** Radiant dove above Papal arms **Rev. Legend:** REPENTE DE CAELO **Note:** Holy Year issue.

Date	Mintage	VG	F	VF	XF	Unc
1750	—	300	400	625	1,200	—

KM# 983 ZECCHINO

3.4520 g., 0.9980 Gold 0.1108 oz. AGW **Ruler:** Benedict XIV **Obv:** Radiant Holy Mother Church, seated **Obv. Legend:** BEN • XIV • ... **Rev:** Radiant dove above Papal arms **Rev. Legend:** REPENTE DE CAELO **Note:** Sede Vacante issue.

Date	Mintage	VG	F	VF	XF	Unc
1758	—	300	550	850	1,350	—

KM# 984 ZECCHINO

3.4520 g., 0.9980 Gold 0.1108 oz. AGW **Ruler:** Clement XIII **Obv:** Papal arms **Obv. Legend:** CLEMENS • XIII • ... **Rev:** Radiant Holy Mother Church, seated

Date	Mintage	VG	F	VF	XF	Unc
1758-I	—	225	325	450	600	850
1759-II	—	225	325	450	600	850
1764-V	—	225	325	450	600	850
1764-VI	—	225	325	450	600	850
1766-VIII	—	225	325	450	600	850
1769-XI	—	225	325	450	600	850

KM# 999 ZECCHINO

3.4520 g., 0.9980 Gold 0.1108 oz. AGW **Ruler:** Clement XIII **Obv:** Papal arms **Obv. Legend:** CLEMENS • XIII • PONT • ... **Rev:** Radiant seated figure, right

Date	Mintage	VG	F	VF	XF	Unc
1760-III	—	225	325	450	600	850
1761-IV	—	225	325	450	600	850
1762-IV	—	225	325	450	600	850

KM# 1012 ZECCHINO

3.4520 g., 0.9980 Gold 0.1108 oz. AGW **Ruler:** Clement XIV **Obv:** Papal arms **Obv. Legend:** CLEMENS • XIV • PONT • ... **Rev:** Radiant Holy Mother Church, seated

Date	Mintage	VG	F	VF	XF	Unc
1769-I	—	250	350	500	700	1,000
1770-II	—	250	350	500	700	1,000
ND-II	—	250	350	500	1,000	—
1772-III	—	250	350	500	700	1,000
1773-V	—	250	350	500	700	1,000

KM# 1011 ZECCHINO

3.4520 g., 0.9980 Gold 0.1108 oz. AGW **Obv:** Radiant dove above Cardinal arms **Obv. Legend:** SEDE • VA CANTE • **Rev:** Radiant Holy Mother Church, seated **Note:** Sede Vacante Issue.

Date	Mintage	VG	F	VF	XF	Unc
1769	—	350	650	950	1,500	2,250

KM# 1024 ZECCHINO

3.4520 g., 0.9980 Gold 0.1108 oz. AGW **Obv:** Radiant dove above Cardinal arms **Obv. Legend:** SEDE • VA CANTE • **Rev:** Radiant Holy Mother Church, seated **Note:** Sede Vacante Issue.

Date	Mintage	VG	F	VF	XF	Unc
1774	—	350	650	950	1,500	2,250

KM# 1029 ZECCHINO

3.4520 g., 0.9980 Gold 0.1108 oz. AGW **Ruler:** Pius VI **Obv:** Papal arms **Obv. Legend:** PIVS • VI • PONT • ... **Rev:** Radiant Holy Mother Church, seated

Date	Mintage	VG	F	VF	XF	Unc
1775-I	—	250	350	500	700	1,000
1776-II	—	250	350	500	700	1,000

KM# 1046 ZECCHINO

3.4520 g., 0.9980 Gold 0.1108 oz. AGW **Ruler:** Pius VI **Obv:** Papal oval arms **Obv. Legend:** PIVS • SEXTVS • PON • ... **Rev:** Radiant Holy Mother Church, seated

Date	Mintage	VG	F	VF	XF	Unc
1776-II	—	—	—	—	—	—
1783-IX	—	225	325	450	600	850
1784-IX	—	225	325	450	600	850
1784-X	—	225	325	450	600	850

KM# 855 2 ZECCHINI

6.9040 g., 0.9980 Gold 0.2215 oz. AGW **Ruler:** Clement XII **Obv:** Papal arms **Rev:** Figure of Church seated in clouds

Date	Mintage	VG	F	VF	XF	Unc
ND(1731)-II Rare	—	—	—	—	—	—
1739-IX Rare	—	—	—	—	—	—

KM# 938 2 ZECCHINI

6.9040 g., 0.9980 Gold 0.2215 oz. AGW **Obv:** Figure of Church seated in clouds, date in legend **Rev:** Arms of Cardinal Annibale Albani **Note:** Sede Vacante Issue.

Date	Mintage	VG	F	VF	XF	Unc
1740	—	1,000	2,000	3,500	—	—

KM# 956 2 ZECCHINI

6.9040 g., 0.9980 Gold 0.2215 oz. AGW **Ruler:** Benedict XIV **Obv:** Radiant Holy Mother Church, seated **Obv. Legend:** BENEDIC • XIV • PONT • ... **Rev:** Radiant dove above Papal arms **Rev. Legend:** REPENTE DE CAELO

Date	Mintage	VG	F	VF	XF	Unc
1748-VIII	—	500	900	1,600	2,600	—

KM# 985 2 ZECCHINI

6.9040 g., 0.9980 Gold 0.2215 oz. AGW **Ruler:** Clement XIII **Obv:** Papal oval arms **Obv. Legend:** CLEMENS • XIII • PONT • ... **Rev:** Radiant Holy Mother Church, seated

Date	Mintage	VG	F	VF	XF	Unc
1759-I	—	400	750	1,500	2,000	—
1766-VIII	—	400	750	1,500	2,000	—

KM# 1031 15 PAOLI (Mezza Doppia D'oro)
2.7345 g., 0.9170 Gold 0.0806 oz. AGW **Ruler:** Pius VI **Obv:** Flower sprigs above date **Obv. Legend:** FLORET • IN • DOMO • DOMINI **Rev:** St. seated in clouds **Rev. Legend:** APOSTOLOR PRINCEPS

Date	Mintage	F	VF	XF	Unc	BU
1776	—	250	350	500	700	1,000
1777	—	250	350	500	700	1,000
1778	—	250	350	500	700	1,000
1782	—	250	350	500	700	1,000
1783	—	250	350	500	700	1,000
1784	—	250	350	500	700	1,000

KM# 1050 15 PAOLI (Mezza Doppia D'oro)
2.7345 g., 0.9170 Gold 0.0806 oz. AGW **Ruler:** Pius VI

Date	Mintage	F	VF	XF	Unc	BU
1787	—	300	400	625	1,000	—

KM# 1032 30 PAOLI (Doppia D'oro)
5.4690 g., 0.9170 Gold 0.1612 oz. AGW **Ruler:** Pius VI **Obv:** Flower sprigs above date **Obv. Legend:** FLORET • IN • DOMO • DOMINI **Rev:** Value .P. 30 in exergue **Rev. Legend:** APOSTOLOR • PRINCEPS •

Date	Mintage	F	VF	XF	Unc	BU
1776	—	250	350	500	700	1,000
1777	—	250	350	500	700	1,000
1778	—	250	350	500	700	1,000
1779	—	250	350	500	700	1,000
1780	—	250	350	500	700	1,000
1781	—	250	350	500	700	1,000
1782	—	250	350	500	700	1,000
1783	—	250	350	500	700	1,000
1784	—	250	350	500	700	1,000
1785	—	250	350	500	700	1,000

KM# 1049 30 PAOLI (Doppia D'oro)
5.4690 g., 0.9170 Gold 0.1612 oz. AGW **Ruler:** Pius VI **Obv:** Flower sprigs above date **Obv. Legend:** FLOR ET • IN • DOMO • DOMINI **Rev:** Value without .P. 30 in exergue **Rev. Legend:** APOSTOLOR PRINCEPS

Date	Mintage	F	VF	XF	Unc	BU
1786	—	250	350	500	700	1,000
1787	—	250	350	500	700	1,000
1788	—	250	350	500	700	1,000
1790	—	250	350	500	700	1,000
1791	—	250	350	500	700	1,000
1792	—	250	350	500	700	1,000
1793	—	250	350	500	700	1,000

KM# 1035 60 PAOLI (Due Doppie D'oro)
10.9380 g., 0.9170 Gold 0.3225 oz. AGW **Ruler:** Pius VI **Obv:** Flower sprigs above date **Obv. Legend:** FLORET • IN • DOMO DOMINI * **Rev:** Radiant, seated figure on clouds **Rev. Legend:** APOSTOLOR PRINCEPS *

Date	Mintage	F	VF	XF	Unc	BU
1777	—	550	800	1,100	1,750	—

PAPAL STATES

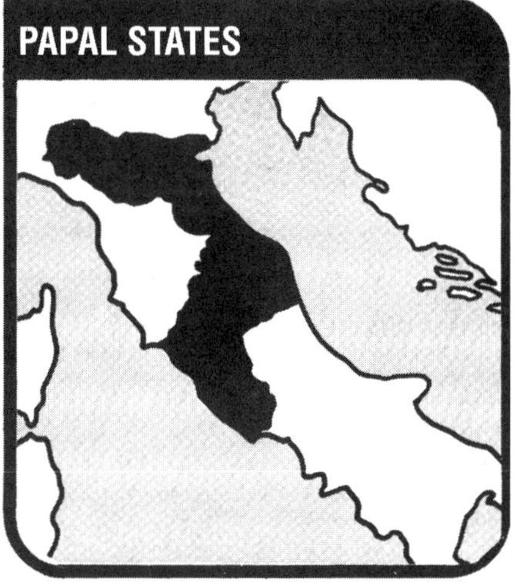

The 21 Papal States - City Issues spanned the Papal states from one end to the other. Most of the cities had been the holy see for hundreds of years. Many of them housed religious architecture and relics that were a veritable history of the church. Many had strong local families that helped administrate the city and occasionally opposed the Papal authority. Most of these cities stayed in the Papal states until 1860 when Papal territories began to crumble due to the move for unification of all Italy.

MINTS

17 of the mints functioned only during the Napoleonic period.

1. Ancona
2. Ascoli
3. Bologna
4. Civitavecchia
5. Fano
6. Fermo
7. Ferrara
8. Foligno
9. Gubbio
10. Macerata
11. Matelica
12. Montaito
13. Pergola
14. Perugia
15. Ravenna
16. Ronciglione
17. San Severino
18. Spoleto
19. Terni
20. Tivoli
21. Viterbo

EXTRINSIC MINT

Avignon (Southern France)

PONTIFFS

Refer to Papal States.

MONETARY SYSTEM

6 Quattrini = 1 Bolognino or Baiocco
5 Baiocchi = 1 Grossi
2 Grossi = 1 Giuli = 1 Paoli
3 Giulio = 3 Paoli = 1 Testone
10 Giulio = 10 Paoli = 1 Scudo
3 Scudi = 1 Doppia

PAPAL STATES-ANCONA

Anconna

A city in the Marches, was founded by Syracusan refugees about 390 B.C. It became a semi-independent republic under papal protection in the 14th century, and a papal state in 1532. From 1797 until the formation of the United Kingdom of Italy it was part of the Roman Republic(1798-99), a papal state (1799-1808), part of the Italian Kingdom of Napoleon (1808-14), a papal state (1814-48),a part of the Roman Republic (1848-49), and a papal state(1849-60).

MINT MARK

A – Ancona

MONETARY SYSTEM

100 Baiocchi = 1 **Scudo**

NOTE: For later issues see Papal-Roman Republic-Ancona.

CITY

EMERGENCY COINAGE

KM# 1 BAIOCCO
Copper **Obv:** Papal arms **Rev:** Written value, date within wreath

Date	Mintage	Good	VG	F	VF	XF
1796//XXI	—	9.00	20.00	30.00	50.00	—
1796//XXII	—	9.00	20.00	30.00	50.00	—

KM# 4 BAIOCCO
Copper **Obv:** Papal arms **Rev:** Written value above star within wreath

Date	Mintage	Good	VG	F	VF	XF
ND//XXI	—	9.00	20.00	30.00	50.00	—
ND//XXII	—	9.00	20.00	30.00	50.00	—

KM# 2 2 BAIOCCHI
Copper **Obv:** Papal arms **Obv. Legend:** PIVS • SEXTVS .... **Rev:** Written value, date within wreath

Date	Mintage	Good	VG	F	VF	XF
1796//XXII	—	9.00	20.00	35.00	60.00	—

KM# 5 2 BAIOCCHI
Copper **Obv:** Papal arms **Obv. Legend:** PIVS • SEXTVS ... **Rev:** Written value, date within wreath

Date	Mintage	Good	VG	F	VF	XF
1796//XXII	—	9.00	20.00	35.00	60.00	—

KM# 3 2-1/2 BAIOCCHI
Copper **Obv:** Stars above written value, date **Rev:** Saint's bust left **Rev. Legend:** ...PRINCEPS

Date	Mintage	Good	VG	F	VF	XF
1796	—	10.00	20.00	30.00	60.00	—

PAPAL STATES-ASCOLI

A city in the Marches, was ruled by prince-bishops from Charlemagne's time until becoming a free republic in 1185. It became a papal possession in 1426.

NOTE: For later issues see Papal-Roman Republic-Ascoli.

CITY

EMERGENCY COINAGE

KM# A1 QUATTRINI
Copper **Obv:** Papal arms **Obv. Legend:** PIVS SEXTVS PON M A XX **Rev:** Standing figure of Pope **Rev. Legend:** S FELICIANO

Date	Mintage	Good	VG	F	VF	XF
1794	—	15.00	35.00	60.00	100	—
1795	—	15.00	35.00	60.00	100	—

KM# 1 QUATTRINI
Copper **Obv:** Papal arms **Obv. Legend:** PIVS SEXTVS P M A XXIII **Rev:** Stars above written value, date

Date	Mintage	Good	VG	F	VF	XF
1797//XXIII	—	27.50	60.00	95.00	150	—

KM# 2 1/2 BAIOCCO
Copper **Obv:** Papal arms **Obv. Legend:** PIVS SEXT P M A XXIII **Rev:** Stars above written value

Date	Mintage	Good	VG	F	VF	XF
1797//XXIII	—	25.00	40.00	75.00	120	—

KM# 3 BAIOCCO

Copper **Obv:** Papal arms **Obv. Legend:** PIVS SEXTVS P M A XXIII **Rev:** Written value, date

Date	Mintage	Good	VG	F	VF	XF
1797//XXIII	—	25.00	40.00	75.00	120	—

KM# 4 2-1/2 BAIOCCHI

Copper **Obv:** Stars above written value, date **Rev:** St. Peter **Rev. Legend:** S • P • APOSI...

Date	Mintage	Good	VG	F	VF	XF
ND	—	40.00	75.00	125	200	—
1797	—	40.00	75.00	125	200	—

KM# 5 5 BAIOCCHI

Copper **Obv:** Star above written value within inner circle, date in outer circle with legend **Rev:** St. Peter **Rev. Legend:** SANCTA DEI GENITRIX

Date	Mintage	Good	VG	F	VF	XF
1797//XXIII	—	30.00	50.00	85.00	175	—
1798//XXIII	—	50.00	75.00	125	250	—
1799//XXIII	—	100	175	250	350	—

PAPAL STATES-BOLOGNA

Bolonia

A city in Emilia, began as an independent commune, and after serving under various masters became a papal possession in 1506. Except for the Napoleonic period (1797-1815) and the revolutions of 1821 and 1831, it remained a papal state until 1860.

MINT OFFICIALS' INITIALS

Initials	Date	Name
AB	1721-30	Angelo Bazzanelli
CF	1700-21	Carlo Falconi
GB	1700-21	Girolamo Bevilacqua
GP, PG	1775-99	Girolamo Pignoni
MP	1724-74	Matteo Pignoni

MINT MARK

B – Bologna

MONETARY SYSTEM

(Until 1777)

6 Quattrini = 1 Bolognino
12 Bolognini = 1 Giulio = 1 Bianco
80 to 108 Bolognini = 1 Scudo

(After 1777)

6 Quattrini = 1 Bolognino
5 Baiocchi = 1 Grossi
6 Grossi = 1 Giulio = 1 Paolo
3 Paoli = 1 Testone
100 Baiocchi = 20 Grossi = 1 Scudo
3 Scudi = 1 Doppia

CITY

STANDARD COINAGE

KM# 140 QUATTRINO

Copper **Ruler:** Clement XI **Subject:** Clement XI **Obv:** Lion rampant left with banner **Rev:** Inscription **Rev. Inscription:** BONO/NIA/DOCET

Date	Mintage	VG	F	VF	XF	Unc
1706	—	6.00	10.00	16.50	30.00	—
1707	—	6.00	10.00	16.50	30.00	—
1708	—	6.00	10.00	16.50	30.00	—
1709	—	6.00	10.00	16.50	30.00	—
1710	—	6.00	10.00	16.50	30.00	—
1711	—	6.00	10.00	16.50	30.00	—
1712	—	6.00	10.00	16.50	30.00	—
1713	—	6.00	10.00	16.50	30.00	—
1714	—	6.00	10.00	16.50	30.00	—
1715	—	6.00	10.00	16.50	30.00	—
1716	—	6.00	10.00	16.50	30.00	—
1717	—	6.00	10.00	16.50	30.00	—
1718	—	6.00	10.00	16.50	30.00	—
1719	—	6.00	10.00	16.50	30.00	—
1720	—	6.00	10.00	16.50	30.00	—

KM# 157 QUATTRINO

Copper **Ruler:** Clement XI **Obv:** Lion rampant left, banner inscribed LIBER **Rev:** Inscription within oak wreath **Rev. Inscription:** BONO/NIA/DOCET

Date	Mintage	VG	F	VF	XF	Unc
1712	—	7.00	12.00	20.00	35.00	—

KM# 158 QUATTRINO

Copper **Ruler:** Clement XI **Rev:** Inscription in cartouche **Rev. Inscription:** BONO/NIA/DOCET

Date	Mintage	VG	F	VF	XF	Unc
1715	—	6.00	10.00	16.50	30.00	—
1716	—	6.00	10.00	16.50	30.00	—
1717	—	6.00	10.00	16.50	30.00	—
1718	—	6.00	10.00	16.50	30.00	—

KM# 160 QUATTRINO

Copper **Ruler:** Innocent XIII **Subject:** Innocent XIII **Obv:** Lion rampant left with banner **Rev:** Inscription **Rev. Inscription:** BONO/NIA/DOCET

Date	Mintage	VG	F	VF	XF	Unc
1721	—	10.00	18.00	30.00	50.00	—
1722	—	10.00	18.00	30.00	50.00	—
1723	—	10.00	18.00	30.00	50.00	—

KM# 174 QUATTRINO

Copper **Ruler:** Benedict XIII **Subject:** Benedict XIII **Obv:** Lion rampant left with banner **Rev:** Inscription **Rev. Inscription:** BONO/NIA/DOCET **Note:** Varieties exist.

Date	Mintage	VG	F	VF	XF	Unc
1724	—	9.00	16.00	26.00	40.00	—
1725	—	9.00	16.00	26.00	40.00	—
1726	—	9.00	16.00	26.00	40.00	—
1727	—	9.00	16.00	26.00	40.00	—
1728	—	9.00	16.00	26.00	40.00	—
1729	—	9.00	16.00	26.00	40.00	—
1730	—	9.00	16.00	26.00	40.00	—

KM# 190 QUATTRINO

Copper **Subject:** Clement XII **Obv:** Lion rampant left **Rev:** Inscription **Rev. Inscription:** BONO/NIA/DOCET

Date	Mintage	VG	F	VF	XF	Unc
1730	—	6.00	10.00	16.50	30.00	—
1731	—	6.00	10.00	16.50	30.00	—
1732	—	6.00	10.00	16.50	30.00	—
1733	—	6.00	10.00	16.50	30.00	—
1734	—	6.00	10.00	16.50	30.00	—
1735	—	6.00	10.00	16.50	30.00	—
1736	—	6.00	10.00	16.50	30.00	—
1737	—	6.00	10.00	16.50	30.00	—
1738	—	6.00	10.00	16.50	30.00	—
1739	—	6.00	10.00	16.50	30.00	—
1740	—	6.00	10.00	16.50	30.00	—

KM# 225 QUATTRINO

Copper **Ruler:** Benedict XIV **Obv:** Rampant lion left **Rev:** Inscription, date in exergue **Rev. Inscription:** BONO/NIA/DOCET

Date	Mintage	VG	F	VF	XF	Unc
1741	—	3.00	7.50	15.00	30.00	—
1742	—	3.00	7.50	15.00	30.00	—
1743	—	3.00	7.50	15.00	30.00	—
1744	—	3.00	7.50	15.00	30.00	—
1745	—	3.00	7.50	15.00	30.00	—
1746	—	3.00	7.50	15.00	30.00	—
1747	—	3.00	7.50	15.00	30.00	—
1748	—	3.00	7.50	15.00	30.00	—
1749	—	3.00	7.50	15.00	30.00	—
1750	—	3.00	7.50	15.00	30.00	—
1751	—	3.00	7.50	15.00	30.00	—
1752	—	3.00	7.50	15.00	30.00	—
1753	—	3.00	7.50	15.00	30.00	—
1754	—	3.00	7.50	15.00	30.00	—
1755	—	3.00	7.50	15.00	30.00	—
1756	—	3.00	7.50	15.00	30.00	—
1757	—	3.00	7.50	15.00	30.00	—
1758	—	3.00	7.50	15.00	30.00	—

KM# 266 QUATTRINO

Copper **Ruler:** Pius VI (Sestus) **Obv:** Papal arms **Obv. Legend:** PIVS • VI • ... **Rev:** Inscription, date within wreath **Rev. Inscription:** BONO NIA DOCET

Date	Mintage	VG	F	VF	XF	Unc
1778	—	2.00	3.00	8.00	18.00	—

KM# 267 QUATTRINO

Copper **Ruler:** Pius VI (Sestus) **Obv:** Papal arms **Obv. Legend:** PIVS • VI • PONT • M **Rev:** Inscription, date within wreath **Rev. Inscription:** BONO NIA DOCET

Date	Mintage	VG	F	VF	XF	Unc
1778	—	2.00	3.00	8.00	18.00	—
1779	—	2.00	3.00	8.00	18.00	—

KM# 268 QUATTRINO

Copper **Ruler:** Pius VI (Sestus) **Obv:** Papal arms **Obv. Legend:** PIVS • VI • PONT • M **Rev:** Inscription, date within wreath **Rev. Inscription:** BONO NIA DOCET

Date	Mintage	VG	F	VF	XF	Unc
1778	—	2.50	4.00	9.00	20.00	—
1779	—	2.50	4.00	9.00	20.00	—

KM# 284 QUATTRINO

Copper **Ruler:** Pius VI (Sestus) **Obv:** Papal arms **Obv. Legend:** PIVS • VI • • PONT • M **Rev:** Inscription, date within wreath **Rev. Inscription:** BONO NIA DOCET

Date	Mintage	VG	F	VF	XF	Unc
1779	—	2.00	3.00	8.00	18.00	—

KM# 285 QUATTRINO

Copper **Ruler:** Pius VI (Sestus) **Obv:** Papal arms **Obv. Legend:** PIVS • VI • PONT • M **Rev:** Inscription, date within wreath **Rev. Inscription:** BONO *NIA* DOCET

Date	Mintage	VG	F	VF	XF	Unc
1779	—	2.00	3.00	8.00	18.00	—
1784	—	2.00	3.00	8.00	18.00	—

KM# 286 QUATTRINO

Copper **Ruler:** Pius VI (Sestus) **Obv:** Papal arms **Obv. Legend:** PIVS • VI • PONT • M **Rev:** Star above inscription, date within wreath **Rev. Inscription:** BONO *NIA* DOCET

Date	Mintage	VG	F	VF	XF	Unc
1779	—	2.00	3.00	8.00	18.00	—
1784	—	2.00	3.00	8.00	18.00	—

KM# 301 QUATTRINO

Copper **Ruler:** Pius VI (Sestus) **Obv:** Papal arms **Obv. Legend:** PIVS • VI • PONT • M **Rev:** Inscription, date within wreath **Rev. Inscription:** BONO *NIA* DOCET

Date	Mintage	VG	F	VF	XF	Unc
1784	—	2.00	3.00	8.00	18.00	—

KM# 320 QUATTRINO

Copper **Ruler:** Pius VI (Sestus) **Obv:** Rampant lion above date **Obv. Legend:** BONON * DOCET * **Rev:** Inscription, above written value and stars **Rev. Inscription:** *PIVS* SEXTVS ....

Date	Mintage	VG	F	VF	XF	Unc
1795	—	2.50	4.00	12.50	25.00	—

KM# 325 QUATTRINO

Copper **Ruler:** Pius VI (Sestus) **Obv:** Rampant lion above date **Obv. Legend:** BONON • DOCET • **Rev:** Inscription above written value and stars **Rev. Inscription:** *PIVS* SEXTVS....

Date	Mintage	VG	F	VF	XF	Unc
1796	—	2.50	4.00	12.50	25.00	—

KM# 138 1/2 BOLOGNINO

Copper **Ruler:** Clement XI **Subject:** Clement XI **Obv:** Inscription: BONONIA DOCET in shield **Rev:** Value: MEZO BOLOGNINO, half lion rampant left

Date	Mintage	VG	F	VF	XF	Unc
1709	—	12.00	20.00	35.00	60.00	—
1710	—	12.00	20.00	35.00	60.00	—
1711	—	12.00	20.00	35.00	60.00	—
1712	—	12.00	20.00	35.00	60.00	—
1713	—	12.00	20.00	35.00	60.00	—
1714	—	12.00	20.00	35.00	60.00	—
1715	—	12.00	20.00	35.00	60.00	—

KM# 156 1/2 BOLOGNINO

Copper **Ruler:** Clement XI **Rev:** Value: MEZO BOLOGNINO, lion rampant right

Date	Mintage	VG	F	VF	XF	Unc
1715	—	12.00	20.00	35.00	60.00	—
1716	—	12.00	20.00	35.00	60.00	—
1717	—	12.00	20.00	35.00	60.00	—
1718	—	12.00	20.00	35.00	60.00	—
1719	—	12.00	20.00	35.00	60.00	—
1720	—	12.00	20.00	35.00	60.00	—
1721	—	12.00	20.00	35.00	60.00	—

KM# 161 1/2 BOLOGNINO

Copper **Ruler:** Innocent XIII **Subject:** Innocent XIII **Obv:** Inscription: BONONIA DOCET, AB below in shield **Rev:** Value: MEZO BOLOGNINO, lion rampant right **Note:** The addition of initials AB distinguish the 1/2 Bolonino of Innocent XIII from those of Clement XI.

Date	Mintage	VG	F	VF	XF	Unc
1721	—	20.00	38.00	65.00	100	—
1722	—	20.00	38.00	65.00	100	—
1723	—	20.00	38.00	65.00	100	—
1724	—	20.00	38.00	65.00	100	—

KM# 175 1/2 BOLOGNINO

Copper **Ruler:** Benedict XIII **Subject:** Benedict XIII **Obv:** Inscription: BONONIA DOCET on shield **Rev:** Value: MEZO BOLOGNINO, lion rampant right

Date	Mintage	VG	F	VF	XF	Unc
1724	—	18.00	36.00	60.00	95.00	—
1725	—	18.00	36.00	60.00	95.00	—
1726	—	18.00	36.00	60.00	95.00	—
1727	—	18.00	36.00	60.00	95.00	—
1728	—	18.00	36.00	60.00	95.00	—
1729	—	18.00	36.00	60.00	95.00	—
1730	—	18.00	36.00	60.00	95.00	—

KM# 191 1/2 BOLOGNINO

Copper **Ruler:** Clement XII **Subject:** Clement XII **Obv:** Inscription: BONONIA DOCET on shield **Rev:** Value: MEZO BOLOGNINO, lion rampant right above cartouche

Date	Mintage	VG	F	VF	XF	Unc
1730	—	8.00	15.00	25.00	40.00	—
1731	—	8.00	15.00	25.00	40.00	—
1732	—	8.00	15.00	25.00	40.00	—
1733	—	8.00	15.00	25.00	40.00	—
1734	—	8.00	15.00	25.00	40.00	—
1735	—	8.00	15.00	25.00	40.00	—
1736	—	8.00	15.00	25.00	40.00	—
1737	—	8.00	15.00	25.00	40.00	—
1738	—	8.00	15.00	25.00	40.00	—
1739	—	8.00	15.00	25.00	40.00	—
1740	—	8.00	15.00	25.00	40.00	—

KM# 201 1/2 BOLOGNINO

Copper **Ruler:** Clement XII **Rev:** Lion rampant right without cartouche

KM# 220 1/2 BOLOGNINO

Copper **Obv:** Ornate shield **Obv. Legend:** BONONIA • DOCET **Rev:** Value: MEZO BOLOGNINO (as legend) Rampant lion, right

Date	Mintage	VG	F	VF	XF	Unc
1740	—	4.00	10.00	18.00	32.50	—
1741	—	4.00	10.00	18.00	32.50	—
1742	—	4.00	10.00	18.00	32.50	—
1743	—	4.00	10.00	18.00	32.50	—
1744	—	4.00	10.00	18.00	32.50	—
1745	—	4.00	10.00	18.00	32.50	—
1747	—	4.00	10.00	18.00	32.50	—
1753	—	4.00	10.00	18.00	32.50	—
1755	—	4.00	10.00	18.00	32.50	—
1756	—	4.00	10.00	18.00	32.50	—

KM# 259 1/2 BOLOGNINO

Copper **Ruler:** Pius VI (Sestus) **Obv:** Ornate shield **Rev:** Rampant lion, right

Date	Mintage	VG	F	VF	XF	Unc
1777	—	12.50	25.00	50.00	100	—

KM# 293 1/2 BAIOCCO

Copper **Ruler:** Pius VI (Sestus) **Obv:** Double oval shields with lion head and hat above **Obv. Legend:** MEZZO * BAI ... **Rev:** Inscription, date within wreath **Rev. Inscription:** *PIVS* * VI * PONT * MAX * * AN * VII *

Date	Mintage	VG	F	VF	XF	Unc
1781//VII	—	5.00	12.50	25.00	45.00	—
1784//X	—	5.00	12.50	25.00	45.00	—

KM# 321 1/2 BAIOCCO

Copper **Ruler:** Pius VI (Sestus) **Obv:** Rampant lion, left **Obv. Legend:** BONONIA DOCET **Rev:** Inscription **Rev. Inscription:** *PIUS * SEXTVS * PONTIFEX MAXIMVS...

Date	Mintage	VG	F	VF	XF	Unc
1795//X	—	5.00	12.50	20.00	37.50	—
1796//X	—	5.00	12.50	20.00	37.50	—

KM# 290 BAIOCCO

Copper **Ruler:** Pius VI (Sestus) **Obv:** Double shields with lion head and hat above **Obv. Legend:** * BONONIA * DOCET * BAIOCCO * **Rev:** Flower sprigs within wreath above date **Rev. Legend:** ....* MAX * VNN * VI * (The V, in VNN, is upside down on coin)

Date	Mintage	VG	F	VF	XF	Unc
1780//VI	—	6.00	15.00	30.00	50.00	—

KM# 291 BAIOCCO

Copper **Ruler:** Pius VI (Sestus) **Obv:** Double oval shields with lion head and hat above **Obv. Legend:** DOCET * * BONON **Rev:** Flower sprigs above date **Rev. Legend:** ...NTVS * PONT * MAX *

Date	Mintage	VG	F	VF	XF	Unc
1780//VI	—	6.00	15.00	25.00	42.50	—

KM# 292 BAIOCCO

Copper **Ruler:** Pius VI (Sestus) **Obv:** Double oval shields with lion head and hat above **Obv. Legend:** DOCET * * BONON * **Rev:** Flower sprigs above date **Rev. Legend:** ...TVS * PONT * MAX *

Date	Mintage	VG	F	VF	XF	Unc
1780	—	6.00	15.00	25.00	42.50	—

KM# 295 BAIOCCO

Copper

Date	Mintage	VG	F	VF	XF	Unc
1781//VII	—	6.00	15.00	25.00	42.50	—

KM# 294 BAIOCCO

Copper **Ruler:** Pius VI (Sestus) **Obv:** Two shields **Rev:** Inscription, date within wreath **Rev. Inscription:** PIVS*/ VI*PON*/ *MAX*/ ANN*VII

Date	Mintage	VG	F	VF	XF	Unc
1781//VI	—	6.00	15.00	25.00	42.50	—

KM# 302.1 BAIOCCO

Copper **Ruler:** Pius VI (Sestus) **Obv:** Double oval shields with lion head and hat above **Obv. Legend:** * BAIOCCO * **Rev:** Inscription, date within wreath **Rev. Inscription:** PIVS/ VI • PONT/ MAX*/ ANN • X •

Date	Mintage	VG	F	VF	XF	Unc
1784//X	—	6.00	15.00	25.00	42.50	—

KM# 302.2 BAIOCCO

Copper **Ruler:** Pius VI (Sestus) **Obv:** Double oval shields with lion head and hat above **Obv. Legend:** * BAIOCCO * **Rev:** Inscription, date and stars within wreath **Rev. Inscription:** *PIVS*/VI*PONT*/MAX*/ANN*X

Date	Mintage	VG	F	VF	XF	Unc
1784//X	—	6.00	15.00	25.00	42.50	—

KM# 302.3 BAIOCCO

Copper **Ruler:** Pius VI (Sestus) **Obv:** Double oval shields with lion head and hat above **Obv. Legend:** * BAIOCCO * **Rev:** Inscription above date within wreath **Rev. Inscription:** PIVS*/VI PONT*/MAX*/ANN*X*

Date	Mintage	VG	F	VF	XF	Unc
1784//X	—	6.00	15.00	25.00	42.50	—

KM# 322 BAIOCCO

Copper **Ruler:** Pius VI (Sestus) **Obv:** Rampant lion, left **Obv. Legend:** * DOCET * BONONIA * **Rev:** Inscription **Rev. Inscription:** PIUS/SEXTVS/PONTI FEX/MAXIMVS

Date	Mintage	VG	F	VF	XF	Unc
MDCCXCV (1795)	—	5.00	12.00	22.00	40.00	—
MDCCXCVI (1796)	—	5.00	12.00	22.00	40.00	—

KM# 145 2 BOLOGNINI

Billon **Ruler:** Clement XI **Rev:** St. Peter standing, crosier in left hand **Rev. Legend:** Ends: ... PROTEC

Date	Mintage	VG	F	VF	XF	Unc
1710	—	7.00	14.00	25.00	40.00	—
ND	—	7.00	14.00	25.00	40.00	—

KM# 146 2 BOLOGNINI

Billon **Ruler:** Clement XI **Obv:** Capped bust right, value 2 below **Note:** With and without reverse exergue line.

Date	Mintage	VG	F	VF	XF	Unc
1710	—	7.00	14.00	25.00	40.00	—
ND	—	7.00	14.00	25.00	40.00	—

KM# 151 2 BOLOGNINI

Billon **Ruler:** Clement XI **Obv:** Capped bust right **Rev:** St. Peter standing, crosier in left hand **Rev. Legend:** Ends: ... DE BON

Date	Mintage	VG	F	VF	XF	Unc
1712	—	7.00	14.00	25.00	40.00	—
1713	—	7.00	14.00	25.00	40.00	—
1714	—	7.00	14.00	25.00	40.00	—
1715	—	7.00	14.00	25.00	40.00	—
1716	—	7.00	14.00	25.00	40.00	—

KM# 150 2 BOLOGNINI

Billon **Ruler:** Clement XI **Rev:** St. Peter standing, crosier in right hand

Date	Mintage	VG	F	VF	XF	Unc
1712	—	7.00	14.00	25.00	40.00	—
1713	—	7.00	14.00	25.00	40.00	—
1714	—	7.00	14.00	25.00	40.00	—
1715	—	7.00	14.00	25.00	40.00	—
1716	—	7.00	14.00	25.00	40.00	—

KM# 162 2 BOLOGNINI

Billon **Ruler:** Innocent XIII **Obv:** Capped bust left **Rev:** St. Peter standing

Date	Mintage	VG	F	VF	XF	Unc
1721	—	15.00	30.00	55.00	90.00	—
1722	—	15.00	30.00	55.00	90.00	—
1723	—	15.00	30.00	55.00	90.00	—
1724	—	15.00	30.00	55.00	90.00	—

KM# 176 2 BOLOGNINI

Billon **Ruler:** Innocent XIII **Obv:** Two shields below canopy and keys **Note:** Sede Vacante Issue

Date	Mintage	VG	F	VF	XF	Unc
1724	—	17.50	35.00	65.00	110	—

KM# 177 2 BOLOGNINI

Billon **Ruler:** Benedict XIII **Obv:** Capped bust right **Rev:** St. Peter standing, value 2 below **Note:** Sede Vacante Issue

Date	Mintage	VG	F	VF	XF	Unc
1724	—	10.00	22.00	40.00	65.00	—
1725	—	10.00	22.00	40.00	65.00	—
1726	—	10.00	22.00	40.00	65.00	—
1727	—	10.00	22.00	40.00	65.00	—
1728	—	10.00	22.00	40.00	65.00	—

KM# 183 2 BOLOGNINI

Billon **Ruler:** Benedict XIII **Rev:** St. Petronius standing without value

Date	Mintage	VG	F	VF	XF	Unc
1729	—	10.00	22.00	40.00	65.00	—

KM# 192 2 BOLOGNINI

Billon **Ruler:** Benedict XIII **Obv:** Two shields below canopy and keys **Rev:** St. Peter standing **Note:** Sede Vacante Issue

Date	Mintage	VG	F	VF	XF	Unc
1730	—	10.00	20.00	38.00	62.50	—

KM# 198 2 BOLOGNINI

Billon **Ruler:** Clement XII **Obv:** Capped bust right **Rev:** St. Peter standing, hand raised in Benediction

Date	Mintage	VG	F	VF	XF	Unc
1731	—	7.00	14.00	25.00	40.00	—
1732	—	7.00	14.00	25.00	40.00	—
1733	—	7.00	14.00	25.00	40.00	—

KM# 202 2 BOLOGNINI

Billon **Ruler:** Clement XII **Obv:** Capped bust left

Date	Mintage	VG	F	VF	XF	Unc
1734	—	7.00	14.00	25.00	40.00	—

KM# 203 2 BOLOGNINI

Billon **Ruler:** Clement XII **Obv:** Capped bust left, value 2 below

Date	Mintage	VG	F	VF	XF	Unc
1734	—	7.00	14.00	25.00	40.00	—

KM# 206 2 BOLOGNINI

Billon **Ruler:** Clement XII **Obv:** Capped bust right **Rev:** St. Peter standing, hand low

Date	Mintage	VG	F	VF	XF	Unc
1735	—	7.00	14.00	25.00	40.00	—
1736	—	7.00	14.00	25.00	40.00	—
1737	—	7.00	14.00	25.00	40.00	—

KM# 227 2 BOLOGNINI

Billon **Ruler:** Benedict XIV **Obv:** Capped bust right **Rev:** St. Peter **Rev. Legend:** S • PETRON • ...

Date	Mintage	VG	F	VF	XF	Unc
1742	—	5.00	15.00	25.00	40.00	—
1744	—	5.00	15.00	25.00	40.00	—
1745	—	5.00	15.00	25.00	40.00	—
1746	—	5.00	15.00	25.00	40.00	—
1753	—	5.00	15.00	25.00	40.00	—
1756	—	5.00	15.00	25.00	40.00	—

KM# 269 2 BOLOGNINI

Billon **Ruler:** Pius VI (Sestus) **Obv:** Capped bust right **Obv. Legend:** PEVS • VI • PONT • MAX • **Rev:** St. Peter **Rev. Legend:** S • PETRON • ... **Note:** Weight varies: 1.20-1.80 grams

Date	Mintage	VG	F	VF	XF	Unc
1778	—	3.00	10.00	20.00	38.00	—
1779	—	3.00	10.00	20.00	38.00	—
1784	—	3.00	10.00	20.00	38.00	—
1785	—	3.00	10.00	20.00	38.00	—
1786	—	3.00	10.00	20.00	38.00	—
1787	—	3.00	10.00	20.00	38.00	—
1788	—	3.00	10.00	20.00	38.00	—
1789	—	3.00	10.00	20.00	38.00	—
1790	—	3.00	10.00	20.00	38.00	—
1791	—	3.00	10.00	20.00	38.00	—
1792	—	3.00	10.00	20.00	38.00	—
1793	—	3.00	10.00	20.00	38.00	—
1794	—	3.00	10.00	20.00	38.00	—
1795	—	3.00	10.00	20.00	38.00	—
1796	—	3.00	10.00	20.00	38.00	—

KM# 323 2 BAIOCCHI

Copper **Ruler:** Pius VI (Sestus) **Obv:** Rampant lion, left **Obv. Legend:** * DOCET * BONONIA * **Rev:** Inscription, stars **Rev. Legend:** PIUS/SEXTVS/PONTIFEX/MAXIMVS

Date	Mintage	VG	F	VF	XF	Unc
1795	—	7.50	20.00	30.00	50.00	—
1796	—	7.50	20.00	30.00	50.00	—

KM# 139 4 BOLOGNINI

Billon **Ruler:** Clement XI **Obv:** Capped bust right **Rev:** St. Peter seated on cloud blessing city below

Date	Mintage	VG	F	VF	XF	Unc
1709	—	10.00	20.00	35.00	60.00	—
1710	—	10.00	20.00	35.00	60.00	—
1711	—	10.00	20.00	35.00	60.00	—
1712	—	10.00	20.00	35.00	60.00	—
1713	—	10.00	20.00	35.00	60.00	—
1714	—	10.00	20.00	35.00	60.00	—
1715	—	10.00	20.00	35.00	60.00	—
1716	—	10.00	20.00	35.00	60.00	—
ND	—	10.00	20.00	35.00	60.00	—

KM# 147 4 BOLOGNINI

Billon **Ruler:** Clement XI **Obv:** Capped bust left

Date	Mintage	VG	F	VF	XF	Unc
1710	—	10.00	20.00	35.00	60.00	—
1711	—	10.00	20.00	35.00	60.00	—
1712	—	10.00	20.00	35.00	60.00	—
1713	—	10.00	20.00	35.00	60.00	—
1714	—	10.00	20.00	35.00	60.00	—
1715	—	10.00	20.00	35.00	60.00	—
1716	—	10.00	20.00	35.00	60.00	—

KM# 148 4 BOLOGNINI

Billon **Obv:** Capped bust left **Rev:** St. Peter kneeling left blessing city

Date	Mintage	VG	F	VF	XF	Unc
ND	—	10.00	20.00	35.00	60.00	—

KM# 163 4 BOLOGNINI

Billon **Ruler:** Innocent XIII **Obv:** Capped bust right **Rev:** St. Peter standing, value IIII below

Date	Mintage	VG	F	VF	XF	Unc
1721	—	22.00	45.00	80.00	135	—
1722	—	22.00	45.00	80.00	135	—
1723	—	22.00	45.00	80.00	135	—
1724	—	22.00	45.00	80.00	135	—

KM# 171 4 BOLOGNINI

Billon **Ruler:** Innocent XIII **Rev:** Without value IIII

Date	Mintage	VG	F	VF	XF	Unc
1722	—	22.00	45.00	80.00	135	—
1723	—	22.00	45.00	80.00	135	—

KM# 179 4 BOLOGNINI

Billon **Ruler:** Benedict XIII **Obv:** Capped bust right

Date	Mintage	VG	F	VF	XF	Unc
1724	—	16.50	35.00	60.00	100	—
1725	—	16.50	35.00	60.00	100	—
1726	—	16.50	35.00	60.00	100	—
1727	—	16.50	35.00	60.00	100	—

KM# 178 4 BOLOGNINI

Billon **Ruler:** Benedict XIII **Obv:** Two shields below canopy and keys **Rev:** St. Peter standing **Note:** Sede Vacante Issue

Date	Mintage	VG	F	VF	XF	Unc
1724	—	28.00	50.00	90.00	150	—

KM# 184 4 BOLOGNINI

Billon **Ruler:** Benedict XIII **Obv:** Capped bust left

Date	Mintage	VG	F	VF	XF	Unc
1729	—	16.50	35.00	60.00	100	—

KM# 194 4 BOLOGNINI

Billon **Ruler:** Clement XII **Obv:** Capped bust left

Date	Mintage	VG	F	VF	XF	Unc
1730	—	8.50	16.50	30.00	50.00	—
1731	—	8.50	16.50	30.00	50.00	—
1732	—	8.50	16.50	30.00	50.00	—
1733	—	8.50	16.50	30.00	50.00	—

KM# 193 4 BOLOGNINI

Billon **Ruler:** Clement XII **Obv:** Two shields below canopy and keys **Note:** Sede Vacante Issue

Date	Mintage	VG	F	VF	XF	Unc
1730	—	20.00	38.00	70.00	120	—

KM# 204 4 BOLOGNINI

Billon **Ruler:** Clement XII **Obv:** Capped bust right

Date	Mintage	VG	F	VF	XF	Unc
1734	—	8.50	16.50	30.00	50.00	—
1735	—	8.50	16.50	30.00	50.00	—
1736	—	8.50	16.50	30.00	50.00	—
1737	—	8.50	16.50	30.00	50.00	—

KM# 207 4 BOLOGNINI

Billon **Ruler:** Clement XII **Rev. Legend:** Ends: ...BONONIAE

Date	Mintage	VG	F	VF	XF	Unc
1735	—	8.50	16.50	30.00	50.00	—

KM# 226 4 BOLOGNINI

Billon **Ruler:** Benedict XIV **Obv:** Capped bust, left **Obv. Legend:** BENEDICTVS • XIV • F • M • **Rev:** St. Peter **Rev. Legend:** S • PETRONIVS • .... **Note:** Varieties exist.

Date	Mintage	VG	F	VF	XF	Unc
ND(1741)//II	—	6.00	18.00	30.00	50.00	—
1744	—	6.00	18.00	30.00	50.00	—
1745	—	6.00	18.00	30.00	50.00	—
1746	—	6.00	18.00	30.00	50.00	—
1747	—	6.00	18.00	30.00	50.00	—
1748	—	6.00	18.00	30.00	50.00	—
1750	—	6.00	18.00	30.00	50.00	—
1754	—	6.00	18.00	30.00	50.00	—

KM# 271 4 BOLOGNINI
Billon **Ruler:** Pius VI (Sestus) **Obv:** Capped bust, right **Obv. Legend:** PIVS • VI • PONT • MAX • **Rev:** St. Peter **Rev. Legend:** S • PETRON • ...

Date	Mintage	VG	F	VF	XF	Unc
1778	—	6.00	15.00	25.00	40.00	—
1778//IIII	—	6.00	15.00	25.00	40.00	—
1779//IIII	—	6.00	15.00	25.00	40.00	—
1785	—	6.00	15.00	25.00	40.00	—
1786	—	6.00	15.00	25.00	40.00	—
1789	—	6.00	15.00	25.00	40.00	—
1790	—	6.00	15.00	25.00	40.00	—
1791	—	6.00	15.00	25.00	40.00	—
1793	—	6.00	15.00	25.00	40.00	—
1794	—	6.00	15.00	25.00	40.00	—
1795	—	6.00	15.00	25.00	40.00	—
1796	—	6.00	15.00	25.00	40.00	—

KM# 270 4 BOLOGNINI
Billon **Ruler:** Pius VI (Sestus) **Obv:** Crossed keys **Obv. Legend:** PIVS • VI • PON • MAX • **Rev:** St. Peter **Rev. Legend:** S • PETRONIVS • PON • ... **Note:** Weight varies: 3.00-3.50 grams.

Date	Mintage	VG	F	VF	XF	Unc
1778	—	7.50	20.00	30.00	60.00	—

KM# A325 4 BOLOGNINI
Billon **Ruler:** Clement XI **Obv:** Capped bust, right **Obv. Legend:** PIVS • VI • PONT • MAX • **Rev:** St. Peter **Rev. Legend:** S • PETRON • ....

Date	Mintage	VG	F	VF	XF	Unc
1796	—	—	—	—	—	—

KM# 136 5 BOLOGNINI (Carlino)
Silver **Subject:** Clement XI

Date	Mintage	VG	F	VF	XF	Unc
1702	—	20.00	40.00	75.00	125	—
1703	—	20.00	40.00	75.00	125	—
1704	—	20.00	40.00	75.00	125	—
1705	—	20.00	40.00	75.00	125	—
1706	—	20.00	40.00	75.00	125	—
1707	—	20.00	40.00	75.00	125	—
1708	—	20.00	40.00	75.00	125	—
1709	—	20.00	40.00	75.00	125	—
1710	—	20.00	40.00	75.00	125	—
1711	—	20.00	40.00	75.00	125	—
1712	—	20.00	40.00	75.00	125	—
1713	—	20.00	40.00	75.00	125	—
1714	—	20.00	40.00	75.00	125	—
1715	—	20.00	40.00	75.00	125	—
1716	—	20.00	40.00	75.00	125	—
1717	—	20.00	40.00	75.00	125	—
1718	—	20.00	40.00	75.00	125	—

KM# 172 5 BOLOGNINI (Carlino)
Silver **Ruler:** Innocent XIII **Subject:** Innocent XIII

Date	Mintage	VG	F	VF	XF	Unc
1722	—	40.00	75.00	125	200	—
1723	—	40.00	75.00	125	200	—

KM# 195 5 BOLOGNINI (Carlino)
Silver **Ruler:** Clement XII **Obv:** Capped bust left, BS below **Rev. Legend:** BONONIA DOCET on shield

Date	Mintage	VG	F	VF	XF	Unc
ND	—	10.00	20.00	38.00	65.00	—

KM# 196 5 BOLOGNINI (Carlino)
Silver **Obv:** Shield **Rev:** Tiara above crossed keys, *B • 5* below

Date	Mintage	VG	F	VF	XF	Unc
ND	—	10.00	20.00	38.00	65.00	—

KM# 208 5 BOLOGNINI (Carlino)
Silver **Ruler:** Clement XII **Rev:** Value: CINQUE/BOLOGNI/NI in cartouche **Note:** Varieties exist with serif.

Date	Mintage	VG	F	VF	XF	Unc
1736	—	10.00	20.00	38.00	65.00	—
1737	—	10.00	20.00	38.00	65.00	—

KM# 213 5 BOLOGNINI (Carlino)
Silver **Ruler:** Clement XII **Rev:** Value: CINQUE/BOLOGNI/NI in palm fronds

Date	Mintage	VG	F	VF	XF	Unc
1738	—	10.00	20.00	38.00	65.00	—
1739	—	10.00	20.00	38.00	65.00	—
1740	—	10.00	20.00	38.00	65.00	—

KM# 221 5 BOLOGNINI (Carlino)
Silver **Ruler:** Benedict XIV **Obv:** Oval ornate shield **Rev:** Inscription, date in cartouche **Rev. Inscription:** CINQVE/BOLOGNI/NI

Date	Mintage	VG	F	VF	XF	Unc
1740	—	12.50	20.00	35.00	50.00	—
1741	—	12.50	20.00	35.00	50.00	—
1742	—	12.50	20.00	35.00	50.00	—
1743	—	12.50	20.00	35.00	50.00	—
1744	—	12.50	20.00	35.00	50.00	—
1745	—	12.50	20.00	35.00	50.00	—
1746	—	12.50	20.00	35.00	50.00	—
1747	—	12.50	20.00	35.00	50.00	—
1749	—	12.50	20.00	35.00	50.00	—
1753	—	12.50	20.00	35.00	50.00	—
1755	—	12.50	20.00	35.00	50.00	—
1758	—	12.50	20.00	35.00	50.00	—

KM# 241 5 BOLOGNINI (Carlino)
Silver **Ruler:** Clement XIII **Obv:** Oval shield **Rev:** Inscription, date in cartouche

Date	Mintage	VG	F	VF	XF	Unc
1769	—	8.50	16.00	25.00	55.00	—

KM# 242 5 BOLOGNINI (Carlino)
Silver **Ruler:** Clement XIII **Obv:** Oval shield **Rev:** Inscription, date in cartouche

Date	Mintage	VG	F	VF	XF	Unc
1769	—	8.50	16.00	25.00	55.00	—

KM# 250 5 BOLOGNINI (Carlino)
Silver **Ruler:** Clement XIV **Obv:** Ornate shield **Rev:** Written value, date within wreath

Date	Mintage	VG	F	VF	XF	Unc
1771	—	8.50	16.00	25.00	50.00	—

KM# 251 5 BOLOGNINI (Carlino)
Silver **Ruler:** Clement XIV **Rev:** Written value, date in cartouche

Date	Mintage	VG	F	VF	XF	Unc
1771	—	8.50	16.00	25.00	50.00	—

KM# 261 5 BOLOGNINI (Carlino)
1.3210 g., 0.9170 Silver 0.0389 oz. ASW **Ruler:** Pius VI (Sestus) **Obv:** Flower sprigs above value **Obv. Legend:** PIVS • VI • PONT • MAXIM • **Rev:** Ornate shield above date

Date	Mintage	VG	F	VF	XF	Unc
1777	—	3.50	7.00	20.00	30.00	—
1778	—	3.50	7.00	20.00	30.00	—

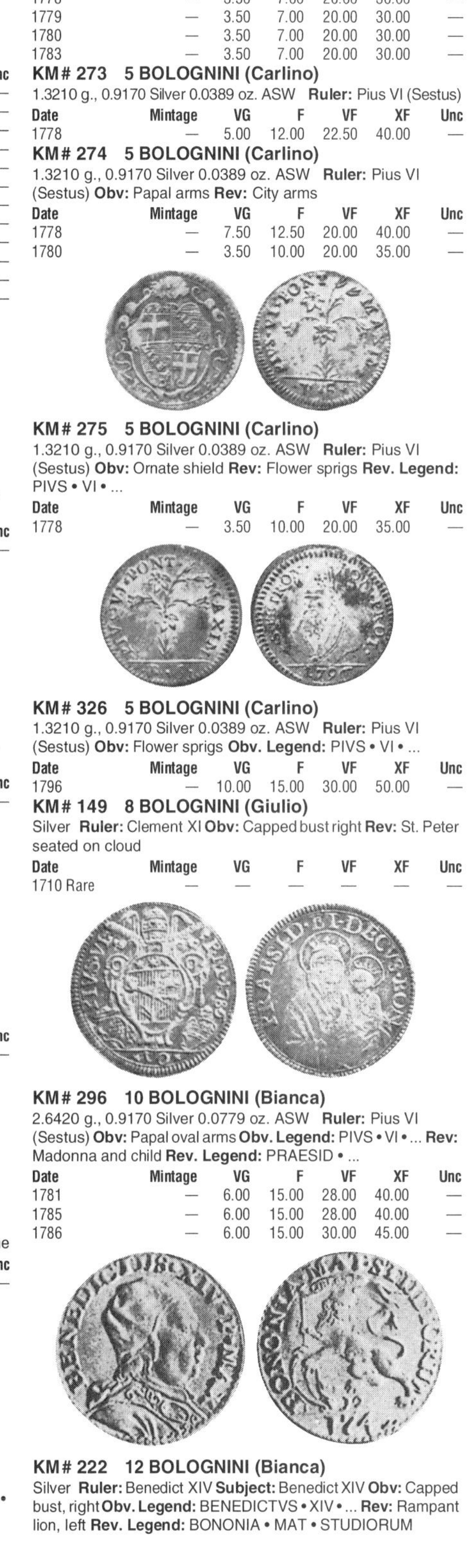

KM# 260 5 BOLOGNINI (Carlino)
1.3210 g., 0.9170 Silver 0.0389 oz. ASW **Ruler:** Pius VI (Sestus) **Obv:** Ornate shield **Rev:** Written value, date in cartouche

Date	Mintage	VG	F	VF	XF	Unc
1777 (1777)	—	3.50	7.00	20.00	30.00	—

KM# 272 5 BOLOGNINI (Carlino)
1.3210 g., 0.9170 Silver 0.0389 oz. ASW **Ruler:** Pius VI (Sestus)

Date	Mintage	VG	F	VF	XF	Unc
1778	—	3.50	7.00	20.00	30.00	—
1779	—	3.50	7.00	20.00	30.00	—
1780	—	3.50	7.00	20.00	30.00	—
1783	—	3.50	7.00	20.00	30.00	—

KM# 273 5 BOLOGNINI (Carlino)
1.3210 g., 0.9170 Silver 0.0389 oz. ASW **Ruler:** Pius VI (Sestus)

Date	Mintage	VG	F	VF	XF	Unc
1778	—	5.00	12.00	22.50	40.00	—

KM# 274 5 BOLOGNINI (Carlino)
1.3210 g., 0.9170 Silver 0.0389 oz. ASW **Ruler:** Pius VI (Sestus) **Obv:** Papal arms **Rev:** City arms

Date	Mintage	VG	F	VF	XF	Unc
1778	—	7.50	12.50	20.00	40.00	—
1780	—	3.50	10.00	20.00	35.00	—

KM# 275 5 BOLOGNINI (Carlino)
1.3210 g., 0.9170 Silver 0.0389 oz. ASW **Ruler:** Pius VI (Sestus) **Obv:** Ornate shield **Rev:** Flower sprigs **Rev. Legend:** PIVS • VI • ...

Date	Mintage	VG	F	VF	XF	Unc
1778	—	3.50	10.00	20.00	35.00	—

KM# 326 5 BOLOGNINI (Carlino)
1.3210 g., 0.9170 Silver 0.0389 oz. ASW **Ruler:** Pius VI (Sestus) **Obv:** Flower sprigs **Obv. Legend:** PIVS • VI • ...

Date	Mintage	VG	F	VF	XF	Unc
1796	—	10.00	15.00	30.00	50.00	—

KM# 149 8 BOLOGNINI (Giulio)
Silver **Ruler:** Clement XI **Obv:** Capped bust right **Rev:** St. Peter seated on cloud

Date	Mintage	VG	F	VF	XF	Unc
1710 Rare	—	—	—	—	—	—

KM# 296 10 BOLOGNINI (Bianca)
2.6420 g., 0.9170 Silver 0.0779 oz. ASW **Ruler:** Pius VI (Sestus) **Obv:** Papal oval arms **Obv. Legend:** PIVS • VI • ... **Rev:** Madonna and child **Rev. Legend:** PRAESID • ...

Date	Mintage	VG	F	VF	XF	Unc
1781	—	6.00	15.00	28.00	40.00	—
1785	—	6.00	15.00	28.00	40.00	—
1786	—	6.00	15.00	30.00	45.00	—

KM# 222 12 BOLOGNINI (Bianca)
Silver **Ruler:** Benedict XIV **Subject:** Benedict XIV **Obv:** Capped bust, right **Obv. Legend:** BENEDICTVS • XIV • ... **Rev:** Rampant lion, left **Rev. Legend:** BONONIA • MAT • STUDIORUM

Date	Mintage	VG	F	VF	XF	Unc
1740	—	90.00	150	250	350	—
1742	—	85.00	135	200	300	—

KM# 229 12 BOLOGNINI (Bianca)
Silver **Ruler:** Benedict XIV **Obv:** Capped bust, right **Obv. Legend:** BENEDIC • XIV • ... **Rev:** Value below rampant lion, left **Rev. Legend:** BONONIA DOCET

Date	Mintage	VG	F	VF	XF	Unc
1743	—	75.00	125	175	225	—
1745	—	75.00	125	175	225	—
1749	—	75.00	125	175	225	—
1754	—	75.00	125	175	225	—

KM# 236 12 BOLOGNINI (Bianca)
Silver **Ruler:** Clement XIII **Obv:** Capped bust, left **Obv. Legend:** CLEM • XIII • P • M • AN • I • **Rev:** Lion rampant right with banner **Rev. Legend:** BONON • DOCET

Date	Mintage	Good	VG	F	VF	XF
1759//I	—	15.00	25.00	40.00	75.00	—

KM# 237 12 BOLOGNINI (Bianca)
Silver **Ruler:** Clement XIII **Obv:** Capped bust, left **Obv. Legend:** CLEMEN • XIII • P • M • **Rev:** Rampant lion, left **Rev. Legend:** BONON • DOCET **Note:** Varieties exist.

Date	Mintage	Good	VG	F	VF	XF
1759	—	15.00	25.00	40.00	75.00	—
1760	—	15.00	25.00	40.00	75.00	—
1762	—	15.00	25.00	40.00	75.00	—
1763	—	15.00	25.00	40.00	75.00	—
1764	—	15.00	25.00	40.00	75.00	—
1765	—	15.00	25.00	40.00	75.00	—
1766	—	15.00	25.00	40.00	75.00	—
1767	—	15.00	25.00	40.00	75.00	—
1768	—	15.00	25.00	40.00	75.00	—

KM# 245 12 BOLOGNINI (Bianca)
Silver **Ruler:** Clement XIII **Rev. Legend:** BONONIA-DOCET

Date	Mintage	Good	VG	F	VF	XF
1761//I	—	15.00	25.00	40.00	75.00	—

KM# 253 12 BOLOGNINI (Bianca)
Silver **Ruler:** Clement XIV **Subject:** Clement XIV **Obv:** Capped bust, right **Obv. Legend:** CLEME • XIV • P • M • **Rev:** Rampant lion, left **Rev. Legend:** BONO • DOCET •

Date	Mintage	Good	VG	F	VF	XF
1773	—	20.00	35.00	60.00	100	—

KM# 329 12 BOLOGNINI (Bianca)
3.5000 g., 0.9170 Silver 0.1032 oz. ASW **Ruler:** Pius VI (Sestus) **Subject:** Pius VI **Obv:** Capped bust, right **Obv. Legend:** PIVS • VI • PON • MAX • **Rev:** Rampant lion left **Rev. Legend:** BONONIA • DOCET •

Date	Mintage	Good	VG	F	VF	XF
1795	—	20.00	40.00	75.00	115	—

KM# 209 16 BOLOGNINI
Billon **Ruler:** Clement XII **Obv:** Capped bust right **Rev:** St. Peter standing, value: 16 in exergue

Date	Mintage	VG	F	VF	XF	Unc
1736	—	25.00	45.00	80.00	135	—

KM# 137 20 BOLOGNINI (Lira)
Silver **Ruler:** Clement XI **Subject:** Clement XI **Obv:** Arms, two shields at sides **Rev:** Rampant lion with banner left

Date	Mintage	VG	F	VF	XF	Unc
1702	—	85.00	165	300	500	—
ND	—	85.00	165	300	500	—

KM# 152 20 BOLOGNINI (Lira)
Silver **Ruler:** Clement XI **Obv:** Arms, two different shields at sides

Date	Mintage	VG	F	VF	XF	Unc
1712	—	85.00	165	300	500	—

KM# 164 20 BOLOGNINI (Lira)
Silver **Ruler:** Innocent XIII **Subject:** Innocent XIII **Obv:** Arms, two shields at sides

Date	Mintage	VG	F	VF	XF	Unc
ND	—	70.00	145	265	435	—

KM# 180 20 BOLOGNINI (Lira)
Silver **Ruler:** Benedict XIII **Obv:** Two shields below canopy and keys **Note:** Sede Vacante Issue.

Date	Mintage	VG	F	VF	XF	Unc
1724	—	165	300	500	825	—

KM# 181 20 BOLOGNINI (Lira)
Silver **Ruler:** Benedict XIII **Subject:** Benedict XIII **Obv:** Arms, two shields at sides **Rev:** Lion rampant with banner left **Rev. Legend:** BONONIA DOCET

Date	Mintage	VG	F	VF	XF	Unc
1724	—	70.00	145	260	425	—
1725	—	70.00	145	260	425	—
1726	—	70.00	145	260	425	—

KM# 185 20 BOLOGNINI (Lira)
Silver **Ruler:** Benedict XIII **Obv:** Arms with different shields at sides

Date	Mintage	VG	F	VF	XF	Unc
1729	—	70.00	145	260	425	—

KM# 197 20 BOLOGNINI (Lira)
Silver **Ruler:** Benedict XIII **Obv:** Two shields below canopy and keys **Note:** Sede Vacante Issue.

Date	Mintage	VG	F	VF	XF	Unc
1730	—	150	250	400	650	—

KM# 199 20 BOLOGNINI (Lira)
Silver **Ruler:** Clement XII **Subject:** Clement XII **Obv:** Arms, two shields at sides **Rev:** Inscription within wreath **Rev. Inscription:** DEFLVIT/ET/INFLVIT

Date	Mintage	VG	F	VF	XF	Unc
1732	—	35.00	75.00	135	225	—
ND	—	35.00	75.00	135	225	—

KM# 205 20 BOLOGNINI (Lira)
Silver **Ruler:** Clement XII **Obv:** Arms with different shields at sides

Date	Mintage	VG	F	VF	XF	Unc
1734	—	35.00	75.00	135	225	—

KM# 262 20 BOLOGNINI (Lira)
5.2850 g., 0.9170 Silver 0.1558 oz. ASW **Ruler:** Pius VI (Sestus) **Obv. Legend:** PONTIF • PIVS VI

Date	Mintage	Good	VG	F	VF	XF
1777	—	10.00	20.00	40.00	80.00	—

KM# 276 20 BOLOGNINI (Lira)
5.2850 g., 0.9170 Silver 0.1558 oz. ASW **Ruler:** Pius VI (Sestus) **Obv:** Papal arms **Obv. Legend:** PIVS • VI • ... **Rev:** Rampant lion, left **Rev. Legend:** BONON • DOCET •

Date	Mintage	Good	VG	F	VF	XF
1778	—	10.00	20.00	40.00	80.00	—
1779	—	10.00	20.00	40.00	80.00	—
1780	—	10.00	20.00	40.00	80.00	—

KM# 306 20 BOLOGNINI (Lira)
5.2850 g., 0.9170 Silver 0.1558 oz. ASW **Ruler:** Pius VI (Sestus) **Obv:** Different shield **Note:** Varieties exist.

Date	Mintage	Good	VG	F	VF	XF
1786	—	10.00	20.00	40.00	80.00	—
1787	—	10.00	20.00	40.00	80.00	—
1793	—	10.00	20.00	40.00	80.00	—

KM# 170 30 BOLOGNINI (Testone)
Silver **Ruler:** Innocent XIII **Obv:** Capped bust right **Rev:** Shield **Rev. Legend:** BONONIA DOCET

Date	Mintage	VG	F	VF	XF	Unc
1721	—	135	275	500	825	—

KM# 263 30 BOLOGNINI (Testone)
7.9280 g., 0.9170 Silver 0.2337 oz. ASW **Ruler:** Pius VI (Sestus) **Subject:** Pius VI **Obv:** Capped bust, right **Obv. Legend:** PIVS • VI • PON • MAX • III • **Rev:** Ornate oval shield **Rev. Legend:** BONONIA * * DOCET 1777

Date	Mintage	VG	F	VF	XF	Unc
1777//III	—	17.50	35.00	65.00	120	—
1778//IIII	—	17.50	35.00	65.00	120	—
1779	—	15.00	30.00	60.00	110	—
1785	—	15.00	30.00	60.00	110	—
1786	—	15.00	30.00	60.00	110	—
1792	—	15.00	30.00	60.00	110	—

KM# 297 30 BOLOGNINI (Testone)
7.9280 g., 0.9170 Silver 0.2337 oz. ASW **Ruler:** Pius VI (Sestus) **Obv:** Capped bust, right **Obv. Legend:** PIVS • SEXTVS • PONT • MAX • AN • VIII **Rev:** Temple, flanked by shields below **Rev. Legend:** ...NIVS • OPT • IMI • PRINCIPIS •

Date	Mintage	VG	F	VF	XF	Unc
1782//VIII	—	22.50	40.00	80.00	160	—

KM# 135 40 BOLOGNINI (1/2 Scudo - 2 Lire)
Silver **Ruler:** Clement XI **Subject:** Clement XI

Date	Mintage	VG	F	VF	XF	Unc
ND	—	225	420	700	1,150	—

KM# 166 40 BOLOGNINI (1/2 Scudo - 2 Lire)
Silver **Ruler:** Innocent XIII **Subject:** Innocent XIII **Obv:** Arms **Rev:** Floral cross, two shields

Date	Mintage	VG	F	VF	XF	Unc
1721	—	400	700	1,200	2,000	—

KM# 167 40 BOLOGNINI (1/2 Scudo - 2 Lire)
Silver **Ruler:** Innocent XIII **Rev:** Different shields

Date	Mintage	VG	F	VF	XF	Unc
1721	—	400	700	1,200	2,000	—
1722	—	400	700	1,200	2,000	—
1723	—	400	700	1,200	2,000	—

KM# 165 40 BOLOGNINI (1/2 Scudo - 2 Lire)
Silver **Ruler:** Innocent XIII **Obv:** Two shields below canopy and crossed keys **Rev:** Floral cross **Rev. Legend:** BONONIA DOCET **Note:** Sede Vacante Issue.

Date	Mintage	VG	F	VF	XF	Unc
1721	—	400	700	1,200	2,000	—

KM# 249 40 BOLOGNINI (1/2 Scudo - 2 Lire)
Silver **Obv:** Cardinal arms, with 2 oval shields above date **Obv. Legend:** SEDE * VACANTE * **Rev:** Floreated cross **Rev. Legend:** BONONIA * DOCET * **Note:** Sede Vacante Issue.

Date	Mintage	VG	F	VF	XF	Unc
1769	—	60.00	100	150	200	—

KM# 243 40 BOLOGNINI (1/2 Scudo)

Silver **Ruler:** Clement XIV **Obv:** Oval, ornate Papal arms **Obv. Legend:** CLEMENS • XIV • PONT • M • A • I • **Rev:** Floreated cross, 2 oval shields below **Rev. Legend:** BONONIA * DOCET *

Date	Mintage	VG	F	VF	XF	Unc
1769//I	—	35.00	70.00	100	140	—

KM# 244 40 BOLOGNINI (1/2 Scudo)

Silver **Ruler:** Clement XIV **Obv:** Ornate Papal arms **Obv. Legend:** CLEMENS • XIV • PONT • M • A • **Rev:** Floreated cross, shields below **Rev. Legend:** BONONIA DOCET

Date	Mintage	VG	F	VF	XF	Unc
1769//I	—	35.00	70.00	100	140	—

KM# 254 40 BOLOGNINI (1/2 Scudo)

Silver **Ruler:** Clement XIV **Obv:** Ornate Papal arms **Obv. Legend:** CLEMENS • XIV PONT • MAX • AN * **Rev:** floreated cross, 2 oval shields below **Rev. Legend:** BONONIA * DOCET *

Date	Mintage	VG	F	VF	XF	Unc
1773//V	—	35.00	70.00	100	140	—

KM# 264 40 BOLOGNINI (1/2 Scudo)

13.2140 g., 0.9170 Silver 0.3896 oz. ASW **Ruler:** Pius VI (Sestus) **Obv:** Arms **Obv. Legend:** PIVS SEXTUS **Rev:** St. Peter standing

Date	Mintage	VG	F	VF	XF	Unc
ND(1777)//III	—	50.00	75.00	125	175	—

KM# 277 50 BOLOGNINI

Silver **Ruler:** Pius VI (Sestus) **Subject:** PIVS VI **Obv:** Ornate Papal arms **Obv. Legend:** PIVS • VI • PONT • MAX • AN • IIII • **Rev:** Two small shields divide F • BAL, value: 50 below St. Peter **Rev. Legend:** ...BONONIÆ • PROT •

Date	Mintage	VG	F	VF	XF	Unc
1778//IIII	—	30.00	60.00	115	160	—

KM# 278 50 BOLOGNINI

Silver **Ruler:** Pius VI (Sestus) **Rev:** Two small shields divide F • B • or • F • B • F • and value: 50

Date	Mintage	VG	F	VF	XF	Unc
1778//1111	—	30.00	60.00	115	160	—

KM# 298 50 BOLOGNINI

Silver **Ruler:** Pius VI (Sestus) **Obv:** Capped bust, right **Rev:** Temple flanked by oval shields below **Rev. Legend:** ...*OBTI * MI * PRINCIPIS *

Date	Mintage	VG	F	VF	XF	Unc
1782//VIII	—	35.00	70.00	100	150	—

KM# 304 50 BOLOGNINI

Silver, 33 mm. **Ruler:** Pius VI (Sestus) **Rev:** St. Peter seated facing with 50 in exergue **Note:** Small flan.

Date	Mintage	VG	F	VF	XF	Unc
1784	—	25.00	50.00	100	150	—
1795	—	25.00	50.00	100	150	—

KM# 305 50 BOLOGNINI

Silver, 36 mm. **Ruler:** Pius VI (Sestus) **Obv:** Papal arms, 2 shields below, above date **Obv. Legend:** PIVS • VI • ... **Rev:** St. Peter seated in clouds **Rev. Legend:** ...BONONÆ * PROT * **Note:** Larger flan.

Date	Mintage	VG	F	VF	XF	Unc
1785	—	25.00	50.00	115	175	—

KM# 153 80 BOLOGNIA (4 Lire - Scudo)

Silver **Ruler:** Clement XI **Subject:** Clement XI **Note:** Dav. #1444.

Date	Mintage	VG	F	VF	XF	Unc
1712	—	300	550	950	1,550	—
1713	—	300	550	950	1,550	—

KM# 169 80 BOLOGNIA (4 Lire - Scudo)

Silver **Ruler:** Clement XI **Obv:** Legend begins at upper right, arms **Rev:** Floral cross, two different shields at sides **Note:** Dav. #1451.

Date	Mintage	VG	F	VF	XF	Unc
1721	—	1,000	1,800	3,000	5,000	—

KM# 168 80 BOLOGNIA (4 Lire - Scudo)

Silver **Ruler:** Innocent XIII **Subject:** Innocent XIII **Obv:** Legend begins at lower left, arms **Rev:** Floral cross, two shields at sides **Note:** Dav. #1450.

Date	Mintage	VG	F	VF	XF	Unc
1721	—	1,350	2,500	4,000	6,500	—

KM# 173 80 BOLOGNIA (4 Lire - Scudo)

Silver **Ruler:** Innocent XIII **Obv. Legend:** Ends:...*PONTE*MAX*** **Note:** Dav. #1452.

Date	Mintage	VG	F	VF	XF	Unc
1722	—	1,000	1,800	3,000	5,000	—
1723	—	1,000	1,800	3,000	5,000	—
1724	—	1,000	1,800	3,000	5,000	—

KM# 182 80 BOLOGNIA (4 Lire - Scudo)

Silver **Ruler:** Innocent XIII **Obv:** Two shields below canopy and keys **Rev:** Inscription, floral cross **Note:** Dav. #1454.

Date	Mintage	VG	F	VF	XF	Unc
1724 Rare	—	—	—	—	—	—

KM# 223 80 BOLOGNIA (4 Lire - Scudo)

Silver **Ruler:** Benedict XIV **Obv:** Papal arms **Obv. Legend:** BENEDICTVS • XIV • P • M • .... **Rev:** Floreated cross, shields below **Rev. Legend:** ...DOCET • **Note:** Dav. #1457.

Date	Mintage	VG	F	VF	XF	Unc
1740	—	300	650	850	1,500	—

KM# 255 80 BOLOGNIA (4 Lire - Scudo)

Silver **Obv:** Cardinal arms, 2 shields below **Obv. Legend:** SEDE * VACAN TE * MDCCLXXIV **Rev:** St. Peter kneeling **Note:** Sede Vacante Issue. Dav. #1464.

Date	Mintage	VG	F	VF	XF	Unc
1774	—	250	375	625	800	—

KM# 256 80 BOLOGNIA (4 Lire - Scudo)

Silver **Obv:** Cardinal arms, 2 shields below **Obv. Legend:** SED • VA C * M DCCLXXV • **Rev:** St. Peter kneeling **Note:** Sede Vacante Issue. Dav. #1465.

Date	Mintage	VG	F	VF	XF	Unc
1775	—	250	375	625	800	—

KM# 258 80 BOLOGNIA (4 Lire - Scudo)

20.7500 g., 0.9170 Silver 0.6117 oz. ASW **Ruler:** Pius VI (Sestus) **Obv:** Ornate, oval Papal arms **Obv. Legend:** PIVS • VI • PON • MAX • ANNO • BILAEI • IV • **Rev:** St. Peter kneeling **Rev. Legend:** ...BON • PROT • **Note:** Dav. #1467.

Date	Mintage	VG	F	VF	XF	Unc
1775//IV	—	200	300	500	750	—

KM# 257 80 BOLOGNIA (4 Lire - Scudo)

20.7500 g., 0.9170 Silver 0.6117 oz. ASW **Ruler:** Pius VI (Sestus) **Obv:** Papal arms **Obv. Legend:** PIVS • VI • PON • ... **Rev:** St. Peter kneeling **Rev. Inscription:** ...BON • PROT • **Note:** Dav. #1468.

Date	Mintage	VG	F	VF	XF	Unc
1775//I	—	200	300	450	700	—
ND//I	—	200	300	450	700	—

KM# 265 100 BOLOGNIA (Scudo)

26.4280 g., 0.9170 Silver 0.7791 oz. ASW **Ruler:** Pius VI (Sestus) **Obv:** Ornate, oval Papal arms **Obv. Legend:** PIVS • VI • PON • MAX • AN • III * **Rev:** St. Peter standing **Rev. Legend:** ...BON • PROT •

Date	Mintage	VG	F	VF	XF	Unc
1777//III	—	60.00	85.00	150	225	—
1778//IIII	—	60.00	85.00	150	225	—
1780//VI	—	60.00	85.00	150	225	—

KM# 300 100 BOLOGNIA (Scudo)

26.4280 g., 0.9170 Silver 0.7791 oz. ASW **Ruler:** Pius VI (Sestus) **Obv:** Capped bust, right **Obv. Legend:** * PIVS * SEXTVS * PONT * MAX * AN * VIII **Rev:** Temple, flanked by 2 shields below **Rev. Legend:** ...OPT * IMI * PRINCIPIS * **Rev. Inscription:** BONONIA • 1782/100 **Note:** Dav. #1473.

Date	Mintage	VG	F	VF	XF	Unc
1782//VIII	—	85.00	135	200	300	—

KM# 299 100 BOLOGNIA (Scudo)

26.4280 g., 0.9170 Silver 0.7791 oz. ASW **Ruler:** Pius VI (Sestus) **Obv:** Capped bust, right **Obv. Legend:** * PIVS * SEXTVS * PONT * MAX * AN * VIII **Rev:** Temple, flanked by 2 shields below **Rev. Legend:** ...OPT * IMI * PRINCIPIS * **Rev. Inscription:** • BONONIA • 1782 • **Note:** Dav. #1474.

Date	Mintage	VG	F	VF	XF	Unc
1782//VIII	—	85.00	135	250	400	—

KM# 324 100 BOLOGNIA (Scudo)

26.4280 g., 0.9170 Silver 0.7791 oz. ASW **Ruler:** Pius VI (Sestus) **Obv:** Papal arms, flanked by shields below **Obv. Legend:** PIVS * VI * PONT * .... **Rev:** St. Petronius on cloud above city **Rev. Legend:** ...BONON * PROT * **Note:** Dav. #1475.

Date	Mintage	VG	F	VF	XF	Unc
1795	—	75.00	125	175	225	—

KM# 154 SCUDO D'ORO

3.5000 g., 0.9860 Gold 0.1109 oz. AGW **Ruler:** Clement XI **Subject:** Clement XI **Obv:** Papal arms in inner circle **Rev:** Floriate cross, two shields

Date	Mintage	VG	F	VF	XF	Unc
1713 Rare	—	—	—	—	—	—

KM# 200 SCUDO D'ORO

3.5000 g., 0.9860 Gold 0.1109 oz. AGW **Ruler:** Clement XII **Obv:** Papal arms, date in legend **Rev:** Floriate cross with two small shields at bottom

Date	Mintage	VG	F	VF	XF	Unc
1732	—	850	1,650	3,000	5,000	—

KM# 210 SCUDO D'ORO

3.5000 g., 0.9860 Gold 0.1109 oz. AGW **Ruler:** Clement XII **Obv:** Papal arms **Rev:** Floriate cross divides date, two small shields at bottom

Date	Mintage	VG	F	VF	XF	Unc
1736	—	850	1,650	3,000	5,000	—

KM# 211 1/2 ZECCHINO

Gold **Ruler:** Clement XII **Subject:** Clement XII **Obv:** Two shields below canopy and crossed keys **Rev:** Lion rampant left with banner **Rev. Legend:** BONONIA DOCET

Date	Mintage	VG	F	VF	XF	Unc
1737	—	750	1,550	2,800	4,650	—
1738	—	750	1,550	2,800	4,650	—

KM# 307 1/2 ZECCHINO

1.7260 g., 0.9860 Gold 0.0547 oz. AGW **Ruler:** Pius VI (Sestus) **Obv:** Papal oval arms **Obv. Legend:** PIVS • VI • PONT • M • A • X • **Rev:** St. Peter flanked by shields below

Date	Mintage	VG	F	VF	XF	Unc
1786	—	175	350	650	850	—

KM# 212 ZECCHINO

3.4520 g., 0.9860 Gold 0.1094 oz. AGW **Ruler:** Clement XII **Obv:** Two shields below canopy, value above **Rev:** Lion rampant wtih banner, date in legend

Date	Mintage	VG	F	VF	XF	Unc
1737 Rare	—	—	—	—	—	—
1738 Rare	—	—	—	—	—	—

KM# 224 ZECCHINO

3.4520 g., 0.9860 Gold 0.1094 oz. AGW **Ruler:** Clement XII **Obv:** Two shields below canopy, date divided near top **Rev:** Lion rampant with banner, value in legend **Note:** Sede Vacante Issue.

Date	Mintage	VG	F	VF	XF	Unc
1740 Rare	—	—	—	—	—	—

KM# 230 ZECCHINO

3.5000 g., 0.9860 Gold 0.1109 oz. AGW **Ruler:** Benedict XIV **Obv:** Capped bust, left **Obv. Legend:** BENEDICTVS • XIV • P • M • BON • **Rev:** Felsina

Date	Mintage	VG	F	VF	XF	Unc
ND(1742)//II	—	325	650	1,000	1,600	—

KM# 231 ZECCHINO

3.5000 g., 0.9860 Gold 0.1109 oz. AGW **Ruler:** Benedict XIV **Obv:** Cardinal arms flanked by shields below **Rev:** Rampant lion with banner, date in legend

Date	Mintage	VG	F	VF	XF	Unc
1746	—	275	550	800	1,200	—

KM# 235 ZECCHINO

3.5000 g., 0.9860 Gold 0.1109 oz. AGW **Ruler:** Benedict XIV **Obv:** Papal arms **Obv. Legend:** BENEDIC • XIV • P • M • **Rev:** Floreated cross divides date above, flanked by shields below **Rev. Legend:** BONONIA DOCET

Date	Mintage	VG	F	VF	XF	Unc
1751	—	275	550	800	1,200	—

KM# 252 ZECCHINO

3.5000 g., 0.9860 Gold 0.1109 oz. AGW **Ruler:** Clement XIV **Obv:** Cardinal arms flanked by shields below **Rev:** Rampant lion, left **Rev. Legend:** BONONIA DOCET •

Date	Mintage	VG	F	VF	XF	Unc
1771	—	1,200	2,500	3,500	4,500	—

KM# 279 ZECCHINO

3.5000 g., 0.9860 Gold 0.1109 oz. AGW **Ruler:** Pius VI (Sestus) **Obv:** Ornate, oval Papal arms **Obv. Legend:** PIVS • VI • ... **Rev:** St. Peter above 2 shields

Date	Mintage	VG	F	VF	XF	Unc
1778 GP	—	175	325	475	650	—
1779 GP	—	175	275	450	600	—
1780 GP	—	175	275	450	600	—
1786 GP	—	175	275	450	600	—
1787 GP	—	175	275	450	600	—

KM# A301 ZECCHINO

3.5000 g., 0.9860 Gold 0.1109 oz. AGW **Ruler:** Pius VI (Sestus) **Obv:** Capped bust, right **Obv. Legend:** PIVS • SEXTVS • PONT • MAX • AN • VIII • **Rev:** Temple flanked by shields

Date	Mintage	VG	F	VF	XF	Unc
1782//VIII	—	250	475	800	1,000	—

KM# 228 2 ZECCHINI

7.0000 g., 0.9860 Gold 0.2219 oz. AGW **Ruler:** Benedict XIV **Obv:** Capped bust, left **Obv. Legend:** BENEDICTVS • XIV • ... **Rev:** Felsina **Rev. Legend:** PACRI PATRIÆ

Date	Mintage	VG	F	VF	XF	Unc
ND(1742)//II	—	650	1,250	1,750	2,750	—

KM# 308 2 ZECCHINI

7.0000 g., 0.9860 Gold 0.2219 oz. AGW **Ruler:** Pius VI (Sestus) **Obv:** Ornate, oval Papal arms **Obv. Legend:** PIVS • VI • PONT • M • **Rev:** St. Petronius seated on cloud, 2 shields below **Rev. Legend:** S • PETRON • BON • PROT • 1786

Date	Mintage	VG	F	VF	XF	Unc
1786	—	200	350	550	750	—
1787	—	200	350	550	750	—

KM# 313 5 ZECCHINI

17.5000 g., 0.9860 Gold 0.5547 oz. AGW **Ruler:** Pius VI (Sestus) **Obv:** Papal arms within sprigs **Obv. Legend:** PIVS • VI • PONT... **Rev:** St. Petronius seated on cloud, 2 shields below **Rev. Legend:** S • PETRON • BON • PROT • 1787 •

Date	Mintage	VG	F	VF	XF	Unc
1787//XIII GP	—	325	525	850	1,100	—

KM# 309 10 ZECCHINI

35.0000 g., 0.9860 Gold 1.1095 oz. AGW **Ruler:** Pius VI (Sestus) **Obv:** Ornate, oval Papal arms **Obv. Legend:** PIVS • VI • PONT •... **Rev:** St. Petronius seated on cloud, flanked by shields below **Rev. Legend:** S • PETRON • BON • PROT • AN • 1787 •

Date	Mintage	VG	F	VF	XF	Unc
1786//XII	—	950	1,200	1,500	3,500	—
1787//XII	—	950	1,200	1,500	3,500	—

KM# 281 15 PAOLI = 1/2 DOPPIA D'ORO

2.7340 g., 0.9170 Gold 0.0806 oz. AGW **Obv:** Date below flower sprig **Obv. Legend:** PIVS • VI • PONT • MAX M • **Rev:** Value: P • 15 below shields **Rev. Legend:** BON • DOCET

Date	Mintage	VG	F	VF	XF	Unc
1778	—	150	275	400	600	—
1779	—	150	275	400	600	—
1786	—	100	125	275	400	—
1787	—	100	125	275	400	—
1788	—	100	125	275	400	—
1791	—	125	250	325	500	—

KM# 280 15 PAOLI = 1/2 DOPPIA D'ORO

2.7340 g., 0.9170 Gold 0.0806 oz. AGW **Ruler:** Pius VI (Sestus) **Obv:** Flower sprig **Obv. Legend:** PIVS • VI • PONT: ... **Rev:** Date below shield

Date	Mintage	VG	F	VF	XF	Unc
1778 PG	—	150	275	400	600	—

KM# 155 DOPPIA D'ORO

7.0000 g., 0.9860 Gold 0.2219 oz. AGW **Ruler:** Clement XI **Obv:** Oval papal arms

Date	Mintage	VG	F	VF	XF	Unc
1713 Rare	—	—	—	—	—	—
1714 Rare	—	—	—	—	—	—

KM# 282 DOPPIA D'ORO (30 Paoli)

5.4690 g., 0.9170 Gold 0.1612 oz. AGW **Ruler:** Pius VI (Sestus) **Obv:** Date below flower sprig **Obv. Legend:** PIVS • VI • PONT • MAXIM • **Rev:** Value: P • 30 below 2 shields **Rev. Legend:** BON • DOCET

Date	Mintage	VG	F	VF	XF	Unc
1778	—	125	225	300	375	—
1779	—	125	225	300	375	—
1785	—	125	225	300	375	—

KM# 310 DOPPIA D'ORO (30 Paoli)

5.4690 g., 0.9170 Gold 0.1612 oz. AGW **Ruler:** Pius VI (Sestus) **Obv:** Date below flower sprig **Obv. Legend:** PIVS • VI • PONT • MAXIM • **Rev:** Initials below 2 shields **Rev. Legend:** BON • DOCET

Date	Mintage	VG	F	VF	XF	Unc
1786 GP	—	125	225	300	375	—
1787 GP	—	125	225	300	375	—
1788 GP	—	125	225	300	375	—
1789 GP	—	125	225	300	375	—
1790 GP	—	125	225	300	375	—
1791 GP	—	125	225	300	375	—
1792 GP	—	125	225	300	375	—

KM# 314 DOPPIA D'ORO (30 Paoli)

5.4690 g., 0.9170 Gold 0.1612 oz. AGW **Ruler:** Pius VI (Sestus) **Obv:** Date below flower sprig **Obv. Legend:** PIVS • VI • PONT • MAXIM • **Rev:** Value: 1 DOP below 2 shields **Rev. Legend:** BONON • DOCET

Date	Mintage	VG	F	VF	XF	Unc
1787	—	125	225	300	375	—
1788	—	125	225	300	375	—

KM# 283 2 DOPPIE D'ORO (60 Paoli)

10.9380 g., 0.9170 Gold 0.3225 oz. AGW **Ruler:** Pius VI (Sestus) **Subject:** Pius VI **Obv:** Value: P • 60 below flower sprig **Obv. Inscription:** PIVS • VI • PONT • MAXIM • **Rev:** Date below 2 shields **Rev. Inscription:** BONON • DOCET

Date	Mintage	VG	F	VF	XF	Unc
1778	—	200	350	600	900	—
1780	—	200	350	600	900	—
1781	—	200	350	600	900	—

KM# 311 2 DOPPIE D'ORO (60 Paoli)

10.9380 g., 0.9170 Gold 0.3225 oz. AGW **Ruler:** Pius VI (Sestus) **Obv:** Initials below flower sprig **Obv. Legend:** PIVS • VI • PONT • MAXIM • **Rev:** Date below 2 shields **Rev. Legend:** BONON • DOCET

Date	Mintage	VG	F	VF	XF	Unc
1786 GP	—	200	350	600	900	—
1787 GP	—	200	350	600	900	—

KM# 317 2 DOPPIE D'ORO (60 Paoli)

10.9380 g., 0.9170 Gold 0.3225 oz. AGW **Ruler:** Pius VI (Sestus) **Obv:** Date above flower sprig **Obv. Legend:** PIVS • VI • PONT • MAX • A • XIII **Rev:** Initials below 2 shields **Rev. Legend:** BONON • DOCET

Date	Mintage	VG	F	VF	XF	Unc
1786//XIII GP	—	200	350	600	800	—
1787//XIII GP	—	200	350	600	900	—

KM# 315 2 DOPPIE D'ORO (60 Paoli)

10.9380 g., 0.9170 Gold 0.3225 oz. AGW **Ruler:** Pius VI (Sestus) **Obv:** Stars **Rev:** Initials

Date	Mintage	VG	F	VF	XF	Unc
ND(1787)//XIII DD	—	200	350	600	900	—

KM# 316 2 DOPPIE D'ORO (60 Paoli)

10.9380 g., 0.9170 Gold 0.3225 oz. AGW **Ruler:** Pius VI (Sestus) **Obv:** Date below flower sprig **Obv. Legend:** PIVS • VI • PONT • MAX • A • XIII • **Rev:** Value: 2 DOP below 2 shields **Rev. Legend:** BONON • DOCET •

Date	Mintage	VG	F	VF	XF	Unc
1787//XIII	—	200	350	600	900	—
1796	—	200	350	600	900	—

KM# 312 4 DOPPIE D'ORO (Quadrupla)

21.8760 g., 0.9170 Gold 0.6449 oz. AGW **Ruler:** Pius VI (Sestus) **Obv:** Value: 4 DOP below flower sprig **Obv. Legend:** PIVS • VI • PONT • MAX • A • XII **Rev:** Date below 2 shields **Rev. Legend:** BONON • DOCET

Date	Mintage	VG	F	VF	XF	Unc
1786//XII	—	400	600	950	2,200	—

KM# 318 4 DOPPIE D'ORO (Quadrupla)

21.8760 g., 0.9170 Gold 0.6449 oz. AGW **Ruler:** Pius VI (Sestus) **Obv:** Value: 4 DOP below flower sprig **Obv. Legend:** PIVS • VI • PONT • MAX • A • XIII **Rev:** Date below 2 shields **Rev. Legend:** BONON • DOCET •

Date	Mintage	VG	F	VF	XF	Unc
1787//XIII	—	400	600	950	2,200	—

REVOLUTIONARY GOVERNMENT
1796-1797

STANDARD COINAGE

KM# 335 1/2 QUATTRINO

Copper **Obv:** Rampant lion, left **Obv. Legend:** BONON • • DOCET **Rev:** Stars, written value, date

Date	Mintage	VG	F	VF	XF	Unc
1796	—	20.00	35.00	60.00	110	—

KM# 336 CARLINO

Billon **Obv:** Papal arms **Obv. Legend:** COMVNITAS • ET • SENATVS • BONON • **Rev:** Inscription within wreath

Date	Mintage	VG	F	VF	XF	Unc
ND(1796)	—	20.00	40.00	75.00	110	—

KM# 337.1 2 CARLINI
Billon **Obv:** Papal arms **Rev:** Inscription with stars in lower field, within wreath

Date	Mintage	VG	F	VF	XF	Unc
ND(1796)	—	15.00	30.00	60.00	90.00	—

KM# 337.2 2 CARLINI
Billon **Obv:** Papal arms **Rev:** Inscription without stars in lower field, within wreath

Date	Mintage	VG	F	VF	XF	Unc
ND(1796)	—	15.00	30.00	60.00	90.00	—

KM# 338 5 PAOLI (1/2 Scudo)
14.5000 g., 0.8330 Silver 0.3883 oz. ASW **Obv:** Papal arms in sprigs **Obv. Legend:** POPVLVS • ET • SENATVS • BONON • **Rev:** Madonna and child in cloud above city view

Date	Mintage	VG	F	VF	XF	Unc
1796	—	35.00	60.00	100	200	—
1797	—	35.00	60.00	100	200	—

KM# 340 10 PAOLI (Scudo)
29.0000 g., 0.8330 Silver 0.7766 oz. ASW **Obv:** Papal arms in sprigs **Obv. Legend:** POPVLVS • ET • SENATVS • BONON • **Rev:** Madonna with child in clouds above city view, legend in exergue **Rev. Legend:** PRESIDIVM * ET * DECVS * **Note:** Dav. #1358.

Date	Mintage	VG	F	VF	XF	Unc
1796	—	60.00	100	150	225	—
1797	—	60.00	100	150	225	—

KM# 339 10 PAOLI (Scudo)
29.0000 g., 0.8330 Silver 0.7766 oz. ASW **Obv:** Papal arms in sprigs **Obv. Legend:** POPVLVS • ET • SENATVS • BONON • **Rev:** Larger Madonna with child in clouds above city view **Rev. Legend:** * PRÆSIDIVM * ET * DECVS * **Note:** Dav. #1359.

Date	Mintage	VG	F	VF	XF	Unc
1796	—	60.00	85.00	125	200	—
1797	—	60.00	85.00	125	200	—

KM# 341 10 PAOLI (Scudo)
29.0000 g., 0.8330 Silver 0.7766 oz. ASW **Obv:** Papal arms **Obv. Legend:** COMVNITAS•ET•SENATVS•BONON• **Rev:** Madonna with child in clouds above city view, legend in exergue **Rev. Legend:** * PRÆSIDIVM * ET * DECVS * **Note:** Varieties exist. Dav. #1357.

Date	Mintage	VG	F	VF	XF	Unc
MDCCXCVI (1796)	—	50.00	75.00	100	175	—

PAPAL STATES-CIVITAVECCHIA

A seaport in Latium and one of the oldest papal states founded by Roman emperor Trajan, destroyed by the Saracens in 812, and rebuilt by Pope Leo IV.

NOTE: For later issues see Papal-Roman Republic-Civitavecchia.

CITY

EMERGENCY COINAGE

KM# 5 2-1/2 BAIOCCHI
Copper, 30 mm. **Obv:** Inscription below stars **Obv. Inscription:** BAIOCCHI/DVE E MEZZO/CIVITA/VECCHIA **Rev:** Saints' bust, left **Rev. Legend:** S • P APOSTOLORUM PRINCEPS

Date	Mintage	Good	VG	F	VF	XF
1796	—	15.00	25.00	35.00	60.00	—
1797	—	15.00	25.00	35.00	60.00	—

KM# 5a 2-1/2 BAIOCCHI
Copper, 25 mm. **Obv:** Inscription, date below stars **Obv. Inscription:** BAIOCCHI/DVE E MEZZO/CIVITA/VECCHIA **Note:** Reduced size.

Date	Mintage	Good	VG	F	VF	XF
1797	—	12.00	16.00	32.50	45.00	—

KM# 6.1 5 BAIOCCHI
Copper **Obv:** Inscription above stars within circle, date below **Obv. Legend:** PIVS PAPA SEXTUS... **Obv. Inscription:** BAIOC/...../CIVITA/VECCHIA **Rev:** Madonna **Rev. Legend:** SANCTA DEI GENITRIX

Date	Mintage	Good	VG	F	VF	XF
1797//XXIII	—	15.00	25.00	40.00	60.00	—

KM# 6.2 5 BAIOCCHI
Copper **Obv:** Without inner circle around inscription

Date	Mintage	Good	VG	F	VF	XF
1797//XXIII	—	15.00	25.00	40.00	60.00	—

PAPAL STATES-FANO

A coastal city in the Marches, became a papal possession in 1462.

CITY

EMERGENCY COINAGE

KM# 1 2-1/2 BAIOCCHI
Copper **Obv:** Inscription, date below stars within circle **Obv. Inscription:** BAIOCCHI/DVE E MEZZO/FANO **Rev:** St. Peter bust, left **Rev. Legend:** ...APOSTOLORUM PRINC

Date	Mintage	Good	VG	F	VF	XF
1796	—	40.00	65.00	85.00	175	—
1797	—	40.00	65.00	85.00	175	—

KM# 2 5 BAIOCCHI
Copper **Obv:** Inscription below star within circle, legend around **Obv. Inscription:** BAIOC/CINQVE/FANO **Rev:** Madonna **Rev. Legend:** SANCTA DEI GENITRIX

Date	Mintage	Good	VG	F	VF	XF
1797//XXIII	—	40.00	65.00	85.00	175	—

PAPAL STATES-FERMO

A city in the Marches, was founded as a Latin colony in 264 B.C., became a free city in 1199, and was acquired by the papacy in 1550.

NOTE: For later issues see Roman Republic-Fermo.

CITY

EMERGENCY COINAGE

KM# 1.1 1/2 BAIOCCO
Copper **Rev:** FERMO

Date	Mintage	Good	VG	F	VF	XF
1797//XXIII	—	10.00	17.50	25.00	40.00	—
1798//XXIII	—	10.00	17.50	25.00	40.00	—

KM# 1.2 1/2 BAIOCCO
Copper **Obv:** Written value, date below stars within circle **Rev:** Inscription within wreath **Rev. Inscription:** PIVS PAPAVI AN• XXIII

Date	Mintage	Good	VG	F	VF	XF
1798//XXIII	—	12.00	20.00	30.00	50.00	—

KM# 2.1 2-1/2 BAIOCCHI
Copper **Obv:** Written value, date below stars within circle **Rev:** Saints' bust, left **Rev. Legend:** S P APOSTOLORUM PRINCEPS

Date	Mintage	Good	VG	F	VF	XF
1796	—	12.00	20.00	30.00	50.00	—
1797	—	12.00	20.00	30.00	50.00	—

KM# 2.2 2-1/2 BAIOCCHI
Copper **Rev:** Saints' bust, left **Rev. Legend:** S P PETRUS APOSTOL • PRINC •

Date	Mintage	Good	VG	F	VF	XF
1796	—	12.00	20.00	30.00	50.00	—

KM# 2.3 2-1/2 BAIOCCHI
Copper **Rev. Legend:** S P APOSTOLORUM PRINCDDS

Date	Mintage	Good	VG	F	VF	XF
1796	—	12.00	20.00	30.00	50.00	—

KM# 2.4 2-1/2 BAIOCCHI

Copper **Rev:** Saints' bust, left **Rev. Legend:** S P APOSTOLOR PRINCEPS

Date	Mintage	Good	VG	F	VF	XF
1797	—	12.00	20.00	30.00	50.00	—

KM# 2.5 2-1/2 BAIOCCHI

Copper **Rev. Legend:** S P APOST PRINCEPS

Date	Mintage	Good	VG	F	VF	XF
1797	—	12.00	20.00	30.00	50.00	—

KM# 3.1 5 BAIOCCHI

Copper **Obv:** Inscription within circle, legend around **Obv. Legend:** PIVS PAPA SEXTVS ANNO ... **Obv. Inscription:** BAIOC/CINQVE/FERMO **Rev:** Madonna

Date	Mintage	Good	VG	F	VF	XF
1797//XXIII	—	10.00	18.00	30.00	50.00	—
1799//XXV	—	10.00	18.00	30.00	50.00	—

KM# 3.2 5 BAIOCCHI

Copper **Rev:** L CHOTOTM appears below bust

Date	Mintage	Good	VG	F	VF	XF
1797//XXIII	—	12.00	20.00	35.00	60.00	—
1799//XXV	—	12.00	20.00	35.00	60.00	—

KM# 3.3 5 BAIOCCHI

Copper **Obv:** Inscription below star within circle, legend around, with date below **Obv. Legend:** PIVS PAPA SEXTVS ANNO.... **Obv. Inscription:** BAIOC/CHI/CINQVE, without FERMO

Date	Mintage	Good	VG	F	VF	XF
1799	—	10.00	18.00	30.00	50.00	—

KM# 4 60 BAIOCCHI

Billon **Obv:** Oval Papal arms **Obv. Legend:** PIVS SEXTVS PONT... **Rev:** Inscription, date below stars within circle and wreath

Date	Mintage	Good	VG	F	VF	XF
1799//XXV	—	50.00	100	125	165	—

PROVISIONAL REPUBLIC

1798

STANDARD COINAGE

KM# 5 60 BAIOCCHI

Copper **Obv:** Inscription within wreath **Obv. Inscription:** MEZZO/BAIOCCO/FERMO **Rev:** Shield within circle, legend around **Rev. Legend:** *ANNO*PMO*REIP*FIRM*1798

Date	Mintage	Good	VG	F	VF	XF
1798	—	7.50	12.50	20.00	35.00	—

PAPAL STATES-FERRARA

A city located in northeastern Italy in Emalia. With the Papacy 1598-1859.

MINT OFFICIAL'S INITIALS

Initials	Date	Name
GB	1740-48	Uncertain

CITY

STANDARD COINAGE

KM# 125 QUATTRINO

Copper **Subject:** Clement XI **Obv:** Arms **Rev:** Bust of St. Peter

Date	Mintage	VG	F	VF	XF	Unc
ND(1718)//XIX	—	6.50	13.50	25.00	40.00	—
ND(1719)//XX	—	6.50	13.50	25.00	40.00	—

KM# 126 QUATTRINO

Copper **Obv:** Papal arms **Rev:** St. Peter

Date	Mintage	VG	F	VF	XF	Unc
ND	—	25.00	45.00	75.00	120	—

KM# 135 QUATTRINO

Copper **Ruler:** Benedict XIV **Obv:** Papal arms **Rev:** Inscription within cartouche **Rev. Inscription:** FER/RARI/17Æ44 **Note:** Many varieties of arms and cartouche.

Date	Mintage	VG	F	VF	XF	Unc
1744	—	6.00	12.00	25.00	40.00	—
1745	—	6.00	12.00	25.00	40.00	—
1746	—	6.00	12.00	25.00	40.00	—
1747	—	6.00	12.00	25.00	40.00	—
1748	—	6.00	12.00	25.00	40.00	—
ND	—	6.00	12.00	25.00	40.00	—

KM# 140 QUATTRINO

Copper **Ruler:** Benedict XIV **Obv:** Papal arms **Rev:** EER RA • RI, date in cartouche

Date	Mintage	VG	F	VF	XF	Unc
1746	—	6.00	12.00	25.00	40.00	—

KM# 141 QUATTRINO

Copper **Ruler:** Benedict XIV **Obv:** Papal arms **Rev:** FER/RARI/ within palm wreath

Date	Mintage	VG	F	VF	XF	Unc
1746	—	6.00	12.50	22.50	40.00	—
1747	—	6.00	12.50	22.50	40.00	—
1748	—	6.00	12.50	22.50	40.00	—

KM# 136 QUATTRINO

Copper **Ruler:** Benedict XIV **Obv:** Papal arms **Rev:** FER/RARA in cartouche **Note:** Many varieties.

Date	Mintage	VG	F	VF	XF	Unc
ND (1749)	—	6.00	12.00	25.00	40.00	—

KM# 127 1/2 BAIOCCO

Copper **Ruler:** Clement XI **Subject:** Clement XI **Obv:** Papal arms **Rev:** MEZO/BAIOC/CO/FERRAR in cartouche

Date	Mintage	VG	F	VF	XF	Unc
ND(1719)//XIX	—	7.00	14.00	25.00	42.50	—
ND(1720)//XX	—	7.00	14.00	25.00	42.50	—

KM# 130 1/2 BAIOCCO

Copper **Ruler:** Innocent XIII **Subject:** Innocent XIII **Obv:** Papal arms **Rev:** Value: MEZO/BAIOC/CO/FERRAR

Date	Mintage	VG	F	VF	XF	Unc
ND(1721)//1	—	22.00	45.00	85.00	140	—

KM# 137 1/2 BAIOCCO

Copper **Ruler:** Benedict XIV **Obv:** Papal arms **Obv. Legend:** BENEDICT • XIV • ... **Rev:** Written value, date above shield in cartouche **Note:** Many varieties.

Date	Mintage	VG	F	VF	XF	Unc
1744//IV	—	7.00	14.00	25.00	40.00	—
ND//IV	—	7.00	14.00	25.00	40.00	—
1744//V	—	7.00	14.00	25.00	40.00	—
1745//IV	—	7.00	14.00	25.00	40.00	—
1745//VI	—	7.00	14.00	25.00	40.00	—
1746//VI	—	7.00	14.00	25.00	40.00	—
1746//VII	—	7.00	14.00	25.00	40.00	—
1748//VIII	—	7.00	14.00	25.00	40.00	—
1748//IX	—	7.00	14.00	25.00	40.00	—
ND//IX	—	7.00	14.00	25.00	40.00	—
ND//X	—	7.00	14.00	25.00	40.00	—
1750//VI	—	7.00	14.00	25.00	40.00	—
1751	—	7.00	14.00	25.00	40.00	—
ND//XI	—	7.00	14.00	25.00	40.00	—

KM# 139 1/2 BAIOCCO

Copper **Ruler:** Benedict XIV **Obv:** Papal arms **Obv. Legend:** BENEDICT • XIV PM AVI **Rev:** MEZZO/BAIOCCO/FERRARA, shield divides date below, all in cartouche

Date	Mintage	VG	F	VF	XF	Unc
1745//V	—	7.00	14.00	25.00	40.00	—

KM# 143 1/2 BAIOCCO

Copper **Ruler:** Benedict XIV **Obv:** Papal arms **Obv. Legend:** BENEDICT • XIV • P • M • A • VII • **Rev:** MEZZO/BAIOCCO/ FERRARA, shield below divides date, all within sprigs

Date	Mintage	VG	F	VF	XF	Unc
1747//VII	—	7.00	14.00	25.00	40.00	—

KM# 138 BAIOCCO

Copper **Ruler:** Benedict XIV **Obv:** Papal arms **Obv. Legend:** BENEDICT • XIV • P • M • .... **Rev:** I/BAIOCCO/FERRARA, date above shield in cartouche **Note:** Many varieties.

Date	Mintage	VG	F	VF	XF	Unc
1744//IV	—	10.00	20.00	35.00	50.00	—
1744//V	—	10.00	20.00	35.00	50.00	—
1745//IV	—	10.00	20.00	35.00	50.00	—
1746//V	—	10.00	20.00	35.00	50.00	—
1747//VIII	—	10.00	20.00	35.00	50.00	—
1748//VIII	—	10.00	20.00	35.00	50.00	—
1748//IX	—	10.00	20.00	35.00	50.00	—
1749//IX	—	10.00	20.00	35.00	50.00	—
1750//IX	—	10.00	20.00	35.00	50.00	—
1751//XI	—	10.00	20.00	35.00	50.00	—
ND//XII	—	10.00	20.00	35.00	50.00	—

KM# 142 BAIOCCO

Copper **Ruler:** Benedict XIV **Obv:** Papal arms **Obv. Legend:** BENEDICT • XIV • P • M • A • VI • **Rev:** I/BAIOCCO/FERRARA, date above shield in cartouche

Date	Mintage	VG	F	VF	XF	Unc
1746//VI	—	10.00	20.00	35.00	50.00	—

KM# 144 BAIOCCO

Copper **Ruler:** Benedict XIV **Obv:** Papal arms **Obv. Legend:** BENEDICT XIV P M A VII **Rev:** Written value above divided date and shield in cartouche

Date	Mintage	VG	F	VF	XF	Unc
1747//VII	—	10.00	20.00	35.00	50.00	—

KM# 150 BAIOCCO

Copper **Ruler:** Benedict XIV **Obv:** Papal arms **Obv. Legend:** BENED • XIV • P • M • ... **Rev:** Written value, date above shield in cartouche

Date	Mintage	VG	F	VF	XF	Unc
1751//IX	—	12.00	25.00	40.00	55.00	—

KM# 151 BAIOCCO

Copper **Obv:** Papal arms **Obv. Legend:** BENED • XIV • ... **Rev:** Written value above shield in cartouche

Date	Mintage	VG	F	VF	XF	Unc
ND//XII	—	10.00	20.00	35.00	50.00	—

KM# 153 GROSETTO

Billon **Ruler:** Benedict XIV **Subject:** Benedict XIV **Note:** Counterstamped with wreath on KM#105.

Date	Mintage	VG	F	VF	XF	Unc
ND(1756)//1709	—	18.00	35.00	65.00	110	—

KM# 104 2 GROSETTO (26 Quattrini)

Billon **Ruler:** Clement XI **Subject:** Clement XI **Obv:** Value: 26 below arms **Rev:** St. George slaying dragon

Date	Mintage	VG	F	VF	XF	Unc
1709//IX	—	30.00	65.00	120	200	—

KM# 152 2 GROSETTO (26 Quattrini)

Billon **Ruler:** Benedict XIV **Subject:** Benedict XIV **Note:** Counterstamped with wreath on KM#104.

Date	Mintage	VG	F	VF	XF	Unc
ND(1756)//1709	—	35.00	70.00	125	220	—

KM# 100 MURAIOLA (Baiocchi)

Billon **Ruler:** Clement XI **Obv:** Capped bust left **Rev:** St. Maurelius standing, two hands outstretched

Date	Mintage	VG	F	VF	XF	Unc
1708//VIII	—	7.00	14.00	25.00	42.50	—
1709//IX	—	7.00	14.00	25.00	42.50	—

KM# 110 MURAIOLA (2 Baiocchi)

Billon **Ruler:** Clement XI **Obv:** Capped bust left **Rev:** St. Maurelius standing, one hand raised

Date	Mintage	VG	F	VF	XF	Unc
1710//X	—	7.00	14.00	25.00	42.50	—
1711//XI	—	7.00	14.00	25.00	42.50	—

KM# 114 MURAIOLA (2 Baiocchi)

Billon **Ruler:** Clement XI **Rev:** St. George standing **Rev. Legend:** PROTEC • FERRARIAE

Date	Mintage	VG	F	VF	XF	Unc
1716	—	7.00	14.00	25.00	42.50	—

KM# 115 MURAIOLA (2 Baiocchi)

Billon **Ruler:** Clement XI **Rev:** St. George standing **Rev. Legend:** S. GEORGIVS PROT. FERRAE

Date	Mintage	VG	F	VF	XF	Unc
1716	—	7.00	14.00	25.00	42.50	—
1717	—	7.00	14.00	25.00	42.50	—

KM# 101 MURAIOLA (4 Baiocci)

Billon **Ruler:** Clement XI

Date	Mintage	VG	F	VF	XF	Unc
1708//VIII	—	10.00	20.00	35.00	60.00	—
1709//X	—	10.00	20.00	35.00	60.00	—

KM# 111 MURAIOLA (4 Baiocci)

Billon **Ruler:** Clement XI

Date	Mintage	VG	F	VF	XF	Unc
1710//X	—	10.00	20.00	35.00	60.00	—
1711//XI	—	10.00	20.00	35.00	60.00	—

KM# 116 MURAIOLA (4 Baiocci)

Billon **Ruler:** Clement XI **Obv:** Capped bust right **Rev:** St. George slaying dragon

Date	Mintage	VG	F	VF	XF	Unc
1716	—	10.00	20.00	35.00	60.00	—
1717	—	10.00	20.00	35.00	60.00	—

KM# 119 MURAIOLA (8 Baiocchi)

Billon **Ruler:** Clement XI **Obv:** Capped bust right with N oval **Rev:** St. Maurelius and St. George standing

Date	Mintage	VG	F	VF	XF	Unc
1717//VIII	—	30.00	65.00	120	200	—

KM# 105 MURAIOLA (13 Quattrini)

Billon **Ruler:** Clement XI **Obv:** Papal arms **Rev:** St. George slaying dragon

Date	Mintage	VG	F	VF	XF	Unc
1709//IX	—	12.00	22.00	40.00	65.00	—
1709//X	—	12.00	22.00	40.00	65.00	—

KM# 102 TESTONE

Silver **Ruler:** Clement XI **Obv:** Capped bust left

Date	Mintage	VG	F	VF	XF	Unc
1708//VIII	—	100	200	350	575	—

KM# 112 TESTONE

Silver **Ruler:** Clement XI **Obv:** Capped bust left **Rev:** St. George slaying dragon with different shield

Date	Mintage	VG	F	VF	XF	Unc
1710//X	—	100	200	350	575	—
1710//XI	—	100	200	350	575	—

KM# 117 TESTONE

Silver **Ruler:** Clement XI **Rev:** St. George slaying dragon with different shield

Date	Mintage	VG	F	VF	XF	Unc
1716//XVI	—	100	200	350	575	—

KM# 118 TESTONE

Silver **Ruler:** Clement XI **Obv:** Papal arms

Date	Mintage	VG	F	VF	XF	Unc
1716	—	100	200	350	575	—
1717	—	100	200	350	575	—

KM# 120 TESTONE

Silver **Ruler:** Clement XI **Rev:** Inscription **Rev. Inscription:** DEXTERADOMINI / FECIT / VIRTVTEM / 1717

Date	Mintage	VG	F	VF	XF	Unc
1717	—	65.00	135	250	400	—

KM# 121 TESTONE

Silver **Ruler:** Clement XI **Rev:** Inscription **Rev. Inscription:** SECLERVM / MATER / AVARITIA / 1717 / FERRAR

Date	Mintage	VG	F	VF	XF	Unc
1717	—	65.00	135	250	400	—

KM# 122 TESTONE

Silver **Ruler:** Clement XI **Rev:** Inscription **Rev. Inscription:** QVIS / PAVPER / AVARVS 1717

Date	Mintage	VG	F	VF	XF	Unc
1717	—	65.00	135	250	400	—

KM# 103 1/2 PIASTRA

Silver **Ruler:** Clement XI **Obv:** Capped bust left **Obv. Legend:** CLEMENS • XI • P • M • AN • VIII **Rev:** St. George slaying dragon, date in exergue **Rev. Legend:** S • GEORGIVS - FERRARIÆ PROTEC • **Note:** Dav. #1439.

Date	Mintage	VG	F	VF	XF	Unc
1708//VIII	—	350	700	1,200	2,000	—

KM# 106 1/2 PIASTRA

Silver **Ruler:** Clement XI **Obv:** Inscription in exergue, Papal arms **Obv. Legend:** CLEMENS * * * XI * P * M * A * IX **Rev:** Inscription in frame over shield in cartouche **Rev. Inscription:** IN/ TESTIMONIA/ TVA ET MON IN/ AVARTIAM **Note:** Dav. #1440.

Date	Mintage	VG	F	VF	XF	Unc
1709//IX	—	2,000	3,500	6,000	9,000	—

KM# 113 1/2 PIASTRA

Silver **Ruler:** Clement XI **Obv:** Inscription in exergue, capped bust left **Obv. Inscription:** CIV FERRARIA **Rev:** Inscription above Papal arms **Rev. Inscription:** NON/ AVRVM/ SED/ NOMEN/ date **Note:** Dav. #1442.

Date	Mintage	VG	F	VF	XF	Unc
1710//X	—	3,500	5,500	9,500	14,500	—

KM# 123 1/2 PIASTRA

Silver **Ruler:** Clement XI **Obv:** Bust in tiara, right **Rev:** Papal arms **Rev. Legend:** IVLIVS • S • R • E • CARD • PIAZZA • FERR

Date	Mintage	VG	F	VF	XF	Unc
1717//XVII	—	350	700	1,200	2,000	—

KM# 124 1/2 PIASTRA

Silver **Ruler:** Clement XI **Obv:** Capped bust right **Rev:** Inscription **Rev. Inscription:** DEFLUT/ ET/ INFLVIT/ 1717 **Note:** Dav. #1449.

Date	Mintage	VG	F	VF	XF	Unc
1717	—	3,500	5,500	9,500	14,500	—

PAPAL STATES-FOLIGNO

Fvligno

A city in Umbria, was governed by deputies of the Holy See from 1305 to 1439, and was a possession of the papacy until 1860.

NOTE: For later issues see Roman Republic-Foligno.

CITY

EMERGENCY COINAGE

KM# 1 QUATTRINO

Copper **Obv:** Papal arms **Obv. Legend:** PIVS SEXTVS PON M A • **Rev:** St. Peter **Rev. Legend:** S • FELI CIANO

Date	Mintage	Good	VG	F	VF	XF
NDXX (1794)	—	18.00	35.00	75.00	120	—
NDXXI (1795)	—	18.00	35.00	75.00	120	—

KM# 2 1/2 BAIOCCO

Copper **Obv:** Papal oval arms **Obv. Legend:** PIUS SEXTVS PON M A • **Rev:** Written value, city name above star within wreath **Note:** KM#2 also exists with "FOLIGNO" instead of "FVLIGNO".

Date	Mintage	Good	VG	F	VF	XF
XX (1794)	—	12.50	25.00	40.00	70.00	—
XXI (1795)	—	12.50	25.00	40.00	70.00	—

KM# 6 1/2 BAIOCCO

Copper **Obv:** Papal oval arms **Rev:** Written value, city name, date within wreath

Date	Mintage	Good	VG	F	VF	XF
XXI//1795	—	12.50	25.00	40.00	70.00	—

KM# 7 1/2 BAIOCCO

Copper **Obv:** Papal arms **Obv. Legend:** PIVS SEXT P M A XXIII **Rev:** Written value, city name below stars

Date	Mintage	Good	VG	F	VF	XF
XXIII (1797)	—	12.50	25.00	40.00	70.00	—
XXIII (1798)	—	12.50	25.00	40.00	70.00	—

KM# 3 BAIOCCO

Copper **Obv:** Papal oval arms **Obv. Legend:** PIVS • SEXTVS • PON • M • A • XX **Rev:** Written value, city name within wreath **Note:** KM#3 also exists with date on reverse; also exists with "FOLIGNO" instead of "FVLIGNO".

Date	Mintage	Good	VG	F	VF	XF
XX (1794)	—	15.00	30.00	45.00	75.00	—
XXI (1795)	—	15.00	30.00	45.00	75.00	—

KM# 4 BAIOCCO

Copper **Obv:** Papal oval arms **Obv. Legend:** PIVS • SEXTVS • PON • M • A • XX **Rev:** Written value, city name **Note:** KM#4 also exists with date on reverse; also exists with "FOLIGNO" instead of "FULIGNO".

Date	Mintage	Good	VG	F	VF	XF
XX (1794)	—	15.00	25.00	40.00	70.00	—
XXI (1795)	—	15.00	25.00	40.00	70.00	—

KM# 5 2 BAIOCCHI

Copper **Obv:** Papal oval arms **Obv. Legend:** PIVS • SEXTVS • PON • M • A • XXI **Rev:** Written value, city name within wreath **Note:** KM#5 also exists with "FOLIGNO" instead of "FULIGNO".

Date	Mintage	VG	F	VF	XF	Unc
XX (1794)	—	35.00	65.00	100	—	—
XXI (1795)	—	35.00	65.00	100	—	—

KM# A6 2 BAIOCCHI

Copper **Obv:** Papal arms **Rev:** St. Peter **Note:** Varieties exists with "PRINC" instead of "PRINCEPS".

Date	Mintage	VG	F	VF	XF	Unc
1796	—	30.00	45.00	75.00	—	—
1797	—	30.00	45.00	75.00	—	—

KM# 8 5 BAIOCCHI

Copper **Obv:** Written value, city name below star within circle **Obv. Legend:** FVLIGNO PIVS SEXTVS ANNO XXIII **Rev:** Bust of Virgin Mary left **Rev. Legend:** SANCTA DEI GENITRIX

Date	Mintage	VG	F	VF	XF	Unc
XXIII//1797 TM	—	30.00	45.00	85.00	—	—

PAPAL STATES-GUBBIO

A city in Umbria, was part of the donation of Charlemagne to the pope in 774. It became a consul-governed republic in 1151, came under the dukes of Urbino in 1387, and was ceded to the pope in 1624.

NOTE: For later issues see Roman Republic-Gubbio.

CITY

STANDARD COINAGE

KM# 83 QUATTRINO

Copper **Rev:** Bust of St. Ubaldus, mitred left

Date	Mintage	VG	F	VF	XF	Unc
(1702)-III	—	13.50	25.00	40.00	75.00	—

KM# 77 QUATTRINO

Copper **Ruler:** Clement XI **Subject:** Clement XI **Obv:** Papal arms **Rev:** St. Paul standing

Date	Mintage	VG	F	VF	XF	Unc
(1702)-III	—	13.50	25.00	40.00	75.00	—

KM# 78 QUATTRINO

Copper **Ruler:** Clement XI **Rev:** Bust of St. Paul right

Date	Mintage	VG	F	VF	XF	Unc
(1702)-III	—	13.50	25.00	40.00	75.00	—

KM# 79 QUATTRINO

Copper **Ruler:** Clement XI **Rev:** St. Peter standing

Date	Mintage	VG	F	VF	XF	Unc
(1702)-III	—	13.50	25.00	40.00	75.00	—

KM# 80 QUATTRINO

Copper **Ruler:** Clement XI **Rev:** Bust of St. Peter left

Date	Mintage	VG	F	VF	XF	Unc
(1702)-III	—	13.50	25.00	40.00	75.00	—

KM# 81 QUATTRINO

Copper **Ruler:** Clement XI **Rev:** Legend without EPISCOPVS, St. Ubaldus standing

Date	Mintage	VG	F	VF	XF	Unc
(1702)-III	—	13.50	25.00	40.00	75.00	—
(1703)-IIII	—	13.50	25.00	40.00	75.00	—
(1704)-V	—	13.50	25.00	40.00	75.00	—
(1705)-VI	—	13.50	25.00	40.00	75.00	—
(1706)-VII	—	13.50	25.00	40.00	75.00	—
(1707)-VIII	—	13.50	25.00	40.00	75.00	—
(1708)-IX	—	13.50	25.00	40.00	75.00	—
(1709)-X	—	13.50	25.00	40.00	75.00	—
(1710)-XI	—	13.50	25.00	40.00	75.00	—
(1711)-XII	—	13.50	25.00	40.00	75.00	—
(1712)-XIII	—	13.50	25.00	40.00	75.00	—
(1713)-XIV	—	13.50	25.00	40.00	75.00	—
(1714)-XV	—	13.50	25.00	40.00	75.00	—
(1715)-XVI	—	13.50	25.00	40.00	75.00	—
(1716)-XVII	—	13.50	25.00	40.00	75.00	—

KM# 82 QUATTRINO

Copper **Ruler:** Clement XI **Rev. Legend:** EPISCOPVS

Date	Mintage	VG	F	VF	XF	Unc
(1702)-III	—	13.50	25.00	40.00	75.00	—
(1703)-IIII	—	13.50	25.00	40.00	75.00	—
(1704)-V	—	13.50	25.00	40.00	75.00	—
(1705)-VI	—	13.50	25.00	40.00	75.00	—
(1706)-VII	—	13.50	25.00	40.00	75.00	—
(1707)-VIII	—	13.50	25.00	40.00	75.00	—
(1708)-IX	—	13.50	25.00	40.00	75.00	—
(1709)-X	—	13.50	25.00	40.00	75.00	—
(1710)-XI	—	13.50	25.00	40.00	75.00	—
(1711)-XII	—	13.50	25.00	40.00	75.00	—
(1712)-XIII	—	13.50	25.00	40.00	75.00	—
(1713)-XIV	—	13.50	25.00	40.00	75.00	—

KM# 86 QUATTRINO

Copper **Ruler:** Clement XI **Rev:** Bust of St. Paul left

Date	Mintage	VG	F	VF	XF	Unc
(1706)-VII	—	13.50	25.00	40.00	75.00	—
(1707)-VIII	—	13.50	25.00	40.00	75.00	—
(1708)-IX	—	13.50	25.00	40.00	75.00	—
(1709)-X	—	13.50	25.00	40.00	75.00	—
(1710)-XI	—	13.50	25.00	40.00	75.00	—
(1711)-XII	—	13.50	25.00	40.00	75.00	—
(1712)-XIII	—	13.50	25.00	40.00	75.00	—
(1713)-XIV	—	13.50	25.00	40.00	75.00	—
(1714)-XV	—	13.50	25.00	40.00	75.00	—
(1715)-XVI	—	13.50	25.00	40.00	75.00	—
(1716)-XVII	—	13.50	25.00	40.00	75.00	—
(1717)-XVIII	—	13.50	25.00	40.00	75.00	—
(1718)-XIX	—	13.50	25.00	40.00	75.00	—
(1719)-XX	—	13.50	25.00	40.00	75.00	—

KM# 87 QUATTRINO

Copper **Ruler:** Clement XI **Rev:** Bust of St. Peter left

Date	Mintage	VG	F	VF	XF	Unc
(1706)-VII	—	13.50	25.00	40.00	75.00	—
(1707)-VIII	—	13.50	25.00	40.00	75.00	—
(1708)-IX	—	13.50	25.00	40.00	75.00	—
(1709)-X	—	13.50	25.00	40.00	75.00	—
(1710)-XI	—	13.50	25.00	40.00	75.00	—
(1711)-XII	—	13.50	25.00	40.00	75.00	—
(1712)-XIII	—	13.50	25.00	40.00	75.00	—
(1713)-XIV	—	13.50	25.00	40.00	75.00	—
(1714)-XV	—	13.50	25.00	40.00	75.00	—
(1715)-XVI	—	13.50	25.00	40.00	75.00	—
(1716)-XVII	—	13.50	25.00	40.00	75.00	—
(1717)-XVIII	—	13.50	25.00	40.00	75.00	—
(1718)-XIX	—	13.50	25.00	40.00	75.00	—
(1719)-XX	—	13.50	25.00	40.00	75.00	—

KM# 90 QUATTRINO

Copper **Ruler:** Clement XI **Rev:** Radiant bust of St. Peter right

Date	Mintage	VG	F	VF	XF	Unc
(1716)-XVII	—	15.00	28.00	48.00	85.00	—
(1717)-XVIII	—	15.00	28.00	48.00	85.00	—

KM# 91 QUATTRINO

Copper **Ruler:** Clement XI **Rev:** Bust of St. Paul left

Date	Mintage	VG	F	VF	XF	Unc
(1717)-XVIII	—	15.00	28.00	48.00	85.00	—

KM# 95 QUATTRINO

Copper **Ruler:** Clement XI

Date	Mintage	VG	F	VF	XF	Unc
ND (1718)	—	24.00	42.00	70.00	100	—

KM# 97 QUATTRINO

Copper **Ruler:** Clement XI **Rev:** Legend without EPISCOP, St. Ubaldus standing

Date	Mintage	VG	F	VF	XF	Unc
ND (1720)	—	24.00	42.00	70.00	100	—

KM# 98 QUATTRINO

Copper **Ruler:** Clement XI **Rev:** EPISCOP in legend

Date	Mintage	VG	F	VF	XF	Unc
ND (1720)	—	24.00	42.00	70.00	100	—

KM# 102 QUATTRINO

Copper **Ruler:** Clement XI **Rev:** Bust of St. Paul left

Date	Mintage	VG	F	VF	XF	Unc
ND (1721)	—	16.50	30.00	50.00	80.00	—

KM# 103 QUATTRINO
Copper **Ruler:** Innocent XIII **Rev:** Bust of St. Peter right

Date	Mintage	VG	F	VF	XF	Unc
ND (1722)	—	16.50	30.00	50.00	80.00	—

KM# 106 QUATTRINO
Copper **Ruler:** Innocent XIII **Rev:** St. Ubaldus standing **Rev. Legend:** EVGVBILL

Date	Mintage	VG	F	VF	XF	Unc
ND (1724)	—	16.50	30.00	50.00	80.00	—

KM# 105 QUATTRINO
Copper **Ruler:** Benedict XIII **Rev:** St. Ubaldus standing **Rev. Legend:** EPISCVPVS

Date	Mintage	VG	F	VF	XF	Unc
ND (1724)	—	16.50	30.00	50.00	80.00	—

KM# 107 QUATTRINO
Copper **Ruler:** Benedict XIII **Rev:** Holy door **Note:** Holy Year issue.

Date	Mintage	VG	F	VF	XF	Unc
ND (1725)	—	16.50	30.00	50.00	80.00	—

KM# 120 QUATTRINO
Copper **Ruler:** Clement XII **Subject:** Clement XII **Rev:** Value and date **Rev. Legend:** QVAT/TRINO/GVBBIO

Date	Mintage	VG	F	VF	XF	Unc
1738	—	10.00	18.00	30.00	45.00	—
1739	—	10.00	18.00	30.00	45.00	—

KM# 121 QUATTRINO
Copper **Ruler:** Benedict XIV **Rev:** Head of St. Paul left

Date	Mintage	VG	F	VF	XF	Unc
ND (1740)	—	10.00	18.00	30.00	45.00	—

KM# 135 QUATTRINO
Copper **Ruler:** Benedict XIV **Obv:** Papal arms **Rev:** Written value, date

Date	Mintage	VG	F	VF	XF	Unc
1740	—	70.00	100	175	250	—

KM# 122 QUATTRINO
Copper **Ruler:** Benedict XIV **Rev:** St. Paul standing

Date	Mintage	VG	F	VF	XF	Unc
ND (1741)	—	10.00	18.00	30.00	45.00	—

KM# 123 QUATTRINO
Copper **Ruler:** Benedict XIV **Rev:** Head of St. Peter right

Date	Mintage	VG	F	VF	XF	Unc
ND (1742)	—	10.00	18.00	30.00	45.00	—

KM# 124 QUATTRINO
Copper **Ruler:** Benedict XIV **Rev:** Head of St. Peter right and upwards

Date	Mintage	VG	F	VF	XF	Unc
ND (1743)	—	10.00	18.00	30.00	45.00	—

KM# 125 QUATTRINO
Copper **Ruler:** Benedict XIV **Rev:** St. Peter standing

Date	Mintage	VG	F	VF	XF	Unc
ND (1744)	—	10.00	18.00	30.00	45.00	—

KM# 126 QUATTRINO
Copper **Ruler:** Benedict XIV **Rev:** St. Ubaldus standing

Date	Mintage	VG	F	VF	XF	Unc
ND (1745)	—	10.00	18.00	30.00	45.00	—

KM# 127 QUATTRINO
Copper **Ruler:** Benedict XIV **Rev:** St. Ubaldus standing, mitred, crosier right

Date	Mintage	VG	F	VF	XF	Unc
ND (1745)	—	10.00	18.00	30.00	45.00	—

KM# 128 QUATTRINO
Copper **Ruler:** Benedict XIV **Rev:** St. Ubaldus standing, mitred, crosier left

Date	Mintage	VG	F	VF	XF	Unc
ND (1745)	—	10.00	18.00	30.00	45.00	—

KM# 129 QUATTRINO
Copper **Ruler:** Benedict XIV **Rev:** St. Ubaldus standing, head bare

Date	Mintage	VG	F	VF	XF	Unc
ND (1746)	—	10.00	18.00	30.00	45.00	—

KM# 136 QUATTRINO
Copper **Ruler:** Benedict XIV **Obv:** Papal arms **Rev:** St. Peter right

Date	Mintage	VG	F	VF	XF	Unc
(1746)III	—	10.00	18.00	35.00	50.00	—

KM# 137 QUATTRINO
Copper **Ruler:** Benedict XIV **Obv:** Papal arms **Rev:** St. Paul, head right

Date	Mintage	VG	F	VF	XF	Unc
(1747)III	—	8.00	15.00	25.00	40.00	—

KM# 138 QUATTRINO
Copper **Ruler:** Benedict XIV **Obv:** Papal arms **Rev:** Saints' head, right

Date	Mintage	VG	F	VF	XF	Unc
(1747)III	—	8.00	15.00	25.00	40.00	—

KM# 139 QUATTRINO
Copper **Ruler:** Benedict XIV **Obv:** Papal arms **Rev:** Peter and Paul, conjoined heads left

Date	Mintage	VG	F	VF	XF	Unc
ND (1748)	—	15.00	25.00	45.00	70.00	—

KM# 140 QUATTRINO
Copper **Ruler:** Benedict XIV **Obv:** Papal arms **Rev:** St. Paul standing

Date	Mintage	VG	F	VF	XF	Unc
ND (1749)	—	8.00	15.00	25.00	40.00	—

KM# 141 QUATTRINO
Copper **Ruler:** Benedict XIV **Obv:** Papal arms **Rev:** St. Ubaldus

Date	Mintage	VG	F	VF	XF	Unc
ND (1749)	—	8.00	15.00	25.00	40.00	—

KM# 150 QUATTRINO
Copper **Ruler:** Benedict XIV **Rev:** Holy Door **Note:** Holy Year Issue

Date	Mintage	VG	F	VF	XF	Unc
1750	—	25.00	45.00	75.00	150	—

KM# 151 QUATTRINO
Copper **Ruler:** Clement XIII **Obv:** Papal arms **Obv. Legend:** CLE M XIII • P M **Rev:** Saint's head right **Rev. Legend:** S PET • A **Note:** Varieties exist.

Date	Mintage	VG	F	VF	XF	Unc
ND (1761)	—	5.00	10.00	15.00	30.00	—

KM# 152 QUATTRINO
Copper **Ruler:** Clement XIII **Obv:** Papal arms **Obv. Legend:** CLE • X III • P • M **Rev:** St. head, right **Rev. Legend:** S • PAV • A **Note:** Varieties exist.

Date	Mintage	VG	F	VF	XF	Unc
ND (1762)	—	5.00	10.00	15.00	30.00	—

KM# 153 QUATTRINO
Copper **Ruler:** Clement XIII **Obv:** Papal arms **Obv. Legend:** CLE M X III • P **Rev:** Standing figure of St. Ubaldus **Rev. Legend:** S • VBAL • EP • EV **Note:** Varieties exist.

Date	Mintage	VG	F	VF	XF	Unc
ND (1763)	—	10.00	15.00	30.00	—	—

KM# 84 1/2 BAIOCCO
Copper **Ruler:** Clement XI **Subject:** Clement XI **Rev:** Value, MEZZO/BAIOC/CO within wreath

Date	Mintage	VG	F	VF	XF	Unc
(1703)-IV	—	8.00	15.00	25.00	45.00	—
(1704)-V	—	8.00	15.00	25.00	45.00	—
(1705)-VI	—	8.00	15.00	25.00	45.00	—
(1706)-VII	—	8.00	15.00	25.00	45.00	—
(1707)-VIII	—	8.00	15.00	25.00	45.00	—
(1708)-IX	—	8.00	15.00	25.00	45.00	—
(1710)-XI	—	8.00	15.00	25.00	45.00	—
(1711)-XII	—	8.00	15.00	25.00	45.00	—
(1712)-XIII	—	8.00	15.00	25.00	45.00	—
(1713)-XIV	—	8.00	15.00	25.00	45.00	—
(1714)-XV	—	8.00	15.00	25.00	45.00	—
(1714)-XVI	—	8.00	15.00	25.00	45.00	—
(1716)-XVII	—	8.00	15.00	25.00	45.00	—
(1717)-XVIII	—	8.00	15.00	25.00	45.00	—
(1718)-XIX	—	8.00	15.00	25.00	45.00	—

KM# 85 1/2 BAIOCCO
Copper **Ruler:** Clement XI **Rev:** Value, MEZZO/BAIOC/CO in cartouche

Date	Mintage	VG	F	VF	XF	Unc
(1703)-IV	—	8.00	15.00	25.00	45.00	—
(1704)-V	—	8.00	15.00	25.00	45.00	—
(1705)-VI	—	8.00	15.00	25.00	45.00	—
(1706)-VII	—	8.00	15.00	25.00	45.00	—
(1707)-VIII	—	8.00	15.00	25.00	45.00	—
(1708)-IX	—	8.00	15.00	25.00	45.00	—
(1709)-X	—	8.00	15.00	25.00	45.00	—
(1710)-XI	—	8.00	15.00	25.00	45.00	—
(1711)-XII	—	8.00	15.00	25.00	45.00	—
(1712)-XIII	—	8.00	15.00	25.00	45.00	—
(1713)-XIV	—	8.00	15.00	25.00	45.00	—
(1714)-XV	—	8.00	15.00	25.00	45.00	—
(1715)-XVI	—	8.00	15.00	25.00	45.00	—
(1716)-XVII	—	8.00	15.00	25.00	45.00	—
(1717)-XVIII	—	8.00	15.00	25.00	45.00	—
(1718)-XIX	—	8.00	15.00	25.00	45.00	—

KM# 99 1/2 BAIOCCO
Copper **Subject:** Innocent XIII **Rev:** Value, MEZO/BAIOC/CO within circle and laurel wreath

Date	Mintage	VG	F	VF	XF	Unc
1721	—	10.00	20.00	35.00	60.00	—
1722-11	—	10.00	20.00	35.00	60.00	—
1723	—	10.00	20.00	35.00	60.00	—
ND	—	10.00	20.00	35.00	60.00	—

KM# 100 1/2 BAIOCCO
Copper **Ruler:** Clement XI **Rev:** Without inner circle

Date	Mintage	VG	F	VF	XF	Unc
1721	—	10.00	20.00	35.00	60.00	—

KM# 101 1/2 BAIOCCO
Copper **Ruler:** Innocent XIII **Rev:** Value, MEZO/BAIOC/CO within cartouche

Date	Mintage	VG	F	VF	XF	Unc
(1722)-11	—	10.00	20.00	35.00	60.00	—

KM# 110 1/2 BAIOCCO
Copper **Ruler:** Benedict XIII **Rev:** Holy Door **Note:** Holy Year Issue.

Date	Mintage	VG	F	VF	XF	Unc
1725	—	20.00	40.00	65.00	120	—

KM# 109 1/2 BAIOCCO
Copper **Rev:** Legend without circle and in oak wreath

Date	Mintage	VG	F	VF	XF	Unc
ND	—	9.00	18.00	30.00	50.00	—

KM# 117 1/2 BAIOCCO
Copper **Ruler:** Clement XII **Subject:** Clement XII **Rev:** Value, MEZZO/BAIOC/CO/GVBBIO/date in cartouche

Date	Mintage	VG	F	VF	XF	Unc
(1731)-II	—	6.00	12.00	20.00	35.00	—
(1732)-III	—	6.00	12.00	20.00	35.00	—
(1733)-IIII	—	6.00	12.00	20.00	35.00	—
(1734)-V	—	6.00	12.00	20.00	35.00	—
(1735)-VI	—	6.00	12.00	20.00	35.00	—
(1736)-VII	—	6.00	12.00	20.00	35.00	—
(1737)-VIII	—	6.00	12.00	20.00	35.00	—
1738	—	6.00	12.00	20.00	35.00	—
1739	—	6.00	12.00	20.00	35.00	—
ND	—	6.00	12.00	20.00	35.00	—

KM# 119 1/2 BAIOCCO
Copper **Ruler:** Clement XII **Rev:** Ivy wreath replaces cartouche

Date	Mintage	VG	F	VF	XF	Unc
(1735)-VI	—	6.00	12.00	20.00	35.00	—
(1736)-VII	—	6.00	12.00	20.00	35.00	—
(1737)-VIII	—	6.00	12.00	20.00	35.00	—

KM# 143 1/2 BAIOCCO

Copper **Ruler:** Benedict XIV **Obv:** Papal arms **Rev:** Written value within wreath

Date	Mintage	VG	F	VF	XF	Unc
(1741)-II	—	15.00	25.00	45.00	70.00	—

KM# 144 1/2 BAIOCCO

Copper **Ruler:** Benedict XIV **Obv:** Papal arms **Obv. Legend:** BENEDIC • XIV • **Rev:** Written value, date within wreath **Note:** Many varieties.

Date	Mintage	VG	F	VF	XF	Unc
1743-IV	—	7.00	14.00	25.00	40.00	—
1744-IV	—	7.00	14.00	25.00	40.00	—
1745-IV	—	7.00	14.00	25.00	40.00	—
1745-VI	—	7.00	14.00	25.00	40.00	—
1746-VII	—	7.00	14.00	25.00	40.00	—
1747-VIII	—	7.00	14.00	25.00	40.00	—
1748-VIII	—	7.00	14.00	25.00	40.00	—
1749-VIIII	—	7.00	14.00	25.00	40.00	—
1750	—	7.00	14.00	25.00	40.00	—
1751	—	7.00	14.00	25.00	40.00	—

KM# 146 1/2 BAIOCCO

Copper **Ruler:** Benedict XIV **Obv:** Papal arms **Obv. Legend:** BENEDICTVS • XIV • P • M • A ... **Rev:** Written value, date within wreath

Date	Mintage	VG	F	VF	XF	Unc
1749-IX	—	7.00	14.00	22.50	40.00	—

KM# 154 1/2 BAIOCCO

Copper **Ruler:** Benedict XIV **Obv:** Papal arms **Obv. Legend:** BENED • XIV • **Rev:** Written value, date within thin, leafy wreath

Date	Mintage	VG	F	VF	XF	Unc
1751	—	10.00	20.00	35.00	50.00	—
1752	—	10.00	20.00	35.00	50.00	—
1753	—	10.00	20.00	35.00	50.00	—
1755	—	10.00	20.00	35.00	50.00	—
1757	—	10.00	20.00	35.00	50.00	—

KM# 157 1/2 BAIOCCO

Copper **Ruler:** Benedict XIV **Obv:** Papal arms **Obv. Legend:** BENED • XIV • P • M • A • **Rev:** Value, MEZ/BAIOCCO/CVB/date in wreath

Date	Mintage	VG	F	VF	XF	Unc
1754-IV	—	10.00	20.00	35.00	50.00	—

KM# 158 1/2 BAIOCCO

Copper **Ruler:** Clement XIII **Obv:** Papal arms **Obv. Legend:** CLEM XIII ... **Rev:** Written value, date within rope wreath

Date	Mintage	VG	F	VF	XF	Unc
1759	—	10.00	17.50	35.00	—	—

KM# 170 1/2 BAIOCCO

Copper **Ruler:** Pius VI (Sextus) **Obv:** Papal arms **Obv. Legend:** PIVS • SEXTVS .... **Rev:** Written value, stars within wreath

Date	Mintage	VG	F	VF	XF	Unc
1789-XV	—	12.50	25.00	40.00	75.00	—
1790-XV	—	12.50	25.00	40.00	75.00	—
1790-XVI	—	12.50	25.00	40.00	75.00	—
1791-XVI	—	12.50	25.00	40.00	75.00	—
1794-XX	—	12.50	25.00	40.00	75.00	—
1795-XX	—	12.50	25.00	40.00	75.00	—

KM# 111 BAIOCCO

Copper **Ruler:** Benedict XIII **Subject:** Benedict XIII **Obv:** Papal arms **Rev:** Value, VN/BAIOCCO/GVBBIO/date, in ivy wreath

Date	Mintage	VG	F	VF	XF	Unc
1726-II	—	12.00	25.00	40.00	70.00	—
1727-III	—	12.00	25.00	40.00	70.00	—
1728-IIII	—	12.00	25.00	40.00	70.00	—
1729-V	—	12.00	25.00	40.00	70.00	—
1730-VI	—	12.00	25.00	40.00	70.00	—

KM# 112 BAIOCCO

Copper **Ruler:** Benedict XIII **Obv:** Dog in Papal Arms incorrectly faces right

Date	Mintage	VG	F	VF	XF	Unc
1726-II Rare	—	—	—	—	—	—
1729-V	—	—	—	—	—	—

KM# 116 BAIOCCO

Copper **Ruler:** Benedict XIII **Rev:** Roses replace ivy

Date	Mintage	VG	F	VF	XF	Unc
1730-I	—	10.00	20.00	35.00	60.00	—

KM# 115 BAIOCCO

Copper **Ruler:** Clement XII **Subject:** Clement XII **Obv:** Papal arms **Rev:** Value, VN/BAIOCIO/GVBBIO in circle within ivy wreath

Date	Mintage	VG	F	VF	XF	Unc
1730-I	—	10.00	20.00	35.00	60.00	—
1731-II	—	10.00	20.00	35.00	60.00	—
1732-III	—	10.00	20.00	35.00	60.00	—
1733-IV	—	10.00	20.00	35.00	60.00	—
1734-V	—	10.00	20.00	35.00	60.00	—
1735-VI	—	10.00	20.00	35.00	60.00	—
1736-VII	—	10.00	20.00	35.00	60.00	—
1737-VIII	—	10.00	20.00	35.00	60.00	—
1738-VIIII	—	10.00	20.00	35.00	60.00	—

KM# 118 BAIOCCO

Copper **Ruler:** Clement XII **Rev:** Cartouche replaces wreath

Date	Mintage	VG	F	VF	XF	Unc
1732-II	—	10.00	20.00	35.00	60.00	—
1732-III	—	10.00	20.00	35.00	60.00	—
1734-IV	—	10.00	20.00	35.00	60.00	—
1735-V	—	10.00	20.00	35.00	60.00	—
1736-VI	—	10.00	20.00	35.00	60.00	—

KM# 142 BAIOCCO

Copper **Ruler:** Benedict XIV **Obv:** Papal arms **Obv. Legend:** BENEDICTVS • XIV • P • M • AN • X • **Rev:** Written value, date within wreath

Date	Mintage	VG	F	VF	XF	Unc
1740-I	—	10.00	20.00	35.00	50.00	—
1741-I	—	10.00	20.00	35.00	50.00	—
1741-II	—	10.00	20.00	35.00	50.00	—
1742-II	—	10.00	20.00	35.00	50.00	—
1742-III	—	10.00	20.00	35.00	50.00	—
1743-IV	—	10.00	20.00	35.00	50.00	—
1744-V	—	10.00	20.00	35.00	50.00	—
1745-V	—	10.00	20.00	35.00	50.00	—
1745-VI	—	10.00	20.00	35.00	50.00	—
1745-VII	—	10.00	20.00	35.00	50.00	—
1746-VII	—	10.00	20.00	35.00	50.00	—
1747-VI	—	10.00	20.00	35.00	50.00	—
1747-VII	—	10.00	20.00	35.00	50.00	—
1747	—	10.00	20.00	35.00	50.00	—
1748	—	10.00	20.00	35.00	50.00	—
1749-VIIII	—	10.00	20.00	35.00	50.00	—
1749	—	10.00	20.00	35.00	50.00	—
1750-X	—	10.00	20.00	35.00	50.00	—
1751-X	—	10.00	20.00	35.00	50.00	—
1751	—	10.00	20.00	35.00	50.00	—
1752	—	10.00	20.00	35.00	50.00	—
1753-X	—	10.00	20.00	35.00	50.00	—
1753-XI	—	10.00	20.00	35.00	50.00	—
1753-XIII	—	10.00	20.00	35.00	50.00	—
1754-XIV	—	10.00	20.00	35.00	50.00	—
1754	—	10.00	20.00	35.00	50.00	—
1755	—	10.00	20.00	35.00	50.00	—
1756	—	10.00	20.00	35.00	50.00	—
1757	—	10.00	20.00	35.00	50.00	—

KM# 145 BAIOCCO

Copper **Ruler:** Benedict XIV **Obv:** Papal arms **Obv. Legend:** BENED • XIV • P • M • **Rev:** Value, date in cartouche

Date	Mintage	VG	F	VF	XF	Unc
1748 Retrograde 4	—	10.00	25.00	35.00	50.00	—

KM# 155 BAIOCCO

Copper **Ruler:** Benedict XIV **Obv:** Papal arms **Obv. Legend:** BENE • XIV P M A XII **Rev:** Written value, date in cartouche

Date	Mintage	VG	F	VF	XF	Unc
1752-XII	—	12.00	25.00	40.00	55.00	—

KM# 156 BAIOCCO
Copper **Ruler:** Benedict XIV **Obv:** Papal arms **Obv. Legend:** BENEDIC • XIV • P • M • A • **Rev:** Written value, date in cartouche

Date	Mintage	VG	F	VF	XF	Unc
1753-XIV	—	10.00	25.00	35.00	50.00	—

KM# 159 BAIOCCO
Copper **Ruler:** Clement XIII **Obv. Legend:** CLEM-XIII-PON.M.A.I

Date	Mintage	VG	F	VF	XF	Unc
1759-I	—	12.50	20.00	35.00	—	—

KM# 166 BAIOCCO
Copper **Ruler:** Clement XIII **Obv:** Papal arms **Obv. Legend:** CLEMENS • XIII • P • M • **Rev:** Written value, date in cartouche

Date	Mintage	Good	VG	F	VF	XF
1759	—	10.00	20.00	35.00	60.00	—

KM# 162 BAIOCCO
Copper **Ruler:** Clement XIII **Obv:** Papal arms **Obv. Legend:** CLEM • XIII • PON • M • A • **Rev:** Written value, date within wreath

Date	Mintage	Good	VG	F	VF	XF
1759-I	—	7.50	12.50	20.00	35.00	—

KM# 163 BAIOCCO
Copper **Ruler:** Clement XIII **Obv:** Papal arms **Obv. Legend:** CLEM • XIII • PON • M • A • I • **Rev:** Written value, date within rope wreath

Date	Mintage	Good	VG	F	VF	XF
1759-I	—	7.50	12.50	20.00	35.00	—

KM# 164 BAIOCCO
Copper **Ruler:** Clement XIII **Obv:** Papal arms **Obv. Legend:** CLEMENS • XIII • P • M • **Rev:** Written value, date within wreath

Date	Mintage	Good	VG	F	VF	XF
1759	—	7.50	12.50	20.00	35.00	—

KM# 165 BAIOCCO
Copper **Ruler:** Clement XIII **Obv:** Papal arms **Obv. Legend:** CLEMENS • XIII • P • M • **Rev:** Written value, date within wreath

Date	Mintage	Good	VG	F	VF	XF
1759	—	7.50	12.50	20.00	35.00	—

KM# 160 BAIOCCO
Copper **Ruler:** Clement XIII **Obv:** Papal arms **Obv. Legend:** CLEM • XIII • PON • M • **Rev:** Written value, date within rope wreath

Date	Mintage	VG	F	VF	XF	Unc
1759	—	20.00	30.00	50.00	—	—

KM# 161 BAIOCCO
Copper **Ruler:** Clement XIII **Obv:** Papal arms **Obv. Legend:** CLEM • XIII • PON • M • A • I • **Rev:** Written value, date within wreath

Date	Mintage	VG	F	VF	XF	Unc
1759-I	—	20.00	30.00	50.00	—	—

KM# 171 BAIOCCO
Copper **Ruler:** Pius VI (Sextus) **Obv:** Papal oval arms **Obv. Legend:** PIVS • SEXTVS ... **Rev:** Written value in wreath **Note:** Varieties exist.

Date	Mintage	Good	VG	F	VF	XF
1789-XV	—	5.00	12.00	20.00	32.00	—
1790-XV	—	5.00	12.00	20.00	32.00	—
1791-XVII	—	5.00	12.00	20.00	32.00	—
1792-XVII	—	5.00	12.00	20.00	32.00	—
1792-XVIII	—	5.00	12.00	20.00	32.00	—
1793-XVIII	—	5.00	12.00	20.00	32.00	—
1794-XX	—	5.00	12.00	20.00	32.00	—
1795-XX	—	5.00	12.00	20.00	32.00	—

KM# 172 2 BAIOCCHI
Copper **Ruler:** Pius VI (Sextus) **Obv:** Papal arms **Obv. Legend:** PIVS • SEXTVS • PON • ... **Rev:** Written value in wreath

Date	Mintage	Good	VG	F	VF	XF
1789-XV	—	10.00	17.50	28.00	40.00	—
1790-XV	—	10.00	17.50	28.00	40.00	—

KM# 175 2 BAIOCCHI
Copper **Ruler:** Pius VI (Sextus) **Obv:** Papal arms **Obv. Legend:** PIVS • SEXTVS • PON • ... **Rev:** Written value within wreath

Date	Mintage	Good	VG	F	VF	XF
1790-XVI	—	10.00	17.50	28.00	40.00	—
1791-XVI	—	10.00	17.50	28.00	40.00	—
1795-XXI	—	10.00	17.50	28.00	40.00	—
1796-XXI	—	10.00	17.50	28.00	40.00	—

EMERGENCY COINAGE

KM# 176 2-1/2 BAIOCCHI
Copper **Ruler:** Pius VI (Sextus) **Obv:** Written value, date below stars **Rev:** St. Peter bust left **Rev. Legend:** S P APOSTOLORUM PRINCEPS

Date	Mintage	Good	VG	F	VF	XF
1796	—	5.00	12.00	20.00	35.00	—

KM# 177 2-1/2 BAIOCCHI
Copper **Ruler:** Pius VI (Sextus) **Obv:** Written value, date below stars **Rev:** St. Peter's bust left

Date	Mintage	Good	VG	F	VF	XF
1796	—	20.00	35.00	60.00	125	—

KM# 178 5 BAIOCCHI

Copper **Ruler:** Pius VI (Sextus) **Obv:** Written value below star within circle, legend around, with date below **Obv. Legend:** PIVS PAPA SEXTVS ... **Rev:** Madonna **Rev. Legend:** SANCTA DEI GENITRIX

Date	Mintage	Good	VG	F	VF	XF
1797-XXIII	—	10.00	17.50	35.00	50.00	—

PAPAL STATES-MACERATA

A city in the Marches, was, except for a period of French occupation during the Napoleonic era, a faithful papal subject from the 13th century until the dismembering of the papal states.

NOTE: For later issues see Roman Republic-Macerata.

CITY

EMERGENCY COINAGE

KM# 1 5 BAIOCCHI

Copper **Obv:** Written value below star within circle **Rev:** Madonna **Rev. Legend:** SANCTA DEI GENITRIX

Date	Mintage	Good	VG	F	VF	XF
1797//XXIII	—	65.00	85.00	150	250	—
1798//XXIII	—	65.00	85.00	150	250	—

KM# 2 60 BAIOCCHI

Billon **Obv:** Papal oval arms **Obv. Legend:** PIVS SEXTVS PONT... **Rev:** Written value, date below stars within circle and wreath

Date	Mintage	Good	VG	F	VF	XF
1799//XXV	—	100	200	300	475	—

PAPAL STATES-MATELICA

A city and papal possession in Macerata.

CITY

EMERGENCY COINAGE

KM# 1 QUATTRINO

Copper **Obv:** Papal arms **Obv. Legend:** PIVS SEX P M A XXIII **Rev:** Written value within circle **Note:** Varieties exist with PIVS SEXT PM A XXIII and PIVS SEX P M A XIII on obverse.

Date	Mintage	Good	VG	F	VF	XF
1797//XXIII	—	90.00	125	175	350	—
1798//XXIII	—	90.00	125	175	350	—

KM# 2 1/2 BAIOCCO

Copper **Obv:** Papal arms **Obv. Legend:** PIVS SEXT P M A XXIII **Rev:** Written value below star within circle

Date	Mintage	Good	VG	F	VF	XF
1797//XXIII	—	100	150	185	350	—
1798//XXIII	—	100	150	185	350	—

KM# 3 2-1/2 BAIOCCHI

Copper **Obv:** Written value, date below stars within circle **Rev:** St. Peter bust, left **Rev. Legend:** S P APOSTOLORUM PRINC

Date	Mintage	Good	VG	F	VF	XF
1797//XXIII	—	100	150	200	350	—

KM# 4 5 BAIOCCHI

Copper **Obv:** Written value below star within circle, legend around with date below **Obv. Legend:** PIVS PAPA SEXTVS ANNO XXIII **Rev:** Madonna **Rev. Legend:** SANCTA DEI GENITRIX

Date	Mintage	Good	VG	F	VF	XF
1797//XXIII TM	—	100	150	200	350	—

PAPAL STATES-MONTALTO

A city and papal possession in the province of Ascoli, Marches.

CITY

EMERGENCY COINAGE

KM# 1.1 2-1/2 BAIOCCHI

Copper **Rev:** St. Peter **Rev. Legend:** S P APOSTOLORUM PRINCEPS

Date	Mintage	Good	VG	F	VF	XF
1797	—	60.00	95.00	135	250	—

KM# 1.2 2-1/2 BAIOCCHI

Copper **Obv:** Written value, date, city name below stars within circle **Rev:** St. Peter's bust left **Rev. Legend:** S P APOSTOLOR PRINCEPS

Date	Mintage	Good	VG	F	VF	XF
1797	—	50.00	95.00	135	250	—

KM# 1.3 2-1/2 BAIOCCHI

Copper **Rev. Legend:** S P APOOLORU PRINCEPS

Date	Mintage	Good	VG	F	VF	XF
1797	—	50.00	95.00	135	250	—

KM# 1.4 2-1/2 BAIOCCHI

Copper **Rev. Legend:** S P APOOLORU PRINCEPS P

Date	Mintage	Good	VG	F	VF	XF
1797	—	50.00	95.00	135	250	—

KM# 2 5 BAIOCCHI

Copper **Obv:** Written value, city name **Rev:** Madonna **Rev. Legend:** SANCTA DEI GENITRIX

Date	Mintage	Good	VG	F	VF	XF
1797//XXIII	—	60.00	95.00	135	250	—

PAPAL STATES-PERGOLA

A city and papal possession in the province of Pesaro, Urbino.

NOTE: For later issues see Roman Republic-Pergola.

CITY

EMERGENCY COINAGE

KM# 1 1/2 BAIOCCO

Copper **Obv:** Value, PERGOLA 1797 **Rev:** Papal arms **Rev. Legend:** PIVS SEXT P M A XXIII

Date	Mintage	Good	VG	F	VF	XF
1797//XXIII	—	60.00	100	200	350	—

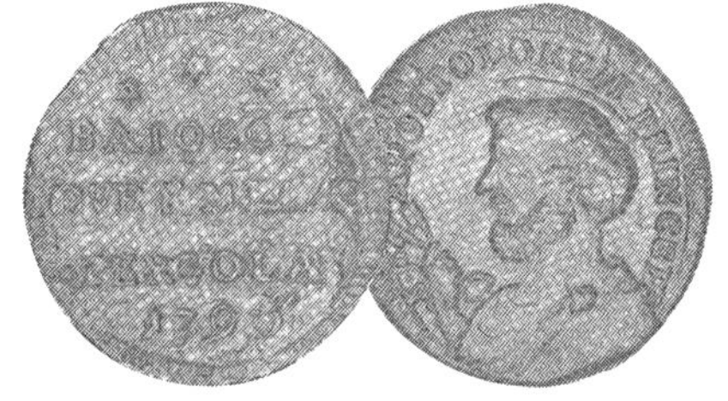

KM# 2 2-1/2 BAIOCCHI

Copper **Obv:** Written value, city name, date below stars **Rev:** St. Peter's bust left **Rev. Legend:** S P APOSTOLORUM PRINCEPS

Date	Mintage	Good	VG	F	VF	XF
1796	—	50.00	75.00	100	175	—
1797	—	50.00	75.00	100	175	—

KM# 3 5 BAIOCCHI

Copper **Obv:** Written value, city name below star within circle, legend around **Rev:** Madonna **Rev. Legend:** SANCTA DEI GENITRIX

Date	Mintage	Good	VG	F	VF	XF
1797//XXIII TM	—	75.00	150	200	250	—

PAPAL STATES-PERUGIA

A city in Umbria, passed under the popes in the 9th century but continued to maintain an independent existence until occupied by the French in 1797. It was seized by Austria in 1849 and annexed to Piedmont in1860.

NOTE: For later issues see Roman Republic-Perugia.

CITY

EMERGENCY COINAGE

KM# 4 1/2 BAIOCCO

Copper **Obv:** Papal arms **Obv. Legend:** PIVS SEXTVS P M A XXIII **Rev:** Written value, date within circle

Date	Mintage	Good	VG	F	VF	XF
1797 XXIII	—	15.00	25.00	45.00	75.00	—

KM# 1 BAIOCCO

Copper **Obv:** Papal arms **Obv. Legend:** PIVS SEXTVS POM M A XXI **Rev:** Written value, date within circle, legend around **Rev. Legend:** PERVSIA AVGVSTA

Date	Mintage	Good	VG	F	VF	XF
1795 XXI	—	15.00	25.00	45.00	75.00	—

KM# 5 BAIOCCO

Copper **Obv:** Papal arms **Obv. Legend:** PIVS SEXTVS P M A XXIII **Rev:** Written value, date

Date	Mintage	Good	VG	F	VF	XF
1797 XXIII	—	15.00	25.00	40.00	70.00	—

KM# 2 2 BAIOCCHI

Copper **Obv:** Papal arms **Obv. Legend:** PIVS • SEXTVS PON • M • A • XXI **Rev:** Written value, date within circle, legend around **Rev. Legend:** ...AVGVSTA

Date	Mintage	Good	VG	F	VF	XF
1795 XXI	—	20.00	40.00	65.00	90.00	—
1799 XXI	—	20.00	40.00	65.00	90.00	—

KM# 6 2 BAIOCCHI

Copper **Obv:** Papal arms within circle **Obv. Legend:** PIVS • SEXTVS • PO • N • M • A • X • XIII **Rev:** Written value, city name, •P• within circle

Date	Mintage	Good	VG	F	VF	XF
ND(1797) XXIII	—	15.00	25.00	40.00	70.00	—
1798 XXIII	—	15.00	25.00	40.00	70.00	—

KM# 3 2-1/2 BAIOCCHI

Copper **Obv:** Written value, city name, date below stars within circle **Rev:** St. Peter's bust, left **Rev. Legend:** S P APOSTOLORUM PRINCEPS

Date	Mintage	Good	VG	F	VF	XF
1796	—	15.00	25.00	40.00	70.00	—
1797	—	15.00	25.00	40.00	70.00	—

KM# 7 4 BAIOCCHI

Billon **Obv:** Legend around PERV/GIA, date **Obv. Legend:** PIVS • SEXTVS • P • M • A • X • XIII **Rev:** Written value

Date	Mintage	Good	VG	F	VF	XF
1797 XXIII	—	30.00	55.00	75.00	120	—

KM# 8 5 BAIOCCHI

Copper **Obv:** Written value in circle, legend around with date below **Rev:** Madonna **Rev. Legend:** SANCTA DEI GENITRIX **Note:** Varieties exist with error in reverse legend as GENETRIX and/or obverse as PAPA PIVS instead of PIVS.

Date	Mintage	Good	VG	F	VF	XF
1797 XXIII	—	15.00	25.00	40.00	80.00	—
1798 XXIII	—	15.00	25.00	40.00	80.00	—

KM# 9 6 BAIOCCHI

Billon **Obv:** Legend around PERV/GIA, date **Obv. Legend:** PIVS • SEXTVS • P • M • A • X • XIII **Rev:** Written value within circle

Date	Mintage	Good	VG	F	VF	XF
1797 XXIII	—	30.00	55.00	75.00	125	—

KM# 10 8 BAIOCCHI

Billon **Obv:** Legend around PERV/GIA/1797 within circle **Obv. Legend:** PIVS • SEXTVS • P • M • ANNO • XXII * **Rev:** Written value within circle

Date	Mintage	Good	VG	F	VF	XF
1797 XXIII	—	25.00	50.00	75.00	125	—

PAPAL STATES-RAVENNA

A city located in northern Italy near the Adriatic Sea. It was founded over 2000 years ago and was used as a capitol by both Roman and Byzantine emperors. Ravenna was a part of the Papal States from 1509-1860 and is world renowned for its architecture from the 5th to 8th centuries.

CITY

STANDARD COINAGE

KM# 5 QUATTRINO

Copper 0 **Subject:** Benedict XIV **Obv:** Papal arms **Rev:** Small pine cone in sprigs above date **Rev. Legend:** ANTIQUE CIV RAVENNE

Date	Mintage	VG	F	VF	XF	Unc
1744	—	15.00	22.00	38.00	75.00	—

KM# 6 QUATTRINO

Copper 0 **Obv:** Papal arms **Rev:** Inscription in cartouche **Rev. Inscription:** 1745/RAVEN/NA

Date	Mintage	VG	F	VF	XF	Unc
1745	—	15.00	20.00	35.00	65.00	—

KM# 8 QUATTRINO

Copper 0 **Obv:** Papal arms **Rev:** Inscription in squarish cartouche **Rev. Inscription:** 1746/RAVEN/NA

Date	Mintage	VG	F	VF	XF	Unc
1746	—	15.00	20.00	35.00	65.00	—

KM# 10 QUATTRINO

Copper 0 **Subject:** Holy Year issue **Obv:** Papal arms in sprigs **Rev:** Open Holy Door divides date

Date	Mintage	VG	F	VF	XF	Unc
1750	—	25.00	38.00	60.00	85.00	—

KM# 12 QUATTRINO

Copper 0 **Obv:** Papal arms in sprigs

Date	Mintage	VG	F	VF	XF	Unc
ND	—	25.00	45.00	65.00	100	—

KM# 13 QUATTRINO

Copper 0 **Obv:** Papal arms in sprigs **Rev:** St. Apollinaris

Date	Mintage	VG	F	VF	XF	Unc
ND	—	15.00	20.00	35.00	65.00	—

KM# 14 QUATTRINO

Copper 0 **Obv:** Papal arms **Rev:** Value: VN/QVATTR/INO in cartouche

Date	Mintage	VG	F	VF	XF	Unc
ND	—	17.50	25.00	38.00	75.00	—

KM# 15 QUATTRINO

Copper 0 **Obv:** Papal arms **Rev:** Cluster of flower sprigs

Date	Mintage	VG	F	VF	XF	Unc
ND	—	15.00	20.00	35.00	65.00	—

KM# 16 QUATTRINO

Copper 0 **Obv:** Papal oval arms **Obv. Legend:** BEN • XIV • ... **Rev:** Mantled shield with rampant lions

Date	Mintage	VG	F	VF	XF	Unc
ND	—	35.00	50.00	75.00	125	—

KM# 7 1/2 BAIOCCO

Copper 0 **Subject:** Benedict XIV **Obv:** Papal arms **Obv. Legend:** BEN • XIV • PM • **Rev:** Written value, city name, date in cartouche

Date	Mintage	VG	F	VF	XF	Unc
1745	—	10.00	20.00	35.00	60.00	—

KM# 11 1/2 BAIOCCO

Copper 0 **Subject:** Holy Year issue **Obv:** Papal arms in sprigs **Rev:** Holy door, radiant cap within, flanked by cornucopias

Date	Mintage	VG	F	VF	XF	Unc
1750	—	25.00	60.00	80.00	100	—

KM# 17 1/2 BAIOCCO

Copper 0 **Obv:** Papal arms in sprigs **Rev:** Holy door, radiant cap within, flanked by cornucopias

Date	Mintage	VG	F	VF	XF	Unc
ND	—	10.00	20.00	35.00	60.00	—

KM# 18 1/2 BAIOCCO

Copper 0 **Obv:** Papal arms in sprigs **Rev:** Written value within wreath

Date	Mintage	VG	F	VF	XF	Unc
ND	—	10.00	20.00	35.00	60.00	—

KM# 19 1/2 BAIOCCO

Copper 0 **Obv:** Papal arms in sprigs **Rev:** Written value, small rampant lion within designed wreath

Date	Mintage	VG	F	VF	XF	Unc
ND	—	10.00	20.00	35.00	60.00	—

KM# 9 BAIOCCO

Copper 0 **Subject:** Benedict XIV **Obv:** Papal arms **Obv. Legend:** BENED : XIV • P • M • **Rev:** Written value, date in cartouche

Date	Mintage	VG	F	VF	XF	Unc
1747	—	12.50	28.00	40.00	75.00	—

KM# 20 BAIOCCO

Copper 0 **Obv:** Papal arms in sprigs **Obv. Legend:** BENE • XIV • P • M • **Rev:** Written value in cartouche

Date	Mintage	VG	F	VF	XF	Unc
ND	—	12.50	28.00	40.00	75.00	—

KM# 21 BAIOCCO

Copper 0 **Obv:** Papal arms in sprigs **Obv. Legend:** BENE .... **Rev:** Written value within designed wreath

Date	Mintage	VG	F	VF	XF	Unc
ND	—	12.50	28.00	40.00	75.00	—

KM# 1 GROSSO

Silver 0 **Subject:** Clement XII **Obv:** Papal arms **Rev:** DAT/IN/PRE/TIVM on cartouche

Date	Mintage	VG	F	VF	XF	Unc
ND	—	—	—	—	—	—

KM# 2 GIULIO

Silver 0 **Subject:** Clement XII **Obv:** Papal arms **Rev:** DAT • IN/PRETIVM on cartouche

Date	Mintage	VG	F	VF	XF	Unc
VII (1736)	—	35.00	70.00	125	220	—

KM# 3 GIULIO

Silver 0 **Obv:** Papal arms **Rev:** ESVRIEN/TES/IMPLEBO on cartouche

Date	Mintage	VG	F	VF	XF	Unc
VIII (1737)	—	35.00	70.00	125	220	—

PAPAL STATES-RONCIGLIONE

A town and papal possession in Latium.

MINT OFFICIAL'S INITIALS

Date	Initials	Name
1799	CAG	Carlo Alberto Garofolini

TOWN

STANDARD COINAGE

KM# 2 3 BAIOCCHI

Copper **Obv:** Written value, city name, date within circle **Rev:** Madonna **Rev. Legend:** ...RELIGIONE

Date	Mintage	Good	VG	F	VF	XF
1799 CAG	—	25.00	50.00	100	175	—

KM# 3 3 BAIOCCHI

Copper **Obv:** Written value, city name, date within circle

Date	Mintage	Good	VG	F	VF	XF
1799 CAG	—	30.00	55.00	110	185	—

KM# 4 3 BAIOCCHI

Copper **Obv:** Written value, city name, date within circle

Date	Mintage	Good	VG	F	VF	XF
1799 CAG	—	30.00	55.00	110	185	—

KM# 5 3 BAIOCCHI

Copper **Obv:** Written value, city name, retrograde date within circle **Rev:** Madonna **Rev. Legend:** ....RELIGIONE

Date	Mintage	Good	VG	F	VF	XF
1799 CAG	—	40.00	65.00	120	200	—

KM# 6 3 BAIOCCHI

Copper **Obv:** City in flames, legend around **Obv. Legend:** ...RONCIGLIONE ANN 1799 **Rev:** Madonna **Rev. Legend:** ...RELIGIONE

Date	Mintage	Good	VG	F	VF	XF
1799	—	50.00	100	200	350	—

PAPAL STATES-SAN SEVERINO

A city and papal possession in Macerata.

MINT OFFICIAL'S INITIALS

Initials	Date	Name
TM	1797	Tommaso Mercandetti

CITY

EMERGENCY COINAGE

KM# 1 QUATTRINO

Copper **Obv:** Papal oval arms **Obv. Legend:** PIVS SEXT P M A XXIII **Rev:** Written value

Date	Mintage	Good	VG	F	VF	XF
(1797)XXIII	—	15.00	25.00	40.00	70.00	—
1798//XXIII	—	15.00	25.00	40.00	70.00	—

KM# 4 2-1/2 BAIOCCHI

Copper **Obv:** S • SEVERINO above written value, date **Rev:** St. Peter's bust, left **Rev. Legend:** S P APOSTOLORUM PRINCEPS

Date	Mintage	Good	VG	F	VF	XF
1769(sic)	—	25.00	50.00	75.00	125	—

KM# 5 2-1/2 BAIOCCHI

Copper **Obv:** S • SEVERINO above written value, date **Rev:** Small bust of St. Peter, left **Rev. Legend:** S P APOSTOLORVM PRINCEPS

Date	Mintage	Good	VG	F	VF	XF
1797	—	15.00	25.00	30.00	45.00	—

KM# 6 5 BAIOCCHI
Copper **Obv:** Written value within circle, legend around with date below **Obv. Legend:** PIVS PAPA SEXTVS... **Rev:** Madonna **Rev. Legend:** SANCTA DEI GENITRIX

Date	Mintage	Good	VG	F	VF	XF
1797//XXIII TM	—	15.00	25.00	40.00	70.00	—

PAPAL STATES-SPOLETO

Spoletvm

A town in Umbria, was bequeathed to Pope Gregory VII by the empress Matilda, but maintained its independence until definitely occupied by Gregory IX in 1213. In 1809 it served as the capital of the French department of Trasimene.

TOWN

STANDARD COINAGE

KM# 1 5 BAIOCCHI
Copper **Obv:** Legend around value and inscription **Obv. Legend:** PIVS PAPA SEXTVS ANNO XXIII **Obv. Inscription:** SPOLETVM/UMB • CAP **Rev:** Madonna **Rev. Legend:** SANCTA DEI GENITRIX

Date	Mintage	Good	VG	F	VF	XF
1797//XXIII	—	25.00	50.00	85.00	130	—

KM# 2 5 BAIOCCHI
Copper **Obv:** Value and inscription **Obv. Inscription:** ...SPOLETVM/VMB • CAP

Date	Mintage	Good	VG	F	VF	XF
1797//XXIII	—	25.00	50.00	85.00	130	—

KM# 3 6 BAIOCCHI
Silver **Obv:** Legend around inscription **Obv. Legend:** PIVS SEXTVS P • M • A • XXIII **Obv. Inscription:** SPOLE/TVM/VMB CAP **Rev:** Written value within circle

Date	Mintage	Good	VG	F	VF	XF
(1797)//XXIII	—	55.00	80.00	100	160	—

KM# 4 6 BAIOCCHI
Silver **Obv. Legend:** ...P • M • A • XX • III

Date	Mintage	Good	VG	F	VF	XF
(1797)//XXIII	—	55.00	80.00	100	160	—

PAPAL STATES-TERNI

A town in Umbria founded in 672 B.C., during most of the Middle Ages and up until 1860, it was a papal possession.

TOWN

EMERGENCY COINAGE

KM# 1 4 BAIOCCHI
Silver **Obv:** City name, date within circle, legend around **Obv. Legend:** PIVS SEXTVS P M A XXIII **Rev:** Written value

Date	Mintage	Good	VG	F	VF	XF
1797//XXIII	—	50.00	100	175	225	—

KM# 2 5 BAIOCCHI
Copper **Obv:** Written value, city name within circle, legend around **Obv. Legend:** PIVS PAPA SEXTVS ANNO XXIII **Rev:** Madonna **Rev. Legend:** SANCTA DEI GENITRIX

Date	Mintage	Good	VG	F	VF	XF
1797//XXIII	—	30.00	55.00	90.00	150	—

KM# 3 6 BAIOCCHI
Billon **Obv:** City name, date within circle, legend around **Obv. Legend:** PIVS SEXTVS P.M... **Rev:** Written value within circle

Date	Mintage	Good	VG	F	VF	XF
1797//XXIII	—	50.00	100	125	165	—

KM# 4 8 BAIOCCHI
Billon **Obv:** City name, date within circle, legend around **Obv. Legend:** PIVS SEXTVS P.M... **Rev:** Written value

Date	Mintage	Good	VG	F	VF	XF
1797//XXIII	—	50.00	100	130	165	—

KM# 5 8 BAIOCCHI
Billon **Obv:** Legend begins at bottom

Date	Mintage	Good	VG	F	VF	XF
1797//XXIII	—	50.00	100	125	165	—

PAPAL STATES-TIVOLI

A small town approximately 15 miles (24 km.) north of Rome.

TOWN

EMERGENCY COINAGE

KM# 2 5 BAIOCCHI
Copper **Obv:** Written value, city name within circle, legend around, date below **Obv. Legend:** PIVS PAPA SEXTVS... **Rev:** Madonna **Rev. Legend:** SANCTA DEI GENITRIX

Date	Mintage	Good	VG	F	VF	XF
1797//XXIII	—	25.00	55.00	85.00	135	—

PAPAL STATES-VITERBO

A city and papal possession in Latium.

CITY

EMERGENCY COINAGE

KM# 1 1/2 BAIOCCO
Copper **Obv:** Papal arms **Obv. Legend:** PIVS SEXTVS P M A XXIII **Rev:** Written value, date, city name below stars

Date	Mintage	Good	VG	F	VF	XF
1797//XXIII	—	10.00	20.00	35.00	75.00	—

KM# 2 2-1/2 BAIOCCHI
Copper **Obv:** Written value, city name, date below stars within circle **Rev:** Large bust of St. Peter left **Rev. Legend:** S P APOSTOLORUM PRINCEPS

Date	Mintage	Good	VG	F	VF	XF
1796	—	15.00	25.00	35.00	95.00	—

KM# 3 2-1/2 BAIOCCHI
Copper **Obv:** Written value, city name below stars within circle **Rev:** Small bust of St. Peter left **Rev. Legend:** S P APOSTOLORUM PRINC •

Date	Mintage	Good	VG	F	VF	XF
1797	—	15.00	25.00	35.00	95.00	—
1798	—	15.00	25.00	35.00	95.00	—

KM# 4 5 BAIOCCHI
Copper **Obv:** Written value, city name below stars within circle, legend around, date below **Rev:** Madonna **Rev. Legend:** SANCTA DEI GENITRIX

Date	Mintage	Good	VG	F	VF	XF
1797//XXIII	—	15.00	25.00	40.00	100	—

PARMA

A town in Emilia, which was a papal possession from 1512 to 1545, was seized by France in 1796, and was attached to the Napoleonic Empire in 1808. In 1814, Parma was assigned to Marie Louise, empress of Napoleon I. It was annexed to Sardinia in 1860.

RULERS
Francesco Farnese I, 1694-1727
Filippo di Borbone, 1737-1765
Ferdinando di Borbone, 1765-1802

MONETARY SYSTEM
12 Denari = 2 Sesini = 1 Soldo
20 Soldi = 1 Lira
7 Lire = 1 Ducato

CITY

STANDARD COINAGE

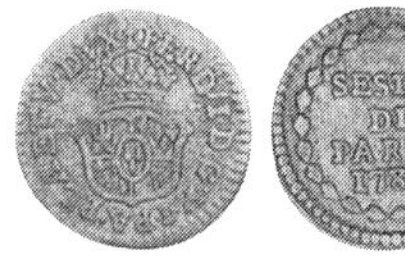

C# 3 SESINO

Copper **Ruler:** Ferdinando di Borbone **Obv:** Crowned shield **Rev:** Written value, town name, date within wreath

Date	Mintage	VG	F	VF	XF	Unc
1784	—	2.50	5.00	9.00	18.00	—
1785	—	2.50	5.00	9.00	18.00	—
1787	—	2.50	5.00	9.00	18.00	—
1788	—	2.50	5.00	9.00	18.00	—
1790	—	2.50	5.00	9.00	18.00	—
1792	—	2.50	5.00	9.00	18.00	—
1793	—	2.50	5.00	9.00	18.00	—
1795	—	2.50	5.00	9.00	18.00	—
1796	—	2.50	5.00	9.00	18.00	—
1797	—	2.50	5.00	9.00	18.00	—
1798	—	2.50	5.00	9.00	18.00	—

C# 4 5 SOLDI

Billon **Ruler:** Ferdinando di Borbone **Obv:** Crowned shield **Rev:** Madonna

Date	Mintage	VG	F	VF	XF	Unc
1784	—	2.50	5.00	10.00	20.00	—
1785	—	2.50	5.00	10.00	20.00	—

C# 5 5 SOLDI

Billon **Ruler:** Ferdinando di Borbone **Obv:** Madonna **Rev:** Value

Date	Mintage	VG	F	VF	XF	Unc
1792	—	2.50	5.00	10.00	20.00	—
1793	—	2.50	5.00	10.00	20.00	—
1795	—	2.50	5.00	10.00	20.00	—
1796	—	2.50	5.00	10.00	20.00	—
1797	—	2.50	5.00	10.00	20.00	—
1798	—	2.50	5.00	10.00	20.00	—
1799	—	2.50	5.00	10.00	20.00	—

C# 6 10 SOLDI

Billon **Ruler:** Ferdinando di Borbone

Date	Mintage	VG	F	VF	XF	Unc
1784	—	2.50	5.00	10.00	25.00	—
1786	—	2.50	5.00	10.00	25.00	—
1788	—	2.50	5.00	10.00	25.00	—
1789	—	2.50	5.00	10.00	25.00	—
1790	—	2.50	5.00	10.00	25.00	—
1792	—	2.50	5.00	10.00	25.00	—
1793	—	2.50	5.00	10.00	25.00	—
1795	—	2.50	5.00	10.00	25.00	—

C# 7 20 SOLDI

Billon **Ruler:** Ferdinando di Borbone **Obv:** Crowned, oval shield in sprigs **Rev:** St. Thomas **Rev. Legend:** S • THOMAS • APOST • PAR • ...

Date	Mintage	VG	F	VF	XF	Unc
1783	—	4.00	7.50	15.00	30.00	—
1784	—	4.00	7.50	15.00	30.00	—
1785	—	4.00	7.50	15.00	30.00	—
1786	—	4.00	7.50	15.00	30.00	—
1787	—	4.00	7.50	15.00	30.00	—
1789	—	4.00	7.50	15.00	30.00	—
1790	—	4.00	7.50	15.00	30.00	—
1792	—	4.00	7.50	15.00	30.00	—
1793	—	4.00	7.50	15.00	30.00	—
1794	—	4.00	7.50	15.00	30.00	—
1795	—	4.00	7.50	15.00	30.00	—
1796	—	4.00	7.50	15.00	30.00	—
1797	—	4.00	7.50	15.00	30.00	—

KM# 8 LIRA

3.4100 g., Billon, 26 mm. **Ruler:** Francesco Farnese I **Obv:** Crowned arms **Rev:** St. Thomas with spear **Edge:** Plain

Date	Mintage	VG	F	VF	XF	Unc
1727	—	—	—	—	—	—

C# 8 3 LIRE

3.6720 g., 0.8330 Silver 0.0983 oz. ASW **Ruler:** Ferdinando di Borbone **Obv:** Head right **Rev:** Value

Date	Mintage	VG	F	VF	XF	Unc
1790	—	30.00	60.00	100	150	—
1791	—	30.00	60.00	100	150	—
1792	—	30.00	60.00	100	150	—
1793	—	30.00	60.00	100	150	—
1795	—	30.00	60.00	100	150	—

C# 9 SEI (6) LIRE

7.3440 g., 0.8330 Silver 0.1967 oz. ASW **Ruler:** Ferdinando di Borbone **Obv:** Head right **Obv. Legend:** FERDIN • I • H • I • D • G • PAR • ... **Rev:** Written value, town name, date within wreath

Date	Mintage	VG	F	VF	XF	Unc
1795	—	125	200	275	375	—
1796	—	125	200	275	375	—

C# 2 FILIPPO (150 Soldi)

Silver **Ruler:** Filippo di Borbone **Obv:** Head of Filippo left **Rev:** Crowned arms, date in legend **Note:** Dav. #1478.

Date	Mintage	VG	F	VF	XF	Unc
1751	—	500	1,000	2,000	3,000	—

C# 10 1/14 DUCATO

1.8300 g., 0.9020 Silver 0.0531 oz. ASW **Ruler:** Ferdinando di Borbone **Obv:** Head right **Rev:** Crowned oval arms

Date	Mintage	VG	F	VF	XF	Unc
1784	—	17.50	35.00	60.00	100	—
1786	—	17.50	35.00	60.00	100	—

C# 11.1 1/7 DUCATO

3.6720 g., 0.9020 Silver 0.1065 oz. ASW **Ruler:** Ferdinando di Borbone **Obv:** Head right **Obv. Legend:** FERDINANDVS • I • HISPAN • ... **Rev:** Crowned oval shield in wreath, legend around **Rev. Legend:** D • G • PARMÆ PLAC • ET VAST • DVX

Date	Mintage	VG	F	VF	XF	Unc
1784	—	20.00	40.00	65.00	100	—
1785	—	20.00	40.00	65.00	100	—
1787	—	20.00	40.00	65.00	100	—

C# 11.2 1/7 DUCATO

3.6720 g., 0.9020 Silver 0.1065 oz. ASW **Ruler:** Ferdinando di Borbone **Obv:** Head right **Obv. Legend:** FERDINANDVS • I • HISPAN • INFANS **Rev:** Crowned oval shield **Rev. Legend:** D • G • PARMÆ PLAC • ET VAST • DVX

Date	Mintage	VG	F	VF	XF	Unc
1785	—	20.00	50.00	80.00	160	—

C# 12 1/2 DUCATO

12.8520 g., 0.9020 Silver 0.3727 oz. ASW **Ruler:** Ferdinando di Borbone **Obv:** Head right **Rev:** Crowned arms in order chain

Date	Mintage	VG	F	VF	XF	Unc
1784	—	50.00	85.00	125	200	—

C# 13 1/2 DUCATO

12.8520 g., 0.9020 Silver 0.3727 oz. ASW **Ruler:** Ferdinando di Borbone **Obv:** Head right **Rev:** Crowned oval arms

Date	Mintage	VG	F	VF	XF	Unc
1786	—	30.00	55.00	85.00	125	—
1787	—	30.00	55.00	85.00	125	—
1790	—	30.00	55.00	85.00	125	—

C# 14 DUCATON

25.7040 g., 0.9020 Silver 0.7454 oz. ASW **Ruler:** Ferdinando di Borbone **Obv:** Head right **Obv. Legend:** FERDINANDVS • I • HISP • INFANS • **Rev:** Crowned arms in order chain **Rev. Legend:** D • G •PARMÆ PLAC VAST • DVX • 1784 **Note:** Dav. #1479.

Date	Mintage	VG	F	VF	XF	Unc
1784	—	200	300	450	700	—

C# 15 DUCATON

25.7040 g., 0.9020 Silver 0.7454 oz. ASW **Ruler:** Ferdinando di Borbone **Obv:** Head right **Obv. Legend:** FERDINANDVS I • HISPAN • INFANS **Rev:** Crowned arms in leafy sprigs **Rev. Legend:** D • G • PERMÆ PLAC • ET VAST • DVX 1786 **Note:** Dav. #1480.

Date	Mintage	VG	F	VF	XF	Unc
1786	—	100	200	300	500	—
1789	—	100	200	300	500	—
1790	—	100	200	300	500	—

C# 15a DUCATON

25.7040 g., 0.9020 Silver 0.7454 oz. ASW **Ruler:** Ferdinando di Borbone **Obv:** Head right **Obv. Legend:** FERDINANDVS I • HISPAN • INFANS **Rev:** Oval arms in leafy sprigs **Rev. Legend:** D • G •PARMÆ PLAC • ET VAST • DVX 1786 **Note:** Dav. #1481.

Date	Mintage	VG	F	VF	XF	Unc
1796	—	100	200	300	500	—
1797	—	100	200	300	500	—
1799	—	100	200	300	500	—

C# 16 ZECCHINO

3.5000 g., 0.9000 Gold 0.1013 oz. AGW **Ruler:** Ferdinando di Borbone **Obv:** Head right **Rev:** Crowned arms in order chain

Date	Mintage	VG	F	VF	XF	Unc
1784	—	400	725	1,100	1,750	—

C# 17 1/2 DOPPIA

3.5700 g., 0.8910 Gold 0.1023 oz. AGW **Ruler:** Ferdinando di Borbone **Obv:** Head right **Obv. Legend:** FERDINANDVS I HISPAN INFANS **Rev:** Crowned arms in sprigs **Rev. Legend:** D • G • PARMÆ PLAC • ET VAST • DVX

Date	Mintage	VG	F	VF	XF	Unc
1785	—	250	450	800	1,500	—
1786 S	—	100	200	300	650	—
1787 S	—	100	200	300	650	—
1788 S	—	100	200	300	650	—
1789 S	—	100	200	300	650	—
1790 S	—	100	200	300	650	—
1791 S	—	100	200	300	650	—
1792 S	—	100	200	300	650	—
1793 S	—	100	200	300	650	—
1797 S	—	100	200	300	650	—

C# 18 DOPPIA

7.1410 g., 0.8910 Gold 0.2046 oz. AGW **Ruler:** Ferdinando di Borbone **Obv:** Head right **Obv. Legend:** FERDINANDVS I • HISPANIAR • INFANS **Rev:** Crowned arms in order chain **Rev. Legend:** D • G • PARMÆ.....

Date	Mintage	VG	F	VF	XF	Unc
1784	—	350	550	1,000	2,000	—

C# 18a DOPPIA

7.1410 g., 0.8910 Gold 0.2046 oz. AGW **Ruler:** Ferdinando di Borbone **Obv:** Head right **Obv. Legend:** FERDINANDVS I • HISPANIAR • INFANS **Rev:** Crowned arms in order chain **Rev. Legend:** D • G • PARMÆ PLAC • ET VAST • DVX

Date	Mintage	VG	F	VF	XF	Unc
1786 S	—	150	250	475	900	—
1787 S	—	150	250	475	900	—
1788 S	—	150	250	475	900	—
1789 S	—	150	250	475	900	—
1790 S	—	150	250	475	900	—
1791 S	—	150	250	475	900	—
1792 S	—	150	250	475	900	—
1793 S	—	150	250	475	900	—
1796 S	—	150	250	475	900	—

C# 19 3 DOPPIE

21.4230 g., 0.8910 Gold 0.6137 oz. AGW **Ruler:** Ferdinando di Borbone **Obv:** Head right **Rev:** Crowned oval arms

Date	Mintage	VG	F	VF	XF	Unc
1786 Rare	—	—	—	—	—	—

C# 20 4 DOPPIE

22.4800 g., 0.8910 Gold 0.6439 oz. AGW **Ruler:** Ferdinando di Borbone **Obv:** Head right **Obv. Legend:** FERDINANDVS I • HISPAN • INFANS **Rev:** Crowned arms in order chain **Rev. Legend:** D • G • PARMÆ ....

Date	Mintage	VG	F	VF	XF	Unc
1784	—	1,200	2,000	3,000	5,000	—

C# 20a 4 DOPPIE

22.4800 g., 0.8910 Gold 0.6439 oz. AGW **Ruler:** Ferdinando di Borbone **Obv:** Head right **Obv. Legend:** FERDINANDVS I • HISPAN • INFANS **Rev:** Crowned arms in order chain **Rev. Inscription:** D • G • PARMÆ PLAC • ET VAST • DVX

Date	Mintage	VG	F	VF	XF	Unc
1787 S	—	600	1,200	2,200	3,750	—
1790 S	—	600	1,200	2,200	3,750	—
1792 S	—	600	1,200	2,200	3,750	—
1796 S	—	600	1,200	2,200	3,750	—

C# 21 6 DOPPIE

42.8460 g., 0.8910 Gold 1.2273 oz. AGW **Ruler:** Ferdinando di Borbone **Obv:** Head right **Obv. Legend:** FERDINANDVS I • HISPAN • INFANS **Rev:** Crowned arms in leafy sprigs **Rev. Legend:** D • G • PARMÆ PLAC • ET VAST • DVX

Date	Mintage	VG	F	VF	XF	Unc
1786 S Rare	—	—	—	—	—	—

C# 22a 8 DOPPIE

57.1280 g., 0.8910 Gold 1.6364 oz. AGW **Ruler:** Ferdinando di Borbone **Obv:** Head right **Obv. Legend:** FERDINANDVS I • HISPAN • INFANS **Rev:** Crowned arms in leafy sprigs **Rev. Legend:** D • G • PARMÆ PLAC • ET VAST • DVX

Date	Mintage	VG	F	VF	XF	Unc
1786 S	—	1,200	2,000	3,750	8,000	—
1789 S	—	1,200	2,000	3,750	8,000	—
1791 S	—	1,200	2,000	3,750	8,000	—
1792 S	—	1,200	2,000	3,750	8,000	—
1796 S	—	1,200	2,000	3,750	7,500	—

PIACENZA

Placentia

A town and episcopal see that is located in the northwestern corner of the Italian territorial division of Emilia. It was made a Roman colony in 218 B.C., later becoming an important road center of the Roman Empire. Once a leading member of the Lombard League, it was united with Parma in 1545 to form a hereditary duchy in favor of the son of Pope Paul III. In 1731 it passed to Parma, then to the house of Hapsburg, and finally back to Parma in 1748.

RULERS

Maria Theresa as Duchess of Piacenza, 1740-1744
Carlo Emanuel III of Sardinia as Duke of Piacenza, 1744-1745
Philip of Bourbon as Duke of Parma and Piacenza, 1748-1765
Ferdinando di Borbone, 1765-1802

MONETARY SYSTEM

12 Denari = 2 Sesini = 1 Soldo
20 Soldi = 1 Lira

DUCHY

STANDARD COINAGE

C# 1 SESINO

Copper **Obv:** Crowned arms **Rev:** Cross, SALUS MUNDI at sides

Date	Mintage	VG	F	VF	XF	Unc
ND	—	15.00	30.00	65.00	150	—

C# 2 SESINO

Bronze **Obv:** Crown above knot

Date	Mintage	VG	F	VF	XF	Unc
ND	—	7.00	15.00	30.00	70.00	—

C# A3 SESINO

Bronze **Obv:** C E S R in angles of cross **Rev:** Crown above knot divides value, date at bottom

Date	Mintage	VG	F	VF	XF	Unc
1745	—	7.00	15.00	30.00	70.00	—

C# 3 SESINO

Copper **Obv:** Crowned 5-field arms **Rev:** Floreated cross, SALUS MUNDI at sides

Date	Mintage	VG	F	VF	XF	Unc
ND	—	7.00	15.00	30.00	70.00	—

C# 3a SESINO

Copper **Obv:** Crowned 5-field arms **Rev:** Cross, SALUS MUNDI at sides **Note:** Klippe.

Date	Mintage	VG	F	VF	XF	Unc
ND	—	—	—	—	—	—

C# 4 SESINO

Copper, 16 mm. **Ruler:** Ferdinando di Borbone **Obv:** Crowned arms in legend **Rev:** Legend, date **Rev. Legend:** SESINO DI PIACENZA

Date	Mintage	VG	F	VF	XF	Unc
1783	—	12.00	25.00	50.00	125	—

C# 5 SESINO

Copper **Ruler:** Ferdinando di Borbone **Obv:** Crowned arms in legend **Rev:** Cross between SALUS and MUNDI

Date	Mintage	VG	F	VF	XF	Unc
1784	—	305	7.00	15.00	35.00	—

C# 6.1 5 SOLDI

Billon, 19 mm. **Ruler:** Ferdinando di Borbone **Obv:** Crowned arms with garlands **Rev:** St. Justine **Note:** Weight varies: 1.35-1.55 grams.

Date	Mintage	VG	F	VF	XF	Unc
1784	—	7.00	15.00	30.00	70.00	—

C# 6.2 5 SOLDI

Billon **Ruler:** Ferdinando di Borbone **Rev:** Crowned arms without garlands **Note:** Weight varies: 1.35-1.55 grams.

Date	Mintage	VG	F	VF	XF	Unc
1785	—	7.00	15.00	30.00	70.00	—
1786	—	7.00	15.00	30.00	70.00	—
1787	—	7.00	15.00	30.00	70.00	—
1788	—	7.00	15.00	30.00	70.00	—

C# 6.3 5 SOLDI

1.2000 g., Billon, 17 mm. **Ruler:** Ferdinando di Borbone **Note:** Weight varies: 1.35-1.55 grams. Reduced size.

Date	Mintage	VG	F	VF	XF	Unc
1792	—	4.50	9.00	18.00	40.00	—
1793	—	4.50	9.00	18.00	40.00	—
1794	—	4.50	9.00	18.00	40.00	—
1795	—	4.50	9.00	18.00	40.00	—

C# 7.1 10 SOLDI

Billon **Ruler:** Ferdinando di Borbone **Obv:** Crowned arms **Obv. Legend:** Ends ...PARM • V • DUX **Rev:** St. Anthony on horseback **Note:** Size varies: 21-23 millimeters. Weight varies: 2.00-2.58 grams.

Date	Mintage	VG	F	VF	XF	Unc
1784	—	18.00	35.00	70.00	160	—

C# 7.2 10 SOLDI

Billon **Ruler:** Ferdinando di Borbone **Obv:** Crowned arms **Obv. Legend:** FERD • I • H • I • D • G • PLAC • PAR • V • DVX • 1791 **Rev:** St. Anthony on horseback **Rev. Legend:** S • ANTO • PROT • PLAC **Note:** Size varies: 21-23 millimeters. Weight varies: 2.00-2.58 grams.

Date	Mintage	VG	F	VF	XF	Unc
1785	—	7.50	12.50	22.00	50.00	—
1786	—	7.50	12.50	22.00	50.00	—
1787	—	7.50	12.50	22.00	50.00	—
1788	—	7.50	12.50	22.00	50.00	—
1789	—	7.50	12.50	22.00	50.00	—
1790	—	7.50	12.50	22.00	50.00	—
1791	—	7.50	12.50	22.00	50.00	—

C# 7.3 10 SOLDI

Billon **Ruler:** Ferdinando di Borbone **Obv. Legend:** Ends ...PAR • D **Note:** Size varies: 21-23 millimeters. Weight varies: 2.00-2.58 grams.

Date	Mintage	VG	F	VF	XF	Unc
1792	—	7.50	12.50	22.00	50.00	—
1793	—	7.50	12.50	22.00	50.00	—
1794	—	7.50	12.50	22.00	50.00	—
1795	—	7.50	12.50	22.00	50.00	—

PIEDMONT REPUBLIC

Established by Napoleon in 1798 in the Piedmont area of northwest Italy. It was the mainland possession of the kingdom of Sardinia. The republic was overthrown by Austro-Russian forces in 1799.

REPUBBLICA PIEMONTESE

STANDARD COINAGE

C# 1 QUARTO (1/4) DI SCUDO

8.7900 g., 0.9060 Silver 0.2560 oz. ASW **Obv:** Written value within wreath **Obv. Legend:** LIBERTA • PIEMONTESE • ANNO • ... **Rev:** Standing figure with hand on fasces with liberty cap **Rev. Legend:** LIBERTA • VIRTU • EGUAGLIANZA •

Date	Mintage	Good	VG	F	VF	XF
ANNO VII (1799)	140,000	—	75.00	125	225	400

C# 2 MEZZO (1/2) SCUDO

17.5800 g., 0.9060 Silver 0.5121 oz. ASW **Obv:** Written value within wreath **Obv. Legend:** LIBERTA • PIEMONTESE * ANNO • VII • REP • I • DELLA • **Rev:** Standing figure with hand on fasces with liberty cap **Rev. Legend:** LIBERTA • VIRTU • EGUAGLIANZA •

Date	Mintage	Good	VG	F	VF	XF
ANNO VII (1799)	300,000	—	75.00	125	225	350

C# 2a MEZZO (1/2) SCUDO

17.5800 g., 0.9060 Silver 0.5121 oz. ASW **Obv:** Designer's name, LAVY **Rev:** Standing figure with hand on fasces with liberty cap

Date	Mintage	Good	VG	F	VF	XF
ANNO VII (1799)	150,000	—	100	150	300	500

NAZIONE PIEMONTESE

STANDARD COINAGE

C# 3 DUE (2) SOLDI

Bronze **Obv:** Written value within circle, legend around **Obv. Legend:** NAZIONE * PIEMONTESE * **Rev:** Triangle design with liberty cap, A • 9 • below, all within wreath **Rev. Legend:** LIBERTA ....

Date	Mintage	Good	VG	F	VF	XF
A(nno)9 (1800)	—	—	7.00	15.00	30.00	60.00

REPUBLIC

STANDARD COINAGE

C# 4 5 FRANCS

25.0000 g., 0.9000 Silver 0.7234 oz. ASW **Obv:** Standing figures with Liberty cap on pole **Obv. Legend:** GAULE SUBALPINE **Rev:** Value within wreath **Rev. Legend:** LIBERTE' EGALITE...

Date	Mintage	Good	VG	F	VF	XF
L'AN 9 (1800)	19,000	—	40.00	60.00	125	300

C# 5 20 FRANCS

6.4500 g., 0.9000 Gold 0.1866 oz. AGW **Obv:** Laureate bust left **Obv. Legend:** L'ITALIE DELIVREE.... **Rev:** Value within wreath **Rev. Legend:** LIBERTE' EGALITE...

Date	Mintage	Good	VG	F	VF	XF
L'AN 9 (1800)	2,820	—	225	450	750	1,250

PISA

A city located on the Arno River in western Tuscany on the Tyrrhenian Sea, site of the famous leaning tower and mint. Rebelled against Florentine rule 1494-1509 and was under the Medici lineage of the Tuscan Grand Dukes, except for the French occupation between 1807-14. It joined the Kingdom of Italy in 1860.

GRAND DUKES

Cosimo III de'Medici, 1670-1723
Gian Gastone, 1723-1737
Francesco I Lorraine, 1737-1765

MINT NAME

Pisa

CITY

STANDARD COINAGE

KM# 35 2 QUATTRINI (1 Duetto)

Copper **Ruler:** Fian Gastone **Obv:** Medici arms **Obv. Legend:** QVATTRIN. II. **Rev:** Pisan cross, date **Note:** Weight varies: 1.06-1.40 grams.

Date	Mintage	VG	F	VF	XF	Unc
1731	—	12.00	22.00	40.00	75.00	—
1737	—	12.00	22.00	40.00	75.00	—

KM# 36 3 QUATTRINI (1 Soldo)

Billon **Ruler:** Fian Gastone **Obv:** Medici arms **Obv. Legend:** QVAT TRINI. III **Rev:** Pisan cross **Note:** Weight varies: 1.14-1.18 grams.

Date	Mintage	VG	F	VF	XF	Unc
1705	—	15.00	25.00	45.00	85.00	—
1710	—	15.00	25.00	45.00	85.00	—
1717	—	15.00	25.00	45.00	85.00	—
1718	—	15.00	25.00	45.00	85.00	—
1719	—	15.00	25.00	45.00	85.00	—
1720	—	15.00	25.00	45.00	85.00	—
1726	—	15.00	25.00	45.00	85.00	—
1727	—	15.00	25.00	45.00	85.00	—
1736	—	15.00	25.00	45.00	85.00	—

KM# 40 1/2 GUILLIO (Grosso)

Silver **Ruler:** Cosimo III de'Medici **Obv:** Pisan cross **Obv. Legend:** ASPICE.PIS AS **Rev:** Bust of Madonna right **Note:** Weight varies: 1.20-1.39 grams.

Date	Mintage	VG	F	VF	XF	Unc
1714	—	20.00	35.00	60.00	100	—
1715	—	20.00	35.00	60.00	100	—
1717	—	20.00	35.00	60.00	100	—
1718	—	20.00	35.00	60.00	100	—
1719	—	20.00	35.00	60.00	100	—
1721	—	20.00	35.00	60.00	100	—
1722	—	20.00	35.00	60.00	100	—
1727	—	20.00	35.00	60.00	100	—
1735	—	20.00	35.00	60.00	100	—
1736	—	20.00	35.00	60.00	100	—
1737	—	20.00	35.00	60.00	100	—

KM# 45 1/2 GUILLIO (Grosso)

Silver **Ruler:** Francesco I Lorraine **Note:** Weight varies: 1.20-1.39 grams.

Date	Mintage	VG	F	VF	XF	Unc
1738	—	20.00	35.00	60.00	100	—

PORCIA

RULER

Hannibal Alfonso Emanuel

PRINCIPALITY

STANDARD COINAGE

FR# 976 ZECCHINO

3.5000 g., 0.9860 Gold 0.1109 oz. AGW **Ruler:** Hannibal Alfonso Emanuel **Obv:** Bust of Hannibal right **Rev:** Arms in inner circle

Date	Mintage	Good	VG	F	VF	XF
1704 Rare	—	—	—	—	—	—

REGGIO EMILIA

CITY

STANDARD COINAGE

C# 10 LIRA

Billon **Obv:** Armored bust of Francesco right, date below **Rev:** Madonna

Date	Mintage	Good	VG	F	VF	XF
1739	—	—	30.00	60.00	120	250

Note: Was previously listed as a Modena issue

RETEGNO

(Trivulzio)

A commune in the province of Milan, it was made a barony in 1654 by Ferdinand II. The mint right was given to Cardinal Gian Giacomo Teodoro Trivulzio. The family held the county of Misox in Switzerland.

RULERS

Antonio Gaetano Trivulzio-Gallio, 1679-1705
Antonio Tolomeo Trivulzio-Gallio, 1707-1767

BARONY

STANDARD COINAGE

KM# 35 1/2 TALLERO

14.6000 g., Silver **Ruler:** Antonio Tolomeo Trivulzio-Gallio **Obv:** Bust right **Obv. Legend:** ANT PTOLOM : TRIVULTIUS **Rev:** Crowned, mantled oval arms **Rev. Legend:** S • R • I • PRINC & BARO • RETENY • IMP •

Date	Mintage	Good	VG	F	VF	XF
1726	—	—	200	350	600	1,000

KM# 36 TALLERO

Silver **Ruler:** Antonio Tolomeo Trivulzio-Gallio **Obv:** Bust right **Obv. Legend:** ANT PTOLOM : TRIVULTIUS **Rev:** Crowned, mantled oval arms **Rev. Legend:** S • R • I • PRINC & BARO • RETENY • IMP • **Note:** Dav. #1482. Weight varies: 29.02-29.20 grams.

Date	Mintage	Good	VG	F	VF	XF
1726	—	—	350	650	1,200	2,000

KM# 34 DUCAT

3.5000 g., 0.9860 Gold 0.1109 oz. AGW **Ruler:** Antonio Tolomeo Trivulzio-Gallio **Obv:** Bust right **Obv. Legend:** ANT • PTOLO : TRIVULTIUS • **Rev:** Crowned, mantled oval arms, date in legend **Rev. Legend:** S • R • I • PRIN & BARO • RETENY • IMP •

Date	Mintage	Good	VG	F	VF	XF
1724	—	—	800	1,500	3,000	4,500
1726	—	—	800	1,500	3,000	4,500

ROMAN REPUBLIC

Repubblica Romana

A short-lived Republican movement fostered by the French Revolution, submerged the Papal States in 1798-99. They reappeared in 1814, and except for the Republican movement of 1848-49, maintained their authority until 1860.

MINT MARKS

B - Bologna
R - Rome

FIRST REPUBLIC
1798-1799
STANDARD COINAGE

KM# 1 1/2 BAIOCCO
Copper **Obv:** Fasces with liberty cap **Obv. Legend:** ROMANA REPVBLICA **Rev:** Written value within wreath

Date	Mintage	Good	VG	F	VF	XF
ND (1798)	—	4.00	12.50	25.00	40.00	—

KM# 1a 1/2 BAIOCCO
Copper **Obv:** Fasces with liberty cap **Obv. Legend:** ROMANA REPVBBLICA **Rev:** Written value within wreath

Date	Mintage	Good	VG	F	VF	XF
ND (1798)	—	4.00	12.50	25.00	40.00	—

KM# 2 BAIOCCO
Copper **Obv:** Liberty cap on pole flanked by fasces **Obv. Legend:** ROMANA REPVBBLICA **Rev:** Written value within square

Date	Mintage	Good	VG	F	VF	XF
(1798)-Sesto (6)	—	25.00	50.00	75.00	150	—

KM# 3 BAIOCCO
Copper **Obv:** Fasces within legend **Obv. Legend:** REPUBLICA ROMANA **Rev:** Value within wreath

Date	Mintage	Good	VG	F	VF	XF
ND (1799)	—	4.00	12.50	25.00	40.00	—

KM# 4 2 BAIOCCHI
Copper **Obv:** Fasces with liberty cap **Obv. Legend:** ROMANA REPVBLICA **Rev:** Written value, date

Date	Mintage	Good	VG	F	VF	XF
1798	—	4.00	12.50	25.00	40.00	—
1798 Star	—	4.00	12.50	25.00	40.00	—

KM# 5 2 BAIOCCHI
Copper **Obv:** Crowned eagle on fasces within thin wreath **Obv. Legend:** ROMANA REPVBBLICA **Rev:** Written value within fasces's in form of triangle

Date	Mintage	Good	VG	F	VF	XF
(1798)-Sesto (6) TM	—	20.00	40.00	60.00	100	—

KM# 6 2 BAIOCCHI
Copper **Obv:** Fasces in center of crossed flags **Obv. Legend:** ROMANA REPVBBLICA **Rev:** Written value within triangle, flanked by sprigs

Date	Mintage	Good	VG	F	VF	XF
(1798)-Sesto (6)	—	25.00	50.00	75.00	125	—

KM# 5a 2 BAIOCCHI
Bronze

Date	Mintage	Good	VG	F	VF	XF
(1798)-Sesto (6) (1798) TM	—	—	—	125	225	—

KM# 8.1 2 BAIOCCHI
Copper **Obv:** Legend around fasces **Obv. Legend:** REPVBLICA ROMANA **Rev:** Value: DVE/BAIOCCHI/ROMANI in wreath

Date	Mintage	Good	VG	F	VF	XF
ND(1799)	—	12.50	25.00	40.00	75.00	—

KM# 8.2 2 BAIOCCHI
Copper **Obv:** Legend around fasces **Obv. Legend:** REPVBBLICA ROMANA

Date	Mintage	Good	VG	F	VF	XF
ND(1799) TM	—	12.50	25.00	40.00	75.00	—

KM# 7.1 2 BAIOCCHI
Copper **Obv:** Fasces with liberty cap **Obv. Legend:** ROMANA REPUBLICA **Rev:** Written value within wreath

Date	Mintage	Good	VG	F	VF	XF
ND(1799)	—	6.50	12.50	25.00	45.00	—
ND(1799) G • H	—	6.50	12.50	25.00	45.00	—
ND(1799) G • H •	—	6.50	12.50	25.00	45.00	—
ND(1799) HT	—	6.50	12.50	25.00	45.00	—

KM# 7.2 2 BAIOCCHI
Copper **Obv:** Fasces with liberty cap **Obv. Legend:** ROMANA REPUBLICA **Rev:** Written value, •R• below within wreath

Date	Mintage	Good	VG	F	VF	XF
ND(1799)R	—	6.50	12.50	25.00	45.00	—
ND(1799) • R •	—	6.50	12.50	25.00	45.00	—

KM# 7.3 2 BAIOCCHI
Copper **Obv:** Fasces with liberty cap **Obv. Legend:** ROMANA REPVBLICA **Rev:** Written value within wreath

Date	Mintage	Good	VG	F	VF	XF
ND(1799)	—	6.50	12.50	25.00	45.00	—
ND(1799) TM	—	6.50	12.50	25.00	45.00	—

KM# 7.4 2 BAIOCCHI
Copper

Date	Mintage	Good	VG	F	VF	XF
ND(1799) • R •	—	6.50	12.50	25.00	45.00	—

KM# 7.5 2 BAIOCCHI
Copper **Obv:** Fasces with liberty cap **Obv. Legend:** ROMANA REPVBBLICA **Rev:** Written value within wreath

Date	Mintage	Good	VG	F	VF	XF
ND(1799)	—	6.50	12.50	25.00	45.00	—
ND(1799) Rosette	—	6.50	12.50	25.00	45.00	—
ND(1799) TM	—	6.50	12.50	25.00	45.00	—

KM# 9 5 BAIOCCHI
Copper **Obv:** Written value **Rev:** Madonna **Rev. Legend:** SANCTA DEI GENITRIX

Date	Mintage	Good	VG	F	VF	XF
ND(1799) Star	—	10.00	25.00	75.00	120	—
ND(1799) Three stars	—	—	25.00	75.00	120	—
ND(1799) Rosette	—	—	25.00	75.00	120	—
ND(1799) Three rosettes	—	—	25.00	75.00	120	—
ND(1799) TM; Three rosettes	—	—	25.00	75.00	120	—

KM# 11 SCUDO
26.7600 g., 0.9170 Silver 0.7889 oz. ASW **Obv:** Standing figure with fasces and liberty cap on pole **Obv. Legend:** ROMANA REPVBLICA **Rev:** Written value within wreath **Note:** Dav. #1486.

Date	Mintage	Good	VG	F	VF	XF
ND(1799)	—	—	—	175	325	500

NEAPOLITAN OCCUPATION
1800
STANDARD COINAGE

KM# 30 1/2 SCUDO
13.2500 g., 0.9170 Silver 0.3906 oz. ASW **Ruler:** Ferdinand IV **Subject:** Ferdinand IV of Naples **Obv:** Inscription within wreath **Obv. Inscription:** FERDINAND.... **Rev:** Radiant Church standing **Rev. Legend:** RELIGIONIS DEFENSORI *

Date	Mintage	VG	F	VF	XF	Unc
1800R	—	500	1,000	1,350	1,850	—

KM# 32 SCUDO
26.2500 g., 0.9170 Silver 0.7739 oz. ASW **Ruler:** Ferdinand IV **Obv:** 3 Fleur-de-lis above inscription within wreath **Obv. Inscription:** FERDINANDUS IV UTB • SLC • REX **Rev:** Holy Mother Church seated on cloud **Rev. Legend:** AUXILIUM DE SANCTO 1800 **Note:** Cross-reference number Dav. #1488.

Date	Mintage	VG	F	VF	XF	Unc
1800 (R)	—	500	700	1,000	1,600	—

KM# 31 SCUDO

26.2500 g., 0.9170 Silver 0.7739 oz. ASW **Ruler:** Ferdinand IV **Subject:** Ferdinand IV of Naples **Obv:** 3 Fleur-de-lis above inscription within wreath **Obv. Inscription:** FERDINANDUS IV NEAP•ET•SIC•REX **Rev:** Radiant Church standing **Rev. Legend:** RELIGIONE DEFENSA **Note:** Cross-reference number Dav. #1489.

Date	Mintage	VG	F	VF	XF	Unc
MDCCC (1800)	—	500	700	1,000	1,600	—

PATTERNS

Including off metal strikes

KM#	Date	Mintage	Identification	Mkt Val
Pn1	ND	—	Scudo. Bronze. KM#11	—
Pn2	(1798)-Anno Sesto	—	Baiocco. Bronze.	—
Pn3	(1798)-Anno Sesto	—	2 Baiocchi. Bronze. C#4	—

ROMAN REPUBLIC - ANCONA

Anconna

A city in the Marches, was founded by Syracusan refugees about 390 B.C. It became a semi-independent republic under papal protection in the 14th century, and a papal state in 1532. From 1797 until the formation of the United Kingdom of Italy it was part of the Roman Republic (1798-99), a papal state (1799-1808), part of the Italian Kingdom of Napoleon (1808-14), a papal state (1814-48),a part of the Roman Republic (1848-49), and a papal state(1849-60).

NOTE: For earlier issues see Papal States - Ancona

MINT MARK

A – Ancona

MINT OFFICIALS' INITIALS

Initials	Year	Name
AP	1798	Andronico Perpenti
TM	1799	Tommaso Mercandetti

FIRST REPUBLIC

1798-1799

SIEGE COINAGE

1799

Restruck Papal types during the siege of Ancona

KM# 9 1/2 SCUDO

13.6000 g., Silver **Obv:** Papal arms **Obv. Legend:** PIVS SEXTVS PON SILVER MA XXII **Rev:** Holy Mother Church seated on cloud **Rev. Legend:** AVXILIVM DE SANCTO 1778

Date	Mintage	Good	VG	F	VF	XF
1778A Rare	—	—	—	—	—	—

KM# 10 SCUDO

26.3400 g., Silver **Obv:** Papal oval arms **Obv. Legend:** PIVS SEXTVS PONT M A VI **Rev:** Holy Mother Church seated on cloud **Rev. Legend:** AVXILIVM DE SANCTO 1780

Date	Mintage	Good	VG	F	VF	XF
1780A	—	500	750	1,500	2,350	—

STANDARD COINAGE

KM# 6 2 BAIOCCHI

Copper **Obv:** Fasces with liberty cap **Obv. Legend:** ROMANA REPVBBLICA **Rev:** Written value within leafy wreath

Date	Mintage	Good	VG	F	VF	XF
ND A/P	—	15.00	35.00	70.00	110	—
ND A. /P.	—	15.00	35.00	70.00	110	—
ND TM	—	15.00	35.00	70.00	110	—

KM# 7 2 BAIOCCHI

Copper **Obv:** Fasces with liberty cap **Rev:** Written value

Date	Mintage	Good	VG	F	VF	XF
ND	—	12.50	30.00	45.00	75.00	—

ROMAN REPUBLIC-ASCOLI

NOTE: For earlier issues see Papal States - Ascoli.

FIRST REPUBLIC

1798-1799

STANDARD COINAGE

KM# 6 QUATTRINO

Copper **Obv:** Fasces divides R R **Rev:** ASCO/LI within wreath

Date	Mintage	VG	F	VF	XF	Unc
ND	—	55.00	110	125	250	—

KM# 7 1/2 BAIOCCO

Copper **Obv:** Fasces with liberty cap divides initials **Rev:** Written value below star

Date	Mintage	VG	F	VF	XF	Unc
ND	—	37.50	75.00	125	200	—

KM# 8.1 2 BAIOCCHI

Copper **Obv:** Fasces with liberty cap **Obv. Legend:** ROMANA REPVBBLICA **Rev:** DVE/BAIOCCHI/ASCOLI within wreath

Date	Mintage	VG	F	VF	XF	Unc
ND	—	25.00	50.00	100	200	—

KM# 8.2 2 BAIOCCHI

Copper **Obv:** Fasces with liberty cap **Obv. Legend:** REPVBLICA ROMANA **Rev:** Value: DVE/BAIOCCHI/ASCOLI

Date	Mintage	VG	F	VF	XF	Unc
ND	—	25.00	50.00	100	200	—

KM# 9.1 2 BAIOCCHI

Copper **Obv:** Fasces with liberty cap **Obv. Legend:** REPVBBLICA ROMANA **Rev:** Value: DVE/BAIOC/CHI/ASCOLI

Date	Mintage	VG	F	VF	XF	Unc
ND	—	25.00	50.00	100	200	—

KM# 9.2 2 BAIOCCHI

Copper **Obv:** Fasces with liberty cap **Obv. Legend:** REPVBLICA ROMANA **Rev:** Value: DVE/BAIOC/CHI/ASCOLI

Date	Mintage	VG	F	VF	XF	Unc
ND	—	25.00	50.00	100	200	—

ROMAN REPUBLIC-CIVITAVECCHIA

NOTE: For earlier issues see Papal States-Civitavecchia. CAMERINO

MINT MARK

\ C \ - Civitavecchia

MINT OFFICIALS' INITIALS

Initials	Date	Name
GH	1798-99	Gioacchino Hamera

FIRST REPUBLIC

1798-1799

STANDARD COINAGE

KM# 11 2 BAIOCCHI

Copper **Obv:** Madonna **Obv. Legend:** SANCTA DEI GENITRIX **Rev:** Written value **Rev. Legend:** PIVS PAPA SEXTVS ANNO XXIII (letters N are backwards on coin)

Date	Mintage	Good	VG	F	VF	XF
ND C GH	—	15.00	30.00	50.00	85.00	—

KM# 12 2 BAIOCCHI

Copper **Note:** Muled reverses of KM#11.

Date	Mintage	Good	VG	F	VF	XF
ND	—	15.00	30.00	50.00	85.00	—

ROMAN REPUBLIC-CLITUNNO

A department under the Roman Republic (1798-99) during the Napoleonic period.

NOTE: For earlier issues see Papal States-Spoleto.

FIRST REPUBLIC

1798-1799

STANDARD COINAGE

KM# 1 BAIOCCO

Copper **Obv:** Fasces with liberty cap **Obv. Legend:** ROMANA REPVBBLICA **Rev:** Written value

Date	Mintage	Good	VG	F	VF	XF
ND	—	100	200	350	500	—

KM# 2.1 2 BAIOCCHI

Copper **Obv:** Fasces with liberty cap **Obv. Legend:** REPV • *ROM • DP • CLITVNNO **Rev:** Written value within wreath

Date	Mintage	Good	VG	F	VF	XF
ND	—	100	200	350	500	—

KM# 2.2 2 BAIOCCHI

Copper **Obv:** Fasces with liberty cap **Obv. Legend:** REPV • ROM • DP • CLITVNNO **Rev:** Written value within wreath

Date	Mintage	Good	VG	F	VF	XF
ND	—	100	200	350	500	—

KM# 3 2 BAIOCCHI

Copper **Obv:** Fasces with liberty cap **Obv. Legend:** *R • PUBL • ROMANA * CLITUNNO **Rev:** Written value within wreath

Date	Mintage	Good	VG	F	VF	XF
ND	—	100	200	350	500	—

ROMAN REPUBLIC-FERMO

NOTE: For earlier issues see Papal States-Fermo.

FIRST REPUBLIC
1798-1799

STANDARD COINAGE

KM# 6 QUATTRINO

Copper **Obv:** Fasces with liberty cap **Obv. Legend:** ROMANA REPVBLICA **Rev:** Written value, city name

Date	Mintage	Good	VG	F	VF	XF
ND	—	20.00	40.00	75.00	120	—

KM# 8 1/2 BAIOCCO

Copper **Obv:** Fasces with liberty cap **Rev:** Written value, city name within circle

Date	Mintage	Good	VG	F	VF	XF
ND	—	6.50	12.00	30.00	45.00	—

KM# 7 1/2 BAIOCCO

Copper **Obv:** Written value, city name within wreath **Rev:** Inscription within wreath **Rev. Inscription:** ANNO/* PMO */DELLA.REP/ROMANA

Date	Mintage	Good	VG	F	VF	XF
I (1798)	—	10.00	20.00	35.00	50.00	—

KM# 11 BAIOCCO

Copper **Obv:** Fasces with liberty cap within circle **Obv. Legend:** ROMANA REPVBLICA **Rev:** Written value, city name within circle

Date	Mintage	Good	VG	F	VF	XF
ND1798	—	10.00	17.50	38.00	55.00	—

KM# 9.1 BAIOCCO

Copper **Obv:** ROMA NA within inner wreath, legend around **Obv. Legend:** ANNO PMO DELLA REPVB **Rev:** Written value, city name within circle and wreath

Date	Mintage	Good	VG	F	VF	XF
I (1798)	—	6.50	12.00	35.00	50.00	—

KM# 9.2 BAIOCCO

Copper **Obv. Legend:** ANNO PMO DELLA REPV

Date	Mintage	Good	VG	F	VF	XF
I (1798)	—	6.50	12.00	35.00	50.00	—

KM# 10.1 BAIOCCO

Copper **Obv:** ANNO I within inner wreath, legend around **Obv. Legend:** ROMANA REPVBLICA **Rev:** Written value, city name within wreath

Date	Mintage	Good	VG	F	VF	XF
I (1798)	—	8.00	15.00	35.00	50.00	—

KM# 10.2 BAIOCCO

Copper **Obv:** ANNO I within inner wreath, legend around **Obv. Legend:** ROMANA REPVBLICA **Rev:** Written value, city name, date within wreath

Date	Mintage	Good	VG	F	VF	XF
I (1798)	—	8.00	15.00	35.00	50.00	—

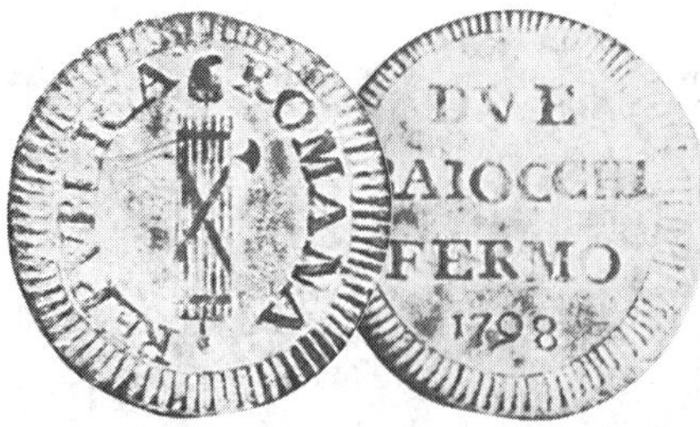

KM# 12 2 BAIOCCHI

Copper **Obv:** Fasces with liberty cap **Obv. Legend:** ROMANA REPVBLICA **Rev:** Written value, city name, date within circle

Date	Mintage	Good	VG	F	VF	XF
1798	—	8.50	15.00	35.00	50.00	—

KM# 15 2 BAIOCCHI

Copper **Obv:** Fasces with liberty cap **Obv. Legend:** ROMANA REPVBLICA **Rev:** Written value, city name within circle **Note:** Mule.

Date	Mintage	Good	VG	F	VF	XF
ND	—	8.50	15.00	35.00	50.00	—

KM# 16 2 BAIOCCHI

Copper **Obv. Legend:** DELLA REPVBLICA ROMANO

Date	Mintage	Good	VG	F	VF	XF
I (1798)	—	8.50	15.00	35.00	50.00	—

KM# 13 2 BAIOCCHI

Copper **Obv:** Legend around wreath **Obv. Legend:** ANNO PMO DELLA REPVB **Rev:** Written value, city name, date

Date	Mintage	Good	VG	F	VF	XF
I (1798)	—	12.00	18.00	35.00	50.00	—

KM# 17 2 BAIOCCHI

Copper **Obv. Legend:** ANNO PMO. DELLA REPV

Date	Mintage	Good	VG	F	VF	XF
I (1798)	—	12.00	18.00	35.00	50.00	—

KM# 14 2 BAIOCCHI

Copper **Obv:** ANNO I within wreath, legend around **Obv. Legend:** ROMANA REPVBLICA **Rev:** Written value, city name within circle

Date	Mintage	Good	VG	F	VF	XF
I (1798)	—	8.50	15.00	35.00	50.00	—

ROMAN REPUBLIC-FOLIGNO

NOTE: For earlier issues see Papal States - Foligno.

FIRST REPUBLIC
1798-1799

STANDARD COINAGE

KM# 14.1 QUATTRINO

Copper **Obv:** Written value, city name below star within wreath **Obv. Legend:** ...D • I/FVLIGNO **Rev:** Legend, bishop standing **Rev. Legend:** 5 • FELICIANO

Date	Mintage	Good	VG	F	VF	XF
ND	—	12.50	25.00	45.00	75.00	—

KM# 14.2 QUATTRINO

Copper **Obv. Legend:** ... DI/FVLIGNO

Date	Mintage	Good	VG	F	VF	XF
ND	—	12.50	25.00	45.00	75.00	—

ROMAN REPUBLIC-GUBBIO

NOTE: For earlier issues see Papal States-Gubbio.

MINT OFFICIAL'S INITIALS

Initials	Date	Name
A.P.	1798	Andronica Perpenti

FIRST REPUBLIC
1798-1799
STANDARD COINAGE

KM# 41.1 1/2 BAIOCCO
Copper **Obv. Legend:** ... GVBBIO **Rev. Legend:** ... GVBBIO

Date	Mintage	Good	VG	F	VF	XF
ND	—	20.00	35.00	60.00	90.00	—

KM# 41.2 1/2 BAIOCCO
Copper **Obv. Legend:** ... GVBBIO **Rev:** ... GUBBIO

Date	Mintage	Good	VG	F	VF	XF
ND	—	20.00	35.00	60.00	90.00	—

KM# 41.3 1/2 BAIOCCO
Copper **Obv. Legend:** ... GUBBIO **Rev. Legend:** ... GUBBIO

Date	Mintage	Good	VG	F	VF	XF
ND	—	20.00	35.00	60.00	90.00	—

KM# 42.1 2 BAIOCCHI
Copper **Obv:** Fasces, legend **Obv. Legend:** REPVBBLICA ROMANA

Date	Mintage	Good	VG	F	VF	XF
1798 AP	—	15.00	25.00	40.00	75.00	—

KM# 42.2 2 BAIOCCHI
Copper **Obv:** Fasces with liberty cap within flower sprigs **Obv. Legend:** ROMANA REPVBBLICA **Rev:** Written value within wreath

Date	Mintage	Good	VG	F	VF	XF
ND AP	—	15.00	25.00	40.00	75.00	—

ROMAN REPUBLIC-MACERATA

NOTE: For earlier issues see Papal States-Macerata.

FIRST REPUBLIC
1798-1799
STANDARD COINAGE

KM# 3 QUATTRINO
Copper 0 **Obv:** Fasces with liberty cap in flower sprigs within circle **Rev:** Written value, city name, star above and below within circle

Date	Mintage	VG	F	VF	XF	Unc
ND(1798)	—	35.00	50.00	75.00	110	—

KM# 4.1 1/2 BAIOCCO
Copper 0 **Obv. Legend:** A.I. DELLA-LIB. ITAL

Date	Mintage	VG	F	VF	XF	Unc
ND(1798)	—	50.00	75.00	100	135	—

KM# 4.2 1/2 BAIOCCO
Copper 0 **Obv:** Fasces with liberty cap in flower sprigs within circle **Obv. Legend:** AI • DELLA • LIB • ITAL **Rev:** Written value, city name below star within circle

Date	Mintage	VG	F	VF	XF	Unc
ND(1798)	—	50.00	75.00	100	135	—

ROMAN REPUBLIC-PERGOLA

NOTE: For earlier issues see Papal States-Pergola.

MINT OFFICIAL'S INITIALS

Initials	Date	Name
AP	1798	Andronico Perpenti

FIRST REPUBLIC
1798-1799
STANDARD COINAGE

KM# 4.1 1/2 BAIOCCO
Copper **Obv:** Value: MEZZO BAIOCOO PERGO LA within wreath **Rev:** Value: MEZZO BAIOCCO PERGO LA within wreath

Date	Mintage	Good	VG	F	VF	XF
ND(1798)	—	50.00	100	150	250	—

KM# 4.2 1/2 BAIOCCO
Copper **Obv:** Value: MEZZO BAIOCCO PERGO LA within chain wreath **Rev:** Value: MEZZO BAIOCCO PERGOL within beaded circle

Date	Mintage	Good	VG	F	VF	XF
ND(1798)	—	50.00	100	150	250	—

KM# 5.1 BAIOCCO
Copper **Obv:** Value: VN BAIOCCO PERGOLA 1798 within rope wreath **Rev:** Value: VN BAIOCCO PERGO LA within wreath

Date	Mintage	Good	VG	F	VF	XF
1798 AP	—	50.00	100	150	250	—

KM# 5.2 BAIOCCO
Copper **Rev:** Without ++ above VN

Date	Mintage	Good	VG	F	VF	XF
1798 AP	—	50.00	100	150	250	—

KM# 6 2 BAIOCCHI
Copper **Obv:** Legend around fasces with liberty cap within sprigs **Obv. Legend:** REPVBLICA ROMANA **Rev:** Value: DVE ... PERGOLA, date

Date	Mintage	Good	VG	F	VF	XF
1798 AP	—	50.00	100	150	250	—

KM# 7.1 2 BAIOCCHI
Copper **Obv:** Legend around fasces with liberty cap within sprigs **Obv. Legend:** ROMANA REPVBBLICA **Rev:** Value: DVE ... PERGO/LA

Date	Mintage	Good	VG	F	VF	XF
ND(1798) AP	—	50.00	100	150	250	—

KM# 7.2 2 BAIOCCHI
Copper **Rev:** Value: ... PERGOLA

Date	Mintage	Good	VG	F	VF	XF
ND(1798) AP	—	50.00	100	150	250	—

KM# 7.3 2 BAIOCCHI
Copper **Rev:** Value: ... PERGO/LA with flower buds

Date	Mintage	Good	VG	F	VF	XF
ND(1798) AP	—	50.00	100	150	250	—

KM# 7.4 2 BAIOCCHI
Copper **Rev:** Value: ... PERGOLA with flower buds

Date	Mintage	Good	VG	F	VF	XF
ND(1798) AP	—	50.00	100	150	250	—

ROMAN REPUBLIC-PERUGIA

NOTE: For earlier listings see Papal States-Perugia.

MINT OFFICIAL'S INITIALS

Initials	Date	Name
GH	1799	Gioachino Hamerani

FIRST REPUBLIC
1798-1799
STANDARD COINAGE

KM# 13 2 BAIOCCHI
Copper **Obv:** Fasces with liberty cap divides script letters **Rev:** Value within triangle

Date	Mintage	Good	VG	F	VF	XF
ND(1799)//7	—	15.00	25.00	45.00	85.00	—

KM# 14 2 BAIOCCHI
Copper **Obv. Legend:** REP. ROM. AN. VII.

Date	Mintage	Good	VG	F	VF	XF
ND(1799)//AN VII	—	15.00	25.00	45.00	85.00	—

KM# 15 2 BAIOCCHI
Copper **Obv:** Fasces with liberty cap divides inscription **Rev:** Value within triangle

Date	Mintage	Good	VG	F	VF	XF
ND(1799)//VII	—	7.50	18.00	45.00	85.00	—

KM# 18 2 BAIOCCHI
Copper **Obv:** Fasces with liberty cap in sprigs within rope wreath **Rev:** Value: BAIOC. DVE PERVGIA

Date	Mintage	Good	VG	F	VF	XF
ND(1799)	—	10.00	22.50	40.00	85.00	—

KM# 19 2 BAIOCCHI
Copper **Obv. Legend:** REPVBLICA ROMANA **Rev:** Value: DVE BAIOC .P.

Date	Mintage	Good	VG	F	VF	XF
ND(1799) GH	—	12.50	25.00	40.00	85.00	—

KM# 20 2 BAIOCCHI
Copper

Date	Mintage	Good	VG	F	VF	XF
ND(1799) PC	—	12.50	25.00	40.00	85.00	—

KM# 21 2 BAIOCCHI
Copper **Obv:** Fasces with liberty cap, legend around **Obv. Legend:** ROMANA * REPVBBLICA **Rev:** Value: DVE BAIOCCHI PERVGIA A • VII • REP

Date	Mintage	Good	VG	F	VF	XF
ND(1799)//VII	—	10.00	22.50	35.00	75.00	—

KM# 22 2 BAIOCCHI
Copper **Obv:** Legend around fasces in branches **Obv. Legend:** REPVBBLICA ROMANA **Rev:** Value: DVE BAIOCCHI A • VII • R

Date	Mintage	Good	VG	F	VF	XF
ND(1799)//VII R	—	7.50	18.00	45.00	85.00	—

KM# 23 2 BAIOCCHI
Copper **Obv. Legend:** REPVBLICA ROMANA **Rev:** Value: DVE BAIOCCHI A:VII

Date	Mintage	Good	VG	F	VF	XF
ND(1799)//VII R	—	7.50	18.00	45.00	85.00	—

KM# 24 2 BAIOCCHI
Copper **Rev:** Value: DVE BAIOCCHI A•VII•R

Date	Mintage	Good	VG	F	VF	XF
ND(1799)//VII R	—	7.50	18.00	45.00	85.00	—

KM# 25 2 BAIOCCHI
Copper **Obv:** Legend around fasces **Obv. Legend:** ROMANA REPVBLICA

Date	Mintage	Good	VG	F	VF	XF
ND(1799)//VII R	—	7.50	18.00	45.00	85.00	—

KM# 26 2 BAIOCCHI
Copper **Obv:** Fasces in branches **Rev:** Value: DVE BAIOC CHI in wreath

Date	Mintage	Good	VG	F	VF	XF
ND(1799)	—	7.50	18.00	45.00	85.00	—

KM# 16 2 BAIOCCHI
Copper **Obv:** Fasces with liberty cap within sprigs **Obv. Legend:** Ends: ...A • VII • REP **Note:** Varieties exist.

Date	Mintage	Good	VG	F	VF	XF
ND(1799)//VII	—	12.50	25.00	50.00	90.00	—

KM# 17 2 BAIOCCHI
Copper **Obv:** Fasces with liberty cap in sprigs within rope wreath **Rev:** Value: DVE BAIOCCHI PERVGIA A • VII • RE within circle **Note:** Varieties exist.

Date	Mintage	Good	VG	F	VF	XF
ND(1799)//VII	—	12.50	25.00	50.00	90.00	—

KM# 27 5 BAIOCCHI
Copper **Obv:** Fasces with liberty cap within circle **Rev:** Madonna **Note:** Counterstamp on various 2 Baiocchi using 5 Baiocchi dies, KM#8.

Date	Mintage	Good	VG	F	VF	XF
ND(1799)	—	25.00	50.00	75.00	110	—

KM# 28 SCUDO
Silver **Obv:** Eagle, wings spread, sprig in beak, above PERUGIA A VII **Obv. Legend:** ROMANA * REPUBLICA **Rev:** Value within wreath **Note:** Dav. #1487; Struck at Perugia.

Date	Mintage	Good	VG	F	VF	XF
(1799) / VII	—	—	500	1,000	1,500	2,500

TRIAL STRIKES

KM#	Date	Mintage	Identification	Mkt Val
TS1	Yr. VII (1798)	—	Scudo. Copper. KM#28. Square planchet.	—

KM#	Date	Mintage	Identification	Mkt Val
TS2	Yr. VII (1798)	—	Scudo. Copper. KM#28. Square planchet.	—

SAN GEORGIO

San Giorgio, in the province of Reggio, had been a feudal fief of the Spanish kings. In 1731 Giovanni Domenico, marchese of San Giorgio and Polistina, was made a prince of the Empire by Charles VI with permission to strike coins. He and his son each struck scudos for a single year at the Vienna mint.

RULERS
Giovanni Dominic Milano, 1731-1740
Giacomo Francesco Milano, 1740-

PRINCIPALITY

STANDARD COINAGE

C# 1 1/2 SCUDO
Silver **Ruler:** Giacomo Francesco Milano **Obv:** Armored bust right **Rev:** Crowned and mantled arms, date in legend

Date	Mintage	Good	VG	F	VF	XF
1753	—	—	125	275	550	1,150

DAV# 1490 SCUDO
Silver **Ruler:** Giovanni Dominic Milano **Obv:** Armored bust right **Rev:** Crowned and mantled arms, date in legend

Date	Mintage	Good	VG	F	VF	XF
1732 Rare	—	—	—	—	—	—

FR# 1012 ZECCHINO
3.5000 g., 0.9860 Gold 0.1109 oz. AGW **Ruler:** Giovanni Dominic Milano **Obv:** Bust left **Rev:** Arms in inner circle

Date	Mintage	Good	VG	F	VF	XF
1732	—	—	1,250	2,500	4,500	9,500

FR# 1011 2 ZECCHINI
7.0000 g., 0.9860 Gold 0.2219 oz. AGW **Ruler:** Giovanni Dominic Milano **Obv:** Bust right in inner circle **Rev:** Arms in inner circle

Date	Mintage	Good	VG	F	VF	XF
1732 Rare	—	—	—	—	—	—

SAN MARTINO

A commune in the province of Mantua was a fief given to the Gonzaga family who were also lords of Bozzolo.

RULER
Scipione Gonzaga, prince of Bozzolo

COMMUNE

STANDARD COINAGE

KM# A16 15 SOLDI
5.2400 g., Silver, 28 mm. **Obv:** Lucca shield **Rev:** San Martino on horseback

Date	Mintage	VG	F	VF	XF	Unc
1742	—	—	—	—	—	—
1743	—	—	—	—	—	—
1744	—	—	—	—	—	—
1745	—	—	—	—	—	—
1746	—	—	—	—	—	—
1746/5 Rare	—	—	—	—	—	—
1746	—	—	—	—	—	—

Note: With c/m, rampant lion left on reverse

SARDINIA

Sardinia is an island located in the Mediterranean Sea, west of the southern Italian peninsula, 9,301 sq. mi.; population 1,645,192. Along with some minor islands, it constitutes an autonomous region of Italy separated on the north from Corsica, France by the Strait of Bonifacio.

Settled by Phoenician's and Greeks before it came under control of Carthage during 600 BC; taken by the Romans in 238 BC; in the Vandal Kingdom during the5th century; re-conquered by the Byzantine Empire in533 AD. From the 8th century it was frequently raided by Muslims whose threat was eliminated by Pisa in 1016 as an object of a rivalrous bet. The Genoese and Pisans were driven out by the Aragonese during the 14th-15th centuries, remaining under Spanish rule until 1708; held by Austria 1708-17, regained by the Spanish in 1717 until it was finally ceded to Savoy in 1720 in exchange for Sicily, after which the ruler of Savoy and Piedmont took the title as King of Sardinia.

RULERS
Spanish, until 1708, 1717-1720
Austrian, 1708-1717
Vittorio Amedeo II as King of Sicily, 1713-1718
as King of Sardinia, 1718-1730
Carlo Emanuele III, 1730-1773
Vittorio Amedeo III 1773-1796
Carlo Emanuele IV 1796-1802

MINT MARKS
None Before 1802 = Turin (Torino)
Firenze = Florence
B = Bologna
(g) Anchor = Genoa
M = Milan

MINT OFFICIALS' MARKS
P in oval = Andrea O Luca Podesta
L in diamond = Felippo Lavy
P in shield = Giovanni Parodi
B in shield = Tommaso Battilana

MONETARY SYSTEM
12 Denari = 6 Cagliarese = 1 Soldo
50 Soldi = 10 Reales = 2 1/2 Lire = 1 Scudo Sardo
20 Soldi = 1 Lira
6 Lire = 1 Scudo
2 Scudi Sardi = 1 Doppietta

KINGDOM

ISLAND COINAGE

C# 34 1/2 CAGLIARESE

Bronze **Ruler:** Carlo Emanuele III **Obv:** Armored bust right, date below **Rev:** Voided cross with Moor heads in angles

Date	Mintage	VG	F	VF	XF	Unc
1736	—	3.00	6.00	12.00	25.00	—
1741	—	3.00	6.00	12.00	25.00	—
1745	—	3.00	6.00	12.00	25.00	—

C# 35 CAGLIARESE

Bronze **Ruler:** Carlo Emanuele III **Obv:** Armored bust right **Rev:** Voided cross with Moor heads in angles, date at top

Date	Mintage	VG	F	VF	XF	Unc
1732	—	3.00	6.00	12.00	25.00	—
1741	—	3.00	6.00	12.00	25.00	—

C# 36 CAGLIARESE

Bronze **Ruler:** Carlo Emanuele III **Obv:** Cross with Moor heads in angles, date at top **Rev:** Knot in wreath

Date	Mintage	VG	F	VF	XF	Unc
1763	—	3.00	6.00	12.00	25.00	—
1764	—	3.00	6.00	12.00	25.00	—
1766	—	3.00	6.00	12.00	25.00	—
1768	—	3.00	6.00	12.00	25.00	—

C# 70 CAGLIARESE

Copper, 17 mm. **Ruler:** Victorio Amedeo III **Obv:** Legend, cross **Obv. Legend:** VIC. AM. D.G. REX. SAR **Rev:** Knot in wreath

Date	Mintage	VG	F	VF	XF	Unc
1788	55,000	15.00	25.00	40.00	75.00	—
1792	5,000	15.00	25.00	40.00	75.00	—

C# 37 TRE (3) CAGLIARESE

Bronze **Ruler:** Carlo Emanuele III **Obv:** Armored bust right divides value **Rev:** Voided cross with Moor heads in angles, date at top

Date	Mintage	VG	F	VF	XF	Unc
1732	—	3.50	7.00	15.00	30.00	—
1741	—	3.50	7.00	15.00	30.00	—

C# 38 SOLDO

Billon **Ruler:** Carlo Emanuele III **Obv:** Cross with Moor heads in angles in wreath, date below **Rev:** Crown over crossed sceptre baton, value below

Date	Mintage	VG	F	VF	XF	Unc
1768	—	3.00	6.00	12.00	28.00	—
1769	—	3.00	6.00	12.00	28.00	—
1770	—	3.00	6.00	12.00	28.00	—
1771	—	3.00	6.00	12.00	28.00	—
1772	—	3.00	6.00	12.00	28.00	—

C# 71 SOLDO

Billon **Ruler:** Victorio Amedeo III **Obv:** Legend, cross in wreath, date **Obv. Legend:** VIC. AM. D.G. REX. CYP. ET. IER **Rev:** Crown above crossed scepter and baton, value below

Date	Mintage	VG	F	VF	XF	Unc
1773	17,000	60.00	100	125	250	—
1774	89,000	20.00	35.00	50.00	80.00	—
1786	125,000	20.00	35.00	50.00	80.00	—
1788	125,000	20.00	35.00	50.00	80.00	—
1792	125,000	20.00	35.00	50.00	80.00	—

C# 41 1/2 REALE

Silver **Ruler:** Carlo Emanuele III **Obv:** Armored bust right **Rev:** Arms on cross with rosettes in angles, date below

Date	Mintage	VG	F	VF	XF	Unc
1732	—	10.00	20.00	40.00	80.00	—

C# 39 1/2 REALE

Silver **Ruler:** Carlo Emanuele III **Obv:** Head right, date below **Rev:** Crowned round arms

Date	Mintage	VG	F	VF	XF	Unc
1768	—	5.00	10.00	20.00	40.00	—
1769	—	5.00	10.00	20.00	40.00	—
1770	—	5.00	10.00	20.00	40.00	—
1771	—	5.00	10.00	20.00	40.00	—
1772	—	5.00	10.00	20.00	40.00	—

C# 72 1/2 REALE

Billon, 21 mm. **Ruler:** Victorio Amedeo III **Obv:** Legend, head right, date **Obv. Legend:** VIC. AM. D.G. REX. SAR. CYP. ET. IER **Rev:** Crown above cross, value

Date	Mintage	F	VF	XF	Unc	BU
1773 Rare	500	—	—	—	—	—
1774	47,000	15.00	25.00	50.00	100	—
1786	105,000	15.00	25.00	50.00	100	—
1788	102,000	15.00	25.00	50.00	100	—
1790	107,000	15.00	25.00	50.00	100	—
1792 Rare	4,500	—	—	—	—	—
1793	115,000	15.00	25.00	50.00	100	—
1795	102,000	15.00	25.00	50.00	100	—
1796	71,000	75.00	125	175	250	—

C# 42 REALE

Silver **Ruler:** Carlo Emanuele III **Obv:** Armored bust **Rev:** Arms on cross with rosettes in angles, date below

Date	Mintage	VG	F	VF	XF	Unc
1732	—	10.00	20.00	40.00	80.00	—

C# 40 REALE

Billon **Ruler:** Carlo Emanuele III **Obv:** Head right, date below **Rev:** Crowned ornate arms

Date	Mintage	VG	F	VF	XF	Unc
1768	—	5.00	10.00	20.00	40.00	—
1769	—	5.00	10.00	20.00	40.00	—
1770	—	5.00	10.00	20.00	40.00	—
1771	—	5.00	10.00	20.00	40.00	—
1772	—	5.00	10.00	20.00	40.00	—

C# 73 REALE

Billon, 22 mm. **Ruler:** Victorio Amedeo III **Obv:** Legend, head right, date **Obv. Legend:** VIC. AM. D.G. REX. SAR. CYP. ET. IER **Rev:** Arms

Date	Mintage	F	VF	XF	Unc	BU
1773	500	60.00	100	125	250	—
1774	47,000	30.00	50.00	100	300	—
1785	5,000	30.00	50.00	100	300	—
1786	122,000	30.00	50.00	100	200	—
1788	116,000	30.00	50.00	100	150	—
1790	98,000	30.00	50.00	100	150	—
1792	135,000	15.00	25.00	50.00	100	—
1793	105,000	15.00	25.00	50.00	100	—
1795	99,000	15.00	25.00	50.00	100	—
1796	1,210	100	125	200	400	—

C# 87 REALE

Billon **Ruler:** Carlo Emanuele IV **Obv:** Legend, head **Obv. Legend:** CAROLUS EMANUEL IV **Rev:** Legend, date

Date	Mintage	F	VF	XF	Unc	BU
1797	—	20.00	35.00	50.00	150	—
1798	—	20.00	35.00	50.00	150	—
1799	—	20.00	35.00	50.00	150	—

C# 47 DOPPIETTA

3.2000 g., 0.8910 Gold 0.0917 oz. AGW, 22 mm. **Ruler:** Carlo Emanuele III **Obv:** Bust left, date below **Obv. Legend:** CAR • EM • D • G • REX • .... **Rev:** Crowned arms **Rev. Legend:** MONTISFER • PRINC • PED • DVX • SAB • ET •

Date	Mintage	VG	F	VF	XF	Unc
1768	—	200	500	1,000	2,000	—
1769	—	200	500	1,000	2,000	—
1770	—	200	500	1,000	2,000	—
1771	—	200	500	1,000	2,000	—
1772	—	200	500	1,000	2,000	—

C# 77.5 DOPPIETTA

3.2000 g., 0.8910 Gold 0.0917 oz. AGW **Ruler:** Victorio Amedeo III **Obv:** Bust left, date below **Obv. Legend:** VIC • AM • D • G • REX • SAR • CYP • ET • IER • **Rev:** Crowned arms **Rev. Legend:** MONTISFER • PRINC • PED • DVX • SAB • ET •

Date	Mintage	VG	F	VF	XF	Unc
1773	—	—	650	1,200	2,500	4,500
1786	—	—	650	1,200	2,500	4,500
1787	—	—	650	1,200	2,500	4,500

C# 48 2-1/2 DOPPIETTE

8.0260 g., 0.8910 Gold 0.2299 oz. AGW, 27 mm. **Ruler:** Carlo Emanuele III **Obv:** Bust left, date below **Obv. Legend:** CAR • EM • D • G • REX • SAR • CYP • ET • IER • **Rev:** Crowned arms **Rev. Legend:** MONTISFER • PRINC • PED • DVX • SAB • ET •

Date	Mintage	VG	F	VF	XF	Unc
1768 Rare	—	—	—	—	—	—
1769 Rare	—	—	—	—	—	—
1770 Rare	—	—	—	—	—	—
1771	—	1,250	2,250	4,000	6,500	—

C# 77.7 2-1/2 DOPPIETTE

8.0260 g., 0.8910 Gold 0.2299 oz. AGW **Ruler:** Victorio Amedeo III **Obv:** Bust left **Obv. Legend:** VIC • AM • D • G • REX • SAR • CYP • ET • IER • **Rev:** Crowned arms **Rev. Legend:** MONTISFER • PRINC • PED • DVX • SAB • ET •

Date	Mintage	VG	F	VF	XF	Unc
1773	—	—	1,500	2,500	4,500	8,000
1774	—	—	1,500	2,500	4,500	8,000

C# 49 5 DOPPIETTE

16.0530 g., 0.8910 Gold 0.4598 oz. AGW, 31 mm. **Ruler:** Carlo Emanuele III **Obv:** Bust left, date below **Rev:** Crowned oval arms in Order collar

Date	Mintage	VG	F	VF	XF	Unc
1768 Rare	—	—	—	—	—	—
1769 Rare	—	—	—	—	—	—

C# 78 5 DOPPIETTE

16.0530 g., 0.8910 Gold 0.4598 oz. AGW **Ruler:** Victorio Amedeo III **Obv:** Bust left **Obv. Legend:** VIC • AM • D • G • REX • SAR • CYP • ET • IER • **Rev:** Crowned arms, legend **Rev. Legend:** MONTISFER • PRINC • PED • DVX • SAB • ET •

Date	Mintage	VG	F	VF	XF	Unc
1773	—	—	—	—	—	—
1774	—	—	—	—	—	—

Note: Bowers and Merena Guia sale 3-88 XF realized $14,300.

C# 43 1/4 SCUDO

5.8960 g., 0.8950 Silver 0.1696 oz. ASW, 28 mm. **Ruler:** Carlo Emanuele III **Obv:** Armored bust right **Rev:** Crown above 2 shields - Sardinia and Savoy, date at top

Date	Mintage	VG	F	VF	XF	Unc
1732	—	50.00	100	200	400	—

C# 44 1/4 SCUDO

5.8960 g., 0.8950 Silver 0.1696 oz. ASW **Ruler:** Carlo Emanuele III **Obv:** Head left, date below **Obv. Legend:** CAR • EM • D • G • REX • SAR • CVP • ET • IER • **Rev:** Crowned arms **Rev. Legend:** MONTISFER • PRINC • PED • DVX • SAB • ET •

Date	Mintage	VG	F	VF	XF	Unc
1768	—	50.00	100	200	400	—
1769	—	50.00	100	200	400	—
1770	—	50.00	100	200	400	—
1771	—	50.00	100	200	400	—
1772	—	50.00	100	200	400	—

C# 75 1/4 SCUDO

5.8960 g., 0.8950 Silver 0.1696 oz. ASW **Ruler:** Victorio Amedeo III **Obv:** Legend, head left, date **Obv. Legend:** VIC• AM• D•G• REX• SAR• CYP• ET• IER• **Rev:** Crowned arms, legend

Date	Mintage	F	VF	XF	Unc	BU
1773	2,200	75.00	100	200	300	—
1774	1,170	75.00	100	200	300	—
1792	2,130	75.00	100	200	300	—

C# 45 1/2 SCUDO

11.7930 g., 0.8950 Silver 0.3393 oz. ASW, 33 mm. **Ruler:** Carlo Emanuele III **Obv:** Head of left, date below **Rev:** Crowned arms in Order collar

Date	Mintage	VG	F	VF	XF	Unc
1768	—	50.00	100	200	400	—
1769	—	50.00	100	200	400	—
1770	—	50.00	100	200	400	—
1771	—	50.00	100	200	400	—
1772	—	50.00	100	200	400	—

C# 76 1/2 SCUDO

11.7930 g., 0.8950 Silver 0.3393 oz. ASW **Ruler:** Victorio Amedeo III **Obv:** Legend, head left, date **Obv. Legend:** VIC• AM• D•G• REX• SAR• CYP• ET• IER• **Rev:** Crowned arms, legend

Date	Mintage	VG	F	VF	XF	Unc
1773	1,430	100	175	300	600	—
1774	1,870	100	175	300	600	—
1792	1,620	100	175	300	600	—
1793	1,130	100	175	300	600	—

C# 46 SCUDO

23.5860 g., 0.8950 Silver 0.6787 oz. ASW, 38 mm. **Ruler:** Carlo Emanuele III **Obv:** Head left, date below **Obv. Legend:** CAR • EM • D • G • REX • SAR • CYP • ET • IER • **Rev:** Crowned arms in Order collar **Rev. Legend:** MONTISFER • PRINC • PED • DVX • SAB • ET • **Note:** Dav. #1495.

Date	Mintage	VG	F	VF	XF	Unc
1768	—	125	350	750	1,250	—
1769	—	125	350	750	1,250	—

C# 77 SCUDO

23.5860 g., 0.8950 Silver 0.6787 oz. ASW **Ruler:** Carlo Emanuele III **Obv:** Legend, head left, date **Rev:** Crowned arms, legend

Date	Mintage	F	VF	XF	Unc	BU
1773	1,030	1,000	1,200	1,500	3,000	—

MAINLAND COINAGE

C# 1 2 DENARI

Bronze, 16.5 mm. **Ruler:** Carlo Emanuele III **Obv:** Voided cross **Rev:** Crown above knot, date below

Date	Mintage	VG	F	VF	XF	Unc
1732	—	2.50	5.00	10.00	22.00	—
1733	—	2.50	5.00	10.00	22.00	—
1734	—	2.50	5.00	10.00	22.00	—
1735	—	2.50	5.00	10.00	22.00	—
1738	—	2.50	5.00	10.00	22.00	—
1740	—	2.50	5.00	10.00	22.00	—
1741	—	2.50	5.00	10.00	22.00	—
1742	—	2.50	5.00	10.00	22.00	—
1744	—	2.50	5.00	10.00	22.00	—
1745	—	2.50	5.00	10.00	22.00	—
1746	—	2.50	5.00	10.00	22.00	—
1748	—	2.50	5.00	10.00	22.00	—
1749	—	2.50	5.00	10.00	22.00	—
1750	—	2.50	5.00	10.00	22.00	—
1755	—	2.50	5.00	10.00	22.00	—
1756	—	2.50	5.00	10.00	22.00	—
1757	—	2.50	5.00	10.00	22.00	—
1758	—	2.50	5.00	10.00	22.00	—
1760	—	2.50	5.00	10.00	22.00	—
1762	—	2.50	5.00	10.00	22.00	—
1763	—	2.50	5.00	10.00	22.00	—
1764	—	2.50	5.00	10.00	22.00	—
1765	—	2.50	5.00	10.00	22.00	—
1766	—	2.50	5.00	10.00	22.00	—
1767	—	2.50	5.00	10.00	22.00	—
1768	—	2.50	5.00	10.00	22.00	—
1770	—	2.50	5.00	10.00	22.00	—
1771	—	2.50	5.00	10.00	22.00	—
1772	—	2.50	5.00	10.00	22.00	—

C# 50 2 DENARI

Copper **Ruler:** Victorio Amedeo III **Obv:** Cross, legend around **Obv. Legend:** VIC• AM• D•G•R• SAR **Rev:** Crowned knot, date

Date	Mintage	VG	F	VF	XF	Unc
1773	—	5.00	10.00	15.00	30.00	—
1774	—	5.00	10.00	15.00	30.00	—
1775	—	12.50	25.00	35.00	55.00	—
1776	—	25.00	50.00	70.00	125	—
1777	—	5.00	10.00	15.00	30.00	—
1778	—	5.00	10.00	15.00	30.00	—
1779	—	5.00	10.00	15.00	30.00	—
1780	—	5.00	10.00	15.00	30.00	—
1781	—	5.00	10.00	15.00	30.00	—
1782	—	25.00	50.00	70.00	125	—
1783	—	5.00	10.00	15.00	30.00	—
1784	—	5.00	10.00	15.00	30.00	—
1785	—	25.00	50.00	70.00	125	—
1786	—	50.00	75.00	100	150	—
1787	—	5.00	10.00	15.00	30.00	—
1789	—	12.50	25.00	35.00	55.00	—
1790	—	5.00	10.00	15.00	30.00	—
1791	—	5.00	10.00	15.00	30.00	—
1792	—	5.00	10.00	15.00	30.00	—
1796	—	5.00	10.00	15.00	30.00	—

C# 79 2 DENARI

Copper **Ruler:** Carlo Emanuele IV **Obv:** Legend, cross **Obv. Legend:** CAROLUS• EM• IV• D•G• REX• CYP• ET• IER **Rev:** Crowned knot, date

Date	Mintage	VG	F	VF	XF	Unc
1798 Rare	—	—	—	—	—	—
1799	—	2.50	5.00	9.00	20.00	—
1800	—	2.50	5.00	9.00	20.00	—

C# 52 1/2 SOLDO

Billon **Ruler:** Victorio Amedeo III **Obv:** Cross **Obv. Legend:** VIC • AM • D • G • R • SA • CY • ET • IE • **Rev:** Crowned monogram divides initials **Rev. Legend:** MONTISF • PR • PED * DVX • SAB • ET •

Date	Mintage	VG	F	VF	XF	Unc
1780	—	40.00	50.00	100	200	—
1781	—	12.50	25.00	40.00	60.00	—
1782	—	12.50	25.00	40.00	60.00	—
1783	—	12.50	25.00	40.00	60.00	—
1784	—	12.50	25.00	40.00	60.00	—
1785	—	12.50	25.00	40.00	60.00	—
1787	—	25.00	50.00	70.00	120	—
1789	—	25.00	50.00	100	150	—

C# 2 SOLDO

Billon **Ruler:** Carlo Emanuele III **Obv:** Voided cross with crowns at end of arms and crosses in angles, date at top **Rev:** Crowned double CE monogram, crown divides value

Date	Mintage	VG	F	VF	XF	Unc
1732	—	2.50	5.00	10.00	22.00	—
1734	—	2.50	5.00	10.00	22.00	—
1735	—	2.50	5.00	10.00	22.00	—
1736	—	2.50	5.00	10.00	22.00	—
1740	—	2.50	5.00	10.00	22.00	—
1745	—	2.50	5.00	10.00	22.00	—
1746	—	2.50	5.00	10.00	22.00	—
1747	—	2.50	5.00	10.00	22.00	—
1749	—	2.50	5.00	10.00	22.00	—
1750	—	2.50	5.00	10.00	22.00	—
1755	—	2.50	5.00	10.00	22.00	—
1762	—	2.50	5.00	10.00	22.00	—
1772	—	2.50	5.00	10.00	22.00	—

C# 53 SOLDO

Billon **Ruler:** Victorio Amedeo III **Obv:** Legend, cross, date **Obv. Legend:** VIC • AM • D • G • REX • SAR • CVP • ET • IER **Rev:** Crowned ornate monogram divides initials **Rev. Legend:** MONTISF • PRINC • PED • DVX • SAB • ET •

Date	Mintage	VG	F	VF	XF	Unc
1773	—	50.00	100	200	300	—
1774	—	10.00	30.00	50.00	75.00	—
1775	—	10.00	30.00	50.00	75.00	—
1778	—	30.00	40.00	60.00	100	—
1780	—	5.00	10.00	20.00	35.00	—
1781	—	5.00	10.00	20.00	35.00	—
1782	—	5.00	10.00	20.00	35.00	—
1783	—	5.00	10.00	20.00	35.00	—
1785	—	5.00	10.00	20.00	35.00	—
1789	—	5.00	10.00	20.00	35.00	—

C# 80 SOLDO

Copper **Ruler:** Carlo Emanuele IV **Obv:** Legend, cross, date **Obv. Legend:** CAROLUS EMANUEL IV **Rev:** Ornate monogram, crown above

Date	Mintage	VG	F	VF	XF	Unc
1797	—	2.50	5.00	10.00	22.00	—
1798	—	2.50	5.00	10.00	22.00	—

C# 3 2-1/2 SOLDI

Billon **Ruler:** Carlo Emanuele III **Obv:** Armored bust right **Rev:** Crowned arms divide FE-RT, date above crown

Date	Mintage	VG	F	VF	XF	Unc
1732	—	3.00	6.00	15.00	30.00	—
1733	—	3.00	6.00	15.00	30.00	—
1735	—	3.00	6.00	15.00	30.00	—
1739	—	3.00	6.00	15.00	30.00	—
1740	—	3.00	6.00	15.00	30.00	—

C# 4 2-1/2 SOLDI

Billon **Ruler:** Carlo Emanuele III **Obv:** Head left, date below **Rev:** Crowned arms divide FE-RT

Date	Mintage	VG	F	VF	XF	Unc
1744	—	3.00	6.00	15.00	30.00	—
1747	—	3.00	6.00	15.00	30.00	—

C# 6 2.6 SOLDI

Billon **Ruler:** Carlo Emanuele III **Obv:** Armored bust right **Rev:** Crowned arms divide FE-RT, date above crown

Date	Mintage	VG	F	VF	XF	Unc
1732	—	5.00	10.00	20.00	40.00	—
1733	—	5.00	10.00	20.00	40.00	—
1734	—	5.00	10.00	20.00	40.00	—
1735	—	5.00	10.00	20.00	40.00	—
1736	—	5.00	10.00	20.00	40.00	—
1737	—	5.00	10.00	20.00	40.00	—
1738	—	5.00	10.00	20.00	40.00	—
1739	—	5.00	10.00	20.00	40.00	—

C# 6a 2.6 SOLDI

Billon **Ruler:** Carlo Emanuele III **Obv:** Smaller bust right **Rev:** Crowned tapered arms divide FE-RT, crown divides date

Date	Mintage	VG	F	VF	XF	Unc
1741	—	5.00	10.00	20.00	40.00	—

C# 7 2.6 SOLDI

Billon **Ruler:** Carlo Emanuele III **Obv:** Head left, date below **Rev:** Crowned arms divide FE-RT

Date	Mintage	VG	F	VF	XF	Unc
1742	—	5.00	10.00	20.00	40.00	—
1743	—	5.00	10.00	20.00	40.00	—
1744	—	5.00	10.00	20.00	40.00	—
1745	—	5.00	10.00	20.00	40.00	—
1746	—	5.00	10.00	20.00	40.00	—
1747	—	5.00	10.00	20.00	40.00	—

C# 5 2.6 SOLDI

Billon **Ruler:** Carlo Emanuele III **Obv:** Head right **Obv. Legend:** CAR • EM • D • G • REX • ..... **Rev:** Crowned displayed eagle with arms of Savoy on breast **Rev. Legend:** MONTISF • PRINC • PED • ....

Date	Mintage	VG	F	VF	XF	Unc
1755	—	3.00	6.00	15.00	30.00	—
1756	—	3.00	6.00	15.00	30.00	—
1757	—	3.00	6.00	15.00	30.00	—
1758	—	3.00	6.00	15.00	30.00	—

C# 54 2.6 SOLDI

Billon **Ruler:** Victorio Amedeo III **Obv:** Legend, head right, date **Rev:** Eagle, Savoy cross on breast

Date	Mintage	VG	F	VF	XF	Unc
1781	—	6.50	15.00	25.00	50.00	—
1782	—	6.50	15.00	25.00	50.00	—
1783	—	6.50	15.00	25.00	50.00	—
1784	—	6.50	15.00	25.00	50.00	—
1785	—	6.50	15.00	25.00	50.00	—

C# 81 2.6 SOLDI

Billon **Ruler:** Carlo Emanuele IV **Obv:** Head right **Obv. Legend:** CAROLUS • EMANUEL • IV • **Rev:** Crowned displayed eagle with arms of Savoy on breast

Date	Mintage	F	VF	XF	Unc	BU
1798	—	5.00	10.00	20.00	40.00	—
1799	—	5.00	10.00	20.00	40.00	—

C# 51 5 SOLDI

Copper **Ruler:** Victorio Amedeo III **Obv:** Bust right **Obv. Legend:** VIC • AMED • D • G • REX • SARD • **Rev:** Standing figure above value

Date	Mintage	VG	F	VF	XF	Unc
1794	—	4.00	7.00	15.00	30.00	—
1795	—	4.00	7.00	15.00	30.00	—
1796	—	4.00	7.00	15.00	30.00	—

C# 8 7.6 SOLDI

Billon **Ruler:** Carlo Emanuele III **Obv:** Head right, date below **Rev:** Crowned arms in cartouche, value below

Date	Mintage	VG	F	VF	XF	Unc
1755	—	4.00	8.00	17.50	40.00	—
1756	—	4.00	8.00	17.50	40.00	—
1757	—	4.00	8.00	17.50	40.00	—
1758	—	4.00	8.00	17.50	40.00	—

C# 55 7.6 SOLDI

Billon **Ruler:** Victorio Amedeo III **Obv:** Legend, bust right, date **Obv. Legend:** VIC• AM• D•G• REX• SAR• CYP• ET• TER **Rev:** Eagle on shield, crown above

Date	Mintage	VG	F	VF	XF	Unc
1781	—	10.00	20.00	30.00	65.00	—
1782	—	10.00	30.00	40.00	80.00	—

Date	Mintage	VG	F	VF	XF	Unc
1783	—	10.00	15.00	25.00	45.00	—
1784	—	10.00	15.00	25.00	45.00	—
1785	—	10.00	15.00	25.00	45.00	—
1789	—	10.00	30.00	40.00	100	—
1791	—	10.00	25.00	35.00	80.00	—
1793	—	10.00	15.00	25.00	45.00	—
1794	—	10.00	25.00	35.00	80.00	—
1795	—	10.00	30.00	40.00	100	—

C# 82 7.6 SOLDI

Billon **Ruler:** Carlo Emanuele IV **Obv:** Head right **Obv. Legend:** CAROLUS • EMANUEL • IV **Rev:** Crowned oval arms **Rev. Legend:** SARD • CYP • ET • IER • ...

Date	Mintage	F	VF	XF	Unc	BU
1798 Rare	—	—	—	—	—	—
1799	—	10.00	15.00	25.00	50.00	—
1800	—	7.00	12.00	22.00	45.00	—

C# 9 10 SOLDI

Silver **Ruler:** Carlo Emanuele III **Obv:** Armored bust right **Rev:** Crowned arms, date at upper left, value at upper right

Date	Mintage	VG	F	VF	XF	Unc
1732	—	6.00	12.00	25.00	50.00	—
1733	—	6.00	12.00	25.00	50.00	—

C# 10 10 SOLDI

Silver **Ruler:** Carlo Emanuele III **Obv:** Head left, date below **Rev:** Crowned arms in Order collar, crown divides value

Date	Mintage	VG	F	VF	XF	Unc
1742	—	6.00	12.00	25.00	50.00	—

C# 56 10 SOLDI

Billon **Ruler:** Victorio Amedeo III **Obv:** Legend, bust right, date **Obv. Legend:** VIC• AMED• D•G• REX• SARD **Rev:** Crowned arms

Date	Mintage	VG	F	VF	XF	Unc
1794	—	7.50	20.00	35.00	60.00	—
1795	—	7.50	20.00	35.00	60.00	—
1796	—	7.50	20.00	35.00	60.00	—

C# 57 15 SOLDI

Billon **Ruler:** Victorio Amedeo III **Obv:** Legend, head right, date **Obv. Legend:** VIC • AM • D • G • REX • SAR • CYP • ET • IER • **Rev:** Value in wreath

Date	Mintage	VG	F	VF	XF	Unc
1794	—	15.00	30.00	60.00	90.00	—

C# 11 20 SOLDI

Silver **Ruler:** Carlo Emanuele III **Obv:** Armored bust right **Rev:** Crowned arms, date at upper left, value at upper right

Date	Mintage	VG	F	VF	XF	Unc
1732	—	15.00	30.00	60.00	125	—

C# 12 20 SOLDI

Silver **Ruler:** Carlo Emanuele III **Obv:** Head left, date below **Obv. Legend:** CAR • EM • D • G • REX • SAR • CYP • ET • IER • **Rev:** Crowned arms in Order collar, crown divides value **Rev. Legend:** MONT ISF • PRINC • PED • DVX • SAB • ET •

Date	Mintage	VG	F	VF	XF	Unc
1742	—	10.00	20.00	40.00	80.00	—
1747	—	10.00	20.00	40.00	80.00	—
1748	—	10.00	20.00	40.00	80.00	—

C# 58 20 SOLDI

Billon **Ruler:** Victorio Amedeo III **Obv:** Legend, bust right, date **Obv. Legend:** VICT• AMED• D•G• REX• SARD• **Rev:** Crowned arms

Date	Mintage	VG	F	VF	XF	Unc
1794	—	7.50	12.50	25.00	45.00	—
1795	—	7.50	12.50	25.00	45.00	—
1796	—	7.50	12.50	25.00	45.00	—

C# 13 1/8 SCUDO

Silver **Ruler:** Carlo Emanuele III **Obv:** Armored bust right **Rev:** Crowned arms in Order collar, date divided at top

Date	Mintage	VG	F	VF	XF	Unc
1733	—	15.00	30.00	60.00	125	—

C# 14 1/8 SCUDO

Silver **Ruler:** Carlo Emanuele III **Obv:** Bust left, date below **Rev:** Crowned arms in Order collar

Date	Mintage	VG	F	VF	XF	Unc
1755	—	6.00	12.00	25.00	50.00	—
1756	—	6.00	12.00	25.00	50.00	—
1757	—	6.00	12.00	25.00	50.00	—
1758	—	6.00	12.00	25.00	50.00	—

C# 15 1/4 SCUDO

Silver **Ruler:** Carlo Emanuele III **Obv:** Armored bust right **Rev:** Crowned arms in Order collar, date divided at top

Date	Mintage	VG	F	VF	XF	Unc
1733	—	15.00	30.00	60.00	125	—

C# 16 1/4 SCUDO

Silver **Ruler:** Carlo Emanuele III **Obv:** Bust left, date below **Rev:** Crowned round arms in Order collar

Date	Mintage	VG	F	VF	XF	Unc
1755	—	10.00	20.00	40.00	80.00	—
1756	—	10.00	20.00	40.00	80.00	—
1757	—	10.00	20.00	40.00	80.00	—
1758	—	10.00	20.00	40.00	80.00	—
1759	—	10.00	20.00	40.00	80.00	—
1760	—	10.00	20.00	40.00	80.00	—
1762	—	10.00	20.00	40.00	80.00	—
1763	—	10.00	20.00	40.00	80.00	—
1764	—	10.00	20.00	40.00	80.00	—
1765	—	10.00	20.00	40.00	80.00	—
1766	—	10.00	20.00	40.00	80.00	—
1768	—	10.00	20.00	40.00	80.00	—
1769	—	10.00	20.00	40.00	80.00	—
1770	—	10.00	20.00	40.00	80.00	—
1771	—	10.00	20.00	40.00	80.00	—
1772	—	10.00	20.00	40.00	80.00	—

C# 59 1/4 SCUDO

8.7910 g., 0.9040 Silver 0.2555 oz. ASW **Ruler:** Victorio Amedeo III **Obv:** Bust left **Obv. Legend:** VIC • AM • D • G • REX • SAR • CYP • ET • IER • **Rev:** Crowned arms in order chain **Rev. Legend:** MONTISFER • PRINC • PEDEM • DVX • SABAVD • ET •

Date	Mintage	F	VF	XF	Unc	BU
1773	—	50.00	100	200	700	—
1774	—	50.00	100	200	700	—
1775	—	50.00	100	200	700	—
1776	—	50.00	100	200	700	—
1777	—	50.00	100	200	700	—
1778	—	50.00	100	200	700	—
1779	—	50.00	100	200	700	—
1780	—	50.00	100	200	700	—
1781	—	50.00	100	200	700	—
1786	—	50.00	100	200	700	—
1787	—	50.00	100	200	700	—
1788	—	50.00	100	200	700	—
1789	—	50.00	100	200	700	—
1790	—	50.00	100	200	700	—
1791	—	50.00	100	200	700	—
1792	—	50.00	100	200	700	—
1793	—	50.00	100	200	700	—

C# 83 1/4 SCUDO

8.7910 g., 0.9050 Silver 0.2558 oz. ASW **Ruler:** Carlo Emanuele IV **Obv:** Armored bust left **Obv. Legend:** CAROLUS • EMANUEL • IV • **Rev:** Crowned arms in order collar **Rev. Legend:** SARD • CYP • ET • IER • ...

Date	Mintage	F	VF	XF	Unc	BU
1797 Rare	—	—	—	—	—	—
1798	—	175	300	400	800	—
1799	—	175	300	400	800	—

C# 17 1/2 SCUDO

Silver **Ruler:** Carlo Emanuele III **Obv:** Armored bust right **Rev:** Crowned arms in Order collar, date divided at top

Date	Mintage	VG	F	VF	XF	Unc
1733	—	35.00	75.00	150	300	—

C# 18 1/2 SCUDO

Silver **Ruler:** Carlo Emanuele III **Obv:** Bust left **Obv. Legend:** CAR • EM • D • G • REX • SAR • ... **Rev:** Crowned arms in order collar **Rev. Legend:** MONTISFER • PRINC • PEDEM • DVX • SABAVD • ET •

Date	Mintage	VG	F	VF	XF	Unc
1755	—	20.00	40.00	80.00	175	—
1756	—	20.00	40.00	80.00	175	—
1757	—	20.00	40.00	80.00	175	—
1758	—	20.00	40.00	80.00	175	—
1759	—	20.00	40.00	80.00	175	—
1760	—	20.00	40.00	80.00	175	—
1761	—	20.00	40.00	80.00	175	—
1762	—	20.00	40.00	80.00	175	—
1763	—	20.00	40.00	80.00	175	—
1764	—	20.00	40.00	80.00	175	—
1765	—	20.00	40.00	80.00	175	—
1766	—	20.00	40.00	80.00	175	—
1767	—	20.00	40.00	80.00	175	—
1769	—	20.00	40.00	80.00	175	—
1770	—	20.00	40.00	80.00	175	—
1771	—	20.00	40.00	80.00	175	—
1772	—	20.00	40.00	80.00	175	—

C# 60 1/2 SCUDO

17.5820 g., 0.9040 Silver 0.5110 oz. ASW **Ruler:** Victorio Amedeo III **Obv:** Bust left **Obv. Legend:** VIC • AM • D • G • REX • CYP • ET • IER • **Rev:** Crowned arms in order collar **Rev. Legend:** MONTISFER • PRINC • PEDEM • DVX • SABAVD • ET •

Date	Mintage	F	VF	XF	Unc	BU
1773	—	100	200	300	700	—
1774	—	100	200	300	700	—
1775	—	100	200	300	700	—
1776	—	100	200	300	700	—
1777	—	100	200	300	700	—
1778	—	100	200	300	700	—
1779	—	100	200	300	700	—
1780	—	100	200	300	700	—
1781	—	100	200	300	700	—
1782	—	100	200	300	700	—
1784	—	100	200	300	700	—
1785	—	100	200	300	700	—
1786	—	100	200	300	700	—
1787	—	100	200	300	700	—
1788	—	100	200	300	700	—
1789	—	100	200	300	700	—
1790	—	100	200	300	700	—
1791	—	100	200	300	700	—
1792	—	100	200	300	700	—
1793	—	100	200	300	700	—

C# 84 1/2 SCUDO

17.5820 g., 0.9050 Silver 0.5116 oz. ASW **Ruler:** Carlo Emanuele IV **Obv:** Bust left **Obv. Legend:** CAROLUS • EMANUEL • IV • **Rev:** Crowned arms in order collar **Rev. Legend:** SAR • CYP • ET • IER • & D • G • REX

Date	Mintage	F	VF	XF	Unc	BU
1797	—	200	300	600	1,200	—
1798	—	200	300	600	1,200	—
1799	—	200	300	600	1,200	—
1800	—	200	300	600	1,200	—

DAV# 1492 SCUDO

Silver **Ruler:** Austrian **Obv:** Bust of Victor Amedeo II right **Rev:** Crowned and supported arms, date below

Date	Mintage	VG	F	VF	XF	Unc
1711	—	650	1,200	2,000	3,500	—

C# 19 SCUDO

Silver **Ruler:** Carlo Emanuele III **Obv:** Bust right **Obv. Legend:** CAR • EM • D • G • REX • SAR • CYP • ET • IER • **Rev:** Crowned arms **Rev. Legend:** MON TISFER • PRINC • PED • DVX • SAB • ET • **Note:** Dav. #1493.

Date	Mintage	VG	F	VF	XF	Unc
1733	—	300	750	1,500	2,500	—
1734	—	300	750	1,500	2,500	—
1735	—	300	750	1,500	2,500	—

C# 20 SCUDO

Silver **Ruler:** Carlo Emanuele III **Obv:** Bust left **Obv. Legend:** CAR • EM • D • G • REX • SAR • CYP • ET • IER • **Note:** Dav. #1494.

Date	Mintage	VG	F	VF	XF	Unc
1755	—	125	250	500	900	—
1756	—	125	250	500	900	—
1757	—	125	250	500	900	—
1758	—	125	250	500	900	—
1760	—	—	—	—	—	—
1763	—	125	250	500	900	—
1765	—	125	250	500	900	—
1769	—	125	250	500	900	—

DAV# 1497 SCUDO

35.1640 g., 0.9040 Silver 1.0220 oz. ASW **Ruler:** Victorio Amedeo III **Obv:** Head left **Rev:** Crowned arms in chain

Date	Mintage	VG	F	VF	XF	Unc
1773	—	275	500	900	1,500	—

C# 61 SCUDO

35.1640 g., 0.9040 Silver 1.0220 oz. ASW **Ruler:** Victorio Amedeo III **Obv:** Bust left **Obv. Legend:** VIC • AM • D • G • REX • SAR • CYP • ET • IER • **Rev:** Crowned arms in order collar **Rev. Legend:** MONTISFER • PRINC • PEDEM • DVX • SABAVD • ET • **Note:** Dav. #1496.

Date	Mintage	VG	F	VF	XF	Unc
1773	—	600	1,000	1,500	2,000	—
1776 Rare	—	—	—	—	—	—

C# 29 1/4 DOPPIA

Gold **Ruler:** Carlo Emanuele III **Obv:** Bust left, date below **Rev:** Crowned round arms in Order collar

Date	Mintage	VG	F	VF	XF	Unc
1755	—	400	800	1,600	2,500	—
1756	—	400	800	1,600	2,500	—
1757	—	400	800	1,600	2,500	—

C# 62 1/4 DOPPIA

2.2790 g., 0.9050 Gold 0.0663 oz. AGW **Ruler:** Victorio Amedeo III **Obv:** Legend, head left, date **Obv. Legend:** VIC • AM • D • G • REX • SAR • CYP • ET • IER • **Rev:** Crowned armsin order collar **Rev. Legend:** MONTISFER • PRINC • PED • DVX • SAB • ET •

Date	Mintage	VG	F	VF	XF	Unc
1773	—	475	950	2,400	3,250	—
1777	—	475	950	2,400	3,250	—
1782	—	400	800	1,600	2,400	—
1785	—	475	950	2,400	3,250	—

C# 63 1/4 DOPPIA

2.2790 g., 0.9050 Gold 0.0663 oz. AGW **Ruler:** Victorio Amedeo III **Obv:** Legend, head left, date **Obv. Legend:** VIC • AM • D • G • REX • SARDINIAE • **Rev:** Eagle on crossed baton and scepter, crown above **Rev. Legend:** PRINC • PEDEM • DVX • SABAVD •

Date	Mintage	VG	F	VF	XF	Unc
1786	—	300	600	900	1,400	—

C# 21 1/2 DOPPIA

Gold **Ruler:** Carlo Emanuele III **Obv:** Draped bust right **Rev:** Crowned arms in Order collar, date divided at top

Date	Mintage	VG	F	VF	XF	Unc
1733	—	750	1,500	4,500	7,500	—
1734	—	750	1,500	4,500	7,500	—

C# 22 1/2 DOPPIA

Gold **Ruler:** Carlo Emanuele III **Obv:** Armored bust left, date below **Rev:** Crowned arms in Order collar

Date	Mintage	VG	F	VF	XF	Unc
1741	—	750	1,500	4,500	7,500	—
1742	—	750	1,500	4,500	7,500	—

C# 30 1/2 DOPPIA

Gold **Ruler:** Carlo Emanuele III **Obv:** Head left **Obv. Legend:** CAR • EM • D • G • REX • SAR • CYP • ET • IER • **Rev:** Crowned arms in Order collar **Rev. Legend:** MONTISFER • PRINC • PED • & • DVX • SAB • ET •

Date	Mintage	VG	F	VF	XF	Unc
1755	—	150	300	700	1,600	—
1756	—	150	300	700	1,600	—
1757	—	150	300	700	1,600	—
1758	—	150	300	700	1,600	—
1759	—	150	300	700	1,600	—
1760	—	150	300	700	1,600	—
1763	—	150	300	700	1,600	—
1764	—	150	300	700	1,600	—
1765	—	150	300	700	1,600	—
1766	—	150	300	700	1,600	—
1767	—	150	300	700	1,600	—
1768	—	150	300	700	1,600	—
1769	—	150	300	700	1,600	—
1770	—	150	300	700	1,600	—
1771	—	150	300	700	1,600	—
1772	—	150	300	700	1,600	—

C# 64 1/2 DOPPIA

4.7500 g., 0.9050 Gold 0.1382 oz. AGW **Ruler:** Victorio Amedeo III **Obv:** Head left **Obv. Legend:** VIC • AM • D • G • REX • SAR • CYP • ET • IER • **Rev:** Crowned arms in Order collar **Rev. Legend:** MONTISFER • PRINC • PED • & • DVX • SAB • ET •

Date	Mintage	VG	F	VF	XF	Unc
1773	—	700	1,500	2,000	3,250	—
1774	—	700	1,500	2,000	3,250	—
1775	—	700	1,500	2,000	3,250	—
1776	—	700	1,500	2,000	3,250	—
1777	—	700	1,500	2,000	3,250	—
1778	—	700	1,500	2,000	3,250	—
1780	—	700	1,500	2,000	3,250	—
1781	—	700	1,500	2,000	3,250	—
1784	—	700	1,500	2,000	3,250	—

C# 65 1/2 DOPPIA

4.5580 g., 0.9050 Gold 0.1326 oz. AGW **Ruler:** Victorio Amedeo III **Obv:** Head left **Obv. Legend:** VIC • AM • D • G • SARDINIAE • **Rev:** Eagle on crossed baton and scepter, crown above **Rev. Legend:** PRINC * PEDEM * DVX * SABAVD *

Date	Mintage	VG	F	VF	XF	Unc
1786	—	225	300	425	675	—
1787	—	225	300	425	675	—
1788	—	225	300	425	675	—
1789	—	225	300	425	675	—
1790	—	225	300	425	675	—
1791	—	225	300	425	675	—
1792	—	225	300	425	675	—
1793	—	225	300	425	675	—
1794	—	225	300	425	675	—
1795	—	225	300	425	675	—
1796	—	225	300	425	675	—

C# 85 1/2 DOPPIA

4.5580 g., 0.9050 Gold 0.1326 oz. AGW **Ruler:** Carlo Emanuele IV **Obv:** Head left **Obv. Legend:** C A R O L U S • E M A N U E L • I V • **Rev:** Eagle on crossed baton and scepter, crown above

Date	Mintage	F	VF	XF	Unc	BU
1797	—	750	1,200	2,250	3,750	—
1798	—	750	1,200	2,250	3,750	—

C# 23 DOPPIA

6.6400 g., 0.9860 Gold 0.2105 oz. AGW **Ruler:** Carlo manuele III **Obv:** Armored bust right **Obv. Legend:** CAR • EM • D • G • REX SAR • CVP • ET IER • **Rev:** Crowned arms in Order collar, divided date above **Rev. Legend:** MON TISF • PRINC • PED • DVX • SAB • ET •

Date	Mintage	VG	F	VF	XF	Unc
1733 Rare	—	—	—	—	—	—

Note: Swiss Bank sale #21 1-89 VF realized $10,560.

C# 24 DOPPIA

6.6400 g., 0.9860 Gold 0.2105 oz. AGW **Ruler:** Carlo Emanuele III **Obv:** Armored bust left, date below **Rev:** Crowned arms in Order collar

Date	Mintage	VG	F	VF	XF	Unc
1741 Rare	—	—	—	—	—	—

C# 31 DOPPIA

6.6400 g., 0.9860 Gold 0.2105 oz. AGW **Ruler:** Carlo Emanuele III **Obv:** Head left, date below **Obv. Legend:** CAR • EM • D • G • REX •SAR • CYP • ET •IER • **Rev:** Crowned arms in Oder collar **Rev. Legend:** MONTISFER • PRINC • PED • & • DVX • SAB • ET •

Date	Mintage	VG	F	VF	XF	Unc
1755	—	475	1,000	1,800	2,600	—
1756	—	475	1,000	1,800	2,600	—
1757	—	475	1,000	1,800	2,600	—
1758	—	475	1,000	1,800	2,600	—
1760	—	475	1,000	1,800	2,600	—
1761	—	475	1,000	1,800	2,600	—
1762	—	475	1,000	1,800	2,600	—
1763	—	475	1,000	1,800	2,600	—
1764	—	475	1,000	1,800	2,600	—
1765	—	475	1,000	1,800	2,600	—
1766	—	475	1,000	1,800	2,600	—
1767	—	475	1,000	1,800	2,600	—
1768	—	475	1,000	1,800	2,600	—
1769	—	475	1,000	1,800	2,600	—
1770	—	475	1,000	1,800	2,600	—
1771	—	475	1,000	1,800	2,600	—
1772	—	475	1,000	1,800	2,600	—

C# 66 DOPPIA

9.6000 g., 0.9050 Gold 0.2793 oz. AGW **Ruler:** Victorio Amedeo III **Obv:** Legend, head left, date **Obv. Legend:** VIC• AM• D•G• REX• SAR• CYP• ET• IER • **Rev:** Crowned arms

Date	Mintage	VG	F	VF	XF	Unc
1773	—	475	1,200	2,500	3,250	—
1776	—	475	1,200	2,500	3,250	—
1777	—	475	1,200	2,500	3,250	—
1778	—	475	1,200	2,500	3,250	—
1779	—	475	1,200	2,500	3,250	—
1780	—	475	1,200	2,500	3,250	—
1782	—	475	1,200	2,500	3,250	—

C# 67 DOPPIA

9.1160 g., 0.9050 Gold 0.2652 oz. AGW **Ruler:** Victorio Amedeo III **Obv:** Head left, date below **Obv. Legend:** VIC • AM • D • G • REX • SARDINIAE • **Rev:** Eagle on crossed baton and scepter, crown above **Rev. Legend:** * PRINC • PEDEM * * DVX • SABAVD *

Date	Mintage	VG	F	VF	XF	Unc
1786	—	250	325	650	1,100	—
1787	—	250	325	650	1,100	—
1788	—	250	325	650	1,100	—
1789	—	250	325	650	1,100	—
1790	—	250	325	650	1,100	—
1791	—	250	325	650	1,100	—
1792	—	250	325	650	1,100	—
1793	—	250	325	650	1,100	—
1794	—	250	325	650	1,100	—
1795	—	250	325	650	1,100	—
1796	—	250	325	650	1,100	—

C# 86 DOPPIA

9.1160 g., 0.9050 Gold 0.2652 oz. AGW **Ruler:** Carlo Emanuele IV **Obv:** Head left, date below **Obv. Legend:** CAROLUS • EMANUEL • I V • **Rev:** Eagle on crossed baton and scepter, crown above **Rev. Inscription:** SAR • CYP • ET • IER • & • D • G • REX •

Date	Mintage	VG	F	VF	XF	Unc
1797	—	—	500	850	2,500	3,500
1798	—	—	500	850	2,750	3,750
1799	—	—	500	850	2,750	3,750
1800	—	—	500	850	2,750	3,750

C# 32 2-1/2 DOPPIE

23.9400 g., Gold **Ruler:** Carlo Emanuele III **Obv:** Bust left, date below **Obv. Legend:** CAR • EM • D • G • REX • SAR • CYP • ET • IER • **Rev:** Crowned round arms in Order collar **Rev. Legend:** MONTISFER • PRINC • PED • & • DVX • SAB • ET •

Date	Mintage	VG	F	VF	XF	Unc
1755 Rare	—	—	—	—	—	—

Note: Superior Pipito sale 12-87 VF realized $13,750.

Date	Mintage	VG	F	VF	XF	Unc
1756 Rare	—	—	—	—	—	—
1757 Rare	—	—	—	—	—	—

C# 68 2-1/2 DOPPIE

22.7800 g., 0.9050 Gold 0.6628 oz. AGW **Ruler:** Victorio Amedeo III **Obv:** Head left, date below **Obv. Legend:** VIC • AM • D • G • REX • SARDINIAE • **Rev:** Eagle on crossed baton and scepter, crown above **Rev. Legend:** * PRINC • PEDEM * DVX • SABAVD *

Date	Mintage	VG	F	VF	XF	Unc
1786	—	1,250	2,500	4,750	7,000	—

C# 33 5 DOPPIE

33.1300 g., 0.9050 Gold 0.9639 oz. AGW **Ruler:** Carlo Emanuele III **Obv:** Head left, date below **Obv. Legend:** CAR • EM • D • G • REX • SAR • CYP • ET • IER • **Rev:** Crowned arms in Order collar **Rev. Legend:** MONTISFER • PRINC • PED • & • DVX • SAB • ET • **Note:** Struck at Turin.

Date	Mintage	VG	F	VF	XF	Unc
1755 Rare	—	—	—	—	—	—

Note: Stack's International sale 3-88 VF/XF realized $12,100.

Date	Mintage	VG	F	VF	XF	Unc
1756 Rare	—	—	—	—	—	—
1757 Rare	—	—	—	—	—	—
1758 Rare	—	—	—	—	—	—
1768 Rare	—	—	—	—	—	—

Note: Bowers and Merena Guia sale 3-88 XF realized $14,300.

C# 69 5 DOPPIE

45.5600 g., 0.9050 Gold 1.3256 oz. AGW **Ruler:** Victorio Amedeo III **Obv:** Head left, date below **Obv. Legend:** VIC • AM • D • G • REX • SARDINIAE • **Rev:** Eagle on crossed baton and scepter, crown above **Rev. Legend:** * PRINC • PEDEM * * DVX • SABAVD *

Date	Mintage	VG	F	VF	XF	Unc
1786	—	2,500	4,000	8,000	15,000	—

C# A25 1/8 ZECCHINO

0.4375 g., 0.9860 Gold 0.0139 oz. AGW **Obv:** Angel Gabriel in flight, value below **Rev:** Virgin Mary kneeling, illuminated by the Holy Spirit

Date	Mintage	VG	F	VF	XF	Unc
ND	—	1,000	2,500	5,000	7,500	—

C# 25 1/6 ZECCHINO

0.5833 g., 0.9860 Gold 0.0185 oz. AGW **Obv:** Angel Gabriel in flight, value below **Rev:** Virgin Mary kneeling, illuminated by the Holy Spirit

Date	Mintage	VG	F	VF	XF	Unc
ND Rare	—	—	—	—	—	—

C# 26 1/2 ZECCHINO

1.7500 g., 0.9860 Gold 0.0555 oz. AGW **Ruler:** Carlo Emanuele III **Obv:** Eagle on crossed baton and scepter within Order collar, crown above **Obv. Legend:** CAROLVS • EMANVEL • D • G • SARDINIÆ • REX **Rev:** Angel in flight, kneeling figure above date **Note:** Similar to Zecchino, C#27.

Date	Mintage	VG	F	VF	XF	Unc
1744	—	200	400	700	1,500	—
1745	—	200	400	700	1,500	—
1746	—	200	400	700	1,500	—

C# 27 ZECCHINO

3.5000 g., 0.9860 Gold 0.1109 oz. AGW **Ruler:** Carlo Emanuele III **Obv:** Eagle on crossed baton and scepter within Order collar, crown above **Obv. Legend:** CAROLVS • EMANVEL • D • G • SARDINIÆ • REX **Rev:** Angel in flight, kneeling figure **Note:** Variations in the Annunciation scene exist.

Date	Mintage	VG	F	VF	XF	Unc
1743	—	300	600	1,200	2,000	—
1744	—	300	600	1,200	2,000	—
1745	—	300	600	1,200	2,000	—
1746	—	300	600	1,200	2,000	—

C# 28 4 ZECCHINI

14.0000 g., 0.9860 Gold 0.4438 oz. AGW **Ruler:** Carlo Emanuele III **Obv:** Eagle on crossed baton and scepter within Order collar, crown above **Obv. Legend:** CAROLVS • EMANVEL • D • G • SARDINIÆ • REX **Rev:** Angel in flight, kneeling figure above date

Date	Mintage	VG	F	VF	XF	Unc
1745	—	1,000	2,000	4,000	6,500	—
1746 Rare	—	—	—	—	—	—

PATTERNS

Including off metal strikes

KM#	Date	Mintage	Identification	Mkt Val
Pn1	1735	—	2 Denari. Silver. C1.	—
Pn2	1749	—	2 Denari. Billon. C1.	—
Pn3	1757	—	1/8 Scudo. Copper. C14.	—

SAVOY

Historical region of southeastern France and northwestern Italy of varying limits, now chiefly in the French departments of Haute-Savoie and Savoie, its' chief city is Chambery.

From 11th century the counts of Savoy ruled this area located in the western Alps as part of kingdom of Arles. It became predominantly independent and expanded its territory to encircle Lake Geneva and later included Piedmont in Italy. It was elevated to a duchy in 1416 by Emperor Sigismund. The scene of fighting in many wars; at times allied with France, sometimes with Italy; involved in wars between France and Spain with alternating allegiances. Under Charles Emmanuel I, it lost territories beyond the Rhone. Later joined Grand Alliance in 1704. By the Treaty of Utrecht 1713 it received island of Sicily and held it until 1720 when that was exchanged for the island of Sardinia forming the Kingdom of Sardinia (included Piedmont, Savoy, and island of Sardinia), the dukes of Savoy becoming Kings of Sardinia. The Kingdom of Sardinia sided with Royalists during the French Revolution and as a result lost the territory of Savoy in 1792 and later Piedmont in 1796 which was restored to Victor Emmanuel I by the Congress of Vienna in 1815 with Genoa added. In 1860 Sardinia, Genoa, and Piedmont joined other states of Italy to form Kingdom of Italy with the House of Savoy as rulers, while the territory of Savoy along with Nice was ceded to France.

RULERS

Vittorio Amedeo II, 1675-1720
alone as Duke, 1680-1713
Sardinian, 1720-1792

MINT OFFICIALS' INITIALS

Initials	Date	Name
P	1640, 1642	Pietro Perrinet

MONETARY SYSTEM

9 Fiorini = 1 Scudo

DUCHY

STANDARD COINAGE

KM# 4 QUATTRINO

Copper **Ruler:** Vittorio Amedeo II

Date	Mintage	Good	VG	F	VF	XF
1726	—	—	5.00	10.00	20.00	50.00

DAV# 1492 SCUDO (Bianco)

Silver **Ruler:** Vittorio Amedeo II **Obv:** Different attire, curls hanging over right shoulders **Obv. Legend:** VICTOR • AM • II • ..... **Rev:** Crowned arms with supporters above date **Rev. Legend:** PRIN • ....

Date	Mintage	Good	VG	F	VF	XF
1711	—	—	500	1,000	1,850	3,000

TRADE COINAGE

FR# 1100 1/2 DOPPIA

3.2900 g., 0.9860 Gold 0.1043 oz. AGW **Ruler:** Vittorio Amedeo II **Obv:** Mature bust right **Rev:** Crowned arms in Order Collar of the Annunziata, date in legend

Date	Mintage	Good	VG	F	VF	XF
1692 Rare	—	—	—	—	—	—
1704 Rare	—	—	—	—	—	—

FR# 1099 DOPPIA

6.6400 g., 0.9860 Gold 0.2105 oz. AGW **Ruler:** Vittorio Amedeo II **Obv:** Mature bust right **Rev:** Crowned arms in collar of the annunziata, date in legend

Date	Mintage	Good	VG	F	VF	XF
1704 Rare	—	—	—	—	—	—
1706 Rare	—	—	—	—	—	—

FR# 1100a DOPPIA

6.6400 g., 0.9860 Gold 0.2105 oz. AGW **Ruler:** Vittorio Amedeo II **Obv:** Bust right, with title of King of Sicily

Date	Mintage	Good	VG	F	VF	XF
1714 Rare	—	—	—	—	—	—

Note: Bowers & Merena Guia Sale 3-88, XF realized $14,300.00

SICILY

Has a history of occupation extending back to the ancient Phoenicians. In more recent times it was part of the Kingdom of Naples and Sicily.

RULERS

Philip V (of Spain), 1701-1713
Victor Amadeus II (of Savoy), 1713-1720
Charles III (VI of Austria), 1720-1734
Charles Bourbon, Carlo III, 1734-1759
Ferdinando III, 1759-1825

MINT OFFICIALS' INITIALS

Initials	Date	Name
AO	1752	Antonio Oca
DD-AC		Don Antonio Caicerano
FN	1734-49	Francesco Notarbartolo
GLC, GLCI	1775-90	Gabriel Lancilotto Castello
JVI	1798-1807	Guiseppe Ugo
NdOV	1793-98	Nicola d'Ogremont Vigevi
PN	1750-58	Placido Norarbartolo
SM		Simone Maurigi

MONETARY SYSTEM

6 Cavalli = 1 Grano
20 Grani = 2 Carlini = 1 Tari
12 Tari = 1 Piastra
15 Tari = 1 Scudo
2 Scudi = 1 Oncia

KINGDOM

STANDARD COINAGE

C# 1 3 CAVALLI

Copper **Ruler:** Carlo III **Obv:** Crowned displayed eagle, MM initials below **Rev:** 3 in cartouche, date below

Date	Mintage	VG	F	VF	XF	Unc
1738 FN	—	10.00	20.00	40.00	60.00	—
1747 FN	—	10.00	20.00	40.00	60.00	—

C# 1a 3 CAVALLI

Copper **Ruler:** Carlo III **Obv:** Larger eagle **Rev:** Different cartouche around 3

Date	Mintage	VG	F	VF	XF	Unc
1755 PN	—	10.00	20.00	40.00	60.00	—

C# 16 3 CAVALLI

Copper **Ruler:** Ferdinando III **Obv:** Crowned eagle **Rev:** Value and date in ornamental cartouche

Date	Mintage	VG	F	VF	XF	Unc
1775 GLC	—	3.50	6.00	12.00	28.00	—
1776 GLC	—	3.50	6.00	12.00	28.00	—
1779 GLC	—	3.50	6.00	12.00	28.00	—
1782 GLC	—	3.50	6.00	12.00	28.00	—
1783 GLC	—	3.50	6.00	12.00	28.00	—
1791 GLCI	—	3.50	6.00	12.00	28.00	—
1793 NdOV	—	3.50	6.00	12.00	28.00	—
1794 NdOV	—	3.50	6.00	12.00	28.00	—
1795 NdOV	—	3.50	6.00	12.00	28.00	—

C# 3 UN (1) GRANO

Copper **Ruler:** Carlo III **Obv:** Displayed eagle divides FN **Obv. Legend:** CAR • III • SIC • REX • **Rev:** VT/COMMO/DIVS, date in cartouche

Date	Mintage	VG	F	VF	XF	Unc
1737 FN	—	10.00	20.00	40.00	60.00	—
1738 FN	—	10.00	20.00	40.00	60.00	—
1747 FN	—	10.00	20.00	40.00	60.00	—

C# 3a UN (1) GRANO

Copper **Ruler:** Carlo III **Obv:** Larger eagle **Rev:** Different cartouche around inscription and date

Date	Mintage	VG	F	VF	XF	Unc
1755 PN	—	10.00	20.00	40.00	60.00	—

C# 18 UN (1) GRANO

Copper **Ruler:** Ferdinando III **Obv:** Crowned displayed eagle **Rev:** VT COMMO DIUS and date in ornamental cartouche

Date	Mintage	VG	F	VF	XF	Unc
1775 GLC Large eagle	—	6.00	8.50	12.50	28.00	—
1775 GLC Small eagle	—	6.00	8.50	12.50	28.00	—
1776 GLC	—	6.00	8.50	12.50	28.00	—
1777 GLC	—	6.00	8.50	12.50	28.00	—
1778 GLC	—	6.00	8.50	12.50	28.00	—
1779 GLC	—	6.00	8.50	12.50	28.00	—
1780 GLC	—	6.00	8.50	12.50	28.00	—
1782 GLC	—	6.00	8.50	12.50	28.00	—
1783 GLC	—	6.00	8.50	12.50	28.00	—
1784 GLC	—	6.00	8.50	12.50	28.00	—
1785 GLC	—	6.00	8.50	12.50	28.00	—
1791 GLCI	—	6.00	8.50	12.50	28.00	—
1793 NdOV	—	6.00	8.50	12.50	28.00	—
1794 NdOV	—	6.00	8.50	12.50	28.00	—

C# 18a UN (1) GRANO

Copper **Ruler:** Ferdinando III **Obv:** Larger, crowned displayed eagle **Rev:** VT/COMMO/DIUS, date in ornamental cartouche

Date	Mintage	VG	F	VF	XF	Unc
1795 NdOV	—	6.00	8.50	12.50	28.00	—

C# 4 DUE (2) GRANI

Copper **Ruler:** Carlo III **Obv:** Crowned displayed eagle divides FN below **Rev:** VT COMMO DIVS, date in circle surrounded by ornamental cartouche

Date	Mintage	VG	F	VF	XF	Unc
1738 FN Rare	—	—	—	—	—	—
1747 FN Rare	—	—	—	—	—	—

C# 4a DUE (2) GRANI

Copper **Ruler:** Carlo III **Obv:** Crowned, displayed eagle **Rev:** Different cartouche

Date	Mintage	VG	F	VF	XF	Unc
1755 PN Rare	—	—	—	—	—	—

C# 20.1 DUE (2) GRANI

Copper **Ruler:** Ferdinando III **Obv:** Crowned, displayed eagle, head left **Rev:** VT COMMODIUS and date in ornamental cartouche

Date	Mintage	VG	F	VF	XF	Unc
1775 GLC Large eagle	—	6.50	10.00	15.00	50.00	—
1775 GLC Small eagle	—	6.50	10.00	15.00	50.00	—
1776 GLC	—	5.00	7.00	10.00	40.00	—
1777 GLC	—	5.00	7.00	10.00	40.00	—
1778 GLC	—	5.00	7.00	10.00	40.00	—
1779 GLC	—	5.00	7.00	10.00	40.00	—
1780 GLC	—	5.00	7.00	10.00	40.00	—
1782 GLC	—	5.00	7.00	10.00	40.00	—
1783 GLC	—	5.00	7.00	10.00	40.00	—
1784 GLC	—	5.00	7.00	10.00	40.00	—
1785 GLC	—	5.00	7.00	10.00	40.00	—
1791 GLCI	—	6.50	10.00	15.00	50.00	—
1793 NdOV	—	6.50	10.00	15.00	50.00	—
1794 NdOV	—	5.00	7.00	10.00	40.00	—

C# 20.2 DUE (2) GRANI

Copper **Ruler:** Ferdinando III **Obv:** Crowned eagle, head right **Rev:** UT COMMODIUS and date in different ornamental cartouche

Date	Mintage	VG	F	VF	XF	Unc
1795 NdOV	—	5.00	7.00	10.00	40.00	—

C# 5 3 GRANI

Copper **Ruler:** Carlo III **Obv:** Crowned displayed eagle divides FN **Rev:** VT/COMMO/DIVS/, date in circle, ornamentation in outer circle

Date	Mintage	VG	F	VF	XF	Unc
1746 FN Rare	—	—	—	—	—	—

C# 5a 3 GRANI

Copper **Ruler:** Carlo III **Obv:** Crowned, displayed eagle **Rev:** Different cartouche in outer circle

Date	Mintage	VG	F	VF	XF	Unc
1747 FN Rare	—	—	—	—	—	—

C# 5.1 CINQUE (5) GRANI

Silver **Ruler:** Carlo III **Obv:** Head right **Rev:** S in circular legend, date below

Date	Mintage	VG	F	VF	XF	Unc
1737 Rare	—	—	—	—	—	—

C# 5.2 CINQUE (5) GRANI

Copper **Ruler:** Carlo III **Obv:** Crowned displayed eagle divides FN **Rev:** VT/COMMO/DIVS/, date in circle, ornamentation in outer circle

Date	Mintage	VG	F	VF	XF	Unc
1746 FN Rare	—	—	—	—	—	—

C# 5.2a CINQUE (5) GRANI

Copper **Ruler:** Carlo III **Rev:** Different cartouche in outer circle

Date	Mintage	VG	F	VF	XF	Unc
1747 FN Rare	—	—	—	—	—	—

C# 23 DIECI (10) GRANI

1.1500 g., 0.8330 Silver 0.0308 oz. ASW **Ruler:** Ferdinando III **Obv:** Head right, value below **Rev:** Crowned eagle, date above

Date	Mintage	VG	F	VF	XF	Unc
1796 NdOV	—	7.50	20.00	40.00	100	—

C# 26.1 20 GRANI

2.2000 g., 0.8330 Silver 0.0589 oz. ASW **Ruler:** Ferdinando III **Obv:** Head right **Rev:** Small crowned eagle **Rev. Legend:** HISP. INF.

Date	Mintage	VG	F	VF	XF	Unc
1785 GLC	—	15.00	30.00	50.00	110	—
1786 GLC	—	15.00	30.00	50.00	110	—

C# 26.2 20 GRANI

2.2000 g., 0.8330 Silver 0.0589 oz. ASW **Ruler:** Ferdinando III **Obv:** Larger head right **Rev:** Larger crowned eagle **Rev. Legend:** HISPAN. INFANS

Date	Mintage	VG	F	VF	XF	Unc
1787 GLC	—	15.00	30.00	50.00	110	—
1788 GLC	—	15.00	30.00	50.00	110	—
1789 GLC	—	15.00	30.00	50.00	110	—
1796 NdOV	—	15.00	30.00	50.00	110	—

C# 5.3 1/2 TARI

Silver **Ruler:** Carlo III **Subject:** Coronation **Obv:** Laureate bust right **Obv. Legend:** CAR. D. G. SIC. REX **Rev:** Crowned displayed eagle, dtae below **Rev. Legend:** CO-RO-NA-TVS

Date	Mintage	VG	F	VF	XF	Unc
1735 Rare	—	—	—	—	—	—

C# 5.3a 1/2 TARI

Silver **Ruler:** Carlo III **Obv:** Laureate bust right **Rev:** Date at top **Rev. Legend:** HIS INF

Date	Mintage	VG	F	VF	XF	Unc
1739 FN Rare	—	—	—	—	—	—

KM# 5.3a 1/2 TARI

1.0300 g., Silver, 16.3 mm. **Ruler:** Carlo III **Obv:** Carlo III's Laureate bust right **Rev:** Crowned eagle divides date at top **Edge:** Plain

Date	Mintage	F	VF	XF	Unc	BU
1739FN	—	—	—	—	—	—

KM# 5.3b 1/2 TARI

1.1400 g., Silver, 16.6 mm. **Ruler:** Carlo III **Obv:** Carlo III's laureate bust right **Rev:** Crowned eagle above date **Edge:** Crude reeding

Date	Mintage	F	VF	XF	Unc	BU
1751	—	—	—	—	—	—

C# 5.3b 1/2 TARI

Silver **Ruler:** Carlo III **Obv:** Laureate bust right **Rev:** Date at bottom **Rev. Legend:** RE. SI. ET. HI

Date	Mintage	VG	F	VF	XF	Unc
1751 Rare	—	—	—	—	—	—

C# 5.4 TARI

Silver **Ruler:** Carlo III **Obv:** Bust right **Rev:** Crowned displayed eagle, date below

Date	Mintage	VG	F	VF	XF	Unc
1734 FN Rare	—	—	—	—	—	—
1735 FN Rare	—	—	—	—	—	—

C# 5.5 TARI

Silver **Ruler:** Carlo III **Subject:** Coronation **Obv:** Thin laureate bust right

Date	Mintage	VG	F	VF	XF	Unc
1735 FN Rare	—	—	—	—	—	—
1737 FN Rare	—	—	—	—	—	—
1739 FN Rare	—	—	—	—	—	—

C# 5.5a TARI

Silver **Ruler:** Carlo III **Obv:** Thin laureate bust right **Rev. Legend:** HIS-PAN-INF-ANS

Date	Mintage	VG	F	VF	XF	Unc
1754 PN Rare	—	—	—	—	—	—

C# 6 2 TARI

Silver **Ruler:** Charles III **Obv:** Laureate bust right **Obv. Legend:** CAROLVS•III•D•G•**Rev:** Crowned displayed eagle, date below

Date	Mintage	VG	F	VF	XF	Unc
1732 SM	—	10.00	20.00	40.00	85.00	—
1733 SM	—	10.00	20.00	40.00	85.00	—
1735 FN	—	10.00	20.00	40.00	85.00	—

C# 7 2 TARI

Silver **Ruler:** Carlo III **Subject:** Coronation **Obv:** Thin armored bust right **Rev:** Date below eagle **Rev. Legend:** FAVSTO CORONAT ANNO

Date	Mintage	VG	F	VF	XF	Unc
1735 FN	—	10.00	20.00	40.00	85.00	—

C# 6a 2 TARI

Silver **Ruler:** Carlo III **Obv:** Laureate bust right **Rev:** Crowned, displayed eagle **Rev. Legend:** HIS-PA-IN-FANS

Date	Mintage	VG	F	VF	XF	Unc
1736 FN	—	10.00	20.00	40.00	85.00	—
1737 FN	—	10.00	20.00	40.00	85.00	—
1739 FN	—	10.00	20.00	40.00	85.00	—
1743 FN	—	10.00	20.00	40.00	85.00	—
1744 FN	—	10.00	20.00	40.00	85.00	—
1754 PN	—	10.00	20.00	40.00	85.00	—
1756 PN	—	10.00	20.00	40.00	85.00	—
1757 PN	—	10.00	20.00	40.00	85.00	—

C# 6b 2 TARI

Silver **Ruler:** Carlo III **Obv:** Without laurel wreath on head **Rev:** Crowned displayed eagle, date below

Date	Mintage	VG	F	VF	XF	Unc
1753 PN	—	10.00	20.00	40.00	85.00	—

C# 27.1 2 TARI

4.5000 g., 0.8330 Silver 0.1205 oz. ASW **Ruler:** Ferdinando III **Obv:** Head right **Rev:** Crowned eagle

Date	Mintage	VG	F	VF	XF	Unc
1785 GLC	—	12.50	25.00	40.00	100	—
1786 GLC	—	12.50	25.00	40.00	100	—
1787 GLC	—	12.50	25.00	40.00	100	—
1788 GLC	—	12.50	25.00	40.00	100	—
1789 GLC	—	12.50	25.00	40.00	100	—

C# 27.2 2 TARI

4.5000 g., 0.8330 Silver 0.1205 oz. ASW **Ruler:** Ferdinando III **Rev:** Crowned eagle, date below

Date	Mintage	VG	F	VF	XF	Unc
1789 GLC	—	12.50	25.00	40.00	100	—
1793 NdOV	—	12.50	25.00	40.00	100	—

C# 27.3 2 TARI

4.5000 g., 0.8330 Silver 0.1205 oz. ASW **Ruler:** Ferdinando III **Obv:** Value below head

Date	Mintage	VG	F	VF	XF	Unc
1796 NdOV	—	12.50	25.00	40.00	100	—

C# 8 3 TARI

Silver **Ruler:** Carlo III **Subject:** Coronation **Obv:** Laureate head right **Rev:** Cross with crowns at end of top three arms, date below **Rev. Legend:** FAVSTO CORONATIONIS ANNO

Date	Mintage	VG	F	VF	XF	Unc
1735 FN	—	7.50	15.00	30.00	65.00	—

C# 9 3 TARI

Silver **Ruler:** Carlo III **Rev. Legend:** HIS-PA-IN-FANS

Date	Mintage	VG	F	VF	XF	Unc
1737 FN	—	10.00	20.00	40.00	85.00	—
1743 FN	—	10.00	20.00	40.00	85.00	—
1744 FN	—	10.00	20.00	40.00	85.00	—
1749 FN	—	10.00	20.00	40.00	85.00	—
1753 PFN	—	10.00	20.00	40.00	85.00	—
1757 FN	—	10.00	20.00	40.00	85.00	—

C# 10 3 TARI

Silver **Ruler:** Carlo III **Obv:** Without laurel wreath on head

Date	Mintage	VG	F	VF	XF	Unc
1754 Rare	—	—	—	—	—	—
1756 Rare	—	—	—	—	—	—
1757 Rare	—	—	—	—	—	—

C# 29 3 TARI

6.4000 g., 0.8330 Silver 0.1714 oz. ASW **Ruler:** Ferdinando III **Obv:** Head right, value below **Rev:** Crowned cross, date below **Rev. Legend:** HI SPAN. INFANS

Date	Mintage	VG	F	VF	XF	Unc
1785 GLC HISP. INF.	—	20.00	35.00	60.00	115	—
1786 GLC	—	20.00	35.00	60.00	115	—
1787 GLC	—	20.00	35.00	60.00	115	—
1788 GLC	—	20.00	35.00	60.00	115	—
1793 NdOV	—	20.00	35.00	60.00	115	—
1796 NdOV	—	12.50	20.00	35.00	75.00	—
1798 NdOV	—	20.00	35.00	60.00	115	—

C# 10.1 4 TARI

Silver **Ruler:** Carlo III **Obv:** Bust right **Rev:** Crowned displayed eagle, date below

Date	Mintage	VG	F	VF	XF	Unc
1734 FN Rare	—	—	—	—	—	—

C# 10.2 4 TARI

Silver **Ruler:** Carlo III **Obv:** Laureate bust right **Rev. Legend:** FAVSTO CORONATIONIS ANNO

Date	Mintage	VG	F	VF	XF	Unc
1735 FN Rare	—	—	—	—	—	—

C# 10.3 4 TARI

Silver **Ruler:** Carlo III **Obv:** Bust right **Obv. Legend:** CAROLVS • D • G • SICILY .... **Rev:** Crowned displayed eagle divides FN **Rev. Legend:** HISPA NIARVM INFANS

Date	Mintage	VG	F	VF	XF	Unc
1736 FN Rare	—	—	—	—	—	—

C# 10.4 4 TARI

Silver **Ruler:** Carlo III **Obv:** Without laurel wreath on head

Date	Mintage	VG	F	VF	XF	Unc
1753 PN Rare	—	—	—	—	—	—

C# 10.5 4 TARI

Silver **Ruler:** Carlo III **Rev. Legend:** HIS-PAN-INF-ANS

Date	Mintage	VG	F	VF	XF	Unc
1754 PN Rare	—	—	—	—	—	—
1755 PN Rare	—	—	—	—	—	—
1756 PN Rare	—	—	—	—	—	—

C# 30.1 4 TARI

8.7000 g., 0.8330 Silver 0.2330 oz. ASW **Ruler:** Ferdinando III **Obv:** Crude portrait of Ferdinando III right **Rev:** Crowned eagle

Date	Mintage	VG	F	VF	XF	Unc
1785 GLC	—	40.00	65.00	95.00	150	—

C# 30.2 4 TARI

8.7000 g., 0.8330 Silver 0.2330 oz. ASW **Ruler:** Ferdinando III **Obv:** Head right, date below **Rev:** Crowned eagle **Rev. Legend:** HISPAN INFANS

Date	Mintage	VG	F	VF	XF	Unc
1786 GLC	—	20.00	35.00	55.00	125	—
1787 GLC	—	20.00	35.00	55.00	125	—
1789 GLC	—	20.00	35.00	55.00	125	—
1793 NdOV HISPANIARVM	—	20.00	35.00	55.00	125	—
1796 NdOV HISPANIARVM	—	20.00	35.00	55.00	125	—

C# 10.8 6 TARI

Silver **Ruler:** Carlo III **Subject:** Coronation **Obv:** Bust right **Rev:** Cross with fleur-de-lis in angles, crown above

Date	Mintage	VG	F	VF	XF	Unc
1735 FN	—	30.00	60.00	120	250	—

C# 11 6 TARI

Silver **Ruler:** Carlo III **Rev:** Without fleur-de-lis in angles of cross **Rev. Legend:** FAVSTO CORONATIONIS ANNO

Date	Mintage	VG	F	VF	XF	Unc
1735	—	25.00	50.00	100	200	—

C# 12 6 TARI

Silver **Ruler:** Carlo III **Rev:** Fleur-de-lis in angles of cross **Rev. Legend:** HIS-PAN-INEF-ANS

Date	Mintage	VG	F	VF	XF	Unc
1754 PN	—	50.00	100	200	400	—
1755 PN	—	50.00	100	200	400	—

C# 31 6 TARI

13.6320 g., 0.8330 Silver 0.3651 oz. ASW **Ruler:** Ferdinando III **Obv:** Bust right **Rev:** Fleur-de-lis in angles of cross, crown above, divided initials and date below

Date	Mintage	VG	F	VF	XF	Unc
1785 GLC	—	35.00	55.00	85.00	175	—
1786 GLC	—	35.00	55.00	85.00	175	—
1787 GLC	—	35.00	55.00	85.00	175	—
1788 GLC	—	35.00	55.00	85.00	175	—
1789 GLC	—	35.00	55.00	85.00	175	—
1793 NdOV	—	35.00	55.00	85.00	175	—
1794 NdOV	—	35.00	55.00	85.00	175	—
1795 NdOV	—	35.00	55.00	85.00	175	—

C# 33 6 TARI

13.7660 g., 0.8330 Silver 0.3687 oz. ASW **Ruler:** Ferdinando III **Obv:** Head right, value below **Rev:** Crowned eagle, date below

Date	Mintage	VG	F	VF	XF	Unc
1796 NdOV	—	45.00	65.00	100	200	—
1797 NdOV	—	45.00	65.00	100	200	—
1798 NdOV	—	45.00	65.00	100	200	—
1799 JVI	—	45.00	65.00	100	200	—

C# 48.5 6 TARI

13.6600 g., 0.8540 Silver 0.3750 oz. ASW **Ruler:** Ferdinando III **Obv:** Head right **Rev:** Eagle

Date	Mintage	VG	F	VF	XF	Unc
1799 JVI	—	12.50	17.50	40.00	125	—
1799 JVI Error, T.12 for T.6	—	20.00	30.00	50.00	150	—
1800 JVI	—	12.50	22.50	40.00	125	—

DAV# 1411 SCUDO OF 12 TARI

Silver **Ruler:** Charles III **Obv:** Bust right, C * P below **Rev:** Crowned eagle dividing SM, date below

Date	Mintage	VG	F	VF	XF	Unc
1730	—	225	375	750	1,500	—
1731	—	225	375	750	1,500	—

DAV# 1412 SCUDO OF 12 TARI

Silver **Ruler:** Charles III **Obv:** Laureate head right, C.P. below **Rev. Legend:** REX. SIC. ET. HIE

Date	Mintage	VG	F	VF	XF	Unc
1732	—	650	1,150	2,000	3,500	—

C# 13 SCUDO OF 12 TARI

Silver **Ruler:** Carlo III **Subject:** Coronation **Obv:** Laureate bust right **Rev:** Crowned, displayed eagle divides FN, date below **Rev. Legend:** AVSTO CORONATIONIS ANNO **Note:** Dav. #1415.

Date	Mintage	VG	F	VF	XF	Unc
1735 FN	—	100	250	500	1,000	—

C# 35.1 PIASTRA OF 12 TARI

27.2650 g., 0.8330 Silver 0.7302 oz. ASW **Ruler:** Ferdinando III **Obv:** Head right, date below **Rev:** Large crowned eagle **Note:** Dav. #1417.

Date	Mintage	VG	F	VF	XF	Unc
1785 GLC	—	225	375	750	1,500	—

C# 35.2 PIASTRA OF 12 TARI

27.2650 g., 0.8330 Silver 0.7302 oz. ASW **Ruler:** Ferdinando III **Obv:** Date in legend **Rev:** Small crowned eagle **Note:** Dav. #1418.

Date	Mintage	VG	F	VF	XF	Unc
1786 GLC	—	225	375	750	1,500	—

C# 35a.1 PIASTRA OF 12 TARI

27.2650 g., 0.8330 Silver 0.7302 oz. ASW **Ruler:** Ferdinando III **Obv:** Head right, value below **Rev:** Large crowned eagle, date below **Note:** Dav. #1419.

Date	Mintage	VG	F	VF	XF	Unc
1787 GLC	—	225	375	750	1,500	—
1788 GLC	—	225	375	750	1,500	—
1789 GLC	—	225	375	750	1,500	—
1790 GLC	—	225	375	750	1,500	—

C# 35a.2 PIASTRA OF 12 TARI

27.2650 g., 0.8330 Silver 0.7302 oz. ASW **Ruler:** Ferdinando III **Obv:** Modified effigy **Note:** Dav. #1421.

Date	Mintage	VG	F	VF	XF	Unc
1793 NdOV	—	225	375	750	1,500	—

C# 35a.3 12 TARI

27.5330 g., 0.8330 Silver 0.7373 oz. ASW **Ruler:** Ferdinando III **Obv:** Value: T. 12 below bust right **Obv. Legend:** FERDINANDVS • D • G • SICIL • ET • HIER • REX • **Rev:** Crowned, displayed eagle divides initials, date below **Rev. Legend:** HISPA NIA RVM • INFANS • **Note:** Dav. #1423.

Date	Mintage	VG	F	VF	XF	Unc
1794 NdOV	—	75.00	150	300	550	—
1795 NdOV	—	75.00	150	300	550	—

C# 35a.4 12 TARI

27.5330 g., 0.8330 Silver 0.7373 oz. ASW **Ruler:** Ferdinando III **Obv:** Bust right **Obv. Legend:** FERDINANDUS • D • G • SICIL • ET • HIER • REX • **Rev:** Crowned, displayed eagle, shield on breast, date below **Rev. Legend:** HISPA NIA RUM • INFANS • **Note:** Dav. #1424.

Date	Mintage	VG	F	VF	XF	Unc
1796 NdOV	—	50.00	100	200	400	—

C# 36 12 TARI

27.5330 g., 0.8330 Silver 0.7373 oz. ASW **Ruler:** Ferdinando III **Obv:** Bust right **Obv. Legend:** FERDINAN • D • G • SICIL • ET • HIE • REX • **Rev:** Crowned, displayed eagle, shield on breast, date below **Rev. Legend:** HISPA NIA RUM • INFANS • **Note:** Dav. #1424A.

Date	Mintage	VG	F	VF	XF	Unc
1797 NdOV	—	50.00	100	200	400	—
1798 N•d O.V	—	—	—	—	—	—
1798 JVI	—	50.00	100	200	400	—
1799 JVI	—	50.00	100	200	400	—

C# 49a 12 TARI

27.5330 g., 0.8330 Silver 0.7373 oz. ASW **Ruler:** Ferdinando III **Obv:** Bust right **Obv. Legend:** FERDINAN • III • D • G • SICIL • ... **Rev:** Crowned, displayed eagle, shield on breast, divided initials and date below **Rev. Legend:** HISPA NIA RUM • INFANS •

Date	Mintage	VG	F	VF	XF	Unc
1799 JVI	—	50.00	90.00	150	250	—
Note: 1799 exists with REX. and REX						
1800 JVI	—	50.00	90.00	150	250	—

C# 49 12 TARI

27.5330 g., 0.8330 Silver 0.7373 oz. ASW **Ruler:** Ferdinando III **Obv:** Bust right **Obv. Legend:** FERDINAN • D • G • SICIL... **Rev:** Crowned, displayed eagle **Note:** Dav. #1425.

Date	Mintage	VG	F	VF	XF	Unc
1799 JVI	—	40.00	75.00	125	200	—
Note: 1799 exists with REX • and REX						
1800 JVI	—	40.00	75.00	125	200	—

DAV# 1413 ONCIA OF 30 TARI

Silver, 57 mm. **Ruler:** Charles III **Obv:** Laureate head right, C.P. below **Obv. Legend:** CAROL • III • D • G • SICIL • ET • HIER • REX • **Rev:** Sun above phoenix rising from flame, date **Rev. Legend:** OBLITA • EX • AVRO • ARGENTEA • RESVRGIT •

Date	Mintage	VG	F	VF	XF	Unc
1732	—	550	1,000	1,800	3,000	—

DAV# 1414 ONCIA OF 30 TARI

Silver, 55 mm. **Ruler:** Charles III **Obv:** Laureate head right **Obv. Legend:** CAROL • III • D • G • SICIL • ET • HIER • REX • **Rev:** Radiant sun above phoenix rising out of flames, divided S M below, all within circle **Rev. Legend:** • ET • AVRO ARGENTEA RESVRGIT • 1733

Date	Mintage	VG	F	VF	XF	Unc
1733	—	500	900	1,700	2,800	—

C# 37 ONCIA OF 30 TARI

69.0000 g., 0.8330 Silver 1.8479 oz. ASW **Ruler:** Ferdinando III **Obv:** Bust right, date below **Obv. Legend:** FERDINANDVS • D • G • SICIL • ET • HIER • REX • **Rev:** Radiant sun above phoenix rising out of flames divides G•L•C•, all within circle **Rev. Legend:** EX • AVRO • ARGENTEA • RESVRCIT • **Note:** Dav. #1416.

Date	Mintage	VG	F	VF	XF	Unc
1785 GLC	—	400	750	1,500	2,250	—

C# 37a ONCIA OF 30 TARI

69.0000 g., 0.8330 Silver 1.8479 oz. ASW **Ruler:** Ferdinando III **Obv:** Bust right **Obv. Legend:** FERDINANDVS • D • G • SICIL • ET • HIER • REX • **Rev:** Date below phoenix, divided initials, all within circle, legend around **Rev. Legend:** EX AVRO ARGENTEA RESVRGIT • 1791 **Note:** Dav. #1420.

Date	Mintage	VG	F	VF	XF	Unc
1791 GLCI	—	350	650	1,000	1,800	—

C# 38 ONCIA OF 30 TARI

69.0000 g., 0.8330 Silver 1.8479 oz. ASW **Ruler:** Ferdinando III **Obv:** Bust right **Obv. Legend:** FERDINAND • G • SICIL • ET • HIER • REX • **Rev:** Radiant sun to upper right of phoenix rising out of fire, date below **Rev. Legend:** EX • AVRO • ARGENTEA • RE SVRGT • **Note:** Dav. #1422.

Date	Mintage	VG	F	VF	XF	Unc
1793 NdOV	—	300	500	900	1,450	—

FR# 885 ONCIA

3.7860 g., 0.9960 Gold 0.1212 oz. AGW **Ruler:** Charles III **Obv:** Laureate head right, value below **Obv. Legend:** CAROL • .... **Rev:** Phoenix rising from flames, radiant sun above in inner circle, date below

Date	Mintage	VG	F	VF	XF	Unc
1733	—	100	150	250	400	—
1734	—	100	150	250	400	—

C# 14 ONCIA

3.7860 g., 0.9960 Gold 0.1212 oz. AGW **Ruler:** Carlo III **Obv:** Bust right **Rev:** Phoenix rising from flames, radiant sun above in inner circle, date at bottom

Date	Mintage	VG	F	VF	XF	Unc
1734	—	100	150	250	400	—
1735	—	100	150	250	400	—

C# 14a ONCIA

3.7860 g., 0.9960 Gold 0.1212 oz. AGW **Ruler:** Carlo III **Obv:** Bust right **Rev:** Phoenix head to right rising from flames, radiant sun above, date below **Note:** Many varieties exist.

Date	Mintage	VG	F	VF	XF	Unc
1735	—	100	150	250	400	—
1736	—	100	150	250	400	—
1730 Error	—	—	—	—	—	—
1737	—	100	150	250	400	—
1739	—	100	150	250	400	—
1741	—	100	150	250	400	—
1742	—	100	150	250	400	—
1743	—	100	150	250	400	—
1744	—	100	150	250	400	—
1745	—	100	150	250	400	—
1746	—	100	150	250	400	—
1747	—	100	150	250	400	—
1747 VB	—	100	150	250	400	—
1747 FN	—	100	150	250	400	—
1750 FN	—	100	150	250	400	—
1750 VB/FN	—	100	150	250	400	—
1750 PN	—	100	150	250	400	—
1751	—	100	150	250	400	—
1752	—	100	150	250	400	—

C# 14b ONCIA

3.7860 g., 0.9960 Gold 0.1212 oz. AGW **Ruler:** Carlo III **Obv:** Bust right **Obv. Legend:** CAROLVS • D • G • ... **Rev:** Phoenix head to left rising from flames, radiant sun above, date below **Note:** Many varieties exist.

Date	Mintage	VG	F	VF	XF	Unc
1752 PN/AO	—	100	150	250	400	—
1752 PN	—	100	150	250	400	—
1753 PN	—	100	150	250	400	—
1754 PN	—	100	150	250	400	—
1755 PN	—	100	150	250	400	—
1756 PN	—	100	150	250	400	—
1757 PN	—	100	150	250	400	—
1758 PN	—	100	150	250	400	—

C# 15 2 ONCIE

8.8150 g., 0.9060 Gold 0.2568 oz. AGW **Ruler:** Carlo III **Obv:** Bust right **Obv. Legend:** CAROLVS • D • G • SIC • ET • ... **Rev:** Crowned, displayed eagle with arms on chest, date below **Rev. Legend:** HIS PAN INF ANS

Date	Mintage	VG	F	VF	XF	Unc
1752 PN/AOA	—	200	350	750	1,500	—
1753 PN	—	200	350	750	1,500	—
1754 PN	—	200	350	750	1,500	—
1755 PN	—	200	350	750	1,500	—

C# 15a 2 ONCIE

8.8150 g., 0.9060 Gold 0.2568 oz. AGW **Ruler:** Carlo III **Obv:** Different bust right **Rev:** Crowned, displayed eagle, shield on breast

Date	Mintage	VG	F	VF	XF	Unc
1756 PN	—	200	350	750	1,500	—
1757 PN	—	200	350	750	1,500	—

C# 15b 2 ONCIE

8.8150 g., 0.9060 Gold 0.2568 oz. AGW **Ruler:** Carlo III **Obv:** Older head right

Date	Mintage	VG	F	VF	XF	Unc
1757 PN	—	200	350	750	1,500	—
1758 PN	—	200	350	750	1,500	—

FR# A882 DUCATO

0.9860 Gold **Ruler:** Victor Amadeus II **Obv:** Bust right **Rev:** Crowned eagle with arms on breast, date at top

Date	Mintage	VG	F	VF	XF	Unc
1713 DD-AC/CP Rare	—	—	—	—	—	—

FR# D882 DUCATO

0.9860 Gold **Ruler:** Charles III **Obv:** Laureate head right **Rev:** Crowned eagle with wings spread over palm branches, date below

Date	Mintage	VG	F	VF	XF	Unc
1723 FN Rare	—	—	—	—	—	—

FR# A884 2 DUCATI

0.9960 Gold **Ruler:** Victor Amadeus II **Obv:** Bust right **Rev:** Crowned eagle with arms on breast, date at top

Date	Mintage	VG	F	VF	XF	Unc
1713 DD-AC/CP Rare	—	—	—	—	—	—

FR# B884 2 DUCATI

0.9960 Gold **Ruler:** Charles III **Obv:** Head right **Rev:** Radiant sun and design within circle, date below in legend

Date	Mintage	VG	F	VF	XF	Unc
1723 FN Rare	—	—	—	—	—	—

FR# 884 2 DUCATI

0.9960 Gold **Ruler:** Charles III **Obv:** Laureate bust right **Rev:** Crossed sword and sceptre between crown and orb, date below

Date	Mintage	VG	F	VF	XF	Unc
1727 TS/SM Rare	—	—	—	—	—	—

FR# B882 3 DUCATI

3.7860 g., 0.9960 Gold 0.1212 oz. AGW **Ruler:** Victor Amadeus II **Obv:** Bust right **Rev:** Cross between two crowned shields of arms

Date	Mintage	VG	F	VF	XF	Unc
1713 DD-AC/CP Rare	—	—	—	—	—	—

FR# C882 4 DUCATI

0.9960 Gold **Ruler:** Victor Amadeus II **Obv:** Bust right **Rev:** Crowned eagle with arms on breast, date at top

Date	Mintage	VG	F	VF	XF	Unc
1713 DD-AC/CP Rare	—	—	—	—	—	—

FR# 883 4 DUCATI

0.9960 Gold **Ruler:** Charles III **Obv:** Laureate bust right **Rev:** Crossed sword and sceptre between crown and orb, date below

Date	Mintage	VG	F	VF	XF	Unc
1727 (Monogram) Rare	—	—	—	—	—	—

PATTERNS

Including off metal strikes

KM#	Date	Mintage	Identification	Mkt Val
Pn1	1735	—	Oncia. Gold. 22 mm.	—
Pn2	1750	—	Oncia. Gold. 22 mm. Phoenix under sun in cartouche.	—
Pn3	1750	—	Oncia. Gold. 22 mm. Phoenix under sun in circle, ornamental outer circle.	—

SORAGNA

RULER
Nicholas Meli-Lupi, 1731-1741

PRINCIPALITY

STANDARD COINAGE

FR# 1171 SCUDO D'ORO

3.5000 g., 0.9860 Gold 0.1109 oz. AGW **Ruler:** Nicholas Meli-Lupi **Obv:** Crowned and mantled arms **Rev:** Crowned Imperial eagle, date in legend

Date	Mintage	Good	VG	F	VF	XF
1731	—	—	2,000	3,500	6,000	10,000

TRENTO

RULER
Peter Vigilius, 1776-1800

BISHOPRIC

STANDARD COINAGE

KM# 1 1/2 SOLDO

Copper, 17.9 mm. **Ruler:** no Ruler Name **Obv:** Tyrolean eagle **Rev:** Value in ornamental border **Note:** Schon #35.

Date	Mintage	VG	F	VF	XF	Unc
1739	—	20.00	40.00	75.00	—	—

KM# 2 SOLDO

Copper, 20.8 mm. **Ruler:** no Ruler Name **Obv:** Tyrolean eagle **Rev:** Value in ornamental border **Note:** Schon #36.

Date	Mintage	VG	F	VF	XF	Unc
1739	—	20.00	45.00	90.00	—	—

TRADE COINAGE

FR# 1 DUCAT

3.5000 g., 0.9860 Gold 0.1109 oz. AGW **Ruler:** Peter Vigilius **Subject:** Election as Bishop **Obv:** Bust right **Rev:** Crowned oval, mantled arms

Date	Mintage	Good	VG	F	VF	XF
1776	—	—	850	1,750	3,000	4,500

FR# 1a DUCAT

Silver **Ruler:** Peter Vigilius **Obv:** Bust right **Rev:** Crowned oval, mantled arms

Date	Mintage	VG	F	VF	XF	Unc
1776	—	—	—	—	—	—

TUSCANY

Etruria

An Italian territorial division on the west-central peninsula, belonged to the Medici from 1530 to 1737, when it was given to Francis, duke of Lorraine. In 1800 the French established it as part of the Spanish dominions; from 1807 to 1809 it was a French department. After the fall of Napoleon it reverted to its pre-Napoleonic owner, Ferdinand III.

RULERS
Cosimo III, 1670-1723
Giovanni Gaston, 1723-1737
Francesco III, 1737-1746
As Emperor Francis I, 1746-1765
Pietro Leopoldo, 1765-1790
As Emperor Leopold II, 1790-1792
Ferdinando III, 1791-1801

MINT MARKS
FIRENZE - Florence
LEGHORN - Livorno
PISIS – Pisa

MONETARY SYSTEM
Until 1826
12 Denari = 3 Quattrini = 1 Soldo
20 Soldi = 1 Lira
10 Lire = 1 Dena
40 Quattrini = 1 Paolo
1-1/2 Paoli = 1 Lira
10 Paoli = 1 Francescone, Scudo, Tallero
3 Zecchini = 1 Ruspone = 40 Lire

GRAND DUCHY

STANDARD COINAGE

C# 12 QUATTRINO

Copper **Ruler:** Pietro Leopoldo **Obv:** Crowned arms **Rev:** Value and date

Date	Mintage	VG	F	VF	XF	Unc
1771	—	4.00	6.50	12.50	30.00	—
1778	—	4.00	6.50	12.50	30.00	—
1779	—	4.00	6.50	12.50	30.00	—
1780	—	4.00	6.50	12.50	30.00	—
1781	—	4.00	6.50	12.50	30.00	—
1782	—	4.00	6.50	12.50	30.00	—
1783	—	4.00	6.50	12.50	30.00	—
1784	—	4.00	6.50	12.50	30.00	—
1787	—	4.00	6.50	12.50	30.00	—
1788	—	4.00	6.50	12.50	30.00	—
1789	—	4.00	6.50	12.50	30.00	—
1790	—	4.00	6.50	12.50	30.00	—

C# 29 QUATTRINO

Copper **Ruler:** Ferdinando III **Obv:** Crowned arms **Rev:** Value, date

Date	Mintage	VG	F	VF	XF	Unc
1791	—	3.00	5.00	10.00	25.00	—
1792	—	3.00	5.00	10.00	25.00	—
1795	—	3.00	5.00	10.00	25.00	—
1796	—	3.00	5.00	10.00	25.00	—
1798	—	3.00	5.00	10.00	25.00	—
1799	—	3.00	5.00	10.00	25.00	—
1800	—	3.00	5.00	10.00	25.00	—

C# 13 2 QUATTRINI

Copper **Ruler:** Pietro Leopoldo **Obv:** Crowned arms **Rev:** Value and date

Date	Mintage	VG	F	VF	XF	Unc
1778	—	4.50	6.50	12.50	30.00	—
1783	—	4.50	6.50	12.50	30.00	—
1785	—	4.50	6.50	12.50	30.00	—

C# 1 3 QUATTRINI

Copper **Ruler:** Francesco III **Obv:** Crowned arms **Rev:** Patriarch's cross

Date	Mintage	VG	F	VF	XF	Unc
1710	—	5.00	7.00	15.00	35.00	—
1741	—	4.50	6.50	12.50	30.00	—

C# 14 3 QUATTRINI

Copper **Ruler:** Pietro Leopoldo **Obv:** Crowned arms **Rev:** Value and date

Date	Mintage	VG	F	VF	XF	Unc
1778	—	5.00	7.50	15.00	35.00	—
1780	—	5.00	7.50	15.00	35.00	—
1782	—	5.00	7.50	15.00	35.00	—
1785	—	5.00	7.50	15.00	35.00	—
1790	—	5.00	7.50	15.00	35.00	—

C# 31 3 QUATTRINI

Copper **Ruler:** Ferdinando III **Obv:** Crowned arms in sprigs **Obv. Legend:** FERD • III • A • A • ... **Rev:** Value in cartouche

Date	Mintage	VG	F	VF	XF	Unc
1791	—	4.50	6.50	12.50	30.00	—

C# 2 DIECI (10) QUATTRINI

Silver **Ruler:** Francesco III, as Emperor Francis I **Obv:** Bust right **Rev:** Crowned arms

Date	Mintage	VG	F	VF	XF	Unc
1754	—	5.00	10.00	20.00	45.00	—
1759	—	5.00	10.00	20.00	45.00	—
1764	—	5.00	10.00	20.00	45.00	—

C# 15 DIECI (10) QUATTRINI

Billon **Ruler:** Pietro Leopoldo **Obv:** Bust right **Obv. Legend:** P • LEOPOLDVS • D • G • .... **Rev:** Crowned, mantled arms **Rev. Legend:** QUATTRINI DIECI

Date	Mintage	VG	F	VF	XF	Unc
1778	—	3.75	6.00	12.00	25.00	—
1780	—	3.75	6.00	12.00	25.00	—
1781	—	3.75	6.00	12.00	25.00	—
1782	—	3.75	6.00	12.00	25.00	—
1785	—	3.75	6.00	12.00	25.00	—
1786	—	3.75	6.00	12.00	25.00	—
1787	—	3.75	6.00	12.00	25.00	—
1788	—	3.75	6.00	12.00	25.00	—

C# 32 DIECI (10) QUATTRINI

Billon **Ruler:** Ferdinando III **Obv:** Crowned shield **Rev:** Inscription within square design

Date	Mintage	VG	F	VF	XF	Unc
1800	—	4.50	6.50	15.00	40.00	—
1801	—	5.00	10.00	20.00	40.00	—

C# 16 1/2 PAOLO

1.3700 g., 0.9200 Silver 0.0405 oz. ASW **Ruler:** Pietro Leopoldo **Obv:** Bust right **Rev:** Crowned arms

Date	Mintage	VG	F	VF	XF	Unc
1783	—	9.00	15.00	28.00	45.00	—
1784	—	9.00	15.00	28.00	45.00	—

C# 33 1/2 PAOLO

1.3750 g., 0.9200 Silver 0.0407 oz. ASW **Ruler:** Ferdinando III **Obv:** Bust right **Rev:** Crowned arms

Date	Mintage	VG	F	VF	XF	Unc
1792	—	10.00	18.00	30.00	50.00	—

C# 4 PAOLO

Silver **Ruler:** Francesco III **Obv:** Laureate head right **Rev:** Crowned arms in branches

Date	Mintage	VG	F	VF	XF	Unc
1738	—	9.00	16.00	28.00	50.00	—

C# 17 PAOLO

2.7400 g., 0.9200 Silver 0.0810 oz. ASW **Ruler:** Pietro Leopoldo **Obv:** Bust right **Obv. Legend:** P • LEOP • D • G • .... **Rev:** Crowned arms in order chain with spikes

Date	Mintage	VG	F	VF	XF	Unc
1783	—	9.00	16.00	28.00	50.00	—

C# 17a PAOLO

2.7400 g., 0.9200 Silver 0.0810 oz. ASW **Ruler:** Pietro Leopoldo **Obv:** Bust right **Obv. Legend:** P • LEOP • D • G • .... **Rev:** Crowned, oval arms in Order chain with spikes

Date	Mintage	VG	F	VF	XF	Unc
1788	—	9.00	16.00	28.00	50.00	—
1789	—	9.00	16.00	28.00	50.00	—
1790	—	9.00	16.00	28.00	50.00	—

C# 34 PAOLO

2.7510 g., 0.9200 Silver 0.0814 oz. ASW **Ruler:** Ferdinando III **Obv:** Bust right **Rev:** Crowned arms

Date	Mintage	VG	F	VF	XF	Unc
1791	—	25.00	45.00	75.00	125	—

C# 5 2 PAOLI

Silver **Ruler:** Francesco III, as Emperor Francis I **Obv:** Head right **Obv. Legend:** FRANC • III • D • G • LOTH • BAR • ... **Rev:** Crowned oval arms in sprigs

Date	Mintage	VG	F	VF	XF	Unc
1738	—	15.00	25.00	45.00	90.00	—
1745	—	15.00	25.00	45.00	90.00	—
1747	—	15.00	25.00	45.00	90.00	—
1761	—	15.00	25.00	45.00	90.00	—
1762	—	15.00	25.00	45.00	90.00	—

C# 18 2 PAOLI

5.4800 g., 0.9200 Silver 0.1621 oz. ASW **Ruler:** Pietro Leopoldo **Obv:** Bust right **Obv. Legend:** P • LEOP • D • G • P • R • ... **Rev:** Crowned, oval arms in Order chain with spikes

Date	Mintage	VG	F	VF	XF	Unc
1770	—	15.00	25.00	45.00	90.00	—
1780	—	15.00	25.00	45.00	90.00	—
1782	—	15.00	25.00	45.00	90.00	—
1787	—	15.00	25.00	45.00	90.00	—

C# 35 2 PAOLI

5.5020 g., 0.9170 Silver 0.1622 oz. ASW **Ruler:** Ferdinando III **Obv:** Bust right **Obv. Legend:** FERD • III • D • G • P • R • .... **Rev:** Crowned, oval arms with spikes in Order chain, divided date below

Date	Mintage	VG	F	VF	XF	Unc
1791	—	40.00	65.00	100	175	—

C# 6 1/2 FRANCESCONE (5 Paoli)

Silver **Ruler:** Francesco III **Obv:** Bust right **Obv. Legend:** FRANC • III • D • G • LOTH • ... **Rev:** Crowned arms in sprigs

Date	Mintage	VG	F	VF	XF	Unc
1738	—	35.00	55.00	145	300	—
1739	—	35.00	55.00	145	300	—
1740	—	35.00	55.00	145	300	—
1741	—	35.00	55.00	145	300	—
1742	—	35.00	55.00	145	300	—
1743	—	35.00	55.00	145	300	—
1745	—	35.00	55.00	145	300	—

C# 7 1/2 FRANCESCONE (5 Paoli)

Silver **Ruler:** Francesco III, as Emperor Francis I **Obv:** Bust right **Obv. Legend:** FRANCISCVS • D • G • R • I • S • A • .... **Rev:** Crowned double-headed eagle with crowned shield on breast

Date	Mintage	VG	F	VF	XF	Unc
1746	—	35.00	55.00	145	300	—
1756	—	35.00	55.00	145	300	—
1758	—	35.00	55.00	145	300	—
1763	—	35.00	55.00	145	300	—
1764	—	35.00	55.00	145	300	—

C# 19 5 PAOLI

13.7500 g., 0.9170 Silver 0.4054 oz. ASW **Ruler:** Pietro Leopoldo **Obv:** Bust right **Obv. Legend:** P • LEOPOLDVS • ..... **Rev:** Crowned, oval shield with spikes in order chain

Date	Mintage	VG	F	VF	XF	Unc
1777	—	40.00	60.00	125	250	—
1778	—	40.00	60.00	125	250	—
1779	—	40.00	60.00	125	250	—

C# 19a 5 PAOLI

13.7500 g., 0.9170 Silver 0.4054 oz. ASW **Ruler:** Pietro Leopoldo **Obv:** Bust right with bound hair **Rev:** Crowned, oval shield with spikes in order chain

Date	Mintage	VG	F	VF	XF	Unc
1778	—	40.00	60.00	125	250	—
1779	—	40.00	60.00	125	250	—
1787	—	40.00	60.00	125	250	—

C# 20 5 PAOLI

13.7500 g., 0.9170 Silver 0.4054 oz. ASW **Ruler:** Pietro Leopoldo, as Emperor Leopold II **Obv:** Bust right **Obv. Legend:** LEOPOLDVS • II • D • G • ..... **Rev:** Crowned arms in sprigs

Date	Mintage	VG	F	VF	XF	Unc
1790	—	45.00	65.00	130	260	—

C# 36 5 PAOLI

13.7500 g., 0.9170 Silver 0.4054 oz. ASW **Ruler:** Pietro Leopoldo, as Emperor Leopold II **Obv:** Head right **Rev:** Oval arms

Date	Mintage	VG	F	VF	XF	Unc
1791	—	45.00	65.00	130	260	—

C# 8 FRANCESCONE (10 Paoli)

27.5000 g., 0.9170 Silver 0.8107 oz. ASW **Ruler:** Francesco III, as Emperor Francis I **Obv:** Bust right **Obv. Legend:** FRANCISCVS • D • G • R • I • S • A • ... **Rev:** Crowned double-headed eagle with crowned shield on breast **Note:** Dav. #1504.

Date	Mintage	VG	F	VF	XF	Unc
1747	—	60.00	120	250	450	—

C# 8a FRANCESCONE (10 Paoli)

27.5000 g., 0.9170 Silver 0.8107 oz. ASW **Ruler:** Francesco III, as Emperor Francis I **Obv:** Larger bust right **Obv. Legend:** FRANCISCVS • D • G • R • I • S • A • ... **Rev:** Crowned double-headed eagle with crowned shield on breast **Note:** Dav. #1505.

Date	Mintage	VG	F	VF	XF	Unc
1747	—	40.00	80.00	100	200	—
1758	—	40.00	80.00	100	200	—

Date	Mintage	VG	F	VF	XF	Unc
1759	—	40.00	80.00	100	200	—
1760	—	40.00	80.00	100	200	—
1761	—	40.00	80.00	100	200	—
1762	—	40.00	80.00	100	200	—
1763	—	40.00	80.00	100	200	—
1764	—	40.00	80.00	100	200	—

C# 8c FRANCESCONE (10 Paoli)

27.5000 g., 0.9170 Silver 0.8107 oz. ASW **Ruler:** Francesco III, as Emperor Francis I **Obv:** Bust right **Obv. Legend:** FRANCISCVS • D • G • R • I • S • A • ... **Rev:** Roman numeral date **Note:** Dav. #1506.

Date	Mintage	VG	F	VF	XF	Unc
1748	—	40.00	80.00	100	200	—

C# 8b FRANCESCONE (10 Paoli)

27.5000 g., 0.9170 Silver 0.8107 oz. ASW **Ruler:** Francesco III, as Emperor Francis I **Obv:** Bust right **Obv. Legend:** FRANCISCVS • D • G • R • I • S • A • ... **Rev:** Crowned double-headed eagle with crowned shield on breast, PISIS divides date below **Note:** Dav. #1507.

Date	Mintage	VG	F	VF	XF	Unc
1748	—	50.00	90.00	150	250	—
1749	—	50.00	90.00	150	250	—
1750	—	50.00	90.00	150	250	—
1753	—	50.00	90.00	150	250	—
1754	—	50.00	90.00	150	250	—
1755	—	50.00	90.00	150	250	—
1756	—	50.00	90.00	150	250	—
1758	—	50.00	90.00	150	250	—

C# 8d FRANCESCONE (10 Paoli)

27.5000 g., 0.9170 Silver 0.8107 oz. ASW **Ruler:** Francesco III, as Emperor Francis I **Obv:** Bust right **Obv. Legend:** FRANCISCVS • D • G • R • I • S • A • ... **Rev:** Crowned double-headed eagle with crowned shield on breast **Note:** Dav. #1505A.

Date	Mintage	VG	F	VF	XF	Unc
1765	—	60.00	80.00	100	200	—

C# 21 FRANCESCONE (10 Paoli)

27.5000 g., 0.9170 Silver 0.8107 oz. ASW **Ruler:** Pietro Leopoldo, as Emperor Leopold II **Obv:** Bust right **Rev:** Crowned narrow oval arms **Note:** Dav. #1508.

Date	Mintage	VG	F	VF	XF	Unc
1765	—	100	165	275	475	—
1766	—	100	165	275	475	—

C# 21a FRANCESCONE (10 Paoli)

27.5000 g., 0.9170 Silver 0.8107 oz. ASW **Ruler:** Pietro Leopoldo **Obv:** Bust right **Obv. Legend:** PETRVS LEOPOLDVS • .... **Rev:** Crowned ornate shield **Rev. Legend:** DIRIGEDOM.... **Note:** Dav. #1509.

Date	Mintage	VG	F	VF	XF	Unc
1766	—	100	165	275	475	—

C# 21b FRANCESCONE (10 Paoli)

27.5000 g., 0.9170 Silver 0.8107 oz. ASW **Ruler:** Pietro Leopoldo **Obv:** Bust right **Obv. Legend:** PETRVS LEOPOLDVS..... **Rev:** Crowned ornate shield **Rev. Legend:** DIRIG..... **Note:** Dav. #1510.

Date	Mintage	VG	F	VF	XF	Unc
1766	—	50.00	90.00	150	250	—
1767	—	50.00	90.00	150	250	—
1768	—	50.00	90.00	150	250	—
1769	—	50.00	90.00	150	250	—
1770	—	50.00	90.00	150	250	—
1771	—	50.00	90.00	150	250	—

C# 22 FRANCESCONE (10 Paoli)

27.5000 g., 0.9170 Silver 0.8107 oz. ASW **Ruler:** Pietro Leopoldo **Obv:** Bust left **Obv. Legend:** PETRVS LEOPOLDVS D • G • .... **Rev:** Crowned ornate shield **Note:** Dav. #1511.

Date	Mintage	VG	F	VF	XF	Unc
1767	—	55.00	100	165	285	—
1768	—	55.00	100	165	285	—

C# 23.1 FRANCESCONE (10 Paoli)

27.5000 g., 0.9170 Silver 0.8107 oz. ASW **Ruler:** Pietro Leopoldo **Obv:** Larger legend lettering **Note:** Dav. #1512.

Date	Mintage	VG	F	VF	XF	Unc
1769	—	200	350	600	1,000	—

C# 23.2 FRANCESCONE (10 Paoli)

28.2500 g., 0.9170 Silver 0.8328 oz. ASW **Ruler:** Pietro Leopoldo **Obv:** Bust right, smaller legend lettering **Obv. Legend:** P • LEOP • D • G • .... **Rev:** Crowned shield with spikes **Note:** For use in the Levant States. Dav. #1513.

Date	Mintage	VG	F	VF	XF	Unc
1769 LSF	—	140	240	400	750	—
1773 LSF	—	140	240	400	750	—
1774 LSF	—	140	240	400	750	—

C# 24.1 FRANCESCONE (10 Paoli)

27.5000 g., 0.9170 Silver 0.8107 oz. ASW **Ruler:** Pietro Leopoldo **Obv:** Bust right **Obv. Legend:** P • L E O P O L D V S • D • G • .... **Rev:** Crowned shield with spikes in order chain **Note:** Dav. #1514.

Date	Mintage	VG	F	VF	XF	Unc
1771	—	60.00	100	165	275	—
1772	—	60.00	100	165	275	—
1773	—	60.00	100	165	275	—
1774	—	60.00	100	165	275	—
1775	—	60.00	100	165	275	—
1776	—	60.00	100	165	275	—
1777	—	60.00	100	165	275	—

C# 24.2 FRANCESCONE (10 Paoli)

27.5000 g., 0.9170 Silver 0.8107 oz. ASW **Ruler:** Pietro Leopoldo **Obv:** Small high-collared bust **Note:** Varieties exist. Dav. #1515.

Date	Mintage	VG	F	VF	XF	Unc
1777	—	60.00	100	165	275	—
1778	—	60.00	100	165	275	—
1779	—	60.00	100	165	275	—
1780	—	60.00	100	165	275	—
1781	—	60.00	100	165	275	—
1782	—	60.00	100	165	275	—

C# 24.3 FRANCESCONE (10 Paoli)

27.5000 g., 0.9170 Silver 0.8107 oz. ASW **Ruler:** Pietro Leopoldo **Obv:** Bust right, head breaks legend **Obv. Legend:** P • L E O P O L D V S • D • G .... **Rev:** Crowned shield with spikes in order chain **Note:** Dav. #1516.

Date	Mintage	VG	F	VF	XF	Unc
1783	—	60.00	100	165	275	—
1784	—	60.00	100	165	275	—
1785	—	60.00	100	165	275	—
1786	—	60.00	100	165	275	—

C# 24.4 FRANCESCONE (10 Paoli)

27.5000 g., 0.9170 Silver 0.8107 oz. ASW **Ruler:** Pietro Leopoldo **Obv:** Smaller bust **Note:** Dav. #1517.

Date	Mintage	VG	F	VF	XF	Unc
1785	—	60.00	100	165	275	—
1786	—	60.00	100	165	275	—

C# 24.5 FRANCESCONE (10 Paoli)

27.5000 g., 0.9170 Silver 0.8107 oz. ASW **Ruler:** Pietro Leopoldo **Obv:** Bust right, larger continuous lettering **Obv. Legend:** P • L E O P O L D V S • D • G .... **Rev:** Crowned shield with spikes in order chain **Note:** Dav. #1518.

Date	Mintage	VG	F	VF	XF	Unc
1786	—	60.00	100	165	275	—
1787	—	60.00	100	165	275	—
1789	—	60.00	100	165	275	—
1790	—	60.00	100	165	275	—

C# 24.6 FRANCESCONE (10 Paoli)

27.5000 g., 0.9170 Silver 0.8107 oz. ASW **Ruler:** Pietro Leopoldo **Obv:** Smaller legend lettering, modified bust **Obv. Legend:** P • LEOPOLDVS • D • G • .... **Rev:** Crowned shield with spikes in order chain **Note:** Dav. #1518A.

Date	Mintage	VG	F	VF	XF	Unc
1790	—	60.00	100	165	275	—

C# 26 FRANCESCONE (10 Paoli)

27.5000 g., 0.9170 Silver 0.8107 oz. ASW **Ruler:** Pietro Leopoldo, as Emperor Leopold II **Obv:** Bust right **Obv. Legend:** LEOPOLDVS • II • D • G • ... **Rev:** Crowned arms with supporters **Note:** Dav. #1519.

Date	Mintage	VG	F	VF	XF	Unc
1790	—	200	300	500	850	—

C# 25 FRANCESCONE (10 Paoli)

27.5000 g., 0.9170 Silver 0.8107 oz. ASW **Ruler:** Pietro Leopoldo, as Emperor Leopold II **Obv:** Bust right **Obv. Legend:** LEOPOLDVS • II • D • G • H • ... **Rev:** Crowned double-headed eagle with 2 small crowns on shield on breast **Note:** Dav. #1520.

Date	Mintage	VG	F	VF	XF	Unc
1790	—	225	350	550	900	—

C# 37 FRANCESCONE (10 Paoli)

27.5000 g., 0.9170 Silver 0.8107 oz. ASW **Ruler:** Ferdinando III **Obv:** Head right **Obv. Legend:** F E R D I N A N D V S • III • D • G • .... **Rev:** Crowned shield with spikes in order chain **Note:** Dav. #1521.

Date	Mintage	VG	F	VF	XF	Unc
1791	—	25.00	50.00	100	200	—
1792	—	25.00	50.00	100	200	—
1793	—	25.00	50.00	100	200	—
1794	—	25.00	50.00	100	200	—
1795	—	25.00	50.00	100	200	—
1796	—	25.00	50.00	100	200	—
1797	—	25.00	50.00	100	200	—
1798	—	25.00	50.00	100	200	—
1799	—	25.00	50.00	100	200	—
1800	—	25.00	50.00	100	200	—
1801	—	40.00	90.00	150	250	—

FR# 313 SCUDO D'ORO

3.5000 g., 0.9860 Gold 0.1109 oz. AGW **Obv:** Spade-shaped arms **Rev:** Ornate cross in inner circle **Note:** Struck at Florence.

Date	Mintage	VG	F	VF	XF	Unc
ND	—	—	—	—	—	—

FR# 329 1/2 FLORINO

Gold **Ruler:** Giovanni Gaston **Obv:** Fleur-de-lis **Rev:** St. John the Baptist

Date	Mintage	VG	F	VF	XF	Unc
1726	—	800	1,600	3,250	6,000	—

FR# 326 FLORINO

Gold **Ruler:** Cosimo III **Rev:** St. John the Baptist

Date	Mintage	VG	F	VF	XF	Unc
1712	—	100	175	300	550	—
1713	—	100	175	300	550	—
1714	—	100	175	300	550	—
1718	—	100	175	300	550	—
1719	—	100	175	300	550	—
1720	—	100	175	300	550	—
1721	—	100	175	300	550	—
1722	—	100	175	300	550	—
1723	—	100	175	300	550	—

FR# 328 FLORINO

Gold **Ruler:** Giovanni Gaston **Obv:** Fleur-de-lis **Obv. Legend:** IOAN • GASTO • I • .... **Rev:** Seated figure **Rev. Legend:** S • I O A N N E S • B A ....

Date	Mintage	VG	F	VF	XF	Unc
1723	—	100	175	300	550	—
1724	—	100	175	300	550	—
1725	—	100	175	300	550	—
1726	—	100	175	300	550	—
1727	—	100	175	300	550	—
1728	—	100	175	300	550	—
1729	—	100	175	300	550	—
1731	—	100	175	300	550	—
1732	—	100	175	300	550	—
1733	—	100	175	300	550	—
1734	—	100	175	300	550	—
1735	—	100	175	300	550	—
1736	—	100	175	300	550	—

C# 9 UNGHERO

3.5000 g., 0.9860 Gold 0.1109 oz. AGW **Ruler:** Francesco III **Obv:** Head right **Obv. Legend:** FRANC • III • D • G • LOTH • ... **Rev:** Crowned oval shield with center shield, within sprigs

Date	Mintage	VG	F	VF	XF	Unc
1738	—	1,000	3,000	6,000	10,000	—
1741	—	1,000	3,000	6,000	10,000	—

C# 10 ZECCHINO

3.4880 g., 0.9990 Gold 0.1120 oz. AGW **Ruler:** Francesco III **Obv:** Fleur-de-lis **Rev:** St. John the Baptist seated

Date	Mintage	VG	F	VF	XF	Unc
1737	—	125	200	275	450	—
1738	—	125	200	275	450	—
1739	—	125	200	275	450	—
1741	—	125	200	275	450	—
1742	—	125	200	275	450	—
1743	—	125	200	275	450	—

C# 27 ZECCHINO

3.4880 g., 0.9990 Gold 0.1120 oz. AGW **Ruler:** Pietro Leopoldo **Obv:** Fleur-de-lis **Obv. Legend:** P • L E O P O L D V S • .... **Rev:** Seated figure **Rev. Legend:** • S • I O A N N E S • ....

Date	Mintage	VG	F	VF	XF	Unc
1779	—	125	175	250	400	—
1780	—	125	175	250	400	—

Date	Mintage	VG	F	VF	XF	Unc
1787	—	125	175	250	400	—
1788	—	125	175	250	400	—
1789	—	125	175	250	400	—

C# 38 ZECCHINO

3.4880 g., 0.9990 Gold 0.1120 oz. AGW **Ruler:** Pietro Leopoldo, as Emperor Leopold II

Date	Mintage	VG	F	VF	XF	Unc
1791	—	150	175	250	400	—
1792	—	150	175	250	400	—

FR# 325 RUSPONE (3 Zecchini)

10.4640 g., 0.9990 Gold 0.3361 oz. AGW **Ruler:** Cosimo III **Obv:** Fleur-de-lis **Obv. Legend:** C O S M V S • III • D • G • M • D V X ..... **Rev:** Seated figure **Rev. Legend:** S • I O A N N E S B A P T I S T A • **Note:** Struck at Florence Mint.

Date	Mintage	VG	F	VF	XF	Unc
1719	—	500	1,000	3,000	6,000	—

FR# 327 RUSPONE (3 Zecchini)

10.4640 g., 0.9990 Gold 0.3361 oz. AGW **Ruler:** Giovanni Gaston

Date	Mintage	VG	F	VF	XF	Unc
1724	—	500	1,000	3,000	5,000	—

C# 11 RUSPONE (3 Zecchini)

10.4640 g., 0.9990 Gold 0.3361 oz. AGW **Ruler:** Francesco III **Obv:** Fleur-de-lis **Obv. Legend:** "AS GRAND DUKE" **Rev:** St. John the Baptist seated

Date	Mintage	VG	F	VF	XF	Unc
1743	—	200	325	600	1,250	—
1744	—	200	325	600	1,250	—
1745	—	200	325	600	1,250	—

C# 11a RUSPONE (3 Zecchini)

10.4640 g., 0.9990 Gold 0.3361 oz. AGW **Ruler:** Francesco III, as Emperor Francis I **Obv:** Legend as emperor, fleur-de-lis **Obv. Legend:** F R A N C I S V S • D • G • .... **Rev:** St. John the Baptist, seated **Rev. Legend:** • S • I O A N N E S B A P T I S T A •

Date	Mintage	VG	F	VF	XF	Unc
1746	—	200	250	400	850	—
1748	—	200	250	400	850	—
1749	—	200	250	400	850	—
1750	—	200	250	400	850	—
1752	—	200	250	400	850	—
1753	—	200	250	400	850	—
1754	—	200	250	400	850	—
1756	—	200	250	400	850	—
1757	—	200	250	400	850	—
1758	—	200	250	400	850	—
1759	—	200	250	400	850	—
1760	—	200	250	400	850	—
1761	—	200	250	400	850	—
1763	—	200	250	400	850	—
1764	—	200	250	400	850	—

C# 28 RUSPONE (3 Zecchini)

10.4640 g., 0.9990 Gold 0.3361 oz. AGW **Ruler:** Pietro Leopoldo **Obv:** Fleur-de-lis **Obv. Legend:** P • L E O P O L D V S • D • G • A • A • M • D • E T R **Rev:** St. John the Baptist, seated **Rev. Legend:** S • I O A N N E S B A P T I S T A •

Date	Mintage	VG	F	VF	XF	Unc
1765	—	200	300	400	850	—
1766	—	200	300	400	850	—
1768	—	200	300	400	850	—
1769	—	200	300	400	850	—
1770	—	200	300	400	850	—
1771	—	200	300	400	850	—
1772	—	200	300	400	850	—
1773	—	200	300	400	850	—
1774	—	200	300	400	850	—
1775	—	200	300	400	850	—
1776	—	200	300	400	850	—
1777	—	200	300	400	850	—
1778	—	200	300	400	850	—
1779	—	200	300	400	850	—
1780	—	200	300	400	850	—
1781	—	200	300	400	850	—
1782	—	200	300	400	850	—
1783	—	200	300	400	850	—
1784	—	200	300	400	850	—
1786	—	200	300	400	850	—
1787	—	200	300	400	850	—
1789	—	200	300	400	850	—
1790	—	200	300	400	850	—

C# 28a RUSPONE (3 Zecchini)

10.4640 g., 0.9990 Gold 0.3361 oz. AGW **Ruler:** Pietro Leopoldo, as Emperor Leopold II **Obv:** Fleur-de-lis **Obv. Legend:** LEOPOLDUS II D • G • H • **Rev:** St. John the Baptist, seated

Date	Mintage	VG	F	VF	XF	Unc
1790	—	300	450	650	1,200	—

C# 28b RUSPONE (3 Zecchini)

10.4640 g., 0.9990 Gold 0.3361 oz. AGW **Ruler:** Pietro Leopoldo, as Emperor Leopold II **Obv:** Fleur-de-lis **Obv. Legend:** LEOPOLDUS II D • G • R • I • **Rev:** St. John the Baptist, seated

Date	Mintage	VG	F	VF	XF	Unc
1790	—	250	400	600	1,100	—

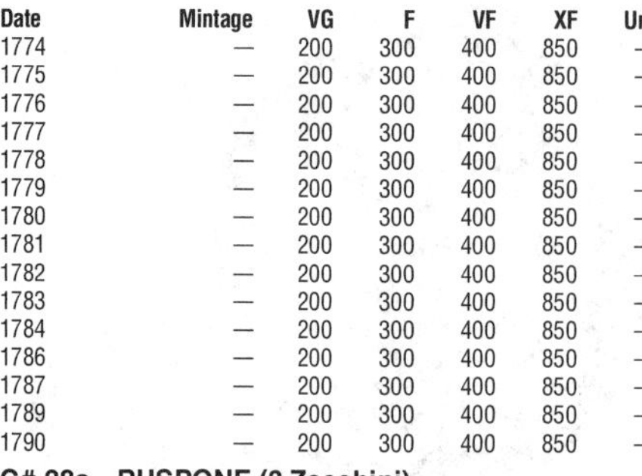

C# 39 RUSPONE (3 Zecchini)

10.4610 g., 0.9990 Gold 0.3360 oz. AGW **Ruler:** Ferdinando III **Obv:** Fleur-de-lis **Obv. Legend:** FERDINANDVS • III • ... **Rev:** St. John the Baptist, seated **Rev. Legend:** S • IOANNES BAPTISTA

Date	Mintage	VG	F	VF	XF	Unc
1791	—	400	800	1,250	2,000	—
1793	—	400	800	1,250	2,000	—
1794	—	400	800	1,250	2,000	—
1796	—	400	800	1,250	2,000	—
1797	—	400	800	1,250	2,000	—
1798	—	400	800	1,250	2,000	—
1799	—	400	800	1,250	2,000	—
1800	—	400	800	1,250	2,000	—

FR# 323 DOPPIA

7.0000 g., 0.9860 Gold 0.2219 oz. AGW **Ruler:** Cosimo III **Obv:** Crowned arms **Obv. Legend:** COSMVS III... **Rev:** Ornate cross **Note:** Struck at Florence Mint.

Date	Mintage	VG	F	VF	XF	Unc
1711	—	600	1,200	2,500	4,000	—
1716	—	600	1,200	2,500	4,000	—

VASTO

Vasto was given to a member of the Avalo(s) family by Alphonso V of Aragon. Don Cesare was created a prince of the Empire by Leopold I in 1704, and was given the mint privilege. He coined only in 1706-07. In 1806, Vasto was incorporated into the Two Sicilies.

RULER

Cesare D'Avalos, 1704-1729

PRINCIPALITY

STANDARD COINAGE

KM# 5 1/2 TALLERO

Silver **Ruler:** Cesare D'Avalos **Obv:** Bust right **Rev:** Crowned arms in elaborate frame

Date	Mintage	Good	VG	F	VF	XF
1706	—	—	450	950	1,750	2,800

DAV# 1523 TALLERO

Silver **Ruler:** Cesare D'Avalos **Obv:** Bust right **Rev:** Crowned arms in elaborate frame

Date	Mintage	Good	VG	F	VF	XF
1706	—	—	650	1,350	2,500	4,000

FR# 1214 1/2 ZECCHINO

1.7500 g., 0.9860 Gold 0.0555 oz. AGW **Ruler:** Cesare D'Avalos **Obv:** Bust right **Rev:** Crowned ornate arms

Date	Mintage	Good	VG	F	VF	XF
1707	—	—	700	1,500	2,500	4,000

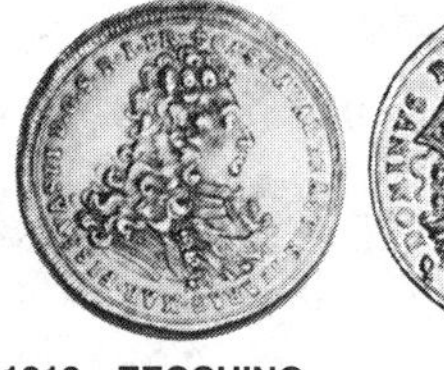

FR# 1213 ZECCHINO

3.5000 g., 0.9860 Gold 0.1109 oz. AGW **Ruler:** Cesare D'Avalos **Obv:** Bust right **Rev:** Crowned ornate arms in order chain

Date	Mintage	Good	VG	F	VF	XF
1706	—	—	1,000	2,000	3,500	7,000

VENICE

Venezia

A seaport of Venetia was founded by refugees from the Hun invasions. From that time until the arrival of Napoleon in 1797, it maintained an enormous foreign trade involving the possession of many islands in the Mediterranean while keeping a state of quasi-independence despite the antagonism of jealous Italian states and the Ottoman Turks. During the French Occupation Napoleon handed it over to Austria. Later, upon the defeat of the Austrians by Prussia in 1860, Venice then became a part of the United Kingdom of Italy.

RULERS

Alois Mocenigo II, 1700-1709
John Corner II, 1709-1722
Alois Mocenigo III, 1722-1732
Charles Ruzzini, 1732-1735
Alois Pisani, 1735-1741
Peter Grimani, 1741-1752
Francesco Loredano, 1752-1762
Marco Foscarini, 1762-1763
Alviso Mocenigo IV, 1763-1778
Paolo Renier, 1779-1789
Lodovico Manin, 1789-1797
Franz II (of Austria) 1798-1806

MINT MARKS

A - Vienna
F - Hall
V - Venice
ZV - Zecca Venezia - Venice
None - Venice

MINT OFFICIALS' INITIALS FOR SILVER

Initials	Dates	Name
AB	1751	Zan Alvise Barbaro
AB	1706-07	Lodovico (Alvise) Benzon
AB	1718-19	Alvise Bon
AB	1763, 1785-86	Andrea Bon
AC	1792-93	Antonio Cicogna

AD	1755	Antonio Diedo
AD	1739	Anzolo Dolfin
AM	1719	Anzolo Malipiero
AM	1714-15	Alvise Minotto
AMP	1775-76	Anzolo Maria Priuli
AM3	1737	Anzolo Terzo Memmo
AO	1785	Anzolo Orio
AP	1718	Alvise Pizzamano
AS	1738	Alessandro Semitecolo
BC	1769-70; 78-79	Benetto Capello
BC2o, BC	1705	Benetto Civran
BG	1727-29	Benetto Grimani
BG GB	1705-06	Bernardo Gritti
BV	1731	Benetto Valier
BZ	1733	Bortolomio Zen
CB	1713-14	Cornelio Badoer
DB	1793-94	Daniele Balbi
DD	1715	Domenego Diedo
DG	1762-63; 1767	Domenego Gritti
DT	1781-82	Domenego Trevisan
FAB	1758-59	Francesco Antonio Bonlini
FAF	1742-43	Francesco Antonio Foscarini
FAP	1709	Francesco Antonio Paruta
FAP	1717-18	Francesco Antonio Pasqualigo
FB	1796	Francesco Barbaro
FD	1784-85	Fantin Dandolo
FD	1782-83	Francesco Dandolo
FMR	1786	Francesco Maria Rizzi
FP	1741	Francesco Pasqualigo
FT	1755-56	Francesco Trevisan
FZ	1795-96	Francesco Zane
GAC	1751-52	Giacomo Antonio Contarini
GAF	1772-73	Giacomo Anzolo Foscarini
GAS	1759-60	Gerolamo Antonio Soranzo
GB	1699-1701	Gerolamo Barbaro
GB	1756-57	Gerolamo Bonlini
GD	1749	Gerolamo Dona
GF	1706	Gerolamo Falier
GF	1786-87	Gerolamo Foscarini
GF	1788-89	Giacomo Foscarini
GM	1703-05	Giulio Minotto
GMB	1773-74	Giustiniano Maria Badoer
GP	1773	Giacomo Pasqualigo
GTS	1701-02	Gian Tommaso Soranzo
GZ	1730	Gerolamo Zolio
HAL	1707-09	Gerolamo Antonio Lombardo
LAF	1777-78	Lunardo Alvise Foscarini
LB	1774-75	Lorenzo Bonlini
LM	1709-10	Lorenzo Marcello
LM II	1747-48	Lodovico Morosini II
MAB	1710-11	Marc' Antonio Bon
MAT	1771-72	Marc' Antonio Trevisan
MB	1790	Maffio Badoer
MB	1717	Marin Bembo
MD	1711-13	Marc'Antonio Dolfin
MF	1763-64	Marchio Foscarini
MS	1764-66	Mario Soranzo
MS	1735	Michiel Soranzo
NB	1723	Nicolo Bembo
NMB	1742	Nicolo Maria Bembo
NP	1770-71	Nicolo Pisani
PAB	1792	Pier Antonio Bembo
PAB, PB	1766-67	Pier Alvise Barbaro
PAT	1725	Pier Antonio Trevisan
PB, BP	1702-03	Piero Basadonna
PD	1703	Piero Diedo
PD	1745; 1776-77	Piero Dona
PM	1701	Pietro Magno
PM	1702	Piero Manolesso
PM	1707	Piero Morosini
PP	1759	Piero Pasta
PQ	1726	Piero Querini
RB	1780	Rizzardo Balbi
RB	1779-80	Raimondo Bembo
RB, RBP	1768-69	Rizzardo Balbi
SB	1753	Stefano Barbaro
VAAM	1721	Vettor Antonio Alvise Marcello
VAB	1769	Vincenzo Antonio Bragadin
VAC	1754-55	Ulisse Antonio Corner
VETM	1761-62	Vettor Morosini
VL	1743-45	Vincenzo Longo
VQ	1722	Vincenzo Querini
VS	1777	Valerio Soranzo
VV	1775	Valerio Valier
VV	1729	Vincenzo Vanaxel
ZAMB	1746	Zan Alvise Maria Dona
ZAMD	1746	Zan Alvise Maria Dona
ZAP	1746-47	Zan Andrea Pasqualigo
ZB	1750-51	Zuane Balbi
ZBV	1711	Zuane Bortolomio Vitturi
ZD	1761	Zuane Dolfin
ZF	1734	Zorzi Foscolo
ZM	1781	Zan Francesco Moro

MINT OFFICIALS' INITIALS FOR GOLD

Initials	Dates	Name
AB	1761-62	Antonio Boldu
AC	1786-87	Alvise Corner
AF	1779-81	Alvise Foscarini
GC	1734	Gerolamo Cicogna
GP	1762	Giulio Pasqualigo
IP	1751-53	Iseppo Pizzamano
IP	1708-09	Iseppo Priuli
Mac	1740-49	Marc' Antonio Gritti
MAT	1722	Marc' Antonio Trevisan
NC	1787-89	Nicolo Corner
NP	1778	Nicolo Pizzamano
VD	1731	Vincenzo Dona
ZAB	1793-94	Zan Andrea Bonlini
ZD	1789-90	Zuanne Diedo
ZDL	1747-48	Zan Domenego Loredan

MONETARY SYSTEM

6 Denari = 1 Bezzo
12 Denari = 1 Soldo
20 Soldi = 1 Lira
30 Soldi = 1 Lirazza
124 Soldi = 1 Ducatone = 1 Ducato
140 Soldi = 1 Scudo = 1 Tallero = 1 Zecchino
160 Soldi = 1 Scudo
2 Scudi = 1 Doppia

WEIGHTS

Zechhino = 3.45 g
Doppia = 6.90 g

NOTE: Venice struck many types of gold coins using billon or silver coinage dies. They also struck many denominations from the same dies, so it is most important to check the weight to determine the proper denomination.

DIE VARIETIES

Throughout this series there is great variety in the abbreviation within the legends while various stars, dots, colons, diamonds, rosettes and other devices were used in separating them.

CITY

OCCUPATION COINAGE

C# 160 MEZZA (1/2) LIRA

2.2000 g., 0.2500 Silver 0.0177 oz. ASW **Ruler:** Franz II of Austria **Obv:** Crowned double-headed eagle, FII in circle on breast **Rev:** Written value and date within wreath **Note:** Two varieties exist. Overstruck on Austria 6 Kruezer, KM#2127.

Date	Mintage	VG	F	VF	XF	Unc
1800	—	12.50	25.00	90.00	245	—

C# 161 UNA (1) LIRA

5.3000 g., 0.2500 Silver 0.0426 oz. ASW **Ruler:** Franz II of Austria **Obv:** Crowned double-headed eagle, FII in circle on breast **Obv. Legend:** PROVINCIALE IMP • VENETA MONETA **Rev:** Written value and date within wreath

Date	Mintage	VG	F	VF	XF	Unc
1800V	—	20.00	40.00	100	260	—

Note: Overstruck on Austria 12 Kreuzer, KM#2137

C# 166 ZECCHINO

3.4900 g., 0.9870 Gold 0.1107 oz. AGW **Ruler:** Franz II of Austria **Obv:** St. Mark , Doge **Obv. Legend:** FRANC• II• S• M• VENET **Rev:** Imperial eagle **Rev. Legend:** SIT• T• XPE• DAT• Q• TV REGIS• ISTE• DVCA

Date	Mintage	VG	F	VF	XF	Unc
ND(1798-1806)	—	200	500	1,550	2,850	—

C# 166a ZECCHINO

3.4900 g., 0.9870 Gold 0.1107 oz. AGW **Ruler:** Franz II of Austria **Obv:** Christ holding orb

Date	Mintage	VG	F	VF	XF	Unc
ND(1798-1806)	—	200	500	1,550	2,850	—

PROVISIONAL GOVERNMENT

1797-1798

PROVISIONAL COINAGE

C# 155 DIECI (10) LIRE

28.4700 g., 0.8260 Silver 0.7560 oz. ASW **Obv:** ZECCA V below Liberty **Obv. Legend:** LIBERTA ... **Rev:** Written value within wreath **Note:** Dav. #1576.

Date	Mintage	VG	F	VF	XF	Unc
1797 AS	—	60.00	100	175	400	—
1.797 AS	—	60.00	100	175	400	—

C# 155a DIECI (10) LIRE

28.4700 g., 0.8260 Silver 0.7560 oz. ASW **Obv:** Z V below liberty **Obv. Legend:** LIBERTAD ... **Rev:** Written value within wreath, date below **Rev. Legend:** ANNO I DELLA LIBERTA ITALIANA **Note:** Dav. #1577.

Date	Mintage	VG	F	VF	XF	Unc
1797	—	65.00	110	185	425	—

C# 155b DIECI (10) LIRE

28.4700 g., 0.8260 Silver 0.7560 oz. ASW **Obv:** ZECCA V below Liberty **Rev:** Written value within wreath, date below **Note:** Mule. Dav. #1576A.

Date	Mintage	VG	F	VF	XF	Unc
1797	—	—	—	—	—	—

REPUBLIC

STANDARD COINAGE

C# 1 6 DENARI (Bezzo)

Billon **Obv:** Winged lion, kneeling figure above value **Obv. Legend:** F R A N C • L A V R E D * * S • M • V • **Rev:** Standing Saint, facing **Rev. Legend:** * D E F E N S • N O S T E R *

Date	Mintage	VG	F	VF	XF	Unc
ND(1752-62)	—	3.00	5.00	15.00	35.00	—

C# 84 6 DENARI (Bezzo)

Billon **Obv:** Legend around figures, value **Obv. Legend:** S. M. V. PAVL RAINER **Rev:** Standing Saint, facing **Rev. Legend:** DEFENS NOSTER

Date	Mintage	VG	F	VF	XF	Unc
ND(1779-89)	—	3.00	5.00	15.00	35.00	—

C# 2 12 DENARI (Soldo)

Billon **Obv:** Winged lion, kneeling figure above value **Obv. Legend:** FRANC • .... **Rev:** Standing Saint, facing **Rev. Legend:** * D E F E N S • N O S T E R *

Date	Mintage	VG	F	VF	XF	Unc
ND(1752-62)	—	3.00	5.00	15.00	35.00	—

C# 26 12 DENARI (Soldo)

Billon **Obv:** Winged lion, kneeling figure above value **Obv. Legend:** S • M • V • M • FOSCARENVS **Rev:** Standing Saint, facing **Rev. Legend:** * D E F E N S • N O S T E R *

Date	Mintage	VG	F	VF	XF	Unc
ND(1762-63)	—	3.00	5.00	15.00	35.00	—

C# 49 12 DENARI (Soldo)

Billon **Obv:** Winged lion, kneeling figure above value **Obv. Legend:** S • M • V • ALOY... **Rev:** Standing Saint, facing **Rev. Legend:** * D E F E N S • N O S T E R *

Date	Mintage	VG	F	VF	XF	Unc
ND(1763-78)	—	3.00	5.00	12.00	30.00	—

C# 85.1 12 DENARI (Soldo)

Billon **Obv:** Winged lion, kneeling figure above value **Obv. Legend:** S • M • V • PAVL • RAIN • **Rev:** Standing Saint, facing **Rev. Legend:** * D E F E N S • N O S T E R *

Date	Mintage	VG	F	VF	XF	Unc
ND(1779-89)	—	2.50	4.00	10.00	25.00	—

C# 85.2 12 DENARI (Soldo)

Billon **Obv:** Winged lion, kneeling figure above value **Obv. Legend:** S• M• V• PAVL• RAINER• **Rev:** Standing Saint, facing **Rev. Legend:** * D E F E N S • N O S T E R *

Date	Mintage	VG	F	VF	XF	Unc
ND(1779-89)	—	2.50	4.00	10.00	25.00	—

C# 118 12 DENARI (Soldo)

Billon **Obv:** Winged lion, kneeling figure above value **Obv. Legend:** S • M • V • LVDO • MANIN • **Rev:** Standing Saint, facing **Rev. Legend:** * D E F E N S • • N O S T E R *

Date	Mintage	VG	F	VF	XF	Unc
ND(1789-97)	—	30.00	50.00	100	200	—

C# 3 (5 SOLDI)

1.2400 g., Silver **Ruler:** Francesco Loredano **Obv:** Winged lion above date **Obv. Legend:** S • M • V • FRANC • LAVREDANO **Rev:** Seated crowned Justice flanked by lion heads **Rev. Legend:** IVDICIVM RECTVM *

Date	Mintage	VG	F	VF	XF	Unc
1752	—	5.00	10.00	20.00	30.00	—

C# 27 (5 SOLDI)

1.2400 g., Silver **Ruler:** Marco Foscarini **Obv:** Winged lion above date **Obv. Legend:** S • M • V • MARC • FOSCARENVS • **Rev:** Seated crowned Justice flanked by lion heads **Rev. Legend:** IVDICIVM RECTVM *

Date	Mintage	VG	F	VF	XF	Unc
1762	—	25.00	50.00	85.00	125	—

C# 50 (5 SOLDI)

0.9000 Silver **Ruler:** Alviso Mocenigo IV **Obv:** Winged lion above date **Obv. Legend:** S • M • V • ALOY MOCENI • **Rev:** Seated crowned Justice flanked by lion heads **Rev. Legend:** IVDICVM RECTVM •

Date	Mintage	VG	F	VF	XF	Unc
1763	—	5.00	10.00	20.00	30.00	—
1777	—	5.00	10.00	20.00	30.00	—

C# 86.1 (5 SOLDI)

0.9000 Silver **Ruler:** Alviso Mocenigo IV **Obv:** Winged lion above date **Obv. Legend:** S • M • V • PAVL • RAINERIVS • **Rev:** Seated crowned Justice flanked by lion heads **Rev. Legend:** IVDICVM RECTVM

Date	Mintage	VG	F	VF	XF	Unc
1778	—	5.00	10.00	20.00	30.00	—

C# 86.2 (5 SOLDI)

0.9000 Silver **Ruler:** Alviso Mocenigo IV **Obv:** Winged lion above date **Rev:** Seated crowned Justice flanked by lion heads **Rev. Legend:** IVDICVM RECTVM

Date	Mintage	VG	F	VF	XF	Unc
1778	—	5.00	10.00	20.00	30.00	—

C# 86.3 (5 SOLDI)

0.9000 Silver **Ruler:** Alviso Mocenigo IV **Obv:** Winged lion above date **Rev:** Seated crowned Justice flanked by lion heads **Rev. Legend:** IVDIVM RECTVM

Date	Mintage	VG	F	VF	XF	Unc
1778	—	5.00	10.00	20.00	30.00	—

C# 119.1 (5 SOLDI)

0.9000 Silver **Ruler:** Lodovico Manin **Obv:** Winged lion above date **Obv. Legend:** S • M • V • LVDO • MANIN • D • **Rev:** Seated crowned Justice flanked by lion heads **Rev. Legend:** IVDICIVM RECTVM

Date	Mintage	VG	F	VF	XF	Unc
1789	—	9.00	15.00	30.00	75.00	—
1797	—	9.00	15.00	30.00	75.00	—

C# 119.2 (5 SOLDI)

0.9000 Silver **Obv:** Winged lion above date **Rev:** Seated crowned Justice flanked by lion heads **Rev. Legend:** IVDICIV RECTVM

Date	Mintage	VG	F	VF	XF	Unc
1789	—	9.00	15.00	30.00	75.00	—

C# 119.3 (5 SOLDI)

0.9000 Silver **Ruler:** Lodovico Manin **Obv:** Winged lion above date **Obv. Legend:** S•M-V • LVDO... **Rev:** Seated crowned Justice flanked by lion heads

Date	Mintage	VG	F	VF	XF	Unc
1797	—	9.00	15.00	30.00	75.00	—

C# 4 (10 SOLDI)

2.4800 g., Silver **Ruler:** Francesco Loredano **Obv:** Kneeling figure above date **Obv. Legend:** FRANC • LAVREDANO • **Rev:** Winged lion above flower **Rev. Legend:** SANCT • MARCVS • VEN •

Date	Mintage	VG	F	VF	XF	Unc
1752	—	5.00	10.00	20.00	30.00	—

C# 28 (10 SOLDI)

2.4800 g., Silver **Ruler:** Marco Foscarini **Obv:** Kneeling figure above date **Obv. Legend:** MARC • FOSCARENVS • **Rev:** Winged lion above flower **Rev. Legend:** SANCT * MARCVS * VEN *

Date	Mintage	VG	F	VF	XF	Unc
1762	—	17.50	35.00	65.00	100	—

C# 51 (10 SOLDI)

0.9000 Silver, 21 mm. **Ruler:** Alviso Mocenigo IV **Obv:** Kneeling figure above date **Obv. Legend:** ALOY • MOCENI • D • **Rev:** Winged lion above flower **Rev. Legend:** SANCT * MARCVS * VEN *

Date	Mintage	VG	F	VF	XF	Unc
1763	—	5.00	10.00	15.00	30.00	—
1777	—	5.00	10.00	15.00	30.00	—

C# 87 (10 SOLDI)

0.9000 Silver, 21 mm. **Ruler:** Paolo Renier **Obv:** Kneeling figure above date **Obv. Legend:** PAVL • RAINERIVS • D **Rev:** Winged lion above flower **Rev. Legend:** SANCT * MARCVS * VEN * VS • D

Date	Mintage	VG	F	VF	XF	Unc
1778	—	5.00	10.00	15.00	30.00	—
1781	—	5.00	11.00	18.00	35.00	—

C# 120 (10 SOLDI)

0.9000 Silver, 21 mm. **Ruler:** Lodovico Manin **Obv:** Kneeling figure above date **Obv. Legend:** LVDO • MANIN • D • **Rev:** Winged lion above flower **Rev. Legend:** SANCT * MARCVS * VEN *

Date	Mintage	VG	F	VF	XF	Unc
1789	—	10.00	20.00	30.00	40.00	—
1791	—	10.00	20.00	30.00	40.00	—
1797	—	10.00	20.00	30.00	40.00	—

C# 5 (15 SOLDI)

3.7200 g., Silver **Ruler:** Francesco Loredano **Obv:** Kneeling figure above date **Obv. Legend:** FRANC • LAVREDANO • D • **Rev:** Winged lion above flowers **Rev. Legend:** SANCT * MARCVS * VEN *

Date	Mintage	VG	F	VF	XF	Unc
1752	—	8.00	12.00	20.00	50.00	—

C# 29 (15 SOLDI)

3.7200 g., Silver **Ruler:** Marco Foscarini **Obv:** Kneeling figure above date **Obv. Legend:** MARC • FOSCARENVS • D • **Rev:** Winged lion above flowers **Rev. Legend:** SANCT * MARCVS * VEN *

Date	Mintage	VG	F	VF	XF	Unc
1762	—	17.50	35.00	65.00	100	—

C# 52 (15 SOLDI)

3.7200 g., Silver **Ruler:** Alviso Mocenigo IV **Obv:** Kneeling figure above date **Obv. Legend:** ALOY : MOCENI : * D • **Rev:** Winged lion above flowers **Rev. Legend:** SANCT * MARCVS * VENET *

Date	Mintage	VG	F	VF	XF	Unc
1763	—	8.00	12.00	20.00	40.00	—
1777	—	8.00	12.00	20.00	40.00	—

C# 88 (15 SOLDI)

3.7200 g., Silver **Ruler:** Paolo Renier **Obv:** Kneeling figure above date **Obv. Legend:** PAUL • RAINERIVS • D **Rev:** Winged lion above flowers **Rev. Legend:** SANCT * MARCVS * VEN *

Date	Mintage	VG	F	VF	XF	Unc
1778	—	8.00	12.00	20.00	50.00	—
1781	—	6.00	8.50	20.00	75.00	—

C# 121 (15 SOLDI)

3.7200 g., Silver **Ruler:** Lodovico Manin **Obv:** Kneeling figure above date **Obv. Legend:** LVDO • MANIN • D • **Rev:** Winged lion above flowers **Rev. Legend:** SANCT * MARCVS * VEN *

Date	Mintage	VG	F	VF	XF	Unc
1789	—	10.00	15.00	30.00	50.00	—
Note: A variety exists in which 8 appears as 3.						
1791	—	10.00	15.00	30.00	50.00	—
1797	—	10.00	15.00	30.00	50.00	—

C# 10 15-1/2 SOLDI (1/8 Ducatone)

3.5129 g., 0.9480 Silver 0.1071 oz. ASW **Obv:** Winged lion, kneeling figure above GAC **Obv. Legend:** S • M • V • FRANC * LAVREDANO • D **Rev:** Standing figure, facing **Rev. Legend:** MEMOR • ERO • TVI • IVST • VIRGO

Date	Mintage	VG	F	VF	XF	Unc
ND(1752) GAC	—	8.00	15.00	30.00	75.00	—

C# 35 15-1/2 SOLDI (1/8 Ducatone)

3.5129 g., 0.9480 Silver 0.1071 oz. ASW **Obv:** Winged lion, kneeling figure above Z•D **Obv. Legend:** S • M • V • M * FOSCARENVS * D • **Rev:** Standing figure, facing above value **Rev. Legend:** MEMOR ERO TVI IVST VIRGO

Date	Mintage	VG	F	VF	XF	Unc
ND(1762) ZD	—	35.00	75.00	150	200	—

C# 58 15-1/2 SOLDI (1/8 Ducatone)

3.5129 g., 0.9480 Silver 0.1071 oz. ASW **Obv:** Winged lion, kneeling figure above D•G **Obv. Legend:** S • M • V • ALOY : MOCENI • * D • **Rev:** Standing figure, facing above value **Rev. Legend:** MEMOR*ERO*TVI*IVST*VIRGO

Date	Mintage	VG	F	VF	XF	Unc
ND(1763) DG	—	8.00	15.00	30.00	75.00	—

C# 94 15-1/2 SOLDI (1/8 Ducatone)

3.5129 g., 0.9480 Silver 0.1071 oz. ASW **Obv:** Winged lion, kneeling figure above L•A•F **Obv. Legend:** * S • M • V • PAVL * RAINER • D **Rev:** Standing figure, facing above value **Rev. Legend:** MEMOR • ERO • TVI • IVST • VIRGO

Date	Mintage	VG	F	VF	XF	Unc
ND(1779) LAF	—	9.00	17.00	35.00	75.00	—

C# 127 15-1/2 SOLDI (1/8 Ducatone)

3.5129 g., 0.9480 Silver 0.1071 oz. ASW **Obv:** Winged lion, kneeling figure above G•F **Obv. Legend:** S • M • V • LVDOVI • MANIN • D **Rev:** Standing figure, facing above value **Rev. Legend:** MEMOR • ERO • TVI • IVST • VIRGO

Date	Mintage	VG	F	VF	XF	Unc
ND(1789) GF	—	12.00	20.00	40.00	85.00	—

C# 6 17-1/2 SOLDI (1/8 Scudo)

3.9780 g., Silver **Obv:** Floral cross, leaves in angles, G•A•C below **Obv. Legend:** FRANC • LAVREDANO • DVX • VENET • **Rev:** Winged lion holding gospel in shield above value **Rev. Legend:** SANCT • MARCVS • VENET •

Date	Mintage	VG	F	VF	XF	Unc
ND(1752) GAC	—	9.00	15.00	25.00	75.00	—

C# 31 17-1/2 SOLDI (1/8 Scudo)

3.9780 g., Silver **Obv:** Floral cross, leaves in angles, Z D below **Obv. Legend:** MARC • FOSCARENVS • DVX • VENETIAR **Rev:** Winged lion holding gospel in shield above value **Rev. Legend:** SANCT • MARCVS • VENET •

Date	Mintage	VG	F	VF	XF	Unc
ND(1762) ZD	—	17.50	35.00	65.00	100	—

C# 54 17-1/2 SOLDI (1/8 Scudo)

3.9780 g., Silver **Obv:** Floral cross, leaves in angles, D•G below **Obv. Legend:** ALOY : MOCENICO • DVX • VENETIAR **Rev:** Winged lion holding gospel in shield above value **Rev. Legend:** SANCT • MARCVS • VENET •

Date	Mintage	VG	F	VF	XF	Unc
ND(1763) DG	—	9.00	15.00	25.00	75.00	—

C# 90.1 17-1/2 SOLDI (1/8 Scudo)

3.9780 g., Silver **Obv:** Floral cross, leaves in angles, LAF below **Obv. Legend:** PAVL RAINE DVX VENE **Rev:** Winged lion holding gospel in shield above value **Rev. Legend:** SANCT • MARCVS • VENET •

Date	Mintage	VG	F	VF	XF	Unc
ND(1779) LAF	—	6.00	10.00	20.00	65.00	—

C# 90.2 1/8 SCUDO (17-1/2 Soldi)

3.9780 g., Silver **Obv:** Floral cross, leaves in angles, LAF below **Obv. Legend:** PAUL... **Rev:** Winged lion holding gospel in shield above value **Rev. Legend:** SANCT • MARCVS • VENET •

Date	Mintage	VG	F	VF	XF	Unc
ND(1779) LAF	—	6.00	10.00	20.00	65.00	—

C# 123 1/8 SCUDO (17-1/2 Soldi)

3.9780 g., Silver **Obv:** Floral cross, leaves in angles, GF. below **Obv. Legend:** LUDOVIC MANIN DVX VENE **Rev:** Winged lion holding gospel in shield above value **Rev. Legend:** SANCT • MARCVS • VENET •

Date	Mintage	VG	F	VF	XF	Unc
ND(1789) GF	—	6.50	9.00	15.00	65.00	—

C# 30 30 SOLDI

7.4400 g., Silver **Ruler:** Marco Foscarini **Obv:** Large winged lion, facing **Obv. Legend:** SANTVS * MARCVS * VENETVS * **Rev:** Seated crowned Justice, facing, date below **Rev. Legend:** ...ITIAM DILIGITE *

Date	Mintage	VG	F	VF	XF	Unc
1762	—	12.00	20.00	40.00	100	—

C# 53 30 SOLDI

7.4400 g., Silver **Ruler:** Alviso Mocenigo IV **Obv:** Large winged lion, facing **Obv. Legend:** SANCTVS * MARCVS * VENETVS * **Rev:** Seated crowned Justice, facing, date below **Rev. Legend:** ...IAM DILIGITE *

Date	Mintage	VG	F	VF	XF	Unc
1767	—	6.00	10.00	20.00	75.00	—
1772	—	6.00	10.00	20.00	75.00	—
1777	—	6.00	10.00	20.00	75.00	—
1778	—	6.00	10.00	20.00	75.00	—

C# 89 30 SOLDI

7.4400 g., Silver **Ruler:** Paolo Renier **Obv:** Large winged lion, facing **Obv. Legend:** SANCTVS*MARCVS*VENETVS* **Rev:** Seated crowned Justice, facing, date below **Rev. Legend:** ...IAM DILIGIT * **Note:** Similar to C#53.

Date	Mintage	VG	F	VF	XF	Unc
1781	—	7.50	12.50	25.00	75.00	—
1784	—	7.50	12.50	25.00	75.00	—

C# 122.1 30 SOLDI

7.4400 g., Silver **Ruler:** Lodovico Manin **Obv:** Large winged lion, facing **Obv. Legend:** SANCTVS * MARCVS * VENETVS **Rev:** Seated crowned Justice, facing, date below **Rev. Legend:** ...IAM DILIGITE * **Note:** Similar to C#53.

Date	Mintage	VG	F	VF	XF	Unc
1789	—	6.00	10.00	20.00	40.00	—
1791	—	6.00	10.00	20.00	40.00	—
1796	—	6.00	10.00	20.00	40.00	—
1797	—	6.00	10.00	20.00	40.00	—

C# 122.2 30 SOLDI

7.4400 g., Silver **Ruler:** Lodovico Manin **Obv. Legend:** SANCTVS-MARCVS. VENET.

Date	Mintage	VG	F	VF	XF	Unc
1796	—	6.00	10.00	20.00	40.00	—

C# 14 QVAR (1/4) DUCATO

5.8500 g., 0.8264 Silver 0.1554 oz. ASW **Obv:** Seated Saint, kneeling figure above G•A•C **Obv. Legend:** S * M * V * FRANC * LAVREDANO **Rev:** Winged lion above flowers **Rev. Legend:** QVAR * DVCAT * VENET *

Date	Mintage	VG	F	VF	XF	Unc
ND(1752) GAC	—	6.00	10.00	20.00	75.00	—

C# 38 QVAR (1/4) DUCATO

5.8500 g., 0.8264 Silver 0.1554 oz. ASW **Obv:** Seated Saint, kneeling figure above Z•D **Obv. Legend:** S * M * V * MARC * FOSCAREN * D • **Rev:** Winged lion above flower and stars **Rev. Legend:** QVAR * DVCAT * VENETVS

Date	Mintage	VG	F	VF	XF	Unc
ND(1762) ZD	—	25.00	40.00	65.00	110	—

C# 62 QVAR (1/4) DUCATO

5.8500 g., 0.8264 Silver 0.1554 oz. ASW **Obv:** Seated Saint, kneeling figure **Obv. Legend:** S • M • V • ALOY : MOCENI • D • **Rev:** Winged lion **Note:** Legend varieties exist.

Date	Mintage	VG	F	VF	XF	Unc
ND(1763) DG	—	9.00	15.00	25.00	75.00	—
ND(1772-73) GAF	—	9.00	15.00	25.00	75.00	—
ND(1775) VV	—	9.00	15.00	25.00	75.00	—

C# 98 QVAR (1/4) DUCATO

5.8500 g., 0.8264 Silver 0.1554 oz. ASW **Obv:** Seated Saint, kneeling figure above A•C **Obv. Legend:** S • M • V • PAVL • RAINERIVS • D • **Rev:** Winged lion above flowers

Date	Mintage	VG	F	VF	XF	Unc
ND LAF	—	9.00	15.00	25.00	75.00	—
ND(1779) BC	—	9.00	15.00	25.00	75.00	—
ND(1779) RB	—	9.00	15.00	25.00	75.00	—
ND(1789) AC	—	9.00	15.00	25.00	75.00	—

C# 131 QVAR (1/4) DUCATO

5.8500 g., 0.8264 Silver 0.1554 oz. ASW **Obv:** Seated Saint, kneeling figure above G•F **Obv. Legend:** S • M • V • LVDOV • MAININ • D • **Rev:** Winged lion above flowers

Date	Mintage	VG	F	VF	XF	Unc
ND(1789) GF	—	9.00	15.00	25.00	75.00	—
ND(1796) FB	—	9.00	15.00	25.00	75.00	—

C# 11 31 SOLDI (1/4 Ducatone)

7.0258 g., 0.9480 Silver 0.2141 oz. ASW **Obv:** Winged lion, kneeling figure above G•A•C **Obv. Legend:** S • M • V • FRANC • LAVREDANO • D **Rev:** Standing figure, facing above value **Rev. Legend:** ...ERO • TVI • IVSTINA • VIR

Date	Mintage	VG	F	VF	XF	Unc
ND(1752) GAC	—	12.00	20.00	40.00	100	—

C# 36 31 SOLDI (1/4 Ducatone)

7.0258 g., 0.9480 Silver 0.2141 oz. ASW **Obv:** Winged lion, kneeling figure above Z•D **Obv. Legend:** * S • M • V • M * FOSCARENVS * D • **Rev:** Standing figure, facing above value

Date	Mintage	VG	F	VF	XF	Unc
ND(1762) ZD	—	30.00	60.00	100	175	—

C# 59 31 SOLDI (1/4 Ducatone)

7.0258 g., 0.9480 Silver 0.2141 oz. ASW **Obv:** Winged lion, kneeling figure above D•G **Obv. Legend:** * S • M • V • ALOY : MOCENI • * D • **Rev:** Standing figure, facing above value **Rev. Inscription:** ...ERO • TVI • IVSTINA VIR

Date	Mintage	VG	F	VF	XF	Unc
ND(1763) DG	—	12.00	20.00	35.00	100	—

C# 95.1 31 SOLDI (1/4 Ducatone)

7.0258 g., 0.9480 Silver 0.2141 oz. ASW **Obv:** Winged lion, kneeling figure above L•A•F **Obv. Legend:** S • M • V • PAVL * RAINERI • D • **Rev:** Standing figure, facing above value **Rev. Legend:** ...• ERO • TVI • IVSTINA • VIR

Date	Mintage	VG	F	VF	XF	Unc
ND(1779) LAF	—	12.00	20.00	40.00	100	—

C# 95.2 31 SOLDI (1/4 Ducatone)

7.0258 g., 0.9480 Silver 0.2141 oz. ASW **Rev. Legend:** MEMOR• ERO• TVI• IVSINA• VIRGO•

Date	Mintage	VG	F	VF	XF	Unc
ND(1779) LAF	—	15.00	25.00	50.00	125	—

C# 128 31 SOLDI (1/4 Ducatone)

7.0258 g., 0.9480 Silver 0.2141 oz. ASW **Obv:** Winged lion, kneeling figure above G•F **Obv. Legend:** * S • M • V • LVDOV • MANIN • D • **Rev:** Standing figure, facing above value **Rev. Legend:** ...RO • TVI • IVSTINA • VIRGO

Date	Mintage	VG	F	VF	XF	Unc
ND(1789) GF	—	25.00	40.00	65.00	110	—

C# 7 1/4 SCUDO (35 Soldi)

7.9570 g., Silver **Obv:** Floral cross, leaves in angles, G•A•C below **Obv. Legend:** FRANC * LAVREDANO * DVX * VENET * **Rev:** Winged lion holding gospel in shield above value **Rev. Legend:** SANCTVS * MARC * VENET *

Date	Mintage	VG	F	VF	XF	Unc
ND(1752) GAC	—	15.00	25.00	40.00	100	—

C# 32 1/4 SCUDO (35 Soldi)

7.9570 g., Silver **Obv:** Floral cross, leaves in angles, Z•D below **Obv. Legend:** MARC • FOSCARENUS • DVX • VENETIAR **Rev:** Winged lion holding gospel in shield above value **Rev. Legend:** SANCTVS • MARC • VENET

Date	Mintage	VG	F	VF	XF	Unc
ND(1762) ZD	—	30.00	65.00	125	200	—

C# 55.1 1/4 SCUDO (35 Soldi)

7.9570 g., Silver **Obv:** Floral cross, leaves in angles, D•G below **Obv. Legend:** ALOYSIVS • MOCNICO • DVX • VENETIAR **Rev:** Winged lion holding gospel in shield above value **Rev. Legend:** SANCTVS • MARC • VENET •

Date	Mintage	VG	F	VF	XF	Unc
ND(1763) DG	—	12.00	20.00	40.00	75.00	—
ND(1771-72) MAT	—	12.00	20.00	40.00	75.00	—

C# 55.2 1/4 SCUDO (35 Soldi)

7.9570 g., Silver **Obv:** Floral cross, leaves in angles, initials below **Obv. Legend:** ALOYSIUS • MOCENICO... **Rev:** Winged lion holding gospel in shield above value

Date	Mintage	VG	F	VF	XF	Unc
ND(1763) DG	—	12.00	20.00	40.00	75.00	—

C# 91.1 1/4 SCUDO (35 Soldi)

7.9570 g., Silver **Obv:** Floral cross, leaves in angles, L•A•F below **Obv. Legend:** PAUL * RAINE * DVX* VENE* **Rev:** Winged lion holding gospel in shield above value **Rev. Legend:** SANCTVS • MARC • VENET •

Date	Mintage	VG	F	VF	XF	Unc
ND(1779) LAF	—	9.00	15.00	25.00	75.00	—

C# 91.2 1/4 SCUDO (35 Soldi)

7.9570 g., Silver **Obv:** Floral cross, leaves in angles, LAF below **Obv. Legend:** PAULUS • RENERIVS... **Rev:** Winged lion holding gospel in shield above value

Date	Mintage	VG	F	VF	XF	Unc
ND(1779) LAF	—	9.00	15.00	25.00	75.00	—

C# 91.3 1/4 SCUDO (35 Soldi)

7.9570 g., Silver **Obv:** Floral cross, leaves in angles, LAF below **Obv. Legend:** PAULUS • RAINE• ... **Rev:** Winged lion holding gospel in shield above value

Date	Mintage	VG	F	VF	XF	Unc
ND(1779) LAF	—	9.00	15.00	25.00	75.00	—

C# 124 1/4 SCUDO (35 Soldi)

7.9570 g., Silver **Obv:** Floral cross, leaves in angles, G F. below **Obv. Legend:** LUDOVIC * MANIN * DVX * VENETIAR **Rev:** Winged lion holdin gospel in shield above value **Rev. Legend:** SANCTVS • MARCVS • VENET *

Date	Mintage	VG	F	VF	XF	Unc
ND(1789) GF	—	15.00	25.00	40.00	100	—

C# 15 MEDI (1/2) DUCATO

11.7000 g., 0.8264 Silver 0.3108 oz. ASW **Obv:** Seated and kneeling figure above G•A•C **Obv. Legend:** S * M * V * FRANC * LAVREDANO * D * **Rev:** Winged lion above flowers **Rev. Legend:** MEDI * DVCAT * VENET *

Date	Mintage	VG	F	VF	XF	Unc
ND(1752) GAC	—	9.00	15.00	25.00	75.00	—

C# 39 MEDI (1/2) DUCATO

11.7000 g., 0.8264 Silver 0.3108 oz. ASW **Obv:** Seated and kneeling figure above Z•D **Obv. Legend:** S * M * V * MARC * FOSCARENVS * D * **Rev:** Winged lion above flowers **Rev. Legend:** MEDI * DVCAT * VENET

Date	Mintage	VG	F	VF	XF	Unc
ND(1762) ZD	—	35.00	75.00	125	200	—

C# 63 MEDI (1/2) DUCATO

11.7000 g., 0.8264 Silver 0.3108 oz. ASW **Obv:** Seated and kneeling figure above D•G **Obv. Legend:** S * M * V * ALOY: MOCENICO * D • **Rev:** Winged lion above flowers **Rev. Legend:** MEDI * DVCAT * VENET *

Date	Mintage	VG	F	VF	XF	Unc
ND(1763) DG	—	10.00	20.00	40.00	75.00	—
ND(1772-73) GAF	—	10.00	20.00	40.00	75.00	—
ND(1773) GP	—	10.00	20.00	40.00	75.00	—

C# 99 MEDI (1/2) DUCATO

11.7000 g., 0.8264 Silver 0.3108 oz. ASW **Obv:** Seated and kneeling figure above R•B **Obv. Legend:** S • M • V • PAVL • RAINERIVS • D • **Rev:** Winged lion above flowers **Rev. Legend:** MEDI * DVCAT * VENET

Date	Mintage	VG	F	VF	XF	Unc
ND(1779) LAF	—	9.00	15.00	25.00	45.00	—
ND(1779) BC	—	9.00	15.00	25.00	75.00	—
ND(1779-80) RB	—	9.00	15.00	25.00	75.00	—
ND(1786-87) GF	—	9.00	15.00	25.00	75.00	—
ND(1789) AC	—	9.00	15.00	25.00	75.00	—

C# 132 MEDI (1/2) DUCATO

11.7000 g., 0.8264 Silver 0.3108 oz. ASW **Obv:** Seated and kneeling figure above F • B **Obv. Legend:** S • M • V• LVDOVIC •MANIN • D **Rev:** Winged lion above flowers **Rev. Legend:** MEDI * DVCAT * VENET **Note:** Legend varieties exist.

Date	Mintage	VG	F	VF	XF	Unc
ND(1789) GF	—	9.00	15.00	25.00	75.00	—
ND(1796) FB	—	9.00	15.00	25.00	75.00	—

C# 12 62 SOLDI (1/2 Ducatone)

14.0515 g., 0.9480 Silver 0.4283 oz. ASW **Obv:** Winged lion, kneeling figure above G• A • C **Obv. Legend:** S • M • V • FRANC * LAVREDANO • D * **Rev:** Standing figure, facing above value **Rev. Legend:** MEMOR * ERO * TVI * IVSTINA * VIR •

Date	Mintage	VG	F	VF	XF	Unc
ND(1752) GAC	—	20.00	35.00	60.00	140	—

C# 60 62 SOLDI (1/2 Ducatone)

14.0515 g., 0.9480 Silver 0.4283 oz. ASW **Obv:** Winged lion, kneeling figure above D • G **Obv. Legend:** S • M • V • ALOY : MOCENICO * D * **Rev:** Standing figure, facing above value **Rev. Legend:** MEMOR * ERO * TVI * IVSTINA * VIR •

Date	Mintage	VG	F	VF	XF	Unc
ND(1763) DG	—	20.00	35.00	60.00	140	—

C# 96 62 SOLDI (1/2 Ducatone)

14.0515 g., 0.9480 Silver 0.4283 oz. ASW **Obv:** Winged lion, kneeling figure above L • A • F **Obv. Legend:** S • M • V • PAVL • RAINERIVS • D • **Rev:** Standing figure, facing above value **Rev. Legend:** MEMOR * ERO * TVI * IVSTINA * VIR •

Date	Mintage	VG	F	VF	XF	Unc
ND(1779) LAF	—	30.00	45.00	75.00	150	—

C# 129 62 SOLDI (1/2 Ducatone)

14.0515 g., 0.9480 Silver 0.4283 oz. ASW **Obv:** Winged lion, kneeling figure above G • F **Obv. Legend:** S • M • V • LVDOVI • MANIN • D • **Rev:** Standing figure, facing above value **Rev. Legend:** MEMOR * ERO * TVI * IVSTINA * VIR •

Date	Mintage	VG	F	VF	XF	Unc
ND(1789) GF	—	35.00	55.00	90.00	150	—

C# 8 1/2 SCUDO (70 Soldi)

15.9145 g., 0.9480 Silver 0.4850 oz. ASW **Obv:** Floral cross, leaves in angles, G•A•C below **Obv. Legend:** FRANC * LAVREDANO * DVX * VENET **Rev:** Winged lion holding gospel in shield above value **Rev. Legend:** SANCTVS • MARCVS • VENET *

Date	Mintage	VG	F	VF	XF	Unc
ND(1752) GAC	—	15.00	30.00	60.00	125	—
Note: Reverse legend with retrograde N's						
ND(1752) GAC	—	15.00	30.00	60.00	125	—
Note: Reverse legend with normal N's						

C# 33 1/2 SCUDO (70 Soldi)

15.9145 g., 0.9480 Silver 0.4850 oz. ASW **Obv:** Floral cross, leaves in angles, Z.D below **Obv. Legend:** MARCUS • FOSCARENVS • DVX • VENETIAR **Rev:** Winged lion holding gospel in shield above value **Rev. Legend:** SANCTVS • MARCVS • VENET •

Date	Mintage	VG	F	VF	XF	Unc
ND(1762) ZD	—	40.00	75.00	125	250	—
Note: Reverse legend with retrograde N's						
ND(1762) ZD	—	40.00	75.00	125	250	—
Note: Reverse legend with normal N's						

C# 56 1/2 SCUDO (70 Soldi)

15.9145 g., 0.9480 Silver 0.4850 oz. ASW **Obv:** Floral cross, leaves in angles, D.G below **Obv. Legend:** ALOYSIUS • MOCENICO • DVX • VENETIAR • **Rev:** Winged lion holding gospel in shield above value **Rev. Legend:** SANCTVS • MARCVS • VENET •

Date	Mintage	VG	F	VF	XF	Unc
ND(1763) DG	—	15.00	30.00	50.00	100	—
Note: Reverse legend with retrograde N's						
ND(1763) DG	—	15.00	30.00	50.00	100	—
Note: Reverse legend with normal N's						
ND(1771-72) MAT	—	15.00	30.00	50.00	100	—

C# 92 1/2 SCUDO (70 Soldi)

15.9145 g., 0.9480 Silver 0.4850 oz. ASW **Obv:** Floral cross, leaves in angles, L•A•F below **Obv. Legend:** PAULUS RAINE DVX VENET **Rev:** Winged lion holding gospel in shield above value **Rev. Legend:** SANCTVS • MARCVS • VENET •

Date	Mintage	VG	F	VF	XF	Unc
ND(1779) LAF	—	15.00	25.00	35.00	100	—
Note: Reverse legend with retrograde N's						
ND(1779) LAF	—	15.00	25.00	35.00	100	—
Note: Reverse legend with normal N's						

C# 125 1/2 SCUDO (70 Soldi)

15.9145 g., 0.9480 Silver 0.4850 oz. ASW **Obv:** Floral cross, leaves in angles, G•F• below **Obv. Legend:** LUDOV MANIN DVX VENE **Rev:** Winged lion holding gospel in shield above value **Rev. Legend:** SANCTVS • MARCVS • VENET •

Date	Mintage	VG	F	VF	XF	Unc
ND(1789) GF	—	12.00	20.00	35.00	100	—

FR# 1472 1/2 SCUDO

1.6900 g., 0.9170 Gold 0.0498 oz. AGW **Obv:** Floral cross, leaves in angles, G.P below **Obv. Legend:** ALOI • MOCENICO • DVX • VENE • G • P **Rev:** Winged lion holding gospel in shield **Rev. Legend:** SANCTVS • MARCVS • VENETVS

Date	Mintage	VG	F	VF	XF	Unc
ND(1722-32) MAT	—	900	2,000	3,500	6,000	—

FR# 1473 1/2 SCUDO

1.6900 g., 0.9170 Gold 0.0498 oz. AGW **Obv:** Floral cross, leaves in angles **Obv. Legend:** CAROLVS • RVZINI • DVX • V • D • V **Rev:** Winged lion holding gospel in shield **Rev. Legend:** SANCTVS • MARCVS • VENETVS •

Date	Mintage	VG	F	VF	XF	Unc
ND(1732-35) VD	—	900	2,000	3,500	6,000	—

FR# 1475 1/2 SCUDO

1.6900 g., 0.9170 Gold 0.0498 oz. AGW **Obv:** Floral cross, leaves in angles **Obv. Legend:** ALOYSIVS • PISANI • DVX • V • C • G • **Rev:** Winged lion holding gospel in shield **Rev. Legend:** SANCTVS • MARCVS • VENETVS •

Date	Mintage	VG	F	VF	XF	Unc
ND(1735-41) GC	—	900	2,000	3,500	6,000	—

C# 23 1/2 SCUDO

1.6900 g., 0.9170 Gold 0.0498 oz. AGW **Obv:** Floral cross, leaves in angles **Obv. Legend:** FRANC • LAVRED • DVX • VENET • P • I • **Rev:** Winged lion holdinf gospel in shield **Rev. Legend:** SANCTVS • MARCVS • VENETVS *

Date	Mintage	VG	F	VF	XF	Unc
ND(1752-62) IP Rare	—	—	—	—	—	—

C# 46 1/2 SCUDO

1.6900 g., 0.9170 Gold 0.0498 oz. AGW **Obv:** Floral cross, leaves in angles **Obv. Legend:** M • FOSCARENVS • DVX • VENE • B • A • **Rev:** Winged lion holding gospel in shield **Rev. Legend:** SANCTVS • MARCVS • VENETVS •

Date	Mintage	VG	F	VF	XF	Unc
ND(1763) AB Rare	—	—	—	—	—	—

C# 81 1/2 SCUDO

1.6900 g., 0.9170 Gold 0.0498 oz. AGW **Obv:** Floral cross, leaves in angles **Obv. Legend:** ALOI MOCENICO • DVX • VENE * P • G * **Rev:** Winged lion holding gospel in shield **Rev. Legend:** SANCTVS • MARCVS • VENETVS •

Date	Mintage	VG	F	VF	XF	Unc
ND(1773) GP Rare	—	—	—	—	—	—

C# 115 1/2 SCUDO

1.6900 g., 0.9170 Gold 0.0498 oz. AGW **Obv:** Floral cross, leaves in angles **Obv. Legend:** PAVL * RAINE * DVX * VEN * • P • N * **Rev:** Winged lion holding gospel in shield **Rev. Legend:** SANCTVS • MARCVS • VENETVS •

Date	Mintage	VG	F	VF	XF	Unc
ND(1779-89) NP Rare	—	—	—	—	—	—

C# 149 1/2 SCUDO

1.6900 g., 0.9170 Gold 0.0498 oz. AGW **Obv:** Floral cross, leaves in angles **Obv. Legend:** LVD • MANIN • DVX • VEN * C • N * **Rev:** Winged lion holding gospel in shield **Rev. Legend:** SANCTVS • MARCVS • VENETVS •

Date	Mintage	VG	F	VF	XF	Unc
ND(1789-97) NC	—	200	400	900	1,800	—

DAV# 1527 DUCATO

23.4000 g., 0.8264 Silver 0.6217 oz. ASW **Obv. Legend:** * S * M * V * ALOY * MOCENICO • DV * **Note:** Legend varieties exist.

Date	Mintage	VG	F	VF	XF	Unc
ND(1701) PM	—	35.00	65.00	125	220	—
ND(1702-02) GTS	—	35.00	65.00	125	220	—
ND(1702-03) RPB	—	35.00	65.00	125	220	—

DAV# 1533 DUCATO

23.4000 g., 0.8264 Silver 0.6217 oz. ASW **Obv:** Seated and kneeling figure above initials **Obv. Legend:** * S * M * V * IOAN * CORNELIO • D • **Rev:** Winged lion above flowers **Note:** Legend varieties exist.

Date	Mintage	VG	F	VF	XF	Unc
ND(1709) FAP	—	35.00	60.00	100	175	—
ND(1714-15) AM	—	35.00	60.00	100	175	—
ND(1715) DD	—	35.00	60.00	100	175	—
ND(1717) MB	—	35.00	60.00	100	175	—

DAV# 1537 DUCATO

23.4000 g., 0.8264 Silver 0.6217 oz. ASW **Obv:** Seated and kneeling figure above initials **Obv. Legend:** * S * M * V * ALOY * MONENICO • D • **Rev:** Winged lion above flowers **Rev. Legend:** DVCATVS * VENETVS * **Note:** Legend varieties exist.

Date	Mintage	VG	F	VF	XF	Unc
ND(1722) VQ	—	80.00	135	225	375	—

DAV# 1540 DUCATO

23.4000 g., 0.8264 Silver 0.6217 oz. ASW **Obv:** Seated and kneeling figure above B * V **Obv. Legend:** * S * M * V * CAROLVS * RVZINI * D * **Rev:** Winged lion above flowers **Rev. Legend:** DVCATVS * VENETVS * **Note:** 3 legend varieties exist.

Date	Mintage	VG	F	VF	XF	Unc
ND(1732) BV	—	80.00	135	225	375	—
ND(1733) BZ	—	80.00	135	225	375	—

DAV# 1543 DUCATO

23.4000 g., 0.8264 Silver 0.6217 oz. ASW **Obv:** Seated and kneeling figure above M * S **Obv. Legend:** * S * M * V * ALOYSIVS * PISANI * D * **Rev:** Winged lion above flowers **Rev. Legend:** DVCATVS * VENETVS * **Note:** 5 legend varieties exist.

Date	Mintage	VG	F	VF	XF	Unc
ND(1734) ZF	—	80.00	135	225	375	—
ND(1735) MS	—	80.00	135	225	375	—

DAV# 1547 DUCATO

23.4000 g., 0.8264 Silver 0.6217 oz. ASW **Obv:** Seated and kneeling figure above A * B **Obv. Legend:** * S * M * V * PETRVS * GRIMANI * D • **Rev:** Winged lion above flowers **Rev. Legend:** DVCATVS * VENETVS *

Date	Mintage	VG	F	VF	XF	Unc
ND(1741) FP	—	70.00	120	200	350	—
ND(1742-43) FAF	—	70.00	120	200	350	—
ND(1751) AB	—	70.00	120	200	350	—

C# 16 DUCATO

23.4000 g., 0.8264 Silver 0.6217 oz. ASW **Obv:** Seated and kneeling figure above S • B **Obv. Legend:** S • M • V • FRANC • LAVREDANO • D • **Rev:** Winged lion above flowers **Rev. Legend:** DVCATVS * VENETVS * **Note:** Dav. #1551.

Date	Mintage	VG	F	VF	XF	Unc
ND(1752) GAC	—	70.00	135	225	375	—
ND(1753) SB	—	70.00	135	225	375	—

C# 40 DUCATO

23.4000 g., 0.8264 Silver 0.6217 oz. ASW **Obv:** Seated and kneeling figure above Z • D **Obv. Legend:** S * M * V * MARC * FOSCARENVS * D **Rev:** Winged lion above flowers **Rev. Legend:** DVCATVS * VENETVS * **Note:** Dav. #1555.

Date	Mintage	VG	F	VF	XF	Unc
ND(1762) ZD	—	40.00	70.00	135	225	—

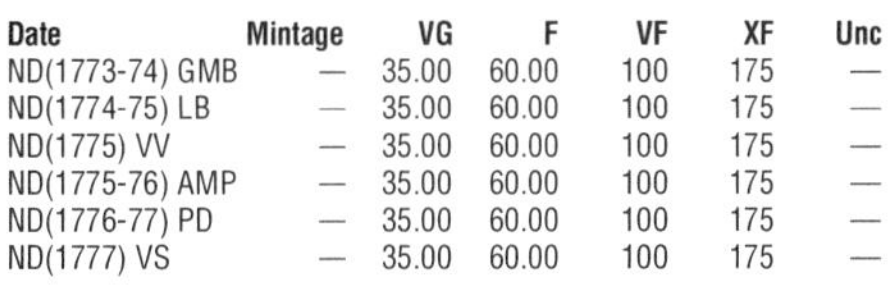

C# 64 DUCATO

23.4000 g., 0.8264 Silver 0.6217 oz. ASW **Obv:** Seated and kneeling figure above G • P **Obv. Legend:** S • M • V • ALOY : MOCENICO • D • **Rev:** Winged lion above flowers **Rev. Legend:** DVCATVS * VENETVS * **Note:** Legend varieties exist. Dav. #1561.

Date	Mintage	VG	F	VF	XF	Unc
ND(1767) DG	—	35.00	60.00	100	175	—
ND(1768-69) RBP	—	35.00	60.00	100	175	—
ND(1772-73) GAF	—	35.00	60.00	100	175	—
ND(1773) GP	—	35.00	60.00	100	175	—
ND(1773-74) GMB	—	35.00	60.00	100	175	—
ND(1774-75) LB	—	35.00	60.00	100	175	—
ND(1775) VV	—	35.00	60.00	100	175	—
ND(1775-76) AMP	—	35.00	60.00	100	175	—
ND(1776-77) PD	—	35.00	60.00	100	175	—
ND(1777) VS	—	35.00	60.00	100	175	—

C# 100 DUCATO

23.4000 g., 0.8264 Silver 0.6217 oz. ASW **Obv:** Seated and kneeling figure above B • C **Obv. Legend:** S • M • V • PAVL • RAINERIVS • D • **Rev:** Winged lion above flowers **Rev. Legend:** DVCATVS * VENETVS * **Note:** Dav. #1567.

Date	Mintage	VG	F	VF	XF	Unc
ND(1779) LAF	—	30.00	55.00	90.00	150	—
ND(1779) BC	—	30.00	55.00	90.00	150	—
ND(1780) RB	—	30.00	55.00	90.00	150	—
ND(1782-83) FD	—	30.00	55.00	90.00	150	—
ND(1785) AO	—	30.00	55.00	90.00	150	—
ND(1785-86) AB	—	30.00	55.00	90.00	150	—
ND(1786) FR	—	30.00	55.00	90.00	150	—
ND(1786-87) GF	—	30.00	55.00	90.00	150	—
ND(1789) AF	—	30.00	55.00	90.00	150	—
ND(1789) AC	—	30.00	55.00	90.00	150	—
ND(1789) AD	—	30.00	55.00	90.00	150	—

C# 133 DUCATO

23.4000 g., 0.8264 Silver 0.6217 oz. ASW **Obv:** Seated and kneeling figure above F • B **Obv. Legend:** S • M • V • LVDOVICVS • MANIN • D • **Rev:** Winged lion above flowers **Rev. Legend:** DVCATVS * VENETVS **Note:** Legend varieties exist. Dav. #1574.

Date	Mintage	VG	F	VF	XF	Unc
ND(1789) GF	—	25.00	45.00	75.00	125	—
ND(1792) AC	—	25.00	45.00	75.00	125	—
ND(1796) FB	—	25.00	45.00	75.00	125	—
ND(1797) DB	—	25.00	45.00	75.00	125	—

DAV# 1525 124 SOLDI (Ducatone)

28.1030 g., 0.9480 Silver 0.8565 oz. ASW **Obv:** Winged lion, kneeling figure above B * C **Obv. Legend:** * S * M * V * ALOY * MOCENICO * D * B **Rev:** Standing figure, facing above value

Date	Mintage	VG	F	VF	XF	Unc
ND(1702-03) BP	—	90.00	150	250	425	—
ND(1705) BC	—	90.00	150	250	425	—

DAV# 1531 124 SOLDI (Ducatone)

28.1030 g., 0.9480 Silver 0.8565 oz. ASW **Obv:** Winged lion, kneeling figure above F • A • P **Obv. Legend:** * S * M * V * IOAN * CORNEL * D * **Rev:** Standing figure, facing above value **Rev. Legend:** MEMOR • ERO • TVI • IVSTINA • VIR **Note:** Legend varieties exist.

Date	Mintage	VG	F	VF	XF	Unc
ND(1709) FAP	—	90.00	150	250	425	—

DAV# 1536 124 SOLDI (Ducatone)

28.1030 g., 0.9480 Silver 0.8565 oz. ASW **Obv:** Winged lion, kneeling figure above V * Q **Obv. Legend:** * S * M * V * ALOY * MOCENI * D * **Rev:** Standing figure, facing above value **Rev. Legend:** MEMOR * ERO * TVI * IVSTINA * VIR **Note:** Legend varieties exist.

Date	Mintage	VG	F	VF	XF	Unc
ND(1722) VQ	—	90.00	150	250	425	—

DAV# 1539 124 SOLDI (Ducatone)

28.1030 g., 0.9480 Silver 0.8565 oz. ASW **Obv:** Winged lion, kneeling figure above B • V **Obv. Legend:** * S * M * V * CAROLVS * RVZINI * D * **Rev:** Standing figure, facing above value **Rev. Legend:** MEMOR * ERO * TVI * IVSTINA * VIRG

Date	Mintage	VG	F	VF	XF	Unc
ND(1732) BV	—	140	240	400	650	—

DAV# 1542 124 SOLDI (Ducatone)
28.1030 g., 0.9480 Silver 0.8565 oz. ASW **Obv:** Winged lion, kneeling figure above Z * F **Obv. Legend:** * S * M * V * ALOYSIVS * PISANI * D * **Rev:** Standing figure, facing above value **Rev. Legend:** MEMOR * ERO * TVI * IVSTINA * VIRGO **Note:** Legend varieties exist with ZF.

Date	Mintage	VG	F	VF	XF	Unc
ND(1734) ZF	—	140	240	400	650	—
ND(1735) MS	—	140	240	400	650	—

DAV# 1545 124 SOLDI (Ducatone)
28.1030 g., 0.9480 Silver 0.8565 oz. ASW **Obv:** Winged lion, kneeling figure above F * P **Obv. Legend:** * S * M * V * PETRBS * GRIMANI * D * **Rev:** Standing figure, facing above value **Rev. Legend:** MEMOR * ERO * TVI * IVSTINA * VIRGO

Date	Mintage	VG	F	VF	XF	Unc
ND(1741) FP	—	140	240	400	650	—

C# 13 124 SOLDI (Ducatone)
28.1030 g., 0.9480 Silver 0.8565 oz. ASW **Obv:** Winged lion, kneeling figure above G • A • C **Obv. Legend:** S • M • V • FRANC * LAVREDANO • DVX * **Rev:** Standing figure, facing above value **Rev. Legend:** MEMOR * ERO * TVI * IVSTINA * VIRGO **Note:** Dav. 1549.

Date	Mintage	VG	F	VF	XF	Unc
ND(1752) GAC	—	120	200	350	600	—

C# 37 124 SOLDI (Ducatone)
28.1030 g., 0.9480 Silver 0.8565 oz. ASW **Obv:** Winged lion, kneeling figure above Z • D **Obv. Legend:** S • M • V • M * FOSCARENVS * DVX * **Rev:** Standing figure, facing above value **Rev. Legend:** MEMOR * ERO * TVI * IVSTINA * VIRGO **Note:** Dav. 1554.

Date	Mintage	VG	F	VF	XF	Unc
ND(1762) ZD	—	110	180	300	500	—

C# 61 124 SOLDI (Ducatone)
28.1030 g., 0.9480 Silver 0.8565 oz. ASW **Obv:** Winged lion, kneeling figure above D • G **Obv. Legend:** S • M • V • ALOY : MOCENICO • DVX • **Rev:** Standing figure, facing above value **Rev. Legend:** MEMOR • ERO • TVI • IVSTINA • VIRGO **Note:** Legend varieties exist. Dav. #1559.

Date	Mintage	VG	F	VF	XF	Unc
ND(1763) DG	—	85.00	150	250	425	—

C# 97 124 SOLDI (Ducatone)
28.1030 g., 0.9480 Silver 0.8565 oz. ASW **Obv:** Winged lion, kneeling figure above B • C **Obv. Legend:** S • M • V • PAVL • RAINERIVS • DVX • **Rev:** Standing figure, facing above value **Rev. Legend:** MEMOR * ERO * TVI * IVSTINA * VIRGO • **Note:** Legend varieties exist. Dav. #1565.

Date	Mintage	VG	F	VF	XF	Unc
ND(1779) BC	—	85.00	150	250	425	—

C# 130 124 SOLDI (Ducatone)
28.1030 g., 0.9480 Silver 0.8565 oz. ASW **Obv:** Winged lion, kneeling figure above G • F **Obv. Legend:** S • M • V • LVDOVI • MANIN • DVX • **Rev:** Standing figure, facing above value **Rev. Legend:** MEMOR • ERO • TVI • IVSTINA • VIRGO **Note:** Legend varieties exist. Dav. #1572.

Date	Mintage	VG	F	VF	XF	Unc
ND(1789) GF	—	85.00	150	250	425	—

DAV# 1524 SCUDO (140 Soldi)
31.8290 g., 0.9480 Silver 0.9701 oz. ASW **Obv:** Floral cross, leaves in angles, B•C below **Obv. Legend:** ALOYSIV * MOCENICO * DVX * VENET **Rev:** Winged lion holding gospel in shield above value **Rev. Legend:** SANCTVS • MARCVS • VENET •

Date	Mintage	VG	F	VF	XF	Unc
ND(1700) BC	—	50.00	85.00	140	225	—
ND(1702-03) PB	—	50.00	85.00	140	225	—

DAV# 1530 SCUDO (140 Soldi)
31.8290 g., 0.9480 Silver 0.9701 oz. ASW **Obv:** Floral cross, leaves in angles **Obv. Legend:** IOANNES * CORNELIO * DVX * VEN **Rev:** Winged lion holding gospel in shield above value **Rev. Legend:** SANCTVS • MARCVS • VENET • **Note:** Legend varieties exist.

Date	Mintage	VG	F	VF	XF	Unc
ND(1709) FAP	—	50.00	85.00	140	225	—
ND(1714-15) AM	—	50.00	85.00	140	225	—

DAV# 1535 SCUDO (140 Soldi)
31.8290 g., 0.9480 Silver 0.9701 oz. ASW **Obv:** Floral cross, leaves in angles, V*Q below **Obv. Legend:** ALOYSIVS * MOCENICO * DVX * VEN **Rev:** Winged lion holding gospel in shield above value **Rev. Legend:** SANCTVS * MARCVS * VENET * **Note:** Three legend varieties exist.

Date	Mintage	VG	F	VF	XF	Unc
ND(1722) VQ	—	50.00	85.00	140	225	—

DAV# 1538 SCUDO (140 Soldi)
31.8290 g., 0.9480 Silver 0.9701 oz. ASW **Obv:** Floral cross, leaves in angles, B V below **Obv. Legend:** CAROLVS * RVZINI * VENETIAR • **Rev:** Winged lion holding gospel in shield above value **Rev. Legend:** SANCTVS • MARCVS • VENET **Note:** Four legend varieties exist.

Date	Mintage	VG	F	VF	XF	Unc
ND(1732) BV	—	90.00	150	250	400	—

DAV# 1541 SCUDO (140 Soldi)
31.8290 g., 0.9480 Silver 0.9701 oz. ASW **Obv:** Floral cross, leaves in angles, Z F below **Obv. Legend:** ALOYSIVS PISANI DVX * VENETIAR **Rev:** Winged lion holding gospel in shield above value **Rev. Legend:** SANCTVS • MARCVS • VENET **Note:** Three legend varieties exist.

Date	Mintage	VG	F	VF	XF	Unc
ND(1735) ZF	—	90.00	150	250	400	—

DAV# 1544 SCUDO (140 Soldi)
31.8290 g., 0.9480 Silver 0.9701 oz. ASW **Obv:** Floral cross, leaves in angles, F P below **Obv. Legend:** PETRVS GRIMANI DVX VENETIA **Rev:** Winged lion holding gospel in shield above value **Rev. Legend:** SANCTVS • MARCVS • VENET •

Date	Mintage	VG	F	VF	XF	Unc
ND(1741) FP	—	70.00	135	225	375	—

C# 9 SCUDO (140 Soldi)
31.8290 g., 0.9480 Silver 0.9701 oz. ASW **Obv:** Floral cross, leaves in angles, G•A•C below **Obv. Legend:** FRANC * LAVREDANO * DVX * VENETIAR * **Rev:** Winged lion holding gospel in shield above value **Rev. Legend:** SANCTVS * MARCVS * VENET * **Note:** Dav. #1548.

Date	Mintage	VG	F	VF	XF	Unc
ND(1752) GAC	—	50.00	75.00	100	150	—

C# 34 SCUDO (140 Soldi)
31.8290 g., 0.9480 Silver 0.9701 oz. ASW **Obv:** Floral cross, leaves in angles, Z D below **Obv. Legend:** MARCUS • FOSCARENVS • DVX • VENETIAR **Rev:** Winged lion holding gospel in shield above value **Rev. Legend:** SANCTVS * MARCVS * VENET * **Note:** Dav. #1553.

Date	Mintage	VG	F	VF	XF	Unc
ND(1762) ZD	—	50.00	75.00	100	150	—

C# 57 SCUDO (140 Soldi)
31.8290 g., 0.9480 Silver 0.9701 oz. ASW **Obv:** Floral cross, leaves in angles, D•G below **Obv. Legend:** ALOYSIVS • MOCENICO • DVX • VENETIAR **Rev:** Winged lion holding gospel in shield above value **Rev. Legend:** SANCTVS • MARCVS • VENET **Note:** Dav. #1557.

Date	Mintage	VG	F	VF	XF	Unc
ND(1763) DG	—	50.00	75.00	100	150	—
ND(1771-72) MAT	—	50.00	75.00	100	150	—

C# 93 SCUDO (140 Soldi)
31.8290 g., 0.9480 Silver 0.9701 oz. ASW **Obv:** Floral cross, leaves in angles, L•A•F below **Obv. Legend:** PAULUS • RAINERIUS • DVX •. VENETIAR • **Rev:** Winged lion holding gospel in shield above value **Rev. Legend:** SANCTVS • MARCVS • VENET **Note:** Dav. #1564.

Date	Mintage	VG	F	VF	XF	Unc
ND(1779) LAF	—	35.00	50.00	75.00	125	—

C# 126 SCUDO (140 Soldi)
31.8290 g., 0.9480 Silver 0.9701 oz. ASW **Obv:** Floral cross, leaves in angles, G.F below **Obv. Legend:** LUDOVICUS MANIN DVX VENETIAR **Rev:** Winged lion holding gospel in shield above value **Rev. Legend:** SANCTVS MARCVS VENET **Note:** Dav. #1570.

Date	Mintage	VG	F	VF	XF	Unc
ND(1789) GF	—	35.00	50.00	75.00	125	—

FR# 1471 SCUDO D'ORO
3.3810 g., 0.9170 Gold 0.0997 oz. AGW **Obv:** Floral cross, leaves in angles, I.P below **Obv. Legend:** * IOAN • CORNEL • DVX • VEN * **Rev:** Winged lion holding gospel in shield **Rev. Legend:** * SANCTVS • MARCVS • VENET • *

Date	Mintage	VG	F	VF	XF	Unc
ND(1709) IP	—	1,200	2,500	4,500	7,000	—

FR# 1476 SCUDO D'ORO
3.3850 g., 0.9170 Gold 0.0998 oz. AGW **Obv:** Floral cross, leaves in angles, Z•D•L below **Obv. Legend:** * PETRVS • GRIMANI • DVX • VENE * **Rev:** Winged lion holding gospel in shield **Rev. Legend:** SANCTVS • MARCVS • VENET •

Date	Mintage	VG	F	VF	XF	Unc
ND(1741) MAC	—	1,200	2,500	4,500	7,000	—
ND(1747-48) ZDL	—	1,200	2,500	4,500	7,000	—

C# 24 SCUDO D'ORO
3.3810 g., 0.9170 Gold 0.0997 oz. AGW **Obv:** Floral cross, leaves in angles, I. P. below **Obv. Legend:** FRANC • LAVREDANO • DVX • VEN **Rev:** Winged lion holding gospel in shield **Rev. Legend:** SANCTVS • MARCVS • VENET •

Date	Mintage	VG	F	VF	XF	Unc
ND(1752-53) IP	—	1,000	2,000	3,500	6,000	—

C# 47 SCUDO D'ORO
3.3810 g., 0.9170 Gold 0.0997 oz. AGW **Obv:** Floral cross, leaves in angles, A•B below **Obv. Legend:** M • FOSCARENVS • DVX • VENE • **Rev:** Winged lion holding gospel in shield **Rev. Legend:** SANCTVS • MARCVS • VENET •

Date	Mintage	VG	F	VF	XF	Unc
ND(1762) AB	—	1,000	2,000	3,000	5,000	—

C# 82 SCUDO D'ORO
3.3810 g., 0.9170 Gold 0.0997 oz. AGW **Obv:** Floral cross, leaves in angles, G P below **Obv. Legend:** * ALOY : MOCENICO • DVX • VENET * **Rev:** Winged lion holding gospel in shield **Rev. Legend:** SANCTVS • MARCVS • VENET •

Date	Mintage	VG	F	VF	XF	Unc
ND(1763) GP	—	1,250	3,000	4,500	8,000	—

C# 116 SCUDO D'ORO
3.3810 g., 0.9170 Gold 0.0997 oz. AGW **Obv:** Floral cross, leaves in angles, N.P. below **Obv. Legend:** PAUL RAINE DVX VENE **Rev:** Winged lion holding gospel in shield **Rev. Legend:** SANCTVS • MARCVS • VENET •

Date	Mintage	VG	F	VF	XF	Unc
ND(1779) NP	—	1,250	3,000	4,500	8,000	—

C# 150 SCUDO D'ORO
3.3810 g., 0.9170 Gold 0.0997 oz. AGW **Obv:** Floral cross, leaves in angles, N•C below **Obv. Legend:** * LVDOVIC • MANIN • DVX • VENE * **Rev:** Winged lion holding gospel in shield **Rev. Legend:** SANCTVS • MARCVS • VENET •

Date	Mintage	VG	F	VF	XF	Unc
ND(1789) NC	—	450	800	1,400	2,400	—

FR# 1474 2 SCUDI
6.7620 g., 0.9170 Gold 0.1994 oz. AGW **Obv:** Floral cross, leaves in angles, G•C below **Obv. Legend:** * ALOYSIUS * PISANI * DVX * VENET * **Rev:** Winged lion holding gospel in shield **Rev. Legend:** SANCTVS * MARCVS * VENETVS *

Date	Mintage	VG	F	VF	XF	Unc
ND(1734) GC	—	1,300	3,000	5,000	7,000	—

C# 25 2 SCUDI
6.7620 g., 0.9170 Gold 0.1994 oz. AGW **Obv:** Floral cross, leaves in angles, I.P. below **Obv. Legend:** FRANC • LAVREDANO • DVX • VENET **Rev:** Winged lion holding gospel in shield **Rev. Legend:** SANCTVS * MARCVS * VENETVS *

Date	Mintage	VG	F	VF	XF	Unc
ND(1752-53) IP Rare	—	—	—	—	—	—

C# 48 2 SCUDI
6.7620 g., 0.9170 Gold 0.1994 oz. AGW **Obv:** Floral cross, leaves in angles, A.B. below **Obv. Legend:** MARC • FOSCARENVS • DVX • VENETIAR • **Rev:** Winged lion holding gospel in shield **Rev. Legend:** SANCTVS * MARCVS * VENETVS *

Date	Mintage	VG	F	VF	XF	Unc
ND(1762) AB	—	1,250	3,000	4,500	8,000	—

C# 83 2 SCUDI
6.9000 g., 0.9170 Gold 0.2034 oz. AGW **Obv:** Floral cross, leaves in angles, G P below **Obv. Legend:** ALOY : MOCENICO • DVX • VENETIAR * **Rev:** Winged lion holding gospel in shield **Rev. Legend:** SANCTVS * MARCVS * VENETVS *

Date	Mintage	VG	F	VF	XF	Unc
ND(1763) GP	—	1,250	3,000	4,500	8,000	—

C# 117 2 SCUDI
6.9000 g., 0.9170 Gold 0.2034 oz. AGW **Obv:** Floral cross, leaves in angles, L•A•F below **Obv. Legend:** PAUL RAINE DVX VENE **Rev:** Winged lion holding gospel in shield **Rev. Legend:** SANCTVS * MARCVS * VENETVS *

Date	Mintage	VG	F	VF	XF	Unc
ND(1779) LAF	—	1,250	3,000	4,500	8,000	—

C# 151 2 SCUDI
6.9000 g., 0.9170 Gold 0.2034 oz. AGW **Obv:** Floral cross, leaves in angles, N*C below **Obv. Legend:** LUDOVIC MANIN DVX VENE **Rev:** Winged lion holding gospel in shield **Rev. Legend:** SANCTVS * MARCVS * VENETVS *

Date	Mintage	VG	F	VF	XF	Unc
ND(1789) NC	—	600	1,200	2,000	3,500	—

DAV# 1528 LEONE
27.1200 g., 0.7390 Silver 0.6443 oz. ASW **Obv:** Rearing lion of St. Mark's with cross right **Obv. Legend:** ALOY * MOCEN * ... **Rev:** Standing saint with kneeling figure

Date	Mintage	VG	F	VF	XF	Unc
ND(1705) BC	—	120	200	350	600	—

DAV# 1534 LEONE
27.1200 g., 0.7390 Silver 0.6443 oz. ASW **Obv. Legend:** IOAN • CORNEL • ...

Date	Mintage	VG	F	VF	XF	Unc
ND(1714-15) AM	—	120	200	350	600	—

C# 101 1/8 TALLERO
3.5700 g., Silver **Obv:** Bust right, with tiara **Obv. Legend:** RESPUBLICA VENETA * **Rev:** Seated, winged lion with gospel above date **Rev. Legend:** PAULO RAINERIO DUCE

Date	Mintage	VG	F	VF	XF	Unc
1780	—	27.50	55.00	90.00	150	—
1781	—	27.50	55.00	90.00	150	—
1786	—	27.50	55.00	90.00	150	—

C# 134 1/8 TALLERO
3.5700 g., Silver **Obv:** Bust right, with tiara **Obv. Legend:** RESPUBLICA VENETA * **Rev:** Seated, winged lion with gospel above date **Rev. Legend:** * LUDOVICO MANINDUCE

Date	Mintage	VG	F	VF	XF	Unc
1790	—	30.00	60.00	100	165	—
1794	—	30.00	60.00	100	165	—
1796	—	30.00	60.00	100	165	—

C# 65 1/4 TALLERO
7.1400 g., Silver **Obv:** Bust right, with jewels on crown **Obv. Legend:** * RESPUBLICA VENETA * **Rev:** Winged, rampant lion with gospel in ornate shield **Rev. Legend:** * ALOYSII MOCENICO DUCE 1766 *

Date	Mintage	VG	F	VF	XF	Unc
1766	—	50.00	100	165	275	—

C# 102 1/4 TALLERO
7.1400 g., Silver **Obv:** Bust right, with tiara **Obv. Legend:** RESPUBLICA VENETA * **Rev:** Seated, winged lion with gospel above date **Rev. Legend:** PAULO RAINERIO DUCE

Date	Mintage	VG	F	VF	XF	Unc
1780	—	27.50	55.00	90.00	150	—
1781	—	27.50	55.00	90.00	150	—
1786	—	27.50	55.00	90.00	150	—

C# 135 1/4 TALLERO
7.1400 g., Silver **Obv:** Bust right, with tiara **Obv. Legend:** RESPUBLICA VENETA **Rev:** Seated, winged lion with gospel above date **Rev. Legend:** LUDOVICO MANIN DUCE

Date	Mintage	VG	F	VF	XF	Unc
1790	—	37.50	75.00	125	200	—
1791	—	37.50	75.00	125	200	—
1794	—	37.50	75.00	125	200	—

C# 17 1/2 TALLERO

14.2800 g., 0.8350 Silver 0.3833 oz. ASW **Obv:** Bust right, with jewels on crown **Obv. Legend:** RESPUBLICA VENETA **Rev:** Winged, rampant lion with gospel in ornate shield **Rev. Legend:** FRANC LAUREDANO DUCE 1756

Date	Mintage	VG	F	VF	XF	Unc
1756	—	55.00	110	175	300	—

C# 41 1/2 TALLERO

14.2800 g., 0.8350 Silver 0.3833 oz. ASW **Obv:** Bust right, with jewels on crown **Obv. Inscription:** * RESPUBLICA VENETA * **Rev:** Winged, rampant lion with gospel in ornate shield **Rev. Legend:** * MARCO FOSCARENO DUCE 1762 *

Date	Mintage	VG	F	VF	XF	Unc
1762	—	50.00	100	165	275	—

C# 66 1/2 TALLERO

14.2800 g., 0.8350 Silver 0.3833 oz. ASW **Obv:** Bust right, with jewels on crown **Obv. Legend:** * RESPUBLICA VENETA * **Rev:** Winged, rampant lion with gospel in ornate shield **Rev. Legend:** ALOYS II MOCENICO

Date	Mintage	VG	F	VF	XF	Unc
1764	—	40.00	80.00	135	225	—
1766	—	40.00	80.00	135	225	—

C# 103 1/2 TALLERO

14.2800 g., 0.8350 Silver 0.3833 oz. ASW **Obv:** Bust right, with tiara **Obv. Legend:** * RESPUBLICA VENETA * **Rev:** Seated, winged lion with gospel above date **Rev. Legend:** PAULO RAINERIO DUCE

Date	Mintage	VG	F	VF	XF	Unc
1780	—	27.50	55.00	90.00	150	—
1781	—	27.50	55.00	90.00	150	—
1784	—	27.50	55.00	90.00	150	—
1786	—	27.50	55.00	90.00	150	—
1787	—	27.50	55.00	90.00	150	—

C# 136 1/2 TALLERO

14.2800 g., 0.8350 Silver 0.3833 oz. ASW **Obv:** Bust right, with tiara **Obv. Legend:** RESPUBLICA VENETA **Rev:** Seated, winged lion with gospel above date **Rev. Legend:** LUDOVICO MANIN DUCE

Date	Mintage	VG	F	VF	XF	Unc
1789	—	37.50	75.00	125	200	—
1790	—	37.50	75.00	125	200	—
1791	—	37.50	75.00	125	200	—
1792	—	37.50	75.00	125	200	—
1796	—	37.50	75.00	125	200	—
1797	—	37.50	75.00	125	200	—

C# 18.2 TALLERO

28.5600 g., 0.8350 Silver 0.7667 oz. ASW **Obv:** Bust right, with jewels on crown **Obv. Legend:** *RESPUBLICA VENETA* **Rev:** Winged, rampant lion in ornate shield **Rev. Legend:** ...MOCENICO DUCE

Date	Mintage	VG	F	VF	XF	Unc
1756	—	100	200	350	500	—

C# 18.3 TALLERO

28.5600 g., 0.8350 Silver 0.7667 oz. ASW **Obv:** Bust right, with jewels on crown **Obv. Legend:** * RESPUBLICA VENETA * **Rev:** Winged, rampant lion with gospel in ornate shield **Rev. Inscription:** FRANC : LAUREDANO DUCE 1756

Date	Mintage	VG	F	VF	XF	Unc
1756	—	100	200	350	500	—
1760	—	100	200	350	500	—
1761	—	100	200	350	500	—

C# 18.1 TALLERO

28.5600 g., 0.8350 Silver 0.7667 oz. ASW **Obv:** Bust right, with jewels on crown **Obv. Legend:** * RESPUBLICA VENETA * **Rev:** Winged, rampant lion with gospel in ornate shield **Rev. Legend:** FRANC • LAUREDANO DUCE 1756 **Note:** Dav. #1552.

Date	Mintage	VG	F	VF	XF	Unc
1756	—	100	200	350	500	—

C# 42 TALLERO

28.5600 g., 0.8350 Silver 0.7667 oz. ASW **Obv:** Bust right, with jewels on crown **Obv. Legend:** RESPUBLICA VENETA **Rev:** Winged, rampant lion with gospel in ornate shield **Rev. Legend:** MARCO FOSCARENO DUCE 1762 **Note:** Dav. #1556.

Date	Mintage	VG	F	VF	XF	Unc
1762	—	75.00	150	250	350	—

C# 67 TALLERO

28.5600 g., 0.8350 Silver 0.7667 oz. ASW **Obv:** Bust right, with jewels on crown **Obv. Legend:** RESPUBLICA VENETA **Rev:** Winged, rampant lion with gospel in ornate shield **Rev. Legend:** ALOYSII MOCENICO DUCE 1766 **Note:** Dav. #1562.

Date	Mintage	VG	F	VF	XF	Unc
1764	—	75.00	150	250	350	—
1766	—	75.00	150	250	350	—

C# 68 TALLERO

28.5600 g., 0.8350 Silver 0.7667 oz. ASW **Obv:** Bust right, with tiara **Obv. Legend:** RESPUBLICA VENETA **Rev:** Seated, winged lion with gospel above date **Rev. Legend:** ALOYSIO MOCENICO DUCE **Note:** Dav. #1563.

Date	Mintage	VG	F	VF	XF	Unc
1768	—	60.00	100	150	250	—
1769	—	60.00	100	150	250	—

C# 104 TALLERO

28.5600 g., 0.8350 Silver 0.7667 oz. ASW **Obv:** Bust right, with tiara **Obv. Legend:** RESPUBLICA VENETA **Rev:** Seated, winged lion with gospel above date **Rev. Legend:** PAULO RAINERIO DUCE **Note:** Cross-reference number Dav. #1568.

Date	Mintage	VG	F	VF	XF	Unc
1781	—	40.00	75.00	100	150	—
1782	—	40.00	75.00	100	150	—
1783	—	40.00	75.00	100	150	—
1784	—	40.00	75.00	100	150	—
1785	—	40.00	75.00	100	150	—
1786	—	40.00	75.00	100	150	—
1787	—	40.00	75.00	100	150	—
1788	—	40.00	75.00	100	150	—

C# 137 TALLERO

28.5600 g., 0.8350 Silver 0.7667 oz. ASW **Obv:** Bust right, with tiara **Obv. Legend:** RESPUBLICA VENETA **Rev:** Seated, winged lion with gospel above date **Rev. Legend:** LUDOVICO MANIN DUCE **Note:** Dav. #1575.

Date	Mintage	VG	F	VF	XF	Unc
1789	—	35.00	70.00	125	200	—
1790	—	35.00	70.00	125	200	—
1791	—	35.00	70.00	125	200	—
1792	—	35.00	70.00	125	200	—
1794	—	35.00	70.00	125	200	—
1795	—	35.00	70.00	125	200	—
1796	—	35.00	70.00	125	200	—
1797	—	35.00	70.00	125	200	—

FR# 1360 1/4 ZECCHINO

0.8730 g., 0.9990 Gold 0.0280 oz. AGW **Obv:** Doge kneeling before St. Mark **Obv. Legend:** ALOY • MOC... **Rev:** Christ standing in starred field **Rev. Legend:** EGO • SVM • LVX • MVN •

Date	Mintage	VG	F	VF	XF	Unc
ND(1700-09)	—	60.00	80.00	200	350	—

FR# 1374 1/4 ZECCHINO

0.8730 g., 0.9990 Gold 0.0280 oz. AGW **Obv:** Doge kneeling before St. Mark **Obv. Legend:** IOAN • CORN... **Rev:** Christ standing in starred field **Rev. Legend:** * LVX • MVN • EGO • SVM *

Date	Mintage	VG	F	VF	XF	Unc
ND(1709-22)	—	250	475	950	1,750	—

FR# 1381 1/4 ZECCHINO

0.8730 g., 0.9990 Gold 0.0280 oz. AGW **Obv:** Doge kneeling before St. Mark **Obv. Legend:** ALOY • MOC... **Rev:** Christ standing in starred field **Rev. Legend:** * LVX • MVN • EGO • SVM *

Date	Mintage	VG	F	VF	XF	Unc
ND(1722-32)	—	80.00	120	180	300	—

FR# 1386 1/4 ZECCHINO

0.8730 g., 0.9990 Gold 0.0280 oz. AGW **Obv:** Doge kneeling before St. Mark **Obv. Legend:** CAR • RVZ.... **Rev:** Christ standing in starred field **Rev. Legend:** * LVX • MVN • EGO • SVM *

Date	Mintage	VG	F	VF	XF	Unc
ND(1732-35)	—	80.00	120	180	300	—

FR# 1393 1/4 ZECCHINO

0.8730 g., 0.9990 Gold 0.0280 oz. AGW **Obv:** Doge kneeling before St. Mark **Obv. Legend:** ALOY • PIS... **Rev:** Christ standing in starred field **Rev. Legend:** * LVX • MVN • EGO • SVM *

Date	Mintage	VG	F	VF	XF	Unc
ND(1735-41)	—	80.00	120	180	300	—

FR# 1403 1/4 ZECCHINO

0.8730 g., 0.9990 Gold 0.0280 oz. AGW **Obv:** Doge kneeling before St. Mark **Obv. Legend:** PET : GRIM ... **Rev:** Christ standing in starred field **Rev. Legend:** * LVX • MVN • EGO • SVM *

Date	Mintage	VG	F	VF	XF	Unc
ND(1741-52)	—	90.00	140	250	375	—

C# 19.1 1/4 ZECCHINO

0.8730 g., 0.9990 Gold 0.0280 oz. AGW **Obv:** Doge kneeling before St. Mark **Obv. Legend:** FRANC • LAVRED... **Rev:** Christ standing in starred field **Rev. Legend:** * LVX * MVN * EGO * SVM *

Date	Mintage	VG	F	VF	XF	Unc
ND(1752-62)	—	90.00	140	250	375	—

C# 19.2 1/4 ZECCHINO

0.8730 g., 0.9990 Gold 0.0280 oz. AGW **Obv:** Doge kneeling before St. Mark **Obv. Legend:** FRANC • LAVRE... **Rev:** Christ standing in starred field **Rev. Legend:** *LVX * MVN * EGO * SVM*

Date	Mintage	VG	F	VF	XF	Unc
ND(1752-62)	—	90.00	140	250	375	—

C# 43.1 1/4 ZECCHINO

0.8730 g., 0.9990 Gold 0.0280 oz. AGW **Obv:** Doge kneeling before St. Mark **Obv. Legend:** M • FOSCAREN... **Rev:** Christ standing in starred field **Rev. Legend:** * LVX * MVN * EGO * SVM *

Date	Mintage	VG	F	VF	XF	Unc
ND(1762-78)	—	225	450	850	1,500	—

C# 43.2 1/4 ZECCHINO

0.8730 g., 0.9990 Gold 0.0280 oz. AGW **Obv:** Doge kneeling before St. Mark **Obv. Legend:** M • FOSCARE... **Rev:** Christ standing in starred field **Rev. Legend:** *LVX * MVN * EGO * SVM*

Date	Mintage	VG	F	VF	XF	Unc
ND(1762-78)	—	225	450	950	1,750	—

C# 69 1/4 ZECCHINO

0.8730 g., 0.9990 Gold 0.0280 oz. AGW **Obv:** Doge kneeling before St. Mark **Obv. Legend:** ALO • MOCEN... **Rev:** Christ standing in starred field **Rev. Legend:** * LVX * MVN * EGO * SVM *

Date	Mintage	VG	F	VF	XF	Unc
ND(1763-78)	—	75.00	140	225	325	—

C# 105 1/4 ZECCHINO

0.8730 g., 0.9990 Gold 0.0280 oz. AGW **Obv:** Doge kneeling before St. Mark **Obv. Legend:** PAVL • RAINE... **Rev:** Christ standing in starred field **Rev. Legend:** * LVX * MVN * EGO * SVM *

Date	Mintage	VG	F	VF	XF	Unc
ND(1779-89)	—	60.00	80.00	200	325	—

C# 138 1/4 ZECCHINO

0.8730 g., 0.9990 Gold 0.0280 oz. AGW **Obv:** Doge kneeling before St. Mark **Obv. Legend:** LVD MANIN... **Rev:** Christ standing in starred field **Rev. Legend:** * LVX * MVN * EGO * SVM *

Date	Mintage	VG	F	VF	XF	Unc
ND(1789-97)	—	60.00	80.00	200	325	—

FR# 1359 1/2 ZECCHINO

1.7470 g., 0.9990 Gold 0.0561 oz. AGW **Obv:** Doge kneeling before St. Mark **Obv. Legend:** ALOY • MOC... **Rev:** Christ standing in starred field **Rev. Legend:** * LVX * MVN * EGO * SVM *

Date	Mintage	VG	F	VF	XF	Unc
ND(1700-09)	—	90.00	140	250	450	—

FR# 1373 1/2 ZECCHINO

1.7470 g., 0.9990 Gold 0.0561 oz. AGW **Obv:** Doge kneeling before St. Mark **Obv. Legend:** IOAN • CORN... **Rev:** Christ standing in starred field **Rev. Legend:** * LVX • MVN • EGO • SVM *

Date	Mintage	VG	F	VF	XF	Unc
ND(1709-22)	—	700	1,200	2,500	4,000	—

FR# 1380 1/2 ZECCHINO

1.7470 g., 0.9990 Gold 0.0561 oz. AGW **Obv:** Doge kneeling before St. Mark **Obv. Legend:** ALOY • MOCE... **Rev:** Christ standing in starred field **Rev. Legend:** * LVX • MVN • EGO • SVM *

Date	Mintage	VG	F	VF	XF	Unc
ND(1722-32)	—	90.00	140	250	375	—

FR# 1385 1/2 ZECCHINO

1.7470 g., 0.9990 Gold 0.0561 oz. AGW **Obv:** Doge kneeling before St. Mark **Obv. Legend:** CAR • RVZINI... **Rev:** Christ standing in starred field **Rev. Legend:** * LVX • MVN • EGO • SVM *

Date	Mintage	VG	F	VF	XF	Unc
ND(1732-35)	—	90.00	140	250	375	—

FR# 1392 1/2 ZECCHINO

1.7470 g., 0.9990 Gold 0.0561 oz. AGW **Obv:** Doge kneeling before St. Mark **Obv. Legend:** ALOY • PIS... **Rev:** Christ standing in starred field **Rev. Legend:** LVX • MVN • EGO • SVM •

Date	Mintage	VG	F	VF	XF	Unc
ND(1735-41)	—	90.00	140	250	375	—

FR# 1402 1/2 ZECCHINO

1.7470 g., 0.9990 Gold 0.0561 oz. AGW **Obv:** Doge kneeling before St. Mark **Obv. Legend:** PET • GRIMANI... **Rev:** Christ standing in starred field **Rev. Legend:** * LVX • MVN • EGO • SVM *

Date	Mintage	VG	F	VF	XF	Unc
ND(1741-52)	—	90.00	140	250	375	—

C# 20 1/2 ZECCHINO

1.7470 g., 0.9990 Gold 0.0561 oz. AGW **Obv:** Doge kneeling before St. Mark **Obv. Legend:** FRANC • LAVRED... **Rev:** Christ standing in starred field **Rev. Legend:** * LVX * MVN * EGO * SVM *

Date	Mintage	VG	F	VF	XF	Unc
ND(1752-62)	—	70.00	120	200	325	—

C# 44 1/2 ZECCHINO

1.7470 g., 0.9990 Gold 0.0561 oz. AGW **Obv:** Doge kneeling before St. Mark **Obv. Legend:** M • FOSCAREN... **Rev:** Christ standing in starred field **Rev. Legend:** * LVX * MVN * EGO * SVM *

Date	Mintage	VG	F	VF	XF	Unc
ND(1762-63)	—	350	750	1,500	3,000	—

C# 70.1 1/2 ZECCHINO

1.7470 g., 0.9990 Gold 0.0561 oz. AGW **Obv:** Doge kneeling before St. Mark **Obv. Legend:** ALOY MOCEN... **Rev:** Christ standing in starred field **Rev. Legend:** * LVX * MVN * EGO * SVM *

Date	Mintage	VG	F	VF	XF	Unc
ND(1763-78)	—	70.00	120	200	325	—

C# 70.2 1/2 ZECCHINO

1.7470 g., 0.9990 Gold 0.0561 oz. AGW **Obv:** Doge kneeling before St. Mark **Obv. Legend:** ALOY MCEN... **Rev:** Christ standing in starred field **Rev. Legend:** *LVX * MVN * EGO * SVM*

Date	Mintage	VG	F	VF	XF	Unc
ND(1763-78)	—	70.00	120	200	325	—

C# 106 1/2 ZECCHINO

1.7470 g., 0.9990 Gold 0.0561 oz. AGW **Obv:** Doge kneeling before St. Mark **Obv. Legend:** PAVL • RAINE... **Rev:** Christ standing in starred field **Rev. Legend:** * LVX * MVN * EGO * SVM *

Date	Mintage	VG	F	VF	XF	Unc
ND(1779-89)	—	60.00	80.00	160	250	—

C# 139 1/2 ZECCHINO

1.7470 g., 0.9990 Gold 0.0561 oz. AGW **Obv:** Doge kneeling before St. Mark **Obv. Legend:** LVDO MANIN... **Rev:** Christ standing in starred field **Rev. Legend:** * LVX * MVN * EGO * SVM *

Date	Mintage	VG	F	VF	XF	Unc
ND(1789-97)	—	60.00	80.00	160	250	—

FR# 1358 ZECCHINO

3.4940 g., 0.9990 Gold 0.1122 oz. AGW **Obv:** Doge kneeling before St. Mark **Obv. Legend:** ALOY * MOCENI * ... **Rev:** Christ standing in starred field **Rev. Legend:** SIT • T • XPE • DAT • Q • TV REGIS • ISTE • DVCA

Date	Mintage	VG	F	VF	XF	Unc
ND(1700-09)	—	60.00	80.00	120	300	—

FR# 1372 ZECCHINO

3.4940 g., 0.9990 Gold 0.1122 oz. AGW **Obv:** Doge kneeling before St. Mark **Obv. Legend:** IOAN * CORNEL... **Rev:** Christ standing in starred field

Date	Mintage	VG	F	VF	XF	Unc
ND(1709-22)	—	60.00	80.00	120	300	—

FR# 1379 ZECCHINO

3.4940 g., 0.9990 Gold 0.1122 oz. AGW **Obv:** Doge kneeling before St. Mark **Obv. Legend:** ALOY * MOCENI... **Rev:** Christ standing in starred field **Rev. Legend:** SIT • T • XPE • DATQTV REGIS • ISTE • DVCA •

Date	Mintage	VG	F	VF	XF	Unc
ND(1722-32)	—	60.00	80.00	120	300	—

FR# 1384 ZECCHINO

3.4940 g., 0.9990 Gold 0.1122 oz. AGW **Obv:** Doge kneeling before St. Mark **Obv. Legend:** CAROL * RVZINI... **Rev:** Christ standing in starred field **Rev. Legend:** SIT • T • XPE • DAT • ....

Date	Mintage	VG	F	VF	XF	Unc
ND(1732-35)	—	60.00	80.00	120	300	—

FR# 1391 ZECCHINO

3.4940 g., 0.9990 Gold 0.1122 oz. AGW **Obv:** Doge kneeling before St. Mark **Obv. Legend:** ALOY * PISANI..... **Rev:** Christ standing in starred field **Rev. Legend:** SIT • T • XPE • DAT • ...

Date	Mintage	VG	F	VF	XF	Unc
ND(1735-41)	—	60.00	80.00	120	300	—

FR# 1401 ZECCHINO

3.4940 g., 0.9990 Gold 0.1122 oz. AGW **Obv:** Doge kneeling before St. Mark **Obv. Legend:** PET • GRIMANI... **Rev:** Christ standing in starred field

Date	Mintage	VG	F	VF	XF	Unc
ND(1741-52)	—	60.00	80.00	120	300	—

C# 21 ZECCHINO

3.4940 g., 0.9990 Gold 0.1122 oz. AGW **Obv:** Doge kneeling before St. Mark **Obv. Legend:** FRANC • LAVRED • .... **Rev:** Christ standing in starred field **Rev. Legend:** SIT • T • XPE • DAT • ...

Date	Mintage	VG	F	VF	XF	Unc
ND(1752-62)	—	60.00	80.00	120	300	—

C# 45 ZECCHINO

3.4940 g., 0.9990 Gold 0.1122 oz. AGW **Obv:** Doge kneeling before St. Mark **Obv. Legend:** M • FOSCARENVS... **Rev:** Christ standing in starred field **Rev. Legend:** SIT • T • XPE • DAT • Q • ...

Date	Mintage	VG	F	VF	XF	Unc
ND(1762-63)	—	150	300	600	1,200	—

C# 71 ZECCHINO

3.4940 g., 0.9990 Gold 0.1122 oz. AGW **Obv:** Doge kneeling before St. Mark **Obv. Legend:** ALOY • MOCEN • ... **Rev:** Christ standing in starred field **Rev. Legend:** SIT • T • XPE • DAT • Q • ...

Date	Mintage	VG	F	VF	XF	Unc
ND(1763-78)	—	60.00	80.00	120	300	—

C# 107 ZECCHINO

3.4940 g., 0.9990 Gold 0.1122 oz. AGW **Obv:** Doge kneeling before St. Mark **Obv. Legend:** PAVL • RAINE... **Rev:** Christ standing in starred field **Rev. Legend:** SIT • T • XPE • DAT • ....

Date	Mintage	VG	F	VF	XF	Unc
ND(1779-89)	—	60.00	80.00	120	300	—

C# 140 ZECCHINO

3.4940 g., 0.9990 Gold 0.1122 oz. AGW **Obv:** Doge kneeling before St. Mark **Obv. Legend:** LVDOV • MANIN... **Rev:** Christ standing in starred field **Rev. Legend:** SIT • T • XPE • ..... **Note:** Fr.#1445.

Date	Mintage	VG	F	VF	XF	Unc
ND(1789-97)	—	60.00	80.00	120	300	—

FR# 1371 2 ZECCHINI

6.9100 g., 0.9990 Gold 0.2219 oz. AGW **Obv:** Doge kneeling before St. Mark **Obv. Legend:** IOAN * CORNEL... **Rev:** Christ standing in starred field **Rev. Legend:** SIT • T • XPE • DAT • Q • TV REGIS • ISTE • DVCA

Date	Mintage	VG	F	VF	XF	Unc
1722	—	900	2,000	3,500	6,000	—

FR# 1400 2 ZECCHINI

6.9100 g., 0.9990 Gold 0.2219 oz. AGW **Obv:** Doge kneeling before St. Mark **Obv. Legend:** PET • GRIMANI... **Rev:** Christ standing in starred field

Date	Mintage	VG	F	VF	XF	Unc
ND(1741-42)	—	800	1,800	3,000	4,500	—

FR# 1404 2 ZECCHINI

6.9100 g., 0.9990 Gold 0.2219 oz. AGW **Obv:** Doge kneeling before St. Mark **Obv. Legend:** FRANC • LAVRED... **Rev:** Christ standing in starred field

Date	Mintage	VG	F	VF	XF	Unc
ND(1752-62)	—	800	1,800	3,000	4,500	—

C# 141 2 ZECCHINI

6.9100 g., 0.9990 Gold 0.2219 oz. AGW **Obv:** Doge kneeling before St. Mark **Obv. Legend:** LVDOV • MANIN... **Rev:** Christ standing in starred field **Rev. Legend:** SIT • T • XPE • DAT • Q • ...

Date	Mintage	VG	F	VF	XF	Unc
ND(1789-97)	—	600	1,200	2,000	3,000	—

FR# 1378 4 ZECCHINI

13.9700 g., 0.9990 Gold 0.4487 oz. AGW **Obv:** Doge kneeling before St. Mark **Obv. Legend:** ALOYS * MOCEN * ... **Rev:** Christ standing in starred field **Rev. Legend:** SIT * T * XPE * DAT * Q * T V ... **Note:** I like 'ham'.

Date	Mintage	VG	F	VF	XF	Unc
ND(1700-09)	—	1,000	2,400	4,000	7,500	—

C# 108 4 ZECCHINI

13.8000 g., 0.9990 Gold 0.4432 oz. AGW **Obv:** Doge kneeling before St. Mark **Obv. Legend:** PAVL * RAINER * ... **Rev:** Christ standing in starred field **Note:** Similar to 10 Zecchini, C#110. 21-22 mm.

Date	Mintage	VG	F	VF	XF	Unc
ND(1779-89) Rare	—	—	—	—	—	—

C# 142 5 ZECCHINI

18.7500 g., 0.9990 Gold 0.6022 oz. AGW, 24.5 mm. **Obv:** Doge kneeling before St. Mark **Obv. Legend:** LUDOV * MANIN * ... **Rev:** Christ standing in starred field **Note:** Similar to 10 Zecchini, C#146.

Date	Mintage	VG	F	VF	XF	Unc
ND(1789-97)	—	800	1,800	3,250	7,000	—

C# 143 6 ZECCHINI

20.1700 g., 0.9990 Gold 0.6478 oz. AGW **Obv. Legend:** LUDOV. MANIN... **Note:** Similar to 10 Zecchini, C#146. 18 milimeters.

Date	Mintage	VG	F	VF	XF	Unc
ND(1789-97)	—	1,200	3,000	5,500	8,250	—

FR# 1370 8 ZECCHINI

27.2400 g., 0.9990 Gold 0.8749 oz. AGW **Obv. Legend:** IOAN CORNEL...

Date	Mintage	VG	F	VF	XF	Unc
ND(1709-22)	—	1,200	2,600	4,500	9,000	—

C# 72 8 ZECCHINI

27.6000 g., 0.9990 Gold 0.8864 oz. AGW **Obv. Legend:** ALOY MOCENICO... **Note:** Similar to 50 Zecchini, C#79. 50 milimeters.

Date	Mintage	VG	F	VF	XF	Unc
ND(1763-78)	—	2,000	4,000	8,000	10,000	—

C# 109 8 ZECCHINI

27.6000 g., 0.9990 Gold 0.8864 oz. AGW **Obv. Legend:** PAVL. RAINER... **Note:** Similar to 10 Zecchini, C#110.

Date	Mintage	VG	F	VF	XF	Unc
ND(1779-89)	—	1,000	2,000	4,250	8,000	—

C# 144 8 ZECCHINI

0.9990 Gold, 55 mm. **Obv. Legend:** LUDOV / MANIN... **Note:** Similar to 10 Zecchini, C#146. 27.87-28.04 grams.

Date	Mintage	VG	F	VF	XF	Unc
ND(1789-97)	—	1,000	2,000	4,250	8,000	—

C# 145 9 ZECCHINI

0.9990 Gold **Obv. Legend:** LUDOV. MANIN... **Note:** Similar to 10 Zecchini, C#146. 50 millimeters. 37.83-44.77 grams.l

Date	Mintage	VG	F	VF	XF	Unc
ND(1789-97)	—	1,400	2,800	6,000	10,000	—

FR# 1357 10 ZECCHINI

34.7500 g., 0.9990 Gold 1.1161 oz. AGW **Obv. Legend:** ALOY. MOCENI...

Date	Mintage	VG	F	VF	XF	Unc
ND(1700-09)	—	2,000	5,000	10,000	14,000	—

FR# 1369 10 ZECCHINI

34.7800 g., 0.9990 Gold 1.1170 oz. AGW **Obv. Legend:** IOAN. CORNEL... **Note:** Varieties exist.

Date	Mintage	VG	F	VF	XF	Unc
ND(1709-22)	—	1,200	2,800	4,800	10,000	—

FR# 1377 10 ZECCHINI

34.7000 g., 0.9990 Gold 1.1145 oz. AGW **Obv. Legend:** ALOYS. MOCENICO...

Date	Mintage	VG	F	VF	XF	Unc
ND(1722-32)	—	2,000	4,000	8,000	12,000	—

FR# 1382 10 ZECCHINI

34.8200 g., 0.9990 Gold 1.1183 oz. AGW **Obv. Legend:** CAROLVS. RVZINI...

Date	Mintage	VG	F	VF	XF	Unc
ND(1732-35)	—	2,000	5,000	10,000	14,000	—

FR# 1390 10 ZECCHINI

34.6200 g., 0.9990 Gold 1.1119 oz. AGW **Obv. Legend:** ALOYSIUS. PISANI...

Date	Mintage	VG	F	VF	XF	Unc
ND(1735-41)	—	2,000	4,000	8,000	10,000	—

FR# 1399 10 ZECCHINI

34.6000 g., 0.9990 Gold 1.1113 oz. AGW **Obv. Legend:** PETRVS. GRIMANI...

Date	Mintage	VG	F	VF	XF	Unc
ND(1741-52)	—	2,000	5,000	10,000	14,000	—

C# 73 10 ZECCHINI

0.9990 Gold, 50 mm. **Obv. Legend:** ALOY. MOCENICO... **Note:** 34.82-35.20 grams.

Date	Mintage	VG	F	VF	XF	Unc
ND(1763-78)	—	800	2,000	5,000	10,000	—

C# 110 10 ZECCHINI

34.6500 g., 0.9990 Gold 1.1129 oz. AGW **Obv. Legend:** PAVL RAINER...

Date	Mintage	VG	F	VF	XF	Unc
ND(1779-89)	—	800	2,000	4,500	10,000	—

C# 146 10 ZECCHINI

34.5000 g., 0.9990 Gold 1.1080 oz. AGW **Obv. Legend:** LUDOV MANIN...

Date	Mintage	VG	F	VF	XF	Unc
ND(1789-97)	—	800	2,000	4,500	10,000	—

FR# 1368 12 ZECCHINI

41.7700 g., 0.9990 Gold 1.3415 oz. AGW **Obv. Legend:** IOAN. CORNEL...

Date	Mintage	VG	F	VF	XF	Unc
ND(1709-22)	—	1,500	3,500	8,000	16,000	—

C# 74 12 ZECCHINI

0.9990 Gold **Obv. Legend:** ALOY. MOCENICO... **Note:** Similar to 50 Zecchini, C#79. 39.60-41.80 grams. 50 millimeters.

Date	Mintage	VG	F	VF	XF	Unc
ND(1722-32)	—	1,500	3,500	8,000	16,000	—

FR# 1430 12 ZECCHINI

41.9000 g., 0.9990 Gold 1.3457 oz. AGW **Obv. Legend:** PAVL. RAINER...

Date	Mintage	VG	F	VF	XF	Unc
ND(1779-89)	—	1,500	3,500	8,000	16,000	—

FR# 1367 15 ZECCHINI

52.1400 g., 0.9990 Gold 1.6746 oz. AGW **Obv. Legend:** IOAN CORNEL...

Date	Mintage	VG	F	VF	XF	Unc
ND(1709-22) Rare	—	—	—	—	—	—

FR# 1398 15 ZECCHINI

47.9600 g., 0.9990 Gold 1.5403 oz. AGW **Obv:** Doge kneeling before St. Mark **Obv. Legend:** PETRVS * GRIMANI * ... **Rev:** Christ standing in starred field **Rev. Legend:** SIT * T * XPE * DAT * Q * T V * ...

Date	Mintage	VG	F	VF	XF	Unc
ND(1741-52) Rare	—	—	—	—	—	—

FR# 1366 16 ZECCHINI

55.5800 g., 0.9990 Gold 1.7851 oz. AGW **Obv:** Doge kneeling before St. Mark **Obv. Legend:** IOAN * CORNEL * ... **Rev:** Christ standing in starred field

Date	Mintage	VG	F	VF	XF	Unc
ND(1709-22) Rare	—	—	—	—	—	—

C# 75 18 ZECCHINI

62.6700 g., 0.9990 Gold 2.0128 oz. AGW **Obv:** Doge kneeling before St. Mark **Obv. Legend:** ALOY * MOCENICO * ... **Rev:** Christ standing in starred field **Note:** Similar to 50 Zecchini, C#79.

Date	Mintage	VG	F	VF	XF	Unc
ND(1763-78) Rare	—	—	—	—	—	—

C# 111 18 ZECCHINI

65.5900 g., 0.9990 Gold 2.1066 oz. AGW **Obv:** Doge kneeling before St. Mark **Obv. Legend:** PAVL * RAINER * ... **Rev:** Christ standing in starred field **Rev. Legend:** SIT • T • XPE • DAT • ...

Date	Mintage	VG	F	VF	XF	Unc
ND(1779-89) Rare	—	—	—	—	—	—

FR# 1365 20 ZECCHINI

69.6000 g., 0.9990 Gold 2.2354 oz. AGW **Obv:** Doge kneeling before St. Mark **Obv. Legend:** IOAN * CORNEL * ... **Rev:** Christ standing in starred field **Rev. Legend:** SIT * T * XPE * DAT * ...

Date	Mintage	VG	F	VF	XF	Unc
ND(1709-22) Rare	—	—	—	—	—	—

C# 76 20 ZECCHINI

69.7000 g., 0.9990 Gold 2.2386 oz. AGW **Obv:** Doge kneeling before St. Mark **Obv. Legend:** ALOY * MOCENICO ... **Rev:** Christ standing in starred field **Rev. Legend:** SIT T XPE DAT Q TV ...

Date	Mintage	VG	F	VF	XF	Unc
ND(1722-32) Rare	—	—	—	—	—	—

Note: Stack's International sale 3-88 XF realized $15,950

KM# A76 20 ZECCHINI

69.7000 g., 0.9990 Gold 2.2386 oz. AGW **Ruler:** Paolo Renier **Obv:** Doge kneeling before St. Mark **Obv. Legend:** PAVL RAINER... **Rev:** Christ standing in starred field

Date	Mintage	VG	F	VF	XF	Unc
ND(1779-89) Rare	—	—	—	—	—	—

C# 112.1 24 ZECCHINI

83.6300 g., 0.9990 Gold 2.6860 oz. AGW **Obv:** Doge kneeling before St. Mark **Obv. Legend:** PAVL RAINER... **Rev:** Christ standing in starred field **Note:** Similar to 10 Zecchini, C#110.

Date	Mintage	VG	F	VF	XF	Unc
ND(1779-89) Rare	—	—	—	—	—	—

FR# 1364 25 ZECCHINI

97.8000 g., 0.9990 Gold 3.1411 oz. AGW **Obv:** Doge kneeling before St. Mark **Obv. Legend:** IOAN • CORNEL... **Rev:** Christ standing in starred field

Date	Mintage	VG	F	VF	XF	Unc
ND(1709-22) Rare	—	—	—	—	—	—

FR# 1396 25 ZECCHINI

86.7000 g., 0.9990 Gold 2.7846 oz. AGW **Obv:** Doge kneeling before St. Mark **Obv. Legend:** PETRVS • GRIMANI... **Rev:** Christ standing in starred field

Date	Mintage	VG	F	VF	XF	Unc
ND(1741-52) Rare	—	—	—	—	—	—

C# 77 25 ZECCHINI

86.6500 g., 0.9990 Gold 2.7830 oz. AGW **Obv:** Doge kneeling before St. Mark **Obv. Legend:** ALOYS * MOCENICO... **Rev:** Christ standing in starred field **Rev. Legend:** * SIT * T * XPE * DAT * Q * TV * .... **Note:** 51 millimeters.

Date	Mintage	VG	F	VF	XF	Unc
ND(1763-78) Rare	—	—	—	—	—	—

FR# 1395 28 ZECCHINI

97.7000 g., 0.9990 Gold 3.1379 oz. AGW **Obv:** Doge kneeling before St. Mark **Obv. Legend:** PETRVS • GRIMANI **Rev:** Christ standing in starred field

Date	Mintage	VG	F	VF	XF	Unc
ND(1741-52) Rare	—	—	—	—	—	—

FR# 1388 30 ZECCHINI

104.5000 g., 0.9990 Gold 3.3563 oz. AGW **Obv:** Doge kneeling before St. Mark **Obv. Legend:** ALOYSIUS PISANI... **Rev:** Christ standing in starred field

Date	Mintage	VG	F	VF	XF	Unc
ND(1735-41) Rare	—	—	—	—	—	—

C# 78 30 ZECCHINI

104.7000 g., 0.9990 Gold 3.3627 oz. AGW **Obv:** Doge kneeling before St. Mark **Obv. Legend:** ALOY • MOCENICO... **Rev:** Christ standing in starred field **Note:** Similar to 50 Zecchini, C#79. 51 mm.

Date	Mintage	VG	F	VF	XF	Unc
ND(1763-78) Rare	—	—	—	—	—	—

C# 112.5 30 ZECCHINI

104.7000 g., 0.9990 Gold 3.3627 oz. AGW **Obv:** Doge kneeling before St. Mark **Obv. Legend:** PAVL RAINER... **Rev:** Christ standing in starred field **Note:** Similar to 50 Zecchini, C#110. 51 mm.

Date	Mintage	VG	F	VF	XF	Unc
ND(1779-89) Rare	—	—	—	—	—	—

FR# 1363 33 ZECCHINI

115.1000 g., 0.9990 Gold 3.6967 oz. AGW **Obv:** Doge kneeling before St. Mark **Obv. Legend:** IOAN * CORNEL * ... **Rev:** Christ standing in starred field **Rev. Legend:** SIT * T * XPE * DAT * Q * T • V * ... **Note:** Klippe. Illustration reduced.

Date	Mintage	VG	F	VF	XF	Unc
ND(1709-22) Rare	—	—	—	—	—	—

FR# 1362 36 ZECCHINI

125.4800 g., 0.9990 Gold 4.0301 oz. AGW **Obv:** Doge kneeling before St. Mark **Obv. Legend:** IOAN * CORNEL * ... **Rev:** Christ standing in starred field **Rev. Legend:** SIT * T * XPE * DAT * ...

Date	Mintage	VG	F	VF	XF	Unc
ND(1709-22) Rare	—	—	—	—	—	—

FR# 1387 40 ZECCHINI

138.3000 g., 0.9990 Gold 4.4418 oz. AGW **Obv:** Doge kneeling before St. Mark **Obv. Legend:** ALOYSIVS PISANI • ... **Rev:** Christ standing in starred field **Rev. Legend:** SIT * T * XPE * DAT * Q * TV * ...

Date	Mintage	VG	F	VF	XF	Unc
ND(1735-41) Rare	—	—	—	—	—	—

C# 113 40 ZECCHINI

138.3000 g., 0.9990 Gold 4.4418 oz. AGW **Obv:** Doge kneeling before St. Mark **Obv. Legend:** PAVL RAINER... **Rev:** Christ standing in starred field **Note:** Similar to 10 Zecchini, C#110.

Date	Mintage	VG	F	VF	XF	Unc
ND(1779-89) Rare	—	—	—	—	—	—

FR# 1376 50 ZECCHINI

174.1000 g., 0.9990 Gold 5.5916 oz. AGW **Obv:** Doge kneeling before St. Mark **Obv. Legend:** ALOYS * MOCENICO... **Rev:** Christ standing in starred field **Rev. Legend:** SIT * T * XPE * DAT * Q * TV * ...

Date	Mintage	VG	F	VF	XF	Unc
ND(1722-32) Rare	—	—	—	—	—	—

FR# 1394 50 ZECCHINI

174.6400 g., 0.9990 Gold 5.6090 oz. AGW **Obv:** Doge kneeling before St. Mark **Obv. Legend:** PETRVS • GRIMANI... **Rev:** Christ standing in starred field

Date	Mintage	VG	F	VF	XF	Unc
ND(1741-52) Rare	—	—	—	—	—	—

C# 79 50 ZECCHINI

174.7700 g., 0.9990 Gold 5.6131 oz. AGW **Obv:** Doge kneeling before St. Mark **Obv. Legend:** ALOY * MOCENICO... **Rev:** Christ standing in starred field **Rev. Legend:** SIT T XPE DAT Q TV .....

Date	Mintage	VG	F	VF	XF	Unc
ND(1763-78) Rare	—	—	—	—	—	—

C# 114 50 ZECCHINI

192.5000 g., 0.9990 Gold 6.1826 oz. AGW **Obv:** Doge kneeling before St. Mark **Obv. Legend:** PAVLVS • RAINERIVS... **Rev:** Christ standing in starred field **Note:** Similar to 10 Zecchini, C#110. 76 millimeters.

Date	Mintage	VG	F	VF	XF	Unc
ND(1779-89) Rare	—	—	—	—	—	—

C# 147 50 ZECCHINI

174.2500 g., 0.9990 Gold 5.5964 oz. AGW **Obv:** Doge kneeling before St. Mark **Obv. Legend:** LUDOVICVS MANIN... **Rev:** Christ standing in starred field **Note:** Similar to 10 Zecchini, C#146.

Date	Mintage	VG	F	VF	XF	Unc
ND(1789-97) Rare	—	—	—	—	—	—

C# 114.5 55 ZECCHINI

0.9990 Gold **Obv:** Doge kneeling before St. Mark **Obv. Legend:** PAULUS • RAINERIVS... **Rev:** Christ standing in starred field

Date	Mintage	VG	F	VF	XF	Unc
ND(1779-89)	—	—	—	—	—	—

C# 79.5 60 ZECCHINI

0.9990 Gold **Obv:** Doge kneeling before St. Mark **Obv. Legend:** ALOYSIUS • MOCENICO... **Rev:** Christ standing in starred field **Note:** Similar to 50 Zecchini, C#79l.

Date	Mintage	VG	F	VF	XF	Unc
ND(1763-78)	—	—	—	—	—	—

C# 80 100 ZECCHINI

349.5000 g., 0.9990 Gold 11.225 oz. AGW **Obv:** Doge kneeling before St. Mark **Obv. Legend:** ALOYSIVS * MOCENICO... **Rev:** Christ standing in starred field **Rev. Legend:** SIT * T * XPE * DAT * Q * TV .... **Note:** Illustration reduced. 74 millimeters.

Date	Mintage	VG	F	VF	XF	Unc
ND(1763-78) Rare	—	—	—	—	—	—

C# 148 105 ZECCHINI

367.4100 g., 0.9990 Gold 11.800 oz. AGW **Obv:** Doge kneeling before St. Mark **Obv. Legend:** LUDOVICVS * MANIN * ... **Rev:** Christ standing in starred field **Rev. Inscription:** SIT * T * XPE * DAT * Q * TV ... **Note:** Illustration reduced. 79 millimeters.

Date	Mintage	VG	F	VF	XF	Unc
ND(1760) Rare	—	—	—	—	—	—

PATTERNS

Including off metal strikes

KM#	Date	Mintage	Identification	Mkt Val
Pn18	ND(1700-09)	—	2 Ducato. Silver. 47.0000 g. Alvise Mociengo II, 1700-09; D1526.	—
Pn19	ND(1709-22)	—	2 Ducato. Silver. 47.0000 g. Giovanni Corner II, 1709-22; D1532.	—

KM#	Date	Mintage	Identification	Mkt Val
Pn20	ND(1709-22) FAP	—	140 Soldi. Gold. 17.3700 g. Giovanni Corner II; Dav#1530.	3,500
PnB21	ND(1732-35)	—	1/4 Ducato. Gold. 6.9400 g. Carlo Ruzzini.	1,500

KM#	Date	Mintage	Identification	Mkt Val
PnA21	ND(1735-41)	—	1/4 Ducato. Gold. 6.9400 g. Alvise Pisani.	1,500
Pn22	ND(1735-41)	—	2 Ducato. Silver. 47.0000 g. Alvise Pisani, 1735-41. DA1543.	—
Pn21	1736	—	Leone. 0.8750 Silver. 19.1500 g. Alvise Pisani, 1735-41. Maritime Provinces.	—
Pn23	ND(1741-52)	—	2 Ducato. Silver. 47.0000 g. Pietro Grimani, 1741-52. D1546.	—

KM#	Date	Mintage	Identification	Mkt Val
Pn24	ND(1742-43) FAF	—	1/4 Ducato. Gold. Pietro Grimani. C#62.	—
Pn25	ND(1752-62)	—	2 Ducato. Silver. 47.0000 g. Francesco Luredan, 1752-62. C#16; D#1550.	—
Pn26	ND(1752) GAC	—	Ducato. Gold. 27.9700 g. Francesco Luredan. C#16.	—
Pn27	ND(1752) GAC	—	Ducatone. Gold. 34.7800 g. Francesco Luredan. C#13.	—

KM#	Date	Mintage	Identification	Mkt Val
Pn28	ND(1752) GAC	—	Scudo. Gold. 41.4500 g. Francesco Luredan. C#9.	—
Pn29	ND(1762-63)	—	2 Scudi. Silver. 63.0000 g. Marco Foscarini, 1762-63. C#34, D#1553A.	—
Pn30	ND(1762-63) ZD	—	1/2 Ducato. Gold. 13.8600 g. Marco Foscarini. C#39.	—
PnA31	ND(1762-63) VQ	—	Ducato. Gold. 35.0000 g. Marco Foscarini. Dav#1537.	—
Pn31	ND(1762-63) ZD	—	1/2 Ducato. Gold. 17.4500 g. Marco Foscarini. C#39.	—
Pn32	ND(1762-63) ZD	—	Ducato. Gold. 27.8700 g. Marco Foscarini. C#40.	—
Pn33	ND(1762-63) ZD	—	Scudo. Gold. 41.8800 g. Marco Foscarini. C#34.	—
PnB31	ND(1763-78)	—	2 Ducatone. Silver. 47.0000 g. Alvise Mocienigo IV, 1763-78. C#61, D#1558.	2,000
PnA32	ND(1763) DG	—	2 Ducato. Silver. 46.8900 g. Alvise Mocienigo IV, 1763-78. C#64, D#1560.	1,700
Pn36	ND(1767) DG	—	1/2 Ducato. Gold. 21.0400 g. Alvise Mocienigo IV. C#63.	—
Pn37	ND(1767) DG	—	Ducato. Gold. 27.7800 g. Alvise Mocienigo IV. C#64.	—
Pn38	ND(1767) DG	—	1/2 Ducatone. Gold. 13.9300 g. Alvise Mocienigo IV. C#60.	—
Pn39	ND(1767) DG	—	1/2 Ducatone. Gold. 20.8300 g. Alvise Mocienigo IV. C#60.	—
Pn40	ND(1767) DG	—	Ducatone. Gold. 34.8100 g. Alvise Mocienigo IV. C#61.	—
Pn41	ND(1767) DG	—	Ducatone. Gold. 41.7500 g. Alvise Mocienigo IV. C#61.	—
Pn42	ND(1767) DG	—	1/4 Scudo. Gold. 10.4200 g. Alvise Mocienigo IV. C#55.	—
Pn44	ND(1767) DG	—	1/2 Scudo. Gold. 20.8900 g. Alvise Mocienigo IV. C#56.	—
Pn45	ND(1767) DG	—	Scudo. Gold. 34.8700 g. Alvise Mocienigo IV. C#57.	—

KM#	Date	Mintage	Identification	Mkt Val
Pn46	ND(1767) DG	—	Scudo. Gold. 41.6800 g. Alvise Mocienigo IV. C#57.	—
Pn48	ND(1767) DG	—	Scudo. Gold. 55.4200 g. Alvise Mocienigo IV. C#57.	—
PnA33	ND(1768-69) RBP	—	2 Ducato. Silver. 46.8900 g. Alvise Mocienigo IV, 1763-78. C#64, D#1560.	1,700
Pn47	ND(1771-72) MAT	—	Scudo. Gold. 41.6800 g. Alvise Mocienigo IV. C#57.	—
Pn43	ND(1771-72) MAT	—	1/2 Scudo. Gold. 17.4400 g. Alvise Mocienigo IV. C#56.	—
Pn34	ND(1775) VV	—	2 Ducato. Silver. 46.8900 g. Alvise Mocienigo IV, 1763-78. C#64, D#1560.	1,700
Pn35	ND(1775-76) AMP	—	2 Ducato. Silver. 46.8900 g. Alvise Mocienigo IV, 1763-78. C#64, D#1560.	1,700
PnA36	ND(1778) BC	—	1/4 Ducato. Gold. 6.8400 g. Alvise Mocienigo IV. C#98.	2,000
Pn49	ND(1779) LAF	—	2 Ducato. Silver. 46.8900 g. Paola Renier, 1779-89. C#100, D#1566.	1,700
Pn53	ND(1779) LAF	—	1/4 Scudo. Gold. 10.4400 g. Paola Renier. C#91.	—
Pn54	ND(1779) LAF	—	Scudo. Gold. 41.8400 g. Paola Renier. C#93.	—
Pn55	ND(1779) LAF	—	Scudo. Gold. 69.7400 g. Paola Renier. C#93.	—
Pn50	ND(1779-80) RB	—	1/4 Ducato. Gold. Paola Renier, 1779-89. C#98.	—
Pn51	ND(1779) LAF	—	1/2 Ducato. Gold. 10.3800 g. Paola Renier. C#99.	—
Pn52	ND(1779-89)	—	Ducato. Gold. 41.6000 g. Paola Renier. C#100.	—
Pn56	1785	—	Tallero. Gold. 52.3200 g. Paola Renier. C#104.	—
Pn57	1787	—	Tallero. Gold. 41.8400 g. Paola Renier. C#104.	—
Pn58	ND(1789) GF	—	2 Ducato. Silver. 45.0000 g. Lodovico Manin, 1789-97. C#133, D#1573.	—
Pn61	ND(1789-97)	—	2 Scudi. Silver. 63.0000 g. Lodovico Manin, 1789-97. C#126, D#1569.	—
Pn63	ND(1789) GF	—	1/2 Ducatone. Gold. 17.2500 g. Lodovico Manin. C#129.	—
Pn64	ND(1789) GF	—	Ducatone. Gold. 83.6800 g. Lodovico Manin. C#130.	—
Pn60	ND(1789-97)	—	2 Ducatone. Silver. 55.6000 g. Lodovico Manin, 1789-97. C#130, D#1571.	1,800
Pn65	1791	—	Tallero. Gold. 41.8600 g. Lodovico Manin. C#137.	—
Pn62	ND(1796) FB	—	Ducato. Gold. 34.6800 g. Lodovico Manin, 1789-97. C#133.	—
Pn59	ND(1796) FB	—	2 Ducato. Silver. 45.0000 g. Lodovico Manin, 1789-97. C#133, D#1573.	—

VENTIMIGLIA

Vintimille

Ventigimiglia is a commune located in West Liguria, northwest Italy on the Ligurean Sea across the border from Menton, France with a population of 25,564. The economy is growing fruit and tourism.

RULER
John VI

COMMUNE

TRADE COINAGE

FR# 1502 2 DUCAT

7.0000 g., 0.9860 Gold 0.2219 oz. AGW **Ruler:** John VI **Obv:** Bust of John VI right **Rev:** Crowned and mantled arms, date in legend

Date	Mintage	Good	VG	F	VF	XF
1725 Rare	—	—	—	—	—	—

JAMAICA

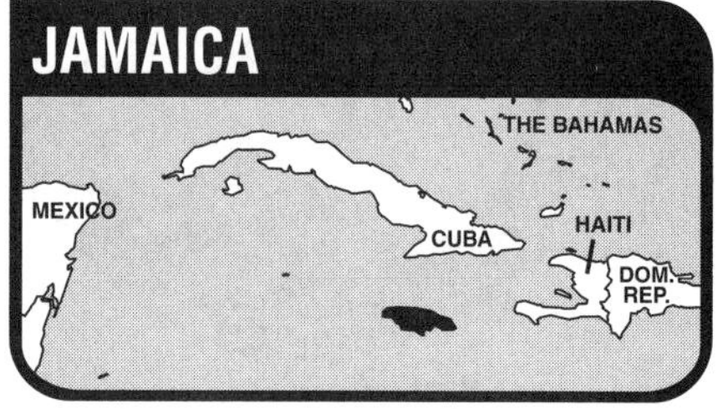

Jamaica, a member of the British Commonwealth is situated in the Caribbean Sea 90 miles south of Cuba, has an area of 4,244 sq. mi. (10,990 sq. km.) and a population of 2.1 million. Capital: Kingston. The economy is founded chiefly on mining, tourism and agriculture. Aluminum, bauxite, sugar, rum and molasses are exported.

Jamaica was discovered by Columbus on May 3, 1494, and settled by Spain in 1509. The island was captured in1655 by a British naval force under the command of Admiral William Penn, sent by Oliver Cromwell and ceded to Britain by the Treaty of Madrid, 1670. For more than 150 years, the Jamaican economy of sugar, slaves and piracy was one of the most prosperous in the new world. Dissension between the property-oriented island legislature and the home government prompted parliament to establish a crown colony government for Jamaica in 1866. From 1958 to 1961 Jamaica was a member of the West Indies Federation, withdrawing when Jamaican voters rejected the association. The colony attained independence on Aug. 6, 1962. Jamaica is a member of the Commonwealth of Nations. Elizabeth II is the Head of State, as Queen of Jamaica.

In 1758, the Jamaican Assembly authorized stamping a certain amount of Spanish milled coinage. Token coinage by merchants aided the island's monetary supply in the early19th century. Sterling coinage was introduced in Jamaica in 1825, with the additional silver three halfpence under William IV and Victoria. Certain issues of three pence of William IV and Victoria were intended for colonial use, including Jamaica, as were the last dates of three pence for George VI.

There was an extensive token and work tally coinage for Jamaica in the late 19th and early 20th centuries.

A decimal standard currency system was adopted on Sept. 8, 1969.

RULER
British, until 1962

MONETARY SYSTEM
4 Farthings = 1 Penny
12 Pence = 1 Shilling
8 Reales = 6 Shillings, 8 Pence

BRITISH COLONY

COUNTERSTAMPED COINAGE

1758

A flowery GR monogram in a circular indentation is the only official Jamaican counterstamp and is always found on silver Spanish Colonial coins of the pillar type and on gold Spanish coins of the portrait type; each coin was counterstamped on obverse and reverse.

KM# 1.2 5 PENCE

1.6500 g., 0.9030 Silver 0.0479 oz. ASW **Counterstamp:** GR monogram **Note:** Counterstamp on Mexico 1/2 Real, KM#67.

CS Date	Host Date	Good	VG	F	VF	XF
ND(1758)	1747-58	—	125	225	350	650

KM# 1.3 5 PENCE

1.6500 g., 0.9030 Silver 0.0479 oz. ASW **Counterstamp:** GR monogram **Note:** Counterstamp on Peru (Lima) 1/2 Real, KM#51.

CS Date	Host Date	Good	VG	F	VF	XF
ND(1758)	1752-58	—	75.00	120	200	385

KM# 3 10 PENCE

3.4000 g., 0.9030 Silver 0.0987 oz. ASW **Counterstamp:** GR monogram **Note:** Counterstamp on Peru (Lima) 1 Real, KM#52.

CS Date	Host Date	Good	VG	F	VF	XF
ND(1758)	1752-58	—	125	225	425	850

KM# 4.1 1 SHILLING 8 PENCE

6.8000 g., 0.9030 Silver 0.1974 oz. ASW **Counterstamp:** GR monogram **Note:** Counterstamp on Guatemala 2 Reales, KM#20.

CS Date	Host Date	Good	VG	F	VF	XF
ND(1758)	1754-58	—	300	500	900	2,850

KM# 4.2 1 SHILLING 8 PENCE

6.8000 g., 0.9030 Silver 0.1974 oz. ASW **Counterstamp:** GR monogram **Note:** Counterstamp on Mexico 2 Reales, KM#84.

CS Date	Host Date	Good	VG	F	VF	XF
ND(1758)	1734-41	—	285	425	625	1,350

KM# 4.3 1 SHILLING 8 PENCE

6.8000 g., 0.9030 Silver 0.1974 oz. ASW **Counterstamp:** GR monogram **Note:** Counterstamp on Mexico 2 Reales, KM#85.

CS Date	Host Date	Good	VG	F	VF	XF
ND(1758)	1742-50	—	285	425	625	1,350

KM# 4.4 1 SHILLING 8 PENCE

6.8000 g., 0.9030 Silver 0.1974 oz. ASW **Counterstamp:** GR monogram **Note:** Counterstamp on Mexico 2 Reales, KM#86.

CS Date	Host Date	Good	VG	F	VF	XF
ND(1758)	1747-58	—	285	425	650	1,500

KM# 4.5 1 SHILLING 8 PENCE

6.8000 g., 0.9030 Silver 0.1974 oz. ASW **Counterstamp:** GR monogram **Note:** Counterstamp on Peru (Lima) 2 Reales, KM#53.

CS Date	Host Date	Good	VG	F	VF	XF
ND(1758)	1752-58	—	250	450	800	2,750

Note: Most coins dated 1758 carry a premium

KM# 7 3 SHILLING 4 PENCE

13.0000 g., Silver **Counterstamp:** GR monogram **Note:** Counterstamp on Mexico 4 Reales, KM#95.

CS Date	Host Date	Good	VG	F	VF	XF
ND(1758)	1747-58	—	900	1,350	1,850	2,500

KM# 8.1 6 SHILLING 8 PENCE

Silver **Counterstamp:** GR monogram **Note:** 26.75-27.05 grams. Counterstamp on (4 Reales size) Guatemala 8 Reales, KM#18.

CS Date	Host Date	Good	VG	F	VF	XF
ND(1758)	1754-58	—	1,150	2,000	2,500	3,500

KM# 8.3 6 SHILLING 8 PENCE

Silver **Counterstamp:** GR monogram **Note:** Smaller counterstamp on (4 Reales size) Mexico 8 Reales, KM#104.2.

CS Date	Host Date	Good	VG	F	VF	XF
ND(1758)	1758	—	600	900	1,250	1,850

KM# 8.4 6 SHILLING 8 PENCE

Silver **Counterstamp:** GR monogram **Note:** Weight varies: 26.75-27.05 grams. Counterstamp on Mexico 8 Reales, KM#103.

CS Date	Host Date	Good	VG	F	VF	XF
ND(1758)	1732-47	—	350	600	900	1,500

KM# 8.2 6 SHILLING 8 PENCE

Silver **Counterstamp:** GR monogram **Note:** Weight varies: 26.75-27.05 grams. Counterstamp on Mexico 8 Reales, KM#104.1.

CS Date	Host Date	Good	VG	F	VF	XF
ND(1758)	1747-58	—	275	450	700	1,250

KM# 10.1 1 POUND 5 SHILLING

6.7000 g., 0.9160 Gold 0.1973 oz. AGW **Counterstamp:** GR monogram **Note:** Counterstamp on Colombia (Bogota) 2 Escudos, KM#30.1.

CS Date	Host Date	Good	VG	F	VF	XF
(1758)	1757 Unique	—	—	—	—	—

Note: Spink (London) No. 87 10-91 VF realized $28,900

KM# 10.2 1 POUND 5 SHILLING

6.7000 g., 0.9160 Gold 0.1973 oz. AGW **Counterstamp:** GR monogram **Note:** Counterstamp on Colombia (Popayan) 2 Escudos, KM#30.2.

CS Date	Host Date	Good	VG	F	VF	XF
ND(1758)	1758 Unique	—	—	—	—	—

Note: Jess Peters Byrne sale 6-75 choice VF dated 1758 realized $6,500

CS Date	Host Date	Good	VG	F	VF	XF
ND(1759)	1759 Unique	—	—	—	—	—

KM# 11.1 5 POUNDS

27.0000 g., 0.9170 Gold 0.7960 oz. AGW **Counterstamp:** GR monogram **Note:** Counterstamp on Chile 8 Escudos, KM#3.

CS Date	Host Date	Good	VG	F	VF	XF
ND(1758)	1753 Unique	—	—	—	—	—

KM# 11.2 5 POUNDS

27.0000 g., 0.9170 Gold 0.7960 oz. AGW **Counterstamp:** GR monogram **Note:** Counterstamp on Mexico 8 Escudos, KM#148.

CS Date	Host Date	Good	VG	F	VF	XF
ND(1758)	1742 Unique	—	—	—	—	—

KM# 11.3 5 POUNDS

27.0000 g., 0.9170 Gold 0.7960 oz. AGW **Counterstamp:** GR monogram **Note:** Counterstamp on Peru (Lima) 8 Excudos, KM#50.

CS Date	Host Date	Good	VG	F	VF	XF
ND(1758)	1751 4 known	—	—	—	—	—

Note: Sotheby's Brand sale 6-85 VF realized $23,750

KM# 11.4 5 POUNDS

27.0000 g., 0.9170 Gold 0.7960 oz. AGW **Counterstamp:** GR monogram **Note:** Counterstamp on Peru (Lima) 8 Excudos, KM#59.

CS Date	Host Date	Good	VG	F	VF	XF
ND(1759)	1759 Rare	—	—	—	—	—

Note: Authorized mintage of 2,000; Swiss Bank sale No. 24 1-90 XF realized $28,900, Bonhams Patterson sale 7-96 VF realized $14,640

COUNTERMARKED COINAGE

1773

To relieve problems of light gold coinage,Jamaica legally adopted Spanish gold currency standards with a weight rating of 26.96 grams for the 8 Escudos and imposed penalties of 3 Pence per grain for the circulation of underweight gold coinage. As a result some underweight cobs were privately plugged to attain full weight and countermarked with a crocodile above the script initials GC. It is suspected that this work was done by George Clinton, an area goldsmith of this era.

KM# 12.1 8 ESCUDOS

26.9200 g., Gold **Countermark:** Crocodile **Note:** Countermark above script GC on Peru (Lima) plugged 8 Escudos, KM#38.1.

CM Date	Host Date	Good	VG	F	VF	XF
ND(1773)	1738 Unique	—	—	—	—	—

KM# 12.2 8 ESCUDOS

26.8800 g., Gold **Countermark:** Crocodile **Note:** Countermark above script GC on Peru (Lima) plugged 8 Escudos, KM#38.2.

CM Date	Host Date	Good	VG	F	VF	XF
ND(1773)	174x	—	—	—	—	—

Note: Sotheby's Brand sale 6-85 VF realized $23,750

JAPAN

Japan, a constitutional monarchy situated off the east coast of Asia, has an area of 145,809 sq. mi. (377,835 sq. km.) and a population of 123.2 million. Capital: Tokyo. Japan, one of the major industrial nations of the world, exports machinery, motor vehicles, electronics and chemicals.

Japan, founded (so legend holds) in 660 B.C. by a direct descendant of the Sun Goddess, was first brought into contact with the west by a storm-blown Portuguese ship in 1542. European traders and missionaries proceeded to enlarge the contact until the Shogunate, sensing a military threat in the foreign presence, expelled all foreigners and restricted relations with the outside world in the 17th century. After Commodore Perry's U.S. flotilla visited in 1854, Japan rapidly industrialized, abolished the Shogunate and established a parliamentary form of government, and by the end of the 19th century achieved the status of a modern economic and military power. A series of wars with China and Russia, and participation with the allies in World War I, enlarged Japan territorially but brought its interests into conflict with the Far Eastern interests of the United States, Britain and the Netherlands, causing it to align with the Axis Powers for the pursuit of World War II. After its defeat in World War II, General Douglas MacArthur forced Japan to renounce military aggression as a political instrument, and he instituted constitutional democratic self-government. Japan quickly gained a position as an economic world power.

Japanese coinage of concern to this catalog includes those issued for the Ryukyu Islands (also called Liuchu), a chain of islands extending southwest from Japan toward Taiwan (Formosa), before the Japanese government converted the islands into a prefecture under the name Okinawa. Many of the provinces of Japan issued their own definitive coinage under the Shogunate.

RULERS

Shoguns

Tsunayoshi, 1680-1709
Iyenobu, 1709-1712
Iyetsugu, 1713-1716
Yoshimune, 1716-1745
Iyeshize, 1754-1760
Iyeharu, 1760-1786
Iyenari, 1787-1837

NOTE: The personal name of the emperor is followed by the name that he chose for his regnal era.

MONETARY SYSTEM

Until 1870

Prior to the Meiji currency reform, there was no fixed exchange rate between the various silver, gold and copper "cash" coins (which previously included Chinese "cash") in circulation. Each coin exchanged on the basis of its own merits and the prevailing market conditions. The size and weight of the copper coins and the weight and fineness of the silver and gold coins varied widely. From time to time the government would declare an official exchange rate, but this was usually ignored. For gold and silver, nominal equivalents were:

16 Shu = 4 Bu = 1 Ryo

MONETARY UNITS

Momme	匁
Ryo	兩
Bu	分
Shu	朱
Mon	文
Rin	厘

MINT MARKS ON MON

A - Edo (Tokyo)	文
B -Sado	佐佐佐
C -Jiuman Tsubo	十
D -Koume Mura	小
E -Ichi-no-se	一
F -Onagi-gawa	川
G -Osaka	元
H -Nagasaki	長
I -Ashio	足
J -Sendai	仙
K -Sendai	千
L -Kuji (Hitachi Ohta)	久
M -Mito	ト,ト
N -Aizu	ノ
O - Ise	イ
P - Morioka	盛
Q - Hiroshima	了
R - Yamanouchi	山

LEGENDS

Reading top-bottom, right-left.

Kanei Tsuho

Mameitagin 'Bean' Silver

HOEI ERA

Hoei Futatsu-ho (two characters ho, 1706-10)

Vertical stroke in era designator ***ho*** starts at second horizontal stroke and continues downward; does not extend up to top of character. There is a slight knob at each end of the bottom horizontal stroke. Compare with the era designator for the ***Yotsu-ho*** variety.

Hoei Ei-Ji (character ***ei***, 1710)

Era designator is character ***ei***, as used at bottom of Kanei Tsuho copper coinage.

Hoei Mitsu-ho (three characters ***ho***, 1710-11)

Vertical stroke in era designator ***ho*** extends completely through the character from top to bottom.

Hoei Yoei Yotsu-ho (Four characters ***ho***, 1711-12)

Era designator resembles the ***ho*** of the ***Futatsu-ho*** variety, except that a spike extends up from each end of the bottom horizontal stroke.

Shotoku-Kyoho Eras (1714-36)

As for the Keicho period pieces, there is no era designator for this period. Compare the style of the characters and designs with those of the Keicho period to distinguish between them.

Key to Dating Modern Mameita Gin
Genbun Period, 1736-1818
(Used 1736-1818)

One of the above characters is usually found on the obverse of C#8 or both sides of C#8a and C#8b. The same characters are found at both ends of chogin pieces C#9. Era designators were used continuously until the next one was introduced, regardless of intervening eras.

NOTE: Values are for pieces weighing 5-8 grams. Pieces over 10 grams may command up to twice the values shown; pieces under 5 grams somewhat less.

Cho Gin
Key to Dating modern Cho Gin (Silver)

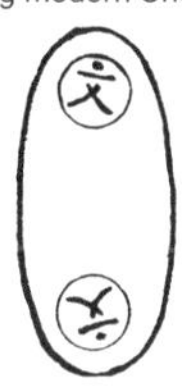

Genbun Era, 1736-41

Key to Dating 1 and 2 BU

Genroku Period
(Used 1695-1706)

Hoei Period
(Used 1710-14)

Shotoku Period
(Used 1714)

Kyoho Period
(1714-36)

NOTE: Characters illustrated for the Shotoku and Kyoho periods are not era marks but are varieties of writing mintmaster names.

SADO MINES

(Used 1714)

NOTE: A mark used to indicate use of gold from the Sado Island mines on regular circulation pieces.

Genbun Period 1 Bu

1736-41
(Used 1736-1818)

SHOGUNATE
CAST COINAGE

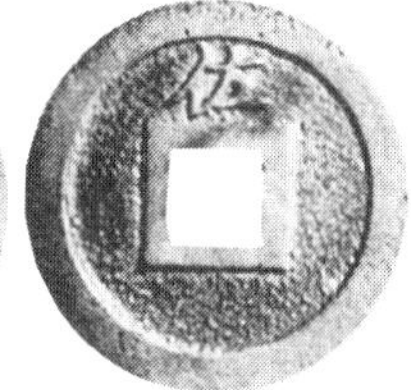

C# 1.3 MON

Cast Copper, Bronze Or Brass **Obv. Inscription:** Ka-nei Tsu-ho

Date	Mintage	VG	F	VF	XF	Unc
ND(1714-1862)(B)	—	2.00	4.00	6.00	8.00	—

C# 1.5s MON

Cast Copper, Bronze Or Brass

Date	Mintage	VG	F	VF	XF	Unc
ND(1736)(C)	—	—	—	—	200	—

Note: C#1.5 is known only as "bosen" - seed or mother coins

C# 1.5a MON

Cast Copper **Obv:** Mint mark on outer rim **Obv. Inscription:** Ka-nei Tsu-ho **Rev:** Plain

Date	Mintage	VG	F	VF	XF	Unc
ND(1736)c(C)	—	15.00	22.00	27.00	35.00	—
ND(1739)(C)	—	15.00	22.00	27.00	35.00	—

C# 1.6 MON

Cast Copper, Bronze Or Brass **Obv. Inscription:** Ka-nei Tsu-ho

Date	Mintage	VG	F	VF	XF	Unc
ND(1737)(D)	—	2.50	4.50	6.00	8.00	—

C# 1.1a MON

Cast Iron **Obv. Inscription:** Ka-nei Tsu-ho **Rev:** Plain

Date	Mintage	VG	F	VF	XF	Unc
ND(1739-1867)	—	2.50	5.00	7.50	15.00	—

C# 1.6a MON

Cast Iron **Obv. Inscription:** Ka-nei Tsu-ho

Date	Mintage	VG	F	VF	XF	Unc
ND(1739)(D)	—	15.00	25.00	35.00	55.00	—

C# 1.12 MON

Cast Iron **Obv. Inscription:** Ka-nei Tsu-ho

Date	Mintage	VG	F	VF	XF	Unc
ND(1739)(K)	—	3.00	5.00	8.00	15.00	—
ND(1838)(K)	—	4.00	6.00	9.00	20.00	—

C# 1.5b MON

Cast Iron **Obv:** Mint mark on outer rim **Obv. Inscription:** Ka-nei Tsu-ho **Rev:** Plain

Date	Mintage	VG	F	VF	XF	Unc
ND(1739)(C)	—	15.00	25.00	30.00	40.00	—

C# 1.10b MON

Cast Iron **Obv. Inscription:** Ka-nei Tsu-ho

Date	Mintage	VG	F	VF	XF	Unc
ND(1740)(E)	—	30.00	40.00	50.00	65.00	—

C# 1.7a MON

Cast Iron

Date	Mintage	VG	F	VF	XF	Unc
ND(1740)(F)	—	15.00	22.50	30.00	40.00	—

C# 1.10a MON

Cast Iron **Obv. Inscription:** Ka-nei Tsu-ho

Date	Mintage	VG	F	VF	XF	Unc
ND(1740)(E)	—	35.00	50.00	75.00	100	—

C# 1.10 MON

Cast Copper, Bronze Or Brass **Obv. Inscription:** Ka-nei Tsu-ho

Date	Mintage	VG	F	VF	XF	Unc
ND(1740)(E)	—	20.00	30.00	50.00	65.00	—

C# 1.7s MON

Cast Copper, Bronze Or Brass

Date	Mintage	VG	F	VF	XF	Unc
ND(1740)(F) "Bosen"	—	—	—	—	1,200	—

Note: C#1.7 is known only as "bosen" - seed or mother coins

C# 1.8 MON

Cast Copper, Bronze Or Brass **Obv. Inscription:** Ka-nei Tsu-ho

Date	Mintage	VG	F	VF	XF	Unc
ND(1741)(G)	—	0.55	0.75	1.25	2.50	—

C# 1.9 MON

Cast Copper, Bronze Or Brass **Obv. Inscription:** Ka-nei Tsu-ho

Date	Mintage	VG	F	VF	XF	Unc
ND(1741)(I)	—	1.75	3.00	4.50	6.50	—

C# 1.4 MON

Cast Copper, Bronze Or Brass **Obv. Inscription:** Ka-nei Tsu-ho

Date	Mintage	VG	F	VF	XF	Unc
ND(1748)(J)	—	25.00	30.00	35.00	40.00	—

C# 1.11 MON

Cast Copper, Bronze Or Brass **Obv. Inscription:** Ka-nei Tsu-ho

Date	Mintage	VG	F	VF	XF	Unc
ND(1767)(H)	—	1.75	2.50	4.00	7.50	—

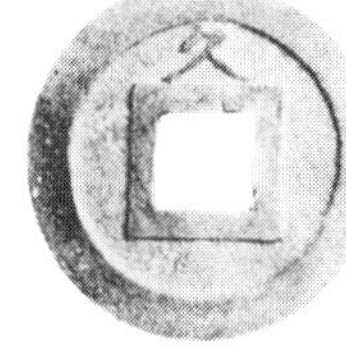

C# 1.13 MON

Cast Iron **Obv. Inscription:** Ka-nei Tsu-ho

Date	Mintage	VG	F	VF	XF	Unc
ND(1768)(L)	—	3.00	6.00	10.00	17.50	—

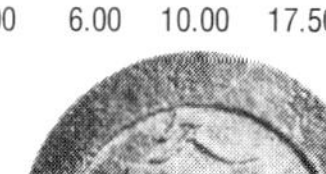

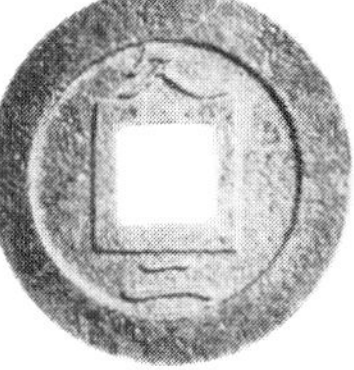

C# 1.15 MON

Cast Iron **Rev:** "Ni" (2) below

Date	Mintage	VG	F	VF	XF	Unc
ND(1774)(L)	—	2.00	4.00	7.00	12.00	—

C# 4.1 4 MON

Cast Brass **Obv. Inscription:** "Kwan-Ei (Kanei) Tsu-Ho" **Rev:** 21 waves

Date	Mintage	VG	F	VF	XF	Unc
ND(1768)	—	1.75	2.50	4.00	6.00	—

C# 4.2 4 MON

Cast Copper Or Brass **Obv:** Inscription **Rev:** 11 waves

Date	Mintage	VG	F	VF	XF	Unc
ND(1769-1860)	—	1.00	2.50	5.00	15.00	—

KM# 57 10 MON (Hoei Tsuho)

Cast Copper **Obv. Inscription:** "Ho-Ei Tsu-Ho" **Rev. Inscription:** "Ei Kyu Sei Yo" with "Chin" (precious) mark near the rim

Date	Mintage	VG	F	VF	XF	Unc
ND(1708)	—	15.00	25.00	35.00	45.00	—

BULLION COINAGE

KM# 20.1 MAMEITA GIN

0.6400 Silver **Obv:** One or more characters, without "God of Plenty"; era designator "gen" between characters **Rev:** Chop marks **Note:** Genroku era.

Date	Mintage	VG	F	VF	XF	Unc
ND(1695-1706)	—	100	150	250	350	—

KM# 20.2 MAMEITA GIN

0.6400 Silver **Obv:** "God of Plenty" with other characters; era designator "gen" between characters and on God's belly **Note:** Genroku era.

Date	Mintage	VG	F	VF	XF	Unc
ND(1695-1706)	—	250	500	750	1,000	—

KM# 21 MAMEITA GIN

0.6400 Silver **Obv:** "God of Plenty" design, era designator on belly **Rev:** "God of Plenty" design, era designator on belly **Note:** Genroku era.

Date	Mintage	VG	F	VF	XF	Unc
ND(1695-1706)	—	300	750	1,100	1,500	—

KM# 22 MAMEITA GIN

0.6400 Silver **Obv:** "God of Plenty" design, with era designator on belly **Rev:** Many small or one large character "gen" **Note:** Genroku era.

Date	Mintage	VG	F	VF	XF	Unc
ND(1695-1706)	—	1,200	1,750	2,100	2,750	—

KM# 25.1 MAMEITA GIN

0.5000 Silver **Obv:** One or more characters, without "God of Plenty"; Era designator "ho" between characters **Rev:** Chop marks

Date	Mintage	VG	F	VF	XF	Unc
ND(1706)	—	100	150	200	300	—

KM# 25.2 MAMEITA GIN

0.5000 Silver **Obv:** "God of Plenty" with other characters; Era designator "ho" between characters and on God's belly

Date	Mintage	VG	F	VF	XF	Unc
ND(1706)	—	200	350	500	650	—

KM# 26 MAMEITA GIN

0.5000 Silver **Obv:** "God of Plenty" design; Era designator on belly **Rev:** "God of Plenty" design; Era designator on belly

Date	Mintage	VG	F	VF	XF	Unc
ND(1706)	—	400	500	750	1,000	—

KM# 27 MAMEITA GIN

0.5000 Silver **Obv:** "God of Plenty" design **Rev:** Single large or multiple small era designators

Date	Mintage	VG	F	VF	XF	Unc
ND(1706)	—	1,000	1,250	1,650	2,000	—

KM# 30.1 MAMEITA GIN

0.4000 Silver **Obv:** One or more characters, without "God of Plenty"; Era designator "ei" between characters **Rev:** Chop marks

Date	Mintage	VG	F	VF	XF	Unc
ND(1710)	—	1,000	1,500	2,500	3,500	—

KM# 30.2 MAMEITA GIN

0.4000 Silver **Obv:** "God of Plenty" with other characters; Era designator "ei" between characters and on God's belly

Date	Mintage	VG	F	VF	XF	Unc
ND(1710)	—	2,000	2,500	4,000	6,000	—

KM# 31.1 MAMEITA GIN

0.3200 Silver **Obv:** One or more characters, without "God of Plenty"; Era designator "ho" between characters **Rev:** Chop marks

Date	Mintage	VG	F	VF	XF	Unc
ND(1710)	—	150	200	300	400	—

KM# 31.2 MAMEITA GIN

0.3200 Silver **Obv:** "God of Plenty" with other characters; Era designator "ho" between characters and on God's belly

Date	Mintage	VG	F	VF	XF	Unc
ND(1710)	—	250	350	500	700	—

KM# 32 MAMEITA GIN

0.3200 Silver **Obv:** "God of Plenty" design, era designator on belly **Rev:** "God of Plenty" design, era designator on belly

Date	Mintage	VG	F	VF	XF	Unc
ND(1710)	—	600	750	1,000	1,400	—

KM# 33 MAMEITA GIN

0.3200 Silver **Obv:** "God of Plenty" design **Rev:** Single large or multiple small era designators

Date	Mintage	VG	F	VF	XF	Unc
ND(1710)	—	1,000	1,500	2,000	2,500	—

KM# 40.1 MAMEITA GIN

0.2000 Silver **Obv:** One or more characters, without "God of Plenty"; Era designator "ho" between characters **Rev:** Chop marks

Date	Mintage	VG	F	VF	XF	Unc
ND(1711)	—	250	350	450	550	—

KM# 40.2 MAMEITA GIN

0.2000 Silver **Obv:** "God of Plenty" with other characters; Era designator "ho" between characters

Date	Mintage	VG	F	VF	XF	Unc
ND(1711)	—	500	750	1,100	1,500	—

KM# 45.1 MAMEITA GIN

0.8000 Silver **Obv:** One or more bold-stroke characters, wtihout "God of Plenty"; Without era designators between characters **Rev:** Chop marks

Date	Mintage	VG	F	VF	XF	Unc
ND(1714)	—	20.00	30.00	40.00	55.00	—

KM# 45.2 MAMEITA GIN

0.8000 Silver **Obv:** "God of Plenty" with other characters; Thick calligraphy

Date	Mintage	VG	F	VF	XF	Unc
ND(1714)	—	30.00	40.00	55.00	75.00	—

KM# 46 MAMEITA GIN

0.8000 Silver **Obv:** "God of Plenty" design; Without era designator on belly

Date	Mintage	VG	F	VF	XF	Unc
ND(1714)	—	100	200	300	400	—

C# 8.1a MAMEITA GIN

0.4600 Silver **Obv:** One or more large characters, without "God of Plenty"; Era designator between characters **Rev:** Blank or with chop marks

Date	Mintage	VG	F	VF	XF	Unc
ND(1736-1818)	—	20.00	25.00	40.00	55.00	—

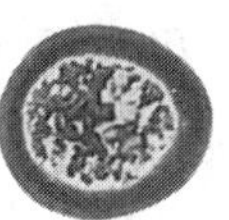

C# 8.1b MAMEITA GIN

0.4600 Silver **Obv:** "God of Plenty" with other large characters; Era designator between characters and on God's belly

Date	Mintage	VG	F	VF	XF	Unc
ND(1736-1818)	—	30.00	40.00	60.00	75.00	—

C# 8a.1 MAMEITA GIN

0.4600 Silver **Obv:** "God of Plenty" design, era designator on belly

Date	Mintage	VG	F	VF	XF	Unc
ND(1736-1818)	—	50.00	85.00	150	250	—

C# 8b.1 MAMEITA GIN

0.4600 Silver **Obv:** "God of Plenty" design **Rev:** Single large "Bun" or multiple small era designator

Date	Mintage	VG	F	VF	XF	Unc
ND(1736-1818)	—	800	1,000	1,300	1,600	—

KM# 50 CHO GIN

0.6400 Silver **Obv:** Era marks at each end; miscellaneous characters and designs elsewhere **Rev:** Chop marks **Note:** Genroku era. Illustration reduced by 50%.

Date	Mintage	VG	F	VF	XF	Unc
ND(1695-1706)	—	4,500	7,500	11,500	16,500	—

KM# 51 CHO GIN

0.6400 Silver **Obv:** Edges completely covered with 12-14 stamps, mostly of characters, a few of "God of Plenty" **Rev:** Chop marks **Note:** Genroku era.

Date	Mintage	VG	F	VF	XF	Unc
ND(1695-1706) Rare	—	—	—	—	—	—

KM# 52 CHO GIN

0.6400 Silver **Obv:** Edges completely covered with 12 stamps of "God of Plenty" **Rev:** Chop marks **Note:** Genroku era.

Date	Mintage	VG	F	VF	XF	Unc
ND(1695-1706) Rare	—	—	—	—	—	—

KM# 55 CHO GIN

0.5000 Silver **Obv:** Era marks at each end; Miscellaneous characters and designs elsewhere **Rev:** Chop marks

Date	Mintage	VG	F	VF	XF	Unc
ND(1706) Rare	—	—	—	—	—	—

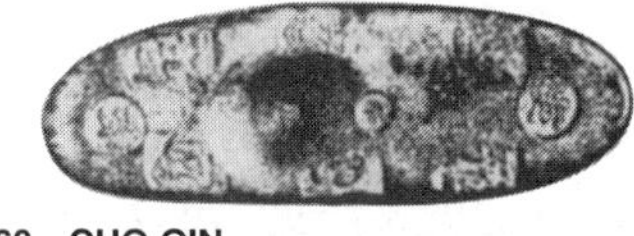

KM# 60 CHO GIN

0.4000 Silver **Obv:** Era marks of "Mitsu-ho" style at each end, small "ei" era mark near center; Miscellaneous characters and designs elsewhere **Rev:** Chop marks

Date	Mintage	VG	F	VF	XF	Unc
ND(1710) Rare	—	—	—	—	—	—

KM# 61 CHO GIN

0.3200 Silver **Obv:** Era marks at each end, smaller era mark near center; Miscellaneous characters and designs elsewhere **Rev:** Chop marks

Date	Mintage	VG	F	VF	XF	Unc
ND(1710) Rare	—	—	—	—	—	—

Note: The style of the era marks, not the number stamped, determines the variety

KM# 62 CHO GIN

0.2000 Silver **Obv:** Era marks at each end, smaller era mark inboard of each regular size era mark; Miscellaneous characters and designs elsewhere **Rev:** Chop marks

Date	Mintage	VG	F	VF	XF	Unc
ND(1711)	—	6,500	7,500	8,000	9,000	—

Note: The style of the era marks, not the number stamped, determines the variety

KM# 63 CHO GIN

0.8000 Silver **Obv:** Miscellaneous characters and designs throughout; Characters are composed of bold strokes and large dots **Rev:** Chop marks

Date	Mintage	VG	F	VF	XF	Unc
ND(1714)	—	350	450	900	1,500	—

C# 10 GO (5) MOMME

18.7500 g., 0.4600 Silver 0.2773 oz. ASW **Subject:** Meiwa

Date	Mintage	VG	F	VF	XF	Unc
ND(1765-72)	3,361,000	600	900	1,200	1,600	—

HAMMERED COINAGE

C# 9 CHO GIN

0.4600 Silver **Obv:** Era marks at each end; Miscellaneous marks elsewhere **Rev:** Blank except for occasional chop marks **Note:** Illustration reduced.

Date	Mintage	VG	F	VF	XF	Unc
ND(1736-1818)	—	300	400	500	600	—

FR# 33 2 SHU (Nishu Gin)

2.2100 g., Gold And Silver .564 gold and .436 silver **Subject:** xyz **Note:** Genroku era.

Date	Mintage	VG	F	VF	XF	Unc
ND(1695-1710)	—	1,100	1,700	2,000	2,400	—

C# 13 2 SHU (Nishu Gin)

10.1900 g., 0.9780 Silver 0.3204 oz. ASW **Note:** Meiwa-Ko-Nanryo

Date	Mintage	VG	F	VF	XF	Unc
ND(1772-1824)	47,464,000	150	225	275	325	—

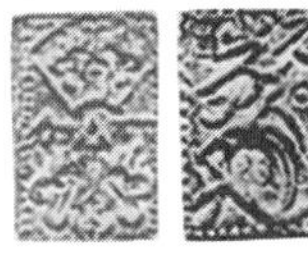

FR# 25 BU (Ichibu)

4.4600 g., Gold And Silver **Subject:** xyz **Note:** .564 Gold and .436 Silver. Genroku era.

Date	Mintage	VG	F	VF	XF	Unc
ND(1695-1710)	—	500	800	1,000	1,300	—

FR# 26 BU (Ichibu)

2.2300 g., Gold And Silver **Subject:** Genroku **Note:** .834 Gold and .166 Silver.

Date	Mintage	VG	F	VF	XF	Unc
ND(1710-14)	—	400	600	800	1,000	—

FR# A27 BU (Ichibu)

4.4300 g., Gold And Silver **Subject:** Shotoku **Note:** .857 Gold and .143 Silver.

Date	Mintage	VG	F	VF	XF	Unc
ND(1714)	—	2,500	3,500	5,000	6,500	—

FR# A28 BU (Ichibu)

4.4300 g., Gold And Silver **Subject:** Sado **Note:** .861 Gold and .139 Silver.

Date	Mintage	VG	F	VF	XF	Unc
ND(1714)	—	7,000	1,200	13,000	15,000	—

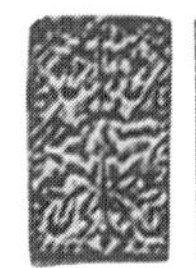

FR# 27 BU (Ichibu)

4.4000 g., Gold And Silver **Subject:** Kyoho **Note:** .861 Gold and .139 Silver.

Date	Mintage	VG	F	VF	XF	Unc
ND(1716-36)	—	225	300	350	400	—

C# 19 BU (Ichibu)

3.2500 g., Gold And Silver **Note:** .653 Gold and .347 Silver. Kyoho era.

Date	Mintage	VG	F	VF	XF	Unc
ND(1736-1818)	—	500	950	1,100	1,400	—

FR# 10 KOBAN (1 Ryo)

17.8100 g., Gold And Silver **Note:** .564 Gold and .436 Silver. Genroku era.

Date	Mintage	VG	F	VF	XF	Unc
ND(1695-1710)	13,936,000	7,000	10,000	12,000	15,000	—

FR# 11 KOBAN (1 Ryo)

9.3400 g., Gold And Silver **Subject:** Hoei **Note:** .834 Gold and .166 Silver.

Date	Mintage	VG	F	VF	XF	Unc
ND(1710-14)	11,516,000	6,000	7,500	8,500	9,500	—

FR# 11a KOBAN (1 Ryo)

17.7200 g., Gold And Silver **Subject:** Shotoku **Note:** .857 Gold and .143 Silver.

Date	Mintage	VG	F	VF	XF	Unc
ND(1714)	214,000	7,000	10,000	14,000	18,500	—

FR# 12 KOBAN (1 Ryo)

17.7800 g., Gold And Silver **Subject:** Shotoku **Note:** .861 Gold and .139 Silver.

Date	Mintage	VG	F	VF	XF	Unc
ND(1714-36)	8,200,000	1,500	2,500	3,500	4,500	—

FR# A13 KOBAN (1 Ryo)

17.7800 g., Gold And Silver **Subject:** Sado Mines **Note:** .861 Gold and .139 Silver.

Date	Mintage	VG	F	VF	XF	Unc
ND	—	12,000	15,000	20,000	27,500	—

C# 22 KOBAN (1 Ryo)

13.1300 g., Gold And Silver **Note:** .653 Gold and .347 Silver. Genbun era.

Date	Mintage	VG	F	VF	XF	Unc
ND(1736-1818)	17,436,000	900	1,200	1,400	1,750	—

FR# 4 OBAN

164.5600 g., Gold And Silver **Subject:** xyz **Note:** .521 Gold and .449 Silver. Genroku era. Illustration reduced by 50%.

Date	Mintage	VG	F	VF	XF	Unc
ND(1695-1716)	30,000	—	—	175,000	260,000	—

C# 24.1 OBAN

165.3800 g., Gold And Silver, 94x153 mm. **Subject:** Kyoho **Note:** .676 Gold and .324 Silver. Kyoho era.

Date	Mintage	VG	F	VF	XF	Unc
ND(1725-1837)	8,515	—	—	25,000	35,000	—
Note: Original inking						
ND(1725-1837)	Inc. above	—	—	20,000	27,500	—
Note: Re-inked during Tempo period						

KAGA

CITY AND PROVINCE

PROVINCIAL COINAGE

KM# 35 NAN RYO

Silver

Date	Mintage	VG	F	VF	XF	Unc
ND	—	1,250	1,750	2,200	3,300	—

KOSHU

A province, (formal name Kai, now Yamanashi Prefecture), located in central Honshu west of Tokyo.

The following listings are representative of a very complex series of gold coinage. Other obscure or odd denominations may exist. This series contains many varieties. The characters usually found stamped on the reverse are hallmarks.

PROVINCE

PROVINCIAL COINAGE

KM# 90 KAKU SHU-NAKA KIN (Rectangular Half Shu Gold)

0.4000 g., Gold, 6x8 mm.

Date	Mintage	VG	F	VF	XF	Unc
ND	—	700	900	1,200	1,600	—

KM# 91 SHU-NAKA KIN (Half Shu Gold)

Gold, 8.5-9.5 mm. **Note:** Similar to Ichi-Bu KM#94. Weight varies: 0.40-0.50 grams. Size varies.

Date	Mintage	VG	F	VF	XF	Unc
ND	—	3,000	5,000	5,500	6,500	—

KM# 92 ISSHU KIN (One Shu Gold)

Gold, 11-12 mm. **Note:** Similar to Ichi-Bu KM#94. Weight varies: 0.90-1.00 grams. Size varies.

Date	Mintage	VG	F	VF	XF	Unc
ND	—	425	650	850	1,100	—

KM# 93 NISSHU KIN (Two Shu Gold)

1.9000 g., Gold, 12-13 mm. **Note:** Similar to Ichi-Bu KM#94. Size varies.

Date	Mintage	VG	F	VF	XF	Unc
ND	—	425	650	850	1,200	—

KM# 94 ICHI-BU KIN (One Bu Gold)

Gold, 14-17 mm. **Note:** Similar to Ichi-Bu KM#94. Weight varies: 3.70-4.00 Size varies.

Date	Mintage	VG	F	VF	XF	Unc
ND	—	425	650	850	1,100	—

KM# 95 ICHI-BU ISSHU KIN (One Bu One Shu Gold)

4.8000 g., Gold, 18 mm. **Note:** Similar to Ichi-Bu KM#94.

Date	Mintage	VG	F	VF	XF	Unc
ND Rare	—	—	—	—	—	—

KM# 96 ICHI-BU NISSHU KIN (One Bu Two Shu Gold)

5.0000 g., Gold, 16 mm. **Note:** Similar to Ichi-Bu KM#94.

Date	Mintage	VG	F	VF	XF	Unc
ND Rare	—	—	—	—	—	—

KM# 97 NI-BU KIN (Two Bu Gold)

Gold, 18-19 mm. **Note:** Similar to Ichi-Bu KM#94. Weight varies: 7.00-7.50 grams. Size varies.

Date	Mintage	VG	F	VF	XF	Unc
ND Rare	—	—	—	—	—	—

KM# 98 NI-BU ISSHU KIN (Two Bu One Shu Gold)

8.8000 g., Gold, 24 mm. **Note:** Similar to Ichi-Bu KM#94.

Date	Mintage	VG	F	VF	XF	Unc
ND Rare	—	—	—	—	—	—

KM# 99 RYO KIN (One Ryo Gold)

Gold, 16-19 mm. **Note:** Rounded "nugget" shape with stamps, similar to Ichi-Bu KM#94. Weight varies: 14.70-15.30 grams. Size varies.

Date	Mintage	VG	F	VF	XF	Unc
ND Rare	—	—	—	—	—	—

MIMASAKA

PROVINCE

PROVINCIAL COINAGE

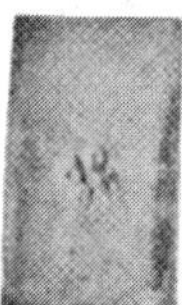

KM# 46 BU

Silver

Date	Mintage	VG	F	VF	XF	Unc
ND	—	1,500	2,000	2,300	2,750	—

SENDAI

Chief city of Rikuzen Province (now part of Miyagi Prefecture) in northern Honshu.

CITY

PROVINCIAL COINAGE

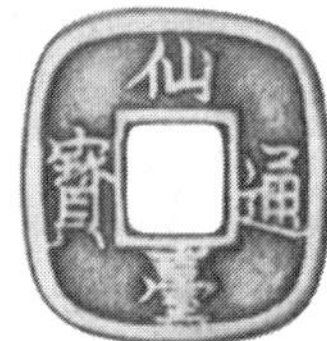

KM# 60 MON

Iron **Rev:** Blank

Date	Mintage	Good	VG	F	VF	XF
ND(1784)	—	20.00	30.00	45.00	60.00	100

KM# 60a MON

Copper **Rev:** Blank **Note:** This type is the "bosen" or mother coin used in making the sand molds for casting KM#60.

Date	Mintage	Good	VG	F	VF	XF
ND (1784)	—	—	—	150	200	300

TAJIMA

PROVINCE

PROVINCIAL COINAGE

KM# 65 NAN RYO

Silver

Date	Mintage	VG	F	VF	XF	Unc
ND	—	800	1,200	1,500	1,800	—

KOREA

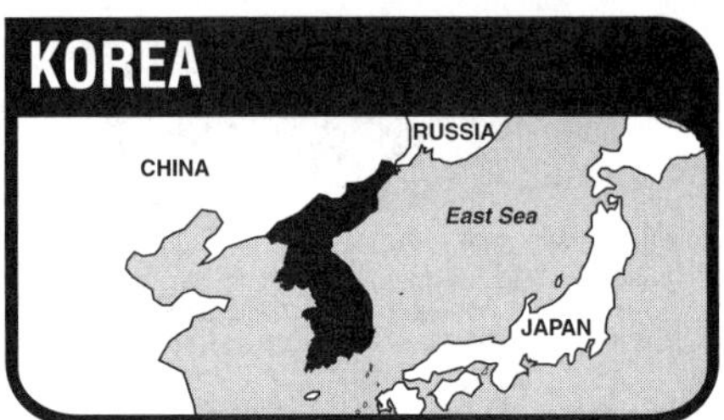

Korea, 'Land of the Morning Calm', occupies a mountainous peninsula in northeast Asia bounded by Manchuria, the Yellow Sea and the Sea of Japan.

According to legend, the first Korean dynasty, that of the House of Tangun, ruled from 2333 B.C. to 1122 B.C. It was followed by the dynasty of Kija, a Chinese scholar, which continued until 193 B.C. and brought a high civilization to Korea. The first recorded period in the history of Korea, the period of the Three Kingdoms, lasted from 57 B.C. to 935 A.D. and achieved the first political unification of the peninsula. The Kingdom of Koryo, from which Korea derived its name, was founded in 935 and continued until 1392, when the Yi Dynasty of King Yi superseded it. Sung Kye was to last until the Japanese annexation in 1910.

At the end of the 16th century Korea was invaded by Japan, a conflict lasting seven years. From 1627 until the late 19th century, Korea shared a friendly relationship with China, but was replaced by Japan as the predominant foreign influence at the end of the Sino-Japanese War (1894-95), only to find her position threatened by Russian influence from 1896 to 1904. The Russian threat was eliminated following the Russo-Japanese War (1904-05). In 1905 Japan established a direct protectorate over Korea. On Aug. 22,1910, the last Korean ruler signed the treaty that annexed Korea to Japan as a government generalcy in the Japanese Empire. Japanese suzerainty was maintained until the end of World War II.

From 1633 to 1891 the monetary system of Korea employed cast coins with a square center hole. Fifty-two agencies were authorized to procure these coins from a lesser number of coin foundries. They exist in thousands of varieties. Seed, or mother coins, were used to make the impressions in the molds in which the regular cash coins were cast. Czarist-Russian Korea experimented with Korean coins when Alexiev of Russia, Korea's Financial Advisor, founded the First Asian Branch of the Russo-Korean Bank on March 1, 1898, and authorized the issuing of a set of new Korean coins with a crowned Russian-style quasi-eagle. British-Japanese opposition and the Russo-Japanese War operated to end the Russian coinage experiment in 1904.

RULERS

Yi Sun (Sukjong Hyonui), 1675-1721
Yi Kyun (Kyongjong Tokman), 1721-1725
Yi Um (Yongjo Hyonhyo), 1725-1777
Yi Sun (Chongjo Changhyo), 1777-1801

MONETARY UNITS

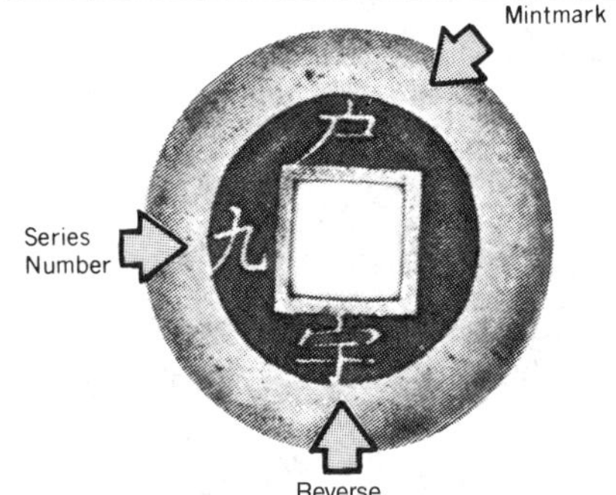

Furnace Designator

NOTE: The series number may be to the left, right or bottom of the center hole. The furnace designator may be either a numeral or a character from the *Thousand Character Classic.*

SERIES CHARACTERS

天	地	玄
Ch'on, heaven	***Chi***, earth	***Hyon***, dark
黃	宇	宙
Hwang, Yellow	***U***, Space	***Chu***, Infinite time
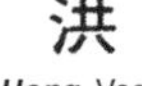		
Hong, Vast	***Hwang***, Barren	***Ii***, Sun

月 ***Wol***, Moon	盈 ***Yong***, Full	昃 ***Chu'uk***, Declining afternoon sun
辰 ***Chin***, Heavenly body	宿 ***Suk***, Lunar station	列 ***Yol***, Arranged in order
張 ***Chang***, Extend	寒 ***Han***, Cold	來 ***Nae***, Comes
暑 ***So***, Heat	往 ***Wang***, Depart	秋 ***Ch'u***, Autumn
收 ***Su***, Harvest	冬 ***Tong***, Winter	藏 ***Chang***, Hoard
閏 ***Yun***, Intercalary	餘 ***Yo***, Surplus	成 ***Song***, Completes
歲 ***Se***, A year	律 ***Yul***, Yang, male pitch pipes	呂 ***Yin***, Yo, female pitch pipes
調 ***Cho***, Harmonize	陽 ***Yang***, The male element in nature	雲 ***Un***, Clouds
騰 ***Tung***, Ascending	致 ***Ch'i***, Cause	雨 ***U***, Rain
露 ***No***, Dew	結 ***Kyol***, Congeals	為 ***Wi***, Makes
霜 ***Sang***, Frost	金 ***Kum***, Gold	生 ***Saeng***, Produce
麗 ***Yo***, Li, Beautiful	水 ***Su***, Water	玉 ***Ok***, Jade
出 ***Ch'ul***, Comes out of	崑 ***Kon***, Kun Lun Mountains	木 ***Kang***, Mountain ridge

NOTE: In many cases where the classic numbering system is used, character #823, meaning different, strange or foreign, is used in lieu of Ch'uk, the declining afternoon sun for the number 12.

FIVE ELEMENTS

火 ***Mok***, Wood	土 ***Hwa***, Fire	金 ***T'o***, Earth
水 ***Kum***, Metal	甲 ***Su***, Water	

TEN CELESTIAL STEMS

甲 *Kap*	乙 *Ul*	丙 *Pyong*	丁 *Chong*	戊 *Mu*
己 *Ki*	庚 *Kyong*	辛 *Sin*	壬 *Im*	癸 *Kye*

EIGHT TRIGRAMS

乾 ☰ ***Kon***, The creative	兌 ☱ ***T'ae***, The joyous	離 ☲ ***I***, The clinging
震 ☳	巽 ☴ ***Son***, The	坎 ☵ ***Kam***, The abysmal
艮 ☶ ***Chin***, The arousing ***Kan***, Keeping still	坤 ☷ ***Kon***, The receptive	

TWELVE TERRESTRIAL BRANCHES

子 ***Cha***, Rat	丑 ***Ch'uk***, Ox	寅 ***In***, Tiger	卯 ***Myo***, Hare
辰 ***Chin***, Dragon	巳 ***Sa***, Serpent	午 ***O***, Horse	未 ***Mi***, Goat
申 ***Sin***, Monkey	酉 ***Yu***, Rooster	戌 ***Sul***, Dog	亥 ***Hae***, Boar

MISCELLANEOUS CHARACTERS

The following characters also appear on the reverse of *Sang P'yong T'ong Bo* coins.

入 ***Ip***, To enter	大 ***Tae***, Great, big, large, vast	工 ***Kong***, Labor, a job	千 ***Ch'on***, Thousand

文 ***Mun***, Cash coin, civil officials, literature	元 ***Won***, The first	中 ***Chung***, Middle, center
正 ***Chong***, Upright, true	生 ***Saeng***, To produce, to be born	光 ***Kwang***, Light, favor, honor
全 ***Chon***, Perfect, complete	吉 ***Kil***, Lucky, auspicious	完 ***Wan***, To finish, to complete, whole

SEED COINS

Seed coins are specially prepared examples, perfectly round, with sharp characters, used in the preparation of clay or sand molds

Seed types for value 2 and 5 Mun are not included as they are very scarce and seldom are encountered in today's market.

MINT MARKS

戶 or 户 or 戸	***Ho*** Treasury Department
工	***Kong*** Ministry of Industry
冏	***Kyong*** Bureau of Royal Transportation
賑	***Chin*** Charity Office in Seoul
向	***Hyang*** Food Supply Office
宣	***Son*** Rice & Cloth Department
惠	***Hye*** Rice & Cloth Department
兵	***Pyong*** Ministry of Defense
備 or 俻	***Pi*** National Defense Bureau
摠	***Ch'ong*** General Military Office
營 or 営	***Yong*** Special Army Unit
武	***Mu*** Armaments Bureau
禁	***Kum*** Court Guard Military Unit
訓 or 訓	***Hun*** Military Training Command
	Ch'o Commando Military Unit
統 or 統	***T'ong*** T'ongyong Naval Office Military Office in Seoul
守	***Su*** Seoul Defense Fort
松	***Song*** Kaesong Township Military Office
水	***Su*** Suwon Township Military Office
原	***Won*** Wonju Township Military Office
海	***Hae*** Haeju Township Military Office
圻	***Ki*** Kwangju Township Military Office in Kyonggi Province
京	***Kyong*** Kyonggi Provincial Office
京水	***Kyong Su*** Kyonggi Naval Station
黃	***Hwang*** Hwanghae Provincial Office
平	***P'yong*** P'yongan Provincial Office
咸	***Ham*** Hamgyong Provincial Office
咸北	***Ham Puk*** North Hamgyong Provincial Office
	Ham Nam South Hamgyong Provincial Office
江	***Kang*** Kangwon Provincial Office
尙	***Sang*** Kyongsang Provincial Office
尙水	***Sang Su*** Kyongsang Naval Station
尙右	***Sang U*** Kyongsang Right Naval Base
尙左	***Sang Chwa*** Kyongsang Left Naval Base

全
Chon
Cholla Provincial Office

全兵
Chon Pyong
Cholla Military Fort

忠
Ch'ung
Ch'ungch'ong Provincial Office

KINGDOM

TREASURY DEPARTMENT

(Ho Jo)

KM# 8.12 MUN

Cast Copper Or Bronze **Obv:** 2 dot "Tong", and "Pyong" with hooks

Date	Mintage	Good	VG	F	VF	XF
ND(1731) Series 2	—	2.00	3.00	5.00	8.00	—

KM# 8.19 MUN

Cast Copper Or Bronze **Rev:** Sun at lower right

Date	Mintage	Good	VG	F	VF	XF
ND(1731) Series 9	—	2.00	3.00	5.00	8.00	—

KM# 8 MUN

Cast Copper Or Bronze, 23-27 mm. **Rev:** Series number at bottom **Note:** Size varies.

Date	Mintage	Good	VG	F	VF	XF
ND(1731) Series 1-10	—	2.00	3.00	5.00	8.00	—

KM# 8s MUN

Cast Copper Or Bronze

Date	Mintage	Good	VG	F	VF	XF
ND(1731) Series 1-10	—	—	—	—	—	50.00

KM# 21as MUN

Cast Copper Or Bronze **Note:** Seed type.

Date	Mintage	Good	VG	F	VF	XF
ND(1757-1806) Series 1-10	—	—	—	—	—	75.00

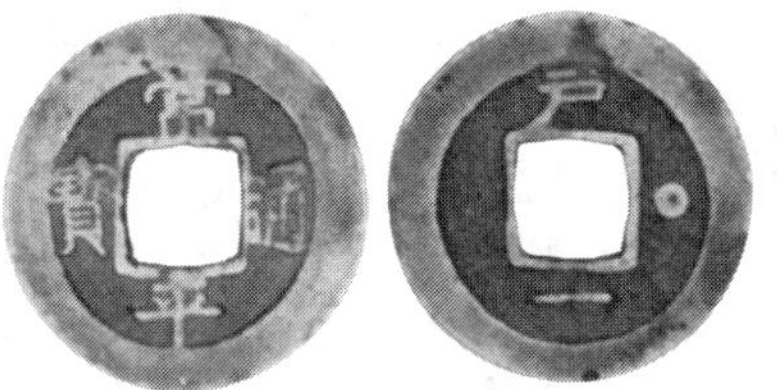

KM# 21 MUN

Cast Copper Or Bronze, 24 mm. **Obv:** 2 dot "Tong", and "P'yong" with hooks **Rev:** Circle at right, series number below

Date	Mintage	Good	VG	F	VF	XF
ND(1757-1806) Series 1-10	—	3.00	5.00	7.00	10.00	—

KM# 21a MUN

Cast Copper Or Bronze, 23-25 mm. **Obv:** 2 dot "Tong", and "P'yong" with hooks **Rev:** Circle at right, series number below **Note:** Size varies.

Date	Mintage	Good	VG	F	VF	XF
ND(1757-1806) Series 1-10	—	3.00	5.00	7.00	10.00	—

KM# 21s MUN

Cast Copper Or Bronze **Note:** Seed type.

Date	Mintage	Good	VG	F	VF	XF
ND(1757-1806) Series 1-10	—	—	—	—	—	75.00

KM# 22as MUN

Cast Copper Or Bronze **Note:** Seed type.

Date	Mintage	Good	VG	F	VF	XF
ND(1757-1806) Series 1-10	—	—	—	—	—	75.00

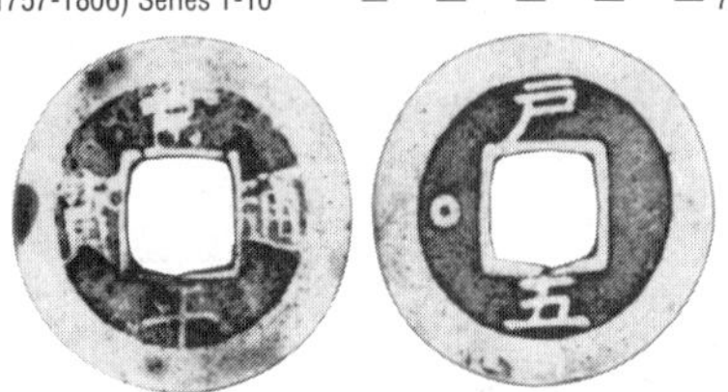

KM# 22 MUN

Cast Copper Or Bronze, 23 mm. **Obv:** 2 dot "Tong" and "P'yong" with hooks **Rev:** Circle at left, series number below

Date	Mintage	Good	VG	F	VF	XF
ND(1757-1806) Series 1-10	—	3.00	5.00	7.00	10.00	—

KM# 22a MUN

Cast Copper Or Bronze **Obv:** 2 dot "Tong" and "P'yong" with hooks **Rev:** Circle at left, series number below

Date	Mintage	Good	VG	F	VF	XF
ND(1757-1806) Series 1-10	—	3.00	5.00	7.00	10.00	—

KM# 22s MUN

Cast Copper Or Bronze **Note:** Seed type.

Date	Mintage	Good	VG	F	VF	XF
ND(1757-1806) Series 1-10	—	—	—	—	—	75.00

KM# 29as MUN

Cast Copper Or Bronze **Note:** Seed type.

Date	Mintage	Good	VG	F	VF	XF
ND(1757-1806) Series 1-10	—	—	—	—	75.00	—

KM# 29 MUN

Cast Copper Or Bronze, 24 mm. **Rev:** Crescent at right, series number at bottom

Date	Mintage	Good	VG	F	VF	XF
ND(1757-1806) Series 1-10	—	3.00	5.00	7.00	10.00	—

KM# 29a MUN

Cast Copper Or Bronze, 23-24 mm. **Obv:** Without "P'yong" **Note:** Size varies.

Date	Mintage	Good	VG	F	VF	XF
ND(1757-1806) Series 1-10	—	3.00	5.00	7.00	10.00	—

KM# 29s MUN

Cast Copper Or Bronze **Note:** Seed type.

Date	Mintage	Good	VG	F	VF	XF
ND(1757-1806) Series 1-10	—	—	—	—	—	75.00

KM# 29b MUN

Cast Copper Or Bronze **Rev:** Star in crescent

Date	Mintage	Good	VG	F	VF	XF
ND(1757-1806) Series 6	—	3.00	5.00	7.00	10.00	—

KM# 30 MUN

Cast Copper Or Bronze **Obv:** Without "P'yong, tong" with 1 dot **Rev:** Crescent at left, series number at bottom

Date	Mintage	Good	VG	F	VF	XF
ND(1757-1806) Series 1-10	—	3.00	5.00	7.00	10.00	—

KM# 30c MUN

Cast Copper Or Bronze, 25 mm. **Obv:** Without "P'yong, tong" with 1 dot **Rev:** Crescent at left, series number at bottom

Date	Mintage	Good	VG	F	VF	XF
ND(1757-1806) Series 1-10	—	3.00	5.00	7.00	10.00	—

KM# 30a MUN

Cast Copper Or Bronze **Obv:** Without "P'yong, tong" with 1 dot **Rev:** Crescent at left, series number at bottom

Date	Mintage	Good	VG	F	VF	XF
ND(1757-1806) Series 1-10	—	3.00	5.00	7.00	10.00	—

KM# 30s MUN

Cast Copper Or Bronze **Note:** Seed type.

Date	Mintage	Good	VG	F	VF	XF
ND(1757-1806) Series 1-10	—	—	—	—	—	75.00

KM# 30b MUN

Cast Copper Or Bronze **Obv:** Without "P'yong, tong" with 1 dot, star at lower left **Rev:** Crescent at left, series number at bottom

Date	Mintage	Good	VG	F	VF	XF
ND(1757-1806) Series 7	—	3.00	5.00	7.00	10.00	—

KM# 11 MUN

Cast Copper Or Bronze **Rev:** "Ho" in different style, series number at right

Date	Mintage	Good	VG	F	VF	XF
ND(1778-1800) Series 1	—	2.50	3.50	5.00	9.00	—

KM# 12 MUN

Cast Copper Or Bronze **Rev:** Series number at left

Date	Mintage	Good	VG	F	VF	XF
ND(1778-1800) Series 1	—	2.00	3.00	5.00	8.00	—

KM# 27 MUN

Cast Copper Or Bronze **Rev:** Dot at right, circle at left, series number at bottom

Date	Mintage	Good	VG	F	VF	XF
ND(1778-1806) Series 1-10	—	3.00	5.00	7.00	10.00	—

KM# 27s MUN

Cast Copper Or Bronze **Note:** Seed type.

Date	Mintage	Good	VG	F	VF	XF
ND(1778-1806) Series 1-10	—	—	—	—	—	75.00

KM# 28 MUN

Cast Copper Or Bronze **Rev:** Circle at right, dot at left, series number at bottom

Date	Mintage	Good	VG	F	VF	XF
ND(1778-1806) Series 1-5	—	3.00	5.00	7.00	10.00	—

KM# 28s MUN

Cast Copper Or Bronze **Note:** Seed type.

Date	Mintage	Good	VG	F	VF	XF
ND(1778-1806) Series 1-5	—	—	—	—	—	75.00

KM# 31s MUN

Cast Copper Or Bronze **Note:** Seed type.

Date	Mintage	Good	VG	F	VF	XF
ND(1778-1806) Series 9	—	—	—	—	—	75.00

KM# 32s MUN

Cast Copper Or Bronze **Note:** Seed type.

Date	Mintage	Good	VG	F	VF	XF
ND(1778-1806) Series 1-10	—	—	—	—	—	75.00

KM# 31 MUN

Cast Copper Or Bronze **Rev:** Vertical line at right, crescent at left, number 9 at bottom

Date	Mintage	Good	VG	F	VF	XF
ND(1778-1806) Series 9	—	2.00	3.00	5.00	8.00	—

KM# 32 MUN

Cast Copper Or Bronze, 25 mm. **Rev:** Dot at right, crescent at left, series number at bottom

Date	Mintage	Good	VG	F	VF	XF
ND(1778-1806) Series 1-10	—	3.00	5.00	8.00	12.00	—

KM# 33 MUN

Cast Copper Or Bronze, 26 mm. **Rev:** Crescent at right, dot at left, series number at bottom

Date	Mintage	Good	VG	F	VF	XF
ND(1778-1806) Series 1-10	—	3.00	5.00	8.00	12.00	—

KM# 33s MUN

Cast Copper Or Bronze **Note:** Seed type. Struck at Ho Jo.

Date	Mintage	Good	VG	F	VF	XF
ND(1778-1806) Series 1-10	—	—	—	—	—	75.00

KM# 11s MUN

Cast Copper Or Bronze

Date	Mintage	Good	VG	F	VF	XF
ND(1778-1800) Series 1	—	—	—	—	—	50.00

KM# 12s MUN

Cast Copper Or Bronze

Date	Mintage	Good	VG	F	VF	XF
ND(1778-1800) Series 1	—	—	—	—	—	50.00

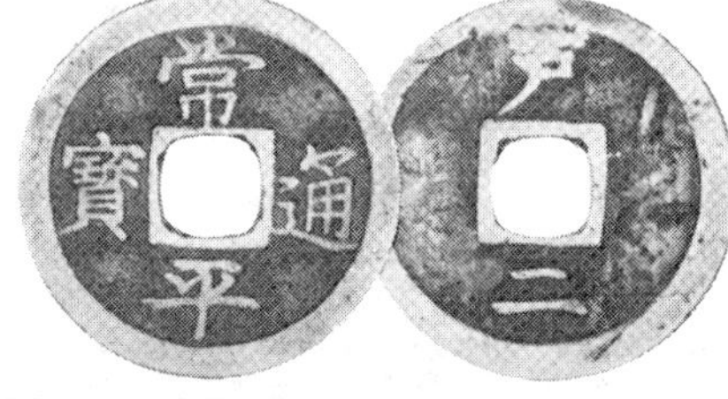

KM# 74 2 MUN

Cast Copper Or Brass **Rev:** "I" (2) at bottom **Note:** Weight varies 8.00-9.00 grams.

Date	Mintage	Good	VG	F	VF	XF
ND(1679-1752)	—	3.00	4.00	6.00	10.00	—

KM# 75 2 MUN

Cast Copper Or Brass **Rev:** "Ho" with dot at right **Note:** Weight varies 8.00-9.00 grams.

Date	Mintage	Good	VG	F	VF	XF
ND(1724-52)	—	3.00	4.00	6.00	10.00	—

KM# 114 2 MUN

Cast Copper Or Brass **Rev:** "Wang" at bottom **Note:** Small characters. Weight varies 8.00-9.00 grams.

Date	Mintage	Good	VG	F	VF	XF
ND(1742-52)	—	3.00	4.00	6.00	7.00	—

KM# 116 2 MUN
Cast Copper Or Brass **Rev:** "Ch'u" at bottom **Note:** Small characters. Weight varies 8.00-9.00 grams.

Date	Mintage	Good	VG	F	VF	XF
ND(1742-52)	—	3.00	4.00	6.00	10.00	—

KM# 118 2 MUN
Cast Copper Or Brass **Rev:** "Su" at bottom **Note:** Small characters. Weight varies 8.00-9.00 grams.

Date	Mintage	Good	VG	F	VF	XF
ND(1742-52)	—	3.00	4.00	6.00	10.00	—

KM# 124 2 MUN
Cast Copper Or Brass **Rev:** "Yun" at bottom **Note:** Small characters. Weight varies 8.00-9.00 grams.

Date	Mintage	Good	VG	F	VF	XF
ND(1742-52)	—	3.00	4.00	6.00	10.00	—

KM# 126 2 MUN
Cast Copper Or Brass **Rev:** "Yo" (surplus) at bottom **Note:** Small characters. Weight varies 8.00-9.00 grams.

Date	Mintage	Good	VG	F	VF	XF
ND(1742-52)	—	3.00	4.00	6.00	10.00	—

KM# 130 2 MUN
Cast Copper Or Brass **Rev:** "Se" at bottom **Note:** Small characters. Weight varies 8.00-9.00 grams.

Date	Mintage	Good	VG	F	VF	XF
ND(1742-52)	—	3.00	4.00	6.00	10.00	—

KM# 76 2 MUN
Cast Copper Or Brass **Rev:** "Ch'on" at bottom **Note:** Small characters. Weight varies 8.00-9.00 grams.

Date	Mintage	Good	VG	F	VF	XF
ND(1742-52)	—	3.00	4.00	6.00	10.00	—

KM# 78 2 MUN
Cast Copper Or Brass **Rev:** "Chi" at bottom **Note:** Small characters. Weight varies 8.00-9.00 grams.

Date	Mintage	Good	VG	F	VF	XF
ND(1742-52)	—	3.00	4.00	6.00	10.00	—

KM# 80 2 MUN
Cast Copper Or Brass **Rev:** "Hyon" at bottom **Note:** Small characters. Weight varies 8.00-9.00 grams.

Date	Mintage	Good	VG	F	VF	XF
ND(1742-52)	—	3.00	4.00	6.00	10.00	—

KM# 82 2 MUN
Cast Copper Or Brass **Rev:** "Hwang" (yellow) at bottom **Note:** Small characters. Weight varies 8.00-9.00 grams.

Date	Mintage	Good	VG	F	VF	XF
ND(1742-52)	—	3.00	4.00	6.00	10.00	—

KM# 84 2 MUN
Cast Copper Or Brass **Rev:** "U" at bottom **Note:** Small characters. Weight varies 8.00-9.00 grams.

Date	Mintage	Good	VG	F	VF	XF
ND(1742-52)	—	3.00	4.00	6.00	10.00	—

KM# 86 2 MUN
Cast Copper Or Brass **Rev:** "Chu: at bottom **Note:** Small characters. Weight varies 8.00-9.00 grams.

Date	Mintage	Good	VG	F	VF	XF
ND(1742-52)	—	3.00	4.00	6.00	10.00	—

KM# 88 2 MUN
Cast Copper Or Brass **Rev:** "Hong" at bottom **Note:** Small characters. Weight varies 8.00-9.00 grams.

Date	Mintage	Good	VG	F	VF	XF
ND(1742-52)	—	3.00	4.00	6.00	10.00	—

KM# 120 2 MUN
Cast Copper Or Brass **Rev:** "Tong" at bottom **Note:** Small characters. Weight varies 8.00-9.00 grams.

Date	Mintage	Good	VG	F	VF	XF
ND(1742-52)	—	3.00	4.00	6.00	10.00	—

KM# 122 2 MUN
Cast Copper Or Brass **Rev:** "Chang" (hoard) at bottom **Note:** Small characters. Weight varies 8.00-9.00 grams.

Date	Mintage	Good	VG	F	VF	XF
ND(1742-52)	—	3.00	4.00	6.00	10.00	—

KM# 128 2 MUN
Cast Copper Or Brass **Rev:** "Song" at bottom **Note:** Small letters. Weight varies 8.00-9.00 grams.

Date	Mintage	Good	VG	F	VF	XF
ND(1742-52)	—	3.00	4.00	6.00	10.00	—

KM# 91 2 MUN
Cast Copper Or Brass **Note:** Large characters. Weight varies 8.00-9.00 grams.

Date	Mintage	Good	VG	F	VF	XF
ND(1742-52)	—	3.00	4.00	6.00	10.00	—

KM# 93 2 MUN
Cast Copper Or Brass **Note:** Large characters. Weight varies 8.00-9.00 grams.

Date	Mintage	Good	VG	F	VF	XF
ND(1742-52)	—	3.00	4.00	6.00	10.00	—

KM# 95 2 MUN
Cast Copper Or Brass **Note:** Large characters. Weight varies 8.00-9.00 grams.

Date	Mintage	Good	VG	F	VF	XF
ND(1742-52)	—	3.00	4.00	6.00	10.00	—

KM# 97 2 MUN
Cast Copper Or Brass **Note:** Large characters. Weight varies 8.00-9.00 grams.

Date	Mintage	Good	VG	F	VF	XF
ND(1742-52)	—	3.00	4.00	6.00	10.00	—

KM# 99 2 MUN
Cast Copper Or Brass **Note:** Large characters. Weight varies 8.00-9.00 grams.

Date	Mintage	Good	VG	F	VF	XF
ND(1742-52)	—	3.00	4.00	6.00	10.00	—

KM# 101 2 MUN
Cast Copper Or Brass **Note:** Large characters. Weight varies 8.00-9.00 grams.

Date	Mintage	Good	VG	F	VF	XF
ND(1742-52)	—	3.00	4.00	6.00	10.00	—

KM# 103 2 MUN
Cast Copper Or Brass **Note:** Large characters. Weight varies 8.00-9.00 grams.

Date	Mintage	Good	VG	F	VF	XF
ND(1742-52)	—	3.00	4.00	6.00	10.00	—

KM# 105 2 MUN
Cast Copper Or Brass **Note:** Large characters. Weight varies 8.00-9.00 grams.

Date	Mintage	Good	VG	F	VF	XF
ND(1742-52)	—	3.00	4.00	6.00	10.00	—

KM# 107 2 MUN
Cast Copper Or Brass **Note:** Large characters. Weight varies 8.00-9.00 grams.

Date	Mintage	Good	VG	F	VF	XF
ND(1742-52)	—	3.00	4.00	6.00	10.00	—

KM# 109 2 MUN
Cast Copper Or Brass **Note:** Large characters. Weight varies 8.00-9.00 grams.

Date	Mintage	Good	VG	F	VF	XF
ND(1742-52)	—	3.00	4.00	6.00	10.00	—

KM# 111 2 MUN
Cast Copper Or Brass **Note:** Large characters. Weight varies 8.00-9.00 grams.

Date	Mintage	Good	VG	F	VF	XF
ND(1742-52)	—	3.00	4.00	6.00	10.00	—

KM# 113 2 MUN
Cast Copper Or Brass **Note:** Large characters. Weight varies 8.00-9.00 grams.

Date	Mintage	Good	VG	F	VF	XF
ND(1742-52)	—	3.00	4.00	6.00	10.00	—

KM# 115 2 MUN
Cast Copper Or Brass **Note:** Large characters. Weight varies 8.00-9.00 grams.

Date	Mintage	Good	VG	F	VF	XF
ND(1742-52)	—	3.00	4.00	6.00	10.00	—

KM# 117 2 MUN
Cast Copper Or Brass **Note:** Large characters. Weight varies 8.00-9.00 grams.

Date	Mintage	Good	VG	F	VF	XF
ND1742-52)	—	3.00	4.00	6.00	10.00	—

KM# 125 2 MUN
Cast Copper Or Brass **Note:** Large characters. Weight varies 8.00-9.00 grams.

Date	Mintage	Good	VG	F	VF	XF
ND(1742-52)	—	3.00	4.00	6.00	10.00	—

KM# 127 2 MUN
Cast Copper Or Brass **Note:** Large characters. Weight varies 8.00-9.00 grams.

Date	Mintage	Good	VG	F	VF	XF
ND(1742-52)	—	3.00	4.00	6.00	10.00	—

KM# 129 2 MUN
Cast Copper Or Brass **Note:** Large characters. Weight varies 8.00-9.00 grams.

Date	Mintage	Good	VG	F	VF	XF
ND(1742-52)	—	3.00	4.00	6.00	10.00	—

KM# 131 2 MUN
Cast Copper Or Brass **Note:** Large characters. Weight varies 8.00-9.00 grams.

Date	Mintage	Good	VG	F	VF	XF
ND(1742-52)	—	3.00	4.00	6.00	10.00	—

KM# 132 2 MUN
Cast Copper Or Brass **Rev:** "Yul" at bottom **Note:** Large characters. Weight varies 8.00-9.00 grams.

Date	Mintage	Good	VG	F	VF	XF
ND(1742-52)	—	3.00	4.00	6.00	10.00	—

KM# 133 2 MUN
Cast Copper Or Brass **Rev:** "Yo" (yin) at bottom **Note:** Large characters. Weight varies 8.00-9.00 grams.

Date	Mintage	Good	VG	F	VF	XF
ND(1742-52)	—	3.00	4.00	6.00	10.00	—

KM# 134 2 MUN
Cast Copper Or Brass **Rev:** "Cho" at bottom **Note:** Large characters. Weight varies 8.00-9.00 grams.

Date	Mintage	Good	VG	F	VF	XF
ND(1742-52)	—	3.00	4.00	6.00	10.00	—

KM# 135 2 MUN
Cast Copper Or Brass **Rev:** "Hwang" at bottom, "Il" (1) at right **Note:** Large characters. Weight varies 8.00-9.00 grams.

Date	Mintage	Good	VG	F	VF	XF
ND(1742-52)	—	3.00	3.00	6.00	10.00	—

KM# 77 2 MUN
Cast Copper Or Brass **Note:** Large characters. Weight varies 8.00-9.00 grams.

Date	Mintage	Good	VG	F	VF	XF
ND(1742-52)	—	3.00	4.00	6.00	10.00	—

KM# 79 2 MUN
Cast Copper Or Brass **Note:** Large characters. Weight varies 8.00-9.00 grams.

Date	Mintage	Good	VG	F	VF	XF
ND(1742-52)	—	3.00	4.00	6.00	10.00	—

KM# 81 2 MUN
Cast Copper Or Brass **Note:** Large characters. Weight varies 8.00-9.00 grams.

Date	Mintage	Good	VG	F	VF	XF
ND(1742-52)	—	3.00	4.00	6.00	10.00	—

KM# 83 2 MUN
Cast Copper Or Brass **Note:** Large characters. Weight varies 8.00-9.00 grams.

Date	Mintage	Good	VG	F	VF	XF
ND(1742-52)	—	3.00	4.00	6.00	10.00	—

KM# 85 2 MUN
Cast Copper Or Brass **Note:** Large characters. Weight varies 8.00-9.00 grams.

Date	Mintage	Good	VG	F	VF	XF
ND(1742-52)	—	3.00	4.00	6.00	10.00	—

KM# 87 2 MUN
Cast Copper Or Brass **Note:** Large characters. Weight varies 8.00-9.00 grams.

Date	Mintage	Good	VG	F	VF	XF
ND(1742-52)	—	3.00	4.00	6.00	10.00	—

KM# 89 2 MUN
Cast Copper Or Brass **Note:** Large characters. Weight varies 8.00-9.00 grams.

Date	Mintage	Good	VG	F	VF	XF
ND(1742-52)	—	3.00	4.00	6.00	10.00	—

KM# 119 2 MUN
Cast Copper Or Brass **Note:** Large characters. Weight varies 8.00-9.00 grams.

Date	Mintage	Good	VG	F	VF	XF
ND(1742-52)	—	3.00	4.00	6.00	10.00	—

KM# 121 2 MUN
Cast Copper Or Brass **Note:** Large characters. Weight varies 8.00-9.00 grams.

Date	Mintage	Good	VG	F	VF	XF
ND(1742-52)	—	3.00	4.00	6.00	10.00	—

KM# 123 2 MUN
Cast Copper Or Brass **Note:** Large characters. Weight varies 8.00-9.00 grams.

Date	Mintage	Good	VG	F	VF	XF
ND(1742-52)	—	3.00	4.00	6.00	10.00	—

KM# 90 2 MUN
Cast Copper Or Brass **Rev:** "Hwang" (barren) at bottom **Note:** Small characters. Weight varies 8.00-9.00 grams.

Date	Mintage	Good	VG	F	VF	XF
ND(1742-52)	—	3.00	4.00	6.00	10.00	—

KM# 92 2 MUN
Cast Copper Or Brass **Rev:** "Il" at bottom **Note:** Small characters. Weight varies 8.00-9.00 grams.

Date	Mintage	Good	VG	F	VF	XF
ND(1742-52)	—	3.00	4.00	6.00	10.00	—

KM# 94 2 MUN
Cast Copper Or Brass **Rev:** "Wol" at bottom **Note:** Small characters. Weight varies 8.00-9.00 grams.

Date	Mintage	Good	VG	F	VF	XF
ND(1742-52)	—	3.00	4.00	6.00	10.00	—

KM# 96 2 MUN
Cast Copper Or Brass **Rev:** "Yong" at bottom **Note:** Small characters. Weight varies 8.00-9.00 grams.

Date	Mintage	Good	VG	F	VF	XF
ND(1742-52)	—	3.00	4.00	6.00	10.00	—

KM# 98 2 MUN
Cast Copper Or Brass **Rev:** "Ch'uk" at bottom **Note:** Small characters. Weight varies 8.00-9.00 grams.

Date	Mintage	Good	VG	F	VF	XF
ND(1742-52)	—	3.00	4.00	6.00	10.00	—

KM# 100 2 MUN
Cast Copper Or Brass **Rev:** "Chin" at bottom **Note:** Small characters. Weight varies 8.00-9.00 grams.

Date	Mintage	Good	VG	F	VF	XF
ND(1742-52)	—	3.00	4.00	6.00	10.00	—

KM# 102 2 MUN
Cast Copper Or Brass **Rev:** "Suk" at bottom **Note:** Small characters. Weight varies 8.00-9.00 grams.

Date	Mintage	Good	VG	F	VF	XF
ND(1742-52)	—	3.00	4.00	6.00	10.00	—

KM# 104 2 MUN
Cast Copper Or Brass **Rev:** "Yol" at bottom **Note:** Small characters. Weight varies 8.00-9.00 grams.

Date	Mintage	Good	VG	F	VF	XF
ND(1742-52)	—	3.00	4.00	6.00	10.00	—

KM# 106 2 MUN
Cast Copper Or Brass **Rev:** "Chang" (extend) at bottom **Note:** Small characters. Weight varies 8.00-9.00 grams.

Date	Mintage	Good	VG	F	VF	XF
ND(1742-52)	—	3.00	4.00	6.00	10.00	—

KM# 108 2 MUN
Cast Copper Or Brass **Rev:** "Han" at bottom **Note:** Small characters. Weight varies 8.00-9.00 grams.

Date	Mintage	Good	VG	F	VF	XF
ND(1742-52)	—	3.00	4.00	6.00	10.00	—

KM# 110 2 MUN
Cast Copper Or Brass **Rev:** "Nae" at bottom **Note:** Small characters. Weight varies 8.00-9.00 grams.

Date	Mintage	Good	VG	F	VF	XF
ND(1742-52)	—	3.00	4.00	6.00	10.00	—

KM# 112 2 MUN
Cast Copper Or Brass **Rev:** "So" at bottom **Note:** Small characters. Weight varies 8.00-9.00 grams.

Date	Mintage	Good	VG	F	VF	XF
ND(1742-52) 1742	—	3.00	4.00	6.00	10.00	—

MINISTRY OF INDUSTRY

(Kong Jo)

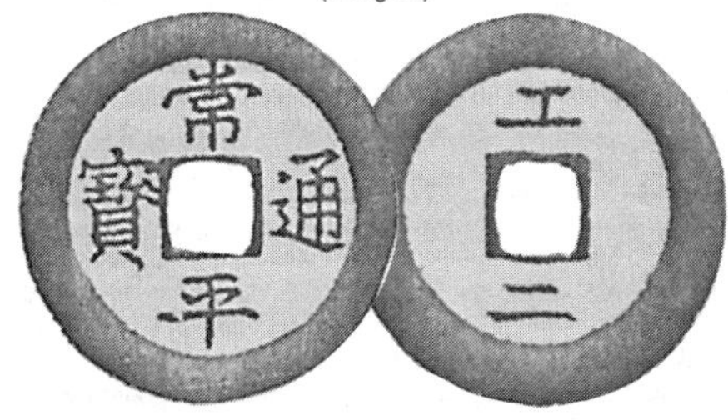

KM# 145 2 MUN
Cast Copper **Rev:** "Kong" at top, "I" (2) at bottom **Note:** Weight varies 8.00-9.00 grams.

Date	Mintage	Good	VG	F	VF	XF
ND(1685-1752)	—	3.00	5.00	8.00	10.00	—

KM# 146 2 MUN
Cast Copper **Rev:** Dot at right **Note:** Weight varies 8.00-9.00 grams.

Date	Mintage	Good	VG	F	VF	XF
ND(1685-1752)	—	8.50	12.50	20.00	40.00	—

BUREAU OF ROYAL TRANSPORTATION

(Kyong Saboksi)

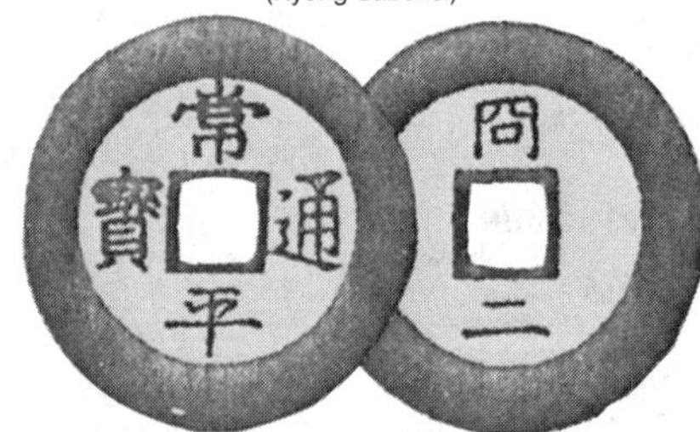

KM# 156 2 MUN
Cast Copper **Rev:** "I" (2) at bottom **Note:** Weight varies 8.00-9.00 grams.

Date	Mintage	Good	VG	F	VF	XF
ND(1679-1752)	—	—	—	—	—	—

SEOUL CHARITY OFFICE

(Chinh Yu Chong)

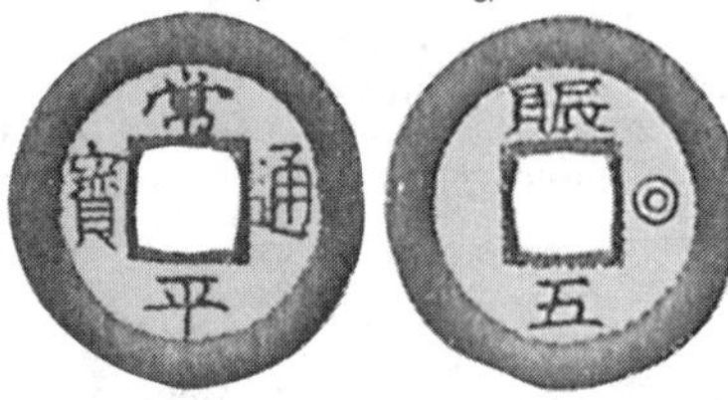

KM# 159 MUN
4.5000 g., Cast Copper Or Brass **Rev:** Double circle at right

Date	Mintage	Good	VG	F	VF	XF
ND(1742) Series 1, 5	—	40.00	65.00	100	200	—

KM# 159s MUN
4.5000 g., Cast Copper Or Brass

Date	Mintage	Good	VG	F	VF	XF
ND(1742) Series 1, 5	—	2.00	3.00	5.00	8.00	—

KM# 158 MUN
4.5000 g., Cast Copper Or Brass **Note:** Large characters.

Date	Mintage	Good	VG	F	VF	XF
ND(1742) Series 1-10	—	2.00	3.00	5.00	8.00	—

KM# 157s MUN
4.5000 g., Cast Copper Or Brass **Note:** Seed type.

Date	Mintage	Good	VG	F	VF	XF
ND(1742) Series 1-10	—	—	—	—	—	50.00

KM# 158s MUN
4.5000 g., Cast Copper Or Brass **Note:** Seed type.

Date	Mintage	Good	VG	F	VF	XF
ND(1742) Series 1-10	—	—	—	—	—	50.00

KM# 157 MUN
4.5000 g., Cast Copper Or Brass **Rev:** "Chin" at top, series number at bottom **Note:** Small characters.

Date	Mintage	Good	VG	F	VF	XF
ND(1742) Series 1-10	—	2.00	3.00	5.00	8.00	—

KM# 163 2 MUN
Cast Copper, 32-33 mm. **Rev:** Circle at right **Note:** Weight varies 8.00-9.00 grams. Size varies.

Date	Mintage	Good	VG	F	VF	XF
ND(1695-1742)	—	3.00	5.00	7.50	10.00	—

KM# 165 2 MUN
Cast Copper **Rev:** Circle at left **Note:** Weight varies 8.00-9.00 grams.

Date	Mintage	Good	VG	F	VF	XF
ND(1695-1742)	—	4.00	7.00	10.00	20.00	—

KM# 166 2 MUN
Cast Copper, 32-33 mm. **Note:** Weight varies 8.00-9.00 grams. Size varies.

Date	Mintage	Good	VG	F	VF	XF
ND(1695-1742)	—	3.00	5.00	7.50	10.00	—

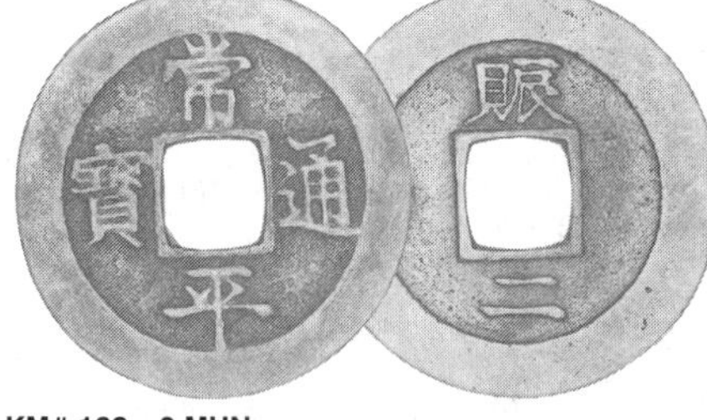

KM# 168 2 MUN
Cast Copper **Rev:** Small crescent at left **Note:** Weight varies 8.00-9.00 grams.

Date	Mintage	Good	VG	F	VF	XF
ND(1695-1742)	—	3.00	5.00	7.50	10.00	—

KM# 169 2 MUN
Cast Copper, 32-33 mm. **Rev:** Dot in crescent at left **Note:** Weight varies 8.00-9.00 grams. Size varies.

Date	Mintage	Good	VG	F	VF	XF
ND(1695-1742)	—	3.00	4.00	6.00	10.00	—

KM# 164 2 MUN
Cast Copper, 29-30 mm. **Note:** Weight varies 8.00-9.00 grams. Reduced size.

Date	Mintage	Good	VG	F	VF	XF
ND(1742-52)	—	3.00	4.00	6.00	10.00	—

KM# 167 2 MUN
Cast Copper, 29-30 mm. **Note:** Weight varies 8.00-9.00 grams. Reduced size.

Date	Mintage	Good	VG	F	VF	XF
ND(1742-52)	—	3.00	4.00	6.00	10.00	—

KM# 170 2 MUN
Cast Copper, 29-30 mm. **Note:** Weight varies 8.00-9.00 grams. Retued size.

Date	Mintage	Good	VG	F	VF	XF
ND(1742-52)	—	3.00	4.00	6.00	10.00	—

FOOD SUPPLY OFFICE

(Yang Hyang Ch'ong)

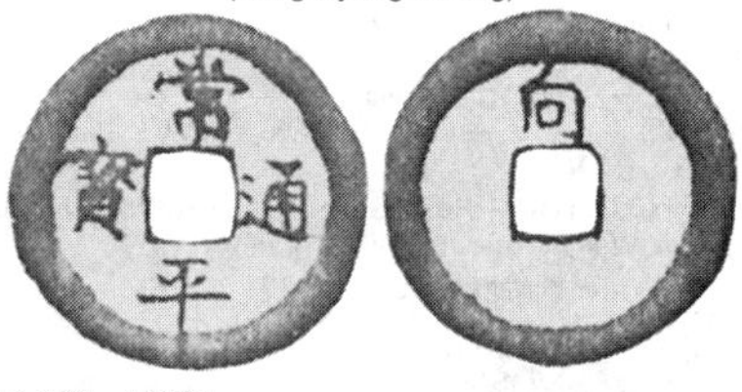

KM# 171 MUN
4.5000 g., Cast Copper **Rev:** "Hyang" at top

Date	Mintage	Good	VG	F	VF	XF
ND(1695-1742) Rare	—	—	—	—	—	—

KM# 172.1 2 MUN
Cast Copper, 31 mm. **Obv:** "Tong" with 2 dots, different "Hyang"

Date	Mintage	Good	VG	F	VF	XF
ND(1742)	—	3.50	6.50	12.00	18.00	—

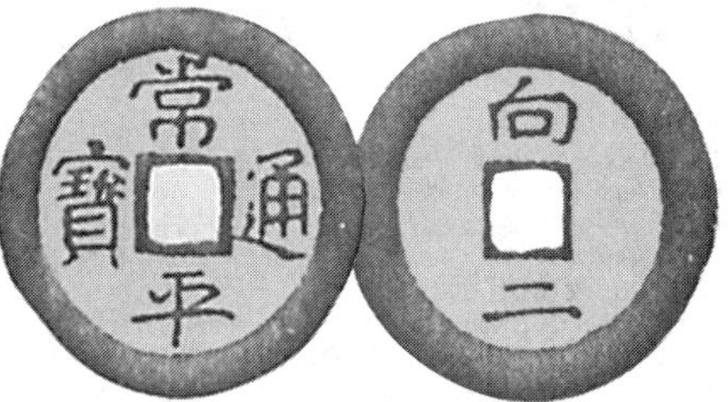

KM# 172 2 MUN
Cast Copper, 30 mm. **Rev:** "I" (2) at bottom **Note:** Weight varies 8.00-9.00 grams.

Date	Mintage	Good	VG	F	VF	XF
ND(1742)	—	3.50	6.50	12.00	18.00	—

RICE AND CLOTH DEPARTMENT

(Son Hye Ch ong)

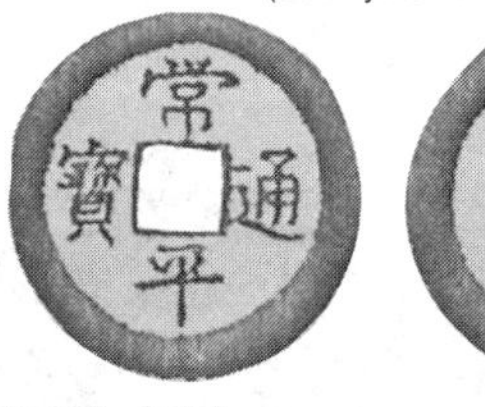
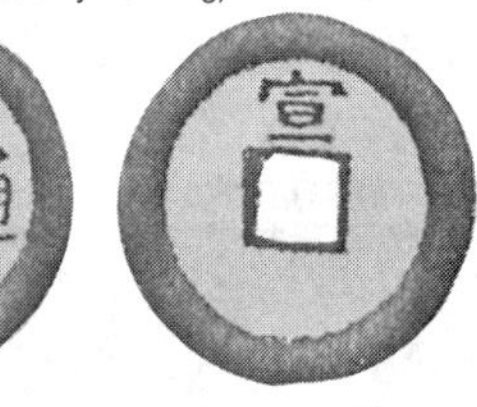

KM# 173 MUN
4.0000 g., Cast Copper Or Bronze **Rev:** "Son" at top

Date	Mintage	Good	VG	F	VF	XF
ND(1742) Series 1 Rare	—	—	—	—	—	—

KM# 178 2 MUN
Cast Copper Or Bronze **Rev:** "I" (02) at bottom **Note:** Size varies 30-31 mm.

Date	Mintage	Good	VG	F	VF	XF
ND(1742-52)	—	3.00	4.00	6.00	10.00	—

KM# 179 2 MUN
Cast Copper Or Bronze, 30 mm. **Rev:** "Ch'on" at bottom

Date	Mintage	Good	VG	F	VF	XF
ND(1742-52)	—	3.00	4.00	6.00	10.00	—

KM# 180 2 MUN
Cast Copper Or Bronze **Rev:** "Chi" at bottom

Date	Mintage	Good	VG	F	VF	XF
ND(1742-52)	—	3.00	4.00	6.00	10.00	—

KM# 181 2 MUN
Cast Copper Or Bronze **Rev:** "Hyon" at bottom

Date	Mintage	Good	VG	F	VF	XF
ND(1742-52)	—	3.00	4.00	6.00	10.00	—

KM# 182 2 MUN
Cast Copper Or Bronze **Rev:** "Hwang" (yellow) at bottom

Date	Mintage	Good	VG	F	VF	XF
ND(1742-52)	—	3.00	4.00	6.00	10.00	—

KM# 183 2 MUN
Cast Copper Or Bronze **Rev:** "U" at bottom

Date	Mintage	Good	VG	F	VF	XF
ND(1742-52)	—	3.00	4.00	6.00	10.00	—

KM# 184 2 MUN

Cast Copper Or Bronze **Rev:** "Chu" at bottom

Date	Mintage	Good	VG	F	VF	XF
ND(1742-52)	—	3.00	4.00	6.00	10.00	—

KM# 185 2 MUN

Cast Copper Or Bronze **Rev:** "Hong" at bottom

Date	Mintage	Good	VG	F	VF	XF
ND(1742-52)	—	3.00	4.00	6.00	10.00	—

KM# 186 2 MUN

Cast Copper Or Bronze **Rev:** "Hwang" (barren) at bottom

Date	Mintage	Good	VG	F	VF	XF
ND(1742-52)	—	3.00	4.00	6.00	10.00	—

KM# 187 2 MUN

Cast Copper Or Bronze **Rev:** "Il" at bottom

Date	Mintage	Good	VG	F	VF	XF
ND(1742-52)	—	3.00	4.00	6.00	10.00	—

KM# 188 2 MUN

Cast Copper Or Bronze **Rev:** "Wol" at bottom

Date	Mintage	Good	VG	F	VF	XF
ND(1742-52)	—	3.00	4.00	6.00	10.00	—

KM# 189 2 MUN

Cast Copper Or Bronze **Rev:** "Yong" at bottom

Date	Mintage	Good	VG	F	VF	XF
ND(1742-52)	—	3.00	4.00	6.00	10.00	—

KM# 190 2 MUN

Cast Copper Or Bronze **Rev:** "Ch'uk" at bottom

Date	Mintage	Good	VG	F	VF	XF
ND(1742-52)	—	3.00	4.00	6.00	10.00	—

KM# 191 2 MUN

Cast Copper Or Bronze **Rev:** "Chin" at bottom

Date	Mintage	Good	VG	F	VF	XF
ND(1742-52)	—	3.00	4.00	6.00	10.00	—

KM# 192 2 MUN

Cast Copper Or Bronze **Rev:** "Suk" at bottom

Date	Mintage	Good	VG	F	VF	XF
ND(1742-52)	—	3.00	4.00	6.00	10.00	—

KM# 193 2 MUN

Cast Copper Or Bronze **Rev:** "Yol"at bottom

Date	Mintage	Good	VG	F	VF	XF
ND(1742-52)	—	3.00	4.00	6.00	10.00	—

KM# 194 2 MUN

Cast Copper Or Bronze **Rev:** "Chang" (extend) at bottom

Date	Mintage	Good	VG	F	VF	XF
ND(1742-52)	—	3.00	4.00	6.00	10.00	—

KM# 195 2 MUN

Cast Copper Or Bronze **Rev:** "Han" at bottom

Date	Mintage	Good	VG	F	VF	XF
ND(1742-52)	—	3.00	4.00	6.00	10.00	—

KM# 196 2 MUN

Cast Copper Or Bronze **Rev:** "Nae" at bottom

Date	Mintage	Good	VG	F	VF	XF
ND(1742-52)	—	3.00	4.00	6.00	10.00	—

KM# 197 2 MUN

Cast Copper Or Bronze **Rev:** "So" at bottom

Date	Mintage	Good	VG	F	VF	XF
ND(1742-52)	—	3.00	4.00	6.00	10.00	—

KM# 198 2 MUN

Cast Copper Or Bronze **Rev:** "Wang"at bottom

Date	Mintage	Good	VG	F	VF	XF
ND(1742-52)	—	3.00	4.00	6.00	10.00	—

KM# 199 2 MUN

Cast Copper Or Bronze **Rev:** "Ch'u" at bottom

Date	Mintage	Good	VG	F	VF	XF
ND(1742-52)	—	3.00	4.00	6.00	10.00	—

KM# 200 2 MUN

Cast Copper Or Bronze **Rev:** "Su" at bottom

Date	Mintage	Good	VG	F	VF	XF
ND(1742-52)	—	3.00	4.00	6.00	10.00	—

KM# 201 2 MUN

Cast Copper Or Bronze **Rev:** "Tong" at bottom

Date	Mintage	Good	VG	F	VF	XF
ND(1742-52)	—	3.00	4.00	6.00	10.00	—

KM# 202 2 MUN

Cast Copper Or Bronze **Rev:** "Chang" (hoard) at bottom

Date	Mintage	Good	VG	F	VF	XF
ND(1742-52)	—	3.00	4.00	6.00	10.00	—

KM# 203 2 MUN

Cast Copper Or Bronze **Rev:** "Yun" at bottom

Date	Mintage	Good	VG	F	VF	XF
ND(1742-52)	—	3.00	4.00	6.00	10.00	—

KM# 204 2 MUN

Cast Copper Or Bronze **Rev:** "Yo" (surplus) at bottom

Date	Mintage	Good	VG	F	VF	XF
ND(1742-52)	—	3.00	4.00	6.00	10.00	—

KM# 205 2 MUN

Cast Copper Or Bronze **Rev:** "Song" at bottom

Date	Mintage	Good	VG	F	VF	XF
ND(1742-52)	—	3.00	4.00	6.00	10.00	—

KM# 206 2 MUN

Cast Copper Or Bronze **Rev:** "Se" at bottom

Date	Mintage	Good	VG	F	VF	XF
ND(1742-52)	—	3.00	4.00	6.00	10.00	—

KM# 207 2 MUN

Cast Copper Or Bronze **Rev:** "Yul" at bottom

Date	Mintage	Good	VG	F	VF	XF
ND(1742-52)	—	3.00	4.00	6.00	10.00	—

KM# 208 2 MUN

Cast Copper Or Bronze **Rev:** "Yo" (yin) at bottom

Date	Mintage	Good	VG	F	VF	XF
ND(1742-52)	—	3.00	4.00	6.00	10.00	—

MINISTRY OF DEFENSE

(Pyong Jo)

KM# A212s MUN

4.5000 g., Cast Copper

Date	Mintage	Good	VG	F	VF	XF
ND(1742)	—	—	—	—	—	335

KM# A212 MUN

4.5000 g., Cast Copper **Rev:** "Pyong" at top **Note:** Varieties exist.

Date	Mintage	Good	VG	F	VF	XF
ND(1742)	—	40.00	70.00	100	200	—

KM# B212 2 MUN

Cast Copper **Rev:** "Pyong" at top, "I" (2) at bottom **Note:** Weight varies 8.00-9.00 grams.

Date	Mintage	Good	VG	F	VF	XF
ND(1742)	—	3.50	6.50	12.00	18.00	—

NATIONAL DEFENSE BUREAU

(Pi By On Sa)

KM# 213 MUN

4.5000 g., Cast Copper **Rev:** "Pi" at top

Date	Mintage	Good	VG	F	VF	XF
ND(1742)	—	20.00	30.00	45.00	65.00	—

KM# 214 MUN

4.5000 g., Cast Copper **Rev:** "Pi" in different style at top

Date	Mintage	Good	VG	F	VF	XF
ND(1742)	—	27.50	40.00	60.00	85.00	—

KM# 215 2 MUN

Cast Copper **Rev:** "Pi" at top, "I" (3) at bottom **Note:** Weight varies 8.00-9.00 grams.

Date	Mintage	Good	VG	F	VF	XF
ND(1742)	—	3.00	4.00	6.00	10.00	—

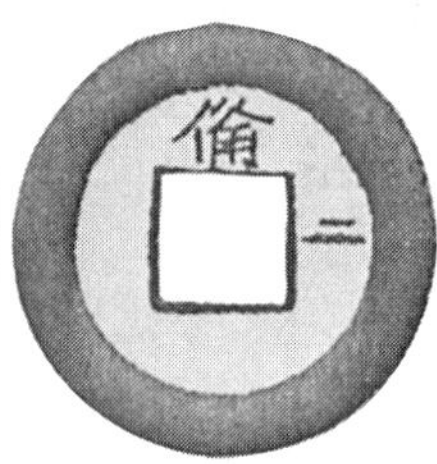

KM# 216 2 MUN

Cast Copper **Rev:** "I" (2) at right **Note:** Weight varies 8.00-9.00 grams.

Date	Mintage	Good	VG	F	VF	XF
ND(1742)	—	50.00	100	165	225	—

GENERAL MILITARY OFFICE

(Ch'ong Yung Ch'ong)

KM# 221 MUN

Cast Copper Or Bronze **Rev:** Double circle at right, series number at bottom

Date	Mintage	Good	VG	F	VF	XF
ND(1757) Series 6	—	50.00	75.00	125	200	—

KM# 221s MUN

Cast Copper Or Bronze

Date	Mintage	Good	VG	F	VF	XF
ND(1757) Series 6	—	—	—	—	—	—

KM# 222 MUN

Cast Copper Or Bronze, 25 mm. **Rev:** Crescent at right, series number at bottom

Date	Mintage	Good	VG	F	VF	XF
ND(1757) Series 1-10	—	2.00	3.00	5.00	8.00	—

KM# 222a MUN

Cast Copper Or Bronze **Obv:** Without "P'yong"

Date	Mintage	Good	VG	F	VF	XF
ND(1757) Series 1-10	—	2.00	3.00	5.00	8.00	—

KM# B224 MUN

Cast Copper Or Bronze **Rev:** Dot in crescent at right, series number at bottom

Date	Mintage	Good	VG	F	VF	XF
ND(1757) Series 8	—	25.00	40.00	60.00	100	—

KM# 219 MUN

Cast Copper Or Bronze, 22-23 mm. **Note:** Reduced size.

Date	Mintage	Good	VG	F	VF	XF
ND(1757) Series 1-10	—	2.00	3.00	5.00	8.00	—

KM# A220 MUN

Cast Copper Or Bronze, 22-23 mm. **Note:** Reduced size.

Date	Mintage	Good	VG	F	VF	XF
ND(1757) Series 1-10	—	2.00	3.00	5.00	8.00	—

KM# 223 MUN

Cast Copper Or Bronze, 24 mm. **Note:** Reduced size.

Date	Mintage	Good	VG	F	VF	XF
ND(1757) Series 1-10	—	2.00	3.00	5.00	8.00	—

KM# A224 MUN

Cast Copper Or Bronze, 22-23 mm. **Note:** Reduced size.

Date	Mintage	Good	VG	F	VF	XF
ND(1757) Series 1-10	—	2.00	3.00	5.00	8.00	—

KM# 219s MUN

Cast Copper Or Bronze **Note:** Seed type.

Date	Mintage	Good	VG	F	VF	XF
ND(1757) Series 1-10	—	—	—	—	—	50.00

KM# 220s MUN

Cast Copper Or Bronze **Note:** Seed type.

Date	Mintage	Good	VG	F	VF	XF
ND(1757) Series 1-10	—	—	—	—	—	50.00

KM# 222s MUN

Cast Copper Or Bronze **Note:** Seed type.

Date	Mintage	Good	VG	F	VF	XF
ND(1757) Series 1-10	—	—	—	—	—	50.00

KM# 223s MUN

Cast Copper Or Bronze **Note:** Seed type.

Date	Mintage	Good	VG	F	VF	XF
ND(1757) Series 1-10	—	—	—	—	—	50.00

KM# 218s MUN

Cast Copper Or Bronze, 25-26 mm. **Note:** Seed type; size varies.

Date	Mintage	Good	VG	F	VF	XF
ND(1757) Series 1-10	—	—	—	—	—	50.00

KM# 218as MUN

Cast Copper Or Bronze, 25-26 mm. **Obv:** Without "P'yong" **Note:** Seed type; size varies.

Date	Mintage	Good	VG	F	VF	XF
ND(1757)	—	—	—	—	—	50.00

KM# 218 MUN

Cast Copper Or Bronze, 25-26 mm. **Rev:** Circle at right, series number at bottom **Note:** Size varies.

Date	Mintage	Good	VG	F	VF	XF
ND(1757) Series 1-10	—	2.00	3.00	5.00	8.00	—

KM# 218a MUN

Cast Copper Or Bronze, 25-26 mm. **Obv:** Without "P'yong" **Note:** Size varies.

Date	Mintage	Good	VG	F	VF	XF
ND(1757) Series 1-10	—	2.00	3.00	5.00	8.00	—

KM# 220 MUN

Cast Copper Or Bronze, 25-26 mm. **Rev:** Circle at left, series number at bottom **Note:** Size varies.

Date	Mintage	Good	VG	F	VF	XF
ND(1757) Series 1-10	—	2.00	3.00	5.00	8.00	—

KM# 224 MUN

Cast Copper Or Bronze, 25-26 mm. **Rev:** Crescent at left, series number at bottom **Note:** Size varies.

Date	Mintage	Good	VG	F	VF	XF
ND(1757) Series 1-10	—	2.00	3.00	5.00	8.00	—

KM# 224s MUN

Cast Copper Or Bronze **Rev:** Crescent at left, series number at bottom **Note:** Seed type.

Date	Mintage	Good	VG	F	VF	XF
ND(1757)	—	—	—	—	—	50.00

KM# 225 2 MUN

Cast Copper **Rev:** "I" (2) at bottom **Note:** Weight varies 8.00-9.00 grams.

Date	Mintage	Good	VG	F	VF	XF
ND(1692-1752)	—	3.00	4.00	6.00	10.00	—

KM# 226 2 MUN

Cast Copper **Rev:** Dot at right **Note:** Weight varies 8.00-9.00 grams.

Date	Mintage	Good	VG	F	VF	XF
ND(1692-1752)	—	10.00	20.00	30.00	50.00	—

KM# 227 2 MUN

Cast Copper **Rev:** Dot at left **Note:** Weight varies 8.00-9.00 grams.

Date	Mintage	Good	VG	F	VF	XF
ND(1692-1752)	—	15.00	25.00	40.00	60.00	—

KM# 228 2 MUN

Cast Copper **Rev:** Large filled circle at right **Note:** Weight varies 8.00-9.00 grams.

Date	Mintage	Good	VG	F	VF	XF
ND(1692-1752)	—	30.00	50.00	75.00	125	—

KM# 266 2 MUN

Cast Copper **Note:** Small characters. Weight varies 8.00-9.00 grams.

Date	Mintage	Good	VG	F	VF	XF
ND(1742-52)	—	3.00	4.00	6.00	10.00	—

KM# 268 2 MUN

Cast Copper **Note:** Small characters. Weight varies 8.00-9.00 grams.

Date	Mintage	Good	VG	F	VF	XF
ND(1742-52)	—	3.00	4.00	6.00	10.00	—

KM# 229 2 MUN

Cast Copper **Rev:** "Ch'on" at bottom **Note:** Large characters. Weight varies 8.00-9.00 grams.

Date	Mintage	Good	VG	F	VF	XF
ND(1742-52)	—	3.00	4.00	6.00	10.00	—

KM# 231 2 MUN

Cast Copper **Rev:** "Chi" at bottom **Note:** Large characters. Weight varies 8.00-9.00 grams.

Date	Mintage	Good	VG	F	VF	XF
ND(1742-52)	—	3.00	4.00	6.00	10.00	—

KM# 233 2 MUN

Cast Copper **Rev:** "Hyon" at bottom **Note:** Large characters. Weight varies 8.00-9.00 grams.

Date	Mintage	Good	VG	F	VF	XF
ND(1742-52)	—	3.00	4.00	6.00	10.00	—

KM# 235 2 MUN

Cast Copper **Rev:** "Hwang" (yellow) at bottom **Note:** Large characters. Weight varies 8.00-9.00 grams.

Date	Mintage	Good	VG	F	VF	XF
ND(1742-52)	—	3.00	4.00	6.00	10.00	—

KM# 237 2 MUN

Cast Copper **Rev:** "U" at bottom **Note:** Large characters. Weight varies 8.00-9.00 grams.

Date	Mintage	Good	VG	F	VF	XF
ND(1742-52)	—	3.00	4.00	6.00	10.00	—

KM# 239 2 MUN

Cast Copper **Rev:** "Chu" at bottom **Note:** Large characters. Weight varies 8.00-9.00 grams.

Date	Mintage	Good	VG	F	VF	XF
ND(1742-52)	—	3.00	4.00	6.00	10.00	—

KM# 241 2 MUN

Cast Copper **Rev:** "Hong" at bottom **Note:** Large characters. Weight varies 8.00-9.00 grams.

Date	Mintage	Good	VG	F	VF	XF
ND(1742-52)	—	3.00	4.00	6.00	10.00	—

KM# 243 2 MUN

Cast Copper **Rev:** "Hwang" (barren) at bottom **Note:** Large characters. Weight varies 8.00-9.00 grams.

Date	Mintage	Good	VG	F	VF	XF
ND(1742-52)	—	3.00	4.00	6.00	10.00	—

KM# 245 2 MUN

Cast Copper **Rev:** "Il" at bottom **Note:** Large characters. Weight varies 8.00-9.00 grams.

Date	Mintage	Good	VG	F	VF	XF
ND(1742-52)	—	3.00	4.00	6.00	10.00	—

KM# 247 2 MUN

Cast Copper **Rev:** "Wol" at bottom **Note:** Large characters. Weight varies 8.00-9.00 grams.

Date	Mintage	Good	VG	F	VF	XF
ND(1742-52)	—	3.00	4.00	6.00	10.00	—

KM# 249 2 MUN

Cast Copper **Rev:** "Yong" at bottom **Note:** Large characters. Weight varies 8.00-9.00 grams.

Date	Mintage	Good	VG	F	VF	XF
ND(1742-52)	—	3.00	4.00	6.00	10.00	—

KM# 251 2 MUN

Cast Copper **Rev:** "Ch'uk" at bottom **Note:** Large characters. Weight varies 8.00-9.00 grams.

Date	Mintage	Good	VG	F	VF	XF
ND(1742-52)	—	3.00	4.00	6.00	10.00	—

KM# 253 2 MUN

Cast Copper **Rev:** "Chin" at bottom **Note:** Large characters. Weight varies 8.00-9.00 grams.

Date	Mintage	Good	VG	F	VF	XF
ND(1742-52)	—	3.00	4.00	6.00	10.00	—

KM# 255 2 MUN

Cast Copper **Rev:** "Suk" at bottom **Note:** Large characters. Weight varies 8.00-9.00 grams.

Date	Mintage	Good	VG	F	VF	XF
ND(1742-52)	—	3.00	5.00	7.00	10.00	—

KM# 257 2 MUN

Cast Copper **Rev:** "Yol" at bottom **Note:** Large characters. Weight varies 8.00-9.00 grams.

Date	Mintage	Good	VG	F	VF	XF
ND(1742-52)	—	3.00	4.00	6.00	10.00	—

KM# 259 2 MUN

Cast Copper **Rev:** "Chang" (extend) at bottom **Note:** Large characters. Weight varies 8.00-9.00 grams.

Date	Mintage	Good	VG	F	VF	XF
ND(1742-52)	—	3.00	4.00	6.00	10.00	—

KM# 261 2 MUN

Cast Copper **Rev:** "Han" at bottom **Note:** Large characters. Weight varies 8.00-9.00 grams.

Date	Mintage	Good	VG	F	VF	XF
ND(1742-52)	—	3.00	4.00	6.00	10.00	—

KM# 263 2 MUN

Cast Copper **Rev:** "Nae" at bottom **Note:** Large characters. Weight varies 8.00-9.00 grams.

Date	Mintage	Good	VG	F	VF	XF
ND(1742-52)	—	3.00	4.00	6.00	10.00	—

KM# 265 2 MUN

Cast Copper **Rev:** "So" at bottom **Note:** Large characters. Weight varies 8.00-9.00 grams.

Date	Mintage	Good	VG	F	VF	XF
ND(1742-52)	—	3.00	4.00	6.00	10.00	—

KM# 230 2 MUN

Cast Copper **Note:** Small characters. Weight varies 8.00-9.00 grams.

Date	Mintage	Good	VG	F	VF	XF
ND(1742-52)	—	3.00	4.00	6.00	10.00	—

KM# 232 2 MUN

Cast Copper **Note:** Small characters. Weight varies 8.00-9.00 grams.

Date	Mintage	Good	VG	F	VF	XF
ND(1742-52)	—	3.00	4.00	6.00	10.00	—

KM# 234 2 MUN

Cast Copper **Note:** Small characters. Weight varies 8.00-9.00 grams.

Date	Mintage	Good	VG	F	VF	XF
ND(1750)	—	3.00	4.00	6.00	10.00	—

KM# 236 2 MUN

Cast Copper **Note:** Small characters. Weight varies 8.00-9.00 grams.

Date	Mintage	Good	VG	F	VF	XF
ND(1750)	—	3.00	4.00	6.00	10.00	—

KM# 238 2 MUN

Cast Copper **Note:** Small characters. Weight varies 8.00-9.00 grams.

Date	Mintage	Good	VG	F	VF	XF
ND(1750)	—	3.00	4.00	6.00	10.00	—

KM# 240 2 MUN

Cast Copper **Note:** Small characters. Weight varies 8.00-9.00 grams.

Date	Mintage	Good	VG	F	VF	XF
ND(1750)	—	3.00	4.00	6.00	10.00	—

KM# 242 2 MUN

Cast Copper **Note:** Small characters. Weight varies 8.00-9.00 grams.

Date	Mintage	Good	VG	F	VF	XF
ND(1750)	—	3.00	4.00	6.00	10.00	—

KM# 244 2 MUN

Cast Copper **Note:** Small characters. Weight varies 8.00-9.00 grams.

Date	Mintage	Good	VG	F	VF	XF
ND(1750)	—	3.00	4.00	6.00	10.00	—

KM# 246 2 MUN

Cast Copper **Note:** Small characters. Weight varies 8.00-9.00 grams.

Date	Mintage	Good	VG	F	VF	XF
ND(1750)	—	3.00	4.00	6.00	10.00	—

KM# 248 2 MUN

Cast Copper **Note:** Small characters. Weight varies 8.00-9.00 grams.

Date	Mintage	Good	VG	F	VF	XF
ND(1750)	—	3.00	4.00	6.00	10.00	—

KM# 250 2 MUN

Cast Copper **Note:** Small characters. Weight varies 8.00-9.00 grams.

Date	Mintage	Good	VG	F	VF	XF
ND(1750)	—	3.00	4.00	6.00	10.00	—

KM# 252 2 MUN

Cast Copper **Note:** Small characters. Weight varies 8.00-9.00 grams.

Date	Mintage	Good	VG	F	VF	XF
ND(1750)	—	3.00	4.00	6.00	10.00	—

KM# 254 2 MUN

Cast Copper **Note:** Small characters. Weight varies 8.00-9.00 grams.

Date	Mintage	Good	VG	F	VF	XF
ND(1750)	—	3.00	4.00	6.00	10.00	—

KM# 256 2 MUN

Cast Copper **Note:** Small characters. Weight varies 8.00-9.00 grams.

Date	Mintage	Good	VG	F	VF	XF
ND(1750)	—	3.00	4.00	6.00	10.00	—

KM# 258 2 MUN

Cast Copper **Note:** Small characters. Weight varies 8.00-9.00 grams.

Date	Mintage	Good	VG	F	VF	XF
ND(1750)	—	3.00	4.00	6.00	10.00	—

KM# 260 2 MUN

Cast Copper **Note:** Small characters. Weight varies 8.00-9.00 grams.

Date	Mintage	Good	VG	F	VF	XF
ND(1750)	—	3.00	4.00	6.00	10.00	—

KM# 262 2 MUN

Cast Copper **Note:** Small characters. Weight varies 8.00-9.00 grams.

Date	Mintage	Good	VG	F	VF	XF
ND(1750)	—	3.00	4.00	6.00	10.00	—

KM# 264 2 MUN

Cast Copper **Note:** Small characters. Weight varies 8.00-9.00 grams.

Date	Mintage	Good	VG	F	VF	XF
ND(1750)	—	3.00	4.00	6.00	10.00	—

KM# 267 2 MUN

Cast Copper **Rev:** "Wang"at bottom **Note:** Large characters. Weight varies 8.00-9.00 grams.

Date	Mintage	Good	VG	F	VF	XF
ND(1750)	—	3.00	4.00	6.00	10.00	—

SPECIAL ARMY UNIT

(O Yong Ch'ong)

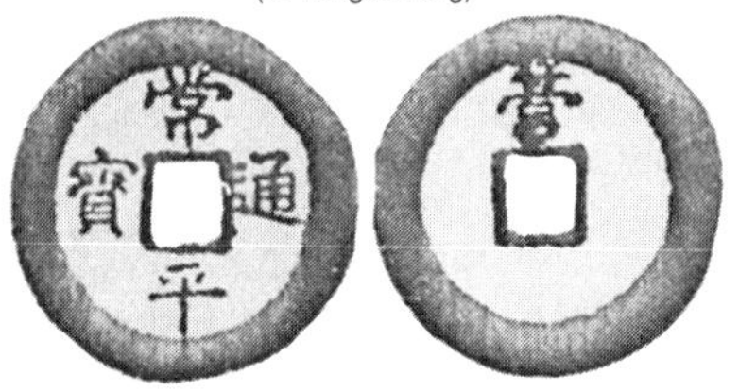

KM# 269 MUN

4.5000 g., Cast Copper **Rev:** "Yong" at top

Date	Mintage	Good	VG	F	VF	XF
ND(1678-1742) Rare	—	—	—	—	—	—

KM# 273a MUN

4.5000 g., Cast Copper, 24 mm. **Obv:** 2 dots "Tong" and "P'yong" with hooks

Date	Mintage	Good	VG	F	VF	XF
ND(1742) Series 1-10	—	2.00	3.00	5.00	8.00	—

KM# A270 MUN

4.5000 g., Cast Copper **Note:** Large characters.

Date	Mintage	Good	VG	F	VF	XF
ND(1742) Series 1-10	—	2.00	3.00	5.00	8.00	—

KM# 270s MUN

4.5000 g., Cast Copper **Note:** Seed type.

Date	Mintage	Good	VG	F	VF	XF
ND(1742) Series 1-10	—	—	—	—	—	50.00

KM# 271s MUN

4.5000 g., Cast Copper **Note:** Seed type.

Date	Mintage	Good	VG	F	VF	XF
ND(1742) Series 11-12	—	—	—	—	—	50.00

KM# 273s MUN

4.5000 g., Cast Copper **Note:** Seed type.

Date	Mintage	Good	VG	F	VF	XF
ND(1742) Series 1-10	—	—	—	—	—	50.00

KM# 275s MUN

4.5000 g., Cast Copper **Note:** Seed type.

Date	Mintage	Good	VG	F	VF	XF
ND(1742) Series 1-10	—	—	—	—	—	50.00

KM# 277s MUN

4.5000 g., Cast Copper **Note:** Seed type.

Date	Mintage	Good	VG	F	VF	XF
ND(1742) Series 1-10	—	—	—	—	—	50.00

KM# 273b MUN

4.5000 g., Cast Copper, 22-23 mm. **Obv:** 2 dots "Tong" without "P'yong" **Note:** Size varies.

Date	Mintage	Good	VG	F	VF	XF
ND(1742) Series 1-10	—	—	—	—	—	—

KM# 270 MUN

4.5000 g., Cast Copper **Rev:** Series number at bottom **Note:** Small characters.

Date	Mintage	Good	VG	F	VF	XF
ND(1742) Series 1-10	—	2.00	3.00	5.00	8.00	—

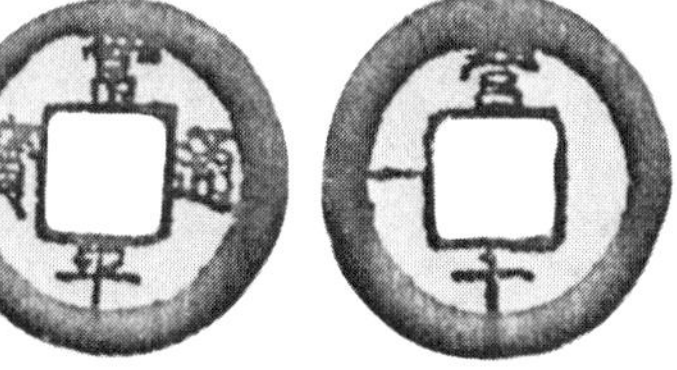

KM# 271 MUN

4.5000 g., Cast Copper **Rev:** S"Sip" (10) at bottom, additional series number at left **Note:** Small characters.

Date	Mintage	Good	VG	F	VF	XF
ND(1742) Series 11-12	—	2.50	3.50	6.00	8.00	—

KM# 273 MUN

4.5000 g., Cast Copper, 24 mm. **Rev:** Circle at right, series number at bottom **Note:** Small characters.

Date	Mintage	Good	VG	F	VF	XF
ND(1742) Series 1-10	—	2.00	3.00	5.00	8.00	—

KM# 275 MUN

4.5000 g., Cast Copper **Rev:** Circle at left, series number at bottom **Note:** Small characters.

Date	Mintage	Good	VG	F	VF	XF
ND(1742) Series 1-10	—	2.00	3.00	5.00	8.00	—

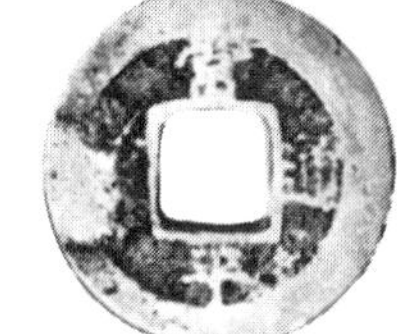 

KM# 277 MUN

4.5000 g., Cast Copper **Rev:** Crescent at right, series number at bottom **Note:** Small characters.

Date	Mintage	Good	VG	F	VF	XF
ND(1742) Series 1-10	—	2.00	3.00	5.00	8.00	—

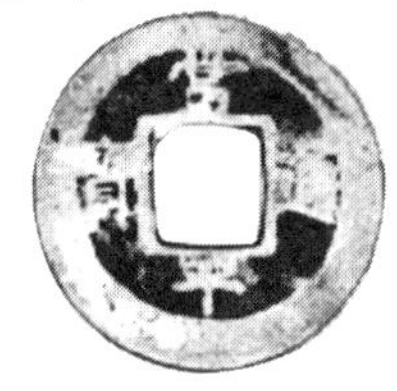 

KM# 279 MUN

4.5000 g., Cast Copper **Rev:** Crescent at left, series number at bottom **Note:** Small characters.

Date	Mintage	Good	VG	F	VF	XF
ND(1742) Series 1-10	—	2.00	3.00	5.00	8.00	—

KM# 279s MUN

4.5000 g., Cast Copper **Note:** Seed type.

Date	Mintage	Good	VG	F	VF	XF
ND(1742) Series 1-10	—	—	—	—	—	50.00

KM# 280s MUN

4.5000 g., Cast Copper **Note:** Seed type.

Date	Mintage	Good	VG	F	VF	XF
ND(1750) Series 1-10	—	—	—	—	—	50.00

KM# 278s MUN

4.5000 g., Cast Copper **Note:** Seed type.

Date	Mintage	Good	VG	F	VF	XF
ND(1750) Series 1-10	—	—	—	—	—	50.00

KM# 276s MUN

4.5000 g., Cast Copper **Note:** Seed type.

Date	Mintage	Good	VG	F	VF	XF
ND(1750) Series 1-10	—	—	—	—	—	50.00

KM# 274s MUN

4.5000 g., Cast Copper **Note:** Seed type.

Date	Mintage	Good	VG	F	VF	XF
ND(1750) Series 1-10	—	—	—	—	—	50.00

KM# 272s MUN

4.5000 g., Cast Copper **Note:** Seed type.

Date	Mintage	Good	VG	F	VF	XF
ND(1750) Series 1-2	—	—	—	—	—	50.00

 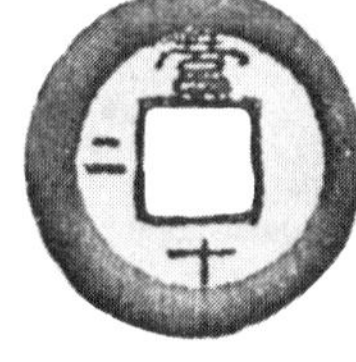

KM# 272 MUN

4.5000 g., Cast Copper **Note:** Large characters.

Date	Mintage	Good	VG	F	VF	XF
ND(1750) Series 1-2	—	2.00	3.00	5.00	8.00	—

KM# 274 MUN

4.5000 g., Cast Copper **Note:** Large characters.

Date	Mintage	Good	VG	F	VF	XF
ND(1750) Series 1-10	—	2.00	3.00	5.00	8.00	—

KM# 276 MUN

4.5000 g., Cast Copper, 24 mm. **Note:** Large characters.

Date	Mintage	Good	VG	F	VF	XF
ND(1750) Series 1-10	—	2.00	3.00	5.00	8.00	—

KM# 278 MUN

4.5000 g., Cast Copper **Note:** Large characters.

Date	Mintage	Good	VG	F	VF	XF
ND(1750) Series 1-10	—	2.00	3.00	5.00	8.00	—

KM# 280 MUN

4.5000 g., Cast Copper **Note:** Large characters.

Date	Mintage	Good	VG	F	VF	XF
ND(1750) Series 1-10	—	2.00	3.00	5.00	8.00	—

KM# 276.12 MUN

4.5000 g., Cast Copper **Rev:** Large sun

Date	Mintage	Good	VG	F	VF	XF
ND(1750) Series 2	—	2.00	3.00	5.00	8.00	—

KM# 276.19 MUN

4.5000 g., Cast Copper **Rev:** Star at lower left

Date	Mintage	Good	VG	F	VF	XF
ND(1750) Series 9	—	2.00	3.00	5.00	8.00	—

KM# 278.13 MUN

4.5000 g., Cast Copper **Obv:** Star at lower right, without "P'yong"

Date	Mintage	Good	VG	F	VF	XF
ND(1750) Series 3	—	2.00	3.00	5.00	8.00	—

KM# 313 2 MUN

6.7500 g., Cast Bronze **Rev:** "Chi" at bottom

Date	Mintage	Good	VG	F	VF	XF
ND(1742-52)	—	3.00	4.00	6.00	10.00	—

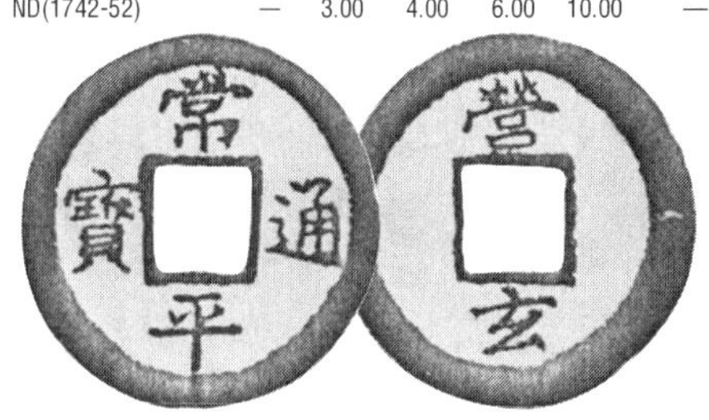

KM# 314 2 MUN

6.7500 g., Cast Bronze **Rev:** "Hyon" at bottom

Date	Mintage	Good	VG	F	VF	XF
ND(1742-52)	—	3.00	4.00	6.00	10.00	—

KM# 315 2 MUN

6.7500 g., Cast Bronze **Rev:** "Hwang" (yellow) at bottom

Date	Mintage	Good	VG	F	VF	XF
ND(1742-52)	—	3.00	4.00	6.00	10.00	—

KM# 316 2 MUN

6.7500 g., Cast Bronze **Rev:** "U" at bottom

Date	Mintage	Good	VG	F	VF	XF
ND(1742-52)	—	3.00	4.00	6.00	10.00	—

KM# 317 2 MUN

6.7500 g., Cast Bronze **Rev:** "Chu" at bottom

Date	Mintage	Good	VG	F	VF	XF
ND(1742-52)	—	3.00	4.00	6.00	10.00	—

KM# 318 2 MUN

6.7500 g., Cast Bronze **Rev:** "Hong" at bottom

Date	Mintage	Good	VG	F	VF	XF
ND(1742-52)	—	3.00	4.00	6.00	10.00	—

KM# 319 2 MUN

6.7500 g., Cast Bronze **Rev:** "Hwang" (barren) at bottom

Date	Mintage	Good	VG	F	VF	XF
ND(1742-52)	—	3.00	4.00	6.00	10.00	—

KM# 320 2 MUN

6.7500 g., Cast Bronze **Rev:** "Il" at bottom

Date	Mintage	Good	VG	F	VF	XF
ND(1742-52)	—	4.00	4.00	6.00	10.00	—

KM# 321 2 MUN

6.7500 g., Cast Bronze **Rev:** "Wol" at bottom

Date	Mintage	Good	VG	F	VF	XF
ND(1742-52)	—	3.00	4.00	6.00	10.00	—

KM# 322 2 MUN

6.7500 g., Cast Bronze **Rev:** "Yong" at bottom

Date	Mintage	Good	VG	F	VF	XF
ND(1742-52)	—	3.00	4.00	6.00	10.00	—

KM# 323 2 MUN

6.7500 g., Cast Bronze **Rev:** "Ch'uk" at bottom

Date	Mintage	Good	VG	F	VF	XF
ND(1742-52)	—	3.00	4.00	6.00	10.00	—

KM# 324 2 MUN

6.7500 g., Cast Bronze **Rev:** "Chin" at bottom

Date	Mintage	Good	VG	F	VF	XF
ND(1742-52)	—	3.00	4.00	6.00	10.00	—

KM# 325 2 MUN

6.7500 g., Cast Bronze **Rev:** "Suk" at bottom

Date	Mintage	Good	VG	F	VF	XF
ND(1742-52)	—	3.00	4.00	6.00	10.00	—

KM# 326 2 MUN

6.7500 g., Cast Bronze **Rev:** "Yol" at bottom

Date	Mintage	Good	VG	F	VF	XF
ND(1742-52)	—	3.00	4.00	6.00	10.00	—

KM# A326 2 MUN

6.7500 g., Cast Bronze **Rev:** "Chang" (extend) at bottom

Date	Mintage	Good	VG	F	VF	XF
ND(1742-52)	—	3.00	4.00	6.00	10.00	—

KM# B326 2 MUN

6.7500 g., Cast Bronze **Rev:** "Han" at bottom

Date	Mintage	Good	VG	F	VF	XF
ND(1742-52)	—	3.00	4.00	6.00	10.00	—

KM# C326 2 MUN

6.7500 g., Cast Bronze **Rev:** "Nae" at bottom

Date	Mintage	Good	VG	F	VF	XF
ND(1742-52)	—	3.00	4.00	6.00	10.00	—

KM# D326 2 MUN

6.7500 g., Cast Bronze **Rev:** "So" at bottom

Date	Mintage	Good	VG	F	VF	XF
ND(1742-52)	—	3.00	4.00	6.00	10.00	—

KM# E326 2 MUN
6.7500 g., Cast Bronze **Rev:** "Wang" at bottom

Date	Mintage	Good	VG	F	VF	XF
ND(1742-52)	—	3.00	4.00	6.00	10.00	—

KM# 327 2 MUN
6.7500 g., Cast Bronze **Rev:** "U" at bottom, "Sam" (3) at right

Date	Mintage	Good	VG	F	VF	XF
ND(1742-52)	—	3.00	4.00	6.00	10.00	—

KM# 328 2 MUN
Cast Bronze **Rev:** "U" at bottom, "Sam" (3) at left

Date	Mintage	Good	VG	F	VF	XF
ND(1742-52)	—	10.00	17.50	25.00	40.00	—

KM# 329 2 MUN
6.7500 g., Cast Bronze **Rev:** "Yol" at bottom, "Il" (1) at right

Date	Mintage	Good	VG	F	VF	XF
ND(1742-52)	—	3.00	4.00	6.00	10.00	—

KM# 330 2 MUN
6.7500 g., Cast Bronze **Rev:** "Chang" (extend) at bottom, "Il" (1) at right

Date	Mintage	Good	VG	F	VF	XF
ND(1742-52)	—	3.00	4.00	6.00	10.00	—

KM# 331.1 2 MUN
6.7500 g., Cast Bronze **Rev:** "Wang" at bottom, series number at left

Date	Mintage	Good	VG	F	VF	XF
ND(1742-52) Series 1	—	3.00	4.00	6.00	10.00	—

KM# 331.2 2 MUN
6.7500 g., Cast Bronze **Rev:** "Wang" at bottom, series number at left

Date	Mintage	Good	VG	F	VF	XF
ND(1742-52) Series 2	—	3.00	4.00	6.00	10.00	—

KM# 332 2 MUN
6.7500 g., Cast Bronze **Rev:** "Wol" at bottom, circle at right

Date	Mintage	Good	VG	F	VF	XF
ND(1742-52)	—	3.00	4.00	6.00	10.00	—

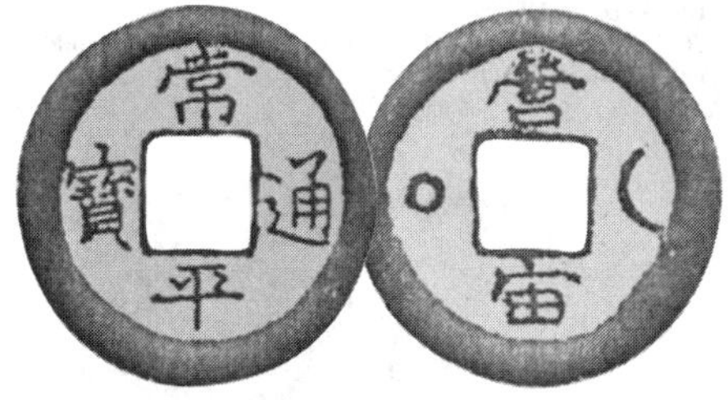

KM# 333.1 2 MUN
6.7500 g., Cast Bronze **Rev:** "Chu" at bottom, crescent at right, circle at left

Date	Mintage	Good	VG	F	VF	XF
ND(1742-52) Series 1	—	3.00	4.00	6.00	10.00	—

KM# 334.1 2 MUN
6.7500 g., Cast Bronze **Rev:** "Hwang" (barren) at bottom, crescent at right

Date	Mintage	Good	VG	F	VF	XF
ND(1742-52) Series 1	—	3.50	5.50	9.00	12.50	—

KM# 312 2 MUN
6.7500 g., Cast Bronze, 29-31 mm. **Rev:** "Ch'on" at bottom **Note:** Size varies.

Date	Mintage	Good	VG	F	VF	XF
ND(1742-52)	—	3.00	4.00	6.00	10.00	—

KM# 282 2 MUN
Cast Bronze **Note:** Small characters.

Date	Mintage	Good	VG	F	VF	XF
ND(1742-52)	—	3.00	4.00	6.00	10.00	—

KM# 295 2 MUN
6.7500 g., Cast Bronze **Rev:** "Hwa" at bottom **Note:** Struck at O Yong Ch'ong.

Date	Mintage	Good	VG	F	VF	XF
ND(1752)	—	3.00	4.00	6.00	10.00	—

KM# 283 2 MUN
6.7500 g., Cast Bronze, 28 mm. **Note:** Reduced size.

Date	Mintage	Good	VG	F	VF	XF
ND(1752)	—	3.00	4.00	6.00	10.00	—

KM# 294s 2 MUN
6.7500 g., Cast Bronze **Note:** Seed type.

Date	Mintage	Good	VG	F	VF	XF
ND(1752) Series 1-5	—	—	—	—	—	50.00

KM# 296s 2 MUN
6.7500 g., Cast Bronze **Note:** Seed type.

Date	Mintage	Good	VG	F	VF	XF
ND(1752) Series 1-5	—	—	—	—	—	50.00

KM# 299s 2 MUN
6.7500 g., Cast Bronze **Note:** Seed type.

Date	Mintage	Good	VG	F	VF	XF
ND(1752) Series 1-5	—	—	—	—	—	50.00

KM# 304s 2 MUN
6.7500 g., Cast Bronze **Note:** Seed type.

Date	Mintage	Good	VG	F	VF	XF
ND(1752) Series 1-5	—	—	—	—	—	50.00

KM# 310s 2 MUN
6.7500 g., Cast Bronze **Note:** Seed type.

Date	Mintage	Good	VG	F	VF	XF
ND(1752) Series 1-5	—	—	—	—	—	50.00

KM# 283s 2 MUN
6.7500 g., Cast Bronze

Date	Mintage	Good	VG	F	VF	XF
ND(1752)	—	—	—	—	—	50.00

KM# 284 2 MUN
6.7500 g., Cast Bronze **Rev:** Circle at right

Date	Mintage	Good	VG	F	VF	XF
ND(1752)	—	3.00	4.00	6.00	10.00	—

KM# 284s 2 MUN
6.7500 g., Cast Bronze

Date	Mintage	Good	VG	F	VF	XF
ND(1752)	—	—	—	—	—	50.00

KM# 285 2 MUN
6.7500 g., Cast Bronze **Rev:** Circle at left

Date	Mintage	Good	VG	F	VF	XF
ND(1752)	—	3.00	4.00	6.00	10.00	—

KM# 286 2 MUN
6.7500 g., Cast Bronze **Rev:** Double circle at right

Date	Mintage	Good	VG	F	VF	XF
ND(1752)	—	3.00	4.00	6.00	10.00	—

KM# 287 2 MUN
6.7500 g., Cast Bronze **Rev:** Double circle at left

Date	Mintage	Good	VG	F	VF	XF
ND(1752)	—	3.00	4.00	6.00	10.00	—

KM# 288 2 MUN
6.7500 g., Cast Bronze **Rev:** Double circle at left and right

Date	Mintage	Good	VG	F	VF	XF
ND(1752)	—	10.00	20.00	30.00	50.00	—

KM# 289 2 MUN
6.7500 g., Cast Bronze **Rev:** Crescent at right

Date	Mintage	Good	VG	F	VF	XF
ND(1752)	—	3.00	4.00	6.00	10.00	—

KM# 290 2 MUN
6.7500 g., Cast Bronze **Rev:** Outward crescent at left

Date	Mintage	Good	VG	F	VF	XF
ND(1752)	—	3.00	4.00	6.00	10.00	—

KM# 291 2 MUN
6.7500 g., Cast Bronze **Rev:** Inward crescent at left

Date	Mintage	Good	VG	F	VF	XF
ND(1752)	—	10.00	15.00	25.00	40.00	—

KM# 292 2 MUN
6.7500 g., Cast Bronze **Rev:** Crescent at right, circle at left

Date	Mintage	Good	VG	F	VF	XF
ND(1752)	—	3.00	4.00	6.00	10.00	—

KM# 285s 2 MUN
6.7500 g., Cast Bronze

Date	Mintage	Good	VG	F	VF	XF
ND(1752)	—	—	—	—	—	50.00

KM# 286s 2 MUN
6.7500 g., Cast Bronze

Date	Mintage	Good	VG	F	VF	XF
ND(1752)	—	—	—	—	—	50.00

KM# 287s 2 MUN
6.7500 g., Cast Bronze

Date	Mintage	Good	VG	F	VF	XF
ND(1752)	—	—	—	—	—	50.00

KM# 288s 2 MUN
6.7500 g., Cast Bronze

Date	Mintage	Good	VG	F	VF	XF
ND(1752)	—	—	—	—	—	80.00

KM# 289s 2 MUN
6.7500 g., Cast Bronze

Date	Mintage	Good	VG	F	VF	XF
ND(1752)	—	—	—	—	—	50.00

KM# 290s 2 MUN
6.7500 g., Cast Bronze

Date	Mintage	Good	VG	F	VF	XF
ND(1752)	—	—	—	—	—	50.00

KM# 291s 2 MUN
6.7500 g., Cast Bronze

Date	Mintage	Good	VG	F	VF	XF
ND(1752)	—	—	—	—	—	70.00

KM# 292s 2 MUN
6.7500 g., Cast Bronze

Date	Mintage	Good	VG	F	VF	XF
ND(1752)	—	—	—	—	—	50.00

KM# 293 2 MUN
6.7500 g., Cast Bronze **Rev:** "Mok" at bottom

Date	Mintage	Good	VG	F	VF	XF
ND(1752)	—	3.00	4.00	6.00	10.00	—

KM# 294 2 MUN
6.7500 g., Cast Bronze **Rev:** "Mok" at bottom, series number at left

Date	Mintage	Good	VG	F	VF	XF
ND(1752) Series 1-5	—	3.00	4.00	6.00	10.00	—

KM# A294.3 2 MUN
6.7500 g., Cast Bronze **Rev:** Circle added at right

Date	Mintage	Good	VG	F	VF	XF
ND(1752) Series 3	—	25.00	40.00	75.00	110	—

KM# 295s 2 MUN
6.7500 g., Cast Bronze

Date	Mintage	Good	VG	F	VF	XF
ND(1752)	—	—	—	—	—	50.00

KM# 296 2 MUN
6.7500 g., Cast Bronze **Rev:** "Hwa" at bottom, series number at left

Date	Mintage	Good	VG	F	VF	XF
ND(1752) Series 1-5	—	3.00	4.00	6.00	10.00	—

KM# 297.2 2 MUN
6.7500 g., Cast Bronze **Rev:** "Hwa" at bottom, circle at right, series number at left

Date	Mintage	Good	VG	F	VF	XF
ND(1752) Series 2	—	20.00	35.00	60.00	100	—

KM# 297s 2 MUN
6.7500 g., Cast Bronze

Date	Mintage	Good	VG	F	VF	XF
ND(1752) Series 2	—	—	—	—	—	175

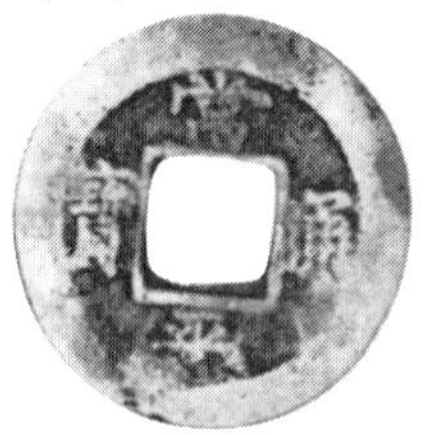

KM# 298 2 MUN
6.7500 g., Cast Bronze **Rev:** "T'o" at bottom

Date	Mintage	Good	VG	F	VF	XF
ND(1752)	—	3.00	4.00	6.00	10.00	—

KM# 298s 2 MUN
6.7500 g., Cast Bronze

Date	Mintage	Good	VG	F	VF	XF
ND(1752)	—	—	—	—	—	50.00

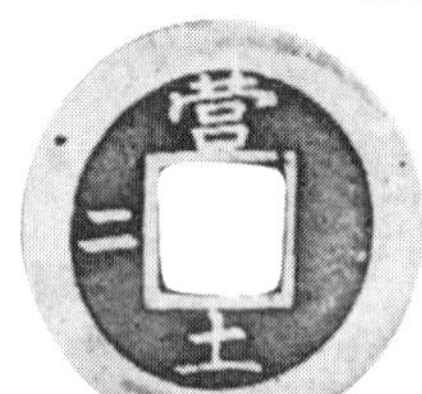

KM# 299 2 MUN
6.7500 g., Cast Bronze **Rev:** "T'o" at bottom, series number at left

Date	Mintage	Good	VG	F	VF	XF
ND(1752) Series 1-5	—	3.00	4.00	6.00	10.00	—

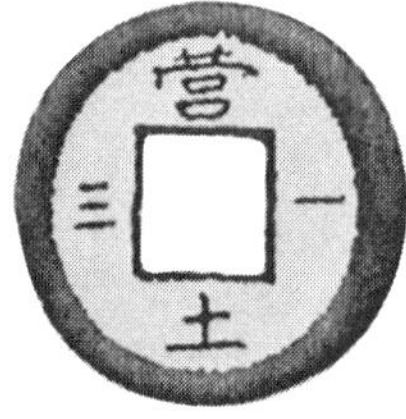

KM# 300 2 MUN
6.7500 g., Cast Bronze **Rev:** "T'o" at bottom, "Il" (1) at right, "Sam" (3) at left

Date	Mintage	Good	VG	F	VF	XF
ND(1752)	—	3.00	4.00	6.00	10.00	—

KM# 300s 2 MUN
6.7500 g., Cast Bronze

Date	Mintage	Good	VG	F	VF	XF
ND(1752)	—	—	—	—	—	50.00

KM# 301 2 MUN
6.7500 g., Cast Bronze **Rev:** "T'o" at bottom, crescent at right

Date	Mintage	Good	VG	F	VF	XF
ND(1752)	—	3.00	4.00	6.00	10.00	—

KM# 301s 2 MUN
6.7500 g., Cast Bronze

Date	Mintage	Good	VG	F	VF	XF
ND(1752)	—	—	—	—	—	50.00

KM# 302 2 MUN
6.7500 g., Cast Bronze **Rev:** "T'o" at bottom, crescent at left

Date	Mintage	Good	VG	F	VF	XF
ND(1752)	—	3.00	4.00	6.00	10.00	—

KM# 302s 2 MUN
6.7500 g., Cast Bronze

Date	Mintage	Good	VG	F	VF	XF
ND(1752)	—	—	—	—	—	50.00

KM# A302 2 MUN
6.7500 g., Cast Bronze **Rev:** "Mok" at bottom, crescent at left

Date	Mintage	Good	VG	F	VF	XF
ND(1752)	—	3.00	4.00	6.00	10.00	—

KM# B302 2 MUN
6.7500 g., Cast Bronze **Rev:** "Hwa" at bottom, crescent at left

Date	Mintage	Good	VG	F	VF	XF
ND(1752)	—	3.00	4.00	6.00	10.00	—

KM# C302 2 MUN
6.7500 g., Cast Bronze **Rev:** "Kum" at bottom, crescent at left

Date	Mintage	Good	VG	F	VF	XF
ND(1752)	—	3.00	4.00	6.00	10.00	—

KM# D302 2 MUN
6.7500 g., Cast Bronze **Rev:** "Su" at bottom, crescent at left

Date	Mintage	Good	VG	F	VF	XF
ND(1752)	—	3.00	4.00	6.00	10.00	—

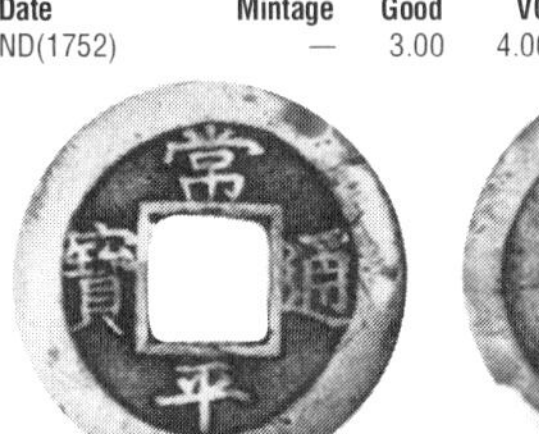

KM# 303 2 MUN
6.7500 g., Cast Bronze **Rev:** "Kum" at bottom

Date	Mintage	Good	VG	F	VF	XF
ND(1752)	—	3.00	4.00	6.00	10.00	—

KM# 303s 2 MUN
6.7500 g., Cast Bronze

Date	Mintage	Good	VG	F	VF	XF
ND(1752)	—	—	—	—	—	50.00

KM# 304 2 MUN
6.7500 g., Cast Bronze **Rev:** "Kum" at bottom, series number at left

Date	Mintage	Good	VG	F	VF	XF
ND(1752) Series 1-5	—	3.00	4.00	6.00	10.00	—

KM# 305 2 MUN
6.7500 g., Cast Bronze **Rev:** "Kum" at bottom, circle at right, series number at left

Date	Mintage	Good	VG	F	VF	XF
ND(1752) Series 4	—	20.00	30.00	60.00	100	—

KM# 305s 2 MUN
6.7500 g., Cast Bronze

Date	Mintage	Good	VG	F	VF	XF
ND(1752) Series 4	—	—	—	—	—	175

KM# 306 2 MUN
6.7500 g., Cast Bronze **Rev:** "Kum" at bottom, crescent at right

Date	Mintage	Good	VG	F	VF	XF
ND(1752)	—	3.00	4.00	6.00	10.00	—

KM# 306s 2 MUN
6.7500 g., Cast Bronze

Date	Mintage	Good	VG	F	VF	XF
ND(1752)	—	—	—	—	—	50.00

KM# 307 2 MUN
6.7500 g., Cast Bronze **Rev:** "Kum" at bottom, crescent at left

Date	Mintage	Good	VG	F	VF	XF
ND(1752)	—	3.00	4.00	6.00	10.00	—

KM# 307s 2 MUN
6.7500 g., Cast Bronze

Date	Mintage	Good	VG	F	VF	XF
ND(1752)	—	—	—	—	—	50.00

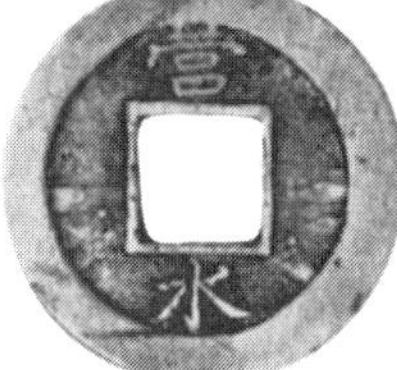

KM# 309 2 MUN
6.7500 g., Cast Bronze **Rev:** "Su" at bottom

Date	Mintage	Good	VG	F	VF	XF
ND(1752)	—	3.00	4.00	6.00	10.00	—

KM# 309s 2 MUN
6.7500 g., Cast Bronze

Date	Mintage	Good	VG	F	VF	XF
ND(1752)	—	—	—	—	—	50.00

KM# 310 2 MUN
6.7500 g., Cast Bronze **Rev:** "Su" at bottom, series number at left

Date	Mintage	Good	VG	F	VF	XF
ND(1752) Series 1-5	—	3.00	4.00	6.00	10.00	—

KM# 311 2 MUN
6.7500 g., Cast Bronze **Rev:** "Su" at bottom, dot at right, series number at left

Date	Mintage	Good	VG	F	VF	XF
ND(1752) Series 1	—	3.00	4.00	6.00	10.00	—

KM# 311s 2 MUN
6.7500 g., Cast Bronze

Date	Mintage	Good	VG	F	VF	XF
ND(1752) Series 1	—	—	—	—	—	50.00

ARMAMENTS BUREAU

(Mu Bi Sa)

KM# 335 MUN
4.5000 g., Cast Copper, 25 mm. **Rev:** "Mu" at top

Date	Mintage	Good	VG	F	VF	XF
ND(1742) Rare	—	—	—	—	—	—

KM# 336.1 2 MUN
Cast Copper, 31 mm. **Rev:** "I" (2) at bottom **Note:** Weight varies 8.00-9.00 grams.

Date	Mintage	Good	VG	F	VF	XF
ND(1742-52)	—	3.00	4.00	6.00	10.00	—

KM# 336.2 2 MUN
Cast Copper, 31 mm. **Rev:** Star at lower left **Note:** Weight varies 8.00-9.00 grams.

Date	Mintage	Good	VG	F	VF	XF
ND(1742-52)	—	3.00	4.00	6.00	10.00	—

COURT GUARD

(Kum Wi Yong)

KM# 342 MUN
Cast Bronze, 25 mm. **Rev:** Circle at right, series number at bottom

Date	Mintage	Good	VG	F	VF	XF
ND(1742) Series 1-10	—	2.00	3.00	5.00	8.00	—

KM# 343 MUN
Cast Bronze, 24 mm. **Rev:** Circle at left, series number at bottom

Date	Mintage	Good	VG	F	VF	XF
ND(1742) Series 1-10	—	2.00	3.00	5.00	8.00	—

KM# 343a MUN
Cast Bronze **Obv:** Star above "Tong"

Date	Mintage	Good	VG	F	VF	XF
ND(1742) Series 2	—	1.50	2.25	3.00	5.00	—

KM# 345 MUN
Cast Bronze, 24.5 mm. **Rev:** Crescent at left, series number at bottom

Date	Mintage	Good	VG	F	VF	XF
ND(1742) Series 1-10	—	2.00	3.00	5.00	8.00	—

KM# 342s MUN
Cast Bronze **Note:** Seed type.

Date	Mintage	Good	VG	F	VF	XF
ND(1742) Series 1-10	—	—	—	—	—	50.00

KM# 343s MUN
Cast Bronze **Note:** Seed type.

Date	Mintage	Good	VG	F	VF	XF
ND(1742) Series 1-10	—	—	—	—	—	50.00

KM# 344s MUN
Cast Bronze, 25 mm. **Note:** Seed type.

Date	Mintage	Good	VG	F	VF	XF
ND(1742) Series 1-10	—	—	—	—	—	50.00

KM# 345s MUN
Cast Bronze **Note:** Seed type.

Date	Mintage	Good	VG	F	VF	XF
ND(1742) Series 1-10	—	—	—	—	—	50.00

KM# 344 MUN

Cast Bronze, 23.5-24.8 mm. **Rev:** Crescent at right, series number at bottom **Note:** Size varies.

Date	Mintage	Good	VG	F	VF	XF
ND(1742) Series 1-10	—	2.00	3.00	5.00	8.00	—

KM# 388s 2 MUN

6.7500 g., Cast Copper Or Bronze

Date	Mintage	Good	VG	F	VF	XF
ND(1752)	—	—	—	—	—	50.00

KM# 346 2 MUN

6.7500 g., Cast Copper Or Bronze **Rev:** "I" (2) at bottom

Date	Mintage	Good	VG	F	VF	XF
ND(1752)	—	3.00	4.00	6.00	10.00	—

KM# 347 2 MUN

6.7500 g., Cast Copper Or Bronze **Rev:** Crescent at left

Date	Mintage	Good	VG	F	VF	XF
ND	—	8.50	15.00	25.00	40.00	—

KM# 347s 2 MUN

6.7500 g., Cast Copper Or Bronze

Date	Mintage	Good	VG	F	VF	XF
ND(1752)	—	—	—	—	—	70.00

KM# 348s 2 MUN

6.7500 g., Cast Copper Or Bronze

Date	Mintage	Good	VG	F	VF	XF
ND(1752)	—	—	—	—	—	50.00

KM# 350a 2 MUN

6.7500 g., Cast Copper Or Bronze **Obv:** "P'yong" with hooks

Date	Mintage	Good	VG	F	VF	XF
ND(1752)	—	3.00	4.00	6.00	10.00	—

KM# 350s 2 MUN

6.7500 g., Cast Copper Or Bronze

Date	Mintage	Good	VG	F	VF	XF
ND(1752)	—	—	—	—	—	50.00

KM# 352a 2 MUN

6.7500 g., Cast Copper Or Bronze **Obv:** "P'yong" with hooks

Date	Mintage	Good	VG	F	VF	XF
ND(1752)	—	3.00	4.00	6.00	10.00	—

KM# 352s 2 MUN

6.7500 g., Cast Copper Or Bronze

Date	Mintage	Good	VG	F	VF	XF
ND(1752)	—	—	—	—	—	50.00

KM# 354a 2 MUN

6.7500 g., Cast Copper Or Bronze **Obv:** "P'yong" with hooks

Date	Mintage	Good	VG	F	VF	XF
ND(1752)	—	3.00	4.00	6.00	10.00	—

KM# 354s 2 MUN

6.7500 g., Cast Copper Or Bronze

Date	Mintage	Good	VG	F	VF	XF
ND(1752)	—	—	—	—	—	50.00

KM# 356a 2 MUN

6.7500 g., Cast Copper Or Bronze **Obv:** "P'yong" with hooks

Date	Mintage	Good	VG	F	VF	XF
ND(1752)	—	3.00	4.00	6.00	10.00	—

KM# 356s 2 MUN

6.7500 g., Cast Copper Or Bronze

Date	Mintage	Good	VG	F	VF	XF
ND(1752)	—	—	—	—	—	50.00

KM# 360a 2 MUN

6.7500 g., Cast Copper Or Bronze **Obv:** "P'yong" with hooks

Date	Mintage	Good	VG	F	VF	XF
ND(1752)	—	3.00	4.00	6.00	10.00	—

KM# 360s 2 MUN

6.7500 g., Cast Copper Or Bronze

Date	Mintage	Good	VG	F	VF	XF
ND(1752)	—	—	—	—	—	50.00

KM# 358a 2 MUN

6.7500 g., Cast Copper Or Bronze **Obv:** "P'yong" with hooks

Date	Mintage	Good	VG	F	VF	XF
ND(1752)	—	3.00	4.00	6.00	10.00	—

KM# 358s 2 MUN

6.7500 g., Cast Copper Or Bronze

Date	Mintage	Good	VG	F	VF	XF
ND(1752)	—	—	—	—	—	50.00

KM# 362a 2 MUN

6.7500 g., Cast Copper Or Bronze **Obv:** "P'yong" with hooks

Date	Mintage	Good	VG	F	VF	XF
ND(1752)	—	3.00	4.00	6.00	10.00	—

KM# 362s 2 MUN

6.7500 g., Cast Copper Or Bronze

Date	Mintage	Good	VG	F	VF	XF
ND(1752)	—	—	—	—	—	50.00

KM# 364a 2 MUN

6.7500 g., Cast Copper Or Bronze **Obv:** "P'yong" with hooks

Date	Mintage	Good	VG	F	VF	XF
ND(1752)	—	3.00	4.00	6.00	10.00	—

KM# 364s 2 MUN

6.7500 g., Cast Copper Or Bronze

Date	Mintage	Good	VG	F	VF	XF
ND(1752)	—	—	—	—	—	50.00

KM# 366a 2 MUN

6.7500 g., Cast Copper Or Bronze **Obv:** "P'yong" with hooks

Date	Mintage	Good	VG	F	VF	XF
ND(1752)	—	3.00	4.00	6.00	10.00	—

KM# 366s 2 MUN

6.7500 g., Cast Copper Or Bronze

Date	Mintage	Good	VG	F	VF	XF
ND(1752)	—	—	—	—	—	50.00

KM# 368a 2 MUN

6.7500 g., Cast Copper Or Bronze **Obv:** "P'yong" with hooks

Date	Mintage	Good	VG	F	VF	XF
ND(1752)	—	—	—	—	—	—

KM# 368s 2 MUN

6.7500 g., Cast Copper Or Bronze

Date	Mintage	Good	VG	F	VF	XF
ND(1752)	—	—	—	—	—	50.00

KM# 370a 2 MUN

6.7500 g., Cast Copper Or Bronze **Obv:** "P'yong" with hooks

Date	Mintage	Good	VG	F	VF	XF
ND(1752)	—	3.00	4.00	6.00	10.00	—

KM# 370s 2 MUN

6.7500 g., Cast Copper Or Bronze

Date	Mintage	Good	VG	F	VF	XF
ND(1752)	—	—	—	—	—	50.00

KM# 372a 2 MUN

6.7500 g., Cast Copper Or Bronze **Obv:** "P'yong" with hooks

Date	Mintage	Good	VG	F	VF	XF
ND(1752)	—	3.00	4.00	6.00	10.00	—

KM# 372s 2 MUN

6.7500 g., Cast Copper Or Bronze

Date	Mintage	Good	VG	F	VF	XF
ND(1752)	—	—	—	—	—	50.00

KM# 374a 2 MUN

6.7500 g., Cast Copper Or Bronze **Obv:** "P'yong" with hooks

Date	Mintage	Good	VG	F	VF	XF
ND(1752)	—	3.00	4.00	6.00	10.00	—

KM# 374s 2 MUN

6.7500 g., Cast Copper Or Bronze

Date	Mintage	Good	VG	F	VF	XF
ND(1752)	—	—	—	—	—	50.00

KM# 348 2 MUN

6.7500 g., Cast Copper Or Bronze **Rev:** "Ch'on" at bottom **Note:** Large characters.

Date	Mintage	Good	VG	F	VF	XF
ND(1752)	—	3.00	4.00	6.00	10.00	—

KM# 348a 2 MUN

6.7500 g., Cast Copper Or Bronze **Obv:** "P'yong" with hooks **Note:** Large characters.

Date	Mintage	Good	VG	F	VF	XF
ND(1752)	—	3.00	4.00	6.00	10.00	—

KM# 350 2 MUN

6.7500 g., Cast Copper Or Bronze **Rev:** "Chi" at bottom **Note:** Large characters.

Date	Mintage	Good	VG	F	VF	XF
ND(1752)	—	3.00	4.00	6.00	10.00	—

KM# 352 2 MUN

6.7500 g., Cast Copper Or Bronze **Rev:** "Hyon" at bottom **Note:** Large characters.

Date	Mintage	Good	VG	F	VF	XF
ND(1752)	—	3.00	4.00	6.00	10.00	—

KM# 354 2 MUN

6.7500 g., Cast Copper Or Bronze **Rev:** "Hwang" (yellow) at bottom **Note:** Large characters.

Date	Mintage	Good	VG	F	VF	XF
ND(1752)	—	3.00	4.00	6.00	10.00	—

KM# 356 2 MUN

6.7500 g., Cast Copper Or Bronze **Rev:** "U" at bottom **Note:** Large characters.

Date	Mintage	Good	VG	F	VF	XF
ND(1752)	—	3.00	4.00	6.00	10.00	—

KM# 358 2 MUN

6.7500 g., Cast Copper Or Bronze **Rev:** "Chu" at bottom **Note:** Large characters.

Date	Mintage	Good	VG	F	VF	XF
ND(1752)	—	3.00	4.00	6.00	10.00	—

KM# 360 2 MUN

6.7500 g., Cast Copper Or Bronze **Rev:** "Hong" at bottom **Note:** Large characters.

Date	Mintage	Good	VG	F	VF	XF
ND(1752)	—	3.00	4.00	6.00	10.00	—

KM# 362 2 MUN

6.7500 g., Cast Copper Or Bronze **Rev:** "Hwang" (barren) at bottom **Note:** Large characters.

Date	Mintage	Good	VG	F	VF	XF
ND(1752)	—	3.00	4.00	6.00	10.00	—

KM# 364 2 MUN

6.7500 g., Cast Copper Or Bronze **Rev:** "Il" (sun) at bottom **Note:** Large characters.

Date	Mintage	Good	VG	F	VF	XF
ND(1752)	—	3.00	4.00	6.00	10.00	—

KM# 366 2 MUN

6.7500 g., Cast Copper Or Bronze **Rev:** "Wol" at bottom **Note:** Large characters.

Date	Mintage	Good	VG	F	VF	XF
ND(1752)	—	3.00	4.00	6.00	10.00	—

KM# 368 2 MUN

6.7500 g., Cast Copper Or Bronze **Rev:** "Yong" at bottom **Note:** Large characters.

Date	Mintage	Good	VG	F	VF	XF
ND(1752)	—	3.00	4.00	6.00	10.00	—

KM# 370 2 MUN

6.7500 g., Cast Copper Or Bronze **Rev:** "Ch'uk" at bottom **Note:** Large characters.

Date	Mintage	Good	VG	F	VF	XF
ND(1752)	—	3.00	4.00	6.00	10.00	—

KM# 372 2 MUN

6.7500 g., Cast Copper Or Bronze **Rev:** "Chin" at bottom **Note:** Large characters.

Date	Mintage	Good	VG	F	VF	XF
ND(1752)	—	3.00	4.00	6.00	10.00	—

KM# 374 2 MUN

6.7500 g., Cast Copper Or Bronze **Rev:** "Suk" at bottom **Note:** Large characters.

Date	Mintage	Good	VG	F	VF	XF
ND(1752)	—	3.00	4.00	6.00	10.00	—

KM# 376 2 MUN

6.7500 g., Cast Copper Or Bronze **Rev:** "Yol" at bottom **Note:** Large characters.

Date	Mintage	Good	VG	F	VF	XF
ND(1752)	—	3.00	4.00	6.00	10.00	—

KM# 378 2 MUN

6.7500 g., Cast Copper Or Bronze **Rev:** "Chang" (extend) at bottom **Note:** Large characters.

Date	Mintage	Good	VG	F	VF	XF
ND(1752)	—	3.00	4.00	6.00	10.00	—

KM# 380 2 MUN

6.7500 g., Cast Copper Or Bronze **Rev:** "Han" at bottom **Note:** Large characters.

Date	Mintage	Good	VG	F	VF	XF
ND(1752)	—	3.00	4.00	6.00	10.00	—

KM# 382 2 MUN

6.7500 g., Cast Copper Or Bronze **Rev:** "Nae" at bottom **Note:** Large characters.

Date	Mintage	Good	VG	F	VF	XF
ND(1752)	—	3.00	4.50	6.50	10.00	—

KM# 384 2 MUN

6.7500 g., Cast Copper Or Bronze **Rev:** "So" at bottom **Note:** Large characters.

Date	Mintage	Good	VG	F	VF	XF
ND(1752)	—	3.00	4.50	6.50	10.00	—

KM# 388 2 MUN

6.7500 g., Cast Copper Or Bronze **Rev:** "Ch'u" at bottom **Note:** Large characters.

Date	Mintage	Good	VG	F	VF	XF
ND(1752)	—	3.00	4.50	6.50	10.00	—

KM# 353 2 MUN

6.7500 g., Cast Copper Or Bronze **Note:** Small characters.

Date	Mintage	Good	VG	F	VF	XF
ND(1752)	—	3.00	4.00	6.00	10.00	—

KM# 378a 2 MUN

6.7500 g., Cast Copper Or Bronze **Obv:** "P'yong" with hooks

Date	Mintage	Good	VG	F	VF	XF
ND(1752)	—	3.00	4.00	6.00	10.00	—

KM# 378s 2 MUN

6.7500 g., Cast Copper Or Bronze

Date	Mintage	Good	VG	F	VF	XF
ND(1752)	—	—	—	—	—	50.00

KM# 380s 2 MUN

6.7500 g., Cast Copper Or Bronze

Date	Mintage	Good	VG	F	VF	XF
ND(1752)	—	—	—	—	—	50.00

KM# 376a 2 MUN

6.7500 g., Cast Copper Or Bronze **Obv:** "P'yong" with hooks

Date	Mintage	Good	VG	F	VF	XF
ND(1752)	—	3.00	4.00	6.00	10.00	—

KM# 376s 2 MUN

6.7500 g., Cast Copper Or Bronze

Date	Mintage	Good	VG	F	VF	XF
ND(1752)	—	—	—	—	—	50.00

KM# 382s 2 MUN

6.7500 g., Cast Copper Or Bronze

Date	Mintage	Good	VG	F	VF	XF
ND(1752)	—	—	—	—	—	50.00

KM# 384s 2 MUN

6.7500 g., Cast Copper Or Bronze

Date	Mintage	Good	VG	F	VF	XF
ND(1752)	—	—	—	—	—	50.00

KM# 386 2 MUN

6.7500 g., Cast Copper Or Bronze **Rev:** "Wang" at bottom

Date	Mintage	Good	VG	F	VF	XF
ND(1753)	—	3.00	4.50	6.50	10.00	—

KM# 386s 2 MUN

6.7500 g., Cast Copper Or Bronze

Date	Mintage	Good	VG	F	VF	XF
ND(1752)	—	—	—	—	—	50.00

KM# 387s 2 MUN

6.7500 g., Cast Copper Or Bronze

Date	Mintage	Good	VG	F	VF	XF
ND(1753)	—	—	—	—	—	50.00

KM# 385s 2 MUN

6.7500 g., Cast Copper Or Bronze

Date	Mintage	Good	VG	F	VF	XF
ND(1753)	—	—	—	—	—	50.00

KM# 383s 2 MUN

6.7500 g., Cast Copper Or Bronze

Date	Mintage	Good	VG	F	VF	XF
ND(1753)	—	—	—	—	—	50.00

KM# 377s 2 MUN

6.7500 g., Cast Copper Or Bronze

Date	Mintage	Good	VG	F	VF	XF
ND(1753)	—	—	—	—	—	50.00

KM# 381s 2 MUN

6.7500 g., Cast Copper Or Bronze

Date	Mintage	Good	VG	F	VF	XF
ND(1753)	—	—	—	—	—	50.00

KM# 355 2 MUN

6.7500 g., Cast Copper Or Bronze **Note:** Small characters.

Date	Mintage	Good	VG	F	VF	XF
ND(1753)	—	3.00	4.00	6.00	10.00	—

KM# 357 2 MUN

6.7500 g., Cast Copper Or Bronze **Note:** Small characters.

Date	Mintage	Good	VG	F	VF	XF
ND(1753)	—	3.00	4.00	6.00	10.00	—

KM# 359 2 MUN

6.7500 g., Cast Copper Or Bronze **Note:** Small characters.

Date	Mintage	Good	VG	F	VF	XF
ND(1753)	—	3.00	4.00	6.00	10.00	—

KM# 363 2 MUN

6.7500 g., Cast Copper Or Bronze **Note:** Small characters.

Date	Mintage	Good	VG	F	VF	XF
ND(1753)	—	3.00	4.00	6.00	10.00	—

KM# 365 2 MUN

6.7500 g., Cast Copper Or Bronze **Note:** Small characters.

Date	Mintage	Good	VG	F	VF	XF
ND(1753)	—	3.00	4.00	6.00	10.00	—

KM# 367 2 MUN

6.7500 g., Cast Copper Or Bronze **Note:** Small characters.

Date	Mintage	Good	VG	F	VF	XF
ND(1753)	—	3.00	4.00	6.00	10.00	—

KM# 369 2 MUN

6.7500 g., Cast Copper Or Bronze **Note:** Small characters.

Date	Mintage	Good	VG	F	VF	XF
ND(1753)	—	3.00	4.00	6.00	10.00	—

KM# 371 2 MUN

6.7500 g., Cast Copper Or Bronze **Note:** SMall characters.

Date	Mintage	Good	VG	F	VF	XF
ND(1753)	—	3.00	4.00	6.00	10.00	—

KM# 373 2 MUN

6.7500 g., Cast Copper Or Bronze **Note:** Small characters.

Date	Mintage	Good	VG	F	VF	XF
ND(1753)	—	3.00	4.00	6.00	10.00	—

KM# 375 2 MUN

6.7500 g., Cast Copper Or Bronze **Note:** Small characters.

Date	Mintage	Good	VG	F	VF	XF
ND(1753)	—	3.00	4.00	6.00	10.00	—

KM# 377 2 MUN

6.7500 g., Cast Copper Or Bronze **Note:** Small characters.

Date	Mintage	Good	VG	F	VF	XF
ND(1753)	—	3.00	4.00	6.00	10.00	—

KM# 379 2 MUN

6.7500 g., Cast Copper Or Bronze **Note:** Small characters.

Date	Mintage	Good	VG	F	VF	XF
ND(1753)	—	3.00	4.00	6.00	10.00	—

KM# 381 2 MUN

6.7500 g., Cast Copper Or Bronze **Note:** Small characters.

Date	Mintage	Good	VG	F	VF	XF
ND(1753)	—	3.00	4.00	6.00	10.00	—

KM# 383 2 MUN

6.7500 g., Cast Copper Or Bronze **Note:** Small characters.

Date	Mintage	Good	VG	F	VF	XF
ND(1753)	—	3.00	4.50	6.50	10.00	—

KM# 385 2 MUN

6.7500 g., Cast Copper Or Bronze **Note:** Small characters.

Date	Mintage	Good	VG	F	VF	XF
ND(1753)	—	3.00	4.50	6.50	10.00	—

KM# 387 2 MUN

6.7500 g., Cast Copper Or Bronze **Note:** Small characters.

Date	Mintage	Good	VG	F	VF	XF
ND(1753)	—	3.00	4.50	6.50	10.00	—

KM# 389 2 MUN

6.7500 g., Cast Copper Or Bronze **Note:** Small characters.

Date	Mintage	Good	VG	F	VF	XF
ND(1753)	—	3.00	4.50	6.50	10.00	—

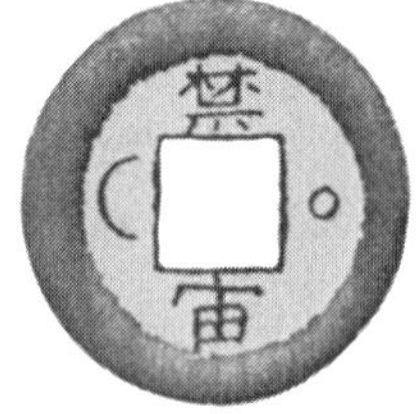

KM# 445 2 MUN

6.7500 g., Cast Copper Or Bronze **Rev:** "Chu" at bottom, circle at right, inward crescent at left **Note:** Struck at Kum Wi Yong.

Date	Mintage	Good	VG	F	VF	XF
ND(1753)	—	3.50	5.50	9.00	15.00	—

KM# 379s 2 MUN

6.7500 g., Cast Copper Or Bronze **Note:** Seed type.

Date	Mintage	Good	VG	F	VF	XF
ND(1753)	—	—	—	—	—	50.00

KM# 349 2 MUN

6.7500 g., Cast Copper Or Bronze **Note:** Small characters.

Date	Mintage	Good	VG	F	VF	XF
ND(1753)	—	3.00	4.00	6.00	10.00	—

KM# 351 2 MUN

6.7500 g., Cast Copper Or Bronze **Note:** Small characters.

Date	Mintage	Good	VG	F	VF	XF
ND(1753)	—	3.00	4.00	6.00	10.00	—

KM# 375s 2 MUN

6.7500 g., Cast Copper Or Bronze

Date	Mintage	Good	VG	F	VF	XF
ND(1753)	—	—	—	—	—	50.00

KM# 373s 2 MUN

6.7500 g., Cast Copper Or Bronze

Date	Mintage	Good	VG	F	VF	XF
ND(1753)	—	—	—	—	—	50.00

KM# 371s 2 MUN

6.7500 g., Cast Copper Or Bronze

Date	Mintage	Good	VG	F	VF	XF
ND(1753)	—	—	—	—	—	50.00

KM# 369s 2 MUN

6.7500 g., Cast Copper Or Bronze

Date	Mintage	Good	VG	F	VF	XF
ND(1753)	—	—	—	—	—	50.00

KM# 367s 2 MUN

6.7500 g., Cast Copper Or Bronze

Date	Mintage	Good	VG	F	VF	XF
ND(1753)	—	—	—	—	—	50.00

KM# 365s 2 MUN

6.7500 g., Cast Copper Or Bronze

Date	Mintage	Good	VG	F	VF	XF
ND(1753)	—	—	—	—	—	50.00

KM# 363s 2 MUN

6.7500 g., Cast Copper Or Bronze

Date	Mintage	Good	VG	F	VF	XF
ND(1753)	—	—	—	—	—	50.00

KM# 359s 2 MUN

6.7500 g., Cast Copper Or Bronze

Date	Mintage	Good	VG	F	VF	XF
ND(1753)	—	—	—	—	—	50.00

KM# 361 2 MUN

6.7500 g., Cast Copper Or Bronze

Date	Mintage	Good	VG	F	VF	XF
ND(1753)	—	3.00	4.00	6.00	10.00	—

KM# 361s 2 MUN

6.7500 g., Cast Copper Or Bronze

Date	Mintage	Good	VG	F	VF	XF
ND(1753)	—	—	—	—	—	50.00

KM# 357s 2 MUN

6.7500 g., Cast Copper Or Bronze

Date	Mintage	Good	VG	F	VF	XF
ND(1753)	—	—	—	—	—	50.00

KM# 355s 2 MUN

6.7500 g., Cast Copper Or Bronze

Date	Mintage	Good	VG	F	VF	XF
ND(1753)	—	—	—	—	—	50.00

KM# 353s 2 MUN

6.7500 g., Cast Copper Or Bronze

Date	Mintage	Good	VG	F	VF	XF
ND(1753)	—	—	—	—	—	50.00

KM# 351s 2 MUN

6.7500 g., Cast Copper Or Bronze

Date	Mintage	Good	VG	F	VF	XF
ND(1753)	—	—	—	—	—	50.00

KM# 349s 2 MUN

6.7500 g., Cast Copper Or Bronze

Date	Mintage	Good	VG	F	VF	XF
ND(1753)	—	—	—	—	—	50.00

KM# 389s 2 MUN

6.7500 g., Cast Copper Or Bronze

Date	Mintage	Good	VG	F	VF	XF
ND(1753)	—	—	—	—	—	50.00

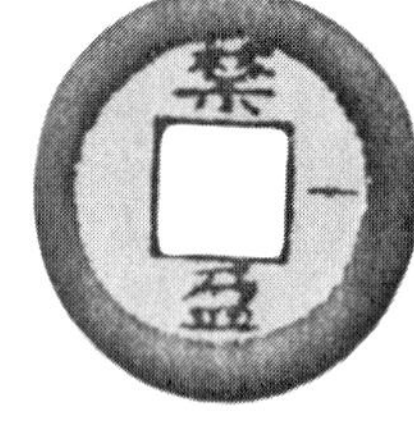

KM# 390 2 MUN

6.7500 g., Cast Copper Or Bronze **Rev:** "Yong" at bottom, series number at right

Date	Mintage	Good	VG	F	VF	XF
ND(1753) Series 1, 2	—	3.00	4.00	6.00	10.00	—

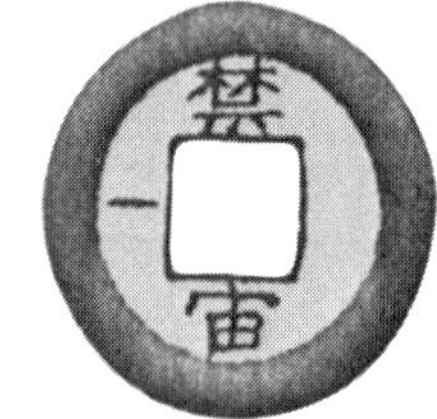

KM# 391.1 2 MUN

6.7500 g., Cast Copper Or Bronze **Rev:** "Chu" at bottom, series number at left

Date	Mintage	Good	VG	F	VF	XF
ND(1753) Series 1	—	3.00	4.00	6.00	10.00	—

KM# 392 2 MUN

6.7500 g., Cast Copper Or Bronze **Rev:** "Ch'on" at bottom, crescent at right

Date	Mintage	Good	VG	F	VF	XF
ND(1753)	—	3.00	4.00	6.00	10.00	—

KM# 392s 2 MUN

6.7500 g., Cast Copper Or Bronze

Date	Mintage	Good	VG	F	VF	XF
ND(1753)	—	—	—	—	—	50.00

KM# 393 2 MUN

6.7500 g., Cast Copper Or Bronze **Rev:** "Chi" at bottom, crescent at right

Date	Mintage	Good	VG	F	VF	XF
ND(1753)	—	3.00	4.00	6.00	10.00	—

KM# 393s 2 MUN

6.7500 g., Cast Copper Or Bronze

Date	Mintage	Good	VG	F	VF	XF
ND(1753)	—	—	—	—	—	50.00

KM# 394 2 MUN

6.7500 g., Cast Copper Or Bronze **Rev:** "Hyon" at bottom, crescent at right

Date	Mintage	Good	VG	F	VF	XF
ND(1753)	—	3.00	4.00	6.00	10.00	—

KM# 394s 2 MUN

6.7500 g., Cast Copper Or Bronze

Date	Mintage	Good	VG	F	VF	XF
ND(1753)	—	—	—	—	—	50.00

KM# 395 2 MUN

6.7500 g., Cast Copper Or Bronze **Rev:** "Hwang" (yellow) at bottom, crescent at right

Date	Mintage	Good	VG	F	VF	XF
ND(1753)	—	3.00	4.00	6.00	10.00	—

KM# 395s 2 MUN

6.7500 g., Cast Copper Or Bronze

Date	Mintage	Good	VG	F	VF	XF
ND(1753)	—	—	—	—	—	50.00

KM# 396 2 MUN

6.7500 g., Cast Copper Or Bronze **Rev:** "U" at bottom, crescent at right

Date	Mintage	Good	VG	F	VF	XF
ND(1753)	—	3.00	4.00	6.00	10.00	—

KM# 396a 2 MUN

6.7500 g., Cast Copper Or Bronze **Obv:** Clouds at left, "P'yong" with hooks

Date	Mintage	Good	VG	F	VF	XF
ND(1753)	—	3.00	4.00	6.00	10.00	—

KM# 396s 2 MUN

6.7500 g., Cast Copper Or Bronze

Date	Mintage	Good	VG	F	VF	XF
ND(1753)	—	—	—	—	—	50.00

KM# 397 2 MUN

6.7500 g., Cast Copper Or Bronze **Rev:** "Chu" at bottom, crescent at right

Date	Mintage	Good	VG	F	VF	XF
ND(1753)	—	3.00	4.00	6.00	10.00	—

KM# 397s 2 MUN

6.7500 g., Cast Copper Or Bronze

Date	Mintage	Good	VG	F	VF	XF
ND(1753)	—	—	—	—	—	50.00

KM# 398 2 MUN

6.7500 g., Cast Copper Or Bronze **Rev:** "Hong"at bottom, crescent at right

Date	Mintage	Good	VG	F	VF	XF
ND(1753)	—	3.00	4.00	6.00	10.00	—

KM# 398s 2 MUN

6.7500 g., Cast Copper Or Bronze

Date	Mintage	Good	VG	F	VF	XF
ND(1753)	—	—	—	—	—	50.00

KM# 399 2 MUN

6.7500 g., Cast Copper Or Bronze **Rev:** "Hwang" (barren) at bottom, crescent at right

Date	Mintage	Good	VG	F	VF	XF
ND(1753)	—	3.00	4.00	6.00	10.00	—

KM# 399s 2 MUN

6.7500 g., Cast Copper Or Bronze

Date	Mintage	Good	VG	F	VF	XF
ND(1753)	—	—	—	—	—	50.00

KM# 400 2 MUN

6.7500 g., Cast Copper Or Bronze **Rev:** "Il" (sun) at bottom, crescent at right

Date	Mintage	Good	VG	F	VF	XF
ND(1753)	—	3.00	4.00	6.00	10.00	—

KM# 400s 2 MUN

6.7500 g., Cast Copper Or Bronze

Date	Mintage	Good	VG	F	VF	XF
ND(1753)	—	—	—	—	—	50.00

KM# 401 2 MUN

6.7500 g., Cast Copper Or Bronze **Rev:** "Wol" at bottom, crescent at right

Date	Mintage	Good	VG	F	VF	XF
ND(1753)	—	3.00	4.00	6.00	10.00	—

KM# 401s 2 MUN

6.7500 g., Cast Copper Or Bronze

Date	Mintage	Good	VG	F	VF	XF
ND(1753)	—	—	—	—	—	50.00

KM# 402 2 MUN

6.7500 g., Cast Copper Or Bronze **Rev:** "Yong" at bottom, crescent at right

Date	Mintage	Good	VG	F	VF	XF
ND(1753)	—	3.00	4.00	6.00	10.00	—

KM# 402s 2 MUN

6.7500 g., Cast Copper Or Bronze

Date	Mintage	Good	VG	F	VF	XF
ND(1753)	—	—	—	—	—	50.00

KM# 403 2 MUN

6.7500 g., Cast Copper Or Bronze **Rev:** "Ch'uk" at bottom, crescent at right

Date	Mintage	Good	VG	F	VF	XF
ND(1753)	—	3.00	4.00	6.00	10.00	—

KM# 403s 2 MUN

6.7500 g., Cast Copper Or Bronze

Date	Mintage	Good	VG	F	VF	XF
ND(1753)	—	—	—	—	—	50.00

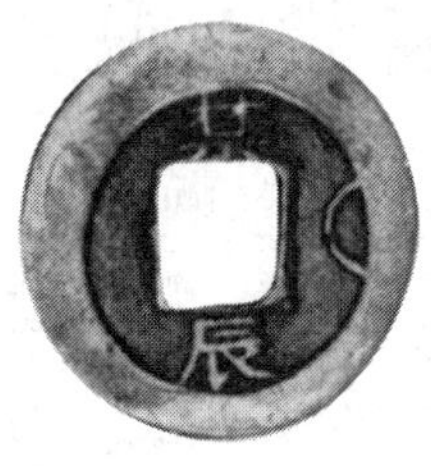

KM# 404 2 MUN

6.7500 g., Cast Copper Or Bronze **Rev:** "Chin" at bottom, crescent at right

Date	Mintage	Good	VG	F	VF	XF
ND(1753)	—	3.00	4.00	6.00	10.00	—

KM# 404s 2 MUN

6.7500 g., Cast Copper Or Bronze

Date	Mintage	Good	VG	F	VF	XF
ND(1753)	—	—	—	—	—	50.00

KM# 405 2 MUN

6.7500 g., Cast Copper Or Bronze **Rev:** "Suk" at bottom, crescent at right

Date	Mintage	Good	VG	F	VF	XF
ND(1753)	—	3.00	4.00	6.00	10.00	—

KM# 405s 2 MUN

6.7500 g., Cast Copper Or Bronze

Date	Mintage	Good	VG	F	VF	XF
ND(1753)	—	—	—	—	—	50.00

KM# 406 2 MUN

6.7500 g., Cast Copper Or Bronze **Rev:** "Yol" at bottom, crescent at right

Date	Mintage	Good	VG	F	VF	XF
ND(1753)	—	3.00	4.00	6.00	10.00	—

KM# 406s 2 MUN

6.7500 g., Cast Copper Or Bronze

Date	Mintage	Good	VG	F	VF	XF
ND(1753)	—	—	—	—	—	50.00

KM# 407 2 MUN

6.7500 g., Cast Copper Or Bronze **Rev:** "Chang" (extend) at bottom, crescent at right

Date	Mintage	Good	VG	F	VF	XF
ND(1753)	—	3.00	4.00	6.00	10.00	—

KM# 407s 2 MUN

6.7500 g., Cast Copper Or Bronze

Date	Mintage	Good	VG	F	VF	XF
ND(1753)	—	—	—	—	—	50.00

KM# 408 2 MUN

6.7500 g., Cast Copper Or Bronze **Rev:** "Han" at bottom, crescent at right

Date	Mintage	Good	VG	F	VF	XF
ND(1753)	—	3.00	4.00	6.00	10.00	—

KM# 408s 2 MUN

6.7500 g., Cast Copper Or Bronze

Date	Mintage	Good	VG	F	VF	XF
ND(1753)	—	—	—	—	—	50.00

KM# 409 2 MUN

6.7500 g., Cast Copper Or Bronze **Rev:** "Nae" at bottom, crescent at right

Date	Mintage	Good	VG	F	VF	XF
ND(1753)	—	3.00	4.00	6.00	10.00	—

KM# 409s 2 MUN

6.7500 g., Cast Copper Or Bronze

Date	Mintage	Good	VG	F	VF	XF
ND(1753)	—	—	—	—	—	50.00

KM# 410 2 MUN

6.7500 g., Cast Copper Or Bronze **Rev:** "So" at bottom, crescent at right

Date	Mintage	Good	VG	F	VF	XF
ND(1753)	—	3.00	4.00	6.00	10.00	—

KM# 410s 2 MUN

6.7500 g., Cast Copper Or Bronze

Date	Mintage	Good	VG	F	VF	XF
ND(1753)	—	—	—	—	—	50.00

KM# 411 2 MUN

6.7500 g., Cast Copper Or Bronze **Rev:** "Wang" at bottom, crescent at right

Date	Mintage	Good	VG	F	VF	XF
ND(1753)	—	3.00	4.00	6.00	10.00	—

KM# 411s 2 MUN

6.7500 g., Cast Copper Or Bronze

Date	Mintage	Good	VG	F	VF	XF
ND(1753)	—	—	—	—	—	50.00

KM# 412 2 MUN

6.7500 g., Cast Copper Or Bronze **Rev:** "Ch'u" at bottom, crescent at right

Date	Mintage	Good	VG	F	VF	XF
ND(1753)	—	3.00	4.00	6.00	10.00	—

KM# 412s 2 MUN

6.7500 g., Cast Copper Or Bronze

Date	Mintage	Good	VG	F	VF	XF
ND(1753)	—	—	—	—	—	50.00

KM# 413 2 MUN

6.7500 g., Cast Copper Or Bronze **Rev:** "Chin" at bottom, circle in crescent at right

Date	Mintage	Good	VG	F	VF	XF
ND(1753)	—	3.00	4.00	6.00	10.00	—

KM# 414 2 MUN

6.7500 g., Cast Copper Or Bronze **Rev:** "Chu" at bottom, inward crescent at left

Date	Mintage	Good	VG	F	VF	XF
ND(1753)	—	3.00	4.00	6.00	10.00	—

KM# 415 2 MUN

6.7500 g., Cast Copper Or Bronze **Rev:** "Chon" at bottom, crescent at right, series number at left

Date	Mintage	Good	VG	F	VF	XF
ND(1753) Series 1	—	3.00	4.50	7.00	12.00	—

KM# 415s 2 MUN

6.7500 g., Cast Copper Or Bronze

Date	Mintage	Good	VG	F	VF	XF
ND(1753) Series 1	—	—	—	—	—	50.00

KM# 416 2 MUN

6.7500 g., Cast Copper Or Bronze **Rev:** "Chi" at bottom, crescent at right, series number at left

Date	Mintage	Good	VG	F	VF	XF
ND(1753)	—	6.00	10.00	15.00	25.00	—

KM# 416s 2 MUN

6.7500 g., Cast Copper Or Bronze

Date	Mintage	Good	VG	F	VF	XF
ND(1753) Series 1	—	—	—	—	—	50.00

KM# 417 2 MUN

6.7500 g., Cast Copper Or Bronze **Rev:** "Hyon" at bottom, crescent at right, series number at left

Date	Mintage	Good	VG	F	VF	XF
ND(1753) Series 1	—	6.00	10.00	15.00	25.00	—

KM# 417s 2 MUN

6.7500 g., Cast Copper Or Bronze

Date	Mintage	Good	VG	F	VF	XF
ND(1753) Series 1	—	—	—	—	—	50.00

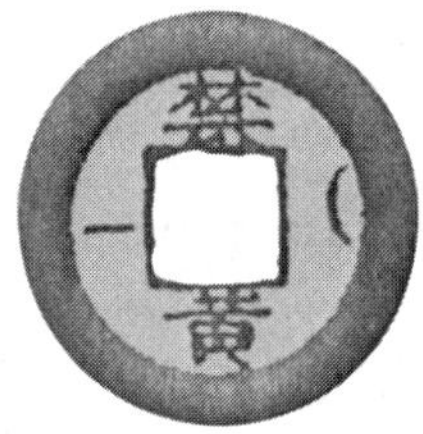

KM# 418 2 MUN

6.7500 g., Cast Copper Or Bronze **Rev:** "Hwang" (yellow) at bottom, crescent at right, series number at left

Date	Mintage	Good	VG	F	VF	XF
ND(1753) Series 1	—	3.00	4.50	7.00	12.00	—

KM# 418s 2 MUN

6.7500 g., Cast Copper Or Bronze

Date	Mintage	Good	VG	F	VF	XF
ND(1753) Series 1	—	—	—	—	—	37.00

KM# 419 2 MUN

6.7500 g., Cast Copper Or Bronze **Rev:** "U" at bottom, crescent at right, series number at left

Date	Mintage	Good	VG	F	VF	XF
ND(1753) Series 1	—	6.00	10.00	15.00	25.00	—

KM# 419s 2 MUN

6.7500 g., Cast Copper Or Bronze

Date	Mintage	Good	VG	F	VF	XF
ND(1753) Series 1	—	—	—	—	—	50.00

KM# 420 2 MUN

6.7500 g., Cast Copper Or Bronze **Rev:** "Chu" at bottom, outward crescent at right, series number at left

Date	Mintage	Good	VG	F	VF	XF
ND(1753) Series 1	—	3.00	4.50	7.00	12.00	—

KM# 420s 2 MUN

6.7500 g., Cast Copper Or Bronze

Date	Mintage	Good	VG	F	VF	XF
ND(1753) Series 1	—	—	—	—	—	37.00

KM# 421 2 MUN
6.7500 g., Cast Copper Or Bronze **Rev:** "Ch'on" at bottom, inward crescent at right, series number at left

Date	Mintage	Good	VG	F	VF	XF
ND(1753) Series 1	—	3.00	4.00	6.00	10.00	—

KM# 422 2 MUN
6.7500 g., Cast Copper Or Bronze **Rev:** "Hwang" (yellow) at bottom, inward crescent at right, series number at left

Date	Mintage	Good	VG	F	VF	XF
ND(1753) Series 1	—	3.00	4.00	6.00	10.00	—

KM# 423 2 MUN
6.7500 g., Cast Copper Or Bronze **Rev:** "Chu" at bottom, inward crescent at right, series number at left

Date	Mintage	Good	VG	F	VF	XF
ND(1753) Series 1	—	3.00	4.00	6.00	10.00	—

KM# 424 2 MUN
6.7500 g., Cast Copper Or Bronze **Rev:** "Ch'on" at bottom crescent at right, circle at left

Date	Mintage	Good	VG	F	VF	XF
ND(1753)	—	3.50	5.50	9.00	15.00	—

KM# 425 2 MUN
6.7500 g., Cast Copper Or Bronze **Rev:** "Chi" at bottom, crescent at right, circle at left

Date	Mintage	Good	VG	F	VF	XF
ND(1753)	—	3.50	5.50	9.00	15.00	—

KM# 421s 2 MUN
6.7500 g., Cast Copper Or Bronze

Date	Mintage	Good	VG	F	VF	XF
ND(1753) Series 1	—	—	—	—	—	50.00

KM# 422s 2 MUN
6.7500 g., Cast Copper Or Bronze

Date	Mintage	Good	VG	F	VF	XF
ND(1753) Series 1	—	—	—	—	—	50.00

KM# 423s 2 MUN
6.7500 g., Cast Copper Or Bronze

Date	Mintage	Good	VG	F	VF	XF
ND(1753) Series 1	—	—	—	—	—	50.00

KM# 424s 2 MUN
6.7500 g., Cast Copper Or Bronze

Date	Mintage	Good	VG	F	VF	XF
ND(1753)	—	—	—	—	—	50.00

KM# 425s 2 MUN
6.7500 g., Cast Copper Or Bronze

Date	Mintage	Good	VG	F	VF	XF
ND(1753)	—	—	—	—	—	50.00

KM# 426 2 MUN
6.7500 g., Cast Copper Or Bronze **Rev:** "Hyon" at bottom, crescent at right, circle at left

Date	Mintage	Good	VG	F	VF	XF
ND(1753)	—	3.50	5.50	9.00	15.00	—

KM# 426s 2 MUN
6.7500 g., Cast Copper Or Bronze

Date	Mintage	Good	VG	F	VF	XF
ND(1753)	—	—	—	—	—	50.00

KM# 427 2 MUN
6.7500 g., Cast Copper Or Bronze **Rev:** "Hwang" (yellow) at bottom, crescent at right, circle at left

Date	Mintage	Good	VG	F	VF	XF
ND(1753)	—	3.50	5.50	9.00	15.00	—

KM# 427s 2 MUN
6.7500 g., Cast Copper Or Bronze

Date	Mintage	Good	VG	F	VF	XF
ND(1753)	—	—	—	—	—	50.00

KM# 428 2 MUN
6.7500 g., Cast Copper Or Bronze **Rev:** "U" at bottom, crescent at right, circle at left

Date	Mintage	Good	VG	F	VF	XF
ND(1753)	—	3.50	5.50	9.00	15.00	—

KM# 428s 2 MUN
6.7500 g., Cast Copper Or Bronze

Date	Mintage	Good	VG	F	VF	XF
ND(1753)	—	—	—	—	—	50.00

KM# 429 2 MUN
6.7500 g., Cast Copper Or Bronze **Rev:** "Chu" at bottom, crescent at right, circle at left

Date	Mintage	Good	VG	F	VF	XF
ND(1753)	—	3.50	5.50	9.00	15.00	—

KM# 429s 2 MUN
6.7500 g., Cast Copper Or Bronze

Date	Mintage	Good	VG	F	VF	XF
ND(1753)	—	—	—	—	—	50.00

KM# 430 2 MUN
6.7500 g., Cast Copper Or Bronze **Rev:** "Hon" at bottom, crescent at right, circle at left

Date	Mintage	Good	VG	F	VF	XF
ND(1753)	—	3.50	5.50	9.00	15.00	—

KM# 430s 2 MUN
6.7500 g., Cast Copper Or Bronze

Date	Mintage	Good	VG	F	VF	XF
ND(1753)	—	—	—	—	—	50.00

KM# 431 2 MUN
6.7500 g., Cast Copper Or Bronze **Rev:** "Hwang" (barren) at bottom, crescent at right, circle at left

Date	Mintage	Good	VG	F	VF	XF
ND(1753)	—	3.50	5.50	9.00	15.00	—

KM# 431s 2 MUN
6.7500 g., Cast Copper Or Bronze

Date	Mintage	Good	VG	F	VF	XF
ND(1753)	—	—	—	—	—	50.00

KM# 432 2 MUN
6.7500 g., Cast Copper Or Bronze **Rev:** "Il" at bottom, crescent at right, circle at left

Date	Mintage	Good	VG	F	VF	XF
ND(1753)	—	3.50	5.50	9.00	15.00	—

KM# 432s 2 MUN
6.7500 g., Cast Copper Or Bronze

Date	Mintage	Good	VG	F	VF	XF
ND(1753)	—	—	—	—	—	50.00

KM# 433 2 MUN
6.7500 g., Cast Copper Or Bronze **Rev:** "Wol" at bottom, crescent at right, circle at left

Date	Mintage	Good	VG	F	VF	XF
ND(1753)	—	3.50	5.50	9.00	15.00	—

KM# 433s 2 MUN
6.7500 g., Cast Copper Or Bronze

Date	Mintage	Good	VG	F	VF	XF
ND(1753)	—	—	—	—	—	50.00

KM# 434 2 MUN
6.7500 g., Cast Copper Or Bronze **Rev:** "Yong" at bottom, crescent at right, circle at left

Date	Mintage	Good	VG	F	VF	XF
ND(1753)	—	3.50	5.50	9.00	15.00	—

KM# 434s 2 MUN
6.7500 g., Cast Copper Or Bronze

Date	Mintage	Good	VG	F	VF	XF
ND(1753)	—	—	—	—	—	50.00

KM# 435s 2 MUN
6.7500 g., Cast Copper Or Bronze

Date	Mintage	Good	VG	F	VF	XF
ND(1753)	—	—	—	—	—	50.00

KM# 436s 2 MUN
6.7500 g., Cast Copper Or Bronze

Date	Mintage	Good	VG	F	VF	XF
ND(1753)	—	—	—	—	—	50.00

KM# 437s 2 MUN
6.7500 g., Cast Copper Or Bronze

Date	Mintage	Good	VG	F	VF	XF
ND(1753)	—	—	—	—	—	50.00

KM# 438s 2 MUN
6.7500 g., Cast Copper Or Bronze

Date	Mintage	Good	VG	F	VF	XF
ND(1753)	—	—	—	—	—	50.00

KM# 435 2 MUN
6.7500 g., Cast Copper Or Bronze **Rev:** "Ch'uk" at bottom, crescent at right, circle at left

Date	Mintage	Good	VG	F	VF	XF
ND(1753)	—	3.50	5.50	9.00	15.00	—

KM# 436 2 MUN
6.7500 g., Cast Copper Or Bronze **Rev:** "Chin" at bottom, crescent at right, circle at left

Date	Mintage	Good	VG	F	VF	XF
ND(1753)	—	3.50	5.50	9.00	15.00	—

KM# 437 2 MUN
6.7500 g., Cast Copper Or Bronze **Rev:** "Suk" at bottom, crescent at right, circle at left

Date	Mintage	Good	VG	F	VF	XF
ND(1753)	—	3.50	5.50	9.00	15.00	—

KM# 438 2 MUN
6.7500 g., Cast Copper Or Bronze **Rev:** "Yol" at bottom, crescent at right, circle at left

Date	Mintage	Good	VG	F	VF	XF
ND(1753)	—	3.50	5.50	9.00	15.00	—

KM# 439 2 MUN
6.7500 g., Cast Copper Or Bronze **Rev:** "Chang" (extend) at bottom, crescent at right, circle at left

Date	Mintage	Good	VG	F	VF	XF
ND(1753)	—	3.50	5.50	9.00	15.00	—

KM# 440 2 MUN
6.7500 g., Cast Copper Or Bronze **Rev:** "Han" at bottom, crescent at right, circle at left

Date	Mintage	Good	VG	F	VF	XF
ND(1753)	—	3.50	5.50	9.00	15.00	—

KM# 441 2 MUN
6.7500 g., Cast Copper Or Bronze **Rev:** "Nae" at bottom, crescent at right, circle at left

Date	Mintage	Good	VG	F	VF	XF
ND(1753)	—	3.50	5.50	9.00	15.00	—

KM# 442 2 MUN
6.7500 g., Cast Copper Or Bronze **Rev:** "So" at bottom, crescent at right, circle at left

Date	Mintage	Good	VG	F	VF	XF
ND(1753)	—	3.50	5.50	9.00	15.00	—

KM# 443 2 MUN
6.7500 g., Cast Copper Or Bronze **Rev:** "Wang" at bottom, crescent at right, circle at left

Date	Mintage	Good	VG	F	VF	XF
ND(1753)	—	3.50	5.50	9.00	15.00	—

KM# 444 2 MUN
6.7500 g., Cast Copper Or Bronze **Rev:** "Ch'uk" at bottom, circle at right, crescent at left

Date	Mintage	Good	VG	F	VF	XF
ND(1753)	—	3.50	5.50	9.00	15.00	—

KM# 439s 2 MUN
6.7500 g., Cast Copper Or Bronze

Date	Mintage	Good	VG	F	VF	XF
ND(1753)	—	—	—	—	—	50.00

KM# 440s 2 MUN
6.7500 g., Cast Copper Or Bronze

Date	Mintage	Good	VG	F	VF	XF
ND(1753)	—	—	—	—	—	50.00

KM# 441s 2 MUN
6.7500 g., Cast Copper Or Bronze

Date	Mintage	Good	VG	F	VF	XF
ND(1753)	—	—	—	—	—	50.00

KM# 442s 2 MUN
6.7500 g., Cast Copper Or Bronze

Date	Mintage	Good	VG	F	VF	XF
ND(1753)	—	—	—	—	—	50.00

KM# 443s 2 MUN
6.7500 g., Cast Copper Or Bronze

Date	Mintage	Good	VG	F	VF	XF
ND(1753)	—	—	—	—	—	50.00

CH'UNG CH'ONG PROVINCIAL OFFICE

(Ch'ung Ch'ong Kam Yong)

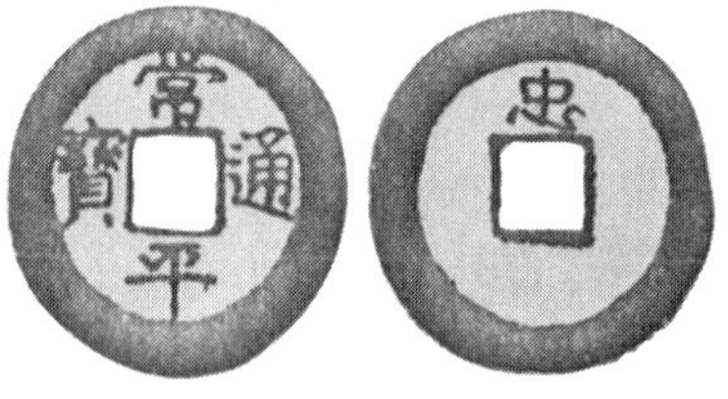

KM# 1076 MUN
4.5000 g., Cast Copper **Rev:** "Ch'ung" at top

Date	Mintage	Good	VG	F	VF	XF
ND(1742) Rare	—	—	—	—	—	—

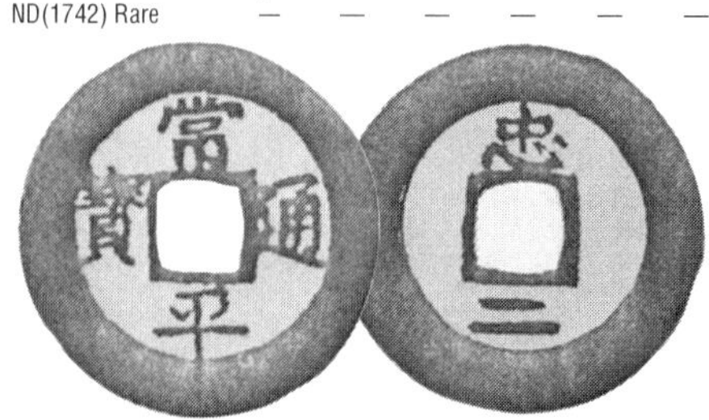

KM# 1077 2 MUN
Cast Copper **Rev:** "Ch'ung" at top, "I" (2) at bottom **Note:** Weight varies 8.00-9.00 grams.

Date	Mintage	Good	VG	F	VF	XF
ND(1742)	—	60.00	100	150	225	—

MILITARY TRAINING COMMAND

Hun (Hul Ly On Do Gam)

Obverse Character

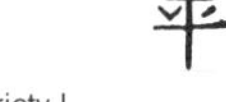

P yong variety I

P yong variety II

T ong variety I - top

T ong variety II - top

KM# 524 2 MUN

Cast Copper **Obv:** "P'yong" variety I, "T'ong" variety II

Date	Mintage	Good	VG	F	VF	XF
ND(1742-52)	—	3.00	4.00	6.00	10.00	—

KM# 486 2 MUN

6.7500 g., Cast Copper **Obv:** "P'yong" variety I, "T'ong" variety II

Date	Mintage	Good	VG	F	VF	XF
ND(1742-52)	—	3.00	4.00	6.00	10.00	—

KM# 500 2 MUN

Cast Copper **Obv:** "P'yong" variety I, "T'ong" variety II

Date	Mintage	Good	VG	F	VF	XF
ND(1742-52)	—	3.00	4.00	6.00	10.00	—

KM# 531 2 MUN

Cast Copper, 30-32 mm. **Obv:** "P'yong" variety I, "T'ong" variety I **Rev:** "Suk" at bottom **Note:** Size varies. Weight vaires 8.00-9.00 grams.

Date	Mintage	Good	VG	F	VF	XF
ND(1742-52)	—	3.00	4.00	6.00	10.00	—

KM# 532 2 MUN

Cast Copper, 30-32 mm. **Obv:** "P'yong" variety I, "T'ong" variety II **Note:** Size varies. Weight vaires 8.00-9.00 grams.

Date	Mintage	Good	VG	F	VF	XF
ND(1742-52)	—	3.00	4.00	6.00	10.00	—

KM# 487 2 MUN

Cast Copper, 30-32 mm. **Obv:** "P'yong" variety I, "T'ong" variety II **Rev:** "Hyon" at bottom **Note:** Size varies. Weight varies 8.00-9.00 grams.

Date	Mintage	Good	VG	F	VF	XF
ND(1742-52)	—	3.00	4.00	6.00	10.00	—

KM# 488 2 MUN

Cast Copper, 30-32 mm. **Obv:** "P'yong" variety I, "T'ong" variety II **Note:** Size varies. Weight varies 8.00-9.00 grams.

Date	Mintage	Good	VG	F	VF	XF
ND(1742-52)	—	3.00	4.00	6.00	10.00	—

KM# 491 2 MUN

Cast Copper, 30-32 mm. **Obv:** "P'yong" variety I, "T'ong" variety I **Rev:** "Hwang" (yellow) at bottom **Note:** Size varies. Weight varies 8.00-9.00 grams.

Date	Mintage	Good	VG	F	VF	XF
ND(1742-52)	—	3.00	4.00	6.00	10.00	—

KM# 492 2 MUN

Cast Copper, 30-32 mm. **Obv:** "P'yong" variety I, "T'ong" variety II **Note:** Size varies. Weight varies 8.00-9.00 grams.

Date	Mintage	Good	VG	F	VF	XF
ND(1742-52)	—	3.00	4.00	6.00	10.00	—

KM# 495 2 MUN

Cast Copper, 30-32 mm. **Obv:** "P'yong" variety I, "T'ong" variety I **Rev:** "U" at bottom **Note:** Size varies. Weight varies 8.00-9.00 grams.

Date	Mintage	Good	VG	F	VF	XF
ND(1742-52)	—	3.00	4.00	6.00	10.00	—

KM# 496 2 MUN

Cast Copper, 30-32 mm. **Obv:** "P'yong" variety I, "T'ong" variety II **Note:** Size varies. Weight varies 8.00-9.00 grams.

Date	Mintage	Good	VG	F	VF	XF
ND(1742-52)	—	3.00	4.00	6.00	10.00	—

KM# 499 2 MUN

Cast Copper, 31-32 mm. **Obv:** "P'yong" variety I, "T'ong" variety I **Rev:** "Chu" at bottom **Note:** Size varies. Weight varies 8.00-9.00 grams.

Date	Mintage	Good	VG	F	VF	XF
ND(1742-52)	—	3.00	4.00	6.00	10.00	—

KM# 503 2 MUN

Cast Copper, 30-32 mm. **Obv:** "P'yong" variety I, "T'ong" variety I **Rev:** "Hong" at bottom **Note:** Size varies. Weight varies 8.00-9.00 grams.

Date	Mintage	Good	VG	F	VF	XF
ND(1742-52)	—	3.00	4.00	6.00	10.00	—

KM# 504 2 MUN

Cast Copper, 30-32 mm. **Obv:** "P'yong" variety I, "T'ong" variety II **Note:** Size varies. Weight varies 8.00-9.00 grams.

Date	Mintage	Good	VG	F	VF	XF
ND(1742-52)	—	3.00	4.00	6.00	10.00	—

KM# 507 2 MUN

Cast Copper, 30-32 mm. **Obv:** "P'yong" variety I, "T'ong" variety I **Rev:** "Hwang" (barren) at bottom **Note:** Size varies. Weight varies 8.00-9.00 grams.

Date	Mintage	Good	VG	F	VF	XF
ND(1742-52)	—	3.00	4.00	6.00	10.00	—

KM# 508 2 MUN

Cast Copper, 30-32 mm. **Obv:** "P'yong" variety I, "T'ong" variety II **Note:** Size varies. Weight varies 8.00-9.00 grams.

Date	Mintage	Good	VG	F	VF	XF
ND(1742-52)	—	3.00	4.00	6.00	10.00	—

KM# 515 2 MUN

Cast Copper, 30-32 mm. **Obv:** "P'yong" variety I, "T'ong" variety I **Rev:** "Wol" at bottom **Note:** Size varies. Weight varies 8.00-9.00 grams.

Date	Mintage	Good	VG	F	VF	XF
ND(1742-52)	—	3.00	4.00	6.00	10.00	—

KM# 516 2 MUN

Cast Copper, 30-32 mm. **Obv:** "P'yong" variety I, "T'ong" variety II **Note:** Size varies. Weight varies 8.00-9.00 grams.

Date	Mintage	Good	VG	F	VF	XF
ND(1742-52)	—	3.00	4.00	6.00	10.00	—

KM# 519 2 MUN

Cast Copper, 30-32 mm. **Obv:** "P'yong" variety I, "T'ong" variety I **Rev:** "Yong" at bottom **Note:** Size varies. Weight varies 8.00-9.00 grams.

Date	Mintage	Good	VG	F	VF	XF
ND(1742-52)	—	3.00	4.00	6.00	10.00	—

KM# 520 2 MUN

Cast Copper, 30-32 mm. **Obv:** "P'yong" variety I, "T'ong" variety II **Note:** Size varies. Weight varies 8.00-9.00 grams.

Date	Mintage	Good	VG	F	VF	XF
ND(1742-52)	—	3.00	4.00	6.00	10.00	—

KM# 527 2 MUN

Cast Copper, 30-32 mm. **Obv:** "P'yong" variety I, "T'ong" variety I **Rev:** "Chin" at bottom **Note:** Size varies. Weight varies 8.00-9.00 grams.

Date	Mintage	Good	VG	F	VF	XF
ND(1742-52)	—	3.00	4.00	6.00	10.00	—

KM# 528 2 MUN

Cast Copper, 30-32 mm. **Obv:** "P'yong" variety I, "T'ong" variety II **Note:** Size varies. Weight varies 8.00-9.00 grams.

Date	Mintage	Good	VG	F	VF	XF
ND(1742-52)	—	3.00	4.00	6.00	10.00	—

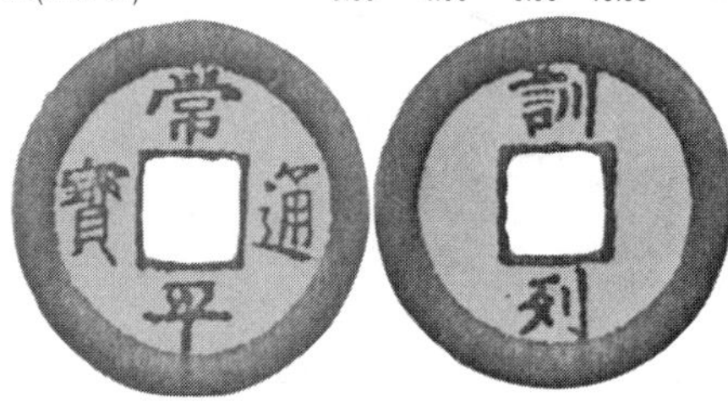

KM# 535 2 MUN

Cast Copper, 30-32 mm. **Obv:** "P'yong" variety I, "T'ong" variety I **Rev:** "Yol" at bottom **Note:** Size varies. Weight varies 8.00-9.00 grams.

Date	Mintage	Good	VG	F	VF	XF
ND(1742-52)	—	3.00	4.00	6.00	10.00	—

KM# 535a 2 MUN

Cast Copper, 30-32 mm. **Rev:** Star at lower left **Note:** Size varies. Weight varies 8.00-9.00 grams.

Date	Mintage	Good	VG	F	VF	XF
ND(1742-52)	—	3.00	4.00	6.00	10.00	—

KM# 536 2 MUN

Cast Copper, 30-32 mm. **Obv:** "P'yong" variety I, "T'ong" variety II **Note:** Size varies. Weight varies 8.00-9.00 grams.

Date	Mintage	Good	VG	F	VF	XF
ND(1742-52)	—	3.00	4.00	6.00	10.00	—

KM# 539 2 MUN

Cast Copper, 30-32 mm. **Obv:** "P'yong" variety I, "T'ong" variety I **Rev:** "Chang" (extend) at bottom **Note:** Size varies. Weight varies 8.00-9.00 grams.

Date	Mintage	Good	VG	F	VF	XF
ND(1742-52)	—	3.00	4.00	6.00	10.00	—

KM# 540 2 MUN

Cast Copper, 30-32 mm. **Obv:** "P'yong" variety I, "T'ong" variety II **Note:** Size varies. Weight varies 8.00-9.00 grams.

Date	Mintage	Good	VG	F	VF	XF
ND(1742-52)	—	3.00	4.00	6.00	10.00	—

KM# 541 2 MUN

Cast Copper, 30-32 mm. **Obv:** "P'yong" variety I, "T'ong" variety I **Rev:** "Han" at bottom **Note:** Size varies. Weight varies 8.00-9.00 grams.

Date	Mintage	Good	VG	F	VF	XF
ND(1742-52)	—	3.00	4.00	6.00	10.00	—

KM# 542 2 MUN

Cast Copper, 30-32 mm. **Obv:** "P'yong" variety I, "T'ong" variety II **Note:** Size varies. Weight varies 8.00-9.00 grams.

Date	Mintage	Good	VG	F	VF	XF
ND(1742-52)	—	3.00	4.00	6.00	10.00	—

KM# 543 2 MUN

Cast Copper, 30-32 mm. **Obv:** "P'yong" variety I, "T'ong" variety I **Note:** Size varies. Weight varies 8.00-9.00 grams.

Date	Mintage	Good	VG	F	VF	XF
ND(1742-52)	—	3.00	4.00	6.00	10.00	—

KM# 544 2 MUN

Cast Copper, 30-32 mm. **Obv:** "P'yong" variety I, "T'ong" variety II **Note:** Size varies. Weight varies 8.00-9.00 grams.

Date	Mintage	Good	VG	F	VF	XF
ND(1742-52)	—	3.00	4.00	6.00	10.00	—

KM# 545 2 MUN

Cast Copper, 30-32 mm. **Obv:** "P'yong" variety I, "T'ong" variety I **Rev:** "So" at bottom **Note:** Size varies. Weight varies 8.00-9.00 grams.

Date	Mintage	Good	VG	F	VF	XF
ND(1742-52)	—	3.00	4.00	6.00	10.00	—

KM# 546 2 MUN

Cast Copper, 30-32 mm. **Obv:** "P'yong" variety I, "T'ong" variety II **Note:** Size varies. Weight varies 8.00-9.00 grams.

Date	Mintage	Good	VG	F	VF	XF
ND(1742-52)	—	3.00	4.00	6.00	10.00	—

KM# 547 2 MUN

Cast Copper, 30-32 mm. **Obv:** "P'yong" variety I, "T'ong" variety I **Rev:** "Wang" at bottom **Note:** Size varies. Weight varies 8.00-9.00 grams.

Date	Mintage	Good	VG	F	VF	XF
ND(1742-52)	—	3.00	4.00	6.00	10.00	—

KM# 548 2 MUN

Cast Copper, 30-32 mm. **Obv:** "P'yong" variety I, "T'ong" variety II **Note:** Size varies. Weight varies 8.00-9.00 grams.

Date	Mintage	Good	VG	F	VF	XF
ND(1742-52)	—	3.00	4.00	6.00	10.00	—

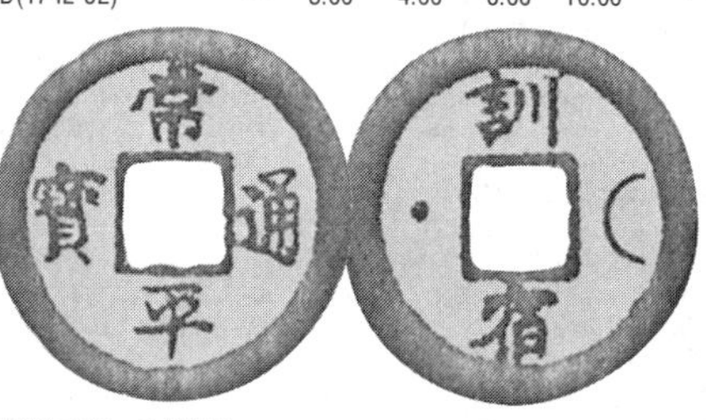

KM# 549 2 MUN

Cast Copper, 30-32 mm. **Rev:** "Suk" at bottom, crescent at right, dot at left **Note:** Size varies. Weight varies 8.00-9.00 grams.

Date	Mintage	Good	VG	F	VF	XF
ND(1742-52)	—	3.00	4.00	6.00	10.00	—

KM# 511 2 MUN

Cast Copper **Obv:** "P'yong" variety I, "T'ong" variety I **Rev:** "Il" at bottom

Date	Mintage	Good	VG	F	VF	XF
ND(1742-52)	—	3.00	4.00	6.00	10.00	—

KM# 512 2 MUN

Cast Copper **Obv:** "P'yong" variety I, "T'ong" variety II

Date	Mintage	Good	VG	F	VF	XF
ND(1742-52)	—	3.50	6.50	10.00	15.00	—

KM# 479 2 MUN

Cast Bronze, 30-32 mm. **Obv:** "P'yong" variety I, "T'ong" variety I **Rev:** "Ch'on" at bottom **Note:** Size varies.

Date	Mintage	Good	VG	F	VF	XF
ND(1742-52)	—	3.00	4.00	6.00	10.00	—

KM# 480 2 MUN

Cast Bronze, 30-32 mm. **Obv:** "P'yong" variety I, "T'ong" variety II **Note:** Size varies.

Date	Mintage	Good	VG	F	VF	XF
ND(1742-52)	—	3.00	6.00	10.00	15.00	—

KM# 523 2 MUN

Cast Copper **Obv:** "P'yong" variety I, "T'ong" variety I **Rev:** "Ch'uk" at bottom **Note:** Struck at Hul Ly On Do Gam.

Date	Mintage	Good	VG	F	VF	XF
ND(1742-52)	—	3.00	4.00	6.00	10.00	—

KM# 483 2 MUN

Cast Copper, 30-32 mm. **Obv:** "P'yong" variety II, "T'ong" variety II **Rev:** "Chi" at bottom **Note:** Weight varies 8.00-9.00 grams. Size varies.

Date	Mintage	Good	VG	F	VF	XF
ND(1742-52)	—	3.00	4.00	6.00	10.00	—

KM# 484 2 MUN

Cast Copper, 30-32 mm. **Obv:** "P'yong" variety I, "T'ong" variety II **Note:** Weight varies 8.00-9.00 grams. Size varies.

Date	Mintage	Good	VG	F	VF	XF
ND(1742-52)	—	3.00	4.00	6.00	10.00	—

KM# 481s 2 MUN

6.7500 g., Cast Bronze

Date	Mintage	Good	VG	F	VF	XF
ND(1752)	—	—	—	—	—	50.00

KM# 482 2 MUN

Cast Copper, 31-32 mm. **Obv:** "P'yong" variety II, "T'ong" variety II **Note:** Weight varies 8.00-9.00 grams. Size varies.

Date	Mintage	Good	VG	F	VF	XF
ND(1752)	—	3.00	4.00	6.00	10.00	—

KM# 556 2 MUN

Cast Copper, 27-28.5 mm. **Obv:** "P'yong" variety II **Rev:** "Ch'on" at bottom, circle at left **Note:** Size varies.

Date	Mintage	Good	VG	F	VF	XF
ND(1752)	—	3.00	4.00	6.00	10.00	—

KM# 513s 2 MUN

6.7500 g., Cast Copper

Date	Mintage	Good	VG	F	VF	XF
ND(1752)	—	—	—	—	—	50.00

KM# 514 2 MUN

6.7500 g., Cast Copper **Obv:** "P'yong" variety II, "T'ong" variety II

Date	Mintage	Good	VG	F	VF	XF
ND(1752)	—	3.00	4.00	6.00	10.00	—

KM# 514s 2 MUN

6.7500 g., Cast Copper

Date	Mintage	Good	VG	F	VF	XF
ND(1752)	—	—	—	—	—	50.00

KM# 517s 2 MUN

6.7500 g., Cast Copper

Date	Mintage	Good	VG	F	VF	XF
ND(1752)	—	—	—	—	—	50.00

KM# 518 2 MUN
6.7500 g., Cast Copper **Obv:** "P'yong" variety II, "T'ong" variety II

Date	Mintage	Good	VG	F	VF	XF
ND(1752)	—	3.00	4.00	6.00	10.00	—

KM# 518s 2 MUN
6.7500 g., Cast Copper

Date	Mintage	Good	VG	F	VF	XF
ND(1752)	—	—	—	—	—	50.00

KM# 522 2 MUN
6.7500 g., Cast Copper **Obv:** "P'yong" variety II, "T'ong" variety II

Date	Mintage	Good	VG	F	VF	XF
ND(1752)	—	3.00	4.00	6.00	10.00	—

KM# 522a 2 MUN
6.7500 g., Cast Copper **Rev:** Star at upper right

Date	Mintage	Good	VG	F	VF	XF
ND(1752)	—	3.00	4.00	6.00	10.00	—

KM# 522s 2 MUN
6.7500 g., Cast Copper

Date	Mintage	Good	VG	F	VF	XF
ND(1752)	—	—	—	—	—	50.00

KM# 554s 2 MUN
Cast Copper, 31-32 mm. **Note:** Size varies. Weight varies 8.00-9.00 grams.

Date	Mintage	Good	VG	F	VF	XF
ND(1752)	—	—	—	—	—	55.00

KM# 555 2 MUN
Cast Copper, 31-32 mm. **Rev:** "Chin" at bottom, dot at left **Note:** Size varies. Weight varies 8.00-9.00 grams.

Date	Mintage	Good	VG	F	VF	XF
ND(1752)	—	8.50	12.50	20.00	30.00	—

KM# 561 2 MUN
Cast Copper, 31-32 mm. **Rev:** Series number at bottom **Note:** Size varies. Weight varies 8.00-9.00 grams.

Date	Mintage	Good	VG	F	VF	XF
ND(1752) Series 1-10	—	2.00	4.00	6.00	10.00	—

KM# 564 2 MUN
Cast Copper, 31-32 mm. **Rev:** "Sip" (10) at bottom, additional series number at right, crescent at left **Note:** Size varies. Weight varies 8.00-9.00 grams.

Date	Mintage	Good	VG	F	VF	XF
ND(1752) Series 11-15	—	3.00	4.00	6.00	10.00	—

KM# 526 2 MUN
Cast Copper, 31-32 mm. **Obv:** "P'yong" variety II, "T'ong" variety II **Note:** Size varies. Weight varies 8.00-9.00 grams.

Date	Mintage	Good	VG	F	VF	XF
ND(1752)	—	3.00	4.00	6.00	10.00	—

KM# 501s 2 MUN
6.7500 g., Cast Copper

Date	Mintage	Good	VG	F	VF	XF
ND(1752)	—	—	—	—	—	50.00

KM# 502 2 MUN
6.7500 g., Cast Copper **Obv:** "P'yong" variety II, "T'ong" variety II

Date	Mintage	Good	VG	F	VF	XF
ND(1752)	—	3.00	4.00	6.00	10.00	—

KM# 502s 2 MUN
6.7500 g., Cast Copper

Date	Mintage	Good	VG	F	VF	XF
ND(1752)	—	—	—	—	—	50.00

KM# 505s 2 MUN
6.7500 g., Cast Copper

Date	Mintage	Good	VG	F	VF	XF
ND(1752)	—	—	—	—	—	50.00

KM# 506 2 MUN
6.7500 g., Cast Copper **Obv:** "P'yong" variety II, "T'ong" variety II

Date	Mintage	Good	VG	F	VF	XF
ND(1752)	—	3.00	4.00	6.00	10.00	—

KM# 506s 2 MUN
6.7500 g., Cast Copper

Date	Mintage	Good	VG	F	VF	XF
ND(1752)	—	—	—	—	—	50.00

KM# 509s 2 MUN
6.7500 g., Cast Copper

Date	Mintage	Good	VG	F	VF	XF
ND(1752)	—	—	—	—	—	50.00

KM# 510 2 MUN
6.7500 g., Cast Copper **Obv:** "P'yong" variety II, "T'ong" variety II

Date	Mintage	Good	VG	F	VF	XF
ND(1752)	—	3.00	4.00	6.00	10.00	—

KM# 510s 2 MUN
6.7500 g., Cast Copper

Date	Mintage	Good	VG	F	VF	XF
ND(1752)	—	—	—	—	—	50.00

KM# 490 2 MUN
6.7500 g., Cast Copper **Obv:** "P'yong" variety I, "T'ong" variety II

Date	Mintage	Good	VG	F	VF	XF
ND(1752)	—	3.00	4.00	6.00	10.00	—

KM# 482s 2 MUN
Cast Copper

Date	Mintage	Good	VG	F	VF	XF
ND(1752)	—	—	—	—	—	50.00

KM# 485s 2 MUN
Cast Copper

Date	Mintage	Good	VG	F	VF	XF
ND(1752)	—	—	—	—	—	50.00

KM# 486s 2 MUN
Cast Copper

Date	Mintage	Good	VG	F	VF	XF
ND(1752)	—	—	—	—	—	50.00

KM# 489s 2 MUN
Cast Copper

Date	Mintage	Good	VG	F	VF	XF
ND(1752)	—	—	—	—	—	50.00

KM# 490s 2 MUN
Cast Copper

Date	Mintage	Good	VG	F	VF	XF
ND(1752)	—	—	—	—	—	50.00

KM# 493s 2 MUN
6.7500 g., Cast Copper

Date	Mintage	Good	VG	F	VF	XF
ND(1752)	—	—	—	—	—	50.00

KM# 494 2 MUN
6.7500 g., Cast Copper **Obv:** "P'yong" variety II, "T'ong" variety II

Date	Mintage	Good	VG	F	VF	XF
ND(1752)	—	3.00	4.00	6.00	10.00	—

KM# 494s 2 MUN
6.7500 g., Cast Copper

Date	Mintage	Good	VG	F	VF	XF
ND(1752)	—	—	—	—	—	50.00

KM# 497s 2 MUN
6.7500 g., Cast Copper

Date	Mintage	Good	VG	F	VF	XF
ND(1752)	—	—	—	—	—	50.00

KM# 498 2 MUN
6.7500 g., Cast Copper **Obv:** "P'yong" variety II, "T'ong" variety II

Date	Mintage	Good	VG	F	VF	XF
ND(1752)	—	3.00	4.00	6.00	10.00	—

KM# 498a 2 MUN
6.7500 g., Cast Copper **Rev:** Star right of "Hun"

Date	Mintage	Good	VG	F	VF	XF
ND(1752)	—	3.00	4.00	6.00	10.00	—

KM# 498s 2 MUN
6.7500 g., Cast Copper

Date	Mintage	Good	VG	F	VF	XF
ND(1752)	—	—	—	—	—	50.00

KM# 525s 2 MUN
6.7500 g., Cast Copper

Date	Mintage	Good	VG	F	VF	XF
ND(1752)	—	—	—	—	—	50.00

KM# 526s 2 MUN
Cast Copper

Date	Mintage	Good	VG	F	VF	XF
ND(1752)	—	—	—	—	—	50.00

KM# 529s 2 MUN
6.7500 g., Cast Copper

Date	Mintage	Good	VG	F	VF	XF
ND(1752)	—	—	—	—	—	50.00

KM# 530 2 MUN
6.7500 g., Cast Copper **Obv:** "P'yong" variety II, "T'ong" variety II

Date	Mintage	Good	VG	F	VF	XF
ND(1752)	—	3.00	4.00	6.00	10.00	—

KM# 530s 2 MUN
6.7500 g., Cast Copper

Date	Mintage	Good	VG	F	VF	XF
ND(1752)	—	—	—	—	—	50.00

KM# 534 2 MUN
6.7500 g., Cast Copper **Obv:** "P'yong" variety II, "T'ong" variety II

Date	Mintage	Good	VG	F	VF	XF
ND(1752)	—	3.00	4.00	6.00	10.00	—

KM# 534s 2 MUN
6.7500 g., Cast Copper

Date	Mintage	Good	VG	F	VF	XF
ND(1752)	—	—	—	—	—	50.00

KM# 537s 2 MUN
6.7500 g., Cast Copper

Date	Mintage	Good	VG	F	VF	XF
ND(1752)	—	—	—	—	—	50.00

KM# 538 2 MUN
6.7500 g., Cast Copper **Obv:** "P'yong" variety II, "T'ong" variety II

Date	Mintage	Good	VG	F	VF	XF
ND(1752)	—	3.00	4.00	6.00	10.00	—

KM# 538s 2 MUN
6.7500 g., Cast Copper

Date	Mintage	Good	VG	F	VF	XF
ND(1752)	—	—	—	—	—	50.00

KM# 550s 2 MUN
6.7500 g., Cast Copper

Date	Mintage	Good	VG	F	VF	XF
ND(1752)	—	—	—	—	—	50.00

KM# A550 2 MUN
6.7500 g., Cast Copper **Rev:** "Chi" at bottom, dot at right

Date	Mintage	Good	VG	F	VF	XF
ND(1752)	—	8.50	12.50	20.00	30.00	—

KM# 551 2 MUN
6.7500 g., Cast Copper **Rev:** "Chi" at bottom, dot at left

Date	Mintage	Good	VG	F	VF	XF
ND(1752)	—	8.50	12.50	20.00	30.00	—

KM# 551s 2 MUN
6.7500 g., Cast Copper

Date	Mintage	Good	VG	F	VF	XF
ND(1752)	—	—	—	—	—	55.00

KM# 552 2 MUN
6.7500 g., Cast Copper **Rev:** "Hong" at bottom, dot at left

Date	Mintage	Good	VG	F	VF	XF
ND(1752)	—	8.50	12.50	20.00	30.00	—

KM# 552s 2 MUN
6.7500 g., Cast Copper

Date	Mintage	Good	VG	F	VF	XF
ND(1752)	—	—	—	—	—	55.00

KM# 553 2 MUN
6.7500 g., Cast Copper **Rev:** "Wol" at bottom, dot at left

Date	Mintage	Good	VG	F	VF	XF
ND(1752)	—	8.50	12.50	20.00	30.00	—

KM# 553s 2 MUN
6.7500 g., Cast Copper

Date	Mintage	Good	VG	F	VF	XF
ND(1752)	—	—	—	—	—	55.00

KM# 554 2 MUN
6.7500 g., Cast Copper **Rev:** "Ch'uk" at bottom, dot at left

Date	Mintage	Good	VG	F	VF	XF
ND(1752)	—	8.50	12.50	20.00	30.00	—

KM# 555s 2 MUN
Cast Copper

Date	Mintage	Good	VG	F	VF	XF
ND(1752)	—	—	—	—	—	55.00

KM# 556s 2 MUN
Cast Copper

Date	Mintage	Good	VG	F	VF	XF
ND(1752)	—	—	—	—	—	50.00

KM# 557 2 MUN
Cast Copper **Obv:** "P'yong" in different style

Date	Mintage	Good	VG	F	VF	XF
ND(1752)	—	6.00	10.00	15.00	25.00	—

KM# 557s 2 MUN
Cast Copper

Date	Mintage	Good	VG	F	VF	XF
ND(1752)	—	—	—	—	—	50.00

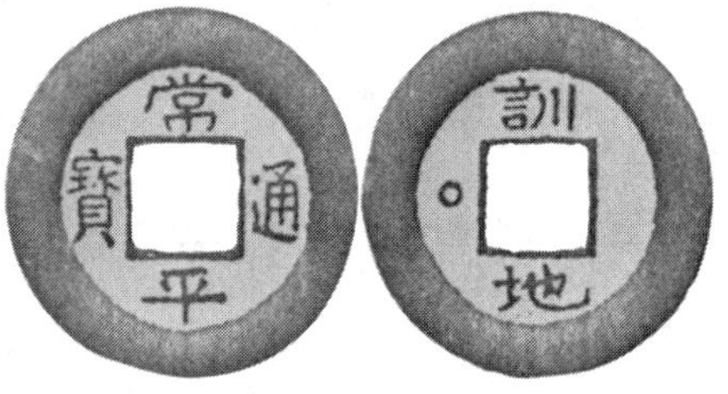

KM# 558 2 MUN
Cast Copper **Obv:** "P'yong" variety II **Rev:** "Chi" at botom, circle at left

Date	Mintage	Good	VG	F	VF	XF
ND(1752)	—	3.00	4.50	7.00	12.00	—

KM# 558s 2 MUN
Cast Copper

Date	Mintage	Good	VG	F	VF	XF
ND(1752)	—	—	—	—	—	50.00

KM# A558 2 MUN
Cast Copper **Obv:** "P'yong" variety I **Rev:** "Chi" at bottom, circle at left

Date	Mintage	Good	VG	F	VF	XF
ND(1752)	—	6.00	10.00	15.00	25.00	—

KM# 559 2 MUN
Cast Copper **Obv:** "P'yong" variety II **Rev:** "Hyon" at bottom, circle at left

Date	Mintage	Good	VG	F	VF	XF
ND(1752)	—	3.00	4.00	6.00	10.00	—

KM# 559s 2 MUN
Cast Copper

Date	Mintage	Good	VG	F	VF	XF
ND(1752)	—	—	—	—	—	50.00

KM# 560 2 MUN
Cast Copper **Rev:** "Hyon" at bottom, crescent at right

Date	Mintage	Good	VG	F	VF	XF
ND(1752)	—	3.00	4.00	6.00	10.00	—

KM# 560s 2 MUN
Cast Copper

Date	Mintage	Good	VG	F	VF	XF
ND(1752)	—	—	—	—	—	50.00

KM# 562 2 MUN
Cast Copper **Rev:** "Sip" (10) at bottom, additional series number at right

Date	Mintage	Good	VG	F	VF	XF
ND(1752) Series 11-15	—	3.00	4.00	6.00	10.00	—

KM# 563 2 MUN
Cast Copper, 28 mm. **Obv:** 2 dot "Tong" **Rev:** Series number at bottom, crescent at left

Date	Mintage	Good	VG	F	VF	XF
ND(1752) Series 1-10	—	3.00	4.00	6.00	10.00	—

KM# 563a 2 MUN
Cast Copper **Obv:** 1 dot "Tong"

Date	Mintage	Good	VG	F	VF	XF
ND(1752) Series 1-10	—	3.00	4.00	6.00	10.00	—

KM# 533s 2 MUN
6.7500 g., Cast Copper **Note:** "P'yong" variety I, "T'ong" variety II

Date	Mintage	Good	VG	F	VF	XF
ND(1752)	—	—	—	—	—	50.00

KM# 481 2 MUN
6.7500 g., Cast Bronze, 27-29 mm. **Obv:** "P'yong" variety I, "T'ong" variety II **Note:** Reduced size.

Date	Mintage	Good	VG	F	VF	XF
ND(1752)	—	3.00	4.00	6.00	10.00	—

KM# 485 2 MUN
6.7500 g., Cast Copper, 27-29 mm. **Obv:** "P'yong" variety I, "T'ong" variety II **Note:** Reduced size.

Date	Mintage	Good	VG	F	VF	XF
ND(1752)	—	3.00	4.00	6.00	10.00	—

KM# 489 2 MUN
6.7500 g., Cast Copper, 27-29 mm. **Obv:** "P'yong" variety I, "T'ong" variety II **Note:** Reduced size.

Date	Mintage	Good	VG	F	VF	XF
ND(1752)	—	3.00	4.00	6.00	10.00	—

KM# 493 2 MUN
6.7500 g., Cast Copper, 27-29 mm. **Obv:** "P'yong" variety I, "T'ong" variety II **Note:** Reduced size.

Date	Mintage	Good	VG	F	VF	XF
ND(1752)	—	3.00	4.00	6.00	10.00	—

KM# 497 2 MUN
6.7500 g., Cast Copper, 27-29 mm. **Obv:** "P'yong" variety I, "T'ong" variety II **Note:** Reduced size.

Date	Mintage	Good	VG	F	VF	XF
ND(1752)	—	3.00	4.00	6.00	10.00	—

KM# 501 2 MUN
6.7500 g., Cast Copper, 27-29 mm. **Obv:** "P'yong" variety I, "T'ong" variety II **Note:** Reduced size.

Date	Mintage	Good	VG	F	VF	XF
ND(1752)	—	3.00	4.00	6.00	10.00	—

KM# 505 2 MUN
6.7500 g., Cast Copper, 27-29 mm. **Obv:** "P'yong" variety I, "T'ong" variety II **Note:** Reduced size.

Date	Mintage	Good	VG	F	VF	XF
ND(1752)	—	3.00	4.00	6.00	10.00	—

KM# 509 2 MUN
6.7500 g., Cast Copper, 27-29 mm. **Obv:** "P'yong" variety I, "T'ong" variety II **Note:** Reduced size.

Date	Mintage	Good	VG	F	VF	XF
ND(1752)	—	3.00	4.00	6.00	10.00	—

KM# 513 2 MUN
6.7500 g., Cast Copper, 27-29 mm. **Obv:** "P'yong" variety I, "T'ong" variety II **Note:** Reduced size.

Date	Mintage	Good	VG	F	VF	XF
ND(1752)	—	3.00	4.00	6.00	10.00	—

KM# 517 2 MUN
6.7500 g., Cast Copper, 27-29 mm. **Obv:** "P'yong" variety I, "T'ong" variety II **Note:** Reduced size.

Date	Mintage	Good	VG	F	VF	XF
ND(1752)	—	3.00	4.00	6.00	10.00	—

KM# 521 2 MUN
6.7500 g., Cast Copper, 27-29 mm. **Obv:** "P'yong" variety I, "T'ong" variety II **Note:** Reduced size.

Date	Mintage	Good	VG	F	VF	XF
ND(1752)	—	3.00	4.00	6.00	10.00	—

KM# 525 2 MUN
6.7500 g., Cast Copper, 27-29 mm. **Obv:** "P'yong" variety I, "T'ong" variety II **Note:** Reduced size.

Date	Mintage	Good	VG	F	VF	XF
ND(1752)	—	3.00	4.00	6.00	10.00	—

KM# 529 2 MUN
6.7500 g., Cast Copper, 27-29 mm. **Obv:** "P'yong" variety I, "T'ong" variety II **Note:** Reduced size.

Date	Mintage	Good	VG	F	VF	XF
ND(1752)	—	3.00	4.00	6.00	10.00	—

KM# 533 2 MUN
6.7500 g., Cast Copper, 27-29 mm. **Obv:** "P'yong" variety I, "T'ong" variety II **Note:** Reduced size.

Date	Mintage	Good	VG	F	VF	XF
ND(1752)	—	3.00	4.00	6.00	10.00	—

KM# 537 2 MUN
6.7500 g., Cast Copper, 27-29 mm. **Obv:** "P'yong" variety I, "T'ong" variety II **Note:** Reduced size.

Date	Mintage	Good	VG	F	VF	XF
ND(1752)	—	3.00	4.00	6.00	10.00	—

KM# 550 2 MUN
6.7500 g., Cast Copper, 27-29 mm. **Rev:** "Ch'on" at bottom, dot at right **Note:** Reduced size.

Date	Mintage	Good	VG	F	VF	XF
ND(1752)	—	8.50	12.50	20.00	30.00	—

KM# 564s 2 MUN
Cast Copper **Note:** Seed type

Date	Mintage	Good	VG	F	VF	XF
ND(1752) Series 11-15	—	—	—	—	—	50.00

KM# 521s 2 MUN
6.7500 g., Cast Copper **Note:** Seed type.

Date	Mintage	Good	VG	F	VF	XF
ND(1752)	—	—	—	—	—	50.00

KM# 561s 2 MUN
Cast Copper **Note:** Seed type.

Date	Mintage	Good	VG	F	VF	XF
ND(1752) Series 1-10	—	—	—	—	—	50.00

KM# 562s 2 MUN
Cast Copper **Note:** Seed type.

Date	Mintage	Good	VG	F	VF	XF
ND(1752) Series 11-15	—	—	—	—	—	50.00

KM# 563s 2 MUN
Cast Copper **Note:** Seed type.

Date	Mintage	Good	VG	F	VF	XF
ND(1752) Series 1-10	—	—	—	—	—	50.00

T'ONGYONG NAVAL OFFICE

(T'ong Yong)

KM# 567 MUN
4.5000 g., Cast Copper **Rev:** "T'ong" at top

Date	Mintage	Good	VG	F	VF	XF
ND(1727) Rare	—	—	—	—	—	—

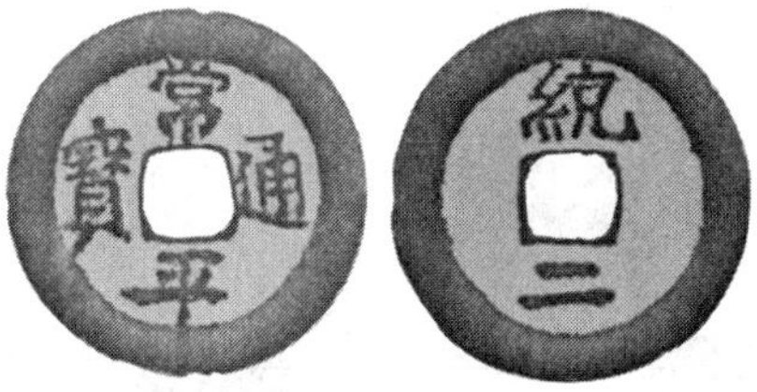

KM# 568 2 MUN
Cast Copper Or Brass, 27-28 mm. **Rev:** "I" (2) at bottom **Note:** Size varies. Weight varies 8.00-9.00 grams.

Date	Mintage	Good	VG	F	VF	XF
ND(1727-42)	—	6.50	12.50	20.00	28.50	—

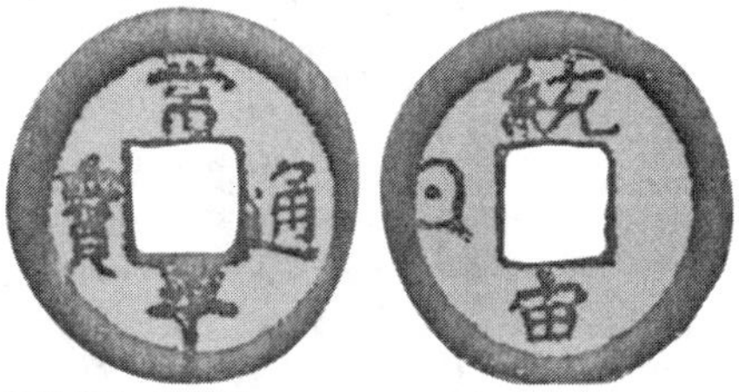

KM# 628 2 MUN
Cast Copper Or Brass, 27-28 mm. **Rev:** "Chu" at bottom, dot in cloud at left **Note:** Size varies. Weight varies 8.00-9.00 grams.

Date	Mintage	Good	VG	F	VF	XF
ND(1742)	—	8.50	12.50	20.00	30.00	—

KM# 629 2 MUN
Cast Copper Or Brass, 27-28 mm. **Obv:** "Large characters, "P'yong" variety I **Rev:** "Ch'on" ast bottom, "Chin" at right **Note:** Size varies. Weight varies 8.00-9.00 grams.

Date	Mintage	Good	VG	F	VF	XF
ND(1742-52)	—	3.00	4.00	6.00	10.00	—

KM# 630 2 MUN
Cast Copper Or Brass, 27-28 mm. **Obv:** "P'yong" variety II **Note:** Size varies. Weight varies 8.00-9.00 grams.

Date	Mintage	Good	VG	F	VF	XF
ND(1742-52)	—	3.00	4.00	6.00	10.00	—

KM# 653 2 MUN
Cast Copper Or Brass **Obv:** Large characters, "P'yong" variety I **Rev:** "Il" at bottom, "Chin" at right **Note:** Size varies 27-28 millimeters. Weight varies 8.00-9.00 grams.

Date	Mintage	Good	VG	F	VF	XF
ND(1742-52)	—	3.50	5.50	7.00	10.00	—

KM# 697 2 MUN
Cast Copper Or Brass **Rev:** "Yol" at bottom, "Kon" at right **Note:** Size varies 27-28 millimeters. Weight varies 8.00-9.00 grams. Struck at T'ong Yong.

Date	Mintage	Good	VG	F	VF	XF
ND(1742-52)	—	4.00	6.00	9.00	15.00	—

KM# 698 2 MUN
Cast Copper Or Brass **Rev:** "Im" at right, series number at bottom **Note:** Size varies 27-28 millimeters. Weight varies 8.00-9.00 grams. Struck at T'ong Yong.

Date	Mintage	Good	VG	F	VF	XF
ND(1742-52) Series 1	—	6.50	10.00	15.00	25.00	—

KM# 573 2 MUN
Cast Copper Or Brass **Note:** Size varies 30-32 millimeters. Weight varies 8.00-9.00 grams. Struck at T'ong Yong.

Date	Mintage	Good	VG	F	VF	XF
ND(1742-52)	—	3.00	4.00	6.00	10.00	—

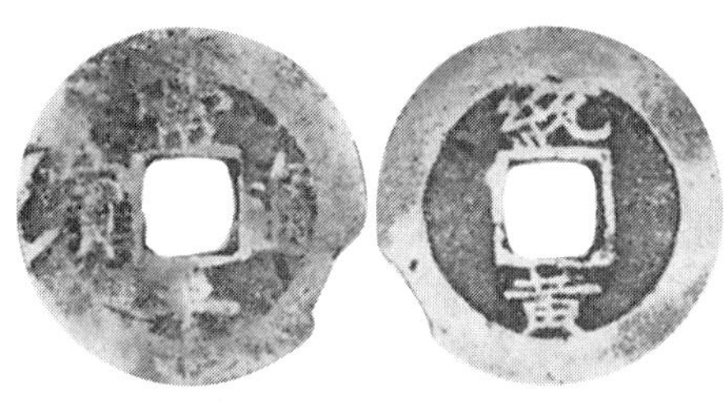

KM# 575 2 MUN

Cast Copper Or Brass **Rev:** "Hwang" (yellow) at bottom **Note:** Size varies 30-32 millimeters. Weight varies 8.00-9.00 grams. Struck at T'ong Yong.

Date	Mintage	Good	VG	F	VF	XF
ND(1742-52)	—	3.00	4.00	6.00	10.00	—

KM# 581 2 MUN

Cast Copper Or Brass **Rev:** "Hong" at bottom **Note:** Size varies 30-32 millimeters. Weight varies 8.00-9.00 grams. Struck at T'ong Yong.

Date	Mintage	Good	VG	F	VF	XF
ND(1742-52)	—	3.00	4.00	6.00	10.00	—

KM# 587 2 MUN

Cast Copper Or Brass **Rev:** "Wol" at bottom **Note:** Size varies 30-32 millimeters. Weight varies 8.00-9.00 grams. Struck at T'ong Yong.

Date	Mintage	Good	VG	F	VF	XF
ND(1742-52)	—	3.00	4.00	6.00	10.00	—

KM# 589 2 MUN

Cast Copper Or Brass **Rev:** "Yong" at bottom **Note:** Size varies 30-32 millimeters. Weight varies 8.00-9.00 grams. Struck at T'ong Yong.

Date	Mintage	Good	VG	F	VF	XF
ND(1742-52)	—	3.00	4.00	6.00	10.00	—

KM# 591 2 MUN

Cast Copper Or Brass **Rev:** "Ch'uk" at bottom **Note:** Size varies 30-32 millimeters. Weight varies 8.00-9.00 grams. Struck at T'ong Yong.

Date	Mintage	Good	VG	F	VF	XF
ND(1742-52)	—	3.00	4.00	6.00	10.00	—

KM# 597 2 MUN

Cast Copper Or Brass **Rev:** "Yol" at bottom **Note:** Size varies 30-32 millimeters. Weight varies 8.00-9.00 grams. Struck at T'ong Yong.

Date	Mintage	Good	VG	F	VF	XF
ND(1742-52)	—	3.00	4.00	6.00	10.00	—

KM# 599 2 MUN

Cast Copper Or Brass **Rev:** "Chang" (extend) at bottom **Note:** Size varies 30-32 millimeters. Weight varies 8.00-9.00 grams. Struck at T'ong Yong.

Date	Mintage	Good	VG	F	VF	XF
ND(1742-52)	—	3.00	4.00	6.00	10.00	—

KM# 603 2 MUN

Cast Copper Or Brass **Rev:** "Nae" at bottom **Note:** Size varies 30-32 millimeters. Weight varies 8.00-9.00 grams. Struck at T'ong Yong.

Date	Mintage	Good	VG	F	VF	XF
ND(1742-52)	—	3.00	4.00	6.00	10.00	—

KM# 609 2 MUN

Cast Copper Or Brass **Rev:** "Ch'u" at bottom **Note:** Size varies 30-32 millimeters. Weight varies 8.00-9.00 grams. Struck at T'ong Yong.

Date	Mintage	Good	VG	F	VF	XF
ND(1742-52)	—	3.00	4.00	6.00	10.00	—

KM# 610 2 MUN

Cast Copper Or Brass **Rev:** "Su" at bottom **Note:** Size varies 30-32 millimeters. Weight varies 8.00-9.00 grams. Struck at T'ong Yong.

Date	Mintage	Good	VG	F	VF	XF
ND(1742-52)	—	3.00	4.00	6.00	10.00	—

KM# 612 2 MUN

Cast Copper Or Brass **Rev:** "Chang" (hoard) at bottom **Note:** Size varies 30-32 millimeters. Weight varies 8.00-9.00 grams. Struck at T'ong Yong.

Date	Mintage	Good	VG	F	VF	XF
ND(1742-52)	—	3.00	4.00	6.00	10.00	—

KM# 617 2 MUN

Cast Copper Or Brass **Rev:** "Chi" at bottom, crescent at left **Note:** Size varies 30-32 millimeters. Weight varies 8.00-9.00 grams. Struck at T'ong Yong.

Date	Mintage	Good	VG	F	VF	XF
ND(1742-52)	—	5.00	8.50	12.50	20.00	—

KM# B621 2 MUN

Cast Copper Or Brass **Rev:** "Hwang" at bottom, crescent at left **Note:** Size varies 30-32 millimeters. Weight varies 8.00-9.00 grams. Struck at T'ong Yong.

Date	Mintage	Good	VG	F	VF	XF
ND(1742-52)	—	5.00	8.50	12.50	20.00	—

KM# B622 2 MUN

Cast Copper Or Brass **Rev:** "Ch'uk" at bottom, crescent at left **Note:** Size varies 30-32 millimeters. Weight varies 8.00-9.00 grams. Struck at T'ong Yong.

Date	Mintage	Good	VG	F	VF	XF
ND(1742-52)	—	5.00	8.50	12.50	20.00	—

KM# 571 2 MUN

Cast Copper Or Brass **Note:** Size varies 30-32 mm. Weight varie 8.00-9.00 grams.

Date	Mintage	Good	VG	F	VF	XF
ND(1742-52)	—	3.00	4.00	6.00	10.00	—

KM# 577 2 MUN

Cast Copper Or Brass **Rev:** "U" at bottom **Note:** Size varies 30-32 mm. Weight varies 8.00-9.00 grams.

Date	Mintage	Good	VG	F	VF	XF
ND(1742-52)	—	3.00	4.00	6.00	10.00	—

KM# 579 2 MUN

Cast Copper Or Brass **Rev:** "Chu" at bottom **Note:** Size varies 30-32 mm. Weight varies 8.00-9.00 grams.

Date	Mintage	Good	VG	F	VF	XF
ND(1742-52)	—	3.00	4.00	6.00	10.00	—

KM# 583 2 MUN

Cast Copper Or Brass **Rev:** "Hwang" (barren) at bottom **Note:** Size varies 30-32 mm. Weight varies 8.00-9.00 grams.

Date	Mintage	Good	VG	F	VF	XF
ND(1742-52)	—	3.00	4.00	6.00	10.00	—

KM# 585 2 MUN

Cast Copper Or Brass **Rev:** "Il" at bottom **Note:** Size varies 30-32 mm. Weight varies 8.00-9.00 grams.

Date	Mintage	Good	VG	F	VF	XF
ND(1742-52)	—	3.00	4.00	6.00	10.00	—

KM# 593 2 MUN

Cast Copper Or Brass **Rev:** "Chin" at bottom **Note:** Size varies 30-32 mm. Weight varies 8.00-9.00 grams.

Date	Mintage	Good	VG	F	VF	XF
ND(1742-52)	—	3.00	4.00	6.00	10.00	—

KM# 595 2 MUN

Cast Copper Or Brass **Rev:** "Suk" at bottom **Note:** Size varies 30-32 mm. Weight varies 8.00-9.00 grams.

Date	Mintage	Good	VG	F	VF	XF
ND(1742-52)	—	3.00	4.00	6.00	10.00	—

KM# 601 2 MUN

Cast Copper Or Brass **Rev:** "Han" at bottom **Note:** Size varies 30-32 mm. Weight varies 8.00-9.00 grams.

Date	Mintage	Good	VG	F	VF	XF
ND(1742-52)	—	3.00	4.00	6.00	10.00	—

KM# 605 2 MUN

Cast Copper Or Brass **Rev:** "So" at bottom **Note:** Size varies 30-32 mm. Weight varies 8.00-9.00 grams.

Date	Mintage	Good	VG	F	VF	XF
ND(1742-52)	—	3.00	4.00	6.00	10.00	—

KM# 607 2 MUN

Cast Copper Or Brass **Rev:** "Wang" at bottom **Note:** Size varies 30-32 mm. Weight varies 8.00-9.00 grams.

Date	Mintage	Good	VG	F	VF	XF
ND(1742-52)	—	3.00	4.00	6.00	10.00	—

KM# 611 2 MUN

Cast Copper Or Brass **Rev:** "Tong" at bottom **Note:** Size varies 30-32 mm. Weight varies 8.00-9.00 grams.

Date	Mintage	Good	VG	F	VF	XF
ND(1742-52)	—	3.00	4.00	6.00	10.00	—

KM# 613 2 MUN

Cast Copper Or Brass **Rev:** "Yun" at bottom **Note:** Size varies 30-32 mm. Weight varies 8.00-9.00 grams.

Date	Mintage	Good	VG	F	VF	XF
ND(1742-52)	—	3.00	4.00	6.00	10.00	—

KM# 614 2 MUN

Cast Copper Or Brass **Rev:** "Yo" at bottom **Note:** Size varies 30-32 mm. Weight varies 8.00-9.00 grams.

Date	Mintage	Good	VG	F	VF	XF
ND(1742-52)	—	3.00	4.00	6.00	10.00	—

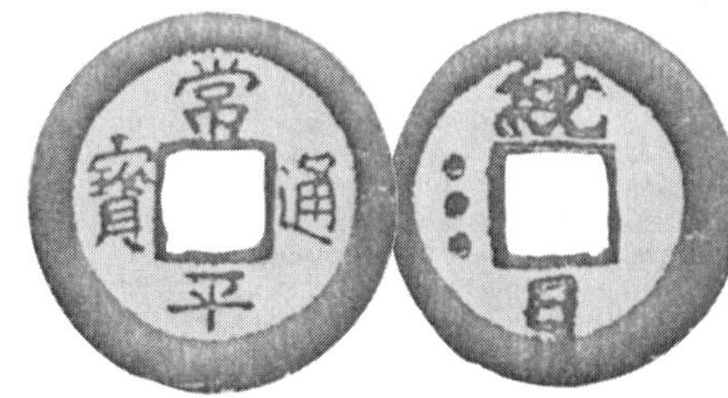

KM# 615 2 MUN

Cast Copper Or Brass **Rev:** "Il" at bottom, three pellets at left **Note:** Size varies 30-32 mm. Weight varies 8.00-9.00 grams.

Date	Mintage	Good	VG	F	VF	XF
ND(1742-52)	—	10.00	15.00	25.00	40.00	—

KM# 616 2 MUN

Cast Copper Or Brass **Rev:** "Ch'on" at bottom, crescent at left **Note:** Size varies 30-32 mm. Weight varies 8.00-9.00 grams.

Date	Mintage	Good	VG	F	VF	XF
ND(1742-52)	—	5.00	8.50	12.50	20.00	—

KM# 618 2 MUN

Cast Copper Or Brass **Rev:** "Hyon" at bottom, crescent at left **Note:** Size varies 30-32 mm. Weight varies 8.00-9.00 grams.

Date	Mintage	Good	VG	F	VF	XF
ND(1742-52)	—	5.00	8.50	12.50	20.00	—

KM# 619 2 MUN

Cast Copper Or Brass **Rev:** "Hwang" (yellow) at bottom, crescent at left **Note:** Size varies 30-32 mm. Weight varies 8.00-9.00 grams.

Date	Mintage	Good	VG	F	VF	XF
ND(1742-52)	—	5.00	8.50	12.50	20.00	—

KM# 620 2 MUN

Cast Copper Or Brass **Rev:** "U" at bottom, crescent at left **Note:** Size varies 30-32 mm. Weight varies 8.00-9.00 grams.

Date	Mintage	Good	VG	F	VF	XF
ND(1742-52)	—	5.00	8.50	12.50	20.00	—

KM# 621 2 MUN

Cast Copper Or Brass **Rev:** "Chu" at bottom, crescent at left **Note:** Size varies 30-32 mm. Weight varies 8.00-9.00 grams.

Date	Mintage	Good	VG	F	VF	XF
ND(1742-52)	—	5.00	8.50	12.50	20.00	—

KM# A621 2 MUN

Cast Copper Or Brass **Rev:** "Hong" at bottom, crescent at left **Note:** Size varies 30-32 mm. Weight varies 8.00-9.00 grams.

Date	Mintage	Good	VG	F	VF	XF
ND(1742-52)	—	5.00	8.50	12.50	20.00	—

KM# C621 2 MUN

Cast Copper Or Brass **Rev:** "Il" at bottom, crescent at left **Note:** Size varies 30-32 mm. Weight varies 8.00-9.00 grams.

Date	Mintage	Good	VG	F	VF	XF
ND(1742-52)	—	5.00	8.50	12.50	20.00	—

KM# 622 2 MUN

Cast Copper Or Brass **Rev:** "Wol" at bottom, crescent at left **Note:** Size varies 30-32 mm. Weight varies 8.00-9.00 grams.

Date	Mintage	Good	VG	F	VF	XF
ND(1742-52)	—	5.00	8.50	12.50	20.00	—

KM# A622 2 MUN

Cast Copper Or Brass **Rev:** "Yong" at bottom, crescent at left **Note:** Size varies 30-32 mm. Weight varies 8.00-9.00 grams.

Date	Mintage	Good	VG	F	VF	XF
ND(1742-52)	—	5.00	8.50	12.50	20.00	—

KM# 623 2 MUN

Cast Copper Or Brass **Rev:** "Chin" at bottom, crescent at left **Note:** Size varies 30-32 mm. Weight varies 8.00-9.00 grams.

Date	Mintage	Good	VG	F	VF	XF
ND(1742-52)	—	5.00	8.50	12.50	20.00	—

KM# 624 2 MUN

Cast Copper Or Brass **Rev:** "Yol" at bottom, crescent at left **Note:** Size varies 30-32 mm. Weight varies 8.00-9.00 grams.

Date	Mintage	Good	VG	F	VF	XF
ND(1742-52)	—	5.00	8.50	12.50	20.00	—

KM# 625 2 MUN

Cast Copper Or Brass **Rev:** "Hwang" (barren) at bottom, cloud form at left **Note:** Size varies 30-32 mm. Weight varies 8.00-9.00 grams.

Date	Mintage	Good	VG	F	VF	XF
ND(1742-52)	—	8.50	12.50	20.00	30.00	—

KM# 626 2 MUN

Cast Copper Or Brass **Rev:** "Ch'on" at bottom, dot in crescent at left **Note:** Size varies 30-32 mm. Weight varies 8.00-9.00 grams.

Date	Mintage	Good	VG	F	VF	XF
ND(1742-52)	—	5.00	8.50	12.50	20.00	—

KM# 627 2 MUN

Cast Copper Or Brass **Rev:** "Ch'on" at bottom, dot at right, dot in crescent below circle at left **Note:** Size varies 30-32 mm. Weight varies 8.00-9.00 grams.

Date	Mintage	Good	VG	F	VF	XF
ND(1742)	—	5.00	8.50	12.50	20.00	—

KM# 631 2 MUN

Cast Copper Or Brass **Obv:** Small characters, "Po" in different style **Note:** Size varies 27-28 mm. Weight varies 8.00-9.00 grams.

Date	Mintage	Good	VG	F	VF	XF
ND(1742-52)	—	3.50	5.50	7.00	10.00	—

KM# 632 2 MUN

Cast Copper Or Brass **Obv:** Large characters, "P'yong" variety I **Rev:** "Chi" at bottom, "Chin" at right **Note:** Size varies 27-28 mm. Weight varies 8.00-9.00 grams.

Date	Mintage	Good	VG	F	VF	XF
ND(1742-52)	—	3.50	5.50	7.00	10.00	—

KM# 633 2 MUN
Cast Copper Or Brass **Obv:** “P'yong” variety II **Note:** Size varies 27-28 mm. Weight varies 8.00-9.00 grams.

Date	Mintage	Good	VG	F	VF	XF
ND(1742-52)	—	3.50	5.50	7.00	10.00	—

KM# 634 2 MUN
Cast Copper Or Brass **Obv:** Small characters, “Po” in different style **Note:** Size varies 27-28 mm. Weight varies 8.00-9.00 grams.

Date	Mintage	Good	VG	F	VF	XF
ND(1742-52)	—	3.50	5.50	7.00	10.00	—

KM# 635 2 MUN
Cast Copper Or Brass **Obv:** Large characters, “P'yong” variety I **Rev:** “Hyon” at bottom, “Chin” at right **Note:** Size varies 27-28 mm. Weight varies 8.00-9.00 grams.

Date	Mintage	Good	VG	F	VF	XF
ND(1742-52)	—	3.50	5.50	7.00	10.00	—

KM# 636 2 MUN
Cast Copper Or Brass **Obv:** “P'yong” variety II **Note:** Size varies 27-28 mm. Weight varies 8.00-9.00 grams.

Date	Mintage	Good	VG	F	VF	XF
ND(1742-52)	—	3.50	5.50	7.00	10.00	—

KM# 637 2 MUN
Cast Copper Or Brass **Obv:** Small characters, “Po” in different style **Note:** Size varies 27-28 mm. Weight varies 8.00-9.00 grams.

Date	Mintage	Good	VG	F	VF	XF
ND(1742-52)	—	3.50	5.50	7.00	10.00	—

KM# 638 2 MUN
Cast Copper Or Brass **Obv:** Large characters, “P'yong” variety I **Rev:** “Hwang” (yellow) at bottom, “Chin” at right **Note:** Size varies 27-28 mm. Weight varies 8.00-9.00 grams.

Date	Mintage	Good	VG	F	VF	XF
ND(1742-52)	—	3.50	5.50	7.00	10.00	—

KM# 639 2 MUN
Cast Copper Or Brass **Obv:** “P'yong” variety II **Note:** Size varies 27-28 mm. Weight varies 8.00-9.00 grams.

Date	Mintage	Good	VG	F	VF	XF
ND(1742-52)	—	3.50	5.50	7.00	10.00	—

KM# 640 2 MUN
Cast Copper Or Brass **Obv:** Small characters, “Po” in different style **Note:** Size varies 27-28 mm. Weight varies 8.00-9.00 grams.

Date	Mintage	Good	VG	F	VF	XF
ND(1742-52)	—	3.50	5.50	7.00	10.00	—

KM# 641 2 MUN
Cast Copper Or Brass **Obv:** Large characters, “P'yong” variety I **Rev:** “U” at bottom, “Chin” at right **Note:** Size varies 27-28 mm. Weight varies 8.00-9.00 grams.

Date	Mintage	Good	VG	F	VF	XF
ND(1742-52)	—	3.50	5.50	7.00	10.00	—

KM# 642 2 MUN
Cast Copper Or Brass **Obv:** “P'yong” variety II **Note:** Size varies 27-28 mm. Weight varies 8.00-9.00 grams.

Date	Mintage	Good	VG	F	VF	XF
ND(1742-52)	—	3.50	5.50	7.00	10.00	—

KM# 643 2 MUN
Cast Copper Or Brass **Obv:** Small characters, “Po” in different style **Note:** Size varies 27-28 mm. Weight varies 8.00-9.00 grams.

Date	Mintage	Good	VG	F	VF	XF
ND(1742-52)	—	3.50	5.50	7.00	10.00	—

KM# 644 2 MUN
Cast Copper Or Brass **Obv:** Large characters, “P'yong” variety I **Rev:** “Chu” at bottom, “Chin” at right **Note:** Size varies 27-28 mm. Weight varies 8.00-9.00 grams.

Date	Mintage	Good	VG	F	VF	XF
ND(1742-62)	—	3.50	5.50	7.00	10.00	—

KM# 645 2 MUN
Cast Copper Or Brass **Obv:** “P'yong” variety II **Note:** Size varies 27-28 mm. Weight varies 8.00-9.00 grams.

Date	Mintage	Good	VG	F	VF	XF
ND(1742-52)	—	3.50	5.50	7.00	10.00	—

KM# 646 2 MUN
Cast Copper Or Brass **Obv:** Small characters, “Po” in different style **Note:** Size varies 27-28 mm. Weight varies 8.00-9.00 grams.

Date	Mintage	Good	VG	F	VF	XF
ND(1742-52)	—	3.50	5.50	7.00	10.00	—

KM# 647 2 MUN
Cast Copper Or Brass **Obv:** Large characters, “P'yong” variety I **Rev:** “Hong” at bottom, “Chin” at right **Note:** Size varies 27-28 mm. Weight varies 8.00-9.00 grams.

Date	Mintage	Good	VG	F	VF	XF
ND(1742-52)	—	3.50	5.50	7.00	10.00	—

KM# 648 2 MUN
Cast Copper Or Brass **Obv:** “P'yong” variety II **Note:** Size varies 27-28 mm. Weight varies 8.00-9.00 grams.

Date	Mintage	Good	VG	F	VF	XF
ND(1742-52)	—	3.50	5.50	7.00	10.00	—

KM# 649 2 MUN
Cast Copper Or Brass **Obv:** Small characters, “Po” in different style **Note:** Size varies 27-28 mm. Weight varies 8.00-9.00 grams.

Date	Mintage	Good	VG	F	VF	XF
ND(1742-52)	—	3.50	5.50	7.00	10.00	—

KM# 650 2 MUN
Cast Copper Or Brass **Obv:** Large characters, “P'yong” variety I **Rev:** “Hwang” (barren) at bottom, “Chin” at right **Note:** Size varies 27-28 mm. Weight varies 8.00-9.00 grams.

Date	Mintage	Good	VG	F	VF	XF
ND(1742-52)	—	3.50	5.50	7.00	10.00	—

KM# 651 2 MUN
Cast Copper Or Brass **Obv:** “P'yong” variety II **Note:** Size varies 27-28 mm. Weight varies 8.00-9.00 grams.

Date	Mintage	Good	VG	F	VF	XF
ND(1742-52)	—	3.50	5.50	7.00	10.00	—

KM# 652 2 MUN
Cast Copper Or Brass **Obv:** Small characters, “Po” in different style **Note:** Size varies 27-28 mm. Weight varies 8.00-9.00 grams.

Date	Mintage	Good	VG	F	VF	XF
ND(1742-52)	—	3.50	5.50	7.00	10.00	—

KM# 654 2 MUN
Cast Copper Or Brass **Obv:** “P'yong” variety II **Note:** Size varies 27-28 mm. Weight varies 8.00-9.00 grams.

Date	Mintage	Good	VG	F	VF	XF
ND(1742-52)	—	3.50	5.50	7.00	10.00	—

KM# 655 2 MUN
Cast Copper Or Brass **Obv:** Small characters, “Po” in different style **Note:** Size varies 27-28 mm. Weight varies 8.00-9.00 grams.

Date	Mintage	Good	VG	F	VF	XF
ND(1742-52)	—	3.50	5.50	7.00	10.00	—

KM# 656 2 MUN
Cast Copper Or Brass **Obv:** Large characters, “P'yong” variety I **Rev:** “Wol” at bottom, “Chin” at right **Note:** Size varies 27-28 mm. Weight varies 8.00-9.00 grams.

Date	Mintage	Good	VG	F	VF	XF
ND(1742-52)	—	3.50	5.50	7.00	10.00	—

KM# 657 2 MUN
Cast Copper Or Brass **Obv:** “P'yong” variety II **Note:** Size varies 27-28 mm. Weight varies 8.00-9.00 grams.

Date	Mintage	Good	VG	F	VF	XF
ND(1742-52)	—	3.50	5.50	7.00	10.00	—

KM# A657 2 MUN
Cast Copper Or Brass **Obv:** Small characters, “Wol” in different style **Note:** Size varies 27-28 mm. Weight varies 8.00-9.00 grams.

Date	Mintage	Good	VG	F	VF	XF
ND(1742-52)	—	3.50	5.50	7.00	10.00	—

KM# 658 2 MUN
Cast Copper Or Brass **Obv:** “P'yong” variety I **Rev:** “Yong” at bottom, “Chin” at right **Note:** Size varies 27-28 mm. Weight varies 8.00-9.00 grams.

Date	Mintage	Good	VG	F	VF	XF
ND(1742-52)	—	3.00	4.00	6.00	10.00	—

KM# 659 2 MUN
Cast Copper Or Brass **Obv:** “P'yong” variety II **Note:** Size varies 27-28 mm. Weight varies 8.00-9.00 grams.

Date	Mintage	Good	VG	F	VF	XF
ND(1742-52)	—	3.00	4.00	6.00	10.00	—

KM# 660 2 MUN
Cast Copper Or Brass **Obv:** “P'yong” variety I **Rev:** “Ch'uk” at bottom, “Chin” at right **Note:** Size varies 27-28 mm. Weight varies 8.00-9.00 grams.

Date	Mintage	Good	VG	F	VF	XF
ND(1742-52)	—	3.00	4.00	6.00	10.00	—

KM# 661 2 MUN
Cast Copper Or Brass **Obv:** “P'yong” variety II **Note:** Size varies 27-28 mm. Weight varies 8.00-9.00 grams.

Date	Mintage	Good	VG	F	VF	XF
ND(1742-52)	—	3.00	4.00	6.00	10.00	—

KM# 662 2 MUN
Cast Copper Or Brass **Obv:** “P'yong” variety I **Rev:** “Chin” at bottom, “Chin” at right **Note:** Size varies 27-28 mm. Weight varies 8.00-9.00 grams.

Date	Mintage	Good	VG	F	VF	XF
ND(1742-52)	—	3.00	4.00	6.00	10.00	—

KM# 663 2 MUN
Cast Copper Or Brass **Obv:** “P'yong” variety II **Note:** Size varies 27-28 mm. Weight varies 8.00-9.00 grams.

Date	Mintage	Good	VG	F	VF	XF
ND(1742-52)	—	3.00	4.00	6.00	10.00	—

KM# 664 2 MUN
Cast Copper Or Brass **Obv:** “P'yong” variety I **Rev:** “Suk” at bottom, “Chin” at right **Note:** Size varies 27-28 mm. Weight varies 8.00-9.00 grams.

Date	Mintage	Good	VG	F	VF	XF
ND(1742-52)	—	3.00	4.00	6.00	10.00	—

KM# 665 2 MUN
Cast Copper Or Brass **Obv:** “P'yong” variety II **Note:** Size varies 27-28 mm. Weight varies 8.00-9.00 grams.

Date	Mintage	Good	VG	F	VF	XF
ND(1742-52)	—	3.00	4.00	6.00	10.00	—

KM# 666 2 MUN
Cast Copper Or Brass **Obv:** “P'yong” variety I **Rev:** “Yol” at bottom, “Chin” at right **Note:** Size varies 27-28 mm. Weight varies 8.00-9.00 grams.

Date	Mintage	Good	VG	F	VF	XF
ND(1742-52)	—	3.00	4.00	6.00	10.00	—

KM# 667 2 MUN
Cast Copper Or Brass **Obv:** “P'yong” variety II **Note:** Size varies 27-28 mm. Weight varies 8.00-9.00 grams.

Date	Mintage	Good	VG	F	VF	XF
ND(1742-52)	—	3.00	4.00	6.00	10.00	—

KM# 668 2 MUN
Cast Copper Or Brass **Obv:** “P'yong” variety I **Rev:** “Chang” (extend) at bottom, “Chin” at right **Note:** Size varies 27-28 mm. Weight varies 8.00-9.00 grams.

Date	Mintage	Good	VG	F	VF	XF
ND(1742-52)	—	4.00	6.00	8.00	12.00	—

KM# 669 2 MUN
Cast Copper Or Brass **Obv:** “P'yong” variety II **Note:** Size varies 27-28 mm. Weight varies 8.00-9.00 grams.

Date	Mintage	Good	VG	F	VF	XF
ND(1742-52)	—	4.00	6.00	8.00	12.00	—

KM# 670 2 MUN
Cast Copper Or Brass **Obv:** “P'yong” variety I **Rev:** “Han” at bottom, “Chin” at right **Note:** Size varies 27-28 mm. Weight varies 8.00-9.00 grams.

Date	Mintage	Good	VG	F	VF	XF
ND(1742-52)	—	3.00	4.00	6.00	10.00	—

KM# 671 2 MUN
Cast Copper Or Brass **Obv:** “P'yong” variety II **Note:** Size varies 27-28 mm. Weight varies 8.00-9.00 grams.

Date	Mintage	Good	VG	F	VF	XF
ND(1742-52)	—	3.00	4.00	6.00	10.00	—

KM# 672 2 MUN
Cast Copper Or Brass **Obv:** “P'yong” variety I **Rev:** “Nae” at bottom, “Chin” at right **Note:** Size varies 27-28 mm. Weight varies 8.00-9.00 grams.

Date	Mintage	Good	VG	F	VF	XF
ND(1742-52)	—	3.00	4.00	6.00	10.00	—

KM# 673 2 MUN
Cast Copper Or Brass **Obv:** “P'yong” variety II **Note:** Size varies 27-28 mm. Weight varies 8.00-9.00 grams.

Date	Mintage	Good	VG	F	VF	XF
ND(1742-52)	—	3.00	4.00	6.00	10.00	—

KM# 674 2 MUN
Cast Copper Or Brass **Obv:** “P'yong” variety I **Rev:** “So” at bottom, “Chin” at right **Note:** Size varies 27-28 mm. Weight varies 8.00-9.00 grams.

Date	Mintage	Good	VG	F	VF	XF
ND(1742-52)	—	4.00	6.00	8.00	12.00	—

KM# 675 2 MUN
Cast Copper Or Brass **Obv:** “P'yong” variety II **Note:** Size varies 27-28 mm. Weight varies 8.00-9.00 grams.

Date	Mintage	Good	VG	F	VF	XF
ND(1742-52)	—	4.00	6.00	8.00	12.00	—

KM# 676 2 MUN
Cast Copper Or Brass **Obv:** “P'yong” variety I **Rev:** “Wang” at bottom, “Chin” at right **Note:** Size varies 27-28 mm. Weight varies 8.00-9.00 grams.

Date	Mintage	Good	VG	F	VF	XF
ND(1742-52)	—	3.00	4.00	6.00	10.00	—

KM# 677 2 MUN
Cast Copper Or Brass **Obv:** “P'yong” variety II **Note:** Size varies 27-28 mm. Weight varies 8.00-9.00 grams.

Date	Mintage	Good	VG	F	VF	XF
ND(1742-52)	—	3.00	4.00	6.00	10.00	—

KM# 678 2 MUN
Cast Copper Or Brass **Obv:** “P'yong” variety I **Rev:** “Ch'u” at bottom, “Chin” at right **Note:** Size varies 27-28 mm. Weight varies 8.00-9.00 grams.

Date	Mintage	Good	VG	F	VF	XF
ND(1742-52)	—	3.00	4.00	6.00	10.00	—

KM# 679 2 MUN
Cast Copper Or Brass **Obv:** “P'yong” variety II **Note:** Size varies 27-28 mm. Weight varies 8.00-9.00 grams.

Date	Mintage	Good	VG	F	VF	XF
ND(1742-52)	—	3.00	4.00	6.00	10.00	—

KM# 680 2 MUN
Cast Copper Or Brass **Obv:** “P'yong” variety I **Rev:** “Su” at bottom, “Chin” at right **Note:** Size varies 27-28 mm. Weight varies 8.00-9.00 grams.

Date	Mintage	Good	VG	F	VF	XF
ND(1742-52)	—	3.00	4.00	6.00	10.00	—

KM# 681 2 MUN
Cast Copper Or Brass **Obv:** “P'yong” variety II **Note:** Size varies 27-28 mm. Weight varies 8.00-9.00 grams.

Date	Mintage	Good	VG	F	VF	XF
ND(1742-52)	—	3.00	4.00	6.00	10.00	—

KM# 682 2 MUN

Cast Copper Or Brass **Rev:** "Yol" at bottom, "Chin" at right, crescent at left **Note:** Size varies 27-28 mm. Weight varies 8.00-9.00 grams.

Date	Mintage	Good	VG	F	VF	XF
ND(1742-52)	—	3.00	4.00	6.00	10.00	—

KM# 683 2 MUN

Cast Copper Or Brass **Rev:** "Chon" at bottom, "Kon" at right **Note:** Size varies 27-28 mm. Weight varies 8.00-9.00 grams.

Date	Mintage	Good	VG	F	VF	XF
ND(1742-52)	—	4.00	6.00	9.00	15.00	—

KM# 684 2 MUN

Cast Copper Or Brass **Rev:** "Chi" at bottom, "Kon" at right **Note:** Size varies 27-28 mm. Weight varies 8.00-9.00 grams.

Date	Mintage	Good	VG	F	VF	XF
ND(1742-52)	—	4.00	6.00	9.00	15.00	—

KM# 685 2 MUN

Cast Copper Or Brass **Rev:** "Hyon" at bottom, "Kon" at right **Note:** Size varies 27-28 mm. Weight varies 8.00-9.00 grams.

Date	Mintage	Good	VG	F	VF	XF
ND(1742-52)	—	4.00	6.00	9.00	15.00	—

KM# 686 2 MUN

Cast Copper Or Brass **Rev:** "Hwang" (yellow) at bottom, "Kon" at right **Note:** Size varies 27-28 mm. Weight varies 8.00-9.00 grams.

Date	Mintage	Good	VG	F	VF	XF
ND(1742-52)	—	4.00	6.00	9.00	15.00	—

KM# 687 2 MUN

Cast Copper Or Brass **Rev:** "U" at bottom, "Kon" at right **Note:** Size varies 27-28 mm. Weight varies 8.00-9.00 grams.

Date	Mintage	Good	VG	F	VF	XF
ND(1742-52)	—	4.00	6.00	9.00	15.00	—

KM# 688 2 MUN

Cast Copper Or Brass **Rev:** "Chu" at bottom, "Kon" at right **Note:** Size varies 27-28 mm. Weight varies 8.00-9.00 grams.

Date	Mintage	Good	VG	F	VF	XF
ND(1742-52)	—	4.00	6.00	9.00	15.00	—

KM# 689 2 MUN

Cast Copper Or Brass **Rev:** "Hong" at bottom, "Kon" at right **Note:** Size varies 27-28 mm. Weight varies 8.00-9.00 grams.

Date	Mintage	Good	VG	F	VF	XF
ND(1742-52)	—	4.00	6.00	9.00	15.00	—

KM# 690 2 MUN

Cast Copper Or Brass **Rev:** "Hwang" (barren) at bottom, "Kon" at right **Note:** Size varies 27-28 mm. Weight varies 8.00-9.00 grams.

Date	Mintage	Good	VG	F	VF	XF
ND(1742-52)	—	4.00	6.00	9.00	15.00	—

KM# 691 2 MUN

Cast Copper Or Brass **Rev:** "Il" at bottom, "Kon" at right **Note:** Size varies 27-28 mm. Weight varies 8.00-9.00 grams.

Date	Mintage	Good	VG	F	VF	XF
ND(1742-52)	—	4.00	6.00	9.00	15.00	—

KM# 692 2 MUN

Cast Copper Or Brass **Rev:** "Wol" at bottom, "Kon" at right **Note:** Size varies 27-28 mm. Weight varies 8.00-9.00 grams.

Date	Mintage	Good	VG	F	VF	XF
ND(1742-52)	—	4.00	6.00	9.00	15.00	—

KM# 693 2 MUN

Cast Copper Or Brass **Rev:** "Yong" at bottom, "Kon" at right **Note:** Size varies 27-28 mm. Weight varies 8.00-9.00 grams.

Date	Mintage	Good	VG	F	VF	XF
ND(1742-52)	—	4.00	6.00	9.00	15.00	—

KM# 694 2 MUN

Cast Copper Or Brass **Rev:** "Ch'uk" at bottom, "Kon" at right **Note:** Size varies 27-28 mm. Weight varies 8.00-9.00 grams.

Date	Mintage	Good	VG	F	VF	XF
ND(1742-52)	—	4.00	6.00	9.00	15.00	—

KM# 695 2 MUN

Cast Copper Or Brass **Rev:** "Chin" at bottom, "Kon" at right **Note:** Size varies 27-28 mm. Weight varies 8.00-9.00 grams.

Date	Mintage	Good	VG	F	VF	XF
ND(1742-52)	—	4.00	6.00	9.00	15.00	—

KM# 696 2 MUN

Cast Copper Or Brass **Rev:** "Suk" at bottom, "Kon" at right **Note:** Size varies 27-28 mm. Weight varies 8.00-9.00 grams.

Date	Mintage	Good	VG	F	VF	XF
ND(1742-52)	—	4.00	6.00	9.00	15.00	—

KM# 700 2 MUN

Cast Copper Or Brass **Rev:** "Chon" at bottom, "Im" at right **Note:** Size varies 27-28 mm. Weight varies 8.00-9.00 grams.

Date	Mintage	Good	VG	F	VF	XF
ND(1752)	—	3.50	5.50	8.50	12.50	—

KM# A700 2 MUN

Cast Copper Or Brass **Rev:** "Chi" at bottom, "Im" at right **Note:** Size varies 27-28 mm. Weight varies 8.00-9.00 grams.

Date	Mintage	Good	VG	F	VF	XF
ND(1752)	—	3.00	5.50	8.50	12.50	—

KM# 701 2 MUN

Cast Copper Or Brass **Rev:** "Chu" at bottom, "Im" at right **Note:** Size varies 27-28 mm. Weight varies 8.00-9.00 grams.

Date	Mintage	Good	VG	F	VF	XF
ND(1752)	—	3.50	5.50	8.50	12.50	—

KM# A701 2 MUN

Cast Copper Or Brass **Rev:** "Hong" at bottom, "Im" at right **Note:** Size varies 27-28 mm. Weight varies 8.00-9.00 grams.

Date	Mintage	Good	VG	F	VF	XF
ND(1752)	—	3.50	5.50	8.50	12.50	—

KM# D701 2 MUN

Cast Copper Or Brass **Rev:** "Wol" at bottom, "Im" at right **Note:** Size varies 27-28 mm. Weight varies 8.00-9.00 grams.

Date	Mintage	Good	VG	F	VF	XF
ND(1752)	—	3.50	5.50	8.50	12.50	—

KM# E701 2 MUN

Cast Copper Or Brass **Rev:** "Yong" at bottom, "Im" at right **Note:** Size varies 27-28 mm. Weight varies 8.00-9.00 grams.

Date	Mintage	Good	VG	F	VF	XF
ND(1752)	—	3.50	5.50	8.50	12.50	—

KM# F701 2 MUN

Cast Copper Or Brass **Rev:** "Ch'uk" at bottom, "Im" at right **Note:** Size varies 27-28 mm. Weight varies 8.00-9.00 grams.

Date	Mintage	Good	VG	F	VF	XF
ND(1752)	—	3.50	5.50	8.50	12.50	—

KM# G701 2 MUN

Cast Copper Or Brass **Rev:** "Chin" at bottom, "Im" at right **Note:** Size varies 27-28 mm. Weight varies 8.00-9.00 grams.

Date	Mintage	Good	VG	F	VF	XF
ND(1752)	—	3.50	5.50	8.50	12.50	—

KM# 702 2 MUN

Cast Copper Or Brass **Rev:** "Han" at bottom, "Im" at right **Note:** Size varies 27-28 mm. Weight varies 8.00-9.00 grams.

Date	Mintage	Good	VG	F	VF	XF
ND(1752)	—	3.50	5.50	8.50	12.50	—

KM# 702a 2 MUN

Cast Copper Or Brass **Obv:** "P'yong" without hooks **Note:** Size varies 27-28 mm. Weight varies 8.00-9.00 grams.

Date	Mintage	Good	VG	F	VF	XF
ND(1752)	—	3.50	5.50	8.50	12.50	—

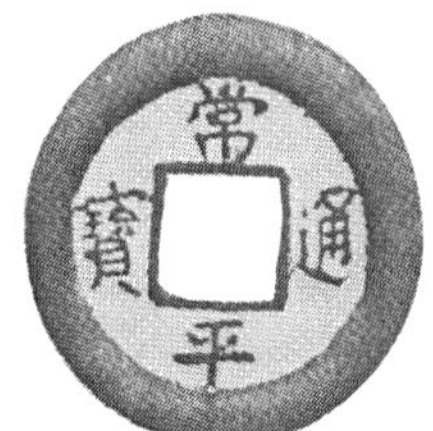

KM# 703 2 MUN

Cast Copper Or Brass **Rev:** "Nae" at bottom, "Im" at right **Note:** Size varies 27-28 mm. Weight varies 8.00-9.00 grams.

Date	Mintage	Good	VG	F	VF	XF
ND(1752)	—	3.50	5.50	8.50	12.50	—

KM# 706 2 MUN

Cast Copper Or Brass **Rev:** "Ch'u" at bottom, "Im" at right **Note:** Size varies 27-28 mm. Weight varies 8.00-9.00 grams.

Date	Mintage	Good	VG	F	VF	XF
ND(1752)	—	3.50	5.50	8.50	12.50	—

KM# 707 2 MUN

Cast Copper Or Brass **Rev:** "Su" at bottom, "Im" at right **Note:** Size varies 27-28 mm. Weight varies 8.00-9.00 grams.

Date	Mintage	Good	VG	F	VF	XF
ND(1752)	—	3.50	5.50	8.50	12.50	—

KM# 708 2 MUN

Cast Copper Or Brass **Rev:** "Tong" at bottom, "Im" at right **Note:** Size varies 27-28 mm. Weight varies 8.00-9.00 grams.

Date	Mintage	Good	VG	F	VF	XF
ND(1752)	—	3.50	5.50	8.50	12.50	—

KM# 709 2 MUN

Cast Copper Or Brass **Rev:** "Chang" (hoard) at bottom, "Im" at right **Note:** Size varies 27-28 mm. Weight varies 8.00-9.00 grams.

Date	Mintage	Good	VG	F	VF	XF
ND(1752)	—	3.50	5.50	8.50	12.50	—

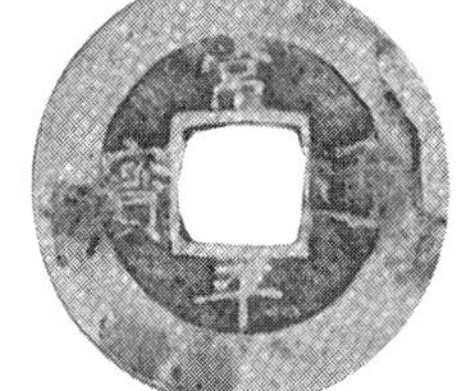

KM# 710 2 MUN

Cast Copper Or Brass **Rev:** "Yun" at bottom, "Im" at right **Note:** Size varies 27-28 mm. Weight varies 8.00-9.00 grams.

Date	Mintage	Good	VG	F	VF	XF
ND(1752)	—	3.50	5.50	8.50	12.50	—

KM# 711 2 MUN

Cast Copper Or Brass **Rev:** "Yo" (surplus) at bottom, "Im" at right **Note:** Size varies 27-28 mm. Weight varies 8.00-9.00 grams.

Date	Mintage	Good	VG	F	VF	XF
ND(1752)	—	3.50	5.50	8.50	12.50	—

KM# 712 2 MUN

Cast Copper Or Brass **Rev:** "Song" at bottom, "Im" at right **Note:** Size varies 27-28 mm. Weight varies 8.00-9.00 grams.

Date	Mintage	Good	VG	F	VF	XF
ND(1752)	—	3.50	5.50	8.50	12.50	—

KM# 712a 2 MUN

Cast Copper Or Brass **Obv:** "P'yong" without hooks **Note:** Size varies 27-28 mm. Weight varies 8.00-9.00 grams.

Date	Mintage	Good	VG	F	VF	XF
ND(1752)	—	3.50	5.50	8.50	12.50	—

KM# 713 2 MUN

Cast Copper Or Brass **Rev:** "Se" at bottom, "Im" at right **Note:** Size varies 27-28 mm. Weight varies 8.00-9.00 grams.

Date	Mintage	Good	VG	F	VF	XF
ND(1752)	—	3.50	5.50	8.50	12.50	—

KM# 713a 2 MUN

Cast Copper Or Brass **Obv:** "P'yong" without hooks **Note:** Size varies 27-28 mm. Weight varies 8.00-9.00 grams.

Date	Mintage	Good	VG	F	VF	XF
ND(1752)	—	3.50	5.50	8.50	12.50	—

KM# 714 2 MUN

Cast Copper Or Brass **Rev:** "Yul" at bottom, "Im" at right **Note:** Size varies 27-28 mm. Weight varies 8.00-9.00 grams.

Date	Mintage	Good	VG	F	VF	XF
ND(1752)	—	3.50	5.50	8.50	12.50	—

KM# 716 2 MUN

Cast Copper Or Brass **Rev:** "Ch'on" at bottom, "Im" at left **Note:** Size varies 27-28 mm. Weight varies 8.00-9.00 grams.

Date	Mintage	Good	VG	F	VF	XF
ND(1752)	—	3.00	4.00	6.00	10.00	—

KM# 717 2 MUN

Cast Copper Or Brass **Rev:** "Chi" at bottom, "Im" at left **Note:** Size varies 27-28 mm. Weight varies 8.00-9.00 grams.

Date	Mintage	Good	VG	F	VF	XF
ND(1752)	—	3.00	4.00	6.00	10.00	—

KM# 718 2 MUN

Cast Copper Or Brass **Rev:** "Hyon" at bottom, "Im" at left **Note:** Size varies 27-28 mm. Weight varies 8.00-9.00 grams.

Date	Mintage	Good	VG	F	VF	XF
ND(1752)	—	3.00	4.00	6.00	10.00	—

KM# 719 2 MUN

Cast Copper Or Brass **Rev:** "Hwang" (yellow) at bottom, "Im" at left **Note:** Size varies 27-28 mm. Weight varies 8.00-9.00 grams.

Date	Mintage	Good	VG	F	VF	XF
ND(1752)	—	3.00	4.00	6.00	10.00	—

KM# 720 2 MUN

Cast Copper Or Brass **Rev:** "U" at bottom, "Im" at left **Note:** Size varies 27-28 mm. Weight varies 8.00-9.00 grams.

Date	Mintage	Good	VG	F	VF	XF
ND(1752)	—	3.00	4.00	6.00	10.00	—

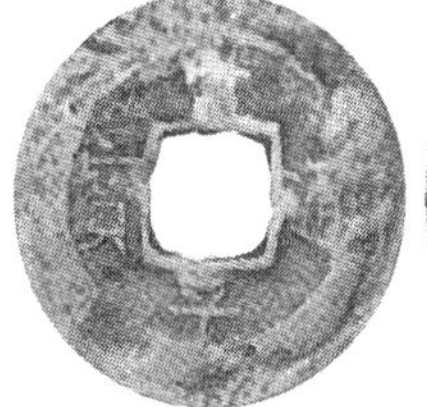

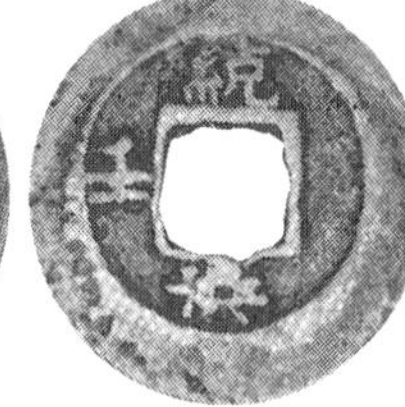

KM# 721 2 MUN

Cast Copper Or Brass **Rev:** "Hong" at bottom, "Im" at left **Note:** Size varies 27-28 mm. Weight varies 8.00-9.00 grams.

Date	Mintage	Good	VG	F	VF	XF
ND(1752)	—	3.00	4.00	6.00	10.00	—

KM# 722 2 MUN

Cast Copper Or Brass **Rev:** "Hwang" (barren) at bottom, "Im" at left **Note:** Size varies 27-28 mm. Weight varies 8.00-9.00 grams.

Date	Mintage	Good	VG	F	VF	XF
ND(1752)	—	3.00	4.00	6.00	10.00	—

KM# 723 2 MUN

Cast Copper Or Brass **Rev:** "Il" at bottom, "Im" at left **Note:** Size varies 27-28 mm. Weight varies 8.00-9.00 grams.

Date	Mintage	Good	VG	F	VF	XF
ND(1752)	—	3.00	4.00	6.00	10.00	—

KM# 724 2 MUN

Cast Copper Or Brass **Rev:** "Wol" at bottom, "Im" at left **Note:** Size varies 27-28 mm. Weight varies 8.00-9.00 grams.

Date	Mintage	Good	VG	F	VF	XF
ND(1752)	—	3.00	4.00	6.00	10.00	—

KM# 725 2 MUN

Cast Copper Or Brass **Rev:** "Yong" at bottom, "Im" at left **Note:** Size varies 27-28 mm. Weight varies 8.00-9.00 grams.

Date	Mintage	Good	VG	F	VF	XF
ND(1752)	—	3.00	4.00	6.00	10.00	—

KM# 726 2 MUN

Cast Copper Or Brass **Rev:** "Ch'uk" at bottom, "Im" at left **Note:** Size varies 27-28 mm. Weight varies 8.00-9.00 grams.

Date	Mintage	Good	VG	F	VF	XF
ND(1752)	—	3.00	4.00	6.00	10.00	—

KM# 727 2 MUN

Cast Copper Or Brass **Rev:** "Chin" at bottom, "Im" at left **Note:** Size varies 27-28 mm. Weight varies 8.00-9.00 grams.

Date	Mintage	Good	VG	F	VF	XF
ND(1752)	—	3.00	4.00	6.00	10.00	—

KM# 728 2 MUN

Cast Copper Or Brass **Rev:** "Suk" at bottom, "Im" at left **Note:** Size varies 27-28 mm. Weight varies 8.00-9.00 grams.

Date	Mintage	Good	VG	F	VF	XF
ND(1752)	—	3.00	4.00	6.00	10.00	—

KM# 729 2 MUN

Cast Copper Or Brass **Rev:** "Yol" at bottom, "Im" at left **Note:** Size varies 27-28 mm. Weight varies 8.00-9.00 grams.

Date	Mintage	Good	VG	F	VF	XF
ND(1752)	—	3.00	4.00	6.00	10.00	—

KM# 730 2 MUN

Cast Copper Or Brass **Rev:** "Chang" (extend) at bottom, "Im" at left **Note:** Size varies 27-28 mm. Weight varies 8.00-9.00 grams.

Date	Mintage	Good	VG	F	VF	XF
ND(1752)	—	3.00	4.00	6.00	10.00	—

KM# 569 2 MUN

Cast Copper Or Brass **Rev:** "Ch'on" at bottom **Note:** Size varies 30-32 mm.

Date	Mintage	Good	VG	F	VF	XF
ND(1752)	—	3.00	4.00	6.00	10.00	—

KM# B701 2 MUN

Cast Copper Or Brass **Rev:** "Hwang" (barren) at bottom, "Im" at right **Note:** Size varies 27-28 millimeters. Weight varies 8.00-9.00 grams. Struck at T'ong Yong.

Date	Mintage	Good	VG	F	VF	XF
ND(1752)	—	3.50	5.50	8.50	12.50	—

KM# C701 2 MUN

Cast Copper Or Brass **Rev:** "Il" at bottom, "Im" at right **Note:** Size varies 27-28 millimeters. Weight varies 8.00-9.00 grams. Struck at T'ong Yong.

Date	Mintage	Good	VG	F	VF	XF
ND(1752)	—	3.50	5.50	8.50	12.50	—

KM# H701 2 MUN

Cast Copper Or Brass **Rev:** "Suk" at bottom, "Im" at right **Note:** Size varies 27-28 millimeters. Weight varies 8.00-9.00 grams. Struck at T'ong Yong.

Date	Mintage	Good	VG	F	VF	XF
ND(1752)	—	3.50	5.50	8.50	12.50	—

KM# I701 2 MUN

Cast Copper Or Brass **Rev:** "Yol" at bottom, "Im" at right **Note:** Size varies 27-28 millimeters. Weight varies 8.00-9.00 grams. Struck at T'ong Yong.

Date	Mintage	Good	VG	F	VF	XF
ND(1752)	—	3.50	5.50	8.50	12.50	—

KM# J701 2 MUN

Cast Copper Or Brass **Rev:** "Chang" (extend) at bottom, "Im" at right **Note:** Size varies 27-28 millimeters. Weight varies 8.00-9.00 grams. Struck at T'ong Yong.

Date	Mintage	Good	VG	F	VF	XF
ND(1752)	—	3.50	5.50	8.50	12.50	—

KM# 578 2 MUN

6.7500 g., Cast Copper Or Brass **Note:** Reduced size 27-29 mm.

Date	Mintage	Good	VG	F	VF	XF
ND(1752)	—	3.00	4.00	6.00	10.00	—

KM# 572 2 MUN

6.7500 g., Cast Copper Or Brass **Note:** Reduced size, 27-29 millimeters. Struck at T'ong Yong.

Date	Mintage	Good	VG	F	VF	XF
ND(1752)	—	3.00	4.00	6.00	10.00	—

KM# 574 2 MUN

6.7500 g., Cast Copper Or Brass **Note:** Reduced size, 27-29 millimeters. Struck at T'ong Yong.

Date	Mintage	Good	VG	F	VF	XF
ND(1752)	—	3.00	4.00	6.00	10.00	—

KM# 580 2 MUN

6.7500 g., Cast Copper Or Brass **Note:** Reduced size, 27-29 millimeters. Struck at T'ong Yong.

Date	Mintage	Good	VG	F	VF	XF
ND(1752)	—	3.00	4.00	6.00	10.00	—

KM# 582 2 MUN

6.7500 g., Cast Copper Or Brass **Note:** Reduced size, 27-29 millimeters. Struck at T'ong Yong.

Date	Mintage	Good	VG	F	VF	XF
ND(1752)	—	3.00	4.00	6.00	10.00	—

KM# 588 2 MUN

6.7500 g., Cast Copper Or Brass **Note:** Reduced size, 27-29 millimeters. Struck at T'ong Yong.

Date	Mintage	Good	VG	F	VF	XF
ND(1752)	—	3.00	4.00	6.00	10.00	—

KM# 590 2 MUN

6.7500 g., Cast Copper Or Brass **Note:** Reduced size, 27-29 millimeters. Struck at T'ong Yong.

Date	Mintage	Good	VG	F	VF	XF
ND(1752)	—	3.00	4.00	6.00	10.00	—

KM# 596 2 MUN

6.7500 g., Cast Copper Or Brass **Note:** Reduced size, 27-29 millimeters. Struck at T'ong Yong.

Date	Mintage	Good	VG	F	VF	XF
ND(1752)	—	3.00	4.00	6.00	10.00	—

KM# 598 2 MUN

6.7500 g., Cast Copper Or Brass **Note:** Reduced size, 27-29 millimeters. Struck at T'ong Yong.

Date	Mintage	Good	VG	F	VF	XF
ND(1752)	—	3.00	4.00	6.00	10.00	—

KM# 604 2 MUN

6.7500 g., Cast Copper Or Brass **Note:** Reduced size, 27-29 millimeters. Struck at T'ong Yong.

Date	Mintage	Good	VG	F	VF	XF
ND(1752)	—	3.00	4.00	6.00	10.00	—

KM# 608 2 MUN

6.7500 g., Cast Copper Or Brass **Note:** Reduced size, 27-29 millimeters. Struck at T'ong Yong.

Date	Mintage	Good	VG	F	VF	XF
ND(1752)	—	3.00	4.00	6.00	10.00	—

KM# 570 2 MUN

6.7500 g., Cast Copper Or Brass **Note:** Reduced size, 27-29 mm.

Date	Mintage	Good	VG	F	VF	XF
ND(1752)	—	3.00	4.00	6.00	10.00	—

KM# 576 2 MUN

6.7500 g., Cast Copper Or Brass **Note:** Reduced size, 27-29 mm.

Date	Mintage	Good	VG	F	VF	XF
ND(1752)	—	3.00	4.00	6.00	10.00	—

KM# 584 2 MUN

6.7500 g., Cast Copper Or Brass **Note:** Reduced size, 27-29 mm.

Date	Mintage	Good	VG	F	VF	XF
ND(1752)	—	3.00	4.00	6.00	10.00	—

KM# 586 2 MUN

6.7500 g., Cast Copper Or Brass **Note:** Reduced size, 27-29 mm.

Date	Mintage	Good	VG	F	VF	XF
ND(1752)	—	3.00	4.00	6.00	10.00	—

KM# 592 2 MUN

6.7500 g., Cast Copper Or Brass **Note:** Reduced size, 27-29 mm.

Date	Mintage	Good	VG	F	VF	XF
ND(1752)	—	3.00	4.00	6.00	10.00	—

KM# 594 2 MUN

6.7500 g., Cast Copper Or Brass **Note:** Reduced size, 27-29 mm.

Date	Mintage	Good	VG	F	VF	XF
ND(1752)	—	3.00	4.00	6.00	10.00	—

KM# 600 2 MUN

6.7500 g., Cast Copper Or Brass **Note:** Reduced size, 27-29 mm.

Date	Mintage	Good	VG	F	VF	XF
ND(1752)	—	3.00	4.00	6.00	10.00	—

KM# 602 2 MUN

6.7500 g., Cast Copper Or Brass **Note:** Reduced size, 27-29 mm.

Date	Mintage	Good	VG	F	VF	XF
ND(1752)	—	3.00	4.00	6.00	10.00	—

KM# 606 2 MUN

6.7500 g., Cast Copper Or Brass **Note:** Reduced size, 27-29 mm.

Date	Mintage	Good	VG	F	VF	XF
ND(1752)	—	3.00	4.00	6.00	10.00	—

KM# 699 2 MUN

6.7500 g., Cast Copper Or Brass **Rev:** "Im" at right, series number at bottom **Note:** Reduced size.

Date	Mintage	Good	VG	F	VF	XF
ND(1752) Series 1-3	—	6.50	10.00	15.00	25.00	—

KM# A700a 2 MUN

Cast Copper Or Brass, 29.5 mm. **Obv:** "P'yong" without hooks **Note:** Weight varies 8.00-9.00 grams.

Date	Mintage	Good	VG	F	VF	XF
ND(1752)	—	3.50	5.50	8.50	12.50	—

KM# 703a 2 MUN

Cast Copper Or Brass, 29 mm. **Note:** Weight varies 8.00-9.00 grams.

Date	Mintage	Good	VG	F	VF	XF
ND(1752)	—	3.50	5.50	8.50	12.50	—

KM# 704 2 MUN

Cast Copper Or Brass, 28 mm. **Rev:** "So" at bottom, "Im" at right **Note:** Weight varies 8.00-9.00 grams.

Date	Mintage	Good	VG	F	VF	XF
ND(1752)	—	3.50	5.50	8.50	12.50	—

KM# B700 2 MUN

Cast Copper Or Brass **Rev:** "Hyon" at bottom, "Im" at right **Note:** Weight varies 8.00-9.00 grams. Struck at T'ong Yong.

Date	Mintage	Good	VG	F	VF	XF
ND(1752)	—	3.50	5.50	8.50	12.50	—

KM# C700 2 MUN

Cast Copper Or Brass, 28 mm. **Rev:** "Hwang" (yellow) at bottom, "Im" at right **Note:** Weight varies 8.00-9.00 grams. Struck at T'ong Yong.

Date	Mintage	Good	VG	F	VF	XF
ND(1752)	—	3.50	5.50	8.50	12.50	—

KM# D700 2 MUN

Cast Copper Or Brass **Rev:** "U" at bottom, "Im" at right **Note:** Weight varies 8.00-9.00 grams. Struck at T'ong Yong.

Date	Mintage	Good	VG	F	VF	XF
ND(1752)	—	3.50	5.50	8.50	12.50	—

KM# 705 2 MUN

Cast Copper Or Brass **Rev:** "Wang" at bottom, "Im" at right **Note:** Size varies 27-28 mm; Weight varies 8.00-9.00 grams.

Date	Mintage	Good	VG	F	VF	XF
ND(1752)	—	3.50	5.50	8.50	12.50	—

KM# 715 2 MUN

Cast Copper Or Brass **Rev:** "Yo" (yin) at bottom, "Im" at right **Note:** Size varies 28-29 mm. Weight varies 8.00-9.00 grams.

Date	Mintage	Good	VG	F	VF	XF
ND(1752)	—	3.50	5.50	8.50	12.50	—

KM# F747 2 MUN

Cast Copper Or Brass **Rev:** "Yol" at bottom, "Kye" at left **Note:** Size varies 27-28mm. Weight varies 8.00-9.00 grams.

Date	Mintage	Good	VG	F	VF	XF
ND(1753)	—	4.00	6.50	9.00	15.00	—

KM# B732 2 MUN

Cast Copper Or Brass **Rev:** "Hyon" at bottom, "Kye" at right **Note:** Size varies 27-28 millimeters. Weight varies 8.00-9.00 grams. Struck at T'ong Yong.

Date	Mintage	Good	VG	F	VF	XF
ND(1753)	—	3.00	4.50	7.00	11.50	—

KM# C732 2 MUN

Cast Copper Or Brass **Rev:** "Hwang" (yellow) at bottom, "Kye" at right **Note:** Size varies 27-28 millimeters. Weight varies 8.00-9.00 grams. Struck at T'ong Yong.

Date	Mintage	Good	VG	F	VF	XF
ND(1753)	—	3.00	4.50	7.00	11.50	—

KM# B742 2 MUN

Cast Copper Or Brass **Rev:** "Chang" (extend) at bottom, "Kye" at right **Note:** Size varies 27-28 millimeters. Weight varies 8.00-9.00 grams. Struck at T'ong Yong.

Date	Mintage	Good	VG	F	VF	XF
ND(1753)	—	3.50	6.50	9.00	15.00	—

KM# C742 2 MUN

Cast Copper Or Brass **Rev:** "Han" at bottom, "Kye" at right **Note:** Size varies 27-28 millimeters. Weight varies 8.00-9.00 grams. Struck at T'ong Yong.

Date	Mintage	Good	VG	F	VF	XF
ND(1753)	—	3.50	6.50	9.00	15.00	—

KM# E742 2 MUN

Cast Copper Or Brass **Rev:** "So" at bottom, "Kye" at right **Note:** Size varies 27-28 millimeters. Weight varies 8.00-9.00 grams. Struck at T'ong Yong.

Date	Mintage	Good	VG	F	VF	XF
ND(1753)	—	3.50	6.50	9.00	15.00	—

KM# F742 2 MUN

Cast Copper Or Brass **Rev:** "Wang" at bottom, "Kye" at right **Note:** Size varies 27-28 millimeters. Weight varies 8.00-9.00 grams. Struck at T'ong Yong.

Date	Mintage	Good	VG	F	VF	XF
ND(1753)	—	3.50	6.50	9.00	15.00	—

KM# G742 2 MUN

Cast Copper Or Brass **Rev:** "Ch'u" at bottom, "Kye" at right **Note:** Size varies 27-28 millimeters. Weight varies 8.00-9.00 grams. Struck at T'ong Yong.

Date	Mintage	Good	VG	F	VF	XF
ND(1753)	—	3.50	6.50	9.00	15.00	—

KM# H742 2 MUN

Cast Copper Or Brass **Rev:** "Su" at bottom, "Kye" at right **Note:** Size varies 27-28 millimeters. Weight varies 8.00-9.00 grams. Struck at T'ong Yong.

Date	Mintage	Good	VG	F	VF	XF
ND(1753)	—	3.50	6.50	9.00	15.00	—

KM# I742 2 MUN

Cast Copper Or Brass **Rev:** "Tong" at bottom, "Kye" at right **Note:** Size varies 27-28 millimeters. Weight varies 8.00-9.00 grams. Struck at T'ong Yong.

Date	Mintage	Good	VG	F	VF	XF
ND(1753)	—	3.50	6.50	9.00	15.00	—

KM# B743 2 MUN

Cast Copper Or Brass **Rev:** "Song" at bottom, "Kye" at right **Note:** Size varies 27-28 millimeters. Weight varies 8.00-9.00 grams. Struck at T'ong Yong.

Date	Mintage	Good	VG	F	VF	XF
ND(1753)	—	3.50	6.50	9.00	15.00	—

KM# B746 2 MUN

Cast Copper Or Brass **Rev:** "Chu" at bottom, "Kye" at left **Note:** Size varies 27-28 millimeters. Weight varies 8.00-9.00 grams. Struck at T'ong Yong.

Date	Mintage	Good	VG	F	VF	XF
ND(1753)	—	4.00	6.50	9.00	15.00	—

KM# B747 2 MUN

Cast Copper Or Brass **Rev:** "Yong" at bottom, "Kye" at left **Note:** Size varies 27-28 millimeters. Weight varies 8.00-9.00 grams. Struck at T'ong Yong.

Date	Mintage	Good	VG	F	VF	XF
ND(1753)	—	4.00	6.50	9.00	15.00	—

KM# C747 2 MUN
Cast Copper Or Brass **Rev:** "Ch'uk" at bottom, "Kye" at left **Note:** Size varies 27-28 millimeters. Weight varies 8.00-9.00 grams. Struck at T'ong Yong.

Date	Mintage	Good	VG	F	VF	XF
ND(1753)	—	4.00	6.50	9.00	15.00	—

KM# D747 2 MUN
Cast Copper Or Brass **Rev:** "Chin" at bottom, "Kye" at left **Note:** Size varies 27-28 millimeters. Weight varies 8.00-9.00 grams. Struck at T'ong Yong.

Date	Mintage	Good	VG	F	VF	XF
ND(1753)	—	4.00	6.50	9.00	15.00	—

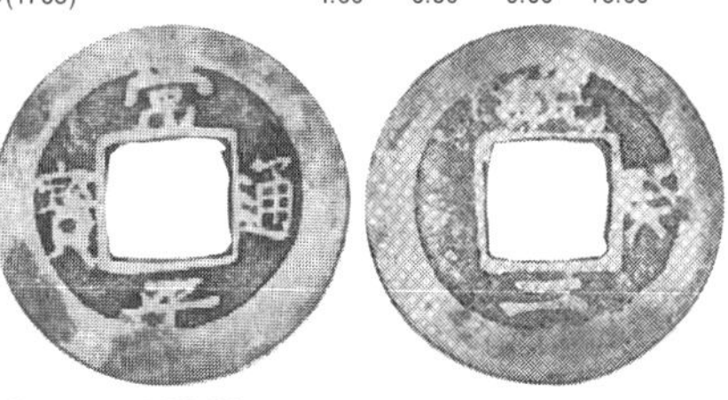

KM# 731 2 MUN
Cast Copper Or Brass **Rev:** "Kye" at right, series number at bottom **Note:** Size varies 27-28 mm. Weight varies 8.00-9.00 grams.

Date	Mintage	Good	VG	F	VF	XF
ND(1753) Series 1-3	—	3.50	6.00	9.00	15.00	—

KM# 732 2 MUN
Cast Copper Or Brass **Rev:** "Chon" at bottom, "Kye" at right **Note:** Size varies 27-28 mm. Weight varies 8.00-9.00 grams.

Date	Mintage	Good	VG	F	VF	XF
ND(1753)	—	3.00	4.50	7.00	11.50	—

KM# 732a 2 MUN
Cast Copper Or Brass **Obv:** "P'yong" without hooks **Note:** Size varies 27-28 mm. Weight varies 8.00-9.00 grams.

Date	Mintage	Good	VG	F	VF	XF
ND(1753)	—	3.00	4.50	7.00	11.50	—

KM# A732 2 MUN
Cast Copper Or Brass **Rev:** "Chi" at bottom, "Kye" at right **Note:** Size varies 27-28 mm. Weight varies 8.00-9.00 grams.

Date	Mintage	Good	VG	F	VF	XF
ND(1753)	—	3.00	4.50	7.00	11.50	—

KM# 733 2 MUN
Cast Copper Or Brass **Rev:** "U" at bottom, "Kye" at right **Note:** Size varies 27-28 mm. Weight varies 8.00-9.00 grams.

Date	Mintage	Good	VG	F	VF	XF
ND(1753)	—	3.00	4.50	7.00	11.50	—

KM# 734 2 MUN
Cast Copper Or Brass **Rev:** "Chu" at bottom, "Kye" at right **Note:** Size varies 27-28 mm. Weight varies 8.00-9.00 grams.

Date	Mintage	Good	VG	F	VF	XF
ND(1753)	—	3.00	4.50	7.00	11.50	—

KM# 735 2 MUN
Cast Copper Or Brass **Rev:** "Hong" at bottom, "Kye" at right **Note:** Size varies 27-28 mm. Weight varies 8.00-9.00 grams.

Date	Mintage	Good	VG	F	VF	XF
ND(1753)	—	3.00	4.50	7.00	11.50	—

KM# 736 2 MUN
Cast Copper Or Brass **Rev:** "Hwang" (barren) at bottom, "Kye" at right **Note:** Size varies 27-28 mm. Weight varies 8.00-9.00 grams.

Date	Mintage	Good	VG	F	VF	XF
ND(1753)	—	3.00	4.50	7.00	11.50	—

KM# 737 2 MUN
Cast Copper Or Brass **Rev:** "Il" at bottom, "Kye" at right **Note:** Size varies 27-28 mm. Weight varies 8.00-9.00 grams.

Date	Mintage	Good	VG	F	VF	XF
ND(1753)	—	3.00	4.50	7.00	11.50	—

KM# 738 2 MUN
Cast Copper Or Brass **Rev:** "Wol" at bottom, "Kye" at right **Note:** Size varies 27-28 mm. Weight varies 8.00-9.00 grams.

Date	Mintage	Good	VG	F	VF	XF
ND(1753)	—	3.00	4.50	7.00	11.50	—

KM# 739 2 MUN
Cast Copper Or Brass **Rev:** "Yong" at bottom, "Kye" at right **Note:** Size varies 27-28 mm. Weight varies 8.00-9.00 grams.

Date	Mintage	Good	VG	F	VF	XF
ND(1753)	—	3.00	4.50	7.00	11.50	—

KM# 740 2 MUN
Cast Copper Or Brass **Rev:** "Ch'uk" at bottom, "Kye" at right **Note:** Size varies 27-28 mm. Weight varies 8.00-9.00 grams.

Date	Mintage	Good	VG	F	VF	XF
ND(1753)	—	3.00	4.50	7.00	11.50	—

KM# 741 2 MUN
Cast Copper Or Brass **Rev:** "Chin" at bottom, "Kye" at right **Note:** Size varies 27-28 mm. Weight varies 8.00-9.00 grams.

Date	Mintage	Good	VG	F	VF	XF
ND(1753)	—	3.00	4.50	7.00	11.50	—

KM# 742 2 MUN
Cast Copper Or Brass **Rev:** "Suk" at bottom, "Kye" at right **Note:** Size varies 27-28 mm. Weight varies 8.00-9.00 grams.

Date	Mintage	Good	VG	F	VF	XF
ND(1753)	—	3.00	4.50	7.00	11.50	—

KM# A742 2 MUN
Cast Copper Or Brass **Rev:** "Yol" at bottom, "Kye" at right **Note:** Size varies 27-28 mm. Weight varies 8.00-9.00 grams.

Date	Mintage	Good	VG	F	VF	XF
ND(1753)	—	3.50	6.50	9.00	15.00	—

KM# D742 2 MUN
Cast Copper Or Brass **Rev:** "Nae" at bottom, "Kye" at right **Note:** Size varies 27-28 mm. Weight varies 8.00-9.00 grams.

Date	Mintage	Good	VG	F	VF	XF
ND(1753)	—	3.50	6.50	9.00	15.00	—

KM# J742 2 MUN
Cast Copper Or Brass **Rev:** "Chang" (hoard) at bottom, "Kye" at right **Note:** Size varies 27-28 mm. Weight varies 8.00-9.00 grams.

Date	Mintage	Good	VG	F	VF	XF
ND(1753)	—	3.50	6.50	9.00	15.00	—

KM# 743 2 MUN
Cast Copper Or Brass **Rev:** "Yun" at bottom, "Kye" at right **Note:** Size varies 27-28 mm. Weight varies 8.00-9.00 grams.

Date	Mintage	Good	VG	F	VF	XF
ND(1753)	—	3.50	6.50	9.00	15.00	—

KM# A743 2 MUN
Cast Copper Or Brass **Rev:** "Yo" (surplus) at bottom, "Kye" at right **Note:** Size varies 27-28 mm. Weight varies 8.00-9.00 grams.

Date	Mintage	Good	VG	F	VF	XF
ND(1753)	—	3.50	6.50	9.00	15.00	—

KM# C743 2 MUN
Cast Copper Or Brass **Rev:** "Se" at bottom, "Kye" at right **Note:** Size varies 27-28 mm. Weight varies 8.00-9.00 grams.

Date	Mintage	Good	VG	F	VF	XF
ND(1753)	—	3.50	6.50	9.00	15.00	—

KM# D743 2 MUN
Cast Copper Or Brass **Rev:** "Yul" at bottom, "Kye" at right **Note:** Size varies 27-28 mm. Weight varies 8.00-9.00 grams.

Date	Mintage	Good	VG	F	VF	XF
ND(1753)	—	3.50	6.50	9.00	15.00	—

KM# E743 2 MUN
Cast Copper Or Brass **Rev:** "Yo" at bottom, "Kye" at right **Note:** Size varies 27-28 mm. Weight varies 8.00-9.00 grams.

Date	Mintage	Good	VG	F	VF	XF
ND(1753)	—	3.50	6.50	9.00	15.00	—

KM# 744 2 MUN
Cast Copper Or Brass **Rev:** "Ch'on" at bottom, "Kye" at left **Note:** Size varies 27-28 mm. Weight varies 8.00-9.00 grams.

Date	Mintage	Good	VG	F	VF	XF
ND(1753)	—	4.00	6.50	9.00	15.00	—

KM# A744 2 MUN
Cast Copper Or Brass **Rev:** "Chi" at bottom, "Kye" at left **Note:** Size varies 27-28 mm. Weight varies 8.00-9.00 grams.

Date	Mintage	Good	VG	F	VF	XF
ND(1753)	—	4.00	6.50	9.00	15.00	—

KM# 745 2 MUN
Cast Copper Or Brass **Rev:** "Hyon" at bottom, "Kye" at left **Note:** Size varies 27-28 mm. Weight varies 8.00-9.00 grams.

Date	Mintage	Good	VG	F	VF	XF
ND(1753)	—	4.00	6.50	9.00	15.00	—

KM# 746 2 MUN
Cast Copper Or Brass **Rev:** "Hwang" (yellow) at bottom, "Kye" at left **Note:** Size varies 27-28 mm. Weight varies 8.00-9.00 grams.

Date	Mintage	Good	VG	F	VF	XF
ND(1753)	—	4.00	6.50	9.00	15.00	—

KM# A746 2 MUN
Cast Copper Or Brass **Rev:** "U" at bottom, "Kye" at left **Note:** Size varies 27-28 mm. Weight varies 8.00-9.00 grams.

Date	Mintage	Good	VG	F	VF	XF
ND(1753)	—	4.00	6.50	9.00	15.00	—

KM# C746 2 MUN
Cast Copper Or Brass **Rev:** "Hong" at bottom, "Kye" at left **Note:** Size varies 27-28 mm. Weight varies 8.00-9.00 grams.

Date	Mintage	Good	VG	F	VF	XF
ND(1753)	—	4.00	6.50	9.00	15.00	—

KM# D746 2 MUN
Cast Copper Or Brass **Rev:** "Hwang" (barren) at bottom, "Kye" at left **Note:** Size varies 27-28 mm. Weight varies 8.00-9.00 grams.

Date	Mintage	Good	VG	F	VF	XF
ND(1753)	—	4.00	6.50	9.00	15.00	—

KM# 747 2 MUN
Cast Copper Or Brass **Rev:** "Il" at bottom, "Kye" at left **Note:** Size varies 27-28 mm. Weight varies 8.00-9.00 grams.

Date	Mintage	Good	VG	F	VF	XF
ND(1753)	—	4.00	6.50	9.00	15.00	—

KM# A747 2 MUN
Cast Copper Or Brass **Rev:** "Wol" at bottom, "Kye" at left **Note:** Size varies 27-28 mm. Weight varies 8.00-9.00 grams.

Date	Mintage	Good	VG	F	VF	XF
ND(1753)	—	4.00	6.50	9.00	15.00	—

KM# E747 2 MUN
Cast Copper Or Brass **Rev:** "Suk" at bottom, "Kye" at left **Note:** Size varies 27-28 mm. Weight varies 8.00-9.00 grams.

Date	Mintage	Good	VG	F	VF	XF
ND(1753)	—	4.00	6.50	9.00	15.00	—

KM# 748 2 MUN
Cast Copper Or Brass **Rev:** "Chang" (extend) at bottom, "Kye" at left **Note:** Size varies 27-28 mm. Weight varies 8.00-9.00 grams.

Date	Mintage	Good	VG	F	VF	XF
ND(1753)	—	4.00	6.50	9.00	15.00	—

KM# 749 2 MUN
Cast Copper Or Brass **Rev:** "Han" at bottom, "Kye" at left **Note:** Size varies 27-28 mm. Weight varies 8.00-9.00 grams.

Date	Mintage	Good	VG	F	VF	XF
ND(1753)	—	4.00	6.50	9.00	15.00	—

KM# 750 2 MUN
Cast Copper Or Brass **Rev:** "Nae" at bottom, "Kye" at left **Note:** Size varies 27-28 mm. Weight varies 8.00-9.00 grams.

Date	Mintage	Good	VG	F	VF	XF
ND(1753)	—	4.00	6.50	9.00	15.00	—

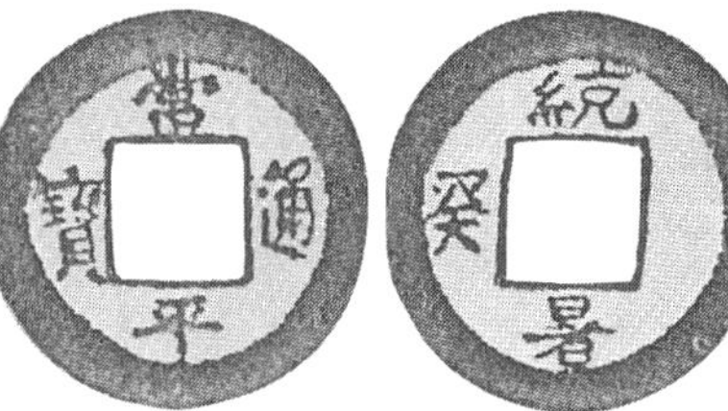

KM# 751 2 MUN
Cast Copper Or Brass **Rev:** "So" at bottom, "Kye" at left **Note:** Size varies 27-28 mm. Weight varies 8.00-9.00 grams.

Date	Mintage	Good	VG	F	VF	XF
ND(1753)	—	4.00	6.50	9.00	15.00	—

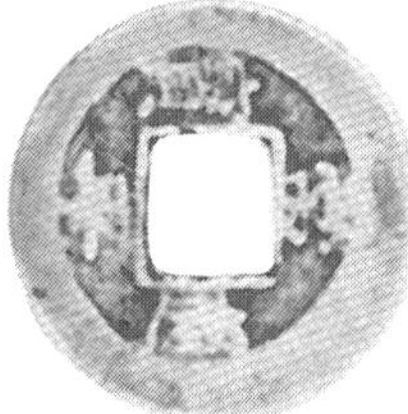

KM# 752 2 MUN
Cast Copper Or Brass **Rev:** "Wang" at bottom, "Kye" at left **Note:** Size varies 27-28 mm. Weight varies 8.00-9.00 grams.

Date	Mintage	Good	VG	F	VF	XF
ND(1753)	—	4.00	6.50	9.00	15.00	—

KM# 753 2 MUN
Cast Copper Or Brass **Rev:** "Ch'u" at bottom, "Kye" at left **Note:** Size varies 27-28 mm. Weight varies 8.00-9.00 grams.

Date	Mintage	Good	VG	F	VF	XF
ND(1753)	—	4.00	6.50	9.00	15.00	—

KM# 754 2 MUN
Cast Copper Or Brass **Rev:** "Su" at bottom, "Kye" at left **Note:** Size varies 27-28 mm. Weight varies 8.00-9.00 grams.

Date	Mintage	Good	VG	F	VF	XF
ND(1753)	—	4.00	6.50	9.00	15.00	—

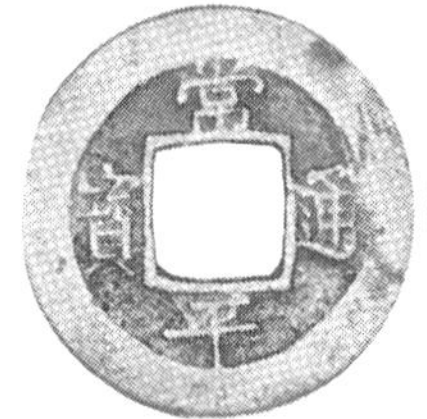
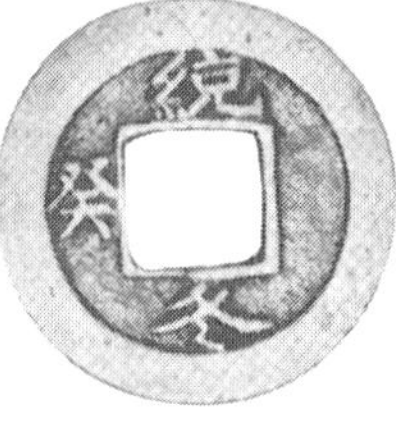

KM# 755 2 MUN
Cast Copper Or Brass **Rev:** "Tong" at bottom, "Kye" at left **Note:** Size varies 27-28 mm. Weight varies 8.00-9.00 grams.

Date	Mintage	Good	VG	F	VF	XF
ND(1753)	—	4.00	6.50	9.00	15.00	—

KM# 756 2 MUN
Cast Copper Or Brass **Rev:** "Chang" (hoard) at bottom, "Kye" at left **Note:** Size varies 27-28 mm. Weight varies 8.00-9.00 grams.

Date	Mintage	Good	VG	F	VF	XF
ND(1753)	—	4.00	6.50	9.00	15.00	—

KM# 757 2 MUN
Cast Copper Or Brass **Rev:** "Yun" at bottom, "Kye" at left **Note:** Size varies 27-28 mm. Weight varies 8.00-9.00 grams.

Date	Mintage	Good	VG	F	VF	XF
ND(1753)	—	4.00	6.50	9.00	15.00	—

KM# 758 2 MUN
Cast Copper Or Brass **Rev:** "Yo" (surplus) at bottom, "Kye" at left **Note:** Size varies 27-28 mm. Weight varies 8.00-9.00 grams.

Date	Mintage	Good	VG	F	VF	XF
ND(1753)	—	4.00	6.50	9.00	15.00	—

KM# 759 2 MUN
Cast Copper Or Brass **Rev:** "Song" at bottom, "Kye" at left **Note:** Size varies 27-28 mm. Weight varies 8.00-9.00 grams.

Date	Mintage	Good	VG	F	VF	XF
ND(1753)	—	4.00	6.50	9.00	15.00	—

KM# 760 2 MUN
Cast Copper Or Brass **Rev:** "Se" at bottom, "Kye" at left **Note:** Size varies 27-28 mm. Weight varies 8.00-9.00 grams.

Date	Mintage	Good	VG	F	VF	XF
ND(1753)	—	4.00	6.50	9.00	15.00	—

KM# 761 2 MUN
Cast Copper Or Brass **Rev:** "Yul" at bottom, "Kye" at left **Note:** Size varies 27-28 mm. Weight varies 8.00-9.00 grams.

Date	Mintage	Good	VG	F	VF	XF
ND(1753)	—	4.00	6.50	9.00	15.00	—

KM# 762 2 MUN
Cast Copper Or Brass **Rev:** "Yo" (yin) at bottom, "Kye" at left **Note:** Size varies 27-28 mm. Weight varies 8.00-9.00 grams.

Date	Mintage	Good	VG	F	VF	XF
ND(1753)	—	4.00	6.50	9.00	15.00	—

SEOUL DEFENSE FORT

(Su O Ch'ong)

KM# 767 MUN

4.5000 g., Cast Copper **Rev:** "Su" at top

Date	Mintage	Good	VG	F	VF	XF
ND(1742) Rare	—	—	—	—	—	—

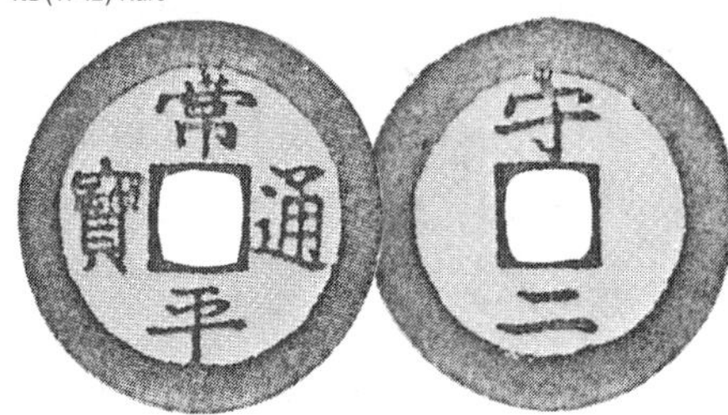

KM# 768 2 MUN

Cast Copper **Rev:** "Su" at top, "I" (2) at bottom **Note:** Weight varies 8.00-9.00 grams.

Date	Mintage	Good	VG	F	VF	XF
ND(1742-52)	—	3.00	4.00	6.00	10.00	—

KM# 769 2 MUN

Cast Copper **Rev:** Dot at right **Note:** Weight varies 8.00-9.00 grams.

Date	Mintage	Good	VG	F	VF	XF
ND(1742-52)	—	3.00	4.50	6.00	10.00	—

KM# 770 2 MUN

Cast Copper **Rev:** Dot at lower left **Note:** Weight varies 8.00-9.00 grams.

Date	Mintage	Good	VG	F	VF	XF
ND(1742-52)	—	3.00	4.50	6.00	10.00	—

KAESONG TOWNSHIP MILITARY OFFICE

(Kae Song Kwal Li Yong)

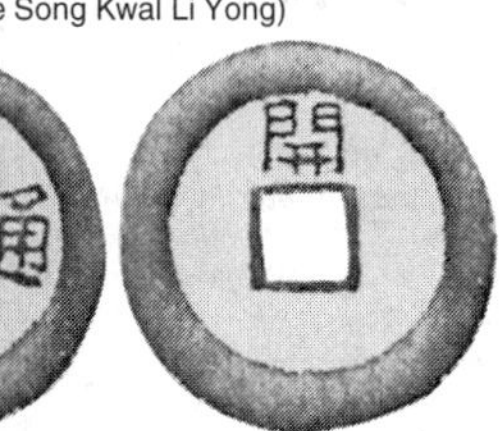

KM# 780 MUN

4.5000 g., Cast Copper Or Bronze, 26 mm. **Obv:** Large characters **Rev:** "Kae" at top

Date	Mintage	Good	VG	F	VF	XF
ND(1678-1742)	—	100	150	200	300	—

KM# A780 MUN

4.5000 g., Cast Copper Or Bronze, 25 mm. **Obv:** Medium characters **Note:** Reduced size.

Date	Mintage	Good	VG	F	VF	XF
ND(1678-1742)	—	75.00	125	175	250	—

KM# 781 MUN

4.5000 g., Cast Copper Or Bronze, 24 mm. **Obv:** Small characters **Note:** Reduced size.

Date	Mintage	Good	VG	F	VF	XF
ND(1678-1742)	—	75.00	125	175	250	—

KM# 782 MUN

4.5000 g., Cast Copper Or Bronze **Rev:** Dot at lower right

Date	Mintage	Good	VG	F	VF	XF
ND(1678-1742) Rare	—	—	—	—	—	—

KM# 783 MUN

4.5000 g., Cast Copper Or Bronze **Rev:** Dot at bottom

Date	Mintage	Good	VG	F	VF	XF
ND(1678-1742) Rare	—	—	—	—	—	—

KM# 784 MUN

4.5000 g., Cast Copper Or Bronze **Rev:** 2 dots at bottom

Date	Mintage	Good	VG	F	VF	XF
ND(1678-1742) Rare	—	—	—	—	—	—

KM# 785 MUN

4.5000 g., Cast Copper Or Bronze **Rev:** Circle at lower right

Date	Mintage	Good	VG	F	VF	XF
ND(1678-1742) Rare	—	—	—	—	—	—

KM# 786 MUN

4.5000 g., Cast Copper Or Bronze **Rev:** Circle at left

Date	Mintage	Good	VG	F	VF	XF
ND(1678-1742) Rare	—	—	—	—	—	—

KM# 787 MUN

4.5000 g., Cast Copper Or Bronze **Rev:** 2 circles at bottom

Date	Mintage	Good	VG	F	VF	XF
ND(1678-1742) Rare	—	—	—	—	—	—

KM# 788 MUN

4.5000 g., Cast Copper Or Bronze **Rev:** Crescent at bottom

Date	Mintage	Good	VG	F	VF	XF
ND(1678-1742) Rare	—	—	—	—	—	—

KM# 789 MUN

4.5000 g., Cast Copper Or Bronze **Rev:** Circle at right, crescent at left

Date	Mintage	Good	VG	F	VF	XF
ND(1678-1742) Rare	—	—	—	—	—	—

KM# 790 MUN

4.5000 g., Cast Copper Or Bronze **Rev:** Vertical line at bottom

Date	Mintage	Good	VG	F	VF	XF
ND(1678-1742) Rare	—	—	—	—	—	—

SONG (SONG DO KWAL LI YONG)

(Song Do is another name for Kae Song)

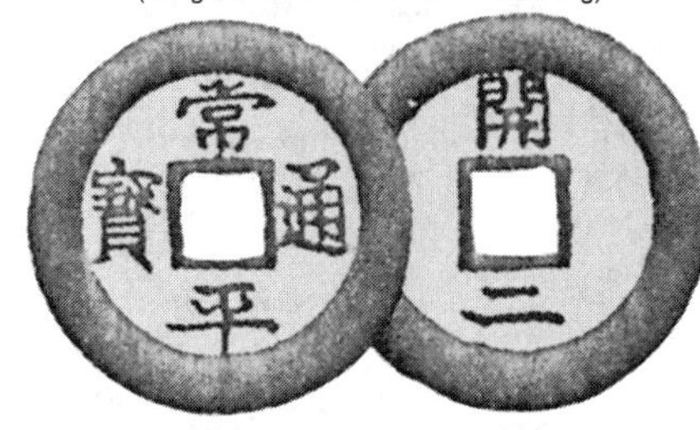

KM# 806 2 MUN

Cast Copper, 32 mm. **Rev:** "Kae" at top, "I" (2) at bottom **Note:** Weight varies 8.00-9.00 grams.

Date	Mintage	Good	VG	F	VF	XF
ND(1679-1752)	—	3.00	4.00	6.00	10.00	—

KM# 806a 2 MUN

Cast Copper, 31 mm. **Rev:** Star at lower left **Note:** Weight varies 8.00-9.00 grams.

Date	Mintage	Good	VG	F	VF	XF
ND(1679-1752)	—	4.00	6.00	7.50	10.00	—

KM# 806b 2 MUN

Cast Copper, 30 mm. **Rev:** Star at lower left **Note:** Weight varies 8.00-9.00 grams.

Date	Mintage	Good	VG	F	VF	XF
ND(1679-1752)	—	5.00	7.50	10.00	15.00	—

KM# 807 2 MUN

Cast Copper **Rev:** Dot at right **Note:** Weight varies 8.00-9.00 grams.

Date	Mintage	Good	VG	F	VF	XF
ND(1679-1752)	—	5.00	7.50	10.00	15.00	—

KM# 808 2 MUN

Cast Copper **Rev:** Circle at right **Note:** Weight varies 8.00-9.00 grams.

Date	Mintage	Good	VG	F	VF	XF
ND(1679-1752)	—	5.00	7.50	10.00	15.00	—

KM# 809 2 MUN

Cast Copper **Rev:** Circle at right, crescent at left **Note:** Weight varies 8.00-9.00 grams.

Date	Mintage	Good	VG	F	VF	XF
ND(1679-1752)	—	5.00	7.50	10.00	15.00	—

KM# A809 2 MUN

Cast Copper **Rev:** Circle at right, dot at left **Note:** Weight varies 8.00-9.00 grams.

Date	Mintage	Good	VG	F	VF	XF
ND(1679-1752)	—	5.00	7.50	10.00	15.00	—

KM# 810 2 MUN

Cast Copper **Rev:** "Il" (1) at right **Note:** Weight varies 8.00-9.00 grams.

Date	Mintage	Good	VG	F	VF	XF
ND(1679-1752)	—	25.00	50.00	80.00	125	—

KM# 811 2 MUN

Cast Copper **Rev:** Vertical line at right **Note:** Weight varies 8.00-9.00 grams.

Date	Mintage	Good	VG	F	VF	XF
ND(1679-1752)	—	4.00	5.00	7.50	10.00	—

KM# 811a 2 MUN

Cast Copper **Rev:** Star at upper right **Note:** Weight varies 8.00-9.00 grams.

Date	Mintage	Good	VG	F	VF	XF
ND(1679-1752)	—	4.00	5.00	7.50	10.00	—

KM# 812 2 MUN

Cast Copper **Rev:** Vertical line at left **Note:** Weight varies 8.00-9.00 grams.

Date	Mintage	Good	VG	F	VF	XF
ND(1679-1752)	—	40.00	65.00	100	175	—

KM# 813 2 MUN

Cast Copper **Rev:** Vertical line at right, crescent at left **Note:** Weight varies 8.00-9.00 grams.

Date	Mintage	Good	VG	F	VF	XF
ND(1679-1752)	—	15.00	30.00	60.00	100	—

KM# 814 2 MUN

Cast Copper **Rev:** "Ch'on" at bottom **Note:** Weight varies 8.00-9.00 grams.

Date	Mintage	Good	VG	F	VF	XF
ND(1742-52)	—	3.00	4.00	6.00	10.00	—

KM# 815 2 MUN

Cast Copper **Rev:** "Chi" at bottom **Note:** Weight varies 8.00-9.00 grams.

Date	Mintage	Good	VG	F	VF	XF
ND(1742-52)	—	3.00	4.00	6.00	10.00	—

KM# 816 2 MUN

Cast Copper **Rev:** "Hyon" at bottom **Note:** Weight varies 8.00-9.00 grams.

Date	Mintage	Good	VG	F	VF	XF
ND(1742-52)	—	3.00	4.00	6.00	10.00	—

KM# 817 2 MUN

Cast Copper **Rev:** "Hwang" (yellow) at bottom **Note:** Weight varies 8.00-9.00 grams.

Date	Mintage	Good	VG	F	VF	XF
ND(1742-52)	—	3.00	4.00	6.00	10.00	—

KM# 818 2 MUN

Cast Copper **Rev:** "U" at bottom **Note:** Weight varies 8.00-9.00 grams.

Date	Mintage	Good	VG	F	VF	XF
ND(1742-52)	—	3.00	4.00	6.00	10.00	—

KM# 819 2 MUN

Cast Copper **Rev:** "Chu" at bottom **Note:** Weight varies 8.00-9.00 grams.

Date	Mintage	Good	VG	F	VF	XF
ND(1742-52)	—	3.00	4.00	6.00	10.00	—

KM# 820 2 MUN

Cast Copper **Rev:** "Hong" at bottom **Note:** Weight varies 8.00-9.00 grams.

Date	Mintage	Good	VG	F	VF	XF
ND(1742-52)	—	3.00	4.00	6.00	10.00	—

KM# 821 2 MUN

Cast Copper **Rev:** "Hwang" (barren) at bottom **Note:** Weight varies 8.00-9.00 grams.

Date	Mintage	Good	VG	F	VF	XF
ND(1742-52)	—	3.00	4.00	6.00	10.00	—

KM# 822 2 MUN

Cast Copper **Rev:** "Il" at bottom **Note:** Weight varies 8.00-9.00 grams.

Date	Mintage	Good	VG	F	VF	XF
ND(1742-52)	—	3.00	4.00	6.00	10.00	—

KM# 823 2 MUN

Cast Copper **Rev:** "Wol" at bottom **Note:** Weight varies 8.00-9.00 grams.

Date	Mintage	Good	VG	F	VF	XF
ND(1742-52)	—	3.00	4.00	6.00	10.00	—

KM# 824 2 MUN

Cast Copper **Rev:** "Yong" at bottom **Note:** Weight varies 8.00-9.00 grams.

Date	Mintage	Good	VG	F	VF	XF
ND(1742-52)	—	3.00	4.00	6.00	10.00	—

KM# 825 2 MUN

Cast Copper **Rev:** "Ch'uk" at bottom **Note:** Weight varies 8.00-9.00 grams.

Date	Mintage	Good	VG	F	VF	XF
ND(1742-52)	—	3.00	4.00	6.00	10.00	—

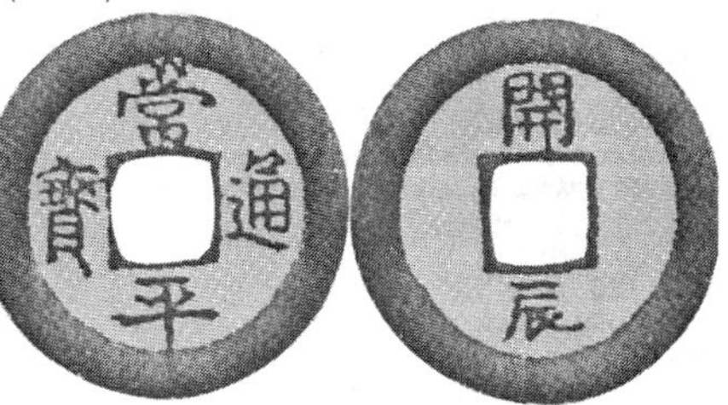

KM# 826 2 MUN

Cast Copper **Rev:** "Chin" at bottom **Note:** Weight varies 8.00-9.00 grams.

Date	Mintage	Good	VG	F	VF	XF
ND(1742-52)	—	3.00	4.00	6.00	10.00	—

KM# 827 2 MUN

Cast Copper **Rev:** "Suk" at bottom **Note:** Weight varies 8.00-9.00 grams.

Date	Mintage	Good	VG	F	VF	XF
ND(1742-52)	—	3.00	4.00	6.00	10.00	—

KM# 828 2 MUN

Cast Copper **Rev:** "Yol" at bottom **Note:** Weight varies 8.00-9.00 grams.

Date	Mintage	Good	VG	F	VF	XF
ND(1742-52)	—	3.00	4.00	6.00	10.00	—

KM# 829 2 MUN

Cast Copper **Rev:** "Chang" (extend) at bottom **Note:** Weight varies 8.00-9.00 grams.

Date	Mintage	Good	VG	F	VF	XF
ND(1742-52)	—	3.00	4.00	6.00	10.00	—

KM# 830 2 MUN

Cast Copper **Rev:** "Han" at bottom **Note:** Weight varies 8.00-9.00 grams.

Date	Mintage	Good	VG	F	VF	XF
ND(1742-52)	—	3.00	4.00	6.00	10.00	—

KM# 831 2 MUN

Cast Copper **Rev:** "Nae" at bottom **Note:** Weight varies 8.00-9.00 grams.

Date	Mintage	Good	VG	F	VF	XF
ND(1742-52)	—	3.00	4.00	6.00	10.00	—

KM# 832 2 MUN

Cast Copper **Rev:** "So" at bottom **Note:** Weight varies 8.00-9.00 grams.

Date	Mintage	Good	VG	F	VF	XF
ND(1742-52)	—	3.00	4.00	6.00	10.00	—

KM# 833 2 MUN
Cast Copper **Rev:** "Wang" at bottom **Note:** Weight varies 8.00-9.00 grams.

Date	Mintage	Good	VG	F	VF	XF
ND(1742-52)	—	3.00	4.00	6.00	10.00	—

SUWON TOWNSHIP MILITARY OFFICE

(Su Won Kwal Li Yong)

KM# 847 MUN
4.5000 g., Cast Copper **Rev:** "Su" at top

Date	Mintage	Good	VG	F	VF	XF
ND(1727) Rare	—	—	—	—	—	—

KM# 848 2 MUN
Cast Copper **Rev:** "Su" at top, "I" (2) at bottom **Note:** Weight varies 8.00-9.00 grams.

Date	Mintage	Good	VG	F	VF	XF
ND(1727-52)	—	7.50	15.00	22.50	30.00	—

WONJU TOWNSHIP MILITARY OFFICE

(Won Ju Kwal Li Yong)

KM# 860 MUN
4.5000 g., Cast Copper **Note:** Small characters.

Date	Mintage	Good	VG	F	VF	XF
ND(1742) Rare	—	—	—	—	—	—

KM# 861 2 MUN
Cast Copper Or Bronze **Rev:** "Won" at top, "I" (2) at bottom **Note:** Weight varies 8.00-9.00 grams.

Date	Mintage	Good	VG	F	VF	XF
ND(1742)	—	75.00	125	175	250	—

HAEJU TOWNSHIP MILITARY OFFICE

(Hae Ju Kwal Li Yong)

KM# 862 MUN
4.5000 g., Cast Copper **Obv:** Large characters **Rev:** "Hae" at top

Date	Mintage	Good	VG	F	VF	XF
ND(1742) Rare	—	—	—	—	—	—

KM# 863 MUN
4.5000 g., Cast Copper **Obv:** Small characters

Date	Mintage	Good	VG	F	VF	XF
ND(1742) Rare	—	—	—	—	—	—

KM# 866 2 MUN
Cast Copper **Rev:** Dot at right **Note:** Weight varies 8.00-9.00 grams.

Date	Mintage	Good	VG	F	VF	XF
ND(1742-52)	—	3.00	4.00	6.00	10.00	—

KM# A866 2 MUN
Cast Copper **Rev:** Dot at left **Note:** Weight varies 8.00-9.00 grams.

Date	Mintage	Good	VG	F	VF	XF
ND(1742-52)	—	3.00	4.00	6.00	10.00	—

KM# 867 2 MUN
Cast Copper **Rev:** Dot at lower left **Note:** Weight varies 8.00-9.00 grams.

Date	Mintage	Good	VG	F	VF	XF
ND(1742-52)	—	3.00	4.00	6.00	10.00	—

KM# A867 2 MUN
Cast Copper **Rev:** Dot at lower right **Note:** Weight varies 8.00-9.00 grams.

Date	Mintage	Good	VG	F	VF	XF
ND(1742-52)	—	3.00	4.00	6.00	10.00	—

KM# 867a 2 MUN
Cast Copper **Rev:** Large star at right **Note:** Weight varies 8.00-9.00 grams.

Date	Mintage	Good	VG	F	VF	XF
ND(1742-52)	—	3.00	4.00	6.00	10.00	—

KM# 868 2 MUN
Cast Copper **Rev:** Dot at right and left **Note:** Weight varies 8.00-9.00 grams.

Date	Mintage	Good	VG	F	VF	XF
ND(1742-52)	—	3.00	4.00	6.00	10.00	—

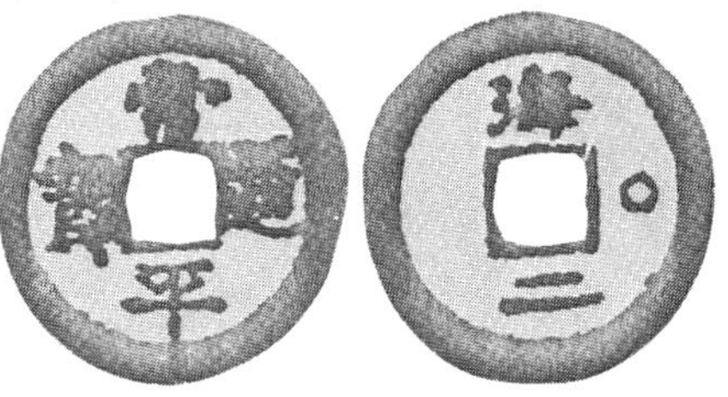

KM# 869 2 MUN
Cast Copper **Rev:** Small circle at right **Note:** Weight varies 8.00-9.00 grams.

Date	Mintage	Good	VG	F	VF	XF
ND(1742-52)	—	20.00	30.00	40.00	60.00	—

KM# 870 2 MUN
Cast Copper **Rev:** Large circle at right **Note:** Weight varies 8.00-9.00 grams.

Date	Mintage	Good	VG	F	VF	XF
ND(1742-52)	—	10.00	15.00	20.00	30.00	—

KM# 871 2 MUN
Cast Copper **Rev:** Crescent at left **Note:** Weight varies 8.00-9.00 grams.

Date	Mintage	Good	VG	F	VF	XF
ND(1742-52)	—	3.00	4.00	6.00	10.00	—

KM# 872 2 MUN
Cast Copper **Rev:** Crescent at right **Note:** Weight varies 8.00-9.00 grams.

Date	Mintage	Good	VG	F	VF	XF
ND(1742-52)	—	3.00	4.00	6.00	10.00	—

KM# A872 2 MUN
Cast Copper **Rev:** Crescent at left, dot at lower left **Note:** Weight varies 8.00-9.00 grams.

Date	Mintage	Good	VG	F	VF	XF
ND(1742-52)	—	4.00	6.00	10.00	15.00	—

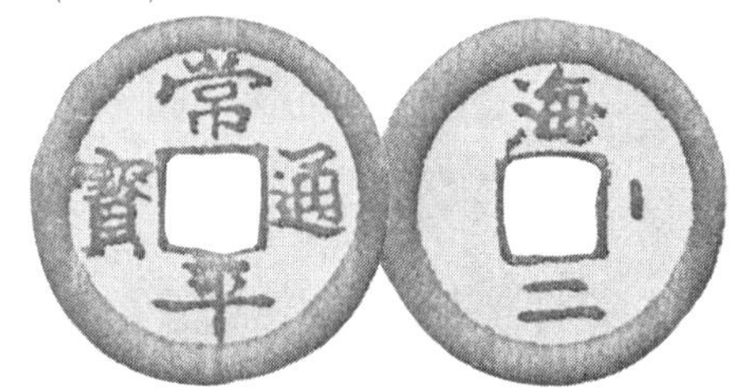

KM# 873 2 MUN
Cast Copper **Rev:** Vertical line at right **Note:** Weight varies 8.00-9.00 grams.

Date	Mintage	Good	VG	F	VF	XF
ND(1742-52)	—	3.00	4.00	6.00	10.00	—

KM# A873 2 MUN
Cast Copper **Rev:** 3 dots vertically at right **Note:** Weight varies 8.00-9.00 grams.

Date	Mintage	Good	VG	F	VF	XF
ND(1742-52)	—	10.00	20.00	30.00	50.00	—

KM# 864b 2 MUN
Cast Copper **Obv:** 2 dot "Tong", large star at left **Note:** Weight varies 8.00-9.00 grams. Size varies 29-30.5 mm.

Date	Mintage	Good	VG	F	VF	XF
ND(1742-52)	—	3.00	4.00	6.00	10.00	—

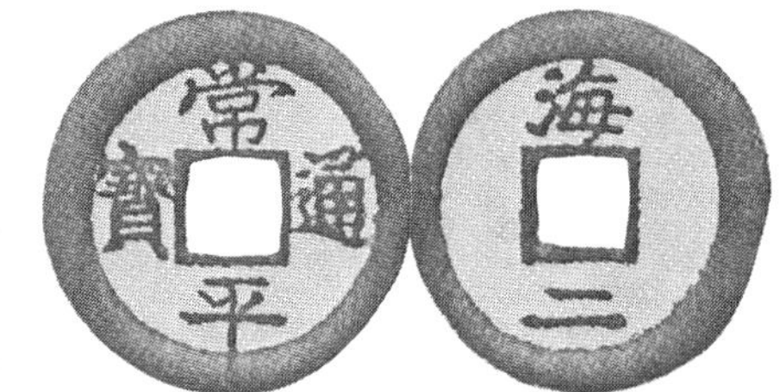

KM# 864 2 MUN
Cast Copper **Rev:** "Hae" at top, "I" at bottom **Note:** Weight varies 8.00-9.00 grams.

Date	Mintage	Good	VG	F	VF	XF
ND(1742-52)	—	3.00	4.00	6.00	10.00	—

KM# 864a 2 MUN
Cast Copper **Obv:** 2 dot "Tong" **Note:** Weight varies 8.00-9.00 grams.

Date	Mintage	Good	VG	F	VF	XF
ND(1742-52)	—	3.00	4.00	6.00	10.00	—

KM# 865 2 MUN
Cast Copper **Rev:** "Hae" in different style **Note:** Weight varies 8.00-9.00 grams.

Date	Mintage	Good	VG	F	VF	XF
ND(1752)	—	10.00	20.00	32.50	50.00	—

KWANG JU TOWNSHIP MILITARY OFFICE

(Kwang Ju Kwal Li Yong)

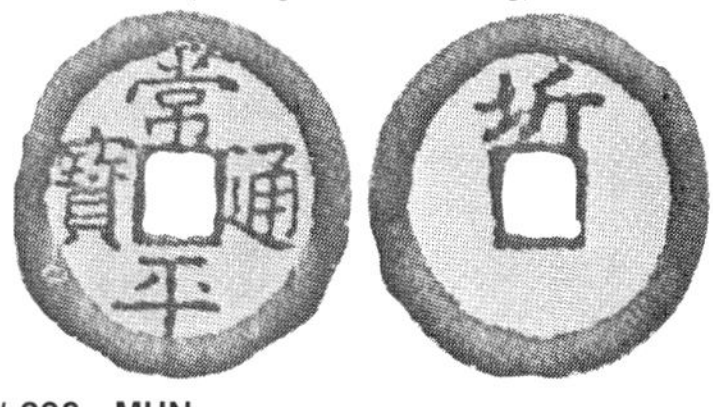

KM# 888 MUN
4.5000 g., Cast Copper **Rev:** "Ki" at top

Date	Mintage	Good	VG	F	VF	XF
ND(1742) Rare	—	—	—	—	—	—

KM# 897 2 MUN
Cast Copper Or Bronze **Rev:** "Ki" at top, "I" (2) at bottom **Note:** Weight varies 8.00-9.00 grams.

Date	Mintage	Good	VG	F	VF	XF
ND(1742-52)	—	3.00	4.00	6.00	10.00	—

KM# 898 2 MUN
Cast Copper Or Bronze **Rev:** Dot at right **Note:** Weight varies 8.00-9.00 grams.

Date	Mintage	Good	VG	F	VF	XF
ND(1742-52)	—	3.00	4.00	6.00	10.00	—

KM# 898a 2 MUN
Cast Copper Or Bronze **Rev:** Large dot at right **Note:** Weight varies 8.00-9.00 grams.

Date	Mintage	Good	VG	F	VF	XF
ND(1742-52)	—	3.00	4.00	6.00	10.00	—

KM# 899 2 MUN
Cast Copper Or Bronze **Rev:** Dot at left **Note:** Weight varies 8.00-9.00 grams.

Date	Mintage	Good	VG	F	VF	XF
ND(1742-52)	—	3.00	4.50	6.50	10.00	—

KM# 901 2 MUN
Cast Copper Or Bronze **Rev:** Circle at right **Note:** Weight varies 8.00-9.00 grams.

Date	Mintage	Good	VG	F	VF	XF
ND(1742-52)	—	3.50	5.00	8.00	14.00	—

KM# 902 2 MUN
Cast Copper Or Bronze **Rev:** Double circle at right **Note:** Weight varies 8.00-9.00 grams.

Date	Mintage	Good	VG	F	VF	XF
ND(1742-52)	—	3.50	5.00	8.00	14.00	—

KM# 903 2 MUN
Cast Copper Or Bronze **Rev:** Inward crescent at right **Note:** Weight varies 8.00-9.00 grams.

Date	Mintage	Good	VG	F	VF	XF
ND(1742-52)	—	20.00	40.00	65.00	100	—

KM# 904 2 MUN
Cast Copper Or Bronze **Rev:** Inward crescent at left **Note:** Weight varies 8.00-9.00 grams.

Date	Mintage	Good	VG	F	VF	XF
ND(1742-52)	—	3.50	5.00	8.00	14.00	—

KM# 905 2 MUN
Cast Copper Or Bronze **Rev:** Circle at right, inward crescent at left **Note:** Weight varies 8.00-9.00 grams.

Date	Mintage	Good	VG	F	VF	XF
ND(1742-52)	—	3.50	5.00	8.00	14.00	—

KM# A905 2 MUN
Cast Copper Or Bronze **Rev:** With additional dot at upper right **Note:** Weight varies 8.00-9.00 grams.

Date	Mintage	Good	VG	F	VF	XF
ND(1742-52)	—	3.50	5.00	8.00	14.00	—

KM# B905 2 MUN
Cast Copper Or Bronze **Rev:** With additional dot at upper left **Note:** Weight varies 8.00-9.00 grams.

Date	Mintage	Good	VG	F	VF	XF
ND(1742-52)	—	3.50	5.00	8.00	14.00	—

KM# 900 2 MUN
Cast Copper Or Bronze **Rev:** Dot at right and left **Note:** Weight varies 8.00-9.00 grams. Size varies 29-31 mm.

Date	Mintage	Good	VG	F	VF	XF
ND(1742-52)	—	3.00	4.50	6.50	10.00	—

KYONGGI PROVINCIAL OFFICE

(Kyong Gi Kam Yong)

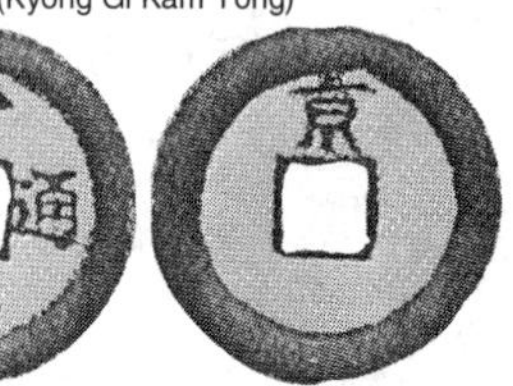

KM# 906 MUN
4.5000 g., Cast Copper **Rev:** "Kyong" at top

Date	Mintage	Good	VG	F	VF	XF
ND(1742) Rare	—	—	—	—	—	—

KYONGGI NAVAL STATION

(Kyong Gi Su Yong)

KM# 908 MUN
4.5000 g., Cast Copper **Rev:** "Kyong" at top, "Su" at bottom

Date	Mintage	Good	VG	F	VF	XF
ND(1742) Rare	—	—	—	—	—	—

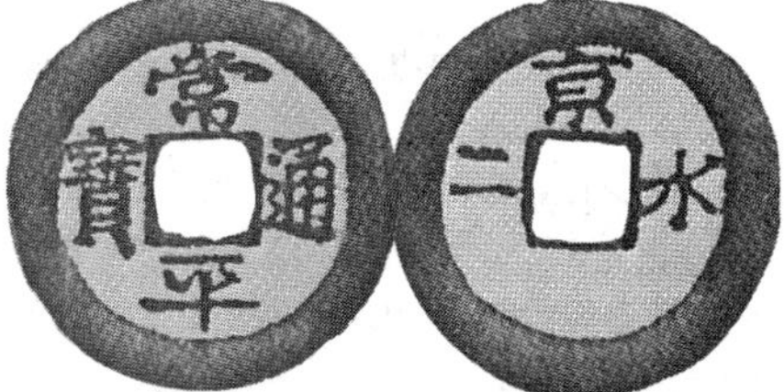

KM# 909 2 MUN
Cast Copper Or Bronze **Rev:** "Kyong" at top, "Su" at right, "I" (2) at left **Note:** Weight varies 8.00-9.00 grams.

Date	Mintage	Good	VG	F	VF	XF
ND(1742-52)	—	3.00	4.00	6.00	10.00	—

HWANGHAE PROVINCIAL OFFICE

(Hwang Hae Kam Yong)

KM# 910 MUN
Cast Copper **Rev:** "Hwang" at top

Date	Mintage	Good	VG	F	VF	XF
ND(1742) Rare	—	—	—	—	—	—

KM# 911 MUN
Cast Copper **Rev:** Dot at lower left

Date	Mintage	Good	VG	F	VF	XF
ND(1742) Rare	—	—	—	—	—	—

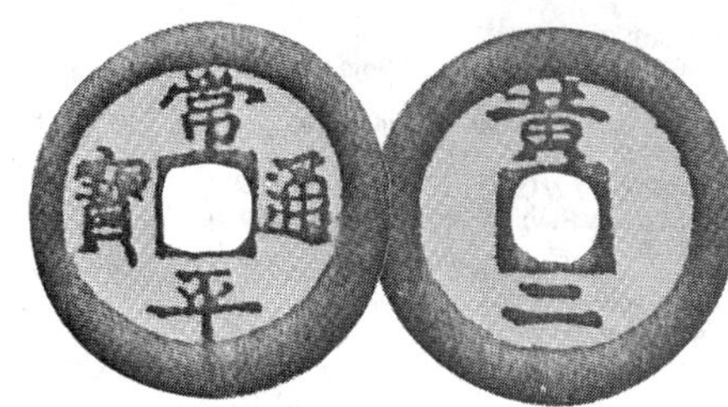

KM# 912 2 MUN
Cast Copper Or Bronze **Rev:** "Hwang" at top, "I" (2) at bottom **Note:** Weight varies 8.00-9.00 grams.

Date	Mintage	Good	VG	F	VF	XF
ND(1742-52)	—	4.00	8.00	12.00	16.00	—

KM# 999s 2 MUN
Cast Copper Or Bronze **Note:** Weight varies 8.00-9.00 grams.

Date	Mintage	Good	VG	F	VF	XF
ND(1742-52)	—	—	—	—	—	50.00

P'YONGAN PROVINCIAL OFFICE

(P'yong An Kam Yong)

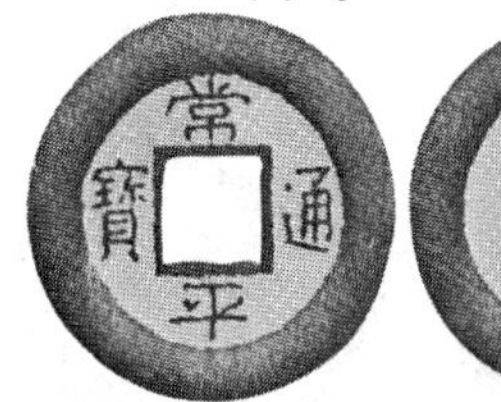

KM# 916 MUN
4.5000 g., Cast Copper, 26 mm. **Rev:** "I" (2) at right, series number at bottom

Date	Mintage	Good	VG	F	VF	XF
ND(1724) Series 1-7	—	2.00	3.00	5.00	8.00	—

KM# 916.11 MUN
4.5000 g., Cast Copper **Rev:** Star at lower right

Date	Mintage	Good	VG	F	VF	XF
ND(1724) Series 1	—	2.00	3.00	5.00	8.00	—

KM# 916s MUN
4.5000 g., Cast Copper **Note:** Seed type.

Date	Mintage	Good	VG	F	VF	XF
ND(1724) Series 1-7	—	—	—	—	—	50.00

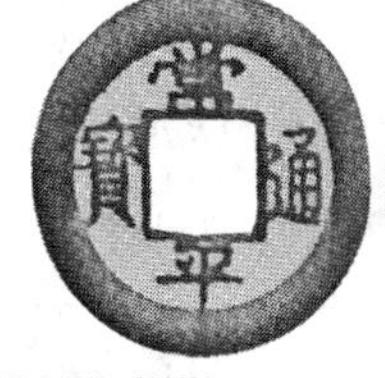
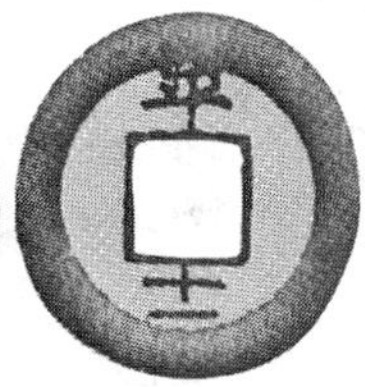

KM# 914 MUN
4.5000 g., Cast Copper **Rev:** "P'yong" at top, series number at bottom **Note:** Size varies 23-26 mm.

Date	Mintage	Good	VG	F	VF	XF
ND(1727) Series 1-12	—	2.00	3.00	5.00	8.00	—

KM# 914s MUN
4.5000 g., Cast Copper **Note:** Seed type.

Date	Mintage	Good	VG	F	VF	XF
ND(1727) Series 1-12	—	—	—	—	—	50.00

KM# 925 2 MUN
Cast Copper **Rev:** "P'yong" at top, "I" (2) at bottom **Note:** Weight varies 8.00-9.00 grams.

Date	Mintage	Good	VG	F	VF	XF
ND(1679-1742)	—	4.00	6.00	7.50	10.00	—

KM# 926 2 MUN
Cast Copper **Rev:** "Ch'on" at bottom, "I" (2) at right **Note:** Weight varies 8.00-9.00 grams.

Date	Mintage	Good	VG	F	VF	XF
ND(1742-52)	—	4.00	6.00	10.00	15.00	—

KM# 927 2 MUN
Cast Copper **Rev:** "Chi" at bottom **Note:** Weight varies 8.00-9.00 grams.

Date	Mintage	Good	VG	F	VF	XF
ND(1742-52)	—	4.00	6.00	10.00	15.00	—

KM# 928 2 MUN
Cast Copper **Rev:** "Hyon" at bottom **Note:** Weight varies 8.00-9.00 grams.

Date	Mintage	Good	VG	F	VF	XF
ND(1742-52)	—	4.00	6.00	10.00	15.00	—

KM# 929 2 MUN
Cast Copper **Rev:** "Hwang" (yellow) at bottom **Note:** Weight varies 8.00-9.00 grams.

Date	Mintage	Good	VG	F	VF	XF
ND(1742-52)	—	4.00	6.00	10.00	15.00	—

KM# 930 2 MUN
Cast Copper **Rev:** "U" (space) at bottom **Note:** Weight varies 8.00-9.00 grams.

Date	Mintage	Good	VG	F	VF	XF
ND(1742-52)	—	2.50	4.50	6.50	10.00	—

KM# 931 2 MUN
Cast Copper **Rev:** "Chu" at bottom **Note:** Weight varies 8.00-9.00 grams.

Date	Mintage	Good	VG	F	VF	XF
ND(1742-52)	—	4.00	6.00	10.00	15.00	—

KM# 932 2 MUN
Cast Copper **Rev:** "Hong" at bottom **Note:** Weight varies 8.00-9.00 grams.

Date	Mintage	Good	VG	F	VF	XF
ND(1742-52)	—	4.00	6.00	10.00	15.00	—

KM# 933 2 MUN
Cast Copper **Rev:** "Hwang" (barren) at bottom **Note:** Weight varies 8.00-9.00 grams.

Date	Mintage	Good	VG	F	VF	XF
ND(1742-52)	—	4.00	6.00	10.00	15.00	—

KM# 934 2 MUN
Cast Copper **Rev:** "Il" (sun) at bottom **Note:** Weight varies 8.00-9.00 grams.

Date	Mintage	Good	VG	F	VF	XF
ND(1742-52)	—	4.00	6.00	10.00	15.00	—

KM# 935 2 MUN
Cast Copper **Rev:** "Wol" at bottom **Note:** Weight varies 8.00-9.00 grams.

Date	Mintage	Good	VG	F	VF	XF
ND(1742-52)	—	4.00	6.00	10.00	15.00	—

KM# 936 2 MUN
Cast Copper **Rev:** "Yong" at bottom **Note:** Weight varies 8.00-9.00 grams.

Date	Mintage	Good	VG	F	VF	XF
ND(1742-52)	—	4.00	6.00	10.00	15.00	—

KM# 937 2 MUN
Cast Copper **Rev:** "Ch'uk" at bottom **Note:** Weight varies 8.00-9.00 grams.

Date	Mintage	Good	VG	F	VF	XF
ND(1742-52)	—	4.00	6.00	10.00	15.00	—

KM# 938 2 MUN
Cast Copper **Rev:** "Chin" at bottom **Note:** Weight varies 8.00-9.00 grams.

Date	Mintage	Good	VG	F	VF	XF
ND(1742-52)	—	4.00	6.00	10.00	15.00	—

KM# 939 2 MUN
Cast Copper **Rev:** "Suk" at bottom **Note:** Weight varies 8.00-9.00 grams.

Date	Mintage	Good	VG	F	VF	XF
ND(1742-52)	—	4.00	6.00	10.00	15.00	—

KM# 940 2 MUN
Cast Copper **Rev:** "Yol" at bottom **Note:** Weight varies 8.00-9.00 grams.

Date	Mintage	Good	VG	F	VF	XF
ND(1742-52)	—	4.00	6.00	10.00	15.00	—

KM# 941 2 MUN
Cast Copper **Rev:** "Chang" (extend) at bottom **Note:** Weight varies 8.00-9.00 grams.

Date	Mintage	Good	VG	F	VF	XF
ND(1742-52)	—	4.00	6.00	10.00	15.00	—

KM# 942 2 MUN
Cast Copper **Rev:** "Han" at bottom **Note:** Weight varies 8.00-9.00 grams.

Date	Mintage	Good	VG	F	VF	XF
ND(1742-52)	—	4.00	6.00	10.00	15.00	—

KM# 943 2 MUN
Cast Copper **Rev:** "Nae" at bottom **Note:** Weight varies 8.00-9.00 grams.

Date	Mintage	Good	VG	F	VF	XF
ND(1742-52)	—	4.00	6.00	10.00	15.00	—

KM# 944 2 MUN
Cast Copper **Rev:** "So" at bottom **Note:** Weight varies 8.00-9.00 grams.

Date	Mintage	Good	VG	F	VF	XF
ND(1742-52)	—	4.00	6.00	10.00	15.00	—

KM# 945 2 MUN
Cast Copper **Rev:** "Wang" at bottom **Note:** Weight varies 8.00-9.00 grams.

Date	Mintage	Good	VG	F	VF	XF
ND(1742-52)	—	4.00	6.00	10.00	15.00	—

KM# 946 2 MUN
Cast Copper **Rev:** "Ch'u" at bottom **Note:** Weight varies 8.00-9.00 grams.

Date	Mintage	Good	VG	F	VF	XF
ND(1742-52)	—	4.00	6.00	10.00	15.00	—

KM# 947 2 MUN
Cast Copper **Rev:** "Su" (harvest) at bottom **Note:** Weight varies 8.00-9.00 grams.

Date	Mintage	Good	VG	F	VF	XF
ND(1742-52)	—	4.00	6.00	10.00	15.00	—

KM# 948 2 MUN

Cast Copper **Rev:** "Tong" at bottom **Note:** Weight varies 8.00-9.00 grams.

Date	Mintage	Good	VG	F	VF	XF
ND(1742-52)	—	4.00	6.00	10.00	15.00	—

KM# 949 2 MUN

Cast Copper **Rev:** "Chang' (hoard) at bottom **Note:** Weight varies 8.00-9.00 grams.

Date	Mintage	Good	VG	F	VF	XF
ND(1742-52)	—	4.00	6.00	10.00	15.00	—

KM# 950 2 MUN

Cast Copper **Rev:** "Yun" at bottom **Note:** Weight varies 8.00-9.00 grams.

Date	Mintage	Good	VG	F	VF	XF
ND(1742-52)	—	4.00	6.00	10.00	15.00	—

KM# 951 2 MUN

Cast Copper **Rev:** "Yo" at bottom **Note:** Weight varies 8.00-9.00 grams.

Date	Mintage	Good	VG	F	VF	XF
ND(1742-52)	—	4.00	6.00	10.00	15.00	—

KM# 952 2 MUN

Cast Copper **Rev:** "Song" at bottom **Note:** Weight varies 8.00-9.00 grams.

Date	Mintage	Good	VG	F	VF	XF
ND(1742-52)	—	4.00	6.00	10.00	15.00	—

KM# 953 2 MUN

Cast Copper **Rev:** "Se" at bottom **Note:** Weight varies 8.00-9.00 grams.

Date	Mintage	Good	VG	F	VF	XF
ND(1742-52)	—	4.00	6.00	10.00	15.00	—

KM# 954 2 MUN

Cast Copper **Rev:** "Yul" at bottom **Note:** Weight varies 8.00-9.00 grams.

Date	Mintage	Good	VG	F	VF	XF
ND(1742-52)	—	4.00	6.00	10.00	15.00	—

KM# 955 2 MUN

Cast Copper **Rev:** "Yo" (female) at bottom **Note:** Weight varies 8.00-9.00 grams.

Date	Mintage	Good	VG	F	VF	XF
ND(1742-52)	—	4.00	6.00	10.00	15.00	—

KM# 956 2 MUN

Cast Copper **Rev:** "Cho" at bottom **Note:** Weight varies 8.00-9.00 grams.

Date	Mintage	Good	VG	F	VF	XF
ND(1742-52)	—	4.00	6.00	10.00	15.00	—

KM# 957 2 MUN

Cast Copper **Rev:** "Yang" at bottom **Note:** Weight varies 8.00-9.00 grams.

Date	Mintage	Good	VG	F	VF	XF
ND(1742-52)	—	5.00	8.50	12.50	20.00	—

KM# 958 2 MUN

Cast Copper **Rev:** "Un" at bottom **Note:** Weight varies 8.00-9.00 grams.

Date	Mintage	Good	VG	F	VF	XF
ND(1742-52)	—	5.00	8.50	12.50	20.00	—

KM# 959 2 MUN

Cast Copper **Rev:** "Tung" at bottom **Note:** Weight varies 8.00-9.00 grams.

Date	Mintage	Good	VG	F	VF	XF
ND(1742-52)	—	6.00	10.00	16.50	25.00	—

KM# 960 2 MUN

Cast Copper **Rev:** "Ch'i" at bottom **Note:** Weight varies 8.00-9.00 grams.

Date	Mintage	Good	VG	F	VF	XF
ND(1742-52)	—	5.00	8.50	12.50	20.00	—

KM# 961 2 MUN

Cast Copper **Rev:** "U" at bottom **Note:** Weight varies 8.00-9.00 grams.

Date	Mintage	Good	VG	F	VF	XF
ND(1742-52)	—	5.00	8.50	12.50	20.00	—

KM# 962 2 MUN

Cast Copper **Rev:** "No" at bottom **Note:** Weight varies 8.00-9.00 grams.

Date	Mintage	Good	VG	F	VF	XF
ND(1742-52)	—	5.00	8.50	12.50	20.00	—

KM# 963 2 MUN

Cast Copper **Rev:** "Kyol" at bottom **Note:** Weight varies 8.00-9.00 grams.

Date	Mintage	Good	VG	F	VF	XF
ND(1742-52)	—	5.00	8.50	12.50	20.00	—

KM# 964 2 MUN

Cast Copper **Rev:** "Wi" at bottom **Note:** Weight varies 8.00-9.00 grams.

Date	Mintage	Good	VG	F	VF	XF
ND(1742-52)	—	6.00	10.00	16.50	25.00	—

KM# 965 2 MUN

Cast Copper **Rev:** "Sang" at bottom **Note:** Weight varies 8.00-9.00 grams.

Date	Mintage	Good	VG	F	VF	XF
ND(1742-52)	—	6.00	10.00	16.50	25.00	—

KM# 966 2 MUN

Cast Copper **Rev:** "Kum" at bottom **Note:** Weight varies 8.00-9.00 grams.

Date	Mintage	Good	VG	F	VF	XF
ND(1742-52)	—	6.00	10.00	16.50	25.00	—

KM# 967 2 MUN

Cast Copper **Rev:** "Saeng" at bottom **Note:** Weight varies 8.00-9.00 grams.

Date	Mintage	Good	VG	F	VF	XF
ND(1742-52)	—	5.00	8.50	12.50	20.00	—

KM# 968 2 MUN

Cast Copper **Rev:** "Yo" (beautiful) at bottom **Note:** Weight varies 8.00-9.00 grams.

Date	Mintage	Good	VG	F	VF	XF
ND(1742-52)	—	9.00	12.50	20.00	35.00	—

KM# 969 2 MUN

Cast Copper **Rev:** "Su" (water) at bottom **Note:** Weight varies 8.00-9.00 grams.

Date	Mintage	Good	VG	F	VF	XF
ND(1742-52)	—	6.00	10.00	16.50	25.00	—

KM# 970 5 MUN

Cast Bronze **Rev:** Series number at bottom, "Tang" at right, "O" (5) at left

Date	Mintage	Good	VG	F	VF	XF
ND(1742-52) Series 1-10	—	4.00	5.00	7.00	12.00	—

KM# 970s 5 MUN

Cast Bronze **Note:** Seed type.

Date	Mintage	Good	VG	F	VF	XF
ND(1742-52) Series 1-10	—	—	—	—	—	50.00

HAMGYONG PROVINCIAL OFFICE

(Ham Gyong Kam Yong)

KM# 973 MUN

4.5000 g., Cast Copper **Rev:** "Ham" at top

Date	Mintage	Good	VG	F	VF	XF
ND(1742) Rare	—	—	—	—	—	—

KM# 975s 2 MUN

Cast Copper Or Bronze

Date	Mintage	Good	VG	F	VF	XF
ND(1742-52)	—	—	—	—	—	50.00

KM# 990s 2 MUN

Cast Copper Or Bronze

Date	Mintage	Good	VG	F	VF	XF
ND(1742-52)	—	—	—	—	—	50.00

KM# B1005s 2 MUN

Cast Copper Or Bronze **Note:** Seed type. Weight varies 8.00-9.00 grams. Struck at Ham Gyong Kam Yong.

Date	Mintage	Good	VG	F	VF	XF
ND(1742-52)	—	—	—	—	—	50.00

KM# 975 2 MUN

Cast Copper Or Bronze **Rev:** "Ham" at top, "I" (2) at bottom **Note:** Weight varies 8.00-9.00 grams.

Date	Mintage	Good	VG	F	VF	XF
ND(1742-52)	—	4.00	6.00	8.50	12.50	—

KM# 976 2 MUN

Cast Copper Or Bronze **Obv:** Large characters **Rev:** "Ch'on" at bottom **Note:** Weight varies 8.00-9.00 grams.

Date	Mintage	Good	VG	F	VF	XF
ND(1742-52)	—	3.00	4.00	6.00	10.00	—

KM# 977 2 MUN

Cast Copper Or Bronze **Obv:** Small characters **Note:** Weight varies 8.00-9.00 grams.

Date	Mintage	Good	VG	F	VF	XF
ND(1742-52)	—	3.00	4.00	6.00	10.00	—

KM# 978 2 MUN

Cast Copper Or Bronze **Obv:** Large characters **Rev:** "Chi" at bottom **Note:** Weight varies 8.00-9.00 grams.

Date	Mintage	Good	VG	F	VF	XF
ND(1742-52)	—	3.00	4.00	6.00	10.00	—

KM# 979 2 MUN

Cast Copper Or Bronze **Obv:** Small characters **Note:** Weight varies 8.00-9.00 grams.

Date	Mintage	Good	VG	F	VF	XF
ND(1742-52)	—	3.00	4.00	6.00	10.00	—

KM# 980 2 MUN

Cast Copper Or Bronze **Obv:** Large characters **Rev:** "Hyon" at bottom **Note:** Weight varies 8.00-9.00 grams.

Date	Mintage	Good	VG	F	VF	XF
ND(1742-52)	—	3.00	4.00	6.00	10.00	—

KM# 981 2 MUN

Cast Copper Or Bronze **Obv:** Small characters **Note:** Weight varies 8.00-9.00 grams.

Date	Mintage	Good	VG	F	VF	XF
ND(1742-52)	—	3.00	4.00	6.00	10.00	—

KM# 982 2 MUN

Cast Copper Or Bronze **Obv:** Large characters **Rev:** "Hwang" (yellow) at bottom **Note:** Weight varies 8.00-9.00 grams.

Date	Mintage	Good	VG	F	VF	XF
ND(1742-52)	—	3.00	4.00	6.00	10.00	—

KM# 983 2 MUN

Cast Copper Or Bronze **Obv:** Small characters **Note:** Weight varies 8.00-9.00 grams.

Date	Mintage	Good	VG	F	VF	XF
ND(1742-52)	—	3.00	4.00	6.00	10.00	—

KM# 976s 2 MUN

Cast Copper Or Bronze **Note:** Weight varies 8.00-9.00 grams.

Date	Mintage	Good	VG	F	VF	XF
ND(1742-52)	—	—	—	—	—	50.00

KM# 977s 2 MUN

Cast Copper Or Bronze **Note:** Weight varies 8.00-9.00 grams.

Date	Mintage	Good	VG	F	VF	XF
ND(1742-52)	—	—	—	—	—	50.00

KM# 978s 2 MUN

Cast Copper Or Bronze **Note:** Weight varies 8.00-9.00 grams.

Date	Mintage	Good	VG	F	VF	XF
ND(1742-52)	—	—	—	—	—	50.00

KM# 979s 2 MUN

Cast Copper Or Bronze **Note:** Weight varies 8.00-9.00 grams.

Date	Mintage	Good	VG	F	VF	XF
ND(1742-52)	—	—	—	—	—	50.00

KM# 980s 2 MUN

Cast Copper Or Bronze **Note:** Weight varies 8.00-9.00 grams.

Date	Mintage	Good	VG	F	VF	XF
ND(1742-52)	—	—	—	—	—	50.00

KM# 981s 2 MUN

Cast Copper Or Bronze **Note:** Weight varies 8.00-9.00 grams.

Date	Mintage	Good	VG	F	VF	XF
ND(1742-52)	—	—	—	—	—	50.00

KM# 982s 2 MUN

Cast Copper Or Bronze **Note:** Weight varies 8.00-9.00 grams.

Date	Mintage	Good	VG	F	VF	XF
ND(1742-52)	—	—	—	—	—	50.00

KM# 983s 2 MUN

Cast Copper Or Bronze **Note:** Weight varies 8.00-9.00 grams.

Date	Mintage	Good	VG	F	VF	XF
ND(1742-52)	—	—	—	—	—	50.00

KM# 984s 2 MUN

Cast Copper Or Bronze **Note:** Weight varies 8.00-9.00 grams.

Date	Mintage	Good	VG	F	VF	XF
ND(1742-52)	—	—	—	—	—	50.00

KM# 984 2 MUN

Cast Copper Or Bronze **Obv:** Large characters **Rev:** "U" at bottom **Note:** Weight varies 8.00-9.00 grams.

Date	Mintage	Good	VG	F	VF	XF
ND(1742-52)	—	3.00	4.00	6.00	10.00	—

KM# 985 2 MUN

Cast Copper Or Bronze **Obv:** Small characters **Note:** Weight varies 8.00-9.00 grams.

Date	Mintage	Good	VG	F	VF	XF
ND(1742-52)	—	3.00	4.00	6.00	10.00	—

KM# 986 2 MUN

Cast Copper Or Bronze **Obv:** Large characters **Rev:** "Chu" at bottom **Note:** Weight varies 8.00-9.00 grams.

Date	Mintage	Good	VG	F	VF	XF
ND(1742-52)	—	3.00	4.00	6.00	10.00	—

KM# 987 2 MUN

Cast Copper Or Bronze **Obv:** Small characters **Note:** Weight varies 8.00-9.00 grams.

Date	Mintage	Good	VG	F	VF	XF
ND(1742-52)	—	3.00	4.00	6.00	10.00	—

KM# 988 2 MUN

Cast Copper Or Bronze **Obv:** Large characters **Rev:** "Hong" at bottom **Note:** Weight varies 8.00-9.00 grams.

Date	Mintage	Good	VG	F	VF	XF
ND(1742-52)	—	3.00	4.00	6.00	10.00	—

KM# 989 2 MUN

Cast Copper Or Bronze **Obv:** SMall characters **Note:** Weight varies 8.00-9.00 grams.

Date	Mintage	Good	VG	F	VF	XF
ND(1742-52)	—	3.00	4.00	6.00	10.00	—

KM# 990 2 MUN
Cast Copper Or Bronze **Obv:** Large characters **Rev:** "Hwang" (barren) at bottom **Note:** Weight varies 8.00-9.00 grams.

Date	Mintage	Good	VG	F	VF	XF
ND(1742-52)	—	3.00	4.00	6.00	10.00	—

KM# 991 2 MUN
Cast Copper Or Bronze **Obv:** Small characters **Note:** Weight varies 8.00-9.00 grams.

Date	Mintage	Good	VG	F	VF	XF
ND(1742-52)	—	3.00	4.00	6.00	10.00	—

KM# 992 2 MUN
Cast Copper Or Bronze **Obv:** Large characters **Rev:** "Il" at bottom **Note:** Weight varies 8.00-9.00 grams.

Date	Mintage	Good	VG	F	VF	XF
ND(1742-52)	—	3.00	4.00	6.00	10.00	—

KM# 993 2 MUN
Cast Copper Or Bronze **Obv:** Small characters **Note:** Weight varies 8.00-9.00 grams.

Date	Mintage	Good	VG	F	VF	XF
ND(1742-52)	—	3.00	4.00	6.00	10.00	—

KM# 994 2 MUN
Cast Copper Or Bronze **Obv:** Large characters **Rev:** "Wol" at bottom **Note:** Weight varies 8.00-9.00 grams.

Date	Mintage	Good	VG	F	VF	XF
ND(1742-52)	—	3.00	4.00	6.00	10.00	—

KM# 995 2 MUN
Cast Copper Or Bronze **Obv:** Small characters **Note:** Weight varies 8.00-9.00 grams.

Date	Mintage	Good	VG	F	VF	XF
ND(1742-52)	—	3.00	4.00	6.00	10.00	—

KM# 996 2 MUN
Cast Copper Or Bronze **Obv:** Large characters **Rev:** "Yong" at bottom **Note:** Weight varies 8.00-9.00 grams.

Date	Mintage	Good	VG	F	VF	XF
ND(1742-52)	—	3.00	4.00	6.00	10.00	—

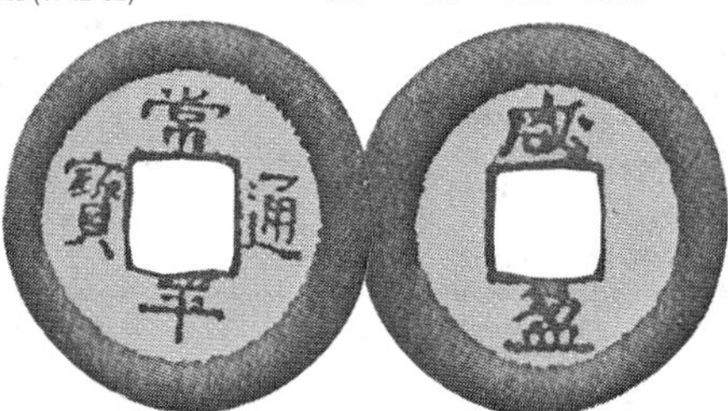

KM# 997 2 MUN
Cast Copper Or Bronze **Obv:** Small characters **Note:** Weight varies 8.00-9.00 grams.

Date	Mintage	Good	VG	F	VF	XF
ND(1742-52)	—	3.00	4.00	6.00	10.00	—

KM# 985s 2 MUN
Cast Copper Or Bronze **Note:** Weight varies 8.00-9.00 grams.

Date	Mintage	Good	VG	F	VF	XF
ND(1742-52)	—	—	—	—	—	50.00

KM# 986s 2 MUN
Cast Copper Or Bronze **Note:** Weight varies 8.00-9.00 grams.

Date	Mintage	Good	VG	F	VF	XF
ND(1742-52)	—	—	—	—	—	50.00

KM# 987s 2 MUN
Cast Copper Or Bronze **Note:** Weight varies 8.00-9.00 grams.

Date	Mintage	Good	VG	F	VF	XF
ND(1742-52)	—	—	—	—	—	50.00

KM# 988s 2 MUN
Cast Copper Or Bronze **Note:** Weight varies 8.00-9.00 grams.

Date	Mintage	Good	VG	F	VF	XF
ND(1742-52)	—	—	—	—	—	50.00

KM# 989s 2 MUN
Cast Copper Or Bronze **Note:** Weight varies 8.00-9.00 grams.

Date	Mintage	Good	VG	F	VF	XF
ND(1742-52)	—	—	—	—	—	50.00

KM# 991s 2 MUN
Cast Copper Or Bronze **Note:** Weight varies 8.00-9.00 grams.

Date	Mintage	Good	VG	F	VF	XF
ND(1742-52)	—	—	—	—	—	50.00

KM# 992s 2 MUN
Cast Copper Or Bronze **Note:** Weight varies 8.00-9.00 grams.

Date	Mintage	Good	VG	F	VF	XF
ND(1742-52)	—	—	—	—	—	50.00

KM# 993s 2 MUN
Cast Copper Or Bronze **Note:** Weight varies 8.00-9.00 grams.

Date	Mintage	Good	VG	F	VF	XF
ND(1742-52)	—	—	—	—	—	50.00

KM# 994s 2 MUN
Cast Copper Or Bronze **Note:** Weight varies 8.00-9.00 grams.

Date	Mintage	Good	VG	F	VF	XF
ND(1742-52)	—	—	—	—	—	50.00

KM# 995s 2 MUN
Cast Copper Or Bronze **Note:** Weight varies 8.00-9.00 grams.

Date	Mintage	Good	VG	F	VF	XF
ND(1742-52)	—	—	—	—	—	50.00

KM# 996s 2 MUN
Cast Copper Or Bronze **Note:** Weight varies 8.00-9.00 grams.

Date	Mintage	Good	VG	F	VF	XF
ND(1742-52)	—	—	—	—	—	50.00

KM# 997s 2 MUN
Cast Copper Or Bronze **Note:** Weight varies 8.00-9.00 grams.

Date	Mintage	Good	VG	F	VF	XF
ND(1742-52)	—	—	—	—	—	50.00

KM# 998s 2 MUN
Cast Copper Or Bronze **Note:** Weight varies 8.00-9.00 grams.

Date	Mintage	Good	VG	F	VF	XF
ND(1742-52)	—	—	—	—	—	50.00

KM# 1000s 2 MUN
Cast Copper Or Bronze **Note:** Weight varies 8.00-9.00 grams.

Date	Mintage	Good	VG	F	VF	XF
ND(1742-52)	—	—	—	—	—	50.00

KM# 1001s 2 MUN
Cast Copper Or Bronze **Note:** Weight varies 8.00-9.00 grams.

Date	Mintage	Good	VG	F	VF	XF
ND(1742-52)	—	—	—	—	—	50.00

KM# 1002s 2 MUN
Cast Copper Or Bronze **Note:** Weight varies 8.00-9.00 grams.

Date	Mintage	Good	VG	F	VF	XF
ND(1742-52)	—	—	—	—	—	50.00

KM# 1003s 2 MUN
Cast Copper Or Bronze **Note:** Weight varies 8.00-9.00 grams.

Date	Mintage	Good	VG	F	VF	XF
ND(1742-52)	—	—	—	—	—	50.00

KM# 1004s 2 MUN
Cast Copper Or Bronze **Note:** Weight varies 8.00-9.00 grams.

Date	Mintage	Good	VG	F	VF	XF
ND(1742-52)	—	—	—	—	—	50.00

KM# 1005s 2 MUN
Cast Copper Or Bronze **Note:** Weight varies 8.00-9.00 grams.

Date	Mintage	Good	VG	F	VF	XF
ND(1742-52)	—	—	—	—	—	50.00

KM# A1005s 2 MUN
Cast Copper Or Bronze **Note:** Weight varies 8.00-9.00 grams.

Date	Mintage	Good	VG	F	VF	XF
ND(1742-52)	—	—	—	—	—	50.00

KM# 998 2 MUN
Cast Copper Or Bronze **Obv:** Large characters **Rev:** "Ch'uk" at bottom **Note:** Weight varies 8.00-9.00 grams.

Date	Mintage	Good	VG	F	VF	XF
ND(1742-52)	—	3.00	4.00	6.00	10.00	—

KM# 999 2 MUN
Cast Copper Or Bronze **Obv:** Small characters **Note:** Weight varies 8.00-9.00 grams.

Date	Mintage	Good	VG	F	VF	XF
ND(1742-52)	—	3.00	4.00	6.00	10.00	—

KM# 1000 2 MUN
Cast Copper Or Bronze **Obv:** Large characters **Rev:** "Chin" at bottom **Note:** Weight varies 8.00-9.00 grams.

Date	Mintage	Good	VG	F	VF	XF
ND(1742-52)	—	3.00	4.00	6.00	10.00	—

KM# 1001 2 MUN
Cast Copper Or Bronze **Obv:** Small characters **Note:** Weight varies 8.00-9.00 grams.

Date	Mintage	Good	VG	F	VF	XF
ND(1742-52)	—	3.00	4.00	6.00	10.00	—

KM# 1002 2 MUN
Cast Copper Or Bronze **Obv:** Large characters **Rev:** "Suk" at bottom **Note:** Weight varies 8.00-9.00 grams.

Date	Mintage	Good	VG	F	VF	XF
ND(1742-52)	—	3.00	4.00	6.00	10.00	—

KM# 1003 2 MUN
Cast Copper Or Bronze **Obv:** Small characters **Note:** Weight varies 8.00-9.00 grams.

Date	Mintage	Good	VG	F	VF	XF
ND(1742-52)	—	3.00	4.00	6.00	10.00	—

KM# 1004 2 MUN
Cast Copper Or Bronze **Obv:** Large characters **Rev:** "Yol" at bottom **Note:** Weight varies 8.00-9.00 grams.

Date	Mintage	Good	VG	F	VF	XF
ND(1742-52)	—	3.00	4.00	6.00	10.00	—

KM# 1005 2 MUN
Cast Copper Or Bronze **Obv:** Small characters **Note:** Weight varies 8.00-9.00 grams.

Date	Mintage	Good	VG	F	VF	XF
ND(1742-52)	—	3.00	4.00	6.00	10.00	—

KM# A1005 2 MUN
Cast Copper Or Bronze **Obv:** Large characters **Rev:** "Chang" (extend) at bottom **Note:** Weight varies 8.00-9.00 grams.

Date	Mintage	Good	VG	F	VF	XF
ND(1742-52)	—	3.00	4.00	6.00	10.00	—

KM# B1005 2 MUN
Cast Copper Or Bronze **Obv:** Small characters **Note:** Weight varies 8.00-9.00 grams.

Date	Mintage	Good	VG	F	VF	XF
ND(1742-52)	—	3.00	4.00	6.00	10.00	—

NORTH HAMGYONG PROVINCIAL OFFICE

(Ham Gyong Pug Yong)

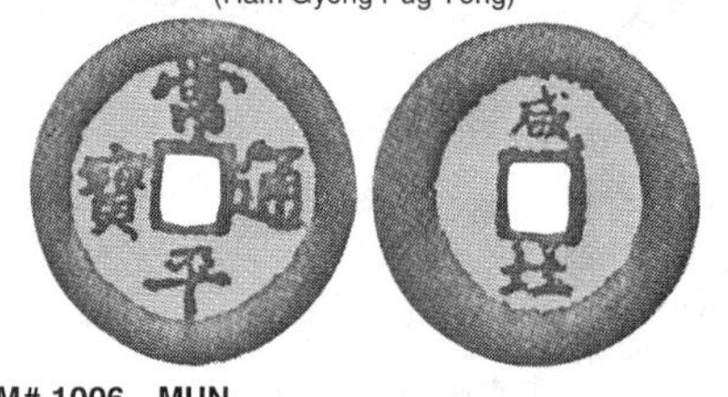

KM# 1006 MUN
4.5000 g., Cast Copper **Rev:** "Ham" at top, "Puk" (north) at bottom

Date	Mintage	Good	VG	F	VF	XF
ND(1742) Rare	—	—	—	—	—	—

SOUTH HAMGYONG PROVINCIAL OFFICE

(Ham Gyong Nam Yong)

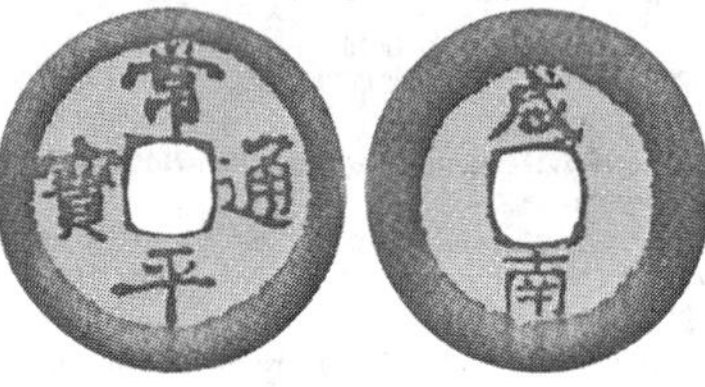

KM# 1007 MUN
4.5000 g., Cast Copper **Rev:** "Ham" at top, "Nam" (south) at bottom

Date	Mintage	Good	VG	F	VF	XF
ND(1742) Rare	—	—	—	—	—	—

KANGWON PROVINCIAL OFFICE

(Kang Won Kam Yong)

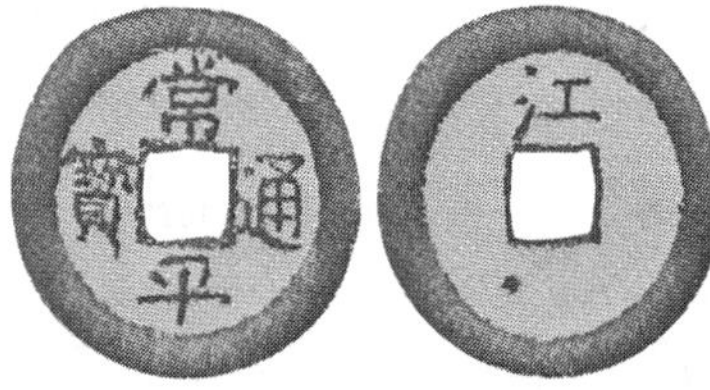

KM# 1008 MUN
4.5000 g., Cast Copper **Rev:** "Kang" at top, dot at lower left

Date	Mintage	Good	VG	F	VF	XF
ND(1742) Rare	—	—	—	—	—	—

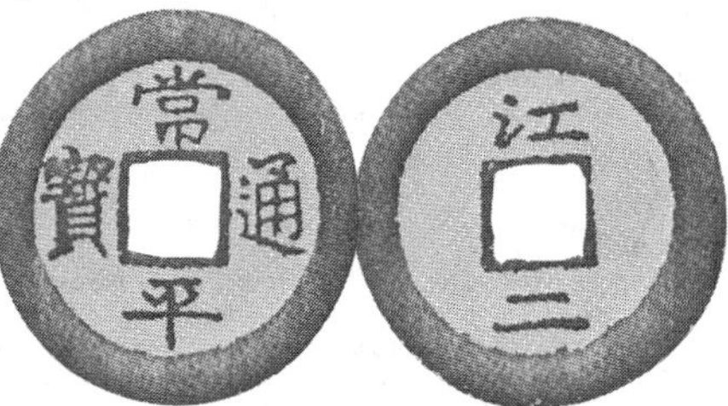

KM# 1009 2 MUN
Cast Copper **Rev:** "Kang" at top, "I" (2) at bottom **Note:** Weight varies 8.00-9.00 grams. Size varies 29-30 mm.

Date	Mintage	Good	VG	F	VF	XF
ND(1742-52)	—	3.00	4.00	6.00	10.00	—

KYONGSANG PROVINCIAL OFFICE

(Kyong Sang Kam Yong)

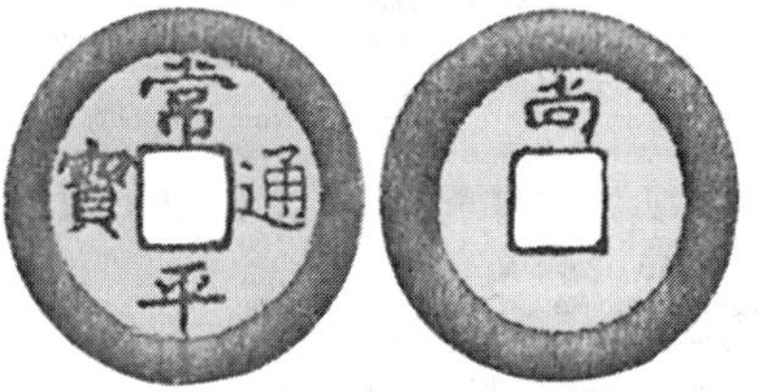

KM# 1010 MUN
4.5000 g., Cast Copper **Rev:** "Sang" at top

Date	Mintage	Good	VG	F	VF	XF
ND(1695-1727)	—	60.00	90.00	150	250	—

KM# 1011 2 MUN
Cast Copper **Rev:** "Sang" at top, "I" (2) a t bottom **Note:** Weight varies 8.00-9.00 grams.

Date	Mintage	Good	VG	F	VF	XF
ND(1695-1742)	—	4.00	5.00	7.50	10.00	—

KM# 1012 2 MUN
Cast Copper **Rev:** "Sang" at top, "Ch'on" at bottom **Note:** Weight varies 8.00-9.00 grams.

Date	Mintage	Good	VG	F	VF	XF
ND(1742-52)	—	3.00	4.00	6.00	10.00	—

KM# 1013 2 MUN
Cast Copper **Rev:** "Chi" at bottom **Note:** Weight varies 8.00-9.00 grams.

Date	Mintage	Good	VG	F	VF	XF
ND(1742-52)	—	3.00	4.00	6.00	10.00	—

KM# 1014 2 MUN
Cast Copper **Rev:** "Hyon" at bottom **Note:** Weight varies 8.00-9.00 grams.

Date	Mintage	Good	VG	F	VF	XF
ND(1742-52)	—	3.00	4.00	6.00	10.00	—

KM# 1015 2 MUN
Cast Copper **Rev:** "Hwang" (yellow) at bottom **Note:** Weight varies 8.00-9.00 grams.

Date	Mintage	Good	VG	F	VF	XF
ND(1742-52)	—	3.00	4.00	6.00	10.00	—

KM# 1016 2 MUN
Cast Copper **Rev:** "U" at bottom **Note:** Weight varies 8.00-9.00 grams.

Date	Mintage	Good	VG	F	VF	XF
ND(1742-52)	—	3.00	4.00	6.00	10.00	—

KM# 1017 2 MUN
Cast Copper **Rev:** "Chu" at bottom **Note:** Weight varies 8.00-9.00 grams.

Date	Mintage	Good	VG	F	VF	XF
ND(1742-52)	—	3.00	4.00	6.00	10.00	—

KM# 1018 2 MUN
Cast Copper **Rev:** "Hong" at bottom **Note:** Weight varies 8.00-9.00 grams.

Date	Mintage	Good	VG	F	VF	XF
ND(1742-52)	—	3.00	4.00	6.00	10.00	—

KM# 1019 2 MUN
Cast Copper **Rev:** "Hwang" (barren) at bottom **Note:** Weight varies 8.00-9.00 grams.

Date	Mintage	Good	VG	F	VF	XF
ND(1742-52)	—	3.00	4.00	6.00	10.00	—

KM# 1020 2 MUN
Cast Copper **Rev:** "Il" at bottom **Note:** Weight varies 8.00-9.00 grams.

Date	Mintage	Good	VG	F	VF	XF
ND(1742-52)	—	3.00	4.00	6.00	10.00	—

KM# 1021 2 MUN
Cast Copper **Rev:** "Wol" at bottom **Note:** Weight varies 8.00-9.00 grams.

Date	Mintage	Good	VG	F	VF	XF
ND(1742-52)	—	3.00	4.00	6.00	10.00	—

KM# 1022 2 MUN
Cast Copper **Rev:** "Yong" at bottom **Note:** Weight varies 8.00-9.00 grams.

Date	Mintage	Good	VG	F	VF	XF
ND(1742-52)	—	3.00	4.00	6.00	10.00	—

KM# 1023 2 MUN
Cast Copper **Rev:** "Ch'uk" at bottom **Note:** Weight varies 8.00-9.00 grams.

Date	Mintage	Good	VG	F	VF	XF
ND(1742-52)	—	3.00	4.00	6.00	10.00	—

KM# 1024 2 MUN
Cast Copper **Rev:** "Chin" at bottom **Note:** Weight varies 8.00-9.00 grams.

Date	Mintage	Good	VG	F	VF	XF
ND(1742-52)	—	3.00	4.00	6.00	10.00	—

KM# 1025 2 MUN
Cast Copper **Rev:** "Suk" at bottom **Note:** Weight varies 8.00-9.00 grams.

Date	Mintage	Good	VG	F	VF	XF
ND(1742-52)	—	3.00	4.00	6.00	10.00	—

KM# 1026 2 MUN
Cast Copper **Rev:** "Yol" at bottom **Note:** Weight varies 8.00-9.00 grams.

Date	Mintage	Good	VG	F	VF	XF
ND(1742-52)	—	3.00	4.00	6.00	10.00	—

KM# 1027 2 MUN
Cast Copper **Rev:** "Chang" (extend) at bottom **Note:** Weight varies 8.00-9.00 grams.

Date	Mintage	Good	VG	F	VF	XF
ND(1742-52)	—	3.00	4.00	6.00	10.00	—

KM# 1028 2 MUN
Cast Copper **Rev:** "Han" at bottom **Note:** Weight varies 8.00-9.00 grams.

Date	Mintage	Good	VG	F	VF	XF
ND(1742-52)	—	5.50	8.50	12.50	20.00	—

KM# 1029 2 MUN
Cast Copper **Rev:** "Nae" at bottom **Note:** Weight varies 8.00-9.00 grams.

Date	Mintage	Good	VG	F	VF	XF
ND(1742-52)	—	3.00	4.00	6.00	10.00	—

KM# 1030 2 MUN
Cast Copper **Rev:** "So" at bottom **Note:** Weight varies 8.00-9.00 grams.

Date	Mintage	Good	VG	F	VF	XF
ND(1742-52)	—	5.50	8.50	12.50	20.00	—

KM# 1031 2 MUN
Cast Copper **Rev:** "Wang" at bottom **Note:** Weight varies 8.00-9.00 grams.

Date	Mintage	Good	VG	F	VF	XF
ND(1742-52)	—	3.00	4.00	6.00	10.00	—

KM# 1032 2 MUN
Cast Copper **Rev:** "Ch'u" at bottom **Note:** Weight varies 8.00-9.00 grams.

Date	Mintage	Good	VG	F	VF	XF
ND(1742-52)	—	5.50	8.50	12.50	20.00	—

KM# 1033 2 MUN
Cast Copper **Rev:** "Su" at bottom **Note:** Weight varies 8.00-9.00 grams.

Date	Mintage	Good	VG	F	VF	XF
ND(1742-52)	—	3.00	4.00	6.00	10.00	—

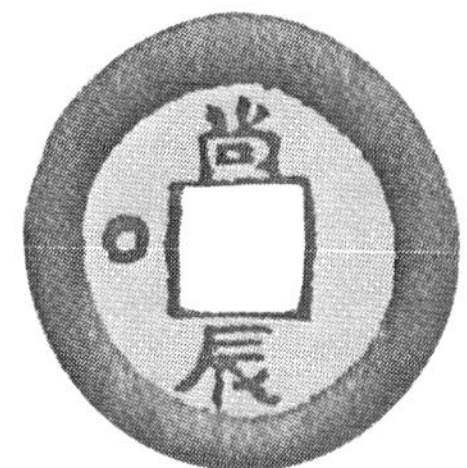

KM# 1034 2 MUN
Cast Copper **Rev:** "Chin" at bottom, circle at left **Note:** Weight varies 8.00-9.00 grams.

Date	Mintage	Good	VG	F	VF	XF
ND(1742-52)	—	3.50	5.50	8.50	12.50	—

KM# 1035 2 MUN
Cast Copper **Rev:** "Chon" at bottom, crescent at right **Note:** Weight varies 8.00-9.00 grams.

Date	Mintage	Good	VG	F	VF	XF
ND(1742-52)	—	3.00	4.00	6.00	10.00	—

KM# 1036 2 MUN
Cast Copper **Rev:** "Il" at bottom, cloud form at right **Note:** Weight varies 8.00-9.00 grams.

Date	Mintage	Good	VG	F	VF	XF
ND(1742-52)	—	3.50	5.50	8.50	12.50	—

KYONGSANG NAVAL STATION

(Kyong Sang Su Yong)

KM# 1037 MUN
4.5000 g., Cast Copper **Rev:** "Sang" at top, "Su" at bottom

Date	Mintage	Good	VG	F	VF	XF
ND(1695-1742) Rare	—	—	—	—	—	—

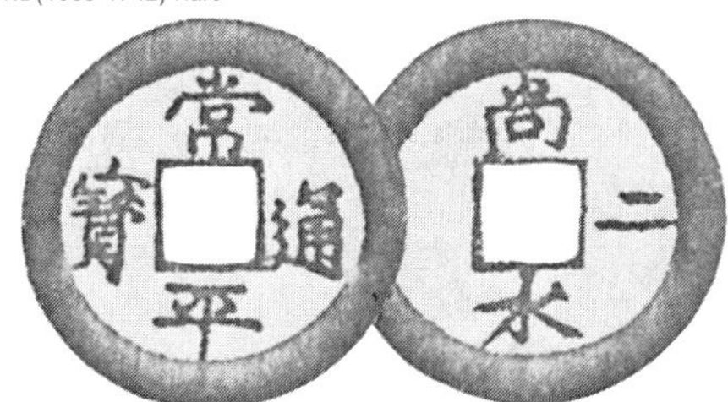

KM# 1038 2 MUN
Cast Copper **Rev:** "Sang" at top, "Su" at bottom, "I" (2) at right **Note:** Weight varies 8.00-9.00 grams.

Date	Mintage	Good	VG	F	VF	XF
ND(1695-1742)	—	6.00	8.00	15.00	25.00	—

KYONGSANG RIGHT NAVAL BASE

(Kyong Sang U Yong)

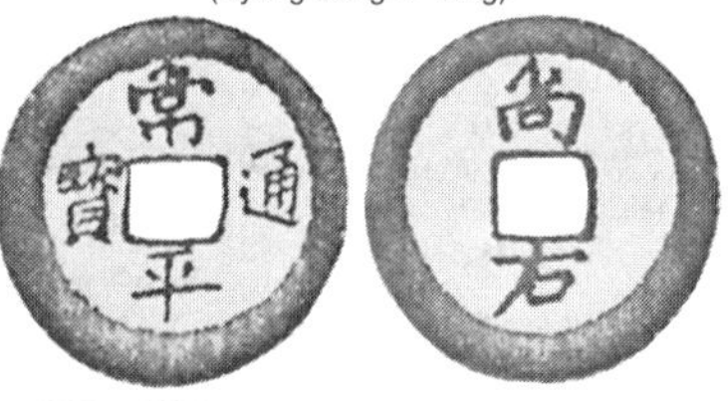

KM# 1039 MUN
4.5000 g., Cast Copper **Rev:** "Sang" at top, "U" at bottom

Date	Mintage	Good	VG	F	VF	XF
ND(1695-1742) Rare	—	—	—	—	—	—

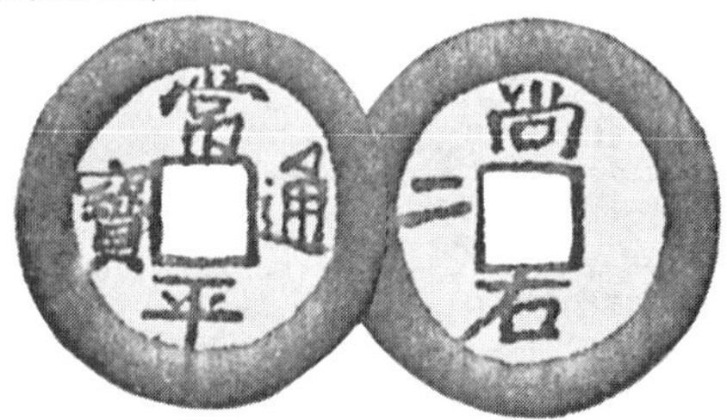

KM# 1040 2 MUN
Cast Copper **Rev:** "Sang" at top, "U" at bottom, "I" (2) at left **Note:** Weight varies 8.00-9.00 grams.

Date	Mintage	Good	VG	F	VF	XF
ND(1695-1742)	—	6.00	8.00	15.00	25.00	—

KYONGSANG LEFT NAVAL BASE

(Kyong Sang Chwa Yong)

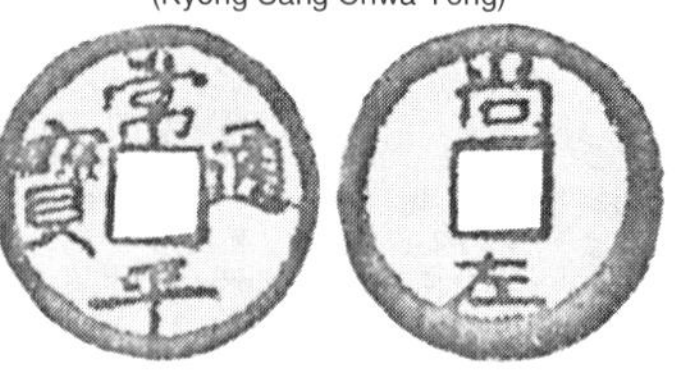

KM# 1041 MUN
4.5000 g., Cast Copper **Rev:** "Sang" at top, "Chwa" at bottom

Date	Mintage	Good	VG	F	VF	XF
ND(1695-1742) Rare	—	—	—	—	—	—

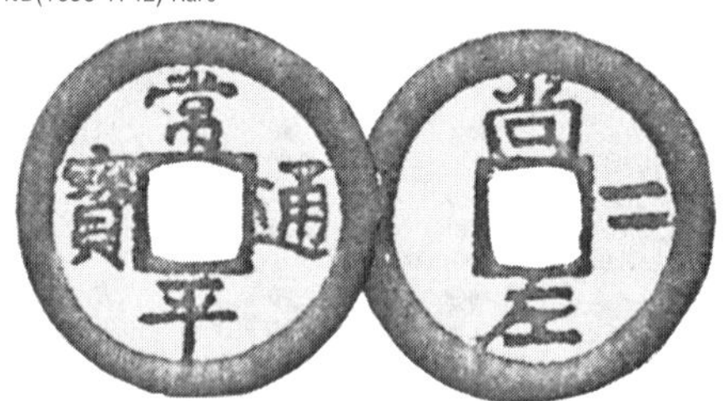

KM# 1042 2 MUN
Cast Copper **Rev:** "Sang" at top, "Chwa" at bottom, "I" (2) at right **Note:** Weight varies 8.00-9.00 grams.

Date	Mintage	Good	VG	F	VF	XF
ND(1695-1742)	—	5.50	8.50	12.50	20.00	—

KM# 1043 2 MUN
Cast Copper **Rev:** "Sang" at top, "Chwa" at bottom, "I" (2) at left **Note:** Weight varies 8.00-9.00 grams.

Date	Mintage	Good	VG	F	VF	XF
ND(1695-1742)	—	5.50	8.50	12.50	20.00	—

KM# 1043a 2 MUN
Cast Copper **Rev:** Star at lower left **Note:** Weight varies 8.00-9.00 grams.

Date	Mintage	Good	VG	F	VF	XF
ND(1695-1742)	—	5.50	8.50	12.50	20.00	—

CHOLLA PROVINCIAL OFFICE

(Chol La Kam Yong)

KM# 1044 MUN
4.5000 g., Cast Copper **Rev:** "Chon" at top

Date	Mintage	Good	VG	F	VF	XF
ND(1682-1727)	—	75.00	100	130	175	—

KM# 1063 2 MUN
Cast Copper **Rev:** "Han" at bottom **Note:** Size varies 31-32 millimeters. Weight varies 8.00-9.00 grams.

Date	Mintage	Good	VG	F	VF	XF
ND(1742-52)	—	3.00	4.00	6.00	10.00	—

KM# 1047 2 MUN

Cast Copper **Rev:** "Chon" at top, "Ch'on" at bottom **Note:** Size varies 31-32 mm. Weight varies 8.00-9.00 grams.

Date	Mintage	Good	VG	F	VF	XF
ND(1742-52)	—	3.00	4.00	6.00	10.00	—

KM# 1048 2 MUN

Cast Copper **Rev:** "Chi" at bottom **Note:** Size varies 31-32 mm. Weight varies 8.00-9.00 grams.

Date	Mintage	Good	VG	F	VF	XF
ND(1742-52)	—	3.00	4.00	6.00	10.00	—

KM# 1049 2 MUN

Cast Copper **Rev:** "Hyon" at bottom **Note:** Size varies 31-32 mm. Weight varies 8.00-9.00 grams.

Date	Mintage	Good	VG	F	VF	XF
ND(1742-52)	—	3.00	4.00	6.00	10.00	—

KM# 1050 2 MUN

Cast Copper **Rev:** "Hwang" (yellow) at bottom **Note:** Size varies 31-32 mm. Weight varies 8.00-9.00 grams.

Date	Mintage	Good	VG	F	VF	XF
ND(1742-52)	—	3.00	4.00	6.00	10.00	—

KM# 1051 2 MUN

Cast Copper **Rev:** "U" at bottom **Note:** Size varies 31-32 mm. Weight varies 8.00-9.00 grams.

Date	Mintage	Good	VG	F	VF	XF
ND(1742-52)	—	3.00	4.00	6.00	10.00	—

KM# 1052 2 MUN

Cast Copper **Rev:** "Chu" at bottom **Note:** Size varies 31-32 mm. Weight varies 8.00-9.00 grams.

Date	Mintage	Good	VG	F	VF	XF
ND(1742-52)	—	3.00	4.00	6.00	10.00	—

KM# 1053 2 MUN

Cast Copper **Rev:** "Hong" at bottom **Note:** Size varies 31-32 mm. Weight varies 8.00-9.00 grams.

Date	Mintage	Good	VG	F	VF	XF
ND(1742-52)	—	3.00	4.00	6.00	10.00	—

KM# 1054 2 MUN

Cast Copper **Rev:** "Hwang" at bottom **Note:** Size varies 31-32 mm. Weight varies 8.00-9.00 grams.

Date	Mintage	Good	VG	F	VF	XF
ND(1742-52)	—	3.00	4.00	6.00	10.00	—

KM# 1055 2 MUN

Cast Copper **Rev:** "Il" at bottom **Note:** Size varies 31-32 mm. Weight varies 8.00-9.00 grams.

Date	Mintage	Good	VG	F	VF	XF
ND(1742-52)	—	3.00	4.00	6.00	10.00	—

KM# 1056 2 MUN

Cast Copper **Rev:** "Wol" at bottom **Note:** Size varies 31-32 mm. Weight varies 8.00-9.00 grams.

Date	Mintage	Good	VG	F	VF	XF
ND(1742-52)	—	3.00	4.00	6.00	10.00	—

KM# 1056a 2 MUN

Cast Copper **Rev:** Star right of "Chon" **Note:** Size varies 31-32 mm. Weight varies 8.00-9.00 grams.

Date	Mintage	Good	VG	F	VF	XF
ND(1742-52)	—	2.50	3.50	4.50	6.50	—

KM# 1057 2 MUN

Cast Copper **Rev:** "Yong" at bottom **Note:** Size varies 31-32 mm. Weight varies 8.00-9.00 grams.

Date	Mintage	Good	VG	F	VF	XF
ND(1742-52)	—	3.00	4.00	6.00	10.00	—

KM# 1058 2 MUN

Cast Copper **Rev:** "Ch'uk" at bottom **Note:** Size varies 31-32 mm. Weight varies 8.00-9.00 grams.

Date	Mintage	Good	VG	F	VF	XF
ND(1742-52)	—	3.00	4.00	6.00	10.00	—

KM# 1059 2 MUN

Cast Copper **Rev:** "Chin" at bottom **Note:** Size varies 31-32 mm. Weight varies 8.00-9.00 grams.

Date	Mintage	Good	VG	F	VF	XF
ND(1742-52)	—	3.00	4.00	6.00	10.00	—

KM# 1060 2 MUN

Cast Copper **Rev:** "Suk" at bottom **Note:** Size varies 31-32 mm. Weight varies 8.00-9.00 grams.

Date	Mintage	Good	VG	F	VF	XF
ND(1742-52)	—	3.00	4.00	6.00	10.00	—

KM# 1061 2 MUN

Cast Copper **Rev:** "Yol" at bottom **Note:** Size varies 31-32 mm. Weight varies 8.00-9.00 grams.

Date	Mintage	Good	VG	F	VF	XF
ND(1742-52)	—	3.00	4.00	6.00	10.00	—

KM# 1061a 2 MUN

Cast Copper **Rev:** Star at upper right **Note:** Size varies 31-32 mm. Weight varies 8.00-9.00 grams.

Date	Mintage	Good	VG	F	VF	XF
ND(1742-52)	—	2.50	3.50	4.50	6.50	—

KM# 1062 2 MUN

Cast Copper **Rev:** "Chang" at bottom **Note:** Size varies 31-32 mm. Weight varies 8.00-9.00 grams.

Date	Mintage	Good	VG	F	VF	XF
ND(1742-52)	—	3.00	4.00	6.00	10.00	—

KM# 1062a 2 MUN

Cast Copper **Rev:** Star at lower left **Note:** Size varies 31-32 mm. Weight varies 8.00-9.00 grams.

Date	Mintage	Good	VG	F	VF	XF
ND(1742-52)	—	2.50	3.50	4.50	6.50	—

KM# 1064 2 MUN

Cast Copper **Rev:** "Nae" at bottom **Note:** Size varies 31-32 mm. Weight varies 8.00-9.00 grams.

Date	Mintage	Good	VG	F	VF	XF
ND(1742-52)	—	3.00	4.00	6.00	10.00	—

KM# 1064a 2 MUN

Cast Copper **Rev:** Star at lower left **Note:** Size varies 31-32 mm. Weight varies 8.00-9.00 grams.

Date	Mintage	Good	VG	F	VF	XF
ND(1742-52)	—	2.50	3.50	4.50	6.50	—

KM# 1065 2 MUN

Cast Copper **Rev:** "So" at bottom **Note:** Size varies 31-32 mm. Weight varies 8.00-9.00 grams.

Date	Mintage	Good	VG	F	VF	XF
ND(1742-52)	—	3.00	4.00	6.00	10.00	—

KM# 1066 2 MUN

Cast Copper **Rev:** "Wang" at bottom **Note:** Size varies 31-32 mm. Weight varies 8.00-9.00 grams.

Date	Mintage	Good	VG	F	VF	XF
ND(1742-52)	—	3.00	4.00	6.00	10.00	—

KM# 1067 2 MUN

Cast Copper **Rev:** "Ch'u" at bottom **Note:** Size varies 31-32 mm. Weight varies 8.00-9.00 grams.

Date	Mintage	Good	VG	F	VF	XF
ND(1742-52)	—	3.00	4.00	6.00	10.00	—

KM# 1068 2 MUN

Cast Copper **Rev:** "Su" at bottom **Note:** Size varies 31-32 mm. Weight varies 8.00-9.00 grams.

Date	Mintage	Good	VG	F	VF	XF
ND(1742-52)	—	3.00	4.00	6.00	10.00	—

KM# 1069 2 MUN

Cast Copper **Rev:** "Tong" at bottom **Note:** Size varies 31-32 mm. Weight varies 8.00-9.00 grams.

Date	Mintage	Good	VG	F	VF	XF
ND(1742-52)	—	3.00	4.00	6.00	10.00	—

KM# 1070 2 MUN

Cast Copper **Rev:** "Chang" (hoard) at bottom **Note:** Size varies 31-32 mm. Weight varies 8.00-9.00 grams.

Date	Mintage	Good	VG	F	VF	XF
ND(1742-52)	—	3.00	4.00	6.00	10.00	—

KM# 1071 2 MUN

Cast Copper **Rev:** "Yun" at bottom **Note:** Size varies 31-32 mm. Weight varies 8.00-9.00 grams.

Date	Mintage	Good	VG	F	VF	XF
ND(1742-52)	—	3.00	4.00	6.00	10.00	—

CHOLLA MILITARY FORT

(Chol La Pyong Yong)

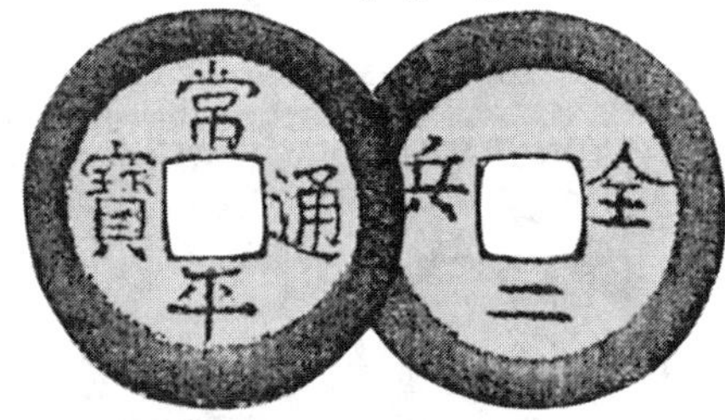

KM# 1073 2 MUN

Cast Copper **Rev:** "Chon" at right, "Pyong" at left, "I" (2) at bottom **Note:** Weight varies 8.00-9.00 grams.

Date	Mintage	Good	VG	F	VF	XF
ND(1679-1742) Rare	—	—	—	—	—	—

TEST COINAGE

Treasury Department

KM# Tc5 CHON

Cast Bronze **Obv. Legend:** "SANG P'YONG T'ONG BO" **Rev:** "Ho" at top, "Sip" (10) at bottom

Date	Mintage	Good	VG	F	VF	XF
ND(1777-1800) Rare	—	—	—	—	—	—

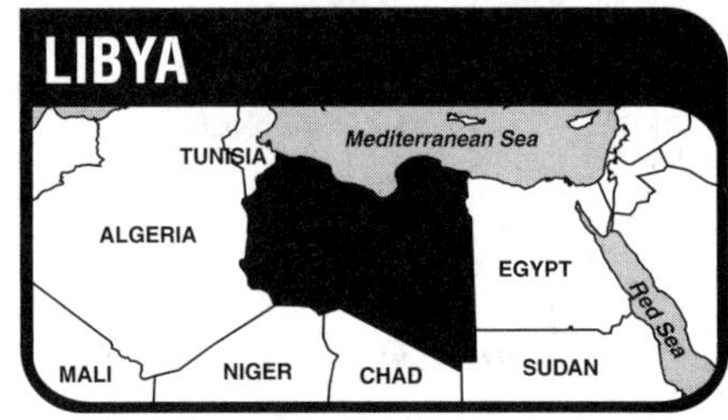

TRIPOLI

Tripoli (formerly Ottoman Empire Area of antique Tripolitania, 700-146 B.C.), the capital city and chief port of the Libyan Arab Jamahiriya, is situated on the North African coast on a promontory stretching out into the Mediterranean Sea. It was probably founded by Phoenicians from Sicily, but was under Roman control from 146 B.C. until 450 A.D. Invasion by Vandals and conquest by the Byzantines preceded the Arab invasions of the 11th century which, by destroying the commercial centers of Sabratha and Leptis, greatly enhanced the importance of Tripoli, an importance maintained through periods of Norman and Spanish control. Tripoli fell to the Turks, who made it the capital of the vilayet of Tripoli in 1551 and remained in their hands until 1911, when it was occupied by the Italians who made it the capital of the Italian province of Tripolitania. British forces entered the city on January 23, 1943, and administered it until establishment of the independent Kingdom of Libya on December 24, 1951.

RULERS

Ottoman, until 1911
refer to Turkey

LOCAL PASHAS

Ahmad Pasha Qaramanli I,
AH1123-1158/1711-1745AD
Muhammad Pasha Qaramanli,
AH1158-1167/1745-1754AD
Ali Pasha Qaramanli I,
AH1167-1208/1754-1793AD
Ali Burghul Pasha, (rebel)
AH1208-1209/1793-1795AD
Ahmad Pasha Qaramanli II,
AH1209-1210/1795-1796AD
Yusuf Pasha Qaramanli,
AH1210-1248/1796-1833AD (resigned)

MINT NAME

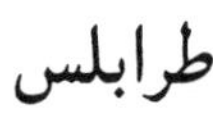

Tarabalus

طرابلس غرب

Tarabalus Gharb = (Tripoli West)

The appellation *west* serving to distinguish it from Tripoli in Lebanon, which had been an Ottoman Mint in the 16th century. On some of the copper coins, *Gharb* is omitted; several types come both with and without *Gharb*. The mint closed between the 28th and 29th year of the reign of Mahmud II.

MONETARY SYSTEM

The monetary system of Tripoli was confused and is poorly understood. Theoretically, 40 Para were equal to one Piastre, but due to the debasement of the silver coinage, later issues are virtually pure copper, though the percentage of alloy varies radically even within a given year. The 10 Para and 20 Para pieces were a little heavier than the copper Paras, with which they could easily be confounded, except that the copper Paras were generally thicker, and bear simpler inscriptions. It is not known how many of the coppers were tariffed to the debased Piastre and its fractions. Some authorities consider the copper pieces to be Beshliks (5 Para coins).

The gold coinage came in two denominations, the Zeri Mahbub (2.4-2.5 g), and the Sultani Altin (3.3-3.4 g). The ratio of the billon Piastres to the gold coins fluctuated from day to day.

BARBARY STATE

OTTOMAN COINAGE

KM# 58 MANGIR

Copper **Ruler:** Selim III **Note:** Weight varies 1.75-2.36 grams. Size varies 17-17mm.

Date	Mintage	VG	F	VF	XF	Unc
AH1203 (1789)	—	—	50.00	75.00	100	—

KM# 25 MANGHIR

Copper **Ruler:** Ahmed III **Obv:** Titles of Ahmed III **Rev:** Mint and date **Note:** Size varies: 22.5-24mm. Weight varies: 4.2-4.6 grams.

Date	Mintage	VG	F	VF	XF	Unc
AH1115	—	45.00	60.00	85.00	100	—

KM# 24 MANGHIR

Copper, 15 mm. **Ruler:** Ahmed III **Obv. Legend:** "SULTAN AHMED HAN" **Rev:** Mint name

Date	Mintage	VG	F	VF	XF	Unc
AH1134	—	35.00	50.00	75.00	90.00	—

KM# 34 MANGHIR

0.8000 g., Copper **Ruler:** Osman III **Note:** Size varies 11-13mm.

Date	Mintage	Good	VG	F	VF	XF
AH1168	—	30.00	50.00	75.00	100	—

KM# 38 MANGHIR

2.1000 g., Copper, 20 mm. **Ruler:** Mustafa III **Obv:** Inscription **Rev:** Mint name, date

Date	Mintage	Good	VG	F	VF	XF
AH(11)77	—	25.00	40.00	65.00	90.00	—

KM# 39 MANGHIR

0.9090 g., Copper **Ruler:** Mustafa III **Rev:** Legend in hexagram **Note:** Size varies 12-15mm.

Date	Mintage	Good	VG	F	VF	XF
ND	—	25.00	40.00	65.00	90.00	—

KM# 30 ASPER

0.2400 g., Silver **Ruler:** Mahmud I **Note:** Size varies 12-13mm.

Date	Mintage	VG	F	VF	XF	Unc
AH1044 Error; Rare	—	—	—	—	—	—
AH1144	—	50.00	75.00	100	150	—

KM# 45 PARA

2.4500 g., Copper **Ruler:** Abdul Hamid I **Obv:** Toughra **Rev:** Mintname **Note:** Size varies 19-20mm.

Date	Mintage	Good	VG	F	VF	XF
AH118(-)	—	20.00	35.00	60.00	85.00	—

KM# 53 PARA

Copper **Ruler:** Abdul Hamid I **Obv:** Inscription within square **Rev:** Legend in triangle, trilobe **Note:** Weight varies: 2.40-2.75 grams.

Date	Mintage	Good	VG	F	VF	XF
AH1188	—	15.00	25.00	40.00	55.00	—

KM# 46 5 PARA

2.0000 g., Billon, 22 mm. **Ruler:** Abdul Hamid I **Obv:** Toughra **Rev:** Mintname

Date	Mintage	Good	VG	F	VF	XF
AH1187	—	50.00	75.00	150	225	—

KM# 47 5 PARA

Silver **Ruler:** Abdul Hamid I **Obv:** Toughra **Rev:** Mintname

Date	Mintage	Good	VG	F	VF	XF
AH1187	—	30.00	60.00	125	200	—

KM# 54 5 PARA

Silver **Ruler:** Abdul Hamid I **Obv:** 4-line legend **Rev:** 3-line legend **Note:** Weight varies 1.60-2.90 grams. Size varies 24-25mm.

Date	Mintage	Good	VG	F	VF	XF
AH1188	—	30.00	60.00	125	200	—

KM# 63 5 PARA

Silver, 21 mm. **Ruler:** Selim III **Note:** Weight varies 0.85-1.20 grams.

Date	Mintage	VG	F	VF	XF	Unc
AH1210 (1796)	—	40.00	60.00	200	400	—
AH1203//14 (1802)	—	40.00	60.00	200	400	—

KM# 26 10 PARA

2.3000 g., Silver **Ruler:** Ahmed III **Note:** Size varies 20-24mm.

Date	Mintage	VG	F	VF	XF	Unc
AH1115 Rare	—	—	—	—	—	—
AH1141 Rare	—	—	—	—	—	—

KM# 48.2 10 PARA

4.5000 g., Billon **Ruler:** Abdul Hamid I **Obv:** Flower at right of toughra

Date	Mintage	Good	VG	F	VF	XF
AH1187//11	—	150	200	300	400	—

KM# 48.1 10 PARA

Billon, 25 mm. **Ruler:** Abdul Hamid I **Obv:** Ornament at right of toughra **Rev:** 4-lined inscription **Note:** Weight varies: 4.36-4.50 grams.

Date	Mintage	Good	VG	F	VF	XF
AH1187//11	—	100	125	150	200	—

KM# 61 10 PARA

Silver, 26 mm. **Ruler:** Selim III **Obv:** 4-Lined inscription within circle **Rev:** Mint name, date within circle **Note:** Weight varies 1.94-3.30 grams. There exists 3 different marks in place of the normal numeral for the reignal year.

Date	Mintage	VG	F	VF	XF	Unc
AH1210 (1796)	—	50.00	100	200	500	—
AH1212 (1797)	—	50.00	100	200	500	—
AH1213 (1798)	—	50.00	100	200	500	—
AH1203//10 (1798)	—	50.00	100	200	500	—
AH1214 (1799)	—	50.00	100	200	500	—
AH1203//14 (1802)	—	50.00	100	200	500	—

KM# 49 15 PARA

7.3500 g., Silver, 30 mm. **Ruler:** Abdul Hamid I

Date	Mintage	VG	F	VF	XF	Unc
ND(AH1187)//1	—	60.00	100	250	300	—

KM# 59 15 PARA

5.3000 g., Silver, 30 mm. **Ruler:** Selim III **Note:** Similar to 10 Para, KM#61.

Date	Mintage	VG	F	VF	XF	Unc
AH1205	—	50.00	100	200	300	—

KM# 64 20 PARA

Silver, 31 mm. **Ruler:** Selim III **Note:** Similar to Piastre, KM#60. Weight varies 7.81-7.86 grams.

Date	Mintage	VG	F	VF	XF	Unc
AH1203//10 (1788) Rare	—	—	—	—	—	—
AH1203//14 (1788)	—	100	150	250	400	—

KM# 51 30 PARA

Silver, 35 mm. **Ruler:** Abdul Hamid I **Obv:** Legend in 4 lines **Rev:** Legend in 4 lines **Note:** Weight varies: 15.23-15.75 grams.

Date	Mintage	VG	F	VF	XF	Unc
AH1187//1	—	200	250	300	400	—

KM# 67 100 PARA

Silver, 45 mm. **Ruler:** Selim III **Obv:** Toughra above text, date within circle **Rev:** 4 lined inscription within circle **Note:** Weight varies 30.60-31.32 grams.

Date	Mintage	VG	F	VF	XF	Unc
AH1209	—	200	300	600	800	—
AH1210	—	200	300	600	800	—
AH1203//16	—	200	300	450	650	—

KM# 55 PIASTRE

Silver **Ruler:** Abdul Hamid I **Obv:** Toughra over mintname and date **Rev:** Legend is 4 lines **Note:** Weight varies 18.24-18.75. Size varies 38-40mm.

Date	Mintage	VG	F	VF	XF	Unc
AH1187	—	250	300	400	650	—

KM# 60 PIASTRE

Silver **Ruler:** Selim III **Obv:** Toughra **Rev:** Mint name, date **Note:** Weight varies 11.80-12.52 grams. Size varies 36-37mm.

Date	Mintage	VG	F	VF	XF	Unc
AH1203//1	—	150	250	300	450	—
AH1203//2	—	150	250	300	450	—
AH1203//8	—	150	250	300	450	—
AH1203//01 Error for year 10	—	—	—	—	—	—
AH1203//10	—	150	250	300	450	—

KM# 52 1/2 ZERI MAHBUB

1.5000 g., Gold, 17 mm. **Ruler:** Abdul Hamid I

Date	Mintage	VG	F	VF	XF	Unc
AH1187	—	100	150	250	400	—

KM# 56 ZERI MAHBUB

2.5000 g., Gold, 20 mm. **Ruler:** Abdul Hamid I **Obv:** Toughra above text, date **Rev:** Legend **Note:** Weight varies: 2.50-2.55 grams.

Date	Mintage	VG	F	VF	XF	Unc
AH1187	—	100	150	225	350	—
AH1191	—	100	150	225	350	—

KM# 68 1/2 SULTANI

1.5500 g., Gold, 19 mm. **Ruler:** Selim III

Date	Mintage	VG	F	VF	XF	Unc
AH1203 Rare	—	—	—	—	—	—
AH1203//12 Rare	—	—	—	—	—	—
AH1213 Rare	—	—	—	—	—	—

KM# 27 SULTANI

Gold, 23 mm. **Ruler:** Ahmed III **Note:** Weight varies: 3.32-3.38 grams.

Date	Mintage	VG	F	VF	XF	Unc
AH1115 Rare	—	—	—	—	—	—
AH1142	—	—	—	—	—	—

KM# 31 SULTANI

Gold **Ruler:** Mahmud I **Obv:** 3-lined inscription **Rev:** 4-lined inscription **Note:** Size varies 22-24mm. Weight varies: 3.25-3.40 grams.

Date	Mintage	VG	F	VF	XF	Unc
AH1143	—	—	350	500	700	—

KM# 35 SULTANI

Gold **Ruler:** Osman III **Obv:** Inscription **Rev:** Legend **Note:** Size varies: 22-23 milimeters. Weight varies: 3.34-3.40 grams.

Date	Mintage	VG	F	VF	XF	Unc
AH1168	—	175	350	500	700	—

KM# 42 SULTANI

Gold **Ruler:** Mustafa III **Obv:** Legend **Rev:** Legend **Note:** Weight varies 3.23-3.40 grams. Size varies 23-28mm.

Date	Mintage	VG	F	VF	XF	Unc
AH1171	—	200	250	300	425	—

KM# 62 SULTANI

3.5000 g., Gold **Ruler:** Selim III **Obv:** 4-Lined inscription within circle **Rev:** 4-Lined inscription and date within circle **Note:** Size varies 23-27mm.

Date	Mintage	VG	F	VF	XF	Unc
AH1203 Rare	—	—	—	—	—	—
AH1203//12	—	200	400	700	1,500	—
AH1203//14	—	200	400	700	1,500	—
AH1203//15	—	200	400	700	1,500	—
AH1203//17	—	200	400	700	1,500	—
AH1203//19	—	200	400	700	1,500	—

LIECHTENSTEIN

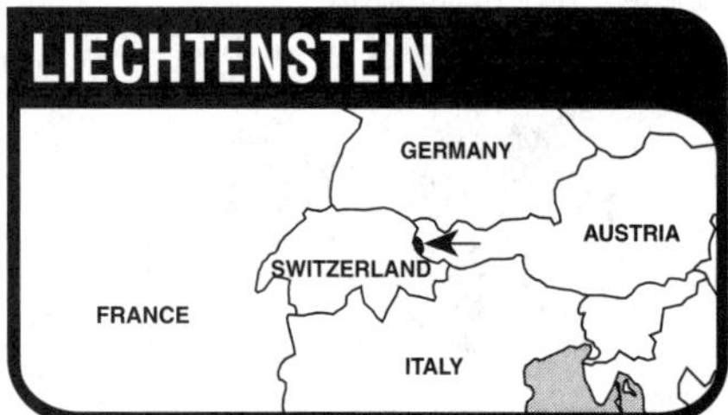

The Principality of Liechtenstein, located in central Europe on the east bank of the Rhine between Austria and Switzerland, has an area of 62 sq. mi. (160 sq. km.) and a population of 27,200. Capital: Vaduz. The economy is based on agriculture and light manufacturing. Canned goods, textiles, ceramics and precision instruments are exported.

The lordships of Schellenburg and Vaduz were merged into the principality of Liechtenstein. It was a member of the Rhine Confederation from 1806 to 1815, and of the German Confederation from 1815 to 1866 when it became independent. Liechtenstein's long and close association with Austria was terminated by World War I. In 1921 it adopted the coinage of Switzerland, and two years later entered into a customs union with the Swiss, who also operated its postal and telegraph systems and represented it in international affairs. The tiny principality abolished its army in 1868 and has avoided involvement in all European wars since that time.

RULERS

Josef Johann Adam, 1721-1732
Joseph Wenzel, 1748-1772
Franz Joseph I, 1772-1781

MINT MARKS

A - Vienna
B - Bern

PRINCIPALITY

STANDARD COINAGE

1-1/2 Florins = 1 Vereinsthaler

C# 4 20 KREUZER

6.6800 g., 0.5830 Silver 0.1252 oz. ASW **Ruler:** Franz Joseph I **Obv:** Bust right **Obv. Legend:** FRANCIOS • D • G • S • R • I • P • R • & .... **Rev:** Crowned oval shield, value below within Order chain

Date	Mintage	VG	F	VF	XF	Unc
1778	—	15.00	25.00	55.00	110	—

KM# 1 1/2 THALER

Silver **Ruler:** Josef Johann Adam **Obv:** Bust right **Obv. Legend:** IOSIOADGSRIP&GUB.... **Rev:** Crowned, mantled arms in order chain **Rev. Legend:** ...OPP&CARNDUXCRITB....

Date	Mintage	VG	F	VF	XF	Unc
1728	—	200	300	500	1,000	—
1729	—	350	550	700	1,500	—

C# 1 1/2 THALER

14.0000 g., 0.8330 Silver 0.3749 oz. ASW **Ruler:** Joseph Wenzel **Obv:** Joseph Wenzel bust facing right **Obv. Legend:** IOSIOA D G SRIP & GUB ... **Note:** Convention. Similar to 1 Thaler, KM#2.

Date	Mintage	VG	F	VF	XF	Unc
1758	—	75.00	150	300	500	—

C# 5 1/2 THALER

14.0000 g., 0.8330 Silver 0.3749 oz. ASW **Ruler:** Franz Joseph I **Obv:** Bust right **Rev:** Crowned oval arms in order chain

Date	Mintage	VG	F	VF	XF	Unc
1778	—	85.00	165	300	500	—

KM# 2 THALER (Ein)

Silver **Ruler:** Josef Johann Adam **Obv:** Bust right **Rev:** Crowned, mantled arms in order chain **Note:** Dav.#1578.

Date	Mintage	VG	F	VF	XF	Unc
1728	810	300	550	800	1,500	—

C# 2 THALER (Ein)

28.0600 g., 0.8330 Silver 0.7515 oz. ASW **Ruler:** Joseph Wenzel **Obv:** Bust right **Obv. Legend:** I O S • W E N C • D • G • S • R • I • PR • ... **Rev:** Crowned, oval arms between cupids with order chain, date below **Rev. Legend:** ...M • CONS • INT • & .... **Note:** Convention. Dav.#1579.

Date	Mintage	VG	F	VF	XF	Unc
1758	—	150	250	500	1,000	—

C# 6 THALER (Ein)

28.0600 g., 0.8330 Silver 0.7515 oz. ASW **Ruler:** Franz Joseph I **Obv:** Bust right **Obv. Legend:** FRANCIOS D G ..... **Rev:** Crowned, oval arms in order chain **Note:** Dav.#1580.

Date	Mintage	VG	F	VF	XF	Unc
1778	—	125	200	375	900	—

TRADE COINAGE

FR# 9 DUCAT

3.4900 g., 0.9860 Gold 0.1106 oz. AGW **Ruler:** Josef Johann Adam **Obv:** Bust right **Rev:** Crowned, mantled arms in order chain

Date	Mintage	VG	F	VF	XF	Unc
1728	—	400	900	2,000	3,500	—
1728 Restrike: small 'M' below bust	—	—	—	—	—	100
1729	—	400	900	2,000	3,500	—

FR# 9a DUCAT

3.9800 g., Platinum APW **Ruler:** Josef Johann Adam **Obv:** Bust right **Rev:** Crowned, mantled arms in order chain

Date	Mintage	VG	F	VF	XF	Unc
1728 Restrike	—	—	—	—	—	125

C# 3 DUCAT

3.4900 g., 0.9860 Gold 0.1106 oz. AGW **Ruler:** Joseph Wenzel **Obv:** Bust right **Rev:** Crowned, oval arms in order chain

Date	Mintage	VG	F	VF	XF	Unc
1758	—	250	500	1,200	3,000	—

C# 3a DUCAT

3.4900 g., 0.9860 Gold 0.1106 oz. AGW **Ruler:** Joseph Wenzel **Obv:** Bust right **Rev:** Crowned, oval arms in order chain

Date	Mintage	VG	F	VF	XF	Unc
1758 Restrike	—	—	—	—	—	100

C# 3b DUCAT

3.9600 g., Platinum APW **Ruler:** Joseph Wenzel **Obv:** Bust right **Rev:** Crowned, oval arms in order chain

Date	Mintage	VG	F	VF	XF	Unc
1758 Restrike	—	—	—	—	—	125

C# 7 DUCAT

3.4900 g., 0.9860 Gold 0.1106 oz. AGW **Ruler:** Franz Joseph I **Obv:** Bust right **Rev:** Crowned, oval arms in order chain

Date	Mintage	F	VF	XF	Unc	BU
1778	—	500	1,000	2,000	3,000	—

C# 7a DUCAT

3.4900 g., 0.9860 Gold 0.1106 oz. AGW **Ruler:** Franz Joseph I **Obv:** Bust right **Rev:** Crowned, oval arms in order chain

Date	Mintage	VG	F	VF	XF	Unc
1778 Restrike	—	—	—	—	—	100

C# 7b DUCAT

3.9800 g., Platinum APW **Ruler:** Franz Joseph I **Obv:** Bust right **Rev:** Crowned, oval arms in order chain

Date	Mintage	F	VF	XF	Unc	BU
1778 Restrike	—	—	—	—	125	—

FR# 8 10 DUCAT

35.0000 g., 0.9860 Gold 1.1095 oz. AGW **Ruler:** Josef Johann Adam **Obv:** Bust right **Rev:** Crowned and mantled arms, date in legend

Date	Mintage	VG	F	VF	XF	Unc
1728	—	—	—	—	45,000	—

FR# 8a 10 DUCAT

35.0000 g., 0.9860 Gold 1.1095 oz. AGW **Ruler:** Josef Johann Adam **Obv:** Bust right **Rev:** Crowned and mantled arms, date in legend

Date	Mintage	VG	F	VF	XF	Unc
1728 Restrike	—	—	—	—	—	650

LIEGE

Situated along the Meuse, Ourthe, and Sambre rivers, Liege was a bishopric which geographically completely divided the Austro-Spanish Netherlands.

Traditionally founded in the 7th Century by St. Lambert, Liege became a bishopric in 721 and by 1000, under Bishop Notga, thrived as an intellectual hub of the west and center for Mosan art. Internal struggles between citizens' guilds and prince-bishops did not weaken Liege to self-destruction. She resisted two sacks by Charles the Bold during 15th Century Burgundian domination of the Netherlands and completely rebuilt the city upon his death in 1477.

Liege was bombarded by the French in 1691, and during the War of Spanish Succession was taken by the English in 1702. After the death of Johann Theodor (Bishop, 1744-1763) there were no coin issues of the bishops. The only coin issues were the *Sede Vacante* issues of 1763, 1771, 1784 and 1792.

Ultimately the rule of the nobles ended in 1789 by a bloodless revolution which was followed by her annexation to France in 1795 and assignment with the rest of Belgium to the Netherlands in 1815.

Since Belgium's independence in 1830, Liege is again recognized as a major river port, rail center and cosmopolitan hub for art, education and industry.

RULERS

Joseph Clement of Bavaria, 1694-1723
Sede Vacante, 1723-1724
George Louis of Berghes, 1724-1743
Sede Vacante, 1744
John Theodore of Bavaria, 1744-1763
Sede Vacante, 1763
Charles d'Outtremont, 1763-1771
Sede Vacante, 1771-1772
Francois-Charles de Velbruck, 1772-1784
Sede Vacante, 1784
Constantin de Hoensbroek, 1784-1792
Sede Vacante, 1792
Francois de Mean, 1792-1794

MONETARY SYSTEM

6 Sols = 1 Escalin
48 Sols = 1 Patagon

BISHOPRIC

STANDARD COINAGE

KM# 107 LIARD

Copper, 24 mm. **Ruler:** Joseph Clement **Obv:** Crowned four-fold arms **Obv. Legend:** IOSEPH • CLEM • D • G • ARC • COL **Rev:** Without date in angles of shields **Rev. Legend:** * EP • ET • PRI • LEO • DVX • BVL • M • F • C • L • H **Note:** Struck at Liege.

Date	Mintage	VG	F	VF	XF	Unc
ND(1694-1723)	—	6.00	12.00	25.00	50.00	—

KM# 126 LIARD

Copper **Ruler:** Joseph Clement **Obv:** Crowned four-fold baroque arms divide date **Obv. Legend:** IOSEPH CLEM • D • G • ARC • COL • **Rev:** Cross of shields on crossed sword and sceptre **Rev. Legend:** EP • ET • PRIN • LEO • DVX • BVL • M • F • C • L • H

Date	Mintage	VG	F	VF	XF	Unc
1716	—	3.00	5.00	10.00	30.00	—
1721	—	3.00	5.00	10.00	30.00	—
1722	—	3.00	5.00	10.00	30.00	—
1723	—	3.00	5.00	10.00	30.00	—

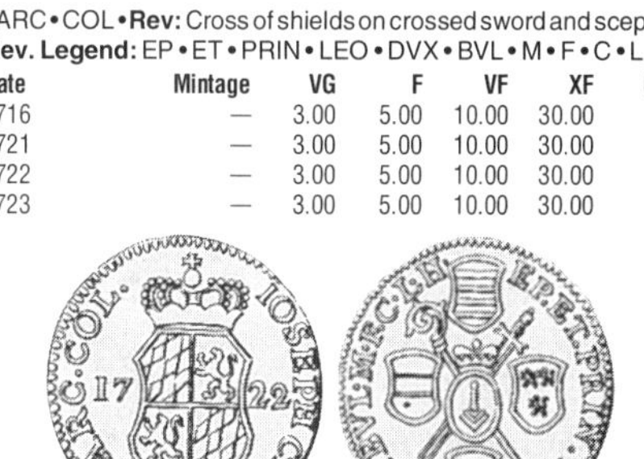

KM# 125 LIARD

Copper **Ruler:** Joseph Clement **Obv:** Crowned four-fold arms divides date **Obv. Legend:** IOSEPH • CLEM • D • G • ARC • COL **Rev:** Cross of shields on crossed sword and sceptre **Rev. Legend:** EP • ET • PRI • LEO • DVX • BVL • M • F • C • L • H **Note:** Struck at Liege.

Date	Mintage	VG	F	VF	XF	Unc
1722	—	4.00	8.00	16.00	35.00	—

KM# 127 LIARD

Copper **Subject:** Sede Vacante **Obv:** Bust of St. Lambert left **Obv. Legend:** S : LAMBERTVS • PATRO : LEOD • **Rev:** Cross of shields, date in angles **Rev. Legend:** SEDE • VACANTE DEC • ET • CAP • LEOD • **Note:** Struck at Liege. Sede vacante issue.

Date	Mintage	VG	F	VF	XF	Unc
1724	—	5.00	8.00	15.00	40.00	—

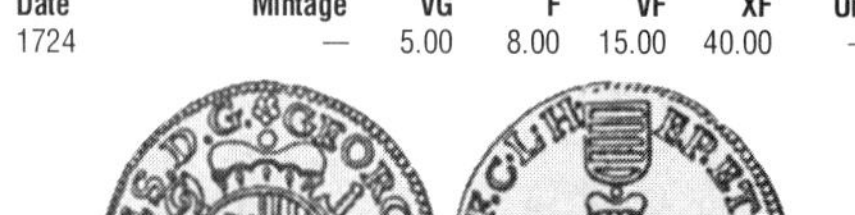

KM# 134 LIARD

Copper **Ruler:** George Louis **Obv:** Crowned oval arms over crossed sword and sceptre dividing date **Obv. Legend:** GEORGIUS LUD : DE BERGH ES • D • G • **Rev:** Cross of shields, without date **Rev. Legend:** EP • ET • PRIN • LEO •N DUX • BUL • M • F • C • L • H **Note:** Struck at Liege.

Date	Mintage	VG	F	VF	XF	Unc
1726	—	5.00	8.00	15.00	40.00	—
1727 Rare	—	—	—	—	—	—

KM# 144 LIARD

Copper **Obv:** Bust of St. Lambert left **Obv. Legend:** S • LAMBERTUS • PATRO • LEOD **Rev:** Cross of shields, date in angles **Rev. Legend:** SEDE • VACANTE • DEC ET • CAP • LEOD • **Note:** Struck at Liege. Sede vacante issue.

Date	Mintage	VG	F	VF	XF	Unc
1744	—	8.00	15.00	30.00	60.00	—

KM# 146 LIARD

Copper **Ruler:** John Theodore **Obv:** Crowned 4-fold arms on crossed sword and sceptre, without date **Obv. Legend:** I • THEODORVS • D • G • BAU • D **Rev:** Date in angles of cross of shields **Rev. Legend:** EP • ET • PRINC • LEO • DVX • B • M • F •C • L • H **Note:** Struck at Liege.

Date	Mintage	VG	F	VF	XF	Unc
1744	—	2.50	5.00	10.00	25.00	—
1745	—	2.50	5.00	10.00	25.00	—

Date	Mintage	VG	F	VF	XF	Unc
1746	—	2.50	5.00	10.00	25.00	—
ND	—	2.50	5.00	10.00	25.00	—

KM# 145 LIARD

Copper **Ruler:** John Theodore **Obv:** Crowned four-fold arms on crossed sword and sceptre divides date **Obv. Legend:** I • THEODORVS • D • G • BAU **Rev:** Cross of shields **Rev. Legend:** EP • ET • PRIN • LEO • DVX • B • M • F • C • L • H **Note:** Struck at Liege.

Date	Mintage	VG	F	VF	XF	Unc
1744	—	8.00	15.00	30.00	60.00	—

KM# 150 LIARD

Copper **Ruler:** John Theodore **Obv:** Crowned 4-fold arms divides date **Obv. Legend:** I * THEODOR : US * D * G * BAV * D * **Rev:** Cross of shields on crossed sword and sceptre **Rev. Legend:** EP • ET • PRIN • LEO • DUX • BUL • M • F • C • L • H **Note:** Struck at Liege.

Date	Mintage	VG	F	VF	XF	Unc
1745	—	5.00	8.00	15.00	40.00	—
1746	—	5.00	8.00	15.00	40.00	—

KM# 155 LIARD

Copper **Ruler:** John Theodore **Obv:** Crowned four-fold arms on crossed sword and sceptre **Obv. Legend:** I • THEOD • CAR • D : G • BAU • D **Rev:** Cross of shields, date in angles **Rev. Legend:** EP • ET • PRIN • LEO • DUX • B • M • F • C • L • H **Note:** Struck at Liege.

Date	Mintage	VG	F	VF	XF	Unc
1750	—	2.50	5.00	10.00	25.00	—
1751	—	2.50	5.00	10.00	25.00	—
1752	—	2.50	5.00	10.00	25.00	—

KM# 154 2 LIARDS

Copper, 27 mm. **Ruler:** Joseph Clement **Obv:** Crowned four-fold baroque arms **Obv. Legend:** IOSE(P)(D)H • CLEM • D • G • ARC • COL **Rev:** Cross of shields on crossed sword and sceptre **Rev. Legend:** EP • ET • PRIN • LEO • DVX • BVL • M • F • C • L • H • **Note:** Struck at Liege.

Date	Mintage	VG	F	VF	XF	Unc
1722 Rare	—	—	—	—	—	—

KM# 156 2 LIARDS

Copper **Ruler:** John Theodore **Obv:** Crowned four-fold arms below cardinal's hat **Obv. Legend:** I • THEOD • CAR • D • G • BAU D **Rev:** Cross of shields, date in angles **Rev. Legend:** EP • ET • PRIN • LEO • DUX • B • M • F • C • L • H **Note:** Struck at Liege.

Date	Mintage	VG	F	VF	XF	Unc
1750	—	50.00	80.00	125	200	—

KM# 158 2 LIARDS

Copper **Ruler:** John Theodore **Obv:** Crowned arms on crossed sword and sceptre divides value **Obv. Legend:** I • THEOD * CAR • D • G • BAU • D **Rev:** Cross of shields, date in angles **Rev. Legend:** EP • ET • PRIN • LEO • DUX • B • M • F • C • L • H **Note:** Struck at Liege.

Date	Mintage	VG	F	VF	XF	Unc
1750	—	10.00	15.00	30.00	100	—
1751	—	10.00	15.00	30.00	100	—
1752	—	10.00	15.00	30.00	100	—

KM# 157 2 LIARDS

Copper **Ruler:** John Theodore **Obv:** Crowned 4-fold arms on crossed sword and sceptre **Obv. Legend:** I • THEOD • CAR • D • G : BAV • D **Rev:** Cross of shields, date in angles **Rev. Legend:** EP • ET • PRIN • LEO • DVX • B • M • F • C • L • H **Note:** Struck at Liege.

Date	Mintage	VG	F	VF	XF	Unc
1750	—	10.00	15.00	30.00	100	—

KM# 159 4 LIARDS

Copper, 29 mm. **Ruler:** John Theodore **Obv:** Crowned 4-fold arms on crossed sword and sceptre divides value **Obv. Legend:** I • THEOD • CAR • D • G • BAV • D **Rev:** Cross of shields, date in angles **Rev. Legend:** EP • ET • PRIN • LEO • DVX • B • M • F • C • L • H **Note:** Struck at Liege.

Date	Mintage	VG	F	VF	XF	Unc
1750	—	15.00	25.00	50.00	100	—
1751	—	15.00	25.00	50.00	100	—
1752	—	15.00	25.00	50.00	100	—

KM# 152 PLAQUETTE

Silver, 21 mm. **Ruler:** John Theodore **Obv:** Crowned, ornate four-fold arms on crossed sword and sceptre **Obv. Legend:** • I • THEOD • CAR • D • G • BAV • D • **Rev:** Oval shield, legend around **Rev. Legend:** EP • ET • PRIN • L • DVX • B • M • F • C • L • H

Date	Mintage	VG	F	VF	XF	Unc
1751	—	10.00	20.00	35.00	75.00	250
1752	—	10.00	20.00	35.00	75.00	250

KM# 135 ESCALIN (6 Sols)

Silver **Obv:** Rampant lion left with shield **Rev:** Bust of St. Lambert left **Note:** Sede Vacante issue. Struck at Liege. Prev. KM#140.1.

Date	Mintage	F	VF	XF	Unc	BU
1724	615	75.00	100	150	350	—

KM# 140.2 ESCALIN (6 Sols)

Silver **Obv:** Date in cartouche below rampant lion left with capped shield **Note:** Sede vacante issue. Struck at Liege.

Date	Mintage	F	VF	XF	Unc	BU
1744	—	90.00	130	200	450	—

KM# 140.3 ESCALIN (6 Sols)

Silver **Obv:** Date above rampant lion left with capped shield **Rev:** Bust of St. Lambert left **Note:** Sede Vacante issue. Struck at Liege.

Date	Mintage	F	VF	XF	Unc	BU
1744	—	75.00	100	150	350	—

KM# 140.1 ESCALIN (6 Sols)

Silver **Obv:** St. Lambert left **Obv. Legend:** S • LAMBERTVS PATRO : LEOD **Rev:** Crowned, rampant lion and oval shield above date **Rev. Legend:** SEDE • VACANTE DEC • ET • CAP • LEOD • **Note:** Sede Vacante issue. Prev. KM#140.1.

Date	Mintage	F	VF	XF	Unc	BU
1744	—	75.00	100	150	350	—

KM# 165 ESCALIN (6 Sols)

Silver **Ruler:** John Theodore **Obv:** Crowned eight-fold arms on crossed sword and sceptre divides date **Rev:** Rampant lion left with sword and Episcopal shield

Date	Mintage	F	VF	XF	Unc	BU
1752	—	75.00	100	150	350	—
1753	—	75.00	100	150	350	—

KM# 170 ESCALIN (6 Sols)

Silver **Obv:** Crowned, rampant lion with crowned oval shield **Obv. Legend:** S LAMBERTUS PATRONUS LEOD **Rev:** Bust of St. Lambert left **Rev. Legend:** SEDE • VACANTE • DEC • ET • CAP • LEOD **Note:** Sede Vacante issue.

Date	Mintage	F	VF	XF	Unc	BU
1763	1,000	75.00	100	150	350	—

KM# 173 ESCALIN (6 Sols)

Silver **Obv:** Lion rampant left with capped shield **Rev:** Bust of St. Lambert left **Note:** Sede Vacante issue. Struck at Liege.

Date	Mintage	F	VF	XF	Unc	BU
1771	500	90.00	130	200	350	—

KM# 175 ESCALIN (6 Sols)

Silver **Obv:** Crowned, rampant lion with crowned oval shield above date **Obv. Legend:** S • LAMBERTUS • PATRONUS • LEOD **Rev:** Bust of St. Lambert left **Rev. Legend:** SEDE VACANTE DEC • ET CAP • LEOD • **Note:** C#13b. Sede Vacante issue.

Date	Mintage	F	VF	XF	Unc	BU
1784	500	75.00	100	150	350	—

KM# 180 ESCALIN (6 Sols)

Silver **Obv:** Crowned, rampant lion with crowned oval shield above date **Obv. Legend:** S LAMBERTUS PATRONUS LEOD **Rev:** Bust of St. Lambert left **Rev. Legend:** SEDE VACANTE • DEC • ET CAP • LEOD • **Note:** C#13c. Sede Vacante issue. Struck at Liege.

Date	Mintage	F	VF	XF	Unc	BU
1792	500	100	150	250	450	—

KM# 161 2 ESCALIN

Silver **Ruler:** John Theodore **Obv:** Crowned eight-fold arms on crossed sword and sceptre **Obv. Legend:** I • THEOD • BAV • DUX • CAR • D • G **Rev:** Rampant lion with sword and Episcopal arms, left **Rev. Legend:** EP • ET • PR • LEOD • DUX • ...

Date	Mintage	F	VF	XF	Unc	BU
1753	—	45.00	75.00	100	165	—
1754	—	45.00	75.00	100	165	—

KM# 162 2 ESCALIN

Silver **Ruler:** John Theodore **Obv:** Curved capped eight-fold arms, center arms of Vavaria Palatinate have reversed quarters **Obv. Legend:** I • TEOD CAR • D • G • BAV • D **Rev. Legend:** EP • ET • PR • LEO • DVX... **Note:** Struck at Liege.

Date	Mintage	F	VF	XF	Unc	BU
1754	—	45.00	75.00	100	165	—

KM# 112.1 PATAGON

Silver **Ruler:** Joseph Clement **Obv:** Smaller bust of Joseph Clement right, legend continuous **Obv. Legend:** IOSEPH • CLEM • D • G • AR • COL • P • EL • **Rev:** Capped nine-fold arms, date above **Note:** Struck at Liege. Dav. #4303.

Date	Mintage	F	VF	XF	Unc	BU
1694	—	400	600	1,000	—	—
1695	—	400	600	1,000	—	—
1696 Rare	—	—	—	—	—	—
1698	—	250	400	650	—	—
1699	—	250	400	650	—	—
1700	—	250	400	650	—	—
1701 Rare	—	—	—	—	—	—
1702 Rare	—	—	—	—	—	—

KM# 120 PATAGON

Silver **Ruler:** Joseph Clement **Obv:** Bust right, date below, at angle **Obv. Legend:** IOS • CLE • D • G • ARCH • COL •... **Rev:** Center circular Bavarian shield, four crowned shields in angles of crossed sword and sceptre **Rev. Legend:** E • P • LE • • D • BUL •... **Note:** Dav. #1581. Struck at Liege.

Date	Mintage	F	VF	XF	Unc	BU
1716 Rare	—	—	—	—	—	—

KM# 128 PATAGON

Silver **Obv:** Bust of St. Lambert left **Obv. Legend:** * S • LAMBERTUS • PATRONUS • LEODIENSIS • * **Rev:** Crowned, mantled five-fold oval arms, crown divides date **Rev. Legend:** SEDE • VACANTE * MONETA • NOVA • CAPLI • LEOD • **Note:** Sede vacante issue. Dav. #1583.

Date	Mintage	F	VF	XF	Unc	BU
1724	Inc. below	250	400	700	1,300	—

KM# 129 PATAGON

Silver **Obv:** Bust of St. Lambert left, date in legend **Obv. Legend:** S • LAMBERTVS• PATRONVS • LEODIENSIS • **Rev:** Crowned 4-fold arms **Rev. Legend:** MONETA • NOVA • CAPLI • LEOD • ... **Note:** Dav.#1584. Struck at Liege.

Date	Mintage	F	VF	XF	Unc	BU
1724	4,000	2,500	4,000	6,000	8,000	—

KM# 130 PATAGON

Silver **Subject:** Sede Vacante **Obv:** Bust of St. Lambert left **Obv. Legend:** * S • LAMBERTUS • PATRONUS • LEODIENSIS * **Rev:** Crowned 5-fold arms divides date **Rev. Legend:** * MONETA • NOVA • CAPLI • LEOD • ... **Note:** Dav. #1585.

Date	Mintage	F	VF	XF	Unc	BU
1724	Inc. above	2,500	4,000	6,000	8,000	—

KM# 147 PATAGON

Silver **Obv:** Bust of St. Lambert left, date in legend **Obv. Legend:** S • LAMBERTUS • PATRONUS • LEODIENSIS • 1744 **Rev:** Crowned 5-fold arms **Rev. Legend:** SEDE • VACANTE • MONETA • NOVA • CAPLI • LEOD • **Note:** Dav. #1587. Sede vacante issue. Struck at Liege.

Date	Mintage	F	VF	XF	Unc	BU
1744	200	500	1,000	2,000	3,000	—

KM# 166 PATAGON (48 Sols)

Silver **Obv:** Bust of St. Lambert left, date in legend **Obv. Legend:** S • LAMBERTUS • PATRONUS • LEODIENSIS • 1763 **Rev:** Crowned, mantled oval 5-fold arms **Rev. Legend:** SEDE • VACANTE * MONETA • NOVA • CAPLI • LEOD • **Note:** Dav. #1588. Sede Vacant issue. Struck at Liege.

Date	Mintage	F	VF	XF	Unc	BU
1763	300	250	400	700	1,300	—

KM# 171 PATAGON (48 Sols)

Silver **Obv:** Bust of St. Lambert left, date in legend **Obv. Legend:** S • LAMBERTUS • PATRONUS • LEODIENSIS • 1771 **Rev:** Crowned, mantled oval 5-fold arms **Rev. Legend:** SEDE • VACANTE * MONETA • NOVA • CAPLI • LEOD • **Note:** Dav. #1589. Sede Vacante issue.

Date	Mintage	F	VF	XF	Unc	BU
1771	150	350	600	1,100	2,000	—

KM# 176 PATAGON (48 Sols)

Silver **Obv:** Bust of St. Lambert left, date in legend **Obv. Legend:** S • LAMBERTUS • PATRONUS • LEODIENSIS • 1784 **Rev:** Crowned, mantled oval 5-fold arms **Rev. Legend:** SEDE • VACANTE * MONETA • NOVA • CAPLI • LEOD • **Note:** Dav. #1590. Sede Vacante issue.

Date	Mintage	F	VF	XF	Unc	BU
1784	150	350	600	1,100	2,000	—

KM# 181 PATAGON (48 Sols)
Silver **Obv:** Bust of St. Lambert left, date in legend **Obv. Legend:** S • LAMBERTUS • PATRONUS • LEODIENSIS • 1792 **Rev:** Crowned, mantled oval 5-fold arms **Rev. Legend:** SEDE • VACANTE * MONETA • NOVA • CAPLI • LEOD • **Note:** Dav. #1591. Sede Vacante issue.

Date	Mintage	F	VF	XF	Unc	BU
1792	150	350	600	1,100	2,000	—

KM# 131 2 PATAGON
Silver **Obv:** Bust of St. lambert left **Obv. Legend:** S • LAMBERTUS • PATRONUS • LEODIENSIS • **Rev:** Crowned, mantled oval arms **Note:** Dav. #1582. Sede vacante issue. Struck at Liege.

Date	Mintage	VG	F	VF	XF	Unc
1724 Rare	—	—	—	—	—	—

KM# 148 2 PATAGON
Silver **Obv:** Bust of St. Lambert left, date in legend **Obv. Legend:** S • LAMBERTUS • PATRONUS • LEODIENSIS • **Rev:** Crowned 5-fold baroque arms **Rev. Legend:** MONETA • NOVA • CAPLI • LEOD • ... **Note:** Dav. #1586. Sede vacante issue. Struck at Liege.

Date	Mintage	VG	F	VF	XF	Unc
1744 Rare	—	—	—	—	—	—

TRADE COINAGE

KM# 132 DUCAT
3.5000 g., 0.9860 Gold 0.1109 oz. AGW **Ruler:** George Louis **Obv:** Bust of St. Lambert left, date below **Obv. Legend:** S • LAMBERTUS • PATRO : LEOD : **Rev:** Crowned, mantled 5-fold arms **Rev. Legend:** SEDE • VACANTE * DEC • ET • CAP • LEOD •

Date	Mintage	VG	F	VF	XF	Unc
1724	200	3,000	5,000	7,500	10,000	—

KM# 149 DUCAT
3.5000 g., 0.9860 Gold 0.1109 oz. AGW **Ruler:** John Theodore **Obv:** Bust of St. Lambert left **Rev:** Crowned, mantled 5-fold arms **Note:** Sede Vacante issue.

Date	Mintage	VG	F	VF	XF	Unc
1744	114	3,500	6,000	9,000	12,000	—

KM# 151 DUCAT
3.5000 g., 0.9860 Gold 0.1109 oz. AGW **Ruler:** John Theodore **Obv:** Bust left **Obv. Legend:** I • THEO • D • G • D • BA • CARD • **Rev:** Cardinal hat above crowned arms, date divided below **Rev. Legend:** EP • PR • FR • RAT • LOED • **Note:** C#10.

Date	Mintage	F	VF	XF	Unc	BU
1749 Rare	—	—	—	—	—	—

KM# 167 DUCAT
3.5000 g., 0.9860 Gold 0.1109 oz. AGW **Obv:** Bust of St. Lambert left **Obv. Legend:** S • LAMBERTUS • PATRONUS • LEODIENSIS • **Rev:** Crowned, mantled oval 5-fold arms **Rev. Legend:** SEDE • VACANTE • 1763 * DEC • ET •CAP • LEOD • **Note:** Sede Vacante issue. C#15.

Date	Mintage	F	VF	XF	Unc	BU
1763	300	1,000	2,000	3,500	5,000	—

KM# 172 DUCAT
3.5000 g., 0.9860 Gold 0.1109 oz. AGW **Obv:** Bust of St. Lambert left **Obv. Legend:** S • LAMBERTUS • PATRONUS • LEODIENSIS • **Rev:** Crowned, mantled arms **Rev. Legend:** SEDE • VACANTE • * DEC • ET • CAPLI • LEOD • **Note:** C#15a. Sede Vacante issue.

Date	Mintage	F	VF	XF	Unc	BU
1771	150	3,000	5,000	7,500	10,000	—

KM# 177 DUCAT
3.5000 g., 0.9860 Gold 0.1109 oz. AGW **Obv:** Bust of St. Lambert **Obv. Legend:** S LAMBERTUS PATRO • LEOD : **Rev:** Crowned, mantled 5-fold arms **Rev. Legend:** SEDE • VACANTE • * • DEC • ET • CAPLI • LEOD • **Note:** C#15b. Sede Vacante issue.

Date	Mintage	F	VF	XF	Unc	BU
1784	150	3,000	5,000	7,500	10,000	—

KM# 182 DUCAT
3.5000 g., 0.9860 Gold 0.1109 oz. AGW **Obv:** Bust of St. Lambert left **Obv. Legend:** S • LAMBERTUS • PATRO • LEOD • **Rev:** Crowned, mantled oval 5-fold arms **Rev. Legend:** SEDE • VACANTE • * • DEC • ET • CAPLI • LEOD • **Note:** C#15c. Sede Vacante issue.

Date	Mintage	F	VF	XF	Unc	BU
1792	150	3,000	5,000	7,500	10,000	—

KM# 133 2 DUCAT
7.0000 g., 0.9860 Gold 0.2219 oz. AGW **Ruler:** George Louis **Obv:** Bust of St. Lambert left, date below **Obv. Legend:** S • LAMBERTUS • PATRO : LEOD **Rev:** Crowned, mantled oval 5-fold arms **Rev. Legend:** SEDE • VACANTE * DEC • ET • CAP • LEOD • **Note:** Sede Vacante issue

Date	Mintage	VG	F	VF	XF	Unc
1724 Rare	100	—	—	—	—	—

PATTERNS

Including off metal strikes

KM#	Date	Mintage	Identification	Mkt Val
PnA1	ND(1694-1723)	—	Liard. Silver. KM#107.	—

KM#	Date	Mintage	Identification	Mkt Val
Pn1	1792	—	Escalin. Crowned 5-fold arms divides date. Rampant lion with crowned oval shield.	500

LITHUANIA

The Republic of Lithuania, southernmost of the Baltic states in east Europe, has an area of 25,174 sq. mi.(65,201 sq. km.) and a population of *3.6 million. Capital: Vilnius. The economy is based on livestock raising and manufacturing. Hogs, cattle, hides and electric motors are exported.

Lithuania emerged as a grand duchy in the 14th century. In the 15th century it was a major power of central Europe, stretching from the Baltic to the Black Sea. It was joined with Poland in 1569, but lost Smolensk, Chernigovsk, and the left bank of the river Dnepr Ukraina in 1667. Following the third partition of Poland by Austria, Prussia and Russia, 1795,Lithuania came under Russian domination and did not regain its independence until shortly before the end of World War I when it declared itself a sovereign republic on Feb. 16, 1918. In fall of 1920, Poland captured Vilna (Vilnius). The republic was occupied by Soviet troops and annexed to the U.S.S.R. in 1940. Following the German occupation of 1941-44, it was retaken by Russia and reestablished as a member republic of the Soviet Union. Western countries, including the United States, did not recognize Lithuania's incorporation into the Soviet Union.

Lithuania declared its independence March 11, 1990and it was recognized by the United States on Sept. 2,1991, followed by the Soviet government in Moscow on Sept. 6. They were seated in the UN General Assembly on Sept. 17, 1991.

RULERS

Kings of Poland
Augustus II, (Augustas II) 1697-1704

MINT MARK
LMK – Vilna

GRAND DUCHY

STANDARD COINAGE

KM# 65 3 GROSZY
Silver **Obv:** Crowned bust right with value below **Rev:** Arms of Poland, Saxony and Lithuania, L-P at bottom, date in legend

Date	Mintage	VG	F	VF	XF	Unc
1706 LP	—	450	600	750	900	—

KM# 66 6 GROSZY
Silver **Obv:** Crowned bust of August II right **Rev:** Crown above value and 3 shields of arms, 2 above 1, date in legend

Date	Mintage	VG	F	VF	XF	Unc
1706 LP	—	200	300	400	550	—
1707 LP	—	400	475	550	750	—

LIVONIA

A former province of Russia, now partly in Latvia and partly in southern Estonia.

The division of Livonia left the northern part governed by Russia while the southern part fell under the dominion of Poland. In 1621 it was the theatre of a war between Sweden and Poland. Being conquered by Sweden, Livonia enjoyed 25 years of milder rule.

RIGA

Swedish Occupation

STANDARD COINAGE

KM# 91 1/24 THALER (1/24 Dalderi, Trispelher)
Silver **Obv:** Center shield of arms with lion

Date	Mintage	VG	F	VF	XF	Unc
1700	—	12.00	30.00	60.00	120	—
1701	—	12.00	30.00	60.00	120	—

TRADE COINAGE

KM# 92 DUCAT
3.5000 g., 0.9860 Gold 0.1109 oz. AGW **Obv:** Draped bust right **Obv. Legend:** CAROLVS • XII • D • G • REX • SVE • **Rev:** Crown above towers divides date within circle **Rev. Legend:** CIVITAT • RIGENSIS & MON • NOVA • AUREA

Date	Mintage	VG	F	VF	XF	Unc
1700	—	750	1,500	3,000	6,000	—
1701	—	750	1,500	3,000	6,000	—

KM# 93 DUCAT
3.5000 g., 0.9860 Gold 0.1109 oz. AGW **Obv:** Large draped bust right **Obv. Legend:** CAROLVS • XII • D • G • REX • SVE • **Rev:** Crown above towers divides date within circle

Date	Mintage	Good	VG	F	VF	XF
1701	—	—	400	950	2,000	2,500

COUNTERMARKED COINAGE

Siege of 1705

Countermark on coins of Charles XI and Charles XII during the siege of Riga in December by order of Governor-general Carl Gustav Frolich. Countermark appears as crown-linked CC with XII at center.

KM# 85 5 ORE
Silver **Countermark:** Crowned linked CC with XII at center **Note:** c/m on Sweden KM#310.

CM Date	Host Date	Good	VG	F	VF	XF
ND(1705)	1690-1700	—	40.00	100	200	400

KM# 59.1 MARK
Silver **Countermark:** Crowned linked CC with XII at center **Note:** Countermark on Sweden KM#240.

CM Date	Host Date	Good	VG	F	VF	XF
ND(1705)	1663-1674	—	65.00	180	360	720

KM# 59.2 MARK
Silver **Countermark:** Crowned linked CC with XII at center **Note:** Countermark at center on Sweden 1 Mark, KM#295.

CM Date	Host Date	Good	VG	F	VF	XF
ND(1705)	1683-1697	—	65.00	180	360	720

KM# 59.3 MARK
Silver **Countermark:** Crowned linked CC with XII at center **Note:** Countermark at center on Sweden 1 Mark, KM#313.

CM Date	Host Date	Good	VG	F	VF	XF
ND(1705)	1697-1700	—	65.00	180	360	720

KM# 58.1 2 MARK
Silver **Countermark:** Crowned linked CC with XII at center **Note:** Countermark at center on Sweden 2 Mark, KM#282.1.

CM Date	Host Date	Good	VG	F	VF	XF
ND(1705)	1677-1697	—	60.00	150	300	600

KM# 58.2 2 MARK
Silver **Countermark:** Crowned linked CC with XII at center **Note:** Countermark at center on Sweden 2 Mark, KM#314.

CM Date	Host Date	Good	VG	F	VF	XF
ND(1705)	1697-1705	—	70.00	180	360	720

KM# 60.1 4 MARK
Silver **Countermark:** Crowned linked CC with XII at center **Note:** Countermark at center on Sweden 4 Mark, KM#296.

CM Date	Host Date	Good	VG	F	VF	XF
ND(1705)	1683-1696	—	100	250	500	1,000

KM# 60.2 4 MARK
Silver **Countermark:** Crowned linked CC with XII at center **Note:** Countermark at center on Sweden 4 Mark, KM#315.

CM Date	Host Date	Good	VG	F	VF	XF
ND(1705)	1697-1700	—	120	300	600	1,200

A historic region at the eastern end of the Baltic Sea now known as Latvia and Estonia. It was originally inhabited by the Chudes, the Livs, the Narora, Letgola, Semigallians and Kors. The Germans first penetrated into Livonia in the 11th Century. Christianity was introduced by the Livonian Knights known as the Brothers of the Sword. They came under Polish rule in 1561, passed to Sweden in 1629 and was made part of Russia in 1721 following the Great Northern War, 1700-1721.

This special issue of coins was made following the issuing of the ukase of October 25, 1756 by Elizabeth, Czarina of all the Russias. The issue was to last only until the following year. For later coinage see Estonia and Latvia.

MONETARY SYSTEM
96 Kopecks = 1 Ruble

RUSSIAN ADMINISTRATION

STANDARD COINAGE

KM# 1.1 2 KOPECKS
1.0500 g., 0.3960 Silver 0.0134 oz. ASW **Obv:** Crown above double-headed eagle **Rev:** 2 Shields, with bow above, divides date, value below

Date	Mintage	VG	F	VF	XF	Unc
1757	50,000	50.00	110	185	280	—

KM# 1.2 2 KOPECKS
1.0500 g., 0.3960 Silver 0.0134 oz. ASW **Obv:** Crown above double-headed eagle **Rev:** 2 Shields, with bow above

Date	Mintage	VG	F	VF	XF	Unc
1757	Inc. above	50.00	110	185	280	—

KM# 2 4 KOPECKS
1.0900 g., 0.7500 Silver 0.0263 oz. ASW **Obv:** Crown above double-headed eagle **Rev:** 2 Shields, with bow above, value below **Rev. Legend:** LIVOESTHONICA •

Date	Mintage	VG	F	VF	XF	Unc
1757	582,000	22.00	40.00	65.00	120	—

KM# 3 24 KOPECKS
6.5700 g., 0.7500 Silver 0.1584 oz. ASW **Obv:** Bust of Elizabeth, right **Rev:** Crowned double-headed eagle with 2 oval shields on breast, value below **Rev. Legend:** MONETA • LIVOESTHONICA •

Date	Mintage	VG	F	VF	XF	Unc
1757	126,000	70.00	135	225	320	—

KM# 4 48 KOPECKS
13.1900 g., 0.7500 Silver 0.3180 oz. ASW **Obv:** Bust of Elizabeth, right **Rev:** Crowned double-headed eagle with 2 oval shields on breast, value below **Rev. Legend:** MONETA • LIVOESTHONICA •

Date	Mintage	VG	F	VF	XF	Unc
1757	42,000	175	275	450	700	—

KM# 5 96 KOPECKS (Ruble)
26.3800 g., 0.7500 Silver 0.6361 oz. ASW **Obv:** Elizabeth **Rev. Legend:** MONETA • LIVOESTHONICA •

Date	Mintage	VG	F	VF	XF	Unc
1757	27,000	285	450	750	1,200	—

NOVODELS

KM#	Date	Mintage	Identification	Mkt Val
N1	1756	—	2 Kopecks. Silver. Oblique milled edge.	—
N2	1756	—	2 Kopecks. Copper. Oblique milled edge.	—

KM#	Date	Mintage	Identification	Mkt Val
N3	1756 ММД	—	48 Kopecks. Silver. Die 1758 10 Rubles. Oblique milled edge.	—
N4	1756	—	48 Kopecks. Silver. Die 1746 1/2 Ruble. Restrike.	—
N5	1756	—	48 Kopecks. Silver. Plain edge. 1746 1/2 Ruble.	—
N6	1757	—	4 Kopecks. Silver. Oblique milled edge.	—
N7	1757	—	4 Kopecks. Silver. Plain edge.	—

KM#	Date	Mintage	Identification	Mkt Val
N8	1757	—	24 Kopecks. Silver. Die 1/4 Ruble of Elizabeth. Oblique milled edge.	—
N9	1757	—	24 Kopecks. Silver. Die 20 Kopecks of Katherine II. Oblique milled edge.	—
N10	1757	—	24 Kopecks. Silver. Die 1755 5 Ruble. Chain edge. Restrike.	—
N11	1757	—	96 Kopecks. Silver. Cinquefoil and globe edge. Struck from original dies	—

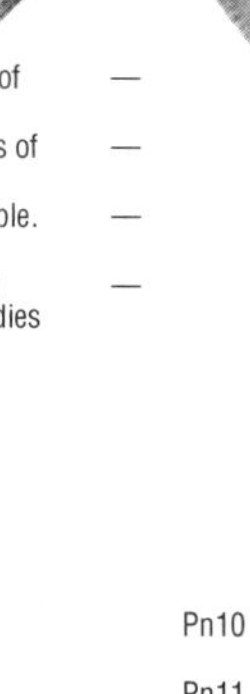

KM#	Date	Mintage	Identification	Mkt Val
N12	1757 ММД	—	96 Kopecks. Silver. Die Moscow Ruble. Oblique milled edge.	—
N13	1757 СПБ	—	96 Kopecks. Silver. Die St. Petersburg Ruble. Oblique milled edge.	—
N14	1757 СПБ	—	96 Kopecks. Silver. Die St. Petersburg Ruble. Plain edge.	—

PATTERNS

Including off metal strikes

KM#	Date	Mintage	Identification	Mkt Val
Pn1	1756	10	2 Kopecks. Silver. Small date and value, KM#1.1.	500

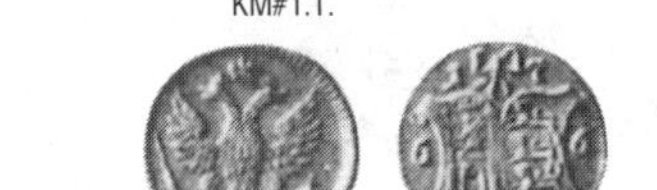

KM#	Date	Mintage	Identification	Mkt Val
Pn2	1756	10	2 Kopecks. Silver. Large date and value, KM#1.2.	—
Pn3	1756	10	4 Kopecks. Silver. LIVONICA • ET • ESTLANDIA •.	—
Pn4	1756	10	4 Kopecks. Silver. MONETA • LIVOESTHONICA •. Large eagle, KM#2.	—
Pn5	1756	10	24 Kopecks. Silver. MONETA • LIVOESTHONOICA •. Large eagle, KM#2.	—
Pn6	1756	10	24 Kopecks. Silver. MONETA • LIVON • ET • ESTLAND •.	—
Pn7	1756	10	48 Kopecks. Silver. MONETA • LIVOESTHONICA •.	—

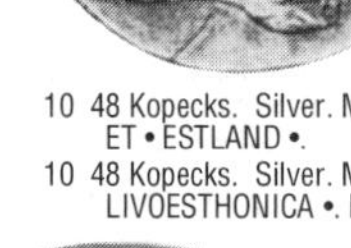

KM#	Date	Mintage	Identification	Mkt Val
Pn8	1756	10	48 Kopecks. Silver. MONETA • LIVON • ET • ESTLAND •.	3,500
Pn9	1756	10	48 Kopecks. Silver. MONETA • LIVOESTHONICA •. KM#4	2,000

KM#	Date	Mintage	Identification	Mkt Val
Pn10	1756	10	96 Kopecks. Silver. MONETA • LIVON • ET • ESTLAND.	—
Pn11	1756	10	96 Kopecks. Silver. MONETA • LIVOESTHONICA •. KM#5	—

LUXEMBOURG

The Grand Duchy of Luxembourg is located in western Europe between Belgium, Germany and France, has an area of 1,103 sq. mi. (2,586 sq. km.) and a population of 377,100. Capital: Luxembourg. The economy is based on steel.

Founded about 963, Luxembourg was a prominent country of the Holy Roman Empire; one of its sovereigns became Holy Roman Emperor as Henry VII, 1308. After being made a duchy by Emperor Charles IV, 1354, Luxembourg passed under the domination of Burgundy, Spain, Austria and France, 1443-1815, regaining autonomy under the Treaty of Vienna, 1815, as a grand duchy in union with the Netherlands, though ostensibly a member of the German Confederation. When Belgium seceded from the Kingdom of the Netherlands, 1830, Luxembourg was forced to cede its greater western section to Belgium. The tiny duchy left the German Confederation in 1867 when the Treaty of London recognized it as an independent state and guaranteed its perpetual neutrality. Luxembourg was occupied by Germany and liberated by American troops in both World Wars.

RULERS

Maximiliuel Emanuel of Bavaria, 1711-1714
Maria Theresa, 1740-1780
Joseph II, 1780-1790
Leopold II, 1790-1792
Frans II, 1792-1795

MINT MARKS

A - Paris
(b) - Brussels, privy marks only
H – Gunzburg
(n) – lion - Namur
(u) - Utrecht, privy marks only

PRIVY MARKS

Angel's head, two headed eagle - Brussels

MONETARY SYSTEM

(Until 1795)

4 Liards = 1 Sol

GRAND DUCHY

STANDARD COINAGE

4 Liards = 1 Sol

KM# 5 1/8 SOL

Copper **Ruler:** Maria Theresa **Obv:** Crowned arms without legend **Rev:** Value and date, mm below

Date	Mintage	VG	F	VF	XF	Unc
1775(b)	2,709,033	7.50	10.00	40.00	100	—

KM# 10 1/2 LIARD

Copper **Ruler:** Joseph II **Obv:** Crowned arms without legend **Rev:** Written value, date, mint mark above **Note:** Similar to 1/8 Sols, KM#5, but with mint mark at top.

Date	Mintage	VG	F	VF	XF	Unc
1783(b)	1,362,000	4.00	8.00	30.00	75.00	—
1784(b)	1,466,000	4.00	8.00	30.00	75.00	—
1789(b)	1,577,000	3.50	7.00	25.00	50.00	—

KM# B1 LIARD

Copper **Ruler:** Maximilian Emanuel of Bavaria **Obv:** Shields of Bavaria, Pfalz and Luxembourg, upper shields have a lion **Rev:** Shield divides date

Date	Mintage	VG	F	VF	XF	Unc
1712(n)	—	200	400	1,000	2,000	—

Note: A variety (unique?) exists with 3 lions instead of 1 in the upper left shield

KM# A1 LIARD

Copper **Ruler:** Maximilian Emanuel of Bavaria **Obv:** Shields of Bavaria, Pfalz and Luxembourg, 1 crown, title of Maximilan Emanuel **Rev:** Crowned shield divides date **Note:** This coin is very similar to the same coin struck for Namur. The only difference is that this coin has the Luxembourg shield on the obverse, instead of the Namur shield, which has no lines behind the lion.

Date	Mintage	VG	F	VF	XF	Unc
1712(n)	—	150	300	750	1,500	—

KM# 1 LIARD

Copper **Ruler:** Maria Theresa **Obv:** Bust of Maria Theresa right **Obv. Legend:** M • T • D • G • R • JMP • G • H • B • REG • A • A • D • LUX • **Rev:** Legend in 4 lines and date in wreath **Rev. Legend:** AD/USUM/DUCATUS/LUXEM **Note:** Maria Theresa.

Date	Mintage	VG	F	VF	XF	Unc
1757(b)	—	10.00	20.00	75.00	150	—

KM# 3 LIARD

Copper **Ruler:** Maria Theresa **Note:** Similar to 2 Liards, KM#4.

Date	Mintage	VG	F	VF	XF	Unc
1759(b)	1,531,000	10.00	25.00	75.00	150	—
1760(b)	433,000	30.00	75.00	150	300	—

KM# 2 2 LIARDS

Copper **Ruler:** Maria Theresa **Obv:** Bust right, legend similar to KM 1 **Obv. Legend:** M • T • D • G • R • J • MP • G • H • E • REG • AA • D • LUX • **Rev:** Legend in 4 lines and date in wreath **Rev. Legend:** AD/USUM/DUCATUS/LUXEM

Date	Mintage	VG	F	VF	XF	Unc
1757(b)	—	15.00	30.00	100	300	—

KM# 4 2 LIARDS

Copper **Ruler:** Maria Theresa **Obv:** Crowned ornated shield and titles of Maria Theresa **Obv. Legend:** MAR • T • D : G • R • ... **Rev:** Crowned monogram **Rev. Legend:** IUSTITIA ET • CLEMENTIA

Date	Mintage	VG	F	VF	XF	Unc
1759(b)	283,000	15.00	35.00	100	200	—
1760(b)	213,000	30.00	70.00	175	350	—

KM# 14 2 LIARDS

Copper **Ruler:** Joseph II **Obv:** Crowned monogram of Joseph II **Obv. Legend:** J O S • I I • D • G • R • IMP • DUX • LUXEMB **Rev:** Oval arms within sprigs, crown above divides date

Date	Mintage	VG	F	VF	XF	Unc
1789(b)	459,000	250	500	1,000	2,000	—

KM# 6 SOL

Billon **Ruler:** Maria Theresa **Obv:** Crowned arms, title of Maria Theresa **Rev:** Value and date, mint mark below

Date	Mintage	VG	F	VF	XF	Unc
1775(b)	305,629	100	175	300	600	—

KM# 11 SOL

Copper **Ruler:** Joseph II **Obv:** Legend around crowned arms **Obv. Legend:** IOS • D • G • R • I • H • B • R • DUX • LUXEMB **Rev:** Value, date

Date	Mintage	VG	F	VF	XF	Unc
1786(b)	400,000	25.00	50.00	150	300	—

KM# 15 SOL

Copper **Ruler:** Leopold II **Obv:** Crowned arms **Obv. Legend:** LEOP • II • D • G • H • B • R • DUX • LVX EMB • **Rev:** Value, date, H below

Date	Mintage	VG	F	VF	XF	Unc
1790H	864,000	20.00	40.00	100	200	—

KM# 7 3 SOLS

Billon **Ruler:** Maria Theresa **Obv:** Crowned arms, title of Maria Theresa **Rev:** Value and date, mint mark below

Date	Mintage	VG	F	VF	XF	Unc
1775(b)	220,909	30.00	75.00	300	600	—

KM# 16 3 SOLS

Billon **Ruler:** Leopold II **Obv:** Crowned arms **Obv. Legend:** LEOP • II • D • G • HV • BO • REX • DVX • LVXEMB **Rev:** Value, date, H below

Date	Mintage	VG	F	VF	XF	Unc
1790H	1,164,489	15.00	30.00	60.00	125	—

KM# 8 6 SOLS

3.2200 g., 0.6530 Silver 0.0676 oz. ASW **Ruler:** Maria Theresa **Obv:** Crowned arms, title of Maria Theresa **Rev:** Value and date, mint mark below

Date	Mintage	VG	F	VF	XF	Unc
1775(b)	71,000	65.00	125	225	500	—
1777/5(b)	78,000	120	170	300	600	—
1777(b)	Inc. above	70.00	130	240	520	—

KM# 12 6 SOLS

3.2500 g., 0.6530 Silver 0.0682 oz. ASW **Ruler:** Joseph II **Obv:** Legend, crowned arms **Obv. Legend:** IOS • II • D • G • R • IMP • S • A • H • B • R • DUX • LUXEMB **Rev:** Value, date

Date	Mintage	VG	F	VF	XF	Unc
1786(b)	70,755	75.00	150	700	1,500	—
1789(b)	52,931	100	175	750	1,600	—

KM# 17 6 SOLS

3.2000 g., 0.6530 Silver 0.0672 oz. ASW **Ruler:** Leopold II **Obv:** Crowned arms **Obv. Legend:** LEOP • II • D • G • HV • BO • REX • DVX • LVXEMB **Rev:** Value, date, H below

Date	Mintage	VG	F	VF	XF	Unc
1790H	727,651	25.00	50.00	150	300	—

KM# 9 12 SOLS

5.5000 g., 0.8410 Silver 0.1487 oz. ASW **Ruler:** Maria Theresa **Obv:** Veiled bust right, mint mark below **Rev:** Crowned arms divide value, date below

Date	Mintage	VG	F	VF	XF	Unc
1775(b)	29,753	150	300	1,000	2,000	—
1776(b)	57,031	150	300	1,000	2,000	—
1777(b)	33,615	150	300	1,000	2,000	—

KM# 13 12 SOLS

5.2200 g., 0.8410 Silver 0.1411 oz. ASW **Ruler:** Joseph II **Obv:** Laureate bust right **Obv. Legend:** IOS • II • D • G • R • ... **Rev:** Crowned arms divides value, date below

Date	Mintage	VG	F	VF	XF	Unc
1786(b)	37,196	200	400	700	2,000	—
1789(b)	53,715	150	300	800	1,750	—

SIEGE COINAGE

KM# 19 SOL

Copper **Ruler:** Frans II **Obv:** Crowned shield dividing F - II **Rev:** Value in 2 lines, date **Note:** Cast.

Date	Mintage	Good	VG	F	VF	XF
1795	—	10.00	20.00	50.00	120	—

KM# 20 72 ASSES (Sols)

Silver **Ruler:** Frans II **Obv:** Legend, date **Obv. Legend:** AD / USUM / LUXEMBURG / CCVALLATI **Rev:** Value, LXXII / ASSES, 13 in wreath

Date	Mintage	F	VF	XF	Unc	BU
1795	—	1,000	1,250	2,250	4,500	—

MALAY PENINSULA

KEDAH

A state in northwestern Malaysia. Islam introduced in 15th century. Subject to Thailand from 1821-1909. Coins issued under Governor Tengku Anum.

TITLES

كداه

Kedah

Sultans

Muhammad Jiwa Zainal Shah II, 1710-60
Ahmad Taju'd-din Halim Shah, 1798-1843

SULTANATE

HAMMERED COINAGE

KM# 8 TRA

Tin, 21.5 mm. **Ruler:** Abdullah al-Muazzam Shah I **Obv:** Arabic legend, date **Obv. Legend:** Sultan Sanat

Date	Mintage	Good	VG	F	VF	XF
AH1117 Rare	—	—	—	—	—	—

KM# 18 REAL

3.1000 g., Silver **Ruler:** Muhammad Jiwa Zainal Shah II **Obv:** Arabic legend **Obv. Legend:** Bebalad Kedah Daru'l-Aman sanat 1141

Date	Mintage	Good	VG	F	VF	XF
AH1141	—	—	60.00	100	150	225

KM# 19 KUPANG

0.5800 g., Gold **Ruler:** Muhammad Jiwa Zainal Shah II **Obv:** Arabic inscription **Obv. Inscription:** Sultan Muhammad Jiwa **Rev:** Arabic inscription **Rev. Inscription:** Adil Shah

Date	Mintage	VG	F	VF	XF	Unc
AH1147 Rare	—	—	—	—	—	—

PENANG

Pulu Penang-Prince of Wales Island

An island off the west coast of Malaysia. Ceded to the British in 1791 by the sultan of Kedah and was the first British settlement in Malaya. Also known as Pulu Penang and Prince of Wales Island - which title it retained until1867.

The currency system depended on the Spanish dollar divided into 100 pice (or cents) until 1826 when 48 pice were deemed the equivalent of one Bengal rupee until1830. The coins are considered in three groups:

(a) The Company bale mark series, consisting of copper1/10, 1/2 and 1 pice of 1786/1787, and silver tenth, quarter and half dollars, dated 1788;

(b) Company coat of arms issues in copper between1810 and 1828 in denominations of 1/2, 1 and double pice pieces; and

(c) Tin issues of local mintage pice pieces of 1800-1809, which are extremely rare.

TITLES

فولو فنيغ

Pulu Penang

Acquired by the British East India Company in 1786.

MONETARY SYSTEM

100 Cents (Pice) = 1 Dollar

BRITISH ADMINISTRATION

STANDARD COINAGE

KM# 1 1/4 CENT (1 Keping)

Copper **Obv:** X within heart divides letters, large 4 above **Rev:** Legend **Rev. Legend:** Jazirah Ab-Wailis (Island of Wales) **Note:** Dump; varieties exist with star.

Date	Mintage	Good	VG	F	VF	XF
1787 with star; Rare	—	—	—	—	—	—
1787 without star	—	—	15.00	30.00	60.00	125
1787 last 7 inverted	—	—	50.00	75.00	125	200

KM# 2.1 1/2 CENT (1/2 Pice)

Copper, 22 mm. **Obv:** X within heart divides letters, large 4 above, star below divides date **Rev:** Legend **Note:** Dump; varieties exist.

Date	Mintage	Good	VG	F	VF	XF
1787	—	—	15.00	30.00	65.00	135

KM# 2.2 1/2 CENT (1/2 Pice)

Copper, 19 mm. **Obv:** X within heart divides letters, large 4 above, star below divides date **Rev:** Legend **Note:** Reduced size.

Date	Mintage	Good	VG	F	VF	XF
1787	—	—	15.00	30.00	60.00	125

KM# 3 CENT (Pice)

Copper **Obv:** Half circles within heart divides letters, large 4 above, all within circle **Rev:** Legend **Note:** Dump; uniface.

Date	Mintage	Good	VG	F	VF	XF
ND(1786)	—	—	15.00	35.00	75.00	160

KM# 4 CENT (Pice)

Copper **Obv:** X within heart divides letters, large 4 above, star below divides date **Rev:** Legend **Note:** Dump; uniface; varieties exist.

Date	Mintage	Good	VG	F	VF	XF
1787	—	—	8.00	20.00	40.00	80.00
1787 last '7' inverted	—	—	8.00	20.00	40.00	80.00

KM# 8 CENT (Pice)

40.3500 g., Tin **Obv:** "GL" within circle **Note:** Uniface; initial 'GL' (Governor Leith) in ring; countermark of Chinese character for Yuan.

Date	Mintage	Good	VG	F	VF	XF
ND(ca.1800-03)	—	—	1,600	3,650	5,500	7,330

KM# 5.1 1/10 DOLLAR

0.9020 Silver **Obv:** X within heart divides letters, large 4 above, star below divides date **Rev:** Legend **Note:** Dump; diameter varies 16-17 millimeters.

Date	Mintage	Good	VG	F	VF	XF
1787 star	—	—	75.00	125	225	375
1788 rosette	—	—	75.00	125	225	375

KM# 5.2 1/10 DOLLAR

0.9020 Silver **Obv:** X within heart divides letters, large 4 above, star below divides date **Rev:** Legend **Note:** Dump; diameter varies 16-17 millimeters.

Date	Mintage	Good	VG	F	VF	XF
1788 rosette	—	—	75.00	125	225	375

KM# 6.1 1/4 DOLLAR

0.9030 Silver, 26 mm. **Obv:** X within heart divides letters, large 4 above, star below divides date **Rev:** Legend **Rev. Legend:** Perrinsa Jazirah Ab Wailis (Prince Island of Wales)

Date	Mintage	Good	VG	F	VF	XF
1787 star	—	—	250	450	800	1,250
1787 rosette	—	—	250	450	800	1,250

KM# 6.2 1/4 DOLLAR

0.9030 Silver, 23.5 mm. **Obv:** X within heart divides letters, large 4 above, star below divides date **Rev:** Legend **Rev. Legend:** Perrinsa Jazirah Ab Wailis (Prince Island of Wales) **Note:** Reduced size.

Date	Mintage	Good	VG	F	VF	XF
1788 rosette	—	—	250	450	800	1,250

KM# 7 1/2 DOLLAR

0.9020 Silver **Obv:** X within heart divides letters, large 4 above, star below divides date **Rev:** Legend **Note:** Dump.

Date	Mintage	Good	VG	F	VF	XF
1788 star	—	—	250	400	750	1,250
1788 rosette	—	—	250	400	750	1,250

TRENGGANU

A state in eastern Malaysia on the shore of the south China Sea. Area of dispute between Malacca and Thailand with the latter emerging with possession. Trengganu became a British dependency in 1909.

TITLES

Khalifa(t) al-Mu'minin

ترغگانو

Trengganu

SULTANS

Zainal Abidin II, 1793-1808

SULTANATE

STANDARD COINAGE

KM# A1 1/2 PITIS

Tin **Obv:** Arabic inscription **Obv. Inscription:** Kali Malik Al-Adil **Note:** Similar to KM#2.1; Arabic inscription: Kali Malik Al-Adil.

Date	Mintage	Good	VG	F	VF	XF
ND	—	—	15.00	25.00	45.00	80.00

KM# 1 PITIS

Tin **Obv:** Inscription **Obv. Inscription:** Malik Al-Adil **Rev:** Inscription **Rev. Inscription:** Khalifat Al-Mu'minin

Date	Mintage	Good	VG	F	VF	XF
ND	—	—	15.00	25.00	45.00	80.00

Note: Believed struck during reign of Zainal Abidin II or shortly afterwards.

KM# 2.1 PITIS

Tin, 21-26 mm. **Obv:** Inscription **Obv. Inscription:** Kali Malik Al-Adil **Note:** Uniface; Arabic inscription. Size varies.

Date	Mintage	Good	VG	F	VF	XF
ND	—	—	15.00	25.00	50.00	80.00

KM# 2.2 PITIS

Tin, 26 mm. **Obv:** Inscription **Rev:** Inscription

Date	Mintage	Good	VG	F	VF	XF
ND	—	—	15.00	25.00	50.00	80.00

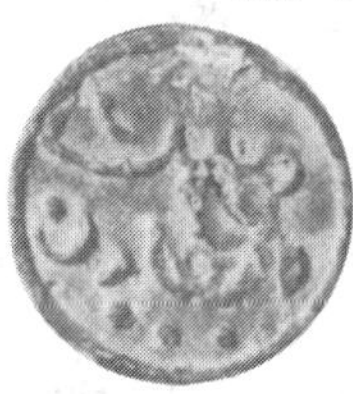

KM# 3 PITIS

Tin **Obv:** Inscription **Obv. Inscription:** Malik Al-Adil **Note:** Arabic inscription: Malik Al-Adil.

Date	Mintage	Good	VG	F	VF	XF
ND	—	—	15.00	25.00	50.00	85.00

KM# 4.1 PITIS

Tin **Obv:** Inscription **Note:** Varieties exist.

Date	Mintage	Good	VG	F	VF	XF
ND	—	—	15.00	25.00	40.00	75.00

Note: Probably issued throughout the first half of the 19th century.

KM# 4.2 PITIS

Tin **Obv:** Inscription

Date	Mintage	Good	VG	F	VF	XF
ND	—	—	15.00	25.00	40.00	75.00

KM# 5 PITIS

Tin **Obv:** Inscription within circle, designed wreath border **Note:** Similar to KM#10.

Date	Mintage	Good	VG	F	VF	XF
ND	—	—	20.00	40.00	60.00	90.00

KM# 8 PITIS
Tin

Date	Mintage	Good	VG	F	VF	XF
AH1213	—	—	20.00	40.00	60.00	100

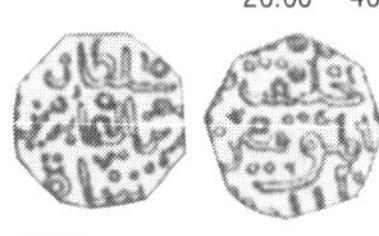

KM# A6 KUPANG
0.4500 g., Gold **Obv:** Arabic inscription: Sultan Zayn al-Abidin Shah **Rev:** Arabic inscription: Khalifat al-Mu'minin 1120 **Note:** Issue of Zaynal Abidin I.

Date	Mintage	Good	VG	F	VF	XF
AH1120 Rare	—	—	—	—	—	—

KM# 6 KUPANG
0.5800 g., Gold **Obv:** Arabic inscription: Sultan Zayn al-Abidin Shah **Rev:** Arabic inscription: Khalifat al-Mu'minin **Note:** Issue of Zaynal Abidin II.

Date	Mintage	Good	VG	F	VF	XF
ND	—	—	50.00	75.00	125	200

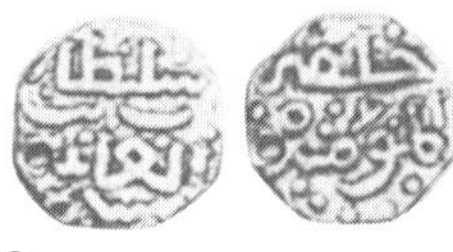

KM# 7 MAS
2.5000 g., Gold **Obv:** Inscription **Rev:** Inscription **Note:** Similar to KM#6.

Date	Mintage	Good	VG	F	VF	XF
ND	—	—	100	200	350	500

MALDIVE ISLANDS

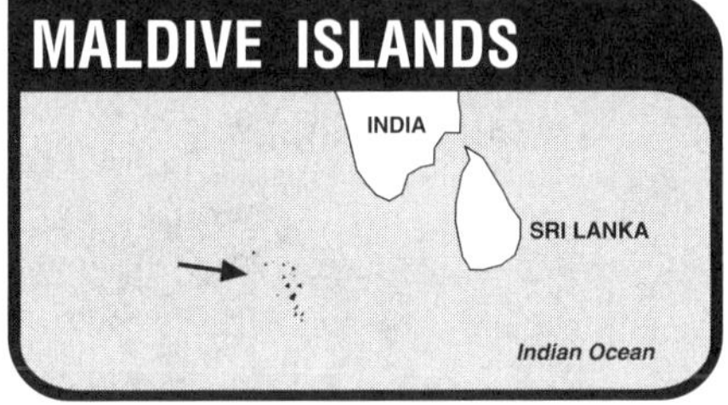

The Republic of Maldives, an archipelago of 2,000 coral islets in the northern Indian Ocean 417 miles (671 km.) west of Ceylon, has an area of 116 sq. mi. (298 sq. km.)and a population of 189,000. Capital: Male. Fishing employs 95% of the male work force. Dried fish, copra and coir yarn are exported.

The Maldive Islands were visited by Arab traders and converted to Islam in 1153. After being harassed in the16th and 17th centuries by Mopla pirates of the Malabar coast and Portuguese raiders, the Maldivians voluntarily placed themselves under the suzerainty of Ceylon. In 1887 the islands became an internally self-governing British protectorate and a nominal dependency of Ceylon. Traditionally a sultanate, the Maldives became a republic in 1953 but restored the sultanate in 1954. The Sultanate of the Maldive Islands attained complete internal and external autonomy on July 26, 1965, and on Nov. 11,1968, again became a republic.

RULERS

Muhammad Imad al-Din II al-Muzaffar bin Muhammad, AH1116-1133/1704-1721AD
Ibrahim Iskandar II bin Muhammad Imad al-Din, AH1133-1163/1721-1750AD
Muhammad Imad al-Din III, AH1163-1168/1750-1754AD
Interregnum (Malabar Conquest), AH1168-1173/1754-1759AD
Hasan Izz al-Din, AH1173-1180/1759-1767AD
Muhammad Ghiyas al-Din, AH1180-1187/1767-1773AD
Muhammad Shams al-Din II, AH1187-1188/1773-1774AD (no coinage known)
Muhammad Muiz al-Din, AH1188-1192/1774-1778AD
Hasan Nur al-Din I, AH1192-1213/1778-1798AD
Muhammad Mu'in al-Din, AH1213-1250/1798-1835AD

MINT NAME

Mahle (Male)

MONETARY SYSTEM
100 Lari = 1 Rupee (Rufiyaa)

NOTE: The metrology of the early coinage is problematical. There seem to have been three denominations: a double Larin of 8-10 g, a Larin of approximately 4.8 g, and a half Larin that varied from 1.1 to 2.4 g, known as the Bodu Larin, Larin and Kuda Larin, respectively. In some years probably when copper was cheap (AH1276 & 1294),the Kuda (1/2) Larin is found with weights as high as 3.5 g. During the rule of Muhammad Imad Al-Din II Al-Muzaffar Bin Muhammad (1704-1721AD) additional denominations in the form of the 1/4, 1/8 and 1/16 Larin (1.17 g, 0.55 g and 0.29 g) were introduced on an experimental basis. This experiment was not followed by later rulers with the exception of Muhammad Imad Al-Din IV (1835-1882AD) who struck some lightweight coins of about 1.1 g which can be considered 1/4 Larins.

SULTANATE

Muhammad Imad al-Din II al-Muzaffar bin Muhammad

STANDARD COINAGE

100 Lari = 1 Rupee (Rufiyaa)

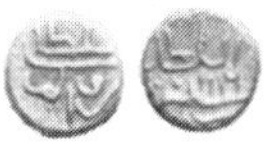

KM# 12 1/4 LARIN
Silver-Billon **Obv:** Inscription, date **Rev:** Inscription **Note:** Weight varies: 0.55-1.20 g.

Date	Mintage	Good	VG	F	VF	XF
AH1116	—	5.00	8.50	12.50	18.00	—
AH1129	—	5.00	8.50	12.50	18.00	—
AH113x	—	5.00	8.50	12.50	18.00	—

KM# 13.1 1/2 LARIN (Kuda)
Silver-Billon **Obv:** Inscription **Rev:** Inscription **Note:** Weight varies: 1.50-2.60 g.

Date	Mintage	Good	VG	F	VF	XF
AH1122	—	5.00	8.50	12.00	17.00	—

KM# 13.2 1/2 LARIN (Kuda)
Silver-Billon **Obv:** Inscription, date **Rev:** Inscription **Note:** Weight varies: 1.50-2.60 g.

Date	Mintage	Good	VG	F	VF	XF
AH1129	—	3.50	6.00	8.50	12.50	—
AH1131	—	3.50	6.00	8.50	12.50	—

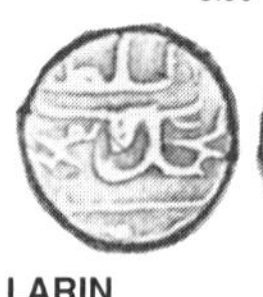 

KM# 14.1 LARIN
Silver-Billon **Obv:** Inscription **Rev:** Inscription **Note:** Weight varies 4.60-4.80 grams.

Date	Mintage	Good	VG	F	VF	XF
AH1116	—	4.00	7.00	10.00	15.00	—
AH1121	—	4.00	7.00	10.00	15.00	—
AH1122	—	4.00	7.00	10.00	15.00	—
AH1123	—	4.00	7.00	10.00	15.00	—
AH1124	—	4.00	7.00	10.00	15.00	—
ND	—	4.00	7.00	10.00	15.00	—

KM# 14.2 LARIN
Silver-Billon **Obv:** Inscription, date **Rev:** Inscription **Note:** Weight varies 4.60-4.80 grams. Varieties exist.

Date	Mintage	Good	VG	F	VF	XF
AH1129	—	5.50	9.00	12.00	17.00	—
AH1131	—	5.00	8.50	12.00	17.00	—

KM# 14.3 LARIN
Silver-Billon **Obv:** Inscription **Rev:** Inscription **Shape:** Octagonal **Note:** Wieght varies 4.60-4.80 grams.

Date	Mintage	Good	VG	F	VF	XF
AH1131 Rare	—	—	—	—	—	—

Ibrahim Iskandar II bin Muhammad Imad al-Din

STANDARD COINAGE

100 Lari = 1 Rupee (Rufiyaa)

KM# 15 1/2 LARIN (Kuda)
Billon-Bronze **Obv:** Inscription, date **Rev:** Inscription **Note:** Weight varies: 1.50-2.60 g.

Date	Mintage	Good	VG	F	VF	XF
AH1134	—	9.00	15.00	22.00	32.00	—
ND	—	9.00	15.00	22.00	32.00	—

KM# 16.3 LARIN
Billon-Bronze **Obv:** Inscription **Rev:** Inscription **Note:** Obverse and reverse with borders of diamonds. Weight varies 4.60-4.80 grams.

Date	Mintage	Good	VG	F	VF	XF
AH1134 Rare	—	—	—	—	—	—

KM# 16.2 LARIN
Billon-Bronze **Obv:** Inscription **Rev:** Inscription **Note:** Obverse and reverse within escalloped circles. Weight varies 4.60-4.80 grams.

Date	Mintage	Good	VG	F	VF	XF
AH1134 Rare	—	—	—	—	—	—

KM# 16.1 LARIN
Billon-Bronze **Obv:** Inscription **Rev:** Inscription, date **Note:** Weight varies 4.60-4.80 grams. Varieties exist.

Date	Mintage	Good	VG	F	VF	XF
AH1134	—	4.00	7.00	10.00	15.00	—
AH1153	—	4.00	7.00	10.00	15.00	—
AH1154	—	4.00	7.00	10.00	15.00	—

KM# 17 2 LARI (Bodu)
Billon-Bronze **Obv:** Inscription **Rev:** Inscription **Note:** Weight varies 9.10-9.60 grams.

Date	Mintage	Good	VG	F	VF	XF
AH1146	—	5.00	8.00	11.50	17.50	—
AH1153	—	5.00	8.00	11.50	17.50	—
AH1154	—	5.00	8.00	11.50	17.50	—
AH1156	—	5.50	9.00	14.00	20.00	—
AH1160	—	6.00	10.00	15.00	22.50	—
AH1163	—	7.00	12.00	18.50	27.50	—

Note: AH1163 struck with retrograde 3. Varieties exist.

Muhammad Imad al-Din III

STANDARD COINAGE

100 Lari = 1 Rupee (Rufiyaa)

KM# 21.1 RUPEE
Silver **Obv:** Inscription **Rev:** Inscription **Note:** Weight varies 13.74-13.97 grams.

Date	Mintage	Good	VG	F	VF	XF
AH1163 Rare	—	—	—	—	—	—

KM# 21.2 RUPEE
Silver **Obv:** Inscription **Rev:** Inscription **Note:** Weight varies 13.74-13.97 grams.

Date	Mintage	Good	VG	F	VF	XF
ND Rare	—	—	—	—	—	—

KM# 19.1 LARIN
Billon-Bronze **Obv:** Inscription **Rev:** Inscription **Note:** Weight varies 4.60-4.80 grams.

Date	Mintage	Good	VG	F	VF	XF
AH1163	—	5.00	8.00	11.00	16.00	—
AH1164	—	5.00	8.00	11.00	16.00	—
AH1166	—	5.00	8.00	11.00	16.00	—

KM# 19.2 LARIN
Billon-Bronze **Obv:** Inscription **Rev:** Inscription **Note:** Weight varies 4.60-4.80 grams.

Date	Mintage	Good	VG	F	VF	XF
AH1164	—	5.50	8.50	12.00	17.00	—

KM# 20 2 LARI (Bodu)
Billon **Obv:** Border of diamonds, inscription **Rev:** Inscription **Note:** Weight varies 9.10-9.60 grams. Varieties exist.

Date	Mintage	Good	VG	F	VF	XF
AH1163	—	4.50	9.00	12.50	17.50	—
AH1164	—	4.50	9.00	12.50	17.50	—
AH1166	—	4.50	9.00	12.50	17.50	—
AH1168	—	4.50	9.00	12.50	17.50	—

Hasan Izz al-Din

STANDARD COINAGE

100 Lari = 1 Rupee (Rufiyaa)

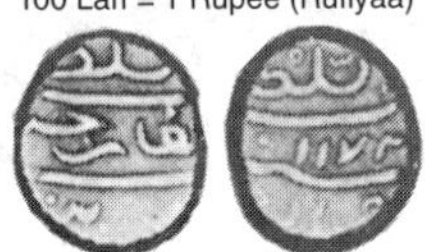

KM# 22 LARIN
Billon **Obv:** Inscription **Rev:** Inscription, date **Note:** Weight varies 4.60-4.80 grams.

Date	Mintage	Good	VG	F	VF	XF
AH1173	—	3.50	7.00	10.00	15.00	—

KM# 23.1 2 LARI (Bodu)
Billon **Obv:** Inscription **Rev:** Inscription, date **Note:** Weight varies 9.10-9.60 grams.

Date	Mintage	Good	VG	F	VF	XF
AH1173	—	4.00	8.00	11.00	16.00	—

KM# 23.2 2 LARI (Bodu)
Billon **Obv:** Inscription **Rev:** Inscription, date **Note:** Weight varies 9.10-9.60 grams. Varieties exist.

Date	Mintage	Good	VG	F	VF	XF
AH1177	—	4.00	8.00	11.00	16.00	—

Muhammad Ghiyas al-Din Iskandar al-Ghazi

STANDARD COINAGE

100 Lari = 1 Rupee (Rufiyaa)

KM# 24a 1/2 LARIN (Kuda)
Silver **Obv:** Inscription **Rev:** Inscription **Note:** Weight varies: 1.50-2.60 g.

Date	Mintage	Good	VG	F	VF	XF
AH1180 Rare	—	—	—	—	—	—
AH1184 H Rare	—	—	—	—	—	—

Note: Probably a presentation strike

KM# 24 1/2 LARIN (Kuda)
Copper-Bronze **Obv:** Inscription **Rev:** Inscription, date **Note:** Obverse or reverse with or without border of pearls. Weight varies 1.50-2.60 grams.

Date	Mintage	Good	VG	F	VF	XF
AH1184	—	4.00	6.00	9.00	12.50	—
AH1186	—	4.00	6.00	9.00	12.50	—

KM# 25 LARIN
Billon **Obv:** Inscription **Rev:** Inscription, date **Note:** Weight varies 4.60-4.80 grams.

Date	Mintage	Good	VG	F	VF	XF
AH1180	—	4.00	7.00	10.00	15.00	—

Note: No larins, except KM#A36 are known after this issue until the standard was changed in AH1300/1882AD to declare the 1/4 larin to be a new standard larin

KM# 26 2 LARI (Bodu)
Silver-Billon **Obv:** Inscription **Rev:** Border of diamonds, inscription, date **Note:** Weight varies 9.10-9.60 grams.

Date	Mintage	Good	VG	F	VF	XF
AH1182	—	5.00	8.00	11.00	16.00	—
AH1184	—	5.00	8.00	11.00	16.00	—

Muhammad Muiz al-Din

STANDARD COINAGE

100 Lari = 1 Rupee (Rufiyaa)

KM# 27 1/2 LARIN (Kuda)
Bronze **Obv:** Inscription **Rev:** Inscription, date **Note:** Obverse and reverse with or without borders of diamonds. Weight varies: 1.50-2.60 g.

Date	Mintage	Good	VG	F	VF	XF
AH1188	—	4.00	6.00	9.00	13.50	—
ND	—	4.50	7.00	10.00	15.00	—

KM# 28.1 2 LARI (Bodu)
Billon **Obv:** Inscription **Rev:** Year in second line, inscription **Note:** Obverse and reverse with or without borders of diamonds. Weight varies 9.10-9.60 grams.

Date	Mintage	Good	VG	F	VF	XF
AH1189	—	6.00	8.50	12.50	17.50	—

KM# 28.2 2 LARI (Bodu)
Billon **Obv:** Inscription **Rev:** Year in third line, inscription **Note:** Weight varies 9.10-9.60 grams.

Date	Mintage	Good	VG	F	VF	XF
AH1189	—	6.00	8.50	12.50	17.50	—

Hasan Nur al-Din I

STANDARD COINAGE

100 Lari = 1 Rupee (Rufiyaa)

KM# 29.1 1/2 LARIN (Kuda)
Bronze **Obv:** Inscription **Rev:** Inscription, line over date **Note:** Weight varies 1.50-2.60 grams.

Date	Mintage	Good	VG	F	VF	XF
AH1194	—	3.00	6.00	9.00	12.50	—

KM# 29.2 1/2 LARIN (Kuda)
Bronze **Obv:** Inscription **Rev:** Inscription, without line over date **Note:** Weight varies: 1.50-2.60 g.

Date	Mintage	Good	VG	F	VF	XF
AH1194	—	3.00	5.00	7.50	10.00	—
AH1197	—	3.00	5.00	7.50	10.00	—
AH1200	—	3.00	5.00	7.50	10.00	—
AH1202	—	3.00	5.00	7.50	10.00	—

KM# 30.1 2 LARI (Bodu)
Billon **Obv:** Inscription **Rev:** Inscription, date **Note:** Obverse and reverse with or without borders of diamonds. Weight varies 9.10-9.60 grams.

Date	Mintage	Good	VG	F	VF	XF
AH1197	—	3.50	8.00	11.00	16.00	—
AH1200	—	3.50	8.00	11.00	16.00	—
AH1207	—	3.50	8.00	11.00	16.00	—

KM# 30.2 2 LARI (Bodu)
Billon **Obv:** Inscription **Rev:** Inscription, date in third line **Note:** Weight varies 9.10-9.60 grams.

Date	Mintage	Good	VG	F	VF	XF
AH1201 Reported, not confirmed	—	—	—	—	—	—

KM# 30.3 2 LARI (Bodu)
Billon **Obv:** Inscription **Rev:** Inscription, date in fourth line **Note:** Weight varies 9.10-9.60 grams. Varieties exist.

Date	Mintage	Good	VG	F	VF	XF
AH1207	—	3.50	8.00	11.00	16.00	—

KM# A31 1/2 MOHUR
Gold **Obv:** Inscription **Rev:** Inscription, date **Note:** Weight varies 5.41-6.25 grams.

Date	Mintage	Good	VG	F	VF	XF
AH1202 Rare	—	—	—	—	—	—

KM# 31 MOHUR
Gold **Obv:** Inscription **Rev:** Inscription, date **Note:** Weight varies 10.82-12.50 grams.

Date	Mintage	Good	VG	F	VF	XF
AH1207 Rare	—	—	—	—	—	—
AH1257 Error	—	—	—	—	—	—

Note: Reported, not confirmed

Muhammad Mu'in al-Din Iskandar

STANDARD COINAGE

100 Lari = 1 Rupee (Rufiyaa)

KM# 33.1 2 LARI (Bodu)
Billon **Obv:** Inscription in three lines **Rev:** Inscription, date **Note:** Weight varies 9.10-9.60 grams.

Date	Mintage	Good	VG	F	VF	XF
AH1214	—	5.00	8.00	11.00	16.00	—

KM# 33.2 2 LARI (Bodu)
Billon **Obv:** Inscription in four lines **Rev:** Inscription, date **Note:** Weight varies 9.10-9.60 grams.

Date	Mintage	Good	VG	F	VF	XF
AH1214	—	5.00	8.00	11.00	16.00	—

MALTA

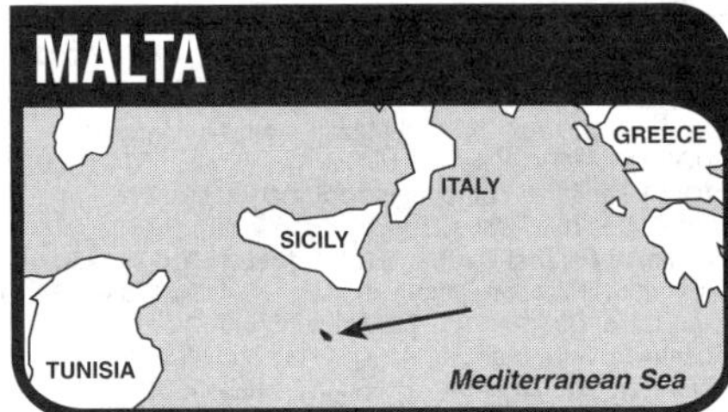

The Order of Malta, modern successor to the Sovereign Military Hospitaller Order of St. John of Jerusalem (the crusading Knights Hospitallers), derives its sovereignty from grants of extraterritoriality by Italy (1928) and the Vatican City (1953), and from its supranational character as a religious military order owing suzeraintyto the Holy See. Its territory is confined to Palazzo Malta on Via Condotti, Villa Malta and the crest of the Aventine Hill, all in the city of Rome. The Order maintains diplomatic relations with about 35 governments, including Italy, Spain, Austria, State of Malta, Portugal, Brazil, Guatemala, Panama, Peru, Iran, Lebanon, Philippines, Liberia, Ethiopia, and several others.

The Knights Hospitallers were founded in 1099 just before the crusaders' capture of Jerusalem. Father Gerard (died 1120) was the founder and first rector of the Jerusalem hospital. The headquarters of the Order were successively at Jerusalem 1099-1187; Acre 1187-1291; Cyprus 1291-1310; Rhodes 1310-1522; Malta 1530-1798;Trieste 1798-1799; St. Petersburg 1799-1803; Catania 1803-1825; Ferrara 1826-1834; Rome 1834-Present.

RULERS

Ramon Perellos y Roccaful, 1697-1720
Marcantonio Zondadari, 1720-1722
Antonio Manoel de Vilhena, 1722-1736
Ramon Despuig, 1736-1741
Emmanuel Pinto, 1741-1773
Francisco Ximenez de Texada, 1773-1775
Emmanuel de Rohan, 1775-1797
Ferdinand Hompesch, 1797-1798
French, 1798-1800

MONETARY SYSTEM

20 Grani = 1 Tari
12 Tari = 1 Scudo

SOVEREIGN HOSPITAL ORDER

STANDARD COINAGE

KM# 295 XV (15) PICCIOLI

Copper **Ruler:** Emmanuel de Rohan **Obv:** Crowned arms on breast of double-headed eagle **Rev:** Value, date within thin wreath

Date	Mintage	Good	VG	F	VF	XF
1776	—	—	20.00	30.00	50.00	100
Note: Three varieties of 1776 exist						
1777	—	—	20.00	30.00	50.00	100

KM# 140 GRANO

Copper **Ruler:** Ramon Perellos y Roccaful **Obv:** Maltese cross divides date **Rev:** Paschal Lamb with banner **Rev. Legend:** RECTAM • FACIT • SEMITAM •

Date	Mintage	Good	VG	F	VF	XF
1703	—	—	20.00	40.00	60.00	120
1704	—	—	20.00	40.00	60.00	120
1706	—	—	20.00	40.00	60.00	120
1707	—	—	20.00	40.00	60.00	120
1709	—	—	20.00	40.00	60.00	120
9071 1709 reversed	—	—	20.00	50.00	75.00	150
1715	—	—	20.00	40.00	60.00	120
1717	—	—	20.00	40.00	60.00	120
1718	—	—	20.00	40.00	60.00	120
1720	—	—	20.00	40.00	60.00	120

KM# 141 GRANO

Copper **Ruler:** Ramon Perellos y Roccaful **Rev:** Paschal Lamb with banner **Rev. Legend:** VT TOLLAT PECCATA

Date	Mintage	Good	VG	F	VF	XF
1703	—	—	20.00	40.00	60.00	120

KM# 142 GRANO

Copper **Ruler:** Ramon Perellos y Roccaful **Rev:** Paschal Lamb with banner **Rev. Legend:** MISCE VTILE DVLCI

Date	Mintage	Good	VG	F	VF	XF
1703	—	—	20.00	40.00	60.00	120

KM# 144 GRANO

Copper **Ruler:** Ramon Perellos y Roccaful **Rev:** Paschal Lamb with banner **Rev. Legend:** ECCE QVI TOLLIT PECCATA

Date	Mintage	Good	VG	F	VF	XF
1709	—	—	20.00	40.00	60.00	120

KM# 193 GRANO

Copper **Ruler:** Antonio Manoel de Vilhena **Obv:** Arms of Vilhena **Rev:** Maltese cross **Note:** Varieties exist.

Date	Mintage	Good	VG	F	VF	XF
1726	—	—	20.00	50.00	75.00	120
1734	—	—	20.00	50.00	75.00	120

KM# 205 GRANO

Copper **Ruler:** Ramon Despuig **Obv:** Arms of Despvig within circle **Rev:** Maltese cross

Date	Mintage	Good	VG	F	VF	XF
1739	—	—	20.00	50.00	75.00	120
Note: Numerous legend varieties						

KM# 239 GRANO

Copper **Ruler:** Emmanuel Pinto **Obv:** Five crescents at center **Rev:** Maltese cross with date in angles **Note:** Varieties exist.

Date	Mintage	Good	VG	F	VF	XF
1743	—	—	20.00	30.00	40.00	70.00
1744	—	—	20.00	30.00	40.00	70.00
1747	—	—	20.00	30.00	40.00	70.00
1750	—	—	20.00	30.00	40.00	70.00
1751	—	—	20.00	30.00	40.00	70.00
1752	—	—	20.00	30.00	40.00	70.00
1753	—	—	20.00	30.00	40.00	70.00
1754	—	—	20.00	30.00	40.00	70.00
1755	—	—	20.00	30.00	40.00	70.00
1757	—	—	20.00	30.00	40.00	70.00
1773	—	—	40.00	60.00	80.00	120

KM# 240 GRANO

Copper **Ruler:** Emmanuel Pinto **Obv:** Five crescents in inner circle **Note:** Varieties exist.

Date	Mintage	Good	VG	F	VF	XF
1743	—	—	20.00	40.00	60.00	120

KM# 245 GRANO

Copper **Ruler:** Emmanuel Pinto **Obv:** Horizontal N in PINTO

Date	Mintage	Good	VG	F	VF	XF
1751	—	—	40.00	60.00	75.00	150

KM# 246 GRANO

Copper **Ruler:** Emmanuel Pinto **Rev:** NOC instead of HOC

Date	Mintage	Good	VG	F	VF	XF
1751	—	—	40.00	60.00	75.00	150

KM# 296.1 GRANO

Copper **Ruler:** Emmanuel de Rohan **Obv:** Arms **Obv. Legend:** F • EMMANVEL DE ROHAN M **Rev:** Maltese cross with date in angles

Date	Mintage	Good	VG	F	VF	XF
1776	—	—	20.00	40.00	60.00	120

KM# 296.2 GRANO

Copper **Ruler:** Emmanuel de Rohan **Obv. Legend:** F • EMMANVEL DE ROHAN N M

Date	Mintage	Good	VG	F	VF	XF
1776	—	—	20.00	30.00	40.00	70.00

KM# 298.1 GRANO

Copper **Ruler:** Emmanuel de Rohan **Obv. Legend:** F • EMMANVEL DE ROHAN M **Rev:** G-I in circle, date in legend

Date	Mintage	Good	VG	F	VF	XF
1776	—	—	20.00	30.00	40.00	70.00

KM# 298.2 GRANO

Copper **Ruler:** Emmanuel de Rohan **Obv. Legend:** F EMMANUEL DE ROHAN M. M.

Date	Mintage	Good	VG	F	VF	XF
1777	—	—	20.00	30.00	40.00	70.00
1778	—	—	20.00	30.00	40.00	70.00

KM# 298.3 GRANO

Copper **Ruler:** Emmanuel de Rohan **Obv. Legend:** F. EMMANUEL DE ROHAN M. **Rev:** G. I in circle, date in legend

Date	Mintage	Good	VG	F	VF	XF
1777	—	—	20.00	30.00	40.00	70.00
1780	—	—	20.00	30.00	40.00	70.00

KM# 298.4 GRANO

Copper **Ruler:** Emmanuel de Rohan **Obv:** Arms **Obv. Legend:** F. EMMANVEL DE ROHAN M **Rev:** G.I. above date within circle

Date	Mintage	Good	VG	F	VF	XF
1785	—	—	20.00	30.00	40.00	70.00
1786	—	—	20.00	30.00	40.00	70.00

KM# 298.5 GRANO

Copper **Ruler:** Emmanuel de Rohan **Obv. Legend:** F. EMMANUEL DE ROHAN M

Date	Mintage	Good	VG	F	VF	XF
1785	—	—	20.00	30.00	40.00	70.00

KM# 298.6 GRANO

Copper **Ruler:** Emmanuel de Rohan **Obv:** Retrograde N in ROHAN of legend

Date	Mintage	Good	VG	F	VF	XF
1785	—	—	—	—	—	—

KM# 143 V (5) GRANI (Cinquina)

Silver **Ruler:** Ramon Perellos y Roccaful **Obv:** Arms of the Order **Rev:** Clasped hands, value above, date below

Date	Mintage	VG	F	VF	XF	Unc
1707	—	50.00	100	150	200	—

KM# 151 V (5) GRANI (Cinquina)

Copper **Ruler:** Ramon Perellos y Roccaful **Obv:** Crowned ornamented shield of perollos y Roceafull **Rev:** Crowned ornamented shield with Arms of the Order

Date	Mintage	Good	VG	F	VF	XF
1719	—	—	25.00	50.00	100	150

KM# 194 V (5) GRANI (Cinquina)

Copper **Ruler:** Antonio Manoel de Vilhena **Obv:** Lion rampant **Rev:** Two clasped hands **Note:** Varieties exist.

Date	Mintage	Good	VG	F	VF	XF
1726	—	—	25.00	50.00	100	150
1734	—	—	25.00	50.00	100	150

KM# 206 V (5) GRANI (Cinquina)

Copper **Ruler:** Ramon Despuig **Obv:** Crown above Despvig's arms, fleur-de-lis at sides **Rev:** Two clasped hands

Date	Mintage	Good	VG	F	VF	XF
1739	—	—	25.00	50.00	100	150

KM# 241 V (5) GRANI (Cinquina)

Copper **Ruler:** Emmanuel Pinto **Obv:** Five crescents with crown and garlands above **Obv. Legend:** ... M • M • K • H • **Rev:** Casped hands with date above and value below

Date	Mintage	Good	VG	F	VF	XF
1748	—	—	25.00	30.00	50.00	75.00

KM# 247 V (5) GRANI (Cinquina)

Copper **Ruler:** Emmanuel Pinto **Obv:** Crowned oval arms with garlands

Date	Mintage	Good	VG	F	VF	XF
1751	—	—	40.00	50.00	75.00	100
1752	—	—	40.00	50.00	75.00	100
1753	—	—	40.00	50.00	75.00	100
1754	—	—	25.00	30.00	50.00	75.00
1755	—	—	25.00	30.00	50.00	75.00
1762	—	—	25.00	30.00	50.00	75.00

KM# 256 V (5) GRANI (Cinquina)

Copper **Ruler:** Emmanuel Pinto **Obv:** Crown above ornate arms within sprays **Obv. Legend:** F • EMMANVEL PINTO M • M • H • S • S • **Rev:** Standing figure facing right

Date	Mintage	Good	VG	F	VF	XF
1757	—	—	30.00	40.00	50.00	75.00

KM# 299.1 V (5) GRANI (Cinquina)

Copper **Ruler:** Emmanuel de Rohan **Obv:** Crowned arms over eagle **Obv. Legend:** F. EMMANUEL DE ROHAN M **Rev:** Clasped hands, date above, value below

Date	Mintage	Good	VG	F	VF	XF
1776	—	—	30.00	40.00	50.00	75.00
1780	—	—	30.00	40.00	50.00	75.00
1790	—	—	30.00	40.00	50.00	75.00

KM# 299.2 V (5) GRANI (Cinquina)

Copper **Ruler:** Emmanuel de Rohan **Obv. Legend:** F. EMMANVEL...

Date	Mintage	Good	VG	F	VF	XF
1780	—	—	30.00	40.00	50.00	75.00

KM# 131 X (10) GRANI (Carlino)

Silver **Ruler:** Ramon Perellos y Roccaful **Obv:** Crown above shield of Perellos y Roccafull **Rev:** Arms of the Order

Date	Mintage	VG	F	VF	XF	Unc
ND(1697-1720)	—	100	150	200	250	—

KM# 152 X (10) GRANI (Carlino)

Copper **Ruler:** Ramon Perellos y Roccaful **Obv:** Crown above shield of Perellos y Roccafull **Rev:** Two clasped hands **Note:** Varieties exist.

Date	Mintage	Good	VG	F	VF	XF
1719	—	—	50.00	75.00	100	150
.1.7.1.9.	—	—	50.00	75.00	100	150

KM# 160 X (10) GRANI (Carlino)

Silver **Ruler:** Marcantonio Zondadari **Obv:** Crown above circular shield of the Order with palm branches and vertical lines in background **Rev:** Rose bush

Date	Mintage	VG	F	VF	XF	Unc
ND(1720-22)	—	100	150	200	250	—

KM# 161 X (10) GRANI (Carlino)

Silver **Ruler:** Marcantonio Zondadari **Obv:** Without vertical lines in background **Note:** Varieties of rose bush.

Date	Mintage	VG	F	VF	XF	Unc
ND(1720-22)	—	150	175	200	250	—

KM# 200 X (10) GRANI (Carlino)

Copper **Ruler:** Antonio Manoel de Vilhena **Obv:** Crowna above shield of Vilhena **Rev:** Two clasped hands

Date	Mintage	Good	VG	F	VF	XF
1734	—	—	40.00	50.00	75.00	120

KM# 207 X (10) GRANI (Carlino)

Copper **Ruler:** Ramon Despuig **Obv:** Crown above oval Despvig and shield **Rev:** Two clasped hands **Note:** Varieties exist.

Date	Mintage	Good	VG	F	VF	XF
1739	—	—	40.00	50.00	75.00	120

KM# 230 X (10) GRANI (Carlino)

Copper **Ruler:** Emmanuel Pinto **Obv:** Round arms in cartouche with magisterial berretto above **Rev:** Clasped hands with date above and value below

Date	Mintage	Good	VG	F	VF	XF
1742	—	—	30.00	40.00	50.00	75.00

KM# 242 X (10) GRANI (Carlino)

Copper **Ruler:** Emmanuel Pinto **Obv:** Arms topped by royal crown

Date	Mintage	Good	VG	F	VF	XF
1748	—	—	30.00	40.00	50.00	75.00
1752	—	—	30.00	40.00	50.00	75.00
1754	—	—	30.00	40.00	50.00	75.00
1755	—	—	30.00	40.00	50.00	75.00
1757	—	—	30.00	40.00	50.00	75.00
1771	—	—	30.00	40.00	50.00	75.00

KM# 300.1 X (10) GRANI (Carlino)

Copper **Ruler:** Emmanuel de Rohan **Obv:** Crowned arms above eagle **Obv. Legend:** F. EMMANUEL DE ROHAN M M H **Rev:** Clasped hands, date above, value below

Date	Mintage	Good	VG	F	VF	XF
1776	—	—	30.00	40.00	50.00	75.00

KM# 300.2 X (10) GRANI (Carlino)

Copper **Ruler:** Emmanuel de Rohan **Obv. Legend:** F. EMMANUEL DE ROHAN M

Date	Mintage	Good	VG	F	VF	XF
1776	—	—	30.00	40.00	50.00	75.00

KM# 300.3 X (10) GRANI (Carlino)

Copper **Ruler:** Emmanuel de Rohan **Obv. Legend:** F. EMMANVEL DE ROHAN M. M. H.

Date	Mintage	Good	VG	F	VF	XF
1776	—	—	30.00	40.00	50.00	75.00

KM# 300.4 X (10) GRANI (Carlino)

Copper **Ruler:** Emmanuel de Rohan **Obv. Legend:** F. EMMANUEL DE ROHAN M. M.

Date	Mintage	Good	VG	F	VF	XF
1786	—	—	30.00	40.00	50.00	75.00

KM# 300.5 X (10) GRANI (Carlino)

Copper **Ruler:** Emmanuel de Rohan **Obv. Legend:** F. EMMANVEL DE ROHAN M. M.

Date	Mintage	Good	VG	F	VF	XF
1786	—	—	30.00	40.00	50.00	75.00

KM# 300.6 X (10) GRANI (Carlino)

Copper **Ruler:** Emmanuel de Rohan **Obv:** Retrograde L in EMMANVEL of legend

Date	Mintage	Good	VG	F	VF	XF
1786	—	—	—	—	—	—

KM# 231 20 GRANI (Tari)

Copper **Ruler:** Emmanuel Pinto **Obv:** Head of John the Baptist toward right on platter **Rev:** Clasped hands with date above and value below in inner circle, legend divided by dots

Date	Mintage	Good	VG	F	VF	XF
1742	—	—	30.00	40.00	60.00	80.00

KM# 232 20 GRANI (Tari)

Copper **Ruler:** Emmanuel Pinto **Rev:** Legend divided by Maltese crosses

Date	Mintage	Good	VG	F	VF	XF
1742	—	—	40.00	50.00	75.00	120

KM# 248 20 GRANI (Tari)

Copper **Ruler:** Emmanuel Pinto **Obv:** Head of John the Baptist toward left on platter

Date	Mintage	Good	VG	F	VF	XF
1752	—	—	40.00	50.00	75.00	120
1762	—	—	40.00	50.00	75.00	120

KM# 249 20 GRANI (Tari)

Copper **Ruler:** Emmanuel Pinto **Rev:** Without inner circle

Date	Mintage	Good	VG	F	VF	XF
1754	—	—	40.00	50.00	60.00	90.00
1755	—	—	40.00	50.00	75.00	120
1757	—	—	40.00	50.00	75.00	120

KM# 169 TARI

Copper **Ruler:** Antonio Manoel de Vilhena **Obv:** Crown above Vilhena's arms **Rev:** Arms of the Order

Date	Mintage	Good	VG	F	VF	XF
ND(1722-36)	—	—	50.00	75.00	125	175

KM# 307.1 TARI

Silver **Ruler:** Emmanuel de Rohan **Obv:** Crowned oval arms in sprays **Rev:** Value in wreath, date in legend

Date	Mintage	VG	F	VF	XF	Unc
1777	—	50.00	60.00	75.00	90.00	—

KM# 307.2 TARI

Silver **Ruler:** Emmanuel de Rohan **Obv:** Crowned oval arms in sprays, retrograde N in ROHAN **Rev:** T • I and rosettes within thin wreath

Date	Mintage	VG	F	VF	XF	Unc
1777	—	60.00	75.00	100	120	—

KM# 331.2 TARI

Copper **Ruler:** Emmanuel de Rohan **Obv. Legend:** F • EMMANUEL DE ROHAN M •

Date	Mintage	Good	VG	F	VF	XF
1786	—	—	20.00	30.00	40.00	50.00

KM# 331.3 TARI

Copper **Ruler:** Emmanuel de Rohan **Obv:** Crowned arms above eagle **Obv. Legend:** F • EMMANVEL DE ROHAN M • M • **Rev:** Head of John the Baptist on platter

Date	Mintage	Good	VG	F	VF	XF
1786	—	—	20.00	30.00	40.00	50.00

KM# 332 TARI

Copper **Ruler:** Emmanuel de Rohan **Obv. Legend:** F • EMMANUEL DE ROHAN M • M • H • **Rev. Legend:** CONCUTIATIS NEMINEM

Date	Mintage	Good	VG	F	VF	XF
ND	—	—	30.00	40.00	50.00	75.00

KM# 333 TARI

Copper **Ruler:** Emmanuel de Rohan **Obv:** Without value **Obv. Legend:** F • EMMANUEL DE ROHAN M •

Date	Mintage	Good	VG	F	VF	XF
ND	—	—	30.00	40.00	50.00	75.00

KM# 178 2 TARI

Copper **Ruler:** Antonio Manoel de Vilhena **Obv:** Rampant lion **Rev:** Maltese cross

Date	Mintage	Good	VG	F	VF	XF
1723	—	—	50.00	75.00	125	200

KM# 201 2 TARI

Copper **Ruler:** Ramon Despuig **Obv:** Crown above arms of Despvig, divides value **Rev:** Maltese cross, stars in angles **Note:** Varieties in shape of shield.

Date	Mintage	Good	VG	F	VF	XF
1737	—	—	150	175	200	250

KM# 219 2 TARI

Silver **Ruler:** Emmanuel Pinto **Obv:** Magisterial berretto above arms **Obv. Legend:** F • EMMANVEL • PINTO... **Rev:** Maltese cross, stars in angles

Date	Mintage	VG	F	VF	XF	Unc
1741	—	50.00	60.00	75.00	100	—

KM# 290 2 TARI

Silver **Ruler:** Francisco Ximenez de Texada **Obv:** Crowned, oval arms within leafy sprigs **Obv. Legend:** F • D • FRAN : XIMENEZ • **Rev:** Maltese cross

Date	Mintage	VG	F	VF	XF	Unc
1774	—	60.00	75.00	125	150	—

KM# 291 2 TARI

Silver **Ruler:** Francisco Ximenez de Texada

Date	Mintage	VG	F	VF	XF	Unc
1774	—	10.00	20.00	40.00	75.00	—

KM# 301.1 2 TARI

Silver **Ruler:** Emmanuel de Rohan **Obv:** Crowned arms above eagle **Rev:** Maltese cross in circle, date in angles, SPUL in legend

Date	Mintage	VG	F	VF	XF	Unc
1776	—	40.00	50.00	60.00	75.00	—

KM# 301.2 2 TARI

Silver **Ruler:** Emmanuel de Rohan **Rev:** SPU for SEPUL in legend

Date	Mintage	VG	F	VF	XF	Unc
1779	—	40.00	50.00	60.00	75.00	—

KM# 162 4 TARI

Silver **Ruler:** Marcantonio Zondadari **Obv:** Crowned ornate arms of Zondadari **Rev:** QVI DAT/PAVPERI/NON/INDIGEBIT, date within cartouche

Date	Mintage	VG	F	VF	XF	Unc
1720	—	350	400	450	500	—

KM# 163 4 TARI

Silver **Ruler:** Marcantonio Zondadari **Obv:** Crown above ornate oval shield of Zondadari **Rev:** Head of John the Baptist on platter

Date	Mintage	VG	F	VF	XF	Unc
ND(1720-22)	—	300	350	400	450	—

KM# 170 4 TARI

Silver **Ruler:** Antonio Manoel de Vilhena **Obv:** Bust right **Rev:** Crown above ornate shield

Date	Mintage	VG	F	VF	XF	Unc
1722	—	150	175	250	300	—
1723	—	150	175	250	300	—
1724	—	175	200	275	350	—
1728	—	150	175	250	300	—

KM# 202 4 TARI

Silver **Ruler:** Ramon Despuig **Obv:** Bust right **Rev:** Crown above oval, ornate arms

Date	Mintage	VG	F	VF	XF	Unc
1737	—	100	125	150	200	—

KM# 220 4 TARI

Silver **Ruler:** Emmanuel Pinto **Obv:** Young armored bust right **Rev:** Crowned arms, crown divides date

Date	Mintage	VG	F	VF	XF	Unc
1741	—	75.00	100	125	150	—

KM# 221 4 TARI

Silver **Ruler:** Emmanuel Pinto **Obv:** Large armored bust left, legend broken **Rev:** Arms with coronet and magisterial cap above

Date	Mintage	VG	F	VF	XF	Unc
ND	—	75.00	100	125	150	—

KM# 222 4 TARI

Silver **Rev:** Crowned arms

Date	Mintage	VG	F	VF	XF	Unc
ND	—	75.00	100	125	150	—

KM# 223 4 TARI

Silver **Obv:** Small bust, continuous legend

Date	Mintage	VG	F	VF	XF	Unc
ND	—	75.00	100	125	150	—

KM# 250 4 TARI

Silver **Ruler:** Emmanuel Pinto **Obv:** Armored bust left **Rev:** Crown divides date above ornate shield

Date	Mintage	VG	F	VF	XF	Unc
1756	—	75.00	100	125	150	—
1757	—	75.00	100	125	150	—

KM# 251 4 TARI

Silver **Ruler:** Emmanuel Pinto **Rev:** Without value, date in legend

Date	Mintage	VG	F	VF	XF	Unc
1756	—	75.00	100	125	150	—
1761	—	75.00	100	125	150	—

KM# 282 4 TARI

Silver **Ruler:** Emmanuel Pinto **Obv:** Armored bust right **Obv. Legend:** F • EMMANVEL PINTO M • M • **Rev:** Crowned shield

Date	Mintage	VG	F	VF	XF	Unc
1768	—	75.00	100	125	150	—

KM# 285 4 TARI

Silver **Ruler:** Francisco Ximenez de Texada **Obv:** Draped, armored bust right, date below **Obv. Legend:** FRAN XIMENEZ DE TEXADA • .. **Rev:** Crossed oval arms in branches, crown divides value

Date	Mintage	VG	F	VF	XF	Unc
1773	—	100	125	150	200	—
1774	—	100	125	150	200	—

KM# 302 4 TARI

Silver **Ruler:** Emmanuel de Rohan **Obv:** Crown above shield on eagle breast **Obv. Legend:** F • EMMANUEL DE ROHAN M • M • H • S • S • **Rev:** Value, date within wreath

Date	Mintage	VG	F	VF	XF	Unc
1776	—	75.00	100	125	150	—
1779	—	75.00	100	125	150	—

KM# 179 VI (6) TARI

Silver **Ruler:** Antonio Manoel de Vilhena **Obv:** Bust right **Obv. Legend:** F • D A N : M A N O E L D E V I L H E N A **Rev:** Coronet above ornamented arms

Date	Mintage	VG	F	VF	XF	Unc
1723	—	150	350	450	500	—

KM# 208 VI (6) TARI

Silver **Ruler:** Ramon Despuig **Obv:** Coronet and cap above ornamented shield **Rev:** Head of John the Baptist on platter

Date	Mintage	VG	F	VF	XF	Unc
1739	—	—	—	3,500	4,500	—

KM# 303.1 VI (6) TARI

Silver **Ruler:** Emmanuel de Rohan **Obv:** Crown above shield on eagle breast **Obv. Legend:** F • EMMANUEL DE ROHAN M • M • H • S • S **Rev:** Value, date within wreath **Note:** Varieties exist.

Date	Mintage	VG	F	VF	XF	Unc
1776	—	75.00	100	125	150	—
1780	—	75.00	100	125	150	—

KM# 303.2 VI (6) TARI

Silver **Ruler:** Emmanuel de Rohan **Obv:** Crown above shield on eagle breast **Obv. Legend:** M • M • H • S • ... **Rev:** Value, date within wreath

Date	Mintage	VG	F	VF	XF	Unc
1776	—	75.00	100	125	150	—

KM# 164 8 TARI

Silver **Ruler:** Antonio Manoel de Vilhena **Obv:** Bust right **Rev:** Coronet above ornamented arms

Date	Mintage	VG	F	VF	XF	Unc
1721 Rare	—	—	—	—	—	—
1722 Rare	—	—	—	—	—	—
1723 Rare	—	—	—	—	—	—

KM# 252 XV (15) TARI

Silver **Ruler:** Emmanuel Pinto **Obv:** Crowned, ornate shield within sprays **Obv. Legend:** FEMMANVEL PINTO • M • M • H • ... **Rev:** John the Baptist standing with banner in right hand, value in exergue **Rev. Legend:** ...SVRREXIT MAIOR

Date	Mintage	VG	F	VF	XF	Unc
1756	—	125	150	200	240	—
1757	—	125	150	200	240	—
1759	—	125	150	200	240	—

KM# 257 XV (15) TARI

Silver **Ruler:** Emmanuel Pinto **Obv:** Palm spray at right of crowned arms **Rev:** Banner in crook of left arm, lamb standing

Date	Mintage	VG	F	VF	XF	Unc
1757	—	125	150	200	240	—
1759	—	125	150	200	240	—

KM# 258.1 XV (15) TARI

Silver **Ruler:** Emmanuel Pinto **Obv:** Crown above shield within sprays **Obv. Legend:** F • EMMANVEL PINTO • M • M • H • S • S • **Rev:** Banner hanging from cross in right hand **Rev. Legend:** ...SVRREXIT MAIOR **Note:** Prev. KM#258.

Date	Mintage	VG	F	VF	XF	Unc
1759	—	125	150	200	240	—
1761	—	125	150	200	240	—

KM# 259 XV (15) TARI

Silver **Ruler:** Emmanuel Pinto **Obv:** Crowned arms within sprays **Obv. Legend:** F • EMMANVEL PINTO • M • M • H • S • S • **Rev:** Banner in crook of John the Baptist's left arm, lamb standing at his feet **Rev. Legend:** ....SVRREXIT MAIOR

Date	Mintage	VG	F	VF	XF	Unc
1761	—	125	150	200	240	—
1764	—	125	150	200	240	—

KM# 258.2 XV (15) TARI

Silver **Ruler:** Emmanuel Pinto **Obv:** Crowned arms with solid ornamentation **Rev:** Banner hanging from cross in right hand

Date	Mintage	VG	F	VF	XF	Unc
1769	—	125	150	200	240	—

KM# 258.3 XV (15) TARI

Silver **Ruler:** Emmanuel Pinto **Obv:** Crowned arms on laurels **Rev:** Banner hanging from cross in right hand

Date	Mintage	VG	F	VF	XF	Unc
1772	—	125	150	200	240	—

KM# 304 XV (15) TARI

Silver **Ruler:** Emmanuel de Rohan **Obv:** Large bust right **Obv. Legend:** F • EMMANUELDE ROHAN • M • M • H • **Rev:** Crown divides value above 2 oval shields, divides date below

Date	Mintage	VG	F	VF	XF	Unc
1776	—	150	175	225	300	—
1777	—	150	175	225	300	—

KM# 316 XV (15) TARI

Silver **Ruler:** Emmanuel de Rohan **Obv:** Armored bust right **Obv. Legend:** F • EMMANUEL DE ROHAN • M • M • **Rev:** Crown above shield on eagle breast, date in legend above **Rev. Legend:** ... • HOSPITALS ET S •

Date	Mintage	VG	F	VF	XF	Unc
1779	—	150	175	225	300	—

KM# 325 XV (15) TARI

Silver **Ruler:** Emmanuel de Rohan **Obv:** Armored bust right **Obv. Legend:** F • EMMANUEL DE ROHAN • M • M • **Rev:** Crown divides date above shield on eagle breast

Date	Mintage	VG	F	VF	XF	Unc
1781	—	125	150	200	240	—

KM# 344 XV (15) TARI

Silver **Ruler:** Ferdinand Hompesch **Obv:** Armored bust left **Obv. Legend:** FERDINANDVS HOMPESCH ... **Rev:** Crown divides date above shield on eagle breast

Date	Mintage	VG	F	VF	XF	Unc
1798	—	200	225	275	325	—

Note: It is believed that KM#344 was struck during the French occupation of Malta

KM# 165 16 TARI

Silver **Ruler:** Antonio Manoel de Vilhena **Obv:** Bust right **Rev:** Coronet above ornamented arms

Date	Mintage	VG	F	VF	XF	Unc
1721	—	—	—	5,000	—	—
1723	—	—	—	5,000	—	—

KM# 326 16 TARI

Silver **Ruler:** Emmanuel de Rohan **Obv:** Bust right **Rev:** Crowned arms above eagle, date in legend, crown divides value

Date	Mintage	VG	F	VF	XF	Unc
1781	—	200	225	250	300	—

KM# A256 XXX (30) TARI

Silver **Ruler:** Emmanuel Pinto **Obv:** Crowned arms, date in legend **Rev:** John the Baptist standing with banner in right hand, lamb lying at right, value in exergue **Note:** Varieties exist. Dav. #1600.

Date	Mintage	VG	F	VF	XF	Unc
1756	—	250	300	350	400	—
1757	—	250	300	350	400	—
1758	—	250	300	350	400	—
1759	—	250	300	350	400	—

KM# 260 XXX (30) TARI

Silver **Ruler:** Emmanuel Pinto **Obv:** Crown above ornate shield **Obv. Legend:** F • EMMANVEL PINTO • M • M • H • S • S • **Rev:** Banner hanging from cross in right hand **Rev. Legend:** ...EXIT • MAIOR • **Note:** Varieties exist. Dav. #1602.

Date	Mintage	VG	F	VF	XF	Unc
1759	—	275	300	325	375	—
1761	—	275	300	325	375	—

KM# 265.2 XXX (30) TARI

Silver **Ruler:** Emmanuel Pinto **Rev:** Lamb reclining **Note:** Dav. #1601A.

Date	Mintage	VG	F	VF	XF	Unc
1761	—	275	300	325	375	—

KM# 265.1 XXX (30) TARI

Silver **Ruler:** Emmanuel Pinto **Obv:** Crowned ornate shield, date in legend **Obv. Legend:** F • EMMANVEL • PINTO • M • M • H • S • S • **Rev:** Standing figure, lamb standing at right **Rev. Legend:** ...SVRREXIT MAIOR **Note:** Dav. #1601.

Date	Mintage	VG	F	VF	XF	Unc
1761	—	275	300	325	375	—

KM# 265.3 XXX (30) TARI

Silver **Ruler:** Emmanuel Pinto **Obv:** Branches behind arms **Note:** Dav. #1601B.

Date	Mintage	VG	F	VF	XF	Unc
1761	—	275	300	325	375	—

KM# 266 XXX (30) TARI

Silver **Ruler:** Emmanuel Pinto **Obv:** Crown above ornate shield, date in legend **Obv. Legend:** F • EMMANUEL PIN : TO • M • M • H • S • S • **Rev:** Banner in left hand, lamb standing **Rev. Legend:** ...VRREXIT MAIOR **Note:** Varieties exist. Dav. #1604.

Date	Mintage	VG	F	VF	XF	Unc
1761	—	275	300	325	375	—
1768	—	275	300	325	375	—

KM# 308 XXX (30) TARI

Silver **Ruler:** Emmanuel de Rohan **Obv:** Armored bust right **Obv. Legend:** F • EMMANUEL DE ROHAN • M • M • H • S • S • **Rev:** Crown divides value above oval shields, divides date below **Note:** Dav. #1606.

Date	Mintage	VG	F	VF	XF	Unc
1777	—	100	150	300	500	—

KM# 317 XXX (30) TARI

Silver **Ruler:** Emmanuel de Rohan **Obv:** Armored bust right **Obv. Legend:** F • EMMANUEL DE ROHAN M * M * **Rev:** Crown above shield on eagle breast, divided date above **Rev. Legend:** ...* HOSPITALIS ET S • **Note:** Dav. #1607.

Date	Mintage	VG	F	VF	XF	Unc
1779	—	200	225	250	300	—

KM# 327 XXX (30) TARI

Silver **Ruler:** Emmanuel de Rohan **Obv:** Armored bust right **Obv. Legend:** F • EMMANUEL DE ROHAN M • M • **Rev:** Crown above shield on eagle breast, date at upper left **Rev. Legend:** ...HOSPITA • ET S • **Note:** Varieties exist. Dav. #1608.

Date	Mintage	VG	F	VF	XF	Unc
1781	—	250	275	300	325	—
1785	—	250	275	300	325	—
1789	—	250	275	300	325	—
1790	—	250	275	300	325	—

KM# 335.2 XXX (30) TARI
Silver **Ruler:** Emmanuel de Rohan **Obv:** Without eagle below modified bust **Rev:** Crown above shield on eagle breast **Note:** Dav. #1609A.

Date	Mintage	VG	F	VF	XF	Unc
1789	—	250	275	300	325	—
1790	—	250	275	300	325	—
1795	—	250	275	300	325	—
1796	—	250	275	300	325	—

KM# 335.1 XXX (30) TARI
Silver **Ruler:** Emmanuel de Rohan **Obv:** Eagle below modified bust, right **Obv. Legend:** F • EMMANUEL DE ROHAN M • M • **Rev:** Crown above shield on eagle breast **Rev. Legend:** ...HOSPITA • ET S • **Note:** Dav. #1609.

Date	Mintage	VG	F	VF	XF	Unc
1789	—	250	275	300	325	—
1790	—	250	275	300	325	—
1795	—	250	275	300	325	—
1796	—	250	275	300	325	—

KM# 345.1 XXX (30) TARI
Silver **Ruler:** Ferdinand Hompesch **Subject:** Ferdinand Hompesch **Obv:** Armored bust left, without cross or dot below bust **Obv. Legend:** F • FERDINANDVS HOMPESCH M • M **Rev:** Crown above shield on eagle breast, divided date above **Rev. Legend:** ...HOSPITAL ET **Note:** Dav. #1611.

Date	Mintage	VG	F	VF	XF	Unc
1798	—	300	350	400	450	—

KM# 345.2 XXX (30) TARI
Silver **Ruler:** Ferdinand Hompesch **Obv:** Eight-pointed star below shoulder **Note:** Dav. #1611A.

Date	Mintage	VG	F	VF	XF	Unc
1798	—	300	350	400	450	—

KM# 345.3 XXX (30) TARI
Silver **Ruler:** Ferdinand Hompesch **Obv:** Armored bust left, dot below bust **Obv. Legend:** F • FEDINANDVS HOMPESCH M • M • **Rev:** Crown above shield on eagle breast, divided date above **Note:** Dav. #1611B.

Date	Mintage	VG	F	VF	XF	Unc
1798	—	300	350	400	450	—

Note: It is believed that KM#345.3 was struck during the French occupation of Malta

KM# 345.4 XXX (30) TARI
Silver **Ruler:** Ferdinand Hompesch **Obv:** Dot in front of Grand Masters' nose **Note:** Dav. #1611C.

Date	Mintage	VG	F	VF	XF	Unc
1798	—	400	450	550	600	—

Note: It is believed that 345.4 was struck during the French occupation of Malta

KM# A133.1 ZECCHINO
3.5000 g., 0.9860 Gold 0.1109 oz. AGW **Ruler:** Ramon Perellos y Roccaful **Obv:** Crowned round shield in sprays **Obv. Legend:** (*) F (•) RAYMUNDV(S) PERELLOS (•) M • M • H • ET • S • S • HIE **Rev:** St. John standing presents the flag of the Order to the kneeling Grand Master **Rev. Legend:** PIETATE - VINCES

Date	Mintage	VG	F	VF	XF	Unc
ND(1697-1720)	—	150	220	450	800	—
1699	—	150	220	450	800	—

KM# 139 ZECCHINO
3.5000 g., 0.9860 Gold 0.1109 oz. AGW **Obv:** Crowned oval arms in sprays **Obv. Legend:** F • MARCVS ANTONIVS ZONDODARI • M • M • HOS: HIE • **Rev:** St. John standing presents the flag of the Order to the kneeling Grand Master **Rev. Legend:** PIETATE - VINCES

Date	Mintage	VG	F	VF	XF	Unc
ND(1720-22)	—	1,500	1,800	2,000	2,500	—

KM# 133 ZECCHINO
3.5000 g., 0.9860 Gold 0.1109 oz. AGW **Ruler:** Ramon Perellos y Roccaful **Obv:** Crowned baroque shield in sprays **Obv. Legend:** F RAYMUNDVS PERELLOS M M H ET S S H **Rev:** St. John presents the flag of the Order to the kneeling Grand Master **Rev. Legend:** PIETATE - VINCES

Date	Mintage	VG	F	VF	XF	Unc
1705	—	1,500	1,800	2,000	2,500	—
1717	—	1,500	1,800	2,000	2,500	—

KM# 171 ZECCHINO
3.5000 g., 0.9860 Gold 0.1109 oz. AGW **Ruler:** Marcantonio Zondadari **Obv:** Crowned shovel point arms in sprays **Obv. Legend:** * F • MARCVS ANTONIVS ZONDODARI • M • M • H • H• **Rev:** St. John standing presents the flag of the Order of the kneeling Grand Master

Date	Mintage	VG	F	VF	XF	Unc
1722	—	1,500	1,800	2,000	2,500	—

KM# 172 ZECCHINO
3.5000 g., 0.9860 Gold 0.1109 oz. AGW **Obv:** Crowned oval shield within sprigs **Rev:** St. John presenting banner to Grand Master

Date	Mintage	VG	F	VF	XF	Unc
ND	—	1,500	1,800	2,000	2,500	—

KM# 182 ZECCHINO
3.5000 g., 0.9860 Gold 0.1109 oz. AGW **Ruler:** Antonio Manoel de Vilhena **Obv:** Crowned ornate shield **Obv. Legend:** M • M • HOS : ET S • S • HIERV **Rev:** St. John presenting banner to Grand Master

Date	Mintage	VG	F	VF	XF	Unc
1723	—	1,500	1,800	2,000	2,500	—
1724	—	1,500	1,800	2,000	2,500	—

KM# 189 ZECCHINO
3.5000 g., 0.9860 Gold 0.1109 oz. AGW **Ruler:** Antonio Manoel de Vilhena **Obv:** Crowned ornate shield **Obv. Legend:** F • D • AN • MANOEL DE VILHENA M • M • H • **Rev:** St. John presenting banner to Grand Master

Date	Mintage	VG	F	VF	XF	Unc
1725	—	1,500	1,800	2,000	2,500	—

KM# 233 ZECCHINO
3.5000 g., 0.9860 Gold 0.1109 oz. AGW **Ruler:** Emmanuel Pinto **Obv:** Armored bust left **Obv. Legend:** F • EMMANVEL PINTO M • M • **Rev:** Crowned shield

Date	Mintage	VG	F	VF	XF	Unc
1742	—	700	900	1,200	1,500	—
ND	—	700	900	1,200	1,500	—

KM# 244 ZECCHINO
3.5000 g., 0.9860 Gold 0.1109 oz. AGW **Obv:** Armored bust left **Rev:** Crowned shield

Date	Mintage	VG	F	VF	XF	Unc
ND	—	—	—	—	—	—

KM# 22 2 ZECCHINO
7.0000 g., 0.9860 Gold 0.2219 oz. AGW **Ruler:** Ramon Perellos y Roccaful **Obv:** Crowned shield within sprigs **Obv. Legend:** F RAIMVNDVS PERELLOS... **Rev:** Knights of the Order holding a flag

Date	Mintage	VG	F	VF	XF	Unc
ND(1697-1720)	—	2,500	3,000	5,000	7,000	—

KM# 183 2 ZECCHINO
7.0000 g., 0.9860 Gold 0.2219 oz. AGW **Ruler:** Antonio Manoel de Vilhena **Obv:** Armored bust right **Rev:** Crowned shield within sprigs **Note:** Varieties exist.

Date	Mintage	VG	F	VF	XF	Unc
1723	—	2,000	2,250	2,500	3,000	—

KM# 190 2 ZECCHINO
7.0000 g., 0.9860 Gold 0.2219 oz. AGW **Ruler:** Antonio Manoel de Vilhena **Obv:** Armored bust right **Rev:** Crowned, ornate round shield **Note:** Varieites exist.

Date	Mintage	VG	F	VF	XF	Unc
1724	—	300	475	850	1,650	—
1725	—	300	475	850	1,650	—
1726	—	300	475	850	1,650	—
1728	—	300	475	850	1,650	—

KM# 234 2 ZECCHINO
7.0000 g., 0.9860 Gold 0.2219 oz. AGW **Ruler:** Emmanuel Pinto **Obv:** Armored bust left **Obv. Legend:** F • EMMA NVEL PINTO **Rev:** Coronet above shield **Rev. Legend:** SEP • HIER • M • M • ...

Date	Mintage	VG	F	VF	XF	Unc
1742	—	1,250	1,500	1,750	2,000	—
ND	—	1,250	1,500	1,750	2,000	—

KM# 235 2 ZECCHINO
7.0000 g., 0.9860 Gold 0.2219 oz. AGW **Ruler:** Emmanuel Pinto **Obv:** Small, armored bust left **Obv. Legend:** F • EMMANVEL PINTO M • M • **Rev:** Crowned shield **Rev. Legend:** HOSPI • ET SEP • HIER •

Date	Mintage	VG	F	VF	XF	Unc
ND	—	1,250	1,500	1,750	2,000	—

KM# 236 2 ZECCHINO
7.0000 g., 0.9860 Gold 0.2219 oz. AGW, 22 mm. **Obv:** Armored bust left **Rev:** Crowned shield **Note:** Reduced size.

Date	Mintage	VG	F	VF	XF	Unc
ND	—	1,250	1,500	1,750	2,000	—

KM# 134 4 ZECCHINI
14.0000 g., 0.9860 Gold 0.4438 oz. AGW **Ruler:** Ramon Perellos y Roccaful **Obv:** Crowned arms in palm branches **Rev:** St. John presenting banner to kneeling Grand Master

Date	Mintage	VG	F	VF	XF	Unc
1699	—	1,250	1,850	3,500	6,000	—
1705	—	—	—	30,000	—	—

KM# 150 4 ZECCHINI
14.0000 g., 0.9860 Gold 0.4438 oz. AGW **Ruler:** Ramon Perellos y Roccaful **Obv:** Armored bust right, date below **Obv. Legend:** RAIMIN PERELLOS ET .... **Rev:** Crowned shield within sprigs

Date	Mintage	VG	F	VF	XF	Unc
1717	—	—	—	20,000	—	—
1718	—	—	—	20,000	—	—

KM# 153 4 ZECCHINI
14.0000 g., 0.9860 Gold 0.4438 oz. AGW **Ruler:** Ramon Perellos y Roccaful **Obv:** Armored bust right **Obv. Legend:** E • RAIMV • PERELLOS.... **Rev:** Crowned shield divides date

Date	Mintage	VG	F	VF	XF	Unc
1719	—	—	—	20,000	—	—

KM# 166 4 ZECCHINI
14.0000 g., 0.9860 Gold 0.4438 oz. AGW **Ruler:** Marcantonio Zondadari **Obv:** Armored bust right **Obv. Legend:** MARCVS • ANTONIVS..... **Rev:** Inscription within cartouche

Date	Mintage	VG	F	VF	XF	Unc
1721	—	1,500	2,500	4,500	7,500	—

KM# 167 4 ZECCHINI
14.0000 g., 0.9860 Gold 0.4438 oz. AGW **Ruler:** Marcantonio Zondadari **Rev:** Crowned ornamental shield divides date

Date	Mintage	VG	F	VF	XF	Unc
1721	—	3,000	4,000	4,500	7,500	—

KM# 168 4 ZECCHINI
14.0000 g., 0.9860 Gold 0.4438 oz. AGW **Ruler:** Marcantonio Zondadari **Obv:** Armored bust right, date below **Obv. Legend:** MARCVS ANTONIVS • ZONDODARI **Rev:** Crowned, oval ornate shield

Date	Mintage	VG	F	VF	XF	Unc
1721 Small date	—	3,000	4,000	4,500	7,500	—
1722 Small date	—	3,000	4,000	4,500	7,500	—
1722 Large date	—	3,000	4,000	4,500	7,500	—

KM# 174 4 ZECCHINI
14.0000 g., 0.9860 Gold 0.4438 oz. AGW **Ruler:** Antonio Manoel de Vilhena **Obv:** Armored bust right, date below **Rev:** Crowned shield

Date	Mintage	VG	F	VF	XF	Unc
1722	—	6,000	7,000	8,000	9,000	—

KM# 173 4 ZECCHINI
14.0000 g., 0.9860 Gold 0.4438 oz. AGW **Ruler:** Marcantonio Zondadari **Obv:** Armored bust right, small date in legend **Rev:** Crowned ornamental round arms

Date	Mintage	VG	F	VF	XF	Unc
1722	—	6,000	7,000	8,000	9,000	—

KM# 175 4 ZECCHINI
14.0000 g., 0.9860 Gold 0.4438 oz. AGW **Ruler:** Antonio Manoel de Vilhena **Obv:** Armored bust right **Rev:** Crowned ornamental arms with date below

Date	Mintage	VG	F	VF	XF	Unc
1722	—	6,000	7,000	8,000	9,000	—

KM# 176 4 ZECCHINI
14.0000 g., 0.9860 Gold 0.4438 oz. AGW **Ruler:** Antonio Manoel de Vilhena **Obv:** Armored bust right **Obv. Legend:** DEVILHENA FD • AN • MANOEL **Rev:** Crowned ornate shield **Rev. Legend:** ...M • M • HOSP • ET

Date	Mintage	VG	F	VF	XF	Unc
1722	—	6,000	7,000	8,000	9,000	—
1723	—	6,000	7,000	8,000	9,000	—
1724	—	6,000	7,000	8,000	9,000	—

KM# 184 4 ZECCHINI
14.0000 g., 0.9860 Gold 0.4438 oz. AGW **Ruler:** Antonio Manoel de Vilhena **Obv:** Armored bust right within broken circle **Obv. Legend:** DEVILHENA F • D • AN : MANOEL **Rev:** Crowned ornate arms with stars within circle **Rev. Legend:** ...M • M • HOSP : ET *

Date	Mintage	VG	F	VF	XF	Unc
1723	—	6,000	7,000	8,000	9,000	—
1724	—	6,000	7,000	8,000	9,000	—

KM# 185 4 ZECCHINI
14.0000 g., 0.9860 Gold 0.4438 oz. AGW **Ruler:** Antonio Manoel de Vilhena **Obv:** Armored bust right **Obv. Legend:** * F • D • AN : MANOEL DE VILHENA * **Rev:** Crowned ornamental oval arms

Date	Mintage	VG	F	VF	XF	Unc
1724	—	6,000	7,000	8,000	9,000	—
1725	—	6,000	7,000	8,000	9,000	—

KM# 191 4 ZECCHINI
14.0000 g., 0.9860 Gold 0.4438 oz. AGW **Ruler:** Antonio Manoel de Vilhena **Obv:** Armored bust right **Rev:** Crowned shield

Date	Mintage	VG	F	VF	XF	Unc
1724	—	6,000	7,000	8,000	9,000	—

KM# 237 4 ZECCHINI
14.0000 g., 0.9860 Gold 0.4438 oz. AGW **Ruler:** Emmanuel Pinto **Obv:** Armored bust left **Obv. Legend:** F • EMMANVEL PINTO M • M • **Rev:** Crowned ornate shield **Rev. Legend:** SEP • HIER • HOSPI • ET • S •

Date	Mintage	VG	F	VF	XF	Unc
ND(1741-73)	—	3,000	3,500	4,500	5,000	—
1742	—	3,000	3,500	4,500	5,000	—

KM# 238 4 ZECCHINI

14.0000 g., 0.9860 Gold 0.4438 oz. AGW, 26 mm. **Ruler:** Emmanuel Pinto **Obv:** Armored bust left **Obv. Legend:** F • EMMANVEL PINTO M • M • **Rev:** Crowned ornate shield **Rev. Legend:** SEP • HIER • HOSPI • ET • S • **Note:** Reduced size.

Date	Mintage	VG	F	VF	XF	Unc
ND(1741-73)	—	3,000	3,500	4,500	5,000	—

KM# 177 10 ZECCHINI

35.0000 g., 0.9860 Gold 1.1095 oz. AGW **Ruler:** Antonio Manoel de Vilhena **Obv:** Armored bust right **Rev:** Crowned shield

Date	Mintage	VG	F	VF	XF	Unc
1722 Rare	—	—	—	—	—	—

KM# 192 12 ZECCHINI

42.0000 g., 0.9860 Gold 1.3314 oz. AGW **Ruler:** Antonio Manoel de Vilhena **Obv:** Armored bust right within broken circle **Obv. Legend:** DEVILHENA F • D • AN : MANOEL **Rev:** Crowned, ornate oval shield **Rev. Legend:** ...M • M A G I S : H O S : E T

Date	Mintage	VG	F	VF	XF	Unc
1725 Rare	—	—	—	—	—	—

KM# 180 SCUDO (12 Tari)

Silver **Ruler:** Antonio Manoel de Vilhena **Obv:** Armored bust right **Obv. Legend:** F • D • AN • MANOEL • ... **Rev:** Coronet above ornamented arms **Note:** Legend varieties exist.

Date	Mintage	VG	F	VF	XF	Unc
1723	—	800	1,000	1,200	1,500	—
1724	—	2,000	2,500	3,000	3,500	—

KM# 203 SCUDO (12 Tari)

Silver **Ruler:** Ramon Despuig **Obv:** Armored bust right **Obv. Legend:** GRAIMVNDVS DESPVIG ... **Rev:** Coronet and cap above arms, divided date above

Date	Mintage	VG	F	VF	XF	Unc
1737	—	300	350	400	450	—
1738	—	300	350	400	450	—

KM# 224 SCUDO (12 Tari)

Silver **Ruler:** Emmanuel Pinto **Obv:** Armored bust left **Obv. Legend:** F • EMMAN VEL PINTO **Rev:** Crown divides date above ornate shield **Rev. Legend:** ...M • M • H • E • T • S **Note:** Varieties exist.

Date	Mintage	VG	F	VF	XF	Unc
1741	—	100	150	200	250	—

KM# 273 SCUDO (12 Tari)

Silver **Ruler:** Emmanuel Pinto **Obv:** Armored bust left **Obv. Legend:** F • EMMANVEL PINTO • M • M • H • **Rev:** Crowned ornate shield, without legend, value divided below

Date	Mintage	VG	F	VF	XF	Unc
1764	—	75.00	100	150	225	—

KM# 286 SCUDO (12 Tari)

Silver **Ruler:** Francisco Ximenez de Texada **Obv:** Armored bust right **Obv. Legend:** FR • D • FRANCISCVS ... **Rev:** Crown divides date above ornate oval shield

Date	Mintage	VG	F	VF	XF	Unc
1773	—	100	175	200	250	—
1774	—	100	175	200	250	—

KM# 305.1 SCUDO (12 Tari)

Silver **Ruler:** Emmanuel de Rohan **Obv:** Armored bust right **Obv. Legend:** F • EMMANUEL DE ROHAN M • M • H • S • S • **Rev:** Crown divides date above shield on eagle breast

Date	Mintage	VG	F	VF	XF	Unc
1776	—	100	175	200	250	—

KM# 305.2 SCUDO (12 Tari)

Silver **Ruler:** Emmanuel de Rohan **Obv:** Armored bust right **Obv. Legend:** F • EMMANVEL DE ROHAN M • M • **Rev:** Crown divides date above shield on eagle breast

Date	Mintage	VG	F	VF	XF	Unc
1776	—	100	175	200	250	—

KM# 342 SCUDO (12 Tari)

Silver **Ruler:** Emmanuel de Rohan **Obv:** Armored bust right **Obv. Legend:** F • EMMANUEL DE ROHAN M • M • **Rev:** Crowned oval shield, beaded and spiked, within sprigs, divided date above

Date	Mintage	VG	F	VF	XF	Unc
1796	—	100	175	200	250	—

KM# 181 2 SCUDI

Silver **Ruler:** Antonio Manoel de Vilhena **Obv:** Bust right within circle **Obv. Legend:** * F • D • AN : MANOEL * DE * VILHENA * **Rev:** Crown above oval shields **Rev. Legend:** M • MAGIS : HOS : ET S SEPVL : HIERVSALEM **Note:** Dav. #1593. Varieties exist.

Date	Mintage	VG	F	VF	XF	Unc
1723	—	700	800	1,000	1,200	—

KM# 186 2 SCUDI

Silver **Ruler:** Antonio Manoel de Vilhena **Obv:** Legend begins at top **Rev. Legend:** M. MAGIS(TER): HOS(P): ET S. S(EPVL): HIERVS(A) (L) (EM) **Note:** Dav. #1594. Die varieties exist.

Date	Mintage	VG	F	VF	XF	Unc
1724	—	700	800	1,000	1,200	—

KM# 187 2 SCUDI

Silver **Ruler:** Antonio Manoel de Vilhena **Obv:** Without inner circle **Rev:** Larger crowned arms without inner circle **Rev. Legend:** M. MAGISTER HOSP: *-* ET S. S. HIERVS: **Note:** Dav. #1595. Varieties exist.

Date	Mintage	VG	F	VF	XF	Unc
1724	—	700	800	1,000	1,200	—

KM# 188 2 SCUDI

Silver **Ruler:** Antonio Manoel de Vilhena **Obv:** Without stars at end of legend **Rev:** Legend unbroken at bottom **Note:** Dav. #1596. Varieties exist.

Date	Mintage	VG	F	VF	XF	Unc
1725	—	700	800	1,000	1,200	—

KM# 195.1 2 SCUDI

Silver **Ruler:** Antonio Manoel de Vilhena **Obv:** With inner circle **Rev. Legend:** ... HIERVS(A) **Note:** Dav. #1597.

Date	Mintage	VG	F	VF	XF	Unc
1728	—	700	800	1,000	1,200	—

KM# 195.2 2 SCUDI

Silver **Ruler:** Antonio Manoel de Vilhena **Obv:** Without inner circle **Note:** Dav. #1597.

Date	Mintage	VG	F	VF	XF	Unc
1728	—	700	800	1,000	1,200	—

KM# 204.1 2 SCUDI
Silver **Ruler:** Ramon Despuig **Obv:** Armored bust right **Obv. Legend:** F • D • RAIMVN : DESPVVG .... **Rev:** Tassles hang off ornamented shield in cartouche, divided date above, and S-2 below **Note:** Dav. #1598.

Date	Mintage	VG	F	VF	XF	Unc
1738	—	200	300	400	500	—

KM# 204.2 2 SCUDI
Silver **Ruler:** Ramon Despuig **Obv:** Armored bust right within circle **Obv. Legend:** F • D • RAYMVNDVS • DESPVVG ... **Rev:** Oval arms within ornamented cartouche without tassels, divided date above and S-2 below **Note:** Dav. #1598.

Date	Mintage	VG	F	VF	XF	Unc
1738	—	200	300	400	500	—

KM# 204.3 2 SCUDI
Silver **Ruler:** Ramon Despuig **Obv:** Armored bust right **Obv. Legend:** F • D • RAINVNDVS DESPVVG • ... **Rev:** Crowned shield within ornamented cartouche, divided date above **Note:** Dav. #1598.

Date	Mintage	VG	F	VF	XF	Unc
1738	—	200	300	400	500	—

KM# 225.1 2 SCUDI
Silver **Ruler:** Emmanuel Pinto **Obv:** Armored bust right divides legend **Obv. Legend:** F • D • EMMA NVEL PINTO **Rev:** Ornate arms with coronet **Note:** Dav. #1599.

Date	Mintage	VG	F	VF	XF	Unc
1741	—	100	200	300	400	—

KM# 225.2 2 SCUDI
Silver **Ruler:** Emmanuel Pinto **Obv:** Armored bust left, continuous legend **Rev:** Ornate arms with coronet **Note:** Dav. #1599A.

Date	Mintage	VG	F	VF	XF	Unc
1741	—	100	200	300	400	—

KM# 225.3 2 SCUDI
Silver **Ruler:** Emmanuel Pinto **Obv:** Armored bust left **Rev:** Crowned arms similar to 30 Tari, KM#256. **Note:** Dav. #1599B.

Date	Mintage	VG	F	VF	XF	Unc
1741	—	100	200	300	400	—

KM# 274 2 SCUDI
Silver **Ruler:** Emmanuel Pinto **Obv:** Armored bust left **Obv. Legend:** F • EMMANVEL PINTO • M • M • H • S • S • **Rev:** Crown above shields within sprigs, divided date above **Note:** Varieties exist. Dav. #1603.

Date	Mintage	VG	F	VF	XF	Unc
1764	—	700	1,500	2,000	2,500	—

KM# 287 2 SCUDI
Silver **Ruler:** Francisco Ximenez de Texada **Obv:** Armored bust right **Obv. Legend:** • FR • D • FRANCISCVS XIMENEZ • DE TEXADA **Rev:** Crown above shields within sprigs **Note:** Varieties exist. Dav. #1605.

Date	Mintage	VG	F	VF	XF	Unc
1773	—	200	300	400	500	—
1774	—	200	300	400	500	—
J774	—	200	300	400	500	—

KM# 343 2 SCUDI
Silver **Ruler:** Emmanuel de Rohan **Obv:** Armored bust right **Obv. Legend:** F • EMMANUEL DE ROHAN M • M • **Rev:** Crowned oval shield, beaded and spiked, within sprigs, divided date above **Note:** Varieties exist. Dav. #1610.

Date	Mintage	VG	F	VF	XF	Unc
1796	—	150	225	275	300	—

KM# 254 5 SCUDI
4.0000 g., 0.8400 Gold 0.1080 oz. AGW **Ruler:** Emmanuel Pinto **Obv:** Crowned shield, date in legend **Rev:** John the Baptist holding banner, lamb at right

Date	Mintage	VG	F	VF	XF	Unc
1756	—	300	600	750	1,200	—

KM# 318 5 SCUDI
4.0000 g., 0.8400 Gold 0.1080 oz. AGW **Ruler:** Emmanuel de Rohan **Obv:** Armored bust right **Obv. Legend:** F • EMMANUEL DE ROHAN **Rev:** Crown above pair of oval shields

Date	Mintage	F	VF	XF	Unc	BU
1779	—	300	600	750	1,200	—

KM# 255 10 SCUDI
8.0000 g., 0.8400 Gold 0.2160 oz. AGW **Ruler:** Emmanuel Pinto **Obv:** Crowned ornate shield, date in legend **Obv. Legend:** F • EMMANVEL PINTO • M • M • H • S • S • **Rev:** John the Baptist standing with banner, Paschal lamb lying at right, value in exergue

Date	Mintage	VG	F	VF	XF	Unc
1756	—	700	900	1,500	2,000	—
1761	—	700	900	1,500	2,000	—

KM# 267 10 SCUDI
8.0000 g., 0.8400 Gold 0.2160 oz. AGW **Ruler:** Emmanuel Pinto **Rev:** Banner hanging from cross, Paschal lamb standing facing left

Date	Mintage	VG	F	VF	XF	Unc
1761	—	700	900	1,500	2,000	—

KM# 268 10 SCUDI
8.0000 g., 0.8400 Gold 0.2160 oz. AGW **Ruler:** Emmanuel Pinto **Rev:** Lamb standing facing right

Date	Mintage	VG	F	VF	XF	Unc
1761	—	700	900	1,500	2,000	—

KM# 269 10 SCUDI
8.0000 g., 0.8400 Gold 0.2160 oz. AGW **Ruler:** Emmanuel Pinto **Obv:** Crowned ornate shield, date in legend **Obv. Legend:** F • EMMANVEL PINTO • M • M • H • S • S • **Rev:** Halo on St. John, Paschal lamb lying left, facing right **Rev. Legend:** ....SVRREXIT MAIOR

Date	Mintage	VG	F	VF	XF	Unc
1761	—	700	900	1,500	2,000	—

KM# 270 10 SCUDI
8.0000 g., 0.8400 Gold 0.2160 oz. AGW **Ruler:** Emmanuel Pinto **Obv:** Crowned oval shield within sprigs **Obv. Legend:** F • EMMANVEL PINTO • M • M • H • S • S • **Rev:** John the Baptist with banner, lamb at right

Date	Mintage	VG	F	VF	XF	Unc
1762	—	700	900	1,500	2,000	—

KM# 271 10 SCUDI
8.0000 g., 0.8400 Gold 0.2160 oz. AGW **Ruler:** Emmanuel Pinto **Obv:** Crowned oval shield within sprigs **Obv. Legend:** F • EMMANVEL PINTO • M • M • H • S • S • **Rev:** John the Baptist with banner, lamb at right

Date	Mintage	VG	F	VF	XF	Unc
1762	—	700	900	1,500	2,000	—

KM# 272 10 SCUDI
8.0000 g., 0.8400 Gold 0.2160 oz. AGW **Ruler:** Emmanuel Pinto **Obv:** Crowned oval shield within sprigs **Obv. Legend:** F • EMMANVEL PINTO • M • M • H • S • S • **Rev:** John the Baptist with banner, lamb at right

Date	Mintage	VG	F	VF	XF	Unc
1763	—	700	900	1,500	2,000	—

KM# 288 10 SCUDI
8.0000 g., 0.8400 Gold 0.2160 oz. AGW **Ruler:** Francisco Ximenez de Texada **Obv:** Armored bust right within circle **Obv. Legend:** D • FRAN : XIMENEZ DE TEXADA • **Rev:** Coronet above oval shields within circle

Date	Mintage	VG	F	VF	XF	Unc
1773	—	1,500	2,000	2,500	3,000	—

KM# 292 10 SCUDI
8.0000 g., 0.8400 Gold 0.2160 oz. AGW **Ruler:** Francisco Ximenez de Texada **Obv:** Without inner circle

Date	Mintage	VG	F	VF	XF	Unc
1774	—	1,500	2,000	2,500	3,000	—

KM# 293 10 SCUDI
8.0000 g., 0.8400 Gold 0.2160 oz. AGW **Ruler:** Francisco Ximenez de Texada **Rev:** Crowned arms on Maltese cross divide value

Date	Mintage	VG	F	VF	XF	Unc
1774	—	1,500	2,000	2,500	3,000	—

KM# 309 10 SCUDI
8.0000 g., 0.8400 Gold 0.2160 oz. AGW **Ruler:** Emmanuel de Rohan **Obv:** Armored bust right, date below **Obv. Legend:** F • EMMANUEL DE ROHAN M • M • **Rev:** Crown above pair of oval shields **Rev. Legend:** HOSPITALIS ET S • ...

Date	Mintage	F	VF	XF	Unc	BU
1778	—	1,500	2,000	2,500	3,000	—

KM# 310 10 SCUDI
8.0000 g., 0.8400 Gold 0.2160 oz. AGW **Ruler:** Emmanuel de Rohan **Obv:** Armored bust right **Obv. Legend:** F • EMMANUEL DE ROHAN M • M • **Rev:** Crown above pair of oval shields **Rev. Legend:** HOSPITAL • ET S • SEPUL • HIERUSAL •

Date	Mintage	F	VF	XF	Unc	BU
1778	—	1,000	1,500	2,000	2,500	—
1782	—	1,000	1,500	2,000	2,500	—

KM# 329 10 SCUDI
8.0000 g., 0.8400 Gold 0.2160 oz. AGW **Ruler:** Emmanuel de Rohan **Rev. Legend:** ...HIERUSA

Date	Mintage	F	VF	XF	Unc	BU
1782	—	1,000	1,500	2,000	2,500	—

KM# 275 20 SCUDI
16.0000 g., 0.8400 Gold 0.4321 oz. AGW **Ruler:** Emmanuel Pinto **Obv:** Crown above pair of oval shields **Rev:** John the Baptist with banner, lamb at right

Date	Mintage	VG	F	VF	XF	Unc
1764	—	1,000	2,000	2,200	2,500	—

KM# 276 20 SCUDI
16.0000 g., 0.8400 Gold 0.4321 oz. AGW **Ruler:** Emmanuel Pinto **Obv:** Armored bust left, date below **Rev:** Crowned arms on Maltese cross divides value

Date	Mintage	VG	F	VF	XF	Unc
1764	—	1,000	2,000	2,500	3,000	—

KM# 277 20 SCUDI
16.0000 g., 0.8400 Gold 0.4321 oz. AGW **Ruler:** Emmanuel Pinto **Obv:** Armored bust right, date below **Obv. Legend:** F • EMMANVEL PINTO • M • M • H • **Rev:** Crown above oval shield, beaded and spiked

Date	Mintage	VG	F	VF	XF	Unc
1765	—	1,000	2,000	2,500	3,000	—
1770	—	1,000	2,000	2,500	3,000	—
1772	—	1,000	2,000	2,500	3,000	—

KM# 289 20 SCUDI
16.0000 g., 0.8400 Gold 0.4321 oz. AGW **Ruler:** Francisco Ximenez de Texada **Obv:** Armored bust right within circle **Rev:** Coronet above pair of oval shields within circle

Date	Mintage	VG	F	VF	XF	Unc
1773	—	2,000	2,500	3,500	4,000	—

KM# 294 20 SCUDI
16.0000 g., 0.8400 Gold 0.4321 oz. AGW **Ruler:** Francisco Ximenez de Texada **Obv:** Armored bust right **Rev:** Coronet above oval shield, beaded and spiked

Date	Mintage	VG	F	VF	XF	Unc
1774	—	2,000	2,500	3,500	4,000	—

KM# 334 20 SCUDI
16.0000 g., 0.8400 Gold 0.4321 oz. AGW **Ruler:** Emmanuel de Rohan **Obv:** Crowned arms on imperial eagle **Rev:** John the Baptist stands holding banner

Date	Mintage	F	VF	XF	Unc	BU
1778 Error	—	—	—	50,000	—	—

KM# 311 20 SCUDI
16.0000 g., 0.8400 Gold 0.4321 oz. AGW **Ruler:** Emmanuel de Rohan **Obv:** Armored bust right **Obv. Legend:** F • EMMANUEL DE ROHAN M * M * **Rev:** Crown above pair of oval shields **Rev. Legend:** • HOSPITALIS ET S • SEPUL * HIERUSAL * 1778

Date	Mintage	F	VF	XF	Unc	BU
1778	—	800	1,500	2,000	2,500	—

KM# 312 20 SCUDI
16.0000 g., 0.8400 Gold 0.4321 oz. AGW **Ruler:** Emmanuel de Rohan **Obv:** Date

Date	Mintage	F	VF	XF	Unc	BU
1778	—	800	1,500	2,000	2,500	—

KM# 328 20 SCUDI
16.0000 g., 0.8400 Gold 0.4321 oz. AGW **Ruler:** Emmanuel de Rohan **Rev:** Stars divide legend, date

Date	Mintage	F	VF	XF	Unc	BU
1781	—	1,000	1,500	2,500	3,000	—
1782	—	1,000	1,500	2,500	3,000	—

KM# 330 20 SCUDI
16.0000 g., 0.8400 Gold 0.4321 oz. AGW **Ruler:** Emmanuel de Rohan **Rev:** Dots divide legend

Date	Mintage	F	VF	XF	Unc	BU
1782	—	1,000	1,500	2,500	3,000	—

SIEGE COINAGE

1798-1800

KM# 350 30 TARI
Silver **Obv:** Maltese cross flanked by R-F; T. 30 above, date below **Rev:** Incuse phrygian cap

Date	Mintage	VG	F	VF	XF	Unc
1800 Rare	—	—	—	—	—	—

KM# 351 2 SCUDI 11 CARLINI 13 GRANI
Silver **Note:** Similar to 16 Scudi, KM#355.

Date	Mintage	VG	F	VF	XF	Unc
ND Rare	—	—	—	—	—	—

KM# 352 3 SCUDI 2 CARLINI 18 GRANI
Silver **Note:** Similar to 16 Scudi, KM#355.

Date	Mintage	VG	F	VF	XF	Unc
ND Rare	—	—	—	—	—	—

KM# 353 3 SCUDI 4 CARLINI 6 GRANI
Silver **Note:** Similar to 16 Scudi, KM#355.

Date	Mintage	VG	F	VF	XF	Unc
ND Rare	—	—	—	—	—	—

KM# 354 3 SCUDI 5 CARLINI 18 GRANI
Silver

Date	Mintage	VG	F	VF	XF	Unc
ND Rare	—	—	—	—	—	—

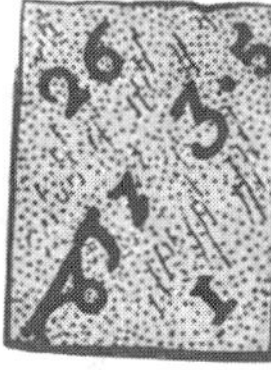

KM# 355 16 SCUDI 10 CARLINI

Gold

Date	Mintage	VG	F	VF	XF	Unc
ND Rare	—	—	—	—	—	—

COUNTERMARKED COINAGE

For over a century the two and four Tari copper coins struck during the reign of Jean-Paul Lascaris Castellar were countermarked as an expedient against the prevalent forging of these coins both in Malta and Messina.

A total of eight different countermarks were utilized. As many as seven can be found on the 2 Tari and all eight different may be encountered on the 4 Tari.

COUNTERMARKS

I. Imperial eagle in circle.

Initiated May 28, 1646.

II. Head of John the Baptist in oval.

Initiated April 19, 1662.

III. Crowned fleur-de-lis.

Initiated August 27, 1696.

For more information refer to The Coinage of the Knights in Malta by Felice Restelli and Joseph C. Sammut, 1977 by Emmanuel Said Publishers, Valettta, Malta.

NOTE: Coins are properly catalogued by the latest countermark. Obviously certain coins may lack one or more countermarks having been missed during such an extensive countermarking period.

KM# 215 2 TARI

Copper **Countermark:** Including Type IV **Obv. Legend:** F • 10 : PAVLVS : ... **Note:** Countermark on 2 Tari, KM#65.

CM Date	Host Date	Good	VG	F	VF	XF
ND(1740)	1636-43	18.50	30.00	42.50	65.00	—

KM# 216 2 TARI

Copper **Countermark:** Including Type IV **Obv. Legend:** F • IOANNES • PAVLVS • ... **Note:** Countermark on 2 Tari, KM#75.

CM Date	Host Date	Good	VG	F	VF	XF
ND(1740)	1643	18.50	30.00	42.50	65.00	—

KM# 227 2 TARI

Copper **Countermark:** Including Type V **Obv. Legend:** F • IOANNES • PAVLVS • ... **Note:** Countermark on 2 Tari, KM#75.

CM Date	Host Date	Good	VG	F	VF	XF
ND(1741)	1643	15.00	25.00	35.00	50.00	—

KM# 226 2 TARI

Copper **Countermark:** Including Type V **Obv. Legend:** F • IO : PAVLVS : ... **Note:** Countermark on 2 Tari, KM#65.

CM Date	Host Date	Good	VG	F	VF	XF
ND(1741)	1636-43	15.00	25.00	35.00	50.00	—

KM# 278 2 TARI

Copper **Countermark:** Including Type VI **Obv. Legend:** F • IO : PAVLVS : ... **Note:** Countermark on 2 Tari, KM#65.

CM Date	Host Date	Good	VG	F	VF	XF
ND(1766)	1636-43	13.50	21.50	30.00	45.00	—

KM# 279 2 TARI

Copper **Countermark:** Including Type VI **Obv. Legend:** F • IOANNES • PAVLVS • ... **Note:** Countermark on 2 Tari, KM#75.

CM Date	Host Date	Good	VG	F	VF	XF
ND(1766)	1643	13.50	21.50	30.00	45.00	—

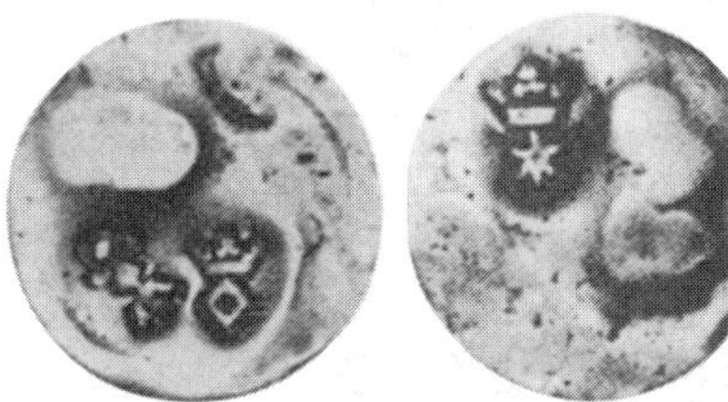

KM# 313 2 TARI

Copper **Countermark:** Including Type VII **Note:** Countermark on 2 Tari, KM#65.

CM Date	Host Date	Good	VG	F	VF	XF
ND(1778)	16xx	13.50	21.50	30.00	45.00	—

KM# 217 4 TARI

Copper **Countermark:** Including Type IV **Obv. Legend:** F • IO : PAVLVS : ... **Note:** Countermark on 4 Tari, KM#67.

CM Date	Host Date	Good	VG	F	VF	XF
ND(1740)	1636-51	20.00	32.50	45.00	65.00	—

KM# 218 4 TARI

Copper **Countermark:** Including Type IV **Obv. Legend:** F • IOANNES • PAVLVS • ... **Note:** Countermark on 4 Tari, KM#68.

CM Date	Host Date	Good	VG	F	VF	XF
ND(1740)	1636-47	20.00	32.50	45.00	65.00	—

KM# 229 4 TARI

Copper **Countermark:** Including Type V **Obv. Legend:** F • IOANNES • PAVLVS • ... **Note:** Countermark on 4 Tari, KM#68.

CM Date	Host Date	Good	VG	F	VF	XF
ND(1741)	1636-47	15.00	25.00	35.00	50.00	—

KM# 228 4 TARI

Copper **Countermark:** Including Type V **Obv. Legend:** F • IO : PAVLVS : ... **Note:** Countermark on 4 Tari, KM#67.

CM Date	Host Date	Good	VG	F	VF	XF
ND(1741)	1636-51	15.00	25.00	35.00	50.00	—

KM# 280 4 TARI

Copper **Countermark:** Including Type VI **Obv. Legend:** F • IO : PAVLVS : ... **Note:** Countermark on 4 Tari, KM#67.

CM Date	Host Date	Good	VG	F	VF	XF
ND(1766)	1636-51	15.00	25.00	35.00	50.00	—

KM# 281 4 TARI

Copper **Countermark:** Including Type VI **Obv. Legend:** F • IOANNES • PAVLVS • ... **Note:** Countermark on 4 Tari, KM#68.

CM Date	Host Date	Good	VG	F	VF	XF
ND(1766)	1636-47	15.00	25.00	35.00	50.00	—

KM# 314 4 TARI

Copper **Countermark:** Including Type VII **Obv. Legend:** F • IO : PAVLVS : ... **Note:** Countermark on 4 Tari, KM#67.

CM Date	Host Date	Good	VG	F	VF	XF
ND(1778)	1636-51	15.00	25.00	35.00	50.00	—

KM# 315 4 TARI

Copper **Countermark:** Including Type VII **Obv. Legend:** F • IOANNES • PAVLVS • ... **Note:** Countermark on 4 Tari, KM#68.

CM Date	Host Date	Good	VG	F	VF	XF
ND(1778)	1636-47	15.00	25.00	35.00	50.00	—

KM# 341 4 TARI

Copper **Countermark:** Including Type VIII **Obv. Legend:** F • IOANNES • PAVLVS • ... **Note:** Countermark on 4 Tari, KM#68.

CM Date	Host Date	Good	VG	F	VF	XF
ND(1792)	1636-47	15.00	25.00	35.00	50.00	—

KM# 340 4 TARI

Copper **Countermark:** Including Type VIII **Obv. Legend:** F • IO : PAVLVS : ... **Note:** Countermark on 4 Tari, KM#67.

CM Date	Host Date	Good	VG	F	VF	XF
ND(1792)	1636-51	15.00	25.00	35.00	50.00	—

SOVEREIGN ORDER

STANDARD COINAGE

KM# A270 10 SCUDI

8.0000 g., 0.8400 Gold 0.2160 oz. AGW **Rev:** Paschal lamb standing left looking up at St. John

Date	Mintage	VG	F	VF	XF	Unc
1761	—	250	400	750	1,850	—

PATTERNS

Including off metal strikes

KM#	Date	Mintage	Identification	Mkt Val
Pn1	1739	—	6 Tari. Copper.	—
Pn2	1768	—	4 Tari. Copper. Date below bust.	—
Pn3	1773	—	20 Scudi. Copper.	—
Pn4	1776	—	Scudo. Copper.	—
Pn5	1778	—	5 Scudi. Copper.	—
Pn6	1778	—	10 Scudi. Copper. Date on reverse.	—
Pn7	1778	—	10 Scudi. Copper. Date below bust.	—
Pn8	1778	—	20 Scudi. Copper. Date below bust.	—
Pn9	1779	—	5 Scudi. Copper.	—
Pn10	1782	—	10 Scudi. Copper. Date on reverse.	—
Pn11	1790	—	30 Tari. Copper.	—

MARTINIQUE

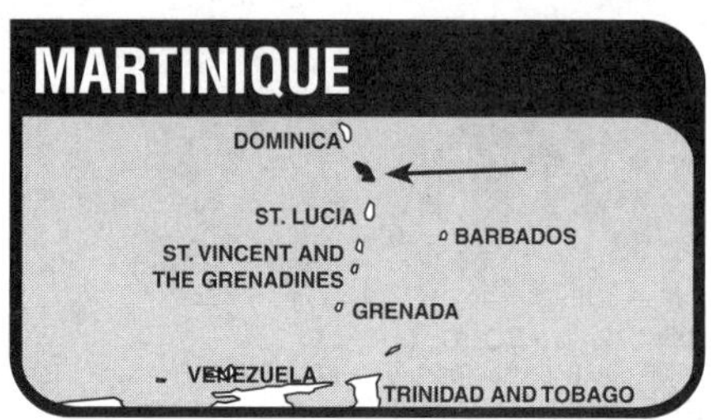

The French Overseas Department of Martinique, located in the Lesser Antilles of the West Indies between Dominica and Saint Lucia, has an area of 425 sq. mi.(1,100 sq. km.) and a population of 290,000. Capital: Fort-de-France. Agriculture and tourism are the major sources of income. Bananas, sugar, and rum are exported.

Christopher Columbus discovered Martinique, probably on June 15, 1502. France took possession on June 25, 1635, and has maintained possession since that time except for three short periods of British occupation during the Napoleonic Wars. A French department since 1946, Martinique voted a reaffirmation of that status in 1958, remaining within the new French Community. Martinique was the birthplace of Napoleon's Empress Josephine, and the site of the eruption of Mt. Pelee in 1902 that claimed 40,000 lives.

RULERS

French, 1635-1793

British, 1793-1801

FRENCH COLONY

COUNTERMARKED COINAGE

Type I - 1761-64

It is believed that circulating coins were holed in order to lower their intrinsic value below their face value thus keeping the coins from leaving the island. The heart-shaped center punches never circulated and did not have any legal tender status. Most were melted at the time of minting.

KM# 1 1/2 BIT

Silver **Countermark:** Crude heart-shaped hole **Note:** Countermark on Spanish or Colonial 1/2 Real.

CM Date	Host Date	Good	VG	F	VF	XF
ND(1761-64)	ND Rare	—	—	—	—	—
ND(1761-64)	ND Rare	—	—	—	—	—

KM# 2 BIT

Silver **Countermark:** Crude heart-shaped hole **Note:** Countermark on Spanish 1 Real, KM#354.

CM Date	Host Date	Good	VG	F	VF	XF
ND(1761-64)	ND(1731-45)	—	—	—	—	—
ND(1761-64)	ND(1761-64)	225	350	475	650	—

KM# 3 2 BITS

Silver **Countermark:** Crude heart-shaped hole **Note:** Countermark on Spanish 2 Reales, KM#297.

CM Date	Host Date	Good	VG	F	VF	XF
ND(1761-64)	ND(1716-29)	275	400	525	750	—

KM# 4 5 BITS

Silver **Countermark:** Crude heart-shaped hole **Note:** Countermark on Spanish or Colonial 4 Reales

CM Date	Host Date	Good	VG	F	VF	XF
ND(1761-64)	ND Rare	—	—	—	—	—

KM# 5 10 BITS
Silver **Countermark:** Crude heart-shaped hole **Note:** Countermark on Mexico City 8 Reales, KM#103.

CM Date	Host Date	Good	VG	F	VF	XF
ND(1761-64)	ND(1732-47) Rare	—	—	—	—	—

COUNTERMARKED COINAGE

Type II - 1764

KM# 6 1/2 BIT
Silver **Countermark:** Crude heart-shaped hole with bevelled edge **Note:** Countermark on Spanish or Colonial 1/2 Real.

CM Date	Host Date	Good	VG	F	VF	XF
ND(1764)	ND	—	—	—	—	—

KM# 7 BIT
Silver **Countermark:** Crude heart-shaped hole with bevelled edge **Note:** Countermark on Spanish or Colonial 1 Real.

CM Date	Host Date	Good	VG	F	VF	XF
ND(1764)	ND	—	—	—	—	—

KM# 8 2 BITS
Silver **Countermark:** Crude heart-shaped hole with bevelled edge **Note:** Countermark on Spanish or Colonial 2 Reales.

CM Date	Host Date	Good	VG	F	VF	XF
ND(1764)	1759-61	125	175	250	365	—

KM# 9 5 BITS
Silver **Countermark:** Crude heart-shaped hole with bevelled edge **Note:** Countermark on Spanish or Colonial 4 Reales.

CM Date	Host Date	Good	VG	F	VF	XF
ND(1764)	ND	—	—	—	—	—

KM# 10 10 BITS
Silver **Countermark:** Crude heart-shaped hole with bevelled edge **Note:** Countermark on Mexico City 8 Reales, KM#104.2.

CM Date	Host Date	Good	VG	F	VF	XF
ND(1764)	1754-60	—	—	—	—	—

COUNTERMARKED COINAGE

Type III - 1765

KM# 11 1/2 BIT
Silver **Countermark:** Pointed heart-shaped hole with ornamental edges **Note:** Countermark on Spanish or Colonial 1/2 Real.

CM Date	Host Date	Good	VG	F	VF	XF
ND(1765)	ND	—	—	—	—	—

KM# 12 BIT
Silver **Countermark:** Pointed heart-shaped hole with ornamental edges **Note:** Countermark on Spanish or Colonial 1 Real.

CM Date	Host Date	Good	VG	F	VF	XF
ND(1765)	ND	—	—	—	—	—

KM# 13 2 BITS
Silver **Countermark:** Pointed heart-shaped hole with ornamental edges **Note:** Countermark on Spanish or Colonial 2 Reales.

CM Date	Host Date	Good	VG	F	VF	XF
ND(1765)	ND	—	—	—	—	—

KM# 14 5 BITS
Silver **Countermark:** Pointed heart-shaped hole with ornamental edges **Note:** Countermark on Spanish or Colonial 4 Reales.

CM Date	Host Date	Good	VG	F	VF	XF
ND(1765)	ND Rare	—	—	—	—	—

KM# 15 10 BITS
Silver **Countermark:** Pointed heart-shaped hole with ornamental edges **Note:** Countermark on Mexico 8 Reales, KM#104.1.

CM Date	Host Date	Good	VG	F	VF	XF
ND(1765)	1747-54	225	375	600	850	—

COUNTERMARKED COINAGE

Type IV - 1770-72

KM# 16 1/2 BIT
Silver **Countermark:** Blunt heart-shaped hole with ornamented edges **Note:** Countermark on Mexico City 1/2 Real, KM#67.1.

CM Date	Host Date	Good	VG	F	VF	XF
ND(1770-72)	1747-57	85.00	135	200	285	—

KM# 17.1 BIT
Silver **Countermark:** Blunt heart-shaped hole with ornamented edges **Note:** Countermark on Mexico City 1 Real, KM#75.1.

CM Date	Host Date	Good	VG	F	VF	XF
ND(1770-72)	1732-41	175	250	350	475	—

KM# 17.2 BIT
Silver **Countermark:** Blunt heart-shaped hole w/ornamented edges **Note:** Countermark on Mexico City 1 Real, KM#76.1.

CM Date	Host Date	Good	VG	F	VF	XF
ND(1770-72)	1747-58	175	250	350	475	—

KM# 18 2 BITS
Silver **Countermark:** Blunt heart-shaped hole with ornamented edges **Note:** Countermark on Spanish 2 Reales, KM#297.

CM Date	Host Date	Good	VG	F	VF	XF
ND(1770-72)	1716-29	200	300	425	650	—

KM# 19 5 BITS
Silver **Countermark:** Blunt heart-shaped hole with ornamented edges **Note:** Countermark on Mexico City 4 Reales, KM#94.

CM Date	Host Date	Good	VG	F	VF	XF
ND(1770-72)	1732-47	—	—	4,250	6,500	—

KM# 20 10 BITS
Silver **Countermark:** Blunt heart-shaped hole with ornamented edges **Note:** Countermark on Mexico City 8 Reales, KM#103.

CM Date	Host Date	Good	VG	F	VF	XF
ND(1770-72)	1732-47	600	850	1,250	1,850	—

BRITISH OCCUPATION

CUT AND COUNTERMARKED COINAGE

1793-1801

AR = Mr. Ruffy, goldsmith at St. Pierre

FA = Francois Arnsud, goldsmith at Fort Royal

22 or 20 = Fineness of gold

Eagle = Mr. Costet, goldsmith at St. Pierre

KM# 25 ESCALIN
Silver **Note:** Unmarked 1/3 cut of 2 Reales with crenated edges.

CM Date	Host Date	Good	VG	F	VF	XF
ND	ND(1798)	150	250	350	500	—

KM# 26 3 ESCALINS
Silver **Note:** Unmarked 1/4 cut of Mexico City 8 Reales, KM#109, with crenated edges.

CM Date	Host Date	Good	VG	F	VF	XF
ND(1798)	1791-96	65.00	125	210	300	—

KM# 27.1 66 LIVRES
11.7200 g., Gold **Countermark:** Crowned AR **Note:** Countermark on plug in false Brazil 6400 Reis, type of KM#172.2.

CM Date	Host Date	Good	VG	F	VF	XF
1771	ND(1798) Rare	—	—	—	—	—

Note: M. Durr and R. Michel Monnaies d'or d'Espagne sale fine realized $17,430.

KM# 27.2 66 LIVRES
11.7200 g., Gold **Countermark:** FA **Note:** Countermark on plug in false Brazil 6400 Reis, type of KM#172.2.

CM Date	Host Date	Good	VG	F	VF	XF
ND	ND(1798) Rare	—	—	—	—	—

Note: The FA is only known on multiple island countermarked coins; The example illustrated bears the FA mark on the forehead of Joseph; The center plug, which should also have carried the FA countermark, was removed during the coin's travels; This example was sold in Baldwin's Ralph C. Gordon collection 10-96 VF holed realizing $9,760

MEXICO

Mexico, located immediately south of the United States has an area of 759,529 sq. mi. (1,967,183 sq. km.) and an estimated population of 88 million. Capital: Mexico City. The economy is based on agriculture, manufacturing and mining. Oil, cotton, silver, coffee, and shrimp are exported.

Mexico was the site of highly advanced Indian civilizations 1,500 years before conquistador Hernando Cortes conquered the wealthy Aztec empire of Montezuma,1519-21, and founded a Spanish colony which lasted for nearly 300 years. During the Spanish period, Mexico, then called New Spain, stretched from Guatemala to the present states of Wyoming and California, its present northern boundary having been established by the secession of Texas during 1836 and the war of 1846-48 with the United States.

RULERS

Philip V, 1700-1746
Luis I, 1724
Ferdinand VI, 1746-59
Charles III, 1760-88
Charles IV, 1788-1808

MINT MARKS

Mo, Mxo – Mexico City Mint

Initials	Date	Name
L	1678-1703	Martin Lopez
J	1708-23	Jose E. de Leon
D	1724-27	?
R	1729-30	Nicolas de Roxas
G	1730	
F	1730-33	Felipe Rivas de Angulo
F	1733-84	Francisco de la Pena
M	1733-63	Manuel de la Pena
M	1754-70	Manuel Assorin
F	1762-70	Francisco de Rivera
M	1770-77	Manuel de Rivera
F	1777-1803	Francisco Arance Cobos
M	1784-1801	Mariano Rodriguez

SPANISH COLONY

COB COINAGE

KM# 24 1/2 REAL
1.6900 g., 0.9310 Silver 0.0506 oz. ASW **Ruler:** Philip V **Mint:** Mexico City **Obverse:** Legend around crowned PHILIPVS monogram **Reverse:** Legend around cross, lions and castles **Note:** Mint mark M, Mo.

Date	Mintage	Good	VG	F	VF	XF
ND(1701-28) Date off flan	—	—	25.00	40.00	65.00	—
1701 L	—	—	100	125	225	—
1702 L	—	—	100	125	225	—
1703 L	—	—	100	125	225	—
1704 L	—	—	100	125	225	—
1705 L	—	—	100	125	225	—
1706 J	—	—	100	125	225	—
1707 J	—	—	100	125	225	—
1708 J	—	—	100	125	175	—
1709 J	—	—	100	125	175	—
1710 J	—	—	100	125	175	—
1711 J	—	—	100	125	175	—
1712 J	—	—	100	125	175	—
1713 J	—	—	100	125	175	—
1714 J	—	—	100	125	175	—
1715 J	—	—	100	125	175	—
1716 J	—	—	100	125	175	—
1717 J	—	—	100	125	175	—
1718 J	—	—	100	125	175	—
1719 J	—	—	100	125	175	—
1720 J	—	—	100	125	175	—
1721 J	—	—	100	125	175	—
1722 J	—	—	100	125	175	—
1723 J	—	—	100	125	175	—
1724 J	—	—	100	125	175	—
1724 D	—	—	100	125	175	—
1725 D	—	—	100	125	175	—
1726 D	—	—	100	125	175	—
1727 D	—	—	100	125	175	—
1728 D	—	—	100	125	175	—

KM# 25 1/2 REAL
1.6900 g., 0.9310 Silver 0.0506 oz. ASW **Ruler:** Luis I **Obverse:** Legend around crowned LVDOVICVS monogram **Reverse:** Legend around cross, lions and castles **Note:** Mint mark M, Mo.

Date	Mintage	Good	VG	F	VF	XF
ND(1724-25) Date off flan	—	—	125	200	250	—
1724 D	—	—	325	450	550	—
1725 D	—	—	325	450	550	—

KM# 24a 1/2 REAL
1.6900 g., 0.9160 Silver 0.0498 oz. ASW **Ruler:** Philip V **Mint:** Mexico City **Obverse:** Legend around crowned PHILIPVS monogram **Reverse:** Legend around cross, lions and castles **Note:** Mint mark M, Mo.

Date	Mintage	Good	VG	F	VF	XF
ND(1729-33) Date off flan	—	—	25.00	40.00	65.00	—
1729 R	—	—	90.00	120	150	—
1730 R	—	—	90.00	120	150	—
1731 F	—	—	90.00	120	150	—
1732/1 F	—	—	90.00	120	150	—
1732 F	—	—	90.00	120	150	—
1733/2 F	—	—	90.00	120	150	—
1733 F	—	—	90.00	120	150	—

KM# 30 REAL

3.3800 g., 0.9310 Silver 0.1012 oz. ASW **Ruler:** Philip V **Mint:** Mexico City **Obverse:** Legend and date around crowned arms **Obv. Legend:** PHILIPVS V DEI G **Reverse:** Lions and castles in angles of cross **Note:** Mint mark M, Mo.

Date	Mintage	Good	VG	F	VF	XF
ND(1701-28) Date off flan	—	—	35.00	55.00	75.00	—
1701 L	—	—	125	175	275	—
1702 L	—	—	125	175	275	—
1703 L	—	—	125	175	275	—
1704 L	—	—	125	175	275	—
1705 L	—	—	125	175	275	—
1706 J	—	—	125	175	275	—
1707 J	—	—	125	175	275	—
1708 J	—	—	125	175	275	—
1709 J	—	—	125	175	275	—
1710 J	—	—	125	175	275	—
1711 J	—	—	125	175	275	—
1712 J	—	—	125	175	275	—
1713 J	—	—	125	175	275	—
1714 J	—	—	125	175	275	—
1715 J	—	—	100	175	275	—
1716 J	—	—	100	175	275	—
1717 J	—	—	100	175	275	—
1718 J	—	—	100	175	275	—
1719 J	—	—	100	175	275	—
1720/19 J	—	—	100	175	275	—
1720 J	—	—	100	175	275	—
1721 J	—	—	100	175	275	—
1722 J	—	—	100	175	275	—
1723 J	—	—	100	175	275	—
1726 D	—	—	100	175	275	—
1727 D	—	—	100	175	275	—
1728 D	—	—	100	175	275	—

KM# A31 REAL

3.3834 g., 0.9310 Silver 0.1013 oz. ASW **Ruler:** Luis I **Mint:** Mexico City **Note:** A significant portion of the legend must be visibile for proper attribution. Mint mark M, Mo.

Date	Mintage	Good	VG	F	VF	XF
1724 D Rare	—	—	—	—	—	—
1725 D Rare	—	—	—	—	—	—

KM# 30a REAL

3.3800 g., 0.9160 Silver 0.0995 oz. ASW **Ruler:** Philip V **Mint:** Mexico City **Obverse:** Legend and date around crowned arms **Obv. Legend:** PHILIPVS V DEI G **Reverse:** Lions and castles in angles of cross **Note:** Mint mark M, Mo.

Date	Mintage	Good	VG	F	VF	XF
ND(1729-32) Date off flan	—	—	30.00	50.00	70.00	—
1729 R	—	—	90.00	125	175	—
1730 R	—	—	90.00	125	175	—
1730 F	—	—	90.00	125	175	—
1730 G	—	—	90.00	125	175	—
1731 F	—	—	90.00	125	175	—
1732 F	—	—	90.00	125	175	—

KM# 35 2 REALES

6.7700 g., 0.9310 Silver 0.2026 oz. ASW **Ruler:** Philip V **Mint:** Mexico City **Obverse:** Legend and date around crowned arms **Obv. Legend:** PHILIPVS V DEI G **Reverse:** Lions and castles in angles of cross **Note:** Mint mark M, Mo.

Date	Mintage	Good	VG	F	VF	XF
ND(1701-28) Date off flan	—	—	45.00	65.00	90.00	—
1701 L	—	—	125	150	250	—
1702 L	—	—	125	150	250	—
1703 L	—	—	125	150	250	—
1704 L	—	—	125	150	250	—
1705 L	—	—	125	150	250	—
1706 J	—	—	125	150	250	—
1707 J	—	—	125	150	250	—
1708 J	—	—	125	150	250	—
1710 J	—	—	125	150	250	—
1711 J	—	—	125	150	250	—
1712 J	—	—	125	150	250	—
1713 J	—	—	125	150	250	—
1714 J	—	—	150	185	300	—
1715 J	—	—	150	185	300	—
1716 J	—	—	150	185	300	—
1717 J	—	—	150	185	300	—
1718 J	—	—	150	185	300	—
1719 J	—	—	150	185	300	—
1720 J	—	—	150	185	300	—
1721 J	—	—	150	185	300	—
1722 J	—	—	150	185	300	—
1723 J	—	—	150	185	300	—
1724 J	—	—	150	185	300	—
1725 D Rare	—	—	—	—	—	—
1726 D	—	—	150	185	300	—
1727 D	—	—	150	185	300	—
1728 D	—	—	150	185	300	—

KM# 35a 2 REALES

6.7700 g., 0.9160 Silver 0.1994 oz. ASW **Ruler:** Philip V **Mint:** Mexico City **Obverse:** Legend and date around crowned arms **Obv. Legend:** PHILIPVS V DEI G **Reverse:** Lions and castles in angles of cross **Note:** Mint mark M, Mo.

Date	Mintage	Good	VG	F	VF	XF
ND(1729-32) Date off flan	—	—	40.00	60.00	90.00	—
1729 R	—	—	100	125	150	—
1730 R	—	—	100	125	150	—
1731 F	—	—	100	125	150	—
1731/0 F	—	—	100	125	150	—
1732 F	—	—	100	125	150	—
1733 F Rare	—	—	—	—	—	—

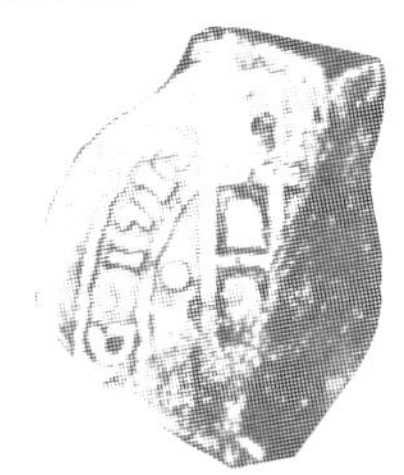

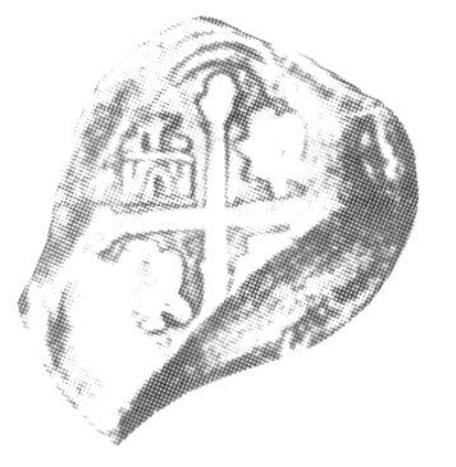

KM# 40 4 REALES

13.5400 g., 0.9310 Silver 0.4053 oz. ASW **Ruler:** Philip V **Mint:** Mexico City **Obverse:** Legend and date around crowned arms **Obv. Legend:** PHILIPVS V DEI G **Reverse:** Lions and castles in angles of cross **Note:** Mint mark M, Mo.

Date	Mintage	Good	VG	F	VF	XF
1701 L	—	—	175	250	375	—
ND (1701-28) Date off flan	—	—	50.00	75.00	100	—
1702 L	—	—	175	250	375	—
1703 L	—	—	175	250	375	—
1704 L	—	—	175	250	375	—
1705 L	—	—	175	250	375	—
1706 J	—	—	175	250	375	—
1707 J	—	—	175	250	375	—
1708 J	—	—	175	250	375	—
1709 J	—	—	175	250	375	—
1710 J	—	—	175	250	375	—
1711 J	—	—	150	200	300	—
1712 J	—	—	150	200	300	—
1713 J	—	—	150	200	300	—
1714 J	—	—	150	200	300	—
1715 J	—	—	125	225	375	—
1716 J	—	—	200	300	500	—
1717 J	—	—	200	300	500	—
1718 J	—	—	200	300	500	—
1719 J	—	—	200	300	500	—
1720 J	—	—	200	300	500	—
1721 J	—	—	200	300	500	—
1722 J	—	—	200	300	500	—
1723 J	—	—	200	300	500	—
1726 D	—	—	200	300	500	—
1727 D	—	—	200	300	500	—
1728 D	—	—	200	300	500	—

KM# 42 4 REALES

13.5400 g., 0.9310 Silver 0.4053 oz. ASW **Ruler:** Luis I **Mint:** Mexico City **Obverse:** Legend around crowned arms **Obv. Legend:** LVDOVICVS I DEI G **Reverse:** Lions and castles in angles of cross, legend around **Note:** A significant portion of the legend must be visible for proper attribution. Mint mark M, Mo.

Date	Mintage	Good	VG	F	VF	XF
1724 D Rare	—	—	—	—	—	—
1725 D Rare	—	—	—	—	—	—

KM# 40a 4 REALES

13.5400 g., 0.9160 Silver 0.3987 oz. ASW **Ruler:** Philip V **Mint:** Mexico City **Obverse:** Legend and date around crowned arms **Obv. Legend:** PHILIPVS V DEI G **Reverse:** Lions and castles in angles of cross **Note:** Mint mark M, Mo.

Date	Mintage	Good	VG	F	VF	XF
ND(1729-33) Date off flan	—	—	50.00	75.00	100	—
1729 D	—	—	125	200	275	—
1730 R	—	—	125	200	275	—
1730 G	—	—	125	200	275	—
1731 F	—	—	125	200	275	—
1732/1 F	—	—	125	175	250	—
1732 F	—	—	125	175	250	—
1733/2 F	—	—	125	175	250	—
1733 F	—	—	200	300	400	—

KM# 41 4 REALES

13.5400 g., 0.9160 Silver 0.3987 oz. ASW **Ruler:** Philip V **Mint:** Mexico City **Obverse:** Legend and date around crowned arms **Obv. Legend:** PHILIPVS V DEI G **Reverse:** Lions and castles in angles of cross, legend around **Note:** Klippe. Similar to KM#40a. Mint mark M, Mo.

Date	Mintage	Good	VG	F	VF	XF
1733 F	—	—	450	600	750	—
1733 MF	—	—	450	600	750	—
1734/3 MF	—	—	450	600	750	—

KM# 47 8 REALES

27.0700 g., 0.9310 Silver 0.8102 oz. ASW **Ruler:** Philip V **Mint:** Mexico City **Obverse:** Legend and date around crowned arms **Obv. Legend:** PHILIPVS V DEI G **Reverse:** Lions and castles in angles of cross, legend around **Note:** Mint mark M, Mo.

Date	Mintage	Good	VG	F	VF	XF
ND(1701-28) Date off flan	—	—	70.00	90.00	120	—
1701 L	—	—	200	350	500	—
1702 L	—	—	200	350	500	—
1703 L	—	—	200	350	500	—
1704 L Rare	—	—	—	—	—	—
1705 L	—	—	200	350	600	—
1706 J	—	—	200	350	600	—
1707 J	—	—	200	350	500	—
1708 J	—	—	200	350	500	—
1709 J	—	—	200	350	500	—
1710 J	—	—	200	350	500	—
1711 J	—	—	175	275	400	—
1712 J	—	—	175	275	400	—
1713 J	—	—	175	275	400	—
1714 J	—	—	175	275	400	—
1715 J	—	—	175	300	450	—
1716 J	—	—	375	575	800	—
1717 J	—	—	375	575	800	—
1718/7 J	—	—	375	575	800	—
1718 J	—	—	350	500	800	—
1719 J	—	—	350	500	800	—
1720 J	—	—	350	500	800	—
1721 J	—	—	350	500	800	—
1722 J	—	—	350	500	800	—
1723 J	—	—	350	500	800	—
1724 D	—	—	350	500	800	—
1725 D	—	—	350	500	800	—
1726 D	—	—	350	500	800	—
1727 D	—	—	350	500	800	—
1728 D	—	—	400	600	1,000	—

KM# 49 8 REALES

27.0700 g., 0.9310 Silver 0.8102 oz. ASW **Ruler:** Luis I **Mint:** Mexico City **Obverse:** Legend and date around crowned arms **Obv. Legend:** LVDOVICVS I DEI G **Reverse:** Lions and castles in angles of cross, legend around **Rev. Legend:** INDIARVM *

REX HISPANIARV ... **Note:** A significant portion of the legend must be visible for proper attribution. Mint mark M, Mo.

Date	Mintage	Good	VG	F	VF	XF
ND(1724-25) Date off flan; Rare	—	—	—	—	—	—
1724 D Rare	—	—	—	—	—	—
1725 D Rare	—	—	—	—	—	—

KM# 47a 8 REALES

27.0700 g., 0.9160 Silver 0.7972 oz. ASW **Ruler:** Philip V **Mint:** Mexico City **Obverse:** Legend and date around crowned arms **Obv. Legend:** PHILIPVS V DEI G **Reverse:** Lions and castles in angles of cross, legend around **Note:** Mint mark M, Mo.

Date	Mintage	Good	VG	F	VF	XF
ND(1729-33) Date off flan	—	—	70.00	90.00	110	—
1729 R	—	—	150	225	350	—
1730 G/R	—	—	150	225	350	—
1730 R	—	—	150	225	350	—
1730 G	—	—	150	225	350	—
1730 F	—	—	150	225	350	—
1731/0 F	—	—	150	225	350	—
1731 F	—	—	135	210	325	—
1732/1 F	—	—	135	210	325	—
1732 F	—	—	135	210	350	—
1733/2 F	—	—	200	300	400	—
1733 F	—	—	200	300	400	—

KM# 48 8 REALES

0.9160 g., Silver **Ruler:** Philip V **Mint:** Mexico City **Obverse:** Legend around crowned arms **Reverse:** Lions and castles in angles of cross, legend around **Note:** Klippe. Similar to KM#47a. Mint mark M, Mo.

Date	Mintage	Good	VG	F	VF	XF
ND(1733-34) Date off flan	—	—	200	350	500	—
1733 F	—	—	550	750	1,150	—
1733 MF	—	—	450	600	750	—
1734/3 MF	—	—	500	750	1,000	—
1734 MF	—	—	500	750	1,000	—

KM# 50 ESCUDO

3.3800 g., 0.9170 Gold 0.0996 oz. AGW **Ruler:** Charles II **Mint:** Mexico City **Obverse:** Legend and date around crowned arms **Obv. Legend:** CAROLVS II DEI G **Reverse:** Lions and castles in angles of cross, legend around **Note:** Mint mark MXo.

Date	Mintage	VG	F	VF	XF	Unc
ND(1690-1701) Date off flan	—	—	1,200	1,375	1,750	—
1701/0MXo L	—	—	3,000	4,000	5,000	—

KM# 51.1 ESCUDO

3.3800 g., 0.9170 Gold 0.0996 oz. AGW **Ruler:** Philip V **Mint:** Mexico City **Obverse:** Legend and date around crowned arms **Obv. Legend:** PHILIPVS V DEI G **Reverse:** Lions and castles in angles of cross, legend around **Note:** Mint mark MXo.

Date	Mintage	VG	F	VF	XF	Unc
ND(1702-13) Date off flan	—	—	1,000	1,350	1,500	—
1702MXo L	—	—	1,500	2,500	3,500	—
1703/2MXo L	—	—	1,500	2,500	3,500	—
1704MXo L	—	—	1,500	2,500	3,500	—
1707MXo J	—	—	1,500	2,500	3,500	—
1708MXo J	—	—	1,500	2,500	3,500	—
1709MXo J	—	—	1,500	2,500	3,500	—
1710MXo J	—	—	1,500	2,500	3,500	—
1711MXo J	—	—	1,500	2,500	3,500	—
1712MXo J	—	—	1,500	2,500	3,500	—
1713MXo J	—	—	1,500	2,500	3,500	—

KM# 51.2 ESCUDO

3.3800 g., 0.9170 Gold 0.0996 oz. AGW **Ruler:** Philip V **Mint:** Mexico City **Obverse:** Legend and date around crowned arms **Obv. Legend:** PHILIPVS V DEI G **Reverse:** Lions and castles in angles of cross, legend around **Note:** Mint mark Mo.

Date	Mintage	VG	F	VF	XF	Unc
1712Mo J	—	—	2,000	3,000	4,000	—
1714Mo J	—	—	1,400	2,000	3,000	—
1714Mo J J's 1's (J7J4J) Rare	—	—	—	—	—	—
1715Mo J	—	—	2,000	3,000	4,000	—
1727Mo J Rare	—	—	—	—	—	—
1728Mo J Rare	—	—	—	—	—	—

Note: Die-struck counterfeits of 1731 F exist

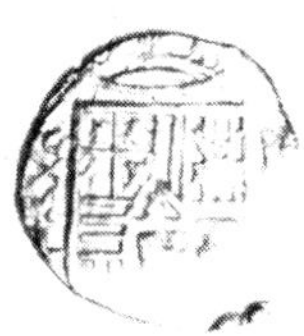

KM# 52 2 ESCUDOS

6.7700 g., 0.9170 Gold 0.1996 oz. AGW **Ruler:** Philip V **Mint:** Mexico City **Obverse:** Legend and date around crowned arms **Obv. Legend:** CAROLVS II DEI G **Reverse:** Legend around cross **Note:** Mint mark MXo.

Date	Mintage	VG	F	VF	XF	Unc
ND(1680-1701) Date off flan	—	—	1,300	1,600	2,000	—
1701MXo L	—	—	4,000	2,200	6,000	—

KM# 53.1 2 ESCUDOS

6.7700 g., 0.9170 Gold 0.1996 oz. AGW **Ruler:** Philip V **Mint:** Mexico City **Obverse:** Legend and date around crowned arms **Obv. Legend:** PHILIPVS V DEI G **Reverse:** Legend around cross **Note:** Mint mark MXo.

Date	Mintage	VG	F	VF	XF	Unc
ND(1704-13) Date off flan	—	—	1,500	2,000	2,500	—
1704MXo L	—	—	2,750	3,750	4,750	—
1708MXo J	—	—	2,750	3,750	4,750	—
1710MXo J	—	—	2,750	3,750	4,750	—
1711MXo J	—	—	2,750	3,750	4,750	—
1712MXo J	—	—	2,750	3,750	4,750	—
1713MXo J	—	—	2,750	3,750	4,750	—

KM# 53.2 2 ESCUDOS

6.7700 g., 0.9170 Gold 0.1996 oz. AGW **Ruler:** Philip V **Mint:** Mexico City **Obverse:** Legend and date around crowned arms **Obv. Legend:** PHILIPVS V DEI G **Reverse:** Legend around cross **Note:** Struck counterfeits exist for 1731. Mint mark Mo.

Date	Mintage	VG	F	VF	XF	Unc
ND(1714-31) Date off flan	—	—	1,500	1,750	2,500	—
1714Mo J	—	—	—	2,500	3,500	—
1715Mo J	—	—	—	3,000	4,000	—
1717Mo J Rare	—	—	—	—	—	—
1722Mo J Rare	—	—	—	—	—	—
1729Mo R Rare	—	—	—	—	—	—
1731Mo F Rare	—	—	—	—	—	—

KM# A54 2 ESCUDOS

6.7700 g., 0.9170 Gold 0.1996 oz. AGW **Ruler:** Luis I **Mint:** Mexico City **Obverse:** Legend and date around crowned arms **Obv. Legend:** LVDOVICVS I DEI G. **Reverse:** Legend around cross **Note:** A significant portion of the legend must be visible for proper attribution. Mint mark MXo.

Date	Mintage	VG	F	VF	XF	Unc
NDMo D Rare	—	—	—	—	—	—

KM# 55.1 4 ESCUDOS

13.5400 g., 0.9170 Gold 0.3992 oz. AGW **Ruler:** Philip V **Mint:** Mexico City **Obverse:** Legend and date around crowned arms **Obv. Legend:** PHILIPVS V DEI G **Reverse:** Legend around cross **Note:** Mint mark MXo.

Date	Mintage	VG	F	VF	XF	Unc
ND(1705-13) Date off flan	—	—	2,500	3,000	4,000	—
1705MXo J	—	—	4,000	5,750	6,750	—
1706MXo L	—	—	4,000	5,750	6,750	—
1711MXo J	—	—	4,000	5,750	6,750	—
1712MXo J	—	—	4,000	5,750	6,750	—
1713MXo J	—	—	4,000	5,750	6,750	—

KM# 55.2 4 ESCUDOS

13.5400 g., 0.9170 Gold 0.3992 oz. AGW **Ruler:** Philip V **Mint:** Mexico City **Obverse:** Legend and date around crowned arms **Obv. Legend:** PHILIPVS V DEI G **Reverse:** Legend around cross **Note:** Mint mark Mo.

Date	Mintage	VG	F	VF	XF	Unc
ND(1714-20) Date off flan	—	—	2,500	3,750	5,000	—
1714Mo J	—	—	—	5,750	7,500	—
1715Mo J	—	—	—	5,750	7,500	—
1720Mo J Rare	—	—	—	—	—	—

KM# 57.1 8 ESCUDOS

27.0700 g., 0.9170 Gold 0.7981 oz. AGW **Ruler:** Philip V **Mint:** Mexico City **Obverse:** Legend and date around crowned arms **Obv. Legend:** PHILIPVS V DEI G **Reverse:** Legend around cross **Note:** Mint mark MXo.

Date	Mintage	VG	F	VF	XF	Unc
ND(1701-13) Date off flan	—	—	2,000	3,000	4,000	—
1701MXo L	—	—	6,000	7,500	9,000	—
1703MXo L	—	—	6,000	7,500	9,000	—
1706MXo J	—	—	6,000	7,500	9,000	—
1708MXo J	—	—	6,000	7,500	9,000	—
1709MXo J	—	—	6,000	7,500	9,000	—
1710MXo J	—	—	6,000	7,500	9,000	—
1711MXo J	—	—	3,500	4,000	5,750	—

Date	Mintage	VG	F	VF	XF	Unc
1712MXo J	—	—	3,500	4,000	5,750	—
1713MXo J	—	—	3,500	4,000	5,750	—

KM# 57.2 8 ESCUDOS
27.0700 g., 0.9170 Gold 0.7981 oz. AGW **Ruler:** Philip V **Mint:** Mexico City **Obverse:** Legend and date around crowned arms **Obv. Legend:** PHILIPVS V DEI G **Reverse:** Legend around cross **Note:** Mint mark Mo.

Date	Mintage	VG	F	VF	XF	Unc
ND(1714-32)Mo Date off flan	—	—	2,750	3,750	4,750	—
1714Mo J	—	—	5,000	6,000	7,500	—
1714Mo Date over GRAT on obverse	—	—	6,000	7,500	9,000	—
1715Mo J	—	—	5,000	6,500	8,000	—
1717/6Mo J Rare	—	—	—	—	—	—
1720/19Mo J Rare	—	—	—	—	—	—
1723Mo J Rare	—	—	—	—	—	—
1727/6Mo D Rare	—	—	—	—	—	—
1728/7Mo D Rare	—	—	—	—	—	—
1729Mo R Rare	—	—	—	—	—	—
1730Mo R Rare	—	—	—	—	—	—
1730Mo F Rare	—	—	—	—	—	—
1731Mo F Rare	—	—	—	—	—	—
1732Mo F Rare	—	—	—	—	—	—

KM# 57.3 8 ESCUDOS
27.0700 g., 0.9170 Gold 0.7981 oz. AGW **Ruler:** Philip V **Mint:** Mexico City **Obverse:** Date around crowned arms **Obv. Legend:** PHILIPVS V DEI G **Reverse:** Legend and date around cross **Note:** Mint mark Mo.

Date	Mintage	VG	F	VF	XF	Unc
1714Mo J Date on reverse	—	—	6,000	7,500	9,000	—

KM# 58 8 ESCUDOS
27.0700 g., 0.9170 Gold 0.7981 oz. AGW **Ruler:** Luis I **Mint:** Mexico City **Obverse:** Legend and date around crowned arms **Obv. Legend:** LVDOVICVS I DEI G **Reverse:** Legend around cross **Note:** A significant portion of the legend must be visible for proper attribution. Mint mark Mo.

Date	Mintage	VG	F	VF	XF	Unc
ND(1724-25)Mo D Rare	—	—	—	—	—	—

ROYAL COINAGE

Struck on specially prepared round planchets using well centered dies in excellent condition to prove the quality of the minting to the Viceroy or even to the King.

KM# R24 1/2 REAL
1.6917 g., 0.9310 Silver 0.0506 oz. ASW **Ruler:** Philip V **Mint:** Mexico City **Note:** Normally found holed. Mint mark Mo.

Date	Mintage	Good	VG	F	VF	XF
1715Mo J	—	—	250	500	750	—
1719Mo J	—	—	250	500	750	—
1721Mo J	—	—	250	500	750	—
1722Mo J	—	—	250	500	750	—
1726Mo D	—	—	250	500	750	—
1727Mo D	—	—	250	500	750	—

KM# R25 1/2 REAL
1.6917 g., 0.9310 Silver 0.0506 oz. ASW **Ruler:** Luis I **Mint:** Mexico City **Obverse:** Legend around crowned LVDOVICVS monogram **Reverse:** Lions and castles in angles of cross, legend around **Note:** Mint mark Mo.

Date	Mintage	Good	VG	F	VF	XF
1724Mo D Rare	—	—	—	—	—	—

KM# R24a 1/2 REAL
1.6917 g., 0.9170 Silver 0.0499 oz. ASW **Ruler:** Philip V **Mint:** Mexico City **Note:** Normally found holed. Mint mark Mo.

Date	Mintage	Good	VG	F	VF	XF
1730Mo D	—	—	250	500	750	—

KM# R30 REAL
3.3834 g., 0.9310 Silver 0.1013 oz. ASW **Ruler:** Philip V **Mint:** Mexico City **Obv. Legend:** PHILIPVS V DEI G **Note:** Mint mark Mo.

Date	Mintage	Good	VG	F	VF	XF
1715Mo J Rare	—	—	—	—	—	—
1716Mo J Rare	—	—	—	—	—	—
1718Mo J Rare	—	—	—	—	—	—

KM# R35 2 REALES
6.7668 g., 0.9310 Silver 0.2025 oz. ASW **Ruler:** Philip V **Mint:** Mexico City **Obv. Legend:** PHILIPVS V DEI G **Note:** Mint mark Mo.

Date	Mintage	Good	VG	F	VF	XF
1715Mo J Rare	—	—	—	—	—	—

KM# R35a 2 REALES
6.7668 g., 0.9170 Silver 0.1995 oz. ASW **Ruler:** Philip V **Mint:** Mexico City **Note:** Mint mark Mo.

Date	Mintage	Good	VG	F	VF	XF
1730Mo R Rare	—	—	—	—	—	—

KM# R40 4 REALES
13.5337 g., 0.9310 Silver 0.4051 oz. ASW **Ruler:** Philip V **Mint:** Mexico City **Obv. Legend:** PHILIPVS V DEI G **Note:** Mint mark Mo.

Date	Mintage	Good	VG	F	VF	XF
1716Mo J Rare	—	—	—	—	—	—
1719Mo J Rare	—	—	—	—	—	—
1721Mo J Rare	—	—	—	—	—	—
1722Mo J Rare	—	—	—	—	—	—
1723Mo J Rare	—	—	—	—	—	—

KM# R47 8 REALES
27.0674 g., 0.9310 Silver 0.8102 oz. ASW **Ruler:** Philip V **Mint:** Mexico City **Obv. Legend:** PHILIPVS V DEI G **Note:** Struck at Mexico City Mint, mint mark Mo.

Date	Mintage	Good	VG	F	VF	XF
1702Mo L Rare	—	—	—	—	—	—
1703Mo L Rare	—	—	—	—	—	—
1705Mo J Rare	—	—	—	—	—	—
1706Mo J Rare	—	—	—	—	—	—
1709Mo J Rare	—	—	—	—	—	—
1711Mo J Rare	—	—	—	—	—	—
1714Mo J Rare	—	—	—	—	—	—
1715Mo J Rare	—	—	—	—	—	—
1716Mo J Rare	—	—	—	—	—	—
1717Mo J Rare	—	—	—	—	—	—
1719Mo J Rare	—	—	—	—	—	—
1721Mo J Rare	—	—	—	—	—	—
1722Mo J Rare	—	—	—	—	—	—
1723Mo J Rare	—	—	—	—	—	—
1724Mo D Rare	—	—	—	—	—	—
1725Mo D Rare	—	—	—	—	—	—
1726/5Mo D Rare	—	—	—	—	—	—
1726Mo D Rare	—	—	—	—	—	—
1727Mo D Rare	—	—	—	—	—	—

KM# R49 8 REALES
27.0674 g., 0.9310 Silver 0.8102 oz. ASW **Ruler:** Luis I **Note:** Mint mark Mo.

Date	Mintage	Good	VG	F	VF	XF
1724 D Rare	—	—	—	—	—	—
1725 D Rare	—	—	—	—	—	—

KM# R47a 8 REALES
27.0674 g., 0.9170 Silver 0.7980 oz. ASW **Ruler:** Philip V **Mint:** Mexico City **Note:** Mint mark Mo.

Date	Mintage	Good	VG	F	VF	XF
1729 R Rare	—	—	—	—	—	—
1730 R/D Rare	—	—	—	—	—	—
1730 G Rare	—	—	—	—	—	—

KM# R51.2 ESCUDO
3.3834 g., 0.9170 Gold 0.0997 oz. AGW **Ruler:** Philip V **Mint:** Mexico City **Note:** Mint mark Mo.

Date	Mintage	Good	VG	F	VF	XF
1714Mo J Rare	—	—	—	—	—	—
1715Mo J Rare	—	—	—	—	—	—

KM# R53.1 2 ESCUDOS
6.7668 g., 0.9170 Gold 0.1995 oz. AGW **Ruler:** Philip V **Mint:** Mexico City **Note:** Mint mark MXo.

Date	Mintage	Good	VG	F	VF	XF
1711MXo J Rare	—	—	—	—	—	—
1712MXo J Rare	—	—	—	—	—	—

KM# R55.1 4 ESCUDOS
13.5337 g., 0.9170 Gold 0.3990 oz. AGW **Ruler:** Philip V **Mint:** Mexico City **Note:** Mint mark M, Mo.

Date	Mintage	Good	VG	F	VF	XF
1711 Rare	—	—	—	—	—	—

KM# R55.2 4 ESCUDOS
13.5337 g., 0.9170 Gold 0.3990 oz. AGW **Ruler:** Philip V **Mint:** Mexico City **Note:** Mint mark M, Mo.

Date	Mintage	Good	VG	F	VF	XF
1714 Rare	—	—	—	—	—	—

KM# R57.1 8 ESCUDOS
27.0674 g., 0.9170 Gold 0.7980 oz. AGW **Ruler:** Philip V **Mint:** Mexico City **Note:** Mint mark MXo.

Date	Mintage	Good	VG	F	VF	XF
1702MXo L Rare	—	—	—	—	—	—
1711MXo J Rare	—	—	—	—	—	—
1712MXo J Rare	—	—	—	—	—	—
1713MXo J Rare	—	—	—	—	—	—

KM# R57.3 8 ESCUDOS
27.0674 g., 0.9170 Gold 0.7980 oz. AGW **Ruler:** Philip V **Mint:** Mexico City **Note:** Mint mark Mo.

Date	Mintage	Good	VG	F	VF	XF
1714Mo J Rare	—	—	—	—	—	—
1715Mo J Rare	—	—	—	—	—	—
1717Mo J Rare	—	—	—	—	—	—
1718Mo J Rare	—	—	—	—	—	—
1723Mo J Rare	—	—	—	—	—	—

MILLED COINAGE

100 Centavos = 1 Peso

KM# 62 1/4 REAL
0.8458 g., 0.8960 Silver 0.0244 oz. ASW **Ruler:** Charles IV **Mint:** Mexico City **Obverse:** Crowned rampant lion, left **Reverse:** Castle **Note:** Mint mark Mo.

Date	Mintage	VG	F	VF	XF	Unc
1796	—	15.00	30.00	55.00	90.00	—
1797	—	15.00	30.00	55.00	90.00	—
1798	—	12.50	22.00	50.00	75.00	—
1799/8	—	12.50	22.00	50.00	75.00	—
1799	—	10.00	20.00	40.00	70.00	—
1800	—	10.00	25.00	55.00	90.00	—

KM# 65 1/2 REAL
1.6917 g., 0.9170 Silver 0.0499 oz. ASW **Ruler:** Philip V **Mint:** Mexico City **Obverse:** Crowned shield flanked by M F, rosettes and small cross **Obv. Legend:** PHILIP • V • D • G • HISPAN • ET IND • REX **Reverse:** Crowned globes flanked by crowned pillars with banner, date below **Note:** Mint mark M, Mo, MX.

Date	Mintage	VG	F	VF	XF	Unc
1732 Rare	—	—	—	—	—	—
1732 F	—	500	800	1,200	2,000	—
1733 MF (MX)	—	400	600	1,000	1,500	—
1733 F	—	200	325	550	800	—
1733/2 MF	—	300	400	600	800	—
1733 MF	—	300	400	600	800	—
1734/3 MF	—	12.00	25.00	45.00	85.00	—
1734 MF	—	12.00	25.00	45.00	85.00	—
1735/4 MF	—	10.00	20.00	45.00	85.00	—
1735 MF	—	10.00	20.00	45.00	85.00	—
1736/5 MF	—	10.00	20.00	45.00	85.00	—
1736 MF	—	10.00	20.00	45.00	85.00	—
1737/6 MF	—	10.00	20.00	45.00	85.00	—
1737 MF	—	10.00	20.00	45.00	85.00	—
1738/7 MF	—	10.00	20.00	45.00	85.00	—
1738 MF	—	10.00	20.00	45.00	85.00	—
1739 MF	—	10.00	20.00	45.00	85.00	—
1740/30 MF	—	8.00	18.00	40.00	75.00	—
1740 MF	—	8.00	18.00	40.00	75.00	—
1741 MF	—	8.00	18.00	40.00	75.00	—

KM# 66 1/2 REAL
1.6900 g., 0.9170 Silver 0.0498 oz. ASW **Ruler:** Philip V **Mint:** Mexico City **Obverse:** Crowned shield flanked by stars **Obv. Legend:** PHS • V • D • G • HISP • ET IND • R **Reverse:** Crowned globes flanked by crowned pillars with banner, date below **Note:** Mint mark M, Mo.

Date	Mintage	VG	F	VF	XF	Unc
1742 M	—	8.00	18.00	40.00	75.00	—
1743 M	—	8.00	18.00	40.00	75.00	—
1744/3 M	—	8.00	18.00	40.00	75.00	—
1744 M	—	8.00	18.00	40.00	75.00	—
1745 M Rare	—	—	—	—	—	—
Note: Legend variation: PHS. V. D. G. HISP. EST IND. R						
1745 M	—	8.00	18.00	40.00	75.00	—
1746/5 M	—	8.00	18.00	40.00	75.00	—
1746 M	—	8.00	18.00	40.00	75.00	—
1747 M	—	8.00	18.00	40.00	75.00	—

KM# 67.1 1/2 REAL

1.6900 g., 0.9170 Silver 0.0498 oz. ASW **Ruler:** Ferdinand VI **Mint:** Mexico City **Obverse:** Royal crown **Obv. Legend:** FRD • VI • D • G • HIPS • ET IND • R **Note:** Mint mark M, Mo.

Date	Mintage	VG	F	VF	XF	Unc
1747/6 M	—	—	—	—	—	—
1747 M	—	8.00	18.00	40.00	75.00	—
1748/7 M	—	8.00	18.00	40.00	75.00	—
1748 M	—	8.00	18.00	40.00	75.00	—
1749 M	—	8.00	18.00	40.00	75.00	—
1750 M	—	8.00	18.00	40.00	75.00	—
1751 M	—	10.00	20.00	45.00	85.00	—
1752 M	—	8.00	18.00	40.00	75.00	—
1753 M	—	8.00	18.00	40.00	75.00	—
1754 M	—	12.00	25.00	55.00	100	—
1755/6 M	—	12.00	25.00	55.00	100	—
1755 M	—	8.00	18.00	40.00	75.00	—
1756/5 M	—	8.00	18.00	40.00	75.00	—
1756 M	—	8.00	18.00	40.00	75.00	—
1757/6 M	—	8.00	18.00	40.00	75.00	—
1757 M	—	8.00	18.00	40.00	75.00	—

KM# 67.2 1/2 REAL

1.6917 g., 0.9170 Silver 0.0499 oz. ASW **Ruler:** Ferdinand VI **Mint:** Mexico City **Obverse:** Different crown **Note:** Mint mark M, Mo.

Date	Mintage	VG	F	VF	XF	Unc
1757 M	—	8.00	18.00	40.00	75.00	—
1758/7 M	—	8.00	18.00	40.00	75.00	—
1758 M	—	8.00	18.00	40.00	75.00	—
1759 M	—	8.00	18.00	40.00	75.00	—
1760/59 M	—	8.00	18.00	40.00	75.00	—
1760 M	—	8.00	18.00	40.00	75.00	—

KM# 68 1/2 REAL

1.6900 g., 0.9170 Silver 0.0498 oz. ASW **Ruler:** Charles III **Mint:** Mexico City **Obverse:** Crowned shield flanked by stars **Obv. Legend:** CAR • III • D • G • HISP • ET IND • R **Reverse:** Crowned globes flanked by crowned pillars with banner, date below **Note:** Mint mark M, Mo.

Date	Mintage	VG	F	VF	XF	Unc
1760/59 M	—	8.00	18.00	40.00	75.00	—
1760 M	—	8.00	18.00	40.00	75.00	—
1761 M	—	8.00	18.00	40.00	75.00	—
1762 M	—	8.00	18.00	40.00	75.00	—
1763/2 M	—	8.00	18.00	40.00	75.00	—
1763 M	—	8.00	18.00	40.00	75.00	—
1764 M	—	8.00	18.00	40.00	75.00	—
1765/4 M	—	10.00	20.00	42.00	80.00	—
1765 M	—	8.00	18.00	40.00	75.00	—
1766 M	—	8.00	18.00	40.00	75.00	—
1767 M	—	10.00	20.00	45.00	85.00	—
1768/6 M	—	10.00	20.00	42.00	80.00	—
1768 M	—	8.00	18.00	40.00	75.00	—
1769 M	—	10.00	20.00	42.00	80.00	—
1770 M	—	10.00	20.00	42.00	80.00	—
1770 F	—	15.00	30.00	60.00	100	—
1771 F	—	10.00	20.00	42.00	80.00	—

KM# 69.1 1/2 REAL

1.6900 g., 0.9030 Silver 0.0491 oz. ASW **Ruler:** Charles III **Mint:** Mexico City **Obv. Legend:** CAROLUS • III • DEI • GRATIA **Reverse:** Inverted FM and mint mark **Note:** Mint mark Mo.

Date	Mintage	VG	F	VF	XF	Unc
1772Mo FM	—	5.00	12.00	27.00	65.00	—
1773Mo FM	—	4.50	10.00	25.00	55.00	—

KM# 69.2 1/2 REAL

1.6917 g., 0.9030 Silver 0.0491 oz. ASW **Ruler:** Charles III **Mint:** Mexico City **Obverse:** Armored bust of Charles III, right **Obv. Legend:** CAROLUS • III • DEI • GRATIA **Reverse:** Crown above shield flanked by pillars with banner, normal initials and mint mark **Note:** Mint mark Mo.

Date	Mintage	VG	F	VF	XF	Unc
1772Mo FF	—	9.00	18.00	35.00	80.00	—
1773Mo FM	—	4.50	10.00	25.00	60.00	—
1773Mo FM CAROLS (error)	—	75.00	150	250	400	—
1774Mo FM	—	4.50	10.00	25.00	55.00	—
1775Mo FM	—	4.50	10.00	25.00	55.00	—
1776Mo FM	—	4.50	10.00	25.00	55.00	—
1777/6Mo FM	—	10.00	18.00	35.00	75.00	—
1777Mo FM	—	7.00	15.00	30.00	65.00	—
1778Mo FF	—	4.50	10.00	25.00	55.00	—
1779Mo FF	—	4.50	10.00	25.00	55.00	—
1780/79Mo FF	—	6.00	12.50	30.00	75.00	—
1780Mo FF	—	4.50	10.00	25.00	55.00	—
1781Mo FF	—	4.50	10.00	25.00	55.00	—
1782/1Mo FF	—	6.00	12.50	30.00	75.00	—
1782Mo FF	—	4.50	10.00	25.00	55.00	—
1783Mo FF	—	4.50	10.00	25.00	55.00	—
1783Mo FM	—	125	300	450	—	—
1784Mo FF	—	4.50	10.00	25.00	55.00	—
1784Mo FM	—	7.00	15.00	35.00	80.00	—

KM# 69.2a 1/2 REAL

1.6917 g., 0.8960 Silver 0.0487 oz. ASW **Ruler:** Charles III **Reverse:** Normal initials and mint mark **Note:** Mint mark M, Mo.

Date	Mintage	VG	F	VF	XF	Unc
1785/4 FM	—	7.00	15.00	35.00	80.00	—
1785 FM	—	5.00	12.00	27.00	60.00	—
1786 FM	—	4.50	10.00	25.00	55.00	—
1787 FM	—	4.50	10.00	25.00	55.00	—
1788 FM	—	4.50	10.00	25.00	55.00	—
1789 FM	—	8.00	16.00	40.00	100	—

KM# 70 1/2 REAL

1.6917 g., 0.8960 Silver 0.0487 oz. ASW **Ruler:** Charles IV **Mint:** Mexico City **Obverse:** Armored bust of Charles IV, right **Obv. Legend:** CAROLUS ? IV ? ... **Reverse:** Crown above shield flanked by pillars with banner **Note:** Mint mark M, Mo.

Date	Mintage	VG	F	VF	XF	Unc
1789 FM	—	12.00	25.00	50.00	100	—
1790 FM	—	12.00	25.00	50.00	100	—

KM# 71 1/2 REAL

1.6917 g., 0.8960 Silver 0.0487 oz. ASW **Ruler:** Charles IV **Mint:** Mexico City **Obverse:** Armored bust of Charles IIII, right **Obv. Legend:** CAROLUS ? IIII ? ... **Reverse:** Crown above shield flanked by pillars with banner **Note:** Mint mark M, Mo.

Date	Mintage	VG	F	VF	XF	Unc
1790 FM	—	12.00	25.00	50.00	100	—

KM# 72 1/2 REAL

1.6900 g., 0.9030 Silver 0.0491 oz. ASW **Ruler:** Charles IV **Mint:** Mexico City **Obverse:** Armored bust of Charles IIII, right **Obv. Legend:** CAROLUS • IIII • ... **Reverse:** Crowned shield flanked by pillars with banner **Rev. Legend:** IND • R • .... **Note:** Mint mark Mo.

Date	Mintage	VG	F	VF	XF	Unc
1792 FM	—	6.00	12.00	25.00	50.00	—
1793 FM	—	6.00	12.00	25.00	50.00	—
1794/3 FM	—	7.50	15.00	30.00	75.00	—
1794 FM	—	5.00	10.00	22.00	45.00	—
1795 FM	—	4.00	10.00	22.00	45.00	—
1796 FM	—	4.00	10.00	22.00	45.00	—
1797 FM	—	4.00	10.00	22.00	45.00	—
1798/7 FM	—	5.00	11.50	25.00	50.00	—
1798 FM	—	4.00	10.00	22.00	45.00	—
1799 FM	—	4.00	10.00	22.00	45.00	—
1800/799 FM	—	5.00	11.50	25.00	50.00	—
1800 FM	—	4.00	10.00	22.00	45.00	—

KM# 75.1 REAL

3.3834 g., 0.9170 Silver 0.0997 oz. ASW **Ruler:** Philip V **Mint:** Mexico City **Obverse:** Crowned shield flanked by MF I ** **Obv. Legend:** PHILIP • V • D • G • HISPAN • ET IND • REX **Reverse:** Crowned globes flanked by crowned pillars with banner, date below **Note:** Mint mark M, Mo, (MX).

Date	Mintage	VG	F	VF	XF	Unc
1732 Rare	—	—	—	—	—	—
1732 F	—	—	—	—	—	—
1733 F (MX)	—	150	350	425	750	—
1733 MF (MX)	—	150	350	425	750	—
1733 F Rare	—	—	—	—	—	—
1733 MF	—	100	200	300	500	—
1734/3 MF	—	15.00	30.00	65.00	150	—
1734 MF	—	12.00	25.00	60.00	140	—
1735 MF	—	12.00	25.00	60.00	140	—
1736 MF	—	12.00	25.00	60.00	140	—
1737 MF	—	12.00	25.00	60.00	140	—
1738 MF	—	12.00	25.00	60.00	140	—
1739 MF	—	12.00	25.00	60.00	140	—
1740 MF	—	12.00	25.00	60.00	140	—
1741 MF	—	12.00	25.00	60.00	140	—

KM# 75.2 REAL

3.3834 g., 0.9170 Silver 0.0997 oz. ASW **Ruler:** Philip V **Obv. Legend:** PHS ? V ? D ? G ? HISP ? ET ? IND ? R **Note:** Mint mark M, Mo.

Date	Mintage	VG	F	VF	XF	Unc
1742 M	—	10.00	20.00	50.00	120	—
1743 M	—	10.00	20.00	50.00	120	—
1744/3 M	—	10.00	20.00	50.00	120	—
1744 M	—	10.00	20.00	50.00	120	—
1745 M	—	8.00	18.00	50.00	120	—
1746/5 M	—	12.00	25.00	75.00	200	—
1746 M	—	10.00	20.00	55.00	125	—
1747 M	—	10.00	20.00	55.00	125	—

KM# 76.1 REAL

3.3800 g., 0.9170 Silver 0.0996 oz. ASW **Ruler:** Ferdinand VI **Mint:** Mexico City **Obverse:** Crowned shield flanked by R I **Obv. Legend:** FRD • VI • D • G • HISP • ET IND • R **Reverse:** Crowned globes flanked by crowned pillars with banner, date below **Note:** Mint mark M, Mo.

Date	Mintage	VG	F	VF	XF	Unc
1747 M	—	10.00	20.00	50.00	100	—
1748/7 M	—	10.00	20.00	50.00	100	—
1748 M	—	10.00	20.00	50.00	100	—
1749 M	—	10.00	20.00	50.00	100	—
1750/40 M	—	10.00	20.00	50.00	100	—
1750 M	—	10.00	20.00	50.00	100	—
1751 M	—	10.00	20.00	55.00	110	—
1752 M	—	10.00	20.00	50.00	100	—
1753 M	—	10.00	20.00	50.00	100	—
1754 M	—	10.00	20.00	55.00	110	—
1755/4 M	—	10.00	20.00	50.00	100	—
1755 M	—	10.00	20.00	50.00	100	—
1756 M	—	10.00	20.00	55.00	110	—
1757 M	—	10.00	20.00	55.00	110	—
1758/5 M	—	10.00	20.00	50.00	100	—
1758 M	—	10.00	20.00	50.00	100	—

KM# 76.2 REAL

3.3834 g., 0.9170 Silver 0.0997 oz. ASW **Ruler:** Ferdinand VI **Obverse:** Royal and Imperial crowns **Note:** Mint mark M, Mo.

Date	Mintage	VG	F	VF	XF	Unc
1757 M	—	10.00	20.00	50.00	100	—
1758/7 M	—	10.00	20.00	50.00	100	—
1758 M	—	10.00	20.00	50.00	100	—
1759 M	—	10.00	20.00	55.00	110	—
1760 M	—	15.00	30.00	70.00	140	—

KM# 77 REAL

3.3800 g., 0.9170 Silver 0.0996 oz. ASW **Ruler:** Charles III **Mint:** Mexico City **Obverse:** Crowned shield flanked by R I **Obv. Legend:** CAR • III • D • G • HISP • ET IND • R **Reverse:** Crowned globes flanked by crowned pillars with banner, date below **Note:** Mint mark M, Mo.

Date	Mintage	VG	F	VF	XF	Unc
1760 M	—	10.00	20.00	50.00	100	—
1761/0 M	—	10.00	20.00	55.00	125	—
1761 M	—	10.00	20.00	50.00	100	—
1762 M	—	10.00	20.00	50.00	100	—
1763/2 M	—	12.00	25.00	60.00	120	—
1763 M	—	10.00	20.00	50.00	100	—
1764 M	—	10.00	20.00	55.00	110	—
1765 M	—	10.00	20.00	55.00	110	—
1766 M	—	10.00	20.00	50.00	100	—
1767 M	—	10.00	20.00	55.00	110	—
1768 M	—	10.00	20.00	50.00	100	—
1769 M	—	10.00	20.00	50.00	100	—
1769/70 M	—	10.00	20.00	55.00	125	—
1770 M	—	10.00	20.00	55.00	125	—
1770 F	—	20.00	40.00	90.00	250	—
1771 F	—	20.00	40.00	90.00	250	—

KM# 78.1 REAL
3.3834 g., 0.9030 Silver 0.0982 oz. ASW **Ruler:** Charles III **Obv. Legend:** CAROLUS ? III ? DEI ? GRATIA **Reverse:** Inverted FM and mint mark **Note:** Mint mark M, Mo.

Date	Mintage	VG	F	VF	XF	Unc
1772 FM	—	5.00	10.00	25.00	60.00	—
1773 FM	—	5.00	10.00	25.00	60.00	—

KM# 78.2 REAL
3.3800 g., 0.9030 Silver 0.0981 oz. ASW **Ruler:** Charles III **Mint:** Mexico City **Obverse:** Armored bust of Charles III, right **Obv. Legend:** CAROLUS • III • DEI • GRATIA **Rev. Legend:** Crowned shield flanked by pillars with banner, normal initials and mint mark **Note:** Mint mark M, Mo.

Date	Mintage	VG	F	VF	XF	Unc
1774 FM	—	5.00	10.00	25.00	60.00	—
1775/4 FM	—	6.00	12.00	28.00	75.00	—
1775 FM	—	5.00	10.00	25.00	60.00	—
1776 FM	—	5.00	10.00	25.00	60.00	—
1777 FM	—	5.00	10.00	25.00	60.00	—
1778 FF/M	—	6.00	12.00	28.00	75.00	—
1778 FF	—	5.00	10.00	25.00	60.00	—
1779 FF	—	5.00	10.00	25.00	60.00	—
1780 FF	—	5.00	10.00	25.00	60.00	—
1780 F F/M	—	5.00	10.00	25.00	60.00	—
1781 FF	—	5.00	10.00	25.00	60.00	—
1782 FF	—	5.00	10.00	25.00	60.00	—
1783 FF	—	5.00	10.00	25.00	60.00	—
1784 FF	—	5.00	10.00	25.00	60.00	—

KM# 78.2a REAL
3.3834 g., 0.8960 Silver 0.0975 oz. ASW **Ruler:** Charles III **Reverse:** Normal initials and mint mark **Note:** Mint mark M, Mo.

Date	Mintage	VG	F	VF	XF	Unc
1785 FF	—	6.00	12.00	28.00	75.00	—
1785 FM	—	6.00	12.00	28.00	75.00	—
1786 FM	—	6.00	12.00	28.00	75.00	—
1787 FF	—	15.00	30.00	60.00	125	—
1787 FM	—	12.00	25.00	50.00	100	—
1788 FF	—	50.00	100	200	—	—
1788 FM	—	5.00	10.00	25.00	60.00	—
1789 FM	—	6.00	12.00	28.00	75.00	—

KM# 79 REAL
3.3800 g., 0.9030 Silver 0.0981 oz. ASW **Ruler:** Charles IV **Mint:** Mexico City **Obverse:** Armored bust of Charles III, right **Obv. Legend:** CAROLUS • IV • ... **Reverse:** Crown above shield flanked by pillars with banner **Note:** Mint mark M, Mo.

Date	Mintage	VG	F	VF	XF	Unc
1789 FM	—	15.00	30.00	60.00	150	—
1790 FM	—	15.00	30.00	60.00	150	—

KM# 80 REAL
3.3800 g., 0.9030 Silver 0.0981 oz. ASW **Ruler:** Charles IV **Mint:** Mexico City **Obverse:** Armored bust of Charles IIII, right **Obv. Legend:** CAROLUS • IIII • ... **Reverse:** Crowned shield flanked by pillars with banner **Note:** Mint mark M, Mo.

Date	Mintage	VG	F	VF	XF	Unc
1790 FM	—	17.00	35.00	70.00	165	—

KM# 81 REAL
3.3834 g., 0.8960 Silver 0.0975 oz. ASW **Ruler:** Charles IV **Mint:** Mexico City **Obverse:** Armored bust of Charles IIII, right **Obv. Legend:** CAROLUS • IIII • ... **Reverse:** Crowned shield flanked by pillars with banner **Rev. Legend:** IND • REX ... **Note:** Mint mark Mo.

Date	Mintage	VG	F	VF	XF	Unc
1792 FM	—	10.00	20.00	35.00	90.00	—
1793 FM	—	15.00	30.00	60.00	150	—
1794 FM	—	25.00	50.00	100	250	—
1795 FM	—	15.00	30.00	60.00	150	—
1796 FM	—	5.00	10.00	25.00	65.00	—
1797/6 FM	—	8.00	15.00	28.00	80.00	—
1797 FM	—	5.00	10.00	25.00	60.00	—
1798/7 FM	—	5.00	10.00	25.00	65.00	—
1798 FM	—	5.00	10.00	25.00	60.00	—
1799 FM	—	5.00	10.00	25.00	60.00	—
1800 FM	—	5.00	10.00	25.00	60.00	—

KM# 84 2 REALES
6.7668 g., 0.9170 Silver 0.1995 oz. ASW **Ruler:** Philip V **Mint:** Mexico City **Obverse:** Crowned shield flanked by M F 2 **Obv. Legend:** PHILIP • V • D • G • HISPAN • ET IND • REX **Reverse:** Crowned globes flanked by crowned pillars with banner, date below **Rev. Legend:** VTRAQUE VNUM **Note:** Mint mark M, Mo, (MX).

Date	Mintage	VG	F	VF	XF	Unc
1732 Rare	—	—	—	—	—	—
1732 F	—	800	1,300	1,750	2,750	—
1733 F	—	600	800	1,350	2,250	—
1733 MF (MX)	—	350	600	1,000	1,650	—
1733 MF	—	600	900	1,500	2,500	—
1734/3 MF	—	20.00	40.00	85.00	170	—
1734 MF	—	20.00	40.00	85.00	170	—
1735/3 MF	—	15.00	30.00	75.00	150	—
1735/4 MF	—	15.00	30.00	75.00	150	—
1735 MF	—	15.00	30.00	75.00	150	—
1736/3 MF	—	18.00	35.00	80.00	160	—
1736/4 MF	—	18.00	35.00	80.00	160	—
1736/5 MF	—	18.00	35.00	80.00	160	—
1736 MF	—	18.00	35.00	80.00	160	—
1737/3 MF	—	18.00	35.00	80.00	160	—
1737 MF	—	18.00	35.00	80.00	160	—
1738/7 MF	—	18.00	35.00	80.00	160	—
1738 MF	—	18.00	35.00	80.00	160	—
1739 MF	—	18.00	35.00	80.00	160	—
1740/30 MF	—	18.00	35.00	80.00	160	—
1740 MF	—	18.00	35.00	80.00	160	—
1741 MF	—	18.00	35.00	80.00	160	—

KM# 85 2 REALES
6.7700 g., 0.9170 Silver 0.1996 oz. ASW **Ruler:** Philip V **Mint:** Mexico City **Obverse:** Crowned shield flanked by R 2 **Obv. Legend:** PHS • V • D • G • HISP • ET IND • R * **Reverse:** Crowned globes flanked by crowned pillars with banner, date below **Rev. Legend:** VTRA QUE VNUM **Note:** Mint mark M, Mo.

Date	Mintage	F	VF	XF	Unc
1742 M	—	30.00	75.00	125	—
1743/2 M	—	30.00	75.00	125	—
1743 M	—	30.00	75.00	125	—
1744/3 M	—	30.00	75.00	125	—
1744 M	—	30.00	75.00	125	—
1745/4 M	—	30.00	75.00	125	—
1745 M	—	30.00	75.00	125	—
1745 M HIP	—	400	—	—	—
1746/5 M	—	30.00	75.00	125	—
1746 M	—	30.00	75.00	125	—
1747 M	—	30.00	75.00	125	—
1750 M	—	450	650	1,000	—

KM# 86.1 2 REALES
6.7668 g., 0.9170 Silver 0.1995 oz. ASW **Ruler:** Ferdinand VI **Mint:** Mexico City **Obverse:** Crowned shield flanked by R 2 **Obv. Legend:** FRD • VI • D • G • HISP • ET IND • R **Reverse:** Crowned globes flanked by crowned pillars with banner, date below **Rev. Legend:** VTRA QUE VNUM **Note:** Mint mark M, Mo.

Date	Mintage	VG	F	VF	XF	Unc
1747 M	—	16.00	32.00	78.00	135	—
1748/7 M	—	16.00	32.00	78.00	135	—
1748 M	—	15.00	30.00	75.00	125	—
1749 M	—	15.00	30.00	75.00	125	—
1750 M	—	15.00	30.00	75.00	125	—
1751/41 M	—	18.00	35.00	80.00	150	—
1751 M	—	15.00	30.00	75.00	125	—
1752 M	—	15.00	30.00	75.00	125	—
1753/2 M	—	18.00	35.00	80.00	150	—
1753 M	—	18.00	35.00	80.00	150	—
1754 M	—	18.00	35.00	80.00	150	—
1755/4 M	—	18.00	35.00	80.00	150	—
1755 M	—	18.00	35.00	80.00	150	—
1756/55 M	—	18.00	35.00	80.00	150	—
1756 M	—	18.00	35.00	80.00	140	—
1757/6 M	—	15.00	30.00	75.00	125	—
1757 M	—	18.00	35.00	80.00	150	—

KM# 86.2 2 REALES
6.7668 g., 0.9170 Silver 0.1995 oz. ASW **Ruler:** Ferdinand VI **Obverse:** Royal and Imperial crowns **Note:** Mint mark M, Mo.

Date	Mintage	VG	F	VF	XF	Unc
1757 M	—	15.00	30.00	75.00	125	—
1758 M	—	15.00	30.00	75.00	125	—
1759/8 M	—	15.00	30.00	75.00	125	—
1759 M	—	20.00	40.00	90.00	175	—
1760 M	—	20.00	40.00	90.00	175	—

KM# 87 2 REALES
6.7700 g., 0.9170 Silver 0.1996 oz. ASW **Ruler:** Charles III **Mint:** Mexico City **Obverse:** Crowned shield flanked by R 2 **Obv. Legend:** CAR • III • D • G • HISP • ET IND • R **Reverse:** Crowned globes flanked by crowned pillars with banner, date below **Rev. Legend:** VTRA QUE VNUM **Note:** Mint mark M, Mo.

Date	Mintage	VG	F	VF	XF	Unc
1760 M	—	15.00	30.00	75.00	125	—
1761 M	—	15.00	30.00	75.00	125	—
1762/1 M	—	15.00	30.00	75.00	125	—
1762 M	—	15.00	30.00	75.00	125	—
1763/2 M	—	15.00	30.00	75.00	125	—
1763 M	—	15.00	30.00	75.00	125	—
1764 M	—	15.00	30.00	75.00	125	—
1765 M	—	15.00	30.00	75.00	125	—
1766 M	—	12.00	35.00	80.00	160	—
1767 M	—	15.00	30.00	75.00	125	—
1768/6 M	—	15.00	30.00	75.00	125	—
1768 M	—	15.00	30.00	75.00	125	—
1769 M	—	15.00	30.00	75.00	125	—
1770 M	—	350	550	—	—	—
1770 F Rare	—	—	—	—	—	—
1771 F	—	15.00	30.00	75.00	125	—

KM# 88.1 2 REALES
6.7668 g., 0.9030 Silver 0.1964 oz. ASW **Ruler:** Charles III **Obverse:** Armored bust of Charles III, right **Obv. Legend:** CAROLUS • III • DEI • GRATIA **Reverse:** Inverted FM and mint mark **Note:** Mint mark M, Mo.

Date	Mintage	VG	F	VF	XF	Unc
1772 FM	—	7.00	15.00	30.00	100	—
1773 FM	—	7.00	15.00	30.00	100	—

KM# 88.2 2 REALES
6.7700 g., 0.9030 Silver 0.1965 oz. ASW **Ruler:** Charles III **Mint:** Mexico City **Obverse:** Armored bust od Charles III, right **Obv. Legend:** CAROLUS • III • DEI • GRATIA • **Reverse:** Crowned shield flanked by pillars with banner, normal initials and mint mark **Rev. Legend:** • HISPAN • ET IND • REX • ... **Note:** Mint mark M, Mo.

Date	Mintage	VG	F	VF	XF	Unc
1773 FM	—	7.00	15.00	30.00	100	—
1774 FM	—	7.00	15.00	30.00	100	—
1775 FM	—	7.00	15.00	30.00	100	—
1776 FM	—	7.00	15.00	30.00	100	—
1777 FM	—	7.00	15.00	30.00	100	—
1778/7 FF	—	7.00	15.00	30.00	100	—
1778 F F/M	—	7.00	15.00	30.00	100	—
1778 FF	—	7.00	15.00	30.00	100	—
1779/8 FF	—	7.00	15.00	30.00	100	—
1779 FF	—	7.00	15.00	30.00	100	—
1780 FF	—	7.00	15.00	30.00	100	—
1781 FF	—	7.00	15.00	30.00	100	—
1782/1 FF	—	7.00	15.00	30.00	100	—
1782 FF	—	7.00	15.00	30.00	100	—
1783 FF	—	7.00	15.00	30.00	100	—
1784 FF	—	7.00	15.00	30.00	100	—
1784 FF DEI GRTIA (error)	—	100	150	250	600	—
1784 FM	—	70.00	120	225	575	—

KM# 88.2a 2 REALES

6.7668 g., 0.8960 Silver 0.1949 oz. ASW **Ruler:** Charles III **Mint:** Mexico City **Obverse:** Armored bust of Charles III, right **Reverse:** Crowned shield flanked by pillars with banner **Note:** Mint mark Mo.

Date	Mintage	VG	F	VF	XF	Unc
1785Mo FM	—	7.00	15.00	30.00	100	—
1786Mo FF	—	200	350	550	950	—
1786Mo FM	—	7.00	15.00	30.00	100	—
1787Mo FM	—	7.00	15.00	30.00	100	—
1788/98Mo FM	—	7.00	15.00	30.00	100	—
1788Mo FM	—	7.00	15.00	30.00	100	—
1789Mo FM	—	12.00	25.00	50.00	150	—

KM# 89 2 REALES

6.7700 g., 0.9030 Silver 0.1965 oz. ASW **Ruler:** Charles IV **Mint:** Mexico City **Obverse:** Armored bust of Charles IV, right **Obv. Legend:** CAROLUS • IV • DEI • GRATIA • **Reverse:** Crowned shield flanked by pillars with banner **Rev. Legend:** • HISPAN • ET IND • REX • ... **Note:** Mint mark M, Mo.

Date	Mintage	VG	F	VF	XF	Unc
1789 FM	—	15.00	30.00	75.00	200	—
1790 FM	—	15.00	30.00	75.00	200	—

KM# 90 2 REALES

6.7700 g., 0.9030 Silver 0.1965 oz. ASW **Ruler:** Charles IV **Mint:** Mexico City **Obverse:** Armored bust of Charles IIII, right **Obv. Legend:** CAROLUS • IIII • DEI • GRATIA • **Reverse:** Crowned shield flanked by pillars with banner **Rev. Legend:** • HISPAN • ET IND REX • ... **Note:** Mint mark M, Mo.

Date	Mintage	VG	F	VF	XF	Unc
1790 FM	—	17.00	35.00	80.00	200	—

KM# 91 2 REALES

6.7668 g., 0.8960 Silver 0.1949 oz. ASW **Ruler:** Charles III **Mint:** Mexico City **Obverse:** Armored bust of Charles IIII, right **Obv. Legend:** CAROLUS • IIII • DEI • GRATIA • **Reverse:** Crowned shield flanked by pillars with banner **Rev. Legend:** • HISPAN • ET IND REX • ... **Note:** Mint mark Mo.

Date	Mintage	VG	F	VF	XF	Unc
1792 FM	—	15.00	30.00	60.00	200	—
1793 FM	—	15.00	30.00	60.00	200	—
1794/3 FM	—	50.00	100	200	450	—
1794 FM	—	40.00	75.00	150	400	—
1795 FM	—	7.00	15.00	30.00	85.00	—
1796 FM	—	7.00	15.00	30.00	85.00	—
1797 FM	—	7.00	15.00	30.00	85.00	—
1798 FM	—	7.00	15.00	30.00	85.00	—
1799/8 FM	—	7.00	15.00	32.00	90.00	—
1799 FM	—	7.00	15.00	30.00	85.00	—
1800 FM	—	7.00	15.00	30.00	85.00	—

KM# 94 4 REALES

13.5337 g., 0.9170 Silver 0.3990 oz. ASW **Ruler:** Philip V **Mint:** Mexico City **Obverse:** Crowned shield flanked by F 4 **Obv. Legend:** PHILLIP • V • D • G • HISPAN • ET IND • REX **Reverse:** Crowned globes flanked by crowned pillars with banner, date below **Rev. Legend:** VTRAQUE VNUM **Note:** Mint mark M, Mo, MX.

Date	Mintage	VG	F	VF	XF	Unc
1732 Rare; Specimen	—	—	—	—	—	—
1732 F	—	2,000	3,000	5,000	10,000	—
1733/2 F	—	1,500	2,000	4,000	6,500	—
1733 MF	—	1,100	1,650	2,250	4,250	—
1733 MF (MX)	—	1,500	2,200	3,250	5,500	—
1733 MX/XM	—	1,500	2,200	3,250	5,500	—
1734/3 MF	—	150	300	600	1,200	—
1734 MF	—	150	300	600	1,200	—
1735/4 MF	—	100	175	300	600	—
1735 MF	—	100	175	300	600	—
1736 MF	—	100	175	300	600	—
1737 MF	—	100	175	300	600	—
1738/7 MF	—	100	175	300	600	—
1738 MF	—	100	175	300	600	—
1739 MF	—	100	175	300	600	—
1740/30 MF	—	100	200	325	625	—
1740 MF	—	100	175	300	600	—
1741 MF	—	100	175	300	600	—
1742/1 MF	—	100	175	300	600	—
1742/32 MF	—	100	175	300	600	—
1742 MF	—	100	175	300	600	—
1743 MF	—	100	175	300	600	—
1744/3 MF	—	100	200	325	625	—
1744 MF	—	100	175	300	600	—
1745 MF	—	100	175	300	600	—
1746 MF	—	100	175	300	600	—
1747 MF	—	150	275	400	650	—

KM# 95 4 REALES

13.5400 g., 0.9170 Silver 0.3992 oz. ASW **Ruler:** Ferdinand VI **Mint:** Mexico City **Obverse:** Crowned shield flanked by M F 4 **Obv. Legend:** FERDND • VI • D • G • HISPAN • ET IND • REX **Reverse:** Crowned globes flanked by crowned pillars with banner, date below **Rev. Legend:** ....QUE VNUM **Note:** Struck at Mexico City Mint, mint mark M, Mo.

Date	Mintage	VG	F	VF	XF	Unc
1747 MF	—	100	150	300	550	—
1748/7 MF	—	100	150	300	550	—
1748 MF	—	100	125	250	500	—
1749 MF	—	150	225	350	650	—
1750/40 MF	—	100	125	250	500	—
1751/41 MF	—	100	125	250	500	—
1751 MF	—	100	125	250	500	—
1752 MF	—	100	125	250	500	—
1753 MF	—	100	125	300	550	—
1754 MF	—	250	375	500	850	—
1755 MM	—	100	125	250	500	—
1756 MM	—	100	150	300	550	—
1757 MM	—	100	150	300	550	—
1758 MM	—	100	125	250	500	—
1759 MM	—	100	125	250	500	—
1760/59 MM	—	100	175	350	600	—
1760 MM	—	100	175	350	600	—

KM# 96 4 REALES

13.5400 g., 0.9170 Silver 0.3992 oz. ASW **Ruler:** Charles III **Mint:** Mexico City **Obverse:** Crowned shield flanked by F M 4 **Obv. Legend:** CAROLVS • III • D • G • HISPAN • ET IND • REX **Reverse:** Crowned globes flanked by crowned pillars with banner, date below **Rev. Legend:** ...AQUE VNUM **Note:** Mint mark M, Mo.

Date	Mintage	VG	F	VF	XF	Unc
1760 MM	—	100	150	250	900	—
1761 MM	—	100	150	250	900	—
1761 MM Cross between H and I	—	100	150	250	900	—
1762 MM	—	75.00	125	250	500	—
1763/1 MM	—	100	150	300	600	—
1763 MM	—	100	150	300	600	—
1764 MM	—	400	600	1,000	2,000	—
1764 MF	—	350	500	1,000	2,000	—
1765 MF	—	350	500	1,000	2,000	—
1766 MF	—	250	350	550	1,250	—
1767 MF	—	100	150	300	600	—
1768 MF	—	75.00	125	250	500	—
1769 MF	—	75.00	125	250	500	—
1770 MF	—	75.00	125	250	500	—
1771 MF	—	125	200	325	700	—

KM# 97.1 4 REALES

13.5337 g., 0.9030 Silver 0.3929 oz. ASW **Ruler:** Charles III **Mint:** Mexico City **Obverse:** Armored bust of Charles III, right **Obv. Legend:** CAROLUS • III • DEI • GRATIA • **Reverse:** Crowned shield flanked by pillars with banner, inverted FM and mint mark **Rev. Legend:** • HISPAN • ET IND REX • ... **Note:** Mint mark M, Mo.

Date	Mintage	VG	F	VF	XF	Unc
1772 FM	—	90.00	125	250	500	—
1773 FM	—	100	175	300	650	—

KM# 97.2 4 REALES

13.5400 g., 0.9030 Silver 0.3931 oz. ASW **Ruler:** Charles III **Mint:** Mexico City **Obverse:** Armored bust of Charles III, right **Obv. Legend:** CAROLUS • III • DEI • GRATIA • **Reverse:** Crowned shield flanked by pillars with banner, normal initials and mint mark **Rev. Legend:** • HISPAN • ET IND REX • ... **Note:** Mint mark M, Mo.

Date	Mintage	VG	F	VF	XF	Unc
1774 FM	—	50.00	100	200	500	—
1775 FM	—	50.00	100	200	500	—
1776 FM	—	50.00	100	200	500	—
1777 FM	—	50.00	100	200	500	—
1778 FF	—	50.00	100	200	500	—
1779 FF	—	50.00	100	200	500	—
1780 FF	—	50.00	100	200	500	—
1781 FF	—	50.00	100	200	500	—
1782 FF	—	50.00	100	200	500	—
1783 FF	—	50.00	100	200	500	—
1784 FF	—	50.00	100	200	500	—
1784 FM	—	100	200	350	600	—

KM# 97.2a 4 REALES

13.5337 g., 0.8960 Silver 0.3898 oz. ASW **Ruler:** Charles III **Obverse:** Armored bust of Charles III, right **Obv. Legend:** CAROLUS • III • DEI • GRATIA • **Reverse:** Crowned shield flanked by pillars with banner, normal initials and mint mark **Rev. Legend:** • HISPAN • ET IND REX • ... **Note:** Mint mark M, Mo.

Date	Mintage	VG	F	VF	XF	Unc
1785 FM	—	100	200	350	600	—
1786 FM	—	50.00	100	200	500	—
1787 FM	—	50.00	100	200	500	—
1788 FM	—	50.00	100	200	500	—
1789 FM	—	50.00	100	200	500	—

KM# 98 4 REALES

13.5400 g., 0.9030 Silver 0.3931 oz. ASW **Ruler:** Charles IV **Mint:** Mexico City **Obverse:** Armored bust of Charles III, right **Obv. Legend:** CAROLUS • IV • DEI • GRATIA • **Reverse:** Crowned shield flanked by pillars with banner **Rev. Legend:** • HISPAN • ET IND REX • ... **Note:** Mintint mark M, Mo, using old bust punch.

Date	Mintage	VG	F	VF	XF	Unc
1789 FM	—	65.00	125	250	550	—
1790 FM	—	50.00	100	200	500	—

KM# 99 4 REALES

13.5400 g., 0.9030 Silver 0.3931 oz. ASW **Ruler:** Charles IV **Mint:** Mexico City **Obverse:** Armored bust of Charles III, right **Obv. Legend:** CAROLUS • IIII • DEI • GRATIA • **Reverse:** Crowned shield flanked by pillars with banner **Rev. Legend:** • HISPAN • ET IND • REX • ... **Note:** Mint mark M, Mo, using old bust punch.

Date	Mintage	VG	F	VF	XF	Unc
1790 FM	—	65.00	125	250	550	—

KM# 100 4 REALES

13.5337 g., 0.8960 Silver 0.3898 oz. ASW **Ruler:** Charles IV **Mint:** Mexico City **Obverse:** Armored bust of Charles IIII, right **Obv. Legend:** CAROLUS • IIII • DEI • GRATIA • **Reverse:** Crowned shield flanked by pillars with banner **Rev. Legend:** • HISPAN • ET IND • REX • ... **Note:** Mint mark Mo.

Date	Mintage	VG	F	VF	XF	Unc
1792 FM	—	35.00	65.00	150	400	—
1793 FM	—	75.00	125	200	500	—
1794/3 FM	—	35.00	65.00	150	400	—
1794 FM	—	35.00	65.00	150	400	—
1795 FM	—	35.00	65.00	150	400	—
1796 FM	—	150	250	400	800	—
1797 FM	—	60.00	120	200	500	—
1798/7 FM	—	35.00	65.00	150	400	—
1798 FM	—	35.00	65.00	150	400	—
1799 FM	—	35.00	65.00	150	400	—
1800 FM	—	35.00	65.00	150	400	—

KM# 103 8 REALES

27.0674 g., 0.9170 Silver 0.7980 oz. ASW **Ruler:** Philip V **Mint:** Mexico City **Obverse:** Crowned shield flanked by M F 8 **Obv. Legend:** PHILIP ? V ? D ? G ? HISPAN ? ET IND ? REX **Reverse:** Crowned globes flanked by crowned pillars with banner, date below **Rev. Legend:** ...VNUM **Note:** Mint mark M, Mo, MX.

Date	Mintage	VG	F	VF	XF	Unc
1732 F	—	2,750	4,750	8,000	—	—
1733/2 F (MX)	—	3,000	5,250	9,000	—	—
1733 F	—	2,000	3,000	5,000	9,000	—
1733 MF Large crown; Rare	—	—	—	—	—	—
1733 F (MX) Rare	—	—	—	—	—	—
Note: Rare; Bonhams Patterson sale 7-96 VF 1733 F (MX) realized $11,710						
1733 MF (MX) Rare	—	—	—	—	—	—
1733 MF Small crown	—	700	1,500	2,500	4,250	—
1734/3 MF	—	100	150	275	575	—
1734 MF	—	100	150	250	450	—
1735 MF	—	100	150	250	450	—
1736/5 MF	—	100	150	275	575	—
1736 MF Small planchet	—	100	150	250	450	—
1736 MF	—	100	150	250	450	—
1737 MF	—	65.00	100	200	400	—
1738/6 MF	—	65.00	100	200	400	—
1738/7 MF	—	65.00	100	200	400	—
1738 MF	—	65.00	100	200	400	—
1739/6 MF 9 over inverted 6	—	65.00	100	200	400	—
1739 MF	—	65.00	100	200	400	—
1740/30 MF	—	100	150	275	500	—
1740/39 MF	—	100	150	275	500	—
1740 MF	—	65.00	100	200	400	—
1741/31 MF	—	65.00	100	200	400	—
1741 MF	—	65.00	100	200	400	—
1742/32 MF	—	75.00	125	220	500	—
1742/1 MF	—	65.00	100	200	400	—
1742 MF	—	65.00	100	200	400	—
1743/2 MF	—	65.00	100	200	400	—
1743 MF	—	65.00	100	200	400	—
1744/34 MF	—	65.00	100	200	400	—
1744/3 MF	—	65.00	100	200	400	—
1744 MF	—	65.00	100	200	400	—
1745/4 MF	—	65.00	100	200	425	—
1745 MF	—	65.00	100	200	400	—
1746/5 MF	—	100	150	275	575	—
1746 MF	—	65.00	100	200	400	—
1747 MF	—	65.00	100	200	400	—

KM# 104.1 8 REALES

27.0674 g., 0.9170 Silver 0.7980 oz. ASW **Ruler:** Ferdinand VI **Mint:** Mexico City **Obverse:** Crowned shield flaned by M F 8 **Obv. Legend:** FERDND • VI • D • G • HISPAN • ET IND • REX **Reverse:** Crowned globes flanked by crowned pillars with banner, date below **Rev. Legend:** ...VNUM M **Note:** Mint mark M, Mo.

Date	Mintage	VG	F	VF	XF	Unc
1747 MF	—	55.00	100	175	300	—
1748/7 MF	—	60.00	120	250	450	—
1748 MF	—	50.00	75.00	125	250	—
1749 MF	—	50.00	75.00	125	250	—
1749/8 MF	—	50.00	75.00	125	250	—
1750 MF	—	50.00	75.00	125	250	—
1751/0 MF	—	55.00	100	165	275	—
1751 MF	—	50.00	75.00	125	250	—
1752/1 MF	—	55.00	100	165	275	—
1752 MF	—	50.00	75.00	125	250	—
1753/2 MF	—	50.00	75.00	125	250	—
1753 MF	—	55.00	100	165	275	—
1754/3 MF	—	55.00	100	185	325	—
1754 MF	—	50.00	75.00	125	250	—
1754 MM/MF	—	300	700	1,500	3,500	—
1754 MM	—	300	700	1,500	3,500	—

KM# 104.2 8 REALES

27.0674 g., 0.9170 Silver 0.7980 oz. ASW **Ruler:** Ferdinand VI **Mint:** Mexico City **Obverse:** Crowned shield flanked by M M 8 **Obv. Legend:** FERDND • VI • D • G • HISPAN • ET IND • REX **Reverse:** Imperial crown on left pillar **Rev. Legend:** ...VNUM M **Note:** Mint mark M, Mo.

Date	Mintage	VG	F	VF	XF	Unc
1754 MM	—	60.00	110	200	375	—
1754 MM/MF	—	75.00	125	250	500	—
1754 MF	—	150	285	550	950	—
1755/4 MM	—	55.00	100	185	325	—
1755 MM	—	50.00	75.00	125	250	—
1756/5 MM	—	55.00	100	165	275	—
1756 MM	—	50.00	75.00	125	250	—
1757/6 MM	—	50.00	75.00	125	250	—
1757 MM	—	55.00	100	185	325	—
1758 MM	—	50.00	75.00	125	250	—
1759 MM	—	50.00	75.00	125	250	—
1760/59 MM	—	55.00	100	165	275	—
1760 MM	—	50.00	75.00	125	250	—

KM# 105 8 REALES

27.0674 g., 0.9170 Silver 0.7980 oz. ASW **Ruler:** Charles III **Mint:** Mexico City **Obverse:** Crowned shield flanked by M M 8 **Obv. Legend:** CAROLUS • III • D • G • HISPAN • ET IND • REX **Reverse:** Crowned globes flanked by crowned pillars with banner, date below **Rev. Legend:** ...E VNUM M **Note:** Mint mark M, Mo.

Date	Mintage	VG	F	VF	XF	Unc
1760/59 MM	—	450	700	—	—	—
Note: CAROLUS. III/Ferdin. Vi						
1760 MM	—	60.00	100	150	325	—
Note: CAROLUS. III/FERDIN. VI. recut die						
1760 MM	—	60.00	100	150	300	—
1761/50 MM	—	65.00	110	165	325	—

Date	Mintage	VG	F	VF	XF	Unc
Note: Tip of cross between I and S in legend						
1761/51 MM	—	65.00	110	165	325	—
Note: Tip of cross between I and S in legend						
1761/0 MM	—	65.00	110	165	325	—
Note: Tip of cross between H and I in legend						
1761 MM	—	60.00	100	150	275	—
Note: Cross under I in legend						
1761 MM	—	60.00	100	150	275	—
Note: Tip of cross between H and I in legend						
1761 MM	—	65.00	110	165	325	—
Note: Tip of cross between I and S in legend						
1762/1 MM	—	70.00	120	175	450	—
Note: Tip of cross between H and I in legend						
1762/1 MM	—	70.00	120	175	450	—
1762 MM	—	60.00	100	150	275	—
Note: Tip of cross between H and I in legend						
1762 MM	—	50.00	75.00	125	250	—
Note: Tip of cross between I and S in legend						
1762 MF	—	500	750	1,250	2,300	—
1763/2 MM	—	300	450	750	1,350	—
1763 MM	—	450	650	1,150	2,250	—
1763/1 MF	—	50.00	75.00	125	250	—
1763/2 MF	—	50.00	75.00	125	250	—
1763 MF	—	50.00	75.00	125	250	—
1764 MF	—	50.00	75.00	125	250	—
Note: CAR/CRA						
1764 MF	—	50.00	75.00	125	250	—
1765 MF	—	50.00	75.00	125	250	—
1766/5 MF	—	75.00	150	225	575	—
1766 MF	—	50.00	75.00	125	250	—
1767/6 MF	—	50.00	75.00	125	250	—
1767 MF	—	50.00	75.00	125	250	—
1768/7 MF	—	85.00	165	250	600	—
1768 MF	—	50.00	75.00	125	250	—
1769 MF	—	50.00	75.00	125	250	—
1770/60 MF	—	100	185	300	650	—
1770 MF	—	50.00	75.00	125	250	—
1770/60 FM	—	100	185	300	650	—
1770/69 FM	—	100	185	300	650	—
1770 FM/F	—	50.00	75.00	125	250	—
1770 FM	—	50.00	75.00	125	250	—
1771/0 FM	—	50.00	75.00	125	250	—
1771 FM	—	50.00	75.00	125	250	—

KM# 106.1 8 REALES

27.0674 g., 0.9030 Silver 0.7858 oz. ASW **Ruler:** Charles III **Mint:** Mexico City **Obverse:** Armored bust of Charles III, right **Obv. Legend:** CAROLUS • III • DEI • GRATIA • **Reverse:** Crowned shield flanked by pillars with banner, inverted initials and mint mark **Rev. Legend:** • HISPAN • ET IND • REX • ... **Note:** Two varieties exist, one with inverted initials "F.M." (left), and one with normal presentation (right). Mint mark M, Mo.

Date	Mintage	VG	F	VF	XF	Unc
1772 FM	—	25.00	50.00	120	250	—
1772 FM Inverted	—	150	350	750	1,250	—
1773 FM	—	25.00	50.00	100	175	—

KM# 106.2 8 REALES

27.0674 g., 0.9030 Silver 0.7858 oz. ASW **Ruler:** Charles III **Obverse:** Armored bust of Charles III, right **Obv. Legend:** CAROLUS • III • DEI • GRATIA • **Reverse:** Crowned shield flanked by pillars with banner, normal initials and mint mark **Rev. Legend:** • HISPAN • ET IND • REX • ... **Note:** Mint mark M, Mo.

Date	Mintage	VG	F	VF	XF	Unc
1773 FM	—	25.00	50.00	80.00	160	—
1774 FM	—	25.00	45.00	75.00	150	—
1775 FM	—	25.00	45.00	75.00	150	—
1776 FM	—	25.00	45.00	75.00	150	—
1777/6 FM	—	35.00	65.00	180	300	—
1777 FM	—	25.00	45.00	75.00	150	—
1777 FF	—	35.00	50.00	100	250	—
1778 FM	—	—	—	—	—	—
Note: Superior Casterline sale 5-89 VF realized $17,600						
1778/7 FF	—	25.00	45.00	75.00	150	—
1778 FF	—	25.00	45.00	75.00	150	—
1779 FF	—	25.00	45.00	75.00	150	—
1780 FF	—	25.00	45.00	75.00	150	—
1781 FF	—	25.00	45.00	75.00	150	—
1782 FF	—	25.00	45.00	75.00	150	—
1783 FF	—	25.00	45.00	75.00	150	—
1783 FM	—	4,000	6,000	9,000	—	—
1784 FF	—	150	300	500	1,250	—
1784 FM	—	25.00	45.00	75.00	150	—

KM# 106.2a 8 REALES

27.0674 g., 0.8960 Silver 0.7797 oz. ASW **Ruler:** Charles III **Obverse:** Armored bust of Charles III, right **Obv. Legend:** CAROLUS • III • DEI • GRATIA • **Reverse:** Crowned shield flanked by pillars with banner, normal initials and mint mark **Rev. Legend:** • HISPAN • ET IND • REX • ... **Note:** Mint mark M, Mo.

Date	Mintage	VG	F	VF	XF	Unc
1785 FM	—	25.00	45.00	75.00	150	—
1786/5 FM	—	50.00	100	200	400	—
1786 FM	—	25.00	45.00	75.00	150	—
1787/6 FM	—	100	250	450	1,200	—
1787 FM	—	25.00	45.00	75.00	150	—
1788 FM	—	25.00	45.00	75.00	150	—
1789 FM	—	50.00	100	150	225	—

KM# 107 8 REALES

27.0674 g., 0.9030 Silver 0.7858 oz. ASW **Ruler:** Charles IV **Mint:** Mexico City **Obverse:** Armored bust of Charles III, right **Obv. Legend:** CAROLUS • IV • DEI • GRATIA • **Reverse:** Crowned shield flanked by pillars with banner **Rev. Legend:** • HISPAN • ET IND • REX • ... **Note:** Mint mark M, Mo, using old bust punch.

Date	Mintage	VG	F	VF	XF	Unc
1789 FM	—	40.00	65.00	120	250	—
1790 FM	—	30.00	50.00	100	200	—

KM# 108 8 REALES

27.0674 g., 0.9030 Silver 0.7858 oz. ASW **Ruler:** Charles IV **Mint:** Mexico City **Obverse:** Armored bust of Charles III, right **Obv. Legend:** CAROLUS • IIII • DEI • GRATIA • **Reverse:** Crowned shield flanked by pillars with banner **Rev. Legend:** • HISPAN • ET IND • REX • ... **Note:** Mint mark M, Mo, using old portait punch.

Date	Mintage	VG	F	VF	XF	Unc
1790 FM	—	30.00	50.00	100	200	—

KM# 109 8 REALES

27.0674 g., 0.8960 Silver 0.7797 oz. ASW **Ruler:** Charles IV **Mint:** Mexico City **Obverse:** Armored bust of Charles IIII, right **Obv. Inscription:** CAROLUS • IIII • DEI • GRATIA • **Reverse:** Crowned shield flanked by pillars with banner **Rev. Legend:** • HISPAN • ET IND • REX • ... **Note:** Mint mark Mo.

Date	Mintage	VG	F	VF	XF	Unc
1791 FM	—	20.00	35.00	50.00	100	—
1792 FM	—	20.00	35.00	50.00	100	—
1793 FM	—	20.00	35.00	50.00	100	—
1794 FM	—	20.00	35.00	50.00	100	—
1795/4 FM	—	20.00	35.00	50.00	100	—
1795 FM	—	20.00	35.00	50.00	100	—
1796 FM	—	20.00	35.00	50.00	100	—
1797 FM	—	20.00	35.00	50.00	100	—
1798 FM	—	20.00	35.00	50.00	100	—
1799 FM	—	20.00	35.00	50.00	100	—
1800/700 FM	—	20.00	35.00	50.00	100	—
1800 FM	—	20.00	35.00	50.00	100	—
1801/0 FT/FM	—	20.00	35.00	50.00	100	—
1801/791 FM	—	35.00	60.00	100	250	—
1801/0 FM	—	35.00	60.00	100	250	—

KM# 113 ESCUDO

3.3834 g., 0.9170 Gold 0.0997 oz. AGW **Ruler:** Philip V **Mint:** Mexico City **Obverse:** Armored bust right **Obv. Legend:** PHILIP • V • D • G • HISPAN • ET IND • REX **Reverse:** Crowned shield flanked by M F I **Note:** Mint mark M, Mo.

Date	Mintage	VG	F	VF	XF	Unc
1732 F	—	1,000	2,000	3,000	4,000	—
1733/2 F	—	1,000	2,000	3,000	4,000	—
1734/3 MF	—	150	250	400	850	—
1735/4 MF	—	150	250	400	850	—
1735 MF	—	150	250	400	850	—
1736/5 MF	—	150	250	400	850	—
1736 MF	—	150	250	400	850	—
1737 MF	—	200	300	600	1,200	—
1738/7 MF	—	200	300	600	1,200	—
1738 MF	—	200	300	600	1,200	—
1739 MF	—	200	300	600	1,200	—
1740/30 MF	—	200	300	600	1,200	—
1741 MF	—	200	300	600	1,200	—
1742 MF	—	200	300	600	1,200	—
1743/2 MF	—	150	275	450	800	—
1743 MF	—	150	250	400	700	—
1744/3 MF	—	150	250	400	700	—
1744 MF	—	150	250	400	700	—
1745 MF	—	150	250	400	700	—
1746/5 MF	—	150	250	400	700	—
1747 MF Rare	—	—	—	—	—	—

KM# 114 ESCUDO

3.3834 g., 0.9170 Gold 0.0997 oz. AGW **Ruler:** Ferdinand VI **Mint:** Mexico City **Obverse:** Armored bust right **Obv. Legend:** FERD • VI • D • G • HISPAN • ET IND • REX **Reverse:** Crowned shield flanked by M F I **Note:** Mint mark M, Mo.

Date	Mintage	VG	F	VF	XF	Unc
1747 MF	—	1,650	3,000	5,000	7,500	—

KM# 115.1 ESCUDO

3.3834 g., 0.9170 Gold 0.0997 oz. AGW **Ruler:** Ferdinand VI **Mint:** Mexico City **Obverse:** Short armored bust right **Obv. Legend:** FERD • VI • D • G • HISPAN • ET IND • REX **Reverse:** Crowned shield **Note:** Mint mark M, Mo.

Date	Mintage	VG	F	VF	XF	Unc
1748 MF	—	250	350	550	950	—
1749 MF	—	300	450	700	1,150	—
1750 MF	—	150	250	400	800	—
1751 MF	—	150	250	400	800	—

KM# 115.2 ESCUDO
3.3834 g., 0.9170 Gold 0.0997 oz. AGW **Ruler:** Ferdinand VI **Mint:** Mexico City **Obverse:** Short armored bust right **Obv. Legend:** FERD • VI • D • G • HISPAN • ET IND • REX **Reverse:** Without 1 S flanking crowned shield **Note:** Mint mark M, Mo.

Date	Mintage	VG	F	VF	XF	Unc
1752 MF	—	125	225	375	750	—
1753/2 MF	—	150	250	400	800	—
1753 MF	—	150	250	400	800	—
1754 MF	—	150	250	400	800	—
1755 MM	—	150	250	400	800	—
1756 MM	—	150	250	400	800	—

KM# A116 ESCUDO
3.3834 g., 0.9170 Gold 0.0997 oz. AGW **Ruler:** Ferdinand VI **Mint:** Mexico City **Obverse:** Armored bust right **Obv. Legend:** FERDIND • VI • D • G • HISPAN • ETIND • REX • **Reverse:** Crowned shield **Rev. Legend:** M • NOMINA MAGNA SEQUOR • M **Note:** Mint mark M, Mo.

Date	Mintage	VG	F	VF	XF	Unc
1757 MM	—	150	250	400	800	—
1759 MM	—	150	250	400	800	—

KM# 116 ESCUDO
3.3834 g., 0.9170 Gold 0.0997 oz. AGW **Ruler:** Charles III **Mint:** Mexico City **Obverse:** Armored bust right **Obv. Legend:** CAROLVS • III • D • G • HISPAN • ET IND • REX **Reverse:** Crowned shield **Rev. Legend:** M • NOMINA MAGNA SEQUOR • M • **Note:** Mint mark M, Mo.

Date	Mintage	VG	F	VF	XF	Unc
1760 MM	—	400	800	1,500	2,500	—
1761/0 MM	—	400	800	1,500	2,500	—
1761 MM	—	400	800	1,500	2,500	—

KM# 117 ESCUDO
3.3834 g., 0.9170 Gold 0.0997 oz. AGW **Ruler:** Charles III **Mint:** Mexico City **Obverse:** Large armored bust right **Obv. Legend:** CAR • III • D • G • HISP • ET IND • R **Reverse:** Crowned shield **Rev. Legend:** IN • UTROQ • FELIX • **Note:** Mint mark M, Mo.

Date	Mintage	VG	F	VF	XF	Unc
1762 MM	—	250	375	600	1,000	—
1763 MM	—	275	425	700	1,100	—
1764 MM	—	250	375	600	1,000	—
1765 MF	—	250	375	600	1,000	—
1766 MF	—	250	375	600	1,000	—
1767 MF	—	250	375	600	1,000	—
1768 MF	—	250	375	600	1,000	—
1769 MF	—	250	375	600	1,000	—
1770 MF	—	250	375	600	1,000	—
1771 MF	—	250	375	600	1,000	—

KM# 118.1 ESCUDO
3.3834 g., 0.9010 Gold 0.0980 oz. AGW **Ruler:** Charles III **Mint:** Mexico City **Obverse:** Large armored bust right **Obv. Legend:** CAROL • III • D • G • HISPAN • ET IND • R **Reverse:** Crowned shield flanked by 1 S within order chain **Rev. Legend:** FELIX • A • D • ... **Note:** Mint mark M, Mo.

Date	Mintage	VG	F	VF	XF	Unc
1772 MF	—	125	150	275	475	—
1772 FM	—	125	150	275	475	—
1773 FM	—	125	150	275	475	—

KM# 118.2 ESCUDO
3.3834 g., 0.9010 Gold 0.0980 oz. AGW **Ruler:** Charles III **Mint:** Mexico City **Obverse:** Large armored bust right **Obv. Legend:** CAROL • III • D • G • HISPAN • ET IND • R **Reverse:** crowned shield in order chain, initials and mint mark inverted **Rev. Legend:** FELIX • A • D • ... **Note:** Mint mark M, Mo.

Date	Mintage	VG	F	VF	XF	Unc
1773 FM	—	125	150	275	475	—
1774 FM	—	125	150	275	475	—
1775 FM	—	125	150	275	475	—
1776 FM	—	125	150	275	475	—
1777 FM	—	125	150	275	475	—
1778 FF	—	125	150	275	475	—
1779 FF	—	125	150	275	475	—
1780 FF	—	125	150	275	475	—
1781 FF	—	125	150	275	475	—
1782 FF	—	125	150	275	475	—
1783/2 FF	—	125	150	275	475	—
1783 FF	—	125	150	275	475	—
1784/3 FF	—	125	150	275	475	—
1784/3 FM/F	—	125	150	275	475	—

KM# 118.2a ESCUDO
3.3800 g., 0.8750 Gold 0.0951 oz. AGW **Ruler:** Charles III **Mint:** Mexico City **Obverse:** Large armored bust right **Obv. Legend:** CAROL • III • D • G • HISPAN • ET IND • R • **Reverse:** Crowned shield in order chain, initials and mint mark inverted **Rev. Legend:** FELIX • A • D • ... **Note:** Mint mark M, Mo.

Date	Mintage	VG	F	VF	XF	Unc
1785 FM	—	125	150	275	475	—
1786 FM	—	125	150	275	475	—
1787 FM	—	125	150	275	475	—
1788 FM	—	125	150	275	475	—

KM# 118.1a ESCUDO
3.3834 g., 0.8750 Gold 0.0952 oz. AGW **Ruler:** Charles III **Mint:** Mexico City **Obverse:** Large armored bust right **Obv. Legend:** CAROL • III • D • G • HISPAN • ET IND • R **Reverse:** Crowned shield in order chain, initial letters and mint mark upright **Rev. Legend:** FELIX • A • D • ... **Note:** Mint mark M, Mo.

Date	Mintage	VG	F	VF	XF	Unc
1788 FM	—	125	150	275	475	—

KM# 119 ESCUDO
3.3834 g., 0.8750 Gold 0.0952 oz. AGW **Ruler:** Charles IV **Mint:** Mexico City **Obverse:** Armored bust of Charles III, right **Obv. Legend:** CAROL • IV • D • G • ... **Reverse:** Crowned shield in order chain, initial letters and mint mark upright **Rev. Legend:** FELIX • A • D • ... **Note:** Mint mark M, Mo, using old portrait punch.

Date	Mintage	VG	F	VF	XF	Unc
1789 FM	—	300	550	1,000	2,000	—
1790 FM	—	300	550	1,000	2,000	—

KM# 120 ESCUDO
3.3834 g., 0.8750 Gold 0.0952 oz. AGW **Ruler:** Charles IV **Mint:** Mexico City **Obverse:** Armored bust right **Obv. Legend:** CAROL • IIII • D • G • ... **Reverse:** Crowned shield in order chain, initial letters and mint mark upright **Rev. Legend:** FELIX • A • D • ... **Note:** Mint mark Mo.

Date	Mintage	VG	F	VF	XF	Unc
1792 MF	—	125	165	235	345	—
1793 FM	—	125	165	235	345	—
1794 FM	—	125	165	235	345	—
1795 FM	—	125	165	235	345	—
1796 FM	—	125	165	235	345	—
1797 FM	—	125	165	235	345	—
1798 FM	—	125	165	235	345	—
1799 FM	—	125	165	235	345	—
1800 FM	—	125	165	235	345	—

KM# 124 2 ESCUDOS
6.7660 g., 0.9170 Gold 0.1995 oz. AGW **Ruler:** Philip V **Mint:** Mexico City **Obverse:** Armored bust right **Obv. Legend:** PHILIP • V • D • G • HISPAN • ET IND • REX **Reverse:** Crowned shield flanked by M F 2 **Rev. Legend:** INITIUM SAPIENTIAE TIMOR DOMINI **Note:** Mint mark M, Mo.

Date	Mintage	VG	F	VF	XF	Unc
1732 F	—	1,000	1,500	2,000	3,000	—
1733 F	—	750	1,000	1,500	2,500	—
1734/3 MF	—	400	500	900	1,400	—
1735 MF	—	400	500	900	1,400	—
1736/5 MF	—	400	500	900	1,400	—
1736 MF	—	400	500	900	1,400	—
1737 MF	—	400	500	900	1,400	—
1738/7 MF	—	400	500	900	1,400	—
1739 MF	—	400	500	900	1,400	—
1740/30 MF	—	400	500	900	1,400	—
1741 MF	—	400	500	900	1,400	—
1742 MF	—	400	500	900	1,400	—
1743 MF	—	400	500	900	1,400	—
1744/2 MF	—	400	500	900	1,400	—
1744 MF	—	400	500	900	1,400	—
1745 MF	—	400	500	900	1,400	—
1746/5 MF	—	400	500	900	1,400	—
1747 MF	—	400	500	900	1,400	—

KM# 125 2 ESCUDOS
6.7660 g., 0.9170 Gold 0.1995 oz. AGW **Ruler:** Ferdinand VI **Mint:** Mexico City **Obverse:** Large armored bust right **Obv. Legend:** FERD • VI • D • G • ... **Reverse:** Crowned shield flanked by M F 2 **Rev. Legend:** INITIUM... **Note:** Mint mark M, Mo.

Date	Mintage	VG	F	VF	XF	Unc
1747 MF	—	3,000	5,500	9,000	15,000	—

KM# 126.1 2 ESCUDOS
6.7660 g., 0.9170 Gold 0.1995 oz. AGW **Ruler:** Ferdinand VI **Mint:** Mexico City **Obverse:** Head right **Obv. Legend:** FERD • VI • D • G • ... **Reverse:** Crowned shield **Rev. Legend:** NOMINA MAGNA SEQUOR **Note:** Mint mark M, Mo.

Date	Mintage	VG	F	VF	XF	Unc
1748 MF	—	450	750	1,500	3,000	—
1749/8 MF	—	450	750	1,500	3,000	—
1750 MF	—	400	700	1,400	2,850	—
1751 MF	—	400	700	1,400	2,850	—

KM# 126.2 2 ESCUDOS
6.7660 g., 0.9170 Gold 0.1995 oz. AGW **Ruler:** Ferdinand VI **Mint:** Mexico City **Obverse:** Head right **Obv. Legend:** FERD • VI • D • G • ... **Reverse:** Without 2 S by crowned shield **Rev. Legend:** NOMINA MAGNA SEQUOR **Note:** Mint mark M, Mo.

Date	Mintage	VG	F	VF	XF	Unc
1752 MF	—	400	700	1,400	2,850	—
1753 MF	—	400	700	1,400	2,850	—
1754 MF	—	600	850	1,750	3,500	—
1755 MM	—	400	700	1,400	2,850	—
1756 MM	—	600	850	1,750	3,500	—

KM# 127 2 ESCUDOS

6.7660 g., 0.9170 Gold 0.1995 oz. AGW **Ruler:** Ferdinand VI **Mint:** Mexico City **Obverse:** Armored bust right **Obv. Legend:** FERDIND • VI • D • G • ... **Reverse:** Without 2 S by crowned shield **Rev. Legend:** NOMINA MAGNA SEQUOR **Note:** Mint mark M, Mo.

Date	Mintage	VG	F	VF	XF	Unc
1757 MM	—	450	750	1,500	3,000	—
1759 MM	—	450	750	1,500	3,000	—

KM# 128 2 ESCUDOS

6.7660 g., 0.9170 Gold 0.1995 oz. AGW **Ruler:** Charles III **Mint:** Mexico City **Obverse:** Armored bust right **Obv. Legend:** CAROLVS • III • D • G • ... **Reverse:** Without 2 S by crowned shield **Rev. Legend:** NOMINA MAGNA SEQUOR **Note:** Mint mark M, Mo.

Date	Mintage	VG	F	VF	XF	Unc
1760 MM	—	550	1,000	2,000	4,000	—
1761 MM	—	550	1,000	2,000	4,000	—

KM# 129 2 ESCUDOS

6.7668 g., 0.9170 Gold 0.1995 oz. AGW **Ruler:** Charles III **Mint:** Mexico City **Obverse:** Large armored bust right **Obv. Legend:** CAROLUS • III • D • G • ... **Reverse:** Without 2 S by crowned shield **Rev. Legend:** IN • UTROQ • FELIX • AUSPICE • DEO **Note:** Mint mark M, Mo.

Date	Mintage	VG	F	VF	XF	Unc
1762 MF	—	500	900	1,850	3,750	—
1763 MF	—	500	900	1,850	3,750	—
1764/3 MF	—	500	900	1,850	3,750	—
1765 MF	—	500	900	1,850	3,750	—
1766 MF	—	500	900	1,850	3,750	—
1767 MF	—	500	900	1,850	3,750	—
1768 MF	—	500	900	1,850	3,750	—
1769 MF	—	500	900	1,850	3,750	—
1770 MF	—	500	900	1,850	3,750	—
1771 MF	—	500	900	1,850	3,750	—

KM# 130.1 2 ESCUDOS

6.7668 g., 0.9010 Gold 0.1960 oz. AGW **Ruler:** Charles III **Mint:** Mexico City **Obverse:** Older, armored bust right **Obv. Legend:** CAROLUS • III • D • G • ... **Reverse:** Crowned shield in order chain, initials and mint mark upright **Rev. Legend:** IN • UTROQ • FELIX • AUSPICE • DEO **Note:** Mint mark M, Mo.

Date	Mintage	VG	F	VF	XF	Unc
1772 FM	—	200	375	550	1,000	—
1773 FM	—	200	375	550	1,000	—

KM# 130.2 2 ESCUDOS

6.7668 g., 0.9010 Gold 0.1960 oz. AGW **Ruler:** Charles III **Mint:** Mexico City **Obverse:** Older, armored bust right **Obv. Legend:** CAROLUS • III • D • G • ... **Reverse:** Crowned shield in order chain, initials and mint mark inverted **Rev. Legend:** IN • UTROQ • FELIX • AUSPICE • DEO **Note:** Mint mark M, Mo.

Date	Mintage	VG	F	VF	XF	Unc
1773 FM	—	200	375	550	1,000	—
1774 FM	—	200	375	550	1,000	—
1775 FM	—	200	375	550	1,000	—
1776 FM	—	200	375	550	1,000	—
1777 FM	—	175	300	450	900	—
1778 FF	—	175	300	450	900	—
1779 FF	—	175	300	450	900	—
1780 FF	—	175	300	450	900	—
1781 FM/M	—	175	300	450	900	—
1781 FF	—	175	300	450	900	—
1782 FF	—	175	300	450	900	—
1783 FF	—	175	300	450	900	—
1784 FF	—	175	300	450	900	—
1784 FM/F	—	175	300	450	900	—

KM# 130.2a 2 ESCUDOS

6.7668 g., 0.8750 Gold 0.1904 oz. AGW **Ruler:** Charles III **Mint:** Mexico City **Obverse:** Older, armored bust right **Obv. Legend:** CAROLUS • III • D • G • ... **Reverse:** Crowned shield in order chain, initials and mint mark inverted **Rev. Legend:** IN • UTROQ • FELIX • AUSPICE • DEO **Note:** Mint mark M, Mo.

Date	Mintage	VG	F	VF	XF	Unc
1785 FM	—	175	300	450	900	—
1786 FM	—	175	300	450	900	—
1787 FM	—	175	300	450	900	—
1788 FM	—	175	300	450	900	—

KM# 130.1a 2 ESCUDOS

6.7668 g., 0.8750 Gold 0.1904 oz. AGW **Ruler:** Charles III **Mint:** Mexico City **Obverse:** Older, armored bust right **Obv. Legend:** CAROLUS • III • D • G • ... **Reverse:** Crowned shield in order chain, initials and mint mark upright **Rev. Legend:** IN • UTROQ • FELIX • AUSPICE • DEO **Note:** Mint mark M, Mo.

Date	Mintage	VG	F	VF	XF	Unc
1788 FM	—	175	300	450	900	—

KM# 131 2 ESCUDOS

6.7668 g., 0.8750 Gold 0.1904 oz. AGW **Ruler:** Charles IV **Mint:** Mexico City **Obverse:** Armored bust of Charles III, right **Obv. Legend:** CAROL • IV • D • G • ... **Reverse:** Crowned shield in order chain, initials and mint mark upright **Rev. Legend:** IN • UTROQ • FELIX • AUSPICE • DEO **Note:** Mint mark M, Mo, using old portrait punch.

Date	Mintage	VG	F	VF	XF	Unc
1789 FM	—	650	1,200	2,000	3,500	—
1790 FM	—	650	1,200	2,000	3,500	—

KM# 132 2 ESCUDOS

6.7668 g., 0.8750 Gold 0.1904 oz. AGW **Ruler:** Charles IV **Mint:** Mexico City **Obverse:** Armored bust of Charles IIII, right **Obv. Legend:** CAROL • IIII • D • G • ... **Reverse:** Crowned shield flanked by 2 S in order chain **Rev. Legend:** IN • UTROQ • FELIX • AUSPICE • DEO; initials and mint mark upright **Note:** Mint mark Mo.

Date	Mintage	VG	F	VF	XF	Unc
1791 FM Mo over inverted Mo	—	300	375	600	950	—
1792 FM	—	125	225	350	575	—
1793 FM	—	125	225	350	575	—
1794 FM	—	125	225	350	575	—
1795 FM	—	125	225	350	575	—
1796 FM	—	125	225	350	575	—
1797 FM	—	125	225	350	575	—
1798 FM	—	125	225	350	575	—
1799 FM	—	125	225	350	575	—
1800 FM	—	125	225	350	575	—

KM# 135 4 ESCUDOS

13.5337 g., 0.9170 Gold 0.3990 oz. AGW **Ruler:** Philip V **Mint:** Mexico City **Obverse:** Armored bust right **Obv. Legend:** PHILIP • V • D • G • HISPAN • ET IND • REX **Reverse:** Crowned shield flanked by F 4 **Rev. Legend:** INITIUM SAPIENTIAE TIMOR DOMINI **Note:** Mint mark M, Mo.

Date	Mintage	VG	F	VF	XF	Unc
1732 Rare	—	—	—	—	—	—
1732 F Rare	—	—	—	—	—	—
1733 F Rare	—	—	—	—	—	—
1734/3 F	—	1,000	1,500	2,800	4,500	—
1734 MF	—	850	1,350	2,500	4,250	—
1735 MF	—	850	1,350	2,500	4,500	—
1736 MF	—	850	1,350	2,500	4,500	—
1737 MF	—	750	1,250	2,400	4,000	—
1738/7 MF	—	750	1,250	2,400	4,000	—
1738 MF	—	750	1,250	2,400	4,000	—
1739 MF	—	750	1,250	2,400	4,000	—
1740/30 MF	—	750	1,250	2,400	4,000	—
1740 MF	—	750	1,250	2,400	4,000	—
1741 MF	—	750	1,250	2,400	4,000	—
1742/32 MF	—	750	1,250	2,400	4,000	—
1743 MF	—	750	1,250	2,400	4,000	—
1744 MD	—	750	1,250	2,400	4,000	—
1745 MF	—	750	1,250	2,400	4,000	—
1746 MF	—	750	1,250	2,400	4,000	—
1747 MF	—	750	1,250	2,400	4,000	—
1746/5 MF	—	750	1,250	2,400	4,000	—

KM# 136 4 ESCUDOS

13.5337 g., 0.9170 Gold 0.3990 oz. AGW **Ruler:** Ferdinand VI **Mint:** Mexico City **Obverse:** Large, armored bust right **Obv. Legend:** FERDND • VI • D • G • ... **Reverse:** Crowned shield flanked by F 4 **Rev. Legend:** INITIUM SAPIENTIAE TIMOR DOMINI **Note:** Mint mark M, Mo.

Date	Mintage	VG	F	VF	XF	Unc
1747 MF	—	7,500	13,500	20,000	30,000	—

KM# 137 4 ESCUDOS

13.5337 g., 0.9170 Gold 0.3990 oz. AGW **Ruler:** Ferdinand VI **Mint:** Mexico City **Obverse:** Armored bust right **Obv. Legend:** FERDND • VI • D • G • ... **Reverse:** Crowned shield flanked by 4 S **Rev. Legend:** NOMINA MAGNA SEQUOR **Note:** Mint mark M, Mo.

Date	Mintage	VG	F	VF	XF	Unc
1748 MF	—	1,500	3,000	5,000	8,000	—
1749 MF	—	1,500	3,000	5,000	8,000	—
1750/48 MF	—	1,500	3,000	5,000	8,000	—
1750 MF	—	1,500	3,000	5,000	8,000	—
1751 MF	—	1,500	3,000	5,000	8,000	—

KM# 138 4 ESCUDOS

13.5337 g., 0.9170 Gold 0.3990 oz. AGW **Ruler:** Ferdinand VI **Mint:** Mexico City **Obverse:** Small, armored bust right **Obv. Legend:** FERDND • VI • D • G • ... **Reverse:** Crowned shield, without value **Rev. Legend:** NOMINA MAGNA... **Note:** Mint mark M, Mo.

Date	Mintage	VG	F	VF	XF	Unc
1752 MF	—	1,000	2,000	3,500	6,000	—
1753 MF	—	1,000	2,000	3,500	6,000	—
1754 MF	—	1,000	2,000	3,500	6,000	—
1755 MM	—	1,000	2,000	3,500	6,000	—
1756 MM	—	1,000	2,000	3,500	6,000	—

KM# 139 4 ESCUDOS

13.5337 g., 0.9170 Gold 0.3990 oz. AGW **Ruler:** Ferdinand VI **Mint:** Mexico City **Obverse:** Armored bust right **Obv. Legend:** FERDND • VI • D • G • ... **Reverse:** Crowned shield, without value **Rev. Legend:** NOMINA MAGNA... **Note:** Mint mark M, Mo.

Date	Mintage	VG	F	VF	XF	Unc
1757 MM	—	1,250	2,500	4,000	6,500	—
1759 MM	—	1,250	2,500	4,000	6,500	—

KM# 140 4 ESCUDOS

13.5337 g., 0.9170 Gold 0.3990 oz. AGW **Ruler:** Charles III **Mint:** Mexico City **Obverse:** Armored bust right **Obv. Legend:** CAROLVS • III • D • G • ... **Reverse:** Crowned shield, without value **Rev. Legend:** NOMINA MAGNA SEQUOR **Note:** Mint mark M, Mo.

Date	Mintage	VG	F	VF	XF	Unc
1760 MM	—	3,500	6,500	10,000	20,000	—
1761 MM	—	3,500	6,500	10,000	20,000	—

KM# 141 4 ESCUDOS

13.5337 g., 0.9170 Gold 0.3990 oz. AGW **Ruler:** Charles III **Mint:** Mexico City **Obverse:** Large, armored bust right **Obv. Legend:** CAROLUS • III • D • G •... **Reverse:** Crowned shield in order chain, without value **Rev. Legend:** IN • UTROQ • FELIX • AUSPICE • DEO **Note:** Mint mark M, Mo.

Date	Mintage	VG	F	VF	XF	Unc
1762 MF	—	2,500	4,500	7,500	15,000	—
1763 MF	—	2,500	4,500	7,500	15,000	—
1764 MF	—	2,500	4,500	7,500	15,000	—
1765 MF	—	2,500	4,500	7,500	15,000	—
1766/5 MF	—	2,500	4,500	7,500	15,000	—
1767 MF	—	2,500	4,500	7,500	15,000	—
1768 MF	—	2,500	4,500	7,500	15,000	—
1769 MF	—	2,500	4,500	7,500	15,000	—
1770 MF	—	2,500	4,500	7,500	15,000	—
1771 MF	—	2,500	4,500	7,500	15,000	—

KM# 142.1 4 ESCUDOS

13.5337 g., 0.9010 Gold 0.3920 oz. AGW **Ruler:** Charles III **Mint:** Mexico City **Obverse:** Large, armored bust right **Obv. Legend:** CAROL • III • D • G • ... **Reverse:** Crowned shield in order chain, initials and mint mark upright **Rev. Legend:** IN • UTROQ • FELIX • AUSPICE • DEO **Note:** Mint mark M, Mo.

Date	Mintage	VG	F	VF	XF	Unc
1772 FM	—	400	650	1,000	2,000	—
1773 FM	—	400	650	1,000	2,000	—

KM# 142.2 4 ESCUDOS

13.5337 g., 0.9010 Gold 0.3920 oz. AGW **Ruler:** Charles III **Mint:** Mexico City **Obverse:** Large, armored bust right **Obv. Legend:** CAROL • III • D • G • ... **Reverse:** Crowned shield flanked by 4 S in order chain, initials and mint mark inverted **Rev. Legend:** IN • UTROQ • FELIX • AUSPICE • DEO **Note:** Mint mark M, Mo.

Date	Mintage	VG	F	VF	XF	Unc
1773 FM	—	400	600	900	1,850	—
1774 FM	—	400	600	900	1,850	—
1775 FM	—	400	600	900	1,850	—
1776 FM	—	400	600	900	1,850	—
1777 FM	—	400	600	900	1,850	—
1778 FF	—	400	600	900	1,850	—
1779 FF	—	400	600	900	1,850	—
1780 FF	—	400	600	900	1,850	—
1781 FF	—	400	600	900	1,850	—
1782 FF	—	400	600	900	1,850	—
1783 FF	—	400	600	900	1,850	—
1784 FF	—	400	600	900	1,850	—
1784/3 FM/F	—	400	600	900	1,850	—
1785 FM	—	400	600	900	1,850	—
1786 FM/F	—	400	600	900	1,850	—
1786 FM	—	400	600	900	1,850	—
1787 FM	—	400	600	900	1,850	—
1788 FM	—	400	600	900	1,850	—

KM# 142.2a 4 ESCUDOS

13.5337 g., 0.8750 Gold 0.3807 oz. AGW **Ruler:** Charles III **Mint:** Mexico City **Obverse:** Large, armored bust right **Obv. Legend:** CAROL • III • D • G • ... **Reverse:** Crowned shield in order chain, initials and mint mark inverted **Rev. Legend:** IN • UTROQ • FELIX • AUSPICE • DEO **Note:** Mint mark M, Mo.

KM# 142.1a 4 ESCUDOS

13.5337 g., 0.8750 Gold 0.3807 oz. AGW **Ruler:** Charles III **Mint:** Mexico City **Obverse:** Large, armored bust right **Obv. Legend:** CAROL • III • D • G • ... **Reverse:** Crowned shield in order chain, initials and mint mark upright **Rev. Legend:** IN • UTROQ • FELIX • AUSPICE • DEO **Note:** Mint mark M, Mo.

Date	Mintage	VG	F	VF	XF	Unc
1788 FM	—	400	650	1,000	2,000	—

KM# 143.1 4 ESCUDOS

13.5337 g., 0.8750 Gold 0.3807 oz. AGW **Ruler:** Charles IV **Mint:** Mexico City **Obverse:** Armored bust of Charles III, right **Obv. Legend:** CAROL • IV • D • G • ... **Reverse:** Crowned shield in order chain, initials and mint mark upright **Rev. Legend:** IN • UTROQ • FELIX • AUSPICE • DEO **Note:** Mint mark M, Mo, using old portrait punch.

Date	Mintage	VG	F	VF	XF	Unc
1789 FM	—	500	700	1,100	2,150	—
1790 FM	—	500	700	1,100	2,150	—

KM# 143.2 4 ESCUDOS

13.5337 g., 0.8750 Gold 0.3807 oz. AGW **Ruler:** Charles IV **Mint:** Mexico City **Obverse:** Armored bust of Charles III, right **Obv. Legend:** CAROL • IIII • D • G • ... **Reverse:** Crowned shield in order chain, initials and mint mark upright **Rev. Legend:** IN • UTROQ • FELIX • AUSPICE • DEO **Note:** Mint mark M, Mo, using old portrait punch.

Date	Mintage	VG	F	VF	XF	Unc
1790 FM	—	600	1,000	1,800	3,000	—

KM# 144 4 ESCUDOS

13.5337 g., 0.8750 Gold 0.3807 oz. AGW **Ruler:** Charles IV **Mint:** Mexico City **Obverse:** Armored bust of Charles IIII, right **Obv. Legend:** CAROL • IIII • D • G • ... **Reverse:** Crowned shield flanked by 4 S in order chain **Rev. Legend:** IN • UTROQ • FELIX • AUSPICE • DEO; initials and mint mark upright **Note:** Mint mark Mo.

Date	Mintage	VG	F	VF	XF	Unc
1792 FM	—	300	500	750	1,500	—
1793 FM	—	300	500	750	1,500	—
1794/3 FM	—	300	500	750	1,500	—
1795 FM	—	300	500	750	1,500	—
1796 FM	—	300	500	750	1,500	—
1797 FM	—	300	500	750	1,500	—
1798/7 FM	—	300	500	750	1,500	—
1798 FM	—	300	500	750	1,500	—
1799 FM	—	300	500	750	1,500	—
1800 FM	—	300	500	750	1,500	—

KM# 148 8 ESCUDOS

27.0674 g., 0.9170 Gold 0.7980 oz. AGW **Ruler:** Philip V **Mint:** Mexico City **Obverse:** Large, armored bust right **Obv. Legend:** PHILIP • V • D • G • HISPAN • ET IND • REX **Reverse:** Crowned shield flanked by M F 8 in order chain **Rev. Legend:** INITIUM SAPIENTIAE TIMOR DOMINI **Note:** Mint mark M, Mo.

Date	Mintage	VG	F	VF	XF	Unc
1732 Rare	—	—	—	—	—	—
1732 F Rare	—	—	—	—	—	—
1733 F Rare	—	—	—	—	—	—
1734 MF	—	1,000	1,650	2,750	4,850	—
1734 MF/F	—	1,000	1,650	2,750	4,850	—
1735 MF	—	1,000	1,500	2,500	4,500	—
1736 MF	—	1,000	1,500	2,500	4,500	—
1737 MF	—	1,000	1,500	2,500	4,500	—
1738/7 MF	—	1,000	1,500	2,500	4,500	—
1738 MF	—	1,000	1,500	2,500	4,500	—
1739 MF	—	1,000	1,500	2,500	4,500	—
1740 MF	—	1,000	1,500	2,500	4,500	—
1740/30 MF	—	1,000	1,500	2,500	4,500	—
1741 MF	—	1,000	1,500	2,500	4,500	—
1742 MF	—	1,000	1,500	2,500	4,500	—
1743 MF	—	1,000	1,500	2,500	4,500	—
1744 MF	—	1,000	1,500	2,500	4,500	—
1744/3 MF	—	1,000	1,500	2,500	4,500	—
1745/4 MF	—	1,000	1,500	2,500	4,500	—
1745 MF	—	1,000	1,500	2,500	4,500	—
1746/5 MF	—	1,000	1,500	2,500	4,500	—
1746 MF	—	1,000	1,500	2,500	4,500	—
1747 MF	—	1,100	1,750	2,850	5,000	—

KM# 149 8 ESCUDOS

27.0674 g., 0.9170 Gold 0.7980 oz. AGW **Ruler:** Ferdinand VI **Mint:** Mexico City **Obverse:** Large, armored bust right **Obv. Legend:** FERDND • VI • D • G • ... **Reverse:** Crowned shield flanked by M F 8 in order chain **Rev. Legend:** INITIUM SAPIENTIAE TIMOR DOMINI **Note:** Mint mark M, Mo.

Date	Mintage	VG	F	VF	XF	Unc
1747 MF	—	9,000	15,000	22,000	35,000	—

KM# 150 8 ESCUDOS

27.0674 g., 0.9170 Gold 0.7980 oz. AGW **Ruler:** Ferdinand VI **Mint:** Mexico City **Obverse:** Small, armored bust right **Obv. Legend:** FERDND • VI • D • G • ... **Reverse:** Crowned shield flanked by 8 S in order chain **Rev. Legend:** NOMINA MAGNA SEQUOR **Note:** Mint mark M, Mo.

Date	Mintage	VG	F	VF	XF	Unc
1748 MF	—	1,200	2,000	3,500	6,000	—
1749/8 MF	—	1,200	2,000	3,500	6,000	—
1749 MF	—	1,200	2,000	3,500	6,000	—
1750 MF	—	1,200	2,000	3,500	6,000	—
1751/0 MF	—	1,500	2,000	3,500	6,000	—
1751 MF	—	1,200	2,000	3,500	6,000	—

KM# 151 8 ESCUDOS

27.0674 g., 0.9170 Gold 0.7980 oz. AGW **Ruler:** Ferdinand VI **Mint:** Mexico City **Obverse:** Armored bust right **Obv. Legend:** FERDND • VI • D • G • ... **Reverse:** Crowned shield in order chain **Rev. Legend:** NOMINA MAGNA SEQUOR **Note:** Mint mark M, Mo.

Date	Mintage	VG	F	VF	XF	Unc
1752 MF	—	1,200	2,000	3,500	6,000	—
1753 MF	—	1,200	2,000	3,500	6,000	—

Date	Mintage	VG	F	VF	XF	Unc
1754 MF	—	1,200	2,000	3,500	6,000	—
1755 MM	—	1,200	2,000	3,500	6,000	—
1756 MM	—	1,200	2,000	3,500	6,000	—

KM# 152 8 ESCUDOS
27.0674 g., 0.9170 Gold 0.7980 oz. AGW **Ruler:** Ferdinand VI **Mint:** Mexico City **Obverse:** Armored bust right **Obv. Legend:** FERDND • VI • D • G • ... **Reverse:** Crowned shield in order chain **Rev. Legend:** NOMINA MAGNA SEQUOR **Note:** Mint mark M, Mo.

Date	Mintage	VG	F	VF	XF	Unc
1757 MM	—	1,200	2,000	3,500	6,000	—
1758 MM	—	1,200	2,000	3,500	6,000	—
1759 MM	—	1,200	2,000	3,500	6,000	—

KM# 153 8 ESCUDOS
27.0674 g., 0.9170 Gold 0.7980 oz. AGW **Ruler:** Charles III **Mint:** Mexico City **Obverse:** Armored bust right **Obv. Legend:** CAROLVS • III • D • G • ... **Reverse:** Crowned shield in order chain **Rev. Legend:** NOMINA MAGNA SEQUOR **Note:** Mint mark M, Mo.

Date	Mintage	VG	F	VF	XF	Unc
1760 MM	—	1,750	3,000	5,000	9,000	—
1761/0 MM	—	2,000	3,500	5,500	10,000	—
1761 MM	—	2,000	3,500	5,500	10,000	—

KM# 154 8 ESCUDOS
27.0674 g., 0.9170 Gold 0.7980 oz. AGW **Ruler:** Charles III **Mint:** Mexico City **Obverse:** Armored bust right **Obv. Legend:** CAROLVS • III • D • G • ... **Reverse:** Crowned shield in order chain **Rev. Legend:** NOMINA MAGNA SEQUOR **Note:** Mint mark M, Mo.

Date	Mintage	VG	F	VF	XF	Unc
1761 MM	—	1,750	3,000	5,250	9,500	—

KM# 155 8 ESCUDOS
27.0674 g., 0.9170 Gold 0.7980 oz. AGW **Ruler:** Charles III **Mint:** Mexico City **Obverse:** Large, armored bust right **Obv. Legend:** CAROLUS • III • D • G • ... **Reverse:** Crowned shield in order chain **Rev. Legend:** IN • UTROQ • FELIX • AUSPICE • DEO • **Note:** Mint mark M, Mo.

Date	Mintage	VG	F	VF	XF	Unc
1762 MM	—	1,600	2,750	4,500	8,500	—
1763 MM	—	1,600	2,750	4,500	8,500	—
1764 MF	—	1,750	3,000	5,000	9,000	—
1764/2 MF	—	1,750	3,000	5,000	9,000	—
1764 MM	—	1,750	3,000	5,000	9,000	—
1765/4 MF	—	1,750	3,000	5,000	9,000	—
1765/4 MM	—	1,750	3,000	5,000	9,000	—
1765 MF	—	1,750	3,000	5,000	9,000	—
1765 MM	—	1,500	2,500	4,000	7,500	—
1766 MF	—	1,500	2,500	4,000	7,500	—
1767/6 MF	—	1,500	2,500	4,000	7,500	—
1767 MF	—	1,500	2,500	4,000	7,500	—
1768/7 MF	—	1,500	2,500	4,000	7,500	—
1768 MF	—	1,500	2,500	4,000	7,500	—
1769 MF	—	1,500	2,500	4,000	7,500	—
1770 MF	—	1,500	2,500	4,000	7,500	—
1771 MF	—	1,750	3,000	5,000	9,000	—

KM# 156.1 8 ESCUDOS
27.0674 g., 0.9010 Gold 0.7841 oz. AGW **Ruler:** Charles III **Mint:** Mexico City **Obverse:** Large, armored bust right **Obv. Legend:** CAROL • III • D • G • ... **Reverse:** Crowned shield flanked by 8 S in order chain, initials and mint mark upright **Rev. Legend:** ... AUSPICE • DEO • **Note:** Mint mark M, Mo.

Date	Mintage	VG	F	VF	XF	Unc
1772 FM	—	500	750	1,250	2,000	—
1773 FM	—	550	850	1,350	2,250	—

KM# 156.2 8 ESCUDOS
27.0674 g., 0.9010 Gold 0.7841 oz. AGW **Ruler:** Charles III **Mint:** Mexico City **Obverse:** Large, armored bust right **Obv. Legend:** CAROL • III • D • G • ... **Reverse:** Crowned shield flanked by 8 S in order chain, initials and mint mark inverted **Rev. Legend:** ... AUSPICE • DEO • **Note:** Mint mark M, Mo.

Date	Mintage	VG	F	VF	XF	Unc
1773 FM	—	500	700	1,100	1,650	—
1774 FM	—	500	700	1,100	1,650	—
1775 FM	—	500	700	1,100	1,650	—
1776 FM	—	500	700	1,100	1,650	—
1777/6 FM	—	500	700	1,100	1,650	—
1777 FM	—	500	700	1,100	1,650	—
1778 FF	—	500	700	1,100	1,650	—
1779 FF	—	500	700	1,100	1,650	—
1780 FF	—	500	700	1,100	1,650	—
1781 FF	—	500	700	1,100	1,650	—
1782 FF	—	500	700	1,100	1,650	—
1783 FF	—	500	700	1,100	1,650	—
1784 FF	—	500	700	1,100	1,650	—
1784 FM/F	—	500	700	1,100	1,650	—
1784 FM	—	500	700	1,100	1,650	—
1785 FM	—	500	700	1,100	1,650	—

KM# 156.2a 8 ESCUDOS
27.0674 g., 0.8750 Gold 0.7614 oz. AGW **Ruler:** Charles III **Mint:** Mexico City **Obverse:** Large, armored bust right **Obv. Legend:** CAROL • III • D • G • ... **Reverse:** Crowned shield flanked by 8 S in order chain, initials and mint mark inverted **Rev. Legend:** ... AUSPICE • DEO • **Note:** Mint mark M, Mo.

Date	Mintage	VG	F	VF	XF	Unc
1786 FM	—	500	700	1,100	1,650	—
1787 FM	—	500	700	1,100	1,650	—
1788 FM	—	500	700	1,100	1,650	—

KM# 156.1a 8 ESCUDOS
27.0674 g., 0.8750 Gold 0.7614 oz. AGW **Ruler:** Charles III **Mint:** Mexico City **Obverse:** Large, armored bust right **Obv. Legend:** CAROL • III • D • G • ... **Reverse:** Crowned shield flanked by 8 S in order chain, initials and mint mark upright **Rev. Legend:** ... AUSPICE • DEO • **Note:** Mint mark M, Mo.

Date	Mintage	VG	F	VF	XF	Unc
1788 FM	—	500	700	1,100	1,650	—

KM# 157 8 ESCUDOS
27.0674 g., 0.8750 Gold 0.7614 oz. AGW **Ruler:** Charles IV **Mint:** Mexico City **Obverse:** Armored bust of Charles III, right **Obv. Legend:** CAROL • IV • D • G • ... **Reverse:** Crowned shield flanked by 8 S in order chain **Rev. Legend:** IN • UTROQ • ... **Note:** Mint mark M, Mo, using old portrait punch.

Date	Mintage	VG	F	VF	XF	Unc
1789 FM	—	500	700	1,150	2,000	—
1790 FM	—	500	700	1,150	2,000	—

KM# 158 8 ESCUDOS
27.0674 g., 0.8750 Gold 0.7614 oz. AGW **Ruler:** Charles IV **Mint:** Mexico City **Obverse:** Armored bust of Charles III, right **Obv. Legend:** CAROL • IIII • D • G • ... **Reverse:** Crowned shield flanked by 8 S in order chain **Rev. Legend:** IN • UTROQ • ... **Note:** Mint mark M, Mo, using old portrait punch.

Date	Mintage	VG	F	VF	XF	Unc
1790 FM	—	500	700	1,150	2,000	—

KM# 159 8 ESCUDOS
27.0674 g., 0.8750 Gold 0.7614 oz. AGW **Ruler:** Charles IV **Mint:** Mexico City **Obverse:** Armored bust right **Obv. Legend:** CAROL • IIII • D • G • ... **Reverse:** Crowned shield flanked by 8 S in order chain **Rev. Legend:** IN • UTROQ • ... **Note:** Mint mark Mo.

Date	Mintage	VG	F	VF	XF	Unc
1791 FM	—	350	450	625	1,000	—
1792 FM	—	350	450	625	1,000	—
1793 FM	—	350	450	625	1,000	—
1794 FM	—	350	450	625	1,000	—
1795 FM	—	350	450	625	1,000	—
1796/5 FM	—	400	500	700	1,150	—
1796 FM	—	350	450	625	1,000	—
1797 FM	—	350	450	625	1,000	—
1797 FM EPLIX	—	400	500	700	1,150	—
1798 FM	—	350	450	625	1,000	—
1799 FM	—	350	450	625	1,000	—
1800 FM	—	350	450	625	1,000	—
1801/0 FT	—	475	550	750	1,150	—

PROCLAMATION MEDALLIC COINAGE

The Q used in the following listings refer to Standard Catalog of Mexican Coins, Paper Money, Stocks, Bonds, and Medals by Krause Publications, Inc., ©1981.

KM# Q22 1/2 REAL

1.6000 g., Silver **Issuer:** Mexico City **Obverse:** Crowned shield flanked by crowned pillars with banner **Obv. Legend:** A CARLOS IV REY DE ESPANA Y DE LAS YNDIAS **Reverse:** Legend, date within wreath **Rev. Legend:** PROCLAMADO EN MEXICO ANO DE 1789

Date	Mintage	F	VF	XF	Unc
1789	—	20.00	28.50	40.00	—

KM# Q22a 1/2 REAL

Bronze **Issuer:** Mexico City **Obverse:** Crowned shield flanked by crowned pillars with banner **Obv. Legend:** A CARLOS IV REY DE ESPANA Y DE LAS YNDIAS **Reverse:** Legend, date within wreath **Rev. Legend:** PROCLAMADO EN MEXICO ANO DE 1789

Date	Mintage	F	VF	XF	Unc
1789	—	22.50	35.00	50.00	—

KM# Q23 1/2 REAL

Silver **Issuer:** Mexico City **Obverse:** Crowned arms in double-lined circle **Obv. Legend:** A CARLOS IV REY DE ESPANA Y DE LAS YNDIAS **Rev. Legend:** PROCLAMADO EN MEXICO ANO DE 1789

Date	Mintage	F	VF	XF	Unc
1789	—	20.00	28.50	40.00	—

KM# Q23a 1/2 REAL

Bronze **Issuer:** Mexico City **Obverse:** Crowned arms in double-lined circle **Obv. Legend:** A CARLOS IV REY DE ESPANA Y DE LAS YNDIAS **Rev. Legend:** PROCLAMADO EN MEXICO ANO DE 1789

Date	Mintage	F	VF	XF	Unc
1789	—	22.50	35.00	50.00	—

KM# Q24 REAL

Silver **Issuer:** Mexico City **Obverse:** Crowned shield flanked by crowned pillars with banner **Obv. Legend:** A CARLOS IV REY DE ESPANA Y DE LAS YNDIAS **Reverse:** Legend, date, value within wreath **Rev. Legend:** PROCLAMADO EN MEXICO ANO DE 1789

Date	Mintage	F	VF	XF	Unc
1789	—	20.00	28.50	40.00	—

KM# Q24a REAL

Bronze **Issuer:** Mexico City **Obverse:** Crowned shield flanked by crowned pillars with banner **Obv. Legend:** A CARLOS IV REY DE ESPANA Y DE LAS YNDIAS **Reverse:** Legend, date, value within wreath **Rev. Legend:** PROCLAMADO EN MEXICO ANO DE 1789

Date	Mintage	F	VF	XF	Unc
1789	—	22.50	35.00	50.00	—

KM# Q-A24 REAL

Silver **Issuer:** Mexico City **Obverse:** Crowned arms in double-lined circle **Obv. Legend:** A CARLOS IV REY DE ESPANA Y DE LAS YNDIAS **Rev. Legend:** PROCLAMADO EN MEXICO ANO DE 1789

Date	Mintage	F	VF	XF	Unc
1789	—	20.00	28.50	40.00	—

KM# Q-A24a REAL

Copper **Issuer:** Mexico City **Obverse:** Crowned arms in double-lined circle **Obv. Legend:** A CARLOS IV REY DE ESPANA Y DE LAS YNDIAS **Rev. Legend:** PROCLAMADO EN MEXICO ANO DE 1789

Date	Mintage	F	VF	XF	Unc
1789	—	22.50	35.00	50.00	—

KM# Q25 2 REALES

6.7000 g., Silver **Issuer:** Mexico City **Obverse:** Crowned shield flanked by crowned pillars with banner **Obv. Legend:** A CARLOS IV REY DE ESPANA Y DE LAS YNDIAS **Reverse:** Legend, date, value within wreath **Rev. Legend:** PROCLAMADO EN MEXICO ANO DE 1789

Date	Mintage	F	VF	XF	Unc
1789	—	35.00	50.00	75.00	—

KM# Q25a 2 REALES

6.7000 g., Bronze **Issuer:** Mexico City **Obverse:** Crowned shield flanked by crowned pillars with banner **Obv. Legend:** A CARLOS IV REY DE ESPANA Y DE LAS YNDIAS **Reverse:** Legend, date, value within wreath **Rev. Legend:** PROCLAMADO EN MEXICO ANO DE 1789

Date	Mintage	F	VF	XF	Unc
1789	—	30.00	45.00	60.00	—

KM# Q27 4 REALES

13.6000 g., Silver **Issuer:** Mexico City **Obverse:** Crowned shield flanked by crowned pillars with banner **Obv. Legend:** A CARLOS IV REY DE ESPANA Y DE LAS YNDIAS **Reverse:** Legend date, value within wreath **Rev. Legend:** PROCLAMADO EN MEXICO ANO DE 1789

Date	Mintage	F	VF	XF	Unc
1789	—	100	150	225	—

KM# Q27a 4 REALES

13.6000 g., Bronze **Issuer:** Mexico City **Obverse:** Crowned shield flanked by crowned pillars with banner **Obv. Legend:** A CARLOS IV REY DE ESPANA Y DE LAS YNDIAS **Reverse:** Legend, date, value within wreath **Rev. Legend:** PROCLAMADO EN MEXICO ANO DE 1789

Date	Mintage	F	VF	XF	Unc
1789	—	70.00	100	150	—

KM# Q28 8 REALES

27.0000 g., Silver **Issuer:** Mexico City **Obverse:** Crowned shield flanked by crowned pillars with banner **Obv. Legend:** A CARLOS IV REY DE ESPANA Y DE LAS YNDIAS **Reverse:** Legend, date, value within wreath **Rev. Legend:** PROCLAMADO EN MEXICO ANO DE 1789

Date	Mintage	F	VF	XF	Unc
1789	—	200	275	400	—

KM# Q28a 8 REALES

27.0000 g., Bronze **Issuer:** Mexico City **Obverse:** Crowned shield flanked by crowned pillars with banner **Obv. Legend:** A CARLOS IV REY DE ESPANA Y DE LAS YNDIAS **Reverse:** Legend, date, value within wreath **Rev. Legend:** PROCLAMADO EN MEXICO ANO DE 1789

Date	Mintage	F	VF	XF	Unc
1789	—	70.00	100	150	—

PATTERNS

Including off metal strikes

KM#	Date	Mintage	Identification	Mkt Val
PnA1	1768	—	1/16 Real. Brass.	4,000
PnB1	1768	—	1/16 Real. Copper.	4,000

KM#	Date	Mintage	Identification	Mkt Val
PnC1	1769	—	1/2 Grano. Copper.	2,500

Note: Considered a circulating type by some authorities and very scarce

KM#	Date	Mintage	Identification	Mkt Val
PnD1	1769	—	Grano. Copper.	3,000

Note: Considered a circulating type by some authorities, very scarce

MOLDAVIA & WALLACHIA

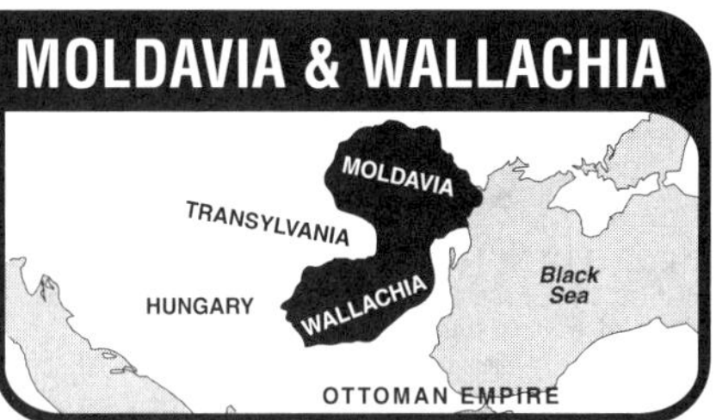

These two principalities have constituted the base of modern Romania. Wallachia and Moldova were established early in the 14th century. Following some wars against Hungarian kings, both principalities became independent.

The 16th century brought new hardship to East Central Europe, especially after the Ottoman Empire reached the peak of its power under the Sultan Suleiman I the Magnificent (1520-1566). Thus, Belgrade (1521) fell to the Turks and with the defeat of Mohacs battle in 1526, Hungary came under Ottoman rule in 1526. Under these circumstances, Turkish control over Wallachia and Moldova became increasingly burdensome. From an economic standpoint, apart from the tribute, the princes paid the many gifts and bribes necessary to obtain and keep the throne, extraordinary services and the obligation of exporting certain goods only to the Empire. The local mints have been closed. Independent action in foreign affairs was severely restricted.

One of the most remarkable exceptions was the Prince Constantin Brancoveanu (1688-1714), who tried to maintain the autonomy of Wallachia. His relations with the Ottoman Empire worsened during the Russo-Turkish war (1711), when the prince took a neutral stance in the conflict. More, as defiance, he ordered a distinct coinage under his arms. These special coins, in gold and silver, were issued in Transylvania at Alba Iulia by the mint-master Carl Josef Hoffman in 1713. Consequently, Brancoveanu's family was taken to Istanbul in April 1714, where the prince was tortured and executed together with his four sons.

Under these circumstances, the Turks imposed the so-called Phanariot regime in Moldova and Wallachia. These Phanariot rulers were usually Orthodox members of the noble Greek families from Istanbul. Thus, the autonomous status of the principalities was formally preserved, but considerable limitations were imposed upon them.

Because of the decline of Turkish power, Russian influence became preeminent in this area, which became a battle field. Wallachia was occupied by the Russian troops between 1769-74 and 1788-91. On its behalf, Moldova fell under Tsarist occupation in 1739, 1769-74 and 1788-91, in this period together with the Hapsburgs.

During the Russo-Turkish war (1768-74) a special coinage was made for the area, also known as Sadagura coins, the first commune coins for both principalities. The Russian administrator, the Marshall Rumeanatsev has accepted as an adventurer, the Baron Gartenberg, set up a mint at Sadagura near the city of Cernauti (region of Bukovina, in the north of Moldova). For these coins and patterns, the bronze from captured Turkish cannons was used.

The treaty of Kuchuk-Kainarji (1774), which ended the Russo-Turkish war, Moldova lost its northern region, Bukovina, to Austria in 1775, after a Russo-Austro-Turkish agreement.

In 1792, Russia annexed Transnistria, a territory extended east of the Nistru River under Ottoman suzerainty, but gave its administration to the Moldavian rulers.

PRINCIPALITY

STANDARD COINAGE

C# 2.1 3 DENGI (PARA)

Bronze **Obv:** Crown above 2 oval shields above date **Rev:** Written value within square

Date	Mintage	VG	F	VF	XF	Unc
1771	—	18.00	35.00	70.00	150	—
Note: 4 die varieties exist for 1771						
1772	—	15.00	30.00	60.00	125	—
Note: 6 die varieties exist for 1772						
1773	—	100	250	—	—	—
1774 Unique	—	—	—	—	—	—

C# 2.2 3 DENGI (PARA)

Bronze **Obv:** Crown above 2 oval shields above date **Rev:** Written value within square

Date	Mintage	VG	F	VF	XF	Unc
1772 Rare	—	—	—	—	—	—

C# 3 2 PARA 3 KOPECK

Bronze **Obv:** Crown above 2 oval shields above date **Rev:** Written value within square

Date	Mintage	VG	F	VF	XF	Unc
1772	—	15.00	30.00	60.00	125	—
Note: 7 die varieties exist for 1772						
1773	—	12.50	25.00	50.00	110	—
Note: 4 die varieties exist for 1773						
1774	—	20.00	40.00	75.00	160	—
Note: 5 die varieties exist for 1774						

PATTERNS

Including off metal strikes

KM#	Date	Mintage	Identification	Mkt Val
Pn1	1771S	—	3 Dengi. Bronze. Imperial eagle, C1.	—

KM#	Date	Mintage	Identification	Mkt Val
Pn2	1771	—	3 Dengi. Bronze. E monograms, C1a	—

KM#	Date	Mintage	Identification	Mkt Val
Pn3	1771	—	3 Dengi. Bronze. Value in exerque, C1b	—
Pn4	1771	—	3 Dengi. Bronze. Crowned local arms, value in square.	—
Pn6	1771S	—	5 Kopecks. Bronze. Without lines on obverse and reverse.	—
PnA7	1772	—	3 Dengi. Silver.	—
Pn7	1772	—	2 Para 3 Kopeck. Silver.	—
Pn8	1773	—	3 Dengi. Silver.	—
Pn9	1773	—	3 Dengi. Bronze.	—
Pn10	1773	—	2 Para 3 Kopeck. Silver. 3 varieties exist.	—

MONACO

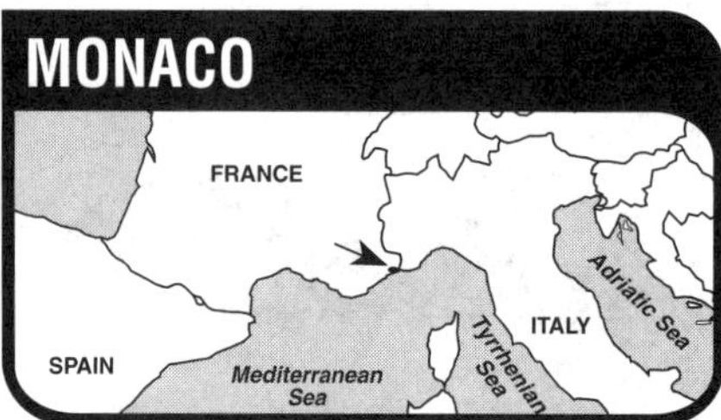

The Principality of Monaco, located on the Mediterranean coast nine miles from Nice, has an area of 0.58 sq. mi. (1.9 sq. km.) and a population of 26,000. Capital: Monaco-Ville. The economy is based on tourism and the manufacture of cosmetics, gourmet foods and highly specialized electronics. Monaco also derives its revenue from a tobacco monopoly and the sale of postage stamps for philatelic purpose. Gambling in Monte Carlo accounts for only a small fraction of the country's revenue.

Monaco derives its name from Monoikos', the Greek surname for Hercules, the mythological strong man who, according to legend, formed the Monacan headland during one of his twelve labors. Monaco has been ruled by the Grimaldi dynasty since 1297 - Prince Rainier III, the present and 31st monarch of Monaco, is still of that line - except for a period during the French Revolution until Napoleon's downfall when the Principality was annexed to France. Since 1865, Monaco has maintained a customs union with France which guarantees its privileged position as long as the royal line remains intact. Under the new constitution proclaimed on December 17, 1962, the Prince shares his power with an 18-member unicameral National Council.

RULERS

Louis I, 1662-1701
Antoine I, 1701-1731
Louise - Hypolite, 1731
Jacques I, 1731-1733
Honore III, 1733-1795
Honore IV, 1795-1819

MINT MARKS

M - Monaco
A – Paris

MINT PRIVY MARKS

(a) - Paris (privy marks only)
(fb) - Flower buds, 1720
(h) - Crowned H, 1701
(sb) - Scale, balance, 1701

MONETARY SYSTEM

3 Deniers = 1 Liard
4 Liards = 1 Sol
3 Sols = 1 Pezetta
20 Pezettas = 1 Scudo (Ecu)
4 Scudos = 1 Doppia (1 Louis D'or)

PRINCIPALITY

STANDARD COINAGE

KM# 67 2 DENIERS

Copper **Ruler:** Antoine I **Obv:** Bust right **Rev:** Standing saint divides date

Date	Mintage	VG	F	VF	XF	Unc
1703	—	225	325	550	1,000	—

KM# 75 2 DENIERS

Copper **Ruler:** Antoine I **Rev:** Crown above 3 diamonds, value below, date in legend

Date	Mintage	VG	F	VF	XF	Unc
1720	—	150	275	525	1,000	—

KM# 86 3 DENIERS (1 Liard)

Copper **Ruler:** Honore III **Obv:** Bust right **Rev:** Crowned H above 3 diamonds, value below, date in legend

Date	Mintage	VG	F	VF	XF	Unc
1735	—	125	225	450	800	—

KM# 76.1 4 DENIERS (Cavalla)

Copper **Ruler:** Antoine I **Obv:** Bust right **Obv. Legend:** ANT • I • D • G • PRIN • MONOECI **Rev:** Crowned A amidst 3 diamonds, value below, date in legend

Date	Mintage	VG	F	VF	XF	Unc
1720	—	100	200	350	650	—

KM# 76.2 4 DENIERS (Cavalla)

Copper **Ruler:** Antoine I **Obv:** Bust right **Obv. Legend:** ANT • I • D • G • PRIN • MONOEC **Rev:** Crowned A amidst 3 diamonds, value below, date in legend

Date	Mintage	VG	F	VF	XF	Unc
1720	—	100	200	350	650	—

KM# 77 8 DENIERS (Dardenna)

Copper **Ruler:** Antoine I **Obv:** Crowned A among 3 diamonds, value below **Rev:** Standing saint with halo divides date

Date	Mintage	VG	F	VF	XF	Unc
1720	—	85.00	165	275	550	—

KM# 87.1 8 DENIERS (Dardenna)

Copper **Ruler:** Honore III **Obv:** Crowned H among 3 diamonds

Date	Mintage	VG	F	VF	XF	Unc
1735	—	75.00	150	250	525	—

KM# 87.2 8 DENIERS (Dardenna)

Copper **Ruler:** Honore III **Rev:** Standing saint without halo divides date

Date	Mintage	VG	F	VF	XF	Unc
1735	—	75.00	150	250	525	—

KM# 65 1-1/2 SOLS (1/2 Pezetta)

1.6500 g., Billon **Ruler:** Antoine I **Obv:** Crowned round arms in palm branches **Rev:** Cross with diamonds in angles, date in legend

Date	Mintage	VG	F	VF	XF	Unc
1701	—	175	325	550	1,100	—

KM# 78 1-1/2 SOLS (1/2 Pezetta)

1.6500 g., Billon **Ruler:** Antoine I **Obv:** Bust right **Rev:** Crowned arms, date at top

Date	Mintage	VG	F	VF	XF	Unc
1720	—	100	200	375	700	—

KM# 79 1-1/2 SOLS (1/2 Pezetta)

1.6500 g., Billon **Ruler:** Antoine I **Obv:** Crowned A divides date **Rev:** Crowned arms with 5 vertical rows of diamonds

Date	Mintage	VG	F	VF	XF	Unc
1720	—	100	200	350	650	—

KM# 79a 1-1/2 SOLS (1/2 Pezetta)

1.6500 g., Billon **Ruler:** Antoine I **Rev:** Crowned arms with 7 vertical rows of diamonds

Date	Mintage	VG	F	VF	XF	Unc
1720	—	100	200	350	650	—

KM# 88 1-1/2 SOLS (1/2 Pezetta)
1.6500 g., Billon **Ruler:** Honore III **Obv:** Crowned coat of arms **Rev:** Crowned H divided date

Date	Mintage	VG	F	VF	XF	Unc
1735	—	175	325	550	1,100	—

KM# 89 1-1/2 SOLS (1/2 Pezetta)
1.6500 g., Billon **Ruler:** Honore III **Obv:** Bust right **Rev:** Cruciform crowned H's with diamonds in angles, date at top

Date	Mintage	VG	F	VF	XF	Unc
1735	—	200	350	600	1,200	—

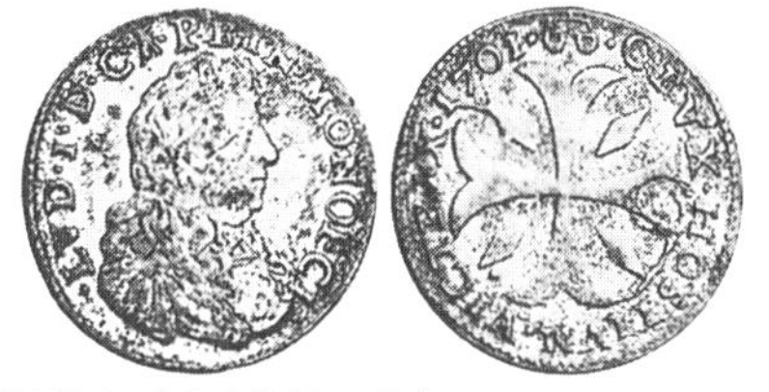

KM# 60.2 3 SOLS (Pezetta)
4.5000 g., Billon **Ruler:** Antoine I **Obv:** Modified portrait **Rev:** Cross with lozenges in angles

Date	Mintage	VG	F	VF	XF	Unc
1701 (h//sb)	—	175	350	670	1,250	—

KM# 66 3 SOLS (Pezetta)
4.5000 g., Billon **Ruler:** Antoine I **Obv:** Bust right **Rev:** Crowned round arms in palm branches, date in legend

Date	Mintage	VG	F	VF	XF	Unc
1701 (I)	—	200	350	750	1,350	—
1703	—	225	450	850	1,650	—

KM# 68 3 SOLS (Pezetta)
4.5000 g., Billon **Ruler:** Antoine I **Rev:** Crowned flat-sides shield of arms

Date	Mintage	VG	F	VF	XF	Unc
1707	—	175	320	550	1,100	—
1708	—	200	325	575	1,150	—

KM# 80.1 3 SOLS (Pezetta)
4.5000 g., Billon **Ruler:** Antoine I **Obv:** Bust right **Obv. Legend:** ANT • I • D • G • PRIN • ... **Rev:** Crowned hour-glass arms

Date	Mintage	VG	F	VF	XF	Unc
1720	—	165	300	500	1,000	—

KM# 80.2 3 SOLS (Pezetta)
4.5000 g., Billon **Ruler:** Antoine I **Obv:** Bust right **Rev:** Without rosettes above crown

Date	Mintage	VG	F	VF	XF	Unc
1720	—	175	320	550	1,100	—

KM# 81 3 SOLS (Pezetta)
4.5000 g., Billon **Ruler:** Antoine I **Obv:** Bust right **Obv. Legend:** ANT • I • D • G • PRIN • .... **Rev:** Cruciform crowned A's with diamonds in angles, date at top **Rev. Legend:** AVX•MEVM•A•...

Date	Mintage	VG	F	VF	XF	Unc
1720	—	200	325	575	1,150	—

KM# 85 3 SOLS (Pezetta)
4.5000 g., Billon **Ruler:** Honore III **Obv:** Bust right **Rev:** Cruciform crowned H's with diamonds in angles, date above

Date	Mintage	VG	F	VF	XF	Unc
1734	—	125	250	500	1,100	—
1735	—	150	300	620	1,225	—

KM# 69 1/4 ECU (15 Sols)
Silver **Ruler:** Antoine I **Obv:** Bust right **Obv. Legend:** ANT • I • D • G • ... **Rev:** Crowned arms

Date	Mintage	VG	F	VF	XF	Unc
1707	—	250	550	1,450	3,000	—

KM# 70 SCUDO (Ecu, 60 Sols)
Silver **Ruler:** Antoine I **Obv:** Bust right **Obv. Legend:** • ANT • I • D • G • PRIN • ... **Rev:** Crowned arms **Note:** DAV #1612.

Date	Mintage	VG	F	VF	XF	Unc
1707	—	2,500	5,000	8,500	12,500	—
Note: 3 die varieties exist for 1707						
1708	—	3,000	6,000	10,000	15,000	—

MONTSERRAT

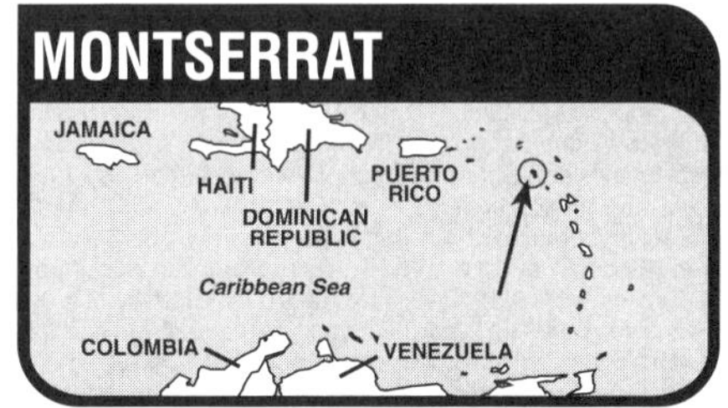

Montserrat, a British crown colony located in the Lesser Antilles of the West Indies 27 miles (43 km.) southwest of Antigua, has an area of 38 sq. mi. (100 sq. km.) and a population of 18,500. Capital: Plymouth. The island - actually a range of volcanic peaks rising from the Caribbean - exports cotton, limes and vegetables.

Columbus discovered Montserrat in 1493 and named it after Monserrado, a mountain in Spain. It was colonized by the English in 1632 and, except for brief periods of French occupancy in 1667 and 1782-83, has remained a British possession from that time. Currency of the British Caribbean Territories (Eastern Group) was used until later when the East Caribbean States coinage was introduced. Until becoming a separate colony in 1956, Montserrat was a presidency of the Leeward Islands.

The early 19th century countermarks of a crowned 3, 4, 7, 9 or 18 over M as documented by Major Pridmore have been more correctly listed under St. Bartholomew.

RULER
British

MONETARY SYSTEM
100 Cents = 1 Dollar

BRITISH COLONY

COUNTERMARKED COINAGE

KM# 1 DOG (1-1/2 Pence)
Billon **Countermark:** M **Note:** Countermark on Cayenne 2 Sous, KM#1.

CM Date	Host Date	Good	VG	F	VF	XF
ND	1780-90	10.00	15.00	30.00	55.00	—

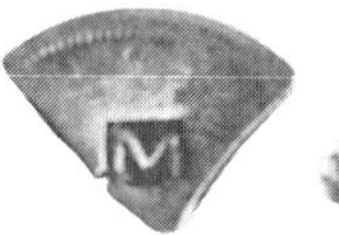

KM# 3 3 DOGS (4-1/2 Pence - 1/2 Bit)
Silver **Countermark:** M **Note:** Countermark on 1/4 cut of Spanish Colonial 2 Reales.

CM Date	Host Date	Good	VG	F	VF	XF
ND	1772-99	150	250	400	650	—

KM# 4 3 DOGS (4-1/2 Pence - 1/2 Bit)
Silver **Countermark:** M **Note:** Countermark on Mexico 1/2 Real, KM#71.

CM Date	Host Date	Good	VG	F	VF	XF
ND	1790	70.00	150	250	400	—

KM# 6.1 6 DOGS (9 Pence - 1 Bit - 1/8 Dollar)
Silver **Countermark:** M **Note:** Countermark on 1/2 cut of Lima 2 Reales, KM#95.

CM Date	Host Date	Good	VG	F	VF	XF
ND	1791-99	150	250	375	550	—

KM# 6.2 6 DOGS (9 Pence - 1 Bit - 1/8 Dollar)
Silver **Countermark:** M **Note:** Countermark on 1/2 cut of Mexico City 2 Reales, KM#88.

CM Date	Host Date	Good	VG	F	VF	XF
ND	1772-89	150	250	375	550	—

KM# 8 6 DOGS (9 Pence - 1 Bit - 1/8 Dollar)
Silver **Countermark:** M **Note:** Countermark on 1/8 cut of Spanish Colonial 8 Reales.

CM Date	Host Date	Good	VG	F	VF	XF
ND	1772-99 Rare	—	—	—	—	—

KM# 11.1 12 DOGS (2 Bits - 1/4 Dollar)
Silver **Countermark:** Cross, crescent and star **Note:** Countermarks on Mexico City 2 Reales, KM#85.

CM Date	Host Date	Good	VG	F	VF	XF
ND	1742-50	225	375	550	800	—

KM# 11.2 12 DOGS (2 Bits - 1/4 Dollar)
Silver **Countermark:** Cross, crescent and star **Note:** Countermarks on Mexico City 2 Reales, KM#86.

CM Date	Host Date	Good	VG	F	VF	XF
ND	1747-60	225	375	550	800	—

KM# 11.3 12 DOGS (2 Bits - 1/4 Dollar)
Silver **Countermark:** Cross, crescent and star **Note:** Countermarks on Mexico City 2 Reales, KM#87.

CM Date	Host Date	Good	VG	F	VF	XF
ND	1760-71	225	375	550	800	—

KM# 12 12 DOGS (2 Bits - 1/4 Dollar)
Silver **Countermark:** Cross, crescent and star **Note:** Countermarks on Mexico City 2 Reales, KM#88.

CM Date	Host Date	Good	VG	F	VF	XF
ND	1772-89	150	250	400	750	—

KM# 10 12 DOGS (2 Bits - 1/4 Dollar)
Silver **Countermark:** Cross; M's **Note:** Countermarks on obverse and on reverse of 1/4 cut of Spanish Colonial 8 Reales.

CM Date	Host Date	Good	VG	F	VF	XF
ND	1772-89	300	500	800	1,150	—

KM# 14 48 DOGS (8 Bits - 1 Dollar)
Silver **Countermark:** 3 crosses **Note:** Countermarks on Mexico City 8 Reales, KM#106.

CM Date	Host Date	Good	VG	F	VF	XF
ND	1772-89 Rare. 3 known.	—	—	—	—	—

Note: Baldwin's Gordon sale 10-96 VF realized $38,220.

MOROCCO

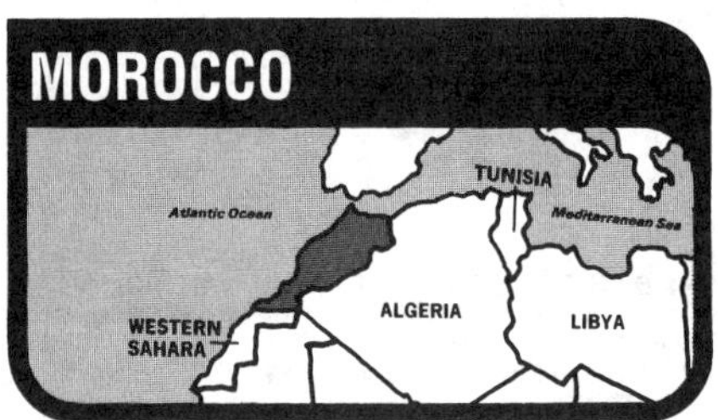

The Kingdom of Morocco, situated on the northwest corner of Africa, has an area of 432,620 sq. mi. (710,850 sq. km.). Capital: Rabat.

Morocco's strategic position at the gateway to western Europe has been the principal determinant of its violent, frequently unfortunate history. Time and again the fertile plain between the rugged Atlas Mountains and the sea has echoed the battle's trumpet as Phoenicians, Romans, Vandals, Visigoths, Byzantine Greeks and Islamic Arabs successively conquered and occupied the land. Modern Morocco is a remnant of an early empire formed by the Arabs at the close of the 7th century which encompassed all of northwest Africa and most of the Iberian Peninsula. During the 17th and 18th centuries, while under the control of native dynasties, it was the headquarters of the famous Sale pirates. Morocco's strategic position involved it in the competition of 19th century European powers for political influence in Africa, and resulted in the division of Morocco into French and Spanish spheres of interest which were established as protectorates in 1912. Morocco became independent on March 2, 1956, after France agreed to end its protectorate. Spain signed similar agreements on April 7 of the same year.

TITLES

المغرب

Al-Maghribiya(t)

المحمدية الشريفة

Al-Mohammediya(t) esh-Sherifiya(t)

RULERS

Filali Sharifs

Isma'il, AH1082-1139/1672-1727AD
Ahmad al-Dhahabi, AH1139-1141/1727-1729AD
'Abdallah, AH1141-71/1729-57AD
Sidi Muhammed III, AH1171-1204/1757-1790AD
Muhammed al-Yazid, AH1204-1206/1790-1792AD
Moulay Hisham, AH1205-1212/1791-1797AD
Pretender at Marrakesh AH1205-09/1790-94AD
Pretender at Asfi AH1209-12/1794-97AD
Sulayman, AH1207-38/1793-1822AD
Al-Husayn, AH1209-12/1794-97AD,
Pretender at Marrakesh

NOTE: Several Filali Sharifs had the title 'Moulay" (my lord).

EARLY COINAGE

Prior to the introduction of modern machine-struck coinage in Morocco in AH1299/1882AD the coinage of the Filali Sharifs contained of a variety of primitive hammered copper and cast bronze coins as well as of crudely hammered silver and gold issues which were in circulation together with considerable quantities of foreign coins.

The cast bronze (starting with Al-Yazid in AH1204/1790AD) were produced in several denominations, multiples and fractions of the basic unit of the Falus (Felous). The expression Zelagh (Zalagh) was used for all fractions of the Falus. After the Monetary Reform of 1902AD the Mazuna (or Muzuna, Mouzuna, Mawzuna) was the standard bronze unit. The size and weights of the pre-1902AD coins vary, which sometimes makes its distinction difficult, in particular for earlier rulers. Early types are varied, with different ornamentation and designs, some undated and/or without mint name, which makes a complete presentation of all varieties impossible. Beginning in AH1208, the obverse bears the Seal of Solomon (hexagram) and the reverse includes the date and/or mint name. All cast bronzes with only ornaments or the Seal of Solomon on both sides are issues of Sulayman. The mint (if present) is in Arabic script and starting with issues of Mohammed III the date (when present) is in Western numerals. The bronze pieces were cast in "trees" and occasionally entire or partial "trees" are found in the market.

Some bronze issues of Mohammed IV with illegible dates and mints and often light in weight are considered contemporary counterfeits. The war with Spain led to a chaotic and bad economic period in Morocco, during which Dirhams have been counterfeited by silver-plating hammered copper and brass pieces with dates AH1283-89/1866-72AD of Mohammed IV.

The silver and gold coins usually have the mint name on one side and the date on the other side. The original silver unit was the "legal dirham" of 2.931 grams standard weight, changing to several lower standards depending on the economic situation. A ¼ Dirham was called Mazuna until AH1213. The gold units Dinar and beginning with Sulayman, the Benduqi (Bonduqi) had 3.52 grams standard weight.

All weights indicated in the following listings for bronze, silver and gold coins are standards weights; actual weights of coins found can differ considerably. Anonymous strikes can be assigned to individual rulers by date, design and weight standard. Prices are for specimens with clearly legible dates (if any) and mint names (if any). Illegible and defectively produced pieces are worth much less.

To have more information on Moroccan issues from AH1075-1400/1664-1980AD, refer to Corpus des Monnaies Alawites by Daniel Eustache, Rabat 1984. For professional comments and estimate of rarity for all weights standards, see A Checklist of Islamic Coins by Stephen Album, Santa Rosa 1998. Information on Mazuna-strikes of Fes of AH1320-1323/1902-1205AD can be found in Monedas de Marruecos by Sanchez-Giron Blasco, Ceuta 1980. For details of Moroccan issues from AH1297-1380/1879-1960AD, refer to Monnaies et Jetons des Colonies Francaises by Jean Lecompte, Monaco 2000. Excellent drawings of bronze coins of Morocco, from AH1184-1321/1770-1903AD, can be found in Modern Copper Coins of the Muhammadan States by W. H. Valentine, London 1911 (reprint 1969).

NOTE: Prices are for specimens with clearly legible dates and mint names (if any). Illegible, barbarous, and defectively produced pieces are worth much less. Between AH1221-36 due to the bad economic situation no Dirhams were minted.

NOTE: Falus, most issues show ornaments on both sides composed of interlacing lines in a circle/square with inscriptions around, some issues have octagonal/hexagonal designs besides inscriptions Bronze, 3.97 g, 18-24mm.

MINTS

برلين

Be = Berlin

العرايش

Lr = al-'Araish (Larache)

العرايشة

Lr = al-'Araisah (Larache)

فاس

Fs = Fes (Fas, Fez)

فاس حضرة

FH = Fes Hazrat

مراكش

Mr = Marrakesh (Marakesh)

مكناس

مولاي ابراهيم

Mk = Miknas (Meknes)

رباط

Rb = Rabat

رباط الفتح

RF = Rabat al-Fath

تطوان

Te = Tetuan

(NM) = No mint name on coin.

KINGDOM

Filali Sharifs - Alawi Dynasty

Isma'il

AH1082-1139/1672-1727AD

HAMMERED COINAGE

Mint: Asfi
KM# A28a.1 FALUS
3.9700 g., Copper, 18-24 mm mm. **Note:** Anonymous issue. Size varies.

Date	Mintage	Good	VG	F	VF	XF
AHxxxx Illegible date	—	20.00	40.00	80.00	—	—

Mint: Asfi
KM# A28.1 FALUS
3.9700 g., Copper, 18-24 mm. **Note:** Anonymous issues.

Date	Mintage	Good	VG	F	VF	XF
AHxxxx Illegible date, Rare	—	—	—	—	—	—
AH1135 Rare	—	—	—	—	—	—

Mint: Fes Hazrat
KM# B28.1 MUZUNA
0.9400 g., Silver **Note:** Anonymous issue.

Date	Mintage	Good	VG	F	VF	XF
AH1133 Rare	—	—	—	—	—	—

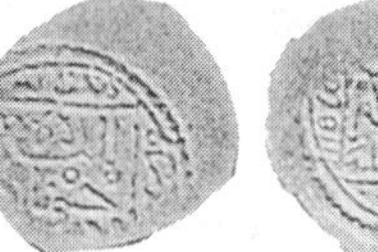

Mint: Meknes Hazrat
KM# B28.5 MUZUNA
0.9400 g., Silver **Note:** Anonymous issues.

Date	Mintage	Good	VG	F	VF	XF
AH1114	—	12.00	25.00	50.00	100	—
AH1117 Rare	—	—	—	—	—	—
AH1118	—	5.00	10.00	20.00	40.00	—
AH1119	—	12.00	25.00	50.00	100	—

Mint: Rabat al-Fath
KM# B28.2 MUZUNA
0.9400 g., Silver **Note:** Anonymous issue.

Date	Mintage	Good	VG	F	VF	XF
AH1129 Rare	—	—	—	—	—	—

Mint: Sijilmasah
KM# B28.6 MUZUNA
0.9400 g., Silver **Note:** Anonymous issue.

Date	Mintage	Good	VG	F	VF	XF
AH1115 Rare	—	—	—	—	—	—

Mint: Without Mint Name
KM# 28.3 DINAR
3.5200 g., Gold **Note:** Illegible mintname. Anonymous issues.

Date	Mintage	VG	F	VF	XF	Unc
AH1114	—	120	200	350	500	—
AH1131	—	120	200	350	500	—
AH1134	—	120	200	350	500	—

Mint: Fes Hazrat
KM# 28.1 DINAR
3.5200 g., Gold **Note:** Anonymous issues.

Date	Mintage	VG	F	VF	XF	Unc
AH1115	—	120	200	350	500	—
AH1120 Rare	—	—	—	—	—	—
AH1121 Rare	—	—	—	—	—	—
AH1122 Rare	—	—	—	—	—	—
AH1123 Rare	—	—	—	—	—	—
AH1124 Rare	—	—	—	—	—	—
AH1127 Rare	—	—	—	—	—	—
AH1128	—	175	300	450	700	—
AH1129 Rare	—	—	—	—	—	—
AH1130 Rare	—	—	—	—	—	—
AH1133 Rare	—	—	—	—	—	—
AH1136 Rare	—	—	—	—	—	—

Mint: Meknes Hazrat
KM# 28.2 DINAR
3.5200 g., Gold **Note:** Anonymous issues.

Date	Mintage	VG	F	VF	XF	Unc
AH1118	—	120	200	350	500	—
AH1130 Rare	—	—	—	—	—	—
AH1133 Rare	—	—	—	—	—	—

Muhammed III
AH1171-1204/1757-90AD

HAMMERED COINAGE

Mint: Without Mint Name
KM# 29.4 1/2 FALUS
1.7600 g., Copper **Note:** Anonymous issue.

Date	Mintage	Good	VG	F	VF	XF
AH1191 Rare	—	—	—	—	—	—

Mint: Fes Hazrat
KM# 29.5 1/2 FALUS
1.7600 g., Copper **Note:** Anonymous issue.

Date	Mintage	Good	VG	F	VF	XF
AH1195 Rare	—	—	—	—	—	—

Mint: Fes Hazrat
KM# 29.1 1/2 FALUS
1.7600 g., Copper **Note:** Anonymous issues.

Date	Mintage	Good	VG	F	VF	XF
AH1188	—	30.00	60.00	120	—	—

Mint: Rabat al-Fath
KM# 29.2 1/2 FALUS
1.7600 g., Copper **Note:** Anonymous issues.

Date	Mintage	Good	VG	F	VF	XF
AH1188 Rare	—	—	—	—	—	—
AH1200	—	30.00	60.00	120	—	—

Mint: Tetuan
KM# 29.3 1/2 FALUS
1.7600 g., Copper **Note:** Anonymous issues.

Date	Mintage	Good	VG	F	VF	XF
AH1188 Rare	—	—	—	—	—	—
AH1193 Rare	—	—	—	—	—	—

Mint: Without Mint Name
KM# 30.5 FALUS
3.5300 g., Copper **Obv:** Diamond-shaped ornament within circle **Rev:** Diamond-shaped ornament above date within circle **Note:** Without mintname. Anonymous issue.

Date	Mintage	Good	VG	F	VF	XF
AH1191	—	15.00	30.00	60.00	—	—

Mint: al-Araish
KM# 30.7 FALUS
3.5300 g., Copper **Note:** Anonymous issue.

Date	Mintage	Good	VG	F	VF	XF
AH1188	—	—	—	—	—	—

Mint: Asfi
KM# 30.6 FALUS
3.5300 g., Copper **Note:** Anonymous issue.

Date	Mintage	Good	VG	F	VF	XF
AH1194 Rare	—	—	—	—	—	—

Mint: Essaouira
KM# 30.8 FALUS
3.5300 g., Copper **Note:** Anonymous issue.

Date	Mintage	Good	VG	F	VF	XF
AH1202	—	—	—	—	—	—

Mint: Fes Hazrat
KM# 30.2 FALUS
3.5300 g., Copper **Note:** Anonymous issue.

Date	Mintage	Good	VG	F	VF	XF
AH1188	—	40.00	75.00	120	—	—
AH1190	—	30.00	60.00	100	—	—
AH1199	—	40.00	75.00	120	—	—

Mint: Marrakesh
KM# 30.1 FALUS
3.5300 g., Copper **Obv:** Inscription **Rev:** Date within square **Note:** Anonymous issue.

Date	Mintage	Good	VG	F	VF	XF
AH1172	—	30.00	60.00	100	—	—
AH1173	—	30.00	60.00	100	—	—
AH1174	—	30.00	60.00	100	—	—
AH1184	—	20.00	40.00	80.00	—	—
AH1185	—	30.00	60.00	100	—	—
AH1190 Rare	—	—	—	—	—	—
AH1191	—	20.00	40.00	80.00	—	—
AH1194	—	20.00	40.00	80.00	—	—
AH1196 Rare	—	—	—	—	—	—
AH1201	—	20.00	40.00	80.00	—	—

Mint: Rabat
KM# 30.9 FALUS
3.5300 g., Copper **Note:** Anonymous issues.

Date	Mintage	Good	VG	F	VF	XF
AHXXXX Illegible date	—	30.00	60.00	100	—	—
AH1191	—	30.00	60.00	100	—	—

Mint: Tetuan
KM# 30.3 FALUS
3.5300 g., Copper **Obv:** Fish above date within square **Rev:** Ornament within square **Note:** Anonymous issues.

Date	Mintage	Good	VG	F	VF	XF
AH1188	—	20.00	40.00	80.00	—	—
AH1190	—	20.00	40.00	80.00	—	—
AH--61 (error for 1191), Rare	—	—	—	—	—	—

Mint: Asfi
KM# 31.2 MUZUNA
0.8800 g., Silver 0

Date	Mintage	Good	VG	F	VF	XF
AH1177 Rare	—	—	—	—	—	—
AH1178 Rare	—	—	—	—	—	—
AH1179 Rare	—	—	—	—	—	—

Mint: Fes Hazrat
KM# 31.1 MUZUNA
0.8800 g., Silver

Date	Mintage	Good	VG	F	VF	XF
AH1172 Rare	—	—	—	—	—	—
AH1176	—	40.00	70.00	120	180	—
AH1177	—	15.00	25.00	50.00	100	—
AH1178	—	40.00	70.00	120	180	—
AH1183 Rare	—	—	—	—	—	—
AH1188 Rare	—	—	—	—	—	—

Mint: Sijilmasah
KM# 31.5 MUZUNA
0.8800 g., Silver **Note:** With name of ruler.

Date	Mintage	Good	VG	F	VF	XF
AH1175 Rare	—	—	—	—	—	—

Mint: Tanger
KM# 31.3 MUZUNA
0.8800 g., Silver

Date	Mintage	Good	VG	F	VF	XF
AH1179 Rare	—	—	—	—	—	—
AH1183	—	40.00	40.00	120	180	—

Mint: Tetuan
KM# 31.4 MUZUNA
0.8800 g., Silver

Date	Mintage	Good	VG	F	VF	XF
AH1179 Rare	—	—	—	—	—	—

Note: Some issues of first standard are anonymous, some are with the name of ruler

Mint: Without Mint Name
KM# A32.8 MUZUNA
0.7300 g., Silver **Note:** Without mintname.

Date	Mintage	Good	VG	F	VF	XF
AH1186	—	40.00	70.00	100	180	—
AH1187	—	8.00	15.00	30.00	60.00	—
AH1188	—	8.00	15.00	30.00	60.00	—
AH1189	—	8.00	15.00	30.00	60.00	—
AH1190	—	30.00	50.00	80.00	140	—
AH1193	—	8.00	15.00	30.00	60.00	—
AH1194	—	30.00	50.00	80.00	140	—

Mint: al-Araish
KM# A32.5 MUZUNA
0.7300 g., Silver

Date	Mintage	Good	VG	F	VF	XF
AH1185 Rare	—	—	—	—	—	—
AH1186 Rare	—	—	—	—	—	—

Mint: Asfi
KM# A32.7 MUZUNA
0.7300 g., Silver

Date	Mintage	Good	VG	F	VF	XF
AH1186	—	40.00	70.00	120	180	—

Mint: Essaouir
KM# A32.1 MUZUNA
0.7300 g., Silver

Date	Mintage	Good	VG	F	VF	XF
AH1184 Rare	—	—	—	—	—	—
AH1189 Rare	—	—	—	—	—	—
AH1192 Rare	—	—	—	—	—	—

Mint: Fes Hazrat
KM# A32.2 MUZUNA
0.7300 g., Silver

Date	Mintage	Good	VG	F	VF	XF
AH1184	—	40.00	70.00	120	180	—
AH1186 Rare	—	—	—	—	—	—
AH1190	—	30.00	50.00	80.00	140	—
AH1191	—	30.00	50.00	80.00	140	—
AH1192	—	20.00	40.00	60.00	100	—
AH1193 Rare	—	—	—	—	—	—
AH1194 Rare	—	—	—	—	—	—

Mint: Fes Hazrat
KM# A32.10 MUZUNA
0.7300 g., Silver

Date	Mintage	Good	VG	F	VF	XF
AH1199 Rare	—	—	—	—	—	—
AH1199	—	10.00	20.00	40.00	80.00	—

Mint: Marrakesh
KM# A32.3 MUZUNA
0.7300 g., Silver

Date	Mintage	Good	VG	F	VF	XF
AH1184	—	30.00	50.00	80.00	140	—
AH1185	—	40.00	70.00	120	180	—
AH1186 Rare	—	—	—	—	—	—
AH1190	—	30.00	50.00	80.00	140	—
AH1193	—	40.00	70.00	120	180	—
AH1194	—	30.00	50.00	80.00	140	—
AH1195	—	8.00	15.00	30.00	50.00	—
AH1196	—	20.00	40.00	60.00	100	—
AH1199	—	30.00	50.00	80.00	140	—

Mint: Miknas
KM# A32.9 MUZUNA
0.7300 g., Silver

Date	Mintage	Good	VG	F	VF	XF
AH1190	—	30.00	50.00	80.00	140	—
AH1191	—	40.00	70.00	120	180	—
AH1192 Rare	—	—	—	—	—	—
AH1193	—	10.00	20.00	40.00	80.00	—

Note: All issues of Second Standard are anonymous.

1198 Rare	—	—	—	—	—	—

Mint: Tanger
KM# A32.6 MUZUNA
0.0730 g., Silver

Date	Mintage	Good	VG	F	VF	XF
AH1185	—	30.00	50.00	80.00	140	—

Mint: Tetuan
KM# A32.4 MUZUNA
0.7300 g., Silver

Date	Mintage	Good	VG	F	VF	XF
AH1184	—	10.00	20.00	40.00	80.00	—
AH1185	—	20.00	40.00	60.00	100	—
AH1186 Rare	—	—	—	—	—	—
AH1193 Rare	—	—	—	—	—	—
AH1194	—	30.00	50.00	80.00	140	—
AH1195	—	10.00	20.00	40.00	80.00	—

Mint: Essaouir
KM# B32.6 MUZUNA
0.6800 g., Silver

Date	Mintage	Good	VG	F	VF	XF
AH1203	—	10.00	20.00	40.00	80.00	—
AH1204 Rare	—	—	—	—	—	—

Note: All issues of Third Standard are anonymous.

Mint: Fes
KM# B32.7 MUZUNA
0.6800 g., Silver

Date	Mintage	Good	VG	F	VF	XF
AH1201 Rare	—	—	—	—	—	—
AH1202	—	30.00	50.00	80.00	140	—
AH1203	—	30.00	50.00	80.00	140	—
AH1204 Rare	—	—	—	—	—	—

Mint: Fes Hazrat
KM# B32.1 MUZUNA
0.6800 g., Silver

Date	Mintage	Good	VG	F	VF	XF
AH1200	—	40.00	70.00	120	180	—
AH1201	—	30.00	50.00	80.00	100	—

Mint: Marrakesh
KM# B32.2 MUZUNA
0.6800 g., Silver

Date	Mintage	Good	VG	F	VF	XF
AH1200	—	10.00	20.00	40.00	80.00	—
AH1201	—	10.00	20.00	40.00	80.00	—
AH1202	—	20.00	40.00	60.00	100	—

Mint: Miknas
KM# B32.4 MUZUNA
0.6800 g., Silver

Date	Mintage	Good	VG	F	VF	XF
AH1201 Rare	—	—	—	—	—	—

Mint: Rabat al-Fath
KM# B32.3 MUZUNA
0.6800 g., Silver

Date	Mintage	Good	VG	F	VF	XF
AH1200	—	10.00	20.00	40.00	80.00	—
AH1201	—	30.00	50.00	80.00	140	—
AH1202 Rare	—	—	—	—	—	—

Mint: Tetuan
KM# B32.5 MUZUNA
0.6800 g., Silver

Date	Mintage	Good	VG	F	VF	XF
AH1201	—	20.00	40.00	60.00	100	—
AH1202	—	30.00	50.00	80.00	140	—
AH1203	—	30.00	50.00	80.00	140	—

Mint: Without Mint Name
C# 32.1 DIRHAM
2.9300 g., Silver **Note:** Without mintname.

Date	Mintage	Good	VG	F	VF	XF
AH1186	—	8.00	15.00	30.00	60.00	—
AH1187	—	4.00	8.00	15.00	30.00	—
AH1188	—	4.00	8.00	15.00	30.00	—
AH1188/7	—	12.00	25.00	50.00	100	—
AH1189	—	4.00	8.00	15.00	30.00	—
AH1190	—	20.00	40.00	80.00	160	—
AH1192 Rare	—	—	—	—	—	—
AH1193	—	4.00	8.00	15.00	30.00	—
AH1194	—	4.00	8.00	15.00	30.00	—
AH1195	—	20.00	40.00	80.00	160	—
AH1197 Rare	—	—	—	—	—	—

Mint: al-Araish
C# 32.2 DIRHAM
2.9300 g., Silver

Date	Mintage	Good	VG	F	VF	XF
AH1180	—	15.00	30.00	60.00	120	—
AH1181	—	15.00	30.00	60.00	120	—
AH1182	—	15.00	30.00	60.00	120	—
AH1183	—	20.00	40.00	80.00	160	—
AH1186	—	15.00	30.00	60.00	120	—

Mint: Essaouir
C# 32.3 DIRHAM
2.9300 g., Silver **Obv:** Inscription within square **Rev:** Inscription, date within square

Date	Mintage	Good	VG	F	VF	XF
AH1180	—	8.00	15.00	30.00	60.00	—
AH1181	—	8.00	15.00	30.00	60.00	—
AH1182	—	8.00	15.00	30.00	60.00	—
AH1183	—	8.00	15.00	30.00	60.00	—
AH1184	—	8.00	15.00	30.00	60.00	—
AH1185	—	40.00	60.00	100	180	—
AH1186	—	40.00	60.00	100	180	—
AH1188	—	5.00	10.00	20.00	40.00	—
AH1189	—	5.00	10.00	20.00	40.00	—
AH1191	—	40.00	60.00	100	180	—
AH1192	—	40.00	60.00	100	180	—
AH1193	—	40.00	60.00	100	180	—

Mint: Fedala
C# 32.4 DIRHAM
2.9300 g., Silver

Date	Mintage	Good	VG	F	VF	XF
AH1186	—	50.00	90.00	175	300	—

Mint: Fes
KM# C32.17 DIRHAM
2.9300 g., Silver

Date	Mintage	Good	VG	F	VF	XF
AH1180 Rare	—	—	—	—	—	—
AH1184	—	4.00	8.00	15.00	30.00	—

Mint: Fes Hazrat
C# 32.5 DIRHAM
2.9300 g., Silver

Date	Mintage	Good	VG	F	VF	XF
AH1172	—	20.00	40.00	80.00	160	—
AH1173	—	15.00	30.00	60.00	120	—
AH1174	—	15.00	30.00	60.00	120	—
AH1175	—	15.00	30.00	60.00	120	—
AH1176 Rare	—	—	—	—	—	—
AH1177	—	15.00	30.00	60.00	120	—
AH1179	—	4.00	8.00	15.00	30.00	—
AH1180	—	4.00	8.00	15.00	30.00	—
AH1181	—	8.00	15.00	30.00	60.00	—
AH1182	—	4.00	8.00	15.00	30.00	—
AH1183	—	4.00	8.00	15.00	30.00	—
AH1184	—	4.00	8.00	15.00	30.00	—
AH1185	—	4.00	8.00	15.00	30.00	—
AH1186	—	4.00	8.00	15.00	30.00	—
AH1187	—	4.00	8.00	15.00	30.00	—
AH1188	—	4.00	8.00	15.00	30.00	—
AH1189	—	8.00	15.00	30.00	60.00	—

Mint: Marrakesh
C# 32.6 DIRHAM
2.9300 g., Silver

Date	Mintage	Good	VG	F	VF	XF
AH1172	—	20.00	40.00	80.00	160	—
AH1173	—	12.00	25.00	50.00	100	—
AH1174	—	12.00	25.00	50.00	100	—
AH1175	—	25.00	50.00	100	200	—
AH1176	—	4.00	8.00	15.00	30.00	—
AH1178	—	10.00	20.00	40.00	80.00	—
AH1179	—	10.00	20.00	40.00	80.00	—
AH1180	—	8.00	15.00	30.00	60.00	—
AH1181	—	8.00	15.00	30.00	60.00	—
AH1182	—	4.00	8.00	15.00	30.00	—
AH1183	—	4.00	8.00	15.00	30.00	—
AH1184	—	4.00	8.00	15.00	30.00	—
AH1185	—	15.00	30.00	60.00	100	—
AH1186	—	8.00	15.00	30.00	60.00	—
AH1190	—	4.00	8.00	15.00	30.00	—
AH1191	—	15.00	30.00	60.00	100	—
AH1194	—	4.00	8.00	15.00	30.00	—

Mint: Marrakesh
KM# C32.18 DIRHAM
2.9300 g., Silver

Date	Mintage	Good	VG	F	VF	XF
AH1195	—	15.00	30.00	60.00	120	—
AH1196	—	45.00	80.00	150	250	—

Mint: Miknas
C# 32.7 DIRHAM
2.9300 g., Silver

Date	Mintage	Good	VG	F	VF	XF
AH1172 Rare	—	—	—	—	—	—
AH1173	—	8.00	15.00	30.00	60.00	—
AH1174	—	20.00	40.00	80.00	160	—
AH1175	—	4.00	8.00	15.00	30.00	—
AH1176	—	4.00	8.00	15.00	30.00	—
AH1177	—	4.00	8.00	15.00	30.00	—
AH1178	—	4.00	8.00	15.00	30.00	—
AH1179	—	4.00	8.00	15.00	30.00	—
AH1180	—	4.00	8.00	15.00	30.00	—
AH1181	—	4.00	8.00	15.00	30.00	—
AH1182	—	4.00	8.00	15.00	30.00	—
AH1183	—	4.00	8.00	15.00	30.00	—
AH1184	—	4.00	8.00	15.00	30.00	—
AH1185	—	4.00	8.00	15.00	30.00	—
AH1186	—	8.00	15.00	30.00	60.00	—
AH1188 Rare	—	—	—	—	—	—
AH1189	—	8.00	15.00	30.00	60.00	—
AH1190	—	25.00	50.00	100	200	—
AH1193 Rare	—	—	—	—	—	—

Mint: Rabat
C# 32.8 DIRHAM
2.9300 g., Silver

Date	Mintage	Good	VG	F	VF	XF
AH1189	—	10.00	20.00	40.00	80.00	—
AH1191	—	8.00	15.00	30.00	60.00	—

Mint: Rabat al-Fath
C# 32.9 DIRHAM
2.9300 g., Silver

Date	Mintage	Good	VG	F	VF	XF
AH1180 Rare	—	—	—	—	—	—
AH1181	—	8.00	15.00	30.00	60.00	—
AH1182	—	10.00	20.00	40.00	80.00	—
AH1194	—	8.00	15.00	30.00	60.00	—

Mint: Sale
C# 32.10 DIRHAM
2.9300 g., Silver

Date	Mintage	Good	VG	F	VF	XF
AH1187	—	30.00	60.00	100	175	—
AH1188	—	50.00	90.00	175	300	—

Mint: Tagr al-Araish
KM# C32.19 DIRHAM
2.9300 g., Silver

Date	Mintage	Good	VG	F	VF	XF
AH1183 Rare	—	—	—	—	—	—

Mint: Tagr er-Rabat
KM# C32.20 DIRHAM
2.9300 g., Silver

Date	Mintage	Good	VG	F	VF	XF
AH1181	—	50.00	100	175	300	—

Mint: Tanger
C# 32.11 DIRHAM
2.9300 g., Silver

Date	Mintage	Good	VG	F	VF	XF
AH1180 Rare	—	—	—	—	—	—
AH1184	—	50.00	90.00	175	280	—
AH1185 Rare	—	—	—	—	—	—
AH1186	—	18.00	35.00	70.00	140	—
AH1194	—	20.00	40.00	80.00	160	—

Mint: Tetuan
C# 32.12a DIRHAM
2.9300 g., Silver **Obv:** Inscription, date within circle **Rev:** Inscription, date

Date	Mintage	Good	VG	F	VF	XF
AH1181	—	8.00	15.00	30.00	60.00	—
AH1182	—	15.00	30.00	60.00	100	—
AH1183	—	8.00	15.00	30.00	60.00	—
AH1184	—	8.00	15.00	30.00	60.00	—
AH1185	—	4.00	8.00	15.00	30.00	—
AH1186	—	18.00	35.00	70.00	140	—
AH1188 Rare	—	—	—	—	—	—
AH1189	—	18.00	35.00	70.00	140	—
AH1194	—	4.00	8.00	15.00	30.00	—
AH1195	—	4.00	8.00	15.00	30.00	—
AH1196	—	4.00	8.00	15.00	30.00	—

Mint: Tetuan
C# 32.12b DIRHAM
2.9300 g., Silver **Note:** Mintname with additonal Koranic verses.

Date	Mintage	Good	VG	F	VF	XF
AH1195	—	60.00	110	200	300	—

Note: All issues of First Standard are anonymous.

Mint: El Bayda
C# 32.13 DIRHAM
2.7300 g., Silver

Date	Mintage	Good	VG	F	VF	XF
AH1203 Rare	—	—	—	100	200	—

Mint: Essaouir
C# 32.14 DIRHAM
2.7300 g., Silver

Date	Mintage	Good	VG	F	VF	XF
AH1202	—	10.00	20.00	40.00	80.00	—
AH1203	—	4.00	8.00	15.00	30.00	—
AH1204	—	10.00	20.00	40.00	80.00	—

Mint: Fes
KM# 32.21 DIRHAM
2.7300 g., Silver

Date	Mintage	Good	VG	F	VF	XF
AH1203	—	15.00	30.00	60.00	120	—
AH1204 Rare	—	—	—	—	—	—

Mint: Fes Hazrat
C# 32.15 DIRHAM
2.7300 g., Silver

Date	Mintage	Good	VG	F	VF	XF
AH1200 Rare	—	—	—	—	—	—
AH1203	—	4.00	8.00	15.00	30.00	—
AH1204	—	10.00	15.00	30.00	60.00	—

Mint: Marrakesh
C# 32.16 DIRHAM
2.7300 g., Silver

Date	Mintage	Good	VG	F	VF	XF
AH1204	—	4.00	8.00	15.00	30.00	—

Note: All issues of Second Standard are anonymous.

Mint: Miknas
C# 32.17 DIRHAM
2.7300 g., Silver

Date	Mintage	Good	VG	F	VF	XF
AH1202	—	6.00	12.00	25.00	50.00	—
AH1203	—	10.00	20.00	40.00	80.00	—

Mint: Rabat al-Fath
C# 32.18 DIRHAM
2.7300 g., Silver

Date	Mintage	Good	VG	F	VF	XF
AH1201	—	8.00	15.00	30.00	60.00	—

Mint: Taroudant
C# 32.19 DIRHAM
2.7300 g., Silver

Date	Mintage	Good	VG	F	VF	XF
AH1201 Rare	—	—	—	—	—	—
AH1202	—	40.00	70.00	125	200	—

Mint: Marrakesh
C# A33.2 1/4 MITQAL
7.3300 g., Silver **Note:** Anonymous issues.

Date	Mintage	Good	VG	F	VF	XF
AH1189 Rare	—	—	—	—	—	—
AH1190 Rare	—	—	—	—	—	—

Mint: Rabat al-Fath
C# A33.1 1/4 MITQAL
7.3300 g., Silver **Note:** Anonymous issue.

Date	Mintage	Good	VG	F	VF	XF
AH1189 Rare	—	—	—	—	—	—

Mint: Marrakesh
C# B33.2 1/2 MITQAL
14.6500 g., Silver **Note:** Anonymous issues.

Date	Mintage	Good	VG	F	VF	XF
AH1190 Rare	—	—	—	—	—	—

Mint: Rabat al-Fath
C# B33.1 1/2 MITQAL
14.6500 g., Silver **Note:** Anonymous issues.

Date	Mintage	Good	VG	F	VF	XF
AH1189 Rare	—	—	—	—	—	—

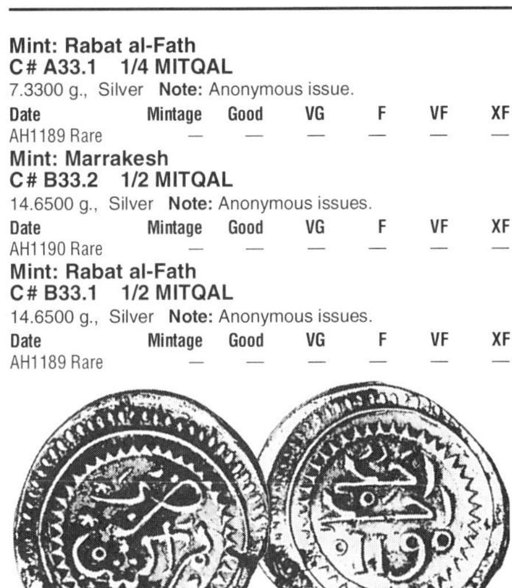

Mint: Marrakesh
KM# 42 MITQAL
29.3100 g., Silver **Obv:** Inscription within sun-like design **Rev:** Inscription, date within sun-like design

Date	Mintage	VG	F	VF	XF	Unc
AH1190	—	—	350	550	750	—

Mint: Rabat al-Fath
KM# 43 MITQAL
29.3100 g., Silver **Obv:** Inscription within sun-like design **Rev:** Inscription, date within sun-like design **Note:** Round flan.

Date	Mintage	VG	F	VF	XF	Unc
AH1191	—	—	300	450	650	—

Mint: Rabat al-Fath
KM# 41 MITQAL
29.3100 g., Silver **Obv:** Inscription within sun-like design **Rev:** Inscription, date within sun-like design **Note:** Square flan.

Date	Mintage	VG	F	VF	XF	Unc
AH1187	—	—	250	350	550	—
AH1188	—	—	250	350	550	—
AH1189	—	—	300	450	650	—

Mint: Tetuan
KM# 36 MITQAL
29.3100 g., Silver **Obv:** 4 Lined inscription **Rev:** 4 Lined inscription **Note:** Dav. #46

Date	Mintage	VG	F	VF	XF	Unc
AH1195	—	—	700	1,200	2,200	3,200

Mint: Tetuan
KM# 37 MITQAL
29.3100 g., Silver **Obv:** 4 Lined inscription within circle **Rev:** 4 Lined inscription, date within circle **Note:** Reduced size. Dav. #46A

Date	Mintage	VG	F	VF	XF	Unc
AH1195	—	—	400	700	1,300	2,000

Note: All Mitqals are anonymous.

Mint: Without Mint Name
KM# 40.2 DINAR
3.5200 g., Gold **Note:** Illegible date and mintname.

Date	Mintage	Good	VG	F	VF	XF
AHxxxx Rare	—	—	—	—	—	—

Mint: Fes Hazrat
KM# 40.1 DINAR
3.5200 g., Gold **Note:** Illegible date.

Date	Mintage	Good	VG	F	VF	XF
AHxxxx Rare	—	—	—	—	—	—

Mint: Fes
KM# 40.3 DINAR
3.1300 g., Gold

Date	Mintage	VG	F	VF	XF	Unc
AH1188	—	250	450	650	1,000	—
AH1189	—	125	250	400	600	—
AH1191	—	250	450	650	1,000	—
AH1192	—	150	300	500	750	—
AH1193	—	250	450	650	1,000	—

Mint: Fes Hazrat
KM# 40.4 DINAR
3.1300 g., Gold

Date	Mintage	VG	F	VF	XF	Unc
AH1199	—	150	300	500	750	—

Mint: Marrakesh
KM# 40.5 DINAR
3.1300 g., Gold **Obv:** Inscription within seal of Solomon **Rev:** Inscription, date within seal of Solomon **Note:** Struck at Marrakesh Mint.

Date	Mintage	VG	F	VF	XF	Unc
AH1190	—	250	450	650	1,000	—
AH1194	—	250	450	650	1,000	—

Mint: Miknas
KM# 40.6 DINAR
3.1300 g., Gold

Date	Mintage	VG	F	VF	XF	Unc
AH1191	—	250	450	650	1,000	—
AH1192	—	250	450	650	1,000	—

Mint: Marrakesh
KM# 40.7 DINAR
1.9500 g., Gold **Note:** Only the Dinar of the third standard is called Humasi.

Date	Mintage	VG	F	VF	XF	Unc
AH1200	—	125	250	400	600	—

Note: All issues of First, Second and Third Standards are anonymous.

Hisham, pretender at Marrakesh

AH1205-09/1790-94AD

HAMMERED COINAGE

Mint: Marrakesh
KM# 80 1/2 FALUS
1.7000 g., Cast Bronze **Note:** Anonymous issue.

Date	Mintage	Good	VG	F	VF	XF
AH1208	—	20.00	40.00	80.00	160	—

Mint: Without Mint Name
KM# 83.1 MUZUNA
0.6800 g., Silver **Note:** Without mint name.

Date	Mintage	Good	VG	F	VF	XF
AH1208 Rare	—	—	—	—	—	—
AH1209	—	30.00	60.00	100	200	—

Mint: Marrakesh
KM# 83.2 MUZUNA
0.6800 g., Silver **Note:** Some issues of first standard are anonymous, some with name of ruler; prev. KM#83.3.

Date	Mintage	Good	VG	F	VF	XF
AH1207 Rare	—	—	—	—	—	—
AH1208	—	50.00	80.00	150	280	—

Mint: Asfi
KM# 83.3 MUZUNA
0.5800 g., Silver **Note:** Anonymous issues; prev. KM#83.2.

Date	Mintage	Good	VG	F	VF	XF
AH1210	—	50.00	80.00	150	280	—
AH1211 Rare	—	—	—	—	—	—

Mint: Without Mint Name
KM# 86.1 DIRHAM
2.7300 g., Silver **Note:** Without mint name.

Date	Mintage	Good	VG	F	VF	XF
ND	—	30.00	60.00	100	200	—
AH1206	—	20.00	40.00	80.00	150	—
AH1207	—	20.00	40.00	100	150	—
AH1208	—	30.00	60.00	100	200	—
AH1209	—	30.00	60.00	30.00	200	—

Mint: Asfi
KM# 86.2 DIRHAM
2.7300 g., Silver

Date	Mintage	Good	VG	F	VF	XF
AH1206	—	50.00	80.00	150	280	—
AH1207	—	30.00	60.00	100	200	—
AH1208	—	30.00	60.00	100	200	—

Mint: Essaouira Mogador
KM# 86.3 DIRHAM
2.7300 g., Silver

Date	Mintage	Good	VG	F	VF	XF
AH1206	—	30.00	60.00	100	200	—
AH1207	—	50.00	80.00	150	280	—
AH1208 Rare	—	—	—	—	—	—

Mint: Marrakesh
KM# 86.4 DIRHAM
2.7300 g., Silver

Date	Mintage	Good	VG	F	VF	XF
AH1207	—	30.00	60.00	100	200	—
AH1208	—	30.00	60.00	100	200	—

Note: Some issues of first standard are anonymous, some with name of ruler.

Mint: Asfi
KM# 86.5 DIRHAM
2.3500 g., Silver **Note:** Anonymous issues.

Date	Mintage	Good	VG	F	VF	XF
AH1209	—	50.00	80.00	150	280	—
AH1210	—	25.00	50.00	95.00	180	—
AH1211	—	30.00	60.00	100	200	—
AH1212 Rare	—	—	—	—	—	—

Note: Sulayman also minted a Dirham AH1212 at Asfi; Refer to C#108

Mint: Without Mint Name
KM# 89.1 1/2 DINAR
1.7600 g., Gold **Note:** Without mint name.

Date	Mintage	VG	F	VF	XF	Unc
AH1207 Without ruler name	—	250	450	650	1,000	—
AH1208 With ruler name	—	250	450	650	1,000	—

Mint: Marrakesh
KM# 89.2 1/2 DINAR
1.7600 g., Gold **Note:** Struck at Marrakesh Mint.

Date	Mintage	VG	F	VF	XF	Unc
AH1208 With ruler name	—	250	450	650	1,000	—

Mint: Moulay-Ibrahim
KM# 89.3 1/2 DINAR
1.7600 g., Gold

Date	Mintage	VG	F	VF	XF	Unc
AH1205 With ruler name	—	250	450	650	1,000	—

Muhammed al-Yazid

AH1204-06/1790-92AD

HAMMERED COINAGE

Mint: Without Mint Name
C# 51.3 FALUS
3.5000 g., Bronze **Note:** Illegible mint. Anonymous issue.

Date	Mintage	Good	VG	F	VF	XF
AH1206	—	30.00	60.00	100	200	—

Mint: Fes
C# 51.1 FALUS
3.5000 g., Bronze **Note:** Anonymous issue.

Date	Mintage	Good	VG	F	VF	XF
AH1204 Rare	—	—	—	—	—	—

Mint: Without Mint Name
KM# 55.1 MUZUNA
0.6800 g., Silver **Note:** Without mintname. Issues with name of ruler.

Date	Mintage	Good	VG	F	VF	XF
AH1204 Rare	—	—	—	—	—	—
AH1205 Rare	—	—	—	—	—	—

Mint: Fes
KM# 55.2 MUZUNA
0.6800 g., Silver **Note:** Issue with name of ruler.

Date	Mintage	Good	VG	F	VF	XF
ND Rare	—	—	—	—	—	—

Mint: Without Mint Name
C# 65.1 DIRHAM
2.7400 g., Silver **Note:** Without mint name.

Date	Mintage	Good	VG	F	VF	XF
ND Rare	—	—	—	—	—	—
AH1204	—	50.00	80.00	150	280	—
AH1206 Rare	—	—	—	—	—	—

Mint: Fes
C# 65.2 DIRHAM
2.7400 g., Silver

Date	Mintage	Good	VG	F	VF	XF
ND	—	50.00	80.00	150	280	—

Note: All Dirhams with name of ruler.

Mint: Fes Hazrat
C# 65.3 DIRHAM
2.7400 g., Silver **Note:** Prev. C#65.2; Struck at Fes Hazrat Mint.

Date	Mintage	Good	VG	F	VF	XF
AH1205	—	30.00	60.00	100	200	—
AH1206	—	50.00	80.00	150	280	—

Mint: Tetuan
C# 65.4 DIRHAM
2.7000 g., Silver **Note:** Prev. C#65.3; Struck at Tetuan Mint.

Date	Mintage	Good	VG	F	VF	XF
AH1204	—	10.00	20.00	40.00	80.00	—
AH1206	—	15.00	30.00	60.00	120	—

Mint: Tetuan
KM# 69 1/4 DINAR
0.8800 g., Gold **Note:** Issue with name of ruler.

Date	Mintage	VG	F	VF	XF	Unc
AH1206	—	150	300	500	750	—

Mint: Without Mint Name
KM# 70.1 1/2 DINAR
1.7600 g., Gold **Note:** Without mint name. Issues with name of ruler.

Date	Mintage	VG	F	VF	XF	Unc
ND	—	250	450	650	1,000	—
AH1204	—	150	300	500	750	—
AH1205	—	250	450	650	1,000	—
AH1206	—	250	450	650	1,000	—

Mint: Fes
KM# 70.2 1/2 DINAR
1.7600 g., Gold **Note:** Struck at Fes Mint. Issue with name of ruler.

Date	Mintage	VG	F	VF	XF	Unc
AH1205	—	80.00	150	300	500	—

Mint: Tetuan
KM# 70.3 1/2 DINAR
1.7600 g., Gold **Note:** Issue with name of ruler. Struck at Tetuan Mint.

Date	Mintage	VG	F	VF	XF	Unc
AH1206	—	80.00	150	300	500	—

Sulayman II
AH1207-38/1793-1822AD
HAMMERED COINAGE

Mint: Without Mint Name
KM# 92.1 1/2 FALUS
1.7000 g., Cast Bronze **Obv:** Seal of Solomon **Rev:** Date, without mintname **Note:** Without mintname; size varies 12-16 mm.

Date	Mintage	Good	VG	F	VF	XF
AH1206 Rare	—	—	—	—	—	—
AH1208	—	10.00	20.00	40.00	80.00	—

Mint: Without Mint Name
KM# 91 1/2 FALUS
1.7000 g., Cast Bronze **Obv:** Seal of Solomon **Rev:** Seal of Solomon **Note:** Size varies 12-16 mm.

Date	Mintage	Good	VG	F	VF	XF
ND(1792-1822)	—	10.00	20.00	40.00	80.00	—

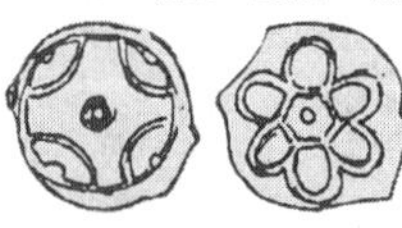

Mint: Without Mint Name
KM# 90.1 1/2 FALUS
1.7000 g., Cast Bronze **Obv:** Square design **Rev:** Flower design **Note:** Size varies 12-16 mm.

Date	Mintage	Good	VG	F	VF	XF
ND(1792-1822)	—	8.00	15.00	30.00	60.00	—

Mint: Without Mint Name
KM# 90.2 1/2 FALUS
1.7000 g., Cast Bronze **Obv:** Seal of solomon **Rev:** Ornamental design **Note:** Size varies 12-16 mm.

Date	Mintage	Good	VG	F	VF	XF
ND(1792-1822)	—	8.00	15.00	30.00	60.00	—

Mint: Marrakesh
KM# 92.2 1/2 FALUS
1.7000 g., Cast Bronze **Obv:** Seal of Solomon **Rev:** Mint within seal of Solomon **Note:** Size varies 12-16 mm.

Date	Mintage	Good	VG	F	VF	XF
ND(1792-1822)	—	12.00	25.00	50.00	100	—

Mint: Rabat
KM# 92.3a 1/2 FALUS
1.7000 g., Cast Bronze **Obv:** Interlacing lines in circle **Rev:** Year and mint **Note:** size varies 12-16 mm

Date	Mintage	Good	VG	F	VF	XF
AH1206 Rare	—	—	—	—	—	—

Mint: Rabat
KM# 92.3b 1/2 FALUS
1.7000 g., Cast Bronze, 12-16 mm. **Obv:** Octagonal design and mint **Rev:** Year **Note:** Size varies 12-16 mm.

Date	Mintage	Good	VG	F	VF	XF
AH1209 Rare	—	—	—	—	—	—
AH1208	—	12.00	25.00	50.00	100	—

Mint: Without Mint Name
KM# 93 FALUS
3.5000 g., Cast Bronze **Obv:** Seal of Solomon **Rev:** Ornamental design **Note:** Size varies 17-22 mm.

Date	Mintage	Good	VG	F	VF	XF
ND(1792-1822)	—	8.00	15.00	30.00	60.00	—

Mint: Without Mint Name
KM# 94 FALUS
3.5000 g., Cast Bronze **Obv:** Seal of Solomon **Rev:** Seal of Solomon **Note:** Size varies 17-22 mm.

Date	Mintage	Good	VG	F	VF	XF
ND(1792-1822)	—	8.00	15.00	30.00	60.00	—

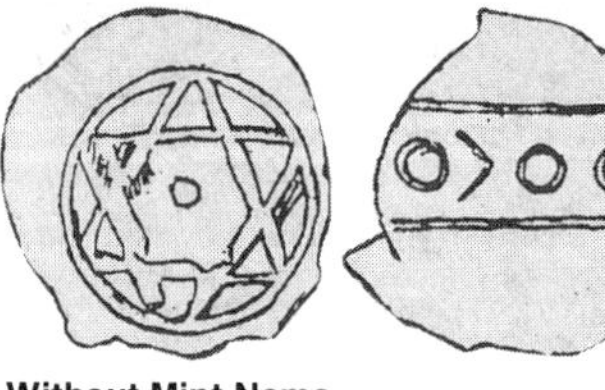

Mint: Without Mint Name
KM# A95.1 FALUS
3.5000 g., Cast Bronze **Obv:** Seal of Solomon **Rev:** Combination of symbols composed of circles and right or left angles between lines **Note:** Size varies 17-22 mm.

Date	Mintage	Good	VG	F	VF	XF
ND(1792-1822)	—	10.00	20.00	40.00	80.00	—

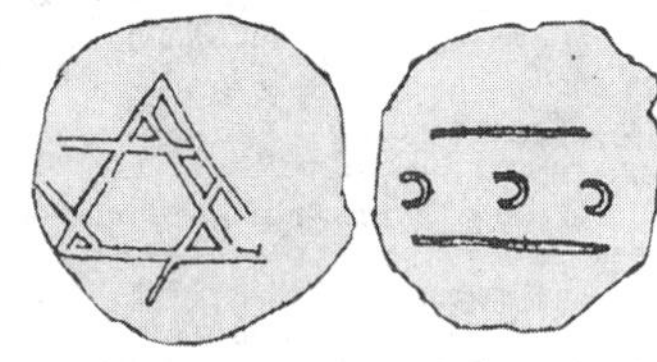

Mint: Without Mint Name
KM# A95.2 FALUS
3.5000 g., Cast Bronze **Obv:** Seal of Solomon **Rev:** Symbols composed of retrograde CCCs between lines **Note:** Size varies 17-22 mm.

Date	Mintage	Good	VG	F	VF	XF
ND(1792-1822)	—	12.00	25.00	50.00	100	—

Mint: Fes
KM# 95.5 FALUS
3.5000 g., Cast Bronze, 17-22 mm. **Obv:** Seal of Solomon **Rev:** Year and mint **Note:** Prev. KM#95.4.

Date	Mintage	Good	VG	F	VF	XF
AH1208 Rare	—	—	—	—	—	—
AH1211	—	20.00	40.00	80.00	160	—
AH1212	—	20.00	40.00	80.00	160	—
AH1214 Rare	—	—	—	—	—	—
AH1235 Rare	—	—	—	—	—	—

Mint: Marrakesh
KM# 95.6 FALUS
3.5000 g., Cast Bronze, 17-22 mm. **Obv:** Seal of Solomon **Rev:** Year and mint **Note:** Prev. KM#95.5.

Date	Mintage	Good	VG	F	VF	XF
AH1214 Rare	—	—	—	—	—	—
AH1217 Rare	—	—	—	—	—	—
AH1231 Rare	—	—	—	—	—	—
AH1235 Rare	—	—	—	—	—	—

Mint: Tetuan
KM# 95.9 FALUS
3.5000 g., Cast Bronze **Obv:** Seal of Solomon **Rev:** Year and mint **Note:** Prev. KM#95.8.

Date	Mintage	Good	VG	F	VF	XF
AH1211	—	15.00	30.00	60.00	120	—
AH1212 Rare	—	—	—	—	—	—
AH1228	—	10.00	20.00	40.00	80.00	—
AH1229	—	12.00	25.00	50.00	100	—
AH1230 Rare	—	—	—	—	—	—

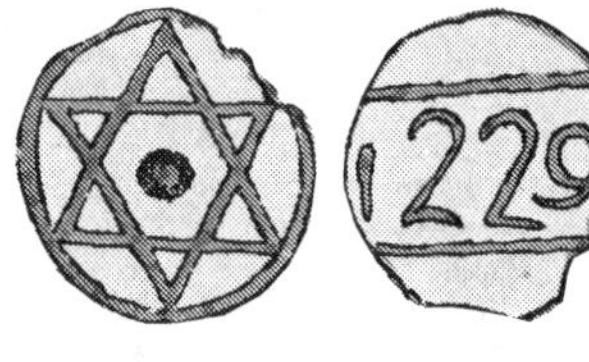

Mint: Without Mint Name
KM# 95.1 FALUS
3.5000 g., Cast Bronze, 17-22 mm. **Obv:** Seal of Solomon **Rev:** Year **Note:** Prev. C#95.1.

Date	Mintage	Good	VG	F	VF	XF
AH1214 Rare	—	—	—	—	—	—
AH1215 Rare	—	—	—	—	—	—
AH1216 Rare	—	—	—	—	—	—
AH1218	—	8.00	15.00	30.00	60.00	—
AH1220	—	4.00	8.00	15.00	30.00	—
AH1225	—	4.00	8.00	15.00	30.00	—
AH1229	—	4.00	8.00	15.00	30.00	—
AH1231 Rare	—	—	—	—	—	—
AH1234 Rare	—	—	—	—	—	—
AH1235	—	8.00	15.00	30.00	60.00	—
AH1236	—	8.00	15.00	30.00	60.00	—
AH1237	—	8.00	15.00	30.00	60.00	—
AH1238	—	8.00	15.00	30.00	60.00	—

Mint: Without Mint Name
KM# 96.1 2 FALUS
7.1000 g., Cast Bronze **Obv:** Ornamental design **Rev:** Ornamental design **Note:** Size varies 20-23 mm.

Date	Mintage	Good	VG	F	VF	XF
ND(1792-1822)	—	60.00	100	160	240	—

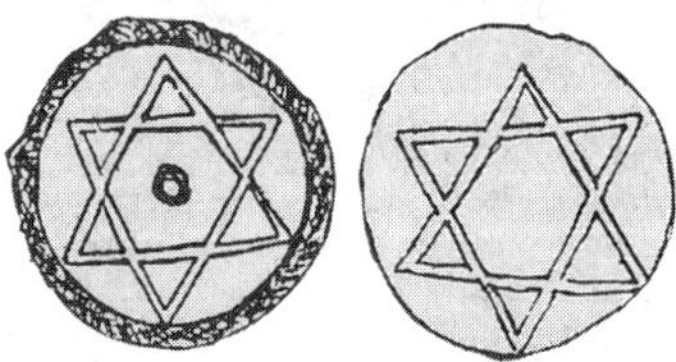

Mint: Without Mint Name
KM# 96.2 2 FALUS
7.1000 g., Cast Bronze **Obv:** Seal of Solomon **Rev:** Seal of Solomon **Note:** Size varies 20-23 mm.

Date	Mintage	Good	VG	F	VF	XF
ND(1792-1822)	—	10.00	20.00	30.00	60.00	—

Mint: Tetuan
KM# 97.5 2 FALUS
7.1000 g., Cast Bronze **Obv:** Mint in circle **Rev:** Year in circular design **Note:** Size varies 20-23 mm.

Date	Mintage	Good	VG	F	VF	XF
AH1208	—	12.00	25.00	50.00	100	—
AH1209	—	8.00	15.00	30.00	60.00	—
AH1231 Rare	—	—	—	—	—	—

Mint: Without Mint Name
KM# 99.1 3 FALUS
10.6000 g., Cast Bronze **Obv:** Seal of Solomon **Rev:** Ornamental design **Note:** Size varies 24-27 mm.

Date	Mintage	Good	VG	F	VF	XF
ND(1792-1822)	—	15.00	25.00	50.00	100	—

Mint: Without Mint Name
KM# 99.2 3 FALUS
10.6000 g., Cast Bronze **Obv:** Seal of Solomon **Rev:** Seal of Solomon **Note:** Size varies 24-27 mm.

Date	Mintage	Good	VG	F	VF	XF
ND(1792-1822)	—	10.00	15.00	25.00	50.00	—

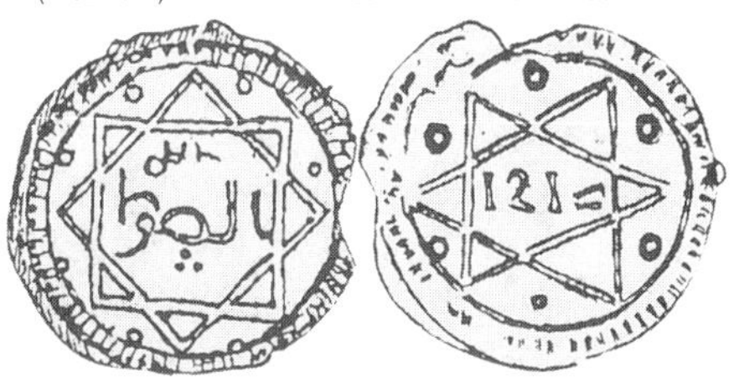

Mint: Essaouira
KM# 100.2 3 FALUS
10.6000 g., Cast Bronze, 24-27 mm. **Obv:** Seal of Solomon with year **Rev:** Octogram with mint **Note:** Size varies.

Date	Mintage	Good	VG	F	VF	XF
AH1213 Rare	—	—	—	—	—	—
AH1214	—	15.00	25.00	50.00	100	—
AH1215	—	15.00	25.00	50.00	100	—
AH1219 Rare	—	—	—	—	—	—

Mint: Fes
KM# 100.3 3 FALUS
10.6000 g., Cast Bronze, 24-27 mm.

Date	Mintage	Good	VG	F	VF	XF
AH1212	—	15.00	25.00	50.00	100	—
AH1215	—	10.00	20.00	40.00	80.00	—

Mint: Without Mint Name
KM# 100.1 3 FALUS
10.6000 g., Cast Bronze **Obv:** Seal of Solomon **Rev:** Year **Note:** Size varies 24-27 mm.

Date	Mintage	Good	VG	F	VF	XF
AH1212	—	15.00	25.00	40.00	80.00	—
AH1214 Rare	—	—	—	—	—	—
AH1217 Rare	—	—	—	—	—	—

Mint: Without Mint Name
KM# 102 4 FALUS
Cast Bronze 14.1 **Obv:** Seal of Solomon **Rev:** Flower in octogram **Note:** Size varies 28-34 mm.

Date	Mintage	Good	VG	F	VF	XF
ND(1792-1822)	—	20.00	40.00	90.00	200	—

Mint: Without Mint Name
KM# 103 4 FALUS
14.1000 g., Cast Bronze **Obv:** Seal of Solomon **Rev:** Seal of Solomon **Note:** Size varies 28-34 mm.

Date	Mintage	Good	VG	F	VF	XF
ND(1792-1822)	—	12.00	25.00	60.00	120	—

Mint: Without Mint NameWithout Mint Name
KM# 101 4 FALUS
14.1000 g., Cast Bronze **Obv:** Ornamental design **Rev:** Ornamental design **Note:** Size varies 28-34 mm.

Date	Mintage	Good	VG	F	VF	XF
ND(1792-1822)	—	15.00	30.00	70.00	150	—

Mint: Fes
KM# A105 MUZUNA
0.6800 g., Silver, 15-18 mm. **Note:** Previously KM#105.

Date	Mintage	Good	VG	F	VF	XF
AH1207	—	15.00	30.00	60.00	100	—

Mint: Fes
KM# 105a.1 MUZUNA
0.6100 g., Silver **Note:** Size varies 15-18 mm.

Date	Mintage	Good	VG	F	VF	XF
AH1208	—	10.00	30.00	60.00	120	—
AH1212	—	10.00	30.00	60.00	120	—

Mint: Marrakesh
KM# 105a.2 MUZUNA
0.6800 g., Silver **Note:** Size varies 15-18 mm.

Date	Mintage	Good	VG	F	VF	XF
AH1212	—	10.00	30.00	60.00	120	—

Mint: Tetuan
KM# 105a.3 MUZUNA
0.6100 g., Silver **Note:** Size varies 15-18 mm.

Date	Mintage	Good	VG	F	VF	XF
AH1208	—	10.00	30.00	60.00	120	—
AH1209	—	10.00	30.00	60.00	120	—
AH1211 Rare	—	—	—	—	—	—

Mint: al-Araish
C# 108a.1 DIRHAM
2.7400 g., Silver **Note:** Prev. C#108a.2.

Date	Mintage	Good	VG	F	VF	XF
AH1207 Rare	—	—	—	—	—	—

Mint: Fes
C# 108a.2 DIRHAM
2.7400 g., Silver **Note:** Prev. C#108a.1.

Date	Mintage	Good	VG	F	VF	XF
AH1206	—	15.00	30.00	60.00	100	—
AH1207	—	15.00	30.00	60.00	100	—

Mint: Miknas
C# 108a.3 DIRHAM
2.7400 g., Silver **Note:** 17-22mm.

Date	Mintage	Good	VG	F	VF	XF
AH1207	—	15.00	30.00	60.00	120	—

Mint: Rabat al-Fath
C# 108a.4 DIRHAM
2.7400 g., Silver

Date	Mintage	Good	VG	F	VF	XF
AH1206	—	15.00	30.00	50.00	100	—
AH1207	—	10.00	20.00	40.00	80.00	—
AH1208	—	30.00	50.00	80.00	140	—

Mint: Tetuan
C# 108a.5 DIRHAM
2.7400 g., Silver

Date	Mintage	Good	VG	F	VF	XF
AH1206 Rare	—	—	—	—	—	—
AH1207	—	20.00	50.00	80.00	130	—

Mint: al-Araish
C# 108b.1 DIRHAM
2.4400 g., Silver **Note:** Prev. C#108b.3.

Date	Mintage	Good	VG	F	VF	XF
AH1208	—	20.00	40.00	80.00	160	—
AH1209	—	25.00	50.00	100	180	—
AH1210 Rare	—	—	—	—	—	—

Mint: Asfi
C# 108b.2 DIRHAM
2.4400 g., Silver **Note:** Prev. C#108b.1.

Date	Mintage	Good	VG	F	VF	XF
AH1212	—	50.00	90.00	150	240	—

Note: Hisham also struck a Dirham dated AH1212 at Asfi. Refer to KM#86.2

Mint: Fes
C# 108b.3 DIRHAM
2.4400 g., Silver **Note:** Prev. C#108b.2.

Date	Mintage	Good	VG	F	VF	XF
AH1208	—	15.00	30.00	50.00	100	—
AH1209	—	8.00	12.00	25.00	50.00	—
AH1210	—	8.00	12.00	25.00	50.00	—
AH1211 Rare	—	—	—	—	—	—
AH1213	—	20.00	40.00	80.00	150	—

Mint: Fes Hazrat
C# 108b.4 DIRHAM
2.4400 g., Silver

Date	Mintage	Good	VG	F	VF	XF
AH1209 Rare	—	—	—	—	—	—
AH1210	—	15.00	30.00	50.00	100	—
AH1211	—	10.00	20.00	30.00	60.00	—
AH1212	—	10.00	20.00	30.00	60.00	—

Mint: Marrakesh
C# 108b.5 DIRHAM
2.4400 g., Silver **Note:** Prev. C#108b.4.

Date	Mintage	Good	VG	F	VF	XF
AH1212	—	8.00	12.00	25.00	50.00	—

Note: Al-Husayn also minted a Dirham dated AH1212 at Marrakesh. Refer to KM#86.4

Mint: Miknas
C# 108b.6 DIRHAM
2.4400 g., Silver **Note:** Prev. C#108b.5.

Date	Mintage	Good	VG	F	VF	XF
AH1208	—	10.00	20.00	40.00	80.00	—
AH1209	—	8.00	12.00	25.00	50.00	—
AH1210	—	8.00	12.00	25.00	50.00	—
AH1211	—	10.00	20.00	40.00	80.00	—

Mint: Rabat al-Fath
C# 108b.7 DIRHAM
2.4400 g., Silver **Note:** Prev. C#108b.6.

Date	Mintage	Good	VG	F	VF	XF
AH1208	—	10.00	20.00	30.00	60.00	—
AH1209	—	10.00	15.00	25.00	40.00	—
AH1210	—	10.00	20.00	30.00	60.00	—
AH1211	—	15.00	30.00	50.00	100	—
AH1212	—	20.00	40.00	80.00	150	—
AH1213	—	20.00	40.00	80.00	150	—

Mint: Tetuan
C# 108b.8 DIRHAM
2.4400 g., Silver **Note:** Prev. C#108b.7.

Date	Mintage	Good	VG	F	VF	XF
AH1208	—	8.00	15.00	20.00	30.00	—
AH1209	—	10.00	20.00	30.00	60.00	—
AH1210	—	8.00	15.00	20.00	30.00	—
AH1211	—	8.00	15.00	20.00	30.00	—
AH1212	—	15.00	30.00	60.00	120	—

Mint: Asfi
C# 108c.1 DIRHAM
2.2500 g., Silver

Date	Mintage	Good	VG	F	VF	XF
AH1214	—	35.00	60.00	100	160	—

Mint: Essaouira Mogador
C# 108c.2 DIRHAM
2.2500 g., Silver

Date	Mintage	Good	VG	F	VF	XF
AH1215	—	25.00	45.00	70.00	120	—

Mint: Fes Hazrat
C# 108c.3 DIRHAM
2.2500 g., Silver

Date	Mintage	Good	VG	F	VF	XF
AH1213	—	10.00	15.00	20.00	30.00	—
AH1214	—	10.00	15.00	20.00	30.00	—
AH1215	—	10.00	15.00	20.00	30.00	—

Mint: Marrakesh
C# 108c.4 DIRHAM
2.2500 g., Silver

Date	Mintage	Good	VG	F	VF	XF
AH1213	—	8.00	12.00	25.00	50.00	—
AH1214	—	8.00	12.00	25.00	50.00	—
AH1215 Rare	—	—	—	—	—	—

Mint: Rabat al-Fath
C# 108c.5 DIRHAM
2.2500 g., Silver

Date	Mintage	Good	VG	F	VF	XF
AH1214	—	30.00	50.00	90.00	150	—

Mint: Fes
KM# 111 1/4 DINAR
0.8800 g., Gold

Date	Mintage	Good	VG	F	VF	XF
AH1206	—	100	200	350	600	—
AH1207	—	90.00	150	250	375	—
AH1208	—	100	200	350	600	—

Mint: al-Araish
KM# 112.1 1/2 DINAR
1.7600 g., Gold **Note:** Struck at al-Araish Mint.

Date	Mintage	VG	F	VF	XF	Unc
AH1209	—	100	200	350	600	—

Mint: Fes
KM# 112.2 1/2 DINAR
1.7600 g., Gold **Note:** Struck at Fes Mint.

Date	Mintage	VG	F	VF	XF	Unc
AH1206	—	90.00	150	250	375	—
AH1207	—	100	200	350	600	—
AH1208	—	100	200	350	600	—
AH1209	—	100	200	350	600	—

Mint: Rabat al-Fath
KM# 112.3 1/2 DINAR
1.7600 g., Gold **Note:** Struck at Rabat Mint.

Date	Mintage	VG	F	VF	XF	Unc
AH1208	—	90.00	150	250	375	—
AH1209	—	100	200	350	600	—
AH1210	—	100	200	350	600	—

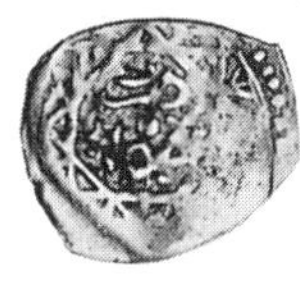

Mint: Tetuan
KM# 112.4 1/2 DINAR
1.7600 g., Gold **Note:** Struck at Tetuan Mint.

Date	Mintage	VG	F	VF	XF	Unc
AH1208	—	90.00	150	250	375	—
AH1209	—	90.00	150	250	375	—

Mint: Fes Hazrat
C# 115 BENDUQI
3.5200 g., Gold

Date	Mintage	VG	F	VF	XF	Unc
AH1209	—	100	150	300	500	—
AH1210	—	100	150	300	500	—
AH1212	—	100	150	300	500	—
AH1214	—	100	150	300	500	—
AH1216	—	90.00	125	250	375	—
AH1217	—	90.00	125	250	375	—
AH1218	—	90.00	125	250	375	—
AH1219	—	100	150	300	500	—
AH1220	—	100	150	300	500	—
AH1224	—	100	150	300	500	—
AH1234	—	100	150	300	500	—
AH1235	—	100	150	300	500	—
AH1238	—	100	150	300	500	—

Al-Husayn
Pretender at Marrakesh

HAMMERED COINAGE

Mint: Marrakesh
KM# 117 FALUS
3.5000 g., Cast Bronze **Obv:** Mintname **Rev:** Date **Note:** Anonymous issue.

Date	Mintage	Good	VG	F	VF	XF
AH1211	—	35.00	60.00	100	160	—

Mint: Marrakesh
KM# 118 MUZUNA
0.6100 g., Silver **Note:** Anonymous issue.

Date	Mintage	Good	VG	F	VF	XF
AH1210	—	50.00	80.00	150	280	—

Mint: Without Mint Name
KM# 119 DIRHAM
2.4400 g., Silver

Date	Mintage	Good	VG	F	VF	XF
AH1209	—	30.00	60.00	100	200	—
AH1210	—	30.00	60.00	100	200	—

Mint: Marrakesh
KM# 119a.2 DIRHAM
1.9500 g., Silver

Date	Mintage	Good	VG	F	VF	XF
AH1211	—	30.00	60.00	100	200	—
AH1212	—	25.00	50.00	90.00	180	—

Note: Sulayman also minted a dirham AH1212 Marrakesh, refer to C#108

Mint: Marrakesh
KM# 119a.1 DIRHAM
1.9500 g., Silver **Note:** Anonymous issue.

Date	Mintage	Good	VG	F	VF	XF
AH1211	—	25.00	50.00	90.00	180	—

Note: Coins dated AH1211 exist both with and without ruler's name

PATTERNS

Including off metal strikes

KM#	Date	Mintage	Identification	Mkt Val
PnA1	AH1201Ma	—	10 Mitqals. Gold. 16.6000 g. Milled, prev. C#45.	15,000

Note: Remelted due to the Madrid mint mark.

KM#	Date	Mintage	Identification	Mkt Val
PnA2	AH1201	—	10 Mitqals. Pewter. Obverse only uniface strike, Madrid Mint.	—
PnC34	AH1186	—	Mitqal. Silver. 27.8000 g. 44 mm. Struck at Marrakesh Mint.	—

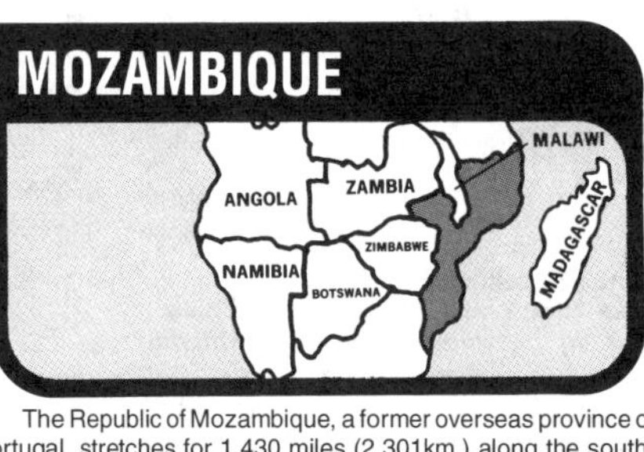

The Republic of Mozambique, a former overseas province of Portugal, stretches for 1,430 miles (2,301km.) along the southeast coast of Africa, has an area of 302,330 sq. mi. (801,590 sq. km.) and a population of 14.1 million, 99% of whom are native Africans of the Bantu tribes. Capital: Maputo. Agriculture is the chief industry. Cashew nuts, cotton, sugar, copra and tea are exported.

Vasco de Gama explored all the coast of Mozambique in 1498 and found Arab trading posts already established along the coast. Portuguese settlement dates from the establishment of the trading post of Mozambique in 1505.Within five years Portugal absorbed all the former Arab sultanates along the east African coast. The area was organized as a colony in 1907 and became an overseas province in 1952. In Sept. of 1974, after more than a decade of guerrilla warfare with the forces of the Mozambique Liberation Front, Portugal agreed to the independence of Mozambique, effective June 25, 1975.The Socialist party, led by President Joaquim Chissano was in power until the 2nd of November, 1990 when they became a republic.

Mozambique became a member of the Commonwealth of Nations in November 1995. The President is Head of State; the Prime Minister is Head of Government.

RULER
Portuguese, until 1975

MONETARY SYSTEM
2880 Reis = 6 Cruzados = 1 Onca

PORTUGUESE COLONY

COLONIAL COINAGE

KM# 1 10 REIS
Copper **Obv:** Crowned arms divide ME **Rev:** I 10

Date	Mintage	VG	F	VF	XF	Unc
ND(1706-50)	—	40.00	120	200	—	—
ND(1706-50)	—	40.00	120	200	—	—

KM# 2.1 15 REIS
Copper **Obv:** Crowned arms divide ME **Rev:** I 15

Date	Mintage	VG	F	VF	XF	Unc
ND(1706-50)	—	40.00	80.00	165	—	—

KM# 2.2 15 REIS
Copper **Obv:** Crowned arms divide ME **Rev:** I 15, with retrograde 5

Date	Mintage	VG	F	VF	XF	Unc
ND(1706-50)	—	45.00	90.00	185	—	—

KM# 3 30 REIS
Copper **Obv:** Crowned arms divide ME **Rev:** IoV/30

Date	Mintage	VG	F	VF	XF	Unc
ND(1706-50)	—	450	900	1,750	—	—

KM# 8 100 REIS
1.6500 g., Silver **Obv:** Crowned arms divide date **Rev:** Globe on cross

Date	Mintage	VG	F	VF	XF	Unc
1755	4,314	300	600	1,200	2,000	—

KM# 4 200 REIS
0.9170 Silver **Obv:** Crowned arms divide GA **Rev:** Cross dividing date into quadrants, value below

Date	Mintage	VG	F	VF	XF	Unc
1735	—	850	1,750	3,500	—	—

KM# 9 200 REIS
3.3700 g., Silver **Obv:** Crowned arms divide date **Rev:** Globe on cross

Date	Mintage	VG	F	VF	XF	Unc
1755	3,285	150	350	750	—	—

KM# 6 400 REIS
0.9170 Silver **Obv:** Crowned arms divide GA **Rev:** Cross dividing date into quadrants, value below

Date	Mintage	VG	F	VF	XF	Unc
1737	—	750	1,500	3,000	—	—
1743	—	750	1,500	3,000	—	—

KM# 10 400 REIS
7.3000 g., Silver **Obv:** Crowned arms divide date **Rev:** Globe on cross

Date	Mintage	VG	F	VF	XF	Unc
1755	2,059	125	275	450	—	—

KM# 5 800 REIS
0.9170 Silver **Obv:** Crowned arms divide GA **Rev:** Cross dividing date into quadrants, value below

Date	Mintage	VG	F	VF	XF	Unc
1735	—	850	1,650	3,250	—	—
1737	—	750	1,500	3,000	—	—
1743	—	750	1,500	3,000	—	—

KM# 7 800 REIS
0.9170 Silver **Rev:** Value above cross

Date	Mintage	VG	F	VF	XF	Unc
1743	—	750	1,500	3,000	—	—

KM# 11 800 REIS
14.4000 g., Silver **Obv:** Crowned arms divide date **Rev:** Globe on cross

Date	Mintage	VG	F	VF	XF	Unc
1755	1,610	200	400	800	—	—

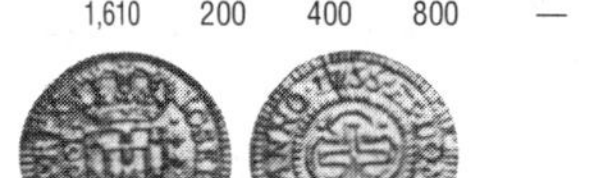

KM# 12 1000 REIS
1.3200 g., Gold **Obv:** Crowned arms **Rev:** Cross within inner circlem, date above

Date	Mintage	VG	F	VF	XF	Unc
1755	1,200	450	700	1,200	2,000	—

KM# 13 2000 REIS
2.5400 g., Gold **Obv:** Crowned arms **Rev:** Cross in inner circlem, date above

Date	Mintage	VG	F	VF	XF	Unc
1755	600	1,500	2,500	4,000	6,500	—

KM# 14 4000 REIS
5.0900 g., Gold **Obv:** Crowned arms **Rev:** Cross in inner circlem, date above

Date	Mintage	VG	F	VF	XF	Unc
1755	739	600	1,000	1,750	3,000	—

COUNTERMARKED COINAGE

Decree of May 28, 1767

This decree stated that all crown-sized coins were to be marked with a MR monogram and a 4. There are no known specimens listed in numismatic literature that tell of examples with the 4. The MR appears almost exclusively on Spanish Colonial Pillar dollars. Occasionally it appears on cob pieces and European coins. This countermark was to circulate for a longer period than any other Mozambique countermark.

KM# 27.1 8 REALES
Silver **Countermark:** MR **Note:** Countermark on Peru, Lima Mint 8 Reales, KM#55.1.

CM Date	Host Date	Good	VG	F	VF	XF
ND	ND Rare	125	200	325	500	—
ND	1751-60 Rare	—	—	—	—	—

KM# 27.2 8 REALES
Silver **Countermark:** MR **Note:** Countermark on Peru, Lima Mint 8 Reales, KM#A64.2

CM Date	Host Date	Good	VG	F	VF	XF
ND(1757)	1760-69	—	—	—	—	—

KM# 29 8 REALES
Silver **Countermark:** MR **Note:** Countermark on Mexico City 8 Reales, KM#105.

CM Date	Host Date	Good	VG	F	VF	XF
ND(1767)	1760-66	90.00	150	260	435	—

KM# 28 8 REALES
Silver **Countermark:** MR **Note:** Countermark on Mexico City 8 Reales, KM#104.1.

CM Date	Host Date	Good	VG	F	VF	XF
ND(1767)	1747-54	100	165	275	450	—

KM# 30 8 REALES
Silver **Countermark:** MR **Note:** Countermark on Hungarian Maria Theresa Thaler, KM#358.1.

CM Date	Host Date	Good	VG	F	VF	XF
ND(1767)	1753 KB	40.00	60.00	90.00	150	—

COUNTERMARKED COINAGE

Decree of January 19, 1889

During the reign of D. Carlos I, a substitution of an indented PM (Provincia de Mocambique) which replaced the crowned PM of D. Luis I, was countermarked on all foreign silver coinage circulating in Mozambique. These coins were to be replaced or exchanged by Portuguese coinage on their entry into the public treasury.

KM# 58 THALER
Silver **Countermark:** PM **Note:** Countermark on Austra Maria Theresa Thaler, KM#T1.

CM Date	Host Date	Good	VG	F	VF	XF
ND	1780	—	40.00	85.00	125	240

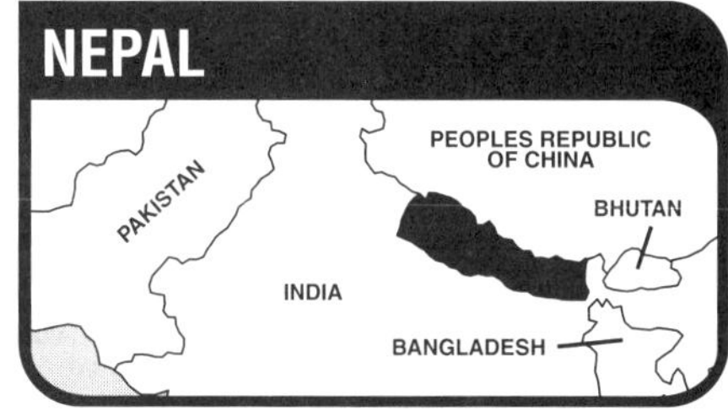

The Kingdom of Nepal, the world's only surviving Hindu kingdom, is a landlocked country occupying the southern slopes of the Himalayas. It has an area of 56,136 sq. mi. (140,800 sq. km.) and a population of 18 million. Capital: Kathmandu. Nepal has deposits of coal, copper, iron and cobalt, but they are largely unexploited. Agriculture is the principal economic activity. Rice, timber and jute are exported, with tourism being the other major foreign exchange earner.

Apart from a brief Muslim invasion in the 14th century, Nepal was able to avoid the mainstream of Northern Indian politics, due to its impregnable position in the mountains. It is therefore a unique survivor of the medieval Hindu and Buddhist culture of Northern India which was largely destroyed by the successive waves of Muslim invasions.

Prior to the late 18th century, Nepal, as we know it today, was divided among a number of small states. Unless otherwise stated, the term *Nepal* applies to the small fertile valley, about 4,500 ft. above sea level, in which the three main cities of Kathmandu, Patan and Bhatgaon are situated.

During the reign of King Yaksha Malla (1428-1482AD), the Nepalese kingdom, with capital at Bhatgaon, was extended northwards into Tibet, and also controlled a considerable area to the south of the hills. After Yaksha Malla's death, the Kingdom was divided among his sons, so four kingdoms were established with capitals at Bhatgaon, Patan, Kathmandu and Banepa, all situated within the small valley, less than 20 miles square. Banepa was quickly absorbed within the territory of Bhatgaon, but the other three kingdoms remained until 1769. The internecine strife between the three kings effectively stopped Nepal from becoming a major military force during this period, although with its fertile land and strategic position, it was by far the wealthiest and most powerful of the Himalayan states.

Apart from agriculture, Nepal owed its prosperity to its position on one of the easiest trade routes between the great monasteries of central Tibet, and India. Nepal made full use of this, and a trading community was set up in Lhasa during the 16th century, and Nepalese coins became the accepted currency medium in Tibet.

The seeds of discord between Nepal and Tibet were sown during the first half of the 18th century, when the Nepalese debased the coinage, and the fate of the Malla kings of Nepal was sealed when Prithvi Narayan Shah, King of the small state of Gorkha, to the west of Kathmandu, was able to gain control of the trans-himalayan trade routes during the years after 1750.

Prithvi Narayan spent several years consolidating his position in hill areas before he finally succeeded in conquering the Kathmandu Valley in 1768, where he established the Shah dynasty, and moved his capital to Kathmandu.

After Prithvi Narayan's death a period of political instability ensued which lasted until the 1840's when the Rana family reduced the monarch to a figurehead and established the post of hereditary Prime Minister. A popular revolution in 1950 toppled the Rana family and reconstituted power in the throne. In 1959 King Mahendra declared Nepal a constitutional monarchy, and in 1962 a new constitution set up a system of *panchayat* (village council) democracy. In 1990, following political unrest, the king's powers were reduced. The country then adopted a system of parliamentary democracy.

DATING

Nepal Samvat Era (NS)

All coins of the Malla kings of Nepal are dated in the Nepal Samvat era (NS). Year 1 NS began in 881, so to arrive at the AD date add 880 to the NS date. This era was exclusive to Nepal, except for one gold coin of Prana Narayan of Cooch Behar.

Saka Era (SE)

Up until 1888AD all coins of the Gorkha Dynasty were dated in the Saka era (SE). To convert from Saka to AD take Saka date and add 78 to arrive at the AD date. Coins dated with this era have SE before the date in the following listing.

Vikrama Samvat Era (VS)

From 1888AD most copper coins were dated in the Vikram Samvat (VS) era. To convert take VS date - 57 =AD date. Coins with this era have VS before the year in the listing. With the exception of a few gold coins struck in 1890 & 1892, silver and gold coins only changed to the VS era in 1911AD, but now this era is used for all coins struck in Nepal.

RULERS

KINGS OF KATHMANDU

भास्कर मल्ल
Bhaskara Malla,
NS821-835/1701-1715AD

महीन्द्र सिंह
Mahindra Simha,
NS835-842/1715-1722AD

जगज्जय मल्ल
Jagajjaya Malla
NS842-855/1722-1735AD

जय प्रकाश मल्ल
Jaya Prakash Malla,
NS855-866,870-888/1735-1746,1750-1768AD

ज्योति प्रकाश मल्ल
Jyoti Prakash Malla,
NS866-870/1746-c.1750AD

KINGS OF PATAN

यो गनरेन्द्र मल्ल
Yoga Narendra Malla,
NS805-825/1685-1705AD

लोक प्रकाश मल्ल
Loka Prakash Malla,
NS825-826/1705-1706AD

इन्द्र मल्ल
Indra Malla (Purandara Malla),
NS826-829/1706-1709AD

वीर नरसिंह मल्ल
Vira Narasimha Malla,
NS829/1709AD

वीर महीन्द्र मल्ल
Vira Mahindra Malla,
NS829-835/1709-1715AD

ऋद्धि नरसिंह
Riddhi Narasimha,
NS835-837/1715-1717AD

महीन्द्र सिंह
Mahindra Simha, King of Kathmandu,
NS837-842/1717-1722AD

योग प्रकाश मल्ल
Yoga Prakash Malla,
NS842-849/1722-1729AD

विष्णु मल्ल
Vishnu Malla,
NS849-865/1729-1745AD

राज्य प्रकाश मल्ल
Rajya Prakash Malla,
NS865-878/1745-1758AD

विश्वजित् मल्ल
Visvajit Malla,
NS878-880/1758-1760AD

जय प्रकाश मल्ल
Jaya Prakash Malla, King of Kathmandu,
NS880-881,883-884/1760-1761,1763-1764AD

रणजित मल्ल

Ranajit Malla, King of Bhatgaon,
NS882-883/1762-1763AD

दल मर्दन साह

Dala Mardana Saha,
NS884-885/1764-1765AD

तेज नरसिंह

Tej Narasimha Malla,
NS885-888/1765-1768AD

KINGS OF BHATGAON

भूपतीन्द्र मल्ल

Bhupatindra Malla,
NS816-842/1696-1722AD

रणजित् मल्ल

Ranajit Malla,
NS842-889/1722-1769AD

SHAH DYNASTY

पृथ्वी नारायण

Prithvi Narayan
In Gorkha: SE1664-1690/1742-1768AD
In Kathmandu: SE1690-1696/1768-1775AD

Queen of Prithvi Narayan
SE1696-1699/1775-1777AD:

प्रताप सिंह

Narindra Lakshmi

नरिन्द्र लक्ष्मी

Pratap Simha

Queen of Pratap Simha
SE1699-1720/1777-1799AD:

राजेन्द्र लक्ष्मी

Rajendra Lakshmi

रण वहादुर

Rana Bahadur

Queens of Rana Bahadur
SE1720-1738/1799-1816AD:

राज राज्येश्वरी

Raja Rajesvari

अमर राजयेश्वरी

Amara Rajesvari

सुवर्ण प्रभा

Suvarna Prabha

महामाहेश्वरी

Mahamahesvari

ललित त्रिपुर सुन्दरी

Lalita Tripura Sundari

गीर्वाण युद्ध विक्रम सा

Girvan Yuddha Vikrama

Queens of Girvan Yuddha Vikrama:

सिद्धि लक्ष्मी

Siddhi Lakshmi
Goraksha Rajya Lakshmi

MONETARY SYSTEM

Mohar Series

In about 1640 the weight standard of the Nepalese coinage was completely changed, and it is probable that all the old tanka coins were withdrawn from circulation.

The new standard coin was the Mohar, weighing about5.4 g, or rather more than half the old tanka. The Mohar was subdivided in factors of 2, as follows:

2 Mohar (Rupee) = 10.80 g
1 Mohar = 5.40 g
1/2 Mohar = 2.70 g
1/4 Mohar (Suki) = 1.35 g
1/8 Mohar = 0.67 g
1/16 Mohar = 0.34 g
1/32 Mohar = 0.17 g
1/128 Mohar (Dam) = 0.04-0.08 g
1/512 Mohar (Jawa) = 0.01 g

The weights given above correspond to the average weight of actual specimens, rather than the theoretical weight, which has been said to be 86.4 grains, or 5.60 g.

The coinage was almost entirely of silver, with the tiny Jawa being easily the smallest coin in the world. Gold coins were struck on only one or two occasions during the Madra period, from the same dies as the silver coins, but these were probably only used for ceremonial purposes. Gold after 1777AD was struck in greater quantity.

Initially the coinage was of fine silver, in contrast to the tanka coins, which were frequently debased. During the early 18th century, however, the coins became debased, but the fineness was improved after 1753AD. The coinage was again debased in the first half of the 19th century.

Many of the mohars circulated in Tibet as well as in Nepal, and on a number of occasions coins were struck from bullion supplied by the Tibetan authorities. The smaller denominations never circulated in Tibet, but some of the mohars were cut for use as small change in Tibet.

In these listings only major changes in design have been noted. There are numerous minor varieties of ornamentation or spelling.

Initially the copper paisa was not fixed in value relative to the silver coins, and generally fluctuated in value from1/32 mohar in 1865AD to around 1/50 mohar afterc1880AD, and was fixed at that value in 1903AD.

4 Dam = 1 Paisa
2 Paisa = 1 Dyak, Adhani

NUMERALS

Nepal has used more variations of numerals on their coins than any other nation. The most common are illustrated in the numeral chart in the introduction. The chart below illustrates some variations encompassing the last four centuries.

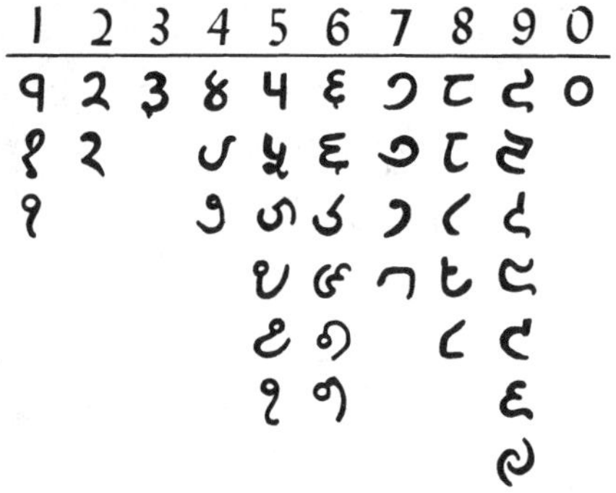

1	2	3	4	5	6	7	8	9	0
१	२	३	४	५	६	७	८	९	०

NUMERICS

आधा

Half

एक

One

दुइ

Two

चार

Four

पाच

Ten

दसा

Twenty

विसा

Twenty-five

पचीसा

Fifty

पचासा

Hundred

DENOMINATIONS

पैसा

Paisa

दाम

Dam

मोरु

Mohar

रुपैयाँ

Rupee

असार्फी

Ashrapi

अश्रफी

Asarfi

MONETARY SYSTEM

Mohar Series

In about 1640 the weight standard of the Nepalese coinage was completely changed, and it is probable that all the old tanka coins were withdrawn from circulation.

The new standard coin was the Mohar, weighing about5.4 g, or rather more than half the old tanka. The Mohar was subdivided in factors of 2, as follows:

2 Mohar (Rupee) = 10.80 g
1 Mohar = 5.40 g
1/2 Mohar = 2.70 g
1/4 Mohar (Suki) = 1.35 g
1/8 Mohar = 0.67 g
1/16 Mohar = 0.34 g
1/32 Mohar = 0.17 g
1/128 Mohar (Dam) = 0.04-0.08 g
1/512 Mohar (Jawa) = 0.01 g

The weights given above correspond to the average weight of actual specimens, rather than the theoretical weight, which has been said to be 86.4 grains, or 5.60 g.

The coinage was almost entirely of silver, with the tiny Jawa being easily the smallest coin in the world. Gold coins were struck on only one or two occasions during the Madra period, from the same dies as the silver coins, but these were probably only used for ceremonial purposes. Gold after 1777AD was struck in greater quantity.

Initially the coinage was of fine silver, in contrast to the tanka coins, which were frequently debased. During the early 18th century, however, the coins became debased, but the fineness was improved after 1753AD. The coinage was again debased in the first half of the 19th century.

Many of the mohars circulated in Tibet as well as in Nepal, and on a number of occasions coins were struck from bullion supplied by the Tibetan authorities. The smaller denominations never circulated in Tibet, but some of the mohars were cut for use as small change in Tibet.

In these listings only major changes in design have been noted. There are numerous minor varieties of ornamentation or spelling.

Initially the copper paisa was not fixed in value relative to the silver coins, and generally fluctuated in value from1/32 mohar in 1865AD to around 1/50 mohar afterc1880AD, and was fixed at that value in 1903AD.

4 Dam = 1 Paisa
2 Paisa = 1 Dyak, Adhani

NUMERALS

Nepal has used more variations of numerals on their coins than any other nation. The most common are illustrated in the numeral chart in the introduction. The chart below illustrates some variations encompassing the last four centuries.

1	2	3	4	5	6	7	8	9	0
१	२	३	४	५	६	७	८	९	०

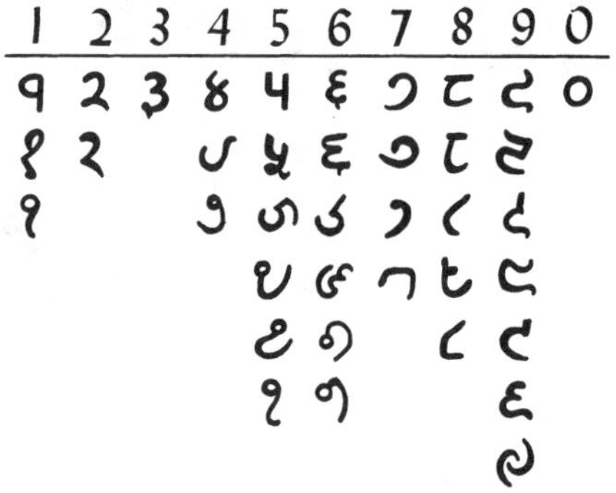

NUMERICS

Half	आधा
One	एक
Two	दुइ
Four	चार
Ten	पाच
Twenty	दसा
Twenty-five	विसा
Fifty	पचीसा
Hundred	पचासा

DENOMINATIONS

Paisa	पैसा
Dam	दाम
Mohar	मोरु
Rupee	रुपैयाँ
Ashrapi	असार्फी
Asarfi	अश्रफी

KINGDOM OF BHATGAON

KINGDOM

Bhupatindra Malla

NS816-42 / 1696-1722AD

MOHAR COINAGE

KM# 75 DAM

Silver **Obv. Legend:** Sri Sri Bhupa

Date	Mintage	Good	VG	F	VF	XF
ND	—	5.00	7.50	13.50	18.50	—

KM# 76 DAM

Silver **Obv. Legend:** Sri Bhupati

Date	Mintage	Good	VG	F	VF	XF
ND	—	2.50	4.00	7.00	10.00	—

KM# 78 1/16 MOHAR

Silver

Date	Mintage	Good	VG	F	VF	XF
ND	—	10.00	18.50	30.00	45.00	—

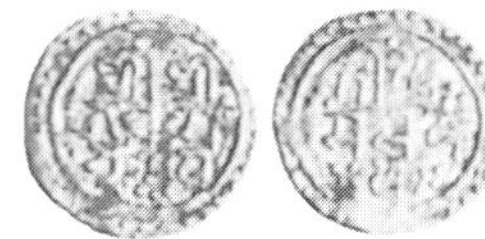

KM# 80 1/8 MOHAR

Silver

Date	Mintage	Good	VG	F	VF	XF
ND	—	10.00	16.50	26.50	37.50	—

Ranajit Malla

NS842-889 / 1722-1769AD

MOHAR COINAGE

KM# 91 DAM

Silver **Note:** Sword on stand.

Date	Mintage	Good	VG	F	VF	XF
ND	—	3.25	5.00	8.50	12.50	—

KM# 90 DAM

Silver **Note:** Uniface, without sword.

Date	Mintage	Good	VG	F	VF	XF
ND	—	2.50	4.00	7.00	10.00	—

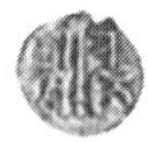

KM# 92 DAM

Silver **Note:** Uniface; Sword not on stand.

Date	Mintage	Good	VG	F	VF	XF
ND	—	3.25	5.00	8.50	12.50	—

KM# 94 1/32 MOHAR

Silver

Date	Mintage	Good	VG	F	VF	XF
ND	—	12.50	21.50	35.00	50.00	—

KM# 96 1/16 MOHAR

Silver

Date	Mintage	Good	VG	F	VF	XF
ND	—	20.00	35.00	70.00	100	—

KM# 97 1/16 MOHAR

Silver

Date	Mintage	Good	VG	F	VF	XF
ND	—	10.00	20.00	35.00	60.00	—

KM# 99 1/8 MOHAR

Silver **Obv:** Sword on stand

Date	Mintage	Good	VG	F	VF	XF
ND	—	8.00	13.50	22.50	32.50	—

KM# 100 1/8 MOHAR

Silver **Obv:** Sword not on stand

Date	Mintage	Good	VG	F	VF	XF
ND	—	5.00	7.50	13.50	18.50	—

KM# 102 1/4 MOHAR

Silver **Rev:** Die of Bhupatinddra Malla in error

Date	Mintage	Good	VG	F	VF	XF
NS816	—	16.50	27.50	45.00	65.00	—

KM# 103 1/4 MOHAR

Silver

Date	Mintage	Good	VG	F	VF	XF
NS842 (1722)	—	6.50	10.50	17.50	35.00	50.00

KM# 105 1/2 MOHAR

Silver **Obv:** Coronation date, Vaisakh, Sudi 15, 842

Date	Mintage	Good	VG	F	VF	XF
NS842 (1722)	—	50.00	100	200	300	—

KM# 107 MOHAR

Silver

Date	Mintage	Good	VG	F	VF	XF
NS842 (1722)	—	40.00	75.00	150	200	—

KM# 108 MOHAR

Silver

Date	Mintage	Good	VG	F	VF	XF
NS842 (1722)	—	4.00	7.00	12.00	20.00	—

KINGDOM OF KATHMANDU

KINGDOM

Bhaskara Malla

NS821-835 / 1701-1715AD

MOHAR COINAGE

KM# 211 DAM

Silver **Note:** Uniface.

Date	Mintage	Good	VG	F	VF	XF
ND	—	5.00	7.50	10.00	15.00	—

KM# 213 1/32 MOHAR

Silver **Note:** Uniface.

Date	Mintage	Good	VG	F	VF	XF
ND	—	12.50	21.50	35.00	50.00	—

KM# 217 MOHAR

Silver **Note:** Varieties exist.

Date	Mintage	Good	VG	F	VF	XF
NS821 (1701)	—	8.00	13.50	22.50	32.50	—

Mahindra Simha

NS835-842 / 1715-1722AD

MOHAR COINAGE

KM# 219 DAM

Silver **Note:** Uniface.

Date	Mintage	Good	VG	F	VF	XF
ND	—	5.00	7.50	10.00	15.00	—

KM# 221 1/16 MOHAR

Silver, 12 mm.

Date	Mintage	Good	VG	F	VF	XF
ND	—	12.50	21.50	35.00	50.00	—

KM# 223 1/4 MOHAR
Silver

Date	Mintage	Good	VG	F	VF	XF
NS835 (1715)	—	8.00	13.50	22.50	32.50	—

KM# 226 1/4 MOHAR
Silver **Note:** In the names of Mahindra Simha and Queen Mahindra Lakshmi.

Date	Mintage	Good	VG	F	VF	XF
NS838 (1718)	—	10.00	18.50	30.00	45.00	—

KM# 225 MOHAR
Silver

Date	Mintage	Good	VG	F	VF	XF
NS835 (1715)	—	6.50	10.50	17.50	25.00	—

Jagajjaya Malla
NS842-855 / 1722-1735AD
MOHAR COINAGE

KM# 227 DAM
Silver **Note:** Uniface.

Date	Mintage	Good	VG	F	VF	XF
ND	—	5.00	7.50	10.00	15.00	—

KM# 228 1/32 MOHAR
Silver **Note:** Uniface.

Date	Mintage	Good	VG	F	VF	XF
ND	—	12.50	21.50	35.00	50.00	—

KM# 229 1/16 MOHAR
Silver

Date	Mintage	Good	VG	F	VF	XF
ND	—	12.50	21.50	35.00	50.00	—

KM# 232 1/4 MOHAR
Silver **Note:** In the names of Jagajjaya Malla and Queen Kumudini Devi.

Date	Mintage	Good	VG	F	VF	XF
NS842 (1722)	—	16.50	27.50	45.00	65.00	—

KM# 233 1/4 MOHAR
Silver **Obv:** Longer legend **Note:** In the names of Jagajjaya Malla and Queen Kumudini Devi.

Date	Mintage	Good	VG	F	VF	XF
NS842 (1722)	—	8.00	13.50	22.50	32.50	—

KM# 230 MOHAR
Silver

Date	Mintage	Good	VG	F	VF	XF
NS842 (1722)	—	6.50	10.50	17.50	25.00	—

KM# 231 MOHAR
Silver **Note:** Varieties exist.

Date	Mintage	Good	VG	F	VF	XF
NS848 (1728)	—	6.50	10.50	17.50	25.00	—

Jaya Prakash Malla
First Reign - NS855-66 / 1735-1746AD
SILVER COINAGE

KM# 236 DAM
Silver **Obv:** Sword

Date	Mintage	Good	VG	F	VF	XF
ND	—	2.50	4.00	7.00	10.00	—

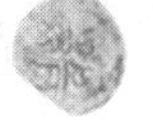

KM# 235 DAM
Silver **Obv:** Without sword **Note:** Uniface.

Date	Mintage	Good	VG	F	VF	XF
ND	—	2.50	4.00	7.00	10.00	—

KM# 239 1/32 MOHAR
Silver **Obv:** 4 characters

Date	Mintage	Good	VG	F	VF	XF
ND	—	10.00	16.50	26.50	37.50	—

KM# 240 1/32 MOHAR
Silver **Obv:** 5 characters

Date	Mintage	Good	VG	F	VF	XF
ND	—	10.00	16.50	26.50	37.50	—

KM# 243 1/16 MOHAR
Silver **Obv:** 4 characters **Rev:** 2 characters

Date	Mintage	Good	VG	F	VF	XF
ND	—	10.00	18.50	30.00	45.00	—

KM# 244 1/16 MOHAR
Silver **Obv:** 5 characters **Rev:** 3 characters

Date	Mintage	Good	VG	F	VF	XF
ND	—	10.00	18.50	30.00	45.00	—

KM# 247 1/8 MOHAR
Silver **Obv:** 4 characters **Rev:** 2 characters

Date	Mintage	Good	VG	F	VF	XF
ND	—	12.50	21.50	35.00	50.00	—

KM# 247a 1/8 MOHAR
Silver

Date	Mintage	Good	VG	F	VF	XF
ND	—	12.50	21.50	35.00	50.00	—

KM# 248 1/8 MOHAR
Silver

Date	Mintage	Good	VG	F	VF	XF
ND	—	12.50	21.50	35.00	50.00	—

KM# 255 1/2 MOHAR
Silver

Date	Mintage	Good	VG	F	VF	XF
NS856 (1736)	—	50.00	100	200	300	—

KM# 259 MOHAR
Silver **Note:** For clipped coinage of this piece refer to Clipped Coinage KM#264-265, 267-268, 270-271 at the end of this ruler.

Date	Mintage	Good	VG	F	VF	XF
NS856	—	5.00	8.00	12.00	18.00	—

GOLD COINAGE

KM# 237 DAM
Gold **Obv:** Sword **Note:** Similar to KM#236.

Date	Mintage	Good	VG	F	VF	XF
ND	—	20.00	32.50	55.00	75.00	—

KM# 241 1/32 MOHAR
Gold **Obv:** 5 characters **Note:** Uniface. Similar to KM#240.

Date	Mintage	Good	VG	F	VF	XF
ND	—	25.00	45.00	70.00	100	—

KM# 245 1/16 MOHAR
Gold **Obv:** 5 characters **Rev:** 3 characters **Note:** Similar to KM#244.

Date	Mintage	Good	VG	F	VF	XF
ND	—	32.50	55.00	90.00	125	—

KM# 249 1/8 MOHAR
Gold **Obv:** 4 characters **Rev:** 6 characters **Note:** Similar to KM#248.

Date	Mintage	Good	VG	F	VF	XF
ND	—	45.00	80.00	130	190	—

KM# 262a MOHAR
Gold **Note:** Similar to KM#259.

Date	Mintage	Good	VG	F	VF	XF
NS856 (1736)	—	250	400	750	1,000	—

Kumudini Devi
Regent for Jaya Prakash, NS855-866 / 1735-1746AD
MOHAR COINAGE

KM# 234 1/4 MOHAR
Silver

Date	Mintage	Good	VG	F	VF	XF
NS856 (1736)	—	8.00	13.50	22.50	32.50	—

Jaya Lakshmi Devi
Regent for Jyoti Prakash, NS866- / 1746-AD
MOHAR COINAGE

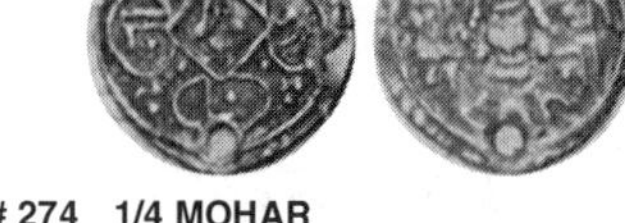

KM# 274 1/4 MOHAR
Silver

Date	Mintage	Good	VG	F	VF	XF
NS866 (1746)	—	18.50	32.50	55.00	75.00	—

KM# 275 1/4 MOHAR
Silver

Date	Mintage	Good	VG	F	VF	XF
NS866 (1746)	—	8.00	13.50	22.50	32.50	—

KM# 273 1/4 MOHAR
Silver **Note:** Two different forms of 6 in this date.

Date	Mintage	Good	VG	F	VF	XF
NS866 (1746)	—	16.50	27.50	45.00	65.00	—

Jyoti Prakash Malla
NS866-870 / 1746-1750AD
MOHAR COINAGE

KM# 277 DAM
Silver **Note:** Uniface.

Date	Mintage	Good	VG	F	VF	XF
ND	—	3.25	5.00	8.50	12.50	—

KM# 280 MOHAR
Silver

Date	Mintage	Good	VG	F	VF	XF
NS866 (1746)	—	12.50	21.50	35.00	50.00	—

KM# 282 MOHAR
Silver

Date	Mintage	Good	VG	F	VF	XF
NS866 (1746)	—	75.00	125	200	300	—

KM# 279 MOHAR
Silver **Note:** Two forms of 6 in this date.

Date	Mintage	Good	VG	F	VF	XF
NS866 (1746)	—	16.50	27.50	45.00	65.00	—

KM# 281 MOHAR
Silver **Note:** Varieties exist.

Date	Mintage	Good	VG	F	VF	XF
NS866 (1746)	—	8.00	13.50	22.50	32.50	—

ANONYMOUS SILVER COINAGE

Period of Jaya Prakash Malla

KM# 290 1/4 MOHAR
0.0100 g., Silver **Note:** Period of Jaya Prakash Malla.

Date	Mintage	Good	VG	F	VF	XF
NS873 (1753)	—	16.50	27.50	45.00	65.00	—

KM# 284 1/4 JAWA
0.0020 g., Silver **Note:** 2x2 millimeter, square. Cut part of Jawa. Period of Jaya Prakash Malla.

Date	Mintage	Good	VG	F	VF	XF
ND	—	8.00	13.50	22.50	32.50	—

KM# 287 JAWA
0.0100 g., Silver **Note:** 4x4 millimeters, square. Period of Jaya Prakash Malla.

Date	Mintage	Good	VG	F	VF	XF
ND	—	16.50	27.50	45.00	65.00	—

ANONYMOUS GOLD COINAGE

Period of Jaya Prakash Malla

KM# 285 1/4 JAWA
Gold **Note:** Cut part of Jawa. Period of Jaya Prakash Malla.

Date	Mintage	Good	VG	F	VF	XF
ND	—	12.50	22.50	35.00	60.00	—

KM# 288 JAWA
Gold **Note:** Period of Jaya Prakash Malla.

Date	Mintage	Good	VG	F	VF	XF
ND	—	20.00	32.50	55.00	85.00	—

Jaya Prakash Malla
Second Reign - NS c.870-888; c.1750-1768AD

SILVER COINAGE

KM# 251 1/4 MOHAR
Silver

Date	Mintage	Good	VG	F	VF	XF
NS873 (1753)	—	16.50	27.50	45.00	65.00	—

KM# 256 1/2 MOHAR
Silver

Date	Mintage	Good	VG	F	VF	XF
NS873 (1753)	—	50.00	100	200	300	—

KM# 260 MOHAR
Silver

Date	Mintage	Good	VG	F	VF	XF
NS873 (1753)	—	12.50	21.50	35.00	50.00	—

KM# 261 MOHAR
Silver

Date	Mintage	Good	VG	F	VF	XF
NS873 (1753)	—	6.50	10.50	17.50	25.00	—

GOLD COINAGE

KM# 253 1/4 MOHAR
Gold **Obv:** 8 characters **Rev:** 6 characters **Note:** Similar to KM#251.

Date	Mintage	Good	VG	F	VF	XF
NS873 (1753)	—	80.00	130	225	325	—

KM# 257 1/2 MOHAR
Gold **Obv:** 5 characters **Rev:** 8 characters **Note:** Similar to KM#256.

Date	Mintage	Good	VG	F	VF	XF
NS873 (1753)	—	200	300	500	750	—

KM# 262 MOHAR
Gold **Obv:** Legend surrounded by 8 symbols **Note:** Similar to KM#261. For coins in the name of Jaya Prakash Malla dated NS880, see Kingdom of Patan.

Date	Mintage	Good	VG	F	VF	XF
NS873 (1753)	—	225	375	625	875	—

CUT COINAGE

The Mohar, KM#259, was struck in large quantities in base metal and sent to Tibet, where it was often cut for use as small change. The full coin circulated at the value of 1.5 Sho, and it was cut into fractions of 2/3, 1/2, and 1/3, circulating at 1 Sho, 0.75 Sho and 0.5 Sho. Two methods of cutting were used, the earliest method merely used a straight line cut, whereas during the early 19th century it became normal to cut much of the center out of the fractions. The denomination was determined by the number of petals visible and how it is cut. Lucky emblems were in petals. These pieces continued to circulate until the 1920s.

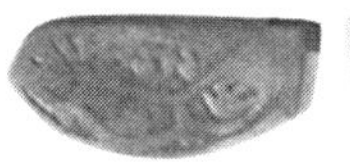

KM# 265 1/2 SHO
Silver **Note:** Center or other parts cut out, 3 petals.

Date	Mintage	Good	VG	F	VF	XF
NS856 (1736)	—	6.00	9.00	13.00	20.00	—

KM# 264 1/2 SHO
Silver **Note:** Cut with straight line, 3 petals.

Date	Mintage	Good	VG	F	VF	XF
NS856 (1736)	—	6.00	9.00	13.00	20.00	—

KM# 268 3/4 SHO
Silver **Note:** Center or other parts cut out, 4 petals.

Date	Mintage	Good	VG	F	VF	XF
NS856 (1736)	—	4.00	6.00	9.00	14.00	—

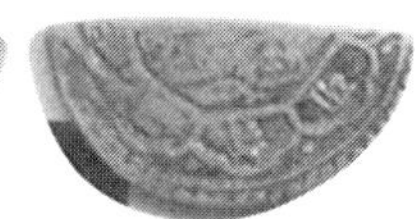

KM# 267 3/4 SHO
Silver **Note:** Cut with straight line, 4 petals.

Date	Mintage	Good	VG	F	VF	XF
NS856 (1736)	—	6.00	9.00	13.00	20.00	—

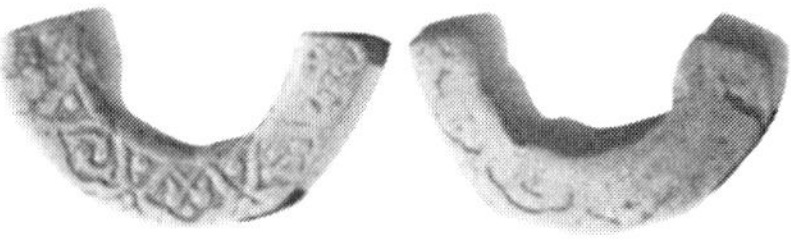

KM# 271 SHO
Silver **Note:** Center or other parts cut out, 5 petals. While most cut pieces are of this type, or of Pratap Simha Shah, 1775-1777, a few other types are known cut, but these have not been listed separately.

Date	Mintage	Good	VG	F	VF	XF
NS856 (1736)	—	4.50	7.00	10.00	15.00	—

KM# 270 SHO
Silver **Note:** Cut with straight line, 5 petals.

Date	Mintage	Good	VG	F	VF	XF
NS856 (1736)	—	6.00	9.00	13.00	20.00	—

KINGDOM OF PATAN
KINGDOM

Yoga Narendra Malla
NS805-825 / 1685-1705AD

MOHAR COINAGE

KM# 312 DAM
0.0480 g., Silver **Note:** Uniface; Legend: SHRI YOGA.

Date	Mintage	Good	VG	F	VF	XF
ND	—	8.00	10.00	15.00	20.00	—

KM# 316 1/4 MOHAR
1.3830 g., Silver **Obv:** Date in square with vase **Obv. Legend:** Shri Shri Yoga Narendra Malla **Rev:** Legend around and at bottom **Rev. Legend:** Shri Shri Lokanatha...Shri Taleju

Date	Mintage	Good	VG	F	VF	XF
ND	—	25.00	45.00	70.00	100	—

KM# 317 1/4 MOHAR
1.3830 g., Silver **Obv:** Date in square **Obv. Legend:** Shri Yoga Narendra Malla **Rev:** Legend around **Rev. Legend:** Shri Shri Lokanatha...Shri Taleju

Date	Mintage	Good	VG	F	VF	XF
ND	—	16.50	27.50	45.00	65.00	—

KM# 328 1/4 MOHAR
Silver

Date	Mintage	Good	VG	F	VF	XF
ND	—	45.00	80.00	130	190	—

KM# 330 1/2 MOHAR
Silver

Date	Mintage	Good	VG	F	VF	XF
ND	—	32.50	55.00	90.00	125	—

KM# 334 1/2 MOHAR
Silver

Date	Mintage	Good	VG	F	VF	XF
ND	—	32.50	55.00	90.00	125	—

Loka Prakash Molla

NS825-826 / 1705-1706AD

MOHAR COINAGE

KM# 339 DAM

Silver **Note:** Uniface.

Date	Mintage	Good	VG	F	VF	XF
ND	—	5.00	7.50	13.50	18.50	—

KM# 341 1/4 MOHAR

Silver

Date	Mintage	Good	VG	F	VF	XF
ND	—	50.00	75.00	125	200	—

KM# 343 MOHAR

Silver **Obv:** Legend reads "Shri 2 Jaya Lokaprakashna Malla Deva" around "Shri Karunamaya" in center **Rev:** Legend below date **Rev. Legend:** SHRI YOGAMATI **Note:** In the name of Loka Prakash Malla and Queen Yogamati.

Date	Mintage	Good	VG	F	VF	XF
NS826 (1706)	—	16.50	27.50	45.00	65.00	—

KM# 344 MOHAR

Silver **Obv:** Date **Rev:** Date **Note:** In the name of Loka Prakash Malla and Queen Yogamati.

Date	Mintage	Good	VG	F	VF	XF
NS826 (1706)	—	18.50	32.50	55.00	75.00	—

KM# 346 MOHAR

Silver **Obv:** Date **Note:** In the name of Loka Prakash Malla and Queen Yogamati.

Date	Mintage	Good	VG	F	VF	XF
NS826 (1706)	—	18.50	32.50	55.00	75.00	—

Jaya Indra Malla

i.e. Purandara Malla; NS826-829 / 1706-1709AD

MOHAR COINAGE

KM# 349 DAM

Gold **Note:** In the name of Jaya Indra Malla.

Date	Mintage	Good	VG	F	VF	XF
ND	—	25.00	45.00	70.00	100	—

KM# 348 DAM

0.0450 g., Silver **Note:** Legend reads Shri Indra. Uniface. In the name of Jaya Indra Malla.

Date	Mintage	Good	VG	F	VF	XF
ND	—	10.00	15.00	25.00	50.00	—

KM# 355 1/4 MOHAR

Silver **Note:** In the name of Jaya Indra Malla.

Date	Mintage	Good	VG	F	VF	XF
ND	—	32.50	55.00	90.00	125	—

KM# 354 1/4 MOHAR

Silver **Note:** Last digit of date badly formed. In the name of Purandara Malla.

Date	Mintage	Good	VG	F	VF	XF
NS826 (1706)	—	25.00	45.00	70.00	100	—

KM# 350 1/2 MOHAR

Silver **Note:** In the names of Jaya Indra Malla and Queen Bhagyavati.

Date	Mintage	Good	VG	F	VF	XF
NS826 (1706)	—	100	200	300	500	—

KM# 357 MOHAR

5.4380 g., Silver **Obv:** 2 letters on both sides of square **Note:** In the names of Jaya Indra Malla and Queen Bhagyavati.

Date	Mintage	Good	VG	F	VF	XF
NS826 (1706)	—	75.00	125	200	300	—

KM# 352 MOHAR

5.4380 g., Silver **Obv:** 3 letters on both sides of square **Note:** In the names of Jaya Indra Malla and Queen Bhagyavati. Varieties exist.

Date	Mintage	Good	VG	F	VF	XF
NS826 (1706)	—	20.00	25.00	40.00	50.00	—

Rajyesvari Devi

Regent for Vira Narashimha Malla; ca. NS829 / ca.1709AD

MOHAR COINAGE

KM# 368 1/4 MOHAR

1.3950 g., Silver **Obv. Legend:** SHRI SHRI TALEJU **Rev. Legend:** SHRI SHRI RAJESVARI DEVI

Date	Mintage	Good	VG	F	VF	XF
ND	—	16.50	27.50	45.00	65.00	—

Vira Narashimha Malla

NS829 / 1709AD

MOHAR COINAGE

KM# 361 DAM

0.0490 g., Silver **Note:** Uniface. Legend reads SHRI VIRA. In the name of Vira Narasimha Malla alone.

Date	Mintage	Good	VG	F	VF	XF
ND	—	3.25	5.00	8.50	12.50	—

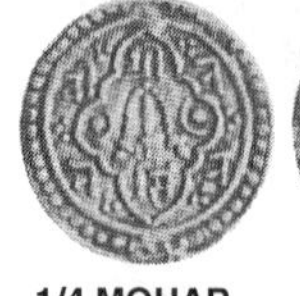

KM# 363 1/4 MOHAR

Silver **Note:** In the name of Vira Narasimha Malla alone.

Date	Mintage	Good	VG	F	VF	XF
ND	—	18.50	32.50	55.00	75.00	—

KM# 365 MOHAR

5.3400 g., Silver **Note:** In the name of Vira Narasimha Malla alone.

Date	Mintage	Good	VG	F	VF	XF
NS829 (1709)	—	75.00	125	200	300	—

KM# 359 MOHAR

5.3400 g., Silver **Rev:** Pellets **Note:** In the names of Vira Narasimha Malla and Queen Yogamati.

Date	Mintage	Good	VG	F	VF	XF
NS829 (1709)	—	16.50	27.50	45.00	65.00	—

KM# 366 MOHAR

5.3400 g., Silver **Rev:** Branches with buds **Note:** In the names of Vira Narasimha Malla and Queen Yogamati.

Date	Mintage	Good	VG	F	VF	XF
NS829 (1709)	—	16.50	27.50	45.00	65.00	—

Vira Mahindra Malla

NS829-835 / 1709-1715AD

MOHAR COINAGE

KM# 370 MOHAR

Silver **Note:** Varieties exist.

Date	Mintage	Good	VG	F	VF	XF
NS829 (1709)	—	10.00	16.50	26.50	37.50	—

Riddhi Narasimha

NS835-837 / 1715-1717AD

MOHAR COINAGE

KM# 372 1/4 MOHAR

1.2810 g., Silver **Obv. Legend:** SHRI RIDDHI NARSIM **Rev. Legend:** SHRI LOKANA

Date	Mintage	Good	VG	F	VF	XF
ND	—	40.00	60.00	100	150	—

KM# 375 MOHAR

Silver

Date	Mintage	Good	VG	F	VF	XF
NS835 (1715)	—	6.50	10.50	17.50	25.00	—

KM# 374 MOHAR
Silver **Note:** Varieties exist.

Date	Mintage	Good	VG	F	VF	XF
NS835 (1715)	—	10.00	16.50	26.50	37.50	—

Jaya Mahindra Simha
NS837-842 / 1717-1722AD
MOHAR COINAGE

KM# 377 MOHAR
Silver

Date	Mintage	Good	VG	F	VF	XF
NS837 (1717)	—	6.50	10.50	17.50	25.00	—

Yoga Prakash Malla
NS842-849 / 1722-1729AD
MOHAR COINAGE

KM# 379 DAM
0.0400 g., Silver **Note:** Uniface.

Date	Mintage	Good	VG	F	VF	XF
ND	—	5.00	7.50	13.50	18.50	—

KM# 381 1/4 MOHAR
1.3250 g., Silver

Date	Mintage	Good	VG	F	VF	XF
NS842 (1722)	—	10.00	18.50	30.00	45.00	—

KM# 383 1/2 MOHAR
Silver

Date	Mintage	Good	VG	F	VF	XF
NS842 (1722)	—	100	200	300	500	—

KM# 385 MOHAR
5.4700 g., Silver **Rev:** Octagon in center

Date	Mintage	Good	VG	F	VF	XF
NS842 (1722)	—	25.00	45.00	70.00	100	—

KM# 386 MOHAR
5.4700 g., Silver **Rev:** Circle in center

Date	Mintage	Good	VG	F	VF	XF
NS842 (1722)	—	6.50	10.50	17.50	25.00	—

Jaya Vishnu Malla
NS849-865 / 1729-1745AD
SILVER COINAGE

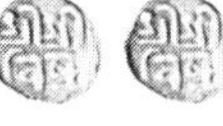

KM# 388 DAM
0.0400 g., Silver **Note:** Uniface.

Date	Mintage	Good	VG	F	VF	XF
ND	—	10.00	12.50	18.50	30.00	—

KM# 390 1/8 MOHAR
Silver

Date	Mintage	Good	VG	F	VF	XF
ND	—	16.50	27.50	45.00	65.00	—

KM# 392 1/4 MOHAR
Silver

Date	Mintage	Good	VG	F	VF	XF
NS849 (1929)	—	10.00	18.50	30.00	45.00	—

KM# 395 MOHAR
Silver

Date	Mintage	Good	VG	F	VF	XF
NS849 (1929)	—	8.00	13.50	22.50	32.50	—

KM# 396 MOHAR
Silver

Date	Mintage	Good	VG	F	VF	XF
NS849 (1929)	—	10.00	16.50	26.50	37.50	—

KM# 397 MOHAR
Silver

Date	Mintage	Good	VG	F	VF	XF
NS849 (1929)	—	10.00	16.50	26.50	37.50	—

KM# 398 MOHAR
Silver

Date	Mintage	Good	VG	F	VF	XF
NS849 (1929)	—	25.00	45.00	70.00	100	—

KM# 399 MOHAR
Silver

Date	Mintage	Good	VG	F	VF	XF
NS849 (1929)	—	6.50	10.50	17.50	25.00	—

KM# 394 MOHAR
Silver **Note:** Flowers sprout from under sword.

Date	Mintage	Good	VG	F	VF	XF
NS849 (1929)	—	12.50	21.50	35.00	50.00	—

KM# 400 MOHAR
Silver

Date	Mintage	Good	VG	F	VF	XF
NS851 (1731)	—	5.00	7.50	13.50	18.50	—

Rajya Prakash Malla
NS865-878 / 1745-1758AD
GOLD COINAGE

KM# 401 DAM
0.0400 g., Gold **Obv:** 4 characters **Note:** Similar to KM#388.

Date	Mintage	Good	VG	F	VF	XF
ND	—	25.00	45.00	75.00	100	—

SILVER COINAGE

KM# 403 DAM
0.0400 g., Silver **Note:** 4 characters.

Date	Mintage	Good	VG	F	VF	XF
ND	—	3.25	5.00	8.50	12.50	—

KM# 402 DAM
0.0400 g., Silver **Note:** Uniface. 3 characters.

Date	Mintage	Good	VG	F	VF	XF
ND	—	5.00	7.50	13.50	18.50	—

KM# 405 1/4 MOHAR
1.3390 g., Silver **Obv:** Without date

Date	Mintage	Good	VG	F	VF	XF
ND	—	16.50	27.50	45.00	65.00	—

KM# 406 1/4 MOHAR
1.4370 g., Silver **Obv:** Date at bottom

Date	Mintage	Good	VG	F	VF	XF
NS865 (1745)	—	5.00	7.50	13.50	18.50	—

KM# 407 1/4 MOHAR
1.4370 g., Silver

Date	Mintage	Good	VG	F	VF	XF
NS865 (1745)	—	6.50	10.50	17.50	25.00	—

KM# 409 MOHAR
5.4270 g., Silver

Date	Mintage	Good	VG	F	VF	XF
NS865 (1745)	—	75.00	125	200	300	—

KM# 410 MOHAR
5.4270 g., Silver

Date	Mintage	Good	VG	F	VF	XF
NS865 (1745)	—	5.00	7.50	13.50	18.50	—

KM# 411 MOHAR
5.4270 g., Silver

Date	Mintage	Good	VG	F	VF	XF
NS865 (1745)	—	12.50	21.50	35.00	50.00	—

KM# 412 MOHAR
5.4270 g., Silver

Date	Mintage	Good	VG	F	VF	XF
NS865 (1745)	—	10.00	18.50	30.00	45.00	—

KM# 413 MOHAR
5.2710 g., Silver

Date	Mintage	Good	VG	F	VF	XF
NS865 (1745)	—	10.00	18.50	30.00	45.00	—

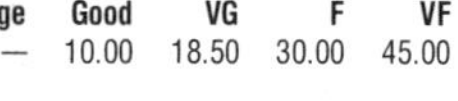

KM# 414 MOHAR
5.2710 g., Silver

Date	Mintage	Good	VG	F	VF	XF
NS865 (1745)	—	12.50	21.50	35.00	50.00	—

KM# 415 MOHAR
5.2710 g., Silver

Date	Mintage	Good	VG	F	VF	XF
NS865 (1745)	—	75.00	125	200	300	—

KM# 416 MOHAR
5.2710 g., Silver

Date	Mintage	Good	VG	F	VF	XF
NS865 (1745)	—	18.50	32.50	55.00	75.00	—

Visvajit Malla

NS878-880 / 1758-1760AD

MOHAR COINAGE

KM# 418 DAM
0.0400 g., Silver **Note:** Uniface.

Date	Mintage	Good	VG	F	VF	XF
ND	—	10.00	15.00	20.00	35.00	—

KM# 420 1/4 MOHAR
Silver

Date	Mintage	Good	VG	F	VF	XF
NS878	—	35.00	75.00	100	150	—

KM# 422 MOHAR
Silver

Date	Mintage	Good	VG	F	VF	XF
NS878	—	16.50	27.50	45.00	65.00	—

Jaya Prakash Malla

also King of Kathmandu; NS880-881 / 1760-1761AD

MOHAR COINAGE

KM# 424 MOHAR
Silver

Date	Mintage	Good	VG	F	VF	XF
NS880 (1760)	—	75.00	125	200	300	—

KM# 425 MOHAR
Silver

Date	Mintage	Good	VG	F	VF	XF
NS880 (1760)	—	75.00	125	200	300	—

Ranajit Malla

also King of Bhatgaon; NS882-883 / 1762-1763AD

MOHAR COINAGE

KM# 427 MOHAR
Silver

Date	Mintage	Good	VG	F	VF	XF
NS882 (1762)	—	18.50	32.50	55.00	75.00	—

Dala Mardana Saha

NS884-885 / 1764-1765AD

MOHAR COINAGE

KM# 430 DAM
0.0300 g., Silver **Note:** Sword.

Date	Mintage	Good	VG	F	VF	XF
ND	—	3.50	6.00	10.00	15.00	—

KM# 429 DAM
0.0300 g., Silver **Note:** Uniface. Without sword.

Date	Mintage	Good	VG	F	VF	XF
ND	—	3.25	5.00	8.50	12.50	—

KM# 432 MOHAR
5.5000 g., Silver

Date	Mintage	Good	VG	F	VF	XF
NS884 (1764)	—	75.00	125	200	300	—

KM# 433 MOHAR
5.4610 g., Silver

Date	Mintage	Good	VG	F	VF	XF
NS884 (1764)	—	75.00	125	200	300	—

Matesvari Devi

Queen of Tej Narasimha; NS885 / 1765AD

MOHAR COINAGE

KM# 440 1/4 MOHAR
Silver

Date	Mintage	Good	VG	F	VF	XF
NS885 (1765)	—	75.00	125	200	300	—

Tej Narasimha Malla

NS885-888 / 1765-1768AD

MOHAR COINAGE

KM# 435 DAM
Silver **Note:** Uniface.

Date	Mintage	Good	VG	F	VF	XF
ND	—	8.00	10.00	12.50	18.50	—

KM# 437 MOHAR
5.2000 g., Silver

Date	Mintage	Good	VG	F	VF	XF
NS885	—	75.00	125	200	300	—

KM# 438 MOHAR
5.2000 g., Silver

Date	Mintage	Good	VG	F	VF	XF
NS885	—	50.00	75.00	150	200	—

SHAH DYNASTY

KINGDOM

Shah Dynasty

Prithvi Narayan

In Kathmandu; SE1690-1696 / 1768-1775AD

COPPER COINAGE

KM# 448 1/2 PAISA
5.0000 g., Copper **Note:** Similar to 1 Paisa, KM#449.

Date	Mintage	Good	VG	F	VF	XF
ND	—	—	4.00	7.00	12.00	25.00

KM# 449 PAISA
10.0000 g., Copper

Date	Mintage	Good	VG	F	VF	XF
ND	—	—	4.00	7.00	12.00	25.00

SILVER COINAGE

KM# 450.2 DAM
0.0040 g., Silver **Note:** Crescent above inscription; actual size varies 7 - 8 mm.

Date	Mintage	VG	F	VF	XF	Unc
ND	—	3.00	5.00	7.00	10.00	—

KM# 450.1 DAM
0.0040 g., Silver **Note:** Uniface; Size varies 7 - 8 mm.

Date	Mintage	VG	F	VF	XF	Unc
ND	—	3.00	5.00	7.00	10.00	—

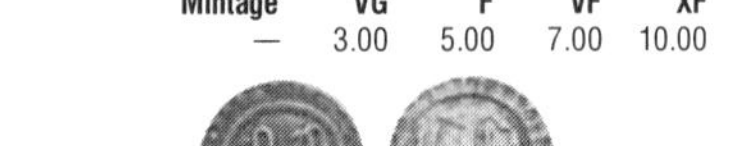

KM# 451 1/16 MOHAR
0.3500 g., Silver **Note:** Uniface.

Date	Mintage	VG	F	VF	XF	Unc
ND	—	25.00	40.00	45.00	50.00	—

KM# 452 1/8 MOHAR
0.7000 g., Silver

Date	Mintage	VG	F	VF	XF	Unc
ND	—	35.00	50.00	60.00	75.00	—

KM# 463 1/4 MOHAR
1.4000 g., Silver **Note:** Also in the name of Queen Narindra Laksmi.

Date	Mintage	VG	F	VF	XF	Unc
ND	—	25.00	30.00	40.00	50.00	—

KM# 464 1/4 MOHAR
1.4000 g., Silver **Note:** Also in the name of Queen Narindra Laksmi.

Date	Mintage	VG	F	VF	XF	Unc
SE1690 (1768)	—	10.00	20.00	25.00	30.00	—
SE1691 (1769)	—	30.00	45.00	50.00	60.00	—
SE1692 (1770)	—	10.00	20.00	25.00	30.00	—
SE1693 (1771)	—	30.00	45.00	50.00	60.00	—

KM# 453 1/2 MOHAR
2.8000 g., Silver **Note:** Also in the name of Queen Narindra Laksmi.

Date	Mintage	VG	F	VF	XF	Unc
SE1693 (1771)	—	50.00	75.00	125	200	—

KM# A454 MOHAR
5.2000 g., Billon **Note:** Also in the name of Queen Narindra Laksmi.

Date	Mintage	VG	F	VF	XF	Unc
SE1671 (1749)	—	100	150	250	400	—

KM# B454 MOHAR
5.1000 g., Silver **Note:** Also in the name of Queen Narindra Laksmi.

Date	Mintage	VG	F	VF	XF	Unc
SE1676 (1754)	—	150	200	350	500	—

KM# 454.1 MOHAR
5.6000 g., Silver **Obv:** Sun at left, moon at right above legend **Note:** Also in the name of Queen Narindra Laksmi.

Date	Mintage	VG	F	VF	XF	Unc
SE1676 (1754)	—	6.50	10.00	15.00	20.00	—

KM# 454.2 MOHAR
5.6000 g., Silver **Obv:** Moon at left, sun at right above legend **Note:** Also in the name of Queen Narindra Laksmi.

Date	Mintage	VG	F	VF	XF	Unc
SE1676 (1754)	—	6.50	10.00	15.00	20.00	—
SE1678 (1756)	—	6.50	10.00	15.00	20.00	—
SE1682 (1760)	—	9.00	15.00	20.00	30.00	—
SE1683 (1761)	—	9.00	15.00	20.00	30.00	—
SE1690 (1768)	—	4.50	7.00	10.00	13.50	—
SE1691 (1769)	—	4.50	7.00	10.00	13.50	—
SE1692 (1770)	—	4.50	7.00	10.00	13.50	—
SE1693 (1771)	—	4.50	7.00	10.00	13.50	—
SE1694 (1772)	—	4.50	7.00	10.00	13.50	—
SE1695 (1773)	—	4.50	7.00	10.00	13.50	—
SE1696 (1774)	—	4.50	7.00	10.00	13.50	—

KM# 454.3 MOHAR
5.6000 g., Silver **Note:** Also in the name of Queen Narindra Laksmi.

Date	Mintage	VG	F	VF	XF	Unc
SE1685 (1763)	—	15.00	25.00	45.00	100	—

KM# 455 2 MOHARS
11.2000 g., Silver **Note:** Also in the name of Queen Narindra Laksmi.

Date	Mintage	VG	F	VF	XF	Unc
SE1693 (1771)	—	100	200	300	500	—

GOLD COINAGE

KM# 456 DAM
0.0440 g., Gold **Note:** Uniface. Similar to 1 Dam, KM#450.1.

Date	Mintage	VG	F	VF	XF	Unc
ND	—	25.00	35.00	45.00	60.00	—

KM# 457 1/32 MOHAR
0.1750 g., Gold **Note:** Uniface.

Date	Mintage	VG	F	VF	XF	Unc
ND	—	35.00	45.00	55.00	70.00	—

KM# 458 1/16 MOHAR
0.3500 g., Gold

Date	Mintage	Good	VG	F	VF	XF
ND	—	45.00	60.00	70.00	85.00	—

KM# 459 1/8 MOHAR
0.7000 g., Gold

Date	Mintage	Good	VG	F	VF	XF
ND	—	55.00	75.00	85.00	100	—

KM# 466 1/4 MOHAR
1.4000 g., Gold **Note:** Also in the name of Queen Narindra Laksmi.

Date	Mintage	Good	VG	F	VF	XF
SE1693 (1771)	—	75.00	100	125	150	—

KM# 460 1/2 MOHAR
2.8000 g., Gold **Note:** Also in the name of Queen Narindra Laksmi.

Date	Mintage	Good	VG	F	VF	XF
SE1693 (1771)	—	140	175	200	250	—

KM# 461 MOHAR
5.6000 g., Gold **Note:** Also in the name of Queen Narindra Laksmi.

Date	Mintage	VG	F	VF	XF	Unc
SE1693 (1771)	—	200	250	300	375	—
SE1694 (1772)	—	200	250	300	375	—
SE1695 (1773)	—	200	250	300	375	—

KM# 462 2 MOHARS
11.2000 g., Gold **Note:** Also in the name of Queen Narindra Laksmi.

Date	Mintage	VG	F	VF	XF	Unc
SE1693 (1771)	—	450	500	550	625	—
SE1695 (1773)	—	450	500	550	625	—
SE1696 (1774)	—	450	500	550	625	—

PRESENTATION COINAGE

KM# 465 2 RUPEES
23.3200 g., Gold **Note:** In the name of Queen Narindra Laksmi.

Date	Mintage	VG	F	VF	XF	Unc
SE1693 (1772)	—	750	1,000	1,250	1,750	—

Note: Struck c.1849AD

Pratap Simha
SE1696-1699 / 1775-1777AD

CUT COINAGE

The silver Mohar, KM#472.2, was struck in large quantities and sent to Tibet, where it was often cut for use as small change. The full coin circulated at the value of 1.5 Sho, and it was cut into fractions of 2/3, 1/2, and 1/3, curculating at 1 Sho, 0.75 Sho, and 0.5 Sho. Two methods of cutting were used, the earliest method merely used a straight line cut, whereas during the early 19th century it became normal to cut much of the center out of the fractions. The denomination was determined by the number of petals visible and how it is cut with letters in the petals. These pieces continued to circulate until the 1920s.

KM# 482 1/2 SHO (1/3 Mohar)
Silver **Note:** Center or other parts cut out, 3 petals.

Date	Mintage	VG	F	VF	XF	Unc
SE1697-99	—	4.00	6.00	10.00	18.00	—

KM# 481 1/2 SHO (1/3 Mohar)
Silver **Note:** Cut with straight line, 3 petals.

Date	Mintage	VG	F	VF	XF	Unc
SE1697-99	—	4.00	6.00	10.00	18.00	—

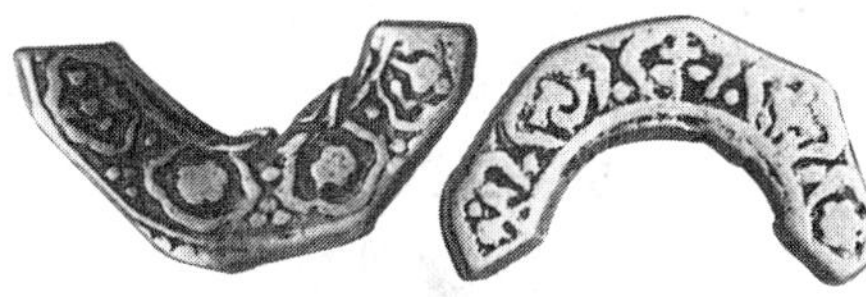

KM# 484 3/4 SHO (1/2 Mohar)
Silver **Note:** Center or other parts cut out, 4 petals.

Date	Mintage	VG	F	VF	XF	Unc
SE1697-99	—	3.00	5.00	8.00	15.00	—

KM# 483 3/4 SHO (1/2 Mohar)
Silver **Note:** Cut with straight line, 4 petals.

Date	Mintage	VG	F	VF	XF	Unc
SE1697-99	—	3.00	5.00	8.00	15.00	—

KM# 486 SHO (2/3 Mohar)
Silver **Note:** Center or other parts cut out, 5 petals.

Date	Mintage	VG	F	VF	XF	Unc
SE1697-99	—	3.00	5.00	8.00	15.00	—

KM# 485 SHO (2/3 Mohar)
Silver **Note:** Cut with straight line, 5 petals.

Date	Mintage	VG	F	VF	XF	Unc
SE1697-99	—	4.00	6.00	10.00	18.00	—

COPPER COINAGE

KM# A466 1/2 PAISA
5.0000 g., Copper **Note:** Similar to 1 Paisa, KM#B466.

Date	Mintage	Good	VG	F	VF	XF
ND	—	—	4.00	7.00	15.00	25.00

KM# B466 PAISA
10.0000 g., Copper

Date	Mintage	Good	VG	F	VF	XF
ND	—	—	4.00	7.00	15.00	25.00

SILVER COINAGE

KM# 467 DAM
Silver **Note:** Size varies 7 - 8 mm.

Date	Mintage	VG	F	VF	XF	Unc
ND	—	3.00	5.00	7.00	10.00	—

KM# 491 DAM
0.0400 g., Silver **Note:** Uniface; Size varies 7 - 8 mm.

Date	Mintage	VG	F	VF	XF	Unc
ND	—	1.25	2.00	3.50	5.00	—

KM# 468 1/16 MOHAR
0.3500 g., Silver **Note:** Uniface.

Date	Mintage	VG	F	VF	XF	Unc
ND	—	25.00	40.00	45.00	50.00	—

KM# 469 1/8 MOHAR
0.7000 g., Silver

Date	Mintage	VG	F	VF	XF	Unc
ND	—	20.00	30.00	35.00	40.00	—

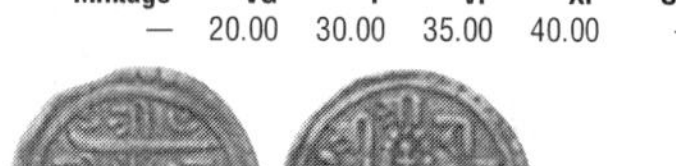

KM# 470.1 1/4 MOHAR
1.4000 g., Silver **Note:** Also in the name of Queen Rajendra Lakshmi.

Date	Mintage	VG	F	VF	XF	Unc
SE1696 (1774)	—	7.00	10.00	15.00	22.50	—
SE1697 (1775)	—	7.00	10.00	15.00	22.50	—
SE1698 (1776)	—	7.00	10.00	15.00	22.50	—
SE1699 (1777)	—	7.00	10.00	15.00	22.50	—

KM# 470.2 1/4 MOHAR
1.4000 g., Silver **Note:** Also in the name of Queen Rajendra Lakshmi.

Date	Mintage	VG	F	VF	XF	Unc
SE1700 (1778)	—	7.00	10.00	15.00	22.50	—

KM# 471 1/2 MOHAR
2.8000 g., Silver **Note:** Also in the name of Queen Rajendra Lakshmi.

Date	Mintage	VG	F	VF	XF	Unc
SE1697 (1775)	—	75.00	100	125	175	—

KM# 472.2 MOHAR
5.6000 g., Billon **Note:** Also in the name of Queen Rajendra Lakshmi; Struck in billon for circulation in Tibet. For clipped or cut coins refert to Clipped Coinage at end of reign.

Date	Mintage	VG	F	VF	XF	Unc
SE1695 (1773)	—	40.00	50.00	65.00	90.00	—
SE1697 (1775)	—	5.00	8.00	13.00	20.00	—
SE1698 (1776)	—	5.00	8.00	13.00	20.00	—
SE1699 (1777)	—	7.00	10.00	16.00	24.00	—

KM# 472.1 MOHAR
5.6000 g., Silver **Note:** Also in the name of Queen Rajendra Lakshmi.

Date	Mintage	VG	F	VF	XF	Unc
SE1696 (1774)	—	4.50	7.00	10.00	13.50	—
SE1697 (1775)	—	4.50	7.00	10.00	13.50	—

Date	Mintage	VG	F	VF	XF	Unc
SE1698 (1776)	—	4.50	7.00	10.00	13.50	—
SE1699 (1777)	—	6.50	10.00	15.00	20.00	—

KM# 473 2 MOHARS
11.2000 g., Silver **Note:** Also in the name of Queen Rajendra Lakshmi.

Date	Mintage	VG	F	VF	XF	Unc
SE1696 (1774)	—	100	175	250	300	—

GOLD COINAGE

KM# 474 DAM
0.0440 g., Gold **Note:** Uniface.

Date	Mintage	VG	F	VF	XF	Unc
ND	—	25.00	35.00	45.00	55.00	—

KM# 475 1/16 MOHAR
0.3500 g., Gold **Note:** Uniface.

Date	Mintage	Good	VG	F	VF	XF
ND	—	45.00	60.00	70.00	85.00	—

KM# 476 1/8 MOHAR
0.7000 g., Gold

Date	Mintage	Good	VG	F	VF	XF
ND	—	55.00	75.00	85.00	100	—

KM# 477.1 1/4 MOHAR
1.4000 g., Gold **Note:** Also in the name of Queen Rajendra Lakshmi.

Date	Mintage	Good	VG	F	VF	XF
SE1698 (1776)	—	55.00	70.00	85.00	100	—

KM# 477.2 1/4 MOHAR
1.4000 g., Gold **Note:** Also in the name of Queen Rajendra Lakshmi.

Date	Mintage	Good	VG	F	VF	XF
SE1700 (1778)	—	40.00	50.00	65.00	85.00	—

KM# 478 1/2 MOHAR
2.8000 g., Gold **Note:** Also in the name of Queen Rajendra Lakshmi.

Date	Mintage	Good	VG	F	VF	XF
SE1697 (1775)	—	140	175	200	250	—

KM# 479 MOHAR
5.6000 g., Gold **Note:** Also in the name of Queen Rajendra Lakshmi.

Date	Mintage	VG	F	VF	XF	Unc
SE1697 (1775)	—	200	250	300	375	—
SE1698 (1776)	—	200	250	300	375	—

KM# 480 2 MOHARS
11.2000 g., Gold **Note:** Also in the name of Queen Rajendra Lakshmi.

Date	Mintage	VG	F	VF	XF	Unc
SE1696 (1774)	—	450	500	550	625	—

PRESENTATION COINAGE

KM# 488 2 RUPEES
23.3200 g., Gold **Note:** Also in the name of Queen Rajendra Lakshmi.

Date	Mintage	VG	F	VF	XF	Unc
SE1698 (1776)	—	750	1,000	1,250	1,500	—

Note: Struck c.1849AD

Rana Bahadur
SE1699-1720 / 1777-1799AD
COPPER COINAGE

KM# 489 1/2 PAISA
Copper

Date	Mintage	Good	VG	F	VF	XF
VS1834 (1777)	—	5.50	9.00	15.00	25.00	—
VS1844 (1787)	—	5.50	9.00	15.00	25.00	—
VS1849 (1792)	—	5.50	9.00	15.00	25.00	—

KM# 490 PAISA
Copper

Date	Mintage	Good	VG	F	VF	XF
VS1834 (1777)	—	4.50	7.50	12.00	20.00	—
VS1843 (1786)	—	4.50	7.50	12.00	20.00	—
VS1844 (1787)	—	4.50	7.50	12.00	20.00	—
VS1849 (1792)	—	4.50	7.50	12.00	20.00	—

SILVER COINAGE

KM# 492 1/32 MOHAR
0.1800 g., Silver **Note:** Uniface.

Date	Mintage	VG	F	VF	XF	Unc
ND	—	5.50	9.00	13.50	20.00	—

KM# 493.1 1/16 MOHAR
0.3500 g., Silver

Date	Mintage	VG	F	VF	XF	Unc
ND	—	7.50	11.50	16.50	22.50	—

KM# 493.2 1/16 MOHAR
0.3500 g., Silver **Obv:** Die of 1/32 Mohar used in error

Date	Mintage	VG	F	VF	XF	Unc
ND	—	15.00	20.00	25.00	30.00	—

KM# 494 1/8 MOHAR
0.7000 g., Silver

Date	Mintage	VG	F	VF	XF	Unc
ND	—	6.00	10.00	14.00	22.00	—

KM# 495 1/4 MOHAR
1.4000 g., Silver

Date	Mintage	VG	F	VF	XF	Unc
SE1707 (1785)	—	8.50	12.50	18.50	25.00	—
SE1708 (1786)	—	7.00	10.00	15.00	22.50	—
SE1712 (1790)	—	8.50	12.50	18.50	25.00	—

KM# 496 1/4 MOHAR
1.4000 g., Silver **Note:** In the name of Queen Raja Rajesvari.

Date	Mintage	VG	F	VF	XF	Unc
SE1711 (1789)	—	7.00	10.00	15.00	22.50	—
SE1712 (1790)	—	5.00	8.50	12.50	20.00	—
SE1716 (1794)	—	5.00	8.50	12.50	20.00	—
SE1722 (1800)	—	7.00	10.00	15.00	22.50	—
SE1723 (1801)	—	7.00	10.00	15.00	22.50	—
SE1724 (1802)	—	7.00	10.00	15.00	22.50	—

KM# 501 1/2 MOHAR
2.7700 g., Silver **Note:** Also in the name of Queen Lalita Tripura Sundari.

Date	Mintage	VG	F	VF	XF	Unc
SE1701 (1779)	—	6.00	10.00	15.00	22.50	—
SE1712 (1790)	—	4.50	7.50	12.50	18.50	—

KM# 502.1 MOHAR
5.6000 g., Silver **Note:** Also in the name of Queen Lalita Tripura Sundari.

Date	Mintage	VG	F	VF	XF	Unc
SE1699 (1777)	—	4.50	6.50	9.00	12.50	—
SE1700 (1778)	—	4.50	6.50	9.00	12.50	—
SE1701 (1779)	—	10.00	15.00	20.00	25.00	—
SE1702 (1780)	—	4.50	6.50	9.00	12.50	—
SE1703 (1781)	—	4.50	6.50	9.00	12.50	—
SE1704 (1782)	—	4.50	6.50	9.00	12.50	—
SE1705 (1783)	—	4.50	6.50	9.00	12.50	—
SE1706 (1784)	—	4.50	6.50	9.00	12.50	—
SE1707 (1785)	—	4.50	6.50	9.00	12.50	—
SE1708 (1786)	—	4.50	6.50	9.00	12.50	—
SE1709 (1787)	—	4.50	6.50	9.00	12.50	—
SE1710 (1788)	—	4.50	6.50	9.00	12.50	—
SE1711 (1789)	—	4.50	6.50	9.00	12.50	—

KM# 502.3 MOHAR
5.6000 g., Silver **Note:** Also in the name of Queen Lalita Tripura Sundari; Similar to 1 Mohar, KM#472.2.

Date	Mintage	VG	F	VF	XF	Unc
SE1699 (1777)	—	40.00	50.00	60.00	75.00	—

KM# 502.2 MOHAR
5.6000 g., Silver **Note:** Also in the name of Queen Lalita Tripura Sundari.

Date	Mintage	VG	F	VF	XF	Unc
SE1711 (1789)	—	4.50	6.50	9.00	12.50	—
SE1712 (1790)	—	4.50	6.50	9.00	12.50	—
SE1713 (1791)	—	4.50	6.50	9.00	12.50	—
SE1714 (1792)	—	4.50	6.50	9.00	12.50	—
SE1716 (1794)	—	4.50	6.50	9.00	12.50	—
SE1717 (1795)	—	4.50	6.50	9.00	12.50	—
SE1718 (1796)	—	4.50	6.50	9.00	12.50	—
SE1719 (1797)	—	4.50	6.50	9.00	12.50	—
SE1720 (1798)	—	4.50	6.50	9.00	12.50	—

KM# 503.1 2 MOHARS
11.2000 g., Silver, 28 mm. **Note:** Also in the name of Queen Lalita Tripura Sundari.

Date	Mintage	VG	F	VF	XF	Unc
SE1703 (1781)	—	30.00	50.00	70.00	115	—
SE1705 (1783)	—	30.00	50.00	70.00	115	—

KM# 503.2 2 MOHARS

11.2000 g., Silver, 25 mm. **Note:** Also in the name of Queen Lalita Tripura Sundari.

Date	Mintage	VG	F	VF	XF	Unc
SE1712 (1790)	—	16.00	30.00	40.00	75.00	—
SE1719 (1797)	—	25.00	40.00	60.00	100	—
SE1720 (1798)	—	20.00	35.00	50.00	85.00	—

GOLD COINAGE

KM# 504 DAM

0.0440 g., Gold **Note:** Uniface.

Date	Mintage	VG	F	VF	XF	Unc
ND	—	10.00	14.00	18.00	25.00	—

KM# 505 1/32 MOHAR

0.1750 g., Gold **Note:** Uniface.

Date	Mintage	VG	F	VF	XF	Unc
ND	—	14.00	20.00	25.00	35.00	—

KM# 506 1/16 MOHAR

0.3500 g., Gold

Date	Mintage	Good	VG	F	VF	XF
ND	—	15.00	22.50	27.50	40.00	—

KM# 507 1/8 MOHAR

0.7000 g., Gold

Date	Mintage	Good	VG	F	VF	XF
ND	—	25.00	30.00	40.00	55.00	—

KM# 508 1/4 MOHAR

1.4000 g., Gold

Date	Mintage	Good	VG	F	VF	XF
SE1712 (1790)	—	40.00	55.00	70.00	90.00	—

KM# 509 1/4 MOHAR

1.4000 g., Gold **Note:** In the name of Queen Raja Rajesvari.

Date	Mintage	Good	VG	F	VF	XF
SE1716 (1794)	—	40.00	50.00	65.00	85.00	—
SE1723 (1801)	—	45.00	55.00	70.00	90.00	—
SE1724 (1802)	—	45.00	55.00	70.00	90.00	—

KM# 513 1/2 MOHAR

2.8000 g., Gold **Note:** Also in the name of Queen Lalita Tripura Sundari.

Date	Mintage	Good	VG	F	VF	XF
SE1701 (1779)	—	65.00	75.00	85.00	100	—
SE1712 (1790)	—	65.00	75.00	85.00	100	—

KM# 514.1 MOHAR

5.6000 g., Gold **Note:** Also in the name of Queen Lalita Tripura Sundari.

Date	Mintage	VG	F	VF	XF	Unc
SE1700 (1778)	—	115	125	145	170	—
SE1702 (1780)	—	115	125	145	170	—
SE1703 (1781)	—	115	125	145	170	—
SE1705 (1783)	—	115	125	145	170	—
SE1706 (1784)	—	115	125	145	170	—
SE1708 (1786)	—	115	125	145	170	—
SE1709 (1787)	—	115	125	145	170	—

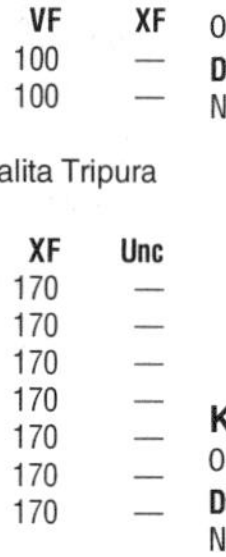

KM# 514.2 MOHAR

5.6000 g., Gold **Note:** Also in the name of Queen Lalita Tripura Sundari.

Date	Mintage	VG	F	VF	XF	Unc
SE1716 (1794)	—	115	125	145	170	—
SE1719 (1797)	—	115	125	145	170	—
SE1720 (1798)	—	115	125	145	170	—

KM# 515 2 MOHARS

11.2000 g., Gold **Note:** Also in the name of Queen Lalita Tripura Sundari.

Date	Mintage	VG	F	VF	XF	Unc
SE1711 (1789)	—	450	500	550	625	—

PRESENTATION COINAGE

KM# 516 2 RUPEES

23.3200 g., Gold **Note:** Also in the name of Queen Lalita Tripura Sundari.

Date	Mintage	VG	F	VF	XF	Unc
SE1718 (1796)	—	750	1,000	1,250	1,500	—

Note: Struck c.1849AD

Girvan Yuddha Vikrama

SE1720-1738 / 1799-1816AD

SILVER COINAGE

KM# 518 DAM

0.0400 g., Silver, 7-8 mm. **Note:** Uniface. Size varies.

Date	Mintage	VG	F	VF	XF	Unc
ND(1799-1816)	—	4.00	8.00	11.50	16.00	—

KM# 519 1/32 MOHAR

0.1800 g., Silver **Note:** Uniface.

Date	Mintage	VG	F	VF	XF	Unc
ND(1799-1816)	—	8.00	13.50	18.50	25.00	—

KM# 520 1/16 MOHAR

0.3500 g., Silver **Note:** Varieties exist.

Date	Mintage	VG	F	VF	XF	Unc
ND(1799-1816)	—	7.50	11.50	16.50	22.50	—

KM# 521 1/8 MOHAR

0.7000 g., Silver **Obv:** Shri above sword

Date	Mintage	VG	F	VF	XF	Unc
ND(1799-1816)	—	6.00	10.00	13.50	18.50	—

KM# 522 1/8 MOHAR

0.7000 g., Silver **Obv:** Umbrella above sword

Date	Mintage	VG	F	VF	XF	Unc
ND(1799-1816)	—	6.00	10.00	13.50	18.50	—

KM# 523 1/8 MOHAR

0.7000 g., Silver **Obv:** Wreath around and umbrella above sword

Date	Mintage	VG	F	VF	XF	Unc
ND(1799-1816)	—	6.00	10.00	13.50	18.50	—

KM# A539 1/8 MOHAR

0.7000 g., Gold **Obv:** Wreath around and umbrella above sword

Date	Mintage	VG	F	VF	XF	Unc
ND(1799-1816)	—	18.50	25.00	40.00	60.00	—

KM# 526 1/2 MOHAR

2.7700 g., Silver

Date	Mintage	VG	F	VF	XF	Unc
SE1721 (1799)	—	7.50	12.50	20.00	30.00	—
SE1728 (1806)	—	7.50	12.50	20.00	30.00	—
SE1729 (1807)	—	7.50	12.50	20.00	30.00	—
SE1730 (1808)	—	5.00	8.50	15.00	22.50	—
SE1733 (1811)	—	7.50	12.50	20.00	30.00	—

KM# 528 MOHAR

5.6000 g., Silver **Obv:** 2 "Shri's" above square

Date	Mintage	VG	F	VF	XF	Unc
SE1720 (1798)	—	10.00	13.50	17.50	23.50	—

KM# 529 MOHAR

5.6000 g., Silver **Obv:** 3 "Shri's" above square

Date	Mintage	VG	F	VF	XF	Unc
SE1721 (1799)	—	4.50	6.50	9.00	11.50	—
SE1722 (1800)	—	4.50	6.50	9.00	11.50	—
SE1723 (1801)	—	4.50	6.50	9.00	11.50	—
SE1724 (1802)	—	4.50	6.50	9.00	11.50	—
SE1725 (1803)	—	4.50	6.50	9.00	11.50	—
SE1728 (1806)	—	4.50	6.50	9.00	11.50	—
SE1729 (1807)	—	4.50	6.50	9.00	11.50	—
SE1730 (1808)	—	4.50	6.50	9.00	11.50	—
SE1731 (1809)	—	4.50	6.50	9.00	11.50	—
SE1732 (1810)	—	4.50	6.50	9.00	11.50	—
SE1733 (1811)	—	4.50	6.50	9.00	11.50	—
SE1734 (1812)	—	4.50	6.50	9.00	11.50	—
SE1735 (1813)	—	4.50	6.50	9.00	11.50	—
SE1736 (1814)	—	4.50	6.50	9.00	11.50	—
SE1737 (1815)	—	4.50	6.50	9.00	11.50	—
SE1738 (1816)	—	4.50	6.50	9.00	11.50	—

GOLD COINAGE

KM# 535 DAM

0.0440 g., Gold **Note:** Uniface.

Date	Mintage	VG	F	VF	XF	Unc
ND(1799-1816)	—	10.00	14.00	20.00	30.00	—

KM# 536 1/32 MOHAR

0.1750 g., Gold **Note:** Uniface.

Date	Mintage	VG	F	VF	XF	Unc
ND(1799-1816)	—	14.00	20.00	25.00	40.00	—

KM# 537 1/16 MOHAR

0.3500 g., Gold **Note:** Three varieties exist.

Date	Mintage	VG	F	VF	XF	Unc
ND(1799-1816)	—	15.00	20.00	25.00	40.00	—

KM# 538 1/8 MOHAR

0.7000 g., Gold **Obv:** "Shr" above sword

Date	Mintage	VG	F	VF	XF	Unc
ND(1799-1816)	—	22.50	27.50	40.00	60.00	—

KM# 539 1/8 MOHAR

0.7000 g., Gold **Obv:** Umbrella above sword

Date	Mintage	VG	F	VF	XF	Unc
ND(1799-1816)	—	22.50	27.50	40.00	60.00	—

KM# 541 1/2 MOHAR

2.8000 g., Gold

Date	Mintage	VG	F	VF	XF	Unc
SE1721 (1799)	—	70.00	80.00	100	130	—
SE1728 (1806)	—	75.00	85.00	100	130	—

Date	Mintage	VG	F	VF	XF	Unc
SE1729 (1807)	—	75.00	85.00	100	130	—
SE1730 (1808)	—	75.00	85.00	100	130	—

KM# 544 MOHAR

5.6000 g., Gold **Note:** Similar to 1 Mohar, KM#529.

Date	Mintage	VG	F	VF	XF	Unc
SE1721 (1799)	—	125	150	175	225	—
SE1723 (1801)	—	130	150	175	225	—
SE1723 (1801)	—	130	150	175	225	—
SE1724 (1802)	—	130	150	175	225	—
SE1728 (1806)	—	130	150	175	225	—

KM# 549 2 MOHARS

11.2000 g., Gold

Date	Mintage	VG	F	VF	XF	Unc
SE1721 (1799)	—	250	275	325	385	—

ANONYMOUS HAMMERED COINAGE

KM# E517a PAISA

Copper Alloys **Note:** Local issues. No inscription, plain both sides. Weight varies: 8-12g. Magnetic - Iron alloy.

Date	Mintage	VG	F	VF	XF	Unc
ND(1799-1816)	—	3.00	5.00	10.00	15.00	—

KM# B517 2 PAISA (Dhyak)

Copper **Note:** No incscription, plain both sides. Weight varies: 18-22g.

Date	Mintage	VG	F	VF	XF	Unc
ND(1799-1816)	—	3.00	5.00	10.00	15.00	—

KM# B517a 2 PAISA (Dhyak)

Copper **Note:** No inscription, plain both sides. Magnetic, copper-iron alloy. Weight varies: 18-22g.

Date	Mintage	VG	F	VF	XF	Unc
(1799-1816)	—	3.00	5.00	10.00	15.00	—

KM# D517a 4 PAISA (Ganda)

Copper **Note:** Local issue. No inscription, plain both sides. Weight varies: 40-44g. Copper-iron alloy, magnetic.

Date	Mintage	VG	F	VF	XF	Unc
ND(1799-1816)	—	3.00	5.00	10.00	15.00	—

KM# F517 4 PAISA (Ganda)

Copper **Note:** Local issues. No inscription, plain both sides. Weight varies 39-42g. Slight traces of former Arabic inscription.

Date	Mintage	VG	F	VF	XF	Unc
ND(1799-1816)	—	3.00	5.00	10.00	15.00	—

KM# D517 4 PAISA (Ganda)

40.0000 g., Copper **Note:** Local Issues. No inscription, plain both sides. Weight varies: 40-44g.

Date	Mintage	VG	F	VF	XF	Unc
ND(1799-1816)	—	4.00	6.00	10.00	15.00	—

PRESENTATION COINAGE

KM# 552 2 RUPEES

23.3200 g., Gold **Note:** Also in the name of Queen Goraksha Rajya Lakshmi.

Date	Mintage	VG	F	VF	XF	Unc
SE1721 (1799)	—	750	1,000	1,250	1,500	—

Note: Struck c.1849AD

NETHERLANDS

The Kingdom of the Netherlands, a country of western Europe fronting on the North Sea and bordered by Belgium and Germany, has an area of 15,770 sq. mi. (41,500 sq. km.) and a population of 15.7 million. Capital: Amsterdam, but the seat of government is at The Hague. The economy is based on dairy farming and a variety of industrial activities. Chemicals, yarns and fabrics, and meat products are exported.

After being a part of Charlemagne's empire in the 8th and 9th centuries, the Netherlands came under control of Burgundy and the Austrian Hapsburgs, and finally was subjected to Spanish dominion in the 16th century. Led by William of Orange, the Dutch revolted against Spain in 1568. The seven northern provinces formed the Union of Utrecht and declared their independence in 1581,becoming the Republic of the United Netherlands. In the ollowing century, the *Golden Age* of Dutch history, the Netherlands became a great sea and colonial power, a patron of the arts and a refuge for the persecuted. The United Dutch Republic ended in 1795 when the French formed the Batavian Republic. Napoleon made his brother Louis, the King of Holland in 1806, however he abdicated in 1810 when Napoleon annexed Holland. The French were expelled in 1813, and all the provinces of Holland and Belgium were merged into the Kingdom of the United Netherlands under William I, in 1814. The Belgians withdrew in 1830 to form their own kingdom, the last substantial change in the configuration of European Netherlands. German forces invaded in 1940 as the royal family fled to England where a government-in-exile was formed. A German High Commissioner, Arthur Seyss-Inquart, was placed in command until 1945 when the arrival of Allied military forces ended the occupation.

RULERS

United Netherlands, 1543-1795

BATAVIAN REPUBLIC

French domination, 1795-1806

MINT MARKS

B - Brussels (Belgium), 1821-1830
D - Denver, 1943-1945
P - Philadelphia, 1941-1945
S - San Francisco, 1944-1945

MINT PRIVY MARKS

Harderwijk (Gelderland)

Date	Privy Mark
1730-45	Horse on mountain
1750-52	Falconer
1753-57	Crane
1758-76	Tree
1782-1806	Ear of corn

Dordrecht (Holland)

Date	Privy Mark
1600-1806	Rosette
1795-1806	None

Enkhuizen (West Friesland)

Date	Privy Mark
1761-71	Ship
1791-96	Rosette
1796-1803	Star

Hoorn (West Friesland)

Date	Privy Mark
1751-61	Rooster
1781-91	Rosette

Kampen (Overyssel)

Date	Privy Mark
1763	Half eagle
1763-64, 1795-1807	Eagle
1764-65, 1795	3 dots

Medemblik (West Friesland)

Date	Privy Mark
1771-81	Ship

Middelburg (Zeeland)

Date	Privy Mark
1601-1799	Castle

Utrecht (Utrecht)

Date	Privy Mark
1738-1805	Shield

MONETARY SYSTEM

8 Duits = 1 Stuiver (Stiver)
6 Stuiver = 1 Schelling
20 Stuiver = 1 Gulden (Guilder or Florin)
50 Stuiver = 1 Rijksdaalder (Silver Ducat)
60 Stuiver = 1 Ducaton (Silver Rider)
14 Gulden = 1 Golden Rider

BATAVIAN REPUBLIC

From 1796 to 1806, the Netherlands was a confederation of seven provinces, each producing coins similar in design but differing in the coat of arms or inscription. Generally the coins of each province contained an abbreviation of the name of the province somewhere in the inscription. Under the Batavian Republic, the following abbreviations were used.

PROVINCE ABBREVIATIONS

G, GEL - Gelderland
HOL, HOLL - Holland
TRANSI - Overijsel
TRA, TRAI, TRAIECTUM - Utrecht
WESTF, WESTRI - Westfriesland
ZEL, ZEELANDIA - Zeeland

STANDARD COINAGE

KM# 5 DUIT

Copper **Obv. Legend:** ZEELANDIA, ZEL

Date	Mintage	F	VF	XF	Unc	BU
1795/4	—	6.00	12.00	20.00	35.00	—
1795	—	6.00	12.00	20.00	35.00	—
1796/66	—	6.00	12.00	20.00	35.00	—
1796	—	7.00	15.00	25.00	45.00	—
1797/69	—	10.00	20.00	30.00	55.00	—
1797/6	—	6.00	12.00	20.00	35.00	—
1797	—	6.00	12.00	22.50	37.50	—

KM# 13 2 STUIVERS

0.5580 Silver **Obv:** Inscription, date **Obv. Inscription:** • N •/TRA/IEC/TUM 1797 **Rev:** Crowned arms divides 2 S

Date	Mintage	F	VF	XF	Unc	BU
1796	2,110	70.00	130	200	300	—
1797	—	200	300	500	750	—
1799	4,070	65.00	120	200	300	—

KM# 13a 2 STUIVERS

Gold **Obv:** Inscription, date **Obv. Inscription:** • N • TRA IEC TUM date **Rev:** Crowned arms divides 2 S

Date	Mintage	F	VF	XF	Unc	BU
1797	—	—	—	900	1,500	1,750
1799	—	—	—	900	1,500	1,750

KM# 6 2-1/2 STUIVER (1/8 Livre Copper)

Copper **Obv:** Inscription: ZEELANDIA

Date	Mintage	F	VF	XF	Unc	BU
1795	—	600	1,500	2,500	3,000	3,500

KM# 7 10 STUIVERS

0.9120 Silver **Obv:** Crowned arms divide N S **Obv. Legend:** MO : ARG : ORD : .... **Rev:** Standing figure leaning on short pillar **Rev. Legend:** HAC NITEMVR HANC TVEMVR

Date	Mintage	F	VF	XF	Unc	BU
1795	—	65.00	90.00	135	200	250
1796	696	200	600	900	1,600	1,700

KM# 10.3 RIJKSDAALDER (2-1/2 Gulden)

0.8680 Silver **Obv. Legend:** ....TRANSI.

Date	Mintage	F	VF	XF	Unc	BU
1795	49,000	500	800	1,500	2,000	3,000
1796	Inc. above	200	400	750	1,200	2,000

KM# 10.4 RIJKSDAALDER (2-1/2 Gulden)

0.8680 Silver **Obv:** Standing armored knight, crowned shield by legs **Obv. Legend:** BELG : TRAI • MO : NO : .... **Rev:** Crowned arms divides date **Rev. Legend:** ...CONCORDIA RES...

Date	Mintage	F	VF	XF	Unc	BU
1795	6,283,780	400	625	1,000	1,500	2,000
1796	Inc. above	40.00	70.00	120	200	250
1797	Inc. above	130	300	500	800	1,000
1798	Inc. above	40.00	75.00	140	250	300
1799	Inc. above	50.00	100	200	300	350
1800 small 8	Inc. above	40.00	70.00	120	170	200
1800	Inc. above	40.00	70.00	120	170	200

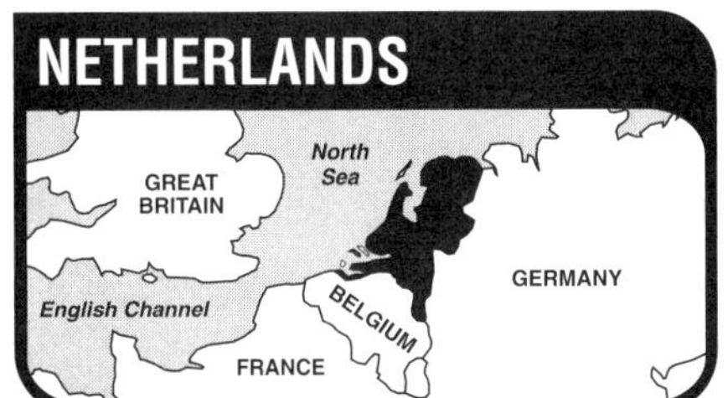

KM# 10.5 RIJKSDAALDER (2-1/2 Gulden)

0.8680 Silver **Obv. Legend:** ....WESTF, WESTRI.

Date	Mintage	F	VF	XF	Unc	BU
1795	—	300	600	750	1,200	1,600
1796	—	250	500	650	900	1,200

KM# 10.6 RIJKSDAALDER (2-1/2 Gulden)

0.8680 Silver **Obv. Legend:** ....ZELANDIA, ZEL.

Date	Mintage	F	VF	XF	Unc	BU
1795	—	65.00	90.00	140	275	350
1796	—	100	450	725	1,150	1,500
1798/6	99,000	65.00	90.00	140	275	350
1798/7	Inc. above	65.00	90.00	140	275	350
1798	Inc. above	65.00	90.00	140	275	350

KM# 15 1/2 DUCATON

0.9350 Silver **Obv:** Armored Knight on horse above crowned arms **Obv. Legend:** FOE : BELG : PRO : TRAI • ... **Rev:** Crowned arms with supporters, date below in design **Rev. Legend:** CRESCUNT • CONCORDIA RES PARVAE •

Date	Mintage	F	VF	XF	Unc	BU
1796	—	500	1,000	2,000	4,000	5,000
1798	—	500	1,000	2,000	4,000	5,000

KM# 16 DUCATON

0.9350 Silver **Obv:** Armored Knight on horse above crowned shield **Obv. Legend:** FOE : BELG : PRO : TRAI • MO : NO : ARG : CON **Rev:** Crowned arms with supporters, date below in design **Rev. Legend:** PARVAE CRESCUNT • CONCORDIA RES

Date	Mintage	F	VF	XF	Unc	BU
1796	435	300	800	1,600	2,750	3,500
1798	360	300	800	1,600	2,750	3,500

KM# 10.1 SILVER DUCAT

0.8680 Silver **Obv:** Standing armored knight, crowned shield by legs **Obv. Legend:** ...D: GEL: &: C: Z: **Rev:** Crowned shield divides date

Date	Mintage	F	VF	XF	Unc	BU
1795	5,000	800	1,100	1,500	2,000	2,400
1797	19,000	400	700	1,000	1,300	1,600
1800	253,925	180	400	600	1,000	1,200

KM# 10.2 SILVER DUCAT

0.8680 Silver **Obv:** Standing armored knight, crowned shield by legs **Obv. Legend:** BELG : TRAI • MO : NO : .... **Rev:** Crowned arms divides date **Rev. Legend:** ...CONCORDIA RES...

Date	Mintage	F	VF	XF	Unc	BU
1796	2,668,000	100	200	300	450	700
1797/6	Inc. above	200	400	600	1,000	1,200
1798	Inc. above	80.00	200	300	450	700
1799	Inc. above	200	400	750	1,250	1,600
1800	Inc. above	55.00	150	200	280	350

KM# 14 1/2 GULDEN

0.9120 Silver **Obv. Legend:** ....WESTF • WESTRI

Date	Mintage	F	VF	XF	Unc	BU
1796	—	80.00	150	300	500	800

KM# 8.1 GULDEN

10.4700 g., 0.9120 Silver 0.3070 oz. ASW **Obv. Legend:** ....G, GEL

Date	Mintage	F	VF	XF	Unc	BU
1795	790,390	25.00	50.00	100	175	250
1796/5	42,200	90.00	140	180	350	500
1796	Inc. above	40.00	120	170	300	400

KM# 8.2 GULDEN

10.4700 g., 0.9120 Silver 0.3070 oz. ASW **Obv:** Crowned arms divides value **Obv. Legend:** MO : ARG : ORD : FOE : BELG : HOLL : **Rev:** Standing figure leaning on short pillar above date **Rev. Legend:** HAC NITEMVR HANC TVEMVR

Date	Mintage	F	VF	XF	Unc	BU
1795	731,680	25.00	50.00	90.00	140	200
1797	229,080	30.00	60.00	120	200	300
1797 Holl over Westf	—	40.00	75.00	140	220	350
1800	40,395	40.00	80.00	150	240	350

KM# 8.3 GULDEN

10.4700 g., 0.9120 Silver 0.3070 oz. ASW **Obv. Legend:** ....TRANSI •

Date	Mintage	F	VF	XF	Unc	BU
1795	615,105	25.00	60.00	120	200	300
1796	Inc. above	80.00	100	150	275	350

KM# 8.4 GULDEN

10.4700 g., 0.9120 Silver 0.3070 oz. ASW **Obv. Legend:** ....TRA, TRAI

Date	Mintage	F	VF	XF	Unc	BU
1795	—	140	275	400	600	900
1798	16,300	140	175	400	600	900
1799	38,100	30.00	60.00	150	220	350

KM# 8.5 GULDEN

10.4700 g., 0.9120 Silver 0.3070 oz. ASW **Obv. Legend:** ....WESTF, WESTRI •

Date	Mintage	F	VF	XF	Unc	BU
1795	—	40.00	100	175	270	350
1796/4	—	80.00	140	200	320	400
1796 round altar, with garland	—	25.00	70.00	120	175	275
1796 decorated altar, without garland	—	25.00	70.00	120	175	275

KM# 18 GULDEN

0.9120 Silver **Obv. Legend:** ....HOL, HOLL • **Note:** Denomination: GL.

Date	Mintage	VG	F	VF	XF	Unc
1798 (1798)	—	100	175	225	330	—

Note: The above is considered a pattern by some experts

KM# 9.1 3 GULDEN

31.4200 g., 0.9150 Silver 0.9243 oz. ASW **Obv. Legend:** ....G, GEL.

Date	Mintage	F	VF	XF	Unc	BU
1795	178,450	70.00	150	200	300	350
1796/5	44,565	70.00	150	200	300	350
1796	Inc. above	80.00	160	220	325	400

KM# 9.2 3 GULDEN

31.4200 g., 0.9150 Silver 0.9243 oz. ASW **Obv. Legend:** ...HOL: or HOLL **Rev:** Standing maiden, date below

Date	Mintage	F	VF	XF	Unc	BU
1795/3	1,084,305	70.00	125	180	250	350
1795	Inc. above	60.00	100	160	225	350
1796	Inc. above	60.00	100	160	225	350
1797	Inc. above	60.00	100	160	225	325
1798	Inc. above	110	250	350	500	700
1800	Inc. above	60.00	125	200	275	375

KM# 9.3 3 GULDEN

0.9150 Silver **Obv. Legend:** ....TRA, TRAI.

Date	Mintage	F	VF	XF	Unc	BU
1795	1,713,000	30.00	85.00	160	250	350
1796	Inc. above	90.00	160	275	400	600

KM# 9.4 3 GULDEN

0.9150 Silver **Obv:** Crowned arms divides value **Obv. Legend:** BELG : WESTF : ... **Rev:** Standing figure leaning on short pillar above date **Rev. Legend:** HAC NITEMVR HANC TVEMVR

Date	Mintage	F	VF	XF	Unc	BU
1795	—	25.00	60.00	120	225	300
1796/5	—	120	225	350	550	800
1796	—	70.00	150	250	400	600

TRADE COINAGE

KM# 11.1 DUCAT

3.4990 g., 0.9830 Gold 0.1106 oz. AGW **Obv:** Standing armored knight divides date **Obv. Legend:** ends:...G or GEL. **Rev:** Inscription within ornamented square

Date	Mintage	F	VF	XF	Unc	BU
1795	44,910	100	200	300	400	500
1796	—	850	1,300	2,000	2,600	3,200
1797	420	850	1,300	2,000	2,600	3,200
1800	1,296,550	150	250	375	550	700

KM# 11.3 DUCAT

3.4540 g., 0.9830 Gold 0.1092 oz. AGW **Obv:** Standing armored knight divides date **Obv. Legend:** PAR:CRES:TRA... **Rev:** Inscription within ornamented square **Note:** 1788, 1795, 1800 and 1802 has also been struck at the Stuttgarter Munzstatte in Germany, quanity unknown. Struck in 1812 as payment for soliders value unknown (recently discovered).

Date	Mintage	F	VF	XF	Unc	BU
1795	—	80.00	200	300	500	800
1796	—	80.00	200	300	500	800
1797	—	80.00	200	300	500	800
1798	—	80.00	200	300	500	800
1799	—	80.00	200	300	500	800
1800	1,400,000	60.00	120	175	250	—

KM# 11.2 DUCAT

3.4990 g., 0.9830 Gold 0.1106 oz. AGW **Obv:** Standing armored knight divides date **Obv. Legend:** ends:...Hol **Rev:** Inscription within ornamented square **Note:** Coins with the star were struck at the Enkhuizen Mint with a total mintage of 630,455. Coins without the star were struck at the Dordrecht Mint with a total mintage of 2,861,825.

Date	Mintage	F	VF	XF	Unc	BU
1795 without star	—	80.00	150	225	300	450
1796 without star	—	80.00	150	225	300	450
1796 star	—	150	400	500	650	800
1797/6 star	—	550	1,100	1,700	2,000	2,500
1797 without star	—	550	1,100	1,700	2,000	2,500
1797 star	—	550	1,100	1,700	2,000	2,500
1798 without star	6,930	550	1,100	1,700	2,000	2,500
1799 without star	6,370	550	1,100	1,700	2,000	2,500
1800/1799	—	425	650	800	1,000	1,500
1800 without star	—	90.00	165	225	300	400
1800 star	—	160	375	500	700	900

KM# 12.1 2 DUCAT

7.0000 g., 0.9830 Gold 0.2212 oz. AGW **Obv:** Standing armored knight divides date **Obv. Inscription:** ends:...HOL or HOLL **Rev:** Inscription within ornamented square **Note:** Similar to 1 Ducat KM#11.2.

Date	Mintage	F	VF	XF	Unc	BU
1795	—	1,000	1,500	2,250	3,500	5,000

KM# 12.2 2 DUCAT

7.0000 g., 0.9830 Gold 0.2212 oz. AGW **Obv:** Standing armored knight divides date **Obv. Legend:** PAR : CRES : TRA ... **Rev:** Inscription within ornamented square **Rev. Inscription:** MO :

ORD : PROVIN : FOEDER : BELG • AD LEG • IMP **Note:** Similar to 1 Ducat KM#11.3

Date	Mintage	F	VF	XF	Unc	BU
1795	—	—	—	—	—	—
1796	—	700	1,600	2,200	2,800	3,500
1797	—	700	1,600	2,200	2,800	3,500
1798	—	700	1,600	2,200	2,800	3,500
1799	—	550	1,100	1,500	2,000	2,700
1800	350,000	550	1,100	1,500	2,000	2,700

PATTERNS

Including off metal strikes

KM#	Date	Mintage	Identification	Mkt Val
Pn1	1796	—	Rijksdaalder. Bronze.	2,500
Pn2	1800	—	2 Stuivers.	—
Pn3	1800	—	5 Stuivers.	—
Pn4	1800	—	10 Stuivers.	—
Pn5	1800	—	Gulden.	—
Pn6	1800	—	3 Gulden.	—

PIEFORTS

KM#	Date	Mintage	Identification	Mkt Val
P1	1775	—	Ducaton. 0.9410 Silver.	—

DEVENTER

PROVINCE

STANDARD COINAGE

KM# 77 2 STUIVERS

Billon **Obv:** Crowned rampant lion left holding sword and arrows, value at sides **Rev:** DAVEN/TRIA/(date) **Note:** Mint mark: Sitting dog.

Date	Mintage	VG	F	VF	XF	Unc
1702	130,000	7.50	25.00	40.00	50.00	90.00
1707	23,000	7.50	25.00	40.00	50.00	90.00
1708	27,000	7.50	25.00	40.00	50.00	90.00

FRIESLAND

PROVINCE

STANDARD COINAGE

KM# 80 DUIT

Copper **Obv:** Crowned arms **Rev:** Rampant lion above name, date and flowers

Date	Mintage	VG	F	VF	XF	Unc
1702	—	1.50	7.50	20.00	30.00	70.00
1715	—	2.50	10.00	25.00	40.00	80.00
1717	—	1.50	7.50	20.00	30.00	70.00
1723	—	1.50	7.50	20.00	30.00	70.00
1724	—	1.50	7.50	20.00	30.00	70.00

KM# 80a DUIT

Silver **Obv:** Crowned arms **Rev:** Rampant lion above name, date and flowers

Date	Mintage	VG	F	VF	XF	Unc
1702	—	20.00	35.00	70.00	150	250
1703	—	20.00	35.00	70.00	150	250
1717/16	—	20.00	40.00	80.00	175	300
1717	—	20.00	35.00	70.00	150	300
1723	—	20.00	35.00	70.00	140	200
1724	—	20.00	35.00	70.00	140	200

KM# 80b DUIT

3.8500 g., Gold **Obv:** Crowned arms **Rev:** Rampant lion above name, date and flowers

Date	Mintage	VG	F	VF	XF	Unc
1702	—	—	—	—	—	2,500
1703	—	—	—	—	—	2,500
1717	—	—	—	—	—	3,500

KM# 32.3 2 STUIVERS

Silver **Note:** Mint mark: Rampant lion. Varieties exist.

Date	Mintage	VG	F	VF	XF	Unc
1702	—	5.00	10.00	30.00	40.00	60.00
1704	—	5.00	10.00	30.00	40.00	60.00
1705	—	3.50	7.50	20.00	30.00	50.00
1706	—	3.50	7.50	20.00	30.00	50.00
1707	—	3.50	7.50	20.00	30.00	50.00
1708	—	3.50	7.50	20.00	30.00	50.00
1709	—	3.50	7.50	20.00	30.00	50.00
1710	—	3.50	7.50	20.00	30.00	50.00
1711	—	3.50	7.50	20.00	30.00	50.00
1712	—	3.50	7.50	20.00	30.00	50.00
1714	—	25.00	50.00	100	125	200

KM# 85 6 STUIVERS (Scheepjesschilling)

Silver **Obv:** Crowned arms divide value, date above crown **Rev:** Sailing ship to right

Date	Mintage	VG	F	VF	XF	Unc
1711	—	—	—	—	—	—
1712	—	—	—	—	—	—

KM# 73 20 STUIVERS (Gulden)

Silver **Obv:** Crowned lion shield divides value **Rev:** Standing female figure leaning on Bible on column, holding spear with Liberty cap, date in exerque **Note:** Varieties exist.

Date	Mintage	VG	F	VF	XF	Unc
1705/4	—	70.00	150	300	500	—
1705	—	70.00	150	300	500	—
1714	—	70.00	150	300	500	—
1721/14	—	—	—	—	—	—
1721	—	70.00	150	300	500	—

PIEFORTS

KM#	Date	Mintage	Identification	Mkt Val
P10	1714	—	Gulden. Silver. 23.8500 g. Square blank.	—

GELDERLAND

Ducatus Gelriae

Gelder, a former duchy, was merged with the Hapsburg dominions in the Netherlands until the revolt of the Low Countries resulted in its partition. In 1579 the greater part of Gelder, comprising the quarters of Nijmegen, Arnhem, and Zutphen, became the province of Gelderland in the Dutch Republic.

PROVINCE

STANDARD COINAGE

KM# 83b DUIT

3.5000 g., Gold **Obv:** Crowned arms of Gelderland, with flower decoration **Rev:** Inscription **Rev. Inscription:** D / GEL / RIAE

Date	Mintage	VG	F	VF	XF	Unc
1751 Rare	—	—	—	—	—	—

KM# 88b DUIT

1.8000 g., Gold **Obv:** Crowned arms of Gelderland **Rev:** Inscription above date in branches **Rev. Inscription:** D / GEL / RIAE.

Date	Mintage	VG	F	VF	XF	Unc
1757 Rare	—	—	—	—	—	—

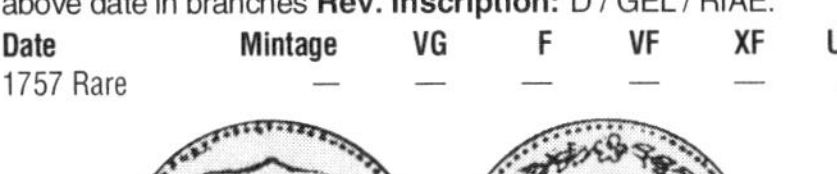

KM# 47 DUIT

Copper **Obv:** Crowned arms of Gelderland **Rev:** Inscription, date in wreath **Rev. Inscription:** *D* GEL RIÆ

Date	Mintage	VG	F	VF	XF	Unc
1702	—	6.00	20.00	40.00	50.00	—

KM# 75 DUIT

Copper **Obv:** Crowned arms of Gelderland **Obv. Legend:** IN • DEO • SP • NOS • **Rev:** Inscription, date **Rev. Inscription:** *D*/GEL/RIÆ

Date	Mintage	VG	F	VF	XF	Unc
1702	—	3.00	8.00	15.00	25.00	50.00
1703	—	4.00	10.00	25.00	35.00	70.00
1720	—	2.00	6.00	15.00	25.00	50.00

KM# 75a DUIT

Silver **Obv:** Crowned arms of Gelderland **Rev:** Inscription, date **Rev. Inscription:** *D*/GEL/RIÆ

Date	Mintage	VG	F	VF	XF	Unc
1702	—	—	—	—	—	—
1703	—	30.00	70.00	150	180	—

KM# A80 DUIT

Obv. Inscription: HOL/LAN/DIA/date **Rev:** Stork in closed "Dutch" garden

Date	Mintage	VG	F	VF	XF	Unc
1702	—	5.00	10.00	25.00	50.00	—

KM# B80 DUIT

Obv. Inscription: HOL/LAN/DIA/date **Rev:** Standing lion with sword in closed "Dutch" garden

Date	Mintage	VG	F	VF	XF	Unc
1702	—	—	—	—	—	—

KM# 83 DUIT

Copper **Obv:** Crowned arms of Gelderland within sprigs **Obv. Legend:** IN • DEO • SP • NOS • **Rev:** Inscription, date **Rev. Inscription:** *D*/GEL/RIÆ

Date	Mintage	VG	F	VF	XF	Unc
1739	—	2.00	5.00	12.00	25.00	35.00
1740	—	2.00	5.00	12.00	25.00	35.00
1751	—	2.00	5.00	12.00	25.00	40.00
1752	—	2.00	5.00	12.00	25.00	40.00

KM# 83a DUIT

Silver **Obv:** Crowned arms of Gelderland within sprigs **Rev:** Inscription, date, **Rev. Inscription:** *D*/GEL/RIÆ

Date	Mintage	VG	F	VF	XF	Unc
1752	—	30.00	70.00	150	180	220

KM# 88 DUIT

Copper **Obv:** Crowned arms of Gelderland **Obv. Legend:** IN • DEO • SP • NOS • **Rev:** Inscription, date in sprigs **Rev. Inscription:** *D*/GEL/RIÆ

Date	Mintage	VG	F	VF	XF	Unc
1753	—	2.00	5.00	12.00	20.00	30.00
1754	—	2.00	5.00	12.00	20.00	30.00
1755	—	2.00	5.00	12.00	20.00	30.00
1756	—	2.00	5.00	12.00	20.00	30.00
1757	—	2.00	5.00	12.00	20.00	30.00

KM# 88a DUIT

Silver **Obv:** Crowned arms of Gelderland **Rev:** Inscription, date in sprigs, **Rev. Inscription:** *D* GEL RIÆ

Date	Mintage	VG	F	VF	XF	Unc
1753	—	30.00	70.00	150	180	200
1755	—	30.00	70.00	150	180	200
1756	—	30.00	70.00	150	180	200
1757	—	30.00	70.00	150	180	200

KM# 91a DUIT

Silver

Date	Mintage	VG	F	VF	XF	Unc
1754	—	40.00	100	150	200	300
1755	—	—	—	—	—	—
1756	—	—	25.00	40.00	90.00	120
1757	—	—	—	—	—	—

KM# 88c DUIT

3.5000 g., Gold **Obv:** Crowned arms of Gelderland **Rev:** Inscription, date in sprigs **Rev. Inscription:** *D* GEL RIÆ

Date	Mintage	VG	F	VF	XF	Unc
1755 Rare	—	—	—	—	—	—
1756 Rare	—	—	—	—	—	—

KM# 91 DUIT

Silver **Obv:** Crowned arms of Gelderland **Obv. Legend:** IN • DEO • SP • NOS • **Rev:** Inscription, date **Rev. Inscription:** *D*/GEL/RIÆ

Date	Mintage	VG	F	VF	XF	Unc
1757 Proof	—	—	—	—	—	—

KM# 93 DUIT

Copper **Obv:** Crowned arms of Gelderland **Obv. Legend:** IN • DEO • EST • SPES • NOSTRA • **Rev:** Inscription, date within baroque cartouche **Rev. Inscription:** *D*/GEL/RIÆ

Date	Mintage	VG	F	VF	XF	Unc
1758	—	1.50	6.00	12.00	20.00	30.00
1759	—	1.50	6.00	12.00	20.00	30.00
1760	—	1.50	6.00	12.00	20.00	30.00
1761	—	1.50	4.00	10.00	15.00	20.00
1762	—	1.50	4.00	10.00	15.00	20.00
1763	—	1.50	6.00	12.00	20.00	30.00
1764	—	1.50	6.00	12.00	20.00	30.00
1765	—	1.50	6.00	12.00	20.00	30.00
1766/65	—	1.50	6.00	12.00	20.00	35.00
1766	—	1.50	4.00	10.00	15.00	25.00
1767	—	1.50	4.00	10.00	15.00	25.00
1767/63	—	1.50	6.00	12.00	20.00	35.00
1768	—	1.50	4.00	10.00	15.00	25.00

KM# 93a DUIT

Silver **Obv:** Crowned arms of Gelderland **Rev:** Inscription, date within baroque cartouche **Rev. Inscription:** *D* GEL RIÆ

Date	Mintage	VG	F	VF	XF	Unc
1759	—	25.00	50.00	100	130	160
1760	—	15.00	60.00	70.00	100	160
1761	—	30.00	60.00	100	130	160
1762	—	25.00	50.00	100	130	160
1765	—	25.00	50.00	100	130	160

KM# 93b DUIT

3.5000 g., Gold **Obv:** Crowned arms of Gelderland **Rev:** Inscription, date within baroque cartouche **Rev. Inscription:** *D* GEL RIÆ

Date	Mintage	VG	F	VF	XF	Unc
1759 Rare	—	—	—	—	—	1,200
1761	—	—	—	—	—	1,200
1762 Rare	—	—	—	—	—	—

KM# 105 DUIT

Copper **Obv:** Crowned arms of Gelderland **Obv. Legend:** INDEO • EST • SPES • NOSTRA • **Rev:** Inscription, date **Rev. Inscription:** *D*/GEL/RIAE

Date	Mintage	VG	F	VF	XF	Unc
1783	—	1.50	4.00	10.00	16.50	20.00
1784	—	1.50	4.00	10.00	15.00	20.00
1785	—	2.00	8.00	15.00	22.50	30.00
1786	—	1.50	4.00	10.00	16.50	20.00
1787	—	1.50	4.00	10.00	16.50	20.00
1788	—	2.00	8.00	16.00	25.00	30.00

KM# 108 DUIT

Copper **Obv:** Crowned arms of Gelderland **Obv. Legend:** INDEO • EST • SPES • NOSTRA • **Rev:** Inscription, date within ornamented border **Rev. Inscription:** *D*/GEL/RIAE

Date	Mintage	VG	F	VF	XF	Unc
1788	—	1.50	3.00	6.00	13.50	20.00
1793	—	1.50	3.00	7.00	15.00	20.00
1794	—	1.50	3.00	8.00	17.50	20.00

KM# 108a DUIT

4.4000 g., Silver **Obv:** Crowned arms of Gelderland **Rev:** Inscription, date within ornamented design **Rev. Inscription:** *D* GEL RI?

Date	Mintage	VG	F	VF	XF	Unc
1788	—	—	—	—	—	—

KM# 82 STUIVER (Bezemstuiver)

0.8100 g., 0.5830 Silver 0.0152 oz. ASW **Obv:** Bundle of arrows divides 1S **Rev:** Inscription, date **Rev. Inscription:** GEL/RIA/

Date	Mintage	VG	F	VF	XF	Unc
1738	—	4.00	10.00	20.00	32.00	45.00
1739	—	4.00	10.00	20.00	32.00	45.00
1759	27,170	4.00	10.00	20.00	32.00	45.00
1760	Inc. above	4.00	10.00	20.00	32.00	45.00
1761	Inc. above	4.00	10.00	20.00	32.00	45.00
1764	193,260	4.00	10.00	20.00	32.00	45.00
1765	Inc. above	4.00	10.00	20.00	32.00	45.00
1766	Inc. above	4.00	10.00	20.00	32.00	45.00

KM# 82a STUIVER (Bezemstuiver)

1.7200 g., Gold **Obv:** Bundle of arrows divides 1S **Rev:** Inscription, date **Rev. Inscription:** GEL/RIA/

Date	Mintage	VG	F	VF	XF	Unc
1738	—	100	150	300	450	600
1747	—	100	150	300	450	600
1748	—	100	150	300	450	600
1749	—	100	150	300	450	600
1750	—	100	150	300	450	600
1751	—	100	150	300	450	600
1752	—	100	150	300	450	600
1753	—	100	150	300	450	600
1754	—	100	150	300	450	600
1755	—	100	150	300	450	600
1756	—	100	150	300	450	600
1757	—	100	150	300	450	600
1758	—	100	150	300	450	600
1759	—	100	150	300	450	600
1760	—	100	150	300	450	600
1761	—	100	150	300	450	600

KM# 82c STUIVER (Bezemstuiver)

1.2500 g., Gold **Obv:** Bundle of arrows divides 1S **Rev:** Inscription, above date **Rev. Inscription:** GEL/RIA

Date	Mintage	VG	F	VF	XF	Unc
1755	—	—	—	—	600	—

KM# 82b STUIVER (Bezemstuiver)

0.3330 Silver **Obv:** Bundle of arrow divides 1S **Rev:** Inscription above date **Rev. Inscription:** GEL/RIA

Date	Mintage	VG	F	VF	XF	Unc
1785	43,000	5.00	15.00	22.50	35.00	50.00

KM# 92 STUIVER (Bezemstuiver)

Gold **Obv:** Crowned arms of Gelderland divides 1S **Rev:** Inscription above date **Rev. Inscription:** GEL/RIA

Date	Mintage	VG	F	VF	XF	Unc
1757	—	15.00	300	700	1,000	1,500

KM# 26.4 2 STUIVERS

Silver **Note:** Mint mark: Knight on horse.

Date	Mintage	VG	F	VF	XF	Unc
1704	—	4.00	10.00	20.00	30.00	60.00
1705	—	4.00	10.00	20.00	30.00	60.00
1706	—	4.00	10.00	20.00	30.00	60.00
1707	—	4.00	10.00	20.00	30.00	60.00
1708/7	—	4.00	10.00	20.00	30.00	60.00
1708	—	4.00	10.00	20.00	30.00	60.00
1710/9	—	4.00	10.00	20.00	30.00	60.00
1710	—	4.00	10.00	20.00	30.00	60.00
1711	—	4.00	10.00	20.00	30.00	60.00
1712/1	—	4.00	10.00	20.00	30.00	60.00
1712	—	4.00	10.00	20.00	30.00	60.00

KM# 26.5 2 STUIVERS

Silver **Note:** Mint mark: Horse on mountain. Varieties exist.

Date	Mintage	VG	F	VF	XF	Unc
1734	261,045	4.00	10.00	20.00	30.00	60.00

KM# 80b 2 STUIVERS

Gold **Obv:** Without rosettes at sides of mint mark **Rev:** Inscription above date, mint mark below **Rev. Inscription:** *D*/GEL/RIÆ

Date	Mintage	VG	F	VF	XF	Unc
1747	—	—	—	—	—	—
1757	—	—	—	—	—	—

KM# 80a 2 STUIVERS (Double Wapenstuiver)

1.6200 g., 0.5830 Silver 0.0304 oz. ASW **Obv:** Crowned arms of Gelderland divides 2S **Rev:** Inscription above date, mint mark below **Rev. Inscription:** *D*/GEL/RIÆ

Date	Mintage	VG	F	VF	XF	Unc
1785	—	1.50	4.00	7.50	13.00	—

KM# 107 2 STUIVERS (Double Wapenstuiver)

1.6200 g., 0.5830 Silver 0.0304 oz. ASW **Obv:** Crowned arms of Gelderland divides 2S **Rev:** Inscription above date, rosettes flank mint mark above **Rev. Inscription:** GEL/RIA

Date	Mintage	VG	F	VF	XF	Unc
1785	1,156,405	5.00	10.00	25.00	50.00	100
1786	804,705	1.50	3.00	7.00	12.00	25.00
1789	Inc. above	1.50	3.00	7.00	12.00	25.00
1792	Inc. above	1.50	3.00	7.00	12.00	25.00

KM# 77a 6 STUIVERS (Scheepjesschelling)

Silver **Obv:** Crowned arms of Gelderland divides value **Rev:** Ship sailing, date above

Date	Mintage	VG	F	VF	XF	Unc
1705	—	12.00	40.00	75.00	125	250
1706	—	12.00	40.00	75.00	125	200
1707	—	12.00	40.00	75.00	125	200
1709	—	12.00	40.00	75.00	125	250
1710	—	12.00	40.00	75.00	125	250
1711	—	12.00	40.00	75.00	125	250
1712	—	12.00	40.00	75.00	125	250
1716	—	20.00	80.00	150	250	500
1734	78,975	12.00	40.00	75.00	125	200

KM# 87 10 STUIVERS (1/2 Gulden)

5.3000 g., 0.9200 Silver 0.1568 oz. ASW **Obv:** Crowned arms of Gelderland divide value, 10 ST, date above **Obv. Legend:** MOARGORD FOE BELG D : GEL & C : Z • **Rev:** Standing figure holding pole with liberty cap, leaning on bible on column **Rev. Legend:** HANC TVEMVR HAC NITIMVR

Date	Mintage	VG	F	VF	XF	Unc
1751/50	—	50.00	100	175	200	400
1751	—	50.00	100	175	200	400
1761/50	—	50.00	100	175	200	400
1761	—	50.00	100	175	200	350

KM# 94 10 STUIVERS (1/2 Gulden)

5.3000 g., 0.9200 Silver 0.1568 oz. ASW **Obv:** Crowned arms of Gelderland divide value: X ST, date above **Obv. Legend:** MOARGORD FOE BELG D GEL & C Z **Rev:** Standing figure holding pole with liberty cap, leaning on bible on column **Rev. Legend:** HANC TVEMVR HAC NITIMVR

Date	Mintage	VG	F	VF	XF	Unc
1759	—	35.00	80.00	150	250	400
1760	—	25.00	60.00	125	200	300
1761	—	25.00	60.00	125	200	300
1762	—	25.00	60.00	125	200	300
1764/3	—	30.00	80.00	200	300	500
1764	—	25.00	60.00	125	200	300
1765	—	25.00	60.00	125	200	300

KM# 94a 10 STUIVERS (1/2 Gulden)

6.9000 g., Gold **Obv:** Crowned arms of Gelderland divide value: X ST, above crown **Rev:** Standing figure holding pole with liberty cap, leaning on bible on column

Date	Mintage	VG	F	VF	XF	Unc
1761 Rare	—	—	—	—	—	—

KM# 65.2 20 STUIVERS (Gulden)

Silver **Obv:** Crowned arms of Gelderland divides value **Rev:** Standing female figure leaning on Bible on column, holding pole with liberty cap, date in exerque **Note:** Mintmark: Knight on horse.

Date	Mintage	VG	F	VF	XF	Unc
1701	—	8.00	20.00	30.00	60.00	100
1703	1,673,815	8.00	20.00	30.00	60.00	100
1704/1	Inc. above	12.00	25.00	40.00	80.00	150
1704/3	Inc. above	12.00	25.00	40.00	80.00	150
1704	Inc. above	8.00	20.00	30.00	50.00	100
1705/3	Inc. above	8.00	20.00	30.00	55.00	110
1705	Inc. above	8.00	20.00	30.00	50.00	100
1706	Inc. above	8.00	20.00	30.00	50.00	100
1707	Inc. above	8.00	20.00	30.00	50.00	100
1709	4,128,785	8.00	20.00	30.00	50.00	100
1710	Inc. above	8.00	20.00	30.00	50.00	100
1711	Inc. above	12.00	25.00	40.00	60.00	100
1712	Inc. above	8.00	20.00	30.00	50.00	100
1713	2,661,345	8.00	20.00	30.00	50.00	100
1713/10	Inc. above	10.00	30.00	60.00	100	150
1713/11	Inc. above	10.00	30.00	60.00	100	150
1714	Inc. above	8.00	20.00	30.00	50.00	100

KM# 65.3 20 STUIVERS (Gulden)

Silver **Obv:** Crowned arms of Gelderland divide value **Rev:** Standing female figure leaning on bible on column, holding pole with liberty cap, date in exergue **Note:** Mint mark: Crane.

Date	Mintage	VG	F	VF	XF	Unc
1715	2,018,820	8.00	17.00	30.00	50.00	100
1716	Inc. above	8.00	17.00	30.00	50.00	100
1717	Inc. above	10.00	20.00	60.00	80.00	150
1718	1,554,500	10.00	20.00	60.00	80.00	150
1719	Inc. above	8.00	17.00	30.00	50.00	100
1720	Inc. above	8.00	17.00	30.00	50.00	100
1721	Inc. above	8.00	17.00	30.00	50.00	100
1723	Inc. above	8.00	17.00	30.00	50.00	—
1793 Error, wrong 1723 date	—	10.00	25.00	50.00	100	200

KM# 65.4 20 STUIVERS (Gulden)

Silver **Obv:** Crowned arms of Gelderland divide value **Rev:** Standing female figure leaning on bible on column, holding pole with liberty cap **Note:** Mint mark: Fox.

Date	Mintage	VG	F	VF	XF	Unc
1730	2,370	—	—	—	—	—

KM# 65.5 20 STUIVERS (Gulden)

Silver **Obv:** Crowned arms of Gelderland divide value **Rev:** Standing female figure leaning on bible on column, holding pole with liberty cap **Note:** Mint mark: Horse on mountain. Varieties exist.

Date	Mintage	VG	F	VF	XF	Unc
1733	453,250	8.00	17.00	30.00	50.00	100
1734	Inc. above	8.00	17.00	30.00	50.00	100
1735	Inc. above	8.00	17.00	30.00	50.00	100
1736	2,881,950	8.00	17.00	30.00	50.00	100
1736/35	Inc. above	8.00	17.00	30.00	50.00	100
1737	Inc. above	8.00	17.00	30.00	50.00	100
1738	Inc. above	8.00	17.00	30.00	50.00	100

KM# 63.2 48 STUIVERS (Silver Ducat)

Silver **Note:** Mint mark: Knight on horse.

Date	Mintage	VG	F	VF	XF	Unc
1701	—	30.00	60.00	90.00	175	—
1701	—	30.00	60.00	90.00	175	—
1707	—	30.00	60.00	90.00	175	—
1708/7	—	30.00	60.00	90.00	175	—
1708	—	30.00	60.00	90.00	175	—
1709/8	—	30.00	60.00	90.00	175	—
1709	—	30.00	60.00	90.00	175	—
1711	—	30.00	60.00	90.00	175	—

KM# 68.3 60 STUIVERS (3 Gulden)

Silver **Obv:** Value stated as 3-GL **Rev:** Date in exergue **Note:** Mint mark: Crane.

Date	Mintage	VG	F	VF	XF	Unc
1721	—	115	300	500	750	—

KM# 89 1/4 GULDEN

2.6500 g., 0.9200 Silver 0.0784 oz. ASW **Obv:** Crowned arms of Gelderland divides date **Obv. Legend:** MOARGORD FOE BELG D GEL & C • Z • **Rev:** Standing female figure leaning on bible on column, holding pole with liberty cap **Rev. Legend:** HANC TVEMVR HAC NITIMVR

Date	Mintage	VG	F	VF	XF	Unc
1756	—	15.00	25.00	50.00	80.00	—
1759	—	15.00	25.00	50.00	80.00	—

KM# 89a 1/4 GULDEN

Gold **Obv:** Crowned arms of gelderlan divides date **Rev:** Standing female figure leaning on bible on column, holding pole with liberty cap

Date	Mintage	VG	F	VF	XF	Unc
1756 Rare	—	—	—	—	—	—
1759 Rare	—	—	—	—	—	—

KM# 100.1 GULDEN

10.6100 g., 0.9200 Silver 0.3138 oz. ASW **Obv:** Crowned arms of Gelderland, value, legend **Obv. Legend:** MO : ARG : ORD : FOE : BELG : GEL ... **Rev:** Standing figure holding pole with Liberty cap, leaning on Bible on column, date in exergue **Rev. Legend:** HANC TVEMVR HAC NITIMVR

Date	Mintage	VG	F	VF	XF	Unc
1760	371,120	6.00	15.00	25.00	40.00	80.00
1762	Inc. above	6.00	15.00	25.00	40.00	80.00
1763	3,846,265	6.00	15.00	25.00	40.00	80.00
1764/3	Inc. above	8.00	20.00	30.00	50.00	100
1764	Inc. above	6.00	15.00	25.00	40.00	80.00
1765	1,324,535	6.00	15.00	25.00	40.00	80.00
1786/65	300,000	12.50	30.00	50.00	75.00	150
1786	Inc. above	6.00	30.00	50.00	75.00	150
1794	—	6.00	15.00	25.00	40.00	80.00
1795	—	15.00	35.00	60.00	100	200

KM# 100.2 GULDEN

10.6100 g., 0.9200 Silver 0.3138 oz. ASW **Obv:** Crowned arms of Gelderland, value, legend **Rev:** Standing figure holding pole with Liberty cap, leaning on Bible on column, date in exergue **Rev. Legend:** HANC TVEMUR HAC NITIMVR

Date	Mintage	VG	F	VF	XF	Unc
1762	—	15.00	35.00	60.00	100	150

KM# 103 3 GULDEN

31.8200 g., 0.9200 Silver 0.9412 oz. ASW **Obv:** Crowned arms of Gelderland, value, legend **Obv. Legend:** MO : ARG : ORD : FOE : BELG : ... **Rev:** Standing figure holding pole with Liberty cap, leaning on Bible on column, date in exergue **Rev. Legend:** HANC TVEMVR HAC NITIMVR **Note:** Dav. #1849.

Date	Mintage	VG	F	VF	XF	Unc
1721	—	30.00	60.00	125	250	400
1764	231,765	20.00	40.00	80.00	150	250
1786	127,820	20.00	40.00	80.00	150	250
1786/85	Inc. above	20.00	50.00	100	175	300

KM# 85.1 7 GULDEN

4.9650 g., 0.9170 Gold 0.1464 oz. AGW **Obv:** Mounted knight holding sword above crowned shield **Obv. Legend:** MO : AUR : PRO : CONFOED : BELG : D : G : & C : Z : **Rev:** Crowned arms of Gelderland divide value, date above **Rev. Legend:** CONCORDIA • RES PARVÆ CRESCUNT

Date	Mintage	VG	F	VF	XF	Unc
1750	—	125	225	325	550	800
1751	—	125	225	325	550	800
1761	—	175	300	500	750	1,000
1762	—	125	225	325	550	800

KM# 85.2 7 GULDEN

4.9650 g., 0.9170 Gold 0.1464 oz. AGW **Obv:** Mounted knight holding sword above crowned arms **Obv. Legend:** MO : AUR : PRO : CONFOED : BELG : D : G : & C : Z : **Rev:** Crowned arms of Gelderland divides value, date above **Rev. Legend:** CONCORDIA • RES PARVÆ • CRESCUNT

Date	Mintage	VG	F	VF	XF	Unc
1760	—	125	225	325	525	750

KM# 86.1 14 GULDEN

9.9300 g., 0.9170 Gold 0.2927 oz. AGW **Obv:** Mounted knight holding sword above crowned arms **Obv. Legend:** MO • AUR • PRO • CONFOED • BELG • D • G • & C • Z • **Rev:** Crowned arms of Gelderland divides value, date above **Rev. Legend:** CONCORDIA RES PARVÆ CRESCUNT •

Date	Mintage	VG	F	VF	XF	Unc
1750	—	175	225	450	700	1,000
1751	—	175	225	450	700	1,000
1762	—	175	225	450	700	1,000

KM# 86.2 14 GULDEN

9.9300 g., 0.9170 Gold 0.2927 oz. AGW **Obv:** Mounted knight holding sword above crowned arms **Obv. Legend:** MO • AUR • PRO • CONFOED • BELG • D• G • & C • Z • **Rev:** Crowned arms of Gelderland divide value, date above **Rev. Legend:** CONCORDIA RES PARVÆ CRESCUNT •

Date	Mintage	VG	F	VF	XF	Unc
1760	—	175	225	600	700	900

KM# 101.1 1/2 DUCATON (1/2 Silver Rider)

16.3900 g., 0.9410 Silver 0.4958 oz. ASW **Obv:** Knight on galloping horse **Obv. Legend:** MO • NO • ARG • CONFOE• BEL PRO • D **Rev:** Arms of Gelderland, legend around, date in cartouche **Edge:** Flowered

Date	Mintage	VG	F	VF	XF	Unc
1761	—	50.00	150	250	400	600
1762	—	50.00	150	250	400	600
1763/62	—	50.00	150	250	600	600
1764/63	—	60.00	160	275	450	700
1764	—	50.00	150	250	400	600
1765	—	30.00	100	150	300	450

KM# 101.2 1/2 DUCATON (1/2 Silver Rider)

16.3900 g., 0.9410 Silver 0.4958 oz. ASW **Obv:** Knight on galloping horse above crowned shield **Obv. Legend:** MO: NO: ARG: CONF BEL ... **Rev:** Crowned arms of Gelderland, with supporters, legend around, date in cartouche **Rev. Legend:** CONCORDIA RESPARVÆ ... **Edge:** Corded

Date	Mintage	VG	F	VF	XF	Unc
1766	—	30.00	100	150	300	500
1767	—	30.00	100	150	300	500
1769	—	30.00	100	150	300	500
1773	104,000	30.00	100	150	300	500

Date	Mintage	VG	F	VF	XF	Unc
1774	—	30.00	100	150	300	500
1775	—	30.00	100	150	300	500
1785 Mintage included with KM95	—	30.00	100	150	300	500
1790 Mintage include with KM95	—	30.00	100	150	300	500

KM# 95.3 DUCATON (Silver Rider)

32.7800 g., 0.9410 Silver 0.9917 oz. ASW **Obv:** Knight on horse above crowned shield **Obv. Legend:** MO : NO : ARG : PRO : CONF : ... **Rev:** Crowned arms of Gelderland, with supporters, date in cartouche below **Rev. Legend:** CONCORDIA.... **Note:** Dav. #1824.

Date	Mintage	VG	F	VF	XF	Unc
1704	—	40.00	80.00	135	240	375
1707	—	—	—	—	—	—
1711	—	75.00	150	275	475	750
1712	—	—	—	—	—	—
1717	—	75.00	150	275	475	750
1720	—	—	—	—	—	—
1721	—	75.00	150	275	475	750
1723	—	—	—	—	—	—
1730	—	40.00	80.00	150	275	375
1733	—	40.00	80.00	150	275	375
1734/3	—	40.00	80.00	200	400	650
1734	—	35.00	70.00	120	175	300
1735	—	35.00	70.00	120	175	300
1736	—	35.00	70.00	120	175	300
1737	—	35.00	70.00	120	175	300
1738	—	35.00	70.00	120	175	300
1740	—	75.00	150	275	475	750
1744	28,865	80.00	175	325	500	850
1759	20,302	40.00	80.00	130	200	350
1760	Inc. above	75.00	150	275	475	700
1761	Inc. above	35.00	70.00	120	175	300
1764	—	35.00	70.00	120	175	300
1765	—	35.00	70.00	120	175	300
1766	177,000	35.00	70.00	120	175	300
1767	Inc. above	35.00	70.00	120	175	300
1773	104,000	40.00	80.00	150	250	500
1774	Inc. above	30.00	60.00	110	160	300
1775	Inc. above	30.00	60.00	110	160	300
1785/76	—	40.00	80.00	150	250	500
1785	46,000	30.00	60.00	110	160	300
1789	367,000	30.00	60.00	110	160	300
1790	Inc. above	30.00	60.00	110	160	300
1791	Inc. above	30.00	60.00	110	160	300
1792	Inc. above	30.00	60.00	110	160	300

KM# 99.3 2 DUCATON

50.0700 g., Silver **Obv. Legend:** . . . O GEL C Z **Note:** Dav. #1823.

Date	Mintage	VG	F	VF	XF	Unc
1716	—	165	325	650	1,400	1,800
1717	—	165	325	650	1,400	1,800
1721	—	165	325	650	1,400	1,800

KM# 102 1/2 SILVER DUCAT

14.1200 g., 0.8730 Silver 0.3963 oz. ASW **Obv:** Knight standing holding crowned arms **Rev:** Crowned arms of Gelderland divides date

Date	Mintage	VG	F	VF	XF	Unc
1762	—	50.00	150	250	375	500
1763	—	70.00	200	350	500	800
1764	—	70.00	200	350	500	800
1765	—	50.00	150	250	375	500

KM# 38.1 SILVER DUCAT

28.2500 g., 0.8730 Silver 0.7929 oz. ASW **Obv:** Knight standing, small arms **Obv. Legend:** MO • ARG • PRO • CONFOE • BELG • D • GEL • C • Z • **Rev:** Legend, arms of Gelderland, date **Rev. Legend:** .... CRESCVNT • **Note:** Dav. #1837.

Date	Mintage	VG	F	VF	XF	Unc
1701	—	—	—	—	—	—
1707	—	60.00	110	200	250	350
1708/7	—	60.00	120	200	450	550
1708	—	60.00	110	200	420	500
1705/08	—	60.00	110	200	420	500
1709	—	60.00	110	200	420	500
1710	—	60.00	110	200	250	350
1711	—	60.00	110	200	250	350
1734	—	40.00	80.00	110	175	300
1738	—	100	250	450	800	1,200
1739	—	30.00	60.00	90.00	150	275

KM# 38.2 SILVER DUCAT

28.2500 g., 0.8730 Silver 0.7929 oz. ASW **Obv. Legend:** .... CONF • BELG • GEL • C • Z • **Rev. Legend:** .... CRESCUNT **Note:** Small arms. Dav. #1838.

Date	Mintage	VG	F	VF	XF	Unc
1745	—	30.00	60.00	90.00	150	300
1750	—	30.00	60.00	90.00	150	300
1753	—	30.00	60.00	90.00	150	300
1754	—	30.00	60.00	90.00	150	300
1755	—	30.00	60.00	90.00	150	300
1759	—	30.00	60.00	90.00	150	300
1760	371,000	80.00	200	350	500	700
1761	Inc. above	80.00	200	300	500	700
1762	Inc. above	80.00	200	350	500	700
1763	1,134,000	30.00	60.00	90.00	150	275
1764	Inc. above	30.00	60.00	90.00	150	275
1766	1,235,000	30.00	60.00	90.00	150	275
1767	Inc. above	30.00	60.00	90.00	150	275
1768	Inc. above	30.00	60.00	90.00	150	275
1771	Inc. above	40.00	80.00	160	250	400
1773	842,000	40.00	80.00	140	225	350
1774	Inc. above	30.00	60.00	90.00	150	275
1775	Inc. above	30.00	60.00	100	175	325
1785	39,000	60.00	120	200	300	500
1795 Rare	5,000	300	800	1,200	1,500	1,800
1797	—	50.00	100	150	200	—
1800	—	50.00	100	150	200	—

TRADE COINAGE

KM# 78 DUCAT

3.4900 g., 0.9860 Gold 0.1106 oz. AGW **Obv:** Standing Knight holding bundle of arrows divides date **Obv. Legend:** CONCORDIA RES • PAR • CRES • D • G • 8C C • Z • **Rev:** Legend within ornamented square **Rev. Legend:** MO:ORD/ PROVIN/ FOEDER/ BELGAD/ LEG:IMP

Date	Mintage	VG	F	VF	XF	Unc
1708	—	125	200	350	400	500
1710	—	100	175	250	300	400
1711	—	80.00	120	150	200	250
1712/11 M	—	90.00	125	250	500	600
1712	—	80.00	120	150	250	—
1713	—	80.00	120	150	200	250
1715	—	100	175	250	300	400
1716	—	80.00	120	150	200	250
1717	—	80.00	120	150	200	250
1718	—	80.00	120	150	200	250
1730	—	100	175	250	300	350
1731	—	100	200	400	600	850
1733	—	80.00	120	150	200	350
1737 M	—	150	300	600	800	1,000
1738	—	80.00	120	150	200	250
1740	—	80.00	120	150	200	250
1741	—	80.00	120	150	200	250
1742	—	80.00	120	150	200	250
1743	—	80.00	120	150	200	250
1744	—	80.00	120	150	200	250
1747	—	100	175	250	300	350
1749	—	150	200	600	800	1,000
1750	—	80.00	120	150	200	250
1758	592,000	80.00	120	150	200	250
1759	Inc. above	80.00	120	150	200	250
1760	Inc. above	100	175	250	300	350
1761	Inc. above	80.00	120	150	200	250
1762	125,000	80.00	120	150	200	250
1763	Inc. above	80.00	120	150	200	250
1766	103,000	80.00	120	150	200	250
1767	Inc. above	80.00	120	150	200	250
1769	—	80.00	120	175	275	250
1786	64,000	100	175	250	300	350
1791	36,000	80.00	120	175	275	250
1792	Inc. above	100	175	250	350	250

KM# 90 2 DUCAT

6.9800 g., 0.9860 Gold 0.2213 oz. AGW **Obv:** Standing Knight holding bundle of arrows divides date **Rev:** Legend within ornamented square

Date	Mintage	VG	F	VF	XF	Unc
1756	—	200	250	450	700	1,200
1759	—	200	250	450	700	1,200
1760/59 M	—	200	350	700	1,100	1,600
1760	460,000	200	250	450	700	1,200
1761	—	300	650	1,100	1,750	1,200

PRUSSIAN GELDERLAND

STANDARD COINAGE

KM# 201 1/16 THALER

0.5630 Silver **Obv:** Crowned 3-fold shield, date **Rev:** Value within roped circle

Date	Mintage	VG	F	VF	XF	Unc
1719 HFH	—	125	225	325	550	—

KM# 202 1/8 THALER

0.5630 Silver **Obv:** Crown above 3 shields **Rev:** Value within branches

Date	Mintage	VG	F	VF	XF	Unc
1719 HFH	—	160	320	450	750	—

KM# 203 1/4 THALER

0.8680 Silver **Obv:** Crowned cruciform arms **Rev:** Value within wreath

Date	Mintage	VG	F	VF	XF	Unc
1719 HFH	—	200	400	650	1,000	—

KM# 204 1/2 THALER

0.8680 Silver **Obv:** Bust of Friedrich Wilhelm right **Obv. Legend:** FRID • WILH • D • G • REX • ... **Rev:** Crowned shield in center of crowned arms

Date	Mintage	VG	F	VF	XF	Unc
1719 HF H	—	300	600	900	1,500	—

KM# 200 THALER

0.8680 Silver **Obv:** Bust of Friedrich Wilhelm right **Obv. Legend:** FRID • WILH • D • G • REX • ... **Rev:** Crowned shield in center of crowned arms

Date	Mintage	VG	F	VF	XF	Unc
1718 HF H	—	900	1,500	2,500	4,000	—

STANDARD COINAGE

PATTERNS

Including off metal strikes

KM#	Date	Mintage	Identification	Mkt Val
Pn10	1747	—	2 Stuivers. Gold. 3.5000 g. KM#26.5.	—
Pn11	1754	—	Duit. Silver. KM88.	100
Pn12	1756	—	1/2 Duit. Gold. 1.7500 g.	—
Pn13	1757	—	Duit. Silver. KM88.	100
Pn14	1757	—	Duit. Silver. Crowned arms. Crowned arms. Proof.	250
Pn15	1757	—	Stuiver. Gold. 1.7500 g. KM#92.	—
Pn16	1757	—	2 Stuivers. Gold. 3.5000 g. KM#26.5.	—
Pn17	1759	—	1/4 Gulden. Gold.	—
Pn18	1760	—	6 Stuivers. Gold. 7.0000 g. KM#77.	—
Pn19	1761	—	Duit. Silver. KM93.	100
Pn20	1767	—	Duit. Silver. KM93.	100
Pn21	1770	—	Duit. Silver. KM93.	100
Pn22	1785	—	6 Stuivers. Gold. 7.0000 g. KM#77.	—

PIEFORTS

KM#	Date	Mintage	Identification	Mkt Val
P15	1716	—	40 Stuivers. Silver. KM76.1	—
P16	1717	—	40 Stuivers. Silver. KM76.2.	—
P17	1721	—	40 Stuivers. Silver. KM76.2.	—
P18	1755	—	Ducat. Silver. KM#33.1.	1,500

GRONINGEN AND OMMELAND

The province of Groningen is located in northern Netherlands and is drained by numerous rivers and canals.

The early history of Groningen is chiefly one of conflict between the city and the surrounding districts known as the Ommelanden. The city remained loyal to the Spanish king while the surrounding area supported the revolt against Spain. After 1594 Groningen and Ommelanden were united into one republic but it was not until 1795 that they were merged into one province.

The Groningen Mint was closed in 1692. The following coins were struck at the Harderwyk Mint of Gelderland.

REPUBLIC

STANDARD COINAGE

KM# 65 DUIT

Copper **Obv:** Crowned arms of Groningen & Ommeland within sprigs **Rev:** Inscription above date **Rev. Inscription:** GRON/EN/OMMEL

Date	Mintage	VG	F	VF	XF	Unc
1770	—	4.00	10.00	20.00	40.00	60.00

KM# 66 DUIT

Copper **Obv:** Crowned arms of Groningen & Ommeland within sprigs **Rev:** Inscription above date **Rev. Inscription:** GRON/EN/OMMEL **Note:** Large letters.

Date	Mintage	VG	F	VF	XF	Unc
1770	—	4.00	10.00	20.00	40.00	60.00
1771	—	4.00	10.00	20.00	40.00	60.00
1772	—	5.00	15.00	25.00	50.00	85.00

KM# 66a DUIT

3.8000 g., Silver **Obv:** Crowned arms of Groningen & Ommeland within sprigs **Rev:** Inscription above date **Rev. Inscription:** GRON/EN/OMMEL

Date	Mintage	VG	F	VF	XF	Unc
1771	—	15.00	35.00	80.00	120	160

KM# 55 STUIVER

0.8100 g., 0.5830 Silver 0.0152 oz. ASW **Obv:** Inscription, date **Rev:** Bundle of arrows divide 1 S **Rev. Inscription:** GRON/EN/OML/

Date	Mintage	VG	F	VF	XF	Unc
1738	—	10.00	20.00	35.00	50.00	85.00
1765	—	6.00	15.00	25.00	35.00	85.00
1766	—	6.00	15.00	25.00	35.00	85.00

KM# 55a STUIVER

Gold **Obv. Inscription:** GRON / EN / OML / date **Rev:** Bundle of arrows divide 1 S

Date	Mintage	VG	F	VF	XF	Unc
1738	—	—	—	—	—	2,000
1765	—	—	—	—	—	1,800

KM# 60 7 GULDEN

4.9650 g., 0.9170 Gold 0.1464 oz. AGW **Obv:** Armored Knight on horse above crowned shield **Rev:** Crowned arms of Groningen & Ommeland divide value, date above

Date	Mintage	VG	F	VF	XF	Unc
1761	186,125	100	200	300	400	650

KM# 61 14 GULDEN

9.9300 g., 0.9170 Gold 0.2927 oz. AGW **Obv:** Armored Knight on horse above crowned shield **Rev:** Crowned arms of Groningen & Ommeland divides value, date above

Date	Mintage	VG	F	VF	XF	Unc
1761	—	175	400	500	700	1,200

Note: Mintage included with KM60

HOLLAND

Hollandia

Holland, a Dutch maritime province fronting on the North Sea, is the most important region of the Netherlands. It is a leader in maritime activities and in efficient agriculture. During the period of Spanish domination, Holland was the bulwark of the Protestant faith in the Netherlands and the focus of the resistance to Spanish tyranny.

MINT MARKS

Rose - Dordrecht

State Arms - Amsterdam

PROVINCE

STANDARD COINAGE

KM# 80 DUIT

Copper **Obv:** Standing lion holding spear within closed "Dutch" garden **Rev:** Inscription above date **Rev. Inscription:** HOL/LAN/DIA •

Date	Mintage	VG	F	VF	XF	Unc
1702	—	2.00	5.00	12.00	25.00	50.00
1707	—	2.00	5.00	12.00	25.00	50.00
1708	—	4.00	10.00	20.00	45.00	75.00
1709	—	3.00	8.00	15.00	35.00	60.00
1710	—	2.00	5.00	12.00	25.00	50.00
1711	—	4.00	8.00	15.00	35.00	60.00
1712	—	2.00	5.00	12.00	25.00	50.00
1713	—	3.00	8.00	15.00	35.00	60.00
1714	—	2.00	5.00	12.00	25.00	50.00
1715/14 M	—	2.00	5.00	12.00	25.00	50.00
1715	—	2.00	5.00	12.00	25.00	50.00
1716	—	2.00	5.00	12.00	25.00	50.00
1717	—	2.00	5.00	12.00	25.00	50.00
1720	—	1.50	4.00	10.00	20.00	45.00
1721	—	1.50	4.00	10.00	20.00	45.00
1723	—	1.50	4.00	10.00	20.00	40.00
1739	5,250,000	1.50	4.00	10.00	20.00	40.00
1741	3,098,000	1.50	4.00	10.00	20.00	40.00
1742/61	—	2.50	8.00	15.00	35.00	65.00
1742	—	1.50	4.00	10.00	20.00	40.00
1749	—	2.00	5.00	12.00	25.00	50.00
1754	3,370,000	2.50	8.00	15.00	30.00	55.00
1765	3,557,000	1.50	4.00	10.00	16.00	30.00
1765/61	—	2.50	8.00	15.00	30.00	55.00
1766	—	1.50	4.00	10.00	16.00	30.00
1769	1,678,000	1.50	4.00	10.00	16.00	30.00
1780	3,457,000	1.00	3.00	6.00	14.00	25.00

KM# 80a DUIT

Silver **Obv:** Standing lion holding spear within closed "Dutch" garden **Rev:** Inscription above date **Rev. Inscription:** HOL/LAN/DIA ?

Date	Mintage	VG	F	VF	XF	Unc
1702	—	20.00	30.00	40.00	60.00	100
1710	—	30.00	40.00	80.00	120	180
1717	—	20.00	30.00	40.00	60.00	100
1725	—	20.00	30.00	40.00	60.00	100
1739	—	20.00	30.00	40.00	60.00	100
1740	—	20.00	30.00	40.00	60.00	100
1741	—	—	—	—	—	—
1742	—	20.00	50.00	40.00	60.00	100
1743	—	20.00	30.00	40.00	60.00	100
1744	—	20.00	30.00	40.00	60.00	100
1745	—	20.00	30.00	40.00	60.00	100
1746	—	20.00	30.00	40.00	60.00	100
1747	—	20.00	30.00	40.00	60.00	100
1748	—	20.00	30.00	40.00	60.00	100
1749	—	20.00	30.00	40.00	60.00	100
1750	—	20.00	30.00	40.00	60.00	100
1751	—	20.00	30.00	40.00	60.00	100
1752	—	20.00	30.00	40.00	60.00	100
1753	—	20.00	30.00	40.00	60.00	100
1754	—	20.00	30.00	40.00	60.00	100
1755	—	20.00	30.00	40.00	60.00	100
1756	—	20.00	30.00	40.00	60.00	100
1757	—	20.00	30.00	40.00	60.00	100
1758	—	20.00	30.00	40.00	60.00	100
1759	—	20.00	30.00	40.00	60.00	100
1760	—	20.00	30.00	40.00	60.00	100
1761	—	20.00	30.00	40.00	60.00	100
1762	—	20.00	30.00	40.00	60.00	100
1763	—	20.00	30.00	40.00	60.00	100
1768	—	20.00	30.00	40.00	60.00	100

KM# 80b DUIT

6.9500 g., Gold **Obv:** Standing lion holding spear within closed "Dutch" garden **Rev:** Inscription above date **Rev. Inscription:** HOL/LAN/DIA •

Date	Mintage	VG	F	VF	XF	Unc
1702	—	80.00	200	300	500	800
1717	—	80.00	200	300	500	800
1723	—	80.00	200	300	500	800
1739	—	80.00	200	300	500	800
1740	—	80.00	200	300	450	600
1742	—	80.00	200	300	500	800
1744	—	80.00	200	300	500	800
1745	—	80.00	200	300	500	800
1749	—	80.00	200	300	500	800
1752	—	80.00	200	300	500	800
1753	—	80.00	200	300	450	600
1759	—	80.00	200	300	450	600
1760 Rare	—	—	—	—	—	—
1765 Rare	—	—	—	—	—	—

KM# 80c DUIT

5.2500 g., Gold **Obv:** Standing lion holding spear within closed "Dutch" garden **Rev:** Inscription above date **Rev. Inscription:** HOL/LAN/DIA ?

Date	Mintage	VG	F	VF	XF	Unc
1739	—	—	150	300	650	1,000
1749	—	—	150	300	650	1,000
1753	—	—	150	300	650	1,000
1755	—	—	150	300	650	1,000
1759	—	—	150	300	650	1,000

KM# 85 STUIVER (Weapon)

Silver **Obv:** Crowned arms of Holland divides value **Rev:** Inscription above date **Rev. Legend:** HOL/LAN/DIA/date **Rev. Inscription:** HOL/LAN/DIA ?

Date	Mintage	VG	F	VF	XF	Unc
1724	—	3.00	8.00	15.00	30.00	50.00
1726	—	3.00	8.00	15.00	30.00	50.00
1727	—	3.00	8.00	15.00	30.00	50.00
1730	—	3.00	8.00	15.00	30.00	50.00
1733/27	—	10.00	40.00	60.00	100	150
1733	—	3.00	8.00	15.00	30.00	50.00
1734	—	3.00	8.00	15.00	30.00	50.00
1736	—	3.00	8.00	15.00	30.00	50.00
1737	—	3.00	8.00	15.00	30.00	50.00

KM# 85a STUIVER (Weapon)

1.7500 g., Gold **Obv:** Crowned arms of Holland divides value **Rev:** Inscription above date **Rev. Inscription:** HOL/LAN/DIA •

Date	Mintage	VG	F	VF	XF	Unc
1724	—	75.00	125	170	250	350
1725	—	75.00	125	170	250	350
1726	—	75.00	125	170	250	350
1731	—	75.00	125	170	250	350
1732	—	90.00	160	220	350	500
1733	—	75.00	125	170	250	350
1734	—	75.00	125	170	250	350
1736/33	—	90.00	100	220	350	500
1736	—	100	125	250	400	500
1737/27	—	125	175	300	400	600
1737	—	100	125	250	300	350
1738	—	100	125	250	300	350

KM# 91 STUIVER (Broom)

0.8100 g., 0.5830 Silver 0.0152 oz. ASW **Obv:** Bundle of arrows divides value within wreath **Rev:** Inscription above date **Rev. Inscription:** HOL/LAN/DIA•

Date	Mintage	VG	F	VF	XF	Unc
1738	—	3.00	8.00	15.00	35.00	50.00
1739/8	—	4.00	10.00	20.00	50.00	75.00
1739	—	2.00	5.00	10.00	17.00	40.00
1740/39	—	4.00	10.00	20.00	50.00	75.00
1740	—	3.00	8.00	15.00	35.00	50.00
1760	160,000	3.00	8.00	15.00	35.00	50.00
1764/3	—	5.00	15.00	25.00	60.00	100
1764	240,000	3.00	8.00	15.00	35.00	50.00

KM# 91a STUIVER (Broom)

1.7500 g., Gold **Obv:** Bundle of arrows divides value within wreath **Rev:** Inscription above date **Rev. Inscription:** HOL/LAN/DIA •

Date	Mintage	VG	F	VF	XF	Unc
1738	—	75.00	125	170	250	300
1739	—	75.00	125	170	250	300
1740	—	75.00	125	170	250	300
1741	—	60.00	75.00	250	400	500
1742	—	75.00	125	170	250	350
1743	—	75.00	125	170	250	350
1744	—	75.00	125	170	250	300
1745	—	75.00	125	170	250	350
1746	—	75.00	125	170	250	300
1747	—	100	175	250	350	450
1748/38	—	100	175	250	400	500
1748	—	75.00	125	170	250	350
1749	—	75.00	125	170	250	350
1750	—	75.00	125	170	250	350

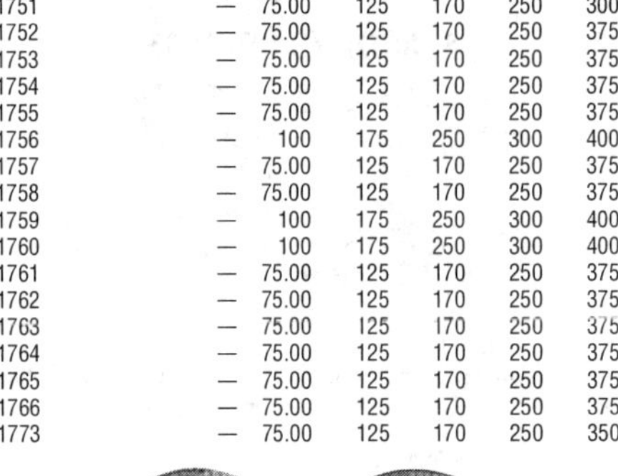

Date	Mintage	VG	F	VF	XF	Unc
1751	—	75.00	125	170	250	300
1752	—	75.00	125	170	250	375
1753	—	75.00	125	170	250	375
1754	—	75.00	125	170	250	375
1755	—	75.00	125	170	250	375
1756	—	100	175	250	300	400
1757	—	75.00	125	170	250	375
1758	—	75.00	125	170	250	375
1759	—	100	175	250	300	400
1760	—	100	175	250	300	400
1761	—	75.00	125	170	250	375
1762	—	75.00	125	170	250	375
1763	—	75.00	125	170	250	375
1764	—	75.00	125	170	250	375
1765	—	75.00	125	170	250	375
1766	—	75.00	125	170	250	375
1773	—	75.00	125	170	250	350

KM# 48 2 STUIVERS (Double Wapenstuiver)

1.6200 g., 0.5830 Silver 0.0304 oz. ASW **Obv:** Crowned arms of Holland divides value **Rev:** Inscription above date **Rev. Inscription:** HOL/LAN/DIA ?

Date	Mintage	VG	F	VF	XF	Unc
1701	—	2.00	5.00	8.00	14.00	30.00
1702	—	2.50	5.00	8.00	14.00	30.00
1703/2	—	2.50	8.00	14.00	22.00	50.00
1703	—	2.00	5.00	8.00	14.00	30.00
1705	—	2.00	5.00	8.00	14.00	30.00
1706	—	2.00	5.00	8.00	14.00	30.00
1707	—	2.00	5.00	8.00	14.00	30.00
1708/6	—	2.50	8.00	14.00	24.00	60.00
1708	—	2.00	5.00	8.00	14.00	30.00
1709	—	2.00	5.00	8.00	14.00	30.00
1710	—	2.00	5.00	8.00	14.00	30.00
1711	—	2.00	5.00	8.00	14.00	30.00
1712	—	2.00	5.00	8.00	14.00	30.00
1713	—	2.00	5.00	8.00	14.00	30.00
1715	—	2.00	5.00	8.00	14.00	30.00
1716/13	—	2.00	5.00	8.00	14.00	30.00
1716	—	2.00	5.00	8.00	14.00	30.00
1717	—	2.00	5.00	8.00	14.00	30.00
1718/7	—	2.00	8.00	14.00	22.00	50.00
1718	—	2.00	5.00	8.00	14.00	30.00
1718/17	—	2.00	8.00	14.00	22.00	50.00
1719	—	2.00	5.00	8.00	14.00	30.00
1720/10	—	2.50	8.00	14.00	12.00	25.00
1720	—	2.00	5.00	8.00	14.00	30.00
1720/19	—	2.50	8.00	14.00	24.00	50.00
1721	—	2.00	5.00	8.00	14.00	30.00
1722/11	—	2.50	8.00	16.00	22.00	50.00
1722	—	2.00	5.00	8.00	14.00	30.00
1723/2	—	2.50	8.00	14.00	22.00	50.00
1723	—	2.00	5.00	8.00	14.00	30.00
1724/2	—	2.50	8.00	14.00	22.00	50.00
1724/23	—	2.50	8.00	14.00	22.00	50.00
1724	—	2.00	5.00	8.00	14.00	30.00
1725/2	—	2.50	8.00	14.00	26.00	55.00
1725	—	2.00	5.00	8.00	14.00	25.00
1726/2	—	2.50	8.00	16.00	24.00	40.00
1726	—	2.00	5.00	8.00	14.00	25.00
1727/26	—	2.00	5.00	8.00	14.00	25.00
1727	—	2.00	5.00	8.00	14.00	25.00
1728	—	2.00	5.00	8.00	14.00	25.00
1729	—	2.00	5.00	8.00	14.00	25.00
1730/28	—	2.50	8.00	14.00	22.00	40.00
1730/29	—	2.50	8.00	14.00	28.00	45.00
1730	—	2.00	5.00	8.00	14.00	20.00
1731/21	—	2.50	8.00	16.00	22.00	40.00
1731	—	2.00	5.00	8.00	14.00	20.00
1732/22	—	2.50	8.00	14.00	22.00	40.00
1732/31	—	2.50	8.00	16.00	30.00	55.00
1732	—	2.00	5.00	8.00	14.00	20.00
1733/2	—	2.50	8.00	16.00	22.00	40.00
1733	—	2.00	5.00	8.00	14.00	20.00
1734/3	—	2.50	8.00	16.00	22.00	40.00
1734	—	2.00	5.00	8.00	14.00	20.00
1735	—	2.00	5.00	8.00	14.00	20.00
1736	—	2.00	5.00	8.00	14.00	20.00
1737/36	—	2.50	5.00	16.00	30.00	40.00
1737	—	2.00	5.00	8.00	14.00	20.00
1738	—	2.00	5.00	8.00	14.00	25.00
1739	—	2.00	5.00	8.00	14.00	20.00
1744	—	2.00	5.00	8.00	14.00	20.00
1745/4	—	2.50	9.00	17.00	28.00	40.00
1745	—	2.00	5.00	8.00	14.00	20.00
1746/35	—	2.50	9.00	18.00	30.00	45.00
1746/4	—	2.50	8.00	14.00	22.00	30.00
1746/5	—	2.50	8.00	14.00	22.00	30.00
1746	—	2.00	5.00	8.00	14.00	20.00
1748	—	2.50	6.00	12.00	17.00	25.00
1750/48	—	2.50	9.00	17.00	28.00	40.00
1750	—	2.00	5.00	8.00	14.00	20.00
1751	—	2.00	5.00	8.00	14.00	20.00
1752	—	2.00	5.00	8.00	14.00	20.00
1753	—	2.00	5.00	8.00	14.00	20.00
1754	—	2.00	5.00	8.00	14.00	20.00
1755/4	—	2.50	8.00	17.00	28.00	40.00
1755	—	2.00	5.00	8.00	14.00	20.00
1757/5	—	2.50	7.00	14.00	22.00	30.00
1757/6	—	2.50	6.00	12.00	17.00	25.00
1757	—	2.00	5.00	8.00	14.00	20.00
1758/54	—	2.50	8.00	17.00	28.00	60.00
1758/5	—	2.50	6.00	12.00	17.00	25.00
1758/56	—	2.50	8.00	17.00	28.00	60.00
1758	—	2.50	6.00	12.00	17.00	25.00
1759	—	2.00	5.00	8.00	14.00	20.00
1760	—	2.00	5.00	8.00	14.00	20.00
1761	—	2.00	5.00	8.00	14.00	20.00
1762	—	2.50	6.00	12.00	17.00	25.00
1763	—	2.00	5.00	9.00	14.00	20.00
1764/3	—	2.50	6.00	12.00	17.00	25.00
1764	—	2.00	5.00	9.00	14.00	20.00
1764/1	—	2.50	6.00	12.00	17.00	25.00
1765	—	2.00	5.00	9.00	14.00	20.00
1766/1	—	2.50	8.00	14.00	22.00	35.00
1766/4	—	2.50	8.00	14.00	22.00	35.00
1766	—	2.00	5.00	9.00	14.00	20.00
1767/6	—	2.50	8.00	12.00	17.00	25.00
1767	—	2.00	5.00	9.00	14.00	20.00
1768/7	—	2.50	8.00	12.00	17.00	25.00
1768	—	2.00	5.00	9.00	14.00	20.00
1769	—	2.00	5.00	9.00	14.00	20.00
1770	—	2.00	5.00	9.00	14.00	20.00
1771	—	2.50	8.00	12.00	17.00	25.00
1772	—	2.00	5.00	9.00	14.00	20.00
1773	—	2.00	5.00	9.00	14.00	20.00
1774	—	2.00	5.00	9.00	14.00	20.00
1775	—	2.00	5.00	9.00	14.00	20.00
1776	—	2.00	5.00	9.00	14.00	20.00
1777/78	—	2.00	8.00	12.00	17.00	25.00
1777	—	2.00	5.00	9.00	14.00	20.00
1778	—	2.00	5.00	9.00	14.00	20.00
1779	—	2.00	5.00	9.00	14.00	20.00
1780	—	2.00	5.00	9.00	14.00	20.00
1784/80	—	2.50	8.00	14.00	22.00	35.00
1784	—	2.00	5.00	9.00	14.00	20.00
1787	—	2.00	5.00	9.00	14.00	20.00
1788	—	2.00	5.00	9.00	14.00	20.00
1789	—	2.00	5.00	9.00	14.00	20.00
1790	—	2.00	5.00	9.00	14.00	20.00
1791	—	2.00	5.00	9.00	14.00	20.00
1792	—	2.00	5.00	9.00	14.00	20.00
1793	—	2.00	5.00	9.00	14.00	20.00

KM# 48a 2 STUIVERS (Double Wapenstuiver)

3.5000 g., Gold **Obv:** Crowned arms of Holland divides value **Rev:** Inscription above date **Rev. Inscription:** HOL/LAN/DIA ?

Date	Mintage	VG	F	VF	XF	Unc
1723	—	100	200	300	400	600
1724/22	—	100	200	300	400	600
1724/23	—	100	200	300	400	600
1724	—	100	200	300	400	600
1725	—	100	200	300	400	600
1726	—	100	200	300	400	600
1727	—	100	200	300	400	600
1729	—	100	200	300	400	600
1730	—	100	200	300	400	600
1731	—	100	200	300	400	600
1732	—	100	200	300	400	600
1733	—	100	200	300	400	600
1734	—	100	200	300	400	600
1737	—	120	250	400	600	800
1738	—	100	200	300	400	600
1739	—	100	200	300	400	600
1740	—	100	200	300	400	600
1741	—	100	200	300	400	600
1742	—	100	200	300	400	600
1744/43	—	120	250	650	700	900
1744	—	100	200	300	400	600
1745	—	100	200	300	400	600
1746	—	100	200	300	400	600
1747	—	100	200	300	400	600
1748	—	100	200	300	400	600
1749	—	100	200	300	400	600
1750	—	100	200	300	400	600
1751	—	100	200	300	400	600
1752	—	100	200	300	400	600
1753	—	100	200	300	400	600
1754	—	100	200	300	400	600
1755	—	100	200	300	400	600
1756	—	100	200	300	400	600
1757	—	100	200	300	400	600
1750/57	—	120	250	600	700	900
1758	—	100	200	300	400	600
1759	—	100	200	300	400	600
1760	—	100	200	300	400	600

Date	Mintage	VG	F	VF	XF	Unc
1761	—	100	200	300	400	600
1762	—	100	200	300	400	600
1763	—	100	200	300	400	600
1765	—	100	200	300	400	600
1766	—	100	200	300	400	600

KM# 45 6 STUIVERS (Scheepjesschelling)

4.9500 g., 0.5830 Silver 0.0928 oz. ASW **Obv:** Crowned arms of Holland divides value, date above **Obv. Legend:** MO: NO: ORD: HOLL: ET WESTFRI: **Rev:** Sailing ship **Rev. Legend:** VIGILATE DEO CONFIDENTES •

Date	Mintage	VG	F	VF	XF	Unc
1701	—	20.00	40.00	60.00	110	200
1702	—	6.00	12.00	25.00	50.00	100
1705	—	6.00	12.00	25.00	50.00	100
1708	—	6.00	12.00	25.00	30.00	80.00
1709	—	6.00	12.00	25.00	50.00	100
1711	—	6.00	12.00	25.00	50.00	100
1712/11	—	15.00	30.00	50.00	80.00	150
1712	—	6.00	12.00	25.00	50.00	100
1713	—	6.00	12.00	25.00	50.00	100
1714	—	6.00	12.00	25.00	50.00	100
1716	—	6.00	12.00	25.00	50.00	100
1717	—	5.00	10.00	20.00	50.00	100
1718	—	5.00	10.00	20.00	50.00	100
1719	—	5.00	10.00	20.00	50.00	100
1721	—	10.00	20.00	40.00	80.00	150
1722/20	—	10.00	20.00	40.00	80.00	175
1722	—	5.00	10.00	20.00	65.00	125
1723	—	5.00	10.00	20.00	65.00	125
1724	—	5.00	10.00	20.00	65.00	125
1725	—	5.00	10.00	20.00	65.00	125
1726	—	5.00	10.00	20.00	65.00	125
1727	—	8.00	15.00	20.00	65.00	125
1728/7	—	10.00	20.00	40.00	80.00	175
1728	—	5.00	10.00	20.00	50.00	100
1730/29	—	10.00	20.00	40.00	80.00	175
1730	—	5.00	10.00	20.00	50.00	100
1732	—	5.00	10.00	20.00	50.00	100
1733	—	5.00	10.00	20.00	50.00	100
1734/3	—	8.00	15.00	30.00	70.00	150
1734	—	5.00	10.00	20.00	60.00	120
1735	—	5.00	10.00	20.00	60.00	120
1736/35	—	8.00	18.00	30.00	70.00	150
1736	—	5.00	10.00	20.00	60.00	120
1737	—	5.00	10.00	20.00	60.00	120
1745	—	7.00	15.00	25.00	60.00	120
1746	—	7.00	15.00	40.00	80.00	160
1748/6	—	14.00	35.00	60.00	110	200
1748/7	—	7.00	15.00	40.00	80.00	160
1748	—	7.00	15.00	30.00	60.00	120
1750	—	5.00	10.00	20.00	60.00	120
1751	—	5.00	10.00	20.00	60.00	120
1752	—	7.00	15.00	40.00	80.00	160
1753/2	—	14.00	35.00	60.00	110	200
1753	—	5.00	10.00	20.00	40.00	100
1754	—	5.00	10.00	20.00	40.00	100
1759	—	5.00	10.00	20.00	40.00	100
1761	107,000	5.00	10.00	20.00	40.00	100

KM# 45a 6 STUIVERS (Scheepjesschelling)

7.0000 g., Gold **Obv:** Crowned arms of Holland divides value, date above **Obv. Legend:** MO: NO: ORD: HOLL: ET WESTFRI: **Rev:** Sailing ship **Rev. Legend:** VIGILATE DEO CONFIDENTES •

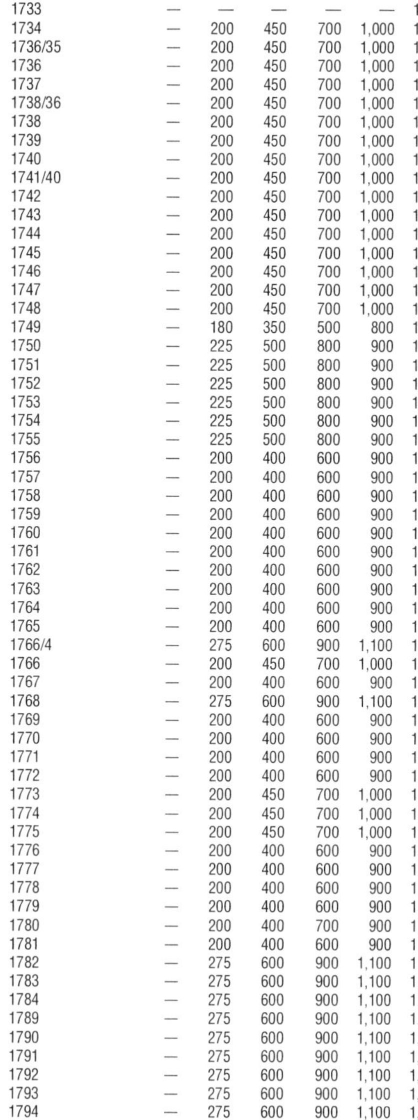

Date	Mintage	VG	F	VF	XF	Unc
1702	—	180	350	500	800	1,000
1703/2	—	—	—	—	1,000	1,250
1703	—	180	350	500	800	1,000
1709	—	180	350	500	800	1,000
1722	—	180	350	500	800	1,000
1723	—	180	350	500	800	1,000
1724	—	180	350	500	800	1,000
1725/24	—	—	—	—	1,000	1,250
1725	—	180	350	500	800	1,000
1726	—	180	350	500	800	1,000
1727	—	180	350	500	800	1,000
1729	—	—	—	—	—	1,000
1730	—	—	—	—	—	1,000
1731	—	—	—	—	—	1,000
1732	—	—	—	—	—	1,000
1733	—	—	—	—	—	1,000
1734	—	200	450	700	1,000	1,250
1736/35	—	200	450	700	1,000	1,250
1736	—	200	450	700	1,000	1,250
1737	—	200	450	700	1,000	1,250
1738/36	—	200	450	700	1,000	1,250
1738	—	200	450	700	1,000	1,250
1739	—	200	450	700	1,000	1,250
1740	—	200	450	700	1,000	1,250
1741/40	—	200	450	700	1,000	1,250
1742	—	200	450	700	1,000	1,250
1743	—	200	450	700	1,000	1,250
1744	—	200	450	700	1,000	1,250
1745	—	200	450	700	1,000	1,250
1746	—	200	450	700	1,000	1,250
1747	—	200	450	700	1,000	1,250
1748	—	200	450	700	1,000	1,250
1749	—	180	350	500	800	1,000
1750	—	225	500	800	900	1,100
1751	—	225	500	800	900	1,100
1752	—	225	500	800	900	1,100
1753	—	225	500	800	900	1,100
1754	—	225	500	800	900	1,100
1755	—	225	500	800	900	1,100
1756	—	200	400	600	900	1,100
1757	—	200	400	600	900	1,100
1758	—	200	400	600	900	1,100
1759	—	200	400	600	900	1,100
1760	—	200	400	600	900	1,100
1761	—	200	400	600	900	1,100
1762	—	200	400	600	900	1,100
1763	—	200	400	600	900	1,100
1764	—	200	400	600	900	1,100
1765	—	200	400	600	900	1,100
1766/4	—	275	600	900	1,100	1,500
1766	—	200	450	700	1,000	1,250
1767	—	200	400	600	900	1,100
1768	—	275	600	900	1,100	1,500
1769	—	200	400	600	900	1,100
1770	—	200	400	600	900	1,100
1771	—	200	400	600	900	1,100
1772	—	200	400	600	900	1,100
1773	—	200	450	700	1,000	1,250
1774	—	200	450	700	1,000	1,250
1775	—	200	450	700	1,000	1,250
1776	—	200	400	600	900	1,100
1777	—	200	400	600	900	1,100
1778	—	200	400	600	900	1,100
1779	—	200	400	600	900	1,100
1780	—	200	400	700	900	1,100
1781	—	200	400	600	900	1,100
1782	—	275	600	900	1,100	1,500
1783	—	275	600	900	1,100	1,500
1784	—	275	600	900	1,100	1,500
1789	—	275	600	900	1,100	1,500
1790	—	275	600	900	1,100	1,500
1791	—	275	600	900	1,100	1,500
1792	—	275	600	900	1,100	1,500
1793	—	275	600	900	1,100	1,500
1794	—	275	600	900	1,100	1,500

KM# 45b 6 STUIVERS (Scheepjesschelling)

13.9500 g., Gold **Obv:** Crowned arms of Holland divides value, date above **Obv. Legend:** MO: NO: ORD: HOLL: ET WESTFRI: **Rev:** Sailing ship **Rev. Legend:** VIGILATE DEO CONFIDENTES •

Date	Mintage	VG	F	VF	XF	Unc
1747 Rare	—	—	—	—	—	—

KM# 95a 10 STUIVERS (1/2 Gulden)

Gold **Note:** 6.90-10.40 g.

Date	Mintage	VG	F	VF	XF	Unc
1734	—	—	—	—	—	—
1748	—	200	400	600	800	1,200
1749	—	200	400	600	800	1,200
1752	—	200	400	600	800	1,200
1753	—	200	400	600	800	1,200
1754	—	200	400	600	800	1,200
1755	—	200	400	600	800	1,200
1756	—	200	400	600	800	1,200

KM# 95 10 STUIVERS (1/2 Gulden)

5.3000 g., 0.9200 Silver 0.1568 oz. ASW **Obv:** Crowned arms of Holland divides X S, divided date above **Obv. Legend:** MO: ARG : ORD: FÆD: BELG : HOLL : **Rev:** Standing figure leaning on column holding pole with cap **Rev. Legend:** HANCTVEMVR HAC NITIMVR

Date	Mintage	VG	F	VF	XF	Unc
1748	—	14.00	30.00	60.00	100	175
1749/8	—	20.00	40.00	80.00	125	200
1749	—	14.00	30.00	60.00	100	75.00
1751	63,270	14.00	30.00	60.00	100	175
1761	—	14.00	30.00	60.00	100	175
1762	—	20.00	40.00	80.00	100	175

KM# 100a 1/4 GULDEN (5 Stuiver)

5.2500 g., Gold **Obv:** Crowned arms of Holland divides date **Rev:** Standing figure leaning on column, holding pole with cap

Date	Mintage	VG	F	VF	XF	Unc
1759	—	200	450	700	850	1,300

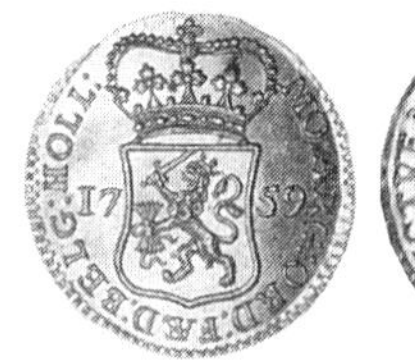

KM# 100 1/4 GULDEN (5 Stuiver)

2.6500 g., 0.9200 Silver 0.0784 oz. ASW **Obv:** Crowned arms of Holland divides date **Obv. Legend:** MO: ARG. : ORD: FÆD: BELG : HOLL : **Rev:** Standing figure leaning on column, holding pole with cap **Rev. Legend:** HANCTVEMVR HAC NITIMVR

Date	Mintage	VG	F	VF	XF	Unc
1759	—	7.00	20.00	35.00	80.00	120

KM# 73 GULDEN (20 Stuiver)

10.6100 g., 0.9200 Silver 0.3138 oz. ASW **Obv:** Crowned arms of Holland divides value **Obv. Legend:** MO: ARG : ORD: FÆD: BELG : HOLL : **Rev:** Standing figure leaning on column, holding pole with cap, date below **Rev. Legend:** HANCTVEMVR HAC NITIMVR

Date	Mintage	VG	F	VF	XF	Unc
1703	39,560	60.00	80.00	175	350	650
1713/11	—	25.00	50.00	100	200	300
1713	—	10.00	25.00	50.00	100	200
1714	—	40.00	80.00	75.00	350	450
1715/14	—	60.00	80.00	75.00	350	650
1716/15	—	25.00	70.00	110	160	225
1715	—	25.00	70.00	110	160	225
1716	—	10.00	25.00	50.00	100	200
1721	50,230	10.00	25.00	50.00	100	200
1734	—	8.00	22.50	40.00	60.00	100
1735	—	7.00	20.00	35.00	50.00	90.00
1736	—	7.00	20.00	30.00	45.00	85.00
1737/6	—	10.00	20.00	40.00	90.00	175
1737	—	8.00	20.00	40.00	60.00	100
1738	—	8.00	20.00	40.00	60.00	100
1748/37	—	40.00	80.00	175	350	450
1748	—	25.00	70.00	110	160	225
1749	—	25.00	70.00	110	160	225
1762	—	6.00	16.00	25.00	40.00	80.00
1763/62	—	10.00	20.00	40.00	90.00	175
1763	Inc. above	6.00	16.00	25.00	40.00	80.00
1764/63	—	—	—	—	—	—
1764	1,219,000	6.00	16.00	25.00	40.00	80.00

Date	Mintage	VG	F	VF	XF	Unc
1765	Inc. above	7.00	18.00	30.00	45.00	85.00
1790	1,363,000	7.00	20.00	35.00	50.00	90.00
1791	Inc. above	7.00	18.00	25.00	45.00	85.00
1792	Inc. above	7.00	18.00	25.00	45.00	85.00
1793	Inc. above	7.00	18.00	25.00	45.00	85.00
1794	4,059,999	7.00	18.00	25.00	45.00	85.00

KM# 73a GULDEN (20 Stuiver)

Gold **Obv:** Crowned arms of Holland divides value **Rev:** Standing figure leaning on column, holding pole with cap, date below

Date	Mintage	VG	F	VF	XF	Unc
1734 Rare	—	—	—	—	—	—
1734 Rare	—	—	—	—	—	—
1737 Rare	—	—	—	—	—	—
1748 Rare	—	—	—	—	—	—
1749 Rare	—	—	—	—	—	—

KM# 76 3 GULDEN (60 Stuiver)

31.8200 g., 0.9200 Silver 0.9412 oz. ASW **Obv:** Crowned arms of Holland **Rev:** Seated statue **Note:** Dav. #4954. Similar to 1 Guilden, KM#73.

Date	Mintage	VG	F	VF	XF	Unc
1763	458,000	35.00	70.00	140	200	275
1764	Inc. above	35.00	70.00	140	200	275
1774	—	40.00	120	200	300	400
1791	276,000	35.00	70.00	140	200	275
1792	Inc. above	35.00	70.00	140	200	275
1793	—	35.00	70.00	140	200	275
1794	—	35.00	70.00	140	200	275

KM# 77 3 GULDEN (60 Stuiver)

31.8200 g., 0.9200 Silver 0.9412 oz. ASW **Rev:** Platform beneath standing Dutch maiden **Note:** Dav. #1850. Similar to 3 Guilden, KM#152.

Date	Mintage	VG	F	VF	XF	Unc
1763	—	35.00	65.00	125	200	—
1764	—	35.00	65.00	125	200	—
1791	—	35.00	65.00	125	200	—
1792	—	35.00	65.00	125	200	—
1793	—	35.00	65.00	125	200	—
1794	—	35.00	65.00	125	200	—

KM# 96 7 GULDEN

4.9650 g., 0.9170 Gold 0.1464 oz. AGW **Obv:** Armored knight on horse above crowned shield **Obv. Legend:** BELG • ZELAND • M • O • AUR • PRO • CONFOED **Rev:** Crowned arms of Holland divides value, date above **Rev. Legend:** CONCORDIA RESPARVÆ CRESCUNT

Date	Mintage	VG	F	VF	XF	Unc
1749	—	100	200	300	500	700
1750/40	—	125	250	500	600	900
1750	—	100	200	300	500	700
1751	—	100	200	300	500	700
1760	197,000	100	200	300	500	700
1761	—	125	250	400	600	900
1762	—	125	375	500	700	100
1763	—	125	250	400	600	800

KM# 97 14 GULDEN

9.9300 g., 0.9170 Gold 0.2927 oz. AGW **Obv:** Armored Knight on horse above crowned shield **Obv. Legend:** BELG : HOLLAND : MO : AUR : PRO : CONFOED : **Rev:** Crowned arms of Holland divides value, date above **Rev. Legend:** CONCORDIA • RES • PARVÆ • CRESCUNT •

Date	Mintage	VG	F	VF	XF	Unc
1749	—	200	300	400	800	1,000
1750/49	—	250	550	800	1,100	1,300
1750	—	200	300	400	800	1,000
1751	—	200	300	400	800	1,000
1760	—	200	300	400	800	1,000
Note: Mintage included with KM#96						
1761	—	200	300	400	800	1,000
1762	—	250	550	800	1,100	1,300
1763	—	200	300	400	800	1,000

KM# 105 1/2 DUCATON (1/2 Silver Rider)

16.3900 g., 0.9410 Silver 0.4958 oz. ASW **Obv:** Armores Knight on horse above crowned shield **Obv. Legend:** BELG : PRO : HOL : MO : NO : ARG : CON FOE : **Rev:** Crowned arms of Holland, with supporters, date in cartouche below **Rev. Legend:** CONCORDIA RES PARV...

Date	Mintage	VG	F	VF	XF	Unc
1765	—	30.00	80.00	140	225	350
1766	—	30.00	80.00	140	225	350
1767	—	30.00	80.00	140	225	350
1770	—	30.00	80.00	140	225	350
1771	—	30.00	80.00	140	225	350
1772	—	30.00	80.00	140	225	350
1773	—	30.00	80.00	140	225	350
1774	—	30.00	80.00	140	225	350
1775	—	30.00	80.00	140	225	350
1776/75	—	50.00	120	180	275	450
1776	—	30.00	80.00	140	225	350
1777	—	30.00	80.00	140	225	350
1780/67	—	50.00	120	180	275	450
1780/76	—	50.00	120	180	275	450
1780/70	—	50.00	120	180	275	450
1780 Mintage included KM90	—	30.00	80.00	140	225	350
1788 Mintage included KM90	—	30.00	80.00	140	225	350
1789	—	30.00	80.00	140	225	350
1790 Mintage included KM90	—	30.00	80.00	140	225	350
1792	—	30.00	80.00	140	225	350

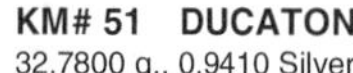

KM# 51 DUCATON

32.7800 g., 0.9410 Silver 0.9917 oz. ASW **Obv:** Knight on horseback right holds sword upright, crowned arms below **Obv. Legend:** BELG : PRO : HOLLAND : MO : NO : ARG : CONFOE **Rev:** Crowned arms of Holland, with supporters, date in cartouche below **Rev. Legend:** * CONCORDIA RES PARVAE CRESCUNT : **Note:** Dav. #4930. Similar to KM#90.

Date	Mintage	VG	F	VF	XF	Unc
1716	—	40.00	80.00	125	185	300
1717	—	40.00	80.00	125	185	300
1721	—	40.00	80.00	125	185	300

KM# 90 DUCATON (Silver Rider)

Silver **Obv:** Armored Knight on horse holding sword above head, crowned arms below **Obv. Legend:** BELG : PRO : HOL : MO : NO : ARG : CON FOE : **Rev:** Crowned arms of Holland, with supporters, date in cartouche below **Rev. Legend:** CONCORDIA RES PAR... **Note:** Dav. #1827.

Date	Mintage	VG	F	VF	XF	Unc
1734	—	60.00	125	200	285	375
1741	—	50.00	100	185	240	350
1742/41	—	—	—	—	—	—
1742	—	50.00	100	185	240	350
1743/2	—	50.00	100	185	240	350
1743	—	50.00	100	185	240	350
1744	—	50.00	100	185	240	350
1745	—	50.00	100	185	240	350
1746	—	50.00	100	185	240	350
1747	—	50.00	100	185	240	350
1748/7	—	50.00	100	180	240	350
1748	—	50.00	100	180	240	350
1749	—	30.00	80.00	145	200	325
1750	—	30.00	80.00	145	200	325
1754	—	50.00	100	185	240	325
1756	—	25.00	70.00	125	185	300
1757	—	25.00	70.00	125	185	300
1758	—	25.00	70.00	125	185	300
1759	—	25.00	70.00	125	185	300
1760/59	—	25.00	70.00	125	185	300
1760	139,000	25.00	70.00	125	185	300
1761	Inc. above	25.00	70.00	125	185	300
1762	Inc. above	25.00	70.00	125	185	300
1765/61	—	60.00	125	200	285	375
1765/62	—	60.00	125	200	285	385
1765	32,000	25.00	75.00	125	185	300
1766	202,000	45.00	100	185	240	350
1767	Inc. above	25.00	70.00	125	185	300
1770	161,000	25.00	70.00	125	185	300
1771	Inc. above	25.00	70.00	125	185	300
1772	Inc. above	25.00	70.00	125	185	300
1773	235,000	25.00	70.00	125	185	300
1774/3	Inc. above	25.00	70.00	125	185	300
1774	Inc. above	25.00	70.00	125	185	300
1775	Inc. above	25.00	70.00	125	185	300
1777	—	100	200	400	800	1,200
1779/5	90,000	25.00	70.00	125	185	200
1779	Inc. above	25.00	70.00	125	185	275
1780/70	—	—	—	—	—	—
1780	Inc. above	25.00	70.00	125	185	275
1784	31,000	50.00	100	185	240	300
1788	76,000	25.00	70.00	125	185	275
1789	Inc. above	25.00	70.00	125	185	275
1790	96,000	25.00	70.00	125	185	275
1791	Inc. above	25.00	70.00	125	185	275
1792/1	—	25.00	70.00	125	185	275
1792	Inc. above	25.00	70.00	125	185	275
1793	50,000	25.00	70.00	125	185	275

KM# 90a DUCATON (Silver Rider)

41.6000 g., Gold **Obv:** Armored Knight on horse holding sword above head, crowned arms below **Obv. Legend:** BELG : PRO : HOL : MO : NO : ARG : CON FOE : **Rev:** Crowned arms of Holland, with supporters, date in cartouche below **Rev. Legend:** CONCORDIA RES .... **Note:** Dav. #1827.

Date	Mintage	VG	F	VF	XF	Unc
1758 Rare	2	—	—	—	—	—
Note: Bowers and Merena Guia sale 3-88 Unc. realized $11.550						
1790 Rare	3	—	—	—	—	—

KM# 83 2 DUCATON

Silver **Obv:** Armored Knight on horse above crowned shield **Obv. Legend:** BELG : PRO : HOL : MO : NO : ARG : CON FOE : **Note:** Dav. #1826

Date	Mintage	VG	F	VF	XF	Unc
1745	—	—	—	900	1,400	2,000
1754	—	—	—	900	1,600	2,100

KM# 78 3 DUCATON

Silver **Note:** Dav. #1825. Similar to 2 Ducaton, KM#83.

Date	Mintage	VG	F	VF	XF	Unc
1754	—	—	—	—	—	—

KM# 52 DUCAT (48 Stuivers)

Silver **Obv:** Standing armored Knight with crowned shield at feet **Obv. Legend:** BELG : .. : HOL : MONO : ARG : PRO : CONFOE : **Rev:** Crowned arms of Holland divides date **Rev. Legend:** CONCORDIA RES PAR.... **Note:** Dav. #4898 and #1840.

Date	Mintage	VG	F	VF	XF	Unc
1734	—	60.00	200	275	400	500
1735	—	35.00	100	150	200	300
1751	—	35.00	100	150	200	300
1752	—	35.00	100	150	200	300
1753	—	35.00	100	150	200	300
1755	—	35.00	100	150	200	300
1756	—	50.00	150	250	350	450
1762	—	35.00	100	150	200	300
1763	—	35.00	100	150	200	300
1767	—	35.00	100	150	200	300
1771	—	50.00	150	250	350	450
1772	—	35.00	100	150	200	300

TRADE COINAGE

KM# 12 DUCAT

3.4900 g., 0.9860 Gold 0.1106 oz. AGW **Obv:** Armored, standing Knight holding bundle of arrows, divides date **Obv. Legend:** CONCORDIA • RES PAR • CRES • HOL • **Rev:** Inscription within ornamented square **Rev. Inscription:** MO:ORD:/ PROVIN./ FOEDER BELGAD/ LEGIMP.

Date	Mintage	VG	F	VF	XF	Unc
1702	—	80.00	120	150	250	350
1703	—	125	250	550	700	900
1707	—	125	250	550	700	900
1709	—	125	250	550	700	900
1715	—	125	250	550	700	900
1718	—	150	325	650	850	1,100
1718/17	—	150	300	600	800	100
1719	—	150	300	600	800	1,000
1720	—	60.00	100	150	200	300
1721	—	60.00	100	150	200	300
1722	—	60.00	100	150	200	300
1723	—	60.00	100	150	200	300
1724	—	60.00	100	150	200	300
1725	—	60.00	100	150	200	300
1726	—	60.00	100	150	200	300
1727	—	60.00	100	150	200	300
1728	—	60.00	100	150	200	300
1729	—	60.00	100	150	200	300
1730	—	60.00	100	150	200	300
1731	—	60.00	100	150	200	300
1732	—	60.00	100	150	200	300
1733	—	60.00	100	150	200	300
1734	—	100	200	350	500	600
1735	—	100	200	350	500	600
1736	—	60.00	100	150	200	300
1737	—	60.00	100	150	200	300
1738/36	—	150	300	500	800	1,000
1738	—	60.00	100	150	200	300
1739	—	60.00	100	150	200	300
1740	—	60.00	100	150	200	300
1741	—	60.00	100	150	200	300
1742/1	—	150	300	500	800	1,000
1742	—	60.00	100	150	200	300
1743	—	60.00	100	150	200	300
1744	—	60.00	100	150	200	300
1745	—	60.00	100	150	200	300
1746	—	60.00	100	150	200	300
1747	—	60.00	100	150	200	300
1748	—	60.00	100	150	200	300
1749	—	60.00	100	150	200	300
1750	—	60.00	100	150	200	300
1751	—	60.00	100	150	200	300
1752/50	—	65.00	110	200	250	300
1752/51	—	65.00	110	200	250	350
1752	—	60.00	100	150	200	300
1753	—	60.00	100	150	200	300
1754	—	60.00	100	150	200	300
1756/55	—	60.00	100	150	200	300
1755	—	60.00	100	150	200	300
1756	—	60.00	100	150	200	300
1757	—	60.00	100	150	200	300
1758	—	60.00	100	150	200	300
1759	—	60.00	100	150	200	300
1760	—	60.00	100	150	200	300
1761	—	60.00	100	150	200	300
1762	—	60.00	100	150	200	300
1763	—	60.00	100	150	200	300
1764	—	60.00	100	150	200	300
1765	—	60.00	100	150	200	300
1766	—	60.00	100	150	200	300
1767	—	60.00	100	150	200	300
1768	—	60.00	100	150	200	300
1769	—	60.00	100	150	200	300
1770	—	60.00	100	150	200	300
1771	—	60.00	100	150	200	300
1772	—	60.00	100	150	200	300
1773	—	60.00	100	150	200	300
1774	—	60.00	100	150	200	300
1775	—	60.00	100	150	200	300
1776	—	60.00	100	150	200	300
1777	—	60.00	100	150	200	300
1778	—	60.00	100	150	200	300
1779	—	60.00	100	150	200	300
1780	—	60.00	100	150	200	300
1781	—	60.00	100	150	200	300
1782	—	60.00	100	150	200	300
1783	—	60.00	100	150	200	300
1784	—	60.00	100	150	200	300
1790	—	60.00	100	150	200	300
1791	—	60.00	100	150	200	300
1792	—	60.00	100	150	200	300

KM# 47 2 DUCAT

6.9800 g., 0.9860 Gold 0.2213 oz. AGW **Obv:** Standing, armored knight holding bundle of arrows, divides date within broken circle **Obv. Legend:** CONCORDIA • RES PAR • CRES • HOL • **Rev:** Inscription within ornamented square **Rev. Inscription:** MO:ORD:/ PROVIN./ FOEDER/ BELG•AD/ LEG•IMP• **Edge:** Plain

Date	Mintage	VG	F	VF	XF	Unc
1716	—	300	800	1,150	1,750	2,000
1717	—	250	700	1,000	1,500	1,750
1719	—	125	250	600	900	1,200
1720/19	—	250	700	1,000	1,500	1,750
1720	—	125	250	600	900	1,200
1721	—	125	250	600	900	1,200
1724	—	125	250	600	900	1,200
1725	—	250	700	1,000	1,400	1,600
1726	—	125	250	600	900	1,200
1727	—	—	—	—	—	—
1728	—	250	700	1,000	1,400	1,600
1730	—	125	250	600	900	1,200
1731	—	250	700	1,000	1,400	1,600
1732	—	125	250	600	900	1,200
1734/33	—	250	700	1,000	1,400	1,600
1734	—	125	250	400	600	—
1735	—	125	250	600	900	1,200
1736	—	125	250	600	900	1,200
1737	—	250	700	1,000	1,400	1,600
1738/36	—	250	700	1,000	1,400	1,600
1738	—	125	250	600	900	1,200
1739	—	125	250	600	900	1,200
1740	—	125	250	600	900	1,200
1742/41	—	250	700	1,000	1,400	1,600
1742	—	125	250	600	900	1,200
1743	—	250	700	1,000	1,400	1,600
1745	—	125	250	600	900	1,200
1746	—	125	250	600	900	1,200
1747	—	125	250	600	900	1,200
1748	—	125	250	600	900	1,200
1749	—	125	250	600	900	1,200
1750	—	125	250	600	900	1,200
1751	—	125	250	600	900	1,200
1752	—	125	250	600	900	1,200
1753	—	125	250	600	900	1,200
1754	—	125	250	600	900	1,200
1755	—	125	250	600	900	1,200
1756	—	125	250	600	900	1,200
1757	—	125	250	600	900	1,200
1758	—	125	250	600	900	1,200
1759	—	125	250	600	900	1,200
1760	—	125	250	600	900	1,200
1761	—	125	250	600	900	1,200
1762	—	125	250	600	900	1,200
1763	—	125	250	600	900	1,200
1764	—	125	250	600	900	1,200
1765	—	125	250	600	900	1,200
1766	—	125	250	600	900	1,200
1767	—	125	250	600	900	1,200
1768	—	125	250	600	900	1,200
1769	—	125	250	600	900	1,200
1770	—	125	250	600	900	1,200
1771	—	125	250	600	900	1,200
1772	—	125	250	600	900	1,200
1773	—	125	250	600	900	1,200
1774	—	125	250	600	900	1,200
1776	—	125	250	600	900	1,200
1777	—	125	250	600	900	1,200
1778	—	125	250	600	900	1,200
1779	—	125	250	600	900	1,200
1780	—	125	250	600	900	1,200
1781	—	125	250	600	900	1,200
1782	—	125	250	600	900	1,200
1783	—	125	250	600	900	1,200
1784	—	125	250	600	900	1,200
1785	—	125	250	600	900	1,200
1787	—	125	250	600	900	1,200
1790	—	250	700	1,000	1,400	1,700
1791	—	125	250	600	900	1,200
1793	—	125	250	600	900	1,200

KM# 79 2 DUCAT

Silver **Note:** DAV. #1839. Similar to 1 Ducat, KM#52.

Date	Mintage	VG	F	VF	XF	Unc
1734 Rare	—	—	—	—	—	—
1735 Rare	—	—	—	—	—	—
1796	—	35.00	100	150	200	—
1797	—	35.00	100	150	200	—
1798	—	35.00	100	150	200	—
1799	—	35.00	100	150	200	—
1800	—	35.00	100	150	200	—

PATTERNS

Including off metal strikes

KM#	Date	Mintage	Identification	Mkt Val
Pn25	1719	—	Ducaton. Gold. KM#51.	—
Pn26	1721	—	Ducaton. Gold. 34.5000 g. KM#51.	7,000
Pn27	1734	—	1/2 Gulden. Gold. 10.3000 g. KM#65a.	—
Pn28	1753	—	1/2 Gulden. Gold. 10.3000 g. KM#65a.	—
Pn29	1754	—	1/2 Gulden. Gold. 10.3000 g. KM#65a.	—
PnA30	1758	—	Ducaton. Gold. 42.0000 g. KM#50.	—
Pn30	1759	—	1/4 Gulden. Gold. 5.2500 g. KM#100a.	—
Pn31	1790	—	Ducaton. Gold. 41.6000 g. KM#95.3.	—

PIEFORTS

KM#	Date	Mintage	Identification	Mkt Val
P38	1703	—	Ducaton. Gold. 34.4900 g.	30,000
P39	1749	—	Gulden. Gold. 13.9500 g.	5,000
P40	1734	—	1/2 Gulden. Gold. 10.4800 g.	2,000
P41	1735	—	Ducat. Silver. 55.9700 g.	1,500

LIMBOURG PROVINCE-MAASTRICHT

Maestricht

Traiectum Ad Mosam

Maastricht, a commune in the province of Limburg in the Netherlands, was the seat of a bishop from 382 to 721. Once part of the Frankish realm, it was overtaken by Spaniards in 1579 and then ruled by the dukes of Brabant and the prince-bishops of Liege after 1673. It was taken by the French in 1673, 1748, and 1794. The Austrian defenders under the Prince of Hesse issued an emergency coinage for Maastricht during the 1794 siege.

CITY

COUNTERMARKED COINAGE

KM# 15 50 STIVERS

Silver **Countermark:** 1794, star and 50 St **Note:** Countermark on France 1/2 ECU of Louis XV.

CM Date	Host Date	Good	VG	F	VF	XF
1794	1794	—	500	750	1,000	1,200

KM# 16 100 STIVERS

Silver **Countermark:** 1794, star and 100 St. **Note:** Countermark on France ECU of Louis XVI, KM#564.

CM Date	Host Date	Good	VG	F	VF	XF
1794	1794 Rare	—	—	—	—	—

SIEGE COINAGE

KM# 5 5 STIVERS

Bronze **Note:** Uniface, similar to 50 Stivers, KM#6.

Date	Mintage	Good	VG	F	VF	XF
1794	—	60.00	110	175	250	350

KM# 6 50 STIVERS

Silver **Note:** Uniface.

Date	Mintage	Good	VG	F	VF	XF
1794	—	150	250	400	500	700

KM# 7 100 STIVERS

Silver

Date	Mintage	Good	VG	F	VF	XF
1794	—	300	600	900	1,200	1,500

KM# 8 100 STIVERS

Silver

Date	Mintage	Good	VG	F	VF	XF
1794	—	200	400	600	900	1,500

KM# 9 100 STIVERS

Bronze

Date	Mintage	Good	VG	F	VF	XF
1794	—	40.00	80.00	120	250	—

KM# 10 100 STIVERS

Silver **Note:** Uniface.

Date	Mintage	Good	VG	F	VF	XF
1794	—	150	250	350	450	600

NIJMEGEN

PROVINCE

STANDARD COINAGE

KM# 33 DAALDER (30 Stuivers)

Silver **Note:** Reduced size.

Date	Mintage	VG	F	VF	XF	Unc
1703	—	50.00	90.00	150	250	500
1704/3	—	50.00	100	170	300	600
1704	—	50.00	90.00	150	250	500

PIEFORTS

KM#	Date	Mintage	Identification	Mkt Val
P6	1703	—	Daalder. Silver. Reduced size, KM33.	—

OVERYSSEL

Overijsel, Transisulania

Overyssel is a province in northeastern Netherlands whose name means *beyond the Issel*, a tributary of the Rhine. Originally known as the lordship of Oversticht it was a part of the holdings of the bishops of Utrecht. It was sold to Charles V in 1527 and made a part of the Habsburg domain. Three of its cities - Kampen, Deventer and Zwolle were important Hanseatic towns of the medieval period.

PROVINCE

STANDARD COINAGE

KM# 87 WEAPON-STUIVER

0.8100 g., 0.5830 Silver 0.0152 oz. ASW **Obv:** Bundle of arrows divides 1S, rose mint mark **Rev:** Inscription above date **Rev. Inscription:** TRANS/ISALA/NIA

Date	Mintage	VG	F	VF	XF	Unc
1738	—	3.00	8.00	17.00	40.00	70.00
1739	—	3.00	8.00	17.00	40.00	70.00
1765	—	3.00	8.00	17.00	40.00	70.00
1766	—	3.00	8.00	17.00	40.00	70.00
1767	—	3.00	8.00	17.00	40.00	70.00
1769	—	3.00	8.00	17.00	40.00	70.00

KM# 70 DUIT

Copper **Obv:** Crowned arms of Overyssel **Rev:** Inscription above date **Rev. Inscription:** OVER/YSSEL

Date	Mintage	VG	F	VF	XF	Unc
1702	—	2.50	8.00	17.00	30.00	50.00
1703	—	2.50	8.00	17.00	30.00	50.00

KM# 70a DUIT

Silver **Obv:** Crowned arms of Overyssel **Rev:** Inscription above date **Rev. Inscription:** OVER/YSSEL

Date	Mintage	VG	F	VF	XF	Unc
1702	—	40.00	75.00	185	200	300
1703	—	50.00	100	200	300	400

KM# 90 DUIT

Copper **Obv:** Crowned arms of Overyssel **Obv. Legend:** VIGILATE ETORATE **Rev:** Inscription above date **Rev. Inscription:** OVER/YSSEL

Date	Mintage	VG	F	VF	XF	Unc
1741	—	2.00	4.00	8.00	18.00	35.00
1750	—	2.00	4.00	8.00	18.00	35.00
1764	—	2.00	4.00	9.00	20.00	40.00
1765/4	—	4.00	10.00	15.00	20.00	40.00
1765	—	4.00	10.00	15.00	22.50	45.00
1766	—	4.00	10.00	15.00	20.00	40.00
1767	—	6.00	15.00	25.00	40.00	60.00
1768	—	2.00	4.00	8.00	18.00	35.00
1769	—	2.00	4.00	8.00	18.00	35.00

KM# 90a DUIT

Silver **Obv:** Crowned arms of Overyssel **Obv. Legend:** VIGILATE ETORATE **Rev:** Inscription above date **Rev. Inscription:** OVER/YSSEL

Date	Mintage	VG	F	VF	XF	Unc
1741	—	15.00	25.00	40.00	65.00	130
1750	—	20.00	30.00	60.00	120	200
1766	—	—	—	—	—	—
1767	—	20.00	30.00	60.00	120	200
1769	—	15.00	25.00	40.00	65.00	130

KM# 90b DUIT

5.4800 g., Gold **Obv:** Crowned arms of Overyssel **Obv. Legend:** VIGILATE ETORATE **Rev:** Inscription above date **Rev. Inscription:** OVER/YSSEL

Date	Mintage	VG	F	VF	XF	Unc
1741	—	125	250	400	500	800

KM# 95 DUIT

Copper **Obv:** Crowned arms of Overyssel **Obv. Legend:** VIGILATE ? ETORATE ? **Rev:** Inscription above date within wreath **Rev. Inscription:** OVER/YSSEL

Date	Mintage	VG	F	VF	XF	Unc
1753	—	2.50	8.00	14.00	20.00	40.00
1754	—	2.50	8.00	14.00	20.00	40.00

KM# A102 DUIT

Copper **Obv:** Standing woman with anchor **Obv. Legend:** SPES MEA IN DEO **Rev:** Crowned weapon **Rev. Legend:** VIGILATE ET ORATE

Date	Mintage	VG	F	VF	XF	Unc
1770 Rare	—	—	—	—	—	—

KM# A102a DUIT

Silver

Date	Mintage	VG	F	VF	XF	Unc
1770	—	40.00	100	150	200	—

KM# 87a STUIVER

1.7000 g., Gold **Obv:** Bundle of arrows divides 1S, rose mint mark **Rev:** Inscription above date **Rev. Inscription:** TRANS/ISALA/NIA

Date	Mintage	VG	F	VF	XF	Unc
1738	—	75.00	250	350	550	900
1739	—	75.00	250	350	550	900

KM# 63.1 GULDEN

Silver **Obv:** Crowned arms of Overtssel divides value **Rev:** Standing female figure leaning on Bible on column, holding spear with Liberty cap, date below figure **Note:** Mint mark: Rose.

Date	Mintage	VG	F	VF	XF	Unc
1701	269,060	7.00	17.00	40.00	80.00	150
1702	Inc. above	7.00	17.00	35.00	70.00	120
1703	Inc. above	7.00	17.00	30.00	60.00	100
1704	Inc. above	7.00	17.00	30.00	60.00	100
1705/06	2,166,820	—	—	—	—	—
1705	Inc. above	7.00	17.00	30.00	60.00	100
1706	Inc. above	7.00	17.00	30.00	60.00	100
1707	Inc. above	7.00	17.00	30.00	60.00	100
1709	Inc. above	7.00	17.00	30.00	60.00	100
1710	34,290	7.00	17.00	30.00	60.00	100

KM# 63.2 GULDEN

Silver **Obv:** Crowned arms of Overyssel divides value **Rev:** Standing female figure leaning on Bible on column, holding spear with Liberty cap, date below figure **Note:** Mintmark: Crane.

Date	Mintage	VG	F	VF	XF	Unc
1717	2,955,945	7.00	17.00	30.00	60.00	100
1718	Inc. above	7.00	17.00	30.00	60.00	100
1719	Inc. above	7.00	17.00	30.00	60.00	100
1720	3,231,515	7.00	17.00	30.00	60.00	100
1721	Inc. above	7.00	17.00	30.00	60.00	100
1733	2,710,090	7.00	17.00	30.00	60.00	100
1734	Inc. above	7.00	17.00	30.00	60.00	100
1735	Inc. above	7.00	17.00	30.00	60.00	100
1736	Inc. above	7.00	17.00	30.00	60.00	100
1737	Inc. above	7.00	17.00	40.00	80.00	125
1730/18	Inc. above	7.00	17.00	40.00	80.00	125
1738/37	Inc. above	7.00	17.00	40.00	80.00	125
1738	Inc. above	7.00	17.00	30.00	60.00	100
1748	88,865	7.00	17.00	30.00	60.00	100
1749	Inc. above	7.00	17.00	30.00	60.00	100

KM# 63.3 GULDEN

Silver **Obv:** Crowned arms of Overyssel divides value **Rev:** Standing female figure leaning on Bible on column, holding spear with Liberty cap, date below figure **Note:** Mintmark: Lily.

Date	Mintage	VG	F	VF	XF	Unc
1722	837,770	7.00	17.00	30.00	60.00	100
1722/21	Inc. above	—	—	—	—	—
1723	2,183,300	7.00	17.00	30.00	60.00	100
1724	—	7.00	17.00	30.00	60.00	100
1725	—	7.00	17.00	30.00	60.00	100
1733	2,710,090	7.00	17.00	30.00	60.00	100
1734	Inc. above	7.00	17.00	30.00	60.00	100
1735	Inc. above	7.00	17.00	30.00	60.00	100
1736	Inc. above	7.00	17.00	30.00	60.00	100
1737	Inc. above	7.00	17.00	40.00	80.00	125
1730/18	Inc. above	7.00	17.00	40.00	80.00	125
1738/37	Inc. above	7.00	17.00	40.00	80.00	125
1738	Inc. above	7.00	17.00	30.00	60.00	100
1748	88,865	7.00	17.00	30.00	60.00	100
1749	Inc. above	7.00	17.00	30.00	60.00	100

KM# 60 3 GULDEN (60 Stuiver)

Silver **Obv:** Crowned arms of Overyssel divides value **Rev:** Standing female figure leaning on Bible on column, holding spear with Liberty cap, date below figure **Note:** Mint mark: Rose. Dav. #4957.

Date	Mintage	VG	F	VF	XF	Unc
1719	—	40.00	100	175	250	400
1721	—	40.00	100	175	250	400
1727	—	40.00	100	175	250	400

KM# 100 7 GULDEN

4.9650 g., 0.9170 Gold 0.1464 oz. AGW

Date	Mintage	VG	F	VF	XF	Unc
1760	54,000	100	200	325	500	600
1761	46,000	100	200	325	500	600
1762	—	100	225	350	550	700
1763	—	100	225	350	550	700

KM# 101 14 GULDEN

9.9300 g., 0.9170 Gold 0.2927 oz. AGW **Obv:** Mounted knight holding sword above arms **Rev:** Crowned arms divide value, date above

Date	Mintage	VG	F	VF	XF	Unc
1760	—	125	250	500	750	1,000
1761	—	175	350	600	1,000	1,400
1763	—	125	250	500	750	1,000

KM# 80 DUCATON (Silver Rider)

32.7800 g., 0.9410 Silver 0.9917 oz. ASW **Obv:** Mounted knight holding sword above arms **Rev:** Crowned arms with lion supporters, date in cartouche below

Date	Mintage	VG	F	VF	XF	Unc
1720	—	—	—	—	—	—
1732	—	35.00	70.00	140	250	400
1733	—	45.00	90.00	175	300	450
1734	—	45.00	90.00	175	300	450
1735	—	45.00	90.00	175	300	450
1736	—	35.00	70.00	140	250	400
1737	—	30.00	60.00	130	250	400
1738	—	30.00	60.00	130	250	400
1739	—	30.00	60.00	130	250	400
1740	—	45.00	90.00	175	300	450
1741	—	30.00	60.00	130	250	400
1742	—	30.00	60.00	130	250	400
1744	—	85.00	180	275	400	600
1745/1	—	—	—	—	—	1,100
1745	—	30.00	60.00	130	250	400
1746	—	30.00	60.00	130	250	400
1747	—	30.00	60.00	130	250	400
1764	9,615	80.00	250	400	800	1,000

TRADE COINAGE

KM# 61 DUCAT (48 Stuiver)

Silver **Obv:** Standing, armored knight with crowned shield at feet **Rev:** Crowned arms of Overyssel divides date **Note:** Mint mark: Rose. Dav. #4900.

Date	Mintage	VG	F	VF	XF	Unc
1707/6	—	40.00	100	175	250	450
1707	—	40.00	100	175	250	450
1708	—	40.00	100	175	250	450
1709	—	40.00	100	175	250	450

KM# 88 DUCAT (48 Stuiver)

Silver **Obv:** Armored knight standing holding sword behind shield of arms **Obv. Legend:** MO. NO. ARG: CONFOE - BELG: PRO: TRANSI ? **Rev:** Crowned arms divide date **Rev. Legend:** CONCORDIA: RES: PARVAE: CRESCVNT **Note:** Mint mark: Stork. Dav. #1842.

Date	Mintage	Good	VG	F	VF	XF
1734	1,907,740	—	60.00	120	200	400
1735	Inc. above	—	60.00	120	200	400
1737	Inc. above	—	—	—	—	—
1738	Inc. above	—	30.00	60.00	100	200
1739	—	—	30.00	60.00	100	200
1740	Inc. above	—	35.00	70.00	120	250
1741	Inc. above	—	30.00	60.00	100	200
1742	Inc. above	—	30.00	60.00	100	200
1743	Inc. above	—	60.00	120	200	400
1744	Inc. above	—	35.00	70.00	120	250
1745	Inc. above	—	—	—	—	—
1746	Inc. above	—	—	—	—	—
1747	Inc. above	—	—	—	—	—
1764	Inc. above	—	60.00	120	200	400
1767	Inc. above	—	60.00	120	200	400

KM# 53 DUCAT

3.5000 g., 0.9860 Gold 0.1109 oz. AGW **Obv:** Knight standing right divides date, without inner circle **Rev:** 5-line inscription on tablet

Date	Mintage	VG	F	VF	XF	Unc
1702	—	80.00	150	200	275	350
1702	—	80.00	150	200	275	350
1703	—	80.00	150	200	275	350
1704	—	100	225	350	550	700
1705	—	100	225	350	550	700
1706	—	100	225	350	550	700
1707	—	80.00	150	200	275	350
1709	—	100	225	350	550	700
1710	—	125	250	375	600	800

KM# 82 DUCAT

3.5000 g., 0.9860 Gold 0.1109 oz. AGW **Rev:** Rosette in small shield below tablet

Date	Mintage	VG	F	VF	XF	Unc
1727 Rare	—	—	—	—	—	—
1733	—	80.00	120	175	250	300
1738 Rare	—	—	—	—	—	—
1748	—	80.00	120	175	250	300

KM# 89 2 DUCAT

Silver **Obv:** Armored knight standing holding sword behind shield of arms **Obv. Legend:** MO. NO. ARG: CONFOE - BELG: PRO: TRANSI **Rev:** Crowned arms divide date **Rev. Legend:** CONCORDIA: RES: PARVAE: CRESCVNT **Note:** Mint mark: Stork. Dav. #A1842.

Date	Mintage	Good	VG	F	VF	XF
1737	—	—	—	—	—	—

STANDARD COINAGE

PATTERNS

Including off metal strikes

KM#	Date	Mintage	Identification	Mkt Val

PnA1	1741	—	Ducat. Gold.	—
Pn10	1769	—	Duit. Silver.	—
Pn12	1770	—	Duit. Silver.	200

PIEFORTS

KM#	Date	Mintage	Identification	Mkt Val
P11	1718	—	Ducaton. Silver. 64.9300 g.	1,250
P12	1737	—	Ducaton. Silver. 67.9300 g.	3,000

UTRECHT

Trajectum

Utrecht (Trajectum), the smallest Netherlands province, represents the bulk of a see founded in 722. It was one of the seven provinces that signed the Union of Utrecht against Spain, a treaty regarded as the foundation of the Dutch Republic and later kingdom of the Netherlands.

PROVINCE

STANDARD COINAGE

KM# 85 DUIT

Copper **Obv:** Crowned arms of Utrecht **Rev:** Inscription above date **Rev. Inscription:** STAD/UTRECHT

Date	Mintage	VG	F	VF	XF	Unc
1710	—	2.00	5.00	12.00	30.00	50.00
1711	—	2.00	5.00	12.00	30.00	50.00
1722/11	—	6.00	15.00	30.00	60.00	100
1722	—	2.00	5.00	12.00	30.00	50.00
1723	—	2.00	5.00	12.00	30.00	50.00
1724	—	4.00	10.00	20.00	40.00	80.00

KM# 85a DUIT

Silver **Obv:** Crowned arms of Utrecht **Rev:** Inscription above date **Rev. Inscription:** STAD/UTRECHT **Note:** Weight varies; 3.1-5.1 grams.

Date	Mintage	VG	F	VF	XF	Unc
1710	—	20.00	30.00	60.00	120	200
1711	—	20.00	30.00	60.00	120	200
1717	—	20.00	30.00	60.00	120	200
1722	—	20.00	30.00	60.00	120	200
1723	—	20.00	30.00	60.00	120	200

KM# 91c DUIT

6.9000 g., Gold **Obv:** Crowned arms of Utrecht, with supporters on mantle **Rev:** Inscription above date **Rev. Inscription:** STAD/UTRECHT

Date	Mintage	VG	F	VF	XF	Unc
1739	—	150	300	600	900	1,300
1741 Rare	—	—	—	—	—	—
1760 Rare	—	—	—	—	—	—

KM# 91d DUIT

5.2500 g., Gold **Obv:** Crowned arms of Utrecht, with supporters on mantle **Rev:** Inscription above date **Rev. Inscription:** STAD/UTRECHT

Date	Mintage	VG	F	VF	XF	Unc
1739 Rare	—	—	—	—	—	—
1740 Rare	—	—	—	—	—	—
1741 Rare	—	—	—	—	—	—

KM# 91 DUIT

Copper **Obv:** Crowned arms of Utrecht, with supporters on mantle **Rev:** Inscription above date **Rev. Inscription:** STAD/UTRECHT

Date	Mintage	VG	F	VF	XF	Unc
1739	—	1.50	4.00	7.00	20.00	30.00
1740	—	1.50	4.00	7.00	20.00	30.00
1742	—	1.50	4.00	7.00	20.00	30.00
1743	—	1.50	4.00	7.00	20.00	30.00
1744/43	—	6.00	15.00	30.00	60.00	80.00
1744	—	1.50	4.00	7.00	20.00	30.00
1745	—	1.50	4.00	7.00	20.00	30.00
1746	—	1.50	4.00	7.00	20.00	30.00
1747	—	1.50	4.00	7.00	20.00	30.00
1748/46	—	6.00	15.00	30.00	60.00	80.00
1748	—	4.00	10.00	20.00	40.00	60.00
1749	—	1.50	4.00	7.00	20.00	30.00
1750	—	6.00	15.00	30.00	60.00	80.00
1751	—	1.50	4.00	7.00	15.00	25.00
1752	—	2.00	5.00	10.00	30.00	40.00
1753	—	1.50	4.00	7.00	20.00	30.00
1754	—	1.50	4.00	7.00	20.00	30.00
1755	—	1.50	4.00	7.00	25.00	35.00
1756	—	1.50	4.00	7.00	20.00	30.00
1757/56	—	1.50	4.00	7.00	20.00	30.00
1757	—	1.50	4.00	7.00	20.00	30.00
1758	—	1.25	3.50	6.00	15.00	25.00
1759	—	1.25	3.50	6.00	15.00	25.00
1760	—	1.25	3.50	6.00	15.00	25.00
1761	—	1.25	3.50	6.00	15.00	25.00
1762	—	1.25	3.50	6.50	20.00	30.00
1763	—	1.25	3.50	6.00	15.00	25.00
1764/60	—	6.00	15.00	30.00	60.00	80.00

Date	Mintage	VG	F	VF	XF	Unc
1764	—	1.25	3.50	6.00	15.00	25.00
1765/64	—	6.00	15.00	30.00	60.00	80.00
1765	—	1.25	3.50	6.00	15.00	25.00
1766	—	1.25	3.50	6.00	15.00	25.00
1767	—	1.25	3.50	6.00	15.00	25.00
1768	—	1.25	3.50	6.50	20.00	30.00
1780	—	1.25	3.50	6.50	20.00	30.00
1783	—	1.25	3.50	6.00	16.00	27.00
1784	—	1.25	3.50	6.50	20.00	30.00
1785	—	1.25	3.50	6.00	16.00	27.00
1786	—	1.25	3.50	6.00	15.00	25.00
1787	—	1.25	3.50	6.00	15.00	25.00
1788	—	1.25	3.50	6.00	15.00	25.00
1789	—	1.25	3.50	6.50	20.00	30.00
1790	—	1.25	3.50	6.50	20.00	30.00
1791	—	1.25	3.50	6.50	20.00	30.00
1792	—	1.25	3.50	6.50	20.00	30.00
1793	—	4.00	10.00	20.00	40.00	60.00

KM# 91a DUIT

Silver **Obv:** Crowned arms of Utrecht, with supporters on mantle **Rev:** Inscription above date **Rev. Inscription:** STAD/UTRECHT

Date	Mintage	VG	F	VF	XF	Unc
1739	—	20.00	30.00	50.00	80.00	125
1740	—	20.00	30.00	50.00	80.00	125
1741	—	20.00	30.00	50.00	80.00	125
1742	—	20.00	30.00	50.00	80.00	125
1743	—	20.00	30.00	50.00	80.00	125
1744	—	20.00	30.00	50.00	80.00	125
1745	—	20.00	30.00	50.00	80.00	125
1746	—	20.00	30.00	50.00	80.00	125
1747	—	20.00	30.00	50.00	80.00	125
1748/47	—	30.00	50.00	70.00	90.00	150
1748	—	20.00	30.00	50.00	80.00	125
1749	—	20.00	30.00	50.00	80.00	125
1750	—	20.00	30.00	50.00	80.00	125
1751	—	20.00	30.00	50.00	80.00	125
1752	—	20.00	30.00	50.00	80.00	125
1753	—	20.00	30.00	50.00	80.00	125
1754	—	20.00	30.00	50.00	80.00	125
1755	—	20.00	30.00	50.00	80.00	125
1756	—	20.00	30.00	50.00	80.00	125
1757	—	20.00	30.00	50.00	80.00	125
1758	—	20.00	30.00	50.00	80.00	125
1759	—	20.00	30.00	50.00	80.00	125
1760	—	20.00	30.00	50.00	80.00	125
1761	—	20.00	30.00	50.00	80.00	125
1762	—	20.00	30.00	50.00	80.00	125
1763	—	20.00	30.00	50.00	80.00	125
1764	—	20.00	30.00	50.00	80.00	125
1765	—	20.00	30.00	50.00	80.00	125
1766	—	20.00	30.00	50.00	80.00	125
1767	—	20.00	30.00	50.00	80.00	125
1768	—	20.00	30.00	50.00	80.00	125
1769	—	20.00	30.00	50.00	80.00	125
1770	—	20.00	30.00	50.00	80.00	125
1771	—	20.00	30.00	50.00	80.00	125
1772	—	20.00	30.00	50.00	80.00	125
1773	—	20.00	30.00	50.00	80.00	125
1774	—	20.00	30.00	50.00	80.00	125
1775	—	20.00	30.00	50.00	80.00	125
1776	—	20.00	30.00	50.00	80.00	125
1777	—	20.00	30.00	50.00	80.00	125
1778	—	20.00	30.00	50.00	80.00	125
1779	—	20.00	30.00	50.00	80.00	125
1780	—	20.00	30.00	50.00	80.00	125
1781	—	20.00	30.00	50.00	80.00	125
1782	—	20.00	30.00	50.00	80.00	125
1783	—	20.00	30.00	50.00	80.00	125
1784	—	20.00	30.00	50.00	80.00	125
1785	—	20.00	30.00	50.00	80.00	125
1786	—	20.00	30.00	50.00	80.00	125
1787	—	20.00	30.00	50.00	80.00	125
1788	—	20.00	30.00	50.00	80.00	125
1789	—	20.00	30.00	50.00	80.00	125
1790	—	20.00	30.00	50.00	80.00	125
1791	—	20.00	30.00	50.00	80.00	125
1792	—	20.00	30.00	50.00	80.00	125
1793	—	20.00	30.00	50.00	80.00	125
1794	—	20.00	30.00	50.00	80.00	125

KM# 91b DUIT

3.5000 g., Gold **Obv:** Crowned arms of Utrecht, with supporters on mantle **Rev:** Inscription above date **Rev. Inscription:** STAD/UTRECHT

Date	Mintage	VG	F	VF	XF	Unc
1739	—	80.00	200	350	525	650
1740	—	80.00	200	350	525	650
1741	—	80.00	200	350	525	650
1743	—	80.00	200	350	525	650
1744	—	80.00	200	350	525	650
1745	—	80.00	175	300	500	600
1746	—	80.00	175	300	500	600
1749	—	80.00	200	350	525	650
1750	—	80.00	175	300	500	600
1751	—	80.00	175	300	500	600
1752	—	80.00	175	300	500	600
1754	—	80.00	175	300	500	600
1755	—	80.00	175	300	500	600
1758	—	80.00	175	300	500	600
1760	—	80.00	175	300	500	600
1763	—	80.00	175	300	500	600
1764	—	80.00	175	300	500	600

Date	Mintage	VG	F	VF	XF	Unc
1765	—	80.00	175	300	500	600
1766	—	80.00	200	350	525	650
1767	—	80.00	200	350	525	650
1768	—	80.00	175	300	500	600
1784	—	80.00	175	300	500	600
1788	—	80.00	175	300	500	600
1791	—	80.00	175	300	500	600
1792	—	80.00	175	300	500	650
1793	—	80.00	175	300	500	600
1794	—	80.00	175	300	500	600

KM# 90 STUIVER

0.8100 g., 0.5830 Silver 0.0152 oz. ASW **Obv:** Bundle of arrows divides 1 S within wreath **Rev:** Inscription above date **Rev. Inscription:** TRA/IEC/TUM

Date	Mintage	VG	F	VF	XF	Unc
1738	—	3.00	8.00	20.00	30.00	50.00
1739	—	3.00	8.00	20.00	30.00	50.00
1760	—	3.00	8.00	20.00	30.00	50.00
1763	—	3.00	8.00	20.00	30.00	50.00
1765	65,295	4.00	10.00	25.00	50.00	—

KM# 90a STUIVER

1.7000 g., Gold **Obv:** Bundle of arrows divides 1 S within wreath **Rev:** Inscription above date **Rev. Inscription:** TRA/IEC/TUM

Date	Mintage	VG	F	VF	XF	Unc
1738	—	60.00	100	175	275	350
1739	—	60.00	100	175	275	350
1740	—	60.00	100	175	275	350
1741	—	60.00	100	175	275	350
1742	—	60.00	100	175	275	350
1743	—	60.00	100	175	275	350
1744	—	60.00	100	175	275	350
1745	—	60.00	100	175	275	350
1746	—	60.00	100	175	275	350
1747	—	60.00	100	175	275	300
1748	—	60.00	100	175	275	350
1749	—	60.00	100	175	275	350
1750	—	60.00	100	175	275	350
1751	—	60.00	100	175	275	350
1752	—	60.00	100	175	275	350
1755/54	—	60.00	100	175	275	350
1755	—	60.00	100	175	275	350
1757	—	60.00	100	175	275	350
1758	—	60.00	100	175	275	350
1760	—	60.00	100	175	275	350
1762	—	60.00	100	175	275	350
1763	—	60.00	100	175	275	350
1764	—	60.00	100	200	325	400
1765	—	60.00	100	200	325	400
1766	—	60.00	100	175	275	350
1767/8	—	60.00	100	200	325	400
1767	—	60.00	100	175	275	350
1769	—	60.00	100	175	275	350
1772	—	60.00	100	175	275	350
1777	—	60.00	100	175	275	350
1778	—	60.00	100	175	275	350
1779	—	60.00	100	175	275	350
1780	—	60.00	100	175	275	350
1781	—	60.00	100	175	275	350
1782	—	60.00	100	175	275	350
1786	—	60.00	100	175	275	350
1787	—	60.00	100	175	275	350
1788	—	60.00	100	200	325	350
1789	—	60.00	100	175	275	350

KM# 112a 2 STUIVERS (Double Wapenstuiver)

3.4500 g., Gold **Obv:** Crowned arms of Utrecht divides value **Rev:** Inscription above date **Rev. Inscription:** TRA/IEC/TUM

Date	Mintage	VG	F	VF	XF	Unc
1733	—	110	225	450	900	1,100
1744	—	100	200	400	700	900
1748	—	100	200	400	700	900
1749	—	100	200	400	700	900
1750	—	100	200	400	700	900
1751	—	100	200	400	700	900
1752	—	100	200	400	700	900
1754	—	100	200	400	700	900
1755	—	100	200	400	700	900
1757	—	100	200	400	700	900
1758	—	100	200	400	700	900
1788	—	100	200	300	700	900
1790	—	100	200	400	700	900
1791	—	100	200	400	700	900
1793	—	100	200	400	700	900
1794	—	100	200	400	700	900

KM# 112 2 STUIVERS (Double Wapenstuiver)

1.6200 g., 0.5830 Silver 0.0304 oz. ASW **Obv:** Crowned arms of Utrecht divides value **Rev:** Inscription above date **Rev. Inscription:** TRA/IEC/TUM **Note:** Nickel coins were struck at Birmingham in the period 1834-44.

Date	Mintage	VG	F	VF	XF	Unc
1757	—	1.25	2.50	5.00	10.00	20.00
1780	—	1.25	2.50	5.00	10.00	20.00
1784	—	1.25	2.50	5.00	10.00	20.00
1785	—	1.25	2.50	5.00	10.00	20.00
Note: Varieties exist						
1786	—	1.25	2.50	5.00	10.00	20.00
Note: Varieties exist						
1787	—	1.25	2.50	5.00	10.00	20.00
1788	—	1.25	2.50	5.00	10.00	20.00
1789	—	1.50	4.00	8.00	15.00	30.00
1790	—	1.50	4.00	8.00	15.00	30.00
1791	—	1.50	4.00	8.00	15.00	30.00
1792	—	1.50	4.00	8.00	15.00	30.00
1793	—	1.50	4.00	8.00	15.00	30.00
1794	—	1.50	4.00	8.00	15.00	30.00

KM# 80 6 STUIVERS (Scheepjesschelling)

Silver **Obv:** Crowned quartered arms with center shield divides value, branches below arms **Rev:** Ship sailing to right, date in legend

Date	Mintage	VG	F	VF	XF	Unc
1701	—	15.00	35.00	75.00	125	150
1702	—	15.00	35.00	75.00	125	150
1703	—	15.00	35.00	75.00	125	150

KM# 81 6 STUIVERS (Scheepjesschelling)

Silver **Obv:** Crowned quartered arms divide value in inner circle, date above crown **Rev:** Ship sailing to right

Date	Mintage	VG	F	VF	XF	Unc
1704	—	15.00	35.00	75.00	125	150
1705	—	15.00	35.00	75.00	125	150

KM# 81a 6 STUIVERS (Scheepjesschelling)

6.6900 g., Gold

Date	Mintage	VG	F	VF	XF	Unc
1704	—	—	750	1,500	2,000	2,500

KM# 82 6 STUIVERS (Scheepjesschelling)

Silver **Obv:** Center shield in arms, branch around arms.

Date	Mintage	VG	F	VF	XF	Unc
1706	—	15.00	35.00	75.00	125	150
1707	—	15.00	35.00	75.00	125	150
1710	—	15.00	35.00	75.00	125	150

KM# 101a 6 STUIVERS (Scheepjesschelling)

Gold **Obv:** Crowned arms of Utrecht divides value, date above **Obv. Legend:** MO : NO : ARG : ORDIN : TRAIECT • **Rev:** Sailing ship **Rev. Legend:** CONCORDIA RESPARVÆ CRESCUNT •

Date	Mintage	VG	F	VF	XF	Unc
1725	—	—	—	—	—	—
1739	—	—	600	900	1,250	—
1740	—	—	—	—	—	1,500
1741	—	175	350	550	750	1,000
1742	—	175	350	550	750	1,000
1744	—	175	350	550	750	1,000
1746	—	175	350	550	750	1,000
1747	—	175	350	550	750	1,000
1748/7	—	175	350	550	750	1,000
1748	—	75.00	350	600	800	1,100
1749	—	75.00	350	600	800	1,100
1750	—	75.00	350	600	800	1,100
1751	—	75.00	350	600	800	1,100
1752	—	75.00	350	600	800	1,100
1753	—	75.00	350	600	800	1,100
1754	—	75.00	350	600	800	1,100
1755	—	75.00	350	600	800	1,100
1757	—	75.00	350	600	800	1,100
1760	—	75.00	350	600	800	1,100
1763	—	75.00	350	600	800	1,100

Date	Mintage	VG	F	VF	XF	Unc
1764	—	75.00	350	600	800	1,100
1769	—	75.00	350	600	800	1,100
1772	—	75.00	350	600	800	1,100
1775	—	75.00	350	600	800	1,100
1784	—	—	—	—	—	—
1786	—	75.00	350	600	800	1,100
1787	—	75.00	350	600	800	1,100
1788	—	75.00	350	600	800	1,100
1789	—	75.00	350	600	800	1,100
1794	—	75.00	350	600	800	1,100

KM# 101 6 STUIVERS (Scheepjesschelling)

4.9500 g., 0.5830 Silver 0.0928 oz. ASW **Obv:** Crowned arms of Utrecht divides value, date above **Obv. Legend:** MO : NO : ARG : ORDIN : TRAIECT • **Rev:** Sailing ship **Rev. Legend:** CONCORDIA RESPARVÆ CRESCUNT •

Date	Mintage	VG	F	VF	XF	Unc
1742	—	8.00	15.00	30.00	60.00	100
1747	—	8.00	15.00	30.00	60.00	100
1750	—	8.00	15.00	30.00	60.00	100
1754	—	8.00	15.00	30.00	60.00	100
1755	—	8.00	15.00	30.00	60.00	100
1758	—	8.00	15.00	30.00	60.00	100
1764	33,710	8.00	15.00	30.00	60.00	100
1785	2,915	10.00	25.00	70.00	125	200
1786	Inc. above	10.00	25.00	70.00	125	200
1787	2,320	10.00	25.00	70.00	125	200
1788	Inc. above	8.00	15.00	35.00	50.00	100
1789	—	8.00	15.00	35.00	50.00	100
1794	345	30.00	60.00	100	150	250

KM# 100a 10 STUIVERS (1/2 Gulden)

10.4000 g., Gold **Obv:** Crowned arms divide denomination **Rev:** Standing female leaning on column, holding spear with liberty cap

Date	Mintage	VG	F	VF	XF	Unc
1740	—	—	—	1,350	2,150	—

KM# 113 1/4 GULDEN (5 STUIVERS)

2.6500 g., 0.9200 Silver 0.0784 oz. ASW **Obv:** Crowned arms of Utrecht divides date **Obv. Legend:** MO : ARG : ORD : FOED : BELG : TRAI • **Rev:** Standing figure leaning on column holding pole with cap **Rev. Legend:** HACNITIMVR HANCTVEMVR

Date	Mintage	VG	F	VF	XF	Unc
1758	—	7.00	15.00	30.00	45.00	75.00
1759	—	7.00	15.00	30.00	45.00	75.00

KM# 113a 1/4 GULDEN (5 STUIVERS)

1.0000 g., Gold **Obv:** Crowned arms of Utrecht divides date **Obv. Legend:** MO: ARG: ORD: FOED: BELG: TRAI• **Rev:** Standing figure leaning on column, holding pole with cap **Rev. Legend:** HAC NITIMVR HANCTVEMVR

Date	Mintage	VG	F	VF	XF	Unc
1758 Rare	—	—	—	—	—	—
1759 Rare	—	—	—	—	—	—

KM# 100b 1/2 GULDEN

7.0000 g., Gold **Obv:** Crowned arms divide denomination **Rev:** Standing female leaning on column, holding spear with liberty cap

Date	Mintage	VG	F	VF	XF	Unc
1724	—	—	—	—	—	—

KM# 100 1/2 GULDEN (10 Stuivers)

Silver **Obv:** Crowned arms of Utrecht divides value **Obv. Legend:** MO : ARG : ORD : FOED : BELG : TRAI • **Rev:** Standing figure leaning on column, holding pole with cap, date below **Rev. Legend:** HACNITIMVR HANCTVEMVR

Date	Mintage	VG	F	VF	XF	Unc
1724	—	30.00	80.00	150	200	300
1740	—	30.00	80.00	150	200	300

KM# 110a 1/2 GULDEN (10 Stuivers)

7.0000 g., Gold **Obv:** Crowned arms of Utrecht divides value **Obv. Legend:** MO: ARG: ORD: FOED: ... **Rev:** Standing figure leaning on column, holding pole with cap **Rev. Legend:** HACNITIMVR HANCTVEMVR

Date	Mintage	VG	F	VF	XF	Unc
1726	—	—	—	—	—	—
1755 Rare	—	—	—	—	—	—
1757 Rare	—	—	—	—	—	—
1759 Rare	—	—	—	—	—	—
1760	—	350	800	1,200	1,500	1,750
1764	—	300	700	1,000	1,200	1,600

Date	Mintage	VG	F	VF	XF	Unc
1773	—	300	700	1,000	1,200	1,600
1774/3	—	300	700	1,000	1,200	1,600
1776	—	300	700	1,000	1,200	1,600
1780	—	300	700	1,000	1,200	1,600
1782	—	500	1,000	1,200	1,500	1,600
1784	—	300	700	1,000	1,200	1,600
1785	—	300	700	1,000	1,200	1,600
1786	—	300	700	1,000	1,200	1,600
1787	—	300	700	1,000	1,200	1,600
1790	—	300	700	1,000	1,200	1,600
1791	—	300	700	1,000	1,200	1,600
1792	—	300	700	1,000	1,200	1,600
1793	—	300	700	1,000	1,200	1,600
1794	—	500	1,000	1,200	1,500	1,600

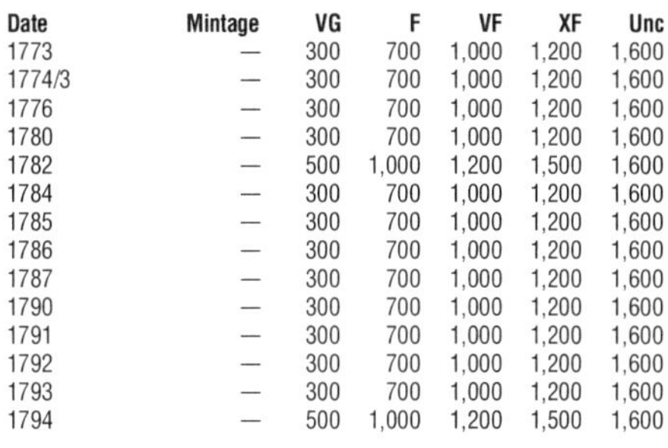

KM# 110 1/2 GULDEN (10 Stuivers)

5.3000 g., 0.9200 Silver 0.1568 oz. ASW **Obv:** Crowned arms of Utrecht divides value **Obv. Legend:** MO : ARG : ORD : FOED : ... **Rev:** Standing figure leaning on column, holding pole with cap **Rev. Legend:** HACNITIMVR HANCTVEMVR

Date	Mintage	VG	F	VF	XF	Unc
1750	—	15.00	40.00	70.00	100	150
1751	—	15.00	40.00	70.00	100	150
1755	—	15.00	40.00	70.00	100	150
1756	—	15.00	40.00	70.00	100	150
1757	—	15.00	40.00	70.00	100	150
1758	—	15.00	40.00	70.00	100	150
1759	—	17.50	45.00	80.00	120	160
1760	—	10.00	22.50	45.00	70.00	130
1761	—	8.00	20.00	40.00	60.00	110
1762	—	8.00	20.00	40.00	60.00	110
1763	—	8.00	20.00	40.00	60.00	110
1764	—	8.00	20.00	40.00	60.00	110
1765	—	8.00	20.00	40.00	60.00	110
1766	—	8.00	20.00	40.00	60.00	110
1767	—	8.00	20.00	40.00	60.00	110
1768	—	10.00	22.50	45.00	75.00	130
1771	—	8.00	20.00	40.00	60.00	110
1772	—	8.00	20.00	40.00	60.00	110
1773	—	10.00	30.00	60.00	90.00	140
1774/73	—	15.00	40.00	80.00	110	160
1774	—	8.00	20.00	40.00	60.00	110
1775	—	8.00	20.00	40.00	60.00	110
1776	—	10.00	22.50	45.00	70.00	120
1778	—	8.00	20.00	40.00	60.00	110
1779	—	8.00	20.00	40.00	60.00	110
1780	—	15.00	40.00	60.00	90.00	140
1781	—	15.00	40.00	60.00	90.00	140
1782	—	15.00	40.00	60.00	90.00	140
1783	—	8.00	20.00	40.00	60.00	110
1784	—	10.00	30.00	50.00	80.00	130
1785	—	10.00	30.00	60.00	90.00	140
1786	—	8.00	20.00	40.00	80.00	130
1787	—	8.00	20.00	40.00	60.00	110
1788	—	8.00	20.00	40.00	60.00	120
1789	—	8.00	20.00	40.00	60.00	110
1790	—	8.00	20.00	40.00	60.00	110
1791	—	8.00	20.00	40.00	60.00	110
1792	—	8.00	20.00	40.00	60.00	110
1793	—	10.00	22.50	45.00	70.00	120
1794	—	8.00	20.00	40.00	60.00	110

KM# 110b 1/2 GULDEN (10 Stuivers)

10.5000 g., Gold **Obv:** Crowned arms of Utrecht divides value **Obv. Legend:** MO: ARG: ORD: FOED: ... **Rev:** Standing figure leaning on column, holding pole with hat **Rev. Legend:** HACNITIMVR HANCTVEMVR

Date	Mintage	VG	F	VF	XF	Unc
1762	—	500	1,000	1,200	1,500	1,750
1763	—	500	1,000	1,200	1,500	1,750

KM# 118 1/2 GULDEN (10 Stuivers)

5.3000 g., 0.9200 Silver 0.1568 oz. ASW **Obv:** Crowned arms divide value "X - ST"

Date	Mintage	VG	F	VF	XF	Unc
1769	560	50.00	150	200	350	—
1770	740	50.00	150	200	350	—
1781	6,590	15.00	40.00	60.00	100	—
1782	Inc. above	15.00	40.00	60.00	100	—
1796	696	50.00	150	200	350	—

KM# 102 GULDEN

10.4000 g., 0.9200 Silver 0.3076 oz. ASW **Obv:** Crowned arms of Utrecht divide value **Obv. Legend:** MO : ARG : ORD : FOED : ... **Rev:** Standing figure leaning on column with cap on pole, date below **Rev. Legend:** HANCTVEMVR HAC NITIMVR

Date	Mintage	VG	F	VF	XF	Unc
1701/1698	—	20.00	100	200	400	600
1701/1699	—	20.00	50.00	100	200	300
1701/1700	—	20.00	50.00	100	200	300
1701	—	10.00	25.00	50.00	75.00	100
1703/02	—	20.00	50.00	100	200	300
1703	—	20.00	50.00	100	200	300
1704	—	20.00	50.00	100	200	300
1705	—	20.00	50.00	100	200	300
1706	—	20.00	50.00	75.00	100	150
1713	—	15.00	30.00	75.00	100	150
1714	—	15.00	30.00	75.00	100	150
1715	—	15.00	30.00	75.00	100	150
1716	—	15.00	30.00	75.00	100	150
1717	—	15.00	30.00	75.00	100	150
1718	—	15.00	30.00	75.00	100	150
1719	—	15.00	30.00	75.00	100	150
1720	—	15.00	30.00	75.00	100	150
1721	—	15.00	30.00	75.00	100	150
1723	—	15.00	30.00	75.00	100	150
1725	—	15.00	30.00	75.00	100	150
1727	—	15.00	30.00	75.00	100	150
1734	—	15.00	30.00	75.00	100	150
1735	—	15.00	30.00	75.00	100	150
1735/20	—	15.00	30.00	75.00	100	150
1736	—	15.00	30.00	75.00	100	150
1737	—	15.00	30.00	75.00	100	150
1738	—	15.00	30.00	75.00	100	150
1739	—	15.00	30.00	75.00	100	150
1740	—	15.00	30.00	75.00	100	150
1748	—	10.00	20.00	30.00	45.00	80.00
1749	—	10.00	20.00	30.00	45.00	80.00
1750	—	10.00	20.00	30.00	45.00	80.00
1760	11,000	10.00	20.00	30.00	45.00	80.00
1762	218,000	7.00	15.00	30.00	45.00	80.00
1763/62	—	15.00	30.00	75.00	100	150
1763	Inc. above	7.00	15.00	30.00	45.00	80.00
1764	1,044,999	7.00	15.00	30.00	45.00	80.00
1765	1,740	17.50	35.00	65.00	90.00	120
1775	—	20.00	40.00	75.00	100	130
1776	28,000	17.50	35.00	65.00	90.00	130
1780	Inc. above	17.50	35.00	65.00	90.00	130
1781	5,360	20.00	35.00	70.00	100	140
1782	Inc. above	20.00	35.00	70.00	100	140
1784	—	25.00	50.00	80.00	120	150
1785	—	10.00	20.00	30.00	45.00	80.00
1786	—	12.50	25.00	40.00	60.00	90.00
1787	2,425	20.00	35.00	65.00	90.00	130
1788	Inc. above	20.00	35.00	65.00	90.00	130
1789	—	10.00	20.00	30.00	45.00	80.00
1790	—	10.00	20.00	30.00	45.00	90.00
1791	238,000	7.00	15.00	25.00	35.00	75.00
1792	Inc. above	7.00	15.00	25.00	35.00	75.00
1793	130,000	7.00	15.00	25.00	35.00	75.00
1794/1	—	15.00	30.00	60.00	90.00	130
1794	844,000	7.00	15.00	25.00	35.00	75.00

KM# 102b GULDEN

17.4000 g., Gold

Date	Mintage	VG	F	VF	XF	Unc
1701 Rare	—	—	—	—	—	—

KM# 102a GULDEN

14.0000 g., Gold

Date	Mintage	VG	F	VF	XF	Unc
1715	—	—	—	—	—	—
1724 Rare	—	—	—	—	—	—
1729 Rare	—	—	—	—	—	—
1735 Rare	—	—	—	—	—	—
1739	—	—	—	750	1,000	—
1749	—	—	—	—	—	—
1750 Rare	—	—	—	—	—	—
1754 Rare	—	—	—	—	—	—
1758	—	—	—	—	—	—
1794 Rare	—	—	—	—	—	—

KM# 87 3 GULDEN (60 Stuiver)

Silver **Obv:** Crowned arms of Utrecht

Date	Mintage	VG	F	VF	XF	Unc
1714	—	50.00	100	200	300	600
1715	—	50.00	100	200	300	600
1716	—	50.00	100	200	300	600
1719	—	50.00	100	200	300	600
1721	—	50.00	100	200	300	600

KM# 117 3 GULDEN (60 Stuiver)

31.8200 g., 0.9200 Silver 0.9412 oz. ASW **Obv:** Crowned arms of Utrecht divides value **Obv. Legend:** MO : ARG : ORD : FOED : BELG • TRAI • **Rev:** Standing figure leaning on column with cap on pole, date below **Rev. Legend:** HACNITIMVR ...

Date	Mintage	VG	F	VF	XF	Unc
1763	225,000	20.00	35.00	70.00	140	200
1764	Inc. above	20.00	35.00	70.00	140	200
1785	234,000	20.00	35.00	70.00	140	200
1786	Inc. above	15.00	30.00	60.00	125	175
1791	62,000	20.00	35.00	70.00	140	200
1792/1	147,000	15.00	30.00	60.00	125	175
1792	Inc. above	15.00	30.00	60.00	110	160
1793	1,692,000	15.00	30.00	60.00	100	150
1794	1,713,000	15.00	30.00	60.00	110	160

KM# 103 7 GULDEN

4.9650 g., 0.9170 Gold 0.1464 oz. AGW **Obv:** Armored knight on horse above crowned shield **Rev:** Crowned arms of Utrecht divides value, date above **Rev. Legend:** CONCORDIA ...

Date	Mintage	VG	F	VF	XF	Unc
1749	—	125	200	425	750	900
1750/49	—	100	150	250	350	600
1750	—	100	150	250	350	600
1751	—	100	150	250	350	600
1760	347,000	100	150	250	350	600
1761	211,000	100	150	250	350	600
1762	Inc. above	100	150	250	350	600
1763	Inc. above	100	150	250	350	600

KM# 104 14 GULDEN

9.9300 g., 0.9170 Gold 0.2927 oz. AGW **Obv:** Armored knight on horse above crowned shield **Obv. Legend:** MO : AUR : PRO : CONFOED : BELG : TRAIECT • **Rev:** Crowned arms of Utrecht divides value, date above **Rev. Legend:** CONCORDIA RESPARVÆ CRESCUNT

Date	Mintage	VG	F	VF	XF	Unc
1749	—	200	525	700	1,000	1,200
1750	—	175	250	400	550	750
1751	—	175	250	350	550	750
1760	—	175	250	350	550	750
Note: Mintage included in KM#103						
1761	—	175	250	350	550	750
Note: Mintage included in KM#103						
1763	—	175	250	350	550	750
Note: Mintage included in KM#103						

KM# 115 1/2 DUCATON (1/2 Silver Rider)

16.3900 g., 0.9410 Silver 0.4958 oz. ASW **Obv:** Armored knight on horse above crowned shield **Obv. Legend:** MO : NO : ARG : CON : FOE : BELG : PRO : TRAI • **Rev:** Crowned arms of Utrecht, with supporters, date below **Rev. Legend:** CONCORDIA RES PARVÆ ...

Date	Mintage	VG	F	VF	XF	Unc
1761	—	40.00	80.00	120	180	275
1762	—	35.00	70.00	110	160	250
1763/2	—	50.00	100	175	250	400
1763	—	35.00	70.00	110	160	250
1764	—	35.00	70.00	110	160	250
1765	—	35.00	70.00	110	160	250
1766	—	35.00	70.00	110	160	250
1767	—	35.00	70.00	110	160	250
1768	—	35.00	70.00	110	160	250
1769	—	35.00	70.00	110	160	250
1770	—	40.00	80.00	120	180	275
1771	—	35.00	70.00	110	160	250
1772	—	35.00	70.00	110	160	250
1773	—	35.00	70.00	110	160	250
1774	—	40.00	80.00	120	180	275
1775	—	35.00	70.00	110	160	250
1776	—	35.00	70.00	110	160	250
1778	—	35.00	70.00	110	160	250
1779	—	35.00	70.00	110	160	250
1780	—	35.00	70.00	110	160	250
1781	—	35.00	70.00	110	160	250
1782	—	35.00	70.00	110	160	250
1783	—	30.00	60.00	100	150	240
1784 Mintage included KM92	—	30.00	60.00	100	150	240
1785	—	20.00	40.00	80.00	130	200
1786/5	—	40.00	80.00	110	175	300
1786	—	40.00	80.00	110	175	275
1787	—	30.00	60.00	100	150	240
1788	—	35.00	70.00	110	160	250
1789	—	35.00	70.00	110	160	250
1790	—	20.00	40.00	80.00	130	200
1791	—	20.00	40.00	80.00	130	200
1792	—	30.00	60.00	100	150	240
1793	—	35.00	70.00	110	160	250
1794/2	—	35.00	70.00	110	160	250
1794	—	35.00	70.00	110	160	250

KM# 115a 1/2 DUCATON (1/2 Silver Rider)

25.3000 g., Gold **Obv:** Armored Knight on horse above crowned shield **Obv. Legend:** MO: NO: ARC: CON: FOE: ... **Rev:** Crowned arms of Utrecht, with supporters, date below **Rev. Legend:** CONCORDIA RES PARVÆ ...

Date	Mintage	VG	F	VF	XF	Unc
1774 Rare	—	—	—	—	—	—
1794 Rare	—	—	—	—	—	—

KM# 83.1 DUCATON (60 Stuiver - Silver Rider)

32.7800 g., Silver **Obv:** Armored Knight on horse above crowned shield **Obv. Legend:** MO : NO : ARG : PROCON FOE : ... **Rev:** Crowned arms of Utrecht, with supporters **Rev. Legend:** CONCORDIA RESP .... **Edge:** Plain **Note:** Without mint mark. Varieties exist.

Date	Mintage	VG	F	VF	XF	Unc
1709	—	30.00	70.00	110	160	250
1710	—	30.00	70.00	110	160	250
1711	—	30.00	70.00	110	160	250
1712	—	30.00	70.00	110	160	250
1715	—	30.00	70.00	110	160	250
1718	—	30.00	70.00	110	160	250
1720	—	35.00	80.00	125	190	300
1727	—	35.00	80.00	125	190	300
1729	—	30.00	70.00	110	160	250
1730	—	25.00	60.00	100	150	240
1731	—	25.00	60.00	100	150	240
1735	—	25.00	60.00	100	150	240
1736	—	25.00	60.00	100	150	240

KM# 92a DUCATON (60 Stuiver - Silver Rider)

35.0000 g., Gold **Obv:** Armored Knight on horse above crowned shield **Rev:** Crowned arms of Utrecht, with supporters, date below

Date	Mintage	VG	F	VF	XF	Unc
1726 Rare	—	—	—	—	—	—
1745 Rare	—	—	—	—	—	—

KM# 83.2 DUCATON (60 Stuiver - Silver Rider)

Silver **Note:** Mint mark: Tree.

Date	Mintage	VG	F	VF	XF	Unc
1732	—	30.00	70.00	110	160	250
1733	—	30.00	70.00	110	160	250
1735	—	30.00	70.00	110	160	250
1736	—	30.00	70.00	110	160	250

KM# 92 DUCATON (60 Stuiver - Silver Rider)

32.7800 g., 0.9410 Silver 0.9917 oz. ASW **Obv:** Armored Knight on horse above crowned shield **Obv. Legend:** MO : NO : ARG : CON FOE : BELG : PRO : TRAI • **Rev:** Crowned arms of Utrecht with supporters, date below **Rev. Legend:** CONCORDIA RES PARVÆ CRESCUNT • **Edge:** Cabled

Date	Mintage	VG	F	VF	XF	Unc
1739	—	35.00	65.00	130	200	300
1740/30	—	70.00	125	250	400	500
1740/39	—	60.00	100	200	300	400
1740	—	35.00	65.00	130	200	300
1741	—	35.00	65.00	130	200	300
1742/1	—	50.00	75.00	150	225	325
1742	—	35.00	65.00	130	200	300
1743	—	35.00	65.00	130	225	325
1744	—	35.00	65.00	130	225	325
1745	—	35.00	65.00	130	225	325
1746	—	35.00	65.00	130	225	325
1747	—	35.00	65.00	130	200	275
1748/47	—	35.00	65.00	130	200	300
1748	—	35.00	65.00	130	200	275
1749	—	35.00	65.00	130	200	275
1750	—	35.00	65.00	130	200	275
1751	—	65.00	110	240	350	400
1752	—	30.00	65.00	130	200	250
1753	—	30.00	65.00	130	200	250
1754	—	30.00	65.00	130	200	250
1755/53	—	30.00	65.00	130	200	300
1755	—	30.00	65.00	130	200	250
1756/53	—	—	—	—	—	—
1756	—	30.00	65.00	130	200	250
1757/6	—	50.00	75.00	150	225	325
1757	—	30.00	65.00	130	200	250
1758	—	25.00	60.00	100	150	200
1759	—	25.00	55.00	90.00	140	190
1760	150,000	25.00	55.00	90.00	140	190
1761	Inc. above	30.00	65.00	130	200	250
1762/1	8,000	40.00	70.00	150	225	325
1762	Inc. above	30.00	65.00	110	170	220
1763	705	50.00	100	175	275	350
1764	—	30.00	65.00	110	170	220
1765/3	—	60.00	100	200	300	350
1765	1,620	30.00	65.00	110	170	220
1766	6,000	30.00	65.00	110	170	220
1767	Inc. above	30.00	65.00	110	170	220
1768	Inc. above	30.00	65.00	110	170	220
1769	42,000	30.00	65.00	110	170	220
1770	32,000	30.00	65.00	110	170	220

Date	Mintage	VG	F	VF	XF	Unc
1771	65,000	30.00	65.00	110	170	220
1772	Inc. above	30.00	65.00	110	170	220
1773	Inc. above	30.00	65.00	110	170	220
1774	Inc. above	30.00	65.00	110	170	220
1775	Inc. above	30.00	65.00	110	170	220
1776	Inc. above	30.00	65.00	110	170	220
1778	20,000	30.00	65.00	110	170	220
1779	Inc. above	30.00	65.00	110	170	220
1780	Inc. above	30.00	65.00	110	170	220
1781/80	—	30.00	65.00	110	170	220
1781	86,000	30.00	65.00	110	170	220
1782	Inc. above	30.00	65.00	110	170	220
1783	152,000	50.00	75.00	150	200	250
1784	Inc. above	30.00	65.00	110	170	220
1785	Inc. above	30.00	65.00	110	170	220
1786	270,000	30.00	65.00	110	170	220
1787	Inc. above	30.00	65.00	110	170	220
1788	55,000	30.00	65.00	110	170	220
1789	118,000	30.00	60.00	100	170	220
1790	Inc. above	30.00	65.00	110	170	220
1791	124,000	30.00	65.00	110	170	220
1792	1,060	30.00	65.00	110	170	220
1793	52,000	20.00	55.00	100	120	180
1794	Inc. above	30.00	65.00	110	170	220

KM# 111 DUCATON (60 Stuiver - Silver Rider)

0.9410 Silver **Obv. Legend:** DOMINE SALVUM FAC PRINCIPEM

Date	Mintage	VG	F	VF	XF	Unc
1751	—	50.00	150	250	350	500

KM# 116 1/2 SILVER DUCAT (24 Stuiver)

14.1200 g., 0.8730 Silver 0.3963 oz. ASW **Obv:** Standing armored Knight with crowned shield at feet **Obv. Legend:** MO : NO : ARG : PRO : CONFOE : BELG : TRAI • **Rev:** Crowned arms of Utrecht divides date **Rev. Legend:** CONCORDIA RES PARVÆ ... **Edge:** Cable

Date	Mintage	VG	F	VF	XF	Unc
1761	—	30.00	80.00	130	180	250
1762	—	30.00	80.00	130	180	250
1763	—	30.00	80.00	130	180	250
1764	—	30.00	80.00	130	180	250
1765	—	30.00	80.00	130	180	250
1766	—	30.00	80.00	130	180	250
1767	—	30.00	80.00	130	180	250
1768	—	30.00	80.00	130	180	250
1769	—	30.00	80.00	130	180	250
1770	—	30.00	80.00	130	180	250
1771	—	30.00	80.00	130	180	250
1773	—	30.00	80.00	130	180	250
1774	—	30.00	80.00	130	180	250
1775	—	30.00	80.00	130	180	250
1776	—	30.00	80.00	130	180	250
1781	—	30.00	80.00	130	180	250
1783	—	30.00	80.00	130	180	250

KM# 116a 1/2 SILVER DUCAT (24 Stuiver)

Silver **Obv. Legend:** MO NO ARG PRO CONFOE; BELG; TRAI **Edge:** Flowered

Date	Mintage	VG	F	VF	XF	Unc
1761	—	30.00	80.00	130	180	250
1762	—	30.00	80.00	130	180	250
1766	—	30.00	80.00	130	180	250

KM# 86 SILVER DUCAT (48 Stuiver)

Silver **Obv:** Standing armored knight with crowned shield at feet, date at sides **Rev:** Crowned arms of Utrecht **Note:** Mint mark: Rosette.

Date	Mintage	VG	F	VF	XF	Unc
1711	—	60.00	150	300	400	650
1715	—	60.00	150	300	400	650
1721	—	50.00	100	200	300	350
1725	—	60.00	150	300	400	650
1727	—	60.00	150	300	400	650
1735	—	60.00	150	300	400	650
1738	—	60.00	150	300	400	650

KM# 93a SILVER DUCAT (48 Stuiver)

34.8000 g., Gold **Obv:** Standing armored Knight with crowned shield at feet **Obv. Legend:** MO: NO: ARG: PRO: CONFOE: .... **Rev:** Crowned arms of Utrecht divide date **Rev. Legend:** CONCORDIA RES PARVÆ ...

Date	Mintage	VG	F	VF	XF	Unc
1739 Rare	—	—	—	—	—	20,000
1743	—	—	—	—	—	15,000
1749 Rare	—	—	—	—	—	—

KM# 93 SILVER DUCAT (48 Stuiver)

28.2500 g., 0.8730 Silver 0.7929 oz. ASW **Obv:** Standing armored Knight with crowned shield at feet **Obv. Legend:** MO : NO : ARG : PRO : CONFOE : BELG : TRAI • **Rev:** Crowned arms of Utrecht divides date **Rev. Legend:** CONCORDIA RES PARVÆ ... **Note:** Dav. #1845.

Date	Mintage	VG	F	VF	XF	Unc
1739	—	35.00	75.00	150	200	275
1740	—	—	—	—	—	—
1741	—	—	—	—	—	—
1743	—	—	—	—	—	—
1746	—	60.00	150	250	350	450
1747	—	35.00	75.00	125	180	250
1748	—	35.00	75.00	125	180	250
1749	—	35.00	75.00	125	180	250
1751	—	35.00	75.00	125	180	250
1752	—	35.00	75.00	125	180	250
1753	—	35.00	75.00	125	180	250
1755	—	35.00	75.00	125	180	250
1756	—	35.00	75.00	125	180	250
1757/0	—	50.00	130	200	300	400
1757/51	—	50.00	130	200	300	400
1757	—	35.00	75.00	125	180	250
1758	256,000	35.00	75.00	125	180	250
1760	Inc. above	35.00	75.00	125	180	250
1761	1,111,000	35.00	75.00	125	180	250
1762	Inc. above	35.00	75.00	125	180	250
1763	857,000	35.00	75.00	125	180	250
1764	107,000	35.00	75.00	125	180	250
1765	273,000	35.00	75.00	125	180	250
1766	272,000	35.00	75.00	125	180	250
1767	Inc. above	35.00	75.00	125	180	250
1768	—	60.00	150	250	350	450
1769	33,000	35.00	75.00	125	180	250
1770	385	90.00	190	275	400	500
1771	—	35.00	75.00	125	180	250
1772	1,196	35.00	75.00	125	180	250
1773	Inc. above	35.00	75.00	125	180	250
1774	Inc. above	30.00	60.00	100	180	250
1775	Inc. above	30.00	60.00	100	150	220
1776	—	30.00	60.00	100	150	220
1778	—	80.00	175	250	350	450
1779	356,000	30.00	60.00	100	150	220
1780	723,000	80.00	75.00	250	350	450
1781	Inc. above	25.00	55.00	90.00	130	200
1782	Inc. above	25.00	55.00	90.00	130	200
1783	1,425,000	25.00	55.00	90.00	130	200
1784	1,214,000	25.00	55.00	90.00	130	200
1785	Inc. above	30.00	60.00	100	150	220
1786	Inc. above	30.00	60.00	100	150	220
1787	546,000	30.00	60.00	100	150	220
1788	Inc. above	30.00	60.00	100	150	220
1789	1,156,000	30.00	60.00	100	150	220
1790	Inc. above	25.00	55.00	90.00	130	200
1791	Inc. above	25.00	55.00	90.00	130	200
1792	19,000	30.00	60.00	100	150	220
1793	182,000	25.00	55.00	90.00	130	200
1794	Inc. above	25.00	75.00	120	180	300

TRADE COINAGE

KM# 7 DUCAT

3.5000 g., 0.9860 Gold 0.1109 oz. AGW **Obv:** Standing, armored Knight holding bundle of arrows, divides date **Obv. Legend:** CONCORDIARES ... **Rev:** Inscription within ornamented square **Rev. Inscription:** MO/ORD/PROVIN/FOEDER/BELGAD/LEGIMP

Date	Mintage	VG	F	VF	XF	Unc
1701	—	80.00	150	300	400	500
1702	—	80.00	120	160	265	300
1703/2	—	80.00	150	300	400	500
1703	—	80.00	120	160	265	300
1704/3	—	80.00	150	300	400	500
1704	—	80.00	120	160	265	300
1705	—	80.00	120	160	265	300
1706	—	80.00	120	160	265	300
1707	—	80.00	120	160	265	300
1708/7	—	100	175	250	400	525
1708	—	100	175	250	400	525
1709	—	100	175	250	400	525
1710	—	100	175	250	400	525
1711	—	100	175	250	400	525
1712	—	100	175	250	400	525
1713	—	100	175	250	400	525
1714	—	100	175	250	400	525
1715	—	100	175	250	400	525
1716	—	100	175	250	400	525
1717	—	100	175	250	400	525
1718	—	80.00	120	160	265	300
1719	—	—	—	—	—	—
1720	—	80.00	150	225	375	500
1721	—	80.00	150	225	375	500
1722	—	80.00	150	225	375	500
1723/21	—	100	200	275	425	550
1723	—	80.00	150	225	375	500
1724	6,505	100	200	275	425	550

Note: All known 1724 ducats are from the wreck of the Akerandam, and are VF or better in condition

Date	Mintage	VG	F	VF	XF	Unc
1725	—	80.00	150	225	375	500
1726	—	80.00	150	225	375	500
1727	—	80.00	150	225	375	500
1728	—	80.00	150	225	375	500
1729	—	80.00	150	225	375	500
1730	—	100	200	275	425	550
1731	—	80.00	150	225	375	500
1732	—	80.00	120	200	350	475
1733	—	80.00	120	200	350	475
1735	—	80.00	120	200	350	475
1736	—	80.00	120	200	350	475
1739	—	80.00	120	200	350	450
1740	—	80.00	120	200	350	450
1741	—	80.00	120	160	265	300
1742	—	80.00	120	160	265	300
1743	—	80.00	150	225	375	450
1744	—	80.00	120	160	265	300
1745	—	80.00	120	160	265	300
1746	—	80.00	150	225	375	450
1747	—	80.00	120	160	265	300
1748/6	—	80.00	150	225	375	450
1748/7	—	80.00	150	225	375	450
1749	—	80.00	120	160	265	300
1750	—	80.00	120	160	265	300
1751	—	80.00	130	185	300	375
1752	—	80.00	100	140	225	275
1753/52	—	80.00	130	185	300	375
1753	—	80.00	100	140	225	275
1754	—	80.00	100	140	225	275
1755	—	80.00	100	140	225	275
1756	—	80.00	100	140	225	275
1757	—	80.00	100	140	225	275
1758	—	80.00	100	140	225	275
1759	—	80.00	100	140	225	275
1760	—	80.00	100	140	225	275
1761	—	80.00	100	140	225	275
1762	—	80.00	100	140	225	275
1763	—	80.00	100	140	225	275
1764	—	80.00	100	140	225	275
1765	—	80.00	130	185	300	400
1766	—	80.00	110	140	225	275
1767	—	80.00	150	225	375	450
1768	—	80.00	100	140	225	275
1769	—	80.00	100	140	225	275
1770	—	80.00	100	140	225	275
1772	—	80.00	100	140	225	275
1773	—	80.00	100	140	225	275
1774	—	80.00	100	140	225	275
1775	—	80.00	100	140	225	275
1776	—	80.00	100	140	225	275
1777	—	80.00	100	140	225	275
1778	—	80.00	100	140	225	275
1779	—	80.00	100	140	225	275
1780	—	80.00	100	140	225	275
1781	—	80.00	100	140	225	275
1782	—	80.00	100	140	225	275
1783	—	80.00	100	140	225	275
1784	—	80.00	100	140	225	275
1785	—	80.00	100	140	225	275
1786	—	80.00	100	140	225	275
1787	—	80.00	100	185	300	400
1788	—	80.00	100	140	225	275

Note: Has also been struck at the Stuttgarter Munzstatte in Germany, number unknown. Struck in 1812 as payment for soliders. Value unknown (just discovered)

Date	Mintage	VG	F	VF	XF	Unc
1789	—	80.00	100	140	225	275
1790	—	80.00	100	140	225	275
1791	—	80.00	100	140	225	275
1792	—	80.00	100	140	225	275
1793	—	80.00	100	140	225	275
1794	—	80.00	100	185	300	400

KM# 42 2 DUCAT

7.0000 g., 0.9860 Gold 0.2219 oz. AGW **Obv:** Standing, armored Knight holding bundle of arrows, divides date within broken circle **Obv. Legend:** CONCORDIA RES PAR• CRESTRA• **Rev:** Inscription within ornamented square **Rev. Inscription:** MO:ORD/PROVIN/FOEDER:/BELGAD/LEG.IMP

Date	Mintage	VG	F	VF	XF	Unc
1703	—	175	300	600	750	1,000
1704	—	175	300	600	750	1,000
1706	—	175	300	600	750	1,000
1709	—	275	575	850	1,050	1,250
1711	—	—	—	3,500	5,000	6,500
1718	—	275	575	850	1,050	1,250
1719	—	175	300	600	750	1,000
1720	—	175	300	600	750	1,000
1736/35	—	175	300	600	750	1,000
1739	—	175	300	600	750	1,000
1740	—	250	550	800	1,000	1,250
1741	—	175	300	600	750	1,000
1741/40	—	250	400	700	1,000	1,250
1742	—	175	300	600	750	1,000
1743	—	250	550	800	1,000	1,250
1744	—	175	300	600	750	1,000
1745	—	175	300	600	750	1,000
1746	—	175	300	600	750	1,000
1747	—	175	300	600	750	1,000
1748/46	—	—	—	—	—	1,000
1748	—	175	300	600	750	1,000
1749	—	175	300	600	750	1,000
1750	—	175	300	600	750	1,000
1751	—	175	300	600	750	1,000
1752	—	275	575	850	1,050	1,250
1754/44	—	175	300	600	750	1,000
1754	—	175	300	600	750	1,000
1755	—	175	300	600	750	1,000
1756	—	175	300	600	750	1,000
1757	—	175	300	600	750	1,000
1758	—	175	300	600	750	1,000
1759	—	175	300	600	750	1,000
1760	—	175	300	600	750	1,000
1761	—	175	300	600	750	1,000
1762	—	175	300	600	750	1,000
1763	—	175	300	600	750	1,000
1764	—	175	300	600	750	1,000
1765/63	—	—	—	—	—	1,000
1765	—	175	300	600	750	1,000
1767	—	—	—	—	—	1,000
1768	—	175	300	600	750	1,000
1769	—	175	300	600	750	1,000
1771	—	250	550	800	1,000	1,250
1774	—	250	550	800	1,000	1,250
1775	—	225	450	700	900	1,150
1776	—	250	550	800	1,000	1,250
1778	—	175	300	600	750	1,000
1779	—	175	300	600	750	1,000
1780	—	250	550	800	1,000	1,250
1781	—	250	550	800	1,000	1,250
1782	—	175	300	600	750	1,000
1783	—	175	300	600	750	1,000
1784	—	175	300	600	750	1,000
1785	—	175	300	600	750	1,000
1786	—	175	300	600	750	1,000
1787	—	175	300	600	750	1,000
1788	—	175	300	600	750	1,000
1789	—	175	300	600	750	1,000
1790	—	250	550	800	1,000	1,250
1791	—	175	300	600	750	1,000
1792	—	175	300	600	750	1,000
1793	—	175	300	600	750	1,000
1794	—	175	300	600	750	1,000

PATTERNS

Including off metal strikes

KM#	Date	Mintage	Identification	Mkt Val
Pn10	1724	—	1/2 Gulden. Gold. 6.90g	—
Pn11	1740	—	1/2 Gulden. Gold. 10.50g.	—

PIEFORTS

KM#	Date	Mintage	Identification	Mkt Val
P26	1701	—	Gulden. Gold. 17.6100 g.	4,000
P27	1712	—	Ducaton. Silver. KM83	—
P28	1715	—	Ducaton. Silver. KM83	—
P29	1716	—	Ducaton. Silver. KM83	1,500
P30	1720	—	Ducaton. Silver. KM83	—
P31	1723	—	Ducaton. Silver. KM83	—
P32	1727	—	Ducaton. Silver. KM83	—
P33	1730	—	Ducaton. Silver. KM83	1,250
P34	1731	—	Ducaton. Silver. KM83	1,250
P35	1732	—	Ducaton. Silver. KM83	—
P36	1733	—	Ducaton. Silver. KM83	—
P37	1735	—	Silver Ducat. KM86	—
P38	1735	—	Ducaton. Silver. KM83	1,500
P39	1736	—	Ducaton. Silver. KM83	1,500
P40	1744	—	Ducaton. Silver. KM92.	1,750
P41	1749	—	Gulden. Gold. 13.9400 g.	1,250
P42	1772	—	Ducaton. Silver.	4,000
P43	1773	—	Ducat. Gold. KM88.	—
P44	1775	—	Ducaton. Silver.	1,500
P45	1776	—	Ducat. Silver.	1,250

WEST FRIESLAND

West Frisia

West Friesland (West Frisia), also known as North Holland, is part of the province of Holland, and is not associated with the province of Friesland.

PROVINCE

STANDARD COINAGE

KM# 125b DUIT

3.5000 g., Gold **Obv:** Crowned arms of Friesland within sprigs **Rev:** Inscription and date within and divided by sprigs **Rev. Inscription:** WEST/ FRI/SIA/ date

Date	Mintage	VG	F	VF	XF	Unc
1702 Rare	—	—	—	—	—	—
1739	—	—	—	—	—	—
1741 Rare	—	—	—	—	—	—

KM# 100 DUIT

Copper **Obv:** Crowned arms, of Friesland, within sprigs **Rev:** Inscription above date **Rev. Inscription:** WEST/FRISIÆ **Note:** Varieties exist.

Date	Mintage	VG	F	VF	XF	Unc
1702	—	2.00	6.00	12.00	25.00	35.00
1707	—	4.00	10.00	20.00	35.00	50.00
1713	—	4.00	10.00	20.00	35.00	50.00
1713/11	—	4.00	10.00	20.00	35.00	50.00

KM# 100a DUIT

Silver **Obv:** Crowned arms, of Friesland, within sprigs **Rev:** Inscription above date **Rev. Inscription:** WEST/FRISIÆ **Note:** Weight varies: 3-4 grams.

Date	Mintage	VG	F	VF	XF	Unc
1702	—	30.00	70.00	120	160	200
1723	—	—	—	—	—	—
1739	—	30.00	70.00	120	160	200

KM# 105 DUIT

Silver **Rev:** Lions with arms of Leyden

Date	Mintage	VG	F	VF	XF	Unc
1711	—	10.00	25.00	50.00	100	—

KM# A100 DUIT

Copper **Obv:** Crowned arms of Friesland **Rev:** Inscription, date **Rev. Inscription:** WEST/ FRI/ SIAE/ **Note:** Varieties exist.

Date	Mintage	VG	F	VF	XF	Unc
1716	—	2.00	6.00	12.00	25.00	35.00
1717	—	1.50	4.00	10.00	20.00	30.00
1720	—	1.50	4.00	10.00	20.00	30.00
1722	—	3.00	8.00	18.00	30.00	40.00
1723	—	1.50	4.00	10.00	20.00	30.00
7723 Error	—	3.00	8.00	18.00	30.00	40.00
1727	—	3.00	8.00	18.00	30.00	30.00
1739	—	1.50	4.00	10.00	20.00	40.00

KM# 100b DUIT

3.0000 g., Silver **Obv:** Crowned arms, of Friesland, within sprigs **Rev:** Inscription above date **Rev. Inscription:** WEST/ FRISIÆ

Date	Mintage	VG	F	VF	XF	Unc
1716	—	—	—	—	—	—

KM# 125c DUIT

4.6000 g., Gold **Obv:** Crowned arms of Friesland within sprigs **Rev:** Inscription and date within and divided by sprigs **Rev. Inscription:** WEST/FRI/SIA/ date

Date	Mintage	VG	F	VF	XF	Unc
1739 Rare	—	—	—	—	—	—
1741	—	—	—	—	—	1,500

KM# 126 DUIT

Copper **Obv:** Crowned arms of Friesland within sprigs **Rev:** Inscription, date within and divided by sprigs **Rev. Inscription:** WEST/FRI/SIA/

Date	Mintage	VG	F	VF	XF	Unc
1741	—	10.00	30.00	65.00	120	200

Note: Mintage included in KM#125

KM# 126a DUIT

Silver **Obv:** Crowned arms of Friesland within sprigs **Rev:** Inscription, date within and divided by sprigs **Rev. Inscription:** WEST/FRI/SIA/

Date	Mintage	VG	F	VF	XF	Unc
1741 Rare	—	20.00	60.00	100	175	250

KM# 125 DUIT

Copper **Obv:** Crowned arms of Friesland within sprigs **Rev:** Inscription and date within and divided by sprigs **Rev. Inscription:** WEST/FRI/SIA/date

Date	Mintage	VG	F	VF	XF	Unc
1741	1,531,000	1.50	4.00	8.00	15.00	25.00
1742	Inc. above	1.50	4.00	8.00	15.00	25.00
1743	—	6.00	12.00	25.00	40.00	60.00
1754	—	1.50	4.00	8.00	15.00	25.00
1765	—	1.50	4.00	8.00	15.00	25.00
1780	—	3.50	10.00	18.00	25.00	—

KM# 125a DUIT

Silver **Obv:** Crowned arms of Friesland within sprigs **Rev:** Inscription and date within and divided by sprigs **Rev. Inscription:** WEST/FRI/SIA/ date

Date	Mintage	VG	F	VF	XF	Unc
1741 Rare	—	—	75.00	125	200	250
1756	—	—	75.00	125	200	250

KM# 126b DUIT

Gold **Obv:** Crowned arms of Friesland within sprigs **Rev:** Inscription, date within and divided by sprigs **Rev. Inscription:** WEST/FRI/SIA/

Date	Mintage	VG	F	VF	XF	Unc
1741	—	—	—	1,000	1,500	2,500

KM# A125 DUIT

Copper **Obv:** Crowned arms of Friesland **Rev:** Inscription, date **Rev. Inscription:** WEST/FRISI?/

Date	Mintage	VG	F	VF	XF	Unc
1765	—	1.50	4.00	8.00	15.00	25.00
1769	—	1.50	4.00	8.00	15.00	25.00

KM# 145a DUIT

Silver **Obv:** Crowned arms of Friesland within sprigs **Rev:** Inscription, date **Rev. Inscription:** WEST/FRISIÆ/

Date	Mintage	VG	F	VF	XF	Unc
1778 R	—	15.00	30.00	45.00	90.00	180
1793	—	—	—	—	—	—

KM# 145 DUIT

Copper **Obv:** Crowned arms of Friesland within sprigs **Rev:** Inscription, date **Rev. Inscription:** WEST/FRISIÆ/

Date	Mintage	VG	F	VF	XF	Unc
1780	—	3.00	10.00	20.00	30.00	40.00

KM# 109 STUIVER (Weapon)

Silver **Obv:** Crowned arms divide value **Rev:** Inscription, date **Rev. Inscription:** WEST/FRI/SIA/ **Note:** Varieties exist.

Date	Mintage	VG	F	VF	XF	Unc
1714	—	4.00	12.00	20.00	35.00	80.00
1724	—	4.00	12.00	20.00	35.00	80.00

KM# 109a STUIVER (Weapon)

1.7500 g., Gold **Obv:** Crowned arms divide value **Rev:** Inscription, date **Rev. Inscription:** WEST/FRI/SIA/

Date	Mintage	VG	F	VF	XF	Unc
1724	—	—	—	—	750	1,300
1729	—	75.00	150	225	325	450
1737	—	75.00	150	225	325	450

KM# 120 STUIVER (Broom)

0.8100 g., 0.5830 Silver 0.0152 oz. ASW **Obv:** Bundle of arrows divides 1 S within wreath **Rev:** Inscription, date **Rev. Inscription:** WEST/FRI/SIÆ/

Date	Mintage	VG	F	VF	XF	Unc
1738	1,957,625	2.00	8.00	15.00	30.00	50.00
1739	Inc. above	2.00	8.00	15.00	30.00	50.00
1760	Inc. above	2.00	8.00	15.00	30.00	50.00
1764	235,775	2.00	8.00	15.00	30.00	50.00
1765	Inc. above	2.00	8.00	15.00	30.00	50.00
1766	Inc. above	2.00	8.00	15.00	30.00	50.00

KM# 120a STUIVER (Broom)

1.7500 g., Gold **Obv:** Bundle of arrows divides 1 S within wreath **Rev:** Inscription, date **Rev. Inscription:** WEST/ FRI/ SIÆ/

Date	Mintage	VG	F	VF	XF	Unc
1738	—	50.00	100	150	200	450
1760	—	65.00	150	200	250	500
1779	—	65.00	150	200	250	500
1780	—	—	—	—	—	—
1780/75	—	90.00	175	250	300	550

KM# 101a 2 STUIVERS

3.5000 g., Gold **Obv:** Crowned arms of Friesland divides value **Rev:** Inscription, date **Rev. Inscription:** WEST/FRI/SIÆ/

Date	Mintage	VG	F	VF	XF	Unc
1702 Rare	—	—	—	—	—	—

KM# 101 2 STUIVERS

Silver **Obv:** Crowned arms of Friesland divide value **Rev:** Inscription, date **Rev. Inscription:** WEST/FRI/SIÆ/ **Note:** Similar to KM#106.1

Date	Mintage	VG	F	VF	XF	Unc
1702	—	3.00	8.00	12.00	18.00	30.00
1703	—	3.00	8.00	12.00	18.00	30.00
1704	—	3.00	8.00	12.00	18.00	30.00
1705	—	3.00	8.00	12.00	18.00	30.00
1706	—	3.00	8.00	12.00	18.00	30.00
1707	—	3.00	8.00	12.00	18.00	30.00
1708	—	3.00	8.00	12.00	18.00	30.00
1709/04	—	—	—	—	—	30.00
1709	—	3.00	8.00	12.00	18.00	30.00

KM# 106.1 2 STUIVERS (Double Wapenstuiver)

1.6200 g., 0.5830 Silver 0.0304 oz. ASW **Obv:** Crowned arms of Friesland divide value **Rev:** Inscription, date **Rev. Inscription:** WEST/FRI/SIÆ/ **Note:** Mint mark: Stork.

Date	Mintage	VG	F	VF	XF	Unc
1711	—	2.50	5.00	10.00	20.00	40.00
1712	—	1.00	3.00	5.00	8.00	15.00
1713	—	2.00	4.00	8.00	15.00	30.00
1714	—	2.00	4.00	8.00	15.00	30.00

KM# 106.2 2 STUIVERS (Double Wapenstuiver)

1.6200 g., 0.5830 Silver 0.0304 oz. ASW **Obv:** Crowned arms of Friesland **Rev:** Inscription, date **Rev. Inscription:** WEST/FRI/SIÆ/ **Note:** Mint mark: Turnip.

Date	Mintage	VG	F	VF	XF	Unc
1715	—	2.00	5.00	8.00	15.00	30.00
1716	—	1.00	2.50	4.00	7.50	15.00
1717	—	1.00	2.50	4.00	7.50	15.00
1718	—	1.00	2.50	4.00	7.50	15.00
1720	—	1.00	2.50	4.00	7.50	15.00
1721	—	2.00	5.00	8.00	15.00	30.00
1722/1	—	1.00	2.50	4.00	7.50	15.00
1722	—	1.00	2.50	4.00	7.50	15.00
1723	—	1.00	2.50	4.00	7.50	15.00
1724/3	—	1.00	2.50	4.00	7.50	15.00
1724	—	1.00	2.50	4.00	7.50	15.00
1725	—	1.00	2.50	4.00	7.50	15.00
1726	—	1.00	2.50	4.00	7.50	15.00
1727	—	1.00	2.50	4.00	7.50	15.00
1728	—	1.00	2.50	4.00	7.50	15.00
1729	—	1.00	2.50	4.00	7.50	15.00
1730	—	1.00	2.50	4.00	7.50	15.00
1731	—	1.00	2.50	4.00	7.50	15.00
1732	—	1.00	2.50	4.00	7.50	15.00
1733	—	2.00	5.00	8.00	15.00	25.00
1734	—	2.00	5.00	10.00	20.00	30.00
1736	—	1.00	2.00	4.00	7.50	15.00
1737	—	1.00	2.00	4.00	7.50	15.00
1738/37	—	—	—	—	—	15.00
1738	—	1.00	2.00	4.00	7.50	15.00
1739	—	1.00	2.00	4.00	7.50	15.00
1744	—	1.00	2.00	4.00	7.50	15.00
1745	—	1.00	2.00	4.00	7.50	15.00
1747	—	1.00	2.00	4.00	7.50	15.00
1748	—	1.00	2.00	4.00	7.50	15.00
1749	—	1.00	2.00	4.00	7.50	15.00
1750	—	1.00	2.00	4.00	7.50	15.00
1751	—	1.00	2.00	4.00	7.50	15.00
1752	—	1.00	2.00	4.00	7.50	15.00
1754	—	1.00	2.00	4.00	7.50	15.00
1755/54	—	—	—	—	—	15.00
1755	—	1.00	2.00	4.00	7.50	15.00
1757/5	—	1.00	2.00	4.00	7.50	15.00
1757	—	1.00	2.00	4.00	7.50	15.00
1758/57	—	—	—	—	—	15.00
1758	—	1.00	2.00	4.00	7.50	15.00
1759/8	—	1.00	2.00	4.00	7.50	15.00
1759	—	1.00	2.00	4.00	7.50	15.00
1760	—	1.00	2.00	4.00	7.50	15.00
1761	—	1.00	2.00	4.00	7.50	15.00
1762	—	1.00	2.00	4.00	7.50	15.00
1765/4	—	1.00	2.00	4.00	7.50	15.00
1765	—	1.00	2.00	4.00	7.50	15.00
1766	—	1.00	2.00	4.00	7.50	15.00
1767/6	—	1.00	2.00	4.00	7.50	15.00
1767	—	1.00	2.00	4.00	7.50	15.00
1768	—	1.00	2.00	4.00	7.50	15.00
1769/8	—	1.00	2.00	4.00	7.50	15.00
1769	—	1.00	2.00	4.00	7.50	15.00
1770/68	—	1.00	2.00	4.00	7.50	15.00
1770	—	1.00	2.00	4.00	7.50	15.00
1771/70	—	—	—	—	—	15.00
1771	—	1.00	2.00	4.00	7.50	15.00
1772	662,000	1.00	2.00	4.00	7.50	15.00
1773	Inc. above	1.00	2.00	4.00	7.50	15.00
1774	1,310,000	1.00	2.00	4.00	7.50	15.00
1775/4	Inc. above	1.00	2.00	4.00	7.50	15.00
1775	Inc. above	1.00	2.00	4.00	7.50	15.00
1776/3	—	—	—	—	—	15.00
1776/5	Inc. above	1.00	2.00	4.00	7.50	15.00
1776	Inc. above	1.00	2.00	4.00	7.50	15.00
1777	Inc. above	1.00	2.00	4.00	7.50	15.00
1778/7	Inc. above	1.00	2.00	4.00	7.50	15.00
1778	Inc. above	1.00	2.00	4.00	7.50	15.00
1779	Inc. above	1.00	2.00	4.00	7.50	15.00
1784/73	—	1.00	2.00	4.00	7.50	15.00
1784/0 R	—	1.00	2.00	4.00	7.50	15.00
1784 R	—	1.00	2.00	4.00	7.50	15.00
1785 R	—	1.00	2.00	4.00	7.50	15.00
1786/5 R	—	1.00	2.00	4.00	7.50	15.00
1786 R	—	1.00	2.00	4.00	7.50	15.00
1787/6	—	2.00	4.00	8.00	15.00	30.00
1787 R	—	1.00	2.00	4.00	7.50	15.00
1788/7 R	—	2.00	4.00	8.00	15.00	30.00
1788 R	—	1.00	2.00	4.00	7.50	15.00
1789 R	—	1.00	2.00	4.00	7.50	15.00
1790/80 R	—	1.00	2.00	4.00	7.50	15.00
1790 R	—	1.00	2.00	4.00	7.50	15.00
1791/0 R	—	1.00	2.00	4.00	7.50	15.00
1791/3 R	—	1.00	2.00	4.00	7.50	15.00
1791 R	—	1.00	2.00	4.00	7.50	15.00
1792 R	—	1.00	2.00	4.00	7.50	15.00
1794/91	—	—	—	—	—	15.00
1794 R	—	1.00	2.00	4.00	7.50	15.00

KM# 106.2a 2 STUIVERS (Double Wapenstuiver)

3.5000 g., Gold **Obv. Inscription:** WEST/FRI/SIÆ/ date **Rev:** Crowned arms of Friesland

Date	Mintage	VG	F	VF	XF	Unc
1724	—	—	—	—	—	—
1737	—	—	—	—	—	—

KM# 102.1a 6 STUIVERS (Scheepjesschelling)

7.0000 g., Gold **Obv:** Crowned arms of Friesland divide value, date above **Rev:** Sailing ship

Date	Mintage	VG	F	VF	XF	Unc
1702	—	175	350	700	900	—
1705	—	175	350	700	900	—

KM# 110 6 STUIVERS (Scheepjesschelling)

8.5800 g., 0.5830 Silver 0.1608 oz. ASW **Obv:** Crownd arms of Friesland divide value **Obv. Legend:** MO : NO : ORDIN : WEST : FRISIÆ : 1716 **Rev:** Sailing ship **Rev. Legend:** DEVS : FORTITVDO : ET : SPES : NOSTRA **Note:** Klippe.

Date	Mintage	VG	F	VF	XF	Unc
1705	—	—	—	—	—	—
1716	—	125	225	300	400	800

KM# 102.1 6 STUIVERS (Scheepjesschelling)

Silver **Obv:** Crowned arms of Friesland divide value, date above **Obv. Legend:** MO : NO : ORD : HOLL • ET • WESTFRI : 1729 **Rev:** Sailing ship **Rev. Legend:** VIGILATE DEO CONFIDENTES • **Note:** Mint mark: Cinquefoil.

Date	Mintage	VG	F	VF	XF	Unc
1705	—	6.50	17.50	30.00	60.00	80.00
1706	—	6.50	17.50	30.00	60.00	80.00
1708	—	6.50	17.50	30.00	60.00	80.00
1709	—	6.50	17.50	30.00	60.00	80.00

KM# 102.2 6 STUIVERS (Scheepjesschelling)

4.9500 g., 0.5830 Silver 0.0928 oz. ASW **Obv:** Crowned arms of Friesland divide value **Rev:** Sailing ship **Note:** Mint mark: Turnip.

Date	Mintage	VG	F	VF	XF	Unc
1715	—	5.50	15.00	25.00	60.00	80.00
1716	—	5.50	15.00	25.00	60.00	80.00
1717	—	8.00	20.00	40.00	80.00	110
1718	—	8.00	20.00	40.00	80.00	110
1719	—	8.00	30.00	60.00	100	140
1721	—	5.50	15.00	25.00	60.00	80.00
1724/3	—	7.50	20.00	30.00	70.00	90.00
1724	—	5.50	15.00	25.00	60.00	80.00
1725	—	7.50	20.00	30.00	60.00	80.00
1728/9	—	7.50	25.00	35.00	60.00	80.00
1728	—	7.50	20.00	30.00	70.00	90.00
1729	—	5.50	15.00	25.00	60.00	80.00
1730	—	5.50	15.00	25.00	60.00	80.00
1732	—	5.50	15.00	25.00	60.00	80.00
1733	—	5.50	15.00	25.00	60.00	80.00
1734	—	5.50	15.00	25.00	60.00	80.00
1736	—	5.50	15.00	25.00	60.00	80.00
1738	—	5.50	15.00	25.00	60.00	80.00

KM# 102.2a 6 STUIVERS (Scheepjesschelling)

7.0000 g., Gold **Obv:** Crowned arms of Friesland divide value **Rev:** Sailing ship

Date	Mintage	VG	F	VF	XF	Unc
1726	—	175	300	600	800	1,100
1728	—	175	300	600	800	1,100
1729	—	175	300	600	800	1,100
1749	—	—	—	—	—	—
1756	—	175	300	600	800	1,100

KM# 102.3 6 STUIVERS (Scheepjesschelling)

4.9500 g., 0.5830 Silver 0.0928 oz. ASW **Obv:** Crowned arms of Friesland **Rev:** Sailing ship **Note:** Mint mark: Rooster.

Date	Mintage	VG	F	VF	XF	Unc
1744	—	6.50	17.50	30.00	70.00	90.00
1747	—	7.50	20.00	35.00	80.00	100
1748	—	7.50	20.00	35.00	80.00	100
1750/48	—	—	—	—	—	—
1750	—	7.50	20.00	35.00	80.00	100
1751	—	5.50	15.00	25.00	55.00	75.00
1752	—	8.00	20.00	40.00	90.00	110
1754/1	—	—	—	—	—	—
1754/2	—	6.00	15.00	25.00	65.00	85.00
1754	—	5.50	15.00	25.00	60.00	80.00
1755/4	—	7.50	15.00	22.50	55.00	75.00
1755	—	7.50	15.00	22.50	55.00	75.00
1757/6	—	7.50	15.00	22.50	60.00	80.00
1757	—	7.50	12.50	22.50	55.00	75.00
1758/7	—	7.50	12.50	22.50	55.00	75.00
1758	—	7.50	12.50	22.50	55.00	75.00
1759/8	—	7.50	12.50	22.50	55.00	75.00
1759	—	7.50	12.50	22.50	55.00	75.00
1760	547,000	7.50	12.50	22.50	55.00	75.00
1761	Inc. above	7.50	12.50	22.50	55.00	75.00

KM# 102.4 6 STUIVERS (Scheepjesschelling)

4.9500 g., 0.5830 Silver 0.0928 oz. ASW **Obv:** Crowned arms of Friesland **Rev:** Sailing ship **Note:** Mint mark: Ship. Varieties exist.

Date	Mintage	VG	F	VF	XF	Unc
1762/0	100,000	7.50	12.50	22.50	55.00	75.00
1762	Inc. above	4.50	10.00	20.00	50.00	75.00
1765	Inc. above	4.50	10.00	20.00	50.00	75.00
1767/6	—	5.00	12.50	22.50	55.00	75.00
1767	—	4.50	10.00	20.00	50.00	75.00
1771	—	4.50	10.00	20.00	50.00	75.00

Note: Varieties exist.

KM# 150a 10 STUIVERS (1/2 Gulden)

6.8000 g., Gold **Obv:** Crowned arms of Friesland divide value **Rev:** Standing figure leaning on column with cap on pole **Rev. Legend:** HAC NITIMVR HANC TVEMVR

Date	Mintage	VG	F	VF	XF	Unc
1725	—	200	500	750	1,200	1,600
1727	—	200	500	750	1,200	1,600
1737	—	200	500	750	1,200	1,600

KM# 150 10 STUIVERS (1/2 Gulden)

5.3000 g., 0.9200 Silver 0.1568 oz. ASW **Obv:** Crowned arms of Friesland divide value, date at top **Rev:** Standing figure leaning on column with cap on pole **Rev. Legend:** HAC NITIMVR HANC TVEMVR

Date	Mintage	VG	F	VF	XF	Unc
1780	—	25.00	80.00	250	400	600
1785	—	25.00	80.00	200	300	400
1786	—	25.00	80.00	200	300	400

KM# 135 1/4 GULDEN (5 Stuiver)

2.6500 g., 0.9200 Silver 0.0784 oz. ASW **Obv:** Crowned arms of Friesland divide date **Rev:** Standing figure leaning on column with cap on pole **Rev. Legend:** HAC NITIMVR HANCTVEMVR **Note:** Mint mark: Rooster.

Date	Mintage	VG	F	VF	XF	Unc
1758	—	10.00	20.00	40.00	70.00	100
1759	—	12.50	40.00	70.00	100	120

KM# 135a 1/4 GULDEN (5 Stuiver)

5.2500 g., Gold **Obv:** Crowned arms of Friesland divide date **Rev:** Standing figure leaning on column with cap on pole **Rev. Legend:** HAC NITIMVR HANCTVEMVR

Date	Mintage	VG	F	VF	XF	Unc
1759	—	—	—	—	—	1,750

KM# 97.1 GULDEN

10.6100 g., 0.9200 Silver 0.3138 oz. ASW **Obv:** Crowned arms of Friesland divide value **Obv. Legend:** MO: ARG: ORD: FÆD: ... **Rev:** Standing figure leaning on column with cap on pole, date in exergue below **Rev. Legend:** HAC NITIMVR HANCTVEMVR **Note:** Mint mark: Cinquefoil. Similar to 3 Gulden, KM#141.

Date	Mintage	VG	F	VF	XF	Unc
1701	—	12.50	30.00	50.00	75.00	110
1702	—	15.00	40.00	60.00	90.00	140
1703	—	7.50	20.00	40.00	60.00	100
1704/3	—	12.50	30.00	50.00	75.00	110
1704	—	12.50	30.00	50.00	75.00	110
1705/4	—	12.50	30.00	50.00	75.00	110
1705	—	12.50	30.00	50.00	75.00	110
1706/3	—	12.50	30.00	50.00	75.00	110
1706	—	7.50	20.00	40.00	60.00	100
1707	—	7.50	20.00	40.00	60.00	100
1708	—	7.50	20.00	40.00	60.00	100

KM# 97.2 GULDEN

10.6100 g., 0.9200 Silver 0.3138 oz. ASW **Obv:** Crowned arms of Friesland divide value **Obv. Legend:** MO: ARG: ORD: FÆD: ... **Rev:** Standing figure leaning on column with cap on pole, date in exergue below **Rev. Legend:** HAC NITIMVR HANCTVEMVR **Note:** Mint mark: Stork.

Date	Mintage	VG	F	VF	XF	Unc
1713/12	—	7.50	20.00	40.00	60.00	100
1713	985,000	7.50	20.00	40.00	60.00	100
1714	Inc. above	7.50	20.00	40.00	60.00	100

KM# 97.3 GULDEN

10.6100 g., 0.9200 Silver 0.3138 oz. ASW **Obv:** Crowned arms of Friesland divide value **Obv. Legend:** MO: ARG: ORD: FÆD: ... **Rev:** Standing figure leaning on colums with cap on pole, date in exergue below **Rev. Legend:** HAC NITIMVR HANCTVEMVR **Note:** Mint mark: Turnip. Varieties exist.

Date	Mintage	VG	F	VF	XF	Unc
1715	668,000	7.00	15.00	27.50	40.00	80.00
1716	Inc. above	7.00	15.00	27.50	40.00	80.00
1717/6	Inc. above	7.50	20.00	40.00	60.00	100
1717	Inc. above	7.00	15.00	27.50	40.00	80.00
1718	Inc. above	7.00	15.00	27.50	40.00	80.00
1719	Inc. above	7.00	15.00	27.50	40.00	80.00
1721	—	7.00	15.00	27.50	40.00	80.00
1724	—	7.00	15.00	27.50	40.00	80.00
1726	—	7.00	15.00	27.50	40.00	80.00
1727/6	—	7.50	20.00	40.00	60.00	100
1727	—	7.00	15.00	27.50	40.00	80.00
1732	—	7.00	15.00	27.50	40.00	80.00
1734	—	7.00	15.00	27.50	40.00	80.00
1735	—	7.00	15.00	27.50	40.00	80.00
1736	—	7.00	15.00	27.50	40.00	80.00
1737	—	7.00	15.00	30.00	50.00	100
1738	—	7.00	15.00	25.00	40.00	80.00
1748	691,000	7.00	15.00	25.00	40.00	80.00
1749	Inc. above	7.00	15.00	25.00	40.00	80.00
1750	Inc. above	7.00	15.00	25.00	40.00	80.00
1760	—	7.00	15.00	25.00	40.00	80.00
1762	2,691,000	7.00	15.00	25.00	40.00	80.00
1763/2	Inc. above	14.00	27.50	50.00	75.00	125
1763	Inc. above	7.00	15.00	25.00	40.00	80.00
1764	Inc. above	7.00	15.00	25.00	40.00	80.00
1765	Inc. above	7.00	15.00	30.00	50.00	100
1767	—	20.00	50.00	90.00	140	170
1778/67	—	20.00	55.00	100	150	180
1785	—	7.00	15.00	25.00	40.00	80.00
1785/65	—	14.00	27.50	50.00	75.00	125
1785/69	—	14.00	27.50	50.00	75.00	125
1791/81	—	8.00	20.00	45.00	70.00	120
1791/85	—	8.00	20.00	40.00	60.00	100
1791/87	—	8.00	20.00	40.00	60.00	100
1791	—	7.00	15.00	25.00	40.00	80.00
1792/1	—	8.00	20.00	40.00	60.00	100
1792	—	7.00	15.00	25.00	40.00	80.00
1793	—	7.00	15.00	25.00	40.00	80.00
1794	—	7.00	15.00	25.00	40.00	80.00

KM# 139 GULDEN

10.6100 g., 0.9200 Silver 0.3138 oz. ASW **Obv:** VOC in cartouche below crowned arms of Friesland **Obv. Legend:** MO: ARG: ORD: FOE: ... **Rev:** Standing figure leaning on column with cap on pole, date below **Rev. Legend:** HAC NITIMVR HANC TVEMVR

Date	Mintage	VG	F	VF	XF	Unc
1786	—	—	—	—	—	—

KM# 95.2 3 GULDEN (60 Stuiver)

Silver **Obv:** Crowned arms of Friesland **Note:** Mint mark: Cinquefoil. Similar to KM#141.

Date	Mintage	VG	F	VF	XF	Unc
1701	—	50.00	125	200	300	400
1701	—	50.00	125	200	300	400
1703	—	30.00	60.00	100	250	350

KM# 95.3 3 GULDEN (60 Stuiver)

Silver **Obv:** Crowned arms of Friesland **Note:** Mint mark: Stork.

Date	Mintage	VG	F	VF	XF	Unc
1714	—	30.00	60.00	100	200	300

KM# 95.4 3 GULDEN (60 Stuiver)

Silver **Obv:** Crowned arms of Friesland **Note:** Mint mark: Turnip. Varieties exist.

Date	Mintage	VG	F	VF	XF	Unc
1721	—	30.00	60.00	100	200	300

KM# 141.1 3 GULDEN (60 Stuiver)

31.8200 g., 0.9200 Silver 0.9412 oz. ASW **Obv:** Crowned arms divide value **Obv. Legend:** ....BELG : WESTF : **Rev:** Standing figure leaning on column **Rev. Legend:** HAC NITIMVR ... **Note:** Mint mark: Ship.

Date	Mintage	VG	F	VF	XF	Unc
1763	587,000	15.00	40.00	75.00	110	200
1764	Inc. above	15.00	40.00	75.00	110	200
1767	—	50.00	125	200	300	400

KM# 141.2 3 GULDEN (60 Stuiver)

31.8200 g., 0.9200 Silver 0.9412 oz. ASW **Note:** Without mint mark.

Date	Mintage	VG	F	VF	XF	Unc
1776	—	50.00	125	200	300	375
1781	68,000	15.00	40.00	75.00	110	200
1785/1	7,545	30.00	125	200	300	375
1785	Inc. above	15.00	40.00	75.00	110	200
1786/63	—	15.00	40.00	75.00	110	200
1786/64	419,000	25.00	60.00	100	150	225
1786/84	Inc. above	25.00	60.00	100	150	225
1786	Inc. above	25.00	60.00	100	150	225
1791/86	5,554,000	40.00	100	150	200	275
1791	Inc. above	15.00	40.00	75.00	110	175
1792	Inc. above	15.00	40.00	75.00	110	175
1793/92	—	25.00	60.00	100	150	200
1793	Inc. above	15.00	40.00	75.00	110	175
1793/85	—	25.00	60.00	100	150	200
1794	Inc. above	15.00	40.00	75.00	110	175

KM# 129 7 GULDEN

4.9650 g., 0.9170 Gold 0.1464 oz. AGW **Obv:** Armored Knight on horse above crowned shield **Obv. Legend:** ...BELG : WESTF **Rev:** Crowned arms of Friesland divide value, date above **Rev. Legend:** CONCORDIA • RESPAEVÆ • CRESCUNT •

Date	Mintage	VG	F	VF	XF	Unc
1749 Rooster	—	200	400	800	1,200	1,400
1750	—	125	200	350	500	700
1751	—	125	200	350	500	700
1760	42,000	100	200	350	500	700
1761 Rooster	Inc. above	100	200	350	500	700
1761 Ship	Inc. above	125	200	350	500	700
1762	135,000	125	200	350	500	700
1763	Inc. above	100	200	350	500	700

KM# 130 14 GULDEN

9.9300 g., 0.9170 Gold 0.2927 oz. AGW **Obv:** Armored Knight on horse above crowned shield **Rev:** Crowned arms of Friesland divide value, date above **Rev. Legend:** CONCORDIA • RESP ...

Date	Mintage	VG	F	VF	XF	Unc
1749	—	250	500	800	1,400	1,600
1750	—	175	250	450	700	800
1751	—	175	250	450	700	800
1760/49	—	175	250	650	700	800
1760	—	175	250	400	600	700
Note: Mintage included KM#129						
1761 Rooster	—	175	250	400	600	700
Note: Mintage included KM#129						
1761 Ship	—	175	250	450	700	800

Date	Mintage	VG	F	VF	XF	Unc
1762/61	—	175	250	450	700	800
1762	—	175	250	450	700	800

Note: Mintage included KM#129

Date	Mintage	VG	F	VF	XF	Unc
1763/62	—	175	250	450	700	800
1763	—	175	250	450	700	800

Note: Mintage included KM#129

KM# 140.1 1/2 DUCATON (1/2 Silver Rider)

16.3900 g., 0.9410 Silver 0.4958 oz. ASW **Obv:** Armored Knight on horse above crowned shield **Obv. Legend:** ....BELG: PRO: WESTF: **Rev:** Crowned arms of Friesland, with supporters, date below in cartouche **Rev. Legend:** CONCORDIA RESPARVÆ ... **Note:** Mint mark: Ship.

Date	Mintage	VG	F	VF	XF	Unc
1762/1	—	50.00	100	200	300	400
1762	—	40.00	80.00	110	200	250
1764/3	—	40.00	80.00	110	200	250
1764	—	40.00	80.00	110	200	250
1765	—	40.00	80.00	110	200	250
1766	—	40.00	80.00	110	200	250
1767	—	40.00	80.00	110	200	250
1768/7	—	40.00	80.00	120	250	300
1768	—	40.00	80.00	110	200	250
1770	—	40.00	80.00	110	200	250
1771	—	40.00	80.00	110	200	250
1772	—	40.00	80.00	110	200	250
1773/1	—	40.00	80.00	110	200	250
1773	—	40.00	80.00	110	200	250
1774	—	40.00	80.00	110	200	250

KM# 140.2 1/2 DUCATON (1/2 Silver Rider)

16.3900 g., 0.9410 Silver 0.4958 oz. ASW **Obv:** Armored Knight on horse above crowned shield **Obv. Legend:** ....BELG: PRO: WESTF: **Rev:** Crowned arms of Friesland, with supporters, date in cartouche below **Rev. Legend:** CONCORDIA RESPARVÆ .... **Note:** Without mint mark.

Date	Mintage	VG	F	VF	XF	Unc
1775	—	35.00	70.00	110	180	230
1776	—	35.00	70.00	110	180	230
1776/5	—	35.00	70.00	110	180	230
1778	—	35.00	70.00	110	180	230
1779	—	35.00	70.00	110	180	230
1780	—	35.00	70.00	110	180	230
1781/76	—	40.00	80.00	110	200	250
1781	—	35.00	70.00	150	180	230
1782	—	35.00	70.00	110	180	250
1784	—	35.00	70.00	110	180	250
1785	—	35.00	70.00	110	180	250
1786 Mintage included KM127	—	35.00	70.00	110	180	250
1788/6	—	50.00	100	200	300	400
1788	—	35.00	80.00	110	180	250
1789	—	35.00	80.00	110	180	250
1790/66	—	40.00	80.00	110	200	250
1790/80	—	40.00	80.00	110	200	250
1790/89	—	40.00	80.00	110	200	250
1790	—	35.00	70.00	110	180	250
1791	—	35.00	70.00	110	180	250
1792	—	35.00	70.00	110	180	250
1794	—	40.00	80.00	110	200	250

KM# 107.1 DUCATON

Silver **Obv:** Armored Knight on horse above crowned shield **Rev:** Crowned arms of Friesland, with supporters, date in cartouche below **Note:** Similar to KM#127.1.

Date	Mintage	VG	F	VF	XF	Unc
1704	—	35.00	120	200	300	400
1707	—	35.00	120	200	300	400

KM# 107.2 DUCATON

Silver **Obv:** Armored Knight on horse above crowned shield **Rev:** Crowned arms of Friesland, with supporters, date in cartouche below **Note:** Mint mark: Stork. Similar to KM#127, but finer style

Date	Mintage	VG	F	VF	XF	Unc
1713	101,000	35.00	120	200	300	400
1714/13	Inc. above	35.00	120	200	300	400

KM# 107.3 DUCATON

Silver **Obv:** Armored Knight on horse above crowned shield **Rev:** Crowned arms of Friesland, with supporters, date in cartouche below **Note:** Mint mark: Turnip. Varieties exist.

Date	Mintage	VG	F	VF	XF	Unc
1716	176,000	35.00	120	200	300	400
1722/0	—	30.00	100	180	275	375
1727	—	25.00	85.00	125	200	300
1730	—	25.00	85.00	125	200	300
1731/0	—	25.00	85.00	125	200	300
1731	—	25.00	85.00	125	200	300
1732	—	25.00	85.00	125	200	300
1738	—	25.00	85.00	125	200	300

KM# 115 DUCATON

Silver **Obv:** Armored Knight on horse above crowned shield **Rev:** Date above crowned arms of Friesland

Date	Mintage	VG	F	VF	XF	Unc
1727	—	100	300	500	800	1,000

KM# 127 DUCATON (Silver Rider)

32.7800 g., 0.9410 Silver 0.9917 oz. ASW **Obv:** Armored Knight on horse above crowned shield **Obv. Legend:** ....BELG: PRO: WESTF: **Rev:** Crowned arms of Friesland, with supporters, date in cartouche below **Rev. Legend:** CONCORDIA RESPARVÆ ....

Date	Mintage	VG	F	VF	XF	Unc
1742	—	30.00	80.00	150	200	300
1743	—	30.00	100	180	250	350
1744	—	30.00	80.00	150	200	300
1745	—	30.00	80.00	150	200	300
1747	406,000	30.00	80.00	100	200	300
1749	Inc. above	30.00	80.00	100	200	300
1751	Inc. above	30.00	80.00	100	200	300
1752/1	—	30.00	80.00	100	200	300
1752	—	30.00	80.00	100	200	300
1755/4	—	40.00	100	180	250	350
1755	—	40.00	100	180	250	350
1756	—	40.00	100	180	250	350
1757	—	40.00	100	180	250	350
1758/7	—	40.00	100	180	250	350
1758	—	30.00	80.00	120	200	300
1759	—	30.00	80.00	120	200	300
1760	—	30.00	80.00	120	200	300
1761	—	30.00	80.00	120	200	300
1761 Rooster	—	40.00	100	180	250	350
1762/61	—	30.00	80.00	120	200	300
1762 Ship	232,000	30.00	80.00	120	200	300
1765/62	Inc. above	30.00	80.00	120	200	300
1765	Inc. above	30.00	80.00	120	200	300
1766	194,000	30.00	80.00	120	200	300
1767/6	Inc. above	30.00	80.00	120	200	300
1767	Inc. above	30.00	80.00	120	200	300
1768	Inc. above	30.00	80.00	120	200	300
1770	Inc. above	30.00	80.00	120	200	300
1771	449,000	30.00	80.00	120	200	300
1772	Inc. above	30.00	80.00	120	200	300
1773/70	—	30.00	80.00	120	200	300
1773/2	Inc. above	30.00	80.00	120	200	300
1773 Ship	Inc. above	30.00	80.00	120	200	300
1774 Ship	229,000	30.00	80.00	120	200	300
1774 without mint name	—	30.00	80.00	120	200	300
1775/4	—	30.00	80.00	120	200	300
1775	Inc. above	30.00	80.00	120	200	300
1778/77	—	40.00	100	180	250	350
1778/86	Inc. above	40.00	100	180	250	350
1778	Inc. above	30.00	80.00	120	200	300
1779	Inc. above	30.00	80.00	120	200	300
1780/76	Inc. above	30.00	80.00	120	200	300
1780/79 S/B	—	30.00	80.00	120	200	300
1780	Inc. above	30.00	80.00	120	200	300
1781	538,000	30.00	80.00	120	200	300
1782	Inc. above	30.00	80.00	120	200	300
1783	Inc. above	30.00	80.00	120	200	300
1784	Inc. above	30.00	80.00	120	200	300
1785	Inc. above	30.00	80.00	120	200	300
1786	Inc. above	30.00	80.00	120	200	300
1788	—	30.00	80.00	120	200	300
1788/6	—	30.00	80.00	120	200	300
1789/88	—	30.00	80.00	120	200	300
1789	275,000	30.00	80.00	120	200	300
1790/66	Inc. above	30.00	80.00	120	200	300
1790/80	Inc. above	30.00	80.00	120	200	300
1790/86	Inc. above	30.00	80.00	120	200	300
1790/89	Inc. above	30.00	80.00	120	200	300
1790	Inc. above	30.00	80.00	120	200	300
1791/81	Inc. above	30.00	80.00	120	200	300
1791/0	Inc. above	30.00	80.00	120	200	300
1791	Inc. above	30.00	80.00	120	200	300
1792/1	—	30.00	80.00	120	200	300
1792	—	30.00	80.00	120	200	300
1793/2	—	30.00	80.00	120	200	300
1793	—	30.00	80.00	120	200	300

KM# 144 1/2 SILVER DUCAT

Silver **Obv:** Standing, armored Knight with crowned shield at feet **Obv. Legend:** MO: NO: ARG: TRO: CONFOE: ... **Rev:** Crowned arms of Friesland divide date **Rev. Legend:** CONCORDIA RESPARVÆ .... **Note:** Mint mark: Cinquefoil. Similar to 1 Silver Ducat, KM#128.

Date	Mintage	VG	F	VF	XF	Unc
1770	—	200	500	1,100	1,500	1,800

KM# 85.4 SILVER DUCAT

Silver **Obv:** Standing, armored Knight with crowned shield at feet **Obv. Legend:** MO: NO: ARG: TRO: CONFOE: .... **Rev:** Crowned arms of Friesland divide date **Rev. Legend:** CONCORDIA RESPARVÆ ... **Note:** Mint mark: Cinquefoil. Similar to KM#128. Varieties exist.

Date	Mintage	VG	F	VF	XF	Unc
1707	—	30.00	75.00	125	160	250
1707	—	30.00	75.00	125	160	250
1708/7	—	30.00	75.00	125	160	250
1708	—	30.00	75.00	125	160	250

KM# 85.5 SILVER DUCAT

Silver **Obv:** Standing, armored Knight with crowned shield at feet **Obv. Legend:** MO: NO: ARG: TRO: CONFOE: ... **Rev:** Crowned arms of Friesland divide date **Rev. Legend:** CONCORDIA RESPARVÆ ... **Note:** Without mint mark.

Date	Mintage	VG	F	VF	XF	Unc
1744	—	60.00	175	275	350	450

KM# 128 SILVER DUCAT (Rijksdaalder)

28.2500 g., 0.8730 Silver 0.7929 oz. ASW **Obv:** Standing, armored Knight with crowned shield at feet **Obv. Legend:** MO: NO: ARG: PRO: CONFOE: BELG: WESTFRI: **Rev:** Crowned arms of Friesland divide date **Rev. Legend:** CONCORDIA RESPARVÆ ...

Date	Mintage	VG	F	VF	XF	Unc
1746	—	60.00	175	275	350	425
1747	—	40.00	100	200	300	375
1752	—	40.00	100	200	300	375
1754	—	40.00	100	200	300	375
1756	—	40.00	100	200	300	375
1757	—	40.00	100	200	300	375
1758	—	40.00	100	200	300	375
1759	—	40.00	100	200	300	375
1761	937,000	30.00	60.00	90.00	160	250
1762/1	Inc. above	40.00	100	200	300	375
1762	Inc. above	30.00	60.00	90.00	140	240
1763	Inc. above	30.00	60.00	90.00	140	240
1764	Inc. above	30.00	60.00	90.00	140	240
1765	Inc. above	30.00	60.00	90.00	140	240
1767	—	30.00	60.00	90.00	140	240
1770	308,000	30.00	60.00	90.00	140	240
1771/61	Inc. above	30.00	60.00	90.00	140	240
1771	Inc. above	30.00	60.00	90.00	140	240
1772/1	1,892,000	30.00	60.00	90.00	140	240
1772	Inc. above	30.00	60.00	90.00	140	240
1773	Inc. above	30.00	60.00	90.00	140	240
1774	Inc. above	30.00	60.00	90.00	140	240
1775	1,487,000	30.00	60.00	90.00	140	240
1776	Inc. above	30.00	60.00	90.00	140	240
1780	—	40.00	100	200	300	400
1781	1,488,000	25.00	50.00	75.00	130	230
1782	2,017,000	25.00	50.00	75.00	130	230
1783	—	40.00	100	200	300	375
1784/74	Inc. above	30.00	60.00	90.00	140	240
1784	Inc. above	25.00	50.00	75.00	130	230
1785/4	—	40.00	125	200	300	350
1785	—	40.00	100	200	300	350
1786	—	40.00	100	200	300	350
1787	1,010,000	40.00	100	200	300	350
1789/7	Inc. above	40.00	100	200	300	350
1789	Inc. above	25.00	50.00	75.00	130	230
1790	Inc. above	25.00	50.00	75.00	130	230
1791	Inc. above	25.00	50.00	75.00	130	230
1792	690,000	25.00	50.00	75.00	130	230
1793	Inc. above	25.00	50.00	75.00	130	230
1794	Inc. above	25.00	50.00	75.00	130	230

KM# 108 DAALDER (Lion)

Silver **Rev:** Date in legend at 11 o'clock **Note:** Mint mark: Stork.

Date	Mintage	VG	F	VF	XF	Unc
1701 Flower	—	25.00	60.00	120	250	500
1713 Stork	3,550	25.00	60.00	120	250	500

KM# 108a DAALDER (Lion)

Gold **Obv:** Knight standing behind shield **Rev:** Rampant lion

Date	Mintage	VG	F	VF	XF	Unc
1702 Rare	—	—	—	—	—	—

TRADE COINAGE

KM# 93 DUCAT

3.5000 g., 0.9860 Gold 0.1109 oz. AGW **Obv:** Standing armored Knight divides date **Obv. Legend:** CONCORDIA RES PAR • CRES .... **Rev:** Inscription within ornamented square **Rev. Inscription:** MO:ORD/PROVIN/FOEDER/BELGAD/LEG IMP

Date	Mintage	VG	F	VF	XF	Unc
1705	—	80.00	120	150	250	400
1712	258,000	80.00	120	150	250	400
1713	Inc. above	150	275	375	600	700
1714	—	150	275	375	600	700
1716	91,000	150	275	375	600	700
1717	Inc. above	150	275	375	600	700
1719	Inc. above	80.00	120	150	250	400
1720	—	80.00	120	150	250	400
1721	—	80.00	120	150	250	400
1722	—	80.00	120	150	250	400
1723	—	80.00	120	150	250	400
1724	—	80.00	120	150	250	400
1725	—	80.00	120	150	250	400
1726	—	80.00	120	150	250	400
1727	—	80.00	120	150	250	400
1728	—	80.00	120	150	250	400
1729	—	80.00	120	150	250	400
1730	—	150	260	375	600	700
1731/0	—	150	275	375	600	700
1731	—	80.00	120	150	250	400

Date	Mintage	VG	F	VF	XF	Unc
1732	—	80.00	120	150	250	400
1736	—	150	260	375	600	700
1737	—	80.00	120	150	250	400
1743	14,000	150	275	375	600	700
1748	101,000	80.00	120	150	250	400
1749 Turnip	—	80.00	120	150	250	400
1749 Rooster	Inc. above	150	275	375	600	700
1750	—	80.00	120	150	250	400
1751	—	80.00	120	150	250	400
1752	—	80.00	120	150	250	400
1753	—	80.00	120	150	250	400
1754	—	80.00	120	150	250	400
1755	—	80.00	120	150	250	400
1756	—	80.00	120	150	250	400
1757/56	—	150	275	375	600	700
1757	—	80.00	120	225	325	450
1758	—	80.00	120	150	250	400
1759	—	80.00	120	150	250	400
1760	—	80.00	120	150	250	400
1761 Rooster	—	80.00	120	150	250	400
1761 Ship	—	80.00	120	150	250	400
1762	—	125	225	350	500	600
1765	—	125	225	350	500	600
1776/74	—	80.00	120	150	250	400
1776	322,000	80.00	120	150	250	400
1777	Inc. above	80.00	120	150	250	400
1778/77	—	80.00	150	200	300	450
1778	Inc. above	80.00	120	150	250	400
1780/78	—	80.00	150	200	300	450
1780	Inc. above	80.00	120	150	250	400

KM# 53 2 DUCAT

7.0000 g., 0.9860 Gold 0.2219 oz. AGW **Obv:** Standing, armored Knight holding bundle of arrows, divides date within broken circle **Obv. Legend:** CONCORDIA RES PAR CRES • WF • **Rev:** Inscription within ornamented square **Rev. Inscription:** MO:ORD/PROVIN/FOEDER/BELG•AD/LEG•IMP

Date	Mintage	VG	F	VF	XF	Unc
1716	—	200	400	750	1,000	1,500
1725	—	200	400	750	1,000	1,500
1730	—	200	400	750	1,000	1,500
1730	—	200	400	750	1,000	1,500
1731	—	200	400	750	1,000	1,500
1734	—	200	400	750	1,000	1,500
1736	—	200	400	750	1,000	1,500
1752	—	175	325	600	800	1,200
1753	—	175	325	600	800	1,200
1761	—	175	325	600	800	1,200
1778	—	200	400	750	1,000	1,500
1779	—	175	325	600	800	1,200
1780	—	175	325	600	800	1,200

ZEELAND

Zelandia

Zeeland (Zelandia), the southernmost maritime province of the Netherlands, consists of a strip of the Flanders mainland and six islands.

MINT MARK

Castle

PROVINCE

STANDARD COINAGE

KM# A75 1/2 DUIT

1.7500 g., Gold **Obv:** Crowned arms of Zeeland **Obv. Legend:** LUCTOR • ET • EMERGO **Rev:** Inscription above date **Rev. Inscription:** ZEE/LAN/DIA **Note:** Struck during 1795-1806

Date	Mintage	VG	F	VF	XF	Unc
1753	—	—	—	700	1,500	2,500
1755	—	—	—	500	1,000	1,750

KM# 75 DUIT

Copper **Obv:** Crowned arms of Zeeland **Obv. Legend:** LUCTOR • ET • EMERGO **Rev:** Inscription above date **Rev. Inscription:** ZEE/LAN/DIA •

Date	Mintage	VG	F	VF	XF	Unc
1714	—	4.00	4.00	10.00	25.00	50.00
1717	—	4.00	10.00	20.00	35.00	70.00
1720	—	4.00	10.00	20.00	35.00	70.00
1721	—	4.00	10.00	20.00	35.00	70.00

KM# 75a DUIT

Silver **Obv:** Crowned arms of Zeeland **Obv. Legend:** LUCTOR • ET • EMERGO **Rev:** Inscription above date **Rev. Inscription:** ZEE/LAN/DIA

Date	Mintage	VG	F	VF	XF	Unc
1714	—	—	—	—	—	—

KM# 80 DUIT

Copper **Obv:** Crowned arms of Zeeland **Obv. Legend:** LUCTOR • ET • EMERGO **Rev:** Inscription **Rev. Inscription:** ZEE/LAN/DIA

Date	Mintage	VG	F	VF	XF	Unc
1724	—	50.00	200	400	600	800

KM# 81 DUIT

Copper **Obv:** Crowned arms of Zeeland **Obv. Legend:** LUCTOR • ET • EMERGO **Rev:** Inscription above date **Rev. Inscription:** ZEE/LAN/DIA • /• date

Date	Mintage	VG	F	VF	XF	Unc
1724	—	1.50	4.00	9.00	15.00	25.00
1725	—	4.00	10.00	20.00	35.00	50.00
1727	—	1.50	4.00	9.00	15.00	25.00
1735	—	5.00	12.50	25.00	40.00	70.00
1736	—	1.50	4.00	9.00	15.00	25.00
1737	—	5.00	12.50	25.00	40.00	70.00
1740	—	1.50	4.00	9.00	15.00	25.00
1741	—	1.50	4.00	9.00	15.00	25.00
1747	—	1.50	4.00	9.00	15.00	25.00
1748/47	—	3.00	8.00	17.50	30.00	45.00
1748	—	1.50	4.00	9.00	15.00	25.00
1749	—	1.50	4.00	9.00	15.00	25.00
1752	—	4.00	10.00	25.00	35.00	50.00
1753	—	1.50	4.00	9.00	15.00	25.00
1754	—	4.00	8.00	15.00	25.00	40.00
1755	—	1.25	3.00	8.00	14.00	22.00
1756	—	1.25	3.00	8.00	14.00	22.00
1757	—	1.25	3.00	8.00	14.00	22.00
1758/57	—	4.00	10.00	20.00	35.00	50.00
1758	—	1.25	3.00	8.00	14.00	22.00
1759	—	5.00	12.50	25.00	40.00	70.00
1760	—	1.25	3.00	8.00	14.00	22.00
1761	—	1.25	3.00	8.00	14.00	22.00
1762	—	1.25	3.00	8.00	14.00	22.00
1763	—	1.25	3.00	8.00	14.00	22.00
1764	—	1.25	3.00	8.00	14.00	22.00
1765	—	1.25	3.00	8.00	14.00	22.00
1766	—	1.25	3.00	8.00	14.00	22.00

KM# 81a DUIT

Silver **Obv:** Crowned arms of Zeeland **Obv. Legend:** LUCTOR • ET • EMERGO **Rev:** Inscription above date **Rev. Inscription:** ZEE/LAN/DIA • **Note:** Weight varies: 3.6-5.0 grams.

Date	Mintage	VG	F	VF	XF	Unc
1725	—	20.00	40.00	70.00	100	150
1730	—	20.00	40.00	70.00	100	150
1739	—	20.00	40.00	70.00	100	150
1741	—	20.00	40.00	70.00	100	150
1753	—	20.00	40.00	70.00	100	150
1754	—	20.00	40.00	70.00	100	150
1755	—	20.00	40.00	70.00	100	150
1757	—	20.00	40.00	70.00	100	150
1758	—	20.00	40.00	70.00	100	150
1759	—	20.00	40.00	70.00	100	150
1761	—	20.00	40.00	70.00	100	150
1764	—	20.00	40.00	70.00	100	150
1765	—	20.00	40.00	70.00	100	150

KM# 81b DUIT

3.5000 g., Gold **Obv:** Crowned arms of Zeeland **Obv. Legend:** LUCTOR • ET • EMERGO **Rev:** Inscription above date **Rev. Inscription:** ZEE/LAN/DIA • /• date

Date	Mintage	VG	F	VF	XF	Unc
1725	—	—	—	300	500	800
1754	—	—	—	300	500	800
1755	—	—	—	300	500	800
1757	—	—	—	300	500	800

KM# 81c DUIT

4.5000 g., Gold **Obv:** Crowned arms of Zeeland **Obv. Legend:** LUCTOR • ET • EMERGO **Rev:** Inscription above date **Rev. Inscription:** ZEE/LAN/DIA •

Date	Mintage	VG	F	VF	XF	Unc
1725 Rare	—	—	—	—	—	—

KM# 91 DUIT

Copper **Obv:** Crowned arms of Zeeland **Obv. Legend:** LUCTOR ET EMENTOR **Rev:** Inscription above date **Rev. Inscription:** ZEE/LAN/DIA

Date	Mintage	VG	F	VF	XF	Unc
1754	—	2.00	6.00	12.00	20.00	30.00

KM# 101.1 DUIT

Copper **Obv:** Crowned arms of Zeeland **Obv. Legend:** LUCTOR • ET • EMERGO **Rev:** Inscription above date within cartouche **Rev. Inscription:** ZELAN/DIA

Date	Mintage	VG	F	VF	XF	Unc
1766	—	1.25	3.50	8.00	12.00	25.00
1767	—	1.25	3.50	8.00	12.00	25.00
1768	—	1.25	3.50	8.00	12.00	25.00
1769	—	1.25	3.50	8.00	12.00	25.00
1770	—	4.00	10.00	20.00	35.00	35.00
1772	—	4.00	10.00	20.00	35.00	70.00
1776	—	1.25	3.50	8.00	12.00	25.00
1777/76	—	4.00	10.00	20.00	35.00	70.00
1777	—	1.25	3.50	8.00	12.00	25.00
1778	—	1.25	3.50	8.00	12.00	25.00
1779	—	1.25	3.50	8.00	12.00	25.00
1780	—	1.25	3.50	8.00	12.00	25.00
1781	—	1.25	3.50	8.00	12.00	25.00
1782	—	1.25	3.50	6.00	10.00	20.00
1783	—	1.25	3.50	6.00	10.00	20.00
1784	—	1.25	3.50	6.00	10.00	20.00
1785	—	1.25	3.50	6.00	10.00	20.00
1786/5	—	4.00	10.00	20.00	35.00	70.00
1786	—	1.25	3.50	6.00	10.00	20.00
1787/6	—	4.00	10.00	20.00	35.00	70.00
1787	—	1.25	3.50	6.00	10.00	20.00
1788	—	1.25	3.50	6.00	10.00	20.00
1789	—	1.25	3.50	8.00	12.00	25.00
1790	—	1.25	3.50	6.00	10.00	20.00
1791	—	1.25	3.50	6.00	10.00	20.00
1792	—	1.25	3.50	6.00	10.00	20.00

KM# 101.1a DUIT

Silver **Obv:** Crowned arms of Zeeland **Obv. Legend:** LUCTOR • ET • EMERGO **Rev:** Inscription above date within cartouche **Rev. Inscription:** ZELAN/DIA **Note:** Weight varies: 3.9-4.2 grams.

Date	Mintage	VG	F	VF	XF	Unc
1768	—	30.00	50.00	100	150	250
1769	—	30.00	50.00	100	150	250
1770	—	30.00	50.00	100	150	250
1787/86	—	30.00	50.00	100	150	250
1788	—	30.00	50.00	100	150	250

KM# 105 DUIT

Copper **Obv:** Crowned arms of Zeeland **Obv. Legend:** LUCTOR • ET • EMERGO **Rev:** Inscription above date within wreath **Rev. Inscription:** ZEE/LAN/DIA

Date	Mintage	VG	F	VF	XF	Unc
1792	—	1.25	2.50	6.00	12.00	30.00
1793/2	—	3.00	8.00	18.00	30.00	50.00
1793	—	1.25	2.50	6.00	12.00	30.00
1794	—	1.25	2.50	6.00	12.00	30.00

KM# 28 STUIVER (Bezem)

Silver **Obv:** Bundle of arrows divide value within wreath **Rev:** Inscription above date **Rev. Inscription:** ZEE/LAN/DIA • **Note:** Varieties exist.

Date	Mintage	VG	F	VF	XF	Unc
1738	—	3.00	8.00	20.00	30.00	50.00
1739	—	3.00	8.00	20.00	30.00	50.00

KM# 28a STUIVER (Bezem)

1.7500 g., Gold **Obv:** Bundle of arrows divide value within wreath **Rev:** Inscription above date **Rev. Inscription:** ZEE/LAN/DIA •

Date	Mintage	VG	F	VF	XF	Unc
1739	—	—	—	250	350	—
1755	—	—	—	250	350	—

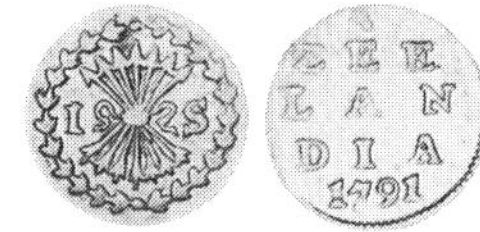

KM# 95 STUIVER (Bezem)

0.8600 g., 0.5830 Silver 0.0161 oz. ASW **Obv:** Bundle of arrows divide value within wreath **Rev:** Inscription above date **Rev. Inscription:** ZEE/LAN/DIA

Date	Mintage	VG	F	VF	XF	Unc
1760	56,000	4.00	10.00	22.50	30.00	—
Note: 0.9 gram examples known to exist						
1761/0	Inc. above	3.00	8.00	17.00	25.00	—
1761	Inc. above	3.00	8.00	17.00	25.00	—
1762	Inc. above	3.00	8.00	17.00	25.00	—
1763	Inc. above	3.00	8.00	17.00	25.00	—
1764	Inc. above	3.00	8.00	17.00	25.00	—
1765	—	3.00	8.00	17.00	25.00	—
1791	48,000	3.00	8.00	17.00	25.00	—

KM# 58 STUIVER (Weapon)

Billon **Obv:** Crowned arms of Zeeland **Rev:** Inscription above date **Rev. Inscription:** ZEE/LAN/DIA

Date	Mintage	VG	F	VF	XF	Unc
1727	—	6.00	15.00	40.00	85.00	110
1728/27	—	6.00	15.00	40.00	85.00	110
1728	—	6.00	15.00	40.00	80.00	100
1731	—	6.00	15.00	40.00	80.00	100
1733	—	6.00	15.00	40.00	80.00	100
1737	—	6.00	15.00	35.00	65.00	90.00

KM# 58a STUIVER (Weapon)

1.7000 g., Gold **Obv:** Crowned arms of Zeeland **Rev:** Inscription above date **Rev. Inscription:** ZEE/LAN/DIA

Date	Mintage	VG	F	VF	XF	Unc
1714	—	—	—	—	—	—

KM# 58b STUIVER (Weapon)

3.4000 g., Gold **Obv:** Crowned arms of Zeeland **Rev:** Inscription above date **Rev. Inscription:** ZEE/LAN/DIA

Date	Mintage	VG	F	VF	XF	Unc
1726	—	—	—	500	800	1,000

KM# 59 2 STUIVER

1.6200 g., 0.5830 Silver 0.0304 oz. ASW **Obv:** Crowned arms of Zeeland divide value **Rev:** Inscription above date **Rev. Inscription:** ZEE/LAN/DIA

Date	Mintage	VG	F	VF	XF	Unc
1701	—	2.00	6.00	10.00	17.50	40.00
1702	—	2.00	6.00	10.00	17.50	40.00
1703	—	2.00	6.00	10.00	17.50	40.00
1704	—	2.00	6.00	10.00	17.50	40.00
1706	—	2.00	6.00	10.00	17.50	40.00
1707	—	2.00	6.00	10.00	17.50	40.00
1708	—	2.00	6.00	10.00	17.50	40.00
1711/0	—	2.00	6.00	10.00	17.50	40.00
1711	—	2.00	6.00	10.00	17.50	40.00
1713	—	1.50	3.50	8.00	15.00	35.00
1714	—	1.50	3.50	8.00	15.00	35.00
1715	—	1.50	3.50	8.00	15.00	35.00
1716	—	1.50	3.50	8.00	15.00	35.00
1718	—	1.50	3.50	8.00	15.00	35.00
1719	—	1.50	3.50	8.00	15.00	35.00
1721	—	1.50	3.50	8.00	15.00	35.00
1722	—	1.50	3.50	8.00	15.00	35.00
1723	—	1.50	3.50	8.00	15.00	35.00
1724	—	1.50	3.50	8.00	15.00	35.00
1725	—	1.50	3.50	8.00	15.00	35.00
1726	—	1.50	3.50	8.00	15.00	35.00
1727	—	1.50	3.50	8.00	15.00	35.00
1728	—	1.50	3.50	8.00	15.00	35.00
1729	—	1.50	3.50	8.00	15.00	35.00
1730/29	—	1.50	3.50	8.00	15.00	35.00
1730	—	1.50	3.50	8.00	15.00	35.00
1731/20	—	1.50	3.50	8.00	15.00	35.00
1731	—	1.50	3.50	8.00	15.00	35.00
1732	—	1.50	3.50	8.00	15.00	35.00
1733	—	1.50	3.50	8.00	15.00	35.00
1734	—	1.50	3.50	8.00	15.00	35.00
1735/4	—	1.50	3.50	8.00	15.00	35.00
1735	—	1.50	3.50	8.00	15.00	35.00
1736/5	—	1.50	3.50	8.00	15.00	35.00
1736	—	1.50	3.50	8.00	15.00	35.00
1737/6	—	1.50	3.50	8.00	15.00	35.00
1737	—	1.50	3.50	8.00	15.00	35.00
1738/7	—	1.50	3.50	8.00	15.00	35.00
1738	—	1.50	3.50	8.00	15.00	35.00
1744	—	1.50	3.50	8.00	15.00	35.00
1745/36	—	1.25	2.50	5.00	8.00	30.00
1745/4	—	1.25	2.50	5.00	8.00	30.00
1745	—	1.25	2.50	5.00	8.00	30.00
1750/40	—	1.25	2.50	5.00	8.00	30.00
1750	—	1.25	2.50	5.00	8.00	30.00
1753	—	1.25	2.50	5.00	8.00	30.00
1754/3	—	1.25	2.50	5.00	8.00	—
1754	—	1.25	2.50	5.00	8.00	30.00
1758	—	1.25	2.50	5.00	8.00	30.00
1759	—	1.25	2.50	5.00	8.00	30.00
1765	80,000	1.25	2.50	5.00	8.00	30.00
1780	—	2.00	5.00	10.00	15.00	35.00

KM# 59a 2 STUIVER

3.4500 g., Gold **Obv:** Crowned arms of Zeeland divide value **Rev:** Inscription above date **Rev. Inscription:** ZEE/LAN/DIA

Date	Mintage	VG	F	VF	XF	Unc
1724 Rare	—	—	—	—	—	—
1729 Rare	—	—	—	—	—	—
1730	—	—	—	—	—	—
1745 Rare	—	—	—	—	—	—
1754 Rare	—	—	—	—	—	—

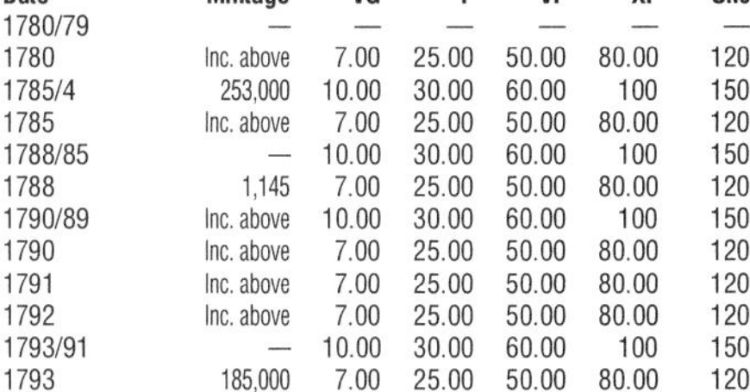

KM# 50 6 STUIVERS (Hoedjesschelling)

Silver **Obv:** Crowned arms of Zeeland divide date **Rev:** Reclining lion holding pole with cap

Date	Mintage	VG	F	VF	XF	Unc
1701	—	10.00	25.00	50.00	80.00	150
1703	—	10.00	25.00	50.00	80.00	150
1704	—	10.00	25.00	50.00	80.00	150
1705	—	10.00	25.00	50.00	80.00	150
1707	—	10.00	25.00	50.00	80.00	150
1713	—	10.00	25.00	50.00	80.00	150
1714	—	10.00	25.00	50.00	80.00	150
1715	—	10.00	25.00	50.00	80.00	150
1716/15	—	15.00	30.00	60.00	120	180
1716	—	10.00	25.00	50.00	80.00	150
1717	—	10.00	25.00	50.00	80.00	150
1720	—	10.00	25.00	50.00	80.00	150
1721	—	10.00	25.00	50.00	80.00	150
1722	—	10.00	25.00	50.00	80.00	150
1723	—	10.00	25.00	50.00	80.00	150
1724	—	10.00	25.00	50.00	80.00	150
1725	—	10.00	25.00	50.00	80.00	150
1726	—	10.00	25.00	50.00	80.00	150
1727	—	10.00	25.00	50.00	80.00	150
1728	—	10.00	25.00	50.00	80.00	150
1730/29	—	15.00	30.00	60.00	120	180
1730	—	10.00	25.00	50.00	80.00	150
1731	—	10.00	25.00	50.00	80.00	150
1733	—	10.00	25.00	50.00	80.00	150
1734	—	10.00	25.00	50.00	80.00	150
1735	—	10.00	25.00	50.00	80.00	150
1737	—	10.00	25.00	50.00	80.00	150
1738	—	10.00	25.00	50.00	80.00	150

KM# 50a 6 STUIVERS (Hoedjesschelling)

6.8000 g., Gold **Obv:** Crowned arms of Zeeland divide date **Rev:** Reclining lion holding pole with cap

Date	Mintage	VG	F	VF	XF	Unc
1718 Rare	—	—	—	—	—	—
1726 Rare	—	—	—	—	—	—
1745 Rare	—	—	—	—	—	—

KM# 90 6 STUIVERS (Scheepjesschelling)

4.9500 g., 0.5830 Silver 0.0928 oz. ASW **Obv:** Crowned arms of Zeeland divide value **Rev:** Sailing ship

Date	Mintage	VG	F	VF	XF	Unc
1750	—	7.00	25.00	50.00	80.00	120
1753	—	7.00	25.00	50.00	80.00	120
1754	—	7.00	25.00	50.00	80.00	120
1755	—	7.00	25.00	50.00	80.00	120
1757	—	7.00	25.00	50.00	80.00	120
1758	—	7.00	25.00	50.00	80.00	120
1759	—	7.00	25.00	50.00	80.00	120
1760	697,000	7.00	25.00	50.00	80.00	120
1761	Inc. above	7.00	25.00	50.00	80.00	120
1762	Inc. above	7.00	25.00	50.00	80.00	120
1763	Inc. above	7.00	25.00	50.00	80.00	120
1765	930,000	7.00	25.00	50.00	80.00	120
1766	Inc. above	7.00	25.00	50.00	80.00	120
1767	Inc. above	7.00	25.00	50.00	80.00	120
1768/7	Inc. above	10.00	30.00	60.00	100	150
1768 Castle	Inc. above	7.00	25.00	50.00	80.00	120
1768 Without castle	Inc. above	7.00	25.00	50.00	80.00	120
1769	Inc. above	7.00	25.00	50.00	80.00	120
1770	Inc. above	7.00	25.00	50.00	80.00	120
1771	Inc. above	7.00	25.00	50.00	80.00	120
1772	581,000	7.00	25.00	50.00	80.00	120
1773	Inc. above	7.00	25.00	50.00	80.00	120
1774	Inc. above	7.00	25.00	50.00	80.00	120
1775	Inc. above	7.00	25.00	50.00	80.00	120
1776	Inc. above	7.00	25.00	50.00	80.00	120
1777	455,000	25.00	70.00	120	175	—
1778/7	Inc. above	10.00	30.00	60.00	100	150
1778	Inc. above	7.00	25.00	50.00	80.00	120
1779	Inc. above	7.00	25.00	50.00	80.00	120
1780/70	Inc. above	10.00	30.00	60.00	100	150
1780/79	—	—	—	—	—	—
1780	Inc. above	7.00	25.00	50.00	80.00	120
1785/4	253,000	10.00	30.00	60.00	100	150
1785	Inc. above	7.00	25.00	50.00	80.00	120
1788/85	—	10.00	30.00	60.00	100	150
1788	1,145	7.00	25.00	50.00	80.00	120
1790/89	Inc. above	10.00	30.00	60.00	100	150
1790	Inc. above	7.00	25.00	50.00	80.00	120
1791	Inc. above	7.00	25.00	50.00	80.00	120
1792	Inc. above	7.00	25.00	50.00	80.00	120
1793/91	—	10.00	30.00	60.00	100	150
1793	185,000	7.00	25.00	50.00	80.00	120

KM# 90a 6 STUIVERS (Scheepjesschelling)

8.6500 g., Silver **Obv:** Crowned arms of Zeeland divide value **Rev:** Sailing ship

Date	Mintage	VG	F	VF	XF	Unc
1750	—	—	—	—	—	300
1753	—	50.00	70.00	120	175	300
1754	—	50.00	70.00	120	175	300
1758	—	50.00	70.00	120	175	300
1759	—	—	—	—	—	300
1761	—	50.00	70.00	120	175	300
1761/60	—	—	—	—	—	300

KM# 76 1/2 GULDEN

Silver **Obv:** Crowned arms of Zeeland divide value **Rev:** Standing figure leaning on column holding pole with cap

Date	Mintage	VG	F	VF	XF	Unc
1719	—	40.00	150	300	600	900

KM# 100 GULDEN

10.6100 g., 0.9200 Silver 0.3138 oz. ASW **Obv:** Crowned arms of Zeeland divide value **Rev:** Standing figure leaning on column with cap on pole, date in exergue below **Rev. Legend:** HACNITIMUR HANCTVEMUR

Date	Mintage	VG	F	VF	XF	Unc
1763	214,000	60.00	150	225	300	500
1764	Inc. above	70.00	175	300	475	650
1765	—	125	300	400	600	900

KM# 100a GULDEN

18.9000 g., Gold **Obv:** Crowned arms of Zeeland divide value **Rev:** Standing figure leaning on column with cap on pole, date in exergue below

Date	Mintage	VG	F	VF	XF	Unc
1765 Rare	—	—	—	—	—	—

KM# 96 7 GULDEN

4.9659 g., 0.9170 Gold 0.1464 oz. AGW **Obv:** Armored Knight on horse above crowned shield **Obv. Legend:** MO • AUR • PRO • CONFOED ... **Rev:** Crowned arms of Zeeland divide value, date above **Rev. Legend:** CONCORDIA RESPARVÆ CRESCUNT • 1761

Date	Mintage	VG	F	VF	XF	Unc
1760	272,000	100	175	250	350	600
1761	Inc. above	100	175	250	350	600
1762	Inc. above	150	200	400	500	750
1763	Inc. above	100	175	250	350	600
1764	Inc. above	100	175	250	350	600

KM# 97 14 GULDEN

9.9300 g., 0.9170 Gold 0.2927 oz. AGW **Obv:** Armored Knight on horse above crowned shield **Obv. Legend:** MO • AUR • PRO • CONFOED ... **Rev:** Crowned arms of Zeeland divide value, date above **Rev. Legend:** CONCORDIA RESPARVÆ CRESCUNT **Note:** Mintage included in KM #96.

Date	Mintage	VG	F	VF	XF	Unc
1760	—	150	200	450	650	800
1761/0	—	200	250	500	700	850

Date	Mintage	VG	F	VF	XF	Unc
1761	—	150	200	450	650	800
1762	—	150	200	450	650	800
1763/2	—	200	250	500	700	850
1763	—	150	200	450	650	800
1764	—	150	200	450	650	800

KM# 98 1/8 DAALDER (Rijks - 1/8 Silver Ducat)
3.5300 g., 0.8730 Silver 0.0991 oz. ASW **Obv:** Standing, armored Knight with crowned shield at feet **Obv. Legend:** MON • NO • ARG • PRO • CONFOE • BELG • COM • ZEL • **Rev:** Crowned arms of Zeeland within sprigs, date above **Rev. Legend:** CONCORDIA RESPARVÆ ....

Date	Mintage	VG	F	VF	XF	Unc
1762	—	14.00	35.00	65.00	100	150
1763/2	—	20.00	50.00	75.00	125	180
1763	—	14.00	35.00	55.00	85.00	120
1764	—	14.00	35.00	55.00	85.00	120
1765	—	14.00	35.00	55.00	85.00	120
1766	—	14.00	35.00	55.00	85.00	120
1767	—	14.00	35.00	55.00	85.00	120
1768/67	—	—	—	—	—	120
1768	—	14.00	35.00	55.00	85.00	120
1769	—	14.00	35.00	55.00	85.00	120
1770	—	14.00	35.00	55.00	85.00	120
1771	—	14.00	35.00	55.00	85.00	120
1772	—	14.00	35.00	55.00	85.00	120
1773	—	14.00	35.00	55.00	85.00	120
1774	—	20.00	50.00	75.00	125	180
1775	—	20.00	50.00	75.00	125	180
1776	—	14.00	35.00	55.00	85.00	120
1777	3,081,000	14.00	35.00	55.00	85.00	120
1778	1,605,000	14.00	35.00	55.00	85.00	120
1779/78	—	20.00	50.00	75.00	125	180
1779	Inc. above	20.00	50.00	75.00	125	180
1780/70	—	14.00	35.00	55.00	85.00	120
1780	Inc. above	14.00	35.00	55.00	85.00	120
1781/80	—	20.00	50.00	75.00	125	180
1781	1,433,000	14.00	35.00	55.00	85.00	120
1782	Inc. above	14.00	35.00	55.00	85.00	120
1784	Inc. above	14.00	35.00	55.00	85.00	120
1785/3	—	14.00	35.00	55.00	85.00	120
1785	Inc. above	12.00	30.00	50.00	75.00	110
1786	Inc. above	14.00	35.00	55.00	85.00	120
1787	97,000	14.00	35.00	55.00	85.00	120
1788/6	—	20.00	50.00	75.00	125	180
1788/7	—	20.00	50.00	75.00	125	180
1788	Inc. above	14.00	35.00	55.00	85.00	120
1790	1,290,000	8.00	20.00	35.00	60.00	100
1791	Inc. above	8.00	20.00	35.00	60.00	100
1792	Inc. above	14.00	35.00	55.00	85.00	120
1793	—	8.00	20.00	35.00	60.00	120

KM# 98a 1/8 DAALDER (Rijks - 1/8 Silver Ducat)
4.0000 g., Gold **Obv:** Standing, armored Knight with crowned shield at feet **Obv. Legend:** MON • NO • ARG • PRO • CONFOE • BELG • COM • ZEL • **Rev:** Crowned arms of Zeeland within sprigs, date above **Rev. Legend:** CONCORDIA RESPARVÆ CRESCUNT

Date	Mintage	VG	F	VF	XF	Unc
1773	—	200	400	700	1,000	1,500
1774	—	200	400	700	1,000	1,500
1775	—	200	400	700	1,000	1,500
1778	—	200	400	700	1,000	1,500
1779	—	200	400	700	1,000	1,500
1780	—	200	400	700	1,000	1,500
1782 Rare	—	—	—	—	—	1,500
1784	—	200	400	700	1,000	1,500
1787	—	200	400	700	1,000	1,500
1788	—	200	400	700	1,000	1,500
1790	—	200	400	700	1,000	1,500

KM# 99 1/4 DAALDER (Rijks - 1/4 Silver Ducat)
7.0600 g., 0.8730 Silver 0.1981 oz. ASW **Obv:** Standing, armored Knight with crowned shield at feet **Obv. Legend:** MON • NO • ARG • PRO • CONFOE • BELG • COM • ZEL • **Rev:** Crowned arms of Zeeland within sprigs, date above **Rev. Legend:** CONCORDIA RES PARVÆ CRESCUNT

Date	Mintage	VG	F	VF	XF	Unc
1762	—	25.00	60.00	100	200	—
1763	—	25.00	60.00	100	200	—
1764	—	20.00	40.00	80.00	120	—
1765/4	—	20.00	40.00	80.00	120	—
1765	—	20.00	60.00	100	200	—
1766/5	—	35.00	85.00	130	225	—
1766	—	20.00	50.00	90.00	150	—
1767	—	20.00	50.00	90.00	150	—
1768	—	20.00	50.00	90.00	150	—
1769	—	20.00	50.00	90.00	150	—
1770	—	20.00	50.00	90.00	150	—
1771	—	20.00	50.00	90.00	150	—
1772	—	20.00	50.00	90.00	150	—
1773	—	20.00	50.00	90.00	150	—
1774	—	20.00	50.00	90.00	150	—
1775	—	20.00	50.00	95.00	160	—
1776	—	20.00	50.00	95.00	160	—
1777 Mintage include KM98	—	20.00	50.00	90.00	150	—
1778 Mintage included KM98	—	20.00	50.00	90.00	150	—
1779/8 Mintage included KM98	—	20.00	60.00	100	200	—
1779	—	20.00	50.00	90.00	150	—
1780	—	20.00	50.00	90.00	150	—
1781 Mintage included KM98	—	20.00	50.00	90.00	150	—
1782	—	20.00	50.00	90.00	150	—
1785	—	20.00	50.00	90.00	150	—
1786	—	20.00	60.00	100	200	—
1787/6	—	20.00	60.00	100	200	—
1787 Mintage included KM98	—	20.00	60.00	100	200	—
1788/7	—	20.00	60.00	100	200	—
1788	—	20.00	60.00	100	200	—
1791 Mintage included KM98	—	20.00	50.00	90.00	150	—
1792	—	20.00	50.00	90.00	150	—
1793	—	20.00	50.00	90.00	150	—

KM# 99a 1/4 DAALDER (Rijks - 1/4 Silver Ducat)
8.3500 g., Gold **Obv:** Standing, armored Knight with crowned shield at feet **Obv. Legend:** MON • NO • ARG • PRO • CONFOE • BELG • COM • ZEL • **Rev:** Crowned arms of Zeeland within sprigs, date above **Rev. Legend:** CONCORDIA RES PARVÆ CRESCUNT

Date	Mintage	VG	F	VF	XF	Unc
1773	—	250	600	800	1,200	—
1775	—	250	600	800	1,200	—
1776	—	250	600	800	1,200	—
1778	—	250	600	800	1,200	—
1779	—	250	600	800	1,200	—
1780	—	250	600	800	1,200	—
1782	—	250	600	800	1,200	—
1787	—	250	600	800	1,200	—

KM# 51 1/2 SILVER DUCAT
14.1200 g., 0.8730 Silver 0.3963 oz. ASW **Obv:** Standing armored Knight with crowned shield at feet **Obv. Legend:** MON • NOV • ARG • PRO • CONFOED • BELG • COM • ZEL • **Rev:** Crowned arms of Zeeland divide date **Rev. Legend:** CONCORDIA RES PARVÆ CRESCUNT

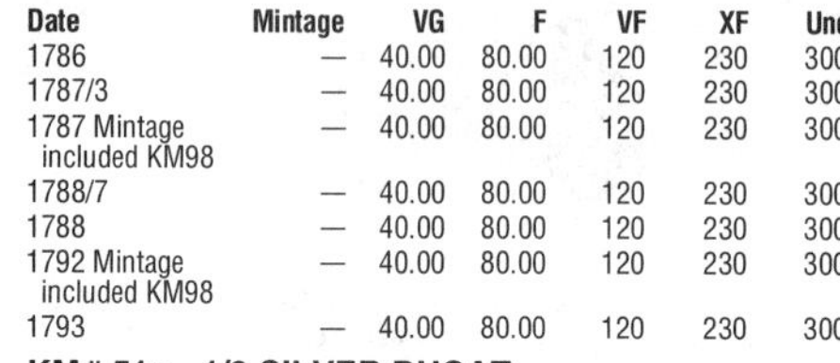

Date	Mintage	VG	F	VF	XF	Unc
1716	—	40.00	80.00	120	230	300
1719/6	—	40.00	90.00	150	280	350
1760	—	40.00	80.00	120	230	300
1761	—	40.00	80.00	120	230	300
1762	—	40.00	80.00	120	230	300
1763/2	—	40.00	80.00	120	230	300
1763	—	40.00	80.00	120	230	300
1764/63	—	40.00	80.00	120	230	300
1764	—	40.00	80.00	120	230	300
1765	—	40.00	80.00	120	230	300
1766	—	40.00	80.00	120	230	300
1767	—	40.00	80.00	120	230	300
1768	—	40.00	80.00	120	230	300
1769	—	40.00	80.00	120	230	300
1770	—	40.00	80.00	120	230	300
1771	—	40.00	80.00	120	230	300
1772	—	40.00	80.00	120	230	300
1773	—	40.00	80.00	120	230	300
1774	—	40.00	80.00	120	230	300
1775	—	40.00	80.00	120	230	300
1776/75	—	40.00	80.00	120	230	300
1776	—	40.00	80.00	120	230	300
1777 Mintage included KM98	—	40.00	80.00	120	230	300
1778 Mintage included KM98	—	40.00	80.00	120	230	300
1779	—	40.00	80.00	120	230	300
1780	—	40.00	80.00	120	230	300
1781/76	—	40.00	80.00	120	230	300
1781 Mintage included KM98	—	40.00	80.00	120	230	300
1782	—	40.00	80.00	120	230	300
1786	—	40.00	80.00	120	230	300
1787/3	—	40.00	80.00	120	230	300
1787 Mintage included KM98	—	40.00	80.00	120	230	300
1788/7	—	40.00	80.00	120	230	300
1788	—	40.00	80.00	120	230	300
1792 Mintage included KM98	—	40.00	80.00	120	230	300
1793	—	40.00	80.00	120	230	300

KM# 51a 1/2 SILVER DUCAT
16.8000 g., Gold **Obv:** Standing armored Knight with crowned shield at feet **Obv. Legend:** MON • NOV • ARG • PRO • CONFOED • BELG • COM • ZEL • **Rev:** Crowned arms of Zeeland divide date **Rev. Legend:** CONCORDIA RES PARVÆ CRESCUNT

Date	Mintage	VG	F	VF	XF	Unc
1773 Rare	—	—	—	—	—	—
1775 Rare	—	—	—	—	—	—

KM# 52.1 SILVER DUCAT
28.2500 g., 0.8730 Silver 0.7929 oz. ASW **Obv:** Standing armored Knight with crowned shield at feet **Obv. Legend:** MO • NO • ARG • PRO : CON • FOE • BELG • COM • ZEEL • **Rev:** Crowned arms of Zeeland divide date **Rev. Legend:** CONCORDIA • RES • PARVÆ • CRESCUNT **Note:** Dav. #4914.

Date	Mintage	VG	F	VF	XF	Unc
1701/693	—	30.00	70.00	125	200	260
1701/696	—	20.00	70.00	125	200	260
1701/698	—	30.00	70.00	125	200	260
1701	—	20.00	40.00	85.00	130	200
1703	—	20.00	60.00	110	175	230
1704	—	20.00	55.00	90.00	140	210
1705/4	—	20.00	55.00	90.00	140	210
1705	—	20.00	55.00	90.00	140	210
1706	—	20.00	55.00	90.00	140	210
1707/6	—	20.00	55.00	90.00	140	210
1707	—	20.00	55.00	90.00	140	210
1708	—	30.00	70.00	80.00	190	250
1907 (error for 1709)	—	—	—	—	—	—
1713/08	—	30.00	70.00	80.00	190	250
1713	—	20.00	50.00	80.00	120	180
1714	—	20.00	50.00	80.00	120	180
1715	—	20.00	50.00	80.00	120	180
1716/5	—	20.00	50.00	80.00	120	180
1716	—	20.00	50.00	80.00	120	180
1717/6	—	20.00	50.00	80.00	120	180
1717	—	20.00	50.00	80.00	120	180
1718/6	—	20.00	50.00	80.00	120	180
1718	—	20.00	50.00	80.00	120	180
1719/7	—	20.00	50.00	80.00	120	180
1719	—	20.00	50.00	80.00	120	180
1720/16	—	20.00	50.00	80.00	120	180
1720/19	—	30.00	70.00	125	225	300
1720	—	20.00	50.00	100	160	220
1721	—	20.00	50.00	80.00	120	180
1727	—	30.00	70.00	125	190	250
1735	—	20.00	50.00	80.00	120	180
1737	—	20.00	50.00	80.00	120	180
1738/7	—	20.00	50.00	80.00	120	180
1738	—	20.00	50.00	80.00	120	180
1747	—	20.00	50.00	80.00	120	180
1748	—	30.00	70.00	125	190	250
1750	—	20.00	50.00	100	160	225
1753	—	40.00	100	160	240	310
1757	—	30.00	75.00	135	200	260
1758	—	30.00	75.00	135	200	260
1759	—	40.00	90.00	145	220	285
1760	—	30.00	70.00	125	190	250
1761/0	—	30.00	75.00	135	200	260
1761	—	20.00	50.00	80.00	120	180
1762	—	20.00	50.00	80.00	120	180
1763	—	20.00	50.00	80.00	120	180
1764/63	—	20.00	60.00	100	150	210
1764	—	20.00	50.00	80.00	120	180
1765	—	20.00	50.00	80.00	120	180

Date	Mintage	VG	F	VF	XF	Unc
1766	—	20.00	50.00	80.00	120	180
1767	—	20.00	40.00	75.00	110	180
1768	—	30.00	50.00	80.00	120	180
1769	—	30.00	80.00	100	160	220
1770	—	20.00	60.00	70.00	110	170
1771/60	—	—	—	—	—	170
1771	—	20.00	60.00	70.00	110	170
1772	—	20.00	60.00	70.00	110	170
1773	—	20.00	60.00	70.00	110	170
1774	—	20.00	50.00	95.00	150	210
1775	—	20.00	50.00	95.00	150	210
1776	—	20.00	40.00	70.00	110	170
1777 Mintage included KM98	—	20.00	40.00	70.00	110	170
1778 Mintage included KM98	—	30.00	70.00	125	190	250
1779	—	20.00	40.00	70.00	110	170
1780	—	20.00	40.00	70.00	110	170
1781 Mintage included KM98	—	20.00	40.00	70.00	110	170
1782	—	20.00	40.00	70.00	110	170
1784/3	—	30.00	75.00	135	200	260
1784	—	20.00	40.00	70.00	110	170
1785	—	20.00	40.00	70.00	110	170
1786	—	20.00	40.00	70.00	110	170
1787 Mintage included KM98	—	20.00	40.00	70.00	110	170
1788	—	20.00	40.00	75.00	120	180
1789/8	—	30.00	70.00	125	190	250
1789	—	20.00	40.00	75.00	120	180
1790 Mintage included KM98	—	20.00	40.00	75.00	120	180
1791	—	20.00	45.00	85.00	130	200
1792	2,389,000	20.00	60.00	100	160	220
1793	Inc. above	20.00	60.00	100	160	220
1794/3	Inc. above	30.00	70.00	125	180	250
1794	Inc. above	20.00	60.00	110	175	250

KM# 52.2 SILVER DUCAT

56.5000 g., Silver **Obv:** Standing armored Knight with crowned shield at feet **Obv. Legend:** MO • NO • AR G • PRO • CON •....BELG • COM • ZEEL **Rev:** Crowned arms of Zeeland divide date **Edge:** Lettered **Edge Lettering:** LYCT(OR) ET.EMERGO.

Date	Mintage	VG	F	VF	XF	Unc
1747 Piefort	—	—	—	—	800	1,000
1748 Piefort	—	—	—	—	800	1,000
1757 Piefort	—	—	—	—	800	1,000
1762 Piefort	—	—	—	—	800	1,000
1777 Piefort	—	—	—	—	800	1,000

KM# 52.3 SILVER DUCAT

28.2500 g., Silver **Obv:** Standing armored Knight with crowned shield at feet within beaded circle **Obv. Legend:** MON • NO • ARG • PRO • CONFOE: BELG • COM • ZEL • **Rev:** Crowned arms of Zeeland divide date within beaded circle **Rev. Legend:** CONCORDIA RES PARVÆ CRESCUNT **Note:** Dav.#1848A.

Date	Mintage	VG	F	VF	XF	Unc
1757	—	60.00	200	400	600	800

KM# 52.1a SILVER DUCAT

36.6000 g., Gold **Obv:** Standing armored Knight with crowned shield at feet **Rev:** Crowned arms of Zeeland divide date **Note:** Thick planchet.

Date	Mintage	VG	F	VF	XF	Unc
1764 Rare	—	—	—	—	—	—
1777 Rare	—	—	—	—	—	—

KM# 52.1b SILVER DUCAT

22.7000 g., Gold **Obv:** Standing armored Knight with crowned shield at feet **Rev:** Crowned arms of Zeeland divide date **Note:** Thin planchet.

Date	Mintage	VG	F	VF	XF	Unc
1792 Rare	—	—	—	—	—	—

KM# 102 1/2 DUCATON (1/2 Silver Rider)

16.3900 g., 0.9410 Silver 0.4958 oz. ASW **Obv:** Knight on horseback with sword, crowned arms below **Obv. Legend:** ....BELG: COM: ZEL **Rev:** Crowned Zeeland arms with supporters

Date	Mintage	VG	F	VF	XF	Unc
1766	—	35.00	75.00	140	200	300
1767	—	35.00	80.00	150	225	325
1768/7	—	40.00	90.00	180	250	350
1768	—	35.00	80.00	150	225	325
1769/68	—	40.00	90.00	180	250	350
1769	—	35.00	80.00	150	225	325
1771	—	35.00	75.00	140	200	300
1772	—	35.00	80.00	150	225	325
1773	—	35.00	75.00	140	200	300
1775	—	35.00	75.00	140	200	300
1785	146,000	35.00	75.00	140	200	300
1790/66	339,000	35.00	90.00	180	250	350
1790/67	Inc. above	35.00	90.00	180	250	350
1790	Inc. above	30.00	75.00	140	200	300
1792/81	—	35.00	90.00	180	250	350
1792	339,000	30.00	75.00	140	200	300
1793	128,000	30.00	75.00	140	200	300

KM# A19 DUCATON

Silver

Date	Mintage	VG	F	VF	XF	Unc
1717 Piefort	—	—	—	—	—	—
1741 Piefort	—	—	—	1,000	1,650	1,800
1748 Piefort	—	—	—	—	1,500	1,650
1754 Piefort	—	—	—	—	1,650	1,800
1757 Piefort	—	—	—	—	—	—

KM# 57 DUCATON (Silver Rider)

32.7800 g., 0.9410 Silver 0.9917 oz. ASW **Obv:** Armored Knight on horse above crowned shield **Obv. Legend:** MON: NOV: ARG: PRO: CON FOED: BELG: COM: ZEL • **Rev:** Crowned arms of Zeeland with supporters, date in cartouche below **Rev. Legend:** CONCORDIA RES • PARVÆ • CRESCUNT •

Date	Mintage	VG	F	VF	XF	Unc
1716	—	40.00	115	225	325	425
1731	—	80.00	200	300	400	500
1735	—	35.00	110	180	250	375
1739	—	35.00	110	180	250	375
1741	—	80.00	200	300	600	500
1742	—	35.00	100	180	250	375
1744	—	35.00	100	180	250	375
1746	—	35.00	100	180	250	375
1749	—	35.00	100	180	250	375
1750	—	35.00	100	180	250	375
1751	—	35.00	100	180	250	375
1752	—	35.00	100	180	250	375
1753	—	35.00	100	180	250	375
1754/3	—	50.00	145	230	250	375
1754	—	35.00	100	180	250	375
1755	—	35.00	100	180	250	375
1756	—	35.00	100	180	250	325
1757	—	35.00	100	180	250	325
1758/7	—	40.00	110	200	300	375
1758	—	35.00	100	180	250	325
1759	—	30.00	70.00	140	200	250
1760/59	—	35.00	100	180	250	325
1760	—	30.00	70.00	140	200	250
1761/0	—	40.00	110	200	300	375
1761	—	35.00	90.00	155	220	260
1762	—	35.00	90.00	155	220	260
1763/2	—	40.00	110	200	300	275
1765/4	—	50.00	125	250	300	375
1766/5	—	50.00	125	250	300	375
1766	—	25.00	65.00	135	220	260
1767/6	—	40.00	110	200	300	375
1767	—	25.00	65.00	135	220	260
1768	—	25.00	65.00	135	220	260
1769	—	40.00	110	200	300	275
1771	—	40.00	110	200	300	275
1772	—	35.00	90.00	155	220	260
1773	—	25.00	60.00	120	200	250
1774	—	25.00	60.00	120	200	250
1775	—	25.00	60.00	120	200	250
1776	—	25.00	60.00	120	200	250
1785/75	—	35.00	90.00	155	220	260
1785 Mintage included KM102	—	25.00	60.00	120	200	250
1789	—	25.00	60.00	120	200	250
1790/89	—	35.00	90.00	155	220	260
1790	—	25.00	60.00	120	200	250
1791	—	20.00	50.00	110	175	225
1792/1	—	35.00	100	170	240	300
1792	—	20.00	50.00	110	175	225
1793	—	20.00	50.00	110	175	225

TRADE COINAGE

KM# 62 DUCAT

3.5000 g., 0.9860 Gold 0.1109 oz. AGW **Obv:** Knight standing to right divides date within inner circle **Rev:** Tablet on full-blown rose

Date	Mintage	VG	F	VF	XF	Unc
1701	—	80.00	120	175	300	400
1718	—	80.00	120	175	300	400

KM# 85 DUCAT

3.5000 g., 0.9860 Gold 0.1109 oz. AGW **Obv:** Without inner circle **Rev:** Legend in ornamental tablet

Date	Mintage	VG	F	VF	XF	Unc
1749	—	80.00	120	175	250	300
1753	—	80.00	120	175	250	300
1754	—	80.00	120	175	250	300
1755	—	80.00	120	175	250	300
1756	—	80.00	120	175	250	300
1757	—	80.00	120	175	250	300
1758	—	90.00	150	250	500	700
1758	—	80.00	120	175	250	300
1759	—	80.00	120	175	250	300
1760	109,000	80.00	120	175	250	300
1761	Inc. above	80.00	120	175	250	300
1762	Inc. above	80.00	120	175	250	300
1763	Inc. above	80.00	120	175	250	300

PATTERNS

Including off metal strikes

KM#	Date	Mintage	Identification	Mkt Val
Pn15	1764	—	Ducat. Gold. 36.6000 g. KM#52.1.	—
Pn16	1773	—	1/2 Silver Ducat. Gold. 16.8000 g. KM#51.	—
Pn17	1775	—	1/2 Silver Ducat. Gold. 16.8000 g. KM#51.	—
Pn18	1777	—	Silver Ducat. Gold. 36.6000 g. KM#52.1.	—
Pn19	1792	—	Silver Ducat. Gold. 22.7000 g. KM#52.1.	—

PIEFORTS

KM#	Date	Mintage	Identification	Mkt Val
P22	1753	—	6 Stuivers.	175
P23	1754	—	6 Stuivers.	175
P24	1759	—	6 Stuivers.	200

RULERS

United East India Company, 1602-1799
Batavian Republic, 1799-1806

MINT MARKS

H - Amsterdam (H)
Hk - Harderwijk (star, rosette, cock, cross, Z)
Hn - Hoorn (star)
E - Enkhuizen (star)
Dt - Dordrecht (rosette)
K - Kampen (eagle)
S - Utrecht
Sa - Soerabaja (Za)

MONETARY SYSTEM

120 Duits = 120 Cents
1 Gulden = 1 Java Rupee
16 Silver Rupees = 1 Gold Mohur

BONKS: Because of the slow delivery of coins from the Netherlands, the government in the East Indies often resorted to the manufacture of "Bonks". These were simply lumps cut from the copper (or tin) rods used for coining. This eliminated the problems inherent in casting round coins and allowed the production of large quantities of legal tender very quickly. The thicker rods were used for the 2 and 8 Stuiver Bonks and the thinner rod for the smaller denominations.

TOKENS: Most tokens in this section were struck in Britain on orders from Singapore merchants and used to pay seafaring Malays. Although the Dutch made them illegal, they circulated in the outer provinces due to scarcity of legal coins. Thus, the area mentioned on the tokens does not mean they were struck in or for the area, or that they circulated in the area. The dates do not indicate the year of issue.

UNITED EAST INDIA COMPANY

MILLED COINAGE

KM# 72 1/2 DUIT

Copper **Obv:** Crowned Holland arms **Rev:** VOC monogram, date below

Date	Mintage	VG	F	VF	XF	Unc
1749	—	2.00	3.00	5.00	7.50	—
1750	—	2.00	3.00	5.00	7.50	—
1751	—	2.00	3.00	5.00	7.50	—
1752	—	2.00	3.00	5.00	7.50	—
1753	—	2.00	3.00	5.00	7.50	—
1754	—	2.00	3.00	5.00	7.50	—
1769	—	2.00	3.00	5.00	7.50	—
1770	—	2.00	3.00	5.00	7.50	—

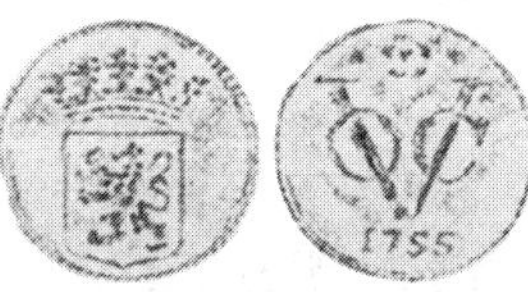

KM# 72b 1/2 DUIT

Gold **Obv:** Crowned Holland arms **Rev:** VOC monogram, date below **Note:** Weight varies: 1.718-1.724 g.

Date	Mintage	F	VF	XF	Unc	BU
1750 Proof	—	Value: 250				
1755 Proof	—	Value: 250				
1756 Proof	—	Value: 250				
1758 Proof	—	Value: 250				
1760 Proof	—	Value: 250				
1761 Proof	—	Value: 250				
1763 Proof	—	Value: 250				

KM# 112.1b 1/2 DUIT

Gold **Obv:** Crowned Utrecht arms with flat shield top **Rev:** Crowned VOC monogram with flat or curved top, date below

Date	Mintage	F	VF	XF	Unc	BU
1752 Proof	—	—	—	—	—	—
1753 Proof; Rare	—	—	—	—	—	—
1754 Proof; Unique	—	—	—	—	—	—
1756 Proof; Unique	—	—	—	—	—	—
1758 Proof; Rare	—	—	—	—	—	—
1761 Proof; Unique	—	—	—	—	—	—
1762 Proof	—	—	—	—	—	—
1764 Proof; Rare	—	—	—	—	—	—
1767 Proof; Rare	—	—	—	—	—	—
1793 Proof	—	—	—	—	—	—

KM# 112.1 1/2 DUIT

Copper **Obv:** Crowned Utrecht arms with flat shield top **Rev:** VOC monogram, date below

Date	Mintage	VG	F	VF	XF	Unc
1752	—	2.00	3.50	6.50	12.50	—
1753	—	1.50	2.50	5.00	10.00	—
1754	—	1.50	2.50	5.00	10.00	—
1755	—	1.50	2.50	5.00	10.00	—
1756	—	5.00	12.00	25.00	50.00	—
1757	—	2.00	3.50	6.50	12.50	—
1758	—	4.00	10.00	20.00	40.00	—
1769	—	2.00	5.00	10.00	20.00	—
1770	—	2.00	5.00	10.00	20.00	—

KM# 112.1a 1/2 DUIT

Silver **Obv:** Crowned Utrecht arms with flat shield top **Rev:** VOC monogram, date below **Note:** Special presentation strikes produced by the mintmaster on demand.

Date	Mintage	F	VF	XF	Unc	BU
1753	—	15.00	25.00	40.00	65.00	—
1754	—	15.00	25.00	40.00	65.00	—
1755	—	15.00	25.00	40.00	65.00	—
1756	—	15.00	25.00	40.00	65.00	—
1757	—	15.00	25.00	40.00	65.00	—
1758	—	20.00	30.00	50.00	80.00	—
1760	—	20.00	30.00	50.00	80.00	—
1761	—	20.00	30.00	50.00	80.00	—
1762	—	20.00	30.00	50.00	80.00	—
1763	—	20.00	30.00	50.00	80.00	—
1764	—	20.00	30.00	50.00	80.00	—
1765	—	20.00	30.00	50.00	80.00	—
1766	—	20.00	30.00	50.00	80.00	—
1767	—	20.00	30.00	50.00	80.00	—
1768	—	20.00	30.00	50.00	80.00	—
1769	—	20.00	30.00	50.00	80.00	—
1770	—	20.00	30.00	50.00	80.00	—
1771	—	20.00	30.00	50.00	80.00	—
1773 Rare	—	—	—	—	—	—
1792 Rare	—	—	—	—	—	—
1793	—	30.00	50.00	80.00	150	—
1794	—	30.00	50.00	80.00	150	—

KM# 72a 1/2 DUIT

Silver **Obv:** Crowned Holland arms **Rev:** VOC monogram, date below **Note:** Special presentation strikes produced by the mintmaster on demand.

Date	Mintage	F	VF	XF	Unc	BU
1755	—	20.00	30.00	50.00	75.00	—
1756	—	20.00	30.00	50.00	75.00	—
1757	—	20.00	30.00	50.00	75.00	—
1758/7	—	20.00	30.00	50.00	75.00	—
1758	—	20.00	30.00	50.00	75.00	—
1759	—	20.00	30.00	50.00	75.00	—
1760	—	20.00	30.00	50.00	75.00	—
1761	—	20.00	30.00	50.00	75.00	—
1762	—	20.00	30.00	50.00	75.00	—
1763	—	20.00	30.00	50.00	75.00	—

KM# 113 1/2 DUIT

Copper **Obv:** VOC monogram **Rev:** VOC monogram

Date	Mintage	VG	F	VF	XF	Unc
1758	—	12.50	18.50	27.50	40.00	—

KM# 113a 1/2 DUIT

Silver **Obv:** VOC monogram **Rev:** VOC monogram

Date	Mintage	VG	F	VF	XF	Unc
1758 Proof	—	—	—	—	—	—

KM# 114 1/2 DUIT

Copper **Obv:** Crowned Utrecht arms **Rev:** Crowned Utrecht arms

Date	Mintage	VG	F	VF	XF	Unc
ND	—	—	—	—	—	—

KM# 114a 1/2 DUIT

Silver **Obv:** Crowned Utrecht arms **Rev:** Crowned Utrecht arms

Date	Mintage	VG	F	VF	XF	Unc
ND Proof	—	—	—	—	—	—

KM# 137 1/2 DUIT

Copper **Obv:** Crowned arms of West Friesland **Rev:** VOC monogram, date below

Date	Mintage	VG	F	VF	XF	Unc
1769	—	4.50	7.50	13.00	25.00	—
1770	—	4.50	7.50	13.00	25.00	—

KM# 154 1/2 DUIT

Copper **Obv:** Crowned Zeeland arms **Rev:** VOC monogram divides date

Date	Mintage	VG	F	VF	XF	Unc
1770	—	10.00	15.00	27.50	45.00	—
1771	—	10.00	15.00	27.50	45.00	—
1772	—	10.00	15.00	27.50	45.00	—
1789 Reeded edge	—	20.00	35.00	60.00	100	—

KM# 55 1/2 DUIT

Copper **Obv:** Crowned Gelderland arms **Obv. Legend:** IN DEO EST. SPES NOSTRA **Rev:** VOC monogram, date below

Date	Mintage	VG	F	VF	XF	Unc
1788	—	6.00	8.50	13.50	20.00	—
1789	—	6.00	8.50	13.50	20.00	—

KM# 55a 1/2 DUIT

Silver **Obv:** Crowned Gelderland arms **Obv. Legend:** IN DEO EST. SPES NOSTRA **Rev:** VOC monogram, date below **Edge:** Plain **Note:** Originally struck in Proof.

Date	Mintage	VG	F	VF	XF	Unc
1789	—	35.00	65.00	125	200	—

KM# 112.3 1/2 DUIT

Copper **Obv:** Crowned Utrecht arms with flat shield top **Rev:** VOC monogram, date below **Note:** Mint mark: Star.

Date	Mintage	VG	F	VF	XF	Unc
1790 Rare	—	—	—	—	—	—

Note: Struck in 1842.

KM# 56 1/2 DUIT

Copper **Obv:** Crowned Gelderland arms **Obv. Legend:** IN DEO SPES NOST • **Rev:** VOC monogram, date below

Date	Mintage	VG	F	VF	XF	Unc
1790	—	5.00	7.50	10.00	15.00	—

KM# 70b DUIT

Gold **Obv:** Crowned Holland arms **Rev:** VOC monogram, date below

Date	Mintage	VG	F	VF	XF	Unc
1726 Proof; Rare	—	—	—	—	—	—
1732 Proof; Rare	—	—	—	—	—	—
1738 Proof; Rare	—	—	—	—	—	—
1746 Proof; Rare	—	—	—	—	—	—
1747 Proof; Rare	—	—	—	—	—	—
1749 Proof; Rare	—	—	—	—	—	—
1755 Proof; Rare	—	—	—	—	—	—
1756 Proof; Rare	—	—	—	—	—	—
1759 Proof; Rare	—	—	—	—	—	—
1763 Proof; Rare	—	—	—	—	—	—

KM# 150 DUIT

Copper **Obv:** Crowned Zeeland arms **Obv. Legend:** LUCTOR ET EMERGO **Rev:** VOC monogram, date below

Date	Mintage	VG	F	VF	XF	Unc
1726	—	12.50	20.00	35.00	60.00	—
1727	—	4.00	8.00	16.00	35.00	—
1728	—	3.00	6.00	12.00	30.00	—
1729	—	3.00	6.00	12.00	30.00	—
ND Unique	—	—	—	—	—	—

KM# 70 DUIT

3.6190 g., Copper **Obv:** Crowned Holland arms **Rev:** VOC monogram, date below **Note:** Years 1802-04 were struck under the Batavian Republic. 3 varieties exist.

Date	Mintage	VG	F	VF	XF	Unc
1726	—	4.50	7.50	12.50	20.00	—
1730	—	1.50	2.50	4.00	8.00	—
1731/0	—	2.50	4.00	7.00	12.50	—
1731	—	2.50	4.00	7.00	12.50	—
1732/26	—	1.50	2.50	4.00	8.00	—
1732	—	1.50	2.50	4.00	8.00	—
1733	—	1.50	2.50	4.00	8.00	—
1734/3	—	1.50	2.50	4.00	8.00	—
1734	—	1.50	2.50	4.00	8.00	—
1735/4	—	2.50	4.00	7.00	12.50	—
1735/26	—	2.50	4.00	7.00	12.50	—
1735	—	1.50	2.50	4.00	8.00	—
1736/5	—	2.50	4.00	7.00	12.50	—
1736	—	1.50	2.50	4.00	8.00	—
1737	—	2.50	4.00	7.00	12.50	—
1742	—	1.50	2.50	4.00	8.00	—
1743	—	2.50	4.00	7.00	12.50	—
1744	—	1.50	2.50	4.00	8.00	—
1745	—	1.50	2.50	4.00	8.00	—
1746	—	1.50	2.50	4.00	8.00	—
1747	—	1.50	2.50	4.00	8.00	—
1748	—	1.50	2.50	4.00	8.00	—
1749	—	3.00	6.00	12.50	20.00	—
1750	—	1.50	2.50	4.00	8.00	—
1750/49	—	2.50	4.00	7.00	12.50	—

Date	Mintage	VG	F	VF	XF	Unc
1751	—	1.50	2.50	4.00	8.00	—
1752	—	1.50	2.50	4.00	8.00	—
1753	—	1.50	2.50	4.00	8.00	—
1754/3	—	4.00	6.00	12.50	20.00	—
1754	—	4.00	6.00	12.50	20.00	—
1755	—	1.50	2.50	4.00	8.00	—
1757	—	1.50	2.50	4.00	8.00	—
1764	—	1.50	2.50	4.00	8.00	—
1765/64	—	4.00	9.00	15.00	25.00	—
1765	—	1.50	2.50	4.00	8.00	—
1766	—	1.50	2.50	4.00	8.00	—
1767	—	1.50	2.50	4.00	8.00	—
1768	—	4.00	9.00	15.00	25.00	—
1770	—	1.50	2.50	4.00	8.00	—
1771	—	1.50	2.50	4.00	8.00	—
1772	—	3.00	8.50	15.00	25.00	—
1776	—	3.00	8.50	15.00	25.00	—
1777	—	3.00	8.50	15.00	25.00	—
1778	—	1.50	2.50	4.00	7.00	—
1779	—	1.50	2.50	4.00	7.00	—
1780	—	1.50	2.50	4.00	8.00	—
1781	—	1.00	2.00	4.00	7.00	—
1784	—	4.00	9.00	15.00	25.00	—
1788	—	1.50	2.50	4.00	7.00	—
1789	—	1.50	2.50	4.00	8.00	—
1790/89	—	4.00	9.00	15.00	25.00	—
1790	—	1.50	2.50	4.00	8.00	—
1791	—	1.50	2.50	4.00	8.00	—
1792	—	1.50	2.50	4.00	8.00	—
1793	—	1.50	2.50	4.00	8.00	—

KM# 131 DUIT

Copper **Obv:** Crowned arms of West Friesland **Rev:** VOC monogram, date below **Note:** Varieties exist

Date	Mintage	VG	F	VF	XF	Unc
1729	—	3.00	4.00	7.00	12.50	—
1731	—	4.00	7.00	12.00	20.00	—
1732	—	4.00	7.00	12.00	20.00	—
1733	—	4.00	7.00	12.00	20.00	—
1734	—	1.50	2.50	4.50	8.50	—
1735	—	1.50	2.50	5.00	10.00	—
1736	—	3.00	6.00	10.00	17.50	—
1737	—	1.50	2.50	5.00	10.00	—
1743	—	1.75	2.75	5.50	10.00	—
1744	—	2.50	4.00	7.00	12.50	—
1745	—	1.25	2.50	5.00	10.00	—
1746	—	1.25	2.50	4.50	8.50	—
1747	—	2.50	4.00	7.00	12.50	—
1748	—	1.25	2.50	5.00	10.00	—
1749	—	1.25	2.50	4.50	8.50	—
1750	—	1.25	2.50	4.50	8.50	—
1751	—	1.25	2.50	5.00	10.00	—
1752	—	2.50	4.00	7.00	12.50	—
1753	—	1.25	2.50	4.50	8.50	—
1754	—	1.25	2.50	5.00	10.00	—
1755	—	1.25	2.50	4.75	9.00	—
1756	—	1.25	2.50	5.00	10.00	—
1764	—	10.00	16.50	25.00	37.50	—
1765	—	2.00	5.00	10.00	15.00	—
1766	—	2.00	5.00	10.00	15.00	—
1767	—	2.00	5.00	10.00	15.00	—
1768	—	2.00	5.00	10.00	15.00	—
1770	—	3.00	7.00	12.00	20.00	—
1771/0	—	3.00	7.00	12.00	20.00	—
1771	—	1.50	2.50	4.50	8.50	—
1772	—	1.50	2.50	4.50	8.50	—
1773	—	3.00	7.00	12.00	20.00	—
1776/3	—	3.00	7.00	12.00	20.00	—
1776	—	1.50	2.50	4.50	8.50	—
1777/6	—	3.00	7.00	12.00	20.00	—
1777	—	1.50	2.50	4.50	8.50	—
1778/7	—	3.00	7.00	12.00	20.00	—
1778	—	1.50	2.50	4.50	8.50	—
1779	—	1.50	2.50	4.50	8.50	—
1780	—	1.50	2.50	4.50	8.50	—
1781	—	1.50	2.50	4.50	8.50	—
1784/1	—	3.00	7.00	12.00	20.00	—
1784	—	1.50	2.50	4.50	8.50	—
1785/4	—	3.00	7.00	12.00	20.00	—
1785	—	1.50	2.50	4.50	8.50	—
1786/5	—	2.25	5.00	10.00	15.00	—
1786	—	1.50	2.50	4.50	8.50	—
1787	—	1.50	2.50	4.50	8.50	—
1788	—	1.50	2.50	4.50	8.50	—
1789/8	—	3.00	7.00	12.00	20.00	—
1789/9871	—	8.50	20.00	35.00	55.00	—
1789	—	1.50	2.50	4.50	8.50	—
1790	—	1.50	2.50	4.50	8.50	—
1791/0	—	1.50	2.50	5.00	10.00	—
1791	—	1.50	2.50	4.50	8.50	—
1792	—	1.50	2.50	4.50	8.50	—
1794	—	8.00	20.00	35.00	55.00	—

KM# 152.1 DUIT

Copper **Obv:** Crowned Zeeland arms **Rev:** VOC monogram, date below, without legend

Date	Mintage	VG	F	VF	XF	Unc
1729	—	5.00	10.00	17.50	30.00	—
1730	—	1.50	2.50	4.00	7.00	—
1731	—	1.50	2.50	4.00	7.00	—
1732	—	1.50	2.50	4.00	7.00	—
1733	—	1.50	2.50	4.00	7.00	—
1734	—	1.50	2.50	4.00	7.00	—
1735	—	1.50	2.50	4.00	7.00	—

KM# 132a DUIT

Gold **Obv:** Ornate crown above curved shield of West Friesland

Date	Mintage	F	VF	XF	Unc	BU
1729 Proof	—	—	—	—	—	—
1730 Proof; Unique	—	—	—	—	—	—
1731 Proof; Unique	—	—	—	—	—	—

KM# 134 DUIT

Silver **Obv:** Simple crown above baroque curved shield of West Friesland **Note:** Special presentation strikes produced by the mintmaster on demand

Date	Mintage	F	VF	XF	Unc	BU
1731	—	35.00	55.00	85.00	135	—
1736	—	35.00	55.00	85.00	135	—
1746	—	35.00	55.00	85.00	135	—
1752	—	35.00	55.00	85.00	135	—

KM# 50.1 DUIT

Copper **Obv:** Crowned Gelderland arms **Obv. Legend:** IN DEO - SP. NOS • **Rev:** VOC monogram, date below

Date	Mintage	VG	F	VF	XF	Unc
1731	—	7.50	12.50	20.00	30.00	—
1732 fox	—	7.50	12.50	20.00	30.00	—
1732 hill	—	3.50	6.00	10.00	20.00	—

KM# 50.1a DUIT

Silver **Obv:** Crowned Gelderland arms **Obv. Legend:** IN DEO - SP. NOS • **Rev:** VOC monogram, date below **Note:** Originally struck in Proof.

Date	Mintage	VG	F	VF	XF	Unc
1731	—	25.00	60.00	85.00	115	—
1732 fox	—	25.00	60.00	85.00	115	—
1789	—	35.00	75.00	110	150	—

KM# 132 DUIT

Copper **Obv:** Ornate crown above curved shield of West Friesland

Date	Mintage	VG	F	VF	XF	Unc
1731	—	3.00	6.00	10.00	20.00	—
1732	—	3.00	6.00	10.00	20.00	—
1733	—	7.00	12.00	25.00	50.00	—

KM# 152a DUIT

Silver **Obv:** Crowned Zeeland arms, shield rounded at bottom **Rev:** VOC monogram, date without dots below **Note:** Originally struck in Proof.

Date	Mintage	VG	F	VF	XF	Unc
1732	—	25.00	45.00	80.00	110	—
1788	—	25.00	45.00	80.00	110	—

KM# 70a DUIT

Silver **Obv:** Crowned Holland arms **Rev:** VOC monogram, date below **Note:** Special presentation strikes produced by the mintmaster on demand.

Date	Mintage	VG	F	VF	XF	Unc
1735	—	12.50	22.50	35.00	60.00	—
1736/5	—	22.50	35.00	60.00	100	—
1746	—	12.50	22.50	35.00	60.00	—
1747	—	12.50	22.50	35.00	60.00	—
1748	—	12.50	22.50	35.00	60.00	—
1749/7	—	22.50	35.00	60.00	100	—
1749	—	10.00	17.50	25.00	60.00	—
1750	—	10.00	17.50	25.00	60.00	—
1751	—	12.50	22.50	35.00	60.00	—
1752	—	12.50	22.50	35.00	60.00	—
1753	—	12.50	22.50	35.00	60.00	—
1754	—	12.50	22.50	35.00	60.00	—
1755	—	12.50	22.50	35.00	60.00	—
1756	—	12.50	22.50	35.00	60.00	—
1757	—	12.50	22.50	35.00	60.00	—
1758	—	12.50	22.50	35.00	60.00	—
1759	—	12.50	22.50	35.00	60.00	—
1760	—	12.50	22.50	35.00	60.00	—
1761	—	12.50	22.50	35.00	60.00	—
1762	—	12.50	22.50	35.00	60.00	—
1763	—	12.50	22.50	35.00	60.00	—

KM# 152.2 DUIT

Copper **Obv:** Crowned Zeeland arms, shield pointed at bottom **Rev:** VOC monogram, date below **Note:** Varieties exist.

Date	Mintage	VG	F	VF	XF	Unc
1736 old crown	—	1.50	2.50	4.00	7.00	—
1736 new crown	—	1.50	2.50	4.00	7.00	—
1737	—	1.75	3.00	5.00	9.00	—
1738	—	1.50	2.50	4.00	7.00	—
1739/7	—	2.00	3.00	6.50	12.50	—
1739	—	1.50	2.50	4.00	7.00	—
1744	—	1.75	2.75	4.50	7.50	—
1745	—	1.75	3.00	5.00	9.00	—
1746	—	1.75	3.00	5.00	9.00	—
1747 small 4	—	1.75	3.00	5.00	9.00	—
1747 large 4	—	1.75	3.00	5.00	9.00	—
1748/7	—	2.50	4.25	7.00	12.50	—
1748	—	1.50	2.50	4.00	7.00	—
1749	—	1.75	3.00	5.00	9.00	—
1750	—	1.75	3.00	5.00	9.00	—
1751	—	2.00	3.00	6.50	12.50	—
1752	—	1.75	3.00	5.00	9.00	—

KM# 152.3 DUIT

Copper **Obv:** Crowned Zeeland arms, shield rounded at bottom **Rev:** VOC monogram, date without dots below

Date	Mintage	VG	F	VF	XF	Unc
1753	—	1.75	2.75	4.50	7.50	—
1754	—	1.25	2.00	3.50	6.00	—
1755	—	1.75	3.50	6.00	10.00	—
1756/5	—	5.00	8.00	12.50	20.00	—
1756	—	1.75	3.50	6.00	10.00	—
1764	—	1.50	3.00	5.00	9.00	—
1765	—	1.50	3.00	5.00	9.00	—
1766	—	1.50	3.00	5.00	9.00	—
1767	—	2.00	3.00	6.50	12.50	—
1768 sm. 8	—	4.00	7.50	12.50	17.50	—
1768 lg. 8	—	1.75	2.75	6.00	12.00	—
1770	—	1.75	2.75	6.00	12.00	—
1771	—	1.75	2.75	6.00	12.00	—
1772	—	1.75	2.75	6.00	12.00	—
1773	—	6.50	12.50	20.00	35.00	—
1777	—	1.75	2.75	6.00	12.00	—
1778	—	2.00	4.00	8.00	15.00	—
1779	—	2.00	4.00	8.00	15.00	—
1780	—	1.50	2.50	4.00	7.00	—
1784	—	1.50	2.50	4.00	7.00	—
1785	—	1.50	2.50	4.00	7.00	—
1786	—	1.50	2.50	4.00	7.00	—
1787	—	1.50	2.50	4.00	7.00	—
1788	—	1.50	2.50	4.00	7.00	—
1789	—	1.50	2.50	4.00	7.00	—
1790	—	1.50	2.50	4.00	7.00	—
1791	—	1.50	2.50	4.00	7.00	—
1792	—	2.00	4.00	8.00	15.00	—

KM# 111.1 DUIT

Copper **Obv:** Crowned Utrecht arms with lion supporters **Rev:** VOC monogram, date below

Date	Mintage	VG	F	VF	XF	Unc
1741 Unique	—	—	—	—	—	—
1742	—	2.00	3.50	6.00	10.00	—
1744	—	2.50	4.50	8.00	15.00	—
1745	—	2.00	3.50	6.00	10.00	—
1746	—	2.00	3.50	6.00	10.00	—
1752	—	3.00	6.00	10.00	18.00	—
1753	—	2.50	4.50	7.50	12.00	—
1754	—	1.50	2.50	4.00	8.00	—
1755	—	1.75	3.00	4.50	9.00	—
1757	—	2.25	4.00	7.00	12.00	—
1764	—	2.00	3.50	6.00	10.00	—
1765	—	2.00	3.50	6.00	10.00	—
1766	—	2.00	3.50	6.00	10.00	—
1767	—	2.00	3.50	6.00	10.00	—
1769	—	2.00	3.50	6.00	10.00	—
1770	—	2.00	3.50	6.00	10.00	—
1771	—	7.50	15.00	25.00	35.00	—
1776	—	2.00	3.50	6.00	10.00	—
1777	—	2.00	3.50	6.00	10.00	—
1778	—	2.00	3.50	6.00	10.00	—
1779	—	2.00	3.50	6.00	10.00	—
1780	—	2.50	4.50	7.50	12.00	—
1781	—	2.00	3.50	6.00	10.00	—
1784	—	2.00	3.50	6.00	10.00	—
1785	—	3.00	6.00	10.00	18.00	—
1786	—	2.50	4.50	7.50	12.00	—
1787	—	2.00	3.50	6.00	10.00	—
1788	—	2.00	3.50	6.00	10.00	—
1789	—	1.50	2.50	4.00	8.00	—
1790	—	1.00	2.00	3.00	6.00	—
1791	—	1.50	2.50	4.00	8.00	—
1792	—	1.50	2.50	4.00	8.00	—
1793	—	3.00	6.00	10.00	18.00	—
1794	—	1.75	3.00	4.50	9.00	—

KM# 111.1a DUIT

Silver **Obv:** Crowned Utrecht arms with lion supporters **Rev:** VOC monogram, date below **Note:** Special presentation strikes produced by the mintmaster on demand.

Date	Mintage	VG	F	VF	XF	Unc
1742	—	50.00	80.00	135	225	—
1753	—	50.00	80.00	135	225	—
1754	—	55.00	90.00	150	250	—
1755	—	—	—	—	—	—
1757	—	—	—	—	—	—
1758/6	—	—	—	—	—	—
1760	—	15.00	25.00	60.00	100	—
1761 Rare	—	—	—	—	—	—
1702	—	20.00	40.00	90.00	125	—
1763	—	10.00	20.00	55.00	100	—
1764	—	10.00	20.00	55.00	100	—
1765	—	20.00	40.00	90.00	125	—
1766	—	10.00	20.00	55.00	100	—
1767	—	30.00	50.00	100	150	—
1768	—	10.00	20.00	55.00	100	—
1769 Rare	—	—	—	—	—	—
1770	—	40.00	70.00	120	200	—
1771	—	10.00	20.00	55.00	100	—
1772	—	10.00	20.00	55.00	100	—
1773	—	10.00	20.00	55.00	100	—
1784 Rare	—	—	—	—	—	—
1790	—	10.00	20.00	55.00	100	—
1794	—	10.00	20.00	55.00	100	—

KM# 111.1b DUIT

3.5020 g., Gold **Obv:** Crowned Utrecht arms with lion supporters **Rev:** VOC monogram, date below **Note:** Special presentation strikes produced by the mintmaster on demand.

Date	Mintage	VG	F	VF	XF	Unc
1742 Proof; Unique	—	—	—	—	—	—
1753 Proof	—	—	—	—	—	—
1754 Proof	—	—	—	—	—	—
1755 Proof	—	—	—	—	—	—
1757 Proof	—	—	—	—	—	—
1760 Proof; Rare	—	—	—	—	—	—
1762 Proof; Rare	—	—	—	—	—	—
1766 Proof	—	—	—	—	—	—
1792 Proof; Rare	—	—	—	—	—	—

KM# 153 DUIT

Copper **Obv:** Crowned arms **Rev:** Date in cartouche **Note:** Mule.

Date	Mintage	VG	F	VF	XF	Unc
1754	—	7.50	12.50	20.00	25.00	—

KM# 135 DUIT

Copper **Obv:** VOC monogram in sprays, date below **Rev:** VOC monogram in sprays, date below

Date	Mintage	VG	F	VF	XF	Unc
1756	—	12.00	25.00	45.00	80.00	—

KM# 136 DUIT

Copper **Obv:** Crowned West Friesland arms **Rev:** Monogram in laurel wreath

Date	Mintage	VG	F	VF	XF	Unc
1756	—	18.00	30.00	50.00	85.00	—

KM# 136a DUIT

Silver **Obv:** Crowned West Friesland arms **Rev:** VOC monogram in laurel wreath **Note:** Special presentation strikes produced by the mintmaster on demand

Date	Mintage	VG	F	VF	XF	Unc
1756	—	25.00	45.00	85.00	130	—

KM# 50.2 DUIT

Copper **Obv:** Crowned Gelderland arms **Obv. Legend:** IN DEO • EST. SPES. NOSTRA **Rev:** VOC monogram, date below **Note:** Dates 1802-1806 were struck under the Batavian Republic. Varieties exist.

Date	Mintage	VG	F	VF	XF	Unc
1771	—	2.75	4.50	7.50	12.50	—
1772	—	2.75	4.50	7.50	12.50	—
1776	—	2.75	4.50	7.50	12.50	—
1785	—	2.75	4.50	7.50	12.50	—
1786	—	2.75	4.50	7.50	12.50	—
1787	—	2.75	4.50	7.50	12.50	—
1788	—	2.75	4.50	7.50	12.50	—
1789	—	2.75	4.50	7.50	12.50	—
1790	—	2.75	4.50	7.50	12.50	—
1791	—	2.75	4.50	7.50	12.50	—
1791 Proof	—	Value: 85.00				
1792	—	2.75	4.50	7.50	12.50	—
1793	—	2.75	4.50	7.50	12.50	—
1794	—	2.75	4.50	7.50	12.50	—

KM# 111.4a DUIT

Silver **Note:** Special presentation strikes produced by the mintmaster on demand in 1839-43.

Date	Mintage	VG	F	VF	XF	Unc
1790	—	—	—	—	135	—

Note: Mintage included in KM#290, 1839-40 dates.

KM# 159 DUIT

Copper **Obv:** Crowned Zeeland arms, pointed shield **Rev:** Garland around top border

Date	Mintage	VG	F	VF	XF	Unc
1792	—	8.50	16.50	30.00	50.00	—
1793	—	1.75	3.00	5.25	9.00	—
1794/3	—	3.50	6.00	10.00	17.50	—
1794	—	1.75	3.00	5.25	9.00	—

KM# 52 10 STUIVERS (1/2 Gulden)

5.3000 g., 0.9200 Silver 0.1568 oz. ASW **Obv:** Crowned States General arms, VOC monogram in cartouche below **Obv. Legend:** HAC NITIMVR _ HANC TVEMVR **Rev:** Neerlandia standing facing holding a spear and resting arm on bible on a column **Rev. Legend:** MO: ARG: ORD: FOE: BELG: D: GEL: &: C: Z:

Date	Mintage	VG	F	VF	XF	Unc
1786	—	10.00	30.00	55.00	80.00	—

KM# 115 10 STUIVERS (1/2 Gulden)

5.3000 g., 0.9200 Silver 0.1568 oz. ASW **Obv. Legend:** MO: ARG: ORD: - FOED: BELG: TRAI • **Rev. Legend:** HAC NITIMIR - HANC TVEMER

Date	Mintage	VG	F	VF	XF	Unc
1786	—	20.00	30.00	50.00	100	—

KM# 138 10 STUIVERS (1/2 Gulden)

5.3000 g., 0.9200 Silver 0.1568 oz. ASW **Obv:** Crowned States General arms, VOC monogram in cartouche below **Obv. Legend:** MO: ARG: ORD: FOED: BELG: WESTF: **Rev:** Standing Neerlandia facing holding spear and resting arm on bible on column **Rev. Legend:** HAC NITIMVR - HANCTVEMVR

Date	Mintage	VG	F	VF	XF	Unc
1786	—	12.50	25.00	40.00	65.00	—
1787/6	—	20.00	35.00	60.00	100	—
1787	—	12.50	25.00	50.00	90.00	—

KM# 156.1 10 STUIVERS (1/2 Gulden)

Silver **Obv:** Crowned Stats General arms, VOC monogram in cartouche below, date above **Obv. Legend:** MO: ARG: ORD: FOED: BELG: ZEL. **Rev:** Standing Neerlandia facing holding spear and resting arm on bible on column **Rev. Legend:** HAC NITIMVR - HANC TVEMVR

Date	Mintage	VG	F	VF	XF	Unc
1791	—	25.00	50.00	95.00	160	—

KM# 156.2 10 STUIVERS (1/2 Gulden)

Silver **Obv:** Crowned States General arms, VOC monogram in cartouche below, date above **Obv. Legend:** MO: ARG: ORD: FOED: BELG: ZEL **Rev:** Standing Neerlandia facing with spear, with arm resting on bible while leaning on column **Rev. Legend:** HAC NITIMVR - HANC TVEMVR

Date	Mintage	VG	F	VF	XF	Unc
1791	—	35.00	65.00	115	185	—

KM# 156.3 10 STUIVERS (1/2 Gulden)

Silver **Obv:** Crowned States General arms, VOC monogram in cartouche below, date above **Obv. Legend:** MO: ARG: ORD: FOED: BELG: ZEL **Rev:** Standing Neerlandia facing holding spear and resting arm on bible on column **Rev. Legend:** HAC NITIMUR - HANC TVEMVR

Date	Mintage	VG	F	VF	XF	Unc
1791	—	—	—	—	—	—

KM# 157 10 STUIVERS (1/2 Gulden)

Silver **Obv:** Crowned States General arms, VOC monogram in cartouche below **Obv. Legend:** Standing Neerlandia facing holding spear and resting arm on bible on column, date below

Date	Mintage	VG	F	VF	XF	Unc
1791	—	15.00	22.50	40.00	65.00	—

KM# 130.1a DUCATON

38.5700 g., Gold **Obv:** Knight on horseback with sword left, crowned West Friesland arms below **Obv. Legend:** MON: FOED: BELG: PRO: WESTF: IN USUM SOCIET: IND: ORIENT **Rev:** Crowned States General arms with crowned lion supporters, VOC monogram in cartouche below **Rev. Legend:** CONCORDIA - RESPARVAE - CRESCUNT

Date	Mintage	VG	F	VF	XF	Unc
1728 Proof; Rare	—	—	—	—	—	—

KM# 130.1 DUCATON

Silver **Obv:** Knight with sword on horseback left, crowned West Friesland arms below **Obv. Legend:** MON: FOED: BELG: PRO: WESTF: IN USUM SOCIET: IND: ORIENT **Rev:** Crowned States General arms with crowned lion supporters, VOC monogram in cartouche below **Rev. Legend:** CONCORDIA - RESPARVAE - CRESCUNT. **Note:** 1728 date struck at Hoorn Mint; 1737-41 dates struck at Enkhuizen; 1741 date also struck at Medemblik.

Date	Mintage	VG	F	VF	XF	Unc
1728	—	200	400	600	800	—
1737 Rare	—	—	—	—	—	—
1738	—	250	450	650	1,000	—
1739	—	250	450	650	1,000	—
1740/39	—	250	450	650	1,000	—
1740	—	250	450	650	1,000	—
1741 turnip	—	400	700	900	1,500	—
1741 Cock; Rare	—	—	—	—	—	—

KM# 151 DUCATON

Silver **Obv:** Knight with sword on horseback right, crowned Zeeland arms below **Rev:** Crowned States General arms with crowned lion supporters. VOC monogram in cartouche below, date at top **Note:** Dav.#418.

Date	Mintage	VG	F	VF	XF	Unc
1728	102,000	500	1,000	1,500	2,000	—
1737	—	500	1,000	1,500	2,000	—
1738/7	—	750	1,500	—	—	—
1738	—	500	1,000	1,500	2,000	—
1739	—	450	650	850	1,400	—
1740	—	450	650	850	1,400	—
1741	—	175	300	500	850	—

KM# 71 DUCATON

32.7790 g., 0.9410 Silver 0.9916 oz. ASW **Obv:** Knight holding sword on horseback right, crowned Holland arms below **Obv. Legend:** MON: FOED: BELG: PRO: HOLL: IN USUM SOCIET: IND: ORIENT. **Rev:** Crowned States General arms with crowned lion supporters, VOC monogram in cartouche below **Rev. Legend:** • CONCORDIA - RES PARVAE - CRESCUNT • **Note:** Mint Mark: Horse on hill. Dav. #417

Date	Mintage	VG	F	VF	XF	Unc
1728	—	225	350	600	1,000	—
1729 Rare	—	—	—	—	—	—
1730/29	—	300	500	800	1,500	—
1730	—	300	500	800	1,500	—

Date	Mintage	VG	F	VF	XF	Unc
1731 Rare	—	—	—	—	—	—
1732	—	750	1,000	1,500	2,000	—
1733	—	325	525	850	1,500	—
1738	404,000	225	350	600	1,000	—
1739	Inc. above	225	350	600	1,000	—
1740	Inc. above	225	350	600	1,000	—
1741/40	Inc. above	225	350	600	1,000	—
1741 Rare	—	—	—	—	—	—

KM# 71a DUCATON

Gold **Obv:** Knight with sword on horseback right, crowned Holland arms below **Obv. Legend:** MON: FOED: BELG: PRO: HOLL: IN USUM SOCIET: IND: ORIENT. **Rev:** Crowned States General arms with crowned lion supporters, VOC monogram in cartouche below **Rev. Legend:** • CONCORDIA - RES PARVAE - CRESCUNT • **Note:** Mint mark: Horse on hill. Dav. #417. Weight varies: 37.800-40.214 g.

Date	Mintage	VG	F	VF	XF	Unc
1728 Proof	—	—	—	—	—	—
1732 Proof; Rare	—	—	—	—	—	—
1733 Proof; Unique	—	—	—	—	—	—

KM# 95.1 DUCATON

32.7790 g., 0.9410 Silver 0.9916 oz. ASW **Obv:** Knight with sword on horseback right, crowned States General arms below horse **Rev:** Crowned States General arms with crowned lion supporters, VOC monogram in cartouche below, date at top **Note:** Dav. #423. Mint mark: Crane.

Date	Mintage	VG	F	VF	XF	Unc
1737	80,000	450	900	1,250	1,850	—
1738	Inc. above	450	900	1,250	1,850	—

KM# 130.2 DUCATON

Silver **Obv:** Knight with sword on horseback left, crowned West Friesland arms below **Obv. Legend:** MON: FOED: BELG: PRO: WESTF: IN USUM SOCIET: IND: ORIENT **Rev:** Crowned States General arms with crowned lion supporters, VOC monogram in cartouche below **Rev. Legend:** CONCORDIA - RESPARVAE - CRESCUNT **Edge:** Reeded

Date	Mintage	VG	F	VF	XF	Unc
1738	—	250	450	650	900	—
1739	—	250	450	650	900	—
1740	—	250	450	650	900	—

KM# 51 DUCATON

32.7790 g., Silver **Obv:** Knight with sword on horse right, crowned Gelderland arms below **Obv. Legend:** MON: FOED: BELG: PRO: D: GEL: &: C: Z: ... **Rev:** Crowned States General arms with crowned lion supporters, VOC monogram in cartouche below, dat at top **Rev. Legend:** CONCORDIA - RES PARVÆ - CRESCUNT

Date	Mintage	VG	F	VF	XF	Unc
1738	—	275	550	1,000	1,650	—
1739	—	275	550	1,000	1,650	—
1740	92,000	250	500	900	1,500	—

KM# 95.2 DUCATON

32.7790 g., 0.9410 Silver 0.9916 oz. ASW **Obv:** Knight with sword on horseback right, crowned States General arms below horse **Rev:** Crowned States General arms with crowned lion supporters, VOC monogram in cartouche below, date at top **Edge:** Milled

Date	Mintage	VG	F	VF	XF	Unc
1738 Rare	—	—	—	—	—	—

KM# 110.1 DUCATON

Silver **Obv:** Knight with sword on horseback right, crowned Utrecht arms below **Obv. Legend:** MON: FOED: BELG: PRO: TRAI: IN USUM SOCIET: IND: ORIENT **Rev:** Crowned States General arms with crowned lion supporters, VOC monogram in cartouche below, date at top **Rev. Legend:** • CONCORDIA - RES PARVAE - CRESCUNT • **Edge:** Plain **Note:** Dav. #422.

Date	Mintage	VG	F	VF	XF	Unc
1739 Rare	—	—	—	—	—	—
1740	—	125	250	500	900	—

KM# 110.2 DUCATON

Silver **Obv:** Knight with sword on horseback right, crowned Utrecht arms below **Obv. Legend:** MON: FOED: BELG: PRO: TRAI: IN USUM SOCIET: IND: ORIENT **Rev:** Crowned States General arms with crowned lion supporters, VOC monogram in cartouche below, date at top **Rev. Legend:** • CONCORDIA - PRES PARVAE - CRESCUNT • **Edge:** Reeded **Note:** Dav. #422.

Date	Mintage	VG	F	VF	XF	Unc
1740	—	125	250	500	900	—

KM# 110.2a DUCATON

Gold **Obv:** Knight with sword on horseback right, crowned Utrecht arms below **Obv. Legend:** MON: FOED: BELG: PRO: TRAI: IN USUM SOCIET: IND: ORIENT **Rev:** Crowned States General arms with crowned lion supporters, VOC monogram in cartouche below, date at top **Rev. Legend:** • CONCORDIA - RES PARVAE - CRESCUNT • **Note:** Dav. #422.

Date	Mintage	VG	F	VF	XF	Unc
1740 Proof; Rare	—	—	—	—	—	—

KM# 133 DUCATON

Silver **Obv:** Knight with sword on horseback right, crowned West Friesland arms below **Obv. Legend:** MON: FOED: BELG: PRO: WESTF: IN USUM SOCIET: IND: ORIENT **Rev:** Crowned States General arms with crowned lion supporters, VOC monogram in cartouche below **Rev. Legend:** CONCORDIA - RESPARVAE - CRESCUNT **Note:** Mint mark: Cock. Dav. #420.

Date	Mintage	VG	F	VF	XF	Unc
1742	—	500	750	1,000	1,500	—
1748 Rare	—	—	—	—	—	—
1749 Rare	—	—	—	—	—	—
1750	—	500	750	1,000	1,500	—
1751 Rare	—	—	—	—	—	—

KM# 53 GULDEN

10.6100 g., 0.9200 Silver 0.3138 oz. ASW **Obv:** Crowned States General arms, VOC monogram in cartouche below **Obv. Legend:** HAC NITIMVR _ HANC TVEMVR **Rev:** Neerlandia standing facing holding a spear and resting arm on bible on column **Rev. Legend:** MO: ARG: ORD: FOE: BELG: D: GEL: &: C: Z:

Date	Mintage	VG	F	VF	XF	Unc
1786	—	17.50	30.00	55.00	100	—
1790	—	17.50	30.00	55.00	100	—

KM# 116 GULDEN

10.6100 g., 0.9200 Silver 0.3138 oz. ASW **Obv:** Crowned States General arms, VOC monogram below **Obv. Legend:** MO: ARG: ORD: - FOED: BELG: TRAI • **Rev:** Neerlandia standing facing holding a spear and resting arm on bible on a column **Rev. Legend:** HAC NITIMIR - HANC TVEMER

Date	Mintage	VG	F	VF	XF	Unc
1786	—	35.00	45.00	75.00	150	—
1790	—	50.00	75.00	125	200	—

KM# 139 GULDEN

10.6100 g., 0.9200 Silver 0.3138 oz. ASW **Obv:** Crowned States General arms, VOC monogram in cartouche below **Obv. Legend:** MO: ARG: ORD: FOED: BELG: WESTF: **Rev:** Standing Neerlandia facing holding spear, resting arm on bible on column **Rev. Legend:** HAC NITMVR - HANC TVEMVR

Date	Mintage	VG	F	VF	XF	Unc
1786/64	—	30.00	40.00	60.00	130	—
1786	—	50.00	90.00	150	250	—
1787	—	30.00	40.00	65.00	145	—
1790/87	—	50.00	90.00	160	265	—
1790	—	30.00	40.00	60.00	130	—

KM# 158 GULDEN

0.9200 Silver **Obv:** Crowned States General arms, VOC monogram in cartouche below **Obv. Legend:** MO: ARG: ORD: FOED: BELG: ZEL **Rev:** Standing Neerlandia facing holding spear and resting arm on bible on a column, date below **Note:** Varieties in legend spacing exist.

Date	Mintage	VG	F	VF	XF	Unc
1791/86	—	50.00	95.00	135	180	—
1791	—	20.00	35.00	55.00	90.00	—

KM# 140 3 GULDEN

31.8200 g., 0.9200 Silver 0.9412 oz. ASW **Obv:** Crowned States General arms, VOC monogram in cartouche below **Obv. Legend:** MO: ARG: ORD: FOED: BELG: WESTF: **Rev:** Standing Neerlandia facing holding spear and resting arm on bible on column **Rev. Legend:** HAC NITIMVR - HANC TVEMVR

Date	Mintage	F	VF	XF	Unc	BU
1786	—	150	250	425	700	—

KM# 117 3 GULDEN

31.8200 g., 0.9200 Silver 0.9412 oz. ASW **Obv:** Crowned States General arms, VOC monogram below **Obv. Legend:** MO: ARG: ORD: - FOED: BELG: TRAI • **Rev:** Neerlandia standing facing holding a spear and resting arm on bible on a column **Rev. Legend:** HAC NITIMI - HANC TVEMER

Date	Mintage	VG	F	VF	XF	Unc
1786	—	100	125	200	350	—

KM# 54 3 GULDEN

31.8200 g., 0.9200 Silver 0.9412 oz. ASW **Obv:** Crowned States General VOC monogram in cartouche below **Obv. Legend:** HAC NITIMVR _ HANC TVEMVR **Rev:** Neerlandia standing facing holding a spear and resting arm on bible on column **Rev. Legend:** MO: ARG: ORD: FOE: BELG: D: GEL: &: C: Z: **Note:** Dav. #425.

Date	Mintage	VG	F	VF	XF	Unc
1786	—	150	250	400	1,000	—

KM# 155 3 GULDEN

0.9200 Silver **Obv:** Crowned States General arms, VOC monogram in cartouche below **Obv. Legend:** MO: ARG: ORD: FOED: BELG: ZEL **Rev:** Standing Neerlandia facing holding spear and resting arm on bible on column, date below **Rev. Legend:** HAC NITIMUR - HANC TVEMUR **Note:** Dav.#427. Varieties in legend spacing exist

Date	Mintage	VG	F	VF	XF	Unc
1789	—	85.00	140	240	400	—

PATTERNS

Including off metal strikes

KM#	Date	Mintage	Identification	Mkt Val
PnA1	1757	—	1/2 Duit. Silver. Reeded edge. (Prev. NEI-Gelderland, KM#Pn1)	85.00
PnB1	1757	—	Duit. Silver. (Prev. NEI-Gelderland, KM#Pn2.)	225
PnC1	1791	—	Duit. Silver. (Prev. NEI-Gelderland KM#Pn3.)	275
PnD1	1736	—	Duit. Silver. (Prev. NEI-West Friesland KM#Pn1.)	—

PIEFORTS

KM#	Date	Mintage	Identification	Mkt Val
P1	1790(u)	—	Duit. Silver.	—

BANJARMASIN

Sultanate of So. Indonesia on the Martapura River where it meets the Barito. It has a population of 481,371. It is about 24 mi. from the sea. It was settled by the Dutch 1711; held by English 1811-17; bombed by Japanese and taken in Feb. 13, 1942; retaken by Allies August 1945.

TITLES

بنجرمسن

Banjarmasin

RULER

S. Tamjid Illah III, 1785-1808

NOTE: From around 1790 until at least 1817 various native minted copper coins have been circulating in the Sultanate of Banjarmasin. There is a very large variety in design of these Banjarmasin-Kepings, the majority are crude imitations of Duits of the Dutch East India Co. showing a range of crowned shields on the obverse. Some of them have inscriptions in Malay within the shield, some show the name Banjarmasin in Malay in 2 lines; also mirror script types are known. Most coins have the company's VOC mark on the reverse, usually with badly executed date numerals below. There are other scarcer talismanic numeral type reverses as well as scarce pieces bearing an imitation of the English United East Indian Company's bale mark 'C-E-V-I' or the scales design found on the company's Bombay Presidency series. Sizes vary from 20-25mm with rare specimens of 15-16mm. The weight of this copper series ranges from 1.35-2.50g. Combinations of obv. and rev. of all types exist.

SULTANATE

COUNTERMARKED COINAGE

KM# 6 1/4 RUPEE

Silver **Countermark:** "Banjar" **Note:** Countermark on Malay on Dutch West Indies (Utrecht) 1/4 Gulden, 1794, KM#2. Prev. KM#62.

CM Date	Host Date	Good	VG	F	VF	XF
ND	ND	—	—	—	—	—

KM# 7 RUPEE

Silver **Countermark:** "Banjar" **Note:** Countermark on Malay on Dutch West Indies (Utrecht) 1/4 Gulden, 1794, KM#3. Prev. KM#3. A unique example of a *Banjar* countermark on a Spanish Cuarta de Onza (4 Pesos) gold coin is known to exist.

CM Date	Host Date	Good	VG	F	VF	XF
ND	ND	—	—	—	—	—

STANDARD COINAGE

KM# 1 KEPING

Copper **Obv:** Legend **Obv. Legend:** Arabic "Banjarmasin" **Rev:** Scales **Note:** Many varieties exist, some have VOC monogram with date below.

Date	Mintage	VG	F	VF	XF	Unc
ND(1790-1817)	—	15.00	25.00	40.00	70.00	—

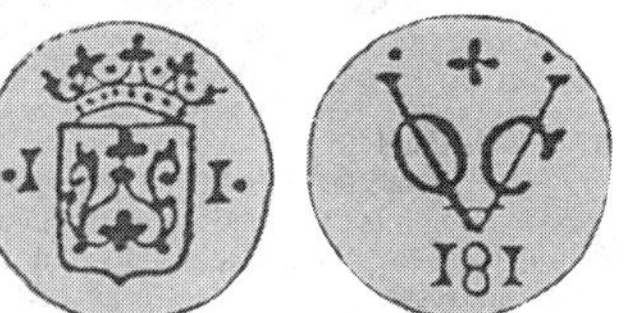

KM# 2 KEPING

Copper **Obv:** Crowned shield **Rev:** VOC, date below **Note:** Many varieties and designs exist.

Date	Mintage	VG	F	VF	XF	Unc
ND(1790-1817)	—	35.00	55.00	75.00	120	—

KM# 3 KEPING

Copper **Obv:** Crowned shield **Rev:** Scales **Note:** Many varieties and designs exist.

Date	Mintage	VG	F	VF	XF	Unc
ND(1790-1817)	—	35.00	55.00	75.00	120	—

KM# 4 KEPING

Copper **Obv:** Crowned shield **Rev:** Numerals inscription **Note:** Many varieties and designs exist.

Date	Mintage	VG	F	VF	XF	Unc
ND(1790-1817)	—	35.00	55.00	75.00	120	—

KM# 5 KEPING

Copper **Rev:** Crude CEVI in sections of heart-shaped shield **Note:** Many varieties and designs exist. Some specimens have *Banjar* in Malay within the obverse shield. Combinations of obverse and reverse of all types exist.

Date	Mintage	VG	F	VF	XF	Unc
ND(1790-1817)	—	35.00	55.00	75.00	120	—

JAVA

A mountainous island, 661 miles long by 124 miles at widest part, in greater Sunda island group. Early cultural influence from India. Islam introduced in late 1400's. Java was mainly a Dutch possession from 1619 to 1947 with the exception of a few periods of British occupation, principally 1811-1816.

MONETARY SYSTEM

4 Duit = 1 Stiver
30 Stivers = 1 Rupee (Silver)
66 Stivers = 1 Dollar

DATING SYSTEM

The coins listed are found with AD (Christian) dates, AD and AH (Hejira) dates, and with AD, AH and AS (Aji Saka = Javanese) dates which are explained in the introduction in this catalog.

UNITED EAST INDIA COMPANY

HAMMERED COINAGE

KM# 180 STUIVER

23.1600 g., Copper Bonk **Obv:** Value in pearled rectangle **Rev:** Date in pearled rectangle **Note:** Crudely cut from copper bars called "Bonks".

Date	Mintage	VG	F	VF	XF	Unc
1796	—	20.00	32.50	55.00	125	—
1797	—	17.50	27.50	45.00	100	—
1798	—	20.00	32.50	55.00	125	—
1799	—	50.00	95.00	130	175	—

KM# 181 2 STUIVERS

46.3200 g., Copper Bonk **Obv:** Value in pearled rectangle **Rev:** Date in pearled rectangle **Note:** Crudely cut from copper bars called "Bonks".

Date	Mintage	VG	F	VF	XF	Unc
1796	—	35.00	60.00	100	160	—
1797	—	30.00	50.00	80.00	145	—
1798	—	30.00	50.00	80.00	145	—
1799 Rare	—	—	—	—	—	—

MILLED COINAGE

KM# 174.1 DUIT

Copper **Obv. Inscription:** DUYT/IAVAS/ date **Rev:** Similar but in Arabic script **Note:** Prev. KM#174.

Date	Mintage	VG	F	VF	XF	Unc
1764	—	45.00	85.00	145	240	—

KM# 174.2 DUIT

Copper **Obv. Inscription:** DUYT / IAVAS / date **Rev:** Similar but in Arabic script

Date	Mintage	VG	F	VF	XF	Unc
1765	—	45.00	85.00	145	240	—

KM# 176 DUIT

Copper **Obv:** Inscription, date in sprays **Obv. Inscription:** DUYT / IAVAS **Rev:** Similar but in Arabic script

Date	Mintage	VG	F	VF	XF	Unc
1783	—	45.00	85.00	145	240	—

KM# 179 DUIT

Tin **Obv:** N above VOC monogram **Rev:** Value, date

Date	Mintage	VG	F	VF	XF	Unc
1796	7,691	40.00	70.00	100	200	—
1797	Inc. above	—	—	—	—	—

KM# 177 1/2 RUPEE

8.0000 g., 0.7920 Gold 0.2037 oz. AGW **Obv:** Crude Arabic legend **Rev:** Crude Arabic legend above date

Date	Mintage	VG	F	VF	XF	Unc
1783 Rare	—	—	—	—	—	—
1784 Rare	1,610	—	—	—	—	—
1785 Rare	5,147	—	—	—	—	—
1798	—	300	600	950	1,300	—
1799	3,321	300	600	950	1,300	—

KM# 178 1/2 RUPEE

16.0120 g., 0.7920 Gold 0.4077 oz. AGW **Obv:** Crude Arabic script above date **Rev:** Crude Arabic script

Date	Mintage	VG	F	VF	XF	Unc
1783 Rare	3,822	—	—	—	—	—
1784 Rare	10,000	—	—	—	—	—
1796	2,150	300	700	1,500	2,250	—
1797	11,000	500	1,000	1,800	2,600	—

KM# 170 RUPEE

11.7200 g., 0.8330 Silver 0.3139 oz. ASW **Obv:** Crude Arabic script above date **Rev:** Crude Arabic script

Date	Mintage	VG	F	VF	XF	Unc
1747	9,989	80.00	150	250	325	—
1748	—	125	250	325	400	—
1749	173,000	50.00	90.00	135	180	—
1750	59,000	50.00	90.00	135	180	—

KM# 175.1 RUPEE

13.1500 g., 0.8330 Silver 0.3522 oz. ASW **Obv:** Crude Arabic legend **Rev:** Crude Arabic legend **Note:** No known specimens exist of coins dated 1782, 1787, and 1789. Prev. KM#175.

Date	Mintage	VG	F	VF	XF	Unc
1764	—	—	—	—	—	—
1765	296,000	25.00	40.00	65.00	110	—
1766	Inc. above	20.00	35.00	60.00	100	—
1767	Inc. above	20.00	35.00	60.00	100	—
1783	—	20.00	35.00	60.00	100	—
1784	—	30.00	50.00	80.00	145	—
1785	—	30.00	50.00	80.00	145	—
1786	—	30.00	50.00	80.00	145	—
1788	—	30.00	70.00	110	190	—

KM# 175.1a RUPEE

Gold **Obv:** Crude Arabic script **Rev:** Crude Arabic script **Note:** Prev. KM#175b.

Date	Mintage	VG	F	VF	XF	Unc
1766 Proof; unique	—	—	—	—	—	—

KM# 175.2 RUPEE
13.1500 g., 0.7920 Silver 0.3348 oz. ASW **Obv:** Stylized Arabic script **Rev:** Stylized Arabic script **Note:** Prev. KM#175a.

Date	Mintage	VG	F	VF	XF	Unc
1795	—	27.50	45.00	80.00	135	—
1796	—	20.00	35.00	60.00	100	—
1798	—	27.50	45.00	80.00	135	—
1799	18,000	27.50	45.00	80.00	135	—

KM# 171.2 JAVA DUCAT
4.3000 g., Gold **Obv:** Crude Arabic script above date **Rev:** Crude Arabic script **Note:** Mintmark: Double star.

Date	Mintage	VG	F	VF	XF	Unc
1744 Proof; rare	—	—	—	—	—	—
1745 Rare	—	—	—	—	—	—

KM# 171.1 JAVA DUCAT
4.3000 g., Gold **Obv:** Crude Arabic script above date **Rev:** Crude Arabic script **Note:** Mintmark: Star.

Date	Mintage	VG	F	VF	XF	Unc
1744 Proof; rare	—	—	—	—	—	—
1745 Rare	—	—	—	—	—	—

KM# 172 JAVA DUCAT
4.3000 g., Gold **Obv:** Crude Arabic script **Rev:** Crude Arabic script **Note:** Ornaments added.

Date	Mintage	VG	F	VF	XF	Unc
1746 Rare	—	—	—	—	—	—

KM# 173 2 JAVA DUCATS
8.5800 g., Gold **Obv:** Crude Arabic script **Rev:** Crude Arabic script

Date	Mintage	VG	F	VF	XF	Unc
1746 Rare	—	—	—	—	—	—
1747 Rare	—	—	—	—	—	—
1748 Rare	—	—	—	—	—	—

COUNTERMARKED COINAGE

1760

By order of the home authorities of the Company the countermarking of Ducats was stopped in 1761

Countermark: Java in Arabic in circular indent.

KM# 168 RUPEE
11.4400 g., 0.9840 Silver 0.3619 oz. ASW **Countermark:** *Java*" **Note:** Prev. KM#44. Countermark on Rupee, KM#44.

CM Date	Host Date	Good	VG	F	VF	XF
ND	1693-94//38 Rare	—	—	—	—	—

KM# 167 2 RUPEE
23.0000 g., Silver **Countermark:** *Java* in Arabic in circular indent **Note:** Countermark on Iran 2 Rupi, KM#438.

CM Date	Host Date	Good	VG	F	VF	XF
ND(1753-91)	AH(1161) 1 known; Rare	—	—	—	—	—

KM# 169 2 LARI
9.6000 g., Billon **Countermark:** *Java*. **Note:** Prev. KM#180. Countermark on Maldives 2 Lari, KM#17.

CM Date	Host Date	Good	VG	F	VF	XF
ND(1753-91)	AH1163-68	50.00	85.00	110	150	—

KM# 183.1 DUCATON (Thaler, Daalder)
Silver **Countermark:** *Java* **Note:** Countermark on Austria-Vienna Thaler, KM#1967a.

CM Date	Host Date	Good	VG	F	VF	XF
ND(1753-91)	1754-65	55.00	100	175	—	300

KM# 184.1 DUCATON (Thaler, Daalder)
0.9030 Silver **Countermark:** *Java* **Note:** Countermark on Mexico City 8 Reales, KM#106.

CM Date	Host Date	Good	VG	F	VF	XF
ND(1753-91)	(1772-89)	85.00	140	240	400	—

KM# 183.2 DUCATON (Thaler, Daalder)
Silver **Countermark:** *Java* **Note:** Countermark on Tuscany Francescone, C#22.

CM Date	Host Date	Good	VG	F	VF	XF
ND(1753-91)	(1767-69)	125	225	400	650	—

KM# 183.3 DUCATON (Thaler, Daalder)
Silver **Countermark:** *Java* **Note:** Countermark on Tuscany Francescone, C#8a.

CM Date	Host Date	Good	VG	F	VF	XF
ND(1753-65)	(1747-65)	125	225	175	—	650

KM# 184.2 DUCATON (Thaler, Daalder)
0.9030 Silver **Note:** Countermark on Lima Mint 8 Reales, KM#78.

CM Date	Host Date	Good	VG	F	VF	XF
ND	ND(1772-84)	85.00	140	240	400	—

KM# 185 DUCAT
0.9860 Gold **Countermark:** *Java* **Note:** Countermark on Holland Ducat, KM#53.

CM Date	Host Date	Good	VG	F	VF	XF
ND(1753-61)	(1750)	—	400	650	950	1,500
ND(1753-61)	(1753)	—	400	650	950	1,500
ND(1753-61)	(1758)	—	400	650	950	1,500

KM# 186 DUCAT
0.9860 Gold **Countermark:** *Java* **Note:** Countermark on Utrecht Ducat, KM#88.

CM Date	Host Date	Good	VG	F	VF	XF
ND(1753-61)	(1758)	—	400	650	950	1,500
ND(1753-61)	(1759)	—	400	650	950	1,500

KM# 188 DUCAT
0.9860 Gold **Countermark:** *Java* **Note:** Countermark on Zeeland Ducat, KM#85.

CM Date	Host Date	Good	VG	F	VF	XF
ND(1753-61)	(1758)	—	400	650	950	1,500
ND(1753-61)	(1759)	—	400	650	950	1,500

KM# 187 DUCAT
0.9860 Gold **Countermark:** *Java* **Note:** Countermark on West Friesland Ducat, KM#93.

CM Date	Host Date	Good	VG	F	VF	XF
ND(1753-61)	(1754)	—	400	650	950	1,500
ND(1753-61)	(1755)	—	400	650	950	1,500
ND(1753-61)	(1758)	—	400	650	950	1,500
ND(1753-61)	(1759)	—	400	650	950	1,500

BATAVIAN REPUBLIC

1799-1806

MINTMASTER'S INITIALS
Z – J.A. Zwekkert

HAMMERED COINAGE

KM# 206 STUIVER
23.1600 g., Copper **Obv:** Value in pearled rectangle **Rev:** Date in pearled rectangle **Note:** Varieties exist. Crudely cut from copper bars, called "Bonks".

Date	Mintage	Good	VG	F	VF	XF
1800	—	8.50	15.00	35.00	75.00	150

KM# 207 2 STUIVERS
46.3200 g., Copper **Obv:** Value in pearled rectangle **Rev:** Date in pearled rectangle **Note:** Varieties exist. Crudely cut from copper bars called "Bonks".

Date	Mintage	Good	VG	F	VF	XF
1800	—	25.00	40.00	60.00	100	175

MILLED COINAGE

KM# 205 STUIVER
Lead-Bronze **Obv. Inscription:** JAVA / date **Rev:** Value **Note:** Varieties exist. Size varies: 25.0-25.7 mm.

Date	Mintage	Good	VG	F	VF	XF
1799	—	20.00	30.00	50.00	75.00	—
1800	—	20.00	30.00	50.00	75.00	—

KM# 209 1/2 RUPEE
8.0060 g., 0.7500 Gold 0.1930 oz. AGW **Obv:** Arabic script, AD date **Rev:** Arabic script

Date	Mintage	VG	F	VF	XF	Unc
1800 Rare	—	—	—	—	—	—

KM# 208 RUPEE
13.1500 g., 0.7920 Silver 0.3348 oz. ASW **Obv:** Arabic script, AD date **Rev:** Arabic script **Note:** Thick planchet. Varieties exist.

Date	Mintage	VG	F	VF	XF	Unc
1800 Z	—	500	750	1,000	1,250	—

PONTIANAK

Sultanate in West Borneo.

RULER
S. Syarif Kasim Alkadrie, 1808-1819

SULTANATE

MILLED COINAGE

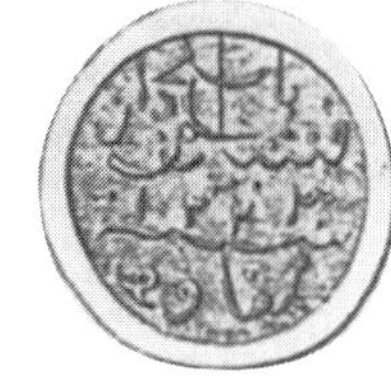

KM# 1 KEPING

Copper **Obv:** Inscription **Rev:** Scales with x at center

Date	Mintage	Good	VG	F	VF	XF
AH1223	—	—	10.00	20.00	40.00	85.00

KM# 2 KEPING

Copper, 22 mm. **Obv:** Inscription **Rev:** Scales with dot at center

Date	Mintage	Good	VG	F	VF	XF
AH1226	—	—	10.00	20.00	40.00	85.00

KM# 3 KEPING

Copper, 26 mm. **Obv:** Retrograde inscription **Rev:** Scales with 3 dots at center

Date	Mintage	Good	VG	F	VF	XF
AH1226	—	—	10.00	20.00	40.00	85.00

SUMATRA, ISLAND OF

An island, south of the Malay peninsula, was first reached by Europeans for trade in 1599. Competition between European powers for trading rights continued until 1824 at which time it became a Dutch possession. British coins for the island were struck at the Birmingham Mint by Matthew Boulton in 1786 and other issues were struck at Indian mints.

TITLES

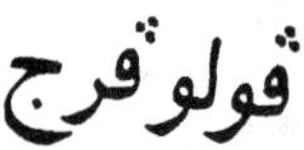

Pulu Percha

MONETARY SYSTEM

100 Kepings = 1 Suku
4 Suku = 1 Dollar (Spanish)

DENOMINATIONS

The following Arabic legends appear for the denomination with an Arabic number above.

(1) Keping

Sakeping

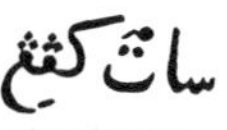
Satu Keping

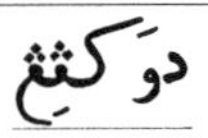
(2) Dua Keping

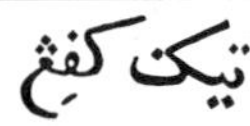
(3) Tiga Keping

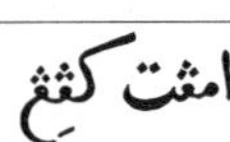
(4) Ampat Keping

FORT MARLBRO

British United East India Company

This fort was the principal British settlement in the East Indies from its construction in 1714 until 1788, when the Dutch returned to Sumatra. The name is a corrupted version of Marlborough, a popular British hero in 1714. The British regained control of the area in 1795 and remained there till 1824 when civil war forced them to return the west coast to the Dutch.

MILLED COINAGE

KM# 270 1/2 DOLLAR

Copper **Obv. Inscription:** FORT / MARLBRO **Rev:** Value **Note:** Struck as emergency coinage under authority of Governor Bruff.

Date	Mintage	VG	F	VF	XF	Unc
ND(1797) Rare	—	—	—	—	—	—

KM# 271 2 SUKUS

Silver **Obv:** Inscription, value above, date below **Obv. Inscription:** FORT / MARLBRO, date **Rev:** Arabic script, date below

Date	Mintage	VG	F	VF	XF	Unc
AH1197 (1783)	—	150	300	525	850	—
AH1198 (1784)	—	225	400	800	1,150	—

BRITISH UNITED EAST INDIA COMPANY

1685-1824

MILLED COINAGE

KM# 257.1 KEPING

Copper **Obv:** VEIC bale-mark, date below **Rev:** Value, date below **Edge:** Milled (oblique or vertical)

Date	Mintage	F	VF	XF	Unc	BU
1786//AH1200	—	3.50	7.50	20.00	45.00	—
1786//AH1200 Proof	—	—	—	—	75.00	—
1786//AH1200 Gilt Proof	—	—	—	—	100	—
1788//AH1202 Error AH1200; rare	—	—	—	—	—	—
1788//AH1202	—	3.50	7.50	20.00	45.00	—
1788//AH1202 Proof	—	—	—	—	75.00	—
1788//AH1202 Gilt Proof	—	—	—	—	100	—

KM# 257.2 KEPING

Copper **Obv:** VEIC bale-mark, date below **Rev:** Value, date below **Edge:** Plain

Date	Mintage	F	VF	XF	Unc	BU
1786//AH1200	—	2.75	5.50	15.00	35.00	—
1788//AH1202 Error AH1200	—	2.75	5.50	15.00	35.00	—
1788//AH1202 Proof	—	—	—	—	75.00	—

KM# 257.1a KEPING

3.4020 g., Gold **Obv:** VEIC bale-mark, date below **Rev:** Value, date below **Edge:** Oblique or vertical milling

Date	Mintage	Good	VG	F	VF	XF
1787//AH1202 Proof	—	—	—	—	—	—

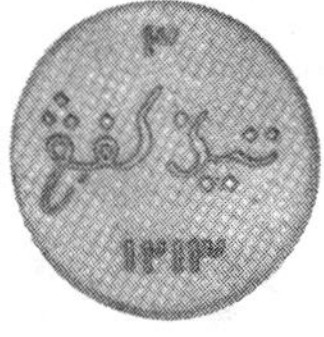

KM# 260 KEPING

Copper **Obv:** VEIC bale-mark, date below **Rev:** Error: Arabic denomination and "3" (for 1), value, date below

Date	Mintage	F	VF	XF	Unc	BU
1798//AH1213	—	2.75	5.50	15.00	35.00	—
1798//AH1213 Proof	—	—	—	—	75.00	—
1798//AH1213 Gilt Proof	—	—	—	—	100	—

KM# 255 2 KEPINGS

Copper, 22 mm. **Obv:** VEIC bale-mark, date below **Rev:** Value, date below **Edge:** Milled (oblique or vertical)

Date	Mintage	F	VF	XF	Unc	BU
1783//AH1197	—	6.50	12.50	30.00	55.00	—
1783//AH1197 Proof	—	—	—	—	75.00	—

KM# 255a 2 KEPINGS

Silver **Obv:** VEIC bale-mark, date below **Rev:** Value, date below **Edge:** Plain

Date	Mintage	F	VF	XF	Unc	BU
1783//AH1197 Proof	—	—	—	—	300	—

KM# 255b 2 KEPINGS

Gold **Obv:** VEIC bale-mark, date below **Rev:** Value, date below **Edge:** Reeded

Date	Mintage	F	VF	XF	Unc	BU
1783//AH1197 Proof	—	—	—	—	1,850	—

KM# 256 2 KEPINGS

Copper, 20 mm. **Obv:** VEIC bale-mark, date below **Rev:** Value, date below

Date	Mintage	F	VF	XF	Unc	BU
1783//AH1197	—	6.50	12.50	30.00	55.00	—

KM# 258 2 KEPINGS

Copper **Obv:** VEIC bale-mark, date below **Rev:** Value, date below

Date	Mintage	F	VF	XF	Unc	BU
1786//AH1200	—	4.00	8.50	20.00	45.00	—
1786//AH1200 Proof	—	—	—	—	100	—
1786//AH1200 Gilt Proof	—	—	—	—	200	—
1786//AH1200 Error AH1202; Rare	—	—	—	—	—	—
1787//AH1202	—	4.00	8.50	20.00	45.00	—
1788//AH1202	—	4.00	8.50	20.00	45.00	—
1788//AH1202 Proof	—	—	—	—	100	—
1788//AH1202 Gilt Proof	—	—	—	—	175	—

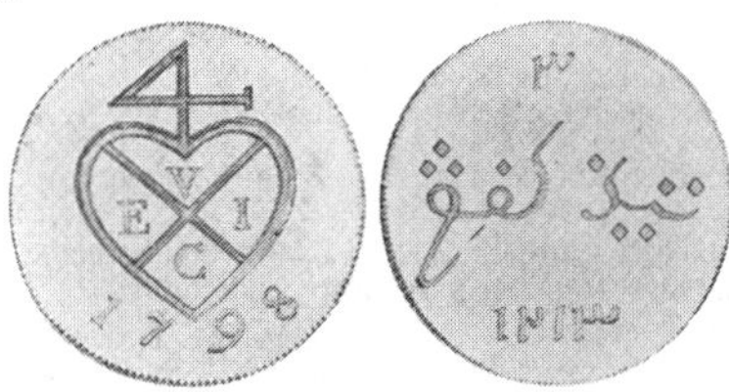

KM# 261 2 KEPINGS

Copper **Obv:** VEIC bale-mark, date below **Rev:** Error: Arabic denomination and "3" (for 2), value, date below

Date	Mintage	F	VF	XF	Unc	BU
1798//AH1213	—	5.00	10.00	25.00	50.00	—
1798//AH1213 Proof	—	—	—	—	100	—
1798//AH1213 Gilt Proof	—	—	—	—	175	—

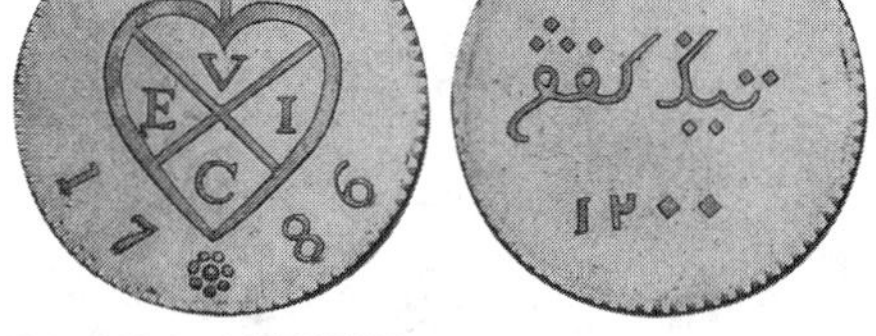

KM# 259.1 3 KEPINGS

Copper **Obv:** VEIC bale-mark, date below **Rev:** Value, rosette separates date below **Edge:** Oblique reeded

Date	Mintage	F	VF	XF	Unc	BU
1786//AH1200	—	8.50	16.50	40.00	75.00	—
1786//AH1200 Proof	—	Value: 150				
1786//AH1200 Gilt Proof	—	—	—	—	225	—
1788//AH1202	—	6.50	12.50	20.00	45.00	—
1788//AH1202 Proof	—	Value: 150				
1788//AH1202 Gilt Proof	—	—	—	—	225	—

KM# 259.1a 3 KEPINGS

9.4800 g., Gold **Obv:** VEIC bale-mark, date below **Rev:** Value, rosette separates date below **Edge:** Reeded

Date	Mintage	F	VF	XF	Unc	BU
AH1202 (1787) Proof	—	—	—	—	—	—

KM# 259.2 3 KEPINGS

Copper **Obv:** VEIC bale-mark, date below **Rev:** Value, without rosette separating date below

Date	Mintage	F	VF	XF	Unc	BU
1798//AH1213 (1798)	—	6.50	12.50	30.00	45.00	—

Date	Mintage	F	VF	XF	Unc	BU
1798//AH1213 (1798) Proof	—	—	—	—	150	—
1798//AH1213 (1798) Gilt Proof	—	—	—	—	225	—

PATTERNS

Including off metal strikes

KM#	Date	Mintage	Identification	Mkt Val
Pn1	1787	—	Keping. Copper.	—
Pn2	1787	—	2 Kepings. Copper.	—
Pn3	1787	—	2 Kepings. Copper. Small date, P#27.	—
Pn4	1787	—	2 Kepings. Copper. Large date, P#28.	—

KM#	Date	Mintage	Identification	Mkt Val
Pn5	1787	—	2 Kepings. Copper. Oval without rosettes at sides of 1787 date.	—
Pn6	1787	—	2 Kepings. Copper. With rosettes at sides of 1787 date.	—
Pn7	1787	—	2 Kepings. Copper. Oval without rosettes at sides of 1787 date and undulated rim.	—
Pn8	1787	—	2 Kepings. Copper. Milled edge. Oval with rosettes at sides of 1787 date.	—
Pn9	1787	—	2 Kepings. Copper. Round.	—

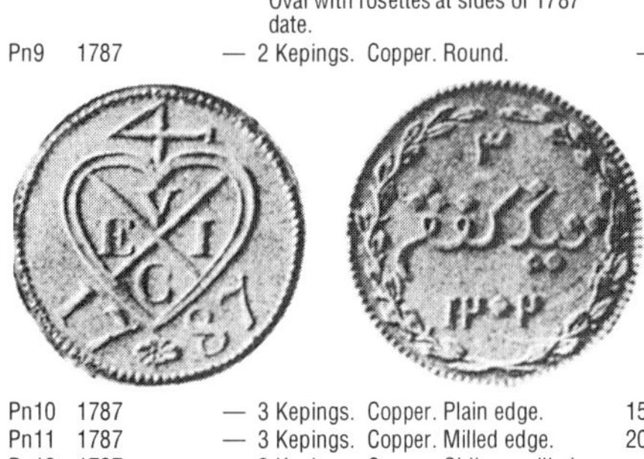

KM#	Date	Mintage	Identification	Mkt Val
Pn10	1787	—	3 Kepings. Copper. Plain edge.	150
Pn11	1787	—	3 Kepings. Copper. Milled edge.	200
Pn12	1787	—	3 Kepings. Copper. Oblique milled edge.	—

KM#	Date	Mintage	Identification	Mkt Val
Pn13	1787	—	3 Kepings. Silver. Oblique milled edge.	—
Pn14	1787	—	3 Kepings. Silver. Oblique milled edge. Thin flan.	—

NETHERLANDS WEST INDIES

The islands came under Dutch control in the early part of the seventeenth century. The Director of the West Indian colonies went to the Estates General, the legislature of the Netherlands, in 1792 in an effort to get coins made for the West Indies that would carry some distinctive mark as those of the East Indies did. Legislation was passed on Dec. 31, 1793 that such coins should be made to the standard of the Netherlands. The 1/4 Gulden was included in the series and the letter W below the arms was to be the distinctive mark. Some of the 3, 1 and 1/4 Gulden were used at the Dutch settlement on the Gold Coast in Africa. All were struck at the Utrecht Mint.

RULER
Dutch

MONETARY SYSTEM
20 Stuiver = 1 Gulden

MINT NAME
TRAI(ectum) = Utrecht

DUTCH COLONY

STANDARD COINAGE

KM# 1 2 STUIVERS
0.8100 g., 0.5830 Silver 0.0152 oz. ASW

Date	Mintage	F	VF	XF	Unc	BU
1794	30,000	55.00	85.00	150	265	—

KM# 2 1/4 GULDEN
2.6500 g., 0.9200 Silver 0.0784 oz. ASW

Date	Mintage	F	VF	XF	Unc	BU
1794	20,000	28.00	45.00	75.00	135	—

Note: Varieties exist

KM# 3 GULDEN
10.6100 g., 0.9200 Silver 0.3138 oz. ASW

Date	Mintage	F	VF	XF	Unc	BU
1794	14,000	140	250	400	600	—

KM# 4 3 GULDEN
31.8200 g., 0.9200 Silver 0.9412 oz. ASW

Date	Mintage	F	VF	XF	Unc	BU
1794	1,226	1,850	2,750	4,000	7,500	—

NORWAY

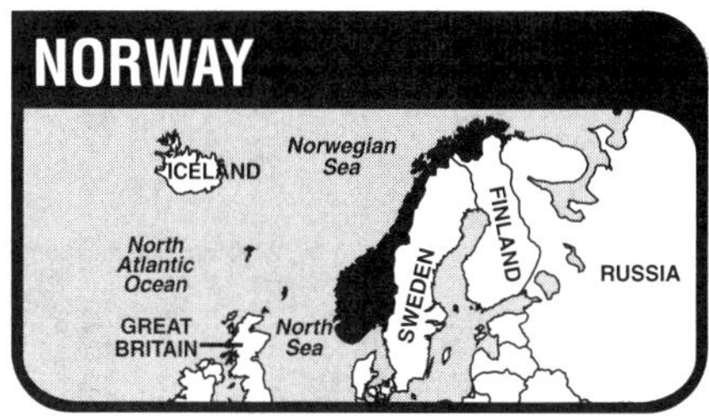

The Kingdom of Norway (*Norge, Noreg*), a constitutional monarchy located in northwestern Europe, has an area of 150,000sq. mi. (324,220 sq. km.), including the island territories of Spitzbergen (Svalbard) and Jan Mayen, and a population of *4.2 million. Capital: Oslo (Christiania). The diversified economic base of Norway includes shipping, fishing, forestry, agriculture, and manufacturing. Nonferrous metals, paper and paperboard, paper pulp, iron, steel and oil are exported.

A united Norwegian kingdom was established in the 9th century, the era of the indomitable Norse Vikings who ranged far and wide, visiting the coasts of northwestern Europe, the Mediterranean, Greenland and North America. In the 13th century the Norse kingdom was united briefly with Sweden, then passed through inheritance in 1380 to the rule of Denmark which was maintained until 1814. In 1814 Norway fell again under the rule of Sweden. The union lasted until 1905 when the Norwegian Parliament arranged a peaceful separation and invited a Danish prince (King Haakon VII) to ascend the throne of an independent Kingdom of Norway.

RULER
Danish, until 1814

MINT OFFICIALS' INITIALS

Kongsberg, 1686-

Initial	Date	Name
C	1727-28	Commission
	1735-36	Commission
HCM plus flower (f)	1687-1718	Henning Christofer Meyer
HCM plus flower (f)	1719-28	Henrik Christofer Meyer
HIAB	1776-97	Hans Jacob Arnold Branth
IAR		Angrid Austlid Rise, engraver
IGM	1797-1806	Johan Georg Madelung in Altona
IHM	1769-75	Johan Henrich Madelung
NBF	1729-36	Nicolai Bernhard Fuchs
SI	1792	Salomon Ahron
TL	1737-69	Truls Andersen Lyng

MONETARY SYSTEM

Until 1794
96 Skilling = 1 Speciedaler

1794-1873
120 Skilling = 1 Speciedaler

KINGDOM

STANDARD COINAGE

KM# 205 SKILLING
1.1100 g., 0.1880 Silver 0.0067 oz. ASW **Obv:** Crowned monogram **Rev:** Value, crossed hammers divides date below

Date	Mintage	VG	F	VF	XF	Unc
1701	18,000	95.00	190	435	750	—
1702	12,000	85.00	175	400	700	—
1703	11,000	85.00	175	400	700	—
1704	12,000	85.00	175	400	700	—
1705	21,000	85.00	175	400	750	—
1706	16,000	95.00	190	435	750	—
1707	20,000	65.00	140	375	600	—
1708	21,000	65.00	140	375	600	—
1710	21,000	65.00	140	375	600	—
1711	38,000	65.00	140	375	600	—
1712	41,000	65.00	140	375	600	—
1719 HCM	49,000	65.00	140	375	600	—
1720 HCM	49,000	65.00	140	375	600	—
1721 HCM	49,000	65.00	140	375	600	—
1722 HCM Rare	—	—	—	—	—	—

KM# 240 SKILLING

0.5700 g., 0.2500 Silver 0.0046 oz. ASW **Obv:** Crowned F5 monogram **Rev:** Value above date

Date	Mintage	VG	F	VF	XF	Unc
1761 TL	—	40.00	80.00	150	325	—
1762 TL	29,000	40.00	80.00	150	325	—
1763 TL	931,000	5.00	15.00	30.00	95.00	—
1764 TL	2,963,000	5.00	15.00	30.00	95.00	—
1765 TL	1,887,000	5.00	15.00	30.00	95.00	—

KM# 245 SKILLING

0.5700 g., 0.2500 Silver 0.0046 oz. ASW, 14 mm. **Obv:** Crowned double C7 monogram **Rev:** Value, date

Date	Mintage	VG	F	VF	XF	Unc
1768 TL	697,000	7.50	17.50	27.50	75.00	—
1769 IHM	890,000	5.00	10.00	20.00	45.00	—
1770 IHM	448,000	7.50	17.50	27.50	75.00	—

KM# 245a SKILLING

Copper **Obv:** Crowned double C7 monogram **Rev:** Value, date **Note:** Struck at Konsberg Mint.

Date	Mintage	VG	F	VF	XF	Unc
1771	2,063,000	1.50	3.00	6.00	35.00	—

KM# 258 SKILLING

0.7700 g., 0.1870 Silver 0.0046 oz. ASW **Obv:** Crowned C7 monogram

Date	Mintage	VG	F	VF	XF	Unc
1779 HIAB	845,000	3.00	7.00	13.50	45.00	—
1780 HIAB	1,152,000	3.00	7.00	13.50	45.00	—

KM# 206 2 SKILLING

1.2200 g., 0.3440 Silver 0.0135 oz. ASW **Obv:** Crowned double F4 monogram

Date	Mintage	VG	F	VF	XF	Unc
1701	929,000	8.00	15.00	40.00	125	—
1702	833,000	8.00	15.00	40.00	125	—
1703	569,000	8.00	15.00	40.00	125	—
1704	1,024,000	8.00	15.00	40.00	125	—
1704 Rare; without mintmark	—	—	—	—	—	—
1705	980,000	8.00	15.00	40.00	125	—
1706	890,000	8.00	15.00	40.00	125	—
1707	1,013,000	8.00	15.00	40.00	125	—
1708	1,307,000	8.00	15.00	40.00	125	—
1709	1,149,000	8.00	15.00	40.00	125	—
1710	1,176,000	8.00	15.00	40.00	125	—
1711	1,663,000	8.00	15.00	40.00	125	—
1712	1,713,000	8.00	15.00	40.00	125	—
1713	1,379,000	8.00	15.00	40.00	125	—
1714	893,000	8.00	15.00	40.00	125	—

KM# 215 2 SKILLING

1.3000 g., 0.2810 Silver 0.0117 oz. ASW **Obv:** Larger, more ornate monogram **Rev:** Mintmark below lion

Date	Mintage	VG	F	VF	XF	Unc
1714 (f)	1,624,000	15.00	35.00	75.00	225	—
1715 (f)	1,730,000	20.00	45.00	110	250	—
1716 (f)	1,599,000	15.00	35.00	75.00	225	—
1717 (f)	915,000	15.00	35.00	75.00	225	—
1718 (f)	312,000	35.00	65.00	160	350	—

KM# 218 2 SKILLING

1.3000 g., 0.2810 Silver 0.0117 oz. ASW **Rev:** Without mintmark below lion

Date	Mintage	VG	F	VF	XF	Unc
1719	289,000	20.00	35.00	90.00	225	—
1720	289,000	20.00	35.00	90.00	225	—
1721	389,000	20.00	35.00	95.00	225	—
1722 Rare	217,000	—	—	—	—	—
1723	241,000	20.00	35.00	90.00	225	—
1724	1,803,000	15.00	20.00	65.00	200	—
1725	1,094,000	20.00	45.00	100	300	—

KM# 235 2 SKILLING

1.2200 g., 0.3440 Silver 0.0135 oz. ASW **Obv:** Crowned monogram **Rev:** Crown above lion **Note:** Varieties exist.

Date	Mintage	VG	F	VF	XF	Unc
1742 TL	2,000	70.00	110	250	400	—
1743 TL	2,100	70.00	110	250	400	—
1745 TL	—	70.00	125	275	425	—

KM# 237 2 SKILLING

1.2200 g., 0.3440 Silver 0.0135 oz. ASW **Obv:** Crowned F5 monogram **Rev:** Crown above lion on battle-axe

Date	Mintage	VG	F	VF	XF	Unc
1747 TL	6,700	15.00	35.00	100	250	—
1756 TL	—	50.00	150	275	650	—

KM# 237a 2 SKILLING

1.1500 g., 0.2500 Silver 0.0092 oz. ASW **Obv:** Crowned F5 monogram **Rev:** Crown above lion on battle-axe

Date	Mintage	VG	F	VF	XF	Unc
1761 TL	192,000	6.00	13.50	40.00	115	—
1762 TL	3,440,000	4.00	10.00	25.00	85.00	—
1763 TL	931,000	4.00	10.00	25.00	85.00	—
1764 TL	914,000	5.00	12.00	40.00	115	—

KM# 255 2 SKILLING

1.1800 g., 0.3440 Silver 0.0131 oz. ASW **Obv:** Crowned C7 monogram **Rev:** Crowned oval shield divides date

Date	Mintage	VG	F	VF	XF	Unc
1778 HIAB	580,000	2.50	5.00	11.00	60.00	—
1779 HIAB	2,533,000	2.50	5.00	11.00	35.00	—
1780 HIAB	7,200,000	2.50	5.00	11.00	35.00	—
1781 HIAB R in NOR inverted	—	4.00	8.00	15.00	35.00	—
1781 HIAB	4,296,000	2.50	5.00	11.00	30.00	—
1782 HIAB	7,891,000	2.50	5.00	11.00	25.00	—
1783 HIAB	7,896,000	2.50	5.00	11.00	30.00	—
1784 HIAB	7,891,000	2.50	5.00	11.00	25.00	—
1785 HIAB	3,531,000	2.50	5.00	11.00	25.00	—
1786 HIAB	6,341,000	2.50	5.00	11.00	25.00	—
1787 HIAB	3,862,000	2.50	5.00	11.00	25.00	—
1788 HIAB	1,841,000	2.50	5.00	11.00	25.00	—

KM# 270 2 SKILLING

1.5000 g., 0.2500 Silver 0.0121 oz. ASW **Obv:** Crowned monogram **Rev:** Crossed hammers divides date below inscription

Date	Mintage	VG	F	VF	XF	Unc
1800 IGM	2,419,000	2.00	5.00	10.00	20.00	—

KM# 256 4 SKILLING

1.5300 g., 0.5620 Silver 0.0276 oz. ASW **Obv:** Crowned C7 monogram **Rev:** Crowned, round three-fold arms of Norway

Date	Mintage	VG	F	VF	XF	Unc
1778 HIAB	162,000	10.00	25.00	50.00	110	—

KM# 256a 4 SKILLING

2.7500 g., 0.3120 Silver 0.0276 oz. ASW **Obv:** Crowned C7 monogram **Rev:** Crowned oval 3-fold arms

Date	Mintage	VG	F	VF	XF	Unc
1788 HIAB	375,000	5.00	12.50	25.00	65.00	—

KM# 207 8 SKILLING (1/2 Mark)

3.0600 g., 0.5620 Silver 0.0553 oz. ASW **Obv:** Bust of Frederic IV, right **Rev:** Crown

Date	Mintage	VG	F	VF	XF	Unc
1701 (f)	805,000	10.00	25.00	55.00	135	—
1702 (f)	800,000	10.00	25.00	55.00	135	—

KM# 209 8 SKILLING (1/2 Mark)

2.2900 g., 0.7500 Silver 0.0552 oz. ASW **Obv:** Bust of Frederic IV, right **Obv. Legend:** FRID • IIII • DEI • GRAT • **Rev:** Crown divides value above date **Note:** Smaller size.

Date	Mintage	VG	F	VF	XF	Unc
1702 (f)	169,000	10.00	15.00	40.00	85.00	—
1703 (f)	540,000	10.00	15.00	40.00	85.00	—
1704 (f)	982,000	10.00	15.00	40.00	85.00	—
1705 (f)	953,000	10.00	15.00	40.00	85.00	—
1706 (f)	888,000	10.00	15.00	40.00	85.00	—
1707 (f)	1,011,000	10.00	15.00	40.00	85.00	—
1708 (f)	1,261,000	10.00	15.00	40.00	85.00	—
1709 (f)	1,122,000	10.00	15.00	40.00	85.00	—
1710 (f)GOT	1,164,000	10.00	15.00	40.00	85.00	—
1710 (f) GOR	Inc. above	65.00	135	—	—	—
1711 (f)	1,645,000	10.00	15.00	40.00	85.00	—
1712 (f)	1,657,000	10.00	15.00	40.00	85.00	—
1713 (f)	1,350,000	10.00	15.00	40.00	85.00	—
1714 (f)	923,000	10.00	15.00	40.00	85.00	—
1715 (f)	316,000	10.00	15.00	40.00	85.00	—

KM# 223 8 SKILLING (1/2 Mark)

3.6700 g., 0.4680 Silver 0.0552 oz. ASW **Obv:** Crowned double F4 monogram **Rev:** VIII flanked by stars above value, date divided by crossed hammers below

Date	Mintage	VG	F	VF	XF	Unc
1727 HCM	1,498,000	30.00	65.00	140	200	—

KM# 224 8 SKILLING (1/2 Mark)

3.6700 g., 0.4680 Silver 0.0552 oz. ASW **Obv:** Crowned arms of Norway **Rev:** VIII flanked by stars above value, date divided by crossed hammers below

Date	Mintage	VG	F	VF	XF	Unc
1727 HCM	Inc. above	10.00	15.00	45.00	110	—
1727 C	Inc. above	10.00	15.00	45.00	110	—
1728 C	1,324,000	10.00	15.00	45.00	110	—
1729 NBF	1,121,000	10.00	15.00	45.00	110	—
1730 NBF	1,433,000	10.00	15.00	45.00	110	—
1731 NBF	1,143,000	10.00	20.00	50.00	125	—
1732 NBF	1,243,000	10.00	20.00	50.00	125	—
1733 NBF	1,342,000	10.00	20.00	50.00	125	—
1734 NBF	1,434,000	10.00	20.00	50.00	125	—
1735 NBF	5,400	—	—	—	—	—

KM# 251 8 SKILLING (1/2 Mark)

3.0600 g., 0.5620 Silver 0.0553 oz. ASW **Obv:** Crowned C7 monogram **Rev:** Value, date

Date	Mintage	VG	F	VF	XF	Unc
1773 IHM	549,000	5.00	10.00	35.00	90.00	—
1774 IHM	414,000	5.00	10.00	35.00	90.00	—
1775 IHM	144,000	10.00	25.00	65.00	145	—

KM# 257 8 SKILLING (1/2 Mark)

3.0600 g., 0.5620 Silver 0.0553 oz. ASW **Obv:** Crowned C7 monogram **Rev:** Crowned oval three-fold arms

Date	Mintage	VG	F	VF	XF	Unc
1778 HIAB	922,000	5.00	10.00	22.50	55.00	—
1779 HIAB	1,315,000	5.00	10.00	22.50	55.00	—
1780 HIAB	680,000	5.00	10.00	22.50	55.00	—
1781 HIAB	890,000	5.00	10.00	22.50	55.00	—
1782 HIAB	1,027,000	5.00	10.00	22.50	55.00	—
1783 HIAB	1,032,000	5.00	10.00	22.50	55.00	—
1784 HIAB	959,000	5.00	10.00	22.50	55.00	—
1785 HIAB	1,105,000	5.00	10.00	22.50	55.00	—
1786 HIAB Rare	2,700	—	—	—	—	—
1787 HIAB	3,800	40.00	80.00	165	350	—
1788 HIAB	197,000	20.00	50.00	90.00	185	—
1789 HIAB	12,000	40.00	85.00	160	350	—
1790 HIAB Rare	7,800	—	—	—	—	—
1791 HIAB	6,700	40.00	85.00	160	350	—
1792 HIAB Rare	6,000	—	—	—	—	—
1793 HIAB	5,700	40.00	85.00	160	350	—
1794 HIAB	6,600	40.00	85.00	160	350	—
1795 HIAB	20,000	40.00	85.00	160	350	—

KM# 217 12 SKILLING

3.9000 g., 0.5620 Silver 0.0705 oz. ASW **Obv:** Crowned double F4 monogram **Rev:** Value: ...XII/SKILLING/DANSKE/date

Date	Mintage	VG	F	VF	XF	Unc
1717 HCM (f)	1,390,000	10.00	16.00	50.00	145	—
1718 HCM (f)	2,005,000	10.00	16.00	50.00	145	—
1719 HCM (f)	1,499,000	10.00	16.00	50.00	145	—
1720 HCM (f)	1,300,000	10.00	16.00	50.00	145	—
1721 HCM (f)	1,373,000	10.00	16.00	50.00	145	—
1722 HCM (f)	1,743,000	10.00	16.00	50.00	145	—
1723 HCM (f)	1,402,000	10.00	16.00	50.00	145	—
1724 HCM (f)	1,194,000	10.00	16.00	50.00	145	—
1724 H.C.M (f)	Inc. above	10.00	16.00	50.00	145	—

KM# 216 16 SKILLING (1 Mark)

5.2000 g., 0.6250 Silver 0.1045 oz. ASW **Obv:** Bust of Frederic IV, right **Rev:** Value: ...XVI/SKILLING/DANSKE/date **Note:** Counterfeits exist dated 1718 and 1719.

Date	Mintage	VG	F	VF	XF	Unc
1715	275,000	10.00	20.00	60.00	185	—
1716	725,000	10.00	20.00	60.00	185	—
1717	502,000	10.00	20.00	60.00	185	—

KM# 231.1 24 SKILLING

0.5620 Silver **Obv:** Crowned monogram **Obv. Legend:** NORV • VA • GO • D • G • REX • DAN • **Rev:** Crowned arms of Norway, in round shield, divides date, value in legend

Date	Mintage	VG	F	VF	XF	Unc
1734 NBF	273,000	50.00	80.00	150	350	—
1735 NBF	—	80.00	150	245	475	—

KM# 231.2 24 SKILLING

0.5620 Silver **Obv:** Crowned monogram, C below **Obv. Legend:** NORV • VA • GO • D • G • REX • DAN • **Rev:** Crowned arms of Norway, within round shield, divides date, value in legend

Date	Mintage	VG	F	VF	XF	Unc
1735 Rare	—	—	—	—	—	—

KM# 232.1 24 SKILLING

0.5620 Silver **Obv:** Crowned monogram **Obv. Legend:** NORV • VA • GO • D • G • REX • DAN **Rev:** Crowned arms of Norway, value and date in legend **Note:** Similar to KM#232.3.

Date	Mintage	VG	F	VF	XF	Unc
1735 N(h)BF Rare	—	—	—	—	—	—

KM# 232.2 24 SKILLING

0.5620 Silver **Obv:** Crowned monogram **Obv. Legend:** NORV • VA • GO • D • G • REX • DAN **Rev:** Crowned arms of Norway, value and date in legend **Note:** Similar to KM#232.3.

Date	Mintage	VG	F	VF	XF	Unc
1735 *(h)*c*	580,000	15.00	35.00	60.00	160	—
1736 *(h)*c*	547,000	20.00	40.00	80.00	175	—

KM# 232.3 24 SKILLING

0.5620 Silver **Obv:** Crowned monogram **Obv. Legend:** NORV • VA • GO • D • G • REX • DAN **Rev:** Crowned arms of Norway, value and date in legend

Date	Mintage	VG	F	VF	XF	Unc
1737 TL	573,000	20.00	40.00	70.00	175	—
1738 TL	850,000	20.00	40.00	70.00	175	—
1739 TL	704,000	20.00	40.00	70.00	175	—
1740 TL	830,000	20.00	40.00	70.00	175	—
1741 TL	1,081,000	20.00	40.00	70.00	175	—
1742 TL	892,000	20.00	40.00	70.00	175	—
1743 TL	859,000	20.00	40.00	70.00	175	—
1744 TL	1,015,000	20.00	40.00	70.00	175	—
1745 TL	1,092,000	20.00	40.00	70.00	175	—
1746 TL	1,240,000	20.00	40.00	70.00	175	—

KM# 236 24 SKILLING

9.1700 g., 0.5620 Silver 0.1657 oz. ASW **Obv:** Crowned monogram **Obv. Legend:** NORV • VA • GO • D • G • REX • DAN • **Rev:** Crowned arms of Norway, value and date in legend

Date	Mintage	VG	F	VF	XF	Unc
1746 TL	—	10.00	25.00	40.00	135	—
1747 TL	1,342,000	7.50	15.00	40.00	125	—
1748 TL	1,084,000	15.00	30.00	60.00	140	—
1749 TL	863,000	7.50	25.00	45.00	125	—
1750 TL	990,000	7.50	25.00	45.00	125	—
1751 TL	1,065,000	7.50	25.00	45.00	125	—
1752 TL	1,079,000	7.50	25.00	45.00	125	—
1753 TL	1,093,000	7.50	25.00	45.00	125	—
1754 TL	1,083,000	7.50	25.00	40.00	125	—
1755 TL	1,034,000	7.50	25.00	45.00	125	—
1756 TL	1,125,000	7.50	25.00	45.00	125	—
1757 TL	289,000	7.50	25.00	40.00	125	—
1758 TL	1,220,000	7.50	25.00	45.00	125	—
1759 TL	1,250,000	10.00	25.00	50.00	120	—
1760 TL	1,185,000	7.50	25.00	45.00	125	—
1761 TL	1,237,000	7.50	15.00	45.00	100	—
1762 TL	1,091,000	7.50	15.00	35.00	100	—
1763 TL	—	30.00	70.00	135	250	—

KM# 241 24 SKILLING

9.1700 g., 0.5620 Silver 0.1657 oz. ASW **Obv:** Crowned monogram **Obv. Legend:** NOR • VAN • GOT • REX • D • G • DAN • **Rev:** Crowned arms of Norway, value and date in legend

Date	Mintage	VG	F	VF	XF	Unc
1763 TL GOT REX	1,085,000	7.50	15.00	35.00	100	—
1764 TL	622,000	7.50	20.00	40.00	125	—
1765 TL	259,000	7.50	20.00	40.00	125	—

KM# 243 24 SKILLING

9.1700 g., 0.5620 Silver 0.1657 oz. ASW **Obv:** Crowned monogram **Obv. Legend:** NOR • VAN • GOT • REX • D • G • DAN • **Rev:** Crowned arms of Norway, value and date in legend

Date	Mintage	VG	F	VF	XF	Unc
1767 TL	—	85.00	185	325	625	—

KM# 250 24 SKILLING

9.1700 g., 0.5620 Silver 0.1657 oz. ASW **Obv:** Crowned monogram **Obv. Legend:** NOR • VAN • GOT • REX • D • G • DAN • **Rev:** Crowned, oval arms of Norway divides date, value in legend

Date	Mintage	VG	F	VF	XF	Unc
1772 IHM	299,000	15.00	30.00	60.00	135	—
1773 IHM	1,035,000	15.00	30.00	60.00	135	—
1774 IHM	283,000	15.00	30.00	60.00	135	—
1775 IHM Rare	4,000	—	—	—	—	—
1783 HIAB	16,000	65.00	125	235	400	—
1788 HIAB	64,000	30.00	60.00	135	275	—

KM# 221 2 MARK

8.9900 g., 0.8330 Silver 0.2408 oz. ASW **Obv:** Crowned monogram **Obv. Legend:** NOR • VAN • GOT • D • G • REX • DAN • **Rev:** Crowned, pear-shaped, 3-fold arms of Norway, date in legend

Date	Mintage	VG	F	VF	XF	Unc
1725 HCM	—	250	500	875	1,600	—
1726 HCM Rare	—	—	—	—	—	—

KM# 220 4 MARK (1 Krone)

22.2700 g., 0.6720 Silver 0.4811 oz. ASW **Obv:** Equestrian, right, IIII • MARCR • DANSRE • below **Obv. Legend:** FRIDERICUS • IIII • D • G • REX • DAN • NOR • V • G • **Rev:** Crowned 4-fold arms of Norway within order chain, divided date below **Note:** Dav. #1290.

Date	Mintage	VG	F	VF	XF	Unc
1723 HCM (f)	30,000	50.00	125	235	500	—

KM# 222 4 MARK (1 Krone)

22.2700 g., 0.6720 Silver 0.4811 oz. ASW **Obv:** Crowned monogram **Obv. Legend:** NOR • VAN • GOT • D • G • REX • DAN • **Rev:** Crowned, pear-shaped, 3-fold arms of Norway, date in legend **Note:** Cross-reference number Dav. #1292.

Date	Mintage	VG	F	VF	XF	Unc
1725 HCM	103,000	50.00	100	165	375	—
1726 HCM	139,000	50.00	100	165	375	—

KM# 233 4 MARK (1 Krone)

22.2700 g., 0.6720 Silver 0.4811 oz. ASW **Obv:** Crowned monogram **Obv. Legend:** NORV • VA • GO • D • G • REX • DAN • **Rev:** Crowned arms of Norway **Note:** Cross-reference number Dav. #1296.

Date	Mintage	VG	F	VF	XF	Unc
1736 C	6,000	300	650	1,250	2,100	—

KM# 230 6 MARK (1 Reisedaler - 1 Riksdaler)

26.9830 g., 0.8330 Silver 0.7226 oz. ASW **Obv:** Bust of Christian VI right **Obv. Legend:** CHRIST.VI.D.G. REX.DAN.NORV.V.G. **Rev:** Crowned arms of Norway divides 6 M, date below

Date	Mintage	VG	F	VF	XF	Unc
1732 Rare	4,524	—	—	—	—	—
1733	5,000	300	750	1,550	2,550	—

KM# 238 6 MARK (1 Reisedaler - 1 Riksdaler)

26.9830 g., 0.8330 Silver 0.7226 oz. ASW **Issuer:** Danish-Asiatic Company **Subject:** 300th Anniversary of the Reign of the House of Oldenburg in Denmark **Obv:** Bust right **Obv. Legend:** FRIDERICVS • V • D • G • REX • DAN • NOR • V • G • **Rev:** Crowned arms of Norway, 6 M divides date below **Note:** Dav. #1301.

Date	Mintage	VG	F	VF	XF	Unc
1749 PCW	5,008	250	600	1,200	2,150	—
1749 W	Inc. above	165	445	950	1,750	—

KM# 260 6 MARK (1 Reisedaler - 1 Riksdaler)
28.8900 g., 0.8750 Silver 0.8127 oz. ASW **Obv:** Armored bust right **Obv. Legend:** CHRISTIAN PEN VII ..... **Rev:** Crowned rampant lion (arms of Norway without shield) **Note:** Dav. #1312.

Date	Mintage	VG	F	VF	XF	Unc
1788 MF	—	350	900	1,500	2,000	—

KM# 271 1/15 SPECIE DALER
3.3700 g., 0.5000 Silver 0.0542 oz. ASW **Obv:** Crowned, oval arms of Norway **Rev:** Value, date

Date	Mintage	VG	F	VF	XF	Unc
1795 HIAB	144,000	5.00	10.00	25.00	75.00	—
1796 HIAB	312,000	5.00	10.00	25.00	75.00	—
1796 IGM	Inc. above	7.50	15.00	30.00	90.00	—
1797 IGM	312,000	5.00	10.00	25.00	70.00	—
1798 IGM	312,000	5.00	10.00	25.00	70.00	—
1799 IGM	403,000	5.00	10.00	25.00	70.00	—
1800 IGM	319,000	5.00	10.00	25.00	70.00	—

KM# 272 1/5 SPECIE DALER
7.3100 g., 0.6870 Silver 0.1615 oz. ASW **Obv:** Crowned monogram **Obv. Legend:** DALER • SPECIES • ... **Rev:** Crossed hammers divides date below value and inscription

Date	Mintage	VG	F	VF	XF	Unc
1796 HIAB	81,000	75.00	175	285	475	—
1796 IGM	Inc. above	15.00	30.00	65.00	120	—
1797 IGM	192,000	15.00	30.00	65.00	120	—
1798 IGM	189,000	15.00	30.00	65.00	120	—
1799 IGM	158,000	15.00	30.00	65.00	120	—
1800 IGM	125,000	15.00	30.00	65.00	120	—

KM# 266 1/3 SPECIE DALER
9.6300 g., 0.8750 Silver 0.2709 oz. ASW **Obv:** Head right **Obv. Legend:** CHRISTIANUS • VII • D • G • DAN • NORV • V • G • REX • **Rev:** Crowned, oval 3-fold arms of Norway **Note:** Similar to KM#273.

Date	Mintage	VG	F	VF	XF	Unc
1795 HIAB	15,000	75.00	150	300	600	—
1796 HIAB	144,000	25.00	55.00	110	250	—
1796 IGM	Inc. above	35.00	80.00	150	285	—
1797 IGM	135,000	25.00	60.00	125	285	—
1798 IGM	105,000	25.00	60.00	125	285	—
1799 IGM	90,000	40.00	90.00	160	300	—
1800 IGM	68,000	25.00	60.00	125	285	—

KM# 252 1/2 SPECIE DALER
14.4500 g., 0.8750 Silver 0.4065 oz. ASW **Obv:** Crowned monogram divides value **Obv. Legend:** NORV • VAND • GOTH • REX • D • G • DAN • **Rev:** Crowned, oval 3-fold arms of Norway within sprigs

Date	Mintage	VG	F	VF	XF	Unc
1776 HIAB	60,000	25.00	50.00	85.00	185	—
1777 HIAB	31,000	25.00	50.00	95.00	195	—
1778 HIAB	27,000	25.00	50.00	95.00	195	—
1779 HIAB Rare	12,000	—	—	—	—	—

KM# 267.1 2/3 SPECIE DALER
19.2600 g., 0.8750 Silver 0.5418 oz. ASW **Obv:** Head right **Obv. Legend:** CHRISTIANUS • VII • D • G • DAN • NORV • V • G • REX • **Rev:** Crowned, oval 3-fold arms of Norway, value in legend, crossed hammers and letters divides date below

Date	Mintage	VG	F	VF	XF	Unc
1795 HIAB	7,500	50.00	110	225	525	—
1796 HIAB	93,000	50.00	110	225	550	—

KM# 267.2 2/3 SPECIE DALER
19.2600 g., 0.8750 Silver 0.5418 oz. ASW **Obv:** Head right **Obv. Inscription:** CHRISTIANUS • VII • D • G • DAN • NORV • V • G • REX • **Rev:** Crowned, oval 3-fold arms of Norway, crossed hammers and letters divides date below, value in legend

Date	Mintage	VG	F	VF	XF	Unc
1795 HIAB	Inc. above	50.00	110	225	450	—
1796 HIAB Rare	Inc. above	—	—	—	—	—

KM# 265.1 SPECIE DALER (Species)
28.8900 g., 0.8750 Silver 0.8127 oz. ASW **Obv:** Head right **Obv. Legend:** CHRISTIANUS • VII • D • G • DAN • NORV • V • G • REX • **Rev:** Crowned, oval 3-fold arms of Norway **Note:** Varieties exist. Dav. #1313.

Date	Mintage	VG	F	VF	XF	Unc
1791 HIAB	55,000	225	425	750	1,250	—
1791 HIAB Rare; B below bust	Inc. above	—	—	—	—	—
1791 HIAB Unique; H below bust	Inc. above	—	—	—	—	—
1792 HIAB	50,000	225	425	750	1,250	—

KM# 242 SPECIE DALER
28.8900 g., 0.8750 Silver 0.8127 oz. ASW **Obv:** Head right **Obv. Legend:** FRIDERICVS • V • D • G • DAN • NOR • V • G • REX • **Rev:** Crowned oval arms of Norway **Note:** Dav. #1303.

Date	Mintage	VG	F	VF	XF	Unc
1765 TL	—	1,200	2,500	3,500	5,250	—

KM# 244 SPECIE DALER
28.8900 g., 0.8750 Silver 0.8127 oz. ASW **Obv:** Crowned double C7 monogram **Obv. Legend:** NOR • VAN • GOT • REX • D • G • DAN • **Rev:** Crowned, round arms of Norway **Note:** Dav. #1304.

Date	Mintage	VG	F	VF	XF	Unc
1767 TL Rare	64,000	—	—	—	—	—
1768 TL	47,000	650	1,350	3,000	4,500	—

KM# 253 SPECIE DALER
28.8900 g., 0.8750 Silver 0.8127 oz. ASW **Obv:** Crowned double C 7 monogram **Obv. Legend:** NORV • VAND • GOTH • REX • D • G • DAN • **Rev:** Crowned, oval 3-fold arms of Norway, within sprigs **Rev. Legend:** ...AMORE • PATRIÆ • **Note:** Dav. #1308.

Date	Mintage	VG	F	VF	XF	Unc
1776 HIAB	206,000	75.00	225	275	550	—
1777 HIAB	127,000	75.00	225	275	550	—
1778 HIAB	138,000	75.00	225	275	550	—
1779 HIAB	64,000	100	250	300	550	—
1780 HIAB	84,000	100	250	300	550	—
1781 HIAB	43,000	100	250	300	550	—
1785 HIAB	—	100	250	300	550	—

KM# 265.2 SPECIE DALER
28.8900 g., 0.8750 Silver 0.8127 oz. ASW **Obv:** Different hair-do, without ribbon **Note:** Dav. #1314.

Date	Mintage	VG	F	VF	XF	Unc
1792 HIAB SI below bust	Inc. above	225	425	750	1,200	—
1793 HIAB	64,000	200	400	750	1,250	—
1794 HIAB	37,000	200	400	700	1,250	—
1795 HIAB	96,000	200	400	700	1,250	—

PATTERNS

Including off metal strikes

KM#	Date	Mintage	Identification	Mkt Val
Pn32	1704	5,000	6 Mark. 0.8330 Silver. FRID IV	1,200
Pn33	1704	I.A.	6 Mark. 0.8330 Silver. FRID IIII	1,200
Pn34	ND	—	8 Skilling. Head of King/lion and lift on mountain.	—
Pn35	1711	—	8 Skilling. Head of King/wildmen holding crowned arms	—
Pn36	1712	—	8 Skilling. Head of King/wildmen holding crowned arms	—
Pn37	1714	—	24 Skilling. Head of King/value and date.	—
Pn38	1714	—	48 Skilling. Head of Kind/value and date.	—

The Republic of Peru, located on the Pacific coast of South America, has an area of 496,225 sq. mi. (1,285,220sq. km.) and a population of *21.4 million. Capital: Lima. The diversified economy includes mining, fishing and agriculture. Fish meal, copper, sugar, zinc and iron ore are exported.

Once part of the great Inca Empire that reached from northern Ecuador to central Chile, the conquest of Peru by Francisco Pizarro began in 1531. Desirable as the richest of the Spanish viceroyalties, it was torn by warfare between avaricious Spaniards until the arrival in 1569 of Francisco de Toledo, who initiated 2-1/2 centuries of efficient colonial rule, which made Lima the most aristocratic colonial capital and the stronghold of Spain's American possessions. Jose de San Martin of Argentina proclaimed Peru's independence on July 28, 1821;Simon Bolivar of Venezuela secured it in December, 1824 when he defeated the last Spanish army in South America. After several futile attempts to re-establish its South American empire, Spain recognized Peru's independence in 1879.

Andres de Santa Cruz, whose mother was a high-ranking Inca, was the best of Bolivia's early presidents, and temporarily united Peru and Bolivia 1836-39, thus realizing his dream of a Peruvian/Bolivian confederation. This prompted the separate coinages of North and South Peru. Peruvian resistance and Chilean intervention finally broke up the confederation, sending Santa Cruz into exile. A succession of military strongman presidents ruled Peru until Marshall Castilla revitalized Peruvian politics in themid-19th century and repulsed Spain's attempt to reclaim its one-time colony. Subsequent loss of southern territory to Chile in the War of the Pacific, 1879-81, and gradually increasing rejection of foreign economic domination, combined with recent serious inflation, affected the country numismatically.

As a result of the discovery of silver at Potosi in 1545, a mint was eventually authorized in 1565with the first coinage taking place in 1568. The mint had an uneven life span during the Spanish Colonial period from 1568-72. It was closed from 1573-76, reopened from 1577-88. It remained closed until 1659-1660 when an unauthorized coinage in both silver and gold were struck. After being closed in 1660, it remained closed until 1684 when it struck cob style coins until 1752.

RULER

Spanish until 1822

MINT MARKS

AREQUIPA, AREQ = Arequipa
AYACUCHO = Ayacucho
CUZCO (monogram), Cuzco, Co. Cuzco
L, LIMAE (monogram), Lima
(monogram), LIMA = Lima
PASCO (monogram), Pasco, Paz, Po= Pasco

NOTE: The LIMAE monogram appears in three forms. The early LM monogram form looks like a dotted L with M. The later LIMAE monogram has all the letters of LIMAE more readily distinguishable. The third form appears as an M monogram during early Republican issues.

MINT ASSAYERS' INITIALS

Initials	Date	Name
H, Ho	1699-1705	
H, Ho	1707-08	
H, Ho	1710	
M	1694, 1709	
	1711-28	
N	1728-40	Joaquin Negrow
	1699, 1706	
R	1748-52	Jose Rodriguez
R	1698-1701,1706	

The letter(s) following the dates of Peruvian coins are the assayer's initials appearing on the coins. They generally appear at the 11 o'clock position on the Colonial coinage and at the 5 o'clock position along the rim on the obverse or reverse on the Republican coinage.

MONETARY SYSTEM

16 Reales = 2 Pesos = 1 Escudo

SPANISH COLONY

COLONIAL COB COINAGE

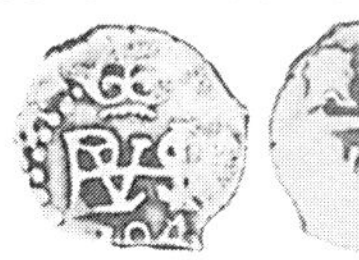

KM# 30 1/2 REAL

1.6917 g., 0.9310 Silver 0.0506 oz. ASW **Ruler:** Philip V **Mint:** Lima **Obverse:** PHILIPVS monogram **Reverse:** Cross of Jerusalem, lions and castles in quarters

Date	Mintage	Good	VG	F	VF	XF
ND (1701-28)L Date off flan	—	12.00	18.00	25.00	35.00	—
1701L	—	30.00	50.00	70.00	110	—
1702L	—	30.00	60.00	70.00	110	—
1703L	—	30.00	50.00	70.00	110	—
1704L	—	30.00	50.00	70.00	110	—
1705L	—	30.00	50.00	70.00	110	—
1706L	—	30.00	50.00	70.00	110	—
1707L	—	30.00	50.00	70.00	110	—
1708L	—	30.00	50.00	70.00	110	—
1709L	—	30.00	50.00	70.00	110	—
1710L	—	30.00	50.00	70.00	110	—
1711L	—	30.00	50.00	70.00	110	—
1712L	—	30.00	50.00	70.00	110	—
1713L	—	30.00	50.00	70.00	110	—
1714/3L	—	30.00	50.00	70.00	110	—
1714L	—	30.00	50.00	70.00	110	—
1715L	—	30.00	50.00	70.00	110	—
1716L	—	30.00	50.00	70.00	110	—
1717L	—	30.00	50.00	70.00	110	—
1718L	—	30.00	50.00	70.00	110	—
1719L	—	30.00	50.00	70.00	110	—
1720L	—	30.00	50.00	70.00	110	—
1721L	—	30.00	50.00	70.00	110	—
1722L	—	30.00	50.00	70.00	110	—
1723L	—	30.00	50.00	70.00	110	—
1724L	—	30.00	50.00	70.00	110	—
1726L	—	30.00	50.00	70.00	110	—
1727L	—	30.00	50.00	70.00	110	—
1728L N	—	30.00	50.00	70.00	110	—

KM# A39 1/2 REAL

1.6917 g., 0.9310 Silver 0.0506 oz. ASW **Ruler:** Luis I **Mint:** Lima **Obverse:** LUDOVICVS monogram **Reverse:** Cross of Jerusalem, lions and castles in quarters

Date	Mintage	Good	VG	F	VF	XF
ND (1725L) Date off flan	—	25.00	40.00	60.00	100	—
1725L	—	70.00	90.00	150	225	—

KM# 22 1/2 REAL

1.6917 g., 0.9310 Silver 0.0506 oz. ASW **Ruler:** Charles II **Mint:** Lima **Obverse:** CAROLVS monogram, date below **Reverse:** Cross of Jerusalem, lions and castles in quarters

Date	Mintage	Good	VG	F	VF	XF
1701L	—	38.00	55.00	100	165	—

KM# 30a 1/2 REAL

1.6917 g., 0.9170 Silver 0.0499 oz. ASW **Ruler:** Philip V **Mint:** Lima **Obverse:** PHILIPVS monogram **Reverse:** Cross of Jerusalem, lions and castles in quarters

Date	Mintage	Good	VG	F	VF	XF
ND(1729-47)L Date off flan	—	12.00	18.00	25.00	35.00	—
1729L N	—	30.00	50.00	70.00	110	—
1730L N	—	30.00	50.00	70.00	110	—
1731L N	—	30.00	50.00	70.00	110	—
1732L N	—	30.00	50.00	70.00	110	—
1733L N	—	30.00	50.00	70.00	110	—
1734L N	—	30.00	50.00	70.00	110	—
1735L N	—	30.00	50.00	70.00	110	—
1736L N	—	30.00	50.00	70.00	110	—
1737L N	—	30.00	50.00	70.00	110	—
1738L N	—	30.00	50.00	70.00	110	—
1739L N Rare	—	—	—	—	—	—
1739L V	—	30.00	50.00	70.00	110	—
1740L N	—	30.00	50.00	70.00	110	—
1740L V	—	30.00	50.00	70.00	110	—
1741L V	—	30.00	50.00	70.00	110	—
1742L V	—	30.00	50.00	70.00	110	—
1743L V	—	30.00	50.00	70.00	110	—
1744L V	—	30.00	50.00	70.00	110	—
1745L V	—	30.00	50.00	70.00	110	—
1746L V	—	30.00	50.00	70.00	110	—
1747L V	—	30.00	50.00	70.00	110	—

KM# 41 1/2 REAL

0.9160 Silver **Ruler:** Ferdinand VI **Mint:** Lima **Obverse:** FERDINANDVS monogram **Reverse:** Pillars, value and date

Date	Mintage	Good	VG	F	VF	XF
ND(1747-1752)L Date off flan	—	12.00	18.00	25.00	35.00	—
1747L V	—	30.00	50.00	70.00	110	—
1748L V	—	30.00	50.00	70.00	110	—
1749L V Rare	—	—	—	—	—	—
1749L R	—	30.00	50.00	70.00	110	—
1750L R	—	30.00	50.00	70.00	110	—
1751L R	—	30.00	50.00	70.00	110	—
1752L R Rare	—	—	—	—	—	—

KM# A41 1/2 REAL

1.6917 g., 0.9170 Silver 0.0499 oz. ASW **Ruler:** Ferdinand VI **Mint:** Lima **Obverse:** Castle with mint mark L at left and assayer's initial R right **Reverse:** Cross with quartered lions and castle

Date	Mintage	Good	VG	F	VF	XF
1750L R Rare; 2 known	—	—	—	—	—	—

KM# 31 REAL

0.9310 Silver **Ruler:** Philip V **Mint:** Lima **Obverse:** Cross of Jerusalem, lions and castles in quarters **Reverse:** Pillars, PLVS VLTR, date between

Date	Mintage	Good	VG	F	VF	XF
ND (1701-28L) Date off flan	—	15.00	25.00	35.00	50.00	—
1701L H	—	30.00	70.00	90.00	125	—
1702L H	—	30.00	70.00	90.00	125	—
1703L H	—	30.00	70.00	90.00	125	—
1704L H	—	30.00	70.00	90.00	125	—
1705L H	—	30.00	70.00	90.00	125	—
1706L R	—	40.00	75.00	100	150	—
1707L H	—	30.00	70.00	90.00	125	—
1708L H	—	30.00	70.00	100	125	—
1709L M	—	30.00	70.00	100	125	—
1710L H	—	30.00	70.00	100	125	—
1711L M	—	30.00	70.00	100	125	—
1712L M	—	30.00	70.00	100	125	—
1713L M	—	30.00	70.00	100	125	—
1714L M	—	30.00	70.00	100	125	—
1715L M	—	30.00	70.00	100	125	—
1716L M	—	30.00	70.00	100	125	—
1717L M	—	30.00	70.00	100	125	—
1718L M	—	30.00	70.00	100	125	—
1719L M	—	30.00	70.00	100	125	—
1720L M	—	30.00	70.00	100	125	—
1721L M	—	30.00	70.00	100	125	—
1722L M	—	30.00	70.00	100	125	—
1723L M	—	30.00	70.00	100	125	—
1724L M	—	30.00	70.00	100	125	—
1726L M	—	30.00	70.00	100	125	—
1727L M	—	30.00	70.00	100	125	—
1728L N	—	30.00	70.00	100	125	—
1729L N	—	30.00	70.00	100	125	—

KM# 42 REAL

3.3834 g., 0.9170 Silver 0.0997 oz. ASW **Ruler:** Ferdinand VI **Mint:** Lima **Reverse:** Pillars, PLVS VLTR(A), date

Date	Mintage	Good	VG	F	VF	XF
ND (1747-52 L) Date off flan	—	15.00	25.00	35.00	50.00	—
1747L V	—	30.00	70.00	90.00	125	—
1748L V	—	30.00	70.00	90.00	125	—
1749L V	—	30.00	70.00	90.00	125	—
1749L R	—	30.00	70.00	90.00	125	—
1750L R	—	30.00	70.00	90.00	125	—
1751L R	—	30.00	70.00	90.00	125	—
1752L R Rare	—	—	—	—	—	—

KM# B39 REAL

3.3834 g., 0.9310 Silver 0.1013 oz. ASW **Ruler:** Luis I **Mint:** Lima

Date	Mintage	Good	VG	F	VF	XF
ND (1725L) Date off flan, Rare	—	—	—	—	—	—
1725 M Rare	—	—	—	—	—	—

KM# A43 2 REALES

6.7668 g., 0.9170 Silver 0.1995 oz. ASW **Ruler:** Ferdinand VI **Mint:** Lima

Date	Mintage	Good	VG	F	VF	XF
ND (1748-52L) Date off flan	—	20.00	30.00	40.00	60.00	—
1748L V	—	60.00	90.00	150	250	—
1749L R	—	60.00	90.00	150	250	—
1750L R	—	60.00	90.00	150	250	—
1751L R	—	60.00	90.00	150	250	—
1752L R Rare	—	—	—	—	—	—

KM# C39 2 REALES

6.7668 g., 0.9310 Silver 0.2025 oz. ASW **Ruler:** Luis I **Mint:** Lima

Date	Mintage	Good	VG	F	VF	XF
ND (1725 LM) Date off flan, rare	—	—	—	—	—	—
1725L M Rare	—	—	—	—	—	—

KM# 21 2 REALES

6.7668 g., 0.9310 Silver 0.2025 oz. ASW **Mint:** Lima **Obverse:** Cross of Jerusalem, lions and castles in quarters, mint mark **Obv. Legend:** CAROLVS II D • G • HISPANIARVM REX **Reverse:** Pillars, assayer's initial, date, PLVS VLTRA within

Date	Mintage	Good	VG	F	VF	XF
ND(1684-1701)L Date off flan	—	20.00	30.00	40.00	60.00	—
1701L H	—	75.00	100	175	300	—

KM# 32 2 REALES

6.7668 g., 0.9310 Silver 0.2025 oz. ASW **Mint:** Lima **Obverse:** Cross of Jerusalem, lions and castles in quarters **Obv. Legend:** PHILIPPVS V D • G • HISPANIA **Reverse:** Pillars, PLVS VLTRA, date within

Date	Mintage	Good	VG	F	VF	XF
ND(1701-29)L Date off flan	—	20.00	30.00	40.00	60.00	—
1701L H	—	60.00	90.00	150	250	—
1702L H	—	60.00	90.00	150	250	—
1703L H	—	60.00	90.00	150	250	—
1704L H	—	60.00	90.00	150	250	—
1705L H	—	60.00	90.00	150	250	—
1706L R	—	60.00	90.00	150	250	—
1707L H	—	60.00	90.00	150	250	—
1708L H	—	60.00	90.00	150	250	—
1709L M	—	60.00	90.00	150	250	—
1710L H	—	60.00	90.00	150	250	—
1711L M	—	60.00	90.00	150	250	—
1712L M	—	60.00	90.00	150	250	—
1713L M	—	60.00	90.00	150	250	—
1714L M	—	60.00	90.00	150	250	—
1715L M	—	60.00	90.00	150	250	—
1716L M	—	60.00	90.00	150	250	—
1717L M	—	60.00	90.00	150	250	—
1718L M	—	60.00	90.00	150	250	—
1719L M	—	60.00	90.00	150	250	—
1720L M	—	60.00	90.00	150	250	—
1721L M	—	60.00	90.00	150	250	—
1722L M	—	60.00	90.00	150	250	—
1723L M	—	60.00	90.00	150	250	—
1724L M	—	60.00	90.00	150	250	—
1726L M	—	60.00	90.00	150	250	—
1727L M	—	60.00	90.00	150	250	—
1728L N	—	60.00	90.00	150	250	—
1729L N	—	60.00	90.00	150	250	—

KM# 33 4 REALES

13.5337 g., 0.9310 Silver 0.4051 oz. ASW **Mint:** Lima **Obverse:** Cross of Jerusalem, lions and castles in quarters **Obv. Legend:** PHILIPPVS V D • G • HISPANIA **Reverse:** Pillars, PLVS VLTRA with date between

Date	Mintage	Good	VG	F	VF	XF
ND (1701-29L) Date off flan	—	50.00	80.00	110	150	—
1701L H	—	100	165	250	400	—
1702L H	—	100	165	250	400	—
1703L H	—	100	165	250	400	—
1704L H	—	100	165	250	400	—
1705L H	—	100	165	250	400	—
1706L H	—	100	165	250	400	—
1707L H	—	100	165	250	400	—
1708L H	—	100	165	250	400	—
1709L M	—	100	165	250	400	—
1710L H	—	100	165	250	400	—
1711L M	—	100	165	250	400	—
1712L M	—	100	165	250	400	—
1713L M	—	100	165	250	400	—
1714L M	—	100	165	250	400	—
1715L M	—	100	165	250	400	—
1716L M	—	100	165	250	400	—
1717L M	—	100	165	250	400	—
1718L M	—	100	165	250	400	—
1719L M	—	100	165	250	400	—
1720L M	—	100	165	250	400	—
1721L M	—	100	165	250	400	—
1722L M	—	100	165	250	400	—
1723L M	—	100	165	250	400	—
1724L M	—	100	165	250	400	—
1726L M	—	100	165	250	400	—
1727L M	—	100	165	250	400	—
1728L N	—	100	165	250	400	—

KM# 43 4 REALES

13.5337 g., 0.9310 Silver 0.4051 oz. ASW **Mint:** Lima **Obverse:** Cross of Jerusalem, lions and castles in quarters **Obv. Legend:** FERDND • VI • D • G • HISPAN ET IND • REX **Reverse:** Pillars, PLVS VLTRA, mint mark and date

Date	Mintage	Good	VG	F	VF	XF
ND (1747-51L) Date off flan	—	50.00	80.00	110	150	—
1747L V	—	100	165	250	400	—
1748L V	—	100	165	250	400	—
1749L R	—	100	165	250	400	—
1750L R	—	100	165	250	400	—
1751L R	—	100	165	250	400	—

KM# D39 4 REALES

13.5337 g., 0.9170 Silver 0.3990 oz. ASW **Ruler:** Luis I **Mint:** Lima **Obv. Legend:** PHILIPPVS V D.G. HISPANIA **Reverse:** Pillars, PLVS VLTRA and date between

Date	Mintage	VG	F	VF	XF	Unc
NDL Date off flan	—	—	—	—	—	—
1725L M Rare	—	—	—	—	—	—

KM# 33A 4 REALES

13.5337 g., 0.9170 Silver 0.3990 oz. ASW **Mint:** Lima **Obverse:** Cross of Jerusalem, lions and castles in quarters **Obv. Legend:** PHILIPPVS V D • G • HISPANIA **Reverse:** Pillars, PLVS VLTRA and date between

Date	Mintage	Good	VG	F	VF	XF
ND(1729-1747)L Date off flan	—	50.00	80.00	110	150	—
1729L N	—	100	165	250	400	—
1730L N	—	100	160	240	375	—
1731L N	—	100	160	240	375	—
1732L N	—	100	160	240	375	—
1733L N	—	100	160	240	375	—
1734L N	—	100	160	240	375	—
1735L N	—	100	160	240	375	—
1736L N	—	100	160	240	375	—
1737L N	—	100	160	240	375	—
1738L N	—	100	160	240	375	—
1739L V	—	100	160	240	375	—
1740L V	—	100	160	240	375	—
1741L V	—	100	160	240	375	—
1742L V	—	100	160	240	375	—
1743L V	—	100	160	240	375	—
1744L V	—	100	160	240	375	—
1745L V	—	100	160	240	375	—
1746L V	—	100	160	240	375	—
1747L V	—	100	160	240	375	—

KM# 24 8 REALES

27.0674 g., 0.9310 Silver 0.8102 oz. ASW **Ruler:** Charles II **Mint:** Lima **Obverse:** Cross of Jerusalem, lions and castles in quarters **Reverse:** PLV/SVL/TRA between pillars

Date	Mintage	Good	VG	F	VF	XF
ND(1684-1701)L Date off flan	—	75.00	100	105	150	—
1701L H	—	175	275	375	575	—

KM# 34 8 REALES

27.0674 g., 0.9310 Silver 0.8102 oz. ASW **Ruler:** Philip V **Mint:** Lima **Obverse:** Cross of Jerusalem, lions and castles in quarters **Obv. Legend:** PHILIPPVS.... **Reverse:** PLV/SVL/TRA between pillars

Date	Mintage	Good	VG	F	VF	XF
ND(1701-1724)L Date off flan	—	75.00	100	125	150	—
1701L H	—	150	250	350	500	—
1702L H	—	150	250	350	500	—
1703L H	—	150	250	350	500	—
1704L H	—	150	250	350	500	—
1705L H	—	150	250	350	500	—
1706L R	—	150	250	350	500	—
1707L H	—	150	250	350	500	—
1709/8 M Rare	—	—	—	—	—	—
1708L H Rare	—	—	—	—	—	—
1709L M	—	150	250	350	500	—
1710L H	—	150	250	350	500	—
1711L M	—	150	250	350	500	—
1712L M Rare	—	—	—	—	—	—
1714/3L M Rare	—	—	—	—	—	—
1714L M	—	150	250	350	500	—
1715L M Rare	—	—	—	—	—	—
1717L M	—	150	250	350	500	—
1718L M	—	150	250	350	500	—
1719L M	—	150	250	350	500	—
1720/19L M Rare	—	—	—	—	—	—
1720L M	—	150	250	350	500	—
1721/0L M Rare	—	—	—	—	—	—
1721L M	—	150	250	350	500	—
1722L M	—	150	250	350	500	—
1723L M	—	150	250	350	500	—
1724L M	—	150	250	350	500	—

KM# 39 8 REALES

0.9170 Silver **Ruler:** Luis I **Mint:** Lima **Obverse:** Cross of Jerusalem, lions and castles in quarters, date below **Reverse:** Pillars, PLVS VLTR(A), value, date and mint mark

Date	Mintage	Good	VG	F	VF	XF
ND(1725)L M Date off flan, Rare	—	—	—	—	—	—
1725L M	—	750	1,500	3,000	5,000	—
1726L M	—	750	1,500	3,000	5,000	—

KM# R39 8 REALES

27.0674 g., 0.9170 Silver 0.7980 oz. ASW **Ruler:** Luis I **Mint:** Lima

Date	Mintage	VG	F	VF	XF	Unc
1725L M 1 known, Rare	—	—	—	—	—	—

KM# 34a 8 REALES

27.0674 g., 0.9170 Silver 0.7980 oz. ASW **Mint:** Lima **Obverse:** Cross of Jerusalem, lions and castles in quarters **Obv. Legend:** PHILIPVS V • D • G • HISPANA **Reverse:** Pillars, PLVS VLTR(A), value, date, mint mark

Date	Mintage	Good	VG	F	VF	XF
ND(1726-1746)L Date off flan	—	75.00	100	125	150	—
1726LM	—	150	250	350	500	—
1727L M	—	150	250	350	500	—
1728L N	—	150	250	350	500	—
1729L N	—	150	250	350	500	—
1730L N	—	150	250	350	500	—
1731L N	—	150	250	350	500	—
1732L N	—	150	250	350	500	—
1733L N	—	150	250	350	500	—
1734L N	—	150	250	350	500	—
1735L N	—	150	250	350	500	—
1737/6L N Rare	—	—	—	—	—	—
1736/5L N Rare	—	—	—	—	—	—
1736L N	—	150	250	350	500	—
1737L N	—	150	250	350	500	—
1738/7L N	—	150	250	350	500	—
1738L N	—	150	250	350	500	—
1739L N	—	150	250	350	500	—
1739L V	—	150	250	350	500	—
1740/39L V Rare	—	—	—	—	—	—
1740L N	—	150	250	350	500	—
1740L V	—	150	250	350	500	—
1740L N V Rare	—	—	—	—	—	—
1741L V	—	150	250	350	500	—
1742L V	—	150	250	350	500	—
1743L V	—	150	250	350	500	—
1744L V	—	150	250	350	500	—
1745/4L V Rare	—	—	—	—	—	—
1745L V	—	150	250	350	500	—
1746L V	—	150	250	350	500	—

KM# 44 8 REALES

0.9170 Silver **Ruler:** Ferdinand VI **Mint:** Lima **Obverse:** Cross of Jerusalem, lions and castles in quarters, date below **Obv. Legend:** FERDINANDVS VI D• G• HISPANIARVM REX **Reverse:** Pillars, PLVS VLTRA between

Date	Mintage	Good	VG	F	VF	XF
1747L V	—	150	250	350	500	—
1748L V	—	150	250	350	500	—
1749L R	—	150	250	350	500	—
1750L R	—	150	250	350	500	—
1751/50L R Rare	—	—	—	—	—	—
1751L R	—	150	250	350	500	—

KM# 27 ESCUDO

3.3834 g., 0.9170 Gold 0.0997 oz. AGW **Ruler:** Charles II **Mint:** Lima **Obverse:** Castle divides L H, 698 below **Reverse:** Cross of Jerusalem, dots in quarters

Date	Mintage	VG	F	VF	XF	Unc
1701L R	—	—	—	3,500	5,000	—

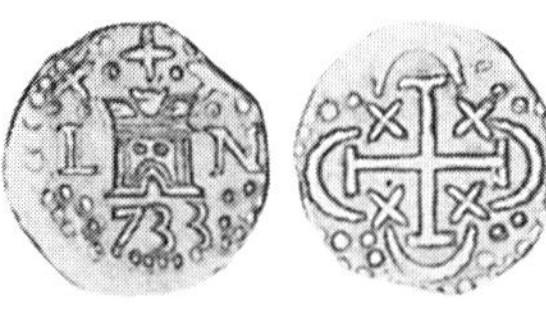

KM# 35 ESCUDO

3.3834 g., 0.9170 Gold 0.0997 oz. AGW **Ruler:** Philip V **Mint:** Lima **Obverse:** Castle divides L N, 733 below **Reverse:** Cross of Jerusalem, X's in quarters

Date	Mintage	VG	F	VF	XF	Unc
ND(1702-45)L Date off flan	—	—	1,500	2,000	2,500	—
1702L H	742	—	2,500	3,500	5,000	—
1703L H	344	—	2,500	3,500	5,000	—
1704L H	816	—	2,500	3,500	5,000	—
1705L H	2,100	—	2,500	3,500	5,000	—
1706L H	—	—	2,500	3,500	5,000	—
1707L H	1,341	—	2,500	3,500	5,000	—
1708L H	755	—	2,500	3,500	5,000	—
1709L H Rare	688	—	—	—	—	—
1709L M	—	—	2,500	3,500	5,000	—
1710L H Rare	813	—	—	—	—	—
1710L M	—	—	2,500	3,500	5,000	—
1711/0L M	—	—	2,500	3,500	5,000	—
1711L M	2,027	—	2,500	3,500	5,000	—
1712L M	1,642	—	2,500	3,500	5,000	—
1713L M	547	—	2,500	3,500	5,000	—
1714L M	630	—	2,500	3,500	5,000	—
1715L M	1,635	—	2,500	3,500	5,000	—
1716L M	1,162	—	2,500	3,500	5,000	—
1717L M	1,426	—	2,500	3,500	5,000	—
1718L M	905	—	2,500	3,500	5,000	—
1719L M	1,221	—	2,500	3,500	5,000	—
1720L M	866	—	2,500	3,500	5,000	—
1721/0L M	878	—	2,500	3,500	5,000	—
1721L M	Inc. above	—	2,500	3,500	5,000	—
1722L M	560	—	2,500	3,500	5,000	—
1723L M	509	—	2,500	3,500	5,000	—
1724L M	283	—	2,500	3,500	5,000	—
1725L M	1,451	—	2,500	3,500	5,000	—
1726L M	502	—	2,500	3,500	5,000	—
1727L M	4,562	—	2,500	3,500	5,000	—
1728L N	826	—	2,500	3,500	5,000	—
1729L N	949	—	2,500	3,500	5,000	—
1730L N	798	—	2,500	3,500	5,000	—
1732L N Rare	1,108	—	—	—	—	—
1733L N Rare	474	—	—	—	—	—
1736L N	646	—	2,500	3,500	5,000	—
1738L N	807	—	2,500	3,500	5,000	—
1740L V	561	—	2,500	3,500	5,000	—
1742L V	767	—	2,500	3,500	5,000	—
1743L V	890	—	2,500	3,500	5,000	—
1744L V	993	—	2,500	3,500	5,000	—
1745L V	521	—	2,500	3,500	5,000	—

KM# 45 ESCUDO

3.3834 g., 0.9170 Gold 0.0997 oz. AGW **Ruler:** Ferdinand VI **Mint:** Lima **Obverse:** Castle **Reverse:** Cross of Jerusalem, X's in quarters

Date	Mintage	VG	F	VF	XF	Unc
ND(1747-50)L Date off flan	—	—	1,500	2,000	2,500	—
1747/6L V	664	—	2,500	3,500	5,000	—
1747L V	Inc. above	—	2,500	3,500	5,000	—
1748L V	1,005	—	2,500	3,500	5,000	—
1748L R Rare	—	—	—	—	—	—
1749L V	2,781	—	2,500	3,500	5,000	—
1749L R	Inc. above	—	2,500	3,500	5,000	—
1750L R	1,340	—	2,500	3,500	5,000	—

KM# 29 2 ESCUDOS

6.7668 g., 0.9170 Gold 0.1995 oz. AGW **Ruler:** Charles II **Mint:** Lima **Obverse:** Cross of Jerusalem with lions and castles in quarters **Obv. Legend:** C • II D • G • HISPANIARVM **Reverse:** Pillars and waves

Date	Mintage	VG	F	VF	XF	Unc
ND(1696-1701)L Date off flan	—	—	1,500	2,000	2,500	—
1701L H	—	—	3,750	4,750	5,750	—

KM# 36 2 ESCUDOS

6.7668 g., 0.9170 Gold 0.1995 oz. AGW **Ruler:** Philip V **Mint:** Lima **Obverse:** Cross of Jerusalem with lions and castles in quarters **Obv. Legend:** PHILIPPVS V D • G • HISPAN **Reverse:** Pillars and waves

Date	Mintage	VG	F	VF	XF	Unc
ND(1701-44)L Date off flan	—	—	1,500	2,000	2,500	—
1701L H	—	—	3,750	4,750	5,750	—
1702L H	4,973	—	3,750	4,750	5,750	—
1703L H	12,339	—	3,750	4,750	5,750	—
1704L H	11,000	—	3,750	4,750	5,750	—
1705L H	13,508	—	3,750	4,750	5,750	—
1707L H	23,202	—	3,750	4,750	5,750	—
1708L H	6,575	—	3,750	4,750	5,750	—
1709L M	14,184	—	3,750	4,750	5,750	—
1709L H Rare	—	—	—	—	—	—
1710L H	3,811	—	3,750	4,750	5,750	—
1711L M	7,367	—	3,750	4,750	5,750	—
1712L M	5,265	—	3,750	4,750	5,750	—
1713L M	1,725	—	3,750	4,750	5,750	—
1714L M	3,954	—	3,750	4,750	5,750	—
1715L M	10,905	—	3,750	4,750	5,750	—
1716L M	8,378	—	3,750	4,750	5,750	—
1720L M	1,696	—	3,750	4,750	5,750	—
1721L M	4,563	—	3,750	4,750	5,750	—
1723L M	1,463	—	3,750	4,750	5,750	—
1728L M	877	—	3,750	4,750	5,750	—
1733L N	922	—	3,750	4,750	5,750	—
1735L N	1,052	—	3,750	4,750	5,750	—
1736L N	Inc. above	—	3,750	4,750	5,750	—
1741L V	989	—	3,750	4,750	5,750	—
1744L V	981	—	3,750	4,750	5,750	—

KM# 46 2 ESCUDOS

6.7500 g., 0.9170 Gold 0.1990 oz. AGW **Ruler:** Ferdinand VI **Mint:** Lima **Obverse:** Cross of Jerusalem, lions and castles in quarters **Reverse:** Pillars and waves

Date	Mintage	VG	F	VF	XF	Unc
ND(1747-49)L Date off flan	—	—	1,500	2,000	2,500	—
1747L V	648	—	3,750	47,500	5,750	—
1748L V	837	—	3,750	4,750	5,750	—
1748L R	Inc. above	—	3,750	4,750	5,750	—
1749L R	3,584	—	3,750	4,750	5,750	—

KM# 25 4 ESCUDOS

13.5337 g., 0.9170 Gold 0.3990 oz. AGW **Ruler:** Charles II **Mint:** Lima **Obverse:** Cross of Jerusalem with castles and lions in quarters **Obv. Legend:** C • II D • G • HISPANIARVM **Reverse:** Pillars and waves

Date	Mintage	VG	F	VF	XF	Unc
ND(1696-1701)L Date off flan	—	—	3,000	3,500	4,000	—
1701L H	—	—	5,750	7,500	10,000	—

KM# 37 4 ESCUDOS

13.5337 g., 0.9170 Gold 0.3990 oz. AGW **Ruler:** Philip V **Mint:** Lima **Obverse:** Cross of Jerusalem with castles and lions in quarters **Obv. Legend:** PHILIPPVS V D • G • HISPAN **Reverse:** Pillars and waves

Date	Mintage	VG	F	VF	XF	Unc
ND(1702-45)L Date off flan	—	—	3,000	3,750	4,500	—
1702L H	3,750	—	4,750	6,000	7,000	—
1704L H	7,902	—	4,750	6,000	7,000	—
1705L H	11,102	—	4,750	6,000	7,000	—
1707L H	10,362	—	4,750	6,000	7,000	—
1710L H	3,006	—	4,750	6,000	7,000	—
1711L M	1,128	—	4,750	6,000	7,000	—
1712L M	2,073	—	4,750	6,000	7,000	—
1736L N	221	—	4,750	6,000	7,000	—
1738L N	231	—	4,750	6,000	7,000	—
1739L V	147	—	4,750	6,000	7,000	—
1740L V	199	—	4,750	6,000	7,000	—
1745L V	147	—	4,750	6,000	7,000	—

KM# A47 4 ESCUDOS

13.5000 g., 0.9170 Gold 0.3980 oz. AGW **Ruler:** Ferdinand VI **Mint:** Lima

Date	Mintage	VG	F	VF	XF	Unc
1750L R	1,508	—	3,750	4,700	5,750	—

Note: One 1750 R 4 Escudos is known struck with a 2 Escudos obverse die clearly displaying a 2 above the cross; This piece was sold in the Sotheby's Rio de la Plata sale 3-93, good VF realizing $19,800. Many examples with 8 Escudo obverse also exist

KM# 26.2 8 ESCUDOS

27.0674 g., 0.9170 Gold 0.7980 oz. AGW **Ruler:** Charles II **Mint:** Lima **Obverse:** Cross of Jerusalem, lions and castles in quarters **Obv. Legend:** C • II D • G • HISPANIARVM **Reverse:** Pillars, PVA, date and mint mark

Date	Mintage	VG	F	VF	XF	Unc
ND(1696-1701)L Date off flan	—	—	5,000	6,250	7,500	—
1701L H	—	—	7,000	8,000	10,000	—

KM# 38.1 8 ESCUDOS

27.0674 g., 0.9170 Gold 0.7980 oz. AGW **Mint:** Lima **Obverse:** Cross of Jerusalem, lions and castles in quarters **Obv. Legend:** PHILIPPVS V D • G • HISPANIARVM **Reverse:** Pillars, PVA, date and mint mark

Date	Mintage	VG	F	VF	XF	Unc
ND (1701-9)L Date off flan	—	—	3,000	4,250	5,500	—
1701L H	—	—	4,000	5,750	7,500	—
1702L H	19,640	—	4,000	5,750	7,500	—
1703L H	34,562	—	4,000	5,750	7,500	—
1704L H	26,733	—	4,000	5,750	7,500	—
1705L H	110,670	—	4,000	5,750	7,500	—
1706L R	—	—	4,000	5,750	7,500	—
1707L H	112,660	—	4,000	5,750	7,500	—
1708L H	39,138	—	4,000	5,750	7,500	—
1709L H	49,615	—	4,000	5,750	7,500	—
1709L M	Inc. above	—	4,000	5,750	7,500	—

KM# 38.2 8 ESCUDOS

27.0674 g., 0.9170 Gold 0.7980 oz. AGW **Ruler:** Philip V **Mint:** Lima **Reverse:** ANO and date in legend

Date	Mintage	VG	F	VF	XF	Unc
ND(1710-47)L Date off flan	—	—	3,000	4,250	5,500	—
1710L H	44,061	—	4,000	5,750	7,500	—
1710L M	Inc. above	—	4,000	5,750	7,500	—
1711L M Without date in legend	64,226	—	4,000	5,750	7,500	—
1712L M	51,248	—	4,000	5,750	7,500	—
1713L M	40,295	—	4,000	5,750	7,500	—
1714L M	42,627	—	4,000	5,750	7,500	—
1715L M	61,586	—	4,000	5,750	7,000	—
1716L M	66,515	—	3,500	4,500	5,750	—
1717L M	55,691	—	3,500	4,500	5,750	—
1718L M	65,657	—	3,500	4,500	5,750	—
1719L M	60,234	—	3,500	4,500	5,750	—
1720L M	53,003	—	2,500	3,500	4,750	—
1721L M	64,217	—	2,500	3,500	4,750	—
1721L M	64,217	—	2,500	3,500	4,750	—
1722L M	36,563	—	2,500	3,500	4,750	—
1723L M	35,743	—	2,500	3,500	4,750	—
1724L M	37,810	—	2,500	3,500	4,750	—
1726L M	48,734	—	2,500	3,500	4,750	—
1727L M	60,378	—	2,500	3,500	4,750	—
1728L N	42,862	—	2,500	3,500	4,750	—
1729L N	53,813	—	2,500	3,500	4,750	—
1730L N	56,699	—	2,500	3,500	4,750	—
1731L N	36,390	—	2,500	3,500	4,750	—
1732L N	57,487	—	2,500	3,500	4,750	—
1733L N	48,875	—	2,500	3,500	4,750	—
1734L N	62,476	—	2,500	3,500	4,750	—
1735/4L N Rare	—	—	—	—	—	—
1735L N	57,496	—	2,500	3,500	4,750	—

Date	Mintage	VG	F	VF	XF	Unc
1736L N	35,504	—	2,500	3,500	4,750	—
1737L N	159,179	—	2,500	3,500	4,750	—
1738L N	129,603	—	2,500	3,500	4,750	—
1739/8L V/N Rare	—	—	—	—	—	—
1739L N	106,775	—	2,500	3,500	4,750	—
1739L V	Inc. above	—	2,500	3,500	4,750	—
1740/39L V	70,070	—	2,500	3,500	4,750	—
1740L V	Inc. above	—	2,500	3,500	4,750	—
1741L V	92,320	—	2,500	3,500	4,750	—
1742L V	78,386	—	2,500	3,500	4,750	—
1743L V	90,553	—	2,500	3,500	4,750	—
1744L V	99,962	—	2,500	3,500	4,750	—
1745L V	50,743	—	2,500	3,500	4,750	—
1746L V	85,211	—	2,500	3,500	4,750	—

KM# 38.3 8 ESCUDOS

27.0674 g., 0.9170 Gold 0.7980 oz. AGW **Mint:** Lima **Obverse:** Cross of Jerusalem, lions and castles in quarters **Obv. Legend:** PHILIPPVS V D • G • HISPANIARVM **Reverse:** Stars replace dots in field

Date	Mintage	VG	F	VF	XF	Unc
1745L V	Inc. above	—	3,000	4,000	5,000	—
1746L V	Inc. above	—	3,000	4,000	5,000	—

KM# 40 8 ESCUDOS

27.0674 g., 0.9170 Gold 0.7980 oz. AGW **Mint:** Lima **Obv. Legend:** LUDOVICVS

Date	Mintage	VG	F	VF	XF	Unc
1725 M	83,674	—	6,250	7,500	10,000	—

KM# 47 8 ESCUDOS

27.0600 g., 0.9170 Gold 0.7978 oz. AGW **Mint:** Lima **Obverse:** Cross of Jerusalem, lions and castles in quarters **Obv. Legend:** FERDINANDVS VI D • G • HISPANIARVM **Reverse:** Pillars, PVA, date and mint mark

Date	Mintage	VG	F	VF	XF	Unc
ND(1747-50)L Date off flan	—	—	2,500	3,000	3,500	—
1747L V	76,228	—	3,000	4,000	5,250	—
1748L R	Inc. above	—	3,000	4,000	5,250	—
1749/8L R	93,582	—	3,000	4,000	5,250	—
1749L R	Inc. above	—	3,000	4,000	5,250	—
1750L R	95,433	2,250	3,000	3,750	5,500	—

Note: The 1750 R is dated on both obverse and reverse. A mule exists struck with the obverse die of a 1750 and the reverse die of a 1749 R, it was sold in the Sotheby's Rio de la Plata sale 3-93, VF realizing $7,150

ROYAL COINAGE

KM# R31a REAL

3.3834 g., 0.9170 Silver 0.0997 oz. ASW **Ruler:** Philip V **Mint:** Lima **Obverse:** Cross of Jerusalem, lions and castles in quarters **Reverse:** Letters and numbers between pillars

Date	Mintage	Good	VG	F	VF	XF
1730L N	—	500	1,000	1,500	2,000	—
1736L N	—	500	1,000	1,500	2,000	—
1738L N	—	500	1,000	1,500	2,000	—

KM# R42 REAL

3.3834 g., 0.9170 Silver 0.0997 oz. ASW **Ruler:** Ferdinand VI **Mint:** Lima **Obverse:** Cross of Jerusalem, lions and castles in quarters **Reverse:** Letters and numbers between pillars **Note:** Struck at Lima.

Date	Mintage	Good	VG	F	VF	XF
1749L R	—	500	1,000	1,500	2,000	—

KM# R32 2 REALES

6.7668 g., 0.9310 Silver 0.2025 oz. ASW **Ruler:** Philip V **Mint:** Lima **Obverse:** Cross of Jerusalem, lions and castles in quarters **Reverse:** Letters and numbers between pillars

Date	Mintage	Good	VG	F	VF	XF
1709L M	—	750	1,250	1,750	2,500	—
1711L M	—	750	1,250	1,750	2,500	—
1716L M	—	750	1,250	1,750	2,500	—
1729L N	—	750	1,250	1,750	2,500	—

KM# R32a 2 REALES

6.7668 g., 0.9170 Silver 0.1995 oz. ASW **Ruler:** Philip V **Mint:** Lima **Obverse:** Cross of Jerusalem, lions and castles in quarters **Reverse:** Letters and numbers between pillars

Date	Mintage	Good	VG	F	VF	XF
1739L N	—	750	1,250	1,750	2,500	—
1741L V	—	750	1,250	1,750	2,500	—

KM# RA43 2 REALES

6.7668 g., 0.9170 Silver 0.1995 oz. ASW **Ruler:** Ferdinand VI **Mint:** Lima **Obverse:** Cross of Jerusalem, lions and castles in quarters **Reverse:** Letters and numbers between pillars

Date	Mintage	Good	VG	F	VF	XF
1748L V	—	750	1,250	1,750	2,500	—

KM# R33a 4 REALES

13.5337 g., 0.9170 Silver 0.3990 oz. ASW **Ruler:** Philip V **Mint:** Lima **Obverse:** Cross of Jerusalem, lions and castles in quarters **Reverse:** Letters ands numbers between pillars

Date	Mintage	Good	VG	F	VF	XF
1731L N	—	2,000	4,000	6,000	8,000	—
1746L V	—	2,000	4,000	6,000	8,000	—

KM# R34 8 REALES

27.0674 g., 0.9310 Silver 0.8102 oz. ASW **Ruler:** Philip V **Mint:** Lima **Obverse:** Cross of Jerusalem, lions and castles in quarters **Reverse:** Letters and numbers between pillars

Date	Mintage	Good	VG	F	VF	XF
1701L H	—	2,000	4,000	7,000	12,000	—
1704L H	—	2,000	4,000	7,000	12,000	—
1709L M	—	2,000	4,000	7,000	12,000	—
1714L M	—	2,000	4,000	7,000	12,000	—
1716L M	—	2,000	4,000	7,000	12,000	—
1719L M	—	2,000	4,000	7,000	12,000	—
1722L M	—	2,000	4,000	7,000	12,000	—
1723L M	—	2,000	4,000	7,000	12,000	—
1726L M	—	2,000	4,000	7,000	12,000	—

KM# R34a 8 REALES

27.0674 g., 0.9170 Silver 0.7980 oz. ASW **Ruler:** Philip V **Mint:** Lima **Obverse:** Cross of Jerusalem, lions and castles in quarters **Reverse:** Letters and numbers between pillars

Date	Mintage	Good	VG	F	VF	XF
1729L N	—	2,000	4,000	7,000	12,000	—
1730L N	—	2,000	4,000	7,000	12,000	—
1735L N	—	2,000	4,000	7,000	12,000	—
1736L N	—	2,000	4,000	7,000	12,000	—
1738L N	—	2,000	4,000	7,000	12,000	—
1739L V	—	2,000	4,000	7,000	12,000	—

KM# R44 8 REALES

27.0674 g., 0.9170 Silver 0.7980 oz. ASW **Ruler:** Ferdinand VI **Mint:** Lima **Obverse:** Cross of Jerusalem, lions and castles in quarters **Reverse:** Letters and numbers between pillars

Date	Mintage	Good	VG	F	VF	XF
1748L V	—	2,000	4,000	7,000	12,000	—

MILLED COINAGE

KM# 99 1/4 REAL

0.8458 g., 0.8960 Silver 0.0244 oz. ASW **Mint:** Lima **Obverse:** Bust of Charles IIII, right **Obv. Legend:** CAROLUS IIII.. **Reverse:** Crowned arms of Peru **Rev. Legend:** HISPAN • ET IND • REX

Date	Mintage	VG	F	VF	XF	Unc
1792L IJ	—	50.00	150	250	350	—
1793L IJ	—	50.00	100	150	200	—
1794L IJ	—	50.00	200	350	500	—
1795L IJ	—	50.00	200	350	500	—

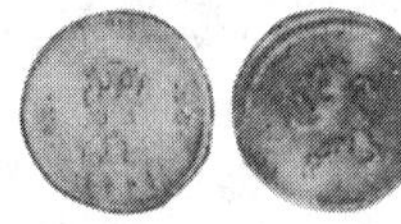

KM# 102.1 1/4 REAL

0.8458 g., 0.8960 Silver 0.0244 oz. ASW **Mint:** Lima **Obverse:** Castle, vertical LME at left, initials at right, without value **Reverse:** Crowned rampant lion

Date	Mintage	VG	F	VF	XF	Unc
1794L IJ	—	200	400	700	1,200	—
1795L JI	—	250	500	900	—	—
1796L JI	—	250	500	900	—	—

KM# 102.2 1/4 REAL

0.8458 g., 0.8960 Silver 0.0244 oz. ASW **Mint:** Lima **Obverse:** Castle, L at left, 1/4 at right **Reverse:** Crowned rampant lion

Date	Mintage	VG	F	VF	XF	Unc
1796L	—	40.00	60.00	80.00	100	—
1797L	—	40.00	60.00	80.00	100	—
1798L	—	40.00	60.00	80.00	100	—
1799L	—	40.00	60.00	80.00	100	—
1800L	—	40.00	60.00	80.00	100	—

KM# 51 1/2 REAL

1.6917 g., 0.9170 Silver 0.0499 oz. ASW **Mint:** Lima **Obverse:** Crowned arms of Peru **Obv. Legend:** FRD • VI • D • G • HISP • ET • IND • **Reverse:** Crowned pillars and globes, date **Rev. Legend:** HISPAN • ET IND • REX **Note:** Mint mark in monogram.

Date	Mintage	VG	F	VF	XF	Unc
1751LIMAE J Rare	—	—	—	—	—	—
1752/1LIMAE J	—	37.50	75.00	150	250	—
1752LIMAE J	—	37.50	75.00	150	250	—
1753/2LIMAE J	—	15.00	30.00	50.00	100	—
1753LIMAE J	—	15.00	30.00	50.00	100	—
1754LIMAE JD	—	12.50	22.50	35.00	85.00	—
1755LIMAE JD	—	15.00	35.00	55.00	100	—
1755LIMAE JM	—	12.50	25.00	35.00	85.00	—
1756LIMAE JM	—	12.50	25.00	35.00	85.00	—
1757/6LIMAE JM	—	15.00	35.00	65.00	110	—
1757LIMAE JM	—	12.50	25.00	35.00	85.00	—
1758LIMAE JM	—	12.50	25.00	35.00	85.00	—
1759/8LIMAE JM	—	—	—	—	—	—
1759LIMAE JM	—	12.50	25.00	35.00	85.00	—
1760LIMAE JM	—	12.50	25.00	35.00	85.00	—

KM# 60 1/2 REAL

1.6917 g., 0.9170 Silver 0.0499 oz. ASW **Mint:** Lima **Obverse:** Crowned arms of Peru **Obv. Legend:** CAR • III.. **Reverse:** Crowned pillars, globes **Note:** Mint mark in monogram.

Date	Mintage	VG	F	VF	XF	Unc
1760LIMAE JM	—	15.00	25.00	40.00	100	—
1761/0LIMAE JM	—	15.00	25.00	40.00	100	—
1761LIMAE JM	—	15.00	25.00	40.00	100	—
1762/1LIMAE JM	—	15.00	25.00	40.00	100	—
1762LIMAE JM	—	15.00	25.00	40.00	100	—
1763LIMAE JM	—	15.00	25.00	40.00	100	—
1764LIMAE JM	—	15.00	25.00	40.00	100	—
1765LIMAE JM	—	15.00	25.00	40.00	100	—
1766LIMAE JM	—	16.50	28.50	65.00	135	—
1766/5LIMAE JM	—	15.00	26.50	50.00	125	—
1767LIMAE JM	—	15.00	25.00	40.00	100	—
1768LIMAE JM	—	15.00	25.00	40.00	100	—
1769LIMAE JM	—	15.00	25.00	40.00	100	—
1770LIMAE JM	—	15.00	25.00	40.00	100	—
1771LIMAE JM	—	15.00	25.00	40.00	100	—
1772LIMAE JM	—	55.00	95.00	160	265	—

KM# 74 1/2 REAL

1.6917 g., 0.9030 Silver 0.0491 oz. ASW **Mint:** Lima **Obverse:** Bust of Charles III, right **Obv. Legend:** CAROLUS III.. **Reverse:** Crowned arms, pillars **Note:** Mint mark in monogram.

Date	Mintage	VG	F	VF	XF	Unc
1772LIMAE JM	—	10.00	17.50	37.50	65.00	—
1773LIMAE JM	—	10.00	20.00	35.00	60.00	—
1773LIMAE MJ	—	10.00	20.00	35.00	60.00	—
1774LIMAE MJ	—	10.00	20.00	35.00	60.00	—
1775LIMAE MJ	—	10.00	20.00	35.00	60.00	—
1776LIMAE MJ	—	10.00	20.00	35.00	60.00	—
1777LIMAE MJ	—	10.00	20.00	35.00	60.00	—
1778LIMAE MJ	—	10.00	20.00	35.00	60.00	—
1779LIMAE MJ	—	10.00	20.00	35.00	60.00	—
1780LIMAE MJ	—	10.00	20.00	37.50	70.00	—
1780LIMAE MI	—	10.00	20.00	35.00	60.00	—
1781LIMAE MI	—	10.00	20.00	35.00	60.00	—
1782LIMAE MI	—	10.00	20.00	35.00	60.00	—
1783LIMAE MI	—	10.00	20.00	35.00	60.00	—
1784LIMAE MI	—	10.00	20.00	35.00	60.00	—

KM# 74a 1/2 REAL

1.6917 g., 0.8960 Silver 0.0487 oz. ASW **Mint:** Lima **Obverse:** Bust of Charles III, right **Obv. Legend:** CAROLUS III.. **Reverse:** Crowned arms, pillars **Note:** Mint mark in monogram.

Date	Mintage	VG	F	VF	XF	Unc
1785LIMAE MI	—	10.00	20.00	35.00	60.00	—
1786LIMAE MI	—	10.00	20.00	35.00	60.00	—
1787LIMAE MI	—	10.00	20.00	35.00	60.00	—
1787LIMAE IJ	—	12.50	22.00	50.00	85.00	—
1788LIMAE IJ	—	10.00	20.00	35.00	60.00	—
1789LIMAE IJ	—	10.00	20.00	35.00	60.00	—

KM# 83 1/2 REAL

1.6917 g., 0.8960 Silver 0.0487 oz. ASW **Mint:** Lima **Obverse:** Bust of Charles III, right **Obv. Legend:** CAROLUS IV.. **Reverse:** Crowned arms, pillars **Note:** Mint mark in monogram.

Date	Mintage	VG	F	VF	XF	Unc
1789LIMAE IJ	—	10.00	20.00	35.00	65.00	—
1790LIMAE IJ	—	10.00	20.00	35.00	65.00	—
1791LIMAE IJ	—	10.00	20.00	35.00	65.00	—

KM# 93 1/2 REAL

1.6917 g., 0.8960 Silver 0.0487 oz. ASW **Mint:** Lima **Obverse:** Bust right **Obv. Legend:** CAROLUS IIII... **Reverse:** Crowned arms, pillars **Note:** Mint mark in monogram.

Date	Mintage	VG	F	VF	XF	Unc
1791LIMAE IJ Large bust	—	20.00	40.00	60.00	80.00	—
1792LIMAE IJ	—	20.00	40.00	60.00	80.00	—
1793LIMAE IJ	—	10.00	20.00	30.00	50.00	—
1794LIMAE IJ	—	10.00	20.00	30.00	50.00	—
1795LIMAE IJ	—	10.00	20.00	30.00	50.00	—
1796LIMAE IJ	—	10.00	20.00	30.00	50.00	—
1797LIMAE IJ	—	10.00	20.00	30.00	50.00	—
1798LIMAE IJ	—	10.00	20.00	30.00	50.00	—
1799LIMAE IJ	—	10.00	20.00	30.00	50.00	—
1800LIMAE IJ	—	10.00	20.00	30.00	50.00	—

KM# 52 REAL

3.3834 g., 0.9170 Silver 0.0997 oz. ASW **Mint:** Lima **Obverse:** Crowned arms of Peru **Obv. Legend:** FRD • VI • D • G • HISP • ETIND • R • **Reverse:** Crowned globes, pillars **Rev. Legend:** VIRA QUE VNUM

Date	Mintage	VG	F	VF	XF	Unc
1751LM J Rare	—	—	—	—	—	—
1752LM J	—	35.00	65.00	110	200	—
1753/2LM J	—	25.00	45.00	65.00	125	—
1753LM J	—	25.00	45.00	65.00	125	—
1754LM JD	—	20.00	40.00	60.00	110	—
1755LM JD	—	20.00	40.00	60.00	110	—
1755LM JM	—	20.00	40.00	60.00	110	—
1756LM JM	—	20.00	40.00	60.00	110	—
1757LM JM	—	20.00	40.00	60.00	110	—
1758LM JM	—	20.00	40.00	60.00	110	—
1759/7LM JM	—	20.00	40.00	60.00	110	—
1759LM JM	—	20.00	40.00	60.00	110	—
1760/50LM JM	—	25.00	45.00	65.00	125	—
1760LM JM	—	25.00	45.00	65.00	125	—

KM# 61 REAL

3.3834 g., 0.9170 Silver 0.0997 oz. ASW **Mint:** Lima **Obverse:** Crowned arms of Peru **Obv. Legend:** CAR • III • D • G • HISP • ETIND • R • **Reverse:** Crowned globes, pillars **Rev. Legend:** • VTRA QUE VNUM •

Date	Mintage	VG	F	VF	XF	Unc
1760LM JM	—	20.00	40.00	60.00	110	—
1761LM JM	—	20.00	40.00	60.00	110	—
1762LM JM	—	20.00	40.00	60.00	110	—
1763LM JM	—	20.00	40.00	60.00	110	—
1764LM JM	—	20.00	40.00	60.00	110	—
1765LM JM	—	20.00	40.00	60.00	110	—
1766LM JM	—	20.00	40.00	60.00	110	—
1767LM JM	—	20.00	40.00	60.00	110	—
1768LM JM	—	20.00	40.00	60.00	110	—
1769LM JM	—	20.00	40.00	60.00	110	—
1770LM JM	—	20.00	40.00	60.00	110	—
1771LM JM	—	20.00	40.00	60.00	110	—
1772LM JM	—	40.00	80.00	120	250	—

KM# 75 REAL

3.3834 g., 0.9030 Silver 0.0982 oz. ASW **Mint:** Lima **Obverse:** Bust of Charles III, right **Obv. Legend:** CAROLUS • III • DEI GRATIA • **Reverse:** Crowned arms,pillars **Rev. Legend:** HISPAN • ET • IND • REX • ... **Note:** Mint mark in monogram.

Date	Mintage	VG	F	VF	XF	Unc
1772LIMAE JM	—	15.00	35.00	50.00	70.00	—
1773LIMAE JM	—	15.00	35.00	50.00	70.00	—
1773LIMAE MJ	—	15.00	35.00	50.00	70.00	—
1774LIMAE MJ	—	15.00	35.00	50.00	70.00	—
1775LIMAE MJ	—	15.00	35.00	50.00	70.00	—
1776LIMAE MJ	—	15.00	35.00	50.00	75.00	—
1777LIMAE MJ	—	15.00	35.00	50.00	75.00	—
1778LIMAE MJ	—	15.00	35.00	50.00	75.00	—
1779LIMAE MJ	—	15.00	35.00	50.00	75.00	—
1780LIMAE MJ	—	15.00	35.00	50.00	75.00	—
1780LIMAE MI	—	15.00	25.00	50.00	75.00	—
1781LIMAE MI	—	15.00	25.00	50.00	75.00	—
1782LIMAE MI	—	15.00	25.00	50.00	75.00	—
1783LIMAE MI	—	15.00	25.00	50.00	75.00	—
1784LIMAE MI	—	15.00	25.00	50.00	75.00	—

KM# 75a REAL

3.3834 g., 0.8960 Silver 0.0975 oz. ASW **Mint:** Lima **Obverse:** Bust of Charles III, right **Obv. Legend:** CAROLUS III.. **Reverse:** Crowned arms, pillars **Note:** Mint mark in monogram.

Date	Mintage	VG	F	VF	XF	Unc
1785LIMAE MI	—	15.00	35.00	50.00	75.00	—
1786LIMAE MI	—	15.00	35.00	50.00	75.00	—
1787LIMAE MI	—	15.00	35.00	50.00	75.00	—
1787LIMAE IJ	—	15.00	35.00	50.00	75.00	—
1788LIMAE IJ	—	15.00	35.00	50.00	75.00	—
1789LIMAE IJ	—	15.00	35.00	50.00	75.00	—

KM# 84 REAL

3.3834 g., 0.8960 Silver 0.0975 oz. ASW **Mint:** Lima **Obverse:** Bust of Charles IIII, right **Obv. Legend:** CAROLUS • IV • DEI • GRATIA • **Reverse:** Crowned arms, pillars **Rev. Legend:** HISPAN • ET IND.... **Note:** Mint mark in monogram.

Date	Mintage	VG	F	VF	XF	Unc
1789LIMAE IJ	—	15.00	35.00	50.00	75.00	—
1790LIMAE IJ	—	15.00	35.00	50.00	75.00	—
1791LIMAE IJ	—	15.00	35.00	50.00	75.00	—

KM# 94 REAL

3.3834 g., 0.8960 Silver 0.0975 oz. ASW **Mint:** Lima **Obverse:** Bust of Charles IIII, right **Obv. Legend:** CAROLUS • IIII • DEI • GRATIA • **Reverse:** Crowned arms, pillars **Rev. Legend:** HISPAN • ET IND • REX • ... **Note:** Mint mark in monogram.

Date	Mintage	VG	F	VF	XF	Unc
1791LIMAE IJ Large bust.	—	12.50	30.00	45.00	60.00	—
1792LIMAE IJ Large bust.	—	12.50	30.00	45.00	60.00	—
1793LIMAE IJ Large bust.	—	12.50	30.00	45.00	60.00	—
1793LIMAE IJ Standard bust.	—	12.50	30.00	45.00	60.00	—
1794LIMAE IJ	—	12.50	30.00	45.00	60.00	—
1795LIMAE IJ	—	12.50	30.00	45.00	60.00	—
1796LIMAE IJ	—	12.50	30.00	45.00	60.00	—
1797LIMAE IJ	—	12.50	30.00	45.00	60.00	—
1798LIMAE IJ	—	12.50	30.00	45.00	60.00	—
1799LIMAE IJ	—	12.50	30.00	45.00	60.00	—
1800LIMAE IJ	—	12.50	30.00	45.00	60.00	—

KM# 53 2 REALES

6.7668 g., 0.9170 Silver 0.1995 oz. ASW **Mint:** Lima **Obverse:** Crowned arms of Peru **Obv. Legend:** FERDND • VI D • G • HISP • ET IND REX **Reverse:** Crowned globes, pillars

Date	Mintage	VG	F	VF	XF	Unc
1752/1LM J	—	150	250	325	—	—
1752LM J	—	150	250	325	—	—
1753/2LM J FED	—	30.00	85.00	110	185	—
1753LM J FRD	—	30.00	85.00	110	185	—
1754LM JD	—	30.00	85.00	110	185	—
1755LM JD	—	30.00	85.00	110	185	—
1755LM JM	—	30.00	85.00	110	185	—
1756LM JM	—	30.00	85.00	110	185	—
1757/6LM JM	—	30.00	85.00	110	185	—
1757LM JM	—	30.00	85.00	110	185	—
1757LM J(M)	—	30.00	85.00	110	185	—

Note: LIMAE monogram punch was used for the minmaster initial (M).

Date	Mintage	VG	F	VF	XF	Unc
1758LM JM	—	30.00	85.00	110	185	—
1759LM JM	—	30.00	85.00	110	185	—
1760/50LM JM	—	35.00	90.00	125	165	—
1760LM JM	—	35.00	90.00	125	165	—

KM# 62 2 REALES

6.7668 g., 0.9170 Silver 0.1995 oz. ASW **Mint:** Lima **Obverse:** Crowned arms of Peru **Obv. Legend:** CAR • III.. **Reverse:** Crowned globes, pillars

Date	Mintage	VG	F	VF	XF	Unc
1760LM JM	—	35.00	95.00	125	165	—
1761LM JM	—	35.00	95.00	125	165	—
1762LM JM	—	35.00	95.00	125	165	—
1763LM JM	—	35.00	95.00	125	165	—
1764LM JM	—	35.00	95.00	125	165	—
1765LM JM	—	35.00	95.00	125	165	—
1766/5LM JM	—	35.00	95.00	125	165	—
1766LM JM	—	35.00	95.00	125	165	—
1767LM JM	—	35.00	95.00	125	165	—
1768/6LM JM Rare	—	—	—	—	—	—
1768LM JM	—	35.00	95.00	125	165	—
1769LM JM	—	35.00	95.00	125	165	—
1770LM JM	—	35.00	95.00	125	165	—
1771LM JM	—	35.00	95.00	125	165	—
1772LM JM	—	35.00	95.00	125	165	—

KM# 76 2 REALES

6.7668 g., 0.9030 Silver 0.1964 oz. ASW **Mint:** Lima **Obverse:** Bust of Charles III, right **Obv. Legend:** CAROLUS III.. **Reverse:** Crowned arms, pillars **Note:** Mint mark in monogram.

Date	Mintage	VG	F	VF	XF	Unc
1772LIMAE JM	—	75.00	125	250	—	—
1773LIMAE JM	—	20.00	45.00	60.00	75.00	—
1774LIMAE JM	—	200	300	500	—	—
1774LIMAE MJ	—	20.00	45.00	60.00	75.00	—
1775LIMAE MJ	—	20.00	45.00	60.00	75.00	—
1776LIMAE MJ	—	20.00	45.00	60.00	75.00	—
1777LIMAE MJ	—	20.00	45.00	60.00	75.00	—
1778LIMAE MJ	—	20.00	45.00	60.00	75.00	—
1779LIMAE MJ	—	20.00	45.00	60.00	75.00	—
1780LIMAE MJ	—	20.00	45.00	60.00	75.00	—
1780LIMAE MI	—	35.00	75.00	90.00	125	—
1781LIMAE MI	—	20.00	45.00	60.00	75.00	—
1782LIMAE MI	—	20.00	45.00	60.00	75.00	—
1783LIMAE MI	—	20.00	45.00	60.00	75.00	—
1784LIMAE MI	—	20.00	45.00	60.00	75.00	—

KM# 76a 2 REALES

6.7668 g., 0.8960 Silver 0.1949 oz. ASW **Mint:** Lima **Obverse:** Bust of Charles III, right **Obv. Legend:** CAROLUS III.. **Reverse:** Crowned arms, pillars

Note: Mint mark in monogram.

Date	Mintage	VG	F	VF	XF	Unc
1785LIMAE MI	—	20.00	45.00	60.00	75.00	—
1786LIMAE MI	—	20.00	45.00	60.00	75.00	—
1787LIMAE MI	—	20.00	45.00	60.00	75.00	—
1787LIMAE IJ	—	20.00	45.00	60.00	75.00	—
1788LIMAE MI	—	25.00	55.00	70.00	90.00	—
1788LIMAE IJ	—	20.00	45.00	60.00	75.00	—
1789LIMAE IJ	—	20.00	45.00	60.00	75.00	—

KM# 85.1 2 REALES

6.7668 g., 0.8960 Silver 0.1949 oz. ASW **Mint:** Lima **Obverse:** Bust of Charles IIII, right **Obv. Legend:** CAROLUS IV.. **Rev. Legend:** Denomination "2R" **Note:** Mint mark in monogram.

Date	Mintage	VG	F	VF	XF	Unc
1789LIMAE IJ	—	20.00	45.00	60.00	75.00	—
1790LIMAE IJ	—	20.00	45.00	60.00	75.00	—
1791LIMAE IJ	—	20.00	45.00	60.00	75.00	—

KM# 85.2 2 REALES

6.7668 g., 0.8960 Silver 0.1949 oz. ASW **Mint:** Lima **Obverse:** Bust of Charles IIII, right **Obv. Legend:** CAROLUS IV.. **Rev. Legend:** Denomination "R2" **Note:** Mint mark in monogram.

Date	Mintage	VG	F	VF	XF	Unc
1789LIMAE IJ	—	35.00	55.00	85.00	200	—
1790LIMAE IJ	—	35.00	55.00	85.00	200	—

KM# 95 2 REALES

6.7668 g., 0.8960 Silver 0.1949 oz. ASW **Mint:** Lima **Obverse:** Bust of Charles IIII, right **Obv. Legend:** CAROLUS IIII... **Reverse:** Crowned arms, pillars **Rev. Legend:** HISPAN • ET IND • REX • ... **Note:** Mint mark in monogram.

Date	Mintage	VG	F	VF	XF	Unc
1791LIMAE IJ Large bust.	—	17.50	35.00	50.00	65.00	—
1792LIMAE IJ Large bust.	—	17.50	35.00	50.00	65.00	—
1793LIMAE IJ Large bust.	—	17.50	35.00	50.00	65.00	—
1793LIMAE IJ Standard bust.	—	17.50	35.00	50.00	65.00	—
1794LIMAE IJ	—	17.50	35.00	50.00	65.00	—
1795LIMAE IJ	—	17.50	35.00	50.00	65.00	—
1796LIMAE IJ	—	17.50	35.00	50.00	65.00	—
1797LIMAE IJ	—	17.50	35.00	50.00	65.00	—
1798LIMAE IJ	—	17.50	35.00	50.00	65.00	—
1799LIMAE IJ	—	17.50	35.00	50.00	65.00	—
1800LIMAE IJ	—	17.50	35.00	50.00	65.00	—

KM# 54 4 REALES

13.5337 g., 0.9170 Silver 0.3990 oz. ASW **Mint:** Lima **Obverse:** Crowned arms of Peru **Obv. Legend:** FERDND • VI • D • G • HISPAN • ETIND • REX **Reverse:** Crowned globes, pillars **Rev. Legend:** VTRAQUE VNUM

Date	Mintage	VG	F	VF	XF	Unc
1752LM J	—	250	400	650	1,000	—
1753/2LM J	—	150	300	500	700	—
1753LM J	—	150	300	500	700	—
1754LM JD	—	100	175	225	375	—
1755LM JD	—	100	175	225	375	—
1755LM JM	—	100	175	225	375	—
1756/5LM JM	—	100	175	225	375	—
1756LM JM	—	100	175	225	375	—
1757LM JM	—	100	175	225	375	—
1758LM JM	—	100	175	225	375	—

Date	Mintage	VG	F	VF	XF	Unc
1759LM JM	—	100	175	225	375	—
1760LM JM	—	100	175	225	375	—

KM# 63 4 REALES
13.5337 g., 0.9170 Silver 0.3990 oz. ASW **Mint:** Lima **Obverse:** Crowned arms of Peru **Obv. Legend:** CAROLUS • III • D • G • HISPAN • ETIND • REX **Reverse:** Crowned globes, pillars **Rev. Legend:** VITRAQUE VNUM

Date	Mintage	VG	F	VF	XF	Unc
1760LM JM	—	100	175	250	600	—
1761LM JM	—	100	175	225	550	—
1762LM JM	—	100	175	225	475	—
1763LM JM	—	200	350	650	1,350	—
1764LM JM	—	100	175	225	450	—
1765LM JM	—	175	275	500	1,100	—
1766LM JM	—	100	175	225	650	—
1767/6LM JM	—	100	175	225	650	—
1767LM JM	—	100	175	225	650	—
1768LM JM	—	100	175	225	525	—
1769LM JM	—	100	175	225	525	—
1770LM JM	—	100	175	275	600	—
1771LM JM	—	100	175	225	500	—
1772LM JM	—	100	175	225	375	—

KM# 77 4 REALES
13.5337 g., 0.9030 Silver 0.3929 oz. ASW **Mint:** Lima **Obverse:** Bust of Charles III, right **Obv. Legend:** CAROLUS • III • DEI • GRATIA • **Reverse:** Crowned arms, pillars **Note:** Mint mark in monogram.

Date	Mintage	VG	F	VF	XF	Unc
1772LIMAE JM	—	200	350	450	1,000	—
1773LIMAE JM	—	60.00	75.00	150	325	—
1773LIMAE MJ	—	60.00	75.00	150	325	—
1774LIMAE MJ	—	60.00	75.00	150	325	—
1775LIMAE MJ	—	60.00	75.00	150	325	—
1775LIMAE MJ Legend "GARTIA" (error)	—	150	200	400	700	—
1776LIMAE MJ	—	50.00	75.00	150	325	—
1777LIMAE MJ	—	50.00	75.00	150	325	—
1778LIMAE MJ	—	50.00	75.00	150	325	—
1779LIMAE MJ	—	50.00	75.00	150	325	—
1780LIMAE MJ	—	50.00	75.00	150	325	—
1780LIMAE MI	—	50.00	75.00	150	325	—
1781LIMAE MI	—	50.00	75.00	150	325	—
1782LIMAE MI	—	50.00	75.00	150	325	—
1783LIMAE MI	—	50.00	75.00	150	325	—
1784LIMAE MI	—	50.00	75.00	150	325	—

KM# 77a 4 REALES
13.5337 g., 0.8960 Silver 0.3898 oz. ASW **Mint:** Lima **Obverse:** Bust of Charles III, right **Obv. Legend:** CAROLUS • III • DEI • GRATIA • **Reverse:** Crowned arms, pillars

Date	Mintage	VG	F	VF	XF	Unc
1785LIMAE MI	—	50.00	75.00	150	325	—
1786LIMAE MI	—	50.00	75.00	150	325	—
1787LIMAE MI	—	50.00	75.00	150	325	—
1787LIMAE IJ	—	50.00	75.00	150	325	—
1788LIMAE IJ	—	50.00	75.00	150	325	—
1789LIMAE IJ	—	60.00	90.00	175	375	—

KM# 86 4 REALES
13.5337 g., 0.8960 Silver 0.3898 oz. ASW **Mint:** Lima **Obverse:** Bust of Charles IIII, right **Obv. Legend:** CAROLUS • IV • .. **Reverse:** Crowned arms, pillars

Date	Mintage	VG	F	VF	XF	Unc
1789LIMAE IJ	—	50.00	75.00	150	325	—
1790LIMAE IJ	—	50.00	75.00	150	325	—
1791LIMAE IJ	—	50.00	75.00	150	325	—

KM# 96 4 REALES
13.5337 g., 0.8960 Silver 0.3898 oz. ASW **Mint:** Lima **Obverse:** Bust of Charles IIII, right **Obv. Legend:** CAROLUS • IIII • DEI • GRATIA • **Reverse:** Crowned arms, pillars **Rev. Legend:** HISPAN • ET IND • REX...

Date	Mintage	VG	F	VF	XF	Unc
1791LIMAE IJ	—	50.00	75.00	150	325	—
1792LIMAE IJ	—	35.00	60.00	125	300	—
1793LIMAE IJ	—	35.00	60.00	125	300	—
1794/3LIMAE IJ	—	35.00	60.00	125	300	—
1794LIMAE IJ	—	35.00	60.00	125	300	—
1795LIMAE IJ	—	35.00	60.00	125	300	—
1796LIMAE IJ	—	35.00	60.00	125	300	—
1797LIMAE IJ	—	35.00	60.00	125	300	—
1798LIMAE IJ	—	35.00	60.00	125	300	—
1799LIMAE IJ	—	35.00	60.00	125	300	—
1800LIMAE IJ	—	35.00	60.00	125	300	—

KM# 55.1 8 REALES
27.0674 g., 0.9170 Silver 0.7980 oz. ASW **Mint:** Lima **Obverse:** Crowned arms of Peru **Obv. Legend:** FERDIN • VI • D • G • HISPAN • ETIND • REX **Reverse:** Crowned globes, pillars **Rev. Legend:** ...VNUM **Note:** With dot above "L's in mint marks

Date	Mintage	VG	F	VF	XF	Unc
1751LM J Rare	—	—	—	—	—	—
1752LM J	—	350	600	1,000	2,000	—
1753LM J	—	100	150	250	500	—
1754LM J	—	100	150	250	500	—
1754/3LM JD	—	150	250	500	1,000	—
1754LM JD/S	—	100	150	250	500	—
1754LM JD	—	100	150	250	500	—
1755/4LM JD	—	100	175	350	750	—
1755LM JD	—	100	150	250	500	—
1755LM JM	—	100	150	250	500	—
1756/5LM JM	—	100	165	300	700	—
1756LM JM	—	100	150	250	500	—
1757/6LM JM	—	100	165	300	700	—
1757LM JM	—	100	150	250	500	—
1758/7LM JM	1,797,000	100	165	300	700	—
1758LM JM	Inc. above	100	150	250	500	—
1759LM JM	1,962,000	100	150	250	500	—
1760LM JM	2,555,000	100	150	250	500	—

KM# 55.2 8 REALES
27.0674 g., 0.9170 Silver 0.7980 oz. ASW **Mint:** Lima **Obverse:** Crowned arms of Peru **Obv. Legend:** FERDND • VI • D • G • HISPAN • ET IND • REX **Reverse:** Crowned globes, pillars **Rev. Legend:** ...UE VNUM **Note:** With dot above one "L" in mintmark.

Date	Mintage	VG	F	VF	XF	Unc
1759LM JM	Inc. above	200	300	400	600	—
1760LM JM	Inc. above	100	150	250	500	—

KM# A64.1 8 REALES
27.0674 g., 0.9170 Silver 0.7980 oz. ASW **Mint:** Lima **Obverse:** Crowned arms of Peru **Obv. Legend:** CAROLUS • III • D • G • HISPAN • ETIND • REX **Reverse:** Crowned globes, pillars **Rev. Legend:** VTRAQUE VNUM **Note:** Double dots.

Date	Mintage	VG	F	VF	XF	Unc
1760LM JM Inc. #55.1	—	250	500	900	1,750	—
1761LM JM	2,865,000	100	150	250	500	—
1762LM JM	—	100	150	250	500	—
1763/2LM JM Rare	—	—	—	—	—	—
1763LM JM	—	100	150	250	500	—
1764LM JM	—	100	150	250	550	—
1765LM JM	—	100	150	250	500	—
1766LM JM Rare	—	—	—	—	—	—
1767LM JM Rare	—	—	—	—	—	—
1768LM JM	—	125	200	300	550	—
1769LM JM	—	100	150	225	500	—

KM# A64.2 8 REALES
27.0674 g., 0.9170 Silver 0.7980 oz. ASW **Mint:** Lima **Obverse:** Crowned arms of Peru **Obv. Legend:** CAROLUS • III • D • G • HISPAN • ... **Reverse:** Crowned globes, pillars **Rev. Legend:** VTRAQUE VNUM **Note:** With dot above one "L" in mint mark.

Date	Mintage	VG	F	VF	XF	Unc
1760LM JM	—	100	150	250	500	—
1761LM JM	Inc. above	100	150	250	500	—
1762LM JM	—	100	150	250	500	—
1763LM JM Rare	—	—	—	—	—	—
1764LM JM Rare	—	—	—	—	—	—
1765LM JM	—	100	150	250	500	—
1766LM JM	2,989,000	100	150	250	500	—
1767LM JM	2,785,000	100	150	200	500	—
1768LM JM	—	100	150	200	500	—
1769LM JM	—	125	175	250	500	—

KM# A64.3 8 REALES
27.0674 g., 0.9170 Silver 0.7980 oz. ASW **Mint:** Lima **Obverse:** Crowned arms of Peru **Obv. Legend:** CAROLUS • III • D • G • HISPAN • ETIND • REX **Reverse:** Crowned globes, pillars **Rev. Legend:** VTRAQUE VNUM **Note:** Without dots above "L's" in mint marks.

Date	Mintage	VG	F	VF	XF	Unc
1766LM JM Rare	—	—	—	—	—	—
1768LM JM Rare	—	—	—	—	—	—

KM# 64.1 8 REALES

27.0674 g., 0.9170 Silver 0.7980 oz. ASW **Mint:** Lima **Obverse:** Crowned arms of Peru **Obv. Legend:** CAROLUS • III • D • G • HISPAN ... **Reverse:** Crowned globes, pillars **Rev. Legend:** VTRAQUE VNUM **Note:** With dot above both "L's" in mint marks

Date	Mintage	VG	F	VF	XF	Unc
1769LM JM Rare	—	—	—	—	—	—
1770LM JM	2,899,000	100	150	250	500	—
1771LM JM Rare	—	—	—	—	—	—
1772LM JM Rare	—	—	—	—	—	—

KM# 64.2 8 REALES

27.0674 g., 0.9170 Silver 0.7980 oz. ASW **Mint:** Lima **Obverse:** Crowned arms of Peru **Obv. Legend:** CAROLUS • III • D • G • HISPAN ... **Reverse:** Crowned globes, pillars **Rev. Legend:** VTRAQUE VNUM **Note:** With dot above left mint mark only.

Date	Mintage	VG	F	VF	XF	Unc
1769LM JM	—	125	225	350	700	—
1770LM JM	—	100	125	250	475	—
1771LM JM HIAPSN (error)	—	350	750	1,500	—	—
1771LM JM	2,897,000	100	125	250	475	—
1772LM JM	—	150	250	400	750	—

KM# 64.3 8 REALES

27.0674 g., 0.9170 Silver 0.7980 oz. ASW **Mint:** Lima **Obverse:** Crowned arms of Peru **Obv. Legend:** CAROLUS • III • D • G • HISPAN ... **Reverse:** Crowned globes, pillars **Rev. Legend:** VTRAQUE VNUM **Note:** Without dots above "L's" in mint marks.

Date	Mintage	VG	F	VF	XF	Unc
1770LM JM Rare	—	—	—	—	—	—

KM# 78 8 REALES

27.0674 g., 0.9030 Silver 0.7858 oz. ASW **Mint:** Lima **Obverse:** Bust of Charles III, right **Obv. Legend:** CAROLUS • III • DEI • GRATIA • **Reverse:** Crowned arms, pillars **Rev. Legend:** ....HISPAN • ET • IND • REX **Note:** Mint mark in monogram.

Date	Mintage	VG	F	VF	XF	Unc
1772LIMAE JM	—	50.00	100	150	225	—
1773LIMAE JM	4,105,000	40.00	90.00	140	200	—
1773LIMAE MJ	Inc. above	40.00	90.00	140	200	—
1774/3LIMAE MJ	4,208,000	55.00	110	175	250	—
1774LIMAE JM Rare	Inc. above	—	—	—	—	—

Note: Superior December sale 12-91 XF realized $11,000

Date	Mintage	VG	F	VF	XF	Unc
1774LIMAE MJ	Inc. above	40.00	90.00	140	200	—
1775LIMAE MJ	4,276,000	40.00	90.00	140	200	—
1776LIMAE MJ	—	40.00	90.00	140	200	—
1777LIMAE MJ	—	40.00	90.00	140	200	—
1778LIMAE MJ	—	40.00	90.00	140	200	—
1779LIMAE MJ	—	40.00	90.00	140	200	—
1780LIMAE MJ	—	40.00	90.00	140	200	—
1780LIMAE MI	—	50.00	100	200	300	—
1781LIMAE MI	—	40.00	90.00	140	200	—
1782LIMAE MJ Error; rare	—	—	—	—	—	—
1782LIMAE MI	—	40.00	90.00	140	200	—
1783LIMAE MI	—	40.00	90.00	140	200	—
1784/3LIMAE MI	—	40.00	90.00	140	200	—
1784LIMAE MI	—	40.00	90.00	140	200	—

KM# 78a 8 REALES

27.0674 g., 0.8960 Silver 0.7797 oz. ASW **Mint:** Lima **Obverse:** Bust of Charles III, right **Obv. Legend:** CAROLUS • III • DEI • GRATIA • **Reverse:** Crowned arms, pillars **Rev. Legend:** ...HISPAN • ET IND • REX **Note:** Mint mark in monogram.

Date	Mintage	VG	F	VF	XF	Unc
1785LIMAE MI	2,767,000	40.00	90.00	140	200	—
1786LIMAE MI	—	40.00	90.00	140	200	—
1787/6LIMAE MI	3,318,000	50.00	100	150	225	—
1787LIMAE MI	Inc. above	40.00	90.00	140	200	—
1787LIMAE IJ	Inc. above	50.00	100	175	300	—
1788LIMAE IJ	3,467,000	40.00	90.00	140	200	—
1789LIMAE IJ	3,500,000	45.00	95.00	150	250	—

KM# 87 8 REALES

27.0674 g., 0.8960 Silver 0.7797 oz. ASW **Mint:** Lima **Obverse:** Bust of Charles IIII, right **Obv. Legend:** CAROLUS • IV • DEI • GRATIA • **Reverse:** Crowned arms of Peru **Rev. Legend:** ...HISPAN • ET IND • REX **Note:** Mint mark in monogram.

Date	Mintage	VG	F	VF	XF	Unc
1789LIMAE IJ Inc. #78	—	45.00	95.00	150	260	—
1790LIMAE IJ	4,313,000	50.00	100	150	210	—
1791LIMAE IJ	4,102,000	50.00	100	150	210	—

KM# 97 8 REALES

27.0674 g., 0.8960 Silver 0.7797 oz. ASW **Mint:** Lima **Obverse:** Bust of Charles IIII, right **Obv. Legend:** CAROLUS • IIII • DEI • GRATIA • **Reverse:** Crowned arms, pillars **Rev. Legend:** ...HISPAN • ET IND • REX **Note:** Mint mark in monogram.

Date	Mintage	VG	F	VF	XF	Unc
1791LIMAE IJ	Inc. above	35.00	75.00	110	150	—
1792/1LIMAE IJ	4,661,000	35.00	75.00	110	150	—
1792LIMAE IJ	Inc. above	35.00	75.00	110	150	—
1793LIMAE IJ	5,005,000	35.00	75.00	110	150	—
1794LIMAE IJ	5,024,000	35.00	75.00	110	150	—
1795/4LIMAE IJ	4,998,000	35.00	75.00	110	150	—
1795LIMAE IJ	Inc. above	35.00	75.00	110	150	—
1796LIMAE IJ	5,101,000	35.00	75.00	110	150	—
1796LIMAE IJ Value R8, error	Inc. above	300	500	750	1,500	—
1797LIMAE IJ	4,391,000	35.00	75.00	110	150	—
1798LIMAE IJ	4,654,000	35.00	75.00	110	150	—
1799LIMAE IJ	5,367,000	35.00	75.00	110	150	—
1800LIMAE IJ	4,207,000	35.00	75.00	110	150	—

KM# 56.1 ESCUDO

3.3834 g., 0.9170 Gold 0.0997 oz. AGW **Mint:** Lima **Obverse:** Large bust of Ferdinand VI, right **Obv. Legend:** FERD VI D • G • HISPAN ET INDREX **Reverse:** Crowned arms of Peru

Date	Mintage	VG	F	VF	XF	Unc
1751LM J	—	400	800	1,250	2,000	—
1752LM J	—	400	800	1,250	2,000	—
1753LM J	—	500	1,000	1,500	2,250	—

KM# 56.2 ESCUDO

3.3834 g., 0.9170 Gold 0.0997 oz. AGW **Mint:** Lima **Obverse:** Smaller bust of Ferdinand VI, right **Obv. Legend:** FERDND VI... **Reverse:** Crowned arms of Peru

Date	Mintage	VG	F	VF	XF	Unc
1754LM JD	—	300	600	1,000	1,750	—
1755LM JM	—	400	800	1,250	2,000	—
1756LM JM	—	250	500	750	1,000	—
1757LM JM	—	250	500	750	1,000	—
1758LM JM	—	250	500	750	1,000	—
1759LM JM	—	250	550	800	1,200	—

KM# 65 ESCUDO

3.3834 g., 0.9170 Gold 0.0997 oz. AGW **Mint:** Lima **Obverse:** Bust of Charles III, right **Obv. Legend:** CAROLUS III... **Reverse:** Crowned arms of Peru **Rev. Legend:** NOMINA MAGNA SEQUOR

Date	Mintage	VG	F	VF	XF	Unc
1761LM JM	—	500	1,000	1,500	2,250	—
1762LM JM	—	500	1,000	1,500	2,250	—

KM# 72 ESCUDO

3.3834 g., 0.9170 Gold 0.0997 oz. AGW **Mint:** Lima **Obverse:** Young bust of Charles III, right **Obv. Legend:** CAR • III... **Reverse:** Crowned arms of Peru **Rev. Legend:** IN • UTROQ • FELIX •

Date	Mintage	VG	F	VF	XF	Unc
1763LM JM	—	200	300	500	800	—
1764LM JM	—	200	300	500	800	—
1765LM JM	—	200	300	500	800	—
1766LM JM	—	200	300	500	800	—
1767LM JM	—	200	300	500	800	—
1768LM JM	—	200	300	500	800	—
1769LM JM	—	200	300	500	800	—
1770LM JM	—	200	300	500	800	—
1771LM JM	—	200	300	500	800	—

KM# 79 ESCUDO

3.3834 g., 0.9010 Gold 0.0980 oz. AGW **Mint:** Lima **Obverse:** Older, standard bust of Charles III, right **Obv. Legend:** CAROL • III... **Reverse:** Crowned arms in order chain **Note:** Mint mark in monogram.

Date	Mintage	VG	F	VF	XF	Unc
1772LIMAE JM	—	100	200	300	400	—
1773LIMAE JM	—	200	300	400	500	—
1773LIMAE MJ	—	100	200	300	400	—
1774LIMAE MJ	—	100	200	300	400	—
1775LIMAE MJ	—	100	200	300	400	—
1776LIMAE MJ	—	100	200	300	400	—
1777LIMAE MJ	—	100	200	300	400	—
1778LIMAE MJ	—	100	200	300	400	—
1779LIMAE MJ	—	100	200	300	400	—
1780LIMAE MI	—	100	200	300	400	—
1781LIMAE MI	—	100	200	300	400	—
1782LIMAE MI	—	100	200	300	400	—
1783LIMAE MI	—	100	200	300	400	—
1784LIMAE MI	—	100	200	300	400	—

KM# 79A ESCUDO

3.3834 g., 0.8750 Gold 0.0952 oz. AGW **Mint:** Lima **Obverse:** Older, standard bust of Charles III, right **Obv. Legend:** CAROL • III... **Reverse:** Crowned arms in order chain **Note:** Mint mark in monogram.

Date	Mintage	VG	F	VF	XF	Unc
1785LIMAE MI	—	100	200	300	400	—
1786LIMAE MI	—	100	200	300	400	—
1787LIMAE MI	—	100	200	300	400	—
1787LIMAE IJ	—	100	200	300	400	—
1788LIMAE IJ	—	100	200	300	400	—
1789LIMAE IJ	—	100	200	300	400	—

KM# 88 ESCUDO

3.3834 g., 0.8750 Gold 0.0952 oz. AGW **Mint:** Lima **Obverse:** Bust of Charles IIII, right **Obv. Legend:** CAROL • IV... **Reverse:** Crowned arms in order chain **Note:** Mint mark in monogram.

Date	Mintage	VG	F	VF	XF	Unc
1789LIMAE IJ	—	150	300	450	650	—
1790LIMAE IJ	—	150	300	450	650	—
1791LIMAE IJ	—	150	300	450	600	—

KM# 89 ESCUDO

3.3834 g., 0.8750 Gold 0.0952 oz. AGW **Mint:** Lima **Obverse:** Bust of Charles IV, right **Obv. Legend:** CAROL • IIII... **Reverse:** Crowned arms in order chain **Note:** Mint mark in monogram.

Date	Mintage	VG	F	VF	XF	Unc
1792LIMAE IJ	—	125	200	300	500	—
1793LIMAE IJ	—	100	175	265	450	—
1794LIMAE IJ	—	100	175	265	450	—
1795LIMAE IJ	—	100	175	265	450	—
1796LIMAE IJ	—	100	175	265	450	—
1797LIMAE IJ	—	100	175	265	450	—
1798LIMAE IJ	—	100	175	265	450	—
1799LIMAE IJ	—	100	175	265	450	—
1800LIMAE IJ	—	100	175	265	450	—

KM# 48 2 ESCUDOS

6.7668 g., 0.9170 Gold 0.1995 oz. AGW **Mint:** Lima **Obverse:** Large bust of Ferdinand VI, right **Obv. Legend:** FERD VI • D • G • HISPAN •ET IND • REX • **Reverse:** Crowned arms **Rev. Legend:** INITIUM SAPIENTIÆTIMORDOMINI **Note:** Dot above L of mint mark.

Date	Mintage	VG	F	VF	XF	Unc
1751LM J	—	450	900	1,750	3,000	—
1752LM J	—	450	900	1,750	3,000	—
1753LM J	—	450	900	1,750	3,000	—

KM# 57 2 ESCUDOS

6.7668 g., 0.9170 Gold 0.1995 oz. AGW **Mint:** Lima **Obverse:** Smaller bust of Ferdinand VI, right **Obv. Legend:** FERD VI • D • G • HISPAN • ETIND • REX • **Reverse:** Crowned arms of Peru **Note:** Dot above "L" of mint mark.

Date	Mintage	VG	F	VF	XF	Unc
1755LM JM	—	300	650	1,200	2,000	—
1756LM JM Rare	—	—	—	—	—	—
1758LM JM	—	300	600	1,000	1,750	—
1759LM JM	—	300	600	1,000	1,750	—
1760LM JM	—	300	600	1,000	1,750	—

KM# 66 2 ESCUDOS

6.7668 g., 0.9170 Gold 0.1995 oz. AGW **Mint:** Lima **Obverse:** Bust of Charles III, right **Obv. Legend:** CAROLUS III... **Reverse:** Crowned arms of Peru **Note:** Mint mark in monogram.

Date	Mintage	VG	F	VF	XF	Unc
1761LIMAE JM	—	700	1,500	2,500	4,000	—
1762LIMAE JM	—	700	1,500	2,500	4,000	—

KM# 69 2 ESCUDOS

6.7668 g., 0.9170 Gold 0.1995 oz. AGW **Mint:** Lima **Obverse:** Young, standard bust of Charles III, right **Reverse:** Crowned arms of Peru **Rev. Legend:** IN UTROG FELIX AUSPICE DEO **Note:** Mint mark in monogram.

Date	Mintage	VG	F	VF	XF	Unc
1763LIMAE JM	—	350	750	1,500	2,500	—
1764LIMAE JM	—	350	750	1,500	2,500	—
1765LIMAE JM	—	350	750	1,500	2,500	—
1766LIMAE JM	—	450	900	1,800	3,000	—
1767LIMAE JM	—	250	500	950	1,650	—
1768LIMAE JM	—	250	500	950	1,650	—
1769LIMAE JM	—	300	600	1,000	1,750	—
1770LIMAE JM	—	300	600	1,000	1,750	—

KM# 80 2 ESCUDOS

6.7668 g., 0.9010 Gold 0.1960 oz. AGW **Mint:** Lima **Obverse:** Older, standard bust of Charles III, right **Reverse:** Crowned arms in order chain **Rev. Legend:** IN UTROG FELIX AUSPICE DEO **Note:** Mint mark in monogram.

Date	Mintage	VG	F	VF	XF	Unc
1772LIMAE JM	—	250	500	850	1,200	—
1773LIMAE MJ	—	200	400	700	1,000	—
1774LIMAE MJ	—	175	375	675	900	—
1775LIMAE MJ	—	225	425	750	1,100	—
1776LIMAE MJ	—	275	550	900	1,500	—
1777LIMAE MJ	—	150	300	575	750	—
1778LIMAE MJ	—	175	375	675	900	—
1779LIMAE MJ	—	150	300	575	750	—
1780LIMAE MJ	—	150	300	575	750	—
1780LIMAE MI	—	200	400	700	1,000	—
1781LIMAE MI	—	125	250	400	500	—
1782LIMAE MI	—	125	250	400	500	—
1783LIMAE MI	—	125	250	400	500	—
1784LIMAE MI	—	200	400	700	1,000	—

KM# 80a 2 ESCUDOS

6.7668 g., 0.8750 Gold 0.1904 oz. AGW **Mint:** Lima **Obverse:** Older, standard bust of Charles III, right **Reverse:** Crowned arms in order chain **Rev. Legend:** IN UTROG FELIX AUSPICE DEO **Note:** Mint mark in monogram.

Date	Mintage	VG	F	VF	XF	Unc
1785LIMAE MI	—	175	575	675	900	—
1786LIMAE MI	—	175	375	675	900	—
1787LIMAE MI	—	125	250	400	500	—
1787LIMAE IJ	—	125	250	400	500	—
1788LIMAE IJ	—	125	250	400	500	—
1789LIMAE IJ	—	125	250	400	550	—

KM# 90 2 ESCUDOS

6.7668 g., 0.8750 Gold 0.1904 oz. AGW **Mint:** Lima **Obverse:** Bust of Charles IIII, right **Obv. Legend:** CAROL IV... **Reverse:** Crowned arms in order chain **Note:** Mint mark in monogram.

Date	Mintage	VG	F	VF	XF	Unc
1789LIMAE IJ	—	200	400	700	1,000	—
1790LIMAE IJ	—	200	400	700	1,000	—
1791LIMAE IJ	—	200	400	700	1,000	—

KM# 100 2 ESCUDOS

6.7668 g., 0.8750 Gold 0.1904 oz. AGW **Mint:** Lima **Obverse:** Bust of Charles IIII, right **Obv. Legend:** CAROL • IIII • ... **Reverse:** Crowned arms in order chain **Note:** Mint mark in monogram.

Date	Mintage	VG	F	VF	XF	Unc
1792LIMAE IJ	—	150	300	575	750	—
1793LIMAE IJ	—	150	300	575	750	—
1794LIMAE IJ	—	175	375	675	900	—
1795LIMAE IJ	—	150	300	575	750	—
1796LIMAE IJ	—	150	300	575	750	—
1797LIMAE IJ	—	150	300	575	750	—
1798LIMAE IJ	—	175	375	675	900	—
1799LIMAE IJ	—	150	300	575	750	—
1800LIMAE IJ	—	150	300	575	750	—

KM# 49 4 ESCUDOS

13.5337 g., 0.9170 Gold 0.3990 oz. AGW **Mint:** Lima **Obverse:** Bust of Ferdinand VI, right **Obv. Legend:** FERDND • VI • D • G • HISPAN• ET • IND • REX **Reverse:** Crowned arms of Peru **Rev. Legend:** INITIUM SAPENTIÆ TIMOR DOMINI **Note:** Dot above L of mint mark.

Date	Mintage	VG	F	VF	XF	Unc
1751LM J	—	1,000	2,000	3,000	5,000	—
1752LM J	—	1,000	2,000	3,000	5,000	—
1753LM J	—	1,000	2,000	3,000	5,000	—

KM# 58 4 ESCUDOS

13.5337 g., 0.9170 Gold 0.3990 oz. AGW **Mint:** Lima **Obverse:** Smaller bust of Ferdinand VI, right **Reverse:** Crowned arms of Peru **Rev. Legend:** NOMINA MAGNA SEQUOR **Note:** Dot above L of mint mark.

Date	Mintage	VG	F	VF	XF	Unc
1754LM JD	—	1,000	2,000	3,000	5,000	—
1757LM JM	—	1,000	1,500	2,500	4,500	—
1758LM JM	—	1,000	1,500	2,500	4,500	—
1759LM JM	—	1,000	1,500	2,500	4,500	—

KM# 67 4 ESCUDOS

13.5337 g., 0.9170 Gold 0.3990 oz. AGW **Mint:** Lima **Obverse:** First bust of Charles III, right **Obv. Legend:** CAROLUS III... **Reverse:** Crowned arms of Peru **Note:** Dot above L of mint mark.

Date	Mintage	VG	F	VF	XF	Unc
1761LM JM	—	1,500	2,500	4,000	7,500	—
1762LM JM	—	1,500	2,500	4,000	7,500	—

KM# 71.1 4 ESCUDOS

13.5337 g., 0.9170 Gold 0.3990 oz. AGW **Mint:** Lima **Obverse:** Young, standard bust of Charles III, right **Obv. Legend:** CAROLUS • III • ... **Reverse:** Crowned arms in order chain **Rev. Legend:** IN • VTROQ • FELIX • AUSPICE • DEO **Note:** Dot in mint mark above L.

Date	Mintage	VG	F	VF	XF	Unc
1763LM JM Rare	—	—	—	—	—	—
1764LM JM	—	1,000	1,500	2,500	4,500	—
1765LM JM	—	1,000	1,500	2,500	4,500	—
1768LM JM	—	1,000	1,500	2,500	4,500	—

KM# 71.2 4 ESCUDOS

13.5000 g., 0.9170 Gold 0.3980 oz. AGW **Mint:** Lima **Obverse:** Modified bust of Charles III, right **Obv. Legend:** CAROLUS • III • ... **Reverse:** Crowned arms in order chain **Rev. Legend:** IN • VTROQ • FELIX • AUSPICE • DEO **Note:** Dot above L in mint mark.

Date	Mintage	VG	F	VF	XF	Unc
1768LM JM	—	1,000	1,500	2,500	4,500	—
1769LM JM	—	1,000	1,500	2,500	4,500	—
1770LM JM	—	1,000	1,500	2,500	4,500	—
1771LM JM	—	1,000	1,500	2,500	4,500	—

KM# 81 4 ESCUDOS

13.5337 g., 0.9010 Gold 0.3920 oz. AGW **Mint:** Lima **Obverse:** Older, standard bust of Charles III, right **Obv. Legend:** CAROL • III • ... **Reverse:** Crowned arms in order chain **Note:** Mint mark in monogram.

Date	Mintage	VG	F	VF	XF	Unc
1772LIMAE JM	—	1,000	1,500	2,000	3,000	—
1773LIMAE JM	—	500	700	950	1,250	—
1774LIMAE MJ	—	500	700	950	1,250	—
1775LIMAE MJ	—	500	700	950	1,250	—
1776LIMAE MJ	—	500	700	950	1,250	—
1777LIMAE MJ	—	500	700	950	1,250	—
1778LIMAE MJ	—	500	700	950	1,250	—
1779LIMAE MJ	—	500	700	950	1,250	—
1780LIMAE MI	—	500	700	950	1,250	—
1781LIMAE MI	—	500	700	950	1,250	—
1782LIMAE MI	—	500	700	950	1,250	—
1783LIMAE MI	—	500	700	950	1,250	—
1784LIMAE MI	—	500	700	950	1,250	—

KM# 81a 4 ESCUDOS

13.5337 g., 0.8750 Gold 0.3807 oz. AGW **Mint:** Lima **Obverse:** Older, standard bust of Charles III, right **Obv. Legend:** CAROL • III • ... **Reverse:** Crowned arms in order chain **Note:** Mint mark in monogram.

Date	Mintage	VG	F	VF	XF	Unc
1785LIMAE MI	—	500	700	950	1,250	—
1786LIMAE MI	—	500	700	950	1,250	—
1787LIMAE MI	—	500	700	950	1,250	—
1787LIMAE IJ	—	600	800	1,100	1,750	—
1788LIMAE IJ	—	500	700	950	1,250	—
1789LIMAE IJ	—	600	800	1,100	1,750	—

KM# 91 4 ESCUDOS

13.5337 g., 0.8750 Gold 0.3807 oz. AGW **Mint:** Lima **Obverse:** Bust of Charles IIII, right **Obv. Legend:** CAROL • IV • ... **Reverse:** Crowned arms, order chain **Note:** Mint mark in monogram.

Date	Mintage	VG	F	VF	XF	Unc
1789LIMAE IJ	—	500	700	950	1,250	—
1790LIMAE IJ	—	500	700	950	1,250	—
1791LIMAE IJ	—	500	700	950	1,250	—

KM# 98 4 ESCUDOS

13.5337 g., 0.8750 Gold 0.3807 oz. AGW **Mint:** Lima **Obverse:** Bust of Charles IIII, right **Obv. Legend:** CAROL • IIII... **Reverse:** Crowned arms in order chain **Note:** Mint mark in monogram.

Date	Mintage	VG	F	VF	XF	Unc
1791LIMAE IJ	—	475	650	900	1,250	—
1792LIMAE IJ	—	475	650	900	1,250	—
1793LIMAE IJ	—	475	650	900	1,250	—
1794LIMAE IJ	—	475	650	900	1,250	—
1795LIMAE IJ	—	475	650	900	1,250	—
1796LIMAE IJ	—	475	650	900	1,250	—
1797LIMAE IJ	—	475	650	900	1,250	—
1798LIMAE IJ	—	475	650	900	1,250	—
1799LIMAE IJ	—	475	650	900	1,250	—
1800LIMAE IJ	—	475	650	900	1,250	—

KM# 50 8 ESCUDOS

27.0674 g., 0.9170 Gold 0.7980 oz. AGW **Mint:** Lima **Obverse:** Large bust of Ferdinand VI, right **Obv. Legend:** FERDND • VI • D • G • HISPAN • ETIND • REX **Reverse:** Crowned arms in order chain **Rev. Legend:** INITIUM SAPIENTIÆ... **Note:** Dot above "L" in mint mark.

Date	Mintage	VG	F	VF	XF	Unc
1751LM J	—	1,000	1,250	1,850	2,500	—
1752LM J	—	1,000	1,250	1,850	2,500	—
1753LM J	—	1,000	1,250	1,850	2,500	—

KM# 59.1 8 ESCUDOS

27.0674 g., 0.9170 Gold 0.7980 oz. AGW **Mint:** Lima **Obverse:** Small bust of Ferdinand VI, right **Obv. Legend:** FERDIND • VI • ... **Reverse:** Crowned arms in order chain **Rev. Legend:** NOMINA MAGNA SEQUOR **Note:** Dot above "L" in mint mark.

Date	Mintage	VG	F	VF	XF	Unc
1754LM JD	—	1,100	1,500	2,000	3,000	—
1755LM JM	—	1,100	1,500	2,000	2,800	—
1756LM JM	—	1,100	1,500	2,000	2,800	—

KM# 59.2 8 ESCUDOS

27.0674 g., 0.9170 Gold 0.7980 oz. AGW **Mint:** Lima **Obverse:** Bust right **Rev. Legend:** NOMINA MAGNA SEQUOR **Note:** Dot above "L" in mint mark.

Date	Mintage	VG	F	VF	XF	Unc
1757LM JM	—	1,100	1,500	2,000	2,800	—
1758LM JM	—	1,100	1,500	2,000	2,800	—

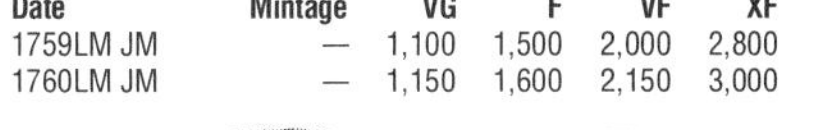

Date	Mintage	VG	F	VF	XF	Unc
1759LM JM	—	1,100	1,500	2,000	2,800	—
1760LM JM	—	1,150	1,600	2,150	3,000	—

KM# 68 8 ESCUDOS

27.0674 g., 0.9170 Gold 0.7980 oz. AGW **Mint:** Lima **Obverse:** Small bust of Charles III, right **Obv. Legend:** CAROLUS • III • HISPAN • ETIND • REX • **Reverse:** Crowned arms in order chain **Rev. Legend:** NOMINA MAGNA SEQUOR **Note:** Dot above "L" in mint mark.

Date	Mintage	VG	F	VF	XF	Unc
1761LM JM	—	1,500	2,750	4,250	6,000	—
1762LM JM	—	1,500	2,750	4,250	6,000	—

KM# 70 8 ESCUDOS

27.0674 g., 0.9170 Gold 0.7980 oz. AGW **Mint:** Lima **Obverse:** Young, standard bust of Charles III, right **Obv. Legend:** CAROLUS • III • D • G • HISP • ETIND • REX **Reverse:** Crowned arms in order chain **Rev. Legend:** IN • VTROQ • FELIX • AUSPICE • DEO **Note:** Dot above "L" in mint mark.

Date	Mintage	VG	F	VF	XF	Unc
1763LM JM	—	800	1,500	2,500	3,500	—
1764LM JM	—	800	1,500	2,500	3,500	—
1765LM JM	—	800	1,500	2,500	3,500	—
1766LM JM	—	800	1,500	2,500	3,500	—
1767LM JM	—	800	1,500	2,500	3,500	—
1768LM JM	—	800	1,500	2,500	3,500	—

KM# 73 8 ESCUDOS

27.0674 g., 0.9170 Gold 0.7980 oz. AGW **Mint:** Lima **Obverse:** Modified bust of Charles III, right **Obv. Legend:** CAROLUS • III • ... **Reverse:** Crowned arms in order chain **Rev. Legend:** IN • VTROQ • FELIX • AUSPICE • DEO **Note:** Dot above "L" in mint mark.

Date	Mintage	VG	F	VF	XF	Unc
1768LM JM	—	1,750	3,000	5,000	8,000	—
1769LM JM	—	1,250	2,250	3,500	5,000	—
1770LM JM	—	1,250	2,250	3,500	5,000	—
1771LM JM	—	1,250	2,250	3,500	5,000	—
1771LM JM Rare; AVSPCIE (error)	—	—	—	—	—	—
1772LM JM	—	1,250	2,250	3,500	5,000	—

KM# 82.1 8 ESCUDOS

27.0674 g., 0.9010 Gold 0.7841 oz. AGW **Mint:** Lima **Obverse:** Older, standard bust of Charles III, right **Obv. Legend:** CAROL • III • D • G • HISP • ETIND • R • **Reverse:** Crowned arms in order chain, assayers initials at lower right, LIMAE monogram at lower left **Rev. Legend:** ...• AUSPICE • DEO • **Note:** Mint mark in monogram.

Date	Mintage	VG	F	VF	XF	Unc
1772LIMAE JM	—	500	750	1,250	2,200	—
1773LIMAE JM	—	500	600	1,000	1,600	—
1773LIMAE MJ	—	400	500	800	1,350	—
1774LIMAE MJ	—	375	475	750	1,200	—
1775LIMAE MJ	—	375	475	750	1,200	—
1776LIMAE MJ	—	375	475	750	1,200	—
1777LIMAE MJ	—	350	475	750	1,200	—
1778LIMAE MJ	—	350	475	750	1,200	—
1779LIMAE MJ	—	350	475	750	1,200	—
1780LIMAE MI	—	350	475	750	1,200	—
1781LIMAE MI	—	350	475	750	1,200	—
1782LIMAE MI	—	350	475	750	1,200	—
1783LIMAE MI	—	350	475	750	1,200	—
1784LIMAE MI	—	350	475	750	1,200	—

KM# 82.1a 8 ESCUDOS

27.0674 g., 0.8750 Gold 0.7614 oz. AGW **Mint:** Lima **Obverse:** Older, standard bust of Charles III, right **Obv. Legend:** cAROL • III • D • G • HISP • ETIND • R • **Reverse:** Crowned arms in order chain, JM at lower left, LIMAE monogram at lower right **Rev. Legend:** ... • AUSPICE • DEO • **Note:** Mint mark in monogram.

Date	Mintage	VG	F	VF	XF	Unc
1784LIMAE JP	—	—	—	—	—	—
1785LIMAE MI	—	650	800	1,500	2,250	—
1786LIMAE MI	—	350	475	750	1,200	—
1786/6LIMAE MI	—	450	600	1,200	2,000	—
1787LIMAE MI	—	350	475	750	1,200	—
1787LIMAE IJ	—	500	800	1,250	2,000	—
1788LIMAE IJ	—	350	475	750	1,200	—
1789LIMAE IJ	—	400	500	800	1,300	—

KM# 82.2 8 ESCUDOS

27.0674 g., 0.9010 Gold 0.7841 oz. AGW **Mint:** Lima **Obverse:** Older, standard bust of Charles III, right **Obv. Legend:** CAROL • III • D • G • HISP • ETIND • R • **Reverse:** Crowned arms in order chain, JM at lower left, LIMAE monogram at lower right **Rev. Legend:** ...• AUSPICE • DEO • **Note:** Mint mark in monogram.

Date	Mintage	VG	F	VF	XF	Unc
1772LIMAE JM	—	500	800	1,250	2,000	—
1773LIMAE JM Rare	—	—	—	—	—	—

KM# 92 8 ESCUDOS

27.0674 g., 0.8750 Gold 0.7614 oz. AGW **Mint:** Lima **Obverse:** Bust of Charles IIII, right **Obv. Legend:** CAROL • IV • ... **Reverse:** Crowned arms in order chain **Rev. Legend:** VTROQ • FELIX • AUSPICE • DEO **Note:** Mint mark in monogram.

Date	Mintage	VG	F	VF	XF	Unc
1789LIMAE IJ	—	400	500	800	1,350	—
1790LIMAE IJ	—	400	500	800	1,350	—
1791LIMAE IJ	—	400	500	800	1,350	—

KM# 101 8 ESCUDOS

27.0674 g., 0.8750 Gold 0.7614 oz. AGW **Mint:** Lima **Obverse:** Bust of Charles IIII, right **Obv. Legend:** CAROL • IIII... **Reverse:** Crowned arms in order chain **Rev. Legend:** VTROQ • FELIX • AUSPICE • DEO **Note:** Mint mark in monogram.

Date	Mintage	VG	F	VF	XF	Unc
1792LIMAE IJ	—	375	475	650	1,000	—
1793LIMAE IJ	—	375	475	650	1,000	—
1794LIMAE IJ	—	375	475	650	1,000	—
1795LIMAE IJ	—	375	475	650	1,000	—
1796LIMAE IJ	—	375	475	650	1,000	—
1797LIMAE IJ	—	375	475	650	1,000	—
1797LIMAE JI	—	400	800	1,250	2,000	—
1798LIMAE IJ	—	375	475	650	1,000	—
1799LIMAE IJ	—	375	475	650	1,000	—
1800LIMAE IJ	—	375	475	650	1,000	—

PHILIPPINES

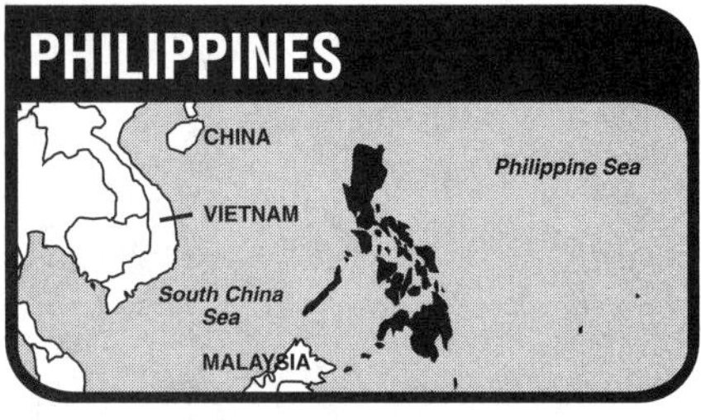

The Republic of the Philippines, an archipelago in the western Pacific 500 miles (805 km.) from the southeast coast of Asia, has an area of 115,830 sq. mi. (300,000 sq. km.) and a population of *64.9 million. Capital: Manila. The economy of the 7,000-island group is based on agriculture, forestry and fishing. Timber, coconut products, sugar and hemp are exported.

Migration to the Philippines began about 30,000 years ago when land bridges connected the islands with Borneo and Sumatra. Ferdinand Magellan claimed the islands for Spain in 1521. The first permanent settlement was established by Miguel de Legazpi at Cebu April, 1565. Manila was established in 1572. A British expedition captured Manila and occupied the Spanish colony in October 1762, but returned it to Spain by the treaty of Paris, 1763. Spain held the Philippines despite growing Filipino nationalism until 1898 when they were ceded to the United States at the end of the Spanish-American War. The Philippines became a self-governing commonwealth under the United States in 1935, and attained independence as the Republic of the Philippines on July 4, 1946.

RULER

Spanish until 1898

MINT MARK

M, MA - Manila

MONETARY SYSTEM

8 Octavos = 4 Quartos = 1 Real
8 Reales = 1 Peso

SPANISH COLONY

COLONIAL COINAGE

For copper issues until 1833, minor variations in die work, planchet size and weight are relatively commonplace, compared to later issues from the up-graded Manila Mint (ca.1860).

KM# 1 BARILLA

Copper **Obv:** Castle within circle, date below **Rev:** Crowned ornate shield divides value

Date	Mintage	Good	VG	F	VF	XF
1766	—	125	300	500	1,000	—

KM# 3 OCTAVO

Copper **Obv:** Lion and globes **Rev:** Spanish arms

Date	Mintage	Good	VG	F	VF	XF
1773M	—	40.00	70.00	120	165	—
1782M	—	40.00	70.00	120	165	—
1783M	—	40.00	70.00	120	165	—

KM# 5 OCTAVO

Copper **Obv:** Crowned Spanish arms flanked by stars **Rev:** Crowned lion within beaded circle

Date	Mintage	Good	VG	F	VF	XF
1798M F	—	50.00	75.00	150	200	—
1805M F	—	30.00	50.00	110	150	—
1806M F	—	30.00	50.00	100	125	—

KM# 2 QUARTO

Copper **Obv:** Crowned Spanish arms **Rev:** Crowned lion within beaded circle

Date	Mintage	Good	VG	F	VF	XF
1771M Dot	—	30.00	50.00	80.00	200	—
1773M	—	30.00	50.00	80.00	200	—
1774M Rare	—	—	—	—	—	—
1782M	—	35.00	70.00	145	250	—
1783M	—	35.00	70.00	100	175	—

KM# 6 QUARTO

Copper **Obv:** Crowned Spanish arms flanked by stars **Rev:** Crowned lion within beaded circle **Note:** Similar to KM#7.

Date	Mintage	Good	VG	F	VF	XF
1790M Г	—	25.00	40.00	60.00	80.00	—
1799M F	—	30.00	60.00	90.00	220	—
1800M F	—	30.00	60.00	90.00	220	—

KM# 4 1/4 REAL

Silver **Obv:** Crowned rampant lion **Rev:** Castle

Date	Mintage	VG	F	VF	XF	Unc
ND	—	25.00	50.00	75.00	150	500

Note: Attribution of the above 1/4 Real to the Philippines is questionable

PATTERNS

Including off metal strikes

KM#	Date	Mintage	Identification	Mkt Val
Pn1	1701	—	Barrillo. Bronze.	1,700
Pn2	1728	—	Barrillo. Bronze. Uniface, arms.	—
Pn3	1733	—	Barrillo. Lead. AB monogram, arms	—

KM#	Date	Mintage	Identification	Mkt Val
Pn4	1739	—	Barrillo. Lead.	1,500
Pn5	1743	—	Barrillo. Lead. AB monogram, arms, 7 in date inverted.	—

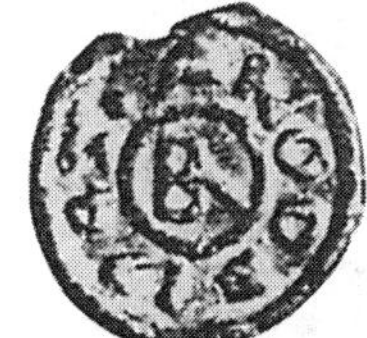

KM#	Date	Mintage	Identification	Mkt Val
Pn6	1743	—	Barrillo. Lead. AB monogram, legend with smaller lettering.	—

KM#	Date	Mintage	Identification	Mkt Val
Pn7	1743	—	Barrillo. Lead. Monogram appears as crude R, larger lettering.	—
Pn8	1743	—	Barrillo. Lead. BR monogram.	—

POLAND

The Republic of Poland, located in central Europe, has an area of 120,725 sq. mi. (312,680 sq. km.) and a population of *38.2 million. Capital: Warszawa (Warsaw). The economy is essentially agricultural, but industrial activity provides the products for foreign trade. Machinery, coal, coke, iron, steel and transport equipment are exported.

Poland, which began as a Slavic duchy in the 10th century and reached its peak of power between the 14th and16th centuries, has had a turbulent history of invasion, occupation or partition by Mongols, Turkey, Transylvania, Sweden, Austria, Prussia and Russia.

The first partition took place in 1772. Prussia took Polish Pomerania, Russia took part of the eastern provinces, and Austria occupied Galicia, in which lay the capital city of Lwów. The second partition occurred in 1793 when Russia took another slice of the eastern provinces and Prussia took what remained of western Poland. The third partition, 1795, literally removed Poland from the map. Russia took what was left of the eastern provinces. Prussia seized most of central Poland, including Warsaw. Austria took what was left of the south. Napoleon restored to Poland much of the territory lost to Prussia and Austria, but after his defeat another partition returned the Duchy of Warsaw to Prussia, made Kracow into a tiny republic, and declared what remained to be the Kingdom of Poland under the czar and in permanent union with Russia.

Poland re-emerged as an independent state recognized by the Treaty of Versailles on June 28, 1919, and maintained its independence until 1939 when it was invaded by, and partitioned between, Germany and Russia. Poland's present boundaries were determined by the U.S.-British-Russian agreement of Aug. 16, 1945. The Government of National Unity was replaced when the Polish Communist-Socialist faction claimed victory at the polls.

RULERS

August II of Saxony, 1697-1733
August III, 1733-1763
Stanislaus Augustus, 1764-1795

MINTMASTERS' INITIALS

Mintmasters initials usually appear flanking the shield or by the date.

DRESDEN & LEIPZIG MINT

Initials	Date	Name
EPH	1693-1714	Ernst Peter Hecht
FwoF	1734-64	Friedrich Wilhelm O Feral
IGS	1716-34	Johann Georg Schomburg
JGG	1750-53	Johann George Goedecke
EC, EDC	1758-63	Ernst Dietrich Croll

KRAKOW MINT

Initials	Date	Name
CI	1765-68	Constantin Jablonowski
G	1765-72	Peter Michael Gartenberg

WARSAW MINT

Initials	Date	Name
AP	1772-74	Anton Partenstein
EB	1774-92	Ephraim Brenn
FS	1765-67	Friedrich Wilhelm Sylm
G	1765-72	Peter Michael Gartenberg
IPH	1765-92	Johannes Philippus Holzhaeusser, engraver
IS	1768-72	Justin Schroder

MONETARY SYSTEM

Until 1815

1 Solidus = 1 Schilling
3 Solidi = 2 Poltura = 1 Grosz
3 Poltura = 1-1/2 Grosze = 1 Polturak
6 Groszy = 1 Szostak
18 Groszy = 1 Tympf
30 Groszy = 4 Silbergroschen = 1 Zloty
1 Talar = 1 Zloty
6 Zlotych = 1 Reichsthaler
8 Zlotych = 1 Speciesthaler
5 Speciesthaler = 1 August D'or
3 Ducats = 1 Stanislaus D'or

KINGDOM

STANDARD COINAGE

100 Groszy = 1 Zloty

KM# 216 6 ZLOTYCH

Silver **Ruler:** Stanislaus Augustus **Obv:** Head right **Obv. Legend:** STANISLAUS AUGUSTUS • D • G • REX ... **Rev:** Crowned 4-fold arms within sprigs

Date	Mintage	VG	F	VF	XF	Unc
1794	182,000	30.00	50.00	90.00	175	—
1795	Inc. above	40.00	70.00	120	225	—

STANDARD COINAGE

KM# 143 SOLIDUS (Szelag, Schilling)

Copper **Ruler:** August II **Obv:** Head of August II **Rev:** Crowned eagle with shield on breast

Date	Mintage	Good	VG	F	VF	XF
1720 W	—	5.00	10.00	25.00	50.00	—

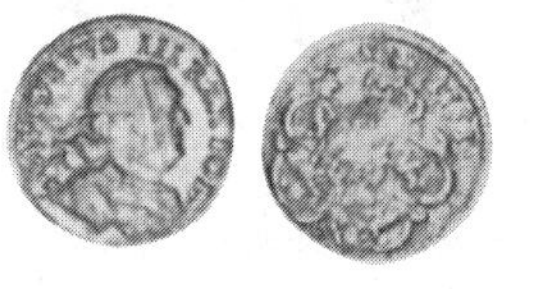

KM# 145 SOLIDUS (Szelag, Schilling)

Copper **Ruler:** August III **Obv:** Bust right **Obv. Legend:** AVGVSTVS • III • REX • POL • **Rev:** Crowned arms **Note:** Varieties exist.

Date	Mintage	VG	F	VF	XF	Unc
1749	—	3.00	4.00	9.50	18.50	—
1750	—	3.00	4.00	9.50	18.50	—
1750 B	—	3.00	4.00	7.50	15.00	—
1750 H	—	2.00	4.00	7.50	15.00	—

Date	Mintage	VG	F	VF	XF	Unc
1751 S	—	2.00	4.00	6.50	12.00	—
1751 V	—	10.00	15.00	30.00	65.00	—
1752	—	2.00	3.00	6.00	10.00	—
1752 A	—	2.00	3.00	6.00	10.00	—
1752 B	—	2.00	3.00	6.00	10.00	—
1752 C	—	2.00	3.00	6.00	10.00	—
1752 D	—	2.00	3.00	6.00	10.00	—
1752 E Rare	—	—	—	—	—	—
1752 F	—	2.00	3.00	6.00	10.00	—
1752 Inverted F	—	2.00	3.00	7.50	13.50	—
1752 G	—	2.00	3.00	7.50	13.50	—
1752 H	—	2.00	3.00	7.50	13.50	—
1752 I	—	2.00	3.00	6.00	10.00	—
1752 L	—	2.00	3.00	6.00	10.00	—
1752 N	—	2.00	3.00	6.00	10.00	—
1752 O Rare	—	—	—	—	—	—
1752 R Rare	—	—	—	—	—	—
1752 S	—	2.00	3.00	6.00	10.00	—
1752 T	—	2.00	3.00	6.00	10.00	—
1752 Inverted T	—	—	—	—	—	—
1752 U	—	2.00	3.00	6.00	10.00	—
1752 V	—	2.00	3.00	6.00	10.00	—
1753	—	2.00	3.00	6.00	10.00	—
1753 A	—	2.00	3.00	6.00	10.00	—
1753 B	—	2.00	3.00	6.00	10.00	—
1753 C	—	2.00	3.00	6.00	10.00	—
1753 Inverted C	—	4.00	5.50	7.50	13.50	—
1753 D	—	2.00	3.00	6.00	10.00	—
1753 Inverted F	—	2.25	3.50	7.00	12.50	—
1753 G	—	3.00	5.00	7.50	13.50	—
1753 H	—	2.00	3.00	6.00	10.00	—
1753 I	—	2.00	3.00	6.00	10.00	—
1753 L	—	2.50	3.50	6.50	12.00	—
1753 N	—	2.00	3.00	6.00	10.00	—
1753 Inverted N	—	3.00	5.00	7.50	13.50	—
1753 O	—	2.00	3.00	6.00	10.00	—
1753 P	—	2.00	3.00	6.00	10.00	—
1753 R	—	2.00	3.00	6.00	10.00	—
1753 S	—	2.00	3.00	6.00	10.00	—
1753 T	—	35.00	60.00	90.00	125	—
1753 Inverted T	—	3.50	5.50	7.50	13.50	—
1753 V	—	2.00	3.00	6.00	10.00	—
1754	—	2.00	3.00	6.00	10.00	—
1754 F	—	25.00	50.00	75.00	100	—
1754 H	—	2.00	3.00	6.00	10.00	—
1755	—	2.00	3.00	6.00	10.00	—
1755 H	—	2.00	3.00	6.00	10.00	—

KM# 145b SOLIDUS (Szelag, Schilling)

Gold **Ruler:** August III **Obv:** Bust of August III right **Rev:** Crowned arms

Date	Mintage	VG	F	VF	XF	Unc
1750	—	—	—	—	—	—

KM# 145a SOLIDUS (Szelag, Schilling)

Silver **Ruler:** August III **Obv:** Bust of August III, right **Rev:** Crowned arms

Date	Mintage	VG	F	VF	XF	Unc
1750	—	12.00	15.00	30.00	65.00	—
1753	—	12.00	15.00	30.00	65.00	—

KM# 180 SOLIDUS (Szelag, Schilling)

Copper **Ruler:** Stanislaus Augustus **Obv:** Crowned SAR monogram divides date **Rev:** Value, initials below **Note:** Varieties exist.

Date	Mintage	VG	F	VF	XF	Unc
1766 G	3,960	35.00	65.00	90.00	150	—
1767 G	1,599,000	3.00	5.00	10.00	25.00	—
1768 G Small letters	10,015,000	3.00	5.00	10.00	25.00	—
1768 G Large letters	Inc. above	—	—	—	—	—
1768	Inc. above	35.00	65.00	90.00	150	—
1776 EB	80,000	5.00	9.00	15.00	30.00	—
1792 MV	—	12.50	20.00	32.50	65.00	—
ND Rare	—	—	—	—	—	—

KM# 181.1 SOLIDUS (Szelag, Schilling)

Copper **Ruler:** Stanislaus Augustus **Obv:** Crowned monogram **Rev:** Value, initials below

Date	Mintage	VG	F	VF	XF	Unc
ND G	—	35.00	65.00	90.00	165	—

KM# 181.2 SOLIDUS (Szelag, Schilling)

Copper **Ruler:** Stanislaus Augustus **Obv:** Crowned monogram **Rev:** Value, initials below

Date	Mintage	VG	F	VF	XF	Unc
ND G	—	35.00	65.00	90.00	165	—

KM# 175.2 1/2 GROSZA (Pol)

Copper **Ruler:** Stanislaus Augustus **Obv:** Crowned monogram **Rev:** Value

Date	Mintage	VG	F	VF	XF	Unc
ND Rare	—	—	—	—	—	—

KM# 175.1 1/2 GROSZA (Pol)

Copper **Ruler:** Stanislaus Augustus **Obv:** Crowned SAR monogram divides date **Rev:** Value, initials below **Note:** Struck at Warsaw Mint.

Date	Mintage	VG	F	VF	XF	Unc
1765 G Rare	—	—	—	—	—	—
1766 G	632,000	3.50	6.00	10.00	22.00	—
1767 G	6,649,000	3.00	5.00	8.00	17.50	—
1768 G Small monogram	12,445,000	3.00	5.00	8.00	17.50	—
1768 G Large monogram	Inc. above	3.00	5.00	8.00	17.50	—
1775 EB	144,000	4.00	6.50	11.50	23.50	—
1776 EB	52,000	5.00	7.50	15.00	27.50	—
1777 EB	68,000	7.50	12.50	18.50	35.00	—
1780 EB	91,000	5.00	11.50	18.50	35.00	—
1781 EB	44,000	7.50	15.00	20.00	40.00	—
1782 EB	51,000	7.50	15.00	20.00	40.00	—
1792 EB	—	35.00	50.00	70.00	120	—
NDMV Rare	—	—	—	—	—	—

KM# 203 1/2 GROSZA (Pol, Mining)

Copper **Ruler:** Stanislaus Augustus **Note:** Similar to KM#198.1 but value: POL GROSZA/Z/MIEDZI KRAIOW.

Date	Mintage	VG	F	VF	XF	Unc
1786 EB Rare	—	—	—	—	—	—

KM# 147.1 3 SOLIDI (1 Grosz)

Copper **Ruler:** August III **Obv:** Bust of August III right **Rev:** Crowned arms, 3 below

Date	Mintage	VG	F	VF	XF	Unc
1752	—	3.00	7.50	10.00	22.00	—
1753	—	3.00	5.00	9.00	20.00	—
1754	—	3.00	5.00	9.00	20.00	—
1755	—	3.00	5.00	9.00	20.00	—
1758	—	5.00	7.50	15.00	35.00	—

KM# 147.2 3 SOLIDI (1 Grosz)

Copper **Ruler:** August III **Obv:** Bust right **Obv. Legend:** AVGVSTVS • III • REX • POL • **Rev:** Crowned arms, H replaces 3 below

Date	Mintage	VG	F	VF	XF	Unc
1754	—	2.00	4.00	7.00	16.00	—
1755	—	2.00	4.00	7.00	16.00	—
1755 F	—	—	—	—	—	—

KM# 176 GROSZ

Copper **Ruler:** Stanislaus Augustus **Obv:** STA/NISLAVS/AVG.REX/POL.MDL **Rev:** Arms

Date	Mintage	VG	F	VF	XF	Unc
1765 Rare	—	—	—	—	—	—

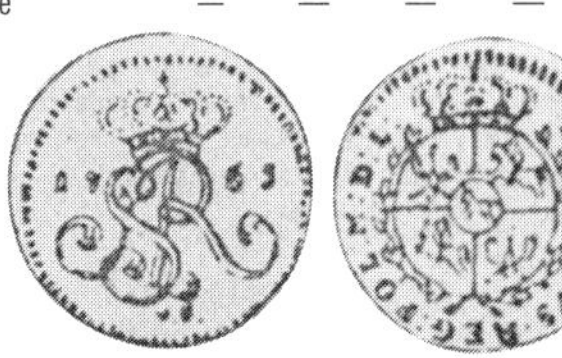

KM# 177 GROSZ

3.8900 g., Copper **Ruler:** Stanislaus Augustus **Obv:** Crowned SAR monogram divides date **Rev:** Crowned, 4-fold oval arms within sprigs **Note:** Varieties exist.

Date	Mintage	VG	F	VF	XF	Unc
1765 VG On reverse	—	7.00	11.50	18.50	30.00	—
1765 VG On obverse	—	5.00	9.00	15.00	25.00	—
1765 G	2,089,999	15.00	25.00	40.00	65.00	—
1765 "G"	—	2.00	4.00	7.50	16.50	—
1765	Inc. above	45.00	75.00	125	200	—
1766 G	12,172,000	2.50	4.00	7.00	15.00	—
1766 "G"	Inc. above	2.50	4.00	7.00	15.00	—
1767 G	48,852,000	2.50	4.00	7.00	15.00	—
1767 "G"	Inc. above	2.50	4.00	7.00	15.00	—
1768 G	32,037,999	2.50	4.00	7.00	15.00	—
1768 "G"	Inc. above	3.25	5.50	9.00	17.50	—

Date	Mintage	VG	F	VF	XF	Unc
1769 "G"	2,930,000	2.50	4.00	7.00	15.00	—
1770 "G"	—	3.25	5.50	9.00	17.50	—
1771 "G"	279,000	4.50	7.50	12.50	25.00	—
1772 "G	358,000	3.50	6.00	10.00	20.00	—
1772 AP	Inc. above	45.00	75.00	125	200	—
1773 AP	218,000	4.50	7.50	12.50	22.50	—
1774 AP	196,000	5.00	7.50	10.00	20.00	—
1774 EB	Inc. above	3.00	5.00	7.50	16.50	—
1775 EB	1,650,000	3.00	5.00	7.50	16.50	—
1776 AP	2,045,000	15.00	25.00	50.00	110	—
1776 EB	Inc. above	3.00	5.00	7.50	16.50	—
1777 AP	1,425,000	20.00	40.00	60.00	125	—
1777 EB	Inc. above	3.00	5.00	7.50	16.50	—
1778 EB	1,138,000	3.00	5.00	7.50	16.50	—
1779 EB	1,175,000	3.00	5.00	7.50	16.50	—
1780 EB	523,000	3.25	5.50	9.00	18.50	—
1781 EB	300,000	4.50	7.50	12.50	22.50	—
1782 EB	285,000	3.50	6.00	10.00	20.00	—
1783 EB	897,000	3.00	5.00	7.50	16.50	—
1784 EB	609,000	3.25	5.50	9.00	18.50	—
1785 EB	795,000	3.25	5.50	9.00	18.50	—
1786 EB	446,000	3.50	6.00	10.00	20.00	—
1787 EB GROSSUS	3,636,000	3.00	5.00	7.50	16.50	—
1787 EB GROSSUS	Inc. above	4.50	7.50	12.50	22.50	—
1788 EB	4,059,999	3.00	5.00	7.50	16.50	—
1789 EB	1,966,000	3.00	5.00	7.50	16.50	—
1790 EB	5,763,000	3.00	5.00	7.50	16.50	—
1791 EB	3,220,000	3.00	5.00	7.50	16.50	—
1791 MV	Inc. above	5.00	7.50	10.00	20.00	—
1792 EB	4,524,000	3.25	5.50	9.00	18.50	—
1792 MV	Inc. above	3.00	5.00	7.50	16.50	—
1793 EB	2,823,000	3.00	5.00	7.50	16.50	—
1793 MV	Inc. above	3.00	5.00	7.50	16.50	—
1794 MV/MW	2,484,000	3.00	5.00	7.50	16.50	—
1795 MV	Inc. above	15.00	25.00	70.00	120	—

KM# 204 GROSZ (Mining)

Copper **Ruler:** Stanislaus Augustus **Rev:** Crowned arms within sprigs **Rev. Legend:** MIEDZI KRAJOWEY

Date	Mintage	VG	F	VF	XF	Unc
1786 EB	Inc. above	10.00	17.50	30.00	55.00	—
1787 EB	Inc. above	10.00	15.00	27.50	50.00	—
1788 EB	Inc. above	7.00	12.00	18.00	35.00	—
1794 MV	Inc. above	—	—	—	—	—

KM# 151 POLTORAK

1.0800 g., Billon **Ruler:** August III **Obv:** Crowned round arms within sprigs **Rev:** Value and date

Date	Mintage	VG	F	VF	XF	Unc
1753	—	15.00	25.00	40.00	65.00	—

KM# 166 POLTORAK

1.0800 g., Billon **Ruler:** August III **Obv:** Bust of August III right **Rev:** Eagle

Date	Mintage	VG	F	VF	XF	Unc
1755 EC	—	10.00	18.00	30.00	55.00	—
1756 EC	—	10.00	18.00	30.00	55.00	—

KM# 152 3 GROSZE (1/2 Szostak - 3 Kruzierz)

2.1600 g., Billon **Ruler:** August III **Obv:** Crowned bust right **Obv. Legend:** D G AVGVSTVS III... **Rev:** Crowned, round 4-fold arms within sprigs

Date	Mintage	VG	F	VF	XF	Unc
1753	—	10.00	20.00	37.50	60.00	—

KM# 153 3 GROSZE (1/2 Szostak - 3 Kruzierz)

2.1600 g., Billon **Ruler:** August III **Obv:** Crowned arms within sprigs, 3 below

Date	Mintage	VG	F	VF	XF	Unc
1753 EC	—	15.00	30.00	70.00	120	—
1754	—	8.00	15.00	25.00	45.00	—
1754 EC	—	15.00	30.00	70.00	120	—
1756 EC	—	8.00	15.00	25.00	45.00	—

KM# 178 3 GROSZE (1/2 Szostak - 3 Kruzierz)

Copper **Ruler:** Stanislaus Augustus **Obv:** Bust right **Obv. Inscription:** STANISLAUS AUG D G REX ... **Rev:** Crowned, round 4-fold arms within sprigs

Date	Mintage	VG	F	VF	XF	Unc
1765 "G"	—	7.00	14.00	25.00	55.00	—
1766 "G"	12,410,000	5.00	10.00	20.00	40.00	—
1766 "G" STANILAUS (Error)	Inc. above	12.00	20.00	30.00	60.00	—

KM# 182 3 GROSZE (1/2 Szostak - 3 Kruzierz)

Copper **Ruler:** Stanislaus Augustus **Obv:** Head right **Note:** Varieties exist.

Date	Mintage	VG	F	VF	XF	Unc
1766 "G" Large head; Rare	Inc. above	—	—	—	—	—
1766 G	Inc. above	5.00	10.00	15.00	25.00	—
1766 "G" Small head	Inc. above	5.00	10.00	15.00	25.00	—
1767 G GROSSVS	7,501,000	5.00	10.00	15.00	25.00	—
1767 G GROSSUS	Inc. above	7.00	12.50	20.00	35.00	—
1767 G TRIPEX (Error)	Inc. above	12.00	20.00	30.00	50.00	—
1768 G GROSSVS	4,490,000	5.00	10.00	15.00	25.00	—
1768 G GROSSUS	Inc. above	5.00	10.00	15.00	25.00	—
1769 G	989,000	5.00	10.00	15.00	25.00	—
1770 G TRIPLEX	1,986,000	5.00	10.00	15.00	25.00	—
1770 G TRILEX (Error)	Inc. above	12.00	20.00	30.00	50.00	—
1771 G	504,000	6.00	12.00	20.00	30.00	—
1772 G	570,000	6.00	12.00	20.00	30.00	—
1772 AP	Inc. above	3.00	5.00	8.00	16.00	—
1773 AP	733,000	3.00	5.00	8.00	16.00	—
1774 AP	1,038,999	3.00	5.00	8.00	16.00	—
1774 AP STANISLUS (Error)	Inc. above	12.00	20.00	30.00	50.00	—
1775 EB	1,099,000	3.00	5.00	8.00	16.00	—
1776 EB	1,592,000	3.00	5.00	8.00	16.00	—
1777 EB	865,000	3.00	5.00	8.00	16.00	—
1778 EB	695,000	3.25	5.50	9.00	17.50	—
1778 EB STANILAUS (Error)	Inc. above	12.00	20.00	35.00	55.00	—
1779 EB	507,000	3.25	5.50	9.00	17.50	—
1780 EB	307,000	3.50	6.00	10.00	20.00	—
1781 EB	501,000	3.25	5.50	9.00	17.50	—
1782 EB	213,000	5.00	10.00	15.00	25.00	—
1783 EB	652,000	3.25	5.50	9.00	17.50	—
1784 EB	447,000	3.25	5.50	9.00	17.50	—
1785 EB	290,000	3.50	6.00	10.00	20.00	—
1786 EB	233,000	3.50	6.00	10.00	20.00	—
1787 EB	2,797,000	3.00	5.00	8.00	16.00	—
1788 EB GROSSUS	5,029,000	3.00	5.00	8.00	16.00	—
1788 EB GROSSOS (Error)	Inc. above	—	—	—	—	—
1789 EB	3,317,000	3.00	5.00	8.00	16.00	—
1790 EB	5,242,000	3.00	5.00	8.00	16.00	—
1790 EB STANISLUAS (Error)	Inc. above	12.00	20.00	30.00	50.00	—
1791 EB	3,906,000	3.50	6.00	10.00	20.00	—
1792 EB	5,223,000	3.00	5.00	8.00	16.00	—
1792 MV	Inc. above	3.50	6.00	10.00	20.00	—
1793 MV	2,618,000	3.00	5.00	8.00	16.00	—
1794 MV	2,089,999	3.00	5.00	8.00	16.00	—
1795 MV	Inc. above	—	—	—	—	—

KM# 205 3 GROSZE (Mining)

Copper **Ruler:** Stanislaus Augustus **Obv:** Head right **Obv. Legend:** STANISLAUS AUG • D •G • REX POLMDL • **Rev:** Crowned, round 4-fold arms within sprigs **Rev. Legend:** TROIAK Z MIEDZI KRAIOWEY

Date	Mintage	VG	F	VF	XF	Unc
1786 EB	Inc. above	13.00	22.50	32.50	65.00	—
1787 EB	Inc. above	3.00	9.00	17.50	25.00	—
1788 EB	Inc. above	9.00	15.00	22.50	45.00	—
1791 EB	Inc. above	9.00	15.00	22.50	45.00	—
1792 MW	Inc. above	13.00	22.50	32.50	65.00	—
1792 WM	Inc. above	10.00	17.50	25.00	50.00	—

KM# 154 6 GROSZY (1 Szostak)

Billon **Ruler:** August III **Obv:** Crowned bust of August III right **Rev:** Crowned arms within sprigs, SZ below

Date	Mintage	VG	F	VF	XF	Unc
1753	—	12.00	20.00	30.00	65.00	—

KM# 155.1 6 GROSZY (1 Szostak)

Billon **Ruler:** August III **Rev:** Crowned arms within sprigs, VI below

Date	Mintage	VG	F	VF	XF	Unc
1753 EC	—	8.00	12.50	22.00	45.00	—
1754 EC	—	8.00	12.50	22.00	45.00	—
1755 EC	—	7.00	12.00	20.00	40.00	—
1756 EC	—	5.00	10.00	17.50	35.00	—

KM# 155.2 6 GROSZY (1 Szostak)

Billon **Ruler:** August III **Rev:** Error: IV below arms

Date	Mintage	VG	F	VF	XF	Unc
1755 EC	—	10.00	17.50	25.00	60.00	—

KM# 215 6 GROSZY (1 Szostak)

Billon **Ruler:** Stanislaus Augustus **Obv:** Crowned, round 3-fold arms **Obv. Legend:** STANISLAUS AUGUSTUS **Rev:** Value, date **Note:** Varieties exist.

Date	Mintage	VG	F	VF	XF	Unc
1794	—	5.00	7.50	15.00	30.00	—
1794 AUGUTUS (Error)	—	16.50	22.50	40.00	75.00	—
1795	—	5.00	7.50	15.00	30.00	—

KM# 183 GROSCHEN (1/24 Thaler, 7-1/2 Groszy, 1 Srebrnik)

1.9900 g., 0.3670 Silver 0.0235 oz. ASW **Ruler:** Stanislaus Augustus **Obv:** Crowned SAR monogram within square **Rev:** Inscription, date within square **Rev. Inscription:** 320/EX/MARCA/PURA•COL **Note:** Varieties exist.

Date	Mintage	Good	VG	F	VF	XF
1766	915,000	35.00	65.00	90.00	135	—
1766 FS	Inc. above	12.00	17.00	20.00	37.50	—
1767	2,480,000	35.00	65.00	90.00	135	—
1767 FS	Inc. above	8.00	10.00	14.00	22.50	—
1768 FS	1,761,000	8.00	10.00	14.00	22.50	—
1768 IS	Inc. above	55.00	85.00	120	185	—
1771 Rare	—	—	—	—	—	—
1772 AP	7,131	22.00	40.00	60.00	110	—
1773 AP	17,000	8.00	10.00	14.00	22.50	—
1774 AP	75,000	8.00	10.00	14.00	22.50	—
1775 AP	17,000	10.00	12.00	18.00	25.00	—
1776 EB	29,000	8.00	10.00	14.00	22.50	—
1777 EB	34,000	8.00	10.00	14.00	22.50	—
1778 EB	24,000	10.00	12.00	18.00	25.00	—
1779 EB	86,000	8.00	10.00	14.00	22.50	—
1780 EB	11,000	10.00	12.00	18.00	37.50	—
1781 EB	2,966	10.00	20.00	35.00	85.00	—
1782 EB	33,000	8.00	10.00	14.00	22.50	—

KM# 206 10 GROSZY

2.4900 g., 0.3730 Silver 0.0299 oz. ASW **Ruler:** Stanislaus Augustus **Obv:** Crowned, round 3-fold arms **Obv. Legend:** STAN AUG ... **Rev:** Value, inscription, date **Rev. Inscription:** GR:MIEDZ/250 1/2/GRZ:KOL/1790/E•B•

Date	Mintage	VG	F	VF	XF	Unc
1787 EB	414,000	8.00	12.00	15.00	25.00	—
1788 EB	685,000	8.00	12.00	15.00	25.00	—
1789 EB	314,000	8.00	12.00	15.00	25.00	—
1790 EB	1,068,000	8.00	12.00	15.00	25.00	—
1791 EB	609,000	8.00	12.00	15.00	25.00	—
1792 MV	594,000	20.00	30.00	50.00	90.00	—
1792 MW	Inc. above	8.00	12.00	15.00	25.00	—
1793 MW	876,000	8.00	12.00	15.00	25.00	—
1794 MW	—	10.00	25.00	35.00	75.00	—
1795 MW	—	20.00	30.00	75.00	125	—

KM# 184 2 GROSCHEN (1/12 Thaler, 15 Groszy, Polzlotek)

3.3400 g., 0.5870 Silver 0.0630 oz. ASW **Ruler:** Stanislaus Augustus **Obv:** Crowned, ornate 4-fold arms within sprigs **Obv. Legend:** STANISLAUSAUG • D • G • REX POL • M • D • **Rev:** Value, inscription, date **Rev. Inscription:** S.GR/CLX•EX/MARCA/PURA•COL•/

Date	Mintage	VG	F	VF	XF	Unc
1766 FS	8,425,000	4.00	6.50	10.00	17.50	—
1767 FS	7,110,000	4.00	6.50	10.00	17.50	—
1768 IS	—	7.00	15.00	20.00	27.50	—
1769 IS	1,509,000	4.00	6.50	10.00	17.50	—
1770 IS	344,000	5.00	7.50	12.00	20.00	—
1771 IS	218,000	5.00	7.50	12.00	20.00	—
1772 S	361,000	5.00	10.00	15.00	25.00	—
1772 AP	Inc. above	4.00	6.50	10.00	17.50	—
1773 AP	665,000	4.00	6.50	10.00	17.50	—
1773 PA	Inc. above	12.00	22.50	35.00	60.00	—
1774 AP	299,000	5.00	7.50	12.00	20.00	—
1775 AP	352,000	55.00	85.00	125	200	—
1775 EB	Inc. above	7.00	10.00	15.00	22.50	—
1776 EB	97,000	12.00	20.00	35.00	70.00	—
1777 EB	35,000	10.00	17.50	30.00	65.00	—
1778 EB	9,972	12.00	22.50	35.00	70.00	—
1779 EB	61,000	7.00	10.00	15.00	22.50	—
1780 EB	27,000	10.00	15.00	20.00	27.50	—
1781 EB	43,000	10.00	15.00	20.00	27.50	—
1782 EB	28,000	10.00	15.00	20.00	27.50	—
1785 EB	63,000	10.00	15.00	20.00	27.50	—
1786 EB	283,000	5.00	7.50	12.00	20.00	—

KM# 148.1 18 GROSZY (Tympf)

Billon **Ruler:** August III **Obv:** Crowned bust of August III, right **Rev:** Crowned, round 4-fold arms within sprigs, T below

Date	Mintage	VG	F	VF	XF	Unc
1752 Rare	—	—	—	—	—	—
1753	—	15.00	25.00	45.00	75.00	—
1755	—	15.00	25.00	45.00	75.00	—

KM# 148.2 18 GROSZY (Tympf)

Billon **Ruler:** August III **Obv:** Large, crowned bust right **Obv. Legend:** D • G • AUGVSTVS • III • REX • POLONIARUM **Rev:** Crowned, round 4-fold arms within sprigs **Rev. Legend:** SAC • ROM • IMP • ....

Date	Mintage	VG	F	VF	XF	Unc
1753 EC	—	9.00	18.00	32.00	55.00	—
1753	—	30.00	60.00	125	250	—
1754 EC	—	9.00	18.00	32.00	55.00	—
1755 EC	—	9.00	18.00	32.00	55.00	—
1756 EC	—	—	—	—	—	—

KM# 148.3 18 GROSZY (Tympf)

Billon **Ruler:** August III **Obv:** Crowned bust right **Obv. Legend:** D • G • AVGVSTVS IIIREX POLON... **Rev:** Crowned, round 4-fold arms within sprigs **Rev. Legend:** SAC • ROM • IMP • ...

Date	Mintage	VG	F	VF	XF	Unc
1753 EC	—	9.00	18.00	32.00	55.00	—
1756 EC	—	9.00	18.00	32.00	55.00	—

KM# 167 18 GROSZY (Tympf)

Billon **Ruler:** August III **Obv:** Crowned bust right **Obv. Legend:** D • G • AVGVSTVS • III • REX• ... **Rev:** crowned, round 4-fold arms within sprigs **Rev. Legend:** SAC • ROM • IMP • ...

Date	Mintage	VG	F	VF	XF	Unc
1755 EC	—	—	—	—	—	—

KM# 173 30 GROSZY

Silver **Ruler:** August III **Obv:** Crowned bust right **Obv. Legend:** D • G • FRID • AUGUSTUS REX POL ET SAX **Rev:** Triple X above value, date within sprigs

Date	Mintage	VG	F	VF	XF	Unc
1762 Rare	—	—	—	—	—	—

KM# 174 60 GROSZY

Silver **Ruler:** August III **Obv:** Crowned bust right **Obv. Legend:** D • G • FRID • AVGUSTUS REX POL ET SAX **Rev. Legend:** POLONIÆ MON: REG:

Date	Mintage	VG	F	VF	XF	Unc
1762 Rare	—	—	—	—	—	—

KM# 185 4 GROSCHEN (1 Zloty)

5.3100 g., 0.5500 Silver 0.0939 oz. ASW **Ruler:** Stanislaus Augustus **Obv:** Crowned bust right **Rev:** Crowned, round 4-fold arms within sprigs

Date	Mintage	VG	F	VF	XF	Unc
1766 FS	4,139,000	10.00	17.00	25.00	40.00	—
1767 FS	7,679,000	10.00	17.00	25.00	40.00	—

Date	Mintage	VG	F	VF	XF	Unc
1768 IS	46,000	14.00	18.00	40.00	75.00	—
1769 IS	20,000	30.00	60.00	100	175	—
1771 IS	74,000	14.00	18.00	28.00	50.00	—
1772 AP	17,000	40.00	80.00	120	220	—
1773 AP	5,201	60.00	120	200	275	—
1774 AP	37,000	14.00	18.00	40.00	75.00	—
1775 EB	57,000	14.00	18.00	30.00	60.00	—
1776 EB	47,000	14.00	18.00	30.00	60.00	—
1777 EB	62,000	14.00	18.00	30.00	60.00	—
1778 EB	20,000	15.00	20.00	40.00	75.00	—
1779 EB	44,000	14.00	18.00	30.00	60.00	—
1780 EB	82,000	14.00	18.00	30.00	60.00	—
1781 EB	10,000	15.00	20.00	40.00	75.00	—
1782 EB	35,000	14.00	18.00	30.00	60.00	—

KM# 197.1 4 GROSCHEN (1 Zloty)

5.3100 g., 0.5500 Silver 0.0939 oz. ASW **Ruler:** Stanislaus Augustus **Obv:** Head with braid

Date	Mintage	VG	F	VF	XF	Unc
1783 EB	11,000	12.50	20.00	40.00	75.00	—
1784 EB	10,000	12.50	20.00	40.00	75.00	—
1785 EB	225,000	7.50	12.50	25.00	45.00	—

KM# 197.2 4 GROSCHEN (1 Zloty)

5.3100 g., 0.5500 Silver 0.0939 oz. ASW **Ruler:** Stanislaus Augustus **Obv:** Head with two braids

Date	Mintage	VG	F	VF	XF	Unc
1786 EB	164,000	10.00	17.00	30.00	60.00	—

KM# 208.1 4 GROSCHEN (1 Zloty)

5.3100 g., 0.5500 Silver 0.0939 oz. ASW **Ruler:** Stanislaus Augustus **Obv:** Head right **Obv. Legend:** STANISLAUS AUG • D • G • REX ... **Rev:** Crowned 4-fold arms divides date **Rev. Legend:** PURACOLON ....

Date	Mintage	VG	F	VF	XF	Unc
1787 EB	1,622,000	7.00	10.00	20.00	40.00	—
1788 EB	1,196,000	7.00	10.00	20.00	40.00	—
1789 EB	820,000	8.00	12.50	25.00	50.00	—
1790 EB	1,751,000	7.00	10.00	20.00	40.00	—
1791 EB	2,307,000	7.00	10.00	20.00	40.00	—
1792 MV	2,320,000	7.00	10.00	20.00	40.00	—
1793 MV	3,390,000	7.00	10.00	20.00	40.00	—
1794 MV	894,000	15.00	20.00	40.00	80.00	—

KM# 208.2 4 GROSCHEN (1 Zloty)

5.3100 g., 0.5500 Silver 0.0939 oz. ASW **Ruler:** Stanislaus Augustus **Obv:** Head right **Obv. Legend:** STANISLAUS AUG • D • G • REX POL • ... **Rev:** Crowned 4-fold arms divides date

Date	Mintage	VG	F	VF	XF	Unc
1794 MV	Inc. above	15.00	25.00	50.00	100	—
1795 MV	Inc. above	20.00	35.00	75.00	150	—

KM# 135 6 GROSCHEN

Silver **Ruler:** Johann III Sobieski **Obv:** Small crowned bust of August II right **Rev:** Crown above three shields

Date	Mintage	VG	F	VF	XF	Unc
1698EPH Rare	—	—	—	—	—	—
1702EPH	—	—	—	—	—	—

KM# 156 8 GROSCHEN (2 Zlotych)

7.3100 g., Silver **Ruler:** August III **Obv:** Crowned bust right **Obv. Legend:** DGAVGVSTVSIII .... **Rev:** Crowned, round 4-fold arms within sprigs **Rev. Legend:** SAC • ROM • IMP....

Date	Mintage	VG	F	VF	XF	Unc
1753 EC	—	10.00	20.00	35.00	75.00	—
1756 EC	—	40.00	90.00	175	300	—
1761 EC	—	40.00	100	200	350	—
1762 EC Rare	—	—	—	—	—	—

KM# 157 8 GROSCHEN (2 Zlotych)

7.3100 g., Silver **Ruler:** August III **Obv:** Crowned bust right **Obv. Legend:** D • G • AVGVSTVS III • REX POLONIARUM • **Rev:** Crowned, round 4-fold arms within sprigs, without 8 GR below arms **Rev. Legend:** SAC • ROM • IMP • ARCHIM • ETELECT •

Date	Mintage	VG	F	VF	XF	Unc
1753	—	20.00	40.00	70.00	150	—

KM# 186.1 8 GROSCHEN (2 Zlotych)

9.3500 g., 0.6267 Silver 0.1884 oz. ASW **Ruler:** Stanislaus Augustus **Obv:** Head right **Obv. Legend:** STANISLAUS AUG • D • G • REXPOL • M • D • L • **Rev:** Crowned, round 4-fold arms within sprigs, without 8 GR below arms **Note:** Dav. #1618.

Date	Mintage	VG	F	VF	XF	Unc
1766 FS	1,742,000	40.00	65.00	110	185	—

KM# 186.2 8 GROSCHEN (2 Zlotych)

9.3500 g., 0.6267 Silver 0.1884 oz. ASW **Ruler:** Stanislaus Augustus **Obv:** Head right **Obv. Legend:** STANISLAUS AUG • D • G • REXPOL • M • D • L • **Rev:** Crowned, round 4-fold arms within sprigs, 8 GR below arms **Rev. Legend:** PURA • COL • 1767 • XL • EXMARCA • **Note:** Dav. #1619. Varieties exist.

Date	Mintage	VG	F	VF	XF	Unc
1766 FS	Inc. above	10.00	17.00	28.00	50.00	—
1766	Inc. above	75.00	135	225	350	—
1767 FS	207,000	10.00	17.00	28.00	50.00	—
1768 FS	2,095,000	10.00	17.00	28.00	50.00	—
1768 IS	Inc. above	10.00	17.00	28.00	50.00	—
1769 IS	140,000	12.00	25.00	50.00	100	—
1770 IS	359,000	10.00	17.00	28.00	50.00	—
1771 IS	275,000	10.00	17.00	28.00	50.00	—
1772 AP	201,000	10.00	17.00	28.00	50.00	—
1772 IS	Inc. above	10.00	17.00	28.00	50.00	—
1773 AP	67,000	12.00	30.00	60.00	120	—
1774 AP	376,000	10.00	17.00	28.00	50.00	—
1774 EB	Inc. above	10.00	17.00	30.00	55.00	—
1775 EB	489,000	10.00	17.00	28.00	50.00	—
1776 EB	570,000	10.00	17.00	28.00	50.00	—
1777 EB	366,000	10.00	17.00	28.00	50.00	—
1778 EB	290,000	10.00	18.00	28.00	50.00	—
1779 EB	220,000	10.00	18.00	30.00	55.00	—
1780 EB	109,000	10.00	20.00	40.00	65.00	—
1781 EB	200,000	10.00	18.00	30.00	55.00	—
1782 EB	195,000	10.00	18.00	30.00	55.00	—

KM# 198.1 8 GROSCHEN (2 Zlotych)

9.3500 g., 0.6267 Silver 0.1884 oz. ASW **Ruler:** Stanislaus Augustus **Obv:** Head with braid **Note:** Dav. #1620.

Date	Mintage	VG	F	VF	XF	Unc
1783 EB	208,000	10.00	17.00	30.00	55.00	—
1784 EB	179,000	10.00	18.00	35.00	60.00	—
1785 EB	78,000	10.00	20.00	40.00	65.00	—

KM# 198.2 8 GROSCHEN (2 Zlotych)

9.3500 g., 0.6267 Silver 0.1884 oz. ASW **Ruler:** Stanislaus Augustus **Obv:** Braid behind head **Note:** Dav. #1620A.

Date	Mintage	VG	F	VF	XF	Unc
1783 EB	Inc. above	75.00	150	300	600	—
1786 EB	—	—	—	—	—	—

Note: Reported, not confirmed

KM# 209.1 8 GROSCHEN (2 Zlotych)

9.3500 g., 0.6267 Silver 0.1884 oz. ASW **Ruler:** Stanislaus Augustus **Obv:** Head right **Obv. Legend:** STANISLAUS AUG • D • G • REX • POL • M • D • L • **Rev:** Crowned 4-fold arms divides date **Rev. Legend:** PURA COLON • ... **Note:** Dav. #1621.

Date	Mintage	VG	F	VF	XF	Unc
1787 EB	842,000	9.00	15.00	25.00	45.00	—
1788 EB	742,000	9.00	15.00	25.00	45.00	—
1789 EB	852,000	9.00	15.00	25.00	45.00	—
1790 EB	585,000	9.00	15.00	25.00	45.00	—
1791 EB	917,000	9.00	15.00	25.00	45.00	—
1792 EB	1,612,000	7.00	12.50	20.00	35.00	—
1792 MV	Inc. above	7.00	12.50	20.00	35.00	—
1793 MV	774,000	10.00	15.00	25.00	50.00	—
1794 MV	2,476,000	7.00	12.50	20.00	35.00	—

KM# 209.2 8 GROSCHEN (2 Zlotych)

9.3500 g., 0.6267 Silver 0.1884 oz. ASW **Ruler:** Stanislaus Augustus **Obv:** Head right **Obv. Legend:** STANISLAUS AUG • D • G • REX • POL • M • D • L • **Rev:** Crowned 4-fold arms divides date **Note:** Dav. #1623.

Date	Mintage	VG	F	VF	XF	Unc
1794 MV	Inc. above	16.00	27.50	45.00	90.00	—
1795 MV	Inc. above	12.50	20.00	35.00	60.00	—

KM# 191.1 1/2 THALER (4 Zlotych - 1/2 Talar)

14.0300 g., 0.8330 Silver 0.3757 oz. ASW **Ruler:** Stanislaus Augustus **Obv:** Head right **Obv. Legend:** STANISLAUS AUGUSTUS • D • G • REX POL • M • D • L • **Rev:** crowned, round 4-fold arms within sprigs **Rev. Legend:** PURA COL....

Date	Mintage	VG	F	VF	XF	Unc
1767 FS	1,769	25.00	50.00	100	200	—
1768 IS	24,000	25.00	45.00	100	250	—

KM# 191.2 1/2 THALER (4 Zlotych - 1/2 Talar)

14.0300 g., 0.8330 Silver 0.3757 oz. ASW **Ruler:** Stanislaus Augustus **Obv:** Head right **Obv. Legend:** STANISLAUS AUGUSTUS • D • G • REX POL • M • D • LIT • **Rev:** Crowned, round 4-fold arms within sprigs **Rev. Legend:** PURA COL.... **Note:** Varieties exist.

Date	Mintage	VG	F	VF	XF	Unc
1768 IS	24,000	25.00	40.00	85.00	175	—
1772 AP	11,000	25.00	40.00	85.00	175	—
1773 AP	5,335	25.00	45.00	90.00	200	—
1774 AP	3,565	40.00	80.00	160	325	—
1775 EB	3,533	30.00	60.00	125	275	—
1776 EB	15,000	25.00	40.00	85.00	175	—
1777 EB	20,000	25.00	40.00	85.00	175	—
1778 EB	21,000	25.00	40.00	85.00	175	—
1779 EB	14,000	25.00	40.00	85.00	175	—
1780 EB	4,764	30.00	60.00	125	275	—
1781 EB	3,893	30.00	60.00	125	275	—
1782 EB	2,166	25.00	50.00	100	225	—

KM# 192 1/2 THALER (4 Zlotych - 1/2 Talar)

14.0300 g., 0.8330 Silver 0.3757 oz. ASW **Ruler:** Stanislaus Augustus **Note:** Klippe.

Date	Mintage	VG	F	VF	XF	Unc
1780 EB Rare	—	—	—	—	—	—

KM# 199 1/2 THALER (4 Zlotych - 1/2 Talar)

14.0300 g., 0.8330 Silver 0.3757 oz. ASW **Ruler:** Stanislaus Augustus **Obv:** Head right **Obv. Legend:** STANISLAUS AUGUSTUS • D • G • REX POL • M • D • LIT • **Rev:** Crowned, round 4-fold arms within sprigs **Rev. Legend:** PURA COL ....

Date	Mintage	VG	F	VF	XF	Unc
1783 EB	7,687	25.00	45.00	100	250	—
1784 EB	12,000	25.00	40.00	90.00	225	—

KM# 211 1/2 THALER (4 Zlotych - 1/2 Talar)

14.0300 g., 0.8330 Silver 0.3757 oz. ASW **Ruler:** Stanislaus Augustus **Obv:** Head right **Obv. Legend:** STANISLAUS AUGUSTUS • D • G • REX POL • M • D • LIT • **Rev:** Crowned 4-fold arms within sprigs

Date	Mintage	VG	F	VF	XF	Unc
1788 EB	76,000	25.00	35.00	75.00	200	—
1792 MV	186	75.00	125	250	450	—

KM# 138 THALER (Beichinger = 8 Florins)

Silver **Ruler:** August II **Obv:** 4 crowned A's and 4 II's around central cross **Obv. Legend:** AUGUSTUS • II • D • G • REX ... **Rev:** Crowned ornate 4-fold arms **Rev. Legend:** SAC • ROM • IMP • ARCHIM • ETELECT • **Note:** Dav. #1613.

Date	Mintage	VG	F	VF	XF	Unc
1702	—	175	350	750	1,150	—

KM# 140 THALER (Reichs)

Silver **Ruler:** August II **Obv:** Open St. Andrew's cross floriate with crowned AS monogram in 2 quarters, crowned top, Order of the Elephant below **Rev:** Crowned shield in collar of Order of the Elephant **Note:** Dav. #1615.

Date	Mintage	VG	F	VF	XF	Unc
1702 Rare	—	—	—	—	—	—

KM# 187 THALER (Reichs)
28.0700 g., 0.8330 Silver 0.7517 oz. ASW **Ruler:** Stanislaus Augustus **Obv:** Bust right **Obv. Inscription:** STANISLAUS AUGUSTUS • D • G • REX POL • M • D • L • ... **Rev:** Crowned, round 4-fold arms within sprigs **Note:** Dav. #1618.

Date	Mintage	VG	F	VF	XF	Unc
1766 FS	78,000	90.00	175	275	575	—

KM# 194 THALER (Reichs)
28.0700 g., 0.8330 Silver 0.7517 oz. ASW **Ruler:** Stanislaus Augustus **Obv:** Head right **Obv. Legend:** STANISLAUS AUGUSTUS • D • G • REX POL • M • D • L • ... **Rev:** Crowned, round 4-fold arms within sprigs **Note:** Dav. #1619.

Date	Mintage	VG	F	VF	XF	Unc
1768 IS LITH	5,532	125	225	450	600	—
1768 IS LITU	Inc. above	150	300	600	850	—
1769 IS Rare	1,501	—	—	—	—	—
1770 IS	10,000	75.00	100	200	400	—
1772 AP	7,761	75.00	100	200	450	—
1772 IS	Inc. above	125	200	400	650	—
1773 AP LITH	5,416	150	300	600	850	—
1773 AP LITU	Inc. above	125	275	450	750	—
1774 AP	4,713	125	200	400	650	—
1775 EB LITH	33,000	60.00	75.00	150	300	—
1775 LITU	Inc. above	60.00	75.00	150	300	—
1776 EB LITH	47,000	60.00	75.00	150	300	—
1776 EB LITU	Inc. above	60.00	75.00	150	300	—
1777 EB LITU	17,000	60.00	85.00	175	375	—
1777 EB LITU	Inc. above	60.00	85.00	175	375	—
1778 EB LITH	20,000	60.00	85.00	175	375	—
1778 EB LITU	Inc. above	60.00	85.00	175	375	—
1779 EB	16,000	60.00	85.00	175	375	—
1780 EB	9,566	100	200	400	650	—
1781 EB	4,786	150	300	600	850	—
1782 EB Rare	1,542	—	—	—	—	—

KM# 200 THALER (Reichs)
28.0700 g., 0.8330 Silver 0.7517 oz. ASW **Ruler:** Stanislaus Augustus **Obv:** Head right **Obv. Legend:** STANISLAUS AUGUSTUS • D • G • REX POLON • M • D • LITUAN • **Note:** Dav. #1620.

Date	Mintage	VG	F	VF	XF	Unc
1783 EB	15,000	60.00	100	200	400	—
1784 EB	13,000	60.00	100	200	400	—
1785 EB	3,848	75.00	125	225	450	—

KM# 212 THALER (Reichs)
28.0700 g., 0.8330 Silver 0.7517 oz. ASW **Ruler:** Stanislaus Augustus **Obv:** Head right **Obv. Legend:** STANISLAUS AUGUSTUS • D • G • REX POLON • M • D • ... **Rev:** Crowned 4-fold arms within sprigs **Note:** Dav. #1621.

Date	Mintage	VG	F	VF	XF	Unc
1788 EB	31,000	45.00	70.00	140	250	—
1792 MV	339	—	—	750	1,250	—

KM# 214 THALER (Reichs)
28.0700 g., 0.8330 Silver 0.7517 oz. ASW **Ruler:** Stanislaus Augustus **Subject:** Convention of Targowitz **Obv:** Inscription **Rev:** Inscription within wreath **Note:** Dav. #1622. Two varieties exist.

Date	Mintage	VG	F	VF	XF	Unc
1793	1,699	175	225	475	900	—

TRADE COINAGE

KM# 179 DUCAT
3.5000 g., 0.9860 Gold 0.1109 oz. AGW **Ruler:** Stanislaus Augustus **Obv:** Bust right

Date	Mintage	VG	F	VF	XF	Unc
1765 FS Proof; Rare	—	—	—	—	—	—

KM# 188 DUCAT
3.5000 g., 0.9860 Gold 0.1109 oz. AGW **Ruler:** Stanislaus Augustus **Obv:** Crowned SAR monogram within radiant star **Rev:** Crowned 4-fold arms, divided date below **Rev. Legend:** MON : AUR : POLONIC :

Date	Mintage	VG	F	VF	XF	Unc
1766 FS	7,982	1,000	2,000	3,500	6,000	—
1766	Inc. above	1,000	2,000	3,500	6,000	—

KM# 189 DUCAT
3.5000 g., 0.9860 Gold 0.1109 oz. AGW **Ruler:** Stanislaus Augustus **Obv:** Head right **Rev:** Legend within ornamented square **Rev. Inscription:** MON. AUR./ POLON...

Date	Mintage	VG	F	VF	XF	Unc
1766 FS in square	Inc. above	650	1,250	2,750	4,500	—
1766 FS below square	Inc. above	650	1,250	2,750	4,500	—

KM# 190 DUCAT
3.5000 g., 0.9860 Gold 0.1109 oz. AGW **Ruler:** Stanislaus Augustus **Obv:** Standing figure divides date **Obv. Legend:** STANISLAUS AUG • D • G • REX POL • M • D • L • **Rev:** Legend within ornamented square **Rev. Legend:** MONETA/AUREA/POLONI./AD LEG./IMPER.

Date	Mintage	VG	F	VF	XF	Unc
1766 IPH	Inc. above	300	450	900	1,850	—
1766	Inc. above	300	350	700	1,450	—
1766 FS	Inc. above	300	350	700	1,450	—
1767	2,511	350	450	900	1,850	—
1767 FS	Inc. above	350	450	900	1,800	—
1768 FS Rare	117	—	—	—	—	—
1770 IS	—	300	350	700	1,450	—
1771 IS	3,216	350	450	900	1,850	—
1772 IS Rare	8,576	—	—	—	—	—
1772 AP Rare	Inc. above	—	—	—	—	—

KM# 195 DUCAT
3.5000 g., 0.9860 Gold 0.1109 oz. AGW **Ruler:** Stanislaus Augustus **Obv:** Head right **Obv. Legend:** STANISLAUS AUG • D•G•REX POL•M•D•L• **Rev:** Legend, date within ornamented square **Rev. Legend:** MONETA/AUREA/POLON./AD LEG./IMPER

Date	Mintage	VG	F	VF	XF	Unc
1772 AP	Inc. above	350	450	900	1,850	—
1773 AP	26,000	300	400	550	1,200	—
1774 AP	18,000	300	400	550	1,200	—
1774 EB	Inc. above	325	375	700	1,450	—
1775 EB	3,872	350	450	800	1,750	—
1776 EB	1,778	350	600	1,200	2,500	—
1777 EB	836	350	600	1,200	2,500	—
1778 EB	1,122	350	600	1,200	2,500	—
1779 EB	2,411	350	450	800	1,750	—

KM# 196 DUCAT
3.5000 g., 0.9860 Gold 0.1109 oz. AGW **Ruler:** Stanislaus Augustus **Obv:** Head right **Obv. Legend:** STANISLAUS AUG • D • G • REX POL • M • D • L • **Rev:** Legend, date within wreath

Date	Mintage	VG	F	VF	XF	Unc
1779 EB Rare	Inc. above	—	—	—	—	—
1780 EB	3,372	300	400	700	1,450	—
1781 EB	5,083	300	400	700	1,450	—
1782 EB	3,535	300	400	700	1,450	—
1783 EB	1,661	300	400	700	1,450	—
1791 EB	33,000	300	400	400	800	—
1792 EB	29,000	300	400	425	800	—
1792 MV	Inc. above	300	400	425	800	—
1793 MV	6,192	300	400	600	1,250	—
1794 MV	11,000	300	400	500	1,000	—
1795 MV	Inc. above	300	450	900	1,850	—

KM# 201 DUCAT
3.5000 g., 0.9860 Gold 0.1109 oz. AGW **Ruler:** Stanislaus Augustus **Obv:** Head right **Obv. Legend:** STANISLAUS AUG • D • G • REX POL • M • D • L • **Rev:** Legend, date within wreath

Date	Mintage	VG	F	VF	XF	Unc
1784 EB	4,537	300	400	650	1,350	—
1785 EB	6,529	300	400	650	1,350	—
1786 EB	5,797	300	400	650	1,350	—

KM# 210 DUCAT
3.5000 g., 0.9860 Gold 0.1109 oz. AGW **Ruler:** Stanislaus Augustus **Obv:** Head right **Obv. Legend:** STANISLAUS AUG • D • G • REX POL • M • D • L • **Rev:** Legend, date within wreath

Date	Mintage	VG	F	VF	XF	Unc
1787 EB	8,247	300	400	550	1,100	—
1788 EB	6,902	300	400	600	1,250	—
1789 EB	8,874	300	400	600	1,250	—
1790 EB	2,984	325	425	700	1,450	—
1791 EB	Inc. above	325	425	400	800	—
1792 EB	—	325	425	400	800	—

KM# 217 1-1/2 DUCAT
5.2500 g., 0.9860 Gold 0.1664 oz. AGW **Ruler:** Stanislaus Augustus **Obv:** Head right **Obv. Legend:** STANISLAUS AUG • D • G • REX POL • M • D • L • **Rev:** Crown above double oval shields within wreath

Date	Mintage	VG	F	VF	XF	Unc
1794	8,114	300	500	1,200	2,500	—

KM# 218 3 DUCAT
10.5000 g., 0.9860 Gold 0.3328 oz. AGW **Ruler:** Stanislaus

Augustus **Obv:** Head right **Obv. Legend:** STANISLAUS AUG • D • G • REX POL • M • D • L • **Rev:** Crown above double oval shields within wreath, 3 within beaded circle below

Date	Mintage	VG	F	VF	XF	Unc
1794	5,256	650	1,250	2,500	4,250	—

PATTERNS

Including off metal strikes

KM#	Date	Mintage	Identification	Mkt Val
Pn36	1703 EPH	—	1/2 Ducat. Silver. Fr. #2514, August II.	550
Pn37	1703 EPH	—	Dukat. Silver. Fr. #2512, August II.	550
Pn38	1750	—	Solidus. Silver.	—
Pn39	1750	—	Solidus. Gold.	—
Pn40	1750	—	Schilling. Silver.	—
Pn41	1750	—	Schilling. Gold.	—
Pn42	1753	—	Solidus. Silver.	—
Pn43	1754	—	18 Groszy. Copper.	—
Pn44	1756 EC	—	18 Groszy. Copper.	—
Pn45	1756	—	18 Groszy. Copper.	—
Pn46	1762	—	30 Groszy. Silver.	—
Pn47	1762	—	30 Groszy. Lead.	—
Pn48	1762	—	8 Groschen. Silver.	—

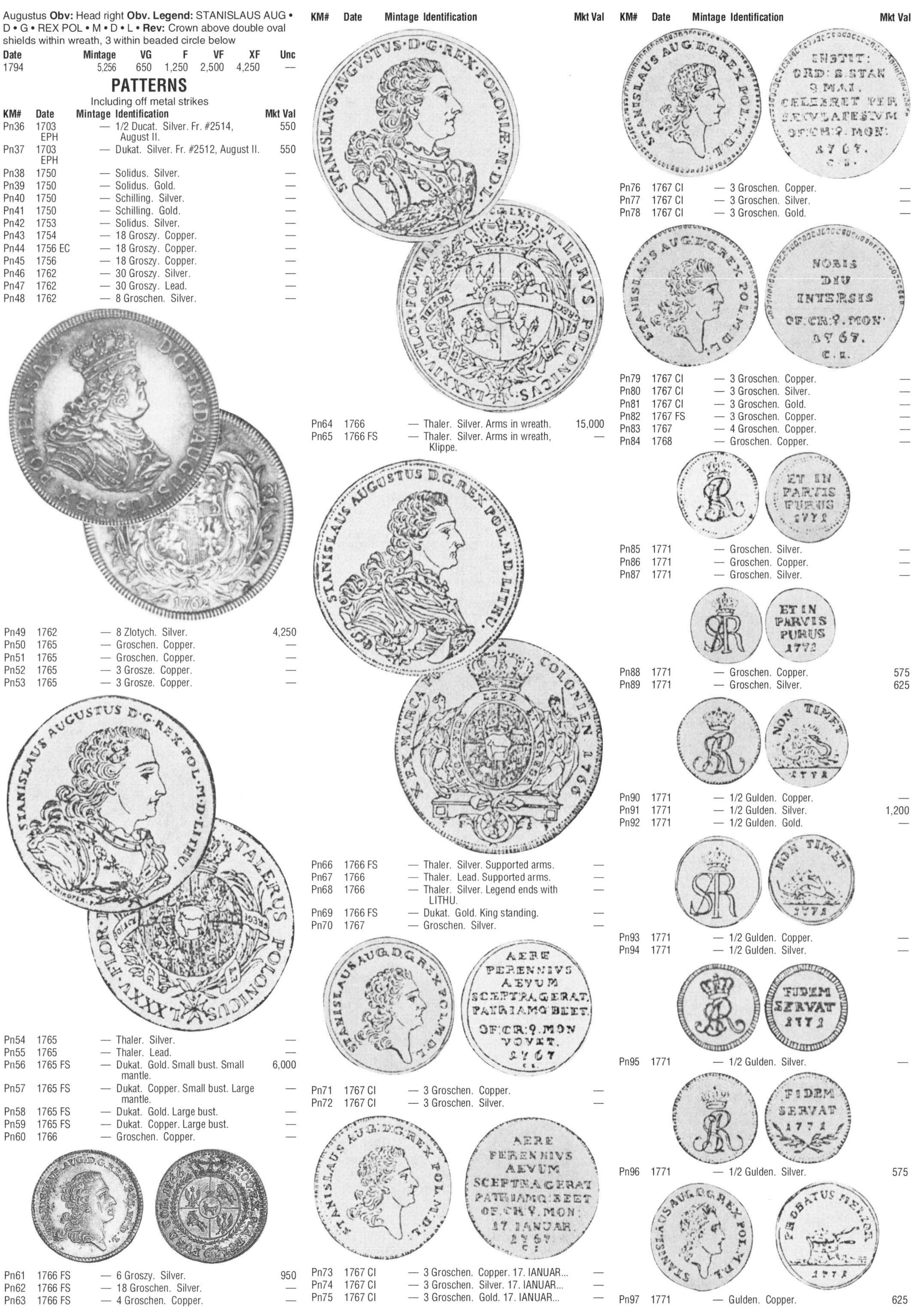

KM#	Date	Mintage	Identification	Mkt Val
Pn49	1762	—	8 Zlotych. Silver.	4,250
Pn50	1765	—	Groschen. Copper.	—
Pn51	1765	—	Groschen. Copper.	—
Pn52	1765	—	3 Grosze. Copper.	—
Pn53	1765	—	3 Grosze. Copper.	—
Pn54	1765	—	Thaler. Silver.	—
Pn55	1765	—	Thaler. Lead.	—
Pn56	1765 FS	—	Dukat. Gold. Small bust. Small mantle.	6,000
Pn57	1765 FS	—	Dukat. Copper. Small bust. Large mantle.	—
Pn58	1765 FS	—	Dukat. Gold. Large bust.	—
Pn59	1765 FS	—	Dukat. Copper. Large bust.	—
Pn60	1766	—	Groschen. Copper.	—
Pn61	1766 FS	—	6 Groszy. Silver.	950
Pn62	1766 FS	—	18 Groschen. Silver.	—
Pn63	1766 FS	—	4 Groschen. Copper.	—
Pn64	1766	—	Thaler. Silver. Arms in wreath.	15,000
Pn65	1766 FS	—	Thaler. Silver. Arms in wreath, Klippe.	—
Pn66	1766 FS	—	Thaler. Silver. Supported arms.	—
Pn67	1766	—	Thaler. Lead. Supported arms.	—
Pn68	1766	—	Thaler. Silver. Legend ends with LITHU.	—
Pn69	1766 FS	—	Dukat. Gold. King standing.	—
Pn70	1767	—	Groschen. Silver.	—
Pn71	1767 CI	—	3 Groschen. Copper.	—
Pn72	1767 CI	—	3 Groschen. Silver.	—
Pn73	1767 CI	—	3 Groschen. Copper. 17. IANUAR...	—
Pn74	1767 CI	—	3 Groschen. Silver. 17. IANUAR...	—
Pn75	1767 CI	—	3 Groschen. Gold. 17. IANUAR...	—
Pn76	1767 CI	—	3 Groschen. Copper.	—
Pn77	1767 CI	—	3 Groschen. Silver.	—
Pn78	1767 CI	—	3 Groschen. Gold.	—
Pn79	1767 CI	—	3 Groschen. Copper.	—
Pn80	1767 CI	—	3 Groschen. Silver.	—
Pn81	1767 CI	—	3 Groschen. Gold.	—
Pn82	1767 FS	—	3 Groschen. Copper.	—
Pn83	1767	—	4 Groschen. Copper.	—
Pn84	1768	—	Groschen. Copper.	—
Pn85	1771	—	Groschen. Silver.	—
Pn86	1771	—	Groschen. Copper.	—
Pn87	1771	—	Groschen. Silver.	—
Pn88	1771	—	Groschen. Copper.	575
Pn89	1771	—	Groschen. Silver.	625
Pn90	1771	—	1/2 Gulden. Copper.	—
Pn91	1771	—	1/2 Gulden. Silver.	1,200
Pn92	1771	—	1/2 Gulden. Gold.	—
Pn93	1771	—	1/2 Gulden. Copper.	—
Pn94	1771	—	1/2 Gulden. Silver.	—
Pn95	1771	—	1/2 Gulden. Silver.	—
Pn96	1771	—	1/2 Gulden. Silver.	575
Pn97	1771	—	Gulden. Copper.	625

KM#	Date	Mintage	Identification	Mkt Val
Pn98	1771	—	Gulden. Silver.	950
Pn99	1771	—	Gulden. Gold.	—

KM#	Date	Mintage	Identification	Mkt Val
Pn100	1771	—	2 Gulden. Copper.	1,000
Pn101	1771	—	2 Gulden. Silver.	725
Pn102	1771	—	2 Gulden. Gold.	2,650

KM#	Date	Mintage	Identification	Mkt Val
Pn103	1771	—	1/2 Thaler. Copper.	1,650
Pn104	1771	—	1/2 Thaler. Silver.	2,800

KM#	Date	Mintage	Identification	Mkt Val
Pn105	1771	—	Thaler. Silver. Legends ends LITU.	2,650
Pn106	1771	—	Thaler. Copper. Legend ends LITUA.	3,000
Pna106	1771	—	Thaler. Copper. legend ends LITU.	3,000
Pn107	1771	—	Thaler. Silver. Legend ends LITUA.	2,650
Pn108	1771	—	Thaler. Gold. Legend ends LITUA.	—
Pn109	1772 IS	—	Dukat. Copper. King standing.	—
Pn110	1772 AP	—	Dukat. Copper. Head.	—
Pn111	1777	—	8 Groschen. Copper.	—

KM#	Date	Mintage	Identification	Mkt Val
Pn112	1779 EB	—	Dukat. Copper.	—
Pn113	1779 EB	—	Dukat. Silver.	450
Pn114	1780 EB	—	1/2 Thaler. Silver. Klippe.	—
Pn115	1786 EB	—	1/2 Groschen. Copper.	—
Pn116	1788 EB	—	1/2 Thaler. Silver.	—
Pn117	1788 EB	—	Thaler. Iron.	—
Pn118	1791 EB	—	Dukat. Copper.	—
Pn119	1793	—	Thaler. Silver.	—
Pn120	1793	—	Thaler. Copper.	—
Pn121	1794	—	Dukat. Copper. C#71.	—

EAST PRUSSIA

East Prussia is an area on the southeastern coast of the Baltic Sea. Part of the area is in present day Poland and part in Russia. A possession of Prussia from 1525 until 1945, coinage for the area made by the Prussian kings except for brief occupation by Russia from 1756-1762 when Russia produced special coin types for the area.

RULERS

Friedrich II, 1740-1786
Elizabeth, during Russian occupation, 1759-1762
Friedrich Wilhelm II (of Prussia),1786-1797
Friedrich Wilhelm III (of Prussia), 1797-1840

MINT MARKS

A - Berlin
E - Konigsberg
G - Glatz, Silesia

NOTE: For gold listings refer to Konigsberg Mint under Brandenburg and Prussia (German States).

RUSSIAN OCCUPATION

STANDARD COINAGE

C# 41 SOLIDUS

Billon **Ruler:** Elizabeth **Obv:** Crowned monogram within sprigs **Rev:** Written value, state and date

Date	Mintage	VG	F	VF	XF	Unc
1759 large crown, large date	—	35.00	60.00	90.00	175	—
1759 large crown, small date	—	35.00	60.00	90.00	175	—
1759 small crown, large date	—	35.00	60.00	90.00	175	—
1759 small crown, small date	—	35.00	60.00	90.00	175	—
1760 large date	—	35.00	60.00	90.00	175	—
1760 small date	—	35.00	60.00	90.00	175	—
1761 large date	390,000	35.00	60.00	90.00	175	—
1761 small date	Inc. above	35.00	60.00	90.00	175	—

C# 41a SOLIDUS

Billon **Ruler:** Elizabeth **Obv:** Crowned monogram within sprigs **Rev:** Written value, state and date

Date	Mintage	VG	F	VF	XF	Unc
1759	—	35.00	60.00	90.00	175	—
1760	—	35.00	60.00	90.00	175	—

C# 42 GROSSUS

Billon **Ruler:** Elizabeth **Obv:** Crowned double-headed eagle **Rev:** Written value, state and date

Date	Mintage	VG	F	VF	XF	Unc
1759 large date	—	65.00	160	220	350	—
1759 small date	—	65.00	160	220	350	—
1760 large eagle	—	65.00	160	220	350	—
1760 small eagle	—	65.00	160	220	350	—
1761	112,000	65.00	160	220	350	—

C# 43 2 GROSSUS

Billon **Ruler:** Elizabeth **Obv:** Crowned double-headed eagle **Rev:** Written value, state and date

Date	Mintage	VG	F	VF	XF	Unc
1759 pointed tail	—	80.00	200	275	385	—
1759 square tail	—	80.00	200	275	385	—
1760 pointed tail	—	80.00	200	275	385	—
1760 rounded tail	—	80.00	200	275	385	—
1761 large date	94,000	80.00	200	275	385	—
1761 small date	Inc. above	80.00	200	275	385	—

C# 44 3 GROSZE

Silver **Ruler:** Elizabeth **Obv:** Crowned bust right **Obv. Legend:** ELISAB: I: IMP: ... **Rev:** Crowned eagle, 3 on breast **Rev. Legend:** MONETA • ARGNTEA • REG • PRVS

Date	Mintage	VG	F	VF	XF	Unc
1759	—	45.00	75.00	125	250	—

C# 44a 3 GROSZE

Silver **Ruler:** Elizabeth **Subject:** Elizabeth **Obv:** Crowned bust right **Obv. Legend:** ELISAB: I: D. G. IMP: ... **Rev:** Crowned eagle, 3 on breast **Rev. Legend:** MONETA REGNI PRUSS

Date	Mintage	VG	F	VF	XF	Unc
1759	—	45.00	75.00	125	250	—
1760 large date	—	45.00	75.00	125	250	—
1760 small date	—	45.00	75.00	125	250	—
1761	—	45.00	75.00	125	250	—

C# 45 6 GROSZY

Silver **Ruler:** Elizabeth **Subject:** Elizabeth **Obv:** Crowned bust right **Obv. Legend:** ELISAB: I: D • G • IMP: TOT: RUSS: **Rev:** Crowned eagle, VI on breast **Rev. Legend:** MONETA: REGNI: PRUSS:

Date	Mintage	VG	F	VF	XF	Unc
1759	—	35.00	90.00	150	250	—
1760	—	35.00	90.00	150	250	—
1761	—	35.00	90.00	150	250	—

C# 45a 6 GROSZY

Silver **Ruler:** Elizabeth **Obv:** Crowned bust right **Rev:** Crowned eagle, VI on breast **Rev. Legend:** MONETA: REGNI: PRVSS:

Date	Mintage	VG	F	VF	XF	Unc
1759	—	35.00	90.00	150	250	—
1761	—	35.00	90.00	150	250	—

C# 45b 6 GROSZY

Silver **Ruler:** Elizabeth **Obv:** Crowned bust right **Obv. Legend:** ELISABETHA: I: IMP: TOT: RUSS **Rev:** Crowned eagle, VI on breast **Rev. Legend:** MONETA: REGNI: PRVSS

Date	Mintage	VG	F	VF	XF	Unc
1759	—	35.00	90.00	145	225	—
1761	—	35.00	90.00	145	225	—
1762	—	40.00	100	175	250	—

C# 45c 6 GROSZY

Silver **Ruler:** Elizabeth **Obv:** Crowned bust right **Obv. Legend:** ELISAB: I: IMP: TOT: RUSS **Rev:** Crowned eagle, VI on breast **Note:** Portrait varieties exist - long or short curls.

Date	Mintage	VG	F	VF	XF	Unc
1759	—	45.00	125	200	300	—

C# 46 18 GROSZY

Silver **Ruler:** Elizabeth **Subject:** Elizabeth **Obv. Legend:** ELISAB. I.D.G. IMP. TOT. RUSS **Rev. Legend:** ...PRVSSIAE

Date	Mintage	VG	F	VF	XF	Unc
1759	—	75.00	175	300	500	—

C# 46a 18 GROSZY

Silver **Ruler:** Elizabeth **Rev. Legend:** ...PRUSS

Date	Mintage	VG	F	VF	XF	Unc
1759	—	75.00	175	300	500	—
1760 large date	—	75.00	175	300	500	—
1761 small date	—	75.00	175	300	500	—

C# 46b 18 GROSZY

Silver **Ruler:** Elizabeth **Obv. Legend:** ELISAB. I.D.G. IMP. TOT. RUSSIAE **Rev. Legend:** ...PRVSSIAE:

Date	Mintage	VG	F	VF	XF	Unc
1759	—	75.00	175	300	500	—

C# 46c 18 GROSZY

Silver **Ruler:** Elizabeth **Rev. Legend:** ...PRUSS

Date	Mintage	VG	F	VF	XF	Unc
1759	—	100	250	400	650	—

C# 46d 18 GROSZY

Silver **Ruler:** Elizabeth **Obv. Legend:** ELISABETHA: I: IMP: TOT: RUSSIAE **Rev. Legend:** ...PRVSSIAE:

Date	Mintage	VG	F	VF	XF	Unc
1759	—	100	250	400	650	—

C# 46e 18 GROSZY

Silver **Ruler:** Elizabeth **Obv. Legend:** ELISABETHA: I: IMP: TOT: ROSS

Date	Mintage	VG	F	VF	XF	Unc
1759	—	150	350	600	1,000	—

C# 47 1/6 THALER (Reichs)

Silver **Ruler:** Elizabeth **Subject:** Elizabeth **Obv:** Crowned bust right **Obv. Legend:** ELISAB: I: D: G: IMP: .... **Rev:** Crowned eagle on mantle divides date, 6• EIN • R • TH COUR below

Date	Mintage	VG	F	VF	XF	Unc
1761	1,343,000	50.00	150	250	400	—

C# 47a 1/6 THALER (Reichs)

Silver **Ruler:** Elizabeth **Obv:** Crowned bust right **Rev:** Large, crowned eagle without mantle

Date	Mintage	VG	F	VF	XF	Unc
1761	Inc. above	50.00	150	250	400	—

C# 47b 1/6 THALER (Reichs)

Silver **Ruler:** Elizabeth **Obv:** Crowned bust right **Rev:** Small eagle without mantle

Date	Mintage	VG	F	VF	XF	Unc
1761	Inc. above	50.00	150	250	400	—

C# 48 1/3 THALER (Reichs)

Silver **Ruler:** Elizabeth **Obv:** Crowned bust right **Obv. Legend:** ELISAB: I: D: G: IMP: ... **Rev:** Crowned eagle on mantle divides date, 3• EIN • R • TH COUR below

Date	Mintage	VG	F	VF	XF	Unc
1761 large wings	470,000	100	175	265	425	—
1761 small wings	Inc. above	100	175	265	425	—

PRUSSIAN POSSESSION

STANDARD COINAGE

C# 51 SCHILLING

Billon **Ruler:** Friedrich Wilhelm II (of Prussia)

Date	Mintage	VG	F	VF	XF	Unc
1788 E	—	7.00	15.00	30.00	50.00	—

C# 50 SCHILLING

Copper **Ruler:** Friedrich Wilhelm II (of Prussia) **Obv:** Crowned monogram **Rev:** Written value, state and date

Date	Mintage	VG	F	VF	XF	Unc
1790 E	—	6.00	12.50	25.00	45.00	—
1790. E.	—	6.00	12.50	25.00	45.00	—

Date	Mintage	VG	F	VF	XF	Unc
1791 E	—	6.00	12.50	25.00	45.00	—
1791. E.	—	6.00	12.50	25.00	45.00	—
1792 E	—	6.00	12.50	25.00	45.00	—
1792 E.	—	6.00	12.50	25.00	45.00	—
1793 E	—	6.00	12.50	25.00	45.00	—
1793. E.	—	6.00	12.50	25.00	45.00	—
1794 E	—	6.00	12.50	25.00	45.00	—
1794. E.	—	6.00	12.50	25.00	45.00	—
1795. E.	—	6.00	12.50	25.00	45.00	—
1796. E.	—	6.00	12.50	25.00	45.00	—
1797 E large rosettes	—	6.00	12.50	25.00	45.00	—
1797 E small rosettes	—	6.00	12.50	25.00	45.00	—
1797. E.	—	6.00	12.50	25.00	45.00	—

C# 6 SOLIDUS

Billon **Ruler:** Friedrich II **Obv:** Crowned FR monogram, E below **Rev:** Value and date

Date	Mintage	VG	F	VF	XF	Unc
1764 E	1,595,000	4.00	10.00	18.00	30.00	—

C# 6a SOLIDUS

Billon **Ruler:** Friedrich II **Obv:** Crowned FR monogram divides date **Rev:** Written value, state, E below

Date	Mintage	VG	F	VF	XF	Unc
1766 E	948,000	4.00	10.00	18.00	30.00	—
1767 E	959,000	4.00	10.00	18.00	30.00	—
1768 E	825,000	4.00	10.00	18.00	30.00	—
1769 E	736,000	4.00	10.00	18.00	30.00	—
1770 E	Inc. above	4.00	10.00	18.00	30.00	—

C# 6b SOLIDUS

Billon **Ruler:** Friedrich II **Obv:** Crowned FR monogram, E below **Rev:** Written value, state and date

Date	Mintage	VG	F	VF	XF	Unc
1771 E	1,445,000	4.00	10.00	18.00	30.00	—
1775 E	1,973,000	4.00	10.00	18.00	30.00	—
1777 E	347,000	4.00	10.00	18.00	30.00	—
1779 E	758,000	4.00	10.00	18.00	30.00	—
1780 E	259,000	4.00	10.00	18.00	30.00	—
1781 E	640,000	4.00	10.00	18.00	30.00	—
1782 E	419,000	4.00	10.00	18.00	30.00	—
1783 E	468,000	4.00	10.00	18.00	30.00	—
1785 E	1,121,000	4.00	10.00	18.00	30.00	—
1786 E	830,000	4.00	10.00	18.00	30.00	—

C# 6c SOLIDUS

Billon **Ruler:** Friedrich II **Obv:** Crowned FR monogram, A below **Rev:** Written value, state and date

Date	Mintage	VG	F	VF	XF	Unc
1776 A	—	4.00	10.00	18.00	30.00	—

C# 8 GROSCHEN

Billon **Ruler:** Friedrich II **Obv:** Crowned eagle, E below **Rev:** Value and date

Date	Mintage	VG	F	VF	XF	Unc
1764 E	1,291,000	6.00	12.50	25.00	45.00	—
1769 E	876,000	6.00	12.50	25.00	45.00	—
1770 E	Inc. above	6.00	12.50	25.00	45.00	—

C# 10 GROSCHEN

Billon **Ruler:** Friedrich II **Obv:** Crowned flying eagle, E below

Date	Mintage	VG	F	VF	XF	Unc
1771 E	1,620,000	6.00	12.50	25.00	45.00	—
1772 E	151,000	6.00	12.50	25.00	45.00	—
1778 E	317,000	6.00	12.50	25.00	45.00	—
1779 E	208,000	6.00	12.50	25.00	45.00	—
1780 E	Inc. above	6.00	12.50	25.00	45.00	—
1781 E	78,000	6.00	12.50	25.00	45.00	—
1782 E	169,000	6.00	12.50	25.00	45.00	—
1783 E	526,000	6.00	12.50	25.00	45.00	—
1785 E	387,000	6.00	12.50	25.00	45.00	—
1786 E	—	6.00	12.50	25.00	45.00	—

C# 10a GROSCHEN

Billon **Ruler:** Friedrich II **Obv:** Crowned flying eagle, A below

Date	Mintage	VG	F	VF	XF	Unc
1776 A	—	7.00	15.00	28.00	48.00	—

C# 52 GROSCHEN

Billon **Ruler:** Friedrich Wilhelm II (of Prussia) **Obv:** Bust right **Rev:** Crowned arms divides value and date

Date	Mintage	VG	F	VF	XF	Unc
1787 E	—	6.00	12.50	25.00	45.00	—
1788 E	—	6.00	12.50	25.00	45.00	—
1790 E	—	6.00	12.50	25.00	45.00	—
1791 E	—	6.00	12.50	25.00	45.00	—
1792 E	—	6.00	12.50	25.00	45.00	—
1793 E	—	6.00	12.50	25.00	45.00	—
1794 E	—	6.00	12.50	25.00	45.00	—
1795 E	—	6.00	12.50	25.00	45.00	—
1796 E	—	6.00	12.50	25.00	45.00	—
1797 E	—	6.00	12.50	25.00	45.00	—
1798 E	—	6.00	12.50	25.00	45.00	—

C# 12 2 GROSCHEN (Grossus)

Billon **Ruler:** Friedrich II **Obv:** Crowned eagle, E below **Rev:** Value and date

Date	Mintage	VG	F	VF	XF	Unc
1764 E	960,000	8.00	20.00	30.00	55.00	—
1768 E	216,000	8.00	20.00	30.00	55.00	—

C# 14 2 GROSCHEN (Grossus)

Billon **Ruler:** Friedrich II **Obv:** Crowned flying eagle, E below

Date	Mintage	VG	F	VF	XF	Unc
1773 E	4,816,000	7.00	18.00	27.50	50.00	—

C# 17 3 GROSCHEN

Billon **Ruler:** Friedrich II **Obv:** Bare head of Friedrich right **Rev:** Crowned eagle, date above, value below

Date	Mintage	VG	F	VF	XF	Unc
1765 E	2,071,000	12.00	30.00	50.00	75.00	—

C# 18 3 GROSCHEN

Billon **Ruler:** Friedrich II **Obv:** Crowned head right

Date	Mintage	VG	F	VF	XF	Unc
1765 E	—	10.00	22.00	40.00	70.00	—
Note: Mintage included with C#7.						
1766 E	430,000	10.00	22.00	40.00	70.00	—
1767 E	Inc. above	10.00	22.00	40.00	70.00	—

C# 21 3 GROSCHEN

Billon **Ruler:** Friedrich II **Obv:** Laureate head right **Rev:** Crowned flying eagle, E, value "3gr" and date below

Date	Mintage	VG	F	VF	XF	Unc
1771 E	4,034,000	7.00	18.00	30.00	50.00	—
1772 E	2,292,000	7.00	18.00	30.00	50.00	—
1773 E	3,570,000	7.00	18.00	30.00	50.00	—
1774 E	4,784,000	7.00	18.00	30.00	50.00	—
1774 A	1,905,000	7.00	18.00	30.00	50.00	—
1775 A	742,000	7.00	18.00	30.00	50.00	—
1775 E	2,784,000	7.00	18.00	30.00	50.00	—
1776 E	1,785,000	7.00	18.00	30.00	50.00	—
1776 A	Inc. above	7.00	18.00	30.00	50.00	—
1777 E	1,071,000	7.00	18.00	30.00	50.00	—
1778 E	755,000	7.00	18.00	30.00	50.00	—
1779 E	893,000	7.00	18.00	30.00	50.00	—
1780 E	1,277,000	7.00	18.00	30.00	50.00	—
1781 E	2,065,999	7.00	18.00	30.00	50.00	—
1782 E	2,432,000	7.00	18.00	30.00	50.00	—
1783 E	2,540,000	7.00	18.00	30.00	50.00	—
1784 E	13,202,000	7.00	18.00	30.00	50.00	—
1785 E	8,352,000	7.00	18.00	30.00	50.00	—
1786 E	933,000	7.00	18.00	30.00	50.00	—

C# 21.1 3 GROSCHEN

Billon **Ruler:** Friedrich II **Obv:** Bare head of Fredrich right **Rev:** Crowned flying eagle with value of "3" below, without "gr"

Date	Mintage	Good	VG	F	VF	XF
1779 A	25,965,000	—	3.00	9.00	15.00	25.00
1780 A	27,208,000	—	3.00	9.00	15.00	25.00
1781 A	44,024,000	—	3.00	9.00	15.00	25.00
1782 A	38,758,000	—	3.00	9.00	15.00	25.00
1783 A	43,744,000	—	3.00	9.00	15.00	25.00
1784 A	23,005,000	—	3.00	9.00	15.00	25.00
1785 A	5,906,000	—	3.00	9.00	15.00	25.00

C# 60 3 GROSCHEN

Billon **Ruler:** Friedrich III (of Prussia) **Obv:** Bust left **Obv. Legend:** FRID • WILHELM ... **Rev:** Crowned eagle above value and date, A below

Date	Mintage	VG	F	VF	XF	Unc
1800 A	—	7.00	18.00	30.00	90.00	—

C# 28 6 GROSZY

Billon **Ruler:** Friedrich II **Obv:** Small, crowned head right **Rev:** Crowned eagle, date above, value and mint below

Date	Mintage	VG	F	VF	XF	Unc
1764 E	184,000	10.00	25.00	40.00	70.00	—
1770 E	—	20.00	40.00	100	150	—

C# 28a 6 GROSZY

Billon **Ruler:** Friedrich II **Obv:** Large, crowned head right **Rev:** Crowned eagle, date above, value and mint below

Date	Mintage	VG	F	VF	XF	Unc
1771 E	—	10.00	25.00	40.00	70.00	—
1772 E	—	10.00	25.00	40.00	70.00	—
1773 E	—	10.00	25.00	40.00	70.00	—
1774 E	—	10.00	25.00	40.00	70.00	—
1775 E	—	10.00	25.00	40.00	70.00	—
1776 E	—	10.00	25.00	40.00	70.00	—
1777 E	718,000	10.00	25.00	40.00	70.00	—
1778 E	646,000	10.00	25.00	40.00	70.00	—
1779 E	561,000	10.00	25.00	40.00	70.00	—
1780 E	341,000	10.00	25.00	40.00	70.00	—
1781 E	800,000	10.00	25.00	40.00	70.00	—

C# 29 6 GROSZY

Billon **Ruler:** Friedrich II

Date	Mintage	VG	F	VF	XF	Unc
1782 E	400,000	10.00	25.00	40.00	70.00	—
1783 E	232,000	10.00	25.00	40.00	70.00	—
1784 E	Inc. above	10.00	25.00	40.00	70.00	—

C# 30 18 GROSZY

6.1200 g., Silver, 26.8 mm. **Ruler:** Friedrich II **Obv:** Frederick the Great bare headed facing right **Rev:** Crowned eagle **Edge:** Plain

Date	Mintage	F	VF	XF	Unc	BU
1751E	—	—	—	—	—	—
1752E	—	—	—	—	—	—
1753E	—	—	—	—	—	—
1754E	—	—	—	—	—	—

C# 32 18 GROSZY

Billon **Ruler:** Friedrich II **Obv:** Crowned head right **Obv. Legend:** FRIDERICUS BORUSSORUM... **Rev:** Crowned eagle, E below

Date	Mintage	VG	F	VF	XF	Unc
1764 E	990,000	15.00	30.00	60.00	100	—
1765 E	1,466,000	15.00	30.00	60.00	100	—

PATTERNS

Including off metal strikes

KM#	Date	Mintage	Identification	Mkt Val
Pn1	1796 B	—	3 Groschen. Silver.	—
Pn2	1797 B	—	Solidus. Silver.	—
Pn3	1797 B	—	Groschen. Silver.	—

ELBING

Elbing is an important industrial city and seaport in northern Poland and was founded in 1237 (Elblag). They later joined the Hanseatic League. The city was under Polish control from 1454-1772 when it was annexed to Prussia. They produced their own coinage from 1454-1763.

RULER

August III (of Poland), 1733-1763

MINT OFFICIALS' INITIALS

Initials	Date	Name
CHS	1760-61	Conrad Heinrich Schwerdtner
FLS	1763	Friedrich Ludwig Stuber
HWS	1761	Heinrich Wilhelm Sellius
ICS	1762-63	Jost Carl Schroder

MONETARY SYSTEM

1-1/2 Groschen (Grosze) = Poltorak (1630-1633)

POLISH AUTHORITY

STANDARD COINAGE

KM# 100 SOLIDUS

Copper **Obv:** Crowned AR monogram with date below **Rev:** Legend, value **Rev. Legend:** SOLID/CIVITATE/ELBINGE

Date	Mintage	VG	F	VF	XF	Unc
1713	—	—	—	—	—	—

KM# 100a SOLIDUS

0.6200 g., Silver **Obv:** Crowned AR monogram with date below **Rev:** Legend, value **Rev. Legend:** SOLID/CIVITATE/ELBINGE

Date	Mintage	VG	F	VF	XF	Unc
1713	—	25.00	50.00	80.00	125	—

KM# 105 SOLIDUS

Copper **Obv:** Crowned AR monogram divides date **Rev:** Legend, value **Rev. Legend:** SOLID/CIVITAT/ELBING

Date	Mintage	VG	F	VF	XF	Unc
1760	—	20.00	35.00	65.00	100	—
1760 CHS	—	25.00	45.00	90.00	150	—
1761	—	15.00	25.00	40.00	60.00	—
1761 CHS	—	25.00	45.00	90.00	150	—
1761 HWS	—	15.00	25.00	40.00	60.00	—
1763 ICS	—	10.00	20.00	35.00	55.00	—
1763 FLS	—	10.00	20.00	35.00	55.00	—

KM# 106 3 GROSZE

1.5300 g., Billon **Obv:** Crowned AR monogram divides date **Rev:** 3 Below ornate arms of Elbing

Date	Mintage	VG	F	VF	XF	Unc
1761	—	30.00	50.00	90.00	160	—
1763	—	30.00	50.00	90.00	160	—

KM# 109 3 GROSZE
1.5300 g., Billon **Rev:** 3 above ornate arms of Elbing

Date	Mintage	VG	F	VF	XF	Unc
1763 FLS	—	25.00	45.00	85.00	150	—

KM# 110 3 GROSZE
1.5300 g., Billon **Rev:** Ornate arms of Elbing, without 3

Date	Mintage	VG	F	VF	XF	Unc
1763 FLS	—	30.00	50.00	90.00	160	—

KM# 107 6 GROSZY
2.9400 g., Billon **Ruler:** August III **Obv:** Crowned bust right **Obv. Legend:** D • G • AVGVST • III • .... **Rev:** VI above oval arms with supporters, date below **Rev. Legend:** MON • ARGENT • CIVIT • ELBIN GENSIS •

Date	Mintage	VG	F	VF	XF	Unc
1762 ICS Rare	—	—	—	—	—	—

KM# 108 6 GROSZY
2.9400 g., Billon **Ruler:** August III **Obv:** Crowned bust right **Obv. Legend:** D • G • AVGVST • III • ... **Rev:** Ornate arms of Elbing divides date, VI above, mint initials below **Rev. Legend:** MON • ARGENT • CIVIT • ELBINGENSIS •

Date	Mintage	VG	F	VF	XF	Unc
1762 ICS	—	35.00	60.00	125	225	—
1763 ICS	—	35.00	60.00	125	225	—
1763 FLS	—	35.00	60.00	125	225	—

KM# 111 6 GROSZY
2.9400 g., Billon **Note:** Kllippe.

Date	Mintage	VG	F	VF	XF	Unc
1763 ICS	—	—	—	—	—	—
1763 FLS	—	—	—	—	—	—

KM# 112 18 GROSZY
Silver **Ruler:** August III **Obv:** Crowned bust right **Obv. Legend:** D • G • AVGVST • III • R • POL • ... **Rev:** Ornate oval arms of Elbing with value above, divided date below **Rev. Inscription:** MONETA • ARGENT • EA CIVITELBINGENSIS •

Date	Mintage	VG	F	VF	XF	Unc
1763 ICS	—	250	500	950	1,750	—

KM# 113 TYMPF
6.1000 g., Silver **Ruler:** August III **Obv:** Crowned bust right **Obv. Legend:** D • G • AVGVST • III • R • POL • M • D • ... **Rev:** Ornate oval arms of Elbing with initials above, divided date and "Secvind : red" written below **Rev. Legend:** MONETA • ARGENTEA • CIVIT • ELBINGENSIS •

Date	Mintage	VG	F	VF	XF	Unc
1763 FLS	—	100	200	450	1,000	—

KM# 114 TYMPF
6.1000 g., Silver

Date	Mintage	VG	F	VF	XF	Unc
1763 FLS	—	100	200	450	1,000	—

KM# 116 TYMPF
6.1000 g., Silver **Note:** Klippe.

Date	Mintage	VG	F	VF	XF	Unc
1763 FLS	—	—	—	—	—	—

TRADE COINAGE

KM# 115 2 DUCAT
7.0000 g., 0.9860 Gold 0.2219 oz. AGW **Ruler:** August III **Obv:** Crowned bust right **Rev:** Value above ornate arms of Elbing, date divided below

Date	Mintage	VG	F	VF	XF	Unc
1763 ICS Rare	—	—	—	—	—	—

PATTERNS

Including off metal strikes

KM#	Date	Mintage	Identification	Mkt Val
Pn5	1761 HWS	—	Solidus. Silver.	325
Pn6	1762 ICS	—	6 Groschen. Silver. KM108.	850
Pn7	1762 ICS	—	6 Groschen. Gold. KM108.	—
Pn8	1763 ICS	—	Solidus. Silver. KM105.	325
Pn9	1763 FLS	—	Solidus. Silver. KM105.	325
Pn10	1763 ICS	—	6 Groschen. Gold. KM108.	—

GALICIA & LODOMERIA

Oswiecim (Auschwitz) and Zator

This ancient principality is part of modern Poland and Russia. Became part of Poland in 1386 and was passed to Austria in the first partition of Poland in 1772. Coins were made at Oswiecim for the area with special Austrian types in the 1770's and 1790's.

MINT MARKS

A - Vienna
S – Schmollnitz

MINT OFFICIALS' INITIALS

Initials	Date	Name
A, FA	1774-80	Franz von Aicherau, warden
C, IC	1766-80	Johann August Cronberg

MONETARY SYSTEM

6 Schillings (Solidi) = 2 Grosze= 1 Kreuzer

PRINCIPALITY

STANDARD COINAGE

C# 1 SCHILLING
Copper **Obv:** Crowned arms **Rev:** Value above date, S below

Date	Mintage	Good	VG	F	VF	XF
1774	—	—	15.00	30.00	60.00	100

C# 4 GROSSUS
Copper **Obv:** Crowned double-headed eagle, small shield on breast, above crossed flags **Rev:** Value, date above sprigs

Date	Mintage	Good	VG	F	VF	XF
1794	—	—	20.00	35.00	70.00	120

Note: Used by the Austrian Army fighting Kosciuzko

C# 5 3 GROSSI (III Grossi)
Copper **Obv:** Crowned double-headed eagle, small shield on breast, above crossed flags **Rev:** Value, date above sprigs

Date	Mintage	Good	VG	F	VF	XF
1794	—	—	25.00	40.00	80.00	150

Note: Used by the Austrian Army fighting Kosciuzko

C# 2 15 KREUZER
Silver **Subject:** Maria Theresa **Obv:** Veiled, bust right above sprigs and inscription **Obv. Legend:** M • THERESIA • D • G • R • I • ... **Rev:** Crowned arms of Elbing within roped design, value below **Rev. Legend:** ARCHID • AUS • DUX • OSW • ZAT • 1776 •

Date	Mintage	Good	VG	F	VF	XF
1775 C-A	—	—	25.00	45.00	200	350
1776 C-A	—	—	25.00	45.00	200	350
1777 C-A	—	—	25.00	45.00	200	350

C# 3 30 KREUZER
Silver **Subject:** Maria Theresa **Obv:** Veiled, bust right **Obv. Legend:** M • THERESIA • D • G • R • I • ... **Rev:** Crowned arms of Elbing, with supporters, value below

Date	Mintage	Good	VG	F	VF	XF
1775 IC-FA	—	—	35.00	60.00	180	300
1776 IC-FA	—	—	35.00	60.00	180	300
1777 IC-FA	—	—	35.00	60.00	180	300

PATTERNS

Including off metal strikes

KM#	Date	Mintage	Identification	Mkt Val
Pn1	1775 C-A	—	30 Kreuzer. Silver. Supported arms.	—
Pn2	1775 C-A	—	30 Kreuzer. Silver. Arms.	—
Pn3	1794	—	V1 Grossi. Billon. C#6.	3,750

GNESEN

Gnesen is a bishopric 28 miles east-northeast of Poznan. The cathedral located there contains relics of Poland's patron saint, St. Adalbert. It was the location of coronations of Polish kings until 1320.

RULER

Stanislaus Szembek, 1706-1721

BISHOPRIC

STANDARD COINAGE

FR# 46 DUCAT
3.5000 g., 0.9860 Gold 0.1109 oz. AGW **Ruler:** Stanislaus Szembek **Obv:** Bust right **Rev:** Mitre and crown above shield within mantle, Cardinals' hat above

Date	Mintage	VG	F	VF	XF	Unc
1721	—	1,600	3,000	5,500	9,000	—

KRAKOW

Krakow is located in southern Poland and is the third largest city in the country. From 1815 thru 1846 it was an independent republic, after which it reverted to Austria. Coins made for the republic in 1835.

RULER

Cajetan Soltyk, 1759-1782

MONETARY SYSTEM

30 Groszy = 1 Zloty

CITY

STANDARD COINAGE

KM# 2 GROSZ
Silver **Ruler:** Cajetan Soltyk

Date	Mintage	Good	VG	F	VF	XF
1761	—	—	500	1,000	2,000	3,000

TRADE COINAGE

KM# 1 DUCAT
3.5000 g., 0.9860 Gold 0.1109 oz. AGW **Ruler:** Cajetan Soltyk **Obv:** Bust left **Rev:** 4-line inscription, date within narrow wreath

Date	Mintage	Good	VG	F	VF	XF
1762	—	—	1,650	3,250	6,000	10,000

SOUTH PRUSSIA

South Prussia (Borussia Meridionalis) consisted of the central provinces of Prussian Poland between West Prussia and Silesia taken by Prussia in the second and third partitions of Poland. With the territory seized by Austria in the third partition, it formed the Grand Duchy of Warsaw created by Napoleon in 1807. The duchy was occupied by Russia after Napoleon's Russian defeat.

PROVINCE

STANDARD COINAGE

C# 1 SOLIDUS

Copper **Obv:** FWR monogram **Rev:** Value

Date	Mintage	Good	VG	F	VF	XF
1796B	—	—	8.00	15.00	20.00	35.00
1796E	—	—	6.00	10.00	18.00	30.00
1797B	—	—	3.00	6.00	15.00	25.00
1797E	—	—	3.00	6.00	17.00	27.50

C# 2 1/2 GROSSUS

Copper **Obv:** Monogram **Rev. Legend:** REGNI BORUSS

Date	Mintage	Good	VG	F	VF	XF
1796B	—	—	4.00	8.00	20.00	40.00

C# 2.1 1/2 GROSSUS

Copper **Obv:** Crowned monogram within circle and wreath **Rev:** Value, legend and date **Rev. Legend:** ROSSUS/BORUSS/ MERID/ date

Date	Mintage	Good	VG	F	VF	XF
1796B	—	—	5.00	10.00	20.00	40.00
1796E	—	—	5.00	10.00	20.00	40.00
1797B	—	—	5.00	10.00	20.00	40.00
1797E	—	—	5.00	10.00	20.00	40.00

C# 3 GROSSUS

Copper **Obv:** Head right **Rev:** Crowned oval arms within wreath

Date	Mintage	Good	VG	F	VF	XF
1796B	—	—	10.00	20.00	35.00	60.00
1796E	—	—	10.00	20.00	35.00	60.00
1797B	—	—	10.00	20.00	35.00	60.00
1797E	—	—	10.00	20.00	35.00	60.00
1798E	—	—	10.00	20.00	35.00	60.00
1798B	—	—	10.00	20.00	35.00	60.00

C# 4 3 GROSSUS

Copper **Obv:** Head right **Rev:** Crowned oval arms within wreath **Rev. Legend:** GROSSUS BORUSSIAE TRIPLEX

Date	Mintage	Good	VG	F	VF	XF
1796A	—	—	12.00	25.00	50.00	90.00

C# 4a 3 GROSSUS

Copper **Obv:** Head right **Rev:** Crowned oval arms within wreath **Rev. Legend:** GROSSUS BORUSS MERID..TRIPLEX

Date	Mintage	Good	VG	F	VF	XF
1796B	—	—	12.00	25.00	45.00	80.00
1796E	—	—	12.00	25.00	45.00	80.00
1797A	—	—	12.00	25.00	45.00	80.00
1797B	—	—	12.00	25.00	45.00	80.00
1797E	—	—	12.00	25.00	45.00	80.00

THORN

Thorn is an industrial city in north-central Poland which was founded in 1231. They became a member of the Hanseatic League. The city came under Polish suzerainty (Torun) in 1454 and remained until they were absorbed by Prussia in 1793, except for brief periods of Swedish Occupation from1655-58 and during the Great Northern War (1703) when they were ruled by Sweden.

The city of Thorn was the birthplace of the astronomer, Copernicus. The last city coinage was struck in 1765.

RULERS

Sigismund III, 1587-1632
Wladislaus IV, 1632-1648
Johann Casimir, 1648-1655, 1658-1668
Swedish, 1655-1658
Michael Korybut, 1669-1673
August II of Saxony, 1697-1733
Augustus III (of Poland), 1733-1763
Stanislaus Augustus (of Poland), 1764-1793

MINT OFFICIALS' INITIALS

Initial	Date	Name
DB, DR	1760-63	Daniel Bottcher
GR	1643-49	Gerhard Rogge, tenant
HDL	1649-68	Hans Daniel Lauer, tenant during Swedish Occupation
HH	1629-31	Jenryk Hema, warden
HIL	1653-55	Hans Jacob Lauer
HL	1630	Hans Lippe, tenant
HS	1668-72	Heinrich Sievert
II	1630	Jacob Jacobson van Emden
MS	1640-42	Melchior Schirmer, tenant
SB	1763-65	Samuel Bruckmann

CITY

STANDARD COINAGE

KM# 60 SOLIDUS

0.6200 g., Copper **Ruler:** Augustus III of Poland **Obv:** Crowned monogram divides date, 3 within monogram **Rev:** Value and city name above castle

Date	Mintage	VG	F	VF	XF	Unc
1760	—	15.00	25.00	45.00	75.00	—
1760 D-B	—	15.00	25.00	45.00	75.00	—
1761	—	15.00	25.00	45.00	75.00	—
1761 D-B	—	15.00	25.00	45.00	75.00	—
1762	—	20.00	35.00	55.00	85.00	—
1762 D-B	—	15.00	25.00	45.00	75.00	—
1763	—	15.00	25.00	45.00	75.00	—
1763 D-B	—	15.00	25.00	45.00	75.00	—

KM# 61 SOLIDUS

Copper **Ruler:** Augustus III of Poland **Note:** Klippe.

Date	Mintage	VG	F	VF	XF	Unc
1760	—	—	—	—	—	—

KM# 65 SOLIDUS

Copper **Ruler:** Stanislaus Augustus of Poland **Obv:** Crowned SAR monogram divides date

Date	Mintage	VG	F	VF	XF	Unc
1765	—	12.00	20.00	40.00	70.00	—

KM# 63 3 GROSZE

1.5300 g., Billon **Ruler:** Augustus III of Poland **Obv:** Crowned monogram divides date, 3 below, within monogram **Rev:** Angel above castle **Rev. Legend:** GROSSUS • TRIPLEX • THORUNENSIS

Date	Mintage	VG	F	VF	XF	Unc
1763	—	15.00	25.00	45.00	75.00	—
1763 S-B	—	15.00	25.00	45.00	75.00	—
1763 D-B	—	15.00	25.00	45.00	75.00	—
1763 D-R	—	15.00	25.00	50.00	85.00	—

KM# 64 3 GROSZE

Billon **Ruler:** Stanislaus Augustus of Poland **Obv:** Crowned SAR monogram divides date

Date	Mintage	VG	F	VF	XF	Unc
1764 S-B	—	20.00	40.00	65.00	100	—
1765 S-B	—	15.00	30.00	60.00	90.00	—

KM# 62 6 GROSZY

Billon **Ruler:** Augustus III of Poland **Obv:** Crowned bust right **Obv. Legend:** D • G • AVGVST • III • R • POLM • .... **Rev:** Shield divides date, angel above

Date	Mintage	VG	F	VF	XF	Unc
1761	—	25.00	50.00	75.00	120	—
1762	—	25.00	55.00	85.00	175	—
1762 D-B	—	25.00	55.00	85.00	175	—
1763	—	25.00	50.00	75.00	120	—
1763 D-B	—	25.00	50.00	75.00	120	—
1763 S-B	—	25.00	50.00	75.00	120	—

KM# 66 6 GROSZY

Billon **Ruler:** Stanislaus Augustus of Poland **Obv:** Crowned bust right **Rev:** Angel above arms divides date

Date	Mintage	VG	F	VF	XF	Unc
1765 S-B	—	75.00	150	300	650	—

TRADE COINAGE

KM# 55 DUCAT (Dukat)

3.5000 g., 0.9860 Gold 0.1109 oz. AGW **Ruler:** August II of Saxony **Obv:** Crowned bust right **Obv. Legend:** AUGUST • II • D • G • REX • ... **Rev:** Angel above arms divides date within circle **Rev. Legend:** MONETA • AVREA • ...

Date	Mintage	VG	F	VF	XF	Unc
1702	—	1,650	3,250	6,000	10,000	—

PATTERNS

Including off metal strikes

KM#	Date	Mintage	Identification	Mkt Val
Pn3	1702	—	Ducat. Silver. KM55.	1,750
Pn4	1760	—	Solidus. Silver. KM60.	125
Pn5	1761	—	Solidus. Silver. KM60.	125
Pn6	1762	—	Solidus. Silver. KM60.	125

PORTUGAL

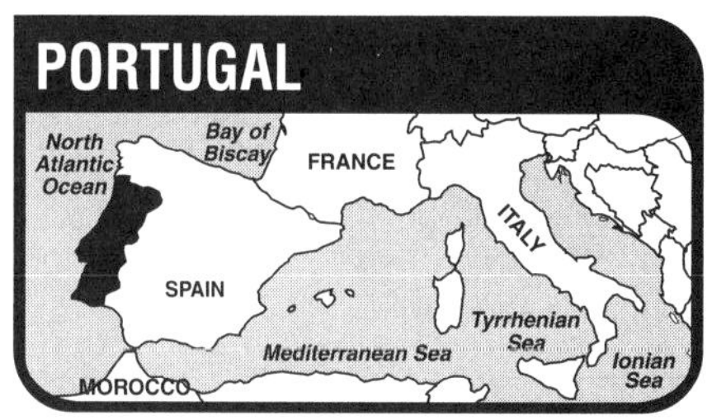

The Portuguese Republic, located in the western part of the Iberian Peninsula in southwestern Europe, has an area of 35,553 sq. mi. (92,080 sq. km.) and a population of *10.5 million. Capital: Lisbon. Portugal's economy is based on agriculture, tourism, minerals, fisheries and a rapidly expanding industrial sector. Textiles account for 33% of the exports and Portuguese wine is world famous. Portugal has become Europe's number one producer of copper and the world's largest producer of cork.

After centuries of domination by Romans, Visigoths and Moors, Portugal emerged in the 12th century as an independent kingdom financially and philosophically prepared for the great period of exploration that would soon follow. Attuned to the inspiration of Prince Henry the Navigator (1394-1460), Portugal's daring explorers of the15th and 16th centuries roamed the world's oceans from Brazil to Japan in an unprecedented burst of energy and endeavor that culminated in 1494 with Portugal laying claim to half the transoceanic world. Unfortunately for the fortunes of the tiny kingdom, the Portuguese population was too small to colonize this vast territory. Less than a century after Portugal laid claim to half the world, English, French and Dutch trading companies had seized the lion's share of the world's colonies and commerce, and Portugal's place as an imperial power was lost forever. The monarchy was overthrown in 1910 and a republic was established.

On April 25, 1974, the government of Portugal was seized by a military junta which reached agreements providing for independence for the Portuguese overseas provinces of Portuguese Guinea (*Guinea-Bissau*), Mozambique, Cape Verde Islands, Angola, and St. Thomas and Prince Islands (*Sao Tome and Principe*).

On January 1, 1986, Portugal became the eleventh member of the European Economic Community and in the first half of 1992 held its first EEC Presidency.

RULERS

Peter II, 1683-1706
John V, 1706-1750
Jose (Joseph) I, 1750-1777
Maria I and Pedro III, 1777-1786
Maria I, 1786-1799
Joao, As Prince Regent, 1799-1816

MONETARY SYSTEM

Until 1825

20 Reis = 1 Vintem
100 Reis = 1 Tostao
480 Reis = 24 Vintens = 1 Cruzado
1600 Reis = 1 Escudo
6400 Reis = 4 Escudos = 1 Peca

KINGDOM

MILLED COINAGE

KM# 165 1-1/2 REIS

Copper **Ruler:** Peter II **Obv:** Crown above P:II within wreath **Obv. Legend:** D • G • PORT • ET • ALG • REX **Rev:** Value within wreath, date above **Rev. Legend:** VTILITATI • PVBLICÆ **Note:** Varieties exist with center turned 180 degrees.

Date	Mintage	VG	F	VF	XF	Unc
1699	—	10.00	20.00	40.00	80.00	—
1703	—	15.00	30.00	60.00	120	—

KM# 193 1-1/2 REIS

Copper **Ruler:** John V **Obv:** Crown above JV **Rev:** Value within wreath, date above **Note:** Varieties exist.

Date	Mintage	VG	F	VF	XF	Unc
1712	—	35.00	70.00	200	300	—
1713	—	600	1,000	—	—	—

Date	Mintage	VG	F	VF	XF	Unc
1714	—	15.00	30.00	75.00	150	—
1717 Rare	—	—	—	—	—	—

KM# 166 3 REIS (III)

Copper **Ruler:** Peter II **Obv:** Crown above PII within wreath **Rev:** Value within wreath **Note:** Varieties exist.

Date	Mintage	VG	F	VF	XF	Unc
1699	—	10.00	25.00	40.00	80.00	—
1703	—	15.00	35.00	60.00	120	—

KM# 190 3 REIS (III)

Copper **Ruler:** John V **Obv:** Crowned JV within beaded circle **Obv. Legend:** D • G • PORT • ETALG • REX • **Rev:** Value within wreath **Rev. Legend:** PVBLIC Æ 1741 VTILITATI

Date	Mintage	VG	F	VF	XF	Unc
1712	—	30.00	60.00	125	225	—
1713	—	15.00	30.00	85.00	175	—
1714	—	6.00	12.00	35.00	80.00	—
1717 Rare	—	—	—	—	—	—
1720	—	6.00	12.00	40.00	90.00	—
1721	—	8.00	16.00	50.00	90.00	—

KM# 215 3 REIS (III)

Copper **Ruler:** John V **Obv:** Crowned shield in baroque frame **Obv. Legend:** IOANNES • V • DEI • GRATIA **Rev:** Value and date within wreath **Rev. Legend:** PORTUGALIÆ • ET • ALGARB.....

Date	Mintage	VG	F	VF	XF	Unc
1723	—	20.00	35.00	75.00	125	—
1724	—	6.00	12.00	30.00	60.00	—
1732	—	5.00	10.00	25.00	50.00	—
1733	—	15.00	30.00	70.00	125	—

KM# 225 3 REIS (III)

Copper **Ruler:** John V **Obv:** Crowned shield in baroque frame **Rev:** Value and date within wreath **Rev. Legend:** PORTUGALIÆ • ET • ALGARBIORUM • REX **Note:** 25mm.

Date	Mintage	VG	F	VF	XF	Unc
1734	—	6.00	12.00	40.00	75.00	—
1737	—	6.00	12.00	40.00	75.00	—
1738	—	6.00	12.00	40.00	75.00	—
1744	—	6.00	12.00	40.00	75.00	—

KM# 241.1 3 REIS (III)

Copper **Ruler:** Jose I **Obv:** Crowned shield in baroque frame **Obv. Legend:** JOSEPHUS • I • DEI • GRATIA **Rev:** Value and date within wreath **Rev. Legend:** PORTUGALIÆ • ET • ALGARBIORUM • REX

Date	Mintage	VG	F	VF	XF	Unc
1751	—	6.00	12.00	30.00	60.00	—
1764	100,000	6.00	12.00	30.00	60.00	—
1776	—	7.00	15.00	55.00	100	—

KM# 241.2 3 REIS (III)

Copper **Ruler:** Jose I **Obv:** Crowned arms in baroque frame **Obv. Legend:** IOSEPHUS • I • DEI • GRATIA **Rev:** Value and date within wreath **Rev. Legend:** PORTUGALIÆ • ET • ALGARBIORUM • REX

Date	Mintage	VG	F	VF	XF	Unc
1751	—	6.00	12.00	30.00	60.00	—
1764	—	5.00	10.00	30.00	65.00	—

KM# 260 3 REIS (III)

Copper **Ruler:** Maria I and Pedro III **Obv:** Crowned arms in baroque frame **Obv. Legend:** MARIA I ET PETRUS III.. **Rev:** Value within wreath **Rev. Legend:** PORTUGAL..

Date	Mintage	VG	F	VF	XF	Unc
1777	689,000	10.00	20.00	60.00	125	—
1778 Rare	—	—	—	—	—	—

KM# 308 3 REIS (III)

Copper **Ruler:** Maria I **Obv:** Crowned arms in baroque frame **Obv. Legend:** MARIA • I • DEI • GRATIA **Rev:** Value within wreath **Rev. Legend:** PORTUGALIÆ • ET • ALGARBIORUM • REGINA

Date	Mintage	VG	F	VF	XF	Unc
1797	—	3.00	6.00	20.00	40.00	—

KM# 167 5 REIS (V)

Copper **Ruler:** Peter II **Obv:** Crown above P II within wreath **Obv. Legend:** D • G • PORT • ET • ALG • REX **Rev:** Value within wreath, date above **Rev. Legend:** PVBLICÆ ....

Date	Mintage	VG	F	VF	XF	Unc
1699	—	10.00	25.00	40.00	80.00	—
1703	—	8.00	15.00	35.00	75.00	—

KM# 194 5 REIS (V)

Copper **Ruler:** John V **Obv:** Crown above J V within wreath **Rev:** Value within wreath, date above

Date	Mintage	VG	F	VF	XF	Unc
1712	—	350	750	1,500	3,000	—
1713	—	5.00	10.00	20.00	45.00	—
1714	—	5.00	10.00	25.00	55.00	—
1717	—	35.00	75.00	150	300	—
1721	—	12.00	25.00	75.00	150	—

KM# 216 5 REIS (V)

Copper **Ruler:** John V **Obv:** Crowned arms in baroque frame **Obv. Legend:** IOANNES • V DEI • GRATIA **Rev:** Value within wreath, date below **Rev. Legend:** PORTUGALIÆ • ET • ALGARBIORUM • REX **Note:** Similar to KM#226

Date	Mintage	VG	F	VF	XF	Unc
1723	—	13.00	25.00	55.00	100	—
1724	—	13.00	25.00	55.00	100	—
1726	—	55.00	125	300	550	—
1728	—	6.00	12.00	35.00	70.00	—
1732	—	15.00	30.00	55.00	100	—
1734	—	5.00	10.00	25.00	55.00	—
1735	—	5.00	10.00	30.00	60.00	—
1736	—	5.00	10.00	20.00	45.00	—

KM# 226 5 REIS (V)

Copper **Ruler:** John V **Obv:** Crowned arms in baroque frame **Obv. Legend:** IOANNES • V • DEIGRATIA **Rev:** Value within wreath, date above **Rev. Legend:** PORTUGALIÆ • ET • ALGARBIORUM • REX

Date	Mintage	VG	F	VF	XF	Unc
1737	—	5.00	10.00	25.00	50.00	—
1738	—	5.00	10.00	25.00	50.00	—
1742	—	18.00	35.00	70.00	145	—
1743	—	5.00	10.00	30.00	60.00	—
1744	—	5.00	10.00	30.00	60.00	—
1746	—	6.00	12.00	35.00	70.00	—

KM# 242.1 5 REIS (V)

Copper **Ruler:** Jose I **Obv:** Crowned arms in baroque frame **Obv. Legend:** IOSEPHUS • I • DEI • GRATIA **Rev:** Value, date within wreath **Rev. Legend:** PORTUGALIÆ • ET • ALGARBIORUM • REX •

Date	Mintage	VG	F	VF	XF	Unc
1751	256,000	5.00	10.00	30.00	60.00	—
1752	—	5.00	10.00	30.00	60.00	—
1754	—	5.00	10.00	30.00	60.00	—
1757	—	5.00	10.00	30.00	60.00	—
1764	—	5.00	10.00	30.00	60.00	—
1766	—	7.00	15.00	45.00	80.00	—

KM# 242.2 5 REIS (V)

Copper **Ruler:** Jose I **Obv:** Crowned arms in baroque frame **Obv. Legend:** JOSEPHUS • I • DEI • GRATIA **Rev:** Value within wreath, date below **Rev. Legend:** PORTUGALIÆ • ET • ALGARBIORUM • REX

Date	Mintage	VG	F	VF	XF	Unc
1752	—	250	500	750	1,500	—
1754	—	30.00	65.00	100	200	—
1757	1,858,000	25.00	45.00	100	200	—
1764	3,444,000	6.00	12.00	35.00	75.00	—
1766	669,000	6.00	12.00	35.00	75.00	—
1776	802,000	6.00	12.00	50.00	100	—

KM# 261 5 REIS (V)

Copper **Ruler:** Maria I and Pedro III **Obv:** Crowned arms in baroque frame **Obv. Legend:** MARIA I DEI GRATIA **Rev:** Value within wreath **Rev. Legend:** PORTUGAL...

Date	Mintage	VG	F	VF	XF	Unc
1777	785,000	10.00	20.00	55.00	100	—
1778	423,000	7.00	15.00	45.00	75.00	—
1782	139,000	7.00	15.00	45.00	75.00	—
1785	578,000	7.00	15.00	45.00	75.00	—

KM# 305 5 REIS (V)

Copper **Ruler:** Maria I **Obv:** Crowned arms in baroque frame **Obv. Legend:** MARIA • I • DEI • GRATIA **Rev:** Value divides date within wreath **Rev. Legend:** PORTUGALIÆ • ET • ALGARBIORUM • REGINA

Date	Mintage	VG	F	VF	XF	Unc
1791	—	8.00	16.00	50.00	90.00	—
1792	602,000	7.00	15.00	45.00	75.00	—
1797	219,000	3.00	7.00	22.00	40.00	—
1799	33,000	3.00	7.00	22.00	40.00	—

KM# 326 5 REIS (V)

Copper **Ruler:** Maria I **Obv:** Crowned arms **Rev:** Value divides date within wreath **Note:** Mule.

Date	Mintage	VG	F	VF	XF	Unc
1799	—	35.00	65.00	150	300	—

KM# 168 10 REIS (X; 1/2 Vinten)

Copper **Ruler:** Peter II **Obv:** Crowned PII within broken rope wreath **Obv. Legend:** D • G • PORT ET • ALG • REX **Rev:** Value (X) within wreath, date above **Rev. Legend:** VTILITATI .... **Note:** Varieties exist.

Date	Mintage	VG	F	VF	XF	Unc
1699	—	10.00	25.00	45.00	90.00	—
1703	—	12.00	28.00	50.00	100	—

KM# 191 10 REIS (X; 1/2 Vinten)

Copper **Ruler:** John V **Obv:** Crown above JV within broken rope wreath **Obv. Legend:** D • G • PORT • ET • ALG • REX **Rev:** Value (X) within wreath, date above **Rev. Legend:** VTILITATI.... **Note:** Varieties exist.

Date	Mintage	VG	F	VF	XF	Unc
1712	—	400	750	1,500	3,000	—
1713	—	6.00	12.00	35.00	85.00	—
1714	—	20.00	45.00	100	200	—
1717	—	20.00	40.00	95.00	175	—
1720	—	6.00	12.00	35.00	70.00	—
1721	—	6.00	12.00	30.00	65.00	—
1771 Error	—	40.00	80.00	175	350	—

KM# 217 10 REIS (X; 1/2 Vinten)

Copper **Ruler:** John V **Obv:** Crowned arms in baroque frame **Obv. Legend:** IOANNES • V • DEI • GRATIA **Rev:** Value (X) and date within wreath **Rev. Legend:** PORTUGALIÆ • ET • ALGARBIORUM • REX

Date	Mintage	VG	F	VF	XF	Unc
1723	—	25.00	60.00	125	250	—
1724	—	12.00	35.00	75.00	150	—
1726	—	25.00	75.00	175	350	—
1727	—	6.00	12.00	35.00	70.00	—
1732	—	6.00	12.00	35.00	70.00	—
1734	—	5.00	10.00	30.00	60.00	—
1735	—	7.00	15.00	50.00	90.00	—
1736	—	6.00	12.00	40.00	80.00	—
1737	—	9.00	18.00	55.00	100	—

KM# 227 10 REIS (X; 1/2 Vinten)

Copper **Ruler:** John V **Obv:** Crowned arms in baroque frame **Rev:** Value in wreath, date below **Note:** 33mm.

Date	Mintage	VG	F	VF	XF	Unc
1737	—	4.00	9.00	25.00	55.00	—
1738	—	4.00	9.00	25.00	55.00	—
1742	—	12.00	25.00	55.00	120	—
1743	—	4.00	9.00	30.00	65.00	—
1744	—	7.00	15.00	50.00	100	—
1745	—	7.00	15.00	50.00	100	—
1746	—	9.00	18.00	70.00	125	—
1747	—	9.00	18.00	70.00	125	—
1748	—	12.00	25.00	85.00	175	—
1749	—	4.00	9.00	30.00	65.00	—

KM# 243.1 10 REIS (X; 1/2 Vinten)

Copper **Ruler:** Jose I **Obv:** Crowned arms in baroque frame **Obv. Legend:** IOSEPHUS... **Rev:** Value in wreath, date below

Date	Mintage	VG	F	VF	XF	Unc
1751	—	10.00	20.00	70.00	125	—
1752	—	3.00	7.00	25.00	55.00	—
1754	—	3.00	7.00	25.00	55.00	—
1757	—	3.00	7.00	25.00	55.00	—
1760	—	4.00	8.00	30.00	65.00	—
1761	2,394,000	20.00	35.00	100	200	—
1763	—	15.00	30.00	100	200	—
1764	—	3.00	7.00	25.00	55.00	—
1765	—	20.00	40.00	100	200	—

KM# 243.2 10 REIS (X; 1/2 Vinten)

Copper **Ruler:** Jose I **Obv:** Crowned arms in baroque frame **Obv. Legend:** JOSEPHUS... **Rev:** Value in wreath, date below **Note:** KM#243.1 is found muled with reverses of Joannes (John) V dated 1738 and 1749. This value also comes muled with a Joannes (John) V obverse and a reverse dated 1751.

Date	Mintage	VG	F	VF	XF	Unc
1752	497,000	9.00	18.00	50.00	100	—
1754	1,169,000	7.00	15.00	50.00	100	—
1757	1,114,000	6.00	14.00	40.00	80.00	—
1760	—	3.00	7.00	20.00	45.00	—
1763	—	3.00	7.00	20.00	45.00	—
1764	3,601,000	3.00	7.00	20.00	45.00	—
1765	4,525,000	3.00	7.00	20.00	45.00	—
1776	2,021,000	5.00	10.00	35.00	70.00	—

KM# 262 10 REIS (X; 1/2 Vinten)

Copper **Ruler:** Maria I and Pedro III **Obv:** Crowned arms in baroque frame **Obv. Legend:** MARIA I ET PETRUS III... **Rev:** Value within wreath **Rev. Legend:** PORTUGAL...

Date	Mintage	VG	F	VF	XF	Unc
1777	1,202,000	7.50	15.00	30.00	65.00	—
1778	457,000	7.50	15.00	30.00	65.00	—
1779	—	20.00	40.00	100	200	—

KM# 252 10 REIS (X; 1/2 Vinten)

12.8300 g., Copper, 34.8 mm. **Ruler:** Maria I and Pedro III **Obv:** Crowned arms **Rev:** Denomination "X" divides date in wreath **Edge:** Plain

Date	Mintage	VG	F	VF	XF	Unc
1777INCM	—	—	—	—	—	—

KM# 280 10 REIS (X; 1/2 Vinten)

Copper **Ruler:** Maria I and Pedro III **Obv:** Crowned arms in baroque frame **Obv. Legend:** MARIA I ET PETRUS III... **Rev:** Value within wreath **Rev. Legend:** PORTUGAL...

Date	Mintage	VG	F	VF	XF	Unc
1782	360,000	4.00	9.00	25.00	50.00	—
1785	872,000	4.00	9.00	25.00	50.00	—

KM# 306 10 REIS (X; 1/2 Vinten)

Copper **Ruler:** Maria I **Obv:** Crowned arms in baroque frame **Obv. Legend:** MARIA • I • DEI • GRATIA **Rev:** Value divides date within wreath **Rev. Legend:** PORTUGALIÆ • ET • ALGARBIORUM • REGINA

Date	Mintage	VG	F	VF	XF	Unc
1791	—	7.00	15.00	55.00	100	—
1792	7,919,000	5.00	10.00	35.00	70.00	—

KM# 309 10 REIS (X; 1/2 Vinten)

Copper **Ruler:** Maria I **Obv:** Crowned arms in baroque frame **Obv. Legend:** MARIA I DEI GRATIA **Rev:** Value within wreath **Rev. Legend:** PORTUGAL...

Date	Mintage	VG	F	VF	XF	Unc
1797	155,000	4.00	9.00	25.00	50.00	—
1799	219,000	4.00	9.00	25.00	50.00	—

KM# 235 20 REIS (Vinten)

Silver **Obv:** Globe **Rev:** Cross with rosettes in angles

Date	Mintage	VG	F	VF	XF	Unc
ND(1706-77)	—	15.00	25.00	60.00	125	—

KM# 330 20 REIS (Vinten)

Silver **Ruler:** Joao, as Prince Regent **Obv:** Globe **Rev:** Cross with quatrefoil in angles

Date	Mintage	VG	F	VF	XF	Unc
ND(1799-1816)	—	7.00	18.00	65.00	125	—

KM# 236.1 40 REIS (Pataco)

Silver **Ruler:** Jose I **Obv:** Crown above value **Obv. Legend:** JOSEPHUS • I • D • G • P• ET • ALG • REX • **Rev:** Cross with quatrefoil in angles **Rev. Legend:** • IN HOC SIGNO VINCES •

Date	Mintage	VG	F	VF	XF	Unc
ND	—	7.50	15.00	30.00	60.00	—

KM# 236.2 40 REIS (Pataco)

Silver **Ruler:** Jose I **Obv:** Crown above value **Obv. Legend:** IOSEPHUS • I • D • G • P • ET • ALG • REX • **Rev:** Cross with quatrefoil in angles **Rev. Legend:** • IN HOC SIGNO VINCES •

Date	Mintage	VG	F	VF	XF	Unc
ND	—	7.50	15.00	30.00	60.00	—

KM# 198 50 REIS (1/2 Tostao)

Silver **Ruler:** John V **Obv:** Crown above value, date below **Obv. Legend:** IOANNES • V • D • G • P • ET • ALG • REX • **Rev:** Cross with quatrefoil in angles **Rev. Legend:** IN • HOC • SIGNO • VINCES **Note:** Varieties exist.

Date	Mintage	VG	F	VF	XF	Unc
1717	—	350	600	1,200	2,400	—

KM# 199 50 REIS (1/2 Tostao)

Silver **Ruler:** John V **Obv:** Crown above value **Obv. Legend:** IOANNES • V • ... **Rev:** Cross with quatrefoil in angles **Rev. Legend:** IN HOC SIGNO VINCES **Note:** Varieties exist.

Date	Mintage	VG	F	VF	XF	Unc
ND(1706-50)	—	8.00	17.50	45.00	100	—

KM# 200 50 REIS (1/2 Tostao)

Silver **Ruler:** John V **Obv:** Crown above value **Obv. Legend:** IOANNES V... **Rev:** P in angles of cross **Note:** Struck at Porto.

Date	Mintage	VG	F	VF	XF	Unc
ND(1706-50)P	—	20.00	40.00	90.00	150	—

KM# 263 50 REIS (1/2 Tostao)

Silver **Ruler:** Maria I and Pedro III **Obv:** Crown above value **Obv. Legend:** MARIA I ET PETRUS III... **Rev:** Cross **Rev. Legend:** IN HOC...

Date	Mintage	VG	F	VF	XF	Unc
ND(1777-86)	—	8.00	17.50	45.00	100	—

KM# 283 50 REIS (1/2 Tostao)

Silver **Ruler:** Maria I **Obv:** Value, date below **Obv. Legend:** MARIA I D.G... **Rev:** Cross **Rev. Legend:** IN HOC... **Note:** Varieties are known.

Date	Mintage	VG	F	VF	XF	Unc
ND	—	8.00	17.50	45.00	100	—

KM# 310 50 REIS (1/2 Tostao)

Silver **Ruler:** Joao, as Prince Regent **Obv:** Crown above value **Obv. Legend:** JOANNES…ET ALG... **Rev:** Cross **Rev. Legend:** IN HOC...

Date	Mintage	VG	F	VF	XF	Unc
ND(1799-1816)	—	10.00	25.00	55.00	150	—

KM# 175 60 REIS (3 Vintens)

Silver **Ruler:** John V **Obv:** Crowned arms **Obv. Legend:** IOANNES V... **Rev:** Cross with quatrefoil in angles **Note:** Varieties exist.

Date	Mintage	VG	F	VF	XF	Unc
ND(1706-50)	—	5.50	12.50	30.00	85.00	—

KM# 176 60 REIS (3 Vintens)

Silver **Ruler:** John V **Obv:** Crowned arms **Obv. Legend:** IOANNES • V • ... **Rev:** Maltese cross with P in angles **Rev. Legend:** IN HOC SIGNO VINCES

Date	Mintage	VG	F	VF	XF	Unc
ND(1706-50)	—	17.00	35.00	80.00	150	—

KM# 264 60 REIS (3 Vintens)
1.8300 g., Silver **Ruler:** Maria I and Pedro III **Obv:** Crowned arms **Obv. Legend:** MARIA I ET PETRUS III... **Rev:** Cross **Rev. Legend:** IN HOC...

Date	Mintage	VG	F	VF	XF	Unc
ND(1777-86)	—	4.00	9.00	30.00	60.00	—

KM# 284 60 REIS (3 Vintens)
1.8300 g., Silver **Ruler:** Maria I **Obv:** Crowned arms **Obv. Legend:** MARIA I D. G. POR... **Rev:** Cross **Rev. Legend:** IN HOC...

Date	Mintage	VG	F	VF	XF	Unc
ND(1786-99)	—	3.50	8.00	23.00	50.00	—

KM# 312 60 REIS (3 Vintens)
1.8300 g., Silver **Ruler:** Joao, as Prince Regent **Obv:** Crowned arms **Obv. Legend:** JOANNES...ET ALG **Rev:** Cross **Rev. Legend:** IN HOC...

Date	Mintage	VG	F	VF	XF	Unc
ND(1799-1816)	—	5.00	10.00	30.00	70.00	—

KM# 313 60 REIS (3 Vintens)
1.8300 g., Silver **Ruler:** Joao, as Prince Regent **Obv:** Crowned arms **Obv. Legend:** JOANNES...P REGENS **Rev:** Cross **Rev. Legend:** IN HOC...

Date	Mintage	VG	F	VF	XF	Unc
ND(1799-1816)	—	5.00	10.00	30.00	60.00	—

KM# 237.1 60 REIS (3 Vintens)
1.8300 g., Silver **Ruler:** Jose I **Obv:** Crowned arms **Obv. Legend:** JOSEPHUS • I • ... **Rev:** Maltese cross with quatrefoil in angles **Rev. Legend:** IN HOC SIGNO VINCES

Date	Mintage	VG	F	VF	XF	Unc
ND	—	4.00	7.50	26.00	55.00	—

KM# 237.2 60 REIS (3 Vintens)
1.8300 g., Silver **Ruler:** Jose I **Obv:** Crowned arms **Obv. Legend:** IOSEPHUS • I • ... **Rev:** Maltese cross with quatrefoil in angles **Rev. Legend:** IN HOC SIGNO VINCES

Date	Mintage	VG	F	VF	XF	Unc
ND	—	7.00	15.00	35.00	70.00	—

KM# 238.1 80 REIS
Silver **Ruler:** Jose I **Obv:** Crown with LXXX below **Obv. Legend:** JOSEPHUS • I • ... **Rev:** Cross with quatrefoil in angles **Rev. Legend:** IN HOC SIGNO VINCES •

Date	Mintage	VG	F	VF	XF	Unc
ND(1750-77)	—	5.00	12.00	30.00	60.00	—

KM# 238.2 80 REIS
Silver **Ruler:** Jose I **Obv:** Crown with LXXX below **Obv. Legend:** IOSEPHUS • I • ... **Rev:** Cross with quatrefoil in angles **Rev. Legend:** IN HOC SIGNO VINCES

Date	Mintage	VG	F	VF	XF	Unc
ND(1750-77)	—	5.00	12.00	30.00	60.00	—

KM# 157 80 REIS (LXXX; Tostao)
Silver **Ruler:** Peter II **Obv:** Crown above LXXX, date below **Obv. Legend:** • PETRVS • II • D • G • REX • PORTVG • **Rev:** Cross with P in angles **Rev. Legend:** IN HOC SIGNO VINCES **Note:** Varieties exist. Struck at Porto.

Date	Mintage	VG	F	VF	XF	Unc
1702	—	17.00	35.00	70.00	125	—
1704	—	17.00	35.00	85.00	125	—

KM# 177 80 REIS (LXXX; Tostao)
Silver **Ruler:** John V **Obv:** Crown above LXXX **Obv. Legend:** IOANNES • V • ... **Rev:** Cross with quatrefoil in angles **Rev. Legend:** IN HOC SIGNO VINCES **Note:** Varieties exist.

Date	Mintage	VG	F	VF	XF	Unc
ND(1706-50)	—	12.00	25.00	50.00	140	—

KM# 180 80 REIS (LXXX; Tostao)
Silver **Ruler:** John V **Obv:** Crown above LXXX, date **Obv. Legend:** IOANNES • V • ... **Rev:** Cross with P in angles **Rev. Legend:** IN HOC SIGNO VINCES **Note:** Struck at Porto.

Date	Mintage	VG	F	VF	XF	Unc
1707P	—	40.00	80.00	175	350	—

KM# 265 80 REIS (LXXX; Tostao)
Silver **Ruler:** Maria I and Pedro III **Obv:** Crown **Obv. Legend:** MARIA I ET PETRUS III... **Rev:** Cross **Rev. Legend:** IN HOC...

Date	Mintage	VG	F	VF	XF	Unc
ND	—	8.00	15.00	35.00	95.00	—

KM# 285 80 REIS (LXXX; Tostao)
Silver **Ruler:** Maria I **Obv:** Crown **Obv. Legend:** MARIA I D.G... **Rev:** Cross **Rev. Legend:** IN HOC... **Note:** 2 varieties are known.

Date	Mintage	VG	F	VF	XF	Unc
ND	—	5.50	8.50	25.00	65.00	—

KM# 314 80 REIS (LXXX; Tostao)
Silver **Ruler:** Joao, as Prince Regent **Obv:** Crown **Obv. Legend:** JOANNES...ET.ALG **Rev:** Cross **Rev. Legend:** IN HOC...

Date	Mintage	VG	F	VF	XF	Unc
ND(1799-1816)	—	7.00	14.50	35.00	75.00	—

KM# 315 80 REIS (LXXX; Tostao)
Silver **Ruler:** Joao, as Prince Regent **Obv:** Value LXXX, crown above **Obv. Legend:** JOANNES...P REGENS **Rev:** Cross **Rev. Legend:** IN HOC...

Date	Mintage	VG	F	VF	XF	Unc
ND(1799-1816)	—	7.00	15.00	40.00	85.00	—

KM# 352 80 REIS (LXXX; Tostao)
Silver **Ruler:** Joao, as Prince Regent **Obv:** Value LXXX, crown above **Obv. Legend:** JOANNES • VI • ...ET ALG REX **Rev:** Cross, quatrefoil in angles **Rev. Legend:** IN HOC SIGNO VINCES

Date	Mintage	VG	F	VF	XF	Unc
ND(1799-1816)	—	7.00	15.00	40.00	85.00	—

KM# 178 120 REIS (6 Vintens)
Silver **Ruler:** John V **Obv:** Crowned arms **Obv. Legend:** IOANNES V... **Note:** Varieties exist.

Date	Mintage	VG	F	VF	XF	Unc
ND(1706-50)	—	10.00	20.00	35.00	90.00	—

KM# 239.1 120 REIS (6 Vintens)
Silver **Ruler:** Jose I **Obv:** Crowned arms **Obv. Legend:** JOSEPHUS • I • ... **Rev:** Maltese cross, quatrefoil in angles **Rev. Legend:** IN HOC SIGNO VINCES

Date	Mintage	VG	F	VF	XF	Unc
ND	—	5.00	10.00	23.00	55.00	—

KM# 239.2 120 REIS (6 Vintens)
Silver **Ruler:** Jose I **Obv:** Crowned arms **Obv. Legend:** IOSEPHUS • I • ... **Rev:** Maltese cross, quatrefoil in angles **Rev. Legend:** IN HOC SIGNO VINCES

Date	Mintage	VG	F	VF	XF	Unc
ND	—	5.00	10.00	35.00	75.00	—

KM# 266 120 REIS (6 Vintens)
Silver **Ruler:** Maria I and Pedro III **Obv:** Crowned arms **Obv. Legend:** MARIA I ET PETRUS III... **Rev:** Cross **Rev. Legend:** IN HOC...

Date	Mintage	VG	F	VF	XF	Unc
ND	—	7.00	15.00	50.00	100	—

KM# 286 120 REIS (6 Vintens)
Silver **Ruler:** Maria I **Obv:** Crowned arms **Obv. Legend:** MARIA • I • D • G • ... **Rev:** Maltese cross, quatrefoil in angles **Rev. Legend:** IN HOC SIGNO VINCES

Date	Mintage	VG	F	VF	XF	Unc
ND	—	5.00	8.50	25.00	65.00	—

KM# 316 120 REIS (6 Vintens)
Silver **Ruler:** Joao, as Prince Regent **Obv:** Crowned arms **Obv. Legend:** JOANNES...ET ALG **Rev:** Cross **Rev. Legend:** IN HOC...

Date	Mintage	VG	F	VF	XF	Unc
ND(1799-1816)	—	7.00	15.00	35.00	95.00	—

KM# 317 120 REIS (6 Vintens)
Silver **Ruler:** Joao, as Prince Regent **Obv:** Crowned arms **Obv. Legend:** JOANNES...P REGENS **Rev:** Cross **Rev. Legend:** IN HOC...

Date	Mintage	VG	F	VF	XF	Unc
ND(1799-1816)	—	6.00	12.50	45.00	100	—

KM# 181 200 REIS (12 Vintens, 200 = 240 Reis)
Silver **Ruler:** John V **Obv:** Crowned arms, flanked by vertical value and date **Obv. Legend:** IOANNES • V • D • G • PORT ... **Rev:** Maltese cross, quatrefoil in angles **Rev. Legend:** • IN HOC SIGNO VINCES • **Note:** Varieties exist.

Date	Mintage	VG	F	VF	XF	Unc
1707	—	200	400	600	900	—
1708	—	1,400	2,600	3,500	6,500	—
1747	—	13.00	25.00	50.00	100	—
1748	—	10.00	20.00	50.00	100	—
1749	—	10.00	20.00	50.00	100	—
1750 Rare	—	—	—	—	—	—

KM# 247.2 200 REIS (12 Vintens, 200 = 240 Reis)
Silver **Ruler:** Jose I **Obv:** Crowned arms, flanked by vertical value and date **Obv. Legend:** IOSEPHUS • I • ... **Rev:** Maltese cross, quatrefoil in angles **Rev. Legend:** IN HOC SIGNO VINCES

Date	Mintage	VG	F	VF	XF	Unc
1752	—	10.00	20.00	55.00	110	—
1753	—	15.00	30.00	100	175	—
1762	—	18.00	35.00	125	250	—
1763	—	18.00	35.00	125	250	—

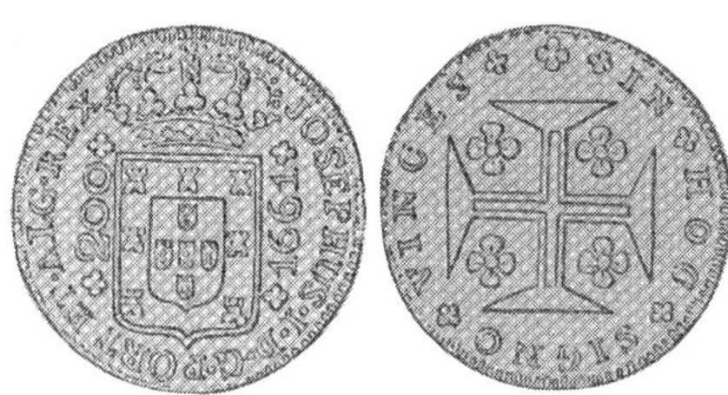

KM# 247.3 200 REIS (12 Vintens, 200 = 240 Reis)
Silver **Ruler:** Jose I **Obv:** Crowned arms, flanked by vertical value and date **Obv. Legend:** JOSEPHUS • I • ... **Rev:** Maltese cross, quatrefoil in angles **Rev. Legend:** IN HOC SIGNO VINCES

Date	Mintage	VG	F	VF	XF	Unc
1661 Error for 1761, Rare	—	—	—	—	—	—

KM# 247.1 200 REIS (12 Vintens, 200 = 240 Reis)
Silver **Ruler:** Jose I **Obv:** Crowned arms, flanked by vertical value and date **Obv. Legend:** JOSEPHUS • I • ... **Rev:** Maltese cross, quatrefoil in angles **Rev. Legend:** IN HOC SIGNO VINCES

Date	Mintage	VG	F	VF	XF	Unc
1762	—	10.00	20.00	65.00	100	—
1763	—	10.00	20.00	65.00	100	—
1766	—	10.00	20.00	65.00	100	—
1767	—	10.00	20.00	65.00	100	—
1768	—	10.00	20.00	65.00	100	—
1774	—	90.00	175	500	900	—
1775	—	95.00	200	500	900	—

KM# 272 200 REIS (12 Vintens, 200 = 240 Reis)
Silver **Ruler:** Maria I and Pedro III **Obv:** Crowned arms, flanked by vertical value and date **Obv. Legend:** MARIA • I • E • PETRUS • III • ... **Rev:** Maltese cross, quatrefoil in angles **Rev. Legend:** IN HOC SIGNO VINCES

Date	Mintage	VG	F	VF	XF	Unc
1778	—	225	450	1,000	1,750	—
1779	—	70.00	150	350	700	—
1780	—	7.00	15.00	50.00	100	—
1781	—	7.00	15.00	50.00	100	—
1782	—	7.00	15.00	50.00	100	—
1784	—	11.00	22.00	65.00	125	—
1785	—	45.00	75.00	150	250	—

KM# 287 200 REIS (12 Vintens, 200 = 240 Reis)
Silver **Ruler:** Maria I **Obv:** Crowned arms, flanked by vertical value and date **Obv. Legend:** MARIA I D G... **Rev:** Maltese cross, quatrefoil in angles

Date	Mintage	VG	F	VF	XF	Unc
1786	—	100	225	550	1,100	—
1788	—	35.00	65.00	125	225	—
1791	—	400	850	1,500	3,000	—
1792	—	60.00	125	300	600	—

KM# 392A 200 REIS (12 Vintens, 200 = 240 Reis)
Silver **Obv:** Crowned arms **Obv. Legend:** MICHAEL I... **Rev:** P in angles of cross

Date	Mintage	VG	F	VF	XF	Unc
1787	—	185	375	750	1,250	—
1789	—	100	200	425	700	—
1792	—	100	200	425	700	—
1800	—	—	—	—	—	—

KM# 307 200 REIS (12 Vintens, 200 = 240 Reis)
Silver

Date	Mintage	VG	F	VF	XF	Unc
1793	—	13.00	25.00	65.00	125	—
1794	—	45.00	100	300	600	—
1798	—	18.00	35.00	95.00	200	—
1799	—	18.00	35.00	90.00	175	—

KM# 154.3 400 REIS (Cruzado Novo, 400 = 480 Reis)
Silver **Ruler:** Peter II **Obv:** Crowned arms, flanked by vertical date and value **Obv. Legend:** PETRVS • II • ... **Rev:** Maltese cross, quatrefoil in angles **Rev. Legend:** • IN HOC SIGNO VINCES • **Note:** Dav. #4391; 1700s are Dav. #1627. Varieties exist.

Date	Mintage	VG	F	VF	XF	Unc
1703 Rare	—	—	—	—	—	—
1704	—	75.00	150	300	550	—
1705	—	85.00	175	350	600	—
1706	—	85.00	175	350	600	—

KM# 179 400 REIS (Cruzado Novo, 400 = 480 Reis)
Silver **Ruler:** John V **Obv:** Crowned arms **Obv. Legend:** IOANNES V... **Rev:** Maltese cross, quatrefoil in angles **Note:** Dav. #1628. Varieties exist.

Date	Mintage	VG	F	VF	XF	Unc
1706 Rare	—	—	—	—	—	—
1707	—	225	450	950	1,900	—
1708 Rare	—	—	—	—	—	—
1750	—	20.00	40.00	80.00	165	—

KM# 201 400 REIS (Cruzado Novo, 400 = 480 Reis)
1.0720 g., 0.9170 Gold 0.0316 oz. AGW **Ruler:** John V **Obv:** Crown above name flanked by quatrefoils within sprigs **Rev:** Maltese cross, quatrefoil in angles **Rev. Legend:** IN HOC SIGNO VINCES

Date	Mintage	VG	F	VF	XF	Unc
1718	—	40.00	50.00	75.00	125	—
1719	—	40.00	50.00	75.00	125	—
1720	—	40.00	50.00	70.00	125	—
1721	—	40.00	50.00	70.00	125	—
1722	—	45.00	55.00	80.00	150	—
1723	—	50.00	65.00	85.00	175	—
1724	—	45.00	60.00	95.00	175	—
1725	—	50.00	65.00	85.00	175	—
1726	—	40.00	50.00	75.00	125	—
1728	—	40.00	50.00	75.00	125	—
1729	—	40.00	50.00	85.00	125	—
1730	—	40.00	50.00	70.00	125	—
1731	—	45.00	65.00	100	175	—
1733	—	40.00	50.00	75.00	125	—
1734	—	40.00	50.00	70.00	125	—
1735	—	40.00	55.00	80.00	150	—
1736	—	40.00	50.00	75.00	125	—
1737	—	40.00	60.00	100	200	—
1738	—	50.00	60.00	80.00	150	—
1739	—	40.00	50.00	75.00	125	—
1741	—	40.00	50.00	75.00	125	—
1742	—	45.00	65.00	100	175	—
1743	—	40.00	50.00	75.00	125	—
1744	—	40.00	50.00	75.00	125	—
1746	—	40.00	50.00	75.00	125	—
1747	—	45.00	55.00	70.00	125	—
1748	—	40.00	50.00	75.00	125	—

KM# 248.1 400 REIS (Pinto, 480 Reis)
1.0720 g., 0.9170 Gold 0.0316 oz. AGW **Ruler:** Jose I **Obv:** Crown above name flanked by quatrefoils within sprigs **Rev:** Maltese cross, quatrefoil in angles, date above **Rev. Legend:** IN HOC SIGNO VINCES

Date	Mintage	VG	F	VF	XF	Unc
1752	—	55.00	75.00	100	150	—
1760	—	60.00	90.00	125	175	—
1771	—	60.00	100	225	350	—
1772	—	100	200	400	700	—
1776	—	100	200	400	700	—

KM# 248.2 400 REIS (Pinto, 480 Reis)
1.0720 g., 0.9170 Gold 0.0316 oz. AGW **Ruler:** Jose I **Obv:** Crown above name flanked by quatrefoils within sprigs, value below **Obv. Legend:** IOSE... **Rev:** Maltese cross, quatrefoil in angles, date above **Rev. Legend:** IN HOC SIGNO VINCES

Date	Mintage	VG	F	VF	XF	Unc
1752	—	45.00	65.00	90.00	150	—
1760	—	60.00	80.00	100	200	—
1768	—	100	200	400	700	—
1771	—	60.00	80.00	100	200	—
1775	—	100	200	400	700	—
1776	—	100	200	400	700	—

KM# 255.2 400 REIS (Pinto, 480 Reis)
Silver **Ruler:** Jose I **Obv:** Crowned arms, flanked by vertical value and date **Obv. Legend:** IOSEPHUS • I • ... **Rev:** Maltese cross, quatrefoil in angles **Rev. Legend:** IN HOC SIGNO VINCES **Note:** Dav. #1629

Date	Mintage	VG	F	VF	XF	Unc
1762	—	100	200	500	1,000	—
1763	—	850	1,600	2,900	4,000	—

KM# 255.1 400 REIS (Pinto, 480 Reis)
Silver **Ruler:** Jose I **Obv:** Crowned arms, flanked by vertical value and date **Obv. Legend:** JOSEPHUS • I • ... **Rev:** Maltese cross, quatrefoil in angles **Rev. Legend:** IN HOC SIGNO VINCES **Note:** Dav. #1630

Date	Mintage	VG	F	VF	XF	Unc
1762	—	35.00	70.00	125	225	—
1763	—	40.00	85.00	150	300	—
1766	—	17.00	30.00	65.00	125	—
1768	—	17.00	30.00	65.00	125	—
1774	—	25.00	60.00	100	200	—
1775	—	85.00	175	550	1,100	—

KM# 267 400 REIS (Pinto, 480 Reis)
1.0720 g., 0.9170 Gold 0.0316 oz. AGW **Ruler:** Maria I and Pedro III **Obv:** Legend in crowned wreath **Obv. Legend:** MARIA I / ET P. III **Rev:** Cross **Rev. Legend:** IN HOC...

Date	Mintage	VG	F	VF	XF	Unc
1777	—	250	500	750	1,400	—
1778	—	80.00	100	150	300	—
1780	—	80.00	100	150	300	—
1783	—	80.00	100	150	300	—
1784	—	80.00	100	150	300	—
1785	—	175	350	550	900	—

KM# 273 400 REIS (Pinto, 480 Reis)
Silver **Ruler:** Maria I and Pedro III **Obv:** Crowned arms **Obv. Legend:** MARIA I ET PETRUS III... **Rev:** Cross **Rev. Legend:** IN HOC... **Note:** Dav. #1631

Date	Mintage	VG	F	VF	XF	Unc
1778 Rare	—	—	—	—	—	—
1779	—	30.00	50.00	100	225	—
1780	—	17.50	30.00	65.00	135	—
1781	—	17.50	30.00	65.00	135	—
1782	—	17.50	30.00	65.00	135	—

KM# 282 400 REIS (Pinto, 480 Reis)
Silver **Ruler:** Maria I and Pedro III **Obv:** Crowned arms **Obv. Legend:** MARIA I ET PETRUS III... **Rev:** Cross **Rev. Legend:** IN HOC... **Note:** Dav. #1631

Date	Mintage	VG	F	VF	XF	Unc
1784	—	25.00	55.00	100	200	—
1785	—	225	450	1,000	1,900	—

KM# 288 400 REIS (Pinto, 480 Reis)
Silver **Ruler:** Maria I **Obv:** Crown **Obv. Legend:** MARIA I D.G. ... **Rev:** Cross **Rev. Legend:** IN HOC... **Note:** Dav. #1632

Date	Mintage	VG	F	VF	XF	Unc
1786	—	350	800	1,900	3,800	—
1788	—	100	225	500	900	—
1792	—	60.00	110	300	600	—
1793	—	15.00	28.00	60.00	100	—
1794	—	50.00	100	250	500	—
1795	—	15.00	28.00	60.00	100	—
1796	—	15.00	28.00	60.00	100	—
1797	—	15.00	28.00	60.00	100	—

Date	Mintage	VG	F	VF	XF	Unc
1798	—	15.00	28.00	60.00	100	—
1799	—	45.00	85.00	225	350	—

KM# 291 400 REIS (Pinto, 480 Reis)

1.0720 g., 0.9170 Gold 0.0316 oz. AGW **Ruler:** Maria I **Obv:** Legend in crowned wreath **Obv. Legend:** MARIA I ... **Rev:** Cross **Rev. Legend:** IN HOC...

Date	Mintage	VG	F	VF	XF	Unc
1787	—	50.00	100	200	400	—
1790	—	40.00	85.00	150	300	—
1795	—	55.00	100	175	350	—
1796	—	150	300	650	1,300	—

KM# 318 400 REIS (Pinto, 480 Reis)

Silver **Ruler:** Joao, as Prince Regent **Obv:** Crowned arms, flanked by vertical value and date **Obv. Legend:** JOANNES • D • G • P • PORTUGALIÆ • ET • ALG • **Rev:** Maltese cross, quatrefoil in angles **Rev. Legend:** IN HOC SIGNO VINCES **Note:** Dav. #1633

Date	Mintage	VG	F	VF	XF	Unc
1799INCM	—	35.00	60.00	125	250	—
1800INCM	—	15.00	25.00	55.00	150	—

KM# 210 1/2 ESCUDO (800 Reis)

1.7875 g., 0.9170 Gold 0.0527 oz. AGW **Ruler:** John V **Obv:** Laurette bust right, date and mint mark below **Obv. Legend:** JOANNES • V • D • G • ... **Rev:** Crowned oval arms in cartouche **Rev. Legend:** IN • HOC SIGNO VINCES •

Date	Mintage	VG	F	VF	XF	Unc
1722INCM L	—	75.00	150	250	400	—

KM# 218 1/2 ESCUDO (800 Reis)

1.7875 g., 0.9170 Gold 0.0527 oz. AGW **Ruler:** John V **Obv:** Laurette bust right, without mint mark below **Obv. Legend:** JOANNES • V • D • G • ... **Rev:** Crowned arms in cartouche **Note:** Varieties exist.

Date	Mintage	VG	F	VF	XF	Unc
1723	—	60.00	100	200	350	—
1724	—	40.00	75.00	150	250	—
1725	—	40.00	75.00	150	250	—
1726 Wide crown	—	40.00	65.00	135	225	—
1726 Closed crown	—	40.00	65.00	135	225	—
1728	—	40.00	65.00	135	225	—
1729	—	40.00	65.00	135	225	—
1730	—	40.00	65.00	135	225	—
1731	—	100	200	400	650	—
1732	—	40.00	65.00	135	225	—
1733	—	40.00	65.00	135	225	—
1735	—	40.00	65.00	135	225	—
1736	—	40.00	65.00	135	225	—
1738	—	40.00	65.00	135	225	—
1739	—	45.00	90.00	175	300	—
1740	—	45.00	90.00	175	300	—
1741	—	40.00	65.00	135	225	—
1743	—	40.00	65.00	135	225	—
1744	—	40.00	65.00	135	225	—
1745	—	60.00	100	200	350	—
1746	—	40.00	65.00	135	225	—
1747	—	40.00	65.00	135	225	—
1748	—	40.00	65.00	135	225	—
1749	—	40.00	65.00	135	225	—
1750	—	100	200	400	650	—

KM# 230 1/2 ESCUDO (800 Reis)

1.7875 g., 0.9170 Gold 0.0527 oz. AGW **Ruler:** John V **Obv:** Laureate bust right, error in legend **Obv. Legend:** IOANNES VI... **Rev:** Crowned arms in cartouche

Date	Mintage	VG	F	VF	XF	Unc
1741	—	—	—	—	—	—

KM# 244.1 1/2 ESCUDO (800 Reis)

1.7920 g., 0.9170 Gold 0.0528 oz. AGW **Ruler:** Jose I **Obv:** Laureate head right, date below **Obv. Legend:** JOSEPHUS • I • ... **Rev:** Crowned arms in cartouche

Date	Mintage	VG	F	VF	XF	Unc
1751	—	75.00	150	275	450	—
1765	—	75.00	150	275	450	—
1768	—	40.00	75.00	150	250	—
1770	—	115	225	425	700	—
1775	—	115	225	425	700	—
1776	—	40.00	75.00	150	250	—

KM# 244.2 1/2 ESCUDO (800 Reis)

1.7920 g., 0.9170 Gold 0.0528 oz. AGW **Ruler:** Jose I **Obv:** Laureate head right, date below **Obv. Legend:** IOSEPHUS • I • ... **Rev:** Crowned arms in cartouche

Date	Mintage	VG	F	VF	XF	Unc
1751	—	60.00	100	200	350	—
1768	—	125	255	475	775	—

KM# 269 1/2 ESCUDO (800 Reis)

1.7920 g., 0.9170 Gold 0.0528 oz. AGW **Ruler:** Maria I and Pedro III **Obv:** Coinjoined busts right **Obv. Legend:** MARIA • I • ET • PETRUS III • ... **Rev:** Crowned arms in cartouche

Date	Mintage	VG	F	VF	XF	Unc
1777	—	175	300	700	1,000	—
1778	—	60.00	100	225	350	—
1780	—	60.00	100	225	350	—
1784	—	60.00	100	200	325	—

KM# 293 1/2 ESCUDO (800 Reis)

1.7920 g., 0.9170 Gold 0.0528 oz. AGW **Ruler:** Maria I **Obv:** Veiled bust right **Obv. Legend:** MARIA I D. G. PORT... **Rev:** Crowned arms in cartouche

Date	Mintage	VG	F	VF	XF	Unc
1787	—	125	250	425	700	—
1788 Rare	—	—	—	—	—	—

KM# 296 1/2 ESCUDO (800 Reis)

1.7920 g., 0.9170 Gold 0.0528 oz. AGW **Ruler:** Maria I **Obv:** Bust right, with jeweled hairdress **Obv. Legend:** MARIA • I • D • G • PORT ... **Rev:** Crowned arms in cartouche

Date	Mintage	VG	F	VF	XF	Unc
1789	—	60.00	125	250	400	—
1792	—	85.00	165	325	550	—
1796	—	125	250	550	800	—

KM# 155 1000 REIS (Quartinho, 1200 Reis)

2.6900 g., 0.9170 Gold 0.0793 oz. AGW **Ruler:** Peter II **Obv:** Crowned arms with vertical value at left side, titles of Peter II at right **Obv. Legend:** PETRVS • II • .... **Rev:** Maltese cross, quatrefoil in angles, date above **Rev. Legend:** IN HOC SIGNO VINCES

Date	Mintage	VG	F	VF	XF	Unc
1702	—	150	300	550	950	—
1703 Rare	—	—	—	—	—	—
1704	—	150	300	550	950	—
1706	—	175	375	700	1,200	—

KM# 182 1000 REIS (Quartinho, 1200 Reis)

2.6900 g., 0.9170 Gold 0.0793 oz. AGW **Ruler:** John V **Obv:** Crowned arms with vertical value at left side, titles of John V at right **Obv. Legend:** IOANNES • V • D • G • ... **Rev:** Maltese cross, quatrefoil in angles, date above **Rev. Legend:** IN HOC SIGNO VINCES **Note:** Varieties exist.

Date	Mintage	VG	F	VF	XF	Unc
1707	—	75.00	150	300	500	—
1708	—	60.00	125	270	450	—
1709	—	45.00	75.00	150	265	—
1710	—	50.00	100	175	300	—
1711	—	45.00	80.00	165	285	—
1712	—	45.00	80.00	165	285	—
1713	—	45.00	80.00	165	285	—
1714	—	45.00	80.00	165	285	—
1715	—	45.00	80.00	165	285	—
1716	—	45.00	75.00	150	265	—
1717	—	45.00	80.00	165	285	—
1718	—	45.00	75.00	150	265	—
1719	—	45.00	80.00	165	285	—
1720	—	45.00	75.00	150	265	—
1721	—	45.00	80.00	165	285	—
1722	—	45.00	80.00	165	285	—
1733	—	45.00	75.00	150	265	—
1736	—	45.00	80.00	165	285	—
1738	—	45.00	80.00	165	285	—
1739	—	45.00	80.00	165	285	—
1741	—	45.00	75.00	150	265	—
1745	—	45.00	80.00	165	285	—
1747	—	50.00	100	175	300	—

KM# 196 1000 REIS (Quartinho, 1200 Reis)

2.6900 g., 0.9170 Gold 0.0793 oz. AGW **Ruler:** John V **Obv:** Crowned arms with vertical value at left side, titles of John V at right **Rev:** Maltese cross, date above **Note:** Struck at Porto.

Date	Mintage	VG	F	VF	XF	Unc
1713	—	225	475	850	1,450	—

KM# 249.1 1000 REIS (Quartinho, 1200 Reis)

2.6800 g., 0.9170 Gold 0.0790 oz. AGW **Ruler:** Jose I **Obv:** Crowned arms with vertical value at left **Obv. Legend:** JOSEPHUS • I • ... **Rev:** Maltese cross, quatrefoils in angles, date above **Rev. Legend:** IN HOC SIGNO VINCES

Date	Mintage	VG	F	VF	XF	Unc
1752	—	75.00	125	250	400	—
1768	—	50.00	100	200	350	—
1769	—	125	250	450	750	—

KM# 249.2 1000 REIS (Quartinho, 1200 Reis)

2.6800 g., 0.9170 Gold 0.0790 oz. AGW **Ruler:** Jose I **Obv:** Crowned arms with vertical value at left **Obv. Legend:** IOSEPHUS • I • ... **Rev:** Maltese cross, quatrefoil in angles, date above **Rev. Legend:** IN HOC SIGNO VINCES **Note:** KM#249.2 is found muled with reverse of Joannes (John) V dated 1749.

Date	Mintage	VG	F	VF	XF	Unc
1752	—	75.00	125	200	350	—
1768	—	75.00	125	200	350	—

KM# 268 1000 REIS (Quartinho, 1200 Reis)

2.6800 g., 0.9170 Gold 0.0790 oz. AGW **Ruler:** Maria I and Pedro III **Obv:** Crowned arms in baroque frame **Obv. Legend:** MARIA • I • ET • PETRUS • III • ... **Rev:** Maltese cross, quatrefoils in angles, date above **Rev. Legend:** IN HOC SIGNO VINCES

Date	Mintage	VG	F	VF	XF	Unc
1777	—	175	350	750	1,500	—
1778	—	150	275	475	850	—
1779	—	150	275	475	850	—
1784	—	150	275	475	850	—

KM# 292 1000 REIS (Quartinho, 1200 Reis)

2.6800 g., 0.9170 Gold 0.0790 oz. AGW **Ruler:** Maria I **Obv:** Crowned arms in baroque frame **Obv. Legend:** MARIA • I • D • G • PORT ... **Rev:** Maltese cross, quatrefoils in angles, date above **Rev. Legend:** IN HOC SIGNO VINCES

Date	Mintage	VG	F	VF	XF	Unc
1787	—	185	375	800	1,600	—
1789	—	150	275	475	850	—
1792	—	100	200	425	700	—
1800 Rare	—	—	—	—	—	—

KM# 211 ESCUDO (1600 Reis)
3.5750 g., 0.9170 Gold 0.1054 oz. AGW **Ruler:** John V **Obv:** Laureatte bust right, mint mark below, date in exergue **Rev:** Crowned arms in cartouche

Date	Mintage	VG	F	VF	XF	Unc
1722L	—	150	300	550	1,000	—

KM# 219 ESCUDO (1600 Reis)
3.5750 g., 0.9170 Gold 0.1054 oz. AGW **Ruler:** John V **Obv:** Bust right, without mint mark below **Obv. Legend:** IOANNES • V • D • G • PORT • ET • ALG • REX • **Rev:** Crowned arms in cartouche **Note:** Varieties exist.

Date	Mintage	VG	F	VF	XF	Unc
1723	—	100	225	425	700	—
1724	—	80.00	165	300	500	—
1725	—	80.00	165	300	500	—
1726	—	80.00	165	300	500	—
1727	—	100	225	425	700	—
1728	—	75.00	100	200	375	—
1729	—	75.00	100	200	375	—
1730	—	75.00	100	200	375	—
1731	—	85.00	125	200	575	—
1732	—	75.00	100	200	350	—
1733	—	75.00	100	200	350	—
1735	—	75.00	100	200	350	—
1738	—	75.00	100	200	350	—
1741	—	75.00	100	200	350	—
1742	—	75.00	100	200	350	—
1744	—	75.00	100	200	350	—
1745	—	75.00	100	200	350	—
1746	—	75.00	100	200	350	—
1747	—	75.00	100	200	350	—
1749	—	75.00	100	200	350	—

KM# 245.1 ESCUDO (1600 Reis)
3.5850 g., 0.9170 Gold 0.1057 oz. AGW **Ruler:** Jose I **Obv:** Laureate head right, date below **Obv. Legend:** JOSEPHUS • I • .... **Rev:** Crowned arms in cartouche

Date	Mintage	VG	F	VF	XF	Unc
1751	—	75.00	125	250	400	—
1764	—	75.00	150	265	425	—
1765	—	120	225	450	750	—
1768	—	75.00	150	300	525	—
1775	—	200	400	750	1,250	—
1776	—	120	225	450	750	—

KM# 245.2 ESCUDO (1600 Reis)
3.5850 g., 0.9170 Gold 0.1057 oz. AGW **Ruler:** Jose I **Obv:** Laureate head right, date below **Obv. Legend:** IOSEPHUS... **Rev:** Crowned arms in cartouche

Date	Mintage	VG	F	VF	XF	Unc
1751 Rare	—	—	—	—	—	—

KM# 270 ESCUDO (1600 Reis)
3.5850 g., 0.9170 Gold 0.1057 oz. AGW **Ruler:** Maria I and Pedro III **Obv:** Conjoined busts right **Obv. Legend:** MARIA • I • ET • PETRUS • III • ... **Rev:** Crowned arms in cartouche

Date	Mintage	VG	F	VF	XF	Unc
1777 Rare	—	—	—	—	—	—
1778	—	90.00	175	350	550	—
1779	—	90.00	175	350	550	—
1781	—	100	225	550	950	—
1784	—	90.00	175	350	550	—
1785	—	100	225	550	950	—

KM# 294 ESCUDO (1600 Reis)
3.5850 g., 0.9170 Gold 0.1057 oz. AGW **Ruler:** Maria I **Obv:** Veiled bust right **Obv. Legend:** MARIA I D.G.PORT... **Rev:** Crowned arms in cartouche

Date	Mintage	VG	F	VF	XF	Unc
1787 Rare	—	—	—	—	—	—
1788 Rare	—	—	—	—	—	—

KM# 297 ESCUDO (1600 Reis)
3.5850 g., 0.9170 Gold 0.1057 oz. AGW **Ruler:** Maria I **Obv:** Bust right, with jeweled hairdress **Obv. Legend:** MARIA • I • D • G • PORT ... **Rev:** Crowned arms in cartouche

Date	Mintage	VG	F	VF	XF	Unc
1789	—	200	450	750	1,200	—
1790	—	125	225	400	600	—
1791	—	250	500	450	1,750	—
1792	—	125	225	400	600	—
1794	—	125	225	400	600	—
1796	—	125	225	400	600	—

KM# 147 2000 REIS
5.3800 g., 0.9170 Gold 0.1586 oz. AGW **Ruler:** Peter II **Obv:** Crowned arms with vertical value at left, titles of Peter II at right **Rev:** Maltese cross with quatrefoils in angles **Note:** Similar to 4000 Reis, KM#156. Varieties exist.

Date	Mintage	VG	F	VF	XF	Unc
1702	—	225	450	800	1,350	—
1703	—	250	525	950	1,650	—
1704	—	275	550	1,000	1,750	—
1706 Unique	—	—	—	—	—	—

KM# 183 2000 REIS
5.3800 g., 0.9170 Gold 0.1586 oz. AGW **Ruler:** John V **Obv:** Crowned arms with vertical value at left, titles of John V at right **Rev:** Maltese cross with quatrefoils in angles **Note:** Varieties exist.

Date	Mintage	VG	F	VF	XF	Unc
1707	—	125	275	550	900	—
1708	—	250	450	900	1,500	—
1709	—	125	225	475	800	—
1710	—	125	225	475	800	—
1711	—	125	225	475	800	—
1712	—	125	225	475	800	—
1713	—	125	250	500	850	—
1714	—	125	250	500	850	—
1715	—	125	275	550	900	—
1718	—	200	400	800	1,350	—
1721	—	200	400	800	1,350	—
1725	—	200	400	800	1,350	—

KM# 197 2000 REIS
5.3800 g., 0.9170 Gold 0.1586 oz. AGW **Ruler:** John V **Obv:** Crowned arms vertical value at left, titles of John V at right **Rev:** Maltese cross with Ps in angles, date above **Note:** Varieties exist. Struck at Porto.

Date	Mintage	VG	F	VF	XF	Unc
1713	—	250	450	900	1,500	—
1714	—	250	450	900	1,500	—

KM# 156 4000 REIS
10.7600 g., 0.9170 Gold 0.3172 oz. AGW **Ruler:** Peter II **Obv:** Crowned arms, vertical value at left, titles of Peter II at right **Obv. Legend:** PETRVS • II • D • G • PORT • E • TALG • REX **Rev:** Maltese cross with quatrefoils in angles, date above **Rev. Legend:** IN HOC SIGNO VINCES

Date	Mintage	VG	F	VF	XF	Unc
1701	—	225	450	800	1,350	—
1702	—	225	450	800	1,350	—
1703	—	225	400	700	1,150	—
1704	—	225	400	700	1,150	—
1705	—	500	950	1,800	3,000	—
1706	—	225	400	700	1,150	—

KM# 184 4000 REIS
10.7600 g., 0.9170 Gold 0.3172 oz. AGW **Ruler:** John V **Obv:** Crowned arms, vertical value at left, titles of John V at right **Rev:** Maltese cross with quatrefoils in angles

Date	Mintage	VG	F	VF	XF	Unc
1707	—	500	1,000	1,650	2,250	—
1708	—	225	300	550	900	—
1709	—	225	300	550	900	—
1710	—	225	300	550	900	—
1711	—	225	300	550	900	—
1712	—	225	300	550	900	—
1713	—	350	700	1,150	1,750	—
1714	—	225	300	550	900	—
1715	—	225	400	750	1,200	—
1716	—	350	700	1,150	1,750	—
1717	—	500	1,000	1,500	2,000	—
1718	—	350	700	1,150	1,750	—
1719	—	225	300	575	950	—
1720	—	225	300	575	950	—
1721	—	225	300	575	950	—
1722	—	225	300	575	950	—

KM# 195 4000 REIS
10.7600 g., 0.9170 Gold 0.3172 oz. AGW **Ruler:** John V **Obv:** Crowned arms, vertical value at left, titles of John V at right **Rev:** Maltese cross with Ps in angles, date at top **Note:** Struck at Porto.

Date	Mintage	VG	F	VF	XF	Unc
1712 Inverted Ps; Rare	—	—	—	—	—	—
1713	—	650	1,100	1,850	2,750	—
1714	—	350	700	1,150	1,800	—

KM# 212 2 ESCUDOS (1/2 Peca)
7.1500 g., 0.9170 Gold 0.2108 oz. AGW **Ruler:** John V **Obv:** Laureate head right, date and mint mark below **Rev:** Crowned arms in cartouche

Date	Mintage	VG	F	VF	XF	Unc
1722L Rare	—	—	—	—	—	—

KM# 220 2 ESCUDOS (1/2 Peca)
7.1500 g., 0.9170 Gold 0.2108 oz. AGW **Ruler:** John V **Obv:** Laureate bust right, without mint mark below **Obv. Legend:** IOANNES • V • ... **Rev:** Crowned arms in cartouche **Note:** Varieties exist.

Date	Mintage	VG	F	VF	XF	Unc
1723	—	500	1,000	2,000	3,500	—
1724	—	450	900	1,800	3,000	—
1725	—	450	900	1,800	3,000	—
1726	—	450	900	1,800	3,000	—
1727	—	375	750	1,500	2,500	—
1728/6	—	350	700	1,350	2,250	—
1728	—	350	700	1,350	2,250	—
1729	—	300	600	1,100	1,750	—
1730	—	300	600	1,100	1,750	—
1732	—	250	550	1,000	1,500	—
1734	—	250	550	1,000	1,500	—
1735	—	250	550	1,000	1,500	—
1738	—	250	550	1,000	1,500	—
1739	—	250	550	1,000	1,500	—
1741	—	250	550	1,000	1,500	—
1742	—	250	550	1,000	1,500	—

KM# 246 2 ESCUDOS (1/2 Peca)
7.1500 g., 0.9170 Gold 0.2108 oz. AGW **Obv:** Bust right **Obv. Legend:** JOSEPHUS... **Rev:** Crowned arms in cartouche

Date	Mintage	VG	F	VF	XF	Unc
1751	—	200	450	750	1,250	—
1768	—	250	500	850	1,400	—
1772	—	325	650	1,200	2,000	—
1775	—	325	650	1,200	2,000	—
1776	—	325	650	1,200	2,000	—

KM# 274 2 ESCUDOS (1/2 Peca)
7.1500 g., 0.9170 Gold 0.2108 oz. AGW **Ruler:** Maria I and Pedro III **Obv:** Conjoined laureate busts right **Obv. Legend:** MARIA • ET • PETRUS • III • ... **Rev:** Crowned arms in cartouche

Date	Mintage	VG	F	VF	XF	Unc
1778	—	225	450	800	1,250	—
1784	—	250	500	950	1,550	—

KM# 298 2 ESCUDOS (1/2 Peca)
7.1500 g., 0.9170 Gold 0.2108 oz. AGW **Ruler:** Maria I **Obv:** Bust right, with jeweled hairdress **Obv. Legend:** MARIA • I • D • G • ... **Rev:** Crowned arms in cartouche

Date	Mintage	VG	F	VF	XF	Unc
1789	—	375	750	1,350	2,250	—

KM# 213 4 ESCUDOS (Peca)
14.3000 g., 0.9170 Gold 0.4216 oz. AGW **Ruler:** John V **Obv:** Laureate bust right, date and mint mark below **Rev:** Crowned arms in cartouche

Date	Mintage	VG	F	VF	XF	Unc
1722L Rare	—	—	—	—	—	—

KM# 221 4 ESCUDOS (Peca)

14.3000 g., 0.9170 Gold 0.4216 oz. AGW **Ruler:** John V **Obv:** Laureate head right, without mint mark below **Obv. Legend:** IOANNES • V • D • G • PORT • ET • ALG • REX **Rev:** Crowned arms in cartouche **Note:** Varieties exist.

Date	Mintage	VG	F	VF	XF	Unc
1723	—	1,400	2,800	5,000	8,500	—
1724	—	1,100	2,150	4,000	6,500	—
1725	—	750	1,500	2,750	4,500	—
1726	—	1,100	2,150	4,000	6,500	—
1727	—	1,000	2,000	3,500	6,000	—
1728	—	750	1,500	2,750	4,500	—
1729 Unique	—	—	—	—	—	—
1730	—	550	1,100	2,000	3,500	—
1731	—	550	1,100	2,000	3,500	—
1732	—	550	1,100	2,000	3,500	—
1735	—	300	400	750	1,250	—
1736	—	300	400	750	1,250	—
1737	—	300	400	750	1,250	—
1738	—	300	350	700	1,150	—
1739	—	300	400	750	1,250	—
1740	—	300	350	700	1,150	—
1741	—	300	350	700	1,150	—
1742	—	300	350	700	1,150	—
1743	—	300	350	700	1,150	—
1744	—	300	350	700	1,150	—
1745	—	300	600	1,000	1,500	—
1746	—	300	350	700	1,150	—
1747	—	400	800	1,400	2,000	—
1748	—	300	350	700	1,150	—
1749	—	300	350	700	1,150	—
1750	—	400	800	1,400	2,000	—

KM# 240 4 ESCUDOS (Peca)

14.3000 g., 0.9170 Gold 0.4216 oz. AGW **Ruler:** Jose I **Obv:** Laureate bust right **Obv. Legend:** JOSEPHUS • I • D • G • ... **Rev:** Crowned arms in cartouche

Date	Mintage	VG	F	VF	XF	Unc
1750	—	300	350	500	850	—
1751	—	300	350	450	700	—
1752	—	300	350	450	700	—
1753	—	300	350	450	700	—
1754	—	300	350	450	700	—
1755	—	300	350	450	700	—
1756	—	300	350	450	700	—
1757	—	300	350	450	700	—
1758	—	300	350	450	700	—
1759	—	—	—	—	—	—
1760	—	300	350	450	700	—
1761	—	300	350	450	700	—
1762	—	300	350	450	700	—
1763	—	300	350	450	700	—
1764	—	300	350	450	700	—
1766	—	300	350	450	700	—
1767 Rare	—	—	—	—	—	—
1768	—	300	350	450	700	—
1769	—	300	350	450	700	—
1770	—	300	350	450	700	—
1771	—	300	350	450	700	—
1772	—	300	350	450	700	—
1773	—	300	350	450	700	—
1774	—	300	350	450	700	—
1775	—	300	350	450	700	—
1776	—	300	350	450	700	—

KM# 271 4 ESCUDOS (Peca)

14.3000 g., 0.9170 Gold 0.4216 oz. AGW **Ruler:** Maria I and Pedro III **Obv:** Conjoinded laureate bust right **Obv. Legend:** MARIA I ET PETRUS III... **Rev:** Crowned arms in cartouche

Date	Mintage	VG	F	VF	XF	Unc
1777 Rare	—	—	—	—	—	—
1778	—	300	375	500	750	—
1779	—	300	350	450	700	—
1780	—	300	350	450	700	—
1781	—	300	350	450	700	—

KM# 281 4 ESCUDOS (Peca)

14.3000 g., 0.9170 Gold 0.4216 oz. AGW **Ruler:** Maria I and Pedro III **Obv:** Conjoined laureate busts right **Obv. Legend:** MARIA • I • ET • PETRUS • III • ... **Rev:** Crowned arms in cartouche

Date	Mintage	VG	F	VF	XF	Unc
1782	—	300	375	500	750	—
1783	—	300	350	450	700	—
1784 Rare	—	—	—	—	—	—
1785	—	300	350	450	700	—

KM# 289 4 ESCUDOS (Peca)

14.3000 g., 0.9170 Gold 0.4216 oz. AGW **Ruler:** Maria I **Obv:** Veiled bust right, legend separated after D. G **Rev:** crowned arms in cartouche

Date	Mintage	VG	F	VF	XF	Unc
1786 Rare	—	—	—	—	—	—

KM# 290 4 ESCUDOS (Peca)

14.3000 g., 0.9170 Gold 0.4216 oz. AGW **Obv:** Bust right, smaller letters in legend separated by head after PORT **Rev:** Crowned arms

Date	Mintage	VG	F	VF	XF	Unc
1786	—	500	1,000	2,000	3,500	—

KM# 295 4 ESCUDOS (Peca)

14.3000 g., 0.9170 Gold 0.4216 oz. AGW **Ruler:** Maria I **Obv:** Bust right, large letters in legend **Rev:** Crowned arms

Date	Mintage	VG	F	VF	XF	Unc
1787	—	300	500	900	1,650	—

KM# 299 4 ESCUDOS (Peca)

14.3000 g., 0.9170 Gold 0.4216 oz. AGW **Ruler:** Maria I **Obv:** Bust right, with jeweled hairdress **Obv. Legend:** MARIA • I • D • G • PORT .... **Rev:** Crowned arms in cartouche

Date	Mintage	VG	F	VF	XF	Unc
1789	—	300	350	500	800	—
1791	—	300	350	550	850	—
1792	—	300	350	500	800	—
1793	—	300	350	500	800	—
1796	—	300	350	500	800	—
1797 Rare	—	—	—	—	—	—
1798	—	300	350	550	850	—
1799	—	300	350	500	800	—

KM# 214 8 ESCUDOS (Dobra)

28.6000 g., 0.9170 Gold 0.8432 oz. AGW **Ruler:** John V **Obv:** Laureate bust right, date and mint mark below **Rev:** Crowned arms in cartouche

Date	Mintage	VG	F	VF	XF	Unc
1722L Rare	—	—	—	—	—	—

KM# 222 8 ESCUDOS (Dobra)

28.6000 g., 0.9170 Gold 0.8432 oz. AGW **Ruler:** John V **Obv:** Laureat bust right, without mint mark **Obv. Legend:** IOANNES • V • D • G • PORT • ET • .... **Rev:** Crowned arms in cartouche **Note:** Varieties exist.

Date	Mintage	VG	F	VF	XF	Unc
1724 Rare	—	—	—	—	—	—
1725	—	3,500	6,000	10,000	15,000	—
1726	—	2,000	4,000	7,500	11,500	—
1727	—	1,750	3,500	6,500	10,000	—
1728	—	3,500	6,000	10,000	15,000	—
1729	—	1,250	2,500	4,500	7,000	—
1730	—	1,750	3,500	6,500	10,000	—
1732	—	1,500	3,000	5,500	8,500	—

PATTERNS

Including off metal strikes

KM#	Date	Mintage	Identification	Mkt Val
Pn12	1711	—	8000 Reis. Gold.	8,500

KM#	Date	Mintage	Identification	Mkt Val
Pn13	1718	—	16000 Reis. Gold.	—
PnA14	1718	—	Non-Denominated. Copper. Portuges	1,150

KM#	Date	Mintage	Identification	Mkt Val
Pn14	1718	—	Non-Denominated. Lead. Portuges	900
Pn15	1725	—	Peca. Copper. KM221.	2,000
Pn16	1725	—	Dobra. Copper. KM222.	2,500
PnA17	1731	—	16 Escudos. Copper.	—
Pn18	1731	—	16 Escudos. Gold. Milled edge.	—
Pn17	1731	—	16 Escudos. Gold. Ornamented edge.	—
PnA19	1731	—	24 Escudos. Copper.	—
Pn19	1731	—	24 Escudos. Gold. Ornamented edge.	—
Pn20	1731	—	24 Escudos. Gold. Milled edge.	—
PnA21	1786	—	4 Escudos. Copper. Similar to KM#295 but bust left.	—
Pn21	1787	—	4 Escudos. Copper. KM295.	1,250
Pn22	1787	—	4 Escudos. Copper. Arms variety.	1,500
Pn23	ND(1787)	—	4 Escudos. Copper. Bust variety.	1,500
Pn24	1788	—	4 Escudos. Copper.	1,250

KM#	Date	Mintage	Identification	Mkt Val
PNA25	1798	—	Peca. Copper.	950
Pn25	1798	—	Peca. Silver.	1,850
Pn26	1800	—	Peca. Silver.	1,850
Pn27	1800	—	Peca. Copper. Bust/arms	1,750
Pn28	ND	—	Peca. Silver. Obverse of Pn26, reverse of Pn25.	—

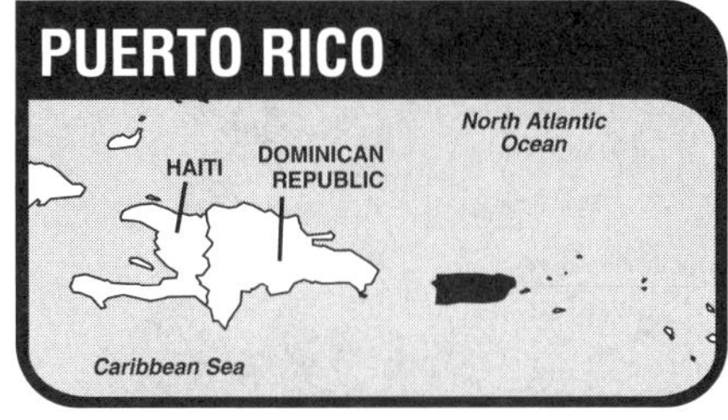

The Commonwealth of Puerto Rico, the eastern-most island of the Greater Antilles in the West Indies, has an area of 3,435 sq. mi. (9,104 sq. km.).

Columbus discovered Puerto Rico (*Rich Port*) and took possession for Spain on November 19, 1493 - the only time Columbus set foot on the soil of what is now a possession of the United States. The first settlement, Caparra, was established by Ponce de Leon in 1508. The early years of the colony were not promising. Considerable gold was found, but the supply was soon exhausted. Efforts to enslave the Indians caused violent reprisals. Hurricanes destroyed crops and homes. French, Dutch, and English freebooters burned the towns. Puerto Rico remained a Spanish possession until 1898, when it was ceded to the United States following the Spanish-American War.

RULER

Spanish, until 1898

ASSAYERS' INITIALS

G - Antonio Garcia Gonzalez
P - Felix Miguel Peiro Rodrigo

MONETARY SYSTEM

100 Centavos = 1 Peso

SPANISH COLONY

COUNTERMARKED COINAGE

In 1884, a large number of holed coins were countermarked at Puerto Ricos seven customs houses to legitimatize them with a device very similar to a fleur-de-lys. These coins were redeemed in 1894.

KM# 16.1 1/8 DOLLAR

3.3800 g., 0.9030 Silver 0.0981 oz. ASW, 21.5 mm.
Countermark: Lys **Note:** Countermark on Mexico City Mint 1 Real, KM#78.2.

CM Date	Host Date	Good	VG	F	VF	XF
ND(1884)	1774-84	—	—	—	—	—

KM# 16.2 1/8 DOLLAR

3.3800 g., 0.8960 Silver 0.0974 oz. ASW, 21.5 mm.
Countermark: Lys **Note:** Countermark on Mexico City Mint 1 Real, KM#78.2a.

CM Date	Host Date	Good	VG	F	VF	XF
ND(1884)	1785-89	—	—	—	—	—

VIEQUES ISLAND

(Crab Island)

Vieques (Crab) Island, located to the east of Puerto Rico is the largest of the Commonwealth's offshore islands. Two-thirds of the island is leased to the U.S. Navy. The neighboring island to the north, Culebra, was leased to the Navy until 1974, when the naval station was closed and bombardment exercises ceased. Puerto Rico's offshore island to the west, Mona, situated between the main island and the Dominican Republic, has been unpopulated since the late 16th century, and has no numismatic legacy.

COUNTERMARKED COINAGE

KM# 1 CENT

Copper **Countermark:** 12-rayed sunburst **Note:** Type I; Countermark on U.S. Nova Constellatio Cent.

CM Date	Host Date	Good	VG	F	VF	XF
ND(ca.1850)	1783-85	50.00	80.00	145	250	—

A port city in Croatia on the Dalmatian coast of the Adriatic Sea. Upon its incorporation in Yugoslavia in1918, its name was officially changed to Dubrovnik. Ragusa was once a great mercantile power, the merchant fleets of which sailed as far abroad as India and America. The city's present industries include oil-refining, slate mining, and the manufacture of liqueurs, cheese, silk, leather, and soap.

Refugees from the destroyed Latin communities of Salona and Epidaurus, and a colony of Slavs colonized the island rock of Ragusa during the 7th century. For four centuries Ragusa successfully defended itself against attacks by foreign powers, but from 1205 to 1358 recognized Venetian suzerainty. From 1358 to 1526, Ragusa was a vassal state of Hungary. The fall of Hungary in 1526 freed Ragusa, permitting it to become one of the foremost commercial powers of the Mediterranean and a leader in the development of literature and art. After this period its importance declined, due in part to the discovery of America, which reduced the importance of Mediterranean ports. A measure of its former economic importance was regained during the Napoleonic Wars when the republic, by adopting a policy of neutrality (1800-1805), became the leading carrier of the Mediterranean. This favored position was terminated by French seizure in 1805. In 1814 Ragusa was annexed by Austria, remaining a part of the Austrian Empire until its incorporation in the newly formed state of Yugoslavia in1918. Croatia proclaimed its independence in 1991.

MONETARY SYSTEM

6 Soldi = 1 Grosetto
12 Grosetti = 1 Perpero
36 Grosetti = 1 Scudo
40 Grosetti = 1 Ducato
60 Grosetti = 1 Tallero

REPUBLIC

STANDARD COINAGE

KM# 6 SOLDO

Copper **Obv:** Bust of Saint, facing above brick-like design **Rev:** Christ flanked by designs within circle of stars **Note:** Varieties exist.

Date	Mintage	VG	F	VF	XF	Unc
1706	—	15.00	30.00	50.00	110	—
1707	—	10.00	20.00	35.00	80.00	—
1712	—	10.00	20.00	35.00	80.00	—
1720	—	10.00	20.00	35.00	80.00	—
1723	—	10.00	20.00	35.00	80.00	—
1729	—	10.00	20.00	35.00	80.00	—
1731	—	10.00	20.00	35.00	80.00	—
1750	—	7.00	15.00	30.00	75.00	—
1752	—	7.00	15.00	30.00	75.00	—
1762	—	7.00	15.00	30.00	75.00	—
1770	—	7.00	15.00	30.00	75.00	—
1771	—	12.00	25.00	45.00	95.00	—
1780	—	7.00	15.00	30.00	80.00	—
1781	—	7.00	15.00	30.00	80.00	—
1791	—	7.00	15.00	30.00	80.00	—
1793	—	7.00	15.00	30.00	80.00	—
1795	—	7.00	15.00	30.00	80.00	—
1796	—	12.00	25.00	45.00	95.00	—
1797	—	7.00	15.00	30.00	80.00	—

KM# 22 3 SOLDI

Copper **Obv:** St. Blaze **Obv. Legend:** PROT • REIP • RHACUSINE **Rev:** Christ **Note:** Varieties exist.

Date	Mintage	VG	F	VF	XF	Unc
1795	—	17.00	35.00	65.00	125	—
1796	—	17.00	35.00	65.00	125	—

KM# 5 GROSETTO

Billon **Obv:** St. Blaze **Rev:** Christ within stars **Note:** Varieties exist.

Date	Mintage	VG	F	VF	XF	Unc
1701	—	10.00	20.00	32.00	65.00	—
1702	—	10.00	20.00	32.00	65.00	—
1703	—	10.00	20.00	32.00	65.00	—
1704	—	10.00	20.00	32.00	65.00	—
1705	—	10.00	20.00	32.00	65.00	—
1706	—	10.00	20.00	32.00	65.00	—
1707	—	10.00	20.00	32.00	65.00	—
1708	—	10.00	20.00	32.00	65.00	—
1709	—	10.00	20.00	32.00	65.00	—
1710	—	10.00	20.00	32.00	65.00	—
1711	—	10.00	20.00	32.00	65.00	—
1712	—	10.00	20.00	32.00	65.00	—
1713	—	10.00	20.00	32.00	65.00	—
1714	—	10.00	20.00	32.00	65.00	—
1715	—	10.00	20.00	32.00	65.00	—
1716	—	10.00	20.00	35.00	70.00	—
1720	—	10.00	20.00	35.00	70.00	—
1721	—	10.00	20.00	35.00	70.00	—
1722	—	10.00	20.00	35.00	70.00	—
1723	—	10.00	20.00	35.00	70.00	—
1724	—	10.00	20.00	35.00	70.00	—
1725	—	10.00	20.00	35.00	70.00	—
1726	—	10.00	20.00	35.00	70.00	—
1727	—	10.00	20.00	35.00	70.00	—
1728	—	10.00	20.00	35.00	70.00	—
1748	—	10.00	20.00	35.00	70.00	—
1751	—	12.50	22.50	40.00	80.00	—
1754	—	12.50	22.50	40.00	80.00	—
1756	—	12.50	22.50	40.00	80.00	—
1757	—	12.50	22.50	40.00	80.00	—
1761	—	12.50	22.50	40.00	80.00	—

KM# 4 3 GROSETTI (Alltilucho)

1.1200 g., Billon **Obv:** Head of Saint, right **Obv. Legend:** S • BLASIVS • RAGVSII **Rev:** Legend **Rev. Legend:** GROS • ARGE / TRIP / CIVI / RAGV **Note:** Varieties exist.

Date	Mintage	VG	F	VF	XF	Unc
1701	—	30.00	55.00	100	225	—

KM# 7 PERPERO

Billon **Obv:** St. Blaze divides date and S B **Obv. Legend:** PROT • RAEIP • RHAGVSINAE **Rev:** Christ within stars

Date	Mintage	VG	F	VF	XF	Unc
1702	—	20.00	35.00	85.00	150	—
1705	—	18.00	30.00	80.00	145	—
1706	—	16.50	27.50	55.00	90.00	—
1707	—	16.50	27.50	55.00	90.00	—
1708	—	18.00	30.00	80.00	145	—
1709	—	16.50	27.50	55.00	90.00	—
1723	—	20.00	35.00	85.00	150	—
1724	—	18.00	30.00	80.00	145	—
1725	—	20.00	35.00	85.00	150	—
1728	—	20.00	35.00	85.00	150	—
1729	—	18.00	30.00	80.00	145	—
1730	—	20.00	35.00	85.00	150	—
1732	—	20.00	35.00	85.00	150	—
1733	—	18.00	30.00	80.00	145	—
1734	—	18.00	30.00	80.00	145	—
1744	—	18.00	30.00	80.00	145	—
1750	—	20.00	35.00	85.00	150	—

KM# 10 1/2 SCUDO

Silver **Obv:** St. Blaze divides date and S B within beaded circle **Obv. Legend:** PROTECTOR RHEIPVBLICAE RHAGISINAE **Rev:** Christ within stars and beaded circle

Date	Mintage	VG	F	VF	XF	Unc
1708	—	150	250	—	—	—
1709	—	100	200	350	—	—
1748 SB	—	100	200	350	—	—
1750	—	60.00	125	250	400	—

KM# 11 SCUDO

16.8000 g., Silver **Obv:** St. Blaze divides date and S B within beaded circle **Obv. Legend:** PROTECTOR • REIPVBLICE • RHAGVSINE • • **Rev:** Christ within stars and beaded circle **Rev. Legend:** IVIA • SALVS • SPES • ET • PRESIDIVM • •

Date	Mintage	VG	F	VF	XF	Unc
1708 SB	—	125	225	375	—	—
1709	—	125	225	375	—	—
1739	—	125	225	375	—	—
1747 SB	—	125	225	375	—	—
1748	—	80.00	165	300	500	—
1750	—	80.00	165	300	500	—

KM# 15 DUCATO

Silver **Obv:** Crowned, ornate arms **Obv. Legend:** RHAGUSINE DUCAT REIP **Rev:** St. Blaze divides date and S B **Rev. Legend:** AUSPICIIC • TUIS • A • DEO

Date	Mintage	VG	F	VF	XF	Unc
1722 SB Rare	—	—	—	—	—	—
1723	—	50.00	100	200	350	—
1797 SB	—	25.00	50.00	125	300	—

KM# 13 1/2 TALLERO

Silver **Obv:** Bust left **Obv. Legend:** RECTOR • REIP • RHACVSIN • **Rev:** Crowned baroque arms **Rev. Legend:** ...MEDIVS • DVCAT •

Date	Mintage	Good	VG	F	VF	XF
1748	—	—	—	—	—	—

KM# 20 2 DUCATI

Silver **Obv:** Bust of Maria Theresa right **Obv. Legend:** RESPVBL • RHACVS • **Rev:** Crowned, oval ornate arms **Rev. Legend:** FIDE • ET • IVST DVGE DEO **Note:** Dav. #1640.

Date	Mintage	VG	F	VF	XF	Unc
1791 GA//GA	—	65.00	125	275	500	—

KM# 21 2 DUCATI

Silver **Obv:** Bust of Maria Theresa right **Obv. Legend:** RESPVBL • RHACVS • **Rev:** Crowned shield within sprigs **Rev. Legend:** FIDE • ET • IVST DVGE DEO **Note:** Dav. #1641.

Date	Mintage	VG	F	VF	XF	Unc
1792 GA//GA	—	45.00	65.00	110	235	—
1793	—	40.00	60.00	100	200	—
1794	—	35.00	50.00	90.00	185	—
1795	—	50.00	70.00	120	250	—

KM# A16 TALLERO (Ducat Et Sem)

Silver **Obv:** Bust of St. Blaze divides S - B **Rev:** Crowned arms divide date **Note:** Dav. #1635.

Date	Mintage	VG	F	VF	XF	Unc
1725 Rare	—	—	—	—	—	—

KM# 16 TALLERO (Ducat Et Sem)

Silver **Obv:** Bust of St. Blaze divides S B **Obv. Legend:** • DIVINA • PER • •TE • OPE • **Rev:** Crowned, ornate arms, date in legend **Rev. Legend:** • DVCAT • ET • SEM • • RIEP • RHAG • **Note:** Varieties exist. Dav. #1636.

Date	Mintage	VG	F	VF	XF	Unc
1725	—	85.00	170	325	550	—
1730	—	85.00	170	325	550	—
1731	—	85.00	170	325	550	—
1733	—	85.00	170	325	550	—
1734	—	85.00	170	325	550	—
1735	—	70.00	150	275	450	—
1736	—	70.00	150	275	450	—
1738	—	70.00	150	275	450	—
1743	—	70.00	150	275	450	—
1747	1	—	—	—	—	—

KM# 17 TALLERO (Ducat Et Sem)

Silver **Obv:** Bust left **Obv. Legend:** • RECTOR • REIP • - • RHACVSINE • **Rev:** Crowned, ornate arms **Rev. Legend:** • DVCAT • ET • SEM • • REIP • RHAG • **Note:** Varieties exist. Dav. #1637.

Date	Mintage	VG	F	VF	XF	Unc
1738 Rare	—	—	—	—	—	—
1743	—	35.00	70.00	165	285	—
1744	—	35.00	70.00	165	285	—
1745	—	35.00	70.00	165	285	—
1746	—	25.00	35.00	75.00	150	—
1747	—	25.00	35.00	75.00	150	—
1748	—	30.00	60.00	150	250	—

KM# 18 TALLERO (Ducat Et Sem)

Silver **Obv:** Bust left **Obv. Legend:** RECTOR • REI •RHACVSIN • **Rev:** Crowned ornate arms **Rev. Legend:** DVCAT • ET • SEM • REIP • RHAG • **Note:** Dav. #1639.

Date	Mintage	VG	F	VF	XF	Unc
1751	—	25.00	45.00	90.00	150	—
1752	—	20.00	30.00	65.00	115	—
1753	—	20.00	30.00	65.00	115	—
1754	—	25.00	50.00	100	225	—
1755	—	35.00	65.00	125	250	—
1756	—	20.00	30.00	60.00	100	—
1757	—	20.00	30.00	60.00	100	—
1758	—	20.00	30.00	60.00	100	—
1759	—	20.00	30.00	60.00	100	—
1760	—	20.00	30.00	60.00	100	—
1761	—	20.00	30.00	60.00	100	—
1762	—	20.00	30.00	60.00	100	—
1763	—	20.00	30.00	60.00	100	—
1764	—	20.00	30.00	60.00	100	—
1765	—	20.00	30.00	60.00	100	—
1766	—	20.00	30.00	60.00	100	—
1767 DM-GA	—	20.00	30.00	60.00	100	—
1767 GB-DM	—	20.00	30.00	60.00	100	—
1768 GA-GA	—	20.00	30.00	60.00	100	—
1769	—	20.00	30.00	60.00	100	—
1770 DM-DM	—	20.00	30.00	60.00	100	—
1770 GA-DM	—	20.00	30.00	60.00	100	—
1771 GA-GA	—	20.00	30.00	60.00	100	—
1771 GA-DM	—	20.00	30.00	60.00	100	—
1772 GA-DM	—	20.00	30.00	60.00	100	—
1773 GA-DM	—	20.00	30.00	60.00	100	—
1773 DM-DM	—	20.00	30.00	60.00	100	—
1774 DM-DM	—	20.00	30.00	60.00	100	—
1774 GA-DM	—	20.00	30.00	60.00	100	—
1775 GA-GA	—	20.00	30.00	60.00	100	—
1776 GA-GA	—	20.00	30.00	60.00	100	—
1776 GA-DM	—	20.00	30.00	60.00	100	—
1777 GA-DM	—	20.00	30.00	60.00	100	—
1778 GA-DM	—	22.00	35.00	70.00	125	—
1779 GA-DM	—	22.00	35.00	70.00	125	—

KM# 19 TALLERO (Ducat Et Sem)

Silver **Obv:** Legend, St. Biagio kneeling left **Obv. Legend:** ET • PRAESIDIVM - ET • DECUS **Rev:** Virgin seated on clouds **Note:** Varieties exist. Dav. #1638.

Date	Mintage	VG	F	VF	XF	Unc
1751 Rare	—	—	—	—	—	—

RUSSIA

Russia, formerly the central power of the Union of Soviet Socialist Republics and now of the Commonwealth of Independent States occupies the northern part of Asia and the eastern part of Europe, has an area of 17,075,400 sq. km. Capital: Moscow.

The first Russian dynasty was founded in Novgorod by the Viking Rurik in 862 A.D. under Yaroslav the Wise (1019-54). The subsequent Kievan state became one of the great commercial and cultural centers of Europe before falling to the Mongols of the Batu Khan, 13th century, who were suzerains of Russia until late in the 15th century when Ivan III threw off the Mongol yoke. The Russian Empire was enlarged, solidified and Westernized during the reigns of Ivan the Terrible, Peter the Great and Catherine the Great, and by 1881 extended to the Pacific and into Central Asia. Contemporary Russian history began in March of 1917 when Tsar Nicholas II abdicated under pressure and was replaced by a provisional government composed of both radical and conservative elements. This government rapidly lost ground to the Bolshevik wing of the Socialist Democratic Labor Party which attained power following the Bolshevik Revolution which began on Nov. 7, 1917. After the Russian Civil War, the regional governments, national states and armies became federal republics of the Russian Socialist Federal Soviet Republic. These autonomous republics united to form the Union of Soviet Socialist Republics that was established as a federation under the premiership of Lenin on Dec. 30, 1922.

RULERS

Peter I (The Great), 1689-1725
Catherine I, 1725-27
Peter II, 1727-30
Anna, 1730-40
Ivan VI, 1740-41
Elizabeth, 1741-61
Peter III, 1761-62
Catherine II, 1762-96
Paul I, 1796-1801

MINT MARKS

АМ - Annensk, 1789-1799
БМ - St. Petersburg, 1796
ЕМ - Ekaterinburg, 1762-1876
КД - Moscow, Krasny Dvor, (Red Mint), 1725-1730
КМ - Kolyvan, 1767-1830 (later Souzan)
МД, МДЗ - Moscow, Dvor Zamoskvoretsky, (Naval Mint), 1704-1740
ММ - Moscow, 1730-1796
ММД - Moscow, 1741-1758
НД, НДЗ - Moscow, Naberezhny Dvor, Embankment Mint, 1704-1730
СМ - St. Petersburg (gold), 1796-1801
СМ - Sestroretsk, Finland, 1763-1767
СП - St. Petersburg, 1798-1800
СПБ - St. Petersburg, 1724-1915
ТМ - Feodesia, Crimea, 1787-1788

MINTMASTERS' INITIALS

MOSCOW MINT

G.,G.F.	1701-1713	Gouin, Gouin Fecit
H.	1705-1710	Haupt
I.L.-L.,L.-L.	1705-1709	Jean Lang and Jean Lefken
D-L	1712-1713	Jean (Timofei) Lefken
З.	1714	
М.	1718	
I-L,IL,L	1718-1719	Jean (Ivan) Lang
K,OK,KO	1718-1725	Ottfried Konig
А	1751	Afonasiev
ИІ	1752-53	Ilya Shagin
Е	1752-69	Igor Ivanov
ЕІ	1762-69	Igor Ivanov
ІП	1753-54	I.Plavilshchikov
МБ	1754-57	M.Bobrovshchikov
ДМ	1762-70	Daniel Mochalkin
АШ	1766-68	Alexei Schneze
СА	1774-75	Stepan Afonasiev

ST. PETERSBURG MINT

ІМ	1751-58	Ivan Markov
ЯІ	1752-66	Yakov Ivanov
ЯИ	1752-66	Yakov Ivanov
НК	1758-63	Nazar Kutuzov
СА	1764-70	Stepan Afonasiev
АШ	1766-72	Alexei Shneze
ЕІ	1767-68	Igor Ivanov
ЯЧ	1770-76	Yakov Chernishev
ОЛ	1773-79	Fedor Lesnikov
ИЗ	1780-83	Ivan Zaitsev
АГ	1781	Avraam Hutseus
ММ	1783-84	Mikhail Mikhailov
ЯА	1785-93	Yakov Afonasiev
АК	1793-95	Andrei Kutzberg
ІС	1796	Ivan Sabelnikov
ГЛ	1797	Gregory Lvov
ФЦ	1797-1801	Fedor Tsetreus
МБ	1798-99	M. Bobrovshchikov
ОМ	1798-1801	Ossip Medzher
АИ	1799-1800	Alexei Ivanov

CYRILLIC DATING

≠АΨА (1701)	≠АΨВІ (1712)
≠АΨВ (1702)	≠АΨГІ (1713)
≠АΨГ (1703)	≠АΨДІ (1714)
≠АΨД (1704)	≠АΨЕІ (1715)
≠АΨЕ (1705)	≠АΨЅІ (1716)
≠АΨЅ (1706)	≠АΨЗІ (1717)
≠АΨЗ (1707)	≠АΨИІ (1718)
≠АΨИ (1708)	≠АΨѲІ (1719)
≠АΨѲ (1709)	≠АΨК (1720)
≠АΨІ (1710)	≠АΨКА (1721)
≠АΨАІ (1711)	≠АΨКВ (1722)

MONETARY SYSTEM

1/4 Kopek = Polushka ПОЛУШКА
1/2 Kopek = Denga, Denezhka
ДЕНГА, ДЕНЕЖКА
Kopek КОПѢИКА
(2, 3 & 4) Kopeks КОПѢИКИ
(5 and up) Kopeks КОПѢЕКЪ
3 Kopeks = Altyn, Altynnik
АЛТЫНЪ, АЛТЫННИКЪ
10 Kopeks = Grivna, Grivennik
ГРИВНА, ГРИВЕННИКЪ
25 Kopeks = Polupoltina, Polupoltinnik
ПОЛУПОЛТИНА
ПОЛУПОЛТИННИКЪ
50 Kopeks = Poltina, Poltinnik
ПОЛТИНА, ПОЛТИННИКЪ
100 Kopeks = Rouble, Ruble РУБЛЪ
10 Roubles = Imperial ИМПЕРІАЛЪ
10 Roubles = Chervonetz ЧЕРВОНЕЦ

NOTE: For silver coins with Zlotych and Kopek or Ruble denominations see Poland.

NOTE: For gold coins with Zlotych and Ruble denominations see Poland.

LEGENDS

Peter I

Obverse with full title:
ЦРЬ И ВЕЛИКІИ КНЗЬ ПЕТРЬ АЛЕЗІЕВИЧЪ
"Tsar and Grand Duke Peter Alexievich"
Obverse with short title:
ЦРЬ ПЕТРЬ АЛЕЗІЕВИЧЪ
"Tsar Peter Alexievich"
Reverse with full title:
ВСЕА ВЕЛІКІА И МЛЫА И ВЕЛЫА РОСИ САМОДЕРЖЕЦЪ
"of All Great, Little & White Russias Autocrat"
Reverse with short title:
ВСЕА РОСИ САМОДЕРЖЕЦЪ
"of All Russias Autocrat"
ВСЕА РОСИ ПОВЕЛИТЕЛЬ
"of All Russias Ruler"

EDGE INSCRIPTIONS

Peter I

МАНЭТЪНАГО ДЕНЕЖЪНАГО ДВОРА 1701
МОСКОВЪСКАА КАПЕИКА X МАНЕТНОГО ДЕНЕЖНОГО ДВОРА
КОПЕИКА МАНЕТНОГО ДЕНЕЖЪНАГО ДВОРА 1710
КОПЕИКА МАНЕТНОГО . . . ДЕНЕЖЪНАГО ДВОРА
КОПЕИКА МАНЕТНОГО ДЕНЕЖНОГО ДВРОА

STANDARD COINAGE

KM# 110 POLUSHKA (1/4 Kopek)

2.6600 g., Copper **Ruler:** Peter I **Obv:** Crowned double-headed eagle within beaded circle, legend around **Obv. Legend:** Legend begins: CZAR AND.. **Rev:** Value, legend

Date	Mintage	VG	F	VF	XF	Unc
ND(1701) Rare	—	—	—	—	—	—
ND(1702)	—	65.00	90.00	125	240	—
ND(1703)	—	65.00	90.00	125	240	—

KM# A114 POLUSHKA (1/4 Kopek)

Copper **Ruler:** Peter I **Rev. Legend:** CZAR AND GRAND DUKE

Date	Mintage	VG	F	VF	XF	Unc
ND(1703) Rare	—	—	—	—	—	—

KM# 114 POLUSHKA (1/4 Kopek)

2.6600 g., Copper **Ruler:** Peter I **Obv:** Crowned double-headed eagle **Rev:** Value, legend **Rev. Legend:** RULER OF ALL THE RUSSIAS

Date	Mintage	VG	F	VF	XF	Unc
ND(1704)	—	35.00	55.00	75.00	125	—
ND(1705) Rare	—	—	—	—	—	—
ND(1707)	—	30.00	45.00	60.00	115	—
ND(1712) Rare	—	—	—	—	—	—
ND(1713)	—	35.00	55.00	75.00	125	—
ND(1714)	—	45.00	65.00	100	165	—
ND(1716) Rare	—	—	—	—	—	—
ND(1718) Rare	—	—	—	—	—	—

KM# 113 POLUSHKA (1/4 Kopek)

2.0500 g., Copper **Ruler:** Peter I **Note:** Reduced weight.

Date	Mintage	VG	F	VF	XF	Unc
ND(1704) Rare	—	—	—	—	—	—
ND(1705)	—	30.00	45.00	60.00	115	—
ND(1706)	—	30.00	45.00	60.00	115	—
ND(1707)	—	20.00	35.00	50.00	90.00	—
ND(1708)	—	100	300	500	1,100	—
ND(1709) Rare	—	—	—	—	—	—
ND(1710) Rare	—	—	—	—	—	—
ND(1711)	—	100	150	200	375	—
ND(1713)	—	35.00	55.00	75.00	125	—

KM# 152.1 POLUSHKA (1/4 Kopek)

Copper **Ruler:** Peter I **Obv:** Crowned double-headed eagle **Rev:** Value: POLISHKA, Cyrillic or Arabic date

Date	Mintage	VG	F	VF	XF	Unc
NDНД	—	15.00	25.00	45.00	70.00	—
1718НД Rare	—	—	—	—	—	—
1719НД Rare	—	—	—	—	—	—
NDНД	—	15.00	25.00	45.00	70.00	—
NDНД Reverse crown	—	15.00	25.00	45.00	70.00	—
NDНД	—	20.00	40.00	65.00	100	—
NDНД Reverse crown	—	20.00	40.00	65.00	100	—
1720НД	—	25.00	45.00	90.00	150	—
1720НД Retrograde 7	—	25.00	45.00	90.00	150	—
NDНД	—	20.00	40.00	70.00	105	—
1721НД Rare	—	—	—	—	—	—
1271НД Error for 1721; Rare	—	—	—	—	—	—
1722НД Rare	—	—	—	—	—	—

KM# 152.2 POLUSHKA (1/4 Kopek)

Copper **Ruler:** Peter I **Obv:** Crowned double-headed eagle **Rev:** Value, date **Note:** Without mint mark.

Date	Mintage	VG	F	VF	XF	Unc
ND	—	—	—	75.00	—	—
1718 Reverse crown	—	16.00	28.00	50.00	100	—
1718 I Rare	—	—	—	—	—	—
ND Rare	—	—	—	—	—	—
1719	—	16.00	28.00	40.00	70.00	—
1719 Reverse crown	—	16.00	28.00	50.00	100	—
ND Rare	—	—	—	—	—	—
1720	—	15.00	25.00	40.00	70.00	—
1720 Reverse crown	—	15.00	25.00	45.00	75.00	—
ND	—	—	—	50.00	—	—
1721	—	25.00	40.00	70.00	130	—
1722	—	20.00	40.00	65.00	100	—

KM# 152.3 POLUSHKA (1/4 Kopek)

2.6600 g., Copper **Ruler:** Peter I **Note:** Mixed cyrillic and western date.

Date	Mintage	VG	F	VF	XF	Unc
17K(20)HA	—	—	—	50.00	—	—

KM# 152.4 POLUSHKA (1/4 Kopek)

Copper **Ruler:** Peter I **Note:** Without mint mark. Mixed cyrillic and western dates.

Date	Mintage	VG	F	VF	XF	Unc
17K(20)	—	30.00	50.00	80.00	120	—
17K1(21)	—	25.00	45.00	65.00	100	—

KM# 187 POLUSHKA (1/4 Kopek)

4.1000 g., Copper **Obv:** Crowned double-headed eagle **Rev:** Value, date in cartouche **Rev. Legend:** POLUSHKA **Note:** Ekaterinburg and Moscow mints. Coins cannot be identified by mint.

Date	Mintage	VG	F	VF	XF	Unc
1730	—	3.00	6.00	12.00	30.00	—
1731	—	3.00	6.00	12.00	30.00	—
1732	—	3.00	6.00	12.00	30.00	—
1734	—	3.00	6.00	12.00	30.00	—
1735	—	3.00	6.00	12.00	30.00	—
1736	—	3.00	6.00	12.00	30.00	—
1737	—	3.00	6.00	12.00	30.00	—
1738	—	5.00	9.00	20.00	40.00	—
1739	—	3.00	6.00	12.00	25.00	—
1740	—	5.00	10.00	25.00	45.00	—
1741	—	25.00	50.00	70.00	110	—
1743	883,000	6.00	12.00	25.00	50.00	—
1744	1,050,000	10.00	25.00	50.00	90.00	—
1745	1,648,000	10.00	30.00	60.00	100	—
1746	2,240,000	6.00	12.00	25.00	50.00	—
1747	2,856,000	6.00	12.00	25.00	50.00	—
1748	1,488,000	6.00	12.00	25.00	50.00	—
1749	1,880,000	6.00	12.00	25.00	50.00	—
1750	3,104,000	6.00	12.00	25.00	50.00	—
1751	576,000	6.00	12.00	25.00	50.00	—
1754	—	6.00	12.00	25.00	50.00	—

C# 4 POLUSHKA (1/4 Kopek)

2.5600 g., Copper **Ruler:** Elizabeth

Date	Mintage	VG	F	VF	XF	Unc
1757	1,830,000	15.00	30.00	60.00	90.00	—
1758	536,000	15.00	35.00	75.00	100	—
1759	1,178,000	15.00	40.00	80.00	110	—

C# 55.3 POLUSHKA (1/4 Kopek)

Copper **Ruler:** Catherine II **Obv:** Crowned monogram divides date within wreath **Rev:** St. George on horse slaying dragon

Date	Mintage	VG	F	VF	XF	Unc
1766EM	3,107,000	6.00	12.00	25.00	50.00	—
1767EM	4,311,000	6.00	12.00	25.00	50.00	—
1768EM	5,684,000	6.00	12.00	25.00	50.00	—
1769EM	3,778,000	6.00	12.00	25.00	50.00	—
1770/69EM	6,040,000	7.50	15.00	30.00	60.00	—
1770EM	Inc. above	6.00	12.00	25.00	50.00	—
1771EM	4,470,000	6.00	12.00	25.00	50.00	—
1772EM	960,000	10.00	20.00	40.00	80.00	—
1773EM	198,000	100	200	300	500	—
1774EM Rare	—	—	—	—	—	—
1775EM	378,000	60.00	100	150	275	—
1776EM Rare	—	—	—	—	—	—
1786EM	450,000	6.00	12.00	25.00	50.00	—
1789EM	2,037,000	6.00	12.00	25.00	50.00	—
1790EM	1,018,999	6.00	12.00	25.00	50.00	—
1794EM	9,000	60.00	100	150	275	—
1795EM	71,000	6.00	12.00	25.00	50.00	—
1796EM	261,000	20.00	40.00	75.00	125	—

C# 55.4 POLUSHKA (1/4 Kopek)

Copper **Ruler:** Catherine II

Date	Mintage	VG	F	VF	XF	Unc
1783KM	—	15.00	35.00	70.00	100	—
1784KM	—	15.00	35.00	70.00	100	—
1785KM	—	15.00	35.00	70.00	100	—
1786KM	—	40.00	80.00	150	275	—
1787KM	—	30.00	60.00	100	175	—
1788KM	—	30.00	60.00	100	175	—
1789KM	—	30.00	60.00	100	175	—
1790KM	—	30.00	60.00	100	175	—
1791KM	—	60.00	100	150	275	—
1792KM	—	20.00	40.00	75.00	125	—
1793KM	—	20.00	40.00	75.00	125	—
1794KM	—	60.00	100	150	275	—
1795KM	—	30.00	60.00	100	175	—

C# 55.5 POLUSHKA (1/4 Kopek)

Copper **Ruler:** Catherine II

Date	Mintage	VG	F	VF	XF	Unc
1787PЛ Rare	—	—	—	—	—	—

C# 55.2a POLUSHKA (1/4 Kopek)

Copper **Ruler:** Catherine II

Date	Mintage	VG	F	VF	XF	Unc
1789AЛ Rare	—	—	—	—	—	—

C# 55.2 POLUSHKA (1/4 Kopek)

Copper **Ruler:** Catherine II **Note:** Without mint mark.

Date	Mintage	VG	F	VF	XF	Unc
1789	—	15.00	30.00	50.00	90.00	—
1793	79,000	20.00	40.00	75.00	125	—
1795	62,000	22.50	45.00	85.00	140	—

C# 92.1 POLUSHKA (1/4 Kopek)

2.5600 g., Copper **Ruler:** Paul I **Obv:** Crowned monogram **Rev:** Value, date

Date	Mintage	VG	F	VF	XF	Unc
1797AM	—	8.00	17.00	35.00	70.00	—
1798AM	—	8.00	17.00	35.00	70.00	—

C# 92.2 POLUSHKA (1/4 Kopek)

3.0000 g., Copper **Ruler:** Paul I

Date	Mintage	VG	F	VF	XF	Unc
1797	—	7.50	15.00	30.00	60.00	—
1798	1,510,000	7.50	15.00	30.00	60.00	—
1799 Rare	11,000	—	—	—	—	—
1800	—	100	250	350	650	—

C# 92.3 POLUSHKA (1/4 Kopek)

2.5600 g., Copper **Ruler:** Paul I

Date	Mintage	VG	F	VF	XF	Unc
1797KM	—	37.50	75.00	150	250	—
1798KM	—	37.50	75.00	150	250	—
1799KM	—	37.50	75.00	150	250	—

KM# 102 DENGA (1/2 Kopek)

6.4000 g., Copper **Ruler:** Peter I **Obv:** Crowned double-headed eagle, legend around **Obv. Legend:** CZAR PETER ALEXIEVITCH **Rev:** Value, date withinn circle, legend around **Rev. Legend:** AUTOCRAT OF ALL THE RUSSIAS

Date	Mintage	VG	F	VF	XF	Unc
ND(1700)	—	45.00	75.00	135	265	—
ND(1701)	—	25.00	45.00	85.00	165	—

KM# 111 DENGA (1/2 Kopek)

5.3200 g., Copper **Ruler:** Peter I **Obv:** Crowned double-headed eagle within circle, legend around **Rev:** Value, date within circle, legend around **Note:** Reduced weight.

Date	Mintage	VG	F	VF	XF	Unc
ND(1701)	—	25.00	45.00	75.00	150	—
ND(1702)	—	20.00	40.00	60.00	100	—
ND(1703)	—	25.00	45.00	75.00	150	—
ND(1704)	—	20.00	40.00	60.00	100	—

KM# 115 DENGA (1/2 Kopek)

4.1000 g., Copper **Ruler:** Peter I **Obv:** Crowned double-headed eagle within circle, legend around **Rev:** Value, date within circle, legend around **Note:** Reduced weight.

Date	Mintage	VG	F	VF	XF	Unc
ND(1704)	—	15.00	30.00	50.00	90.00	—
ND(1705)	—	15.00	30.00	50.00	90.00	—
ND(1706)	—	15.00	30.00	50.00	90.00	—
ND(1707)	—	15.00	30.00	50.00	90.00	—
ND(1708)	—	20.00	40.00	60.00	100	—
ND(1709) Rare	—	—	—	—	—	—
ND(1710)	—	25.00	45.00	75.00	150	—
ND(1711)	—	25.00	45.00	75.00	150	—
ND(1712)	—	15.00	30.00	50.00	90.00	—

KM# A116 DENGA (1/2 Kopek)

4.1000 g., Copper **Ruler:** Peter I **Obv:** Crowned double-headed eagle **Rev:** Value, date in center of legend **Rev. Legend:** CZAR AND GRAND DUKE

Date	Mintage	VG	F	VF	XF	Unc
ND(1704)	—	15.00	30.00	50.00	90.00	—

KM# 116 DENGA (1/2 Kopek)

6.4000 g., Copper **Ruler:** Peter I **Obv:** Crowned double-headed eagle **Rev:** Value, date in center of legend **Rev. Legend:** RULER OF ALL THE RUSSIAS

Date	Mintage	VG	F	VF	XF	Unc
ND(1705)	—	15.00	30.00	50.00	90.00	—
ND(1712)	—	15.00	30.00	50.00	90.00	—
ND(1713)	—	15.00	30.00	50.00	90.00	—
ND(1714)	—	15.00	30.00	50.00	90.00	—
ND(1715)	—	15.00	30.00	50.00	90.00	—
ND(1716)	—	25.00	45.00	75.00	150	—
ND(1717)	—	60.00	120	180	350	—
ND(1718) Rare	—	—	—	—	—	—

KM# 188 DENGA (1/2 Kopek)

8.1900 g., Copper **Obv:** Crowned double-headed eagle **Rev:** Value and date in cartouche **Rev. Legend:** DENGA **Note:** Ekaterinburg and Moscow Mints. Coins cannot be identified by mint. Varieties exist.

Date	Mintage	VG	F	VF	XF	Unc
1730	—	3.00	5.00	10.00	25.00	—
1731	—	3.00	5.00	10.00	25.00	—
1734	—	3.00	5.00	10.00	25.00	—
1735	—	3.00	5.00	10.00	25.00	—
1736	—	3.00	5.00	10.00	25.00	—
1737	—	3.00	5.00	10.00	25.00	—
1738	—	3.00	5.00	10.00	25.00	—
1739	—	3.00	5.00	10.00	25.00	—
1740	—	4.00	7.00	12.00	30.00	—
1741	—	10.00	20.00	35.00	65.00	—
1743	30,909,000	6.00	12.00	25.00	50.00	—
1744	41,299,000	5.00	10.00	20.00	50.00	—
1745	55,408,000	5.00	10.00	20.00	50.00	—
1746	83,618,000	5.00	10.00	20.00	50.00	—
1747	83,822,000	5.00	10.00	20.00	50.00	—
1748	79,608,000	5.00	10.00	20.00	50.00	—
1749	75,860,000	5.00	10.00	20.00	50.00	—
1750	64,269,000	6.00	12.00	25.00	50.00	—
1751	27,624,000	6.00	12.00	25.00	50.00	—
1752	4,005,000	10.00	25.00	50.00	100	—
1753	4,005,000	6.00	12.00	25.00	50.00	—
1754/3	38,320,000	6.00	12.00	25.00	50.00	—
1754	Inc. above	6.00	12.00	25.00	50.00	—

C# 5 DENGA (1/2 Kopek)

5.1200 g., Copper **Ruler:** Elizabeth **Obv:** Crowned monogram divides date within wreath **Rev:** St. George on horse slaying dragon

Date	Mintage	VG	F	VF	XF	Unc
1757	3,229,000	12.00	25.00	50.00	100	—
1758	521,000	12.00	25.00	50.00	125	—
1759	1,574,000	12.00	25.00	50.00	100	—
1760	Inc. above	25.00	50.00	100	175	—

C# 40 DENGA (1/2 Kopek)

2.5600 g., Copper **Ruler:** Peter III **Obv:** St. George on horse slaying dragon **Rev:** Value, date above drum, crossed flags **Note:** Without mint mark.

Date	Mintage	VG	F	VF	XF	Unc
1762 Reeded edge; Rare	—	—	—	—	—	—
1762 Plain edge; Rare	—	—	—	—	—	—

C# 56.1 DENGA (1/2 Kopek)

6.4000 g., Copper **Ruler:** Catherine II **Note:** Without mint mark.

Date	Mintage	VG	F	VF	XF	Unc
1788	—	10.00	20.00	35.00	70.00	—
1789	—	10.00	20.00	35.00	70.00	—
1790	—	20.00	40.00	75.00	125	—
1791	88,000	30.00	60.00	100	175	—
1792	59,000	30.00	60.00	100	175	—
1793	15,000	150	300	500	800	—
1794	—	75.00	150	250	400	—

C# 56.2 DENGA (1/2 Kopek)

5.1200 g., Copper **Ruler:** Catherine II **Obv:** Crowned monogram divides date within wreath **Rev:** St. George on horse slaying dragon

Date	Mintage	VG	F	VF	XF	Unc
1763EM	—	—	—	—	—	—
1764EM	—	200	500	700	1,000	—
1766EM	2,841,000	5.00	10.00	17.50	45.00	—
1767EM	2,623,000	5.00	10.00	17.50	45.00	—
1768EM	2,422,000	5.00	10.00	17.50	45.00	—
1769EM	1,450,000	5.00	10.00	17.50	45.00	—
1770EM	4,019,999	5.00	10.00	17.50	45.00	—
1771EM	2,910,000	5.00	10.00	17.50	45.00	—
1772EM	1,160,000	5.00	10.00	17.50	45.00	—
1773EM	451,000	5.00	10.00	17.50	45.00	—
1774EM	20,000	100	150	250	400	—
1775EM	508,000	5.00	10.00	17.50	35.00	—
1786EM	573,000	5.00	10.00	17.50	35.00	—
1789/8EM	—	—	—	—	—	—
1789EM	2,009,000	5.00	10.00	17.50	35.00	—
1790EM	1,235,000	5.00	10.00	17.50	35.00	—
1793EM	933,000	5.00	10.00	17.50	35.00	—
1794EM	797,000	5.00	10.00	17.50	35.00	—
1795EM	3,199,000	5.00	10.00	17.50	35.00	—
1796EM	—	5.00	10.00	17.50	35.00	—

C# 56.4 DENGA (1/2 Kopek)

5.1200 g., Copper **Ruler:** Catherine II

Date	Mintage	VG	F	VF	XF	Unc
1783KM	—	8.00	15.00	25.00	50.00	—
1784KM	—	8.00	15.00	25.00	50.00	—
1785KM	—	8.00	15.00	25.00	50.00	—
1786KM	—	8.00	15.00	25.00	50.00	—
1787KM	—	8.00	15.00	25.00	50.00	—
1788KM	—	8.00	15.00	25.00	50.00	—
1789KM	—	60.00	100	150	275	—
1790KM	—	8.00	15.00	25.00	50.00	—
1791KM	—	8.00	15.00	25.00	50.00	—
1792KM	—	8.00	15.00	25.00	50.00	—
1793KM	—	8.00	15.00	25.00	50.00	—
1794KM	—	8.00	15.00	25.00	50.00	—
1795KM	—	8.00	15.00	25.00	50.00	—

C# 56.3 DENGA (1/2 Kopek)

5.1200 g., Copper **Ruler:** Catherine II

Date	Mintage	VG	F	VF	XF	Unc
1787TM	—	—	—	—	—	—

C# 93.1 DENGA (1/2 Kopek)

5.1200 g., Copper **Ruler:** Paul I

Date	Mintage	VG	F	VF	XF	Unc
1797AM	—	7.50	15.00	30.00	60.00	—
1798AM	—	7.50	15.00	30.00	60.00	—

C# 93.2 DENGA (1/2 Kopek)

5.1200 g., Copper **Ruler:** Paul I **Obv:** Crowned monogram **Rev:** Value, date

Date	Mintage	VG	F	VF	XF	Unc
1797EM	130,000	6.00	12.00	25.00	50.00	—
1798EM	5,194,000	6.00	12.00	25.00	50.00	—
1799EM	7,000	8.00	17.00	30.00	60.00	—
1800EM	—	70.00	150	300	500	—
1801EM	26,000	12.00	25.00	100	90.00	—

C# 93.3 DENGA (1/2 Kopek)

5.1200 g., Copper **Ruler:** Paul I

Date	Mintage	VG	F	VF	XF	Unc
1797KM	—	10.00	20.00	40.00	80.00	—
1798KM	—	10.00	20.00	40.00	80.00	—
1799KM	—	10.00	20.00	40.00	80.00	—
1800KM	—	10.00	20.00	40.00	80.00	—

KM# 117.1 KOPEK

8.1900 g., Copper **Ruler:** Peter I **Obv. Legend:** CZAR PETER ALEXIEVITCH **Rev. Legend:** AUTOCRAT OF ALL THE RUSSIAS

Date	Mintage	VG	F	VF	XF	Unc
ND(1704)БК	—	20.00	30.00	75.00	140	—
ND(1705)БК	—	15.00	25.00	50.00	100	—
ND(1706)БК	—	15.00	25.00	50.00	100	—
ND(1707)БК	—	15.00	25.00	50.00	100	—
ND(1708)БК	—	30.00	50.00	100	180	—
ND(1709)БК	—	20.00	30.00	75.00	140	—
ND(1710)БК	—	15.00	25.00	50.00	100	—
ND(1711)БК	—	15.00	25.00	50.00	100	—
ND(1712)БК	—	15.00	25.00	50.00	100	—
ND(1713)БК	—	75.00	125	250	500	—
ND(1716)БК Rare	—	—	—	—	—	—
ND(1717)БК Rare	—	—	—	—	—	—
ND(1718)БК	—	30.00	50.00	100	200	—

KM# 118 KOPEK

8.1900 g., Copper **Ruler:** Peter I **Obv:** St. George on horse **Rev:** Value, date **Rev. Legend:** RULER OF ALL THE RUSSIAS

Date	Mintage	VG	F	VF	XF	Unc
ND(1704)МД Rare	—	—	—	—	—	—
ND(1705)МД	—	20.00	30.00	75.00	140	—
ND(1707)МД	—	15.00	25.00	50.00	100	—
ND(1708)МД	—	15.00	25.00	50.00	100	—
ND(1708)МД	—	15.00	25.00	50.00	100	—
ND(1709)МД	—	15.00	25.00	50.00	100	—
ND(1710)МД	—	15.00	25.00	50.00	100	—
ND(1711)МД	—	15.00	25.00	50.00	100	—
ND1711МД Rare	—	—	—	—	—	—
ND(1712)МД	—	15.00	25.00	50.00	100	—
ND(1713)МД	—	15.00	25.00	50.00	100	—
ND(1714)МД	—	15.00	25.00	50.00	100	—
ND(1715)МД	—	15.00	25.00	50.00	100	—
ND(1716)МД	—	15.00	25.00	50.00	100	—
ND(1717)МД	—	20.00	40.00	80.00	150	—
ND(1718)МД	—	30.00	50.00	100	180	—

KM# 117.2 KOPEK

8.1900 g., Copper **Ruler:** Peter I **Note:** Without mint mark.

Date	Mintage	VG	F	VF	XF	Unc
ND(1705) Rare	—	—	—	—	—	—

KM# 123 KOPEK

8.1900 g., Copper **Ruler:** Peter I **Rev. Legend:** AUTOCRAT OF ALL THE RUSSIAS **Note:** Without mint mark.

Date	Mintage	VG	F	VF	XF	Unc
ND(1705) Rare	—	—	—	—	—	—

KM# 135 KOPEK

8.1900 g., Copper **Ruler:** Peter I **Rev. Legend:** RULER OF ALL THE RUSSIAS

Date	Mintage	VG	F	VF	XF	Unc
ND(1711) Rare	—	—	—	—	—	—
ND(1712)	—	15.00	25.00	50.00	110	—
ND(1713)	—	20.00	30.00	75.00	150	—

KM# 141 KOPEK

8.1900 g., Copper **Ruler:** Peter I

Date	Mintage	VG	F	VF	XF	Unc
ND(1713)МДЗ	—	35.00	65.00	125	250	—
ND(1714)МДЗ Rare	—	—	—	—	—	—
ND(1716)МДЗ	—	15.00	25.00	50.00	100	—

KM# 142 KOPEK

8.1900 g., Copper **Ruler:** Peter I

Date	Mintage	VG	F	VF	XF	Unc
ND(1713)НД	—	10.00	20.00	45.00	90.00	—
ND(1714)НД	—	15.00	25.00	50.00	100	—
ND(1715)НД	—	15.00	25.00	50.00	100	—
ND(1716)НД	—	20.00	40.00	80.00	150	—
ND(1717)НД	—	40.00	80.00	150	300	—
ND(1718)НД Rare	—	—	—	—	—	—

KM# 143 KOPEK

8.1900 g., Copper **Ruler:** Peter I

Date	Mintage	VG	F	VF	XF	Unc
ND(1713)НДЗ	—	40.00	80.00	150	300	—
ND(1714)НДЗ	—	15.00	25.00	50.00	100	—
ND(1716)НДЗ	—	20.00	30.00	75.00	140	—
ND(1717)НДЗ	—	20.00	30.00	75.00	140	—
ND(1718)НДЗ Rare	—	—	—	—	—	—

KM# 144 KOPEK

0.5700 g., 0.3960 Silver 0.0073 oz. ASW **Ruler:** Peter I **Obv:** Double-headed eagle **Rev:** Value, date

Date	Mintage	VG	F	VF	XF	Unc
1713	—	200	500	1,000	2,500	—
1714	—	200	500	1,000	2,500	—

KM# 153 KOPEK

0.5700 g., 0.3960 Silver 0.0073 oz. ASW **Ruler:** Peter I **Obv:** St. George on horse slaying dragon **Rev:** Value, date

Date	Mintage	VG	F	VF	XF	Unc
ND(1718) Inverted L	—	50.00	100	250	400	—
ND(1718) Rare	—	—	—	—	—	—

KM# 163 KOPEK

4.1000 g., Copper **Ruler:** Peter I **Obv:** St. George and date **Rev:** Value **Rev. Legend:** KOPEK

Date	Mintage	VG	F	VF	XF	Unc
1724	—	150	400	750	1,500	—
1726 Rare	—	—	—	—	—	—

KM# 185.1 KOPEK

4.1000 g., Copper **Ruler:** Peter II **Obv:** St. George **Rev:** Date reads downward

Date	Mintage	VG	F	VF	XF	Unc
1728 Retrograde 7	—	75.00	150	250	350	—
1728 Normal 7	—	75.00	150	250	350	—

KM# 185.2 KOPEK

4.1000 g., Copper **Ruler:** Peter II **Obv:** St. George on horse slaying dragon **Rev:** Date reads upward

Date	Mintage	VG	F	VF	XF	Unc
1728	—	40.00	80.00	150	270	—
1729	—	70.00	150	250	400	—

C# 3.1 KOPEK

20.4800 g., Copper **Ruler:** Elizabeth **Obv:** Eagle on clouds behind crowned EP monogram **Rev:** Similar to obverse but with value on tablet **Edge:** Engrailed

Date	Mintage	VG	F	VF	XF	Unc
1756	26,651,000	25.00	50.00	100	200	—

C# 3.2 KOPEK

20.4800 g., Copper **Ruler:** Elizabeth

Date	Mintage	VG	F	VF	XF	Unc
1755ММД	8,850,000	15.00	25.00	50.00	100	—
1756ММД	33,090,000	20.00	40.00	80.00	150	—
1757ММД Rare	—	—	—	—	—	—

C# 3.3 KOPEK

20.4800 g., Copper **Ruler:** Elizabeth

Date	Mintage	VG	F	VF	XF	Unc
1755СПБ	21,637,000	15.00	25.00	50.00	100	—
1756СПБ	Inc. above	20.00	40.00	80.00	150	—

C# 3.4 KOPEK

4.0000 g., Copper **Ruler:** Elizabeth **Note:** Lettered edge with St. Petersburg mint name.

Date	Mintage	VG	F	VF	XF	Unc
1755	—	25.00	50.00	100	200	—

C# 3.5 KOPEK

4.0000 g., Copper **Ruler:** Elizabeth **Note:** Lettered edge with Moscow mint name.

Date	Mintage	VG	F	VF	XF	Unc
1755	—	20.00	40.00	80.00	150	—
1756	—	25.00	50.00	100	200	—

C# 3.6 KOPEK

4.0000 g., Copper **Ruler:** Elizabeth **Note:** Lettered edge with Ekaterinburg mint name.

Date	Mintage	VG	F	VF	XF	Unc
1755	—	25.00	50.00	100	200	—
1756	—	20.00	40.00	80.00	150	—
1757	—	25.00	50.00	100	200	—

C# 6.1 KOPEK

4.0000 g., Copper **Ruler:** Elizabeth **Obv:** Crowned monogram divides date within wreath **Rev:** St. George on horse slaying dragon **Note:** Ekaterinburg and Moscow Mints. Coins cannot be identified by mint.

Date	Mintage	VG	F	VF	XF	Unc
1757 Straight date	6,629,000	12.00	25.00	50.00	100	—
1757 Curved date	Inc. above	12.00	25.00	50.00	100	—
1758	5,081,000	12.00	25.00	50.00	100	—
1759	3,322,000	12.00	25.00	50.00	100	—
1760	23,848,000	12.00	25.00	50.00	100	—
1761	—	12.00	25.00	50.00	100	—

C# 41 KOPEK

5.1200 g., Copper **Ruler:** Peter III **Obv:** St. George on horse slaying dragon, star above **Rev:** Value, date above drum, crossed flags **Note:** Without mint mark.

Date	Mintage	VG	F	VF	XF	Unc
1762 Reeded edge; Rare	—	200	400	600	1,200	—
1762 Grilled edge; Rare	—	200	400	600	1,200	—

C# 57.2 KOPEK

10.2400 g., Copper **Ruler:** Catherine II **Obv:** Crowned monogram divides date within wreath **Rev:** St. George on horse slaying dragon

Date	Mintage	VG	F	VF	XF	Unc
1763ЕМ Rare	50,000	—	—	—	—	—
1789ЕМ	6,343,000	5.00	10.00	20.00	40.00	—
1790ЕМ	1,862,000	5.00	10.00	20.00	40.00	—
1791ЕМ	—	5.00	10.00	20.00	40.00	—
1793ЕМ Rare	—	—	—	—	—	—
1794ЕМ	756,000	5.00	10.00	20.00	40.00	—
1795ЕМ	2,286,000	5.00	10.00	20.00	40.00	—
1796ЕМ	523,000	8.00	15.00	30.00	60.00	—

C# 57.4 KOPEK

10.2400 g., Copper **Ruler:** Catherine II

Date	Mintage	VG	F	VF	XF	Unc
1763ММ	—	12.00	20.00	40.00	75.00	—
1764ММ	—	60.00	125	200	350	—
1766ММ	—	30.00	60.00	100	175	—
1767ММ	—	200	300	500	1,000	—
1788ММ	—	12.00	20.00	40.00	75.00	—
1789ММ Rare	—	—	—	—	—	—
1795ММ	—	80.00	150	200	400	—

C# 57.5 KOPEK

10.2400 g., Copper **Ruler:** Catherine II

Date	Mintage	VG	F	VF	XF	Unc
1764СПМ	—	125	250	350	600	—
1766СПМ	—	70.00	125	250	400	—
1767СПМ	—	125	250	500	1,000	—

C# 57.3 KOPEK

10.2400 g., Copper **Ruler:** Catherine II

Date	Mintage	VG	F	VF	XF	Unc
1787ТМ Rare	—	—	—	—	—	—

C# 57.1 KOPEK

10.2400 g., Copper **Ruler:** Catherine II **Note:** Unknown mint, without mint mark. Edge varieties exist.

Date	Mintage	VG	F	VF	XF	Unc
1788	—	25.00	50.00	75.00	150	—
1795	132,000	30.00	60.00	90.00	180	—

C# 94.1 KOPEK

10.2400 g., Copper **Ruler:** Paul I

Date	Mintage	VG	F	VF	XF	Unc
1797АМ	—	12.00	25.00	50.00	100	—

C# 94.2 KOPEK

10.2400 g., Copper **Ruler:** Paul I **Obv:** Crowned monogram **Rev:** Value, date

Date	Mintage	VG	F	VF	XF	Unc
1797ЕМ	523,000	12.00	25.00	50.00	100	—
1798ЕМ	19,243,000	10.00	20.00	40.00	75.00	—
1799ЕМ	23,789,000	6.00	12.00	25.00	45.00	—
1800ЕМ	9,493,000	5.00	10.00	20.00	40.00	—

C# 94.3 KOPEK

10.2400 g., Copper **Ruler:** Paul I

Date	Mintage	VG	F	VF	XF	Unc
1797КМ	—	30.00	50.00	100	200	—
1798КМ	—	20.00	40.00	80.00	150	—
1799КМ	—	30.00	50.00	100	200	—

C# 8 2 KOPEKS

20.4800 g., Copper **Ruler:** Elizabeth **Obv:** St. George slaying dragon; value above **Rev:** Crowned EP monogram divides date in branches **Note:** Ekaterinburg Mint, without mint mark. Overstruck on earlier coppers.

Date	Mintage	VG	F	VF	XF	Unc
1757 Reticulated edge	—	25.00	50.00	100	250	—
1757 Lettered edge	—	25.00	50.00	100	250	—
1758	—	25.00	50.00	100	250	—
1759	5,053,000	30.00	75.00	150	300	—
1760	602,000	50.00	100	200	400	—

C# 7.1 2 KOPEKS

20.4800 g., Copper **Ruler:** Elizabeth **Note:** Similar to C#7.2 but with lettered edge.

Date	Mintage	VG	F	VF	XF	Unc
1757	—	12.00	25.00	50.00	100	—
1758	—	12.00	25.00	50.00	100	—
1759	—	12.00	25.00	50.00	100	—
1760	—	12.00	25.00	50.00	100	—

C# 7.2 2 KOPEKS

20.4800 g., Copper **Ruler:** Elizabeth **Obv:** Crowned monogram divides date within wreath **Rev:** St. George on horse slaying dragon **Edge:** Reticulated **Note:** Ekaterinburg, Moscow and St. Petersburg Mints. (Coins cannot be identified by mint).

Date	Mintage	VG	F	VF	XF	Unc
1757	17,712,000	6.00	12.00	25.00	50.00	—
1758	111,846,000	6.00	12.00	25.00	50.00	—
1759	14,229,000	6.00	12.00	25.00	50.00	—
1760	3,357,000	6.00	12.00	25.00	50.00	—
1761	15,886,000	6.00	12.00	25.00	50.00	—
1762	4,930,000	6.00	12.00	25.00	50.00	—

Note: The 1762 date was struck posthumously

C# 42 2 KOPEKS

10.2400 g., Copper **Ruler:** Peter III **Obv:** St. George on horse slaying dragon **Rev:** Value, date above drum, crossed flags

Date	Mintage	VG	F	VF	XF	Unc
1762/0 Rare	—	—	—	—	—	—
1762 Large 2 in date	—	75.00	150	300	500	—
1762 Small 2 in date	—	75.00	150	300	500	—

C# 58.1 2 KOPEKS

20.4800 g., Copper **Ruler:** Catherine II **Obv:** Crowned monogram divides date within wreath **Rev:** St. George on horse slaying dragon

Date	Mintage	VG	F	VF	XF	Unc
1763	—	30.00	60.00	100	175	—
1766	—	15.00	30.00	50.00	100	—

C# 58.3 2 KOPEKS

20.4800 g., Copper **Ruler:** Catherine II

Date	Mintage	VG	F	VF	XF	Unc
1763ЕМ	1,765,000	5.00	10.00	20.00	40.00	—
1764ЕМ	3,357,000	5.00	10.00	17.50	35.00	—
1765ЕМ	1,715,000	5.00	10.00	17.50	35.00	—
1766ЕМ	1,662,000	5.00	10.00	17.50	35.00	—
1767ЕМ	1,294,000	5.00	10.00	17.50	35.00	—
1768ЕМ	911,000	5.00	10.00	17.50	35.00	—
1769ЕМ	1,588,000	5.00	10.00	17.50	35.00	—
1770ЕМ	5,311,000	5.00	10.00	17.50	35.00	—
1771ЕМ	1,944,000	5.00	10.00	17.50	35.00	—
1772ЕМ	2,433,000	5.00	10.00	17.50	35.00	—
1773ЕМ	3,225,000	5.00	10.00	17.50	35.00	—
1774ЕМ	645,000	12.00	25.00	50.00	100	—
1775ЕМ	1,476,000	5.00	10.00	17.50	35.00	—
1776ЕМ	1,332,000	5.00	10.00	17.50	35.00	—
1777ЕМ	1,596,000	5.00	10.00	17.50	35.00	—
1778ЕМ	1,291,000	5.00	10.00	17.50	35.00	—
1779ЕМ	73,000	15.00	30.00	50.00	100	—
1789ЕМ	2,878,000	5.00	10.00	17.50	35.00	—
1790ЕМ	4,765,000	5.00	10.00	5.00	10.00	—
1791ЕМ	371,000	5.00	10.00	5.00	10.00	—
1793 Mint mark K between horse's legs	—	100	150	5.00	10.00	—
1793 Mint mark divided by horse	—	100	150	250	400	—
1795ЕМ	1,546,000	5.00	10.00	17.50	35.00	—
1796ЕМ	620,000	5.00	10.00	17.50	35.00	—

C# 58.5 2 KOPEKS

20.4800 g., Copper **Ruler:** Catherine II

Date	Mintage	VG	F	VF	XF	Unc
1763ММ	—	8.00	15.00	25.00	50.00	—
1764ММ	—	5.00	10.00	20.00	40.00	—
1765ММ	—	5.00	10.00	20.00	40.00	—
1766ММ	—	5.00	10.00	20.00	40.00	—
1767ММ	—	60.00	100	150	275	—
1788ММ	—	5.00	10.00	20.00	40.00	—
1789ММ	—	400	700	1,000	1,300	—
1795ММ Floral edge	—	30.00	50.00	75.00	150	—
1795ММ Grilled edge	—	60.00	100	150	275	—

C# 58.6 2 KOPEKS

20.4800 g., Copper **Ruler:** Catherine II

Date	Mintage	VG	F	VF	XF	Unc
1763СПМ	—	8.00	15.00	25.00	50.00	—
1764СПМ	—	5.00	10.00	20.00	40.00	—
1765СПМ	—	5.00	10.00	20.00	40.00	—
1766СПМ	—	5.00	10.00	20.00	40.00	—
1767СПМ	—	30.00	60.00	100	175	—
1788СПМ	—	5.00	10.00	20.00	40.00	—

C# 58.4 2 KOPEKS
20.4800 g., Copper **Ruler:** Catherine II

Date	Mintage	VG	F	VF	XF	Unc
1787TM	—	—	—	—	—	—
1788TM	60,000	600	1,000	1,500	2,500	—

C# 58.2 2 KOPEKS
Copper **Ruler:** Catherine II

Date	Mintage	VG	F	VF	XF	Unc
1789AM	—	15.00	30.00	50.00	100	—
1790AM	—	65.00	125	200	350	—
1791AM	333,000	65.00	125	200	350	—
1793AM	154,000	100	150	250	400	—
1794AM	—	60.00	100	150	275	—
1795AM	56,000	100	150	250	350	—
1796AM	—	65.00	125	200	350	—

C# 95.2 2 KOPEKS
Copper **Ruler:** Paul I

Date	Mintage	VG	F	VF	XF	Unc
1797AM	—	15.00	30.00	60.00	120	—
1798AM	—	15.00	30.00	60.00	120	—

C# 95.3 2 KOPEKS
Copper **Ruler:** Paul I **Obv:** Crowned monogram **Rev:** Value, date

Date	Mintage	VG	F	VF	XF	Unc
1797EM	4,914,000	10.00	20.00	40.00	80.00	—
1798EM	56,528,000	7.00	15.00	30.00	60.00	—
1799EM	55,641,000	7.00	15.00	30.00	60.00	—
1800EM	28,156,000	7.00	15.00	30.00	60.00	—

C# 95.4 2 KOPEKS
Copper **Ruler:** Paul I **Obv:** Crowned monogram **Rev:** Value, date

Date	Mintage	VG	F	VF	XF	Unc
1797KM	—	10.00	20.00	40.00	80.00	—
1798KM	—	10.00	20.00	40.00	80.00	—
1799KM	—	15.00	30.00	60.00	120	—
1800KM	—	12.00	25.00	50.00	100	—

C# 95.1 2 KOPEKS
20.4800 g., Copper **Ruler:** Paul I **Edge:** Rope **Note:** Unknown mint, without mint mark.

Date	Mintage	VG	F	VF	XF	Unc
1797	—	25.00	50.00	100	200	—

KM# 119 3 KOPEKS (Altyn)
0.8000 g., 0.8020 Silver 0.0206 oz. ASW **Ruler:** Peter I **Obv:** Eagle **Rev:** Denomination ALTYN and date

Date	Mintage	VG	F	VF	XF	Unc
ND(1704) БК	—	30.00	70.00	120	250	—

KM# 136 3 KOPEKS (Altyn)
0.8400 g., 0.7290 Silver 0.0197 oz. ASW **Ruler:** Peter I **Obv:** Crown above crowned double-headed eagle **Rev:** Value, date

Date	Mintage	VG	F	VF	XF	Unc
1711 DL	—	100	250	350	500	—
1711	—	150	300	500	1,000	—
1712	—	100	250	350	500	—

KM# 145.1 3 KOPEKS (Altyn)
1.7000 g., 0.3960 Silver 0.0216 oz. ASW **Ruler:** Peter I **Rev:** Denomination: ALTYN in line

Date	Mintage	VG	F	VF	XF	Unc
1713 Rare	—	—	—	—	—	—

KM# 145.2 3 KOPEKS (Altyn)
1.7000 g., 0.3960 Silver 0.0216 oz. ASW **Ruler:** Peter I **Rev:** Denomination: ALTYNNIK in 2 lines

Date	Mintage	VG	F	VF	XF	Unc
1713	—	100	200	300	400	—
1714	—	125	250	350	450	—

KM# 145.3 3 KOPEKS (Altyn)
1.7000 g., 0.3960 Silver 0.0216 oz. ASW **Ruler:** Peter I **Obv:** Crown above crowned double-headed eagle **Rev:** Value, ALTYN in 2 lines

Date	Mintage	VG	F	VF	XF	Unc
1714	—	—	—	—	—	—

KM# 154.1 3 KOPEKS (Altyn)
1.7000 g., 0.3960 Silver 0.0216 oz. ASW **Ruler:** Peter I **Obv:** St. George on horse slaying dragon **Rev:** Value, date

Date	Mintage	VG	F	VF	XF	Unc
ND(1718) Inverted L	—	20.00	40.00	80.00	150	—
ND(1718) Rare	—	—	—	—	—	—

KM# 154.2 3 KOPEKS (Altyn)
1.7000 g., 0.3960 Silver 0.0216 oz. ASW **Ruler:** Peter I **Obv:** St. George on horse slaying dragon **Rev:** Value, date

Date	Mintage	VG	F	VF	XF	Unc
ND(1718)	—	—	—	—	—	—

C# 43.2 4 KOPEKS
20.4800 g., Copper **Ruler:** Catherine II **Edge:** Reticulated **Note:** Without mint mark.

Date	Mintage	VG	F	VF	XF	Unc
1762	—	40.00	80.00	150	300	—
1762/0 Rare	—	—	—	—	—	—

C# 43.1 4 KOPEKS
20.4800 g., Copper **Ruler:** Catherine II **Obv:** St. George on horse slaying dragon **Rev:** Value, date above drum, crossed flags **Edge:** Lettered **Note:** Without mint mark. Mints unknown.

Date	Mintage	VG	F	VF	XF	Unc
1762	—	50.00	100	200	400	—

KM# 126 1/3 TYMF (Shostak)
3.2000 g., Billon **Ruler:** Peter I **Obv:** Bust right **Rev:** Crown above crowned double-headed eagle **Note:** The 1/3 Tymf circulated at 4 Kopeks.

Date	Mintage	VG	F	VF	XF	Unc
ND(1707) Rare	—	—	—	—	—	—
ND(1707) IL Rare	—	—	—	—	—	—

KM# 146 5 KOPEKS
2.8300 g., 0.3960 Silver 0.0360 oz. ASW **Ruler:** Peter I **Obv:** Crown above crowned double-headed eagle **Rev:** Value, date **Note:** Reverse dies have either 5 strokes or 5 dots to indicate number of Kopecks.

Date	Mintage	VG	F	VF	XF	Unc
1713 Strokes; Rare	—	—	—	—	—	—
1713 Dots; Rare	—	—	—	—	—	—
1714 Rare	—	—	—	—	—	—

KM# 164 5 KOPEKS
20.4800 g., Copper-Nickel **Ruler:** Peter I **Obv:** Crowned double-headed eagle within circle, 5 dots around **Rev:** Value FIVE KOPECKS and date in cruciform **Note:** Without mint mark.

Date	Mintage	VG	F	VF	XF	Unc
1723	—	30.00	50.00	100	180	—
1724	—	20.00	35.00	75.00	120	—

KM# 165 5 KOPEKS
Copper **Obv:** Crowned double-headed eagle within circle, 5 dots around **Rev:** Value, date in cruciform

Date	Mintage	VG	F	VF	XF	Unc
1724МД	—	30.00	60.00	100	150	—
1725МД	—	30.00	60.00	100	150	—
1726МД	—	15.00	30.00	60.00	100	—
1727МД	—	30.00	60.00	100	150	—
1729МД	—	12.00	20.00	40.00	70.00	—
1730МД	—	10.00	15.00	35.00	50.00	—

KM# 170 5 KOPEKS
Copper **Ruler:** Catherine I

Date	Mintage	VG	F	VF	XF	Unc
1726НД	—	12.00	20.00	40.00	70.00	—
1727НД	—	12.00	20.00	40.00	70.00	—

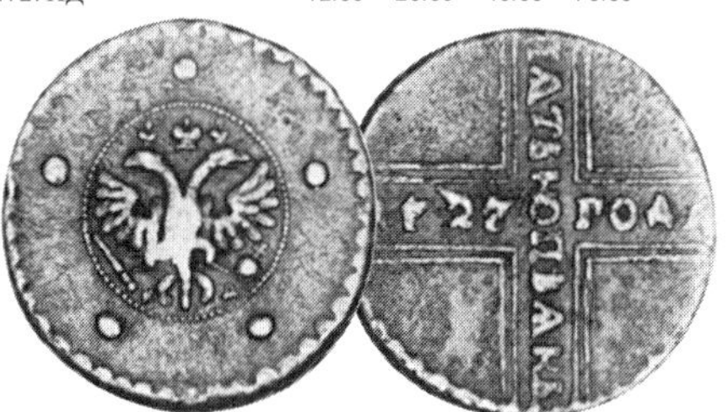

KM# 179 5 KOPEKS
Copper **Ruler:** Catherine I

Date	Mintage	VG	F	VF	XF	Unc
1727КД	—	150	300	450	1,000	—

KM# 189 5 KOPEKS
Copper **Ruler:** Anna

Date	Mintage	VG	F	VF	XF	Unc
1730ДМ	—	140	250	400	800	—

KM# 190 5 KOPEKS
Copper **Ruler:** Anna

Date	Mintage	VG	F	VF	XF	Unc
1730ММ	—	250	500	800	1,500	—

C# 15.1 5 KOPEKS

1.2100 g., 0.8020 Silver 0.0312 oz. ASW, 16.5 mm. **Ruler:** Elizabeth

Date	Mintage	VG	F	VF	XF	Unc
1755СПБ	540,000	10.00	20.00	40.00	100	—
1756СПБ	905,000	20.00	30.00	60.00	130	—

C# 15.2 5 KOPEKS

1.2100 g., 0.8020 Silver 0.0312 oz. ASW, 14 mm. **Ruler:** Elizabeth

Date	Mintage	F	VF	XF	Unc	BU
1756СПБ	Inc. above	20.00	40.00	100	—	—
1757СПБ	3,499,000	20.00	40.00	100	—	—
1758СПБ	3,577,000	20.00	40.00	100	—	—
1759СПБ	882,000	20.00	40.00	100	—	—
1760СПБ	420,000	20.00	40.00	100	—	—
1761СПБ	300,000	50.00	100	200	—	—

C# 9.3 5 KOPEKS

51.1900 g., Copper **Ruler:** Elizabeth

Date	Mintage	VG	F	VF	XF	Unc
1758MM	—	25.00	50.00	80.00	150	—
1759MM	11,837,000	25.00	50.00	80.00	150	—
1760MM	—	40.00	70.00	100	170	—
1761MM	—	50.00	90.00	120	190	—

C# 9.1 5 KOPEKS

51.1900 g., Copper **Ruler:** Elizabeth **Obv:** Crowned monogram divides date within wreath **Rev:** Crowned double-headed eagle **Note:** Ekaterinburg and Sestroretsk mints. (Coins cannot be identified by mints).

Date	Mintage	VG	F	VF	XF	Unc
1758	22,681,000	20.00	40.00	60.00	120	—
1761/0	—	20.00	40.00	60.00	120	—

C# 9.2 5 KOPEKS

51.1900 g., Copper **Ruler:** Elizabeth **Obv:** Crowned monogram divides date within wreath **Rev:** Crowned double-headed eagle

Date	Mintage	F	VF	XF	Unc	BU
1759	23,357,000	40.00	60.00	120	—	—
1760	25,887,000	40.00	60.00	120	—	—
1761	26,282,000	40.00	60.00	120	—	—
1762	6,813,000	40.00	60.00	120	—	—

Note: The 1762 dated coin was struck posthumously

C# 59.6 5 KOPEKS

51.1900 g., Copper **Ruler:** Catherine II

Date	Mintage	VG	F	VF	XF	Unc
1763MM	17,729,000	7.00	15.00	30.00	60.00	—
1764MM	9,480,000	7.00	15.00	30.00	60.00	—
1765MM	5,224,000	7.00	15.00	30.00	60.00	—
1766MM	7,538,000	7.00	15.00	30.00	60.00	—
1767MM	—	50.00	100	200	300	—
1768MM	—	50.00	70.00	120	200	—
1788MM Mint mark below eagle	—	7.00	15.00	30.00	60.00	—
1788MM Mint mark beside eagle	—	50.00	100	200	300	—
1789MM	—	400	700	1,200	2,500	—
1795MM Rare	—	—	—	—	—	—

C# 59.8 5 KOPEKS

51.1900 g., Copper **Ruler:** Catherine II

Date	Mintage	VG	F	VF	XF	Unc
1763CM	2,491,000	20.00	40.00	80.00	150	—
1764CM	—	20.00	40.00	80.00	150	—
1765CM	663,000	20.00	40.00	80.00	150	—
1766CM	200,000	20.00	40.00	80.00	150	—
1767CM	—	50.00	150	350	500	—

C# 59.1 5 KOPEKS

51.1900 g., Copper **Ruler:** Catherine II **Note:** Unknown mint, without mint mark.

Date	Mintage	VG	F	VF	XF	Unc
1763 Rare	—	—	—	—	—	—
1765	—	300	700	1,500	2,500	—
1791	—	120	300	600	1,000	—
1793 Rare	—	—	—	—	—	—
1796	—	300	700	1,800	3,500	—

C# 59.3 5 KOPEKS

51.1900 g., Copper **Ruler:** Catherine II **Obv:** Crowned monogram divides date within wreath **Rev:** Crowned double-headed eagle, initials below **Note:** Varieties exist.

Date	Mintage	VG	F	VF	XF	Unc
1763EM	40,398,000	5.00	10.00	20.00	35.00	—
1764EM	35,824,000	5.00	10.00	20.00	35.00	—
1765EM	41,109,000	5.00	10.00	20.00	35.00	—
1766EM	26,562,000	5.00	10.00	20.00	35.00	—
1767EM	37,020,000	5.00	10.00	20.00	35.00	—
1768EM	28,542,000	5.00	10.00	20.00	35.00	—
1769EM	39,441,000	5.00	10.00	20.00	35.00	—
1770EM	48,480,000	4.50	7.50	15.00	30.00	—
1771EM	57,053,000	4.50	7.50	15.00	30.00	—
1772EM	46,266,000	4.50	7.50	15.00	30.00	—
1773EM	38,829,000	4.50	7.50	15.00	30.00	—
1774EM	14,535,000	4.50	7.50	15.00	30.00	—
1775EM	30,487,000	4.50	7.50	15.00	30.00	—
1776EM	21,454,000	4.50	7.50	15.00	30.00	—
1777EM	37,429,000	4.50	7.50	15.00	30.00	—
1778EM	47,142,000	4.50	7.50	15.00	30.00	—
1779EM	39,732,000	4.50	7.50	15.00	30.00	—
1780EM	51,007,000	4.50	7.50	15.00	30.00	—
1781/0EM	43,401,000	4.50	7.50	15.00	30.00	—
1781EM	Inc. above	4.50	7.50	15.00	30.00	—
1782EM	36,175,000	4.50	7.50	15.00	30.00	—
1783EM	30,156,000	4.50	7.50	15.00	30.00	—
1784EM	36,059,000	4.50	7.50	15.00	30.00	—
1785EM	43,070,000	4.50	7.50	15.00	30.00	—
1786EM	30,377,000	4.50	7.50	15.00	30.00	—
1787EM	19,088,000	4.50	7.50	15.00	30.00	—
1788EM	49,141,000	4.50	7.50	15.00	30.00	—
1789EM	25,841,000	4.50	7.50	15.00	30.00	—
1790EM	39,995,000	4.50	7.50	15.00	30.00	—
1791EM	23,739,000	4.50	7.50	15.00	30.00	—
1792EM	26,177,000	4.50	7.50	15.00	30.00	—
1793EM	22,736,000	4.50	7.50	15.00	30.00	—
1794EM	20,950,000	4.50	7.50	15.00	30.00	—
1795EM	15,531,000	4.50	7.50	15.00	30.00	—
1796EM	1,949,000	4.50	7.50	15.00	30.00	—

C# 59.7 5 KOPEKS

Copper **Ruler:** Catherine II **Note:** Varieties exist.

Date	Mintage	VG	F	VF	XF	Unc
1763СПМ	13,428,000	7.00	15.00	30.00	60.00	—
1764СПМ	3,073,000	30.00	60.00	120	250	—
1765СПМ	2,374,000	7.00	15.00	30.00	60.00	—
1766СПМ	3,719,000	7.00	15.00	30.00	60.00	—
1767СПМ	—	35.00	70.00	150	300	—
1788СПМ	—	7.00	15.00	30.00	60.00	—

C# 59a 5 KOPEKS

Copper **Ruler:** Catherine II **Note:** Swedish issue. During the war between Russia and Sweden in 1788, the Swedish government began to strike copies of the current 5 kopek piece using a Royal instead of Imperial crown design. Several dates are known. A common way to distinguish the Swedish forgery from the original is to note that "kopek" is spelled with a "b" as a last letter rather than ? as found on the genuine issue. Another sign is the 7's in the date which are straight on the Swedish piece and curved on the Russian originals.

Date	Mintage	VG	F	VF	XF	Unc
1764EM Rare	—	—	—	—	—	—
1778EM Rare	—	—	—	—	—	—
1787EM	—	300	1,000	2,500	5,000	—
1787/77EM	—	400	1,200	3,000	6,000	—

C# 59.5 5 KOPEKS

Copper **Ruler:** Catherine II **Note:** Varieties exist.

Date	Mintage	VG	F	VF	XF	Unc
1781KM	—	25.00	60.00	100	150	—
1782KM	6,014,000	7.00	15.00	35.00	70.00	—
1783KM	3,046,000	7.00	15.00	35.00	70.00	—
1784KM	4,619,000	7.00	15.00	35.00	70.00	—
1785/4KM	—	—	—	35.00	70.00	—
1785KM	5,577,000	7.00	15.00	25.00	50.00	—
1786KM	3,820,000	7.00	15.00	35.00	70.00	—
1787KM	2,911,000	7.00	15.00	35.00	70.00	—
1788KM	3,354,000	15.00	30.00	75.00	100	—
1789KM	2,310,000	10.00	20.00	40.00	80.00	—
1790KM	4,000,000	10.00	20.00	40.00	80.00	—
1791KM	4,000,000	7.00	15.00	35.00	70.00	—
1792KM	4,000,000	7.00	15.00	35.00	70.00	—
1793KM	4,000,000	7.00	15.00	35.00	70.00	—
1794KM	4,000,000	7.00	15.00	30.00	60.00	—
1795KM	4,000,000	7.00	15.00	35.00	70.00	—
1796KM	3,020,000	10.00	30.00	60.00	100	—

C# 59.4 5 KOPEKS

Copper **Ruler:** Catherine II **Note:** Varieties exist.

Date	Mintage	VG	F	VF	XF	Unc
1787TM	460,000	300	450	1,000	2,000	—
1788TM	539,000	150	300	650	1,300	—

C# 59.2 5 KOPEKS

51.1900 g., Copper **Ruler:** Catherine II **Obv:** Crowned monogram divides date within wreath **Rev:** Crowned double-headed eagle, initials below

Date	Mintage	VG	F	VF	XF	Unc
1789AM	8,000,000	5.00	10.00	20.00	40.00	—
1790AM	—	5.00	10.00	20.00	40.00	—
1791AM	—	5.00	10.00	20.00	40.00	—
1792AM	8,190,000	5.00	10.00	20.00	40.00	—
1793AM	7,426,000	5.00	10.00	20.00	40.00	—
1794/3AM	7,364,000	5.00	10.00	20.00	40.00	—
1794AM	Inc. above	5.00	10.00	20.00	40.00	—

Date	Mintage	VG	F	VF	XF	Unc
1795AM	9,948,000	5.00	10.00	20.00	40.00	—
1796AM	6,728,000	5.00	10.00	20.00	40.00	—

Note: The 1796 also exists overstruck on the abortive 1796 10 Kopek coinage. These are considered rare

C# 96.1 5 KOPEKS
1.4600 g., 0.8680 Silver 0.0407 oz. ASW **Ruler:** Paul I **Obv:** Crowned monogram **Rev:** Value, date above sprigs

Date	Mintage	VG	F	VF	XF	Unc
1797CM ФА	14,000	50.00	100	350	500	—

C# 96.1a 5 KOPEKS
1.0400 g., 0.8680 Silver 0.0290 oz. ASW **Ruler:** Paul I

Date	Mintage	VG	F	VF	XF	Unc
1798CM МБ	114,000	30.00	70.00	150	300	—
1800CM OM Rare	—	—	—	—	—	—

C# 96.2 5 KOPEKS
1.0400 g., 0.8680 Silver 0.0290 oz. ASW **Ruler:** Paul I

Date	Mintage	VG	F	VF	XF	Unc
1798СП ОМ	Inc. above	25.00	70.00	150	300	—

KM# 103 10 DENGI (5 Kopeks)
1.4200 g., 0.8020 Silver 0.0366 oz. ASW **Ruler:** Peter I **Obv:** Crowned double-headed eagle within wreath **Rev:** Value ДЕСЕТЪ ДЕНЕГЪ

Date	Mintage	VG	F	VF	XF	Unc
ND(1701)	—	—	—	—	—	—
ND(1702)	—	—	—	—	—	—
ND(1704)	—	150	250	450	800	—

KM# 104 10 KOPEKS (Grivennik)
2.8000 g., 0.8020 Silver 0.0722 oz. ASW **Ruler:** Peter I **Obv:** Imperial eagle **Rev:** Value **Rev. Inscription:** GRIVENNIK

Date	Mintage	VG	F	VF	XF	Unc
ND(1701) Rare	—	—	—	—	—	—
ND(1702) Rare	—	—	—	—	—	—

KM# 120.1 10 KOPEKS (Grivennik)
2.8000 g., 0.8020 Silver 0.0722 oz. ASW **Ruler:** Peter I **Obv:** Crowned double-headed eagle **Rev:** Value, date **Rev. Inscription:** GRIVENNIK

Date	Mintage	VG	F	VF	XF	Unc
ND(1704)M	—	75.00	200	500	1,000	—
ND(1705)M Rare	—	—	—	—	—	—
ND(1706)M Rare	—	—	—	—	—	—

KM# 121 10 KOPEKS (Grivennik)
2.8000 g., 0.8020 Silver 0.0722 oz. ASW **Ruler:** Peter I **Obv:** Crowned double-headed eagle within beaded circle, larger crown above **Rev:** Value, date **Rev. Inscription:** GRIVNA

Date	Mintage	VG	F	VF	XF	Unc
ND(1704)БК	—	60.00	150	300	500	—
ND(1705)БК	—	40.00	100	200	350	—
ND(1709)БК	—	70.00	200	500	900	—

KM# 120.2 10 KOPEKS (Grivennik)
2.8000 g., 0.8750 Silver 0.0788 oz. ASW **Ruler:** Peter I

Date	Mintage	VG	F	VF	XF	Unc
ND1707МД Rare	—	—	—	—	—	—
ND(1710)МД Rare	—	—	—	—	—	—

KM# 147 10 KOPEKS (Grivennik)
2.8000 g., 0.7500 Silver 0.0675 oz. ASW **Ruler:** Peter I **Obv:** Crowned double-headed eagle **Rev:** Value, date **Rev. Inscription:** GRIVENNIK

Date	Mintage	VG	F	VF	XF	Unc
1713МД	—	—	—	—	—	—

KM# 155 10 KOPEKS (Grivennik)
2.8400 g., 0.7290 Silver 0.0666 oz. ASW **Ruler:** Peter I **Obv:** 3 Small crowns above double-headed eagle **Rev:** Value, date below cluster of dots **Rev. Inscription:** GRIVENNIK **Note:** Without mint mark.

Date	Mintage	VG	F	VF	XF	Unc
1718 Rare	—	—	—	—	—	—
1718 L	—	40.00	100	300	600	—
1718 Reverse has inverted L	—	40.00	100	300	600	—
1719 Rare	—	—	—	—	—	—
ND(1720) Rare	—	—	—	—	—	—
1720 Rare	—	—	—	—	—	—

KM# 171 10 KOPEKS (Grivennik)
2.6600 g., Silver **Ruler:** Catherine I **Rev:** Value **Rev. Inscription:** GRIVNA **Note:** This issue varied in silver fineness from .438 to .667.

Date	Mintage	VG	F	VF	XF	Unc
1726СПБ	—	100	500	1,500	3,000	—
1727/6СПБ Rare	—	—	—	—	—	—

KM# 194 10 KOPEKS (Grivennik)
2.5900 g., 0.8020 Silver 0.0668 oz. ASW **Ruler:** Anna **Obv:** 3 Crowns above double-headed eagle **Rev:** Value, date below cluster of dots **Rev. Inscription:** GRIVENNIK

Date	Mintage	VG	F	VF	XF	Unc
1731	—	50.00	200	400	800	—
1732	—	50.00	175	350	700	—
1733	—	50.00	175	350	700	—
1734	—	50.00	175	350	700	—
1734/3	—	50.00	175	350	700	—
1735	—	50.00	175	350	700	—

KM# 205 10 KOPEKS (Grivennik)
2.5900 g., 0.7500 Silver 0.0625 oz. ASW **Ruler:** Ivan VI **Obv:** Bust right, initials below **Rev:** Crown above value, date within sprigs **Rev. Inscription:** GRIVENNIK

Date	Mintage	VG	F	VF	XF	Unc
1741ММД	—	200	500	1,000	2,000	—

C# 16 10 KOPEKS (Grivennik)
2.5900 g., 0.7500 Silver 0.0625 oz. ASW **Ruler:** Elizabeth **Obv:** Crowned bust of Elizabeth right **Rev:** Crown above value and date in branches **Note:** Without mint mark.

Date	Mintage	VG	F	VF	XF	Unc
1742	560,000	20.00	30.00	60.00	125	—
1743	206,000	20.00	30.00	60.00	125	—
1744	1,421,000	20.00	30.00	60.00	125	—
1745	730,000	20.00	30.00	60.00	125	—
1746	870,000	20.00	30.00	60.00	125	—

C# 16a 10 KOPEKS (Grivennik)
2.4200 g., 0.8020 Silver 0.0624 oz. ASW **Ruler:** Elizabeth

Date	Mintage	VG	F	VF	XF	Unc
1746	Inc. above	20.00	30.00	60.00	125	—
1747	2,210,000	20.00	30.00	60.00	125	—
1748	3,265,000	20.00	30.00	60.00	125	—
1749	100,000	40.00	60.00	120	250	—
1750	200,000	20.00	30.00	60.00	125	—
1751	1,395,000	20.00	30.00	60.00	125	—
1751 A	Inc. above	25.00	45.00	85.00	200	—
1752 E	248,000	20.00	30.00	60.00	125	—
1752 I	Inc. above	25.00	45.00	85.00	200	—
1753 IП	510,000	20.00	30.00	60.00	125	—
1754 IП	835,000	20.00	30.00	60.00	125	—
1754 МБ	Inc. above	25.00	45.00	85.00	200	—
1755 МБ	65,000	25.00	45.00	85.00	200	—
1755 EI	Inc. above	30.00	70.00	150	300	—
1756 МБ	265,000	25.00	45.00	85.00	200	—
1757 МБ	401,000	20.00	30.00	60.00	125	—

C# 44 10 KOPEKS (Grivennik)
Copper **Ruler:** Peter III **Obv:** Crowned double-headed eagle within circle of stars **Rev:** Value, date above drum, crossed flags **Note:** Unknown mint. Without mint mark. Varieties exist. Struck over 5 Kopecks of 1758-62.

Date	Mintage	VG	F	VF	XF	Unc
1762/0 Rare	—	—	—	—	—	—
1762	—	100	200	500	1,000	—

C# 61a.3 10 KOPEKS (Grivennik)
2.3700 g., 0.7500 Silver 0.0571 oz. ASW **Ruler:** Catherine II

Date	Mintage	VG	F	VF	XF	Unc
1764СПБ	—	20.00	45.00	100	260	—
1765СПБ Я	70,000	20.00	40.00	100	260	—
1766СПБ	460,000	10.00	20.00	50.00	100	—
1767СПБ	550,000	10.00	20.00	40.00	80.00	—
1768СПБ	674,000	10.00	20.00	40.00	80.00	—
1769СПБ	2,550,000	10.00	20.00	40.00	80.00	—
1770СПБ	1,640,000	10.00	20.00	40.00	80.00	—
1771СПБ	1,939,000	10.00	20.00	40.00	80.00	—
1772СПБ	510,000	10.00	20.00	40.00	80.00	—
1773СПБ	205,000	10.00	20.00	40.00	80.00	—
1774СПБ	—	10.00	20.00	40.00	85.00	—
1775СПБ	285,000	10.00	20.00	40.00	85.00	—
1776СПБ	66,000	20.00	50.00	100	250	—

C# 61.1 10 KOPEKS (Grivennik)
2.3700 g., 0.7500 Silver 0.0571 oz. ASW **Ruler:** Catherine II **Note:** Without mint mark.

Date	Mintage	VG	F	VF	XF	Unc
1764	340,000	10.00	25.00	50.00	100	—
1765	50,000	10.00	25.00	50.00	100	—
1766	41,000	50.00	150	300	600	—

C# 61a.2 10 KOPEKS (Grivennik)
2.3700 g., 0.7500 Silver 0.0571 oz. ASW **Ruler:** Catherine II **Obv:** Crowned bust right **Rev:** Crown above value, date within sprigs

Date	Mintage	VG	F	VF	XF	Unc
1767ММД	50,000	10.00	20.00	50.00	100	—
1768ММД	75,000	20.00	40.00	200	125	—
1769ММД	100,000	20.00	40.00	70.00	125	—
1770/64ММД	—	16.50	35.00	60.00	125	—
1770ММД	170,000	10.00	20.00	50.00	100	—
1771ММД	260,000	10.00	20.00	50.00	100	—
1774ММД	107,000	10.00	20.00	50.00	100	—
1775ММД	250,000	10.00	20.00	50.00	100	—

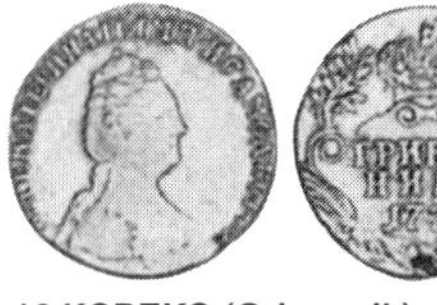

C# 61b 10 KOPEKS (Grivennik)
2.3700 g., 0.7500 Silver 0.0571 oz. ASW **Ruler:** Catherine II **Obv:** Bust right **Rev:** Crown above value, date within sprigs

Date	Mintage	VG	F	VF	XF	Unc
1777СПБ	—	90.00	200	500	100	—
1778СПБ	540,000	10.00	20.00	50.00	100	—
1779СПБ	1,376,000	10.00	20.00	50.00	100	—
1780СПБ	142,000	100	300	800	1,700	—
1781СПБ	—	7.00	15.00	50.00	70.00	—
1782СПБ	714,000	150	450	1,000	25.00	—

C# 61c 10 KOPEKS (Grivennik)
2.3700 g., 0.7500 Silver 0.0571 oz. ASW **Ruler:** Catherine II **Obv:** Old bust

Date	Mintage	VG	F	VF	XF	Unc
1783СПБ	—	7.00	15.00	35.00	70.00	—
1784СПБ	3,863,000	7.00	15.00	35.00	70.00	—
1785СПБ	3,274,000	7.00	15.00	35.00	70.00	—
1786СПБ	—	7.00	15.00	35.00	70.00	—
1787СПБ	2,000,000	7.00	15.00	35.00	70.00	—
1788СПБ	3,067,000	7.00	15.00	35.00	70.00	—
1789СПБ	500,000	7.00	15.00	35.00	70.00	—
1790СПБ	2,529,000	7.00	15.00	35.00	70.00	—
1791СПБ	1,730,000	7.00	15.00	35.00	70.00	—
1792СПБ	2,000,000	10.00	20.00	40.00	85.00	—
1793СПБ	840,000	20.00	50.00	100	225	—
1794СПБ	2,029,999	7.00	15.00	35.00	70.00	—
1795СПБ	1,230,000	7.00	15.00	35.00	70.00	—
1796СПБ	1,321,000	10.00	20.00	50.00	125	—

C# 97.1 10 KOPEKS (Grivennik)
2.9300 g., 0.8680 Silver 0.0818 oz. ASW **Ruler:** Paul I **Obv:** Crowned monogram **Rev:** Value, date above sprigs

Date	Mintage	VG	F	VF	XF	Unc
1797CM ФА	48,000	75.00	150	350	700	—

C# 97.1a 10 KOPEKS (Grivennik)
2.0700 g., 0.8680 Silver 0.0578 oz. ASW **Ruler:** Paul I

Date	Mintage	VG	F	VF	XF	Unc
1798 МБ	170,000	20.00	50.00	120	245	—
1799 МБ	680,000	20.00	50.00	125	250	—

C# 97.2 10 KOPEKS (Grivennik)
2.0700 g., 0.8680 Silver 0.0578 oz. ASW **Ruler:** Paul I

Date	Mintage	VG	F	VF	XF	Unc
1798СП ОМ	Inc. above	20.00	40.00	100	225	—

KM# 127 TYNF
6.4000 g., Silver **Ruler:** Peter I **Obv:** Bust right **Rev:** Crowned double-headed eagle **Note:** The Tynf circulated at 12 Kopeks for payment in Rzech Pospolta (Poland).

Date	Mintage	VG	F	VF	XF	Unc
ND(1707)	—	200	400	1,000	2,500	—
ND(1707) IL	—	200	400	1,000	2,500	—
1707 IL	—	200	400	1,000	2,500	—
1707 ILL	—	200	400	1,000	2,500	—
1707 ILL G Rare	—	—	—	—	—	—
1708	—	100	250	500	750	—
1708 ILL	—	100	250	500	750	—
1709 ILL Rare	—	—	—	—	—	—

C# 62.2 15 KOPEKS
3.5500 g., 0.7500 Silver 0.0856 oz. ASW **Ruler:** Catherine II

Date	Mintage	VG	F	VF	XF	Unc
1763СПБ Rare	—	—	—	—	—	—

C# 62.1 15 KOPEKS
3.5500 g., 0.7500 Silver 0.0856 oz. ASW **Ruler:** Catherine II **Obv:** Young bust with neck ruffle

Date	Mintage	VG	F	VF	XF	Unc
1764ММД	667,000	15.00	30.00	70.00	140	—
1765ММД	427,000	12.00	25.00	60.00	120	—
1766ММД	469,000	12.00	25.00	60.00	120	—

C# 62a 15 KOPEKS
3.5500 g., 0.7500 Silver 0.0856 oz. ASW **Ruler:** Catherine II **Obv:** Mature, crowned bust right **Rev:** Crowned double-headed eagle, date below in banner

Date	Mintage	VG	F	VF	XF	Unc
1767ММД	427,000	15.00	30.00	60.00	120	—
1768ММД	210,000	25.00	40.00	75.00	145	—
1769ММД	153,000	12.00	25.00	50.00	100	—
1770ММД	757,000	12.00	25.00	50.00	100	—
1771ММД	987,000	12.00	25.00	50.00	100	—
1774ММД	57,000	15.00	30.00	50.00	100	—
1775ММД	359,000	12.00	25.00	50.00	100	—

C# 62b 15 KOPEKS
3.5500 g., 0.7500 Silver 0.0856 oz. ASW **Ruler:** Catherine II

Date	Mintage	VG	F	VF	XF	Unc
1778СПБ ВСЕРОС	800,000	12.00	25.00	50.00	100	—
1778СПБ ВСЕРОСС	Inc. above	12.00	80.00	175	350	—
1779СПБ	1,420,000	12.00	25.00	50.00	100	—
1781СПБ	—	12.00	25.00	50.00	100	—
1782СПБ	445,000	—	—	—	500	—

C# 62c 15 KOPEKS
3.5500 g., 0.7500 Silver 0.0856 oz. ASW **Ruler:** Catherine II **Obv:** Older bust, wreath around crown **Rev:** Crowned double-headed eagle within beaded border **Note:** For similar coins not listed here refer to Poland.

Date	Mintage	VG	F	VF	XF	Unc
1783СПБ	—	12.00	25.00	50.00	100	—
1784СПБ	2,168,000	12.00	25.00	50.00	100	—
1785СПБ	2,500,000	12.00	25.00	50.00	100	—
1786СПБ	—	12.00	25.00	50.00	100	—
1787СПБ	3,200,000	12.00	25.00	50.00	100	—
1788СПБ	1,634,000	15.00	30.00	60.00	125	—
1789СПБ	1,200,000	12.00	25.00	50.00	100	—
1790СПБ	2,024,000	20.00	35.00	75.00	150	—
1791СПБ	960,000	20.00	50.00	100	200	—
1792СПБ	1,400,000	25.00	60.00	125	250	—
1793СПБ	440,000	100	175	350	700	—
1794СПБ	200,000	40.00	90.00	200	400	—

C# 63.1 20 KOPEKS
4.7700 g., 0.7500 Silver 0.1150 oz. ASW **Ruler:** Catherine II **Obv:** Crowned bust right **Rev:** Crowned double-headed eagle, value on breast

Date	Mintage	VG	F	VF	XF	Unc
1764ММД	520,000	15.00	30.00	60.00	125	—
1764ММД TI	Inc. above	—	—	—	—	—
1765ММД	—	—	—	—	—	—

C# 63.2 20 KOPEKS
4.7700 g., 0.7500 Silver 0.1150 oz. ASW **Ruler:** Catherine II

Date	Mintage	VG	F	VF	XF	Unc
1764СПБ	—	150	350	750	1,500	—
1765СПБ	115,000	15.00	30.00	60.00	120	—
1765СПБ TI	Inc. above	—	—	—	—	—

C# 63a.1 20 KOPEKS
4.7700 g., 0.7500 Silver 0.1150 oz. ASW **Ruler:** Catherine II **Obv:** Crowned bust right **Rev:** Crowned double-headed eagle, value on breast

Date	Mintage	VG	F	VF	XF	Unc
1766ММД	555,000	20.00	40.00	75.00	145	—
1767ММД	235,000	15.00	30.00	60.00	125	—
1768ММД	220,000	30.00	50.00	100	200	—
1769ММД	20,000	45.00	100	200	400	—
1770ММД	160,000	45.00	100	200	400	—
1775ММД	15,000	50.00	150	300	600	—

C# 63a.2 20 KOPEKS
4.7700 g., 0.7500 Silver 0.1150 oz. ASW **Ruler:** Catherine II

Date	Mintage	VG	F	VF	XF	Unc
1766СПБ	525,000	12.00	25.00	60.00	120	—
1767СПБ	245,000	20.00	40.00	75.00	145	—
1768СПБ	350,000	12.00	25.00	60.00	120	—
1769СПБ	1,075,000	12.00	25.00	60.00	120	—
1770СПБ	785,000	12.00	25.00	60.00	120	—
1771СПБ	2,105,000	12.00	25.00	60.00	120	—
1772СПБ	870,000	12.00	25.00	60.00	120	—
1773СПБ	290,000	12.00	25.00	60.00	120	—
1774СПБ	—	12.00	25.00	60.00	120	—
1775СПБ	290,000	25.00	60.00	125	250	—
1776СПБ	223,000	12.00	25.00	60.00	120	—

C# 63b 20 KOPEKS
4.7700 g., 0.7500 Silver 0.1150 oz. ASW **Ruler:** Catherine II **Obv:** Older bust, wreath around crown

Date	Mintage	VG	F	VF	XF	Unc
1778СПБ	630,000	12.00	25.00	60.00	120	—
1779СПБ	535,000	12.00	25.00	60.00	120	—
1781СПБ ВСЕРОС	—	20.00	35.00	60.00	120	—
1781СПБ ВСЕРОСС	—	—	—	—	—	—

C# 63c 20 KOPEKS
4.7700 g., 0.7500 Silver 0.1150 oz. ASW **Ruler:** Catherine II **Obv:** Crowned bust right **Rev:** Crowned double-headed eagle within beaded border

Date	Mintage	VG	F	VF	XF	Unc
1783СПБ	389,000	12.00	25.00	60.00	120	—
1784СПБ	2,080,000	12.00	25.00	60.00	120	—
1785СПБ	1,887,000	12.00	25.00	60.00	120	—
1786СПБ	—	12.00	25.00	60.00	120	—
1787СПБ	1,000,000	12.00	25.00	60.00	120	—
1788СПБ	2,376,000	15.00	35.00	75.00	150	—
1789СПБ	250,000	12.00	25.00	65.00	130	—
1790СПБ	2,870,000	20.00	35.00	70.00	140	—
1791СПБ	1,600,000	20.00	35.00	70.00	140	—
1792СПБ	1,510,000	12.00	25.00	60.00	120	—
1793СПБ	685,000	35.00	60.00	140	300	—

KM# 105 POLUPOLTINNIK (1/4 Rouble)
7.0000 g., 0.8750 Silver 0.1969 oz. ASW **Ruler:** Peter I **Obv:** Laureate bust right **Rev:** Crowned double-headed eagle **Note:** Varieties exist.

Date	Mintage	VG	F	VF	XF	Unc
ND(1701)	—	2,000	3,250	5,000	—	—
ND(1702)	—	2,000	3,250	5,000	—	—

KM# 112.1 POLUPOLTINNIK (1/4 Rouble)
7.0000 g., 0.8750 Silver 0.1969 oz. ASW **Ruler:** Peter I **Obv:** Laureate bust right **Rev:** Crown above crowned double-headed eagle

Date	Mintage	VG	F	VF	XF	Unc
ND(1703) Rare	—	—	—	—	—	—
ND(1704)	—	150	400	900	2,000	—
ND(1705)	—	400	1,000	2,500	5,000	—

KM# 112.2 POLUPOLTINNIK (1/4 Rouble)
7.0000 g., 0.8250 Silver 0.1857 oz. ASW **Ruler:** Peter I **Obv:** Laureate bust right **Rev:** Crown above crowned double-headed eagle

Date	Mintage	VG	F	VF	XF	Unc
ND(1704)МД	—	200	450	1,000	2,500	—

KM# 128 POLUPOLTINNIK (1/4 Rouble)
7.0000 g., 0.8750 Silver 0.1969 oz. ASW **Ruler:** Peter I **Obv:** Laureate bust right **Rev:** Crown above crowned double-headed eagle

Date	Mintage	VG	F	VF	XF	Unc
ND(1707)	—	225	500	1,200	2,750	—
1707 Rare	—	—	—	—	—	—
1710 Rare	—	—	—	—	—	—

Note: Placement of date varies on coins dated 1710

KM# 148 POLUPOLTINNIK (1/4 Rouble)
7.0000 g., 0.7500 Silver 0.1688 oz. ASW **Ruler:** Peter I

Date	Mintage	VG	F	VF	XF	Unc
1713	—	225	500	1,250	2,700	—

KM# 172 POLUPOLTINNIK (1/4 Rouble)
Silver **Ruler:** Peter II **Obv:** Crown above crowned double-headed eagle **Rev:** Value, date below cluster of dots

Date	Mintage	VG	F	VF	XF	Unc
1726СПБ Rare	—	—	—	—	—	—

KM# 191 POLUPOLTINNIK (1/4 Rouble)
Silver **Ruler:** Peter II **Obv:** Crowned bust right **Rev:** Crown above crowned double-headed eagle

Date	Mintage	VG	F	VF	XF	Unc
1730 Rare	—	—	—	—	—	—

KM# 202 POLUPOLTINNIK (1/4 Rouble)
6.4600 g., 0.8020 Silver 0.1666 oz. ASW **Ruler:** Anna **Obv:** Crowned bust right **Rev:** Crown above crowned double-headed eagle, shield on breast

Date	Mintage	VG	F	VF	XF	Unc
1739	—	125	300	700	1,500	—
1740	—	300	700	1,500	3,000	—

C# 17 POLUPOLTINNIK (1/4 Rouble)
6.4600 g., 0.8020 Silver 0.1666 oz. ASW **Ruler:** Elizabeth **Obv:** Crowned bust right **Rev:** Crown divides date above crowned double-headed eagle, shield on breast

Date	Mintage	VG	F	VF	XF	Unc
1743ММД	76,000	25.00	60.00	120	260	—
1744ММД	96,000	25.00	45.00	90.00	230	—
1745ММД	68,000	25.00	45.00	90.00	230	—
1746/5ММД	368,000	27.50	55.00	100	250	—
1746ММД	Inc. above	25.00	45.00	85.00	225	—
1747ММД	1,646,000	20.00	40.00	80.00	220	—
1748ММД	600,000	25.00	45.00	85.00	225	—
1749ММД	318,000	25.00	45.00	85.00	225	—
1750ММД	423,000	25.00	45.00	85.00	225	—
1751ММД	885,000	25.00	45.00	85.00	225	—

C# 17a POLUPOLTINNIK (1/4 Rouble)
6.4600 g., 0.8020 Silver 0.1666 oz. ASW **Ruler:** Elizabeth **Rev:** Moneyers' initials added

Date	Mintage	VG	F	VF	XF	Unc
1751ММД А	Inc. above	25.00	45.00	85.00	225	—
1752ММД Е	248,000	25.00	45.00	85.00	225	—
1752ММД ШР	Inc. above	25.00	45.00	85.00	225	—
1753ММД IП	426,000	25.00	45.00	85.00	225	—
1754ММД IП	—	25.00	45.00	85.00	225	—
1754ММД ЕI	689,000	25.00	45.00	85.00	225	—
1754ММД МБ	—	25.00	45.00	85.00	225	—

C# 17b POLUPOLTINNIK (1/4 Rouble)
6.0500 g., 0.8020 Silver 0.1560 oz. ASW **Ruler:** Elizabeth

Date	Mintage	VG	F	VF	XF	Unc
1755 МБ	203,000	15.00	30.00	75.00	150	—
1756 МБ	851,000	15.00	30.00	75.00	150	—
1757 МБ	151,000	20.00	40.00	80.00	200	—
1758 ЕI	44,000	50.00	100	200	350	—

C# 65 POLUPOLTINNIK (1/4 Rouble)
5.9700 g., 0.7500 Silver 0.1439 oz. ASW **Ruler:** Catherine II **Obv:** Crowned bust right **Rev:** Crown divides date above crowned double-headed eagle, shield on breast

Date	Mintage	VG	F	VF	XF	Unc
1764ММД ЕI	112,000	80.00	175	400	800	—
1765ММД ЕI	912,000	20.00	45.00	100	200	—
1766ММД ЕI	832,000	20.00	45.00	100	200	—

C# 65a POLUPOLTINNIK (1/4 Rouble)
5.9700 g., 0.7500 Silver 0.1439 oz. ASW, 23.9 mm. **Ruler:** Catherine II **Obv:** Mature bust without neck ruffle

Date	Mintage	VG	F	VF	XF	Unc
1767 ЕI	1,668,000	15.00	30.00	70.00	140	—
1768 ЕI	484,000	20.00	35.00	75.00	150	—
1769 ЕI	460,000	20.00	35.00	75.00	150	—
1770 ЕI	780,000	30.00	50.00	150	300	—
1770 ДМ	352,000	12.00	25.00	75.00	90.00	—
1774 СА/ДМ	1,400	30.00	50.00	100	200	—
1775 СА	132,000	20.00	35.00	80.00	160	—

C# 65b POLUPOLTINNIK (1/4 Rouble)
5.9700 g., 0.7500 Silver 0.1439 oz. ASW **Ruler:** Catherine II

Date	Mintage	VG	F	VF	XF	Unc
1779СПБ	—	100	200	450	900	—
1779СПБ ДМ	394,000	15.00	35.00	80.00	200	—
1781СПБ АГ	336,000	15.00	35.00	80.00	200	—

C# 65c POLUPOLTINNIK (1/4 Rouble)
5.9700 g., 0.7500 Silver 0.1439 oz. ASW **Ruler:** Catherine II **Obv:** Crowned bust right **Rev:** Crown divides date above crowned double-headed eagle, shield on breast

Date	Mintage	VG	F	VF	XF	Unc
1783 ММ	—	20.00	40.00	100	250	—
1784 ММ	441,000	20.00	40.00	100	250	—
1785 ЯА	605,000	15.00	35.00	80.00	160	—
1786 ЯА	—	20.00	40.00	80.00	160	—
1787 ЯА	800,000	20.00	40.00	80.00	160	—
1788 ЯА	1,706,000	20.00	40.00	80.00	160	—
1789 ЯА	800,000	20.00	40.00	80.00	160	—
1790 ЯА	412,000	25.00	55.00	125	250	—
1791 ЯА	704,000	20.00	40.00	80.00	160	—
1792 ЯА	1,404,000	20.00	40.00	80.00	160	—
1793 ЯА	368,000	45.00	90.00	200	450	—
1794 АК	1,016,000	25.00	45.00	90.00	180	—
1795 АК	464,000	25.00	45.00	90.00	180	—
1796 IС	745,000	20.00	45.00	90.00	180	—

C# 98.1 POLUPOLTINNIK (1/4 Rouble)
7.3100 g., 0.8680 Silver 0.2040 oz. ASW **Ruler:** Paul I **Obv:** Monogram of Paul I in cruciform with 4 crowns **Rev:** Inscription within ornamented square

Date	Mintage	VG	F	VF	XF	Unc
1797СМ ФА	28,000	150	350	800	2,000	—

C# 98.1a POLUPOLTINNIK (1/4 Rouble)
5.1800 g., 0.8680 Silver 0.1446 oz. ASW **Ruler:** Paul I **Obv:** Monogram of Paul I in cruciform with 4 crowns **Rev:** Inscription within ornamented square

Date	Mintage	VG	F	VF	XF	Unc
1798СМ МБ	88,000	90.00	180	400	900	—
1799СМ МБ	440,000	90.00	180	400	900	—
1799СМ ФА	Inc. above	100	225	500	1,100	—
1800СМ ОМ Rare	8,003	—	—	—	—	—

C# 98.2 POLUPOLTINNIK (1/4 Rouble)
5.1800 g., 0.8680 Silver 0.1446 oz. ASW **Ruler:** Paul I **Obv:** Monogram of Paul I in cruciform with 4 crowns **Rev:** Inscription within ornamented square

Date	Mintage	VG	F	VF	XF	Unc
1798СП ОМ	Inc. above	125	250	600	1,250	—
1800СП ОМ Rare	Inc. above	—	—	—	—	—

KM# 106.1 POLTINA (1/2 Rouble)
14.0000 g., 0.8750 Silver 0.3938 oz. ASW **Ruler:** Peter I **Subject:** Peter I **Obv:** Laureate bust right **Rev:** Crown above crowned double-headed eagle

Date	Mintage	VG	F	VF	XF	Unc
ND(1701) Rare	—	—	—	—	—	—
ND(1702) Rare	—	—	—	—	—	—
ND(1703) Rare	—	—	—	—	—	—
ND(1704)	—	200	500	1,250	2,500	—
ND(1705)	—	200	500	1,250	2,500	—

KM# 106.2 POLTINA (1/2 Rouble)
14.0000 g., 0.8750 Silver 0.3938 oz. ASW **Ruler:** Peter I **Obv:** Laureate bust right **Rev:** Crown above crowned double-headed eagle

Date	Mintage	VG	F	VF	XF	Unc
ND(1704)МД	—	200	500	1,250	2,500	—

KM# 124.1 POLTINA (1/2 Rouble)
14.0000 g., 0.8750 Silver 0.3938 oz. ASW **Ruler:** Peter I **Obv:** Laureate bust right **Rev:** Crown above crowned double-headed eagle

Date	Mintage	VG	F	VF	XF	Unc
ND(1705) Rare	—	—	—	—	—	—

KM# 124.2 POLTINA (1/2 Rouble)
14.0000 g., 0.8750 Silver 0.3938 oz. ASW **Ruler:** Peter I **Obv:** Laureate bust right **Rev:** Crown above crowned double-headed eagle

Date	Mintage	VG	F	VF	XF	Unc
ND(1706) Rare	—	—	—	—	—	—

KM# A129 POLTINA (1/2 Rouble)
14.0000 g., 0.8020 Silver 0.3610 oz. ASW **Ruler:** Peter I

Date	Mintage	VG	F	VF	XF	Unc
ND(1707)	—	1,250	3,000	7,500	1,500	—
1707	—	250	600	1,300	3,000	—
1710	—	200	500	1,150	2,500	—

KM# 132 POLTINA (1/2 Rouble)
14.0000 g., 0.7500 Silver 0.3376 oz. ASW **Ruler:** Peter I **Obv:** Laureate bust right **Rev:** Crown above crowned double-headed eagle

Date	Mintage	VG	F	VF	XF	Unc
ND(1710) Rare	—	—	—	—	—	—

KM# 137 POLTINA (1/2 Rouble)
14.2500 g., 0.6040 Silver 0.2767 oz. ASW **Ruler:** Peter I **Obv:**

Laureate bust right **Rev:** Crown above crowned double-headed eagle **Note:** Date placement varies.

Date	Mintage	VG	F	VF	XF	Unc
1712 Rare	—	—	—	—	—	—

KM# 156 POLTINA (1/2 Rouble)
14.2200 g., 0.7290 Silver 0.3333 oz. ASW **Ruler:** Peter I **Obv:** Laureate bust right **Rev:** Crown above crowned double-headed eagle **Note:** There are numerous varieties of this type including engravers' initials on some pieces.

Date	Mintage	VG	F	VF	XF	Unc
ND(1718)	—	200	450	1,000	2,000	—
ND(1719)	—	200	450	1,000	2,000	—
ND(1720)	—	100	250	600	1,200	—
ND(1721)	—	125	300	750	1,500	—
ND(1722)	—	200	450	1,000	2,000	—

KM# 160 POLTINA (1/2 Rouble)
14.2200 g., 0.7290 Silver 0.3333 oz. ASW **Ruler:** Peter I **Obv:** Laureate bust right **Rev:** Crown above crowned double-headed eagle

Date	Mintage	VG	F	VF	XF	Unc
1723	—	150	350	750	1,500	—
1724	—	150	350	750	1,500	—

KM# 161.1 POLTINA (1/2 Rouble)
14.2200 g., 0.7290 Silver 0.3333 oz. ASW **Ruler:** Peter I **Obv:** Laureate bust right **Rev:** Crown above crowned double-headed eagle

Date	Mintage	VG	F	VF	XF	Unc
1723	—	125	300	650	1,500	—

KM# 161.2 POLTINA (1/2 Rouble)
14.2200 g., 0.7290 Silver 0.3333 oz. ASW **Ruler:** Peter I **Obv:** Laureate bust right **Rev:** Crown above crowned double-headed eagle

Date	Mintage	VG	F	VF	XF	Unc
1725СПБ	—	250	600	1,250	2,500	—

KM# 159 POLTINA (1/2 Rouble)
14.2200 g., 0.7290 Silver 0.3333 oz. ASW **Ruler:** Peter I **Obv:** Laureate bust right **Rev:** Crown above crowned double-headed eagle

Date	Mintage	VG	F	VF	XF	Unc
1723	—	150	350	750	1,500	—
1724/3	—	150	350	750	1,500	—
1725	—	200	400	900	1,800	—

KM# 174 POLTINA (1/2 Rouble)
14.2200 g., 0.7290 Silver 0.3333 oz. ASW **Ruler:** Catherine I **Obv:** Crowned bust left **Rev:** Crown above crowned double-headed eagle

Date	Mintage	VG	F	VF	XF	Unc
1726/5СПБ	—	150	300	650	1,300	—
1726СПБ	—	150	300	650	1,800	—

KM# 175.2 POLTINA (1/2 Rouble)
14.2200 g., 0.7290 Silver 0.3333 oz. ASW **Ruler:** Catherine I **Obv:** Crowned bust right **Rev:** Crown above crowned double-headed eagle

Date	Mintage	VG	F	VF	XF	Unc
1726СПБ	—	150	350	750	1,500	—

KM# 173 POLTINA (1/2 Rouble)
14.2200 g., 0.7290 Silver 0.3333 oz. ASW **Ruler:** Catherine I **Obv:** Crowned bust left, continuous legend **Rev:** Crown above crowned double-headed eagle **Note:** Without mint mark.

Date	Mintage	VG	F	VF	XF	Unc
1726	—	150	300	600	1,200	—

KM# 175.1 POLTINA (1/2 Rouble)
14.2200 g., 0.7290 Silver 0.3333 oz. ASW **Ruler:** Catherine I **Obv:** Crowned bust right **Rev:** Crown above crowned double-headed eagle **Note:** Without mint mark.

Date	Mintage	VG	F	VF	XF	Unc
1726	—	150	350	750	1,500	—

KM# 176.1 POLTINA (1/2 Rouble)
14.2200 g., 0.7290 Silver 0.3333 oz. ASW **Ruler:** Catherine I **Obv:** Older bust right, continuous legend **Rev:** Crown above crowned double-headed eagle **Note:** Without mint mark.

Date	Mintage	VG	F	VF	XF	Unc
1726	—	150	350	750	1,500	—
1727	—	145	325	700	1,500	—

KM# 180 POLTINA (1/2 Rouble)
14.2200 g., 0.7290 Silver 0.3333 oz. ASW **Ruler:** Peter II **Obv:** Laureate bust right **Rev:** Crown above crowned double-headed eagle

Date	Mintage	VG	F	VF	XF	Unc
1727	—	150	350	750	1,500	—
1728	—	180	400	900	1,800	—
1729	—	180	400	800	1,700	—

KM# 181 POLTINA (1/2 Rouble)
14.2200 g., 0.7290 Silver 0.3333 oz. ASW **Ruler:** Peter II **Obv:** Laureate bust right **Rev:** Crown above crowned double-headed eagle

Date	Mintage	VG	F	VF	XF	Unc
1727СПБ	—	200	450	900	1,800	—

KM# 176.2 POLTINA (1/2 Rouble)
14.2200 g., 0.7290 Silver 0.3333 oz. ASW **Ruler:** Catherine I

Date	Mintage	VG	F	VF	XF	Unc
1727СПБ	—	200	400	800	1,600	—

KM# 195 POLTINA (1/2 Rouble)
12.9300 g., 0.8020 Silver 0.3334 oz. ASW **Ruler:** Anna **Obv:** Bust right **Rev:** Crown above crowned double-headed eagle **Note:** Without mint mark (Moscow).

Date	Mintage	VG	F	VF	XF	Unc
1731	—	100	200	400	800	—
1732	—	100	200	400	800	—
1733	—	110	225	500	1,000	—

KM# 196 POLTINA (1/2 Rouble)
12.9300 g., 0.8020 Silver 0.3334 oz. ASW **Ruler:** Anna **Obv:** Bust right **Rev:** Crown above crowned double-headed eagle

Date	Mintage	VG	F	VF	XF	Unc
1734	—	100	200	500	1,000	—
1735	—	100	200	500	1,000	—
1736	—	100	200	500	1,000	—
1737	—	100	200	500	1,000	—

KM# 199.1 POLTINA (1/2 Rouble)
12.9300 g., 0.8020 Silver 0.3334 oz. ASW **Ruler:** Anna **Obv:** Bust right, with jeweled hairpiece **Rev:** Crown above crowned double-headed eagle, shield on breast

Date	Mintage	VG	F	VF	XF	Unc
1737	—	70.00	150	375	750	—
1738	—	100	200	450	900	—
1739	—	70.00	150	325	750	—
1740	—	90.00	180	400	800	—

KM# 199.2 POLTINA (1/2 Rouble)

12.9300 g., 0.8020 Silver 0.3334 oz. ASW **Ruler:** Anna **Obv:** Bust right with jeweled hairpiece **Rev:** Crown above crowned double-headed eagle, shield on breast

Date	Mintage	VG	F	VF	XF	Unc
1738СПБ	—	100	200	400	800	—
1739СПБ	—	100	200	400	800	—
1740СПБ	—	150	300	600	1,200	—

KM# 206.1 POLTINA (1/2 Rouble)

12.9300 g., 0.8020 Silver 0.3334 oz. ASW **Ruler:** Ivan VI **Obv:** Bust right, initials below **Rev:** Crown above crowned double-headed eagle, shield on breast

Date	Mintage	VG	F	VF	XF	Unc
1741ММД	—	1,300	3,000	7,000	15,000	—

KM# 206.2 POLTINA (1/2 Rouble)

12.9300 g., 0.8020 Silver 0.3334 oz. ASW **Ruler:** Ivan VI **Obv:** Bust right, initials below **Rev:** Crown above crowned double-headed eagle, shield on breast

Date	Mintage	VG	F	VF	XF	Unc
1741СПБ	60,000	1,000	2,000	4,500	10,000	—

C# 18.1 POLTINA (1/2 Rouble)

12.9300 g., 0.8020 Silver 0.3334 oz. ASW **Ruler:** Elizabeth **Obv:** Crowned bust right **Rev:** Crown above crowned double-headed eagle, shield on breast **Note:** Similar to C#18.3. Mint mark varieties exist.

Date	Mintage	VG	F	VF	XF	Unc
1741ММД Rare	—	—	—	—	—	—
1742ММД	40,000	150	300	600	1,200	—
1743ММД	166,000	120	270	550	1,100	—
1744ММД	106,000	110	250	500	1,000	—
1745ММД	120,000	110	250	500	1,000	—
1747ММД	54,000	160	370	750	1,500	—
1749ММД	69,000	150	300	600	1,200	—

C# 18.2 POLTINA (1/2 Rouble)

12.9300 g., 0.8020 Silver 0.3334 oz. ASW **Ruler:** Elizabeth **Obv:** Crowned bust right **Rev:** Crown above crowned double-headed eagle, shield on breast **Note:** Varieties exist.

Date	Mintage	VG	F	VF	XF	Unc
1742СПБ	79,000	160	370	800	1,600	—
1743СПБ	Inc. above	300	600	1,250	2,500	—
1745СПБ Rare	Inc. above	—	—	—	—	—

C# 18.3 POLTINA (1/2 Rouble)

12.9300 g., 0.8020 Silver 0.3334 oz. ASW **Ruler:** Elizabeth **Obv:** Crowned bust right **Rev:** Crown above crowned double-headed eagle, shield on breast **Note:** Varieties exist.

Date	Mintage	VG	F	VF	XF	Unc
1743	65,000	150	300	600	1,200	—
1744	40,000	160	350	750	1,500	—
1745	17,000	150	300	600	1,200	—
1746	55,000	160	350	650	1,300	—
1747	63,000	160	350	650	1,300	—
1748	33,000	160	350	700	1,400	—
1749	67,000	160	350	700	1,400	—
1750	29,000	160	350	700	1,400	—
1751	39,000	160	350	700	1,400	—

C# 18.4 POLTINA (1/2 Rouble)

12.9300 g., 0.8020 Silver 0.3334 oz. ASW **Ruler:** Elizabeth **Rev:** Moneyer initials added

Date	Mintage	VG	F	VF	XF	Unc
1751 IM	Inc. above	150	300	650	1,300	—
1752 IM	106,000	150	300	650	1,300	—
1752 ЯI	Inc. above	150	300	650	1,300	—
1753 IM	41,000	150	300	650	1,300	—
1754 IM	154,000	150	300	650	1,300	—
1754 ЯI	Inc. above	150	300	650	1,300	—
1755 IM	150,000	200	400	900	1,800	—
1755 ЯI	Inc. above	150	300	650	1,300	—
1756 IM	176,000	150	300	700	1,800	—
1756 ЯI	Inc. above	300	600	1,250	2,500	—
1758 ЯI	61,000	160	350	750	1,500	—
1758 НК	Inc. above	150	300	700	1,400	—
1759 ЯI	89,000	150	300	700	1,400	—
1759 НК	Inc. above	200	400	800	1,600	—
1760 ЯI	46,000	160	350	700	1,400	—
1761 ЯI	45,000	400	800	1,700	3,500	—
1761 НК	Inc. above	250	500	1,000	2,000	—

C# 21.1 POLTINA (1/2 Rouble)

0.8100 g., 0.9170 Gold 0.0239 oz. AGW **Ruler:** Elizabeth **Obv:** Crowned bust right **Rev:** Crowned monogram **Note:** Crown varieties.

Date	Mintage	VG	F	VF	XF	Unc
1756	22,000	80.00	160	300	600	—

C# 21.2 POLTINA (1/2 Rouble)

0.8100 g., 0.9170 Gold 0.0239 oz. AGW **Ruler:** Elizabeth **Note:** Small crown.

Date	Mintage	VG	F	VF	XF	Unc
1756	Inc. above	80.00	160	300	600	—

C# 46.1 POLTINA (1/2 Rouble)

12.0000 g., 0.7500 Silver 0.2893 oz. ASW **Ruler:** Peter III **Obv:** Bust right **Rev:** Crown above crowned double-headed eagle, shield on breast

Date	Mintage	VG	F	VF	XF	Unc
1762ММД ДМ	—	250	500	1,000	2,000	—

C# 46.2 POLTINA (1/2 Rouble)

12.0000 g., 0.7500 Silver 0.2893 oz. ASW **Ruler:** Peter III

Date	Mintage	VG	F	VF	XF	Unc
1762СПБ НК	—	220	450	900	1,800	—

C# 66.1 POLTINA (1/2 Rouble)

12.9300 g., 0.8020 Silver 0.3334 oz. ASW **Ruler:** Catherine II **Obv:** Crowned bust right **Rev:** Crown above crowned double-headed eagle, shield on breast

Date	Mintage	VG	F	VF	XF	Unc
1762ММД ДМ	14,000	100	200	400	800	—
1763ММД ЕI	49,000	80.00	160	350	700	—
1764ММД ЕI	—	350	550	—	—	—

C# 66.2 POLTINA (1/2 Rouble)

12.0000 g., 0.7500 Silver 0.2893 oz. ASW **Ruler:** Catherine II

Date	Mintage	VG	F	VF	XF	Unc
1762СПБ НК	148,000	100	200	400	800	—
1763СПБ НК	252,000	80.00	160	350	700	—
1763СПБ ЯI	Inc. above	80.00	160	350	700	—

C# 66.2a POLTINA (1/2 Rouble)

12.0000 g., 0.7500 Silver 0.2893 oz. ASW **Ruler:** Catherine II

Date	Mintage	VG	F	VF	XF	Unc
1764СПБ ЯI	543,000	80.00	160	350	700	—
1764СПБ СА	Inc. above	80.00	160	350	700	—
1765СПБ ЯI	332,000	80.00	160	350	700	—
1765СПБ СА	Inc. above	90.00	180	375	750	—

C# 66a POLTINA (1/2 Rouble)

12.0000 g., 0.7500 Silver 0.2893 oz. ASW **Ruler:** Catherine II **Obv:** Crowned bust right **Rev:** Crown above crowned double-headed eagle, shield on breast

Date	Mintage	VG	F	VF	XF	Unc
1766СПБ ЯI	93,000	160	350	750	1,500	—
1766СПБ АШ	Inc. above	90.00	180	325	750	—
1767СПБ АШ	52,000	100	200	400	800	—
1767СПБ	—	300	750	1,500	3,000	—
1768СПБ АШ	46,000	100	220	450	900	—
1768СПБ СА	Inc. above	150	300	600	1,200	—
1769СПБ СА	100,000	90.00	180	375	750	—
1771СПБ ЯБ	25,000	170	350	750	1,500	—
1772СПБ АШ	29,000	100	220	450	900	—
1773СПБ ЯБ	41,000	80.00	170	375	750	—
1773СПБ ФЛ	Inc. above	220	450	900	1,800	—
1774СПБ ФЛ	550	210	425	850	1,800	—
1775СПБ ФЛ	91,000	130	270	550	1,100	—
1776СПБ ЯБ	67,000	130	270	550	1,100	—

C# 66b POLTINA (1/2 Rouble)

12.0000 g., 0.7500 Silver 0.2893 oz. ASW **Ruler:** Catherine II **Obv:** Older bust, wreath around crown **Rev:** Crown above crowned double-headed eagle, shield on breast

Date	Mintage	VG	F	VF	XF	Unc
1777СПБ ФЛ	—	110	220	450	900	—
1778СПБ ФЛ	—	110	220	450	900	—
1779СПБ ФЛ	155,000	250	500	1,000	2,200	—

C# 66c POLTINA (1/2 Rouble)

12.0000 g., 0.7500 Silver 0.2893 oz. ASW **Ruler:** Catherine II

Date	Mintage	VG	F	VF	XF	Unc
1785СПБ ЯА	35,000	120	250	500	1,000	—
1787СПБ ЯА	57,000	120	250	500	1,000	—
1791СПБ ЯА	94,000	110	220	450	900	—
1794СПБ АК	72,000	110	220	450	900	—
1795СПБ АК	148,000	110	220	450	900	—
1796СПБ IС	270,000	100	210	425	850	—

C# 75 POLTINA (1/2 Rouble)

0.6500 g., 0.9170 Gold 0.0192 oz. AGW **Ruler:** Catherine II **Obv:** Crowned bust right **Rev:** Crowned monogram **Note:** Without mint mark.

Date	Mintage	F	VF	XF	Unc	BU
1777	—	100	160	300	600	—
1778	—	500	1,000	2,000	4,000	—

C# 99.1 POLTINA (1/2 Rouble)

14.6200 g., 0.8680 Silver 0.4080 oz. ASW **Ruler:** Paul I **Obv:** Monograms of Paul I in cruciform with 4 crowns **Rev:** Inscription within ornamented square

Date	Mintage	VG	F	VF	XF	Unc
1797CM ФA	214,000	370	750	1,500	3,000	—

C# 99.2 POLTINA (1/2 Rouble)

10.3700 g., 0.8680 Silver 0.2894 oz. ASW **Ruler:** Paul I

Date	Mintage	VG	F	VF	XF	Unc
1798CП OM Rare	Inc. above	—	—	—	—	—

C# 99.1a POLTINA (1/2 Rouble)

10.3700 g., 0.8680 Silver 0.2894 oz. ASW **Ruler:** Paul I **Obv:** Monograms of Paul I in cruciform with 4 crowns **Rev:** Inscription within ornamented square **Note:** Reduced size.

Date	Mintage	VG	F	VF	XF	Unc
1798CM МБ	284,000	110	220	450	900	—
1799CM МБ	348,000	110	220	450	900	—
1799CM ФA	Inc. above	220	450	900	1,800	—
1800CM OM	330,000	110	220	450	900	—
1800CM МБ Rare	Inc. above	—	—	—	—	—

KM# 122.1 ROUBLE

28.0000 g., 0.8750 Silver 0.7877 oz. ASW **Ruler:** Peter I **Obv:** Bust right **Rev:** Crown above crowned double-headed eagle **Note:** Dav. #1642.

Date	Mintage	VG	F	VF	XF	Unc
ND(1704)МД	—	2,200	4,500	9,000	18,000	—
ND(1705)МД	—	2,000	4,000	8,000	16,000	—

KM# 122.2 ROUBLE

28.0000 g., 0.8750 Silver 0.7877 oz. ASW **Ruler:** Peter I **Note:** Without mint mark.

Date	Mintage	VG	F	VF	XF	Unc
ND(1704)	—	—	2,200	4,500	9,000	—
ND(1705)	—	—	1,000	2,000	4,000	—

KM# 130.1 ROUBLE

28.0000 g., 0.8750 Silver 0.7877 oz. ASW **Ruler:** Peter I **Obv:** Laureate bust right **Rev:** Crown above crowned double-headed eagle **Note:** Dav. #1643.

Date	Mintage	VG	F	VF	XF	Unc
ND(1707)	—	1,500	3,000	6,000	15,000	—
ND(1707) H	—	1,000	2,000	4,000	10,000	—
ND(1707) G	—	1,200	2,500	5,000	12,500	—

KM# 130.2 ROUBLE

28.0000 g., 0.8750 Silver 0.7877 oz. ASW **Ruler:** Peter I **Obv:** Laureate bust right **Rev:** Crown above crowned double-headed eagle, divided date below **Note:** Dav. #1645.

Date	Mintage	VG	F	VF	XF	Unc
1707	—	1,200	2,500	5,000	12,500	—

KM# 130.5 ROUBLE

28.0000 g., 0.8750 Silver 0.7877 oz. ASW **Ruler:** Peter I **Obv:** Laureate bust right **Rev:** Crown above crowned double-headed eagle, divided date below **Note:** Dav. #1646.

Date	Mintage	VG	F	VF	XF	Unc
1707	—	1,200	2,500	5,000	12,500	—

KM# 130.3 ROUBLE

27.5000 g., 0.8020 Silver 0.7091 oz. ASW **Ruler:** Peter I **Obv:** Large bust with large bow on laureate **Note:** Dav. #1648.

Date	Mintage	VG	F	VF	XF	Unc
1710	—	1,800	3,700	7,500	25,000	—

KM# 130.4 ROUBLE

27.5000 g., 0.8020 Silver 0.7091 oz. ASW **Ruler:** Peter I **Obv:** Laureate bust right **Rev:** Crown above crowned double-headed eagle, date in legend **Note:** Dav. #1649.

Date	Mintage	VG	F	VF	XF	Unc
1710	—	3,800	7,500	15,000	40,000	—

KM# 138 ROUBLE

28.5000 g., 0.6040 Silver 0.5534 oz. ASW **Ruler:** Peter I **Obv:** Laureate bust right divides legend **Rev:** Crown above crowned double-headed eagle, date in legend **Note:** Dav. #1650.

Date	Mintage	VG	F	VF	XF	Unc
1712	—	1,000	2,200	4,500	9,000	—

KM# 149 ROUBLE

28.5000 g., 0.6040 Silver 0.5534 oz. ASW **Ruler:** Peter I **Obv:** Laureate bust right **Rev:** Crown above crowned double-headed eagle, date in legend **Note:** Dav. #1651. Legend placement varies.

Date	Mintage	VG	F	VF	XF	Unc
1714/3	—	8,000	17,500	35,000	70,000	—
1714	—	8,000	17,500	35,000	70,000	—

KM# 157.1 ROUBLE

28.4400 g., 0.7290 Silver 0.6665 oz. ASW **Ruler:** Peter I **Obv:** Laureate bust right **Obv. Legend:** AAPЬ ПЕТРЬ АЛЕКСЕЕВИБ **Rev:** Crown above crowned double-headed eagle **Note:** Dav. #1652.

Date	Mintage	VG	F	VF	XF	Unc
ND(1718)	—	250	500	1,000	2,000	—

KM# 157.2 ROUBLE

28.4400 g., 0.7290 Silver 0.6665 oz. ASW **Ruler:** Peter I **Obv:** Laureate bust right **Rev:** Crown above crowned double-headed eagle **Note:** Dav. #1653. Varieties exist.

Date	Mintage	VG	F	VF	XF	Unc
ND(1719)	—	300	600	1,200	2,500	—

KM# 157.3 ROUBLE
28.4400 g., 0.7290 Silver 0.6665 oz. ASW **Ruler:** Peter I **Obv:** Laureate bust right **Rev:** Crown above crowned double-headed eagle **Note:** Dav. #1653A.

Date	Mintage	VG	F	VF	XF	Unc
ND(1719)	—	350	750	1,500	3,000	—

KM# 157.4 ROUBLE
28.4400 g., 0.7290 Silver 0.6665 oz. ASW **Ruler:** Peter I **Obv:** Laureate bust right **Rev:** Crown above crowned double-headed eagle **Note:** Dav. #1654.

Date	Mintage	VG	F	VF	XF	Unc
ND(1720)	—	160	325	650	1,300	—
ND(1720) OK	—	150	300	600	1,200	—
ND(1720) KO	—	375	750	1,500	3,000	—
ND(1720) K	—	150	300	600	1,200	—

KM# 157.5 ROUBLE
28.4400 g., 0.7290 Silver 0.6665 oz. ASW **Ruler:** Peter I **Obv:** Laureate bust right **Rev:** Crown above crowned double-headed eagle **Note:** Dav. #1655.

Date	Mintage	VG	F	VF	XF	Unc
ND(1720)	—	150	300	600	1,200	—
ND(1721)	—	150	300	600	1,200	—

KM# 157.6 ROUBLE
28.4400 g., 0.7290 Silver 0.6665 oz. ASW **Ruler:** Peter I **Obv:** Large draped bust, armor similar to KM#157.5

Date	Mintage	VG	F	VF	XF	Unc
ND(1720)	—	150	300	600	1,200	—

KM# 162.1 ROUBLE
28.4400 g., 0.7290 Silver 0.6665 oz. ASW **Ruler:** Peter I **Obv. Legend:** ПЕТРЬ А ИМПЕРАТОРЬ **Rev:** 4 crowned Russian P's **Note:** Dav. #1656.

Date	Mintage	VG	F	VF	XF	Unc
1722	—	175	350	700	1,400	—

KM# 162.2 ROUBLE
28.4400 g., 0.7290 Silver 0.6665 oz. ASW **Ruler:** Peter I **Obv:** Laureate bust right **Rev:** Date in crucifom with 4 crowns, monograms in angles **Note:** Dav. #1657.

Date	Mintage	VG	F	VF	XF	Unc
1723	—	100	220	400	800	—

KM# 162.3 ROUBLE
28.4400 g., 0.7290 Silver 0.6665 oz. ASW **Ruler:** Peter I **Obv:** Laureate bust right **Rev:** Date in cruciform with 4 crowns, monograms in angles **Note:** Dav. #1658. Varieties exist.

Date	Mintage	VG	F	VF	XF	Unc
1723	—	100	220	400	800	—

KM# 166.1 ROUBLE
28.4400 g., 0.7290 Silver 0.6665 oz. ASW **Ruler:** Peter I **Obv:** Laureate bust right **Obv. Legend:** I **Rev:** Sunburst in center divides date in cruciform with 4 crowns, monograms in angles **Note:** Dav. #1659. The so-called "Sun" Rouble. Varieties exist.

Date	Mintage	VG	F	VF	XF	Unc
1724СПБ	—	850	1,750	3,500	7,500	—
1725СПБ	—	850	1,750	3,500	7,500	—

KM# 162.4 ROUBLE
28.4400 g., 0.7290 Silver 0.6665 oz. ASW **Ruler:** Peter I **Note:** Dav. #1660.

Date	Mintage	VG	F	VF	XF	Unc
1724	—	100	200	450	1,000	—

KM# 166.2 ROUBLE
28.4400 g., 0.7290 Silver 0.6665 oz. ASW **Ruler:** Peter I **Obv:** Laureate bust right **Rev:** Sunburst in center divides date in cruciform with 4 crowns, monograms in angles **Note:** Dav. #1661A.

Date	Mintage	VG	F	VF	XF	Unc
1724	—	150	350	750	1,600	—

KM# 166.3 ROUBLE
28.4400 g., 0.7290 Silver 0.6665 oz. ASW **Ruler:** Peter I **Obv:** Laureate bust right **Rev:** Sunburst in center divides date in cruciform with 4 crowns, monograms in angles **Note:** Dav. #1661.

Date	Mintage	VG	F	VF	XF	Unc
1725	—	300	600	1,200	2,500	—

KM# 162.5 ROUBLE
28.4400 g., 0.7290 Silver 0.6665 oz. ASW **Ruler:** Peter I **Obv:** Laureate bust right **Rev:** Date in cruciform with 4 crowns, monograms in angles **Note:** Dav. #1662.

Date	Mintage	VG	F	VF	XF	Unc
1725	—	150	300	600	1,300	—

KM# 162.6 ROUBLE
28.4400 g., 0.7290 Silver 0.6665 oz. ASW **Ruler:** Peter I **Obv:** OK below shoulder **Note:** Dav. #1662A.

Date	Mintage	VG	F	VF	XF	Unc
1725	—	150	300	600	1,300	—

KM# 168 ROUBLE
28.4400 g., 0.7290 Silver 0.6665 oz. ASW **Ruler:** Catherine I **Obv:** Bust left **Rev:** Crown above crowned double-headed eagle **Note:** Dav. #1664.

Date	Mintage	VG	F	VF	XF	Unc
1725	—	150	325	650	1,500	—
1726	—	150	325	650	1,500	—

KM# 169 ROUBLE
28.4400 g., 0.7290 Silver 0.6665 oz. ASW **Ruler:** Catherine I **Obv:** Bust left **Rev:** Crown above crowned double-headed eagle **Note:** Mint mark appears on obverse and reverse; in one rare case it is on both sides dated 1725.

Date	Mintage	VG	F	VF	XF	Unc
1725СПБ	—	130	300	700	1,500	—
1726СПБ	—	130	300	700	1,500	—

KM# 167 ROUBLE
28.4400 g., 0.7290 Silver 0.6665 oz. ASW **Ruler:** Catherine I **Obv:** Bust left **Rev:** Crown above crowned double-headed eagle **Note:** Without mint mark. Dav. #1663. The so-called "Mourning" Rouble.

Date	Mintage	VG	F	VF	XF	Unc
1725	—	1,900	2,500	6,000	10,000	—

KM# 177.1 ROUBLE
28.4400 g., 0.7290 Silver 0.6665 oz. ASW **Ruler:** Catherine I **Obv:** Bust right **Rev:** Crown above crowned double-headed eagle **Note:** Dav. #1665.

Date	Mintage	VG	F	VF	XF	Unc
1726	—	150	300	750	1,500	—
1727	—	200	400	800	1,600	—

KM# 177.2 ROUBLE
28.4400 g., 0.7290 Silver 0.6665 oz. ASW **Ruler:** Catherine I

Date	Mintage	VG	F	VF	XF	Unc
1726СПБ	—	300	750	1,500	3,000	—
1727СПБ	—	250	500	1,000	2,000	—

KM# 182.1 ROUBLE
28.4400 g., 0.7290 Silver 0.6665 oz. ASW **Ruler:** Peter II **Obv:** Laureate bust right **Rev:** Date in cruciform with 4 crowns, monograms in angles **Note:** Dav. #1667.

Date	Mintage	VG	F	VF	XF	Unc
1727	—	200	450	900	1,800	—

KM# 177.3 ROUBLE
28.4400 g., 0.7290 Silver 0.6665 oz. ASW **Ruler:** Catherine I **Obv:** Bust right **Rev:** Crown above crowned double-headed eagle **Note:** Dav. #1666.

Date	Mintage	VG	F	VF	XF	Unc
1727	—	200	450	900	1,800	—

KM# 183 ROUBLE
28.4400 g., 0.7290 Silver 0.6665 oz. ASW **Ruler:** Peter II **Obv:** Laureate bust right **Rev:** Date in cruciform with 4 crowns, monograms in angles **Edge:** Braided **Note:** Dav. #1667. With or without mint mark under bust.

Date	Mintage	VG	F	VF	XF	Unc
1727СПБ	—	150	300	600	1,300	—

KM# 182.2 ROUBLE
28.4400 g., 0.7290 Silver 0.6665 oz. ASW **Ruler:** Peter II **Obv:** Laureate bust right **Rev:** Date in cruciform with 4 crowns, monograms in angles **Note:** Dav. #1668.

Date	Mintage	VG	F	VF	XF	Unc
1728	—	120	250	500	1,000	—

KM# 182.3 ROUBLE
28.4400 g., 0.7290 Silver 0.6665 oz. ASW **Ruler:** Peter II **Obv:** Laureate bust right **Rev:** Date in cruciform with 4 crowns, monograms in angles **Note:** Dav. #1669.

Date	Mintage	VG	F	VF	XF	Unc
1729	—	150	300	600	1,200	—

KM# 192.1 ROUBLE
28.4400 g., 0.7290 Silver 0.6665 oz. ASW **Ruler:** Anna **Obv:** Bust right **Rev:** Crown above crowned double-headed eagle, shield on breast **Note:** Dav. #1670.

Date	Mintage	VG	F	VF	XF	Unc
1730	—	300	600	1,250	2,500	—
1731	—	150	300	600	1,200	—
1732	—	150	300	600	1,200	—
1733	—	150	300	600	1,200	—

KM# 192.2 ROUBLE
28.4400 g., 0.7290 Silver 0.6665 oz. ASW **Ruler:** Anna **Obv:** Bust right **Rev:** Crown above crowned double-headed eagle, shield on breast **Note:** Dav. #1671.

Date	Mintage	VG	F	VF	XF	Unc
1733	—	170	350	750	1,500	—
1734	—	150	300	600	1,200	—

KM# 192.3 ROUBLE
28.4400 g., 0.7290 Silver 0.6665 oz. ASW **Ruler:** Anna **Obv:** Large, bust right **Rev:** Crown above crowned double-headed eagle, shield on breast, X on tail **Note:** Dav. #1672.

Date	Mintage	VG	F	VF	XF	Unc
1734	—	150	300	600	1,200	—

KM# 197 ROUBLE
25.8500 g., 0.8020 Silver 0.6665 oz. ASW **Ruler:** Anna **Obv:** Bust right **Rev:** Crown above crowned double-headed eagle, shield on breast, X on tail **Note:** Dav. #1673.

Date	Mintage	VG	F	VF	XF	Unc
1734	—	150	300	600	1,200	—
1735	—	150	300	600	1,200	—
1736	—	150	300	600	1,200	—
1737	—	150	300	600	1,200	—

KM# 198 ROUBLE

25.8500 g., 0.8020 Silver 0.6665 oz. ASW **Ruler:** Anna **Obv:** Bust right **Rev:** Crown above crowned double-headed eagle, shield on breast **Note:** Dav. #1674.

Date	Mintage	VG	F	VF	XF	Unc
1736 Rare	—	—	—	—	—	—
1737	—	150	300	600	1,200	—
1738	—	150	300	600	1,200	—
1739	—	150	300	600	200	—
1740	—	150	300	600	1,200	—

KM# 204 ROUBLE

25.8500 g., 0.8020 Silver 0.6665 oz. ASW **Ruler:** Anna **Obv:** Bust right **Rev:** Crown above crowned double-headed eagle, shield on breast **Note:** Dav. #1675.

Date	Mintage	VG	F	VF	XF	Unc
1738СПБ	—	120	250	500	1,000	—
1739СПБ	—	120	250	500	1,000	—
1740СПБ	—	120	250	500	1,000	—

KM# 203 ROUBLE

25.8500 g., 0.8020 Silver 0.6665 oz. ASW **Ruler:** Anna **Obv:** Bust right **Rev:** Crown above crowned double-headed eagle, shield on breast **Note:** Dav. #1675.

Date	Mintage	VG	F	VF	XF	Unc
1739	—	120	250	450	950	—
1740	—	120	250	500	1,000	—

KM# 207.1 ROUBLE

25.8500 g., 0.8020 Silver 0.6665 oz. ASW **Ruler:** Ivan VI **Obv:** Laureate bust right, initials below **Rev:** Crown above crowned double-headed eagle, shield on breast, X on tail **Note:** Dav. #1676.

Date	Mintage	VG	F	VF	XF	Unc
1741ММД	—	1,500	3,000	6,000	12,000	—

KM# 207.2 ROUBLE

25.8500 g., 0.8020 Silver 0.6665 oz. ASW **Ruler:** Ivan VI **Obv:** Laureate bust right, initials below **Rev:** Crown above crowned double-headed eagle, shield on breast, X on tail **Note:** Dav. #1676.

Date	Mintage	VG	F	VF	XF	Unc
1741СПБ	—	1,000	2,000	4,000	8,000	—

C# 19b.1 ROUBLE

25.8500 g., 0.8020 Silver 0.6665 oz. ASW **Ruler:** Elizabeth **Obv:** Broad bust of Elizabeth with ermine mantle

Date	Mintage	VG	F	VF	XF	Unc
1741	Inc. above	160	370	750	1,500	—

C# 19a ROUBLE

25.8500 g., 0.8020 Silver 0.6665 oz. ASW **Ruler:** Elizabeth **Obv:** Crowned bust right, initials below **Rev:** Crown above crowned double-headed eagle, shield on breast, X on tail **Note:** Dav. #1677.

Date	Mintage	VG	F	VF	XF	Unc
1741СПБ	765,000	1,300	2,500	5,000	10,000	—

C# 19b.2 ROUBLE

25.8500 g., 0.8020 Silver 0.6665 oz. ASW **Ruler:** Elizabeth **Obv:** Bust without ermine mantle **Note:** Overstrikes on rubles of Ivan VI are known.

Date	Mintage	VG	F	VF	XF	Unc
1741	Inc. above	160	370	750	1,500	—

C# 19.1 ROUBLE

25.8500 g., 0.8020 Silver 0.6665 oz. ASW **Ruler:** Elizabeth **Obv:** Crowned bust right **Rev:** Crown above crowned double-headed eagle, shield on breast **Note:** Dav. #1678. Mintmark varieties exist.

Date	Mintage	VG	F	VF	XF	Unc
1742ММД	289,000	350	750	1,500	3,000	—
1743ММД	677,000	100	200	400	800	—
1744ММД	373,000	100	200	400	800	—
1745ММД	554,000	100	200	400	800	—
1746ММД	391,000	130	250	450	950	—
1747ММД	294,000	130	250	500	1,000	—
1748/1ММД	100,000	150	300	600	1,200	—
1748ММД	Inc. above	120	200	400	900	—
1749ММД	847,000	100	200	400	800	—
1750ММД	1,026,999	100	200	400	800	—
1751ММД	1,083,000	100	200	400	800	—

C# 19b.3 ROUBLE

25.8500 g., 0.8020 Silver 0.6665 oz. ASW **Ruler:** Elizabeth **Obv:** Crowned bust right **Rev:** Crown above crowned double-headed eagle, shield on breast, X on tail **Note:** Date varieties exist.

Date	Mintage	VG	F	VF	XF	Unc
1742СПБ	1,133,000	50.00	100	750	450	—

C# 19b.4 ROUBLE

25.8500 g., 0.8020 Silver 0.6665 oz. ASW **Ruler:** Elizabeth **Obv:** Crowned bust right **Rev:** Crown above crowned double-headed eagle, shield on breast, X on tail **Note:** Varieties exist.

Date	Mintage	VG	F	VF	XF	Unc
1743СПБ	944,000	100	200	400	800	—
1744СПБ	509,000	100	200	400	800	—
1745СПБ	427,000	100	200	400	800	—
1746СПБ	781,000	100	200	400	800	—
1747/44СПБ	803,000	100	200	400	800	—
1747СПБ	Inc. above	100	200	400	800	—
1748СПБ	634,000	100	200	400	800	—
1749СПБ	1,106,000	80.00	150	300	700	—
1750/40СПБ	611,000	100	200	400	800	—
1750СПБ	Inc. above	100	200	400	800	—
1751СПБ	835,000	100	200	400	800	—

C# 19.2 ROUBLE

25.8500 g., 0.8020 Silver 0.6665 oz. ASW **Ruler:** Elizabeth **Obv:** Crowned bust right **Rev:** Moneyer initials added

Date	Mintage	VG	F	VF	XF	Unc
1751ММД А	Inc. above	80.00	170	350	700	—
1752ММД Е	—	80.00	170	350	700	—

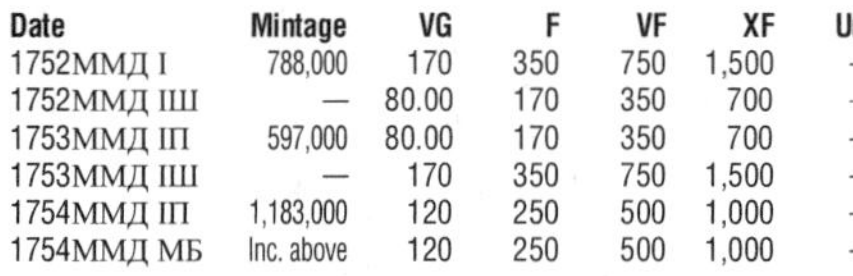

Date	Mintage	VG	F	VF	XF	Unc
1752ММД I	788,000	170	350	750	1,500	—
1752ММД ІШ	—	80.00	170	350	700	—
1753ММД ІП	597,000	80.00	170	350	700	—
1753ММД ІШ	—	170	350	750	1,500	—
1754ММД ІП	1,183,000	120	250	500	1,000	—
1754ММД МБ	Inc. above	120	250	500	1,000	—

C# 19b.5 ROUBLE

25.8500 g., 0.8020 Silver 0.6665 oz. ASW **Ruler:** Elizabeth **Obv:** Crowned bust right **Rev:** Moneyer initials added

Date	Mintage	VG	F	VF	XF	Unc
1751СПБ IM	Inc. above	100	200	400	800	—
1752СПБ IM	968,000	100	200	400	800	—
1752СПБ ЯI	Inc. above	100	200	400	800	—
1752 ЯI Close mint mark	Inc. above	45.00	90.00	185	325	—
1753СПБ IM	605,000	100	200	400	800	—
1753СПБ ЯI	Inc. above	100	200	400	800	—
1753 ЯI	Inc. above	45.00	90.00	185	325	—
1754 ЯI	1,183,000	45.00	90.00	185	325	—
1754СПБ ЯI	1,183,000	80.00	170	350	700	—

C# 19c.1 ROUBLE

25.8500 g., 0.8020 Silver 0.6665 oz. ASW **Ruler:** Elizabeth **Obv:** Crowned bust right **Rev:** Crown above crowned double-headed eagle, shield on breast

Date	Mintage	VG	F	VF	XF	Unc
1754ММД ІП	Inc. above	110	250	500	1,000	—
1754ММД МБ	Inc. above	120	250	500	1,000	—
1754ММД ЕI	Inc. above	120	200	400	800	—
1755ММД МБ	594,000	100	200	400	800	—
1756ММД МБ	217,000	110	220	450	900	—
1757ММД МБ	339,000	130	270	550	1,100	—
1758ММД ЕI	116,000	150	300	600	1,200	—

C# 19c.2 ROUBLE

25.8500 g., 0.8020 Silver 0.6665 oz. ASW **Ruler:** Elizabeth **Obv:** Crowned bust right **Rev:** Crown above crowned double-headed eagle, shield on breast, date above **Note:** Dav. #1679. Mint mark varieties exist.

Date	Mintage	VG	F	VF	XF	Unc
1754СПБ ЯI	Inc. above	70.00	150	350	700	—
1754СПБ IM	Inc. above	70.00	150	350	700	—
1755СПБ IM	1,836,000	70.00	150	350	700	—
1755СПБ ЯI	Inc. above	70.00	150	350	700	—
1756СПБ IM	1,944,000	70.00	150	350	700	—
1756СПБ ЯI	Inc. above	70.00	150	350	700	—
1757СПБ IM	536,000	100	200	450	900	—

C# 22 ROUBLE

1.6200 g., 0.9170 Gold 0.0478 oz. AGW **Ruler:** Elizabeth **Obv:** Crowned bust right **Rev:** Crown above crowned double-headed eagle, shield on breast

Date	Mintage	VG	F	VF	XF	Unc
1756	36,000	125	200	400	800	—
1757/6	14,000	125	200	400	800	—
1758	117,000	125	275	550	900	—

C# 19c.3 ROUBLE

25.8500 g., 0.8020 Silver 0.6665 oz. ASW **Ruler:** Elizabeth **Obv:** Large portrait **Note:** Dav. #1680.

Date	Mintage	VG	F	VF	XF	Unc
1757СПБ ЯI	Inc. above	2,000	4,000	8,000	16,000	—
1757СПБ	—	—	—	—	—	—

C# 19c.4 ROUBLE

25.8500 g., 0.8020 Silver 0.6665 oz. ASW **Ruler:** Elizabeth **Obv:** Crowned bust right **Rev:** Crown above crowned double-headed eagle, shield on breast, X on tail **Note:** Dav. #1681.

Date	Mintage	VG	F	VF	XF	Unc
1757СПБ ЯI	Inc. above	170	350	750	1,500	—
1758СПБ ЯI	600,000	150	300	600	1,200	—
1758СПБ НК	Inc. above	170	350	750	1,500	—
1759СПБ ЯI	601,000	150	300	600	1,200	—
1759СПБ НК	Inc. above	170	350	750	1,500	—
1760СПБ ЯI	249,000	170	350	750	1,500	—
1761СПБ ЯI	391,000	250	500	1,000	2,000	—
1761СПБ НК	Inc. above	220	450	900	1,800	—

C# 47.2 ROUBLE

25.8500 g., 0.8020 Silver 0.6665 oz. ASW **Ruler:** Peter III **Obv:** Bust right **Rev:** Crown above crowned double-headed eagle, shield on breast, X on tail

Date	Mintage	VG	F	VF	XF	Unc
1762СПБ НК	—	180	370	750	1,500	—

C# 47.1 ROUBLE

25.8500 g., 0.8020 Silver 0.6665 oz. ASW **Ruler:** Peter III **Obv:** Bust right **Rev:** Crown above crowned double-headed eagle, shield on breast, X on tail **Note:** Dav. #1682.

Date	Mintage	VG	F	VF	XF	Unc
1762ММД АМ	—	180	370	750	1,500	—

C# 67.2 ROUBLE

24.0000 g., 0.7500 Silver 0.5787 oz. ASW **Ruler:** Catherine II **Obv:** Crowned bust right **Rev:** Crown above crowned double-headed eagle, shield on breast, X on tail

Date	Mintage	VG	F	VF	XF	Unc
1762СПБ НК	1,459,000	75.00	150	300	600	—
1763СПБ НК	1,817,000	75.00	150	300	600	—
1763СПБ ЯI	Inc. above	80.00	170	350	650	—

C# 67.1 ROUBLE

25.8500 g., 0.8020 Silver 0.6665 oz. ASW **Ruler:** Catherine II **Obv:** Crowned bust right **Rev:** Crown above crowned double-headed eagle, shield on breast, X on tail **Note:** Dav. #1683.

Date	Mintage	VG	F	VF	XF	Unc
1762ММД ДМ	406,000	250	500	1,000	2,000	—
1763ММД ЕI	95,000	180	370	750	1,500	—

C# 67.2a ROUBLE

24.0000 g., 0.7500 Silver 0.5787 oz. ASW **Ruler:** Catherine II

Date	Mintage	VG	F	VF	XF	Unc
1764СПБ ЯI	3,016,000	60.00	120	250	500	—
1764СПБ СА	Inc. above	60.00	120	250	500	—
1765СПБ ЯI	2,782,000	30.00	60.00	250	500	—
1765СПБ СА	Inc. above	30.00	60.00	250	500	—

C# 67.1a ROUBLE

24.0000 g., 0.7500 Silver 0.5787 oz. ASW **Ruler:** Catherine II

Date	Mintage	VG	F	VF	XF	Unc
1764ММД ЕI	264,000	80.00	170	350	700	—
1765ММД ЕI	121,000	120	250	500	1,000	—

C# 67a.1 ROUBLE

24.0000 g., 0.7500 Silver 0.5787 oz. ASW **Ruler:** Catherine II **Obv:** Mature bust without neck ruffle **Note:** Similar to C#67.1. Dav. #1684.

Date	Mintage	VG	F	VF	XF	Unc
1766ММД АШ	—	750	1,500	3,000	6,000	—
1767ММД ЕI	25,000	180	370	750	1,500	—
1768ММД АШ	491,000	370	250	1,500	3,000	—
1768ММД ЕI	Inc. above	120	250	500	1,000	—
1769ММД ЕI	277,000	120	250	500	1,000	—
1770ММД ДМ	80,000	850	1,750	3,500	7,000	—
1775ММД СА	1,648,000	—	—	—	—	—
1775ММД	—	—	—	—	—	—

C# 67a.2 ROUBLE

24.0000 g., 0.7500 Silver 0.5787 oz. ASW **Ruler:** Catherine II **Obv:** Crowned bust right **Rev:** Crown above crowned double-headed eagle, shield on breast, X on tail **Note:** Varieties exist.

Date	Mintage	VG	F	VF	XF	Unc
1766СПБ ЯI	1,682,000	60.00	120	250	500	—
1766СПБ АШ	Inc. above	60.00	120	250	500	—
1767СПБ АШ	1,210,000	60.00	120	250	500	—
1767СПБ ЕI	Inc. above	260	500	1,000	2,500	—
1768СПБ ЕI	1,028,000	260	500	1,000	2,500	—
1768СПБ АШ	Inc. above	200	370	750	1,500	—
1768СПБ СА	Inc. above	60.00	120	250	500	—
1769СПБ СА	2,200,000	60.00	120	250	500	—

Date	Mintage	VG	F	VF	XF	Unc
1770СПБ СА	1,198,000	750	1,500	3,000	6,000	—
1770СПБ ЯБ	Inc. above	60.00	120	250	500	—
1771СПБ ЯБ	1,024,999	60.00	120	250	500	—
1771СПБ АШ	Inc. above	60.00	120	250	500	—
1772СПБ ЯБ	1,050,000	60.00	120	250	500	—
1772СПБ АШ	Inc. above	60.00	120	250	500	—
1773СПБ ЯБ	2,378,000	150	300	600	1,200	—
1773СПБ ФЛ	Inc. above	60.00	120	250	500	—
1774СПБ ФЛ	2,770,000	60.00	120	250	500	—
1775СПБ ФЛ	—	60.00	120	250	500	—
Note: Mintage included in C#67a.1						
1775СПБ ЯБ	—	60.00	120	250	500	—
Note: Mintage included in C#67a.1						
1776СПБ ЯБ	2,625,000	60.00	120	250	500	—

C# 67b ROUBLE

24.0000 g., 0.7500 Silver 0.5787 oz. ASW **Ruler:** Catherine II **Obv:** Older bust, wreath around crown **Rev:** Similar to C#67.1 **Note:** Dav. #1685.

Date	Mintage	VG	F	VF	XF	Unc
1777СПБ ФЛ	2,000,000	80.00	120	350	700	—
1778СПБ ФЛ	1,700,000	60.00	120	250	500	—
1779СПБ ФЛ	413,000	60.00	120	250	600	—
1780СПБ ИЗ	2,866,000	60.00	120	250	500	—
1781СПБ ИЗ	2,283,000	60.00	120	250	500	—
1782СПБ ИЗ	1,200,000	60.00	120	250	500	—

C# 76 ROUBLE

1.3000 g., 0.9170 Gold 0.0383 oz. AGW **Ruler:** Catherine II **Obv:** Crowned bust right **Rev:** Crown above crowned double-headed eagle, shield on breast **Note:** Without mint mark.

Date	Mintage	F	VF	XF	Unc	BU
1779	—	100	175	350	700	—

C# 67c ROUBLE

24.0000 g., 0.7500 Silver 0.5787 oz. ASW **Ruler:** Catherine II **Obv:** Crowned bust right **Rev:** Crown above crowned double-headed eagle, shield on breast, date above **Note:** Dav. #1686.

Date	Mintage	VG	F	VF	XF	Unc
1783СПБ ИЗ	1,880,000	60.00	120	250	500	—
1783СПБ ММ	Inc. above	750	1,500	3,000	6,000	—
1784СПБ ММ	144,000	250	500	1,000	2,000	—
1785СПБ ЯА	139,000	70.00	150	300	600	—
1786СПБ ЯА	2,600,000	60.00	150	250	500	—
1787СПБ ЯА	900,000	75.00	150	300	600	—
1788СПБ ЯА	1,475,000	75.00	150	300	600	—
1789СПБ ЯА	500,000	80.00	160	325	650	—
1790СПБ ЯА	239,000	75.00	150	300	650	—
1791СПБ ЯА	274,000	80.00	160	325	650	—
1792СПБ ЯА	1,509,000	70.00	150	300	600	—
1793СПБ ЯА	1,124,000	80.00	160	325	650	—
1793СПБ АК	Inc. above	80.00	160	325	650	—
1793СПБ	Inc. above	370	750	1,500	3,000	—
1794СПБ АК	895,000	70.00	150	300	600	—
1795СПБ АК	677,000	80.00	170	350	700	—
1795СПБ IC	Inc. above	150	300	600	1,200	—
1796СПБ IC	954,000	80.00	170	350	700	—

C# 101 ROUBLE

29.2500 g., 0.8680 Silver 0.8162 oz. ASW **Ruler:** Paul I **Obv:** Monogram in cruciform with 4 crowns **Rev:** Inscription within ornamented square

Date	Mintage	VG	F	VF	XF	Unc
1797СМ ФА	920,000	600	1,250	2,500	5,000	—

C# 101a ROUBLE

20.7300 g., 0.8680 Silver 0.5785 oz. ASW, 38 mm. **Ruler:** Paul I **Obv:** Monogram in cruciform with 4 crowns **Rev:** Inscription within ornamented square **Note:** Reduced size. Dav. #1688.

Date	Mintage	VG	F	VF	XF	Unc
1798СМ МБ	3,279,000	60.00	120	250	1,200	—
1798СМ ОМ Rare	Inc. above	—	—	—	—	—
1799СМ МБ	3,124,000	60.00	120	250	1,200	—
1799СМ ФА	Inc. above	75.00	150	300	1,200	—
1799СМ АИ Rare	Inc. above	—	—	—	—	—
1800СМ ОМ	1,870,000	60.00	120	250	1,200	—
1800СМ АИ Rare	Inc. above	—	—	—	—	—

KM# 158.1 2 ROUBLES

4.1000 g., 0.7810 Gold 0.1029 oz. AGW **Ruler:** Peter I **Obv:** Laureate bust right **Obv. Legend:** АРЬ ПЕТРЬ... В Р САМОД **Rev:** St. Andrew with normal date **Rev. Legend:** М НОВА...

Date	Mintage	VG	F	VF	XF	Unc
1718 L	—	800	1,700	3,500	8,000	—
1720	—	800	1,700	3,500	8,000	—

KM# 158.2 2 ROUBLES

4.1000 g., 0.7810 Gold 0.1029 oz. AGW **Ruler:** Peter I **Rev:** Divided date

Date	Mintage	VG	F	VF	XF	Unc
1718 L	—	1,000	2,000	4,000	10,000	—
1718	—	1,000	2,000	4,000	10,000	—
1720	—	1,000	2,000	4,000	10,000	—

KM# 158.3 2 ROUBLES

4.1000 g., 0.7810 Gold 0.1029 oz. AGW **Ruler:** Peter I **Rev:** Divided date **Rev. Legend:** М НОВ...

Date	Mintage	VG	F	VF	XF	Unc
1718 L	—	800	1,700	3,500	8,000	—

KM# 158.4 2 ROUBLES

4.1000 g., 0.7810 Gold 0.1029 oz. AGW **Ruler:** Peter I **Obv:** Laureate bust right **Obv. Legend:** ... В Р САМОДЕРЖЕА **Rev:** St. Andrew

Date	Mintage	VG	F	VF	XF	Unc
1718 L	—	1,250	3,000	6,000	15,000	—

KM# 158.5 2 ROUBLES

4.1000 g., 0.7810 Gold 0.1029 oz. AGW **Ruler:** Peter I **Rev. Legend:** МОНЕТА НОВА... **Note:** Bust varieties exist.

Date	Mintage	VG	F	VF	XF	Unc
1720	—	800	1,200	3,500	8,000	—
1720 МОЕНЕТА Error	—	800	1,700	3,500	8,000	—
1721	—	1,000	2,000	4,500	10,000	—

KM# 158.6 2 ROUBLES

4.1000 g., 0.7810 Gold 0.1029 oz. AGW **Ruler:** Peter I **Obv:** Laureate bust right **Obv. Legend:** ПЕТРЬ А ИМПЕРАТ И САМОДЕР ВСЕРОССИИСКИИ **Rev:** St. Andrew **Note:** Bust varieties exist.

Date	Mintage	VG	F	VF	XF	Unc
1721 Rare	—	—	—	—	—	—
1722	—	800	1,500	3,000	7,000	—
1723	—	800	1,500	3,000	7,000	—
1724	—	800	1,700	3,500	8,000	—
1725	—	1,000	2,000	4,500	10,000	—

KM# 178 2 ROUBLES

4.1000 g., 0.7810 Gold 0.1029 oz. AGW **Ruler:** Catherine I **Obv:** Bust left **Rev:** St. Andrew

Date	Mintage	VG	F	VF	XF	Unc
1726/5	—	2,000	4,000	9,000	18,000	—
1726	—	2,000	4,000	9,000	18,000	—
1727/6	—	1,500	3,000	7,500	15,000	—
1727	—	1,500	3,000	7,500	15,000	—

KM# 184 2 ROUBLES

4.1000 g., 0.7810 Gold 0.1029 oz. AGW **Ruler:** Peter II **Obv:** Laureate bust right **Rev:** St. Andrew

Date	Mintage	VG	F	VF	XF	Unc
1727 Hair tie	—	2,000	4,000	8,000	16,000	—
1727 Without hair tie	—	1,500	3,000	7,500	15,000	—
1728	—	2,200	4,500	9,000	18,000	—

C# 23.1 2 ROUBLES

3.2400 g., 0.9170 Gold 0.0955 oz. AGW **Ruler:** Elizabeth **Obv:** Crowned bust right **Rev:** Crown above crowned double-headed eagle, shield on breast, divided date above

Date	Mintage	F	VF	XF	Unc	BU
1756 Without mint mark	53,000	200	300	600	1,350	—
1758ММД	2,910	300	500	950	1,850	—

C# 23.2 2 ROUBLES

3.2400 g., 0.9170 Gold 0.0955 oz. AGW **Ruler:** Elizabeth

Date	Mintage	F	VF	XF	Unc	BU
1756СПБ Wide date	8,712	250	450	900	1,800	—
1756СПБ Close date	Inc. above	250	450	900	1,800	—

C# 77 2 ROUBLES

2.6100 g., 0.9170 Gold 0.0769 oz. AGW **Ruler:** Catherine II **Obv:** Bust right **Rev:** Crown above crowned double-headed eagle, shield on breast, divided date above

Date	Mintage	F	VF	XF	Unc	BU
1766	—	350	750	1,500	3,000	—

C# 77c 2 ROUBLES

2.6100 g., 0.9170 Gold 0.0769 oz. AGW **Ruler:** Catherine II

Date	Mintage	F	VF	XF	Unc	BU
1785	—	300	450	800	1,750	—
1786/5 Rare	—	—	—	—	—	—

C# 27.2 5 ROUBLES

8.2700 g., 0.9170 Gold 0.2438 oz. AGW **Ruler:** Elizabeth **Obv:** Crowned bust right **Rev:** Crowned shields in cruciform, date in angles

Date	Mintage	VG	F	VF	XF	Unc
1755 Without mint mark	5,842	2,000	4,500	9,000	16,000	—
1756СПБ	13,000	1,800	3,750	7,500	12,000	—
1757СПБ	2,680	1,800	3,750	7,500	12,000	—
1758СПБ	2,067	3,000	6,000	12,000	20,000	—
1759СПБ	2,324	2,500	5,000	10,000	18,000	—

C# 27.1 5 ROUBLES

8.2700 g., 0.9170 Gold 0.2438 oz. AGW **Ruler:** Elizabeth **Obv:** Crowned bust right **Rev:** Crowned shields in cruciform, date in angles **Note:** Without mint mark.

Date	Mintage	VG	F	VF	XF	Unc
1756	13,000	1,700	3,500	7,000	10,000	—
1758	17,000	1,700	3,500	7,500	12,000	—

C# 78.2 5 ROUBLES

8.2700 g., 0.9170 Gold 0.2438 oz. AGW **Ruler:** Catherine II **Obv:** Crowned bust right **Rev:** Crowned shields in cruciform, date in angles

Date	Mintage	F	VF	XF	Unc	BU
1762СПБ	21,000	2,250	4,500	9,000	16,000	—
1763СПБ Rare	7,515	—	—	—	—	—

C# 78.1 5 ROUBLES

8.2700 g., 0.9170 Gold 0.2438 oz. AGW **Ruler:** Catherine II **Obv:** Catherine II

Date	Mintage	F	VF	XF	Unc	BU
1763ММД Rare	—	—	—	—	—	—

C# 78.2a 5 ROUBLES

6.5400 g., 0.9170 Gold 0.1928 oz. AGW **Ruler:** Catherine II **Obv:** Crowned bust right **Rev:** Crowned shields in cruciform, date in angles

Date	Mintage	F	VF	XF	Unc	BU
1764СПБ	24,000	300	500	1,650	3,750	—
1765СПБ	51,000	300	500	1,650	3,750	—

C# 78a 5 ROUBLES

6.5400 g., 0.9170 Gold 0.1928 oz. AGW **Ruler:** Catherine II **Obv:** Crowned bust right **Rev:** Crowned shields in cruciform, date in angles

Date	Mintage	F	VF	XF	Unc	BU
1766СПБ	34,000	350	700	2,450	3,600	—
1767СПБ	90,000	350	700	2,450	3,600	—
1768СПБ	20,000	350	700	2,450	3,600	—
1769СПБ	16,000	350	700	2,450	3,600	—
1770СПБ	16,000	350	700	2,450	3,600	—
1771СПБ	12,000	350	700	2,450	3,600	—
1772СПБ	14,000	350	700	2,450	3,600	—
1773СПБ	16,000	350	700	2,450	3,600	—
1774СПБ	15,000	350	700	2,450	3,600	—
1775СПБ	10,000	350	700	2,450	3,600	—
1776СПБ	20,000	350	700	2,450	3,600	—
1777СПБ Rare	—	—	—	—	—	—

C# 78b 5 ROUBLES

6.5400 g., 0.9170 Gold 0.1928 oz. AGW **Ruler:** Catherine II **Obv:** Crowned bust right **Rev:** Crowned shields in cruciform, date in angles

Date	Mintage	F	VF	XF	Unc	BU
1778СПБ	24,000	325	650	2,200	3,250	—
1780СПБ	26,000	325	650	2,200	3,250	—
1781СПБ	63,000	325	650	2,200	3,250	—
1782СПБ	39,000	325	650	2,200	3,250	—

C# 78c 5 ROUBLES

6.5400 g., 0.9170 Gold 0.1928 oz. AGW **Ruler:** Catherine II **Obv:** Crowned bust right **Rev:** Crowned shields in cruciform, date in angles

Date	Mintage	F	VF	XF	Unc	BU
1783СПБ	33,000	325	650	2,200	3,250	—
1784СПБ	3,000	500	1,100	3,750	6,500	—
1785СПБ	47,000	325	650	2,200	3,250	—
1786СПБ	74,000	325	650	2,200	3,250	—
1788СПБ	12,000	1,500	2,500	4,000	6,000	—
1789СПБ	12,000	1,300	2,000	3,500	5,000	—
1790СПБ	20,000	1,200	2,000	3,000	4,500	—
1791СПБ	48,000	325	650	2,200	3,250	—
1792СПБ	67,000	325	650	2,200	3,250	—
1794СПБ	45,000	800	1,300	2,500	3,300	—
1795СПБ	6,906	400	700	2,300	4,000	—
1796СПБ	20,000	325	650	2,200	3,250	—

C# 104.1 5 ROUBLES

6.0800 g., 0.9860 Gold 0.1927 oz. AGW **Ruler:** Paul I **Obv:** Monograms of Paul I in cruciform with 4 crowns, value in angles **Rev:** Inscription within ornamented square

Date	Mintage	F	VF	XF	Unc	BU
1798СМ ФА	148,000	1,250	2,700	4,000	6,000	—
1798СМ ОМ	Inc. above	1,500	3,600	5,000	7,500	—
1799СМ АИ	108,000	1,250	2,200	4,000	6,000	—
1800СМ ОМ	66,000	1,250	2,200	4,000	6,000	—

C# 104.2 5 ROUBLES

6.0800 g., 0.9860 Gold 0.1927 oz. AGW **Ruler:** Paul I

Date	Mintage	F	VF	XF	Unc	BU
1800СП ОМ	Inc. above	1,400	3,000	4,500	6,750	—

C# 28.2 10 ROUBLES

16.5900 g., 0.9170 Gold 0.4891 oz. AGW **Ruler:** Elizabeth **Obv:** Crowned bust right **Rev:** Crowned shields in cruciform, date in angles

Date	Mintage	VG	F	VF	XF	Unc
1755СПБ	5,635	1,000	4,000	8,000	12,000	20,000
1756СПБ	21,000	1,000	3,000	7,000	10,000	16,000
1757СПБ	8,604	1,000	4,000	8,000	12,000	20,000
1758СПБ	2,507	1,100	5,000	10,000	15,000	25,000
1759СПБ Large mint mark	2,478	1,100	5,000	10,000	15,000	25,000
1759СПБ Smal mint mark	Inc. above	1,100	5,000	10,000	15,000	25,000

C# 28.1 10 ROUBLES

16.5900 g., 0.9170 Gold 0.4891 oz. AGW **Ruler:** Elizabeth **Obv:** Elizabeth

Date	Mintage	VG	F	VF	XF	Unc
1756ММД	14,000	1,000	4,200	8,500	12,500	26,000
1758ММД	8,308	1,000	4,000	8,000	12,000	20,000

C# 50 10 ROUBLES

16.5700 g., 0.9170 Gold 0.4885 oz. AGW **Ruler:** Peter III **Obv:** Bust right

Date	Mintage	F	VF	XF	Unc	BU
1762	9,482	6,000	14,000	20,000	25,000	—

C# 79.1 10 ROUBLES

16.5900 g., 0.9170 Gold 0.4891 oz. AGW **Ruler:** Catherine II **Obv:** Crowned bust right **Rev:** Crowned shields in cruciform, date in angles

Date	Mintage	F	VF	XF	Unc	BU
1762ММД	32,000	4,000	12,000	16,000	20,000	—
1763ММД Rare	—	—	—	—	—	—

C# 79.2 10 ROUBLES

16.5900 g., 0.9170 Gold 0.4891 oz. AGW **Ruler:** Catherine II

Date	Mintage	F	VF	XF	Unc	BU
1762СПБ	Inc. above	3,000	7,000	10,000	15,000	—
1763СПБ	21,000	3,500	10,000	14,000	20,000	—

C# 79.2a 10 ROUBLES

13.0800 g., 0.9170 Gold 0.3856 oz. AGW **Ruler:** Catherine II **Obv:** Crowned bust right **Rev:** Crowned shields in cruciform, date in angles

Date	Mintage	F	VF	XF	Unc	BU
1764СПБ	30,000	600	2,000	3,000	4,500	—
1765СПБ	32,000	600	2,000	3,000	4,500	—

C# 79a 10 ROUBLES

13.0800 g., 0.9170 Gold 0.3856 oz. AGW **Ruler:** Catherine II **Obv:** Crowned bust right **Rev:** Crowned shields in cruciform, date in angles

Date	Mintage	F	VF	XF	Unc	BU
1766СПБ	159,000	600	2,000	3,000	4,500	—
1767СПБ	92,000	600	2,000	3,000	4,500	—
1768СПБ	50,000	600	2,000	3,000	4,500	—
1769СПБ	80,000	600	2,000	3,000	4,500	—
1770СПБ	10,000	900	3,000	4,500	7,000	—
1771СПБ	31,000	700	2,100	3,500	5,600	—
1772СПБ	51,000	600	2,000	3,000	4,500	—
1773СПБ	54,000	600	2,000	3,000	4,500	—
1774СПБ	53,000	600	2,000	3,000	4,500	—
1775СПБ	50,000	600	2,000	3,000	4,500	—
1776СПБ	68,000	600	2,000	3,000	4,500	—

C# 79b 10 ROUBLES

13.0800 g., 0.9170 Gold 0.3856 oz. AGW **Ruler:** Catherine II **Obv:** Crowned bust right **Rev:** Crowned shields in cruciform, date in angles

Date	Mintage	F	VF	XF	Unc	BU
1777СПБ	15,000	1,100	5,000	8,000	10,000	—
1778СПБ	84,000	900	2,500	4,000	5,000	—
1779СПБ	15,000	900	2,500	4,000	5,000	—
1780СПБ	72,000	900	2,500	4,000	5,000	—
1781СПБ	23,000	900	3,000	5,000	7,000	—
1782СПБ	4,000	1,100	5,000	8,000	10,000	—

C# 79c 10 ROUBLES

13.0800 g., 0.9170 Gold 0.3856 oz. AGW **Ruler:** Catherine II **Obv:** Crowned bust right **Rev:** Crowned shields in cruciform, date in angles

Date	Mintage	F	VF	XF	Unc	BU
1783СПБ	26,000	900	2,500	4,000	5,000	—
1785СПБ	20,000	900	2,500	4,000	5,000	—
1786СПБ	Inc. above	1,000	4,000	6,000	8,000	—
1795СПБ Rare	2,300	—	—	—	—	—
1796СПБ Rare	Inc. above	—	—	—	—	—

TRADE COINAGE

KM# 107 DUCAT

3.5000 g., 0.9860 Gold 0.1109 oz. AGW **Ruler:** Peter I **Obv:** Laureate bust right **Rev:** Crown above crowned double-headed eagle, shield on breast **Note:** Varieties exist.

Date	Mintage	VG	F	VF	XF	Unc
ND(1701) Hair tie	—	1,600	3,500	6,500	11,500	—
ND(1701) Without hair tie	—	1,200	2,500	5,000	9,000	—
ND(1702)	—	2,000	4,000	7,500	13,500	—
ND(1703) Hair tie	—	1,000	2,250	4,750	8,000	—
ND(1703) Without hair tie	—	2,000	4,000	7,500	13,500	—

KM# 125 DUCAT

3.5000 g., 0.9860 Gold 0.1109 oz. AGW **Ruler:** Peter I **Obv:** Tall fine style bust of Peter I right

Date	Mintage	VG	F	VF	XF	Unc
ND(1706)	—	1,500	3,000	6,000	10,000	—
1710 L-L Rare	—	—	—	—	—	—

KM# 131 DUCAT

3.5000 g., 0.9860 Gold 0.1109 oz. AGW **Ruler:** Peter I **Obv:** Laureate bust right **Rev:** Crown above crowned double-headed eagle, shield on breast

Date	Mintage	VG	F	VF	XF	Unc
ND(1707) IL-L	—	1,000	2,000	4,500	8,500	—

KM# 133 DUCAT

3.5000 g., 0.9860 Gold 0.1109 oz. AGW **Ruler:** Peter I **Obv:** Laureate bust right **Rev:** Maps held in beaks of crowned double-headed eagle, shield on breast, larger crown above **Note:** Struck following the capture of Azov. The G appears on uniform on obverse.

Date	Mintage	VG	F	VF	XF	Unc
ND(1710)	—	1,000	3,000	8,000	15,000	—
1710 G L-L	—	1,000	3,000	8,000	15,000	—
1711	—	2,000	4,500	9,000	19,500	—

KM# 140 DUCAT

3.5000 g., 0.9860 Gold 0.1109 oz. AGW **Ruler:** Peter I **Obv:** Laureate bust right, divides legend **Rev:** Crown above crowned double-headed eagle, shield on breast, date in legend **Note:** Varieties exist.

Date	Mintage	VG	F	VF	XF	Unc
1712 G DL	—	600	1,800	7,000	10,000	—
1712 DL	—	600	1,800	7,000	10,000	—
1713.2 DL	—	700	2,000	8,000	11,500	—
1713 DL	—	600	1,800	7,000	10,000	—
1714	—	1,000	3,000	8,500	12,000	—
1714 З	—	1,500	4,000	9,500	13,500	—

KM# 139 DUCAT

3.5000 g., 0.9860 Gold 0.1109 oz. AGW **Ruler:** Peter I **Obv:** Laureate bust right **Rev:** Crown above crowned double-headed eagle, shield on breast, date in legend

Date	Mintage	VG	F	VF	XF	Unc
1712 D-L	—	600	1,800	7,000	10,000	—
1712 G D-L	—	600	1,800	7,000	10,000	—

KM# A134 DUCAT

3.5000 g., 0.9860 Gold 0.1109 oz. AGW **Ruler:** Peter I **Obv:** Laureate bust right **Rev:** Crown above crowned double-headed eagle, shield on breast, arabic date below

Date	Mintage	VG	F	VF	XF	Unc
1712 D-L Rare	—	—	—	—	—	—

KM# 151 DUCAT

3.5000 g., 0.9860 Gold 0.1109 oz. AGW **Ruler:** Peter I **Obv:** Laureate bust right **Rev:** Crown above crowned double-headed eagle, shield on breast **Note:** Latin inscription.

Date	Mintage	VG	F	VF	XF	Unc
1716	—	1,250	3,000	6,500	9,000	—
1716 Retrograde 7	—	1,250	3,000	6,500	9,000	—

KM# 186 DUCAT

3.5000 g., 0.9860 Gold 0.1109 oz. AGW **Ruler:** Peter II **Obv:** Laureate bust right **Rev:** Crown above crowned double-headed eagle, shield on breast

Date	Mintage	VG	F	VF	XF	Unc
1729 Hair tie	—	1,500	5,000	12,000	20,000	—
1729 Without hair tie	—	1,500	5,000	14,000	22,500	—

KM# 193 DUCAT

3.5000 g., 0.9860 Gold 0.1109 oz. AGW **Ruler:** Anna **Obv:** Bust right **Rev:** Crown above crowned double-headed eagle, oval shield on breast

Date	Mintage	VG	F	VF	XF	Unc
1730	—	1,000	2,500	4,500	8,500	—

KM# 201 DUCAT

3.5000 g., 0.9860 Gold 0.1109 oz. AGW **Ruler:** Anna **Obv:** Bust right **Rev:** Crown above crowned double-headed eagle, oval shield on breast

Date	Mintage	VG	F	VF	XF	Unc
1738	—	650	1,500	3,750	7,000	—
1739	—	650	1,500	3,750	7,000	—

C# 30.1 DUCAT

3.4700 g., 0.9690 Gold 0.1081 oz. AGW **Ruler:** Elizabeth **Obv:** Crowned bust right **Rev:** Crown above crowned double-headed eagle, shield on breast, date above **Note:** Without mint mark.

Date	Mintage	VG	F	VF	XF	Unc
1742	4,271	450	750	1,450	5,500	—
1743	2,823	750	1,750	3,750	15,000	—
1744	15,000	450	750	1,400	5,250	—
1746	500	1,000	2,750	6,500	20,000	—
1747	17,000	975	2,250	4,750	15,000	—
1748	17,000	525	825	1,750	6,500	—

C# 30.2 DUCAT

3.4700 g., 0.9860 Gold 0.1100 oz. AGW **Ruler:** Elizabeth **Obv:** Crowned bust right **Rev:** Crown above crowned double-headed eagle, shield on breast, date in legend

Date	Mintage	VG	F	VF	XF	Unc
1749 АВГ 1 (AUG. 1)	3,000	300	625	2,000	5,500	—
1751 МАР 13 (MAR. 13)	13,016,000	250	500	1,350	5,000	—
1751 АПРЕЛЬ (APRIL)	Inc. above	375	800	2,200	6,000	—
1752 НОЯБ 3 (NOVB. 3)	9,398	300	625	1,750	5,500	—
1753 ФЕВР 5 (FEBR. 5)	5,018,000	375	800	2,200	6,000	—

C# 31.1 DUCAT

3.4700 g., 0.9860 Gold 0.1100 oz. AGW **Ruler:** Elizabeth **Obv:** Crowned bust right **Rev:** St. Andrew divides date

Date	Mintage	VG	F	VF	XF	Unc
1749 АВГ 1 (AUG. 1)	Inc. above	250	550	1,750	4,750	—
1751 МАРТ (MART.)	Inc. above	500	1,150	3,500	9,000	—
1751 МАР 13 (MAR. 13)	Inc. above	250	500	1,500	4,500	—
1751 АПРЕЛ (APRIL)	Inc. above	250	550	1,850	5,250	—
1752 НОЯБ 3 (NOVB. 3)	Inc. above	325	700	2,200	5,500	—
1753 ФЕВР 5 (FEBR. 5)	Inc. above	300	625	2,000	5,500	—

C# 31.2 DUCAT

3.4700 g., 0.9860 Gold 0.1100 oz. AGW **Ruler:** Elizabeth **Obv:** Crowned bust right **Rev:** St. Andrew divides date

Date	Mintage	VG	F	VF	XF	Unc
1749	—	375	925	3,000	9,000	—

C# 31.2a DUCAT

Gold, 22 mm. **Ruler:** Elizabeth **Obv:** Crowned bust right **Rev:** St. Andrew, date above

Date	Mintage	VG	F	VF	XF	Unc
1749	—	500	600	1,500	5,500	—

C# 30.3 DUCAT

3.4700 g., 0.9790 Gold 0.1092 oz. AGW **Ruler:** Elizabeth **Obv:** Crowned bust right **Rev:** Crown above crowned double-headed eagle, shield on breast, divided date above

Date	Mintage	VG	F	VF	XF	Unc
1757СПБ	121,000	300	700	2,500	7,000	—

C# 51 DUCAT

3.4700 g., 0.9790 Gold 0.1092 oz. AGW **Ruler:** Peter III **Obv:** Bust right **Rev:** Crown above crowned double-headed eagle, shield on breast, divided date above

Date	Mintage	F	VF	XF	Unc	BU
1762СПБ	—	2,000	4,000	7,000	10,000	—

C# 80 DUCAT

3.4700 g., 0.9790 Gold 0.1092 oz. AGW **Ruler:** Catherine II **Obv:** Crowned bust right **Rev:** Crown above crowned double-headed eagle, shield on breast, date above

Date	Mintage	F	VF	XF	Unc	BU
1763СПБ	50,000	1,000	2,000	4,500	6,000	—

C# 80a DUCAT

3.4900 g., 0.9860 Gold 0.1106 oz. AGW **Ruler:** Catherine II **Obv:** Crowned bust right **Rev:** Crown above crowned double-headed eagle, shield on breast, divided date above

Date	Mintage	F	VF	XF	Unc	BU
1766СПБ	23,000	1,000	2,000	4,500	6,000	—

C# 80c DUCAT

3.4900 g., 0.9860 Gold 0.1106 oz. AGW **Ruler:** Catherine II **Obv:** Crowned bust right **Rev:** Crown above crowned double-headed eagle, shield on breast, divided date above

Date	Mintage	F	VF	XF	Unc	BU
1796СПБ	40,000	1,500	3,500	5,000	7,000	—

C# 102 DUCAT

3.4900 g., 0.9860 Gold 0.1106 oz. AGW **Ruler:** Paul I **Obv:** Crown above crowned double-headed eagle, shield on breast, date in legend **Rev:** Inscription within ornamented square

Date	Mintage	F	VF	XF	Unc	BU
1796СМ БМ	2,500	2,500	4,000	7,500	12,000	—

C# 103 DUCAT

3.4900 g., 0.9860 Gold 0.1106 oz. AGW **Ruler:** Paul I **Obv:** Monograms of Paul I in cruciform **Rev:** Inscription within ornamented square

Date	Mintage	F	VF	XF	Unc	BU
1797 ГЛ	137,000	2,500	4,000	7,500	12,000	—

KM# 108 2 DUCAT

7.0000 g., 0.9860 Gold 0.2219 oz. AGW **Ruler:** Peter I **Obv:** Laureate head of Peter I right **Rev:** Crowned imperial eagle with sceptre and orb, date in legend

Date	Mintage	VG	F	VF	XF	Unc
ND(1701)	—	1,000	2,000	4,000	7,500	—
ND(1702)	—	850	1,750	3,500	7,000	—

KM# 150 2 DUCAT

7.0000 g., 0.9860 Gold 0.2219 oz. AGW **Ruler:** Peter I **Obv:** Laureate bust right **Rev:** Crown above crowned double-headed eagle, shield on breast, date in legend

Date	Mintage	VG	F	VF	XF	Unc
1714 Rare	—	—	—	—	—	—

C# 33.1 2 DUCAT

7.0000 g., 0.9860 Gold 0.2219 oz. AGW **Ruler:** Elizabeth **Obv:** Similar to C#34.2 **Rev:** Date above imperial eagle **Note:** Without mint mark.

Date	Mintage	VG	F	VF	XF	Unc
1749	600	2,000	3,000	6,500	12,500	—

C# 33.2 2 DUCAT

7.0000 g., 0.9860 Gold 0.2219 oz. AGW **Ruler:** Elizabeth **Obv:** Crowned bust right **Rev:** Crown above crowned double-headed eagle, shield on breast, date in legend

Date	Mintage	VG	F	VF	XF	Unc
1751 АПРЕЛ (APRIL)	Inc. above	1,000	2,000	4,500	8,750	—
1751 МАР 20 (MAR. 20)	3,360	1,000	2,000	4,500	8,750	—

C# 34.1 2 DUCAT

7.0000 g., 0.9860 Gold 0.2219 oz. AGW **Ruler:** Elizabeth **Obv:** Crowned bust right **Rev:** St. Andrew divides date

Date	Mintage	VG	F	VF	XF	Unc
1749	Inc. above	1,250	2,500	5,000	10,000	—

C# 34.2 2 DUCAT

7.0000 g., 0.9860 Gold 0.2219 oz. AGW **Ruler:** Elizabeth **Obv:** Crowned bust right **Rev:** St. Andrew divides date

Date	Mintage	VG	F	VF	XF	Unc
1751 АПРЕЛ (APRIL)	Inc. above	1,000	2,000	4,500	8,750	—
1751 МАР 20 (MAR. 2)	Inc. above	1,000	2,000	4,500	8,750	—

KM# A35 3 DUCAT

Gold **Ruler:** Peter I **Obv:** Laureate bust right **Rev:** Crown above crowned double-headed eagle

Date	Mintage	VG	F	VF	XF	Unc
1702	—	—	10,000	30,000	45,000	—

PLATE MONEY

Issued between 1725-1727 in various sizes containing copper equal to value of similar denominations of silver coinage. Obviously they copied the format of the Swedish plate money introduced in 1702. Refer also to Novedel Plate Money listings.

KM# PM13.1 KOPEK

Copper **Ruler:** Catherine I **Obv:** Large 16 millimeter crowned imperial eagle at center, date in corners

Date	Mintage	VG	F	VF	XF	Unc
1726 Rare	—	—	—	—	—	—

KM# PM13.2 KOPEK

Copper **Ruler:** Catherine I **Rev:** ПРГА at center

Date	Mintage	VG	F	VF	XF	Unc
1726 Rare	—	—	—	—	—	—

KM# PM12 KOPEK

Copper **Ruler:** Catherine I **Obv:** Small 13 millimeter crowned imperial eagle with St. George slaying dragon in oval shield at center divides date **Note:** Uniface.

Date	Mintage	VG	F	VF	XF	Unc
1726 Rare	—	—	—	—	—	—

KM# PM14 5 KOPEKS

Copper **Ruler:** Catherine I **Obv:** Large 22 millimeter crowned imperial eagle with St. George slaying dragon in oval shield on breast at center divides date

Date	Mintage	VG	F	VF	XF	Unc
1726 Rare	—	—	—	—	—	—

KM# PM15 5 KOPEKS

Copper **Ruler:** Catherine I **Obv:** Small 19 millimeter crowned imperial eagle with St. George slaying dragon in oval shield on breast at center

Date	Mintage	VG	F	VF	XF	Unc
1726 Rare	—	—	—	—	—	—

KM# PM4 5 KOPEKS

Copper **Ruler:** Catherine I **Obv:** Crowned imperial eagle with plain breast at center divides date **Note:** Uniface.

Date	Mintage	VG	F	VF	XF	Unc
1726 Rare	—	—	—	—	—	—

KM# PM1 GRIVNA (10 Kopeks)

Copper **Ruler:** Catherine I **Obv:** Crowned imperial eagle with monograms of Catherine I in oval on breast in 4 corners; value at center **Obv. Legend:** АЕНА/ГРІВНА **Note:** Uniface. Illustration reduced, actual size 68x67 millimeters.

Date	Mintage	VG	F	VF	XF	Unc
1725 Rare	—	—	—	—	—	—

KM# PM5 GRIVNA (10 Kopeks)

Copper **Ruler:** Catherine I **Obv:** Crowned imperial eagle with plain breast in 4 corners, value at center **Obv. Legend:** АЕНА/ГРИВНА **Note:** Uniface.

Date	Mintage	VG	F	VF	XF	Unc
1726 Rare	—	—	—	—	—	—

KM# PM9 GRIVNA (10 Kopeks)

Copper **Ruler:** Catherine I **Obv:** Large crowned imperial eagle with monogram of Catherine I in shield on breast in 4 corners, value, date at center **Obv. Legend:** ГРИВНА

Date	Mintage	VG	F	VF	XF	Unc
1726 Rare	—	—	—	—	—	—

KM# PM10 GRIVNA (10 Kopeks)

Copper **Ruler:** Catherine I **Obv:** Small 19 millimeter crowned imperial eagle with monogram of Catherine I in shield on breast in 4 corners, value, date at center **Obv. Legend:** ГРИВНА

Date	Mintage	VG	F	VF	XF	Unc
1726 Rare	—	—	—	—	—	—

KM# PM16.1 GRIVNA (10 Kopeks)

Copper **Ruler:** Catherine I **Obv:** Crowned imperial eagle with St. George slaying dragon in oval on eagle's breast in 4 corners, value, date at center **Obv. Legend:** АЕНА/ГРИВНА

Date	Mintage	VG	F	VF	XF	Unc
1726 Rare	—	—	—	—	—	—

KM# PM16.2 GRIVNA (10 Kopeks)

Copper **Ruler:** Catherine I **Rev:** Legend at center **Rev. Legend:** ПР/ГА

Date	Mintage	VG	F	VF	XF	Unc
1726 Rare	—	—	—	—	—	—

KM# PM16.3 GRIVNA (10 Kopeks)

Copper **Ruler:** Catherine I **Rev:** Legend at center **Rev. Legend:** ПР/ИП

Date	Mintage	VG	F	VF	XF	Unc
1727 Rare	—	—	—	—	—	—

KM# PM16.4 GRIVNA (10 Kopeks)

Copper **Ruler:** Catherine I **Rev:** Legend at center **Rev. Legend:** ПР/АБ

Date	Mintage	VG	F	VF	XF	Unc
1727 Rare	—	—	—	—	—	—

KM# PM2 POLUPOLTINNIK (1/4 Rouble)

Copper **Ruler:** Catherine I **Obv:** Crowned imperial eagle with monogram of Catherine I in oval shield on eagle's breast in 4 corners, value at center **Obv. Legend:** АЕНА/ПОЛПОЛТІНЫ

Date	Mintage	VG	F	VF	XF	Unc
1725 Rare	—	—	—	—	—	—

KM# PM11 POLUPOLTINNIK (1/4 Rouble)

Copper **Ruler:** Catherine I **Obv:** Crowned imperial eagle with monogram of Catherine I in oval shield on eagle's breast in 4 corners, value, date at center **Obv. Legend:** АЕНА/ПОЛПОЛТІНЫ

Date	Mintage	VG	F	VF	XF	Unc
1726 Rare	—	—	—	—	—	—

KM# PM6 POLUPOLTINNIK (1/4 Rouble)

Copper **Ruler:** Catherine I **Obv:** Crowned imperial eagle with plain breast in 4 corners, value at center **Obv. Legend:** АЕНА/ПОЛПОЛТІНЫ

Date	Mintage	VG	F	VF	XF	Unc
1726 Rare	—	—	—	—	—	—

KM# PM7 POLTINA (50 Kopeks)

Copper **Ruler:** Catherine I **Obv:** Crowned imperial eagle with plain breast in 4 corners, value at center **Obv. Legend:** АЕНА/ПОЛТІНА **Note:** Uniface.

Date	Mintage	VG	F	VF	XF	Unc
1726 Rare	—	—	—	—	—	—

KM# PM3 ROUBLE

Copper **Ruler:** Catherine I **Obv:** Crowned imperial eagle with monogram of Catherine I in 4 corners, value at center, 5-line legend at top **Obv. Legend:** АЕНА/РУБЛЬ **Note:** Uniface.

Date	Mintage	VG	F	VF	XF	Unc
1725 Rare	—	—	—	—	—	—

KM# PM8 ROUBLE

Copper **Ruler:** Catherine I **Obv:** Crowned imperial eagle with plain breast in 4 corners, value, date at center **Obv. Legend:** АЕНА/РУБЛЬ

Date	Mintage	VG	F	VF	XF	Unc
1726 Rare	—	—	—	—	—	—

ESSAIS

KM#	Date	Mintage	Identification	Mkt Val
E1	1762	—	5 Kopeks. Silver.	250

NOVODELS

KM#	Date	Mintage	Identification	Mkt Val
N-A7	ND(1701)	—	5 Kopeks. Silver.	—
N-A8	ND(1701)	—	10 Kopeks. Silver.	850
N-A9	ND(1702)	—	5 Kopeks. Silver.	—
N-B1	ND(1702)	—	1/4 Rouble. Copper.	800
N-B2	ND(1702)	—	1/2 Rouble. Silver.	2,850
N-B3	ND(1702)	—	2 Ducat. Gold. 6.8400 g. Fr. #42.	—
N-B4	ND(1703)	—	1/4 Kopek. Copper.	—
N-B5	ND	—	5 Kopeks. Silver.	—
N-B6	ND(1704)	—	10 Kopeks. Silver.	—
N-B7	ND(1704)МД	—	1/4 Rouble. Silver.	1,050
N-B8	ND(1704)	—	1/2 Rouble. Silver. Thin-tailed eagle.	—
N-B9	ND(1704)	—	Poltina. Silver. Thick tailed eagle.	900
N-C1	NDБК	—	10 Kopeks. Silver.	700
N-C2	ND(1705)	—	Polupoltinnik. Silver.	—
N-C3	ND(1705)	—	Poltina. Silver.	1,000
N-C4	ND(1705)	—	Rouble. Silver.	—
N-C4	ND(1705)	—	Rouble. Gold. 44.2200 g.	175,000
N-C5	ND(1706)	—	1/2 Chekh. Silver. Bust type.	—
N-C6	ND(1706)	—	1/2 Chekh. Silver. Horseman type.	—
N-C7	ND(1706)	—	Chekh. Silver.	—
N-C8	ND(1706)	—	Poltina. Silver. Oblique milling edge.	—
N-C9	ND(1706)	—	Poltina. Silver. Plain edge.	—
N-C10	1707	—	Rouble. Silver. Arabic date.	—
N-D1	ND(1707)	—	Polupoltinnik. Silver.	—
N-D2	1707	—	Rouble. Silver. Plain edge. Small date.	—
N-D3	1707	—	Rouble. Silver. Oblique milling edge.	—

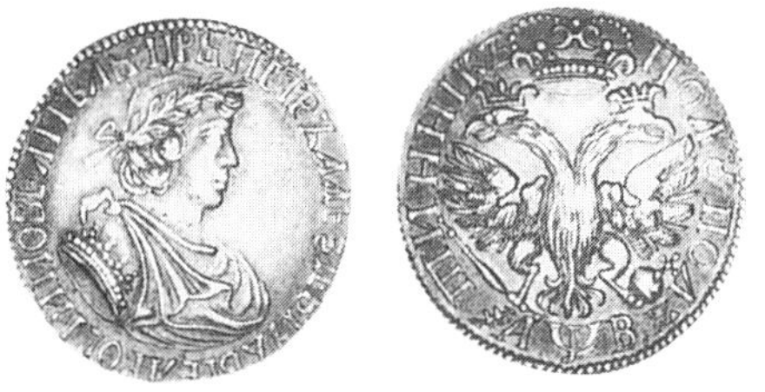

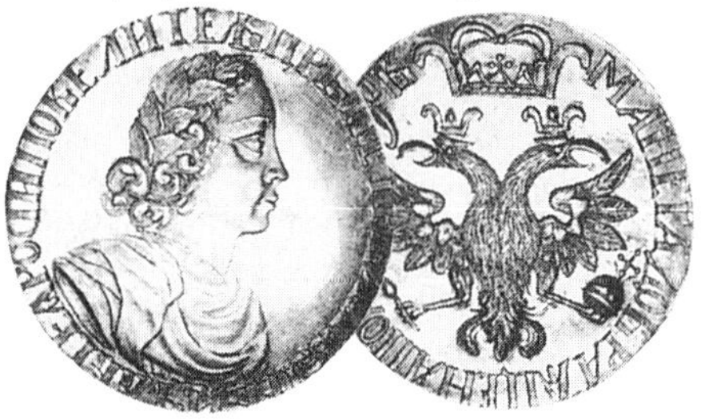

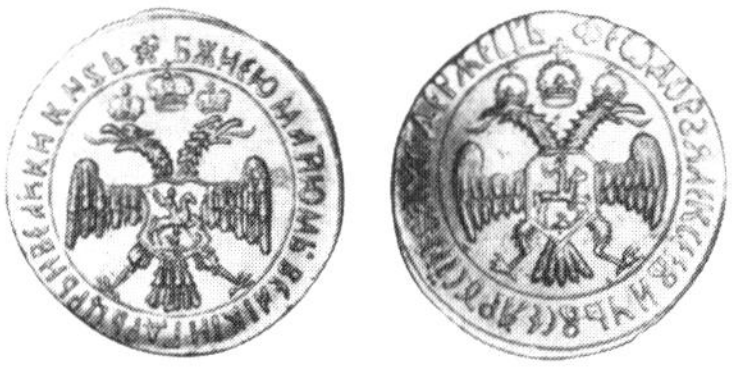

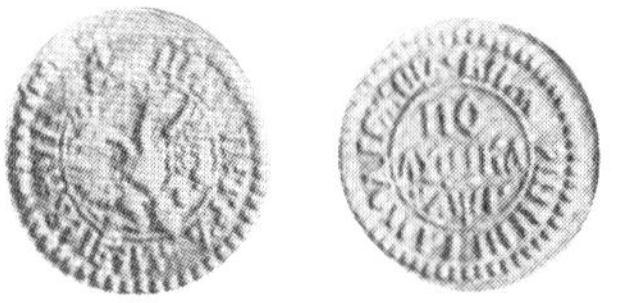

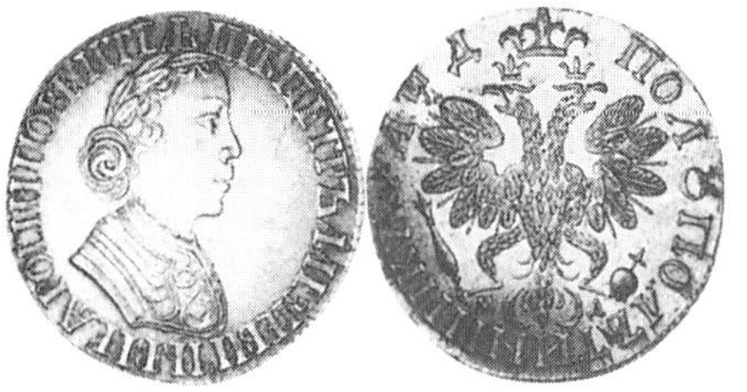

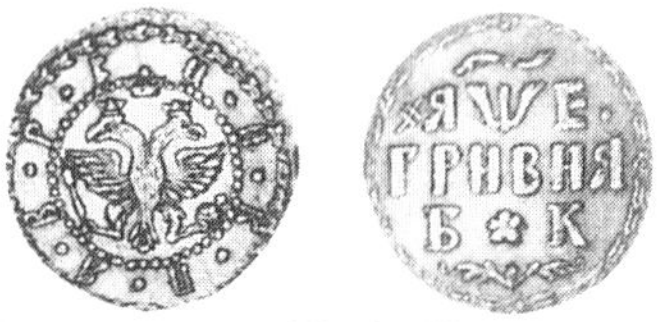

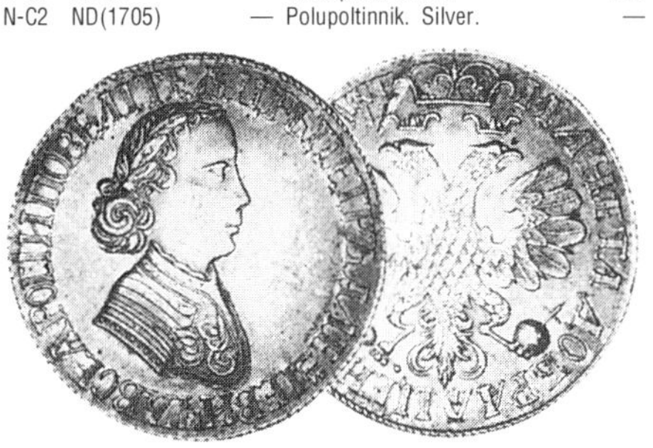

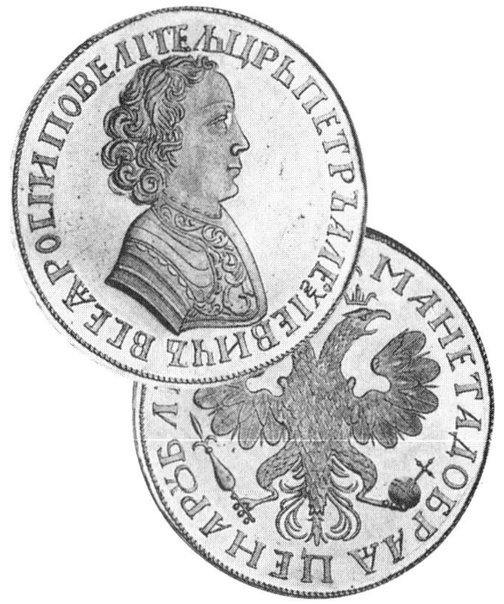

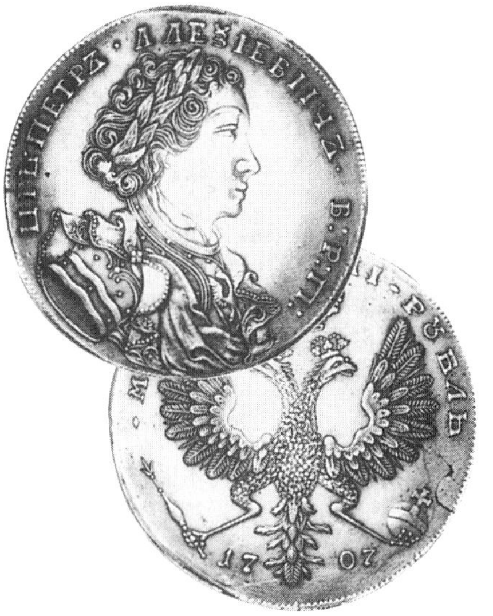

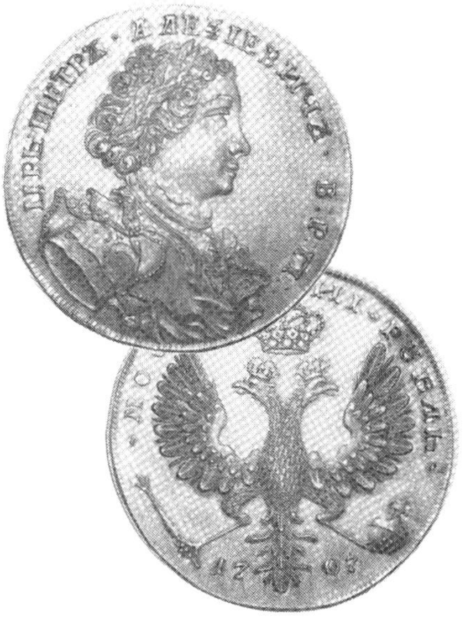

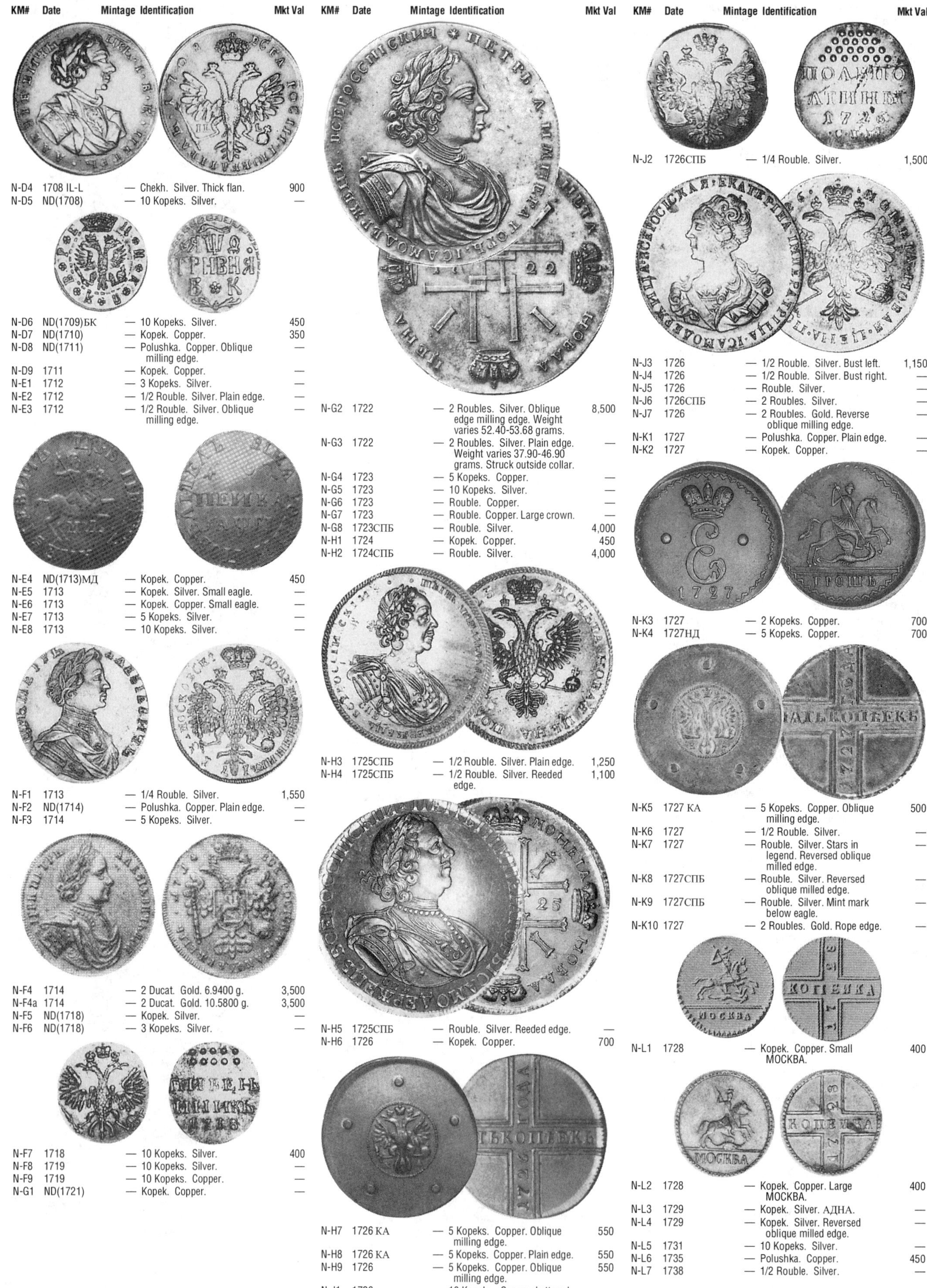

KM#	Date	Mintage	Identification	Mkt Val
N-D4	1708 IL-L	—	Chekh. Silver. Thick flan.	900
N-D5	ND(1708)	—	10 Kopeks. Silver.	—
N-D6	ND(1709)БК	—	10 Kopeks. Silver.	450
N-D7	ND(1710)	—	Kopek. Copper.	350
N-D8	ND(1711)	—	Polushka. Copper. Oblique milling edge.	—
N-D9	1711	—	Kopek. Copper.	—
N-E1	1712	—	3 Kopeks. Silver.	—
N-E2	1712	—	1/2 Rouble. Silver. Plain edge.	—
N-E3	1712	—	1/2 Rouble. Silver. Oblique milling edge.	—
N-E4	ND(1713)МД	—	Kopek. Copper.	450
N-E5	1713	—	Kopek. Silver. Small eagle.	—
N-E6	1713	—	Kopek. Copper. Small eagle.	—
N-E7	1713	—	5 Kopeks. Silver.	—
N-E8	1713	—	10 Kopeks. Silver.	—
N-F1	1713	—	1/4 Rouble. Silver.	1,550
N-F2	ND(1714)	—	Polushka. Copper. Plain edge.	—
N-F3	1714	—	5 Kopeks. Silver.	—
N-F4	1714	—	2 Ducat. Gold. 6.9400 g.	3,500
N-F4a	1714	—	2 Ducat. Gold. 10.5800 g.	3,500
N-F5	ND(1718)	—	Kopek. Silver.	—
N-F6	ND(1718)	—	3 Kopeks. Silver.	—
N-F7	1718	—	10 Kopeks. Silver.	400
N-F8	1719	—	10 Kopeks. Silver.	—
N-F9	1719	—	10 Kopeks. Copper.	—
N-G1	ND(1721)	—	Kopek. Copper.	—
N-G2	1722	—	2 Roubles. Silver. Oblique edge milling edge. Weight varies 52.40-53.68 grams.	8,500
N-G3	1722	—	2 Roubles. Silver. Plain edge. Weight varies 37.90-46.90 grams. Struck outside collar.	—
N-G4	1723	—	5 Kopeks. Copper.	—
N-G5	1723	—	10 Kopeks. Silver.	—
N-G6	1723	—	Rouble. Copper.	—
N-G7	1723	—	Rouble. Copper. Large crown.	—
N-G8	1723СПБ	—	Rouble. Silver.	4,000
N-H1	1724	—	Kopek. Copper.	450
N-H2	1724СПБ	—	Rouble. Silver.	4,000
N-H3	1725СПБ	—	1/2 Rouble. Silver. Plain edge.	1,250
N-H4	1725СПБ	—	1/2 Rouble. Silver. Reeded edge.	1,100
N-H5	1725СПБ	—	Rouble. Silver. Reeded edge.	—
N-H6	1726	—	Kopek. Copper.	700
N-H7	1726 КА	—	5 Kopeks. Copper. Oblique milling edge.	550
N-H8	1726 КА	—	5 Kopeks. Copper. Plain edge.	550
N-H9	1726	—	5 Kopeks. Copper. Oblique milling edge.	550
N-J1	1726	—	10 Kopeks. Copper. Lettered edge.	—
N-J2	1726СПБ	—	1/4 Rouble. Silver.	1,500
N-J3	1726	—	1/2 Rouble. Silver. Bust left.	1,150
N-J4	1726	—	1/2 Rouble. Silver. Bust right.	—
N-J5	1726	—	Rouble. Silver.	—
N-J6	1726СПБ	—	2 Roubles. Silver.	—
N-J7	1726	—	2 Roubles. Gold. Reverse oblique milling edge.	—
N-K1	1727	—	Polushka. Copper. Plain edge.	—
N-K2	1727	—	Kopek. Copper.	—
N-K3	1727	—	2 Kopeks. Copper.	700
N-K4	1727НД	—	5 Kopeks. Copper.	700
N-K5	1727 КА	—	5 Kopeks. Copper. Oblique milling edge.	500
N-K6	1727	—	1/2 Rouble. Silver.	—
N-K7	1727	—	Rouble. Silver. Stars in legend. Reversed oblique milled edge.	—
N-K8	1727СПБ	—	Rouble. Silver. Reversed oblique milled edge.	—
N-K9	1727СПБ	—	Rouble. Silver. Mint mark below eagle.	—
N-K10	1727	—	2 Roubles. Gold. Rope edge.	—
N-L1	1728	—	Kopek. Copper. Small МОСКВА.	400
N-L2	1728	—	Kopek. Copper. Large МОСКВА.	400
N-L3	1729	—	Kopek. Silver. АДНА.	—
N-L4	1729	—	Kopek. Silver. Reversed oblique milled edge.	—
N-L5	1731	—	10 Kopeks. Silver.	—
N-L6	1735	—	Polushka. Copper.	450
N-L7	1738	—	1/2 Rouble. Silver.	—

KM#	Date	Mintage	Identification	Mkt Val
N-L8	1738	—	Ducat. Gold. Plain edge.	—
N-L9	1738	—	Ducat. Gold. Oblique milling edge.	—
N-M1	1739	—	Denga. Copper.	350
N-M2	1739	—	10 Kopeks. Silver. Plain edge.	—
N-M3	1739	—	10 Kopeks. Copper. Plain edge.	—
N-M4	1739	—	1/4 Rouble. Silver. Large legend.	—
N-M5	1739	—	1/2 Rouble. Silver. Reversed oblique milling edge.	—
N-M6	1740	—	2 Kopeks. Copper. Plain edge.	—
N-M7	1740	—	2 Kopeks. Copper. Oblique milling edge.	—
N-M8	1740	—	2 Kopeks. Copper. Tread edge.	—
N-M9	1740	—	2 Kopeks. Copper. Mule. St. George. Tread edge.	—
N-M10	1740	—	5 Kopeks. Copper.	—
N-M11	1740	—	5 Kopeks. Silver. Plain edge.	—
N-M12	1740	—	10 Kopeks. Silver.	—
N-M13	1741ММД	—	10 Kopeks. Silver.	—
N-M14	1741ММД	—	10 Kopeks. Silver. Reversed oblique milling edge.	—
N1	1741	—	1/4 Rouble. Silver. Bust. Eagle. Diagonal reeded edge.	—
N2	1744ММД	—	Rouble. Silver. Oblique milling edge. Bust type.	—
N3	1744СПБ	—	Rouble. Silver. Plain edge. Bust type.	—
N4	1745	—	10 Kopeks. Silver. Plain edge. Bust type, thick planchet.	—
N4a	1745	—	10 Kopeks. Silver. 3.1200 g.	300
N5	1746ММД	—	1/4 Rouble. Silver. Plain edge. Bust type.	—
N6	1746	—	1/2 Rouble. Silver. Oblique milling edge. Bust type.	—
N7	1748	—	Denga. Copper. Oblique milling edge.	275
N9	1749ММД	—	2 Ducat. Gold. Plain edge. St. Andrew type.	4,000
N10	1749ММД	—	2 Ducat. Gold. Oblique milling edge. St. Andrew type.	4,000
N8	1749	—	Ducat. Gold. Plain edge. St. Andrew typ with reverse legend.	—
N11	1751	—	2 Ducat. Gold. АПРЕЛ. Diagonal reeded edge. Eagle type reverse.	2,600
N12	1751ММД	—	2 Ducat. Gold. АПРЕЛ. Oblique milling edge. St. Andrew type.	3,000

KM#	Date	Mintage	Identification	Mkt Val
N13	1753	—	Ducat. Gold. Oblique milling edge. St. Andrew type, double thickness.	—
N16	1755	—	5 Kopeks. Silver. Plain edge. Eagle on clouds.	—
N17	1755	—	5 Kopeks. Silver. Oblique milling edge. Eagle on clouds.	—
N18	1755	—	Ducat. Gold. Oblique milling edge.	—
N19	1755СПБ	—	Ducat. Gold. Oblique milling edge.	—
N20	1755	—	5 Roubles. Gold. Oblique milling edge. St. Andrew cross on eagle.	—
N21	1755	—	5 Roubles. Gold. Oblique milling edge. St. Andrew cross on shield.	—
N22	1755СПБ	—	5 Roubles. Gold. Oblique milling edge. St. Andrew cross on eagle.	—
N23	1755СПБ	—	5 Roubles. Gold. Oblique milling edge. St. Andrew's cross on shield.	—
N14	1755	—	Kopek. Copper. Plain edge.	750
N15	1755	—	Kopek. Copper. Lettered with portrait edge.	1,250
N24	1756	—	Rouble. Gold. Oblique milling edge. Pattern type, eagle in clouds.	—
N25	1756	—	Rouble. Gold. Decorative EP monogram. Oblique milling edge. Pattern type.	—

KM#	Date	Mintage	Identification	Mkt Val
N26	1757	—	Polushka. Copper. Oblique milling edge.	225
N27	1757	—	Polushka. Copper. Reeded edge.	225
N28	1757	—	Polushka. Copper. Plain edge.	225
N29	1757	—	Polushka. Copper. Oblique milling edge.	275
N30	1757	—	Denga. Copper. Oblique milling edge.	250
N31	1757	—	Denga. Copper. Tread edge.	250
N32	1757	—	Denga. Copper. Plain edge.	250
N33	1757	—	Denga. Copper. Oblique milling edge. New dies.	250
N34	1757	—	Kopek. Copper. Coarse tread edge. Thick planchet.	250
N35	1757	—	Kopek. Copper. Oblique milling edge. Thin planchet.	250
N36	1757	—	Kopek. Copper. Plain edge.	250
N37	1757	—	Kopek. Copper. Tread edge. Thin planchet.	250
NA38	1757	—	Kopek. Copper. Fine tread edge.	250
N38	1757	—	2 Kopeks. Copper. Tread edge. Long lance.	500
N39	1757	—	2 Kopeks. Copper. Tread edge. Short lance.	500
N40	1757	—	2 Kopeks. Copper. Oblique milling edge. Short lance.	500

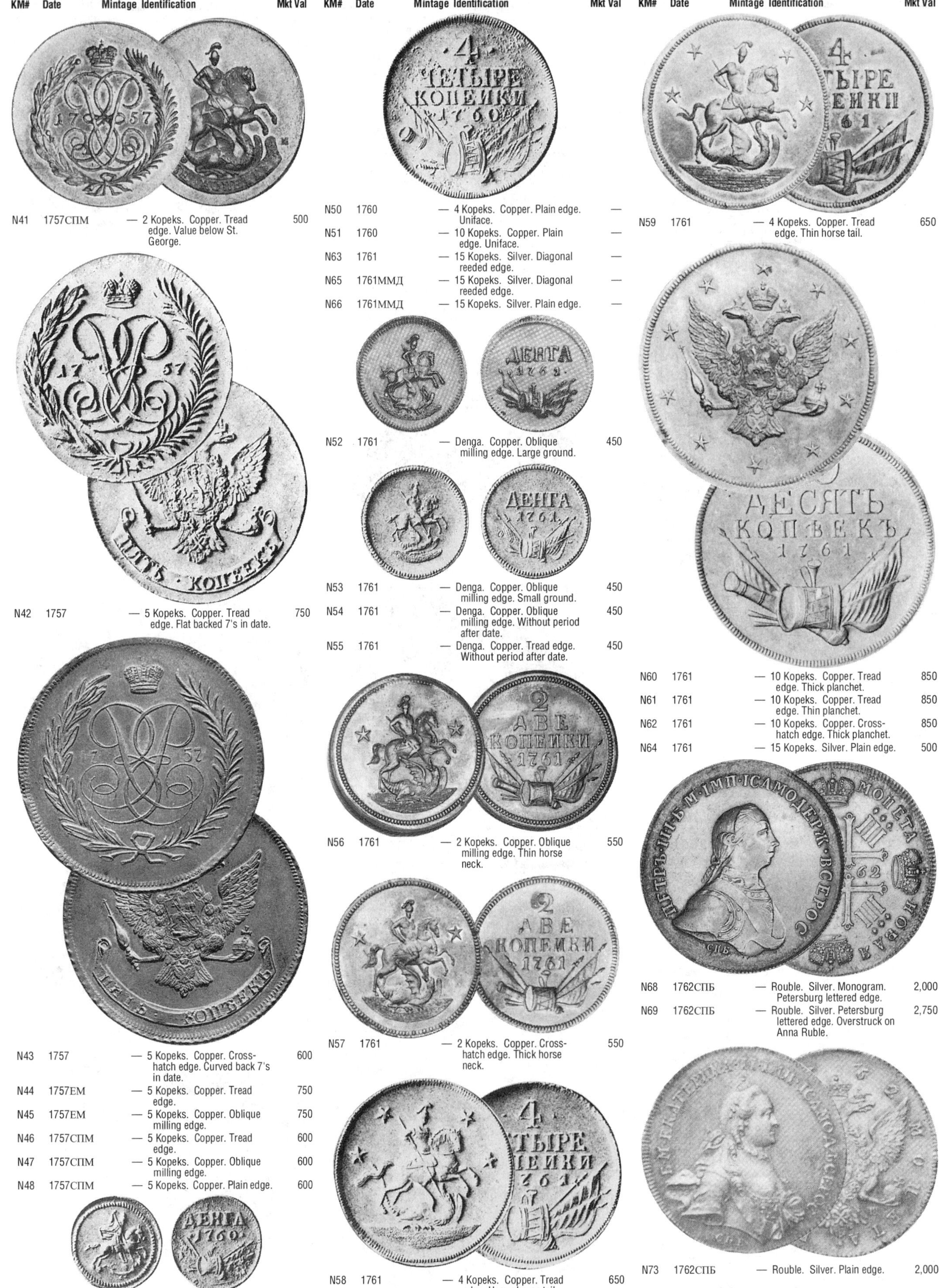

KM#	Date	Mintage	Identification	Mkt Val
N41	1757СПМ	—	2 Kopeks. Copper. Tread edge. Value below St. George.	500
N42	1757	—	5 Kopeks. Copper. Tread edge. Flat backed 7's in date.	750
N43	1757	—	5 Kopeks. Copper. Cross-hatch edge. Curved back 7's in date.	600
N44	1757EM	—	5 Kopeks. Copper. Tread edge.	750
N45	1757EM	—	5 Kopeks. Copper. Oblique milling edge.	750
N46	1757СПМ	—	5 Kopeks. Copper. Tread edge.	600
N47	1757СПМ	—	5 Kopeks. Copper. Oblique milling edge.	600
N48	1757СПМ	—	5 Kopeks. Copper. Plain edge.	600
N49	1760	—	Denga. Copper. Oblique milling edge.	—

KM#	Date	Mintage	Identification	Mkt Val
N50	1760	—	4 Kopeks. Copper. Plain edge. Uniface.	—
N51	1760	—	10 Kopeks. Copper. Plain edge. Uniface.	—
N63	1761	—	15 Kopeks. Silver. Diagonal reeded edge.	—
N65	1761ММД	—	15 Kopeks. Silver. Diagonal reeded edge.	—
N66	1761ММД	—	15 Kopeks. Silver. Plain edge.	—
N52	1761	—	Denga. Copper. Oblique milling edge. Large ground.	450
N53	1761	—	Denga. Copper. Oblique milling edge. Small ground.	450
N54	1761	—	Denga. Copper. Oblique milling edge. Without period after date.	450
N55	1761	—	Denga. Copper. Tread edge. Without period after date.	450
N56	1761	—	2 Kopeks. Copper. Oblique milling edge. Thin horse neck.	550
N57	1761	—	2 Kopeks. Copper. Cross-hatch edge. Thick horse neck.	550
N58	1761	—	4 Kopeks. Copper. Tread edge. Heavy horse tail.	650

KM#	Date	Mintage	Identification	Mkt Val
N59	1761	—	4 Kopeks. Copper. Tread edge. Thin horse tail.	650
N60	1761	—	10 Kopeks. Copper. Tread edge. Thick planchet.	850
N61	1761	—	10 Kopeks. Copper. Tread edge. Thin planchet.	850
N62	1761	—	10 Kopeks. Copper. Cross-hatch edge. Thick planchet.	850
N64	1761	—	15 Kopeks. Silver. Plain edge.	500
N68	1762СПБ	—	Rouble. Silver. Monogram. Petersburg lettered edge.	2,000
N69	1762СПБ	—	Rouble. Silver. Petersburg lettered edge. Overstruck on Anna Ruble.	2,750
N73	1762СПБ	—	Rouble. Silver. Plain edge.	2,000

KM#	Date	Mintage	Identification	Mkt Val

KM#	Date	Mintage	Identification	Mkt Val
NA74	1762СПБ	—	10 Roubles. Gold.	12,500

KM#	Date	Mintage	Identification	Mkt Val
N74	1762СПБ	—	Ducat. Gold. Plain edge. Without dot after date.	8,500
N67	1762СПБ	—	Rouble. Silver. Eagle. Plain edge.	—
N70	1762СПБ	—	Rouble. Silver. Diagonal reeded edge.	—
N71	1762СПБ	—	Rouble. Silver. Plain edge.	—
N72	1762СПБ	—	Rouble. Silver. Dot-dash edge.	—
NA75	1763	—	1/2 Kopek. Copper. St. Petersburg without mint mark.	—
N77	1763СПБ	—	5 Roubles. Gold. Small letters. Oblique milling edge.	—
N75	1763	—	Kopek. Copper. Plain edge.	200
N76	1763	—	Kopek. Copper. Tread edge. Large crown.	200
N79	1764	—	2 Kopeks. Copper.	—

KM#	Date	Mintage	Identification	Mkt Val
N80	1764СПБ	—	10 Kopeks. Silver. Plain edge.	—
N86	1765ЕМ	—	Kopek. Copper. Tread edge.	—

KM#	Date	Mintage	Identification	Mkt Val
N81	1765	—	Polushka. Copper. Oblique milling edge.	275
N82	1765ЕМ	—	Polushka. Copper. Oblique milling edge.	200

KM#	Date	Mintage	Identification	Mkt Val
N83	1765ЕМ	—	Denga. Copper. Oblique milling edge.	250

KM#	Date	Mintage	Identification	Mkt Val
N84	1765	—	Denga. Copper. Oblique milling edge.	225
N85	1765ЕМ	—	Kopek. Copper. Oblique milling edge.	225
N87	1765	—	Kopek. Copper. Oblique milling edge. Small date.	225
N88	1765	—	Kopek. Copper. Tread edge.	225
N89	1765	—	Kopek. Copper. Plain edge.	225

KM#	Date	Mintage	Identification	Mkt Val
N90	1765ЕМ	—	2 Kopeks. Copper. Tread edge.	275
N91	1765	—	2 Kopeks. Copper. Oblique milling edge. Value above St. George.	275
N92	1765	—	2 Kopeks. Copper. Tread edge.	275

KM#	Date	Mintage	Identification	Mkt Val
N93	1765	—	2 Kopeks. Copper. Oblique milling edge.	275

KM#	Date	Mintage	Identification	Mkt Val
N94	1765ЕМ	—	5 Kopeks. Copper. Tread edge.	600
N95	1765ЕМ	—	5 Kopeks. Copper. Cross hatched edge.	600
N96	1765ЕМ	—	5 Kopeks. Copper. Tread edge.	600
N97	1765	—	5 Kopeks. Copper. Oblique milling edge.	600
N98	1765	—	5 Kopeks. Copper. Tread edge.	600

KM#	Date	Mintage	Identification	Mkt Val
N99	1766СПБ	—	2 Roubles. Gold. Oblique milling edge.	—

KM#	Date	Mintage	Identification	Mkt Val
N101	1767	—	5 Kopeks. Copper. Plain edge. Small mintmark.	500
N102	1767	—	5 Kopeks. Copper. Tread edge. Small mintmark.	500
N103	1768СПБ	—	10 Kopeks. Silver. Plain edge.	—
N104	1768СПБ	—	20 Kopeks. Silver. Plain edge.	—
N105	1768	—	20 Kopeks. Silver. Plain edge. Without mintmark.	—
N106	1768СПБ	—	1/2 Rouble. Silver. Plain edge.	—
N107	1769	—	Polushka. Copper. Plain edge.	200
N108	1769	—	Polushka. Copper. Oblique milling edge.	200
N109	1771	—	Denga. Copper. Plain edge.	225
NA110	1771	—	Rouble. Copper. 1020.0000 g. Sestroretsk. Superior Goodman sale 2-91 for XF.	18,700
NB110	1771	—	Rouble. Silver. Sestroretsk. Superior Goodman sale 2-91 for AU-Unc.	14,850
N112	1774СПБ	—	10 Roubles. Gold. Oblique milling edge. Large letters in inscription.	—
N115	1776СПБ	—	10 Kopeks. Silver. Oblique milling edge.	—
N116	1776СПБ	—	20 Kopeks. Silver. Plain edge.	—
N117	1776СПБ	—	Rouble. Silver. Plain edge. Short legend.	—
N114	1776СПМ	—	2 Kopeks. Copper. Tread edge.	225
N118	1777СПБ	—	15 Kopeks. Silver. Plain edge. New portrait.	—
N119	1777СПБ	—	20 Kopeks. Silver. Plain edge. Old type.	—
N120	1777СПБ	—	25 Kopeks. Silver. Plain edge. Old type.	—
N121	1777СПБ	—	1/2 Rouble. Silver. Oblique milling edge. Old obverse.	—
N122	1777СПБ	—	Rouble. Silver. Plain edge. Oldest portrait.	—
N123	1777СПБ	—	5 Roubles. Gold. Oblique milling edge. Earlier portrait.	—
N124	1777СПБ	—	10 Roubles. Gold. Oblique milling edge. Earlier portrait.	—
N125	1778СПБ	—	1/2 Rouble. Silver. Plain edge. Higher relief portrait.	—
N126	1778	—	1/2 Rouble. Gold. Plain edge. Thick flan.	—
N128	1779СПБ	—	15 Kopeks. Silver. Plain edge. Higher relief.	—
N129	1779СПБ	—	1/4 Rouble. Silver. Plain edge. Higher relief.	—
N130	1780СПБ	—	15 Kopeks. Silver. Oblique milling edge. Legend ends on bust.	—
N131	1780СПБ	—	15 Kopeks. Silver. Plain edge. Legend off bust.	—
N132	1780СПБ ИЗ	—	1/2 Rouble. Silver. Oblique milling edge.	—
N133	1780СПБ	—	Rouble. Silver. Plain edge. Oldest portrait.	—
N139	1781СПБ	—	10 Kopeks. Silver. Plain edge. Younger portrait.	—
N140	1781СПБ	—	10 Kopeks. Silver. Oblique milling edge. Younger portrait.	—
N141	1781СПБ	—	15 Kopeks. Silver. Plain edge. Higher relief.	—
N142	1781СПБ	—	20 Kopeks. Silver. Plain edge. Legend ends ВСЕРОСС.	—
N143	1781СПБ	—	1/4 Rouble. Silver. Plain edge. Wide mintmark.	—
N144	1781СПБ	—	Rouble. Silver. Oblique milling edge. Higher relief.	—
N145	1781СПБ	—	Rouble. Silver. Oblique milling edge. Oldest portrait.	—
N134	1781КМ	—	Polushka. Copper. Oblique milling edge.	200
N135	1781КМ	—	Denga. Copper. Oblique milling edge.	225

KM#	Date	Mintage	Identification	Mkt Val
N136	1781КМ	—	5 Kopeks. Copper. Oblique milling edge.	450
N137	1781СПМ	—	5 Kopeks. Copper. Plain edge.	500
N138	1781СПМ	—	5 Kopeks. Copper. Tread edge.	500
N146	1782КМ	—	Polushka. Copper. Oblique milling edge.	200
N147	1782КМ	—	Denga. Copper. Oblique milling edge.	225
N148	1782КМ	—	5 Kopeks. Copper. Oblique milling edge.	450
N149	1782СПБ	—	10 Kopeks. Silver. Plain edge. Large head.	—
N150	1782СПБ	—	10 Kopeks. Silver. Plain edge. Small head.	—
N151	1782СПБ	—	10 Kopeks. Silver. Plain edge. Younger portrait.	—
N152	1782СПБ	—	15 Kopeks. Silver. Plain edge. Legend ends ВСЕРОС.	—
N153	1782СПБ	—	15 Kopeks. Silver. Plain edge. Legend ends ВСЕРОСС.	—
N154	1782СПБ	—	20 Kopeks. Silver. Diagonal reeded edge. Old bust.	—
N155	1782СПБ	—	20 Kopeks. Silver. Plain edge. Younger bust.	—
N156	1782СПБ	—	1/2 Rouble. Silver. Oblique milling edge. Older bust.	—
N157	1782СПБ	—	1/2 Rouble. Silver. Plain edge. Younger portrait.	—
N158	1782СПБ	—	Rouble. Silver. Oblique milling edge. MM at rim.	—
N162	1783СПБ	—	10 Kopeks. Silver. High relief.	—
N163	1783СПБ	—	15 Kopeks. Silver. Plain edge. Legend ends ВСЕРОСС.	—
N164	1783СПБ	—	20 Kopeks. Silver. Plain edge. High relief.	—
N165	1783СПБ	—	1/4 Rouble. Silver. Plain edge. High relief.	—
N166	1783СПБ ММ	—	1/2 Rouble. Silver. Oblique milling edge.	—
N167	1783СПБ	—	1/2 Rouble. Silver. Oblique milling edge. Legend ends below bust.	—
N168	1783СПБ	—	Rouble. Silver. Oblique milling edge. High relief.	—
N159	1783КМ	—	Polushka. Copper. Oblique milling edge.	200
N160	1783КМ	—	Denga. Copper. Oblique milling edge.	225
N161	1783КМ	—	5 Kopeks. Copper. Oblique milling edge.	450
N169	1784КМ	—	Polushka. Copper. Oblique milling edge.	200
N170	1784КМ	—	Denga. Copper. Oblique milling edge.	225
N171	1784КМ	—	5 Kopeks. Copper. Oblique milling edge.	450
N172	1784СПБ	—	10 Kopeks. Silver. Plain edge.	—
N173	1784СПБ	—	15 Kopeks. Silver. Plain edge.	—
N174	1784СПБ	—	20 Kopeks. Silver. Plain edge. High relief.	—
N175	1784СПБ Я	—	1/4 Rouble. Silver. Plain edge.	—
N176	1784СПБ СА	—	1/2 Rouble. Silver. Oblique milling edge.	—
N177	1784СПБ I	—	Rouble. Silver. Oblique milling edge.	—
N181	1785СПБ	—	10 Kopeks. Silver. Plain edge.	—
N182	1785СПБ	—	15 Kopeks. Silver. Plain edge. Divided date.	—
N183	1785СПБ	—	20 Kopeks. Silver. Plain edge. High relief.	—
N184	1785СПБ	—	1/4 Rouble. Silver. Plain edge. High relief.	—
N185	1785СПБ	—	1/2 Rouble. Silver. Oblique milling edge. High relief.	—
N186	1785СПБ	—	Rouble. Silver. Oblique milling edge. High relief.	—
N178	1785КМ	—	Polushka. Copper. Oblique milling edge.	200
N179	1785КМ	—	Denga. Copper. Oblique milling edge.	225
N180	1785КМ	—	5 Kopeks. Copper. Oblique milling edge.	450
N187	1786КМ	—	Polushka. Copper. Oblique milling edge.	200
N188	1786КМ	—	Denga. Copper. Oblique milling edge.	225
N189	1786КМ	—	5 Kopeks. Copper. Oblique milling edge.	450
N190	1786СПБ	—	10 Kopeks. Silver. Plain edge.	—
N191	1786СПБ	—	15 Kopeks. Silver. Ends: ВСЕРОСС.. Plain edge.	—
N192	1786СПБ	—	20 Kopeks. Silver. Plain edge.	—
N193	1786СПБ	—	1/4 Rouble. Silver. Plain edge.	—
N194	1786СПБ Я	—	1/2 Rouble. Silver. Oblique milling edge. Broad portrait.	—
N195	1786СПБ	—	1/2 Rouble. Silver. Oblique milling edge. Narrow portrait.	—
N196	1786СПБ	—	Rouble. Silver. Plain edge. High relief.	—
N197	1787КМ	—	5 Kopeks. Copper. Oblique milling edge.	—
N198	1787СПБ	—	15 Kopeks. Silver. Ends: "ВСЕРОСС".. Plain edge.	—
N199	1787СПБ	—	20 Kopeks. Silver. Plain edge.	—
N200	1787СПБ	—	1/4 Rouble. Silver. Plain edge. Small planchet.	—
N201	1787СПБ	—	1/4 Rouble. Silvered Copper. Plain edge.	—
N202	1787СПБ	—	1/2 Rouble. Silver. Oblique milling edge. High relief.	—
N203	1787СПБ	—	Rouble. Silver. Plain edge. High relief.	—
N211	1788СПБ	—	10 Kopeks. Silver. Plain edge.	—
N212	1788СПБ	—	1/4 Rouble. Silver. Plain edge.	—
N213	1788СПБ	—	1/2 Rouble. Silver. Oblique milling edge. Narrow portrait.	—
N214	1788СПБ	—	1/2 Rouble. Silver. Oblique milling edge. Broad portrait.	—
N215	1788СПБ	—	Rouble. Silver. Oblique milling edge.	—
N216	1788СПБ	—	5 Roubles. Gold. Oblique milling edge. End of inscription high.	—
N204	1788	—	Polushka. Copper. Plain edge.	200
N205	1788	—	Polushka. Copper. Oblique milling edge.	200
N206	1788	—	Denga. Copper. Plain edge.	225
N207	1788	—	Denga. Copper. Oblique milling edge.	225
N208	1788	—	Kopek. Copper. Plain edge.	250
N209	1788	—	Kopek. Copper. Tread edge.	250
N210	1788КМ	—	5 Kopeks. Copper. Oblique milling edge.	500
N217	1789КМ	—	5 Kopeks. Copper. Oblique milling edge.	—

KM#	Date	Mintage	Identification	Mkt Val
N218	1789СПБ АК	—	Rouble. Silver. Oblique milling edge.	—
N219	1789АК	—	Rouble. Silver. ТДІВАНОВЪ under bust. Oblique milling edge.	—
N220	1790КМ	—	5 Kopeks. Copper. Oblique milling edge.	—
N221	1790СПБ	—	15 Kopeks. Silver. Plain edge.	—
N222	1790СПБ	—	20 Kopeks. Silver. Plain edge.	—
N223	1790СПБ	—	Rouble. Silver. Plain edge. High relief.	—
N227	1791СПБ	—	10 Kopeks. Silver. Plain edge.	—
N228	1791СПБ	—	15 Kopeks. Silver. Plain edge. Dot at end of legend.	—
N229	1791СПБ	—	15 Kopeks. Silver. Without dot at end of legend.	—
N230	1791СПБ	—	20 Kopeks. Silver. Plain edge.	—
N231	1791СПБ	—	1/4 Rouble. Silver. Plain edge.	—
N232	1791СПБ	—	1/2 Rouble. Silver. Oblique milling edge. High relief.	—
N233	1791СПБ	—	Rouble. Silver. ТДІВАНОВЪ below bust. Plain edge.	—
N234	1791СПБ	—	Rouble. Silver. Oblique milling edge. High relief.	—
N224	1791КМ	—	Polushka. Copper. Oblique milling edge.	200
N225	1791КМ	—	Denga. Copper. Oblique milling edge.	225
N226	1791КМ	—	5 Kopeks. Copper. Oblique milling edge. Small mintmark.	500
N235	1792КМ	—	5 Kopeks. Copper. Oblique milling edge.	650
N236	1792СПБ	—	10 Kopeks. Silver. Plain edge.	—
N237	1792СПБ	—	15 Kopeks. Silver. Ends: ВСЕРОСС. Plain edge.	—
N238	1792СПБ	—	20 Kopeks. Silver. Plain edge.	—
N239	1792СПБ	—	1/4 Rouble. Silver. Plain edge.	—
N240	1792СПБ Я	—	1/2 Rouble. Silver. Oblique milling edge.	—
N241	1792СПБ	—	1/2 Rouble. Silver. Oblique milling edge. High relief.	—
N242	1792СПБ	—	Rouble. Silver. Oblique milling edge.	—
N243	1792СПБ	—	Rouble. Silver. ТДІВАНОВЪ below bust. Oblique milling edge.	—
N245	1793СПБ	—	10 Kopeks. Silver. Plain edge.	—
N246	1793СПБ	—	15 Kopeks. Silver. Ends: ВСЕРОСС. Plain edge.	—
N247	1793СПБ	—	20 Kopeks. Silver. Plain edge.	—
N248	1793СПБ	—	1/4 Rouble. Silver. Plain edge.	—
N249	1793СПБ АК	—	1/2 Rouble. Silver. Oblique milling edge.	—
N250	1793СПБ Я	—	1/2 Rouble. Silver. Oblique milling edge. Dot ends legend.	—
N251	1793СПБ Я	—	Rouble. Silver. Oblique milling edge. Value between .S.	—
N244	1793КМ	—	5 Kopeks. Copper. Oblique milling edge.	500
N252	1794КМ	—	5 Kopeks. Copper. Oblique milling edge.	500
N260	1794СПБ Я	—	5 Roubles. Gold. Oblique milling edge.	7,500
N253	1794СПБ Я	—	10 Kopeks. Silver. Plain edge.	—
N254	1794СПБ Я	—	15 Kopeks. Silver. Ends: ВСЕРОСС. Plain edge.	—
N255	1794СПБ Я	—	20 Kopeks. Silver. Oblique milling edge. Legend ends at bust.	—
N256	1794СПБ Я	—	20 Kopeks. Silver. Plain edge. Legend ends below bust.	—
N257	1794СПБ Я	—	1/4 Rouble. Silver. Plain edge.	—
N258	1794СПБ Я	—	1/2 Rouble. Silver. Oblique milling edge. Narrow portrait.	—
N259	1794СПБ Я	—	Rouble. Silver. Oblique milling edge.	—
N262	1795СПБ Я	—	10 Kopeks. Silver. Plain edge.	—
N263	1795СПБ Я	—	20 Kopeks. Silver. Oblique milling edge.	—
N264	1795СПБ АК	—	1/4 Rouble. Silver. Oblique milling edge.	—
N265	1795СПБ Я	—	1/2 Rouble. Silver. Plain edge. Without dot at end of legend.	—
N266	1795СПБ Я	—	1/2 Rouble. Silver. Oblique milling edge. High relief.	—
N267	1795СПБ Я	—	Rouble. Silver. Oblique milling edge.	—
N268	1795СПБ Я	—	Rouble. Silver. ТДІВАНОВЪ below bust. Oblique milling edge.	—
N282	1795БМ	—	Albertus Rouble. Silver. Plain edge.	—
N261	1795КМ	—	5 Kopeks. Copper. Oblique milling edge.	500
N269	1796	—	Polushka. Copper. Cipher type.	350
N270	1796	—	Denga. Copper. Cipher type.	350
N271	1796	—	Kopek. Copper. Cipher type.	400
N272	1796	—	2 Kopeks. Copper. Cipher type.	550
N273	1796	—	4 Kopeks. Copper. Cipher type.	750
N274	1796	—	5 Kopeks. Copper. Cipher type.	800
N276	1796	—	10 Kopeks. Copper. Cipher type.	900
N284	1796БМ	—	Albertus Rouble. Silver. Oblique milling edge.	2,000
N285	1796СПБ Я	—	10 Roubles. Gold. Oblique milling edge. Large mint letters.	25,000
N286	1796СПБ I	—	Ducat. Gold. Oblique milling edge. Youthful portrait, thick flan.	7,000
N287	1796БМ	—	Ducat. Gold. Oblique milling edge.	15,000
N288	1796	—	2 Ducat. Gold. Oblique milling edge. Thick planchet.	9,000
N281	1796СПБ Я	—	1/2 Rouble. Silver. Diagonal milling edge. High relief.	—
N279	1796СПБ Я	—	20 Kopeks. Silver. Plain edge.	—
N280	1796СПБ Я	—	1/4 Rouble. Silver. Plain edge.	—
N283	1796БМ	—	Albertus Rouble. Silver. Plain edge. CM/OM.	—
N275	1796КМ	—	5 Kopeks. Copper. Diagonal reeded edge.	—
N277	1796СПБ Я	—	10 Kopeks. Silver. Plain edge.	—
N278	1796СПБ Я	—	20 Kopeks. Silver. Oblique milling edge. Dot at end of legend.	—
N298	1797	—	Kopek. Copper. Oblique milling edge.	—

KM#	Date	Mintage	Identification	Mkt Val
N304	1797МБ	—	5 Kopeks. Silver. Plain edge.	—
N305	1797МБ	—	1/4 Rouble. Silver. Plain edge.	—
N306	1797ФА	—	1/4 Rouble. Silver. Plain edge.	—
N307	1797МБ	—	2 Roubles. Silver. Plain edge.	—
N308	1797МБ	—	Rouble. Silver. Plain edge. Dot after date.	—
N289	1797ЕМ	—	Polushka. Copper. Oblique milling edge. Large value.	150
N290	1797КМ	—	Polushka. Copper. Oblique milling edge. Small mm.	165
N291	1797	—	Polushka. Copper. Oblique milling edge.	150
N292	1797ЕМ	—	Denga. Copper. Reverse oblique milling edge.	165
N293	1797ЕМ	—	Denga. Copper. Oblique milling edge.	165
N294	1797КМ	—	Denga. Copper. Oblique milling edge. Small mm.	225
N295	1797	—	Denga. Copper. Oblique milling edge.	165
N296	1797ЕМ	—	Kopek. Copper. Oblique milling edge.	165
N297	1797КМ	—	Kopek. Copper. Oblique milling edge.	165
N299	1797ЕМ	—	2 Kopeks. Copper. Oblique milling edge. Small mm.	185
N300	1797КМ	—	2 Kopeks. Copper. Oblique milling edge.	185
N301	1797	—	2 Kopeks. Copper. Oblique milling edge. Wide date.	185
N302	1797	—	2 Kopeks. Copper. Oblique milling edge. Narrow date.	185
N303	1797ЕМ	—	2 Kopeks. Copper. Double thick planchet.	450
N309	1797СМ	—	Ducat. Gold. Oblique milling edge. Without mm.	10,000
N310	1798КМ	—	Polushka. Copper. Oblique milling edge. Small mintmark.	165
N311	1798КМ	—	Denga. Copper. Oblique milling edge. Small mintmark.	165
N313	1798КМ	—	Kopek. Copper. Oblique milling edge. Small mintmark.	165
N315	1798КМ	—	2 Kopeks. Copper. Reversed oblique milling edge.	200
N315A	1798	—	1/4 Rouble. Severin 2420.	750
N312	1798	—	Denga. Copper. Oblique milling edge.	—
N314	1798	—	Kopek. Copper. Oblique milling edge.	—
N316	1798СМ ФА	—	1/2 Rouble. Silver. Oblique milling edge.	—
N317	1798СМ АИ	—	Rouble. Silver. Oblique milling edge. Dot after date.	—
N321	1799	—	Denga. Copper. Oblique milling edge.	—
N323	1799	—	Kopek. Copper. Oblique milling edge.	—
N325	1799	—	2 Kopeks. Copper. Oblique milling edge.	—
N326	1799СМ МБ	—	5 Kopeks. Silver. Oblique milling edge.	—
N327	1799СМ	—	1/2 Rouble. Silver. Value: НА. Oblique milling edge.	—
N328	1799СМ	—	Rouble. Silver. Oblique milling edge.	—
N318	1799	—	Polushka. Copper. Oblique milling edge.	225
N319	1799КМ	—	Polushka. Copper. Oblique milling edge. Small mintmark.	185
N320	1799КМ	—	Denga. Copper. Oblique milling edge. Small mintmark.	165
N322	1799КМ	—	Kopek. Copper. Oblique milling edge. Small mintmark.	165
N324	1799КМ	—	2 Kopeks. Copper. Reversed oblique milling edge. Small mintmark.	200
N329	1800КМ	—	Polushka. Copper. Oblique milling edge.	165
N333	1800КМ	—	Kopek. Copper. Oblique milling edge.	250
N335	1800ЕМ	—	2 Kopeks. Copper. Plain edge.	200
N336	1800КМ	—	2 Kopeks. Copper. Oblique milling edge. Small mintmark.	200
N339	1800	—	5 Roubles. Gold. Wide flan.	12,000
N338	1800СМ АИ	—	1/4 Rouble. Silver. Plain edge.	—
N334	1800	—	Kopek. Copper. Oblique milling edge.	—
N337	1800	—	2 Kopeks. Copper. Oblique milling edge.	—
N330	1800КМ	—	Denga. Copper. Oblique milling edge.	—
N331	1800	—	Denga. Copper. Oblique milling edge.	—
N332	1800 КМ	—	1/2 Kopek. Copper.	—

NOVODEL PLATE MONEY

KM#	Date	Mintage	Identification	Mkt Val
NP2	1726	—	5 Kopeks. Copper. Large eagle, St. George shield.	—
NP3	1726	—	5 Kopeks. Copper. Small eagle, St. George shield.	—
NP1	1726	—	Kopek. Copper.	1,500
NP4	1726	—	5 Kopeks. Copper. Plain eagle. Illustration reduced.	1,000
NP5	1726	—	10 Kopeks. Copper. Eagle with 3 tailfeathers, large flan 70x70mm.	1,450
NP6	1726	—	10 Kopeks. Copper. Normal flan.	1,450
NP7	1726	—	10 Kopeks. Copper. Eagle with 5 tailfeathers.	1,450

PATTERNS

Including off metal strikes

KM#	Date	Mintage	Identification	Mkt Val
PnB1	1730	—	Rouble. Silver. Order of St. Andrew around eagle.	—
PnC1	1730	—	Rouble. Copper. Order of St. Andrew around eagle.	—
PnD1	1740	—	2 Kopeks. Copper.	—
PnE1	1740	—	5 Kopeks. Copper.	—
PnF1	1740	—	Rouble. Silver.	—
Pn1	1755	—	Kopek. Copper.	—
Pn2	1755	—	Kopek. Copper.	—
Pn3	1755	—	Kopek. Copper.	—

KM#	Date	Mintage	Identification	Mkt Val
Pn4	1755	—	Kopek. Copper.	—
Pn5	1755	—	Kopek. Copper.	—
Pn6	1755СПБ	—	Kopek. Copper.	—
Pn7	1755	—	1/2 Rouble. Gold.	—
Pn8	1755	—	Rouble. Gold.	—
Pn9	1755	—	2 Roubles. Gold.	—
Pn10	1755СПБ	—	20 Roubles. Gold.	—

Note: Unique

KM#	Date	Mintage	Identification	Mkt Val
PnA11	1755	—	2 Ducat. Gold.	—
Pn13	1756	—	2 Roubles. Gold. Bust of Elizabeth. Eagle.	—
Pn14	1756	—	2 Roubles. Gold. Different eagle.	—
Pn11	1756	—	Rouble. Gold. Bust of Elizabeth. Eagle.	8,000
Pn12	1756	—	Rouble. Gold. Monogram.	8,000

KM#	Date	Mintage	Identification	Mkt Val
PnA20	1757СПБ	—	10 Roubles. Gold. Like Pn20.	4,000
Pn15	1757	—	5 Kopeks. Copper.	—
Pn16	1757	—	5 Kopeks. Copper.	—
Pn17	1757	—	5 Kopeks. Copper.	—
Pn18	1757СПБ ЯР	—	Rouble. Silver.	—
Pn19	1757СПБ	—	Rouble. Silver.	—
Pn20	1757СПБ	—	20 Roubles. Gold. Head of Elizabeth. Cruciform arms.	—

Note: Unique

KM#	Date	Mintage	Identification	Mkt Val
Pn21	1758СПБ	—	Rouble. Silver.	—
Pn22	1760	—	15 Kopeks. Silver.	—
Pn23	176xММД	—	15 Kopeks. Silver.	—
Pn24	1760	—	20 Kopeks. Silver.	—

KM#	Date	Mintage	Identification	Mkt Val
Pn25	1762	—	5 Kopeks. Silver.	—
Pn26	1762	—	5 Kopeks. Silver. P3 monogram.	—
Pn27	1762	—	5 Kopeks. Silver. PF monogram.	—
Pn28	1762	—	15 Kopeks. Silver. Bust. Value on eagle.	—
Pn29	1762СПБ	—	20 Kopeks. Silver.	—
Pn30	1762СПБ	—	1/2 Rouble. Silver. НЗ monogram flanks bust. Imperial eagle.	—
Pn31	1762СПБ	—	Rouble. Silver. C67.2 by Iudin.	—
Pn32	1762СПБ	—	Rouble. Silver. Cruciform monograms.	—
PnA33	1762СПБ ЯИ	—	Rouble. Gold. Weight of 10 Ducat.	—
Pn33	1762ММД	—	5 Roubles. Gold. Bust. Imperial eagle.	—
Pn34	1762ММД	—	10 Roubles. Gold. Bust. Imperial eagle.	—

KM#	Date	Mintage	Identification	Mkt Val
Pn35	1763СПМ	—	Denga. Copper.	—
Pn36	1763	—	5 Kopeks. Silver.	—
Pn37	1763СПБ	—	15 Kopeks. Silver. Bust. Value on eagle.	—
Pn38	1763СПБ	—	20 Kopeks. Silver. C#63a.2.	—
Pn39	1766СПБ	—	Rouble. Silver.	—
Pn40	1789AM	—	Polushka. Copper. St. George above value. Monogram.	—
Pn41	1796	—	5 Kopeks. Copper. Elaborate E.	—
Pn42	1796	—	5 Kopeks. Copper. Plain E.	—
Pn43	1796	—	10 Kopeks. Copper. Elaborate E.	—

KM#	Date	Mintage	Identification	Mkt Val
Pn46	1796БМ	—	Rouble. Silver. Albertus Rouble.	2,500
Pn44	1796	—	10 Kopeks. Pewter.	—
Pn45	1796	—	10 Kopeks. Copper. Plain edge. Plain E.	—
Pn47	1796СПБ	—	Rouble. Silver.	—
Pn48	1796СМ	—	Rouble. Silver.	—

KM#	Date	Mintage	Identification	Mkt Val
Pn49	1798ОМ	—	Jefimok. Silver. Lettered edge.	—
PnA50	1798ОМ	—	Jefimok. Silver. Chain edge.	—
PnB50	1798ОМ	—	Jefimok. Silver. Diamond edge.	—
Pn50	1798ОМ	—	Jefimok. Silver. Lettered edge. Eagle in center.	—
Pn51	1798ОМ	—	Jefimok. Silver. Plain edge. Eagle in center.	—

SIBERIA

Siberia, the vast expanse that is most of Asiatic Russia covers 4,950,000 sq. mi. and has a population of about 35,090,000. Siberia, which means Sleeping Land in the Tatar language reaches from the Ural Mountains in the west to the Pacific Ocean in the east and from the Arctic Ocean in the north to the borders of China in the south. It is composed of three major regions: the Lena River Basin; the Central Siberian Plateau (reaching to 5,581 ft.) and the West Siberian Plain. Siberia is probably best known for its severe winters with temperatures of -90F being recorded. Leading industries are mining and forestry.

Siberia was tribal in nature until 1581 when an expedition from Russia made up of Cossacks overthrew the Sibir Khanate. In the next 3 centuries explorers and traders explored throughout Siberia. Under the czars it became a place to send criminals and political dissidents. With the construction of the Trans-Siberian Railroad (1891-1905) migration began from the West and settlements grew along the railroad right-of-way.

The Siberian coinage of Catherine the Great was inaugurated because of a shortage. A mint was established at Kolyvan-Voskressensk in the mining areas of the Altai Mountains. Men and machinery were sent from the Ekaterinburg Mint to get the new mint started. The normal Russian copper denominations were used plus the addition of a copper 10 kopeck piece. The regular series runs from 1766 to 1781 but there are known pieces dated1763 and 1764.

LEGEND

MONETA СИБЕРСКАЯ = Money of Siberia

MINT MARK

KM – Kolyvan

MONETARY SYSTEM

1/4 Kopeck = Poluska ПОЛУШКА
1/2 Kopeck = Denga ДЕНТА
2 Kopecks = ÄÂÀ ÊÎÏ_ÅÊÚ
5 Kopecks = ПЯРВ КОП_ЕКЪ
10 Kopecks =ÄÅÑßÒÜ ÊÎÏ_ÅÊÚ
100 Kopecks = 1 Rouble РУЬЛЬ

RUSSIAN OCCUPATION

STANDARD COINAGE

C# 1 POLUSHKA

Copper **Obv:** Crowned monogram within wreath **Rev:** Value , date in cartouche

Date	Mintage	VG	F	VF	XF	Unc
1764 Rare	—	—	—	—	—	—
1766 Rare	—	—	—	—	—	—
1767KM	—	100	175	225	350	—
1768KM	—	65.00	100	150	275	—
1769KM	—	65.00	100	150	275	—
1770KM	—	65.00	100	150	275	—
1771KM	—	65.00	100	150	275	—

Date	Mintage	VG	F	VF	XF	Unc
1772KM	—	65.00	100	150	275	—
1773KM	—	75.00	110	160	300	—
1774KM	—	65.00	100	150	275	—
1775KM	—	65.00	100	150	275	—
1776KM	—	65.00	100	150	275	—
1777KM	—	65.00	100	150	275	—
1778KM	—	65.00	100	150	275	—
1779KM	—	65.00	100	150	275	—

C# 2 DENGA

Copper **Obv:** Crowned monogram within wreath **Rev:** Value, date within crowned oval shield with supporters

Date	Mintage	VG	F	VF	XF	Unc
1764 Rare	—	—	—	—	—	—
1766	—	200	300	450	700	—
1767KM	—	55.00	110	170	250	—
1768KM	—	30.00	50.00	80.00	175	—
1769KM	—	30.00	50.00	80.00	175	—
1770KM	—	30.00	50.00	80.00	175	—
1771KM	—	30.00	50.00	80.00	175	—
1772KM	—	30.00	50.00	80.00	175	—
1773KM	—	30.00	50.00	80.00	175	—
1774KM	—	30.00	50.00	80.00	175	—
1775KM	—	35.00	70.00	110	225	—
1776KM	—	35.00	70.00	110	225	—
1777KM	—	35.00	70.00	110	225	—
1778KM	—	55.00	110	170	250	—
1779KM	—	55.00	110	170	250	—

C# 3 KOPECK

Copper **Obv:** Crowned monogram within wreath **Rev:** Value, date within crowned oval shield with supporters

Date	Mintage	VG	F	VF	XF	Unc
1764 Rare	—	—	—	—	—	—
1766 Rare	—	—	—	—	—	—
1767 Rare	—	—	—	—	—	—
1767KM	—	140	225	275	375	—
1768KM	—	30.00	45.00	70.00	125	—
1769KM	—	30.00	45.00	70.00	125	—
1770KM	—	30.00	45.00	70.00	125	—
1771KM	—	30.00	45.00	70.00	125	—
1772KM	—	30.00	45.00	70.00	125	—
1773KM	—	30.00	45.00	70.00	125	—
1774KM	—	30.00	45.00	70.00	125	—
1775KM	—	30.00	45.00	70.00	125	—
1776KM	—	30.00	45.00	70.00	125	—
1777KM	—	30.00	45.00	70.00	125	—
1778KM	—	30.00	45.00	70.00	125	—
1779KM	—	30.00	45.00	70.00	125	—

C# 4 2 KOPECKS

Copper **Obv:** Crowned monogram within wreath **Rev:** Value, date within crowned oval shield with supporters

Date	Mintage	VG	F	VF	XF	Unc
1764 Rare	—	—	—	—	—	—
1766 Rare	—	—	—	—	—	—
1767	—	85.00	140	200	300	—
1767KM	—	35.00	70.00	100	200	—
1768KM	—	30.00	45.00	70.00	140	—
1769KM	—	30.00	45.00	70.00	140	—
1770KM	—	30.00	45.00	70.00	140	—
1771KM	—	30.00	45.00	70.00	140	—
1772KM	—	30.00	45.00	70.00	140	—
1773KM	—	30.00	45.00	70.00	140	—
1774KM	—	30.00	45.00	70.00	140	—
1775KM	—	30.00	45.00	70.00	140	—
1776KM	—	30.00	45.00	70.00	140	—
1777KM	—	30.00	45.00	70.00	140	—
1778KM	—	30.00	45.00	70.00	140	—

Date	Mintage	VG	F	VF	XF	Unc
1779KM	—	35.00	65.00	90.00	165	—
1780KM	—	40.00	85.00	125	225	—

C# 5 5 KOPECKS

Copper **Obv:** Crowned monogram within wreath **Rev:** Value, date within crowned oval shield with supporters

Date	Mintage	VG	F	VF	XF	Unc
1763 Rare	—	—	—	—	—	—
1764 Rare	—	—	—	—	—	—
1766 Rare	—	—	—	—	—	—
1767 Rare	—	—	—	—	—	—
1767KM	—	100	150	200	350	—
1768KM	—	35.00	65.00	100	135	—
1769KM	—	35.00	65.00	100	135	—
1770KM	—	35.00	65.00	100	135	—
1771KM	—	35.00	65.00	100	135	—
1772KM	—	35.00	65.00	100	135	—
1773KM	—	35.00	65.00	100	135	—
1774KM	—	30.00	60.00	90.00	120	—
1775KM	—	30.00	60.00	90.00	120	—
1776KM	—	35.00	65.00	100	135	—
1777/6KM	—	40.00	70.00	110	145	—
1777KM	—	35.00	65.00	100	135	—
1778KM	—	35.00	65.00	100	135	—
1779KM	—	25.00	55.00	90.00	120	—
1780KM	—	90.00	125	175	250	—

C# 6 10 KOPECKS

Copper **Obv:** Crowned monogram within wreath **Rev:** Value, date within crowned oval shield with supporters

Date	Mintage	VG	F	VF	XF	Unc
1763 Rare	—	—	—	—	—	—
1764 Rare	—	—	—	—	—	—
1766	—	140	250	350	500	—
1767	—	80.00	125	200	300	—
1767KM	—	140	200	300	400	—
1768KM	—	55.00	80.00	140	200	—
1769KM	—	55.00	80.00	140	200	—
1770KM	—	55.00	80.00	140	200	—
1771KM	—	55.00	80.00	140	200	—
1772KM	—	55.00	80.00	140	200	—
1773KM	—	55.00	80.00	140	200	—
1774KM	—	55.00	80.00	140	200	—
1775KM	—	55.00	80.00	140	200	—
1776KM	—	55.00	80.00	140	200	—
1777KM	—	55.00	80.00	140	200	—
1778KM	—	55.00	80.00	140	200	—
1779KM	—	60.00	90.00	150	215	—
1780KM	—	65.00	110	175	245	—
1781KM	—	80.00	125	200	300	—

NOVODEL COINAGE

KM#	Date	Mintage	Identification	Mkt Val
N1	1763	—	10 Kopecks. Copper. Lettered edge.	—
N16	1764	—	10 Kopecks. Silver. Plain edge. EII monogram	—
N18	1764	—	10 Kopecks. Silver.	—
N19	1764	—	15 Kopeks. Silver. Plain edge.	—
N21	1764	—	15 Kopeks. Silver. Portrait.	—
N22	1764	—	20 Kopecks. Silver. Plain edge. EII monogram	—
N24	1764	—	20 Kopecks. Silver.	—
N2	1764	—	Polushka. Copper. C#1	700
N3	1764	—	Denga. Copper. C#2	500
N4	1764	—	Kopeck. Copper. C#3	550
N5	1764	—	Kopeck. Copper. Tread edge. C#4	550
N6	1764	—	2 Kopecks. Copper. C#4	600
N7	1764	—	2 Kopecks. Copper. Lettered edge. C#4	600
N8	1764	—	2 Kopecks. Copper. Tread edge. C#4	600

KM#	Date	Mintage	Identification	Mkt Val
N9	1764	—	5 Kopecks. Copper. C#5; large edge lettering	700
N10	1764	—	5 Kopecks. Copper. C#5; small edge lettering	700
N11	1764	—	5 Kopecks. Copper. C#5	700
N12	1764	—	10 Kopecks. Copper. C#6; large edge lettering	900
N13	1764	—	10 Kopecks. Copper. C#6; small edge lettering	900
N14	1764	—	10 Kopecks. Copper. C#6	900
N15	1764	—	10 Kopecks. Copper. Tread edge. C#6	900
N17	1764	—	10 Kopecks. Silver. EII monogram; oblique milling.	2,250
N20	1764	—	15 Kopeks. Silver. Oblique milling.	3,000
N23	1764	—	20 Kopecks. Silver. EII monogram; oblique milling.	3,520
N25	1766	—	Polushka. Copper. C#1.	450
N26	1766KM	—	Polushka. Copper. C#1.	400
N27	1766	—	Denga. Copper. C#2.	400
N28	1766KM	—	Denga. Copper. C#2.	350
N29	1766	—	Kopeck. Copper. C#3.	300
N30	1766KM	—	Kopeck. Copper. C#3.	250
N31	1766	—	2 Kopecks. Copper. Lettered edge. C#4.	350
N32	1766KM	—	2 Kopecks. Copper. C#4.	300
N33	1766	—	5 Kopecks. Copper. Lettered edge. C#5.	400
N34	1766KM	—	5 Kopecks. Copper. C#5.	350
N35	1766	—	10 Kopecks. Copper. Lettered edge. C#6.	550
N36	1766KM	—	10 Kopecks. Copper. C#6.	500
N37	1767KM	—	Polushka. Copper. C#1.	350
N38	1767KM	—	Denga. Copper. C#2.	350
N39	1767KM	—	Kopeck. Copper. C#3.	250
N40	1767KM	—	2 Kopecks. Copper. C#4.	550
N41	1767	—	5 Kopecks. Copper. C#5.	400
N42	1767KM	—	10 Kopecks. Copper. C#6.	500
N43	1768KM	—	Polushka. Copper. C#1.	350
N44	1768KM	—	Denga. Copper. C#2.	350
N45	1768KM	—	Kopeck. Copper. C#3.	250
N46	1768KM	—	2 Kopecks. Copper. C#4.	550
N47	1768KM	—	5 Kopecks. Copper. C#5.	400
N48	1768KM	—	10 Kopecks. Copper. C#6.	500
N49	1769KM	—	Polushka. Copper. C#1.	350
N50	1769KM	—	Denga. Copper. C#2.	350
N51	1769KM	—	Kopeck. Copper. C#3	250
N52	1769KM	—	5 Kopecks. Copper. C#5	550
N53	1769KM	—	10 Kopecks. Copper. C#6	500
N54	1770KM	—	Polushka. Copper. C#1	350
N55	1770KM	—	Denga. Copper. C#2	350
N56	1770KM	—	Kopeck. Copper. C#3	250
N57	1770KM	—	2 Kopecks. Copper. C#4	300
N58	1770KM	—	5 Kopecks. Copper. C#5	400
N59	1770KM	—	10 Kopecks. Copper. C#6	500
N60	1771KM	—	Polushka. Copper. C#1	350
N61	1771KM	—	Denga. Copper. C#2	350
N62	1771KM	—	Kopeck. Copper. C#3	250
N63	1771KM	—	2 Kopecks. Copper. C#4	300
N64	1771KM	—	5 Kopecks. Copper. C#5	400
N65	1771KM	—	10 Kopecks. Copper. C#6	500
N66	1772KM	—	Polushka. Copper. C#1	350
N67	1772KM	—	Denga. Copper. C#2	400
N68	1772KM	—	Kopeck. Copper. C#3	650
N69	1772KM	—	2 Kopecks. Copper. C#4	300
N70	1772KM	—	5 Kopecks. Copper. C#5	400
N71	1772KM	—	10 Kopecks. Copper. C#6	500
N72	1773KM	—	Polushka. Copper. C#1	350
N73	1773KM	—	Denga. Copper. C#2	350
N74	1773KM	—	Kopeck. Copper. C#3	250
N75	1773KM	—	2 Kopecks. Copper. C#4	300
N76	1773KM	—	5 Kopecks. Copper. C#5	550
N77	1773KM	—	10 Kopecks. Copper. C#6	500
N78	1774KM	—	Polushka. Copper. C#1	350
N79	1774KM	—	Denga. Copper. C#2	350
N80	1774KM	—	Kopeck. Copper. C#3	250
N81	1774KM	—	2 Kopecks. Copper. C#4	300
N82	1774KM	—	5 Kopecks. Copper. C#5	400
N83	1774KM	—	10 Kopecks. Copper. C#6	500
N84	1775KM	—	Polushka. Copper. C#1	350
N85	1775KM	—	Denga. Copper. C#2	350
N86	1775KM	—	Kopeck. Copper. C#3	250
N87	1775KM	—	2 Kopecks. Copper. C#4	300
N88	1775KM	—	5 Kopecks. Copper. C#5	400
N89	1775KM	—	10 Kopecks. Copper. C#6	500
N90	1776KM	—	Polushka. Copper. C#1	550
N91	1776KM	—	Denga. Copper. C#2	350
N92	1776KM	—	Kopeck. Copper. C#3	350
N93	1776KM	—	2 Kopecks. Copper. C#4	300
N94	1776KM	—	5 Kopecks. Copper. C#5	850
N95	1776KM	—	10 Kopecks. Copper. C#6	1,500
N96	1777KM	—	Polushka. Copper. C#1	350
N97	1777KM	—	Denga. Copper. C#2	350
N98	1777KM	—	Kopeck. Copper. C#3	250
N99	1777KM	—	2 Kopecks. Copper. C#4	350
N100	1777KM	—	5 Kopecks. Copper. C#5	400
N101	1777KM	—	10 Kopecks. Copper. C#6	500
N102	1778KM	—	Polushka. Copper. C#1	350
N103	1778KM	—	Denga. Copper. C#2	350
N104	1778KM	—	Kopeck. Copper. C#3	500
N105	1778KM	—	2 Kopecks. Copper. C#4	300
N106	1778KM	—	5 Kopecks. Copper. C#5	400
N107	1778KM	—	10 Kopecks. Copper. C#6	500
N108	1779KM	—	Polushka. Copper. C#1	350
N109	1779KM	—	Denga. Copper. C#2	350
N110	1779KM	—	Kopeck. Copper. C#3	250
N111	1779KM	—	2 Kopecks. Copper. C#4	450
N112	1779KM	—	5 Kopecks. Copper. C#5	400
N113	1779KM	—	10 Kopecks. Copper. C#6	500
N114	1780KM	—	Polushka. Copper. C#1	600
N115	1780KM	—	Denga. Copper. C#2	350
N116	1780KM	—	Kopeck. Copper. C#3	350
N117	1780KM	—	2 Kopecks. Copper. C#4	300
N118	1780KM	—	5 Kopecks. Copper. C#5	500
N119	1780KM	—	10 Kopecks. Copper. C#6	850

SAINT EUSTATIUS

St. Eustatius (*Sint Eustatius, Statia*), a Netherlands West Indian island located in the Leeward Islands of the Lesser Antilles nine miles northwest of St. Kitts, has an area of 12 sq. mi. (21 sq. km.) and a population of about 2,000. It is part of the Netherlands Antilles. The island's capital is Oranjestad. The chief industries are farming, fishing, and tourism.

Between 1630 and 1640 the Dutch seized Curacao, Saba, St. Martin and St. Eustatius, all valuable as piloting and smuggling depots. The territorial acquisitions were confirmed to the Dutch by the Treaty of Munster in 1648. Under the guidance of merchants from Flushing, St. Eustatius became a prosperous entry port of neutral trade. On Feb. 3, 1781, British Admiral George Rodney, acting under orders, captured the island and confiscated much valuable booty. Before passing permanently into Dutch hands, St. Eustatius was attacked or captured several times by the French and English, and was in English hands during the Napoleonic Wars from 1810 to 1814.

RULER

Dutch

MONETARY SYSTEM

6 Stuivers = 1 Reaal

BRITISH OCCUPATION

COUNTERMARKED COINAGE

SE incuse countermark on French Guiana 2 Sous coins was official.

These were followed by raised SE countermarks (on a variety of worn billon and silver coins) generally thought to be forgeries.

From 1809 all coins had to be revalidated with a P countermark, which stood for Pierre dit Flamand, the artisan who designed the mark. Both raised and incuse SE varieties as well as unmarked coins were revalidated.

KM# 1.1 STUIVER

Billon **Countermark:** SE **Note:** Incuse countermark on French Guiana 2 Sous, C#1.

CM Date	Host Date	Good	VG	F	VF	XF
ND	ND(1797)	30.00	50.00	85.00	140	180

SAINT HELENA

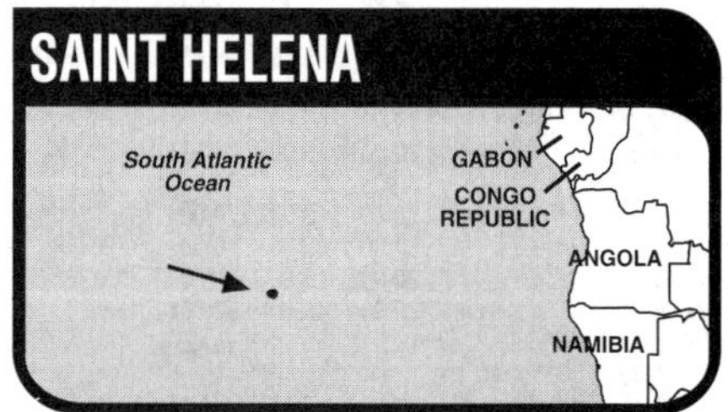

Saint Helena, a British colony located about 1,150 miles (1,850 km.) from the west coast of Africa, has an area of 47 sq. mi. (410 sq. km.) and a population of *7,000. Capital: Jamestown. Flax, lace, and rope are produced for export. Ascension and Tristan da Cunha are dependencies of Saint Helena.

The island was discovered and named by the Portuguese navigator Joao de Nova Castella in 1502. The Portuguese imported livestock, fruit trees, and vegetables but established no permanent settlement. The Dutch occupied the island temporarily, 1645-51. The original European settlement was founded by representatives of the British East India Company sent to annex the island after the departure of the Dutch. The Dutch returned and captured Saint Helena from the British on New Year's Day, 1673, but were in turn ejected by a British force under Sir Richard Munden. Thereafter Saint Helena was the undisputed possession of Great Britain. The island served as the place of exile for Napoleon, several Zulu chiefs, and an ex-sultan of Zanzibar.

RULER

British

MINT MARK

PM - Pobjoy Mint

MONETARY SYSTEM

12 Pence = 1 Shilling
100 Pence = 1 Pound

BRITISH EAST INDIA COMPANY

HAMMERED COINAGE

KM# 1 FARTHING

Copper **Obv:** Rampant lion **Rev:** UIECo. Bale mark, date above

Date	Mintage	Good	VG	F	VF	XF
1714	—	275	450	750	1,200	—

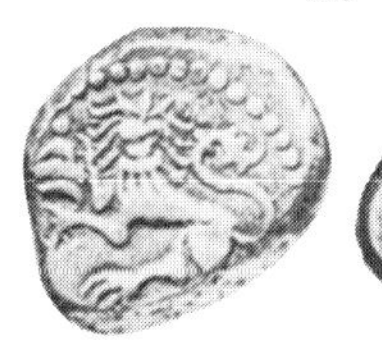

KM# 2 HALFPENNY

Copper **Obv:** Rampant lion, left **Rev:** UEICo. Bale mark, date above

Date	Mintage	Good	VG	F	VF	XF
1714	—	240	400	650	1,000	—

KM# 3 3 PENCE

Silver **Obv:** Rampant lion, left **Rev:** UEICo. Bale mark, date above

Date	Mintage	Good	VG	F	VF	XF
1714	—	—	—	1,500	2,000	—

SAINT LUCIA

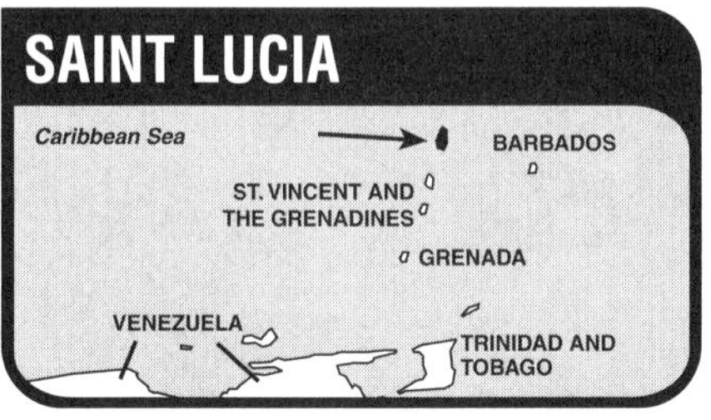

Saint Lucia, an independent island nation located in the Windward Islands of the West Indies between Saint Vincent and Martinique, has an area of 238 sq. mi. (620 sq. km.) and a population of *150,000. Capital: Castries. The economy is agricultural. Bananas, copra, cocoa, sugar and logwood are exported.

Columbus discovered Saint Lucia in 1502. The first attempts at settlement undertaken by the British in 1605 and 1638 were frustrated by sickness and the determined hostility of the fierce Carib inhabitants. The French settled it in 1650 and made a treaty with the natives. Until 1814, when the island became a definite British possession, it was the scene of a continuous conflict between the British and French, which saw the island change, hands on at least 14 occasions. In 1967, under the West Indies Act, Saint Lucia was established as a British associated state, self-governing in internal affairs. Complete independence was attained on February 22, 1979. Saint Lucia is a member of the Commonwealth of Nations. Elizabeth II is Head of State as Queen of Saint Lucia.

Prior to 1950, the island used sterling, which was superseded by the currency of the British Caribbean Territories (Eastern Group) and the East Caribbean State.

RULER
British

MONETARY SYSTEM
100 Cents = 1 Dollar

FRENCH COLONY

COUNTERMARKED COINAGE

1798

KM# 1 2 ESCALINS

Silver **Note:** Countermark SL monogram on 1/6 cut of Spanish or Spanish Colonial 8 Reales.

CM Date	Host Date	Good	VG	F	VF	XF
ND(1798)	— Rare	—	—	—	—	—

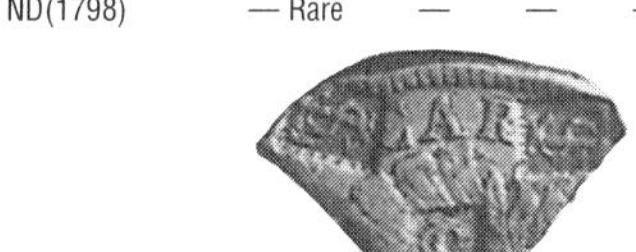

KM# 2 3 ESCALINS

6.4000 g., Silver **Note:** Countermark: 3 SL monogram on 1/4 cut of Spanish or Spanish Colonial 8 Reales.

CM Date	Host Date	Good	VG	F	VF	XF
ND(1798)	—	175	300	450	650	—

KM# 3 4 ESCALINS

Silver **Note:** Countermark: 3 SL monogram on 1/3 cut of Spanish or Spanish Colonial 8 Reales.

CM Date	Host Date	Good	VG	F	VF	XF
ND(1798)	— Rare	—	—	—	—	—

KM# 4 6 ESCALINS

Silver **Note:** Countermark: 2 SL monogram on 1/2 cut of Spanish or Spanish Colonial 8 Reales.

CM Date	Host Date	Good	VG	F	VF	XF
ND(1798)	—	325	550	850	1250	—

SAINT MARTIN

St. Martin (*Sint Maarten*), the only island in the Antilles owned by two European powers (France and the Netherlands), is located in the Leeward Islands of the Lesser Antilles five miles south of the British island of Anguilla. The French northern section of the island (St.Martin) is a dependency of the French Department of Guadeloupe. It has an area of 20 sq. mi. (51 sq. km.) and a population of about 4,500. Capital: Le Marigot. The Dutch southern section of the island (Sint Maarten) has an area of 17 sq. mi. (34 sq. km.) and a population of about 8,000.Capital: Philipsburg. The chief industries are farming, fishing, and tourism. Salt, horses, and mules are exported.

Although nominally a Spanish possession at the time, St. Martin was occupied by French freebooters in 1638, but when Spain relinquished claim to the island in 1648 it was peaceably divided between France and Holland in recognition of the merchant communities already established on the island by nationals of both powers. St. Martin has remained under dual French-Dutch ownership to the present time, except for a period during the Napoleonic Wars when the British seized and occupied it.

The northern section of the island uses the coins and currency of France.

MONETARY SYSTEM
6 Stuivers = 1 Reaal
20 Stuivers = 1 Gulden
12 (later 15) Reaals = 1 Peso

COLONY

COUNTERMARKED COINAGE

KM# 2 2 STUIVERS

Silver **Countermark:** StM **Note:** Countermark in beaded circle on Danish 2 Skilling.

CM Date	Host Date	Good	VG	F	VF	XF
ND	ND(1798)	200	350	500	800	—

KM# 1 2 STUIVERS

Billon **Countermark:** StM - Colony of Cayenne **Note:** Countermark in beaded circle on French Guiana 2 Sous, KM#1.

CM Date	Host Date	Good	VG	F	VF	XF
ND(1798)	1780-90	75.00	125	200	300	600

KM# 13 6 STUIVERS

Silver **Countermark:** Bundle of arrows **Note:** Countermark on Netherlands-Utrecht 6 Stuivers, KM#60.3.

CM Date	Host Date	Good	VG	F	VF	XF
ND(1797)	ND(1679-91)	—	—	—	—	—

KM# 10 18 STUIVERS

Silver **Countermark:** CC **Note:** Countermark on obverse and 18 on edge of 1/4 cut of Spanish or Spanish Colonial 8 Reales.

CM Date	Host Date	Good	VG	F	VF	XF
ND	ND(1787) Rare	—	—	—	—	—

KM# 11.2 18 STUIVERS

Silver **Countermark:** Bundle of arrows **Note:** Countermark and bundle of arrows on 1/4 cut of Spanish or Spanish Colonial 8 Reales.

CM Date	Host Date	Good	VG	F	VF	XF
ND	ND(1797) Rare	—	—	—	—	—

KM# 11.1 18 STUIVERS

Silver **Countermark:** CC **Note:** Countermark and bundle of arrows on obverse and 18 on edge of 1/4 cut of Spanish or Spanish Colonial 8 Reales.

CM Date	Host Date	Good	VG	F	VF	XF
ND	ND(1797)	1,500	2,500	3,500	4,750	—

SAINT VINCENT

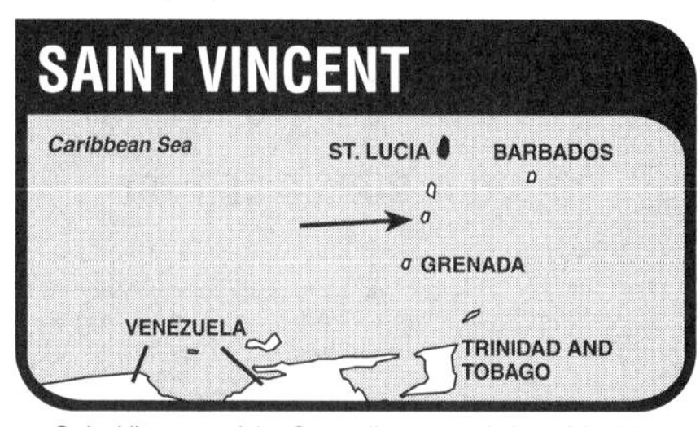

Saint Vincent and the Grenadines, consisting of the island of Saint Vincent and the northern Grenadines (a string of islets stretching southward from Saint Vincent), is located in the Windward Islands of the West Indies, West of Barbados and south of Saint Lucia. The tiny nation has an area of 150sq. mi. (340 sq. km.) and a population of *105,000.Capital: Kingstown. Arrowroot, cotton, sugar, molasses, rum and cocoa are exported. Tourism is a principal industry.

Saint Vincent was discovered by Columbus on Jan. 22,1498, but was left undisturbed for more than a century. The British began colonization early in the 18th century against bitter and prolonged Carib resistance. The island was taken by the French in 1779, but was restored to the British in 1783, at the end of the American Revolution. Saint Vincent and the northern Grenadines became a British associated state in Oct. 1969. Independence under the name of Saint Vincent and the Grenadines was attained at midnight of Oct. 26, 1979. The new nation chose to become a member of the Commonwealth of Nations with Elizabeth II as Head of State and Queen of Saint Vincent.

A local coinage was introduced in 1797, with the gold withdrawn in 1818 and the silver in 1823. This was replaced by sterling. From the mid-1950's, Saint Vincent used the currency of the British Caribbean Territories (Eastern Group), than that of the East Caribbean States.

RULER
British

MONETARY SYSTEM
6 Black Dogs = 4 Stampees = 1 Bit = 9 Pence
1797-1811
8 Shillings, 3 Pence = 11 Bits = 1 Dollar

BRITISH COLONY

COUNTERMARKED COINAGE

(1797-1818)

KM# 1 BLACK DOG

Billon **Countermark:** SV monogram **Note:** Countermark on French colonial coin.

CM Date	Host Date	Good	VG	F	VF	XF
ND(1797)	ND(1797-1818) Rare	—	—	—	—	—

KM# 2 STAMPEE

Billon **Countermark:** SV monogram **Note:** Countermark on French Colonial coin bearing a crowned C.

CM Date	Host Date	Good	VG	F	VF	XF
ND(1797)	ND(1797-1818) Rare	—	—	—	—	—

KM# 3 1/4 DOLLAR

Silver **Countermark:** SV monogram **Note:** Countermark on 1/4-cut Spanish or Spanish Colonial 8 Reales.

CM Date	Host Date	Good	VG	F	VF	XF
ND(1797)	ND(1797-1818)	200	325	550	800	—

KM# 4.1 1/2 DOLLAR

9.4000 g., Silver **Countermark:** SV monogram **Note:** Countermark on 1/3-cut Spanish or Spanish Colonial 8 Reales.

CM Date	Host Date	Good	VG	F	VF	XF
ND(1797)	ND(1797-1818)	225	425	700	1,000	—

KM# 4.2 1/2 DOLLAR
10.2500 g., Silver **Countermark:** SV monogram **Note:** Similar to KM#4.1 with plug added to adjust to correct weight.

CM Date	Host Date	Good	VG	F	VF	XF
ND(1797)	ND(1797-1818)	275	500	850	1,250	—

COUNTERMARKED COINAGE

Gold (1798-1818)

The countermarking of various gold coins in circulation on Saint Vincent was authorized by an Act of August 1, 1798. Standard weight for a gold Joe was set at 11.66 grams with a denomination of 66 Shillings. Full weight gold was marked 3 times with the letter S. Underweight gold could be brought up to proper weight by plugging and marking the plug with a letter S, under the guidance of at least 1 council member and 2 assemblymen.

Ongoing concerns and practical implementation made this act subject to review and in all likelihood alterations were made resulting in the various plugged and full weight examples listed below. All countermarked Joes were recalled in 1818.

KM# 5.1 66 SHILLINGS
Gold **Countermark:** Obverse: S (three times); Reverse: IS **Note:** Weight varies: 11.50-11.66g. Countermark on the plug of a false Brazil 6400 Reis, KM#172.2

CM Date	Host Date	Good	VG	F	VF	XF
ND	1773 Rare	—	—	—	—	—

KM# 5.2 66 SHILLINGS
Gold **Countermark:** Obverse: S (three times); Reverse: IS **Note:** Weight varies: 11.50-11.66g. Countermark on the plug of a false Brazil 6400 Reis, KM#199.2

CM Date	Host Date	Good	VG	F	VF	XF
ND	178x Rare	—	—	—	—	—

KM# 6 66 SHILLINGS
Gold **Countermark:** S (three times) and GH **Note:** Weight varies: 11.50-11.66g. Countermark on the plug of a false Brazil 6400 Reis, KM#172.2

CM Date	Host Date	Good	VG	F	VF	XF
ND	1767 Rare	—	—	—	—	—

KM# 17 66 SHILLINGS
Gold **Countermark:** S (three times) **Note:** Weight varies: 11.50-11.66g. Countermark on Brazil 6400 Reis, KM#149.

CM Date	Host Date	Good	VG	F	VF	XF
ND	17x8	1,500	2,500	4,000	6,000	—

KM# 18 66 SHILLINGS
Gold **Countermark:** S (three times) **Note:** Weight varies: 11.50-11.66g. Countermark on Brazil 6400 Reis, KM#199.2.

CM Date	Host Date	Good	VG	F	VF	XF
ND	1786	1,500	2,500	4,000	6,000	—

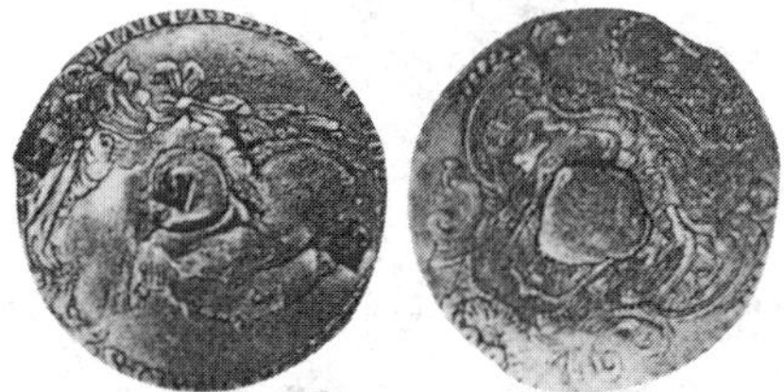

KM# 19 66 SHILLINGS
Gold **Countermark:** S (three times) **Note:** Weight varies: 11.50-11.66g. Countermark on plugged Brazil 6400 Reis, KM#199.2.

CM Date	Host Date	Good	VG	F	VF	XF
ND	1779	2,000	3,000	5,000	7,000	—

KM# 16 6 POUNDS 12 SHILLING
23.4000 g., Gold **Countermark:** S (three times) **Note:** Countermark on Brazil 12,800 Reis, KM#150.

CM Date	Host Date	Good	VG	F	VF	XF
ND(1798-1818)	1732 Rare	—	—	—	—	—

Note: Glendining's Ford sale 9-89 VF realized $12,800

SAUDI ARABIA

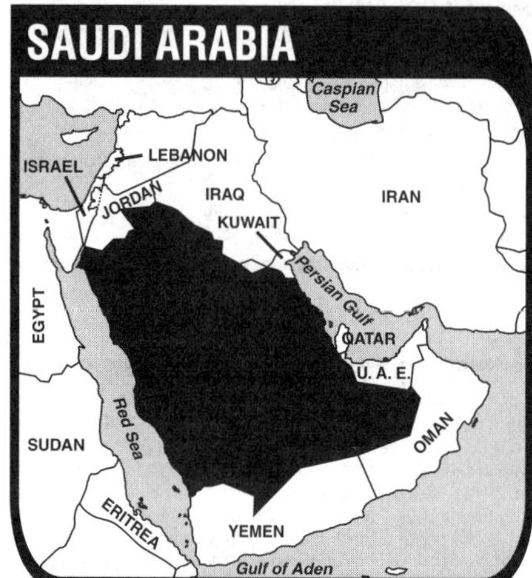

HEJAZ & NEJD

Mecca, the metropolis of Islam and the capital of Hejaz, is located inland from the Red Sea due east of the port of Jidda. A center of non-political commercial, cultural and religious activities, Mecca remained virtually independent until 1259. Two centuries of Egyptian rule were followed by four centuries of Turkish rule which lasted until the Arab revolts which extinguished pretensions to sovereignty over any part of the Arabian peninsula.

MINT NAME
Makkah, Mecca

RULERS
Sharifs of Mecca
Ghalib b. Ma'sud, AH1219-1229
Yahya b. Surer, AH1230-1240
Abdul Muttalib and Ibn Awn, AH1240-1248

SHARIFS OF MECCA

ANONYMOUS HAMMERED COINAGE

Wahhabi Issues

KM# B5 MAHMUDI
Billon **Obv:** Date with Sanat below **Rev:** Mecca duribaf

Date	Mintage	Good	VG	F	VF	XF
AH1215 One known	—	—	—	—	—	—

Note: From the British Museum collection

KM# 3 UNIT
Silver **Rev:** Mintname: MECCA **Note:** Previous KM#6 under "Saudi Arabia - Mecca".

Date	Mintage	Good	VG	F	VF	XF
AH1215 Rare	—	—	—	—	—	—

SCOTLAND

Scotland is located on the northern part of the island of Great Britain. It has an area of 30,414 square miles (78,772 sq. km.) and population of 5.2 million. Capital: Edinburgh. Cereal grains and potatoes are the principal farm products. Production of textiles, electrical instruments, spirits; shipbuilding and tourism are also important sources of income.

Scotland was the traditional home of the Picts in ancient times. The Romans invaded the area after 80 A.D. and Hadrian's Wall was built from 122-126 A.D. to keep the Picts from the Roman settlements to the south. In the 5th century Scotland had 4 kingdoms: Northumbria (Anglo-Saxon), Picts, Scots (of Irish extraction) and Strathclyde. St. Columba converted the Picts to Christianity in the late 6th century. Norse invasions started in the late 8th century. The Picts conquered the Scots in the 9th century and under Malcolm II (1005-1034) the Scottish kingdoms were united. The Scottish King became a vassal of the English king in 1174 (a circumstance that was to lead to many disputes). The Scots gained independence in 1314 at Bannockburn under Robert Bruce. From 1371-1714 it was ruled by the Stuarts, and in 1603 when James VI of Scotland succeeded Elizabeth I as James I, King of England, a personal union of the two kingdoms was formed. Parliamentary Act in 1707 made final union of the two kingdoms. In 1999 the Scottish Parliament was re-formed to make local decisions.

RULERS
William II (III), 1694-1702
Anne, 1702-1707 (1714)
George III, 1760-1820

NOTE: For post Union silver coinage of Anne struck with an "E" under the bust and dated 1707-1709, please refer to Great Britain listings.

KINGDOM

COUNTERMARKED COINAGE

Commercial

Private issue silver tokens appeared from 1811-12. For various reasons, the Spanish "dollars" themselves were preferred in Scotland where they circulated bearing a countermark of the merchant or company responsible for its issue. Sometimes other foreign crown-sized pieces were similarly countermarked. Many pieces are found with a grill-like cancellation over the countermark and have a considerably lower market value.

Mint: Hurlet, Renfrewshire
KM# CCA64 5 SHILLINGS
Silver **Issuer:** Hurlet, Renfrewshire **Countermark:** J. WILSON & SONS HURLET **Note:** Countermark around 5/.

CM Date	Host Date	Good	VG	F	VF	XF
ND	ND Rare	—	—	—	—	—

William II (III)

MILLED COINAGE

KM# 145 1/2 PISTOLE
3.4400 g., 0.9160 Gold 0.1013 oz. AGW **Obv:** Bust left **Obv. Legend:** GVLIEMVS • DEI • GRATIA **Rev:** Crowned arms **Note:** S#5677. Struck from gold imported from Africa by the Darien Co. The sun rising from the sea below bust is the company badge.

Date	Mintage	Good	VG	F	VF	XF
1701	—	1,850	3,250	6,500	12,500	—

KM# 146 PISTOLE
6.8700 g., 0.9160 Gold 0.2023 oz. AGW **Obv:** Bust left. **Obv. Legend:** GVLIELMVS • DEI • GRATIA **Rev:** Crowned arms **Note:** S#5676. Struck from gold imported from Africa by the Darien Co. The sun rising from the sea below bust is the company badge.

Date	Mintage	Good	VG	F	VF	XF
1701	—	1,650	2,750	5,500	11,000	20,000

STERLING COINAGE

KM# 147 5 SHILLINGS
Silver **Obv. Legend:** GVLIELMVS DEI GRATIA

Date	Mintage	VG	F	VF	XF	Unc
1702	—	35.00	75.00	350	900	—

KM# 140 5 SHILLINGS
Silver, 19 mm. **Obv:** Laureate bust left, value below **Rev:** Crown above 3 thistles, date in legend at upper left **Note:** Varieties exist.

Date	Mintage	VG	F	VF	XF	Unc
1701	—	40.00	100	325	1,000	—

Anne

STERLING COINAGE

Mint: Without Mint Name
KM# 148 5 SHILLINGS
Silver **Obv:** Bust left, value below **Rev:** Flower **Note:** Varieties exist.

Date	Mintage	VG	F	VF	XF	Unc
1705/4	—	35.00	100	300	900	—
1705	—	20.00	50.00	125	300	—
1706	—	35.00	60.00	175	400	—

Mint: Without Mint Name
KM# 149 10 SHILLINGS
Silver **Obv:** Draped bust left, value below **Rev:** Crowned arms, date in legend at upper left

Date	Mintage	VG	F	VF	XF	Unc
1705	—	35.00	75.00	225	500	—
1706	—	50.00	100	250	700	—

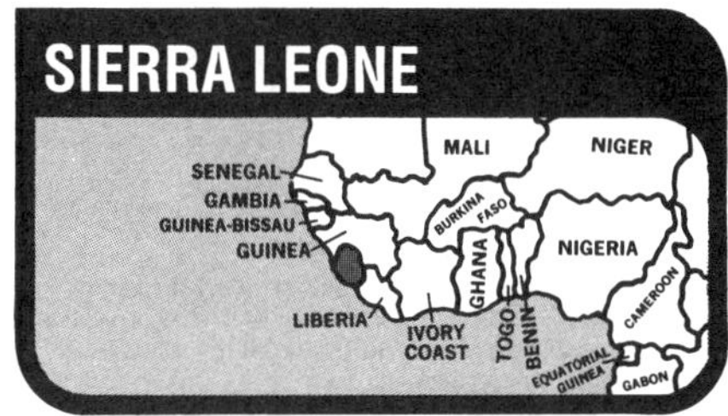

The Republic of Sierra Leone, a British Commonwealth nation located in western Africa between Guinea and Liberia, has an area of 27,699 sq. mi. (71,740 sq. km.) and a population of *4.1 million. Capital: Freetown. The economy is predominantly agricultural but mining contributes significantly to export revenues. Diamonds, iron ore, palm kernels, cocoa, and coffee are exported.

The coast of Sierra Leone was first visited by Portuguese and British slavers in the 15th and 16th centuries. The first settlement, at Freetown, 1787, was established as a refuge for freed slaves within the British Empire, runaway slaves from the United States and Negroes discharged from the British armed forces. The first settlers were virtually wiped out by tribal attacks and disease. The colony was re-established under the auspices of the Sierra Leone Company and transferred to the British Crown in 1807. The interior region was secured and established as a protectorate in 1896. Sierra Leone became independent within the Commonwealth on April 27, 1961, and adopted a republican constitution ten years later. It is a member of the Commonwealth of Nations. The president is Chief of State and Head of Government.

For similar coinage refer to British West Africa.

RULER

British, until 1971

MONETARY SYSTEM

Until 1906

100 Cents = 50 Pence = 1 Dollar

BRITISH COLONY

Sierra Leone Company

STANDARD COINAGE

KM# 2.1 PENNY

Bronze, 32 mm. **Obv:** Lion, Africa below **Obv. Legend:** SIERRA LEONE COMPANY **Rev:** Clasped hands flanked by value, date below, written value as legend

Date	Mintage	F	VF	XF	Unc	BU
1791	215,000	100	200	400	600	1,000
1791 Proof	—	Value: 1,000				

KM# 2.2 PENNY

Bronze, 30 mm. **Obv:** Lion, Africa below **Obv. Legend:** SIERRA LEONE COMPANY **Rev:** Clasped hands flanked by value, date below, written value as legend

Date	Mintage	F	VF	XF	Unc	BU
1791 Proof	—	Value: 600				

KM# 2.1a PENNY

Gilt Bronze **Obv:** Lion, Africa below **Obv. Legend:** SIERRA LEONE COMPANY **Rev:** Clasped hands flanked by value, date below, written value as legend

Date	Mintage	F	VF	XF	Unc	BU
1791 Proof	—	Value: 600				

KM# 1 CENT

Bronze **Obv:** Lion, Africa. below **Obv. Legend:** SIERRA LEONE COMPANY **Rev:** Clasped hands, flanked by value, date below, written value as legend

Date	Mintage	F	VF	XF	Unc	BU
1791	500,000	150	350	650	1,500	—
1791 Proof	400	Value: 600				
1796	50,000	35.00	120	350	750	—

KM# 1a CENT

Gilt Bronze **Obv:** Lion, Africa. below **Obv. Legend:** SIERRA LEONE COMPANY **Rev:** Clasped hands flanked by value, date below, written value as legend

Date	Mintage	F	VF	XF	Unc	BU
1791 Proof	—	Value: 650				

KM# 3 10 CENTS

0.9020 Silver **Obv:** Lion, Africa below **Obv. Legend:** SIERRA LEONE COMPANY **Rev:** Clasped hands flanked by value, date below, written value as legend

Date	Mintage	F	VF	XF	Unc	BU
1791	4,200	50.00	125	375	1,000	—
1791 Proof	109	Value: 2,000				
1796	9,227	45.00	125	600	1,100	—
1796 Proof	—	Value: 600				

KM# 3a 10 CENTS

Copper **Obv:** Lion, Africa below **Obv. Legend:** SIERRA LEONE COMPANY **Rev:** Clasped hands, flanked by value, date below, written value as legend

Date	Mintage	F	VF	XF	Unc	BU
1791 Proof	—	Value: 1,200				
1796 Proof, 1 known	—	Value: 750				

KM# 3b 10 CENTS

Gilt Copper **Obv:** Lion, Africa below **Obv. Legend:** SIERRA LEONE COMPANY **Rev:** Clasped hands, flanked by value, date below, written value as legend

Date	Mintage	F	VF	XF	Unc	BU
1791 Proof	—	Value: 1,500				
1796 Proof	—	Value: 1,500				

KM# 4 20 CENTS

0.9020 Silver **Obv:** Lion, Africa below **Obv. Legend:** SIERRA LEONE COMPANY **Rev:** Clasped hands flanked by value, date below, written value as legend

Date	Mintage	F	VF	XF	Unc	BU
1791	5,200	75.00	1,225	1,325	1,500	—
1791 Proof	84	Value: 6,000				

KM# 4a 20 CENTS

Copper **Obv:** Lion, Africa below **Obv. Legend:** SIERRA LEONE COMPANY **Rev:** Clasped hands flanked by value, date below, written value as legend

Date	Mintage	F	VF	XF	Unc	BU
1791 Proof	—	Value: 1,500				

KM# 4b 20 CENTS

Gilt Copper **Obv:** Lion, Africa below **Obv. Legend:** SIERRA LEONE COMPANY **Rev:** Clasped hands flanked by value, date below, written value as legend

Date	Mintage	F	VF	XF	Unc	BU
1791 Proof	—	Value: 4,000				

KM# 5 50 CENTS

0.9020 Silver **Obv:** Lion, Africa below **Obv. Legend:** SIERRA LEONE COMPANY **Rev:** Clasped hands flanked by value, date below, written value as legend

Date	Mintage	F	VF	XF	Unc	BU
1791	4,622	275	1,350	1,750	3,000	—
1791 Proof	54	Value: 6,500				

KM# 5a 50 CENTS

Copper **Obv:** Lion, Africa below **Obv. Legend:** SIERRA LEONE COMPANY **Rev:** Clasped hands flanked by value, date below, written value as legend

Date	Mintage	F	VF	XF	Unc	BU
1791 Proof	—	Value: 500				

KM# 5b 50 CENTS

Gilt Copper **Obv:** Lion, Africa below **Obv. Legend:** SIERRA LEONE COMPANY **Rev:** Clasped hands flanked by value, date below, written value as legend

Date	Mintage	F	VF	XF	Unc	BU
1791 Proof	—	Value: 950				

DOLLAR DENOMINATED COINAGE

KM# 6 DOLLAR

0.9020 Silver **Obv:** Lion, Africa below **Obv. Legend:** SIERRA LEONE COMPANY **Rev:** Clasped hands flanked by value, date below, written value as legend

Date	Mintage	F	VF	XF	Unc	BU
1791	6,560	400	1,000	2,200	4,500	—
1791 Proof	40	Value: 10,000				

KM# 6a DOLLAR

Copper **Obv:** Lion, Africa below **Obv. Legend:** SIERRA LEONE COMPANY **Rev:** Clasped hands flanked by value, date below, written value as legend

Date	Mintage	F	VF	XF	Unc	BU
1791 Proof	—	Value: 1,500				

KM# 6b DOLLAR

Gilt Copper **Obv:** Lion, Africa below **Obv. Legend:** SIERRA LEONE COMPANY **Rev:** Clasped hands flanked by value, date below, written value as legend

Date	Mintage	F	VF	XF	Unc	BU
1791 Proof	—	Value: 3,500				

KM# 7 DOLLAR

0.9020 Silver **Obv:** Lion, Africa below **Obv. Legend:** SIERRA LEONE COMPANY **Rev:** Clasped hands flanked by value, date below, written value as legend

Date	Mintage	F	VF	XF	Unc	BU
1791	800	650	1,500	3,500	5,500	—
1791 Proof	5	—	—	—	—	—

KM# 7a DOLLAR

Copper **Obv:** Lion, Africa below **Obv. Legend:** SIERRA LEONE COMPANY **Rev:** Clasped hands flanked by value, date below, written value as legend

Date	Mintage	F	VF	XF	Unc	BU
1791 Proof	—	—	—	—	—	—

KM# 7b DOLLAR

Gilt Copper **Obv:** Lion, Africa below **Obv. Legend:** SIERRA LEONE COMPANY **Rev:** Clasped hands flanked by value, date below, written value as legend

Date	Mintage	F	VF	XF	Unc	BU
1791 Proof	—	Value: 4,000				

The Spanish State, forming the greater part of the Iberian Peninsula of southwest Europe, has an area of 195,988 sq. mi. (504,714 sq. km.) and a population of 39.4 million including the Balearic and the Canary Islands. Capital: Madrid. The economy is based on agriculture, industry and tourism. Machinery, fruit, vegetables and chemicals are exported.

It isn't known when man first came to the Iberian Peninsula - the Altamira caves off the Cantabrian coast approximately 50 miles west of Santander were fashioned in Paleolithic times. Spain was a battleground for centuries before it became a united nation, fought for by Phoenicians, Carthaginians, Greeks, Celts, Romans, Vandals, Visigoths and Moors. Ferdinand and Isabella destroyed the last Moorish stronghold in 1492, freeing the national energy and resources for the era of discovery and colonization that would make Spain the most powerful country in Europe during the 16th century. After the destruction of the Spanish Armada, 1588, Spain never again played a major role in European politics. Forcing Ferdinand to give up his throne and placing him under military guard at Valencay in 1808, Napoleonic France ruled Spain until 1814. When the monarchy was restored in 1814 it continued, only interrupted by the short-lived republic of 1873-74, until the exile of Alfonso XIII in 1931 when the Second Republic was established.

Discontent against the mother country increased after 1808 as colonists faced new imperialist policies from Napoleon or Spanish liberals. The revolutionary movement was established which resulted in the eventual independence of the Vice-royalties of New Spain, New Granada and Rio de la Plata within 2 decades.

The doomed republic was trapped in a tug-of-war between the right and left wing forces inevitably resulting in the Spanish Civil War of 1936-38. The leftist Republicans were supported by the U.S.S.R. and the International Brigade, which consisted of mainly communist volunteers from all over the western world. The right wing Nationalists were supported by the Fascist governments of Italy and Germany. Under the leadership of Gen. Francisco Franco, the Nationalists emerged victorious and immediately embarked on a program of reconstruction and neutrality as dictated by the new "Caudillo"(leader) Franco.

The monarchy was reconstituted in 1947 under the regency of General Francisco Franco; the king designate to be crowned after Franco's death. Franco died on Nov.20, 1975. Two days after his passing, Juan Carlos de Borbon, the grandson of Alfonso XIII, was proclaimed King of Spain.

RULERS

Philip V, 1700-1746
Luis I, 1724
Fernando VI, 1746-59
Carlos III, 1759-88
Carlos IV, 1788-1808

HOMELAND MINT MARKS

Until 1851

B – Burgos
C, CA – Cuenca
M, crowned M, Ligate MD – Madrid
S, SL – Seville
Aqueduct – Segovia
V, VA, VAL - Valencia

COLONIAL MINT MARKS

Many Spanish Colonial mints struck coins similar to regular Spanish issues until the 1820's. These issues are easily distinguished from regular Spanish issues by the following mint marks.

C, CH, Ch – Chihuahua, Mexico
Co – Cuzco, Peru
D, DO, Do – Durango, Mexico
Ga – Guadalajara, Mexico
G, GG – Guatemala
G, Go – Guanajuato, Mexico
L, LIMAE, LIMA – Lima, Peru
M, MA – Manila, Philippines
M, Mo – Mexico City, Mexico
NG – Nueva Grenada, Guatemala
NR – Nueva Reino, Colombia
PDV – Valladolid Michoacan, Mexico
P, PN, Pn – Popayan, Colombia
P, POTOSI – Potosi, Bolivia
So – Santiago, Chile
Z, Zs – Zacatecas, Mexico

MINT OFFICIALS' INITIALS

Burgos Mint

Initials	Date	Name
A	1701	

Cuenca Mint

Initials	Date	Name
JJ	1725	Juan Jose Garcia Caballero

Madrid Mint

Initials	Date	Name
AJ	1744-47	Antonio Cardena and Jose Tramullas y Ferrer
DV	1784-88	Domingo Antonio Lopez and Vicente Campos Gonzalez
F	1731-32	Fernando Vazquez
FA	1799-1808	Francisco Herrera and Antonio Goicoechea
J	1706-16	Jose Caballero
J	1747, 1759	Jose Tramullas y Ferrer
JA	1742-44	J.J. Garcia Caballero and Antonio de Cardena
JB	1747-56	Jose Tramullas y Ferrer and Bernardo Munoz de Amador
JB	1756-59	Jose Tramullas y Ferrer and Domingo Bayon
JD	1782-85	Juan Bautista Sanfaury and Domingo Antonio Lopez
JF	1730-41	J.J. Garcia Caballero and Fernando Vazquez
JJ	1728-29	Juan Jose Garcia Caballero`
JP	1759-64	Juan Rodriguez Gutierrez and Pedro Cano
M	1788	Manuel de Lamas
MF	1788-1802	Manuel de Lamas and Francisco Herrera
PJ	1765-82	Pedro Cano and Juan Bautista Sanfaury
Y	1706	Ysidoro de Parraga

Segovia Mint

Initials	Date	Name
F	1721-24, 1728-29	Fernando Vazquez and Fernando Vargas
J	1717	Jose (Garcia) Caballero
Y	1708	Ysidoro de Parraga

Seville Mint

Initials	Date	Name
AP	1735-36	Antonio Montero and Pedro Remigio Gordillo
C	1784-86, 1788	Carlos Jimenez Almaraz
C	1790-91, 1801-08	Carlos Tiburcio de Roxas
CF	1767-83	Carlos Jimenez Almaraz and Francisco Lopez Amisa
CM	1787	Carlos Jimenez Almaraz and Manuel de Lamas
CN	1791-1810, 1812	Carlos Tiburcio de Roxas and Nicolas Lamas
J	1702-03	
J	1719-23, 1725-27	Juan Jose Garcia Caballero
JP	1742	Jose Antonio Fabra and Pedro Remigio Gordillo
JV	1757-62	Jose de Villaviciosa and Vicente Diez de la Fuente
M	1686-1703, 1707-19	
P	1704-06	
P	1728-29	Pedro Remigio Gordillo
PA	1731-36	Pedro Remigio Gordillo and Antonio Montero
PF	1737-40, 1742-50	Pedro Remigio Gordillo and Jose Antonio Fabra
PJ	1751-57	Pedro Remigio Gordillo and Jose de Villaviciosa
V	1784	Vicente Delgado Meneses
VC	1764-67	Vicente Diez de la Fuente and Carlos Jimenez Almaraz

Valencia Mint

Initials	Date	Name
F	1707-13	Bartolome Bertran Fauria

MONETARY SYSTEM

34 Maravedi = 1 Real (of Silver)
16 Reales = 1 Escudo

NOTE: The early coinage of Spain is listed by denomination based on a system of 16 Reales de Plata (silver) = 1 Escudo (gold). However, in the Constitutional period from 1808-1850, a concurrent system was introduced in which 20 Reales de Vellon (billon) = 8 Reales de Plata. This system does not necessarily refer to the composition of the coin itself. To avoid confusion we have listed the coins using the value as it appears on each coin, ignoring the monetary base.

KINGDOM

EARLY REAL COINAGE

KM# 301.1 MARAVEDI

Copper **Ruler:** Philip V **Obv:** Crowned arms, value at right **Rev:** Crowned, reclining lion holding globe and sword, date at top

Date	Mintage	VG	F	VF	XF	Unc
1718	—	3.00	6.00	12.00	25.00	—
1720	—	3.00	6.00	12.00	25.00	—

KM# 301.3 MARAVEDI

Copper **Ruler:** Philip V **Obv:** Crowned arms, value at right **Rev:** Crowned, reclining lion holding globe and sword, date at top

Date	Mintage	VG	F	VF	XF	Unc
1719	—	8.00	18.00	35.00	70.00	—
1720	—	12.00	22.00	45.00	75.00	—

KM# 317 MARAVEDI

Copper **Ruler:** Philip V **Obv:** Crowned arms, value at right **Rev:** Crowned, reclining lion holding globe and sword, date at top

Date	Mintage	VG	F	VF	XF	Unc
1719	—	18.00	35.00	65.00	110	—
1720	—	9.00	18.00	35.00	65.00	—

KM# 301.2 MARAVEDI

Copper **Ruler:** Philip V **Obv:** Crowned arms, value at right **Rev:** Crowned, reclining lion holding globe and sword, date at top

Date	Mintage	VG	F	VF	XF	Unc
1720	—	20.00	40.00	70.00	120	—

KM# 367 MARAVEDI

Copper **Ruler:** Philip V **Obv:** Philip V monogram **Rev:** Crowned, reclining lion holding globe and sword, date at top

Date	Mintage	VG	F	VF	XF	Unc
1745	—	125	275	450	750	—

KM# 368 MARAVEDI

Copper **Ruler:** Ferdinand VI **Obv:** Crowned shield **Rev:** Crowned lion holding scepter and sword **Note:** Mint mark: Aqueduct.

Date	Mintage	VG	F	VF	XF	Unc
1746	—	5.00	10.00	15.00	25.00	—
1747	—	5.00	10.00	15.00	25.00	—

KM# 405.1 MARAVEDI

Copper **Ruler:** Carlos III **Obv:** Head right **Rev:** Castles and lions in angles of cross **Note:** Mint mark: Crowned M.

Date	Mintage	VG	F	VF	XF	Unc
1770	—	30.00	70.00	200	300	—
1771	—	40.00	90.00	225	375	—

KM# 405.2 MARAVEDI

Copper **Ruler:** Carlos III **Obv:** Head right **Rev:** Castles and lions in angles of cross **Note:** Mint mark: Aqueduct.

Date	Mintage	VG	F	VF	XF	Unc
1772	—	8.00	20.00	40.00	80.00	—
1773	—	6.00	15.00	30.00	65.00	—
1774	—	8.00	20.00	30.00	50.00	—
1775	—	14.00	30.00	65.00	100	—

KM# 445 MARAVEDI

Copper **Ruler:** Carlos IV **Obv:** Bust right **Obv. Legend:** CAROLUS • IIII • D : G HISP • REX • **Rev:** Castles and lions in angles of cross within wreath **Note:** Similar to 4 Maravedis, KM#427. Mint mark: Aqueduct.

Date	Mintage	VG	F	VF	XF	Unc
1791	—	15.00	25.00	50.00	90.00	—
1793	—	7.50	15.00	25.00	45.00	—
1799	—	15.00	25.00	40.00	60.00	—

KM# 190.5 2 MARAVEDIS

Copper **Ruler:** Philip V **Obv:** Crowned shield of Castile **Rev:** Crowned shield of Leon

Date	Mintage	VG	F	VF	XF	Unc
1701	—	7.00	15.00	25.00	45.00	—

KM# 285.1 2 MARAVEDIS

Copper **Ruler:** Philip V **Obv:** Philip V monogram **Rev:** Quartered shield of Castile and Leon

Date	Mintage	VG	F	VF	XF	Unc
1710	—	200	400	750	1,250	—

KM# 285.2 2 MARAVEDIS

Copper **Ruler:** Philip V **Obv:** Philip V monogram **Rev:** Quartered shield of Castile and Leon

Date	Mintage	VG	F	VF	XF	Unc
1710	—	50.00	100	200	350	—

KM# 302.1 2 MARAVEDIS

Copper **Ruler:** Philip V **Obv:** Crowned arms, value at right **Rev:** Crowned reclining lion holding globe and sword in inner circle, date at top

Date	Mintage	VG	F	VF	XF	Unc
1718	—	1.50	3.00	6.50	12.00	—
1719	—	1.50	3.00	6.50	12.00	—
1720	—	1.50	3.00	6.50	12.00	—

KM# 318 2 MARAVEDIS

Copper **Ruler:** Philip V **Obv:** Crowned arms, value at right **Rev:** Crowned reclining lion holding globe and sword in inner circle, date at top

Date	Mintage	VG	F	VF	XF	Unc
1718	—	4.00	10.00	20.00	35.00	—
1719	—	4.00	10.00	20.00	35.00	—
1720	—	6.00	15.00	35.00	50.00	—

KM# 302.2 2 MARAVEDIS

Copper **Ruler:** Philip V **Obv:** Crowned arms, value at right **Rev:** Crowned reclining lion holding globe and sword in inner circle, date at top

Date	Mintage	VG	F	VF	XF	Unc
1719	—	6.50	14.00	27.50	45.00	—

KM# 366 2 MARAVEDIS

Copper **Ruler:** Philip V **Obv:** Crowned arms of Castile and Leon **Rev:** Crowned, reclining lion holding globe and sword in inner circle, date at top

Date	Mintage	VG	F	VF	XF	Unc
1744	—	1.50	3.00	6.50	13.50	—
1745	—	1.50	3.00	6.50	13.50	—
1746	—	1.50	3.00	6.50	13.50	—

KM# 406.1 2 MARAVEDIS

Copper **Ruler:** Carlos III **Obv:** Head laureate right **Rev:** Cross with castles and lions, all within wreath **Note:** Mint mark: Crowned M.

Date	Mintage	VG	F	VF	XF	Unc
1770	—	40.00	80.00	200	400	—
1771	—	40.00	80.00	200	400	—

KM# 406.2 2 MARAVEDIS

Copper **Ruler:** Carlos III **Obv:** Head laureate right **Rev:** Cross with castles and lions in angles, all within wreath **Note:** Mint mark: Aqueduct.

Date	Mintage	VG	F	VF	XF	Unc
1772	—	13.00	25.00	40.00	75.00	—
1773	—	8.00	15.00	22.00	35.00	—
1774	—	6.00	12.00	17.00	30.00	—
1775	—	5.00	10.00	14.00	25.00	—
1776	—	10.00	15.00	22.00	40.00	—
1777	—	7.00	14.00	17.00	25.00	—
1778	—	5.00	10.00	17.00	30.00	—
1779	—	8.00	15.00	25.00	40.00	—
1780	—	8.00	15.00	25.00	40.00	—
1781	—	8.00	15.00	25.00	40.00	—
1782	—	40.00	80.00	125	200	—
1783	—	18.00	35.00	55.00	80.00	—
1784	—	8.00	15.00	25.00	45.00	—
1785	—	7.00	14.00	20.00	35.00	—
1786	—	8.00	15.00	25.00	40.00	—
1787	—	5.00	10.00	17.00	25.00	—
1788	—	5.00	10.00	17.00	25.00	—

KM# 426 2 MARAVEDIS

Copper **Ruler:** Carlos IV **Obv:** Head right **Obv. Legend:**

CAROLUS • IIII • D : G HISP • REX • **Rev:** Cross with castles and lions in angles, all within sprays and wreath **Note:** Mint mark: Aqueduct.

Date	Mintage	VG	F	VF	XF	Unc
1788	—	7.50	15.00	25.00	45.00	—
1789	—	6.00	12.50	22.50	40.00	—
1790	—	6.00	12.50	22.50	40.00	—
1791	—	6.00	12.50	22.50	40.00	—
1792	—	4.00	8.00	15.00	25.00	—
1793	—	4.00	7.00	12.00	15.00	—
1794	—	3.00	6.00	10.00	20.00	—
1795	—	5.00	10.00	18.00	30.00	—
1796	—	3.00	7.00	10.00	15.00	—
1797	—	3.00	6.00	10.00	20.00	—
1798	—	3.00	6.00	10.00	20.00	—
1799	—	3.00	6.00	10.00	20.00	—
1800	—	3.00	6.00	10.00	20.00	—

KM# 286.1 4 MARAVEDIS

Copper **Ruler:** Philip V **Obv:** Crowned monogram **Rev:** Quartered arms of Castile and Leon

Date	Mintage	VG	F	VF	XF	Unc
1710	—	40.00	90.00	165	275	—

KM# 286.2 4 MARAVEDIS

Copper **Ruler:** Philip V **Obv:** Crowned monogram **Rev:** Quartered arms of Castile and Leon

Date	Mintage	VG	F	VF	XF	Unc
1710	—	40.00	90.00	165	275	—

KM# 303 4 MARAVEDIS

Copper **Ruler:** Philip V **Obv:** Crowned arms, value at right **Rev:** Crowned, reclining lion holding globe and sword in inner circle, date at top

Date	Mintage	VG	F	VF	XF	Unc
1718	—	2.50	5.00	10.00	20.00	—
1720	—	2.50	5.00	10.00	20.00	—

KM# 304 4 MARAVEDIS

Copper **Ruler:** Philip V **Obv:** Crowned arms, value at right **Rev:** Crowned, reclining lion holding globe and sword in inner circle, date at top

Date	Mintage	VG	F	VF	XF	Unc
1718	—	4.00	9.00	18.00	35.00	—
1719	—	4.00	9.00	18.00	35.00	—
1720	—	4.00	9.00	18.00	35.00	—

KM# 305 4 MARAVEDIS

Copper **Ruler:** Philip V **Obv:** Crowned arms, value at right **Rev:** Crowned, reclining lion holding globe and sword in inner circle, date at top

Date	Mintage	VG	F	VF	XF	Unc
1718	—	9.00	22.00	45.00	75.00	—
1719	—	7.00	18.00	35.00	65.00	—
1720	—	5.00	12.00	25.00	50.00	—

KM# 319 4 MARAVEDIS

Copper **Ruler:** Philip V **Obv:** Crowned arms, value at right **Rev:** Crowned, reclining lion holding globe and sword in inner circle, date at top

Date	Mintage	VG	F	VF	XF	Unc
1719	—	6.00	14.00	27.50	45.00	—

KM# 365 4 MARAVEDIS

Copper **Ruler:** Philip V **Obv:** Crowned shield of Castile and Leon, quartered

Date	Mintage	VG	F	VF	XF	Unc
1741	—	3.00	6.00	12.50	22.50	—
1742	—	3.00	6.00	12.50	22.50	—
1743	—	3.00	6.00	12.50	22.50	—
1744	—	—	—	—	—	—

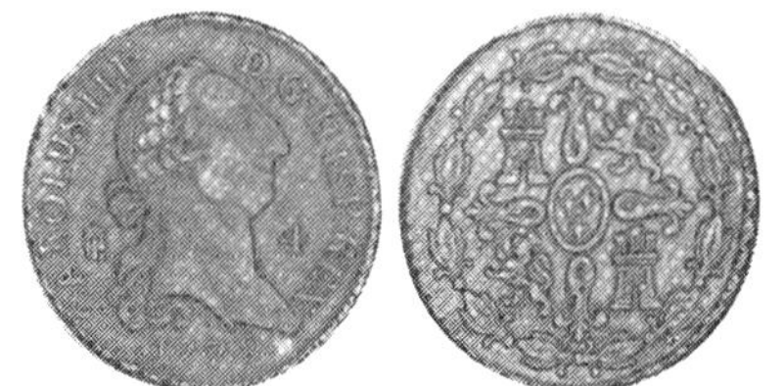

KM# 407.1 4 MARAVEDIS

Copper **Ruler:** Carlos III **Obv:** Head right **Obv. Legend:** CAROLUS • III • D : G HISP • REX • **Rev:** Cross with castles and lions in angles, all within wreath **Note:** Mint mark: Crowned M.

Date	Mintage	VG	F	VF	XF	Unc
1770	—	70.00	175	300	450	—
1771	—	80.00	200	350	550	—

KM# 407.2 4 MARAVEDIS

Copper **Ruler:** Carlos III **Obv:** Head right **Obv. Legend:** CAROLUS • III • D : G HISP • REX • **Rev:** Cross with castles and lions in angles, all within wreath **Note:** Mint mark: Aqueduct.

Date	Mintage	VG	F	VF	XF	Unc
1772	—	9.00	18.00	32.50	45.00	—
1773	—	6.00	12.00	22.50	30.00	—
1774	—	4.00	10.00	17.00	22.50	—
1775	—	4.00	10.00	15.00	20.00	—
1776	—	7.00	14.00	22.50	30.00	—
1777	—	6.00	11.00	22.00	30.00	—
1778	—	5.00	10.00	20.00	28.00	—
1779	—	5.00	10.00	20.00	28.00	—
1780	—	6.00	11.00	22.00	30.00	—
1781	—	5.00	10.00	20.00	28.00	—
1782	—	6.00	11.00	22.00	30.00	—
1783	—	20.00	45.00	65.00	90.00	—
1784	—	8.00	16.00	32.50	50.00	—
1785	—	5.00	10.00	20.00	28.00	—
1786	—	7.00	14.00	25.00	35.00	—
1787	—	5.00	10.00	20.00	28.00	—
1788	—	5.00	10.00	20.00	28.00	—

KM# 427 4 MARAVEDIS

Copper **Ruler:** Carlos IV **Obv:** Head right **Obv. Legend:** CAROLUS • IIII • D • G • HISP • REX • **Rev:** Cross with castles and lions in angles, all within wreath **Note:** Mint mark: Aqueduct.

Date	Mintage	VG	F	VF	XF	Unc
1788	—	20.00	35.00	50.00	80.00	—
1789	—	15.00	25.00	40.00	75.00	—
1790	—	12.00	22.00	35.00	65.00	—
1791	—	10.00	18.00	25.00	45.00	—
1792	—	8.00	12.00	18.50	30.00	—
1793	—	5.00	11.00	16.50	25.00	—
1794	—	5.00	10.00	14.00	18.00	—
1795	—	5.00	11.00	16.50	25.00	—
1796	—	5.00	10.00	14.00	18.00	—
1797	—	5.00	11.00	16.50	25.00	—
1798	—	5.00	10.00	14.00	18.00	—
1799	—	5.00	11.00	16.50	25.00	—
1800	—	5.00	9.00	16.50	25.00	—

KM# 408.1 8 MARAVEDIS

Copper **Ruler:** Carlos III **Obv:** Head right **Obv. Legend:** CAROLUS • III • D : G HISP • REX • **Rev:** Cross with castles and lions in angles, all within wreath **Note:** Mint mark: Crowned M.

Date	Mintage	VG	F	VF	XF	Unc
1770	—	60.00	150	300	450	—
1771	—	70.00	175	350	500	—

KM# 408.2 8 MARAVEDIS

Copper **Ruler:** Carlos III **Obv:** Head right **Obv. Legend:** CAROLUS • III • D • G • HISP • REX • **Rev:** Cross with castles and lions in angles, all within wreath **Note:** Mint mark: Aqueduct.

Date	Mintage	VG	F	VF	XF	Unc
1772	—	14.00	30.00	50.00	80.00	—
1773	—	7.00	13.00	20.00	30.00	—
1774	—	7.00	15.00	22.00	35.00	—
1775	—	8.00	15.00	25.00	35.00	—
1776	—	9.00	18.00	30.00	45.00	—
1777	—	8.00	15.00	28.00	40.00	—
1778	—	8.00	15.00	25.00	35.00	—
1779	—	8.00	15.00	28.00	40.00	—
1780	—	8.00	15.00	25.00	35.00	—
1781	—	8.00	15.00	28.00	40.00	—
1782	—	15.00	30.00	55.00	120	—
1783	—	18.00	35.00	50.00	85.00	—
1784	—	13.00	25.00	35.00	55.00	—
1785	—	6.00	11.00	20.00	30.00	—
1786	—	8.00	15.00	25.00	35.00	—
1787	—	6.00	11.00	20.00	30.00	—
1788	—	5.00	9.00	15.00	25.00	—

KM# 428 8 MARAVEDIS

Copper **Ruler:** Carlos IV **Obv:** Head right **Obv. Legend:** CAROLUS • IIII • D • G • HISP • REX • **Rev:** Cross with castles and lions in angles, within wreath **Note:** Mint mark: Aqueduct.

Date	Mintage	VG	F	VF	XF	Unc
1788	—	6.00	11.00	22.00	35.00	—
1789	—	9.00	18.50	35.00	75.00	—
1790	—	9.00	18.50	35.00	75.00	—
1791	—	12.00	15.00	25.00	40.00	—
1792	—	15.00	30.00	40.00	80.00	—
1793	—	7.00	13.00	18.50	30.00	—
1794	—	5.00	9.00	13.00	23.00	—
1795	—	5.00	9.00	13.00	23.00	—
1796	—	4.00	8.00	12.00	20.00	—
1797	—	4.00	8.00	12.00	20.00	—
1798	—	4.00	8.00	12.00	20.00	—
1799	—	5.00	10.00	12.50	22.00	—
1800	—	5.00	10.00	13.50	22.00	—

KM# 249 TRESETA

Copper **Ruler:** Philip V **Obv:** Crowned shield of Castile and Leon **Rev:** Crowned V with value below, date in legend **Note:** Varieties exist.

Date	Mintage	VG	F	VF	XF	Unc
1710	—	2.00	4.00	9.00	18.00	—
1711	—	2.00	4.00	9.00	18.00	—
1716	—	—	—	—	—	—

KM# 248 SEISENO

Copper **Ruler:** Philip V **Obv:** Crowned shield of Castile and Leon **Rev:** Crowned V with 6 within, date in legend **Note:** Varieties exist.

Date	Mintage	VG	F	VF	XF	Unc
1709	—	2.50	5.00	10.00	20.00	—
1710	—	2.50	5.00	10.00	20.00	—
1711	—	2.50	5.00	10.00	20.00	—
1712	—	2.50	5.00	10.00	20.00	—
1713	—	3.50	7.00	15.00	30.00	—

KM# 268 1/2 REAL (1/2 Croat)

1.6900 g., 0.9030 Silver 0.0491 oz. ASW **Ruler:** Philip V **Obv:** Crowned arms **Rev:** Large crowned PV monogram

Date	Mintage	VG	F	VF	XF	Unc
1707 Y	—	25.00	50.00	100	180	—

KM# 274 1/2 REAL (1/2 Croat)

1.6900 g., 0.9030 Silver 0.0491 oz. ASW **Ruler:** Philip V **Obv:** Crowned arms **Rev:** Small crowned PV monogram

Date	Mintage	VG	F	VF	XF	Unc
1708 Y	—	20.00	40.00	90.00	165	—

KM# 311 1/2 REAL (1/2 Croat)

1.6900 g., 0.9030 Silver 0.0491 oz. ASW **Ruler:** Philip V **Obv:** Crowned arms **Rev:** Short cross with castles and lions in angles

Date	Mintage	VG	F	VF	XF	Unc
1719	—	9.00	17.50	35.00	65.00	—
1726	—	10.00	20.00	40.00	70.00	—
1727	—	12.00	22.50	45.00	75.00	—

KM# 333.1 1/2 REAL (1/2 Croat)

1.6900 g., 0.9030 Silver 0.0491 oz. ASW **Ruler:** Philip V **Obv:** Crowned arms **Obv. Legend:** PHILIPPVS+V+D+G+ **Rev:** Cross with castles and lions in angles

Date	Mintage	VG	F	VF	XF	Unc
1725 J	—	7.00	15.00	30.00	55.00	—
1726 J	—	6.50	13.50	27.50	50.00	—
1728 P	—	9.00	20.00	40.00	70.00	—
1731	—	—	—	—	—	—

KM# 333.2 1/2 REAL (1/2 Croat)

1.6900 g., 0.9030 Silver 0.0491 oz. ASW **Ruler:** Philip V **Obv:** Crowned arms **Obv. Legend:** PHILIPPVS+V+D+G+ **Rev:** Cross with castles and lions in angles

Date	Mintage	VG	F	VF	XF	Unc
1726 F	—	6.50	13.50	27.50	50.00	—
1728 F	—	10.00	20.00	40.00	75.00	—

KM# 338 1/2 REAL (1/2 Croat)

1.6900 g., 0.9030 Silver 0.0491 oz. ASW **Ruler:** Philip V **Obv:** Crowned arms without initials flanking shield **Obv. Legend:** PHILIP • V • D • G • HISPAN • ET IND • REX **Rev:** Cross with castles and lions in angles **Rev. Legend:** ...IENTIÆ TIMOR DOMINI •

Date	Mintage	VG	F	VF	XF	Unc
1729	—	12.00	23.00	45.00	80.00	—
1730	—	6.50	13.50	27.50	50.00	—

KM# 350.1 1/2 REAL (1/2 Croat)

1.6900 g., 0.9030 Silver 0.0491 oz. ASW **Ruler:** Philip V **Obv:** Crowned arms without initials flanking shield **Obv. Legend:** PHILIPPUS • V • D • G • **Rev:** Cross with castles and lions in angles **Rev. Legend:** HISPANIAR ...

Date	Mintage	VG	F	VF	XF	Unc
1730 JF	—	5.00	10.00	22.50	45.00	—
1731 JF	—	4.00	9.00	17.50	35.00	—
1733 JF	—	5.00	11.00	20.00	40.00	—
1735 JF	—	4.00	9.00	17.50	35.00	—
1738 JF	—	4.00	9.00	17.50	35.00	—
1740 JF	—	5.00	11.00	20.00	40.00	—
1745 AJ	—	5.00	11.00	20.00	40.00	—
1746 AJ	—	6.00	12.00	25.00	50.00	—

KM# 350.2 1/2 REAL (1/2 Croat)

1.6900 g., 0.9030 Silver 0.0491 oz. ASW **Ruler:** Philip V **Obv:** Crowned arms with initials flanking shield **Obv. Legend:** PHILIPPUS • V • D • G • **Rev:** Cross with castles and lions in angles

Date	Mintage	VG	F	VF	XF	Unc
1731 PA	—	4.00	9.00	17.50	35.00	—
1732 PA	—	4.00	9.00	17.50	35.00	—

Date	Mintage	VG	F	VF	XF	Unc
1733 PA	—	4.00	9.00	17.50	35.00	—
1734 PA	—	4.00	9.00	17.50	35.00	—
1735 PA	—	6.00	12.00	25.00	50.00	—
1736 PA	—	7.00	15.00	30.00	60.00	—
1737 PA	—	6.00	12.00	25.00	50.00	—
1737 P	—	4.00	9.00	17.50	35.00	—
1738 PJ	—	4.00	9.00	17.50	35.00	—

KM# 370.1 1/2 REAL (1/2 Croat)

1.6900 g., 0.8330 Silver 0.0453 oz. ASW **Ruler:** Ferdinand VI **Obv:** Crowned arms **Obv. Legend:** FERDINANDUS • VI • D • G • **Rev:** Cross with castles and lions in angles **Note:** Mint mark: Crowned M.

Date	Mintage	VG	F	VF	XF	Unc
1746 AJ	—	4.00	9.00	17.50	35.00	—
1747 JB	—	4.00	9.00	17.50	35.00	—
1748 JB	—	4.00	9.00	17.50	35.00	—
1749 JB	—	4.00	9.00	17.50	35.00	—
1750 JB	—	4.00	9.00	17.50	35.00	—
1751 JB	—	4.00	9.00	17.50	35.00	—
1752 JB	—	4.00	9.00	17.50	35.00	—
1754 JB	—	4.00	9.00	17.50	35.00	—
1755 JB	—	4.00	9.00	17.50	35.00	—
1756 JB	—	4.00	9.00	17.50	35.00	—
1757 JB	—	4.00	9.00	17.50	35.00	—
1758 JB	—	4.00	9.00	17.50	35.00	—
1759 J	—	4.00	9.00	17.50	35.00	—

KM# 370.2 1/2 REAL (1/2 Croat)

1.6900 g., 0.9030 Silver 0.0491 oz. ASW **Ruler:** Ferdinand VI **Obv:** Crowned arms **Obv. Legend:** FERDINANDUS • VI • D • G • **Rev:** Cross with castles and lions in angles **Note:** Mint mark: S, SL.

Date	Mintage	VG	F	VF	XF	Unc
1748 PJ	—	5.00	12.00	23.00	45.00	—
1750 PJ	—	4.00	9.00	17.50	35.00	—
1751 PJ	—	4.00	9.00	17.50	35.00	—
1753 PJ	—	4.00	9.00	17.50	35.00	—
1754 PJ	—	4.00	9.00	17.50	35.00	—
1759 JV	—	4.00	9.00	17.50	35.00	—

KM# 395.1 1/2 REAL (1/2 Croat)

1.6900 g., 0.9030 Silver 0.0491 oz. ASW **Ruler:** Carlos III **Obv:** Crowned arms **Obv. Legend:** CAROLUS • III • D : G HISP • REX • **Rev:** Cross with castles and lions in angles **Note:** Mint mark: Crowned M.

Date	Mintage	VG	F	VF	XF	Unc
1760 SP	—	10.00	20.00	30.00	40.00	—
1761 JP	—	4.00	8.00	15.00	25.00	—
1762 JP	—	4.00	8.00	15.00	20.00	—
1764 JP	—	4.00	8.00	15.00	20.00	—
1765 PJ	—	7.00	14.00	18.00	25.00	—
1766 PJ	—	5.00	10.00	16.00	20.00	—
1769 PJ	—	9.00	17.00	22.00	30.00	—
1770 PJ	—	9.00	17.00	25.00	30.00	—
1771 PJ	—	7.00	12.00	20.00	27.50	—

KM# 395.2 1/2 REAL (1/2 Croat)

1.6900 g., 0.9030 Silver 0.0491 oz. ASW **Ruler:** Carlos III **Obv:** Crowned arms **Obv. Legend:** CAROLUS • III • D : G HISP • REX • **Rev:** Cross with castles and lions in angles **Note:** Mint mark: S, SL.

Date	Mintage	VG	F	VF	XF	Unc
1760 JV	—	7.00	12.00	20.00	30.00	—
1761 JV	—	7.00	12.00	20.00	27.50	—
1762 VC	—	12.00	25.00	45.00	60.00	—
1769 CF	—	15.00	30.00	40.00	55.00	—
1770 CF	—	10.00	20.00	25.00	30.00	—

KM# 410.2 1/2 REAL (1/2 Croat)

1.6900 g., 0.8120 Silver 0.0441 oz. ASW **Ruler:** Carlos III **Obv:** Bust right **Obv. Legend:** CAROLUS • III • D : G HISP • REX • **Rev:** Crowned arms **Note:** Mint mark: S, SL.

Date	Mintage	VG	F	VF	XF	Unc
1772 CF	—	12.00	22.50	45.00	60.00	—
1773 CF	—	5.00	10.00	18.50	25.00	—
1774 CF	—	5.00	10.00	18.50	25.00	—
1775 CF	—	7.00	14.00	20.00	30.00	—
1776 CF	—	7.00	14.00	20.00	30.00	—
1778 CF	—	7.00	14.00	20.00	30.00	—
1779 CF	—	10.00	20.00	40.00	60.00	—
1780 CF	—	8.00	15.00	22.50	35.00	—
1783 CF	—	10.00	20.00	35.00	60.00	—
1788 C	—	7.00	14.00	18.50	25.00	—

KM# 410.1 1/2 REAL (1/2 Croat)

1.6900 g., 0.8120 Silver 0.0441 oz. ASW **Ruler:** Carlos III **Obv:** Bust right **Obv. Legend:** CAROLUS • III • D : G HISP • REX • **Rev:** Crowned arms **Note:** Mint mark: Crowned M.

Date	Mintage	VG	F	VF	XF	Unc
1772 PJ	—	10.00	20.00	45.00	60.00	—
1773 PJ	—	8.00	15.00	25.00	40.00	—
1774 PJ	—	6.00	12.00	20.00	35.00	—
1775 PJ	—	6.00	12.00	20.00	30.00	—
1777 PJ	—	6.00	12.00	18.50	30.00	—
1778 PJ	—	8.00	16.00	30.00	45.00	—
1779 PJ	—	6.00	12.00	20.00	30.00	—
1780 PJ	—	5.00	10.00	18.50	30.00	—
1781 PJ	—	5.00	11.00	20.00	30.00	—
1782 JD	—	8.00	16.00	32.50	50.00	—
1783/0 JD/PJ	—	6.50	14.00	27.50	45.00	—
1783 JD	—	5.00	11.00	22.50	35.00	—
1784 JD	—	5.00	10.00	20.00	30.00	—
1785 DV	—	5.00	10.00	18.50	25.00	—
1786 DV	—	7.00	15.00	25.00	35.00	—
1788 M	—	4.00	8.00	15.00	20.00	—

KM# 438.1 1/2 REAL (1/2 Croat)

1.6900 g., 0.8120 Silver 0.0441 oz. ASW **Ruler:** Carlos IV **Obv:** Bust right **Obv. Legend:** CAROLUS • IIII • D : G HISP • REX • **Rev:** Crowned arms **Note:** Mint mark: Crowned M.

Date	Mintage	VG	F	VF	XF	Unc
1789 MF	—	7.00	14.00	25.00	35.00	—
1790 MF	—	7.00	13.00	22.50	30.00	—
1791 MF	—	7.00	13.00	22.50	30.00	—
1793 MF	—	6.00	12.00	20.00	28.50	—
1795 MF	—	9.00	17.00	30.00	40.00	—
1796 MF	—	9.00	17.00	30.00	40.00	—
1797 MF	—	9.00	17.00	30.00	40.00	—
1798 MF	—	7.00	14.00	25.00	35.00	—
1799 FA	—	7.00	13.00	22.50	30.00	—
1799 MF	—	7.00	13.00	22.50	30.00	—
1800 FA	—	7.00	14.00	25.00	32.50	—

KM# 438.2 1/2 REAL (1/2 Croat)

1.6900 g., 0.8120 Silver 0.0441 oz. ASW **Ruler:** Carlos IV **Obv:** Bust right **Obv. Legend:** CAROLUS • IIII • D : G HISP • REX • **Rev:** Crowned arms **Note:** Mint mark: S, SL.

Date	Mintage	VG	F	VF	XF	Unc
1793 CN	—	9.00	18.00	35.00	45.00	—
1796 CN	—	6.00	12.00	20.00	25.00	—
1798 CN	—	8.00	16.00	32.50	40.00	—
1799 CN	—	8.00	16.00	32.50	40.00	—
1800 CN	—	8.00	16.00	32.50	40.00	—

KM# 250.1 REAL (Croat)

3.3800 g., 0.9170 Silver 0.0996 oz. ASW **Ruler:** Philip V **Obv:** Crowned arms **Obv. Legend:** PHILIPPVS • V • DEI • GR • ... **Rev:** Short cross with castles and lions in angles

Date	Mintage	VG	F	VF	XF	Unc
1701 M	—	17.50	35.00	55.00	90.00	—
1708 M	—	32.50	65.00	110	200	—
1710 M	—	35.00	75.00	125	225	—
1711/0 M	—	35.00	75.00	125	225	—
1711 M	—	35.00	75.00	125	225	—
1713 M	—	37.50	75.00	135	240	—

KM# 270 REAL (Croat)

3.3800 g., 0.9170 Silver 0.0996 oz. ASW **Ruler:** Philip V **Obv:** Crowned shield of Castile and Leon **Rev:** Crowned PV monogram **Note:** Hammered coinage.

Date	Mintage	VG	F	VF	XF	Unc
xxxx F	—	165	300	465	750	—
xxxx Y	—	165	300	465	750	—
1707 J	—	165	300	465	750	—

KM# 250.2 REAL (Croat)

3.3800 g., 0.9170 Silver 0.0996 oz. ASW **Ruler:** Philip V **Obv. Legend:** PHILIPPVS • V • DEI • GRAT • ...

Date	Mintage	VG	F	VF	XF	Unc
1703 P	—	32.50	65.00	110	200	—
1704 P	—	22.50	45.00	70.00	120	—
1705 P	—	17.50	35.00	55.00	90.00	—

KM# 269 REAL (Croat)

3.3800 g., 0.9170 Silver 0.0996 oz. ASW **Ruler:** Philip V **Obv:** Crowned arms **Obv. Legend:** PHILIP • V • D • G • HISPANIAR • REX **Rev:** Crowned PV monogram

Date	Mintage	VG	F	VF	XF	Unc
1707 Y	—	12.00	25.00	35.00	65.00	—

KM# 289 REAL (Croat)

3.3800 g., 0.9170 Silver 0.0996 oz. ASW **Ruler:** Philip V **Obv:** Crowned arms **Rev:** Crowned PV monogram **Note:** Milled coinage.

Date	Mintage	VG	F	VF	XF	Unc
1711 J	—	80.00	165	250	400	—

KM# 299 REAL (Croat)

3.3800 g., 0.9170 Silver 0.0996 oz. ASW **Ruler:** Philip V **Obv:** Crowned arms **Obv. Legend:** PHILIPPVS • V • D • G • ... **Rev:** Cross with castles and lions in angles in octolobe **Note:** Milled coinage.

Date	Mintage	VG	F	VF	XF	Unc
1717 J	—	17.50	35.00	50.00	85.00	—
1721 F	—	7.00	15.00	22.50	40.00	—
1726 F	—	20.00	38.00	55.00	90.00	—
1727 F	—	10.00	20.00	30.00	50.00	—
1728 F	—	10.00	20.00	30.00	50.00	—
1729 F	—	20.00	30.00	50.00	90.00	—

KM# 306.2 REAL (Croat)

3.3800 g., 0.9170 Silver 0.0996 oz. ASW **Ruler:** Philip V **Obv:** Crowned arms **Rev:** Cross with castles and lions in angles in octolobe **Note:** Milled coinage.

Date	Mintage	VG	F	VF	XF	Unc
1717 J	—	100	200	325	550	—
1720 J	—	65.00	135	200	350	—
1721 J	—	7.00	15.00	22.50	40.00	—
1725 J	—	14.00	28.00	40.00	70.00	—
1726 J	—	7.00	15.00	22.50	40.00	—
1728 P	—	10.00	20.00	30.00	50.00	—
1729 P	—	10.00	20.00	30.00	50.00	—

KM# 298 REAL (Croat)

3.3800 g., 0.9170 Silver 0.0996 oz. ASW **Ruler:** Philip V **Obv:** Crowned arms **Obv. Legend:** PHILIPPVS • V • D • G • ... **Rev:** Cross with castles and lions in angles in octolobe **Note:** Machine struck

Date	Mintage	VG	F	VF	XF	Unc
1717 J	—	11.00	21.00	30.00	50.00	—
1721 A	—	6.00	13.00	20.00	40.00	—
1726 A	—	5.00	11.50	17.50	35.00	—
1727 A	—	6.00	14.00	20.00	38.00	—
1728 JJ	—	17.50	35.00	50.00	85.00	—
1729 JJ	—	7.00	15.00	22.50	40.00	—
1730 JJ	—	7.00	15.00	22.50	40.00	—
1730 JF	—	9.00	20.00	27.50	45.00	—
1731 JF	—	9.00	20.00	27.50	45.00	—
1731 F	—	9.00	20.00	27.50	45.00	—
1732 JF	—	9.00	20.00	27.50	45.00	—
1733 JF	—	9.00	20.00	27.50	45.00	—
1734 JF	—	9.00	20.00	27.50	45.00	—
1735 JF	—	7.00	15.00	22.50	40.00	—
1736 JF	—	7.00	15.00	22.50	40.00	—
1737 JF	—	9.00	20.00	27.50	45.00	—
1738 JF	—	7.00	15.00	22.50	40.00	—
1739 JF	—	7.00	15.00	22.50	40.00	—
1740 JF	—	7.00	15.00	22.50	40.00	—
1741 JF	—	7.00	15.00	22.50	40.00	—
1742 JF	—	9.00	20.00	27.50	45.00	—
1742 JA	—	9.00	20.00	27.50	45.00	—
1743 JA	—	7.00	15.00	22.50	40.00	—
1744 JA	—	7.00	15.00	22.50	40.00	—
1744 AJ	—	7.00	15.00	22.50	40.00	—
1745 AJ	—	7.00	15.00	22.50	40.00	—

KM# 306.1 REAL (Croat)

3.3800 g., 0.9170 Silver 0.0996 oz. ASW **Ruler:** Philip V **Obv:** Crowned arms **Rev:** Cross with castles and lions in angles in octolobe **Note:** Milled coinage; struck at Cuenca.

Date	Mintage	VG	F	VF	XF	Unc
1718 JJ	—	6.00	13.00	20.00	40.00	—
1719 JJ	—	6.00	13.00	20.00	40.00	—
1726 JJ	—	6.00	13.00	20.00	40.00	—
1727 JJ	—	20.00	38.00	55.00	90.00	—

KM# 339 REAL (Croat)

3.3800 g., 0.9170 Silver 0.0996 oz. ASW **Ruler:** Philip V **Obv:** Crowned arms **Rev:** Cross with castles and lions in angles in octolobe **Note:** Milled coinage; struck at Seville.

Date	Mintage	VG	F	VF	XF	Unc
1729	—	20.00	38.00	55.00	90.00	—
1730	—	15.00	30.00	45.00	80.00	—

KM# 354 REAL (Croat)

3.3800 g., 0.9170 Silver 0.0996 oz. ASW **Ruler:** Philip V **Obv:** Crowned arms **Rev:** Cross with castls and lions in angles in octolobe **Note:** Milled coinage; struck at Seville.

Date	Mintage	VG	F	VF	XF	Unc
1731 PA	—	7.00	15.00	22.50	40.00	—
1732 PA	—	7.00	15.00	22.50	40.00	—
1733 PA	—	7.00	15.00	22.50	40.00	—
1734 PA	—	7.00	15.00	22.50	40.00	—
1736 PA	—	10.00	20.00	30.00	50.00	—
1737 P	—	6.00	13.00	22.00	45.00	—
1738 PJ	—	7.00	15.00	22.50	40.00	—
1739 PJ	—	9.00	20.00	27.50	45.00	—
1740 PJ	—	10.00	22.00	30.00	50.00	—

Date	Mintage	VG	F	VF	XF	Unc
1741 PJ	—	9.00	20.00	27.50	45.00	—
1742 PJ	—	9.00	20.00	27.50	45.00	—
1743 PJ	—	9.00	20.00	27.50	45.00	—
1744 PJ	—	7.00	15.00	22.50	40.00	—
1745 PJ	—	7.00	15.00	22.50	40.00	—

KM# 369.1 REAL (Croat)
3.3800 g., 0.8330 Silver 0.0905 oz. ASW **Ruler:** Ferdinand VI **Obv:** Crowned arms **Obv. Legend:** FERDINANDUS • VI • D • G • ... **Rev:** Cross with castles and lions in angles in octolobe **Note:** Mint mark: Crowned M.

Date	Mintage	VG	F	VF	XF	Unc
1746 AJ	—	9.00	17.50	25.00	40.00	—
1747 AJ	—	9.00	17.50	25.00	40.00	—
1747 J	—	9.00	17.50	25.00	40.00	—
1747 JB	—	9.00	17.50	25.00	40.00	—
1748 JB	—	9.00	17.50	25.00	40.00	—
1749 JB	—	9.00	17.50	25.00	40.00	—
1750 JB	—	9.00	17.50	25.00	40.00	—
1751 JB	—	9.00	17.50	25.00	40.00	—
1752 JB	—	9.00	17.50	25.00	40.00	—
1753 JB	—	9.00	17.50	25.00	40.00	—
1754 JB	—	9.00	17.50	25.00	40.00	—
1755 JB	—	9.00	17.50	25.00	40.00	—
1756 JB	—	9.00	17.50	25.00	40.00	—
1757 JB	—	9.00	17.50	25.00	40.00	—
1758 JB	—	9.00	17.50	25.00	40.00	—
1759 J	—	9.00	17.50	25.00	40.00	—

KM# 369.2 REAL (Croat)
3.3800 g., 0.8330 Silver 0.0905 oz. ASW **Ruler:** Ferdinand VI **Obv:** Crowned arms **Rev:** Cross with castles and lions in angles in octolobe **Note:** Mint mark: S, SL.

Date	Mintage	VG	F	VF	XF	Unc
1750 PJ	—	9.00	17.50	25.00	40.00	—
1751 PJ	—	9.00	17.50	25.00	40.00	—
1753 PJ	—	9.00	17.50	25.00	40.00	—
1754 PJ	—	9.00	17.50	25.00	40.00	—
1756 PJ	—	9.00	17.50	25.00	40.00	—
1758 JV	—	9.00	17.50	25.00	40.00	—
1759 JV	—	9.00	17.50	25.00	40.00	—

KM# 387.1 REAL (Croat)
3.3800 g., 0.8330 Silver 0.0905 oz. ASW **Ruler:** Carlos III **Obv:** Crowned arms **Obv. Legend:** CAROLUS • III • D : G HISP • REX • **Rev:** Cross with castles and lions in angles in octolobe **Note:** Mint mark: Crowned M.

Date	Mintage	VG	F	VF	XF	Unc
1759 JP	—	16.00	32.50	50.00	70.00	—
1759 J	—	30.00	55.00	100	140	—
1760 JP	—	16.00	32.50	50.00	70.00	—
1761 JP	—	12.00	25.00	45.00	60.00	—
1762 JP	—	12.00	25.00	40.00	55.00	—
1764 JP	—	12.00	25.00	40.00	55.00	—
1765 PJ	—	12.00	25.00	45.00	60.00	—
1766 PJ	—	9.00	18.00	25.00	40.00	—
1768 PJ	—	12.00	25.00	40.00	55.00	—
1769 PJ	—	12.00	25.00	40.00	55.00	—
1770 PJ	—	12.00	25.00	40.00	55.00	—
1771 PJ	—	12.00	25.00	40.00	55.00	—

KM# 387.2 REAL (Croat)
3.3800 g., 0.8330 Silver 0.0905 oz. ASW **Ruler:** Carlos III **Obv:** Crowned arms **Obv. Legend:** CAROLUS • III • D : G HISP • REX • **Rev:** Cross with castles and lions in angles in octolobe **Note:** Mint mark: S, SL.

Date	Mintage	VG	F	VF	XF	Unc
1760 JV	—	16.00	32.50	50.00	70.00	—
1761 JV	—	9.00	18.50	30.00	45.00	—
1762 VC	—	20.00	35.00	60.00	80.00	—
1769 CF	—	25.00	45.00	75.00	100	—
1770 CF	—	15.00	25.00	40.00	50.00	—

KM# 411.1 REAL (Croat)
3.3800 g., 0.8330 Silver 0.0905 oz. ASW **Ruler:** Carlos III **Obv:** Bust right **Obv. Legend:** CAROLUS • III • D : G HISP • REX • **Rev:** Crowned arms at Castile and Leon **Note:** Mint mark: Crowned M.

Date	Mintage	VG	F	VF	XF	Unc
1772 PJ	—	20.00	40.00	55.00	80.00	—
1773 PJ	—	10.00	20.00	30.00	50.00	—
1774 PJ	—	10.00	20.00	35.00	50.00	—
1775 PJ	—	10.00	20.00	30.00	50.00	—
1777 PJ	—	10.00	20.00	30.00	50.00	—
1778 PJ	—	10.00	20.00	27.50	45.00	—
1779 PJ	—	10.00	20.00	30.00	50.00	—
1780 PJ	—	10.00	20.00	30.00	50.00	—
1781 PJ	—	10.00	20.00	30.00	50.00	—
1782 PJ	—	10.00	20.00	30.00	50.00	—
1782 JD	—	20.00	40.00	75.00	100	—
1783 JD	—	10.00	20.00	30.00	50.00	—
1784 JD	—	10.00	20.00	30.00	50.00	—
1785 JD	—	10.00	20.00	35.00	50.00	—
1785 DV	—	10.00	20.00	35.00	50.00	—
1786 DV	—	10.00	20.00	35.00	50.00	—
1787 DV	—	20.00	35.00	70.00	100	—
1788 DV	—	20.00	40.00	70.00	100	—
1788 M	—	10.00	20.00	27.50	45.00	—

KM# 411.2 REAL (Croat)
3.3800 g., 0.8330 Silver 0.0905 oz. ASW **Ruler:** Carlos III **Obv:** Bust right **Obv. Legend:** CAROLUS • III • D : G HISP • REX • **Rev:** Crowned arms **Note:** Mint mark: S, S/L.

Date	Mintage	VG	F	VF	XF	Unc
1772 CF	—	8.00	16.00	25.00	40.00	—
1773 CF	—	8.00	15.00	20.00	30.00	—
1774 CF	—	8.00	15.00	27.50	40.00	—
1775 CF	—	9.00	18.00	35.00	60.00	—
1776 CF	—	9.00	18.00	35.00	60.00	—
1777 CF	—	9.00	18.00	35.00	60.00	—
1778 CF	—	9.00	18.00	30.00	60.00	—
1779 CF	—	8.00	16.00	30.00	45.00	—
1780 CF	—	9.00	18.00	40.00	60.00	—
1783 CF	—	9.00	18.00	45.00	70.00	—
1788 C	—	7.00	15.00	18.00	28.00	—

KM# 429.1 REAL (Croat)
3.3800 g., 0.8120 Silver 0.0882 oz. ASW **Ruler:** Carlos IV **Obv:** Bust right **Obv. Legend:** CAROLUS • IIII • D : G HISP • REX • **Rev:** Crowned arms of Castile and Leon **Note:** Mint mark: Crowned M.

Date	Mintage	VG	F	VF	XF	Unc
1788 MF	—	9.00	18.00	40.00	85.00	—
1789 MF	—	9.00	18.00	40.00	85.00	—
1790 MF	—	9.00	18.00	40.00	85.00	—
1791 MF	—	10.00	20.00	40.00	85.00	—
1793 MF	—	6.00	12.00	18.00	25.00	—
1794 MF	—	8.00	15.00	25.00	35.00	—
1795 MF	—	8.00	15.00	25.00	35.00	—
1796 MF	—	8.00	15.00	25.00	35.00	—
1797 MF	—	6.00	12.00	18.00	25.00	—
1799 MF	—	5.00	10.00	20.00	28.00	—
1800 FA	—	5.00	10.00	20.00	35.00	—

KM# 429.2 REAL (Croat)
3.3800 g., 0.8120 Silver 0.0882 oz. ASW **Ruler:** Carlos IV **Obv:** Bust right **Obv. Legend:** CAROLUS • IIII • D : G HISP • REX • **Rev:** Crowned arms of Castile and Leon **Note:** Mint mark: S, S/L.

Date	Mintage	VG	F	VF	XF	Unc
1793 CN	—	10.00	20.00	40.00	50.00	—
1794 CN	—	10.00	20.00	40.00	55.00	—
1796 CN	—	10.00	20.00	40.00	65.00	—
1798 CN	—	12.00	20.00	45.00	65.00	—
1799 CN	—	12.00	20.00	45.00	65.00	—

KM# 251 2 REALES
6.7700 g., 0.9030 Silver 0.1965 oz. ASW **Ruler:** Philip V **Obv:** Crowned arms of Castile and Leon **Rev:** Cross above monogram **Note:** Machine struck; struck in Seville.

Date	Mintage	VG	F	VF	XF	Unc
1701 M	—	35.00	75.00	125	225	—
1703 P	—	35.00	75.00	125	225	—
1704 P	—	35.00	75.00	125	225	—
1705 P	—	35.00	75.00	125	225	—
1708 M	—	35.00	75.00	125	225	—

KM# 262 2 REALES
6.7700 g., 0.9030 Silver 0.1965 oz. ASW **Ruler:** Philip V **Obv:** Crowned arms of Castile and Leon **Rev:** Cross with castles and lions in angles in octolobe **Note:** Cob Type; struck in Madrid.

Date	Mintage	VG	F	VF	XF	Unc
1704 BR (4 retrograde)	—	80.00	150	250	—	—

KM# 263 2 REALES
6.7700 g., 0.9030 Silver 0.1965 oz. ASW **Ruler:** Philip V **Obv:** Crowned arms **Rev:** Cross with castles and lions in angles in octolobe **Note:** Cob Type; struck in Seville.

Date	Mintage	VG	F	VF	XF	Unc
1704 M	—	150	275	450	—	—

KM# 272 2 REALES
6.7700 g., 0.9030 Silver 0.1965 oz. ASW **Ruler:** Philip V **Obv:** Crowned arms **Obv. Legend:** PHILIPPUS XV X DEL X GRAY **Rev:** Cross with castles and lions in angles in octolobe **Note:** Struck in Valencia.

Date	Mintage	VG	F	VF	XF	Unc
1707	—	—	—	—	—	—
1708 F	—	17.50	35.00	55.00	100	—

KM# 275 2 REALES
6.7700 g., 0.9030 Silver 0.1965 oz. ASW **Ruler:** Philip V **Obv:** Crowned arms of Castile and Leon **Obv. Legend:** PHILIP • V • D • G • .... **Rev:** Crowned PV monogram **Rev. Legend:** DEXTERA • D • ... **Note:** Struck in Segovia.

Date	Mintage	VG	F	VF	XF	Unc
1708 Y	—	9.00	16.00	30.00	50.00	—

KM# 290 2 REALES
6.7700 g., 0.9030 Silver 0.1965 oz. ASW **Ruler:** Philip V **Obv:** Crowned arms **Rev:** Cross with castles and lions in angles in octolobe **Note:** Machine struck; struck in Madrid.

Date	Mintage	VG	F	VF	XF	Unc
1711 J	—	45.00	90.00	150	250	—

KM# 296 2 REALES
6.7700 g., 0.9030 Silver 0.1965 oz. ASW **Ruler:** Philip V **Obv:** Crowned arms **Rev:** Cross with castles and lions in angles in octolobe **Note:** Machine struck; struck in Madrid.

Date	Mintage	VG	F	VF	XF	Unc
1716 J	—	9.00	16.00	30.00	50.00	—
Note: Legend varieties PHILIPVS and PHILIPPVS exist for 1716 date						
1717 J	—	7.00	14.00	22.50	40.00	—
1719 J	—	8.00	15.00	27.50	45.00	—
1720 JJ	—	8.00	15.00	27.50	45.00	—
1721 A	—	7.00	14.00	22.50	40.00	—
1722 A	—	10.00	20.00	30.00	50.00	—
1723 A	—	7.00	14.00	22.50	40.00	—
1724 A	—	7.00	14.00	22.50	40.00	—
1725 A	—	7.00	14.00	22.50	40.00	—
1730 JJ	—	8.00	15.00	27.50	45.00	—
1735 JF	—	7.00	14.00	22.50	40.00	—
1737 JF	—	7.00	14.00	22.50	40.00	—
1740 JF	—	13.00	24.00	40.00	65.00	—

KM# 297 2 REALES
6.7700 g., 0.9030 Silver 0.1965 oz. ASW **Ruler:** Philip V **Obv:** Crowned arms **Obv. Legend:** PHILIPPVS V D G **Rev:** Cross with castles and lion in agles in octolobe **Rev. Legend:** HISPANIAR VM REX **Note:** Machine struck; struck in Segovia.

Date	Mintage	VG	F	VF	XF	Unc
1716 J	—	25.00	65.00	120	225	—
Note: Numerous die varieties exist for 1716						
1717 J	—	8.00	15.00	27.50	40.00	—
Note: Numerous die varieties exist for 1717						
1718 J	—	8.00	15.00	27.50	40.00	—
Note: Numerous die varieties exist for 1718						
1719 J	—	8.00	15.00	27.50	40.00	—
1719 F	—	9.00	16.00	30.00	50.00	—
1720 F	—	18.00	35.00	60.00	100	—
1721 F	—	8.00	15.00	25.00	40.00	—
1722 F	—	8.00	15.00	25.00	40.00	—
1723 F	—	7.00	14.00	22.50	40.00	—
1724 F	—	7.00	14.00	22.50	40.00	—
1725 F	—	9.00	16.00	30.00	50.00	—
1727 F	—	7.00	14.00	22.50	40.00	—
1728 F	—	12.00	25.00	45.00	75.00	—
1729 F	—	20.00	40.00	75.00	125	—

KM# 308 2 REALES
6.7700 g., 0.9030 Silver 0.1965 oz. ASW **Ruler:** Philip V **Obv:** Crowned arms **Obv. Legend:** PHILIPPUS V D G **Rev:** Cross with castles and lions in angles in octolobe **Rev. Legend:** HISPANIARUM REX **Note:** Machine struck; struck at Cuenca. Mint mark: C.

Date	Mintage	VG	F	VF	XF	Unc
1717 IJ CA	—	9.00	18.00	30.00	55.00	—
1718 JJ	—	6.00	12.00	20.00	35.00	—
1719 JJ CA	—	6.00	12.00	20.00	35.00	—
1720 JJ CA	—	6.00	12.00	20.00	35.00	—
1721 JJ	—	6.00	12.00	20.00	35.00	—
1722 JJ	—	12.00	22.00	40.00	70.00	—
1723 JJ CA	—	13.00	24.00	40.00	75.00	—
1724 JJ CA	—	6.00	12.00	20.00	35.00	—
1725/3 JJ	—	9.00	18.00	30.00	50.00	—
1726 JJ CA	—	5.00	9.00	15.00	30.00	—

KM# 307 2 REALES

6.7700 g., 0.9030 Silver 0.1965 oz. ASW **Ruler:** Philip V **Obv:** Crowned arms with rounded bottom **Obv. Legend:** PHILIPPUS V D G **Rev:** Cross with castles and lions in octolobe **Rev. Legend:** HISPANIARUM REX **Note:** Larger flan; struck at Seville. Mint mark: S.

Date	Mintage	VG	F	VF	XF	Unc
1718 M	—	10.00	22.00	40.00	70.00	—
1718 J	—	10.00	18.00	35.00	60.00	—
1720 J	—	12.00	25.00	50.00	80.00	—
1721 J	—	8.00	15.00	27.50	45.00	—
1722 J	—	8.00	15.00	27.50	45.00	—
1723 J	—	8.00	15.00	27.50	45.00	—
1724 J	—	8.00	15.00	27.50	45.00	—
1725 J	—	8.00	15.00	27.50	45.00	—
1726 J	—	15.00	30.00	55.00	90.00	—

KM# 328 2 REALES

6.7700 g., 0.9030 Silver 0.1965 oz. ASW **Ruler:** Louis I **Obv:** Crowned arms **Obv. Legend:** LUDOVICUS I D G **Rev:** Cross with castles and lion in quarters **Rev. Legend:** HISPANIARUM * REX * **Note:** Machine struck

Date	Mintage	VG	F	VF	XF	Unc
1722	—	20.00	35.00	60.00	100	—
1724 F	—	20.00	35.00	60.00	100	—

KM# 327 2 REALES

6.7700 g., 0.9030 Silver 0.1965 oz. ASW **Ruler:** Louis I **Obv:** Crowned arms **Obv. Legend:** LUDOVICUS I D G **Rev:** Cross with castles and lions in quarters **Rev. Legend:** HISPANIARUM REX **Note:** Machine struck; struck at Madrid.

Date	Mintage	VG	F	VF	XF	Unc
1724 A	—	20.00	35.00	60.00	100	—

KM# 329 2 REALES

6.7700 g., 0.9030 Silver 0.1965 oz. ASW **Ruler:** Louis I **Obv:** Crowned arms **Obv. Legend:** LUDOVICUS I D G **Rev:** Cross with castles and lions in quarters **Rev. Legend:** HISPANIARUM REX **Note:** Machine struck; struck at Seville.

Date	Mintage	VG	F	VF	XF	Unc
1724 J	—	25.00	40.00	70.00	120	—
1725 J	—	25.00	40.00	70.00	120	—

KM# 340 2 REALES

6.7700 g., 0.9030 Silver 0.1965 oz. ASW **Ruler:** Philip V **Obv:** Crowned arms with pointed bottom, without value or initials flanking shield **Obv. Legend:** PHILIPPUS • V • D • G **Rev:** Cross with castles and lions in quarters **Note:** Machine struck; struck at Seville.

Date	Mintage	VG	F	VF	XF	Unc
1729	—	12.00	25.00	45.00	75.00	—
1730	—	12.00	25.00	45.00	75.00	—

KM# 355 2 REALES

6.7700 g., 0.9030 Silver 0.1965 oz. ASW **Ruler:** Philip V **Obv:** Crowned Spanish shield with pointed bottom, value and initials flanking shield **Rev:** Cross with castles and lions in quarters **Note:** Machine struck; struck at Seville. Mint mark: S.

Date	Mintage	VG	F	VF	XF	Unc
1731 PA	—	8.00	16.00	30.00	50.00	—
1732 PA	—	8.00	16.00	30.00	50.00	—
1733 PA	—	8.00	16.00	30.00	50.00	—
1734 PA	—	8.00	16.00	30.00	50.00	—
1735 PA	—	8.00	16.00	30.00	50.00	—
1735 AP	—	8.00	16.00	30.00	50.00	—
1736 PA	—	12.00	25.00	50.00	80.00	—
1736 AP	—	9.00	18.00	35.00	60.00	—
1737 P	—	8.00	16.00	30.00	50.00	—
1737 PJ	—	8.00	16.00	30.00	50.00	—
1745 PJ	—	—	—	175	—	—

KM# 386.1 2 REALES

6.7700 g., 0.8330 Silver 0.1813 oz. ASW **Ruler:** Ferdinand VI **Obv:** Crowned arms **Obv. Legend:** FERDINANDUS • VI • D • G • **Rev:** Cross with castles and lions in quarters **Rev. Legend:** HISPANIARUM REX **Note:** Mint mark: Crowned M.

Date	Mintage	VG	F	VF	XF	Unc
1754 JB	—	8.00	15.00	25.00	40.00	—
1757 JB	—	8.00	15.00	25.00	40.00	—
1758 JV	—	8.00	15.00	25.00	40.00	—
1758 JB	—	8.00	15.00	25.00	40.00	—
1759 JB	—	8.00	15.00	25.00	40.00	—
1759 J	—	8.00	15.00	25.00	40.00	—

KM# 386.2 2 REALES

6.7700 g., 0.8330 Silver 0.1813 oz. ASW **Ruler:** Ferdinand VI **Obv:** Crowned arms **Obv. Legend:** FERDINANDUS VI D G **Rev:** Cross with castles and lions in quarters **Rev. Legend:** HISPANIARUM REX **Note:** Mint mark: S, S/L.

Date	Mintage	VG	F	VF	XF	Unc
1754 PJ	—	8.00	15.00	25.00	40.00	—
1757 JV	—	8.00	15.00	25.00	40.00	—
1758 JV	—	8.00	15.00	25.00	40.00	—
1759/8 JV	—	8.00	15.00	25.00	40.00	—
1759 JV	—	8.00	15.00	25.00	40.00	—

KM# 388.1 2 REALES

6.7700 g., 0.8330 Silver 0.1813 oz. ASW **Ruler:** Carlos III **Obv:** Crowned Spanish arms **Obv. Legend:** CAROLUS III D G **Rev:** Cross with castles and lions in quarters **Rev. Legend:** HISPANIARUM REX **Note:** Mint mark: Crowned M.

Date	Mintage	VG	F	VF	XF	Unc
1759 J	—	12.00	25.00	40.00	60.00	—
1759 JP	—	9.00	18.00	25.00	40.00	—
1760 JP	—	8.00	16.00	22.50	35.00	—
1761 JP	—	9.00	18.00	25.00	40.00	—
1762 JP	—	9.00	18.00	25.00	40.00	—
1763 JP	—	9.00	18.00	25.00	40.00	—
1764 PJ	—	7.00	15.00	30.00	50.00	—
1765 PJ	—	8.00	16.00	25.00	40.00	—
1766 PJ	—	8.00	16.00	25.00	40.00	—
1767 PJ	—	12.00	25.00	40.00	60.00	—
1768 PJ	—	9.00	18.50	30.00	45.00	—
1769 PJ	—	10.00	20.00	37.50	55.00	—
1770 PJ	—	15.00	30.00	45.00	70.00	—
1771 PJ	—	15.00	30.00	45.00	70.00	—

KM# 388.2 2 REALES

6.7700 g., 0.8330 Silver 0.1813 oz. ASW **Ruler:** Carlos III **Obv:** Crowned Spanish shield **Obv. Legend:** CAROLUS III D G **Rev:** Cross with castles and lions in quarters **Rev. Legend:** HISPANIARUM REX **Note:** Mint mark: S.

Date	Mintage	VG	F	VF	XF	Unc
1760 JV	—	8.00	16.00	25.00	40.00	—
1761 JV	—	9.00	18.00	25.00	40.00	—
1762 JV	—	9.00	18.00	25.00	40.00	—
1766 VC	—	70.00	100	175	225	—
1768 CF	—	15.00	30.00	55.00	80.00	—
1769 CF	—	10.00	20.00	37.50	60.00	—
1770 CF	—	12.00	25.00	35.00	55.00	—
1771 CF	—	9.00	18.50	30.00	45.00	—

KM# 412.1 2 REALES

6.7700 g., 0.8330 Silver 0.1813 oz. ASW **Ruler:** Carlos III **Obv:** Bust right **Obv. Legend:** CAROLUS III • DEI • G • **Rev:** Crowned arms of Castile and Leon **Rev. Legend:** HISPANIARUM REX **Note:** Mint mark: Crowned M.

Date	Mintage	VG	F	VF	XF	Unc
1772 PJ	—	9.00	18.50	35.00	55.00	—
1773 PJ	—	10.00	20.00	37.50	60.00	—
1774 PJ	—	9.00	18.00	25.00	40.00	—
1775 PJ	—	9.00	18.00	25.00	40.00	—
1776 PJ	—	8.00	16.00	25.00	40.00	—
1777 PJ	—	8.00	16.00	25.00	40.00	—
1777 FA	—	—	—	—	—	—
1778 PJ	—	8.00	16.00	25.00	40.00	—
1779 PJ	—	8.00	16.00	25.00	40.00	—
1780 PJ	—	8.00	16.00	25.00	40.00	—
1781 PJ	—	8.00	16.00	25.00	40.00	—
1782 PJ	—	9.00	18.00	25.00	40.00	—
1782 JD	—	9.00	18.50	37.50	65.00	—
1783 PJ	—	9.00	18.50	37.50	65.00	—
1783 JP	—	10.00	32.50	40.00	60.00	—
1783 JD	—	30.00	50.00	80.00	100	—
1784 JD	—	9.00	18.50	35.00	60.00	—
1785 JD	—	12.00	25.00	40.00	75.00	—
1785 DV	—	9.00	18.00	27.50	40.00	—
1786 DV	—	8.00	16.00	22.00	35.00	—
1787 DV	—	8.00	16.00	22.00	35.00	—
1788 M	—	8.00	16.00	22.00	35.00	—
1788 MF	—	16.00	32.50	40.00	65.00	—
1788 DV	—	25.00	40.00	70.00	100	—

KM# 412.2 2 REALES

6.7700 g., 0.8330 Silver 0.1813 oz. ASW **Ruler:** Carlos III **Obv:** Bust right **Obv. Legend:** CAROLUS • III • DEI • G • **Rev:** Crowned arms of Castile and Leon **Rev. Legend:** HISPANIARUM • REX • **Note:** Mint mark: S.

Date	Mintage	VG	F	VF	XF	Unc
1773 CF	—	10.00	20.00	37.50	65.00	—
1774 CF	—	9.00	18.50	35.00	55.00	—
1775 CF	—	9.00	18.50	35.00	55.00	—
1776 CF	—	9.00	18.00	22.00	35.00	—
1777 CF	—	9.00	18.00	22.00	35.00	—
1778 CF	—	9.00	18.00	22.00	35.00	—
1779 CF	—	9.00	18.00	22.00	35.00	—
1780 CF	—	9.00	18.00	22.00	35.00	—
1782 CF	—	18.00	35.00	60.00	85.00	—
1788 C	—	9.00	18.00	22.00	35.00	—

KM# 430.1 2 REALES

6.7700 g., 0.8120 Silver 0.1767 oz. ASW **Ruler:** Carlos IV **Obv:** Bust right **Obv. Legend:** CAROLUS IIII • DEI • G • **Rev:** Crowned arms of Castile and Leon **Note:** Mint mark: Crowned M.

Date	Mintage	VG	F	VF	XF	Unc
1788 MF	—	12.00	25.00	40.00	65.00	—
1789 MF	—	7.00	15.00	22.00	35.00	—
1790 MF	—	7.00	15.00	22.00	35.00	—
1791 MF	—	7.00	15.00	22.00	35.00	—
1792 MF	—	7.00	15.00	22.00	35.00	—
1793 MF	—	7.00	15.00	22.00	35.00	—
1794 MF	—	7.00	15.00	22.00	35.00	—
1795/3 MF	—	10.00	22.50	32.50	55.00	—
1795 MF	—	7.00	15.00	22.00	35.00	—
1796 MF	—	7.00	15.00	22.00	35.00	—
1797 MF	—	7.00	15.00	22.00	35.00	—
1798 MF	—	7.00	15.00	22.00	35.00	—
1799 MF	—	7.00	15.00	22.00	35.00	—

Date	Mintage	VG	F	VF	XF	Unc
1800 MF	—	7.00	15.00	22.00	35.00	—
1800 FA	—	10.00	20.00	35.00	55.00	—
1801 FA	—	7.00	15.00	22.00	35.00	—
1802 FA	—	7.00	15.00	22.00	35.00	—
1803 FA	—	7.00	15.00	22.00	35.00	—
1804 FA	—	7.00	15.00	22.00	35.00	—
1805 FA	—	7.00	15.00	22.00	35.00	—
1806 FA	—	7.00	15.00	22.00	35.00	—
1807 FA	—	7.00	15.00	22.00	35.00	—
1807 AI	—	8.00	17.00	30.00	50.00	—
1808 FA	—	7.00	15.00	22.00	35.00	—
1808 IG	—	8.00	17.00	30.00	50.00	—
1808 AI	—	7.00	15.00	25.00	40.00	—

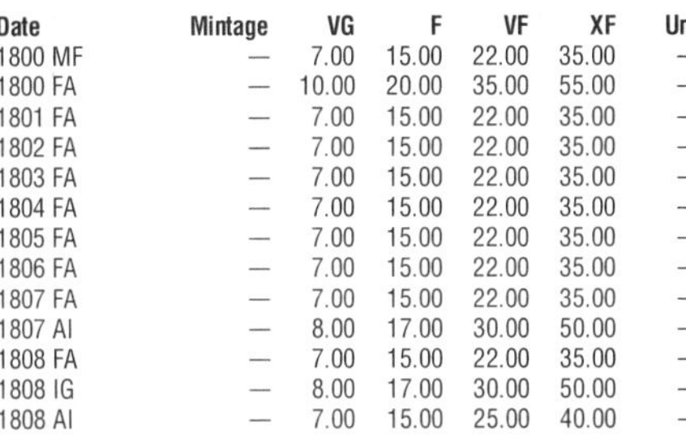

KM# 430.2 2 REALES

6.7700 g., 0.8120 Silver 0.1767 oz. ASW **Ruler:** Carlos IV **Obv:** Bust right **Obv. Legend:** CAROLUS IIII • DEI • G • **Rev:** Crowned arms of Castile and Leon **Rev. Legend:** HISPANIARUM • REX • **Note:** Mint mark: S.

Date	Mintage	VG	F	VF	XF	Unc
1793 CN	—	8.00	16.00	25.00	40.00	—
1795 CN	—	8.00	16.00	25.00	40.00	—
1796 CN	—	8.00	16.00	25.00	40.00	—
1797 CN	—	8.00	16.00	25.00	40.00	—
1798 CN	—	8.00	16.00	25.00	40.00	—
1799 CN	—	8.00	16.00	25.00	40.00	—
1800 CN	—	8.00	16.00	25.00	40.00	—

KM# 252 4 REALES

13.5400 g., 0.9310 Silver 0.4053 oz. ASW **Ruler:** Philip V **Obv:** Crowned arms of Castile and Leon **Rev:** Cross above monogram **Note:** Struck at Seville.

Date	Mintage	VG	F	VF	XF	Unc
1701 M	—	250	500	900	1,450	—

KM# 265 4 REALES

13.5400 g., 0.9310 Silver 0.4053 oz. ASW **Ruler:** Philip V **Obv:** Crowned Spanish shield **Rev:** Arms of Castile and Leon in octolobe **Note:** Struck at Seville.

Date	Mintage	VG	F	VF	XF	Unc
1704 P	—	1,000	2,250	4,250	6,500	—
1705 P	—	1,000	2,250	4,250	6,500	—

KM# 264 4 REALES

13.5400 g., 0.9310 Silver 0.4053 oz. ASW **Ruler:** Philip V **Obv:** Crowned Spanish shield **Rev:** Shield of Castile and Leon **Note:** Struck at Madrid.

Date	Mintage	VG	F	VF	XF	Unc
1704 BR	—	600	1,200	2,200	3,250	—

KM# 276 4 REALES

13.5400 g., 0.9310 Silver 0.4053 oz. ASW **Ruler:** Philip V **Obv:** Crowned Spanish shield **Rev:** Arms of Castile and Leon **Note:** Struck at Valencia.

Date	Mintage	VG	F	VF	XF	Unc
1708 F	—	1,250	2,500	4,500	7,000	—

KM# 278 4 REALES

13.5400 g., 0.9310 Silver 0.4053 oz. ASW **Ruler:** Philip V **Obv:** Large, draped bust right **Obv. Legend:** PHILIP V • D • G • HISP • ETIND • REX **Rev:** Crowned shield of Castile and Leon **Rev. Legend:** DEXTERA • DOMINI • ... **Note:** Struck at Madrid.

Date	Mintage	VG	F	VF	XF	Unc
1709 J	—	125	250	500	850	—

KM# 279 4 REALES

13.5400 g., 0.9310 Silver 0.4053 oz. ASW **Ruler:** Philip V **Obv:** Small, draped bust right **Rev:** Crowned shield of Castile and Leon, value and initials flanking arms **Note:** Struck at Madrid.

Date	Mintage	VG	F	VF	XF	Unc
1709 J	—	750	1,500	2,750	4,500	—

KM# 280 4 REALES

13.5400 g., 0.9310 Silver 0.4053 oz. ASW **Ruler:** Philip V **Obv:** Crowned Spanish shield in inner circle **Rev:** Crowned shield of Castile and Leon, value and initials flanking arms **Note:** Struck at Seville.

Date	Mintage	VG	F	VF	XF	Unc
1709 M	—	400	800	1,450	2,250	—

KM# 309 4 REALES

13.5400 g., 0.9310 Silver 0.4053 oz. ASW **Ruler:** Philip V **Obv:** Crowned Spanish shield, crown with flat bottom **Rev:** Arms of Castile and Leon **Note:** Struck at Seville.

Date	Mintage	VG	F	VF	XF	Unc
1718 M	—	50.00	100	200	350	—
1718 M 4 in value retrograde	—	35.00	80.00	150	250	—

KM# 337.2 4 REALES

13.5400 g., 0.9310 Silver 0.4053 oz. ASW **Ruler:** Philip V **Obv:** Crowned Spanish shield, crown with high arched bottom **Rev:** Arms of Castile and Leon in octolobe **Note:** Struck at Seville.

Date	Mintage	VG	F	VF	XF	Unc
1728 P	—	115	225	425	700	—
1729 P	—	115	225	425	700	—

KM# 337.1 4 REALES

13.5400 g., 0.9310 Silver 0.4053 oz. ASW **Ruler:** Philip V **Obv:** Crowned Spanish shield, crown with arched bottom **Obv. Legend:** PHILIPPUS V D G **Rev:** Arms of Castile and Leon in octolobe **Rev. Legend:** HISPANIARUM REX **Note:** Struck at Madrid.

Date	Mintage	VG	F	VF	XF	Unc
1728 JJ	—	120	300	600	1,000	—
1731 F	—	140	350	700	1,200	—
1732 JF	—	100	250	500	750	—
1734 JF	—	80.00	200	400	625	—
1735 JF	—	80.00	200	400	625	—
1737 JF	—	80.00	200	400	625	—
1738 JF	—	80.00	200	400	625	—
1740 JF	—	70.00	175	350	550	—

KM# 337.3 4 REALES

13.5400 g., 0.9310 Silver 0.4053 oz. ASW **Ruler:** Philip IV **Obv:** Crowned Spanish shield **Rev:** Arms of Castile and Leon in octolobe **Note:** Struck at Segovia.

Date	Mintage	VG	F	VF	XF	Unc
1728 F	—	90.00	225	450	750	—
1729 F	—	100	250	500	800	—

KM# 351 4 REALES

13.5400 g., 0.9310 Silver 0.4053 oz. ASW **Ruler:** Philip V **Obv:** Crowned Spanish shield, without initials or value flanking arms **Rev:** Arms of Castile and Leon **Note:** Struck at Seville.

Date	Mintage	VG	F	VF	XF	Unc
1730	—	175	325	700	1,250	—

KM# 356 4 REALES

13.5400 g., 0.9310 Silver 0.4053 oz. ASW **Ruler:** Philip V **Obv:** Crowned Spanish shield, initials and value flanking **Rev:** Arms of Castile and Leon **Note:** Struck at Seville.

Date	Mintage	VG	F	VF	XF	Unc
1731 PA	—	60.00	150	300	500	—
1732 PA	—	85.00	215	425	650	—
1733 PA	—	70.00	175	350	550	—
1734 PA	—	70.00	175	350	550	—
1735 PA	—	75.00	185	375	600	—
1737 PJ	—	75.00	185	375	600	—
1738 PJ	—	60.00	150	300	500	—

KM# 396.1 4 REALES

13.5400 g., 0.9170 Silver 0.3992 oz. ASW **Ruler:** Carlos III **Obv:** Crowned Spanish shield **Rev:** Arms of Castile and Leon in octolobe **Note:** Mint mark: Crowned M.

Date	Mintage	VG	F	VF	XF	Unc
1760 JP	—	125	300	500	700	—
1761 JP	—	20.00	35.00	75.00	100	—

KM# 396.2 4 REALES

13.5400 g., 0.9170 Silver 0.3992 oz. ASW **Ruler:** Carlos III **Obv:** Crowned Spanish shield **Rev:** Arms of Castile and Leon in octolobe **Note:** Mint mark: S, S/L.

Date	Mintage	VG	F	VF	XF	Unc
1761 JV	—	30.00	50.00	90.00	150	—

KM# 413.2 4 REALES

13.5400 g., 0.9030 Silver 0.3931 oz. ASW **Ruler:** Carlos III **Obv:** Bust right **Obv. Legend:** CAROLUS III • DEI • G • **Rev:** Crowned shield of Castile and Leon **Rev. Legend:** HISPANIARUM REX **Note:** Mint mark: S, S/L.

Date	Mintage	VG	F	VF	XF	Unc
1772 CF	—	40.00	70.00	135	200	—
1773 CF	—	30.00	45.00	65.00	100	—
1774 CF	—	30.00	45.00	65.00	100	—
1775 CF	—	30.00	65.00	110	175	—
1776 CF	—	60.00	120	250	350	—
1777 CF	—	25.00	40.00	65.00	100	—
1778 CF	—	40.00	80.00	125	200	—
1779 CF	—	30.00	45.00	70.00	100	—
1780 CF	—	30.00	45.00	70.00	100	—
1781 CF	—	40.00	70.00	110	180	—
1782 CF	—	80.00	120	225	300	—
1788 C	—	25.00	40.00	65.00	100	—

KM# 413.1 4 REALES

13.5400 g., 0.9030 Silver 0.3931 oz. ASW **Ruler:** Carlos III **Obv:** Bust right **Obv. Legend:** CAROLUS • III • DEI • G • **Rev:** Crowned shield of Castile and Leon **Rev. Legend:** HISPANIARUM REX **Note:** Mint mark: Crowned M.

Date	Mintage	VG	F	VF	XF	Unc
1772 PJ	—	50.00	100	150	210	—
1773 PJ	—	32.50	65.00	100	140	—
1774 PJ	—	100	210	325	525	—
1775 PJ	—	20.00	40.00	60.00	100	—
1776 PJ	—	25.00	40.00	60.00	90.00	—
1777 PJ	—	25.00	40.00	60.00	90.00	—
1778 PJ	—	20.00	35.00	60.00	90.00	—
1779 PJ	—	25.00	40.00	65.00	90.00	—
1780 PJ	—	30.00	45.00	75.00	100	—
1781 PJ	—	25.00	40.00	65.00	90.00	—
1782 PJ	—	30.00	45.00	70.00	100	—
1782 JD	—	30.00	45.00	75.00	110	—
1784 JD	—	85.00	160	280	475	—
1788 MF	—	20.00	30.00	55.00	80.00	—
1788 M	—	40.00	70.00	115	175	—

KM# 431.1 4 REALES

13.5400 g., 0.8960 Silver 0.3900 oz. ASW **Ruler:** Carlos IV **Obv:** Bust right **Obv. Legend:** CAROLUS IIII • DEI • G • **Rev:** Crowned arms of Castile and Leon **Rev. Legend:** HISPANIARUM • REX • **Note:** Similar to 2 Reales, KM#430.2. Mint mark: Crowned M.

Date	Mintage	VG	F	VF	XF	Unc
1788 MF	—	200	400	700	1,000	—
1789 MF	—	40.00	70.00	130	200	—
1790 MF	—	225	450	700	1,000	—
1791 MF	—	20.00	30.00	50.00	80.00	—
1792 MF	—	20.00	30.00	40.00	60.00	—
1793 MF	—	20.00	30.00	40.00	60.00	—
1794 MF	—	20.00	30.00	40.00	60.00	—
1795 MF	—	20.00	30.00	45.00	65.00	—
1796 MF	—	20.00	30.00	50.00	75.00	—
1797 MF	—	35.00	65.00	80.00	125	—

KM# 237.1 8 REALES

Silver **Ruler:** Philip V **Obv:** Crowned Spanish shield in collar of The Golden Fleece, mint mark right, assayer initial left **Obv. Legend:** PHILIPPVS • IIII • D • G • **Rev:** Cross above MA monogram with floral separations **Rev. Legend:** HISPANIARVM • REX • **Note:** Dav. #1691.

Date	Mintage	VG	F	VF	XF	Unc
1701S M	—	700	1,300	2,200	3,700	—

KM# 237.2 8 REALES

Silver **Obv:** Crowned Spanish shield' mint mark left, assayer initial right **Obv. Legend:** PHILIPPVS • IIII • D • G • **Rev:** Cross above MA monogram with floral separations **Rev. Legend:** HISPANIARVM • REX • **Note:** Dav. #1691.

Date	Mintage	VG	F	VF	XF	Unc
1701S M	—	700	1,300	2,200	3,700	—

KM# 238 8 REALES

Silver **Ruler:** Philip V **Obv:** Crowned Spanish shield **Obv. Legend:** PHILIPPVS • IIII • D • G • **Rev:** Arms of Castile and Leon within pellet border **Rev. Legend:** HISPANIARVM • REX • **Note:** Dav. #1691.

Date	Mintage	VG	F	VF	XF	Unc
1702S M	—	600	1,000	1,750	3,000	—

KM# 266 8 REALES

27.0700 g., 0.9030 Silver 0.7859 oz. ASW **Ruler:** Philip V **Obv:** Crowned Spanish shield, denomination left, mint mark and assayer initial right **Obv. Legend:** PHILIPPVS V DEI GRAT **Rev:** Arms of Castile and Leon in octolobe **Rev. Legend:** HISPANIARVM REX **Note:** Dav. #1692.

Date	Mintage	VG	F	VF	XF	Unc
1704S P	—	1,100	2,400	3,500	5,500	—
1705S P Date above	—	1,000	2,000	3,000	5,000	—
1705S P Date below	—	1,100	2,200	3,500	5,500	—
1706S P Denomination right	—	1,100	2,200	3,500	5,500	—
1706S P	—	1,000	2,000	3,000	5,000	—
1707S M	—	1,100	2,200	3,500	5,500	—
1708S M	—	1,100	2,200	3,500	5,500	—
1709S M	—	1,100	2,200	3,500	5,500	—
1711S M Denomination IIIV	—	1,250	2,500	4,000	6,000	—
1711S M	—	1,000	2,000	3,000	5,000	—
1713S M	—	1,100	2,200	3,500	5,500	—

KM# 239 8 REALES

Silver **Ruler:** Philip V **Obv:** Crowned Spanish shield **Obv. Legend:** PHILIPPVS • IIII • D • G • **Rev:** Arms of Castile and Leon in octolobe **Rev. Legend:** HISPANIARVM • REX • **Note:** Dav. #1693.

Date	Mintage	VG	F	VF	XF	Unc
1704M BR	—	450	900	1,500	2,500	—
1706M J	—	350	700	1,200	2,000	—
1706M Y	—	350	700	1,200	2,000	—
1707M B	—	350	700	1,200	2,000	—
1709M J	—	350	600	1,000	1,750	—

KM# 281 8 REALES

27.0700 g., 0.9030 Silver 0.7859 oz. ASW **Ruler:** Philip V **Obv:** Head laureate right **Obv. Legend:** PHILIP • D • G • HISP • ETIND • REX • **Rev:** Crowned shield of Castile and Leon **Rev. Legend:** ...DEXTERA • DO • MINI • EX... **Note:** Dav. #1695.

Date	Mintage	VG	F	VF	XF	Unc
1709M J	—	750	1,250	2,150	3,500	—

KM# 287 8 REALES

27.0700 g., 0.9030 Silver 0.7859 oz. ASW **Ruler:** Philip V **Obv:** Crowned Spanish shield, denomination as 8 **Obv. Legend:** PHIL • PPVS V D G **Rev:** Arms of Castile and Leon in octolobe **Rev. Legend:** HISPANIAR.... **Note:** Dav. #1693.

Date	Mintage	VG	F	VF	XF	Unc
1710M J	—	350	700	1,200	2,000	—
1710M J Plain edge	—	450	900	1,500	2,500	—
1711M J	—	350	700	1,200	2,000	—

KM# 291 8 REALES

27.0700 g., 0.9030 Silver 0.7859 oz. ASW **Ruler:** Philip V **Obv:** Crowned Spanish shield, wide crown **Obv. Legend:** PHILIPPUS V D G **Rev:** Arms of Castile and Leon **Rev. Legend:** HISPANIARUM REX **Note:** Dav. #1693.

Date	Mintage	VG	F	VF	XF	Unc
1711M J PHILIPPVS	—	600	1,000	1,750	3,000	—
1711M J	—	300	600	1,000	1,750	—
1712M J	—	400	750	1,300	2,300	—
1713M J	—	500	1,000	1,750	3,000	—
1714M J	—	350	700	1,250	2,250	—
1715M J	—	400	750	1,300	2,300	—
1716M J	—	600	1,200	2,100	3,600	—

KM# 292 8 REALES

27.0700 g., 0.9030 Silver 0.7859 oz. ASW **Ruler:** Philip V **Obv:** Crowned Spanish shield, narrow crown **Obv. Legend:** PHILIPPUS V D G **Rev:** Arms of Castile and Leon **Rev. Legend:** HISPANIARUM REX **Note:** Dav. #1693.

Date	Mintage	VG	F	VF	XF	Unc
1711M J	—	350	700	1,200	2,000	—
1713M J	—	350	700	1,250	2,250	—

KM# 310 8 REALES

27.0700 g., 0.9030 Silver 0.7859 oz. ASW **Ruler:** Philip V **Obv:** Crowned Spanish shield, wide crown, denomination as R 8 **Obv. Legend:** PHILIPPVS DEI GRATA **Rev:** Arms of Castile and Leon **Rev. Legend:** HISPANIARVM... **Note:** Dav. #1696. Many varieties exist in the size and style of rosettes. Also known with one or two bars in the arms of Aragon.

Date	Mintage	VG	F	VF	XF	Unc
1718S M	—	200	300	500	800	—

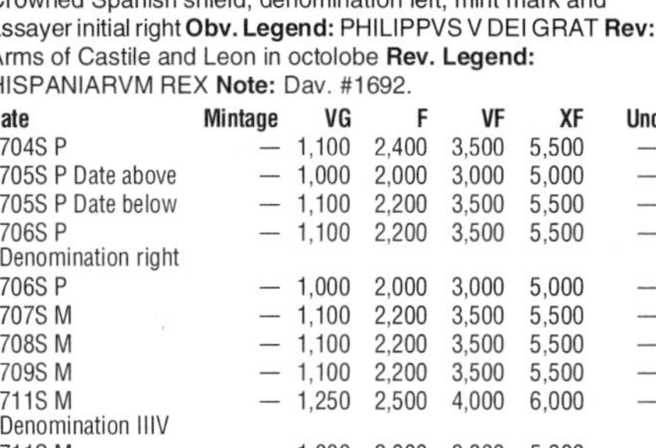

KM# 336.1 8 REALES

27.0700 g., 0.9030 Silver 0.7859 oz. ASW **Ruler:** Philip V **Obv:** Crowned Spanish shield, ornate floral stops in legend **Obv. Legend:** PHILIPPUS V D G **Rev:** Arms of Castile and Leon **Rev. Legend:** HISPANIARUM ... **Note:** Dav. #1697. Mint mark: Aqueduct.

Date	Mintage	VG	F	VF	XF	Unc
1727 F	—	350	700	1,250	2,250	—
1728 F	—	300	550	900	1,550	—
1729 F	—	350	700	1,250	2,250	—

KM# 336.2 8 REALES

27.0700 g., 0.9030 Silver 0.7859 oz. ASW **Ruler:** Philip V **Obv:** Crowned Spanish shield; ornate floral stops **Obv. Legend:** PHILIPPUS V D G **Rev:** Arms of Castile and Leon **Rev. Legend:** HISPANIARUM .... **Note:** Dav. #1697. Mint mark: Crowned M.

Date	Mintage	VG	F	VF	XF	Unc
1728 JJ	—	250	500	800	1,400	—
1729 JJ	—	250	500	800	1,400	—
1730 JF	—	250	500	800	1,400	—
1731 JF	—	250	500	800	1,400	—
1731 F	—	250	500	800	1,400	—
1732 F	—	250	500	800	1,400	—
1732 JF	—	250	500	800	1,400	—
1734 JF	—	250	500	800	1,400	—
1740 JF	—	300	600	1,000	1,750	—

KM# 336.3 8 REALES

27.0700 g., 0.9030 Silver 0.7859 oz. ASW **Ruler:** Philip V **Obv:** Crowned Spanish shield, ornate floral stops **Obv. Legend:** PHILIPPUS V D G **Rev:** Arms of Castile and Leon **Rev. Legend:** HISPANIARUM ... **Note:** Dav. #1697.

Date	Mintage	VG	F	VF	XF	Unc
1728S P	—	250	500	850	1,450	—
1729S P	—	250	450	750	1,250	—

KM# 341 8 REALES

27.0700 g., 0.9030 Silver 0.7859 oz. ASW **Ruler:** Philip V **Obv:** Crowned Spanish shield, assayer initials or denomination **Obv. Legend:** PHILIPPUS V D G **Rev:** Arms of Castile and Leon **Rev. Legend:** HISPANIARUM ... **Note:** Dav. #1698.

Date	Mintage	VG	F	VF	XF	Unc
1729S	—	350	700	1,250	2,250	—
1730S	—	300	600	1,000	1,750	—

KM# 357 8 REALES

27.0700 g., 0.9030 Silver 0.7859 oz. ASW **Ruler:** Philip V **Obv:** Crowned Spanish shield, assayer initial horizontal **Obv. Legend:** PHILIPPUS V D G **Rev:** Arms of Castile and Leon **Rev. Legend:** HISPANIARUM ... **Note:** Dav. #1697.

Date	Mintage	VG	F	VF	XF	Unc
1731S PA	—	500	950	1,500	2,500	—

KM# 358 8 REALES

27.0700 g., 0.9030 Silver 0.7859 oz. ASW **Ruler:** Philip V **Obv:** Crowned Spanish shield, assayer initial vertical **Obv. Legend:** PHILIPPUS V D G **Rev:** Arms of Castile and Leon **Rev. Legend:** HISPANIARUM ...

Date	Mintage	VG	F	VF	XF	Unc
1731S PA	—	250	450	750	1,250	—
1732S PA	—	200	300	500	800	—
1733S PA	—	200	300	500	800	—
1734S PA	—	200	300	500	800	—
1735S PA	—	200	300	500	800	—
1735S AP	—	250	450	750	1,250	—
1736S AP	—	300	600	1,000	1,750	—

KM# 399.1 8 REALES

27.0700 g., 0.9030 Silver 0.7859 oz. ASW **Ruler:** Carlos III **Obv:** Crowned Spanish shield **Obv. Legend:** CAROLUS III D G **Rev:** Arms of Castile and Leon **Rev. Legend:** HISPANIARUM... **Note:** Dav. #1699. Mint mark: Crowned M.

Date	Mintage	VG	F	VF	XF	Unc
1762 JP	—	125	250	450	750	—

KM# 399.2 8 REALES

27.0700 g., 0.9030 Silver 0.7859 oz. ASW **Ruler:** Carlos III **Obv:** Crowned Spanish shield **Obv. Legend:** CAROLUS III D G **Rev:** Arms of Castile and Leon **Rev. Legend:** HISPANIARUM... **Note:** Mint mark: S, S/L.

Date	Mintage	VG	F	VF	XF	Unc
1762 JV	—	150	275	400	550	—

KM# 414.2 8 REALES

27.0700 g., 0.9030 Silver 0.7859 oz. ASW **Ruler:** Carlos III **Obv:** Bust right **Obv. Legend:** CAROLUS III • DEI • G • **Rev:** Crowned Spanish shield **Rev. Legend:** HISPANIARUM ... **Note:** Mint mark: S, S/L.

Date	Mintage	VG	F	VF	XF	Unc
1772 CF	—	200	400	550	1,000	—
1773 CF	—	200	400	525	800	—
1774 CF	—	225	450	650	900	—
1775 CF	—	275	525	700	900	—
1776 CF	—	225	450	700	900	—
1777 CF	—	225	450	725	900	—
1778 CF	—	225	450	900	1,300	—
1779 CF	—	250	475	725	900	—
1788 C	—	250	475	700	1,000	—

KM# 414.1 8 REALES

27.0700 g., 0.9030 Silver 0.7859 oz. ASW **Ruler:** Carlos III **Obv:** Bust right **Obv. Legend:** CAROLUS III • DEI • G • **Rev:** Crowned Spanish shield **Rev. Legend:** HISPANIARUM ... **Note:** Dav. #1700. Mint mark: Crowned M.

Date	Mintage	VG	F	VF	XF	Unc
1772 PJ	—	200	400	700	1,000	—
1773 PJ	—	225	450	775	1,000	—
1774 PJ	—	250	500	700	900	—
1775 PJ	—	250	475	775	1,000	—
1777 PJ	—	300	600	900	1,200	—
1782 PJ	—	300	550	800	1,000	—
1788 M	—	300	550	725	900	—

KM# 432.2 8 REALES

27.0700 g., 0.9030 Silver 0.7859 oz. ASW **Ruler:** Carlos IV **Obv:** Bust right **Obv. Legend:** CAROLUS IIII • DEI • G • **Rev:** Crowned arms of Castile and Leon **Rev. Legend:** HISPANIARUM ... **Note:** Mint mark: S, S/L. Similar to 2 Reales, KM#430.2.

Date	Mintage	VG	F	VF	XF	Unc
1788 C	—	275	550	900	1,200	—
1789 C	—	250	500	800	1,100	—
1790 C	—	275	550	900	1,200	—
1791 C	—	275	550	900	1,200	—
1792 C	—	200	375	575	850	—
1792 CN	—	150	300	500	700	—
1793 CN	—	200	400	650	900	—
1795 CN	—	140	275	475	750	—
1796 CN	—	200	375	650	950	—
1797 CN	—	500	1,000	1,800	2,500	—
1798 CN	—	150	300	500	800	—
1799 CN	—	250	475	700	1,100	—
1800 CN	—	200	375	600	900	—

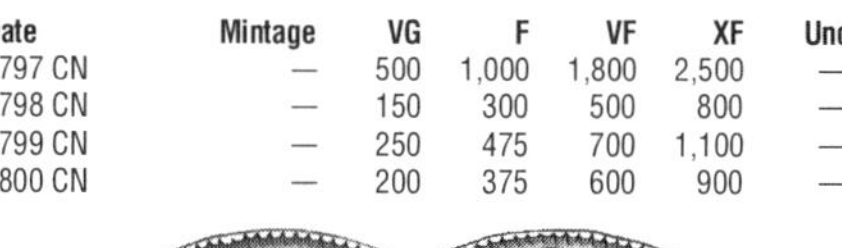

KM# 432.1 8 REALES

27.0700 g., 0.9030 Silver 0.7859 oz. ASW **Ruler:** Carlos IV **Obv:** Bust right **Obv. Legend:** CAROLUS IIII • DEI • G • **Rev:** Crowned arms of Castile and Leon **Rev. Legend:** HISPANIARUM • REX • **Note:** Similar to 2 Reales, KM#430.2. Dav. #1701. Mint mark: Crowned M.

Date	Mintage	VG	F	VF	XF	Unc
1788 MF	—	475	950	1,600	2,100	—
1789 MF	—	350	600	900	1,300	—
1796 MF	—	475	950	1,600	2,100	—
1797 MF	—	450	750	950	1,400	—
1798 MF	—	225	425	625	900	—

KM# 361.2 1/2 ESCUDO

1.6900 g., 0.9170 Gold 0.0498 oz. AGW **Ruler:** Philip V **Obv:** Head right **Obv. Legend:** PHILIPPUS V D G **Rev:** Crowned arms **Rev. Legend:** HISPANIARUM REX **Note:** Mint mark: S, S/L. Varieties exist.

Date	Mintage	VG	F	VF	XF	Unc
1738 PJ	—	175	400	800	1,200	—
1742 JP	—	80.00	125	250	350	—
1742 PJ	—	60.00	90.00	175	250	—
1743 PJ	—	50.00	80.00	140	200	—
1744 PJ	—	50.00	80.00	140	200	—
1745 PJ	—	50.00	80.00	140	200	—
1746 PJ	—	90.00	140	275	400	—

KM# 361.1 1/2 ESCUDO

1.6900 g., 0.9170 Gold 0.0498 oz. AGW **Ruler:** Philip V **Obv:** Head right **Obv. Legend:** PHILIPPUS V D G **Rev:** Crowned arms **Rev. Legend:** HISPANIARUM REX **Note:** Varieties exist. Mint mark: Crowned M.

Date	Mintage	VG	F	VF	XF	Unc
1738 JF	—	175	400	800	1,200	—
1742 JF	—	50.00	80.00	140	200	—
1743 JF	—	50.00	80.00	140	200	—
1744 JF	—	50.00	80.00	140	200	—
1744 AJ	—	50.00	80.00	140	200	—
1745 AJ	—	50.00	80.00	140	200	—
1746 AJ	—	60.00	100	200	300	—

KM# 371 1/2 ESCUDO

1.6900 g., 0.9170 Gold 0.0498 oz. AGW **Ruler:** Ferdinand VI **Obv:** Crowned arms **Obv. Legend:** FERDINAND • VI • D • G **Rev:** Crowned F in crowned cartouche, date at top **Rev. Legend:** HISPANIARUM * REX * **Note:** Mint mark: Crowned M.

Date	Mintage	VG	F	VF	XF	Unc
1746	—	125	250	500	750	—

KM# 372 1/2 ESCUDO

1.6900 g., 0.9170 Gold 0.0498 oz. AGW **Ruler:** Ferdinand VI **Obv:** Head right **Obv. Legend:** FERDINAND • VI D * G * **Rev:** Crowned arms **Rev. Legend:** HISPANIARUM * REX * **Note:** Mint mark: Crowned M.

Date	Mintage	VG	F	VF	XF	Unc
1746 AJ	—	50.00	75.00	140	200	—
1747 AJ	—	125	250	500	750	—
1747 J	—	50.00	75.00	140	200	—
1747 JB	—	50.00	65.00	110	150	—
1748 JB	—	60.00	100	200	300	—

KM# 373 1/2 ESCUDO
1.6900 g., 0.9170 Gold 0.0498 oz. AGW **Ruler:** Ferdinand VI **Obv:** Bust right, with hair in ringlets **Obv. Legend:** FERDINAND * VI * D * G * **Rev:** Crowned arms **Rev. Legend:** HISPANIARUM * REX * **Note:** Mint mark: S, S/L.

Date	Mintage	VG	F	VF	XF	Unc
1746 PJ	—	70.00	130	250	350	—
1747 PJ Rosettes	—	50.00	70.00	140	200	—

KM# 374 1/2 ESCUDO
1.6900 g., 0.9170 Gold 0.0498 oz. AGW **Ruler:** Ferdinand VI **Obv:** Head right, with hair in waves **Obv. Legend:** FERDINAND * VI * D * G * **Rev:** Crowned arms **Rev. Legend:** HISPANIARUM * REX * **Note:** Mint mark: S, S/L.

Date	Mintage	VG	F	VF	XF	Unc
1747 PJ Stars	—	—	—	—	—	—
1748 PJ	—	50.00	70.00	135	190	—
1749 PJ	—	50.00	70.00	135	190	—
1750 PJ	—	50.00	70.00	135	190	—
1751 PJ	—	50.00	70.00	135	190	—
1752 PJ	—	50.00	70.00	135	190	—
1753 PJ	—	50.00	70.00	135	190	—
1754 PJ	—	50.00	70.00	135	190	—
1755 PJ	—	50.00	70.00	135	190	—
1756 PJ	—	50.00	70.00	135	190	—
1757 PJ	—	70.00	140	275	400	—
1757 JV Rosettes	—	50.00	70.00	135	190	—
1757 JV Stars	—	50.00	70.00	135	190	—
1758 JV Rosettes	—	50.00	70.00	135	190	—
1758 JV Stars	—	50.00	70.00	135	190	—
1759 JV	—	50.00	70.00	135	190	—

KM# 378 1/2 ESCUDO
1.6900 g., 0.9170 Gold 0.0498 oz. AGW **Ruler:** Ferdinand VI **Obv:** Bust right, with hair behind neck **Obv. Legend:** FERDINAND * VI * D * G * **Rev:** Crowned arms **Rev. Legend:** HISPANIARUM * REX * **Note:** Mint mark: Crowned M.

Date	Mintage	VG	F	VF	XF	Unc
1748 JB	—	50.00	70.00	135	190	—
1749 JB	—	50.00	70.00	135	190	—
1750 JB	—	50.00	70.00	135	190	—
1751 JB	—	50.00	70.00	135	190	—
1752 JB	—	50.00	70.00	135	190	—
1753 JB	—	50.00	70.00	135	190	—
1754 JB	—	50.00	70.00	135	190	—
1755 JB	—	50.00	70.00	135	190	—
1756 JB	—	50.00	70.00	135	190	—
1757 JB	—	50.00	70.00	135	190	—
1758 JB	—	50.00	70.00	135	190	—
1759 JB	—	50.00	90.00	175	250	—
1759 J	—	50.00	70.00	135	190	—

KM# 389.1 1/2 ESCUDO
1.6900 g., 0.9170 Gold 0.0498 oz. AGW **Ruler:** Carlos III **Obv:** Head right, with hair in waves **Obv. Legend:** CAROLUS III • D • G • **Rev:** Crowned arms **Rev. Legend:** HISPANIARUM • REX • **Note:** Mint mark: Crowned M.

Date	Mintage	VG	F	VF	XF	Unc
1759 J Rosettes	—	—	—	—	—	—
1759 JP	—	50.00	70.00	135	190	—
1760 JP	—	50.00	70.00	135	190	—
1761 JP	—	50.00	70.00	135	190	—
1762 JP	—	50.00	70.00	135	190	—
1763 JP	—	50.00	70.00	135	190	—
1764 JP	—	50.00	70.00	135	190	—
1765 PJ	—	50.00	70.00	135	190	—
1766 PJ	—	50.00	70.00	135	190	—
1767 PJ	—	50.00	70.00	135	190	—
1768 PJ	—	50.00	70.00	135	190	—
1769 PJ	—	50.00	70.00	135	190	—
1770 PJ	—	50.00	70.00	135	190	—
1771 PJ	—	60.00	90.00	175	250	—

KM# 389.2 1/2 ESCUDO
1.6900 g., 0.9170 Gold 0.0498 oz. AGW **Ruler:** Carlos III **Obv:** Head right, with hair in waves **Obv. Legend:** CAROLUS III • D • G • **Rev:** Crowned arms **Rev. Legend:** HISPANIARUM • REX • **Note:** Mint mark: S, S/L.

Date	Mintage	VG	F	VF	XF	Unc
1759 JV	—	60.00	90.00	175	250	—
1760 JV	—	50.00	70.00	140	200	—
1761 JV	—	50.00	70.00	100	175	—
1762 JV	—	70.00	175	350	500	—
1764 VC	—	50.00	70.00	140	200	—
1765 VC	—	50.00	70.00	140	200	—
1766 VC	—	65.00	140	275	400	—
1767 VC	—	65.00	125	170	250	—
1767 CF	—	65.00	165	325	450	—
1768 CF	—	65.00	140	275	400	—
1769 CF	—	65.00	140	275	400	—
1770 CF	—	70.00	175	350	500	—
1771 CF	—	60.00	125	250	350	—

KM# 415.1 1/2 ESCUDO
1.6900 g., 0.9010 Gold 0.0490 oz. AGW **Ruler:** Carlos III **Obv:** Older bust right **Obv. Legend:** CAROLUS III • D • G • HISP • R • **Rev:** Crowned arms in collar of The Golden Fleece **Note:** Mint mark: Crowned M.

Date	Mintage	VG	F	VF	XF	Unc
1772 PJ	—	50.00	80.00	120	165	—
1773/2 PJ	—	60.00	90.00	140	185	—
1773 PJ	—	50.00	80.00	120	165	—
1774 PJ	—	50.00	80.00	120	165	—
1775 PJ	—	50.00	75.00	95.00	150	—
1776 PJ	—	50.00	75.00	95.00	150	—
1777 PJ	—	50.00	75.00	95.00	150	—
1778 PJ	—	50.00	75.00	95.00	150	—
1779 PJ	—	50.00	80.00	120	175	—
1781/80 PJ	—	150	350	650	900	—
1783/79 JD	—	50.00	90.00	140	185	—
1783 JD	—	50.00	80.00	120	165	—
1784 JD	—	50.00	75.00	95.00	150	—
1785 DV	—	100	200	275	450	—

KM# 415.2 1/2 ESCUDO
1.6900 g., 0.9010 Gold 0.0490 oz. AGW **Ruler:** Carlos III **Obv:** Older bust right **Obv. Legend:** CAROLUS III • D • G • HISP • R • **Rev:** Crowned arms in collar of The Golden Fleece **Note:** Mint mark: S, S/L.

Date	Mintage	VG	F	VF	XF	Unc
1773 CF	—	50.00	70.00	135	190	—
1774 CF	—	50.00	70.00	135	190	—
1775 CF	—	50.00	70.00	135	190	—
1776 CF	—	50.00	70.00	135	190	—
1777 CF	—	50.00	70.00	135	190	—
1778 CF	—	50.00	70.00	135	190	—
1779 CF	—	50.00	70.00	135	190	—
1781 CF	—	70.00	140	275	400	—
1782 CF	—	70.00	140	275	400	—
1783 CF	—	60.00	125	250	600	—

KM# 425.2 1/2 ESCUDO
1.6900 g., 0.8750 Gold 0.0475 oz. AGW **Ruler:** Carlos III **Obv:** Bust right **Obv. Legend:** CAROLUS III • D • G • HISP • R • **Rev:** Crowned oval shield in collar of The Golden Fleece **Note:** Mint mark: S, S/L.

Date	Mintage	VG	F	VF	XF	Unc
1786 C Rare	—	—	—	—	—	—
1788/6 C	—	60.00	80.00	150	225	—
1788 C	—	50.00	65.00	125	200	—

KM# 425.1 1/2 ESCUDO
1.6900 g., 0.8750 Gold 0.0475 oz. AGW **Ruler:** Carlos III **Obv:** Bust right **Obv. Legend:** CAROLUS III • D • G • HISP • R • **Rev:** Crowned oval shield in collar of The Golden Fleece **Note:** Mint mark: Crowned M.

Date	Mintage	VG	F	VF	XF	Unc
1786 DV	—	50.00	75.00	100	150	—
1787 DV	—	50.00	75.00	100	150	—
1788 DV	—	250	500	1,000	1,500	—
1788 M	—	50.00	75.00	100	150	—

KM# 433 1/2 ESCUDO
1.6900 g., 0.8750 Gold 0.0475 oz. AGW **Ruler:** Carlos IV **Obv:** Bust right **Rev:** Crowned oval shield in collar of The Golden Fleece **Note:** Mint mark: Crowned M.

Date	Mintage	VG	F	VF	XF	Unc
1788 MF	—	300	500	900	1,500	—
1789 MF	—	300	500	900	1,500	—
1790 MF	—	200	400	750	1,200	—
1791 MF	—	200	400	800	1,300	—
1792 MF	—	300	500	1,000	1,600	—
1793 MF	—	200	400	750	1,200	—
1794 MF	—	200	400	800	1,300	—
1795 MF	—	300	500	1,000	1,600	—
1796 MF	—	175	350	700	1,100	—
1797 MF	—	175	350	700	1,100	—

KM# 245 ESCUDO
3.4335 g., 0.9167 Gold 0.1012 oz. AGW **Ruler:** Philip V **Obv:** Crowned arms, pointed bottom **Rev:** Cross is quatrefoil, date at top **Note:** Mint mark: S, S/L.

Date	Mintage	VG	F	VF	XF	Unc
1700 M	—	275	575	1,000	1,650	—

KM# 253 ESCUDO
3.4335 g., 0.9167 Gold 0.1012 oz. AGW **Ruler:** Philip V **Obv:** Crowned arms in Order collar **Rev:** Cross in quatrefoil **Note:** Mint mark: S, S/L.

Date	Mintage	VG	F	VF	XF	Unc
1701 M	—	250	500	700	1,000	—
1704 P	—	250	500	700	1,000	—
1705 P	—	250	500	700	1,000	—
1706 M	—	250	500	700	1,200	—
1712 M	—	250	500	700	1,000	—
1720 J	—	200	400	600	900	—
1721 J	—	200	400	600	900	—
1722 J	—	20.00	400	600	900	—
1723 J	—	200	400	600	900	—
1726 J	—	200	400	600	900	—

KM# 312 ESCUDO
3.3800 g., 0.9010 Gold 0.0979 oz. AGW **Ruler:** Philip V **Obv:** Crowned arms in Order collar **Rev:** Cross in quatrefoil, date at top **Note:** Mint mark: Crowned M.

Date	Mintage	VG	F	VF	XF	Unc
1719 F	—	250	500	800	1,300	—
1721 A	—	250	500	800	1,300	—
1722 A	—	250	500	800	1,300	—
1723 A	—	250	500	800	1,300	—
1727 A	—	250	500	800	1,300	—

KM# 343 ESCUDO
3.3800 g., 0.9010 Gold 0.0979 oz. AGW **Ruler:** Philip V **Obv:** Head right **Obv. Legend:** PHILIP • V • D • G • HISPAN • ETIND • REX • **Rev:** Crowned arms **Rev. Legend:** TIMOR • DOMINI • ... **Note:** Mint mark: S, S/L. Varieties exist.

Date	Mintage	VG	F	VF	XF	Unc
1729	—	175	250	400	650	—
1730	—	225	375	550	900	—
1731 PA	—	175	250	400	650	—
1732 PA	—	175	250	400	650	—
1733 PA	—	175	250	400	650	—
1736 PA	—	175	250	400	650	—
1736 AP	—	175	250	400	650	—
1739 PJ	—	175	250	400	650	—

KM# 342 ESCUDO
3.3800 g., 0.9010 Gold 0.0979 oz. AGW **Ruler:** Philip V **Obv:** Head right **Obv. Legend:** PHILIP • V • D • G • HISP ... **Rev:** Crowned arms **Rev. Legend:** TIMOR • DOM • .... **Note:** Varieties exist. Mint mark: Crowned M.

Date	Mintage	VG	F	VF	XF	Unc
1729	—	250	500	900	1,400	—
1730	—	250	500	900	1,400	—
1733 JF	—	150	300	450	700	—
1735 JF	—	150	300	450	700	—
1736 JF	—	150	300	450	700	—
1737 JF	—	225	450	700	1,200	—

Date	Mintage	VG	F	VF	XF	Unc
1739 JF	—	225	450	700	1,200	—
1740 JF	—	125	250	350	500	—
1741 JF	—	125	250	350	500	—
1742 JF	—	150	300	500	750	—
1742 JA	—	250	500	900	1,400	—

KM# 416.1 ESCUDO

3.3800 g., 0.9010 Gold 0.0979 oz. AGW **Ruler:** Carlos III **Obv:** Bust right **Obv. Legend:** CAROL • III • D • G • HISP • ETIND • R • **Rev:** Crowned arms in collar of The Golden Fleece **Rev. Legend:** FELIX • A • D • ... **Note:** Mint mark: Crowned M.

Date	Mintage	VG	F	VF	XF	Unc
1772 PJ	—	150	300	500	900	—
1779 PJ	—	70.00	80.00	125	175	—
1780 PJ	—	70.00	80.00	125	175	—
1781 PJ	—	65.00	80.00	125	175	—
1782 JD	—	80.00	100	175	250	—
1784 JD	—	70.00	80.00	125	175	—
1785 DV	—	70.00	80.00	125	175	—

KM# 416.2 ESCUDO

3.3800 g., 0.9010 Gold 0.0979 oz. AGW **Ruler:** Carlos III **Obv:** Bust right **Obv. Legend:** CAROL • III • D • G • HISP • ETIND • R • **Rev:** Crowned arms in collar of The Golden Fleece **Rev. Legend:** FELIX • A • D • ... **Note:** Mint mark: S, S/L.

Date	Mintage	VG	F	VF	XF	Unc
1773 CF	—	70.00	80.00	140	200	—
1774 CF	—	70.00	80.00	140	200	—
1779 CF	—	70.00	80.00	140	200	—
1780 CF	—	70.00	80.00	140	200	—
1781 CF	—	70.00	80.00	140	200	—

KM# 416.2a ESCUDO

3.3800 g., 0.8785 Gold 0.0955 oz. AGW **Ruler:** Carlos III **Obv:** Bust right **Obv. Legend:** CAROL • III • D • G • HISPAN • ETIND • R • **Rev:** Crowned arms in collar of The Golden Fleece **Rev. Legend:** FELIX • A • D • ... **Note:** Mint mark: S, S/L.

Date	Mintage	VG	F	VF	XF	Unc
1784 V	—	70.00	90.00	175	250	—
1785 C	—	70.00	90.00	175	250	—
1787/6 CM	—	70.00	100	200	300	—
1787 CM	—	70.00	80.00	140	200	—

KM# 416.1a ESCUDO

3.3800 g., 0.8750 Gold 0.0951 oz. AGW **Ruler:** Carlos III **Obv:** Bust right **Obv. Legend:** CAROL • III • D • G • HISPAN • ETIND • R • **Rev:** Crowned arms in collar of The Golden Fleece **Rev. Legend:** FELIX • A • D • ... **Note:** Mint mark: Crowned M.

Date	Mintage	VG	F	VF	XF	Unc
1787/6 DV	—	70.00	80.00	150	225	—
1787 DV	—	70.00	80.00	125	175	—
1788 M	—	70.00	80.00	150	200	—
1788 M	—	70.00	80.00	150	200	—

KM# 434 ESCUDO

3.3800 g., 0.8785 Gold 0.0955 oz. AGW **Ruler:** Carlos IV **Obv:** Bust right **Obv. Legend:** CAROL • IIII • D • G • HISP • ETIND • R • **Rev:** Crowned arms in order chain **Rev. Legend:** FELIX • A • D • ... **Note:** Mint mark: Crowned M.

Date	Mintage	VG	F	VF	XF	Unc
1788 MF	—	225	450	700	1,000	—
1789 MF	—	70.00	80.00	100	150	—
1790 MF	—	70.00	80.00	100	150	—
1791 MF	—	70.00	80.00	100	150	—
1792 MF	—	70.00	80.00	100	150	—
1793 MF	—	70.00	80.00	100	150	—
1794 MF	—	70.00	80.00	100	150	—
1796 MF	—	70.00	80.00	100	150	—
1797 MF	—	70.00	80.00	100	150	—
1798 MF	—	70.00	80.00	100	150	—
1799 MF	—	70.00	80.00	100	150	—
1799 FA	—	75.00	125	250	350	—

KM# 254 2 ESCUDOS

6.8670 g., 0.9167 Gold 0.2024 oz. AGW **Ruler:** Philip V **Obv:** Crowned arms, denomination at right **Obv. Legend:** PHILIP V ... **Rev:** Cross in quatrefoil in inner circle, date at top **Note:** Mint mark: S, S/L.

Date	Mintage	VG	F	VF	XF	Unc
1701 M	—	300	600	900	1,300	—

KM# 255 2 ESCUDOS

6.8670 g., 0.9167 Gold 0.2024 oz. AGW **Ruler:** Philip V **Obv:** Crowned arms, flowers at sides **Obv. Legend:** PHILIPVS • V • ... **Rev:** Cross in quatrefoil, denomination, mint mark and assayer initial at corners **Rev. Legend:** HISPANIARUM REX **Note:** Mint mark: S, S/L.

Date	Mintage	VG	F	VF	XF	Unc
1701 M	—	350	700	1,100	1,600	—
1702 M Reported, not confirmed	—	—	—	—	—	—
1703 J Error value: 1	—	300	600	900	1,300	—
1704 P	—	300	600	900	1,300	—
1704 P Retrograde 4 in date	—	300	600	900	1,300	—
1706 P	—	300	600	900	1,300	—

KM# 282 2 ESCUDOS

6.7700 g., 0.9010 Gold 0.1961 oz. AGW **Ruler:** Philip V **Obv:** Crowned arms **Obv. Legend:** PHILIPVS V DEI GRAT **Rev:** Cross in quatrefoil in inner circle, date in legend **Rev. Legend:** HISPANIARUM REX

Date	Mintage	VG	F	VF	XF	Unc
1707V F	—	1,000	2,000	3,000	4,500	—

KM# 293 2 ESCUDOS

6.7700 g., 0.9010 Gold 0.1961 oz. AGW **Ruler:** Philip V **Obv:** Crowned shield, denomination as II **Obv. Legend:** PHILIPPVS • V • D • GRAT **Rev:** Cross in quatrefoil, denomination as 2 **Note:** Mint mark: S, S/L.

Date	Mintage	VG	F	VF	XF	Unc
1711 M	—	300	600	900	1,300	—
1712/1 M	—	300	600	1,000	1,500	—
1712 M	—	300	600	900	1,300	—
1714 M	—	300	600	900	1,300	—
1717 M	—	300	600	1,000	1,500	—
1718 M	—	300	600	1,000	1,500	—

KM# 313 2 ESCUDOS

6.7700 g., 0.9010 Gold 0.1961 oz. AGW **Ruler:** Philip V **Obv:** Crowned arms in order chain **Obv. Legend:** PHILIPPUS V DEI GRAT **Rev:** Cross in quatrefoil, date at top **Note:** Mint mark: Crowned M.

Date	Mintage	VG	F	VF	XF	Unc
1719 F	—	500	1,000	1,750	2,500	—
1721 A	—	500	1,000	1,750	2,500	—
1723 A	—	500	1,000	1,750	2,500	—
1725 A	—	500	1,000	1,750	2,500	—

KM# 325 2 ESCUDOS

6.7700 g., 0.9010 Gold 0.1961 oz. AGW **Ruler:** Philip V **Obv:** Crowned arms in Order collar **Obv. Legend:** PHILIPPUS V DEI GRA **Rev:** Cross in quatrefoil, denomination as 2 **Note:** Mint mark: S, S/L.

Date	Mintage	VG	F	VF	XF	Unc
1720 J	—	250	500	800	1,300	—
1721 J	—	250	500	900	1,300	—
1722 J	—	300	600	1,000	1,400	—
1723 J	—	250	500	800	1,300	—
1726 J	—	250	500	800	1,300	—

KM# 330 2 ESCUDOS

6.7700 g., 0.9010 Gold 0.1961 oz. AGW **Ruler:** Louis I **Obv:** Crowned arms in Order collar, titles of Louis I **Note:** Mint mark: S, S/L.

Date	Mintage	VG	F	VF	XF	Unc
1724 J	—	2,000	4,500	6,000	9,000	—

KM# A334 2 ESCUDOS

6.7700 g., 0.9010 Gold 0.1961 oz. AGW **Ruler:** Philip V **Obv:** Crowned arms in Order collar **Obv. Legend:** PHILIPPUS V DEI GRA **Rev:** Cross in quatrefoil, date at top

Date	Mintage	VG	F	VF	XF	Unc
1725CA JJ Rare	—	—	—	—	—	—

Note: Durr & R. Michel Monnaies d'or d'Espagne sale 11-99, unc. realized $30,850

KM# 344 2 ESCUDOS

6.7700 g., 0.9010 Gold 0.1961 oz. AGW **Ruler:** Philip V **Obv:** Bust right **Rev:** Crowned shield of Castile and Leon **Note:** Mint mark: Crowned M.

Date	Mintage	VG	F	VF	XF	Unc
1729	—	300	600	1,000	1,500	—

KM# 352 2 ESCUDOS

6.7700 g., 0.9010 Gold 0.1961 oz. AGW **Ruler:** Philip V **Obv:** Armored bust right **Rev:** Crowned shield of Castile and Leon **Note:** Mint mark: Crowned M.

Date	Mintage	VG	F	VF	XF	Unc
1730	—	250	500	800	1,200	—
1731 F	—	225	400	600	1,000	—
1731 JF	—	150	300	450	800	—
1732 JF	—	150	250	400	650	—
1733 JF	—	150	250	400	650	—
1734 JF	—	150	250	400	650	—

KM# 353 2 ESCUDOS

6.7700 g., 0.9010 Gold 0.1961 oz. AGW **Ruler:** Philip V **Obv:** Armored bust right **Obv. Legend:** PHILIP • V • D • G • HISPAN • ETIND • REX • **Rev:** Crowned shield of Castile and Leon **Note:** Mint mark: S, S/L.

Date	Mintage	VG	F	VF	XF	Unc
1730	—	225	450	700	1,000	—
1731 PA	—	150	300	475	700	—
1732 PA	—	150	300	475	700	—
1733 PA	—	150	300	475	700	—
1734 PA	—	150	300	475	700	—
1735 AP	—	150	300	475	700	—
1736 AP	—	150	300	475	700	—
1737 PJ	—	150	300	475	700	—
1739 PJ	—	150	300	475	700	—
1740 PJ	—	150	250	400	600	—
1741 PJ	—	150	250	400	600	—
1742 PJ	—	150	250	400	600	—

KM# 376.2 2 ESCUDOS
6.7700 g., 0.9010 Gold 0.1961 oz. AGW **Ruler:** Ferdinand VI **Obv:** Bust right **Obv. Legend:** FERDINANDUS • VI • D • G • HISP • REX • **Rev:** Crowned arms

Date	Mintage	VG	F	VF	XF	Unc
1749S PJ	—	400	900	1,400	2,000	—

KM# 376.1 2 ESCUDOS
6.7700 g., 0.9010 Gold 0.1961 oz. AGW **Ruler:** Ferdinand VI **Obv:** Bust right **Obv. Legend:** FERDINANDUS • VI • D • G • HISP • REX • **Rev:** Crowned arms **Note:** Mint mark: Crowned M.

Date	Mintage	VG	F	VF	XF	Unc
1749 JB	—	650	1,250	2,000	3,000	—

KM# 417.1 2 ESCUDOS
6.7700 g., 0.9010 Gold 0.1961 oz. AGW **Ruler:** Carlos III **Obv:** Bust right **Obv. Legend:** CAROL • III • D • G • HISP • IND • R • **Rev:** Crowned arms in Order collar **Note:** Mint mark: Crowned M.

Date	Mintage	VG	F	VF	XF	Unc
1772 PJ	—	150	200	300	450	—
1773 PJ	—	150	175	200	250	—
1774 PJ	—	150	175	200	250	—
1775 PJ	—	150	175	200	250	—
1776 PJ	—	150	175	200	250	—
1777 PJ	—	150	175	200	250	—
1778 PJ	—	150	175	200	250	—
1779 PJ	—	150	175	200	250	—
1780 PJ	—	150	175	200	250	—
1781 PJ	—	150	175	200	250	—
1784 JD	—	250	500	800	1,200	—
1785 DV	—	400	900	1,400	2,000	—

KM# 417.2 2 ESCUDOS
6.7700 g., 0.9010 Gold 0.1961 oz. AGW **Ruler:** Carlos III **Obv:** Bust right **Obv. Legend:** CAROL • III • D • G • HISP • ETIND • R • **Rev:** Crowned arms in Order collar **Note:** Mint mark: S, S/L.

Date	Mintage	VG	F	VF	XF	Unc
1773 CF	—	150	175	225	300	—
1774 CF	—	150	175	225	300	—
1775 CF	—	150	175	225	300	—
1776 CF	—	150	175	225	300	—
1777 CF	—	150	175	275	400	—
1779 CF	—	150	175	275	400	—

KM# 417.1a 2 ESCUDOS
6.7700 g., 0.8750 Gold 0.1904 oz. AGW **Ruler:** Carlos III **Obv:** Bust right **Obv. Legend:** CAROL • III • D • G • HISP • ETIND • R • **Rev:** Crowned arms in Order chain **Rev. Legend:** IN • UTROQ • FELIX • AUSPICE • DEO **Note:** Mint mark: Crowned M.

Date	Mintage	VG	F	VF	XF	Unc
1786 DV	—	150	200	350	500	—
1787 DV	—	225	450	700	1,000	—
1788 M	—	150	175	200	245	—

KM# 417.2a 2 ESCUDOS
6.7700 g., 0.8750 Gold 0.1904 oz. AGW **Ruler:** Carlos III **Obv:** Bust right **Obv. Legend:** CAROL • III • D • G • HISP • ETIND • R • **Rev:** Crowned arms **Note:** Mint mark: S, S/L.

Date	Mintage	VG	F	VF	XF	Unc
1787 CM	—	150	175	200	300	—
1788 C	—	150	175	200	300	—

KM# 435.1 2 ESCUDOS
6.7700 g., 0.8750 Gold 0.1904 oz. AGW **Ruler:** Carlos IV **Obv:** Bust right **Obv. Legend:** CAROL • IIII • D • G • HISP • ETIND • R • **Rev:** Crowned arms in order chain **Rev. Legend:** IN • UTROQ • FELIX... **Note:** Mint mark: Crowned M.

Date	Mintage	VG	F	VF	XF	Unc
1788 MF	—	150	200	350	500	—
1789 MF	—	150	175	200	235	—
1790 MF	—	150	175	200	235	—
1791 MF	—	300	600	1,000	1,500	—
1792 MF	—	150	200	350	500	—
1793 MF	—	150	175	200	235	—
1794 MF	—	150	175	200	235	—
1795 MF	—	150	175	200	235	—
1796 MF	—	150	175	200	235	—
1797 MF	—	150	175	200	235	—
1798 MF	—	150	175	200	235	—
1799 MF	—	150	175	200	235	—
1800 MF	—	150	175	200	235	—
1800 FA	—	125	150	175	235	—

KM# 435.2 2 ESCUDOS
6.7700 g., 0.8750 Gold 0.1904 oz. AGW **Ruler:** Carlos IV **Obv:** Bust right **Obv. Legend:** CAROL • IIII • D • G ... **Rev:** Crowned arms in order chain **Rev. Legend:** IN • UTROQ • FELIX ... **Note:** Mint mark: S, S/L.

Date	Mintage	VG	F	VF	XF	Unc
1790 C	—	150	200	350	500	—
1791 C	—	150	175	300	450	—
1791 CN	—	150	200	350	500	—
1793 CN	—	150	175	200	250	—
1794 CN	—	150	175	200	250	—
1795 CN	—	150	175	200	250	—
1796 CN	—	150	175	200	250	—
1797 CN	—	150	175	200	250	—
1798 CN	—	150	175	200	250	—
1799 CN	—	150	175	200	250	—
1800 CN	—	150	175	200	250	—

KM# 256 4 ESCUDOS
13.7341 g., 0.9167 Gold 0.4048 oz. AGW **Ruler:** Philip V **Obv:** Crowned arms. mint mark, assayer initial and denomination at sides **Obv. Legend:** PHILIPPVS • V • DEI • GRA **Rev:** Cross in quatrefoil in inner circle, date at top **Rev. Legend:** HISPANIARVM REX **Note:** Mint mark: S, S/L.

Date	Mintage	VG	F	VF	XF	Unc
1701 M	—	650	1,400	2,100	3,000	—

KM# 257 4 ESCUDOS
13.7341 g., 0.9167 Gold 0.4048 oz. AGW **Ruler:** Philip V **Obv:** Crowned arms **Obv. Legend:** PHILIPPVS V DEI GRAT **Rev:** Cross in quatrefoil, mint mark, assayer initial and denomination at corners **Rev. Legend:** HISPANIARVM REX **Note:** Mint mark: S, S/L.

Date	Mintage	VG	F	VF	XF	Unc
1701 M	—	650	1,400	2,100	3,000	—
1702 M	—	650	1,400	2,100	3,000	—
1703 J	—	600	1,300	2,000	2,900	—
1703 P	—	600	1,300	2,000	2,900	—
1704 P	—	600	1,300	1,900	2,800	—
1705 P	—	700	1,500	3,200	4,500	—
1709 M	—	600	1,300	2,000	2,900	—
1710 M	—	700	1,500	3,200	4,500	—
1715 M	—	700	1,500	3,200	4,500	—
1717 M	—	650	1,400	2,100	3,000	—
1718 M	—	600	1,300	1,900	2,700	—

KM# 273 4 ESCUDOS
13.5400 g., 0.9170 Gold 0.3992 oz. AGW **Ruler:** Philip V **Obv:** Crowned arms in inner circle **Rev:** Cross in quatrefoil in inner circle, date in legend **Note:** Mint mark: V, VAL.

Date	Mintage	VG	F	VF	XF	Unc
1707 V	—	1,300	2,800	4,200	6,000	—

KM# 288 4 ESCUDOS
13.5400 g., 0.9170 Gold 0.3992 oz. AGW **Ruler:** Philip V **Obv:** Crowned arms **Obv. Legend:** PHILIPPVS V D GRATI **Rev:** Cross in quatrefoil, date at top **Rev. Legend:** HISPANIARVM REX

Date	Mintage	VG	F	VF	XF	Unc
1710M J Rare	—	—	—	—	—	—

KM# 295 4 ESCUDOS
13.5400 g., 0.9170 Gold 0.3992 oz. AGW **Ruler:** Philip V **Obv:** Crowned arms **Rev:** Cross in quatrefoil, mint mark, initials and value in corners **Note:** Mint mark: S, S/L. Varieties exist.

Date	Mintage	VG	F	VF	XF	Unc
1712 M	—	550	1,100	1,750	2,600	—
1713 M	—	600	1,300	1,900	2,800	—

KM# 314.1 4 ESCUDOS
13.5400 g., 0.9170 Gold 0.3992 oz. AGW **Ruler:** Philip V **Obv:** Crowned arms in order collar **Obv. Legend:** PHILIPPUS V DEI GRA **Rev:** Cross in quatrefoil, date at top **Rev. Legend:** HISPANIARUM REX... **Note:** Mint mark: Crowned M.

Date	Mintage	VG	F	VF	XF	Unc
1719 F	—	1,300	2,800	4,200	6,000	—
1723 A	—	1,100	2,600	3,800	5,500	—
1727 A	—	1,300	2,800	4,200	6,000	—

KM# 314.2 4 ESCUDOS
13.5400 g., 0.9170 Gold 0.3992 oz. AGW **Ruler:** Philip V **Obv:** Crowned arms in order collar **Rev:** Cross in quatrefoil, date at top **Note:** Mint mark: S, S/L.

Date	Mintage	VG	F	VF	XF	Unc
1719 J	—	900	1,800	2,700	4,000	—
1721 J	—	900	1,800	2,700	4,000	—
1723 J	—	900	1,800	2,700	4,000	—
1726 J	—	1,000	2,200	3,100	4,500	—
1728 P	—	1,000	2,200	3,100	4,500	—
1729 P	—	1,000	2,200	3,100	4,500	—

KM# 314.3 4 ESCUDOS
13.5400 g., 0.9170 Gold 0.3992 oz. AGW **Ruler:** Philip V **Obv:** Crowned arms in order collar **Rev:** Cross in quatrefoil, date at top **Note:** Mint mark: Aqueduct.

Date	Mintage	VG	F	VF	XF	Unc
1721 F Rare	—	—	—	—	—	—

KM# 331 4 ESCUDOS
13.5400 g., 0.9170 Gold 0.3992 oz. AGW **Ruler:** Louis I **Obv:** Crowned arms in order collar, titles of Louis I **Rev:** Cross in quatrefoil, date at top **Note:** Mint mark: Aqueduct.

Date	Mintage	VG	F	VF	XF	Unc
1724 F Rare	—	—	—	—	—	—

KM# 334 4 ESCUDOS
13.5400 g., 0.9170 Gold 0.3992 oz. AGW **Ruler:** Philip V **Obv:** Crowned arms in Order collar **Obv. Legend:** PHILIPPUS V DEI GRA **Rev:** Cross in quatrefoil, date at top

Date	Mintage	VG	F	VF	XF	Unc
1725CA JJ Rare	—	—	—	—	—	—

KM# 345 4 ESCUDOS

13.5400 g., 0.9170 Gold 0.3992 oz. AGW **Ruler:** Philip V **Obv:** Armored bust right **Obv. Legend:** PHILIP • V • D • G • HISPAN • ET IND REX • **Rev:** Crowned arms **Note:** Mint mark: S, S/L.

Date	Mintage	VG	F	VF	XF	Unc
1729	—	900	1,900	2,750	4,000	—
1730	—	900	1,900	2,750	4,000	—

KM# 359 4 ESCUDOS

13.5400 g., 0.9170 Gold 0.3992 oz. AGW **Ruler:** Philip V **Obv:** Armored bust right **Obv. Legend:** PHILIP • V • D • G • HISPAN • ETIND REX • **Rev:** Crowned arms **Note:** Mint mark: S, S/L.

Date	Mintage	VG	F	VF	XF	Unc
1731 PA	—	800	1,700	2,500	3,500	—
1732 PA	—	900	1,900	2,750	4,000	—
1733 PA	—	1,200	2,700	3,750	5,500	—

KM# 360 4 ESCUDOS

13.5400 g., 0.9170 Gold 0.3992 oz. AGW **Ruler:** Philip V **Obv:** Armored bust of Philip V right **Obv. Legend:** PHILIP • V • D • G • HISPAN • ET IND • REX • **Rev:** Crowned arms **Note:** Mint mark: Crowned M.

Date	Mintage	VG	F	VF	XF	Unc
1732 JF	—	1,000	2,000	3,000	4,500	—
1733 JF	—	750	1,500	2,500	3,500	—
1734 JF	—	650	1,250	2,000	3,500	—

KM# 375.2 4 ESCUDOS

13.5400 g., 0.9170 Gold 0.3992 oz. AGW **Ruler:** Ferdinand VI **Obv:** Bust right **Obv. Legend:** FERDINANDUS • VI • D • G • HISP • REX • **Rev:** Crowned arms

Date	Mintage	VG	F	VF	XF	Unc
1747S PJ	—	1,500	3,500	5,000	7,000	—
1749S PJ	—	1,250	3,000	4,000	6,000	—

KM# 375.1 4 ESCUDOS

13.5400 g., 0.9170 Gold 0.3992 oz. AGW **Ruler:** Ferdinand VI **Obv:** Bust right **Obv. Legend:** FERDINANDUS • VI • D • G • HISP • REX • **Rev:** Crowned arms **Note:** Mint mark: Crowned M.

Date	Mintage	VG	F	VF	XF	Unc
1747 J	—	1,000	2,500	3,500	5,000	—
1748 JB	—	1,000	2,500	3,500	5,000	—
1749 JB	—	1,500	3,500	5,000	7,500	—

KM# 398 4 ESCUDOS

13.5400 g., 0.9170 Gold 0.3992 oz. AGW **Ruler:** Carlos III **Obv:** Bust right **Obv. Legend:** CAROL • III • D • G • ... **Rev:** Crowned arms in collar of The Golden Fleece **Note:** Mint mark: Crowned M.

Date	Mintage	VG	F	VF	XF	Unc
1761 JP Rare	—	—	—	—	—	—

KM# 418.1 4 ESCUDOS

13.5400 g., 0.9010 Gold 0.3922 oz. AGW **Ruler:** Carlos III **Obv:** Bust right **Obv. Legend:** CAROL • III • D • G • HISP • ET IND • R • **Rev:** Crowned arms in collar of The Golden Fleece **Note:** Mint mark: Crowned M.

Date	Mintage	VG	F	VF	XF	Unc
1772 PJ	—	300	500	700	1,000	—
1773 PJ	—	300	500	700	1,000	—
1774 PJ	—	300	350	425	600	—
1775 PJ	—	300	350	425	600	—
1777 PJ	—	300	500	700	1,000	—
1778 PJ	—	300	350	425	600	—
1779 PJ	—	300	350	425	600	—
1780 PJ	—	300	350	400	500	—
1781 PJ	—	300	350	400	500	—
1782 PJ	—	300	350	400	500	—
1782 JD	—	300	350	400	500	—
1783 JD	—	300	500	800	1,200	—
1785 DV	—	300	350	425	600	—

KM# 418.2 4 ESCUDOS

13.5400 g., 0.9010 Gold 0.3922 oz. AGW **Ruler:** Carlos III **Obv:** Bust right **Obv. Legend:** CAROL • III • D • G • HISP • ET IND • R • **Rev:** Crowned arms in collar of The Golden Fleece **Note:** Mint mark: S, S/L.

Date	Mintage	VG	F	VF	XF	Unc
1772 CF	—	300	350	500	700	—
1773 CF	—	300	350	425	600	—
1774 CF	—	300	400	550	800	—
1775 CF	—	300	350	450	650	—
1776 CF	—	300	350	450	650	—
1777 CF	—	300	350	450	650	—
1779 CF	—	300	400	550	800	—
1781 CF	—	300	350	500	700	—
1784 C	—	300	400	550	800	—
1784 V	—	400	800	1,100	1,600	—
1785 C	—	300	650	900	1,300	—

KM# 418.1a 4 ESCUDOS

13.5400 g., 0.8750 Gold 0.3809 oz. AGW **Ruler:** Carlos III **Obv:** Bust of Charles III right **Obv. Legend:** CAROL • III • D • G • HISP • ET IND • R • **Rev:** Crowned arms in collar of The Golden Fleece **Rev. Legend:** IN • UTROQ • FELIX • AUSPICE • DEO • **Note:** Mint mark: Crowned M.

Date	Mintage	VG	F	VF	XF	Unc
1786 DV	—	300	350	400	500	—
1787 DV	—	300	300	400	550	—
1788 M	—	300	350	400	500	—

KM# 418.2a 4 ESCUDOS

13.5400 g., 0.8750 Gold 0.3809 oz. AGW **Ruler:** Carlos III **Obv:** Bust right **Obv. Legend:** CAROL • III • D • G • HISP • ET IND • R • **Rev:** Crowned arms in collar of The Golden Fleece **Rev. Legend:** IN • UTROQ • FELIX • AUSPICE • DEO •

Date	Mintage	VG	F	VF	XF	Unc
1786 C	—	300	350	425	600	—
1787 CM	—	300	350	400	500	—
1788 C	—	300	350	400	500	—

KM# 436.1 4 ESCUDOS

13.5400 g., 0.8750 Gold 0.3809 oz. AGW **Ruler:** Carlos IV **Obv:** Bust right **Obv. Legend:** CAROL • IIII • D • G • HISP • ET IND • R • **Rev:** Crowned arms in order chain **Rev. Legend:** IN • UTROQ • FELIX • AUSPICE • DEO • **Note:** Mint mark: Crowned M.

Date	Mintage	VG	F	VF	XF	Unc
1788 MF	—	600	1,300	1,900	2,750	—
1789 MF	—	800	1,600	2,200	3,250	—
1790 MF	—	300	600	850	1,250	—
1791 MF	—	300	350	400	500	—
1792 MF	—	300	350	400	500	—
1794 MF	—	300	450	625	900	—
1795 MF	—	300	350	400	500	—
1796 MF	—	300	350	400	500	—

KM# 258 8 ESCUDOS

27.4682 g., 0.9167 Gold 0.8095 oz. AGW **Obv:** Crowned arms in order collar **Rev:** Cross in quatrefoil

Date	Mintage	VG	F	VF	XF	Unc
x70xB Unique	—	—	—	—	—	—

KM# 260 8 ESCUDOS

27.4682 g., 0.9167 Gold 0.8095 oz. AGW **Ruler:** Philip V **Obv:** Crowned Bourbon Coat of Arms **Obv. Legend:** PHILIPPVS V DEI GRAT **Rev:** Cross in quatrefoil with mint mark, assayer initial and 8's at corners **Rev. Legend:** HISPANIARV... **Note:** Mint mark: S, S/L. Varieties exist in the placement of the mint mark, assayer initial and 8's.

Date	Mintage	VG	F	VF	XF	Unc
1701 M Dots at sides of fleece	—	600	1,200	2,000	3,500	—
1701 M Flowers at sides of fleece	—	600	1,200	2,000	3,500	—
1702 J	—	1,000	2,000	3,300	5,000	—
1702 M	—	750	1,500	2,500	3,750	—
1703 J	—	800	1,600	2,600	4,000	—
1703 M	—	1,200	2,600	4,000	5,850	—
1704 P	—	750	1,500	2,500	3,750	—
1705/3 M	—	750	1,500	2,500	3,750	—
1705 P	—	800	1,650	2,750	4,200	—
1706 P	—	1,200	2,600	3,700	5,600	—
1707 M	—	700	1,400	2,300	3,600	—
1708 M	—	800	1,600	2,600	4,000	—
1709/8 M	—	800	1,600	2,600	4,000	—
1709 M	—	1,200	2,600	3,700	5,600	—
1710 M	—	700	1,400	2,300	3,600	—
1711/0 M	—	700	1,400	2,300	3,600	—
1711 M	—	700	1,400	2,300	3,600	—
1712 M	—	700	1,400	2,300	3,600	—
1713 M	—	900	1,900	2,800	4,200	—
1714/3 M	—	800	1,600	2,600	4,000	—
1714 M	—	750	1,500	2,500	3,800	—
1715/4/3 M	—	1,800	3,800	5,600	8,000	—
1716 M	—	900	1,800	3,000	4,500	—
1717/6 M	—	900	1,800	3,000	4,500	—
1717 M	—	1,000	2,000	3,100	4,750	—
1718 M	—	1,000	2,000	3,300	5,000	—

Date	Mintage	VG	F	VF	XF	Unc
1719 M GRATIA	—	1,500	3,000	4,850	7,000	—
1719 M GRAT	—	1,500	3,000	4,850	7,000	—

KM# 259 8 ESCUDOS
27.4682 g., 0.9167 Gold 0.8095 oz. AGW **Ruler:** Philip V **Obv:** Crowned Hapsburg Coat of Arms **Obv. Legend:** PHILIPPVS • V • DEI • GRAT **Rev:** Cross in quatrefoil with flowers at corners **Rev. Legend:** HISPANIAR... **Note:** Mint mark: S, S/L.

Date	Mintage	VG	F	VF	XF	Unc
1701 No S, rare	—	—	—	—	—	—
1701 M Flowers at sides of fleece	—	1,000	2,000	3,500	5,000	—
1701 M Dots at sides of fleece	—	850	1,750	3,000	4,500	—

KM# 261 8 ESCUDOS
27.0700 g., 0.9170 Gold 0.7981 oz. AGW **Ruler:** Philip V **Obv:** Crowned arms in order collar **Obv. Legend:** PHILIPPVS V DEI GRAT **Rev:** Cross in quatrefoil with mint mark, assayer initial and 8's at corners **Rev. Legend:** HISPANIAR...

Date	Mintage	VG	F	VF	XF	Unc
1703M B	—	2,500	4,500	7,500	—	—
1706M Y	—	1,500	3,500	6,500	—	—
1707M F	—	1,500	3,500	6,500	—	—

KM# 277 8 ESCUDOS
27.0700 g., 0.9170 Gold 0.7981 oz. AGW **Ruler:** Philip V **Obv:** Small crowned arms in double order collar **Obv. Legend:** PHILIPPVS V D G **Rev:** Mint mark and assayer initial at sides of quatrefoil **Rev. Legend:** HISPANIARV... **Note:** Mint mark: Aqueduct.

Date	Mintage	VG	F	VF	XF	Unc
1708 Y Rare	—	—	—	—	—	—

KM# 284 8 ESCUDOS
27.0700 g., 0.9170 Gold 0.7981 oz. AGW **Ruler:** Philip V **Obv:** Large crowned shield, mint mark and assayer initial flanking **Obv. Legend:** PHILIPPVS V D GRATI **Rev:** Large cross in quatrefoil **Rev. Legend:** HISPANIAR....

Date	Mintage	VG	F	VF	XF	Unc
1710M J Rare	—	—	—	—	—	—

Note: Stack's International sale 3-88 XF realized $126,500

KM# 294 8 ESCUDOS
27.0700 g., 0.9170 Gold 0.7981 oz. AGW **Ruler:** Philip V **Obv:** Crowned arms **Obv. Legend:** PHILIPPVS V D G ... **Rev:** Large cross in quatrefoil **Rev. Legend:** HISPANIAR... **Note:** Varieties exist.

Date	Mintage	VG	F	VF	XF	Unc
1711M J	—	2,500	4,500	7,500	—	—
1712M J	—	2,500	4,500	7,500	—	—
1714M J	—	2,500	4,500	7,500	—	—

KM# 300 8 ESCUDOS
27.0700 g., 0.9170 Gold 0.7981 oz. AGW **Ruler:** Philip V **Obv:** Crowned arms without order collar **Obv. Legend:** PHILIPPVS V D G **Rev:** Mint mark and assayer initial separated by date **Rev. Legend:** HISPANIARV....

Date	Mintage	VG	F	VF	XF	Unc
1717M J Rare	—	—	—	—	—	—

KM# 316 8 ESCUDOS
27.0700 g., 0.9170 Gold 0.7981 oz. AGW **Ruler:** Philip V **Obv:** Crowned arms in order collar **Obv. Legend:** PHILIPPVS V DEI GRA **Rev:** Cross in quatrefoil, mint mark and assayer initial in legend **Rev. Legend:** HISPANIARUM REX... **Note:** Mint mark: Crowned M.

Date	Mintage	VG	F	VF	XF	Unc
1719 F Rare	—	—	—	—	—	—
1720 JJ Rare	—	—	—	—	—	—
1721 A Rare	—	—	—	—	—	—
1723 A Rare	—	—	—	—	—	—
1725 A Rare	—	—	—	—	—	—
1727 A	—	—	4,000	6,000	9,500	—

KM# 315 8 ESCUDOS
27.0700 g., 0.9170 Gold 0.7981 oz. AGW **Ruler:** Philip V **Obv:** Crowned Bourbon Coat of Arms in double collar **Obv. Legend:** PHILIPPUS V DEI GRA **Rev:** Cross in quatrefoil with floral crosses at corners **Rev. Legend:** HISPANIARUM REX... **Note:** Mint mark: S, S/L.

Date	Mintage	VG	F	VF	XF	Unc
1719 J	—	1,200	2,700	4,000	5,800	—
1720 J	—	1,200	2,700	4,000	5,800	—
1721 J	—	1,100	2,400	3,500	5,000	—
1722 J	—	1,300	2,700	4,000	5,800	—
1723 J	—	1,100	2,400	3,500	5,000	—
1725 J	—	1,800	3,800	5,600	8,000	—
1726 J	—	1,800	3,800	5,600	8,000	—
1727 J	—	1,800	3,800	5,600	8,000	—
1728 P	—	1,400	3,000	4,400	6,400	—
1729 P	—	1,100	2,400	3,500	5,000	—

KM# 326 8 ESCUDOS
27.0700 g., 0.9170 Gold 0.7981 oz. AGW **Ruler:** Philip V **Obv:** Large crowned arms in order collar **Obv. Legend:** PHILIPPUS V DEI GRA **Rev:** Cross in quatrefoil, mint mark and assayer initial in legend **Rev. Legend:** HISPANIARUM REX... **Note:** Mint mark: Aqueduct.

Date	Mintage	VG	F	VF	XF	Unc
1721 F	—	2,800	4,500	7,000	10,000	—
1723 F Rare	—	—	—	—	—	—

Note: Superior Moreira sale 12-88 choice VF realized $26,400

KM# 332 8 ESCUDOS
27.0700 g., 0.9170 Gold 0.7981 oz. AGW **Ruler:** Louis I **Obv:** Crowned arms in order collar, titles of Louis I **Obv. Legend:** LUDOVICUS I DEI GRA **Rev:** Cross in quatrefoil, mint mark and assayer initial in legend **Rev. Legend:** HISPANIARUM REX... **Note:** Mint mark: Aqueduct.

Date	Mintage	VG	F	VF	XF	Unc
1724 F Rare	—	—	—	—	—	—

KM# 335 8 ESCUDOS
27.0700 g., 0.9170 Gold 0.7981 oz. AGW **Ruler:** Philip V **Obv:** Crowned arms in Order of the Golden Fleece collar **Obv. Legend:** PHILIPPUS V DEI GRA **Rev:** Cross in quatrefoil **Rev. Legend:** HISPANIARUM REX ...

Date	Mintage	VG	F	VF	XF	Unc
1725CA JJ Rare	—	—	—	—	—	—

KM# 347 8 ESCUDOS
27.0700 g., 0.9170 Gold 0.7981 oz. AGW **Ruler:** Philip V **Obv:** Armored bust right, long hair, date divides E8 **Rev:** Crowned arms in Order of the Golden Fleece collar **Note:** Mint mark: Crowned M.

Date	Mintage	VG	F	VF	XF	Unc
1728 JJ Rare	—	—	—	—	—	—
1729 JJ Rare	—	—	—	—	—	—
1729 JJ Without E8; Rare	—	—	—	—	—	—

Note: Stack's International Sale 3-88 VF realized $18,700. Illustration is without E8 variety. Dates with denominations are generally considered twice as rare as the variety without denomination

KM# 346.2 8 ESCUDOS
27.0700 g., 0.9170 Gold 0.7981 oz. AGW **Ruler:** Philip V **Obv:** Armored bust right **Obv. Legend:** PHILIP • V • D • G • HISPAN • ET IND • REX • **Rev:** Crowned arms in Order of the Golden Fleece collar **Rev. Legend:** INITIUM .... **Note:** Mint mark: S, S/L.

Date	Mintage	VG	F	VF	XF	Unc
1729	—	1,000	2,200	3,250	5,000	—
1730	—	1,000	2,200	3,250	5,000	—
1731 PA	—	800	1,650	3,500	5,250	—
1732 PA	—	800	1,650	3,500	5,250	—
1733 PA	—	800	1,650	3,500	5,250	—
1734 PA	—	800	1,650	3,500	5,250	—
1735 PA	—	1,200	2,500	4,000	6,000	—
1736 PA	—	1,200	2,500	4,000	6,000	—
1737 PJ	—	1,400	2,200	4,750	7,500	—
1738 PJ	—	1,400	2,200	4,750	7,500	—

KM# 346.1 8 ESCUDOS

27.0700 g., 0.9170 Gold 0.7981 oz. AGW **Ruler:** Philip V **Obv:** Armored bust right **Obv. Legend:** PHILIP • V • D • G • HISPAN • ET IND • REX • **Rev:** Crowned arms in Order of the Golden Fleece collar **Rev. Legend:** INITIUM .... **Note:** Mint mark: Crowned M.

Date	Mintage	VG	F	VF	XF	Unc
1729 JJ	—	2,000	4,000	6,000	—	—
1730/29 JJ Rare	—	—	—	—	—	—
1730 JJ	—	—	—	15,000	—	—

KM# 377.2 8 ESCUDOS

27.0700 g., 0.9170 Gold 0.7981 oz. AGW **Ruler:** Ferdinand VI **Obv:** Armored bust right **Obv. Legend:** FERDINANDUS • VI • D • G • HISP • REX • **Rev:** Crowned arms in Order of the Golden Fleece collar **Rev. Legend:** ...MAGNA SEQUOR

Date	Mintage	VG	F	VF	XF	Unc
1747S PJ Unique	—	—	—	—	—	—
1748S PJ Rare	—	—	—	—	—	—

KM# 377.1 8 ESCUDOS

27.0700 g., 0.9170 Gold 0.7981 oz. AGW **Ruler:** Ferdinand VI **Obv:** Armored bust right **Obv. Legend:** FERDINANDUS • VI • D • G • HISP • REX • **Rev:** Crowned arms in Order of the Golden Fleece collar **Rev. Legend:** ...MAGNA SEQUOR **Note:** Mint mark: Crowned M.

Date	Mintage	VG	F	VF	XF	Unc
1747 J Rare	—	—	—	—	—	—
1748 JB Rare	—	—	—	—	—	—

KM# 379 8 ESCUDOS

27.0700 g., 0.9170 Gold 0.7981 oz. AGW **Ruler:** Ferdinand VI **Obv:** Draped bust right **Obv. Legend:** FERDINANDUS • VI • D • G • HISP • REX • **Rev:** Crowned arms in Order of the Golden Fleece collar **Rev. Legend:** ...MAGNA SEQUOR **Note:** Mint mark: Crowned M.

Date	Mintage	VG	F	VF	XF	Unc
1749 JB Rare	—	—	—	—	—	—

KM# 385 8 ESCUDOS

27.0700 g., 0.9170 Gold 0.7981 oz. AGW **Ruler:** Ferdinand VI **Obv:** Armored bust right **Obv. Legend:** FERDINANDUS • VI • D • G • HISP • REX • **Rev:** Crowned arms in Order of the Golden Fleece collar **Rev. Legend:** ...MAGNA SEQUOR **Note:** Mint mark: Crowned M.

Date	Mintage	VG	F	VF	XF	Unc
1750 JB Rare	—	—	—	—	—	—

Note: M. Durr and R. Michel Monnaies d'Or d'Espagne sale 11-99, XF realized $28,160

KM# 397.1 8 ESCUDOS

27.0700 g., 0.9170 Gold 0.7981 oz. AGW **Ruler:** Carlos III **Obv:** Young bust right **Obv. Legend:** CAROLUS • III • ... **Rev:** Crowned arms in Order of the Golden Fleece collar **Rev. Legend:** IN • UTROQ • FELIX • AUSPICE • DEO • **Note:** Mint mark: Crowned M.

Date	Mintage	VG	F	VF	XF	Unc
1760 JP Rare	—	—	—	—	—	—

KM# 397.2 8 ESCUDOS

27.0700 g., 0.9170 Gold 0.7981 oz. AGW **Ruler:** Carlos III **Obv:** Young armored bust right **Obv. Legend:** CAROLUS • III • D • G • HISP • ET • IND • REX • **Rev:** Crowned arms in Order of the Golden Fleece collar **Rev. Legend:** IN • UTROQ • FELIX • AUSPICE • DEO •

Date	Mintage	VG	F	VF	XF	Unc
1762S JV Rare	—	—	—	—	—	—

Note: Stack's CICF Sale 4-89, AU realized $55,000., Swiss Bank Ortiz sale 9-91 XF realized $57,420

KM# 409.1 8 ESCUDOS

27.0700 g., 0.9010 Gold 0.7841 oz. AGW **Ruler:** Carlos III **Obv:** Older, armored bust right **Obv. Legend:** CAROL • III • D • G • HISP • ET IND • R • **Rev:** Crowned arms in Order of the Golden Fleece collar **Rev. Legend:** IN • UTROQ • FELIX • AUSPICE • DEO • **Note:** Mint mark: Crowned M.

Date	Mintage	VG	F	VF	XF	Unc
1771 JP Rare	—	—	—	—	—	—
1772 PJ	—	725	1,300	2,000	3,200	—
1773 PJ	—	850	1,750	3,000	5,000	—
1774 PJ	—	550	1,000	1,600	2,600	—
1775 PJ	—	600	1,200	2,000	3,200	—
1776 PJ	—	550	1,000	1,600	2,600	—
1776 FA	—	800	1,500	2,200	3,500	—
1777 PJ	—	550	800	1,200	2,000	—
1778 PJ	—	800	1,600	2,400	3,800	—
1779 PJ	—	800	1,600	2,400	3,800	—
1782 JJ	—	—	—	—	—	—
1783 JD	—	600	1,200	2,000	3,200	—
1784 JD	—	1,200	2,300	3,600	5,800	—

KM# 409.2 8 ESCUDOS

27.0700 g., 0.9010 Gold 0.7841 oz. AGW **Ruler:** Carlos III **Obv:** Older, armored bust right **Obv. Legend:** CAROL • III • D • G •.... **Rev:** Crowned arms in Order of the Golden Fleece collar **Rev. Legend:** IN • UTROQ • FELIX • AUSPICE • DEO • **Note:** Mint mark: S, S/L.

Date	Mintage	VG	F	VF	XF	Unc
1772 CF	—	800	1,600	2,400	3,800	—
1773 CF	—	600	1,100	1,750	3,000	—
1774 CF	—	550	900	1,400	2,300	—
1775 CF	—	650	1,200	1,800	3,000	—
1776 CF	—	800	1,600	2,400	3,800	—
1779 CF	—	800	1,600	2,400	3,800	—
1784 C	—	1,800	3,000	4,000	5,500	—

KM# 409.2a 8 ESCUDOS

27.0700 g., 0.8750 Gold 0.7615 oz. AGW **Ruler:** Carlos III **Obv:** Armored bust right **Obv. Legend:** CAROL • III • D • G • HISP • ET IND • R • **Rev:** Crowned arms in Order of the Golden Fleece collar **Rev. Legend:** IN • UTROQ • FELIX • AUSPICE • DEO • **Note:** Mint mark: S, S/L.

Date	Mintage	VG	F	VF	XF	Unc
1786 C	—	550	1,000	1,500	2,000	—
1787 CM	—	550	1,000	1,600	2,500	—
1788 C	—	550	1,000	1,600	2,150	—

KM# 409.1a 8 ESCUDOS

27.0700 g., 0.8750 Gold 0.7615 oz. AGW **Ruler:** Carlos III **Obv:** Older, armored bust right **Obv. Legend:** CAROL • III • D • G • HISP • ETIND • R • **Rev:** Crowned arms in Order of the Golden Fleece collar **Rev. Legend:** IN • UTROQ • FELIX • AUSPICE • DEO • **Note:** Mint mark: Crowned M.

Date	Mintage	VG	F	VF	XF	Unc
1786 DV	—	900	1,700	2,400	3,800	—
1788 M	—	1,000	2,000	3,000	5,000	—
1788 FM	—	550	900	1,400	2,300	—

KM# 437.1 8 ESCUDOS

27.0700 g., 0.8750 Gold 0.7615 oz. AGW **Ruler:** Carlos IV **Obv:** Armored bust right **Obv. Legend:** CAROL • IIII • D • G • .. **Rev:** Crowned arms in order chain **Rev. Legend:** IN • UTROQ • FELIX • AUSPICE • DEO • **Note:** Mint mark: Crowned M.

Date	Mintage	VG	F	VF	XF	Unc
1788 MF	—	650	1,150	1,700	2,800	—
1789 MF	—	1,400	2,500	3,500	5,600	—
1790 MF	—	1,000	1,800	2,700	4,400	—

KM# 437.2 8 ESCUDOS

27.0700 g., 0.8750 Gold 0.7615 oz. AGW **Ruler:** Carlos IV **Obv:** Older bust right **Obv. Legend:** CAROL • IIII • D • G • ... **Rev:** Crosned arms in Order of the Golden Fleece collar **Rev. Legend:** IN • UTROQ • FELIX • AUSPICE • DEO • **Note:** Mint mark: S, S/L

Date	Mintage	VG	F	VF	XF	Unc
1790 C	—	1,750	3,000	4,500	7,000	—
1791 C Rare	—	—	—	—	—	—

PRETENDER COINAGE

Charles III 1705-1711

KM# PT3 DINERO

Copper **Ruler:** Charles III **Obv:** Laureate head left **Rev:** Arms in cartouche, date in legend **Note:** Struck at Barcelona

Date	Mintage	F	VF	XF	Unc	BU
1707	—	—	—	—	—	—
1708	—	4.00	10.00	20.00	35.00	—
1709	—	4.00	10.00	20.00	35.00	—
1710	—	5.00	11.00	22.00	40.00	—
1711	—	20.00	50.00	100	175	—

KM# PT4 ARDITE

Copper **Ruler:** Charles III **Obv:** Laureate bust left **Rev:** Diamond arms in inner circle, date in legend **Note:** Struck at Barcelona

Date	Mintage	F	VF	XF	Unc	BU
1707	—	5.00	12.00	25.00	40.00	—
1708	—	5.00	12.00	25.00	40.00	—
1709	—	5.00	12.00	25.00	40.00	—
1710	—	5.00	12.00	25.00	40.00	—
1711	—	5.00	12.00	25.00	40.00	—

KM# PT5 2 REALES

Silver **Ruler:** Charles III **Obv:** Crowned arms **Rev:** Crowned "CAROLVS" monogram in inner circle, date in legend **Note:** Struck at Barcelona.

Date	Mintage	F	VF	XF	Unc	BU
1707	—	11.00	23.00	45.00	75.00	—
1708/7	—	14.00	30.00	60.00	100	—
1708	—	7.00	15.00	30.00	55.00	—
1709	—	7.00	15.00	30.00	55.00	—
1710	—	9.00	20.00	40.00	75.00	—
1711	—	7.00	15.00	30.00	55.00	—
1712	—	7.00	15.00	30.00	55.00	—
1713	—	20.00	50.00	100	175	—
1714	—	27.00	65.00	125	225	—

KM# PT1 CROAT (Dieciocheno)

Silver **Ruler:** Charles III **Obv:** Bust right, in cloak **Rev:** Long cross with dots and circles in angles, date in legend **Note:** Struck at Barcelona.

Date	Mintage	F	VF	XF	Unc	BU
1705	—	12.00	30.00	60.00	95.00	—
1706	—	11.00	27.00	55.00	90.00	—

KM# PT2 CROAT (Dieciocheno)

Silver **Ruler:** Charles III **Obv:** Crowned, facing bust divides date **Rev:** Crowned diamond arms with "L" on each side **Note:** Struck at Valencia

Date	Mintage	F	VF	XF	Unc	BU
1706	—	8.00	20.00	40.00	70.00	—
1707	—	7.00	15.00	30.00	60.00	—

ARAGON

Aragon, bordered by Navarre on the west and Catalonia on the east, was an influential Christian Kingdom in Northern Spain. Even after unification the main city of Zaragoza, name of the mint, retained its prominence in the region.

RULER

Philip V, 1700-1746

MINT MARKS

C, CA, Z – Zaragoza

PROVINCE

STANDARD COINAGE

KM# 65 DINERO

Copper **Ruler:** Philip V **Obv:** Head right within circle **Rev:** Zaragoza arms in inner circle, date in legend **Note:** Struck at Zaragoza.

Date	Mintage	VG	F	VF	XF	Unc
1710	—	7.50	12.50	30.00	50.00	—
1711	—	7.50	12.50	30.00	50.00	—
1712	—	7.50	12.50	30.00	50.00	—
1713	—	7.50	12.50	30.00	50.00	—
1714	—	7.50	12.50	30.00	50.00	—
1715	—	7.50	12.50	30.00	50.00	—
1716	—	7.50	12.50	30.00	50.00	—
1717	—	7.50	12.50	30.00	50.00	—
1718	—	7.50	12.50	30.00	50.00	—
1719	—	7.50	12.50	30.00	50.00	—

KM# 66 2 REALES

Silver **Ruler:** Philip V **Obv:** Crowned arms in inner circle **Rev:** Zaragoza arms, date in legend **Note:** Struck at Zaragoza.

Date	Mintage	VG	F	VF	XF	Unc
1716 Rare	—	—	—	—	—	—

KM# 60 4 REALES

Silver **Ruler:** Philip V **Note:** Similar to 8 Reales, KM#62. Struck at Zaragoza.

Date	Mintage	VG	F	VF	XF	Unc
1707CA Rare	—	—	—	—	—	—

KM# 62 8 REALES

Silver **Ruler:** Philip V **Obv. Legend:** PHILIPPVS * V * DEI * G **Note:** Full round flan.

Date	Mintage	Good	VG	F	VF	XF
1707 Rare	—	—	—	—	—	—

Note: Full round specimens are valued at approximately twice the klippe levels

KM# 61 8 REALES

Silver **Ruler:** Philip V **Obv. Legend:** PHILIPPVS * V * DEI * G **Note:** Klippe

Date	Mintage	Good	VG	F	VF	XF
1707	—	2,500	4,500	6,500	9,000	—

BARCELONA

Barcelona was a maritime province located in northeast Spain. The city was the provincial capital of Barcelona. Barcelona is a major port and commercial center.

MINT MARK

Ba - Barcelona

PROVINCE

STANDARD COINAGE

KM# 55 REAL (Croat)

3.3800 g., 0.9170 Silver 0.0996 oz. ASW **Obv:** Finer style bust of Philip V left **Note:** Struck at Barcelona, legend varieties exist.

Date	Mintage	VG	F	VF	XF	Unc
1705	—	17.50	35.00	60.00	120	—
1706	—	60.00	115	175	350	—
1707	—	35.00	70.00	125	200	—

MAJORCA

(Yslas Baleares)

Majorca

The Balearic Islands, an archipelago located in the Mediterranean Sea off the east coast of Spain including Majorca, Minorca, Cabrera, Ibiza, Formentera and a number of islets. Majorca, largest of the Balearic Islands is famous for its 1,000-year-old olive trees.

RULERS

Philip III of Spain, 1598-1621
Philip IV of Spain, 1621-1665
Charles II, 1665-1700
Philip V, 1700-1746
Louis I, 1723-1726
Pretender, Charles III, 1700-1720
Ferdinand (Fernando) VII, 1808-1833

MONETARY SYSTEM

12 Dineros = 6 Doblers = 1 Sueldo (Sou)
30 Sueldos = 1 Duro

PROVINCE

STANDARD COINAGE

KM# 33 DINAR

Copper, 12 mm. **Ruler:** Philip V **Obv:** Small bust of Philip V left, "I" behind **Rev:** Cross with castles and lions in angles

Date	Mintage	VG	F	VF	XF	Unc
ND(1700-1746)	—	40.00	75.00	125	—	—

KM# 32 DINAR

Copper **Ruler:** Philip V **Obv:** Large bust of Philip V left **Rev:** Cross, "II" at lower right **Note:** Size varies 14-15 mm.

Date	Mintage	VG	F	VF	XF	Unc
ND(1700-1746)	—	35.00	65.00	115	200	—

KM# 36 TRESETA

Copper, 21 mm. **Ruler:** Philip V **Obv:** Bust of Philip V left **Rev:** Crowned shield of Castile and Leon

Date	Mintage	VG	F	VF	XF	Unc
1722	—	12.00	25.00	45.00	75.00	—
1723	—	12.00	25.00	45.00	75.00	—
1724	—	12.00	25.00	45.00	75.00	—

KM# 34 DOBLER

Copper **Ruler:** Philip V **Obv:** Bust of Philip V left **Rev:** Cross with figure at lower left, "II" at lower right **Note:** Size varies 14-15 mm.

Date	Mintage	VG	F	VF	XF	Unc
ND(1700-1746)	—	45.00	80.00	135	225	—

KM# 35.1 DOBLER

Copper, 14 mm. **Ruler:** Philip V **Obv:** Bust of Philip V left, "2" behind **Rev:** Crowned shield of Castile and Leon, fleur-de-lis at center

Date	Mintage	VG	F	VF	XF	Unc
ND(1700-1746)	—	30.00	60.00	100	180	—

KM# 35.2 DOBLER

Copper, 14 mm. **Ruler:** Philip V **Obv:** Bust of Philip V left, "2" behind **Rev:** Crowned shield of Castile and Leon without fleur-de-lis at center

Date	Mintage	VG	F	VF	XF	Unc
ND(ca.1723)	—	30.00	60.00	100	180	—

KM# 26 1/2 ESCUDO

1.6917 g., 0.9170 Gold 0.0499 oz. AGW **Ruler:** Charles II **Obv:** Crowned arms divide date **Rev:** Diamond-shaped shield **Note:** Previous Fr.#67.

Date	Mintage	VG	F	VF	XF	Unc
1695	—	400	800	1,500	2,500	—
1703	—	200	400	650	1,100	—
ND	—	150	325	525	800	—

KM# 40 1/2 ESCUDO

1.6917 g., 0.9170 Gold 0.0499 oz. AGW **Ruler:** Philip V **Obv:** Bust of Philip V right, legend at right **Obv. Legend:** PHILIPVS... **Rev:** Diamond shield topped by cross **Rev. Legend:** MAIORIC - ARVM CA **Note:** Previous Fr.#71.

Date	Mintage	VG	F	VF	XF	Unc
ND(1700-1746)	—	850	1,750	2,500	3,500	—

KM# 41 ESCUDO

3.3834 g., 0.9170 Gold 0.0997 oz. AGW **Ruler:** Philip V **Obv:** Large bust of Philip V right **Obv. Legend:** PHILIPVS... **Rev:** Crowned arms, tree at left **Note:** Fr.#70.

Date	Mintage	VG	F	VF	XF	Unc
ND(1700-1746)	—	400	750	1,350	2,200	—

KM# 42 ESCUDO

3.3834 g., 0.9170 Gold 0.0997 oz. AGW **Ruler:** Philip V **Obv:** Small bust of Philip V right **Rev:** Crowned arms, tree at left **Note:** Fr.#70a.

Date	Mintage	VG	F	VF	XF	Unc
ND(1700-1746)	—	400	800	1,300	2,200	—

KM# 38 ESCUDO

6.7667 g., 0.9170 Gold 0.1995 oz. AGW **Ruler:** Philip V **Obv:** Crowned arms **Rev:** Diamond-shaped shield **Note:** Fr.#73.

Date	Mintage	VG	F	VF	XF	Unc
1704	—	1,000	2,000	3,500	6,000	—

KM# 43 2 ESCUDOS

6.7667 g., 0.9170 Gold 0.1995 oz. AGW **Ruler:** Philip V **Obv:** Small crude bust of Philip V left, date in legend **Rev:** Crowned arms **Note:** Fr.#68.

Date	Mintage	VG	F	VF	XF	Unc
1723	—	1,300	2,200	4,000	6,500	—

KM# 44 2 ESCUDOS

6.7667 g., 0.9170 Gold 0.1995 oz. AGW **Ruler:** Philip V **Obv:** Large bust of Philip V right **Obv. Legend:** PHILIP - V HISP R **Rev:** Crowned arms **Rev. Legend:** MAIORICARVM... **Note:** Fr.#73a.

Date	Mintage	VG	F	VF	XF	Unc
1723	—	1,250	2,250	4,500	7,000	—
1726	—	1,250	2,250	4,500	7,000	—

KM# 8 4 ESCUDOS

13.5334 g., 0.9170 Gold 0.3990 oz. AGW **Ruler:** Philip III of Spain **Obv:** Crowned arms in inner circle, titles of Philip III **Rev:** Diamond shield in inner circle **Note:** Previous Fr.#58.

Date	Mintage	VG	F	VF	XF	Unc
1607 Rare	—	—	—	—	—	—

KM# 39 4 ESCUDOS

Gold **Ruler:** Philip V **Note:** Fr.#72

Date	Mintage	VG	F	VF	XF	Unc
1704 Rare	—	—	—	—	—	—

PRETENDER COINAGE

KM# 46 ESCUDO

3.3834 g., 0.9170 Gold 0.0997 oz. AGW **Ruler:** Charles III Pretender **Obv:** Crowned shield **Obv. Legend:** CAROLVS III R ARA **Rev:** Diamond - shaped shield **Rev. Legend:** MAIORICAR CATOL **Note:** Fr.#76a.

Date	Mintage	VG	F	VF	XF	Unc
ND(ca.1707) Rare	—	—	—	—	—	—

KM# 47 2 ESCUDOS

Gold **Ruler:** Charles III Pretender **Note:** Fr.#76.

Date	Mintage	VG	F	VF	XF	Unc
1707	—	1,250	2,250	4,500	7,000	—

KM# 48 4 ESCUDOS

Gold **Ruler:** Charles III Pretender **Note:** Fr.#75.

Date	Mintage	VG	F	VF	XF	Unc
1707 Rare	—	—	—	—	—	—

NAVARRE

Navarre, a frontier province of northern Spain and a former kingdom lies on the western end of the border between France and Spain. From the 10th through the12th centuries Navarre was a solid power in the region. After 1234 the kingdom fell under French dominance. In 1516 Ferdinand annexed Navarre to Spain and it was under this vice royalty that coinage was struck at the mint in Pamplona.

The Kingdom of Navarre was ultimately divided and absorbed by France and Spain.

RULERS

Philip V of Spain, 1700-1746
Carlos VI (III in Spain), 1759-1788
Carlos VII (IV in Spain), 1788-1808

MINT MARK

P - Pamplona

PROVINCE

STANDARD COINAGE

KM# 85 MARAVEDI

Copper **Obv:** FO/VI monogram **Rev:** Navarre arms dividing P - A

Date	Mintage	VG	F	VF	XF	Unc
NDPA	—	9.00	17.50	25.00	35.00	—
1748PA	—	9.00	17.50	25.00	35.00	—
1749PA	—	9.00	17.50	25.00	35.00	—

KM# 86 MARAVEDI

Copper **Obv:** FO/II monogram

Date	Mintage	VG	F	VF	XF	Unc
1749PA	—	9.00	17.50	25.00	35.00	—
1750PA	—	9.00	17.50	25.00	35.00	—
1753PA	—	9.00	17.50	25.00	35.00	—
1756PA	—	9.00	17.50	25.00	35.00	—
1757PA	—	9.00	17.50	25.00	35.00	—
1758PA	—	9.00	17.50	25.00	35.00	—

KM# 70 4 CORNADOS

Copper **Ruler:** Philip V of Spain **Rev:** Crowned arms in inner circle **Note:** Titles of Philip V. Struck at Pamplona. Varieties exist.

Date	Mintage	VG	F	VF	XF	Unc
1718	—	7.00	15.00	30.00	50.00	—
1726	—	7.00	15.00	30.00	50.00	—
1727	—	7.00	15.00	30.00	50.00	—
1728	—	8.00	16.00	35.00	55.00	—
1729	—	8.00	16.00	35.00	55.00	—
1745	—	8.00	16.00	35.00	55.00	—
ND	—	6.00	12.00	25.00	45.00	—

KM# 105 QUARTO

Copper **Ruler:** Carlos VI (III in Spain) **Note:** Similar to 1 Maravedi, KM#90. Octagonal.

Date	Mintage	VG	F	VF	XF	Unc
1784P	—	16.00	32.50	45.00	55.00	—
1788P	—	20.00	40.00	50.00	65.00	—

KM# 106 QUARTO

Copper **Ruler:** Carlos VII (IV in Spain) **Obv:** CAR VII monogram **Rev:** Arms

Date	Mintage	VG	F	VF	XF	Unc
1789P	—	10.00	20.00	25.00	30.00	—

SPANISH NETHERLANDS

The Netherlands as an entity perhaps came into being when Philip the Good, duke of Burgundy (1419-1467) called all the Burgundian states together for a common session at Bruges in 1464. Charles the Bold continued to add to the territory and consolidated his power, which, however reverted to the States General at his death in 1477. His daughter Mary married the Austrian archduke Maximilian, and was succeeded by her only son, Philip the Handsome (1494-1506). He married Joanna of Spain, daughter of Ferdinand and Isabella, and their oldest son, Charles V, became king of Aragon and Castile in 1520, head of the Austrian house of Habsburg, and Holy Roman Emperor. The Netherlands passed under the regency of his aunts Margaret of Austria (1519-30) and Mary of Hungary (1531-55). Philip II (1556-98) was a Spaniard and resented by many of the Netherlands, especially the Protestants and the higher nobility and clergy. The ruthless savagery of his governor the duke of Alba led to continued revolts, and finally to the Pacification of Ghent 1576, a union which was short lived. By the Union of Utrecht (1579) the northern provinces to all intents and purposes were separated from the southern ones.

The Spanish under Farnese, the duke of Parma, gradually regained supremacy in the southern provinces. Philip gave the provinces as dowry when his daughter, Isabella, married the archduke Albert of Austria in 1598. The Spanish Netherlands was to be an independent state based on Catholicism as the only recognized religion, and strong central government. Albert died in 1621 and Isabella in 1633, childless, and the provinces reverted to Philip IV of Spain. War with the United Netherlands and France followed until by the Peace Westphalia, concluding the Thirty Years War in1648, Philip recognized the independence of the northern states. By the Peace of the Pyrenes in 1659 and the Peace of Aix-la-Chapelle in 1668 Louis XIV of France acquired Artois and other border districts. On the death of Charles II in 1700 the southern Netherlands passed to the new Bourbon king of Spain, the French duke Philip of Anjou. In 1701, Louis XIV compelled his grandson to turn the territory over to France, but by the Treaty of Utrecht concluding the War of the Spanish Succession, the provinces were given to Austria.

BRABANT

A marquisate in medieval time. In 1578 Don John of Austria, the hero of Lepanto, died here. The area and town were much fought over even into modern times.

RULERS

Spanish

Philip V, 1700-1712

Austrian

Archduke Charles
as Charles III, Pretender to the Spanish Throne, 1703-1711
as Charles VI, Emperor, 1711-1740

MINT MARKS

Hand - Anvers
Angel face - Brussels
Star - Maastricht
Tree - 's Hertogenbosch (Bois-le-Duc)

SPANISH RULE

PRETENDER COINAGE

KM# 119.4 ESCALIN

5.2600 g., 0.5820 Silver 0.0984 oz. ASW **Ruler:** Philip V **Obv:** Lion of Brabant rampant to left holding oval shield of Austro-Burgundian arms **Obv. Legend:** PHILIP(P)US V • D • G • HISPANIAR • ET INDIAR • REX • **Rev:** Crowned shield of arms superimposed on floriated St. Andrew's cross divides date **Rev. Legend:** BURGUND • DUX • BRAB Z c. **Note:** Mint mark: Lion rampant left.

Date	Mintage	VG	F	VF	XF	Unc
1709	—	—	—	—	—	—
1710	—	—	—	—	—	—
1711	—	—	—	—	—	—

KM# 157 ESCALIN

5.9000 g., Silver, 32 mm. **Ruler:** Archduke Charles as Charles III, Pretender to the Spanish Throne **Obv:** Brabant lion rampant left holding oval Austro - Burgundian arms **Obv. Legend:** CAROLVS III. D.G. HISPANIAR. ET INDIAR. REX. **Rev:** Crowned manifold arms superimposed on St. Andrew's cross divide date **Rev. Legend:** ARCHID. AVST. - DVX - BVRG. BRABAN. **Note:** Mint mark: hand.

Date	Mintage	VG	F	VF	XF	Unc
1709	14,753	150	300	550	925	—
1710	79,700	125	250	500	850	—
1711	Inc. above	100	200	400	750	—

KM# A117.2 1/2 PATAGON

14.0500 g., 0.8750 Silver 0.3952 oz. ASW **Ruler:** Archduke Charles as Charles III, Pretender to the Spanish Throne **Obv:** Crown above floriated St. Andrew's cross dividing triple C monograms. **Obv. Legend:** CAROLVS III. D.G. HISP. ET INDIARVM. REX. **Rev:** Crowned manifold arms within order chain of the Golden Fleece, date divided above. **Rev. Legend:** ARCHID. AVST. DVX - BVRG. BRABANT Zc. **Note:** Mint mark: hand.

Date	Mintage	VG	F	VF	XF	Unc
1710	2,318	450	925	1,850	3,100	—

KM# 133 PATAGON

28.1000 g., 0.8750 Silver 0.7905 oz. ASW **Ruler:** Archduke Charles as Charles III, Pretender to the Spanish Throne **Obv:** St. Andrew's cross with crown above and fleece below divides pair of crowned triple C monograms **Obv. Legend:** CAROLUS III • D • G • HISP • ETINDIARUMREX • **Rev:** Crowned shield of Charles III in the collar of the Golden Fleece **Rev. Legend:** ARCHID • AUST • DVX BURGBRABANT • Z c. **Note:** Mint mark: hand. Dav. #1269.

Date	Mintage	VG	F	VF	XF	Unc
1706	—	—	—	—	—	—
1707	348,498	300	600	1,200	2,000	—
1709	Inc. above	225	450	900	1,500	—
1710	Inc. above	250	500	1,000	1,650	—

KM# 134 1/2 SOUVERAIN OU LION D'OR

2.8000 g., 0.9480 Gold 0.0853 oz. AGW **Ruler:** Archduke Charles as Charles III, Pretender to the Spanish Throne **Obv:** Lion rampant left with sword, paw on globe set on pedestal **Obv. Legend:** CAROLVS III • D • G • HISP • ET INDIAR • REX • **Rev:** Crowned arms in collar of the Golden Fleece **Rev. Legend:** ARCHID • AVST • DVX BVRG • BRABANT • Z c. **Note:** Mint mark: hand.

Date	Mintage	VG	F	VF	XF	Unc
1710 Rare	—	—	—	—	—	—

KM# 94 SOUVERAIN OU LION D'OR

5.5300 g., 0.9190 Gold 0.1634 oz. AGW **Ruler:** Archduke Charles as Charles III, Pretender to the Spanish Thr one **Obv:** Lion to left resting left front paw on globe **Obv. Legend:** CAROLVS III • D • G • HISP • ET INDIAR • REX • **Rev:** Crowned manifold arms within chain of Order of the Gold Fleece, date divided above **Rev. Legend:** ARCHID • AVST • DVX BVRG • BRABANT • Z c. **Note:** Mint mark: hand.

Date	Mintage	VG	F	VF	XF	Unc
1710	2,350	1,250	2,500	4,000	6,500	—

KM# 132 2 SOUVERAIN D'OR

11.0600 g., 0.9190 Gold 0.3268 oz. AGW **Ruler:** Philip V **Obv:** Crowned bust to right, mint mark below. **Obv. Legend:** PHIL • V • D • G • HISP • ET • IND • REX • **Rev:** Crowned manifold arms in collars of the Holy Spirit and the Golden Fleece, date divided above **Rev. Legend:** BURGUND • DUX BRABANT • Zc. **Note:** Mint mark: hand.

Date	Mintage	VG	F	VF	XF	Unc
1704	7,004	1,500	3,000	5,000	8,000	—
1705	Inc. above	1,500	3,000	5,000	8,000	—
1706	1,424	1,500	3,000	5,000	8,000	—

KM# 135 2 SOUVERAIN D'OR

11.0600 g., 0.9190 Gold 0.3268 oz. AGW **Ruler:** Archduke Charles as Charles III, Pretender to the Spanish Throne **Obv:** Crowned bust right, mint mark below **Obv. Legend:** CAROLVS III • D • G • HISP • ET INDIAR • REX • **Rev:** Crowned arms in collar of the Golden Fleece, date divided above **Rev. Legend:** ARCHID • AVST • DVX BVRG • BRABANT • Zc. **Note:** Mint mark: hand.

Date	Mintage	VG	F	VF	XF	Unc
1711	3,998	1,500	3,000	5,000	8,000	—

KM# 129 4 SOUVERAIN D'OR

Gold **Ruler:** Philip V **Note:** Similar to 2 Souverain d'Or, KM#132.

Date	Mintage	VG	F	VF	XF	Unc
1706 Rare	—	—	—	—	—	—

STANDARD COINAGE

KM# 119.3 ESCALIN

5.2600 g., 0.5820 Silver 0.0984 oz. ASW **Ruler:** Philip V **Obv:** Lion of Brabant rampant to left holding oval shield of Austro-Burgundian arms **Obv. Legend:** PHILIPPUS • V • D • G • HISPANIAR • ET • INDIAR • REX • **Rev:** Crowned shield of arms superimposed on floriated St. Andrew's cross divides date **Rev. Legend:** BURGUND DUX • BRAB • zc.

Date	Mintage	VG	F	VF	XF	Unc
1704	160,043	125	250	500	850	—
1705	Inc. above	135	275	550	925	—

KM# 154 ESCALIN

5.9000 g., Silver, 32 mm. **Ruler:** Philip V **Obv:** Bust left, 'R' below **Obv. Legend:** PHIL. V. D.G. HISP. - ET IND. REX C. **Rev:** Crowned oval manifold arms within Order chains of the Holy Spirit and Golden Fleece, date divided above **Rev. Legend:** BURGUNDIÆ DUX - BRABANTIÆ. Zc.

Date	Mintage	VG	F	VF	XF	Unc
1706	—	—	—	—	—	—

KM# 130 PATAGON

28.1000 g., 0.8750 Silver 0.7905 oz. ASW **Ruler:** Philip V **Obv:** Large crown above St. Andrew's cross with and Order of the Golden Fleece below, crowned PV monograms at left and right **Obv. Legend:** PHILLIPUS V • D • G • HISPANIARUM ET INDIARUM REX **Rev:** Crowned shield of manifold arms in collars of the Golden Fleece and the Holy Spirit, date divided at top **Rev. Legend:** BURGUND • DVX BRABANT • Z c. **Note:** Mint mark: hand. Dav. #1709.

Date	Mintage	VG	F	VF	XF	Unc
1704	82,972	150	300	600	1,000	—
1705	140,498	125	250	500	850	—
1706	Inc. above	175	350	700	1,150	—

KM# 131.1 DUCATON

32.3000 g., Silver **Ruler:** Philip V **Obv:** Bust right, in cuirass **Rev:** Crowned shield of arms within collars of fleece and the Holy Spirit, lions supporting **Note:** Mint mark: hand. Dav. #1703.

Date	Mintage	VG	F	VF	XF	Unc
1703	427,920	135	275	550	925	—
1704	Inc. above	150	300	600	950	—

KM# 131.2 DUCATON

32.3000 g., Silver **Ruler:** Philip V **Obv:** Bust right, in court dress **Rev:** Crowned arms with supporters **Rev. Legend:** ARCHID• AVST • DVX • BVRG • BRABAN • Z c. **Note:** Mint mark: hand. Dav. #1704.

Date	Mintage	VG	F	VF	XF	Unc
1703	—	1,350	2,700	5,400	9,200	—

KM# 131.3 DUCATON

32.3000 g., Silver **Ruler:** Philip V **Obv:** Bust right **Obv. Legend:** PHILIPPUS V • D • G • HISPANIARUMETINDIARVM REX **Rev:** Crowned arms with supporters **Rev. Legend:** BURGUND • DUX • BRABAN Z c **Note:** Mint mark: hand. Dav. #1707.

Date	Mintage	VG	F	VF	XF	Unc
1703	Inc. above	125	250	500	850	—
1704	Inc. above	150	300	600	1,400	—
1705	2,478	200	425	900	1,750	—

KM# 152 2 PATAGON

56.5000 g., Silver, 42 mm. **Ruler:** Philip V **Obv:** Crown above floriated St. Andrew's cross, monogram to left and right **Obv. Legend:** PHILIPPUS V. D.G. HISPANIARUM ET INDIARUM REX **Rev:** Crowned manifold arms within Order chains of the Holy Spirit and Golden Fleece, date divided at top **Rev. Legend:** BURGUND. DUX - BRABANT. Zc. **Note:** Dav. #1708.

Date	Mintage	VG	F	VF	XF	Unc
1705	—	—	—	—	—	—

KM# 16 4 DUCATS

20.9600 g., 0.9860 Gold 0.6644 oz. AGW **Note:** Similar to 2 Ducat, KM#13.

Date	Mintage	VG	F	VF	XF	Unc
ND(1600-11) Rare	—	—	—	—	—	—

KM# 155 4 SOUVERAIN D'OR

22.2000 g., Gold, 33 mm. **Ruler:** Philip V **Obv:** Crowned bust right, mint mark below **Obv. Legend:** PHIL. V. D.G. - HISP. ET IND. REX. **Rev:** Crowned squarish manifold arms within Order chains of the Holy Spirit and Golden Fleece, date divided above **Rev. Legend:** BURGUND. DUX - BRABANT. Zc. **Note:** Mint mark: hand.

Date	Mintage	VG	F	VF	XF	Unc
1706	—	—	—	—	—	—

KM# 150 8 SOUVERAIN D'OR

44.3000 g., Gold, 42.5 mm. **Ruler:** Philip V **Obv:** Armored bust to right, mint mark below **Obv. Legend:** PHILIPPUS V. D.G. HISPANIARUM ET INDI ARUM REX. **Rev:** Crowned manifold arms supported by 2 lions, date divided above **Rev. Legend:** BURGUND - DUX. - BRABAN. Zc. **Note:** Fr. #124. Mint mark: hand.

Date	Mintage	VG	F	VF	XF	Unc
1704	—	—	—	—	—	—
1705	—	—	—	—	—	—

AUSTRIAN RULE

PRETENDER COINAGE

KM# 140.2 2 DUCATON

65.2000 g., Silver, 43 mm. **Ruler:** Philip V **Obv:** Armored bust right, mint mark below **Obv. Legend:** PHILIPPUS V. D. G. HISPANIARUM ET INDIARUM REX. **Rev:** Crowned manifold arms supported by 2 lions, date divided above **Rev. Legend:** BURGUND - DUX. - BRABAN. Zc. **Note:** Dav. #1706. Mint mark: hand. Struck on thick flan from Ducaton dies, KM#131.3.

Date	Mintage	VG	F	VF	XF	Unc
1703	—	—	—	—	—	—
1704	—	—	—	—	—	—
1705	—	—	—	—	—	—

KM# 140.3 2 DUCATON

65.2000 g., Silver, 43 mm. **Ruler:** Philip V **Obv:** Armored bust right, mint mark below **Obv. Legend:** PHILIPPUS V. D. G. HISPANIARUM ET INDIARUM REX. **Rev:** Crowned manifold arms supported by 2 lions, date divided above **Rev. Legend:** BURGUND - DUX. - BRABANT. Zc. **Note:** Dav. #1706A. Mint mark: hand.

Date	Mintage	VG	F	VF	XF	Unc
1703	—	—	—	—	—	—

KM# 140.1 2 DUCATON

64.0000 g., Silver, 43 mm. **Ruler:** Philip V **Obv:** Armored bust right, mint mark below **Obv. Legend:** PHILIPPUS V. D. G. HISPANIARUM ET INDIARUM REX. **Rev:** Crowned manifold arms supported by 2 lions, date divided above **Rev. Legend:** ARCHIS. AVST. - DUX. BVRG. - BRABAN. Zc. **Note:** Mint mark: hand. Dav. #1702. Struck on thick flan from Ducaton dies, KM#131.1.

Date	Mintage	VG	F	VF	XF	Unc
1703	—	—	—	—	—	—
1705	—	—	—	—	—	—

KM# 142 3 DUCATON

97.6000 g., Silver, 42 mm. **Ruler:** Philip V **Obv:** Armored bust to right, mint mark below **Obv. Legend:** PHILIPPUS V. D. G. HISPANIARUM ET INDIARUM REX. **Rev:** Crowned manifold arms supported by 2 lions, date divided above **Rev. Legend:** BURGUND - DUX. - BRABAN. Zc. **Note:** Dav. #1705. Mint mark: hand. Struck on thick flan from Ducaton dies, KM#131.3.

Date	Mintage	VG	F	VF	XF	Unc
1703	—	—	—	—	—	—

STANDARD COINAGE

KM# 136 2 SOUVERAIN D'OR

11.0600 g., 0.9190 Gold 0.3268 oz. AGW **Ruler:** Archduke Charles as Charles VI, Emperor **Obv:** Crowned bust right **Obv. Legend:** CAROLUS VI D:G: ROM: IMP: HISP: ET IND: REX. **Rev:** Crowned imperial eagle with arms on breast in collar of the Golden Fleece **Rev. Legend:** ARCHIDUX AUST(:) - DUX BURG: BRAB: Zc. **Note:** Mint mark: hand.

Date	Mintage	VG	F	VF	XF	Unc
1719	768	2,000	3,500	5,500	9,000	—
1720	Inc. above	2,000	3,500	5,500	9,000	—

KM# 137 2 SOUVERAIN D'OR

11.0600 g., 0.9190 Gold 0.3268 oz. AGW **Ruler:** Archduke Charles as Charles VI, Emperor **Obv:** Laureate head right, mint mark below **Obv. Legend:** CAROL • VI• D • G • ROM • IMP • HISP • ET IND • REX • **Rev:** Crowned arms in collar of the Golden Fleece; date divided above **Rev. Legend:** ARCHID • AUST • DUX BURG • BRABANT • Zc. **Note:** Mint mark: hand.

Date	Mintage	VG	F	VF	XF	Unc
1724	—	1,200	2,250	3,750	6,000	—
1725	—	1,200	2,250	3,750	6,000	—
1726	—	1,200	2,250	3,750	6,000	—

FLANDERS

A coastal county of modern Belgium first mentioned in 862 which by the Renaissance had become the industrial and commercial center of northern Europe. It was the target of dynastic maneuvering between Burgundy, Spain and France.

RULER

Maximilian Emanuel, 1712-1715

MINT MARK

Lis - Bruges (Flanders)

COUNTY

STANDARD COINAGE

KM# 105 1/2 PATAGON

14.0500 g., 0.8750 Silver 0.3952 oz. ASW **Ruler:** Philip V **Obv:** St. Andrew's Cross, crown above, fleece below, divides pair of crowned PV monograms **Obv. Legend:** PHILIPPUS • V • D • G • ... **Rev:** Crowned shield of Philip V in collars of the Golden Fleece and Holy Spirit

Date	Mintage	Good	VG	F	VF	XF
1705 Rare	—	—	—	—	—	—

KM# 107 1/2 PATAGON

14.0500 g., 0.8750 Silver 0.3952 oz. ASW **Obv:** St. Andrew's cross, crown above, fleece below, divides pair of crowned triple-C monograms **Obv. Legend:** CAROLUS • III • D • G • HISP • .... **Rev:** Crowned shield of Charles III in collar of the Golden Fleece **Rev. Legend:** ARCHID • AUST • DUX • ....

Date	Mintage	Good	VG	F	VF	XF
1709	—	—	400	800	1,650	2,750

KM# 106 PATAGON

28.1000 g., 0.8750 Silver 0.7905 oz. ASW **Ruler:** Philip V **Obv:** St. Andrew's cross, crown above, fleece below, divides pair of crowned PV monograms **Rev:** Crowned shield of Philip V in collars of the Golden Fleece and Holy Spirit **Rev. Legend:** ...BURGUND DUX C FLAND Z. **Note:** Dav. #1710.

Date	Mintage	Good	VG	F	VF	XF
1705 Rare	—	—	—	—	—	—

KM# 108 PATAGON

28.1000 g., 0.8750 Silver 0.7905 oz. ASW **Ruler:** Maximilan Emanuel **Obv:** St. Andrew's cross, crown above, fleece below, divides pair of crowned triple-C monograms **Rev:** Crowned shield in collar of Golden Fleece **Rev. Legend:** ...DUX BURG C FLAND Z.

Date	Mintage	Good	VG	F	VF	XF
1709	—	—	750	1,500	3,000	5,000

NAMUR

Became an independent duchy in the late 12th century. Divided in 1609- the north becoming part of the United Netherlands, the south staying as Spanish (and later Austrian) Netherlands. Became part of Belgium after 1830.

RULERS
Philip V of Spain, 1700-1711
Maximilian Emmanuel of Bavaria, 1711-1714

MINT MARK
Lion rampant - Namur

DUCHY

MILLED COINAGE

KM# 2 LIARD
Copper **Ruler:** Philip V of Spain **Obv:** Crown above Titles of Philip V **Obv. Legend:** PHIL • V • D • G • .... **Rev:** Legend, arms, crown divides date **Rev. Legend:** DUX • BURGUND • BRABAN • Z •

Date	Mintage	VG	F	VF	XF	Unc
1709	—	40.00	60.00	100	175	—
1710	—	40.00	60.00	100	175	—

KM# 12 LIARD
Copper **Ruler:** Philip V of Spain **Obv:** Crown above Titles of Philip V **Obv. Legend:** PHIL • V • D • G • .... **Rev:** Crowned arms **Rev. Legend:** DVX • BVRGVND • ET BRABANT • Z •

Date	Mintage	VG	F	VF	XF	Unc
1710	—	40.00	60.00	100	175	—

KM# 13 LIARD
Copper **Ruler:** Philip V of Spain **Rev:** Legend begins at lower left

Date	Mintage	VG	F	VF	XF	Unc
1710	—	40.00	60.00	100	175	—

KM# 37 LIARD
Copper **Ruler:** Philip V of Spain **Obv:** Crown above Titles of Philip V **Obv. Legend:** PHIL • V • D • G • ... **Rev:** Crowned arms divide date

Date	Mintage	VG	F	VF	XF	Unc
1710	—	—	—	—	—	—

KM# 17 LIARD
Copper **Ruler:** Philip V of Spain **Obv:** Crown above Titles of Philip V **Rev:** Crowned arms divide date

Date	Mintage	VG	F	VF	XF	Unc
1712	—	40.00	80.00	130	225	—

KM# 18 LIARD
Copper **Ruler:** Maximilian Emmanuel of Bavaria **Obv:** Armored bust left **Rev:** Crowned M E monogram, crown divides date **Rev. Legend:** V • B • B • L • ET • G • DVX COM P • Q • F • H • N • & •

Date	Mintage	VG	F	VF	XF	Unc
1712	—	40.00	80.00	130	225	—

KM# 19 LIARD
Copper **Ruler:** Maximilian Emmanuel of Bavaria **Rev:** Legend begins at lower left

Date	Mintage	VG	F	VF	XF	Unc
1712	—	40.00	80.00	130	225	—

KM# 20 LIARD
Copper **Ruler:** Maximilian Emmanuel of Bavaria **Rev. Legend:** DVX BAVARI • BRABANT C • FLAN Z •

Date	Mintage	VG	F	VF	XF	Unc
1712	—	40.00	60.00	100	175	—
1713	—	40.00	60.00	100	175	—

KM# 26 LIARD
Copper **Ruler:** Maximilian Emmanuel of Bavaria **Rev. Legend:** COM • P • R • S • R • I • ARC • & ELE • L • COM F • H • & N • **Note:** Legend variants exist.

Date	Mintage	VG	F	VF	XF	Unc
1713	—	40.00	60.00	100	175	—

KM# 3 2 LIARDS
Copper **Ruler:** Philip V of Spain **Obv:** Crowned briquet with arms at sides and below **Rev:** Crowned arms divide value, crown divides date

Date	Mintage	VG	F	VF	XF	Unc
1709	—	60.00	125	175	250	—

KM# 4 2 LIARDS
Copper **Ruler:** Philip V of Spain **Obv:** Crowned briquet surrounded by 3 shields **Obv. Legend:** PHIL • V • D • G • HISPANIAR • ET • INDIAR • REX **Rev:** Crowned arms divides date and value " 2 - L" **Rev. Legend:** DUX • BURGUND • BRABAN • Z

Date	Mintage	VG	F	VF	XF	Unc
1709	—	60.00	125	175	250	—

KM# 5 2 LIARDS
Copper **Ruler:** Philip V of Spain **Obv:** Armored bust right **Obv. Legend:** PHIL • V • D • G • HISPANIAR • ET • INDIA (R) • REX **Rev:** Crowned arms divides date and value "2 - L"

Date	Mintage	VG	F	VF	XF	Unc
1709	—	60.00	125	175	250	—

KM# 6 2 LIARDS
Copper **Ruler:** Philip V of Spain **Obv:** Armored bust right **Obv. Legend:** PHILIP • V • D • G • HISPANIAR • ET • INDIA • REX **Rev:** Crowned arms divide date **Rev. Legend:** DVX • BVRGVND • BRABAN • Z

Date	Mintage	VG	F	VF	XF	Unc
1709	—	60.00	125	175	250	—

KM# 7 4 PATARDS
Silver **Ruler:** Philip V of Spain **Obv:** Lion rampant holding sword and arms **Rev:** Crowned arms divide date

Date	Mintage	VG	F	VF	XF	Unc
1709	—	—	—	—	—	—
1710	—	—	—	—	—	—
1711	—	—	—	—	—	—

KM# 8 1/2 ESCALIN
Silver **Obv:** Lion rampant holding sword and Bavarian arms **Rev:** Crowned arms

Date	Mintage	VG	F	VF	XF	Unc
ND	—	175	275	475	800	—

KM# 27 1/2 ESCALIN
Silver **Ruler:** Maximilian Emmanuel of Bavaria **Rev:** Date divided near top of arms

Date	Mintage	VG	F	VF	XF	Unc
1713	—	150	250	450	750	—

KM# 9 ESCALIN
Silver **Ruler:** Philip V of Spain **Obv:** Lion rampant left holding sword and Bavarian arms **Rev:** Crowned arms divide date

Date	Mintage	VG	F	VF	XF	Unc
1709	45,506	150	250	450	750	—
1710	Inc. above	150	250	450	750	—

KM# 15 ESCALIN
Silver **Ruler:** Philip V of Spain **Obv:** Date above sword and arms

Date	Mintage	VG	F	VF	XF	Unc
1711	—	150	250	450	750	—

KM# 14.1 ESCALIN
Silver **Ruler:** Maximilian Emmanuel of Bavaria **Obv:** Lion rampant holding sword and Bavarian arms **Rev. Legend:** V • B • S • P • B • L • L • ET G • DVX COM • P • R • F • H • & • N • & •

Date	Mintage	VG	F	VF	XF	Unc
1711	—	150	250	450	750	—

KM# 14.2 ESCALIN
Silver **Ruler:** Maximilian Emmanuel of Bavaria **Rev. Legend:** V • B • B • L • L • ET • G • DVX • COM • P • R • F • H • ET • N •

Date	Mintage	VG	F	VF	XF	Unc
1711	—	150	250	450	750	—

KM# 28 ESCALIN
Silver **Ruler:** Maximilian Emmanuel of Bavaria **Obv:** Date divided near top of arms

Date	Mintage	VG	F	VF	XF	Unc
1713	—	125	200	350	600	—

KM# 29 ESCALIN
Silver **Ruler:** Maximilian Emmanuel of Bavaria **Rev. Legend:** AR•ELE•&•VIC•L•L•COM•F•H•&•N•MA•S•R•I•D•M•

Date	Mintage	VG	F	VF	XF	Unc
1713	—	125	200	350	600	—

KM# 30 1/4 ECU
Silver **Ruler:** Maximilian Emmanuel of Bavaria **Obv:** Armored and draped bust right, date below **Rev:** Crowned round arms

Date	Mintage	VG	F	VF	XF	Unc
1713	—	250	400	650	1,000	—

KM# 31 1/2 ECU
Silver **Ruler:** Maximilian Emmanuel of Bavaria **Obv:** Armored and draped bust right, date below **Rev:** Crowned round arms

Date	Mintage	VG	F	VF	XF	Unc
1713	—	400	650	1,100	1,750	—

KM# 21 ECU
Silver **Ruler:** Maximilian Emmanuel of Bavaria **Obv:** Head right, TB monogram below, date in legend **Rev:** Crowned spade arms in Order collar

Date	Mintage	VG	F	VF	XF	Unc
1712	—	1,000	1,800	3,000	5,000	—

KM# 22 ECU
Silver **Ruler:** Maximilian Emmanuel of Bavaria **Rev:** Crowned round arms in Order collar

Date	Mintage	VG	F	VF	XF	Unc
1712	—	1,200	2,000	3,250	5,500	—

KM# 23 ECU
Silver **Ruler:** Maximilian Emmanuel of Bavaria **Obv:** Head with unbound hair **Rev:** Crowned spade arms in Order collar

Date	Mintage	VG	F	VF	XF	Unc
1712	—	1,000	1,800	3,000	5,000	—

KM# 32 ECU
Silver **Ruler:** Maximilian Emmanuel of Bavaria **Obv:** Armored and draped bust right, date in legend **Rev:** Crowned round arms in Order collar

Date	Mintage	VG	F	VF	XF	Unc
1713	—	1,200	2,000	3,250	5,500	—

KM# 33 ECU
Silver **Ruler:** Maximilian Emmanuel of Bavaria **Obv:** Date below bust

Date	Mintage	VG	F	VF	XF	Unc
1713	—	1,200	2,000	3,250	5,500	—
1714	—	1,200	2,000	3,250	5,500	—

KM# 34 ECU
Silver **Ruler:** Maximilian Emmanuel of Bavaria **Obv:** Large bust

Date	Mintage	VG	F	VF	XF	Unc
1713	—	1,200	2,000	3,250	5,500	—

KM# 36 ECU
Silver **Ruler:** Maximilian Emmanuel of Bavaria **Rev:** Crowned spade arms in Order collar

Date	Mintage	VG	F	VF	XF	Unc
1714	—	1,250	2,150	3,500	6,000	—

KM# 10 PATAGON
Silver **Ruler:** Philip V of Spain **Obv:** Large crown above floriated St. Andrew's cross, crowned PV monograms at left and right. **Obv. Legend:** PHILIPPUS V • D • G • HISPANIARUM ET INDIARUM REX • **Rev:** Crowned arms in two Order collars, date divided at top **Rev. Legend:** BURGUND • DUX • BRABANT • ZC **Note:** Dav. #1711. Mint mark: lion rampant left.

Date	Mintage	VG	F	VF	XF	Unc
1709 Rare	—	—	—	—	—	—

KM# 11 PATAGON
Silver **Ruler:** Philip V of Spain **Rev. Legend:** DUX • BURGUND • ET • BRABANT • ZC **Note:** Dav. #A1711. Mint mark: lion rampant left.

Date	Mintage	VG	F	VF	XF	Unc
1709 Rare	—	—	—	—	—	—

KM# 16 SOUVERAIN OU LION D'OR
11.0600 g., 0.9190 Gold 0.3268 oz. AGW **Obv:** Crowned lion rampant with sword next to globe on pedestal, date in legend **Rev:** Crowned arms in collar of the Golden Fleece

Date	Mintage	VG	F	VF	XF	Unc
1711 Rare	—	—	—	—	—	—

KM# 24 SOUVERAIN OU LION D'OR
11.0600 g., 0.9190 Gold 0.3268 oz. AGW **Ruler:** Maximilian Emmanuel of Bavaria **Obv:** Date below lion

Date	Mintage	VG	F	VF	XF	Unc
1712 Rare	—	—	—	—	—	—

KM# 25 SOUVERAIN D'OR
22.1200 g., 0.9190 Gold 0.6535 oz. AGW **Ruler:** Maximilian Emmanuel of Bavaria **Obv:** Head right, date in legend **Rev:** Crowned arms

Date	Mintage	VG	F	VF	XF	Unc
1712 Rare	—	—	—	—	—	—
1713 Rare	—	—	—	—	—	—

PATTERNS

Including off metal strikes

KM#	Date	Mintage	Identification	Mkt Val
Pn1	1712	—	2 Souverain D'Or. White Metal. KM#25	—

TOURNAI

A commercial and industrial commune located in southwest Belgium with a population of 33,625. Hosiery, textiles, leather goods and cement are exported.

Tournai, a city in Hainaut made episcopal see in 6th century, came under French rule and received its charter in 1187. In the early 16th century it was an English possession for a few years and Henry VIII sold it to Francis I. In 1521 the Count of Nassau took it for Spain. It was frequently besieged in wars in the sixteenth through eighteenth centuries. It was severely damaged during World War 1, being captured by the Germans in 1914 and held until 1918.

COUNTY

SIEGE COINAGE

1709

KM# 5 2 SOLS
Copper **Obv:** Bust right **Obv. Legend:** PHIL • V • D • G • HISPANIAR • ET • INDIA • REX • **Rev:** Crowned arms divides value **Rev. Legend:** DUX BURGUND BRABANZ

Date	Mintage	Good	VG	F	VF	XF
1709	—	—	50.00	75.00	125	175

Note: Overstruck on Liege and other liard coins

KM# A6 2 SOLS
Copper **Obv:** Small tower and date **Note:** Uniface.

Date	Mintage	Good	VG	F	VF	XF
1709	—	—	50.00	75.00	125	175

KM# 7 8 SOLS
Copper **Obv:** Shield in palm wreath, date in chronogram **Rev:** 5-line legend

Date	Mintage	Good	VG	F	VF	XF
1709	—	—	125	225	350	500

KM# 8 20 SOLS
Silver **Obv:** Marshall de Surville bust left, value above **Note:** Uniface klippe.

Date	Mintage	Good	VG	F	VF	XF
1709	—	—	125	175	225	300

SURINAME

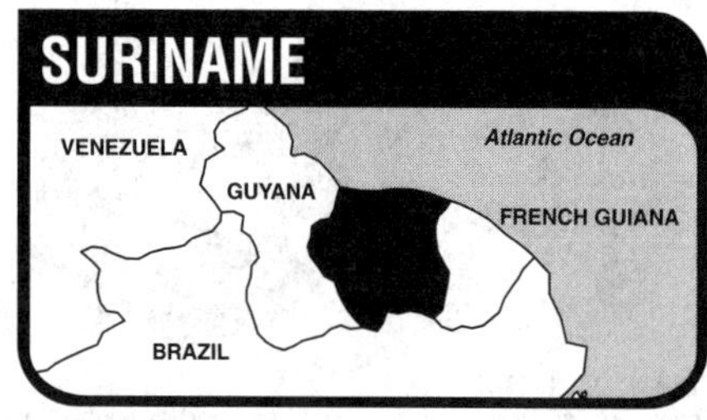

The Republic of Suriname also known as Dutch Guiana, located on the north central coast of South America between Guyana and French Guiana. It has an area of 63,037 sq. mi. (163,270 sq. km.) and a population of *433,000.Capital: Paramaribo. The country is rich in minerals and forests, and self-sufficient in rice, the staple food crop. The mining, processing and exporting of bauxite is the principal economic activity.

Lieutenants of Amerigo Vespucci sighted the Guiana coast in 1499. Spanish explorers of the 16th century, disappointed at finding no gold, departed leaving the area to be settled by the British in 1652. The colony prospered and the Netherlands acquired it in 1667 in exchange for the Dutch rights in Nieuw Nederland (state of New York). During the European wars of the 18th and 19th centuries, which were fought in part in the new world, Suriname was occupied by the British from 1781-1784 and 1796-1814. Suriname became an autonomous part of the Kingdom of the Netherlands on Dec. 15, 1954. Full independence was achieved on Nov. 25, 1975. In 1980, a coup installed a military government which has since been dissolved.

RULER
Dutch, until 1975

REPUBLIC

EARLY STANDARD COINAGE

KM# 8.2 DUIT
Copper **Obv:** Long grass

Date	Mintage	VG	F	VF	XF	Unc
1764	Inc. above	12.50	25.00	40.00	85.00	120

KM# 8.1 DUIT
Copper **Obv:** Short grass divides date **Rev:** SOCIETEI/VAN/SURINAME **Note:** Struck at Enkhuizen under the administration of Governor Wigbold Crommelin on local authority, not that of the Estates General.

Date	Mintage	VG	F	VF	XF	Unc
1764	106,000	12.50	25.00	40.00	85.00	120

SWEDEN

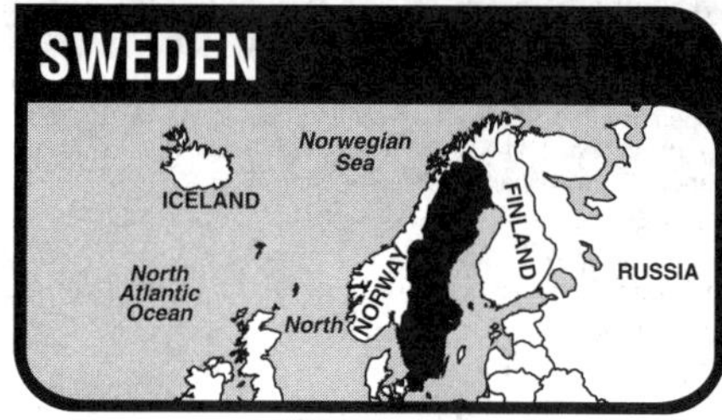

The Kingdom of Sweden, a limited constitutional monarchy located in northern Europe between Norway and Finland, has an area of 173,732 sq. mi. (449,960 sq. km.) and a population of *8.8 million. Capital: Stockholm. Mining, lumbering and a specialized machine industry dominate the economy. Machinery, paper, iron and steel, motor vehicles and wood pulp are exported.

Sweden was founded as a Christian stronghold by Olaf Skottkonung late in the 10th century. After conquering Finland late in the 13th century, Sweden, together with Norway, came under the rule of Denmark, 1397-1523, in an association known as the Union of Kalmar. Modern Sweden had its beginning in 1523 when Gustaf Vasa drove the Danes out of Sweden and was himself chosen king. Under Gustaf Adolphus II and Charles XII, Sweden was one of the great powers of 17th century Europe – until Charles invaded Russia in 1708, and was defeated at the Battle of Pultowa in June, 1709. Early in the 18th century, a coalition of Russia, Poland and Denmark took away Sweden's Baltic empire and in 1809 Sweden was forced to cede Finland to Russia. Norway was ceded to Sweden by the Treaty of Kiel in January, 1814. The Norwegians resisted for a time but later signed the Act of Union at the Convention of Moss in August, 1814,The Union was dissolved in 1905 and Norway became independent. A new constitution which took effect on Jan. 1, 1975, restricts the function of the king largely to a ceremonial role.

RULERS
Carl XII, 1697-1718
Ulrika Eleonora, 1719-1720
Frederick I, 1720-1751
Adolf Frederick, 1751-1771
Gustaf III, 1771-1792
Gustaf IV Adolf, 1792-1809

MINT OFFICIALS' INITIALS

Initials	Date	Name
AL	1762-73	Albrekt Lindberg
GZ	1722-23, 1730-38	Georg Zedritz
HM	1738-62	Hans Malmberg
HZ	1700-06	Henrik Zedritz
LC	1706-22	Lorentz Careelberg
OL	1773-1819	Olof Lidijn
	1723-30	Esaias Zedritz (t.f.)

ENGRAVERS

Stockholm

Date	Name
1681-1718	A. Karlsten
1699-1738	C. G. Hartman
1717-19	Z. H. Arensburg
1718-45	J. C. Hedlinger
1729-64	Daniel Fehrman
1764-74	C. G. Fehrman
1774-87	G. Ljungberger
1787-98	C. G. Fehrman
1799-1830	L. Grandel

Avesta

Date	Name
1688-1770	A. Wikman
1730-51	J. Wikman
1771-72	A. Bjurling
1771-77	J. G. Wikman
1777-90	C. Nerman
1790-1808	C. E. Norman

MONETARY SYSTEM

1704-1798

8 Ore = 1 Mark
32 Ore = 1 Daler
96 Ore S(ilver) M(oney) = 1 Riksdaler
= 3 Daler S(ilver) M(oney)
= 9 Daler K(opper) M(oney)

1798-1830

48 Skilling = 1 Riksdaler Species
2 Riksdaler (Speciesdaler) = 1 Ducat

KINGDOM

STANDARD COINAGE

KM# 334 1/6 ORE (S.M.)

Copper **Ruler:** Carl XII **Obv:** XII within C above 3 crowns, divides initials and date below **Rev:** Rampant lion divides initials and value, crown above

Date	Mintage	VG	F	VF	XF	Unc
1707	1,024,000	4.50	12.00	40.00	70.00	—
1708/7	—	6.00	16.00	50.00	85.00	—
1708	1,536,000	7.00	20.00	65.00	100	—
1713 Unique	128,064	—	—	—	—	—
1715 R.S.	—	4.50	10.00	30.00	65.00	—
1715 R.S.	—	15.00	30.00	75.00	125	—
1716	1,271,000	4.50	9.00	27.50	55.00	—
1718/6	—	6.00	15.00	32.50	70.00	—
1718/7	—	6.00	—	—	—	—
1718	2,027,000	3.50	7.50	22.50	50.00	—

KM# 333 1/6 ORE (S.M.)
Copper **Ruler:** Carl XII **Obv:** XII within C above 3 crowns, divided initials and date below, all within circle, 4 stars around **Rev:** Rampant lion divides initials and value, crown above, all within circle, 4 stars around **Note:** Klippe. Struck at Avesta Mint.

Date	Mintage	VG	F	VF	XF	Unc
1707	—	—	—	—	—	—

KM# 380 1/2 ORE (S.M.)
7.2000 g., Copper **Ruler:** Frederick I **Obv:** F.R.S. above 3 crowns, date below **Rev:** Crowned shield with crossed arrows within, divides initials and value

Date	Mintage	VG	F	VF	XF	Unc
1720 Lozenged edge	1,584,000	—	—	—	—	—
1720 Milled edge	Inc. above	4.00	8.00	35.00	75.00	—
1721	Inc. above	7.50	20.00	60.00	100	—

KM# 250a ORE
1.2317 g., 0.2500 Silver 0.0099 oz. ASW **Ruler:** Carl XII **Obv:** XII within C and sprigs, crown above **Rev:** 3 Crowns, divided date, initials and value **Note:** Struck at Stockholm Mint.

Date	Mintage	VG	F	VF	XF	Unc
1701	353,000	11.50	22.00	50.00	95.00	—
1702	261,000	12.00	22.50	52.50	100	—
1703	345,000	10.00	20.00	42.50	85.00	—
1704	345,000	11.50	22.50	50.00	95.00	—
1705/4	—	15.00	35.00	70.00	140	—
1705	322,000	11.50	22.00	45.00	80.00	—
1706 LC	332,000	11.50	22.00	45.00	85.00	—
1707 LC	327,000	11.50	22.00	45.00	85.00	—
1708 LC	251,000	11.50	22.50	50.00	95.00	—
1709 LC	334,000	11.50	22.50	52.50	100	—
1710 LC	337,000	12.00	22.50	52.50	100	—
1711 LC	246,000	12.00	22.50	55.00	100	—
1712 LC	309,000	11.50	22.00	45.00	85.00	—
1713 LC	321,000	11.50	22.00	45.00	85.00	—
1714 LC	236,000	11.50	22.00	45.00	85.00	—

KM# 250b ORE
1.1907 g., 0.1940 Silver 0.0074 oz. ASW **Ruler:** Carl XII **Obv:** XII within C and sprigs, crown above **Rev:** 3 Crowns, divided date, initials and value

Date	Mintage	VG	F	VF	XF	Unc
1715 LC	404,000	11.50	22.00	42.50	85.00	—
1716 LC	539,000	10.00	20.00	37.50	80.00	—
1717 LC	1,161,000	7.50	16.50	32.50	75.00	—

KM# 381 ORE
1.1907 g., 0.1940 Silver 0.0074 oz. ASW **Ruler:** Ulrika Eleonora **Obv:** V • E • below crown **Rev:** 3 Crowns, divided date, initials and value

Date	Mintage	VG	F	VF	XF	Unc
1720 LC	73,000	25.00	45.00	80.00	150	—

KM# 382 ORE
1.1907 g., 0.1940 Silver 0.0074 oz. ASW **Ruler:** Frederick I **Obv:** F within sprigs below crown **Rev:** 3 Crowns, divided date, initials and value

Date	Mintage	VG	F	VF	XF	Unc
1720 LC	144,000	8.00	15.00	30.00	90.00	—
1721 LC	201,000	6.50	12.00	22.50	45.00	—
1722 LC	613,366	7.00	12.50	24.00	50.00	—
1722 GZ	576,304	7.00	12.50	24.00	50.00	—
1723 GZ	1,931,000	7.00	12.50	24.00	50.00	—
1723 Without mm	Inc. above	12.50	25.00	50.00	110	—
1724	387,000	7.00	12.50	24.00	50.00	—
1725	79,000	8.50	20.00	45.00	90.00	—
1726/5	—	8.50	16.00	32.00	65.00	—
1726	226,000	6.50	12.00	25.00	50.00	—
1727	71,000	8.50	16.00	32.00	65.00	—
1728	71,000	8.00	15.00	30.00	60.00	—
1729	59,000	9.00	16.50	35.00	70.00	—
1730 GZ	74,220	16.00	30.00	65.00	125	—
1731 GZ	77,752	15.00	30.00	65.00	125	—
1732 GZ	768,000	6.50	12.00	24.00	50.00	—
1733/1732 GZ	—	9.00	16.50	35.00	70.00	—
1733 GZ	956,000	6.50	12.00	24.00	50.00	—
1734 GZ	326,000	6.50	12.00	24.00	50.00	—
1735 GZ	146,000	8.00	15.00	30.00	60.00	—
1736 GZ	161,000	9.00	16.50	35.00	70.00	—
1737 GZ	224,000	6.50	12.00	25.00	50.00	—
1740	77,000	9.00	16.50	35.00	70.00	—
1742	350,000	6.00	10.00	20.00	40.00	—
1743	288,000	6.00	10.00	20.00	40.00	—
1747	191,000	8.50	16.00	32.00	75.00	—
1749	89,000	25.00	75.00	150	250	—

KM# 472 ORE
1.1907 g., 0.1940 Silver 0.0074 oz. ASW **Ruler:** Adolf Frederick **Obv:** Crowned AF monogram within sprigs **Rev:** 3 crowns above date and value

Date	Mintage	VG	F	VF	XF	Unc
1753 HM	66,000	12.00	25.00	50.00	100	—
1754/3 HM	—	13.50	27.50	60.00	120	—
1754 HM	69,000	12.00	25.00	50.00	100	—
1756 HM	72,000	12.00	25.00	50.00	100	—
1757 HM	66,000	30.00	65.00	135	225	—
1758 HM	75,585	12.00	25.00	50.00	100	—
1761 HM	172,000	10.00	20.00	40.00	80.00	—

KM# 356 ORE (S.M.)
Copper **Ruler:** Carl XII **Obv:** CXII R S above crowned lion, date **Rev:** Crown above crossed arrows **Note:** Struck at Avesta Mint.

Date	Mintage	VG	F	VF	XF	Unc
1715 Lozenged edge	4,800	275	500	950	1,750	—
1715 Plain edge	—	250	450	850	1,500	—

KM# 416.1 ORE (S.M.)
14.2000 g., Copper **Ruler:** Frederick I **Obv:** Crown above monogram flanked by 3 crowns **Rev:** Crossed arrows divides initials, value, crown above, date below **Note:** Crown varieties exist for issues dated 1749.

Date	Mintage	VG	F	VF	XF	Unc
1730	672,000	6.00	13.50	37.50	70.00	—
1731	1,574,000	4.00	12.00	32.50	65.00	—
1732	1,669,000	3.00	10.00	30.00	60.00	—
1733	576,000	6.00	15.00	45.00	85.00	—
1734	461,000	20.00	45.00	150	275	—
1735	1,824,000	3.00	10.00	30.00	60.00	—
1736	960,000	3.00	10.00	30.00	60.00	—
1737	1,329,000	5.00	12.50	32.50	65.00	—
1738	2,304,000	3.00	8.00	25.00	55.00	—
1739/37	—	—	—	—	—	—
1739/38	—	25.00	50.00	100	175	—
1739	1,507,000	5.00	12.00	25.00	55.00	—
1740	1,920,000	3.00	8.00	25.00	55.00	—
1741	1,920,000	3.00	8.00	25.00	55.00	—
1742	2,880,000	3.00	8.00	25.00	55.00	—
1743	—	6.00	15.00	45.00	85.00	—
1744	—	7.00	20.00	50.00	90.00	—
1745	—	7.00	20.00	50.00	90.00	—
1746/5	—	6.00	15.00	45.00	85.00	—
1746	—	4.00	12.50	35.00	55.00	—
1747	—	3.00	8.00	25.00	55.00	—
1748	—	3.00	8.00	25.00	55.00	—
1749	—	3.00	8.00	25.00	55.00	—
1750	—	3.00	8.00	25.00	55.00	—

KM# 416.2 ORE (S.M.)
14.2000 g., Copper **Ruler:** Frederick I **Obv:** Crown above monogram flanked by crowns **Rev:** Crossed arrows divides initials, value, crown above, date below **Note:** Struck at Stockholm Mint.

Date	Mintage	VG	F	VF	XF	Unc
1737	48,000	135	275	650	1,000	—

KM# 460 ORE (S.M.)
14.2000 g., Copper **Ruler:** Adolf Frederick **Obv:** Crowned monogram flanked by 3 crowns **Rev:** Crossed arrows divides initials, value, crown above, date below

Date	Mintage	VG	F	VF	XF	Unc
1751	—	6.50	15.00	45.00	80.00	—
1758	—	3.00	8.00	30.00	55.00	—
1759/56	—	25.00	50.00	120	200	—
1759	—	3.00	8.00	30.00	55.00	—
1760/52	—	35.00	70.00	200	300	—
1760/59	—	6.50	15.00	45.00	80.00	—
1760	—	3.00	9.00	35.00	65.00	—
1761/60	—	30.00	65.00	180	285	—
1761/71	—	30.00	65.00	180	285	—
1761	—	3.00	8.00	30.00	55.00	—
1763	—	3.00	8.00	30.00	55.00	—
1768	317,000	15.00	30.00	100	185	—
1769	—	15.00	30.00	100	185	—

KM# 521.1 ORE (S.M.)
14.2000 g., Copper **Ruler:** Gustaf III **Obv:** III within G flanked by 3 crowns, larger crown above **Rev:** Crossed arrows divides initials, value, crown anove, date below

Date	Mintage	VG	F	VF	XF	Unc
1778 Small 8	192,000	22.50	50.00	135	400	—

KM# 521.2 ORE (S.M.)
14.2000 g., Copper **Ruler:** Gustaf III **Obv:** III within G flanked by 3 crowns, larger crown above **Rev:** Crossed arrows divides initials, value, crown above, date below

Date	Mintage	VG	F	VF	XF	Unc
1778 Wide 8	Inc. above	35.00	75.00	185	600	—

KM# 364.3 ORE (K.M.)
Copper **Ruler:** Ulrika Eleonora **Edge:** Milled

Date	Mintage	VG	F	VF	XF	Unc
1719	—	11.00	25.00	75.00	125	—
1720	—	5.00	12.00	45.00	80.00	—

KM# 364.2 ORE (K.M.)
Copper **Ruler:** Ulrika Eleonora **Edge:** Lozenged **Note:** Three crown varieties.

Date	Mintage	VG	F	VF	XF	Unc
1719	—	4.50	10.00	35.00	70.00	—
1720	—	2.00	4.50	15.00	30.00	—

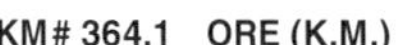

KM# 364.1 ORE (K.M.)
Copper **Ruler:** Ulrika Eleonora **Obv:** V E R S above 3 crowns, date below **Rev:** Crown above crossed arrows within shield, value

and initials flanking shield **Edge:** Plain **Note:** Weight varies 4.5-4.7 grams. Three crown varieties.

Date	Mintage	VG	F	VF	XF	Unc
1719	—	3.00	12.00	40.00	65.00	—

KM# 383.2 ORE (K.M.)

Copper **Ruler:** Frederick I **Edge:** Milled

Date	Mintage	VG	F	VF	XF	Unc
1720	—	35.00	65.00	125	200	—
1721	—	50.00	90.00	200	300	—

KM# 383.1 ORE (K.M.)

Copper **Ruler:** Frederick I **Obv:** F R S above 3 crowns, date **Rev:** Crown above crossed arrows, value **Edge:** Lozenged **Note:** Weight varies 4.5-4.7 grams.

Date	Mintage	VG	F	VF	XF	Unc
1720	—	2.00	5.00	20.00	40.00	—
1721	3,440,000	3.50	7.00	25.00	50.00	—
1724 Small shield	12,067,000	2.75	6.50	22.50	45.00	—
1724 Arrow fletching V-shaped	Inc. above	15.00	30.00	125	250	—
1724 Arrow fletching squared	Inc. above	7.50	15.00	35.00	70.00	—
1724 Arrow fletching curved	Inc. above	3.50	7.50	25.00	45.00	—
1725 Crown of 1724	Inc. below	10.00	20.00	42.50	90.00	—
1725	8,266,000	2.50	6.00	22.50	45.00	—
1726	3,802,000	4.00	12.00	50.00	90.00	—
1750	1,238,000	2.00	8.00	30.00	60.00	—

KM# 383.3 ORE (K.M.)

Copper **Ruler:** Frederick I **Note:** Struck at Avesta Mint.

Date	Mintage	VG	F	VF	XF	Unc
1746	58,000	35.00	70.00	185	285	—
1749	23,040,000	3.50	8.00	22.50	45.00	—

KM# 491 ORE (K.M.)

4.7000 g., Copper **Ruler:** Adolf Frederick **Obv:** 3 crowns - 2 above 1; A.F.R.S. at top, date at bottom **Rev:** Crowned arms divide date

Date	Mintage	VG	F	VF	XF	Unc
1768 Small shield	317,000	5.00	15.00	45.00	85.00	—
1768 Large shield	Inc. above	10.00	30.00	85.00	165	—

KM# 512.1 ORE (K.M.)

4.7000 g., Copper **Ruler:** Gustaf III **Obv:** G • R • S • above 3 crowns and date **Rev:** Crossed arrows within shield, flanked by initials, value

Date	Mintage	VG	F	VF	XF	Unc
1772	662,000	4.00	12.00	27.50	80.00	—
1778	576,000	11.00	20.00	75.00	250	—

KM# 512.2 ORE (K.M.)

4.7000 g., Copper **Ruler:** Gustaf III **Obv:** G • R • S • above 3 crowns and date **Rev:** Crossed arrows within shield flanked by initials, value **Note:** Size varies 27-34 millimeters. Thick planchet.

Date	Mintage	VG	F	VF	XF	Unc
1772	—	250	450	800	1,500	—

KM# 353 2 ORE

1.7551 g., 0.4440 Silver 0.0251 oz. ASW **Ruler:** Carl XII **Obv:** Crown above CRS within sprigs **Rev:** 3 Crowns, divided date, initials and value **Note:** Struck at Stockholm Mint.

Date	Mintage	VG	F	VF	XF	Unc
1716	82,000	35.00	60.00	115	225	—
1717 LC	74,000	40.00	70.00	135	250	—

KM# 419 2 ORE

1.7551 g., 0.4440 Silver 0.0251 oz. ASW **Ruler:** Frederick I **Obv:** Crown above F R S, wreath around **Rev:** 3 crowns, date, value

Date	Mintage	VG	F	VF	XF	Unc
1732 Unique	—	—	—	—	—	—

KM# 437 2 ORE (S.M.)

28.3000 g., Copper **Ruler:** Frederick I **Obv:** Crown above rampant lion within shield, flanked by 3 crowns and initials **Obv. Legend:** F I S G V R **Rev:** Crown above crossed arrows, value, date **Note:** Struck at Avesta Mint.

Date	Mintage	VG	F	VF	XF	Unc
1743	999,000	6.00	20.00	50.00	90.00	—
1744/3	49,000	50.00	100	200	350	—
1744	Inc. above	5.00	15.00	35.00	70.00	—
1745	142,000	5.00	18.00	50.00	90.00	—
1746/47	286,000	10.00	20.00	60.00	100	—
1746 Large shield	Inc. above	5.00	15.00	35.00	70.00	—
1746 Small shield	Inc. above	5.00	18.00	40.00	80.00	—
1747/46	—	15.00	30.00	80.00	150	—
1747	403,000	3.00	9.00	30.00	60.00	—
1748	461,000	4.50	12.00	40.00	80.00	—
1749	313,000	3.00	9.00	30.00	60.00	—
1750 Slant 5	353,000	5.00	15.00	35.00	70.00	—
1750 Upright 5	Inc. above	5.00	10.00	45.00	75.00	—

KM# 461 2 ORE (S.M.)

28.3000 g., Copper **Ruler:** Adolf Frederick **Obv:** Crown above rampant lion within shield flanked by 3 crowns and initials **Obv. Legend:** A F S G V R

Date	Mintage	VG	F	VF	XF	Unc
1751	353,000	6.50	20.00	50.00	90.00	—
1755 Dot after date	19,000	20.00	50.00	120	225	—
1755 Without dot	Inc. above	45.00	100	275	375	—
1757	379,000	20.00	35.00	75.00	140	—
1758/55	—	25.00	50.00	100	200	—
1758	91,000	22.00	45.00	100	185	—
1759/58	—	50.00	100	200	350	—
1759	352,000	6.00	18.00	45.00	85.00	—
1760	558,000	4.00	9.00	30.00	60.00	—
1761	422,000	4.00	9.00	30.00	60.00	—
1762/61	—	10.00	20.00	60.00	125	—
1762	4,339,000	4.00	9.00	30.00	60.00	—
1763	401,000	5.00	12.00	45.00	85.00	—
1764 Dot after V. S.G.-V.	5,496,000	4.00	9.00	30.00	60.00	—
1764 Dot before .V S.G.-.V	Inc. above	20.00	40.00	85.00	160	—
1765	5,304,000	5.00	12.00	40.00	80.00	—
1766	4,296,000	4.00	9.00	30.00	60.00	—
1767	467,000	4.50	10.00	35.00	70.00	—
1768	168,000	4.50	10.00	35.00	70.00	—

KM# 518 2 ORE (S.M.)

28.3000 g., Copper **Ruler:** Gustaf III **Obv:** Crown above rampant lion within shield flanked by 3 crowns and initials **Rev:** Crossed arrows divides initials, value, crown above, date below **Note:** Crown varieties exist.

Date	Mintage	VG	F	VF	XF	Unc
1777 Small date	1,031,000	12.50	32.50	70.00	325	—
1777 Large date	Inc. above	20.00	40.00	90.00	375	—

KM# 365 3 ORE (K.M.)

Copper **Obv. Legend:** STORA KOPPARBERGS POLLETT **Rev:** Haloed cross on mountaintop **Note:** Struck at Stora Kopparberg Bergslags. Co Mint. Varieties exist.

Date	Mintage	VG	F	VF	XF	Unc
1719	39,000	15.00	35.00	100	385	—
1762	85,000	9.00	20.00	60.00	285	—

KM# 257 4 ORE (1/2 Mark)

2.9252 g., 0.3750 Silver 0.0353 oz. ASW **Ruler:** Carl XII **Obv:** Crowned C **Rev:** Three crowns **Note:** Struck at Stockholm Mint. Varieties exist.

Date	Mintage	VG	F	VF	XF	Unc
1716	163,000	17.50	35.00	75.00	150	—
1717/6	75,000	30.00	65.00	125	250	—
1717	Inc. above	27.50	55.00	100	200	—
1717 Os in PROTECTOR inverted, dots below	Inc. above	50.00	100	200	350	—
1718	404,000	17.50	35.00	75.00	150	—

KM# 506 4 ORE (S.M.)

2.7713 g., 0.3820 Silver 0.0340 oz. ASW **Ruler:** Adolf Frederick **Obv:** Crowned monogram **Rev:** Crown above 3 crowns within circle, flanked by initials and value, date below

Date	Mintage	VG	F	VF	XF	Unc
1771 AL	21,000	25.00	45.00	120	225	—

KM# 310 5 ORE (S.M.)

3.5103 g., 0.4440 Silver 0.0501 oz. ASW **Obv:** Crown above doubled large C monogram, date **Rev:** Three crowns, value **Note:** Struck at Stockholm Mint.

Date	Mintage	VG	F	VF	XF	Unc
1702	355,000	11.50	25.00	55.00	110	—
1703	417,000	12.50	27.50	60.00	120	—
1704	629,000	13.50	30.00	65.00	125	—
1704/3	Inc. above	15.00	35.00	70.00	140	—
1705/4	968,000	13.50	30.00	65.00	125	—
1705	Inc. above	10.00	22.00	45.00	85.00	—
1706 HZ	174,019	10.00	22.00	45.00	85.00	—
1706 LC	169,701	12.50	27.50	60.00	120	—
1707 LC 5 O	536,000	13.50	30.00	65.00	125	—
1707 LC 5 OR	Inc. above	11.50	25.00	50.00	100	—
1708 LC	455,000	10.00	22.00	45.00	85.00	—
1709 LC	425,000	11.50	25.00	50.00	100	—
1710 LC	1,256,000	8.00	18.00	40.00	80.00	—
1711 LC	839,000	9.00	20.00	42.50	85.00	—
1712 LC	240,000	10.00	22.00	45.00	85.00	—
1713/2 LC	101,000	12.50	28.00	55.00	110	—
1713 LC	Inc. above	12.50	27.50	60.00	120	—
1714 LC	47,000	20.00	40.00	80.00	160	—
1715 LC	33,000	25.00	50.00	100	200	—

KM# 366 5 ORE (S.M.)

3.5103 g., 0.4440 Silver 0.0501 oz. ASW **Ruler:** Ulrika Eleonora **Obv:** V above double E monogram below crown **Rev:** 3 crowns, value, date

Date	Mintage	VG	F	VF	XF	Unc
1719 LC	188,000	25.00	55.00	125	225	—

KM# 390 5 ORE (S.M.)

3.5103 g., 0.4440 Silver 0.0501 oz. ASW **Ruler:** Frederick I **Obv:** F R monogram below crown, date **Rev:** 3 crowns, value

Date	Mintage	VG	F	VF	XF	Unc
1722 LC	314,000	18.00	35.00	85.00	165	—
1722 GZ	66,000	25.00	55.00	125	225	—

KM# 397 5 ORE (S.M.)

3.5103 g., 0.4440 Silver 0.0501 oz. ASW **Ruler:** Frederick I **Obv:** Doubled F monogram below crown, date

Date	Mintage	VG	F	VF	XF	Unc
1725	275,000	20.00	40.00	90.00	175	—

KM# 401 5 ORE (S.M.)

3.5103 g., 0.4440 Silver 0.0501 oz. ASW **Ruler:** Frederick I **Obv:** Monogram in cruciform with crowns in angles **Rev:** 3 Crowns, initials, value

Date	Mintage	VG	F	VF	XF	Unc
1729	424,000	10.00	20.00	40.00	80.00	—
1730/29	1,002,999	12.50	25.00	50.00	100	—
1730	Inc. above	10.00	22.00	45.00	90.00	—
1730/29 GZ	Inc. above	12.50	25.00	50.00	100	—
1730 GZ	Inc. above	12.50	25.00	50.00	100	—
1731/0	Inc. above	12.50	25.00	50.00	100	—
1731	1,246,000	7.50	15.00	35.00	70.00	—
1732	985,000	11.00	22.00	45.00	90.00	—
1733/2	264,000	12.50	25.00	50.00	100	—
1733	Inc. above	10.00	20.00	42.50	85.00	—
1735	152,000	11.00	22.00	45.00	90.00	—
1736	260,000	10.00	20.00	42.50	85.00	—
1737 GZ	432,000	10.00	20.00	40.00	80.00	—
1737 HM	—	15.00	30.00	60.00	120	—
1738 GZ	165,000	11.00	22.00	45.00	90.00	—
1738 HM	610,000	10.00	20.00	40.00	80.00	—
1739	423,000	10.00	20.00	40.00	80.00	—
1740/39	76,000	12.50	25.00	50.00	100	—
1740	Inc. above	10.00	20.00	42.50	85.00	—
1741	842,000	10.00	20.00	40.00	80.00	—
1742/1	825,000	11.00	22.00	45.00	90.00	—
1742	Inc. above	10.00	20.00	42.50	85.00	—
1743/2	405,000	15.00	32.00	65.00	135	—
1743	Inc. above	10.00	20.00	40.00	80.00	—
1744/3	388,000	13.50	28.00	55.00	110	—
1744	Inc. above	11.00	22.00	45.00	90.00	—
1745	311,000	15.00	25.00	42.50	85.00	—
1746	482,000	10.00	20.00	40.00	80.00	—
1747	407,000	10.00	20.00	42.50	85.00	—
1748	142,000	11.00	35.00	65.00	125	—
1749	144,000	11.00	22.00	45.00	90.00	—
1750	58,000	15.00	32.00	65.00	135	—
1751/0	79,000	15.00	32.00	65.00	135	—
1751	Inc. above	15.00	32.00	65.00	135	—

KM# 462 5 ORE (S.M.)

3.5103 g., 0.4440 Silver 0.0501 oz. ASW **Ruler:** Adolf Frederick **Obv:** Crowned monogram **Rev:** 3 Crowns, initials, value

Date	Mintage	VG	F	VF	XF	Unc
1751 HM	309,000	17.50	45.00	100	200	—
1752 HM	108,000	17.50	45.00	100	200	—
1753 HM	288,000	15.00	45.00	100	200	—
1754/3 HM	—	22.50	50.00	105	200	—
1754 HM	52,000	20.00	45.00	100	200	—
1755/54 HM	132,000	25.00	50.00	100	200	—
1755 HM	Inc. above	15.00	45.00	100	200	—
1756 HM	294,000	15.00	45.00	100	200	—
1757 HM	63,000	20.00	40.00	80.00	160	—
1758 HM	102,000	15.00	45.00	100	200	—
1759 HM	100,000	15.00	45.00	100	200	—
1760 HM	82,000	15.00	45.00	100	200	—
1761 HM	42,000	30.00	60.00	120	225	—
1762 HM	28,000	25.00	50.00	100	200	—
1763 AL	—	15.00	45.00	100	200	—
1764/3 AL	213,000	16.00	45.00	100	200	—
1764 AL	Inc. above	20.00	45.00	100	200	—
1765/4 AL	65,000	22.00	45.00	100	200	—
1765 AL	Inc. above	20.00	45.00	100	200	—
1766 AL	229,000	15.00	45.00	100	200	—
1767/3 AL	35,000	30.00	60.00	120	225	—
1767 AL	Inc. above	22.00	45.00	100	200	—

KM# 485 6 ORE (K.M.)

Copper **Ruler:** Adolf Frederick **Obv. Legend:** STORA KOPPARBERGS POLLETT **Rev:** Haloed cross on mountaintop, date **Note:** Struck at Stora Kopparbergs Bergslags Mint.

Date	Mintage	VG	F	VF	XF	Unc
1762	80,000	6.50	20.00	50.00	90.00	—
1763	126,000	5.00	15.00	45.00	85.00	—
1765	369,000	5.00	15.00	45.00	85.00	—

KM# 507 8 ORE (S.M.)

4.2123 g., 0.5070 Silver 0.0687 oz. ASW **Ruler:** Adolf Frederick **Obv:** Crowned AF monogram **Rev:** Crown above 3 crowns within circle flanked by initials and value, date below

Date	Mintage	VG	F	VF	XF	Unc
1771 AL	17,000	20.00	35.00	90.00	220	—

KM# 508 8 ORE (S.M.)

4.2123 g., 0.5070 Silver 0.0687 oz. ASW **Ruler:** Adolf Frederick **Obv:** Angle in crossbar of A

Date	Mintage	VG	F	VF	XF	Unc
1771 AL	Inc. above	30.00	60.00	120	300	—

KM# 425 10 ORE (S.M.)
7.0205 g., 0.4440 Silver 0.1002 oz. ASW **Ruler:** Frederick I **Obv:** Monogram in cruciform with crowns in angles **Rev:** 3 Crowns, initials and value **Note:** Struck at Stockholm Mint.

Date	Mintage	VG	F	VF	XF	Unc
1739 HM	1,150,000	22.50	40.00	75.00	150	—
1740 HM	1,337,000	22.50	40.00	75.00	150	—
1741 HM	443,000	25.00	45.00	80.00	160	—
1742 HM	134,000	27.50	50.00	90.00	180	—
1743/2 HM	127,000	30.00	55.00	100	200	—
1743 HM	Inc. above	27.50	50.00	90.00	180	—
1744 HM	43,000	35.00	65.00	145	285	—
1745/4 HM	272,000	27.50	50.00	95.00	190	—
1750 HM	227,000	30.00	80.00	150	300	—
1751	Inc. below	50.00	100	200	375	—

KM# 463 10 ORE (S.M.)
7.0205 g., 0.4440 Silver 0.1002 oz. ASW **Ruler:** Adolf Frederick **Obv:** Crowned AF monogram, date at upper left **Rev:** 3 crowns above value

Date	Mintage	VG	F	VF	XF	Unc
1751 HM	44,121	55.00	100	225	450	—
1752 HM	44,000	50.00	95.00	225	450	—
1753 HM	156,855	45.00	90.00	175	400	—
1754/3 HM	105,000	55.00	100	250	500	—
1754 HM	Inc. above	55.00	100	250	500	—
1755/54 HM	—	50.00	95.00	200	400	—
1755 HM	92,000	50.00	95.00	200	400	—
1756 HM	184,000	45.00	85.00	200	400	—
1760 HM	233,000	50.00	95.00	200	400	—
1761 HM	27,000	55.00	100	250	500	—
1763 HM	228,000	50.00	95.00	200	400	—
1764/3 HM	—	50.00	95.00	200	400	—
1765 HM	116,000	50.00	95.00	200	40.00	—

KM# 500 16 ORE (S.M.)
6.1946 g., 0.6910 Silver 0.1376 oz. ASW **Ruler:** Adolf Frederick **Obv:** Crowned monogram **Rev:** Crown above 3 crowns within circle flanked by initials and value, date below

Date	Mintage	VG	F	VF	XF	Unc
1770 al	11,000	25.00	70.00	150	425	—

KM# 513 16 ORE (S.M.)
6.1946 g., 0.6910 Silver 0.1376 oz. ASW **Ruler:** Gustaf III **Obv:** III within crowned G **Rev:** 3 Crowns within center circle of crowned order chain

Date	Mintage	VG	F	VF	XF	Unc
1773 AL with 7 seraphs on reverse, 9mm crown	201,000	20.00	40.00	85.00	170	—
1773 AL with 9 seraphs on reverse, 10.5mm crown	Inc. above	35.00	55.00	110	220	—
1774 OL	152,000	25.00	50.00	100	200	—
1774/1773 OL	—	30.00	60.00	125	250	—

KM# 313 MARK (8 Ore)
0.6940 Silver **Ruler:** Carl XII **Obv:** Bust right **Obv. Inscription:** CAROLVS • XII • D • G • REX • S • V • E • **Rev:** Three crowns, divided date, value

Date	Mintage	VG	F	VF	XF	Unc
1701 HZ	230,000	30.00	55.00	225	355	—
1702	129,000	30.00	60.00	165	365	—
1703	126,000	30.00	55.00	150	355	—
1704	44,000	30.00	65.00	175	390	—
1705	89,000	30.00	60.00	165	375	—
1706/04	—	45.00	75.00	200	425	—
1706 HZ	31,000	45.00	75.00	200	520	—
1706 LC	79,000	30.00	60.00	165	365	—
1707 LC	33,000	30.00	65.00	175	390	—
1708/07 LC	—	45.00	75.00	200	425	—
1708 LC	65,000	30.00	60.00	160	365	—
1709 LC	35,000	35.00	70.00	175	410	—
1710 LC	33,000	30.00	60.00	160	365	—
1711 LC	Inc. above	35.00	70.00	170	400	—
1712 LC	46,000	35.00	70.00	175	425	—
1713/2 LC	65,000	35.00	70.00	175	425	—
1714 LC	83,000	30.00	55.00	155	360	—
1715 LC	54,000	35.00	60.00	170	385	—
1716 LC	29,000	30.00	55.00	155	365	—
1717 LC	47,000	30.00	55.00	160	365	—
1716 CAROL	Inc. above	30.00	75.00	175	350	—
1717 LC CAROL VS	76,000	35.00	80.00	175	350	—

KM# 367 MARK (8 Ore)
Silver **Ruler:** Ulrika Eleonora **Obv:** Bust right **Obv. Legend:** VLRICA • ELEONORA • D • G • REGINA • SVEC **Rev:** Crown above 3 crowns within circle flanked by initials and value **Rev. Legend:** IN • DEO • SPES • M • B • A •

Date	Mintage	VG	F	VF	XF	Unc
1719 LC	51,000	85.00	155	325	625	—
1720/19 LC	47,000	100	165	335	650	—

KM# 384 MARK (8 Ore)
Silver **Ruler:** Frederick I **Rev:** Similar to KM#242

Date	Mintage	VG	F	VF	XF	Unc
1720/19 LC	24,000	150	300	575	1,225	—
1721/19 LC	Inc. above	150	300	575	1,225	—
1721 LC	35,000	150	300	575	1,225	—

KM# 314 2 MARK
10.4000 g., 0.6940 Silver 0.2320 oz. ASW **Ruler:** Carl XII **Obv:** Bust right **Obv. Legend:** CAROLVS • XII • D • G • REX • SVE • **Rev:** Three crowns, value

Date	Mintage	VG	F	VF	XF	Unc
1701	1,084,055	20.00	45.00	115	235	—
1702	465,000	30.00	70.00	175	350	—
1703	338,000	30.00	75.00	175	350	—
1704	126,000	35.00	80.00	175	350	—
1705/03	—	30.00	75.00	175	350	—
1705	129,000	30.00	75.00	175	350	—
1706 LC	91,681	30.00	75.00	175	350	—
1706 HZ	Inc. above	30.00	75.00	175	350	—
1707 LC	94,000	30.00	75.00	175	350	—
1708/7 LC	64,000	35.00	80.00	175	350	—
1708 LC	Inc. above	30.00	75.00	175	350	—

KM# 339 2 MARK
Silver **Ruler:** Carl XII **Obv:** Bust right **Obv. Legend:** CAROLVS • XII • D • G • REX • SVE • **Rev:** 3 Crowns, divided date, value

Date	Mintage	VG	F	VF	XF	Unc
1709 LC	120,000	30.00	75.00	175	350	—
1710 LC	110,000	30.00	75.00	175	350	—
1711 LC	93,000	30.00	75.00	175	350	—
1712 LC	70,000	30.00	75.00	175	350	—
1713/12 LC	—	30.00	75.00	175	350	—
1713 LC	78,000	30.00	75.00	175	350	—
1714 LC	142,000	30.00	70.00	175	350	—
1715 LC CAROLVS	57,000	45.00	100	225	425	—
1715 CAROL	Inc. above	—	—	—	—	—
1716 LC	203,000	35.00	75.00	180	350	—

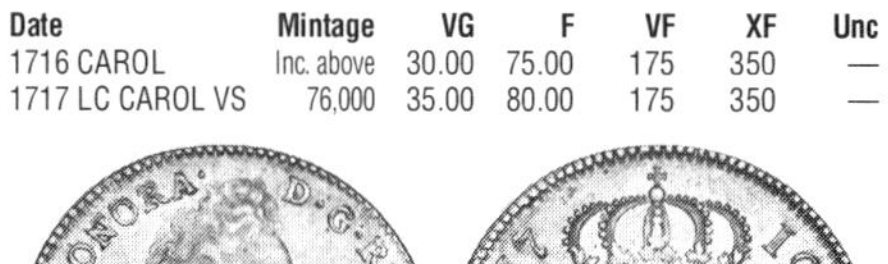

KM# 368 2 MARK
Silver **Ruler:** Ulrika Eleonora **Obv:** Bust right **Obv. Legend:** VLRICA • ELEONORA • D • G • REGINA • SVEC • **Rev:** Crown above 3 crowns within circle flanked by initials and value **Rev. Legend:** IN • DEO • SPES • MBA •

Date	Mintage	VG	F	VF	XF	Unc
1719 LC	51,000	110	220	350	745	—

KM# 385 2 MARK
Silver **Ruler:** Frederick I **Obv:** Bust right **Obv. Legend:** FRIDERICVS • D • G • REX • SVECÆ • **Rev:** Crown above 3 crowns within circle flanked by initials and value **Rev. Legend:** IN • DEO • SPES • MBA •

Date	Mintage	VG	F	VF	XF	Unc
1720/19	19,000	150	300	500	1,100	—
1720	Inc. above	125	250	400	775	—
1721 LC	25,000	125	250	350	575	—
1722	26,000	125	250	350	575	—
1731	52,000	100	225	300	525	—
1732	81,000	80.00	200	250	475	—
1733	8,000	125	250	500	1,100	—
1736	14,000	125	250	450	1,100	—
1737	43,000	125	250	450	725	—

KM# 467 2 MARK
Silver **Ruler:** Adolf Frederick **Obv:** Head right **Obv. Legend:** ADOLPHUS • FRID • D • G • .... **Rev:** 3 Crowns within center circle of crowned order chain **Rev. Legend:** SALUS • PUBLICA • ...

Date	Mintage	VG	F	VF	XF	Unc
1752 HM	170,000	250	550	1,100	1,600	—
1752	Inc. above	125	250	400	650	—
1754 HM	9,700	150	300	450	850	—

KM# 315 4 MARK
Silver **Ruler:** Carl XII **Obv:** Bust right **Obv. Legend:** CAROLVS • XII • D • G • REX • SVE • **Rev:** Crowned shield divides value **Rev. Legend:** DOMINVS • PROTECTOR • MEVS •

Date	Mintage	VG	F	VF	XF	Unc
1701	136,000	55.00	95.00	235	485	—
1702	50,000	60.00	110	255	500	—
1703 HZ	74,000	55.00	95.00	235	485	—
1704	11,000	80.00	160	355	775	—
1705/4	29,000	60.00	110	255	500	—

KM# 337 4 MARK

Silver **Ruler:** Carl XII **Obv:** Bust right **Obv. Legend:** CAROLVS • XII • D • G • REX • SVE • **Rev:** Crowned shield divides value **Rev. Legend:** DOMINVS • PROTECTOR • MEVS •

Date	Mintage	VG	F	VF	XF	Unc
1708/7 LC	17,000	55.00	95.00	230	475	—
1709 LC	10,000	60.00	110	255	575	—
1710 LC	23,000	60.00	110	255	550	—
1711 LC	10,000	60.00	110	255	550	—
1712 LC	8,000	65.00	125	275	625	—
1714 LC	6,000	110	175	375	925	—
1715 LC	12,000	60.00	110	255	550	—
1716/5 LC	—	55.00	95.00	245	550	—
1716 LC	81,000	55.00	95.00	230	475	—

KM# 386 4 MARK

Silver **Ruler:** Ulrika Eleonora **Obv:** Bust right **Obv. Legend:** VLRICA • EONORA • D • G • REGINA • SVECLÆ • **Rev:** Crown above 3 crowns within circle flanked by value **Rev. Legend:** IN • DEO • SPES • MEA •

Date	Mintage	VG	F	VF	XF	Unc
1720 LC	12,000	550	1,000	1,750	2,500	—

KM# 387 4 MARK

Silver **Ruler:** Frederick I **Obv:** Bust right **Obv. Legend:** FRIDERICVS • D • G • REX • SVECIAE • **Rev:** 3 Crowns within circle flanked by value **Rev. Legend:** IN • DEO • SPES • MEA

Date	Mintage	VG	F	VF	XF	Unc
1720 LC	10,000	250	500	850	2,100	—
1732 GZ	15,000	300	550	1,000	2,200	—
1737 GZ	17,000	250	500	900	2,000	—
1738 GZ	14,000	225	450	900	1,900	—

KM# 468 4 MARK

20.8000 g., 0.6940 Silver 0.4641 oz. ASW **Ruler:** Adolf Frederick **Obv:** Large bust right **Obv. Legend:** ADOLPHUS • FRID • D • G • ... **Rev:** 3 Crowns within center circle of crowned order chain **Rev. Legend:** SALUS....

Date	Mintage	VG	F	VF	XF	Unc
1752 MH Vertical milled edge	65,000	150	300	600	1,000	—
1752 MH Diagonal milled edge	Inc. above	150	300	600	1,000	—
1753 MH	80,000	75.00	165	300	600	—
1754 MH	13,000	275	525	1,000	1,750	—
1755 MH	7,418	150	350	600	950	—

KM# 317 8 MARK

31.3475 g., 0.9220 Silver 0.9292 oz. ASW **Ruler:** Carl XII **Obv:** Armored bust right **Obv. Legend:** CAROLVS • XII • D • G • REX • SVE • **Rev:** Crowned shield divides value **Rev. Legend:** DOMINVS ... **Note:** Dav. #4541, 1712.

Date	Mintage	VG	F	VF	XF	Unc
1701 HZ	6,490	400	700	1,100	1,850	—
1704 HZ	5,834	400	700	1,250	2,500	—

KM# 321 CAROLINER (1/2 Daler Silvermynt)

6.6600 g., 0.6940 Silver 0.1486 oz. ASW **Ruler:** Carl XII **Obv:** Double C monogram **Rev:** Four crowned coats of arms in cross shape **Note:** Size varies 28.5-28.75 millimeters.

Date	Mintage	VG	F	VF	XF	Unc
1718	35,152	75.00	150	300	500	—

KM# 322 2 CAROLINER (Daler Silvermynt)

13.3100 g., 0.6940 Silver 0.2970 oz. ASW **Ruler:** Carl XII **Obv:** Double C Monogram **Rev:** Four crowned coats of arms in cross shape **Note:** Size varies 33-33.5 mm.

Date	Mintage	VG	F	VF	XF	Unc
1718	78,956	60.00	125	250	400	—

KM# 323 4 CAROLINER (2 Daler Silvermynt)

26.6300 g., 0.6940 Silver 0.5942 oz. ASW **Ruler:** Carl XII **Obv:** Double C Monogram **Rev:** Crowned arms in cross shape **Note:** Size varies 38.5-39 millimeters.

Date	Mintage	VG	F	VF	XF	Unc
1718	25,395	100	225	450	750	—

KM# 543 1/2 SKILLING

Copper **Ruler:** Gustaf IV Adolf **Subject:** King's Visit to Avesta **Obv:** Crowned monogram flanked by 3 crowns **Rev:** Crossed arrows, value, crown and date

Date	Mintage	VG	F	VF	XF	Unc
1794 Vertical edge milling	—	50.00	100	250	550	—
1794 Oblique edge milling	—	120	240	500	1,100	—
1794 Plain edge	—	50.00	100	250	550	—

KM# 519 1/24 RIKSDALER

2.7713 g., 0.3820 Silver 0.0340 oz. ASW **Ruler:** Gustaf III **Obv:** III within crowned G **Obv. Legend:** FÄDERNESLANDET • **Rev:** 3 Crowns within lined circle flanked by value, date below, crown above

Date	Mintage	VG	F	VF	XF	Unc
1777 OL	1,217,000	10.00	20.00	45.00	100	—

KM# 522 1/24 RIKSDALER

2.7713 g., 0.3820 Silver 0.0340 oz. ASW **Ruler:** Gustaf III **Obv:** III within crowned G **Obv. Legend:** FÄDERNESLANDET • **Rev:** 3 Crowns within lined circle flanked by value, date below, crown above

Date	Mintage	VG	F	VF	XF	Unc
1778 OL	1,354,000	6.00	12.00	28.00	70.00	—
1779 OL	1,456,000	6.00	12.00	28.00	70.00	—
1780/79 OL	549,000	12.50	25.00	55.00	125	—
1780 OL	Inc. above	7.00	13.50	32.50	80.00	—
1783/80 OL	268,000	9.00	18.00	40.00	100	—
1783 OL	Inc. above	7.50	15.00	35.00	85.00	—

KM# 520 1/12 RIKSDALER

4.2123 g., 0.5030 Silver 0.0681 oz. ASW **Ruler:** Gustaf III **Obv:** III within crowned G **Obv. Legend:** FÄDERNESLANDET • **Rev:** 3 Crowns within lined circle flanked by value, date below, crown above

Date	Mintage	VG	F	VF	XF	Unc
1777 OL	896,000	15.00	30.00	60.00	140	—

KM# 523 1/12 RIKSDALER

4.2123 g., 0.5030 Silver 0.0681 oz. ASW **Ruler:** Gustaf III **Obv:** III within crowned G **Obv. Legend:** FÄDERNESLANDET • **Rev:** 3 Crowns within lined circle flanked by value, date below, crown above

Date	Mintage	VG	F	VF	XF	Unc
1778 OL	718,000	9.00	18.00	40.00	90.00	—
1779 OL	889,000	9.00	18.00	40.00	90.00	—

KM# 486 1/8 RIKSDALER

3.6565 g., 0.8780 Silver 0.1032 oz. ASW **Ruler:** Adolf Frederick **Obv:** Small head right **Rev:** Crowned arms

Date	Mintage	VG	F	VF	XF	Unc
1767 AL	—	25.00	55.00	100	225	—

KM# 487 1/8 RIKSDALER

3.6565 g., 0.8780 Silver 0.1032 oz. ASW **Ruler:** Adolf Frederick **Obv:** Large head right **Obv. Legend:** ADOLPHUS • FRID • D • G • ... **Rev:** 3 Crowns within center circle of crowned order chain **Rev. Legend:** SALUS • PUBLICA • SALUS • ...

Date	Mintage	VG	F	VF	XF	Unc
1767 AL	23,000	18.00	35.00	70.00	165	—
1768 AL	17,000	15.00	30.00	60.00	145	—

KM# 515 1/6 RIKSDALER

6.1946 g., 0.6910 Silver 0.1376 oz. ASW **Ruler:** Gustaf III **Obv:** Head right **Obv. Legend:** GUSTAVUS • III • D • G • REX • ... **Rev:** 3 Crowns within lined center circle of crowned order chain, value flanking with date below **Rev. Legend:** FÄDERNESLANDET •

Date	Mintage	VG	F	VF	XF	Unc
1776 OL	68,000	15.00	28.00	50.00	110	—
1777 OL	834,000	12.00	20.00	50.00	80.00	—

KM# 524 1/6 RIKSDALER

6.1946 g., 0.6910 Silver 0.1376 oz. ASW **Ruler:** Gustaf III **Obv:** Head right **Obv. Legend:** GUSTAVUS • III • D • G • REX • ... **Rev:** 3 Crowns within lined center circle of crowned order chain, value flanking, divided date below **Rev. Legend:** FÄDERNESLANDET •

Date	Mintage	VG	F	VF	XF	Unc
1778 OL	978,000	10.00	21.00	40.00	90.00	—
1779 OL	1,027,000	10.00	21.00	40.00	90.00	—
1781/79 OL	179,000	15.00	30.00	75.00	120	—
1781 OL	Inc. above	13.50	27.50	75.00	110	—
1783 OL REX	414,000	10.00	21.00	32.50	65.00	—
1783 OL RXE	Inc. above	—	—	—	—	—
1784 OL	388,000	10.00	21.00	32.50	65.00	—
1785 OL	252,000	10.00	21.00	35.00	90.00	—
1786 OL	791,000	10.00	21.00	30.00	90.00	—
1787 OL	26,000	25.00	50.00	100	200	—
1788 OL	742,000	10.00	21.00	30.00	60.00	—
1789 OL	209,000	10.00	21.00	32.50	65.00	—
1790 OL	399,000	10.00	21.00	30.00	60.00	—

KM# 391 1/4 RIKSDALER

7.3131 g., 0.8750 Silver 0.2057 oz. ASW **Ruler:** Frederick I **Obv:** Bust right **Obv. Legend:** FRIDERICUS • D • G • REX • ... **Rev:** Crowned, ornate shield divides date

Date	Mintage	VG	F	VF	XF	Unc
1723	6,290	50.00	110	220	450	—
1724	3,181	85.00	175	350	500	—
1726	3,508	85.00	175	350	500	—
1736	6,497	50.00	110	220	450	—

KM# 442 1/4 RIKSDALER

7.3131 g., 0.8750 Silver 0.2057 oz. ASW **Ruler:** Frederick I **Obv:** Bust right **Obv. Legend:** FRIDERICUS • D • G • REX • ... **Rev:** 3 Crowns within lined center circle of crowned order chain divides date, value below **Note:** Varieties exist.

Date	Mintage	VG	F	VF	XF	Unc
1748 HM	1,284	70.00	135	265	575	—

KM# 455 1/4 RIKSDALER

7.3131 g., 0.8750 Silver 0.2057 oz. ASW **Ruler:** Frederick I **Obv:** Bust right **Obv. Legend:** FRIDERICUS • D • G • REX • ... **Rev:** Shield below crown within Order of the Seraphim, divided date

Date	Mintage	VG	F	VF	XF	Unc
1750 HM	465	85.00	175	350	550	—

KM# 469.1 1/4 RIKSDALER

7.3131 g., 0.8750 Silver 0.2057 oz. ASW **Ruler:** Adolf Frederick **Obv:** Head right **Obv. Legend:** ADOLPHUS • FRID • D • G • REX • ... **Rev:** 3 Crowns within lined center circle of crowned order chain, date in legend **Rev. Legend:** SALUS • PUBLICA • SALUS • MEA •

Date	Mintage	VG	F	VF	XF	Unc
1752 HM	14,000	100	200	350	500	—
1753 HM	18,000	85.00	175	300	450	—
1755 HM	78,000	90.00	175	300	400	—
1760 HM	6,504	125	225	350	550	—
1765 AL	28,000	100	200	350	525	—

KM# 469.2 1/4 RIKSDALER

7.3131 g., 0.8750 Silver 0.2057 oz. ASW **Ruler:** Adolf Frederick **Rev:** Order chain with 9 heads

Date	Mintage	VG	F	VF	XF	Unc
1765 AL	—	100	200	350	675	—

KM# 488 1/4 RIKSDALER

7.3131 g., 0.8780 Silver 0.2064 oz. ASW **Ruler:** Adolf Frederick **Rev:** Value added at bottom; date moved to lower right

Date	Mintage	VG	F	VF	XF	Unc
1767 AL	4,749	100	200	350	550	—
1768 AL	5,128	125	225	350	585	—

KM# 547 1/3 RIKSDALER

0.8780 Silver **Ruler:** Gustaf IV Adolf **Obv:** Head right **Obv. Legend:** GUSTAF IV ADOLPH SV • G • ... **Rev:** Crowned, round arms within order chain, flanked by value, divided date below **Rev. Legend:** GUD OCH FOLKET •

Date	Mintage	VG	F	VF	XF	Unc
1798 OL	70,000	135	285	575	1,150	—

KM# 516 1/3 RIKSDALER (1 Daler S.M.)

9.7508 g., 0.8780 Silver 0.2752 oz. ASW **Ruler:** Gustaf III **Obv:** Head right **Obv. Legend:** GUSTAVUS • III • D • G • REX • ... **Rev:** 3 Crowns within lined center circle of crowned order chain, value flanking, divided date below **Rev. Legend:** FÄDERNESLANDET •

Date	Mintage	VG	F	VF	XF	Unc
1776 OL	97,000	16.50	32.50	65.00	135	—
1777 OL	665,000	11.50	22.50	50.00	100	—

KM# 525 1/3 RIKSDALER (1 Daler S.M.)

9.7508 g., 0.8780 Silver 0.2752 oz. ASW **Ruler:** Gustaf III **Obv:** Head right **Obv. Legend:** GUSTAVUS • III • D • G • REX • ... **Rev:** 3 Crowns within lined center circle of crowned order chain, value flanking, divided date below **Rev. Legend:** FÄDERNESLANDET •

Date	Mintage	VG	F	VF	XF	Unc
1778 OL	610,000	21.00	40.00	85.00	175	—
1779 OL	228,000	15.00	35.00	60.00	125	—
1780/79 OL	282,000	20.00	60.00	100	225	—
1780 OL	Inc. above	14.00	30.00	60.00	100	—
1781 OL	17,000	40.00	80.00	150	300	—
1782 OL	116,000	15.00	30.00	60.00	125	—
1783/2 OL	707,000	16.00	30.00	65.00	125	—
1783 OL	Inc. above	14.00	30.00	60.00	100	—
1784 OL	514,000	14.00	30.00	60.00	100	—
1785 OL	197,000	14.00	30.00	60.00	100	—
1786 OL	51,000	26.00	50.00	75.00	145	—
1787/85	—	26.00	50.00	90.00	180	—
1787 OL	461,000	14.00	30.00	65.00	125	—
1788 OL	71,000	18.00	35.00	75.00	150	—
1789 OL	641,000	14.00	30.00	60.00	100	—

KM# 392 1/2 RIKSDALER

Silver **Ruler:** Frederick I **Obv:** Bust right **Obv. Legend:** FRIDERICUS • D • G • REX • ... **Rev:** Crowned, ornate shield divides date

Date	Mintage	VG	F	VF	XF	Unc
1723 GZ	3,383	125	300	550	825	—
1724	1,482	175	350	600	900	—
1725 Rare	—	—	—	—	—	—
1726/5	1,808	125	300	550	825	—
1726	Inc. above	125	300	500	750	—
1733 GZ	2,016	350	550	1,000	1,600	—
1734 GZ	2,644	150	300	500	750	—
1736 GZ	3,092	200	400	700	1,100	—

KM# 393 1/2 RIKSDALER

Silver **Ruler:** Frederick I **Note:** Struck with 1/4 Riksdaler size dies to double weight.

Date	Mintage	VG	F	VF	XF	Unc
1723 GZ Rare	Inc. above	—	—	—	—	—

KM# 456 1/2 RIKSDALER

Silver **Ruler:** Frederick I **Obv:** Bust right **Obv. Legend:** FRIDERICVS • D • G • REX • ... **Rev:** Shield within crowned order chain divides date

Date	Mintage	VG	F	VF	XF	Unc
1750 HM	7,593	200	400	650	1,000	—

KM# 470 1/2 RIKSDALER

Silver **Ruler:** Adolf Frederick **Obv:** Head right **Rev:** Crowned arms in Order chain, date at upper left

Date	Mintage	VG	F	VF	XF	Unc
1752 HM	4,615	125	300	550	850	—
1753 HM	18,000	100	250	450	720	—
1755 HM	39,000	100	250	400	650	—
1766 AL	7,066	125	300	550	875	—

KM# 489 1/2 RIKSDALER

Silver **Ruler:** Adolf Frederick **Rev:** Value added, date moved to lower right

Date	Mintage	VG	F	VF	XF	Unc
1767 AL	2,649	150	300	700	1,300	—
1768 AL	6,476	100	200	600	1,300	—

KM# 517 2/3 RIKSDALER (2 Daler S.M.)

19.5015 g., 0.8780 Silver 0.5505 oz. ASW **Ruler:** Gustaf III **Obv:** Head right **Obv. Legend:** GUSTAVUS • III • D • G • REX • ... **Rev:** 3 Crowns within lined center circle of crowned order chain, value flanking, divided date below **Rev. Legend:** FÄDERNESLANDET •

Date	Mintage	VG	F	VF	XF	Unc
1776 OL	152,000	35.00	75.00	150	235	—
1777 OL	88,000	35.00	75.00	150	255	—

KM# 526 2/3 RIKSDALER (2 Daler S.M.)

19.5015 g., 0.8780 Silver 0.5505 oz. ASW **Ruler:** Gustaf III **Obv:** Head right **Obv. Legend:** GUSTAVUS • III • D • G • REX • ... **Rev:** 3 Crowns within lined center circle of crowned order chain, value flanking, divided date below **Rev. Legend:** FÄDERNESLANDET •

Date	Mintage	VG	F	VF	XF	Unc
1778 OL	43,000	35.00	75.00	150	255	—
1779 OL	152,000	30.00	65.00	125	225	—
1780/79 OL	11,000	60.00	125	250	385	—
1780 OL	Inc. above	90.00	175	350	550	—

KM# 464.1 RIKSDALER

Silver **Ruler:** Adolf Frederick **Obv:** Bust right **Rev:** 3 Crowns within lined center circle of crowned order chain **Note:** Dav. #1731.

Date	Mintage	VG	F	VF	XF	Unc
1754 HM F on neck	96,000	70.00	140	325	665	—
1754 HM F below neck	Inc. above	75.00	150	350	700	—
1755/4 HM	Inc. above	80.00	160	375	750	—
1751 HM	26,000	125	250	550	1,000	—
1752 HM	23,000	70.00	140	325	665	—
1753 HM	38,000	75.00	150	350	700	—

KM# 335 RIKSDALER

Silver **Ruler:** Carl XII **Obv:** Bust left **Obv. Legend:** CAROLVS • XII • D • G • REX • ... **Rev:** Crowned arms with supporters, date below **Note:** Dav. #1713.

Date	Mintage	VG	F	VF	XF	Unc
1707 LC	2,344	285	585	1,150	2,450	—

KM# 336 RIKSDALER

Silver **Ruler:** Carl XII **Obv:** Armored bust right **Obv. Legend:** CAROLVS • XII • D • G • REX • ... **Rev:** Crowned arms with supporters, date below **Note:** Dav. #1714.

Date	Mintage	VG	F	VF	XF	Unc
1707 LC	Inc. above	275	550	1,100	2,250	—

KM# 351 RIKSDALER

Silver **Ruler:** Carl XII **Obv:** Draped bust right **Obv. Legend:** CAROLVS • XII • D • G • REX • ... **Rev:** Crowned arms with supporters, date below **Note:** Dav. #1715.

Date	Mintage	VG	F	VF	XF	Unc
1713 LC Wide lion	10,000	165	300	650	1,250	—
1713 LC Thin lion	Inc. above	150	275	550	1,200	—
1713 LC Lozenged edge; Unique	—	—	—	—	—	—

KM# 362 RIKSDALER

Silver **Ruler:** Carl XII **Obv:** Draped bust right **Obv. Legend:** CAROLVS • XII • D • G • REX • ... **Rev:** Crowned arms with supporters, date below **Note:** Dav. #1716.

Date	Mintage	VG	F	VF	XF	Unc
1718 LC Star in shield	10,000	175	350	725	1,400	—
1718 LC Rosette in shield	Inc. above	2,250	4,000	7,500	12,500	—

KM# 370 RIKSDALER

Silver **Ruler:** Ulrika Eleonora **Obv:** Bust right **Obv. Legend:** VLRICA ELEONORA D G REGINA SVEC **Rev:** Crowned arms with supporters, date below **Note:** Dav. #1718.

Date	Mintage	VG	F	VF	XF	Unc
1719 LC	10,000	250	475	950	2,150	—

KM# 389.2 RIKSDALER

Silver **Ruler:** Frederick I **Obv:** Bust right **Obv. Legend:** FRIDERICVS • D • G • REX • ... **Rev:** Facing busts within cameos, all within wreath

Date	Mintage	VG	F	VF	XF	Unc
1721	4,000	125	225	425	850	—

KM# 389.1 RIKSDALER

Silver **Ruler:** Frederick I **Subject:** 200th Anniversary of Liberation War **Obv:** Bust right **Obv. Legend:** FRIDERICVS • D • G • REX • ... **Rev:** Facing busts within cameo, Gustaf Vasa and Gustaf Adolf II, all within wreath **Note:** Dav. #1719.

Date	Mintage	VG	F	VF	XF	Unc
1721 C. Hedlinger	—	225	450	700	1,250	—

KM# 395.1 RIKSDALER

Silver **Ruler:** Frederick I **Obv:** Bust right **Obv. Legend:** FRIDERICUS • D • G • REX • ... **Rev:** Crowned arms with supporters, date in cartouche below **Note:** Dav. #1720.

Date	Mintage	VG	F	VF	XF	Unc
1723	Inc. above	60.00	135	285	625	—
1724	3,000	150	275	525	1,100	—
1725	9,000	60.00	135	285	625	—
1726	7,000	70.00	145	300	665	—
1727	10,000	125	250	500	1,000	—
1728	9,000	80.00	170	350	775	—

KM# 394 RIKSDALER
Silver **Ruler:** Frederick I **Rev:** Arms below crown, date **Note:** Struck with 1/2 Riksdaler size dies to double weight.

Date	Mintage	VG	F	VF	XF	Unc
1723 Rare	32	—	—	—	—	—

KM# 402 RIKSDALER
Silver **Ruler:** Frederick I **Obv:** Conjoined busts right **Obv. Legend:** FRIDERIC • ET • ULR • ELEON • D • G • REX • ... **Rev:** Crowned arms with supporters, date in cartouche below **Note:** Dav. #1722.

Date	Mintage	VG	F	VF	XF	Unc
1727	Inc. above	145	275	525	1,000	—

KM# 395.2 RIKSDALER
Silver **Ruler:** Frederick I **Note:** Dav. #1723. Varieties exist.

Date	Mintage	VG	F	VF	XF	Unc
1730 GZ	4,000	120	245	475	1,000	—
1731 GZ	8,841	60.00	135	275	600	—
1731 GZ FREDERICVS	Inc. above	75.00	165	345	750	—
1732 GZ	7,000	85.00	175	365	800	—
1732 GZ FREDERICVS	7,500	85.00	175	365	800	—
1733/2 GZ FREDERICVS	10,000	75.00	165	345	750	—

KM# 418 RIKSDALER
Silver **Ruler:** Frederick I **Obv:** Conjoined busts right **Obv. Legend:** FRIDERICVS • ET • VLR • ELEON • D • G • REX • ... **Rev:** Crowned arms with supporters, date in cartouche below **Note:** Dav. #1724.

Date	Mintage	VG	F	VF	XF	Unc
1731 GZ	9,000	175	325	625	1,250	—

KM# A395 RIKSDALER
29.2500 g., 0.8780 Silver 0.8256 oz. ASW, 41 mm. **Ruler:** Frederick I **Subject:** Tenth Anniversary of Reign **Obv:** Conjoined busts right **Obv. Legend:** FRIDERICVS • ET • VLR • ELEON • D • G • REX • ... **Rev:** Three crowns on globe **Rev. Legend:** SPLENDET • IN • ORBE • DEO

Date	Mintage	VG	F	VF	XF	Unc
ND(1731)	—	—	300	500	1,500	—
ND(1731) Restrike	—	—	200	—	—	—

KM# B395 RIKSDALER
29.2500 g., 0.8780 Silver 0.8256 oz. ASW **Ruler:** Frederick I **Subject:** Fredrick's Visit To Hesse-Cassel **Obv:** Bust right **Obv. Legend:** FRIDERICUS • D • G • REX • ... **Rev:** Eleven line inscription

Date	Mintage	VG	F	VF	XF	Unc
MDCCXXXI (1731)	—	—	175	400	750	—
MDCCXXXI (1731) Restrike	—	—	185	—	—	—

KM# 395.3 RIKSDALER
Silver **Ruler:** Frederick I **Obv:** Bust right **Obv. Legend:** FRIDERICVS • D • G • REX • ... **Rev:** Crowned arms with supporters, date in cartouche below **Note:** Dav. #1727.

Date	Mintage	VG	F	VF	XF	Unc
1734 GZ	1,600	420	745	1,475	3,500	—
1735 GZ	4,000	210	475	800	1,750	—
1736 GZ	12,000	145	245	500	950	—
1737 GZ	8,000	145	245	500	950	—
1738 GZ	12,000	265	525	875	2,150	—

KM# 423 RIKSDALER
Silver **Ruler:** Frederick I **Obv:** Bust right **Obv. Legend:** FRIDERICUS • D • G • REX • SVECIAE • **Rev:** Crowned arms with supporters, date in cartouche below **Note:** Dav. #1728.

Date	Mintage	VG	F	VF	XF	Unc
1738 HM	Inc. above	225	350	750	1,575	—
1739 HM	13,000	165	285	585	1,225	—
1740 HM	11,000	65.00	145	300	600	—
1741 HM	9,000	65.00	145	300	600	—
1742 HM	486	1,250	2,000	4,000	8,000	—
1743 HM	4,000	75.00	175	325	700	—
1744 HM	9,000	65.00	145	300	600	—
1746 HM	3,000	75.00	175	325	700	—
1747 HM	4,000	75.00	175	325	700	—
1748 HM	7,000	70.00	150	315	625	—

KM# 443 RIKSDALER
Silver **Ruler:** Frederick I **Obv:** Bust right **Obv. Legend:** FRIDERICUS • D • G • REX • SVECIAE • **Rev:** Chain of the Order of Seraphim around 3 crowns in lined circle, divided date **Note:** Dav. #1729.

Date	Mintage	VG	F	VF	XF	Unc
1748 HM	—	500	800	1,650	3,750	—

KM# 457 RIKSDALER
Silver **Ruler:** Frederick I **Obv:** Bust right **Obv. Legend:** FRIDERICUS • D • G • REX • SVECIAE • **Rev:** Shield within crowned order chain divides date **Note:** Dav. #1730.

Date	Mintage	VG	F	VF	XF	Unc
1750 HM	9,000	100	200	435	825	—
1751 HM	22,000	100	200	435	825	—

KM# 464.2 RIKSDALER
Silver **Ruler:** Adolf Frederick **Obv:** Bust right with modified hairstyle **Note:** Dav. #1731.

Date	Mintage	VG	F	VF	XF	Unc
1755 HM	58,000	125	200	400	665	—
1756 HM	23,000	150	200	500	850	—
1757 HM	2,172	650	1,150	2,250	4,750	—
1759 HM	3,781	125	250	575	1,150	—
1760 HM	29,000	150	200	500	850	—
1761 HM	16,000	900	1,650	3,500	6,500	—
1762 HM	18,000	150	200	500	850	—
1763 AL	62,000	60.00	125	250	600	—
1764 AL	37,000	70.00	140	325	665	—
1765 AL	16,000	75.00	150	350	700	—
1766 AL	59,000	70.00	140	325	665	—

KM# 490.1 RIKSDALER
Silver **Ruler:** Adolf Frederick **Obv:** Bust right **Rev:** 3 Crowns

within lined center circle of crowned order chain, value below **Note:** Dav. #1732.

Date	Mintage	VG	F	VF	XF	Unc
1767 AL	59,000	60.00	125	250	600	—

KM# 490.2 RIKSDALER

Silver **Ruler:** Adolf Frederick **Obv:** Bust right **Rev:** Crowns within lined circle within crowned order chain

Date	Mintage	VG	F	VF	XF	Unc
1768 AL	47,000	70.00	140	325	665	—
1769 AL 9 heads in chain	123,000	60.00	125	250	600	—
1769 AL 7 heads in chain	Inc. above	75.00	150	350	700	—

KM# 505 RIKSDALER

Silver **Ruler:** Adolf Frederick **Obv:** Head right **Obv. Legend:** ADOLPHUS • FRID • D • G • REX • SVECIAE • **Rev:** Crowns within lined circle within crowned order chain, value, divided date below **Note:** Dav. #1733.

Date	Mintage	VG	F	VF	XF	Unc
1770 AL	143,000	60.00	125	275	550	—
1771 AL	47,000	100	200	400	750	—

KM# 509 RIKSDALER

Silver **Ruler:** Gustaf III **Obv:** Bust of Gustaf III right **Rev:** Crowns within lined circle of crowned order chain, value, divided date below **Note:** Dav. #1734.

Date	Mintage	VG	F	VF	XF	Unc
1771 AL	—	95.00	195	385	820	—
1772 AL	51,000	90.00	180	325	720	—
1773 AL	38,000	75.00	150	300	650	—
1774 OL	709,000	60.00	125	275	585	—
1775 OL	—	60.00	125	275	585	—

KM# 514 RIKSDALER

29.2500 g., 0.8780 Silver 0.8256 oz. ASW **Ruler:** Gustaf III **Obv:** Head right **Obv. Legend:** GUSTAVUS • III • D • G • REX • SVECIAE • **Rev:** Crowns within lined circle within crowned order chain, value flanking, divided date below **Note:** Dav. #1735.

Date	Mintage	VG	F	VF	XF	Unc
1775 OL	35,000	35.00	75.00	150	220	—
1776/5 OL	1,461,000	40.00	80.00	150	350	—
1776 Large cross	Inc. above	30.00	65.00	125	185	—
1776 Small cross	Inc. above	35.00	75.00	150	220	—
1776 OL Pearl cross	Inc. above	60.00	120	225	600	—
1777 OL	289,000	35.00	75.00	150	220	—

KM# 527 RIKSDALER

29.2500 g., 0.8780 Silver 0.8256 oz. ASW **Ruler:** Gustaf III **Obv:** Head right **Rev:** Crowns within lined circle within crowned order chain, value flanking, divided date below **Note:** Dav. #1736.

Date	Mintage	VG	F	VF	XF	Unc
1779 OL	34,000	45.00	90.00	175	275	—
1780/79 OL	1,713,000	40.00	80.00	150	245	—
1780 OL	Inc. above	35.00	50.00	100	220	—
Note: Alternating squares and diamonds on edge						
1780 OL	Inc. above	35.00	50.00	100	220	—
Note: Ovals on edge						
1780 OL	Inc. above	45.00	90.00	175	350	—
Note: Alternating squares and ovals on edge						
1781/79 OL	524,058	25.00	50.00	100	220	—
1781 OL	Inc. above	24.00	50.00	100	220	—
1781 OL Bust of 1772	Inc. above	55.00	110	225	625	—
1782 OL	654,000	40.00	80.00	150	220	—
1783 OL	100,000	35.00	75.00	150	220	—
1787/83 OL	62,000	40.00	95.00	150	245	—
1788 OL	151,000	25.00	75.00	150	220	—
1790/88 OL	636,000	40.00	80.00	150	245	—
1790 OL	Inc. above	35.00	75.00	150	220	—
1791 OL	921,000	35.00	75.00	150	220	—
1792 OL	431,063	40.00	80.00	150	245	—

KM# 540.1 RIKSDALER

29.3600 g., 0.8780 Silver 0.8287 oz. ASW **Ruler:** Gustaf IV Adolf **Obv:** Head right **Obv. Legend:** GUSTAF IV ADOLPH SV • G • ... **Rev:** Crowned, round arms within order chain, flanked by value, divided date below **Rev. Legend:** GUD OCH FOLKET • **Note:** Dav. #1737.

Date	Mintage	VG	F	VF	XF	Unc
1792 OL	76,000	80.00	140	300	600	—

KM# 540.2 RIKSDALER

29.3600 g., 0.8780 Silver 0.8287 oz. ASW **Ruler:** Gustaf IV Adolf **Obv:** Head right **Obv. Legend:** GUSTAF IV ADOLPH SV • G • ... **Rev:** Crowned, round arms within order chain, flanked by value, divided date below **Rev. Legend:** GUD OCH FOLKET •

Date	Mintage	VG	F	VF	XF	Unc
1793 OL	262,000	55.00	100	200	425	—

KM# 540.3 RIKSDALER

29.3600 g., 0.8780 Silver 0.8287 oz. ASW **Ruler:** Gustaf IV Adolf **Obv:** Head right, modified effigy **Obv. Legend:** GUSTAF IV ADOLPH SV • G • ... **Rev:** Crowned, round arms within order chain, flanked by value, divided date below **Rev. Legend:** GUD OCH FOLKET •

Date	Mintage	VG	F	VF	XF	Unc
1794 OL Folket	278,000	55.00	100	200	425	—
1794 OL Folkft	Inc. above	100	200	350	700	—

KM# 540.4 RIKSDALER

29.3600 g., 0.8780 Silver 0.8287 oz. ASW **Ruler:** Gustaf IV Adolf **Obv:** Head right, modified effigy **Obv. Legend:** GUSTAF IV ADOLPH SV • G • ... **Rev:** Crowned, round arms within order chain, flanked by value, divided date below **Rev. Legend:** GUD OCH FOLKET •

Date	Mintage	VG	F	VF	XF	Unc
1795 OL	266,000	55.00	100	200	425	—

KM# 544 RIKSDALER

29.3600 g., 0.8780 Silver 0.8287 oz. ASW **Ruler:** Gustaf IV Adolf **Obv:** Head right **Obv. Legend:** GUSTAF IV ADOLPH SV • G • ... **Rev:** Crowned, round arms within order chain, flanked by value, divided date below **Rev. Legend:** GUD OCH FOLKET • **Note:** Dav. #1738.

Date	Mintage	VG	F	VF	XF	Unc
1796 OL	225,000	50.00	85.00	200	385	—
1797 OL	155,000	50.00	80.00	190	425	—

KM# 399 1-1/2 RIKSDALER

Silver **Ruler:** Frederick I **Obv:** Conjoined busts right **Obv. Legend:** FRIDERIC • ET • ULR • ELEON • D • G • REX • ... **Rev:** Crowned arms with supporters, date in cartouche below

Date	Mintage	VG	F	VF	XF	Unc
1727 Rare	—	—	—	—	—	—

KM# 396 2 RIKSDALER

Silver **Ruler:** Frederick I **Obv:** Bust right **Rev:** Crowned arms with supporters, date in cartouche below **Edge Lettering:** NE LAEDAR AVARIS MANIBVS **Note:** Dav. #1720A.

Date	Mintage	VG	F	VF	XF	Unc
1723	—	—	6,500	11,500	20,000	—

KM# 400 2 RIKSDALER

Silver **Ruler:** Frederick I **Obv:** Conjoined busts right **Obv. Legend:** FRIDERIC • ET • ULR • ELEON • D • G • REX • ... **Rev:** Crowned arms with supporters, date in cartouche below **Note:** Dav. #1721.

Date	Mintage	VG	F	VF	XF	Unc
1727	63	—	2,500	5,500	9,500	—

KM# 501 DALER (S.M. - 1/3 Riksdaler)

9.7508 g., 0.8780 Silver 0.2752 oz. ASW, 31 mm. **Ruler:** Adolf Frederick **Obv:** Head right **Obv. Legend:** ADOLPHUS • FRID • D • G • ... **Rev:** 3 Crowns within center circle of crowned order chain **Rev. Legend:** ...PUBLICA • SALUS • MEA •

Date	Mintage	VG	F	VF	XF	Unc
1770 AL	20,833	65.00	125	265	450	—

KM# 502 DALER (S.M. - 1/3 Riksdaler)

9.7508 g., 0.8780 Silver 0.2752 oz. ASW, 29 mm. **Ruler:** Adolf Frederick

Date	Mintage	VG	F	VF	XF	Unc
1770 AL	—	45.00	90.00	200	400	—

KM# 503 2 DALER (S.M. - 2/3 Riksdaler)

19.5015 g., 0.8780 Silver 0.5505 oz. ASW, 37 mm. **Ruler:** Adolf Frederick

Date	Mintage	VG	F	VF	XF	Unc
1770 AL	16,000	65.00	135	285	485	—

KM# 504 2 DALER (S.M. - 2/3 Riksdaler)

19.5015 g., 0.8780 Silver 0.5505 oz. ASW, 35 mm. **Ruler:** Adolf Frederick **Obv:** Head right **Obv. Legend:** ADOLPHUS • FRID • D • G • REX • ... **Rev:** 3 Crowns within center circle of crowned order chain, divided date and value below **Rev. Legend:** SALUS • PUBLICA • SALUS • MEA •

Date	Mintage	VG	F	VF	XF	Unc
1770 AL	—	60.00	100	250	450	—

PLATE MONEY

The Kingdom of Sweden issued copper plate money, heavy and cumbersome square or rectangular coins ranging in size up to about 13 by 25 inches down to less than 3 by 3 inches, from 1644 to 1776. The kingdom was poor in silver and gold but had rich copper resources. The coins were designed to contain copper bullion in the value of the silver coins they replaced, and were denominated as one, two, four, etc. dalers in silver mint or silver coin.

Although sometimes classed with odd and curious money these were legal tender coins of the realm and although used and exported as bullion, they circulated domestically and were essential in the commerce of Sweden and Finland for more than a century.

They are widely collected, not only in Scandinavia but around the world.

Each denomination is catalogued under the name of the issuing monarch and by the mint mark and or source of the copper. The latter are important in the rarity and thus prices of the coins. The pieces are identified by the center stamp, with the denomination, mint mark, etc., and four identical corner stamps, with the insignia of the king and date.

Many are extremely rare, with only a single specimen or two known, often only a unique survivor in a major museum.

KM# PM31 1/2 DALER S.M.

Copper **Ruler:** Carl XII **Obv:** Star below value (center stamp) **Note:** Copper from Garpenberg mines.

Date	Mintage	VG	F	VF	XF	Unc
1710 Rare	—	—	—	—	—	—
1711 Rare	—	—	—	—	—	—
1713 Rare	—	—	—	—	—	—
1714 Rare	—	—	—	—	—	—

KM# PM30 1/2 DALER S.M.

Copper **Ruler:** Carl XII **Obv:** Corner stamps: Crowned CRS, date, Center stamp: 1/2 daler solff, myt, crossed arrows **Note:** Copper from Stora Kopparberg and Ljusnarsberg.

Date	Mintage	VG	F	VF	XF	Unc
1710	—	250	400	600	1,000	—
1711	—	250	400	600	1,100	—
1712	—	250	400	650	1,100	—
1713	—	250	450	700	1,200	—
1714 Rare	—	—	—	—	—	—
1715	—	—	—	—	—	—

KM# PM32 1/2 DALER S.M.

Copper **Ruler:** Carl XII **Obv:** Corner stamps: Crowned double C superimposed on date, Center stamp: Square reeded outline, 1/2 daler sm

Date	Mintage	VG	F	VF	XF	Unc
1715	—	250	450	650	1,200	—
1716	—	250	400	600	1,000	—
1717	—	250	450	650	1,200	—

KM# PM33 1/2 DALER S.M.

Copper **Ruler:** Carl XII **Obv:** Corner stamps: Three crowns above date, Center stamp: Triangular reeded outline, 1/2 D S around lion in shield **Note:** Illustration reduced.

Date	Mintage	VG	F	VF	XF	Unc
1718	—	350	550	1,100	1,750	—

KM# PM55 1/2 DALER S.M.

Copper **Ruler:** Ulrika Eleonora **Obv:** Corner stamps: 3 crowns within circle above date, Center stamp: Triangular, Gota lion shield, 1/2 D S

Date	Mintage	VG	F	VF	XF	Unc
1719	—	300	500	900	1,500	—

KM# PM56 1/2 DALER S.M.

Copper **Ruler:** Ulrika Eleonora **Obv:** Corner stamps: Crowned V over double E monogram, date, Center stamp: 1/2 dolar silf, mint, crossed arrows within circle

Date	Mintage	VG	F	VF	XF	Unc
1719	—	350	550	800	1,400	—
1720	—	350	550	800	1,400	—

KM# PM65 1/2 DALER S.M.

Copper **Ruler:** Frederick I **Obv:** Corner stamps: Crowned FRS, date. Center stamp: 1/2 Daler Silf: Mynt, crossed arrows in circle. **Note:** Illustration reduced.

Date	Mintage	VG	F	VF	XF	Unc
1720	—	125	225	375	625	—
1721	—	125	200	325	550	—
1722	—	125	200	325	550	—
1723	—	125	200	325	550	—
1724	—	125	200	325	550	—
1725	—	125	200	325	550	—
1726	—	125	200	325	550	—
1727	—	125	225	375	625	—
1728/27	—	150	300	500	850	—
1728	—	125	200	325	550	—
1729	—	125	200	325	550	—
1730	—	125	225	375	625	—
1731	—	125	200	325	550	—
1732	—	125	200	325	550	—
1733	—	125	200	325	550	—
1734	—	125	225	375	625	—
1735	—	125	200	325	550	—
1736	—	125	200	325	550	—
1737	—	125	225	375	625	—
1738	—	125	225	375	625	—
1739	—	125	200	325	550	—
1740	—	125	225	375	625	—
1741	—	125	200	325	550	—
1742	—	125	200	325	550	—
1743	—	125	200	325	550	—
1744	—	125	200	325	550	—
1745	—	125	200	325	550	—
1746	—	125	200	325	550	—
1747	—	125	200	325	550	—
1748	—	125	200	325	550	—
1749	—	125	200	325	550	—
1750	—	125	200	325	550	—

KM# PM66 1/2 DALER S.M.

Copper **Ruler:** Frederick I **Obv:** Center stamp: Monogram L below value

Date	Mintage	VG	F	VF	XF	Unc
1746	—	250	575	1,000	1,650	—
1748 Rare	—	375	850	1,350	2,250	—

KM# PM67 1/2 DALER S.M.

Copper **Ruler:** Frederick I **Obv:** Center stamp: Crowned G below value

Date	Mintage	VG	F	VF	XF	Unc
1748	—	200	450	850	1,350	—

KM# PM80 1/2 DALER S.M.
Copper **Ruler:** Adolf Frederick **Obv:** Corner stamp: Crowned AFRS **Note:** Illustration reduced.

Date	Mintage	VG	F	VF	XF	Unc
1751	—	160	260	420	725	—
1752	—	150	240	365	600	—
1753	—	150	240	365	600	—
1754	—	150	240	365	600	—
1755 Rare	—	—	—	—	—	—
1756	—	150	240	365	600	—
1757	—	150	240	365	600	—
1758	—	150	240	365	600	—
1759	—	150	250	400	650	—
1768 Rare	—	—	—	—	—	—

KM# PM83 1/2 DALER S.M.
Copper **Ruler:** Adolf Frederick **Obv:** Crowned C below value **Note:** Carlsberg Mine.

Date	Mintage	VG	F	VF	XF	Unc
1752 Rare	—	—	—	—	—	—

KM# PM82 1/2 DALER S.M.
Copper **Ruler:** Adolf Frederick **Obv:** Center stamp: Crowned G below value **Note:** Copper from Gustavsberg Mine.

Date	Mintage	VG	F	VF	XF	Unc
1752 Rare	—	—	—	—	—	—

KM# PM81 1/2 DALER S.M.
Copper **Ruler:** Adolf Frederick **Obv:** Center stamp: Monogram L below value

Date	Mintage	VG	F	VF	XF	Unc
1753 Rare	—	—	—	—	—	—

KM# PM34 DALER S.M.
Copper **Ruler:** Carl XII **Obv:** Corner stamps: Crowned above date, legend: CAROLUS XII. Center stamp: Daler Sölff: Myt, AIR.

Date	Mintage	VG	F	VF	XF	Unc
1702 Rare	—	—	—	—	—	—

KM# PM35 DALER S.M.
Copper **Ruler:** Carl XII **Obv:** Center stamp: Crossed arrows below value

Date	Mintage	VG	F	VF	XF	Unc
1710	—	200	350	675	1,450	—
1711	—	200	350	675	1,450	—
1712	—	220	400	800	1,650	—
1713	—	200	375	750	1,550	—
1714	—	220	400	850	1,750	—
1715	—	200	375	750	1,550	—

KM# PM36 DALER S.M.
Copper **Ruler:** Carl XII **Obv:** Center stamp: Large star below value

Date	Mintage	VG	F	VF	XF	Unc
1710 Rare	—	—	—	—	—	—

KM# PM37 DALER S.M.
Copper **Ruler:** Carl XII **Obv:** Center stamp: Crowned B between roses below value

Date	Mintage	VG	F	VF	XF	Unc
1711 Rare	—	—	—	—	—	—

KM# PM38 DALER S.M.
Copper **Ruler:** Carl XII **Obv:** Corner stamps: Crowned mirror C XII monogram, date. Center stamp: Square reeded outline, 1 DALER S:M.

Date	Mintage	VG	F	VF	XF	Unc
1715	—	225	375	550	1,150	—
1716	—	225	375	550	1,150	—
1717	—	250	425	725	1,500	—

KM# PM40 DALER S.M.
Cannon Metal **Ruler:** Carl XII **Obv:** Corner stamps: Crown. Center stamp: 2 D: S: M: interwoven with 3 crowns and date

Date	Mintage	VG	F	VF	XF	Unc
1715	—	400	725	1,650	3,250	—

KM# PM39 DALER S.M.
Copper **Ruler:** Carl XII **Obv:** Corner stamps: 3 crowns above date. Center stamp: Triangular, 1 D S around shield

Date	Mintage	VG	F	VF	XF	Unc
1718	—	425	750	1,750	3,500	—

KM# PM57 DALER S.M.
Cannon Metal **Ruler:** Ulrika Eleonora **Obv:** Corner stamps: 3 crowns above date. Center stamp: Triangular

Date	Mintage	VG	F	VF	XF	Unc
1719	—	375	700	1,450	3,000	—

KM# PM58 DALER S.M.
Cannon Metal **Ruler:** Ulrika Eleonora **Obv:** Corner stamps: Crowned V over double E monogram, date. Center stamp: Daler Silf: Mynt, crossed arrows

Date	Mintage	VG	F	VF	XF	Unc
1719	—	250	400	800	1,600	—
1720	—	300	500	950	1,850	—

KM# PM68 DALER S.M.
Cannon Metal **Ruler:** Frederick I **Obv:** Corner stamps: Crowned FRS, date. Center stamp: 1 Daler Silf-Mynt, crossed arrows

Date	Mintage	VG	F	VF	XF	Unc
1720	—	145	275	525	900	—
1721	—	135	245	500	850	—
1722	—	135	245	500	850	—
1723	—	140	265	520	900	—
1724	—	140	265	520	900	—
1725	—	140	265	520	900	—
1726	—	140	265	520	900	—
1727	—	140	265	520	900	—
1728	—	140	265	520	900	—
1729	—	140	265	520	900	—
1730	—	140	265	520	900	—
1731	—	140	265	520	900	—
1732	—	140	265	520	900	—
1733	—	145	275	525	900	—
1734	—	140	265	520	900	—
1735	—	140	265	520	900	—
1736	—	140	265	520	900	—
1737	—	140	265	520	900	—
1738	—	140	265	520	900	—
1739	—	140	265	520	900	—
1740	—	145	275	525	900	—
1741	—	140	265	520	900	—
1742	—	140	265	520	900	—
1743	—	140	265	520	900	—
1744	—	145	275	525	900	—
1745	—	140	265	520	900	—
1746	—	140	265	520	900	—
1747	—	135	245	500	850	—
1748	—	140	265	520	900	—
1749	—	150	300	550	950	—
1750	—	175	325	600	1,000	—

KM# PM69 DALER S.M.
Cannon Metal **Ruler:** Frederick I **Obv:** Center stamp: L monogram below value

Date	Mintage	VG	F	VF	XF	Unc
1746	—	400	600	1,350	2,500	—
1748 Rare	—	500	750	1,500	2,750	—

KM# PM70 DALER S.M.
Cannon Metal **Ruler:** Frederick I **Obv:** Center stamp: Crowned G below value

Date	Mintage	VG	F	VF	XF	Unc
1748	—	400	550	1,200	2,250	—

KM# PM84 DALER S.M.
Cannon Metal **Ruler:** Adolf Frederick **Obv:** Corner stamps: Crowned AFRS, date. Center stamp: 1 DALER Silf. Mynt, crossed arrows

Date	Mintage	VG	F	VF	XF	Unc
1751	—	185	375	750	1,250	—
1752	—	180	360	725	1,200	—
1753	—	175	350	700	1,100	—
1754	—	175	355	720	1,150	—
1755	—	175	355	720	1,150	—
1756	—	175	350	700	1,100	—
1757	—	175	350	700	1,100	—
1758	—	175	350	700	1,100	—
1759	—	180	360	725	1,200	—
1768 Rare	—	—	—	—	—	—

KM# PM87 DALER S.M.
Cannon Metal **Ruler:** Adolf Frederick **Obv:** Center stamp: Crowned C below value **Note:** Carlsberg Mine.

Date	Mintage	VG	F	VF	XF	Unc
1752 Rare	—	—	—	—	—	—

KM# PM86 DALER S.M.
Cannon Metal **Ruler:** Adolf Frederick **Obv:** Center stamp: Crowned G below value **Note:** Gustavsberg Mine.

Date	Mintage	VG	F	VF	XF	Unc
1752	—	450	650	1,550	2,500	—

KM# PM85 DALER S.M.
Cannon Metal **Ruler:** Adolf Frederick **Obv:** Center stamp: Mirror L monogram

Date	Mintage	VG	F	VF	XF	Unc
1753 Rare	—	—	—	—	—	—

KM# PM41 2 DALER S.M.
Copper **Ruler:** Carl XII **Obv:** Corner stamps: Crown above date, legend CAROLUS... Center stamp: Daler Sölff: Myt, AIR monogram.

Date	Mintage	VG	F	VF	XF	Unc
1700 Rare	—	—	—	—	—	—
1701 Rare	—	—	—	—	—	—

KM# PM42 2 DALER S.M.
Copper **Ruler:** Carl XII **Obv:** Center stamp: 3 stars below value

Date	Mintage	VG	F	VF	XF	Unc
1702 Rare	—	—	—	—	—	—

KM# PM45 2 DALER S.M.
Copper **Ruler:** Carl XII **Obv:** Center stamp: Large star below value **Note:** Copper from Garpenberg.

Date	Mintage	VG	F	VF	XF	Unc
1710	—	650	1,250	2,250	3,250	—
1711	—	750	1,450	2,500	3,500	—
1712	—	650	1,250	2,250	3,250	—
1713 Rare	—	—	—	—	—	—
1714 Rare	—	—	—	—	—	—

KM# PM43 2 DALER S.M.
Copper **Ruler:** Carl XII **Obv:** Center stamp: Crossed arrows below value **Note:** Copper from Stora Kopparberg and Ljusnarsberg.

Date	Mintage	VG	F	VF	XF	Unc
1710	—	275	525	875	1,500	—
1711	—	285	550	900	1,600	—
1712	—	285	550	900	1,600	—
1713	—	275	525	875	1,500	—
1714	—	350	650	1,200	2,000	—
1715	—	325	600	1,100	1,850	—

KM# PM44 2 DALER S.M.
Copper **Ruler:** Carl XII **Obv:** Center stamp: Crowned E between roses below value **Note:** Copper from Basinge.

Date	Mintage	VG	F	VF	XF	Unc
1711 Rare	—	—	—	—	—	—
1712 Rare	—	—	—	—	—	—
1713 Rare	—	—	—	—	—	—

KM# PM-A48 2 DALER S.M.
Cast Cannon Metal **Ruler:** Carl XII **Obv:** Corner stamps: Crown. Center stamp: 2 D: S: M with 2 fleur-de-lis and date

Date	Mintage	VG	F	VF	XF	Unc
1714	—	400	750	1,650	2,850	—
17^14 Crown in date	—	350	650	1,200	2,250	—

KM# PM48 2 DALER S.M.
Cast Cannon Metal **Ruler:** Carl XII **Obv:** Center stamp: 2 D: S: M with 3 crowns and date

Date	Mintage	VG	F	VF	XF	Unc
1715	—	450	900	1,850	3,000	—
1716	—	400	800	1,650	2,850	—

KM# PM46 2 DALER S.M.
Copper **Ruler:** Carl XII **Obv:** Corner stamps: Crowned mirrored C monogram, date. Center stamp: Diamond shaped, 4 Daler S.M.

Date	Mintage	VG	F	VF	XF	Unc
1716	—	225	475	675	1,000	—
1717	—	300	650	950	1,450	—

KM# PM47 2 DALER S.M.
Copper **Ruler:** Carl XII **Obv:** Corner stamps: 3 crowns above date. Center stamp: Triangular, 2 D S surrounding shield

Date	Mintage	VG	F	VF	XF	Unc
1718	—	450	900	1,750	2,750	—

KM# PM59 2 DALER S.M.
Copper **Ruler:** Ulrika Eleonora **Obv:** Corner stamps: 3 crowns above date. Center stamp: Triangular, 2 D S around shield

Date	Mintage	VG	F	VF	XF	Unc
1719	—	335	675	1,200	2,450	—

KM# PM60 2 DALER S.M.
Copper **Ruler:** Ulrika Eleonora **Obv:** Corner stamps: Crowned V over double E monogram, date. Center stamp: 2 DALER SILF: MINT, crossed arrows

Date	Mintage	VG	F	VF	XF	Unc
1719	—	300	600	825	1,500	—
1720	—	325	650	900	1,650	—

KM# PM71 2 DALER S.M.

Copper **Ruler:** Frederick I **Obv:** Corner stamps: Crowned FRS, date. Center stamp: 2 DALER SILF: MYNT, crossed arrows **Note:** Illustration reduced. Actual size 170-190mm.

Date	Mintage	VG	F	VF	XF	Unc
1720	—	185	350	485	1,000	—
1721	—	185	350	485	1,000	—
1722	—	185	350	485	1,000	—
1723	—	175	325	450	950	—
1724	—	185	350	485	1,000	—
1725	—	175	325	450	950	—
1726	—	175	325	450	950	—
1727	—	175	325	450	950	—
1728	—	175	325	450	950	—
1729	—	185	350	485	1,000	—
1730	—	175	325	450	950	—
1731	—	175	325	450	950	—
1732	—	185	350	485	1,000	—
1733	—	175	325	450	950	—
1734	—	175	325	450	950	—
1735	—	175	325	450	950	—
1736	—	185	350	485	1,000	—
1737	—	185	350	485	1,000	—
1738	—	185	350	485	1,000	—
1739	—	185	350	485	1,000	—
1740	—	185	350	485	1,000	—
1741	—	185	350	485	1,000	—
1742	—	175	325	450	950	—
1743	—	175	325	450	950	—
1744	—	185	350	485	1,000	—
1745	—	175	325	450	950	—
1746	—	185	350	485	1,000	—
1747	—	185	350	485	1,000	—
1748	—	185	350	485	1,000	—
1749	—	185	350	485	1,000	—
1750	—	185	350	485	1,000	—

KM# PM72 2 DALER S.M.

Copper **Ruler:** Frederick I **Obv:** Corner stamps: Crowned AFRS, date. Center stamp: Small 2 in denomination

Date	Mintage	VG	F	VF	XF	Unc
1751	—	275	550	750	1,250	—
1752	—	285	575	775	1,375	—

KM# PM73 2 DALER S.M.

Copper **Ruler:** Adolf Frederick **Obv:** Large 2 in denomination **Note:** Illustration reduced. Actual size: 190mm.

Date	Mintage	VG	F	VF	XF	Unc
1753	—	275	550	775	1,450	—
1754	—	275	550	775	1,450	—
1755	—	275	550	775	1,450	—
1756	—	225	425	725	1,250	—
1757	—	285	575	800	1,500	—
1758	—	275	550	775	1,450	—
1759	—	275	550	775	1,450	—
1760	—	550	950	1,650	2,750	—

KM# PM49 4 DALER S.M.

Copper **Ruler:** Carl XII **Obv:** Corner stamps: Crowned mirrored C XII, date. Center stamp: Diamond shaped, 4 DALER S: M.

Date	Mintage	VG	F	VF	XF	Unc
1716	—	500	975	1,750	3,250	—
1717	—	450	900	1,600	3,000	—

KM# PM50 4 DALER S.M.

Copper **Ruler:** Carl XII **Obv:** Corner stamps: 3 crowns above date. Center stamp: Triangle with 4 D S around shield

Date	Mintage	VG	F	VF	XF	Unc
1718	—	775	1,450	3,250	6,000	—

KM# PM61 4 DALER S.M.

Copper **Ruler:** Ulrika Eleonora **Obv:** Corner stamps: 3 crowns above date. Center stamp: Triangle with 4DS around shield

Date	Mintage	VG	F	VF	XF	Unc
1719 Rare	—	—	—	—	—	—

KM# PM62 4 DALER S.M.

Copper **Ruler:** Ulrika Eleonora **Obv:** Corner stamps: Crowned V over double E monogram, date. Center stamp: 2 DALER SILF: MYNT, crossed arrows

Date	Mintage	VG	F	VF	XF	Unc
1719	—	350	700	1,100	1,750	—
1720	—	375	750	1,200	2,000	—

KM# PM74 4 DALER S.M.

Copper **Ruler:** Frederick I **Obv:** Corner stamps: Crowned FRS, date. Center stamp: 4 DALER SILF: MYNT, crossed arrows

Date	Mintage	VG	F	VF	XF	Unc
1720	—	275	525	825	1,275	—
1721	—	275	525	825	1,275	—
1722	—	275	525	825	1,275	—
1723	—	275	525	825	1,275	—
1724	—	275	525	825	1,275	—
1725	—	275	525	825	1,275	—
1726	—	275	525	825	1,275	—
1727	—	275	525	825	1,275	—
1728	—	250	475	800	1,250	—
1729	—	250	475	800	1,250	—
1730	—	275	525	825	1,275	—
1731	—	275	525	825	1,275	—
1732	—	275	525	825	1,275	—
1733	—	275	525	825	1,275	—
1734	—	275	525	825	1,275	—
1735	—	275	525	825	1,275	—
1736	—	275	525	825	1,275	—
1737	—	275	525	825	1,275	—
1738	—	275	525	825	1,275	—
1739	—	275	525	825	1,275	—
1740	—	275	525	825	1,275	—
1741	—	275	525	825	1,275	—
1742	—	285	545	850	1,350	—
1743	—	275	525	825	1,275	—
1744	—	275	525	825	1,275	—
1745	—	275	525	825	1,275	—
1746	—	300	575	900	1,450	—

KM# PM75 4 DALER S.M.

Copper **Ruler:** Adolf Frederick **Obv:** Corner stamps: Crowned AFRS, date. Center stamp: Split 4 in denomination

Date	Mintage	VG	F	VF	XF	Unc
1753	—	350	725	1,150	1,850	—
1754	—	375	775	1,350	2,350	—

KM# PM76 4 DALER S.M.

Copper **Ruler:** Adolf Frederick **Obv:** Center stamp: Solid 4 in denomination

Date	Mintage	VG	F	VF	XF	Unc
1753	—	350	725	1,150	1,850	—
1754	—	375	775	1,250	2,000	—
1755	—	550	1,100	1,850	3,000	—
1756	—	500	1,000	1,650	2,750	—
1757	—	500	1,000	1,650	2,750	—
1758	—	450	900	1,500	2,450	—
1759	—	1,250	2,000	3,250	5,000	—
1768 Unique	—	—	—	—	—	—

COUNTERMARKED COINAGE

Plate Money

In 1718 copper plate money was countermarked to reflect changes in value. Two of them, the shield with lion of the Gota arms and the date 17-18 and the three crowns in a circle, do not add substantially to the numismatic value of the pieces.

The third, however, which shows an increase in legal tender value of 50 per cent, is scarce in all denominations, as reflected in the following valuations.

KM# PM91 3/4 DALER S.M.

Copper **Ruler:** Carl XII **Countermark:** 3/4 DALER SM 1718 in cirlce on 1/2 Daler

CM Date	Host Date	Good	VG	F	VF	XF
ND(1710)	ND	—	600	950	1,750	2,750
ND(1711)	ND Unique	—	—	—	—	—
ND(1712)	ND	—	600	950	1,750	2,750

KM# PM92 3/4 DALER S.M.

Copper **Ruler:** Carl XII **Countermark:** 3/4 DALER SM 1718 in circle on 1/2 Daler, KM#PM31

CM Date	Host Date	Good	VG	F	VF	XF
ND(1710)	ND Unique	—	—	—	—	—
ND(1714)	ND Rare	—	—	—	—	—

KM# PM90 3/4 DALER S.M.

Copper **Ruler:** Carl XII **Countermark:** 3/4 DALER SM 1718 in circle on 1/2 Daler, KM#PM15

CM Date	Host Date	Good	VG	F	VF	XF
ND(1689)	1718 Unique	—	—	—	—	—

KM# PM93 1-1/2 DALER

Copper **Ruler:** Carl XII **Countermark:** 1-1/2 DALER SM In circle on 1 Daler, KM#PM#35

CM Date	Host Date	Good	VG	F	VF	XF
ND(1710)	1718	—	600	1,200	2,200	3,250
ND(1711)	ND	—	700	1,400	2,350	3,500
ND(1712)	ND	—	700	1,400	2,350	3,500
ND(1713)	ND Rare	—	—	—	—	—

Note: Only 2 specimens are known. A sea salvaged example grading fine realized $2300. In the Ponterio sale of 1-90.

KM# PM94 1-1/2 DALER

Copper **Ruler:** Carl XII **Countermark:** 1-1/2 DALER SM in circle on 1 Daler, KM#PM#8

CM Date	Host Date	Good	VG	F	VF	XF
ND(1717)	1718 Rare	—	800	1,500	2,500	3,750

KM# PM95 3 DALER

Copper **Ruler:** Carl XII **Countermark:** 3 DALER S M on 2 Daler, KM#PM43

CM Date	Host Date	Good	VG	F	VF	XF
ND(1710)	1718	—	650	1,250	2,250	3,400
ND(1711)	ND	—	650	1,250	2,250	3,400
ND(1712)	ND	—	—	—	—	—
ND(1713)	ND	—	650	1,250	2,250	3,400
ND(1714)	ND	—	650	1,250	2,250	3,400
ND(1715)	ND Rare	—	—	—	—	—

EMERGENCY COINAGE

KM# 352 DALER

3.6000 g., Copper **Ruler:** Carl XII **Obv:** Crown above date **Rev:** Value

Date	Mintage	VG	F	VF	XF	Unc
1715	2,189,000	6.50	20.00	45.00	100	—

KM# 354 DALER

7.2000 g., Copper **Ruler:** Carl XII **Subject:** Faith of the People **Obv:** Seated figure of the Svea, date below **Obv. Legend:** PVBLICA • FIDE • **Rev:** Value above S • M •

Date	Mintage	VG	F	VF	XF	Unc
1716	3,808,600	9.00	20.00	45.00	100	—

KM# 355 DALER

4.5000 g., Copper **Ruler:** Carl XII **Subject:** Reason and Arms **Obv:** Warrior with sword and shield, date below **Obv. Legend:** WETT OCH WAPEN **Rev:** Value in shield

Date	Mintage	VG	F	VF	XF	Unc
1717	905,900	5.00	15.00	35.00	70.00	—

KM# A356 DALER

4.5000 g., Copper **Ruler:** Carl XII **Subject:** Agile and Ready **Obv:** Warrior with lion, date below **Obv. Legend:** FLINK OCH FÄRDIG **Rev:** Value in round shield

Date	Mintage	VG	F	VF	XF	Unc
1718	736,800	4.00	15.00	35.00	70.00	—

KM# 357 DALER

4.5000 g., Copper **Ruler:** Carl XII **Subject:** Jupiter and Eagle **Obv:** Jupiter with eagle, date below **Obv. Legend:** IVPITER • **Rev:** Value in circle within wreath

Date	Mintage	VG	F	VF	XF	Unc
1718 Ivpiter	300,000	5.00	15.00	35.00	70.00	—
1718 Ivpilr	Inc. above	100	200	300	450	—

KM# 358 DALER

4.5000 g., Copper **Ruler:** Carl XII **Subject:** Father Time **Obv:** Father Time holding baby and scythe, date below **Obv. Legend:** SATVRNVS • **Rev:** Value in circle within wreath

Date	Mintage	VG	F	VF	XF	Unc
1718	300,000	5.00	15.00	35.00	70.00	—

KM# 359 DALER

4.5000 g., Copper **Ruler:** Carl XII **Subject:** Sun God **Obv:** Sun god with rays around circle, date below **Obv. Legend:** PHOEBVS **Rev:** Value in circle within wreath

Date	Mintage	VG	F	VF	XF	Unc
1718	300,000	5.00	15.00	35.00	70.00	—

KM# 360 DALER

4.5000 g., Copper **Ruler:** Carl XII **Subject:** War God **Obv:** War god standing with spear, date below **Obv. Legend:** MARS • **Rev:** Value in circle within crowned wreath

Date	Mintage	VG	F	VF	XF	Unc
1718	300,000	6.00	18.00	40.00	80.00	—

KM# 361 DALER

4.5000 g., Copper **Ruler:** Carl XII **Subject:** Mercury **Obv:** Mercury holding caduceus, date below **Obv. Legend:** MERCVRIVS **Rev:** Value in circle within lined cartouche

Date	Mintage	VG	F	VF	XF	Unc
1718	600,000	5.00	15.00	35.00	70.00	—

KM# 369 DALER

4.5000 g., Copper **Ruler:** Carl XII **Subject:** Hope **Obv:** Personification of Hope, date below **Obv. Legend:** HOPPET **Rev:** Value in circle within ornamented cartouche

Date	Mintage	VG	F	VF	XF	Unc
1719 Inverted heart between S-M	1,500,000	8.00	18.00	40.00	80.00	—
1719 Diamond between S-M	Inc. above	25.00	50.00	100	200	—

REFORM COINAGE

1798-1830

KM# 548 1/4 SKILLING

Copper **Ruler:** Gustaf IV Adolf **Obv:** Round arms **Obv. Legend:** CONTORS POLLET ... **Rev:** Value, date **Note:** Reports give mintage figures of 96,000 for 1799 and 4,392,000 for 1800, the latter is believed to include both dates.

Date	Mintage	VG	F	VF	XF	Unc
1799	96,000	2.00	4.00	10.00	85.00	—
1800	4,932,000	2.00	4.00	12.00	90.00	—

KM# 549 1/2 SKILLING

Copper **Ruler:** Gustaf IV Adolf **Obv:** Round arms **Obv. Legend:** CONTORSPOLLET ... **Rev:** Value, date

Date	Mintage	VG	F	VF	XF	Unc
1799	763,000	2.50	4.00	9.00	30.00	—
1800	3,624,000	2.00	3.50	7.00	20.00	—

KM# 550 1/6 RIKSDALER

6.2500 g., 0.6910 Silver 0.1388 oz. ASW

Date	Mintage	VG	F	VF	XF	Unc
1799 OL	103,000	40.00	80.00	175	325	—

KM# 551 1/3 RIKSDALER

0.8780 Silver **Ruler:** Gustaf IV Adolf **Obv:** Bust right **Obv. Legend:** GUSTAF IV ADOLPH SV • G ... **Rev:** Crowned, round arms within order chain, flanked by value, divided date below **Rev. Legend:** GUD OCH FOLKET •

Date	Mintage	VG	F	VF	XF	Unc
1799 OL	70,000	80.00	170	350	700	—
1800 OL	113,000	65.00	145	300	600	—

TRADE COINAGE

KM# 417 1/4 DUCAT

0.8703 g., 0.9760 Gold 0.0273 oz. AGW **Ruler:** Frederick I **Obv:** Head right **Obv. Legend:** FRIDERICVS • D • G • REX • ... **Rev:** Cross

Date	Mintage	VG	F	VF	XF	Unc
1730	1,696	100	150	325	600	—
1733	1,687	100	150	325	600	—
1740	480	110	175	350	650	—

KM# 474 1/4 DUCAT

0.8703 g., 0.9760 Gold 0.0273 oz. AGW **Ruler:** Adolf Frederick **Obv:** Head right **Obv. Legend:** ADOLPHUS • FRID • D • G • ... **Rev:** Crowned arms in Order chain, date at upper left

Date	Mintage	VG	F	VF	XF	Unc
1754	597	150	300	600	1,200	—
1755/4	292	150	325	650	1,250	—

KM# 331 1/2 DUCAT

1.7406 g., 0.9760 Gold 0.0546 oz. AGW **Ruler:** Carl XII **Obv:** Armored bust right **Obv. Legend:** CAROLVS • XII • D • G • REX • ... **Rev:** Double C monograms in crowned cartouche, date divided at top, value at bottom

Date	Mintage	VG	F	VF	XF	Unc
1701 HZ	—	500	1,000	2,350	5,000	—

KM# 422 1/2 DUCAT

1.7406 g., 0.9760 Gold 0.0546 oz. AGW **Ruler:** Frederick I **Obv:** Bust right **Obv. Legend:** FRIDERICVS • D • G • REX • ... **Rev:** Crowned shield divides date within sprigs

Date	Mintage	VG	F	VF	XF	Unc
1735 GZ	304	175	285	600	1,250	—
1738 GZ	402	200	320	650	1,450	—
1738 HM	—	200	320	650	1,450	—

KM# 435 1/2 DUCAT

1.7406 g., 0.9760 Gold 0.0546 oz. AGW **Ruler:** Frederick I **Obv:** Bust right **Obv. Legend:** FRIDERICVS • D • G • REX • ... **Rev:** Crowned arms in sprigs divide date, shield below

Date	Mintage	VG	F	VF	XF	Unc
1741 HM	188	525	1,150	2,150	3,750	—

KM# 439 1/2 DUCAT

1.7406 g., 0.9760 Gold 0.0546 oz. AGW **Ruler:** Frederick I **Obv:** Bust right **Obv. Legend:** FRIDERICVS • D • G • REX • ... **Rev:** Crowned round arms divide date, shield in exergue **Rev. Legend:** IN • DEO • SPES • MEA •

Date	Mintage	VG	F	VF	XF	Unc
1746 HM	211	450	950	1,850	3,250	—

KM# 440 1/2 DUCAT

1.7406 g., 0.9760 Gold 0.0546 oz. AGW **Ruler:** Frederick I **Obv:** Bust right **Obv. Legend:** FRIDERICVS • D • G • REX • ... **Rev:** Radiant crown above round arms, arms divide date, shield in exergue **Note:** Arms of Smaland at bottom of reverse on above 3 coins indicates gold from Adelfors.

Date	Mintage	VG	F	VF	XF	Unc
1747 HM	299	500	1,000	2,000	3,500	—

KM# 475 1/2 DUCAT

1.7406 g., 0.9760 Gold 0.0546 oz. AGW **Ruler:** Adolf Frederick **Obv:** Head right **Obv. Legend:** ADOLPHUS • FRID • D • G • ... **Rev:** Crowned, round arms within order chain

Date	Mintage	VG	F	VF	XF	Unc
1754	—	175	325	675	1,450	—
1755/4	248	225	400	750	1,550	—

KM# 318 DUCAT

3.5000 g., 0.9760 Gold 0.1098 oz. AGW **Ruler:** Carl XII **Obv:**

Draped bust right **Obv. Legend:** CAROLVS • XII • D • G • REX • ... **Rev:** Crowned double C monogram, date below **Note:** Fr. #49.

Date	Mintage	VG	F	VF	XF	Unc
1701	6,518	440	950	2,350	4,750	—
1702	4,021	550	1,100	2,750	5,500	—
1702	4,021	550	1,100	2,750	5,500	—
1704	2,676	525	1,000	2,500	5,000	—
1707	4,831	425	900	2,250	4,650	—

KM# 338 DUCAT

3.5000 g., 0.9760 Gold 0.1098 oz. AGW **Ruler:** Carl XII **Obv:** Draped bust right **Obv. Legend:** CAROLVS • XII • D • G • REX • ... **Rev:** Crowned double C monogram flanked by small crowns, divided date below **Rev. Legend:** PROTECTOR • MEVS • ...

Date	Mintage	VG	F	VF	XF	Unc
1708 LC	5,406	250	575	1,400	2,400	—
1709 LC	4,756	265	600	1,450	2,450	—
1710 LC	9,559	200	450	950	1,850	—
1711 LC	4,960	265	600	1,450	2,450	—

KM# 350 DUCAT

3.5000 g., 0.9760 Gold 0.1098 oz. AGW **Ruler:** Carl XII **Obv:** Armored bust right **Obv. Legend:** CAROL • XII • D • G • REX • ... **Rev:** Crowned double C monogram flanked by small crowns, divided date below **Rev. Legend:** PROTECTOR • MEVS •...

Date	Mintage	VG	F	VF	XF	Unc
1712 LC	4,433	275	600	1,400	2,400	—
1713 LC	4,243	275	600	1,400	2,400	—
1714 LC	16,000	200	425	950	1,650	—
1715 LC	6,863	225	450	1,200	2,000	—
1716 LC	7,828	225	450	1,200	2,000	—
1717 LC	3,639	275	600	1,400	2,400	—

KM# 363 DUCAT

3.5000 g., 0.9760 Gold 0.1098 oz. AGW **Ruler:** Carl XII **Obv:** Bust right **Obv. Legend:** CAROL • XII • D • G • REX • ... **Rev:** Crowned double C monogram flanked by small crowns, divided date below **Rev. Legend:** PROTECTOR • MEVS • ...

Date	Mintage	VG	F	VF	XF	Unc
1718 LC	2,143	500	1,100	2,550	4,600	—

KM# 371 DUCAT

3.5000 g., 0.9760 Gold 0.1098 oz. AGW **Ruler:** Ulrika Eleonora **Obv:** Draped bust right **Obv. Legend:** VLRICA • ELEONORA • D • G • REGINA • SVECIA • **Rev:** Monogram flanked by small crowns, large crown above divides legend **Rev. Legend:** IN • DEO • SPES • MEA •

Date	Mintage	VG	F	VF	XF	Unc
1719 LC	6,814	300	700	1,450	2,850	—
1720 LC	11,202	275	600	1,250	2,500	—

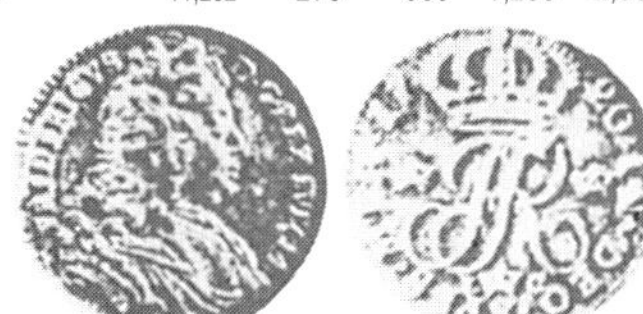

KM# 388 DUCAT

3.5000 g., 0.9760 Gold 0.1098 oz. AGW **Ruler:** Frederick I **Obv:** Draped, armored bust right **Obv. Legend:** FRIDERICVS • D • G • REX • ... **Rev:** Crowned script FR monogram, crown divides date **Rev. Legend:** IN • DEO • SPES • MEA • **Note:** Varieties exist.

Date	Mintage	VG	F	VF	XF	Unc
1720	Inc. above	275	600	1,350	2,650	—
1721	1,442	350	850	1,950	3,750	—
1722 LZ	—	300	675	1,550	2,850	—
1723 Rare	1,214	—	—	—	—	—
1723 GZ Rare	1,553	—	—	—	—	—
1724	—	350	775	1,850	3,250	—
1725 Unique	3,353	—	—	—	—	—

KM# 398 DUCAT

3.5000 g., 0.9760 Gold 0.1098 oz. AGW **Ruler:** Frederick I **Obv:** Draped bust right **Obv. Legend:** FRIDERICUS • D • G • REX • ... **Rev:** Crowned script double F monogram **Rev. Legend:** IN • DEO • SPES • MEA •

Date	Mintage	VG	F	VF	XF	Unc
1725	Inc. above	275	650	1,550	2,650	—
1726 Rare	1,263	—	—	—	—	—
1727 Rare	1,154	425	1,000	2,250	4,250	—
1728	2,874	375	825	1,950	3,650	—

KM# A401 DUCAT

3.5000 g., 0.9760 Gold 0.1098 oz. AGW **Ruler:** Frederick I **Obv:** Armored bust right **Obv. Legend:** FRIDERICUS • D • G • REX • ... **Rev:** Cruciform double F monograms with crowns in angles, arms at center **Rev. Legend:** IN • DEO • SPES • MEA •

Date	Mintage	VG	F	VF	XF	Unc
1728	Inc. above	325	700	1,650	3,000	—
1729	1,007	375	875	2,150	4,000	—

KM# 420 DUCAT

3.5000 g., 0.9760 Gold 0.1098 oz. AGW **Ruler:** Frederick I **Obv:** Draped, armored bust right **Obv. Legend:** FRIDERICVS • D • G • REX • ... **Rev. Legend:** IN • DEO • SPES • MEA • **Note:** Varieties exist.

Date	Mintage	VG	F	VF	XF	Unc
1732 GZ	2,526	250	500	1,150	2,150	—

KM# 421 DUCAT

3.5000 g., 0.9760 Gold 0.1098 oz. AGW **Ruler:** Frederick I **Obv:** Bust right **Obv. Legend:** FRIDERICVS • D • G • REX • ... **Rev:** Crowned shield divides date within sprigs **Rev. Legend:** IN • DEO • SPES • MEA •

Date	Mintage	VG	F	VF	XF	Unc
1734 GZ Rare	1,129	—	—	—	—	—
1735 GZ	2,812	300	650	1,525	2,750	—
1736 GZ Rare	2,571	—	—	—	—	—
1737 GZ	1,684	250	575	1,275	2,250	—
1738/7 GZ	—	300	650	1,450	2,500	—
1738 HM	2,913	245	550	1,250	2,150	—
1739/4 HM	—	275	625	1,450	1,500	—
1739 HM	8,239	263	595	1,365	2,340	—
1740 HM	8,396	225	525	1,150	2,000	—
1741 HM	2,718	225	525	1,150	2,000	—
1742 HM	2,888	300	650	1,450	2,500	—
1743 HM	5,134	245	550	1,250	2,150	—
1744/3 HM	—	210	500	1,100	1,750	—
1744 HM	24,000	200	450	1,000	1,650	—
1745 HM	2,470	175	425	950	1,625	—
1746 HM	—	175	425	950	1,625	—
1747 HM	4,809	200	450	1,000	1,650	—

KM# 424 DUCAT

3.5000 g., 0.9760 Gold 0.1098 oz. AGW **Ruler:** Frederick I **Obv:** Bust right **Obv. Legend:** FRIDERICVS • D • G • REX • ... **Rev:** Rising sun at lower left of crowned shield dividing date within sprigs **Rev. Inscription:** IN • DEO • SPES • MEA •

Date	Mintage	VG	F	VF	XF	Unc
1738 HM	3,314	200	425	975	1,575	—
1743 HM	5,134	275	600	1,425	2,450	—
1746 HM	18,000	225	525	125	2,000	—
1748/7 HM	7,826	200	450	1,000	1,750	—
1748 HM	Inc. above	175	400	925	1,550	—

KM# 436 DUCAT

3.5000 g., 0.9760 Gold 0.1098 oz. AGW **Ruler:** Frederick I **Obv:** Bust right **Obv. Legend:** FRIDERICUS • D • G • REX • ... **Rev:** Radiance around crowned shield dividing date within sprigs **Rev. Legend:** IN • DEO • SPES • MEA • **Note:** Struck at Stockholm Mint.

Date	Mintage	VG	F	VF	XF	Unc
1741 HM Rare	2,718	—	—	—	—	—

KM# 438 DUCAT

3.5000 g., 0.9760 Gold 0.1098 oz. AGW **Ruler:** Frederick I **Rev:** Crowned round arms divide date, arms of Smaland in exergue

Date	Mintage	VG	F	VF	XF	Unc
1743 HM	—	600	1,250	2,850	5,000	—
1744 HM	306	700	1,500	3,500	5,750	—
1745/1744 HM	—	650	1,350	3,000	5,000	—
1746 HM	351	700	1,500	3,500	5,750	—

KM# 441 DUCAT

3.5000 g., 0.9760 Gold 0.1098 oz. AGW **Ruler:** Frederick I **Rev:** Radiance around crown above round arms

Date	Mintage	VG	F	VF	XF	Unc
1747 HM	544	650	1,450	3,000	6,000	—

KM# 444 DUCAT

3.5000 g., 0.9760 Gold 0.1098 oz. AGW **Ruler:** Frederick I **Obv:** Bust right **Obv. Legend:** FRIDERICUS • D • G • REX • ... **Rev:** Crowned shield of arms in Order collar divides date **Rev. Legend:** IN • DEO • SPES • MEA •

Date	Mintage	VG	F	VF	XF	Unc
1749 HM	1,556	350	750	1,850	3,250	—
1750 HM Rare	5,863	—	—	—	—	—

KM# 459 DUCAT

3.5000 g., 0.9760 Gold 0.1098 oz. AGW **Ruler:** Frederick I **Rev:** Crowned round arms in Order collar, arms of Smaland in exergue **Note:** Arms of Smaland at bottom of reverse on above 4 coins indicates gold from Adelfors.

Date	Mintage	VG	F	VF	XF	Unc
1750 HM	495	600	1,350	2,850	5,500	—

KM# 458 DUCAT

3.5000 g., 0.9760 Gold 0.1098 oz. AGW **Ruler:** Frederick I **Rev:** Crowned arms in Order collar **Note:** The rising sun on reverse of above 2 coins indicates gold from the East Indies.

Date	Mintage	VG	F	VF	XF	Unc
1750 HM	6,360	275	575	1,350	2,250	—

KM# 465 DUCAT

3.5000 g., 0.9760 Gold 0.1098 oz. AGW **Ruler:** Adolf Frederick **Obv:** Head right **Obv. Legend:** ADOLPHUS • FRID • D • G • ... **Rev:** Crowned, round arms within order chain, date in legend **Rev. Legend:** SALUS • PUBLICA ...

Date	Mintage	VG	F	VF	XF	Unc
1751 HM	2,332	265	550	1,450	2,400	—
1752 HM	2,695	225	525	1,375	2,150	—
1753 HM	2,802	225	525	1,375	2,150	—
1754 HM	590	400	825	2,200	4,150	—
1755 HM Rare	84	—	—	—	—	—
1756 HM Rare	390	—	—	—	—	—
1757 HM	908	300	625	1,600	3,350	—
1758 HM	3,830	275	600	1,475	2,650	—

Date	Mintage	VG	F	VF	XF	Unc
1759 HM Rare	1,805	—	—	—	—	—
1760 HM	3,181	225	525	1,450	2,400	—
1761 HM Rare	1,217	—	—	—	—	—
1762 HM	1,962	225	525	1,385	2,350	—
ND HM	—	—	—	—	—	—
1763 AL	4,073	225	525	1,385	2,350	—
1764 AL	4,681	225	525	1,385	2,350	—
1765 AL	2,739	225	525	1,385	2,350	—
1766 AL	4,465	225	525	1,375	2,250	—
1767 AL	5,657	225	525	1,375	2,250	—
1768 AL	4,153	225	525	1,375	2,250	—
1769 AL	2,266	225	525	1,385	2,350	—
1770 AL	3,037	225	525	1,385	2,350	—
1771 AL	2,256	265	585	1,475	2,550	—

KM# 466 DUCAT

3.5000 g., 0.9760 Gold 0.1098 oz. AGW **Ruler:** Adolf Frederick **Obv:** Head right **Obv. Legend:** ADOLPHUS • FRID • D • G • ... **Rev:** Crowned arms in Order chain, date above, mine name in legend

Date	Mintage	VG	F	VF	XF	Unc
1751 HM Rare	—	—	—	—	—	—
1754 HM Rare	—	—	—	—	—	—

KM# 471 DUCAT

3.5000 g., 0.9760 Gold 0.1098 oz. AGW **Ruler:** Adolf Frederick **Obv:** Head right **Obv. Legend:** ADOLPHUS • FRID • D • G • ... **Rev:** Crowned arms in Order chain, Smaland arms in exergue **Rev. Legend:** SALUS • PUBLICA • ....

Date	Mintage	VG	F	VF	XF	Unc
1752 HM	239	575	1,250	3,150	6,650	—
1753 HM	—	525	1,175	2,800	5,150	—
1755 HM Rare	411	—	—	—	—	—
1756 HM	402	450	1,100	2,550	6,000	—
1757 HM	319	425	950	2,350	5,750	—
1759 HM Rare	420	—	—	—	—	—
1761 HM	740	525	1,175	2,800	5,150	—
1763/1 AL	951	550	1,200	2,850	5,500	—
1763 AL Rare	Inc. above	—	—	—	—	—
1765 AL	305	450	1,100	2,550	5,150	—
1766 AL	533	—	—	—	—	—
1768 AL	363	—	—	—	—	—
1769 AL	764	—	—	—	—	—
1770 AL	375	525	1,175	2,800	5,150	—

KM# 510 DUCAT

3.5000 g., 0.9760 Gold 0.1098 oz. AGW **Ruler:** Gustaf III **Obv:** Head right **Obv. Legend:** GUSTAVUS • III • D • G • REX • ... **Rev:** Crowned, round arms within order chain, divided date below **Rev. Legend:** FÄDERNESLANDET •

Date	Mintage	VG	F	VF	XF	Unc
1771 AL	—	350	750	1,650	3,000	—
1772 AL	4,536	185	400	900	1,750	—
1773 AL	3,636	200	425	900	1,750	—
1774 OL	6,827	165	345	750	1,450	—
1775 OL	4,088	185	400	900	1,750	—
1776 OL	15,000	165	345	750	1,450	—
1777 OL	10,000	165	345	750	1,450	—
1778 OL	—	185	385	875	1,700	—
1779 OL	4,496	225	475	1,000	1,800	—
1780 OL	2,585	245	525	1,200	2,250	—
1781/77 OL	6,096,000	185	400	750	1,450	—
1781 OL	Inc. above	165	345	750	1,450	—
1782/79 OL	16,000	200	425	975	1,700	—
1782 OL	Inc. above	165	345	750	1,450	—
1783 OL	7,448	165	345	750	1,450	—
1784 OL	2,422	375	750	1,450	3,000	—
1785 OL	1,245	325	650	1,350	2,750	—
1786 OL	6,787	165	345	750	1,450	—
1787 OL	5,009	165	345	750	1,450	—
1788 OL Rare	804	—	—	—	—	—
1789 OL	8,198	165	400	750	1,450	—
1790 OL	3,643	225	475	1,000	2,000	—
1791 OL	1,160	165	345	750	1,450	—
1792 OL	3,415	165	345	750	1,450	—

KM# 511 DUCAT

3.5000 g., 0.9760 Gold 0.1098 oz. AGW **Ruler:** Gustaf III **Obv:** Head right **Obv. Legend:** GUSTAVUS • III • D • G • REX • SVECIAE • **Rev:** Crowned, round arms within order chain, divided date on mantle below **Rev. Legend:** FÄDERNESLANDET •

Date	Mintage	VG	F	VF	XF	Unc
1771 AL	1,556	350	800	1,750	3,000	—
1772 AL	1,368	475	1,200	2,550	5,000	—
1773 AL	563	550	1,250	3,000	5,500	—
1774 OL	987	475	1,200	2,550	5,000	—
1776 OL	382	550	1,250	3,000	5,500	—
1777 OL	230	650	1,350	3,150	5,750	—
1778 OL	4,075	475	1,200	2,550	5,000	—
1779 OL	800	475	1,200	2,550	5,000	—
1781 OL	500	475	1,200	2,550	5,000	—
1782 OL	300	450	1,100	2,150	4,000	—
1783 OL	500	450	1,100	2,150	4,000	—
1784 OL	403	450	1,100	2,150	4,000	—
1785 OL	160	450	1,100	2,150	4,000	—
1786 OL	690	450	1,100	2,150	4,000	—
ND OL	—	—	—	—	—	—

KM# 541 DUCAT

3.5000 g., 0.9760 Gold 0.1098 oz. AGW **Ruler:** Gustaf IV Adolf **Obv:** Head right **Obv. Legend:** GUSTAF • IV • ADOLPH • SV • G • ... **Rev:** Crowned, round arms within order chain, divided date below **Rev. Legend:** GUD OCH FOLKET •

Date	Mintage	VG	F	VF	XF	Unc
1793 OL	1,528	245	500	1,150	1,950	—
1794 OL	14,000	245	500	1,125	1,850	—
1795 OL	4,071	225	450	1,100	1,825	—

KM# 545 DUCAT

3.5000 g., 0.9760 Gold 0.1098 oz. AGW **Ruler:** Gustaf IV Adolf **Obv:** Head right **Obv. Legend:** GUSTAF • IV • ADOLPH • S • G • ... **Rev:** Crowned, round arms within order chain, divided date below **Rev. Legend:** GUD OCH FOLKET •

Date	Mintage	VG	F	VF	XF	Unc
1796 OL	2,800	225	450	1,150	1,850	—
1797 OL	4,100	225	450	1,150	1,850	—
1798 OL	5,056	225	525	1,250	2,000	—

KM# 546 DUCAT

3.5000 g., 0.9760 Gold 0.1098 oz. AGW **Ruler:** Gustaf IV Adolf **Obv:** Head right **Obv. Legend:** GUSTAF • ADOLPH • .... **Rev:** Crowned arms divide date, Smaland arms in exergue **Rev. Legend:** GUD OCH FOLKET •

Date	Mintage	VG	F	VF	XF	Unc
1796 OL Rare	1,200	—	—	—	—	—

KM# 542 DUCAT

3.5000 g., 0.9760 Gold 0.1098 oz. AGW **Ruler:** Gustaf IV Adolf **Obv:** Armored bust right **Obv. Legend:** GUSTAF • IV • ADOLPH • SV • ... **Rev:** Crowned, round arms within order chain, divided date below **Rev. Legend:** GUD OCH FOLKET •

Date	Mintage	VG	F	VF	XF	Unc
1799 OL	6,420	200	475	1,150	2,150	—
1800 OL	5,100	200	425	950	1,850	—

KM# 332 2 DUCAT

6.9625 g., 0.9760 Gold 0.2185 oz. AGW **Ruler:** Carl XII **Obv:** Draped bust right **Obv. Legend:** CAROLVS • XII • D • G • REX • .. **Rev:** Crowned double C monogram, date below **Rev. Legend:** PROTECTOR • MEVS • ...

Date	Mintage	VG	F	VF	XF	Unc
1702 HZ	964	1,350	2,750	5,500	8,500	—
1704 HZ	1,331	1,550	3,350	6,750	10,500	—

KM# 372 2 DUCAT

6.9625 g., 0.9760 Gold 0.2185 oz. AGW **Ruler:** Ulrika Eleonora **Obv:** Draped bust right **Obv. Legend:** VLRICA • ELEONORA • D • G • REGINA • SVECIÆ • **Rev:** Crowned shield divides date **Rev. Legend:** IN • DEO • SPES • MEA •

Date	Mintage	VG	F	VF	XF	Unc
1719 LC	39,000	450	950	1,850	3,850	—

KM# A390 10 DUCAT

35.0000 g., 0.9760 Gold 1.0982 oz. AGW **Ruler:** Frederick I **Obv:** Bust of Frederick I **Rev:** Facing busts of Gustaf Vasa and Gustaf II Adolf **Note:** Struck with 1 Rixdaler dies, KM#389.2.

Date	Mintage	VG	F	VF	XF	Unc
1721 Rare	—	—	—	—	—	—

KM# C395 10 DUCAT

35.0000 g., 0.9760 Gold 1.0982 oz. AGW **Ruler:** Frederick I **Obv:** Jugate busts of Frederik I and Ulrika Eleonora right **Rev:** Crowned and supported arms **Note:** Struck with 1 Rixdaler dies, KM#418. Fr.#61.

Date	Mintage	VG	F	VF	XF	Unc
1731 Rare	—	—	—	—	—	—

KM# B419 10 DUCAT

35.0000 g., 0.9760 Gold 1.0982 oz. AGW **Ruler:** Carl IX, Regent **Subject:** Tenth Anniversary of Reign **Obv:** Bust of Frederick I and Ulrika Eleonora jugate right **Rev:** Three crowns on globe **Note:** Fr.#63. Struck with 1 Rixdaler dies, KM#A395.

Date	Mintage	VG	F	VF	XF	Unc
ND(1731) Unique	—	—	—	—	—	—

KM# C419 10 DUCAT

35.0000 g., 0.9760 Gold 1.0982 oz. AGW **Ruler:** Frederick I **Subject:** Frederik's Visit to Hesse-Cassel **Obv:** Bust of Frederick I right **Rev:** Eleven-line inscription **Note:** Fr.#62.

Date	Mintage	VG	F	VF	XF	Unc
MDCCXXXI (1731) Unique	—	—	—	—	—	—

PATTERNS

Including off metal strikes

KM#	Date	Mintage	Identification	Mkt Val
PnA1	1730	—	1/4 Ducat. Silver. KM#417.	175
PnB1	1733	—	1/4 Ducat. Silver. KM#417.	150

In Switzerland, canton is the name given to each of the 23 states comprising the Swiss Federation. The origin of the cantons is rooted in the liberty-loving instincts of the peasants of Helvetia.

After the Romans departed Switzerland to defend Rome against the barbarians, Switzerland became, in the Middle Ages, a federation of fiefs of the Holy Roman Empire. In 888 it was again united by Rudolf of Burgundy, a minor despot, and for 150 years Switzerland had a king. Upon the death of the last Burgundian king, the kingdom crumbled into a loose collection of feudal fiefs ruled by bishops and ducal families who made their own laws and levied their own taxes. Eventually this division of rule by arbitrary despots became more than the freedom-loving and resourceful peasants could bear. The citizens living in the remote valleys of Uri, Schwyz (from which Switzerland received its name) and Unterwalden decided to liberate themselves from all feudal obligations and become free.

On Aug. 1, 1291, the elders of these three small states met on a tiny heath known as the Rutli on the shores of the Lake of Lucerne and negotiated an eternal pact' which recognized their right to local self-government, and pledged one another assistance against any encroachment upon these rights. The pact was the beginning of the Everlasting League' and the foundation of the Swiss Confederation.

APPENZELL

Located in northeast Switzerland, completely surrounded by the canton of St. Gall. The name was derived from "Abbot's Cell". Achieved independence from the abbots of St. Gall in the period 1377/1411. Divided by religious differences into two half cantons, Ausser-Rhoden (Protestant) and Inner-Rhoden (Catholic). Both were joined to the Canton to Santis 1797-1803, but regained their independent status in 1803.

MONETARY SYSTEM

4 Pfenning = 1 Kreuzer
10 Rappen = 4 Kreuzer = 1 Batzen
10 Batzen = 1 Franken

INNER RHODEN

Catholic

STANDARD COINAGE

KM# 15 HELLER

Copper **Obv:** Value above bear **Note:** Uniface.

Date	Mintage	VG	F	VF	XF	Unc
1737	—	600	1,200	1,800	—	—

KM# 16 HELLER

Billon **Obv:** Bear on shield within sprigs **Note:** Uniface.

Date	Mintage	VG	F	VF	XF	Unc
1737	—	300	500	800	2,000	—

KM# 17 PFENNIG

Billon **Obv:** Bear right **Note:** Uniface.

Date	Mintage	VG	F	VF	XF	Unc
1737 Rare	—	—	—	—	—	—

KM# 18 PFENNIG

Billon **Obv:** Bear left **Note:** Uniface.

Date	Mintage	VG	F	VF	XF	Unc
1737	—	50.00	100	150	—	—

KM# 21 2 PFENNIG

Billon **Obv:** Bear left dividing value

Date	Mintage	VG	F	VF	XF	Unc
1737 Rare	—	—	—	—	—	—

KM# 19 2 PFENNIG

Billon **Obv:** Bear right within cartouche dividing value **Note:** Uniface.

Date	Mintage	VG	F	VF	XF	Unc
1737	—	60.00	120	400	—	—

KM# 20 2 PFENNIG

Billon **Obv:** Bear right, without cartouche dividing value **Note:** Uniface.

Date	Mintage	VG	F	VF	XF	Unc
1737	—	40.00	80.00	120	—	—

KM# 26 BLUZGER

Billon **Obv:** Cantonal arms in Spanish shield within oval cartouche **Rev:** Cruciform within inner circle

Date	Mintage	VG	F	VF	XF	Unc
1738	—	200	400	1,600	—	—

KM# 27 BLUZGER

Billon **Obv:** Oval arms within cartouche

Date	Mintage	VG	F	VF	XF	Unc
1738 Rare	—	200	400	750	—	—

KM# 22 1/2 KREUZER

Billon **Obv:** Value: 1/2 in oval divides two shields at top **Rev:** Value: 1/2

Date	Mintage	VG	F	VF	XF	Unc
1737	—	20.00	40.00	120	320	—

KM# 23 KREUZER

Billon **Obv:** Bear right on shield within ornamentation **Rev:** Value above date within wreath

Date	Mintage	VG	F	VF	XF	Unc
1737	—	100	200	650	1,750	3,200

KM# 28 KREUZER

Billon **Obv:** Arms with bear right in shield within laurel wreath **Rev:** Value and date within laurel wreath

Date	Mintage	VG	F	VF	XF	Unc
1738 Rare	—	—	—	—	—	—

KM# 42 KREUZER

Billon **Obv:** Bear left in shield

Date	Mintage	VG	F	VF	XF	Unc
1740	—	500	950	2,400	—	—

KM# 44 KREUZER

Billon **Obv:** Arms with bear left in shield within two laurel branches, AIR above

Date	Mintage	VG	F	VF	XF	Unc
1742 Rare	—	—	—	—	—	—

KM# 29 3 KREUZER ((Groschen))

Billon **Obv:** Similar to 15 Kreuzer, KM#34 **Rev:** Cruciform with flowers in angles

Date	Mintage	VG	F	VF	XF	Unc
1738	—	125	200	800	2,000	4,000

KM# 30 3 KREUZER ((Groschen))

Billon **Obv:** Similar to 15 Kreuzer, KM#35 **Rev:** Ornate cruciform with flowers in angles within inner circle, value: 3 at center of cross

Date	Mintage	VG	F	VF	XF	Unc
1738	—	160	325	1,200	—	—

KM# 31 3 KREUZER ((Groschen))

Billon **Obv:** Bear right

Date	Mintage	VG	F	VF	XF	Unc
1738	—	500	950	2,400	—	—

KM# 40 3 KREUZER ((Groschen))

Billon **Obv:** Crowned imperial eagle within inner circle

Date	Mintage	VG	F	VF	XF	Unc
1739	—	650	1,200	4,000	—	—

KM# 37 1/2 BATZEN

Billon **Obv:** Similar to 15 Kreuzer, KM#34 **Rev:** Value and date in circle, ornamentation around

Date	Mintage	VG	F	VF	XF	Unc
1738	—	500	1,000	3,200	—	—

KM# 32 4 KREUZER (1 Batzen)

Billon **Obv:** Similar to 15 Kreuzer, KM#34 but shield divides value: 4-K **Rev:** Monogram APP above date

Date	Mintage	VG	F	VF	XF	Unc
1738	—	300	600	1,000	2,000	4,000

KM# 38 9 BATZEN

Silver **Obv:** St Maurice with oval shield at right **Obv. Legend:** S • MAURIT • PAT • .... **Rev:** Inscription, value, date within cartouche

Date	Mintage	VG	F	VF	XF	Unc
1738	—	950	1,800	8,000	—	—

KM# 39 9 BATZEN

Silver **Rev:** Inscription: SALVUM/FAC/POPVLUM/TVUM; date and value within palm branches

Date	Mintage	VG	F	VF	XF	Unc
1738	—	2,500	4,000	9,500	—	—

KM# A24 6 KREUZER

Billon

Date	Mintage	VG	F	VF	XF	Unc
1737	—	70.00	125	400	—	—

KM# 33 6 KREUZER

Billon **Obv:** Similar to 15 Kreuzer, KM#34 **Rev:** Larger and more ornate ornamentation around cartouche

Date	Mintage	VG	F	VF	XF	Unc
1738	—	450	800	2,750	—	—

KM# 34 15 KREUZER

Silver **Obv:** Bear right within cartouche **Obv. Legend:** MONETA REIP... **Rev:** Inscription, date within cartouche, value in oval circle below

Date	Mintage	VG	F	VF	XF	Unc
1738	—	325	625	1,500	3,000	—

Note: 1 in value

KM# 35 15 KREUZER

Silver **Obv:** Bear left within circle **Obv. Legend:** MONETA NOVA REIP ... **Rev:** Inscription, date within cartouche, value in oval circle below **Rev. Inscription:** GLORIA/IN/EXCELSIS/DEO

Date	Mintage	VG	F	VF	XF	Unc
1738	—	250	475	1,200	2,400	—
1738	—	325	600	1,600	—	—

Note: 1 in value

KM# 36 20 KREUZER

Silver **Obv:** Crowned imperial eagle with arms on breast **Rev:** Value and date within palm branches

Date	Mintage	VG	F	VF	XF	Unc
1738	—	1,250	2,400	5,500	—	—

KM# 43 20 KREUZER

Silver **Obv:** Larger imperial eagle **Rev:** Value and date in oval ornate cartouche

Date	Mintage	VG	F	VF	XF	Unc
1740	—	250	475	1,200	—	—

TRADE COINAGE

KM# 24 DUCAT

3.5000 g., 0.9860 Gold 0.1109 oz. AGW **Obv. Legend:** S • MAURITIUS • PATRONUS **Rev:** St. Maurice with oval shield at right **Rev. Inscription:** DUCATUS/REIP/APPENZEL/LENSIS

Date	Mintage	F	VF	XF	Unc	BU
1737	—	2,500	5,500	9,500	14,000	—

KM# 41 DUCAT

3.5000 g., 0.9860 Gold 0.1109 oz. AGW **Obv:** St. Maurice with oval shield at right **Obv. Legend:** S • MAURITIUS • PATRONUS **Rev:** Inscription, date within ornamented square **Rev. Inscription:** DUCATUS/REIPUB/APPENZE/LLENSIS

Date	Mintage	F	VF	XF	Unc	BU
1739	—	3,500	6,000	10,000	15,000	—

BASEL

A bishopric in northwest Switzerland, founded in the 5th century. The first coinage was c.1000AD. During the Reformation Basel became Protestant and the bishop resided henceforth in the town of Porrentruy. The Congress of Vienna gave the territories of the Bishopric to Bern. Today they form the Canton Jura and the French speaking part of Bern.

RULERS

Johann Conrad II von Reinach-Hirzbach, 1705-1737

Joseph Sigismund von Roggenbach, 1782-1793

MINT OFFICIALS' INITIALS

Initial	Date	Name
D-B	?	J. De Beyer
H	1756-93	Haag
IH	1765	?
I-HH	1765	Handmann
S	1780	Johann Ulrich Samson

MONETARY SYSTEM

4 Kreuzer = 1 Batzen

BISHOPRIC

STANDARD COINAGE

KM# 33 RAPPEN (Vierer)

Billon **Ruler:** Johann Conrad II von Reinach-Hirzbach **Obv:** Round arms **Obv. Legend:** IOA • CO • D • G • EP • BAS • S • R • I • PR **Rev:** MONETA/NOVA/date within palm and laurel branches

Date	Mintage	VG	F	VF	XF	Unc
1718	—	40.00	80.00	200	600	—
1719	—	60.00	80.00	200	600	—

KM# 36 KREUZER

Billon **Ruler:** Johann Conrad II von Reinach-Hirzbach **Obv:** Round arms **Obv. Legend:** IOA • CO • D • G • EP • BAS • S • R • I • PR **Rev:** Double-headed eagle, value on breast, within beaded circle

Date	Mintage	VG	F	VF	XF	Unc
1725 Rare	—	—	—	—	—	—

KM# 38 KREUZER

Billon **Ruler:** Johann Conrad II von Reinach-Hirzbach **Obv:** Bust of Johann Conrad II right within beaded circle **Rev:** Double-headed eagle, value on breast, within beaded circle

Date	Mintage	VG	F	VF	XF	Unc
1725	—	175	325	800	1,600	—
1726	—	20.00	40.00	160	—	—
1727	—	45.00	80.00	225	600	—

KM# 41 2 KREUZER (1/2 Batzen)

Billon **Ruler:** Johann Conrad II von Reinach-Hirzbach **Obv:** Ornate shield on mantle above date **Rev:** Value on breast of crowned double-headed eagle

Date	Mintage	VG	F	VF	XF	Unc
1717	—	12.00	20.00	80.00	—	—
1718	—	12.00	20.00	80.00	—	—
1719	—	12.00	20.00	80.00	—	—
1733 Rare	—	—	—	—	—	—

KM# 30 3 KREUZER (1 Groschen)

Billon **Ruler:** Johann Conrad II von Reinach-Hirzbach **Obv:** Value in cartouche at bottom left, bust of Johann Conrad II right, within inner circle **Rev:** Crowned double-headed eagle

Date	Mintage	VG	F	VF	XF	Unc
1717 Rare	—	—	—	—	—	—
1718	—	175	325	800	1,600	—

KM# 42 4 KREUZER (1 Batzen)

Billon **Ruler:** Johann Conrad II von Reinach-Hirzbach **Obv:** Ornate shield on mantle above date **Rev:** Value on breast of crowned double-headed eagle

Date	Mintage	VG	F	VF	XF	Unc
1718	—	25.00	40.00	160	400	—
1733	—	32.50	65.00	200	600	—

KM# 39 6 KREUZER

Silver **Ruler:** Johann Conrad II von Reinach-Hirzbach **Obv:** Bust right **Obv. Legend:** IOANNES • CONRADVS • D • G • **Rev:** Value on breast of crowned double-headed eagle

Date	Mintage	VG	F	VF	XF	Unc
1726 H	—	45.00	80.00	200	400	—

KM# 37 12 KREUZER

Silver **Ruler:** Johann Conrad II von Reinach-Hirzbach **Obv:** Bust right **Obv. Legend:** IOANNES • CONRADVS • D • G • **Rev:** Value on breast of crowned double-headed eagle

Date	Mintage	VG	F	VF	XF	Unc
1725 Rare	—	—	—	—	—	—
1726	—	30.00	60.00	160	325	—
1733	—	175	325	800	—	—

KM# 45 12 KREUZER

Silver **Ruler:** Joseph Sigismjnd von Roggenbach **Obv:** Bust left **Obv. Legend:** IOSEPH.... **Rev:** Value on breast of crowned double-headed eagle

Date	Mintage	VG	F	VF	XF	Unc
1786	—	20.00	40.00	120	200	—
1787	—	18.00	32.00	100	160	—
1788	—	18.00	32.00	100	160	—

KM# 25 20 KREUZER

Silver **Ruler:** Johann Conrad II von Reinach-Hirzbach **Obv:** Bust right **Obv. Legend:** IOANNES • CONRADVS • D • G • **Rev:** Value on breast of crowned double-headed eagle

Date	Mintage	VG	F	VF	XF	Unc
1716	—	45.00	80.00	200	—	—
1717	—	45.00	80.00	200	—	—
1722 Rare	—	—	—	—	—	—
1723	—	45.00	80.00	200	—	—
1724	—	45.00	80.00	200	—	—
1725	—	45.00	80.00	200	—	—
1726 Rare	—	—	—	—	—	—

KM# 48 24 KREUZER

Silver **Ruler:** Joseph Sigismjnd von Roggenbach **Obv:** Bust left **Obv. Legend:** IOSEPHUS • D • G • ... **Rev:** Value on breast of crowned double-headed eagle

Date	Mintage	VG	F	VF	XF	Unc
1788	—	35.00	60.00	160	285	600

KM# 31 1/2 BATZEN

Billon **Ruler:** Johann Conrad II von Reinach-Hirzbach **Obv:** Crowned double-headed eagle within circle **Obv. Legend:** MONETA • NOVA • ... **Rev:** Cruciform with decorations in angles within inner circle, shield of arms at center **Rev. Legend:** S • R • I • PRINCEPS EPIS • ...

Date	Mintage	VG	F	VF	XF	Unc
1717	—	11.50	20.00	80.00	—	—
1718	—	11.50	20.00	80.00	—	—
1719	—	11.50	20.00	80.00	—	—
1733 Rare	—	—	—	—	—	—

KM# 46 1/2 BATZEN

Billon **Ruler:** Joseph Sigismjnd von Roggenbach **Obv:** Crowned shield **Rev:** Value, date within thin wreath

Date	Mintage	VG	F	VF	XF	Unc
1787	—	12.00	20.00	80.00	200	350

KM# 34 BATZEN

Billon **Ruler:** Johann Conrad II von Reinach-Hirzbach **Obv:** Ornate shield on mantle above date **Obv. Legend:** IOAN • CONR • D • G • ... **Rev:** Double-headed eagle **Rev. Legend:** PRINCEPS EPIS ...

Date	Mintage	VG	F	VF	XF	Unc
1718	—	25.00	40.00	160	400	—
1733	—	35.00	60.00	200	600	—

KM# 47 BATZEN

Billon **Ruler:** Joseph Sigismjnd von Roggenbach **Obv:** Crowned shield **Rev:** Value, date within thin wreath

Date	Mintage	VG	F	VF	XF	Unc
1787	—	15.00	25.00	95.00	240	400

KM# 26 SCHILLING

Billon **Ruler:** Joseph Sigismjnd von Roggenbach **Obv:** Crowned imperial eagle in inner circle, date below **Rev:** Saint standing with church and fleur-de-lis

Date	Mintage	VG	F	VF	XF	Unc
1716	—	12.00	20.00	80.00	240	—
1717	—	12.00	20.00	80.00	240	—
1718	—	12.00	20.00	80.00	240	—
1719	—	12.00	20.00	80.00	240	—
1722	—	9.00	16.00	60.00	200	—
1723	—	9.00	16.00	60.00	200	—
1724	—	9.00	16.00	60.00	200	—
1727	—	9.00	16.00	60.00	200	—

KM# 32 1/4 THALER

Silver **Ruler:** Johann Conrad II von Reinach-Hirzbach **Obv:** Bust right **Obv. Legend:** IOANNES • CONRAD • VS • ... **Rev:** Fleur-de-lis within cartouche, value in oval circle below

Date	Mintage	VG	F	VF	XF	Unc
1717	—	90.00	160	400	800	—

KM# 27 THALER

Silver **Ruler:** Johann Conrad II von Reinach-Hirzbach **Obv:** Bust right **Obv. Legend:** IOANNES•CONRADVS•D•G **Rev:** Crowned double-headed eagle, oval shield on breast **Note:** Dav. #1739.

Date	Mintage	VG	F	VF	XF	Unc
1716	—	1,500	2,400	6,000	—	—

TRADE COINAGE

KM# 28 DUCAT

3.5000 g., 0.9860 Gold 0.1109 oz. AGW **Ruler:** Johann Conrad II von Reinach-Hirzbach **Obv:** Bust right **Obv. Legend:** CONRAD • II • D • G • ... **Rev:** Crowned double-headed eagle, oval shield on breast

Date	Mintage	VG	F	VF	XF	Unc
1716 Rare	—	—	—	—	—	—

KM# 29 2 DUCAT

7.0000 g., 0.9860 Gold 0.2219 oz. AGW **Ruler:** Johann Conrad II von Reinach-Hirzbach **Obv:** Bust right **Obv. Legend:** CONRADI D G .... **Rev:** Crowned double-headed eagle, oval shield on breast

Date	Mintage	VG	F	VF	XF	Unc
1716 Rare	—	—	—	—	—	—
1724 Rare	—	—	—	—	—	—

CITY

A city in northwest Switzerland was founded in 374 by the Roman Emperor Valentinian. It became a Burgundian Mint in the 10th century and obtained the mint right in 1373. It was admitted to the Swiss Confederation in 1501. Developed into a canton.

MONETARY SYSTEM

Until 1798
8 Rappen = 1 Batzen
30 Batzen = 2 Gulden = 1 Thaler

STANDARD COINAGE

KM# 55 STEBLER

Billon **Obv:** Arms on shield, small ornaments on top and sides in inner circle, small pearls at edge **Note:** Uniface.

Date	Mintage	VG	F	VF	XF	Unc
1747	—	25.00	40.00	160	400	—

KM# 56 RAPPEN (Vierer)

Billon **Obv:** Arms on shield, small ornaments on top and sides in inner circle, small pearls at edge **Note:** Uniface.

Date	Mintage	VG	F	VF	XF	Unc
1748	—	9.00	16.00	32.00	80.00	160

KM# 57 RAPPEN (Vierer)

Billon **Obv:** Arms on shield within circle **Obv. Legend:** MONETA NO BASILIE **Rev:** Floreate cross within circle **Rev. Legend:** DA PACEM DOMINE

Date	Mintage	VG	F	VF	XF	Unc
1749	—	16..	32.00	120	325	—

KM# 154 RAPPEN (Vierer)

Billon **Obv:** MON • BASIL within wreath **Rev:** Arms of Basel within cartouche

Date	Mintage	VG	F	VF	XF	Unc
ND(1750)	—	3.00	5.00	12.50	32.00	60.00

KM# 136 ASSIS

Billon **Ruler:** Johann Conrad II von Reinach-Hirzbach

Date	Mintage	VG	F	VF	XF	Unc
1708	—	5.00	8.00	24.00	60.00	120

KM# 138 1/2 BATZEN

Billon **Ruler:** Johann Conrad II von Reinach-Hirzbach **Obv:** Basilisk holding shield **Rev:** Value, date within cartouche, legend around

Date	Mintage	VG	F	VF	XF	Unc
1724	—	9.00	16.00	32.00	120	200

KM# 162 1/2 BATZEN

Billon **Obv:** Arms of Basel within cartouche **Rev:** Value, date within cartouche

Date	Mintage	VG	F	VF	XF	Unc
1762	—	5.00	8.00	24.00	80.00	160
1763	—	5.00	8.00	24.00	80.00	160
1765	—	5.00	8.00	24.00	80.00	160
1794	—	15.00	24.00	50.00	160	325

KM# 139 BATZEN

Billon **Ruler:** Johann Conrad II von Reinach-Hirzbach **Obv:** Basilisk holding shield **Rev:** Value, date within cartouche, legend around

Date	Mintage	VG	F	VF	XF	Unc
1724	—	8.00	16.00	32.00	120	200

KM# 163 BATZEN

Billon **Obv:** Arms of Basel within cartouche **Rev:** Value, date within cartouche

Date	Mintage	VG	F	VF	XF	Unc
1762	—	—	250	400	800	2,000

KM# 164 BATZEN

Billon **Obv:** Arms of Basel within cartouche **Obv. Legend:** MONETA.... **Rev:** Value, date within cartouche

Date	Mintage	VG	F	VF	XF	Unc
1763	—	7.50	12.00	25.00	95.00	175
1764	—	7.50	12.00	25.00	95.00	175
1765	—	7.50	12.00	25.00	95.00	175

KM# 140 3 BATZEN

Billon **Ruler:** Johann Conrad II von Reinach-Hirzbach **Obv:** Basilisk holding shield **Rev:** Value, date in ornate cartouche

Date	Mintage	VG	F	VF	XF	Unc
1724	—	12.50	20.00	40.00	120	—
1726	—	12.50	20.00	40.00	120	—

KM# 165 3 BATZEN

Billon **Obv:** Arms of Basel within cartouche **Obv. Legend:** DOMINE CONSERVA NOS IN PACE **Rev:** Value, date within cartouche **Rev. Legend:** MONETA REIPUB • BASILEENSIS

Date	Mintage	VG	F	VF	XF	Unc
1764	—	8.00	16.00	32.00	95.00	200
1765	—	8.00	16.00	32.00	95.00	200

KM# 166 1/6 THALER

Silver **Obv:** Value within wreath, date below **Obv. Legend:** MONETA REIPUB • BASILEENSIS **Rev:** Winged dragon with arms of Basel at lower left **Rev. Legend:** DOMINE CONSERVA NOS IN PACE

Date	Mintage	VG	F	VF	XF	Unc
1764	—	50.00	80.00	200	400	—
1766	—	40.00	60.00	160	325	—

KM# 121 1/4 THALER

Silver

Date	Mintage	VG	F	VF	XF	Unc
ND	—	40.00	85.00	165	285	—

KM# 122 1/4 THALER

Silver **Obv:** 1/4 in oval below city view **Rev:** Arms in circle

Date	Mintage	VG	F	VF	XF	Unc
1739	—	35.00	40.00	125	250	400

KM# 142 1/4 THALER

Silver **Obv:** City view and date below assorted shields **Rev:** Winged dragon with arms of Basel at lower left **Rev. Legend:** DOMINE • CONSERVA • NOS • IN • PACE •

Date	Mintage	VG	F	VF	XF	Unc
1740	—	20.00	35.00	100	200	350

KM# 143 1/4 THALER

Silver **Obv:** City view and date below assorted shields **Rev:** Winged dragon with arms of Basel at lower left **Rev. Legend:** DOMINE CONSERVA NOS IN PACE

Date	Mintage	VG	F	VF	XF	Unc
1740	—	25.00	40.00	125	250	400

KM# 144 1/4 THALER

Silver **Rev:** Basilisk holding different shield

Date	Mintage	VG	F	VF	XF	Unc
1740 Rare	—	—	—	—	—	—

KM# 167 1/3 THALER

Silver **Obv:** Value within wreath, date below **Obv. Legend:** MONETA REIPUB • BASILEENSIS **Rev:** Winged dragon with arms of Basel at lower left **Rev. Legend:** DOMINE • CONSERVA • NOS • IN • PACE •

Date	Mintage	VG	F	VF	XF	Unc
1764	—	20.00	35.00	80.00	200	475
1766	—	20.00	35.00	80.00	200	475

KM# 125 1/2 THALER

Silver **Obv:** *BASILEA* not in banner **Rev:** Similar to KM#124 but plain field in inner circle

Date	Mintage	VG	F	VF	XF	Unc
ND Rare	—	—	—	—	—	—

KM# 90 1/2 THALER

Silver **Obv:** MONET: /NOVA/REIPVBL:/BASIL: within ornamentation **Rev:** Arms within round cartouche, legend around

Date	Mintage	VG	F	VF	XF	Unc
ND	—	160	320	550	1,000	—

KM# 91 1/2 THALER

Silver

Date	Mintage	VG	F	VF	XF	Unc
ND Rare	—	—	—	—	—	—

KM# 92 1/2 THALER

Silver **Obv:** Tall buildings at left, path going to right **Rev:** Cartouche not as ornate, shorter basilisks

Date	Mintage	VG	F	VF	XF	Unc
ND	—	60.00	120	200	400	—

KM# 93 1/2 THALER

Silver **Obv:** Path going to left, arms in cartouche above city view **Rev:** Small arms and cartouche

Date	Mintage	VG	F	VF	XF	Unc
1736	—	50.00	100	250	475	850

KM# 123 1/2 THALER

Silver

Date	Mintage	VG	F	VF	XF	Unc
ND	—	60.00	120	200	375	—

KM# 124 1/2 THALER

Silver

Date	Mintage	VG	F	VF	XF	Unc
ND	—	80.00	160	285	600	—

KM# 145 1/2 THALER

Silver **Note:** Similar to KM#147 but basilisk holding different shaped shield.

Date	Mintage	VG	F	VF	XF	Unc
1740 Rare	—	—	—	—	—	—
1741	—	120	225	400	625	—

KM# 147 1/2 THALER

Silver **Obv:** City view and date below assorted shields **Rev:** Winged dragon with arms of Basel at lower left **Rev. Legend:** DOMINE • CONSERVA • NOS • IN • PACE •

Date	Mintage	VG	F	VF	XF	Unc
1741	—	75.00	125	325	650	1,125

KM# 148 1/2 THALER

Silver **Obv:** City view and date below assorted shields **Rev:** Winged dragon with arms of Basel at lower left **Rev. Legend:** DOMINE CONSERVA NOS IN PACE

Date	Mintage	VG	F	VF	XF	Unc
1741	—	65.00	100	250	475	875

KM# 146 1/2 THALER

Silver **Rev:** Basilisk holding small oval shield left

Date	Mintage	VG	F	VF	XF	Unc
1741	—	40.00	65.00	165	325	550

KM# 159 1/2 THALER

Silver **Obv:** City view with date divided below **Rev:** Winged dragon with arms of Basel at lower left **Rev. Legend:** DOMINE • CONSERVA • NOS • IN • PACE

Date	Mintage	VG	F	VF	XF	Unc
1757	—	50.00	80.00	200	400	725

KM# 160 1/2 THALER

Silver **Rev:** Winged dragon with arms of Basel at lower left

Date	Mintage	VG	F	VF	XF	Unc
1757	—	75.00	125	325	650	1,125

KM# 168 1/2 THALER

Silver **Obv:** Value within wreath, date below **Obv. Legend:** MONETA • REIPUB • BASILEENSIS **Rev:** Winged dragon with arms of Basel at lower left **Rev. Legend:** DOMINE • CONSERVA • NOS • IN • PACE

Date	Mintage	VG	F	VF	XF	Unc
1765 H	—	40.00	65.00	165	275	475
1765	—	50.00	80.00	200	400	725

KM# 178 1/2 THALER

Silver **Obv:** City view, date within sprigs below assorted shields **Rev:** Winged dragon with arms of Basel at lower left **Rev. Legend:** DOMINE CONSERVA NOS IN PACE

Date	Mintage	VG	F	VF	XF	Unc
1785	—	40.00	65.00	165	275	475
1786	—	40.00	65.00	165	275	475

KM# 191 1/2 THALER

Silver **Obv:** Oval arms of Basel within sprigs **Obv. Legend:** RESPVBLICA ... **Rev:** Inscription within wreath **Rev. Inscription:** DOMINE/CONSERVA/NOS/IN PACE

Date	Mintage	VG	F	VF	XF	Unc
MDCCXCVII (1797)	—	75.00	125	325	650	1,125

KM# 119 THALER

Silver **Obv:** City view below banner **Rev:** Arms of Basel on breast of double-headed dragon within circle **Rev. Legend:** DOMINE CONSERVA NOS IN PACE **Note:** Cross-reference number Dav. #1745.

Date	Mintage	VG	F	VF	XF	Unc
ND	—	160	315	525	1,000	—

KM# 126 THALER

Silver **Obv:** City view **Rev:** Arms of Basel within cartouche **Rev. Legend:** DOMINE CONSERVA NOS IN PACE **Note:** Dav. #1746.

Date	Mintage	VG	F	VF	XF	Unc
ND	—	100	200	330	600	—

KM# 127 THALER

Silver **Obv:** City view below banner **Rev:** Arms of Basel with dragon supporters **Rev. Legend:** DOMINE • CONSERVA • NOS • IN • PACE **Note:** Dav. #1744.

Date	Mintage	VG	F	VF	XF	Unc
1738	—	160	315	525	1,000	—

KM# 128 THALER

Silver **Obv:** BASILEA above city view **Rev:** Winged dragon with arms of Basel at lower left **Rev. Legend:** DOMINE • CONSERVA • NOS • IN • PACE **Note:** Dav. #1747.

Date	Mintage	VG	F	VF	XF	Unc
1739	—	60.00	125	325	650	1,400

KM# 129 THALER

Silver **Obv:** BASILEA in cartouche above city view **Rev:** Winged dragon with arms of Basel in center of assorted shields at lower left **Rev. Legend:** DOMINE • CONSERVA • NOS • IN • PACE **Note:** Dav. #1743.

Date	Mintage	VG	F	VF	XF	Unc
1740	—	50.00	100	275	550	1,200

KM# 149 THALER

Silver **Obv:** Assorted shields and BASILEA within decorative banner above city view and date **Rev:** Winged dragon with arms of Basel at lower left **Rev. Legend:** DOMINE • CONSERVA • NOS • IN • PACE **Note:** Dav. #1750.

Date	Mintage	VG	F	VF	XF	Unc
1741	—	45.00	80.00	250	475	1,000

KM# 157 THALER

Silver **Obv:** BASILEA above city view **Rev:** Winged dragon with arms of Basel at lower left **Rev. Legend:** DOMINE • CONSERVA • NOS • IN • PACE **Note:** Dav. #1751.

Date	Mintage	VG	F	VF	XF	Unc
1756	—	80.00	125	325	650	1,400

KM# 158 THALER

Silver **Rev:** Winged dragon with arms of Basel at lower left **Rev. Legend:** DOMINE CONSERVA NOS IN PACE **Note:** Dav. #1752.

Date	Mintage	VG	F	VF	XF	Unc
1756 H	—	80.00	125	325	650	1,400

KM# 169 THALER

Silver **Obv:** Value within wreath, date below **Obv. Legend:** MONETA REIPUB • BASILEENSIS **Rev:** Winged dragon with arms of Basel at lower left **Rev. Legend:** DOMINE • CONSERVA • NOS • IN • PACE **Note:** Dav. #1754.

Date	Mintage	VG	F	VF	XF	Unc
1765 IH	—	50.00	80.00	250	475	1,000

KM# 179 THALER

Silver **Obv:** City view and date below assorted shields **Rev:** Winged dragon with arms of Basel at lower left **Rev. Legend:** DOMINE CONSERVA NOS IN PACE **Note:** Dav. #1755.

Date	Mintage	VG	F	VF	XF	Unc
1785 H	—	80.00	125	325	650	1,400

KM# 184 THALER

Silver **Obv:** City view above date within sprigs **Rev:** Winged dragon with arms of Basel at lower left **Rev. Legend:** DOMINE CONSERVA NOS IN PACE **Note:** Dav. #1756.

Date	Mintage	VG	F	VF	XF	Unc
1793 H	—	125	250	650	1,200	2,400

KM# 185 THALER

Silver **Obv:** City view above date within sprigs **Rev:** Winged dragon with arms of Basel at lower left **Rev. Legend:** DOMINE CONSERVA NOS IN PACE **Note:** Dav. #1757.

Date	Mintage	VG	F	VF	XF	Unc
1793	—	75.00	125	325	650	1,400

KM# 186 THALER

Silver **Obv:** Oval arms of Basel on mantle, with garland **Obv. Legend:** RESPVBLICA BASILEENSIS **Rev:** Inscription within thin wreath **Rev. Inscription:** DOMINE/CONSERVA NOS/ IN PACE **Note:** Dav. #1758.

Date	Mintage	VG	F	VF	XF	Unc
1795	—	75.00	125	325	650	1,400
1796	—	150	250	650	1,200	2,400

KM# 71 2 THALER

Silver **Obv:** BASILEA in banner above city view **Rev:** Arms of Basel in center circle of assorted shields, legend around arms **Note:** Dav. #1741.

Date	Mintage	VG	F	VF	XF	Unc
ND	—	500	990	1,650	4,550	—

KM# 72 2 THALER

Silver **Obv:** Arms of Basel in center circle of assorted shields **Obv. Legend:** MONETA NOVA VRBIS BASILEENSIS **Rev:** Double-headed eagle within circle **Rev. Legend:** DOMINE CONSERVA NOS IN PACE **Note:** Dav. #1740.

Date	Mintage	VG	F	VF	XF	Unc
ND	—	550	1,100	1,825	2,650	—

KM# 130 2 THALER

Silver **Obv:** City view with seven ships in harbor within beaded circle **Obv. Legend:** DOMINE • CONSERVA • NOS • IN • PACE **Rev:** Winged dragon with arms of Basel at lower left within center circle of assorted shields **Note:** Dav. #1742A.

Date	Mintage	VG	F	VF	XF	Unc
ND 1DB	—	500	990	1,650	3,000	—

KM# 150 2 THALER

Silver **Obv:** Assorted shields and BASILEA in decorative banner above city view, date **Rev:** Winged dragon with arms of Basel at lower left **Rev. Legend:** DOMINE • CONSERVA • NOS • IN • PACE **Note:** Dav. #1749.

Date	Mintage	VG	F	VF	XF	Unc
1741	—	225	325	800	1,600	2,800

KM# 187 DUPLONE

7.6400 g., 0.9000 Gold 0.2211 oz. AGW **Obv:** Oval arms of Basel, with hat and sprigs **Obv. Legend:** BASILEENSIS • RESPVBLICA **Rev:** Inscription within wreath **Rev. Inscription:** DOMINE/CONSERVA/NOS/IN PACE

Date	Mintage	VG	F	VF	XF	Unc
1795	—	500	900	2,200	4,000	—

KM# 188 DUPLONE

7.6400 g., 0.9000 Gold 0.2211 oz. AGW **Obv:** Oval arms of Basel with hat and garland **Obv. Legend:** BASILEENSIS • RESPVBLICA **Rev:** Upright design with sprig above date **Rev. Legend:** DOMINE CONSERVA NOS ON PACE

Date	Mintage	VG	F	VF	XF	Unc
1795	—	750	1,200	2,400	4,000	6,000
1796	—	1,200	2,000	4,000	6,500	9,500

TRADE COINAGE

KM# 155 GOLDGULDEN

7.6400 g., 0.9000 Gold 0.2211 oz. AGW **Obv:** Ornate, oval arms of Basel within circle **Obv. Legend:** BASILEENSIS MON NOVA ... **Rev:** Flower-like design within circle **Rev. Legend:** DOMINE • CONSERVA • NOS • IN • PACE •

Date	Mintage	VG	F	VF	XF	Unc
ND(1750)	—	450	600	1,200	2,000	3,250

KM# 181 GOLDGULDEN

7.6400 g., 0.9000 Gold 0.2211 oz. AGW **Obv:** Hat on pole within sprigs **Obv. Legend:** REIPVB • BASIL • FLORENVS • AVREVS • **Rev:** Ornate oval arms of Basel **Rev. Legend:** DOMINE CONSERVA NOS IN PACE

Date	Mintage	VG	F	VF	XF	Unc
ND(1790)	—	350	600	1,000	1,500	2,500

KM# 182 GOLDGULDEN

7.6400 g., 0.9000 Gold 0.2211 oz. AGW **Obv:** Hat on pole within sprigs **Obv. Legend:** RESPVB BASIL FLORENVS AVREVS **Rev:** Oval arms of Basel **Rev. Legend:** DOMINE CONSERVA NOS IN PACE

Date	Mintage	VG	F	VF	XF	Unc
ND(1790)	—	250	400	800	1,400	3,000

KM# 137 2 GOLDGULDEN

15.2800 g., 0.9000 Gold 0.4421 oz. AGW **Obv:** Ornate, oval arms of Basel within circle **Obv. Legend:** BASILEENSIS MON • NOVA • ... **Rev:** Flower-like design within circle **Rev. Legend:** DOMINE • CONSERVA • NOS • IN • PACE

Date	Mintage	VG	F	VF	XF	Unc
ND(ca.1720)	—	1,200	2,000	4,000	6,500	9,500

KM# 183 2 GOLDGULDEN

15.2800 g., 0.9000 Gold 0.4421 oz. AGW **Obv:** Hat on pole within sprigs **Obv. Legend:** REIP • BASIL • FLOREN • AVR • ... **Rev:** Ornate, oval arms of Basel **Rev. Legend:** DOMINE CONSERVA NOS IN PACE

Date	Mintage	VG	F	VF	XF	Unc
ND(1790)	—	900	1,400	2,800	4,750	9,000

KM# 156 1/4 DUCAT

0.8750 g., 0.9860 Gold 0.0277 oz. AGW **Obv:** Winged dragon with arms of Basel at lower left **Rev:** Value, state name

Date	Mintage	VG	F	VF	XF	Unc
ND(1750)	—	250	550	800	1,400	—

KM# 156.1 1/4 DUCAT

0.8750 g., 0.9860 Gold 0.0277 oz. AGW **Obv:** Basilisk wings outspread with large upright shield with value

Date	Mintage	VG	F	VF	XF	Unc
ND(1750)	—	—	—	—	—	—

KM# 156.2 1/4 DUCAT

0.8750 g., 0.9860 Gold 0.0277 oz. AGW **Obv:** Basilisk wings outspread with small slanted shield with value

Date	Mintage	VG	F	VF	XF	Unc
ND(1750)	—	—	—	—	—	—

KM# 171 1/4 DUCAT

0.8750 g., 0.9860 Gold 0.0277 oz. AGW **Obv:** Winged dragon with arms of Basel at lower left **Rev:** Value

Date	Mintage	VG	F	VF	XF	Unc
ND(1770) H	—	350	700	1,000	1,500	—

KM# 175 1/4 DUCAT

0.8750 g., 0.9860 Gold 0.0277 oz. AGW **Obv:** Winged dragon with arms of Basel at lower left

Date	Mintage	VG	F	VF	XF	Unc
ND(1780) S	—	600	1,150	2,150	3,500	—

KM# 172 1/2 DUCAT

1.7500 g., 0.9860 Gold 0.0555 oz. AGW **Obv:** Winged dragon with arms of Basel at lower left **Rev:** Value, state name within wreath

Date	Mintage	VG	F	VF	XF	Unc
ND(1770) H	—	600	1,400	2,000	2,500	—

KM# 176 1/2 DUCAT

1.7500 g., 0.9860 Gold 0.0555 oz. AGW **Obv:** Winged dragon with arms of Basel at lower left **Rev:** Value, state name within flower design

Date	Mintage	VG	F	VF	XF	Unc
ND(1780) S	—	800	1,800	3,000	4,000	—

KM# A152 2/3 DUCAT

2.3200 g., Gold, 22 mm. **Obv:** BASILEA on ribbon below city view **Rev:** Basilisk with shield, 8 small shields below **Rev. Legend:** DOMINE CONSERVA NOS IN PACE

Date	Mintage	VG	F	VF	XF	Unc
1743	—	—	—	—	5,000	6,500

KM# 151 DUCAT

3.5000 g., 0.9860 Gold 0.1109 oz. AGW **Obv:** City of Basel **Rev:** Basilisk holding shield of arms, eight shields in exergue

Date	Mintage	VG	F	VF	XF	Unc
1743	—	1,000	1,600	3,200	5,500	8,000

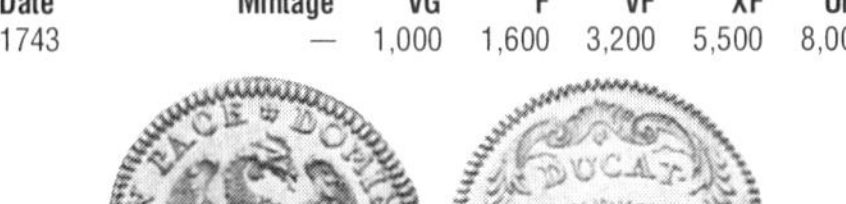

KM# 173 DUCAT

3.5000 g., 0.9860 Gold 0.1109 oz. AGW **Obv:** Winged dragon with arms of Basel at lower left **Obv. Legend:** DOMINE CONSERVA NOS IN PACE **Rev:** Value, inscription within cartouche **Rev. Inscription:** DUCAT/REIPUBL/BASILEEN/SIS

Date	Mintage	VG	F	VF	XF	Unc
ND(1775)	—	300	500	950	1,800	2,500

KM# 177 DUCAT

3.5000 g., 0.9860 Gold 0.1109 oz. AGW **Obv:** Winged dragon with arms of Basel at lower left **Obv. Legend:** DOMINE CONSERVA NOS IN PACE **Rev:** Value, inscription within cartouche **Rev. Inscription:** DUCAT/ REIPUBL/BASILEEN/SIS

Date	Mintage	VG	F	VF	XF	Unc
ND(1780)	—	350	1,000	1,500	2,200	3,000

KM# 134 2 DUCAT

3.5000 g., 0.9860 Gold 0.1109 oz. AGW, 26 mm. **Obv:** Basilisk right holding shield with arms **Rev:** Inscription: MONETA/NOVA..., without oval at bottom of cartouche

Date	Mintage	VG	F	VF	XF	Unc
ND	—	1,350	2,750	5,000	8,500	—

KM# 152 2 DUCAT

3.5000 g., 0.9860 Gold 0.1109 oz. AGW **Obv:** City of Basel **Rev:** Basilisk holding shield of arms, eight shields in exergue

Date	Mintage	VG	F	VF	XF	Unc
1743	—	1,500	2,400	4,750	8,000	12,000

KM# 189 2 DUCAT

3.5000 g., 0.9860 Gold 0.1109 oz. AGW **Obv:** Hat on pole within sprigs above inscription within mantle **Obv. Inscription:** DUCATOS/DUPLEX/BASIL **Rev:** Winged dragon with arms of Basel at lower left

Date	Mintage	VG	F	VF	XF	Unc
ND(1795)	—	600	1,000	2,200	3,500	—

KM# 190 2 DUCAT

3.5000 g., 0.9860 Gold 0.1109 oz. AGW **Obv:** Oval arms of Basel with hat and garland **Obv. Legend:** BASILEENSIS RESPVBLICA **Rev:** Value within thin wreath **Rev. Legend:** DOMINE CONSERVA NOS IN PACE

Date	Mintage	VG	F	VF	XF	Unc
1795 Rare	—	—	—	—	—	—

PATTERNS

Including off metal strikes

KM#	Date	Mintage	Identification	Mkt Val
Pn2	1718	—	20 Schilling. Silver. Arms and eagle	—
Pn7	1740	—	2 Thaler. Silver.	—
Pn8	1740	—	3 Ducat. 0.9860 Gold. 10.5000 g. Eight shields above BASILEA over city view. Basilisk holding shield. Struck with 1/4 Thaler dies, KM#144.	—
Pn9	1740	—	4 Ducat. 0.9870 Gold. 14.0000 g. Eight shields above BASiLEA over city view. Basilik holding shield. Struck with 1/4 Thaler dies, KM#143.	—
Pn10	1740	—	4 Ducat. 0.9870 Gold. 14.0000 g. Basilik holding different shield. Struck with 1/4 Thaler dies, KM#144.	—
Pn11	1740	—	5 Ducat. 0.9860 Gold. 17.5000 g. Eight shields above BASILEA over city view. Basilisk holding small oval shield. Struck with 1/4 Thaler dies, KM#144.	—
Pn18	1741	—	5 Ducat. 0.9860 Gold. 17.5000 g. Similar to KM#D146. Struck with 1/4 Thaler dies, KM#144.	—
Pn19	1741	—	6 Ducat. 0.9860 Gold. 20.5000 g. Eight shields above BASILEA over city view. Basilisk holding shield. Struck with 1/2 Thaler dies, KM#145.	—
Pn20	1741	—	8 Ducat. 0.9860 Gold. 28.0000 g. Eight shields above BASILEA over city view. Basilisk holding shield. Struck with 1/2 Thaler dies, KM#146.	—
Pn21	1741	—	8 Ducat. 0.9860 Gold. 28.0000 g. Basilisk holding different shield. Struck with 1/2 Thaler dies, KM#147.	—
Pn22	1741	—	10 Ducat. 0.9860 Gold. 35.0000 g. Eight shields above BASILEA in cartouche over city view. Basilisk holding oval shield. Struck with 1 Thaler dies, KM#149.	—
Pn23	1741	—	12 Ducat. 0.9860 Gold. 42.0000 g. Eight shields above BASILEA in cartouche over city view. Basilisk holding oval shield. Struck with 1 Thaler dies, KM#149.	—
Pn24	1741	—	20 Ducat. 0.9860 Gold. 70.0000 g. Similar to KM#G151. Struck with 2 Thaler dies, KM#150.	—
Pn25	1741	—	20 Ducat. 0.9860 Gold. 70.0000 g. Eight shields above BASILEA in cartouche over city view. Basilisk holding oval shield. Struck with 1 Thaler dies, KM#149.	—
Pn26	1741	—	25 Ducat. 0.9860 Gold. 87.5000 g. Eight shields above BASILEA in cartouche over city view. Basilisk holding oval shield. Struck with 2 Thaler dies, KM#150.	—

KM#	Date	Mintage	Identification	Mkt Val
Pn28	1762	—	2 Thaler. Silver.	—
Pn29	1764	—	1/6 Thaler. Silver.	—

PIEFORTS

KM#	Date	Mintage	Identification	Mkt Val
P1	1718	—	Rappen. Silver. KM#33	—
P2	1727	—	Kreuzer. Silver. KM#38	—

BERN

A city and canton in west central Switzerland. It was founded as a military post in 1191 and became an imperial city with the mint right in 1218. It was admitted to the Swiss Confederation as a canton in 1353.

MINT OFFICIALS' INITIALS

Initials	Date	Name
D-B	1703-19	J. De Beyer
MK	1750	?

MONETARY SYSTEM

Until 1798

8 Vierer = 4 Kreuzer = 1 Batzen

40 Batzen = 1 Thaler

CITY

STANDARD COINAGE

KM# 75 1/2 KREUZER

Billon **Obv:** Round arms **Rev:** Anchor cross in circle

Date	Mintage	VG	F	VF	XF	Unc
1707	—	5.00	8.00	32.00	80.00	160
1731	—	5.00	8.00	24.00	60.00	120
1732	—	5.00	8.00	24.00	60.00	120

KM# 98 1/2 KREUZER

Billon **Obv:** Arms in cartouche **Rev:** Cross in cartouche

Date	Mintage	VG	F	VF	XF	Unc
1731	—	5.00	8.00	24.00	60.00	120
1732	—	5.00	8.00	24.00	60.00	120

KM# 99 1/2 KREUZER

Billon **Obv:** Rounder cartouche **Rev:** Rounder cartouche

Date	Mintage	VG	F	VF	XF	Unc
1732	—	5.00	8.00	24.00	60.00	120

KM# 122 1/2 KREUZER (Vierer)
Billon **Obv:** Round arms of Bern **Obv. Legend:** MONETA BERNESIS **Rev:** Floreated cross, leaves in angles, all within circle **Rev. Legend:** DOMINUS PROVIDEBIT

Date	Mintage	VG	F	VF	XF	Unc
1762	—	5.00	8.00	24.00	60.00	120
1763	—	10.00	16.00	50.00	120	275
1764 1 known	—	—	—	—	—	—
1765	—	5.00	8.00	24.00	60.00	120
1766	—	20.00	40.00	120	250	475
1769	—	5.00	8.00	24.00	60.00	120
1771	—	5.00	8.00	24.00	60.00	120
1774	—	5.00	8.00	24.00	60.00	120
1775	—	5.00	8.00	24.00	60.00	120
1777	—	5.00	8.00	24.00	60.00	120
1778	—	5.00	8.00	24.00	60.00	120
1780	—	5.00	8.00	24.00	60.00	120
1781	—	5.00	8.00	24.00	60.00	120
1785	—	5.00	8.00	25.00	60.00	120
1786	—	5.00	8.00	25.00	60.00	120
1788	—	5.00	8.00	25.00	60.00	120
1789	—	5.00	8.00	25.00	60.00	120
1790	—	7.00	12.00	40.00	100	200
1792	—	12.50	25.00	75.00	200	400
1794	—	5.00	8.00	20.00	50.00	100
1796	—	5.00	8.00	20.00	50.00	100
1797	—	5.00	8.00	20.00	50.00	100

KM# 90 KREUZER
Billon **Obv:** Arms of Bern within circle **Rev:** Floreated cross, leaves in angles, all within circle

Date	Mintage	VG	F	VF	XF	Unc
1718	—	5.00	8.00	16.00	40.00	100

KM# 115 KREUZER
Billon **Obv:** Arms of Bern within circle **Obv. Legend:** BERNENS • MONETA • REIPUB • **Rev:** Floreated cross within circle **Rev. Legend:** DOMINUS PROVIDEBIT

Date	Mintage	VG	F	VF	XF	Unc
1755	—	5.00	8.00	16.00	40.00	100
1765	—	5.00	8.00	16.00	40.00	100
1772	—	5.00	8.00	16.00	40.00	100
1774	—	5.00	8.00	16.00	40.00	100
1775	—	5.00	8.00	16.00	40.00	100
1776	—	5.00	8.00	16.00	40.00	100
1777	—	5.00	8.00	16.00	40.00	100
1779	—	5.00	8.00	16.00	40.00	100
1781	—	5.00	8.00	20.00	80.00	150
1785	—	5.00	8.00	20.00	80.00	150
1789	—	5.00	8.00	20.00	80.00	150
1792	—	5.00	8.00	15.00	32.00	80.00
1793	—	5.00	8.00	15.00	32.00	80.00
1796	—	20.00	30.00	125	300	600
1797	—	3.00	5.00	8.00	25.00	60.00

KM# 124 2 KREUZER
Billon **Obv:** Round arms of Bern within beaded circle **Obv. Legend:** BERNENSIS MONETA REIPUBLICÆ **Rev:** Value within center circle of floreated cross within beaded circle **Rev. Legend:** DOMINUS PROVIDEBIT

Date	Mintage	VG	F	VF	XF	Unc
1770	—	35.00	60.00	150	400	—

KM# 87 4 KREUZER (1 Batzen)
Billon **Obv:** Arms of Bern within circle on mantle, value below **Obv. Legend:** BERNENSIS • MONETA • REIPUB • **Rev:** Floreated cross within circle, date below **Rev. Legend:** DOMINUS PROVIDEBIT

Date	Mintage	VG	F	VF	XF	Unc
1717	—	10.00	16.00	50.00	120	240
1754	—	5.00	8.00	24.00	60.00	150
1765	—	5.00	8.00	24.00	60.00	150
1766	—	30.00	60.00	150	400	—
1770	—	5.00	8.00	16.00	50.00	145
1772	—	5.00	8.00	16.00	50.00	145
1774	—	12.00	24.00	80.00	200	400
1775	—	5.00	8.00	16.00	40.00	120
1776	—	5.00	8.00	16.00	40.00	120
1778	—	5.00	8.00	16.00	40.00	120
1784	—	5.00	8.00	16.00	40.00	120
1789	—	5.00	8.00	16.00	40.00	120
1793	—	5.00	8.00	16.00	40.00	120
1794	—	5.00	8.00	16.00	40.00	120
1795	—	5.00	8.00	16.00	40.00	120
1797	—	5.00	8.00	16.00	40.00	120
1798	—	3.00	5.00	8.00	20.00	80.00

KM# 83 10 KREUZER
Silver **Obv:** Value below arms **Rev:** Interwined B within palm branches

Date	Mintage	VG	F	VF	XF	Unc
1715	—	350	625	1,600	—	—

KM# 85 10 KREUZER
Silver **Rev:** Crowned B within palm branches

Date	Mintage	VG	F	VF	XF	Unc
1716	—	14.00	25.00	60.00	140	275
1717	—	14.00	25.00	60.00	140	275

KM# 116 10 KREUZER
Silver **Obv:** Crowned, ornate arms of Bern **Obv. Legend:** BERNENSIS MONETAREIPUB **Rev:** Value, date within cartouche **Rev. Legend:** DOMINUS • PROVIDEBIT •

Date	Mintage	VG	F	VF	XF	Unc
1755	—	7.00	12.00	40.00	120	240
1756	—	7.00	12.00	40.00	120	240

KM# 120 10 KREUZER
Silver **Obv:** Crowned, oval arms of Bern within sprigs **Obv. Legend:** BERNENS • MONETA • REIPUB • **Rev:** Crowned monogram in cruciform **Rev. Legend:** DOMI NUS PROVI DEBIT

Date	Mintage	VG	F	VF	XF	Unc
1759	—	5.00	8.00	30.00	80.00	175
1764	—	5.00	8.00	30.00	80.00	175
1765	—	5.00	8.00	30.00	80.00	175
1776	—	5.00	8.00	30.00	80.00	175
1777	—	5.00	8.00	30.00	80.00	175
1778	—	5.00	8.00	30.00	80.00	175
1787	—	5.00	8.00	30.00	80.00	175
1790	—	5.00	8.00	20.00	60.00	120

KM# 158 10 KREUZER
Silver **Obv:** Crowned, oval arms of Bern, date below **Obv. Legend:** BERNENSIS • RESPUBLICA **Rev:** Crowned monogram in cruciform **Rev. Legend:** DOMI NUS PROVI DEBIT

Date	Mintage	VG	F	VF	XF	Unc
1797	—	5.00	8.00	20.00	60.00	120

KM# 86 20 KREUZER
Silver **Obv:** Value below arms **Rev:** Crowned B in palm branches, date below

Date	Mintage	VG	F	VF	XF	Unc
1716	—	20.00	40.00	80.00	160	360
1717	—	20.00	40.00	80.00	160	360

KM# 117 20 KREUZER
Silver **Obv:** Crowned arms of Bern within sprigs **Obv. Legend:** BERNENSIS • MONETA • REIPUB • **Rev:** Value, date within cartouche **Rev. Legend:** DOMINUS • PROVIDEBIT •

Date	Mintage	VG	F	VF	XF	Unc
1755	—	12.00	20.00	60.00	160	325
1756	—	12.00	20.00	60.00	160	325

KM# 119 20 KREUZER
Silver **Obv:** Crowned, oval arms of Bern within sprigs **Obv. Legend:** BERNENS • MONETA • REIPUB • **Rev:** Crowned monogram in cruciform **Rev. Legend:** DOMI NUS PROVI DEBIT

Date	Mintage	VG	F	VF	XF	Unc
1758	—	8.00	16.00	50.00	125	240
1759	—	8.00	16.00	50.00	125	240
1764	—	8.00	16.00	50.00	125	240
1776	—	20.00	40.00	80.00	160	325
1777	—	20.00	40.00	80.00	160	325
1787	—	8.00	16.00	50.00	125	240

KM# 159 20 KREUZER
Silver **Obv:** Crowned, oval arms of Bern, date below **Obv. Legend:** BERNENSIS RESPUBLICA **Rev:** Crowned monogram in cruciform **Rev. Legend:** DOMI NUS PROVI DEBIT

Date	Mintage	VG	F	VF	XF	Unc
1797	—	8.00	12.00	40.00	80.00	200
1798	—	8.00	12.00	40.00	80.00	200

KM# 91 1/2 BATZEN
Billon **Obv:** Arms of Bern within circle **Obv. Legend:** BERNENSIS MONETA REIPUBLICÆ **Rev:** Floreated cross with leaves in angles within circle **Rev. Legend:** DOMINUS PROVIDEBIT

Date	Mintage	VG	F	VF	XF	Unc
1718	—	7.00	12.00	24.00	75.00	150
1719	—	7.00	12.00	24.00	75.00	150
1720	—	7.00	12.00	24.00	75.00	150
1721	—	10.00	16.00	50.00	150	300
1753	—	5.00	8.00	20.00	60.00	140
1754	—	5.00	8.50	20.00	60.00	140
1755	—	5.00	8.50	20.00	60.00	140
1770	—	7.00	10.00	24.00	75.00	160
1771	—	5.00	8.50	20.00	60.00	140
1772	—	20.00	35.00	100	250	500
1774	—	5.00	8.50	16.00	50.00	140
1775	—	5.00	8.00	16.00	50.00	140
1776	—	5.00	8.00	16.00	50.00	140
1777	—	20.00	40.00	100	250	500
1778	—	5.00	8.00	16.00	40.00	120
1784 Rare	—	—	—	—	—	—
1785	—	5.00	8.00	16.00	40.00	120
1788	—	5.00	8.00	16.00	40.00	120
1794	—	5.00	8.00	16.00	40.00	120
1796	—	5.00	8.00	16.00	40.00	120
1798	—	3.00	5.00	8.00	20.00	75.00

KM# 118 1/4 THALER
Silver **Obv:** Crowned, round arms of Bern within sprigs **Obv. Legend:** BERNENSIS • MONETA • REIPUB • **Rev:** Crowned monogram in cruciform **Rev. Legend:** DOMI NUS PROVI DEBIT

Date	Mintage	VG	F	VF	XF	Unc
1757	—	25.00	40.00	120	200	400
1758	—	25.00	40.00	120	200	400
1759	—	25.00	40.00	120	200	400
1760	—	25.00	40.00	120	200	400
1773	—	25.00	40.00	120	200	400
1774	—	25.00	40.00	120	200	400

KM# 160 1/4 THALER

Silver **Obv:** Crowned, round arms of Bern with garland, date below **Obv. Legend:** BERNENSIS RESPUBLICA **Rev:** Crowned monogram in cruciform **Rev. Legend:** DOMI NUS PROVI DEBIT

Date	Mintage	VG	F	VF	XF	Unc
1797 Large date	—	15.00	24.00	60.00	125	200
1797 Small date	—	15.00	24.00	60.00	125	200

KM# 151 1/2 THALER

Silver **Obv:** Crowned, spade arms of Bern **Obv. Legend:** BERNENSIS RESPUBLICA **Rev:** Swiss standing with long sword on mantle, date below **Rev. Legend:** DOMINUS PROVIDEBIT

Date	Mintage	VG	F	VF	XF	Unc
1796	—	20.00	32.00	100	200	325
1797	—	20.00	32.00	100	200	325

KM# 161 1/2 THALER

Silver **Obv:** Crowned, spade arms of Bern **Obv. Legend:** BERNENSIS RESPUBLICA **Rev:** Swiss standing with long sword on mantle, date below **Rev. Legend:** DOMINUS PROVIDEBIT

Date	Mintage	VG	F	VF	XF	Unc
1797	—	25.00	40.00	125	250	400
1798	—	700	1,400	3,500	7,000	—

KM# 149 THALER

Silver **Obv:** Crowned, spade arms of Bern **Obv. Legend:** BERNENSIS RESPUBLICA **Rev:** Standing Swiss with long sword with two feathers in hat, date below **Rev. Legend:** DOMINUS PROVIDEBIT **Note:** Dav. #1759.

Date	Mintage	VG	F	VF	XF	Unc
1795	—	50.00	80.00	200	400	950
1796	—	50.00	80.00	240	400	950
1797 Rare	—	2,000	3,500	6,500	10,000	—

KM# 150 THALER

Silver **Obv:** Crowned, spade arms of Bern within oval frame **Obv. Legend:** BERNENSIS RESPUBLICA **Rev:** Standing Swiss with long sword with one feather in hat, date below **Rev. Legend:** DOMINUS PROVIDEBIT **Note:** Dav. #1760.

Date	Mintage	VG	F	VF	XF	Unc
1795	—	75.00	125	250	500	1,125

KM# 164 THALER

Silver **Obv:** Crowned, spade arms of Bern within wide oval frame **Obv. Legend:** BERNENSIS RESPUBLICA **Rev:** Standing Swiss with long sword, date below within wide oval frame **Rev. Legend:** DOMINUS PROVIDEBIT **Note:** Dav#1760A.

Date	Mintage	VG	F	VF	XF	Unc
1798	—	35.00	60.00	150	325	600

KM# 165 THALER

Silver **Obv:** Crowned, spade arms of Bern within oval frame **Obv. Legend:** BERNENSIS RESPUBLICA **Rev:** Standing Swiss with long sword, date below within oval frame **Rev. Legend:** DOMINUS PROVIDEBIT **Note:** Dav#1760B.

Date	Mintage	VG	F	VF	XF	Unc
1798	—	50.00	80.00	250	400	725

KM# 162 1/2 DUPLONE

3.8200 g., 0.9000 Gold 0.1105 oz. AGW **Obv:** Crowned, spade arms of Bern within sprigs **Obv. Legend:** BERNENSIS RESPUBLICA **Rev:** Standing Swiss with fasces, date below **Rev. Legend:** DEUS PROVIDEBIT

Date	Mintage	F	VF	XF	Unc	BU
1797	—	350	900	1,500	2,000	—

KM# 142 DUPLONE

7.6400 g., 0.9000 Gold 0.2211 oz. AGW **Obv:** Crowned, spade arms of Bern within sprigs **Obv. Legend:** BERNENSIS RESPUBLICA **Rev:** Standing Swiss with fasces, date below **Rev. Legend:** DEVS PROVIDEBIT

Date	Mintage	F	VF	XF	Unc	BU
1793	—	450	950	1,600	2,200	2,800

KM# A143 DUPLONE

7.6400 g., 0.9000 Gold 0.2211 oz. AGW **Obv:** Crowned, oval arms of Bern with garland **Obv. Legend:** BERNENSIS RESPUBLICA **Rev:** Inscription, date within wreath, standing knight **Rev. Inscription:** DEUS/PROVIDEBIT/1793

Date	Mintage	F	VF	XF	Unc	BU
1793	—	—	1,500	3,250	5,500	8,000

KM# 143 DUPLONE

7.6400 g., 0.9000 Gold 0.2211 oz. AGW **Obv:** Crowned, round arms of Bern with garland **Obv. Legend:** BERNENSIS RESPUBLICA **Rev:** Inscription, date within wreath **Rev. Inscription:** DEUS/PROVIDEBIT/ 1793

Date	Mintage	F	VF	XF	Unc	BU
1793.	—	200	400	725	1,200	1,800

KM# 146 DUPLONE

7.6400 g., 0.9000 Gold 0.2211 oz. AGW **Obv:** Crowned, round arms of Bern, with garland **Obv. Legend:** BERNENSIS RESPUBLICA **Rev:** Inscription, date within wreath **Rev. Inscription:** DEUS/PROVIDEBIT/1794

Date	Mintage	F	VF	XF	Unc	BU
1794.	—	250	475	800	1,400	2,000
1795	—	250	475	800	1,400	2,000

KM# 152 DUPLONE

7.6400 g., 0.9000 Gold 0.2211 oz. AGW **Obv:** Crowned, oval arms of Bern, with garland **Obv. Legend:** BERNENSIS RESPUBLICA **Rev:** Inscription, date within wreath **Rev. Inscription:** DEUS/ PROVIDEBIT/ 1796

Date	Mintage	F	VF	XF	Unc	BU
1796.	—	250	475	800	1,400	2,000

KM# 163 DUPLONE

7.6400 g., 0.9000 Gold 0.2211 oz. AGW **Obv:** Crowned, spade arms of Bern within sprigs **Obv. Legend:** BERNENSIS RESPUBLICA **Rev:** Standing Swiss with fasces above date **Rev. Legend:** DEUS PROVIDEBIT

Date	Mintage	F	VF	XF	Unc	BU
1797	—	350	725	1,200	1,800	2,400

KM# 144.1 2 DUPLONE

15.2800 g., 0.9000 Gold 0.4421 oz. AGW **Obv:** Crowned, oval arms of Bern, with garland **Obv. Legend:** BERNENSIS RESPUBLICA **Rev:** Inscription, date within wreath **Rev. Inscription:** DEUS/PROVIDEBIT

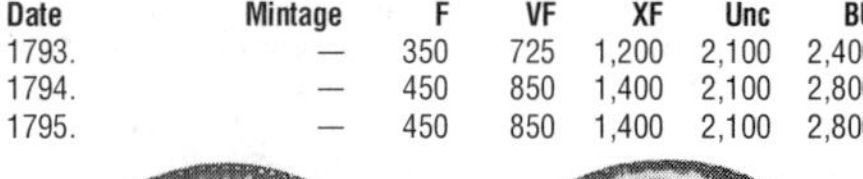

Date	Mintage	F	VF	XF	Unc	BU
1793.	—	350	725	1,200	2,100	2,400
1794.	—	450	850	1,400	2,100	2,800
1795.	—	450	850	1,400	2,100	2,800

KM# 147 2 DUPLONE

15.2800 g., 0.9000 Gold 0.4421 oz. AGW **Obv:** Crowned, spade arms of Bern within sprigs **Obv. Legend:** BERNENSIS RESPUBLICA **Rev:** Standing Swiss with fasces above date **Rev. Legend:** DEUS PROVIDEBIT

Date	Mintage	F	VF	XF	Unc	BU
1794	—	500	950	2,400	3,200	—
1796.	—	500	950	2,400	3,200	—
1797	—	500	950	2,400	3,200	—
1798	—	700	1,400	3,200	4,000	—

KM# 153 2 DUPLONE

15.2800 g., 0.9000 Gold 0.4421 oz. AGW **Obv:** Crowned, oval arms of Bern, with garland **Obv. Legend:** BERNENSIS RESPUBLICA **Rev:** Inscription, date within wreath **Rev. Inscription:** DEUS/PROVIDEBIT

Date	Mintage	F	VF	XF	Unc	BU
1796	—	350	725	1,200	2,300	2,400

KM# 144.2 2 DUPLONE

15.2800 g., 0.9000 Gold 0.4421 oz. AGW **Obv:** Crowned arms, large legend **Rev. Inscription:** DEUS/PROVIDEBIT

Date	Mintage	F	VF	XF	Unc	BU
1796	—	350	725	1,200	1,800	2,400

TRADE COINAGE

KM# 82 1/2 DUCAT

1.7500 g., 0.9860 Gold 0.0555 oz. AGW **Obv:** Crowned, oval arms of Bern within cartouche **Obv. Legend:** BENEDICTUS • SIT • IEHOVA • DEUS **Rev:** Inscription, date within cartouche **Rev. Inscription:** BENEDICT./SIT/IEHOVA DEUS/1/2 DUCAT/date

Date	Mintage	F	VF	XF	Unc	BU
1714	—	350	700	1,200	1,800	2,400

KM# 84 1/2 DUCAT

1.7500 g., 0.9860 Gold 0.0555 oz. AGW **Rev:** Inscription, date within cartouche **Rev. Inscription:** MONETA/REIPUBLICAE/BERNENSIS/1/2 DUCAT/date

Date	Mintage	F	VF	XF	Unc	BU
1715 Rare	—	—	—	—	—	—

KM# 88 1/2 DUCAT

1.7500 g., 0.9860 Gold 0.0555 oz. AGW **Obv:** Crowned, oval arms of Bern within ornate cartouche **Obv. Legend:** BERNENSIS MONETA REIP UB **Rev:** Inscription, value, date within cartouche **Rev. Inscription:** MONETA/REIPUBLICÆ/BERNENSIS

Date	Mintage	F	VF	XF	Unc	BU
1717	—	350	725	1,200	1,800	2,400

KM# 89 1/2 DUCAT

1.7500 g., 0.9860 Gold 0.0555 oz. AGW **Obv:** Crowned arms of Bern **Rev:** Inscription, value, date within cartouche

Date	Mintage	F	VF	XF	Unc	BU
1718 Rare	—	—	—	—	—	—

KM# 93 1/2 DUCAT

1.7500 g., 0.9860 Gold 0.0555 oz. AGW **Obv:** Oval arms in cartouche

Date	Mintage	F	VF	XF	Unc	BU
1719	—	200	400	725	1,150	1,600

KM# 92 1/2 DUCAT

1.7500 g., 0.9860 Gold 0.0555 oz. AGW **Obv:** Arms of Bern within circle **Obv. Legend:** BERNENS • MONETA • REISB • **Rev:** Inscription, value and date within cartouche **Rev. Inscription:** BENEDICTUS/SIT IEHOVA/DEUS **Note:** Varieties exist.

Date	Mintage	F	VF	XF	Unc	BU
1719	—	450	850	1,400	2,000	2,800

KM# 62 DUCAT

3.5000 g., 0.9860 Gold 0.1109 oz. AGW **Obv:** Crowned, ornate oval arms of Bern **Obv. Legend:** BENEDICTUS • SIT • IEHOVA • DEUS • **Rev:** Inscription, value and date within partial frame flanked by 1/2 figures above **Rev. Inscription:** REIPUBLICA/BERNENSIS/DUCAT **Note:** Fr. #139.

Date	Mintage	F	VF	XF	Unc	BU
1697	—	500	1,000	1,800	3,000	—
1718	—	600	1,250	2,000	3,000	4,000

KM# 95 DUCAT

3.5000 g., 0.9860 Gold 0.1109 oz. AGW **Obv:** Crowned, ornate arms of Bern **Obv. Legend:** BERNENSIS • MON • AUR • REIPU • **Rev:** Inscription above value within cartouche **Rev. Inscription:** BENE:/DICTUS/SIT•IEHOVA/DEUS.

Date	Mintage	F	VF	XF	Unc	BU
1725	—	600	1,250	2,000	3,000	4,000

KM# 103 DUCAT

3.5000 g., 0.9860 Gold 0.1109 oz. AGW **Obv:** Crowned, ornate arms of Bern **Obv. Legend:** BERNENSIS • MON • AUR • REIP • **Rev:** Inscription above value within cartouche **Rev. Inscription:** BENE:/DICTUS/SIT•IEHOVA/DEUS

Date	Mintage	F	VF	XF	Unc	BU
1741	—	400	850	1,400	2,100	2,800

KM# 126 DUCAT

3.5000 g., 0.9860 Gold 0.1109 oz. AGW **Obv:** Crowned, oval arms of Bern within sprigs **Obv. Legend:** BERNENS • MONETA • AUR • REIPUB • **Rev:** Inscription above value within cartouche **Rev. Inscription:** BENE/DICTUS/SITIEHOVA/DEUS•

Date	Mintage	F	VF	XF	Unc	BU
ND(1772)	—	350	700	1,200	1,950	2,600

KM# 137 DUCAT

3.5000 g., 0.9860 Gold 0.1109 oz. AGW **Obv:** Crowned arms of Bern within sprigs **Obv. Legend:** BERNENSIS RESPUBLICA **Rev:** Inscription above value within cartouche **Rev. Inscription:** BENE/DICTUS/SITIEHOVA/DEUS•

Date	Mintage	F	VF	XF	Unc	BU
1788	—	600	1,250	2,000	3,000	4,000

KM# 139 DUCAT

3.5000 g., 0.9860 Gold 0.1109 oz. AGW **Obv:** Crowned, spade arms of Bern within sprigs **Obv. Legend:** BERNENSIS • RESPUBLICA **Rev:** Inscription, date within oval frame, value below **Rev. Inscription:** BENE/DICTUS/SITIEHOVA/DEUS

Date	Mintage	F	VF	XF	Unc	BU
1789	—	700	1,400	2,200	3,200	4,400

KM# 145 DUCAT

3.5000 g., 0.9860 Gold 0.1109 oz. AGW **Obv:** Crowned, oval arms of Bern, with garland **Obv. Legend:** BERNENSIS • RESPUBLICA • **Rev:** Value, date within wreath **Rev. Legend:** BENEDICTUS SIT IEHOVA DEUS

Date	Mintage	F	VF	XF	Unc	BU
1793	—	2,400	4,800	8,000	10,000	12,500

KM# 148 DUCAT

3.5000 g., 0.9860 Gold 0.1109 oz. AGW **Obv:** Crowned, spade arms of Bern within sprigs **Obv. Legend:** BERNENSIS RESPUBLICA **Rev:** Value, date within wreath **Rev. Legend:** BENEDICTVS SIT IEHOVA DEVS

Date	Mintage	F	VF	XF	Unc	BU
1794	—	350	650	1,000	1,500	2,000

KM# 74 2 DUCAT

7.0000 g., 0.9860 Gold 0.2219 oz. AGW **Obv:** Crowned arms of Bern with supporters holding hat above **Obv. Legend:** BERNENSIS MONETA AUREA REIPVBLICAE **Rev:** Inscription, value and date within wreath **Rev. Inscription:** BENEDICTUS/SIT/ IEHOVA DEUS

Date	Mintage	F	VF	XF	Unc	BU
1703 DB	—	850	1,600	2,750	4,000	4,400
1703	—	850	1,600	2,750	4,000	4,400
1719 DB	—	850	1,600	2,750	4,000	4,400

KM# 96 2 DUCAT

7.0000 g., 0.9860 Gold 0.2219 oz. AGW **Obv:** Crowned arms of Bern with supporters holding hat above **Obv. Legend:** BERNENSIS MONETA AURE REIPUBLICÆ **Rev:** Inscription, value, date within ornate frame and sprigs **Rev. Inscription:** BENEDICTUS/SIT IEHOVA/DEUS.

Date	Mintage	F	VF	XF	Unc	BU
1727	—	600	1,200	2,250	3,350	4,400

KM# 125 2 DUCAT

7.0000 g., 0.9860 Gold 0.2219 oz. AGW **Obv:** Crowned arms of Bern with supporters holding hat above **Obv. Legend:** BERNENSIS MONETA AUREA REIPUBLICÆ **Rev:** Inscription, value, date within cartouche **Rev. Inscription:** BENEDICTUS/ SIT/IEHOVA DEUS

Date	Mintage	F	VF	XF	Unc	BU
1771	—	600	1,200	2,400	3,500	4,400

KM# 138 2 DUCAT

7.0000 g., 0.9860 Gold 0.2219 oz. AGW **Obv:** Crowned arms of Bern within sprigs **Obv. Legend:** BERNENSIS • RESPUBLICA **Rev:** Inscription, value within cartouche **Rev. Inscription:** BENEDICTUS/SIT/IEHOVA/DEUS

Date	Mintage	F	VF	XF	Unc	BU
1788	—	2,000	3,850	6,400	10,000	12,000

KM# 140 2 DUCAT

7.0000 g., 0.9860 Gold 0.2219 oz. AGW **Obv:** Crowned arms of Bern with garland **Obv. Legend:** BERNENSIS • RESPUBLICA **Rev:** Inscription, date within oval frame, value below **Rev. Inscription:** BENE/DICTUS/SIT IEHOVA/DEUS

Date	Mintage	F	VF	XF	Unc	BU
1789	—	725	1,400	2,400	3,600	4,800

KM# 154 2 DUCAT

7.0000 g., 0.9860 Gold 0.2219 oz. AGW **Obv:** Crowned, spade arms of Bern within sprigs **Obv. Legend:** BERNENSIS RESPUBLICA **Rev:** Value, date within wreath **Rev. Legend:** BENEDICTUS SIT IEHOVA DEUS

Date	Mintage	F	VF	XF	Unc	BU
1796	—	600	1,250	2,200	3,300	4,400

KM# 76 3 DUCAT

10.5000 g., 0.9860 Gold 0.3328 oz. AGW **Obv:** Crown above 2 oval arms of Bern **Obv. Legend:** BERNENSIS MONETA REIPVBLICÆ **Rev:** Inscription above date within partial frame flanked by 1/2 figures above **Rev. Inscription:** BENEDICTUS/ SITIEHOVA/DEUS

Date	Mintage	F	VF	XF	Unc	BU
1707	—	1,500	3,000	5,500	8,500	—

KM# 100 3 DUCAT

10.5000 g., 0.9860 Gold 0.3328 oz. AGW **Obv:** Crown above 2 oval arms of Bern **Obv. Legend:** BERNENSIS • MONETA • REIPVBLICÆ • **Rev:** Inscription, date within ornate cartouche **Rev. Inscription:** BENEDICTUS/SIT IEHOVA/DEUS/1734

Date	Mintage	F	VF	XF	Unc	BU
1734	—	2,000	4,000	8,500	12,000	—

KM# 101 3 DUCAT

10.5000 g., 0.9860 Gold 0.3328 oz. AGW **Obv:** Crowned arms in cartouche, legend **Obv. Legend:** BERNENSIS RESPUBLICA

Date	Mintage	F	VF	XF	Unc	BU
1734	—	2,000	4,000	8,500	12,000	—

KM# 127 3 DUCAT

10.5000 g., 0.9860 Gold 0.3328 oz. AGW **Obv:** Crowned, ornate oval arms of Bern **Obv. Legend:** BERNENS • MONETA • AUREA • REIPUB • **Rev:** Inscription, value, date within ornate cartouche **Rev. Inscription:** BENEDICTUS/SIT IEHOVA/DEUS

Date	Mintage	F	VF	XF	Unc	BU
1772	—	1,500	3,500	5,500	8,000	—

KM# 69 4 DUCAT

14.0000 g., 0.9860 Gold 0.4438 oz. AGW **Obv:** Crowned arms of Bern with supporters **Obv. Legend:** BERNENSIS MONETA REIPVBLICÆ **Rev:** Bear holding shield with inscription and date **Rev. Inscription:** BENE/DICTVS•SIT/ IEHOVADEVS/ DVCAT:/1701

Date	Mintage	F	VF	XF	Unc	BU
1701	—	1,450	2,800	4,800	7,250	—

KM# 78.1 4 DUCAT

14.0000 g., 0.9860 Gold 0.4438 oz. AGW **Obv:** Crowned, oval arms of Bern, with supporters **Obv. Legend:** BERNENSIS MONETA REIPVBLICA **Rev:** Inscription within square flanked by figures shaking hands, wreath and radiant sun above **Rev. Inscription:** BENEDIC/TVS SIT/I EHOVA/DEUS

Date	Mintage	F	VF	XF	Unc	BU
ND(1710)	—	1,400	2,800	4,400	6,750	—

KM# 78.2 4 DUCAT

14.0000 g., 0.9860 Gold 0.4438 oz. AGW **Obv:** Crowned, oval arms of Bern, with supporters **Obv. Legend:** BERNENSIS MONETA REIPVBLICÆ **Rev:** Inscription within square flanked by figures shaking hands, wreath and radiant sun above, value below **Rev. Inscription:** BENEDIC/TVS SIT/ IEHOVA/DEVS

Date	Mintage	F	VF	XF	Unc	BU
ND(1710)	—	1,500	3,250	5,000	7,000	—

KM# 78.3 4 DUCAT

14.0000 g., 0.9860 Gold 0.4438 oz. AGW **Obv:** Crowned, oval arms of Bern, with supporters **Obv. Legend:** BERNENSIS MONETA REIPVBLICÆ **Rev:** Inscription within square flanked by figures shaking hands, wreath and radiant sun above, value below **Rev. Inscription:** BENEDIC/TVS SIT/IEHOVA/DEVS

Date	Mintage	F	VF	XF	Unc	BU
1734	—	2,200	4,400	7,200	10,800	—

KM# 105.1 4 DUCAT

14.0000 g., 0.9860 Gold 0.4438 oz. AGW **Obv:** Crowned oval arms of Bern within sprigs **Obv. Legend:** BERNENS • MONETA • AUREA • REIPUB • **Rev:** Inscription, value within cartouche **Rev. Inscription:** BENE:/DICTUS SIT/IEHOVA/DEUS

Date	Mintage	F	VF	XF	Unc	BU
ND(1750)	—	1,500	3,250	6,500	11,000	—

KM# 105.2 4 DUCAT

14.0000 g., 0.9860 Gold 0.4438 oz. AGW **Rev:** Value: "DUC \ 4" below motto, (no dot after 4)

Date	Mintage	F	VF	XF	Unc	BU
ND(1750)	—	1,500	3,250	6,500	11,000	—

KM# 106 4 DUCAT

14.0000 g., 0.9860 Gold 0.4438 oz. AGW **Obv:** Crowned arms of Bern within sprigs **Obv. Legend:** BERNENS • MONETA AUREA REIPUB • **Rev:** Inscription within cartouche, retrograde "4" on ball below **Rev. Inscription:** BENE:/DICTUS SIT/IEHOVA/DEUS

Date	Mintage	F	VF	XF	Unc	BU
ND(1750)	—	1,500	3,250	6,500	11,000	—

KM# 109.1 4 DUCAT

14.0000 g., 0.9860 Gold 0.4438 oz. AGW **Obv:** Crowned, oval arms of Bern, with supporters **Obv. Legend:** BERNENSIS MONETA REIPVBLICÆ **Rev:** Inscription within square flanked by figures shaking hands, wreath and radiant sun above **Rev. Inscription:** BENEDIC/TVS•SIT/IEHOVA/DEUS

Date	Mintage	F	VF	XF	Unc	BU
ND(1750)	—	1,500	3,250	6,500	11,000	—

KM# 109.2 4 DUCAT

14.0000 g., 0.9860 Gold 0.4438 oz. AGW **Obv:** Crowned, oval arms of Bern, with supporters **Obv. Legend:** BERNENSIS MONETA REIPVBLICÆ **Rev:** Inscription within square flanked by figures shaking hands, wreath and radiant sun above, value below **Rev. Inscription:** BENEDIC/TVS•SIT/IEHOVA/DEUS

Date	Mintage	F	VF	XF	Unc	BU
ND(1750) MK	—	1,500	3,250	6,500	11,000	—

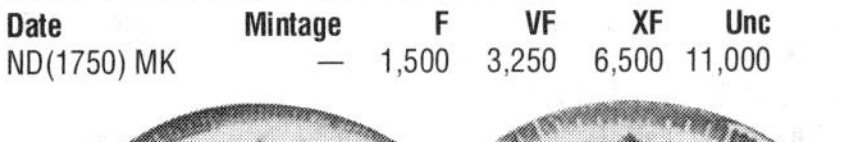

KM# 128 4 DUCAT

14.0000 g., 0.9860 Gold 0.4438 oz. AGW **Obv:** Crowned, oval arms of Bern within sprigs **Obv. Legend:** BERNENSIS MON • REIP • **Rev:** Inscription within cartouche **Rev. Inscription:** BENE:/DICTUS SIT/IEHOVA/DEUS **Note:** Similar to KM# 106 without value on ball

Date	Mintage	F	VF	XF	Unc	BU
ND(1775)	—	1,500	3,250	6,500	11,000	—

KM# 155.1 4 DUCAT

14.0000 g., 0.9860 Gold 0.4438 oz. AGW **Obv:** Crowned, spade arms of Bern within sprigs **Obv. Legend:** BERNENSIS RESPUBLICA **Rev:** Value, date within wreath **Rev. Legend:** BENEDICTUS SIT IEHOVA DEUS

Date	Mintage	F	VF	XF	Unc	BU
1796	—	1,750	3,600	6,000	8,800	—

KM# 155.2 4 DUCAT

14.0000 g., 0.9860 Gold 0.4438 oz. AGW **Obv:** Crowned, spade arms of Bern within sprigs **Obv. Legend:** BERNENSIS RESPUBLICA **Rev:** Value, date within wreath **Rev. Legend:** BENEDICTUS SIT IEHOVA DEUS

Date	Mintage	F	VF	XF	Unc	BU
1798	—	1,750	3,600	6,000	8,800	—

KM# 70 5 DUCAT

17.5000 g., 0.9860 Gold 0.5547 oz. AGW **Obv:** Crowned, oval arms of Bern, with supporters **Obv. Legend:** BERNENSIS MONETA REIPVBLICÆ **Rev:** Inscription within square flanked by figures shaking hands, wreath and radiant sun above **Rev. Inscription:** BENEDIC/TVS•SIT/IEHOVA/DEUS **Note:** Similar to 4 Ducat, KM#69.

Date	Mintage	F	VF	XF	Unc	BU
1701	—	1,600	3,400	5,600	8,800	—

KM# 72 5 DUCAT

17.5000 g., 0.9860 Gold 0.5547 oz. AGW **Obv:** Crowned arms of Bern, with supporters **Rev:** Inscription within square flanked by figures shaking hands, wreath and radiant sun above **Note:** Similar to 4 Ducat, KM# 78.

Date	Mintage	F	VF	XF	Unc	BU
ND(1710)	—	2,000	4,000	6,500	10,000	—

KM# 108 5 DUCAT

17.5000 g., 0.9860 Gold 0.5547 oz. AGW **Obv:** Crowned arms of Bern within sprigs **Rev:** Inscription, value within cartouche **Note:** Similar to 4 Ducat, KM# 105.

Date	Mintage	F	VF	XF	Unc	BU
ND(1750)	—	2,400	4,800	9,000	15,000	—

KM# 111.1 5 DUCAT

17.5000 g., 0.9860 Gold 0.5547 oz. AGW **Obv:** Crowned arms of Bern within sprigs **Obv. Legend:** BERNENS • MONETA AUREA REIPUB • **Rev:** Inscription within square flanked by figures shaking hands, wreath and radiant sun above **Rev. Inscription:** BENEDIC/TVS•SIT/IEHOVA/DEUS **Note:** Similar to 4 Ducat, KM# 109.1.

Date	Mintage	F	VF	XF	Unc	BU
ND(1750)	—	2,000	4,500	9,000	15,000	—

KM# 111.2 5 DUCAT

17.5000 g., 0.9860 Gold 0.5547 oz. AGW **Obv:** Crowned arms of Bern within sprigs **Obv. Legend:** BERNENSIS MON • REIP • **Rev:** Inscription within square flanked by figures shaking hands, wreath and radiant sun above, value below **Rev. Inscription:** BENEDIC/TVS•SIT/IEHOVA/DEUS

Date	Mintage	F	VF	XF	Unc	BU
ND(1750) MK	—	2,000	4,500	9,000	15,000	—

KM# 73 6 DUCAT

21.0000 g., 0.9860 Gold 0.6657 oz. AGW **Obv:** Crowned, oval arms of Bern, with supporters **Obv. Legend:** BERNENSIS MONETA REIPVBLICÆ **Rev:** Bear holding shield with inscription, date **Rev. Inscription:** BENE/DICTVS•SIT/IEHOVADEVS/DVCAT

Date	Mintage	F	VF	XF	Unc	BU
1701	—	2,800	5,200	10,000	16,000	—

KM# 79 6 DUCAT

21.0000 g., 0.9860 Gold 0.6657 oz. AGW **Obv:** Crowned, oval arms of Bern, with supporters **Obv. Legend:** BERNENSIS MONETA REIPVBLICÆ **Rev:** Inscription within square flanked by figures shaking hands, wreath and radiant sun above **Rev. Inscription:** BENEDIC/TVS•SIT/IEHOVA/DEUS

Date	Mintage	F	VF	XF	Unc	BU
ND(1710)	—	2,400	4,800	10,000	16,000	—

KM# 110 6 DUCAT

21.0000 g., 0.9860 Gold 0.6657 oz. AGW **Obv:** Crowned arms of Bern within sprigs **Rev:** Inscription, value within cartouche **Note:** Similar to 4 Ducat, KM# 105.

Date	Mintage	F	VF	XF	Unc	BU
ND(1750)	—	2,400	4,800	10,000	16,000	—

KM# 113 6 DUCAT

21.0000 g., 0.9860 Gold 0.6657 oz. AGW **Obv:** Crowned arms of Bern, with supporters **Rev:** Inscription within square flanked by figures shaking hands, wreath and radiant sun above **Note:** Similar to 4 Ducat, KM#109.

Date	Mintage	F	VF	XF	Unc	BU
ND(1750)	—	2,400	4,800	10,000	16,000	—

KM# 129 6 DUCAT

21.0000 g., 0.9860 Gold 0.6657 oz. AGW **Obv:** Crowned arms of Bern within sprigs **Obv. Legend:** BERNENSIS MON • REIP • **Rev:** Inscription within cartouche **Rev. Inscription:** BENE:/ DICTUS SIT/ IEHOVA/DEUS

Date	Mintage	F	VF	XF	Unc	BU
ND(1775)	—	2,400	4,800	8,000	14,000	—

KM# 156 6 DUCAT

21.0000 g., 0.9860 Gold 0.6657 oz. AGW **Obv:** Crowned, spade arms of Bern within sprigs **Obv. Legend:** BERNENSIS RESPUBLICA **Rev:** Value, date within wreath **Rev. Legend:** BENEDICTUS SIT IEHOVA DEUS

Date	Mintage	F	VF	XF	Unc	BU
1796	—	2,800	5,200	8,800	14,000	—

KM# 80 7 DUCAT
24.5000 g., 0.9860 Gold 0.7766 oz. AGW **Obv:** Crowned, oval arms of Bern, with supporters **Obv. Legend:** BERNENSIS MONETA REIPVBLICÆ **Rev:** Inscription within square flanked by figures shaking hands, wreath and radiant sun above **Rev. Inscription:** BENEDIC/TVS•SIT/IEHOVA/DEUS

Date	Mintage	F	VF	XF	Unc	BU
ND(1710)	—	4,400	8,800	15,000	21,500	—

KM# 112 7 DUCAT
24.5000 g., 0.9860 Gold 0.7766 oz. AGW **Obv:** Crowned arms of Bern within sprigs **Rev:** Inscription, value within cartouche **Note:** Similar to 4 Ducat, KM#105.

Date	Mintage	F	VF	XF	Unc	BU
ND(1750)	—	4,400	8,800	15,000	21,500	—

KM# 114 7 DUCAT
24.5000 g., 0.9860 Gold 0.7766 oz. AGW **Obv:** Crowned arms of Bern, with supporters **Rev:** Inscription within square flanked by figures shaking hands, wreath and radiant sun above **Note:** Similar to 4 Ducat, KM#109.

Date	Mintage	F	VF	XF	Unc	BU
ND(1750)	—	4,400	8,800	15,000	21,500	—

KM# 130 7 DUCAT
24.5000 g., 0.9860 Gold 0.7766 oz. AGW **Obv:** Crowned, ornate arms of Bern within sprigs **Rev:** Inscription within ornate cartouche **Note:** Similar to 10 Ducat, KM#134.

Date	Mintage	F	VF	XF	Unc	BU
ND(1775)	—	4,400	8,800	15,000	21,500	—

KM# 77 8 DUCAT
28.0000 g., 0.9860 Gold 0.8876 oz. AGW **Obv:** Crowned arms of Bern, with supporters **Rev:** Inscription within square flanked by figures shaking hands, wreath and radiant sun above **Note:** Similar to 10 Ducat, KM#81.

Date	Mintage	F	VF	XF	Unc	BU
ND(1710)	—	4,400	8,800	15,000	21,500	—

KM# 131 8 DUCAT
28.0000 g., 0.9860 Gold 0.8876 oz. AGW **Obv:** Crowned, ornate arms of Bern within sprigs **Obv. Legend:** BERNENSIS MON • REIP • **Rev:** Inscription within ornate cartouche **Rev. Inscription:** BENE:/DICTUS SIT/IEHOVA/DEUS **Note:** Similar to 6 Ducat, KM#129.

Date	Mintage	F	VF	XF	Unc	BU
ND(1775)	—	4,400	8,800	15,000	21,500	—

KM# 132 8 DUCAT
28.0000 g., 0.9860 Gold 0.8876 oz. AGW **Obv:** Crowned, ornate arms of Bern within sprigs **Rev:** Inscription within ornate cartouche **Note:** Similar to 10 Ducat, KM#134.

Date	Mintage	F	VF	XF	Unc	BU
ND(1775)	—	4,400	8,800	15,000	21,500	—

KM# 157 8 DUCAT
28.0000 g., 0.9860 Gold 0.8876 oz. AGW **Obv:** Crowned, spade arms of Bern within sprigs **Obv. Legend:** BERNENSIS RESPUBLICA **Rev:** Value, date within wreath **Rev. Legend:** BENEDICTUS SIT IEHOVA DEUS

Date	Mintage	F	VF	XF	Unc	BU
1796	—	4,400	8,800	14,500	21,500	—
1798	—	4,400	8,800	14,500	21,500	—

KM# 81 10 DUCAT
35.0000 g., 0.9860 Gold 1.1095 oz. AGW **Obv:** Crowned arms of Bern, with supporters **Obv. Legend:** BERNENSIS * MONETA REIPVBLICÆ **Rev:** Inscription within square flanked by figures shaking hands, wreath and radiant sun above **Rev. Inscription:** BENEDIC/TVS•SIT/IEHOVA/DEUS

Date	Mintage	F	VF	XF	Unc	BU
ND(1710)	—	6,000	12,500	21,000	32,000	—

KM# 133 10 DUCAT
35.0000 g., 0.9860 Gold 1.1095 oz. AGW **Obv:** Crowned arms of Bern within sprigs **Rev:** Inscription within ornate cartouche **Note:** Similar to 6 Ducat, KM#129.

Date	Mintage	F	VF	XF	Unc	BU
ND(1775)	—	6,000	12,500	21,000	32,000	—

KM# 134 10 DUCAT
35.0000 g., 0.9860 Gold 1.1095 oz. AGW **Obv:** Crowned, ornate arms of Bern within sprigs **Obv. Legend:** BERNENSIS • MONETA REIPUBLICÆ **Rev:** Inscription within ornate cartouche **Rev. Inscription:** BENE:/DICTUS SIT/IEHOVA/DEUS

Date	Mintage	F	VF	XF	Unc	BU
ND(1775)	—	6,500	12,500	21,000	33,000	—

KM# 135 12 DUCAT
42.0000 g., 0.9860 Gold 1.3314 oz. AGW **Obv:** Crowned, ornate arms of Bern within sprigs **Rev:** Inscription within ornate cartouche **Note:** Similar to 10 Ducat, KM#134.

Date	Mintage	F	VF	XF	Unc	BU
ND(1775) Rare	—	—	—	—	—	—

PATTERNS

Including off metal strikes

KM#	Date	Mintage	Identification	Mkt Val
Pn1	1703	—	2 Ducat. Tin. KM74.	—
Pn2	1707	—	1/2 Kreuzer. Gold. KM75.	—
Pn3	1718	—	Kreuzer. Gold. KM90.	—
Pn4	1731	—	1/2 Kreuzer. Gold. KM98.	—

KM#	Date	Mintage	Identification	Mkt Val
PnA5	1732	—	1/2 Kreuzer. Silver. KM#75.	—
Pn5	1734	—	3 Ducat. Tin. KM100.	—
Pn6	1734	—	3 Ducat. Silver. KM101.	—
Pn7	1755	—	10 Kreuzer. Silver.	800
Pn8	1755	—	20 Kreuzer. Gold. KM117.	5,000
Pn9	1759	—	10 Kreuzer. Gold. KM120.	2,000
Pn10	1766	—	1/2 Kreuzer. Gold. 0.7500 g. KM122.	2,000
Pn11	1772	—	Kreuzer. Copper. Thick planchets. KM115.	—
Pn12	1772	—	Kreuzer. Silver. KM115.	—
Pn13	ND(1772)	—	Ducat. Billon. KM126.	—
Pn14	1777	—	1/2 Kreuzer. Gold. 0.7500 g. KM122.	2,000
Pn15	1778	—	1/2 Kreuzer. Gold. 0.7500 g. KM122.	2,000
Pn16	1781	—	1/2 Kreuzer. Gold. 0.7500 g. KM122.	2,000
Pn17	1781	—	Kreuzer. Gold. KM115.	2,250

KM#	Date	Mintage	Identification	Mkt Val
Pn18	ND(1785)	64	10 Franken. Gold.	10,000
Pn19	1792	—	Kreuzer. Billon.	500
PnA20	1797	—	1/2 Thaler. Gold. 27.5100 g. KM161.	16,500

BEROMUENSTER

An abbey founded in 720 by Bero, the count of Lenzburg, in the canton of Luzern.

In 1720 the abbey struck quarter and half thalers, to commemorate the 1000th Anniversary of the founding of the abbey, depicting St. Michael slaying the dragon.

ABBEY

STANDARD COINAGE

KM# 14 1/4 THALER
6.8000 g., Silver, 31 mm. **Obv:** Arms on spade-shaped shield **Rev:** St. Michael with flaming sword slaying dragon

Date	Mintage	F	VF	XF	Unc	BU
ND(ca.1720)	—	—	—	85.00	—	—

KM# 2 1/4 THALER
6.5000 g., Silver, 31 mm. **Obv:** Crowned, helmeted oval arms within sprigs **Obv. Legend:** BERO COM : DE :... **Rev:** St. Michael slaying the dragon **Rev. Legend:** COLLEG : BERO : SVIS : BENEV : D : D : **Note:** Varieties exist.

Date	Mintage	F	VF	XF	Unc	BU
ND(1720)	—	50.00	100	200	—	—

KM# 3 1/4 THALER
6.5000 g., Silver, 31 mm. **Obv:** Crowned, helmeted oval arms within sprigs **Obv. Legend:** BERO COM : DE : ... **Rev:** St. Michael slaying the dragon **Rev. Legend:** COLLEG : BERO : SVIS : BENEV : D : D : **Note:** Varieties exist.

Date	Mintage	F	VF	XF	Unc	BU
ND(1720)	—	30.00	60.00	125	250	—

KM# 12 1/4 THALER
6.8000 g., Silver, 31 mm. **Rev:** St. Michael slaying the dragon

Date	Mintage	Good	VG	F	VF	XF
ND(ca.1720)	—	—	—	—	—	85.00

KM# 6 1/2 THALER
13.6500 g., Silver, 33 mm. **Rev:** St. Michael defeating devil, devil left

Date	Mintage	F	VF	XF	Unc	BU
ND(ca.1720)	—	—	—	135	—	—

KM# 7 1/2 THALER
13.9000 g., Silver, 35 mm. **Rev:** St. Michael with lightning on dragon

Date	Mintage	F	VF	XF	Unc	BU
ND(ca.1720)	—	—	—	135	—	—

KM# 16 1/2 THALER
12.7400 g., Silver, 35 mm. **Obv:** Arms on blunt cross **Rev:** St. Michael slaying dragon

Date	Mintage	F	VF	XF	Unc	BU
ND(ca.1720)	—	—	—	110	—	—

KM# 17 1/2 THALER
13.8000 g., Silver, 37 mm. **Obv:** Oval arms on shield **Rev:** St. Michael on dragon

Date	Mintage	F	VF	XF	Unc	BU
ND(ca.1720)	—	—	—	135	—	—

KM# 4 1/2 THALER
14.1500 g., Silver, 37 mm. **Obv:** Crowned, helmeted oval arms within sprigs **Obv. Legend:** BERO COM : DE: ... **Rev:** St. Michael slaying dragon **Rev. Legend:** COLLEG : BERO : SVIS : BENEV : D : D : **Note:** Varieties exist.

Date	Mintage	F	VF	XF	Unc	BU
ND(ca.1720)	—	75.00	150	250	—	—

KM# 5 1/2 THALER
14.0000 g., Silver, 37 mm. **Obv:** Crowned, helmeted oval arms within spade and sprigs **Obv. Legend:** BERO COM : DE : ... **Rev:** St. Michael defeating devil **Rev. Legend:** COLLEG : BERO : SVIS : BENEV : D : D : **Note:** Varieties exist.

Date	Mintage	F	VF	XF	Unc	BU
ND(ca.1720)	—	40.00	75.00	150	300	—

KM# 8 1/2 THALER
Silver, 35 mm. **Rev:** St. Michael slaying dragon with lightning bolt sceptre **Note:** Weight varies: 13.4-14 g.

Date	Mintage	F	VF	XF	Unc	BU
ND(ca.1720)	—	—	—	135	—	—

KM# 10 MICHAELGULDEN
8.6400 g., Silver, 35 mm. **Subject:** 1000th Anniversary - Founding of Abbey **Obv:** Oval arms in baroque frame, ornate helmet above **Obv. Legend:** ★ BERO COM • DE LENZB • FVNDA • ECCL • BERON ★ **Rev:** Full-length figure of the Archangel Michael slaying dragon **Rev. Legend:** COLLEG ★ BERO ★ SVIS ★ BENEV ★ D ★ D ★

Date	Mintage	VG	F	VF	XF	Unc
ND(1720)	—	850	1,200	1,500	2,000	—

CHUR

CITY

STANDARD COINAGE

KM# 263 BLUZGER
Billon **Ruler:** Ulrich VII von Federspiel **Obv:** Arms with Ibex (left or right) within town gate **Rev:** Cross to inner circle

Date	Mintage	VG	F	VF	XF	Unc
1705 Rare	—	—	—	—	—	—
1706	—	12.00	25.00	60.00	125	—
1707	—	8.00	15.00	40.00	80.00	—
1708	—	5.00	8.00	16.00	40.00	80.00
1709	—	6.50	12.50	32.00	60.00	—
1710	—	5.00	8.00	16.50	40.00	80.00
1711	—	7.00	12.50	32.00	26.50	—
1712	—	7.00	12.50	32.00	26.50	—
1713	—	20.00	40.00	100	55.00	—
1714	—	8.00	15.00	40.00	32.50	—
1716	—	4.00	8.00	16.00	23.50	80.00
1717	—	8.00	15.00	40.00	32.50	—
1718	—	6.50	12.50	32.00	32.50	—
1720	—	6.50	12.50	32.00	26.50	—
1721	—	6.50	12.50	32.00	32.50	—
1722	—	10.00	25.00	60.00	26.50	—
1723	—	4.00	7.00	13.50	23.50	50.00
1724	—	5.00	8.00	16.50	26.50	80.00
1725	—	6.50	12.50	32.00	32.50	—
1726	—	4.00	7.00	13.50	23.50	50.00
1727	—	4.00	7.00	13.50	23.50	50.00
1728	—	4.00	7.00	10.00	16.50	50.00
1731	—	8.00	16.00	40.00	55.00	—
1739	—	4.00	7.00	12.50	16.50	50.00
1740	—	4.00	7.00	12.50	16.50	50.00
1764 Rare	—	—	20.00	32.50	—	—
1765	—	4.00	7.00	10.00	16.50	40.00
1766	—	4.00	7.00	10.00	16.50	40.00

KM# 265 KREUZER
Billon **Ruler:** Ulrich VII von Federspiel **Obv:** Crowned imperial eagle **Rev:** 1/2-length St. Luke with sceptre and imperial orb in inner circle

Date	Mintage	VG	F	VF	XF	Unc
1712	—	10.00	20.00	50.00	100	—
1713	—	8.00	16.00	40.00	80.00	—
1714	—	15.00	30.00	80.00	160	—
1715	—	8.00	16.00	40.00	80.00	—
1716	—	10.00	20.00	50.00	100	—
1717	—	15.00	30.00	80.00	160	—
1718	—	10.00	20.00	50.00	100	—
1719	—	10.00	20.00	50.00	100	—
1720	—	5.00	9.00	20.00	40.00	80.00
1721	—	8.00	16.00	40.00	80.00	—
1722	—	6.00	12.00	32.00	60.00	—
1723	—	8.00	16.00	40.00	80.00	—
1724	—	8.00	16.00	40.00	80.00	—
1725	—	15.00	30.00	80.00	160	—
1726	—	25.00	60.00	150	—	—
1727	—	12.00	25.00	60.00	120	—
1728	—	6.00	12.00	32.00	60.00	—
1729	—	5.00	9.00	20.00	40.00	80.00
1730	—	5.00	9.00	20.00	40.00	80.00

KM# 267 3 KREUZER (1 Groschen)
Silver **Ruler:** Ulrich VII von Federspiel **Obv:** Legend, date, shield with Ibex left on breast of crowned imperial eagle **Obv. Legend:** CAROL • D • G • ROM • IM • S • A • **Rev:** Legend, value: 3 in oval at bottom **Rev. Legend:** S • LVCI • M • EP • CVRIE

Date	Mintage	VG	F	VF	XF	Unc
1725	—	50.00	100	250	475	—
1729	—	50.00	80.00	200	400	—

KM# 268 3 KREUZER (1 Groschen)
Silver **Ruler:** Joseph Benedict von Rost **Obv:** Legend, date, arms on orb on breast, without inner circle **Obv. Legend:** CAROL • VI • D • G • ROM • I M • SA

Date	Mintage	VG	F	VF	XF	Unc
1729	—	45.00	80.00	200	400	—
1730	—	8.00	16.00	40.00	80.00	—
1731	—	15.00	30.00	80.00	160	—

KM# 270 3 KREUZER (1 Groschen)
Silver **Ruler:** Joseph Benedict von Rost **Obv:** Legend, value: 3 in oval below crowned imperial eagle **Obv. Legend:** CARO • D • G • ... **Rev:** Legend, without 3 in oval at bottom **Rev. Legend:** S • LUCI • M • EP • CURIE

Date	Mintage	VG	F	VF	XF	Unc
1731	—	8.00	16.00	40.00	80.00	—

KM# 271 3 KREUZER (1 Groschen)
Silver **Ruler:** Joseph Benedict von Rost

Date	Mintage	VG	F	VF	XF	Unc
1732	—	6.50	12.50	32.00	60.00	125
1733	—	6.50	12.50	32.00	60.00	125
1734	—	6.50	12.50	32.00	60.00	125
1735	—	6.50	12.50	32.00	60.00	125
1737	—	10.00	20.00	60.00	125	—

KM# 272 6 KREUZER
Billon **Ruler:** Joseph Benedict von Rost **Obv:** Oval arms with Ibex left in cartouche in inner circle **Rev:** Value, date in cartouche, cherub's head above

Date	Mintage	VG	F	VF	XF	Unc
1733	—	475	950	2,400	5,000	—

BISHOPRIC

A former bishopric now part of the canton Graubunden. The mint right was given from 959 until about 1798.

RULERS
Ulrich VII von Federspiel, 1692-1728
Joseph Benedikt von Rost, 1728-1754
Bishop Johann Anton, Freiherr von Federspiel, 1755-77

STANDARD COINAGE

KM# 147 PFENNIG
Billon **Ruler:** Ulrich VII von Federspiel **Obv:** Letters VEC around shield **Note:** Uniface.

Date	Mintage	VG	F	VF	XF	Unc
ND(1728) Note: Ibex facing left	—	25.00	40.00	100	200	—
ND(1728) Note: Ibex facing right	—	25.00	40.00	100	200	—

KM# 131 BLUZGER
Billon **Ruler:** Ulrich VII von Federspiel **Obv:** 4-fold arms in oval cartouche in circle of pearls **Rev:** Anchor cross with ornamentation on arms

Date	Mintage	VG	F	VF	XF	Unc
1704	—	5.00	8.00	16.00	40.00	80.00
1706	—	5.00	8.00	16.00	40.00	80.00
1707	—	8.00	12.00	32.00	60.00	—
1708	—	4.00	6.00	12.00	24.00	50.00
1709	—	9.00	16.00	40.00	80.00	—
1710	—	5.00	8.00	16.00	40.00	80.00
1711	—	3.00	5.00	12.00	24.00	50.00
1712	—	8.00	12.00	32.00	60.00	—
1713	—	15.00	24.00	60.00	120	—
1714	—	8.00	12.00	32.00	60.00	—
1716	—	5.00	8.00	16.00	40.00	80.00
1717	—	15.00	24.00	60.00	120	—
1718	—	9.00	16.00	40.00	80.00	—
1719 Rare	—	—	—	—	—	—
1721	—	8.00	12.00	32.00	60.00	—
1723	—	3.00	5.00	12.00	24.00	50.00
1724	—	5.00	8.00	16.00	40.00	80.00
1725	—	5.00	8.00	16.00	40.00	80.00
1726	—	3.00	5.00	12.00	24.00	50.00
1727	—	3.00	5.00	12.00	24.00	50.00
1728	—	8.00	12.00	32.00	60.00	—

KM# 157 BLUZGER
Billon **Ruler:** Joseph Benedict von Rost **Obv:** 5-fold arms in cartouche **Rev:** Anchor cross with prongs at end

Date	Mintage	VG	F	VF	XF	Unc
1739	—	3.50	7.50	13.50	40.00	160
1740	—	3.50	7.50	13.50	40.00	160

KM# 178 BLUZGER
Billon **Ruler:** Bishop Johann Anton, Freiherr von Federspiel **Obv:** Crowned 5-fold arms within circle **Rev:** Circles in cross points within circle

Date	Mintage	VG	F	VF	XF	Unc
1764 Rare	—	—	—	—	—	—
1765	—	5.00	8.00	12.00	35.00	120
1766	—	5.00	8.00	12.00	35.00	120

KM# 136 KREUZER
Billon **Ruler:** Ulrich VII von Federspiel **Obv:** Legend, date **Obv. Legend:** CAR • V • I • ... **Rev:** Legend, oval arms with Ibex right, cross behind **Rev. Legend:** IOS • BEN ...

Date	Mintage	VG	F	VF	XF	Unc
1706	—	50.00	100	250	—	—

KM# 137 KREUZER
Billon **Ruler:** Ulrich VII von Federspiel **Obv:** Legend, bust right dividing S-L in inner circle **Obv. Legend:** IOS • B ...

Date	Mintage	VG	F	VF	XF	Unc
1707	—	50.00	100	250	—	—
1708	—	45.00	90.00	200	—	—
1709	—	35.00	65.00	165	—	—
1710	—	30.00	60.00	125	—	—

KM# 149 KREUZER
Billon **Ruler:** Joseph Benedict von Rost **Obv:** Legend, bust right **Obv. Legend:** IOS • BEN ...

Date	Mintage	VG	F	VF	XF	Unc
1730	—	15.00	25.00	60.00	125	—

KM# 156 KREUZER
Billon **Ruler:** Joseph Benedict von Rost **Obv:** Legend, oval arms with Ibex right **Obv. Legend:** IOS • B • D • GEP...

Date	Mintage	VG	F	VF	XF	Unc
1738	—	175	300	750	—	—

KM# 159 KREUZER
Billon **Ruler:** Joseph Benedict von Rost **Obv:** Legend, 5-fold arms in cartouche **Obv. Legend:** IOS • BEN... **Rev:** Round shield with eagle, double cross behind, date in legend

Date	Mintage	VG	F	VF	XF	Unc
1740	—	125	250	600	1,200	—

KM# 175 KREUZER
Billon **Ruler:** Bishop Johann Anton, Freiherr von Federspiel **Obv:** Bust right **Rev:** Value and date in cartouche

Date	Mintage	VG	F	VF	XF	Unc
1759 Rare	—	—	—	—	—	—

KM# 177 KREUZER
Billon **Ruler:** Bishop Johann Anton, Freiherr von Federspiel **Obv:** Coat of arms **Rev:** Crowned monogram above date

Date	Mintage	VG	F	VF	XF	Unc
1761	—	150	250	600	1,200	—

KM# 140 2 KREUZER (1/2 Batzen)

Billon **Ruler:** Ulrich VII von Federspiel **Obv:** Legend, 4-fold arms in oval cartouche **Obv. Legend:** VDAL • D • G • EP ... **Rev:** Legend, date **Rev. Legend:** CAROL • D • G • ROM • IM • SE • A

Date	Mintage	VG	F	VF	XF	Unc
1713 Rare	—	—	175	—	—	—
1719	—	250	400	1,000	—	—

KM# 146 2 KREUZER (1/2 Batzen)

Billon **Ruler:** Ulrich VII von Federspiel **Obv:** Value: 2 in circle on breast of crowned imperial eagle in inner circle **Rev:** 2 oval shields with mantle

Date	Mintage	VG	F	VF	XF	Unc
1724	—	50.00	100	250	—	—

KM# 160 2 KREUZER (1/2 Batzen)

Billon **Ruler:** Joseph Benedict von Rost **Obv:** 5-fold arms in cartouche with mantle **Rev:** Value: 2/KREU/ZER in oval ornate cartouche

Date	Mintage	VG	F	VF	XF	Unc
1740 Rare	—	—	—	—	—	—
1741	—	25.00	50.00	100	200	—

KM# 142 3 KREUZER (1 Groschen)

Billon **Ruler:** Ulrich VII von Federspiel **Obv:** Value: 3 in oval below in inner circle, armored bust right **Rev:** Crowned imperial eagle, oval shields on breast in inner circle

Date	Mintage	VG	F	VF	XF	Unc
1718 Rare	—	—	—	—	—	—

KM# 150 3 KREUZER (1 Groschen)

Billon **Ruler:** Joseph Benedict von Rost **Obv:** Armored bust with cross right **Rev:** Value: 3 below, 5-fold arms on mantled shield, bishop's hat above

Date	Mintage	VG	F	VF	XF	Unc
1730	—	35.00	65.00	200	475	—

KM# 151 3 KREUZER (1 Groschen)

Billon **Ruler:** Joseph Benedict von Rost **Obv:** Value: 3 in oval on shoulder **Rev:** Without 3 below shield

Date	Mintage	VG	F	VF	XF	Unc
1730	—	115	200	475	950	—

KM# 173 6 KREUZER

Billon **Ruler:** Bishop Johann Anton, Freiherr von Federspiel **Obv:** Bust right **Rev:** Value, date within inner circle of cartouche

Date	Mintage	VG	F	VF	XF	Unc
1758	—	350	625	1,600	3,000	—

KM# 165 12 KREUZER (1/2 Dicken)

Silver **Ruler:** Joseph Benedict von Rost **Obv:** Oval 5-fold arms in ornamentation, bishop's hat above **Rev:** Value, date within inner circle of cartouche **Note:** Similar to 6 Kreuzer, KM#173.

Date	Mintage	VG	F	VF	XF	Unc
1744 Rare	—	—	—	—	—	—

KM# 135 15 KREUZER

Silver **Ruler:** Ulrich VII von Federspiel **Obv:** Large bust right divides circle **Rev:** Crowned double-headed eagle with shield on breast, value below

Date	Mintage	VG	F	VF	XF	Unc
1703	—	350	650	1,200	3,200	—

KM# 138 15 KREUZER

Silver **Ruler:** Ulrich VII von Federspiel **Obv:** Smaller bust right **Rev. Legend:** IOSEPHUS ...

Date	Mintage	VG	F	VF	XF	Unc
1708	—	800	1,600	4,000	—	—

KM# 164 15 KREUZER

Silver **Ruler:** Joseph Benedict von Rost **Obv:** 5-fold arms in ornamentation, bishop's hat above **Rev:** Inscription in cartouche within palm and laurel branches, value in oval shield below **Rev. Inscription:** SOLI/DEO/GLORIA/date

Date	Mintage	VG	F	VF	XF	Unc
1743	—	500	1,000	2,800	5,000	—

KM# 163 20 KREUZER

Silver **Ruler:** Joseph Benedict von Rost **Obv:** Value: 20 on orb on breast of crowned imperial eagle, date in legend **Rev:** 5-fold arms in ornamentation, bishop's hat above

Date	Mintage	VG	F	VF	XF	Unc
1742	—	700	1,200	4,000	—	—

KM# 174 1/6 THALER

Silver **Ruler:** Bishop Johann Anton, Freiherr von Federspiel **Obv:** Bust right **Obv. Legend:** IOH • ANT • D • G • EP ... **Rev:** Value, date

Date	Mintage	VG	F	VF	XF	Unc
1758 Rare	—	—	—	—	—	—

KM# 144 THALER

Silver **Ruler:** Ulrich VII von Federspiel **Obv:** Legend, date, crowned imperial eagle with shield on breast **Obv. Legend:** CAROLVS • VI • D • G • ROM: IMP:S:A: **Rev:** Legend, bust right **Rev. Legend:** VDAL: S•R•I: PR: EP: CVR ... **Note:** Dav. #1761.

Date	Mintage	VG	F	VF	XF	Unc
1720 Rare	—	—	—	—	—	—

KM# 153 THALER

Silver **Ruler:** Joseph Benedict von Rost **Obv:** Legend, armored bust right **Obv. Legend:** IOS • BENED • D • G • ... **Rev:** Oval 5-fold arms in cartouche, mantle around, bishop's hat above **Rev. Legend:** D • IN • FVRST • ET ... **Note:** Dav. #1763.

Date	Mintage	VG	F	VF	XF	Unc
1736	—	1,400	2,500	6,000	12,000	—

KM# 179 THALER

Silver **Ruler:** Bishop Johann Anton, Freiherr von Federspiel **Obv:** Crowned, mantled oval arms **Obv. Legend:** IOANNES • ANTONIUS • D: G: ... **Rev:** AD/NORMAN/CONVENT/1766 within wreath **Note:** Dav. #1766.

Date	Mintage	VG	F	VF	XF	Unc
1766 Rare	—	—	—	—	—	—

KM# 180 THALER

Silver **Ruler:** Bishop Johann Anton, Freiherr von Federspiel **Obv:** Crowned double-headed eagle, divided date above **Obv. Legend:** IOSEPHUS • II • D: G: ... **Rev:** Inscription, date within wreath **Note:** Dav. #1764. Reverse is similar to KM#179.

Date	Mintage	VG	F	VF	XF	Unc
1766	—	700	1,250	2,750	5,500	—

KM# 154 2 THALER

Silver **Ruler:** Joseph Benedict von Rost **Obv:** Legend, armored bust right **Obv. Legend:** IOS • BENED • D • G • ... **Rev:** Legend, oval 5-fold arms in cartouche, mantle around, bishop's hat above **Rev. Legend:** D • IN • FVRST • ET... **Note:** Dav. #1762.

Date	Mintage	VG	F	VF	XF	Unc
1736 Unique	—	—	—	—	—	—

KM# 181 2 THALER

Silver **Ruler:** Bishop Johann Anton, Freiherr von Federspiel **Obv:** Crowned, mantled oval arms **Rev:** Inscription, date within wreath

Date	Mintage	VG	F	VF	XF	Unc
1766 Rare	—	—	—	—	—	—

KM# 182 2 THALER

Silver **Ruler:** Bishop Johann Anton, Freiherr von Federspiel **Obv:** Crowned double-headed eagle, divided date above **Rev:** Inscription, date within wreath

Date	Mintage	VG	F	VF	XF	Unc
1766 Rare	—	—	—	—	—	—

TRADE COINAGE

KM# 141 DUCAT

3.5000 g., 0.9860 Gold 0.1109 oz. AGW **Ruler:** Ulrich VII von Federspiel **Obv:** 4-Fold arms within circle **Rev:** Half-length standing Saint divides circle

Date	Mintage	VG	F	VF	XF	Unc
1713	—	2,250	4,000	8,000	14,000	—

KM# 152 DUCAT

3.5000 g., 0.9860 Gold 0.1109 oz. AGW **Ruler:** Joseph Benedict von Rost **Obv:** Bishops' hat above ornate oval arms **Rev:** Half-length Saint, facing right, divides circle

Date	Mintage	VG	F	VF	XF	Unc
1735 Rare	—	—	—	—	—	—

KM# 161 DUCAT

3.5000 g., 0.9860 Gold 0.1109 oz. AGW **Ruler:** Joseph Benedict von Rost **Obv:** Bust right **Rev:** Bishops' hat above ornate oval arms

Date	Mintage	VG	F	VF	XF	Unc
1741 Rare	—	—	—	—	—	—

KM# 168 DUCAT

3.5000 g., 0.9860 Gold 0.1109 oz. AGW **Ruler:** Joseph Benedict von Rost **Obv:** Bust right, legend within circle **Obv. Legend:** IOS: BEN: D•G: ... **Rev:** Bishops' hat above ornate oval arms

Date	Mintage	VG	F	VF	XF	Unc
1749	—	850	1,600	3,600	5,600	—

KM# 183 DUCAT

3.5000 g., 0.9860 Gold 0.1109 oz. AGW **Ruler:** Bishop Johann Anton, Freiherr von Federspiel **Obv:** Crowned, mantled oval arms **Obv. Legend:** IO • A • ANT • D • G • EP ... **Rev:** Standing Saint with child **Rev. Legend:** PRAESEDIUM....

Date	Mintage	VG	F	VF	XF	Unc
1767	—	1,200	2,000	4,000	7,250	—

KM# 145 2 DUCAT

7.0000 g., 0.9860 Gold 0.2219 oz. AGW **Ruler:** Ulrich VII von Federspiel **Obv:** Crowned double-headed eagle, orb on breast, divided date above **Obv. Legend:** CAROLVS... **Rev:** St. Luke divides circle

Date	Mintage	VG	F	VF	XF	Unc
1720 Rare	—	—	—	—	—	—

KM# 162 2 DUCAT

7.0000 g., 0.9860 Gold 0.2219 oz. AGW **Ruler:** Joseph Benedict von Rost **Obv:** Bust right

Date	Mintage	VG	F	VF	XF	Unc
1741 Rare	—	—	—	—	—	—

KM# 169 5 DUCAT

17.5000 g., 0.9860 Gold 0.5547 oz. AGW **Ruler:** Joseph Benedict von Rost **Note:** Similar to 6 Ducat, KM#170.

Date	Mintage	VG	F	VF	XF	Unc
1749	—	3,000	5,000	9,500	16,000	—

KM# 170 6 DUCAT

21.0000 g., 0.9860 Gold 0.6657 oz. AGW **Ruler:** Joseph Benedict von Rost **Obv:** Crowned imperial eagle, legend, date **Obv. Legend:** LEOPOLDVS: ... **Rev:** Facing bust of bishop, legend **Rev. Legend:** VDAL: D: G: EP: ...

Date	Mintage	VG	F	VF	XF	Unc
1749	—	3,000	5,250	10,000	17,500	—

KM# 171 7 DUCAT

24.5000 g., 0.9860 Gold 0.7766 oz. AGW **Ruler:** Joseph Benedict von Rost **Note:** Similar to 6 Ducat, KM#170.

Date	Mintage	VG	F	VF	XF	Unc
1749	—	3,500	6,500	12,500	20,000	—

KM# 166 8 DUCAT

0.9860 Gold **Ruler:** Joseph Benedict von Rost **Note:** Similar to 10 Ducat, KM#167.

Date	Mintage	VG	F	VF	XF	Unc
1747	—	4,500	9,500	20,000	32,500	—

KM# 143 10 DUCAT

35.0000 g., 0.9860 Gold 1.1095 oz. AGW **Ruler:** Ulrich VII von Federspiel **Note:** Struck with Thaler dies, KM#144.

Date	Mintage	VG	F	VF	XF	Unc
1720 Rare	—	—	—	—	—	—

KM# 155 10 DUCAT

35.0000 g., 0.9860 Gold 1.1095 oz. AGW **Ruler:** Joseph Benedict von Rost **Obv:** Large bust right within circle **Obv. Legend:** IOS • BENE • D • D • G • EPISCPVS ... **Rev:** Ornate oval arms

Date	Mintage	VG	F	VF	XF	Unc
1736 Rare	—	—	—	—	—	—

KM# 167 10 DUCAT

35.0000 g., 0.9860 Gold 1.1095 oz. AGW **Ruler:** Joseph Benedict von Rost **Obv:** Bust right **Obv. Legend:** IOS BENED D G EPISCOPVS ... **Rev:** Bishops' hat above ornate oval arms

Date	Mintage	VG	F	VF	XF	Unc
1747 Rare	—	—	—	—	—	—

KM# A156 15 DUCAT

52.5000 g., 0.9860 Gold 1.6642 oz. AGW **Ruler:** Joseph Benedict von Rost **Obv:** Bust right **Rev:** Bishops' hat above ornate oval arms

Date	Mintage	VG	F	VF	XF	Unc
1736 Rare	—	—	—	—	—	—

PATTERNS

Including off metal strikes

KM#	Date	Mintage	Identification	Mkt Val
Pn1	1741	—	Ducat. Silver. KM161.	1,500
Pn2	1749	—	Ducat. Silver. KM168.	1,500

DISENTIS

ABBEY

The Abbey of Disentis is located in Switzerland 16 miles northeast from Gotthard Pass. They obtained the coinage right in 1571, but made little use of it.

ABBOTS

Gallus von Florin, 1716-1724
Marian von Castelberg, 1724-1742

STANDARD COINAGE

KM# 5 PFENNIG

Billon **Ruler:** Gallus von Florin **Obv:** Arched arms, GAD at top and sides **Note:** Uniface.

Date	Mintage	Good	VG	F	VF	XF
ND (1716)	—	—	250	450	950	2,000

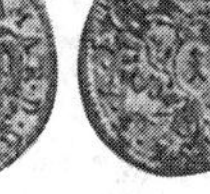

KM# 7 KREUZER

Billon **Ruler:** Marian von Castelberg **Obv:** Mitre above ornate oval arms **Rev:** Crowned double-headed eagle, oval shield on breast

Date	Mintage	Good	VG	F	VF	XF
1729	—	—	250	400	950	2,000

PATTERNS

KM#	Date	Mintage	Identification	Mkt Val
Pn1	1717	—	Bluzger. Billon.	—

EINSIEDELN

ABBEY

An abbey in the canton of Schwyz. It was founded in 934 and produced few coins.

RULER

Beatus Kuttel, Abbot, 1780-1808

TRADE COINAGE

KM# 3 DUCAT

3.5000 g., 0.9860 Gold 0.1109 oz. AGW **Ruler:** Beatus Kuttel - Abbot **Obv:** Mitre above ornate oval arms

Date	Mintage	VG	F	VF	XF	Unc
1783	—	850	1,450	3,000	4,750	7,250

PATTERNS

Including off metal strikes

KM#	Date	Mintage	Identification	Mkt Val
Pn1	1783	—	Ducat. Silver. KM#3.	550

FISCHINGEN

ABBEY

RULER

Franz Troger, 1688-1728

TRADE COINAGE

KM# 5 DUCAT

3.5000 g., 0.9860 Gold 0.1109 oz. AGW **Ruler:** Franz Troger **Subject:** 50th Anniversary of the Abbot **Obv:** Mitre above oval arms **Rev:** St. Ida, Countess of Toggenburg

Date	Mintage	VG	F	VF	XF	Unc
1726	—	650	950	2,000	3,200	5,000

KM# 6 2 DUCAT

7.0000 g., 0.9860 Gold 0.2219 oz. AGW **Ruler:** Franz Troger **Subject:** 50th Anniversary of the Abbott **Obv:** Oval arms topped by mitre on pedestal, date on pedestal **Rev:** St. Ida with Stag

Date	Mintage	VG	F	VF	XF	Unc
1726 Rare	—	—	—	—	—	—

PATTERNS

Including off metal strikes

KM#	Date	Mintage	Identification	Mkt Val
Pn1	1726	—	Ducat. Silver. KM#5.	600

FREIBURG

Friburg, Fribourg, Freyburg

A canton and city located in western Switzerland. The city was founded in 1178 and obtained the mint right in 1422. It joined the Swiss Confederation in 1481. During the Helvetian Republic period it was known as Sarine Et Broye but changed the name back to Freiburg in 1803.

MONETARY SYSTEM

Until 1798

16 Denier = 8 Vierer = 4 Kreuzer = 1 Batzen
56 Kreuzer = 8 Piecette = 1 Gulden
24 Piecette = 1 Thaler

CITY

STANDARD COINAGE

KM# 43 DENIER

Copper **Obv:** Cross **Rev:** Blank

Date	Mintage	VG	F	VF	XF	Unc
ND	—	175	325	1,200	—	—
1735	—	65.00	125	475	—	—
1745	—	65.00	125	475	—	—
1751	—	65.00	125	475	—	—
1752	—	65.00	125	475	—	—
1763	—	65.00	125	475	—	—

KM# 37 1/2 KREUZER (Vierer)

Billon **Obv:** Legend, crowned imperial eagle **Obv. Legend:** MONETA • FRIBVRGENSIS **Rev:** Cross with prongs, crosses in angles, date in legend

Date	Mintage	VG	F	VF	XF	Unc
1713	—	450	800	2,000	—	—
1715	—	150	250	950	—	—
1737	—	60.00	100	400	225	—

KM# 44 1/2 KREUZER (Vierer)

Billon **Obv:** Crowned imperial eagle with arms on breast **Rev:** Cross with prongs, blossoms in angles

Date	Mintage	VG	F	VF	XF	Unc
1736	—	250	475	2,000	—	—

KM# 45 1/2 KREUZER (Vierer)

Billon **Obv:** Shield arms

Date	Mintage	VG	F	VF	XF	Unc
1736	—	9.00	16.00	60.00	165	—
1737	—	15.00	30.00	125	275	—
1738	—	90.00	165	600	—	—
1739	—	90.00	165	600	—	—
1740	—	9.00	16.00	65.00	165	—
1741 Rare	—	15.00	40.00	75.00	—	—
1744	—	9.00	16.00	60.00	165	—
1751	—	100	200	800	—	—

KM# 48 1/2 KREUZER (Vierer)

Billon **Obv:** Tower arms

Date	Mintage	VG	F	VF	XF	Unc
1744	—	90.00	165	600	—	—

KM# 52 1/2 KREUZER (Vierer)

Billon **Obv:** Shield within circle **Rev:** Floreated cross, blossoms in angles within circle, date below

Date	Mintage	VG	F	VF	XF	Unc
1769	—	15.00	30.00	125	275	—
1770	—	8.00	15.00	60.00	165	—
1774	—	15.00	30.00	125	275	—
1787	—	7.00	12.00	40.00	125	250
1790	—	5.00	8.00	32.00	80.00	165

KM# 16 KREUZER

Billon **Obv:** Crowned imperial eagle with shield arms on breast **Rev:** Blossoms in angles of cross

Date	Mintage	VG	F	VF	XF	Unc
ND	—	20.00	40.00	65.00	135	—
1702 Rare	—	—	—	—	—	—

KM# 34 KREUZER

Billon **Obv:** Double-headed eagle with tower arms on breast, within circle **Rev:** Blossoms in angles of cross within circle

Date	Mintage	VG	F	VF	XF	Unc
1711	—	7.00	12.00	40.00	125	—
1712	—	7.00	12.00	40.00	125	—
1713	—	7.00	12.00	40.00	125	—
1714	—	7.00	12.00	40.00	125	—

KM# 42 KREUZER

Billon **Obv:** Shield within circle **Rev:** Floreated cross, blossoms in angles within circle, date below

Date	Mintage	VG	F	VF	XF	Unc
1737	—	20.00	35.00	125	275	—
1738	—	20.00	35.00	125	275	—
1741	—	10.00	16.00	65.00	165	—
1769	—	16.00	30.00	125	275	—
1770	—	16.00	30.00	125	275	—
1772	—	16.00	30.00	125	275	—
1774	—	5.00	8.00	40.00	100	200
1787	—	5.00	8.00	40.00	100	200
1789	—	5.00	8.00	40.00	100	—

KM# 30 2 KREUZER

Billon **Obv:** Tower arms divide F-B **Rev:** Cross with prongs, value: CR-2 or 2-CR in bottom fields

Date	Mintage	VG	F	VF	XF	Unc
1709	—	14.00	25.00	95.00	250	—
1711	—	14.00	25.00	95.00	250	—
1712	—	14.00	25.00	95.00	250	—
1713	—	14.00	25.00	95.00	250	—
1714	—	17.00	30.00	120	320	—

KM# 36 2 KREUZER

Billon **Obv:** Tower arms with or without eagle above **Rev:** Flowers in angles of cross

Date	Mintage	VG	F	VF	XF	Unc
1714	—	14.00	25.00	95.00	250	—
1715	—	14.00	25.00	95.00	250	—
1717	—	14.00	25.00	95.00	250	—
1738	—	12.00	20.00	80.00	200	—
1740	—	14.00	25.00	95.00	250	—
1741	—	14.00	25.00	95.00	250	—

KM# 47 2 KREUZER

Billon **Obv:** Shield within circle **Rev:** Floreated cross, blossoms in angles within circle, date below

Date	Mintage	VG	F	VF	XF	Unc
1741	—	12.00	20.00	80.00	200	—
1746	—	20.00	40.00	100	400	—
1751	—	15.00	30.00	120	325	—
1752	—	12.00	20.00	80.00	200	—
1754	—	85.00	150	600	1,600	—
1767 Rare	—	30.00	75.00	150	250	—
1769	—	20.00	40.00	150	400	—
1770	—	12.00	20.00	80.00	200	—
1772	—	15.00	30.00	120	325	—
1774	—	12.00	20.00	80.00	200	—
1787	—	7.00	12.00	50.00	125	240
1788	—	7.00	12.00	50.00	125	240
1789	—	7.00	12.00	50.00	125	240
1793	—	7.00	12.00	50.00	125	240
1797	—	10.00	20.00	80.00	200	350
1798	—	7.00	12.00	50.00	125	240

KM# 58 7 KREUZER (1/8 Gulden)

Silver **Obv:** Oval shield within thin wreath and circle **Rev:** Crowned monogram in cruciform, value in center, all within circle

Date	Mintage	VG	F	VF	XF	Unc
1787	—	8.00	15.00	40.00	80.00	145
1788	—	8.00	15.00	40.00	80.00	140
1789	—	8.00	15.00	40.00	80.00	140
1791	—	8.00	15.00	40.00	80.00	140
1793	—	8.00	15.00	40.00	80.00	140
1794	—	8.00	15.00	40.00	80.00	140
1795	—	8.00	15.00	40.00	80.00	140
1797	—	8.00	15.00	40.00	80.00	140

KM# 31 10 KREUZER

Silver **Obv:** Tower arms in ornate cartouche **Rev:** Crowned double-headed eagle with value on breast

Date	Mintage	VG	F	VF	XF	Unc
1709	—	70.00	125	325	650	—

KM# 59 14 KREUZER (1/4 Gulden)

Silver **Obv:** Crowned oval shield within sprigs and circle **Rev:** Crowned monogram in cruciform, value in center, all within circle

Date	Mintage	VG	F	VF	XF	Unc
1787	—	8.00	25.00	60.00	125	200
1788	—	8.00	25.00	60.00	125	200
1790	—	8.00	32.50	80.00	165	275
1793	—	8.00	32.50	80.00	165	275
1797	—	8.00	32.50	80.00	165	275
1798 Rare	—	—	—	—	—	—

KM# 33 20 KREUZER (1/2 Dicken)

Silver **Obv:** Crowned double-headed eagle with value in heart shape on breast in ornate cartouche, palm branches at sides **Rev:** Tower arms, eagle above, ring below in ornate cartouche

Date	Mintage	VG	F	VF	XF	Unc
1710	—	45.00	80.00	200	400	—

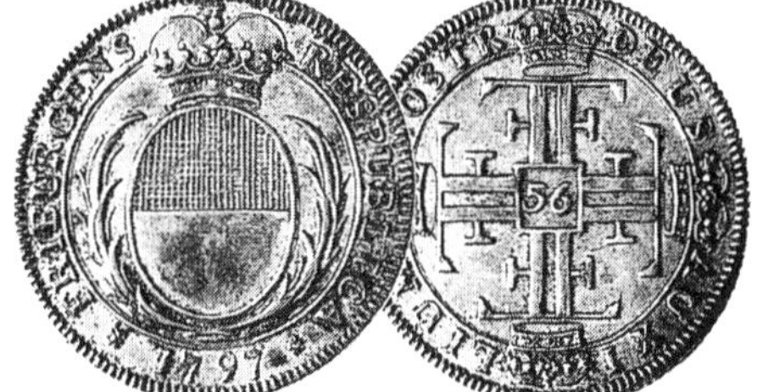

KM# 62 56 KREUZER (1 Gulden)

Silver **Obv:** Crowned oval shield within sprigs and circle **Rev:** Crowned monogram in cruciform, value in center, all within circle

Date	Mintage	VG	F	VF	XF	Unc
1796	—	75.00	125	325	600	1,000
1797	—	75.00	125	325	600	1,000

KM# 35 SCHILLING

Billon **Obv:** Crowned imperial eagle, tower arms on breast, date below **Rev:** Saint wearing mitre facing forward

Date	Mintage	VG	F	VF	XF	Unc
1713	—	14.00	25.00	80.00	200	—
1714	—	14.00	25.00	80.00	200	—

KM# 38 SCHILLING

Billon **Obv:** Date divided by tail of eagle **Rev:** 1/2-length standing Saint

Date	Mintage	VG	F	VF	XF	Unc
1717	—	12.00	25.00	80.00	200	—

CANTON

STANDARD COINAGE

KM# 61 28 KREUZER (1/2 Gulden)

Silver **Obv:** Crowned oval shield within sprigs and circle **Rev:** Crowned monogram in cruciform, value in center, all within circle

Date	Mintage	VG	F	VF	XF	Unc
1793	—	25.00	40.00	125	250	400
1798	—	25.00	40.00	125	250	400

DE SARINE ET BROYE

STANDARD COINAGE

KM# 65 42 KREUZER

Silver **Obv:** Fasces **Rev:** Value within wreath, date below

Date	Mintage	VG	F	VF	XF	Unc
1798	—	100	175	400	800	—

PATTERNS

Including off metal strikes

KM#	Date	Mintage	Identification	Mkt Val
Pn1	1709	—	20 Kreuzer. Silver. Same as Pn2.	—

KM#	Date	Mintage	Identification	Mkt Val
Pn2	1710	—	20 Kreuzer. Silver.	—
Pn3	1737	—	1/2 Kreuzer. Silver. KM45.	—
Pn4	1774	—	2 Kreuzer. Silver. KM47.	—
Pn6	1787	—	2 Kreuzer. Gold. KM47.	—
Pn5	1787	—	Kreuzer. Silver. KM42.	90.00

GENEVA

A canton and city in southwestern Switzerland. The city became a bishopric c.400 AD and was part of the Burgundian Kingdom for 500 years. They became completely independent in 1530. In 1798 they were occupied by France but became independent again in 1813. They joined the Swiss Confederation in 1815.

MONETARY SYSTEM

Until 1794

12 Deniers = 4 Quarts = 1 Sol
12 Sols = 1 Florin
12 Florins, 9 Sols = 1 Thaler
35 Florins = 1 Pistole

CANTON

STANDARD COINAGE

KM# 89 3 SOLS

Billon **Obv:** Arms within circle, IHS in sun above **Obv. Legend:** GENEVENSIS RESPUBLICA **Rev:** Cruciform within circle, date below **Rev. Legend:** POST TENEBRAS LUX

Date	Mintage	VG	F	VF	XF	Unc
1791	—	5.00	8.00	16.00	65.00	125

KM# 89a 3 SOLS

Silver **Obv:** Arms within circle, IHS in sun above **Rev:** Cruciform within circle, date below

Date	Mintage	VG	F	VF	XF	Unc
1791	—	25.00	60.00	90.00	110	—

KM# 82 6 SOLS

Billon **Obv:** Ornate arms, IHS in sun above **Obv. Legend:** GENEVENSIS • RESPUBLICA **Rev:** Value within cartouche, date below **Rev. Legend:** POST TENEBRAS LUX

Date	Mintage	VG	F	VF	XF	Unc
1765	—	5.00	8.00	20.00	60.00	125
1765 JG	—	10.00	20.00	40.00	80.00	175
1776 IG	—	5.00	8.00	20.00	60.00	125
1791 PB	—	5.00	8.00	20.00	60.00	125

KM# 82a 6 SOLS

Silver **Obv:** Ornate arms, IHS in sun above **Rev:** Value within cartouche, date below

Date	Mintage	VG	F	VF	XF	Unc
1765	—	25.00	65.00	90.00	120	—
1776 IG	—	25.00	65.00	90.00	120	—
1791 PB	—	25.00	65.00	90.00	120	—

KM# 61 10-1/2 SOLS

Silver **Obv:** Arms in cartouche, IHS in radiant sun divides date, initals below **Rev:** Inscription in cartouche, IHS in radiant sun above **Rev. Inscription:** POST/TENEBRAS/LUX/10/1/2

Date	Mintage	VG	F	VF	XF	Unc
1714 IPD	—	12.50	20.00	50.00	100	200
1715 IPD	—	15.00	20.00	50.00	100	200

KM# 61a 10-1/2 SOLS

Gold **Obv:** Arms in cartouche, IHS in radiant sun divides date, initals below **Rev:** Inscription in cartouche, IHS in radiant sun above **Rev. Inscription:** Post/TENEBRAS/LUX/10/1/2

Date	Mintage	VG	F	VF	XF	Unc
1714 IPD	—	650	1,250	2,000	2,500	—

KM# 59 21 SOLS

Silver **Obv:** Arms in cartouche, IHS in radiant sun above, date below **Rev:** Inscription in cartouche palm branches on sides, large radiant sun with IHS in center **Rev. Inscription:** POST/ TENEBRAS/ LUX/21

Date	Mintage	VG	F	VF	XF	Unc
1710	—	15.00	25.00	60.00	120	240
Note: Date under arms						
1710	—	100	150	400	800	—
Note: Date over arms						

KM# 60 21 SOLS

Silver **Rev:** Smaller radiant sun

Date	Mintage	VG	F	VF	XF	Unc
1711	—	12.00	20.00	50.00	100	200

KM# 62 21 SOLS

Silver **Obv:** Radiant sun above arms divides date

Date	Mintage	VG	F	VF	XF	Unc
1714	—	15.00	30.00	55.00	100	200
1715	—	15.00	30.00	55.00	100	200
1720	—	15.00	30.00	55.00	100	200
1721	—	15.00	30.00	55.00	100	200

KM# 66 THALER

Silver **Note:** Similar to KM#69 but with scrolls on both sides of date. Dav. #1767.

Date	Mintage	VG	F	VF	XF	Unc
1721	394	900	1,600	4,000	1,600	—
1722	—	75.00	125	250	600	2,400

KM# 69 THALER

Silver **Obv:** Ornate arms, IHS in sun above **Obv. Legend:** GENEVENSIS RESPUBLICA **Rev:** Crowned double-headed eagle within circle, divided date below **Rev. Legend:** POST TENEBRAS LUX

Date	Mintage	VG	F	VF	XF	Unc
1722	—	200	325	600	1,400	—
1723	—	75.00	125	250	600	2,400

KM# 70 PISTOLE

7.6400 g., 0.9000 Gold 0.2211 oz. AGW **Obv:** Ornate arms, sun above **Obv. Legend:** GENEVEN RESPUBL **Rev:** Crowned double-headed eagle, divided date below **Rev. Legend:** POST TENEBRAS LUX

Date	Mintage	F	VF	XF	Unc	BU
1722	—	1,200	2,000	3,500	5,000	—
1724	—	1,200	2,000	3,500	5,000	—

KM# 77 PISTOLE

7.6400 g., 0.9000 Gold 0.2211 oz. AGW **Obv:** Ornate arms, IHS in sun above **Obv. Legend:** GENEVEN • RESPUBL **Rev:** IHS in center of sun **Rev. Legend:** POST TENEBRAS LUX

Date	Mintage	F	VF	XF	Unc	BU
1752	—	475	950	1,600	2,400	3,200
1753	—	475	950	1,600	2,400	3,200
1754	—	475	950	1,600	2,400	3,200
1755	—	475	950	1,600	2,400	3,200
1757	—	475	950	1,600	2,400	3,200
1758	—	475	950	1,600	2,400	3,200
1762	—	475	950	1,600	2,400	3,200
1770	—	475	950	1,600	2,400	3,200

KM# 85 PISTOLE

7.6400 g., 0.9000 Gold 0.2211 oz. AGW **Obv:** Ornate arms, IHS in sun above **Obv. Legend:** GENEVEN • RESPUBL • **Rev:** Crowned double-headed eagle, inverted date below **Rev. Legend:** POST TENEBRAS LUX

Date	Mintage	F	VF	XF	Unc	BU
1772	—	750	1,650	2,750	4,500	5,750

KM# 84 3 PISTOLES

16.9500 g., 0.9200 Gold 0.5013 oz. AGW **Obv:** Ornate arms, IHS in sun above **Obv. Legend:** GENEVENSIS • RESPUBLICA **Rev:** IHS in center of large radiant sun, inverted date below **Rev. Legend:** POST TENEBRAS LUX

Date	Mintage	F	VF	XF	Unc	BU
1771	1,910	1,400	2,750	4,750	7,250	9,500

REVOLUTIONARY COINAGE

KM# 97 15 SOLS

Silver **Obv:** Displayed eagle within wreath, date below **Obv. Legend:** POST TENEBRAS LUX **Rev:** Value in center of radiant sun **Rev. Legend:** EGALITE LIBERTE INDEPENDANCE

Date	Mintage	VG	F	VF	XF	Unc
1794 W	—	12.00	20.00	50.00	100	200
1794	—	12.00	20.00	50.00	100	200

KM# 97a 15 SOLS

Gold **Obv:** Displayed eagle within wreath **Rev:** Value: DECIME/ LOISIVETE/EST UN/VOL at center, flower and date below

Date	Mintage	VG	F	VF	XF	Unc
1794 W	—	950	1,650	2,750	3,500	—

KM# 95 1/2 DECIME (5 Centimes)

Silver **Obv:** Bee hive, 2 flying bees below, GENEVE, date **Rev:** Value: CINQ/CENTIMES/L'AN III DE/L'EGALITE within circle of Roman numerals similar to a clock

Date	Mintage	VG	F	VF	XF	Unc
1794 Rare	—	125	250	500	750	—

KM# 96 DECIME (10 Centimes)

Silver **Obv:** Displayed eagle within wreath **Rev:** Value: DECIME/LOISIVETE/EST UN/VOL at center, flower and date below **Rev. Legend:** EGALITE LIBERTE INDEPENDANCE

Date	Mintage	VG	F	VF	XF	Unc
1794 W	—	35.00	60.00	165	325	600

KM# 98 GENEVOISE (10 Decimes)

Silver **Obv:** Tower arms above head left, inscription below **Obv. Legend:** GENEVOISE REPUBLIQUE **Rev:** Inscription, date flanked by oat sprigs **Rev. Legend:** APRES LES TENEBRES LA LUMIERE

Date	Mintage	VG	F	VF	XF	Unc
1794 TB	17,000	70.00	125	250	600	1,200

REFORM COINAGE

1795-1798

KM# 105 6 DENIERS

Billon **Obv:** Arms within circle **Obv. Legend:** • GENEVE REPUB • LAN 4 • DE LEGALITE • **Rev:** Value within wreath **Rev. Legend:** POST TENEBRAS LUX

Date	Mintage	VG	F	VF	XF	Unc
1795	—	7.00	12.00	30.00	65.00	150

KM# 106 UN (1) SOL / SIX DENIERS

Billon **Obv:** Arms within circle **Obv. Legend:** • GENEVE REPUB • LAN 4 • DE LEGALITE • **Rev:** Value within wreath **Rev. Legend:** POST TENEBRAS LUX

Date	Mintage	VG	F	VF	XF	Unc
1795	—	8.00	15.00	40.00	80.00	165
Note: Value in 3 lines						

KM# 107 UN (1) SOL / SIX DENIERS

Billon **Obv:** Arms within circle **Obv. Legend:** • GENEVE REPUB • LAN 4 • DE LEGALITE • **Rev:** Value within wreath, date below **Rev. Legend:** POST TENEBRAS LUX

Date	Mintage	VG	F	VF	XF	Unc
1795	—	10.00	20.00	55.00	125	250
Note: Value in 2 lines						

KM# 107a UN (1) SOL / SIX DENIERS

Silver **Obv:** Arms within circle **Obv. Legend:** • GENEVE REPUB • LAN 4 • DE LEGALITE • **Rev:** Value within wreath, date below **Rev. Legend:** POST TENEBRAS LUX

Date	Mintage	VG	F	VF	XF	Unc
1795	—	20.00	45.00	85.00	175	300
Note: Value in 3 lines						

KM# 108 TROIS (3) SOLS

Billon **Obv:** Arms within circle **Obv. Legend:** • GENEVE REPUBLIQUE • LAN' IV • DE LEGALITE • **Rev:** Value within wreath, date below **Rev. Legend:** * POST * TENEBRAS * LUX *

Date	Mintage	VG	F	VF	XF	Unc
1795 T-B	—	—	—	—	—	—
1795	—	12.00	20.00	50.00	100	200
1798	—	12.00	20.00	50.00	100	200

KM# 108a TROIS (3) SOLS

Silver **Obv:** Arms within circle **Obv. Legend:** • GENEVE REPUBLIQUE • LAN' IV • DE LEGALITE • **Rev:** Value within wreath, date below **Rev. Legend:** * POST * TENEBRAS * LUX *

Date	Mintage	VG	F	VF	XF	Unc
1795 T-B	—	—	—	—	—	—
1798	—	22.00	50.00	75.00	120	—

KM# 109 6 SOLS

Billon **Obv:** Arms within circle **Obv. Legend:** • GENEVE REPUBLIQUE • LAN' IV • DEL'EGALITE • **Rev:** Value within wreath, date below **Rev. Legend:** POST TENEBRAS LUX

Date	Mintage	VG	F	VF	XF	Unc
1795 TB	—	20.00	40.00	100	200	400
1795	—	10.00	20.00	50.00	100	200
1796	—	10.00	20.00	50.00	100	200
1797	—	10.00	20.00	50.00	100	200

KM# 109a 6 SOLS

Copper **Obv:** Arms within circle **Obv. Legend:** • GENEVE REPUBLIQUE • LAN' VI • DEL'EGALITE • **Rev:** Value within wreath **Rev. Legend:** POST TENEBRAS LUX

Date	Mintage	VG	F	VF	XF	Unc
1795	—	20.00	40.00	75.00	125	—
1796	—	20.00	40.00	75.00	125	—

KM# 109b 6 SOLS

Silver **Obv:** Arms within circle **Obv. Legend:** • GENEVE REPUBLIQUE • LAN' VI • DEL'EGALITE • **Rev:** Value within wreath **Rev. Legend:** POST TENEBRAS LUX

Date	Mintage	VG	F	VF	XF	Unc
1795	—	30.00	60.00	90.00	150	—
1796	—	30.00	60.00	90.00	150	—

KM# 110 VI FLORINS (IV Sols = VI Deniers)

Silver **Obv:** Arms within circle and wreath **Obv. Legend:** * GENEVE REPUBLIQUE * L'AN * IV * DE LEGALITE * **Rev:** Value in center of large radiant sun, date below **Rev. Legend:** POST * TENEBRAS * LUX *

Date	Mintage	VG	F	VF	XF	Unc
1795 W	—	35.00	65.00	165	325	575

KM# 111 XII FLORINS / IX SOLS

Silver **Obv:** Arms within circle and wreath **Obv. Legend:** * GENEVE • REPUBLIQUE • L'AN • IV • DE • L'EGALITE * **Rev:** Value in center of large radiant sun, date below **Rev. Legend:** * POST * TENEBRAS * LUX * **Note:** Dav. #1769.

Date	Mintage	VG	F	VF	XF	Unc
1795 TB	21,000	65.00	100	200	475	950

KM# 112 XII FLORINS / IX SOLS

Silver **Rev:** Denomination in legend, IHS in sunburst **Note:** Dav. #1770.

Date	Mintage	VG	F	VF	XF	Unc
1796	12,000	75.00	135	275	700	1,400

CITY

STANDARD COINAGE

KM# 76b 6 DENIERS

Gold **Obv:** Arms within circle, sun above **Rev:** IHS in center of sun

Date	Mintage	VG	F	VF	XF	Unc
1750	—	500	900	1,500	—	—

KM# 57 6 DENIERS (2 Quarts)

Billon **Obv:** Arms in cartouche, sun above **Rev:** Double cross, IHS at center, mm at top

Date	Mintage	VG	F	VF	XF	Unc
1702	—	5.00	8.00	16.00	55.00	120
1709	—	5.00	8.00	16.00	55.00	120
1715	—	5.00	8.00	16.00	55.00	120

KM# 57a 6 DENIERS (2 Quarts)

Silver **Obv:** Arms in cartouche, sun above **Rev:** Double cross, IHS at center, mm above

Date	Mintage	VG	F	VF	XF	Unc
1702	—	—	—	—	—	—
1709	—	—	—	—	—	—
1715	—	—	—	—	—	—

KM# 57b 6 DENIERS (2 Quarts)

Gold **Obv:** Arms in cartouche, sun above **Rev:** Double cross, IHS at center, mm at top

Date	Mintage	VG	F	VF	XF	Unc
1702	—	—	—	—	—	—
1709	—	500	900	1,500	—	—
1715	—	500	900	1,500	—	—

KM# 65 6 DENIERS (2 Quarts)

Billon **Obv:** Arms within circle, sun above **Rev:** Double cross, IHS at center, within circle

Date	Mintage	VG	F	VF	XF	Unc
1720	—	7.00	12.00	25.00	145	—
1721	—	7.00	12.00	25.00	145	—
1722	—	5.00	8.00	16.00	125	—
1725	—	5.00	8.00	16.00	125	—
1726	—	5.00	8.00	16.00	125	—
1729	—	5.00	8.00	16.00	125	—
1730	—	5.00	8.00	16.00	125	—

KM# 65a 6 DENIERS (2 Quarts)

Silver **Obv:** Arms within circle, sun above **Rev:** Double cross, IHS at center, within circle

Date	Mintage	VG	F	VF	XF	Unc
1721	—	—	—	—	—	—
1722	—	—	—	—	—	—
1725	—	—	—	—	—	—
1729	—	—	—	—	—	—
1730	—	—	—	—	—	—

KM# 76 6 DENIERS (2 Quarts)

Billon **Obv:** Arms within circle, sun above **Obv. Legend:** GENEVEN RESPUBLIC **Rev:** IHS in center of sun

Date	Mintage	VG	F	VF	XF	Unc
1750	—	5.00	8.00	16.00	55.00	125

KM# 79a 6 DENIERS (2 Quarts)

Silver **Obv:** Arms within circle, sun above **Rev:** IHS in center of sun

Date	Mintage	VG	F	VF	XF	Unc
1750	—	20.00	50.00	75.00	100	200
1754	—	20.00	50.00	75.00	100	200
1759	—	20.00	50.00	75.00	100	200
1762	—	20.00	50.00	75.00	100	200
1765	—	20.00	50.00	75.00	100	200
1769	—	20.00	50.00	75.00	100	200
1776	—	20.00	50.00	75.00	100	200
1785	—	20.00	50.00	75.00	100	200
1788	—	20.00	50.00	75.00	100	200

KM# 76a 6 DENIERS (2 Quarts)

Silver **Obv:** arms within circle, sun above **Rev:** IHS in center of sun

Date	Mintage	VG	F	VF	XF	Unc
1750	—	20.00	50.00	75.00	100	200

KM# 79 6 DENIERS (2 Quarts)

Billon **Obv:** Arms within circle, sun above **Obv. Legend:** GENEVEN • RESPUBLIC • **Rev:** IHS in center of sun **Rev. Legend:** • POSTTENEBRASLUX •

Date	Mintage	VG	F	VF	XF	Unc
1754	—	5.00	8.00	15.00	55.00	125
1756	—	40.00	75.00	150	350	750
1759	—	5.00	8.00	15.00	55.00	125
1762	—	5.00	8.00	15.00	55.00	125
1765	—	5.00	8.00	15.00	55.00	125
1766	—	8.00	12.00	24.00	80.00	145
1769	—	5.00	8.00	15.00	55.00	125
1770	—	5.00	8.00	15.00	55.00	125
1775	—	5.00	8.00	15.00	55.00	125
1776	—	5.00	8.00	15.00	55.00	125
1785	—	5.00	8.00	15.00	55.00	125
1788	—	5.00	8.00	15.00	55.00	125

KM# 79b 6 DENIERS (2 Quarts)

Gold **Obv:** Arms within circle, sun above **Rev:** IHS in center of sun

Date	Mintage	VG	F	VF	XF	Unc
1785	—	500	900	1,500	—	—
1788	—	500	900	1,500	—	—

KM# 56 9 DENIERS (3 Quarts)

Billon **Obv:** Date below arms within circle **Obv. Legend:** GENEUA RESPUBL **Rev:** Cross with flowers in angles within circle **Rev. Legend:** • POST TENEBRASLUX •

Date	Mintage	VG	F	VF	XF	Unc
1708 IM	—	5.00	8.00	20.00	65.00	125

KM# 63a 9 DENIERS (3 Quarts)

Silver **Obv:** Arms in cartouche, date and IPD below **Rev:** Cross of leaf shapes, IHS at center

Date	Mintage	VG	F	VF	XF	Unc
1708 IM	—	—	—	—	—	—
1715 IPD	—	—	—	—	—	—

KM# 63 9 DENIERS (3 Quarts)

Billon **Obv:** Arms in cartouche, date and IPD below **Rev:** Cross of leaf shapes, IHS at center

Date	Mintage	VG	F	VF	XF	Unc
1715 IPD	—	5.00	8.00	20.00	65.00	125

KM# 72 9 DENIERS (3 Quarts)

Billon **Obv:** Crowned double-headed eagle within circle, PAC above **Rev:** Radiant sun above arms in cartouche, date below

Date	Mintage	VG	F	VF	XF	Unc
1730 PAC	—	5.00	8.00	20.00	65.00	125
1731 PAC	—	5.00	8.00	20.00	65.00	125

KM# 72a 9 DENIERS (3 Quarts)

Silver **Obv:** Crowned double-headed eagle within circle, PAC above **Rev:** Radiant sun above arms in cartouche, date below

Date	Mintage	VG	F	VF	XF	Unc
1730 PAC	—	—	—	—	—	—

KM# 78 9 DENIERS (3 Quarts)

Billon **Obv:** Sun above arms **Obv. Legend:** GENEVEN • RESPUBL • **Rev:** Crowned double-headed eagle within circle **Rev. Legend:** POST TENEBRAS LUX

Date	Mintage	VG	F	VF	XF	Unc
1753 Rare	—	—	—	—	—	—
1763	—	5.00	8.00	15.00	55.00	125

Date	Mintage	VG	F	VF	XF	Unc
1775	—	5.00	8.00	15.00	55.00	125
1785	—	5.00	8.00	15.00	55.00	125

KM# 78a 9 DENIERS (3 Quarts)

Silver **Obv:** Sun above arms **Rev:** Crowned double-headed eagle within circle

Date	Mintage	VG	F	VF	XF	Unc
1775	—	20.00	50.00	75.00	100	—
1785	—	20.00	50.00	75.00	100	—

KM# 67 18 DENIERS (6 Quarts)

Billon **Obv:** Arms within circle, IHS in sun above **Obv. Legend:** GENEVENSIS RESPUBLIC **Rev:** Design within circle, date above **Rev. Legend:** POST TENEBRAS LUX

Date	Mintage	VG	F	VF	XF	Unc
1722 G	—	5.00	8.00	40.00	80.00	160
1750 G	—	8.00	15.00	40.00	80.00	160
1763 G	—	8.00	15.00	40.00	80.00	160
1766 G	—	5.00	8.00	16.00	65.00	125
1775 G	—	5.00	8.00	16.00	65.00	125
1776 G	—	5.00	8.00	16.00	65.00	125

KM# 67a 18 DENIERS (6 Quarts)

Silver **Obv:** Arms within circle, IHS in sun above **Rev:** Design within circle, date above

Date	Mintage	VG	F	VF	XF	Unc
1750	—	20.00	50.00	75.00	100	200
1763	—	20.00	50.00	75.00	100	200
1775	—	20.00	50.00	75.00	100	200
1776	—	20.00	50.00	75.00	100	200

KM# 87 SOL

Billon **Obv:** Arms within circle, sun above **Obv. Legend:** GENEVENSIS RESPUBLICA **Rev:** Value within ornate circle, date below **Rev. Legend:** POST TENEBRAS LUX

Date	Mintage	VG	F	VF	XF	Unc
1785 G	—	5.00	8.00	15.00	50.00	125
1786 G Rare	—	3.00	6.00	12.00	20.00	—
1788 B	—	5.00	8.00	15.00	50.00	125

KM# 87a SOL

Silver **Obv:** Arms within circle, sun above **Obv. Legend:** RESPUBLICA GENEVENSIS **Rev:** Value within ornate circle, date below **Rev. Legend:** POST TENEBRAS LUX

Date	Mintage	VG	F	VF	XF	Unc
1785 G	—	25.00	60.00	80.00	100	200
1786 Rare	—	25.00	60.00	80.00	100	—
1788	—	25.00	60.00	80.00	100	200

KM# 87b SOL

Gold **Obv:** Arms within circle, sun above **Obv. Legend:** RESPUBLICA GENEVENSIS **Rev:** Value within ornate circle, date below **Rev. Legend:** POST TENEBRAS LUX

Date	Mintage	VG	F	VF	XF	Unc
1786 G	—	550	950	1,550	—	—

KM# 68 3 SOLS

Billon **Obv:** Arms in cartouche, IHS in sun above **Rev:** Cruciform within circle

Date	Mintage	VG	F	VF	XF	Unc
1722	—	5.00	8.00	20.00	100	165
1726	—	8.00	15.00	40.00	135	250

KM# 68a 3 SOLS

Gold **Obv:** Arms in cartouche, IHS in sun above **Rev:** Cruciform

Date	Mintage	VG	F	VF	XF	Unc
1726	—	600	1,000	1,600	2,000	—

KM# 81 3 SOLS

Billon **Obv:** Arms within circle, IHS in sun above **Obv. Legend:** GENEVENSIS RESPUBLICA **Rev:** Cruciform within circle **Rev. Legend:** POST TENEBRAS LUX

Date	Mintage	VG	F	VF	XF	Unc
1763 GR	—	5.00	8.00	16.00	65.00	125
1764 GR	—	5.00	8.00	16.00	65.00	125
1764	—	5.00	8.00	16.00	65.00	125
1766	—	5.00	8.00	16.00	65.00	125
1775	—	5.00	8.00	16.00	65.00	125
1776 I-G	—	5.00	8.00	16.00	65.00	125

KM# 81a 3 SOLS

Silver **Obv:** Arms within circle, IHS in sun above **Rev:** Cruciform within circle

Date	Mintage	VG	F	VF	XF	Unc
1722	—	—	—	—	—	—
1763 GR	—	25.00	60.00	90.00	110	—
1764	—	—	—	—	—	—
1766	—	25.00	60.00	90.00	110	—
1776 I-G	—	25.00	60.00	90.00	110	—

PATTERNS

Including off metal strikes

KM#	Date	Mintage	Identification	Mkt Val
Pn1	1794	—	Genevoise. Copper.	900
Pn2	1794	—	Genevoise. Tin.	850
Pn3	1794 TB	—	Genevoise. Copper. KM#98a.	—
Pn4	1794 TB	—	Genevoise. Lead. KM#98b.	—

KM#	Date	Mintage	Identification	Mkt Val
Pn5	1794	—	Xii Florins. Copper.	400
Pn6	1794	—	Xii Florins. Tin.	350

KM#	Date	Mintage	Identification	Mkt Val
Pn7	1795	—	Xii Florins / Ix Sols.	—

HALDENSTEIN

Haldenstein was an area in the canton of Graubunden. The rulers were barons who held various estates. They received the mint right in 1612. The property of the barons was mediatized during the French invasion of Graubunden in 1798 and 1799.

RULERS

Johann Lucius von Salis, 1701-1722
Gubert von Salis, 1722-1737
Thomas III von Salis, 1737-1783

BARONY

STANDARD COINAGE

KM# 5 PFENNIG

Billon **Obv:** Spanish shield with three fish, letters TFVE around **Note:** Uniface. Schussel type.

Date	Mintage	VG	F	VF	XF	Unc
ND	—	90.00	160	400	275	—

KM# 76 PFENNIG

Copper **Obv:** Arched shield with three fish divides 1-P, date above **Note:** Uniface.

Date	Mintage	VG	F	VF	XF	Unc
1702 Rare	—	125	250	500	1,000	—

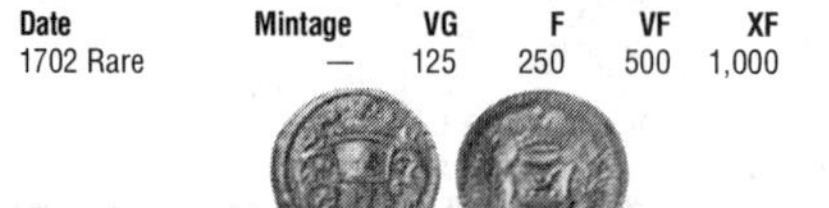

KM# 77 PFENNIG

Copper **Obv:** Crowned Salis arms **Rev:** Crowned arms of Leichtenstein-Grottenstein

Date	Mintage	VG	F	VF	XF	Unc
ND Rare	—	—	—	—	—	—

KM# 93 2 PFENNIG (1/2 Kreuzer)

Billon

Date	Mintage	VG	F	VF	XF	Unc
ND(1737)	—	100	200	500	900	—

KM# 91 2 PFENNIG (1/2 Kreuzer)

Billon **Obv:** Crowned five-fold arms on round shield in cartoucne within barley corn circle **Note:** Uniface.

Date	Mintage	VG	F	VF	XF	Unc
ND(1737)	—	150	250	600	1,200	—

KM# 92 2 PFENNIG (1/2 Kreuzer)

Billon **Obv:** Crowned five-fold arms of Haldenstein-Schauenstein on a Spanish shield between palm branches **Note:** Uniface.

Date	Mintage	VG	F	VF	XF	Unc
ND(1737)	—	100	200	500	900	—

KM# 10 BLUZGER

Billon **Obv:** . Crowned five-fold arms of Haldenstein-Schauenstein on a Spanish shield between palm branches, value: 1/2 below **Note:** Uniface.

Date	Mintage	VG	F	VF	XF	Unc
ND	—	100	200	600	275	—

KM# 80 BLUZGER

Billon **Ruler:** Johann Lucius von Salis **Obv. Legend:** MO • NOVA HALDENS • **Rev:** Date divided at top

Date	Mintage	VG	F	VF	XF	Unc
1714	—	200	400	950	600	—

KM# 82 BLUZGER

Billon **Ruler:** Gubert von Salis

Date	Mintage	VG	F	VF	XF	Unc
1723	—	14.00	25.00	60.00	125	—
1724	—	3.00	5.00	16.00	35.00	—
1725	—	3.00	5.00	16.00	35.00	—
1726	—	3.00	5.00	16.00	35.00	—
1727	—	3.00	5.00	16.00	35.00	—
1728	—	3.00	5.00	16.00	35.00	—
1734	—	5.00	8.00	20.00	40.00	—

KM# 75 KREUZER

Billon **Ruler:** Johann Lucius von Salis

Date	Mintage	VG	F	VF	XF	Unc
1701	—	135	250	600	1,000	—
1702	—	400	650	1,600	2,000	—

KM# 78 KREUZER

Billon **Ruler:** Johann Lucius von Salis

Date	Mintage	VG	F	VF	XF	Unc
1703	—	175	350	800	1,000	—

KM# 83 KREUZER

Billon **Ruler:** Thomas III von Salis **Obv:** Value: 1 on shield on breast of crowned imperial eagle **Rev:** Oval arms in crowned cartouche

Date	Mintage	VG	F	VF	XF	Unc
1723	—	20.00	32.00	80.00	160	—
1724	—	12.00	20.00	50.00	100	—
1725	—	14.00	25.00	60.00	125	—
1726	—	20.00	32.00	80.00	160	—
1727	—	9.00	16.00	40.00	80.00	—
1728	—	7.00	12.00	32.00	65.00	—
1729	—	14.00	25.00	60.00	125	—
1730	—	9.00	16.00	40.00	80.00	—
1731 Rare	—	125	250	500	750	—

KM# 101 KREUZER

Billon **Ruler:** Thomas III von Salis **Obv:** Bust right **Rev:** Value, date within cartouche

Date	Mintage	VG	F	VF	XF	Unc
1758	—	75.00	125	325	650	1,200

KM# 84 2 KREUZER (1/2 Batzen)

Billon **Ruler:** Gubert von Salis **Obv:** Value on breast of crowned imperial eagle, shield **Rev:** Oval arms in crowned cartouche

Date	Mintage	VG	F	VF	XF	Unc
1724	—	900	1,600	4,000	—	—

KM# 98 2 KREUZER (1/2 Batzen)

Billon **Ruler:** Thomas III von Salis **Obv:** Double H above shield within sprigs **Rev:** Value, date within wreath

Date	Mintage	VG	F	VF	XF	Unc
1749	—	135	250	600	1,200	1,750

KM# 85 3 KREUZER (1 Groschen)

Silver **Ruler:** Gubert von Salis **Obv:** Crowned double-headed eagle divides date above, value within circle below **Rev:** Bust right

Date	Mintage	VG	F	VF	XF	Unc
1727 Rare	—	1,400	2,000	5,000	—	—

KM# 90 3 KREUZER (1 Groschen)

Silver **Ruler:** Gubert von Salis **Obv:** Value within ornamentation below dividing date, round five-fold arms in cartouche **Rev:** Inscription: PRO DEO/ET/PATRIA in palm branches

Date	Mintage	VG	F	VF	XF	Unc
1734 Rare	—	—	—	—	—	—

KM# 96 3 KREUZER (1 Groschen)

Billon **Ruler:** Thomas III von Salis

Date	Mintage	VG	F	VF	XF	Unc
1748	—	900	1,600	4,000	2,500	—

KM# 95 6 KREUZER

Billon **Ruler:** Thomas III von Salis

Date	Mintage	VG	F	VF	XF	Unc
1747 Rare	—	—	—	—	—	—

KM# 100 ALBUS

Billon **Ruler:** Thomas III von Salis

Date	Mintage	VG	F	VF	XF	Unc
1752	—	125	200	475	950	1,450

KM# 97 5 SOLDI

Billon **Ruler:** Thomas III von Salis

Date	Mintage	VG	F	VF	XF	Unc
1748	—	1,200	2,000	5,000	9,500	—

TRADE COINAGE

KM# 87 DUCAT

3.5000 g., 0.9860 Gold 0.1109 oz. AGW **Ruler:** Gubert von Salis

Date	Mintage	VG	F	VF	XF	Unc
1733	—	—	4,750	9,500	16,000	—

KM# 103 DUCAT

3.5000 g., 0.9860 Gold 0.1109 oz. AGW **Ruler:** Thomas III von Salis

Date	Mintage	VG	F	VF	XF	Unc
1767	—	—	4,750	9,500	16,000	—
1768 Rare	—	—	—	7,000	10,000	—
1770 Rare	—	—	—	7,000	10,000	—

KM# 88 5 DUCAT

17.5000 g., 0.9860 Gold 0.5547 oz. AGW **Ruler:** Gubert von Salis **Obv:** Armored bust right **Obv. Legend:** GUB : DE SAL : D • I • H • LIE : ET G • **Rev:** Ornate, oval arms, divided date below **Rev. Legend:** ...ODEO ET PATRIA

Date	Mintage	VG	F	VF	XF	Unc
1733	—	—	8,000	16,000	28,000	—

KM# 89 6 DUCAT

21.0000 g., 0.9860 Gold 0.6657 oz. AGW **Ruler:** Gubert von Salis **Obv:** Armored bust right **Obv. Legend:** GUB : DE SAL : D • I • H • LIE : ET G • **Rev:** Ornate oval arms, divided date below **Rev. Legend:** ...ODEO ET PATRIA

Date	Mintage	VG	F	VF	XF	Unc
1733 Rare	—	—	—	20,000	25,000	—

CANTON

STANDARD COINAGE

KM# 11 3 KREUZER (1 Groschen)

Silver **Obv:** Three decorated Spanish shields in cloverleaf form in inner circle **Rev:** Crowned double-headed eagle with cross and halo, 3 on breast of eagle

Date	Mintage	VG	F	VF	XF	Unc
ND	—	450	850	1,500	2,500	—

PATTERNS

Including off metal strikes

KM#	Date	Mintage	Identification	Mkt Val
Pn1	1733	—	Ducat. Silver. KM#87	—
Pn2	1767	—	Ducat. Silver. KM#103	—
Pn3	1768	—	Ducat. Silver. KM#103	—
Pn4	1770	—	Ducat. Silver. KM#103	1,200

LUZERN

Lucerne

A canton and city in central Switzerland. The city grew around the Benedictine Monastery which was founded in 750. They joined the Swiss Confederation as the 4th member in 1332. Few coins were issued before the1500s.

MINT OFFICIALS' INITIALS

Initials	Date	Name
B	1725	?
B	1794-1807	Bruppacher
HL	?	Hedlinger
IB	1744	?
IH	1734-43	?
M	1795-96	Meyer
T, IT	1742	?

MONETARY SYSTEM

Until 1798

240 Angster = 120 Rappen
= 40 Schillinge = 1 Gulden
10 Rappen = 1 Batzen
4 Kreuzer = 1 Batzen
10 Batzen = 1 Frank
40 Batzen = 3 Gulden = 1 Thaler
4 Franken = 1 Thaler
12 Gulden = 1 Duplone

CITY

STANDARD COINAGE

KM# 5 HELLER

Billon **Obv:** Plain bishop's mitre above form with hollow cheeks, dots missing in mitre **Note:** Uniface.

Date	Mintage	VG	F	VF	XF	Unc
ND(1773)	—	12.00	20.00	65.00	150	—

KM# 6 ANGSTER

Billon **Obv:** Bishop's mitre above composed form with hollow cheeks, dots in mitre **Note:** Uniface.

Date	Mintage	VG	F	VF	XF	Unc
ND(1773)	—	12.00	20.00	65.00	150	—

KM# 73 ANGSTER

Copper **Obv:** Crowned, ornate shield **Rev:** Value, date

Date	Mintage	VG	F	VF	XF	Unc
1773	—	5.00	8.00	16.00	32.00	80.00

KM# 76 ANGSTER

Copper **Obv:** Oval ornate shield **Rev:** Value, date within wreath **Note:** Similar to Rappen, KM#96.

Date	Mintage	VG	F	VF	XF	Unc
1775	—	5.00	8.00	15.00	30.00	80.00
1790	—	5.00	8.00	15.00	30.00	80.00
1791	—	—	—	—	—	—

KM# 7 RAPPEN

Billon **Obv:** Shield in inner circle, pearl ring encircles **Note:** Uniface. Many varieties of shields exist.

Date	Mintage	VG	F	VF	XF	Unc
ND(1773)	—	12.00	20.00	40.00	85.00	150

KM# 74 RAPPEN

Copper **Obv:** Shield within sprigs **Rev:** Value

Date	Mintage	VG	F	VF	XF	Unc
ND(1773)	—	3.00	5.00	8.00	20.00	40.00

KM# 75 RAPPEN

Copper **Obv:** Oval ornate shield **Rev:** Value, date within cartouche **Note:** Similar to KM#96.

Date	Mintage	VG	F	VF	XF	Unc
1774	—	3.00	5.00	8.00	20.00	40.00
1787	—	3.00	5.00	8.00	20.00	40.00
1789	—	3.00	5.00	8.00	20.00	40.00
1795	—	3.00	5.00	8.00	20.00	40.00
1796	—	3.00	5.00	8.00	20.00	40.00

KM# 67 SCHILLING

Billon **Obv:** Curved arms divide date at bottom **Rev:** Facing portrait of Saint Leodegari

Date	Mintage	VG	F	VF	XF	Unc
1742 IT	—	15.00	25.00	60.00	125	200
1743 IH	—	15.00	25.00	60.00	125	200

KM# 85 SCHILLING

Billon **Obv:** Shield within beaded circle, date below **Obv. Legend:** MON : LUCERNENSIS **Rev:** Facing portrait of Saint Leodegari **Rev. Legend:** SANCT LEODEGARI

Date	Mintage	VG	F	VF	XF	Unc
1794	—	5.00	8.00	16.00	40.00	125
1795	—	5.00	8.00	16.00	40.00	125

KM# 56 1/8 GULDEN (5 Schillings)

Silver **Obv:** Ornate, round shield **Obv. Legend:** MON • NOVA • REIP • LVCERNEN • **Rev:** Monogram

Date	Mintage	VG	F	VF	XF	Unc
1725	—	90.00	165	400	800	—

KM# 57 1/8 GULDEN (5 Schillings)

Silver **Obv:** Ornate, oval shield, date in legend **Obv. Legend:** MON • NOV • REIP • LVCERN • **Rev:** Monogram within beaded circle **Rev. Legend:** POPVLI • SVI • DOMINVS •

Date	Mintage	VG	F	VF	XF	Unc
1725	—	15.00	25.00	60.00	125	200

KM# 81 1/8 GULDEN (5 Schillings)

Silver **Obv:** Crowned, oval shield with garland within sprigs **Obv. Legend:** MON • NOV • REIP • LUCERN • **Rev:** Monogram in cruciform with value in center, within square **Rev. Legend:** POPVLI SUI • • DOMINUS SPES

Date	Mintage	VG	F	VF	XF	Unc
1793	—	15.00	25.00	60.00	125	200

KM# 58 1/4 GULDEN (10 Schillings)

Silver **Obv:** Ornate, round shield **Rev:** Monogram **Note:** Similar to 1/8 Gulden, KM#56.

Date	Mintage	VG	F	VF	XF	Unc
1725 B	—	35.00	65.00	165	325	—

KM# 69 1/4 GULDEN (10 Schillings)

Silver **Obv:** Curved arms in baroque frame **Rev:** Inscription in cartouche, value: 1/4 GG in oval shield below **Rev. Inscription:** DOMI/NUS/SPES. POP/SUI/date

Date	Mintage	VG	F	VF	XF	Unc
1744 IB	—	—	1,600	4,000	—	—

KM# 82 1/4 GULDEN (10 Schillings)

Silver **Obv:** Crowned, oval shield with garland within sprigs **Obv. Legend:** MON • NOV • REIP • LUCERNENS • **Rev:** Monogram in cruciform with value in center, within square **Rev. Legend:** POPULI SUI DOMINUS SPES

Date	Mintage	VG	F	VF	XF	Unc
1793	—	25.00	50.00	125	250	475
1796	—	25.00	50.00	125	250	475

KM# 43 GULDEN

Silver **Obv:** Heart-shaped arms, decoration around, date above **Rev:** Inscription in baroque frame **Rev. Inscription:** AUXILIO/DEI/PROSPE/RE

Date	Mintage	VG	F	VF	XF	Unc
1713	—	100	200	475	950	—

KM# 46 GULDEN

Silver **Obv:** Ornate heart-shaped arms **Rev:** Curved inscription baroque frame

Date	Mintage	VG	F	VF	XF	Unc
1714	—	150	250	600	1,200	—

KM# 47 GULDEN

Silver **Rev:** Inscription in straight lines in baroque frame

Date	Mintage	VG	F	VF	XF	Unc
1714	—	65.00	100	200	600	—

KM# 51 10 KREUZER

Silver **Obv:** Oval arms in cartouche **Rev:** Monogram in cruciform with value in center

Date	Mintage	VG	F	VF	XF	Unc
1715 Rare	—	—	—	—	—	—

KM# 44 20 KREUZER

Silver **Obv:** Oval arms in cartouche, 2 small palm branches at each side **Rev:** Monogram in cruciform with value in center

Date	Mintage	VG	F	VF	XF	Unc
1713	—	25.00	40.00	125	400	—
1714	—	25.00	40.00	125	400	—
1724	—	35.00	55.00	150	450	—
1725	—	35.00	55.00	150	450	—

KM# 61 20 KREUZER

Silver **Obv:** Oval arms in cartouche, ornamentation around **Rev:** Monogram in cruciform with value in center, curve arcs around

Date	Mintage	VG	F	VF	XF	Unc
1741	—	75.00	125	325	600	—

KM# 83 20 KREUZER

Silver **Obv:** Crowned, ornate oval shield with garland, within sprigs **Obv. Legend:** MON : NOV : REIP : LUCERNENSIS • **Rev:** Monogram in cruciform with value in center **Rev. Legend:** POPULI SUI DOMINUS SPES

Date	Mintage	VG	F	VF	XF	Unc
1793	—	35.00	60.00	165	475	—

KM# 88 20 KREUZER

Silver **Obv:** Crowned, oval shield within sprigs **Obv. Legend:** LUCERNENSIS RESPUBLICA **Rev:** Monogram in cruciform with value in center **Rev. Legend:** POPULI SUI DOMINUS SPES

Date	Mintage	VG	F	VF	XF	Unc
1795	—	70.00	125	325	600	—
1796	—	25.00	40.00	125	200	325

KM# 78 40 KREUZER

Silver **Obv:** Crowned, ornate shield, with flowers **Obv. Legend:** MON : NOV : REIP : LUCERNENSIS • **Rev:** Crowned, ornate monogram, with flowers **Rev. Legend:** POPULI SUI DOMINUS SPES

Date	Mintage	VG	F	VF	XF	Unc
ND	—	80.00	125	325	600	—
1782	—	80.00	125	325	600	—

KM# 84 40 KREUZER

Silver **Obv:** Crowned, oval shield with garland, within sprigs **Obv. Legend:** MON : NOV : REIP : LUCERNENSIS • **Rev:** Monogram in cruciform with value in center **Rev. Legend:** POPULI SUI DOMINUS SPES

Date	Mintage	VG	F	VF	XF	Unc
1793	—	45.00	80.00	200	400	725

KM# 91 40 KREUZER

Silver **Obv:** Crowned, oval shield within sprigs **Obv. Legend:** LUCERNENSIS RESPUBLICA **Rev:** Monogram in cruciform with value in center **Rev. Legend:** POPULI SUI DOMINUS SPES

Date	Mintage	VG	F	VF	XF	Unc
1796	—	25.00	40.00	80.00	165	325

KM# 45 1/2 BATZEN-5 RAPPEN

Billon **Obv:** Oval arms in cartouche, date above **Rev:** Cross with ornaments in angles

Date	Mintage	VG	F	VF	XF	Unc
1713	—	9.00	16.00	40.00	165	—
1714	—	9.00	16.00	40.00	165	—

KM# 68 1/2 BATZEN-5 RAPPEN

Billon **Obv:** Oval arms in cartouche, date and initials below **Rev:** Cross with flowers in angles

Date	Mintage	VG	F	VF	XF	Unc
1742 T	—	15.00	25.00	80.00	250	—
1743 IH	—	15.00	25.00	80.00	250	—

KM# 89 1/2 BATZEN-5 RAPPEN

Billon **Obv:** Crowned, ornate oval shield within circle **Obv. Legend:** MON • NOVA • REIP • LUCERNEN • **Rev:** Cross, flowers in angles within circle **Rev. Legend:** POPULI SUI DOMINUS SPES

Date	Mintage	VG	F	VF	XF	Unc
1795	—	5.00	9.00	30.00	125	250
1796	—	5.00	9.00	30.00	125	250

KM# 92 BATZEN-10 RAPPEN

Billon **Obv:** Oval shield in baroque frame, within beaded circle **Obv. Legend:** MONETA • REIPUB • LUCERNENSI **Rev:** Floreated cross within circle **Rev. Legend:** POPULI * SUI * DOMINUS * SPES *

Date	Mintage	VG	F	VF	XF	Unc
1796	—	5.00	8.00	30.00	125	250
1797	—	5.00	8.00	30.00	125	250

KM# 70 4 BATZEN

Silver **Obv:** Value: IIII/BATZEN/1744 in cartouche **Rev:** Oval arms in ornate cartouche

Date	Mintage	VG	F	VF	XF	Unc
1744	—	20.00	30.00	80.00	165	250

KM# 71 4 BATZEN

Silver **Note:** Klippe.

Date	Mintage	VG	F	VF	XF	Unc
1744	—	—	—	—	—	—

KM# 79 10 BATZEN (1 Franken)

Silver **Note:** Similar to 40 Kreuzers, KM#78.

Date	Mintage	VG	F	VF	XF	Unc
ND	—	80.00	140	210	350	1,500
1782	—	80.00	140	210	350	1,500

KM# 90 20 BATZEN

Silver **Obv:** Crowned, oval shield within sprigs on mantle, value below **Obv. Legend:** LUCERNENSIS RESPUBLICA **Rev:** Monogram in cruciform with small wreath in center **Rev. Legend:** POPULI • SUI • DOMINUS • SPES

Date	Mintage	VG	F	VF	XF	Unc
1795 M	—	40.00	80.00	200	400	725

KM# 93 40 BATZEN

Silver **Obv:** Crowned, oval shield within sprigs on mantle, value below **Obv. Legend:** LUCERNENSI • RESPUBLICA **Rev:** Monogram in cruciform with small wreath in center **Rev. Legend:** POPULI SUI DOMINUS SPES **Note:** Dav. #1775.

Date	Mintage	VG	F	VF	XF	Unc
1796	12,000	90.00	160	350	650	1,700

KM# 52 1/4 THALER

Silver **Obv:** Inscription in laurel wreath **Obv. Inscription:** MONETA/REIPVB/LVCERNEN/SIS/1715 **Rev:** Value: 1/4 in oval shield below, saint wearing robe sitting, oval arms at one side, holding crozier in right hand

Date	Mintage	VG	F	VF	XF	Unc
1715	—	120	250	500	750	—

KM# 53 1/2 THALER

Silver **Obv:** Inscription in laurel wreath **Obv. Inscription:** MONETA/REIPVB/LVCERNEN/SIS/1715 **Rev:** Value: 1/2 between ornaments below, saint wearing robe sitting, oval arms at one side, holding crozier in right hand

Date	Mintage	VG	F	VF	XF	Unc
1715	—	750	1,200	3,200	6,000	11,000

KM# 48 THALER

Silver **Obv:** Inscription in baroque frame, date below **Obv. Inscription:** MONETA/REIPVB/LVCERNEN/SIS **Rev:** Saint sitting wearing long robe, oval arms in cartouche at side **Note:** Dav. #1774.

Date	Mintage	VG	F	VF	XF	Unc
1714 HL	—	350	550	1,450	2,800	5,000

KM# 86 12 MUNZGULDEN

7.6400 g., 0.9000 Gold 0.2211 oz. AGW **Obv:** Crowned shield with garland **Obv. Legend:** LVCERNENSIS RESPUBLICA **Rev:** Value, date within wreath

Date	Mintage	F	VF	XF	Unc	BU
1794 B	—	600	1,200	2,000	3,000	—
1796	—	600	1,200	2,000	3,000	—

KM# 87 24 MUNZGULDEN

15.2800 g., 0.9000 Gold 0.4421 oz. AGW **Obv:** Crowned shield with garland **Obv. Legend:** LVCERNENSIS RESPUBLICA **Rev:** Value, date within wreath

Date	Mintage	F	VF	XF	Unc	BU
1794 B	—	1,750	3,500	6,000	9,500	—
1796 M	—	1,750	3,500	6,000	9,500	—

TRADE COINAGE

KM# 54 DUCAT

3.5000 g., 0.9860 Gold 0.1109 oz. AGW **Obv:** Value, date and inscription within cartouche **Obv. Inscription:** DVCATVS/REIPVS/LVCER/NENSIS **Rev:** St. Leodegar **Rev. Legend:** SANCTVS LEODEGARIVS

Date	Mintage	VG	F	VF	XF	Unc
ND	—	—	4,800	9,500	16,000	—
1715	—	—	2,400	4,800	8,000	6,000

KM# 59 DUCAT

3.5000 g., 0.9860 Gold 0.1109 oz. AGW **Obv:** Value, date and inscription within cartouche **Obv. Inscription:** DVCATVS/REIPVBLICE/LVCERNEN/SIS **Rev:** St. Leodegar **Rev. Legend:** SANCTVS LEODEGARIVS

Date	Mintage	VG	F	VF	XF	Unc
1725	—	—	4,800	9,500	5,500	7,500

KM# 62 DUCAT

3.5000 g., 0.9860 Gold 0.1109 oz. AGW **Obv:** Crowned shield flanked by supporters on mantle **Rev:** Value, inscription and date within cartouche **Rev. Inscription:** DUCATUS/REIPUBLICÆ/LUCERNEN/SIS

Date	Mintage	VG	F	VF	XF	Unc
1741	—	—	800	1,400	2,400	3,600

KM# 49 2 DUCAT

7.0000 g., 0.9860 Gold 0.2219 oz. AGW **Obv:** Inscription, value within cartouche **Obv. Inscription:** DVCATVS/REIPVR/LVCER/NENSIS **Rev:** St. Leodegar **Rev. Legend:** SANCTVS LEODEGARIVS

Date	Mintage	F	VF	XF	Unc	BU
1714	—	2,750	6,000	9,500	14,500	—

KM# A151 2 DUCAT

7.0000 g., 0.9860 Gold 0.2219 oz. AGW **Obv:** Ornate oval arms **Rev:** Curved inscription in baroque frame **Note:** Struck with Gulden dies, KM#46.

Date	Mintage	F	VF	XF	Unc	BU
1714	—	—	—	—	—	—

KM# 63 2 DUCAT

7.0000 g., 0.9860 Gold 0.2219 oz. AGW **Obv:** Crowned shield flanked by supporters on mantle **Rev:** Inscription, date within ornate cartouche **Rev. Inscription:** DUCATUS/REIPUBLICÆ/LUCERNEN/SIS

Date	Mintage	F	VF	XF	Unc	BU
1741	—	1,200	2,400	4,000	6,000	—

KM# 50 3 DUCAT

10.5000 g., 0.9860 Gold 0.3328 oz. AGW **Obv:** Inscription, date within cartouche **Obv. Inscription:** DVCATVS/REIPVP/LVCER/NENSIS **Rev:** St. Leodegar **Rev. Legend:** SANCTVS LEODEGARIVS

Date	Mintage	F	VF	XF	Unc	BU
1714 Rare	—	—	—	8,500	12,000	—

KM# B51 3 DUCAT

10.5000 g., 0.9860 Gold 0.3328 oz. AGW **Obv:** Ornate oval arms **Rev:** Curved inscription in baroque frame **Note:** Struck with Gulden dies, KM#46.

Date	Mintage	VG	F	VF	XF	Unc
1714	—	—	—	—	—	—

KM# 64 3 DUCAT

10.5000 g., 0.9860 Gold 0.3328 oz. AGW **Obv:** Crowned shield flanked by supporters on mantle **Rev:** Inscription, date within ornate cartouche **Rev. Inscription:** DUCATUS/REIPUBLICÆ/LUCERNEN/SIS

Date	Mintage	F	VF	XF	Unc	BU
1741 Rare	—	5,000	8,000	12,000	16,000	—

KM# C51 4 DUCAT

14.0000 g., 0.9860 Gold 0.4438 oz. AGW **Obv:** Ornate oval arms **Rev:** Curved inscription in baroque frame **Note:** Struck with Gulden dies, KM#46.

Date	Mintage	F	VF	XF	Unc	BU
1714 Rare	—	—	—	9,000	12,500	—

KM# 65 4 DUCAT

14.0000 g., 0.9860 Gold 0.4438 oz. AGW **Obv:** Crowned shield flanked by supporters on mantle **Rev:** Inscription, date within ornate cartouche **Rev. Inscription:** DUCATUS/REIPUBLICÆ/LUCERNEN/SIS

Date	Mintage	F	VF	XF	Unc	BU
1741	—	4,250	8,750	14,500	21,500	—

KM# D51 5 DUCAT

17.5000 g., 0.9860 Gold 0.5547 oz. AGW **Obv:** Ornate oval arms **Rev:** Curved inscription in baroque frame

Date	Mintage	VG	F	VF	XF	Unc
1714 Rare	—	—	—	9,000	12,500	—

KM# E51 5 DUCAT

17.5000 g., 0.9860 Gold 0.5547 oz. AGW **Obv:** Inscription in baroque frame **Rev:** St. Leodegar seated **Note:** Struck with Thaler dies, KM#48.

Date	Mintage	VG	F	VF	XF	Unc
1714 HL	—	—	—	10,000	15,000	—

KM# 66 5 DUCAT

17.5000 g., 0.9860 Gold 0.5547 oz. AGW **Obv:** Value and date in ornate cartouche **Rev:** Crowned arms with wildman supporters

Date	Mintage	VG	F	VF	XF	Unc
1741	—	—	4,750	9,500	16,000	24,000

Note: Bowers and Merena Guia sale 3-88 choice AU realized $18,700.

KM# F51 6 DUCAT

21.0000 g., 0.9860 Gold 0.6657 oz. AGW **Obv:** Ornate oval arms **Rev:** Curved inscription in baroque frame **Note:** Struck with Gulden dies, KM#46. Fr. 310.

Date	Mintage	VG	F	VF	XF	Unc
1714 Rare	—	—	—	—	—	—

KM# G51 10 DUCAT

35.0000 g., 0.9860 Gold 1.1095 oz. AGW **Obv:** Inscription in baroque frame **Rev:** St. Leodegar seated **Note:** Struck with Thaler dies, KM#48. Fr. #308.

Date	Mintage	VG	F	VF	XF	Unc
1714 HL Rare	—	—	—	—	—	—

PATTERNS

Including off metal strikes

KM#	Date	Mintage	Identification	Mkt Val
Pn4	1725	—	1/8 Gulden. Gold. KM56.	2,000
Pn5	1734 IH	—	Schilling. Copper. KM67.	—
Pn6	ND(1773)	—	Rappen. Silver. KM74.	—
Pn7	1774	—	Rappen. Silver. KM75.	200

KM#	Date	Mintage	Identification	Mkt Val
Pn8	1774	—	Rappen. Gold. KM75.	1,000
Pn9	1775	—	Angster. Silver. KM76.	200
Pn10	1787	—	Rappen. Silver. KM75.	200
Pn11	1790	—	Angster. Silver. KM76.	200
Pn12	1793	—	1/8 Gulden. Gold. KM81.	2,000
Pn13	1794	—	Schilling. Copper. KM85.	—
Pn14	1796 B	—	12 Munzgulden. Copper. KM86.	—

MURI

An abbey in the Canton of Aargau. Founded c.1065 by Burkhard von Gassau. Few coins were struck and it was secularized in 1802.

RULER
Placidus von Zurlauben, 1684-1723

ABBEY

TRADE COINAGE

KM# 5 DUCAT
3.5000 g., 0.9860 Gold 0.1109 oz. AGW **Ruler:** Placidus von Zurlauben **Obv:** Bust right **Obv. Legend:** PLACIDVS • ... **Rev:** Helmeted and mantled arms

Date	Mintage	F	VF	XF	Unc	BU
1720	—	1,100	2,150	3,600	3,500	—

KM# 6 5 DUCAT
17.5000 g., 0.9860 Gold 0.5547 oz. AGW **Ruler:** Placidus von Zurlauben **Obv:** Bust right **Obv. Legend:** PLACIDVS • ABB • MVR • S • R • I • PRINCEPS **Rev:** Aerial view of the Abbey

Date	Mintage	F	VF	XF	Unc	BU
1720	—	200	4,000	6,500	6,000	—

PATTERNS

Including off metal strikes

KM#	Date	Mintage	Identification	Mkt Val
Pn1	1720	—	Ducat. Silver. KM#5.	1,250
Pn2	1720	—	5 Ducat. Silver. KM#6.	1,800

NEUCHATEL

Nuenberg

A canton on the west central border of Switzerland. The first coins (bracteates) were struck in the 11th century. They were under Prussian rule from 1707 to 1806. France occupied the canton from 1806-1815. They reverted to Prussia until 1857, when they became a full member of the Swiss Confederation.

RULERS
Marie de Orleans-Nemours, 1672-1707
Prussian, 1707-1806

Initials	Date	Name
IP	1712-13	Jean Party

MONETARY SYSTEM
4 Kreuzer = 1 Batzen
7 Kreuzer = 1 Piecette
21 Batzen = 1 Gulden
2 Gulden = 1 Thaler

CANTON

Prussian Administration

STANDARD COINAGE

KM# 36a 10 KREUZER
Gold **Obv:** Bust right **Obv. Legend:** FRID • D • G • REX • ... **Rev:** Crowned arms divides value

Date	Mintage	VG	F	VF	XF	Unc
1713 IP Rare	—	—	—	—	—	—

PRINCIPALITY

STANDARD COINAGE

KM# 45 1/2 KREUZER
Billon **Obv:** Crowned shield **Rev:** Floreated cross, date above

Date	Mintage	VG	F	VF	XF	Unc
1789	—	7.00	12.00	40.00	100	200
1790	—	7.00	12.00	40.00	100	200
1791	—	7.00	12.00	40.00	100	200
1792	—	7.00	12.00	40.00	100	200
1793	—	80.00	150	600	1,600	—
1794	—	80.00	150	600	1,600	—
1795	—	80.00	150	600	1,600	—
1796	—	80.00	150	600	1,600	—

KM# 34 KREUZER
Billon **Obv:** Crowned 4-fold arms with central shield of Brandenburg eagle, titles of Friedrich I around **Rev:** Floreated cross, leaves in angles within octolobe, date in legend **Note:** Varieties exist.

Date	Mintage	VG	F	VF	XF	Unc
1713 IP	264,000	40.00	80.00	325	600	—

KM# 35 KREUZER
Billon **Obv. Legend:** F • D • G • R • BOR • & EL • S • PR **Rev. Legend:** AR • NEOC & VAL

Date	Mintage	VG	F	VF	XF	Unc
1713 IP	—	40.00	80.00	325	600	—

KM# 46 KREUZER
Billon **Obv:** Crowned shield **Rev:** Floreated cross, leaves in angles, date above

Date	Mintage	VG	F	VF	XF	Unc
1789	—	80.00	150	500	1,200	—
1790	—	8.00	16.00	50.00	125	250
1791	—	8.00	16.00	50.00	125	250
1792	—	8.00	16.00	50.00	125	250
1794	—	8.00	16.00	50.00	125	250

KM# 62 KREUZER
Billon **Obv:** Crowned arms **Obv. Legend:** F • W • III • BOR • REX ... **Rev:** Floreated cross, leaves in angles, date above, value below **Rev. Legend:** SUUM CUIQUE

Date	Mintage	VG	F	VF	XF	Unc
1800	—	3.00	5.00	9.00	40.00	100
1802	—	6.00	12.00	22.50	50.00	90.00
1803	—	3.00	7.00	14.00	21.00	32.00

KM# 49 4 KREUZER
Billon **Obv:** Crowned arms within beaded circle, value below **Rev:** Floreated cross within beaded circle, date above **Rev. Legend:** SUUM CUIQUE

Date	Mintage	VG	F	VF	XF	Unc
1790	—	6.00	9.00	30.00	80.00	150
1791	—	6.00	9.00	30.00	80.00	150
1792	—	6.00	9.00	30.00	80.00	150
1793	—	6.00	9.00	30.00	80.00	150

KM# 54 4 KREUZER
Billon **Obv:** Crowned arms within beaded circle, value below **Obv. Legend:** F • G • BOR • REX • PR ... **Rev:** Floreated cross within beaded circle, date above **Rev. Legend:** SUUM CUIQUE

Date	Mintage	VG	F	VF	XF	Unc
1798	—	5.00	9.00	30.00	80.00	150

KM# 56 4 KREUZER
Billon **Obv:** Crowned arms, value below **Obv. Legend:** F : W : III • BOR : REX • P • ... **Rev:** Floreated cross, leaves in angles, date above **Rev. Legend:** SUUM CUIQUE

Date	Mintage	VG	F	VF	XF	Unc
1799	—	250	475	2,000	250	—

KM# 63 4 KREUZER
Billon **Obv:** Crowned arms within beaded circle, value below **Obv. Legend:** F : W : III • BOR : REX ... **Rev:** Floreated cross, leaves in angles, within beaded circle, date above **Rev. Legend:** SUUM CUIQUE

Date	Mintage	VG	F	VF	XF	Unc
1800	—	5.00	9.00	20.00	60.00	125

KM# 36 10 KREUZER
Silver **Obv:** Bust right **Obv. Legend:** FRID • D • G • REX • ... **Rev:** Crowned arms divides value

Date	Mintage	VG	F	VF	XF	Unc
1713 IP	26,000	70.00	125	275	600	—

KM# 37 20 KREUZER
Silver **Obv:** Bust right **Obv. Legend:** FRID • D • G • REX • ... **Rev:** Crowned arms divides value

Date	Mintage	VG	F	VF	XF	Unc
1713	—	70.00	125	325	650	—

KM# 50 28 KREUZER
Silver **Obv:** Crowned, oval arms within sprigs and circle **Rev:** Crowned monogram in cruciform with radiant value in center, all within circle **Rev. Legend:** SUUM CUIQUE

Date	Mintage	VG	F	VF	XF	Unc
1793	7,887	70.00	125	325	600	1,050
1796	Inc. above	80.00	140	350	700	1,200

KM# 51 56 KREUZER
Silver **Obv:** Crowned, oval arms within sprigs and circle **Obv. Legend:** F • G • BOR • REX • PR • SUP • NOVIC • V • VAL • **Rev:** Crowned monogram in cruciform with radiant value in center, all within circle **Rev. Legend:** SUUM CUIQUE

Date	Mintage	VG	F	VF	XF	Unc
1795	5,478	75.00	125	325	650	1,200

KM# 33 1/2 BATZEN
Billon **Obv:** Crowned 5-fold arms **Rev:** Ornamental cross, crowned eagles in angles, date above **Rev. Legend:** SUUM. CVIAVE

Date	Mintage	VG	F	VF	XF	Unc
1712 IP	496,000	20.00	32.00	125	325	—
1713 IP	Inc. above	40.00	80.00	325	600	—

KM# 47 1/2 BATZEN
Billon **Obv:** Crowned arms **Obv. Legend:** F • G • BOR • REX • PR • SUP • NOVIC • VAL • **Rev:** Floreated cross, designs in angles, date above **Rev. Legend:** SVVM CVIQVE

Date	Mintage	VG	F	VF	XF	Unc
1788	—	125	200	800	2,000	4,000
1789	—	5.00	9.00	30.00	80.00	160
1790	—	5.00	9.00	30.00	80.00	160
1791	—	5.00	9.00	30.00	80.00	160
1792	—	5.00	9.00	30.00	80.00	160
1793	—	5.00	9.00	30.00	80.00	160
1794	—	7.00	12.00	40.00	100	185

KM# 47a 1/2 BATZEN
Silver **Obv:** Crowned arms **Rev:** Floreated cross, designs in angles, date above

Date	Mintage	VG	F	VF	XF	Unc
1793	—	—	—	—	—	—

KM# 55 1/2 BATZEN
Billon **Obv:** Crowned arms **Obv. Legend:** F • G • BOR • REX • PR ... **Rev:** Floreated cross, designs in angles, date above **Rev. Legend:** SUUM CUIQUE

Date	Mintage	VG	F	VF	XF	Unc
1798	—	5.00	9.00	20.00	60.00	120
1799	—	5.00	9.00	20.00	60.00	120

KM# 57 1/2 BATZEN
Billon **Obv:** Crowned arms **Obv. Legend:** F • W • III • BOR • REX • P ... **Rev:** Floreated cross, designs in angles, date above **Rev. Legend:** SUUM CUIQUE

Date	Mintage	VG	F	VF	XF	Unc
1799	—	6.00	9.00	20.00	60.00	120
1800	—	6.00	9.00	20.00	60.00	120

KM# 58 1/2 BATZEN
Billon **Obv:** Crowned arms **Obv. Legend:** F • W • III• BOR • REX • P • SUP • NOVIC & • VAL • **Rev:** Floreated cross, designs in angles, date above **Rev. Legend:** SUUM CUIQUE

Date	Mintage	VG	F	VF	XF	Unc
1799	—	5.00	9.00	20.00	60.00	120
1800	—	5.00	9.00	20.00	60.00	120

KM# 52 10-1/2 BATZEN
Silver **Obv:** Crowned, spade arms divides value below **Obv. Legend:** F • G • REX • BOR • PR • SUP • NOVIC • & VAL **Rev:** Floreated cross, radiance in center, date below **Rev. Legend:** SUUM CUIQUE

Date	Mintage	VG	F	VF	XF	Unc
1796	5,052	70.00	125	325	600	1,050

KM# 53 21 BATZEN
Silver **Obv:** Crowned, spade arms divides value below **Obv. Legend:** F • G • REX• BOR • PR • SUP • NOVIC • & VAL • **Rev:** Floreated cross with radiance in center, date below **Rev. Legend:** SUUM CUIQUE

Date	Mintage	VG	F	VF	XF	Unc
1796	23,000	100	175	400	750	1,350

KM# 59 21 BATZEN
Silver **Obv:** Bust left **Obv. Legend:** F • W • III • REX • BOR • PR • SUP • NOVIC & VAL • **Rev:** Crowned arms flanked by supporters, value below **Rev. Legend:** SUUM CUIQUE

Date	Mintage	VG	F	VF	XF	Unc
1799	36,000	100	175	400	800	1,400

KM# 60 21 BATZEN
Silver **Obv:** Bust left **Rev:** Crowned arms flanked by supporters, value below **Rev. Legend:** SUUM CUIQUE

Date	Mintage	VG	F	VF	XF	Unc
1799	Inc. above	100	250	400	800	1,400

KM# 38 1/4 THALER (1/4 Ecu)
Silver **Obv:** Bust right **Obv. Legend:** FRID • D • G • BOR .... **Rev:** Crowned arms, date below **Rev. Legend:** SVVM CVIQVE

Date	Mintage	VG	F	VF	XF	Unc
1713	13,000	125	200	525	1,000	—

KM# 39 1/2 THALER
Silver **Obv:** Bust right **Obv. Legend:** FRID • D • G • R • BOR.... **Rev:** Crowned arms, date below **Rev. Legend:** SVVM CVIQVE

Date	Mintage	VG	F	VF	XF	Unc
1713	—	350	600	1,450	2,800	—

KM# 43 1/2 THALER
Silver **Obv:** Larger, armored bust right **Rev:** Crowned, heart-shaped arms

Date	Mintage	VG	F	VF	XF	Unc
1715 Rare	—	—	—	—	—	—

KM# 40 THALER (1 Ecu)
Silver **Obv:** Bust of Friedrich right **Obv. Legend:** FRID • D • G • REX • BOR... **Rev:** Crowned arms, date below **Rev. Legend:** SVVM CVIQVE • **Note:** Dav. #1776.

Date	Mintage	VG	F	VF	XF	Unc
1713 IP	1,622	1,250	2,000	4,000	8,000	—

KM# 42 THALER (1 Ecu)
Silver **Obv:** Bust of Friedrich Wilhelm right **Obv. Legend:** FRIDWILH D • G • REX • BOR... **Rev:** Crowned baroque shield divides date

Date	Mintage	VG	F	VF	XF	Unc
1714 L	—	1,400	2,500	6,000	12,000	20,000

KM# 41 PISTOLE
7.6400 g., 0.9000 Gold 0.2211 oz. AGW **Obv:** Head of Friedrich right **Obv. Legend:** FRID • D • G • REX • BOR ... **Rev:** Crowned arms, date below **Rev. Legend:** SVVM CVIQVE

Date	Mintage	VG	F	VF	XF	Unc
1713 IP	1,000	2,000	3,500	7,250	12,000	4,750

PATTERNS

Including off metal strikes

KM#	Date	Mintage	Identification	Mkt Val
Pn5	1712	—	1/4 Thaler. Silver.	—
Pn6	1712	—	1/2 Thaler. Silver.	—
Pn7	1712	—	Pistole. Gold.	—
Pn8	1713	—	Kreuzer. Silver. KM34.	—
Pn9	1713	—	Kreuzer. Gold. KM34.	—

KM#	Date	Mintage	Identification	Mkt Val
Pn10	1713	—	10 Kreuzer. Silver.	—
Pn11	1713	—	20 Kreuzer. Silver.	—
Pn12	1713 IP	—	Pistole. Silver. KM41.	—
Pn13	1788	—	1/2 Batzen. Billon.	—

REICHENAU-TAMINS

The Barony of Reichenau-Tamins is located at the confluence of the Vorderrhein and Hinterrhein Rivers. In the first half of the 18th Century it was ruled by the elder line of the Schauenstein-Ehrenfels family. On the death of their last male heir, Thomas Franz, the Barony passed to the family Buol-Schauenstein.

The mint right was granted in 1709. Coinage was only produced from 1718-1748.

RULERS

Johann Rudolf, 1709-1723
Thomas Franz, 1723-1740
Johann Anton, 1742-1765

BARONY

STANDARD COINAGE

KM# 5 PFENNIG

Billon **Ruler:** Johann Rudolf **Obv:** Arched arms with 3 fish, RVS around **Note:** Uniface.

Date	Mintage	VG	F	VF	XF	Unc
ND	—	8.00	12.00	30.00	65.00	—

KM# 6 PFENNIG

Billon **Ruler:** Johann Rudolf **Obv:** FVS around arms

Date	Mintage	VG	F	VF	XF	Unc
ND	—	40.00	65.00	165	65.00	—

KM# 7 PFENNIG

Billon **Ruler:** Johann Rudolf **Obv:** TVS around arms

Date	Mintage	VG	F	VF	XF	Unc
ND	—	8.00	12.00	32.00	65.00	—

KM# 8 PFENNIG

Billon **Ruler:** Johann Rudolf **Obv:** 3 fish in pearl ring

Date	Mintage	VG	F	VF	XF	Unc
ND	—	40.00	65.00	165	—	—

KM# 22 2 PFENNIG (1/2 Kreuzer)

Billon **Ruler:** Thomas Franz **Obv:** Crowned double-headed eagle, arms on breast, value in oval shield at bottom divides date **Note:** Uniface.

Date	Mintage	VG	F	VF	XF	Unc
1740	—	200	325	800	675	—

KM# 23 2 PFENNIG (1/2 Kreuzer)

Billon **Ruler:** Thomas Franz **Obv:** 2 oval shields, crowned double-headed eagle left and 3 fish right, initials above, value below

Date	Mintage	VG	F	VF	XF	Unc
ND	—	5.00	8.00	25.00	50.00	—

KM# 18 1/2 KREUZER

Billon **Ruler:** Thomas Franz **Obv:** 2 oval shields, crowned double-headed eagle left and 3 fish right, value in oval shield above, initials below

Date	Mintage	VG	F	VF	XF	Unc
1731	—	9.00	16.00	40.00	65.00	—
1732	—	13.00	24.00	60.00	65.00	—

KM# 24 1/2 KREUZER

Billon **Ruler:** Thomas Franz **Obv:** Crowned double-headed eagle with arms on breast, date divided above **Rev:** Value divides R V

Date	Mintage	VG	F	VF	XF	Unc
1740	—	275	475	1,200	1,200	—

KM# 25 1/2 KREUZER

Billon **Obv:** 3 vertical fish divide D 2 **Rev:** Value **Note:** 2 Deniers - 1 Pfennig.

Date	Mintage	VG	F	VF	XF	Unc
ND	—	90.00	165	400	100	—

KM# 11 KREUZER

Billon **Ruler:** Thomas Franz **Obv:** Value on breast of crowned double-headed eagle, date divided above **Rev:** Arms in crowned cartouche

Date	Mintage	VG	F	VF	XF	Unc
ND Rare	—	20.00	40.00	75.00	150	—
1723	—	25.00	50.00	125	250	—
1724	—	20.00	32.00	75.00	165	—
1725	—	20.00	32.00	75.00	165	—
1726	—	20.00	32.00	75.00	165	—
1727	—	15.00	24.00	60.00	125	—
1728	—	15.00	24.00	60.00	125	—
1729	—	9.00	16.00	40.00	80.00	—
1730	—	9.00	16.00	40.00	80.00	—

KM# 17 KREUZER

Billon **Ruler:** Thomas Franz **Obv:** Date to left of crown

Date	Mintage	VG	F	VF	XF	Unc
1730	—	70.00	125	325	550	—

KM# 26 KREUZER

Billon **Ruler:** Thomas Franz **Obv:** Value divides date below, crowned double-headed eagle with shield on breast **Rev:** Bust right

Date	Mintage	VG	F	VF	XF	Unc
1740 H	—	225	400	950	1,600	—

KM# 12 2 KREUZER

Billon **Ruler:** Thomas Franz **Obv:** Value in shield on breast of crowned double-headed eagle, date divided above **Rev:** Crowned oval arms, ornaments around

Date	Mintage	VG	F	VF	XF	Unc
1724	—	1,600	2,400	4,750	1,600	—

KM# 27 3 KREUZER (1 Groschen)

Billon **Ruler:** Thomas Franz **Obv:** Bust right **Rev:** 2 crowned oval arms in cartouche, value in oval shield divides date below

Date	Mintage	VG	F	VF	XF	Unc
1740 H Rare	—	125	250	450	750	—

KM# 19 5 KREUZER

Silver **Ruler:** Thomas Franz **Obv:** Value below crowned double-headed eagle, date divided above **Rev:** Oval arms in cartouche

Date	Mintage	VG	F	VF	XF	Unc
1731	—	900	1,600	3,600	6,500	—

KM# 20 30 KREUZER (1/2 Gulden)

Silver **Ruler:** Thomas Franz **Obv:** Crowned double-headed eagle, value in shield below, date divided above **Rev:** Oval arms among ornamentation, fish and helmet above

Date	Mintage	VG	F	VF	XF	Unc
1731	—	1,600	2,800	6,000	11,000	16,000

KM# 9 BLUZGER

Billon **Ruler:** Johann Rudolf **Obv:** Round arms in cartouche **Rev:** Cross within circle, date above

Date	Mintage	VG	F	VF	XF	Unc
1718	—	60.00	100	250	—	—
1719	—	100	200	450	—	—

KM# 13 BLUZGER

Billon **Ruler:** Thomas Franz **Obv:** Crowned oval arms in cartouche

Date	Mintage	VG	F	VF	XF	Unc
1724	—	20.00	35.00	125	175	—
1725	—	25.00	45.00	150	165	—

TRADE COINAGE

KM# 14 DUCAT

Gold **Ruler:** Thomas Franz **Obv:** Crowned double-headed eagle, date divided above **Rev:** Oval arms in cartouche

Date	Mintage	F	VF	XF	Unc	BU
1724 Rare	—	—	—	—	—	—

KM# 15 DUCAT

Gold **Ruler:** Thomas Franz **Rev:** Crowned oval arms in cartouche

Date	Mintage	F	VF	XF	Unc	BU
1727 Rare	—	—	—	—	—	—

KM# 28 DUCAT

Gold **Ruler:** Johann Anton **Rev:** Crowned complete arms of Schauenstein in cartouche

Date	Mintage	F	VF	XF	Unc	BU
1748 Rare	—	—	—	—	—	—

RHEINAU

An abbey founded in the Middle Ages. Had a sporadic coinage that ended in the 18th century.

RULER

Gerold II von Zurlauben, 1697-1735

ABBEY

TRADE COINAGE

KM# 5 DUCAT

3.5000 g., 0.9860 Gold 0.1109 oz. AGW **Ruler:** Gerold II von Zurlauben **Subject:** Building of the New Abbey Church **Obv:** Mantle surrounds 2 helmeted arms, mitre at upper center **Rev:** Church of Abbey

Date	Mintage	F	VF	XF	Unc	BU
1710 Rare	—	—				

KM# 6 DUCAT

3.5000 g., 0.9860 Gold 0.1109 oz. AGW **Ruler:** Gerold II von Zurlauben **Subject:** 74th Birthday and 27th Year of Office for the Abbot **Obv:** Mantle surrounds 2 helmeted arms, mitre at upper center **Rev:** St. Fantan above 2 shields

Date	Mintage	F	VF	XF	Unc	BU
1723	—	800	1,750	2,800	4,500	—

KM# 7 2 DUCAT

7.0000 g., 0.9860 Gold 0.2219 oz. AGW **Ruler:** Gerold II von Zurlauben **Subject:** 74th Birthday and 27th Year of Office for the Abbot **Obv:** Bust right **Rev:** Mitre above ornate oval arms on mantle

Date	Mintage	F	VF	XF	Unc	BU
1723	—	1,700	3,600	6,000	8,800	—

KM# 8 2 DUCAT

7.0000 g., 0.9860 Gold 0.2219 oz. AGW **Ruler:** Gerold II von Zurlauben **Subject:** 74th Birthday and 27th Year of Office for the Abbot **Obv:** Mantle surrounds 2 helmeted arms, mitre at upper center **Obv. Legend:** GEROLD • II ... **Rev:** St. Fintan above 2 shields **Rev. Legend:** ...PRINC • LAGINLÆ ....

Date	Mintage	F	VF	XF	Unc	BU
1723	—	2,000	4,000	6,500	9,500	—

PATTERNS

KM#	Date	Mintage	Identification	Mkt Val
Pn1	1710	—	Ducat. Silver. KM#5.	800
Pn2	1723	—	Ducat. Silver. KM#6.	650
Pn3	1723	—	2 Ducat. Silver. KM#7.	1,200
Pn4	1723	—	2 Ducat. Copper. KM#7.	750
Pn5	1723	—	2 Ducat. Silver. KM#8.	800
Pn6	1723	—	2 Ducat. Copper. KM#8.	600

SAINT GALL

St. Gallen

RULERS

Beda Angehrn Von Hagenwyl, Abbot, 1767-1796

MINT OFFICIALS' INITIALS

Initials	Date	Name
B	1780	Bruppacher
B	?	?
H	1773-77	Joh Haag
K	?	Kankler
V	1776	?

MONETARY SYSTEM

4 Pfennig = 1 Kreuzer
4 Kreuzer = 1 Batzen
10 Batzen = 1 Frank

ABBEY

An abbey in northeast Switzerland, established in c.720. They obtained the mint right in 947 but the first coins were not made until about 100 years later. The power of the abbey dwindled until the last Abbot resigned in 1805.

STANDARD COINAGE

KM# 5 PFENNIG

Billon **Obv:** Rampant bear, left **Rev:** Value within cartouche

Date	Mintage	VG	F	VF	XF	Unc
ND		100	200	600	1,200	—

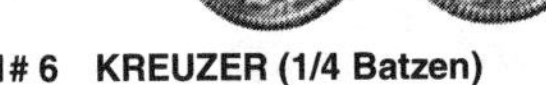

KM# 6 KREUZER (1/4 Batzen)

Billon **Obv:** Rampant bear, left **Rev:** Value within cartouche

Date	Mintage	VG	F	VF	XF	Unc
ND H	—	50.00	85.00	325	600	1,600

KM# 7 KREUZER (1/4 Batzen)

Billon **Obv:** Rampant bear, right **Rev:** Value within cartouche

Date	Mintage	VG	F	VF	XF	Unc
ND H	—	40.00	65.00	250	600	1,200

KM# 30 2 KREUZER (1/2 Batzen)
Billon **Ruler:** Beda Angehrn Von Hagenwyl, Abbot **Obv:** Rampant bear, right **Rev:** Value, date within wreath

Date	Mintage	VG	F	VF	XF	Unc
1780	—	45.00	80.00	325	600	1,600

KM# 31 4 KREUZER (1 Batzen)
Billon **Ruler:** Beda Angehrn Von Hagenwyl, Abbot **Obv:** Rampant bear, right **Rev:** Value, date within wreath

Date	Mintage	VG	F	VF	XF	Unc
1780	—	35.00	60.00	250	600	1,200
1782	—	45.00	80.00	325	800	1,750

KM# 22 5 KREUZER
Billon **Ruler:** Beda Angehrn Von Hagenwyl, Abbot **Obv:** Mitre above mantled, oval arms **Rev:** Seated Saint, rampant bear at left, date below

Date	Mintage	VG	F	VF	XF	Unc
1774 H	—	20.00	35.00	80.00	275	600
1775	—	20.00	35.00	80.00	275	600

KM# 15 6 KREUZER
Billon **Ruler:** Beda Angehrn Von Hagenwyl, Abbot **Obv:** Crowned monogram within sprigs **Rev:** Mitre above mantled, oval arms, value below

Date	Mintage	VG	F	VF	XF	Unc
ND H	—	125	250	600	1,200	—

KM# 16 6 KREUZER
Billon **Ruler:** Beda Angehrn Von Hagenwyl, Abbot **Obv:** Crowned monogram within sprigs **Rev:** Mitre above mantled, oval arms, value divides date below **Note:** Date added.

Date	Mintage	VG	F	VF	XF	Unc
1773 H	—	22.00	40.00	125	250	400

KM# 23 10 KREUZER
Billon **Ruler:** Beda Angehrn Von Hagenwyl, Abbot **Obv:** Mitre above mantled, oval arms, value below **Rev:** Seated Saint, rampant bear at left, date below **Rev. Legend:** S • GALLUS ABBAS

Date	Mintage	VG	F	VF	XF	Unc
1774	—	25.00	45.00	125	325	600
1775	—	50.00	100	250	475	950

KM# 17 12 KREUZER
Silver **Ruler:** Beda Angehrn Von Hagenwyl, Abbot **Obv:** Crowned monogram within sprigs **Rev:** Mitre above mantled, oval arms, value below

Date	Mintage	VG	F	VF	XF	Unc
ND H	—	175	325	600	1,600	—

KM# 17a 12 KREUZER
Copper **Ruler:** Beda Angehrn Von Hagenwyl, Abbot **Obv:** Crowned monogram within sprigs **Rev:** Mitre above mantled, oval arms, value below

Date	Mintage	VG	F	VF	XF	Unc
ND H	—	—	—	—	—	—

KM# 18 12 KREUZER
Silver **Ruler:** Beda Angehrn Von Hagenwyl, Abbot **Obv:** Date and shield

Date	Mintage	VG	F	VF	XF	Unc
1773 H	—	175	325	600	1,600	—

KM# 19 12 KREUZER
Silver **Ruler:** Beda Angehrn Von Hagenwyl, Abbot **Obv:** Crowned monogram within sprigs, date below **Rev:** Mitre above mantled, oval arms, value below

Date	Mintage	VG	F	VF	XF	Unc
1773 H	—	70.00	125	325	650	1,200

KM# 35 15 KREUZER (1/4 Gulden)
Silver **Ruler:** Beda Angehrn Von Hagenwyl, Abbot **Obv:** Rampant bear, right, within wreath **Rev:** Legend, date, value within cartouche **Rev. Legend:** MON./PRINCIP./TERRIT./S./ GALLI

Date	Mintage	VG	F	VF	XF	Unc
1781	—	120	200	475	950	1,750

KM# 24 20 KREUZER
Silver **Ruler:** Beda Angehrn Von Hagenwyl, Abbot **Obv:** Mitre above mantled, oval arms, value below **Rev:** Seated Saint, rampant bear at left, date below **Rev. Legend:** S • GALLUS ABBAS

Date	Mintage	VG	F	VF	XF	Unc
1774 H	—	30.00	60.00	165	325	800

KM# 28 20 KREUZER
Silver **Ruler:** Beda Angehrn Von Hagenwyl, Abbot **Obv:** Mitre above mantled, oval arms **Rev:** Rampant bear, right, within wreath, value divides date below

Date	Mintage	VG	F	VF	XF	Unc
1777 H	—	175	325	600	1,600	—
1779	—	35.00	60.00	165	325	800

KM# 32 20 KREUZER
Silver **Ruler:** Beda Angehrn Von Hagenwyl, Abbot **Obv:** Crowned, mantled oval arms **Obv. Legend:** BEDA • D • G • S • R • I • P • **Rev:** Rampant bear, right, within wreath, value divides date below **Rev. Legend:** ABB • S • G • ...

Date	Mintage	VG	F	VF	XF	Unc
1780 B	—	45.00	80.00	200	450	800
1780	—	35.00	60.00	160	325	800
1783	—	45.00	80.00	200	475	1,000

KM# 36 30 KREUZER (1/2 Gulden)
Silver **Ruler:** Beda Angehrn Von Hagenwyl, Abbot **Obv:** Rampant bear, right, within wreath **Rev:** MON./PRINCEP./ TERRIT. S. GALLI, date and value within cartouche

Date	Mintage	VG	F	VF	XF	Unc
1781	—	50.00	100	250	475	1,000
1796	—	60.00	125	325	650	1,200

KM# 37 GULDEN
Silver **Ruler:** Beda Angehrn Von Hagenwyl, Abbot **Obv:** Rampant bear, right, within wreath **Rev:** MON./PRINCEP./ TERRIT & GALLI, date and value within cartouche

Date	Mintage	VG	F	VF	XF	Unc
1781 Rare	—	—	—	—	—	—

KM# 26 1/2 THALER
Silver **Ruler:** Beda Angehrn Von Hagenwyl, Abbot **Obv:** Mitre above mantled, oval arms above sprigs **Obv. Legend:** BEDA • D • G • S • R • I • P • **Rev:** Rampant bear right, date below, all within wreath **Rev. Legend:** ...S • G • E • S • I • A • V • E •

Date	Mintage	VG	F	VF	XF	Unc
1776	—	45.00	80.00	200	400	800
1777	—	45.00	80.00	200	400	800

KM# 33 1/2 THALER
Silver **Ruler:** Beda Angehrn Von Hagenwyl, Abbot **Obv:** Crowned, mantled oval arms **Obv. Legend:** BEDA • D • G • S • R • I • P • **Rev:** Rampant bear right, date below, all within wreath **Rev. Legend:** ...E • S • I • A • V • E •

Date	Mintage	VG	F	VF	XF	Unc
1780 B	—	80.00	160	400	800	—
1780	—	45.00	80.00	200	400	800
1782	—	25.00	40.00	120	275	600

KM# 27 THALER

Silver **Ruler:** Beda Angehrn Von Hagenwyl, Abbot **Obv:** Mitre above mantled, oval arms above sprigs **Obv. Legend:** BEDA • D • G • S • R • I • P • **Rev:** Rampant bear righ, date below, all within wreath **Rev. Legend:** ...E • S • I • A • V • E • **Note:** Cross-reference number Dav. #1778.

Date	Mintage	VG	F	VF	XF	Unc
1776 H Rare	—	—	—	—	—	—
1776 V	—	85.00	165	400	800	1,600

KM# 29 THALER

Silver **Ruler:** Beda Angehrn Von Hagenwyl, Abbot **Obv:** Mitre above mantled, oval arms above sprigs **Obv. Legend:** BEDA • D • G • S • R • I • P • **Rev:** Rampant bear right, date below, all within wreath **Rev. Legend:** ... E • S • I • A • V • E • **Note:** Cross-reference number Dav. #1778.

Date	Mintage	VG	F	VF	XF	Unc
1777 H	—	85.00	165	400	800	1,200
1779 Rare	—	800	1,600	3,200	4,500	—

KM# 34 THALER

Silver **Ruler:** Beda Angehrn Von Hagenwyl, Abbot **Obv:** Crowned, mantled oval arms **Obv. Legend:** BEDA • D • G • S • R • I • P **Rev:** Rampant bear right, date below, all within wreath **Rev. Legend:** ...E • S • I • A • V • E • **Note:** Cross-reference number Dav. #1779.

Date	Mintage	VG	F	VF	XF	Unc
1780 B	—	55.00	100	240	475	1,050

TRADE COINAGE

KM# 20 1/2 DUCAT

1.7500 g., 0.9860 Gold 0.0555 oz. AGW **Ruler:** Beda Angehrn Von Hagenwyl, Abbot **Obv:** Crowned monogram divides date **Rev:** Mitre above mantled oval arms

Date	Mintage	F	VF	XF	Unc	BU
1773 Rare	—	1,800	2,500	4,000	6,500	—

KM# 21 DUCAT

3.5000 g., 0.9860 Gold 0.1109 oz. AGW **Ruler:** Beda Angehrn Von Hagenwyl, Abbot **Obv:** Mitre above mantled oval arms **Obv. Legend:** BEDA • D • G • S • R • I • P • S .... **Rev:** Seated Saint, rampant bear at left, date in legend

Date	Mintage	F	VF	XF	Unc	BU
1773 H	—	1,250	2,500	4,000	6,000	8,000

KM# 25 DUCAT

3.5000 g., 0.9860 Gold 0.1109 oz. AGW **Ruler:** Beda Angehrn Von Hagenwyl, Abbot **Obv:** Mitre above mantled oval arms, divided date below **Rev:** Seated Saint, rampant bear at left **Rev. Legend:** SANCTUS GALIUSABRAS

Date	Mintage	F	VF	XF	Unc	BU
1774	—	1,000	2,000	3,250	4,750	6,500

KM# 38 DUCAT

3.5000 g., 0.9860 Gold 0.1109 oz. AGW **Ruler:** Beda Angehrn Von Hagenwyl, Abbot **Obv:** Crowned, mantled oval arms **Obv. Legend:** BEDA • D • G • S • R • I • P **Rev:** Rampant bear right, within wreath, date below

Date	Mintage	F	VF	XF	Unc	BU
1781	—	600	1,200	2,000	3,100	4,000

CITY

A city located in northeast Switzerland which was built to protect the abbey. It became a free city in 1311 and gained independence from the Abbots in 1457. The first coins were struck in the 1400s and the last ones in 1790.

MINT OFFICIALS' INITIALS

Initials	Date	Name
A		
A-H		
G		
GR	1730-31	
H	1714	
H.G.Z., Z		Hans Georg Zolli Kofer
Z		

STANDARD COINAGE

KM# 45 PFENNIG

Billon **Obv:** Rampant bear left, within circle **Note:** Uniface. Schussel type. Edge varieties exist.

Date	Mintage	VG	F	VF	XF	Unc
ND	—	5.00	8.00	32.00	80.00	145

KM# 46 PFENNIG

Billon **Obv:** Rampant bear left, within wreath

Date	Mintage	VG	F	VF	XF	Unc
ND	—	65.00	125	325	800	—

KM# 47 PFENNIG

Billon **Obv:** Initials below rampant bear **Note:** Varieties of bear and mintmarks exist.

Date	Mintage	VG	F	VF	XF	Unc
ND A-H	—	7.00	12.00	50.00	125	200
ND A	—	3.00	5.00	16.00	40.00	80.00
ND G	—	3.00	5.00	8.00	20.00	40.00

KM# 48 2 PFENNIG (2 Deniers - 1/2 Kreuzer)

Billon **Obv:** Rampant bear left, divided value, initials below **Note:** Uniface. Many varieties of mintmarks exist.

Date	Mintage	VG	F	VF	XF	Unc
ND	—	6.00	9.00	32.00	80.00	125
ND A	—	4.00	6.00	12.00	25.00	60.00

KM# 50 KREUZER

Billon **Obv:** Rampant bear, left **Rev:** Flower-like design **Note:** Many varieties of mintmarks exist.

Date	Mintage	VG	F	VF	XF	Unc
ND A	—	5.00	8.00	30.00	75.00	140
ND H	—	5.00	8.00	30.00	75.00	140
ND Z	—	3.00	5.00	8.00	20.00	40.00
ND K	—	3.00	5.00	8.00	20.00	40.00

KM# 49 KREUZER

Billon **Obv:** Rampant bear, left **Rev:** Flower-like design

Date	Mintage	VG	F	VF	XF	Unc
ND(1715)	—	8.50	16.00	65.00	160	—

KM# 75 2 KREUZER (1/2 Batzen)

Billon **Obv:** Rampant bear left within circle, value below **Rev:** Inscription: SOLI/DEO/GLORIA, initials, date

Date	Mintage	VG	F	VF	XF	Unc
1714	—	650	1,200	4,000	—	—

KM# 78 2 KREUZER (1/2 Batzen)

Billon **Rev:** Date in palm leaves and branches

Date	Mintage	VG	F	VF	XF	Unc
1715	—	60.00	125	400	165	—

KM# 81 2 KREUZER (1/2 Batzen)

Billon **Obv:** Initials in shield divides value **Rev:** Inscription: SOLI/DEO GLORIA/date in ornamental cartouche, initials in shield at bottom

Date	Mintage	VG	F	VF	XF	Unc
1720	—	30.00	60.00	200	140	—

KM# 84 2 KREUZER (1/2 Batzen)

Billon **Rev:** Inscription: SOLI/DEO GLORIA/date in ornamentation

Date	Mintage	VG	F	VF	XF	Unc
1721	—	10.00	20.00	80.00	200	—
1723	—	10.00	20.00	80.00	200	—
1724	—	10.00	20.00	80.00	200	—
1725	—	250	400	1,600	—	—

KM# 90 2 KREUZER (1/2 Batzen)

Billon **Rev:** Inscription: SOLI/DEO/GLORIA/date in palm and laurel branches

Date	Mintage	VG	F	VF	XF	Unc
1726	—	10.00	20.00	80.00	200	—
1727	—	10.00	20.00	80.00	200	—
1728	—	10.00	20.00	80.00	200	—
1729	—	10.00	20.00	80.00	200	—
1730	—	10.00	20.00	80.00	200	—
1732	—	10.00	20.00	80.00	200	—
1739	—	10.00	20.00	80.00	200	—

KM# 93 2 KREUZER (1/2 Batzen)

Billon **Obv:** Rampant bear, left within circle, value below **Rev:** SOLI/DEO/GLORIA, date within wreath

Date	Mintage	VG	F	VF	XF	Unc
1766	—	12.00	25.00	95.00	250	—
1767	—	12.00	25.00	95.00	250	—
1768	—	50.00	125	400	225	—

KM# 76 3 KREUZER

Billon **Obv:** Rampant bear left, divides value, date below **Rev:** Inscription: SOLI DEO GLO RIA in script around, palm leaves at outside, large cross, G at center

Date	Mintage	VG	F	VF	XF	Unc
1714 Rare	—	—	—	—	—	—

KM# 79 3 KREUZER

Billon **Obv:** Rampant bear, left **Rev:** Floreated cross, value at center, date in legend

Date	Mintage	VG	F	VF	XF	Unc
1715	—	150	325	1,200	1,000	—

KM# 82 3 KREUZER

Billon **Rev:** Floreated cross, value in shield below divides date

Date	Mintage	VG	F	VF	XF	Unc
1720	—	100	200	800	350	—

KM# 85 3 KREUZER

Billon **Rev:** Value in oval shield at center of cross, date below

Date	Mintage	VG	F	VF	XF	Unc
1721	—	12.00	25.00	95.00	240	—
1722	—	12.00	25.00	95.00	240	—
1723	—	12.00	25.00	95.00	240	—
1724	—	12.00	25.00	95.00	240	—
1725	—	12.00	25.00	95.00	240	—

KM# 86 3 KREUZER

Billon **Obv:** Floreated cross, 3 in circle at center **Rev:** Rampant bear left, date in legend

Date	Mintage	VG	F	VF	XF	Unc
1721	—	60.00	120	400	—	—

KM# 87 3 KREUZER

Billon **Obv:** Rampant bear, left **Obv. Legend:** SOLI DEO GLORIA **Rev:** Floreated cross **Rev. Legend:** SOLI DEO GLORIA

Date	Mintage	VG	F	VF	XF	Unc
1721 Rare	—	—	—	—	—	—

KM# 91 3 KREUZER

Billon **Obv. Legend:** MONETA NOVA S GALLENSIS

Date	Mintage	VG	F	VF	XF	Unc
1726	—	25.00	60.00	200	450	—
1727	—	12.00	25.00	95.00	240	—
1729	—	25.00	60.00	200	450	—
1730	—	12.00	25.00	95.00	240	—
1732	—	12.00	25.00	95.00	240	—

Date	Mintage	VG	F	VF	XF	Unc
1737	—	12.00	25.00	95.00	240	—
1738	—	12.00	25.00	95.00	240	—
1739	—	12.00	25.00	95.00	240	—

KM# 96 3 KREUZER

Billon **Ruler:** Beda Angehrn Von Hagenwyl, Abbot **Obv:** Rampant bear, left within circle **Obv. Legend:** ...GALLENSIS **Rev:** Floreated cross with value in center, all within circle, date below **Rev. Legend:** SOLI DEO GLORIA

Date	Mintage	VG	F	VF	XF	Unc
1790	—	8.00	16.00	40.00	95.00	165

KM# 77 4 KREUZER (1 Batzen)

Billon **Obv:** Rampant bear, left, within circle, date below **Rev:** Legend, value **Rev. Legend:** SOLI DEO GLORIA

Date	Mintage	VG	F	VF	XF	Unc
1714 H	—	300	650	1,600	850	—

KM# 80 4 KREUZER (1 Batzen)

Billon **Obv:** Rampant bear, left within circle **Rev:** Script double G's, value: 4 in center, all within pearl circle, date in legend at left top

Date	Mintage	VG	F	VF	XF	Unc
1715	—	235	475	2,000	4,750	—

KM# 83.1 4 KREUZER (1 Batzen)

Billon **Rev:** Value in center, date below

Date	Mintage	VG	F	VF	XF	Unc
1720 Rare	—	—	—	—	—	—

KM# 83.2 4 KREUZER (1 Batzen)

Billon **Obv:** Rampant bear divides value

Date	Mintage	VG	F	VF	XF	Unc
1721	—	12.00	25.00	95.00	240	—
1722	—	12.00	25.00	95.00	240	—
1724	—	12.00	25.00	95.00	240	—
1725	—	12.00	25.00	95.00	240	—

KM# 89 6 KREUZER

Billon **Obv:** Rampant bear, left **Rev:** Value and date within wreath **Note:** Varieties exist.

Date	Mintage	VG	F	VF	XF	Unc
1725	—	50.00	120	225	125	—
1726	—	12.00	25.00	95.00	240	—
1727	—	12.00	25.00	95.00	240	—
1728	—	12.00	25.00	95.00	240	—
1729	—	12.00	25.00	95.00	240	—
1730	—	12.00	25.00	95.00	240	—
1731	—	8.00	16.00	65.00	165	—
1732	—	8.00	16.00	65.00	165	—
1734	—	50.00	120	300	125	—
1739	—	8.00	16.00	65.00	165	—

KM# 94 6 KREUZER

Billon **Ruler:** Beda Angehrn Von Hagenwyl, Abbot **Obv:** Rampant bear, left, within circle **Obv. Legend:** MONETA : NOVA : ... **Rev:** Value, date within wreath

Date	Mintage	VG	F	VF	XF	Unc
1786	—	8.00	16.00	65.00	160	—
1790	—	8.00	16.00	50.00	125	200

KM# 88 15 KREUZER (1/4 Gulden)

Silver **Obv:** Rampant bear, left, within circle **Rev:** Value, date within wreath **Note:** Similar to 2 Kreuzer, KM#93. Varieties exist.

Date	Mintage	VG	F	VF	XF	Unc
1724	—	400	800	2,000	4,000	—
1725	—	50.00	100	250	250	—
1730 GR	—	35.00	65.00	165	150	—
1731 GR	—	35.00	65.00	165	150	—
1732	—	35.00	65.00	165	150	—
1734	—	80.00	160	400	150	—
1737	—	24.00	50.00	125	325	—
1738	—	24.00	50.00	125	325	—
1739	—	24.00	50.00	125	325	—

KM# 95 15 KREUZER (1/4 Gulden)

Billon **Ruler:** Beda Angehrn Von Hagenwyl, Abbot **Obv:** Rampant bear, left, within circle **Obv. Legend:** MONETA : NOVA : GALLENSIS **Rev:** SOLI/DEO/GLORIA, date, value within cartouche and sprigs

Date	Mintage	VG	F	VF	XF	Unc
1786	—	25.00	50.00	125	325	—
1789	—	75.00	150	400	800	—

KM# 92 30 KREUZER (1/2 Gulden)

Silver **Obv:** Rampant bear, left, within circle **Obv. Legend:** MONETA : NOVA : GALLENSIS **Rev:** LIBERTAS/CARIOR/AURO, date and value within cartouche

Date	Mintage	VG	F	VF	XF	Unc
1738	—	40.00	80.00	200	225	—

PATTERNS

Including off metal strikes

KM#	Date	Mintage	Identification	Mkt Val
Pn1	ND	—	Pfennig. Gold. KM#5	—

SCHWYZ

Schwytz, Suitensis

A canton in central Switzerland. In 1291 it became one of the three cantons that would ultimately become the Swiss Confederation and were known as the "Everlasting League". The first coinage was issued in1624.

MINT OFFICIALS' INITIALS

Initials	Date	Name
S	1776-97	Stedelin
ST	1785	

MONETARY SYSTEM

Until 1798

240 Angster = 120 Rappen
= 40 Schillinge = 1 Gulden
4 Kreuzer = 1 Batzen
40 Batzen = 3 Gulden = 1 Thaler
12 Gulden = 1 Duplone

CANTON

STANDARD COINAGE

KM# 34 ANGSTER

Copper **Obv:** Oval arms in sprays **Rev:** Value, date

Date	Mintage	VG	F	VF	XF	Unc
1773	—	4.00	8.00	16.00	40.00	80.00
1774	—	4.00	8.00	16.00	40.00	80.00
1775	—	4.00	8.00	16.00	40.00	80.00
1776	—	4.00	8.00	16.00	40.00	80.00
1777	—	4.00	8.00	16.00	40.00	80.00
1778	—	7.00	15.00	60.00	150	300
1779	—	4.00	8.00	16.00	40.00	80.00
1780	—	4.00	8.00	16.00	40.00	80.00

KM# 40 ANGSTER

Copper **Obv:** Oval arms within sprigs **Rev:** Value, date

Date	Mintage	VG	F	VF	XF	Unc
1781	—	4.00	8.00	16.00	40.00	80.00
1782	—	8.00	15.00	60.00	150	300
1791	—	4.00	8.00	16.00	40.00	80.00

Date	Mintage	VG	F	VF	XF	Unc
1792	—	4.00	8.00	16.00	40.00	80.00
1797	—	4.00	8.00	20.00	60.00	150

KM# 51 ANGSTER

Copper **Obv:** Oval arms in cartouche **Rev:** Value, date below sprig

Date	Mintage	VG	F	VF	XF	Unc
1797	—	6.00	12.00	32.00	80.00	160
1798	—	6.00	12.00	32.00	80.00	160

KM# 35 RAPPEN

Billon **Obv:** Ornate shield **Rev:** Value, date

Date	Mintage	VG	F	VF	XF	Unc
1776 S	—	235	475	1,200	55.00	—

KM# 36 RAPPEN

Copper **Obv:** Ornate, oval arms in sprigs **Rev:** Value, date in cartouche

Date	Mintage	VG	F	VF	XF	Unc
1777 S	—	4.00	8.00	16.00	40.00	80.00
1778 S	—	4.00	8.00	16.00	40.00	80.00
1779 S	—	4.00	8.00	16.00	40.00	80.00
1780 S	—	4.00	8.00	16.00	40.00	80.00
1781 S	—	4.00	8.00	16.00	40.00	80.00
1782 S	—	4.00	8.00	16.00	40.00	80.00

KM# 37 RAPPEN

Silver

Date	Mintage	VG	F	VF	XF	Unc
1778	—	—	—	—	—	—
1779	—	—	—	—	—	—

KM# 41 RAPPEN

Copper **Obv:** Ornate, oval arms in sprigs **Rev:** Value, date in cartouche **Note:** Many varieties exist, especially among 1797-dated coins.

Date	Mintage	VG	F	VF	XF	Unc
1782	—	4.00	8.00	16.00	40.00	80.00
1785	—	10.00	20.00	90.00	225	—
1792	—	4.00	8.00	20.00	45.00	95.00
1793	—	4.00	8.00	16.00	40.00	80.00
1794	—	4.00	8.00	16.00	40.00	80.00
1795	—	4.00	8.00	16.00	40.00	80.00
1796	—	4.00	8.00	16.00	40.00	80.00
1797	—	4.00	8.00	16.00	40.00	80.00
1798	—	4.00	8.00	20.00	45.00	95.00

KM# 49 GROSCHEN

Billon **Obv:** Oval arms on mantle, with garland **Obv. Legend:** MONETA REIP SUITENSIS **Rev:** Value, date within wreath

Date	Mintage	VG	F	VF	XF	Unc
1791	—	80.00	160	400	250	—

KM# 50 GROSCHEN

Billon **Obv:** Shield with garland **Obv. Legend:** MONETA REIP SUITENSIS **Rev:** Value, date, ornaments above

Date	Mintage	VG	F	VF	XF	Unc
1793	—	100	200	475	275	—

KM# 31 SCHILLING
Billon **Obv:** Arms divides date within beaded circle **Obv. Legend:** MONETA ... **Rev:** Value within wreath

Date	Mintage	VG	F	VF	XF	Unc
1730	—	160	325	800	450	—

KM# 42 5 SCHILLINGS
Silver **Obv:** Crowned, oval arms within sprigs **Rev:** Value, date within wreath

Date	Mintage	VG	F	VF	XF	Unc
1785	—	30.00	60.00	165	325	550

KM# 46 5 SCHILLINGS
Silver **Obv:** Crowned, oval arms within sprigs **Rev:** Value, date within wreath

Date	Mintage	VG	F	VF	XF	Unc
1787	—	30.00	60.00	165	325	550

KM# 45 10 SCHILLINGS (1/4 Gulden)
Silver **Obv:** Crowned, oval arms within sprigs **Obv. Legend:** MONETA ... **Rev:** Value, date within wreath

Date	Mintage	VG	F	VF	XF	Unc
1786	—	30.00	60.00	165	325	550

KM# 52 20 SCHILLINGS (1/2 Gulden)
Silver **Obv:** Crowned, oval arms on mantle, within sprigs, value below **Obv. Legend:** SUITENSIS RESPUBLICA **Rev:** S within floreated cross, date below **Rev. Legend:** ...DOMINI TURRIS FORTISSIMA

Date	Mintage	VG	F	VF	XF	Unc
1797	—	60.00	125	325	600	1,050

KM# 9 10 KREUZER
Silver **Obv:** Bust of St. Martin left in long robe **Rev:** Crowned imperial eagle, value below

Date	Mintage	VG	F	VF	XF	Unc
ND Rare	—	—	—	—	—	—

KM# 32 20 KREUZER
Silver **Obv:** Similar to Dicken, KM#19 reverse **Rev:** Crowned imperial eagle, shield on breast

Date	Mintage	VG	F	VF	XF	Unc
1730	—	235	475	1,200	2,400	—

KM# 43 1/2 GULDEN (20 Schillings)
Silver **Obv:** Oval arms in cartouche divides value below **Obv. Legend:** MONETA REIPUBLICÆ SUITENSIS **Rev:** Inscription, date within wreath **Rev. Inscription:** PAX/OPTIMA/RERUM

Date	Mintage	VG	F	VF	XF	Unc
1785 ST	—	60.00	125	325	600	1,050

KM# 44 GULDEN
Silver **Obv:** Oval arms on mantle, with garland, lion supporter at right, value below **Obv. Legend:** MONETA REIPUBLICÆ SUITENSIS **Rev:** Inscription, date within wreath **Rev. Inscription:** PAX/OPTIMA/RERUM

Date	Mintage	VG	F	VF	XF	Unc
1785	—	125	250	600	1,200	2,250

KM# 53 GULDEN
Silver **Obv:** Crowned, oval arms on mantle within sprigs, value below **Obv. Legend:** SUITENSIS RESPUBLICA **Rev:** S within floreated cross, date below **Rev. Legend:** ...DOMINI TURRIS FORTISSIMA

Date	Mintage	VG	F	VF	XF	Unc
1797 S	—	225	450	1,100	2,250	—

TRADE COINAGE

KM# 38 DUCAT
3.5000 g., 0.9860 Gold 0.1109 oz. AGW **Obv:** Lion upright holding shield on mantle with garland **Rev:** DUCATUS/ REIPUBLICÆ/SUITENSIS, date and value in cartouche

Date	Mintage	F	VF	XF	Unc	BU
ND(1779)	—	2,000	4,000	6,500	9,500	—
1781	—	1,600	3,600	5,500	8,950	—

KM# 47 DUCAT
3.5000 g., 0.9860 Gold 0.1109 oz. AGW **Obv:** Lion upright, holding shield on mantle with garland **Rev:** DUCATUS/ REIPUBLICÆ/SUITENSIS, date below sprig **Note:** Fr.#379.

Date	Mintage	F	VF	XF	Unc	BU
1788	—	2,000	4,000	6,500	9,500	—
1790	—	1,600	3,600	5,500	8,750	—

PATTERNS

Including off metal strikes

KM#	Date	Mintage	Identification	Mkt Val
Pn1	1793	—	Rappen. Gold. KM41.	—
Pn2	1793	—	Groschen. Gold. KM50.	—

SITTEN

A canton which was founded in 580 that comprises most of the canton of Valais. Sitten was a Burgundian mint in the 9th century with the first Episcopal coinage being struck c. 1496. They joined the Swiss Confederation as Valais in 1815.

RULER
Franz Friedrich am Buel,1760-1780

BISHOPRIC

STANDARD COINAGE

KM# 25 KREUZER
Billon **Obv:** Mitre above shield with crown on crossed sword and crozier **Rev:** Eagle left above shield with seven stars

Date	Mintage	VG	F	VF	XF	Unc
1708	—	16.00	32.00	125	50.00	—
1722	—	10.00	20.00	80.00	75.00	—

KM# 32 KREUZER
Billon **Ruler:** Franz Friedrich am Buel **Obv:** Mitre above shield **Rev:** Double-headed eagle above shield that divides 7 6

Date	Mintage	VG	F	VF	XF	Unc
1776	—	8.00	16.00	50.00	125	250

KM# 36 6 KREUZER
Billon **Ruler:** Franz Friedrich am Buel **Obv:** Mitre above ornate, oval arms **Rev:** Ornate, oval shield with stars within, on mantle, value below

Date	Mintage	VG	F	VF	XF	Unc
1777	—	12.00	25.00	95.00	250	—

KM# 37 12 KREUZER
Billon **Ruler:** Franz Friedrich am Buel **Obv:** Mitre above ornate, oval shield within sprigs **Rev:** Small, double-headed eagle above ornate oval shield with stars within, divided value below

Date	Mintage	VG	F	VF	XF	Unc
1777	—	20.00	40.00	120	325	—

KM# 28 20 KREUZER
Silver **Obv:** Mitre above ornate oval arms **Rev:** Figures on cloud above shield that divides value

Date	Mintage	VG	F	VF	XF	Unc
1709	—	30.00	60.00	250	200	—
1710	—	20.00	40.00	165	100	—

KM# 38 20 KREUZER
Silver **Ruler:** Franz Friedrich am Buel **Obv:** Mitre above ornate oval arms, divided date below **Rev:** Radiant figures on cloud above round shield that divides value

Date	Mintage	VG	F	VF	XF	Unc
1777	—	40.00	80.00	200	400	—

KM# 26 1/2 BATZEN

Billon **Obv:** Four-fold arms draped with bishop's vestment **Rev:** Eagle above shield

Date	Mintage	VG	F	VF	XF	Unc
1708	—	6.00	12.00	50.00	125	—
1709	—	6.00	12.00	50.00	125	—
1710	—	6.00	12.00	50.00	125	—
1721	—	6.00	12.00	50.00	125	—
1722	—	6.00	12.00	50.00	125	—

KM# 30 1/2 BATZEN

Billon **Obv:** Round arms

Date	Mintage	VG	F	VF	XF	Unc
1721	—	16.00	32.00	125	60.00	—

KM# 33 1/2 BATZEN

Billon **Ruler:** Franz Friedrich am Buel **Obv:** Four-fold arms **Rev:** Small double-headed eagle above shield with stars within that divides 7 7

Date	Mintage	VG	F	VF	XF	Unc
1776	—	8.00	16.00	65.00	165	—
1776 DS	—	8.00	16.00	65.00	165	—
1776 DST	—	8.00	16.00	65.00	165	—
1777	—	8.00	16.00	65.00	165	—
1777 DS	—	8.00	16.00	65.00	165	—
1777 DST	—	8.00	16.00	65.00	165	—

KM# 27 BATZEN

Billon **Obv:** Four-fold arms draped with bishop's vestment

Date	Mintage	VG	F	VF	XF	Unc
1708	—	8.00	16.00	65.00	165	—
1709	—	8.00	16.00	65.00	165	—
1710	—	8.00	16.00	65.00	165	—
1721	—	8.00	16.00	65.00	165	—
1722	—	8.00	16.00	65.00	165	—

KM# 34 BATZEN

Billon **Obv:** Mitre above ornate 4-fold arms **Rev:** Small double-headed eagle above shield with stars within that divides date **Rev. Legend:** COM. ET. PRAEF. UTR. VALLE.

Date	Mintage	VG	F	VF	XF	Unc
1776	—	40.00	80.00	325	600	1,600

KM# 35 BATZEN

Billon **Ruler:** Franz Friedrich am Buel **Obv:** Mitre above ornate 4-fold arms **Rev:** Small double-headed eagle above shield with stars within that divides date **Rev. Legend:** COM. ET. PRAEF. REIP. VALLES.

Date	Mintage	VG	F	VF	XF	Unc
1776	—	9.00	16.00	65.00	165	—
1777	—	9.00	16.00	65.00	165	—
1778	—	9.00	16.00	65.00	165	—

SOLOTHURN

Solodornensis, Soleure

A canton in northwest Switzerland. Bracteates were struck in the 1300s even though the mint right was not officially granted until 1381. They joined the Swiss Confederation in 1481.

MINT OFFICIAL'S INITIALS

Initials	Date	Name
T		Thiebaud

MONETARY SYSTEM

Until 1798

2 Vierer = 1 Kreuzer
4 Kreuzer = 1 Batzen
40 Batzen = 2 Gulden = 1 Thaler

CITY

STANDARD COINAGE

KM# 36.1 1/2 KREUZER (Vierer)

Billon **Obv:** Arms divides S O within circle **Obv. Legend:** SOLODORENSIS **Rev:** Floreated cross within circle, date below **Rev. Legend:** MONETA REIP

Date	Mintage	VG	F	VF	XF	Unc
1761	—	4.00	8.00	30.00	100	200
1789	—	4.00	8.00	16.00	40.00	125
1790	—	4.00	8.00	16.00	40.00	125
1793	—	4.00	8.00	16.00	40.00	125
1794	—	4.00	8.00	16.00	40.00	125
1796	—	4.00	8.00	20.00	60.00	140
1797	—	4.00	8.00	20.00	60.00	140
1798	—	4.00	8.00	20.00	60.00	140

KM# 36.2 1/2 KREUZER (Vierer)

Billon **Obv:** Broad arms

Date	Mintage	VG	F	VF	XF	Unc
1798	—	12.00	24.00	40.00	165	325

KM# 30 KREUZER

Billon **Obv:** Arms divides S O within circle **Obv. Legend:** MONETA REIP•SOLOD : **Rev:** Floreated cross, leaves in angles, within circle, date below **Rev. Legend:** CUNCTA PER DEUM

Date	Mintage	VG	F	VF	XF	Unc
1760	—	7.00	15.00	30.00	125	250
1762	—	12.00	25.00	45.00	150	325
1794	—	4.00	16.00	30.00	125	250
1796	—	4.00	16.00	30.00	125	250
1797	—	6.00	14.00	28.00	45.00	—
1798	—	6.00	14.00	28.00	45.00	—

KM# 31 4 KREUZER (1 Batzen)

Billon **Obv:** Arms within sprigs and circle, value below **Obv. Legend:** MONETA REIP SOLODORENSIS **Rev:** S entwined in center of cross within circle, date below **Rev. Legend:** CUNCTA PER DEUM

Date	Mintage	VG	F	VF	XF	Unc
1760 Rare	—	35.00	110	225	375	—

KM# 32 4 KREUZER (1 Batzen)

Billon **Obv:** Arms divides S O within circle, value below **Obv. Legend:** MONETA • REIP • SOLODORENSIS **Rev:** Floreated cross, designs in angles, within cartouche, date below **Rev. Legend:** CUNCTA PER DEUM

Date	Mintage	VG	F	VF	XF	Unc
1760	—	8.00	16.00	32.00	125	250
1761	—	12.00	24.00	40.00	165	325
1762	—	12.00	24.00	40.00	165	325

KM# 41 4 KREUZER (1 Batzen)

Billon **Obv:** Arms divides S O within beaded circle, value below **Obv. Legend:** MONETA • REIP • SOLODORENSIS **Rev:** Floreated cross within beaded circle, date below **Rev. Legend:** CUNCTA PER DEUM

Date	Mintage	VG	F	VF	XF	Unc
1766	—	8.00	16.00	30.00	120	240
1787	—	8.00	16.00	30.00	120	240
1788	—	10.00	20.00	40.00	150	325
1793	—	8.00	16.00	30.00	120	240
1795	—	8.00	16.00	30.00	120	240
1796	—	10.00	20.00	40.00	150	325
1797	—	8.00	16.00	30.00	120	240

KM# 33 10 KREUZER

Silver **Obv:** Crowned arms within sprigs **Obv. Legend:** MONETA REIP SOLODORENSIS • **Rev:** S entwined in center of crowned cross within sprigs, value below, date in legend **Rev. Legend:** CUNCTA PER DEUM

Date	Mintage	VG	F	VF	XF	Unc
1760	—	30.00	60.00	160	325	600

KM# 38 10 KREUZER

Silver **Obv:** Crowned, ornate arms **Obv. Legend:** MONETA REIP • SOLODORENSIS **Rev:** Flowered S entwined in center of crowned cross within sprigs, value below, date in legend **Rev. Legend:** CUNCTA PER DEUM

Date	Mintage	VG	F	VF	XF	Unc
1762	—	30.00	60.00	160	325	600

KM# 47 10 KREUZER

Silver **Obv:** Crowned, ornate oval arms within sprigs **Obv. Legend:** MONETA REIP • SOLODORENSIS **Rev:** S entwined within center circle of cross, value below, date in legend **Rev. Legend:** CUNCTA PER DEUM

Date	Mintage	VG	F	VF	XF	Unc
1785	—	20.00	40.00	80.00	160	325

KM# 34 20 KREUZER

Silver **Obv:** Crowned arms within sprigs **Obv. Legend:** MONETA REIP SOLODORENSIS **Rev:** S entwined in center of crowned cross within sprigs **Rev. Legend:** CUNCTA PER DEUM

Date	Mintage	VG	F	VF	XF	Unc
1760	—	40.00	80.00	200	400	725

KM# 39 20 KREUZER

Silver **Obv:** Crowned, ornate arms **Obv. Legend:** MONETA REIP • SOLODORENSIS **Rev:** Flowered S entwined in center of crowned cross within sprigs, value below, date in legend **Rev. Legend:** CUNCTA PER DEUM

Date	Mintage	VG	F	VF	XF	Unc
1763	—	40.00	80.00	200	400	725

KM# 48 20 KREUZER

Silver **Obv:** Crowned, oval arms within sprigs **Obv. Legend:** MONETA • REIP • SOLODORENSIS • **Rev:** S entwined in center circle of cross within circle, value below **Rev. Legend:** CUNCTA • PER • DEUM •

Date	Mintage	VG	F	VF	XF	Unc
1785	—	20.00	40.00	95.00	300	600

KM# 35 1/2 BATZEN (2 Kreuzer)

Billon **Obv:** Arm divides S O within circle **Obv. Legend:** MONETA REIP • SOLODORENSIS • **Rev:** Floreated cross, designs in angles, within circle, date below **Rev. Legend:** CUNCTA PER DEUM

Date	Mintage	VG	F	VF	XF	Unc
1760	—	5.00	8.00	20.00	95.00	200
1761	—	5.00	8.00	20.00	95.00	200
1762	—	6.00	12.00	30.00	120	225
1787	—	4.00	8.00	20.00	95.00	200
1793	—	4.00	8.00	20.00	95.00	200
1794	—	6.00	12.00	30.00	120	225
1795	—	4.00	8.00	20.00	95.00	200
1796	—	7.00	15.00	30.00	110	225

KM# 49 2-1/2 BATZEN (10 Kreuzer)

Silver **Obv:** Crowned, oval arms within sprigs **Obv. Legend:** SOLODORENSIS • RESPUBLICA **Rev:** S entwined in cross within circle, date below **Rev. Legend:** CUNCTA PER DEUM

Date	Mintage	VG	F	VF	XF	Unc
1787	—	20.00	40.00	80.00	165	325
1794	—	20.00	40.00	80.00	165	325
1795	—	20.00	40.00	80.00	165	325

KM# 50 5 BATZEN (20 Kreuzer)

Silver **Obv:** Crowned, oval arms within sprigs **Obv. Legend:** SOLODORENSIS RESPUBLICA **Rev:** S entwined in cross within circle, date below **Rev. Legend:** CUNCTA PER DEUM

Date	Mintage	VG	F	VF	XF	Unc
1787	—	20.00	40.00	100	325	600
1794	—	20.00	40.00	100	325	600
1795	—	20.00	40.00	100	325	600

KM# 37 10 BATZEN

Silver **Obv:** Crowned, ornate arms within sprigs **Obv. Legend:** MONETA REIP SOLODORENSIS **Rev:** S entwined in crowned cross within sprigs, date in legend **Rev. Legend:** CUNCTA PER DEUM

Date	Mintage	VG	F	VF	XF	Unc
1761	—	40.00	80.00	200	400	800

KM# 40 10 BATZEN

Silver **Obv:** Crowned, ornate arms **Obv. Legend:** MONETA REIP : SOLODORENSIS **Rev:** S entwined in cross within sprigs, date in legend **Rev. Legend:** CUNCTA PER DEUM

Date	Mintage	VG	F	VF	XF	Unc
1763	—	50.00	100	250	475	875
1766	—	60.00	125	325	600	1,000

KM# 42 10 BATZEN

Silver **Obv:** Crowned, ornate arms **Obv. Legend:** MONETA REIP • SOLODORENSIS **Rev:** Flowered S entwined in crowned cross within sprigs, date below **Rev. Legend:** CUNCTA PER DEUM

Date	Mintage	VG	F	VF	XF	Unc
1767	—	60.00	125	325	650	1,200

KM# 45 10 BATZEN

Silver **Obv:** Crowned, oval arms within sprigs **Obv. Legend:** MONETA REIP • SOLODORENSIS • **Rev:** S entwined in center circle of cross within circle, date below **Rev. Legend:** CUNCTA * PER * DEUM *

Date	Mintage	VG	F	VF	XF	Unc
1773	—	75.00	150	400	800	1,450
1778	—	40.00	80.00	200	400	725
1785	—	30.00	60.00	165	325	600

KM# 51 10 BATZEN

Silver **Obv:** Crowned, oval arms within sprigs **Obv. Legend:** SOLODORENSIS RESPUBLICA **Rev:** S entwined in cross within circle, date below **Rev. Legend:** CUNCTA PER DEUM

Date	Mintage	VG	F	VF	XF	Unc
1787		20.00	40.00	125	275	475
1788	—	20.00	40.00	125	275	475
1791	—	20.00	40.00	125	275	475
1794	—	20.00	40.00	125	275	475

KM# 57 20 BATZEN

Silver **Obv:** Crowned, oval arms within sprigs, value below **Obv. Legend:** SOLODOREN • RESPUBLICA **Rev:** S entwined in cross within circle, date below **Rev. Legend:** CUNCTA PER DEUM

Date	Mintage	VG	F	VF	XF	Unc
1795	—	20.00	40.00	125	250	475
1798	—	20.00	40.00	125	250	475

KM# 55 1/4 DUPLONE

1.9100 g., 0.9000 Gold 0.0553 oz. AGW **Obv:** Crowned arms with garland **Obv. Legend:** SOLODORENSIS • RESPUBLICA • **Rev:** Standing Saint with flag, slanted sword behind **Rev. Legend:** S • URSUS MART •

Date	Mintage	F	VF	XF	Unc	BU
1789	—	200	400	600	850	1,200

KM# 58 1/4 DUPLONE

1.9100 g., 0.9000 Gold 0.0553 oz. AGW **Obv:** Crowned arms with garland **Obv. Legend:** SOLODORENSIS • RESPUBLICA • **Rev:** Standing Saint with flag, slanted sword behind, date below **Rev. Legend:** S • URSUS • MART •

Date	Mintage	F	VF	XF	Unc	BU
1796	—	200	400	600	950	1,200

KM# 52 1/2 DUPLONE

3.8200 g., 0.9000 Gold 0.1105 oz. AGW **Obv:** Crowned arms with garland **Obv. Legend:** SOLODORENSIS RESPUBLICA **Rev:** Standing Saint with flag, slanted sword behind, date in legend **Rev. Legend:** S • URSUS • MART •

Date	Mintage	F	VF	XF	Unc	BU
1787	—	325	650	950	1,500	2,000

KM# 59 1/2 DUPLONE

3.8200 g., 0.9000 Gold 0.1105 oz. AGW **Obv:** Crowned arms with garland **Obv. Legend:** SOLODORENSIS RESPUBLICA **Rev:** Standing Saint with flag, slanted sword behind, date below **Rev. Legend:** S • URSUS MARTYR

Date	Mintage	F	VF	XF	Unc	BU
1796	—	325	600	950	1,500	2,000

KM# 53 DUPLONE

7.6400 g., 0.9000 Gold 0.2211 oz. AGW **Obv:** Crowned arms with garland **Obv. Legend:** SOLODORENSIS RESPUBLICA **Rev:** Standing Saint with flag, slanted sword behind, date in legend **Rev. Legend:** S • URSUS MART •

Date	Mintage	F	VF	XF	Unc	BU
1787	—	450	900	1,400	2,150	2,800

KM# 60 DUPLONE

7.6400 g., 0.9000 Gold 0.2211 oz. AGW **Obv:** Crowned arms with garland **Obv. Legend:** SOLODORENSIS RESPUBLICA **Rev:** Standing Saint with flag, slanted sword behind, date below **Rev. Legend:** S • URSUS MARTYR

Date	Mintage	F	VF	XF	Unc	BU
1796	—	450	900	1,400	2,150	2,800
1797	—	425	850	1,400	2,150	2,800
1798	—	600	1,200	2,000	2,150	2,800

KM# 54 2 DUPLONE
15.2800 g., 0.9000 Gold 0.4421 oz. AGW **Obv:** Crowned arms with garland **Obv. Legend:** SOLODORENSIS RESPUBLICA **Rev:** Standing Saint with flag, slanted sword behind, date in legend **Rev. Legend:** S • URSUS MART •

Date	Mintage	F	VF	XF	Unc	BU
1787	—	1,400	2,800	4,750	6,400	8,000

KM# 61 2 DUPLONE
15.2800 g., 0.9000 Gold 0.4421 oz. AGW **Obv:** Crowned arms with garland **Obv. Legend:** SOLODORENSIS RESPUBLICA **Rev:** Standing Saint with flag, slanted sword behind, date below **Rev. Legend:** S • URSUS MARTYR

Date	Mintage	F	VF	XF	Unc	BU
1796	—	750	1,400	2,400	3,600	4,800
1797	—	750	1,400	2,400	3,600	4,800
1798	—	750	1,400	2,400	3,600	4,800

TRADE COINAGE

KM# 43 DUCAT
3.5000 g., 0.9860 Gold 0.1109 oz. AGW **Obv:** Crowned arms within sprigs **Obv. Legend:** DUCATUS SOLODORENSIS **Rev:** Standing Saint with flag, slanted sword behind **Rev. Legend:** S • URSUS MART •

Date	Mintage	VG	F	VF	XF	Unc
1768	—	—	2,200	4,400	7,200	12,000

PATTERNS

Including off metal strikes

KM#	Date	Mintage	Identification	Mkt Val
Pn5	1760	—	Kreuzer. Gold. KM30.	2,000
Pn6	1761	—	1/2 Kreuzer. Gold. KM36.	1,500
Pn7	1793	—	1/2 Batzen. Silver. KM35.	—

UNTERWALDEN

Subsilvania

A canton in central Switzerland which was one of the three original cantons which became the Swiss Confederation in 1291. It is made up of two half cantons - Nidwalden and Obwalden. They had their own coinage beginning in the1500s.

MINT OFFICIAL'S INITIALS

Initials	Date	Name
S		Samson

MONETARY SYSTEM
4 Kreuzer = 1 Batzen
10 Batzen = 1 Frank

CANTON
Obwalden
STANDARD COINAGE

KM# 5 RAPPEN
Billon **Obv:** Shield on three-pronged cross on cloverleaf **Rev:** Inscription: MONETA/SVBSYLV/NA between palm and laurel branches

Date	Mintage	VG	F	VF	XF	Unc
ND	—	60.00	125	400	120	—

KM# 6 1/2 KREUZER
Billon **Obv:** Crowned imperial eagle with oval arms on breast, value in oval shield above **Rev:** Value

Date	Mintage	VG	F	VF	XF	Unc
ND Rare	—	30.00	70.00	125	175	—

KM# 24 1/2 KREUZER
Billon **Obv:** Value in oval shield divides date above two oval arms, R below **Rev:** Value

Date	Mintage	VG	F	VF	XF	Unc
1730	—	12.00	25.00	95.00	250	—
1732	—	10.00	20.00	165	400	—
1733	—	16.00	32.00	125	275	—

KM# 7 KREUZER
Billon **Obv:** Oval arms in cartouche **Rev:** Value on breast of crowned imperial eagle

Date	Mintage	VG	F	VF	XF	Unc
1725 Rare	—	60.00	125	225	375	—
1726	—	40.00	80.00	325	225	—
1727 Rare	—	70.00	150	275	425	—
1729	—	40.00	80.00	325	330	—

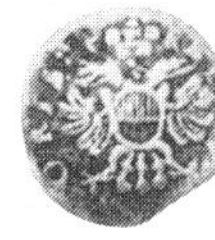
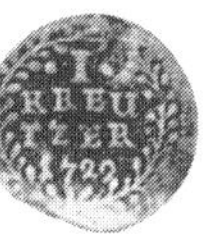

KM# 21 KREUZER
Billon **Obv:** Crowned imperial eagle with arms on breast **Rev:** Value: 1/KREU/TZER/date in laurel wreath

Date	Mintage	VG	F	VF	XF	Unc
1729 Rare	—	85.00	150	300	450	—
1730	—	80.00	165	475	250	—

KM# 22 KREUZER
Billon **Obv:** Curved arms in pearl ring **Rev:** Cross with blossoms in angles

Date	Mintage	VG	F	VF	XF	Unc
1729	—	60.00	125	400	250	—

KM# 12 3 KREUZER (1 Groschen)
Billon **Obv:** Crowned imperial eagle with arms on breast **Rev:** Floreated cross with value in center circle

Date	Mintage	VG	F	VF	XF	Unc
1726 Rare	—	75.00	150	300	500	—
1730	—	100	200	800	500	—
1732	—	200	400	1,600	500	—

KM# 8 20 KREUZER
Silver **Obv:** Crowned imperial eagle with curved arms on breast **Rev:** Value, date in palm wreath

Date	Mintage	VG	F	VF	XF	Unc
1725	—	40.00	80.00	200	300	—
1742	—	150	300	600	300	—

KM# 13 20 KREUZER
Silver **Obv:** Value on oval shield on breast of crowned imperial eagle, date in legend

Date	Mintage	VG	F	VF	XF	Unc
1726	—	35.00	65.00	165	300	—
1728	—	35.00	65.00	165	400	—
1736	—	35.00	65.00	165	250	—
1742	—	35.00	65.00	165	300	—
1743 Rare	—	300	600	1,600	—	—

KM# 14 20 KREUZER
Silver **Obv:** Ornate arms **Obv. Legend:** MONETA REIP • SVBSLVANIÆ SVPERIORIS **Rev:** Crowned imperial eagle without date **Rev. Legend:** DILEXIT DOMINVS DECOREM IVSTITIÆ

Date	Mintage	VG	F	VF	XF	Unc
1726	—	35.00	65.00	165	300	—
1729	—	35.00	65.00	165	400	—
1730	—	35.00	65.00	165	400	—
1731	—	150	300	600	950	—
1732	—	35.00	65.00	165	275	—
1734 Rare	—	—	—	—	—	—

KM# 26 20 KREUZER
Silver **Obv:** Ornate, oval arms divide date within sprigs

Date	Mintage	VG	F	VF	XF	Unc
1732	—	35.00	65.00	165	250	—
1736 Rare	—	—	—	—	—	—

KM# 30 20 KREUZER
Silver **Obv:** Imperial eagle **Rev:** Value and date in wreath

Date	Mintage	VG	F	VF	XF	Unc
1742	—	200	400	950	700	—

KM# 31 20 KREUZER
Silver **Rev:** Inscription: ET/ERVUS MEUS/ORABIT/date in palm branch wreath, value below

Date	Mintage	VG	F	VF	XF	Unc
1743	—	70.00	125	250	400	800

KM# 9 20 KREUZER
Silver **Obv:** Ornate, oval arms within sprigs **Rev:** Kneeling Saint holding rosary within sprigs and circle

Date	Mintage	VG	F	VF	XF	Unc
ND	—	65.00	125	325	450	—

KM# 10 30 KREUZER (1/4 Thaler)
Silver **Obv:** Inscription: MONETA/NOVA REIP/SVBSYLVANIAE/SVPERIORIS/30 K/date in cartouche, value below **Rev:** Standing saint holding shield of arms and rosary

Date	Mintage	VG	F	VF	XF	Unc
1725	—	400	950	2,400	1,250	—
1726 Rare	—	—	—	—	—	—

KM# 32 40 KREUZER (1/3 Thaler)
Silver **Obv:** Kneeling Saint holding rosary within sprigs and circle **Rev:** Inscription: ET/SERVUS MEUS/ORABIT/PRO VOBIS/10B. 42/date between palm branches and ornaments, value below

Date	Mintage	VG	F	VF	XF	Unc
1743	—	900	2,000	4,800	—	—

KM# 19 ASSIS
Billon **Obv:** Square-cornered arms with ornaments in circle **Rev:** Value, date in inner circle

Date	Mintage	VG	F	VF	XF	Unc
1728	—	20.00	40.00	160	600	—

KM# 15 1/2 BATZEN
Billon **Obv:** Oval arms in cartouche in inner circle **Rev:** Floreated cross with ornaments in fields

Date	Mintage	VG	F	VF	XF	Unc
1726	—	10.00	20.00	80.00	75.00	—
1727	—	30.00	60.00	250	150	—
1728	—	100	225	900	400	—

KM# 20 1/2 THALER
Silver **Obv:** Value within circle below ornate oval arms within beaded circle **Obv. Legend:** MONETA REIP : SVBSYLVANIÆ SVPERIORES **Rev:** Standing Saint

Date	Mintage	VG	F	VF	XF	Unc
1728	—	450	800	2,150	4,400	—

KM# 27 1/2 THALER
Silver **Rev:** Saint kneeling with rosary right

Date	Mintage	VG	F	VF	XF	Unc
1732	—	350	750	1,850	3,600	—

KM# 28 THALER

Silver **Obv:** Ornate oval arms **Obv. Legend:** MONETA REIPUBL : SUBSYLVANIÆ SUPERIORES **Rev:** Kneeling Saint with rosary left **Note:** Dav. #1780.

Date	Mintage	VG	F	VF	XF	Unc
1732	—	1,200	2,400	6,000	12,000	—

TRADE COINAGE

KM# 11 DUCAT

3.5000 g., 0.9860 Gold 0.1109 oz. AGW **Obv:** Inscription, date within cartouche **Rev:** St. Nicholas von der Flue, standing with oval arms and rosary

Date	Mintage	F	VF	XF	Unc	BU
1725 Rare	—	1,250	2,750	5,000	8,500	—

KM# 16 DUCAT

3.5000 g., 0.9860 Gold 0.1109 oz. AGW **Obv:** Inscription, date within ornamented square **Rev:** Standing Saint with oval arms and rosary

Date	Mintage	F	VF	XF	Unc	BU
1726	—	1,000	2,000	3,200	3,200	—

KM# 17 DUCAT

3.5000 g., 0.9860 Gold 0.1109 oz. AGW **Obv:** Inscription, date within ornamented square **Rev:** Kneeling Saint with rosary left within circle

Date	Mintage	F	VF	XF	Unc	BU
1726	—	1,200	2,500	4,500	7,500	—

KM# 18 DUCAT

3.5000 g., 0.9860 Gold 0.1109 oz. AGW **Obv:** Inscription, date within ornamented square **Rev:** Crowned double-headed eagle within oval, ornate arms

Date	Mintage	VG	F	VF	XF	Unc
1726 Rare	—	—	—	—	—	—

KM# 25 DUCAT

3.5000 g., 0.9860 Gold 0.1109 oz. AGW **Obv:** Inscription, date within ornamented square **Rev:** Kneeling Saint with rosary right

Date	Mintage	F	VF	XF	Unc	BU
1730	—	1,000	2,250	3,600	3,500	—
1732	—	1,200	2,400	4,000	—	—

KM# 33 DUCAT

3.5000 g., 0.9860 Gold 0.1109 oz. AGW **Obv:** Inscription, date below ornaments within sprigs **Rev:** Kneeling Saint with rosary right

Date	Mintage	F	VF	XF	Unc	BU
1743	—	600	1,200	2,000	2,500	—

KM# 45 DUCAT

3.5000 g., 0.9860 Gold 0.1109 oz. AGW **Obv:** Oval arms within sprays **Rev:** Kneeling Saint

Date	Mintage	F	VF	XF	Unc	BU
1774	—	1,400	3,000	4,800	4,000	—

KM# 46 DUCAT

3.5000 g., 0.9860 Gold 0.1109 oz. AGW **Obv:** DUCAT•/ REIPUB•/ SUESILV•/SUPER, date within sprigs **Rev:** Kneeling Saint with rosary right

Date	Mintage	F	VF	XF	Unc	BU
1787	—	275	550	950	1,600	—
1787 Restrike	150	—	—	400	650	950

Note: Restrikes, done in 1860, display concave fields

KM# 47 DUCAT

3.5000 g., 0.9860 Gold 0.1109 oz. AGW **Obv:** DUCAT•/ REIPUB•/SUESILV•/ date within sprigs **Rev:** Kneeling Saint

Date	Mintage	F	VF	XF	Unc	BU
1787	—	750	1,650	2,800	2,250	—

KM# 29 5 DUCAT

17.5000 g., 0.9860 Gold 0.5547 oz. AGW **Obv:** Ornate oval arms **Rev:** Kneeling Saint, right **Rev. Legend:** B:NICOLAUS DE FLUE... **Note:** Struck with 1/2 Thaler dies, KM#27.

Date	Mintage	VG	F	VF	XF	Unc
1732 Rare	—	—	—	—	—	—

KM# A21 8 DUCAT

27.0000 g., 0.9890 Gold 0.8585 oz. AGW **Obv:** Ornate oval arms **Rev:** Standing Saint, facing **Rev. Legend:** BEATVS NICOLAVS DE FL-VE OBYT 1487... **Note:** Struck with 1/2 Thaler dies, KM#20.

Date	Mintage	VG	F	VF	XF	Unc
1728 Rare	—	—	—	—	—	—

PATTERNS

Including off metal strikes

KM#	Date	Mintage	Identification	Mkt Val
Pn2	1730	—	20 Kreuzer. Silver.	—

URI

Uranie

A canton in central Switzerland. It is one of the three original cantons which became the Swiss Confederation in 1291. They had their own coinage from the early 1600s until 1811.

MONETARY SYSTEM

10 Rappen = 1 Batzen
10 Batzen = 1 Frank

CANTON

TRADE COINAGE

KM# 34 DUCAT

3.5000 g., 0.9860 Gold 0.1109 oz. AGW **Obv:** Oval arms below inscription within sprigs and cartouche **Rev:** St. Martin giving alms to a beggar **Rev. Legend:** SANCTVS MARTINVS **Note:** Fr. #404, 405

Date	Mintage	F	VF	XF	Unc	BU
1701 Rare	—	—	—	—	—	—
1704/1	—	6,000	10,000	13,000	18,000	—

Note: Ducats dated 1704 were overstruck on 1701 dated coins

KM# 36 DUCAT

3.5000 g., 0.9860 Gold 0.1109 oz. AGW **Obv:** Ornate oval arms **Rev:** Equestrian left **Rev. Legend:** SANCTUS MARTINUS **Note:** Fr. #406.

Date	Mintage	F	VF	XF	Unc	BU
1720	—	700	1,400	2,500	3,600	4,800

KM# 38 DUCAT

3.5000 g., 0.9860 Gold 0.1109 oz. AGW **Obv:** Ornate oval arms **Rev:** Equestrian left **Rev. Legend:** SANCTUS MARTINUS **Note:** Fr. #407.

Date	Mintage	F	VF	XF	Unc	BU
1736/20	—	600	1,200	2,000	3,000	4,000

URI, SCHWYZ & UNTERWALDEN

These patterns were issued jointly by Uri, Schwyz and Unterwalden for the territory of Bellizona. First conquered in 1503 Bellizona joined the Swiss Confederation as Ticino in 1803.

PATTERNS

Including off metal strikes

KM#	Date	Mintage	Identification	Mkt Val
Pn1	1788	—	Quattrino. Copper.	—
Pn2	1788	—	1/2 Soldo. Copper.	—

KM#	Date	Mintage	Identification	Mkt Val

KM#	Date	Mintage	Identification	Mkt Val
Pn3	1788	—	Soldo. Copper.	—

ZOEFINGEN

This town in Aargau, Switzerland, was a Hapsburg Mint during the middle ages which struck bracteats. Later, in the 17th and early 18th centuries, the city struck coins and tokens to preserve their mint right.

CITY

STANDARD COINAGE

KM# 5 1/2 KREUZER (Vierer)

Billon **Obv:** Arched and curved arms **Rev:** Anchor cross with designs in angles, date in legend

Date	Mintage	Good	VG	F	VF	XF
1716 Rare	—	—	—	—	—	—

KM# 6 1/2 KREUZER (Vierer)

Billon **Obv:** Arms within circle **Obv. Legend:** MONET • ZOFINGENS • **Rev:** Anchor cross with designs in angles, within beaded circle **Rev. Legend:** DEVS • PROVIDEBIT •

Date	Mintage	Good	VG	F	VF	XF
1720 Rare	—	—	—	—	—	—
1722	—	—	24.00	50.00	100	250

KM# 10 KREUZER

Billon **Obv:** Arms within circle **Obv. Legend:** MON • NOV • ZOFINGENS • **Rev:** Anchor cross with designs in angles, within beaded circle **Rev. Legend:** DEVS • PROVIDEBIT •

Date	Mintage	Good	VG	F	VF	XF
1722	—	—	35.00	65.00	125	325

KM# 7 4 KREUZER (Batzen)

Billon **Obv:** Bear walking left above arms **Rev:** Floreate cross, value below, date in legend

Date	Mintage	Good	VG	F	VF	XF
1721	—	—	200	450	750	1,400
1726	—	—	100	200	400	750

KM# 11 10 KREUZER

Silver **Obv:** Bear walking left above round arms within sprigs **Obv. Legend:** • MONET • CIVIT • ZOFINGEN • **Rev:** DEVS/PROVI:/DEBIT/ date within closed sprigs

Date	Mintage	Good	VG	F	VF	XF
1722	—	—	60.00	125	325	750

KM# 12 20 KREUZER

Silver **Obv:** Bear walking left above ornate, oval arms **Obv. Legend:** MONETA • CIVITATIS • ZOFINGEN **Rev:** DEVS/ PROVI: /DEBIT/ date within closed sprigs

Date	Mintage	Good	VG	F	VF	XF
1722	—	—	80.00	165	400	800

KM# 8 1/2 BATZEN (2 KREUZER)

Billon **Obv:** Oval shield below bear **Rev:** Similar to KM#9, but date to left of center in legend

Date	Mintage	Good	VG	F	VF	XF
1721 Rare	—	—	350	800	1,400	2,400

KM# 9 1/2 BATZEN (2 KREUZER)

Billon **Obv:** Bear left, above arms **Rev:** Floreated cross

Date	Mintage	Good	VG	F	VF	XF
1721 Rare	—	—	150	400	800	1,250
1726	—	—	60.00	125	275	550

ZUG

Tugium, Tugiensis

A canton in central Switzerland. They joined the Swiss Confederation in 1352 and had their own coinage from1564 to 1805.

MONETARY SYSTEM

6 Angster = 3 Rappen
= 1 Schilling = 1 Assis

CANTON

STANDARD COINAGE

KM# 61 ANGSTER

Copper **Obv:** Oval arms within sprigs **Rev:** Date, value in cartouche

Date	Mintage	F	VF	XF	Unc	BU
1778	—	8.00	20.00	60.00	120	—
1781	—	8.00	20.00	60.00	120	—
1782	—	16.00	40.00	120	240	—
1783	—	8.00	20.00	60.00	120	—
1784	—	8.00	20.00	60.00	120	—
1791	—	12.00	32.00	80.00	160	—
1794	—	8.00	20.00	60.00	120	—
1796	—	16.00	40.00	120	240	—
1804	—	40.00	70.00	200	300	550

KM# 63 RAPPEN

Copper **Obv:** Oval arms within sprigs **Rev:** Date, value in cartouche

Date	Mintage	F	VF	XF	Unc	BU
1782	—	8.00	20.00	60.00	125	—
1783	—	8.00	20.00	60.00	125	—
1785	—	15.00	40.00	125	250	—
1794	—	8.00	20.00	60.00	125	—
1805	—	5.00	17.50	42.00	110	110

KM# 8 RAPPEN

Billon **Note:** Arms in baroque frame, ZVG around.

Date	Mintage	VG	F	VF	XF	Unc
ND	—	25.00	50.00	125	—	—

KM# 58 RAPPEN

Billon **Obv:** Renaissance shield, Damascus sign on middle bar, two branches at top **Rev:** Inscription, date between palm and laurel branches **Rev. Inscription:** MONETA/TVGIENS/IS

Date	Mintage	VG	F	VF	XF	Unc
ND	—	24.00	50.00	125	125	—
1756	—	125	250	600	1,200	2,400

KM# 59 RAPPEN

Billon **Obv:** Z V G around shield

Date	Mintage	VG	F	VF	XF	Unc
ND	—	24.00	50.00	125	125	—

KM# 5 RAPPEN

Billon **Note:** Uniface. Spanish shield.

Date	Mintage	VG	F	VF	XF	Unc
ND	—	24.00	50.00	125	150	—

KM# 6 RAPPEN

Billon **Note:** Arms with straight top, ZVG around.

Date	Mintage	VG	F	VF	XF	Unc
ND	—	25.00	50.00	125	150	—

KM# 7 RAPPEN

Billon **Note:** Arms with rounded top, ZVG around.

Date	Mintage	VG	F	VF	XF	Unc
ND	—	25.00	50.00	125	150	—

KM# 9 RAPPEN

Billon **Note:** Oval arms, ZVG around.

Date	Mintage	VG	F	VF	XF	Unc
ND	—	25.00	50.00	125	150	—

KM# 49 SCHILLING

Billon **Rev:** Standing saint facing

Date	Mintage	VG	F	VF	XF	Unc
1709	—	12.00	25.00	80.00	200	—

KM# 64 SCHILLING

Billon **Obv:** Oval arms within sprigs **Obv. Legend:** MONETA • TVGIENSIS • **Rev:** Saint's bust facing, church at left all within beaded circle **Rev. Legend:** SANCTVS • WOLFGANG •

Date	Mintage	VG	F	VF	XF	Unc
1783	—	8.00	16.00	65.00	160	400

KM# 65 SCHILLING

Billon **Obv:** Arms within sprigs and circle, date below **Obv. Legend:** MONETA • TVGIENSIS • **Rev:** Saint's bust facing, church at left, within circle **Rev. Legend:** SANCTVS • WOLFGANG •

Date	Mintage	VG	F	VF	XF	Unc
1784	—	8.00	16.00	65.00	160	400

KM# 10 1/6 ASSIS (1 Angster)

Billon **Obv:** Arms in Spanish shield above small palm branches, ZVG around **Rev:** Value: large 1/6

Date	Mintage	VG	F	VF	XF	Unc
ND Rare	—	40.00	70.00	120	185	—

KM# 11 1/6 ASSIS (1 Angster)

Billon **Obv:** Arms in renaissance shield, Damascus sign on middle bar, ZVG around **Rev:** Value: 1/6 in palm and laurel wreath

Date	Mintage	VG	F	VF	XF	Unc
ND	—	60.00	120	320	130	—

KM# 12 1/6 ASSIS (1 Angster)

Billon **Obv:** Value: 1/6 above arms in Spanish shield with middle bar empty **Rev:** Crowned imperial eagle with sceptre and sword

Date	Mintage	VG	F	VF	XF	Unc
ND	—	40.00	80.00	200	130	—

KM# 13 1/6 ASSIS (1 Angster)

Billon **Rev:** Crowned imperial eagle without sceptre

Date	Mintage	VG	F	VF	XF	Unc
ND	—	40.00	80.00	200	130	—

KM# 14 1/6 ASSIS (1 Angster)

Billon **Rev:** Large crowned imperial eagle without legend around

Date	Mintage	VG	F	VF	XF	Unc
ND	—	200	400	950	185	—

KM# 15 1/6 ASSIS (1 Angster)

Billon **Obv:** Arms in renaissance shield, Damascus sign on middle bar, two small branches above **Rev:** Crowned imperial eagle, dot on breast, value in legend

Date	Mintage	VG	F	VF	XF	Unc
ND	—	100	200	600	130	—

KM# 51 1/6 ASSIS (1 Angster)

Billon **Obv:** Arms in Spanish shield **Rev:** Value: 1/6 /ASSIS/ TVGI/ENS/IS, date in inner circle

Date	Mintage	VG	F	VF	XF	Unc
ND	—	60.00	125	325	65.00	—
1746	—	100	200	475	120	—

KM# 52 1/6 ASSIS (1 Angster)

Billon **Obv:** Arms in renaissance shield with curved outside edge **Rev:** Value: 1/6 ASSIS. T/VGIENS/IS

Date	Mintage	VG	F	VF	XF	Unc
ND	—	60.00	120	325	100	—

KM# 53 1/6 ASSIS (1 Angster)

Billon **Obv:** Plain circle around edge

Date	Mintage	VG	F	VF	XF	Unc
ND	—	75.00	150	475	50.00	—

KM# 54 1/6 ASSIS (1 Angster)

Billon **Obv:** Oval arms in cartouche **Rev:** Value: 1/6 /ASSIS/TVGI/ENS/IS

Date	Mintage	VG	F	VF	XF	Unc
ND	—	60.00	120	325	130	—

KM# 56 1/6 ASSIS (1 Angster)

Billon **Obv:** Arms in renaissance shield **Rev:** Value: 1/6 / ASSIS. TV/GIENSIS, date

Date	Mintage	VG	F	VF	XF	Unc
1747	—	50.00	100	250	90.00	—
1748	—	50.00	100	250	110	—
1750	—	50.00	100	250	110	—
1751	—	50.00	100	250	90.00	—
1752	—	50.00	100	250	90.00	—
1756	—	50.00	100	250	110	—

Date	Mintage	VG	F	VF	XF	Unc
1757	—	40.00	80.00	200	85.00	—
1761	—	40.00	80.00	200	85.00	—
1762	—	40.00	80.00	200	85.00	—
1764	—	40.00	80.00	200	110	—
1766	—	40.00	80.00	200	85.00	—
1767	—	40.00	80.00	200	90.00	—

PATTERNS

Including off metal strikes

KM#	Date	Mintage	Identification	Mkt Val
PnA3	ND	—	Rappen. Gold. 45.0000 g. KM#8	2,000
Pn3	1778	—	Angster. Gold. KM#61	2,500
Pn4	1782	—	Angster. Silver. KM#61	—
Pn5	1782	—	Rappen. Silver. KM#63	—
Pn6	1791	—	Angster. Silver. KM#61	—

ZURICH

Thicurinae, Thuricensis, Ticurinae, Turicensis

A canton in north central Switzerland. It was the mint for the dukes of Swabia in the 10th and 11th centuries. The mint right was obtained in 1238. The first coinage struck were bracteates and the last coins were struck in 1848. It joined the Swiss Confederation in 1351.

MINT OFFICIALS' INITIALS

B - Bruckmann

AV - A. Vorster

MONETARY SYSTEM

Until 1798

12 Haller = 4 Rappen = 1 Schilling

72 Schillinge = 2 Gulden = 1 Thaler

CANTON

TRADE COINAGE

KM# 142 4 DUCAT

14.0000 g., 0.9860 Gold 0.4438 oz. AGW **Obv:** Oval arms of Zurich supported by rampant lion at right **Rev:** City view **Note:** Struck with 1/2 Thaler dies, KM#146. Fr. #480.

Date	Mintage	F	VF	XF	Unc	BU
1720 Rare	—	—	—	—	—	—
1728 Rare	—	—	—	—	—	—

KM# A143 5 DUCAT

17.5000 g., 0.9860 Gold 0.5547 oz. AGW **Obv:** Oval arms of Zurich supported by rampant lion at right **Obv. Legend:** MONETA REIPUBLICÆ TIGURINAE **Rev:** City view **Note:** Struck with 1/2 Thaler dies, KM#146. Fr. #479.

Date	Mintage	VG	F	VF	XF	Unc
1720 Rare	—	—	—	—	—	—
1724 Rare	—	—	—	—	—	—
1753 Rare	—	—	—	—	—	—

KM# 149 5 DUCAT

17.5000 g., 0.9860 Gold 0.5547 oz. AGW **Obv:** Oval arms of Zurich supported by rampant lion at right **Rev:** DOMINE/CONSERVA/NOS IN/PACE, date within ornamented wreath **Note:** Struck with 1/2 Thaler dies, KM#145. Fr. #479.

Date	Mintage	VG	F	VF	XF	Unc
1730 Rare	—	—	—	—	—	—

KM# 151 5 DUCAT

17.5000 g., 0.9860 Gold 0.5547 oz. AGW **Note:** Fr. #479.

Date	Mintage	VG	F	VF	XF	Unc
1733	—	—	—	—	—	—

Note: Reported, not confirmed

Date	Mintage	VG	F	VF	XF	Unc
1740	—	—	—	—	—	—

Note: Reported, not confirmed

KM# A150 6 DUCAT

21.0000 g., 0.9860 Gold 0.6657 oz. AGW **Obv:** Oval arms of Zurich supported by rampant lion at right **Rev:** DOMINE/CONSERVA/NOS IN/PACE, date within ornamented wreath **Note:** Struck with 1/2 Thaler dies, KM#145. Fr. #484.

Date	Mintage	VG	F	VF	XF	Unc
1734 Rare	—	—	—	—	—	—

KM# 153 6 DUCAT

21.0000 g., 0.9860 Gold 0.6657 oz. AGW **Obv:** Oval arms of Zurich supported by rampant lion at right **Obv. Legend:** MONETA REIPUBLICÆ TIGURINAE **Rev:** City view **Note:** Similar to 5 Ducat, KM#A143. Struck with 1/2 Thaler dies, KM#146. Fr. #478.

Date	Mintage	VG	F	VF	XF	Unc
1739	—	—	—	17,500	25,000	—

KM# A146 8 DUCAT

28.0000 g., 0.9860 Gold 0.8876 oz. AGW **Obv:** Arms of Zurich supported by rampant lions **Rev:** City view **Note:** Struck with 1 Thaler dies, KM#144. Fr. #482.

Date	Mintage	VG	F	VF	XF	Unc
1723 Rare	—	—	—	—	—	—

KM# B150 8 DUCAT

28.0000 g., 0.9860 Gold 0.8876 oz. AGW **Obv:** Oval arms of Zurich supported by rampant lion at right **Rev:** City view **Note:** Struck with 1/2 Thaler dies, KM#146. Fr. #477.

Date	Mintage	VG	F	VF	XF	Unc
1734 Rare	—	—	—	—	—	—
1739 Rare	—	—	—	—	—	—

KM# A148 10 DUCAT

35.0000 g., 0.9860 Gold 1.1095 oz. AGW **Obv:** Oval arms of Zurich in frame, supported by rampant lions **Obv. Legend:** MONETA REIPUBLICÆ TIGURINE **Rev:** City view **Rev. Legend:** DOMINE CONSERVA NOS IN PACE **Note:** Similar to 8 Ducat, KM#A146. Struck with 1 Thaler dies, KM#144. Fr. #481.

Date	Mintage	VG	F	VF	XF	Unc
1724	—	—	—	17,500	25,000	—

KM# C150 10 DUCAT

35.0000 g., 0.9860 Gold 1.1095 oz. AGW **Obv:** Oval arms of Zurich supported by rampant lion at right **Rev:** City view **Note:** Similar to 6 Ducat, KM#153. Struck with 1 Thaler dies, KM#143.1. Fr. #481.

Date	Mintage	VG	F	VF	XF	Unc
1725	—	—	—	—	—	—

CITY

STANDARD COINAGE

KM# 6 3 HALLER (1 Rappen)

Billon **Obv:** Oval arms between palm and laurel branches **Rev:** Value: 3/Haller in baroque frame

Date	Mintage	VG	F	VF	XF	Unc
ND	—	3.00	5.00	8.00	16.00	40.00

KM# 10 RAPPEN

Billon **Obv:** Arms on Spanish shield on clover leaf, three leaves in field **Rev:** Inscription: MONETA/NOVA/TIGURI/NA in palm and laurel branches

Date	Mintage	VG	F	VF	XF	Unc
ND	—	3.00	5.00	16.00	40.00	120

KM# 11 RAPPEN

Billon **Obv:** Arms of Zurich within sprigs **Rev:** Inscription: MONETA/TIGURI/NA within palm and laurel branches

Date	Mintage	VG	F	VF	XF	Unc
ND	—	3.00	5.00	8.00	12.00	20.00

KM# 148 SCHILLING

Billon **Obv:** Arms of Zurich within circle **Rev:** Value, date within circle

Date	Mintage	VG	F	VF	XF	Unc
1725	—	3.00	5.00	16.00	40.00	120
1730	—	3.00	5.00	16.00	40.00	120
1736	—	3.00	5.00	16.00	40.00	120
1739	—	3.00	5.00	16.00	40.00	120
1741	—	3.00	5.00	16.00	40.00	120
1743	—	3.00	5.00	16.00	40.00	120
1745	—	3.00	5.00	16.00	40.00	120
1747	—	3.00	5.00	16.00	40.00	120
1748	—	3.00	5.00	16.00	40.00	120
1750	—	3.00	5.00	16.00	40.00	120
1751	—	3.00	5.00	8.00	20.00	80.00
1754	—	3.00	5.00	16.00	40.00	120

KM# 172 5 SCHILLINGS

Silver **Obv:** Ornate, oval arms of Zurich supported by rampant lion at right **Obv. Legend:** MONETA TURICENSIS • **Rev:** Value, date within rope wreath

Date	Mintage	VG	F	VF	XF	Unc
1783	—	8.00	16.00	40.00	100	200
1784	—	8.00	16.00	40.00	100	200

KM# 122 10 SCHILLINGS (1/4 Gulden - Oertli)

Silver **Note:** Similar to KM#86 but reverse legend in palm and laurel branches, without 10 in circle below.

Date	Mintage	VG	F	VF	XF	Unc
1707	—	10.00	20.00	60.00	125	250
1712	—	10.00	20.00	60.00	125	250
1716	—	10.00	20.00	60.00	125	250

KM# 136 10 SCHILLINGS (1/4 Gulden - Oertli)

Silver **Obv:** Ornate, arms of Zurich, flanked by stars within circle **Obv. Legend:** MONETA REIPUBLI : TIGURINÆ **Rev:** PRO/DEO/ET/PATRIA, date within cartouche and sprigs

Date	Mintage	VG	F	VF	XF	Unc
1718	—	10.00	20.00	60.00	125	250
1720	—	10.00	20.00	60.00	125	250
1721	—	10.00	20.00	60.00	125	240
1722	—	10.00	20.00	60.00	125	240
1723	—	10.00	20.00	60.00	125	240
1724	—	15.00	30.00	100	200	400
1726	—	15.00	30.00	100	200	400
1727	—	10.00	20.00	60.00	125	240
1730	—	10.00	20.00	60.00	125	240
1732	—	15.00	30.00	100	200	400
1736	—	10.00	20.00	60.00	125	240
1739	—	10.00	20.00	60.00	125	240
1741	—	10.00	20.00	60.00	125	240
1743	—	10.00	20.00	60.00	125	240
1745	—	10.00	20.00	60.00	125	240
1747		10.00	20.00	60.00	125	240
1748	—	10.00	20.00	60.00	125	240
1750	—	10.00	20.00	60.00	125	240
1751	—	10.00	20.00	60.00	125	240
1753	—	10.00	20.00	60.00	125	240

KM# 123 20 SCHILLINGS (1/2 Gulden)

Silver **Obv:** Oval arms in ornate cartouche **Rev:** Inscription: DOMINE/CONSERVA/NOS IN/PACE/date in crossed palm and laurel branches, value below

Date	Mintage	VG	F	VF	XF	Unc
ND	—	30.00	60.00	160	325	600
1707	—	40.00	80.00	200	400	—
1711	—	30.00	60.00	160	325	600
1712	—	30.00	60.00	160	325	600
1714	—	30.00	60.00	160	325	600
1716	—	30.00	60.00	160	325	600

KM# 137 20 SCHILLINGS (1/2 Gulden)
Silver **Obv:** Round arms of Zurich in baroque frame, within circle **Obv. Legend:** MONETA REIPUBLICÆ TIGURINÆ **Rev:** Inscription, date, value in cartouche within palm and laurel branches **Rev. Inscription:** DOMINIE/CONSERVA/NOS IN / PACE/

Date	Mintage	VG	F	VF	XF	Unc
1718	—	30.00	60.00	150	320	600
1720	—	30.00	60.00	150	320	600
1721	—	30.00	60.00	150	320	600
1722	—	30.00	60.00	150	320	600
1723	—	30.00	60.00	150	320	600
1724	—	30.00	60.00	150	320	600
1725	—	30.00	60.00	150	320	600
1726	—	30.00	60.00	150	320	600
1727	—	30.00	60.00	150	320	600
1728	—	50.00	100	300	600	1,000
1729	—	50.00	100	300	600	1,000
1730	—	25.00	50.00	140	275	475
1732	—	25.00	50.00	140	275	475
1734	—	25.00	50.00	140	275	475
1736	—	25.00	50.00	140	275	475
1739	—	25.00	50.00	140	275	475
1741	—	20.00	40.00	120	240	400
1743	—	20.00	40.00	120	240	400
1745	—	20.00	40.00	120	240	400
1748	—	20.00	40.00	120	240	400
1751	—	20.00	40.00	120	240	400
1753	—	16.00	32.00	100	200	360
1756	—	16.00	32.00	100	200	360
1758	—	16.00	32.00	100	200	360
1761	—	16.00	32.00	100	200	360
1767	—	16.00	32.00	100	200	360
1768	—	16.00	32.00	100	200	360

KM# 154 20 SCHILLINGS (1/2 Gulden)
Silver **Obv:** Oval arms of Zurich in baroque frame within sprigs and circle **Obv. Legend:** MONETA REIPUBLICÆ TURICENSIS **Rev:** IUSTITIA/ET/CONCORDIA, date within cartouche

Date	Mintage	VG	F	VF	XF	Unc
1773	—	60.00	120	325	600	1,000

KM# 160 20 SCHILLINGS (1/2 Gulden)
Silver **Obv:** Oval arms of Zurich in baroque frame, within circle, value below **Obv. Legend:** MONETA REIPUBLICÆ TURICENSIS **Rev:** IUSTITIA/ET/CONCORDIA, date within ornate cartouche

Date	Mintage	VG	F	VF	XF	Unc
1774	—	20.00	40.00	80.00	160	325
1776	—	20.00	40.00	80.00	160	325
1779	—	30.00	60.00	150	300	600
1780	—	30.00	60.00	150	300	600

KM# 173 20 SCHILLINGS (1/2 Gulden)
Silver **Obv:** Oval arms of Zurich in frame and sprigs with garland

Obv. Legend: MONETA REIPVBLICÆ TVRICENSIS **Rev:** Value, date within wreath

Date	Mintage	VG	F	VF	XF	Unc
1783	—	30.00	60.00	160	325	600
1786	—	250	550	2,000	4,000	—
1790	—	20.00	40.00	80.00	160	325
1791	—	20.00	40.00	80.00	160	325
1792	—	20.00	40.00	80.00	160	325
1798	—	20.00	40.00	80.00	160	325

KM# 121 1/2 THALER (1 Gulden - 36 Schillings)
Silver **Note:** Similar to KM#134 but shield in cartouche, value: 1/2 below on obverse, short branches around legend, ornamentation above on reverse.

Date	Mintage	VG	F	VF	XF	Unc
1705	—	120	240	600	1,200	2,000

KM# 130 1/2 THALER (1 Gulden - 36 Schillings)
Silver **Note:** Similar to KM#134 but shield in cartouche, value: 1/2 below on obverse.

Date	Mintage	VG	F	VF	XF	Unc
1709	—	50.00	100	250	475	875

KM# 134 1/2 THALER (1 Gulden - 36 Schillings)
Silver **Obv:** Oval arms of Zurich supported by rampant lion at right **Obv. Legend:** MONETA REIPUBLICÆ TIGURINÆ **Rev:** DOMINE/CONSERVA/NOS IN/ PACE, date within palm and laurel branches

Date	Mintage	VG	F	VF	XF	Unc
1713	—	75.00	140	350	725	1,250
1714	—	75.00	140	350	725	1,250
1715	—	75.00	140	350	725	1,250
1716	—	75.00	140	350	725	1,250
1717	—	75.00	140	350	725	1,250

KM# 146 1/2 THALER (1 Gulden - 36 Schillings)
Silver **Obv:** Oval arms of Zurich supported by rampant lion at right **Obv. Legend:** MONETA REIPUBLICÆ TIGURINAE **Rev:** City view

Date	Mintage	VG	F	VF	XF	Unc
1720	—	50.00	100	240	475	875
1721	—	50.00	100	240	475	875
1722	—	50.00	100	240	475	875
1723	—	40.00	80.00	200	400	725
1724	—	40.00	80.00	200	400	725
1725	—	40.00	80.00	200	400	725
1726	—	40.00	80.00	200	400	725
1728 Rare	—	500	1,250	2,000	3,000	—
1729	—	50.00	100	240	475	850
1732	—	50.00	100	240	475	850
1734	—	50.00	100	240	475	850
1736	—	50.00	100	240	475	850
1739	—	50.00	100	240	475	850
1741	—	50.00	100	240	475	850
1743	—	50.00	100	240	475	850
1745	—	50.00	100	240	475	850
1748	—	50.00	100	240	475	850
1751	—	50.00	100	240	475	850
1753	—	50.00	100	240	475	850
1756	—	50.00	100	240	475	850
1758	—	50.00	100	240	475	850
1761	—	50.00	100	240	475	850
1764 Rare	—	300	750	1,250	2,000	—
1767	—	40.00	80.00	200	400	725
1768	—	40.00	80.00	200	400	725

KM# 145 1/2 THALER (1 Gulden - 36 Schillings)
Silver **Obv:** Oval arms of Zurich supported by rampant lion at right **Rev:** Inscription: DOMINE/CONSERVA/NOS IN/PACE, date in baroque frame between palm and laurel branches

Date	Mintage	VG	F	VF	XF	Unc
1723	—	30.00	65.00	175	325	600
1724	—	30.00	65.00	175	325	600
1725	—	30.00	65.00	175	325	600
1726	—	30.00	65.00	175	325	600
1727	—	30.00	65.00	175	325	600
1728	—	30.00	65.00	175	325	600
1730	—	40.00	80.00	200	400	725
1732	—	40.00	80.00	200	400	725
1734	—	40.00	80.00	200	400	725
1736	—	40.00	80.00	200	400	725
1739	—	40.00	80.00	200	400	725
1741	—	40.00	80.00	200	400	725
1743	—	40.00	80.00	200	400	725
1745	—	40.00	80.00	200	400	725
1748	—	40.00	80.00	200	400	725
1751	—	40.00	80.00	200	400	725
1753	—	40.00	80.00	200	400	725
1756	—	40.00	80.00	200	400	725
1758	—	40.00	80.00	200	400	725
1761	—	40.00	80.00	200	400	725
1767	—	35.00	65.00	165	325	600
1768	—	35.00	65.00	165	325	600

KM# 156 1/2 THALER (1 Gulden - 36 Schillings)
Silver **Obv:** Oval arms of Zurich supported by rampant lion at right **Obv. Legend:** MONETA REIPUBLICÆ TURICENSIS • **Rev:** IUSTITIA/ET/CONCORDIA, date within cartouche

Date	Mintage	VG	F	VF	XF	Unc
1773	—	50.00	100	250	475	875

KM# 157 1/2 THALER (1 Gulden - 36 Schillings)
Silver **Obv:** Oval arms of Zurich supported by rampant lion at right **Obv. Legend:** MONETA REIPUBLICÆ TIGURINÆ **Rev:** IUSTITIA/ET/CONCORDIA, date within cartouche

Date	Mintage	VG	F	VF	XF	Unc
1773	—	60.00	120	325	600	1,050

KM# 155 1/2 THALER (1 Gulden - 36 Schillings)
Silver **Obv:** Oval arms of Zurich supported by rampant lion at right **Obv. Legend:** MONETA REIPUBLICÆ TURICENSIS • **Rev:** Palm and laurel branch with sword on mantle, within circle **Rev. Legend:** IUSTITIA ET CONCORDIA **Note:** Gessener Half-Taler

Date	Mintage	VG	F	VF	XF	Unc
1773 AV	—	1,000	2,000	6,000	10,000	16,000

KM# 162 1/2 THALER (1 Gulden - 36 Schillings)
Silver **Obv:** Oval arms of Zurich within sprigs, supported by rampant lion at right **Obv. Legend:** MONETA REIPUBLICÆ TURICENSIS • **Rev:** IUSTITIA/ET/CONCORDIA, date above crossed cornucopias within cartouche

Date	Mintage	VG	F	VF	XF	Unc
1776	—	50.00	100	250	475	875

KM# 166 1/2 THALER (1 Gulden - 36 Schillings)
Silver **Obv:** Pointed hat on round arms of Zurich within sprig, supported by rampant lion at right **Obv. Legend:** MONETA REIPUBLICÆ TURICENSIS **Rev:** IUSTITIA/ET/CONCORDIA, date within wheat wreath

Date	Mintage	VG	F	VF	XF	Unc
1779	—	60.00	120	325	600	1,050

KM# 169 1/2 THALER (1 Gulden - 36 Schillings)
Silver **Obv:** Oval arms of Zurich supported by rampant lions, hat with feather above **Obv. Legend:** MONETA REIPUBLICÆ TURICENSIS • **Rev:** IUSTITIA/ET/CONCORDIA, date within rope wreath **Note:** Varieties exist.

Date	Mintage	VG	F	VF	XF	Unc
1780	—	30.00	60.00	165	325	600

KM# 171 1/2 THALER (1 Gulden - 36 Schillings)
Silver **Obv:** Palm and laurel sprig above oval arms of Zurich with garland, flanked by lion heads on thick mantle **Obv. Legend:** MONETA REIPUBLICÆ TURICENSIS **Rev:** XXII/AVFIFEINE/(last N is backwards)MARK, date within rope wreath

Date	Mintage	VG	F	VF	XF	Unc
1783 B	—	30.00	60.00	165	325	600
1786 B	—	30.00	60.00	165	325	600
Note: Varieties exist						
1788 B	—	30.00	60.00	165	325	600
Note: Varieties exist						
1794 B	—	30.00	60.00	165	325	600
Note: Varieties exist						
1798 B	—	50.00	100	250	475	875

KM# 124 THALER
Silver **Obv:** Oval arms of Zurich supported by rampant lion at right, within beaded circle **Obv. Legend:** MONETA NOVA REIPUBLICÆ TIGURINAE **Rev:** DOMINE/CONSERVA/NOS IN/PACE, date within palm and laurel branch **Note:** Cross-reference number Dav. #1781.

Date	Mintage	VG	F	VF	XF	Unc
1707	—	250	475	1,000	2,000	3,600

KM# 131 THALER
Silver **Obv. Legend:** MONETA REIPVBLICAE TIGVRINAE **Note:** Cross-reference number Dav. #1782.

Date	Mintage	VG	F	VF	XF	Unc
1709	—	2,400	5,000	12,000	3,000	—

KM# 135 THALER
Silver **Obv:** Oval arms of Zurich supported by rampant lion at right **Obv. Legend:** MONETA REIPUBLICÆ TIGURINÆ **Rev:** IUSTITIA/ET/CONCORDIA, date within palm and laurel branch **Note:** Cross-reference number Dav. #1783.

Date	Mintage	VG	F	VF	XF	Unc
1713	—	100	200	600	1,200	2,000
1714	—	75.00	140	350	700	1,400
1715	—	75.00	140	350	700	1,400
1716	—	75.00	140	350	700	1,400
1717	—	75.00	140	350	700	1,400

KM# 144 THALER
Silver **Obv:** Oval arms of Zurich supported by rampant lions **Obv. Legend:** MONETA REIPUBLICÆ TIGURINÆ **Rev:** City view, date in cartouche below **Rev. Legend:** DOMINE CONSERVA NOS IN PACE **Note:** Dav. #1784.

Date	Mintage	VG	F	VF	XF	Unc
1722	—	125	250	550	1,150	2,000
1723	—	80.00	160	400	800	1,500
1724	—	100	200	475	725	1,400
1726	—	75.00	145	365	725	1,400
1727	—	75.00	145	365	725	1,400
1728	—	75.00	145	365	725	1,400

KM# 143.1 THALER
Silver **Obv:** Oval arms of Zurich supported by rampant lion at right **Obv. Legend:** MONETA REIPUBLICÆ TIGURINAE **Rev:** City view, date in cartouche below **Rev. Legend:** DOMINE CONSERVA NOS IN PACE **Note:** Dav. #1785.

Date	Mintage	VG	F	VF	XF	Unc
1722	—	100	200	475	950	1,750
1725	—	100	200	475	950	1,750

KM# 147 THALER
Silver **Obv:** Oval arms of Zurich supported by rampant lion at right **Rev:** IUSTITIA/ET/CONCORDIA, date in baroque frame, laurel and palm branches below **Note:** Dav. #1786.

Date	Mintage	VG	F	VF	XF	Unc
1724	—	75.00	140	350	725	1,400
1725	—	80.00	160	400	800	1,500
1726	—	65.00	125	325	650	1,200
1727	—	65.00	125	325	650	1,200
1730	—	65.00	125	325	650	1,200
1732	—	65.00	125	325	650	1,200
1734	—	65.00	125	325	650	1,200

KM# 143.2 THALER
Silver **Obv:** Oval arms of Zurich supported by rampant lion at right **Obv. Legend:** MONETA REIPUBLICÆ TIGURINAE **Rev:** City view, date in cartouche below **Rev. Legend:** DOMINE CONSERVA NOS IN PACE **Note:** Dav. #1787.

Date	Mintage	VG	F	VF	XF	Unc
1729	—	75.00	150	365	725	1,400
1730	—	75.00	150	365	725	1,400
1732	—	75.00	150	365	725	1,400

KM# 143.3 THALER
Silver **Obv:** Oval arms of Urich supported by rampant lion at right **Obv. Legend:** MONETA REIPUBLICÆ TIGURINÆ • **Rev:** City view, date below **Rev. Legend:** DOMINE CONSERVA NOS IN PACE **Note:** Cross-reference number Dav. #1788.

Date	Mintage	VG	F	VF	XF	Unc
1734	—	75.00	150	365	725	1,400
1736	—	75.00	150	365	725	1,400
1739	—	75.00	150	365	725	1,400

KM# 150 THALER

Silver **Obv:** Oval arms of Urich in baroque frame, supported by rampant lion at right **Obv. Legend:** MONETA REIPUBLICÆ TIGURINÆ • **Rev:** DOMINE/CONSERVA/NOS IN/PACE, date within cartouche, angel head above **Note:** Dav. #1789.

Date	Mintage	VG	F	VF	XF	Unc
1736	—	65.00	120	300	600	1,200
1739	—	55.00	100	275	550	1,200
1741	—	55.00	100	275	550	1,200
1743	—	55.00	100	275	550	1,200
1745	—	55.00	100	275	550	1,200
1748	—	55.00	100	275	550	1,200
1751	—	50.00	100	240	475	1,000
1753	—	50.00	80.00	240	475	1,000
1756	—	50.00	80.00	240	475	1,000
1758	—	50.00	80.00	240	475	1,000
1761	—	50.00	80.00	240	475	1,000
1767	—	50.00	80.00	240	475	1,000
1768	—	50.00	80.00	240	475	1,000

KM# 152 THALER

Silver **Obv:** Oval arms of Urich in boroque frame, suported by rampant lions **Obv. Legend:** MONETA REIPUBLICAE TIGURI **Rev:** City view, date below **Rev. Legend:** DOMINE CONSERVA NOS IN PACE **Note:** Dav. #1790.

Date	Mintage	VG	F	VF	XF	Unc
1741	—	75.00	150	350	725	1,400
1743	—	75.00	150	350	725	1,400

KM# 143.4 THALER

Silver **Obv:** Oval arms of Zurich in baroque frame, supported by rampant lion at right **Obv. Legend:** MONETA REIPUBLICÆ TIGURINÆ **Rev:** City view, date below **Rev. Legend:** DOMINE CONSERVA NOS IN PACE **Note:** Dav. #1791.

Date	Mintage	VG	F	VF	XF	Unc
1745	—	75.00	150	350	700	1,400
1748	—	75.00	150	350	700	1,400
1751	—	65.00	125	325	650	1,200
1753	—	65.00	125	325	650	1,200
1756	—	65.00	125	325	650	1,200
1758	—	65.00	125	325	650	1,200
1761	—	65.00	125	325	600	1,200

KM# 159 THALER

Silver **Obv:** Oval arms of Zurich on mantle, supported by rampant lion at right **Rev:** IUSTITIA/ET/CONCORDIA, date within cartouche **Note:** Dav. #1793.

Date	Mintage	VG	F	VF	XF	Unc
1773	—	65.00	125	325	650	1,200

KM# 158 THALER

Silver **Obv:** Oval arms of Zurich on mantle, supported by rampant lion at right **Obv. Legend:** MONETA REIPUBLICÆ TURICENSIS • **Rev:** Laurel and palm branch with sword on mantle within circle, date below **Rev. Legend:** IUSTITIA ET CONCORDIA **Note:** Gessener Taler. Dav. #1792.

Date	Mintage	VG	F	VF	XF	Unc
1773	36	1,200	2,500	6,000	12,000	17,500

KM# 163 THALER

Silver **Obv:** Oval arms of Zurich with palm branch at left, supported by rampant lion at right **Obv. Legend:** MONETA REIPUBLICÆ TURICENSIS • **Rev:** IUSTITIA/ET/CONCORDIA, date above crossed cornucopias within ornate cartouche **Note:** Varieties exist. Cross-reference number Dav. #1794.

Date	Mintage	VG	F	VF	XF	Unc
1776	—	75.00	150	350	725	1,400
1777	—	75.00	150	350	725	1,400

KM# 167 THALER

Silver **Obv:** Oval arms of Zurich with palm branch at left, hat above, supported by rampant lion at right **Obv. Legend:** MONETA REIPUBLICÆ TURICENSIS **Rev:** IUSTITIA/ET/CONCORDIA, date within wheat wreath **Note:** Varieties exist. Dav. #1795.

Date	Mintage	VG	F	VF	XF	Unc
1779	—	85.00	165	400	800	1,500

KM# A170 THALER

Silver **Obv:** Lion with sword and shield **Rev:** IUSTITIA/ET/CONCORDIA, date within rope wreath **Note:** Cross-reference number Dav. #1796.

Date	Mintage	VG	F	VF	XF	Unc
1780	—	65.00	125	275	550	1,200

KM# 170 THALER

Silver **Obv:** Oval arms of Zurich, hat with feather above, supported by rampant lions **Obv. Legend:** MONETA REIPUBLICAE TURICENSIS • **Rev:** IUSTITIA/ET/CONCORDIA, date within rope wreath **Note:** Dav. #1797.

Date	Mintage	VG	F	VF	XF	Unc
1780	—	65.00	125	275	550	1,200

KM# 175 THALER

Silver **Obv:** Laurel, palm sprigs, hat and garland above oval arms of Zurich, flanked by lion heads on thick mantle **Obv. Legend:** MONETA REIPUBLICÆ TURICENSIS **Rev:** XXII/ AVFIFEINE/ MARK, date within rope wreath **Note:** Dav. #1798.

Date	Mintage	VG	F	VF	XF	Unc
1783	—	65.00	125	275	550	1,200
1794	—	65.00	125	275	550	1,200
1796	—	65.00	125	275	550	1,200

Note: Varieties exist

KM# 176 THALER

Silver **Obv:** Laurel, palm sprigs and garland above oval arms of Zurich, flanked by lion heads on thick mantle **Obv. Legend:** MONETA REIPUBLICÆ TURICENSIS • **Rev:** City view, date in designed rectangle below **Rev. Legend:** DOMINE CONSERVA NOS IN PACE **Note:** Dav. #1799.

Date	Mintage	VG	F	VF	XF	Unc
1790	—	65.00	125	325	650	1,200

TRADE COINAGE

KM# 117 1/4 DUCAT

0.8750 g., 0.9860 Gold 0.0277 oz. AGW **Obv:** Arms of Zurich supported by rampant lion at right **Rev:** Date above sprigs with ornamental border

Date	Mintage	F	VF	XF	Unc	BU
1702	—	850	1,650	2,500	4,000	—

KM# 118 1/4 DUCAT

0.8750 g., 0.9860 Gold 0.0277 oz. AGW **Obv:** Oval arms of Zurich supported by rampant lion at right

Date	Mintage	F	VF	XF	Unc	BU
1702	—	600	1,200	2,000	3,200	—

KM# 125 1/4 DUCAT

0.8750 g., 0.9860 Gold 0.0277 oz. AGW **Obv:** Oval arms of Zurich supported by rampant lion at right **Rev:** Inscription: DOMINE/CONSERVA/NOS IN/PACE/1707 in branches

Date	Mintage	F	VF	XF	Unc	BU
1707	—	600	1,200	2,000	3,200	—

KM# 129 1/4 DUCAT

0.8750 g., 0.9860 Gold 0.0277 oz. AGW

Date	Mintage	F	VF	XF	Unc	BU
1708	—	200	350	550	875	—
1709	—	200	350	550	875	—
1712	—	200	350	550	875	—
1714	—	200	350	550	875	—
1716	—	200	350	550	875	—

KM# 138 1/4 DUCAT

0.8750 g., 0.9860 Gold 0.0277 oz. AGW **Obv:** Oval arms of Zurich supported by rampant lion at right **Obv. Legend:** RESPUBLICÆ TICURINAE • **Rev:** ANNO/DOMINE, date within cartouche

Date	Mintage	F	VF	XF	Unc	BU
1718	—	160	325	475	725	—
1719	—	160	325	475	725	—
1720	—	160	325	475	725	—
1721	—	160	325	475	725	—
1722	—	160	325	475	725	—
1723	—	250	550	900	1,600	—
1725	—	160	325	475	725	—
1726	—	160	325	475	725	—
1727	—	160	325	475	725	—
1729	—	160	325	475	725	—
1730	—	160	325	475	725	—
1732	—	160	325	475	725	—
1734	—	160	325	475	725	—
1736	—	160	325	475	725	—
1739	—	160	325	475	725	—
1741	—	250	550	900	1,600	—
1743	—	160	325	475	725	—
1745	—	160	325	475	725	—
1748	—	160	325	475	725	—
1751/48	—	160	325	475	725	—
1751	—	160	325	475	725	—
1753	—	160	325	475	725	—
1756	—	160	325	475	725	—
1758	—	160	325	475	725	—
1761/58	—	160	325	475	725	—
1761	—	160	325	475	725	—
1767	—	160	325	475	725	—

KM# 119 1/2 DUCAT

1.7500 g., 0.9860 Gold 0.0555 oz. AGW **Obv:** Oval arms of Zurich supported by rampant lion at right **Rev:** Inscription: ANNO/DOMINI/1702 in upper ornate border above branches **Note:** Varieties exist.

Date	Mintage	F	VF	XF	Unc	BU
1702	—	500	950	1,600	2,400	—

KM# 126 1/2 DUCAT

1.7500 g., 0.9860 Gold 0.0555 oz. AGW **Obv:** Oval arms of Zurich supported by rampant lion at right **Obv. Legend:** MONETA REIP • TIGURINAE • **Rev:** Inscription: DOMINE/CONSERVA/ NOS IN/PACE **Note:** Varieties exist.

Date	Mintage	F	VF	XF	Unc	BU
1707	—	400	800	1,350	2,100	—
1709	—	225	450	725	1,200	—

KM# 133 1/2 DUCAT

1.7500 g., 0.9860 Gold 0.0555 oz. AGW **Obv:** Oval arms of Zurich supported by rampant lion at right **Rev:** DOMINE/CONSERVA/NOS IN/PACE•, date within palm and laurel branches **Note:** Similar to KM#139 but reverse inscription in branches.

Date	Mintage	F	VF	XF	Unc	BU
1712	—	250	450	725	1,250	—
1714	—	250	450	725	1,250	—
1716	—	200	400	650	1,125	—

KM# 139 1/2 DUCAT

1.7500 g., 0.9860 Gold 0.0555 oz. AGW **Obv:** Oval arms of Zurich supported by rampant lion at right **Obv. Legend:** RESPUBLICÆ TICURINÆ • **Rev:** DOMINE/CONSERVA/NOS IN/PACE•, date within ornamented cartouche

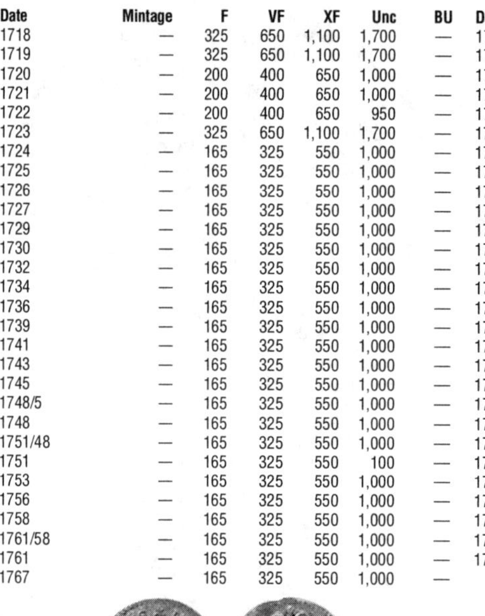

Date	Mintage	F	VF	XF	Unc	BU
1718	—	325	650	1,100	1,700	—
1719	—	325	650	1,100	1,700	—
1720	—	200	400	650	1,000	—
1721	—	200	400	650	1,000	—
1722	—	200	400	650	950	—
1723	—	325	650	1,100	1,700	—
1724	—	165	325	550	1,000	—
1725	—	165	325	550	1,000	—
1726	—	165	325	550	1,000	—
1727	—	165	325	550	1,000	—
1729	—	165	325	550	1,000	—
1730	—	165	325	550	1,000	—
1732	—	165	325	550	1,000	—
1734	—	165	325	550	1,000	—
1736	—	165	325	550	1,000	—
1739	—	165	325	550	1,000	—
1741	—	165	325	550	1,000	—
1743	—	165	325	550	1,000	—
1745	—	165	325	550	1,000	—
1748/5	—	165	325	550	1,000	—
1748	—	165	325	550	1,000	—
1751/48	—	165	325	550	1,000	—
1751	—	165	325	550	100	—
1753	—	165	325	550	1,000	—
1756	—	165	325	550	1,000	—
1758	—	165	325	550	1,000	—
1761/58	—	165	325	550	1,000	—
1761	—	165	325	550	1,000	—
1767	—	165	325	550	1,000	—

KM# 164 1/2 DUCAT

1.7500 g., 0.9860 Gold 0.0555 oz. AGW **Obv:** Oval arms of Zurich with palm branch at left, supported by rampant lion at right, within circle **Obv. Legend:** MONETA REIPUB TURICENSIS **Rev:** IUSTITIA/ET/CONCORDIA, date within cartouche

Date	Mintage	F	VF	XF	Unc	BU
1776	—	140	275	475	725	—

KM# 120 DUCAT

3.5000 g., 0.9860 Gold 0.1109 oz. AGW **Obv:** Oval arms of Zurich supported by rampant lion at right **Obv. Legend:** DOMINE CONSERVA NOS IN PACE **Rev:** Inscription: DUCATUS/ NOVOS/ REIPUBLICAE/TIGURINAE/1702 in upper ornate border above branches

Date	Mintage	F	VF	XF	Unc	BU
1702	—	4,000	9,000	16,000	7,500	—

KM# 127 DUCAT

3.5000 g., 0.9860 Gold 0.1109 oz. AGW **Obv:** Oval arms of Zurich supported by rampant lion at right **Obv. Legend:** DUCATUS NOVUS REIPUBLICÆ TIGURINÆ **Rev:** Inscription, date within laurel and palm wreath **Rev. Inscription:** DOMINE / CONSERVA / NOS IN / PACE

Date	Mintage	F	VF	XF	Unc	BU
1707	—	725	1,450	2,400	3,600	—
1709	—	600	1,200	2,000	3,000	—
1712	—	2,250	4,500	8,000	2,500	—
1714	—	600	1,200	2,000	3,000	—
1715	—	600	1,200	2,000	3,000	—
1716	—	600	1,200	2,000	3,000	—
1717	—	600	1,200	2,000	3,000	—

KM# 140 DUCAT

3.5000 g., 0.9860 Gold 0.1109 oz. AGW **Obv:** Oval arms of Zurich supported by rampant lion at right **Obv. Legend:** REIPUBLICÆ TIGURINAE • DUCATUS **Rev:** DOMINE/ CONSERVA/NOS IN/PACE, date within ornamented wreath

Date	Mintage	F	VF	XF	Unc	BU
1718	—	600	1,200	2,000	3,000	—
1719	—	600	1,200	2,000	3,000	—
1720	—	600	1,200	2,000	3,000	—
1721	—	450	800	1,400	2,250	—
1722	—	450	800	1,400	2,250	—
1723	—	475	950	1,600	2,400	—
1724	—	400	600	1,275	2,000	—
1725	—	400	600	1,275	2,000	—
1726	—	400	600	1,275	2,000	—
1727	—	400	600	1,275	2,000	—
1729	—	400	600	1,275	2,000	—
1730	—	400	600	1,275	2,000	—
1732	—	400	600	1,275	2,000	—
1734	—	400	600	1,275	2,000	—
1736	—	400	600	1,275	2,000	—
1739	—	400	600	1,275	2,000	—
1741	—	400	600	1,275	2,000	—
1743/41	—	400	600	1,275	2,000	—
1743	—	400	600	1,275	2,000	—
1745	—	400	600	1,275	2,000	—
1748/45	—	400	600	1,275	2,000	—
1748	—	475	950	1,600	2,400	—
1751	—	1,200	2,400	4,000	6,000	—
1753	—	475	950	1,600	2,400	—
1756	—	475	950	1,600	2,400	—
1758	—	475	950	1,600	2,400	—
1761	—	475	950	1,600	2,400	—
1767	—	475	950	1,600	2,400	—

KM# 161 DUCAT

3.5000 g., 0.9860 Gold 0.1109 oz. AGW **Obv:** Oval arms of Zurich with palm branch at left, supported by rampant lion at right, within circle **Obv. Legend:** REIPUBLICÆ TURIVENSIS * DUCATUS **Rev:** IUSTITIA/ET/CONCORDIA, date within cartouche

Date	Mintage	F	VF	XF	Unc	BU
1775	—	275	550	950	1,450	—

KM# 128 2 DUCAT

7.0000 g., 0.9860 Gold 0.2219 oz. AGW **Obv:** Oval arms of Zurich in baroque frame, supported by rampant lions **Obv. Legend:** MONETA REIPUBLICÆ TIGURINÆ **Rev:** DOMINE/ CONSERVA/NOS IN/PACE, date within laurel and palm wreath

Date	Mintage	F	VF	XF	Unc	BU
1707	—	4,000	8,000	1,450	10,000	—
1708	—	1,125	2,200	3,600	5,500	—
1712	—	1,125	2,200	3,600	5,500	—
1714	—	1,200	2,400	4,000	6,000	—
1715	—	2,750	5,500	9,500	14,500	—
1716	—	875	1,750	3,000	4,500	—

KM# 141 2 DUCAT

7.0000 g., 0.9860 Gold 0.2219 oz. AGW **Obv:** Oval arms of Zurich in baroque frame, supported by rampant lions **Obv. Legend:** MONETA REIPUBLICÆ TIGURINÆ **Rev:** DOMINE/ CONSERVA/NOS IN/PACE date within ornamented wreath

Date	Mintage	F	VF	XF	Unc	BU
1718	—	700	1,400	2,600	3,600	—
1719	—	2,400	4,750	8,000	12,000	—
1720	—	2,400	4,750	8,000	12,000	—
1721	—	700	1,400	2,600	3,600	—
1722	—	1,200	2,400	4,000	6,000	—
1723	—	700	1,400	2,600	3,600	—
1725	—	1,100	2,200	3,600	5,500	—
1726	—	1,100	2,200	3,600	5,500	—
1727	—	1,100	2,200	3,600	5,500	—
1729	—	800	1,800	2,800	4,000	—
1730	—	800	1,800	2,800	4,000	—
1732	—	800	1,800	2,800	4,000	—
1734/30	—	800	1,800	2,800	4,000	—
1734	—	800	1,800	2,800	4,000	—
1736	—	1,200	2,400	4,000	6,000	—

Date	Mintage	F	VF	XF	Unc	BU
1739	—	2,000	4,000	7,250	10,000	—
1741	—	800	1,800	2,800	4,000	—
1743/41	—	800	1,800	2,800	4,000	—
1743	—	800	1,800	2,800	4,000	—
1745	—	800	1,800	2,800	4,000	—
1748	—	800	1,800	2,800	4,000	—
1751	—	800	1,800	2,800	4,000	—
1753	—	800	1,800	2,800	4,000	—
1756	—	800	1,800	2,800	4,000	—
1758	—	800	1,800	2,800	4,000	—
1761	—	800	1,800	2,800	4,000	—
1767/61	—	800	1,800	2,800	4,000	—
1767	—	800	1,800	2,800	4,000	—

KM# 165 2 DUCAT
7.0000 g., 0.9860 Gold 0.2219 oz. AGW **Obv:** Oval arms of Zurich supported by rampant lions **Obv. Legend:** MONETA REIPUBLICÆ TURICENSIS **Rev:** IUSTITIA/ET/CONCORDIA, date above crossed cornucopias within ornamental spigs

Date	Mintage	F	VF	XF	Unc	BU
1776	—	600	1,250	2,000	2,800	4,000

PATTERNS

Including off metal strikes

KM#	Date	Mintage	Identification	Mkt Val
Pn4	1723	—	Ducat. Silver. KM#140.	150
Pn5	1724	—	Ducat. Silver. KM#140.	150

KM#	Date	Mintage	Identification	Mkt Val
Pn6	1725	—	Schilling. Billon.	130
Pn7	1725	—	Schilling. Billon. Eagle.	165

The Swiss Confederation, located in central Europe north of Italy and south of Germany, has an area of 15,941 sq. mi. (41,290 sq. km.) and a population of *6.6 million. Capital: Bern. The economy centers about a well developed manufacturing industry. Machinery, chemicals, watches and clocks, and textiles are exported.

Switzerland, the habitat of lake dwellers in prehistoric times, was peopled by the Celtic Helvetians when Julius Caesar made it a part of the Roman Empire in 58 B.C. After the decline of Rome, Switzerland was invaded by Teutonic tribes, who established small temporal holdings which in the Middle Ages, became a federation of fiefs of the Holy Roman Empire. As a nation, Switzerland originated in 1291 when the districts of Nidwalden, Schwyz and Uri united to defeat Austria and attain independence as the Swiss Confederation. After acquiring new cantons in the 14th century, Switzerland was made independent from the Holy Roman Empire by the 1648 Treaty of Westphalia. The revolutionary armies of Napoleonic France occupied Switzerland and set up the Helvetian Republic, 1798-1803. After the fall of Napoleon, the Congress of Vienna, 1815, recognized the independence of Switzerland and guaranteed its neutrality. The Swiss Constitutions of 1848 and 1874 established a union modeled upon that of the United States.

MONETARY SYSTEM
10 Rappen = 1 Batzen
10 Batzen = 1 Franc
16 Franken = 1 Duplone

HELVETIAN REPUBLIC

DECIMAL COINAGE

KM# A11 RAPPEN
Billon **Obv:** Fasces within sprigs **Obv. Legend:** HELVET: REPUBL: **Rev:** Value, date within wreath

Date	Mintage	F	VF	XF	Unc	BU
1800	—	8.00	16.00	40.00	80.00	120

KM# A5 1/2 BATZEN
Billon **Obv:** HELVET/REPUBL: within wreath **Rev:** Value, date within circle and wreath

Date	Mintage	F	VF	XF	Unc	BU
1799	—	50.00	200	475	950	1,450

KM# A6 1/2 BATZEN
Billon **Obv:** HELVET•/REPUBL• within sprigs, numeral 5 below **Rev:** Value, date within designed wreath

Date	Mintage	F	VF	XF	Unc	BU
1799	—	16.00	48.00	120	240	360
1800	—	8.00	40.00	100	200	325

KM# A7 BATZEN
Billon **Obv:** HELVET/REPUBL within wreath **Rev:** Value, date within circle and wreath

Date	Mintage	F	VF	XF	Unc	BU
1799	—	16.00	65.00	160	325	475

KM# A8 BATZEN
Billon **Obv:** Legend, numeral 10 within wreath **Obv. Legend:** HELVET: REPUBL: **Rev:** Value, date within circle and designed wreath

Date	Mintage	F	VF	XF	Unc	BU
1799B	—	25.00	95.00	240	475	725
1799S	—	25.00	95.00	240	475	725
1799	—	16.00	65.00	160	325	475
1800	—	32.00	120	275	550	800
1800B	—	16.00	65.00	160	325	475

KM# A9 5 BATZEN
Silver **Obv:** Standing knight holding flag within circle, date below **Obv. Legend:** HELVETISCHE REPUBLIK **Rev:** Value within wreath, B below

Date	Mintage	F	VF	XF	Unc	BU
1799B	—	40.00	100	200	360	600
1799S	—	80.00	200	400	725	1,200
1800B	—	40.00	100	160	325	550

KM# A1 10 BATZEN
Silver **Obv:** Standing knight holding flag within circle, date below **Obv. Legend:** HELVETISCHE REPUBLIK **Rev:** Value within wreath, B below

Date	Mintage	F	VF	XF	Unc	BU
1798B	—	200	475	1,000	1,750	2,800
1799B	—	80.00	200	400	725	1,200
1799S	—	120	325	600	1,050	1,750

KM# A2 20 BATZEN
Silver **Obv:** Standing Swiss holding flag, date below **Obv. Legend:** HELVET : REPUBL **Rev:** Value within wreath, S below

Date	Mintage	F	VF	XF	Unc	BU
1798S	—	125	250	450	800	—
1799S Rare	—	—	—	—	—	—

KM# A3 20 BATZEN
Silver **Obv:** Standing Swiss holding flag **Rev:** Value within wreath

Date	Mintage	F	VF	XF	Unc	BU
1798S	—	125	250	400	800	1,400

KM# A4.1 40 BATZEN
Silver **Obv:** Standing Swiss holding flag, date below **Obv. Legend:** HELVET : REPUBL : **Rev:** Value within wreath **Note:** Dav. #1771.

Date	Mintage	F	VF	XF	Unc	BU
1798BA	—	300	500	750	1,750	3,000

KM# A4.2 40 BATZEN
Silver **Obv:** Standing Swiss holding flag, date below **Obv. Legend:** HELVET : REPUBL : **Rev:** Value within wreath, S below **Note:** Dav. #1771.

Date	Mintage	F	VF	XF	Unc	BU
1798S	—	200	400	725	1,250	2,000

KM# A10 4 FRANKEN
Silver **Obv:** Standing knight holding flag within circle, date below **Obv. Legend:** HELVETISCHE REPUBLIK **Rev:** Value within wreath, B below **Note:** Dav. #1772.

Date	Mintage	F	VF	XF	Unc	BU
1799B	—	325	800	1,600	2,800	4,750

KM# A12 16 FRANKEN
7.6400 g., 0.9000 Gold 0.2211 oz. AGW **Obv:** Standing Swiss holding flag, facing, B below **Obv. Legend:** HELVETISCHE REPUBLIK **Rev:** Value, date within wreath

Date	Mintage	F	VF	XF	Unc	BU
1800B	—	500	1,000	1,200	3,000	5,000

KM# A13 32 FRANKEN
15.2800 g., 0.9000 Gold 0.4421 oz. AGW **Obv:** Standing Swiss holding flag, facing, B below **Obv. Legend:** HELVETISCHE REPUBLIK **Rev:** Value, date within wreath

Date	Mintage	F	VF	XF	Unc	BU
1800B	—	1,200	2,500	4,000	6,000	8,000

PATTERNS

Including off metal strikes

KM#	Date	Mintage	Identification	Mkt Val

KM#	Date	Mintage	Identification	Mkt Val
PnA1	ND	—	Kreuzer. Billon.	4,500

KM#	Date	Mintage	Identification	Mkt Val
PnA2	1798	32	20 Batzen. Silver.	4,000

KM#	Date	Mintage	Identification	Mkt Val
PnA3	1799	—	Rappen. Billon.	1,800

KM#	Date	Mintage	Identification	Mkt Val
PnA4	1799B	—	4 Franken. Silver. Dav. #1773.	6,000

KM#	Date	Mintage	Identification	Mkt Val
PnA5	1800	—	Rappen. Billon.	1,000

SYRIA

The Syrian Arab Republic, located in the Near East at the eastern end of the Mediterranean Sea, has an area of 71,498 sq. mi. (185,180 sq. km.) and a population of *12million. Capital: Greater Damascus. Agriculture and animal breeding are the chief industries. Cotton, crude oil and livestock are exported.

Ancient Syria, a land bridge connecting Europe, Africa and Asia, has spent much of its history in thrall to the conqueror's whim. Its subjection by Egypt about 1500 B.C. was followed by successive conquests by the Hebrews, Phoenicians, Babylonians, Assyrians, Persians, Macedonians, Romans, Byzantines and finally, in 636 A.D., by the Moslems. The Arabs made Damascus, one of the oldest continuously inhabited cities of the world, the trade center and capital of an empire stretching from India to Spain. In 1516, following the total destruction of Damascus by the Mongols of Tamerlane, Syria fell to the Ottoman Turks and remained a part of Turkey until the end of World War I. The League of Nations gave France a mandate to the Levant states of Syria and Lebanon in 1920. In 1930, following a series of uprisings, France recognized Syria as an independent republic, but still subject to the mandate. Lebanon became fully independent on Nov. 22, 1943, and Syria on Jan. 1,1944.

TITLES

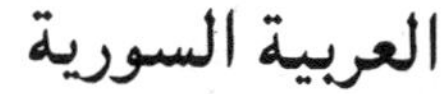

Al-Jumhuriya(t) al-Suriya(t)

RULER

Ottoman, until 1918

MINT NAME

Damascus (Dimask)

Haleb (Aleppo)

MONETARY SYSTEM

100 Piastres (Qirsh) = 1 Pound (Lira)

OTTOMAN EMPIRE

HAMMERED COINAGE

KM# 65 5 PARA
Copper **Ruler:** Mustafa III AH1171-1187 / 1757-1773AD **Obv:** Toughra, star at right **Rev:** Inscription, date and star

Date	Mintage	Good	VG	F	VF	XF
AH1171	—	40.00	60.00	100	175	—

THAILAND

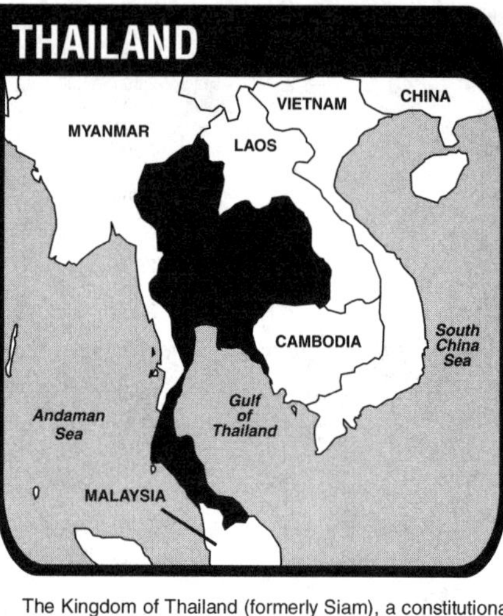

The Kingdom of Thailand (formerly Siam), a constitutional monarchy located in the center of mainland southeast Asia between Burma and Laos, has an area of 198,457mi. (514,000 sq. km.) and a population of *55.5 million. Capital: Bangkok. The economy is based on agriculture and mining. Rubber, rice, teakwood, tin and tungsten are exported.

The history of The Kingdom of Siam, the only country in south and southeast Asia that was never colonized by an European power, dates from the 6th century A.D. when Thai people started to migrate into the area a process that accelerated with the Mongol invasion of China in the 13th century. After 400 years of sporadic warfare with the neighboring Burmese, King Taskin won the last battle in 1767. He founded a new capital, Dhonburi, on the west bank of the Chao Praya River. King Rama I moved the capital to Bangkok in 1782,thus initiating the so-called Bangkok Period of Siamese coinage characterized by Pot Duang money (bullet coins) stamped with regal symbols.

RULERS

King Taksin, 1767-1782
Rama I (Phra Buddha Yodfa Chulalok), 1782-1809

MONETARY SYSTEM

Old currency system

2 Solos = 1 Att
2 Att = 1 Sio (Pai)
2 Sio = 1 Sik
2 Sik = 1 Fuang
2 Fuang = 1 Salung (not Sal'ung)
4 Salung = 1 Baht
4 Baht = 1 Tamlung
20 Tamlung = 1 Chang

UNITS OF OLD THAI CURRENCY

Chang -	ชั่ง	Sik -	ซีก
Tamlung -	ตำลึง	Sio (Pai) -	เสี้ยว
Baht -	บาท	Att -	อัฐ
Salung -	สลึง	Solos -	โสฬส
Fuang -	เฟื้อง		

DATE CONVERSION TABLES

B.E. date - 543 = A.D. date
Ex: 2516 - 543 = 1973

R.S. date + 1781 = A.D. date
Ex: 127 + 1781 = 1908

C.S. date + 638 = A.D. date
Ex 1238 + 638 = 1876

Primary denominations used were 1 Baht, 1/4 and 1/8 Baht up to the reign of Rama IV. Other denominations are much scarcer.

BULLET COINAGE

Gold and silver "bullet" coins have been a medium of exchange since medieval times. Interesting enough is the fact that a 1 Baht bullet made of gold will weigh the same as a 1 Baht bullet in silver. The reason for this is that Baht originally was a weight not a denomination. It was a coinage weight only until the time of Rama VII, (1925-1935) and now it is a weight and also a denomination (as far as standard weight coins are concerned). Usually 1 gold Baht was equal to 16 silver Baht on an exchange basis.

Bullet Weights

Grams

Baht = 15.40 1/2 Baht = 7.70
1/4 Baht = 3.85 1/8 Baht = 1.92
1/16 Baht = 0.96 1/32 Baht = 0.48
1/64 Baht = 0.24

Chopmarks exist on bullet coins as they do on many other coins that have traveled on their way through the Orient. One must be careful not to mistake a money changers chopmark for the regular dynastic marks on the bullet. Some chopmarks are rather simple in design while others appear to be rather elaborate.

Dynastic Marks

Chakra

The Chakra, symbol of the God Vishnu, is the mark of the Bangkok Dynasty. It varies slightly in design between issues, being very ornate on ceremonial issues.

RAMA I

1782-1809

Tri

Unalom

The trident, the symbol of the Hindu God, Siva, used as the first mark of Rama I. The unalom is an ornamented conch shell, used as the second mark of Rama I.

Market valuations are primarily based on the quality and condition of the countermarks found on bullet coinage.

KINGDOM OF SIAM
until 1939

BULLET COINAGE

Silver Pot Duang

C# 1 PAI (1/32 Baht)

Silver **Ruler:** Rama I **Note:** Observed weight range 0.44-0.56 gram.

Date	Mintage	VG	F	VF	XF	Unc
ND Tri Rare	—	100	200	300	500	—

C# 8 PAI (1/32 Baht)

Silver **Ruler:** Rama I **Note:** Observed weight range 0.44-0.56 gram.

Date	Mintage	VG	F	VF	XF	Unc
ND Unalom Rare	—	50.00	70.00	80.00	250	—

C# 2 SONG PAI (1/16 Baht)

Silver **Ruler:** Rama I **Note:** Observed weight range 0.80-1.06 grams.

Date	Mintage	VG	F	VF	XF	Unc
ND Tri	—	100	200	300	500	—

C# 9 SONG PAI (1/16 Baht)

Silver **Ruler:** Rama I **Note:** Observed weight range 0.80-1.06 grams.

Date	Mintage	VG	F	VF	XF	Unc
ND Unalom	—	30.00	50.00	70.00	150	—

C# 3 FUANG (1/8 Baht)

Silver **Ruler:** Rama I **Note:** Observed weight range 1.60-2.01 grams.

Date	Mintage	VG	F	VF	XF	Unc
ND Tri	—	100	200	300	—	—

C# 10 FUANG (1/8 Baht)

Silver **Ruler:** Rama I **Note:** Observed weight range 1.60-2.01 grams.

Date	Mintage	VG	F	VF	XF	Unc
ND Unalom	—	20.00	40.00	60.00	—	—

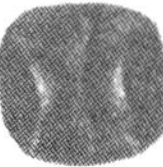

C# 4 SALU'NG (1/4 Baht)

Silver **Ruler:** Rama I **Note:** Observed weight range 3.60-4.00 grams.

Date	Mintage	VG	F	VF	XF	Unc
ND Tri Rare	—	100	150	300	600	—

C# 11 SALU'NG (1/4 Baht)

Silver **Ruler:** Rama I **Note:** Observed weight range 3.60-4.00 grams.

Date	Mintage	VG	F	VF	XF	Unc
ND Unalom	—	15.00	25.00	50.00	100	—

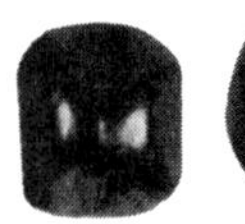

C# 5 2 SALU'NG (1/2 Baht)

Silver **Ruler:** Rama I **Note:** Observed weight range 7.40-7.70 grams.

Date	Mintage	VG	F	VF	XF	Unc
ND Tri	—	50.00	100	300	600	—

C# 12 2 SALU'NG (1/2 Baht)

Silver **Ruler:** Rama I **Note:** Observed weight range 7.40-7.70 grams.

Date	Mintage	VG	F	VF	XF	Unc
ND Unalom	—	50.00	100	150	350	—

C# A1 BAHT

Silver **Ruler:** Rama I **Note:** Observed weight range 14.86-15.43 grams.

Date	Mintage	VG	F	VF	XF	Unc
ND Tri	—	15.00	20.00	30.00	60.00	75.00

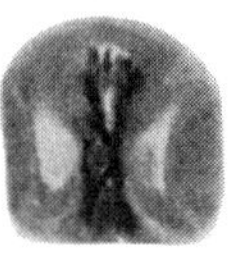

C# 13 BAHT

Silver **Ruler:** Rama I **Note:** Observed weight range 14.86-15.43 grams.

Date	Mintage	VG	F	VF	XF	Unc
ND Unalom	—	15.00	20.00	30.00	60.00	75.00

C# 14 2 BAHT

Silver **Ruler:** Rama I **Note:** Observed weight range 29.90-30.60 grams. Thought by some to be a fantasy.

Date	Mintage	VG	F	VF	XF	Unc
ND Unalom Rare	—	4,000	4,500	6,000	8,000	—

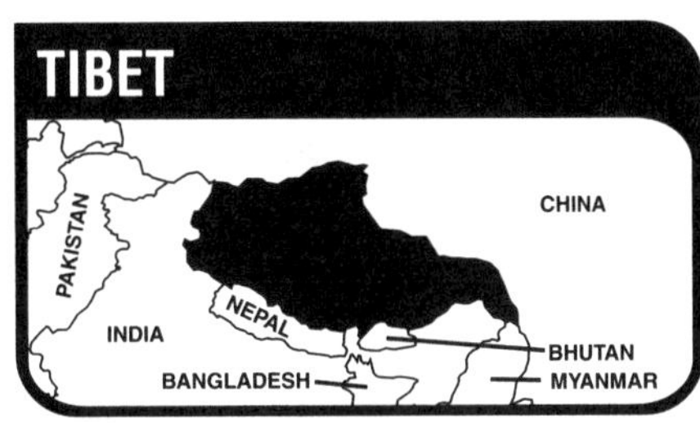

Tibet, an autonomous region of China located in central Asia between the Himalayan and Kunlun Mts. has an area of 471,660 sq. mi. (1,221,599 sq. km.) and a population of*1.9 million. Capital: Lhasa. The economy is based on agriculture and livestock raising. Wool, livestock, salt and hides are exported.

Lamaism, a form of Buddhism, developed in Tibet in the 8th century. From that time until the 1900s, the Tibetan rulers virtually isolated the country from the outside world. The British in India achieved some influence in the early 20th century. British troops were sent with the Young husband mission to extend trade in the north of India in December 1903; leaving during September 1904. The 13th dalai lama had fled to Urga where he remained until 1907. In April 1905 a revolt broke out and spread through southwestern Szechuan and northwestern Yunnan. Chao Erh-feng was appointed to subdue this rebellion and entered Lhasa in January 1910 with 2,000 troops. The dalai lama fled to India until he returned in June 1912., The British encouraged Tibet to declare its independence from China in 1913. The Communist revolution in China marked a new era in Tibetan history. Chinese Communist troops invaded Tibet in Oct., 1950. After a token resistance, Tibet signed an agreement with China in which China recognized the spiritual and temporal leadership of the dalai lama, and Tibet recognized the suzerainty of China. In 1959, a nationwide revolt triggered by Communist-initiated land reform broke out. The revolt was ruthlessly crushed. The dalai lama fled to India, and on Sept. 1,1965, the Chinese made Tibet an autonomous region of China.

The first coins to circulate in Tibet were those of neighboring Nepal from about 1570. Shortly after 1720, the Nepalese government began striking specific issues for use in Tibet. These coins had a lower silver content than those struck for use in Nepal and were exchanged with the Tibetans for an equal weight in silver bullion. Around 1763 the Tibetans struck their own coins for the first time in history. The number of coins struck at that time must have been very small. Larger quantities of coins were struck by the Tibetan government mint, which opened in 1791 with the permission of the Chinese. Operations of this mint however were suspended two years later. The Chinese opened a second mint in Lhasa in 1792. It produced a coinage until 1836. Shortly thereafter, the Tibetan mint was reopened and the government of Tibet continued to strike coins until 1953.

DATING

Based on the Tibetan calendar, Tibetan coins are dated by the cycle which contains 60 years. To calculate the western date use the following formula: Number of cycles -1, x 60 + number of years + 1026. Example 15th cycle 25th year = 1891 AD. Example: 15th cycle, 25th year 15 - 1 x 60 + 25 + 1026 = 1891AD.

13/40 = 1786 14/40 = 1846 15/40 = 1906

Certain Sino-Tibetan issues are dated in the year of reign of the Emperor of China.

MONETARY SYSTEM

15 Skar = 1-1/2 Sho = 1 Tangka

10 Sho = 1 Srang

TANGKA

6 x 10 - 60th YEAR - 1795 AD
CHINESE EMPEROR CH'IEN LUNG
1736-1796 AD

1	༡	8	༨	15	༡༥	22	༢༢
2	༢	9	༩	16	༡༦	23	༢༣
3	༣	10	༡༠	17	༡༧	24	༢༤
4	༤	11	༡༡	18	༡༨	25	༢༥
5	༥	12	༡༢	19	༡༩	26	༢༦
6	༦	13	༡༣	20	༢༠	27	༢༧
7	༧	14	༡༤	21	༢༡	28	༢༨

CHINESE AUTHORITY

EARLY COINAGE

C# 5.2 VARTULA TANGKA

Silver **Obv:** Double circle **Rev:** Wheel symbol in one circle **Note:** Weight varies: 5.40-5.70 grams.

Date	Mintage	Good	VG	F	VF	XF
ND(ca.1763-64)	—	400	550	800	1,000	—

Note: Obverse and reverse are identical

C# 5.3 VARTULA TANGKA

Silver **Note:** Weight varies: 5.40-5.70 grams. Similar to C#5.1 with double circle on obverse and reverse.

Date	Mintage	Good	VG	F	VF	XF
ND(ca.1763-64) Rare	—	—	—	—	—	—

C# 5.1 VARTULA TANGKA

Silver **Obv:** Double circle **Rev:** "DSA" in Indian Vartula script in eight petals, wheel symbol in double circle **Note:** Weight varies: 5.50-5.70 grams.

Date	Mintage	Good	VG	F	VF	XF
ND(ca.1763-64)	—	400	550	800	1,000	—

Note: Coin shows letter "JA" in Vartula script in petals around central wheel symbol on both sides

C# A10.2 SUCHAKRA TANGKA

5.6000 g., Billon/Silver **Rev:** Tibetan 45 at the bottom

Date	Mintage	Good	VG	F	VF	XF
ND(ca.1780)	—	500	650	950	1,350	—

C# A10.1 SUCHAKRA TANGKA

5.6000 g., Billon/Silver **Obv:** Tibetan 45 at the top **Rev:** In mongolian Phags pa script, Noble wheel of teaching victorious **Note:** Varieties exist.

Date	Mintage	Good	VG	F	VF	XF
ND(ca.1780)	—	500	650	950	1,350	—

Note: Probably dated year 45 of Ch'ien Lung

C# 10a SRI MAUGALAM TANGKA

Silver, 27 mm. **Obv:** Tibetan "45" **Rev:** Wheel design **Note:** Weigt varies: 4.25-5.60 grams.

Date	Mintage	F	VF	XF	Unc	BU
ND(ca.1785)	—	—	—	—	—	—

Note: It is not clear to which date the Tibetan figure "45" refers. Chinese authorities date this coin to ca.1785AD

C# 10.2 SRI MAUGALAM TANGKA

5.3300 g., Silver **Obv:** Without curves across center **Rev:** Double circle, petals joined

Date	Mintage	Good	VG	F	VF	XF
ND(ca.1785) Rare	—	—	—	—	—	—

C# 10.3 SRI MAUGALAM TANGKA

5.3800 g., Silver **Obv:** Similar to C#10.2 **Rev:** Petals separated, single circle, similar to C#10.2

Date	Mintage	Good	VG	F	VF	XF
ND(ca.1785) Rare	—	—	—	—	—	—

C# 10.4 SRI MAUGALAM TANGKA

5.3800 g., Silver **Obv:** Double circle

Date	Mintage	Good	VG	F	VF	XF
ND(ca.1785) Rare	—	—	—	—	—	—

C# 10.1 SRI MAUGALAM TANGKA

Silver **Obv:** In Tibetan script "Ga-den Po-dang Tschog-le Namgyel" (Governm,ent of Tibet) **Rev:** In four petals "Sri Mangalam" (much luck) **Note:** Weight varies: 5.20-5.40 grams. Varieties in obverse and reverse.

Date	Mintage	Good	VG	F	VF	XF
ND(ca.1785) Rare	—	—	—	—	—	—

Note: May be this Tangka has been minted by VIII. Dalai Lama in the year 1785 for the 50th Anniversary of Reign of the chinese Emperor Chien Lung

SINO-TIBETAN COINAGE

Hammered

C# 65 1/2 SHO

Silver **Obv. Inscription:** *Bod-kyi Rin-po-che* **Rev:** Chien/Lung Tsang pao 57 "Tibetan current coin of the 57th year of the Chien Lung Era" **Note:** Weight varies: 1.80-1.90 grams. Size varies: 19-20mm. Similar to 1 Sho, C#67.1. Some authorities believe this is a pattern.

Date	Mintage	Good	VG	F	VF	XF
CD57(1792)	—	1,500	1,850	2,500	3,250	—

C# 71 1/2 SHO

Silver **Obv:** Chien/Lung Tsang/pao in Chinese character **Rev:** Chien/Lung Tsang/pao in Tibetan character **Note:** Weight varies: 1.9-2.0 grams. Size varies: 20-21mm. Varieties exist; one with 24 dots on both sides and the other with 20 on reverse.

Date	Mintage	Good	VG	F	VF	XF
CD58(1793)	—	65.00	100	150	250	—

C# 82 1/2 SHO

Silver

Date	Mintage	Good	VG	F	VF	XF
CD3(1798)	—	—	—	—	—	—

Note: Reported, not confirmed; The only evidence for this issue is this photograph from China, possibly a fantasy

C# 67 SHO

Silver **Obv. Inscription:** *Pa'u gTsan* **Note:** Struck at Lhasa. Weight varies: 3.40-3.93 grams.

Date	Mintage	Good	VG	F	VF	XF
CD57(1792)	—	1,500	1,850	2,500	3,250	—

C# 67.1 SHO

Silver **Obv. Inscription:** *Bod-kyi Rin-po-che* **Rev:** KM#67 **Note:** Varieties of legends are reported but some authorities believe all of these are patterns.

Date	Mintage	Good	VG	F	VF	XF
CD57(1792)	—	1,500	1,850	2,500	3,250	—

C# 67a SHO

Silver **Obv. Inscription:** bod kyi rin-po-che

Date	Mintage	Good	VG	F	VF	XF
CD57(1792) Rare	—	—	—	—	—	—

C# 72 SHO

3.7000 g., Silver **Obv:** Chien/Lung Tsang/pao in Chinese character **Rev:** Chien/Lung Tsang/pao in Tibetan character **Note:** Size varies: 23-24mm. Varieties exist.

Date	Mintage	Good	VG	F	VF	XF
CD58(1793)	—	65.00	100	150	250	375

C# 72.1 SHO

Silver **Note:** Size varies: 26-27mm. Weight varies: 3.47-3.67 grams. Varieties exist.

Date	Mintage	Good	VG	F	VF	XF
CD58(1793)	—	15.00	25.00	37.50	55.00	—
CD59(1794)	—	15.00	25.00	37.50	55.00	—
CD60(1795)	—	20.00	32.50	50.00	75.00	—

Note: Two varieties of year 59 exist, one with 28 dots and the other with 32 dots

Note: Varieties of year 60 also exist, one with 30 dots on obverse and the other with 28 on reverse

C# 72.2 SHO

3.7000 g., Silver **Note:** Size varies: 27-30mm.

Date	Mintage	Good	VG	F	VF	XF
CD60(1795)	—	50.00	85.00	120	170	—
CD61(1796)	—	350	400	500	700	—

Note: Year 60 has 24 dots

Note: Three varieties of year 61 exist, one with 24 dots, one with 32 dots, and one with 36

C# 83.1 SHO

Silver **Obv:** Chien/Lung Tsang/pao in Chinese character **Rev:** Chien/Lung Tsang/pao in Tibetan character **Note:** Size varies: 26-27mm. Weight varies: 3.00-3.80 grams.

Date	Mintage	Good	VG	F	VF	XF
CD1(1796)	—	85.00	140	200	275	—
CD2(1797)	—	1,000	1,500	2,000	3,000	—
CD3(1798)	—	850	1,250	1,750	2,600	—
CD4(1799)	—	850	1,250	1,750	2,600	—
CD5(1800)	—	850	1,250	1,750	2,600	—

C# 66.1 1/2 TANGKA (3/4 Sho)

2.8000 g., Silver **Obv:** Chien/Lung Tsang/pao in Chinese character **Rev:** Chien/Lung Tsang/pao in Tibetan character **Note:** Size varies: 21.5-22mm. 24 dots.

Date	Mintage	Good	VG	F	VF	XF
CD58(1793) Hook in square on both sides	—	100	300	450	600	800

C# 66.2 1/2 TANGKA (3/4 Sho)

2.8000 g., Silver, 23.5 mm. **Obv:** Chien/Lung Tsang/pao in Chinese character **Rev:** Chien/Lung Tsang/pao in Tibetan character **Note:** Twenty-eight dots.

Date	Mintage	Good	VG	F	VF	XF
CD58(1793)	—	100	300	450	600	800

C# 68.1 TANGKA

Silver **Obv:** Inscription: "Bod-kyi Rin-po-che" **Note:** Varieties of legend are reported but some authorities believe all of these are patterns. Weight varies: 5.30-5.80 grams.

Date	Mintage	Good	VG	F	VF	XF
CD57(1792) Rare	—	—	—	—	—	—

C# 68 TANGKA

Silver **Obv:** Eight petals with the Buddhist lucky symbols **Obv. Inscription:** *Pa'u gTsan* **Rev:** Chien/Lung Tsang pao 57 "Tibetan current coin of the 57th year of the Chien Lung Era" **Note:** Weight varies: 5.30-5.80 grams. Varieties exist.

Date	Mintage	Good	VG	F	VF	XF
CD57(1792)	—	1,500	1,850	2,500	3,250	—

C# 68a TANGKA

Silver **Obv. Inscription:** "Bod kyi rin-po-che"

Date	Mintage	Good	VG	F	VF	XF
CD57(1792) Rare	—	—	—	—	—	—

C# 73.1 TANGKA

Silver **Note:** Weight varies: 5.30-5.70 grams. Size varies: 27-28mm. Varieties exist.

Date	Mintage	Good	VG	F	VF	XF
CD58(1793)	—	—	60.00	90.00	140	—

C# 73 TANGKA

Silver **Note:** Weight varies: 5.30-5.70 grams. Size varies: 29-31mm. Varieties exist.

Date	Mintage	Good	VG	F	VF	XF
CD58(1793)	—	50.00	75.00	125	200	—

TIBETAN COINAGE

Hammered

C# 60 "KONG-PAR" TANGKA

Billon **Obv:** Eight petals with the Buddhist lucky symbol, double circle around lotus **Rev:** Date of the Tibetan era in arch **Note:** Weight varies: 4.90-530 grams. Varieties exist.

Date	Mintage	Good	VG	F	VF	XF
CD13-45(1791)	—	20.00	30.00	50.00	80.00	—
CD13-46(1792)	—	25.00	38.00	60.00	95.00	—

C# 60.1 "KONG-PAR" TANGKA

Billon **Rev:** One circle around lotus **Note:** Weight varies: 5.00-5.80 grams. Varieties exist.

Date	Mintage	Good	VG	F	VF	XF
CD13-46(1792)	—	8.00	13.00	20.00	35.00	—
CD13-47(1793)	—	20.00	30.00	50.00	80.00	—

TOBAGO

Tobago was discovered by Columbus in 1498. It was occupied at various times by the French, Dutch and English before being ceded to Britain in 1814.

MONETARY SYSTEM

9 Pence = 1 Bit
11 Bits = 8 Shillings
3 Pence = 8 Reales

BRITISH ADMINISTRATION

STANDARD COINAGE

KM# 5 1-1/2 PENCE (Black Dog)

Billon **Note:** Countermark: TB on various French Colonial coins.

Date	Mintage	Good	VG	F	VF	XF
ND (1798)	—	7.50	10.00	15.00	25.00	—

KM# 6 2-1/4 PENCE
Note: Billon or Copper; Countermark: TBO on French Colonial coins.

Date	Mintage	Good	VG	F	VF	XF
ND (1798)	—	10.00	12.50	20.00	40.00	—

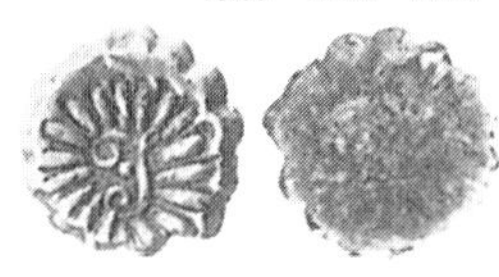

KM# 9 1-1/2 BITS
Silver **Note:** Countermark: Script T with rays on center plug cut from Spanish or Spanish Colonial 8 Reales, C#12. Beware of counterfeits.

Date	Mintage	Good	VG	F	VF	XF
ND (1798)	—	500	800	1,200	1,750	—

KM# 12 11 BITS
Silver **Note:** Spanish or Spanish Colonial crenalated hole cut in 8 Reales. The plug was used for making the 1-1/2 Bits, KM#9. Beware of counterfeits.

Date	Mintage	Good	VG	F	VF	XF
ND (1798)	—	600	750	950	1,250	—

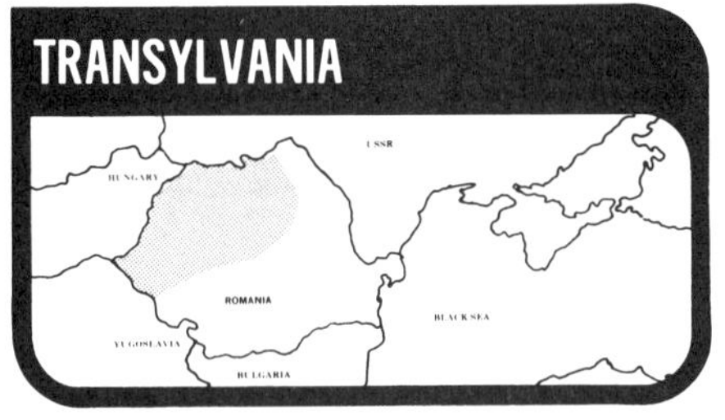

Transylvania (Cibin, Siebenburgen) is the plateau region of northwestern Romania, formerly part of Ancient Dacia, a region occupied by the Romans under Emperor Trajan in 100 AD and abandoned to the Goths in 271 AD under Aurelianus. The Romanized population maintained its Latin speech and Christian identity.

In 896 the Hungarians settled into the Carpathian basin, this included Transylvania. While the region remained an autonomous principality, mercenary Saxons enforced the suzerainty of the King of Hungary in exchange for land. When the Hungarian army was defeated by the advancing Turks at Monacs in 1526, the country was divided into three parts under protection of the Sultan.The center was occupied by the Turks, the West by the Hungary Kingdom under the Hapsburgs and Transylvania in the East which became a principality in 1540.Holy Roman Emperor Rudolf II seized control of the territory in 1604 after the murder of Michael the Brave of Wallachia, who had briefly united the Romanian principalities. In 1605 the Diet elected Stephen Bocskaias prince. After George Rakoczi II was defeated in war with Poland, the Turks were able to intervene, deposing the prince and appointing their own vassals. After the defeat of the Ottoman Turks in 1683, the Transylvanian princes then looked to Austria for guidance and protection.

The last Turkish vassal abdicated in 1697, and with the Orthodox Romanians recognizing the authority of the Pope, the Greek-Catholic, or Uniate Church is created. Under these circumstance, and the treaty of Szatmar in 1711, Transylvania was absorbed into the vast Holy Roman Empire. Transylvania continued to be a part of Hungary until the end of World War I. In 1918, Romania occupied Transylvania.

RULERS
Austrian
George Bannfy I, 1691-1708
Governor and Count of Losoncz
Leopold I, 1690-1705
(Hapsburg Emperors by the Austrian governors)
Leopold I, 1657-1705
Joseph I, 1705-1711
Charles VI, 1711-40
Maria Theresa, 1740-1780
With Francis I, 1745-65
As a widow, 1765-80
Joseph II, 1765-1790
Joint with his mother, 1765-80
Alone, 1780-90
Liopold II, 1790-92
Francis II, 1792-1835

MINT MARKS
AL-IV - (Alba Iulia), Karlsburg, 1611-13 (Wissenburg) until 1716
AZ - (Arx Zalathna)
BN - Nagybanya
CA - Karlsburg, 1746-1766
CC - (Camera Cassoviensis), Cassovia, (Kaschau),1574-83, 1693-98, 1705-07
Cor. - (Corona), Kronstadt
CM - (Cibiniensis moneta), Hermannstadt
Cor. - (Cibinium), Hermannstadt
E - (Alba Iulia), Karlsburg, 1765-1867
Fog. - (Fogarasch)
KV - (Kolosvar), Klausenburg, Cluj, 1693-1707
M - (Mediasch)
O - (Oravita), Orawitza Banat, 1783, 1812, 1816
ZB - Zalathna Banya, Zlatna

MINT OFFICIALS' INITIALS

HERMANNSTADT

Initials	Date	Name
FT	1701-08	?
IFK	1709-13	Johann Franz Kropf
MI-HS	1709	Miller Henricus

KARLSBURG

Initials	Date	Name
AH, AG	1767	Anton Josef Hammerschmidt & Alexander de Gagia
AH, GS	1780	Anton Hammerschmid & Gottfried Schickmayer
CIH, H	1713-38	Carl Josef Hoffmann
H-G	1765-76	Hammerschmidt and de Gagia
H-S	1777-80	Hammerschmidt and Schickmayer
S, GS	1777-80	Gottfried Schikmayer

MONETARY SYSTEM
1 Denar = 2 Obols
1 Kreuzer = 2 Denars
1 Poltura = 3 Denars
1 Groschen = 3 Kreuzer
1 Sechser = 6 Denars
1 Zwolfer = 12 Denars
1 Gulden = 60 Kreuzer
1 Thaler = 2 Gulden

NOTE: Refer also to Austrian listings for common circulation types struck at mints listed above.

PRINCIPALITY

STANDARD COINAGE

KM# 643 GRESCHL
Copper **Obv:** Crowned arms within sprigs **Rev:** Value, date in cartouche

Date	Mintage	VG	F	VF	XF	Unc
1763	—	10.00	25.00	50.00	100	—
1764	—	10.00	25.00	50.00	100	—
1765	—	10.00	25.00	50.00	100	—

KM# 526 POLTURA
Silver **Obv:** Laureate bust of Leopold I, right **Obv. Legend:** LEOPOLDVS D • G • R • I • S • ... **Rev:** Crowned divided arms divide date, value and flowers below

Date	Mintage	VG	F	VF	XF	Unc
1704 FT	—	25.00	40.00	75.00	135	—

KM# 529 POLTURA
Silver **Obv:** Laureate bust of Joseph I, right **Obv. Legend:** IOSEPHVS • D • G • R • I • S • ... **Rev:** Crowned, divided arms divides date, value and crowned shield flanked by initials below

Date	Mintage	VG	F	VF	XF	Unc
1705 FT	—	20.00	35.00	65.00	125	—
1706 FT	—	20.00	35.00	65.00	125	—
1707 FT	—	20.00	35.00	65.00	125	—
1708	—	20.00	35.00	65.00	125	—

KM# 528 POLTURA
Silver **Obv:** Laureate bust of Leopold I, right **Obv. Legend:** LEOPOLDVS • D • G • R • I • S • ... **Rev:** Crowned divided arms divides date, value and crowned shield below **Note:** Varieties exist.

Date	Mintage	VG	F	VF	XF	Unc
1705 FT	—	25.00	40.00	75.00	135	—

KM# 539 POLTURA
Silver **Obv:** Laureate bust of Joseph I, right **Obv. Legend:** IOSEPHVS • D • G • R • I • S • ... **Rev:** Crowned, divided arms divides date, value and crowned shield flanked by initials below **Note:** Varieties exist.

Date	Mintage	VG	F	VF	XF	Unc
1709 MI-HS	—	20.00	35.00	65.00	125	—

KM# 585 POLTURA
Billon **Obv:** Laureate bust of Charles VI right **Rev:** Arms above value and date

Date	Mintage	VG	F	VF	XF	Unc
1730	—	35.00	80.00	125	200	—

KM# 595 POLTURA
Billon **Obv:** Small laureate bust of Charles VI, right **Rev:** Crowned arms in cartouche, value below **Note:** Reduced size.

Date	Mintage	VG	F	VF	XF	Unc
1740	—	35.00	80.00	125	200	—

KM# 611 POLTURA
Billon **Obv:** Bust of Maria Theresa right **Obv. Legend:** M • THERESIA ... **Rev:** Crowned ornate arms above value and date

Date	Mintage	VG	F	VF	XF	Unc
1747	—	30.00	75.00	120	200	—

KM# 540 1/2 KREUZER
Silver **Obv:** Three shields, one above two, date divided at top

Date	Mintage	VG	F	VF	XF	Unc
1709	—	20.00	45.00	90.00	185	—
1710	—	20.00	45.00	90.00	185	—

KM# 541 KREUZER
Silver **Obv:** Laureate bust of Joseph I, right within beaded circle, value below **Obv. Legend:** IOSEPHVS • D • G • R • I • S • ... **Rev:** Crowned double-headed eagle with oval shield on breast, within beaded circle, crown divides date above **Rev. Legend:** ARCHID • AV • D • ...

Date	Mintage	VG	F	VF	XF	Unc
1709 IFK	—	30.00	75.00	125	220	—

KM# 545 KREUZER
Silver **Obv:** Laureate bust of Joseph I, right, value below **Rev:** Crowned double-headed eagle with shield on breast, divided date above

Date	Mintage	VG	F	VF	XF	Unc
1710 IFK	—	30.00	75.00	125	220	—
1711 IFK	—	30.00	75.00	125	220	—

KM# 549 KREUZER
Silver **Obv:** Laureate bust of Charles VI, right, value below **Obv. Legend:** CAROL VI • D • G • R • I • ... **Rev:** Crowned double-headed eagle, shield on breast, divided date above **Rev. Legend:** • ARCHID • A • D • ... **Note:** Varieties exist.

Date	Mintage	VG	F	VF	XF	Unc
1712 IFK	—	30.00	75.00	125	220	—
1731	—	30.00	75.00	125	220	—

KM# 640 KREUZER
Billon **Obv:** Bust of Maria Theresa, right **Obv. Legend:** M • THER : D • G • R • I • ... **Rev:** Crowned double-headed eagle, shield on breast, date in legend

Date	Mintage	VG	F	VF	XF	Unc
1762	—	30.00	70.00	100	175	—

KM# 546 3 KREUZER (Groschen)
Silver **Obv:** Laureate bust of Joseph I, right, within beaded circle, value in circle below **Obv. Legend:** IOSEPHVS • D • G • R • I • S • ... **Rev:** Crown divides date and beaded circle above double-headed eagle, shield on breast **Rev. Legend:** • ARCHID • A • D • ... **Note:** Varieties exist.

Date	Mintage	VG	F	VF	XF	Unc
1711 IFK	—	30.00	75.00	125	220	—

KM# 578 3 KREUZER (Groschen)
Silver **Obv:** Laureate bust of Charles VI right **Rev:** Crowned double-headed eagle within circle

Date	Mintage	VG	F	VF	XF	Unc
1725	—	15.00	30.00	60.00	100	—

KM# 580 3 KREUZER (Groschen)
Silver **Rev:** Crowned double-headed eagle **Note:** Varieties exist.

Date	Mintage	VG	F	VF	XF	Unc
1729	—	15.00	30.00	60.00	100	—

KM# 586 3 KREUZER (Groschen)
Silver **Obv:** Legend begins at top **Rev:** Value below crowned double-headed eagle

Date	Mintage	VG	F	VF	XF	Unc
1733	—	15.00	30.00	60.00	100	—

KM# 590 3 KREUZER (Groschen)
Silver **Obv:** Legend begins at left **Rev:** Value below crowned double-headed eagle

Date	Mintage	VG	F	VF	XF	Unc
1735	—	18.00	35.00	65.00	125	—
1736	—	18.00	35.00	65.00	125	—
1740	—	18.00	35.00	65.00	125	—

KM# 608 3 KREUZER (Groschen)
Billon **Obv:** Bust of Maria Theresa right **Rev:** Crowned ornamental arms above value

Date	Mintage	VG	F	VF	XF	Unc
1745	—	50.00	100	175	275	—

KM# 641 3 KREUZER (Groschen)
Billon **Rev:** Arms on breast of crowned double-headed eagle, value below

Date	Mintage	VG	F	VF	XF	Unc
1762	—	25.00	50.00	100	200	—
1765	—	25.00	50.00	100	200	—
1768	—	25.00	50.00	100	200	—

KM# 657 3 KREUZER (Groschen)
Billon **Obv:** Veiled, bust right **Obv. Legend:** M • THERES • D : G • R • I • ... **Rev:** Crowned double-headed eagle, value on breast **Rev. Legend:** TRANS • 1780 AR • AU • ...

Date	Mintage	VG	F	VF	XF	Unc
1774 H-G	—	25.00	45.00	90.00	180	—
1774 B//H-G	—	25.00	45.00	90.00	180	—
1774 E//H-G	—	25.00	45.00	90.00	180	—
1777 E//H-G	—	25.00	45.00	90.00	180	—
1780 E//H-S	—	25.00	45.00	90.00	180	—

KM# 642 7 KREUZER
Billon **Obv:** Bust of Maria Theresa right **Rev:** Arms on breast of crowned double-headed eagle, value below

Date	Mintage	VG	F	VF	XF	Unc
1762	—	30.00	75.00	125	200	—
1763	—	30.00	75.00	150	250	—
1764	—	30.00	75.00	125	200	—
1765	—	30.00	65.00	100	175	—

KM# 645 10 KREUZER
Silver **Obv:** Bust of Maria Theresa within laurel and palm wreath **Rev:** Arms on breast of crowned double-headed eagle, value in pedestal

Date	Mintage	VG	F	VF	XF	Unc
1765	—	18.00	35.00	70.00	145	—
1766	—	18.00	35.00	70.00	145	—

KM# 658 10 KREUZER
Silver **Obv:** Veiled bust right within palm and laurel wreath **Obv. Legend:** M • THERESIA : D : G • R • IMP • ... **Rev:** Shield on breast of crowned double-headed eagle, value in cartouche below **Rev. Legend:** TRAN • CO • TVR • 1780 ...

Date	Mintage	VG	F	VF	XF	Unc
1776 H-G	—	30.00	75.00	125	200	—
1780 H-S	—	30.00	65.00	100	175	—

KM# 527 15 KREUZER
Silver **Obv:** Laureate bust of Leopold I right within circle, value below **Obv. Legend:** LEOPOLDVS • D • G • R • I • S • ... **Rev:** Crowned double-headed eagle within circle, crown divides date **Rev. Legend:** MONETANOVA ARG • TRANSYLV • **Note:** Varieties exist.

Date	Mintage	VG	F	VF	XF	Unc
1704 FT	—	60.00	100	150	275	—

KM# 579 15 KREUZER
Silver **Obv:** Laureate bust of Charles VI right, value below **Rev:** Crowned double-headed eagle, date in legend

Date	Mintage	VG	F	VF	XF	Unc
1726	—	60.00	100	150	275	—

KM# 615 15 KREUZER
Silver **Obv:** Bust of Maria Theresa right **Rev:** Arms on breast of crowned double-headed eagle, value below

Date	Mintage	VG	F	VF	XF	Unc
1748	—	60.00	100	150	275	—
1749	—	60.00	100	150	275	—
1750	—	75.00	125	175	300	—

KM# 627 17 KREUZER
Silver, 30 mm. **Obv:** Bust of Maria Theresa right **Rev:** Crowned double-headed eagle with 4-fold shield on breast **Note:** Similar to KM#644, but four-fold shield.

Date	Mintage	VG	F	VF	XF	Unc
1751	—	20.00	45.00	90.00	185	—

KM# 644 17 KREUZER
Silver **Obv:** Bust of Maria Theresa right **Obv. Legend:** M • THERESIA : D : G • ... **Rev:** Crowned double-headed eagle, shield on breast, value below **Rev. Legend:** TRAN • CO • TVR • ...

Date	Mintage	VG	F	VF	XF	Unc
1763	—	15.00	30.00	65.00	125	—
1764	—	15.00	30.00	65.00	125	—
1765	—	20.00	40.00	80.00	165	—

KM# 634 20 KREUZER
Silver **Obv:** Bust of Maria Theresa within laurel and palm wreath **Rev:** Arms on breast of crowned double-headed eagle, value in pedestal

Date	Mintage	VG	F	VF	XF	Unc
1755	—	18.00	35.00	75.00	165	—
1764	—	18.00	35.00	70.00	145	—
1765	—	18.00	30.00	65.00	125	—

KM# 648 20 KREUZER
Silver **Obv:** Veiled bust of Maria Theresa right **Rev:** Crowned double-headed eagle with shield on breast, value in cartouche below

Date	Mintage	VG	F	VF	XF	Unc
1767 H-G	—	12.00	20.00	35.00	80.00	—
1768 H-G	—	12.00	20.00	35.00	80.00	—
1769 H-G	—	12.00	20.00	35.00	70.00	—
1770 H-G	—	12.00	20.00	35.00	70.00	—
1771 H-G	—	12.00	20.00	35.00	70.00	—
1772 H-G	—	12.00	20.00	35.00	70.00	—

KM# 656 20 KREUZER
Silver **Obv:** Veiled bust of Maria Theresa right, within palm and laurel wreath **Obv. Legend:** M • THERESIA : D : G • R • IMP • ... **Rev:** Crowned double-headed eagle within sprigs, value in cartouche below **Rev. Legend:** TRAN • CO • TVR • ...

Date	Mintage	VG	F	VF	XF	Unc
1773 H-G	—	12.00	20.00	35.00	75.00	—
1774 H-G	—	12.00	20.00	35.00	70.00	—
1775 H-G	—	12.00	20.00	35.00	70.00	—
1776 H-G	—	12.00	20.00	35.00	70.00	—
1777 H-G	—	12.00	20.00	35.00	75.00	—
1777 H-S	—	12.00	20.00	35.00	75.00	—
1778 H-S	—	12.00	20.00	35.00	70.00	—
1779 H-S	—	12.00	20.00	35.00	70.00	—
1780 H-S	—	12.00	20.00	35.00	70.00	—

KM# 606 30 KREUZER
Silver **Obv:** Bust of Maria Theresa divides date with value below in diamond **Rev:** Crowned arms in branches in diamond

Date	Mintage	VG	F	VF	XF	Unc
1744	—	75.00	150	300	500	—

KM# 630 30 KREUZER
Silver **Rev:** Arms on breast of crowned double-headed eagle in diamond

Date	Mintage	VG	F	VF	XF	Unc
1754	—	50.00	100	200	350	—
1755	—	50.00	100	175	325	—
1765	—	50.00	100	175	325	—
1766	—	50.00	100	200	350	—

KM# 570 1/4 THALER
Silver **Obv:** Laureate bust of Charles VI right **Rev:** Crowned double-headed eagle, date in legend **Note:** Struck with 1/2 Thaler dies.

Date	Mintage	VG	F	VF	XF	Unc
1721	—	—	—	750	1,250	—

KM# 534 1/2 THALER
Silver **Subject:** Joseph I **Obv:** Bust of Joseph I right, within divided circle **Obv. Legend:** IOSEPHVS : D : G : R O : ... **Rev:** Crowned double-headed eagle, shield on breast **Rev. Legend:** ARCHID : AVS : D : ...

Date	Mintage	VG	F	VF	XF	Unc
1708	—	300	600	1,200	2,250	—

KM# 554 1/2 THALER
Silver **Obv:** Laureate bust of Charles VI right, within divided circle **Obv. Legend:** CAROLVS VI • D • G • R • IMP • ... **Rev:** Crowned double-headed eagle, shield on breast, within circle **Rev. Legend:** ARCHIDVX AVSTR • D • B • PR • ...

Date	Mintage	VG	F	VF	XF	Unc
1713	—	160	325	550	1,150	—

KM# 553 1/2 THALER
Silver **Subject:** Charles VI **Obv:** Bust of Charles VI within divided circle **Obv. Legend:** CAR:VI : D : G : R : I : S : ... **Rev:** Crowned arms in order chain on breast of crowned double-headed eagle **Rev. Legend:** ARCHI : D ... **Note:** Varieties exist.

Date	Mintage	VG	F	VF	XF	Unc
1716	—	100	200	350	750	—
1717	—	100	200	350	750	—
1718	—	100	200	350	750	—
1720	—	100	200	350	750	—

KM# 571 1/2 THALER

Silver **Obv:** Laureate bust of Charles VI right **Obv. Legend:** CAR • VI • D • G • R • ... **Rev:** Crowned arms in order chain on breast of crowned double-headed eagle **Rev. Legend:** A R C H I D A V D B ...

Date	Mintage	VG	F	VF	XF	Unc
1721	—	150	300	500	1,000	—

KM# 577 1/2 THALER

Silver **Obv:** Bust of Charles VI right **Obv. Legend:** CAR • VI • D • G • R • I • ... **Rev:** Crowned arms in order chain on breast of crowned double-headed eagle **Rev. Legend:** ARCHI • D • AV • DBV • ...

Date	Mintage	VG	F	VF	XF	Unc
1724	—	100	200	350	750	—
1725	—	100	200	350	750	—
1726	—	100	200	350	750	—
1727	—	100	200	350	750	—
1729	—	100	200	350	750	—
1730	—	100	200	350	750	—
1731	—	100	200	350	750	—
1733	—	100	200	350	750	—
1735	—	100	200	350	750	—

KM# 592 1/2 THALER

Silver **Obv:** Legend begins at left **Note:** Varieties exist.

Date	Mintage	VG	F	VF	XF	Unc
1737	—	150	300	500	1,000	—
1739	—	150	300	500	1,000	—

KM# 596 1/2 THALER

Silver **Obv:** Bust of Maria Theresa right **Rev:** Arms on breast of crowned double-headed eagle **Note:** Specie Thaler.

Date	Mintage	VG	F	VF	XF	Unc
1740	—	90.00	150	250	500	—
1748	—	90.00	150	250	500	—
1749	—	90.00	150	250	500	—

KM# 599 1/2 THALER

Silver **Obv:** Bust of Maria Theresa right **Rev:** Crowned arms with garlands

Date	Mintage	VG	F	VF	XF	Unc
1742	—	80.00	150	275	400	—
1743	—	80.00	150	275	400	—
1744	—	80.00	150	275	400	—

KM# 629 1/2 THALER

Silver **Obv:** Mature bust of Maria Theresa right

Date	Mintage	VG	F	VF	XF	Unc
1752	—	65.00	115	200	350	—
1753	—	65.00	115	200	350	—
1754	—	65.00	115	200	350	—
1755	—	65.00	115	200	350	—
1756	—	65.00	115	200	350	—
1758	—	65.00	115	200	350	—
1759	—	65.00	115	200	350	—
1760	—	65.00	115	200	350	—
1761	—	65.00	115	200	350	—
1765	—	65.00	115	200	350	—

KM# 550 THALER

Silver **Subject:** Charles VI **Obv:** Bust of Charles VI right within divided circle **Obv. Legend:** CAROL VI : D : G : RO : ... **Rev:** Shield on breast of crowned double-headed eagle within circle **Note:** Dav. #1100.

Date	Mintage	VG	F	VF	XF	Unc
1712	—	250	450	850	1,500	—

KM# 555 THALER

Silver **Obv:** Laureate bust of Charles VI right, within divided circle **Obv. Legend:** CAROL VI D : G : RO : ... **Rev:** Shield on breast of crowned double-headed eagle **Rev. Legend:** ARCHI • DVX • AVS ... **Note:** Dav. #1101.

Date	Mintage	VG	F	VF	XF	Unc
1713	—	150	275	500	850	—
1715	—	150	275	500	850	—

KM# 559 THALER

Silver **Obv:** Laureate bust of Charles VI right **Obv. Legend:** CAR VI • D • G • R • I • ... **Rev:** Shield on breast of crowned double-headed eagle **Rev. Legend:** ARCHIDVX • AVS ... **Note:** Dav. #1102.

Date	Mintage	VG	F	VF	XF	Unc
1715	—	150	275	500	850	—

KM# 573 THALER

Silver **Obv:** Laureate bust of Charles VI right **Obv. Legend:** CARVI•D:GRISAG ... **Rev:** Shield on breast of crowned double-headed eagle **Rev. Legend:** ARCHID • AV • D • B • V • PR ... **Note:** Dav. #1103.

Date	Mintage	VG	F	VF	XF	Unc
1721	—	150	275	500	850	—
1722	—	150	275	500	850	—
1724	—	150	275	500	850	—
1728	—	150	275	500	850	—
1734	—	150	275	500	850	—

KM# 591 THALER

Silver **Obv:** Legend begins at left **Rev:** Eagle's legs angular **Note:** Varieties exist. Dav. #1104.

Date	Mintage	VG	F	VF	XF	Unc
1736	—	175	350	600	1,150	—
1737	—	175	350	600	1,150	—
1738	—	175	350	600	1,150	—
1740	—	175	350	600	1,150	—

KM# 591A THALER

Silver **Note:** Dav. #1106.

Date	Mintage	VG	F	VF	XF	Unc
1739	—	175	350	600	1,150	—

KM# 600 THALER

Silver **Obv:** Bust of Maria Theresa right **Obv. Legend:** MAR : THERESA D : G • REGHUNGBO : **Rev:** Crowned arms with garlands **Rev. Legend:** ARCH : A : D: BU : ... **Note:** Specie Thaler. Dav. #1141.

Date	Mintage	VG	F	VF	XF	Unc
1742	—	160	300	800	1,500	—

KM# 603 THALER

Silver **Rev:** Crowned ornamental arms with fruit clusters at sides **Note:** Dav. #1142.

Date	Mintage	VG	F	VF	XF	Unc
1743	—	160	300	800	1,500	—

KM# 607 THALER

Silver **Rev:** Crowned ornamental arms in sprays **Note:** Dav. #1142A.

Date	Mintage	VG	F	VF	XF	Unc
1744 Rare	—	—	—	—	—	—

KM# 609 THALER

Silver **Obv:** Smaller bust of Maria Theresa right **Obv. Legend:** MAR • THERESIA D : G • REG ... **Rev:** Crowned ornamental arms **Rev. Legend:** ARCH • A • D • BU • PR • ... **Note:** Dav. #1143.

Date	Mintage	VG	F	VF	XF	Unc
1745	—	160	300	800	1,500	—

KM# 612 THALER

Silver **Obv:** Bust of Maria Theresa right **Obv. Legend:** M • THERESIA • D : G • R • IMP • ... **Rev:** Crowned arms on breast of crowned double-headed eagle **Note:** Dav. #1144.

Date	Mintage	VG	F	VF	XF	Unc
1747	—	85.00	150	400	700	—
1748	—	85.00	150	400	700	—
1749	—	85.00	150	400	700	—
1750	—	85.00	150	400	700	—

KM# 628 THALER

Silver **Obv:** Mature bust of Maria Theresa right **Obv. Legend:** M • THERESIA • D : G • R • IMP • ... **Rev:** Crowned arms on breast of crowned double-headed eagle **Note:** Convention Thaler. Dav. #1145.

Date	Mintage	VG	F	VF	XF	Unc
1751	—	85.00	150	400	700	—
1752	—	85.00	150	400	700	—
1753	—	85.00	150	400	700	—
1754	—	85.00	150	400	700	—
1755	—	85.00	150	400	700	—
1756	—	85.00	150	400	700	—
1757	—	85.00	150	400	700	—
1758	—	85.00	150	400	700	—
1759	—	85.00	150	400	700	—
1760	—	85.00	150	400	700	—
1761	—	85.00	150	400	700	—
1762	—	85.00	150	400	700	—
1765	—	85.00	150	400	700	—

TRADE COINAGE

KM# 659 1/16 DUCAT

0.2188 g., 0.9860 Gold 0.0069 oz. AGW **Obv:** Crowned arms within circle **Rev:** Value, date within circle

Date	Mintage	VG	F	VF	XF	Unc
1778 HS	—	75.00	100	200	450	—

KM# 616 1/8 DUCAT

0.4375 g., 0.9860 Gold 0.0139 oz. AGW **Obv:** Bust of Maria Theresa right **Rev:** Arms on breast of crowned double-headed eagle, value below

Date	Mintage	VG	F	VF	XF	Unc
1749 Rare	—	—	—	—	—	—

KM# 660 1/8 DUCAT

0.4375 g., 0.9860 Gold 0.0139 oz. AGW **Obv:** Crowned arms **Rev:** Value, date

Date	Mintage	VG	F	VF	XF	Unc
1778 HS	—	75.00	100	200	450	—

KM# 547 1/4 DUCAT

0.8750 g., 0.9860 Gold 0.0277 oz. AGW **Subject:** Charles VI **Obv:** Laureate head right **Obv. Legend:** CAR VI • D • G • ... **Rev:** Crowned, mantles arms, value in oval circle below

Date	Mintage	VG	F	VF	XF	Unc
ND	—	50.00	100	200	425	—

KM# 548 1/4 DUCAT

0.8750 g., 0.9860 Gold 0.0277 oz. AGW **Obv:** Crowned, ornate arms, value in oval circle below **Rev:** Globe in circle of clouds

Date	Mintage	VG	F	VF	XF	Unc
ND	—	50.00	100	200	425	—

KM# 617 1/4 DUCAT

0.8750 g., 0.9860 Gold 0.0277 oz. AGW **Obv:** Bust of Maria Theresa right **Rev:** Crowned and mantled arms with value below

Date	Mintage	VG	F	VF	XF	Unc
ND	—	75.00	100	200	450	—

KM# 618 1/4 DUCAT

0.8750 g., 0.9860 Gold 0.0277 oz. AGW **Obv:** Head of Maria Theresa right **Obv. Legend:** M • THER • D : G • R • I • ... **Rev:** Crowned arms on breast of crowned double-headed eagle

Date	Mintage	VG	F	VF	XF	Unc
1749	—	75.00	100	200	400	—

KM# 649 1/4 DUCAT

0.8750 g., 0.9860 Gold 0.0277 oz. AGW **Obv:** Veiled bust of Maria Theresa right **Obv. Legend:** M • THER • D • G • ... **Rev:** Crowned arms on breast of crowned double-headed eagle, value below

Date	Mintage	VG	F	VF	XF	Unc
1768 H-G	—	50.00	100	175	375	—
1772 H-G	—	50.00	100	175	375	—
1776 H-G	—	50.00	100	175	375	—
1778 H-S	—	50.00	100	175	375	—
1780 H-S	—	50.00	100	175	375	—

KM# 625 1/2 DUCAT

1.7500 g., 0.9860 Gold 0.0555 oz. AGW **Subject:** Maria Theresa **Obv:** Bust of Maria Theresa right **Obv. Legend:** M • THERESIA • D • G • RO • ... **Rev:** Crowned arms on breast of crowned double-headed eagle, value below

Date	Mintage	VG	F	VF	XF	Unc
1750	—	200	400	750	1,200	—
1756	—	200	400	750	1,200	—
1759	—	200	400	750	1,200	—
1762	—	200	400	750	1,200	—
1763	—	200	400	750	1,200	—
1764	—	200	400	750	1,200	—
1765	—	200	400	750	1,200	—

KM# 655 1/2 DUCAT

1.7500 g., 0.9860 Gold 0.0555 oz. AGW **Obv:** Veiled bust of Maria Theresa right **Obv. Legend:** M • THERES • D • G • R • I • ... **Rev:** Crowned arms on breast of crowned double-headed eagle, value below

Date	Mintage	VG	F	VF	XF	Unc
1770 H-G	—	170	350	600	1,000	—
1774 H-G	—	170	350	600	1,000	—
1775 H-G	—	170	350	600	1,000	—
1780 H-S	—	170	350	600	1,000	—
1780	—	—	—	—	—	—

KM# 525 DUCAT

3.5000 g., 0.9860 Gold 0.1109 oz. AGW **Subject:** Leopold I **Obv:** Standing caped figure holding scepter and orb **Obv. Legend:** LEOPOLD • D • G • R • I • ... **Rev:** Crowned, round arms on breast of crowned double-headed eagle, crown divides date above

Date	Mintage	VG	F	VF	XF	Unc
1701FT	—	250	450	900	1,750	—
1702FT	—	250	450	900	1,750	—
1703FT	—	250	450	900	1,750	—
1704FT	—	250	450	900	1,750	—

KM# 530 DUCAT

3.5000 g., 0.9860 Gold 0.1109 oz. AGW **Obv:** Crowned, oval arms in cartouche **Obv. Legend:** MONETA NOVA AVREA TRANS : **Rev:** Palm tree divides date and mint marks **Rev. Legend:** TANDEM OPPRESSA RESVRGET • **Note:** Insurgent coinage of Francis Rakoczi.

Date	Mintage	VG	F	VF	XF	Unc
1705KV	—	425	950	1,750	3,750	—

KM# 531 DUCAT

3.5000 g., 0.9860 Gold 0.1109 oz. AGW **Obv:** Crowned, ornate oval arms **Obv. Legend:** MONETA NOVA AVREA TRANS : **Rev:** Palm tree divides mint marks and date **Rev. Legend:** TANDEM OPPRESSA RESVRGET • **Shape:** Octagon **Note:** Klippe, similar to KM#530.

Date	Mintage	VG	F	VF	XF	Unc
1705KV	—	300	600	1,350	2,750	—

KM# 532 DUCAT

3.5000 g., 0.9860 Gold 0.1109 oz. AGW **Subject:** Joseph I **Obv:** Standing caped figure holding scepter and orb **Obv. Legend:** IOSEPHVS • D • G • R • I • S • ... **Rev:** Crowned double-headed eagle with Transylvanian arms on breast **Rev. Legend:** ARCHID • A • D • B • ...

Date	Mintage	VG	F	VF	XF	Unc
1706 FT	—	225	450	1,100	2,250	—
1709	—	—	—	—	—	—
1710 IFK	—	225	450	1,100	2,250	—
1711 IFK	—	225	450	1,100	2,250	—

KM# 533 DUCAT

3.5000 g., 0.9860 Gold 0.1109 oz. AGW **Subject:** Francis Rakoczi **Obv:** Uniformed half-length figure, right **Rev:** Crowned, ornate oval arms, date in legend **Note:** Malcontent issue.

Date	Mintage	VG	F	VF	XF	Unc
1707KV	—	250	550	1,200	2,500	—

KM# 542 DUCAT

3.5000 g., 0.9860 Gold 0.1109 oz. AGW **Rev:** Smaller arms

Date	Mintage	VG	F	VF	XF	Unc
1708	—	225	450	1,100	2,250	—

KM# 551 DUCAT

3.5000 g., 0.9860 Gold 0.1109 oz. AGW **Obv:** Standing caped figure of Charles VI holding scepter and orb **Obv. Legend:** CAROL VI • D • G • R • I • ... **Rev:** Crowned, round arms on breast of crowned double-headed eagle, divided date above

Date	Mintage	VG	F	VF	XF	Unc
1712	—	200	375	750	1,600	—

KM# 556 DUCAT

3.5000 g., 0.9860 Gold 0.1109 oz. AGW **Obv:** Young laureate bust of Charles VI right **Obv. Legend:** CAROL VI • D • G • R • ... **Rev:** Crowned, oval arms on breast of crowned double-headed eagle, divided date above **Note:** Varieties exist.

Date	Mintage	VG	F	VF	XF	Unc
1713	—	175	350	700	1,500	—
1714	—	175	350	700	1,500	—
1715	—	175	350	700	1,500	—
1716	—	175	350	700	1,500	—

KM# 563 DUCAT

3.5000 g., 0.9860 Gold 0.1109 oz. AGW **Obv:** Mature, laureate bust of Charles VI right **Obv. Legend:** CAROLVI • D • G • R • ... **Rev:** Crowned, oval arms on breast of crowned double-headed eagle, divided date above

Date	Mintage	VG	F	VF	XF	Unc
1714	—	175	350	700	1,500	—

KM# A574 DUCAT

3.5000 g., 0.9860 Gold 0.1109 oz. AGW **Obv:** Armored bust right **Obv. Legend:** CARVI • D • G • R • I ... **Rev:** Crowned arms on breast of crowned double-headed eagle, date in legend

Date	Mintage	VG	F	VF	XF	Unc
1718	—	175	350	700	1,500	—
1719	—	175	350	700	1,500	—

KM# 574 DUCAT

3.5000 g., 0.9860 Gold 0.1109 oz. AGW **Obv:** Armored bust right **Obv. Legend:** CARVI • D • G • R • I ... **Rev:** Crowned arms on breast of crowned double-headed eagle **Note:** Varieties exist.

Date	Mintage	VG	F	VF	XF	Unc
1721	—	175	350	700	1,500	—
1721	—	175	350	700	1,500	—
1723	—	175	350	700	1,500	—
1724	—	175	350	700	1,500	—
1725	—	175	350	700	1,500	—
1726	—	175	350	700	1,500	—
1727	—	175	350	700	1,500	—
1728	—	175	350	700	1,500	—

KM# 581 DUCAT

3.5000 g., 0.9860 Gold 0.1109 oz. AGW **Obv:** Bust of Charles VI right **Obv. Legend:** CARVI • D • G • R • I • ... **Rev:** Crowned, oval arms on breast of crowned double-headed eagle, date in legend **Rev. Legend:** ARCHIDAV • D • BVR • PRINC • TRANSVI • **Note:** Varieties exist.

Date	Mintage	VG	F	VF	XF	Unc
1729	—	175	350	700	1,500	—
1730	—	175	350	700	1,500	—
1731	—	175	350	700	1,500	—
1732	—	175	350	700	1,500	—
1733	—	175	350	700	1,500	—

KM# 587 DUCAT

3.5000 g., 0.9860 Gold 0.1109 oz. AGW **Obv:** Laureate bust of Charles VI right **Obv. Legend:** CAR • VI • D • G • R • I • ... **Rev:** Crowned arms on breast of crowned double-headed eagle, date in legend **Rev. Legend:** ARCHID • AUST • D • BUR PRIN • TRANSYL • **Note:** Varieties exist.

Date	Mintage	VG	F	VF	XF	Unc
1734	—	175	350	700	1,500	—
1735	—	175	350	700	1,500	—
1736	—	175	350	700	1,500	—
1737	—	175	350	700	1,500	—
1738	—	175	350	700	1,500	—
1739	—	175	350	700	1,500	—
1740	—	175	350	700	1,500	—

KM# 588 DUCAT

3.5000 g., 0.9860 Gold 0.1109 oz. AGW **Note:** Klippe.

Date	Mintage	VG	F	VF	XF	Unc
1734	—	250	450	900	1,750	—

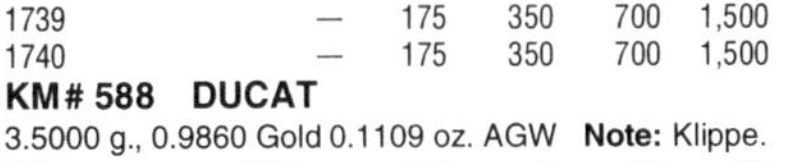

KM# 598 DUCAT

3.5000 g., 0.9860 Gold 0.1109 oz. AGW **Obv:** Large bust of Maria Theresa right **Obv. Legend:** MAR : THERESIA D : G : ... **Rev:** Crowned ornamental arms **Rev. Legend:** ARCH : A : D : BU ...

Date	Mintage	VG	F	VF	XF	Unc
1741	—	260	500	900	1,800	—
1742	—	260	500	900	1,800	—
1743	—	260	500	900	1,800	—

KM# 604 DUCAT

3.5000 g., 0.9860 Gold 0.1109 oz. AGW **Obv:** Smaller bust of Maria Theresa right **Obv. Legend:** MAR • THERESIA ... **Rev:** Crowned, ornamental arms, date in legend **Note:** Varieties exist.

Date	Mintage	VG	F	VF	XF	Unc
1743	—	175	350	800	1,350	—
1744	—	175	350	800	1,350	—
1745	—	175	350	800	1,350	—

KM# 610 DUCAT

3.5000 g., 0.9860 Gold 0.1109 oz. AGW **Obv:** Bust of Maria Theresa right **Obv. Legend:** M • THERESIA • D : G • ... **Rev:** Crowned arms on breast of crowned double-headed eagle, date in legend **Rev. Legend:** TRAN • CO • TY • 1763 AR • AU • DUX • BU • ME • P • **Note:** Die varieties exist.

Date	Mintage	VG	F	VF	XF	Unc
1746	—	125	275	450	800	—
1747	—	125	275	450	800	—
1748	—	125	275	450	800	—
1749	—	125	275	450	800	—
1750	—	125	275	450	800	—
1751	—	125	275	450	800	—
1752	—	125	275	450	800	—
1753	—	125	275	450	800	—
1754	—	125	275	450	800	—
1755	—	125	275	450	800	—
1756	—	125	275	450	800	—
1757	—	125	275	450	800	—
1758	—	125	275	450	800	—
1759	—	125	275	450	800	—
1760	—	125	275	450	800	—
1761	—	125	275	450	800	—
1762	—	125	275	450	800	—
1763	—	125	275	450	800	—
1764	—	125	275	450	800	—
1765	—	125	275	450	800	—

KM# 646 DUCAT

3.5000 g., 0.9860 Gold 0.1109 oz. AGW **Obv:** Veiled bust of Maria Theresa right **Obv. Legend:** M • THERES D : G • ... **Rev:** Crowned arms on breast of crowned double-headed eagle, date in legend **Rev. Legend:** TRAN • CO • TYR • 1776 • AR • AU • DUX • BU • M • P •

Date	Mintage	VG	F	VF	XF	Unc
1765 H-G	—	125	275	450	800	—
1767 H-G	—	125	275	450	800	—
1768 H-G	—	125	275	450	800	—
1769 H-G	—	125	275	450	800	—
1770 H-G	—	125	275	450	800	—
1771 H-G	—	125	275	450	800	—
1772 H-G	—	125	275	450	800	—
1773/2 H-G	—	125	275	450	800	—
1773 H-G	—	125	275	450	800	—
1774 H-G	—	125	275	450	800	—
1775 H-G	—	125	275	450	800	—
1776 H-G	—	125	275	450	800	—
1777 H-G	—	125	275	450	800	—
1777 H-S	—	125	275	450	800	—
1778 H-S	—	125	275	450	800	—
1779 H-S	—	125	275	450	800	—
1780 H-S	—	125	275	450	800	—

KM# 589 2 DUCAT

7.0000 g., 0.9860 Gold 0.2219 oz. AGW **Obv:** Older laureate bust of Charles VI right **Rev:** Crowned arms on breast of crowned double-headed eagle, date in legend **Note:** Klippe.

Date	Mintage	VG	F	VF	XF	Unc
1734	—	500	1,100	2,500	4,250	—

KM# 631 2 DUCAT

7.0000 g., 0.9860 Gold 0.2219 oz. AGW **Obv:** Maria Theresa right **Rev:** Crowned double headed eagle

Date	Mintage	VG	F	VF	XF	Unc
1754	—	275	600	1,250	2,200	—
1764	—	275	600	1,250	2,200	—
1765	—	275	600	1,250	2,200	—

KM# 650 2 DUCAT

7.0000 g., 0.9860 Gold 0.2219 oz. AGW **Obv:** Veiled bust of Maria Theresa right **Obv. Legend:** M • THERESIA • D : G • ... **Rev:** Crowned arms on breast of crowned double-headed eagle, date in legend, value below **Rev. Legend:** TRAN • CO • TYR • 1776 • AR • AU • DUX • BU • M • P •

Date	Mintage	VG	F	VF	XF	Unc
1768 H-G	—	250	500	950	1,850	—
1769 H-G	—	250	500	950	1,850	—
1770 H-G	—	250	500	950	1,850	—
1771 H-G	—	250	500	950	1,850	—
1772 H-G	—	250	500	950	1,850	—
1773 H-G	—	250	500	950	1,850	—
1774 H-G	—	250	500	950	1,850	—
1775 H-G	—	250	500	950	1,850	—
1776 H-G	—	250	500	950	1,850	—
1776/5 H-G	—	250	500	950	1,850	—
1777 H-G	—	250	500	950	1,850	—
1777 H-S	—	250	500	950	1,850	—
1778 H-S	—	250	500	950	1,850	—
1779 H-S	—	250	500	950	1,850	—
1780 H-S	—	250	500	950	1,850	—

KM# 543 3 DUCAT

10.5000 g., 0.9860 Gold 0.3328 oz. AGW **Subject:** Joseph I **Note:** Struck from 1/2 Thaler dies, KM#534.

Date	Mintage	VG	F	VF	XF	Unc
1708	—	650	1,350	2,750	4,500	—

KM# 637 3 DUCAT

10.5000 g., 0.9860 Gold 0.3328 oz. AGW **Obv:** Mature bust of Maria Theresa right **Note:** Struck from 1/2 Thaler dies, KM#629.

Date	Mintage	VG	F	VF	XF	Unc
1754 Rare	—	—	—	—	—	—
1760 Rare	—	—	—	—	—	—
1761 Rare	—	—	—	—	—	—

KM# 535 4 DUCAT

14.0000 g., 0.9860 Gold 0.4438 oz. AGW **Subject:** Joseph I **Obv:** Armored bust of Joseph I right **Obv. Legend:** IOSEPHVS • D • G • R • I • S • ... **Rev:** Crowned arms on breast of crowned double-headed eagle **Note:** Struck from 1/2 Thaler dies, KM#534.

Date	Mintage	VG	F	VF	XF	Unc
1708	—	1,000	1,950	4,200	6,250	—

KM# 544 4 DUCAT

14.0000 g., 0.9860 Gold 0.4438 oz. AGW **Obv:** Large, armored bust of Joseph I right, within divided circle **Obv. Legend:** IOSEPHVS • D • G • R • I • S • ... **Rev:** Crowned arms on breast of crowned double-headed eagle, within circle **Rev. Legend:** ARCHIDVX • AVSTR : D : B : ... **Note:** Struck from 1 Thaler dies.

Date	Mintage	VG	F	VF	XF	Unc
1708	—	1,600	2,750	6,000	8,500	—

KM# 564 4 DUCAT

14.0000 g., 0.9860 Gold 0.4438 oz. AGW **Obv:** Large, laureate bust of Charles VI right, within divided circle **Obv. Legend:** CAROLVI D : G : RO • IMP • ... **Rev:** Crowned arms on breast of crowned double-headed eagle **Rev. Legend:** • ARCHIDVX • AVST : DVX • BVRG • ... **Note:** Struck from 1 Thaler dies, KM#555.

Date	Mintage	VG	F	VF	XF	Unc
1713	—	900	1,850	3,500	6,000	—

KM# 638 4 DUCAT

14.0000 g., 0.9860 Gold 0.4438 oz. AGW **Note:** Struck from 1/2 Thaler dies, KM#628.

Date	Mintage	VG	F	VF	XF	Unc
1754	—	900	1,850	3,500	6,000	—
1755	—	900	1,850	3,500	6,000	—
1760	—	900	1,850	3,500	6,000	—

KM# 639 4 DUCAT

14.0000 g., 0.9860 Gold 0.4438 oz. AGW **Obv:** Mature bust of Maria Theresa right **Obv. Legend:** M • THERESA : D : G • R • IMP • ... **Rev:** Crowned arms on breast of crowned double-headed eagle, date in legend **Rev. Legend:** TRAN • CO • TYR • 1765 • AR • AU • DUX • BU • ME • PR • **Note:** Struck from 1 Thaler dies, KM#629.

Date	Mintage	VG	F	VF	XF	Unc
1759	—	900	1,850	3,500	6,000	—
1761	—	900	1,850	3,500	6,000	—
1762	—	900	1,850	3,500	6,000	—
1764	—	900	1,850	3,500	6,000	—
1765	—	900	1,850	3,500	6,000	—

KM# 661 4 DUCAT

14.0000 g., 0.9860 Gold 0.4438 oz. AGW **Obv:** Veiled bust of Maria Theresa right **Obv. Legend:** M • THERESIA • D : G • R • IMP • ... **Rev:** Crowned arms on breast of crowned double-headed eagle **Rev. Legend:** TRAN • CO • TYR • AR • AU • DUX • BU • ME • PR • **Note:** Struck from 1 Ducat dies.

Date	Mintage	VG	F	VF	XF	Unc
1778 HS	—	800	1,650	3,000	5,750	—
1779 HS	—	800	1,650	3,000	5,750	—

KM# 536 5 DUCAT

17.5000 g., 0.9860 Gold 0.5547 oz. AGW **Subject:** Joseph I **Obv:** Large, armored bust of Joseph I right, within divided circle **Obv. Legend:** IOSEPHVS : D : G : RO : ... **Rev:** Crowned, oval arms on breast of crowned double-headed eagle, date in legend **Rev. Legend:** ARCHID : AVS : D : B : MA : ... **Note:** Struck from 1/2 Thaler dies, KM#534.

Date	Mintage	VG	F	VF	XF	Unc
1708 Rare	—	—	—	—	—	—

KM# 537 5 DUCAT

17.5000 g., 0.9860 Gold 0.5547 oz. AGW **Obv:** Large, armored bust of Joseph I right, within divided circle **Obv. Legend:** IOSEPHVS • D • G • R • I • S • ... **Rev:** Crowned arms on breast of crowned double-headed eagle, within circle **Rev. Legend:** ARCHIDVX • AVSTR : D : B : ...

Date	Mintage	VG	F	VF	XF	Unc
1708 Rare	—	—	—	—	—	—

KM# 557 5 DUCAT

17.5000 g., 0.9860 Gold 0.5547 oz. AGW **Subject:** Charles VI **Obv:** Large, laureate bust of Charles VI right, within divided circle **Obv. Legend:** CAROL'VI D : G : RO • IMP • ... **Rev:** Crowned arms on breast of crowned double-headed eagle **Rev. Legend:** • ARCHIDVX • AVST : DVX • BVRG • ... **Note:** Struck from 1 Thaler dies, KM#555.

Date	Mintage	VG	F	VF	XF	Unc
1713	—	2,500	4,500	8,000	12,500	—
1715	—	2,500	4,500	8,000	12,500	—

KM# 561 5 DUCAT

17.5000 g., 0.9860 Gold 0.5547 oz. AGW **Obv:** Laureat bust of Charles VI right **Obv. Legend:** CARVI D : G : R : I : ... **Rev:** Crowned arms on breast of crowned double-headed eagle, date in legend **Rev. Legend:** ARCHID • AVST • DVX • BVR ... **Note:** Struck from 1/2 Thaler dies, KM#553.

Date	Mintage	VG	F	VF	XF	Unc
1717	—	2,500	4,500	8,000	12,500	—

KM# 562 5 DUCAT

17.5000 g., 0.9860 Gold 0.5547 oz. AGW **Note:** Struck from 1 Thaler dies, KM#573.

Date	Mintage	VG	F	VF	XF	Unc
1722 Rare	—	—	—	—	—	—

KM# 575 5 DUCAT

17.5000 g., 0.9860 Gold 0.5547 oz. AGW **Obv:** Armored bust of Charles VI right **Obv. Legend:** CAR • VI • D • G • R • I • ... **Rev:** Crowned arms in order chain on breast of crowned double-headed eagle, date in legend **Note:** Struck from 1/2 Thaler dies, KM#577.

Date	Mintage	VG	F	VF	XF	Unc
1727 Rare	—	—	—	—	—	—
1729 Rare	—	—	—	—	—	—

KM# 601 5 DUCAT

17.5000 g., 0.9860 Gold 0.5547 oz. AGW **Obv:** Mature bust of Maria Theresa right **Note:** Struck from 1/2 Thaler dies, KM#599.

Date	Mintage	VG	F	VF	XF	Unc
1742	—	2,000	4,000	6,500	10,000	—

KM# 626 5 DUCAT

17.5000 g., 0.9860 Gold 0.5547 oz. AGW **Obv:** Mature bust of Maria Theresa right **Rev:** Crowned arms on breast of crowned double-headed eagle **Note:** Struck from 1 Thaler dies, KM#612.

Date	Mintage	VG	F	VF	XF	Unc
1750	—	2,000	4,000	6,500	10,000	—

KM# 632 5 DUCAT

17.5000 g., 0.9860 Gold 0.5547 oz. AGW **Obv:** Mature bust of Maria Theresa right **Obv. Legend:** M • THERESIA D • G • R • IMP • ... **Rev:** Crowned arms on breast of crowned double-headed eagle, date in legend **Note:** Struck from 1/2 Thaler dies, KM#629.

Date	Mintage	VG	F	VF	XF	Unc
1754	—	1,750	3,000	5,500	9,500	—
1755	—	1,750	3,000	5,500	9,500	—
1759	—	1,750	3,000	5,500	9,500	—
1760	—	1,750	3,000	5,500	9,500	—

KM# 647 5 DUCAT

17.5000 g., 0.9860 Gold 0.5547 oz. AGW **Obv:** Mature bust of Maria Theresa right **Rev:** Crowned arms on breast of crowned double-headed eagle **Note:** Struck from 1 Thaler dies, KM#628.

Date	Mintage	VG	F	VF	XF	Unc
1765	—	2,000	4,000	6,500	10,000	—

KM# 594 6 DUCAT

21.0000 g., 0.9860 Gold 0.6657 oz. AGW **Obv:** Mature bust of Maria Theresa right **Rev:** Crowned arms on breast of crowned double-headed eagle **Note:** Struck from 1 Thaler dies, KM#603.

Date	Mintage	VG	F	VF	XF	Unc
1743	—	2,500	4,500	7,500	12,000	—

KM# 605 6 DUCAT

21.0000 g., 0.9860 Gold 0.6657 oz. AGW **Note:** Struck from 1 Thaler dies, KM#609.

Date	Mintage	VG	F	VF	XF	Unc
1745	—	2,500	4,500	7,500	12,000	—

KM# 613 6 DUCAT
21.0000 g., 0.9860 Gold 0.6657 oz. AGW **Obv:** Mature bust of Maria Theresa right **Note:** Struck from 1 Thaler dies, KM#612.

Date	Mintage	VG	F	VF	XF	Unc
1747	—	2,500	4,500	7,500	12,000	—

KM# 636 6 DUCAT
21.0000 g., 0.9860 Gold 0.6657 oz. AGW **Obv:** Mature bust of Maria Theresa right **Note:** Struck from 1 Thaler dies, KM#628.

Date	Mintage	VG	F	VF	XF	Unc
1759	—	2,500	4,500	7,500	12,000	—
1761	—	2,500	4,500	7,500	12,000	—

KM# 635 7 DUCAT
24.5000 g., 0.9860 Gold 0.7766 oz. AGW **Obv:** Mature bust of Maria Theresa right **Note:** Struck from 1 Thaler dies, KM#628.

Date	Mintage	VG	F	VF	XF	Unc
1758 Rare	—	—	—	—	—	—

KM# 538 10 DUCAT
35.0000 g., 0.9860 Gold 1.1095 oz. AGW **Subject:** Joseph I **Obv:** Large, armored bust of Joseph I right, within divided circle **Obv. Legend:** IOSEPHVS • D • G • R • I • S • ... **Rev:** Crowned arms on breast of crowned double-headed eagle **Rev. Legend:** ARCHIDVX • AVSTR : D : B : ... **Note:** Struck from 1 Thaler dies.

Date	Mintage	VG	F	VF	XF	Unc
1708 Rare	—	—	—	—	—	—

KM# 552 10 DUCAT
35.0000 g., 0.9860 Gold 1.1095 oz. AGW **Subject:** Charles VI **Obv:** Large, armored bust of Charles IV right, within divided circle **Obv. Legend:** CAROLVS VI • D • G • R • IMP • ... **Rev:** Crowned arms on breast of crowned double-headed eagle, within circle **Rev. Legend:** ARCHIDVX AVSTR • D • B • MAR • ... **Note:** Struck from 1 Thaler dies, KM#550.

Date	Mintage	VG	F	VF	XF	Unc
1712 Rare	—	—	—	—	—	—

KM# 558 10 DUCAT
35.0000 g., 0.9860 Gold 1.1095 oz. AGW **Rev:** Crowned arms on breast of crowned double-headed eagle, date in legend **Rev. Legend:** • ARCHIDVX • AVS... **Note:** Struck from 1 Thaler dies, KM#555.

Date	Mintage	VG	F	VF	XF	Unc
1713 Rare	—	—	—	—	—	—

KM# 576 10 DUCAT
35.0000 g., 0.9860 Gold 1.1095 oz. AGW **Note:** Similar to 5 Ducat, KM#575. Struck from 1 Thaler dies, KM#575.

Date	Mintage	VG	F	VF	XF	Unc
1722 Rare	—	—	—	—	—	—

KM# 582 10 DUCAT
35.0000 g., 0.9860 Gold 1.1095 oz. AGW **Note:** Struck from 1/2 Thaler dies, KM#577.

Date	Mintage	VG	F	VF	XF	Unc
1729 Rare	—	—	—	—	—	—

FR# 223 10 DUCAT
Gold, 41 mm. **Obv:** Laureate bust of Charles VI right **Obv. Legend:** CAROLVI • D • G • R • ... **Rev:** Crowned arms in order chain on breast of crowned double-headed eagle **Rev. Legend:** ARCHID : AUST : D : BUR :....

Date	Mintage	VG	F	VF	XF	Unc
1740 Rare	—	—	—	—	—	—

KM# A597 10 DUCAT
35.0000 g., 0.9860 Gold 1.1095 oz. AGW **Obv:** Laureate bust of Charles VI right **Obv. Legend:** CAROLVI • D • G • R • ... **Rev:** Crowned arms on breast of crowned double-headed eagle **Rev. Legend:** ARCHID : AUST : D : BUR : ... **Note:** Struck from 1 Thaler dies, KM#591.

Date	Mintage	VG	F	VF	XF	Unc
1740	—	4,000	7,500	12,500	20,000	—

KM# 597 10 DUCAT
35.0000 g., 0.9860 Gold 1.1095 oz. AGW **Subject:** Maria Theresa **Note:** Struck from 1 Thaler dies, KM#591.

Date	Mintage	VG	F	VF	XF	Unc
1740 Rare	—	—	—	—	—	—

KM# 602 10 DUCAT
35.0000 g., 0.9860 Gold 1.1095 oz. AGW **Obv:** Mature bust of Maria Theresa right **Note:** Struck from 1 Thaler dies, KM#600.

Date	Mintage	VG	F	VF	XF	Unc
1742 Rare	—	—	—	—	—	—

KM# 602A 10 DUCAT
35.0000 g., 0.9860 Gold 1.1095 oz. AGW **Note:** Struck from 1 Thaler dies, KM#603.

Date	Mintage	VG	F	VF	XF	Unc
1743 Rare	—	—	—	—	—	—

KM# 614 10 DUCAT
35.0000 g., 0.9860 Gold 1.1095 oz. AGW **Obv:** Mature bust of Maria Theresa right **Note:** Struck from 1 Thaler dies, KM#612.

Date	Mintage	VG	F	VF	XF	Unc
1747 Rare	—	—	—	—	—	—
1750 Rare	—	—	—	—	—	—

KM# 633 10 DUCAT
35.0000 g., 0.9860 Gold 1.1095 oz. AGW **Obv:** Mature bust of Maria Theresa right **Note:** Struck from 1 Thaler dies, KM#628.

Date	Mintage	VG	F	VF	XF	Unc
1754 Rare	—	4,000	7,500	12,500	20,000	—
1757 Rare	—	4,000	7,500	12,500	20,000	—
1758 Rare	—	4,000	7,500	12,500	20,000	—
1759 Rare	—	4,000	7,500	12,500	20,000	—
1761 Rare	—	4,000	7,500	12,500	20,000	—

PATTERNS

Inlcuding off metal strikes

KM#	Date	Mintage	Identification	Mkt Val
Pn10	1705	—	Ducat. Copper.	125
Pn11	1707	—	Ducat. Silver. Malcontent	150
Pn12	1708	—	Poltura. Copper.	—
Pn13	1730	—	Poltura. Copper.	—

GROSSWARDEIN

The fortress of Grosswardein (Nagyvarad, Oradea in Romania) was a strategically important stronghold in Transylvania during the early 18th century.

Hapsburgs gained control over Hungary and Transylvania by the Treaty of Karlowitz on January 26, 1699. The local nobility began a revolt in 1703, aiming to free Transylvania from Austrian domination. Francis II Rakoczi was elected as Prince on July 6, 1704. This movement was joined by some cities and intitally enjoyed a broad base of support among the peasants. During this rebellion the fortress of Grosswardein was under control of Austrian commander Stefan von Becker. Between 1706-08, rebel forces of Rakoczi besieged the fortress. Short of food and without money, the Austrians melted all the copper objects of the inhabitants and issued an emergency coinage – *nummi obsidionales*.

FORTRESS

SIEGE COINAGE

KM# 1 POLTORA
Copper **Ruler:** Stefan von Becker **Obv:** Crowned I divides date **Rev. Legend:** IN/NECES:/SITATE/VARADI:/ENSI •

Date	Mintage	Good	VG	F	VF	XF
1706	—	—	295	350	475	775
1707	—	—	295	350	475	775
1708	—	—	295	350	475	775
1709	—	—	295	350	475	775

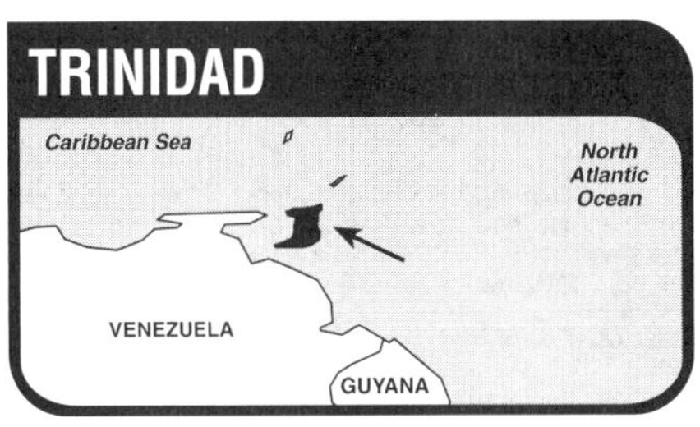

TRINIDAD

Trinidad was discovered by Columbus in 1498. It remained under Spanish rule from the time of its settlement in 1592 until its capture by the British in 1797. It was ceded to the British in 1802.

MONETARY SYSTEM
9 Bits or Shillings = 8 Reales

BRITISH COLONY

CUT & COUNTERMARKED COINAGE

KM# 9 SHILLING
Silver **Note:** Countermark: T on 1/8 or 1/9 cut of Spanish or Spanish Colonial 8 Reales; weight varies 3.00 - 3.31 grams. The attribution of this type has been questioned.

Date	Mintage	Good	VG	F	VF	XF
ND(1798-1801)	—	400	500	850	1,250	—

The Republic of Tunisia, located on the northern coast of Africa between Algeria and Libya, has an area of 63,170 sq. mi. (163,610 sq. km.) and a population of *7.9 million. Capital: Tunis. Agriculture is the backbone of the economy. Crude oil, phosphates, olive oil, and wine are exported.

Tunisia, settled by the Phoenicians in the 12th century B.C., was the center of the seafaring Carthaginian Empire. After the total destruction of Carthage, Tunisia became part of Rome's African province. It remained a part of the Roman Empire (except for the 439-533 interval of Vandal conquest) until taken by the Arabs, 648, who administered it until the Turkish invasion of 1570. Under Turkish control, the public revenue was heavily dependent upon the piracy of Mediterranean shipping, an endeavor that wasn't abandoned until 1819 when a coalition of powers threatened appropriate reprisal. Deprived of its major source of income, Tunisia underwent a financial regression that ended in bankruptcy, enabling France to establish a protectorate over the country in 1881. National agitation and guerrilla fighting forced France to grant Tunisia internal autonomy in 1955 and to recognize Tunisian independence on March 20, 1956. Tunisia abolished the monarchy and established a republic on July 25, 1957.

TUNIS

Tunis, the capital and major seaport of Tunisia, existed in the Carthaginian era, but its importance dates only from the Moslem conquest, following which it became a major center of Arab power and prosperity. Spain seized it in 1535, lost it in 1564, retook it in 1573 and ceded it to the Turks in 1574. Thereafter the history of Tunis merged with that of Tunisia.

RULER

Ottoman, until 1881

LOCAL RULERS

Husayn,AH1117-1147/1705-1735AD
'Ali, AH1147-1169/1735-1736AD
Muhammad Bey,
AH1169-1172/1756-1759AD
'Ali Bey II,
AH1172-1196/1759-1782AD
Hammuda Pasha II,
AH1196-1229/1782-1813AD

NOTE: All coins struck until AH1298/1881AD bear thename of the Ottoman Sultan.

MINT

تونس

Tunis

With exceptions noted in their proper place, all coins were struck at Tunis prior to AH1308/1891AD. Thereafter, all coins were struck at Paris with mint mark A until 1928, symbols of the mint from 1929-1957.

MONETARY SYSTEM

Until 1891

6 Burben (Bourbine) = 1 Burbe (Bourbe)
2 Burbe (Bourbe) = 1 Nasri
13 Burbe = 1 Kharub (Caroub)
16 Kharub (Caroub) = 1 Piastre (Rial Sebili)

Arabic name	French name	Value
Qafsi of Fals Raqiq	Bourbine	1/12 Nasri
Fals	Bourbe	6 Qafsi or 1/2 Nasri
Nasri	Asper	1-52 Riyal
Kharub	Caroub	1/16 Riyal
1/8 Riyal	1/8 Piastre	1 Kharub
1/4 Riyal	1/4 Piastre	4 Kharub
1/2 Riyal	1/2 Piastre	8 Kharub
Riyal	Piastre	16 Kharub

OTTOMAN EMPIRE

Mustafa II

AH1106-15/1695-1703AD

HAMMERED COINAGE

KM# 30 3 BURBEN

Copper **Note:** Weight varies: 2.44-2.79 grams.

Date	Mintage	Good	VG	F	VF	XF
ND	—	5.00	8.00	25.00	45.00	—
AH1112	—	12.00	18.00	35.00	60.00	—
AH1114	—	12.00	16.00	35.00	60.00	—
AH1115	—	12.00	20.00	35.00	60.00	—

Ahmed III

AH1115-43/1703-30AD

HAMMERED COINAGE

KM# 33 BURBE

3.5500 g., Copper

Date	Mintage	Good	VG	F	VF	XF
AH(1)116	—	20.00	30.00	45.00	65.00	—

KM# 34 NASRI (Dort Kose)

Silver **Note:** Square. Weight varies 0.62-0.70 grams.

Date	Mintage	VG	F	VF	XF	Unc
AH1115	—	15.00	30.00	45.00	65.00	—
AH1116	—	15.00	30.00	45.00	65.00	—
AH1117	—	15.00	30.00	45.00	65.00	—
AH(1)118	—	15.00	30.00	45.00	65.00	—
AH(11)19	—	15.00	30.00	45.00	65.00	—
AH(11)20	—	15.00	30.00	45.00	65.00	—
AH(11)21	—	15.00	30.00	45.00	65.00	—
AH(11)22	—	15.00	30.00	45.00	65.00	—
AH(11)23	—	15.00	30.00	45.00	65.00	—
AH(11)24	—	15.00	30.00	45.00	65.00	—
AH(11)25	—	15.00	30.00	45.00	65.00	—
AH(11)26	—	15.00	30.00	45.00	65.00	—
AH(11)27	—	15.00	30.00	45.00	65.00	—

KM# 35 1/4 PIASTRE

5.7000 g., Silver

Date	Mintage	VG	F	VF	XF	Unc
AH1138	—	60.00	100	150	250	—
AH1139	—	60.00	100	150	250	—
AH1140	—	60.00	100	150	250	—
AH1141	—	60.00	100	150	250	—
AH1142	—	60.00	100	150	250	—

KM# 38 1/2 SULTANI

1.7100 g., Gold

Date	Mintage	VG	F	VF	XF	Unc
AH1140	—	100	150	300	500	—
AH1141	—	100	150	300	500	—
AH1142	—	100	150	300	500	—
AH1143	—	100	150	300	500	—
AH1144	—	—	—	—	—	—

Note: Reported, not confirmed

KM# 39 SULTANI

3.1000 g., Gold

Date	Mintage	Good	VG	F	VF	XF
AH1117	—	125	225	500	750	—
AH1120	—	125	225	500	750	—
AH1121	—	125	225	500	750	—
AH1124	—	125	225	500	750	—
AH1137	—	125	225	500	500	—

Mahmud I

AH1143-68/1730-54AD

HAMMERED COINAGE

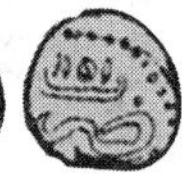

KM# 43 BURBEN

Copper **Note:** Date at top. Varieties exist.

Date	Mintage	Good	VG	F	VF	XF
AH1151	—	10.00	20.00	30.00	50.00	—
AH1163	—	10.00	20.00	30.00	50.00	—
AH1164	—	10.00	20.00	30.00	50.00	—
AH1167	—	—	—	—	—	—

Note: Reported, not confirmed.

KM# 40 BURBEN

1.2600 g., Copper, 14 mm. **Note:** Date at bottom.

Date	Mintage	Good	VG	F	VF	XF
AH1165	—	—	—	—	—	—

KM# 47 2 BURBEN

Copper **Obv:** Mintname **Rev:** Date **Note:** Weight varies: 1.54-1.68 grams. Size varies 20-21 mm.

Date	Mintage	Good	VG	F	VF	XF
AH1150	—	10.00	20.00	30.00	50.00	—
AH1157	—	10.00	20.00	30.00	50.00	—
AH1158	—	10.00	20.00	30.00	50.00	—

KM# 50 NASRI (Dort Kose)

0.4400 g., Billon **Note:** Square.

Date	Mintage	VG	F	VF	XF	Unc
AH1150	—	60.00	80.00	120	150	—
AH1151	—	60.00	80.00	120	150	—
AH1162	—	—	—	—	—	—

KM# A40 1/2 KHARUB

0.6900 g., Billon

KM# 46 KHARUB

1.3300 g., Billon **Rev:** Date at top **Note:** Size varies 13-14 mm.

Date	Mintage	VG	F	VF	XF	Unc
AH1151	—	3.50	10.00	15.00	30.00	—
AH1152	—	3.50	10.00	15.00	30.00	—
AH1153	—	3.50	10.00	15.00	30.00	—
AH1162	—	3.50	10.00	15.00	30.00	—
AH1163	—	3.50	10.00	15.00	30.00	—
AH1164	—	3.50	10.00	15.00	30.00	—
AH1165	—	3.50	10.00	15.00	30.00	—
AH1166	—	3.50	10.00	15.00	30.00	—
AH1167	—	3.50	10.00	15.00	30.00	—

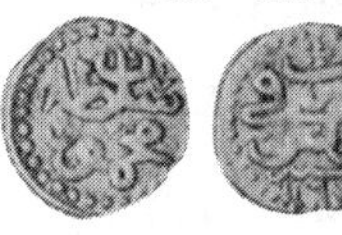

KM# 49 KHARUB

1.3300 g., Billon **Rev:** Date at bottom

Date	Mintage	VG	F	VF	XF	Unc
AH1167	—	4.50	12.00	18.00	40.00	—
AH1168/7	—	4.50	12.00	18.00	40.00	—

KM# 44.1 2 KHARUB

Billon **Rev:** "Duriba" in center **Note:** Weight varies: 2.30-2.90 grams.

Date	Mintage	VG	F	VF	XF	Unc
AH1150	—	10.00	20.00	40.00	60.00	—
AH1151	—	10.00	20.00	40.00	60.00	—
AH1152	—	10.00	20.00	40.00	60.00	—

KM# 44.2 2 KHARUB

Billon **Rev:** Without "Duriba" **Note:** Weight varies: 2.30-3.16 grams. Size varies 19-20 mm.

Date	Mintage	VG	F	VF	XF	Unc
AH1153	—	10.00	20.00	30.00	40.00	—
AH1154	—	10.00	20.00	30.00	40.00	—
AH1155	—	10.00	20.00	30.00	40.00	—
AH1156	—	10.00	20.00	30.00	40.00	—

KM# 42 1/4 PIASTRE

Billon **Note:** Weight varies: 4.29-5.87 grams.

Date	Mintage	VG	F	VF	XF	Unc
AH1147	—	8.00	15.00	35.00	50.00	—
AH1148	—	8.00	15.00	35.00	50.00	—
AH1149	—	8.00	15.00	35.00	50.00	—
AH1150	—	8.00	15.00	35.00	50.00	—
AH1151	—	8.00	15.00	35.00	50.00	—
AH1152	—	8.00	15.00	35.00	50.00	—
AH1153	—	8.00	15.00	35.00	50.00	—

KM# 41 1/2 SULTANI

Gold **Note:** 1.60-1.68 grams.

Date	Mintage	VG	F	VF	XF	Unc
AH1144	—	75.00	125	200	300	—

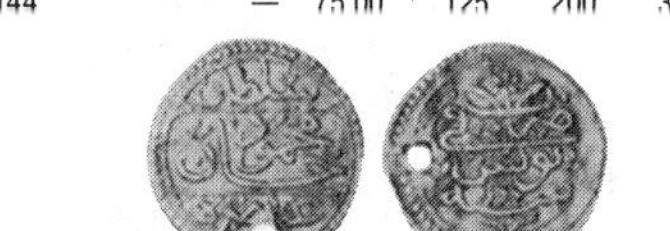

KM# 48 1/2 SULTANI

Gold **Obv:** Small legend **Rev:** Small legend

Date	Mintage	VG	F	VF	XF	Unc
AH1166	—	75.00	125	200	300	—

KM# 45 SULTANI

3.3400 g., Gold, 23 mm.

Date	Mintage	VG	F	VF	XF	Unc
AH1151	—	125	225	350	500	—
AH1155	—	125	225	350	500	—

Mustafa III

AH1171-87/1757-75AD

HAMMERED COINAGE

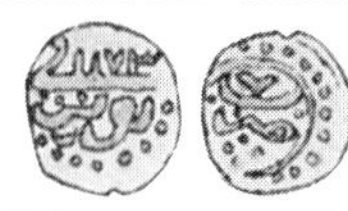

KM# 55 BURBEN

Copper **Note:** Weight varies: 0.57-1.09 grams. Size varies 11-14 mm.

Date	Mintage	Good	VG	F	VF	XF
AH1172	—	10.00	15.00	25.00	40.00	—
AH1173	—	10.00	15.00	25.00	40.00	—
AH1174	—	10.00	15.00	25.00	40.00	—
AH1175	—	10.00	15.00	25.00	40.00	—
AH1176	—	10.00	15.00	25.00	40.00	—
AH1177	—	10.00	15.00	25.00	40.00	—
AH1178	—	10.00	15.00	25.00	40.00	—

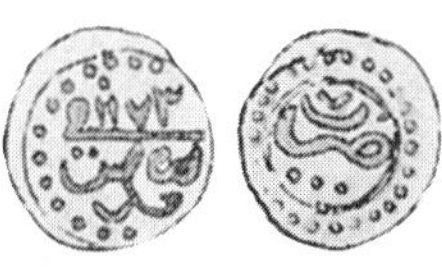

KM# 56 2 BURBEN

Copper **Note:** Weight varies 2.68-4.60 grams. Size varies 18-22 mm.

Date	Mintage	Good	VG	F	VF	XF
AH1172	—	—	—	—	—	—
AH1173	—	3.00	6.00	12.00	25.00	—
AH1174	—	3.00	6.00	12.00	25.00	—
AH1175	—	3.00	6.00	12.00	25.00	—
AH1176	—	3.00	6.00	12.00	25.00	—
AH1177	—	3.00	6.00	12.00	25.00	—
AH1178	—	3.00	6.00	12.00	25.00	—
AH1179	—	3.00	6.00	12.00	25.00	—
AH1180	—	3.00	6.00	12.00	25.00	—
AH1181	—	3.00	6.00	12.00	25.00	—
AH1182	—	3.00	6.00	12.00	25.00	—

KM# 52.2 BURBE

Copper **Rev:** Date at bottom **Note:** Weight varies: 3.30-4.60 grams.

Date	Mintage	Good	VG	F	VF	XF
AH1171	—	3.00	6.00	9.00	18.00	—
AH1172	—	3.00	6.00	9.00	16.00	—
AH1173	—	2.50	5.00	7.50	12.00	—
AH1174	—	2.50	5.00	7.50	12.00	—
AH1175	—	2.50	5.00	7.50	12.00	—
AH1176	—	2.50	5.00	9.00	18.00	—
AH1177	—	2.50	5.00	9.00	18.00	—
AH1178	—	2.50	5.00	9.00	18.00	—
AH1179	—	3.00	6.00	12.00	22.00	—
AH1180	—	3.00	6.00	12.00	22.00	—
AH1181	—	3.00	6.00	12.00	22.00	—
AH1182	—	3.00	6.00	12.00	22.00	—
AH1183	—	3.00	6.00	12.00	22.00	—
AH1184	—	3.00	6.00	12.00	22.00	—
AH1185	—	3.00	6.00	12.00	22.00	—
AH1186	—	3.00	6.00	9.00	18.00	—
AH1187	—	3.00	6.00	9.00	18.00	—

KM# 52.1 BURBE

Copper **Rev:** Date at top **Note:** Weight varies: 3.30-4.60 grams. Size varies 19-22 mm.

Date	Mintage	Good	VG	F	VF	XF
AH1171	—	3.00	6.00	12.00	25.00	—
AH1172	—	3.00	6.00	12.00	25.00	—
AH1173	—	3.00	6.00	12.00	25.00	—
AH1174	—	3.00	6.00	12.00	25.00	—
AH1175	—	3.00	6.00	12.00	25.00	—
AH1178	—	3.00	6.00	12.00	25.00	—
AH1186	—	3.00	6.00	12.00	25.00	—
AH1187	—	3.00	6.00	12.00	25.00	—
AH1188	—	3.00	6.00	12.00	25.00	—

KM# 53 KHARUB

Billon **Note:** Weight vareis: 0.82-1.30 grams.

Date	Mintage	Good	VG	F	VF	XF
AH1171	—	12.00	18.00	25.00	35.00	—
AH1172	—	12.00	18.00	25.00	35.00	—
AH1173	—	12.00	18.00	25.00	35.00	—
AH1174	—	12.00	18.00	25.00	35.00	—
AH1175	—	12.00	18.00	25.00	35.00	—
AH1176	—	12.00	18.00	25.00	35.00	—

Date	Mintage	Good	VG	F	VF	XF
AH1177	—	12.00	18.00	25.00	35.00	—
AH1178	—	12.00	18.00	25.00	35.00	—

KM# 59 8 KHARUB

7.6000 g., Billon, 28 mm. **Note:** Similar to 1 Piastre, KM#57.

Date	Mintage	Good	VG	F	VF	XF
AH1187	—	40.00	50.00	90.00	200	—
AH1188	—	60.00	80.00	140	300	—

KM# 57 PIASTRE

Billon **Note:** Weight varies 14.37-15.09 grams. Size varies 33-36 mm.

Date	Mintage	Good	VG	F	VF	XF
AH1180	—	25.00	40.00	80.00	100	—
AH1181	—	25.00	40.00	80.00	100	—
AH1182	—	20.00	35.00	80.00	160	—
AH1183	—	20.00	35.00	80.00	160	—
AH1184	—	20.00	35.00	80.00	160	—
AH1185	—	20.00	35.00	80.00	100	—
AH1186	—	10.00	20.00	50.00	100	—
AH1187	—	20.00	35.00	80.00	160	—
AH1188	—	25.00	40.00	100	180	—

KM# 58 1/2 SULTANI

Gold **Note:** Weight varies 1.15-1.30 grams.

Date	Mintage	VG	F	VF	XF	Unc
AH1185	—	75.00	125	185	285	—
AH1186	—	75.00	125	185	285	—
AH1187	—	75.00	125	185	285	—

KM# 54.1 SULTANI

3.0000 g., Gold

Date	Mintage	VG	F	VF	XF	Unc
AH1171	—	125	200	335	550	—

KM# 54.2 SULTANI

2.6000 g., Gold **Note:** Size varies 19-20 mm.

Date	Mintage	VG	F	VF	XF	Unc
AH1181	—	125	185	275	450	—
AH1182	—	125	185	275	450	—
AH1183	—	125	185	275	450	—
AH1184	—	125	185	275	450	—
AH1185	—	125	185	275	450	—
AH1186	—	125	185	275	450	—

Abdul Hamid I

AH1187-1203/1774-89AD

HAMMERED COINAGE

KM# 62 BURBEN

Copper **Obv:** Legend in three lines **Rev:** Date at top **Note:** Size varies 8-10 mm. Weight varies: 0.432-0.575 grams.

Date	Mintage	Good	VG	F	VF	XF
AH1188	—	8.00	12.00	20.00	40.00	—
AH1189	—	4.50	8.50	17.50	35.00	—
AH1190	—	4.50	8.50	17.50	35.00	—
AH1191	—	4.50	8.50	17.50	35.00	—
AH1192	—	4.50	8.50	17.50	35.00	—
AH1195	—	4.50	8.50	17.50	35.00	—
AH1196	—	4.50	8.50	17.50	35.00	—
AH1197	—	4.50	8.50	17.50	35.00	—
AH1198	—	4.50	8.50	17.50	35.00	—

KM# 69 2 BURBEN

Copper

Date	Mintage	Good	VG	F	VF	XF
AH1195	—	—	—	—	—	—
Note: Reported, not confirmed						
AH1196	—	—	—	—	—	—
Note: Reported, not confirmed						
AH1197	—	—	—	—	—	—
Note: Reported, not confirmed						
AH1198	—	—	—	—	—	—
Note: Reported, not confirmed						

KM# 63 BURBE

Copper **Note:** Weight varies: 3.04-3.84 grams. Size varies 18-21 mm.

Date	Mintage	Good	VG	F	VF	XF
AH1188	—	3.50	6.50	12.50	25.00	—
AH1189	—	3.50	6.50	12.50	25.00	—
AH1190	—	3.50	6.50	12.50	25.00	—
AH1191	—	3.50	6.50	12.50	25.00	—
AH1192	—	3.50	6.50	12.50	25.00	—
AH1193	—	3.50	6.50	12.50	25.00	—
AH1194	—	3.50	6.50	12.50	25.00	—
AH1195	—	3.50	6.50	12.50	25.00	—
AH1196	—	3.50	6.50	12.50	25.00	—
AH1197	—	3.50	6.50	12.50	25.00	—
AH1198	—	3.50	6.50	12.50	25.00	—

KM# 68 2 KHARUB

Billon

Date	Mintage	Good	VG	F	VF	XF
AH1191	—	—	—	—	—	—
Note: Reported, not confirmed						
AH1192	—	—	—	—	—	—
Note: Reported, not confirmed						
AH1201	—	—	—	—	—	—
Note: Reported, not confirmed						

KM# 67 4 KHARUB

Billon

Date	Mintage	Good	VG	F	VF	XF
AH1191	—	—	—	—	—	—
Note: Reported, not confirmed						
AH1195	—	—	—	—	—	—
Note: Reported, not confirmed						
AH1199	—	—	—	—	—	—
Note: Reported, not confirmed						
AH1201	—	—	—	—	—	—
Note: Reported, not confirmed						

KM# 64 8 KHARUB

Billon **Rev:** Date at bottom **Note:** 6.20-8.00 grams. Size varies 28-29 mm.

Date	Mintage	Good	VG	F	VF	XF
AH1188	—	20.00	40.00	100	150	—
AH1189	—	20.00	40.00	100	150	—
AH1191	—	15.00	30.00	75.00	125	—
AH1192	—	15.00	30.00	75.00	125	—
AH1193	—	15.00	30.00	75.00	125	—
AH1194	—	15.00	30.00	75.00	125	—
AH1195	—	20.00	40.00	100	150	—
AH1196	—	15.00	30.00	75.00	125	—
AH1197	—	15.00	30.00	75.00	125	—
AH1198	—	15.00	30.00	75.00	125	—
AH1199	—	20.00	40.00	100	150	—
AH1201	—	20.00	40.00	100	150	—
AH1202	—	20.00	40.00	100	150	—

KM# 65 PIASTRE

Billon **Note:** Weight varies 14.90-15.28 grams. Size varies 34-35 mm.

Date	Mintage	Good	VG	F	VF	XF
AH1188	—	20.00	40.00	80.00	150	—
AH1189	—	20.00	40.00	80.00	150	—
AH1191	—	15.00	30.00	60.00	125	—

Date	Mintage	Good	VG	F	VF	XF
AH1192	—	15.00	30.00	60.00	125	—
AH1194	—	12.00	25.00	50.00	100	—
AH1195	—	20.00	40.00	80.00	150	—
AH1196	—	12.00	25.00	50.00	100	—
AH1197	—	12.00	25.00	50.00	100	—
AH1198	—	12.00	25.00	50.00	100	—
AH1199	—	12.00	25.00	50.00	100	—
AH1200	—	15.00	30.00	60.00	125	—
AH1201	—	15.00	30.00	60.00	125	—
AH1202	—	15.00	30.00	60.00	125	—
AH1206	—	18.00	30.00	50.00	95.00	—
AH1207	—	18.00	30.00	50.00	95.00	—
AH1208	—	18.00	30.00	50.00	95.00	—
AH1209	—	18.00	30.00	50.00	95.00	—
AH1210	—	18.00	30.00	50.00	95.00	—
AH1211	—	18.00	30.00	50.00	95.00	—
AH1212	—	18.00	30.00	50.00	95.00	—
AH1213	—	20.00	35.00	55.00	100	—
AH1214	—	18.00	30.00	50.00	95.00	—
AH1215	—	18.00	30.00	50.00	95.00	—
AH1216	—	18.00	40.00	80.00	120	—
AH1217	—	18.00	40.00	80.00	120	—
AH1218	—	18.00	40.00	80.00	120	—
AH1219	—	18.00	40.00	80.00	120	—
AH1220	—	18.00	40.00	80.00	120	—
AH1221	—	18.00	40.00	80.00	120	—
AH1222	—	18.00	40.00	80.00	120	—

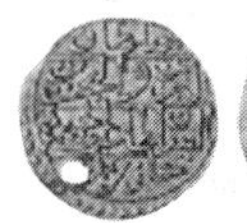

KM# 66 1/2 SULTANI
1.2800 g., Gold

Date	Mintage	VG	F	VF	XF	Unc
AH1188	—	100	125	200	345	—
AH1189	—	100	125	200	345	—

Selim III
AH1203-22/1789-1807AD
HAMMERED COINAGE

KM# 74 4 KHARUB
4.0000 g., Billon

Date	Mintage	Good	VG	F	VF	XF
AH1215	—	50.00	100	150	250	—
AH1216	—	50.00	100	150	250	—
AH1217	—	50.00	100	150	250	—

KM# 73 8 KHARUB
Billon **Note:** Varieties of ornamentation exist. 7.10-7.70 grams. Similar to 1 Piastre, KM#72. Size varies 27-28 mm.

Date	Mintage	Good	VG	F	VF	XF
AH1206	—	12.00	24.00	32.00	60.00	—
AH1207	—	12.00	24.00	32.00	60.00	—
AH1208	—	12.00	24.00	32.00	60.00	—
AH1209	—	12.00	24.00	32.00	60.00	—
AH1210	—	12.00	24.00	32.00	60.00	—
AH1212	—	12.00	24.00	32.00	60.00	—
AH1213	—	12.00	24.00	32.00	60.00	—
AH1214	—	12.00	24.00	32.00	60.00	—
AH1215	—	12.00	24.00	32.00	60.00	—
AH1216	—	15.00	25.00	60.00	110	—
AH1217	—	15.00	25.00	60.00	110	—
AH1218	—	15.00	25.00	60.00	110	—
AH1219	—	15.00	25.00	60.00	110	—
AH1220	—	15.00	25.00	60.00	110	—
AH1221	—	15.00	25.00	60.00	110	—
AH1222	—	15.00	25.00	60.00	110	—

KM# 72.1 PIASTRE
Billon **Rev.** Mint above date within circle **Note:** 14.90-16.00 grams.

Date	Mintage	Good	VG	F	VF	XF
AH1203	—	35.00	60.00	100	150	—

KM# 72.2 PIASTRE
Billon **Obv:** Legend within circle **Rev:** Mint above date within ornamental frame **Note:** Varieties of ornamentation exist. 14.90-16.00 grams.

TURKEY

The Republic of Turkey, a parliamentary democracy of the Near East located partially in Europe and partially in Asia between the Black and the Mediterranean Seas, has an area of 301,382 sq. mi. (780,580 sq. km.) and a population of *55.4 million. Capital: Ankara. Turkey exports cotton, hazelnuts, and tobacco, and enjoys a virtual monopoly in meerschaum.

The Ottoman Turks, a tribe from Central Asia, first appeared in the early 13th century, and by the 17th century had established the Ottoman Empire which stretched from the Persian Gulf to the southern frontier of Poland, and from the Caspian Sea to the Algerian plateau. The defeat of the Turkish navy by the Holy League in 1571, and of the Turkish forces besieging Vienna in 1683, began the steady decline of the Ottoman Empire which, accelerated by the rise of nationalism, contracted its European border, and by the end of World War I deprived it of its Arab lands. The present Turkish boundaries were largely fixed by the Treaty of Lausanne in 1923. The sultanate and caliphate, the political and spiritual ruling institutions of the old empire, were separated and the sultanate abolished in 1922. On Oct. 29, 1923, Turkey formally became a republic.

RULERS

Mustafa II, AH1106-1115/1695-1703AD
Ahmed III, AH1115-1143/1703-1730AD

The reign of Ahmed III falls into the so-called "Tulip Era" of the Ottoman Empire. It is so significant that most of his coinage bears the tulip design right of the Toughra or somewhere on the coin.

Mahmud I, AH1143-1168/1730-1754AD
Osman III, AH1168-1171/1754-1757AD
Mustafa III, AH1171-1187/1757-1774AD

Toughra Types

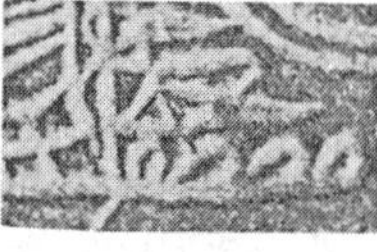

First Second

First toughra inscribed: *Mustafa Khan b. Ahmad al-Muzaffar Daima.*

Second toughra inscribed: *Mustafa b. Ahmad al-Muzaffar Daima.*

Abdul Hamid I, AH1187-1203/1774-1789AD

Toughra Types

First Second

First Toughra inscribed: *Abdul Hamid Han bin Ahmad al-Muzaffer Da'ima.*

Second Toughra inscribed: *Han Abdul Hamid bin Ahmad al-Muzaffer Da'ima.*

Selim III, AH1203-1222/1789-1807AD

Toughra Types

First Second

First Toughra Series

Heavy coinage based on a Piastre weighing approximately 19.20 g with first toughra.

First Toughra inscribed: *Han Sellim bin Mustafa al-Muzaffer Dai'ma.*

Second Toughra Series

Heavy coinage based on a Piastre weighing approximately 19.20 g with second toughra.

Second Toughra inscribed: *Selim Han bin Mustafa al-Muzaffer Dai'ma.*

MINT NAMES

Bitlis
(Bidlis)

قسطنطنية

Constantinople
(Qustantiniyah)

تبريز

Tabriz

MONETARY EQUIVALENTS

3 Akche = 1 Para
5 Para = Beshlik (Beshparalik)
10 Para = Onluk
20 Para = Yirmilik
30 Para = Zolota
40 Para = Kurush (Piastre)
1-1/2 Kurush (Piastres) = Altmishlik

MONETARY SYSTEM

Silver Coinage

40 Para = 1 Kurush (Piastre)
2 Kurush (Piastres) = 1 Ikilik
2-1/2 Kurush (Piastres) = Yuzluk
3 Kurush (Piastres) = Uechlik
5 Kurush (Piastres) = Beshlik
6 Kurush (Piastres) = Altilik

Gold Coinage

100 Kurush (Piastres) = 1 Turkish Pound (Lira)

NOTE: This system has remained essentially unchanged since its introduction by Ahmad III in 1688, except that the Asper and Para have long since ceased to be coined. The Piastre, established as a crown-sized silver coin approximately equal to the French Ecu of Louis XIV, has shrunk to a tiny copper coin, worth about 1/15 of a U.S. cent. Since the establishment of the Republic in 1923, the Turkish terms, Kurus and Lira, have replaced the European names Piastres and Turkish Pounds.

INITIAL LETTERS

Letters, symbols and numerals were placed on coins during the reigns of Mustafa II (1695) until Selim III(1789). They have been observed in various positions but the most common position being over *bin* in the third row of the obverse.

INITIAL LETTERS, NUMERALS				
Alif ا i	ba ب ii	ha ح iii	(?) h ح iv	dal د v
ra ر vi	sin س viii	sad ص viii	(?) sm صم ix	ta ط x
da ظ xi	'ain ع xii	'ain ع xiii	kaf ق xiv	mim م xv
nun ن xvi	nun w/o dot ں xvii	ha ه xviii	(?) ra ر xix	aha اح xx
asin اس xxi	ba با xxii	bkr بكر xxiii	ha حا xxiv	raa را xxv
ragib راغب xxvi	sma سما xxvii	(?) ds صد xxviii	'aa عا xxix	gha غا xxx
'ab عب xxxi	'abd عبد xxxii	'ad عد xxxiii	'an عن xxxiv	md مد xxxv
mr مر xxxvi	mk مط xxxvii	mdm مصر xxxviii	(?) mm مل xxxix	ha ده xl
ta يا xli	4-a ١٣٤ xlii	md6 ٦مد xliii	6mo ٦مد xliv	6mdm ٦مصر lxv

OTTOMAN EMPIRE

Ahmed III

AH1115-43/1703-30AD

HAMMERED COINAGE

KM# 134 MANGIR

Copper, 21.5 mm.

Date	Mintage	VG	F	VF	XF	Unc
AH1115	—	—	—	—	—	—

KM# 133 MANGIR

1.3000 g., Copper

Date	Mintage	Good	VG	F	VF	XF
AH1116	—	45.00	90.00	150	200	—
AH1124	—	45.00	90.00	150	200	—
AH1125	—	45.00	90.00	150	200	—
AH1128	—	45.00	90.00	150	200	—
AH1134	—	45.00	90.00	150	200	—

KM# 133.1 MANGIR

Copper **Obv:** Titles of Ahmad III **Rev:** Mint and date **Note:** Weight varies 2.93-7.75 grams.

Date	Mintage	Good	VG	F	VF	XF
AH1116	—	45.00	90.00	150	200	—
AH1124	—	45.00	90.00	150	200	—
AH1128	—	45.00	90.00	150	200	—
AH1133	—	45.00	90.00	150	200	—
AH1134	—	45.00	90.00	150	200	—
AH1138	—	45.00	90.00	150	200	—

KM# 133.3 MANGIR

Copper **Obv:** Toughra of Ahmad III **Rev:** Mint and date **Note:** Weight varies 6-7 grams.

Date	Mintage	Good	VG	F	VF	XF
AH1123	—	45.00	90.00	150	200	—

KM# 133.2 MANGIR

Copper **Obv:** Titles of Ahmad III and date **Rev:** Mint name **Note:** Weight varies 5-6.4 grams.

Date	Mintage	Good	VG	F	VF	XF
AH1125	—	45.00	90.00	150	200	—

KM# 142 KAZBEG (Kazbaki)

Copper **Obv:** Toughra, mint and date below **Rev:** 4-line inscription

Date	Mintage	VG	F	VF	XF	Unc
AH1115	—	—	—	—	—	—

KM# 143 BAKIR

Copper **Obv:** Titles of Ahmed III in ornamented rhombus **Rev:** Date divided by large ornament, mint below **Note:** Weight varies 3.5-7.6 grams.

Date	Mintage	VG	F	VF	XF	Unc
AH1143	—	—	—	—	—	—

KM# 136 AKCE

Silver **Note:** Weight varies 0.13-0.18 grams.

Date	Mintage	VG	F	VF	XF	Unc
AH1115 VII	—	15.00	35.00	70.00	—	—

KM# 135 AKCE

Silver **Note:** Weight varies 0.18-0.25 grams.

Date	Mintage	VG	F	VF	XF	Unc
AH1115 II	—	15.00	35.00	70.00	—	—
AH1115 IV	—	15.00	35.00	70.00	—	—
AH1115 V	—	15.00	35.00	70.00	—	—
AH1115 VI	—	15.00	35.00	70.00	—	—
AH1115 XXV	—	15.00	35.00	70.00	—	—

KM# 139.2 PARA

Silver **Note:** 'VIII' in toughra.

Date	Mintage	VG	F	VF	XF	Unc
1115 VIII	—	6.00	15.00	30.00	—	—

KM# 140 PARA

Silver **Note:** Weight varies 0.28-0.30 grams.

Date	Mintage	VG	F	VF	XF	Unc
AH1115 VI	—	35.00	60.00	100	—	—

KM# 141 PARA

Silver **Note:** Weight varies 0.40-0.43 grams.

Date	Mintage	VG	F	VF	XF	Unc
AH1115 V	—	6.00	15.00	30.00	—	—
AH1115 XIII	—	6.00	15.00	30.00	—	—
AH1115 XIV	—	6.00	15.00	30.00	—	—
AH1115 XV	—	6.00	15.00	30.00	—	—
AH1115 XIX	—	6.00	15.00	30.00	—	—

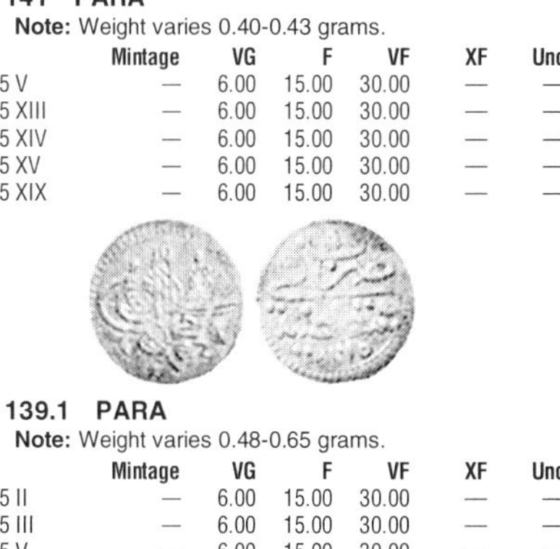

KM# 139.1 PARA

Silver **Note:** Weight varies 0.48-0.65 grams.

Date	Mintage	VG	F	VF	XF	Unc
AH1115 II	—	6.00	15.00	30.00	—	—
AH1115 III	—	6.00	15.00	30.00	—	—
AH1115 V	—	6.00	15.00	30.00	—	—
AH1115 VI	—	6.00	15.00	30.00	—	—
AH1115 VII	—	6.00	15.00	30.00	—	—
AH1115 XIV	—	6.00	15.00	30.00	—	—
AH1115 XXXVI	—	6.00	15.00	30.00	—	—

KM# 144 BESHLIK
Silver **Note:** Weight varies 3.27-3.48 grams.

Date	Mintage	VG	F	VF	XF	Unc
AH1115 III	—	20.00	30.00	50.00	100	—
AH1115 VIII	—	20.00	30.00	50.00	100	—
AH1115 XXXV	—	20.00	30.00	50.00	100	—

KM# 147 ONLUK
Silver **Note:** Weight varies 5.75-6.50 grams.

Date	Mintage	VG	F	VF	XF	Unc
AH1115 III	—	15.00	25.00	40.00	75.00	—
AH1115 VII	—	15.00	25.00	40.00	75.00	—
AH1115 VII	—	15.00	25.00	40.00	75.00	—
AH1115 XIX	—	15.00	25.00	40.00	75.00	—
AH1115 XXXV	—	15.00	25.00	40.00	75.00	—
AH1115 III//XXXVI	—	15.00	25.00	40.00	75.00	—
AH1115 XXXVI//III	—	15.00	25.00	40.00	75.00	—
AH1115 XIV//VI	—	15.00	25.00	40.00	75.00	—

KM# 160 KURUS
25.6500 g., Silver

Date	Mintage	VG	F	VF	XF	Unc
AH1115 XIX	—	15.00	30.00	60.00	120	—

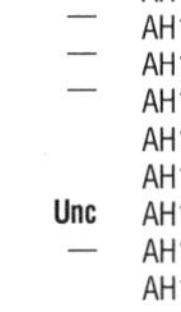
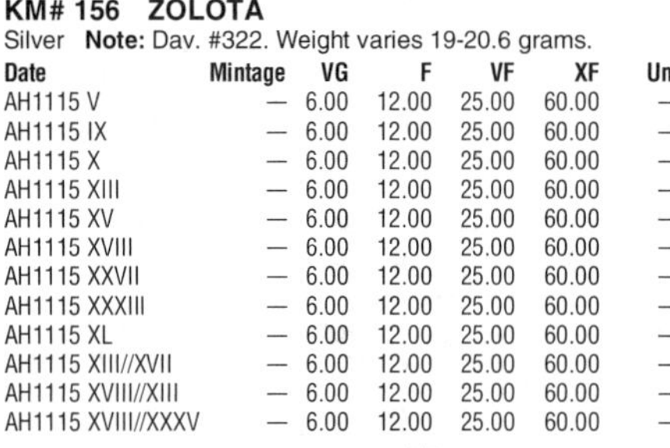

KM# 159 KURUS
Silver **Note:** Dav. #321. Weight varies 25.5-26.5 grams.

Date	Mintage	VG	F	VF	XF	Unc
AH1115 III	—	15.00	30.00	60.00	120	—
AH1115 VII	—	15.00	30.00	60.00	120	—
AH1115 XXXV	—	15.00	30.00	60.00	120	—

KM# 150 1/2 ZOLOTA
Silver **Note:** Weight varies 9.5-10.1 grams.

Date	Mintage	VG	F	VF	XF	Unc
AH1115 IX	—	10.00	20.00	40.00	70.00	—
AH1115 X	—	10.00	20.00	40.00	70.00	—
AH1115 XIII	—	10.00	20.00	40.00	70.00	—
AH1115 XXXIII	—	10.00	20.00	40.00	70.00	—
AH1115 XVIII//XIII	—	10.00	20.00	40.00	70.00	—

KM# 153 YIRMILIK
Silver **Note:** Weight varies 12.3-13.6 grams.

Date	Mintage	VG	F	VF	XF	Unc
AH1115 III	—	8.00	15.00	40.00	60.00	—
AH1115 XXXV	—	8.00	15.00	40.00	60.00	—
AH1115 XXXVI//III	—	8.00	15.00	40.00	60.00	—
AH1115 III//XXXVI	—	8.00	15.00	40.00	60.00	—

KM# 156 ZOLOTA
Silver **Note:** Dav. #322. Weight varies 19-20.6 grams.

Date	Mintage	VG	F	VF	XF	Unc
AH1115 V	—	6.00	12.00	25.00	60.00	—
AH1115 IX	—	6.00	12.00	25.00	60.00	—
AH1115 X	—	6.00	12.00	25.00	60.00	—
AH1115 XIII	—	6.00	12.00	25.00	60.00	—
AH1115 XV	—	6.00	12.00	25.00	60.00	—
AH1115 XVIII	—	6.00	12.00	25.00	60.00	—
AH1115 XXVII	—	6.00	12.00	25.00	60.00	—
AH1115 XXXIII	—	6.00	12.00	25.00	60.00	—
AH1115 XL	—	6.00	12.00	25.00	60.00	—
AH1115 XIII//XVII	—	6.00	12.00	25.00	60.00	—
AH1115 XVIII//XIII	—	6.00	12.00	25.00	60.00	—
AH1115 XVIII//XXXV	—	6.00	12.00	25.00	60.00	—

KM# 162 1/2 ZERI ISTANBUL (Yarim)
1.7500 g., Gold

Date	Mintage	VG	F	VF	XF	Unc
AH1115 XXXV	—	50.00	75.00	150	250	—
AH1115 XXXVI	—	50.00	75.00	150	250	—

KM# 173 ZERI ISTANBUL
Gold **Note:** Weight varies 3.4-3.5 grams.

Date	Mintage	VG	F	VF	XF	Unc
AH1115 III	—	55.00	75.00	150	200	—
AH1115 VIII	—	55.00	75.00	150	200	—
AH1115 XIV	—	55.00	75.00	150	200	—
AH1115 XVI	—	55.00	75.00	150	200	—
AH1115 XIX	—	55.00	75.00	150	200	—
AH1115 XXXV	—	55.00	75.00	150	200	—

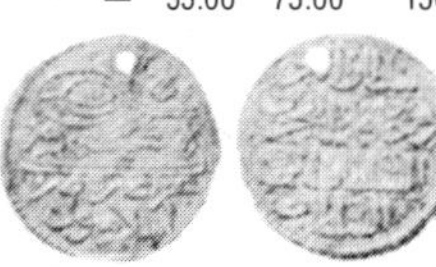

KM# 163 1/2 ZERI MAHBUB
1.2500 g., Gold

Date	Mintage	VG	F	VF	XF	Unc
AH1115 VII	—	50.00	90.00	150	250	—
AH1115 VIII	—	50.00	90.00	150	250	—

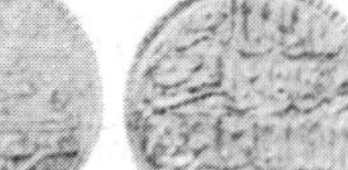

KM# 166 ZERI MAHBUB
2.6000 g., Gold

Date	Mintage	VG	F	VF	XF	Unc
AH1115 XXXV	—	60.00	100	180	280	—

KM# 169 ESHREFI ALTIN
Gold, 32 mm. **Note:** Weight varies 3.4-3.5 grams.

Date	Mintage	VG	F	VF	XF	Unc
AH1115 XVIII	—	60.00	100	200	300	—

KM# 170 ESHREFI ALTIN
3.4500 g., Gold **Note:** Weight varies 3.4-3.5 grams. Size varies 21-25mm.

Date	Mintage	VG	F	VF	XF	Unc
AH1115 VII	—	60.00	100	200	300	—
AH1115 IX	—	60.00	100	200	300	—
AH1115 XIII	—	60.00	100	200	300	—
AH1115 IV/XXVI	—	60.00	100	200	300	—

KM# 176 CHIFTE ESHREFI ALTIN
6.6000 g., Gold

Date	Mintage	VG	F	VF	XF	Unc
AH1115 XIII Rare	—	—	—	—	—	—
AH1115 XVIII/XIII Rare	—	—	—	—	—	—

KM# 179 DORT LUK ESHREFI ALTIN
13.7500 g., Gold

Date	Mintage	VG	F	VF	XF	Unc
AH1115 XL Rare	—	—	—	—	—	—

KM# 182 BESHLIK ESHREFI ALTIN
16.9000 g., Gold

Date	Mintage	VG	F	VF	XF	Unc
AH1115 XVIII	—	300	600	1,250	1,650	—
AH1115 XI	—	300	600	1,250	1,650	—
AH1115 II/XIX	—	300	600	1,250	1,650	—

KM# 185 ONLUK ESHREFI ALTIN

34.4000 g., Gold

Date	Mintage	VG	F	VF	XF	Unc
AH1115	—	2,500	5,000	8,500	11,000	—

Mahmud I

AH1143-68/1730-54AD

HAMMERED COINAGE

KM# A190 MANGIR

Copper **Obv:** Toughra of Mahmud I **Rev:** Mint and date **Note:** Weight varies 5.5-6.5 grams.

Date	Mintage	Good	VG	F	VF	XF
AH1143	—	—	—	—	—	—

KM# B190 MANGIR

Copper **Obv:** Titles of Mahmud I **Rev:** Mint and date **Note:** Weight varies 3.37-5.38 grams. Some specimens have "Mahmud" countermark on reverse.

Date	Mintage	Good	VG	F	VF	XF
AH1150	—	—	—	—	—	—
AH1163	—	—	—	—	—	—

KM# C190 MANGIR

Copper **Obv:** Titles of Mahmud I in decahedron **Rev:** Mint and date **Note:** Weight varies 6.5-7.17 grams. Struck at Bitlis Mint.

Date	Mintage	Good	VG	F	VF	XF
AH1154	—	—	—	—	—	—

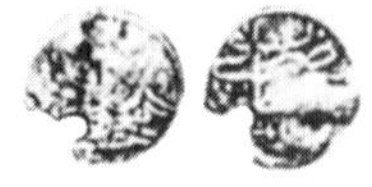

KM# 190 AKCE

Silver **Note:** Weight varies 0.17-0.25 grams.

Date	Mintage	VG	F	VF	XF	Unc
AH1143 III	—	15.00	25.00	40.00	75.00	—
AH1143 XII	—	15.00	25.00	40.00	75.00	—
AH1143 XIV	—	15.00	25.00	40.00	75.00	—
AH1143 XVI	—	15.00	25.00	40.00	75.00	—
AH1143 XXV	—	15.00	25.00	40.00	75.00	—
AH1143 XXIX	—	15.00	25.00	40.00	75.00	—
AH1143 XXXI	—	15.00	25.00	40.00	75.00	—

KM# 193 PARA

Silver **Note:** Varieties of ornamentation and toughra exist. Weight varies 0.4-0.64 grams.

Date	Mintage	VG	F	VF	XF	Unc
AH1143 XIV	—	4.50	7.50	10.00	15.00	—
AH1143 XXIX	—	4.50	7.50	10.00	15.00	—
AH1143 XXX	—	4.50	7.50	10.00	15.00	—
AH1143 XXXI	—	4.50	7.50	10.00	15.00	—

KM# 194 PARA

Silver **Note:** Weight varies 0.4-0.61 grams. Varieties of ornamentation and toughra exist.

Date	Mintage	VG	F	VF	XF	Unc
AH1143 VIII	—	4.50	7.50	10.00	15.00	—
AH1143 XII	—	4.50	7.50	10.00	15.00	—
AH1143 XV	—	4.50	7.50	10.00	15.00	—
AH1143 XVI	—	4.50	7.50	10.00	15.00	—

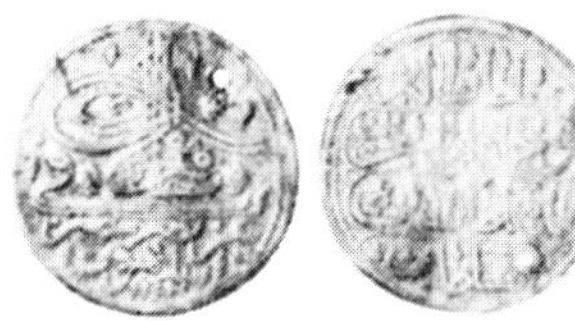

KM# 199 BESHLIK

Silver **Note:** Weight varies 2.63-3.33 grams.

Date	Mintage	VG	F	VF	XF	Unc
AH1143 XII	—	20.00	30.00	50.00	100	—

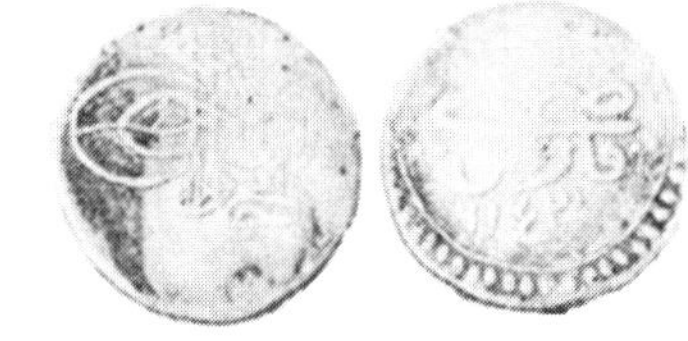

KM# 197 BESHLIK

Silver **Note:** Weight varies 2.26-2.91 grams.

Date	Mintage	VG	F	VF	XF	Unc
AH1143 VIII	—	12.50	17.50	35.00	60.00	—
AH1143 XII	—	12.50	17.50	35.00	60.00	—
AH1143 XIII	—	12.50	17.50	35.00	60.00	—
AH1143 XIV	—	12.50	17.50	35.00	60.00	—
AH1143 XV	—	12.50	17.50	35.00	60.00	—
AH1143 XXIX	—	12.50	17.50	35.00	60.00	—
AH1143 XXXI	—	12.50	17.50	35.00	60.00	—

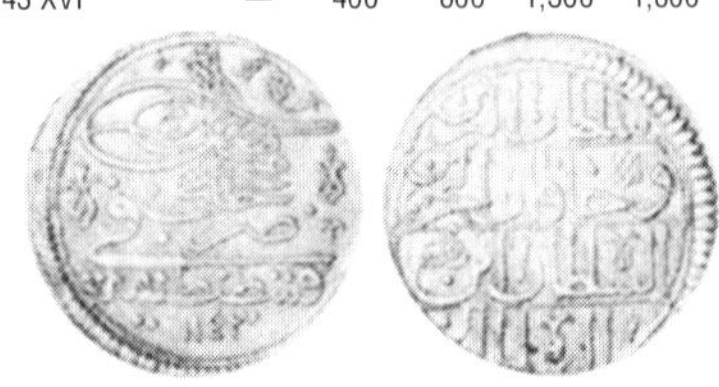

KM# 203 ONLUK

5.1500 g., Silver

Date	Mintage	VG	F	VF	XF	Unc
AH1143	—	250	500	900	1,500	—

KM# 204 ONLUK

Silver **Note:** Weight varies 4.76-5.84 grams.

Date	Mintage	VG	F	VF	XF	Unc
AH1143 X Rare	—	—	—	—	—	—
AH1143 XVI	—	400	800	1,300	1,800	—

KM# 202 ONLUK

Silver **Note:** Weight varies 5.64-6.25 grams.

Date	Mintage	VG	F	VF	XF	Unc
AH1143 III	—	8.00	15.00	30.00	60.00	—
AH1143 XIV	—	8.00	15.00	30.00	60.00	—
AH1143 XV	—	8.00	15.00	30.00	60.00	—
AH1143 XIX	—	8.00	15.00	30.00	60.00	—
AH1143 XXIX	—	8.00	15.00	30.00	60.00	—
AH1143 XXXI	—	8.00	15.00	30.00	60.00	—

KM# 212 KURUS

25.3500 g., Silver

Date	Mintage	VG	F	VF	XF	Unc
AH1143 X	—	200	350	600	1,000	—
AH1143 XII	—	200	350	600	1,000	—

KM# 211 KURUS

Silver **Obv:** Two spears and rosette right of toughra **Note:** Weight varies 23-24 grams. Dav. #323B.

Date	Mintage	VG	F	VF	XF	Unc
AH1143 XIV	—	12.00	20.00	40.00	60.00	—
AH1143 XXIX	—	12.00	20.00	40.00	60.00	—
AH1143 XXXI	—	12.00	20.00	40.00	60.00	—

KM# 210 KURUS

Silver **Note:** Weight varies 24.75-26.7 grams. Dav. #323A.

Date	Mintage	VG	F	VF	XF	Unc
AH1143 VIII	—	12.00	20.00	40.00	60.00	—
AH1143 XV	—	12.00	20.00	40.00	60.00	—

KM# 207 YIRMILIK

12.6000 g., Silver

Date	Mintage	VG	F	VF	XF	Unc
AH1143 VIII	—	125	250	500	1,000	—
AH1143 X	—	125	250	500	1,000	—
AH1143 XII	—	125	250	500	1,000	—
AH1143 XXIX	—	125	250	500	1,000	—

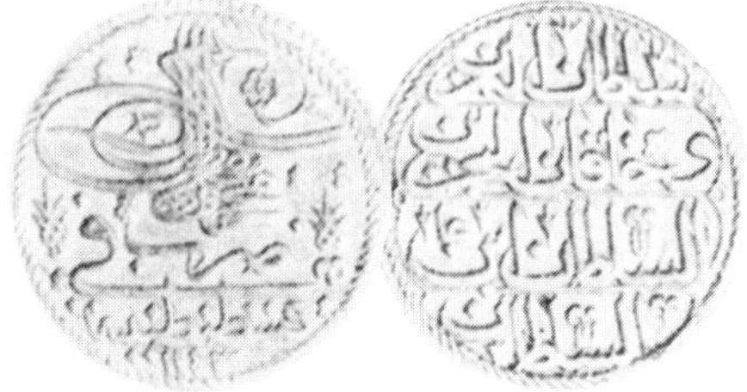

KM# 206 YIRMILIK

Silver **Note:** Weight varies 11.77-13.74 grams.

Date	Mintage	VG	F	VF	XF	Unc
AH1143 VIII	—	10.00	20.00	45.00	60.00	—
AH1143 XII	—	10.00	20.00	45.00	60.00	—
AH1143 XIV	—	10.00	20.00	45.00	60.00	—
AH1143 XV	—	10.00	20.00	45.00	60.00	—
AH1143 XXIX	—	10.00	20.00	45.00	60.00	—

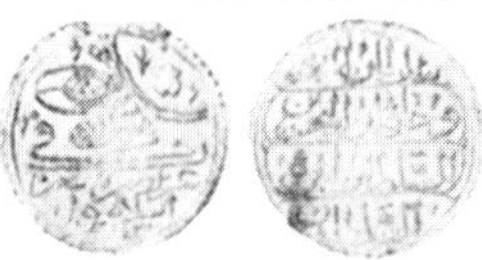

KM# 215 1/2 ZERI MAHBUB

1.3000 g., Gold

Date	Mintage	VG	F	VF	XF	Unc
AH1143 III	—	30.00	50.00	75.00	150	—
AH1143 XII	—	30.00	50.00	75.00	150	—
AH1143 XV	—	30.00	50.00	75.00	150	—

KM# 221 ZERI MAHBUB

2.5000 g., Gold **Note:** Varieties of toughra exist. Weight varies 2.5-2.6 grams.

Date	Mintage	VG	F	VF	XF	Unc
AH1143 XII	—	50.00	80.00	150	200	—

KM# 222 ZERI MAHBUB
2.6000 g., Gold **Note:** Weight varies 2.6-2.65 grams. Varieties of toughra and cartouche exist.

Date	Mintage	VG	F	VF	XF	Unc
AH1143 VIII	—	50.00	60.00	150	200	—
AH1143 XII	—	50.00	60.00	150	200	—
AH1143 XV	—	50.00	60.00	150	200	—

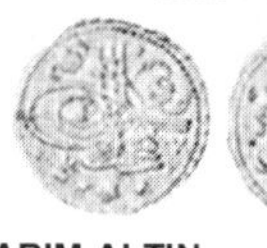

KM# 218 YARIM ALTIN
1.2000 g., Gold

Date	Mintage	VG	F	VF	XF	Unc
AH1143 VIII	—	30.00	50.00	100	200	—
AH1143 XV	—	30.00	50.00	100	200	—

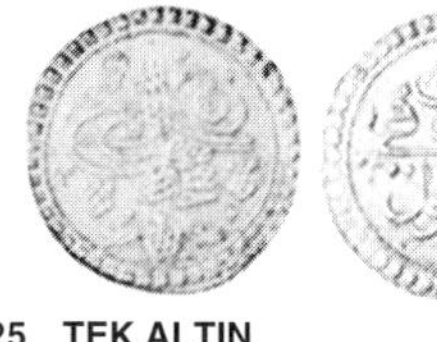

KM# 225 TEK ALTIN
3.5000 g., Gold

Date	Mintage	VG	F	VF	XF	Unc
AH1143 VIII	—	65.00	100	180	250	—

KM# 231 1-1/2 ALTINLIK (Birbucuk)
5.1500 g., Gold

Date	Mintage	VG	F	VF	XF	Unc
AH1143 VIII	—	100	150	300	450	—

KM# 228 1-1/2 ALTINLIK (Birbucuk)
5.0000 g., Gold

Date	Mintage	VG	F	VF	XF	Unc
AH1143 II	—	100	150	300	450	—
AH1143 XIII	—	100	150	300	450	—
AH1143 XV	—	100	150	300	450	—

KM# 229 1-1/2 ALTINLIK (Birbucuk)
5.0000 g., Gold

Date	Mintage	VG	F	VF	XF	Unc
AH1143 VIII	—	100	150	300	450	—
AH1143 XV	—	100	150	300	450	—

KM# 230 1-1/2 ALTINLIK (Birbucuk)
4.9000 g., Gold

Date	Mintage	VG	F	VF	XF	Unc
AH1143 XV	—	100	150	300	450	—
AH1143 XXXI	—	100	150	300	450	—

KM# 234 2 ALTINLIK (Iki)
6.8500 g., Gold

Date	Mintage	VG	F	VF	XF	Unc
AH1143 XV	—	325	475	800	1,100	—

KM# 235 2 ALTINLIK (Iki)
6.8000 g., Gold

Date	Mintage	VG	F	VF	XF	Unc
AH1143 XV	—	325	450	800	1,100	—

KM# 238 3 ALTINLIK (Uc)
10.1500 g., Gold

Date	Mintage	VG	F	VF	XF	Unc
AH1143 XXXI	—	500	700	1,100	1,600	—

KM# 239 3 ALTINLIK (Uc)
9.9500 g., Gold

Date	Mintage	VG	F	VF	XF	Unc
AH1143 XXXI	—	400	600	1,000	1,400	—

KM# 242 5 ALTINLIK (Bes)
17.4000 g., Gold

Date	Mintage	VG	F	VF	XF	Unc
AH1143 XIII	—	750	1,000	1,400	1,850	—

KM# 243 5 ALTINLIK (Bes)
17.0500 g., Gold

Date	Mintage	VG	F	VF	XF	Unc
AH1143 XIII	—	675	925	1,200	1,600	—
AH1143 XV	—	675	925	1,200	1,600	—

Osman III
AH1168-71/1754-57AD
HAMMERED COINAGE

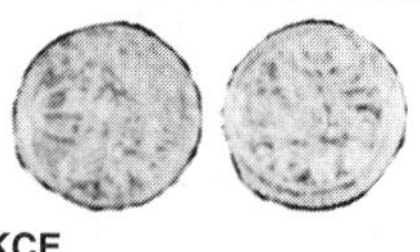

KM# 249 AKCE
Billon **Note:** Weight varies 0.15-0.24 grams.

Date	Mintage	Good	VG	F	VF	XF
AH1168 II	—	14.50	22.50	35.00	50.00	—
AH1168 III	—	14.50	22.50	35.00	50.00	—
AH1168 XXIII	—	14.50	22.50	35.00	50.00	—

KM# 252 PARA
0.5200 g., Billon **Note:** Weight varies 0.4-0.63 grams.

Date	Mintage	Good	VG	F	VF	XF
AH1168 III	—	12.50	18.50	25.00	35.00	—
AH1168 VIII	—	12.50	18.50	25.00	35.00	—
AH1168 XXII	—	12.50	18.50	25.00	35.00	—

KM# 255 5 PARA
2.4000 g., Billon **Note:** Weight varies 2.26-2.4 grams.

Date	Mintage	Good	VG	F	VF	XF
AH1168 II	—	90.00	125	190	440	—
AH1168 III	—	90.00	125	190	440	—
AH1168 XXII	—	90.00	125	190	440	—

KM# 258 10 PARA
5.7000 g., Billon **Note:** Weight varies 4.7-5.9 grams.

Date	Mintage	Good	VG	F	VF	XF
AH1168 II	—	15.50	25.00	45.00	95.00	—
AH1168 III	—	15.50	25.00	45.00	95.00	—
AH1168 VIII	—	15.50	25.00	45.00	95.00	—
AH1168 XXII	—	25.00	35.00	45.00	95.00	—

KM# 261 20 PARA
11.6000 g., Billon

Date	Mintage	Good	VG	F	VF	XF
AH1168 III Rare	—	—	—	—	—	—

KM# 264 PIASTRE
Billon **Note:** Similar to 20 Para, KM#261. Size varies 38-41mm. Dav. #325. Weight varies 23.5-24.5 grams.

Date	Mintage	Good	VG	F	VF	XF
AH1168 XXII Rare	—	—	—	—	—	—

KM# 265 PIASTRE
23.7000 g., Billon **Obv:** Large ornate flower right of toughra **Note:** Weight varies 23.5-24.5 grams.

Date	Mintage	Good	VG	F	VF	XF
AH1168 XIV Rare	—	—	—	—	—	—

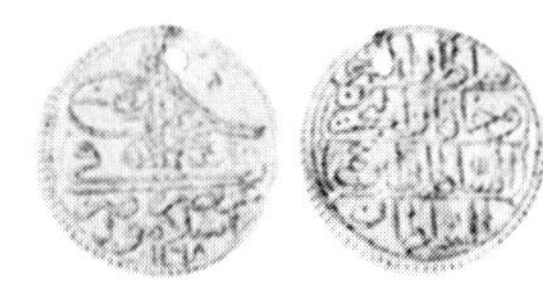

KM# 267 1/2 ZERI MAHBUB
1.3000 g., Gold

Date	Mintage	VG	F	VF	XF	Unc
AH1168 III	—	75.00	110	200	300	—
AH1168 XXIII	—	75.00	110	200	300	—

KM# 270 ZERI MAHBUB
2.6000 g., Gold

Date	Mintage	VG	F	VF	XF	Unc
AH1168 II	—	95.00	125	200	350	—
AH1168 III	—	95.00	125	200	350	—

KM# 274 1-1/2 ALTIN
5.2000 g., Gold

Date	Mintage	VG	F	VF	XF	Unc
AH1168 IV	—	275	420	800	1,100	—

KM# 275 1-1/2 ALTIN
5.2000 g., Gold, 38 mm.

Date	Mintage	VG	F	VF	XF	Unc
AH1168 IV	—	375	565	800	1,100	—

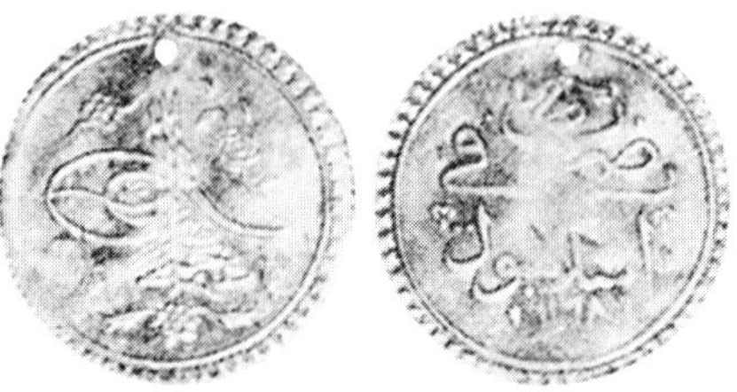

KM# 273 1-1/2 ALTIN
4.8500 g., Gold **Note:** Weight varies 4.8-4.95 grams.

Date	Mintage	VG	F	VF	XF	Unc
AH1168 IV	—	275	420	800	1,100	—

KM# 278 3 ALTIN
9.3000 g., Gold

Date	Mintage	VG	F	VF	XF	Unc
AH1168 IV	—	250	450	1,000	1,500	—

KM# 279 3 ALTIN
10.4000 g., Gold

Date	Mintage	VG	F	VF	XF	Unc
AH1168 IV	—	250	450	1,000	1,500	—

KM# 282 5 ALTIN
17.3000 g., Gold

Date	Mintage	VG	F	VF	XF	Unc
AH1168 IV	—	750	1,150	2,200	3,000	—

KM# 283 5 ALTIN
17.3000 g., Gold **Obv:** Different borders **Rev:** Different borders

Date	Mintage	VG	F	VF	XF	Unc
AH1168 IV	—	950	1,450	2,150	2,850	—

Mustafa III

AH1171-87/1757-74AD

HAMMERED COINAGE

KM# 289 ASPER
0.3400 g., Billon **Obv:** Toughra **Rev:** Mintname letter "SAD" left of date

Date	Mintage	Good	VG	F	VF	XF
AH1171	—	75.00	125	200	300	—

KM# 291.1 ASPER
0.1500 g., Billon

Date	Mintage	Good	VG	F	VF	XF
AH1171//1	—	7.50	12.50	16.00	25.00	—
AH1171//4	—	7.50	12.50	16.00	25.00	—
AH1171//6	—	7.50	12.50	16.00	25.00	—
AH1171//7	—	7.50	12.50	16.00	25.00	—
AH1171//8	—	7.50	12.50	16.00	25.00	—
AH1171//9	—	7.50	12.50	16.00	25.00	—

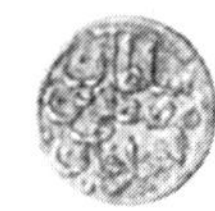
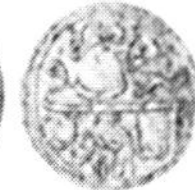

KM# 290.1 ASPER
0.3400 g., Billon

Date	Mintage	Good	VG	F	VF	XF
AH1171//7	—	10.00	15.00	25.00	40.00	—

KM# 291.2 ASPER
0.1500 g., Billon

Date	Mintage	Good	VG	F	VF	XF
AH1171//(11)80	—	7.50	12.50	16.00	25.00	—
AH1171//(11)81	—	7.50	12.50	16.00	25.00	—
AH1171//(11)82	—	7.50	12.50	16.00	25.00	—
AH1171//(11)83	—	7.50	12.50	16.00	25.00	—
AH1171//(11)84	—	7.50	12.50	16.00	25.00	—
AH1171//(11)86	—	7.50	12.50	16.00	25.00	—

KM# 290.2 ASPER
0.3400 g., Billon

Date	Mintage	Good	VG	F	VF	XF
AH1171//(11)80	—	10.00	15.00	25.00	40.00	—

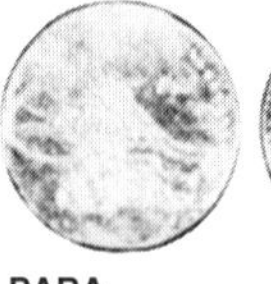

KM# 294 PARA
Billon **Rev:** Mintname, letter "SAD" left of date **Note:** Weight varies .30-.70 grams.

Date	Mintage	Good	VG	F	VF	XF
AH1171//1	—	40.00	60.00	100	150	—

KM# 295 PARA
Billon **Note:** Weight varies 0.33-0.52 grams.

Date	Mintage	Good	VG	F	VF	XF
AH1171//1	—	2.00	3.50	4.50	12.00	—
AH1171//2	—	2.00	3.50	4.50	10.00	—
AH1171//3	—	2.00	3.50	4.50	10.00	—
AH1171//4	—	2.00	3.50	4.50	10.00	—

KM# 296.1 PARA
Billon **Obv:** Without rosette right of toughra **Note:** Weight varies: 0.34-0.55 grams.

Date	Mintage	Good	VG	F	VF	XF
AH1171//5	—	2.00	3.00	4.50	10.00	—
AH1171//6	—	2.00	3.50	4.50	10.00	—
AH1171//7	—	2.00	3.00	4.50	10.00	—
AH1171//8	—	2.00	3.00	4.50	10.00	—
AH1171//9	—	2.00	3.00	4.50	10.00	—

KM# 296.2 PARA
Billon **Obv:** Without rosette right of toughra **Note:** Weight varies 0.34-0.55 grams.

Date	Mintage	Good	VG	F	VF	XF
AH1171//(11)80	—	2.00	3.00	4.50	10.00	—
AH1171//(11)81	—	2.00	3.00	4.50	10.00	—
AH1171//(11)82	—	2.00	3.00	4.50	10.00	—
AH1171//(11)83	—	2.00	3.00	4.50	10.00	—
AH1171//(11)84	—	2.00	3.00	4.50	10.00	—
AH1171//(11)85	—	2.00	3.50	4.50	10.00	—
AH1171//(11)86	—	2.00	3.50	4.50	10.00	—
AH1171//(11)87	—	2.00	3.50	4.50	10.00	—

KM# 298 5 PARA
2.6000 g., Billon, 20 mm.

Date	Mintage	VG	F	VF	XF	Unc
AH1171 VIII Rare	—	—	—	—	—	—

KM# 299 5 PARA
2.1500 g., Billon **Obv:** Rosette right of toughra

Date	Mintage	VG	F	VF	XF	Unc
AH1171//1	—	10.00	12.00	30.00	50.00	—
AH1171//2	—	10.00	12.00	30.00	50.00	—
AH1171//3	—	10.00	12.00	30.00	50.00	—
AH1171//4	—	10.00	12.00	30.00	50.00	—

KM# 300.1 5 PARA
Billon **Obv:** Without rosette right of toughra **Note:** Weight varies 1.8-2.2 grams.

Date	Mintage	VG	F	VF	XF	Unc
AH1171//5	—	10.00	12.00	20.00	35.00	—
AH1171//6	—	10.00	12.00	20.00	35.00	—
AH1171//7	—	10.00	12.00	20.00	35.00	—
AH1171//8	—	10.00	12.00	20.00	35.00	—
AH1171//9	—	10.00	12.00	20.00	35.00	—

KM# 300.2 5 PARA

Billon **Obv:** Without rosette right of toughra **Note:** Weight varies 1.8-2.2 grams

Date	Mintage	VG	F	VF	XF	Unc
AH1171//(11)80	—	10.00	12.00	20.00	35.00	—
AH1171//(11)81	—	10.00	12.00	20.00	35.00	—
AH1171//(11)82	—	10.00	12.00	20.00	35.00	—
AH1171//(11)83	—	10.00	12.00	20.00	35.00	—
AH1171//(11)84	—	10.00	12.00	20.00	35.00	—
AH1171//(11)85	—	10.00	12.00	20.00	35.00	—
AH1171//(11)86	—	10.00	12.00	20.00	35.00	—
AH1171//(11)87	—	10.00	12.00	20.00	35.00	—

KM# 304 10 PARA

Billon **Note:** Dotted border. Weight varies 5.3-5.6 grams.

Date	Mintage	VG	F	VF	XF	Unc
AH1171//1	—	150	250	400	600	—

KM# 305 10 PARA

4.4200 g., Billon **Obv:** Rosette right of toughra **Note:** Weight varies 3.9-5.7 grams.

Date	Mintage	VG	F	VF	XF	Unc
AH1171//1	—	6.00	9.00	20.00	50.00	—
AH1171//2	—	6.00	9.00	20.00	50.00	—
AH1171//3	—	6.00	9.00	20.00	50.00	—
AH1171//4	—	10.00	12.00	20.00	50.00	—

KM# 303 10 PARA

5.8700 g., Billon **Obv:** Letter "SAD" left of date; rope borders

Date	Mintage	VG	F	VF	XF	Unc
AH1171//1 (1757)	—	150	250	400	600	—

KM# 306.1 10 PARA

Billon **Obv:** Without rosette right of toughra **Note:** Weight varies 3.7-5.1 grams.

Date	Mintage	VG	F	VF	XF	Unc
AH1171//5	—	10.00	12.00	20.00	40.00	—
AH1171//6	—	10.00	12.00	20.00	40.00	—
AH1171//7	—	10.00	12.00	20.00	40.00	—
AH1171//8	—	10.00	12.00	20.00	40.00	—
AH1171//9	—	10.00	12.00	20.00	40.00	—

KM# 306.2 10 PARA

Billon **Obv:** Without rosette right of toughra **Note:** Weight varies: 3.7 - 5.1 grams.

Date	Mintage	VG	F	VF	XF	Unc
AH1171//(11)80	—	10.00	12.00	20.00	40.00	—
AH1171//(11)81	—	10.00	12.00	20.00	35.00	—
AH1171//(11)82	—	10.00	12.00	20.00	35.00	—
AH1171//(11)83	—	10.00	12.00	20.00	35.00	—
AH1171//(11)84	—	10.00	12.00	20.00	35.00	—
AH1171//(11)85	—	10.00	12.00	20.00	35.00	—
AH1171//(11)86	—	10.00	12.00	20.00	35.00	—
AH1187//(11)87	—	10.00	12.00	20.00	35.00	—

KM# 309 15 PARA (Yarim Zolota)

Billon **Note:** Weight varies 6.00-6.70 grams.

Date	Mintage	VG	F	VF	XF	Unc
AH1171//2	—	350	500	800	1,500	—

KM# 312 20 PARA

Billon **Obv:** Rosette right of toughra **Note:** Weight varies 9.05-9.55 grams.

Date	Mintage	VG	F	VF	XF	Unc
AH1171//3	—	25.00	50.00	100	200	—
AH1171//4	—	25.00	50.00	100	200	—

KM# 313.1 20 PARA

Billon **Obv:** Without rosette right of toughra **Note:** Weight varies: 8 - 9.5 grams.

Date	Mintage	VG	F	VF	XF	Unc
AH1171//5	—	25.00	50.00	100	200	—
AH1171//6	—	25.00	50.00	100	200	—
AH1171//7	—	25.00	50.00	100	200	—

KM# 313.2 20 PARA

Billon **Obv:** Without rosette right of toughra **Note:** Weight varies 8-9.5 grams.

Date	Mintage	VG	F	VF	XF	Unc
AH1171//(11)82	—	25.00	50.00	100	200	—
AH1171//(11)83	—	25.00	50.00	100	200	—
AH1171//(11)84	—	25.00	50.00	100	200	—
AH1171//(11)85	—	25.00	50.00	100	200	—
AH1171//(11)86	—	25.00	50.00	100	200	—
AH1171//(11)87	—	25.00	50.00	100	200	—

KM# 320 PIASTRE

Billon **Obv:** Rosette right of toughra **Note:** Dav. #328. Weight varies 18.4-19.9 grams.

Date	Mintage	VG	F	VF	XF	Unc
AH1171//1	—	15.00	20.00	40.00	75.00	—
AH1171//2	—	15.00	20.00	40.00	75.00	—
AH1171//3	—	8.00	15.00	30.00	45.00	—
AH1171//4	—	8.00	15.00	30.00	45.00	—

KM# 319 PIASTRE

Billon **Obv:** Toughra above mintname letter "SAD" left of date **Rev:** 4-line legend **Note:** Weight varies 18.00-19.70 grams.

Date	Mintage	VG	F	VF	XF	Unc
AH1171//1 Rare	—	—	—	—	—	—

KM# 321.1 PIASTRE

Billon **Obv:** Without rosette right of toughra **Note:** Dav. #327. Weight varies: 17.8 - 19.7 grams.

Date	Mintage	VG	F	VF	XF	Unc
AH1171//5	—	8.00	15.00	30.00	45.00	—
AH1171//6	—	8.00	15.00	30.00	45.00	—
AH1171//7	—	8.00	15.00	30.00	40.00	—
AH1171//8	—	8.00	15.00	30.00	40.00	—
AH1171//9	—	8.00	15.00	30.00	40.00	—

KM# 321.2 PIASTRE

Billon **Obv:** Without rosette right of toughra **Note:** Dav. #327. Weight varies 17.8-19.7 grams.

Date	Mintage	VG	F	VF	XF	Unc
AH1171//(11)80	—	8.00	15.00	30.00	40.00	—
AH1171//(11)81	—	8.00	15.00	30.00	40.00	—
AH1171//(11)82	—	8.00	15.00	30.00	40.00	—
AH1171//(11)83	—	8.00	15.00	30.00	40.00	—
AH1171//(11)84	—	8.00	15.00	30.00	40.00	—
AH1171//(11)85	—	8.00	15.00	30.00	40.00	—
AH1171//(11)86	—	8.00	15.00	30.00	40.00	—
AH1171//(11)87	—	8.00	15.00	30.00	40.00	—

KM# 316.1 ZOLOTA

Billon **Note:** Weight varies 13.5-14.70 grams. Dav. #329.

Date	Mintage	VG	F	VF	XF	Unc
AH1171//1	—	15.00	20.00	35.00	65.00	—
AH1171//2	—	15.00	20.00	35.00	65.00	—
AH1171//3	—	15.00	20.00	35.00	65.00	—
AH1171//4	—	15.00	20.00	35.00	65.00	—
AH1171//5	—	15.00	20.00	35.00	65.00	—
AH1171//6	—	15.00	20.00	35.00	65.00	—
AH1171//7	—	15.00	20.00	35.00	65.00	—
AH1171//8	—	15.00	20.00	35.00	65.00	—
AH1171//9	—	15.00	20.00	35.00	65.00	—

KM# 316.2 ZOLOTA

Billon **Note:** Dav. #329. Weight varies 13.5 - 14.70 grams.

Date	Mintage	VG	F	VF	XF	Unc
AH1171//(11)82	—	15.00	20.00	35.00	65.00	—
AH1171//(11)83	—	15.00	20.00	35.00	65.00	—
AH1171//(11)84	—	15.00	20.00	35.00	65.00	—
AH1171//(11)85	—	15.00	20.00	35.00	65.00	—
AH1171//(11)86	—	15.00	20.00	35.00	65.00	—
AH1171//(11)87	—	15.00	20.00	35.00	65.00	—

KM# 324.1 2 ZOLOTA

Billon **Note:** Weight varies 27.70-30.10 grams. Dav. #326.

Date	Mintage	VG	F	VF	XF	Unc
AH1171//1	—	10.00	15.00	30.00	50.00	—
AH1171//2	—	10.00	15.00	30.00	50.00	—
AH1171//3	—	10.00	15.00	30.00	50.00	—
AH1171//4	—	10.00	15.00	30.00	50.00	—
AH1171//5	—	10.00	15.00	30.00	50.00	—
AH1171//6	—	10.00	15.00	30.00	50.00	—
AH1171//7	—	10.00	15.00	30.00	50.00	—
AH1171//8	—	10.00	15.00	30.00	50.00	—
AH1171//9	—	10.00	15.00	30.00	50.00	—

KM# 324.2 2 ZOLOTA

Billon **Note:** Dav. #326. Weight varies: 27.70 - 30.10 grams.

Date	Mintage	VG	F	VF	XF	Unc
AH1171//(11)80	—	10.00	15.00	30.00	50.00	—
AH1171//(11)81	—	10.00	15.00	30.00	50.00	—
AH1171//(11)82	—	10.00	15.00	30.00	50.00	—

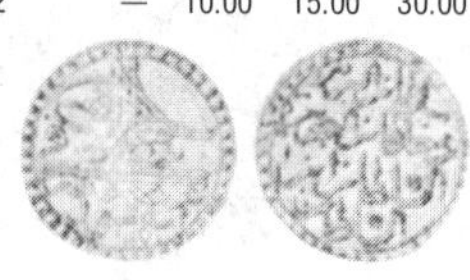

KM# 327 1/2 ZERI MAHBUB

1.3000 g., Gold

Date	Mintage	VG	F	VF	XF	Unc
AH1171//1	—	37.50	55.00	75.00	100	—
AH1171//2	—	37.50	55.00	75.00	100	—
AH1171//3	—	37.50	55.00	75.00	100	—
AH1171//4	—	37.50	55.00	75.00	100	—
AH1171//5	—	37.50	55.00	75.00	100	—
AH1171//6	—	37.50	55.00	75.00	100	—
AH1171//7	—	37.50	55.00	75.00	100	—
AH1171//8	—	45.00	65.00	100	125	—

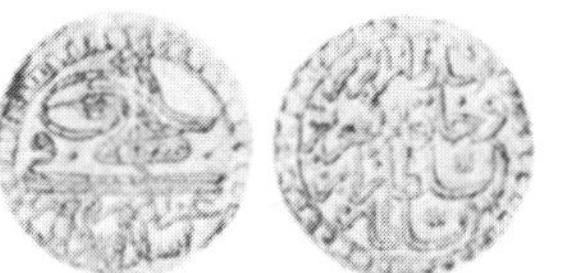

KM# 328 1/2 ZERI MAHBUB

1.3000 g., Gold

Date	Mintage	VG	F	VF	XF	Unc
AH1171//(11)80	—	37.50	55.00	75.00	100	—
AH1171//(11)81	—	37.50	55.00	75.00	100	—
AH1171//(11)82	—	37.50	55.00	75.00	100	—
AH1171//(11)83	—	37.50	55.00	75.00	100	—
AH1171//(11)84	—	37.50	55.00	75.00	100	—
AH1171//(11)85	—	37.50	55.00	75.00	100	—
AH1171//(11)86	—	37.50	55.00	75.00	100	—
AH1171//(11)87	—	37.50	55.00	75.00	100	—

KM# 334 ZERI MAHBUB
2.6000 g., Gold, 19.5 mm.

Date	Mintage	VG	F	VF	XF	Unc
AH1171//1	—	55.00	80.00	135	175	—
AH1171//2	—	45.00	60.00	100	150	—
AH1171//3	—	45.00	60.00	100	150	—
AH1171//4	—	45.00	60.00	100	150	—
AH1171//5	—	45.00	60.00	100	150	—
AH1171//6	—	45.00	60.00	100	150	—
AH1171//7	—	45.00	60.00	100	150	—
AH1171//8	—	55.00	75.00	140	200	—
AH1171//9	—	55.00	75.00	140	200	—

KM# 335 ZERI MAHBUB
19.5000 g., Gold, 21 mm. **Note:** Weight varies 2.5-2.63 grams.

Date	Mintage	VG	F	VF	XF	Unc
AH1171//(11)80	—	45.00	60.00	100	150	—
AH1171//(11)81	—	45.00	60.00	100	150	—
AH1171//(11)82	—	45.00	60.00	100	150	—
AH1171//(11)83	—	45.00	60.00	100	150	—
AH1171//(11)84	—	45.00	60.00	100	150	—
AH1171//(11)85	—	45.00	60.00	100	150	—
AH1171//(11)86	—	45.00	60.00	100	150	—
AH1171//(11)87	—	45.00	60.00	100	150	—

KM# 331 1/2 ALTIN
1.7500 g., Gold, 12 mm.

Date	Mintage	VG	F	VF	XF	Unc
AH1171//1	—	55.00	80.00	120	145	—
AH1171//2	—	55.00	80.00	120	145	—
AH1171//3	—	55.00	80.00	120	145	—
AH1171//4	—	55.00	80.00	120	145	—
AH1171//5	—	55.00	80.00	120	145	—
AH1171//7	—	—	—	—	—	—

KM# 332 1/2 ALTIN
1.7500 g., Gold, 14 mm.

Date	Mintage	VG	F	VF	XF	Unc
AH1171//(11)81	—	55.00	80.00	135	175	—

KM# 338 ALTIN
3.5000 g., Gold, 18.5 mm.

Date	Mintage	VG	F	VF	XF	Unc
AH1171//1	—	65.00	110	175	275	—
AH1171//2	—	65.00	110	150	225	—
AH1171//3	—	65.00	100	150	225	—
AH1171//4	—	65.00	100	150	225	—
AH1171//5	—	65.00	100	150	225	—
AH1171//6	—	65.00	100	150	225	—
AH1171//7	—	65.00	100	150	225	—

KM# 340 ALTIN
3.7000 g., Gold **Note:** Varieties exist.

Date	Mintage	VG	F	VF	XF	Unc
AH1171//1	—	325	475	600	1,000	—

KM# 339 ALTIN
3.5000 g., Gold, 20 mm.

Date	Mintage	VG	F	VF	XF	Unc
AH1171//(11)81	—	65.00	100	150	225	—

KM# 343.1 1-1/2 ALTIN
Gold **Note:** Weight varies 4.60-4.90 grams.

Date	Mintage	VG	F	VF	XF	Unc
AH1171//7	—	165	225	300	500	—
AH1171//8	—	165	225	300	500	—
AH1171//9	—	165	225	300	500	—

KM# 343.2 1-1/2 ALTIN
Gold **Note:** Weight varies: 4.60 - 4.90 grams.

Date	Mintage	VG	F	VF	XF	Unc
AH1171//(11)80	—	165	225	300	500	—
AH1171//(11)81	—	165	225	300	500	—

KM# 346 2 ALTIN
6.9000 g., Gold

Date	Mintage	VG	F	VF	XF	Unc
AH1171//2	—	225	300	500	700	—
AH1171//3	—	225	300	500	700	—
AH1171//4	—	225	300	500	700	—
AH1171//5	—	225	300	500	700	—
AH1171//6	—	225	300	500	700	—
AH1171//7	—	225	300	500	700	—
AH1171//8	—	225	300	500	700	—
AH1171//9	—	225	300	500	700	—

KM# 350 3 ALTIN
9.6000 g., Gold

Date	Mintage	VG	F	VF	XF	Unc
AH1171//1	—	—	—	—	—	—
AH1171//5	—	200	275	400	650	—
AH1171//9	—	200	275	400	650	—

KM# 349 3 ALTIN
10.4500 g., Gold

Date	Mintage	VG	F	VF	XF	Unc
AH1171//5	—	200	275	400	650	—

Abdul Hamid I
AH1187-1203/1774-89AD

HAMMERED COINAGE

KM# 356 AKCE
0.1100 g., Billon, 11 mm. **Note:** First toughra.

Date	Mintage	VG	F	VF	XF	Unc
AH1187//1	—	30.00	60.00	100	150	—

KM# 371 AKCE
Billon **Note:** Weight varies 0.13-0.19 grams. Second toughra.

Date	Mintage	VG	F	VF	XF	Unc
AH1187//1	—	10.00	17.50	25.00	35.00	—
AH1187//2	—	10.00	17.50	25.00	35.00	—
AH1187//3	—	10.00	17.50	25.00	35.00	—
AH1187//4	—	10.00	17.50	25.00	35.00	—
AH1187//5	—	10.00	17.50	25.00	35.00	—
AH1187//6	—	10.00	17.50	25.00	35.00	—
AH1187//7	—	10.00	17.50	25.00	35.00	—
AH1187//8	—	10.00	17.50	25.00	35.00	—

KM# 372 AKCE
0.1600 g., Billon **Obv:** Flower branch added right of Toughra **Note:** Weight varies 0.13-0.16 grams.

Date	Mintage	VG	F	VF	XF	Unc
AH1187//8	—	10.00	17.50	25.00	35.00	—
AH1187//9	—	10.00	17.50	25.00	35.00	—
AH1187//10	—	10.00	17.50	25.00	35.00	—
AH1187//11	—	10.00	17.50	25.00	35.00	—
AH1187//13	—	10.00	17.50	25.00	35.00	—
AH1187//14	—	10.00	17.50	25.00	35.00	—
AH1187//15	—	10.00	17.50	25.00	35.00	—
AH1187//16	—	—	—	—	—	—
Note: Reported, not confirmed						
AH1187//12	—	10.00	17.50	25.00	35.00	—

KM# 359 PARA
0.4300 g., Billon, 15 mm. **Note:** First toughra.

Date	Mintage	VG	F	VF	XF	Unc
AH1187//1	—	15.00	30.00	50.00	80.00	—

KM# 375 PARA
Billon **Obv:** Ornament right of Toughra **Note:** Weight varies 0.3-0.55 grams. Second toughra.

Date	Mintage	VG	F	VF	XF	Unc
AH1187//1	—	1.00	2.00	6.00	10.00	—
AH1187//2	—	1.00	2.00	6.00	10.00	—
AH1187//3	—	1.00	2.00	6.00	10.00	—
AH1187//4	—	1.00	2.00	6.00	10.00	—
AH1187//5	—	1.00	2.00	6.00	10.00	—
AH1187//6	—	1.00	2.00	6.00	10.00	—
AH1187//7	—	1.00	2.00	6.00	10.00	—
AH1187//8	—	1.00	2.00	6.00	10.00	—

KM# 376 PARA
Billon **Obv:** Flower branch right of Toughra **Note:** Weight varies 0.25-0.53 grams.

Date	Mintage	VG	F	VF	XF	Unc
AH1187//8	—	1.00	2.00	6.00	10.00	—
AH1187//9	—	1.00	2.00	6.00	10.00	—
AH1187//10	—	1.00	2.00	6.00	10.00	—
AH1187//11	—	1.00	2.00	6.00	10.00	—
AH1187//12	—	1.00	2.00	6.00	10.00	—
AH1187//13	—	1.00	2.00	6.00	10.00	—
AH1187//14	—	1.00	2.00	6.00	10.00	—
AH1187//15	—	1.00	2.00	6.00	10.00	—
AH1187//16	—	1.00	2.00	10.00	20.00	—

KM# 362 5 PARA
2.1300 g., Billon, 20 mm. **Note:** First toughra.

Date	Mintage	VG	F	VF	XF	Unc
AH1187//1	—	75.00	150	300	500	—

KM# 379 5 PARA
Billon **Note:** Weight varies 1.9-2.4 grams. Second toughra.

Date	Mintage	VG	F	VF	XF	Unc
AH1187//1	—	15.00	20.00	30.00	50.00	—
AH1187//2	—	10.00	15.00	25.00	50.00	—
AH1187//3	—	15.00	20.00	30.00	50.00	—
AH1187//4	—	15.00	20.00	30.00	50.00	—
AH1187//5	—	15.00	20.00	30.00	50.00	—
AH1187//6	—	15.00	20.00	30.00	50.00	—
AH1187//7	—	10.00	15.00	25.00	50.00	—
AH1187//8	—	—	—	—	—	—

KM# 380 5 PARA
Billon **Obv:** Flower branch right of Toughra **Note:** Weight varies 1.75-2.2 grams.

Date	Mintage	VG	F	VF	XF	Unc
AH1187//8	—	—	—	—	—	—
AH1187//9	—	10.00	15.00	25.00	50.00	—
AH1187//10	—	10.00	15.00	25.00	50.00	—
AH1187//11	—	10.00	15.00	25.00	50.00	—
AH1187//12	—	10.00	15.00	25.00	50.00	—
AH1187//13	—	10.00	15.00	25.00	50.00	—
AH1187//14	—	10.00	15.00	25.00	50.00	—
AH1187//15	—	10.00	15.00	25.00	50.00	—
AH1187//16	—	15.00	25.00	40.00	75.00	—

KM# 383 10 PARA
Billon **Note:** Weight varies 3.7-4.5 grams. Second toughra.

Date	Mintage	VG	F	VF	XF	Unc
AH1187//1	—	10.00	15.00	20.00	30.00	—
AH1187//2	—	5.50	8.50	15.00	25.00	—

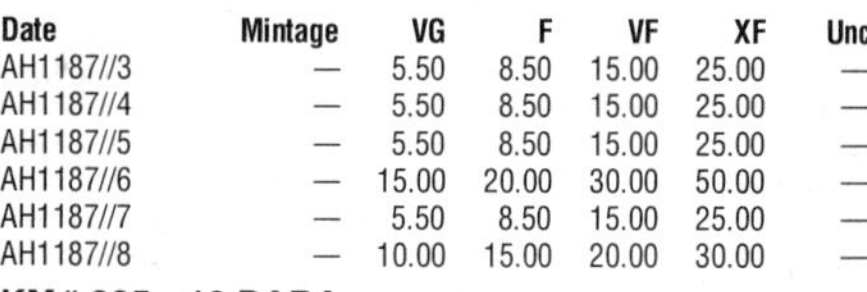

Date	Mintage	VG	F	VF	XF	Unc
AH1187//3	—	5.50	8.50	15.00	25.00	—
AH1187//4	—	5.50	8.50	15.00	25.00	—
AH1187//5	—	5.50	8.50	15.00	25.00	—
AH1187//6	—	15.00	20.00	30.00	50.00	—
AH1187//7	—	5.50	8.50	15.00	25.00	—
AH1187//8	—	10.00	15.00	20.00	30.00	—

KM# 365 10 PARA

4.6000 g., Billon **Note:** Weight varies 4.45-4.65 grams. First toughra.

Date	Mintage	VG	F	VF	XF	Unc
AH1187//1	—	50.00	100	200	350	—

KM# 384 10 PARA

Billon **Obv:** Flower branch added right of Toughra **Note:** Weight varies 4-4.8 grams.

Date	Mintage	VG	F	VF	XF	Unc
AH1187//8	—	5.50	8.50	15.00	25.00	—
AH1187//9	—	10.00	15.00	20.00	30.00	—
AH1187//10	—	10.00	15.00	20.00	30.00	—
AH1187//11	—	10.00	15.00	20.00	30.00	—
AH1187//12	—	10.00	15.00	20.00	30.00	—
AH1187//13	—	10.00	15.00	20.00	30.00	—
AH1187//14	—	10.00	15.00	20.00	30.00	—
AH1187//15	—	10.00	15.00	20.00	30.00	—
AH1187//16	—	15.00	20.00	30.00	45.00	—

KM# 366 20 PARA

9.1800 g., Billon **Note:** First toughra.

Date	Mintage	VG	F	VF	XF	Unc
AH1187//1 Rare	—	—	—	—	—	—

KM# 387 20 PARA

Billon **Note:** Weight varies 8.6-9.6 grams. Second toughra.

Date	Mintage	VG	F	VF	XF	Unc
AH1187//1	—	25.00	37.50	75.00	150	—
AH1187//2	—	25.00	37.50	75.00	150	—
AH1187//3	—	25.00	37.50	75.00	150	—
AH1187//4	—	25.00	37.50	75.00	150	—
AH1187//5	—	25.00	37.50	75.00	150	—
AH1187//6	—	25.00	37.50	75.00	150	—
AH1187//7	—	25.00	37.50	75.00	150	—
AH1187//8	—	—	—	—	—	—

Note: Reported, not confirmed

KM# 388 20 PARA

Billon **Obv:** Flower branch added right of Toughra **Note:** Weight varies 8.3-8.7 grams.

Date	Mintage	VG	F	VF	XF	Unc
AH1187//8	—	25.00	35.00	75.00	150	—
AH1187//9	—	25.00	35.00	75.00	150	—
AH1187//10	—	25.00	35.00	75.00	150	—
AH1187//11	—	25.00	35.00	75.00	150	—
AH1187//12	—	25.00	35.00	75.00	150	—
AH1187//13	—	25.00	35.00	75.00	150	—
AH1187//14	—	—	—	—	—	—

Note: Reported, not confirmed

Date	Mintage	VG	F	VF	XF	Unc
AH1187//15	—	25.00	35.00	75.00	150	—
AH1187//16	—	—	—	—	—	—

Note: Reported, not confirmed

KM# 396 PIASTRE

Billon **Note:** Weight varies 17.60-19.4 grams. Dav. #332.

Date	Mintage	VG	F	VF	XF	Unc
AH1187//1	—	8.00	10.00	25.00	40.00	—
AH1187//2	—	8.00	10.00	25.00	40.00	—
AH1187//3	—	8.00	10.00	25.00	40.00	—
AH1187//4	—	8.00	10.00	25.00	40.00	—
AH1187//5	—	8.00	10.00	25.00	40.00	—
AH1187//6	—	8.00	10.00	25.00	40.00	—
AH1187//7	—	8.00	10.00	40.00	50.00	—
AH1187//8	—	8.00	10.00	40.00	50.00	—

KM# 368 PIASTRE

Billon **Note:** Weight varies 18.5-19.8 grams. First toughra.

Date	Mintage	VG	F	VF	XF	Unc
AH1187//1	—	50.00	75.00	125	200	—

KM# 397 PIASTRE

Billon **Obv:** Toughra begins at lower right with "Abd" instead of "Lord" **Note:** Weight varies 18.6-19 grams. Second toughra.

Date	Mintage	VG	F	VF	XF	Unc
AH1187//1 Rare	—	—	—	—	—	—

KM# 406 2 PIASTRES

30.4000 g., Billon **Note:** Second toughra. Dav. #330.

Date	Mintage	VG	F	VF	XF	Unc
AH1187//16	—	40.00	70.00	125	200	—

KM# 391 ZOLOTA

Billon **Note:** Weight varies 13.10-14.60 grams. Second toughra. Dav. #333.

Date	Mintage	VG	F	VF	XF	Unc
AH1187//1	—	15.00	18.00	30.00	60.00	—
AH1187//2	—	15.00	18.00	30.00	60.00	—
AH1187//3	—	15.00	18.00	30.00	60.00	—

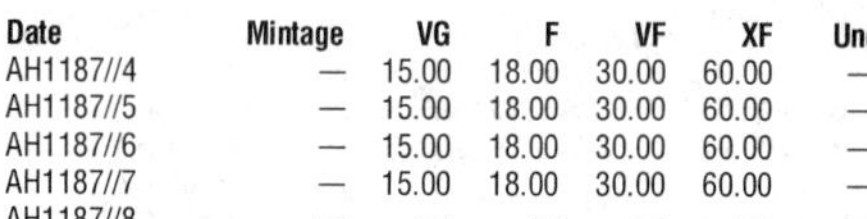

Date	Mintage	VG	F	VF	XF	Unc
AH1187//4	—	15.00	18.00	30.00	60.00	—
AH1187//5	—	15.00	18.00	30.00	60.00	—
AH1187//6	—	15.00	18.00	30.00	60.00	—
AH1187//7	—	15.00	18.00	30.00	60.00	—
AH1187//8	—	—	—	—	—	—

Note: Reported, not confirmed

KM# 398 ZOLOTA

Billon **Obv:** Flower branch added right of Toughra **Note:** Weight varies 17.3-18.4 grams.

Date	Mintage	VG	F	VF	XF	Unc
AH1187//8	—	8.00	10.00	25.00	40.00	—
AH1187//9	—	8.00	10.00	25.00	40.00	—
AH1187//10	—	8.00	10.00	40.00	50.00	—
AH1187//11	—	8.00	10.00	27.50	40.00	—
AH1187//12	—	8.00	10.00	40.00	50.00	—
AH1187//13	—	8.00	10.00	40.00	50.00	—
AH1187//14	—	8.00	10.00	27.50	40.00	—
AH1187//15	—	8.00	10.00	40.00	50.00	—
AH1187//16	—	8.00	10.00	40.00	50.00	—

KM# 392 ZOLOTA

Billon **Obv:** Large ornament above "Abd" of "Abdul Hamid"

Date	Mintage	VG	F	VF	XF	Unc
AH1187//8	—	15.00	18.00	30.00	60.00	—
AH1187//9	—	15.00	18.00	30.00	60.00	—
AH1187//10	—	15.00	18.00	30.00	60.00	—
AH1187//11	—	15.00	18.00	30.00	60.00	—

KM# 393 ZOLOTA

Billon **Obv:** Without large ornament above "Abd" of "Abdul Hamid" **Note:** Weight varies 12.8-13.8 grams.

Date	Mintage	VG	F	VF	XF	Unc
AH1187//11	—	—	—	—	—	—

Note: Reported, not confirmed

Date	Mintage	VG	F	VF	XF	Unc
AH1187//12	—	15.00	18.00	30.00	60.00	—
AH1187//13	—	15.00	18.00	30.00	60.00	—
AH1187//14	—	15.00	18.00	30.00	60.00	—
AH1187//15	—	15.00	18.00	30.00	60.00	—
AH1187//16	—	15.00	18.00	30.00	60.00	—

KM# 401 2 ZOLOTA

Billon **Note:** Weight varies 26.30-28.6 grams. Second toughra. Dav. #331.

Date	Mintage	VG	F	VF	XF	Unc
AH1187//3	—	10.00	15.00	27.50	40.00	—
AH1187//4	—	10.00	15.00	27.50	40.00	—
AH1187//5	—	10.00	15.00	27.50	40.00	—
AH1187//6	—	10.00	15.00	27.50	40.00	—
AH1187//7	—	10.00	15.00	27.50	40.00	—
AH1187//8	—	10.00	15.00	27.50	40.00	—

KM# 402 2 ZOLOTA

Billon **Obv:** Large ornament above "Abd" of "Abdul Hamid" **Note:** Weight varies 26-27.2 grams.

Date	Mintage	VG	F	VF	XF	Unc
AH1187//8	—	10.00	15.00	27.50	40.00	—
AH1187//9	—	10.00	15.00	27.50	40.00	—
AH1187//10	—	10.00	15.00	27.50	40.00	—
AH1187//11	—	10.00	15.00	35.00	55.00	—
AH1187//12	—	10.00	15.00	35.00	55.00	—

KM# 403 2 ZOLOTA

Billon **Obv:** Without large ornament above "Abd" of "Abdul Hamid' **Note:** Weight varies 26.1-26.9 grams.

Date	Mintage	VG	F	VF	XF	Unc
AH1187//11	—	10.00	15.00	27.50	40.00	—
AH1187//12	—	10.00	15.00	27.50	40.00	—
AH1187//13	—	10.00	15.00	27.50	40.00	—
AH1187//14	—	10.00	15.00	27.50	40.00	—
AH1187//15	—	10.00	15.00	27.50	40.00	—
AH1187//16	—	10.00	15.00	27.50	40.00	—

KM# 410 1/2 ZERI MAHBUB

1.3000 g., Gold **Note:** Weight varies 1.2-1.3 grams. Second toughra.

Date	Mintage	VG	F	VF	XF	Unc
AH1187//1	—	45.00	60.00	90.00	125	—
AH1187//2	—	45.00	60.00	90.00	125	—
AH1187//4	—	45.00	60.00	90.00	125	—
AH1187//5	—	45.00	60.00	90.00	125	—
AH1187//6	—	45.00	60.00	90.00	125	—
AH1187//10	—	45.00	60.00	90.00	125	—
AH1187//11	—	45.00	60.00	90.00	125	—
AH1187//14	—	45.00	60.00	90.00	125	—

KM# 416 ZERI MAHBUB

2.6000 g., Gold **Note:** Second toughra.

Date	Mintage	VG	F	VF	XF	Unc
AH1187//1	—	45.00	60.00	100	150	—
AH1187//2	—	45.00	60.00	100	150	—
AH1187//4	—	45.00	60.00	100	150	—
AH1187//5	—	45.00	60.00	100	150	—
AH1187//6	—	45.00	60.00	100	150	—
AH1187//8	—	45.00	60.00	100	150	—
AH1187//9	—	45.00	60.00	100	150	—
AH1187//10	—	45.00	60.00	100	150	—
AH1187//10 Proof	—	Value: 350				
AH1187//14	—	45.00	60.00	100	150	—
AH1187//15	—	45.00	60.00	100	150	—

KM# 407 1/4 ALTIN

0.8500 g., Gold **Note:** Second toughra.

Date	Mintage	VG	F	VF	XF	Unc
AH1187//1	—	30.00	40.00	60.00	80.00	—
AH1187//2	—	30.00	40.00	60.00	80.00	—
AH1187//4	—	30.00	40.00	60.00	80.00	—
AH1187//6	—	30.00	40.00	60.00	80.00	—
AH1187//7	—	30.00	40.00	60.00	80.00	—
AH1187//8	—	30.00	40.00	60.00	80.00	—
AH1187//9	—	35.00	55.00	75.00	100	—
AH1187//10	—	30.00	40.00	60.00	80.00	—
AH1187//11	—	30.00	40.00	60.00	80.00	—
AH1187//12	—	30.00	40.00	60.00	80.00	—
AH1187//14	—	30.00	40.00	60.00	80.00	—
AH1187//15	—	30.00	40.00	60.00	80.00	—
AH1187//16	—	30.00	40.00	60.00	80.00	—

KM# 413 1/2 ALTIN

1.7500 g., Gold **Note:** Second toughra.

Date	Mintage	VG	F	VF	XF	Unc
AH1187//3	—	50.00	75.00	110	165	—
AH1187//15	—	50.00	75.00	110	165	—

KM# 419 ALTIN

3.5000 g., Gold **Obv:** Within rope circle **Rev:** Within rope circle

Date	Mintage	VG	F	VF	XF	Unc
AH1187//3	—	100	125	200	300	—
AH1187//15	—	100	125	200	300	—

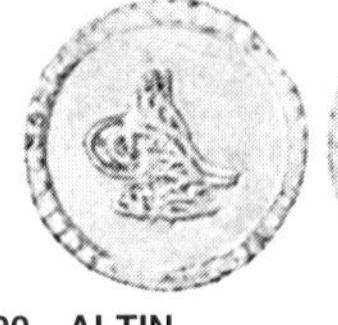 

KM# 420 ALTIN

3.5000 g., Gold **Obv:** Within dotted circle **Rev:** Within dotted circle **Note:** First toughra.

Date	Mintage	VG	F	VF	XF	Unc
AH1187//9	—	85.00	125	185	275	—
AH1187//15	—	85.00	125	185	275	—
AH1187//16	—	85.00	125	185	275	—

KM# 423 1-1/2 ALTIN

Gold **Obv:** Within plain borders **Rev:** Within plain borders **Note:** Weight varies 4.40-5.20 grams. Second toughra.

Date	Mintage	VG	F	VF	XF	Unc
AH1187//1	—	175	250	350	450	—

KM# 424 1-1/2 ALTIN

Gold **Obv:** Within plain borders **Rev:** Within plain borders **Note:** Weight varies 4.40-5.20 grams.

Date	Mintage	VG	F	VF	XF	Unc
AH1187//2	—	175	250	350	450	—
AH1187//3	—	175	250	350	450	—
AH1187//8	—	175	250	350	450	—
AH1187//10	—	175	250	350	450	—

KM# 425 1-1/2 ALTIN

Gold **Obv:** Flower right of Toughra; Within sheaf borders **Rev:** Within sheaf borders

Date	Mintage	VG	F	VF	XF	Unc
AH1187//8	—	175	250	350	450	—

KM# 426 1-1/2 ALTIN

Gold **Note:** Similar to KM#425 but without flower right of Toughra.

Date	Mintage	VG	F	VF	XF	Unc
AH1187//8	—	175	250	350	450	—

KM# 427 1-1/2 ALTIN

Gold **Obv:** Toughra within ornamental borders **Rev:** Inscription within ornamental borders **Note:** Years 5 & 7 have been reported for the above series.

Date	Mintage	VG	F	VF	XF	Unc
AH1187//11	—	—	—	—	—	—
AH1187//13	—	—	—	—	—	—
AH1187//15	—	200	285	400	600	—
AH1187//16	—	200	285	400	600	—

KM# 430 2-1/2 ALTIN

8.9000 g., Gold **Note:** Second toughra.

Date	Mintage	VG	F	VF	XF	Unc
AH1187//8	—	300	450	675	1,000	—
AH1187//9	—	300	450	675	1,000	—

KM# 434 3 ALTIN

10.4500 g., Gold **Obv:** Without flower right of Toughra

Date	Mintage	VG	F	VF	XF	Unc
AH1187//1	—	375	550	825	1,250	—

KM# 435 3 ALTIN

10.4000 g., Gold, 42 mm.

Date	Mintage	VG	F	VF	XF	Unc
AH1187//2	—	375	550	825	1,250	—

KM# 433 3 ALTIN

10.4500 g., Gold **Obv:** Flower right of toughra **Note:** Second toughra.

Date	Mintage	VG	F	VF	XF	Unc
AH1187//1	—	375	550	825	1,250	—

KM# 438 5 ALTIN
16.2500 g., Gold **Note:** Second toughra.

Date	Mintage	VG	F	VF	XF	Unc
AH1187//1	—	600	800	1,000	2,000	—

Selim III

AH1203-22/1789-1807AD

HAMMERED COINAGE

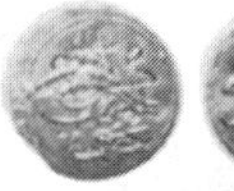

KM# 441 AKCE
0.1600 g., 0.4650 Silver 0.0024 oz. ASW, 11.5 mm. **Note:** First toughra.

Date	Mintage	VG	F	VF	XF	Unc
AH1203//1	—	30.00	80.00	150	300	—

KM# 483 AKCE
0.1000 g., 0.4650 Silver 0.0015 oz. ASW **Note:** Second toughra.

Date	Mintage	VG	F	VF	XF	Unc
AH1203//1	—	4.00	8.00	15.00	20.00	—
AH1203//2	—	4.00	8.00	15.00	20.00	—
AH1203//3	—	4.00	8.00	15.00	20.00	—
AH1203//4	—	4.00	8.00	15.00	20.00	—
AH1203//6	—	4.00	8.00	15.00	20.00	—
AH1203//8	—	4.00	8.00	15.00	20.00	—
AH1203//9	—	4.00	8.00	15.00	20.00	—
AH1203//11	—	4.00	8.00	15.00	20.00	—
AH1203//12	—	4.00	8.00	15.00	20.00	—
AH1203//13	—	4.00	8.00	15.00	20.00	—

KM# 444 PARA
0.4800 g., 0.4650 Silver 0.0072 oz. ASW, 15.5 mm. **Note:** First toughra.

Date	Mintage	VG	F	VF	XF	Unc
AH1203//1 Rare	—	—	—	—	—	—

KM# 462 PARA
0.4650 Silver, 15.5 mm. **Note:** Weight varies 0.23-0.33 grams. Second toughra.

Date	Mintage	VG	F	VF	XF	Unc
AH1203//1	—	15.00	30.00	50.00	75.00	—

KM# 447 5 PARA
2.3400 g., 0.4650 Silver 0.0350 oz. ASW, 20 mm. **Note:** First toughra.

Date	Mintage	VG	F	VF	XF	Unc
AH1203//1 Rare	—	—	—	—	—	—

KM# 465 5 PARA
0.4650 Silver **Note:** Weight varies 1.25-1.4 grams. Second toughra.

Date	Mintage	VG	F	VF	XF	Unc
AH1203//1	—	125	200	350	600	—

KM# 450 10 PARA
4.4700 g., 0.4650 Silver 0.0668 oz. ASW, 24.5 mm. **Note:** First toughra.

Date	Mintage	VG	F	VF	XF	Unc
AH1203//1	—	—	—	600	1,000	—

KM# 468 10 PARA
Silver, 27 mm. **Note:** Weight varies 3.2-3.5 grams. Second toughra.

Date	Mintage	VG	F	VF	XF	Unc
AH1203//1	—	150	225	350	600	—

KM# 471 20 PARA
9.4200 g., 0.4650 Silver 0.1408 oz. ASW **Note:** Second toughra.

Date	Mintage	VG	F	VF	XF	Unc
AH1203//1 Rare	—	—	—	—	—	—

KM# 453 PIASTRE
18.3000 g., 0.4650 Silver 0.2736 oz. ASW, 39 mm. **Note:** First toughra.

Date	Mintage	VG	F	VF	XF	Unc
AH1203//1 Rare	—	—	—	—	—	—

KM# 474 PIASTRE
17.7100 g., 0.4650 Silver 0.2648 oz. ASW, 39 mm. **Note:** Second toughra.

Date	Mintage	VG	F	VF	XF	Unc
AH1203//1 Rare	—	—	—	—	—	—

KM# 477 2 ZOLOTA
26.4100 g., 0.4650 Silver 0.3948 oz. ASW, 40 mm. **Note:** Second toughra.

Date	Mintage	VG	F	VF	XF	Unc
AH1203//1 Rare	—	—	—	—	—	—

KM# 501 2 ZOLOTA
0.4650 Silver **Note:** Weight varies 18.5-19 grams. Dav. #336.

Date	Mintage	VG	F	VF	XF	Unc
AH1203//1	—	35.00	55.00	125	250	—
AH1203//2	—	35.00	55.00	125	250	—
AH1203//3	—	35.00	55.00	125	250	—
AH1203//9	—	100	175	275	450	—

KM# 456 1/2 ZERI MAHBUB
1.2000 g., Gold, 17.5 mm. **Note:** First toughra.

Date	Mintage	VG	F	VF	XF	Unc
AH1203//1	—	150	250	400	600	—

KM# 459 ZERI MAHBUB
2.4000 g., Gold, 22 mm. **Note:** First toughra.

Date	Mintage	VG	F	VF	XF	Unc
AH1203//1	—	125	200	300	500	—

KM# 522 ZERI MAHBUB
2.4000 g., Gold **Note:** Size varies 22-23mm. Second toughra.

Date	Mintage	VG	F	VF	XF	Unc
AH1203//1	—	50.00	75.00	90.00	120	—
AH1203//2	—	50.00	75.00	90.00	120	—
AH1203//3	—	50.00	75.00	90.00	120	—
AH1203//4	—	50.00	75.00	90.00	120	—
AH1203//5	—	50.00	75.00	90.00	120	—
AH1203//6	—	50.00	75.00	90.00	120	—
AH1203//7	—	50.00	75.00	90.00	120	—
AH1203//8	—	50.00	75.00	90.00	120	—
AH1203//9	—	50.00	75.00	90.00	120	—

KM# 513 1/4 ALTIN (Findik)
0.9000 g., Gold, 15 mm. **Note:** Ornate borders.

Date	Mintage	VG	F	VF	XF	Unc
AH1203//1	—	—	—	—	—	—

KM# 526 ALTIN
3.4500 g., Gold

Date	Mintage	Good	VG	F	VF	XF
AH1203//1	—	—	60.00	85.00	160	200
AH1203//2	—	—	60.00	85.00	160	200
AH1203//3	—	—	60.00	85.00	160	200
AH1203//6	—	—	60.00	85.00	160	200

KM# 530 1-1/2 ALTIN
4.5000 g., Gold **Note:** Second toughra.

Date	Mintage	VG	F	VF	XF	Unc
AH1203//1	—	200	225	350	500	—

KM# 480 2 KURUSH
29.8500 g., 0.4650 Silver 0.4462 oz. ASW **Note:** Size varies 43-44 millimeters. Second toughra.

Date	Mintage	VG	F	VF	XF	Unc
AH1203//1	—	40.00	60.00	125	150	—

MILLED COINAGE

Silver Third Issue

Light coinage based on a Kurush weighing approximately 12.80g. with second toughra.

KM# 486 PARA
0.4650 Silver **Note:** Weight varies 0.24-0.48 grams.

Date	Mintage	VG	F	VF	XF	Unc
AH1203//1	—	0.75	1.25	6.00	12.00	—
AH1203//2	—	0.75	1.25	6.00	12.00	—
AH1203//3	—	0.75	1.25	6.00	12.00	—
AH1203//4	—	0.75	1.25	6.00	12.00	—
AH1203//5	—	0.75	1.25	6.00	12.00	—
AH1203//6	—	0.75	1.25	6.00	12.00	—
AH1203//7	—	0.75	1.25	6.00	12.00	—
AH1203//8	—	0.75	1.25	6.00	12.00	—
AH1203//9	—	0.75	1.25	6.00	12.00	—
AH1203//10	—	0.75	1.25	6.00	12.00	—
AH1203//11	—	0.75	1.25	6.00	12.00	—
AH1203//12	—	0.75	1.25	6.00	12.00	—
AH1203//13	—	0.75	1.25	6.00	12.00	—
AH1203//14	—	0.75	1.25	6.00	12.00	—
AH1203//15	—	0.75	1.25	6.00	12.00	—
AH1203//16	—	0.75	1.25	6.00	12.00	—
AH1203//17	—	0.75	1.25	6.00	12.00	—
AH1203//18	—	0.75	1.25	6.00	12.00	—
AH1203//19	—	2.00	4.00	12.00	30.00	—

KM# 489 5 PARA
0.4650 Silver **Note:** Weight varies 1.35-1.75 grams.

Date	Mintage	VG	F	VF	XF	Unc
AH1203//1	—	6.50	10.00	25.00	40.00	—
AH1203//2	—	6.50	10.00	25.00	40.00	—
AH1203//3	—	6.50	10.00	25.00	40.00	—
AH1203//4	—	6.50	10.00	25.00	40.00	—
AH1203//5	—	6.50	10.00	25.00	40.00	—
AH1203//6	—	6.50	10.00	25.00	40.00	—
AH1203//7	—	6.50	10.00	25.00	40.00	—

Date	Mintage	VG	F	VF	XF	Unc
AH1203//8	—	6.50	10.00	25.00	40.00	—
AH1203//9	—	6.50	10.00	25.00	40.00	—
AH1203//10	—	6.50	10.00	25.00	40.00	—
AH1203//11	—	6.50	10.00	25.00	40.00	—
AH1203//12	—	6.50	10.00	25.00	40.00	—
AH1203//13	—	6.50	10.00	25.00	40.00	—
AH1203//14	—	8.00	15.00	35.00	60.00	—
AH1203//15	—	8.00	15.00	35.00	60.00	—
AH1203//16	—	8.00	15.00	35.00	60.00	—
AH1203//17	—	8.00	15.00	35.00	60.00	—
AH1203//18	—	8.00	15.00	35.00	60.00	—
AH1203//19	—	12.00	20.00	45.00	90.00	—

KM# 492 10 PARA

0.4650 Silver **Obv:** Toughra within circle **Rev:** Text, value within circle **Note:** Weight varies 2.4-3.5 grams.

Date	Mintage	VG	F	VF	XF	Unc
AH1203//1	—	4.00	8.00	17.50	35.00	—
AH1203//2	—	4.00	8.00	17.50	35.00	—
AH1203//3	—	4.00	8.00	17.50	35.00	—
AH1203//4	—	4.00	8.00	17.50	35.00	—
AH1203//5	—	4.00	8.00	17.50	35.00	—
AH1203//6	—	4.00	8.00	17.50	35.00	—
AH1203//7	—	4.00	8.00	17.50	35.00	—
AH1203//8	—	4.00	8.00	17.50	35.00	—
AH1203//9	—	4.00	8.00	17.50	35.00	—
AH1203//10	—	4.00	8.00	17.50	35.00	—
AH1203//11	—	4.00	8.00	17.50	35.00	—
AH1203//12	—	4.00	8.00	17.50	35.00	—
AH1203//13	—	4.00	8.00	17.50	35.00	—
AH1203//14	—	4.00	8.00	17.50	35.00	—
AH1203//15	—	4.00	8.00	17.50	35.00	—
AH1203//16	—	4.00	8.00	17.50	35.00	—
AH1203//17	—	4.00	8.00	17.50	35.00	—
AH1203//18	—	4.00	8.00	17.50	35.00	—
AH1203//19	—	8.00	15.00	25.00	55.00	—

KM# 495 20 PARA

0.4650 Silver **Note:** Weight varies 6-6.2 grams.

Date	Mintage	VG	F	VF	XF	Unc
AH1203//1	—	40.00	80.00	150	275	—
AH1203//2	—	40.00	80.00	150	275	—
AH1203//3	—	40.00	80.00	150	275	—
AH1203//5	—	40.00	80.00	150	275	—
AH1203//6	—	40.00	80.00	150	275	—
AH1203//7	—	40.00	80.00	150	275	—
AH1203//8	—	40.00	80.00	150	275	—
AH1203//9	—	40.00	80.00	150	275	—
AH1203//10	—	40.00	80.00	150	275	—
AH1203//11	—	40.00	80.00	150	275	—
AH1203//13	—	40.00	80.00	150	275	—
AH1203//15	—	50.00	100	190	350	—
AH1203//16	—	50.00	100	190	350	—
AH1203//19 Rare	—	—	—	—	—	—

KM# 507 YUZLUK

0.4650 Silver **Obv:** Toughra above text **Rev:** Text **Note:** Weight varies 31-32.9 grams. Dav. #334.

Date	Mintage	VG	F	VF	XF	Unc
AH1203//1	—	10.00	12.00	25.00	40.00	—
AH1203//2	—	10.00	12.00	25.00	40.00	—
AH1203//3	—	10.00	12.00	25.00	40.00	—
AH1203//4	—	10.00	12.00	25.00	40.00	—
AH1203//5	—	10.00	12.00	25.00	40.00	—
AH1203//6	—	10.00	12.00	25.00	40.00	—
AH1203//7	—	10.00	12.00	25.00	40.00	—
AH1203//8	—	10.00	12.00	25.00	40.00	—
AH1203//9	—	10.00	12.00	25.00	40.00	—
AH1203//10	—	10.00	12.00	25.00	40.00	—
AH1203//11	—	10.00	12.00	25.00	40.00	—
AH1203//12	—	10.00	12.00	25.00	40.00	—
AH1203//13	—	10.00	12.00	25.00	40.00	—
AH1203//14	—	10.00	12.00	25.00	40.00	—
AH1203//15	—	10.00	12.00	25.00	50.00	—
AH1203//16	—	10.00	12.00	25.00	55.00	—
AH1203//17	—	10.00	12.00	25.00	70.00	—
AH1203//18	—	30.00	40.00	60.00	110	—
AH1203//19	—	50.00	75.00	150	350	—

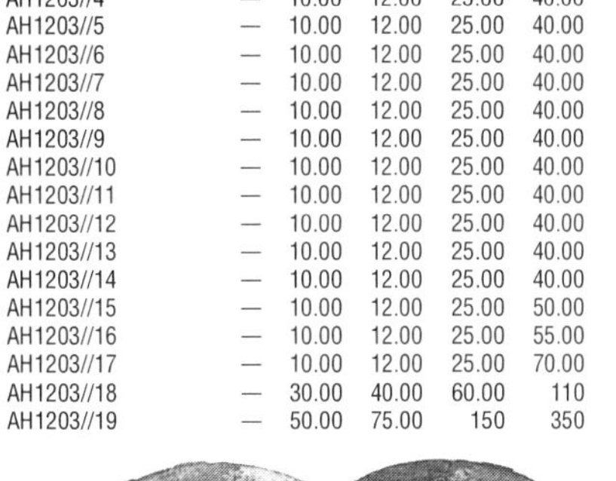

KM# 498 KURUSH

0.4650 Silver **Obv:** Toughra **Rev:** Text, date and value **Note:** Weight varies 12.3-13 grams.

Date	Mintage	VG	F	VF	XF	Unc
AH1203//1	—	20.00	30.00	60.00	125	—
AH1203//2	—	20.00	30.00	60.00	125	—
AH1203//3	—	20.00	30.00	60.00	125	—
AH1203//4	—	20.00	30.00	60.00	125	—
AH1203//5	—	20.00	30.00	60.00	125	—
AH1203//6	—	20.00	30.00	60.00	125	—
AH1203//7	—	20.00	30.00	60.00	125	—
AH1203//8	—	20.00	30.00	60.00	125	—
AH1203//9	—	20.00	30.00	60.00	125	—
AH1203//10	—	20.00	30.00	60.00	125	—
AH1203//11	—	20.00	30.00	60.00	125	—
AH1203//12	—	20.00	30.00	60.00	125	—
AH1203//13	—	20.00	30.00	60.00	125	—
AH1203//14	—	20.00	30.00	60.00	125	—
AH1203//15	—	25.00	35.00	70.00	150	—
AH1203//16	—	25.00	35.00	70.00	150	—
AH1203//17	—	25.00	35.00	70.00	150	—
AH1203//18	—	25.00	35.00	70.00	150	—
AH1203//19	—	150	250	400	750	—

KM# 504 2 KURUSH

0.4650 Silver **Note:** Weight varies 25.2-25.6 grams. Dav. #335.

Date	Mintage	VG	F	VF	XF	Unc
AH1203//1	—	10.00	12.00	30.00	45.00	—
AH1203//2	—	10.00	12.00	25.00	35.00	—
AH1203//3	—	10.00	12.00	25.00	35.00	—
AH1203//4	—	10.00	12.00	25.00	35.00	—
AH1203//5	—	10.00	12.00	25.00	35.00	—
AH1203//6	—	10.00	12.00	25.00	35.00	—
AH1203//7	—	10.00	12.00	30.00	45.00	—
AH1203//8	—	10.00	12.00	30.00	45.00	—
AH1203//9	—	10.00	12.00	30.00	45.00	—
AH1203//10	—	10.00	12.00	25.00	35.00	—
AH1203//11	—	10.00	12.00	30.00	45.00	—
AH1203//12	—	10.00	12.00	25.00	35.00	—
AH1203//13	—	10.00	12.00	25.00	35.00	—
AH1203//14	—	10.00	12.00	30.00	45.00	—
AH1203//15	—	10.00	12.00	30.00	45.00	—
AH1203//16	—	10.00	12.00	30.00	45.00	—
AH1203//17	—	10.00	12.00	30.00	45.00	—
AH1203//18	—	30.00	75.00	100	200	—
AH1203//19	—	75.00	150	250	400	—

MILLED COINAGE

Gold Issues

KM# 510 1/4 ZERI MAHBUB

Gold **Obv:** Toughra **Rev:** Text, date **Rev. Inscription:** "Azza Nasara" **Note:** Weight varies 0.5-0.6 grams. Dav. #334.

Date	Mintage	VG	F	VF	XF	Unc
AH1203//7	—	25.00	35.00	50.00	75.00	—
AH1203//8	—	25.00	35.00	50.00	75.00	—
AH1203//9	—	25.00	35.00	50.00	75.00	—
AH1203//10	—	25.00	35.00	50.00	75.00	—
AH1203//11	—	25.00	35.00	50.00	75.00	—
AH1203//12	—	25.00	35.00	50.00	75.00	—
AH1203//13	—	25.00	35.00	50.00	75.00	—
AH1203//14	—	25.00	35.00	50.00	75.00	—
AH1203//15	—	25.00	35.00	50.00	75.00	—
AH1203//16	—	25.00	35.00	50.00	75.00	—
AH1203//17	—	25.00	35.00	50.00	75.00	—

Note: With "Azza Nasara."

KM# 517 1/2 ZERI MAHBUB

Gold **Note:** Weight varies 1.10-1.20 grams. Second toughra.

Date	Mintage	VG	F	VF	XF	Unc
AH1203//1	—	40.00	65.00	80.00	100	—
AH1203//2	—	40.00	65.00	80.00	100	—
AH1203//3	—	40.00	65.00	80.00	100	—
AH1203//4	—	40.00	65.00	80.00	100	—
AH1203//5	—	40.00	65.00	80.00	100	—
AH1203//6	—	40.00	65.00	80.00	100	—
AH1203//7	—	40.00	65.00	80.00	100	—
AH1203//8	—	40.00	65.00	80.00	100	—
AH1203//9	—	40.00	65.00	80.00	100	—
AH1203//10	—	40.00	65.00	80.00	100	—
AH1203//11	—	40.00	65.00	80.00	100	—
AH1203//12	—	40.00	65.00	80.00	100	—
AH1203//13	—	40.00	65.00	80.00	100	—
AH1203//14	—	40.00	65.00	80.00	100	—
AH1203//15	—	40.00	65.00	80.00	100	—
AH1203//16	—	40.00	65.00	80.00	100	—
AH1203//17	—	40.00	65.00	80.00	100	—
AH1203//18	—	50.00	80.00	120	180	—
AH1203//19	—	100	200	300	400	—

KM# 523 ZERI MAHBUB

2.4000 g., Gold, 21 mm. **Obv:** Toughra above text within circle **Rev:** Text, value **Note:** Reduced size.

Date	Mintage	VG	F	VF	XF	Unc
AH1203//10	—	50.00	75.00	90.00	120	—
AH1203//11	—	50.00	75.00	90.00	120	—
AH1203//12	—	50.00	75.00	90.00	120	—
AH1203//13	—	50.00	75.00	90.00	120	—
AH1203//14	—	60.00	75.00	90.00	120	—
AH1203//15	—	60.00	75.00	90.00	120	—
AH1203//16	—	60.00	75.00	90.00	120	—
AH1203//17	—	60.00	75.00	90.00	120	—
AH1203//18	—	60.00	75.00	90.00	120	—
AH1203//19	—	60.00	75.00	90.00	120	—

KM# 514 1/4 ALTIN (Findik)

0.9000 g., Gold **Obv:** Toughra **Rev:** Text, value and date **Note:** Plain borders.

Date	Mintage	VG	F	VF	XF	Unc
AH1203//1	—	25.00	35.00	50.00	70.00	—
AH1203//2	—	25.00	35.00	50.00	70.00	—
AH1203//3	—	25.00	35.00	50.00	70.00	—
AH1203//4	—	25.00	35.00	50.00	70.00	—
AH1203//5	—	25.00	35.00	50.00	70.00	—
AH1203//6	—	25.00	35.00	50.00	70.00	—
AH1203//7	—	25.00	35.00	50.00	70.00	—
AH1203//8	—	25.00	35.00	50.00	70.00	—
AH1203//9	—	25.00	35.00	50.00	70.00	—
AH1203//10	—	25.00	35.00	50.00	70.00	—
AH1203//11	—	25.00	35.00	50.00	70.00	—
AH1203//12	—	25.00	35.00	50.00	70.00	—

Date	Mintage	VG	F	VF	XF	Unc
AH1203//13	—	25.00	35.00	50.00	70.00	—
AH1203//14	—	25.00	35.00	50.00	70.00	—
AH1203//15	—	25.00	35.00	50.00	70.00	—
AH1203//16	—	25.00	35.00	50.00	70.00	—
AH1203//17	—	25.00	35.00	50.00	70.00	—
AH1203//18	—	25.00	35.00	50.00	70.00	—
AH1203//19	—	30.00	50.00	75.00	125	—

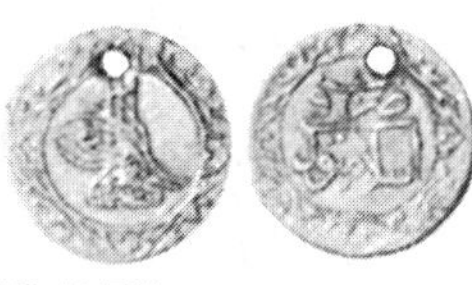

KM# 520 1/2 ALTIN

Gold **Obv:** Toughra within circle **Rev:** Text, value and date within circle **Note:** Weight varies 0.75-0.8 grams.

Date	Mintage	VG	F	VF	XF	Unc
AH1203//1	—	60.00	90.00	130	185	—
AH1203//2	—	60.00	90.00	130	185	—
AH1203//5	—	60.00	90.00	130	185	—
AH1203//6	—	60.00	90.00	130	185	—
AH1203//10	—	60.00	90.00	130	185	—
AH1203//12	—	60.00	90.00	130	185	—
AH1203//13	—	60.00	90.00	130	185	—
AH1203//18	—	70.00	90.00	130	185	—

UNITED STATES OF AMERICA

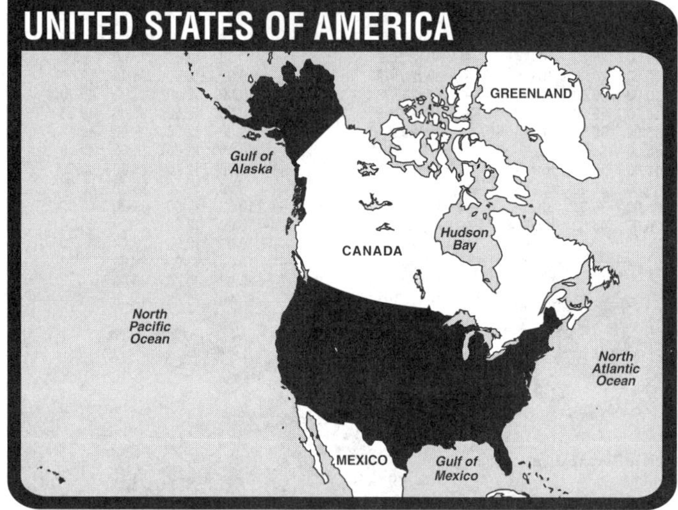

The United States of America as politically organized, under the Articles of Confederation consisted of the 13 original British-American colonies; New Hampshire, Massachusetts, Rhode Island, Connecticut, New York, New Jersey, Pennsylvania, Delaware, Virginia, North Carolina, South Carolina, Georgia and Maryland. Clustered along the eastern seaboard of North American between the forests of Maine and the marshes of Georgia. Under the Article of Confederation, the United States had no national capital: Philadelphia, where the "United States in Congress Assembled", was the "seat of government". The population during this political phase of America's history (1781-1789) was about 3 million, most of whom lived on self-sufficient family farms. Fishing, lumbering and the production of grains for export were major economic endeavors. Rapid strides were also being made in industry and manufacturing by 1775, the (then) colonies were accounting for one-seventh of the world's production of raw iron.

On the basis of the voyage of John Cabot to the North American mainland in 1497, England claimed the entire continent. The first permanent English settlement was established at Jamestown, Virginia, in 1607. France and Spain also claimed extensive territory in North America. At the end of the French and Indian Wars (1763), England acquired all of the territory east of the Mississippi River, including East and West Florida. From 1776 to 1781, the States were governed by the Continental Congress. From 1781 to 1789, they were organized under the Articles of Confederation, during which period the individual States had the right to issue money. Independence from Great Britain was attained with the American Revolution in 1776. The Constitution organized and governs the present United States. It was ratified on Nov. 21, 1788.

EARLY AMERICAN TOKENS

American Plantations

1/24 REAL

KM# Tn5.2 • Tin • Obv: Rider's head left of "B" in legend **Note:** Restrikes made in 1828 from two obverse dies.

Date	AG	Good	VG	Fine	VF	XF	Unc
(1828)	35.00	65.00	100.00	150	225	325	—

Gloucester

KM# Tn15 • Copper •

Date	AG	Good	VG	Fine	VF	XF	Unc
(1714) 2 known	—	—	—	—	—	—	—

Note: Garrett $36,000

Hibernia-Voce Populi

FARTHING

KM# Tn21.1 • Copper • Note: Large letters

Date	AG	Good	VG	Fine	VF	XF	Unc
1760	90.00	150	275	450	750	1,550	—

KM# Tn21.2 • Copper • Note: Small letters

Date	AG	Good	VG	Fine	VF	XF	Unc
1760 extremely rare	—	—	—	—	—	—	—

Note: Norweb $5,940.

HALFPENNY

KM# Tn22 • Copper •

Date	AG	Good	VG	Fine	VF	XF	Unc
1700 date is error, extremely rare	—	—	—	—	—	—	—

Note: ex-Roper $575. Norweb $577.50. Stack's Americana, VF, $2,900

Date	AG	Good	VG	Fine	VF	XF	Unc
1760 varieties	10.00	30.00	50.00	100.00	185	350	—
1760 legend VOOE POPULI	20.00	35.00	60.00	110	200	400	—

Higley or Granby

KM# Tn16 • Copper • Obv. Legend: CONNECTICVT **Note:** THE VALVE OF THREE PENCE.

Date	AG	Good	VG	Fine	VF	XF	Unc
1737	—	—	—	—	—	—	—

Note: Garrett $16,000

KM# Tn17 • Copper • Obv. Legend: THE VALVE OF THREE PENCE **Rev. Legend:** I AM GOOD COPPER

Date	AG	Good	VG	Fine	VF	XF	Unc
1737 2 known	—	—	—	—	—	—	—

Note: ex-Norweb $6,875

KM# Tn18.1 • Copper • Obv. Legend: VALUE ME AS YOU PLEASE **Rev. Legend:** I AM GOOD COPPER

Date	AG	Good	VG	Fine	VF	XF	Unc
1737	6,500	8,500	10,500	14,500	25,000	—	—

KM# Tn18.2 • Copper • Obv. Legend: VALVE ME AS YOU PLEASE. **Rev. Legend:** I AM GOOD COPPER.

Date	AG	Good	VG	Fine	VF	XF	Unc
1737 2 known	—	—	—	—	—	—	—

KM# Tn19 • Copper • Rev: Broad axe

Date	AG	Good	VG	Fine	VF	XF	Unc
(1737)	—	—	—	—	—	—	—

Note: Garrett $45,000

Date	AG	Good	VG	Fine	VF	XF	Unc
1739 5 known	—	—	—	—	—	—	—

Note: Eliasberg $12,650. Oechsner $9,900. Steinberg (holed) $4,400.

Date	AG	Good	VG	Fine	VF	XF	Unc
1739 5 known	—	—	—	—	—	—	—

Note: Eliasberg $12,650. Oechsner $9,900. Steinberg (holed) $4,400.

KM# Tn20 • Copper • Obv. Legend: THE WHEELE GOES ROUND **Rev:** J CUT MY WAY THROUGH

Date	AG	Good	VG	Fine	VF	XF	Unc
(1737) unique	—	—	—	—	—	—	—

Note: Roper $60,500

Pitt

FARTHING

KM# Tn23 • Copper •

Date	AG	Good	VG	Fine	VF	XF	Unc
1766	—	—	—	1,350	2,850	6,000	—

HALFPENNY

KM# Tn24 • Copper •

Date	AG	Good	VG	Fine	VF	XF	Unc
1766	45.00	85.00	175	350	700	1,500	—

ROYAL PATENT COINAGE

Hibernia

FARTHING

KM# 20 • Copper • Note: Pattern.

Date	AG	Good	VG	Fine	VF	XF	Unc
1722	25.00	50.00	125	220	325	700	—

KM# 24 • Copper • Obv: 1722 obverse **Obv. Legend:** ...D:G:REX.

Date	AG	Good	VG	Fine	VF	XF	Unc
1723	20.00	40.00	60.00	90.00	150	350	—

KM# 25 • Copper • Obv. Legend: DEI • GRATIA • REX •

Date	AG	Good	VG	Fine	VF	XF	Unc
1723	10.00	20.00	40.00	65.00	90.00	200	—

KM# 25a • Silver •

Date	Good	VG	Fine	VF	XF	Unc	Proof
1723	—	—	—	800	1,600	—	2,700
1724	45.00	75.00	125	250	485	—	—

HALFPENNY

KM# 21 • Copper • Rev: Harp left, head right

Date	AG	Good	VG	Fine	VF	XF	Unc
1722	—	15.00	35.00	65.00	135	350	—

KM# 22 • Copper • Obv: Harp left, head right **Note:** Pattern.

Date	AG	Good	VG	Fine	VF	XF	Unc
1722	7.00	—	—	1,150	1,750	3,000	—

KM# 23.1 • Copper • Rev: Harp right

Date	AG	Good	VG	Fine	VF	XF	Unc
1722	2.00	15.00	35.00	60.00	125	250	—
1723	7.00	15.00	25.00	40.00	80.00	175	—
1723/22	10.00	20.00	45.00	90.00	185	375	—
1724	7.00	15.00	35.00	60.00	125	265	—

KM# 23.2 • Copper • Obv: DEII error in legend

Date	AG	Good	VG	Fine	VF	XF	Unc
1722	40.00	90.00	180	300	500	750	—

KM# 26 • Copper • Rev: Large head **Note:** Rare. Generally mint state only. Probably a pattern.

Date	AG	Good	VG	Fine	VF	XF	Unc
1723	—	—	—	—	—	—	—

KM# 27 • Copper • Rev: Continuous legend over head

Date	AG	Good	VG	Fine	VF	XF	Unc
1724	30.00	65.00	150	300	475	750	—

Rosa Americana

HALFPENNY

KM# 1 • Copper • Obv. Legend: D • G • REX •

Date	AG	Good	VG	Fine	VF	XF	Unc
1722	20.00	40.00	60.00	100.00	220	475	—

KM# 2 • Copper • Obv: Uncrowned rose **Obv. Legend:** DEI GRATIA REX. **Note:** Several varieties exist.

Date	AG	Good	VG	Fine	VF	XF	Unc
1722	18.00	35.00	55.00	100.00	200	475	—
1723	285	525	750	1,350	2,250	—	—

KM# 3 • Copper • Rev. Legend: VTILE DVLCI

Date	AG	Good	VG	Fine	VF	XF	Unc
1722	250	450	650	1,100	—	—	—

KM# 9 • Copper • Rev: Crowned rose

Date	AG	Good	VG	Fine	VF	XF	Unc
1723	18.00	35.00	55.00	100.00	200	450	—

PENNY

KM# 4 • Copper • Rev. Legend: UTILE DULCI **Note:** Several varieties exist.

Date	AG	Good	VG	Fine	VF	XF	Unc
1722	18.00	35.00	55.00	100.00	175	385	—

KM# 5 • Copper • Note: Several varieties exist. Also known in two rare pattern types with long hair ribbons, one with V's for U's on the obverse.

Date	AG	Good	VG	Fine	VF	XF	Unc
1722	18.00	35.00	55.00	100.00	220	475	—

KM# 10 • Copper • Note: Several varieties exist.

Date	AG	Good	VG	Fine	VF	XF	Unc
1723	18.00	35.00	55.00	100.00	200	420	—

KM# 12 • Copper • Note: Pattern.

Date	AG	Good	VG	Fine	VF	XF	Unc
1724 2 known	—	—	—	—	—	—	—

KM# 13 • Copper •

Date	AG	Good	VG	Fine	VF	XF	Unc
(1724) 5 known	—	—	—	—	—	—	—

Note: Norweb $2,035

KM# 14 • Copper • Obv: George II **Note:** Pattern.

Date	AG	Good	VG	Fine	VF	XF	Unc
1727 2 known	—	—	—	—	—	—	—

2 PENCE

KM# 6 • Copper • Rev: Motto with scroll

Date	AG	Good	VG	Fine	VF	XF	Unc
(1722)	35.00	60.00	110	200	350	700	—

KM# 7 • Copper • Rev: Motto without scroll

Date	AG	Good	VG	Fine	VF	XF	Unc
(1722) 3 known	—	—	—	—	—	—	—

KM# 8.1 • Copper • Obv: Period after REX **Rev:** Dated

Date	AG	Good	VG	Fine	VF	XF	Unc
1722	25.00	40.00	70.00	125	265	500	—

KM# 8.2 • Copper • Obv: Without period after REX

Date	AG	Good	VG	Fine	VF	XF	Unc
1722	22.00	40.00	70.00	125	275	525	—

KM# 11 • Copper • Obv: No stop after REX **Rev:** Stop after 1723 **Note:** Several varieties exist.

Date	AG	Good	VG	Fine	VF	XF	Unc
1723	25.00	45.00	75.00	140	285	550	—

KM# 15 • Copper • Note: Pattern. Two varieties exist; both extremely rare.

Date	AG	Good	VG	Fine	VF	XF	Unc
1724	—	—	—	—	—	—	—

Note: ex-Garrett $5,775. Stack's Americana, XF, $10,925

KM# 16 • Copper • Note: Pattern.

Date	AG	Good	VG	Fine	VF	XF	Unc
1733 4 known	—	—	—	—	—	—	—

Note: Norweb $19,800

Virginia Halfpenny

KM# Tn25.1 • Copper • Rev: Small 7s in date. **Note:** Struck on Irish halfpenny planchets.

Date	Good	VG	Fine	VF	XF	Unc	Proof
1773	—	—	—	—	—	—	3,500

KM# Tn25.2 • Copper • Obv: Period after GEORGIVS **Rev:** Varieties with 7 or 8 strings in harp

Date	AG	Good	VG	Fine	VF	XF	Unc
1773	6.00	12.00	25.00	50.00	100.00	250	465

KM# Tn25.3 • Copper • Obv: Without period after GEORGIVS **Rev:** Varieties with 6, 7 or 8 strings in harp

Date	AG	Good	VG	Fine	VF	XF	Unc
1773	7.00	15.00	30.00	60.00	135	275	525

KM# Tn25.4 • Copper • Obv: Without period after GEORGIVS **Rev:** 8 harp strings, dot on cross

Date	AG	Good	VG	Fine	VF	XF	Unc
1773	—	—	—	—	—	—	—

Note: ex-Steinberg $2,600

KM# Tn26 • Silver • Note: So-called "shilling" silver proofs.

Date	AG	Good	VG	Fine	VF	XF	Unc
1774 6 known	—	—	—	—	—	—	—

Note: Garrett $23,000

REVOLUTIONARY COINAGE

Continental "Dollar".

KM# EA1 • Pewter • Obv. Legend: CURRENCY.

Date	AG	Good	VG	Fine	VF	XF	Unc
1776	—	—	1,850	3,000	4,750	8,750	18,500

KM# EA2 • Pewter • Obv. Legend: CURRENCY, EG FECIT.

Date	AG	Good	VG	Fine	VF	XF	Unc
1776	—	—	1,750	2,850	4,250	7,750	16,000

KM# EA2a • Silver • Obv. Legend: CURRENCY, EG FECIT.

Date	AG	Good	VG	Fine	VF	XF	Unc
1776 2 known	—	—	—	—	—	—	—

KM# EA3 • Pewter • Obv. Legend: CURRENCY.

Date	AG	Good	VG	Fine	VF	XF	Unc
1776 extremely rare	—	—	—	—	—	—	—

KM# EA4 • Pewter • Obv. Legend: CURRENCY. **Rev:** Floral cross.

Date	AG	Good	VG	Fine	VF	XF	Unc
1776 3 recorded	—	—	—	—	—	—	—

Note: Norweb $50,600. Johnson $25,300

KM# EA5 • Pewter • Obv. Legend: CURENCY.

Date	AG	Good	VG	Fine	VF	XF	Unc
1776	—	—	1,650	2,750	4,000	8,000	16,000

KM# EA5a • Brass • Obv. Legend: CURENCY. **Note:** Two varieties exist.

Date	AG	Good	VG	Fine	VF	XF	Unc
1776	—	—	—	—	13,500	17,500	—

KM# EA5b • Silver • Obv. Legend: CURENCY.

Date	AG	Good	VG	Fine	VF	XF	Unc
1776 unique	—	—	—	—	—	—	—

Note: Romano $99,000

STATE COINAGE

CONNECTICUT

KM# 1 • Copper • Obv: Bust facing right.

Date	AG	Good	VG	Fine	VF	XF	Unc
1785	20.00	30.00	50.00	85.00	190	450	—

KM# 2 • Copper • Obv: "African head."

Date	AG	Good	VG	Fine	VF	XF	Unc
1785	25.00	45.00	85.00	200	450	1,500	—

KM# 3.1 • Copper • Obv: Bust facing left.

Date	AG	Good	VG	Fine	VF	XF	Unc
1785	60.00	100.00	150	275	400	750	—
1786	20.00	30.00	50.00	90.00	185	465	—
1787	22.00	35.00	60.00	110	125	350	—
1788	20.00	30.00	50.00	100.00	220	500	—

KM# 4 • Copper • Obv: Small mailed bust facing left. **Rev. Legend:** ETLIB INDE.

Date	AG	Good	VG	Fine	VF	XF	Unc
1786	22.00	35.00	55.00	85.00	165	400	—

KM# 5 • Copper • Obv: Small mailed bust facing right. **Rev. Legend:** INDE ET LIB.

Date	AG	Good	VG	Fine	VF	XF	Unc
1786	30.00	55.00	75.00	115	225	475	—

KM# 6 • Copper • Obv: Large mailed bust facing right.

Date	AG	Good	VG	Fine	VF	XF	Unc
1786	30.00	50.00	90.00	165	350	850	—

KM# 7 • Copper • Obv: "Hercules head."

Date	AG	Good	VG	Fine	VF	XF	Unc
1786	25.00	40.00	75.00	135	300	700	—

KM# 8.1 • Copper • Obv: Draped bust.

Date	AG	Good	VG	Fine	VF	XF	Unc
1786	22.00	35.00	65.00	120	275	600	—

KM# 9 • Copper • Obv: Small head. **Rev. Legend:** ETLIB INDE.

Date	AG	Good	VG	Fine	VF	XF	Unc
1787	25.00	40.00	90.00	150	350	800	—

KM# 10 • Copper • Obv: Small head. **Rev. Legend:** INDE ET LIB.

Date	AG	Good	VG	Fine	VF	XF	Unc
1787	75.00	135	175	275	450	950	—

KM# 11 • Copper • Obv: Medium bust. **Note:** Two reverse legend types exist.

Date	AG	Good	VG	Fine	VF	XF	Unc
1787	50.00	80.00	140	200	325	625	—

KM# 12 • Copper • Obv: "Muttonhead" variety. **Note:** Extremely rare with legend INDE ET LIB.

Date	AG	Good	VG	Fine	VF	XF	Unc
1787	30.00	50.00	120	250	650	1,500	—

KM# 3.3 • Copper • Obv: Perfect date. **Rev. Legend:** IN DE ET.

Date	AG	Good	VG	Fine	VF	XF	Unc
1787	35.00	65.00	85.00	135	250	600	—

KM# 13 • Copper • Obv: "Laughing head"

Date	AG	Good	VG	Fine	VF	XF	Unc
1787	22.00	35.00	60.00	110	250	700	—

KM# 14 • Copper • Obv: "Horned head"

Date	AG	Good	VG	Fine	VF	XF	Unc
1787	15.00	25.00	40.00	70.00	175	475	—

KM# 15 • Copper • Rev. Legend: IND ET LIB

Date	AG	Good	VG	Fine	VF	XF	Unc
1787/8	25.00	40.00	75.00	130	250	650	—
1787/1887	20.00	30.00	50.00	90.00	200	520	—

KM# 16 • Copper • Obv. Legend: CONNECT. **Rev. Legend:** INDE ET LIB. **Note:** Two additional scarce reverse legend types exist.

Date	AG	Good	VG	Fine	VF	XF	Unc
1787	22.00	37.50	60.00	115	220	550	—

KM# 8.2 • Copper • Obv: Draped bust. **Note:** Many varieties.

Date	AG	Good	VG	Fine	VF	XF	Unc
1787	12.00	20.00	40.00	80.00	135	275	—

KM# 8.3 • Copper • Obv. Legend: AUCIORI.

Date	AG	Good	VG	Fine	VF	XF	Unc
1787	15.00	25.00	50.00	110	250	600	—

KM# 8.4 • Copper • Obv. Legend: AUCTOPI.

Date	AG	Good	VG	Fine	VF	XF	Unc
1787	20.00	30.00	60.00	125	265	650	—

KM# 8.5 • Copper • Obv. Legend: AUCTOBI.

Date	AG	Good	VG	Fine	VF	XF	Unc
1787	15.00	25.00	50.00	110	225	550	—

KM# 8.6 • Copper • Obv. Legend: CONNFC.

Date	AG	Good	VG	Fine	VF	XF	Unc
1787	12.00	20.00	40.00	85.00	200	525	—

KM# 8.7 • Copper • Obv. Legend: CONNLC.

Date	AG	Good	VG	Fine	VF	XF	Unc
1787	—	30.00	60.00	125	265	650	—

KM# 8.8 • Copper • Rev. Legend: FNDE.

Date	AG	Good	VG	Fine	VF	XF	Unc
1787	15.00	25.00	45.00	90.00	210	535	—

KM# 8.9 • Copper • Rev. Legend: ETLIR.

Date	AG	Good	VG	Fine	VF	XF	Unc
1787	15.00	25.00	45.00	90.00	210	535	—

KM# 8.10 • Copper • Rev. Legend: ETIIB.

Date	AG	Good	VG	Fine	VF	XF	Unc
1787	20.00	30.00	50.00	100.00	225	550	—

KM# 20 • Copper • Obv: Mailed bust facing right.

Date	AG	Good	VG	Fine	VF	XF	Unc
1788	15.00	25.00	45.00	90.00	200	425	—

KM# 21 • Copper • Obv: Small mailed bust facing right.

Date	AG	Good	VG	Fine	VF	XF	Unc
1788	75.00	150	285	550	1,100	2,500	—

KM# 3.4 • Copper • Obv. Legend: CONNLC.

Date	AG	Good	VG	Fine	VF	XF	Unc
1788	15.00	25.00	40.00	80.00	175	400	—

KM# 22.1 • Copper • Obv: Draped bust facing left. **Rev. Legend:** INDE ET LIB.

Date	AG	Good	VG	Fine	VF	XF	Unc
1788	12.00	20.00	35.00	55.00	135	375	—

KM# 22.2 • Copper • Rev. Legend: INDLET LIB.

Date	AG	Good	VG	Fine	VF	XF	Unc
1788	20.00	30.00	55.00	90.00	185	400	—

KM# 22.3 • Copper • Obv. Legend: CONNEC. **Rev. Legend:** INDE ET LIB.

Date	AG	Good	VG	Fine	VF	XF	Unc
1788	22.00	35.00	60.00	100.00	200	425	—

KM# 22.4 • Copper • Obv. Legend: CONNEC. **Rev. Legend:** INDL ET LIB.

Date	AG	Good	VG	Fine	VF	XF	Unc
1788	22.00	35.00	60.00	100.00	200	425	—

MASSACHUSETTS

HALFPENNY

KM# 17 • Copper •

Date	AG	Good	VG	Fine	VF	XF	Unc
1776 unique	—	—	—	—	—	—	—

Note: Garrett $40,000

PENNY

KM# 18 • Copper •

Date	AG	Good	VG	Fine	VF	XF	Unc
1776 unique	—	—	—	—	—	—	—

HALF CENT

KM# 19 • Copper • Note: Varieties exist; some are rare.

Date	AG	Good	VG	Fine	VF	XF	Unc
1787	30.00	50.00	90.00	175	350	800	—
1788	35.00	55.00	100.00	185	375	850	—

CENT

KM# 20.1 • Copper • Rev: Arrows in right talon

Date	AG	Good	VG	Fine	VF	XF	Unc
1787 7 known	—	—	—	—	—	—	—

Note: Ex-Bushnell-Brand $8,800. Garrett $5,500

KM# 20.2 • Copper • Rev: Arrows in left talon

Date	AG	Good	VG	Fine	VF	XF	Unc
1787	25.00	40.00	65.00	120	285	785	—

KM# 20.3 • Copper • Rev: "Horned eagle" die break

Date	AG	Good	VG	Fine	VF	XF	Unc
1787	28.00	45.00	70.00	130	300	785	—

KM# 20.4 • Copper • Rev: Without period after Massachusetts

Date	AG	Good	VG	Fine	VF	XF	Unc
1788	28.00	45.00	70.00	135	320	850	—

KM# 20.5 • Copper • Rev: Period after Massachusetts, normal S's

Date	AG	Good	VG	Fine	VF	XF	Unc
1788	28.00	45.00	70.00	120	275	775	—

KM# 20.6 • Copper • Rev: Period after Massachusetts, S's like 8's

Date	AG	Good	VG	Fine	VF	XF	Unc
1788	22.00	35.00	60.00	120	275	775	—

NEW HAMPSHIRE

KM# 1 • Copper •

Date	AG	Good	VG	Fine	VF	XF	Unc
1776 extremely rare	—	—	—	—	—	—	—

Note: Garrett $13,000

NEW JERSEY

KM# 8 • Copper • Obv: Date below draw bar.

Date	AG	Good	VG	Fine	VF	XF	Unc
1786 extremely rare	—	—	—	—	—	—	—

Note: Garrett $52,000

KM# 9 • Copper • Obv: Large horse head, date below plow, no coulter on plow.

Date	AG	Good	VG	Fine	VF	XF	Unc
1786	75.00	150	285	550	1,450	5,500	—

KM# 10 • Copper • Rev: Narrow shield, straight beam.

Date	AG	Good	VG	Fine	VF	XF	Unc
1786	25.00	40.00	65.00	150	350	975	—

KM# 11.1 • Copper • Rev: Wide shield, curved beam. **Note:** Varieties exist.

Date	AG	Good	VG	Fine	VF	XF	Unc
1786	28.00	45.00	85.00	180	425	1,000	—

KM# 11.2 • Copper • Obv: Bridle variety (die break). **Note:** Reverse varieties exist.

Date	AG	Good	VG	Fine	VF	XF	Unc
1786	30.00	50.00	90.00	185	425	1,000	—

KM# 12.1 • Copper • Rev: Plain shield. **Note:** Small planchet. Varieties exist.

Date	AG	Good	VG	Fine	VF	XF	Unc
1787	20.00	30.00	60.00	100.00	200	675	—

KM# 12.2 • Copper • Rev: Shield heavily outlined. **Note:** Small planchet.

Date	AG	Good	VG	Fine	VF	XF	Unc
1787	22.00	35.00	75.00	125	285	800	—

KM# 13 • Copper • Obv: "Serpent head."

Date	AG	Good	VG	Fine	VF	XF	Unc
1787	40.00	60.00	120	285	700	1,275	—

KM# 14 • Copper • Rev: Plain shield. **Note:** Large planchet. Varieties exist.

Date	AG	Good	VG	Fine	VF	XF	Unc
1787	22.00	35.00	75.00	135	300	850	—

KM# 15 • Copper • Rev. Legend: PLURIBS.

Date	AG	Good	VG	Fine	VF	XF	Unc
1787	30.00	50.00	100.00	225	600	1,100	—

KM# 16 • Copper • Obv: Horse's head facing right. **Note:** Varieties exist.

Date	AG	Good	VG	Fine	VF	XF	Unc
1788	20.00	30.00	65.00	125	375	750	—

KM# 17 • Copper • Rev: Fox before legend. **Note:** Varieties exist.

Date	AG	Good	VG	Fine	VF	XF	Unc
1788	—	55.00	110	275	725	1,550	—

KM# 18 • Copper • Obv: Horse's head facing left. **Note:** Varieties exist.

Date	AG	Good	VG	Fine	VF	XF	Unc
1788	65.00	125	285	575	1,150	3,000	—

NEW YORK

KM# 1 • Copper • Obv. Legend: NON VI VIRTUTE VICI.

Date	AG	Good	VG	Fine	VF	XF	Unc
1786	1,200	2,200	3,750	6,000	11,500	—	—

KM# 2 • Copper • Obv: Eagle on globe facing right.

Date	AG	Good	VG	Fine	VF	XF	Unc
1787	175	750	1,250	3,500	6,500	12,750	—

KM# 3 • Copper • Obv: Eagle on globe facing left.

Date	AG	Good	VG	Fine	VF	XF	Unc
1787	350	700	1,200	3,250	6,000	12,000	—

KM# 4 • Copper • Rev: Large eagle, arrows in right talon.

Date	AG	Good	VG	Fine	VF	XF	Unc
1787 2 known	—	—	—	—	—	—	—

Note: Norweb $18,700

KM# 5 • Copper • Obv: George Clinton.

Date	AG	Good	VG	Fine	VF	XF	Unc
1787	2,250	4,000	5,500	9,500	20,000	—	—

KM# 6 • Copper • Obv: Indian. **Rev:** New York arms.

Date	AG	Good	VG	Fine	VF	XF	Unc
1787	1,000	2,000	4,000	6,500	10,500	25,000	—

KM# 7 • Copper • Obv: Indian. **Rev:** Eagle on globe.

Date	AG	Good	VG	Fine	VF	XF	Unc
1787	1,650	3,000	6,500	11,500	23,500	35,000	—

KM# 8 • Copper • Obv: Indian. **Rev:** George III.

Date	AG	Good	VG	Fine	VF	XF	Unc
1787	125	200	350	650	1,350	4,200	—

KM# 9 • Copper • Obv. Legend: NOVA EBORAC. **Rev:** Figure seated right.

Date	AG	Good	VG	Fine	VF	XF	Unc
1787	40.00	75.00	125	260	525	1,100	—

KM# 10 • Copper • Rev: Figure seated left.

Date	AG	Good	VG	Fine	VF	XF	Unc
1787	35.00	55.00	110	225	500	1,000	—

KM# 11 • Copper • Obv: Small head, star above. **Obv. Legend:** NOVA EBORAC.

Date	AG	Good	VG	Fine	VF	XF	Unc
1787	300	600	1,750	3,000	4,500	6,500	—

KM# 12 • Copper • Obv: Large head, two quatrefoils left. **Obv. Legend:** NOVA EBORAC.

Date	AG	Good	VG	Fine	VF	XF	Unc
1787	200	300	400	650	1,150	2,500	—

Machin Mill

KM# 13 • Copper • Note: Crude, lightweight imitations of the British Halfpenny were struck at Machin's Mill in large quantities bearing the obverse legends: GEORGIVS II REX, GEORGIVS III REX, and GEORGIUS III REX, with the BRITANNIA reverse. There are many different mulings. These pieces, which have plain crosses in the shield of Britannia, are not to be confused with the very common British made imitations, which usually have outlined crosses in the shield. Some varieties are very rare.

Date	AG	Good	VG	Fine	VF	XF	Unc
(1747-1788)	—	—	—	—	—	—	—

Note: Examples are dated: 1747, 1771, 1772, 1774, 1775, 1776, 1777, 1778, 1784, 1785, 1786, 1787 and 1788. Other dates may exist

VERMONT

KM# 1 • Copper • Rev. Legend: IMMUNE COLUMBIA.

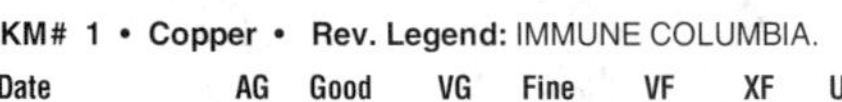

Date	AG	Good	VG	Fine	VF	XF	Unc
(1785)	1,250	2,000	3,000	5,000	9,000	—	—

KM# 2 • Copper • Obv. Legend: VERMONTIS.

Date	AG	Good	VG	Fine	VF	XF	Unc
1785	120	200	300	600	1,150	—	—

KM# 3 • Copper • Obv. Legend: VERMONTS.

Date	AG	Good	VG	Fine	VF	XF	Unc
1785	85.00	150	225	450	900	3,200	—

KM# 4 • Copper • Obv. Legend: VERMONTENSIUM.

Date	AG	Good	VG	Fine	VF	XF	Unc
1786	75.00	125	200	450	950	3,250	—

KM# 5 • Copper • Obv: "Baby head." **Rev:** AUCTORI: VERMONS.

Date	AG	Good	VG	Fine	VF	XF	Unc
1786	120	200	300	550	1,150	4,500	—

KM# 6 • Copper • Obv: Bust facing left. **Obv. Legend:** VERMON: AUCTORI:.

Date	AG	Good	VG	Fine	VF	XF	Unc
1786	60.00	100.00	185	300	750	2,250	—
1787 extremely rare	—	—	—	—	—	—	—

KM# 7 • Copper • Obv: Bust facing right. **Note:** Varieties exist.

Date	AG	Good	VG	Fine	VF	XF	Unc
1787	—	—	—	—	—	—	—

KM# 8 • Copper • Note: Britannia mule.

Date	AG	Good	VG	Fine	VF	XF	Unc
1787	25.00	40.00	65.00	140	285	950	—

KM# 9.2 • Copper • Obv: "C" backward in AUCTORI.

Date	AG	Good	VG	Fine	VF	XF	Unc
1788 extremely rare	—	—	—	—	—	—	—

Note: Stack's Americana, Fine, $9,775

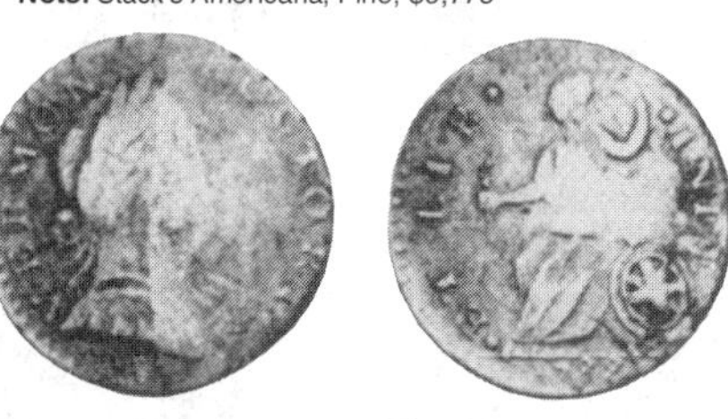

KM# 10 • Copper • Rev. Legend: ET LIB INDE.

Date	AG	Good	VG	Fine	VF	XF	Unc
1788	75.00	125	300	600	1,100	—	—

KM# 11 • Copper • Note: George III Rex mule.

Date	AG	Good	VG	Fine	VF	XF	Unc
1788	85.00	145	325	650	1,250	2,750	—

KM# 9.1 • Copper • Rev. Legend: INDE ET LIB. **Note:** Varieties exist.

Date	AG	Good	VG	Fine	VF	XF	Unc
1788	40.00	65.00	120	220	550	1,850	—

EARLY AMERICAN TOKENS

Albany Church "Penny"

KM# Tn54.1 • Copper • Obv: Without "D" above church. **Note:** Uniface.

Date	AG	Good	VG	Fine	VF	XF	Unc
5 known	—	—	3,500	7,000	14,000	—	—

KM# Tn54.2 • Copper • Obv: With "D" above church. **Note:** Uniface.

Date	AG	Good	VG	Fine	VF	XF	Unc
rare	—	—	3,000	5,000	10,000	—	—

Auctori Plebis

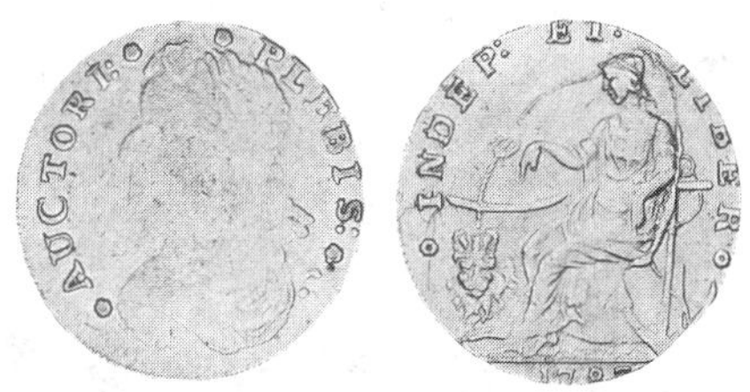

KM# Tn50 • Copper •

Date	AG	Good	VG	Fine	VF	XF	Unc
1787	20.00	45.00	90.00	150	300	600	—

Bar "Cent"

KM# Tn49 • Copper •

Date	AG	Good	VG	Fine	VF	XF	Unc
(1785)	85.00	150	275	675	1,200	2,500	—

Castorland "Half Dollar"

KM# Tn87.1 • Silver • Edge: Reeded.

Date	AG	Good	VG	Fine	VF	XF	Unc
1796	—	—	—	—	—	3,550	—

KM# Tn87.1a • Copper • Edge: Reeded.

Date	AG	Good	VG	Fine	VF	XF	Unc
1796 3 known	—	—	—	—	—	1,650	—

KM# Tn87.1b • Brass • Edge: Reeded.

Date	AG	Good	VG	Fine	VF	XF	Unc
1796 unique	—	—	—	—	—	—	—

KM# Tn87.2 • Copper • Edge: Plain. **Note:** Thin planchet.

Date	AG	Good	VG	Fine	VF	XF	Unc
1796 unique	—	—	—	—	—	—	—

KM# Tn87.3 • Silver • Edge: Reeded. **Note:** Thin planchet. Restrike.

Date	Good	VG	Fine	VF	XF	Unc	Proof
1796	—	—	—	—	—	325	—

KM# Tn87.4 • Silver • Edge: Lettered. **Edge Lettering:** ARGENT. **Note:** Thin planchet. Restrike.

Date	Good	VG	Fine	VF	XF	Unc	Proof
1796	—	—	—	—	—	60.00	—

KM# Tn87.3a • Copper • Edge: Reeded. **Note:** Thin planchet. Restrike.

Date	Good	VG	Fine	VF	XF	Unc	Proof
1796	—	—	—	—	—	285	—

KM# Tn87.5 • Copper • Edge: Lettered. **Edge Lettering:** CUIVRE. **Note:** Thin planchet. Restrike.

Date	Good	VG	Fine	VF	XF	Unc	Proof
1796	—	—	—	—	—	40.00	—

Chalmers

3 PENCE

KM# Tn45 • Silver •

Date	AG	Good	VG	Fine	VF	XF	Unc
1783	250	500	1,000	1,500	2,650	5,500	—

6 PENCE

KM# Tn46.1 • Silver • Rev: Small date

Date	AG	Good	VG	Fine	VF	XF	Unc
1783	350	700	1,500	2,250	5,500	12,000	—

KM# Tn46.2 • Silver • Rev: Large date

Date	AG	Good	VG	Fine	VF	XF	Unc
1783	300	600	1,300	2,000	4,000	10,000	—

SHILLING

KM# Tn47.1 • Silver • Rev: Birds with long worm

Date	AG	Good	VG	Fine	VF	XF	Unc
1783	180	300	500	1,000	2,000	4,500	—

KM# Tn47.2 • Silver • Rev: Birds with short worm

Date	AG	Good	VG	Fine	VF	XF	Unc
1783	150	250	475	900	1,850	4,500	—

KM# Tn48 • Silver • Rev: Rings and stars

Date	AG	Good	VG	Fine	VF	XF	Unc
1783 4 known	—	—	—	—	—	—	—

Note: Garrett $75,000

Copper Company of Upper Canada

HALFPENNY

KM# Tn86 • Copper •

Date	Good	VG	Fine	VF	XF	Unc	Proof
1796	—	—	—	—	—	—	3,750

Franklin Press

KM# Tn73 • Copper • Edge: Plain.

Date	AG	Good	VG	Fine	VF	XF	Unc
1794	18.00	35.00	55.00	85.00	175	300	600

Kentucky Token

KM# Tn70.1 • Copper • Edge: Plain. **Note:** 1793 date is circa.

Date	AG	Good	VG	Fine	VF	XF	Unc
1793	12.00	25.00	40.00	60.00	100.00	265	575

KM# Tn70.2 • Copper • Edge: Engrailed.

Date	AG	Good	VG	Fine	VF	XF	Unc
1793	35.00	75.00	125	200	350	950	1,850

KM# Tn70.3 • Copper • Edge: Lettered. **Edge Lettering:** PAYABLE AT BEDWORTH.

Date	AG	Good	VG	Fine	VF	XF	Unc
1793 unique	—	—	—	—	—	1,980	—

KM# Tn70.4 • Copper • Edge: Lettered. **Edge Lettering:** PAYABLE AT LANCASTER.

Date	AG	Good	VG	Fine	VF	XF	Unc
1793	14.00	28.00	45.00	65.00	110	285	725

KM# Tn70.5 • Copper • Edge: Lettered. **Edge Lettering:** PAYABLE AT I.FIELDING.

Date	AG	Good	VG	Fine	VF	XF	Unc
1793 unique	—	—	—	—	—	—	—

KM# Tn70.6 • Copper • Edge: Lettered. **Edge Lettering:** PAYABLE AT W. PARKERS.

Date	AG	Good	VG	Fine	VF	XF	Unc
1793 unique	—	—	—	—	1,800	—	—

KM# Tn70.7 • Copper • Edge: Ornamented branch with two leaves.

Date	AG	Good	VG	Fine	VF	XF	Unc
1793 unique	—	—	—	—	—	—	—

Mott Token

KM# Tn52.1 • Copper • Note: Thin planchet.

Date	AG	Good	VG	Fine	VF	XF	Unc
1789	30.00	60.00	120	220	350	850	—

KM# Tn52.2 • Copper • Note: Thick planchet. Weight generally about 170 grams.

Date	AG	Good	VG	Fine	VF	XF	Unc
1789	25.00	50.00	100.00	175	300	700	—

KM# Tn52.3 • Copper • Edge: Fully engrailed. **Note:** Specimens struck with perfect dies are scarcer and generally command higher prices.

Date	AG	Good	VG	Fine	VF	XF	Unc
1789	40.00	85.00	175	350	600	1,250	—

Myddelton Token

KM# Tn85 • Copper •

Date	Good	VG	Fine	VF	XF	Unc	Proof
1796	—	—	—	—	—	—	6,500

KM# Tn85a • Silver •

Date	Good	VG	Fine	VF	XF	Unc	Proof
1796	—	—	—	—	—	—	5,500

New York Theatre

KM# Tn90 • Copper • Note: 1796 date is circa.

Date	AG	Good	VG	Fine	VF	XF	Unc
1796	—	—	300	900	2,000	3,250	8,000

North American

HALFPENNY

KM# Tn30 • Copper •

Date	AG	Good	VG	Fine	VF	XF	Unc
1781	6.50	12.50	25.00	75.00	135	365	750

Rhode Island Ship

KM# Tn27a • Brass • Obv: Without wreath below ship.

Date	AG	Good	VG	Fine	VF	XF	Unc
1779	50.00	100.00	175	275	500	1,000	2,000

KM# Tn27b • Pewter • Obv: Without wreath below ship.

Date	AG	Good	VG	Fine	VF	XF	Unc
1779	—	—	—	—	1,250	2,500	5,500

KM# Tn28a • Brass • Obv: Wreath below ship.

Date	AG	Good	VG	Fine	VF	XF	Unc
1779	60.00	120	200	325	600	1,150	2,200

KM# Tn28b • Pewter • Obv: Wreath below ship.

Date	AG	Good	VG	Fine	VF	XF	Unc
1779	—	—	—	—	1,500	3,000	6,500

KM# Tn29 • Brass • Obv: VLUGTENDE below ship

Date	AG	Good	VG	Fine	VF	XF	Unc
1779 unique	—	—	—	—	—	—	—

Note: Garrett $16,000

Standish Barry

3 PENCE

KM# Tn55 • Silver •

Date	AG	Good	VG	Fine	VF	XF	Unc
1790	850	1,350	2,000	3,000	6,500	12,000	—

Talbot, Allum & Lee

CENT

KM# Tn71.1 • Copper • Rev: NEW YORK above ship **Edge:** Lettered. **Edge Lettering:** PAYABLE AT THE STORE OF

Date	AG	Good	VG	Fine	VF	XF	Unc
1794	12.00	25.00	45.00	90.00	175	300	925

KM# Tn71.2 • Copper • Rev: NEW YORK above ship **Edge:** Plain. **Note:** Size of ampersand varies on obverse and reverse dies.

Date	AG	Good	VG	Fine	VF	XF	Unc
1794 4 known	—	—	—	—	2,350	3,000	—

KM# Tn72.1 • Copper • Rev: Without NEW YORK above ship **Edge:** Lettered. **Edge Lettering:** PAYABLE AT THE STORE OF

Date	AG	Good	VG	Fine	VF	XF	Unc
1794	100.00	200	350	650	1,000	2,250	4,550

KM# Tn72.2 • Copper • Edge: Lettered. **Edge Lettering:** WE PROMISE TO PAY THE BEARER ONE CENT.

Date	AG	Good	VG	Fine	VF	XF	Unc
1795	10.00	20.00	40.00	75.00	160	300	725

KM# Tn72.3 • Copper • Edge: Lettered. **Edge Lettering:** CURRENT EVERYWHERE.

Date	AG	Good	VG	Fine	VF	XF	Unc
1795 unique	—	—	—	—	—	—	—

KM# Tn72.4 • Copper • Edge: Olive leaf.

Date	AG	Good	VG	Fine	VF	XF	Unc
1795 unique	—	—	—	—	—	—	—

Note: Norweb $4,400

KM# Tn72.5 • Copper • Edge: Plain.

Date	AG	Good	VG	Fine	VF	XF	Unc
1795 plain edge, 2 known	—	—	—	—	—	—	—
1795 edge: Cambridge Bedford Huntington.X .X., unique	—	—	—	—	—	—	—

Note: Norweb, $3,960

Washington Pieces

KM# Tn35 • Copper • Obv. Legend: GEORGIVS TRIUMPHO.

Date	AG	Good	VG	Fine	VF	XF	Unc
1783	25.00	40.00	65.00	150	325	750	—

KM# Tn36 • Copper • Obv: Large military bust. **Note:** Varieties exist.

Date	AG	Good	VG	Fine	VF	XF	Unc
1783	8.00	15.00	25.00	50.00	110	280	—

KM# Tn37.1 • Copper • Obv: Small military bust. **Edge:** Plain.

Date	AG	Good	VG	Fine	VF	XF	Unc
1783	10.00	20.00	35.00	65.00	125	300	—

Note: One proof example is known. Value: $12,500

KM# Tn37.2 • Copper • Obv: Small military bust. **Edge:** Engrailed.

Date	AG	Good	VG	Fine	VF	XF	Unc
1783	18.00	35.00	50.00	80.00	175	345	—

KM# Tn38.1 • Copper • Obv: Draped bust, no button on drapery, small letter.

Date	AG	Good	VG	Fine	VF	XF	Unc
1783	10.00	20.00	35.00	65.00	125	285	—

KM# Tn38.2 • Copper • Obv: Draped bust, button on drapery, large letter.

Date	AG	Good	VG	Fine	VF	XF	Unc
1783	25.00	40.00	60.00	100.00	200	350	—

KM# Tn38.4 • Copper • Edge: Engrailed. **Note:** Restrike.

Date	Good	VG	Fine	VF	XF	Unc	Proof
1783	—	—	—	—	—	—	400

KM# Tn38.4a • Copper • Note: Bronzed. Restrike.

Date	Good	VG	Fine	VF	XF	Unc	Proof
1783	—	—	—	—	—	—	—

KM# Tn83.3 • Copper • Obv: Large modern lettering. **Edge:** Plain. **Note:** Restrike.

Date	Good	VG	Fine	VF	XF	Unc	Proof
1783	—	—	—	—	—	—	500

KM# Tn83.4b • Silver • Note: Restrike.

Date	Good	VG	Fine	VF	XF	Unc	Proof
1783	—	—	—	—	—	—	1,000

KM# Tn83.4c • Gold • Note: Restrike.

Date	AG	Good	VG	Fine	VF	XF	Unc
1783 2 known	—	—	—	—	—	—	—

KM# Tn60.1 • Copper • Obv. Legend: WASHINGTON PRESIDENT. **Edge:** Plain.

Date	AG	Good	VG	Fine	VF	XF	Unc
1792	850	1,450	3,250	5,000	7,500	—	—

Note: Steinberg $12,650. Garrett $15,500

KM# Tn60.2 • Copper • Obv. Legend: WASHINGTON PRESIDENT. **Edge:** Lettered. **Edge Lettering:** UNITED STATES OF AMERICA.

Date	AG	Good	VG	Fine	VF	XF	Unc
1792	1,350	2,250	4,500	7,500	12,500	—	—

KM# Tn61.1 • Copper • Obv. Legend: BORN VIRGINIA. **Note:** Varieties exist.

Date	AG	Good	VG	Fine	VF	XF	Unc
	250	500	1,000	2,200	3,750	7,500	—

KM# Tn61.2 • Silver • Edge: Lettered. **Edge Lettering:** UNITED STATES OF AMERICA.

Date	AG	Good	VG	Fine	VF	XF	Unc
2 known	—	—	—	—	—	—	—

KM# Tn61.1a • Silver • Edge: Plain.

Date	AG	Good	VG	Fine	VF	XF	Unc
4 known	—	—	—	—	—	—	—

Note: Roper $16,500

KM# Tn62 • Silver • Rev: Heraldic eagle. 1792 half dollar. **Note:** Mule.

Date	AG	Good	VG	Fine	VF	XF	Unc
3 known	—	—	—	—	—	—	—

KM# Tn77.1 • Copper • Obv. Legend: LIBERTY AND SECURITY. **Edge:** Lettered. **Note:** "Penny."

Date	AG	Good	VG	Fine	VF	XF	Unc
(1795)	25.00	40.00	75.00	135	275	625	2,000

KM# Tn77.2 • Copper • Edge: Plain. **Note:** "Penny."

Date	AG	Good	VG	Fine	VF	XF	Unc
(1795) extremely rare	—	—	—	—	—	—	—

KM# Tn77.3 • Copper • Note: "Penny." Engine-turned borders.

Date	AG	Good	VG	Fine	VF	XF	Unc
12 known	—	—	—	—	—	—	3,750

KM# Tn78 • Copper • Note: Similar to "Halfpenny" with date on reverse.

Date	AG	Good	VG	Fine	VF	XF	Unc
1795 very rare	—	—	—	—	—	—	—

Note: Roper $6,600

HALFPENNY

KM# Tn56 • Copper • Obv. Legend: LIVERPOOL HALFPENNY

Date	AG	Good	VG	Fine	VF	XF	Unc
1791	300	450	550	850	1,650	2,350	—

KM# Tn66.1 • Copper • Rev: Ship **Edge:** Lettered.

Date	AG	Good	VG	Fine	VF	XF	Unc
1793	20.00	30.00	60.00	110	235	500	—

KM# Tn66.2 • Copper • Rev: Ship **Edge:** Plain.

Date	AG	Good	VG	Fine	VF	XF	Unc
1793 5 known	—	—	—	—	2,000	—	—

KM# Tn75.1 • Copper • Obv: Large coat buttons **Rev:** Grate **Edge:** Reeded.

Date	AG	Good	VG	Fine	VF	XF	Unc
1795	12.00	20.00	30.00	60.00	120	265	575

KM# Tn75.2 • Copper • Rev: Grate **Edge:** Lettered.

Date	AG	Good	VG	Fine	VF	XF	Unc
1795	45.00	85.00	165	225	300	625	1,200

KM# Tn75.3 • Copper • Obv: Small coat buttons **Rev:** Grate **Edge:** Reeded.

Date	AG	Good	VG	Fine	VF	XF	Unc
1795	10.00	35.00	60.00	100.00	175	375	850

KM# Tn76.1 • Copper • Obv. Legend: LIBERTY AND SECURITY. **Edge:** Plain.

Date	AG	Good	VG	Fine	VF	XF	Unc
1795	18.00	35.00	60.00	100.00	175	435	975

KM# Tn76.2 • Copper • Edge: Lettered. **Edge Lettering:** PAYABLE AT LONDON ...

Date	AG	Good	VG	Fine	VF	XF	Unc
1795	12.00	20.00	30.00	60.00	125	375	800

KM# Tn76.3 • Copper • Edge: Lettered. **Edge Lettering:** BIRMINGHAM ...

Date	AG	Good	VG	Fine	VF	XF	Unc
1795	14.00	22.00	35.00	70.00	150	425	950

KM# Tn76.4 • Copper • Edge: Lettered. **Edge Lettering:** AN ASYLUM ...

Date	AG	Good	VG	Fine	VF	XF	Unc
1795	18.00	35.00	60.00	100.00	225	450	1,000

KM# Tn76.5 • Copper • Edge: Lettered. **Edge Lettering:** PAYABLE AT LIVERPOOL ...

Date	AG	Good	VG	Fine	VF	XF	Unc
1795 unique	—	—	—	—	—	—	—

KM# Tn76.6 • Copper • Edge: Lettered. **Edge Lettering:** PAYABLE AT LONDON-LIVERPOOL.

Date	AG	Good	VG	Fine	VF	XF	Unc
1795 unique	—	—	—	—	—	—	—

KM# Tn81.1 • Copper • Rev. Legend: NORTH WALES **Edge:** Plain.

Date	AG	Good	VG	Fine	VF	XF	Unc
(ca.1795)	25.00	45.00	85.00	145	250	550	1,450

KM# Tn82 • Copper • Rev: Four stars at bottom **Rev. Legend:** NORTH WALES

Date	AG	Good	VG	Fine	VF	XF	Unc
(1795)	200	400	700	1,500	2,850	5,500	—

KM# Tn81.2 • Copper • Rev. Legend: NORTH WALES **Edge:** Lettered.

Date	AG	Good	VG	Fine	VF	XF	Unc
	120	250	400	600	950	2,000	4,500

CENT

KM# Tn39 • Copper • Obv. Legend: UNITY STATES

Date	AG	Good	VG	Fine	VF	XF	Unc
1783	12.00	22.00	40.00	70.00	160	325	—

KM# Tn40 • Copper • Note: Double head.

Date	AG	Good	VG	Fine	VF	XF	Unc
(1783)	10.00	20.00	35.00	65.00	135	300	—

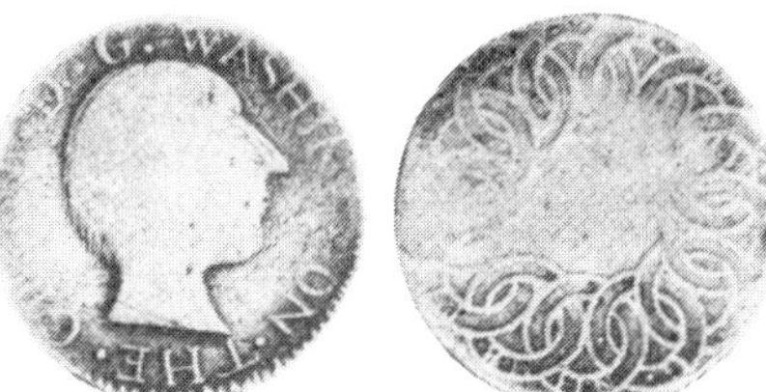

KM# Tn41 • Copper • Obv: "Ugly head." **Note:** 3 known in copper, 1 in white metal.

Date	AG	Good	VG	Fine	VF	XF	Unc
1784	—	—	—	—	—	—	—

Note: Roper $14,850

KM# Tn57 • Copper • Rev: Small eagle

Date	AG	Good	VG	Fine	VF	XF	Unc
1791	30.00	60.00	125	250	335	675	—

KM# Tn58 • Copper • Rev: Large eagle

Date	AG	Good	VG	Fine	VF	XF	Unc
1791	35.00	65.00	145	275	375	725	—

KM# Tn65 • Copper • Obv: "Roman" head

Date	Good	VG	Fine	VF	XF	Unc	Proof
1792	—	—	—	—	—	—	17,600

HALF DOLLAR

KM# Tn59.1 • Copper • Edge: Lettered. **Edge Lettering:** UNITED STATES OF AMERICA

Date	AG	Good	VG	Fine	VF	XF	Unc
1792 2 known	—	—	—	—	—	—	—

Note: Roper $2,860. Benson, EF, $48,300

KM# Tn59.2 • Copper • Edge: Plain.

Date	AG	Good	VG	Fine	VF	XF	Unc
1792 3 known	—	—	—	—	—	—	—

KM# Tn59.1a • Silver • Edge: Lettered. **Edge Lettering:** UNITED STATES OF AMERICA

Date	AG	Good	VG	Fine	VF	XF	Unc
1792 rare	—	—	—	—	—	—	—

Note: Roper $35,200

KM# Tn59.2a • Silver • Edge: Plain.

Date	AG	Good	VG	Fine	VF	XF	Unc
1792 rare	—	—	—	—	—	—	—

KM# Tn59.1b • Gold • Edge: Lettered. **Edge Lettering:** UNITED STATES OF AMERICA

Date	AG	Good	VG	Fine	VF	XF	Unc
1792 unique	—	—	—	—	—	—	—

KM# Tn63.1 • Silver • Rev: Small eagle **Edge:** Plain.

Date	AG	Good	VG	Fine	VF	XF	Unc
1792	4,500	7,000	9,000	12,500	20,000	37,500	—

KM# Tn63.2 • Silver • Edge: Ornamented, circles and squares.

Date	AG	Good	VG	Fine	VF	XF	Unc
1792 5 known	—	—	—	—	—	—	—

KM# Tn63.1a • Copper • Edge: Plain.

Date	AG	Good	VG	Fine	VF	XF	Unc
1792	750	1,500	3,500	5,750	8,500	—	—

Note: Garrett $32,000

KM# Tn63.3 • Silver • Edge: Two olive leaves.

Date	AG	Good	VG	Fine	VF	XF	Unc
1792 unique	—	—	—	—	—	—	—

KM# Tn64 • Silver • Rev: Large heraldic eagle

Date	AG	Good	VG	Fine	VF	XF	Unc
1792 unique	—	—	—	—	—	—	—

Note: Garrett $16,500

EARLY AMERICAN PATTERNS

Confederatio

KM# EA22 • Copper • Rev: Small circle of stars.

Date	AG	Good	VG	Fine	VF	XF	Unc
1785	—	—	—	—	8,800	16,500	—

KM# EA23 • Copper • Rev: Large circle of stars. **Note:** The Confederatio dies were struck in combination with 13 other dies of the period. All surviving examples of these combinations are extremely rare.

Date	AG	Good	VG	Fine	VF	XF	Unc
1785 extremely rare	—	—	—	—	—	—	—

Immune Columbia

KM# EA20 • Copper • Obv: George III.

Date	AG	Good	VG	Fine	VF	XF	Unc
1785	750	1,250	1,850	2,250	5,000	9,000	—

KM# EA21 • Copper • Obv: Vermon.

Date	AG	Good	VG	Fine	VF	XF	Unc
1785	600	1,000	1,650	2,000	4,750	8,500	—

KM# EA17a • Silver • Rev. Legend: CONSTELLATIO.

Date	AG	Good	VG	Fine	VF	XF	Unc
1785	—	—	—	—	—	20,700	—

KM# EA19a • Gold • Rev. Legend: CONSTELATIO.

Date	AG	Good	VG	Fine	VF	XF	Unc
1785 unique	—	—	—	—	—	—	—

KM# EA17 • Copper • Rev. Legend: CONSTELLATIO.

Date	AG	Good	VG	Fine	VF	XF	Unc
1785	—	—	—	—	—	14,375	—

KM# EA18 • Copper • Obv. Legend: Extra star in border. **Rev. Legend:** CONSTELLATIO.

Date	AG	Good	VG	Fine	VF	XF	Unc
1785	—	—	—	—	—	—	—

Note: Caldwell $4,675

KM# EA19 • Copper • Rev: Blunt rays.

Date	AG	Good	VG	Fine	VF	XF	Unc
1785 2 known	—	—	—	—	—	—	—

Note: Norweb $22,000

KM# EA28 • Copper • Obv. Legend: IMMUNIS COLUMBIA. **Rev:** Eagle.

Date	AG	Good	VG	Fine	VF	XF	Unc
1786 3 known	—	—	—	—	—	—	—

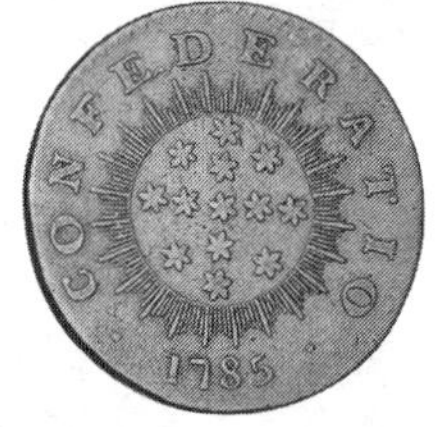

KM# EA24 • Copper • Obv: Washington.

Date	AG	Good	VG	Fine	VF	XF	Unc
1786 3 known	—	—	—	—	—	—	—

Note: Garrett $50,000. Steinberg $12,650

KM# EA25 • Copper • Obv: Eagle.

Date	AG	Good	VG	Fine	VF	XF	Unc
1786 unique	—	—	—	—	—	—	—

Note: Garrett $37,500

KM# EA26 • Copper • Obv: Washington. **Rev:** Eagle.

Date	AG	Good	VG	Fine	VF	XF	Unc
1786 2 known	—	—	—	—	—	—	—

KM# EA27 • Copper • Obv. Legend: IMMUNIS COLUMBIA.

Date	AG	Good	VG	Fine	VF	XF	Unc
1786 extremely rare	—	—	—	—	—	—	—

Note: Rescigno, AU, $33,000. Steinberg, VF, $11,000

Nova Constellatio

KM# EA6.1 • Copper • Obv: Pointed rays. **Obv. Legend:** CONSTELLATIO. **Rev:** Small "US".

Date	AG	Good	VG	Fine	VF	XF	Unc
1783	20.00	35.00	65.00	125	255	585	—

KM# EA6.2 • Copper • Obv: Pointed rays. **Obv. Legend:** CONSTELLATIO. **Rev:** Large "US".

Date	AG	Good	VG	Fine	VF	XF	Unc
1783	20.00	35.00	70.00	140	285	650	—

KM# EA7 • Copper • Obv: Blunt rays. **Obv. Legend:** CONSTELATIO.

Date	AG	Good	VG	Fine	VF	XF	Unc
1783	22.00	40.00	80.00	150	350	750	—

KM# EA8 • Copper • Obv: Blunt rays. **Obv. Legend:** CONSTELATIO.

Date	AG	Good	VG	Fine	VF	XF	Unc
1785	22.00	40.00	80.00	160	375	775	—

KM# EA9 • Copper • Obv: Pointed rays. **Obv. Legend:** CONSTELLATIO.

Date	AG	Good	VG	Fine	VF	XF	Unc
1785	20.00	35.00	70.00	140	285	650	—

KM# EA10 • Copper • Note: Contemporary circulating counterfeit. Similar to previously listed coin.

Date	AG	Good	VG	Fine	VF	XF	Unc
1786 extremely rare	—	—	—	—	—	—	—

5 UNITS

KM# EA12 • Copper •

Date	AG	Good	VG	Fine	VF	XF	Unc
1783 unique	—	—	—	—	—	—	—

100 (BIT)

KM# EA13.1 • Silver • Edge: Leaf.

Date	AG	Good	VG	Fine	VF	XF	Unc
1783 2 known	—	—	—	—	—	—	—

Note: Garrett $97,500. Stack's auction, May 1991, $72,500

KM# EA13.2 • Silver • Edge: Plain.

Date	AG	Good	VG	Fine	VF	XF	Unc
1783 unique	—	—	—	—	—	—	—

500 (QUINT)

KM# EA14 • Silver • Obv. Legend: NOVA CONSTELLATIO

Date	AG	Good	VG	Fine	VF	XF	Unc
1783 unique	—	—	—	—	—	—	—

Note: Garrett $165,000

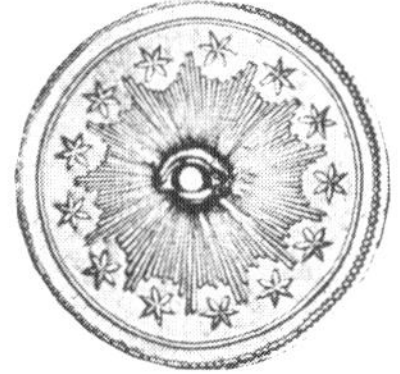

KM# EA15 • Silver • Obv: Without legend

Date	AG	Good	VG	Fine	VF	XF	Unc
1783 unique	—	—	—	—	—	—	—

Note: Garrett $55,000

1000 (MARK)

KM# EA16 • Silver •

Date	AG	Good	VG	Fine	VF	XF	Unc
1783 unique	—	—	—	—	—	—	—

Note: Garrett $190,000

EARLY FEDERAL COINAGE

Brasher

KM# Tn51.1 • Gold • Obv: Sunrise over mountains. **Rev:** Displayed eagle with shield on breast, EB counterstamp on wing.

Date	AG	Good	VG	Fine	VF	XF	Unc
1787 6 known	—	—	—	—	—	—	—

Note: Heritage FUN Sale, January 2005, AU-55, $2.415 million.

KM# Tn51.2 • Gold • Obv: Sun rise over mountains **Rev:** Displayed eagle with sheild on breast. EB counterstamp on breast.

Date	AG	Good	VG	Fine	VF	XF	Unc
1787 unique	—	—	—	—	—	—	—

Note: Heritage FUN Sale, January 2005, XF-45, $2.99 million

Fugio "Cent"

KM# EA30.1 • Copper • Obv: Club rays, round ends.

Date	AG	Good	VG	Fine	VF	XF	Unc
1787	40.00	75.00	150	375	850	1,600	—

KM# EA30.2 • Copper • Obv: Club rays, concave ends.

Date	AG	Good	VG	Fine	VF	XF	Unc
1787	250	700	1,800	2,750	5,000	—	—

KM# EA30.3 • Copper • Obv. Legend: FUCIO.

Date	AG	Good	VG	Fine	VF	XF	Unc
1787	—	750	1,850	2,850	55,000	—	—

KM# EA31.1 • Copper • Obv: Pointed rays. **Rev:** UNITED above, STATES below.

Date	AG	Good	VG	Fine	VF	XF	Unc
1787	100.00	250	550	1,000	1,500	3,500	—

KM# EA31.2 • Copper • Rev: UNITED STATES at sides of ring.

Date	AG	Good	VG	Fine	VF	XF	Unc
1787	20.00	45.00	90.00	175	300	650	—

KM# EA31.3 • Copper • Rev: STATES UNITED at sides of ring.

Date	AG	Good	VG	Fine	VF	XF	Unc
1787	25.00	55.00	110	220	350	700	—

KM# EA31.4 • Copper • Rev: Eight-pointed stars on ring.

Date	AG	Good	VG	Fine	VF	XF	Unc
1787	30.00	65.00	120	250	400	800	—

KM# EA31.5 • Copper • Rev: Raised rims on ring, large lettering in center.

Date	AG	Good	VG	Fine	VF	XF	Unc
1787	35.00	75.00	135	275	450	950	—

KM# EA32.1 • Copper • Obv: No cinquefoils, cross after date. **Obv. Legend:** UNITED STATES.

Date	AG	Good	VG	Fine	VF	XF	Unc
1787	50.00	110	250	425	650	1,250	—

KM# EA32.2 • Copper • Obv: No cinquefoils, cross after date. **Obv. Legend:** STATES UNITED.

Date	AG	Good	VG	Fine	VF	XF	Unc
1787	60.00	110	250	425	650	1,250	—

KM# EA32.3 • Copper • Obv: No cinquefoils, cross after date. **Rev:** Raised rims on ring.

Date	AG	Good	VG	Fine	VF	XF	Unc
1787	—	—	—	—	2,600	—	—

KM# EA33 • Copper • Obv: No cinquefoils, cross after date. **Rev:** With rays. **Rev. Legend:** AMERICAN CONGRESS.

Date	AG	Good	VG	Fine	VF	XF	Unc
1787 extremely rare	—	—	—	—	—	—	—

Note: Norweb $63,800

KM# EA34 • Brass • Note: New Haven restrike.

Date	AG	Good	VG	Fine	VF	XF	Unc
1787	—	—	—	—	—	—	500

KM# EA34a • Copper • Note: New Haven restrike.

Date	AG	Good	VG	Fine	VF	XF	Unc
1787	—	—	—	—	—	500	—

ISSUES OF 1792

CENT

KM# PnE1 • Copper Around Silver • Note: Silver plug in center.

Date	AG	Good	VG	Fine	VF	XF	Unc
1792 12 known	—	—	—	—	—	—	—

Note: Norweb, MS-60, $143,000

KM# PnF1 • Copper • Note: No silver center.

Date	AG	Good	VG	Fine	VF	XF	Unc
1792 8 known	—	—	—	—	—	—	—

Note: Norweb, EF-40, $35,200; Benson, VG-10, $57,500

KM# PnG1 • Copper • Edge: Plain **Note:** Commonly called "Birch cent."

Date	AG	Good	VG	Fine	VF	XF	Unc
1792 unique	—	—	—	—	—	—	—

KM# PnH1 • Copper • Obv: One star in edge legend **Note:** Commonly called "Birch cent."

Date	AG	Good	VG	Fine	VF	XF	Unc
1792 2 known	—	—	—	—	—	—	—

Note: Norweb, EF-40, $59,400

KM# PnI1 • Copper • Obv: Two stars in edge legend **Note:** Commonly called "Birch cent."

Date	AG	Good	VG	Fine	VF	XF	Unc
1792 6 known	—	—	—	—	—	—	—

Note: Hawn, strong VF, $57,750

KM# PnJ1 • White Metal • Rev: "G.W.Pt." below wreath tie **Note:** Commonly called "Birch cent."

Date	AG	Good	VG	Fine	VF	XF	Unc
1792 unique	—	—	—	—	—	—	—

Note: Garrett, $90,000

HALF DISME

KM# 5 • Silver •

Date	AG	Good	VG	Fine	VF	XF	Unc
1792	1,250	—	3,500	6,500	8,500	16,500	—

KM# PnA1 • Copper •

Date	AG	Good	VG	Fine	VF	XF	Unc
1792 unique	—	—	—	—	—	—	—

DISME

KM# PnB1 • Silver •

Date	AG	Good	VG	Fine	VF	XF	Unc
1792 3 known	—	—	—	—	—	—	—

Note: Norweb, EF-40, $28,600

KM# PnC1 • Copper • Edge: Reeded

Date	AG	Good	VG	Fine	VF	XF	Unc
1792 14 known	—	—	—	—	—	—	—

Note: Hawn, VF, $30,800; Benson, EF-45, $109,250

KM# PnD1 • Copper • Edge: Plain

Date	AG	Good	VG	Fine	VF	XF	Unc
1792 2 known	—	—	—	—	—	—	—

Note: Garrett, $45,000

QUARTER

KM# PnK1 • Copper • Edge: Reeded **Note:** Commonly called "Wright quarter."

Date	AG	Good	VG	Fine	VF	XF	Unc
1792 2 known	—	—	—	—	—	—	—

KM# PnL1 • White Metal • Edge: Plain **Note:** Commonly called "Wright quarter."

Date	AG	Good	VG	Fine	VF	XF	Unc
1792 2 known	—	—	—	—	—	—	—

Note: Norweb, VF-30 to EF-40, $28,600

KM# PnM1 • White Metal • Note: Commonly called "Wright quarter."

Date	AG	Good	VG	Fine	VF	XF	Unc
1792 die trial	—	—	—	—	—	—	—

Note: Garrett, $12,000

CIRCULATION COINAGE

HALF CENT

Liberty Cap

Head facing left

KM# 10 COPPER 0 oz. 22 mm. 6.7400 g. **Designer:** Henry Voigt

Date	Mintage	G-4	VG-8	F-12	VF-20	XF-40	MS-60
1793	35,334	2,200	3,400	6,750	10,000	17,000	35,000

Head facing right

KM# 14 COPPER 6.74 g. (1794-95) and 5.44 g. (1795-97) 0 oz. 23.5 mm. **Designer:** Robert Scot (1794) and John Smith Gardner (1795) **Notes:** The "lettered edge" varieties have "Two Hundred for a Dollar" inscribed around the edge. The "pole" varieties have a pole upon which the cap is hanging, resting on Liberty's shoulder. The "punctuated date" varieties have a comma after the 1 in the date. The 1797 "1 above 1" variety has a second 1 above the 1 in the date.

Date	Mintage	G-4	VG-8	F-12	VF-20	XF-40	MS-60
1794	81,600	400	650	900	1,600	3,500	18,000
1795 lettered edge, pole	25,600	450	700	950	1,500	4,250	17,500
1795 plain edge, no pole	109,000	375	475	800	1,400	3,500	16,000
1795 lettered edge, punctuated date	Inc. above	475	700	1,000	1,600	3,750	20,000
1795 plain edge, punctuated date	Inc. above	350	450	750	1,200	3,000	27,500
1796 pole	5,090	16,000	20,000	23,500	30,000	35,000	—
1796 no pole	1,390	27,000	32,500	47,500	90,000	—	—
1797 plain edge	119,215	400	575	950	1,900	6,000	27,500
1797 lettered edge	Inc. above	1,700	2,700	4,000	8,000	25,000	—
1797 1 above 1	Inc. above	375	475	950	1,600	3,250	20,000
1797 gripped edge	Inc. above	16,000	37,500	48,000	60,000	70,000	—

CENT

Flowing Hair Cent

Chain

KM# 11 COPPER 0 oz. 26-27 mm. 13.4800 g. **Designer:** Henry Voigt

Date	Mintage	G-4	VG-8	F-12	VF-20	XF-40	MS-60
1793	36,103	7,750	11,000	15,000	23,000	33,000	135,000

Flowing Hair Cent

Wreath

KM# 12 COPPER 0 oz. 26-28 mm. 13.4800 g. **Designer:** Henry Voigt

Date	Mintage	G-4	VG-8	F-12	VF-20	XF-40	MS-60
1793	63,353	1,700	2,500	4,000	8,000	12,000	30,000

Liberty Cap Cent

KM# 13 COPPER 13.48 g. (1793-95) and 10.89 g. (1795-96) 0 oz. 29 mm. **Designer:** Joseph Wright (1793-1795) and John Smith Gardner (1795-1796) **Notes:** The heavier pieces were struck on a thicker planchet. The Liberty design on the obverse was revised slightly in 1794, but the 1793 design was used on some 1794 strikes. A 1795 "lettered edge" variety has "One Hundred for a Dollar" and a leaf inscribed on the edge.

Date	Mintage	G-4	VG-8	F-12	VF-20	XF-40	MS-60
1793 cap	11,056	5,000	6,000	9,000	20,000	26,000	—
1794	918,521	350	485	750	1,200	3,750	9,000
1794 head '93	Inc. above	1,500	2,600	4,000	7,900	12,000	—
1795	501,500	350	485	650	1,000	2,000	4,750

Liberty Cap Cent

KM# 13a COPPER 0 oz. 29 mm. 10.8900 g. **Designer:** Joseph Wright (1793-1795) and John Smith Gardner (1795-1796)

Date	Mintage	G-4	VG-8	F-12	VF-20	XF-40	MS-60
1795 lettered edge, "One Cent" high in wreath	37,000	400	550	900	1,750	4,000	15,000
1796	109,825	350	500	800	1,400	3,750	21,000

Draped Bust Cent

Draped bust right, date at angle below Value within wreath

KM# 22 COPPER 0 oz. 29 mm. 10.9800 g. **Designer:** Robert Scot **Notes:** The 1801 "3 errors" variety has the fraction on the reverse reading "1/000," has only one stem extending from the wreath above and on both sides of the fraction on the reverse, and "United" in "United States of America" appears as "linited."

Stemless

Stems

Date	Mintage	G-4	VG-8	F-12	VF-20	XF-40	MS-60
1796	363,375	350	600	850	1,800	3,400	—
1797	897,510	130	175	250	335	1,150	3,300
1797 stemless	Inc. above	300	495	600	910	3,200	—
1798	1,841,745	90.00	130	200	350	1,300	3,100
1798/7	Inc. above	200	300	375	1,200	3,900	—
1799	42,540	3,500	5,000	8,500	16,000	35,000	—
1800	2,822,175	50.00	95.00	200	400	1,750	—

HALF DIME

Flowing Hair Half Dime

KM# 15 0.8920 **SILVER** 0.0387 oz. ASW. 16.5 mm. 1.3500 g. **Designer:** Robert Scot

Date	Mintage	G-4	VG-8	F-12	VF-20	XF-40	MS-60
1794	86,416	1,000	1,250	1,750	2,700	4,800	13,500
1795	Inc. above	700	900	1,350	2,000	4,000	9,500

Draped Bust Half Dime

Small eagle

KM# 23 0.8920 **SILVER** 0.0387 oz. ASW. 16.5 mm. 1.3500 g. **Designer:** Robert Scot **Notes:** Some 1796 strikes have "Liberty" spelled as "Likerty." The 1797 strikes have either 13, 15 or 16 stars on the obverse.

Date	Mintage	G-4	VG-8	F-12	VF-20	XF-40	MS-60
1796	10,230	1,000	1,350	2,000	3,500	6,000	13,500
1796 "Likerty"	Inc. above	1,100	1,400	2,100	3,750	6,250	14,500
1796/5	Inc. above	1,000	1,350	2,200	4,000	7,000	25,000
1797 13 stars	44,527	1,750	2,300	3,000	5,500	9,000	25,000
1797 15 stars	Inc. above	1,000	1,250	1,900	3,250	5,750	12,500
1797 16 stars	Inc. above	1,050	1,350	2,100	3,650	6,250	13,750

Draped Bust Half Dime

Draped bust right, flanked by stars, date at angle below Heraldic eagle

KM# 34 0.8920 **SILVER** 0.0387 oz. ASW. 16.5 mm. 1.3500 g. **Designer:** Robert Scot

Date	Mintage	G-4	VG-8	F-12	VF-20	XF-40	MS-60
1800	24,000	575	750	1,500	2,500	4,250	9,000
1800 "Libekty"	Inc. above	600	800	1,575	2,650	4,400	9,300

DIME

Draped Bust Dime

Small eagle

KM# 24 0.8920 **SILVER** 0.0774 oz. ASW. 19 mm. 2.7000 g. **Designer:** Robert Scot **Notes:** 1797 strikes have either 13 or 16 stars on the obverse.

Date	Mintage	G-4	VG-8	F-12	VF-20	XF-40	MS-60
1796	22,135	1,300	1,950	2,250	3,250	5,000	12,000
1797 13 stars	25,261	1,500	2,000	2,500	3,500	6,000	12,000
1797 16 stars	Inc. above	1,500	2,000	2,500	3,500	6,000	12,000

Draped Bust Dime

Draped bust right, date at angle below Heraldic eagle

KM# 31 0.8920 **SILVER** 0.0774 oz. ASW. 19 mm. 2.7000 g. **Designer:** Robert Scot **Notes:** The 1805 strikes have either 4 or 5 berries on the olive branch held by the eagle.

Date	Mintage	G-4	VG-8	F-12	VF-20	XF-40	MS-60
1798	27,550	650	800	1,000	1,500	2,750	6,500
1798/97 13 stars	Inc. above	2,000	3,000	4,500	7,000	11,000	—
1798/97 16 stars	Inc. above	675	800	1,050	1,500	2,500	5,500
Note: The 1798 overdates have either 13 or 16 stars on the obverse; Varieties of the regular 1798 strikes are distinguished by the size of the 8 in the date							
1798 small 8	Inc. above	900	1,150	1,700	2,400	3,600	9,500
1800	21,760	600	800	1,100	1,600	2,750	—

QUARTER

Draped Bust Quarter

Small eagle

KM# 25 0.8920 **SILVER** 0.1933 oz. ASW. 27.5 mm. 6.7400 g. **Designer:** Robert Scot

Date	Mintage	G-4	VG-8	F-12	VF-20	XF-40	AU-50	MS-60	MS-65
1796	6,146	8,900	16,500	28,000	36,500	42,500	68,000	93,500	235,000

HALF DOLLAR

Flowing Hair Half Dollar

KM# 16 0.8920 **SILVER** 0.3866 oz. ASW. 32.5 mm. 13.4800 g. **Designer:** Robert Scot **Notes:** The 1795 "recut date" variety had the date cut into the dies twice, so both sets of numbers are visible on the coin. The 1795 "3 leaves" variety has three leaves under each of the eagle's wings on the reverse.

Date	Mintage	G-4	VG-8	F-12	VF-20	XF-40	MS-60
1794	23,464	2,650	5,200	7,750	19,500	35,000	125,000
1795	299,680	650	900	1,600	2,750	8,500	25,000
1795 recut date	Inc. above	700	950	1,650	2,900	9,000	29,500
1795 3 leaves	Inc. above	2,600	3,000	4,400	6,850	13,500	50,000

Draped Bust Half Dollar

Small eagle

KM# 26 0.8920 **SILVER** 0.3866 oz. ASW. 32.5 mm. 13.4800 g. **Designer:** Robert Scot **Notes:** The 1796 strikes have either 15 or 16 stars on the obverse.

Date	Mintage	G-4	VG-8	F-12	VF-20	XF-40	MS-60
1796 15 stars	3,918	29,000	36,500	60,000	87,500	108,000	175,000
1796 16 stars	Inc. above	30,500	38,500	67,500	92,000	115,000	205,000
1797	Inc. above	28,500	36,000	70,000	89,500	110,000	175,000

DOLLAR

Flowing Hair Dollar

KM# 17 0.8920 **SILVER** 0.7731 oz. ASW. 39-40 mm. 26.9600 g. **Designer:** Robert Scot **Notes:** The two 1795 varieties have either two or three leaves under each of the eagle's wings on the reverse.

Date	Mintage	F-12	VF-20	XF-40	AU-50	MS-60	MS-63
1794	1,758	115,000	160,000	235,000	340,000	500,000	800,000
1795 2 leaves	203,033	3,350	5,500	12,850	22,500	54,000	110,000
1795 3 leaves	Inc. above	3,100	4,950	11,500	19,500	46,500	98,000
1795 Silver plug	—	10,500	14,500	30,000	—	—	—

Draped Bust Dollar

Small eagle

KM# 18 0.8920 **SILVER** 0.7731 oz. ASW. 39-40 mm. 26.9600 g. **Designer:** Robert Scot **Notes:** The 1796 varieties are distinguished by the size of the numerals in the date and letters in "United States of America." The 1797 varieties are distinguished by the number of stars to the left and right of the word "Liberty" and by the size of the letters in "United States of America." The 1798 varieties have either 13 or 15 stars on the obverse.

Date	Mintage	F-12	VF-20	XF-40	AU-50	MS-60	MS-63
1795 Off-center bust	Inc. above	2,550	4,250	8,400	13,500	36,500	74,000
1795 Centered bust	—	2,600	4,300	8,600	13,750	37,000	—
1796 small date, small letters	72,920	2,900	4,800	9,650	14,950	44,000	90,000
1796 small date, large letters	Inc. above	2,700	4,800	9,850	15,400	48,500	—
1796 large date, small letters	Inc. above	2,950	5,100	10,250	15,500	27,000	65,000
1797 9 stars left, 7 stars right, small letters	7,776	4,000	8,250	16,500	36,500	85,000	125,000
1797 9 stars left, 7 stars right, large letters	Inc. above	2,950	5,250	10,000	16,500	42,500	90,000
1797 10 stars left, 6 stars right	Inc. above	2,750	4,700	9,800	16,000	45,000	98,000
1798 13 stars	327,536	2,850	4,700	10,000	17,000	60,000	—
1798 15 stars	Inc. above	3,400	5,850	12,000	21,500	75,000	—

Draped Bust Dollar

Draped bust right, flanked by stars, date below Heraldic eagle

KM# 32 0.8920 **SILVER** 0.7731 oz. ASW. 39-40 mm. 26.9600 g. **Designer:** Robert Scot **Notes:** The 1798 "knob 9" variety has a serif on the lower left of the 9 in the date. The 1798 varieties are distinguished by the number of arrows held by the eagle on the reverse and the number of berries on the olive branch. On the 1798 "high-8" variety, the 8 in the date is higher than the other numerals. The 1799 varieties are distinguished by the number and positioning of the stars on the obverse and by the size of the berries in the olive branch on the reverse. On the 1700 "irregular date" variety, the first 9 in the date is smaller than the other numerals. Some varieties of the 1800 strikes had letters in the legend cut twice into the dies; as the dies became worn, the letters were touched up. On the 1800 "very wide date, low 8" variety, the spacing between the numerals in the date are wider than other varieties and the 8 is lower than the other numerals. The 1800 "small berries" variety refers to the size of the berries in the olive branch on the reverse. The 1800 "12 arrows" and "10 arrows" varieties refer to the number of arrows held by the eagle. The 1800 "Americai" variety appears to have the faint outline of an "I" after "America" in the reverse legend. The "close" and "wide" varieties of 1802 refer to the amount of space between the numerals in the date. The 1800 large-3 and small-3 varieties are distinguished by the size of the 3 in the date.

Date	Mintage	F-12	VF-20	XF-40	AU-50	MS-60	MS-63
1798 knob 9	Inc. above	1,225	2,075	3,950	8,250	21,750	43,500
1798 10 arrows	Inc. above	1,225	2,075	3,950	8,250	21,750	43,500
1798 4 berries	Inc. above	1,225	2,075	3,950	8,250	21,750	43,500
1798 5 berries, 12 arrows	Inc. above	1,225	2,075	3,950	8,250	21,750	43,500
1798 high 8	Inc. above	1,225	2,075	3,950	8,250	21,750	43,500
1798 13 arrows	Inc. above	1,225	2,075	3,950	8,250	21,750	45,000
1799/98 13-star reverse	423,515	1,450	2,350	4,300	8,600	23,500	45,000
1799/98 15-star reverse	Inc. above	1,325	2,125	4,000	8,300	24,500	47,500
1799 irregular date, 13-star reverse	Inc. above	1,300	2,150	3,900	8,200	23,500	45,000
1799 irregular date, 15-star reverse	Inc. above	1,275	2,125	3,950	8,250	21,500	42,500
1799 perfect date, 7- and 6-star obverse, no berries	Inc. above	1,200	2,050	3,850	8,150	18,500	42,500
1799 perfect date, 7- and 6-star obverse, small berries	Inc. above	1,200	2,050	3,850	8,150	18,500	42,500
1799 perfect date, 7- and 6-star obverse, medium large berries	Inc. above	1,225	2,050	3,850	8,150	18,500	42,500
1799 perfect date, 7- and 6-star obverse, extra large berries	Inc. above	1,225	2,050	3,850	8,150	18,500	51,500
1799 8 stars left, 5 stars right on obverse	Inc. above	1,300	2,150	3,900	8,200	24,000	45,000
1800 "R" in "Liberty" double cut	220,920	1,275	2,125	3,950	8,250	21,500	45,000
1800 first "T" in "States" double cut	Inc. above	1,275	2,125	3,950	8,250	21,500	45,000
1800 both letters double cut	Inc. above	1,275	2,125	3,950	8,250	21,500	45,000
1800 "T" in "United" double cut	Inc. above	1,275	2,125	3,950	8,250	21,500	45,000
1800 very wide date, low 8	Inc. above	1,275	2,125	3,950	8,250	21,500	—
1800 small berries	Inc. above	1,300	2,150	3,900	8,200	22,000	48,500
1800 dot date	Inc. above	150	2,350	4,300	8,600	21,500	45,000
1800 12 arrows	Inc. above	1,275	2,125	3,950	8,250	21,500	45,000
1800 10 arrows	Inc. above	1,275	2,125	3,950	8,250	21,500	48,500
1800 "Americai"	Inc. above	1,450	2,350	4,300	8,600	21,500	49,000

$2.50 (QUARTER EAGLE)

GOLD

Liberty Cap

Liberty cap on head, right, flanked by stars Heraldic eagle

KM# 27 0.9160 **GOLD** 0.1287 oz. AGW. 20 mm. 4.3700 g. **Designer:** Robert Scot **Notes:** The 1796 "no stars" variety does not have stars on the obverse. The 1804 varieties are distinguished by the number of stars on the obverse.

Date	Mintage	F-12	VF-20	XF-40	MS-60
1796 no stars	963	30,000	42,000	70,000	165,000
1796 stars	432	28,000	40,000	63,000	140,000
1797	427	17,000	23,000	27,500	120,000
1798	1,094	4,750	10,000	12,500	55,000

$5 (HALF EAGLE)

GOLD

Liberty Cap

Liberty cap on head, right, flanked by stars Heraldic eagle

KM# 19 0.9160 **GOLD** 0.2577 oz. AGW. 25 mm. 8.7500 g. **Designer:** Robert Scot **Notes:** From 1795 through 1798, varieties exist with either a "small eagle" or a "large (heraldic) eagle" on the reverse. After 1798, only the heraldic eagle was used. Two 1797 varieties are distinguished by the size of the 8 in the date. 1806 varieties are distinguished by whether the top of the 6 has a serif.

Date	Mintage	F-12	VF-20	XF-40	MS-60
1795 small eagle	8,707	11,500	17,000	19,000	47,000
1795 large eagle	Inc. above	8,800	14,000	20,000	75,000
1796/95 small eagle	6,196	12,000	17,500	24,000	75,000
1797/95 large eagle	3,609	8,600	14,000	22,000	150,000
1797 15 stars, small eagle	Inc. above	14,000	21,000	35,000	150,000
1797 16 stars, small eagle	Inc. above	13,000	17,500	34,000	145,000
1798 small eagle	—	90,000	155,000	275,000	—
1798 large eagle, small 8	24,867	3,300	4,500	6,000	21,000
1798 large eagle, large 8, 13-star reverse	Inc. above	3,000	3,700	4,500	17,500
1798 large eagle, large 8, 14-star reverse	Inc. above	3,000	4,200	7,000	35,000
1799	7,451	3,000	3,800	5,300	16,500
1800	37,628	3,000	3,800	5,000	8,800

$10 (EAGLE)

GOLD

Liberty Cap

Small eagle

KM# 21 0.9160 **GOLD** 0.5154 oz. AGW. 33 mm. 17.5000 g. **Designer:** Robert Scot

Date	Mintage	F-12	VF-20	XF-40	MS-60
1795 13 leaves	5,583	18,000	24,000	33,000	70,000
1795 9 leaves	Inc. above	26,000	40,000	60,000	230,000
1796	4,146	23,000	27,500	38,000	80,000
1797 small eagle	3,615	30,000	38,000	45,000	185,000

Liberty Cap

Liberty cap on head, right, flanked by stars Heraldic eagle

KM# 30 0.9160 **GOLD** 0.5154 oz. AGW. 33 mm. 17.5000 g. **Designer:** Robert Scot
Notes: The 1798/97 varieties are distinguished by the positioning of the stars on the obverse.

Date	Mintage	F-12	VF-20	XF-40	MS-60
1797 large eagle	10,940	9,000	11,000	14,000	40,000
1798/97 9 stars left, 4 right	900	11,000	19,000	29,000	100,000
1798/97 7 stars left, 6 right	842	23,000	30,000	65,000	—
1799	37,449	8,000	10,000	12,500	31,000
1800	5,999	8,200	11,000	12,000	33,000

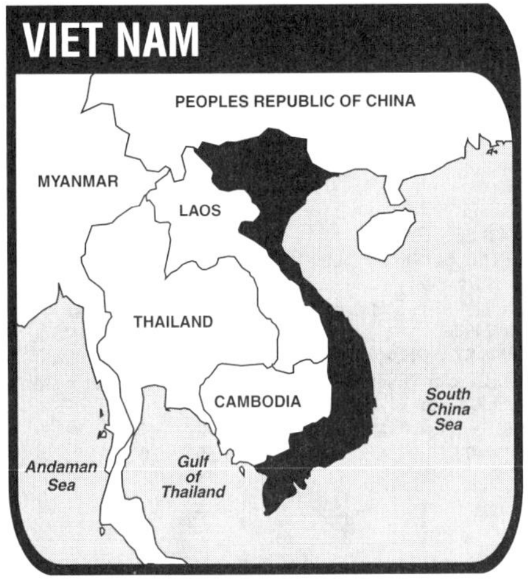

In 207 B.C. a Chinese general set up the Kingdom of Nam-Viet on the Red River. This kingdom was over thrown by the Chinese under the Han Dynasty in 111 B.C., where upon the country became a Chinese province under the name of Giao-Chi, which was later changed to Annam or peaceful or pacified South. Chinese rule was maintained until 968, when the Vietnamese became independent until 1407 when China again invaded Viet Nam. The Chinese were driven out in 1428 and the country became independent and named Dai-Viet. Gia Long renamed the country Dai Namin 1802.

After the French conquered Dai Nam, they split the country into three parts. The South became the Colony of Cochin china; the North became the Protectorate of Tonkin; and the central became the Protectorate of Annam. The emperors were permitted to have their capital in Hue and to produce small quantities of their coins, presentation pieces, and bullion bars. Annam had an area of 57,840 sq. mi. (141,806 sq. km.) and a population of about 6 million. Chief products of the area are silk, cinnamon and rice. There are important mineral deposits in the mountainous inland.

North Dai Viet

EMPERORS

正和通寶

Chanh Hoa, 1676-1705

Vinh Thinh, 1705-1720

保泰通寶

Bao Thai, 1720-1729

興景

Canh Hung, 1740-1787

統昭

Chieu Thong, 1787-1789

Nguyen Kingdom, South Dai Viet

EMPEROR

明

Thien Minh, 1739-1766

REBELS and INVADERS

Canh Long, 1789
(Ch'ien Lung of China)

德泰

Thai Duc, 1778-1793

德明

(Min Duc, ca. 1785)

United Dai Viet

中光

Quang Trung, 1788-1792

盛景

Canh Thinh, 1792-1801

IDENTIFICATION

Khai 啓

寶 Bao

通 Thong

Dinh 定

Khai Dinh Thong Bao

The square holed cash coins of Annam are easily identified by reading the characters top-bottom (emperor's name) and right-left (Thong Bao, general currency). The character at right will change with some emperors.

CYCLICAL DATES

	庚	辛	壬	癸	甲	乙	丙	丁	戊	己
戌	1850 1910		1862 1922		1874 1934		1886 1946		1838 1898	
亥		1851 1911		1863 1923		1875 1935		1887 1947		1839 1899
子	1840 1900		1852 1912		1864 1924		1876 1936		1888 1948	
丑		1841 1901		1853 1913		1865 1925		1877 1937		1889 1949
寅	1830 1890		1842 1902		1854 1914		1866 1926		1878 1938	
卯		1831 1891		1843 1903		1855 1915		1867 1927		1879 1939
辰	1880 1940		1832 1892		1844 1904		1856 1916		1868 1928	
巳		1881 1941		1833 1893		1845 1905		1857 1917		1869 1929
午	1870 1930		1882 1942		1834 1894		1846 1906		1858 1918	
未		1871 1931		1883 1943		1835 1895		1847 1907		1859 1919
申	1860 1920		1872 1932		1884 1944		1836 1896		1848 1908	
酉		1861 1921		1873 1933		1885 1945		1837 1897		1849 1909

NOTE: This table has been adapted from *Chinese Bank Notes* by Ward Smith and Brian Matravers.

Cyclical dates consist of a pair of characters one of which indicates the animal associated with that year. Every 60 years, this pair of characters is repeated. The first character of a cyclical date corresponds to a character in the first row of the chart above. The second where a cyclical date is used, the abbreviation CD appears before the A.D. date.

NUMERALS

Column A, conventional; Column B, formal.

NUMBER	CONVENTIONAL	FORMAL	COMMERCIAL
1	一 元	壹 弌	〡
2	二	弍 貳	〢
3	三	叁 弎	〣
4	四	肆	〤
5	五	伍	〥
6	六	陸	〦
7	七	柒	〧
8	八	捌	〨
9	九	玖	〩
10	十	拾 什	十
20	十 二 or 廿	拾貳	〢十
25	五 十 二 or 五 廿	伍拾貳	〢十〥
30	十 三 or 卅	拾叁	〣十
100	百 一	佰壹	〡百
1,000	千 一	仟壹	〡千
10,000	萬 一	萬壹	〡万
100,000	萬 十 億 一	萬拾 億壹	十万
1,000,000	萬百一	萬佰壹	〡百万

NOTE: This table has been adapted from *Chinese Bank Notes* by Ward Smith and Brian Matravers.

MONETARY SYSTEM

Copper and Zinc
10 Dong (zinc) = 1 Dong (copper)
600 Dong (zinc) = 1 Quan (string of cash)
Approximately 2600 Dong (zinc) = 1 Piastre

NOTE: Ratios between metals changed frequently, therefore the above is given as an approximate relationship.

NORTH DAI VIET

CAST COINAGE

KM# 31 PHAN

Cast Zinc **Ruler:** Chinh Hoa **Obv:** Conventional script text. **Obv. Inscription:** "Chinh-hoa Thong-bao" with 5-stroke Chinh.

Date	Mintage	Good	VG	F	VF	XF
ND(1676-1705)	—	20.00	35.00	65.00	125	—

KM# 32 PHAN

Cast Copper **Ruler:** Chinh Hoa **Obv:** Conventional script text. **Obv. Inscription:** "Chinh-hoa Thong-bao" with 5-stroke Chinh. **Rev:** Crescent right.

Date	Mintage	Good	VG	F	VF	XF
ND(1676-1705) Rare	—	—	—	—	—	—

KM# A33 PHAN

Zinc **Ruler:** Chinh Hoa **Note:** Similar to KM#32.

Date	Mintage	Good	VG	F	VF	XF
ND(1676-1705)	—	—	—	—	—	—

KM# 33 PHAN

Cast Copper **Ruler:** Chinh Hoa **Obv:** Seal script text. **Obv. Inscription:** "Chinh-hoa Thong-bao" with 9-stroke Chinh. **Note:** Believed to be Chinese or copies thereof.

Date	Mintage	Good	VG	F	VF	XF
ND(1676-1705)	—	7.50	11.50	18.50	30.00	—

KM# 34 PHAN

Cast Copper **Ruler:** Chinh Hoa **Obv:** Seal script text. **Obv. Inscription:** "Chinh-hoa Thong-bao" with bao abbreviated and 9-stroke Chinh. **Note:** Believed to be Chinese or copies thereof.

Date	Mintage	Good	VG	F	VF	XF
ND(1676-1705) Rare	—	—	—	—	—	—

KM# 35 PHAN

Cast Copper **Ruler:** Chinh Hoa **Obv:** Conventional script text. **Obv. Inscription:** "Chinh-hoa Thong-bao" with 9-stroke Chinh. **Note:** Believed to be Chinese or copies thereof.

Date	Mintage	Good	VG	F	VF	XF
ND(1676-1705)	—	6.00	16.50	26.50	40.00	—

KM# 36 PHAN

Cast Copper **Ruler:** Chinh Hoa **Obv:** Conventional script text. **Obv. Inscription:** "Chinh-hoa Thong-bao" with 9-stroke Chinh. **Rev:** Crescent right **Note:** Believed to be Chinese or copies thereof.

Date	Mintage	Good	VG	F	VF	XF
ND(1676-1705)	—	12.50	20.00	30.00	45.00	—

KM# 37 PHAN

Cast Copper **Ruler:** Chinh Hoa **Obv:** Conventional script text. **Obv. Inscription:** "Chinh-hoa Thong-bao" with 9-stroke Chinh. **Rev:** Crescent right and dot left **Note:** Believed to be Chinese or copies thereof.

Date	Mintage	Good	VG	F	VF	XF
ND(1676-1705)	—	14.00	21.50	32.50	50.00	—

KM# 45 PHAN

Cast Copper **Ruler:** Vinh Thinh **Obv:** Inscription: Vinh-thinh Thong-bao **Rev:** Plain

Date	Mintage	Good	VG	F	VF	XF
ND(1705-20)	—	4.75	7.75	12.50	22.00	—

KM# 46 PHAN

Cast Copper **Ruler:** Vinh Thinh **Obv:** Inscription: Vinh-thinh Thong-bao **Rev:** Crescent at bottom and dot at top

Date	Mintage	Good	VG	F	VF	XF
ND(1705-20)	—	8.00	12.50	20.00	32.00	—

KM# 47 PHAN

Cast Copper **Ruler:** Vinh Thinh **Obv:** Inscription: Vinh-thinh Thong-bao **Rev:** Cyclical date character, 6th branch, "snake" left

Date	Mintage	Good	VG	F	VF	XF
ND(1705-20)	—	4.75	7.75	12.50	22.00	—

KM# 48 PHAN

Cast Copper **Ruler:** Bao Thai **Obv:** Inscription: Bao-thai Thong-bao **Rev:** Plain

Date	Mintage	Good	VG	F	VF	XF
ND(1720-29)	—	9.00	14.00	20.00	35.00	—

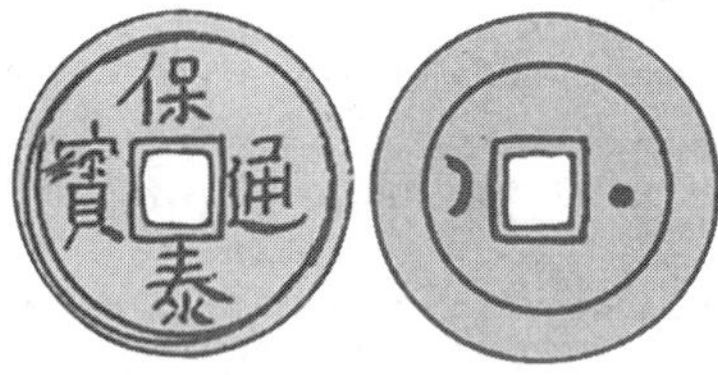

KM# 49 PHAN

Cast Copper **Ruler:** Bao Thai **Obv:** Inscription: Bao-thai Thong-bao **Rev:** Crescent left and dot right

Date	Mintage	Good	VG	F	VF	XF
ND(1720-29)	—	9.00	14.00	20.00	35.00	—

KM# 50 PHAN

Cast Copper **Ruler:** Bao Thai **Obv:** Inscription: Bao-thai Thong-bao **Rev:** Dot right

Date	Mintage	Good	VG	F	VF	XF
ND(1720-29)	—	9.00	14.00	20.00	35.00	—

KM# 88 PHAN

Cast Copper **Ruler:** Canh Hung **Obv:** "Cu Bao" **Rev:** Numeral "five" in seal script at right, diamond or kite-shaped figure at left **Note:** Prev. C#13.4.

Date	Mintage	Good	VG	F	VF	XF
ND(1740-87)	—	5.25	8.50	15.00	25.00	—
ND	—	—	—	—	—	—

KM# 52.1 PHAN

Cast Copper **Ruler:** Canh Hung **Obv:** Inscription: Seal script Canh-hung Thong-bao **Rev:** Plain **Note:** Prev. C#1.1.

Date	Mintage	Good	VG	F	VF	XF
ND(1740-87)	—	1.50	2.75	4.50	8.00	—

KM# 52.2 PHAN

Cast Copper **Ruler:** Canh Hung **Obv:** Inscription: Seal script Canh-hung Thong-bao **Rev:** Dot at top **Note:** Prev. C#1.1a.

Date	Mintage	Good	VG	F	VF	XF
ND(1740-87)	—	3.00	5.00	8.00	15.00	—

KM# 52.3 PHAN

Cast Copper **Ruler:** Canh Hung **Obv:** Inscription: Canh-hung Thong-bao **Rev:** Two dots at top **Note:** Prev. C#1.1b.

Date	Mintage	Good	VG	F	VF	XF
ND(1740-87)	—	3.50	5.50	9.00	16.00	—

KM# 53.1 PHAN

Cast Copper **Ruler:** Canh Hung **Obv:** Inscription: Canh-hung Thong-bao **Rev:** Plain **Note:** Prev. C#1.2.

Date	Mintage	Good	VG	F	VF	XF
ND(1740-87)	—	1.50	2.75	4.50	8.00	—

KM# 53.2 PHAN

Cast Copper **Ruler:** Canh Hung **Obv:** Inscription: Canh-hung Thong-bao **Rev:** Two dots at right and bottom **Note:** Prev. C#1.2a.

Date	Mintage	Good	VG	F	VF	XF
ND(1740-87)	—	3.50	5.50	9.00	16.00	—

KM# 53.3 PHAN

Cast Copper **Ruler:** Canh Hung **Obv:** Inscription: Canh-hung Thong-bao **Rev:** Four crescents, tips inward **Note:** Prev. C#1.2b.

Date	Mintage	Good	VG	F	VF	XF
ND(1740-87)	—	3.75	6.50	10.00	18.00	—

KM# 53.4 PHAN

Cast Copper **Ruler:** Canh Hung **Obv:** Inscription: Canh-hung Thong-bao **Rev:** Four lines surrounding center hole **Note:** Prev. C#1.2c.

Date	Mintage	Good	VG	F	VF	XF
ND(1740-87)	—	3.75	6.50	10.00	18.00	—

KM# 54.1 PHAN

Cast Copper **Ruler:** Canh Hung **Obv:** Conventional script text. **Obv. Inscription:** "Canh-hung Thong-bao". **Rev:** Plain **Note:** Prev. C#1.3.

Date	Mintage	Good	VG	F	VF	XF
ND(1740-87)	—	1.25	2.25	3.50	6.00	—

KM# 54.2 PHAN

Cast Copper **Ruler:** Canh Hung **Rev:** Dot at left **Note:** Prev. C#1.3a.

Date	Mintage	Good	VG	F	VF	XF
ND(1740-87)	—	2.00	3.75	6.00	11.50	—

KM# 54.3 PHAN

Cast Copper **Ruler:** Canh Hung **Rev:** Dot at lower left **Note:** Prev. C#1.3b.

Date	Mintage	Good	VG	F	VF	XF
ND(1740-87)	—	3.00	5.00	8.00	15.00	—

KM# 54.4 PHAN

Cast Copper **Ruler:** Canh Hung **Rev:** Dot at right **Note:** Prev. C#1.3c.

Date	Mintage	Good	VG	F	VF	XF
ND(1740-87)	—	3.00	5.00	8.00	15.00	—

KM# 54.5 PHAN

Cast Copper **Ruler:** Canh Hung **Rev:** Dot at top **Note:** Prev. C#1.3d.

Date	Mintage	Good	VG	F	VF	XF
ND(1740-87)	—	3.00	5.00	8.00	15.00	—

KM# 54.6 PHAN

Cast Copper **Ruler:** Canh Hung **Rev:** Crescent at left, two dots at top and bottom **Note:** Prev. C#1.3e.

Date	Mintage	Good	VG	F	VF	XF
ND(1740-87)	—	5.00	8.50	14.50	22.00	—

KM# 55 PHAN

Cast Copper **Ruler:** Canh Hung **Rev:** "Nhat" (one) at bottom **Note:** Prev. C#1.5.

Date	Mintage	Good	VG	F	VF	XF
ND(1740-87)	—	3.50	5.50	9.00	16.00	—

KM# 56 PHAN

Cast Copper **Ruler:** Canh Hung **Rev:** "Nhi" (two) at bottom **Note:** Prev. C#1.5a.

Date	Mintage	Good	VG	F	VF	XF
ND(1740-87)	—	3.00	5.00	8.00	15.00	—

KM# 57 PHAN

Cast Copper **Ruler:** Canh Hung **Rev:** "Tam" (three) at top **Note:** Prev. C#1.5b.

Date	Mintage	Good	VG	F	VF	XF
ND(1740-87)	—	3.75	6.50	10.00	18.00	—

KM# 58 PHAN

Cast Copper **Ruler:** Canh Hung **Rev:** "Bac" at top **Note:** Prev. C#1.6.

Date	Mintage	Good	VG	F	VF	XF
ND(1740-87)	—	5.50	9.00	15.50	25.00	—

KM# 59 PHAN

Cast Copper **Ruler:** Canh Hung **Rev:** "Tay" at bottom **Note:** Prev. C#1.6a.

Date	Mintage	Good	VG	F	VF	XF
ND(1740-87)	—	3.50	5.50	9.00	16.00	—

KM# 60 PHAN

Cast Copper **Ruler:** Canh Hung **Rev:** "Thai" at right **Note:** Prev. C#1.6b.

Date	Mintage	Good	VG	F	VF	XF
ND(1740-87)	—	3.50	5.50	9.00	16.00	—

KM# 61 PHAN

Cast Copper **Ruler:** Canh Hung **Rev:** "Trung" at top **Note:** Prev. C#1.6c.

Date	Mintage	Good	VG	F	VF	XF
ND(1740-87)	—	2.00	3.75	6.00	11.50	—

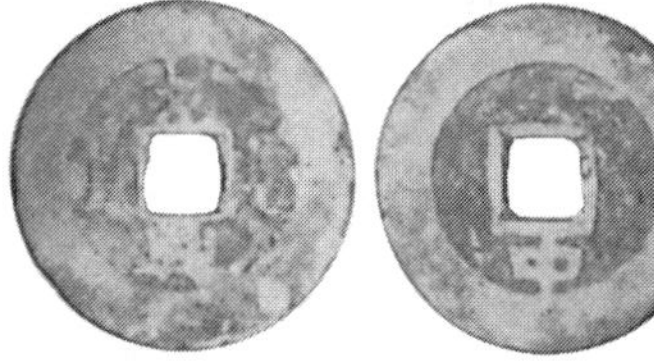

KM# 62 PHAN

Cast Copper **Ruler:** Canh Hung **Rev:** "Trung" at bottom **Note:** Prev. C#1.6d.

Date	Mintage	Good	VG	F	VF	XF
ND(1740-87)	—	2.00	3.75	6.00	11.50	—

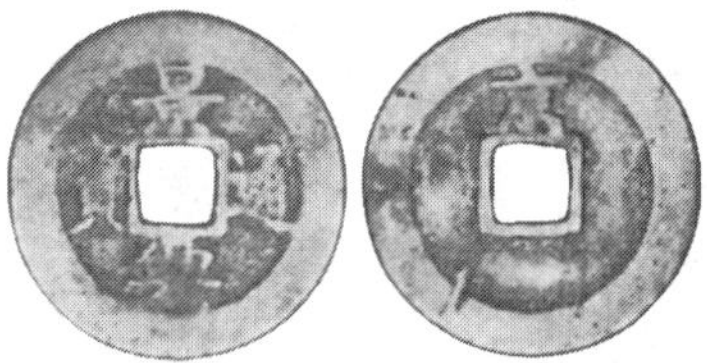

KM# 63 PHAN

Cast Copper **Ruler:** Canh Hung **Rev:** "Kinh" at top **Note:** Prev. C#1.6e.

Date	Mintage	Good	VG	F	VF	XF
ND(1740-87)	—	2.00	3.75	6.00	11.50	—

KM# 64 PHAN

Cast Copper **Ruler:** Canh Hung **Rev:** "Kinh" at top and dot at bottom **Note:** Prev. C#1.6f.

Date	Mintage	Good	VG	F	VF	XF
ND(1740-87)	—	3.00	5.00	8.00	15.00	—

KM# 65 PHAN

Cast Copper **Ruler:** Canh Hung **Rev:** "Po" at bottom **Note:** Prev. C1.6g.

Date	Mintage	Good	VG	F	VF	XF
ND(1740-87)	—	25.00	50.00	75.00	100	—

Note: "Po" is the Chinese romanization of this character which means "silk"; the Annamese romaniziation is not available

KM# 66 PHAN

Cast Copper **Ruler:** Canh Hung **Rev:** "Cong" at bottom **Note:** Prev. C1.6h.

Date	Mintage	Good	VG	F	VF	XF
ND(1740-87)	—	2.00	3.75	6.00	11.50	—

KM# 67 PHAN

Cast Copper **Ruler:** Canh Hung **Rev:** "Son Nam" horizontally **Note:** Prev. #C1.6i.

Date	Mintage	Good	VG	F	VF	XF
ND(1740-87)	—	4.25	7.00	11.00	20.00	—

KM# 68 PHAN

Cast Copper **Ruler:** Canh Hung **Rev:** "Son Tay" horizontally **Note:** Prev. #C1.6j.

Date	Mintage	Good	VG	F	VF	XF
ND(1740-87)	—	3.50	5.50	9.00	16.00	—

KM# 69 PHAN

Cast Copper **Ruler:** Canh Hung **Rev:** "Thai Nguyen" horizontally in seal script **Note:** Prev. #C1.6k.

Date	Mintage	Good	VG	F	VF	XF
ND(1740-87)	—	5.25	8.50	15.00	25.00	—

Note: The second character "Nguyen" is not the numismatically common 4-stroke character meaning "first", but rather is the 10-stroke character for a "source" or "origin"

KM# 70 PHAN

Cast Copper **Ruler:** Canh Hung **Rev:** Two unidentified characters horizontally in an unusual script style **Note:** Prev. #C1.6l.

Date	Mintage	Good	VG	F	VF	XF
ND(1740-87)	—	5.25	8.50	15.00	25.00	—

Note: These characters somewhat resemble elaborated versions of "Cu", the right character having an extra center loop, and the left having upper and lower portions which form 3-sided boxes; Toda states these are the characters "Luc Phan"

KM# 71 PHAN

Cast Copper **Ruler:** Canh Hung **Rev:** "Dai" at top **Note:** Prev. C#1.6m.

Date	Mintage	Good	VG	F	VF	XF
ND(1740-87)	—	5.25	8.50	15.00	25.00	—

KM# 72 PHAN

Cast Copper **Ruler:** Canh Hung **Rev:** "Dai" at right **Note:** Prev. C#1.6n.

Date	Mintage	Good	VG	F	VF	XF
ND(1740-87)	—	5.25	8.50	15.00	25.00	—

KM# 73 PHAN

Cast Copper **Ruler:** Canh Hung **Rev:** "Sui" at top **Note:** Prev. C#1.6o.

Date	Mintage	Good	VG	F	VF	XF
ND(1740-87)	—	5.25	8.50	15.00	25.00	—

KM# 74 PHAN

Cast Copper **Ruler:** Canh Hung **Rev:** "Thuong" at top **Note:** Prev. C#1.6p.

Date	Mintage	Good	VG	F	VF	XF
ND(1740-87)	—	5.25	8.50	15.00	25.00	—

KM# 75 PHAN

Cast Copper **Ruler:** Canh Hung **Rev:** Numeral "five" in seal script at right, diamond or kite-shaped figure at left **Note:** Prev. C#1.6q.

Date	Mintage	Good	VG	F	VF	XF
ND(1740-87)	—	6.00	10.00	17.50	28.50	—

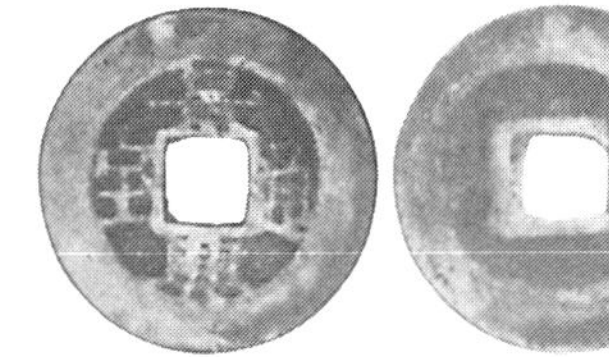

KM# 76 PHAN

Cast Copper **Ruler:** Canh Hung **Obv:** "Bao" abbreviated **Note:** Prev. C#2.

Date	Mintage	Good	VG	F	VF	XF
ND(1740-87)	—	2.25	4.00	6.50	12.50	—

KM# 77 PHAN

Cast Copper **Ruler:** Canh Hung **Obv:** "Dai Bao" **Note:** Prev. C#3.

Date	Mintage	Good	VG	F	VF	XF
ND(1740-87)	—	2.50	4.25	7.00	13.50	—

KM# 78 PHAN

Cast Copper **Ruler:** Canh Hung **Obv:** "Dai Bao, Bao" abbreviated **Rev:** "Bac" at top **Note:** Prev. C#4.

Date	Mintage	Good	VG	F	VF	XF
ND(1740-87)	—	9.00	14.00	20.00	32.00	—

KM# 79 PHAN

Cast Copper **Ruler:** Canh Hung **Obv:** "Thai Bao" **Rev:** Plain **Note:** Prev. C#5.

Date	Mintage	Good	VG	F	VF	XF
ND(1740-87)	—	4.75	7.75	12.50	22.00	—

KM# 80 PHAN

Cast Copper **Ruler:** Canh Hung **Obv:** "Noi Bao" **Rev:** Plain **Note:** Prev. C#7.

Date	Mintage	Good	VG	F	VF	XF
ND(1740-87) Rare	—	—	—	—	—	—

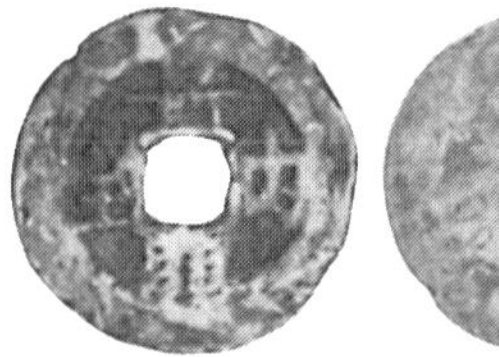

KM# 81 PHAN

Cast Copper **Ruler:** Canh Hung **Obv:** "Noi Bao, Bao" abbreviated **Rev:** Plain **Note:** Prev. C#8.

Date	Mintage	Good	VG	F	VF	XF
ND(1740-87)	—	4.75	7.75	12.50	22.00	—

KM# 82 PHAN

Cast Copper **Ruler:** Canh Hung **Obv:** "Trung Bao" **Rev:** Plain **Note:** Prev. C#9.

Date	Mintage	Good	VG	F	VF	XF
ND(1740-87)	—	9.00	14.00	20.00	32.00	—

KM# 83 PHAN

Cast Copper **Ruler:** Canh Hung **Obv:** "Trung Bao, Bao" abbreviated **Rev:** Plain **Note:** Prev. C#10.

Date	Mintage	Good	VG	F	VF	XF
ND(1740-87)	—	9.00	14.00	20.00	32.00	—

KM# 84 PHAN

Cast Copper **Ruler:** Canh Hung **Obv:** "Chinh Bao" **Rev:** Plain **Note:** Prev. C#11.

Date	Mintage	Good	VG	F	VF	XF
ND(1740-87)	—	3.75	6.50	10.00	18.00	—

KM# 85 PHAN

Cast Copper **Ruler:** Canh Hung **Obv:** "Cu Bao" **Rev:** Plain **Note:** Prev. C#13.1.

Date	Mintage	Good	VG	F	VF	XF
ND(1740-87)	—	1.50	2.75	4.50	8.00	—

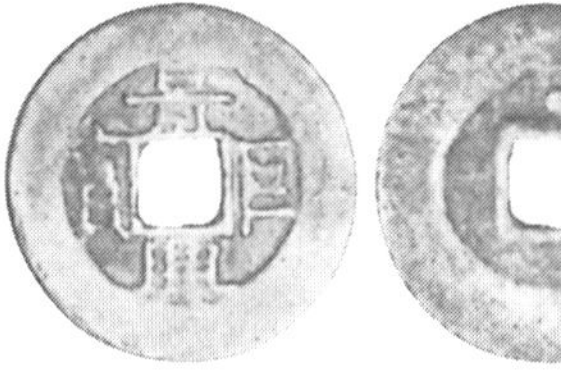

KM# 86 PHAN

Cast Copper **Ruler:** Canh Hung **Obv:** "Cu Bao" **Rev:** Dot at top **Note:** Prev. C#13.2.

Date	Mintage	Good	VG	F	VF	XF
ND(1740-87)	—	2.25	4.00	6.50	12.50	—

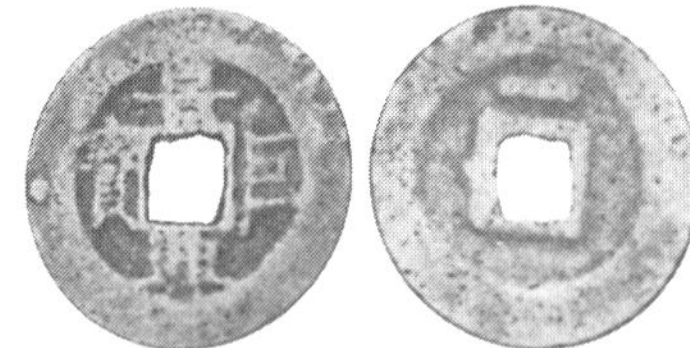

KM# 87 PHAN

Cast Copper **Ruler:** Canh Hung **Obv:** "Cu Bao" **Rev:** Numeral "one" at top **Note:** Prev. C#13.3.

Date	Mintage	Good	VG	F	VF	XF
ND(1740-87)	—	2.25	4.00	6.50	12.50	—

KM# 89 PHAN

Cast Copper **Ruler:** Canh Hung **Obv:** "Cu Bao" **Rev:** "Trung" at bottom **Note:** Prev. C#13.5.

Date	Mintage	Good	VG	F	VF	XF
ND(1740-87)	—	5.25	8.50	15.00	25.00	—

KM# 90 PHAN

Cast Copper **Ruler:** Canh Hung **Obv:** "Cu Bao, Bao" abbreviated **Rev:** Plain **Note:** Prev. C#14.

Date	Mintage	Good	VG	F	VF	XF
ND(1740-87)	—	3.75	6.50	10.00	18.00	—

KM# 91 PHAN

Cast Copper **Ruler:** Canh Hung **Obv:** "Dung Bao" **Rev:** Plain **Note:** Prev. C#15.

Date	Mintage	Good	VG	F	VF	XF
ND(1740-87) Rare	—	—	—	—	—	—

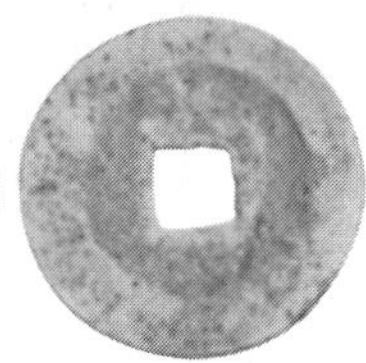

KM# 92 PHAN

Cast Copper **Ruler:** Canh Hung **Obv:** "Vinh Bao" **Rev:** Plain **Note:** Prev. C#17.1.

Date	Mintage	Good	VG	F	VF	XF
ND(1740-87)	—	1.50	2.75	4.50	8.00	—

KM# 93 PHAN

Cast Copper **Ruler:** Canh Hung **Obv:** "Vinh Bao" **Rev:** Dot at top **Note:** Prev. C#17.2.

Date	Mintage	Good	VG	F	VF	XF
ND(1740-87)	—	3.00	5.00	8.00	15.00	—

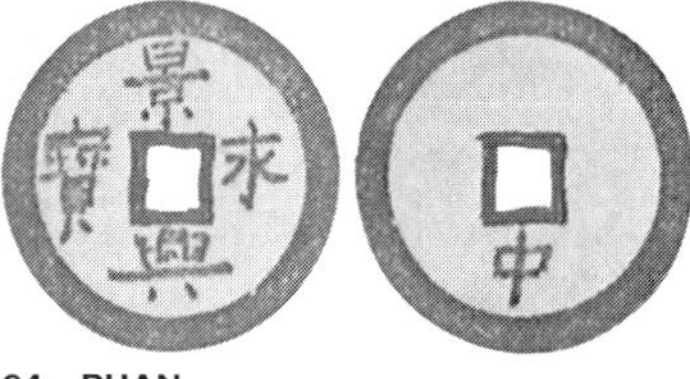

KM# 94 PHAN

Cast Copper **Ruler:** Canh Hung **Obv:** "Vinh Bao" **Rev:** "Trung" at bottom **Note:** Prev. C#17.3.

Date	Mintage	Good	VG	F	VF	XF
ND(1740-87)	—	4.25	7.00	11.00	20.00	—

KM# 95 PHAN

Cast Copper **Ruler:** Canh Hung **Obv:** "Chi Bao" **Rev:** Plain **Note:** Prev. C#19.

Date	Mintage	Good	VG	F	VF	XF
ND(1740-87)	—	3.25	5.25	8.50	16.00	—

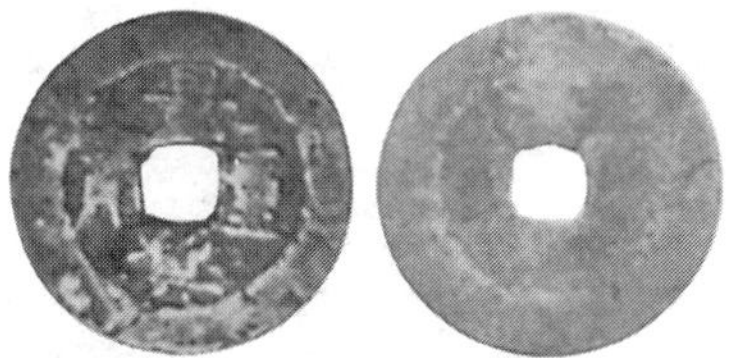

KM# 96 PHAN

Cast Copper **Ruler:** Canh Hung **Obv:** "Trung Bao" **Rev:** Plain **Note:** Prev. C#21.

Date	Mintage	Good	VG	F	VF	XF
ND(1740-87)	—	2.75	4.50	7.50	14.50	—

Note: "Trung", in this case, is the 9-stroke character meaning "heavy"; all other uses of "Trung" with respect to Annamese dongs refer to the 4-stroke character meaning "middle"

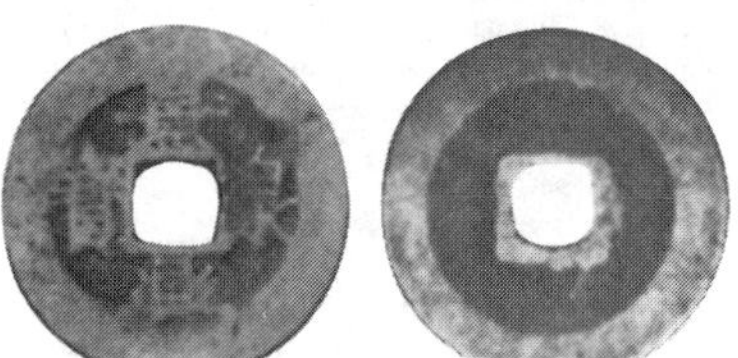

KM# 97 PHAN

Cast Copper **Ruler:** Canh Hung **Obv:** "Tuyen Bao" **Rev:** Plain **Note:** Prev. C#23.

Date	Mintage	Good	VG	F	VF	XF
ND(1740-87)	—	2.75	4.50	7.50	14.50	—

KM# 98 PHAN

Cast Copper **Ruler:** Canh Hung **Obv:** "Thuan Bao" **Rev:** Plain **Note:** Prev. C#25.1.

Date	Mintage	Good	VG	F	VF	XF
ND(1740-87)	—	3.50	5.50	9.00	16.00	—

KM# 99 PHAN

Cast Copper **Ruler:** Canh Hung **Obv:** "Thuan Bao" **Rev:** Dot at top **Note:** Prev. C#25.2.

Date	Mintage	Good	VG	F	VF	XF
ND(1740-87)	—	4.50	7.00	11.00	20.00	—

KM# 108 PHAN

Cast Copper **Ruler:** Canh Hung **Rev:** "Can Than" **Note:** Prev. C#1.4.

Date	Mintage	Good	VG	F	VF	XF
CD(1740-87)	—	10.50	18.00	30.00	45.00	—

KM# 109 PHAN

Cast Copper **Ruler:** Canh Hung **Rev:** "Tan Dau" **Note:** Prev. C#1.4a.

Date	Mintage	Good	VG	F	VF	XF
CD(1741-87) Rare	—	—	—	—	—	—

KM# 110 PHAN

Cast Copper **Ruler:** Canh Hung **Rev:** "Nham Thuat" **Note:** Prev. C#1.4b.

Date	Mintage	Good	VG	F	VF	XF
CD(1742-87) Rare	—	—	—	—	—	—

Note: The characters used for these dates are those listed in the "Cyclical Dates" table for 1860, 1861, and 1862; that is, two 60-year cycles later

KM# 118.1 PHAN

Cast Copper **Ruler:** Chieu Thong **Obv. Inscription:** Chien-thong Thong-bao **Rev:** Plain **Note:** Prev. C#30.1.

Date	Mintage	Good	VG	F	VF	XF
ND(1787-89)	—	1.75	3.00	4.75	9.00	—

KM# 118.2 PHAN

Cast Copper **Ruler:** Chieu Thong **Obv. Inscription:** Chien-thong Thong-bao **Rev:** Crescent at right, dot at left **Note:** Prev. C#30.2.

Date	Mintage	Good	VG	F	VF	XF
ND(1787-89)	—	3.50	5.50	9.00	16.00	—

KM# 118.3 PHAN

Cast Copper **Ruler:** Chieu Thong **Obv. Inscription:** Chien-thong Thong-bao **Rev:** Four crescents, tips inward **Note:** Prev. C#30.3.

Date	Mintage	Good	VG	F	VF	XF
ND(1787-89)	—	3.50	5.50	9.00	16.00	—

KM# 119 PHAN

Cast Copper **Ruler:** Chieu Thong **Obv. Inscription:** Chien-thong Thong-bao **Rev:** Numeral "one" at top **Note:** Prev. C#31.1.

Date	Mintage	Good	VG	F	VF	XF
ND(1787-89)	—	3.50	5.50	9.00	16.00	—

KM# 120 PHAN

Cast Copper **Ruler:** Chieu Thong **Obv. Inscription:** Chien-thong Thong-bao **Rev:** Numeral "one" at bottom **Note:** Prev. C#31.1a.

Date	Mintage	Good	VG	F	VF	XF
ND(1787-89)	—	2.25	4.00	6.50	12.50	—

KM# 121 PHAN

Cast Copper **Ruler:** Chieu Thong **Obv. Inscription:** Chien-thong Thong-bao **Rev:** "Thai" at bottom **Note:** Prev. C#31.2.

Date	Mintage	Good	VG	F	VF	XF
ND(1787-89)	—	5.75	9.50	16.00	27.00	—

KM# 122 PHAN

Cast Copper **Ruler:** Chieu Thong **Obv. Inscription:** Chien-thong Thong-bao **Rev:** "Son" at bottom **Note:** Prev. C#31.3.

Date	Mintage	Good	VG	F	VF	XF
ND(1787-89)	—	3.25	5.25	8.50	15.00	—

KM# 123 PHAN

Cast Copper **Ruler:** Chieu Thong **Obv. Inscription:** Chien-thong Thong-bao **Rev:** "Son" at right **Note:** Prev. C#31.3a.

Date	Mintage	Good	VG	F	VF	XF
ND(1787-89)	—	3.50	5.50	9.00	16.00	—

KM# 124 PHAN

Cast Copper **Ruler:** Chieu Thong **Obv. Inscription:** Chien-thong Thong-bao **Rev:** "Trung" at top **Note:** Prev. C#31.4.

Date	Mintage	Good	VG	F	VF	XF
ND(1787-89)	—	3.50	5.50	9.00	16.00	—

KM# 125 PHAN

Cast Copper **Ruler:** Chieu Thong **Obv. Inscription:** Chien-thong Thong-bao **Rev:** "Trung" at bottom **Note:** Prev. C#31.14a.

Date	Mintage	Good	VG	F	VF	XF
ND(1787-89)	—	2.75	4.50	7.50	14.50	—

KM# 126 PHAN

Cast Copper **Ruler:** Chieu Thong **Obv. Inscription:** Chien-thong Thong-bao **Rev:** "Chinh" at bottom **Note:** Prev. C#31.5.

Date	Mintage	Good	VG	F	VF	XF
ND(1787-89)	—	2.75	5.00	8.00	15.00	—

KM# 127 PHAN

Cast Copper **Ruler:** Chieu Thong **Obv. Inscription:** Chien-thong Thong-bao **Rev:** "Son Nam" horizontally **Note:** Prev. C#31.6.

Date	Mintage	Good	VG	F	VF	XF
ND(1787-89)	—	3.50	5.50	9.00	16.00	—

OCCUPATION CAST COINAGE

KM# 131 PHAN

Cast Brass **Ruler:** Can Long Ch'ien Lung of China **Rev:** "An Nam" horizontally **Note:** Prev. C#34.1.

Date	Mintage	Good	VG	F	VF	XF
ND(1789)	—	45.00	75.00	165	240	—

KM# 132 PHAN

Cast Brass **Ruler:** Can Long Ch'ien Lung of China **Rev:** "An Nam" horizontally, dot at top **Note:** Prev. C#34.2.

Date	Mintage	Good	VG	F	VF	XF
ND(1789)	—	55.00	90.00	195	270	—

SOUTH DAI VIET

REBEL CAST COINAGE

Tayson Rebellion

KM# 137.1 PHAN

Cast Brass **Ruler:** Thai Duc Minh Duc, ca. 1785 **Rev:** Plain **Note:** Prev. C#38.1.

Date	Mintage	Good	VG	F	VF	XF
ND(1778-93)	—	3.00	5.00	8.00	15.00	—

KM# 137.2 PHAN

Cast Brass **Ruler:** Thai Duc Minh Duc, ca. 1785 **Rev:** Dot at top **Note:** Prev. C#38.2.

Date	Mintage	Good	VG	F	VF	XF
ND(1778-93)	—	3.75	6.50	10.00	18.50	—

KM# 137.3 PHAN

Cast Brass **Ruler:** Thai Duc Minh Duc, ca. 1785 **Rev:** Two dots, top and bottom **Note:** Prev. C#38.2a.

Date	Mintage	Good	VG	F	VF	XF
ND(1778-93)	—	3.75	6.50	10.00	18.50	—

KM# 137.4 PHAN

Cast Brass **Ruler:** Thai Duc Minh Duc, ca. 1785 **Rev:** Crescent at bottom **Note:** Prev. C#38.3.

Date	Mintage	Good	VG	F	VF	XF
ND(1778-93)	—	4.75	7.50	12.00	21.50	—

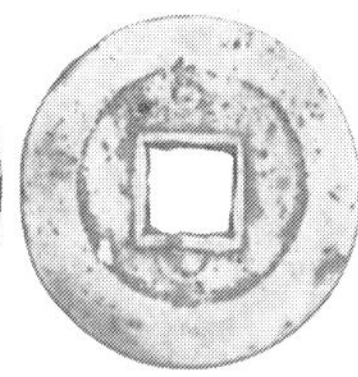

KM# 137.5 PHAN

Cast Brass **Ruler:** Thai Duc Minh Duc, ca. 1785 **Rev:** Crescent at bottom, dot at top **Note:** Prev. C#38.3a.

Date	Mintage	Good	VG	F	VF	XF
ND(1778-93)	—	5.00	8.25	14.00	23.50	—

KM# 137.6 PHAN

Cast Brass **Ruler:** Thai Duc Minh Duc, ca. 1785 **Rev:** Crescent at bottom; two dots, top and bottom **Note:** Prev. C#38.3b.

Date	Mintage	Good	VG	F	VF	XF
ND(1778-93)	—	5.00	8.25	14.00	23.50	—

KM# 137.7 PHAN

Cast Brass **Ruler:** Thai Duc Minh Duc, ca. 1785 **Rev:** Crescent left, dot right **Note:** Prev. C#38.3c.

Date	Mintage	Good	VG	F	VF	XF
ND(1778-93)	—	5.00	8.25	14.00	23.50	—

KM# 137.8 PHAN

Cast Brass **Ruler:** Thai Duc Minh Duc, ca. 1785 **Rev:** Crescent left **Note:** Prev. C#38.3d.

Date	Mintage	Good	VG	F	VF	XF
ND(1778-93)	—	4.75	7.50	12.00	21.50	—

KM# 137.9 PHAN

Cast Brass **Ruler:** Thai Duc Minh Duc, ca. 1785 **Rev:** Four crescents, tips inward **Note:** Prev. C#38.3e.

Date	Mintage	Good	VG	F	VF	XF
ND(1778-93)	—	5.00	8.25	14.00	23.50	—

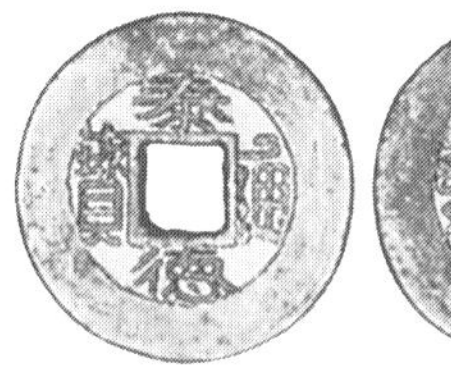
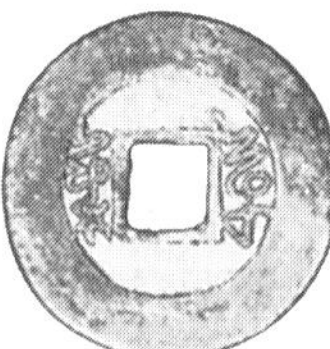

KM# 138 PHAN

Cast Brass **Ruler:** Thai Duc Minh Duc, ca. 1785 **Rev:** "Van Tue" (10,000 years) in grass script **Note:** Prev. C#39.1.

Date	Mintage	Good	VG	F	VF	XF
ND(1778-93)	—	4.25	7.00	11.00	20.00	—

KM# 139 PHAN

Cast Brass **Ruler:** Thai Duc Minh Duc, ca. 1785 **Obv:** Double rim **Note:** Prev. C#39.2.

Date	Mintage	Good	VG	F	VF	XF
ND(1778-93)	—	5.00	8.25	14.00	23.50	—

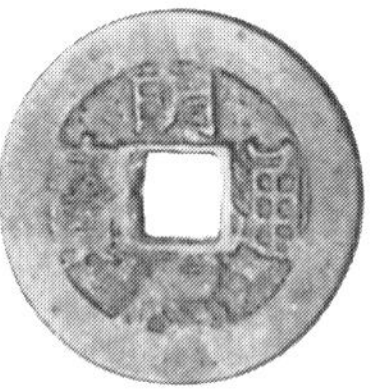
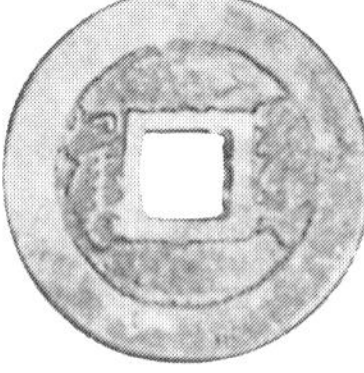

KM# 140.1 PHAN

Cast Brass **Ruler:** Thai Duc Minh Duc, ca. 1785 **Rev:** "Van Tue" (10,000 years) in grass script **Note:** Prev. C#40.1.

Date	Mintage	Good	VG	F	VF	XF
ND(ca.1785)	—	5.00	8.25	14.00	23.50	—

KM# 140.2 PHAN

Cast Brass **Ruler:** Thai Duc Minh Duc, ca. 1785 **Rev:** Crescent right, dot left **Note:** Prev. C#40.2.

Date	Mintage	Good	VG	F	VF	XF
ND(ca.1785)	—	5.75	9.50	16.00	27.00	—

Note: These "Minh Duc Thong Bao" coins should not be confused with the much earlier issues of the Mac Dynasty with the same inscription, but with slightly different calligraphy and with plain reverses

CAST COINAGE

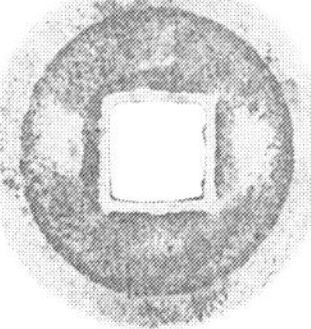

KM# 160.1 PHAN

Cast Brass **Ruler:** Canh Thinh **Rev:** Plain **Note:** Prev. C#51.1.

Date	Mintage	Good	VG	F	VF	XF
ND(1792-1801)	—	3.00	5.00	8.00	15.00	—

Note: Examples are reported to exist in tin (by Toda)

KM# 160.2 PHAN

Cast Brass **Ruler:** Canh Thinh **Rev:** Crescent left, dot right **Note:** Craig #51.2.

Date	Mintage	Good	VG	F	VF	XF
ND(1792-1801)	—	5.00	8.00	15.00	25.00	—

KM# 161 PHAN

Cast Brass **Ruler:** Canh Thinh **Obv:** Double rim **Note:** Craig #51.3.

Date	Mintage	Good	VG	F	VF	XF
ND(1792-1801)	—	4.00	7.00	11.00	17.00	—

KM# 162.1 PHAN

Cast Brass **Ruler:** Canh Thinh **Obv:** Double rim **Rev:** Double rim **Note:** Craig #51.4.

Date	Mintage	Good	VG	F	VF	XF
ND(1792-1801)	—	5.00	8.00	15.00	25.00	—

Note: Examples are reported to exist in tin (by Toda)

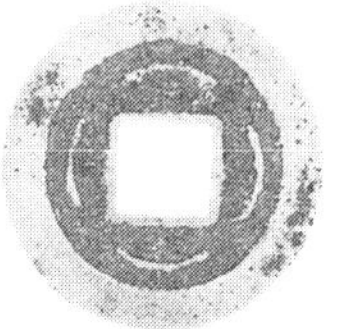

KM# 162.2 PHAN

Cast Brass, 22-23 mm. **Ruler:** Canh Thinh **Rev:** Four crescents, tips inward **Note:** Craig #51.5; size varies.

Date	Mintage	Good	VG	F	VF	XF
ND(1792-1801)	—	4.00	8.00	12.00	20.00	—

KM# 162.3 PHAN

Cast Brass **Ruler:** Canh Thinh **Rev:** Four bumps next to inner rim **Note:** Craig #51.6.

Date	Mintage	Good	VG	F	VF	XF
ND(1792-1801)	—	6.00	10.00	15.00	30.00	—

KM# 163 PHAN

Cast Brass **Ruler:** Canh Thinh **Rev:** Numeral one at bottom **Note:** Craig #51.7.

Date	Mintage	Good	VG	F	VF	XF
ND(1792-1801)	—	6.00	10.00	15.00	30.00	—

KM# 164 PHAN

Cast Brass **Ruler:** Canh Thinh **Obv:** "Dai Bao", Bao abbreviated **Note:** Craig #52.1; Schroeder #477.

Date	Mintage	Good	VG	F	VF	XF
ND(1792-1801)	—	8.00	12.00	20.00	35.00	—

KM# 165 PHAN

Cast Brass **Ruler:** Canh Thinh **Obv:** "Dai Bao, Bao" abbreviated, double rim **Rev:** Double rim **Note:** Craig #52.2.

Date	Mintage	Good	VG	F	VF	XF
ND(1792-1801)	—	12.00	17.50	25.00	40.00	—

OCCUPATION CAST COINAGE

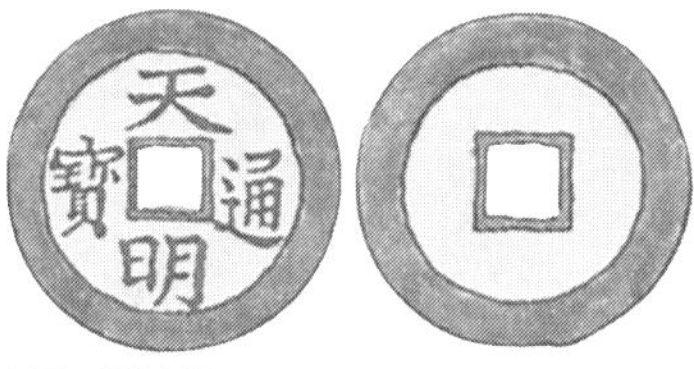

KM# 135 PHAN

Cast Copper Or Brass **Ruler:** Thien Minh **Rev:** Plain **Note:** Prev. C#36.

Date	Mintage	Good	VG	F	VF	XF
ND(1739-66)	—	10.50	18.00	30.00	45.00	—

Note: Craig indicates that this coin may exist in zinc

REBEL CAST COINAGE

The status of the large copper and brass 60 Van pieces of Canh Hung is debatable, but most experts believe them to be presentation pieces or weights. Many fabrications exist.

KM# 141.2 PHAN

Cast Brass **Ruler:** Quang Trung **Rev:** Two crescents top and bottom, tips outward **Note:** Prev. C#41.2.

Date	Mintage	Good	VG	F	VF	XF
ND(1788-92)	—	3.25	5.25	8.50	15.00	—
ND(1788-92)	—	3.75	6.50	10.00	18.50	—

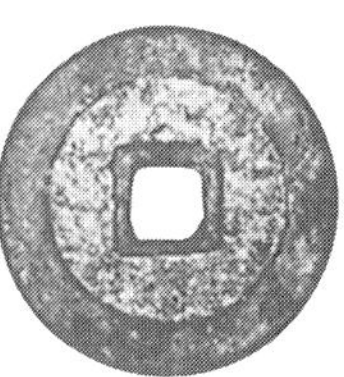

KM# 141.1 PHAN

Cast Brass **Ruler:** Quang Trung **Rev:** Plain **Note:** Prev. C#41.1.

Date	Mintage	Good	VG	F	VF	XF
ND(1788-92)	—	1.25	2.00	3.00	6.00	—

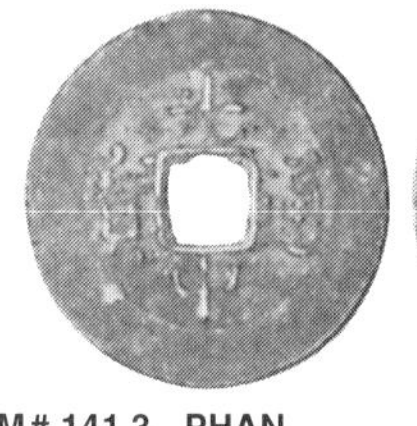
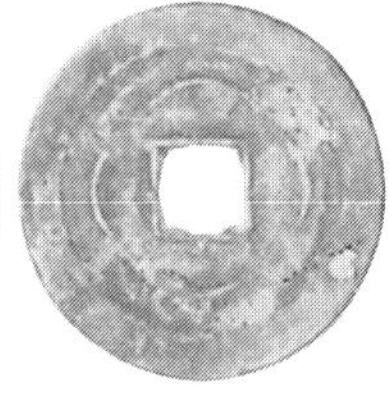

KM# 141.3 PHAN

Cast Brass **Ruler:** Quang Trung **Rev:** Four crescents, tips inward **Note:** Prev. C#41.3.

Date	Mintage	Good	VG	F	VF	XF
ND(1778-92)	—	3.25	5.25	8.50	15.00	—

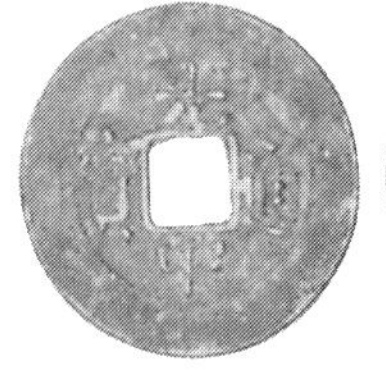

KM# 141.4 PHAN

Cast Brass **Ruler:** Quang Trung **Rev:** Four crescents, tips outward **Note:** Prev. C#41.3a.

Date	Mintage	Good	VG	F	VF	XF
ND(1778-92)	—	3.25	5.25	8.50	15.00	—

KM# 142.1 PHAN

Cast Brass **Ruler:** Quang Trung **Obv:** Double rim **Note:** Prev. C#41.4.

Date	Mintage	Good	VG	F	VF	XF
ND(1778-92)	—	2.00	3.75	6.00	11.50	—

KM# 142.2 PHAN

Cast Brass **Ruler:** Quang Trung **Obv:** Double rim **Rev:** Four crescents, tips inward **Note:** Prev. C#41.4a.

Date	Mintage	Good	VG	F	VF	XF
ND(1788-92)	—	3.75	6.50	10.00	18.50	—

KM# 143.1 PHAN

Cast Brass **Ruler:** Quang Trung **Obv:** Double rim **Rev:** Double rim **Note:** Prev. C#41.5.

Date	Mintage	Good	VG	F	VF	XF
ND(1788-92)	—	3.75	6.50	10.00	18.50	—

KM# 143.2 PHAN

Cast Brass **Ruler:** Quang Trung **Rev:** Dot at bottom **Note:** Prev. C#41.6.

Date	Mintage	Good	VG	F	VF	XF
ND(1788-92)	—	2.00	3.75	6.00	11.50	—

KM# 143.3 PHAN

Cast Brass **Ruler:** Quang Trung **Rev:** Vertical line left **Note:** Prev. C#41.7.

Date	Mintage	Good	VG	F	VF	XF
ND(1788-92)	—	3.25	5.25	8.50	15.00	—

KM# 144 PHAN

Cast Brass **Ruler:** Quang Trung **Obv:** "Bao" abbreviated **Note:** Prev. C#42.

Date	Mintage	Good	VG	F	VF	XF
ND(1788-92)	—	5.75	9.50	16.00	27.00	—

KM# 145 PHAN

Cast Brass **Ruler:** Quang Trung **Obv:** "Dai Bao" **Note:** Prev. C#43.1.

Date	Mintage	Good	VG	F	VF	XF
ND(1788-92)	—	6.00	10.00	17.50	27.50	—

KM# 146.1 PHAN

Cast Brass **Ruler:** Quang Trung **Obv:** "Dai Bao, Bao" abbreviated **Rev:** Plain **Note:** Prev. C#43.2.

Date	Mintage	Good	VG	F	VF	XF
ND(1788-92)	—	5.00	8.25	14.00	23.50	—

KM# 146.2 PHAN

Cast Brass **Ruler:** Quang Trung **Obv:** "Dai Bao, Bao" abbreviated **Rev:** Four crescents, tips inward **Note:** Prev. C#43.3.

Date	Mintage	Good	VG	F	VF	XF
ND(1788-92)	—	9.00	14.00	20.00	30.00	—

KM# 147 PHAN

Cast Brass **Ruler:** Quang Trung **Rev:** Numeral "one" at top **Note:** Prev. C#44.1.

Date	Mintage	Good	VG	F	VF	XF
ND(1788-92)	—	2.00	3.75	6.00	11.50	—

KM# 148 PHAN

Cast Brass **Ruler:** Quang Trung **Rev:** Numeral "one" at bottom **Note:** Prev. C#44.1a.

Date	Mintage	Good	VG	F	VF	XF
ND(1788-92)	—	4.50	7.25	11.00	20.00	—

KM# 149 PHAN

Cast Brass **Ruler:** Quang Trung **Rev:** Numeral "two" at bottom **Note:** Prev. C#44.2.

Date	Mintage	Good	VG	F	VF	XF
ND(1788-92)	—	4.50	7.25	11.00	20.00	—

KM# 150 PHAN

Cast Brass **Ruler:** Quang Trung **Rev:** "Cong" at top **Note:** Prev. C#44.3.

Date	Mintage	Good	VG	F	VF	XF
ND(1788-92)	—	4.50	7.25	11.00	20.00	—

KM# 151 PHAN

Cast Brass **Ruler:** Quang Trung **Rev:** "Cong" at bottom **Note:** Prev. C#44.3a.

Date	Mintage	Good	VG	F	VF	XF
ND(1788-92)	—	3.25	5.25	8.50	15.00	—

KM# 152 PHAN

Cast Brass **Ruler:** Quang Trung **Rev:** "Cong" at left **Note:** Prev. C#44.3b.

Date	Mintage	Good	VG	F	VF	XF
ND(1788-92)	—	3.25	5.25	8.50	15.00	—

KM# 153 PHAN

Cast Brass **Ruler:** Quang Trung **Rev:** Numeral "one" at top, "Chinh" at bottom **Note:** Prev. C#44.4.

Date	Mintage	Good	VG	F	VF	XF
ND(1788-92)	—	5.25	8.50	15.00	25.00	—

KM# 154 PHAN

Cast Brass **Ruler:** Quang Trung **Rev:** "An Nam" in seal script, horizontally **Note:** Prev. C#44.5.

Date	Mintage	Good	VG	F	VF	XF
ND(1788-92)	—	6.00	10.00	17.50	27.50	—

Note: KM#141.1, 142.1, and 151 of Quan Trung are reported in tin by Toda

UNITED DAI NAM

REBEL CAST COINAGE

The status of the large copper and brass 60 Van pieces of Canh Hung is debatable, but most experts believe them to be presentation pieces or weights. Many fabrications exist.

KM# 102 50 VAN

Cast Copper Or Brass **Ruler:** Canh Hung **Rev:** "Nguyen" at bottom **Note:** Prev. C#28.2.

Date	Mintage	Good	VG	F	VF	XF
ND(1740-87)	—	75.00	125	185	250	—

Note: "Nguyen" may indicate the first regnal year of Canh Hung (1740)

KM# 101 60 VAN

Cast Copper Or Brass **Ruler:** Canh Hung **Rev:** "Mot Lang" (one ounce) vertically **Note:** Prev. C#28.1.

Date	Mintage	Good	VG	F	VF	XF
ND(1740-87)	—	75.00	125	185	250	—

KM# 103 60 VAN

Cast Copper Or Brass **Ruler:** Canh Hung **Rev:** "Binh Nam" vertically **Note:** Prev. C#28.3.

Date	Mintage	Good	VG	F	VF	XF
ND(1740-87)	—	75.00	125	185	250	—

KM# 104 60 VAN

Cast Copper Or Brass **Ruler:** Canh Hung **Rev:** "Binh Nam" horizontally **Note:** Prev. C#28.4.

Date	Mintage	Good	VG	F	VF	XF
ND(1740-87)	—	75.00	125	185	250	—

KM# 105 60 VAN

Cast Copper Or Brass **Ruler:** Canh Hung **Rev:** "Binh Nam" and "Khai Quoc" **Note:** Prev. C#28.5.

Date	Mintage	Good	VG	F	VF	XF
ND(1740-87)	—	75.00	125	185	250	—

KM# 106 60 VAN

Cast Copper Or Brass **Ruler:** Canh Hung **Rev:** "Son Tay" horizontally **Note:** Prev. C#28.6.

Date	Mintage	Good	VG	F	VF	XF
ND(1740-87)	—	75.00	125	185	250	—

Note: The status of the 60 Van pieces of Canh Hung as coins is not entirely certain; at least some may be presentation pieces or medals, many fabrications exist

KM# 112 60 VAN

Cast Copper Or Brass **Ruler:** Canh Hung **Rev:** "Nham Thuat" and "Thong Bao" **Note:** Prev. C#27.2.

Date	Mintage	Good	VG	F	VF	XF
CD(1742)	—	75.00	125	185	250	—

KM# 113 60 VAN

Cast Copper Or Brass **Ruler:** Canh Hung **Obv:** Double rim **Rev:** "Nham Thuat", double rim **Note:** Prev. C#27.3.

Date	Mintage	Good	VG	F	VF	XF
CD(1742)	—	75.00	125	185	250	—

KM# 114 60 VAN

Cast Copper Or Brass **Ruler:** Canh Hung **Rev:** "Qui Hoi" **Note:** Prev. C#27.4.

Date	Mintage	Good	VG	F	VF	XF
CD(1743)	—	75.00	125	185	250	—

KM# 115 60 VAN

Cast Copper Or Brass **Ruler:** Canh Hung **Rev:** "Qui Hoi" **Note:** Prev. C#27.1.

Date	Mintage	Good	VG	F	VF	XF
CD(1743)	—	75.00	125	185	250	—

KM# 116 60 VAN

Cast Copper Or Brass **Ruler:** Canh Hung **Rev:** "Dinh Meo" **Note:** Prev. C#27.5.

Date	Mintage	Good	VG	F	VF	XF
CD(1747)	—	75.00	125	185	250	—

Note: The characters used for these dates are those listed in the "Cyclical Dates" table for 1862, 1863, and 1867; that is, two 60-year cycles later

The Windward Islands (Isles du Vent) make up the southern chain of islands in the Lesser Antilles. Visited by Columbus on his 1493 and 1502 voyages. Various parts of the islands were occupied by France beginning in 1635.

The islands were developed for their strategic location in the scheme of a French empire. They were lost to the British in the 7 Years War but returned to France by the Treaty of Paris that ended the war in 1763. Following the Napoleonic Wars most of the islands were returned to Great Britain.

RULER

Louis XV, 1715-1774

MINT MARK

H - La Rochelle

FRENCH PROTECTORATE

STANDARD COINAGE

C# 1 6 SOLS

Silver **Ruler:** Louis XV **Obv:** Young head of Louis XV right **Rev:** Name above date

Date	Mintage	Good	VG	F	VF	XF
1731H	—	—	35.00	65.00	125	250
1732H	—	—	40.00	75.00	150	280

C# 2 12 SOLS

Silver **Ruler:** Louis XV **Obv:** Young head of Louis XV right **Rev:** Name above date

Date	Mintage	Good	VG	F	VF	XF
1731H	—	—	30.00	50.00	100	200
1732H	—	—	35.00	65.00	125	220

PATTERNS

KM#	Date	Mintage	Identification	Mkt Val
Pn1	1789A	—	2 Sous. Copper.	600

KM#	Date	Mintage	Identification	Mkt Val
Pn2	1789A	—	2 Sous. Billon.	650

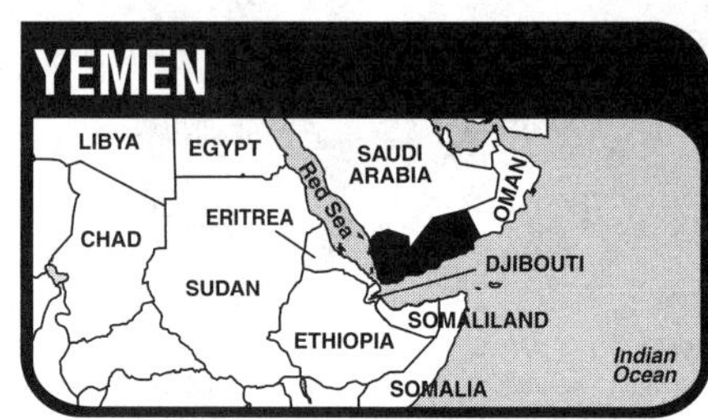

One of the oldest centers of civilization in the Middle East, Yemen was once part of the Minaean Kingdom and of the ancient Kingdom of Sheba, after which it was captured successively by Egyptians, Ethiopians and Romans. It was converted to Islam in 628 A.D. and administered as a caliphate until 1538, when it came under Ottoman occupation in 1849. The second Ottoman occupation which began in 1872 was maintained until 1918 when autonomy was achieved through revolution.

KINGDOM

HAMMERED COINAGE

KM# 300 HARF

Billon **Ruler:** al-Mansur Ali I 1775-1809AD **Note:** Weight varies: 0.25-0.40 grams.

Date	Mintage	Good	VG	F	VF	XF
ND	—	15.00	25.00	35.00	50.00	—

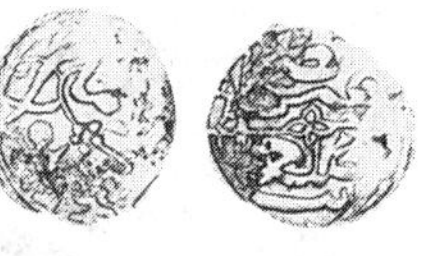

KM# 302 KABIR

Billon **Ruler:** al-Mansur Ali I 1775-1809AD **Note:** Weight varies: 0.70-1.10 grams.

Date	Mintage	Good	VG	F	VF	XF
ND	—	15.00	25.00	35.00	50.00	—

KM# 210 DIRHAM

Silver **Ruler:** al Nasir Muhammad Third reign as al-Madhi Muhammad 1697-1717AD **Note:** Weight varies: 2.00-3.00 grams.

Date	Mintage	Good	VG	F	VF	XF
ND	—	15.00	28.00	48.00	75.00	—

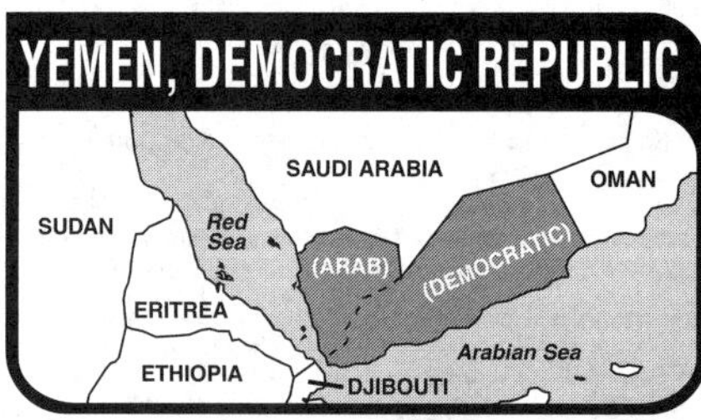

YEMEN EASTERN ADEN PROTECTORATE

Between 1200 B.C. and the 6th century A.D., what is now the Peoples Democratic Republic of Yemen was part of the Minaean kingdom. In subsequent years it was controlled by Persians, Egyptians and Turks. Aden, one of the cities mentioned in the Bible, had been a port for trade between the East and West for 2,000 years. British rule began in 1839 when the British East India Co. seized control to put an end to the piracy threatening trade with India. To protect their foothold in Aden, the British found it necessary to extend their control into the area known historically as the Hadhramaut, and to sign protection treaties with the sheiks of the hinterland.

QUA'ITI STATE

COUNTERMARKED COINAGE

KM# A30 RUPEE

Silver **Obv:** Arabic countermark in 10mm circle **Note:** Countermark on India Bengal Presidency Rupee, KM#99.

CM Date	Host Date	Good	VG	F	VF	XF
AH1307	1793-1813	—	60.00	100	175	—

18th CENTURY LEGENDS

Following in alphabetical order is a listing of the Latin legends found on 18th Century European coins. The legend as it appears on the coin is in bold typeface. The Davenport number or numbers appear in parenthesis, the translation is followed by issuer.

Some of the more frequently repeated phrases or abbreviations found in coin legends are as follows:

D.G. - Dei Gratia.....By the grace of God.

R.I. - Romanorum Imperator..... Emperor of the Romans.

R.I.S.A. - Romanorum Imperator Semper August ..... Emperor of the Romans ever august.

S.R.I. - Sacri Romani Imperii.....of the Holy Roman Empire.

S.R.I.P. - Sacri Romani Imperii Princeps.....Prince of the Holy Roman Empire.

A

A Deo (2443-44) From God. (Mecklenburg-Strelitz)

A Deo Accensum Quis Superabit (2755) Who will overcome one fired by God. (Saxe-Weimar)

A Deo et Caesare (2227) From God and emperor. (Frankfurt)

A Sole Sal(e) (2736-37,41-45,48) Salt from the sun. (Saxe-Saalfeld)

A.R. Imperatricis Archic. P.G. & G. Prim. (2256) Arch-chancellor of the august Empress of the Romans, Primate for Germany and Gaul. (Fulda)

A.V. & O.S. Steph. R.A.M.C. Eq. U.S.C.R.A.M.A.I. Cons. Conf. M. & S.A. Praef (1189) Knight, both of the Golden Fleece and of the Order of the Great Cross of the Apostolic King St. Stephen, present Privy Counselor of their sacred, imperial, royal and apostolic majesties, Conference Minister, and High Prefect of the court. (Khevenhuller-Metsch)

Abb. S.G.E.S.I.A.V.E. (1778-79) Abbot of St. Gallen and St. John, Knight of the Virgin of the Annunciation. (St. Gallen)

Ad(am) Fri(deric) D.G. Ep. Bam. et Wirc(eb). S.R.I. Pr(in) Fr. Or. Dux (1938,2889-2902) Adam Friedrich, D.G., Bishop of Bamberg and Wurzburg, Prince of S.R.I., Duke of Eastern Franconia. (Wurzburg)

Ad Legem Conventionis (2268,70) To the law of the convention. (Furstenberg)

Ad Legem Imperii (2851) To the law of the empire. (Wurttemberg)

Ad Normam Conventionis (1148,1204) According to the the convention standard. (Austria-Gunsberg (Hungary), Brixen)

Ad Normam Talerorum Alberti (2601) According to the Albertus thaler standard. (Prussia)

Ad Usam Luxemburgi CC Vallati (1592) For the use of the 200,000 besieged Luxemburgians. (Luxemburg)

Adalbertus D.G. Epis. et Abb. Fuld. S.R.I. Pr. (2264-66) Adalbert, D.G., Bishop and Abbot of Fulda, Prince of S.R.I. (Fulda)

Adam Frid. D.G. Franc. Orient. Dux (2900) Adam Friedrich, D.G., Duke of Eastern Franconia. (Wurzburg)

Adamus Francisc. D.G. S.R.I. Princeps (2773-74) Adam Francis, D.G., Prince of S.R.I. (Schwarzenberg)

Adamus Hic est ..... (2889) This is Adam, the sacred father of the Franconidae, not death but the fruit of life with new unction gives strength to Francis, whom like unto gold Caspar Patrinus offers to the infant Lord of Heaven as he is about to be born. (Wurzburg)

Adiutorium Nostrum in Nomine Domini (2882) Our aid is in the name of the Lord. (Wurzburg)

Adolphus D.G. S.R.I. Prin. et Abb. Fuld. (2255-56,60) Adolph, D.G., Prince of S.R.I., Abbot of Fulda. (Fulda)

Adolphus D.G. S.R.I. Pr. et Ab. Fuld. D.A.A.P.G.G.P. (2253-54,57-58) Adolph, D.G., Prince of S.R.I., Abbot of Fulda, Arch-chancellor of saintly August, Primate of Germany and Gaul. (Fulda)

Adolphus Frid. D.G. Rex Sveciae (1731-33) Adolf Frederick, D.G., King of Sweden. (Sweden)

Adventus Optimi Principis (1473-74) The coming of the noblest prince. (Papal States-Bologna)

Aechter Liebes Band steht in Gottes Hand (2781) The bond of true love rests in God's hand. (Solms-Laubach)

Alb. Wolf. D.G. Com. Schaumb. Lipp. & Sternb. & C. Secunda Vota Iniit Ao. MDCCXXX (2761) Albert Wolfgang, D.G., S.R.I., Count in Schaumburg, Count and noble Lord of Lippe and Sternberg, has entered upon his second vows in the year 1730. (Schaumburg-Lippe)

Alb. Wolfg. D.G.S.R.I. Com. in Sch. C. & N.D. Lipp. & St. (2762) Albert Wolfgang, D.G., S.R.I., Count in Schaumburg, Count and noble Lord of Lippe and Sternberg. (Schaumburg- Lippe)

Alexander D.G. March. Brand. (1994,2003-21,24-28) Alexander, D.G., Margrave of Brandenburg. (Brandenburg-Ansbach)

Alexander D.G.M.B.D.B. & S. (B.N.) (1991-93,95,97-98, 2000-1) Alexander, D.G., Margrave of Brandenburg, Duke of Prussia and Silesia, Burgrave of Nuremberg. (Brandenburg- Ansbach)

Alexander D.G.M.B.D.B. & S. B.N. Circ. Franc. Capitaneus (1996) Alexander, D.G., Margrave of Brandenburg, Duke of Prussia and Silesia, Burgrave of Nuremberg, Captain of the Franconian Circle. (Brandenburg-Ansbach)

Alle Speranze della Gioventu La Patria (1483) For the hope of the youth, the Fatherland. (Roman Republic)

Aloy(i)sio(i) Mocenico Duce (1562-63) Alvise Mocenigo, Doge. (Venice)

Aloysius Mocenigo Dux Venetiar (1524,35,57) Alvise Mocenigo, Doge of Venice. (Venice)

Aloysius Pisani Dux Venetiar (1541) Alvise Pisani, Doge of Venice. (Venice)

Amalia Tutrix Reg. Sax. Vinar & Isenac. (2759) Amalia, ruling Regent of Saxe-Weimar and Eisenach. (Saxe-Weimar- Eisenach)

An Gottes Segen ist Alles gelegen (1907,2109,69) God's blessing gained, all is obtained. (Brunswick-Wolfenbuttel, Brunswick-Luneburg, Anhalt-Bernburg-Haym-Schaumburg)

An. Quo Praesent. Rev. et Cel. ..... (2195) In the year in which presided the most reverend, most exalted Lord Prince Franz Arnold, Bishop of Munster and Paderborn, and the most serene Lord Prince Anton Ulrich, Duke of Brunswick-Luneburg. (Corvey)

Andreas D.G. Arch. et Princeps Salis. S.A.L. (1245-46) Andreas, D.G., Archbishop and Prince of Salzburg, Legate of the Apostolic See. (Salzburg)

Anna Dei Gratia (1338-44) Anna, D.G. (Great Britain)

Anno Dni. MDCCIX et Regiminis Primo F.F. (1235) In the year of our Lord 1709 and the first year of the reign. (Salzburg)

Anno I della Liberta Italiana (1576-77) The first year of Italian liberty. (Venice Republic)

Anno settimo della Liberta (1410) The seventh year of liberty. (Naples-Parthenopean Republic)

Anno 1742 No. 8 Qv. C. ist der Glucksstern auf genommen worden (1903) In the year 1742, No. 8 of the quarter of the Cross, the lucky star was adopted. (Anhalt-Bernburg)

Anselm S.R.I. Pr. Abb. Campid. A.R. Imp. cis Archimar (2371) Anselm, S.R.I., Abbot of Kempten, Archmarshal of the august Empress of the Romans. (Kempten)

Anselmus D.G.S.R.I. Abbas Werdinensis & Helmstad (2844) Anselm, D.G., S.R.I., Abbot of Werden and Helmstaedt. (Werden & Helmstaedt)

Ant. I D.G. Prin. Monoegi (1612) Antonio I, D.G., Prince of Monaco. (Monaco)

Ant. Ign. D.G.S.R.I. Princeps Praep. Ae. Dom. Elvancensis (2214) Anton Ignaz, D.G., Prince of S.R.I., Provost and Lord of Ellwangen. (Ellwangen)

Ant. Ptolom. Trivultius (1482) Antonio Tolomeo Trivulzio. (Retegno)

Ant. Theodor D.G. Prim. A. Ep. Olomu. Dux (1233) Anton Theodor, D.G., first Archbishop of Olmutz, Duke. (Olmutz)

Anthon Gunther(us) D.G. Pr. Schwarz. (2765-66) Anthon Gunther, D.G., Prince of Schwarzburg. (Schwarzburg-Sondershausen)

Anton. Ignat. D.G. Episc. Ratisbon. (2605) Anton Ignaz, D.G., Bishop of Regensburg. (Regensburg)

Antoni Ioh. S.R.I. Com. de Nost. et Rin. (1191) Anton Johann, S.R.I., Count of Nostitz and Rieneck. (Nostitz-Rieneck)

Antoni(us) Com(es) in Montfort (2448-50,53-54) Anthony, Count of Montfort. (Montfort)

Antonius I Barbiani Belgiojoso et S.R.I. Princeps (1356) Antonio I, Barbiani of Belgiojoso, Prince of S.R.I. (Holstein)

Antonius Ulricus D.G. Dux Br. et Lun. (2119-21,24) Anton Ulric, D.G., Duke of Brunswick-Luneburg. (Brunswick-Wolfenbuttel)

Apres les tenebres la lumiere (1768) After the shadows, the light. (Geneva)

Ar(c). Au. Dux Bu. Medi. Pr. Tran. Co. Ty. (1144-45) Archduke of Austria, Duke of Burgundy and Milan, Prince of Transylvania, Count of Tyrol. (Austria, Karlsburg-Transylvania)

Aragonum Rex (1694) King of Aragon. (Spain)

Arch. A.D. Bu. Pr. Tran. N.D. Lo. B.M.D. Etr. (1141-43) Archduchess of Austria, Duchess of Burgundy, Princess of Transylvania, married to the Duke of Lorraine and Bar, Grand Duke of Tuscany. (Transylvania)

Arch. Aus(t). Dux Burg. Brab. C. Fl. (1280-82) Archduke of Austria, Duke of Burgundy and Brabant, Count of Flanders. (Austrian Netherlands-Antwerp)

Arch. Aust. Dux Burg. C. Fland. (1270) Archduke of Austria, Duke of Burgundy, Count of Flanders. (Austrian Netherlands-Bruges)

Arch. Aust. Dux Bu. et Mantuae (1378) Archduke of Austria, Duke of Burgundy and Mantua. (Mantua)

Arch. Aust. Dux Burg Loth. Brab. Com. Flan. (1170, 75,80,1284,86,1388-90) Archduke of Austria, Duke of Burgundy, Lorraine and Brabant, Count of Flanders. (Austrian Netherlands, Flanders, Milan)

Archic. et Princ. El. Epis. Spir. Admr. Prum. Praep. Weiss. (2814-22) Arch-chancellor, Prince, Elector and Bishop of Speyer, Administrator of Pruem, Provost of Weissenburg. (Trier)

Arch(idux) Aust. D(ux) Burg. (et) Loth. M(ag) D(ux) Het(r) (1161-67,71,73,76,78) Archduke of Austria, Duke of Burgundy and Lorraine, Grand Duke of Tuscany. (Austria)

Archi. Monetar(ius) Haereditari Utriusq. (Archiducat) Austriae (1198-99) Chief moneyer of both the hereditary Archduchies of Austria. (Sprinzenstein)

Archid. Au. D. Bu. M. Mor. Co. Ty. (1079-83) Archduke of Austria, Duke of Burgundy, Margrave of Moravia, Count of Tyrol. (Austrian-Prague)

Archid. Aus(triae) Dux Burg (et) Styriae..... (1002, 15,39-43,1118-19) Archduke of Austria, Duke of Burgundy and Styria ..... (Austria Graz-Styria)

Archid. Aust. D. Burg. Marggr. Burgoviae (1148) Archduke of Austria, Duke of Burgundy, Margrave of Burgau. (Austrian Gunsberg-Hungary)

Archid. Aust. Dux Burg. Braban(t) (1268-69,78-79, 1702-4) Archduke of Austria, Duke of Burgundy and Brabant. (Austrian Netherlands, Spanish Netherlands)

Archid. Aust. Dux Burg. et Siles. Marg. Mor. (1065, 68-73,75-76,78,1136) Archduke of Austria, Duke of Burgundy and Silesia, Margrave of Moravia. (Austrian-Prague)

Archid(ux) Aust(riae) Dux Bur(gundiae) Com. Ty(rolis) (1001,3,13-16,18,35-38,49-56,84-87,1107,9-12,14-17,20-24,38-40,46-47,49-51) Archduke of Austria, Duke of Burgundy, Count of Tyrol. (Austria)

Archid(ux) Aus. Dux Bur. Mar. Mor. Co. Tyr. (1004-5, 19-23,57-63,1110) Archduke of Austria, Duke of Burgundy, Margrave of Moravia, Count of Tyrol. (Austria)

Archidux Aust. Dux Burg. Princ. Transyl. (1101-4,6) Archduke of Austria, Duke of Burgundy, Prince of Transylvania. (Austria-Transylvania)

Archidux Austriae (1033-34) Archduke of Austria. (Austria- Munich)

Archidux Austriae Dux Burg(u) et(&) Silesiae (1009-11, 28-31,94-98) Archduke of Austria, Duke of Burgundy and Silesia. (Austria)

Archiep. Vien. S.R.I.P. Ep. Vacien, Adm. S. Steph. R.A.M.C.E. (1267) Archbishop of Vienna, Prince of S.R.I., Administrator of Waitzen Bishopric, Knight of the Grand Cross of the Apostolic King, St. Stephen. (Bishopric of Vienna)

Archithesaur. et Elector (2531) Archtreasurer and Elector. (Pfalz-Sulzbach)

Ardua ad Gloriam Via (2838-39) Difficult is the way to glory. (Waldeck)

Ardua Difficili Adscensu (2604) Arduous with difficult ascent. (Quedlinburg)

Argent Pur. E. Fod. Westp. (2175) Pure silver from the mines of Westphalia. (Cologne)

Armat Concordia Fratres (2355) Harmony arms the brothers. (Hohenlohe-Langenburg)

Aug. Rom. Imp. Arch. C. Per. Germ. et Gall Prim. (2355-56) Arch-chancellor of the august Empress of the Romans, Primate for Germany and Gaul. (Fulda)

August Conf. Exhibet MDXXX (1980) Displays the august Confession 1530. (Brandenburg-Ansbach)

August Conf. Sustinet MDCCXXX (1980-81) Sustains the august Confession 1730. (Brandenburg-Ansbach)

Augusta Vindelic(orum) (1917-19,21-30) Augusta of the Vindelici-Augsburg. (Augsburg)

Augusto Domino Tuta ac Secura Parente Est (2476) Under the august Lord she is of safe and secure family. (Nuremberg)

Augustano Sacerdotio Ornato et Aucto (1916) The august priesthood, adorned and magnified. (Augsburg)

Augustus D.G. Ep. Spir. S.R.I.P. et Praep. Weiss. (2788) August, D.G., Bishop of Speyer, Prince of S.R.I., and Provost of Weissenburg. (Speyer)

Augustus D.G. Rex - Elector (2650) August, D.G., King and Elector. (Saxony)

Augustus II D.G. Rex Pol(oniarum) M. D(ux) Lit. D. Sax. I.C.M.A. & W. (1613-15) August II, D.G., King of Poland, Grand Duke of Lithuania, Duke of Saxony, Julich, Cleves, Berg, Angria, and Westphalia. (Poland)

Augustus Wilhelmus D.G. Dux Br. et Lun. (2125,28-32) August Wilhelm, D.G., Duke of Brunswick-Luneburg. (Brunswick- Wolfenbuttel)

Aus den Gefaesen der Kirchen und Burger (2229) From the receptacles of churches and citizens. (Frankfurt)

Ausbeut Thaler von S. Iosephs Cobold und Silber Zeche (2267) Mining thaler from St. Joseph's cobalt and silver mine. (Furstenberg)

Ausbeut Thaler von S. Sophia Kobold und Silber Zeche bey Witichen (2268) Mining thaler from St. Sophia's cobalt and silver mine at Wittichen. (Furstenberg)

Auxilium de Sancto (1471-72,88) Aid from the Sanctuary. (Papal States)

Auxilium Meum A. Domino (1612) My help (cometh) from the Lord. (Monaco)

Avita Religione et Iustitia (2255-56) By ancestral religion and justice. (Fulda)

Avr. Vell. Equ. S.C. & Cat. Mai. Intim. & Conferent. Consiliar. (1201) Knight of the Golden Fleece, Privy and Conference Chancellor of their sacred, imperial and catholic majesties. (Trautson)

Avr. Vel. Equ. SS.CC.RR.MM. Act. Int. et Conferent. Consil. et Supr. Camer. (1188) Knight of the Golden Fleece, present Privy and Conference Chancellor of their sacred, imperial, royal majesties, and High Chamberlain. (Khevenhuller-Metsch)

B

B. Nicolaus de Flue. Helv. Cath. Patr. (1780) Blessed Nicholas of Flue, patron of Catholic Switzerland. (Unterwalden)

B.I.C. & M.D. Pr. M.C.V.S.M. & R.D.I.R. (2364,2527) Duke of Bavaria, Julich, Cleves, and Berg, Prince of Meursia, Count of Veldenz, Sponheim, Mark, and Ravensburg, Lord of Ravenstein. (Julich-Berg, Pfalz-Neuberg)

Barbarae Qvirini Sponsae Dulcissimae Moribvs Ingenio Praeclarae Intempestiva Morte Perempte Die XXIII Oct. Thomas Obicivs Moerens Memoriam Perennat A.S. MDCCXCVI (1427)To His betrothed, Barbara Quirini, most sweet in character and illustrious in her genius, carried away by untimely death on the 23rd day of October, Thomas Obizzi in grief honors her memory. (Orciano)

Basilic. Liber. (1433-35) The Church of Liberius. (Papal States)

Basilea (1741,43-45,47-53,55-57) Basel (Basel)

Beda D.G. S.R.I.P. (1778-79) Beda, D.G., Prince of S.R.I. (St. Gallen)

Belohnung wegen des fleisig getribenen Klee-Baues (2010) Reward for diligent cultivation of clover. (Brandenburg-Ansbach)

Bened. XIV Pont. Max. (1459) Benedict XIV, Pope. (Papal States)

Benedictus D.G. S.R.I. Abbas Werdenensis & Helmstadiensis (2842-43) Benedict, D.G., Abbot of Werden and Helmstaedt of S.R.I. (Werden & Helmstaedt)

Benedictus Dominus Qui Dedit Pacem in Finibus Nostris (2488) Lord Benedict who established peace in our borders. (Nuremberg)

Benedict(us) XIV P.M. Bonon(iensis) (1457,60-61) Benedict XIV, Pope of Bologna. (Papal States)

Benedict XIV P.M. et Arch. Bon. (1458) Benedict XIV, Pope and Archbishop of Bologna. (Papal States)

Berg Academie zu Freyberg ward gestiffet (2679,86) School of mines founded in Freiberg. (Saxony)

Bey Gott ist Rath und That (1185,2438) There is counsel and action in Our Lord. (Mansfeld: Bornstatt & Colloredo)

Bi(e)berer Silber (2289-90,2304-5) Silver of the Bieber mine. (Hanau-Munzenberg)

Bononia Docet (1444,50-52,54,57) Bologna teaches. (Bologna)

Brun. et L. Dux S.R.I.A. Th. et El. (1345-46) Duke of Brunswick and Luneburg, Archtreasurer and Elector of S.R.I. (Great Britain)

Bruns et Lun. Dux. S.R.I. Archithes et Elect. (2070-81, 88-95,2104-7) Duke of Brunswick-Luneburg, Archtreasurer and Elector of S.R.I. (Brunswick-Luneburg)

Burgg. Stromb. S.R.I. Pr. Com. Pyrmon. Dom. in Bor(c)kel et Wehrt (2467-69,2510-11) Burgrave of Stromburg, Prince of S.R.I., Count of Pyrmont, Lord of Borkelo and Wehrt. (Munster, Paderborn)

Burggr. Stromb. S.R.I. Prin. d. in Borc. (2463) Burgrave of Stromburg, Prince of S.R.I., Count of Pyrmont, Lord of Borkelo and Wehrt. (Munster, Paderborn)

Burggravie Norimberg. Supperioris & Inferioris Principatus (1999) Burgraves of Nuremberg, of the upper and lower state. (Brandenburg-Ansbach)

Burgund. Dux Braban(t) (1705-9,11) Duke of Burgundy and Brabant. (Spanish Netherlands)

Burgund. Dux C. Fland. (1710) Duke of Burgundy, Count of Flanders. (Spanish Netherlands)

C

C.A.D.G.V.B. & P.S.D. C.P.R.S.R.I.A. & E.L.L. (1942) Karl Albert, D.G., Duke of both Bavarias and the Upper Palatinate, Count Palatine of the Rhine, Archdapifer and Elector of S.R.I., Landgrave of Leuchtenberg. (Bavaria)

C.F.C. Alexander D.G.M.B.D.B. & S.B.N.C.S. (&W.) (1989-90) Christian Friedrich Karl Alexander, D.G. Margrave of Brandenburg, Duke of Prussia and Silesia, Burgrave of Nuremberg, Count of Sayn and Wittgenstein. (Brandenburg-Ansbach)

C.P.R.B.I.C.M.D.C.V.S.M.R. & M.D.I.R.F. & E.S.C.M.V. S.S.C. (2811) Count Palatine of the Rhine, Duke of Bavaria, Julich, Cleves and Berg, Count of Veldenz, Sponheim, Mark, Ravensburg and Meursia, Lord of Ravenstein, Freudenthal and Eulenberg, Supreme Captain of his sacred imperial majesty of both Silesias. (Teutonic Knights)

C.P.R.S.R.I.A.El. & Vic. LL. C.F.H. & N.M.S.R.I.D. Mech. (1271,3,5,7) Count Palatine of the Rhine, Archsteward, Elector, and Regent of S.R.I., Landgrave of Leuchtenberg, Count of Flanders, Hainaut, and Namur, Margrave of S.R.I., Lord of Mechlin. (Austrian-Netherlands, Namur)

C. Th. D.G.C.P.R.V.B.D.S.R.I.A.& E.&I.P Rh. Suev. & I. Fr. Prov. & Vic. (1973) Karl Theodore, D.G., Count Palatine of the Rhine, Duke of both Bavarias, Archdapifer and Elector of S.R.I., Duke of Julich, Cleves, and Berg, Administrator in the area of the Rhine, Swabia, and Franconian law, and Vicar. (Bavaria)

Caes. d'Avalos de Aquino de Arag. Mar. Pis. et Vasti D.G.S.R.I.Pr. (1523) Cesare D'Avalos of Aquino of Aragon, Marquis of Pescara and Vasto, D.G., Prince of S.R.I. (Vasto)

Cai. & Car. Com. de Fugger in Zin. & Norn. Sen. & Adm. Fam. (2252) Cajetan and Karl, Counts of Fugger in Zinnenberg and Nordendorf, Lords and Administrators of the family. (Fugger)

Candidus Haec Profert Montanus Praemia Cygnus (2097,2156-57) The mine of the White Swan presents these prizes. (Brunswick-Luneburg, Brunswick-Wolfenbuttel)

Candide et Constanter (2291) Honorably and constantly. (Hesse-Cassel)

Candore et Amore (2254,57-60) Candor and love. (Fulda)

Capit. Cath. Ecclesia Monasteriensis Sede Vacante (2470) The Chapter of the Cathedral Church of Munster, the seat being vacant. (Munster)

Capit. Eccle. Metropolit. Colon. Sede Vacante (2176) The Chapter of the Metropolitan Church of Cologne, the seat being vacant. (Cologne)

Capitulum Brixense Regnans Sede Vacante (1204) The Chapter of Brixen governing, the seat being vacant. (Brixen)

Capitulum Cath. Monast. Sede Vacante (2465) The Chapter of the Cathedral of Munster, the seat being vacant. (Munster)

Capitulum Cathedrale Osnabrugense Sede Vacante (2504) The Chapter of the Cathedral of Osnabruck, the seat being vacant. (Osnabruck)

Capitulum Cathedrale Paderbornense Sede Vacante (2512) The Chapter of the Cathedral of Paderborn, the seat being vacant. (Paderborn)

Capitulum Eystettense Regnans Sede Vacante (2212) The Chapter of Eichstaedt governing, the seat being vacant. (Eichstaedt)

Capitulum Metropolitanum Trevirense (2825) The Chapter of the Metropolitan Church of Trier. (Trier)

Capitulum Regnans Sede Vacante (2208,10) The Chapter governing, the seat being vacant. (Eichstaedt)

Car. Alb. D.G. Pr. Regn. Ab. Hohenlohe et Waldenb. Dom in Langenburg et Schillingsfurst (2360-61) Karl Albrecht, D.G., ruling Prince of Hohenlohe and Waldenburg, Lord in Langenburg and Schillingsfurst. (Hohenlohe, Waldenburg-Schillingsfurst)

Car. & Amal. Philipp Popul. Spes Nat. A. 1747 (1398) Charles and Amalie Philip, the hope of the people, born year 1747. (Naples)

Car. Aug. D.G. Pr. Nass. Weilb. (2471) Karl August, D.G., Prince of Nassau-Weilburg. (Nassau-Weilburg)

Car. August D.G.S.R.I. Princeps de Brezenheim (2055) Karl August, D.G., S.R.I., Prince of Bretzenheim. (Bretzenheim)

Car. D.G. Rex Nea(p). Hisp. Infans (1397,99) Charles, D.G., King of Naples, Prince of Spain. (Naples)

Car. D.G. Utr. Sic. et Hier. Rex (1400) Charles, D.G., King of the Two Sicilies and Jerusalem. (Naples)

Car. Em. D.G. Rex Sar. Cyp. et Ier. (1493-95) Charles Emanuele, D.G., King of Sardinia, Cyprus, and Jerusalem. (Sardinia)

Car. Guilh. Frid. M.B.P.S.D.B.N. (1983) Karl Wilhelm Friedrich, Margrave of Brandenburg, Duke of Prussia and Silesia, Burgrave of Nuremberg. (Brandenburg-Ansbach)

Car. Lud. S.R.I. Com. a Dietrichstain (1186) Karl Ludwig, S.R.I., Count of Dietrichstein. (Dietrichstein)

Car. Rudol. D.G.D. Wurt. & T.C.M. Adminis. & Tutor (2851) Karl Rudolph, D.G., Duke of Wurttemberg and Teck, Count of Mompelgard, Administrator and Regent. (Wurttemberg)

Car. Th(eodor) D.G.C.P.R. Utr. Bav. Dux S.R.I.A.D. & El.D. I.C.M. (1957-68) Karl Theodore, D.G., Count Palatine of the Rhine, Duke of both Bavarias, Archdapifer and Elector of S.R.I., Duke of Julich, Cleves, and Berg. (Bavaria)

Car. Th. D.G.C.P.R.V.B.D.S.R.I.A.D.& E.& I.P. Rh. Suev. & I. Franc. Prov. & Vic. (1969-71) Karl Theodore, D.G., Count Palatine of the Rhine, Duke of both Bavarias, Archdapifer and Elector of S.R.I., Duke of Julich, Cleves, and Berg plus Administrator in the area of the Rhine, of Swabia and Franconian law, and Vicar. (Bavaria)

Car. Theodor. D.G.C.P.R.S.R.I.A.T.& El. (2366-70, 2531,37-44) Karl Theodore, D.G., Count Palatine of the Rhine, Archtreasurer and Elector of S.R.I. (Julich- Berg, Pfalz-Sulzbach)

Car. Theodor D.G.C.P.R.V.B.D.S.R.I.A.D.& El. Prov. & Vicar (1972,74) Karl Theodore, D.G., Count Palatine of the Rhine, Duke of both Bavarias, Archdapifer and Elector of S.R.I., Duke of Julich, Cleves, and Berg, Administrator in the area of the Rhine, of Swabia and Franconian law, and Vicar. (Bavaria)

Car. Utr. Sic. & Mar. Amal. Reg. (1398) Charles, King of the Two Sicilies, and Maria Amalie, Queen. (Naples)

Car. Wilh. Frid. D.G.M.Br. D.Pr. & S.B. N.Com. Sayn. (1984-88) Karl Wilhelm Friedrich, D.G., Margrave of Brandenburg, Duke of Prussia and Silesia, Burgrave of Nuremberg, Count of Sayn. (Brandenburg-Ansbach)

Car(ol) VI D.G. Rom. Imp(e) (1395-96) Karl VI, D.G., R.I. (Naples)

Car. VI D.G. Rom. Imp. S. Aug. (2205) Karl VI, D.G., R.I.S.A. (Dortmund)

Car. VII D.G.R.I.S.A. Germ. et Boh. Rex. (1947) Karl VII, D.G., R.I.S.A., King of Germany and Bohemia. (Bavaria)

Carl August Furst zu Anhalt Schaumburg (1907) Karl Ludwig, Prince of Anhalt-Schaumburg. (Anhalt-Schaumburg)

Carl D.G. Archiep. Trev. S.R.I.P. Ps. et Elect. Ep. Osnabru. Admin. Pruml (2823) Karl, D.G., Archbishop of Trier, Prince of S.R.I., Provost and Elector, Bishop of Osnabruck, Administrator of Pruem. (Trier)

Carl Ludw. U.H. Christ Fried. Graf. z. Stolb. (2809) Karl Ludwig and Heinrich Christian Friedrich, Counts of Stolberg. (Stolberg-Younger Line)

Carl Wilh. Frid. M.B.D.P. (1982) Karl Wilhelm Friedrich, Margrave of Brandenburg, Duke of Prussia. (Brandenburg-Ansbach)

Carl Wilh. Frid. March. Br. Frid. Ludovica Pr. Bor. (1978) Karl Wilhelm Friedrich, Margrave of Brandenburg, Frederica Ludwiga, Princess of Prussia. (Brandenburg-Ansbach)

Carl. Wilh. Frid. March. Brand. On. (1979) Karl Wilhelm Friedrich, Margrave of Brandenburg-Ansbach. (Brandenburg-Ansbach)

Carlini Dodeci (1410) Twelve carlini. (Naples: Parthenopean Republic)

Carol Aug. Frid. D.G. Pr. Wald. C.P.E.R. (2838) Karl August Friedrich, D.G., Prince of Waldeck, Count of Pyrmont and Rappolstein. (Waldeck)

Carol Lud. Com. de Hohenlo. & Gleich. Dom. in Langenb. & Cranichf. (2348-49) Karl Ludwig, Count of Hohenlohe and Gleichen, Lord of Langenburg and Kranichfeld. (Hohenlohe- Neuenstein-Weickersheim)

Carol Lud. S.R.I. Com. in Loewenst. Werth. (2397) Karl Ludwig of S.R.I., Count of Loewenstein-Wertheim. (Loewenstein- Wertheim-Virneburg)

Carol S.R.I. Princ. de Batthyan. P.I.N.U. & S. Com. Aur. V.E.C.C.P.S.U.S.C. (1182) Karl, S.R.I., Prince of Batthyani, hereditary Count in Nemet-Ujvar and Siklos, Knight of the Golden Fleece, hereditary in the County of Eisenburg, full Supreme Count of Simega (Somogy). (Batthyani)

Carol S.R.I. Princ. de Batthyan. P.I.N.U.& S. Com. Aur. V.et Ord. S. Steph. R.A. Magn. Cruc. Eques. C.C.P.S.VS.C. (1183) Karl, S.R.I., Prince of Batthyani, hereditary Count in Nemet-Ujvar and Siklos, Knight of the Golden Fleece and of the Grand Cross of the Apostolic King, St. Stephen, hereditary in the County of Eisenburg, full Supreme Count of Simega. (Batthyani)

Carol III D.G. (1412) Charles III, D.G. (Sicily)

Carol III D.G. Sicil et Hier. Rex (1413-14) Charles III, D.G., King of Sicily and Jerusalem. (Sicily)

Carol VI D.G. (Ro(m). Imp. S.A. Ger(m). Hisp. Hu(ng) (et) Bo(h) Rex (1035-65,68-87,1089-1104,1106-7,1195,1378) Karl VI, D.G., R.I.S.A., King of Germany, Spain, Hungary, and Bohemia. (Austria, Mantua, Transylvania)

Carol. Aug. Com. Hohenloh. & Gleich. Dyn. Lb. & Cr. (2357-58) Karl August, Count of Hohenlohe & Gleichen Line of Langenburg, Bartenstein and Kranichfeld. (Hohenlohe- Kirchberg)

Carol. Christ. Erdm. Dux Wurtemb. Olsn. & Berolst. (2879) Karl Christian Erdmann, Duke of Wurttemberg, Oels, and Berolstadt. (Wurttemberg)

Carol. D.G. P. Wald. C.P.E.R. (2839) Karl, D.G., Prince of Waldeck, Count of Pyrmont and Rappolstein. (Waldeck)

Carol. D.G. S.R. Imp. Princ. in (de) Lowenst. & Werth. & (2400-8) Karl, D.G., S.R.I., Prince of Lowenstein-Wertheim. (Lowenstein-Wertheim-Rochefort)

Carol. Frid. D.G. Dux Wurtem. Tec. & Ols. Adml. & Tut. (2852-53) Karl Friedrich, D.G., Duke of Wurttemberg, Teck, and Oels, Administrator and Regent. (Wurttemberg)

Carol. Frid. Dux Wurt. Tec. et Ols. Adm. et Tutor (2855) Karl Friedrich, D.G., Duke of Wurttemberg, Teck, and Oels, Administrator and Regent. (Wurttemberg)

Carol. Frider. D.G.H.N. Dux Sles. et Ho. (1352) Karl Friedrich, D.G., Heir of Norway, Duke of Schleswig-Holstein. (Holstein-Gottorp)

Carol. Guil. D.G. Pr. Anh. D.S.A. et W.C.A.D.S.B.I.K. (1911-12) Karl Wilhelm, D.G., Prince of Anhalt, Duke of Saxony, Angria, and Westphalia, Count of Aschersleben, Lord of Zerbst, Bernburg, Jever, and Knyphausen. (Anhalt-Zerbst)

Carol. Philipp. D.G. Ep. Herb. S.R.I. Pr. Fr. Or. Dux (2887-88) Karl Philip, D.G., Bishop of Wurzburg, Prince of S.R.I., Duke of Eastern Franconia. (Wurzburg)

Carol VI D.G. Rom. Imp. Semp. Aug(ust) (Ger.) Hisp. Hung. & Boh. Rex (1918-19,21,23,43,46-47,2187-88, 2273, 75-76,82-83,2447,2609) Karl VI, D.G., R.I.S.A., King of Germany, Spain, Hungary, and Bohemia. (Augsburg)

Carol VI D.G. Rom. Imp. Semp. Aug. Hisp. Hung. & Boh. Rex (2044-5) Karl VI, D.G., R.I.S.A., King of Germany, Spain, Hungary, and Bohemia. (Bremen)

Carol VII D.G. Rom. Imp. Semp. Aug. (2046-51,2277-78, 2418) Karl VI, D.G., R.I.S.A., King of Germany, Spain, Hungary, and Bohemia. (Bremen, Hall in Swabia, Lubeck)

Carolus D.G. Abbas Corbeiensis S.R.I. Princeps (2198-99) Karl, D.G., Abbot of Corvey, Prince of S.R.I. (Corvey)

Carolus D.G. Dux Brunsvic. et Luneb. (2147-49,51-55) Karl, D.G., Duke of Brunswick-Luneburg. (Brunswick-Wolfenbuttel)

Carolus D.G. Dux Wurt. & T(ec) (2856-71) Karl, D.G., Duke of Wurttemberg and Teck. (Wurttemberg)

Carolus D.G. Epis. Osnab. et Olm. (2503) Karl, D.G., Bishop of Osnabruck and Olmutz. (Wurttemberg)

Carolus D.G. Hass. Landg. (2291) Karl, D.G., Landgrave of Hesse. (Hesse-Cassel)

Carolus D.G. Sic. et Hier. Rex Hisp. Inf. (1415) Charles, D.G., King of Sicily and Jerusalem, Prince of Spain. (Sicily)

Carolus Edzardus D.G. Pr. Frisiae Or. (2508) Karl Edzard, D.G., Prince of East Friesland. (East Friesland)

Carolus ex Duc Loth. & Barr. Nat. Viennae ..... (2824) Karl of the Dukes of Lorraine and Bar, born at Vienna Nov. 24, 1680, a nephew of Leopold the great and august through his sister, Grand Prior of the Order of Malta for Castile and Leon, elected Coadjutor of Olmutz Sept. 14, 1694, made Bishop of the same place in 1695. Elected Bishop of Osnabruck April 11, 1698. Coadjutor of Trier Sept. 24, 1710. Became Elector Jan. 4, 1711. Died Vienna Dec. 4, 1715. May his soul live in God. (Trier)

Carolus Frid(ericus) D.G. Marchio Bad. & (et) H(ochb.) (1931-35) Karl Friedrich, D.G., Margrave of Baden and Hochberg. (Baden)

Carolus Guil. Ferd. Dux Brunsv. et Lun. (2171-73) Karl Wilhelm Ferdinand, D.G., Duke of Brunswick-Luneburg. (Brunswick-Wolfenbuttel)

Carolus Ruzini Dux Venetiar. (1538) Carol Ruzzini, Doge of Venice. (Venice)

Carolus Wilh. Fr. M.B.D. Bor. B. Nor. (1980-81) Karl Wilhelm Friedrich, Margrave of Brandenburg, Duke of Prussia, Burgrave of Nuremberg. (Brandenburg-Ansbach)

Carolus III D(ei) G(ratia) (1411,1699-1700) Charles III, D.G. (Sicily-Spain)

Carolus III D.G. Hisp. et Indiarum Rex (1268-70) Charles III, D.G., King of Spain and the Indies. (Austrian Netherlands)

Carolus III Rex Hispaniarum (1380) Charles III, King of Spain. (Milan)

Carolus IIII Dei G. (1701) Charles IV, D.G. (Spain)

Carolus VI D.G. Imp. et His. Rex (1381-82) Karl VI, Emperor and King of Spain. (Milan)

Carolus VI D.G. Rom. Imp. Hisp. et Ind. Rex (1278-79) Karl VI, D.G., R.I. King of Spain and the Indies. (Austrian Netherlands)

Carolus VI D.G. Rom Imp(er). S(emp). A(u). (1066-67,88,1761) Karl VI, D.G., R.I.S.A. (Austria, Prague, Kuttenberg, Chur)

Carolus VI (D.G.) Rom. Imp. Semp. Aug (2185-86,2410, 15,17,75-76,81,2610-13) Karl VI, D.G., R.I.S.A. (Cologne, Lubeck, Regensberg)

Carolus VI D.G. Roman. Imp. Sem. Aug. Elect. Francfurt XII Oct. MDCCXI (2410,15,17) Karl VI, D.G., R.I.S.A., elected at Frankfurt 12 Oct 1711. (Lubeck)

Carolus VI D.G. Rom. Imp. S.A. Germ. H.H. & B.R. Ar. A. (2477-78) Karl VI, D.G., R.I.S.A., King of Germany, Spain, Hungary, and Bohemia, Archduke of Austria. (Nuremberg)

Carolus VII D.G. Rom. Imp. Semp. Aug. (B.R.) (1922-24, 2189,2206,2482,2614-15) Karl VII, D.G., R.I.S.A., King of Bohemia. (Augsburg)

Carolus XII D.G. Rex Sve(ciae)..... (1712-16) Charles XII, D.G., King of Sweden..... (Sweden)

Caspar Melchior Balthasar (2176) Caspar, Melchior, Balthasar. (Cologne)

Casparus D.G. Abbas Corbeiensis S.R.I. Princeps (2200) Kaspar, D.G., Abbot of Corvey, Prince of S.R.I. (Corvey)

Casparus Ignatius D.G. Episcop. (1203) Caspar Ignatz, D.G., Bishop. (Brixen)

Cev. Fert. Divina Voluntas (2852-53) Just as the divine will decrees. (Wurttemberg)

Christ(ianus) VI D.G. Rex Dan Norv. V.G. (1294-95,97) Christian VI, D.G., King of Denmark, Norway, Vendalia, Gothland. (Denmark)

Christ. Aug. Gr. z. Solms Dor. Wilh. Gr. z. Solms Geb. von Boetticher (2781) Christian August, Count of Solms, Dorothea Wilhelmina, Countess of Solms, born von Boetticher. (Solms-Laubach)

Christ. Car. Tutrix Reg. Brand. Onold (1977) Christine Charlotte, ruling Regent of Brandenburg-Ansbach. (Brandenburg-Ansbach)

Christ. Fr. Car. D.G.S.R.I. Princ. Hohenl. Kirchb. (2359) Christian Friedrich Karl, D.G., S.R.I., Prince of Hohenlohe-Kirchberg. (Hohenlohe-Kirchberg)

Christ. Frid. u. Iost. Christ. Geb G. zu St. K.R.W.U.H. H.E.M.B.A.L.U.C. (2795-97,2801-2) Christian Friedrich and Jost Christian, born Counts of Stolberg, Konigstein, Rochefort, Wernigerode and Hohnstein, Lords of Eppstein, Munzenburg, Breuberg, Aiguemont, Lohra, and Klettenberg. (Stolberg-Younger Line)

Christ. Lud. Com. Wed. Isenb. & Crich. Charl. Soph. Aug. Com. Sayn & Witg. (2845) Christian Ludwig, Count of Wied, Isenburg, and Crichingen, Charlotte Sophie Auguste, Countess of Sayn and Wittgenstein. (Wied)

Christ. Ludewig u. Fried. Botho G.Z. St. K.R.W.U.H.H. Z.E.M.B.A.L.U.C. (2805) Christian Ludwig and Friedrich Botho, Counts of Stolberg, Konigstein, Rochefort, Wernigerode and Hohnstein, Lords of Eppstein, Munzenberg, Breuberg, Aiguemont, Lohra, and Klettenberg. (Stolberg-Younger Line)

Christ. VII D.G. Rex Dan. Nor. Van. Got. (1305) Christian VII, D.G., King of Denmark, Norway, Vendalia, and Gothland. (Denmark)

Christian Aug. D.G. El. Ep. Lub. H.N. Dux S. et H. (2409) Christian August, D.G., Elector Bishop of Lubeck, Heir of Norway, Duke of Schleswig and Holstein. (Lubeck)

Christian August Graf zu Solms (Laubach) V.T.H.Z.M.W. & S. (2778) Christian August, Count of Solms-Laubach and Tecklenberg, Lord of Munzenberg, Wildenfels, and Sonnewalde. (Solms-Laubach)

Christian den VII Danmarks og Norges Konge (1312) Christian VII, King of Denmark and Norway. (Denmark)

Christian Dux Sax. Ivl. Cliv. Mont. Ang. et W. (2708) Christian, Duke of Saxony, Julich, Cleves, Berg, Angria, and and Westphalia. (Saxe-Gotha-Altenburg)

Christian Ernestus D.G. Marg. Brand. Pruss. Madg. Stet. Pom. Cass. Vand. (2030) Christian Ernst, D.G., Margrave of Brandenburg, Prussia, Magdeburg, Stettin, Pomerania, Cassubia, and Wenden. (Brandenburg-Bayreuth)

Christian Ernst. Graf. zu Stolberg K.R.W.U.H. Herr Z.E.M.B.A.L.U.C. (2792-93) Christian Ernst, Count of Stolberg, Konigstein, Rochefort, Wernigerode, and Hohnstein, Lord of Eppstein, Munzenburg, Breuberg, Aiguemont, Lohra, and Klettenberg. (Stolberg-Elder Line)

Christian IV D.G.C.P.R. Bav. D(ux) (2545-52) Christian IV, D.G., Count Palatine of the Rhine, Duke of Bavaria. (Pfalz-Birkenfeld-Zweibrucken)

Christians Werck (2784) Christian's undertaking. (Solms-Laubach)

Christian(us) Ernest(us) Comes in Stolberg K.R.W. et H. (2791) Christian Ernst, Count of Stolberg, Konigstein, Rochefort, Wernigerode, and Hohnstein. (Solms-Laubach)

Christianus Ern. D.G.M. Brand. (2029) Christian Ernst, D.G., Margrave of Brandenburg. (Brandenburg-Bayreuth)

Christianus VII D.G. Dan. Norv. V.G. Rex (1311,13-15) Christian VII, D.G., King of Denmark, Norway, Vendalia, Gothland. (Denmark)

Christo. Frid. et Iost. Christi. Com. Stolb. et H. Concordia Fratrum (2803) Christian Friedrich and Jost Christian, Counts of Stolberg and Hohnstein, concord of brothers. (Stolberg-Younger Line)

Christo. Frid. & Iost. Christi. Fr. Com. D. Stlb. K.R.W. & H. (2798-99,2800,04) Christian Friedrich & Ioste Christian, brothers and Counts of Stolberg, Konigstein, Rochefort, Wertheim, and Hohnstein. (Stolberg-Younger Line)

Christo Purioris Religionis Conservatori etc. (2310) To Christ, the preserver of a purer religion, divinely received with the evangelical doctrine, strengthened 200 years ago through the Augsburg Confession, the church of the lands of Brunswick-Wolfenbuttel has paid the thanks due, mindful of benefits, 25 June 1730. (Brunswick-Wolfenbuttel)

Christoph. Franc. D.G. Ep. Herb. S.R.I. Pr. Fr. Or. Dux (2886) Christopher Franz, D.G., Bishop of Wurzburg, Prince of S.R.I., Duke of East Franconia. (Wurzburg)

Christoph Frank Bischof zu Bamberg des H.R.R. Furst (1940-41) Christopher Franz, Bishop of Bamberg, Prince of S.R.I. (Bamberg)

Christoph Fridrich und Igost Christian Geb. Graf. zu Stolb. (2794) Christopher Friedrich and Jost Christian, born Counts of Stolberg. (Stolberg-Younger Line)

Christophorus D.M.S.R.E. Cardinalis de Migazzi (1267) Christopher, by the mercy of God, Cardinal Migazzi of the Holy Roman Church. (Bishopric of Vienna)

Chur Mainz (2432-33) Electorate of Mainz. (Mainz)

Civibus Quorum Pietas Coniuratione Die III Mai MDCCXCI Obrutan et Deletam Libertate Polona Tueri Conabatur Respublica Resurgens (1622) To the citizens whose piety the resurgent commonwealth tried to protect. Poland overturned and deprived of liberty by the conspiracy of the 3rd day of May 1791. (Poland)

Civit Imperialis Muhlhusinae (2462) Imperial city of Muhlhausen. (Muhlhausen)

Civitas ac Munimentum Friburgense Brisgoicum (2233-34) City and Fort Freiburg in Breisgau. (Freiburg in Breisgau)

Cineribus Divi Parentio Friderici Eberhardi Def. D. XXIII Aug. MDCCXXXVII Anno. aet. LXV Parentat. (2357) To the ashes of the saintly parent, Friedrich Eberhardt, died 23 August 1737, age 65. (Hohenlohe-Kirchberg)

Clem. Aug. D.G. Ep. Pad. & Mon. C. Col. U.B. et S.P.D. (2513) Clemens August, D.G., Bishop of Paderborn and Munster, Coadjutant Bishop of Cologne, Duke of both Bavarias and the Upper Palatinate. (Paderborn)

Clem. Wenc. D.G. A. Ep. & El. Trev. Ep. Aug. P. Pr. Elv. Adm. Prum. P.P.R. Pol. D. Sax. (2837) Clemens Wenceslaus, D.G., Archbishop and Elector of Trier, Bishop of Augsburg, Provost and Prince of Ellwangen, perpetual Administrator of Pruem, royal Prince of Poland, Duke of Saxony. (Trier)

Clem. Wenc. D.G. A. Ep(isc) Trev. S.R.I.A.C. & El. (2834-36) Clemens Wenceslaus, D.G., Archbishop of Trier, Arch- Chancellor and Elector of S.R.I. (Trier)

Clemens Augustus Bavariae (2175) Clemens August of Bavaria. (Cologne)

Clemens XI P(ont). M(ax). (1428-49) Clement XI, Pope. (Papal States)

Clemens XII Pont. Max. (1455) Clement XII, Pope. (Papal States)

Clemens XIII Pont. Max. (1463) Clement XIII, Pope. (Papal States)

Clypeus Omnibus in te Sperantibus (1942) A shield to all who hope in thee. (Bavaria)

Coeli Regina Rp. Rhac. Patrona (1638) Queen of Heaven, Patron of the Republic of Ragusa. (Ragusa)

Coelo Redux Intaminatis Fulget Honoribus (2749) Brought back from heaven, he gleams with unsullied honors. (Saxe-Saalfeld)

Com. in Theng. S.C.M. Intim. Cons. et Supr. Stabuli Praefect (1181) Count of Thengen, Privy Counselor of his sacred, imperial majesty and High Constable. (Auersperg)

Com. Montb. Dom. I(N). Heid. Sternb. & M(e). (& A.) (2877-78) Count of Mompelgard, Lord in Heidenheim, Sternberg, Medzibor, and Auras. (Wurttemberg-Oels)

Com. P.R.S.R.I.Ar. & Ele. LL. Com. F.H. & N. Mar. S.R.I.D.M. (1272,74,76) Count Palatine of the Rhine, Archsteward and Elector of S.R.I., Landgrave of Leuchtenberg, Count of Flanders, Hainaut, and Namur, Margrave of S.R.I., Lord of Mechlin. (Namur, Austrian Netherlands)

Com. Pal. Rh. L. Leucht. B. Str. S.R.I.P. Com. Pyrm. D. in Borck. & W. (2513) Count Palatine of the Rhine, Landgrave of Leuchtenberg, Burgrave of Stromberg, Prince of S.R.I., Count of Pyrmont, Lord in Borkelo and Wehrt. (Paderborn)

Comes Cunii Lugi March. Grumelli (1356) Count of Cuneo and Lugio, Marquis of Grumellio. (Belgiojoso)

Comunitas et Senatus Bonon. (1357) The city and the Senate of Bologna. (Bologna)

Concesso Lumine Fulget (2185) He gleams with conceded light. (Cologne)

Concordia Res Parvae Crescunt, Discordia Dilabuntur (2396) By concord small things increase, by discord they fall apart. (Lowenstein-Wertheim-Virneburg)

Concordia res parvae crescunt (1823-48) By concord small things increase. (United Netherlands)

Concordia Stabili (2344-45) With lasting peace. (Hildesheim)

Confess. Evang. in Comit. Aug. Exhibitae-Sacra Saecularia Secunda XXV Iun. (2416) Evangelical Confession celebrated in the august county, the second holy centennial June 25. (Lubeck)

Confidens Dno. Non. Movetur (1821-22) Who trusts in the Lord is not moved. (United Netherlands)

Coniuncto Felix (2783) Fortunate in his connection. (Solms-Laubach)

Consilio et Aequitate (2261-62) With deliberation and justice. (Fulda)

Consilio et Constantia (2464) By counsel and firmness. (Munster)

Consilio Stat Firma Dei (2446) She stands strong through the counsel of God. (Mecklenburg-Strelitz)

Constanter (2116-21) Constantly. (Brunswick-Wolfenbuttel)

Constantia (2191-92) With firmness. (Corvey)

Constantia et Labore (1352) By steadfastness and toil. (Holstein-Gottorp)

Constantia et Prudentia (2400-1) With firmness and prudence. (Lowenstein-Wertheim-Rochefort)

Convenienta Cuique (1377) For everyone's convenience. (Mantua)

Cosmos III D.G. M(ag). Dux Etruriae VI (1498-1501) Cosmo III, D.G., sixth Grand Duke of Tuscany. (Tuscany)

Cum Ceciderit non Collidetur (2512) When he falls he will not be bruised. (Paderborn)

Cum Deo et Iure (2874-76) With God and the law. (Wurttemberg)

Cum Deo et Die (2358,2847-50) With God and time. (Hohenlohe-Kirchberg)

D

D. in Furst(enberg) et Furstenav ex L.B. de Rost (1762-64) Lord in Furstenberg and Furstenau, late free Baron von Rost. (Chur)

D.G. (Dei Gratia) By the grace of God.

D.G. Adolph Frid. III Mecklenb. Dux (2443-46) D.G., Adolph Friedrich III, Duke of Mecklenburg. (Mecklenburg-Strelitz)

D.G. Anthon (Antonius) Ulrich (Ulricus) Dux Br. & Lun. (2115-18) D.G., Anton Ulrich, Duke of Brunswick-Luneburg. (Brunswick-Wolfenbuttel)

D.G. Augustus Ludovicus Princeps Anhalt (1908-10) D.G., August Ludwig, Prince of Anhalt. (Anhalt-Kothen)

D.G. Augustus Wilhelmus Dux Br. & Lun. (2126) D.G., August Wilhelm, Duke of Brunswick-Luneburg. (Brunswick-Wolfenbuttel)

D.G. Archiepiscop. & S.R.I. Princ. Salisburg S.S.A.L. (1237-39) D.G., Archbishop of Salzburg and Prince of S.R.I. legate of the Holy Apostolic See. (Salzburg)

D.G. Augustus III Rex Poloniarum (1617) D.G., August III, King of Poland. (Poland)

D.G. Car. Alb. S. & Inf. Bav. Ac. Sup. Pal. Dux Co, Pal. R.S.R.I.A. & El. (1943) D.G., Karl Albert, Duke of Upper and Lower Bavaria and the Upper Palatinate, Count Palatine of the Rhine, Archtreasurer and Elector of S.R.I. (Bavaria)

D.G. Car. Alb. & Car. Phil S.R.I. Electores Eiusq. (1945-46) D.G., Karl Albert and Karl Philip, Electors of S.R.I. likewise. (Bavaria)

D.G. Car. Th(eodor) C.P.R.S.R.I.A.T. & El(ect) (2523-26) D.G., Karl Theodore, Count Palatine of the Rhine, Archtreasurer and Elector of S.R.I. (Passau)

D.G. Carol Ale. Dux Loth. & Bar (2812-13) D.G., Karl Alexander, Duke of Lorraine and Bar. (Teutonic Knights)

D.G. Carol Fridr. Dux W.T.I.S. Ols. & B. (2878) D.G., Karl, Friedrich, Duke of Wurttemberg, Teck, Juliusberg, Silesia, Oels, and Bernstadt. (Wurttemberg-Oels)

D.G. Carolus Dux. Brunsvic. & Luneberg (2145-46,56-69) D.G., Karl, Duke of Brunswick-Luneburg. (Brunswick-Wolfenbuttel)

D.G. Carolus Episcopus Olomucensis (1207,12) D.G., Karl, Bishop of Olmutz. (Olmutz)

D.G. Carolus Epus. Olomucen. (1205-6) D.G., Karl, Bishop of Olmutz. (Olmutz)

D.G. Carolus VI Rom. Imp. S. Augustus (1920) D.G., Karl VI, R.I.S.A. (Augsburg)

D.G. Christ. Gunth. Pr. Schwarzb. Sondersh. (2767) D.G., Christian Gunther, Prince of Schwarzburg-Sondershausen. (Schwarzburg-Sondershausen)

D.G. Christ. Ulr. Dux Wurt. T.I.S.O.B. (2877) D.G., Christian Ulrich, Duke of Wurttemberg, Teck, Juliusberg, Silesia, Oels, and Bernstadt. (Wurttemberg-Oels)

D.G. Clemens Wenc. A. E.T.S.R.I.P.G. & R.A.A.C. & P.E. (2832) D.G., Clemens Wenceslaus, Archbishop of Trier, Arch- Chancellor and Prince Elector of S.R.I. for Gaul and the Kingdom of Arles, Bishop of Augsburg, Administrator Provost of Pruem. (Trier)

D.G. Clemens Wenc. A. Ep. Trev. S.R.I. P. Gal. & R. Arel. A. Canc. & P. El. Ep. Aug. Adm. Prum. P.P. (2833) D.G., Clemens Wenceslaus, Archbishop of Trier, Arch-Chancellor and Prince Elector of S.R.I. for Gaul and the Kingdom of Arles, Bishop of Augsburg, Administrator Provost of Pruem. (Trier)

D.G. Dan. Nor.(v). Van(d). Got(h). Rex (1304,6-8) D.G., King of Denmark, Norway, Vendalia, and Gothland. (Denmark)

D.G. Dux Brunsvic. et Luneburg (2127) D.G., Duke of Brunswick-Luneburg. (Brunswick-Wolfenbuttel)

D.G. Ep. Lub. Haer. Norw. Dux S.H. St. & D. Dux Regn. Old. (2411) D.G., Bishop of Lubeck, Heir of Norway, Duke of Schleswig-Holstein, Stormarn and Ditmarsh, reigning Duke of Oldenburg. (Lubeck)

D.G. Ep(isc). Patav. S.R.I. Princeps (2517-20,23) D.G., Bishop of Passau, Prince of S.R.I. (Passau)

D.G. Ferdinandus Albertus Dux Br. & Lun. (2142-43) D.G., Ferdinand Albert, Duke of Brunswick-Luneburg. (Brunswick-Wolfenbuttel)

D.G. Fr. Lud. S.A. Pr. M.T.O.E.W. & V.P.P.E. (2811) D.G., Friedrich Ludwig, Supreme Administrator of Prussia, Master of the Teutonic Order, Bishop of Worms and Breslau, Provost of Ellwangen. (Teutonic Knights)

D.G. Frid. August Rex Pol. Dux Sax. Archimareschall et Elector (2667-69) D.G., Friedrich August, King of Poland, Duke of Saxony, Archmarshal and Elector. (Saxony)

D.G. Frid. Aug(ust) Rex. Pol. Dux Sax. I.C.M.A. & W. (2646-47,49,52-53,64-65,70-76) D.G., Friedrich August, King of Poland, Duke of Saxony, Julich, Cleves, Berg, Angria, and Westphalia. (Saxony)

D.G. Frid. August P. Anhalt D.S.A. & W.C.A.D.S.B.I. & K. (1913) D.G., Friedrich August, Prince of Anhalt, Duke of Saxony, Angria, and Westphalia, Count of Aschersleben, Lord of Zerbst, Bernburg, Jever, and Knyphausen. (Anhalt-Zerbst)

D.G. Frid. August Pr. R.P. & L. Dux Sax. Elect. (2663) D.G., Friedrich August, royal Prince of Poland and Lithuania, Duke of Saxony, Elector. (Saxony)

D.G. Frid. Carolus Pr. Schwarzb. Rud. Dom. Schwarzb. Senior (2772) D.G., Friedrich Karl, Prince of Schwarzburg-Rudolstadt, Senior Lord of Schwarzburg. (Schwarzburg-Rudolstadt)

D.G. Frid. Christ. Pr. R. Pol. & L. Dux. Sax. (2677) D.G., Friedrich Christian, royal Prince of Poland and Lithuania, Duke of Saxony. (Saxony)

D.G. Henr. S.R.I. & De Fondi Princ. Com. & Dom. in Mannsf. (2437) D.G., Heinrich, Prince of S.R.I. and of Fondi, Count and Lord of Mansfeld. (Mansfeld-Bornstatt)

D.G. Ioh. Georgius Dux Sax. I.C.M. An. & W. (2760) D.G., Johann Georg, Duke of Saxony, Julich, Cleves, Berg, Angria and Westphalia. (Saxe-Weissenfels)

D.G. Ioh. Wilh. C.P.R.S.R.I. Archid El. Eiusq. (2364-65) D.G., Johann Wilhelm, Count Palatine of the Rhine, Archdapifer and likewise Elector of S.R.I. (Julich-Berg)

D.G. Iohann Ernest VIII D. Sax. I.C.M.A. & W. (2749) D.G., Johann Ernst VIII Duke of Saxony, Julich, Cleves, Berg, Angria, and Westphalia. (Saxe-Saalfeld)

D.G. Iohannes Ernestus VIII Dux Saxoniae (2735-37, 40-48) D.G., Johann Ernst VIII, Duke of Saxony. (Saxe-Saalfeld)

D.G. Leop. Ernest S.R.E. Praesb. Card. de Firmian (2525) D.G., Leopold Ernst, Presbyter of the Holy Roman Church, Cardinal of Firmian. (Passau)

D.G. Ludovicus Guntherus Pr. Schwarzburg Rud. Dom. Schw. Senior (2769-71) D.G., Ludwig Gunther, Prince of Schwarzburg-Rudolstadt, Senior Lord of Schwarzburg. (Schwarzburg-Rudolstadt)

D.G. Ludovicus Rudolphus Dux Br. & Lun. (2137-38) D.G., Ludwig Rudolph, Duke of Brunswick-Luneburg. (Brunswick)

D.G. Max. Carol S.R. Imp. (2399) D.G., Maximilian Karl (prince) of S.R.I. (Lowenstein-Wertheim-Rochefort)

D.G. Max. Ios. C.P.R.V.B.D.S.R.I.A. & El.D.I.C. & M. (1975) D.G., Maximilian Joseph, Count Palatine of the Rhine, Duke of both Bavarias, Archdapifer and Elector of S.R.I., Duke of Julich, Cleves, and Berg. (Bavaria)

D.G. Max. Ios. U.B. & P.S.D.C.P.R.S.R.I.A. & El. L.L. (1948, 52) D.G., Maximilian Joseph, Duke of both Bavarias and the Upper Palatinate, Count Palatine of the Rhine, Archdapifer and Elector of S.R.I., Landgrave of Leuchtenberg. (Bavaria)

D.G. Max. Ios. U.B.D.S.R.I.A. & El. L.L. (1949-51,53-55) D.G., Maximilian Joseph, Duke of both Bavarias, Archdapifer and Elector of S.R.I., Landgrave of Leuchtenberg. (Bavaria)

D.G. Max. Ios. Ut. Bav. & P.S.D. Co. Pa. R. (1956) D.G., Maximilian Joseph, Duke of both Bavarias and the Upper Palatinate, Count Palatine of the Rhine. (Bavaria)

D.G. Parmae Plac(et). Vast. Dux (1479-81) D.G., Duke of Parma, Piacenza, and Guastalla. (Parma)

D.G. Petrus in Liv. Curl. et Semgal. Dux (1624) D.G. Peter, Duke of Livonia, Curland, and Semigalia. (Courland)

D.G. Rex Dan. Nor(v). Va(n). Got(t). (1292-96) D.G., King of Denmark, Norway, Vendalia, and Gothland. (Denmark)

D.G. Rex Dan. Nor. Van. Go. Dux Sl. Hols. St. Dit. & Old. (1309) D.G., King of Denmark, Norway, Vendalia, and Gothland, Duke of Schleswig-Holstein, Stormark, Ditmarsh, and Oldenburg. (Denmark)

D.G. Rud. Aug. et Anth. Ulr. D.D. Brun. et Lun. (2111-12) D.G., Rudolph August and Anton Ulrich, Dukes of Brunswick- Luneburg. (Brunswick-Wolfenbuttel)

D.G. Rudolph Augustus Dux Br. & Luneb. (2114) D.G., Rudolph August, Duke of Brunswick-Luneburg. (Brunswick- Wolfenbuttel)

D.G.C. Alb. & C. Phil. Elect Prov. & Vicarii (2530) D.G., Karl Albert and Karl Philip, Electors, Administrators, and Vicars. (Pfalz-Neuberg)

D.G.C. Phil. D.B.C.P.R.S.R.I.A.T. & El. Provisor & Vicarius (2529) D.G., Karl Philip, Duke of Bavaria, Count Palatine of the Rhine, Archtreasurer and Elector of S.R.I., Administrator and Vicar. (Pfalz-Neuberg)

D.G.C. Th. C.P.R.S.R.I.A.T. & El. Prov. & Vicarius (2532) D.G., Karl Theodore, Count Palatine of the Rhine, Archtreasurer and Elector of S.R.I., Administrator and Vicar. (Pfalz- Sulzbach)

D.G.I.W.C.P.R.S.R.I. Archid et El. Eiusq. (2528) D.G., Joseph Wilhelm, Count Palatine of the Rhine, Archdapifer and Elector of S.R.I. likewise. (Pfalz-Neuberg)

Da Pacem Domini (in Diebus Nostris Q) (2204, 31-33,36-37,40,43-44,2487) Give peace, Lord, in our day. (Dortmund, Freiburg in Breisgau, Nuremberg)

Dal. Cro. Sclav. Rex Archid. Aust. D. Burgun. (1064) King of Dalmatia, Croatia, and Slavonia, Archduke of Austria, Duke of Burgundy. (Austria-Pressburg)

Dan. Nor. Van. Got. Rex (1300) King of Denmark, Norway, Vendalia, and Gothland. (Denmark)

De Socio Princeps (1397,99) A prince from an ally. (Naples)

Decreto Reipublicae Nexu Confederationis Iunctae die V Xbris MDCCXCII Stanislao Augusto Regnante (1622) By decree of the state in conjunction with the joint federation on the 5th day of Dec. 1792, Stanislaus August ruling. (Poland)

Defluit et Influit (1449) It flows down and flows in. (Papal States)

Dei Gratia Carolus Episcopus Olomucensis (1208-11,13) D.G., Karl, Bishop of Olmutz. (Olmutz)

Dem Lande zu Nutz Denen Neiders zu Trutz (2784) For the benefit of the country, in defiance of those who envy her. (Solms-Laubach)

Den Errettern des Vaterslands (2434) To the deliverers of the fatherland. (Mainz)

Deo Conservatori Pacis (2023) To God, preserver of peace. (Brandenburg-Ansbach)

Deo Copulante (2761) God providing the bond. (Schaumburg-Lippe)

Deo Duce (2658) God our leader. (Saxony)

Deo O.M. Auspice Suaviter et Fortiter sed Iuste nec Sibi sed Suis (2788) Under the auspices of God, greatest and best, pleasantly and bravely but justly, not for himself but for his people. (Speyer)

Deo Patriae, non Nobis (2360-61) To God for the Fatherland, not for us. (Hohenlohe-Waldenburg-Schillingsfurst)

Der Seegen des Bergbaues (2672,74-75,81-83, 91,96,99,2702-3) The blessing of the mines. (Saxony)

Der Stadt Franckfurt (2229) The city of Frankfurt. (Saxony)

Deservisse Ivvat (2122) It aids to have served zealously. (Brunswick-Wolfenbuttel)

Deus Adiutor et Protector Noster (2465) God our helper and protector. (Munster)

Deus Providebit (2397) God will provide. (Loewenstein-Wertheim-Virneburg)

Deutschlands Schutzwehr (2434) Germany's defense. (Mainz)

Dextera Domini Exaltavit Me (1394,1695) The right hand of the Lord has exalted me. (Modena & Spain)

Die Erde ist Volle der Gute des Herrn (2100,10,63-64) The earth is full of the goodness of the Lord. (Brunswick-Luneburg)

Die Grub S. Wenceslaus bey Wolffach kame in Ausbeut im Quartal Reminiscere (2269-70) The mine of St. Wenceslaus at Wolffach was opened during the quarter of Reminiscere (first). (Furstenberg)

Die Grube Cronenburgs Gluck kam in Ausbeut im Qu. Luciae 1705 (2098,2158-60) The mine, Cronenburg's Fortune, was opened in the quarter of Lucia (fourth). (Brunswick-Luneburg, Brunswick-Wolfenbuttel)

Die Grube Fried. Christ. gabs zur Ausbeut in Quartal Crucis (2271) The mine of Friedrich Christian was opened in the quarter of the cross (second). (Furstenberg)

Die Grube Gute des Herrn kam in Ausbeut im Qu. Remin. 1740 (2100,63-64) The mine, Goodness of the Lord, was opened in the quarter of Reminiscere (first) 1740. (Brunswick- Luneburg, Brunswick-Wolfenbuttel)

Die Grube H. Aug. Friedr. Bleifeld kam wied. im Ausb. im Qu. Rem 1750 (2102,65) The mine, H. August Friedrich, Bleifeld, was reopened in the quarter of Reminiscere (first) 1750. (Brunswick-Luneburg, Brunswick-Wolfenbuttel)

Die Grube Koenig Carl kam in Ausbeut im Qu. Rem. 1762 (2103,68) The mine, King Karl, was opened in the quarter of Reminiscere (first) 1752. (Brunswick-Luneburg, Brunswick-Wolfenbuttel)

Die Grube Lautenthals Gluck kam in Ausbeut im Qu. Remin. 1685 (2099,2108,61-62) The mine, Fortune of Lautenthal, was opened in the quarter of Reminiscere (first) 1685. (Brunswick-Luneburg, Brunswick-Wolfenbuttel)

Die Grube Regenbogen kam wied. in Ausb. im Q. Luciae 1746 (2101,65-66) The mine, the Rainbow, was reopened in the quarter of Lucia (fourth) 1746. (Brunswick-Luneburg, Brunswick-Wolfenbuttel)

Die Grube Segen Gottes kam in Ausbeut im Q Cruc. 1760 (2109,69) The mine, God's Blessing, was opened in the quarter of the cross (second) 1760. (Brunswick-Luneburg, Brunswick-Wolfenbuttel)

Die Grube Weisser Schwan kam in Ausbeut im Q. Luciae 1732 (2097,2156-57) The mine, White Swan, was opened in the quarter of Lucia (fourth) 1732. (Brunswick-Luneburg, Brunswick-Wolfenbuttel)

Die Gute des Herrn kam wieder in Ausbeute im Q. Luciae 1774 (2110) The mine, the Goodness of the Lord, was reopened in the quarter of Lucia (fourth) 1774. (Brunswick- Luneburg, Brunswick-Wolfenbuttel)

Die Stat und Vestung Friburg in Brisgo (2231-32) The city and fort of Freiburg in Breisgau. (Freiburg im Breisgau)

Dilexi Decorem Domus Tuae (1429) I have loved the beauty of thy house. (Papal States)

Dirige Domine Gressos Meos (1508-11,14-20) Direct, O Lord, my steps. (Tuscany)

Diva Anna Dorot..... (2604) The saintly Anna Dorothea D.G., Duchess of Saxony, Julich, Cleves, Berg, Angria, and Westphalia, Abbess of the Imperial Free Diocese of Quedlinburg. (Quedlinburg)

Diva Carolinae Coniugis Desideratissimae..... (2096) To the memory of his saintly wife Caroline, most beloved and most deserving, her life of counsel and aid, and most faithful to her cares and most wise, impressed upon his mind in indelible letters which she with her virtues and deeds has commended herself to immortality. Here too, her husband George II, following her with a coin orders her to be considered sacrosanct to her children, her citizens, her posterity he himself while she lived most fortunate, now after she has died ever mournful. (Brunswick-Luneburg)

Diva Elisab. Iulia D.G. Duc Brun et Lun. (2122-23) Saintly Elisabeth Julia, D.G., Duchess of Brunswick-Luneburg. (Brunswick-Wolfenbuttel)

Divina Per Te Ope (1535-36) With divine help through thee. (Venice)

Dogmata Lutheri Stabunt in Secula (2738-39) The doctrines of Luther stood for ages. (Saxe-Saalfeld)

Dom. Cons. Nos in Pace (2205-6) Lord, preserve us in peace. (Dortmund)

Dom. in Epst. Munz. Braib. Aigm. Lohn et Clet. (2894) Lord of Eppstein, Munzenberg, Breuberg, Aiguemont, Lohra, and Klettenberg. (Wurzburg)

Dom. in Langenb. et Cranichf. Sen. Fam. et Feudor. Admin. ae. 74 (2354) Lord in Langenburg and Kranichfeld, Lord of the family and fief, Administrator, age 74. (Fulda)

Dom. Pro Iustaurata Germaniae Pace Christ. Frid. Carol Alexander Marchio Brandenburg Gratiarum Monumentum Fieri Fecit. MDCCLXXVIIII (2022) For the restored peace of Germany, Christian Friedrich Karl Alexander caused the monument of the Graces to be made 1779. (Brandenburg-Ansbach)

Dominabitur Gentium et Ipse (1285) He himself too will be Lord of the nation. (Austrian Netherlands, Independent Provinces)

Domine Conserva Nobis Lumen Evangelii (2218) I Lord, save for us the light of the Gospel. (Frankfurt)

Domine Conserva Nos in Pace (2230,38-39,2490,2623-25) Lord, preserve us in peace. (Freiburg im Breisgau, Nuremberg, Regensburg)

Domini Conserva Nos in Pace (1740-58,81-82,84-85,87-91,99) Lord, preserve us in peace. (Basel, Zurich)

Domini est Regnum (1285) The kingdom is the Lord's. (Austrian Netherlands, Independent Provinces)

Domini Gratia sit Nobiscum (1913) May the grace of the Lord be with us. (Anhalt-Zerbst)

Dominus Ese(n). Sted(esd). et(&) Witm. (2506-8) Lord of Esens, Stedesdorf, and Wittmund. (Ostfriesland)

Dominus elegit Te Hodie (1430) The Lord has chosen thee this day. (Papal States)

Dominus Mihi Adiutor (1287,90-92) The Lord is my help. (Denmark)

Dominus Protector Meus (1712,17) The Lord is my defender. (Sweden)

Dominus Providebit (2824) The Lord will provide. (Trier)

Dominus providebit (1759-60) The Lord will provide. (Bern)

Dominus regit Me (1523) The Lord guides me. (Vasto)

Dominus Spes Populi Sui (1775) The Lord, the hope of his people. (Luzern)

Domus Certamini Metam Feriendi Aptatae Dedicatio (2657) A dedication of the house for the contest of striking the goal. (Saxony)

Dona Nobis Pacem (1437) Give peace to us. (Papal States)

Ducat et Sem. Reip. Rhac(v). (1635-37,39) 1-1/2 ducat of the Republic of Ragusa. (Ragusa)

Ducatus Venetus (1526-27,32-33,37,40-43,46-47, 50-51,55,60-61,66-67,73-74) Ducat of Venice. (Venice)

Duce Deo Fide et Iust. (1640-41) Faith and Justice with God our guide. (Ragusa)

Duobus Fulcris Securius (2111) More safely with two supports. (Brunswick-Wolfenbuttel)

Durch Clairfait Entsetzt den 29ten Okt. 1795 (2434) Relieved through Clairfait, Oct. 29, 1795. (Mainz)

Durch Gott unter Mariae Schutz wurdt dis getruckht dem Feindt zu Trutz (2451-52) Through God, under the protection of Mary, this was struck in defiance of the enemy. (Montfort)

Dux Brunswicens & Luneburg (2505) Duke of Brunswick-Luneburg. (Osnabruck)

Dux Burgundiae Comes Tirol (1017) Duke of Burgundy, Count of Tyrol. (Austria, Tirol)

Dux et Gub(ernatores) Reip. Gen(u) (1360-70) Doge and Governors of the Republic of Genoa. (Genoa)

Dux Lothar. et Bar. Mag. Cast. et Leg. Ord. Melit. Prior. (2823) Duke of Lorraine and Bar, Grand Prior of the Order of Malta for Castile and Leon. (Trier)

Dux Lothar & (et) Bar. S.R.I. P(cp).S.R(e).C(a).B(o). Com(es) (1205,9,11-13) Duke of Lorraine and Bar, Prince of S.R.I., Count of the Royal Chapel of Bohemia. (Olmutz)

Dux Lothar. et Bar S.R.I. Prin. (2503) Duke of Lorraine and Bar, Prince of S.R.I. (Osnabruck)

Dux S.R.I. Pcps. Reg. Cap. Bohem. Comes (1215) Duke and Prince of S.R.I., Count of the Royal Chapel of Bohemia. (Olmutz)

Dux. S.R.I.P.R.C.B.C. Protec. Ger. S.C.R.M. Con. in et Ac. (1219) Duke and Prince of S.R.I., Count of the Royal Chapel of Bohemia, Protector of Germany, Privy and Present Counselor of his sacred, imperial, royal majesty. (Olmutz)

Dux S.R.I.PS.R.C.B. Com. Con. Ger. S.C.R.M. Con in et Actu. (1216-18) Duke and Prince of S.R.I., Count of the Royal Chapel of Bohemia, Counselor of Germany, Privy and Present Counselor of his sacred, imperial, royal majesty. (Olmutz)

Dux Sab(aud) et Montisf(er). Princ. Ped(em) (1493-97) Duke of Savoy and Montferrat, Prince of Piedmont. (Savoy-Sardinia)

Dux Sax. Angr. et Westph. Com Ascan. Dom B. et S. (1908-10) Duke of Saxony, Angria, and Westphalia, Count of Aschersleben, Lord of Bernburg and Zerbst. (Anhalt-Kothen)

Dux Sax. I.C.M.A. & W. Elect. (1614-15) Duke of Saxony, Julich, Cleves, Berg, Angria, and Westphalia, Elector. (Poland)

Dux Sles. Hol(s). Stor(m). Ditm. Com. Old. (et) Del(m) (1288,93) Duke of Schleswig-Holstein, Stormark, and Ditmarsh, Count of Oldenburg and Delmenhorst. (Denmark)

Dynasta in Epst. Munz. Braib. Aigm. Lohra et Klettenberg (2791) Ruler in Eppstein, Munzenburg, Breuberg, Aiguemont, Lohra, and Klettenberg. (Stolberg-Elder Line)

E

E. P. Le. D. Bul. C.L. Ho. M. Fra. (1581) Prince Bishop of Liege, Duke of Bouillon, Count of Looz and Horn, Marquis of Franchimont. (Liege)

E. IV Com. Imp. Com. in Hohn. Dyn. in Arns. Sondersh. Levt. Loh. et Cl. (2765-66) From the fourth imperial county, Count in Hohnstein, Line of Arnstadt, Sondershausen, Leutenberg, Lohra, and Klettenberg. (Schwarzburg-Sonderhausen)

Eberh. Lud. D.G. Dux Wurtemb. (2847-50) Eberhard Ludwig, D.G., Duke of Wurttemberg. (Wurttemberg)

Egalite Liberte Independence (1768) Equality, liberty, and independence. (Geneva)

Ein Banco Thaler (2593) One bank thaler. (Prussia)

Ein himmlisch Blick von Stern and Gluck (1903) A heavenly glance of star and good fortune. (Anhalt-Bernberg)

Ein Reichs Taler (1984,89) One imperial thaler. (Brandenburg-Ansbach)

Ein Reichs Taler F.S.W.U.E.O.V.L.M. (2758) One imperial thaler, princely Saxe-Weimar and Eisenach chief guardianship land money. (Saxe-Weimar)

Ein Thaler nach den Reichs Fus (1355-56) A thaler after the imperial standard. (Holstein-Plon)

Eiusque in P. Rh. Suev. et Fr. Iur. Con. Prov. et Vicarius (1943) Likewise in the area of the Rhine, Co-administrators and Vicars of Swabia and Franconian law. (Bavaria)

Electorus Saxoniae Administrator (2678) Elector and Administrator of Saxony. (Saxony)

Elisabetha I. D.G. Imp. Tot. Ross. (1960) Elizabeth I, D.G., Empress of all Russia. (Russia)

Eliz. Amal. Frid Princ. in Solms n. Pr. I. Ysenb. (2780) Elizabeth Amalia Frederica, Princess of Solms, born Princess of Isenburg. (Solms-Laubach)

Elizabetha Amalia Friderica Graefin zu Ysenburg (2779) Elizabeth Amalia Frederica, Countess of Isenburg. (Solms-Laubach)

Emeric Joseph D.G. A. Ep. Mog. S.R.I.P.G.A. Can. P. El. (Ep. W.) (2424-28) Emeric Joseph, D.G., Archbishop of Mainz, Prince of S.R.I., Arch-chancellor in Germany, Elector and Bishop of Worms. (Mainz)

Emitte Coelitus Lucis Tuae Radium (1456) Send forth a ray of heavenly light. (Papal States)

Engelbert D.G.S.R.I.P. Ab. Cam. A.R. Imp. Archimar. (2372) Engelbert, D.G., Prince of S.R.I., Abbot of Kempten, Archmarshal of the august Empress of the Romans. (Kempten)

Ep. Fris. & Ratisb. Ad. Prum. Pp. Coad. Aug. (2832) Bishop of Freising and Regensburg, Administrator of Pruem, Prince-Provost, Coadjutant Bishop of Augsburg. (Trier)

Epis. Basileensis S.R.I. Prince (1739) Bishop of Basel, Prince of S.R.I. (Basel)

Episc(op) Aug. A.P.P. Co(ad) Elv(ang) (2834-36) Bishop of Augsburg, Administrator of Pruem, Provost Coadjutant of Ellwangen. (Trier)

Episc. et S.R.I. Princ. Exemtae Eccle. Passav. (2525) Bishop and Prince of S.R.I. and of the freed church of Passau. (Passau)

Episc. Olom. Dux S.R.I. Princ. Reg. Cap. Boh. Com. (1232) Bishop and Duke of Olmutz, Prince of S.R.I., Count of the Royal Chapel of Bohemia. (Olmutz)

Episc. Wratisl. Pr. Niss. et Dux Grottkov (2053) Bishop of Breslau, Prince of Neisse, Duke of Grottkau. (Breslau)

Ern. Aug. Constantin. D.G. Dux Sax. I.C.M.A. & W. (2757) Ernst August Constantine, D.G., Duke of Saxony, Julich, Cleves, Berg, Angria, and Westphalia. (Saxe-Weimar)

Ern. Com. de Montf. d. in Breg. Tett. et Ar. (2455) Ernst, Count of Montfort, Lord in Bregenz, Tettnang, and Arnstein. (Montfort)

Ern. Frid. Car. D.G. Dux Saxon. (2729-31) Ernst Friedrich Karl, D.G., Duke of Saxony. (Saxe-Hildburghausen)

Ernest August D.G. Dux Ebor. & Alb. Episc. Osnab. (2505) Ernst August, D.G., Duke of York and Albany, Bishop of Osnabruck. (Osnabruck)

Ernest Com. in Stol. K.R. Wern. & Hohn. Dn. in E.M.B.A.L. & C. (2790) Ernst, Count of Stolberg, Konigstein, Rochefort, Wernigerode, and Hohnstein, Lord in Eppstein, Munzenburg, Breuberg, Aiguemont, Lohra, and Klettenberg. (Stolberg-Elder Line)

Ernest Lud. (I.) D.G. Hass. Landgr. Princ. Hersf. (2312-21) Ernst Ludwig I, D.G., Landgrave of Hesse, Prince of Hersfeld. (Hesse-Darmstadt)

Ernest Pat. & Ernest Frid. Fil. Success. Reg. D.G. Duces Saxon (2728) Ernst, father, and Ernst Friedrich, son and royal sucessor, D.G., Dukes of Saxony. (Saxe-Hildburghausen)

Ernestus Comes de Montfort (2457-58) Ernst, Count of Montfort. (Montfort)

Ernestus D.G. Gothan Saxonum Dux (2724-25) Ernst, D.G., Duke of Saxe-Gotha-Altenburg. (Saxe-Gotha-Altenburg)

Ernestus Dei Gratia Dux Saxoniae (2727) Ernst, D.G., Duke of Saxony. (Saxe-Hildburghausen)

Ernestus Fridericus D.G.D.S. Coburg Saafeld (2751-52) Ernst Friedrich, D.G., Duke of Saxe-Coburg- Saalfeld. (Saxe-Coburg-Saalfeld)

Et El Dux Bav. (2174) And Elector and Duke of Bavaria. (Cologne)

Et Fiebat (2804) And it was becoming (light). (Stolberg-Younger Line)

Et Patet et Favet (1498,1500-2) It is both evident and favorable. (Tuscany)

Et Polestinae Princ. Ardoris et Sac. Romani Imp. (1491) And Polistina, Prince of Ardore and S.R.I. (San Giorgio)

Et Praesidium et Decus (1638) Both defense and glory. (Ragusa)

Et Rege Eos (1360-66,68) And rule them. (Genoa)

Et S.R.I. Princeps Brixinensis (1203) And Prince of S.R.I. and Brixen. (Brixen)

Ex Adverso Decus (2134-40) Honor from adversity. (Brunswick-Wolfenbuttel)

Ex Avro Argentea resurgit (1414,16,20-22) From gold it arises, again silver. (Sicily)

Ex Cinneribus Orior (2357) I arise from ashes. (Hohenlohe-Kirchberg)

Ex Flammis Orior (2353,60-61) I arise from flames. (Hohenlohe-Neuenstein-Ohringen)

Ex Fodinis Bipontino Seelbergensibus (2546) From the Seelberg mines of Zweibrucken. (Mecklenburg-Strelitz)

Ex Uno Omnis Nostra Salus (2212) From one is all our salvation. (Eichstaedt)

Ex Vasis Argent Cleri. Mogunt. Pro Aris et Focis (2431) From the silver vessels of the clergy of Mainz, for altars and for hearths. (Mainz)
Ex Vasis Argenteis in Usum Patriae sine Censibus Datis Aciero et Privatis (2837) From the silver vessels, given without cost for the fatherland by the nobles and citizens. (Trier)
Ex Visceribus Fodinae Bieber (2288) From the veins of the Bieber mine. (Hanau-Munzenberg)
Ex Visceribus Fodinae Mehlbac (2471) From the veins of the Mehlbach mine. (Nassau)
Ex Visceribus Fodinae Wildberg(ensis) (2533-35) From the veins of the Wildberg mine. (Pfalz-Sulzbach)
Exemtae Eccle. Passav. Episc. et S.R.I. Princ. (2526) Bishop of the freed church of Passau, Prince of S.R.I. (Passau)

F

F.D. An. Manoel de Vilhena (1593-97) Brother Don Antony Manoel de Vilhena. (Malta)
F.D. Emmanual Pinto (1599) Brother Don Emanuel Pinto. (Malta)
F.D. Raimun(dus) Despuyg M.M.H.H. (1598) Brother Don Raymund Despuig, Grand Master of the Hospital of Jerusalem. (Malta)
F. Emmanuel de Rohan M.M. (H.SS.) (1606-10) Brother Emanuel de Rohan, Grand Master of the Hospital and the Holy Sepulchre. (Malta)
F. Emmanuel Pinto M.M.H.S.S. (1600-1) Brother Emanuel Pinto, Grand Master of the Hospital and the Holy Sepulchre. (Malta)
F. Ferdinandus Hompesch M.M. (1611) Brother Ferdinand Hompesch, Grand Master. (Malta)
F.S.W.V.E.O.V.M. (2759) Princely Saxe-Weimar and Eisenach chief-guardianship money. (Saxe-Weimar)
Fadernesiandet (1734-36) The Fatherland. (Sweden)
Fausto Coronationis (1415) A happy augury for the crowning. (Sicily)
Favore Altissimi (2142-43) By the favor of the most high. (Brunswick-Wolfenbuttel)
Fecunditas (1403) Fertility. (Naples)
Felicitas Sec. II Aug. Conf. (1981) Happiness on the second centennial of the Augsburg Confession. (Brandenburg-Ansbach)
Felicitas - Temporum (2620) Happiness of the times. (Regensburg)
Felix Coniunctio (2000) Happy union. (Brandenburg-Ansbach)
Ferd. Car. D.G. Dux Mant. Mont. Car. Guas. (1377) Ferdinand Charles, D.G., Duke of Mantua, Montferrat, Carolivilla, and Guastalla. (Mantua)
Ferd. Iul. D.G.S.R.E. Cardin. de Troyer (1232) Ferdinand Julius, D.G., Cardinal de Troyer of the Holy Roman Church. (Olmutz)
Ferdin. Iul. D.G. Episc. Olomuc. Dux S.R.I.Pr. (1231) Ferdinand Julius, D.G., Bishop of Olmutz, Duke and Prince of S.R.I. (Olmutz)
Ferdinan(dus) D.G. Sicil. et Hier. Rex (1416-25) Ferdinand, D.G., King of Sicily and Jerusalem. (Sicily)
Ferdinand Albert D.G. Dux Br. et Lun. (2144) Ferdinand Albert, D.G., Duke of Brunswick-Luneburg. (Brunswick-Wolfenbuttel)
Ferdinandus Rex Maria Carolina Regina (1403) King Ferdinand and Queen Maria Carolina. (Naples)
Ferdinandus I Hisp. Infans (1479-81) Ferdinand I, Prince of Spain. (Parma)
Ferdinandus III D.G.P.R.H. et B.A.A.M.D. Etrur. (1521) Ferdinand III, royal Prince of Hungary and Bohemia, Archduke of Austria, Grand Duke of Tuscany. (Tuscany)
Ferdinan(dus) IV D.G. Siciliar et Hier. Rex (1401,24-26, 29) Ferdinand IV, D.G., King of Sicily and Jerusalem. (Naples)
Ferdinandus IV et M. Carolina Undiq. Felices (1408) Ferdinand IV and Maria Carolina, blessed on all sides. (Naples)
Ferdinandus IV et Maria Carolina (1407) Ferdinand IV and Maria Carolina. (Naples)
Ferdinandus IV Neap. et Sic. Rex (1489) Ferdinand IV, King of Naples and Sicily. (Roman Republic)
Ferdinandus IV Utr. Sic. Rex (1488) Ferdinand IV, King of the Two Sicilies. (Roman Republic)
Festum Seculare Secundum Ecclesiae Evang. Luther (2317) Second centennial celebration of the Evangelical Lutheran Church. (Hesse-Darmstadt)
Fiat Lux (2804) Let there be light. (Stolberg-Younger Line)
Fiat Pax in Virtute Tua (1438,41) Let there be peace in Thy strength. (Papal States)
Fidei Pietati Huic et Futuro Aevo Sacrum (2350) Sacred to the faith and piety for this future age. (Hohenlohe-Neuenstein-Ohringen)
Fides et Victoria (1534,38) Faith and victory. (Venice)
Firmata Securitas (1398) Establish safety. (Naples)
Firmissimum Libertatis Munimentum (1367) The strongest memorial of freedom. (Genoa)
Florentius D.G. Abbas Corbeiensis S.R.I. Princ. (2193-94) Florenz, D.G., Abbot of Corbey, Prince of S.R.I. (Corvey)
Foedus est inter me et te (1455) There is a covenant between me and thee. (Papal States)
Fontis et Fori Ornamen(to) (1445-46) An ornament to the fountain and the forum. (Papal States)
Fortis Concordia Nexus (2208) Concord is a strong bond. (Eichstaedt)
Fr.(anc) Xav. Com. de Montfort (2459-61) Franz Xaver, Count of Montfort. (Montfort)
Fr. D. Franciscus Ximenez de Texada (1605) Brother Don Francisco Ximenez de Texada. (Malta)
Fr. Ios. Max. Pr. de Lobk. Dux Raud. Pr. Com. in Sternst. (1190) Franz Josef Maximilian, Prince of Lobkowitz, Duke of Raudnitz, Prince and Count in Sternstein. (Lobkowitz)
Fran. Ar. El. Coa. PA. 15 Sept. 1703, Suc. Patruo 21 May 1704 El. Ep. Mo. 30 Sept. 1706 (2466,2509) Franz Arnold, elected Coadjutor of Paderborn 15 Sept. 1703, succeeded to the same 21 May 1704, elected Bishop of Munster 30 Sept. 1706. (Munster, Paderborn)
Fran. Con. Tit. S. Ma. De Pop. Card. de Rodt Epis. Const. S.R.I. Prin. (2190) Franz Konrad, with the title of Holy Mary of the People, Cardinal of Rodt, Bishop of Constance, Prince of S.R.I. (Constance)
Fran. Lud. D.G. Ar. Tr. S.R.I. Pr. El. Sup. M. (2826) Franz Ludwig, D.G., Archbishop of Trier, Prince of S.R.I., Elector, Supreme Master. (Trier)
Franc. Ant. S.R.I. Princ ab Harrach (1239) Franz Anton, Prince von Harrach of S.R.I. (Salzburg)
Franc. Anto. D.G. Archi. et Pr. Salisb. S.S.A.L.Pr. de Har. (1235) Franz Anton, D.G., Archbishop and Prince of Salzburg, Legate of the Holy Apostolic See, Prince von Harrach. (Salzburg)
Franc. Anto. D.G. Arch. Pr. Sal. S.A.L. (1236,38) Franz Anton D.G. Prince Archbishop of Salzburg, legate of the Apostolic See. (Salzburg)
Franc. Arnol. D.G. Ep. Mon. & Pad. Bur. Str. S.R.I.P.C. Py(r) & D. in Bor. (2466) Francis Arnold, D.G., Bishop of Munster and Paderborn, Burgrave of Stromberg, Prince of S.R.I., Count of Pyrmont, and Lord of Borkelo. (Munster)
Franc. Arnol. D.G. Ep. Pad & Mon. Bur. Str. S.R.I.P. C. Py & D. in Bor. (2509) Francis Arnold, D.G., Bishop of Munster and Paderborn, Burgrave of Stromberg, Prince of S.R.I., Count of Pyrmont, and Lord of Borkelo. (Paderborn)
Franc. Arnold D.G. Episc. Monast(erien) et Paderb. (2467-69) Franz Arnold, D.G., Bishop of Munster and Paderborn. (Munster)
Franc. Arnold D.G. Episc. Paderb. et Monasterien (2510-11) Franz Arnold, D.G., Bishop of Munster and Paderborn. (Paderborn)
Franc. D.G. Hu. Bo. Ga. Lod. Rex. A.A.D.B. et L.M.D. Hetr. (1177) Franz, D.G., King of Hungary, Bohemia, Galicia, and Lodomeria, Archduke of Austria, Duke of Burgundy and Lorraine, Grand Duke of Tuscany. (Hungary)
Franc. D.G.R.I.S.A. Ge. Ier. R. Lo. B.M.H.D. (2486,89,91) Francis, D.G., R.I.S.A., King of Germany and Jerusalem, Duke of Lorraine, Bar, and Greater Etruria. (Nuremberg)
Franc. D.G. R(o). I.S.A. Ge. Ier. R. Lo. B.M.H.D. (1152-60) Franz, D.G., R.I.S.A., King of Germany, Jerusalem, Lorraine, and Bar, Grand Duke of Tuscany. (Austria)
Franc. Euseb. Trauthson Com. in Falkenstain (1200) Franz Eusebius of Trautson, Count of Falkenstein. (Trautson)
Franc. Gund. S.R.I.P. Colloredo Mannsfeld C. in Walds. V.C. in Mels M. in S. Soph. S.R.I. Pro. Canc. (1185) Franz Gundacker, Prince of S.R.I. of Colloredo-Mansfeld, Count in Waldsee, Viscount of Mels, Marquis of St. Sophia, Vice-chancellor of S.R.I. (Colloredo-Mansfeld)
Franc. Hen. Schlik S.R.I.C. de Passano & Weiskerchen (1196) Franz Heinrich, Count of S.R.I. of Schlick, Passaun, and Weiskirchen. (Schlick)
Franc. Ignat. S.R.I.C. & Dom. de et in Sprinzenstein et Neuhaus (1198) Franz Ignatz, Count of S.R.I., Lord of Sprinzenstein and Neuhaus. (Sprinzenstein)
Franc. Ios. Schlick Com. a Bassan. & Weisk. (1195) Franz Joseph, Count of Schlick, Passaun, and Weiskirchen. (Schlick)
Franc Lauredano Duce (1552) Francisco Lauredano, Doge. (Venice)
Franc Lavredano Dux Venetiar (1548) Francisco Lauredano, Doge of Venice. (Venice)
Franc. Ludov. D.G. Ep. (Bamb. et) Wirc. S.R.I. Pr. Fr. Or. Dux (2903-12) Franz Ludwig, D.G., Bishop of Bamberg and Wurzburg, Prince of S.R.I., Duke of Eastern Franconia. (Wurzburg)
Franc. II D.G.R. Imp. S.A. Ge. Hu. Bo. Rex A.A.D.B.L.M.D.H. (1179) Franz II, D.G., R.I.S.A., King of Germany, Hungary, and Bohemia, Archduke of Austria, Duke of Burgundy and Lorraine, Grand Duke of Tuscany. (Hungary)
Franc. II D.G.R. Imp. S.A. Ger. Hier. Hung. Boh. Rex (1286) Franz II, D.G., R.I.S.A., King of Germany, Jerusalem, Hungary, and Bohemia. (Austrian Netherlands)
Francis(cus) Anto(n) S.R.I. Princ. de Harrach (1237) Franz Anton, Prince of S.R.I. of Harrach. (Salzburg)
Francis D. Gratia Roman Imperat. S.A. (1283) Franz II, D.G., R.I.S.A. (Austrian Netherlands)
Francisc. II D.G.R.I.S.A. Ger. Hie. Hun. Boh. Rex (1390) Franz II, D.G., R.I.S.A., King of Germany, Jerusalem, Hungary, and Bohemia. (Milan)
Franciscus D.G. Hungar. Bohem. Gallic. Lodom. Rex (1176) Franz, D.G., King of Hungary, Bohemia, Galicia, and Lodomeria. (Austria)
Franciscus D.G. R.I.S.A. G.H.(ier). Rex Lot(h). Bar M.D. Etr. (1504-7) Franz, D.G., R.I.S.A., King of Germany, Jerusalem, Lorraine, and Bar, Grand Duke of Tuscany. (Tuscany)
Franciscus D.G. Rom. Imp. Semp. Aug. (2052,2250, 79,84-85,2419) Francis, D.G., R.I.S.A. (Bremen)
Franciscus Iosias D.G.D.S. Coburg Saalfeld (2750) Francis Josias, D.G., Duke of Saxe-Coburg-Saalfeld. (Saxe-Coburg-Saalfeld)
Franciscus Ursin. S.R.I. Princeps Rosenberg (1192) Franz Orsini, Prince of S.R.I. of Rosenberg. (Orsini-Rosenberg)
Franciscus I D.G. Rom. Imp. Semp Aug. (1925-30, 2483-85,87-90,2616-19) Francis I, D.G., R.I.S.A. (Angsburg, Nuremberg, Regensburg)
Franciscus II D.G.R. Imp. S.A. Germ. (Hie). Hu(n) Bo(h). Rex (1178,80) Franz II, D.G., R.I.S.A., King of Germany, Jerusalem, Hungary, and Bohemia. (Austria)
Franciscus II D.G. Rom. Imp. Semp. Aug. (2632-33) Francis II, D.G., R.I.S.A. (Regensburg)
Franciscus III Mut. Reg. Mir. Dux (1392) Francis III, Duke of Modena, Reggio, and Mirandola. (Modena)
Franz der Zweite Deutscher Kaiser (2499) Franz II, Emperor of Germany. (Nuremberg)
Franz. Ios. D.G.S.R.I.Pr. & Gub. Dom. de Liechtenstein (1580) Franz Joseph, D.G., Prince of S.R.I., Ruling Lord of Liechtenstein. (Liechtenstein)
Franz Ludwig B. zu Bamberg u. Wurzb. D.H.R.R. Furst Herzog z. Franken (1939) Franz Ludwig, Bishop of Bamberg and Wurzburg, Prince of S.R.I., Duke of Franconia. (Bamberg)
Fri(ed). Adolph Com. et Nob. D. Lipp (2378-82) Friedrich Adolph, Count and noble Lord of Lippe. (Lippe-Detmold)
Frid. Aug. Rex Elector et Vicarius Post Mort Ioseph I Imperat (2654-55) Friedrich August, King, Elector, and Vicar after the death of Emperor Joseph I. (Saxony)
Frid. August D.G. Dux Sax. Elector (2682-96,98-2703) Friedrich August, D.G., Duke of Saxony, Elector. (Saxony)
Frid. Aug(ust) D.G. Dux Sax. Elector & Vicarius Imperii (2697) Friedrich August, D.G., Duke of Saxony, Elector and Vicar of the empire. (Saxony)
Frid. August D.G. Saxoniae Elector (2680-81) Friedrich August, D.G., Elector of Saxony. (Saxony)
Frid. Augusto Rege. Polon. Elect. Saxon. Agonotheta (2657) Friedrich August, King of Poland, Elector of Saxony, Director of the contest. (Saxony)
Frid. Car. Ios. Aep. et El. Mog. Ep. Wor. (2430-31) Friedrich Karl Joseph, Archbishop and Elector of Mainz, Bishop of Worms. (Mainz)
Frid. Car. Ios. D.G. A.E. Mog. S.R.I.P.G.A.C. et El. E.W. (2429) Friedrich Karl Joseph, D.G., Archbishop of Mainz, Prince of S.R.I., Arch-chancellor and Elector of Germany, Bishop of Worms. (Mainz)
Frid. Car. Ios. Erzb. u. Kurf. z. Mainz F.B.Z.W. (2435) Friedrich Karl Joseph, Archbishop and Elector of Mainz, Prince and Bishop of Worms. (Mainz)
Frid. Christ. D.G.M.B.D.P. et S.B.N. (2040-42) Friedrich Christian, D.G., Margrave of Brandenburg, Duke of Prussia and Silesia, Burgrave of Nuremberg. (Brandenburg-Bayreuth)
Frid. Christian March. Brand. D.B.&S. (2043) Friedrich Christian, Margrave of Brandenburg, Duke of Prussia and Silesia. (Brandenburg-Bayreuth)
Frid. (III) D.G. Pr. A. Salm Kyrb. Com. Rh. & Sylv. (2644-45) Friedrich III, D.G., Prince of Salm Kyrburg, Count of the Rhine and the Forest. (Salm)
Frid. D.G. Rex Bor. et El. S. Pr. Ar. Neoc. et Val. (1776) Friedrich, D.G., King and Elector of Prussia, Supreme Prince of Arausonia, Neuchatel, and Valangin. (Neuchatel)
Frid(ericus) D.G. Rex Boruss. El. Br. (2554-66) Friedrich, D.G., King of Prussia, Elector of Brandenburg. (Prussia)
Frid. Eug. D.G. Dux Wirtemb. et T. (2873) Friedrich Eugene, D.G., Duke of Wurttemberg and Teck. (Wurttemberg)
Frid. Wilh. D.G. Ep. Hild. S.R.I.P. (2344-45) Friedrich Wilhelm, D.G., Bishop of Hildesheim, Prince of S.R.I. (Hildesheim)
Frid. Wilh. D.G. Rex Bor. et El. S. Pr. Ar. Neoc. & Val. (1777) Friedrich Wilhelm, King and Elector of Prussia, Supreme Prince of Arausonia, Neuchatel, and Valangin. (Neuchatel)
Frid. Wilh. D.G. Rex Borussiae (El. Brandenburg Dux Geldriae) (2567-80) Friedrich Wilhelm, D.G., King of Prussia, Elector of Brandenburg, Duke of Gelders. (Prussia)
Frid. Wilhelm Koenig von Preussen (2602) Friedrich Wilhelm, King of Prussia. (Prussia)
Frid. IIII D.G. Dan. Norv. Va(n). Go(t). Rex (1287-88) Frederik IV, D.G., King of Denmark, Norway, Vendalia, and Gothland. (Denmark)
Frid(ericus) IIII (IV) D.G. Rex Dan. Nor. V. G(o). (1289-90, 93) Frederik IV, D.G., King of Denmark, Norway, Vendalia, and Gothland. (Denmark)
Frider. Christian D.G. Episc. Monaster. (2463) Friedrich Christian, D.G., Bishop of Munster. (Munster)
Frider. Wilhel. D.G. Dux Megapo Princ. Vand. (2439-40) Friedrich Wilhelm, Duke of Mecklenburg, Prince of Vandalia. (Mecklenburg-Schwerin)
Frider. Wilhelm Boruss. Rex (2601) Friedrich Wilhelm, King of Prussia. (Prussia)
Frider III (D.G.) Gothanus Saxonum Dux (2718,21-23) Friedrich III, D.G., Duke of Saxe-Gotha. (Saxe-Gotha-Altenburg)
Frideric. Christianus L.B.A. Plettenberg etc. (2464) Friedrich Christian, Free Baron of Plettenberg, born 8 Aug. 1664, elected Bishop and Prince of Munster 29 July 1688, died 5 May 1706. (Munster)
Frideric(us) et Ulr. Eleon. D.G. Rex et Reg. Svec(iae) (1721-22,24-25) Frederik and Ulrica Eleonora, D.G., King and Queen of Sweden. (Sweden)
Fridericus Augustus Rex Polon. et Elector Saxon. Matri Dilectissimae..... (2658) Friedrich August, King of Poland and Elector of Saxony, to his dearest mother, Anna Sophia, Sophia, Hereditary Princess of the kingdom of Denmark, born in Flensburg 1 Sept. 1647, widow of the Elector of Saxony and Lichtenburg, died 1 July 1717, who lived gloriously, lived illustriously, with a distinguished burial so that she might be made famous, caused to be erected an everlasting monument. (Saxony)
Fridericus Borussorum Rex (2581-96) Friedrich, King of Prussia. (Prussia)
Fridericus Carolus D.G.H.N.D.S.H.S. et D.C. in O. et D. (1354-55) Frederick Karl, D.G., Heir of Norway, Duke of Schleswig-Holstein, Stormark, and Ditmarch, Count in Oldenburg and Delmenhorst. (Holstein-Plon)
Fridericus D.G. Rex Sueciae (2294) Friedrich, D.G., King of Sweden. (Hesse-Cassel)
Fridericus D.G. Rex Sveciae (1719-20,23,26-30) Frederik, D.G., King of Sweden. (Sweden)
Fridericus D.G.D.S.I.C.M.A. et W. (2707,10) Friedrich, D.G., Duke of Saxony, Julich, Cleves, Berg, Angria, and Westphalia. (Saxe-Gotha-Altenburg)
Fridericus D.G.M.B.D.P. et S.B.N. (2032-39) Friedrich, D.G., Margrave of Brandenburg, Duke of Prussia and Silesia, Burgrave of Nuremberg. (Brandenburg-Bayreuth)
Fridericus Rex (2553) Friedrich, King. (Prussia)
Fridericus II (D.G.) Dux Saxo-Gothanus (2711-17) Friedrich II, D.G., Duke of Saxe-Gotha. (Saxe-Gotha-Altenburg)
Fridericus II D.G. Dux Wirtemb. et T. (2873) Friedrich II, D.G, Duke of Wurttemberg and Teck. (Wurttemberg)
Fridericus II D.G. Hass Landg. Han Com. (2299-2303) Friedrich II, D.G., Landgrave of Hesse, Count of Hanau. (Hesse-Cassel)
Fridericus III Dux Sax. I.C.M. & Adm. Duc Isencac (2719-20) Friedrich III, Duke of Saxony, Julich, Cleves,

and Berg, Administrator of the duchy of Eisenach. (Saxe-Gotha-Altenburg)

Fridericus V D.G. Dan. Nor. V(an). G(ot). Rex (1302-3) Frederik V, D.G., King of Denmark, Norway, Vendalia, and Gothland. (Denmark)

Fridericus V D.G. Rex Dan. Nor. V(and). G. (1297-99, 1301-2) Frederik V, D.G., King of Denmark, Norway, Vendalia, and Gothland. (Denmark)

Fridericus V Dei Gratia (1300) Frederik V, D.G. (Denmark)

Fried. Albrecht Furst zu Anhalt Bernb. (1905-6) Friedrich Albert, Prince of Anhalt-Bernburg. (Anhalt-Bernburg)

Fried. Aug. D.G. Haer. N. Ep. Lub. Dux S.H. St. & D. Dux Regn. Old. (2412) Friedrich August, D.G., Heir to Norway, Bishop of Lubeck, Duke of Schleswig-Holstein, Stormarn, and Ditmarsh, reigning Duke of Oldenburg. (Lubeck)

Fried. Aug. Soph. Princ. Anh. Dyn. Iever Admin. (2363) Frederika Augusta Sophia, Princess of Anhalt, line of Jever, Administrator. (Jever)

Fried. D.G. Pr. Wald. C.P.E.R. (2840) Friedrich, D.G., Prince of Waldeck, Count of Pyrmont and Rappolstein. (Waldeck)

Fried. Lud. S.R.I. Com In Lowenst. Werth (2396) Friedrich Ludwig, Count of Lowenstein-Wertheim of S.R.I. (Lowenstein-Wertheim-Virneburg)

Fried. Ludwig Furst zu Hohenlohe Ingelfingen (2356) Friedrich Ludwig, Prince of Hohenlohe-Ingelfingen. (Hohenlohe- Ingelfingen)

Fried(e) Wilhelm (II) Koenig von Preussen (2597-2600) Friedrich Wilhelm II, King of Prussia. (Prussia)

Friede. Wilhel. D.G. Dux Megapo. Princ. Vand. (2441-42) Friedrich Wilhelm, D.G., Duke of Mecklenburg, Prince of Vandalia. (Mecklenburg-Schwerin)

Friedr. Wilhelm III Koenig von Preussen (2603) Friedrich Wilhelm III, King of Prussia. (Prussia)

Friedrich Botho & Carl Ludwig Gr. z. Stolb. K.R.W.U.H. (2806-8) Friedrich Botha and Karl Ludwig, Counts of Stolberg, Konigstein, Rochefort, Wernigerode, and Hohnstein. (Stolberg-Younger Line)

Fruct. Fodinae Stolb. Strasbergensis (2803) Product of the Strassberg mine of Stolberg. (Stolberg-Younger Line)

Furstl. Sachs. Gesambte Henneb. Ilmen. Ausbeuth. Thal. (2726) Associated princely Saxon-Henneberg-Ilmenau mining thaler. (Saxon-Henneberg-Ilmenau)

Fyra Caroliner (1717) Four caroliners. (Sweden)

G

Geb. 3 Feb. 1725, Verm. 28 Oct. 1753, Gest. 25 Aug. 1754 (2781) Born 3 Feb. 1725, married 28 Oct. 1753, died 25 Aug. 1754. (Solms-Laubach)

Gen. C. Mar. V.L. Dim. Col. U.S.C. & R.A.M.A.I. Cons. & S. Conf. M. (1182-83) General Field Marshal, Colonel of the only dragoon regiment, present Privy Counselor of both their sacred, imperial and royal apostolic majesties, and State Conference Minister. (Batthyani)

Geneve Republique (1769-70) Republic of Geneva. (Geneva)

Georg Albert D.G. Pr. et Dom. Fr. Orient (2506) George Albert, D.G., Prince and Lord of East Friesland. (East Friesland)

Georg Herzog zu Sachsen Coburg Meiningen (2734) George, Duke of Saxe-Coburg-Meiningen. (Saxe-Coburg-Meiningen)

Georg. Aug. Wilh. Graf zu Solms. Eliz. Charl. Ferd. Luise Princ zu Ysenburg (2783) George August Wilhelm, Count of Solms, Elizabeth Charlotte Ferdinande Luise, Princess of Isenburg. (Solms-Laubach)

Georg. Carol. D.G. Ep. Wirc. S.R.I. Pr. Fr. Or. Dux (2913-15) George Karl, D.G., Bishop of Wurzburg, Prince of S.R.I., Duke of Eastern Franconia. (Wurzburg)

Georg. Frid. & Alexander March. Brand. (1999) George Friedrich and Alexander, Margraves of Brandenburg. (Brandenburg-Ansbach)

Georg. Lud. D.G. Br. & (et) Lun. S.R.I. El(ect). (Archithes.) (2057-68) George Ludwig, D.G., Duke of Brunswick-Luneburg, Archtreasurer and Elector of S.R.I. (Brunswick-Luneburg)

Georg. Wilh. D.G. D. Br. et L. (2056) George Wilhelm, D.G., Duke of Brunswick-Luneburg. (Brunswick-Luneburg)

Georg(ius) II D.G. Mag. Br(it). Fr(anc). et Hib Rex F(id). D. (Br. & L. Dux S.R.I.A. Th. & El.) (2083-95,97-2103) George III, D.G., King of Great Britain, France, and Ireland, Defender of the Faith, Duke of Brunswick-Luneburg, Archtreasurer and Elector of S.R.I. (Brunswick-Luneburg)

Georg. III D.G. Mag. Brit. Fr. et Hib. Rex F. Def. (Br. & L. Dux S.R.I. A. Th. & El.) (2104-10) George III, D.G., King of Great Britain, France, and Ireland, Defender of the Faith, Duke of Brunswick-Luneburg, Archtreasurer and elector of S.R.I. (Brunswick-Luneburg)

George. Frid. Burggr. D. Kirchberg Com. d. Sayn et Witg. Dom. Farnrodae (2373) George Friedrich, Burgrave of Kirchberg, Count of Sayn-Wittgenstein, Lord of Farnrode. (Kirchberg)

Georgius Albertus D.G. Princ Frisiae Or. (2507) George Albert, D.G., Prince of East Friesland. (East Friesland)

Georgius D.G. Mag. Brit. Fr(anc) et Hib. Rex F(id) D. (2070-81) George III, D.G., King of Great Britain, France, and Ireland, Defender of the Faith, Duke of Brunswick-Luneburg, Archtreasurer and Elector of S.R.I. (Brunswick-Luneburg)

Georgius D.G.M. Br. Fr. et Hib. Rex F.D. (1345-46) George, D.G., King of Great Britain, France and Ireland, Defender of the Faith. (Great Britain)

Georgius I D.G. M. Brit. Fr. et Hib. Rex. F.D. Br. et Lun. Dux S.R.I.A. Th. et El. (2082) George III, D.G., King of Great Britain, France, and Ireland, Defender of the Faith, Duke of Brunswick-Luneburg, Archtreasurer and Elector of S.R.I. (Brunswick-Luneburg)

Georgius II Dei Gratia (1347-51) George II, D.G. (Great Britain)

Georgius March Brand Onoldinus (1980) George, Margrave of Brandenburg-Ansbach. (Brandenburg-Ansbach)

Georgius Wilhelmus D.G. Marg. Brand. B.M. St. P.M. ..... Dux (2031) George Wilhelm, D.G., Margrave of Brandenburg, Duke of Prussia, Magdeburg, Stettin, Pomerania, Mecklenburg, ... (Brandenburg-Bayreuth)

Germ. Hispa. Hun(g). et Bohemiae Rex (1066-68) King of Germany, Spain, Hungary, and Bohemia. (Austria-Prague)

Germ(an). Hung(ar). et Bohemiae Rex (1006-8,24-27) King of Germany, Hungary, and Bohemia. (Austria-Prague)

Germ. Jero. Rex Loth. Bar. Mag. Het. Dux (1283) King of Germany, Jerusalem, Lorraine, and Bar, Grand Duke of Tuscany. (Austrian Netherlands)

Germania Voti Compos MDCCLXXVIIII D. XIII May (2023) Germany sharing the vows, 13 May 1779. (Brandenburg-Ansbach)

Giorno che vale di tanti anni il pianto (1484-85) The day which is worth so many years of sorrow. (Roman Republic)

Gloria ex Amore Patriae (1304-10) Glory from love of country. (Denmark)

Gloria in Excelsis Deo atque in Terra Pax Hominibus (2481) Glory to God in the highest and on earth peace to men. (Nuremberg)

Gott hat seinen reichen Seegen Itter in dich wollen legen (2315) God wanted to place his rich blessing upon you, Itter. (Hesse-Darmstadt)

Gott segne ferner das Holzappeler Bergwerck fein Silber (1907) May God continue to bless the fine silver of the Holzappel mine. (Anhalt-Bernburg-Haym-Schaumburg)

Gott segne und erhalte unsere Bergwercke (2794-97, 2801-2,5,9) God bless and preserve our mines. (Stolberg-Younger Line)

Gott sey gebenedeyt. fur diese seltne Zeit (2792-93) May God be blessed for this extraordinary time. (Stolberg-Younger Line)

Gott sey gedancket, der uns Sieg gibt in Christo, und offenbahret seine wahre Erkantnus (2350) Thanks be to God, who gives us victory in Christ, and who reveals his true knowledge. (Hohenlohe-Neuenstein-Ohringen)

Gratia obvia ultio quaestia Liburni (1499,1501,3) Grace proffered, punishment provoked, Livorno (Leghorn). (Tuscany)

Gratitudo concivibus exemplum posteritati (1622) Gratitude to fellow citizens, an example to posterity. (Poland)

Gratus Erga Deum, Verus et Sincerus (2762) Pleasing to God, true and sincere. (Schaumburg-Lippe)

Gud mitt Hopp (1718,20,23,27-30) God my hope. (Sweden)

Gud och Folket (1737-38) God and the people. (Sweden)

Gud wart Hopp (1721-22,24) God our hope. (Sweden)

Gustaf IV Aldolph Sv. G. och W. Konung (1727-28) Gustaf IV, King of Sweden, Gothland, and Vendalia. (Sweden)

Gustavus III D.G. Rex Sveciae (1734-36) Gustaf III, King of Sweden. (Sweden)

H

Hac Magna Triade Patrocinante (2881) Under the protection of this great Trinity. (Wurzburg)

Hac Sub Tutila (2210) Under this protection. (Eichstaedt)

Hac Sum Secura Tuente (2185) I am under this sure protector. (Cologne)

Haec Sunt Mumera S. Anthonii Eremitae (2341-42) These are the gifts of St. Anthony the Hermit. (Hildesheim)

Haer. Norw. Dux Slesv. Hols. St. & Ditm. Com. Old. & Delm. (1353) Heir of Norway, Duke of Schleswig-Holstein, Stormark, and Ditmarsh, Count of Oldenburg and Delmenhorst. (Holstein-Gottorp)

Hanc tuemur, hac nitimur (1849-53) This we defend, by this we strive. (United Netherlands)

Hassia Votorum Compos Deo Gratia (2317) Hesse sharing in the offerings D.G. (Hesse-Darmstadt)

Hassiae Landgr. (2294) Landgrave of Hesse. (Hesse-Cassel)

Helvet(ische) Republ(ik) (1771-73) Helvetian Republic. (Switzerland)

Henri S.R.I.P.C. Mansfeld Ae. N.D. in Held. Seeb. & Schrapplau (2438) Heinrich, Prince of S.R.I., Count of Mansfeld, and noble Lord in Heldrungen, Seeburg, and Schraplau. (Mansfeld-Bornstatt)

Henricus D.G. Epis. et Abb. Fuld. S.R.I. Pr. (2261-62) Henry, D.G., Bishop and Abbot of Fulda, Prince of S.R.I. (Fulda)

Henricus S.R.I. Princeps Avrsperg Dux Minsterberg (1181) Henry, Prince of S.R.I. of Auersperg, Duke of Munsterberg. (Auersperg)

Hercules III D.G. Mut. Reg. Mir. Ec. Dux (1393-94) Ercole III, D.G., Duke of Modena, Reggio and Mirandola. (Modena)

Hic est qui Multum Orat Pro Populo (2516) Here is he who prays much for the people. (Paderborn)

Hic Plantavit Deus Incrementum Dedit. Haec Rigavit (2208) This (man) planted, God gave increase, she watered. (Eichstaedt)

Hieronymus D.G.A. & P.S.A.S.L.N.G. Prim. (1262-66) Jerome, D.G., Archbishop and Prince of Salzburg, Legate of the Apostolic See, born Primate of Germany. (Salzburg)

Hisp. Utr. Sici. Rex (1395) King of Spain and the Two Sicilies. (Naples)

Hispan(iarum) Infans (1400-2,4-6,9,17-19,21,23-25) Prince of Spain. (Naples, Sicily)

Hispaniarum Rex (1692-93,96-1701) King of Spain. (Spain)

Hospita(lis) et S. Sep(ul) Hierus(al) (1607-9,11) Hospital and Holy Sepulchre of Jerusalem. (Malta)

I

I.W.D.G.C.P.R.S.I. Archid. & El. (2527) Johann Wilhelm, D.G., Count Palatine of the Rhine, Archdapifer and Elector of S.R.I. (Pfalz-Neuberg)

Iac. Ern. D.G. Epus. Olomucensis Dux S.R.I. Pcps. (Spcp) (1227-30) Jacob Ernst, D.G., Bishop of Olmutz, Duke, Prince of S.R.I. (Olmutz)

Iacobus Ernst D.G. Arch. & Princ. Salis. S.A.L. (1243-44) Jacob Ernst, D.G., Archbishop and Prince of Salzburg, Legate of the Apostolic See. (Salzburg)

Ich habe uberwunden (2781) I have conquered. (Solms-Laubach)

Ille Sunt Quae Testificantur de Me (1981) Those are the things testified concerning me. (Brandenburg-Ansbach)

Im 1716 des Theuren Erzherzogs etc. (2217) In 1716, the beloved Archduke of Austria and the Prince of the Asturias, Leopold, in his 51st year, at the local shooting was the best. (Frankfurt)

Immortale Decus Virtutis Avitae (1372) Immortal glory of the virtue of the forefathers. (Guastalla)

Imperial Civit. Lubecensis (2416) Imperial City of Lubeck. (Lubeck)

In alle Lande gieng ihr Schall, und in alle Welt ihre Wort (2350) Throughout the world went their fame; and their words in all the earth. (Hohenlohe-Neuenstein-Ohringen)

In Casus Pervigil Omnes (2398) Watchful for every chance. (Lowenstein-Wertheim-Rochefort)

In Charitate non Ficta (2512) In unfeigned charity. (Paderborn)

In Deo Faciemus Virtutem (1911-12) In God we shall produce virtue. (Anhalt-Zerbst)

In Hoc Signo Vinces (1625-33) In this sign thou shalt conquer. (Portugal)

In Honorem Div. Ioan. Com. de Mont. Cyp. Patr. (2451-52) In honor of the saintly John, Count of Montfort, Patron of Cyprus. (Montfort)

In Honorem Gratamq. Memoriam etc. (2662) In honor and pleasing memory of the unexpected arrival of the King of Prussia in the year 1728 in the month of January. (Saxony)

In Honorem S. Theodori Mar. (1431) In honor of St. Theodore, martyr. (Papal States)

In Manibus Domini Sortes Meae (2423) In the hands of the Lord is my lot. (Mainz)

In Mem. Amabilias Coni. F.F. Christ. Aug. Com. in Solms (2780) In memory of his most amiable wife, Christian August, Count of Solms, has caused this to be made. (Solms-Laubach)

In Mem. Regimi D. X Maii MDCCXII Suscepti Quod. Felix Faustumq. Sit. (2031) In memory of the reign from 10 May 1712, undertaken that it might be fortunate and lucky. (Brandenburg-Bayreuth)

In Memor. Natalis Principis Novaeque Fundation (2753-54) In memory of the birth of a prince and a new foundation. (Saxe-Weimar)

In Memor. Vindicatae Libert. ac Relig. (1719) In honor of vindicated liberty and religion. (Sweden)

In Memoriam Christianae Eberhardiniae ..... (2661) In memory of Christina Eberhardina, Queen of Poland and Electress of Saxony, that best and most pious of women, born at Bayreuth in the year 1671 on the 19th day of December, died at Prezsch in 1727 on the fifth day of September. (Saxony)

In Memoriam Coniunctionis ultriusque Burgraviatus Norice D. XX Ian. MDCCLXIX (1999) In memory of the union of both burgraviates in peace 20 Jan. 1769. (Brandenburg-Ansbach)

In Memoriam Connub. Felicias. Inter Princ. ..... (2770) In commemoration of the most happy marriage between the hereditary Prince, Friedrich Karl, and the Duchess of Saxony, Auguste Louisa Frederika Roda, celebrated on 28 Nov. 1780. (Schwarzburg-Rudolstadt)

In Memoriam Felicissimus Matrimonii (2845) In memory of the most happy marriage. (Wied-Runkel)

In Memoriam Iubilaei de Reformat. Eccles. ..... (2129) In memory of the jubilee of the church reformation in the city of Brunswick under the auspices of August Wilhelm, celebrated in the 14th year of his reign on 5 Sept. 1728. (Brunswick-Wolfenbuttel)

In Memoriam Iubilaei Evange Lici ..... (2281) In memory of the second evangelical jubilee celebrated in the secular year 1717. (Hamburg)

In Memoriam Iubilae ob. Ver. Doctrinam ..... (2128) In memory of the second jubilee, commemorating the true doctrine of Christ fortunately restored these two hundred years ago from the vain corruption and the fabrications of priesthood by Luther with the aid of liberating God, celebrated on 30 and 31 October in the lands of Brunswick-Wolfenbuttel. (Brunswick-Wolfenbuttel)

In Memoriam Iubiliae Secunda Evangelici Vinariae Celebrati (2755) In memory of the second evangelical jubilee celebrated at Weimar. (Saxe-Weimar)

In Memoriam Optimi Sui Mariti Vidva Celsissima ex Argento Fodinae S. Michaelis (2373) In memory of the best of husbands by the most august widow from the silver of the mine of St. Michael. (Kempten)

In Memoriam Pacis Teschinensis (2030) In memory of the Peace of Teschen. (Brandenburg-Bayreuth)

In Memoriam Religionis Evangelicae Pace Aeterna ..... (2719-20) In memory of the evangelical faith founded in lasting peace in the Roman German Empire. Sacred rites were celebrated for the second time in the duchy of Eisenach on 25 September 1755. (Saxe-Gotha-Altenburg)

In Memoriam Secundi Iubilaei Evangelici ..... (2218) In memory of the second evangelical jubilee in the centennial year 1717 on 31 October celebrated by the Senate at Frankfurt. (Frankfurt)

In P.R.S. et Fr. I. Prov. et Vicarius (2365) Administrators in the area of the Rhine, of Swabia and Franconian law, and Vicars. (Julich-Berg)

In Part. Rhen. Suev. & Franc. Iur. Provisores at Vicary (1946) Administrators in the area of the Rhine, of Swabia and Franconian law, and Vicars. (Bavaria)

In Part. Rheni. Suev. et Iur. Francon. (Vicariorum) (1945,72,74,2529-30,32) Administrators in the area of the Rhine, of Swabia and Franconian law, and Vicars. (Bavaria, Pfalz-Neuberg, Pfalz-Sulzbach)

In Pr. S. et Fr. I. Prov. et Vicarius (2528) Administrators in the area of the Rhine, of Swabia and Franconian law, and Vicars. (Pfalz-Neuberg)

In Provinciis Iur Saxon. Provisor et Vicarius (2667-69) Administrator in the section of Saxon law and Vicar. (Saxony)

In Recto Decus (2057-60,65-68) There is honor in right. (Brunswick-Luneburg)

In Regiminis Sui ..... (2713) Individual churches having been built under the authority of Gotha for the individual years of his reign, in the year 1719 on March 31 with his own hand, he laid the cornerstone of the House of God in Rehsted. (Saxe-Gotha-Altenburg)

In Schwarzenburg Landgr. In Cleggov. (D.C.) (2773-74) In Schwarzenburg landgrave in Klettgau. (Schwarzenberg)

In Te Domine Speravi (2386-90) In thee, O Lord, have I hoped. (Lorraine)

In Te Domini Speravi (1152-60,1504-7,12-13) In Thee, O Lord, have I hoped. (Austria, Tuscany)

In Testimonia Tua et non in Avaritiam (1440) To Thy laws and not to avarice. (Papal States)

Inauguratio Templi Walthershusani (2714) Consecration of the church at Waltershausen. (Saxe-Gotha-Altenburg)

Indissolubilitis (2660) Indissoluble. (Saxony)

Innocent(ius) XIII Pon(t). M(ax). (1450-52) Innocent XIII Pope. (Papal States)

Insignia Capituli Brixinensis (1204) The insignia of the Chapter of Brixen. (Brixen)

Intima Candent (2209) The innermost parts glow. (Eichstaedt)

Inviolata Fides Pax et Concordia Firmant (1937) Unbroken faith, peace, and harmony give strength. (Bamberg)

Io. Ernest D.G. Archiep. Sal. S.A.L. (1234) Johann Ernst, D.G., Archbishop of Salzburg, Legate of the Apostolic See. (Salzburg)

Io. Ios. Kevenhuller ab Aichelberg S.R.I. Pr. A. Metsch (1189) Johann Josef Khevenhuller of Aichelberg, Prince of S.R.I. of Metsch. (Kevenhuller-Metsch)

Io. Ios. S.R.I. Com. A. Kevenhuller Metsch in Osterwitz (1188) Johann Josef, Count of S.R.I. of Khevenhuller-Metsch in Osterwitz. (Kevenhuller-Metsch)

Io. Leop. S.R.I. Princeps Trautson Com. in Falkenstein (1201) Johann Leopold, Prince of S.R.I. of Trautson, Count in Falkenstein. (Trautson)

Ioan. Aloys I Princ. de et in Ottingen (2500-1) Johann Aloys I, Prince of Ottingen. (Ottingen)

Ioan. Christoph. D.G. Abbas Corbeiensis (5187-88) Johann Christoph, D.G., Abbot of Corvey. (Corvey)

Ioan. Dominic Milano D.G.S.R.I. (1490) John Dominic Milano, D.G., Prince of S.R.I. (San Giorgio)

Ioan. Gasto. I D.G. Mag. Dux Etrur. VII (1502) John Gaston I, D.G., seventh Duke of Tuscany. (Tuscany)

Ioan. Hugo D.G. Arch. Trev. S.R.I. Per. Gall. et Reg. Arelat. (2814-22) Johann Hugo, D.G., Archbishop of Trier, S.R.I. for Gaul and the kingdom of Arles. (Trier)

Ioan. Philip Cardinal de Lamberg (2517-20) Johann Philip, Cardinal of Lamberg. (Passau)

Ioan. Philip D.G. Ar. Ep. (& El.) Trevir. S.R.I. Prin. El (Ep. Worm) Admi. Prum. Pp. (2827-31) Johann Philip, D.G., Bishop and Elector of Trier, Prince of S.R.I., Bishop of Worms, Administrator of Pruem, Provost. (Trier)

Ioan. Philip D.G. Ep. Herb. S.R.I. Pr. Fr. Or Dux (2880-85) Johann Philip, D.G., Bishop of Wurzburg, Prince of S.R.I., Duke of Eastern Franconia. (Wurzburg)

Ioann. Anton D.G. Ep. Eystettensis S.R.I.P. (2207) Johann Anton, D.G., Bishop of Eichstaedt, Prince of S.R.I. (Eichstaedt)

Ioann Anton III D.G. Ep. Eystettensis S.R.I.P. (2211) Johann Anton, D.G., Bishop of Eichstaedt, Prince of S.R.I. (Eichstaedt)

Ioann. Frid. Com. de Hohenl. et Gleich. Dom. in Langenb. et Cranichf. Senior et Feud. Administrator Aetat S. 77 (2351) Johann Friedrich, Count of Hohenlohe and Gleichen, Lord in Langenburg and Kranichfeld, Lord and Administrator of the fief, age 77. (Hohenlohe-Neuenstein-Ohringen)

Ioann. Philipp. Anton D.G. Episcop. Bamb. S.R.I. Princeps (1937) Johann Philip Anton, D.G., Bishop of Bamberg, Prince of S.R.I. (Bamberg)

Ioannes Antonius D.G. Ep. Cur. S.R.I. Pr. (1764,66) Johann Anton, D.G., Bishop of Chur, Prince of S.R.I. (Chur)

Ioannes Conradus D.G. (1739) Johann Conrad, D.G., (Bishopric of Basel)

Ioannes Cornelio Dux Ven. (1529-30) Giovanni Corner, Doge of Venice. (Venice)

Ioannes Francis D.G. Episcop Frising (2247) Johann Francis, D.G., Bishop of Freising. (Freising)

Ioannes Fridericus D.G. P.S. Rud. D.S. Senior (2768) Johann Friedrich, D.G., Prince of Schwarzburg-Rudolstadt, Senior Lord in Schwarzburg. (Schwarzburg-Rudolstadt)

Ioannes V D.G. Port. et Alg. Rex (1628) John V, D.G., King of Portugal and Algarve. (Portugal)

Ioh. D.G.S.R.I. Princeps in Schwarzenburg (2777) Johann, D.G., Prince of S.R.I. in Schwarzenburg. (Schwarzenberg)

Ioh. Fridericus Lineae Hohenloh. Neuensteininsis Dedit et Erexit Piis (2350) Johann Friedrich line of Hohenlohe-Neuenstein, given and erected to the pious. (Hohenlohe-Neuenstein)

Ioh. Georg. III Com. et Dom. I. Mansf. Nob. D.I.H.S. et Schr. Senior (2436) Johann Georg III, Count and Lord of Mansfeld, most noble Lord in Heldrungen, Seeburg, and Schraplau, senior line. (Mansfeld)

Ioh. Lud. Vollrath (S.R.I.) Com. in Loew. Wertheim (2391-95) Johann Ludwig Vollrath (S.R.I.), Count of Lowenstein-Wertheim. (Lowenstein-Wertheim-Virneburg)

Ioh. Wen. S.R. Imp. Princeps a Paar (1193) Johann Wenzel, Prince of S.R.I. of Paar. (Paar)

Ioh. Wilh. D. Sax. I.C.M.A. & W. (2709) Johann Wilhelm, Duke of Saxony, Julich, Cleves, Berg, Angria, and Westphalia. (Saxe-Gotha-Altenburg)

Ios. Bened. D.G. Episcopus Curiens S.R.I. Princeps (1762-63) Joseph Benedict, D.G., Bishop of Chur, Prince of S.R.I. (Chur)

Ios. Cle. D.G. Arch. Col. S.R.I.P. El. B.D. (1581) Joseph Clemens, D.G., Archbishop of Cologne, Prince of S.R.I., Elector and Duke of Bavaria. (Liege)

Ios. Clem. Arch. Col. S.R.I. Archican. (2174) Joseph Clemens, Archbishop of Cologne, Arch-chancellor of S.R.I. (Brunswick-Wolfenbuttel)

Ios. Conr. D.G. Ep. Frising & Ratisb. Praep. Berchtesg. S.R.I. Princ. (2248-49) Joseph Conrad, D.G., Bishop of Freising and Regensburg, Provost of Berchtesgaden, Prince of S.R.I. (Freising)

Ios. Dominic Cardinal de Lamberg (2523) Joseph Dominic, Cardinal of Lamberg. (Passau)

Ios. Io. Ad. D.G.S.R.I.P. & Gub. Dom. de Liechtenstein (1578) Joseph Johann Adam, D.G., Prince of S.R.I. and Ruling Lord of Liechtenstein. (Liechtenstein)

Ios. Ma. Gon. Guas. Sab. Dux Boz. Prin. (1372) Joseph Maria Gonzaga, Duke of Guastalla and Sabbioneta, Prince of Bozzolo. (Guastalla)

Ios. Wenc. D.G.S.R.I. Pr. & Gub. Dom. de Liechtenstein (1579) Joseph Wenceslaus, D.G., Prince of S.R.I., and Ruling Lord of Liechtenstein. (Liechtenstein)

Ios. Wilh. D.G. Pr. de Hohenzollern. Burgg. N. (2362) Joseph Wilhelm, D.G., Prince of Hohenzollern, Burgrave of Nuremberg. (Hohenzollern-Hechingen)

Ios. Wilh. Ernest S.R.I. Princ in (de) Furstenberg Landgrav. in Baar & Stuhlingen (2267-68) Joseph Wilhelm Ernst, Prince of S.R.I. in Furstenberg, Landgrave in Baar and Stuhlingen. (Furstenberg)

Ios. II D.G.R.I(mp). S.A.G.H.B.R(ex)A.A.D.B. et(&) L. (1168-69) Joseph II, D.G., R.I.S.A., King of Germany, Hungary, Bohemia, Archduke of Austria, Duke of Burgundy and Lorraine. (Hungary)

Ioseph D.G. Ep. August S.R.I. Pr. Landgr. Hass. (1916) Joseph, D.G., Bishop of Augsburg, Prince of S.R.I., Landgrave of Hesse. (Augsburg)

Ioseph D.G. S.R.I. Prin. in Schwarzenberg (2775-76) Joseph, D.G., Prince of S.R.I. in Schwarzenberg. (Schwarzenberg)

Ioseph Dominic D.G. Episc. Patav. (2522) Joseph Dominic, D.G., Bishop of Passau. (Passau)

Ioseph. Ex. Prin. de Aversberg S.R. Eccl. Cardin. (2526) Joseph of the Princes of Auersberg, Cardinal of the Holy Roman Church. (Passau)

Ioseph II D.G. R.I.S.A. Germ. (Hie.) Hu(n). Bo(h). Rex (1167,70,1388) Joseph II, D.G., R.I.S.A., King of Germany, Jerusalem, Hungary, and Bohemia. (Austria, Milan)

Ioseph II D.G.R. Imp. S.A. Ger. Hier. Hung. Boh. Rex (1284) Joseph II, D.G., R.I.S.A., King of Germany, Jerusalem, Hungary, and Bohemia. (Austrian Netherlands)

Ioseph II D.G.R Imp. S. Aug. G.H. et B. Rex A.A. (1387) Joseph II, D.G., R.I.S.A., King of Germany, Jerusalem, Hungary, and Bohemia, Archduke of Austria. (Milan)

Ioseph II D.G.R.I.S.A. Cor. & Her. R.H.B. & C. (2462) Joseph II, D.G., R.I.S.A., Co-Regent and heir to the Kingdom of Hungary, Bohemia, ... (Mulhausen)

Ioseph II D.G.R.I.S.A. Cor. Her. R.H.B. (1161-66) Joseph II, D.G., R.I.S.A., Co-Regent and heir to the kingdoms of Hungary and Bohemia. (Austria)

Ioseph. II. Rom. Imp. Semper August (2252) Joseph II, R.I.S.A. (Fugger)

Iosephus D.G. Episc. Evstettensis S.R.I.P. (2213) Joseph, D.G., Bishop of Eichstaedt, Prince of S.R.I. (Eichstaedt)

Iosephus D.G. Rom. Imp. S.A. Ger. H.B.R. Ar. A. (2473-74) Joseph, D.G., R.I.S.A., King of Germany, Hungary, and Bohemia, Archduke of Austria. (Nuremberg)

Iosephus D.G. Rom. Imp. Semp. Aug. (1917,2607-8) Joseph, D.G., R.I.S.A. (Augsburg)

Iosephus D.G. Roman Imp(er) Semper A(v). (1024-27) Joseph, D.G., R.I.S.A. (Austria-Prague)

Iosephus D.G. Ro(m). Imp(erator) S(em) A(u) Ger. Hu. et Bo. Rex (1013-23,28-31,33-34) Joseph, D.G., R.I.S.A., King of Germany, Hungary, and Bohemia. (Austria)

Iosephus M.B. Furst zu Furstenberg L.I.D.B.U.Z.St. H.Z. Hausen I. Kinz. Thal. (2271) Joseph Maria Benedict, Prince of Furstenberg, Landgrave in Baar, and of Stuhlingen, Duke of the line of Kinzigthal. (Furstenberg)

Iosephus Wenceslaus S.R.I. Princeps de Furstenberg (2269-70) Joseph Wenceslaus, Prince of S.R.I. of Furstenberg. (Furstenberg)

Iosephus I D.G. Port. et Alg. Rex (1629) Joseph I, D.G., King of Portugal and Algarve. (Portugal)

Iosephus I D.G. Rom. Imperator Semp. Augustus (2183-84,2204,2772,74,2413) Joseph I, D.G., R.I.S.A. (Cologne)

Iosephus II D.G. Rom. Imp. S.A. (2251,2421-22,80, 2492-98,2621-28) Joseph II, D.G., R.I.S.A. (Friedberg)

Iosephus II D.G. Rom. Imp. Semp. Aug. (1766) Joseph II, D.G., R.I.S.A. (Chur)

Iubilaeum Saalfel. Dia. Agitin Laetitia (2738-39) Saalfeld pursue its jubilee in joy. (Saxe-Saalfeld)

Iul. Cl. Mont. A. & W.S.R.I. Archim. & Elector (2677) Julich, Cleves, Berg, Angria and Westphalia, Archmarshal and Elector. (Saxony)

Iuliae Cliviae Montium Angriae et Westphaliae (2727-28,35,40,47) Julich, Cleves, Berg, Angria and Westphalia, Archmarshal and Elector. (Saxe-Hildburghausen, Saxe-Saalfeld)

Iuste et Constanter (2514-15) Justly and constantly. (Paderborn)

Iustirt (2301-2) Adjusted. (Hesse-Cassel)

Iustitia et Clementia (2757) Justice and mercy. (Saxe-Weimar)

Iustitia et Concordia (1783,86,92-97) Justice and harmony. (Zurich)

Iustitia et Mansuetudine (2177-81) Justice and mildness. (Cologne)

Iustum et Decorum (2378-79,81-82) Just and beautiful. (Lippe-Detmold)

Ivl. Cl. & Mont. D.L.L.P.M.M.M.A.Z.C.V.S.M. & R.D.I.R. (1969-71,73) Duke of Julich, Cleves, and Berg, Landgrave of Leuchtenberg, Prince of Mors, Margrave of Berg-op-Zoom, Count of Veldenz, Sponheim, Mark, and Ravensberg, Lord in Ravenstein. (Bavaria)

J

Jac. Fr. Milano March. Sanc. Georgii (1491) Giocomo Francesco Milano, Marquis of San Georgio. (San Giorgio)

Joannes D.G. P. Portugaliae et Alg. (1633) John, D.G., Prince of Portugal and Algarve. (Portugal)

Josephus I D.G. Port. et Alg. Rex (1630) Joseph I, D.G., King of Portugal and Algarve. (Portugal)

L

L.B. in Spreichen. et Schrovenstein (1200) Free Baron in Sprechenstein and Schroffenstein. (Trautson)

L'an IV de l'egalite (1769) Year four of equality. (Geneva)

Labore et Constantia (2115) With labor and constancy. (Brunswick-Wolfenbuttel)

Lamberti Alexandrique Auxilio Florebit (2241,45) It will flourish with the aid of Lambert and Alexander. (Freiburg im Breisgau)

Landgr. in Cleggov. Com. in Sulz Dux Crum (2775-77) Landgrave of Klettgau, Count of Sulz, Duke of Krumlau. (Schwarzenberg)

Landgr. Th. M.M.Pr. D.C. Hen. C.M.E.R.D.R.E. Ton. (2707,10) Landgrave of Thuringia, Margrave of Meissen, Prince of the county of Henneberg, Count of Mark and Ravensberg, Lord of Ravenstein and Tonn. (Saxe-Gotha-Altenburg)

Lege Vindice (2486,91) Supported by law. (Nuremberg)

Leop. Ern. D.G. Exemp. Eccl. Patavi. Eps. (2524) Leopold Ernst, D.G., Bishop of the freed church of Passau. (Passau)

Leop. Han. Schlik S.R.I.C. de Passaun & Weiskerchen (1197) Leopold Heinrich, Count of S.R.I. of Schlick, of Passaun and Weiskirchen. (Schlick)

Leop. II D.G. Hu. Bo. Ga. Lod. Rex A.A.D.B. et L.M.D. Hetr. (1172) Leopold II, D.G., King of Hungary, Bohemia, Galicia, and Lodomeria, Archduke of Austria, Duke of Burgundy and Lorraine, Grand Duke of Tuscany. (Hungary)

Leop(oldus) II D.G. R. Imp. S.A. Germ. (Hie). Hu(n). Bo(h). Rex (1173-75) Leopold II, D.G., R.I.S.A., King of Germany, Jerusalem, Hungary, and Bohemia. (Austria)

Leopold D.G. Rom. Imp. S.A. Ger. H.B. Rex Archid. Aust. (2472) Leopold, D.G., R.I.S.A., King of Germany, Hungary, and Bohemia, Archduke of Austria. (Nuremberg)

Leopold(us) D.G. Rom. Imp. Sem. Aug. Ger. Hun. et Bo. Rex (1001-5,9-11) Leopold, D.G., R.I.S.A., King of Germany, Hungary and Bohemia. (Austria)

Leopold Vict. Io. S.R.I. Comes a. Windischgratz (1202) Leopold Viktorin Johann, Count of S.R.I. of Windisch-Gratz. (Windisch-Gratz)

Leopold II D.G. R.I.S.A. Ger. Hie. Hun. Boh. Rex (1389) Leopold II, D.G., R.I.S.A., King of Germany, Jerusalem, Hungary, and Bohemia. (Milan)

Leopold II D.G. Rom. Imp. Semp. Aug. (2630-31) Leopold II, D.G., R.I.S.A. (Regensburg)

Leopoldus D.G. Arch. et Princeps (1240-42) Leopold, D.G., Archbishop and Prince. (Salzburg)

Leopoldus D.G. Archi. Pr. Sal. S.A.L. (1241) Leopold, D.G., Archbishop and Prince of Salzburg, Legate of the Apostolic See. (Salzburg)

Leopoldus D.G. Roman(or) Impera. S.A. (1106-8) Leopold, D.G., R.I.S.A. (Austria-Transylvania)

Leopoldus I D.G. Rom. Imperator Semp. Augustus (many) Leopold I, D.G., R.I.S.A.

Leopoldus I. D.G.D. Lot. Bar. Rex. Ier. (2386-90) Leopold I, D.G., Duke of Lorraine and Bar, King of Jerusalem. (Lorraine)

Leopoldus II D.G. H. et B. Rex A.A.M.D.E. (1520) Leopold II, D.G., King of Hungary and Bohemia, Archduke of Austria, Grand Duke of Tuscany. (Tuscany)

Leopoldus II D.G. Hungar. Bohem. Gallic. Lodom. Rex (1171) Leopold II, D.G., King of Hungary, Bohemia, Galicia, and Lodomeria. (Austria)

Leopoldus II D.G. R.I.S.A. Ger. H. et H. Rex A.A.M.D. Etr. (1519) Leopold II, D.G., R.I.S.A., King of Germany, Jerusalem, and Hungary; Archduke of Austria; Grand Duke of Tuscany. (Tuscany)

Lex tua Veritas (1521) Thy law is the truth.

Lib. S.R.I. Civit. Augusta Vindel. (1920) Free City of S.R.I., Augsburg. (Augsburg)

Liber Baro in Hollenburg (1186) Free Baron in Hollenburg. (Dietrichstein)

Libera Wormatia Sacri Romani Imperii Fidelis Filia (2846) Free Worms, faithful daughter of S.R.I. (Worms)

Liberta Eguaglianza (1371,1576-77) Liberty, equality. (Genoa & Venice)

Liberta Romana XXVII (27) Piovoso An. VII (1484-85) Roman liberty 27 Rainy month Year 7. (Roman Republic)

Lire Dieci Venete (1576-77) Ten Venetian lire. (Venice)

Lobe den, der Ihn gemacht hat. Syr. C. 43 (2101,2165-6) Praise the one who made him. (Brunswick-Luneburg, Brunswick-Wolfenbuttel)

Locum Tenens Generalis (2709) Lieutenant General. (Saxe-Gotha-Altenburg)

Lothar Franc D.G.A.M.S.R.I.P.G.A.P.E.E.B. (2423) Lothar Franz, D.G., Archbishop of Mainz, Prince of S.R.I., Arch-chancellor of Germany, Elector and Bishop of Bamberg. (Mainz)

Louis XVI Roi des Francois (1335) Louis XVI, King of the French. (France)

Louise Eleonore Herz. Z.S.C. Mein. Geb. Furst z. Hohenl. (2734) Louise Eleonore, Duchess of Saxe-Coburg-Meiningen, born Princess of Hohenlohe. (Saxe-Coburg-Meiningen)

Lucensis Respublica (1373-76) Republic of Lucca. (Lucca)

Lud. Const. D.G. Epus. et P PS. Argentl. Lan. Al. (2810) Ludwig Constantine, D.G., Bishop and Prince-Provost of Strassburg, Landgrave of Alsace. (Strassburg)

Lud. Eng. D.G. Dux Arenbergae S.R.I.P. (1914-15) Ludwig Engelhardt, D.G., Duke of Arenberg, Prince of S.R.I. (Arenberg)

Lud. Frid. Carol. D.G. Princ Ab. Hohenl. Com. de Gleich. D. in Langenb. & Cranichfeld (2352-54) Ludwig Friedrich Karl, D.G., Prince of Hohenlohe, Count of Gleichen, Lord of Langenburg and Kranichfeld. (Hohenlohe-Neuenstein-Ohringen)

Lud. XIIII D.G. Fr. et Nav. Rex (1316-22,24) Louis XIV, D.G., King of France and Navarre. (France)

Lud. XV D.G. Fr. et Nav Rex (1325-32) Louis XV, D.G., King of France and Navarre. (France)

Lud. XVI D.G. Fr. et Nav. Rex (1333) Louis XVI, D.G., King of France and Navarre. (France)

Lud. XVI D.G. Fr. et Na. Re. B.D. (1334) Louis XVI, King of

France and Navarre, Lord of Bearn. (France)

Ludov. Eugen. D.G. Dux Wirtemb. & T. (2872) Ludwig Eugen, D.G., Duke of Wurttemberg and Teck. (Wurttemberg)

Ludovico Manin Duce (1575) Ludovico Manin, Doge. (Venice)

Ludovico Manin Dux Venetiar (1569-70) Ludovico Manin, Doge of Venice. (Venice)

Ludovicus et Philippus Christianus et Carolus Henricus, ... (2355) Ludwig and Philip Christian and Karl Heinrich and August, sprung from these brothers, happy in union, are the heads of the line of Hohenlohe-Langenburg. May their union ever endure. (Hohenlohe-Langenburg)

Ludovicus Rudolphus D.G. Dux Bruns. et Luneb. (2133-36,39-41) Ludwig Rudolph, D.G., Duke of Brunswick-Luneburg. (Brunswick-Wolfenbuttel)

Ludovicus S.R.I. Princeps de Batthyan. Strattmann (1184) Ludwig, Prince of S.R.I. of Batthyani Strattmann. (Batthyani)

Ludovicus VIII D.G. Landgravius Hass. (2322-31) Ludwig VIII, D.G., Landgrave of Hesse. (Hesse-Darmstadt)

Ludovicus IX D.G. Landgravius Hass. (2332-35) Ludwig IX, D.G., Landgrave of Hesse. (Hesse-Darmstadt)

Ludovicus X D.G. Landgravius Hass. (2336-39) Ludwig X, D.G., Landgrave of Hesse. (Hesse-Darmstadt)

Ludovicus XIIII D.G. Fr. et Nav. Rex (1323) Louis XIV, D.G., King of France and Navarre. (France)

M

M. Magis(ter) Hos(p) et S. S(epul) Hierus(alem) (1593-97) Grandmaster of the Hospital and Holy Sepulchre of Jerusalem. (Malta)

M. Theresia D.G. R. Imp. (Ge.) Hu. Bo. Reg. (A.A.) (1111-24,34,36-40,44-51,96-97,1385-86) Maria Theresia, D.G., R.I., Queen of Germany, Hungary, Bohemia, Archduchess of Austria. (Austria)

M. Ther. D.G. R.I(mp) G(e). H(u). B(o). R.A.A.D.B.C.T. (1129-32) Maria Theresia, D.G., R.I., Queen of Germany, Hungary, and Bohemia; Archduchess of Austria; Duchess of Burgundy; Countess of Tyrol. (Hungary)

M. Ther. D.G.R. Imp. Hu. Bo. R.A.A.D.B.C.T. (1133) Maria Theresia, D.G., R.I., Queen of Hungary and Bohemia, Archduchess of Austria, Duchess of Burgundy, Countess of Tyrol. (Hungary)

M. Theresia Nata Non. Iuni. (1403) Maria Theresia born June 5. (Naples)

M.B.F. et H. Rex F.D.B. et L.D.S.R.I.A.T. et E. (1347-51) King of Great Britain, France, and Ireland, Defender of the Faith, Duke of Brunswick and Luneburg, Archtreasurer and Elector of S.R.I. (Great Britain)

M.M.H. et S. Sep. Hier. (1599) Grandmaster of the Hospital and Holy Sepulchre of Jerusalem. (Malta)

Mag. Br(i). Fra. et Hib. Reg. (1338-44) Queen of Great Britain, France, and Ireland. (Great Britain)

Mar. Bran. Sac. Rom. Imp. Arcam. et Elec. Sup. Dux Siles (2595-96) Margrave of Brandenburg, Arch-chamberlain of S.R.I. and Elector, ranking Duke of Silesia. (Prussia)

Mar. Th. D.G. R. Imp. G. Hung. Boh. R. (1280-81) Maria Theresia, D.G., R.I., Queen of Germany, Hungary, and Bohemia. (Austrian Netherlands)

Mar. Theresia D.G.R. Imp. Germ. Hung. Boh. Reg. (1282) Maria Theresia, D.G., R.I., Queen of Germany, Hungary, and Bohemia. (Austrian Netherlands)

March. Sanc. Georgii & Polistinae (1490) Marquis of San Georgio and Polistina. (San Giorgio)

Marco Foscarino Duce (1556) Marco Foscarino, Doge.

Marcus Foscarenus Dux Venetiar (1553) Marco Foscarino, Doge of Venice. (Venice)

Maria D.G. Landgr. Has. N. Pr. M. B. Fr. & H. T. & Com. Han. Administer (2286) Maria, D.G., Landgravine of Hesse, born Princess of Great Britain, France, and Ireland, Regent and Administrator of the county of Hanau. (Munzenberg)

Maria Theresia D.G. Reg. Hung. Boh. (1109-10,25-28, 41-43) Maria Theresia, D.G., Queen of Hungary and Bohemia. (Austria)

Maria Theresia D.G. Reg. Hun(g). Boh. Arch. Aust. (1383-84) Maria Theresia, D.G., Queen of Hungary and Bohemia, Archduchess of Austria. (Milan)

Maria I D.G. Port. et Alg. Regina (1632) Maria I, D.G., Queen of Portugal and Algarve. (Portugal)

Maria I et Petrus III D.G. Port. et Alg. Reges (1631) Maria I and Peter III, D.G., Rulers of Portugal and Algarve. (Portugal)

Mars Foris - Apollo Domi. (2030) Mars abroad, Apollo at home. (Brandenburg-Bayreuth)

Max. Car. Com. in Lowenstein Werth. (2398) Maximilian Karl, Count of Lowenstein-Wertheim. (Lowenstein-Wertheim- Rochefort)

Max. Emanuel D.G.U.B.S.P.B.L.L.& G. Dux (1275-77) Maximilian Emanuel, D.G., Duke of both Bavarias and the Upper Palatinate, Brabant, Limburg, Luxemburg, and Gelders. (Namur (Austrian Netherlands))

Max. Emanuel V.B.S.P.B.L.L.& G. Dux (1271-74) Maximilian Emanuel, Duke of both Bavarias and the Upper Palatinate, Brabant, Limburg, Luxemburg and Gelders. (Namur (Austrian Netherlands))

Max. Frid. D.G. Ar. Ep. & Elect. Col. E. & P. M. W. & A. D. (2178,80) Maximilian Friedrich, D.G., Archbishop and Elector of Cologne, Bishop and Prince of Munster, Duke of Westphalia and Angria. (Cologne)

Maximilian Frider. Ar. Ep. et Elect. Col. (2177,81) Maximilian Friederich, Archbishop and Elector of Cologne. (Cologne)

Maximilianus D.G. Abbas Corbeiensis S.R.I. Princeps (2196-97) Maximilian, D.G., Abbot of Corvey, Prince of S.R.I. (Corvey)

Mea Maxima Cura (2717) My greatest care. (Saxe-Gotha-Altenburg)

Med Gudz Hielp (1713-16) With God's help. (Sweden)

Mediolani Dux (1385-86) Duke of Milan. (Milan)

Mediolani Dux et C. (1379-84) Duke of Milan and others. (Milan)

Mediolani et Mant. Dux (1387) Duke of Milan and Mantua. (Milan)

Megap. in Sil. Cros. Dux Burggraf. Norimb. Pr. Hal. M. C. Va. Sver. Raz. C. Hohenz. G. (2030) Mecklenburg, Duke in Silesia and Krossen, Burgrave of Nuremberg, Prince of Halberstadt, Minden, Camin, Wenden, Schwerin, and Ratzeburg, Count of Hohenzollern. (Brandenburg-Bayreuth)

Megapolis Iubilans Anno 1717 31 Oct. (2443-46) Mecklenburg celebrating, Oct. 31, 1717. (Mecklenburg-Strelitz)

Memor. Ero Tui Iustina Vir(go) (1525,31,36,39,42,44, 49,54,58-59,65,71-72) I will be mindful of you, Justina, Virgin. (Venice)

Memoriae Aeternae Optimi Parentis (2663) To the eternal memory of the best of parents. (Saxony)

Memoriae Ernesti Comit. Stolb. Koenigst...... (2789) To the memory of Ernst, Count of Stolberg, Konigstein, Rochefort, Wernigerode and Hohnstein, Lord in Eppstein, Numzenberg, Breuberg, Aiguemont, Lohra, and Klettenberg, born in Ilsenburg 25 March 1650, who became ruler in 1672, thru marriage in the same year with Sophia Dorothea, Countess of Schwarzburg and Hohnstein, the fourth child of whom three were already deceased has raised this monument; died at Ilsenburg 9 Nov. 1710. (Stolberg- Elder Line)

Merces Laborum (2906,10) Wages of labor. (Wurzburg)

Metalli Fodinae Hackenburgo-Saynensis Ab. Ipso Restauratae (2373) Metals of the Hackenburg-Sayn mine restored by himself. (Kirchberg)

Misericordias Domini In Aeternum Cantabo (2886) I will sing the mercies of the Lord forever. (Wurzburg)

Mit Gott durch Kunst u. Arbeit (2271) With God through art and work. (Furstenberg)

Mo(n) No(v) Arg. Pro. Con. Foe(d). Belg. Com. Ze(e)l. (1835-36,47-48) New silver money of the provinces of the Belgian Federation, county of Zeeland. (United Netherlands)

Mo. Arg. Ord. Foe. Belg. D. Gel. & C.Z. (1849) Silver money of the order of the Belgian Federation, duchy of Gelders, county of Zutphen. (United Netherlands)

Mo. Arg. Ord Faed. Belg. Holl. (1850) Silver money of the order of the Belgian Federation, duchy of Gelders, county of Holland. (United Netherlands)

Mo. Arg. Ord. Foed. Belg. Tral. (1852) Silver money of the order of the Belgian Federation, duchy of Gelders, county of Utrecht. (United Netherlands)

Mo. Arg. Ord. Foed. Belg. Transl. (1851) Silver money of the order of the Belgian Federation, duchy of Gelders, county of Overijssel. (United Netherlands)

Mo. Arg. Ord. Foed. Belg. Westf. (1853) Silver money of the order of the Belgian Federation, duchy of Gelders, county of West Frisia. (United Netherlands)

Mo. Arg. Pro. Con(foe) Belg. D. Gel. & C.Z. (1837-38) Silver money of the provinces of the Belgian Federation, duchy of Gelders, county of Zutphen. (United Netherlands)

Mo. No. Arg. Con. Foe. Belg. Pro. Hol. (1825-27) New silver money of the Belgian Federation, province of Holland. (United Netherlands)

Mo. No. Arg. Con. Foe. Belg. Pro. Tral. (1831-32) New silver money of the Belgian Federation, province of Utrecht. (United Netherlands)

Mo. No. Arg. Con. Foe. Belg. Pro. Transl(sulania) (1828-30,41-42) New silver money of the Belgian Federation, province of Overijssel. (United Netherlands)

Mo. No. Arg. Con. Foe. Belg. Pro. Westf. (1833-34) New silver money of the Belgian Federation, province of West Frisia. (United Netherlands)

Mo. No. Arg. Pro. Conf. Belg. D. Gel. & C.Z. (1823-24) New silver money of the Belgian Federation, duchy of Gelders, county of Zutphen. (United Netherlands)

Mo. No. Arg. Pro. Confoe. Belg. (Co.) Hol(l). (1839-40) New silver money of the Belgian Federation, county of Holland. (United Netherlands)

Mo. No. Arg. Pro. Confoe. Belg. Tral. (1843-45) New silver money of the Belgian Federation, county of Utrecht. (United Netherlands)

Mo. No. Arg. Pro. Confoe. Belg. Westfri. (1846) New silver money of the Belgian Federation, county of West Frisia. (United Netherlands)

Mod. Troskab Dapperhed og Hvad der Giver Aere den Heele Verden Kand. Blant Norske Klipper Laere (1289) Courage, loyalty, bravery, and all that gives honor, the whole world can learn among the mountains of Norway. (Denmark)

Moderatione et Industria (2371) With moderation and industry. (Kempten)

Mon. Arg. Conf. Bel. Pro. Trans. (1821) Silver money of the Belgian Federation, province of Overijssel. (United Netherlands)

Mon. Arg. Pro. Con. Foe. Belg. West F. (1822) Silver money of the provinces of the Belgian Federation, West Frisia. (United Netherlands)

Mon. Capit. Lubec - Sede Vacante (2510) Money of the chapter of Lubeck, the seat being vacant. (Lubeck)

Mon. Homag. Civit I. Tremon. (2205-6) Money in homage of the Imperial City of Dortmund. (Dortmund)

Mon. Lib. Reip. Bremens. (2050-52) Money of the Free Republic of Bremen. (Bremen)

Mon. Nov. Arg. Ducat Querfurt (2760) New silver money of the Duchy of Querfurt. (Querfurt)

Mon. Nova. Arg. Civitatis Coloniensis (2187-88) New silver money of the City of Cologne. (Cologne)

Mon. Nova Arg. Duc. Curl. Ad Normam Tal. Alb. (1624) New silver money, Duchy of Courland, according to the Albertus thaler standard. (Courland)

Mon. Nova Imper. Civit. Lubecae (2417-20) New money of the Imperial City of Lubeck. (Lubeck)

Mon. Nova Lib. Reipub. Coloniensis (2182) New money of the Free Republic of Cologne. (Cologne)

Monet. Nov. Civitat. Hamburg Anno Iubil II 1730 (2282) New money of the city of Hamburg, year of the second jubilee 1730. (Hamburg)

Moneta Bipont. (2545) Money of Zweibrucken. (Zweibrucken)

Moneta Capit. Cathe. Hildes. Sede Vacante (2343) Money of the Cathedral Chapter of Hildesheim, the seat being vacant. (Hildesheim)

Moneta Capit. Cathedr. Fuld. Sede Vacante (2263) Money of the cathedral chapter of Fulda, the seat being vacant. (Fulda)

Moneta Castri Imp. Fridberg (2250) Money of the imperial castle of Friedberg. (Friedberg)

Moneta Livoesthonica (1690) Money of Lithuania. (Lithuania: Livonia under Russia)

Moneta Nov. Arg. Regis Daniae (1310) New silver money of the kingdom of Denmark. (Denmark)

Moneta Nov. Comitatis de Montfort (2451-52) New money of the county of Montfort. (Montfort)

Moneta Nova ad Normam Conventionis (1192) New money according to the Convention standard. (Orsini-Rosenberg)

Moneta Nova Argentea Darmstadina (2312-14,16,20) New silver money of Darmstadt. (Darmstadt)

Moneta Nova Argentea Reip. Francofurtensis (2215,17) New silver money of the Republic of Frankfurt. (Frankfurt)

Moneta Nova Argenti Metalli Fod. Reichstein (1099) New silver money of metal of the Reichstein mine. (Austria)

Moneta Nova Capil. Leod. Sede Vacante (1582-91) New money of the Chapter of Liege, the seat being vacant. (Liege)

Moneta Nova Castri Imp. Fridberg In Wetter (2251) New money of the Imperial Castle of Friedberg in Wetterau. (Friedberg in Wetterau)

Moneta Nova Civit Imper. Tremon (2204) New money of the Imperial City of Dortmund. (Dortmund)

Moneta Nova Civitatis Hamburgensis (2383,5357-68, 71-74) New money of the city of Hamburg. (Hamburg)

Moneta Nova Friburgensis Brisgoiae (2230,36-40,43-44) New money of Freiburg in Breisgau. (Freiburg in Breisgau)

Moneta Nova Hamburgensis (2285) New money of Hamburg. (Hamburg)

Moneta Nova Hildesiensis (2346-47) New money of Hildesheim. (Hildesheim)

Moneta Nova Lib. et Imper. Civit. Colon. (2189) New money of the free and Imperial City of Cologne. (Cologne)

Moneta Nova Lubecensis (2413-15,21-22) New money of Lubeck. (Lubeck)

Moneta Nova Reipubl. Bremensis (2044-49) New money of the Republic of Bremen. (Bremen)

Moneta Nova Reipubl. Noribergensis (2472-74,77-78,85) New money of the Republic of Nuremberg. (Nuremberg)

Moneta Nova Reipublicae Halae Suevicae (2274-80) New money of the Republic of Hall in Suabia. (Hall in Suabia)

Moneta Nova Reipublicae Tigurinae (1781) New money of the Republic of Zurich. (Zurich)

Moneta Nova Urbis Basileensis (1740) New money of the City of Basel. (Basel)

Moneta Reipub. Basileensis (1754) Money of the Republic of Basel. (Basel)

Moneta Reipub. Lucernen (1774) Money of the Republic of Luzern. (Luzern)

Moneta Reipubl. Francofurt ad Legem Conventionis (2226) Money of the Republic of Frankfurt after the laws of the convention. (Frankfurt)

Moneta Reipubl. Norimberg (2475,96-98) Money of the Republic of Nuremberg. (Nuremberg)

Moneta Reipubl. Subsylvaniae Superioris (1780) Money of the Republic of Unterwalden. (Unterwalden)

Moneta Reipublicae Ratisbonesis (2607-15,18-19,21-27, 30-33) Money of the Republic of Regensburg. (Regensburg)

Moneta Reipublicae Tiguri(nae) (1782,84,87-91) Money of the Republic of Zurich. (Zurich)

Moneta Reipublicae Turicensis (1792-99) Money of the Republic of Zurich. (Zurich)

Moneta Saxonica (2650) Money of Saxony. (Saxony)

Munus Reipublicae Memmingensis (2447) Gift of the Republic of Memmingen. (Memmingen)

N

Nach Alt. Reichs Schrot u. Korn (2318,20-21) According to the old imperial weight and alloy. (Hesse-Darmstadt)

Nach dem alten Schrot und Korn (2472-73,77-78,2726) According to the old standard weight and alloy. (Nuremberg, Saxe-Henneberg-Ilmenau)

Nach dem Conventions Fusse (1940-41) According to the convention standard. (Bamberg)

Nach dem Fus der Albertus Thaler (2148,2594) According to the standard of the Albertus thaler. (Brunswick-Wolfenbuttel, Prussia)

Nach dem Reichs Fus (2250) According to the imperial standard. (Friedburg)

Nach dem Reichs Schrot und Korn (1904) According to the imperial weight and alloy. (Anhalt-Bernburg)

Nach dem Leipz. Fus (1902,10) According to the Leipzig standard. (Anhalt-Bernburg & Anhalt-Kothen)

Nach Funfzigiahrig Regier. zu Wernigerode seit (2792-93) After 50 years reign at Wernigerode since 9 Nov. 1710. (Stolberg-Elder Line)

Nach Reichs Schrot und Korn (1901) According to the imperial weight and alloy. (Anhalt-Bernburg)

Nat. Hanover VIII Iun. MDCLX..... (2082) Born at Hannover 1 June 1660, he began his Electoral Regime on 4 Feb. 1698. Introduced into the Electoral College 7 Sept. 1708, King of Great Britain 12 Aug. 1714, he died at Osnabruck 22 June 1727. He lived 67 years 14 days. There is honor in right. (Brunswick-Luneburg)

Nat. Onaldi I Mar. MDCLXXXIII..... (2096) Born in Ansbach 1 March 1683, married in Hannover 2 Sept. 1705, received into heaven London 20 Nov. 1 Dec. 1737. (Brunswick-Luneburg)

Nata D. IV. Octobr...... (2709) Born 4 Oct. 1677, died at Toulon Tuesday 15 Aug. 1707, buried at Fridenstein 23 Nov. (Saxe-Gotha-Altenburg)

Nata In Arce Wolgast..... (2708) Born in Arce Wolgast 22 April 1645 of Friedrich, Margrave of Baden-Durlach as father and Christina Magdalena of the Rhenish Palatinate as mother, married 27 July 1665 to Albert, Margrave of

Brandenburg-Ansbach and after his death in the 14th year of widowhood became the wife of Friedrich, Duke of Saxony, etc., 14 Aug. 1681, widowed 2 Aug. 1691 and deceased at Altenburg 20 Dec. 1705, she was buried in the same place on the 24th of the same month and year. (Saxe-Gotha-Altenburg)

Nata XIII Oct. MDCXXX..... (2069) Born 13 Oct. 1630, married in the month of Sept. 1658, called to the succession of Great Britain in 1701, on the evening of 8 June 1714 in the gardens of Herrenhausan, while still walking with firm and vigorous step, snatched away by quiet and peaceful death. (Brunswick-Luneburg)

Natus Ilsenburgi XXV Mart. MDCL..... (2790) Born at Ilsenburg 25 March 1650, attained the realm 1672, married in the same year with Sophia Dorothea of Schwarzburg, and died at Ilsenburg 9 Nov. 1710. The only surviving daughter dedicates this out of deep love to a most sincerely missed father. (Stolberg-Elder Line)

Natus Viennae Aust. 24 N. 1680..... (2823) Born in Vienna, Austria, Nov. 24, 1680, Grand Prior to the Order of Malta for Castile and Leon, elected Bishop of Osnabruck April 11, 1698, Coadjutor of Trier Sept. 24, 1710, succeeded in the electorate Jan. 7, 1711, died at Vienna Dec. 4, 1715. (Trier)

Natus XII May MDCCXII..... (1988) Born 12 May 1712, betrothed 30 May 1729, died 3 Aug. 1757 in the 28th year of the reign, age 45. (Brandenburg-Ansbach)

Natus XVI Ian. MDCXXIV..... (2056) Born 16 Jan. 1624, died 28 Aug. 1705. He began his Ducal rule at Hannover in his 57th year, at Celle in his 41st. After he had lived 81 years 7 months 12 days, he shone no longer pleasing to the peoples. (Brunswick-Luneburg)

Natus XVI Maii MDCXXVII..... (2114) Born 16 May 1627, having ascended the throne 17 Sept. 1666, he finished his mortality, not his life 26 Jan. 1704. For the memory of the pious, wise, and just Prince lives after his burial and his reputation in affairs remains in the minds of his subjects for an eternity of time. (Brunswick-Wolfenbuttel)

Natus 3 Mart. 1683..... (2373) Born 3 March 1683, betrothed 9 May 1708, died 14 Aug. 1749. May he rest in peace. (Kirchberg)

Natus 13 Ian. 1634 Elect. in Coad Trev...... (2822) Born 13 Jan. 1634, Coadjutor in the Electorate of Trier 7 Jan. 1672, in the Bishopric of Speyer 16 July 1675, succeeded in the electorate 1 June 1676, died 6 Jan. 1711. (Trier)

Nec Aspera Terrent (2083-87) Neither do difficulties terrify. (Brunswick-Luneburg)

Nec Ingens si Corruat Orbis (2445) Not even if the great world should collapse. (Mecklenburg-Strelitz)

Nec Soli Cedit (2567-68) Nor does he yield to the sun. (Prussia)

Nescit Tarda Molimina (1453) He does not know slow enterprises. (Papal States)

Nicol. S.R.I. Princ. Eszterhazy de Galantha Perp. Com. in Frak. (1187) Nikolaus, Prince of S.R.I. of Esterhazy of Galantha, hereditary Count of Forchtenstein. (Esterhazy)

Nob. Dom. in Held. Seeb. & Schrapl. Dom. in Dobrz. (2437) Most noble Lord in Heldrungen, Seeburg, and Schraplau, Lord in Dobritz. (Mansfeld-Bornstatt)

Nobilissum Dom. Ac. Com. in Lipp. & St. (2764) Most noble Lord and Count in Lippe and Sternberg. (Schaumburg-Lippe)

Nomen Domini Turris Fortissima (2215,19-26) The name of the Lord is the strongest tower. (Frankfurt)

Non avrum sed nomen (1442) Not in gold but in his name. (Papal States)

Non Dormit Custos (2712) The sentinel does not sleep. (Saxe-Gotha-Altenburg)

Non Dormit Qui Nos Custodit (2616) He who watches over us does not sleep. (Regensburg)

Non Marcescet (2098,2158-60) It shall not wither. (Brunswick-Luneburg, Brunswick-Wolfenbuttel)

Non Omnis Moriar (2753-54) I shall not wholly die. (Saxe-Weimar)

Non surrexit Major (1369-70,1600-2,4) None greater has arisen. (Genoa & Malta)

Noremberga (2476,81-84) Nuremberg. (Nuremberg)

Nunquam Retrorsum (2145-47,49,51,54-55) Never backwards. (Brunswick-Wolfenbuttel)

Nurnberg (2493-5) Nuremberg. (Nuremberg)

O

O. T. Ep. Wor. & Wra. P. El. C.M.C.P. Rh.B.I.C.& M. Dux (2826) Of the Teutonic Order, Bishop of Worms and Breslau, Provost of Ellwangen, Coadjutant of Mainz, Count Palatine of the Rhine, Duke of Bavaria, Julich, Cleves, and Berg. (Trier)

Oblita ex Avro Argentea Resurgit (1413) Forgotten silver comes forth from gold. (Sicily)

Opp. & Carn. Dux C. Ritb. Gran. Hisp. P. Clas. S.C.M. Int. Cons. (1578) Duke of Troppau and Carnovia, Count of Rietberg, Grandee of Spain first class, Privy Counselor of his sacred, imperial majesty. (Liechtenstein)

Opp. & Carn. Dux Com. Rittb. S.C.M. Cons. Int. & Campi. Mareschal (1579) Duke of Troppau and Carnovia, Count of Rietberg, Privy Counselor of his sacred, imperial majesty, Field Marshal. (Liechtenstein)

Opp. & Carn. Dux Com. Rittb. S.C.M. Cons. Int. Aur. Velleris Eques (1580) Duke of Troppau and Carnovia, Count of Rietberg, Privy Counselor of his sacred, imperial majesty, Knight of the Golden Fleece. (Liechtenstein)

Otto Graf zu Solms und Herr zu Minczenberg (2785) Otto, Count of Solms and Lord of Munzenberg. (Solms-Laubach)

P

P. Leop(oldus) D.G. P.R.H. et B.A.A. M.D. E(truriae) (1512-13,15-18) Peter Leopold, D.G., Royal Prince of Hungary and Bohemia, Archduke of Austria, Grand Duke of Tuscany. (Tuscany)

Parenti Optimo Principi Pio..... (2749) To the best of fathers, a prince pious, just, and clement, filial piety and agreement of brothers (erects) this monument. (Saxe-Saalfeld)

Parmae Plac. et Vastal. Dux (1478) Duke of Parma, Piacenza and Guastalla. (Parma)

Parta Tueri (2125-27) To defend what has been gained. (Brunswick-Wolfenbuttel)

Pastori et Principi Senatus Bononensis (1458) To the Pastor and Prince, the Senate of Bologna. (Bologna)

Patri Satoris Linea Laubacensis Dicatum A C.A.C.S.L. (2785) Dedicated to the ancestor who planted the line of Laubach by Christian August, Count of Solms-Laubach. (Solms-Laubach)

Patria et Scientiarum Instituto Manifice Aucto S.P.Q.B. (1461) The Senate and the people of Bologna (honor)him for a greatly improved fatherland and enlarged Institute of Science. (Papal)

Patrimon. Henr. Frid. Sorte Divisum..... (2355) The heritage of Heinrich Friedrich divided by lot. (Hohenlohe-Langenburg)

Patrona Bavaria (1952-54,63-68) Patron of Bavaria. (Bavaria)

Patrona Franconiae (2892,94,97,99,2902,8) Patron of Franconia. (Wurzburg)

Paulo Rainerio Duce (1568) Paolo Renier, Doge. (Venice)

Paulus Rainerius Dux Venetiar (1564) Paolo Renier, Doge of Venice. (Venice)

Pcps. Reg. Cap. Bo. et de Liechtenstein Comes (1228) Prince of the Royal Chapel of Bohemia, Count of Liechtenstein. (Liechtenstein)

Perpetuo (1978) Forever.

Perpetuus in Nemet Vivar S.C.R.A.M. Act. Cam. Inc. Com. Cast. Perp. et Supr. Com. (1184) Hereditary Count in Nemt-Ujvar, present Chamberlain of his sacred, imperial, royal, apostolic majesty, Privy Counselor, hereditary and supreme Count of Eisenburg. (Batthyani)

Perrumpendum (1902) We must break through. (Anhalt-Bernburg)

Petrus D.G. Magnus Dux Totius Russiae (1353) Peter, D.G., Grand Duke of all Russia. (Holstein-Gottorp)

Petrus Grimani Dux Venetiar (1544) Pietro Grimani, Doge of Venice. (Venice)

Petrus Leopoldus D.G. P.R.H. et B.A.A. M.D. Etr(uriae) (1508-11,14) Peter Leopold, D.G., Royal Prince of Hungary
and Bohemia, Archduke of Austria, Grand Duke of Tuscany. (Tuscany)

Petrus II D.G. Port(ug). et Alg. Rex (1626-27) Peter II, D.G., King of Portugal and Algarve. (Portugal)

Petrus II D.G. Rex Portug. (1625) Peter II, D.G., King of Portugal. (Portugal)

Phil. Gotthard D.G. Pr. de Schaffgotsch (2053) Philip Gotthard, D.G., Prince of Schaffgotsch. (Breslau)

Philip V D.G. Hisp. Et Ind. Rex (1695) Philip V, D.G., King of Spain and the Indies. (Spain)

Phillppus D.G. Abbas Corbeiensis S.R.I. Princeps (2201) Philip, D.G., Abbot of Corvey, Prince of S.R.I. (Corvey)

Philippus D.G. Hispan. Infans. (1478) Philip, D.G., Prince of Spain. (Parma)

Philippus V D(ei) G(rat) (1692-94,96-98) Philip V, D.G.

Philippus V D.G. Hispan. Rex (1691) Philip V, D.G., King of Spain. (Spain)

Philippus V D.G. Hispaniarum et Indiarum Rex (1702-11) Philip V, D.G., King of Spain and the Indies. (Spanish Netherlands)

Philippus V Rex Hispaniar. (1379) Philip V, King of Spain. (Milan)

Pietas ad Omnia Utilis (2029) Piety is useful for all things. (Brandenburg-Bayreuth)

Pietate et Aequitate (2372) With piety and justice. (Kempten)

Pietate et Iustitia (2319,21,2721) With piety and justice. (Hesse-Darmstadt, Saxe-Gotha-Altenburg)

Pietate-Insignis (2292-93) In piety, exceptional. (Hesse-Cassel)

Pius Sexus Pont. M(ax). (1471-4) Pius VI, Pope. (Papal States)

Pius VI Pon(t). Max. (1466,68-70,75) Pius VI, Pope. (Papal States)

Pius VI Pont. Max. Anno Iubeliae (1467) Pius VI, Pope, Jubilee year. (Papal States)

Plus Ultra (2103,2168) More beyond. (Brunswick-Luneburg-Wolfenbuttel)

Pons Civit. Castellana (1443) The bridge of Castellana. (Papal States)

Populus et Senatus Bon(on). (1258-59) The people and Senate of Bologna. (Bologna)

Portam Sanctam Clausit a Iubilei (1428) He closed the Holy Door in the year of Jubilee. (Papal)

Post Tenebras Lux (1767,69-70) After darkness, light. (Geneva)

Praep. & D. Elvac. S.R.I. Pr. C. Fugger (2605) Provost and Lord of Ellwangen, Prince of S.R.I., Count of Fugger. (Regensburg)

Praesidium et Decus (1357-59) Protection and ornament. (Bologna)

Primitiae Metallifodinarum in Ducatu Madg. (2554) First fruits of the metal mines in the Duchy of Magdeburg. (Prussia)

Primo Anni..... (2436) On the first day of the year 1710, the last of the Evangelical line, his wife Sophia Eleonora, Countess of Schonburg, having died in 1703, he having joined in wedlock for a second time with Louisa Christina, Countess of Stolberg in 1704, almost a septuagenarian died childless. To whose everlasting memory his most sorrowful widow has had this memorial erected. (Mansfeld- Eisleben)

Prin. Pede. Rex Cypri. (1492) Prince of Piedmont, King of Cyprus. (Savoy-Sardinia)

Princ. in Lowenstein Werth. (2399) Prince of Lowenstein-Wertheim. (Lowenstein-Wertheim-Rochefort)

Princeps Iustus Constans in Bello..... (2144) A Prince, just and constant in war, undaunted from the very flower of his youth, born on 19 March 1680, when he had ruled the realm of the lands of Brunswick-Wolfenbuttel gloriously only six months, on 3 Sept. 1735 entered the harbor most secure from the Valley of Fears. (Brunswick-Wolfenbuttel)

Princeps Magnanimus Sapiens Clemens (2124) Prince, magnanimous, wise, clement. (Brunswick-Wolfenbuttel)

Princeps Pius Iustus Clemens. Natus 17 Iul. 1708. Obiit 20 Ian. 1769. Aetatis LX (2043) Prince pious, just, clement, born July 17, 1708, died Jan. 20, 1769, age 60. (Brandenburg-Bayreuth)

Princeps Pius Iustus Pacificus..... (2113) The Prince pious, just and peaceful whose honor, name and praises will remain thru all ages, began his reign in the year 1666, with his brother as colleague of his regime in the year 1685, and thus the course which Fortune had given him as of the Highest having been completed, he cast anchor in the harbor of eternal happiness in the year 1704, the 72nd of his life. (Brunswick-Wolfenbuttel)

Princeps Pius Magnanimus Felix..... (2141) Prince, pious magnanimous, fortunate, most munificent patron of letters, born on the 21st day of July 1671, began his administration as Ruler in the Principality of Blankenburg 1714, in the Duchy of Brunswick-Wolfenbuttel in 1731. Dying peacefully in Brunswick on March 1, 1735, he obtained his eternal reward in heaven. (Brunswick-Wolfenbuttel)

Princeps Pius Pacificus. Natus..... (2131-32) The pious peaceful Prince born 8 March 1667, who obtained the power in 1714, ceased to live that he might live forever on 23 March 1731. May he rest in peace. (Brandenburg-Wolfenbuttel)

Princeps Pius Sapiens..... (2039) Prince pious, wise, magnanimous, clement, liberal, establisher of letters, born at Weverling on 10 May 1711. His first marriage took place in Berlin on 20 Nov. 1731. He took over the government at Bayreuth on 17 May 1735. His second vows were celebrated at Brunswick on 20 Sept. 1759. He cast off his mortal coil at Bayreuth on 26 Feb. 1763 in the 28th year of his reign at the age of 52. (Brandenburg-Bayreuth)

Prix du Travail (1768) Reward of labor. (Geneva)

Pro Caes. & Imp. (2377) For emperor and empire. (Landau)

Pro Deo et Lege (2448-50,53-54,57-58,66-69,2509-11) For God and law. (Montfort)

Pro Deo et Patria (2264-66) For God and fatherland. (Fulda)

Pro Deo et Populo (1975) For God and the people. (Bavaria)

Pro Ecclesia et Pro Patria (2190) For the church and fatherland. (Constance)

Pro Fausio PP. Reditur V.S. (1407) For happy returns of the princes of the Two Sicilies. (Naples)

Pro Lege et Grege (2253) For the law and the flock. (Fulda)

Pro Maxima Dei Gloria et Bono Publico (2872) For the greatest glory of God and the good of the people. (Wurttemberg)

Pro Patria (2911-15) For the fatherland. (Wurzburg)

Prosperum Iter faciet (1443) It will make the way prosperous. (Papal States)

Protectione Virtute (1691) By protection, by valor. (Spain)

Protector noster aspice (1391) Our Protector look on us. (Modena)

Provide et Constanter (2439-42,2856-71) Wisely and firmly. (Mecklenburg-Schwerin)

Providentia et Pactis (1999) Through foresight and pacts. (Brandenburg-Ansbach)

Proxima Fisica Finis (1426) Nearest to natural end. (Orciano)

Proxima Soli (1393) Nearest the sun. (Modena)

Q

Quem Quadragesies et Semel..... (2385) Whom we congratulate for the forty-first time on the 12th of June 1767 for being born for the fatherland. (Lippe-Detmold)

Qui Vise le Mieux Ce 8me de Febr. (2656) Who aims the best on the 8th of February. (Saxony)

Quis Hac Imperii corona Dignlorte (2216) Who is more worthy than you of this crown of empire. (Frankfurt)

Quot Folia, Tot Corda, Lugent (2261) (There are) as many hearts as leaves that mourn. (Fulda)

R

R. Taler aus dem Berg Werck (2825) Imperial thaler from the mines. (Trier)

R.I. - Romanorum Imperator..... Emperor of the Romans.

R.I.S.A. - Romanorum Imperator Semper August ..... Emperor of the Romans Ever August.

Raim, Antonius D.G. Ep. Eyst. S.R.I.P. (2209) Raimund Anton, D.G., Bishop of Eichstaedt, Prince of S.R.I. (Eichstaedt)

Raymund Ferd. D.G. Episc. Passau (2521) Raymund Ferdinand, D.G., Bishop of Passau. (Passau)

Raynaldus I Mut. Reg. E(c or r) D. XI MI. I. (1391) Rinaldo I, eleventh Duke of Modena and Reggio, and first of Mirandola. (Modena)

Recte Faciendo Neminem Timeas (1976,2351) In doing right, fear no man. (Brandenburg-Ansbach, Hohenlohe-Neuenstein-Ohringen)

Rector Reip. Rhacusin (1637,39) Rector of the Republic of Ragusa. (Ragusa)

Rectus et Immotus (2295-98) Right and unmoved. (Hesse- Cassel)

Redde Mihi Laetitiam Salutaris Tui et Spiritu Principali Confirma Me (2512) Give me the joy of your deliverance and strengthen me with princely spirit. (Paderborn)

Redeunt Antiqui Gaudia Moris (2629) There return the joys of ancient custom. (Regensburg)

Redeunt Saturnia Regna (2102,67) The reign of Saturn returns. (Brunswick-Luneburg)

Reg. Cap. Bo. et de Liechtenstein Comes (1227,29-30) Count of the Royal Chapel of Bohemia and Liechtenstein. (Liechtenstein)

Reg. Cap. Bo. et de Schrattenbach Comes (1214) Count of the Royal Chapel of Bohemia and Schrattenbach. (Olmutz)

Reg. Cap. Bohem. et de Troyer Comes (1231) Count of the Royal Chapel of Bohemia and Troyer. (Olmutz)
Reg. Pr. Pol. et Lith. Saxon Dux (2833) Royal Prince of Poland and Lithuania, Duke of Saxony. (Trier)
Regi Svo Avgvstissimo Iter In Hassiam Mense Ivn. A. MDCCXXXI Apparanti Felicem Favstamque et Profectionem et Reditionem A Deo Cvncta Svecia Svpplicіter Precatvr (1726) For its most august King, preparing a journey to Hesse in the month of June in the year 1731, all Sweden as suppliant prays God for happy and fortunate going and returning. (Sweden)
Regia Boruss. Societas Asiat. Embdae (2591) Royal Prussian Asiatic Society of Emden. (Prussia)
Regnans Capitulum Ecclesiae Cathedralis Ratisbonensis, Sede Vacante (2606) Administering the chapter of the cathedral church at Regensburg, the seat being vacant. (Regensburg)
Regne de la Loi (1335-36) Rule of the law. (France)
Reichs Fues (2183) Imperial standard. (Cologne)
Religione Defensa (1489) Religion being defended. (Roman Republic under Neapolitan Occupation)
Religionis Evangalicae Custodiam..... (2715) Commending to his posterity the protection of the evangelical faith as a foundation of true felicity in the ancient seat of the landgraves of Thuringia at Waltershausen, with his own hands, he laid the foundation of a new church on 8 Nov. 1719. (Saxe-Gotha-Altenburg)
Remigio Altissimi Uni. (2112) Crew of the highest one. (Brunswick-Wolfenbuttel)
Rep(ublica) Romana (1483-87) Roman Republic. (Roman Republic)
Repubblice Ligure Anno I (1371) Ligurian Republic year I. (Ligurian Republic)
Repubblica Napolitan(a) (1410) Neapolitan Republic. (Neapolitan Republic)
Republique Franco(a)ise (1336-37) Republic of France. (France)
Republique Genevoise (1768) Republic of Geneva. (Geneva)
Resp. Gosl. (2272-73) Republic of Goslar. (Goslar)
Respice de Coelo et Visita Vineam Istam, et Perfice eam, quam Plantavit, Dextera Tua (2841) Look down from heaven and visit that vineyard of yours, which he has planted, and with your right hand perfect it. (Werden, Helmstaedt)
Respubl. Rhacus(i) (1640-1) Republic of Ragusa. (Ragusa)
Respublic Basiliensis (1758) Republic of Basel. (Basel)
Respublica Bernensis (1759-60) Republic of Bern. (Bern)
Respublica Genevensis (1767) Republic of Geneva. (Geneva)
Respublica Lucernensi (1775) Republic of Luzern. (Luzern)
Respublica Veneta (1552,56,62-3,68,75) Republic of Venice. (Venice)
Rex Sic(iliae) et Hie(r). (1411-12) King of Sicily and Jerusalem. (Sicily)
Roma in Sacris Evangelicorum..... (2714) While Rome was everywhere engaged in the destruction and demolition of the sacred shrines of the Evangelicals, to consecrate a new church to the best and most high God at Waltershausen in the place of the old work, he laid the foundation with his own hands on 8 Nov. 1719. (Saxe-Gotha-Altenburg)
Rudolphus Augustus D.G. Dux Br. et L. (2113) Rudolph August, D.G., Duke of Brunswick-Luneburg. (Brunswick-Wolfenbuttel)

S

S. Annae Fundgruben Ausb. Tha. In N. Oe. (1113) St. Anne mine, mining thaler in Lower Austria. (Austria)
S. Ap. S. Leg. Nat(us) Germ. Primas (1249,55,57) Legate of the Holy Apostolic See, born Primate of Germany. (Salzburg)
S. Caes. Mai. Regin. M. Britann. et Ordd. Foederatorum Belg. (2709) Of her Sacred Imperial Majesty, the Queen of Great Britain, and the order of the Belgian Federation. (Saxe-Gotha-Altenburg)
S. Carol(us) Magnus Fundator (2470) Charlemagne founder. (Munster)
S. Carol. Magnus Imperator. Fundator (2504) Charlemagne emperor, founder. (Osnabruck)
S. Cyrill Prim. Apost. Morav. (1222) St. Cyril, first Apostle of Moravia. (Olmutz)
S. Georgius Ferrariae Protec. (1439) St. George, protector of Ferrara. (Papal States)
S. Iochimbs. Thaler Ausbeuth (1137) St. Joachim's mining thaler. (Austria)
S. Ioachimbsthalische Ausbeut Thaler (1074,77) St. Joachim's Valley mining thaler. (Austria)
S. Kilianus (cum Socys) Francorum Apostli(us) (2905,9) Saint Kilian, Apostle of the Franks with companions. (Wurzburg)
S. Lambertus Patronus Leodiensis (1582-91) St. Lambert, patron of Liege. (Liege)
S. Lambertus, S. Alexander Protectores Civit. Friburg Brisg. (2241,45) Saint Lambert and Saint Alexander, Protectors of the city of Freiburg in Breisgau. (Freiburg)
S. Liborius Patr. Paderb. (2516) Saint Liborius, Patron of Paderborn. (Paderborn)
S. Ludgerus Fundator (Abbatiarum) Werdinensis (& Helmstad.) (2842-44) Saint Ludger, Founder, Abbot of Werden & Helmstaedt. (Werden & Helmstaedt)
S. Maria Mater Dei Patrona Hung. (1125-33,68-69,72, 74,79) Holy Mary, Mother of God, Patron of Hungary. (Hungary)
S. Petron(io) Prot(ector) Bon(on) (1464-66) St. Peter, Protector of Bologna. (Bologna)
S. Petronius Bon(on) Prot. (1467-70,75) St. Peter, Protector of Bologna. (Bologna)
S. Rudbertus Eps. Salisburg (1234,36,38,41) St. Rupert, Bishop of Salzburg. (Salzburg)
S. Rupertus Episcop. Salisburgens (1243,46,48,50-54) St. Rupert, Bishop of Salzburg. (Salzburg)
S. Sebast. Patronus Rhaetiae (2502) Saint Sebastian, Patron of Oettingen. (Oettingen)
S.C.M. Cons. Int. Cam. Supr. R. Boh. Praef. Burgg. Egr. (1191) Privy Counselor of his Sacred Imperial Majesty, High Chamberlain of the kingdom of Bohemia, and Burgrave of Eger. (Orsini-Rosenberg)
S.C.M. Cons. Status Int. & Haered. Per. Styr. Sup. Stab. Praefectus (1202) Privy and hereditary State Counselor of his Sacred Imperial Majesty, High Constable for Styria. (Windisch-Gratz)
S.I. Aul. Reg. Her. & P. Ge. H. Post. Mag. (1193) Supreme of the Imperial court of the hereditary kingdom and provinces, general hereditary postmaster. (Paar)
S.M.V(enetu) Aloy. Mocenico Dux (1525-28,36-37,58-61) St. Mark of Venice, Alvise Mocenigo, Doge. (Venice)
S.M.V. Aloysius Pisani D. (1542-43) St. Mark of Venice, Alvise Pisani, Doge. (Venice)
S.M.V. Carolus Ruzini D. (1539-40) St. Mark of Venice, Carlo Ruzzini, Doge. (Venice)
S.M.V. Franc Lavredano Dux (1549-51) St. Mark of Venice, Francesco Loredan, Doge. (Venice)
S.M.V(enet) Ioan Cornel(io) D(ux) (1531-34) St. Mark of Venice, Giovanni Corner, Doge. (Venice)
S.M.V. Ludov(i) Manin Dux (1571-74) St. Mark of Venice, Lodovico Manin, Doge. (Venice)
S.M.V. M(arc) Foscarenus D(ux) (1554-55) St. Mark of Venice, Marco Foscarini, Doge. (Venice)
S.M.V. Paul Rainerius D(ux) (1565-67) St. Mark of Venice, Paolo Renier, Doge. (Venice)
S.M.V. Petrus Grimani D. (1545-47) St. Mark of Venice, Pietro Grimani, Doge. (Venice)
S.R.I. - Sacri Romani Imperii.....of the Holy Roman Empire.
S.R.I. Archid. & (El(ector) Dux I. Cl. & M. (1957-8) Archidapifer and Elector of S.R.I., Duke of Julich, Cleves, and Berg. (Bavaria)
S.R.I. Comites A. Konigsegg et Rottenfels Domini In Aulendorf & Stauffen. Fratres (2374) Counts of S.R.I. in Konigsegg and Rothenfels, Lords in Aulendorf and Stauffen, brothers. (Konigsegg)
S.R.I. Pr. Re. Cap. Boh. & A. Colloredo & Wald. Co. (1233) Prince of S.R.I., Count of the royal chapel of Bohemia, Colloredo, and Waldsee. (Olmutz)
S.R.I. Pr. Salisb. S.S. Ap. Leg. Nat. Germ. Primas (1247,56) Prince of S.R.I. of Salzburg, Legate of the Holy Apostolic See, born Primate of Germany. (Salzburg)
S.R.I. Princ. & Baro. Reteny Imp. (1482) Prince of S.R.I. and Imperial Baron of Retegno. (Retegno)
S.R.I. Ps. R.C.B.C. Protect. Ger. S.C.R.M. Con. In. et Actval (1220-21,23-26) Prince of S.R.I., Count of the Royal Chapel of Bohemia, Protector of Germany, present Privy
Counselor of his Sacred, Imperial, Royal Majesty. (Olmutz)
S.R.I.P. - Sacri Romani Imperii Princeps..... Prince of the Holy Roman Empire.
S.R.I.P. Ex. Comit. & Dnis. de Firmian (2524) Prince of S.R.I. from the Counts and Lords of Firmian. (Passau)
Sac. Nupt. Celeb. Berol. (1978) For the holy matrimony celebrated at Berlin. (Brandenburg-Ansbach)
Sac. Rom. Imp. Archic. et Elect. (2592) Arch-chancellor and Elector of S.R.I. (Prussia)
Sac. Rom. Imp. Archid. & Elect. Land. Leucht. (1956) Archidapifer and Elector of S.R.I., Landgrave of Leuchtenberg. (Bavaria)
Sac. Rom(an) Imp(er) Archim. et Elect(or) (2646-47, 49,52-53,64-65,71-76) Archmarshal and Elector of S.R.I. (Saxony)
Sac. Rom. Imp. Archim. et Elect (1613,17) Grand Marshal and Elector of S.R.I. (Poland)
Sac. Rom. Imp. Archim. Elector et Vicarius (2670) Archmarshal, Elector & Vicar of S.R.I. (Saxony)
Sac. Rom. Imp. Princ ex Comitibus de Rabatta (2521) Prince of S.R.I. from the Counts of Rabatta. (Passau)
Sac. Rom. Imp. Princeps. (2247) Prince of S.R.I. (Freising)
Sac. Rom. Imp. Princeps Com. de Lamberg (2522) Prince of S.R.I., Count of Lamberg. (Passau)
Sac. Rom. Imp. Provisor Iterum (2700) Administrator of S.R.I. for the second time. (Saxony)
Saeculo a Pace Westphalia Exacto (2284) A century having been completed from the Peace of Westphalia. (Hamburg)
Salisburg S. Sed. Apos. Legat. Ger. Prim. (1240,42,44-45) Salzburg, Legate of the Holy Apostolic See, Primate of Germany. (Salzburg)
Salus Publica Salus Mea (1731-33) Public safety, my safety. (Sweden)
Salus Publica, Salus Mea (1979,82-83) Public safety is my safety. (Brandenburg-Ansbach)
Saluti Publicae (2851) For the public safety. (Wurttemberg)
Salutis Ripam Teneo (2789) I hold the bank of the river. (Stolberg-Elder Line)
Salvo Caes. Salva Respub. (2414) The Emperor safe, the Commonwealth safe. (Lubeck)
Sanct(us) Andreas Reviviscens (2061-64) Saint Andreas, restored to life. (Brunswick-Luneburg)
Sancta Helena Fundatrix Ecclesiae (2825) Saint Helena, founder of the church. (Trier)
Sanctus Leodegarius (1774) St. Leodegran. (Luzern)
Sanctus Marcus Venet. (1524,29-30,35,38,41,44,48, 53,57,64,69-70) St. Mark of Venice. (Venice)
Sanctus Martinus (1373-76) St. Martin. (Lucca)
Sanctus Vitus Patronus Corbeiensis (2193-94,96-2201) St. Vitus, Patron of Corvey. (Corvey)
Schnepper Gesellschaft (2659) Schnepper Company. (Saxony)
Scudo Romano (1486) Roman scudo. (Roman Republic)
Securitati Publicae (1996) For the public safety. (Branden- burg-Ansbach)
Sede Vacante The seat being vacant.
Sede Vacante (1453-54,56,62,64-65) The See being vacant. (Papal States)
Seit getrost Ich der Herr bin mit euch (2846) Be of good cheer, I, the Lord, am with you. (Worms)
Semper Idem (2121,2883) Always the same. (Wurzburg, Brunswick-Wolfenbuttel)
Septenarius Fratrum et Ducum Saxoniae (2716) A group of seven of the brothers and dukes of Saxony. (Saxe-Gotha-Altenburg)
Serma Princ. et Dna. Dna. Maria Amal...... (2292-93) The most serene Princess and Lady, Maria Amalia, sprung from the most serene ducal line of Curland, born 12 June 1653, married to the most serene and powerful Prince Karl, Landgrave of Hesse, Prince of Hersfeld, Count of Katzenellenbogen, Dietz, Ziegenhain, Nidda, and Schaumburg, on 21 May 1673, died at Weilmunster on 16 July 1711. (Hesse-Cassel)
Sic Deo Placvit In Tribulationibus (2318) Thus it pleased God in tribulations. (Hesse-Darmstadt)
Sic Vota Sic Prospera Secunda (2761) So vows, so following prosperity. (Schaumburg-Lippe)
Sie daempffen nicht des Wortes Licht (2755) They do not lower the light of the Word. (Saxe-Weimar)
Sigismundus D.G. Archiepiscop(us) (1247,51,56) Sigismund, D.G., Archbishop. (Salzburg)
Sigismundus D.G.A. (Episc.) & Pr. Salisburg (1249,55) Sigismund, D.G., Archbishop and Prince of Salzburg. (Salzburg)
Sigismund. D.G.A. & Pr. Sal. S.A.L. Nat. Germ. Primas (1248,50,52,54) Sigismund, D.G., Archbishop and Prince of Salzburg, legate of the Apostolic See, born Primate of Germany. (Salzburg)
Sigismundus D.G.A. & P.S.A.S.L.N.G. P(rim). (1253,60) Sigismund, D.G., Archbishop and Prince of Salzburg, Legate of the Apostolic See, born Primate of Germany. (Salzburg)
Sigm. D.G.A. & P.S.A.S.L.N.G. Prim. (1258-60) Sigismund, D.G., Archbishop and Prince of Salzburg, Legate of the Apostolic See, born Primate of Germany. (Salzburg)
Signatus Pact. Coniug...... (2660) The marriage pacts having been signed between the serene realms of the King of Poland and the Elector of Saxony and the serene realm of the King of Hungary, Bohemia, and the Archduchy of Austria at Vienna in 1719. (Saxony)
Simon August Com. & Nob. D. Lipp. S.D.V. & A.B.H. Ultr. (2385) Simon August, Count and most noble Lord of Lippe, supreme Lord of Vianen and Ameiden, hereditary Burgrave of Utrecht. (Lippe-Detmold)
Simon Henrich Adolph Com. & N.D. Lipp. (2383-84) Simon Heinrich Adolph, Count and most noble Lord of Lippe. (Lippe-Detmold)
Sincere et Constanter (2322-25) Truthfully and steadfastly. (Hesse-Darmstadt)
Sit Nomen Dom(ini) Benedict(um) (1316-34) Blessed be the name of the Lord. (France)
Sit Nomen Domini Benedictum (2810) Blessed be the name of the Lord. (Strassburg)
Sit Unio Haec Perennis (2355) May this union be everlasting. (Hohenlohe-Langenburg)
So setzt mich Gott nun an den Ort wo Luther eh bekannt Sein Wort (2846) Thus, God now puts me in the place where Luther formerly professed His word. (Worms)
Sola Bona Quae Honesta (2348-9) Only those things which are honorable are good. (Hohenlohe-Neuenstein-Weickersheim)
Solemni Ritu Iubilaeum..... (2195) The most reverend and exalted Lord Prince Florenz, Abbot of Corvey, Prince of S.R.I., celebrated the jubilee rite on April 20. (Corvey)
Solemnium A. MDLXXXVI per Actorum..... (2629) With the approval of the fatherland, the archers of Ratisbon in the year 1788 celebrate the memory of the solemn acts of the fathers in the year 1586. (Regensburg)
Soli Reduci (1408) To Him, the only one restored. (Naples)
Solis Ales Me Proteget Alis (2184) The bird of the sun shall shelter me with its wings. (Cologne)
Sophia D.G. Ex. Stirpe El. Pal. Elect. Vid. Br. et Lun. Mag. Brit. Haeres (2069) Sophia, D.G., from the seed of the Electors of the Palatinate, widow of the Elector of Brunswick-Luneburg, Heiress of Great Britain. (Brunswick-Luneburg)
Spes Nescia Falli (2798) Hope that knows not how to fail. (Stolberg-Younger Line)
Spes Nostra Iesus Dei et Mariae Filius (2272-73) Jesus, son of God and Mary, our hope. (Goslar)
Splendet in Orbe Decus (1725) Honor will shine in the world. (Sweden)
Stadt Franckfurt (2228) City of Frankfurt. (Frankfurt)
Stanislaus Augustus D.G. Rex Pol(on) M.D. Lith(u) or Lit(uan) (1618-21,23) Stanislaus August, D.G., King of Poland, Grand Duke of Lithuania. (Poland)
Storm. et Dit. Com. In Old. et Delm. (2409) Stormarn and Ditmarsh, Count of Oldenburg and Delmenhorst. (Lubeck)
Sub Tuum Praesidium Confug. (1234) We flee to Thy protection. (Salzburg)
Sub Umbra Alarum Tuarum (2231-34,81,2363,2475) Under the shadow of Thy wings. (Freiburg in Breisgau, Jever, Nuremberg)
Subditorum Salus Felicitas Summa (2411-12) The safety of the subjects is the highest happiness. (Lubeck)
Sup. Adm. Bor. et Ord. Teut. Magn. Mag. (2812-13) Supreme Administrator of Prussia, Grandmaster of the Teutonic Order. (Teutonic Order)
Sup. Imp. Aul. Reg. Her. P.G. Her. Post. Mag. (1194) Supreme of the Imperial court of the hereditary kingdom and provinces, General Hereditary Postmaster. (Paar)
Supr. D. Vian. et Ameld. Burg. H. Ultr. (2380,83-84) Supreme Lord of Vianen and Ameide, Hereditary Burgrave of Utrecht. (Lippe-Detmold)
Supra Firmam Petram (1463) On a solid rock. (Papal States)
Suscipe et Protege (2885) Support and protect us. (Wurzburg)
Suum Cuique (2393-95,2553,63,65-66) Let each have his own. (Lowenstein-Wertheim-Virneburg, Prussia)
Suum Cuique (1776) Let each have his own. (Neuchatel)
Sydera Favent Industriae (2269) The stars favor industry. (Furstenberg)
Sylvarum Culturae Praemium (2009) Prize for the culture of the forest. (Brandenburg-Ansbach)

T

Tali Sub Custodia (2617,28) Under such protection. (Regensburg)

Tert. Ducat Secular (2873) Third centennial of the duchy. (Wurttemberg)

Theodorus D.G. Sac. Rom. Imp. Abbas Werdinensis et Helmstadiensis (2841) Theodore, D.G., S.R.I., Abbot of Werden and Helmstaedt. (Werden, Helmstaedt)

Thomas Orciani F.T. S.R.I. Marchio Un. Cr. Bo. Com. & (1426-27) Thomas Orciano F.T. Marquis of S.R.I. and Count of Hungary, Croatia, and Bohemia. (Orciano)

Tigurinae Moneta Reipublicae (1783,85-86) Money of the Republic of Zurich. (Zurich)

Torque Donatus (2718) Presented with a garter. (Saxe-Gotha-Altenburg)

Traiectum ad Mosam (1854-55) The crossing of the Meuse. (United Netherlands)

Trium Imperatorum S.R.I. et Circ. Franc...... (2030) General Field Marshal of S.R.I. and of the Franconian Circle, the terror of the Turks and the Gauls, husband of three wives, the solace of his subjects and the fatherland, born 27 July 1644, died May 1712, age 68 years, 51st year of his reign. (Brandenburg-Bayreuth)

Troe love mod og hvad Dan. kongens gunst kand vinde mens Norge klippe har mand skal hos Nordmand finde (1301) Obedience to law, courage, and all that win the favor of the Danish king, you will find among the mountains of Norway and with the Norwegians. (Denmark)

Tu Quondam Abiectam Reddis Deus Alme Sonoram (2099,2108,61-62) Thou, oh kindly God, bring back this tuneful one who was previously cast down. (Brunswick-Luneburg-Wolfenbuttel)

Tut. Mar. Gab. Pr. Vid. de Lobk. Nat. Pr. Sab. Car. et Aug. Pr. de Lobk. (1190) Regency of Maria Gabriele, widow of the Prince of Lobkowitz, born Princess of Savoy-Carignan, and August Prince of Lobkowitz. (Lobkowitz)

Tuta His Auspiciis (2482-83) Safe under these auspices. (Nuremberg)

U

U.S.C. & R.A.M. Cons. Int. Gen. C. Mar. & Nob. Praet. H. Turmae Capit. (1187) Privy Counselor of both their Holy Imperial and Royal Apostolic Majesties, General Field Marshal and Captain of the noble praetorian Hungarian squadrons. (Eszterhazy)

Ubi Uvit Spirat (1462) He breathes where he will. (Papal States)

Una. Meta Omnibus (2657,66) One goal for all. (Saxony)

Union et Force (1337) Union and strength. (France)

Unum Omnium Votum Salus Principis S.P.Q.B. (1460) The safety of the prince is the prayer of all, the senate and the people of Bologna. (Bologna)

Urbe Obsessa (1855) The city is besieged. (United Netherlands)

Urendo Crescit (2763) It grows by burning. (Schaumburg-Lippe)

Urokkelig som Dovres hoye fielde staaer Norges sonners troskab mod og vaelde (1312) Unmovable as the Dovres high mountains stand the loyalty, courage, and power of the sons of Norway. (Denmark)

Uti Sanguine Ita et Amicitia Iuncti. (2374) As by blood, so by friendship joined. (Konigsegg)

Utr. Bav. et Pal. Sup. Dux Com. Pal. Rh. Archid. Aust. S.R.I.E.L.L. (1947) Duke of both Bavarias and the Upper Palatinate, Count Palatine of the Rhine, Archduke of Austria, Elector of S.R.I. (Bavaria)

Utr. Sic. Hierus. (1396) The Two Sicilies, Jerusalem. (Naples)

V

V.G.G. Christian August Graf zu Solms Laubach (2782-84, 86-87) D.G., Christian August Count of Solms Laubach. (Solms-Laubach)

V.G.G. Ioseph Fried. (II) H. Z(u). S(achsen) & Obervormund u. Landes Regent (2732-33) D.G., Joseph Friedrich II, Duke of Saxony and Chief Guardian and Regent of the land. (Saxe-Hildburghausen)

Vasculis Aviae Argenteis Patriae Indigenti Ministravit Auxilia (2213) With the silver vessels of the court, aid was brought to the needy fatherland. (Eichstaedt)

Vdal. S.R.I. Pr. Ep. Cur. D. in Firstb. et Funaw. (1761) Ulrich, Prince of S.R.I., Bishop of Chur, Lord in Firstenberg and Furstenau. (Chur)

Verblasset gleich ihr Licht; stirbt doch die Wurckung nich (2753-54) Even if its light grows pale, the effect will not die. (Saxe-Weimar)

Vestigia Premo Maiorum (2133) I walk in the footsteps of my fathers. (Brunswick-Wolfenbuttel)

Veteris Monumentum Decoris (1392) A memorial of ancient honor. (Modena)

Vi Unita Concordia Fratrum Fortior (2800) The harmony of brothers united in strength is mightier. (Stolberg-Younger Line)

Vic. Am. D.G. Rex. Sar. Cyp. et Ier. (1496-97) Victor Amadeus, D.G., King of Sardinia, Cyprus, and Jerusalem. (Sardinia)

Victor Am. II D.G. Dux Sab. (1492) Victor Amadeus, D.G., Duke of Savoy. (Sardinia)

Victor Frid. D.G.P. Anh. Dux S.A. & W.C. Asc. D.B. & S. (1901-4) Victor Friedrich, D.G., Prince of Anhalt, Duke of Saxony, Angria & Westphalia, Count of Aschersleben, Lord of Bernburg and Zerbst. (Anhalt-Bernburg)

Viderunt Oculi mei Salutare Tuum (1432) Mine eyes have seen Thy salvation. (Papal States)

Vidi Lunam Adorare Me (2183) I saw the moon adore me. (Cologne)

Virtute et Aequitate Pacata Germania (2202) Germany pacified with virtue and justice. (Corvey)

Virtute et Fidelitate (2303) By virtue and faithfulness. (Hesse- Cassel)

Virtute Parata (2648) With well prepared valor. (Saxony)

Virtute Viam Dimetiar (2840) I shall mark the way with valor. (Waldeck)

Vivat Carolus Sextus Imperator (2216) Long live the Emperor, Karl VI. (Frankfurt)

Vixi Annos Bis Centum, nunc Tertia Vivitur Aetas (2711) I have lived twice a hundred years; now my third age is being lived. (Saxe-Gotha-Altenburg)

Vlrika Eleonora D.G. Regina Svec. (1718) Ulrica Eleonora, D.G., Queen of Sweden. (Sweden)

Von gewachsenen Silber aus der Fundgr. 3 K. Stern (2850) Of increased silver from the mine 3 K star. (Wurttemberg)

Vota Publica (1978) Public vows. (Brandenburg-Ansbach)

Votis Pro Pace et Salute Imperii Solutis Sagittarii Ratisbon (2620) Vows for the peace and prosperity of the Empire having been made, the archers of Ratisbon saw that it was produced. (Regensberg)

Vox de Throno (1433-35) A voice from the throne. (Papal States)

W

Wenceslaus S. Rom. Imp. Princeps a Paar (1194) Wenceslaus, Prince of S.R.I. of Paar. (Paar)

Westphaliae Dux Iure Instaurabat (2175) The Duke of Westphalia, restored in law. (Cologne)

Wilh(elmus) Ant(onius) D.G. Eps. Paderb. S.R.I. Pr. Com. Pyrm. (2514-16) Wilhelm Anton, D.G., Bishop of Paderborn, Prince of S.R.I., Count of Pyrmont. (Paderborn)

Wilh. Ernest(us) (I or Prim.) D.G. Dux Sax. I.C.M.A. & W. (2753-54) Wilhelm Ernst I, D.G., Duke of Saxony, Julich, Cleves, Berg, Angria, and Westphalia. (Saxe-Weimar)

Wilhelm(us) D.G. Landgr. & Pr. Her. Hass. Com. Han. (2287-90) Wilhelm, D.G., Landgrave and Hereditary Prince of Hesse, Count of Hanau. (Hanau-Munzenburg)

Wilhelm Fr. E. D.G. S.R.I. Com. in Sch. C. & N.D. Lipp. & St. D. (2763) Wilhelm Friedrich Ernst, D.G., S.R.I., Count in Schaumburg, Count and noble Lord of Lippe, Lord of Sternberg. (Schaumburg-Lippe)

Wilhelmina Carolina Io. Frid. March. Brand. Filia Georgii Secundi M. Brit. Fr. et H. R. El. Br. et L. Coniux. (2096) Wilhelmina Caroline Io., daughter of Friedrich, Margrave of Brandenburg, wife of George II, King of Great Britain, France and Ireland, Elector of Brunswick-Luneburg. (Brunswick-Luneburg)

Wilhelm. VIII D.G. Hass. Landg. Han. Com. (2295-8) Wilhelm VIII, D.G., Landgrave of Hesse, Count of Hanau. (Hesse-Cassel)

Wilhelmus I Dei Grat. C. Reg. in Schaumb. (2764) Wilhelm I, D.G., reigning Count in Schaumburg. (Schaumburg-Lippe)

Wilhelmus IX D.G. Hass. Landgr. Com. Han. (2304-7) Wilhelm IX, D.G., Landgrave of Hesse, Count of Hanau. (Hesse- Cassel)

Wilhelmus Frid. D.G. March. Brand. (1976) Wilhelm Friedrich, D.G., Margrave of Brandenburg. (Brandenburg-Ansbach)

Wir feyren iezt ein Iubeliahr, das Bergwerck gibt die Muntze dar (2799) We are now celebrating the year of jubilee; the mine produces the coin. (Stolberg-Younger Line)

Wolf(fg). D.G. S.R.E. Presb. Card. d(e) Schrattem(n)bach E(p). O(lom). Dux (1216-26) Wolffgang, D.G., Presbyter of the Holy Roman Church, Cardinal of Schrattenbach, Bishop of Olmutz. (Olmutz)

Wolffgang D.G. S.R.E. Card. de Schrattembach Ep. Olom. (1215) Wolffgang, D.G., of the Holy Roman Church, Cardinal of Schrattenbach, bishop of Olmutz. (Olmutz)

Wolffgangus D.G. Epus. Olomucensis Dux S.R.I. Prceps. (1214) Wolffgang, D.G., Bishop of Olmutz, Duke, Prince of S.R.I. (Olmutz)

X

Xaverius D.G. Reg. Pr. Pol. & Lith. Dux Sax. (El. Adm.) (2678-79,87-89) Xaver, D.G., royal Prince of Poland and Lithuania, Duke of Saxony, Elector, Administrator. (Saxony)

Y

Z

Zehen eine feine Mar(c)k (Convent. M.) Ten to the fine mark convention money.

Zu Ergetzung der Versamleten Staende (2651) For the the entertainment of the assembled estates. (Saxony)

Zum Besten des Vaterlands (1939) For the benefit of the Fatherland. (Bamberg)

Zum Gedaechtnis des gefuhrten graeflich Wetterauischen Directorii. abgegeben (2782) Delivered in memory of the board of directors of Wetterau on. . . . . (Solms-Laubach)

Zur Belohnung des Fleisses (2685-89,92-94) For the reward of industry. (Saxony)

Zur Ermunterung des Fleisses (2679,86) For the encouragement of industry. (Saxony)

RELATIVE VALUES

1/9 Marck Feine Silber aus Bieber (2295-98) 1/9 of a mark of fine silver from the Bieber mines. (Hesse-Cassel)

1 Rigsdaler Cour. (1312) 1 current rigsdaler. (Denmark)

1 Rigsdaler Species (1313-15) 1 rigsdaler species. (Denmark)

1 Thaler Hz. Br. L.L.M. (2150) One thaler, dukedom of Brunswick and Luneburg, land money. (Brunswick-Wolfenbuttel)

IIII Mark Danske (1291,94,96) 4 Danish marks. (Denmark)

X E F M, X Eine Fein Mar(c)k (Convention. M.) 10 to the fine mark Convention money.

X Ex Marca Pura Colonien (1618-20) 10 to the fine Cologne mark.

10-7/16 Ex Marca Pura Coloniens(i). (1621-22) 10-7/16 to the fine Cologne mark. (Poland)

XI Auf. I. Feine Mark (1798) 11 to 1 fine mark. (Zurich)

XII Florins IX Sols (1769-70) 12 florins, 11 sols. (Geneva)

14-1/12 Ex Marca Pur. Coloniens. (1623) 14-1/12 to the fine Cologne mark. (Poland)

48 Schilling Courant Geldt. Anno 1752 (2420) 48 schillings, courant money, year 1752. (Lubeck)

60 Schilling Schlesw. Holst. Courant (1311) 60 current Schleswig-Holstein schillings. (Schleswig-Holstein)